THE RISK MANAGEMENT ASSOCIATION

Serving the Financial Services Industry

ANNUAL STATEMENT STUDIES 2005 2006

RMA
Annual Statement Studies®
Copyright, Ordering, Licensing, and Use of Data

All of the information contained herein is obtained from sources believed to be accurate and reliable.

ALL REPRESENTATIONS CONTAINED HEREIN ARE BELIEVED BY RMA TO BE AS ACCURATE AS THE DATA AND METHODOLOGIES WILL ALLOW. HOWEVER, BECAUSE OF THE POSSIBILITIES OF HUMAN AND MECHANICAL ERROR, AS WELL AS UNFORESEEN FACTORS BEYOND RMA'S CONTROL, THE INFORMATION HEREIN IS PROVIDED "AS IS" WITHOUT WARRANTY OF ANY KIND. RMA MAKES NO REPRESENTATIONS OR WARRANTIES EXPRESS OR IMPLIED TO A SUBSCRIBER OR LICENSEE OR ANY OTHER PERSON OR ENTITY AS TO THE ACCURACY, TIMELINESS, COMPLETENESS, MERCHANTABILITY OR FITNESS FOR ANY PARTICULAR PURPOSE OF ANY OF THE INFORMATION CONTAINED IN THIS BOOK. MOREOVER, INFORMATION IS SUPPLIED WITHOUT WARRANTY ON THE UNDERSTANDING THAT ANY PERSON WHO ACTS UPON IT OR OTHERWISE CHANGES POSITION IN RELIANCE THEREON DOES SO ENTIRELY AT SUCH PERSON'S OWN RISK.

This Annual Statement Studies® book and information is not intended to provide loan advice or recommendations of any kind. The information contained herein is intended for educational, informational, and research purposes only. Accordingly, RMA does not offer any advice regarding the suitability of any loan, of any debtor or of any other business determination related to the information contained in this Annual Statement Studies® book. You use this book and information at your own risk, and RMA assumes no responsibility or liability for any advice or other guidance that you may take from this book or the information contained therein. Prior to making any business decisions, you should conduct all necessary due diligence as may be appropriate under the circumstances, and RMA assumes no responsibility or liability for any business decisions, including but not limited to loan decisions, or other services rendered by you based upon the Statement Studies® data or results obtained therefrom.

The Annual Statement Studies® book is a copyrighted product of RMA.

© The Risk Management Association

ALL RIGHTS RESERVED. No part of this product may be reproduced, replicated, disseminated, distributed in any form or by any means, or utilized in any form, electronic or mechanical, including photocopying, recording or by any information storage and retrieval system without the express permission of The Risk Management Association.

To **obtain permission** to copy, quote, reproduce, replicate, disseminate, or distribute the Statement Studies® data/material please fax or e-mail a brief letter stating who you are and how you intend to use the Statement Studies® data to: Statement Studies Information Products at fax number 215-446-4101 or via e-mail to studies@rmahq.org. Depending on the requested use, RMA may require a license agreement and royalty fee.

A **License Agreement is required** if you wish to use or incorporate any portion of the data, in whole or in part in other products that will in turn be sold to others, such as in software oriented or derived products, scholarly publications, or training materials.

To **purchase** a copy, or additional copies, of the Statement Studies® data in book or online format, contact RMA's Customer Relations at 1-800-677-7621. Regional data presented in the same fashion as you see in this book is only available in eStatement Studies.

If you have a **question regarding** the data please reference the detailed explanatory notes provided in the Help section of the enclosed product. If you are unable to find the answer to your question please contact us by e-mail at: studies@rmahq.org. Be sure to include your detailed question along with your telephone number, fax number, and e-mail address.

TABLE OF CONTENTS

*General Industries Format means that a valid construction NAICS was assigned to the subject companies contained in the sample; however, the financial statements were prepared using a general or traditional manufacturing or service industries presentation of results versus using a percentage-of-completion method of accounting. Industries found in the percentage-of-completion presentation follow the presentation used by RMA in the past.

THE RISK MANAGEMENT ASSOCIATION (RMA)

Founded in 1914, RMA is a member-driven professional association whose sole purpose is to advance the use of sound risk principles in the financial services industry. RMA promotes an enterprise-wide approach to risk management that focuses on credit risk, market risk, and operational risk.

Headquartered in Philadelphia, RMA has 2,850 institutional members that include banks of all sizes as well as nonbank institutions. They are represented in the Association by 16,000 risk management professionals in North America and numerous cities overseas, including Hong Kong, Singapore, Melbourne, Sydney, and London.

RMA has taken a leadership role in providing industry input to regulators as they reform the Basel Capital Accord, first instituted in 1988. This input from RMA provides regulators with information about how the Accord's proposals would impact bank capital and overall operations.

RMA's strong relationship with members and regulators helps us develop new risk management techniques and innovative products. Our education and training programs are geared to risk management professionals at every stage of their careers. Over 70% of the Association's revenue is derived from providing products and services to members.

RMA ACKNOWLEDGES AND THANKS THE FOLLOWING MEMBER INSTITUTIONS, CONTRIBUTORS TO THE 2005 RECORD-BREAKING STATEMENT STUDIES DATA SUBMISSIONS PROGRAM.

ALABAMA
AmSouth Bank
Compass Bank
Regions Financial Corp.

ALASKA
Northrim Bank

ARIZONA
JPMorgan Chase AZ
Mohave State Bank
Northern Trust Bank of Arizona

ARKANSAS
Malvern National Bank
Metropolitan National Bank
Pulaski Bank & Trust Company
Simmons First National Bank

CALIFORNIA
Bank of Agriculture & Commerce
California Bank and Trust
Citizens Business Bank
City National Bank
Desert Community Bank
Exchange Bank
Farmers & Merchants Bank
   Central CA
First Commerce Bank
First National Bank
First Northern Bank of Dixon
Greater Bay Bancorp
Rabobank, N.A.
Sonoma National Bank
The Mechanics Bank
Tri Counties Bank
United Mizrahi Bank Ltd.
Valley Community Bank
Wells Fargo Bank N.A.
Westamerica Bank

COLORADO
American National Bank
Citywide Banks
CoBank
Collegiate Peaks Bank
Colorado Business Bank N.A.
First National Bank

CONNECTICUT
Chelsea Groton Savings Bank
Milford Bank
Naugatuck Savings Bank
Northwest Community Bank
People's Bank

DELAWARE
Delaware National Bank
Wilmington Trust Co.

FLORIDA
Bank of Tampa
Capital City Bank
City National Bank of Florida
First National Bank and Trust of the
   Treasure Coast
First Peoples Bank
SunTrust Banks, Inc.
United Bank & Trust Co.

GEORGIA
Athens First Bank & Trust Co.
Cohutta Banking Co.
Columbus Bank & Trust
First Bank of the South
Georgia Bank & Trust Co.
Heritage Bank
Riverside Bank
Security Bank of Bibb County

HAWAII
American Savings Bank
Bank of Hawaii, Credit & Risk
   Training
Central Pacific Bank
Finance Factors Ltd.
First Hawaiian Bank
Hawaii National Bank

IDAHO
Mountain West Bank

ILLINOIS
Albany Bank & Trust Co. N.A.
AMCORE Bank N.A.
America United Bank and Trust
   Company, USA
American National Bank DeKalb
   County

Busey Bank
Cole Taylor Bank
First National Bank of La Grange
First National Bank-Employee
   Owned
Glenview State Bank
Harris Trust & Savings Bank
JPMorgan Chase
LaSalle Bank N.A.
Main Street Bank & Trust
Northern Trust Company
Prairie Bank & Trust Company
The National Bank & Trust Company

INDIANA
1st Source Bank
Campbell & Fetter Bank
Irwin Union Bank & Trust Co.
Lafayette Bank & Trust Co.
Lake City Bank
STAR Financial Bank

IOWA
American Trust & Savings Bank
Farmers State Bank
Heartland Financial USA
Security National Bank
Wells Fargo Bank Iowa N.A.

KANSAS
Bankers Bank of Kansas
Central Bank & Trust Co.
Citizens National Bank
Cornerstone Bank
Emprise Bank
Fidelity Bank
First Bank
First National Bank of Hutchinson
First State Bank Kansas City
Intrust Bank
Legacy Bank
Midland National Bank
Sunflower Bank
Verus Bank N.A.

KENTUCKY
Central Bank & Trust Co.
Community Trust Bank, N.A.

LOUISIANA
Hibernia National Bank
Jeff Davis Bank & Trust Co.
Omni Bank
Progressive Bank
South Louisiana Bank
Whitney National Bank

MAINE
TD Banknorth, N.A.
First Citizens Bank
Gardiner Savings Institution FSB
Kennebunk Savings Bank
Norway Savings Bank
The First, N.A.

MARYLAND
Annapolis Banking & Trust Co.
Bank of Glen Burnie
Chevy Chase Bank FSB
Citizens National Bank
F&M Bank
Farmers & Mechanics Bank
Frederick County Bank
Hagerstown Trust Company
K Bank
Mercantile County Bank
Mercantile Potomac Bank
Peninsula Bank
Peoples Bank of Elkton
Provident Bank of Maryland
Queenstown Bank of Maryland
Westminster Union Bank

MASSACHUSETTS
Bank of Western Massachusetts
Beverly National Bank
Boston Private Bank & Trust Co.
Bristol County Savings Bank
Cape Cod Five Cents Savings Bank
Central Co-Operative Bank
Commerce Bank & Trust Company
Community Bank
Eastern Bank
Enterprise Bank and Trust Co.
Fall River Five Cents Savings Bank
Flagship Bank & Trust Company
Legacy Banks
North Middlesex Savings Bank
Randolph Savings Bank
Slade's Ferry Trust Co.
South Shore Savings Bank
Sovereign Bank
The Bank of Canton
The Milford National Bank and Trust

Webster Five Cents Savings Bank
Westbank
Westfield Bank
Winchester Savings Bank

MICHIGAN
Capitol National Bank
Citizens Bank
Citizens National Bank
Comerica Bank
Commercial Bank
CSB Bank
F&M Bank
Flagstar Bank, FSB
Honor State Bank
Huron Community Bank
Ionia County National Bank
Mercantile Bank of West Michigan
Republic Bank
Southern Michigan Bank & Trust
State Bank
United Bank & Trust
United Bank of Michigan

MINNESOTA
AgriBank FCB
American Bank of St. Paul
Anchor Bank Heritage
Anchor Bank Saint Paul
Beacon Bank
Bremer Bank National
  Association
Cherokee State Bank of St. Paul
Citizens Independent Bank
Community Bank Corp.
Community National Bank
Crown Bank
Excel Bank of Minnesota
First Minnetonka City Bank
Mainstreet Bank
Merchants Bank, N.A.
North Shore Bank of Commerce
Northeast Bank of Minneapolis
Roundbank
StearnsBank, N.A.
TCF National Bank
The Business Bank
US Bank National Association
Western Bank

MISSISSIPPI
BanCorp South Bank
Merchants & Farmers Bank
Renasant Bank
Trustmark National Bank

MISSOURI
Cass Commercial Bank
Central Bank of Lake of the Ozarks
Central Trust Bank
Commerce Bank N.A.
Empire Bank
Exchange National Bank Jeff City
First Bank
Jefferson Bank of Missouri
Midwest Bank Centre
UMB Bank N.A.
UMB Bank of St. Louis N.A.

MONTANA
American Bank
First Interstate Bank
Three Rivers Bank of Montana

NEBRASKA
First National Bank & Trust Co.
First National Bank of Omaha
Security National Bank Omaha
Union Bank & Trust Company
Washington County Bank

NEVADA
BankWest of Nevada

NEW HAMPSHIRE
Ledyard National Bank

NEW JERSEY
Allaire Community Bank
Commerce Bank N.A.
First Washington State Bank
Hudson United Bank
Peapack-Gladstone Bank
Skylands Community Bank
Somerset Valley Bank
Sun National Bank
The Bank
Two River Community Bank
Union Center National Bank
Yardville National Bank

NEW MEXICO
Charter Bank
Lea County State Bank

NEW YORK
Adirondack Bank N.A.
Adirondack Trust Company
Alliance Bank N.A.
Bank Leumi USA
Bank of Castile
Canandaigua National Bank
Champlain National Bank

Chemung Canal Trust Co.
Community Bank N.A.
Fulton Savings Bank
Glens Falls National Bank
HSBC Bank USA, National
   Association
National Union Bank of Kinderhook
NBT Bank N.A.
Partners Trust Bank
Saratoga National Bank
Steuben Trust Co.
Suffolk County National Bank
Tioga State Bank
Tompkins Trust Co.

NORTH CAROLINA
Bank of America
BB&T
Capital Bank
East Carolina Bank
First Charter Bank
First Citizens Bank & Trust Co.
Lexington State Bank

NORTH DAKOTA
Alerus Financial, N.A.
Bank of North Dakota
Bremer Bank, N.A.
State Bank & Trust

OHIO
Fifth Third Bank
Fifth Third Bank Northwestern OH
First Financial Bancorp
FirstMerit Bank, N.A.
Home Savings & Loan Co. of
   Youngstown
Huntington National Bank
Key Bank
Liberty Savings Bank FSB
National City Corp.
North Side Bank & Trust Co.
Second National Bank
Sky Bank
Unizan Bank

OKLAHOMA
Bank of Oklahoma N.A.
Stillwater National Bank

OREGON
Albina Community Bank
Pacific Continental Bank
West Coast Bank

PENNSYLVANIA
AmeriServ Bank

Blue Ball National Bank
Bryn Mawr Trust Co.
Clearfield Bank & Trust Co.
Commerce Bank/Harrisburg
Commercial Bank of Pennsylvania
Community Bank
Community Banks
County National Bank
Dollar Bank
East Penn Bank
Fidelity Bank PA SB
First Columbia Bank & Trust Co.
First Commonwealth Bank
First Federal Bank
First Liberty Bank & Trust
First National Bank Pennsylvania
First National Bank of Chester
   County
FNB Bank
Fulton Bank
Harleysville National Bank
Jersey Shore State Bank
Lafayette Ambassador Bank
Lebanon Valley Farmers Bank
Luzerne National Bank
Mellon Bank N.A.
National Penn Bank
Northwest Savings Bank
Orrstown Bank
Peoples Bank
PNC Bank
Portage National Bank
Premier Bank
Somerset Trust Company
Sterling Financial
Swineford National Bank
Univest National Bank & Trust Co.
Washington Federal Savings
West Milton State Bank
Woodlands Bank

RHODE ISLAND
Bank Rhode Island
Citizens Trust Company
Washington Trust Company

SOUTH CAROLINA
Bank of South Carolina
Carolina First Bank
Conway National Bank
First Citizens Bank
Geer State Bank

SOUTH DAKOTA
First Bank & Trust
First National Bank in Sioux Falls
First National Bank South Dakota

First Premier Bank
Home Federal Bank

TENNESSEE
Bank of Nashville
First Farmers and Merchants
   National Bank
First Tennessee Bank N.A.
INSOUTH Bank

TEXAS
Amarillo National Bank
Amegy Bank National Association
Bank of the West
Broadway National Bank
Extraco Banks N.A.
Frost National Bank
Partner's Bank of Texas
Southside Bank

UTAH
Bank of Utah
First Utah Bank
State Bank of Southern Utah
Zions First National Bank

VERMONT
Chittenden Bank
Community National Bank
Lyndonville Savings B&T Co.
Merchants Bank
National Bank of Middlebury

VIRGINIA
Bank of Lancaster
First National Bank
Freedom Bank of Virginia
Monarch Bank
Old Point National Bank
Virginia Commerce Bank
Virginia National Bank

WASHINGTON
Banner Bank
City Bank
Columbia Bank
Evergreen Bank
First Heritage Bank Snohomish
Northwest Farm Credit Services
   (ACA)
Pacifica Bank
Security State Bank
Washington First International Bank
Washington Mutual
Washington Trust Bank
Whidbey Island Bank

WEST VIRGINIA
First Century Bank N.A.
Progressive Bank N.A.
United Bank

WISCONSIN
Anchor Bank, FSB
Associated Bank Green Bay N.A.
Bank of Elmwood
Community Business Bank
Coulee State Bank

Fidelity National Bank
First Bank Financial Centre
First Bank of Baldwin
First National Bank & Trust
First National Bank Fox Valley
First National Bank of Hudson
Grafton State Bank c/o Merchants & Manufacturers Bancorp
Horicon State Bank
M&I Bank
M&I Marshall & Ilsley Bank

Park Bank
Southport Bank
St. Francis Bank
State Financial Bank
TCF National Bank
The Business Bank of the Fox River Valley

WYOMING
Jackson State Bank

Introduction to
Annual Statement Studies: Financial Ratio Benchmarks, 2005-2006
and
General Organization of Content

The notes below will explain the presentation of *Annual Statement Studies: Financial Ratio Benchmarks,* show clearly how the book is organized, and answer most of your questions.

- **The Quality You Expect from The Risk Management Association (RMA):** RMA is the most respected source of objective, unbiased information on issues of importance to credit risk professionals. For over 85 years, RMA's *Annual Statement Studies®* has been the industry standard for comparison financial data. Material contained in today's *Annual Statement Studies®* was first published in the March 1919 issue of the *Federal Reserve Bulletin.* In the days before computers, the *Annual Statement Studies®* data was recorded in pencil on yellow ledger paper! Today, it features data for over 710 industries derived <u>directly</u> from more 190,000 statements of financial institutions' borrowers and prospects.

- **Data That Comes Straight from Its Source:** The more than 190,000 statements used to produce the composites presented here come directly from RMA member institutions and represent the financials from their commercial customers and prospects. RMA does not know the names of the individual entities. In fact, to ensure confidentiality, company names are removed before the data is even delivered to RMA. The raw data making up each composite is not available to any third party.

- **Data Presented in Common Size:** *The Annual Statement Studies: Financial Ratio Benchmarks* contains composite financial data. Balance sheet and income statement information is shown in common size format, with each item a percentage of total assets and sales. RMA computes common size statements for each individual statement in an industry group, and then aggregates and averages all the figures. In some cases, because of computer rounding, the figures to the right of the decimal point do not balance exactly with the totals shown. A minus sign beside the value indicates credits and losses.

- **Most Widely Used Ratios Included:** Nineteen of the most widely used ratios in the financial services industry accompany the balance sheet information, including various types of liquidity, coverage, leverage, and operating ratios.

- **Organized by the NAICS for Ease of Use:** This edition is organized according to the North American Industry Classification System (NAICS), a product of the U.S. Office of Management and Budget. At the top of each page of data, you will find both the NAICS with cross-references to the Standard Industrial Classification (SIC) codes. An NAICS code may correspond to more than one SIC, so there may be several SICs listed. If an NAICS code maps to more than three SIC codes, only the first three SICs will be listed at the top of the page, with all corresponding SIC codes found in the NAICS description index.

- **Twenty Sections Outline Major Types of Businesses:** To provide further delineation, the book is divided into 20 sections outlining major lines of businesses. If you know the NAICS number you are looking for, use the NAICS-page guide provided in the front of this book. If you know the SIC number you are looking for, refer to the SIC-page guide also provided in the front of the book. In general, the book is arranged in ascending NAICS numerical order. For your convenience, full descriptions of each NAICS are presented in this book. In addition, you will find a text-based index near the end of the book.

- **If You Do Not Know the NAICS or SIC Code You Are Looking for...** If you do not know the precise industry NAICS/SIC you are looking for, contact the Census Bureau at 1-888-75NAICS or naics@census.gov. Describe the activity of the establishment for which you need an industry code and you will receive a reply. Another source to help you assign the correct NAICS/SIC industry name and number can be found at www.census.gov/epcd/www/naics.html.

- **Can't Find the Industry You Want?** There are a number of reasons you may not find the industry you are looking for (i.e., you know you need industry xxxxxx but it is not in the product). Many times we have information on an industry, but it is not published because the sample size was too small or there were significant questions concerning the data.** In other instances, we simply do not have the data. Generally, most of what we receive is published.

**For an industry to be displayed in the *Annual Statement Studies: Financial Ratio Benchmarks,* there must be at least 30 valid statements submitted to RMA.

- **Composite Data Not Shown?** When there are fewer than 10 financial statements in a particular asset or sales size category, the composite data is not shown because a sample this small is not considered representative and could be misleading. However, all the data for that industry is shown in the All Sizes column. The total number of statements for each size category is shown in bold print at the top of each column. In addition, the number of statements used in a ratio array will differ from the number of statements in a sample because certain elements of data may not be present in all financial statements. In these cases, the number of statements used is shown in parentheses to the left of the array.

• **Presentation of the Data on Each Page Spread:** For all non-contracting spread statements, the data for a particular industry appears on both the left and right pages. The heading Current Data Sorted by Assets is in the five columns on the left side. The center section of the double-page presentation contains the Comparative Historical Data, with the All Sizes column for the current year shown under the heading 4/1/xx-3/31/xx. Comparable data from past editions of the *Annual Statement Studies: Financial Ratio Benchmarks* also appears in this section. Current Data Sorted by Sales is displayed in the five columns to the far right.

• **Companies with Less than $250 Million in Total Assets:** In our presentation, we used companies having less than $250 million in total assets—except in the case of contractors who use the percentage-of-completion method of accounting. *The section for contractors using the percentage-of-completion method of accounting contains data only sorted by revenue.* There is no upper limit placed on revenue size for any industry. Its information is found on only one page.

• **Page Headers:** The information shown at the top of each page includes the following: 1) the identity of the industry group; 2) its North American Industry Classification System (NAICS) number and its Standard Industrial Classification (SIC) number; 3) a breakdown by size categories of the types of financial statements reported; 4) the number of statements in each category; 5) the dates of the statements used; and 6) the size categories. For instance, 16 (4/1-9/30/03) means that 16 statements with fiscal dates between April 1 and September 30, 2003, make up part of the sample.

• **Page Footers:** At the bottom of each page, we have included the sum of the sales (or revenues) and total assets for all the financial statements in each size category. This data allows recasting of the common-size statements into dollar amounts. To do this, divide the number at the bottom of the page by the number of statements in that size category. Then multiply the result by the percentages in the common-size statement.

• **Our Thanks to CFMA:** RMA appreciates the cooperation of the Construction Financial Management Association (CFMA) in permitting us to reproduce excerpts from its *Construction Industry Annual Financial Survey*. This data complements the RMA contractor industry data.

• **Recommended for Use as General Guidelines:** RMA recommends you use *Annual Statement Studies: Financial Ratio Benchmarks* data only as general guidelines and not as absolute industry norms. There are several reasons why the data may not be fully representative of a given industry:

1. **Data Not Random**—The financial statements used in the *Annual Statement Studies: Financial Ratio Benchmarks* are not selected by any random or statistically reliable method. RMA member banks voluntarily submit the raw data they have available each year with no limitation on company size.

2. **Categorized by Primary Product Only**—Many companies have varied product lines; however, the *Annual Statement Studies: Financial Ratio Benchmarks* categorizes them by their primary product NAICS/SIC number only.

3. **Small Samples**—Some of the industry samples are small in relation to the total number of firms for a given industry. A relatively small sample can increase the chances that some composites do not fully represent an industry.

4. **Extreme Statements**—An extreme or outlier statement can occasionally be present in a sample, causing a disproportionate influence on the industry composite. This is particularly true in a relatively small sample.

5. **Operational Differences**—Companies within the same industry may differ in their method of operations, which in turn can directly influence their financial statements. Since they are included in the sample, these statements can significantly affect the composite calculations.

6. **Additional Considerations**—There are other considerations that can result in variations among different companies engaged in the same general line of business. These include different labor markets, geographical location, different accounting methods, quality of products handled, sources and methods of financing, and terms of sale.

For these reasons, RMA does not recommend using the *Annual Statement Studies: Financial Ratio Benchmarks* figures as absolute norms for a given industry. Rather, you should use the figures only as general guidelines and as a supplement to the other methods of financial analysis. RMA makes no claim regarding how representative the figures printed in this book are.

DEFINITION OF RATIOS
INTRODUCTION

Below the common size balance sheet and income statement information presented on each data page, you will find a series of ratios—computed from the financial statement data.

Here is how these figures are calculated for any given ratio...

1. The ratio is computed for each financial statement in the sample.

2. Next, these values are arrayed (listed) in an order from the strongest to the weakest. In interpreting ratios, the "strongest" or "best" value is not always the largest numerical value, nor is the "weakest" always the lowest numerical value. (For certain ratios, there may be differences of opinion concerning what is a strong or a weak value. RMA follows general banking guidelines consistent with sound credit practice to resolve this problem.)

3. Finally, the array of values is divided into four groups of equal size. The description of each ratio appearing in the *Statement Studies* provides details regarding the arraying of the values.

What Are Quartiles?

Each ratio has three points or "cut-off values" that divide an array of values into four equal-sized groups called quartiles as shown below. The quartiles include the upper quartile, upper middle quartile, lower middle quartile, and the lower quartile. The upper quartile is the cut-off value where one-quarter of the array of ratios falls between it and the strongest ratio. The median is the mid-point; that is, the middle cut-off value where half of the array falls above it and half below it. The lower quartile is the point where one-quarter of the array falls between it and the weakest ratio. In many cases, the average of two values is used to arrive at the quartile value. You will find the median and quartile values on all Statement Studies data pages in the order indicated in the chart provided below.

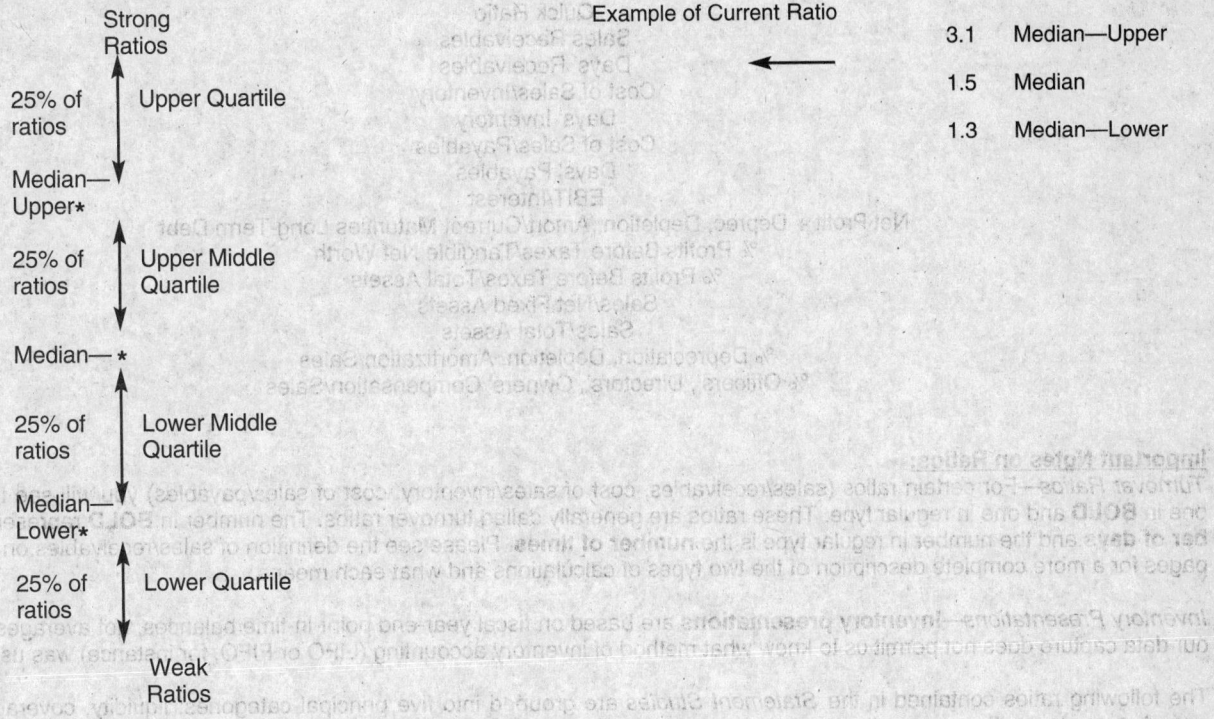

Why Use Medians/Quartiles Instead of the Average?

There are several reasons medians and quartiles are used instead of an average. Medians and quartiles eliminate the influence an "outlier" (or an extremely high or low value when compared to the rest of the values) would have. They also reflect more accurately the ranges of ratio values than a straight averaging method.

It is important to understand that the spread (range) between the upper and lower quartiles represents the middle 50% of all the companies in a sample. Therefore, ratio values greater than the upper quartile or less than the lower quartile may begin to approach "unusual" values.

Non-Conventional Values:

For some ratio values, you will occasionally see an entry that is other than a conventional number. These entries are defined as follows:

(1) <u>UND</u>—This stands for "undefined," the result of the denominator in a ratio calculation approaching zero.

(2) <u>NM</u>—This may occasionally appear as a quartile or median for the ratios sales/working capital, debt/worth, and fixed/worth. It stands for "no meaning" in cases where the dispersion is so small that any interpretation is meaningless.

(3) <u>999.8</u>—When a ratio value equals 1,000 or more, it also becomes an "unusual" value and is given the "999.8" designation. This is considered to be a close enough approximation to the actual unusually large value.

Linear versus Non-Linear Ratios:

An array that is ordered from highest positive to the highest negative is linear. An array that is NOT ordered from highest positive to highest negative is *non-linear*. The ratio values could be arrayed from the lowest positive to the highest positive, to undefined (UND), and then from the highest negative to the lowest negative.

A specific example of a non-linear ratio would be the Sales/Working Capital ratio. In other words, when the Sales/Working Capital ratio is positive, then the top quartile would be represented by the *lowest positive* ratio. However, if the ratio is negative, the top quartile will be represented by the *highest negative* ratio! In a non-linear array such as this, the median could be either positive or negative because it is whatever the middle value is in the particular array of numbers.

Non-Linear Ratios

Sales/Working Capital
Fixed/Worth
Debt/Worth

Linear Ratios

Current Ratio
Quick Ratio
Sales Receivables
Days' Receivables
Cost of Sales/Inventory
Days' Inventory
Cost of Sales/Payables
Days' Payables
EBIT/Interest
Net Profit + Deprec, Depletion, Amort/Current Maturities Long-Term Debt
% Profits Before Taxes/Tangible Net Worth
% Profits Before Taxes/Total Assets
Sales/Net Fixed Assets
Sales/Total Assets
% Depreciation, Depletion, Amortization/Sales
% Officers', Directors', Owners' Compensation/Sales

Important Notes on Ratios:

Turnover Ratios—For certain ratios (sales/receivables, cost of sales/inventory, cost of sales/payables) you will see two numbers, one in **BOLD** and one in regular type. These ratios are generally called turnover ratios. The number in **BOLD** represents **the number of days** and the number in regular type is the **number of times**. Please see the definition of sales/receivables on the following pages for a more complete description of the two types of calculations and what each means.

Inventory Presentations—**Inventory presentations** are based on fiscal year-end point-in-time balances, not averages. In addition, our data capture does not permit us to know what method of inventory accounting (LIFO or FIFO, for instance) was used.

The following ratios contained in the *Statement Studies* are grouped into five principal categories: liquidity, coverage, leverage, operating, and specific expense items.

LIQUIDITY RATIOS

Liquidity is a measure of the quality and adequacy of current assets to meet current obligations as they come due. In other words, can a firm quickly convert its assets to cash - without a loss in value - in order to meet its immediate and short-term obligations? For firms such as utilities that can readily and accurately predict their cash inflows, liquidity is not nearly as critical as it is for firms like airlines or manufacturing businesses that can have wide fluctuations in demand and revenue streams. These ratios provide a level of comfort to lenders in case of liquidation.

1. Current Ratio

How to Calculate: Divide total current assets by total current liabilities.

$$\frac{\text{Total Current Assets}}{\text{Total Current Liabilities}}$$

How to Interpret: This ratio is a rough indication of a firm's ability to service its current obligations. Generally, the higher the current ratio, the greater the "cushion" between current obligations and a firm's ability to pay them. While a stronger ratio shows that the numbers for current assets exceed those for current liabilities, the composition and quality of current assets are critical factors in the analysis of an individual firm's liquidity.

The ratio values are arrayed from the highest positive to the lowest positive.

2. Quick Ratio

How to Calculate: Add cash and equivalents to trade receivables. Then, divide by total current liabilities.

$$\frac{\text{Cash \& Equivalents + Trade Receivables – (net)}}{\text{Total Current Liabilities}}$$

How to Interpret: Also known as the "acid test" ratio, this is a stricter, more conservative measure of liquidity than the current ratio. This ratio reflects the degree to which a company's current liabilities are covered by its most liquid current assets, the kind of assets that can be converted quickly to cash and at amounts close to book value. Inventory and other less liquid current assets are removed from the calculation. Generally, if the ratio produces a value that's less than 1 to 1, it implies a "dependency" on inventory or other "less" current assets to liquidate short-term debt.

The ratio values are arrayed from the highest positive to the lowest positive.

3. Sales/Receivables

How to Calculate: Divide net sales by trade receivables.

$$\frac{\text{Net Sales}}{\text{Trade Receivables (net)}}$$

Please note—In the contractor section, both accounts receivable-progress billings and accounts receivable-current retention are included in the receivables figure used in calculating the revenues/receivables and receivables/payables ratios.

How to Interpret: This ratio measures the number of times trade receivables turn over during the year. The higher the turnover of receivables, the shorter the time between sale and cash collection.

> For example, a company with sales of $720,000 and receivables of $120,000 would have a sales/receivables ratio of 6.0. This means receivables turn over six times a year. If a company's receivables appear to be turning more slowly than the rest of the industry, further research is needed and the quality of the receivables should be examined closely.

Cautions—A problem with this ratio is that it compares one day's receivables, shown at statement date, to total annual sales and does not take into consideration seasonal fluctuations. An additional problem in interpretation may arise when there is a large proportion of cash sales to total sales.

When the receivables figure is zero, the quotient will be undefined (UND) and represents the best possible ratio. The ratio values are therefore arrayed starting with undefined (UND) and then from the numerically highest value to the numerically lowest value. The only time a zero will appear in the array is when the sales figure is low and the quotient rounds off to zero. By definition, this ratio cannot be negative.

4. Days' Receivables

The sales/receivables ratio will have a figure printed in bold type directly to the left of the array. This figure is the days' receivables.

How to Calculate the Days' Receivables: Divide the sales/receivables ratio into 365 (the number of days in one year).

$$\frac{365}{\text{Sales/Receivable ratio}}$$

How to Interpret the Days' Receivables: This figure expresses the average number of days that receivables are outstanding. Generally, the greater number of days outstanding, the greater the probability of delinquencies in accounts receivable. A comparison of a company's daily receivables may indicate the extent of a company's control over credit and collections.

Please note—You should take into consideration the terms offered by a company to its customers because these may differ from terms within the industry.

For example, using the sales/receivable ratio calculated above, 365 ÷ 6 = 61 (i.e., the average receivable is collected in 61 days).

5. Cost of Sales/Inventory

How to Calculate: Divide cost of sales by inventory.

$$\frac{\text{Cost of Sales}}{\text{Inventory}}$$

How to Interpret: This ratio measures the number of times inventory is turned over during the year.

High Inventory Turnover—On the positive side, high inventory turnover can indicate greater liquidity or superior merchandising. Conversely, it can indicate a shortage of needed inventory for sales.

Low Inventory Turnover—Low inventory turnover can indicate poor liquidity, possible overstocking, or obsolescence. On the positive side, it could indicate a planned inventory buildup in the case of material shortages.

Cautions—A problem with this ratio is that it compares one day's inventory to cost of goods sold and does not take seasonal fluctuations into account. When the inventory figure is zero, the quotient will be undefined (UND) and represents the best possible ratio. The ratio values are arrayed starting with undefined (UND) and then from the numerically highest value to the numerically lowest value. The only time a zero will appear in the array is when the figure for cost of sales is very low and the quotient rounds off to zero.

Please note—For service industries, the cost of sales is included in operating expenses. In addition, please note that the data collection process does not differentiate the method of inventory valuation.

6. Days' Inventory

The days' inventory is the figure printed in bold directly to the left of the cost of sales/inventory ratio.

How to Calculate the Days' Inventory: Divide the cost of sales/inventory ratio into 365 (the number of days in one year).

$$\frac{365}{\text{Cost of Sales/Inventory ratio}}$$

How to Interpret: Division of the inventory turnover ratio into 365 days yields the average length of time units are in inventory.

7. Cost of Sales/Payables

How to Calculate: Divide cost of sales by trade payables.

$$\frac{\text{Cost of Sales}}{\text{Trade Payables}}$$

Please note—In the contractor section, both Accounts Payable-Trade and Accounts Payable-Retention are included in the payables figure used in calculating the Cost of Revenues/Payables and Receivables/Payables ratios.

How to Interpret: This ratio measures the number of times trade payables turn over during the year. The higher the turnover of payables, the shorter the time between purchase and payment. If a company's payables appear to be turning more slowly than the industry, then the company may be experiencing cash shortages, disputing invoices with suppliers, enjoying extended terms, or deliberately expanding its trade credit. The ratio comparison of company to industry suggests the existence of these or other possible causes. If a firm buys on 30-day terms, it is reasonable to expect this ratio to turn over in approximately 30 days.

Cautions—A problem with this ratio is that it compares one day's payables to cost of goods sold and does not take seasonal fluctuations into account. When the payables figure is zero, the quotient will be undefined (UND) and represents the best possible ratio. The ratio values are arrayed starting with undefined (UND) and then from the numerically highest to the numerically lowest value. The only time a zero will appear in the array is when the figure for cost of sales is very low and the quotient rounds off to zero.

8. Days' Payables

The days' payables is the figure printed in bold type directly to the left of the cost of sales/payables ratio.

How to Calculate the Days' Payables: Divide the cost of sales/payables ratio into 365 (the number of days in one year).

$$\frac{365}{\text{Cost of Sales/Payables ratio}}$$

How to Interpret: Division of the payables turnover ratio into 365 days yields the average length of time trade debt is outstanding.

9. Sales/Working Capital

How to Calculate: Divide net sales by net working capital (current assets less current liabilities equals net working capital).

$$\frac{\text{Net Sales}}{\text{Net Working Capital}}$$

How to Interpret: Because it reflects the ability to finance current operations, working capital is a measure of the margin of protection for current creditors. When you relate the level of sales resulting from operations to the underlying working capital, you can measure how efficiently working capital is being used.

Low ratio (close to zero)—A low ratio may indicate an inefficient use of working capital.

High ratio (high positive or high negative)—A very high ratio often signifies overtrading, which is a vulnerable position for creditors.

Please note—Sales/Working Capital ratio is a non-linear array. In other words, an array that is NOT ordered from highest positive to highest negative as is the case for linear arrays. The ratio values are arrayed from the lowest positive to the highest positive, to undefined (UND), and then from the highest negative to the lowest negative. If working capital is zero, the quotient is undefined (UND).

If the Sales/Working Capital ratio is positive, then the top quartile would be represented by the *lowest positive* ratio. However, if the ratio is negative, the top quartile will be represented by the *highest negative* ratio! In a non-linear array such as the Sales/Working Capital ratio, the median could be either positive or negative because it is whatever the middle value is in the particular array of numbers.

Cautions—When analyzing this ratio, you need to focus on working capital, not on the sales figure. Although sales cannot be negative, working capital can be. If you have a large, positive working capital number, the ratio will be small and positive—which is good. Because negative working capital is bad, if you have a large, negative working capital number, the Sales/Working Capital ratio will be small and negative—which is NOT good. Therefore, the lowest positive ratio is the best and the lowest negative ratio, the worst. If working capital is a small negative number, the ratio will be large, which is the best of the negatives.

COVERAGE RATIOS

Coverage ratios measure a firm's ability to service its debt. In other words, how well does the flow of a company's funds cover its short-term financial obligations? In contrast to liquidity ratios that focus on the possibility of liquidation, coverage ratios seek to provide lenders a comfort level based on the belief the firm will remain a viable enterprise.

1. Earnings Before Interest and Taxes (EBIT)/Interest

How to Calculate: Divide earnings (profit) before annual interest expense and taxes by annual interest expense.

$$\frac{\text{Earnings Before Interest \& Taxes}}{\text{Annual Interest Expense}}$$

How to Interpret: This ratio measures a firm's ability to meet interest payments. A high ratio may indicate that a borrower can easily meet the interest obligations of a loan. This ratio also indicates a firm's capacity to take on additional debt.

Please note—Only statements reporting annual interest expense were used in the calculation of this ratio. The ratio values are arrayed from the highest positive to the lowest positive and then from the lowest negative to the highest negative.

2. Net Profit + Depreciation, Depletion, Amortization/Current Maturities Long-Term Debt

How to Calculate: Add net profit to depreciation, depletion, and amortization expenses. Then, divide by the current portion of long-term debt.

$$\frac{\text{Net Profit} + \text{Depreciation, Depletion, Amortization Expenses}}{\text{Current Portion of Long-Term Debt}}$$

How to Interpret: This ratio reflects how well cash flow from operations covers current maturities. Because cash flow is the primary source of debt retirement, the ratio measures a firm's ability to service principal repayment and take on additional debt. Even though it is a mistake to believe all cash flow is available for debt service, this ratio is still a valid measure of the ability to service long-term debt.

Please note—Only data for corporations with the following items was used:

(1) Profit or loss after taxes (positive, negative, or zero).

(2) A positive figure for depreciation/depletion/amortization expenses.

(3) A positive figure for current maturities of long-term debt.

Ratio values are arrayed from the highest to the lowest positive and then from the lowest to the highest negative.

LEVERAGE RATIOS

How much protection does a company's assets provide for the debt held by its creditors? Highly leveraged firms are companies with heavy debt in relation to their net worth. These firms are more vulnerable to business downturns than those with lower debt-to-worth positions. While leverage ratios help measure this vulnerability, keep in mind that these ratios vary greatly depending on the requirements of particular industry groups.

1. Fixed/Worth

How to Calculate: Divide fixed assets (net of accumulated depreciation) by tangible net worth (net worth minus intangibles).

$$\frac{\text{Net Fixed Assets}}{\text{Tangible Net Worth}}$$

How to Interpret: This ratio measures the extent to which owner's equity (capital) has been invested in plant and equipment (fixed assets). A lower ratio indicates a proportionately smaller investment in fixed assets in relation to net worth and a better "cushion" for creditors in case of liquidation. Similarly, a higher ratio would indicate the opposite situation. The presence of a substantial number of fixed assets that are leased - and not appearing on the balance sheet - may result in a deceptively lower ratio.

Fixed assets may be zero, in which case the quotient is zero. If tangible net worth is zero, the quotient is undefined (UND). If tangible net worth is negative, the quotient is negative.

Please note—Like the Sales/Working Capital ratio discussed above, this Fixed/Worth ratio is a non-linear array. In other words, an array that is NOT ordered from highest positive to highest negative as is the case for linear arrays. The ratio values are arrayed from the lowest positive to the highest positive, to undefined (UND), and then from the highest negative to the lowest negative.

If the Fixed/Worth ratio is positive, then the top quartile would be represented by the *lowest positive* ratio. However, if the ratio is negative, the top quartile will be represented by the *highest negative* ratio! In a non-linear array such as this, the median could be either positive or negative because it is whatever the middle value is in the particular array of numbers.

2. Debt/Worth

How to Calculate: Divide total liabilities by tangible net worth.

$$\frac{\text{Total Liabilities}}{\text{Tangible Net Worth}}$$

How to Interpret: This ratio expresses the relationship between capital contributed by creditors and that contributed by owners. Basically, it shows how much protection the owners are providing creditors. The higher the ratio, the greater the risk being assumed by creditors. A lower ratio generally indicates greater long-term financial safety. Unlike a highly leveraged firm, a firm with a low debt/worth ratio usually has greater flexibility to borrow in the future.

Tangible net worth may be zero, in which case the ratio is undefined (UND). Tangible net worth may also be negative, which results in the quotient being negative. The ratio values are arrayed from the lowest to highest positive, undefined, and then from the highest to lowest negative.

Please note—Like the Sales/Working Capital ratio discussed above, this Debt/Worth ratio is a non-linear array. In other words, an array that is NOT ordered from highest positive to highest negative as is the case for linear arrays. The ratio values are arrayed from the lowest positive to the highest positive, to undefined (UND), and then from the highest negative to the lowest negative.

If the Debt/Worth ratio is positive, then the top quartile would be represented by the *lowest positive* ratio. However, if the ratio is negative, the top quartile will be represented by the *highest negative* ratio! In a non-linear array such as this, the median could be either positive or negative because it is whatever the middle value is in the particular array of numbers.

OPERATING RATIOS

Operating ratios are designed to assist in the evaluation of management performance.

1. % Profits Before Taxes/Tangible Net Worth

How to Calculate: Divide profit before taxes by tangible net worth. Then, multiply by 100.

$$\frac{\text{Profit Before Taxes}}{\text{Tangible Net Worth}} \times 100$$

How to Interpret: This ratio expresses the rate of return on tangible capital employed. While it can serve as an indicator of management performance, you should always use it in conjunction with other ratios. Normally associated with effective management, a high return could actually point to an undercapitalized firm. Conversely, a low return that's usually viewed as an indicator of inefficient management performance could actually reflect a highly capitalized, conservatively operated business.

This ratio has been multiplied by 100 because it is shown as a percentage.

Profit before taxes may be zero, in which case the ratio is zero. Profits before taxes may be negative, resulting in negative quotients. Firms with negative tangible net worth have been omitted from the ratio arrays. Negative ratios will therefore only result in the case of negative profit before taxes. If the tangible net worth is zero, the quotient is undefined (UND). If there are fewer than 10 ratios for a particular size class, the result is not shown. The ratio values are arrayed starting with undefined (UND), then from the highest to the lowest positive values, and finally from the lowest to the highest negative values.

2. % Profits Before Taxes/Total Assets

How to Calculate: Divide profit before taxes by total assets and multiply by 100.

$$\frac{\text{Profit Before Taxes}}{\text{Total Assets}} \times 100$$

How to Interpret: This ratio expresses the pre-tax return on total assets and measures the effectiveness of management in employing the resources available to it. If a specific ratio varies considerably from the ranges found in this book, the analyst will need to examine the makeup of the assets and take a closer look at the earnings figure. A heavily depreciated plant and a large amount of intangible assets or unusual income or expense items will cause distortions of this ratio.

This ratio has been multiplied by 100 since it is shown as a percentage. If profit before taxes is zero, the quotient is zero. If profit before taxes is negative, the quotient is negative. These ratio values are arrayed from the highest to the lowest positive and then from the lowest to the highest negative.

3. Sales/Net Fixed Assets

How to Calculate: Divide net sales by net fixed assets (net of accumulated depreciation).

$$\frac{\text{Net Sales}}{\text{Net Fixed Assets}}$$

How to Interpret: This ratio is a measure of the productive use of a firm's fixed assets. Largely depreciated fixed assets or a labor-intensive operation may cause a distortion of this ratio.

If the net fixed figure is zero, the quotient is undefined (UND). The only time a zero will appear in the array will be when the net sales figure is low and the quotient rounds off to zero. These ratio values cannot be negative.

They are arrayed from undefined (UND) and then from the highest to the lowest positive values.

4. Sales/Total Assets

How to Calculate: Divide net sales by total assets.

$$\frac{\text{Net Sales}}{\text{Total Assets}}$$

How to Interpret: This ratio is a general measure of a firm's ability to generate sales in relation to total assets. It should be used only to compare firms within specific industry groups and in conjunction with other operating ratios to determine the effective employment of assets.

The only time a zero will appear in the array will be when the net sales figure is low and the quotient rounds off to zero. The ratio values cannot be negative. They are arrayed from the highest to the lowest positive values.

EXPENSE TO SALES RATIOS

The following two ratios relate specific expense items to net sales and express this relationship as a percentage. Comparisons are convenient because the item, net sales, is used as a constant. Variations in these ratios are most pronounced between capital- and labor-intensive industries.

1. % Depreciation, Depletion, Amortization/Sales

How to Calculate: Divide annual depreciation, amortization, and depletion expenses by net sales and multiply by 100.

$$\frac{\text{Depreciation, Amortization, Depletion Expenses}}{\text{Net Sales}} \times 100$$

2. % Officers', Directors', Owners' Compensation/Sales

How to Calculate: Divide annual officers', directors', owners' compensation by net sales and multiply by 100. Include total salaries, bonuses, commissions, and other monetary remuneration to all officers, directors, and/or owners of the firm during the year covered by the statement. This includes drawings of partners and proprietors.

$$\frac{\text{Officers', Directors', Owners' Compensation}}{\text{Net Sales}} \times 100$$

Only statements showing a positive figure for each of the expense categories shown above were used. The ratios are arrayed from the lowest to highest positive values.

Explanation of Noncontractor Balance Sheet and Income Data

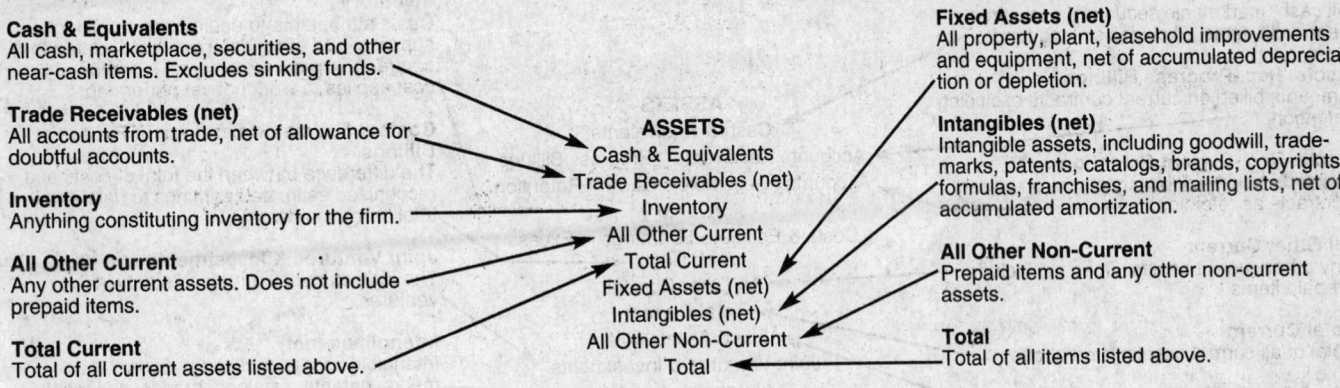

Cash & Equivalents
All cash, marketplace, securities, and other near-cash items. Excludes sinking funds.

Trade Receivables (net)
All accounts from trade, net of allowance for doubtful accounts.

Inventory
Anything constituting inventory for the firm.

All Other Current
Any other current assets. Does not include prepaid items.

Total Current
Total of all current assets listed above.

Fixed Assets (net)
All property, plant, leasehold improvements and equipment, net of accumulated depreciation or depletion.

Intangibles (net)
Intangible assets, including goodwill, trademarks, patents, catalogs, brands, copyrights, formulas, franchises, and mailing lists, net of accumulated amortization.

All Other Non-Current
Prepaid items and any other non-current assets.

Total
Total of all items listed above.

ASSETS
Cash & Equivalents
Trade Receivables (net)
Inventory
All Other Current
Total Current
Fixed Assets (net)
Intangibles (net)
All Other Non-Current
Total

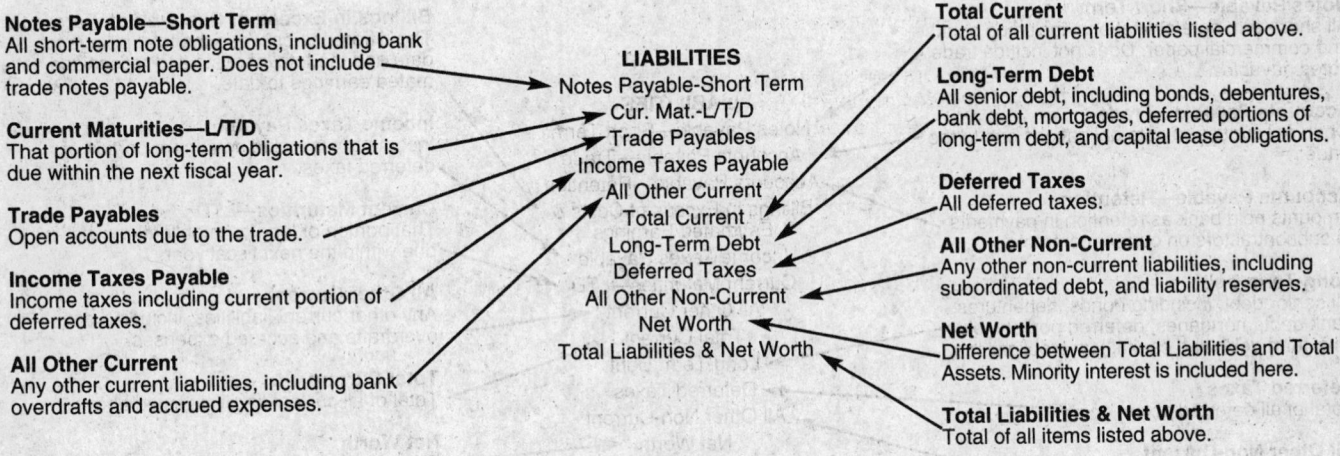

Notes Payable—Short Term
All short-term note obligations, including bank and commercial paper. Does not include trade notes payable.

Current Maturities—L/T/D
That portion of long-term obligations that is due within the next fiscal year.

Trade Payables
Open accounts due to the trade.

Income Taxes Payable
Income taxes including current portion of deferred taxes.

All Other Current
Any other current liabilities, including bank overdrafts and accrued expenses.

Total Current
Total of all current liabilities listed above.

Long-Term Debt
All senior debt, including bonds, debentures, bank debt, mortgages, deferred portions of long-term debt, and capital lease obligations.

Deferred Taxes
All deferred taxes.

All Other Non-Current
Any other non-current liabilities, including subordinated debt, and liability reserves.

Net Worth
Difference between Total Liabilities and Total Assets. Minority interest is included here.

Total Liabilities & Net Worth
Total of all items listed above.

LIABILITIES
Notes Payable-Short Term
Cur. Mat.-L/T/D
Trade Payables
Income Taxes Payable
All Other Current
Total Current
Long-Term Debt
Deferred Taxes
All Other Non-Current
Net Worth
Total Liabilities & Net Worth

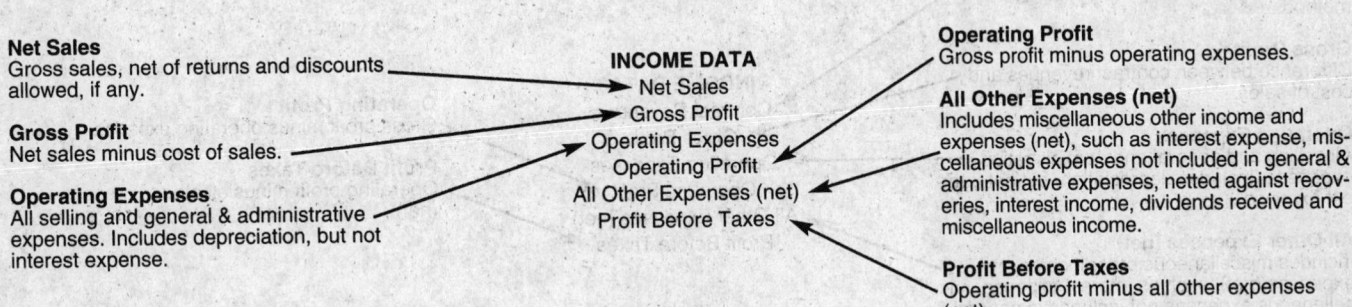

Net Sales
Gross sales, net of returns and discounts allowed, if any.

Gross Profit
Net sales minus cost of sales.

Operating Expenses
All selling and general & administrative expenses. Includes depreciation, but not interest expense.

Operating Profit
Gross profit minus operating expenses.

All Other Expenses (net)
Includes miscellaneous other income and expenses (net), such as interest expense, miscellaneous expenses not included in general & administrative expenses, netted against recoveries, interest income, dividends received and miscellaneous income.

Profit Before Taxes
Operating profit minus all other expenses (net).

INCOME DATA
Net Sales
Gross Profit
Operating Expenses
Operating Profit
All Other Expenses (net)
Profit Before Taxes

Explanation of Contractor Percentage-of-Completion Basis of Accounting
Balance Sheet and Income Data

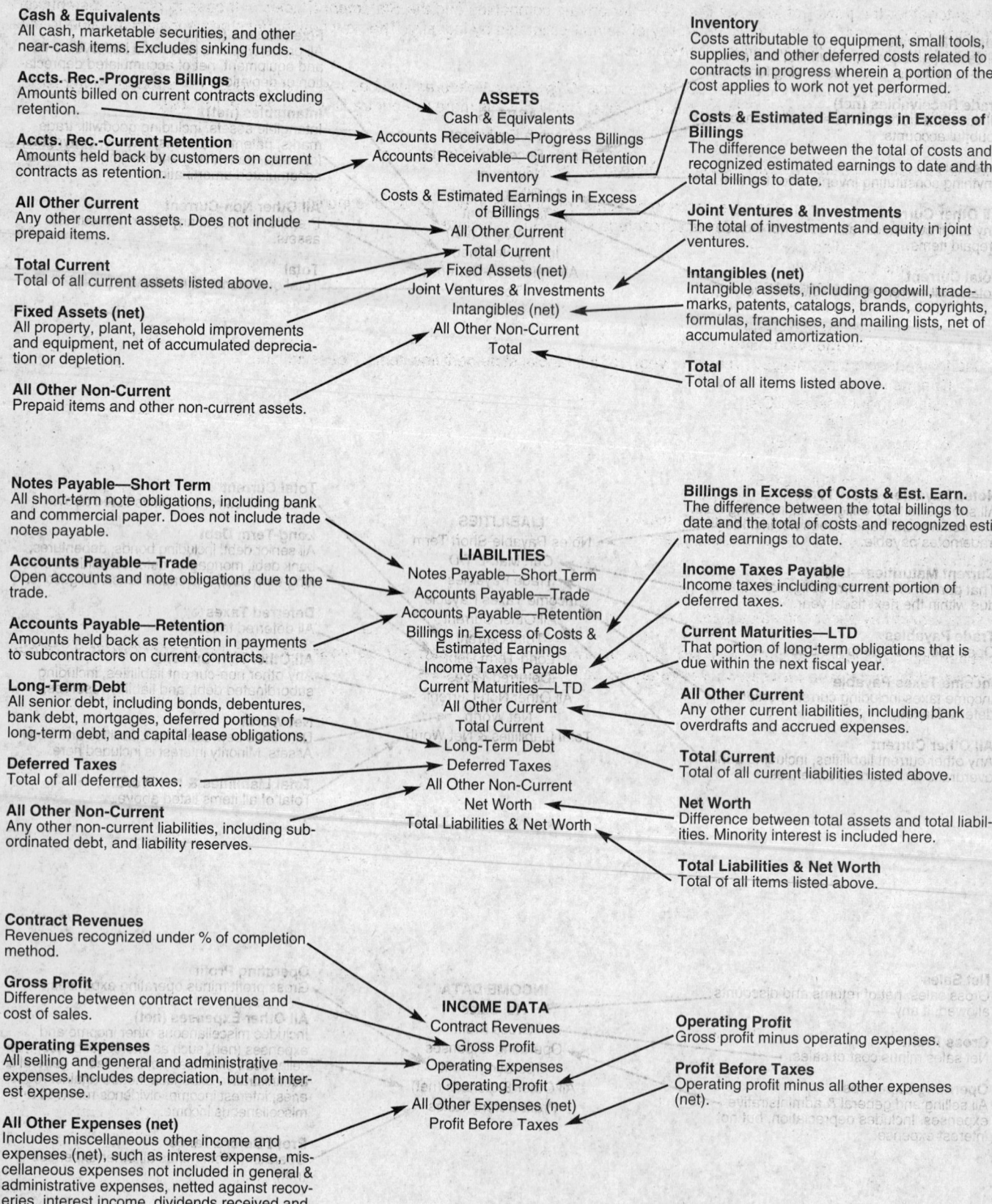

Cash & Equivalents
All cash, marketable securities, and other near-cash items. Excludes sinking funds.

Accts. Rec.-Progress Billings
Amounts billed on current contracts excluding retention.

Accts. Rec.-Current Retention
Amounts held back by customers on current contracts as retention.

All Other Current
Any other current assets. Does not include prepaid items.

Total Current
Total of all current assets listed above.

Fixed Assets (net)
All property, plant, leasehold improvements and equipment, net of accumulated depreciation or depletion.

All Other Non-Current
Prepaid items and other non-current assets.

Inventory
Costs attributable to equipment, small tools, supplies, and other deferred costs related to contracts in progress wherein a portion of the cost applies to work not yet performed.

Costs & Estimated Earnings in Excess of Billings
The difference between the total of costs and recognized estimated earnings to date and the total billings to date.

Joint Ventures & Investments
The total of investments and equity in joint ventures.

Intangibles (net)
Intangible assets, including goodwill, trademarks, patents, catalogs, brands, copyrights, formulas, franchises, and mailing lists, net of accumulated amortization.

Total
Total of all items listed above.

ASSETS
Cash & Equivalents
Accounts Receivable—Progress Billings
Accounts Receivable—Current Retention
Inventory
Costs & Estimated Earnings in Excess of Billings
All Other Current
Total Current
Fixed Assets (net)
Joint Ventures & Investments
Intangibles (net)
All Other Non-Current
Total

Notes Payable—Short Term
All short-term note obligations, including bank and commercial paper. Does not include trade notes payable.

Accounts Payable—Trade
Open accounts and note obligations due to the trade.

Accounts Payable—Retention
Amounts held back as retention in payments to subcontractors on current contracts.

Long-Term Debt
All senior debt, including bonds, debentures, bank debt, mortgages, deferred portions of long-term debt, and capital lease obligations.

Deferred Taxes
Total of all deferred taxes.

All Other Non-Current
Any other non-current liabilities, including subordinated debt, and liability reserves.

Billings in Excess of Costs & Est. Earn.
The difference between the total billings to date and the total of costs and recognized estimated earnings to date.

Income Taxes Payable
Income taxes including current portion of deferred taxes.

Current Maturities—LTD
That portion of long-term obligations that is due within the next fiscal year.

All Other Current
Any other current liabilities, including bank overdrafts and accrued expenses.

Total Current
Total of all current liabilities listed above.

Net Worth
Difference between total assets and total liabilities. Minority interest is included here.

Total Liabilities & Net Worth
Total of all items listed above.

LIABILITIES
Notes Payable—Short Term
Accounts Payable—Trade
Accounts Payable—Retention
Billings in Excess of Costs & Estimated Earnings
Income Taxes Payable
Current Maturities—LTD
All Other Current
Total Current
Long-Term Debt
Deferred Taxes
All Other Non-Current
Net Worth
Total Liabilities & Net Worth

Contract Revenues
Revenues recognized under % of completion method.

Gross Profit
Difference between contract revenues and cost of sales.

Operating Expenses
All selling and general and administrative expenses. Includes depreciation, but not interest expense.

All Other Expenses (net)
Includes miscellaneous other income and expenses (net), such as interest expense, miscellaneous expenses not included in general & administrative expenses, netted against recoveries, interest income, dividends received and miscellaneous income.

INCOME DATA
Contract Revenues
Gross Profit
Operating Expenses
Operating Profit
All Other Expenses (net)
Profit Before Taxes

Operating Profit
Gross profit minus operating expenses.

Profit Before Taxes
Operating profit minus all other expenses (net).

For Further Analysis, Please Refer to *Industry Default Probabilities and Cash Flow Measures*

If you think *Financial Ratio Benchmarks* is a valuable resource, wait till you see its companion study. Now in its fifth year and bigger than ever, *Industry Default Probabilities and Cash Flow Measures* is a major expansion of our *Annual Statement Studies.* It brings together the power of Moody's RiskCalc® for private companies and the *Statement Studies* database to provide distribution statistics on one-year and five-year probability of default estimates by industry. The new benchmarks add substantial value to the critical analysis of cash flow for private companies.

The latest edition of *Industry Default Probabilities and Cash Flow Measures* includes many new industries, stronger statements, two-years of historical data sorted by assets and sales… in short, it is more like our traditional *Statement Studies.*

Industry Default Probabilities and Cash Flow Measures includes:

• Probability of default estimates on a percentage scale, mapped to a "dot" pd bond rating scale.
• Cash flow measures on a common-size percentage scale. Ratios include:
  - Cash from Trading
  - Cash after Operations
  - Net Cash after Operations
  - Cash after Debt Amortization
  - Debt Service P&I Coverage
  - Interest Coverage (Operating Cash)
• Change in position, normalized, year over year, for 8 financial statement line items. Ratios include:
  - Change in Inventory
  - Total Current Assets (TCA)
  - Total Assets (TA)
  - Retained Earnings (RE)
  - Net Sales (NS)
  - Cost of Goods Sold (CGS)
  - Profit before Interest & Taxes (PBIT)
  - Depreciation/Depletion/Amortization (DDA)
• Trend data available for the past three years.
• Other ratios.
  - Sustainable Growth Rate
  - Funded Debt/EBITDA
• Data arrayed by asset and sales size.

Please see the inside front cover for more information, or you can set up your standing order for *Industry Default Probabilities and Cash Flow Measures* **today by calling 1-800-677-7621!**

NAICS CODES APPEARING IN THE STATEMENT STUDIES

NAICS Codes	Page	NAICS Codes	Page	NAICS Codes	Page
515120	1094-1095	541320	1208-1209	611110	1322-1323
515210	1096-1097	541330	1210-1211	611210	1324-1325
517110	1098-1099	541370	1212-1213	611310	1326-1327
517212	1100-1101	541380	1214-1215	611519	1328-1329
517910	1102-1103	541410	1216-1217	611610	1330-1331
518111	1104-1105	541430	1218-1219	611699	1332-1333
518210	1106-1107	541511	1220-1221	611710	1334-1335
522210	1110-1111	541512	1222-1223	621111	1338-1339
522220	1112-1113	541519	1224-1225	621112	1340-1341
522291	1114-1115	541611	1226-1227	621210	1342-1343
522292	1116-1117	541612	1228-1229	621310	1344-1345
522294	1118-1119	541613	1230-1231	621320	1346-1347
522298	1120-1121	541614	1232-1233	621330	1348-1349
522310	1122-1123	541618	1234-1235	621340	1350-1351
522390	1124-1125	541620	1236-1237	621399	1352-1353
523120	1126-1127	541690	1238-1239	621410	1354-1355
523910	1128-1129	541710	1240-1241	621420	1356-1357
523920	1130-1131	541810	1242-1243	621492	1358-1359
523930	1132-1133	541820	1244-1245	621493	1360-1361
523991	1134-1135	541850	1246-1247	621498	1362-1363
524113	1136-1137	541860	1248-1249	621511	1364-1365
524114	1138-1139	541870	1250-1251	621512	1366-1367
524126	1140-1141	541890	1252-1253	621610	1368-1369
524127	1142-1143	541910	1254-1255	621910	1370-1371
524128	1144-1145	541921	1256-1257	621991	1372-1373
524210	1146-1147	541922	1258-1259	621999	1374-1375
525910	1148-1149	541940	1260-1261	622110	1376-1377, 1378-1379
525930	1150-1151	541990	1262-1263	622210	1380-1381
525990	1152-1153	551111	1266-1267	622310	1382-1383
531110	1156-1157	551112	1268-1269	623110	1384-1385
531120	1158-1159	561110	1272-1273	623210	1386-1387
531130	1160-1161	561210	1274-1275	623220	1388-1389
531190	1162-1163	561310	1276-1277	623311	1390-1391
531210	1164-1165	561320	1278-1279	623312	1392-1393
531311	1166-1167	561439	1280-1281	623990	1394-1395
531312	1168-1169	561440	1282-1283	624110	1396-1397
531390	1170-1171	561499	1284-1285	624120	1398-1399
532111	1172-1173	561510	1286-1287	624190	1400-1401
532112	1174-1175	561520	1288-1289	624310	1402-1403
532120	1176-1177	561599	1290-1291	624410	1404-1405
532210	1178-1179	561612	1292-1293	711110	1408-1409
532230	1180-1181	561621	1294-1295	711130	1410-1411
532291	1182-1183	561710	1296-1297	711211	1412-1413
532310	1184-1185	561720	1298-1299	711212	1414-1415
532411	1186-1187	561730	1300-1301	711310	1416-1417
532412	1188-1189	561740	1302-1303	712110	1418-1419
532420	1190-1191	561790	1304-1305	713110	1420-1421
532490	1192-1193	561990	1306-1307	713120	1422-1423
533110	1194-1195	562111	1308-1309	713210	1424-1425
541110	1198-1199	562211	1310-1311	713910	1426-1427
541191	1200-1201	562212	1312-1313	713920	1428-1429
541211	1202-1203	562910	1314-1315	713930	1430-1431
541219	1204-1205	562920	1316-1317	713940	1432-1433
541310	1206-1207	562998	1318-1319	713950	1434-1435

If more than three SIC codes map to one NAICS code, then only the first three SIC will appear at the top of the page listed above. For a complete listing of the SIC codes, see the Description of Industries beginning on page 35.

NAICS CODES APPEARING IN THE STATEMENT STUDIES

NAICS Codes	Page	NAICS Codes	Page	NAICS Codes	Page
111140	96-97	238210	208-209, 1558	315299	318-319
111150	98-99	238220	210-211, 1559	315999	320-321
111199	100-101	238290	212-213	316110	322-323
111211	102-103	238310	214-215, 1560	321113	324-325
111219	104-105	238320	216-217, 1561	321114	326-327
111310	106-107	238330	218-219, 1562	321211	328-329
111331	108-109	238340	220-221	321214	330-331
111332	110-111	238350	222-223	321911	332-333
111335	112-113	238910	224-225, 1563	321912	334-335
111411	114-115	238990	226-227, 1564	321918	336-337
111421	116-117	311119	230-231	321920	338-339
111920	118-119	311211	232-233	321991	340-341
111998	120-121	311330	234-235	321992	342-343
112111	122-123	311411	236-237	321999	344-345
112112	124-125	311412	238-239	322121	346-347
112120	126-127	311421	240-241	322211	348-349
112210	128-129	311423	242-243	322212	350-351
112310	130-131	311511	244-245	322213	352-353
112920	132-133	311513	246-247	322221	354-355
113110	134-135	311611	248-249	322222	356-357
113310	136-137	311612	250-251	322223	358-359
114111	138-139	311613	252-253	322232	360-361
114112	140-141	311615	254-255	322291	362-363
115111	142-143	311712	256-257	322299	364-365
115112	144-145	311811	258-259	323110	366-367
115114	146-147	311812	260-261	323112	368-369
115210	148-149	311821	262-263	323113	370-371
211111	152-153	311919	264-265	323114	372-373
212111	154-155	311920	266-267	323116	374-375
212312	156-157	311930	268-269	323117	376-377
212319	158-159	311941	270-271	323119	378-379
212321	160-161	311999	272-273	323121	380-381
213111	162-163	312111	274-275	323122	382-383
213112	164-165, 1542	312112	276-277	324110	384-385
221122	168-169	312120	278-279	324121	386-387
221210	170-171	312130	280-281	324191	388-389
221310	172-173	312229	282-283	324199	390-391
236115	176-177, 1543	313111	284-285	325188	392-393
236116	178-179, 1544	313210	286-287	325199	394-395
236117	180-181, 1545	313221	288-289	325211	396-397
236118	1546	313311	290-291	325311	398-399
236210	182-183, 1547	313320	292-293	325314	400-401
236220	184-185, 1548	314110	294-295	325320	402-403
237110	186-187, 1549	314129	296-297	325411	404-405
237120	188-189	314912	298-299	325412	406-407
237210	190-191, 1550	314999	300-301	325510	408-409
237310	192-193, 1551	315119	302-303	325520	410-411
237990	194-195, 1552	315191	304-305	325611	412-413
238110	196-197, 1553	315211	306-307	325612	414-415
238120	198-199, 1554	315212	308-309	325620	416-417
238130	200-201	315222	310-311	325910	418-419
238140	202-203, 1555	315228	312-313	325991	420-421
238150	204-205, 1556	315233	314-315	325998	422-423
238160	206-207, 1557	315239	316-317	326113	424-425

If more than three SIC codes map to one NAICS code, then only the first three SIC will appear at the top of the page listed above. For a complete listing of the SIC codes, see the Description of Industries beginning on page 35.

NAICS CODES APPEARING IN THE STATEMENT STUDIES

If more than three SIC codes map to one NAICS code, then only the first three SIC will appear at the top of the page listed above. For a complete listing of the SIC codes, see the Description of Industries beginning on page 35.

NAICS CODES APPEARING IN THE STATEMENT STUDIES

If more than three SIC codes map to one NAICS code, then only the first three SIC will appear at the top of the page listed above. For a complete listing of the SIC codes, see the Description of Industries beginning on page 35.

NAICS CODES APPEARING IN THE STATEMENT STUDIES

NAICS Codes	Page	NAICS Codes	Page	NAICS Codes	Page
713990	1436-1437				
721110	1440-1441				
721120	1442-1443				
721211	1444-1445				
721214	1446-1447				
722110	1448-1449				
722211	1450-1451				
722213	1452-1453				
722320	1454-1455				
722410	1456-1457				
811111	1460-1461				
811112	1462-1463				
811118	1464-1465				
811121	1466-1467				
811122	1468-1469				
811192	1470-1471				
811198	1472-1473				
811212	1474-1475				
811219	1476-1477				
811310	1478-1479				
811412	1480-1481				
812112	1482-1483				
812210	1484-1485				
812220	1486-1487				
812310	1488-1489				
812320	1490-1491				
812331	1492-1493				
812332	1494-1495				
812921	1496-1497				
812930	1498-1499				
812990	1500-1501				
813110	1502-1503				
813212	1504-1505				
813319	1506-1507				
813410	1508-1509				
813910	1510-1511				
813920	1512-1513				
813930	1514-1515				
813990	1516-1517				
814110	1518-1519				
921110	1522-1523				
921140	1524-1525				
921190	1526-1527				
922160	1528-1529				
923110	1530-1531				
924110	1532-1533				
925110	1534-1535				
925120	1536-1537				
926110	1538-1539				

If more than three SIC codes map to one NAICS code, then only the first three SIC will appear at the top of the page listed above. For a complete listing of the SIC codes, see the Description of Industries beginning on page 35.

NAICS CODES APPEARING IN THE STATEMENT STUDIES

If more than three SIC codes map to one NAICS code, then only the first three SIC will appear at the top of the page listed above. For a complete listing of the SIC codes, see the Description of Industries beginning on page 35.

NAICS CODES APPEARING IN THE STATEMENT STUDIES

If more than three SIC codes map to one NAICS code, then only the first three SIC will appear at the top of the page listed above. For a complete listing of the SIC codes, see the Description of Industries beginning on page 35.

NAICS CODES APPEARING IN THE STATEMENT STUDIES

If more than three SIC codes map to one NAICS code, then only the first three SIC will appear at the top of the page listed above. For a complete listing of the SIC codes, see the Description of Industries beginning on page 35.

NAICS CODES APPEARING IN THE STATEMENT STUDIES

If more than three SIC codes map to one NAICS code, then only the first three SIC will appear at the top of the page listed above. For a complete listing of the SIC codes, see the Description of Industries beginning on page 35.

NAICS CODES APPEARING IN THE STATEMENT STUDIES

If more than three SIC codes map to one NAICS code, then only the first three SIC will appear at the top of the page listed above. For a complete listing of the SIC codes, see the Description of Industries beginning on page 35.

SIC NUMBERS APPEARING IN THE STATEMENT STUDIES

SIC No.	Page	SIC No.	Page	SIC No.	Page
0111	96-97	1623	186-187, 188-189, 1549	2099	242-243, 266-267, 270-271, 272-273
0115	98-99	1629	182-183, 186-187, 188-189, 194-195, 224-225, 1547, 1549, 1552, 1563	2121	282-283
0119	98-99, 100-101			2131	282-283
0131	118-119	1711	208-209, 210-211, 1558, 1559	2141	286-287
0134	102-103	1721	192-193, 216-217, 1551, 1561	2211	286-287
0139	100-101, 104-105, 120-121			2221	286-287
0161	104-105	1731	208-209, 1558	2231	286-287
0172	110-111	1741	202-203, 1555	2241	288-289
0173	112-113	1742	214-215, 1560	2252	302-303
0174	106-107	1743	214-215, 220-221, 1560	2253	304-305
0175	108-109	1751	200-201, 222-223	2259	304-305
0181	116-117	1752	218-219, 1562	2261	290-291
0182	114-115	1761	206-207, 1557	2262	290-291
0191	120-121	1771	196-197, 202-203, 1553, 1555	2269	290-291
0211	124-125			2273	294-295
0212	122-123	1781	186-187, 1549	2281	284-285
0213	128-129	1791	198-199, 210-211, 1554, 1559	2295	292-293
0241	122-123, 126-127			2298	284-285
0252	130-131	1793	204-205, 1556	2299	284-285, 288-289, 300-301
0272	132-133	1794	224-225, 1563	2311	306-307, 310-311
0711	144-145	1795	224-225, 1563	2321	306-307
0721	144-145	1796	210-211, 212-213, 1559	2326	306-307
0723	146-147, 230-231	1799	194-195, 204-205, 212-213, 216-217, 222-223, 226-227, 1304-1305, 1314-1315, 1552, 1556, 1561, 1564	2329	312-313, 318-319
0724	142-143			2331	308-309
0741	1260-1261			2335	308-309, 314-315
0742	1260-1261			2337	308-309
0751	148-149, 248-249	2011	248-249	2339	316-317, 318-319, 320-321
0752	148-149	2013	250-251, 252-253	2361	314-315
0781	1208-1209, 1238-1239	2015	254-255	2369	310-311, 312-313, 316-317
0782	1300-1301	2022	246-247	2385	310-311, 312-313, 316-317, 318-319
0783	1300-1301	2023	244-245		
0811	116-117, 134-135	2026	244-245	2387	320-321
0831	120-121	2032	272-273	2389	320-321
0912	138-139	2033	240-241	2392	296-297, 742-743
0913	140-141	2034	232-233, 242-243, 272-273	2394	298-299
0919	140-141	2035	240-241, 270-271	2395	300-301
1221	154-155	2037	236-237	2396	676-677
1311	152-153	2038	238-239	2399	300-301, 676-677
1381	162-163	2041	232-233	2411	136-137
1382	164-165, 1542	2048	230-231, 248-249	2421	324-325, 334-335, 336-337, 344-345
1389	164-165, 188-189, 1542	2051	260-261		
1422	156-157	2052	260-261, 262-263, 264-265	2426	324-325, 334-335, 336-337
1429	158-159	2064	234-235	2429	324-325, 344-345
1442	160-161	2066	234-235	2431	332-333, 336-337
1499	158-159	2077	252-253, 256-257	2434	696-697
1521	176-177, 1543, 1546	2082	278-279	2435	328-329
1522	178-179, 1544, 1546	2084	280-281	2439	330-331
1531	180-181, 182-183, 184-185, 1545, 1546, 1547, 1548	2085	280-281	2441	338-339
		2086	274-275, 276-277	2448	338-339
1541	182-183, 184-185, 1547, 1548	2087	266-267, 268-269	2449	338-339
		2092	256-257	2451	340-341
1542	184-185, 1548	2095	266-267	2452	342-343
1611	192-193, 1551	2096	264-265	2491	326-327
1622	192-193, 194-195, 1551, 1552			2499	344-345, 702-703, 744-745

See pages 23-28 for corresponding NAICS look-up table.

SIC NUMBERS APPEARING IN THE STATEMENT STUDIES

SIC No.	Page	SIC No.	Page	SIC No.	Page
2511	700-701	2911	384-385	3444	502-503, 504-505, 508-509,
2512	698-699	2951	386-387		574-575
2514	698-699	2992	388-389	3446	506-507
2515	698-699, 712-713	2999	390-391	3448	496-497
2519	702-703	3052	440-441	3449	498-499, 506-507
2521	706-707	3053	738-739	3451	518-519
2522	708-709	3061	442-443	3452	520-521
2531	704-705	3069	292-293, 444-445, 732-733,	3462	490-491
2541	696-697, 710-711		734-735	3465	678-679
2542	704-705, 710-711	3081	424-425	3469	492-493
2591	714-715	3082	426-427	3471	526-527
2599	704-705, 716-717	3083	430-431	3479	524-525, 728-729, 730-731
2611	346-347	3084	428-429	3491	528-529
2621	346-347	3085	434-435	3492	530-531
2652	352-353	3086	432-433	3494	534-535, 540-541
2653	348-349	3087	420-421	3495	512-513
2657	350-351	3089	426-427, 428-429, 436-437	3496	514-515, 600-601
2671	354-355	3111	322-323	3498	538-539
2672	356-357	3172	730-731	3499	508-509, 510-511, 534-535,
2673	358-359	3231	448-449		540-541, 676-677, 710-711
2675	364-365	3251	446-447, 452-453	3519	680-681
2676	362-363	3271	452-453	3523	506-507, 542-543, 596-597
2677	360-361	3272	454-455, 460-461	3524	544-545
2679	348-349, 356-357, 364-365	3273	450-451	3531	546-547, 598-599, 686-687
2711	1074-1075	3281	458-459	3532	548-549
2721	1076-1077	3291	456-457	3533	550-551
2731	1078-1079	3292	460-461	3535	596-597
2732	376-377	3299	460-461	3536	598-599
2741	1076-1077, 1078-1079,	3312	390-391, 462-463, 466-467	3537	600-601
	1080-1081, 1082-1083	3315	468-469, 514-515	3541	578-579
2752	366-367, 372-373	3316	466-467	3542	580-581
2759	368-369, 370-371, 372-373,	3317	464-465	3544	576-577, 582-583
	378-379	3321	478-479	3545	494-495, 584-585
2761	374-375	3322	478-479	3548	602-603, 656-657
2771	366-367, 368-369, 370-371,	3325	480-481	3549	586-587
	378-379	3341	476-477	3552	556-557
2782	374-375	3354	470-471	3554	554-555
2789	380-381	3356	474-475	3555	558-559
2791	382-383	3357	472-473, 474-475	3556	560-561
2796	382-383	3363	482-483	3559	542-543, 552-553, 562-563,
2819	392-393, 422-423	3364	484-485		568-569
2821	396-397	3365	486-487	3561	592-593
2833	404-405	3369	488-489	3562	536-537
2834	406-407	3398	522-523	3563	594-595
2835	406-407	3399	462-463, 466-467, 476-477,	3564	570-571
2841	412-413		514-515, 526-527	3565	604-605
2842	414-415	3412	508-509	3566	588-589
2844	412-413, 416-417	3421	494-495	3567	606-607
2851	408-409	3423	494-495	3568	590-591
2869	392-393, 394-395, 422-423	3429	510-511, 520-521, 540-541,	3569	572-573, 608-609
2873	398-399		598-599	3571	610-611
2875	400-401	3432	532-533, 534-535	3577	612-613
2879	402-403	3433	572-573	3578	612-613
2891	410-411	3441	498-499	3585	574-575
2893	418-419	3442	502-503	3589	568-569
2899	394-395, 408-409, 422-423	3443	500-501, 574-575		

See pages 23-28 for corresponding NAICS look-up table.

SIC NUMBERS APPEARING IN THE STATEMENT STUDIES

SIC No.	Page
3599	516-517, 526-527, 568-569, 608-609, 648-649
3612	656-657
3613	660-661
3621	658-659
3625	662-663
3629	666-667
3634	572-573, 744-745
3639	562-563
3643	664-665
3645	650-651
3646	652-653
3648	654-655
3651	620-621
3661	614-615
3663	616-617
3669	618-619
3671	622-623
3672	624-625
3674	626-627
3677	628-629
3678	630-631
3679	616-617, 620-621, 632-633
3699	602-603, 654-655, 666-667
3711	668-669, 670-671
3713	670-671
3714	670-671, 680-681
3715	672-673
3721	1240-1241
3724	682-683
3728	530-531, 684-685
3731	688-689, 1050-1051
3732	690-691
3743	592-593, 686-687
3751	692-693
3792	674-675
3799	600-601, 674-675, 680-681, 694-695
3812	636-637
3821	716-717
3822	638-639
3823	640-641
3824	642-643
3825	642-643, 644-645
3826	646-647
3827	564-565
3829	642-643, 648-649, 718-719
3841	716-717, 718-719
3842	362-363, 634-635, 720-721
3843	722-723
3845	634-635
3851	720-721, 724-725
3861	566-567
3911	728-729
3931	740-741

SIC No.	Page
3944	692-693, 734-735
3949	732-733
3961	730-731
3991	742-743
3993	370-371, 736-737
3999	322-323, 436-437, 524-525, 650-651, 734-735, 744-745
4011	1012-1013
4111	1036-1037
4119	1030-1031, 1032-1033, 1036-1037, 1038-1039, 1370-1371
4121	1028-1029
4141	1034-1035
4142	1034-1035
4151	1032-1033
4173	1054-1055
4212	1016-1017, 1022-1023, 1024-1025, 1308-1309
4213	1018-1019, 1020-1021, 1022-1023, 1026-1027
4214	1016-1017, 1022-1023, 1024-1025
4215	1062-1063
4221	1068-1069
4222	1066-1067
4225	1064-1065, 1160-1161
4226	1064-1065, 1066-1067, 1070-1071
4231	1054-1055
4449	1014-1015
4489	1040-1041
4491	1046-1047
4492	1048-1049
4493	1430-1431
4499	1014-1015, 1048-1049, 1050-1051, 1186-1187
4512	1006-1007
4513	1062-1063
4522	1008-1009, 1010-1011, 1370-1371
4581	1042-1043, 1044-1045
4724	1286-1287
4725	1288-1289
4729	1060-1061, 1290-1291
4731	1056-1057, 1232-1233
4741	1186-1187
4783	1058-1059
4785	1054-1055
4789	1038-1039, 1060-1061
4812	1100-1101
4813	1098-1099
4822	1098-1099
4832	1092-1093
4833	1094-1095
4841	1096-1097

SIC No.	Page
4899	1028-1029, 1100-1101, 1102-1103
4911	168-169
4923	170-171
4924	170-171
4925	170-171
4931	168-169
4939	168-169
4941	172-173
4953	1310-1311, 1312-1313, 1316-1317
4959	1042-1043, 1296-1297, 1304-1305, 1314-1315, 1318-1319
4971	172-173
5012	748-749
5013	750-751, 902-903
5014	752-753, 904-905
5015	754-755, 902-903
5021	756-757, 906-907
5023	758-759, 908-909
5031	760-761, 920-921
5032	762-763, 926-927
5033	764-765, 926-927
5039	760-761, 766-767, 926-927
5043	768-769
5044	770-771, 984-985
5045	772-773, 916-917
5046	774-775
5047	776-777
5048	778-779
5049	780-781
5051	782-783
5052	784-785
5063	786-787
5064	788-789, 912-913, 914-915
5065	790-791
5072	792-793, 924-925
5074	794-795
5075	796-797
5078	798-799
5082	800-801
5083	802-803, 928-929
5084	804-805
5085	804-805, 806-807
5087	808-809, 948-949
5088	810-811
5091	812-813, 970-971
5092	814-815, 972-973
5093	816-817
5094	818-819, 968-969
5099	820-821, 886-887, 972-973
5111	822-823
5112	824-825, 984-985
5113	826-827
5122	828-829, 946-947, 948-949

See pages 23-28 for corresponding NAICS look-up table.

SIC NUMBERS APPEARING IN THE STATEMENT STUDIES

SIC No.	Page	SIC No.	Page	SIC No.	Page
5131	830-831	5621	958-959, 964-965	6351	1140-1141, 1144-1145
5136	812-813, 832-833, 956-957	5632	962-963, 964-965	6361	1142-1143
5137	812-813, 834-835, 958-959	5651	960-961	6371	1130-1131, 1152-1153
5139	836-837, 966-967	5661	966-967	6399	1144-1145
5141	838-839, 932-933	5699	962-963, 964-965	6411	1146-1147
5142	840-841	5712	906-907	6512	1158-1159
5143	842-843	5713	908-909	6513	1156-1157
5144	844-845, 936-937	5719	910-911	6514	1156-1157
5145	846-847, 940-941	5722	912-913	6515	1162-1163
5146	848-849	5731	914-915	6517	1162-1163
5147	850-851, 936-937	5734	916-917	6519	1162-1163
5148	852-853, 938-939	5736	974-975	6531	1156-1157, 1164-1165,
5149	854-855	5812	1408-1409, 1448-1449,		1166-1167, 1168-1169,
5153	856-857		1450-1451, 1452-1453, 1454-1455		1170-1171, 1486-1487
5154	858-859	5813	1456-1457	6541	1200-1201
5159	860-861	5912	946-947	6552	190-191, 1549
5162	862-863	5921	944-945	6553	1486-1487
5169	864-865	5932	988-989	6712	1266-1267
5171	866-867, 998-999, 1000-1001	5941	970-971	6719	1268-1269
5172	868-869	5942	976-977	6722	1148-1149
5181	870-871, 944-945	5943	984-985	6726	1152-1153
5182	872-873, 944-945	5944	968-969	6733	1130-1131, 1134-1135
5191	874-875, 930-931	5945	972-973	6792	1194-1195
5192	876-877, 976-977	5946	918-919	6794	1194-1195
5193	878-879, 930-931	5947	986-987	6798	1150-1151
5194	880-881	5961	994-995	6799	1128-1129
5198	882-883	5962	996-997	7011	1440-1441, 1442-1443
5199	830-831, 836-837, 862-863,	5963	1002-1003	7032	1446-1447
	884-885, 986-987	5983	998-999	7033	1444-1445
5211	920-921	5984	1000-1001	7041	1440-1441
5231	922-923	5992	982-983	7211	1490-1491
5251	924-925	5995	950-951	7212	1490-1491
5261	928-929, 930-931	5999	948-949, 992-993	7213	1492-1493
5271	990-991	6019	1120-1121	7215	1488-1489
5311	978-979	6021	1110-1111	7216	1490-1491
5331	980-981	6022	1110-1111	7217	1302-1303
5399	980-981	6091	1134-1135	7218	1494-1495
5411	932-933, 934-935, 952-953,	6099	1124-1125	7219	1492-1493
	1002-1003	6111	1116-1117, 1118-1119	7221	1256-1257
5421	936-937	6141	1110-1111, 1112-1113,	7231	1482-1483
5431	938-939, 1002-1003		1114-1115	7251	1500-1501
5441	940-941	6153	1112-1113, 1120-1121,	7261	1484-1485, 1486-1487
5451	942-943		1128-1129	7299	1262-1263, 1306-1307,
5461	258-259, 1452-1453	6159	1112-1113, 1116-1117,		1498-1499, 1500-1501
5499	942-943		1118-1119, 1120-1121	7311	1242-1243
5511	890-891	6162	1116-1117, 1124-1125	7312	1246-1247
5521	892-893	6163	1122-1123	7319	1010-1011, 1246-1247,
5531	902-903, 904-905, 980-981	6211	1126-1127, 1128-1129		1250-1251, 1252-1253
5541	952-953, 954-955	6282	1130-1131, 1132-1133	7322	1282-1283
5551	898-899	6289	1134-1135	7331	1080-1081, 1248-1249
5561	894-895	6311	1136-1137	7334	372-373, 1280-1281
5571	896-897	6321	1136-1137, 1138-1139	7335	1258-1259
5599	900-901	6324	1138-1139	7336	1218-1219
5611	956-957, 962-963	6331	1140-1141, 1144-1145	7342	1296-1297, 1298-1299

See pages 23-28 for corresponding NAICS look-up table.

SIC NUMBERS APPEARING IN THE STATEMENT STUDIES

SIC No.	Page	SIC No.	Page	SIC No.	Page
7349	1298-1299, 1304-1305	7841	1180-1181	8412	1418-1419
7352	1182-1183, 1192-1193	7911	1330-1331	8611	1510-1511
7353	1188-1189	7922	1408-1409, 1416-1417	8621	1512-1513
7359	1178-1179, 1184-1185,	7929	1410-1411	8631	1514-1515
	1186-1187, 1188-1189,	7933	1434-1435	8641	1506-1507, 1508-1509,
	1190-1191, 1192-1193	7941	1412-1413, 1416-1417		1516-1517
7361	1228-1229, 1276-1277	7948	1414-1415	8661	1502-1503
7363	1278-1279	7991	1432-1433	8699	1290-1291, 1508-1509,
7371	1220-1221	7992	1426-1427		1510-1511, 1516-1517
7372	1084-1085	7993	1422-1423, 1436-1437	8711	1210-1211
7373	1222-1223	7996	1420-1421	8712	1206-1207
7374	1106-1107	7997	1010-1011, 1426-1427,	8713	1212-1213
7375	1104-1105		1432-1433, 1436-1437	8721	1202-1203, 1204-1205
7377	1190-1191	7999	1416-1417, 1424-1425,	8731	1240-1241
7378	916-917, 1474-1475		1428-1429, 1432-1433,	8732	1254-1255
7379	1106-1107, 1222-1223,		1436-1437	8733	1240-1241
	1224-1225	8011	1338-1339, 1340-1341,	8734	1214-1215, 1260-1261
7381	1292-1293		1360-1361	8741	1272-1273
7382	1294-1295	8021	1342-1343	8742	1226-1227, 1228-1229,
7384	1496-1497	8031	1338-1339, 1340-1341		1230-1231, 1232-1233
7389	1106-1107, 1212-1213,	8041	1344-1345	8743	1244-1245
	1216-1217, 1250-1251,	8042	1346-1347	8744	1274-1275
	1252-1253, 1262-1263,	8049	1348-1349, 1350-1351,	8748	1208-1209, 1210-1211,
	1280-1281, 1282-1283,		1352-1353		1234-1235, 1238-1239,
	1284-1285, 1290-1291,	8051	1384-1385, 1386-1387,		1334-1335
	1306-1307		1390-1391	8811	1518-1519
7513	1176-1177	8052	1384-1385, 1386-1387,	8999	1236-1237, 1262-1263
7514	1172-1173		1390-1391	9111	1522-1523
7515	1174-1175	8059	1384-1385, 1390-1391	9131	1524-1525
7519	1176-1177	8062	1376-1377, 1378-1379	9199	1526-1527
7521	1498-1499	8063	1380-1381	9224	1528-1529
7532	1466-1467	8069	1380-1381, 1382-1383	9411	1530-1531
7533	1462-1463	8071	1364-1365, 1366-1367	9511	1532-1533
7534	438-439, 1472-1473	8072	726-727	9531	1534-1535
7536	1468-1469	8082	1368-1369	9532	1536-1537
7538	1460-1461	8092	1358-1359	9611	1538-1539
7539	1464-1465, 1472-1473	8093	1352-1353, 1354-1355,		
7542	1470-1471		1356-1357, 1362-1363		
7549	1052-1053, 1468-1469,	8099	1354-1355, 1372-1373,		
	1472-1473		1374-1375		
7622	914-915	8111	1198-1199		
7623	1478-1479, 1480-1481	8211	1322-1323		
7629	1474-1475, 1476-1477,	8221	1326-1327		
	1480-1481	8222	1324-1325		
7631	968-969	8243	1328-1329		
7692	1478-1479	8249	1328-1329		
7694	658-659, 1478-1479	8299	1328-1329, 1330-1331,		
7699	970-971, 1474-1475,		1332-1333, 1334-1335		
	1476-1477, 1480-1481	8322	1396-1397, 1398-1399,		
7812	1086-1087		1400-1401		
7819	1090-1091, 1192-1193,	8331	1402-1403		
	1238-1239	8351	1404-1405		
7822	820-821	8361	1386-1387, 1388-1389,		
7829	1090-1091		1392-1393, 1394-1395		
7832	1088-1089	8399	1504-1505, 1506-1507		

See pages 23-28 for corresponding NAICS look-up table.

AGRICULTURE, FORESTRY, FISHING AND HUNTING

NAICS #　　　　　　　　　　　　　　　　　　　　　　　　　　　　　　　　　　　**Page**

111140　**Wheat Farming.** This industry comprises establishments primarily engaged in growing wheat and/or producing wheat seeds. (SIC: 0111) 96-97

111150　**Corn Farming.** This industry comprises establishments primarily engaged in growing corn (except sweet corn) and/or producing corn seeds. (SIC: 0115, 0119) 98-99

111199　**All Other Grain Farming.** This U.S. industry comprises establishments primarily engaged in growing grains and/or producing grain(s) seeds (except wheat, corn, rice, and oilseed(s) and grain(s) combinations). (SIC: 0119, 0139) 100-101

111211　**Potato Farming.** This U.S. industry comprises establishments primarily engaged in growing potatoes and/or producing seed potatoes (except sweet potatoes). (SIC: 0134) 102-103

111219　**Other Vegetable (except Potato) and Melon Farming.** This U.S. industry comprises establishments primarily engaged in one or more of the following: (1) growing melons and/or vegetables (except potatoes; dry peas; dry beans; field, silage, or seed corn; and sugar beets); (2) producing vegetable and/or melon seeds; and (3) growing vegetable and/or melon bedding plants. (SIC: 0139, 0161) 104-105

111310　**Orange Groves.** This industry comprises establishments primarily engaged in growing oranges. (SIC: 0174) 106-107

111331　**Apple Orchards.** This U.S. industry comprises establishments primarily engaged in growing apples. (SIC: 0175) 108-109

111332　**Grape Vineyards.** This U.S. industry comprises establishments primarily engaged in growing grapes and/or growing grapes to sun dry into raisins. (SIC: 0172) 110-111

111335　**Tree Nut Farming.** This U.S. industry comprises establishments primarily engaged in growing tree nuts. (SIC: 0173) 112-113

111411　**Mushroom Production.** This U.S. industry comprises establishments primarily engaged in growing mushrooms under cover in mines underground, or in other controlled environments. (SIC: 0182) 114-115

111421　**Nursery and Tree Production.** This U.S. industry comprises establishments primarily engaged in (1) growing nursery products, nursery stock, shrubbery, bulbs, fruit stock, sod, and so forth, under cover or in open fields and/or (2) growing short rotation woody trees with a growth and harvest cycle of 10 years or less for pulp or tree stock. (SIC: 0181, 0811) 116-117

111920　**Cotton Farming.** This industry comprises establishments primarily engaged in growing cotton. (SIC: 0131) 118-119

111998　**All Other Miscellaneous Crop Farming.** This U.S. industry comprises establishments primarily engaged in one of the following: (1) growing crops (except oilseeds and/or grains; vegetables and/or melons; fruits and/or tree nuts; greenhouse, nursery and/or floriculture products; tobacco; cotton; sugarcane; hay; sugar beets; or peanuts); (2) growing a combination of crops (except a combination of oilseed(s) and grain(s); and a combination of fruit(s) and tree nut(s)) with no one crop or family of crop(s) accounting for one-half of the establishment's agricultural production (i.e., value of crops for market); or (3) gathering tea or maple sap. (SIC: 0139, 0191, 0831) 120-121

112111　**Beef Cattle Ranching and Farming.** This U.S. industry comprises establishments primarily engaged in raising cattle (including cattle for dairy herd replacements). (SIC: 0212, 0241) . . . 122-123

112112　**Cattle Feedlots.** This U.S. industry comprises establishments primarily engaged in feeding cattle for fattening. (SIC: 0211) 124-125

112120　**Dairy Cattle and Milk Production.** This industry comprises establishments primarily engaged in milking dairy cattle. (SIC: 0241) 126-127

112210　**Hog and Pig Farming.** This industry comprises establishments primarily engaged in raising hogs and pigs. These establishments may include farming activities, such as breeding, farrowing, and the raising of weanling pigs, feeder pigs, or market size hogs. (SIC: 0213) 128-129

MINING

MINING

CONSTRUCTION—GENERAL

UTILITIES

CONSTRUCTION—GENERAL

CONSTRUCTION—GENERAL

CONSTRUCTION—GENERAL

MANUFACTURING

MANUFACTURING

MANUFACTURING

MANUFACTURING

MANUFACTURING

MANUFACTURING

MANUFACTURING

MANUFACTURING

MANUFACTURING

MANUFACTURING

MANUFACTURING

MANUFACTURING

MANUFACTURING

MANUFACTURING

MANUFACTURING

MANUFACTURING

MANUFACTURING

MANUFACTURING

MANUFACTURING

MANUFACTURING

WHOLESALE TRADE

WHOLESALE TRADE

WHOLESALE TRADE

WHOLESALE TRADE

WHOLESALE TRADE

WHOLESALE TRADE

RETAIL TRADE

RETAIL TRADE

RETAIL TRADE

RETAIL TRADE

RETAIL TRADE

TRANSPORTATION AND WAREHOUSING

TRANSPORTATION AND WAREHOUSING

TRANSPORTATION AND WAREHOUSING

TRANSPORTATION AND WAREHOUSING

INFORMATION

INFORMATION

FINANCE AND INSURANCE

FINANCE AND INSURANCE

FINANCE AND INSURANCE

REAL ESTATE AND RENTAL AND LEASING

REAL ESTATE AND RENTAL AND LEASING

REAL ESTATE AND RENTAL AND LEASING

PROFESSIONAL, SCIENTIFIC, AND TECHNICAL SERVICES

541110 **Offices of Lawyers.** This industry comprises offices of legal practitioners known as lawyers or attorneys (i.e., counselors-at-law) primarily engaged in the practice of law. Establishments in this industry may provide expertise in a range or in specific areas of law, such as criminal law, corporate law, family and estate law, patent law, real estate law, or tax law. (SIC: 8111) 1198-1199

541191 **Title Abstract and Settlement Offices.** This U.S. industry comprises establishments (except offices of lawyers and attorneys) primarily engaged in one or more of the following activities: (1) researching public land records to gather information relating to real estate titles; (2) preparing documents necessary for the transfer of the title, financing, and settlement; (3) conducting final real estate settlements and closings; and (4) filing legal and other documents relating to the sale of real estate. Real estate settlement offices, title abstract companies, and title search companies are included in this industry. (SIC: 6541) 1200-1201

541211 **Offices of Certified Public Accountants.** This U.S. industry comprises establishments of accountants that are certified to audit the accounting records of public and private organizations and to attest to compliance with generally accepted accounting practices. Offices of certified public accountants (CPAs) may provide one or more of the following accounting services: (1) auditing financial statements; (2) designing accounting systems; (3) preparing financial statements; (4) developing budgets; and (5) providing advice on matters related to accounting. These establishments may also provide related services, such as bookkeeping, tax return preparation, and payroll processing. (SIC: 8721) 1202-1203

541219 **Other Accounting Services.** This U.S. industry comprises establishments (except offices of CPAs) engaged in providing accounting services (except tax return preparation services only or payroll services only). These establishments may also provide tax return preparation or payroll services. Accountant (except CPA) offices, bookkeeper offices, and billing offices are included in this industry. (SIC: 8721) 1204-1205

541310 **Architectural Services.** This industry comprises establishments primarily engaged in planning and designing residential, institutional, leisure, commercial, and industrial buildings and structures by applying knowledge of design, construction procedures, zoning regulations, building codes, and building materials. (SIC: 8712) 1206-1207

541320 **Landscape Architectural Services.** This industry comprises establishments primarily engaged in planning and designing the development of land areas for projects, such as parks and other recreational areas; airports; highways; hospitals; schools; land subdivisions; and commercial, industrial, and residential areas, by applying knowledge of land characteristics, location of buildings and structures, use of land areas, and design of landscape projects. (SIC: 0781, 8748) 1208-1209

541330 **Engineering Services.** This industry comprises establishments primarily engaged in applying physical laws and principles of engineering in the design, development, and utilization of machines, materials, instruments, structures, processes, and systems. The assignments undertaken by these establishments may involve any of the following activities: provision of advice, preparation of feasibility studies, preparation of preliminary and final plans and designs, provision of technical services during the construction or installation phase, inspection and evaluation of engineering projects, and related services. (SIC: 8711, 8748) 1210-1211

541370 **Surveying and Mapping (except Geophysical) Services.** This industry comprises establishments primarily engaged in performing surveying and mapping services of the surface of the earth, including the sea floor. These services may include surveying and mapping of areas above or below the surface of the earth, such as the creation of view easements or segregating rights in parcels of land by creating underground utility easements. (SIC: 7389, 8713) 1212-1213

541380 **Testing Laboratories.** This industry comprises establishments primarily engaged in performing physical, chemical, and other analytical testing services, such as acoustics or vibration testing, assaying, biological testing (except medical and veterinary), calibration testing, electrical and electronic testing, geotechnical testing, mechanical testing, nondestructive testing, or thermal testing. The testing may occur in a laboratory or on-site. (SIC: 8734) 1214-1215

PROFESSIONAL, SCIENTIFIC, AND TECHNICAL SERVICES

PROFESSIONAL, SCIENTIFIC, AND TECHNICAL SERVICES

ADMINISTRATIVE SUPPORT AND WASTE MANAGEMENT

MANAGEMENT OF COMPANIES AND ENTERPRISES

ADMINISTRATIVE AND SUPPORT AND WASTE MANAGEMENT AND REMEDIATION SERVICES

ADMINISTRATIVE SUPPORT AND WASTE MANAGEMENT

EDUCATIONAL SERVICES

EDUCATIONAL SERVICES

HEALTH CARE AND SOCIAL ASSISTANCE

HEALTH CARE AND SOCIAL ASSISTANCE

HEALTH CARE AND SOCIAL ASSISTANCE

HEALTH CARE AND SOCIAL ASSISTANCE

Page

ARTS, ENTERTAINMENT, AND RECREATION

ACCOMMODATION AND FOOD SERVICES

ACCOMMODATION AND FOOD SERVICES

OTHER SERVICES (EXCEPT PUBLIC ADMINISTRATION)

OTHER SERVICES
(EXCEPT PUBLIC ADMINISTRATION)

OTHER SERVICES (EXCEPT PUBLIC ADMINISTRATION)

PUBLIC ADMINISTRATION

PUBLIC ADMINISTRATION

CONSTRUCTION—PERCENTAGE OF COMPLETION

CONSTRUCTION—PERCENTAGE OF COMPLETION

CONSTRUCTION—PERCENTAGE OF COMPLETION

CONSTRUCTION—PERCENTAGE OF COMPLETION

AGRICULTURE, FORESTRY, FISHING AND HUNTING

AGRICULTURE—Wheat Farming NAICS 111140 (SIC 0111)

Current Data Sorted By Assets

Comparative Historical Data

0-500M	500M-2MM	2-10MM	10-50MM	50-100MM	100-250MM	Type of Statement	4/1/00-3/31/01 ALL	4/1/01-3/31/02 ALL
	2	1	7	1	5	Unqualified	3	1
2	1	5	2			Reviewed	1	1
1	8	6	1			Compiled	6	7
7	12	8				Tax Returns	2	
7	10	18	11	2		Other	11	14
21 (4/1-9/30/04)	21 (4/1-9/30/04)	96 (10/1/04-3/31/05)	96 (10/1/04-3/31/05)					
17	33	38	21	3	5	NUMBER OF STATEMENTS	23	24
%	%	%	%	%	%	ASSETS	%	%
25.7	3.7	8.3	20.7			Cash & Equivalents	8.3	11.1
22.0	20.8	24.4	13.4			Trade Receivables (net)	6.0	7.0
10.3	18.1	19.5	12.7			Inventory	14.9	14.1
6.7	2.7	3.7	5.3			All Other Current	10.7	9.8
64.8	45.4	55.9	52.1			Total Current	39.9	42.0
29.9	41.4	35.2	34.5			Fixed Assets (net)	47.4	31.3
1.3	2.7	3.5	4.7			Intangibles (net)	3.9	5.5
4.0	10.5	5.4	8.7			All Other Non-Current	8.8	21.2
100.0	100.0	100.0	100.0			Total	100.0	100.0
						LIABILITIES		
26.7	13.3	13.0	10.9			Notes Payable-Short Term	31.7	21.8
1.2	2.1	3.8	2.3			Cur. Mat.-L/T/D	3.1	2.4
16.4	11.5	9.9	9.5			Trade Payables	11.4	11.0
.2	.2	.4	.4			Income Taxes Payable	.2	.1
12.9	8.9	8.5	12.9			All Other Current	7.4	6.3
57.5	36.0	35.6	36.0			Total Current	53.8	41.6
19.1	24.1	30.1	17.6			Long-Term Debt	22.1	11.4
.0	.0	.3	.7			Deferred Taxes	.7	1.5
2.9	3.3	5.3	-10.2			All Other Non-Current	2.1	4.7
20.5	36.7	28.8	35.6			Net Worth	21.2	40.7
100.0	100.0	100.0	100.0			Total Liabilities & Net Worth	100.0	100.0
						INCOME DATA		
100.0	100.0	100.0	100.0			Net Sales	100.0	100.0
						Gross Profit		
98.8	82.2	88.9	87.1			Operating Expenses	83.7	82.6
1.2	17.8	11.1	12.9			Operating Profit	16.3	17.4
.7	8.3	5.1	2.4			All Other Expenses (net)	6.1	5.2
.5	9.6	6.0	10.5			Profit Before Taxes	10.2	12.2
						RATIOS		
3.2	2.0	2.4	2.4			Current	1.8	3.2
1.2	1.1	1.7	1.3			Current	1.0	1.4
.6	.7	1.0	1.0			Current	.7	.9
1.9	1.0	1.5	1.4			Quick	.6	1.3
.9	.5	.8	.9			Quick	.4	.2
.2	.2	.4	.3			Quick	.2	.0
0 UND	0 UND	4 88.8	3 125.0			Sales/Receivables	0 UND	0 UND
0 UND	17 21.0	31 11.8	21 17.7			Sales/Receivables	20 18.0	1 251.0
38 9.6	46 7.9	57 6.4	53 6.9			Sales/Receivables	36 10.1	32 11.2
						Cost of Sales/Inventory		
						Cost of Sales/Payables		
8.4	5.2	3.6	3.5			Sales/Working Capital	5.0	2.1
123.8	36.6	6.9	13.8			Sales/Working Capital	-70.0	8.7
-8.7	-34.2	277.0	NM			Sales/Working Capital	-5.4	-11.8
15.7	7.7	7.6	20.8			EBIT/Interest	4.9	7.1
(13) 1.0	(26) 3.9	(31) 2.9	(15) 4.0			EBIT/Interest	(21) 1.2	(21) 3.2
-3.5	2.3	1.4	1.2			EBIT/Interest	-.1	-.5
						Net Profit + Depr., Dep., Amort./Cur. Mat. L /T/D		
.0	.3	.3	.1			Fixed/Worth	.8	.3
.5	.9	1.1	.6			Fixed/Worth	1.4	.8
NM	4.2	NM	1.3			Fixed/Worth	6.6	1.1
1.1	.5	1.0	.5			Debt/Worth	.6	.5
2.5	1.5	3.0	2.1			Debt/Worth	1.6	.8
-5.6	13.3	NM	4.2			Debt/Worth	16.6	14.4
48.7	32.8	45.4	45.8			% Profit Before Taxes/Tangible Net Worth	22.3	25.8
(12) 1.7	(29) 18.0	(29) 21.1	(19) 21.1			% Profit Before Taxes/Tangible Net Worth	(19) 6.8	(20) 15.3
-9.6	8.5	2.1	5.7			% Profit Before Taxes/Tangible Net Worth	-17.0	2.8
22.4	8.2	9.9	14.3			% Profit Before Taxes/Total Assets	8.4	12.5
2.2	5.5	4.4	7.3			% Profit Before Taxes/Total Assets	3.1	8.7
-5.1	2.1	.5	1.2			% Profit Before Taxes/Total Assets	-6.3	.0
UND	56.0	36.9	59.7			Sales/Net Fixed Assets	5.1	7.0
24.5	2.9	7.7	5.2			Sales/Net Fixed Assets	1.4	1.7
6.7	.6	1.9	1.5			Sales/Net Fixed Assets	.5	.9
5.6	3.2	2.7	2.5			Sales/Total Assets	1.6	1.5
3.3	1.0	1.5	1.5			Sales/Total Assets	.5	.5
2.8	.3	.6	.4			Sales/Total Assets	.3	.2
	.9	.8	.7			% Depr., Dep., Amort./Sales	2.8	1.1
	(28) 5.7	(29) 1.8	(18) 3.1			% Depr., Dep., Amort./Sales	(21) 6.1	(21) 4.9
	12.6	5.5	7.1			% Depr., Dep., Amort./Sales	8.2	9.8
	1.6					% Officers', Directors', Owners' Comp/Sales		
	(11) 4.4					% Officers', Directors', Owners' Comp/Sales		
	8.4					% Officers', Directors', Owners' Comp/Sales		
25365M	70691M	266219M	888715M	204002M	769260M	Net Sales ($)	106131M	234987M
4431M	37960M	153779M	506883M	225725M	1048886M	Total Assets ($)	136266M	136825M

M = $ thousand   MM = $ million
See Pages 11 through 21 for Explanation of Ratios and Data

AGRICULTURE—Wheat Farming NAICS 111140 (SIC 0111)

Comparative Historical Data				**Current Data Sorted By Sales**					
7	2	16	Type of Statement Unqualified	2	1	2	1	3	8
6	7	10	Reviewed	4	1	1	2	1	1
14	10	16	Compiled	4	3	3	5	1	
12	12	27	Tax Returns	13	5	3	4	2	
34	37	48	Other	7	10	4	9	12	6
4/1/02- 3/31/03 ALL	4/1/03- 3/31/04 ALL	4/1/04- 3/31/05 ALL		21 (4/1-9/30/04)			96 (10/1/04-3/31/05)		
				0-1MM	1-3MM	3-5MM	5-10MM	10-25MM	25MM & OVER
73	68	117	**NUMBER OF STATEMENTS**	30	19	13	21	19	15
%	%	%	**ASSETS**	%	%	%	%	%	%
9.9	6.8	11.7	Cash & Equivalents	10.7	9.7	5.2	10.8	16.6	16.7
11.5	15.3	20.1	Trade Receivables (net)	6.6	35.4	16.8	28.0	21.4	18.2
14.8	17.0	15.7	Inventory	7.2	19.6	28.6	21.2	8.6	17.6
6.3	6.2	4.2	All Other Current	3.8	3.4	1.0	4.1	9.0	2.8
42.5	45.3	51.7	Total Current	28.3	68.2	51.6	64.0	55.6	55.3
37.1	32.4	36.5	Fixed Assets (net)	60.8	22.8	27.1	29.1	29.3	32.6
3.9	5.0	3.6	Intangibles (net)	.2	3.6	5.8	4.0	5.6	5.1
16.5	17.3	8.3	All Other Non-Current	10.7	5.5	15.5	2.9	9.4	6.9
100.0	100.0	100.0	Total	100.0	100.0	100.0	100.0	100.0	100.0
			LIABILITIES						
12.2	21.3	13.9	Notes Payable-Short Term	17.4	17.9	19.6	10.2	6.1	11.6
3.4	3.0	2.5	Cur. Mat.-L/T/D	2.5	1.0	2.8	3.4	4.0	1.1
9.3	9.4	11.1	Trade Payables	2.1	19.7	12.2	13.5	10.8	14.4
.2	.5	.3	Income Taxes Payable	.2	.2	.1	.4	.7	.4
8.7	7.9	10.1	All Other Current	3.8	13.4	3.6	13.8	16.2	10.8
33.8	42.1	37.8	Total Current	26.0	52.2	38.3	41.2	37.7	38.3
33.9	18.4	25.3	Long-Term Debt	35.5	15.5	17.3	24.8	27.4	22.6
.0	.1	.2	Deferred Taxes	.0	.0	.0	.4	.5	.6
2.6	7.4	5.0	All Other Non-Current	4.9	2.1	1.4	3.8	4.2	15.0
29.6	31.9	31.5	Net Worth	33.6	30.2	43.0	29.8	30.1	23.5
100.0	100.0	100.0	Total Liabilities & Net Worth	100.0	100.0	100.0	100.0	100.0	100.0
			INCOME DATA						
100.0	100.0	100.0	Net Sales	100.0	100.0	100.0	100.0	100.0	100.0
			Gross Profit						
89.1	88.6	87.5	Operating Expenses	76.1	94.6	82.6	95.2	88.1	94.1
10.9	11.4	12.5	Operating Profit	23.9	5.4	17.4	4.8	11.9	5.9
4.9	4.6	4.8	All Other Expenses (net)	12.3	4.3	1.8	1.7	.7	2.7
6.0	6.9	7.7	Profit Before Taxes	11.7	1.1	15.6	3.1	11.2	3.2
			RATIOS						
2.5	1.8	2.4		1.9	2.8	4.6	2.4	2.3	2.4
1.2	1.1	1.3	Current	1.1	1.2	1.2	1.3	1.9	1.3
.8	.8	.9		.6	.9	.7	1.1	1.0	.9
1.0	.7	1.4		1.0	1.8	1.9	1.5	1.5	1.3
.7	.4	.7	Quick	.5	.9	.4	.8	.9	.8
.2	.1	.3		.1	.5	.2	.4	.5	.3
0 UND	0 UND	0 UND		0 UND	3 124.2	0 UND	0 UND	21 17.7	3 116.6
18 20.4	18 20.9	21 17.7	Sales/Receivables	0 UND	34 10.6	6 63.2	37 9.8	45 8.1	18 20.5
42 8.8	50 7.3	50 7.4		11 33.0	56 6.5	49 7.4	47 7.8	61 5.9	73 5.0
			Cost of Sales/Inventory						
			Cost of Sales/Payables						
5.1	5.3	4.4		3.5	4.3	5.7	4.5	3.7	4.5
30.4	33.2	19.1	Sales/Working Capital	447.4	23.8	16.2	20.9	6.8	13.8
-18.8	-19.2	-42.3		-8.5	-99.9	-18.5	258.6	250.5	-16.9
5.5	5.5	7.9		7.2	24.4	8.2	8.3	27.9	5.3
(58) 1.8	(55) 3.2	(93) 3.3	EBIT/Interest	(20) 3.8	(14) 2.9	(12) 3.2	(19) 2.5	(15) 4.0	(13) 2.9
.7	1.1	1.1		.8	.6	1.6	1.7	1.5	.8
		4.3							
	(15) 1.5		Net Profit + Depr., Dep., Amort./Cur. Mat. L/T/D						
	.8								
.3	.3	.2		.6	.0	.2	.1	.1	.1
.9	.7	1.0	Fixed/Worth	1.2	.4	.6	1.1	1.0	.6
14.5	5.2	4.6		17.6	2.4	NM	NM	3.1	4.3
.5	.6	.6		.6	.5	.2	1.0	.9	1.8
1.4	1.7	2.5	Debt/Worth	1.9	3.0	3.0	2.2	1.6	4.1
23.2	22.7	8.6		UND	7.3	NM	NM	5.0	6.9
20.1	30.8	36.8		21.2	41.1	72.1	39.6	66.0	25.6
(59) 5.7	(54) 7.3	(96) 15.2	% Profit Before Taxes/Tangible Net Worth	(24) 10.9	(17) 21.0	(10) 5.9	(16) 11.1	(16) 45.4	(13) 14.2
-2.8	.5	3.5		2.7	1.0	-3.1	1.9	21.6	4.3
6.8	9.0	10.6		8.5	16.2	14.9	11.2	24.8	8.4
2.8	3.7	4.8	% Profit Before Taxes/Total Assets	3.7	6.2	4.8	4.1	9.8	3.5
-.4	-.2	.5		-1.1	.5	1.0	.8	2.9	.6
25.8	26.0	53.2		3.0	559.3	115.0	95.7	40.3	61.1
4.0	6.0	7.7	Sales/Net Fixed Assets	.6	21.7	24.4	24.5	6.3	11.2
.7	1.0	1.1		.2	5.5	1.2	4.2	3.6	2.9
3.2	2.9	2.9		1.1	3.7	3.5	4.0	3.1	2.8
1.2	1.1	1.6	Sales/Total Assets	.4	2.7	1.3	2.1	1.8	1.7
.3	.3	.4		.2	.8	.3	1.4	.7	1.0
1.5	1.3	.8		5.9	1.1	.5	.4	.8	.1
(60) 5.2	(55) 3.5	(86) 3.1	% Depr., Dep., Amort./Sales	(23) 11.4	(11) 1.7	(10) 1.7	(17) .9	(14) 2.0	(11) 3.2
12.4	13.6	9.2		21.7	7.3	7.7	2.1	7.0	6.4
3.2	1.8	1.2			1.2				
(20) 7.8	(20) 3.1	(31) 4.4	% Officers', Directors', Owners' Comp/Sales		(11) 4.4				
13.3	6.5	11.0			8.4				
1297854M	852801M	2224252M	Net Sales ($)	12616M	33160M	52017M	146897M	297699M	1681869M
613071M	549436M	1977664M	Total Assets ($)	36227M	26502M	161644M	96109M	258903M	1398279M

M = $ thousand   MM = $ million
See Pages 11 through 21 for Explanation of Ratios and Data

AGRICULTURE—Corn Farming NAICS 111150 (SIC 0115, 0119)

Current Data Sorted By Assets   **Comparative Historical Data**

Type of Statement

Type of Statement	0-500M	500M-2MM	2-10MM	10-50MM	50-100MM	100-250MM		4/1/00-3/31/01 ALL	4/1/01-3/31/02 ALL
Unqualified	1		2			1		1	2
Reviewed		2	2	3				3	2
Compiled		2	5	2				1	8
Tax Returns	6	6	10					2	3
Other	2				1			11	15
	2 (4/1-9/30/04)		43 (10/1/04-3/31/05)						
	0-500M	500M-2MM	2-10MM	10-50MM	50-100MM	100-250MM			
NUMBER OF STATEMENTS	9	15	19	1	1			18	30

Columns 10-50MM, 50-100MM, and 100-250MM current data marked "DATA NOT AVAILABLE."

ASSETS (%)

	500M-2MM	2-10MM		4/1/00-3/31/01 ALL	4/1/01-3/31/02 ALL
Cash & Equivalents	6.3	5.0		7.1	7.3
Trade Receivables (net)	11.7	10.4		3.4	8.8
Inventory	11.6	17.3		12.7	17.8
All Other Current	2.8	4.1		.5	5.7
Total Current	32.4	36.8		23.6	39.6
Fixed Assets (net)	52.0	54.7		56.5	47.5
Intangibles (net)	1.5	1.0		1.8	.0
All Other Non-Current	14.1	7.5		18.1	12.9
Total	100.0	100.0		100.0	100.0

LIABILITIES

	500M-2MM	2-10MM		4/1/00-3/31/01 ALL	4/1/01-3/31/02 ALL
Notes Payable-Short Term	13.6	14.0		28.1	23.8
Cur. Mat.-L/T/D	3.4	1.9		.6	3.5
Trade Payables	.9	6.1		1.1	9.5
Income Taxes Payable	.1	.0		1.4	.7
All Other Current	6.1	14.4		4.6	3.8
Total Current	24.0	36.5		35.8	41.3
Long-Term Debt	22.3	15.7		19.1	17.1
Deferred Taxes	.0	1.3		.9	.5
All Other Non-Current	2.2	1.2		4.9	3.5
Net Worth	51.5	45.3		39.2	37.6
Total Liabilities & Net Worth	100.0	100.0		100.0	100.0

INCOME DATA

	500M-2MM	2-10MM		4/1/00-3/31/01 ALL	4/1/01-3/31/02 ALL
Net Sales	100.0	100.0		100.0	100.0
Gross Profit					
Operating Expenses	86.9	90.9		76.7	91.3
Operating Profit	13.1	9.1		23.3	8.7
All Other Expenses (net)	3.4	5.2		9.0	4.3
Profit Before Taxes	9.7	3.9		14.3	4.4

RATIOS

	500M-2MM	2-10MM		4/1/00-3/31/01 ALL	4/1/01-3/31/02 ALL
Current	2.4	1.8		1.4	2.2
	1.3	1.1		1.1	1.3
	.6	.9		.6	.8
Quick	1.3	.8		.8	.8
	.2	.2		.4	.3
	.1	.2		.0	.1
Sales/Receivables	0 UND	0 UND		0 UND	0 UND
	13 27.5	32 11.5		2 200.4	12 30.6
	35 10.5	77 4.7		29 12.4	43 8.6
Cost of Sales/Inventory					
Cost of Sales/Payables					
Sales/Working Capital	3.7	3.1		5.2	2.7
	8.2	11.5		NM	7.4
	-3.7	-5.3		-10.6	-27.6
EBIT/Interest	7.7	4.8		6.4	3.0
	4.8	(16) 2.8		(13) 2.0	(28) 2.0
	1.2	-1.1		-.7	1.0
Net Profit + Depr., Dep., Amort./Cur. Mat. L./T/D					
Fixed/Worth	.4	.8		.6	.6
	.8	1.1		1.0	1.0
	1.5	1.7		1.5	1.3
Debt/Worth	.4	.4		.5	.4
	.8	.8		.7	.8
	1.7	2.7		2.7	3.5
% Profit Before Taxes/Tangible Net Worth	23.3	14.8		24.1	17.1
	(13) 9.2	(17) 3.2		(17) 3.2	(28) 3.4
	.3	-1.3		-12.3	.8
% Profit Before Taxes/Total Assets	10.6	4.7		17.0	6.0
	5.1	2.4		1.8	1.8
	.4	-2.5		-3.7	.3
Sales/Net Fixed Assets	4.9	2.8		2.2	3.6
	1.0	.6		.9	1.5
	.4	.2		.5	.3
Sales/Total Assets	.9	1.1		1.0	1.0
	.6	.3		.4	.6
	.3	.2		.3	.2
% Depr., Dep., Amort./Sales	4.2	4.9		3.4	3.8
	(14) 7.1	(18) 11.7		(17) 7.0	(28) 5.7
	15.2	19.6		16.8	11.3
% Officers', Directors', Owners' Comp/Sales					

Net Sales / Total Assets ($)

	0-500M	500M-2MM	2-10MM	10-50MM	50-100MM		4/1/00-3/31/01 ALL	4/1/01-3/31/02 ALL
Net Sales ($)	7238M	16402M	40111M	91987M	30671M		61244M	102581M
Total Assets ($)	2516M	22557M	83449M	46899M	66015M		82860M	113567M

© RMA 2005

M = $ thousand   MM = $ million

See Pages 11 through 21 for Explanation of Ratios and Data

Comparative Historical Data / Current Data Sorted By Sales

4/1/02-3/31/03 ALL	4/1/03-3/31/04 ALL	4/1/04-3/31/05 ALL	Type of Statement	0-1MM	1-3MM	3-5MM	5-10MM	10-25MM	25MM & OVER
	3	4	Unqualified	1	1	1			1
4	2	4	Reviewed		2	1	1		
6	10	5	Compiled	1	2	2			
2	9	13	Tax Returns	11	1	1			
17	27	19	Other	11	5	2			1
				2 (4/1-9/30/04)			43 (10/1/04-3/31/05)		
29	51	45	**NUMBER OF STATEMENTS**	24	11	7	1		2
%	%	%	**ASSETS**	%	%	%	%	%	%
7.5	6.2	6.0	Cash & Equivalents	4.5	8.6			D	
5.1	2.6	10.4	Trade Receivables (net)	.9	19.2			A	
16.8	15.7	14.2	Inventory	10.6	13.1			T	
4.8	5.3	3.5	All Other Current	3.2	2.0			A	
34.1	29.9	34.2	Total Current	19.3	42.9				
44.4	49.6	52.3	Fixed Assets (net)	60.9	52.9			N	
.0	.6	2.0	Intangibles (net)	1.0	1.5			O	
21.5	19.9	11.6	All Other Non-Current	18.8	2.8			T	
100.0	100.0	100.0	Total	100.0	100.0			A	
			LIABILITIES					V	
25.3	24.7	24.3	Notes Payable-Short Term	20.4	40.1			A	
1.4	2.0	3.0	Cur. Mat.-L/T/D	2.0	4.5			I	
4.3	1.6	2.9	Trade Payables	.6	.7			L	
.4	.1	.1	Income Taxes Payable	.2	.0			A	
8.5	5.3	9.3	All Other Current	3.4	17.0			B	
39.8	33.9	39.6	Total Current	26.6	62.2			L	
16.8	22.1	22.2	Long-Term Debt	22.2	32.1			E	
.0	.2	.6	Deferred Taxes	.8	.7				
3.9	4.4	2.9	All Other Non-Current	3.7	1.0				
39.4	39.4	34.7	Net Worth	46.7	4.0				
100.0	100.0	100.0	Total Liabilities & Net Worth	100.0	100.0				
			INCOME DATA						
100.0	100.0	100.0	Net Sales	100.0	100.0				
			Gross Profit						
86.5	88.1	85.1	Operating Expenses	85.1	83.7				
13.5	11.9	14.9	Operating Profit	14.9	16.3				
3.1	4.4	4.7	All Other Expenses (net)	5.6	4.7				
10.5	7.4	10.2	Profit Before Taxes	9.3	11.6				
			RATIOS						
1.7	2.3	1.8	Current	1.8	1.5				
1.3	1.4	1.2		1.2	1.1				
.9	.8	.6		.3	.1				
.5	.8	.9	Quick	.2	1.0				
.3	.2	(44) .2		(23) .2	.6				
.1	.0	.1		.1	.0				
0 UND	0 UND	0 UND	Sales/Receivables	0 UND	0 UND				
6 57.0	0 976.7	3 134.0		0 UND	3 135.2				
34 10.8	22 16.2	50 7.3		14 26.2	122 3.0				
			Cost of Sales/Inventory						
			Cost of Sales/Payables						
3.1	3.3	4.1	Sales/Working Capital	3.8	8.0				
9.4	8.5	10.2		9.3	18.3				
-22.9	-13.7	-4.0		-3.7	-3.5				
4.3	7.5	7.0	EBIT/Interest	5.8	11.6				
(26) 2.7	(46) 2.9	(42) 3.8		(22) 3.6	(10) 5.0				
1.6	1.3	1.2		.9	2.3				
			Net Profit + Depr., Dep., Amort./Cur. Mat. L/T/D						
.6	.6	.7	Fixed/Worth	.7	1.1				
1.0	1.0	1.2		1.1	1.7				
1.3	2.0	3.1		1.8	-1.1				
.5	.4	.5	Debt/Worth	.4	1.2				
1.0	.9	1.4		.7	1.8				
2.0	2.8	34.7		3.8	-10.5				
14.6	17.7	25.2	% Profit Before Taxes/Tangible Net Worth	8.4					
(27) 7.2	(47) 5.1	(35) 6.0		(20) 2.5					
1.5	.8	.7		-2.3					
8.9	7.1	11.1	% Profit Before Taxes/Total Assets	8.6	18.8				
3.8	2.3	4.0		2.6	9.1				
1.1	.0	.5		-.6	4.0				
5.1	3.7	5.4	Sales/Net Fixed Assets	3.2	6.7				
1.2	1.2	2.0		.4	2.5				
.4	.3	.4		.2	.8				
1.2	1.1	1.9	Sales/Total Assets	.8	2.5				
.4	.4	.6		.3	1.0				
.2	.2	.3		.2	.6				
4.2	4.8	4.6	% Depr., Dep., Amort./Sales	6.2	3.5				
(26) 5.9	(47) 7.9	(40) 8.5		(22) 11.3	(10) 5.8				
15.3	13.3	13.8		18.9	14.9				
			% Officers', Directors', Owners' Comp/Sales						
60720M	135061M	186409M	Net Sales ($)	14091M	16200M	28162M	5298M		122658M
99585M	223808M	221436M	Total Assets ($)	49923M	25546M	23897M	9156M		112914M

M = $ thousand   MM = $ million
See Pages 11 through 21 for Explanation of Ratios and Data

Current Data Sorted By Assets / Comparative Historical Data

0-500M	500M-2MM	2-10MM	10-50MM	50-100MM	100-250MM	Type of Statement	4/1/00-3/31/01 ALL	4/1/01-3/31/02 ALL
		4	5	5		Unqualified	4	2
		2	1			Reviewed	1	5
	5	13	7		1	Compiled	10	8
4	13	6				Tax Returns	8	6
1	10	9	1	1	1	Other	10	17
	14 (4/1-9/30/04)		61 (10/1/04-3/31/05)					
5	28	28	7	5	2	NUMBER OF STATEMENTS	33	38
%	%	%	%	%	%	**ASSETS**	%	%
	7.1	4.3				Cash & Equivalents	8.0	8.2
	7.5	11.2				Trade Receivables (net)	8.5	8.9
	18.0	16.2				Inventory	21.2	23.0
	1.5	4.2				All Other Current	4.7	3.6
	34.1	35.9				Total Current	42.5	43.7
	48.8	54.7				Fixed Assets (net)	44.9	42.9
	2.5	.4				Intangibles (net)	4.1	.5
	14.5	8.9				All Other Non-Current	8.5	12.9
	100.0	100.0				Total	100.0	100.0
						LIABILITIES		
	26.0	12.0				Notes Payable-Short Term	20.8	21.3
	3.0	7.4				Cur. Mat.-L/T/D	6.2	7.1
	4.3	4.8				Trade Payables	9.2	5.0
	.6	.6				Income Taxes Payable	1.0	.9
	1.5	6.6				All Other Current	12.1	6.4
	35.3	31.4				Total Current	49.4	40.7
	38.7	25.5				Long-Term Debt	22.9	16.8
	.0	.1				Deferred Taxes	1.6	.7
	6.8	2.4				All Other Non-Current	3.6	1.4
	19.2	40.6				Net Worth	22.5	40.4
	100.0	100.0				Total Liabilities & Net Worth	100.0	100.0
						INCOME DATA		
	100.0	100.0				Net Sales	100.0	100.0
						Gross Profit		
	88.1	91.7				Operating Expenses	90.8	94.1
	11.9	8.3				Operating Profit	9.2	5.9
	4.4	5.1				All Other Expenses (net)	4.7	2.7
	7.6	3.2				Profit Before Taxes	4.6	3.2
						RATIOS		
	2.0	1.6					1.2	2.3
	1.5	1.1				Current	1.0	1.1
	.6	.6					.6	.8
	.7	.9					.6	1.0
	.2	.4				Quick	.3 (37)	.5
	.1	.1					.2	.1
0 UND	0 UND						0 UND	0 UND
	0 UND	5 71.5				Sales/Receivables	14 25.5	15 24.0
	27 13.8	31 11.8					46 8.0	39 9.3
						Cost of Sales/Inventory		
						Cost of Sales/Payables		
	5.0	6.9					9.6	5.4
	13.0	38.1				Sales/Working Capital	-91.9	40.8
	-4.9	-7.4					-8.5	-19.1
	5.9	8.2					2.6	3.8
	(26) 2.3	(21) 2.9				EBIT/Interest	(27) 1.2	(35) 1.9
	1.0	-.3					.5	.9
						Net Profit + Depr., Dep., Amort./Cur. Mat. L/T/D		
	.7	.5					.7	.5
	1.6	1.2				Fixed/Worth	1.4	1.1
	NM	2.4					NM	1.7
	.6	.6					1.0	.4
	1.3	1.0				Debt/Worth	2.3	1.2
	NM	8.4					-7.5	3.2
	75.1	17.1					14.8	22.6
	(21) 10.6	(23) 4.9				% Profit Before Taxes/Tangible Net Worth	(23) 3.8	(35) 5.4
	1.5	.8					-.6	.8
	12.2	7.0					6.2	7.8
	4.0	1.4				% Profit Before Taxes/Total Assets	1.0	2.5
	.0	-3.8					-2.6	.0
	6.0	14.5					7.6	6.4
	2.2	.7				Sales/Net Fixed Assets	3.5	2.7
	.6	.4					.7	1.3
	1.7	3.1					3.0	2.4
	.9	.6				Sales/Total Assets	1.1	1.3
	.4	.3					.4	.5
	4.4	1.4					1.3	1.9
	(26) 12.0	(24) 7.3				% Depr., Dep., Amort./Sales	(28) 4.7	(35) 4.5
	17.2	15.1					11.5	10.5
	1.5	.9					2.5	.9
	(12) 3.0	(10) 1.9				% Officers', Directors', Owners' Comp/Sales	(10) 5.1	(18) 2.1
	4.6	6.2					9.1	5.2
8033M	46933M	165388M	386908M	909382M	110098M	Net Sales ($)	340867M	305923M
1374M	32110M	112118M	218232M	387089M	282185M	Total Assets ($)	261175M	236499M

© RMA 2005

M = $ thousand   MM = $ million
See Pages 11 through 21 for Explanation of Ratios and Data

Comparative Historical Data   Current Data Sorted By Sales

			Type of Statement				14 (4/1-9/30/04)	61 (10/1/04-3/31/05)	
6	8	14	Unqualified				1	3	10
7	5	3	Reviewed					2	1
5	15	13	Compiled	4	5	2	1	1	1
7	17	23	Tax Returns	10	9	1	1	2	
11	9	22	Other	8	7	3		1	2
4/1/02-3/31/03 ALL	4/1/03-3/31/04 ALL	4/1/04-3/31/05 ALL		0-1MM	1-3MM	3-5MM	5-10MM	10-25MM	25MM & OVER
36	54	75	NUMBER OF STATEMENTS	22	21	6	3	9	14
%	%	%	ASSETS	%	%	%	%	%	%
8.1	7.4	6.5	Cash & Equivalents	5.4	5.2				6.8
19.2	11.1	11.0	Trade Receivables (net)	2.2	3.4				20.2
18.0	17.9	17.9	Inventory	15.4	8.2				27.3
3.9	7.4	2.7	All Other Current	1.1	1.2				3.2
49.2	43.9	38.1	Total Current	24.1	17.9				57.5
39.3	46.3	47.4	Fixed Assets (net)	64.8	61.2				29.5
1.2	1.2	1.4	Intangibles (net)	.1	3.7				.8
10.4	8.6	13.1	All Other Non-Current	11.0	17.3				12.1
100.0	100.0	100.0	Total	100.0	100.0				100.0
			LIABILITIES						
14.7	19.6	22.6	Notes Payable-Short Term	18.6	36.2				18.2
4.3	12.7	5.3	Cur. Mat.-L/T/D	2.0	8.4				1.4
12.4	4.9	6.2	Trade Payables	1.3	1.3				15.1
1.0	.2	.5	Income Taxes Payable	.1	.1				.2
10.3	4.7	5.2	All Other Current	1.6	2.1				10.9
42.6	42.1	39.7	Total Current	23.6	48.0				45.7
40.6	31.9	28.1	Long-Term Debt	34.7	47.2				11.9
.0	.4	.2	Deferred Taxes	.0	.0				1.1
1.8	4.6	3.8	All Other Non-Current	2.4	9.2				1.6
15.0	21.0	28.2	Net Worth	39.3	-4.4				39.7
100.0	100.0	100.0	Total Liabilities & Net Worth	100.0	100.0				100.0
			INCOME DATA						
100.0	100.0	100.0	Net Sales	100.0	100.0				100.0
			Gross Profit						
94.6	94.1	88.9	Operating Expenses	76.6	94.4				89.0
5.4	5.9	11.1	Operating Profit	23.4	5.6				11.0
2.2	3.4	3.6	All Other Expenses (net)	10.1	3.6				-.4
3.1	2.5	7.4	Profit Before Taxes	13.3	2.0				11.4
			RATIOS						
2.0	2.3	1.9		2.0	1.3				2.6
1.1	1.1	1.2	Current	1.4	.6				1.3
.8	.7	.6		.5	.1				1.0
1.6	.8	.9		.3	.5				1.3
.6	.4	.3	Quick	.2	.2				.7
.3	.1	.1		.1	.0				.4
6 65.2	0 UND	0 UND		0 UND	0 UND				6 61.1
30 12.3	7 50.1	4 81.8	Sales/Receivables	0 UND	0 UND				30 12.1
99 3.7	31 11.7	41 8.8		18 20.3	7 49.1				60 6.1
			Cost of Sales/Inventory						
			Cost of Sales/Payables						
8.4	4.3	7.7		2.7	13.0				7.3
37.2	51.2	30.6	Sales/Working Capital	10.7	-15.0				23.2
-17.2	-17.4	-6.1		-2.5	-4.1				NM
3.8	3.0	7.4		5.0	4.5				13.9
(31) 2.2	(45) 1.2	(62) 2.6	EBIT/Interest	(17) 2.7	(20) 2.3			(11) 3.6	
.9	-4.3	1.0		1.1	-.6				1.7
		6.1	Net Profit + Depr., Dep.,						
	(13) 3.1		Amort./Cur. Mat. L/T/D						
		.9							
.3	.5	.5		.9	1.2				.4
1.1	1.2	1.1	Fixed/Worth	1.6	9.6				.7
2.1	5.3	3.1		3.8	-2.0				1.1
.6	.4	.6		.4	1.1				.8
1.8	1.5	1.3	Debt/Worth	.9	102.5				1.6
6.7	10.3	18.5		4.1	-3.4				3.6
17.1	11.8	39.3	% Profit Before Taxes/Tangible	16.5	161.4				30.4
(33) 5.1	(44) 2.8	(60) 10.3	Net Worth	(20) 6.0	(11) 16.3				15.4
-1.7	-7.9	2.4		.2	1.7				7.6
8.9	5.3	9.6	% Profit Before Taxes/Total	7.4	8.4				11.1
2.9	1.0	3.3	Assets	2.4	3.3				3.7
-.1	-5.2	.0		-.3	-6.6				2.2
13.4	12.7	12.1		1.0	3.7				13.8
4.8	5.4	3.2	Sales/Net Fixed Assets	.5	2.4				6.4
.9	.7	.6		.2	.6				4.2
2.7	2.9	3.0		.5	2.0				2.6
1.3	1.2	1.2	Sales/Total Assets	.3	1.1				1.7
.4	.5	.4		.2	.4				1.3
1.6	1.3	2.1		7.5	6.5				1.3
(33) 4.8	(44) 4.9	(66) 5.9	% Depr., Dep., Amort./Sales	(20) 14.4	(19) 10.4			(13) 1.7	
9.8	10.6	13.9		25.0	14.1				3.5
1.3	1.5	1.3	% Officers', Directors',						
(14) 3.4	(20) 3.5	(24) 2.6	Owners' Comp/Sales						
21.2	6.2	4.6							
1305351M	996527M	1626742M	Net Sales ($)	10661M	35017M	23670M	18547M	132459M	1406388M
917211M	547539M	1033108M	Total Assets ($)	38271M	46481M	19393M	7621M	33836M	887506M

© RMA 2005   **M = $ thousand   MM = $ million**
See Pages 11 through 21 for Explanation of Ratios and Data

AGRICULTURE—Potato Farming NAICS 111211 (SIC 0134)

Current Data Sorted By Assets							Comparative Historical Data	
			2	2		Type of Statement		3
	2	6	1	1		Unqualified		4
2	2	6	3			Reviewed		8
4	3					Compiled		7
		2	3		1	Tax Returns		9
	8 (4/1-9/30/04)		32 (10/1/04-3/31/05)			Other	4/1/00-3/31/01 ALL	4/1/01-3/31/02 ALL
0-500M	500M-2MM	2-10MM	10-50MM	50-100MM	100-250MM			
6	7	14	9	3	1	NUMBER OF STATEMENTS		31
%	%	%	%	%	%		%	%
						ASSETS		
		2.0				Cash & Equivalents		7.1
		9.4				Trade Receivables (net)	D	12.0
		19.2				Inventory	A	14.4
		2.1				All Other Current	T	8.8
		32.7				Total Current	A	42.4
		55.9				Fixed Assets (net)		45.9
		.1				Intangibles (net)	N	1.4
		11.3				All Other Non-Current	O	10.3
		100.0				Total	T	100.0
						LIABILITIES	A	
		15.7				Notes Payable-Short Term	V	23.0
		11.0				Cur. Mat.-L/T/D	A	2.5
		2.5				Trade Payables	I	3.6
		1.0				Income Taxes Payable	L	.1
		5.8				All Other Current	A	5.8
		35.9				Total Current	B	35.0
		28.1				Long-Term Debt	L	33.9
		.0				Deferred Taxes	E	1.6
		1.3				All Other Non-Current		2.9
		34.7				Net Worth		26.6
		100.0				Total Liabilities & Net Worth		100.0
						INCOME DATA		
		100.0				Net Sales		100.0
						Gross Profit		
		102.0				Operating Expenses		93.8
		-2.0				Operating Profit		6.2
		2.0				All Other Expenses (net)		4.7
		-4.1				Profit Before Taxes		1.4
						RATIOS		
		1.3						3.1
		1.0				Current		1.3
		.4						.8
		.4						1.7
		.1				Quick		.5
		.0						.2
	0	UND					0	UND
	11	32.7				Sales/Receivables	36	10.2
	42	8.7					78	4.7
						Cost of Sales/Inventory		
						Cost of Sales/Payables		
		7.5						4.1
		NM				Sales/Working Capital		7.5
		-4.7						-5.2
		5.9						5.5
	(11)	2.8				EBIT/Interest	(27)	1.6
		-5.4						.1
						Net Profit + Depr., Dep., Amort./Cur. Mat. L /T/D		
		.7						.5
		1.3				Fixed/Worth		1.5
		3.0						4.7
		.8						.6
		1.7				Debt/Worth		1.7
		2.8						7.4
		11.2						46.2
	(13)	.7				% Profit Before Taxes/Tangible Net Worth	(28)	6.8
		-20.4						-4.7
		4.9						9.8
		-.1				% Profit Before Taxes/Total Assets		1.3
		-13.6						-5.6
		2.5						6.0
		2.0				Sales/Net Fixed Assets		2.1
		.7						1.2
		1.5						1.2
		.9				Sales/Total Assets		.8
		.4						.4
		5.5						2.0
	(13)	7.8				% Depr., Dep., Amort./Sales		3.5
		14.7						8.3
						% Officers', Directors', Owners' Comp/Sales		
4187M	13758M	66408M	425073M	228308M	96481M	Net Sales ($)		247749M
2067M	9492M	65317M	170105M	211999M	103428M	Total Assets ($)		388586M

© RMA 2005

M = $ thousand   MM = $ million
See Pages 11 through 21 for Explanation of Ratios and Data

Comparative Historical Data | Current Data Sorted By Sales

			Type of Statement						
2	7	4	Unqualified		6	1	1	1	3
6	6	10	Reviewed					1	1
9	16	13	Compiled	2	2	3	3	3	
8	8	7	Tax Returns	2	4	1			
8	6	6	Other	2	1			1	2

				8 (4/1-9/30/04)			32 (10/1/04-3/31/05)		
4/1/02-3/31/03	4/1/03-3/31/04	4/1/04-3/31/05		0-1MM	1-3MM	3-5MM	5-10MM	10-25MM	25MM & OVER
ALL	ALL	ALL							
33	43	40	NUMBER OF STATEMENTS	6	13	5	4	6	6
%	%	%	ASSETS	%	%	%	%	%	%
5.8	2.8	4.3	Cash & Equivalents		3.8				
13.6	15.3	9.6	Trade Receivables (net)		6.8				
16.0	14.8	20.0	Inventory		16.9				
6.9	8.4	2.4	All Other Current		2.2				
42.3	41.3	36.3	Total Current		29.7				
49.9	51.8	52.8	Fixed Assets (net)		59.1				
.3	.7	.3	Intangibles (net)		.5				
7.5	6.2	10.6	All Other Non-Current		10.8				
100.0	100.0	100.0	Total		100.0				
			LIABILITIES						
17.8	21.1	20.0	Notes Payable-Short Term		31.3				
9.6	9.7	12.9	Cur. Mat.-L/T/D		19.2				
4.3	5.9	2.6	Trade Payables		1.9				
.7	.2	.6	Income Taxes Payable		.8				
11.1	8.3	9.6	All Other Current		14.3				
43.4	45.3	45.6	Total Current		67.5				
40.3	37.8	37.5	Long-Term Debt		63.8				
1.6	.9	.1	Deferred Taxes		.0				
1.4	.9	4.8	All Other Non-Current		1.4				
13.3	15.1	12.0	Net Worth		−32.7				
100.0	100.0	100.0	Total Liabilities & Net Worth		100.0				
			INCOME DATA						
100.0	100.0	100.0	Net Sales		100.0				
			Gross Profit						
90.9	97.8	99.2	Operating Expenses		105.5				
9.1	2.2	.8	Operating Profit		−5.5				
2.6	1.8	2.4	All Other Expenses (net)		.6				
6.5	.3	−1.6	Profit Before Taxes		−6.1				
			RATIOS						
2.4	1.7	1.7			2.2				
1.1	1.1	1.0	Current		.6				
.7	.6	.5			.2				
1.0	.9	.6			.3				
.6	.3	.2	Quick		.1				
.1	.0	.0			.0				
0 UND	0 999.8	0 UND		0 UND					
25 14.9	28 13.2	13 28.3	Sales/Receivables	1 296.8					
48 7.6	59 6.2	45 8.1		22 16.4					
			Cost of Sales/Inventory						
			Cost of Sales/Payables						
4.2	5.1	5.0			2.7				
25.3	177.5	NM	Sales/Working Capital		−5.0				
−5.8	−11.1	−5.0			−2.3				
6.5	3.2	10.4			4.9				
(32) 3.0	(40) 1.8	(35) 2.8	EBIT/Interest		1.0				
1.5	−.8	−.8			−4.7				
			Net Profit + Depr., Dep., Amort./Cur. Mat. L/T/D						
.7	1.0	.7			.8				
1.6	1.7	1.4	Fixed/Worth		4.8				
46.8	3.6	7.2			−2.5				
.8	.9	.8			.7				
2.1	2.9	1.7	Debt/Worth		8.2				
73.7	13.5	11.5			−4.1				
49.2	10.9	15.7	% Profit Before Taxes/Tangible Net Worth						
(27) 19.5	(36) 6.9	(33) 5.9							
6.0	−8.5	−11.6							
13.2	5.0	5.7	% Profit Before Taxes/Total Assets		5.2				
8.1	1.5	1.6			.6				
1.8	−3.5	−6.1			−14.6				
5.1	7.4	4.9			3.0				
2.6	2.9	2.3	Sales/Net Fixed Assets		1.9				
1.4	1.3	.9			.8				
2.0	2.6	1.6			1.5				
1.1	1.0	1.0	Sales/Total Assets		1.0				
.7	.7	.5			.5				
2.5	3.0	4.1	% Depr., Dep., Amort./Sales		3.5				
(32) 4.5	(38) 4.8	(37) 6.6		(12) 6.2					
6.2	8.1	11.8			12.5				
	3.1		% Officers', Directors', Owners' Comp/Sales						
	(11) 5.5								
	7.9								
695707M	797728M	834215M	Net Sales ($)	2822M	21277M	21368M	29625M	103843M	655280M
673286M	604860M	562408M	Total Assets ($)	17634M	30834M	19928M	48345M	74532M	371135M

M = $ thousand   MM = $ million
See Pages 11 through 21 for Explanation of Ratios and Data

Current Data Sorted By Assets   **Comparative Historical Data**

						Type of Statement		
	2	11	2 8	2	1	Unqualified	9	9
	3	6	3		1	Reviewed	24	15
7	8	4				Compiled	25	11
3	5	6	7	4		Tax Returns	9	10
						Other	38	21
	20 (4/1-9/30/04)		63 (10/1/04-3/31/05)				4/1/00-3/31/01	4/1/01-3/31/02
0-500M	500M-2MM	2-10MM	10-50MM	50-100MM	100-250MM		ALL	ALL
10	18	27	20	6	2	**NUMBER OF STATEMENTS**	105	66
%	%	%	%	%	%	**ASSETS**	%	%
23.2	6.9	7.0	2.7			Cash & Equivalents	6.3	4.7
6.5	11.5	19.4	22.2			Trade Receivables (net)	15.6	19.3
3.2	7.8	10.5	19.5			Inventory	12.3	15.0
.1	6.9	7.9	6.2			All Other Current	6.0	6.2
33.0	33.1	44.8	50.6			Total Current	40.3	45.1
59.7	62.1	34.1	39.5			Fixed Assets (net)	46.2	44.4
.0	1.7	.9	.4			Intangibles (net)	2.5	2.3
7.4	3.1	20.2	9.5			All Other Non-Current	11.1	8.2
100.0	100.0	100.0	100.0			Total	100.0	100.0
						LIABILITIES		
15.3	30.5	18.7	17.4			Notes Payable-Short Term	16.8	18.4
19.3	1.9	3.0	3.9			Cur. Mat.-L/T/D	3.9	3.0
5.2	11.5	6.4	5.8			Trade Payables	7.8	11.7
.0	.0	1.4	.0			Income Taxes Payable	.2	.2
7.4	10.6	9.4	6.0			All Other Current	6.2	7.6
47.3	54.5	38.9	33.2			Total Current	34.9	40.8
46.1	30.8	17.2	21.9			Long-Term Debt	27.7	18.4
.0	.0	2.0	.1			Deferred Taxes	1.3	1.6
15.6	9.1	2.4	1.4			All Other Non-Current	3.1	2.6
-9.1	5.6	39.5	43.4			Net Worth	32.9	36.6
100.0	100.0	100.0	100.0			Total Liabilities & Net Worth	100.0	100.0
						INCOME DATA		
100.0	100.0	100.0	100.0			Net Sales	100.0	100.0
						Gross Profit		
97.3	86.8	99.4	90.0			Operating Expenses	94.2	95.5
2.7	13.2	.6	10.0			Operating Profit	5.8	4.5
.8	3.4	-.4	1.9			All Other Expenses (net)	1.9	2.3
1.9	9.8	1.0	8.1			Profit Before Taxes	3.9	2.2
						RATIOS		
1.7	1.6	4.3	2.2				2.7	2.0
1.0	.8	1.1	1.6			Current	1.3	1.2
.1	.2	.7	1.1				.7	.7
1.6	1.4	2.9	1.3				1.4	1.1
.5	(17) .2	1.0	.6			Quick	.8	.7
.1	.1	.3	.4				.2	.1
0 UND	0 UND	9 39.8	24 15.2				0 UND	5 79.6
0 UND	0 UND	30 12.0	66 5.5			Sales/Receivables	25 14.3	31 11.8
12 29.6	26 13.9	51 7.1	120 3.1				55 6.6	65 5.6
						Cost of Sales/Inventory		
						Cost of Sales/Payables		
29.8	22.6	5.2	2.8				5.3	5.8
NM	NM	67.8	6.2			Sales/Working Capital	18.1	18.3
-9.2	-8.4	-13.7	41.3				-21.8	-14.2
	14.4	5.4	10.2				4.8	5.4
(14)	(14) 2.8	(25) .9	(19) 6.4			EBIT/Interest	(90) 2.4	(60) 2.1
	.1	-3.2	1.6				-.8	.7
						Net Profit + Depr., Dep.,	4.7	6.3
						Amort./Cur. Mat. L./T/D	(18) 2.7	(10) 2.1
							.7	1.3
.7	.8	.3	.5				.5	.5
-5.0	2.0	.6	.7			Fixed/Worth	1.1	1.1
-1.4	-5.9	2.0	2.1				2.9	3.8
.4	.6	.5	.6				.5	.6
-6.8	5.4	2.1	1.7			Debt/Worth	1.2	1.5
-2.6	-7.3	3.6	3.9				4.1	6.5
	52.9	25.5	31.0			% Profit Before Taxes/Tangible	24.6	18.9
(12)	(12) 30.8	(26) .8	14.0			Net Worth	(90) 8.1	(57) 7.7
	20.1	-9.8	1.4				-3.5	-1.1
27.2	23.6	8.0	9.6			% Profit Before Taxes/Total	12.3	11.8
1.0	6.4	-.2	3.5			Assets	4.1	2.6
-16.5	-.3	-5.6	1.1				-3.7	-.9
28.6	11.5	14.7	7.0				9.1	13.0
6.6	4.7	7.1	3.3			Sales/Net Fixed Assets	3.8	4.0
3.8	1.0	3.0	1.4				1.6	1.8
5.3	5.3	3.0	1.5				2.4	2.4
3.7	3.0	2.0	1.1			Sales/Total Assets	1.4	1.4
3.0	.7	1.2	.6				.8	.7
	1.8	1.2	2.1				1.6	1.5
(16)	(16) 4.1	(24) 3.0	(18) 3.9			% Depr., Dep., Amort./Sales	(88) 3.4	(62) 3.1
	8.6	5.5	5.7				6.3	5.5
		1.0					1.4	1.1
	(11) 1.8					% Officers', Directors',	(26) 2.5	(11) 3.0
	3.5					Owners' Comp/Sales	6.3	4.7
7991M	79467M	315665M	440588M	562924M	480129M	Net Sales ($)	2804038M	1777679M
2145M	20156M	130895M	376042M	424580M	345308M	Total Assets ($)	2107249M	1166343M

M = $ thousand   MM = $ million
See Pages 11 through 21 for Explanation of Ratios and Data

Comparative Historical Data | **Current Data Sorted By Sales**

			Type of Statement						
12	7	5	Unqualified		5		1	8	5
26	27	22	Reviewed		3	2	4	2	8
23	18	12	Compiled			2	2		2
14	9	19	Tax Returns	8	6	2	2	7	1
17	22	25	Other	5		4	5		4
4/1/02-3/31/03	4/1/03-3/31/04	4/1/04-3/31/05			20 (4/1-9/30/04)			63 (10/1/04-3/31/05)	
ALL	ALL	ALL		0-1MM	1-3MM	3-5MM	5-10MM	10-25MM	25MM & OVER
92	83	83	**NUMBER OF STATEMENTS**	13	14	8	12	17	19
%	%	%	**ASSETS**	%	%	%	%	%	%
7.4	7.6	8.0	Cash & Equivalents	17.8	8.2		5.0	8.4	4.5
15.5	18.0	16.5	Trade Receivables (net)	3.0	10.2		18.7	21.9	22.9
12.8	12.3	11.6	Inventory	2.6	10.4		13.3	11.9	20.2
7.2	8.3	6.0	All Other Current	.9	1.4		8.5	9.1	10.2
42.9	46.2	42.1	Total Current	24.2	30.2		45.6	51.3	57.8
44.5	41.5	44.7	Fixed Assets (net)	69.8	49.1		46.3	34.2	27.3
.9	.5	1.9	Intangibles (net)	.3	2.1		.1	.1	6.4
11.6	11.8	11.3	All Other Non-Current	5.7	18.6		8.1	14.3	8.5
100.0	100.0	100.0	Total	100.0	100.0		100.0	100.0	100.0
			LIABILITIES						
16.6	18.4	19.3	Notes Payable-Short Term	14.5	11.1		25.3	17.2	15.9
5.3	4.2	4.8	Cur. Mat.-L/T/D	3.4	14.7		1.5	2.7	1.8
9.7	11.0	7.7	Trade Payables	4.7	4.7		7.0	4.1	15.7
.5	.3	.5	Income Taxes Payable	.0	.0		.0	1.6	.5
7.1	5.4	8.2	All Other Current	8.2	10.4		15.9	5.4	6.1
39.0	39.3	40.4	Total Current	30.8	41.0		49.8	31.0	40.1
32.1	20.4	25.3	Long-Term Debt	44.9	38.7		14.4	14.4	20.2
.7	1.3	.9	Deferred Taxes	.0	.9		2.3	.9	.8
2.0	3.7	5.4	All Other Non-Current	12.0	3.9		1.4	.7	4.3
26.2	35.3	28.0	Net Worth	12.2	15.4		32.1	53.0	34.5
100.0	100.0	100.0	Total Liabilities & Net Worth	100.0	100.0		100.0	100.0	100.0
			INCOME DATA						
100.0	100.0	100.0	Net Sales	100.0	100.0		100.0	100.0	100.0
			Gross Profit						
92.7	94.6	93.4	Operating Expenses	82.8	93.1		98.7	96.9	93.4
7.3	5.4	6.6	Operating Profit	17.2	6.9		1.3	3.1	6.6
2.5	1.2	1.3	All Other Expenses (net)	3.9	3.1		.8	.1	.7
4.8	4.1	5.3	Profit Before Taxes	13.3	3.9		.5	3.0	5.8
			RATIOS						
2.4	1.8	2.1		1.7	2.2		2.0	4.6	2.3
1.3	1.3	1.3	Current	.8	.9		1.1	1.8	1.4
.7	.9	.6		.1	.2		.4	1.0	1.2
1.3	1.2	1.4		1.5	2.0		1.3	2.9	1.0
.6	.6	(82) .6	Quick	(12) .5	.2		.4	1.1	.6
.2	.2	.2		.1	.1		.2	.4	.5
1 313.9	1 277.7	0 UND		0 UND	0 UND		0 UND	18 20.1	22 16.2
27 13.3	32 11.5	28 13.2	Sales/Receivables	0 UND	0 UND		29 12.6	30 12.0	45 8.2
48 7.5	59 6.2	54 6.7		0 UND	41 8.8		51 7.2	67 5.4	76 4.8
			Cost of Sales/Inventory						
			Cost of Sales/Payables						
5.8	5.5	5.2		19.0	9.6		5.2	5.1	4.5
19.2	13.2	26.2	Sales/Working Capital	-69.9	NM		156.9	9.5	9.9
-16.0	-34.1	-22.0		-7.6	-4.6		-16.1	144.4	31.1
11.0	13.3	9.4			4.7		24.1	9.9	16.6
(84) 3.5	(77) 3.1	(72) 2.5	EBIT/Interest	(11) .9			(11) .4	(16) 2.6	(17) 3.3
1.3	1.1	.2			-1.0		-2.1	-3.8	2.1
7.6	6.0	5.0	Net Profit + Depr., Dep.,						
(17) 1.5	(18) 2.2	(13) 2.4	Amort./Cur. Mat. L/T/D						
.5	-1.3	1.2							
.5	.5	.5		.8	.5		.3	.3	.5
.9	1.0	1.2	Fixed/Worth	8.1	2.0		.8	.7	.7
2.6	2.8	4.8		-2.5	-19.5		2.2	1.5	4.4
.6	.8	.5		.4	.4		.3	.3	1.4
1.3	1.8	2.1	Debt/Worth	7.4	2.6		1.7	1.0	2.4
4.5	3.7	8.8		-4.3	-46.5		3.6	1.7	17.8
32.1	26.8	31.4	% Profit Before Taxes/Tangible		35.4		25.0	19.6	102.2
(81) 14.2	(78) 12.8	(69) 14.7	Net Worth	(10) 12.8		(11) -2.0	2.9	(18) 27.9
3.6	-.4	-.6			-6.0		-13.1	-11.6	9.9
13.2	11.0	11.0	% Profit Before Taxes/Total	19.2	23.6		13.3	8.7	16.3
6.1	4.2	3.0	Assets	7.4	.4		-1.6	1.8	5.1
1.2	-.7	-1.6		.9	-7.1		-7.1	-6.0	3.0
9.1	11.1	11.2		10.1	9.3		14.6	12.0	11.0
4.2	4.3	5.5	Sales/Net Fixed Assets	3.7	3.4		7.1	7.1	7.1
2.2	2.1	2.0		.6	1.5		2.9	4.3	4.1
3.1	2.6	3.1		3.7	3.1		4.6	3.0	2.3
1.7	1.3	1.7	Sales/Total Assets	2.8	.9		2.3	2.0	1.5
.7	.8	.8		.6	.5		1.7	1.3	1.0
1.6	2.2	1.6		5.2	1.9		1.9	1.2	1.5
(88) 3.2	(75) 3.4	(73) 3.6	% Depr., Dep., Amort./Sales	(10) 8.0	(12) 4.3		(10) 3.1	(16) 2.1	(18) 2.3
5.1	6.3	6.4		11.4	7.0		5.4	5.4	4.1
1.3	1.2	1.5	% Officers', Directors',						
(25) 3.2	(24) 2.6	(25) 3.3	Owners' Comp/Sales						
7.1	4.7	7.7							
2096052M	1588551M	1886764M	Net Sales ($)	7086M	23256M	32066M	87886M	292982M	1443488M
1253450M	1161488M	1299126M	Total Assets ($)	6577M	33682M	63408M	49822M	211666M	933971M

© RMA 2005

M = $ thousand   MM = $ million
See Pages 11 through 21 for Explanation of Ratios and Data

Current Data Sorted By Assets   Comparative Historical Data

0-500M	500M-2MM	2-10MM	10-50MM	50-100MM	100-250MM	Type of Statement	4/1/00-3/31/01 ALL	4/1/01-3/31/02 ALL
		3	3	3	2	Unqualified	6	10
	1	5		2	2	Reviewed	5	6
5	2	2	1	1		Compiled	34	21
	2	6	1			Tax Returns	3	14
	1	1	4			Other	7	8

28 (4/1-9/30/04)   19 (10/1/04-3/31/05)

0-500M	500M-2MM	2-10MM	10-50MM	50-100MM	100-250MM		ALL	ALL
5	6	17	9	6	4	**NUMBER OF STATEMENTS**	55	59
%	%	%	%	%	%	**ASSETS**	%	%
		9.3				Cash & Equivalents	4.3	7.1
		12.4				Trade Receivables (net)	8.5	10.7
		7.0				Inventory	6.1	8.6
		1.7				All Other Current	17.1	7.8
		30.4				Total Current	35.9	34.2
		57.1				Fixed Assets (net)	49.4	54.6
		.6				Intangibles (net)	2.1	.8
		11.9				All Other Non-Current	12.6	10.4
		100.0				Total	100.0	100.0
						LIABILITIES		
		9.3				Notes Payable-Short Term	15.1	11.1
		2.9				Cur. Mat.-L/T/D	6.7	3.2
		2.8				Trade Payables	7.0	5.0
		.1				Income Taxes Payable	.1	.1
		14.9				All Other Current	12.9	8.9
		30.1				Total Current	41.8	28.3
		31.3				Long-Term Debt	35.7	34.7
		.0				Deferred Taxes	.9	.7
		8.1				All Other Non-Current	2.8	6.2
		30.5				Net Worth	18.9	30.1
		100.0				Total Liabilities & Net Worth	100.0	100.0
						INCOME DATA		
		100.0				Net Sales	100.0	100.0
						Gross Profit		
		88.9				Operating Expenses	92.0	96.1
		11.1				Operating Profit	8.0	3.9
		1.2				All Other Expenses (net)	4.0	5.9
		9.9				Profit Before Taxes	4.0	−2.0
						RATIOS		
		2.6					2.0	2.2
		1.1				Current	1.0	1.2
		.5					.3	.6
		1.7					.6	1.2
		1.0				Quick	.2	.5
		.2					.0	.2
	0 UND						0 UND 0 UND	
	7 52.7					Sales/Receivables	0 999.8 12 29.4	
	37 9.8						18 20.7 38 9.5	
						Cost of Sales/Inventory		
						Cost of Sales/Payables		
		3.3					5.2	5.2
		60.5				Sales/Working Capital	−252.2	32.0
		−6.3					−4.5	−6.7
		7.0					4.2	5.2
	(13) 2.3					EBIT/Interest	(46) 1.7	(44) .9
		−1.2					.6	−.1
						Net Profit + Depr., Dep., Amort./Cur. Mat. L /T/D		
		.8					.5	.7
		1.5				Fixed/Worth	1.6	1.6
		8.6					−9.7	−525.0
		.6					.5	.5
		2.1				Debt/Worth	2.4	1.6
		505.9					−15.0	−529.0
		36.7				% Profit Before Taxes/Tangible Net Worth	26.0	33.0
	(14) 10.8						(40) 7.6	(43) .5
		−2.3					.0	−5.1
		11.3				% Profit Before Taxes/Total Assets	8.8	9.6
		4.6					1.4	.0
		−2.5					−3.0	−3.6
		3.5				Sales/Net Fixed Assets	8.2	7.0
		1.0					3.1	1.8
		.6					.8	.7
		1.8				Sales/Total Assets	2.5	2.0
		.7					.9	.8
		.3					.4	.4
		4.0				% Depr., Dep., Amort./Sales	.1	.7
	(16) 5.5						(52) 1.0	(52) 3.4
		12.2					7.5	11.0
						% Officers', Directors', Owners' Comp/Sales	1.5	1.0
							(22) 2.7	(15) 2.8
							7.0	8.5
4154M	11058M	119061M	227601M	335597M	530071M	Net Sales ($)	1302393M	1763565M
1503M	7795M	73085M	211727M	525669M	702864M	Total Assets ($)	828361M	1228327M

M = $ thousand   MM = $ million
See Pages 11 through 21 for Explanation of Ratios and Data

Comparative Historical Data | **Current Data Sorted By Sales**

			Type of Statement	0-1MM	1-3MM	3-5MM	5-10MM	10-25MM	25MM & OVER
16	17	11	Unqualified		1			1	9
15	9	8	Reviewed		3		1	4	
19	20	5	Compiled		2	1	1		1
23	10	14	Tax Returns	9	2	3			
8	4	9	Other		2		3		4
4/1/02-3/31/03 ALL	4/1/03-3/31/04 ALL	4/1/04-3/31/05 ALL			28 (4/1-9/30/04)			19 (10/1/04-3/31/05)	
81	60	47	**NUMBER OF STATEMENTS**	9	10	4	5	5	14
%	%	%	**ASSETS**	%	%	%	%	%	%
8.5	7.3	12.6	Cash & Equivalents		9.0				8.3
6.5	10.4	7.6	Trade Receivables (net)		4.8				16.4
6.5	9.1	8.1	Inventory		8.1				16.1
4.5	12.2	1.6	All Other Current		4.0				2.3
26.1	39.1	29.9	Total Current		26.0				43.1
58.4	47.8	57.7	Fixed Assets (net)		66.6				41.8
1.6	1.4	1.5	Intangibles (net)		.2				3.6
13.9	11.7	10.8	All Other Non-Current		7.2				11.5
100.0	100.0	100.0	Total		100.0				100.0
			LIABILITIES						
10.8	14.3	9.2	Notes Payable-Short Term		9.5				10.6
4.4	2.7	3.3	Cur. Mat.-L/T/D		2.7				3.7
3.8	5.0	2.8	Trade Payables		2.0				2.0
.1	.1	.1	Income Taxes Payable		.0				.1
12.4	10.8	18.0	All Other Current		44.4				15.3
31.4	33.0	33.3	Total Current		58.6				31.8
32.6	32.8	38.0	Long-Term Debt		41.0				23.6
.8	.8	.8	Deferred Taxes		.0				1.9
4.2	4.7	4.4	All Other Non-Current		2.6				4.4
31.0	28.7	23.4	Net Worth		−2.2				38.3
100.0	100.0	100.0	Total Liabilities & Net Worth		100.0				100.0
			INCOME DATA						
100.0	100.0	100.0	Net Sales		100.0				100.0
			Gross Profit						
94.4	95.0	90.4	Operating Expenses		90.5				90.8
5.6	5.0	9.6	Operating Profit		9.5				9.2
4.0	3.6	1.7	All Other Expenses (net)		2.6				2.2
1.6	1.4	7.9	Profit Before Taxes		6.9				7.0
			RATIOS						
2.1	2.7	2.5			2.6				2.3
1.0	1.1	1.2	Current		1.1				1.5
.4	.7	.7			.7				1.1
1.1	1.1	1.6			1.6				1.4
.5	.4	.8	Quick		1.0				.9
.1	.1	.2			.2				.4
0 UND	0 UND	0 UND			0 UND				11 32.2
3 133.7	5 79.6	5 76.2	Sales/Receivables		3 117.0				28 12.9
22 17.0	27 13.4	36 10.3			22 16.4				43 8.5
			Cost of Sales/Inventory						
			Cost of Sales/Payables						
8.1	4.7	4.1			2.7				5.4
−480.9	65.0	30.3	Sales/Working Capital		NM				11.1
−5.9	−9.0	−8.1			−24.7				283.4
5.8	4.0	3.7			3.2				16.2
(67) 2.1	(51) 1.2	(38) 2.5	EBIT/Interest		1.3			(11)	3.1
.5	−.5	−.5			−.8				1.3
4.3			Net Profit + Depr., Dep.,						
(12) 3.5			Amort./Cur. Mat. L/T/D						
.1									
.8	.7	.8			1.1				.6
1.3	1.5	1.3	Fixed/Worth		1.5				1.0
16.4	−270.9	5.5			NM				3.1
.5	.6	.7			.7				.7
1.4	3.0	1.5	Debt/Worth		1.5				1.4
23.0	−365.6	8.4			NM				5.6
25.3	20.2	28.0	% Profit Before Taxes/Tangible						30.4
(63) 9.3	(44) 1.5	(40) 6.5	Net Worth						15.9
.1	−9.3	−2.0							1.5
9.2	8.2	8.5	% Profit Before Taxes/Total		7.6				9.3
1.9	.9	4.2	Assets		2.2				3.9
−1.3	−2.2	−1.7			−4.5				.8
5.9	8.3	3.4			1.7				6.5
2.0	2.7	1.1	Sales/Net Fixed Assets		.8				2.3
.6	.6	.6			.6				1.2
2.4	2.4	1.6			1.0				1.7
1.1	1.1	.7	Sales/Total Assets		.6				1.4
.3	.3	.3			.4				.6
3.1	2.8	4.0			3.9				
(76) 6.1	(54) 6.4	(40) 6.6	% Depr., Dep., Amort./Sales		5.8				
11.3	11.9	13.8			13.7				
1.5		1.6	% Officers', Directors',						
(20) 2.5		(10) 2.7	Owners' Comp/Sales						
5.4		5.4							
971767M	1123498M	1227542M	Net Sales ($)	3203M	17135M	17087M	32642M	89648M	1067827M
1306677M	1450367M	1522643M	Total Assets ($)	10739M	27232M	18717M	85471M	220280M	1160204M

© RMA 2005   M = $ thousand   MM = $ million
See Pages 11 through 21 for Explanation of Ratios and Data

Current Data Sorted By Assets   Comparative Historical Data

M = $ thousand   MM = $ million

0-500M	500M-2MM	2-10MM	10-50MM	50-100MM	100-250MM	Type of Statement	4/1/00-3/31/01 ALL	4/1/01-3/31/02 ALL
		3			1	Unqualified	3	2
	2	5	1		1	Reviewed	9	14
1	3	4	2			Compiled	12	7
2	1	1	2			Tax Returns	7	3
1		5	2		1	Other	7	4
\<-- 15 (4/1-9/30/04) --\>			\<-- 21 (10/1/04-3/31/05) --\>					
3	7	14	9		3	**NUMBER OF STATEMENTS**	38	30
%	%	%	%	%	%	**ASSETS**	%	%
		4.9				Cash & Equivalents	10.1	5.6
		8.6		D		Trade Receivables (net)	8.6	12.3
		18.5		A		Inventory	9.6	12.0
		2.8		T		All Other Current	3.6	5.3
		34.8		A		Total Current	32.0	35.1
		56.2				Fixed Assets (net)	56.6	56.6
		.3		N		Intangibles (net)	.6	1.0
		8.7		O		All Other Non-Current	10.9	7.3
		100.0		T		Total	100.0	100.0
				A		**LIABILITIES**		
		7.3		V		Notes Payable-Short Term	17.8	22.9
		3.0		A		Cur. Mat.-L/T/D	2.5	4.6
		11.0		I		Trade Payables	3.8	5.6
		.0		L		Income Taxes Payable	.1	.7
		2.2		A		All Other Current	8.0	6.3
		23.4		B		Total Current	32.1	40.1
		22.7		L		Long-Term Debt	29.7	34.3
		.1		E		Deferred Taxes	.8	.4
		.0				All Other Non-Current	3.6	4.1
		53.8				Net Worth	33.7	21.2
		100.0				Total Liabilities & Net Worth	100.0	100.0
						INCOME DATA		
		100.0				Net Sales	100.0	100.0
						Gross Profit		
		92.5				Operating Expenses	95.2	94.8
		7.5				Operating Profit	4.8	5.2
		–.6				All Other Expenses (net)	5.3	8.1
		8.1				Profit Before Taxes	–.5	–2.9
						RATIOS		
		4.1					1.9	1.7
		1.5				Current	1.3	1.0
		.6					.7	.6
		1.8					1.2	.9
		.6				Quick	.5	.4
		.2					.2	.2
	0	UND					0 UND	0 UND
	19	19.4				Sales/Receivables	27 13.4	30 12.0
	37	9.8					46 8.0	73 5.0
						Cost of Sales/Inventory		
						Cost of Sales/Payables		
		1.8					5.5	12.0
		10.4				Sales/Working Capital	16.8	UND
		–14.5					–6.7	–6.6
		9.0					2.7	2.4
	(11)	4.3				EBIT/Interest	(33) 1.0	(26) 1.4
		2.2					–.4	–.6
						Net Profit + Depr., Dep., Amort./Cur. Mat. L /T/D		
		.6					.8	.9
		1.0				Fixed/Worth	1.6	2.0
		2.0					5.1	42.7
		.3					.8	.9
		.8				Debt/Worth	1.6	2.3
		1.8					5.7	63.4
		51.5					15.5	10.9
	(13)	22.3				% Profit Before Taxes/Tangible Net Worth	(33) 1.9	(24) 3.2
		2.8					–9.5	–12.9
		14.4					6.3	4.1
		9.0				% Profit Before Taxes/Total Assets	.9	–.2
		1.1					–4.8	–7.7
		3.6					3.5	3.2
		1.5				Sales/Net Fixed Assets	1.2	1.5
		.9					.8	.9
		2.4					1.5	1.4
		1.0				Sales/Total Assets	.7	.8
		.5					.5	.5
		3.4					3.0	3.2
	(10)	7.4				% Depr., Dep., Amort./Sales	(29) 6.1	4.9
		9.0					10.2	9.1
						% Officers', Directors', Owners' Comp/Sales		
5141M	17003M	110783M	284959M		481929M	Net Sales ($)	394812M	352860M
1236M	10130M	68215M	191243M		417306M	Total Assets ($)	537157M	471106M

M = $ thousand   MM = $ million
See Pages 11 through 21 for Explanation of Ratios and Data

Comparative Historical Data | Current Data Sorted By Sales

			Type of Statement	0-1MM	1-3MM	3-5MM	5-10MM	10-25MM	25MM & OVER
2	3	4	Unqualified					1	3
13	11	9	Reviewed	2	3			2	2
9	10	10	Compiled	1	3	3	2	1	
8	9	4	Tax Returns	1		1	1		
2	6	9	Other	1	2		1	3	2
4/1/02-3/31/03 ALL	4/1/03-3/31/04 ALL	4/1/04-3/31/05 ALL		15 (4/1-9/30/04)			21 (10/1/04-3/31/05)		
34	39	36	NUMBER OF STATEMENTS	5	9	4	4	7	7
%	%	%	ASSETS	%	%	%	%	%	%
12.9	11.9	6.2	Cash & Equivalents						
12.4	11.0	12.9	Trade Receivables (net)						
7.2	9.6	17.6	Inventory						
4.5	2.4	2.5	All Other Current						
36.9	34.9	39.2	Total Current						
53.5	57.4	52.6	Fixed Assets (net)						
.4	.7	.3	Intangibles (net)						
9.2	7.0	7.8	All Other Non-Current						
100.0	100.0	100.0	Total						
			LIABILITIES						
13.1	23.6	8.5	Notes Payable-Short Term						
4.2	4.9	3.5	Cur. Mat.-L/T/D						
5.7	6.1	8.4	Trade Payables						
.1	.2	.0	Income Taxes Payable						
7.8	5.1	6.1	All Other Current						
30.9	40.0	26.5	Total Current						
35.2	19.8	19.9	Long-Term Debt						
.4	.4	.1	Deferred Taxes						
4.7	2.2	2.2	All Other Non-Current						
28.8	37.7	51.3	Net Worth						
100.0	100.0	100.0	Total Liabilities & Net Worth						
			INCOME DATA						
100.0	100.0	100.0	Net Sales						
			Gross Profit						
93.7	93.5	94.0	Operating Expenses						
6.3	6.5	6.0	Operating Profit						
8.2	3.1	1.6	All Other Expenses (net)						
-1.9	3.4	4.5	Profit Before Taxes						
			RATIOS						
2.5	2.1	3.1	Current						
1.5	1.3	1.5							
.7	.6	.7							
2.1	1.4	1.5	Quick						
.8	.6 (35)	.6							
.3	.3	.3							
0 UND	0 UND	3 129.3	Sales/Receivables						
26 14.1	22 16.8	26 13.8							
52 7.1	53 6.8	49 7.4							
			Cost of Sales/Inventory						
			Cost of Sales/Payables						
4.4	4.1	2.8	Sales/Working Capital						
9.3	75.7	8.7							
-10.2	-16.6	-24.9							
3.1	7.9	8.1	EBIT/Interest						
(31) 1.1	(36) 2.7	(30) 2.9							
.1	.5	.9							
			Net Profit + Depr., Dep., Amort./Cur. Mat. L/T/D						
.7	.8	.6	Fixed/Worth						
1.4	1.2	1.1							
9.8	1.9	1.5							
.8	.5	.4	Debt/Worth						
1.3	1.0	1.0							
13.8	2.5	1.7							
21.6	29.1	26.2	% Profit Before Taxes/Tangible Net Worth						
(29) 2.4	(36) 14.0	(34) 11.9							
-7.7	2.2	1.2							
7.6	13.4	12.8	% Profit Before Taxes/Total Assets						
.7	4.7	5.9							
-2.9	-.5	.8							
5.0	5.1	6.1	Sales/Net Fixed Assets						
1.9	2.6	1.7							
1.0	.9	1.1							
2.2	2.7	2.3	Sales/Total Assets						
1.2	1.1	1.1							
.6	.6	.7							
3.6	2.2	2.8	% Depr., Dep., Amort./Sales						
(32) 5.2	(35) 4.5	(32) 4.6							
9.9	8.6	7.6							
1.2	2.3	1.9	% Officers', Directors', Owners' Comp/Sales						
(11) 2.4	(13) 3.0	(11) 3.7							
10.8	9.0	11.9							
402127M	560486M	899815M	Net Sales ($)	3306M	17803M	17632M	28233M	109254M	723587M
461357M	534703M	688130M	Total Assets ($)	11996M	21285M	16787M	48638M	71932M	517492M

M = $ thousand   MM = $ million
See Pages 11 through 21 for Explanation of Ratios and Data

Current Data Sorted By Assets   Comparative Historical Data

0-500M	500M-2MM	2-10MM	10-50MM	50-100MM	100-250MM	Type of Statement	4/1/00-3/31/01 ALL	4/1/01-3/31/02 ALL
		1	2		2	Unqualified	3	5
1	3	8	3	1		Reviewed	15	13
1	1	3	2			Compiled	16	14
5	7	8				Tax Returns	5	9
1	5	8	7	3		Other	35	22
	8 (4/1-9/30/04)		64 (10/1/04-3/31/05)					
8	16	28	14	4	2	**NUMBER OF STATEMENTS**	74	63
%	%	%	%	%	%	**ASSETS**	%	%
	8.8	8.0	8.9			Cash & Equivalents	6.1	4.2
	7.5	8.5	17.6			Trade Receivables (net)	12.5	12.3
	4.7	3.3	13.0			Inventory	5.9	6.0
	2.3	9.7	2.8			All Other Current	5.0	5.7
	23.3	29.5	42.2			Total Current	29.6	28.1
	72.2	63.7	38.6			Fixed Assets (net)	60.1	62.6
	.7	.5	1.1			Intangibles (net)	.7	.4
	3.9	6.3	18.1			All Other Non-Current	9.7	8.9
	100.0	100.0	100.0			Total	100.0	100.0
						LIABILITIES		
	25.1	14.6	9.0			Notes Payable-Short Term	15.8	12.9
	3.8	5.0	7.7			Cur. Mat.-L/T/D	3.4	3.5
	1.9	1.5	6.1			Trade Payables	2.9	3.0
	.0	.0	.0			Income Taxes Payable	.3	.5
	2.2	7.4	10.1			All Other Current	4.2	6.0
	32.9	28.5	32.9			Total Current	26.6	25.9
	65.8	36.6	22.9			Long-Term Debt	40.2	36.6
	.0	.0	.0			Deferred Taxes	.1	.3
	7.1	2.5	9.4			All Other Non-Current	4.2	5.6
	−5.7	32.4	34.8			Net Worth	28.8	31.6
	100.0	100.0	100.0			Total Liabilities & Net Worth	100.0	100.0
						INCOME DATA		
	100.0	100.0	100.0			Net Sales	100.0	100.0
						Gross Profit		
	84.7	83.3	92.5			Operating Expenses	83.3	83.2
	15.3	16.7	7.5			Operating Profit	16.7	16.8
	9.0	9.5	5.4			All Other Expenses (net)	4.8	9.6
	6.3	7.3	2.1			Profit Before Taxes	11.9	7.2
						RATIOS		
	2.0	3.6	4.2				2.7	2.1
	.5	1.7	1.5			Current	1.2	1.2
	.1	.5	1.0				.4	.7
	1.6	2.2	2.5				1.8	1.6
	.5	1.1	1.0			Quick	.6	.8
	.1	.1	.4				.2	.2
0 UND	0 UND	26 13.9					0 UND	0 UND
0 UND	29 12.8	55 6.7				Sales/Receivables	24 15.3	35 10.4
32 11.5	121 3.0	112 3.3					160 2.3	134 2.7
						Cost of Sales/Inventory		
						Cost of Sales/Payables		
	10.2	3.0	2.4				3.0	2.9
	−6.5	7.1	4.7			Sales/Working Capital	11.4	17.7
	−2.9	−13.0	NM				−5.6	−8.9
	2.7	6.1	3.6				5.3	6.8
	(13) 1.7	(23) 1.8	(12) 1.0			EBIT/Interest	(50) 3.3	(47) 2.4
	.5	1.0	.6				1.8	.7
								4.0
						Net Profit + Depr., Dep., Amort./Cur. Mat. L /T/D		(13) 1.6
								.2
	1.4	.9	.3				.8	.8
	NM	1.9	1.1			Fixed/Worth	1.8	1.8
	−2.9	5.1	5.6				9.2	6.4
	1.4	.5	.7				1.0	.9
	NM	1.7	2.2			Debt/Worth	2.0	1.6
	−5.8	9.5	14.8				16.6	6.3
		27.5	22.5				37.1	29.8
	(24)	23.2 (12)	−.2			% Profit Before Taxes/Tangible Net Worth	(61) 18.5	(51) 10.5
		2.0	−2.5				6.7	.9
	6.8	16.2	3.2				12.1	11.6
	3.4	4.6	.3			% Profit Before Taxes/Total Assets	6.3	3.4
	−3.5	.4	−.7				.8	−1.7
	3.8	2.1	11.6				2.8	2.4
	.9	.9	2.7			Sales/Net Fixed Assets	.9	1.1
	.6	.5	.5				.5	.5
	2.0	1.1	1.2				1.0	1.0
	.7	.5	.6			Sales/Total Assets	.5	.6
	.4	.4	.2				.3	.3
	3.8	5.3	6.1				4.3	4.5
	(14) 11.3	(26) 11.2	(11) 8.8			% Depr., Dep., Amort./Sales	(64) 7.8	(53) 7.9
	16.3	18.6	16.4				17.1	13.9
								1.6
						% Officers', Directors', Owners' Comp/Sales		(10) 7.2
								13.1
4196M	21932M	100389M	352029M	95558M	144774M	Net Sales ($)	885028M	991351M
2643M	19765M	120020M	415680M	282902M	335539M	Total Assets ($)	1214302M	1381432M

© RMA 2005

M = $ thousand   MM = $ million
See Pages 11 through 21 for Explanation of Ratios and Data

Comparative Historical Data | Current Data Sorted By Sales

			Type of Statement						
5	1	5	Unqualified					3	2
18	19	16	Reviewed	5	3	2	1	2	3
15	7	7	Compiled	2	2	2	1		
15	16	20	Tax Returns	10	5	2	3	2	
27	21	24	Other	7	6	1	4	2	4
4/1/02-3/31/03 ALL	4/1/03-3/31/04 ALL	4/1/04-3/31/05 ALL		0-1MM	8 (4/1-9/30/04) 1-3MM	3-5MM	64 (10/1/04-3/31/05) 5-10MM	10-25MM	25MM & OVER
80	64	72	**NUMBER OF STATEMENTS**	24	16	7	9	7	9
%	%	%	**ASSETS**	%	%	%	%	%	%
6.1	5.5	9.2	Cash & Equivalents	8.7	10.9				
12.1	11.7	9.4	Trade Receivables (net)	5.5	8.8				
6.6	5.1	7.2	Inventory	2.7	10.5				
3.8	8.5	5.6	All Other Current	3.2	2.8				
28.5	30.8	31.4	Total Current	20.0	32.9				
61.4	58.6	58.8	Fixed Assets (net)	73.3	57.3				
1.0	.8	1.3	Intangibles (net)	.5	.2				
9.2	9.8	8.5	All Other Non-Current	6.1	9.5				
100.0	100.0	100.0	Total	100.0	100.0				
			LIABILITIES						
14.3	15.1	15.6	Notes Payable-Short Term	11.9	24.6				
4.0	3.7	5.4	Cur. Mat.-L/T/D	7.4	2.9				
3.9	4.2	2.5	Trade Payables	.1	1.7				
.3	.1	.0	Income Taxes Payable	.0	.0				
5.8	4.0	5.8	All Other Current	2.1	9.6				
28.3	27.2	29.3	Total Current	21.4	38.9				
42.2	40.2	43.3	Long-Term Debt	72.5	36.3				
.2	.0	.0	Deferred Taxes	.0	.0				
4.4	5.0	4.5	All Other Non-Current	5.3	3.5				
24.9	27.6	22.9	Net Worth	.8	21.3				
100.0	100.0	100.0	Total Liabilities & Net Worth	100.0	100.0				
			INCOME DATA						
100.0	100.0	100.0	Net Sales	100.0	100.0				
			Gross Profit						
86.2	90.9	88.5	Operating Expenses	89.7	81.7				
13.8	9.1	11.5	Operating Profit	10.3	18.3				
7.9	8.0	7.1	All Other Expenses (net)	10.7	9.5				
5.9	1.1	4.3	Profit Before Taxes	−.3	8.9				
			RATIOS						
2.3	3.2	2.8		2.2	4.7				
1.2	1.4	1.5	Current	1.3	1.6				
.6	.7	.5		.2	.3				
1.6	2.3	1.9		1.7	4.7				
.8	.8	.8	Quick	.6	.9				
.2	.2	.2		.1	.1				
0 UND	0 UND	0 UND		0 UND	0 UND				
36 10.2	27 13.5	24 15.1	Sales/Receivables	0 UND	20 17.8				
124 2.9	127 2.9	107 3.4		133 2.7	121 3.0				
			Cost of Sales/Inventory						
			Cost of Sales/Payables						
4.1	2.5	3.4		4.8	1.7				
41.2	7.1	9.4	Sales/Working Capital	13.0	6.3				
−7.8	−12.1	−7.2		−2.9	−6.8				
5.7	6.2	5.0		2.8	3.8				
(63) 2.7	(51) 1.8	(60) 1.6	EBIT/Interest	(19) 1.4	(13) 1.3				
.9	−.1	.5		−1.1	−.2				
1.8	5.1		Net Profit + Depr., Dep., Amort./Cur. Mat. L/T/D						
(15) .5	(12) 2.4								
−1.8	.6								
.9	1.0	.9		1.3	1.0				
2.1	2.1	1.9	Fixed/Worth	3.1	3.9				
12.7	66.9	13.7		−9.6	−8.4				
.9	.6	.8		1.3	.4				
2.2	2.4	2.5	Debt/Worth	5.5	5.3				
15.6	69.3	38.3		−7.1	−13.0				
42.5	31.1	25.8		16.4	31.1				
(65) 10.2	(49) 8.7	(55) 11.8	% Profit Before Taxes/Tangible Net Worth	(14) 3.8	(11) 24.5				
−4.2	−8.5	−2.6		−28.2	.1				
14.6	7.4	10.8		6.8	11.1				
3.2	.6	2.1	% Profit Before Taxes/Total Assets	1.4	2.6				
−3.7	−4.8	−1.6		−7.6	−.2				
4.3	3.3	3.7		1.3	4.0				
1.1	.8	1.0	Sales/Net Fixed Assets	.8	.8				
.5	.5	.6		.3	.6				
1.4	.8	1.3		.9	.7				
.6	.5	.6	Sales/Total Assets	.6	.5				
.3	.3	.4		.3	.4				
3.8	4.8	5.5		6.3	8.0				
(71) 8.1	(57) 11.3	(63) 9.0	% Depr., Dep., Amort./Sales	(22) 11.3	(13) 14.3				
15.9	19.8	16.6		20.0	17.3				
3.0	4.4	1.5							
(13) 4.6	(12) 7.2	(16) 4.4	% Officers', Directors', Owners' Comp/Sales						
11.6	10.4	6.3							
1009107M	633557M	718878M	Net Sales ($)	14250M	27802M	26364M	63854M	101092M	485516M
1165442M	784067M	1176549M	Total Assets ($)	37258M	114528M	41101M	135750M	220154M	627758M

© RMA 2005

M = $ thousand   MM = $ million

See Pages 11 through 21 for Explanation of Ratios and Data

Current Data Sorted By Assets   Comparative Historical Data

0-500M	500M-2MM	2-10MM	10-50MM	50-100MM	100-250MM		4/1/00-3/31/01 ALL	4/1/01-3/31/02 ALL
						Type of Statement		
		1	2			Unqualified		2
		4	1			Reviewed		2
		3	1			Compiled		7
	1	2				Tax Returns		3
2	2		3	1		Other		8
		7 (4/1-9/30/04)	16 (10/1/04-3/31/05)					
2	3	10	7	1		**NUMBER OF STATEMENTS**		22
%	%	%	%	%	%	**ASSETS**	%	%
		2.0				Cash & Equivalents		7.6
		17.0				Trade Receivables (net)		12.8
		11.5				Inventory		16.1
		21.0				All Other Current		7.3
		51.5				Total Current		43.8
		44.8				Fixed Assets (net)		50.1
		.1				Intangibles (net)		1.4
		3.6				All Other Non-Current		4.8
		100.0				Total		100.0
						LIABILITIES		
		20.7				Notes Payable-Short Term		19.7
		2.5				Cur. Mat.-L/T/D		1.2
		1.6				Trade Payables		8.8
		.2				Income Taxes Payable		.1
		6.5				All Other Current		5.6
		31.3				Total Current		35.4
		29.8				Long-Term Debt		45.8
		1.7				Deferred Taxes		.3
		1.1				All Other Non-Current		2.6
		36.0				Net Worth		15.9
		100.0				Total Liabilities & Net Worth		100.0
						INCOME DATA		
		100.0				Net Sales		100.0
						Gross Profit		
		77.9				Operating Expenses		95.8
		22.1				Operating Profit		4.2
		3.0				All Other Expenses (net)		6.4
		19.1				Profit Before Taxes		−2.2
						RATIOS		
		5.9						2.0
		2.5				Current		1.1
		1.3						.8
		2.7						1.6
		.7				Quick		.5
		.1						.2
		6 61.9					0 UND	
		30 12.3				Sales/Receivables	33 11.0	
		151 2.4					77 4.7	
						Cost of Sales/Inventory		
						Cost of Sales/Payables		
		1.7						3.4
		3.0				Sales/Working Capital		54.6
		9.8						−18.0
		10.5						4.0
		7.4				EBIT/Interest	(20) 1.5	
		4.1						−.4
						Net Profit + Depr., Dep., Amort./Cur. Mat. L/T/D		
		.4						.4
		.9				Fixed/Worth		1.4
		1.6						16.3
		.5						1.0
		1.1				Debt/Worth		3.8
		2.0						30.6
								19.3
						% Profit Before Taxes/Tangible Net Worth	(18) 9.4	
								−18.3
		27.9						7.1
		14.3				% Profit Before Taxes/Total Assets		2.3
		8.8						−7.0
		4.8						7.6
		1.4				Sales/Net Fixed Assets		2.6
		1.3						.7
		1.5						1.8
		.8				Sales/Total Assets		.9
		.5						.4
								3.0
						% Depr., Dep., Amort./Sales	(19) 4.9	
								9.0
						% Officers', Directors', Owners' Comp/Sales		
644M	1582M	62845M	230919M	42059M		Net Sales ($)		251763M
799M	5021M	63892M	151801M	52863M		Total Assets ($)		213942M

M = $ thousand   MM = $ million
See Pages 11 through 21 for Explanation of Ratios and Data

Comparative Historical Data			Type of Statement	Current Data Sorted By Sales					
1	4	3	Unqualified					1	2
3	6	5	Reviewed		2	2		1	
6	6	5	Compiled	1		1	3		
5	6	4	Tax Returns	4					
9	8	6	Other		1	2		1	2
4/1/02- 3/31/03	4/1/03- 3/31/04	4/1/04- 3/31/05		7 (4/1-9/30/04)			16 (10/1/04-3/31/05)		
ALL	ALL	ALL		0-1MM	1-3MM	3-5MM	5-10MM	10-25MM	25MM & OVER
24	30	23	NUMBER OF STATEMENTS	5	3	5	3	3	4
%	%	%	ASSETS	%	%	%	%	%	%
5.5	3.6	1.6	Cash & Equivalents						
10.4	16.8	15.6	Trade Receivables (net)						
7.2	5.2	9.7	Inventory						
8.9	6.2	11.2	All Other Current						
32.0	31.9	38.2	Total Current						
58.2	59.2	54.5	Fixed Assets (net)						
.2	.3	.5	Intangibles (net)						
9.5	8.5	6.8	All Other Non-Current						
100.0	100.0	100.0	Total						
			LIABILITIES						
19.0	19.5	14.1	Notes Payable-Short Term						
1.7	2.0	1.5	Cur. Mat.-L/T/D						
1.5	2.9	4.1	Trade Payables						
1.0	.4	.4	Income Taxes Payable						
12.5	13.1	7.4	All Other Current						
35.6	37.9	27.5	Total Current						
30.4	35.8	24.7	Long-Term Debt						
1.5	1.0	.8	Deferred Taxes						
9.3	3.5	12.9	All Other Non-Current						
23.2	21.9	34.2	Net Worth						
100.0	100.0	100.0	Total Liabilities & Net Worth						
			INCOME DATA						
100.0	100.0	100.0	Net Sales						
			Gross Profit						
92.7	87.8	84.6	Operating Expenses						
7.3	12.2	15.4	Operating Profit						
6.0	4.9	2.8	All Other Expenses (net)						
1.3	7.4	12.6	Profit Before Taxes						
			RATIOS						
1.8	2.7	3.8							
1.0	1.4	1.6	Current						
.1	.3	.3							
1.0	2.1	1.8							
.3	.7	.6	Quick						
.0	.2	.1							
0 UND	0 UND	0 UND							
4 85.4	36 10.2	31 11.7	Sales/Receivables						
66 5.6	159 2.3	137 2.7							
			Cost of Sales/Inventory						
			Cost of Sales/Payables						
3.2	2.4	1.8							
NM	7.4	9.5	Sales/Working Capital						
-3.6	-5.9	-9.1							
4.0	5.8	9.8							
(21) 1.2	(27) 2.5	4.8	EBIT/Interest						
-.5	.9	1.0							
			Net Profit + Depr., Dep., Amort./Cur. Mat. L/T/D						
.9	.7	.5							
2.0	1.3	1.1	Fixed/Worth						
-56.6	59.0	2.5							
.7	.7	.5							
2.1	2.1	1.6	Debt/Worth						
-65.9	61.0	3.1							
22.0	35.0	50.9	% Profit Before Taxes/Tangible Net Worth						
(17) .9	(24) 13.5	(21) 14.0							
-4.5	1.9	2.8							
12.1	8.8	17.7	% Profit Before Taxes/Total Assets						
1.2	4.9	9.9							
-3.9	.0	.0							
6.3	4.7	4.2	Sales/Net Fixed Assets						
.7	1.1	1.4							
.5	.3	.6							
1.8	1.1	1.3	Sales/Total Assets						
.6	.5	.7							
.3	.3	.5							
4.3	4.1	2.1	% Depr., Dep., Amort./Sales						
(20) 7.9	(25) 5.2	(20) 4.9							
17.5	17.3	9.6							
			% Officers', Directors', Owners' Comp/Sales						
90422M	345776M	338049M	Net Sales ($)	2226M	6637M	21890M	24068M	43737M	239491M
106122M	354233M	274376M	Total Assets ($)	5820M	27117M	47185M	30448M	21847M	141959M

M = $ thousand   MM = $ million
See Pages 11 through 21 for Explanation of Ratios and Data

Current Data Sorted By Assets   Comparative Historical Data

0-500M	500M-2MM	2-10MM	10-50MM	50-100MM	100-250MM	Type of Statement	4/1/00-3/31/01 ALL	4/1/01-3/31/02 ALL
		1	2	1		Unqualified		
	1	3	1			Reviewed		
	3	4	1	1		Compiled		
2	3	4	1			Tax Returns		
7	2				1	Other		
16 (4/1-9/30/04)			22 (10/1/04-3/31/05)					
9	9	12	5	2	1	NUMBER OF STATEMENTS		
%	%	%	%	%	%	**ASSETS**	%	%
		1.7				Cash & Equivalents	D	D
		12.7				Trade Receivables (net)	A	A
		13.4				Inventory	T	T
		2.8				All Other Current	A	A
		30.7				Total Current		
		58.5				Fixed Assets (net)	N	N
		1.5				Intangibles (net)	O	O
		9.3				All Other Non-Current	T	T
		100.0				Total		
						LIABILITIES	A	A
		9.4				Notes Payable-Short Term	V	V
		6.4				Cur. Mat.-L/T/D	A	A
		6.8				Trade Payables	I	I
		2.9				Income Taxes Payable	L	L
		2.5				All Other Current	A	A
		28.0				Total Current	B	B
		40.3				Long-Term Debt	L	L
		.3				Deferred Taxes	E	E
		6.1				All Other Non-Current		
		25.3				Net Worth		
		100.0				Total Liabilities & Net Worth		
						INCOME DATA		
		100.0				Net Sales		
						Gross Profit		
		96.4				Operating Expenses		
		3.6				Operating Profit		
		1.8				All Other Expenses (net)		
		1.8				Profit Before Taxes		
						RATIOS		
		1.4						
		1.1				Current		
		.8						
		.7						
		.4				Quick		
		.1						
		0 UND						
		24 15.1				Sales/Receivables		
		39 9.4						
						Cost of Sales/Inventory		
						Cost of Sales/Payables		
		31.3						
		261.0				Sales/Working Capital		
		-32.8						
		4.1						
		(10) 1.6				EBIT/Interest		
		-.8						
						Net Profit + Depr., Dep., Amort./Cur. Mat. L./T/D		
		1.4						
		3.6				Fixed/Worth		
		7.6						
		1.9						
		4.7				Debt/Worth		
		7.6						
		50.3						
		(11) 31.3				% Profit Before Taxes/Tangible Net Worth		
		1.8						
		10.8						
		3.4				% Profit Before Taxes/Total Assets		
		-2.9						
		6.5						
		3.0				Sales/Net Fixed Assets		
		2.4						
		2.8						
		1.7				Sales/Total Assets		
		1.5						
		3.2						
		(11) 4.3				% Depr., Dep., Amort./Sales		
		5.3						
						% Officers', Directors', Owners' Comp/Sales		
29152M	55135M	118618M	318511M	201775M	32394M	Net Sales ($)		
1793M	9322M	56357M	105560M	143077M	139537M	Total Assets ($)		

M = $ thousand   MM = $ million
See Pages 11 through 21 for Explanation of Ratios and Data

Comparative Historical Data   **Current Data Sorted By Sales**

			Type of Statement						
3	5	4	Unqualified			1			3
4	4	5	Reviewed		1			2	2
2	15	10	Compiled	1	1	1	1	5	1
2	1	11	Tax Returns	1	3	4	3		
1	5	8	Other		2	1	1	1	3
4/1/02-3/31/03 ALL	4/1/03-3/31/04 ALL	4/1/04-3/31/05 ALL		0-1MM	16 (4/1-9/30/04) 1-3MM	3-5MM	22 (10/1/04-3/31/05) 5-10MM	10-25MM	25MM & OVER
12	30	38	**NUMBER OF STATEMENTS**	2	6	7	6	8	9
%	%	%	**ASSETS**	%	%	%	%	%	%
.7	2.2	4.3	Cash & Equivalents						
23.8	20.3	16.7	Trade Receivables (net)						
11.6	13.3	10.9	Inventory						
9.0	7.2	3.2	All Other Current						
45.2	42.9	35.1	Total Current						
42.9	48.8	52.1	Fixed Assets (net)						
1.8	2.2	3.1	Intangibles (net)						
10.1	6.1	9.7	All Other Non-Current						
100.0	100.0	100.0	Total						
			LIABILITIES						
8.6	6.9	17.6	Notes Payable-Short Term						
4.7	4.9	16.1	Cur. Mat.-L/T/D						
16.1	12.4	8.9	Trade Payables						
.1	.4	1.7	Income Taxes Payable						
3.6	2.9	6.1	All Other Current						
33.3	27.6	50.4	Total Current						
31.7	36.4	37.7	Long-Term Debt						
.7	1.1	.2	Deferred Taxes						
.0	2.6	4.6	All Other Non-Current						
34.4	32.4	7.2	Net Worth						
100.0	100.0	100.0	Total Liabilities & Net Worth						
			INCOME DATA						
100.0	100.0	100.0	Net Sales						
			Gross Profit						
96.2	93.9	98.8	Operating Expenses						
3.8	6.1	1.2	Operating Profit						
.8	3.0	1.0	All Other Expenses (net)						
3.1	3.1	.1	Profit Before Taxes						
			RATIOS						
2.1	2.5	1.4							
1.1	1.6	1.1	Current						
.9	1.1	.6							
.9	1.4	1.1							
.7	.7	.6	Quick						
.4	.5	.1							
21 17.1	25 14.8	0 UND							
27 13.3	31 11.7	15 24.3	Sales/Receivables						
31 11.8	48 7.6	31 11.9							
			Cost of Sales/Inventory						
			Cost of Sales/Payables						
13.2	5.8	31.5							
104.2	17.0	261.0	Sales/Working Capital						
−47.0	67.2	−33.3							
5.7	8.4	6.6							
(11) 2.4	(28) 3.8	(33) 1.5	EBIT/Interest						
1.8	1.3	−1.3							
			Net Profit + Depr., Dep., Amort./Cur. Mat. L/T/D						
.6	.8	1.0							
1.7	1.4	3.6	Fixed/Worth						
3.9	3.8	UND							
.9	.9	1.7							
2.5	1.5	6.1	Debt/Worth						
9.4	5.2	UND							
54.8	32.4	70.6							
(11) 14.8	(25) 15.4	(30) 29.3	% Profit Before Taxes/Tangible Net Worth						
11.8	7.7	−1.5							
8.7	14.7	12.6							
5.0	4.9	3.4	% Profit Before Taxes/Total Assets						
2.4	1.3	−5.2							
13.1	7.9	24.3							
7.1	3.4	8.4	Sales/Net Fixed Assets						
2.7	1.9	3.6							
5.3	2.5	7.9							
2.1	1.8	3.5	Sales/Total Assets						
1.6	1.0	1.7							
1.7	2.0	1.1							
3.1 (28)	3.9 (34)	2.8	% Depr., Dep., Amort./Sales						
5.0	7.4	4.9							
		1.3	% Officers', Directors', Owners' Comp/Sales						
	(16)	2.2							
		4.0							
450685M	826799M	755585M	Net Sales ($)	624M	10836M	26685M	45528M	92693M	579219M
206899M	488503M	455646M	Total Assets ($)	111M	7433M	6894M	11544M	35883M	393781M

M = $ thousand   MM = $ million
See Pages 11 through 21 for Explanation of Ratios and Data

Current Data Sorted By Assets   Comparative Historical Data

Type of Statement

	0-500M	500M-2MM	2-10MM	10-50MM	50-100MM	100-250MM	Type of Statement	ALL 4/1/00-3/31/01	ALL 4/1/01-3/31/02
	1	1	2	7	2	4	Unqualified	16	15
	7	3	18	8	1		Reviewed	22	19
	13	12	14	2			Compiled	33	39
	8	15	2			3	Tax Returns	15	12
		4	15	14			Other	42	31
	37 (4/1-9/30/04)			119 (10/1/04-3/31/05)					
	29	35	51	31	6	4	NUMBER OF STATEMENTS	128	116
	%	%	%	%	%	%	**ASSETS**	%	%
	7.3	8.7	4.8	2.7			Cash & Equivalents	7.7	5.8
	9.3	13.7	12.6	15.6			Trade Receivables (net)	14.7	15.0
	30.3	19.5	30.2	34.2			Inventory	28.6	28.1
	6.8	2.1	2.4	3.7			All Other Current	3.9	3.4
	53.6	44.0	50.0	56.2			Total Current	54.8	52.4
	39.5	45.9	37.4	29.7			Fixed Assets (net)	37.3	38.7
	1.7	1.0	2.2	3.6			Intangibles (net)	2.4	1.6
	5.2	9.1	10.4	10.5			All Other Non-Current	5.6	7.4
	100.0	100.0	100.0	100.0			Total	100.0	100.0
							LIABILITIES		
	32.0	16.6	11.4	13.2			Notes Payable-Short Term	11.4	11.3
	4.9	4.7	3.0	5.7			Cur. Mat.-L/T/D	4.4	3.8
	7.4	10.9	7.8	9.3			Trade Payables	11.9	10.3
	.2	.1	.9	2.5			Income Taxes Payable	.9	1.2
	3.0	5.3	5.5	8.3			All Other Current	9.4	6.5
	47.6	37.7	28.7	39.1			Total Current	38.0	33.0
	31.0	25.9	21.0	20.1			Long-Term Debt	18.1	22.0
	.0	.3	.8	1.5			Deferred Taxes	1.1	1.7
	8.0	9.1	8.4	8.4			All Other Non-Current	4.5	3.8
	13.4	27.1	41.1	30.9			Net Worth	38.2	39.5
	100.0	100.0	100.0	100.0			Total Liabilities & Net Worth	100.0	100.0
							INCOME DATA		
	100.0	100.0	100.0	100.0			Net Sales	100.0	100.0
	53.0	50.5	39.4	32.4			Gross Profit	39.3	38.5
	48.6	47.3	32.7	28.5			Operating Expenses	34.0	32.4
	4.4	3.2	6.6	3.9			Operating Profit	5.3	6.1
	1.2	.3	2.0	2.7			All Other Expenses (net)	.3	1.8
	3.2	2.9	4.6	1.3			Profit Before Taxes	5.0	4.3
							RATIOS		
	4.4	4.6	4.8	2.0				3.0	3.3
	1.2	1.2	1.9	1.4			Current	1.5	1.5
	.7	.4	1.0	1.1				1.0	.9
	2.0	1.4	1.1	.7				1.1	1.1
	.2	.4	.5	.5			Quick	(127) .6	(115) .6
	.0	.2	.2	.3				.2	.2
	0 UND	0 999.8	3 124.3	21 17.7				7 51.5	6 63.1
	0 UND	10 35.1	26 14.1	33 11.1			Sales/Receivables	26 14.0	25 14.5
	8 48.0	31 11.8	47 7.8	51 7.2				55 6.6	53 6.9
	16 22.4	0 UND	0 UND	70 5.2				9 41.9	8 44.8
	78 4.7	28 12.8	113 3.2	144 2.5			Cost of Sales/Inventory	90 4.0	92 4.0
	146 2.5	84 4.4	288 1.3	247 1.5				240 1.5	222 1.6
	0 UND	0 UND	4 81.2	14 27.0				8 45.6	5 72.2
	0 902.0	16 22.7	11 33.0	30 12.1			Cost of Sales/Payables	26 14.2	23 16.1
	41 8.9	50 7.4	71 5.1	63 5.8				54 6.7	55 6.7
	5.9	7.3	2.1	4.4				3.1	3.4
	32.2	28.5	7.6	8.9			Sales/Working Capital	11.7	9.7
	−21.1	−12.1	−426.8	23.3				388.0	−168.7
	6.3	4.6	5.7	6.3				7.3	6.0
	(23) 3.7	(33) 1.2	(45) 2.5	(30) 3.2			EBIT/Interest	(116) 2.9	(113) 2.9
	.1	−4.3	1.1	.7				1.5	1.4
			4.5	8.6			Net Profit + Depr., Dep.,	5.5	4.2
		(14)	1.9	(12) 2.7			Amort./Cur. Mat. L/T/D	(33) 2.7	(33) 3.0
			1.1	.3				1.3	1.1
	.9	.6	.3	.3				.4	.4
	6.2	1.4	.9	1.0			Fixed/Worth	.9	1.0
	−1.4	15.4	1.7	2.5				2.5	2.0
	1.0	.6	.5	.9				.6	.6
	7.0	1.9	1.7	2.1			Debt/Worth	1.3	1.6
	−4.8	22.0	4.9	5.0				5.0	3.4
	46.9	28.3	23.1	28.4			% Profit Before Taxes/Tangible	37.0	34.1
	(18) 17.5	(27) 4.0	(49) 10.2	(27) 14.7			Net Worth	(112) 17.1	(105) 12.9
	−6.7	−15.5	1.7	2.4				5.4	5.3
	12.3	7.6	7.6	8.3			% Profit Before Taxes/Total	13.6	11.7
	3.6	1.2	4.1	4.9			Assets	5.9	5.5
	−7.7	−7.2	.4	−.6				1.5	1.7
	18.5	11.9	10.2	10.9				10.9	8.8
	11.0	6.4	4.7	5.9			Sales/Net Fixed Assets	4.5	4.9
	3.1	3.2	2.9	2.1				2.9	3.0
	5.1	3.5	2.5	1.9				2.7	2.7
	2.8	2.5	1.4	1.1			Sales/Total Assets	1.7	1.7
	1.3	1.7	.8	.6				.9	.9
	1.3	1.7	1.8	2.7				1.5	1.7
	(20) 3.0	(31) 2.7	(49) 3.1	(27) 3.5			% Depr., Dep., Amort./Sales	(117) 2.9	(111) 2.7
	7.1	6.6	5.7	8.1				4.7	4.9
	2.7	2.0	.9					2.0	1.9
	(17) 8.6	(19) 3.2	(20) 2.2				% Officers', Directors',	(50) 3.4	(53) 3.7
	16.1	10.3	4.9				Owners' Comp/Sales	5.2	6.9
	31823M	124566M	431636M	789135M	483773M	1294524M	Net Sales ($)	1802128M	1640816M
	8725M	39054M	258583M	665391M	375055M	676997M	Total Assets ($)	1550855M	1363896M

M = $ thousand   MM = $ million
See Pages 11 through 21 for Explanation of Ratios and Data

Comparative Historical Data   **Current Data Sorted By Sales**

			Type of Statement	0-1MM	1-3MM	3-5MM	5-10MM	10-25MM	25MM & OVER
12	16	17	Unqualified	1			3	3	10
16	17	30	Reviewed		2	5	13	3	7
28	43	35	Compiled	7	16	4	5	3	
18	14	30	Tax Returns	13	8	1	6	2	
31	38	44	Other	5	7	3	8	9	12
4/1/02-3/31/03	4/1/03-3/31/04	4/1/04-3/31/05		37 (4/1-9/30/04)			119 (10/1/04-3/31/05)		
ALL	ALL	ALL							
105	128	156	**NUMBER OF STATEMENTS**	26	33	13	35	20	29
%	%	%	**ASSETS**	%	%	%	%	%	%
8.1	6.4	5.5	Cash & Equivalents	4.2	6.7	5.3	7.4	6.3	2.3
12.7	13.5	13.3	Trade Receivables (net)	8.4	8.5	18.6	11.3	17.4	20.4
31.6	28.4	28.9	Inventory	37.4	26.7	18.0	28.9	24.4	31.5
1.9	4.5	3.4	All Other Current	7.5	.7	1.3	2.7	4.4	4.2
54.3	52.8	51.1	Total Current	57.4	42.7	43.3	50.2	52.5	58.4
36.7	37.5	37.8	Fixed Assets (net)	39.3	45.2	47.2	33.9	34.8	30.6
1.4	2.8	2.4	Intangibles (net)	1.7	1.8	1.9	1.1	4.5	4.0
7.6	6.9	8.8	All Other Non-Current	1.6	10.4	7.6	14.8	8.2	7.0
100.0	100.0	100.0	Total	100.0	100.0	100.0	100.0	100.0	100.0
			LIABILITIES						
17.3	15.9	16.4	Notes Payable-Short Term	21.8	21.1	16.9	15.0	6.1	14.7
4.2	4.3	4.3	Cur. Mat.-L/T/D	4.3	4.1	3.8	3.6	4.3	5.6
8.1	8.3	8.9	Trade Payables	8.0	7.4	13.7	6.7	10.0	11.1
1.2	1.1	1.0	Income Taxes Payable	.0	.4	.0	1.6	.5	2.3
8.2	5.7	6.0	All Other Current	1.9	4.5	4.0	6.0	6.0	12.3
39.1	35.2	36.6	Total Current	36.0	37.6	38.4	33.0	27.0	46.0
16.7	23.5	23.5	Long-Term Debt	39.2	23.3	33.0	17.6	16.9	17.4
1.1	1.0	.7	Deferred Taxes	.0	.7	.0	1.2	1.3	.7
7.2	11.2	8.7	All Other Non-Current	9.2	13.4	11.1	8.3	2.6	6.4
35.9	29.1	30.5	Net Worth	15.6	25.0	17.5	39.9	52.3	29.5
100.0	100.0	100.0	Total Liabilities & Net Worth	100.0	100.0	100.0	100.0	100.0	100.0
			INCOME DATA						
100.0	100.0	100.0	Net Sales	100.0	100.0	100.0	100.0	100.0	100.0
39.2	40.4	42.6	Gross Profit	62.2	48.7	40.9	36.4	34.6	32.1
34.4	35.3	37.5	Operating Expenses	54.3	46.3	36.3	31.0	29.2	26.6
4.8	5.1	5.1	Operating Profit	7.8	2.4	4.6	5.4	5.4	5.5
1.7	1.9	1.7	All Other Expenses (net)	3.5	1.2	1.9	1.0	1.0	1.7
3.0	3.2	3.4	Profit Before Taxes	4.3	1.2	2.7	4.4	4.4	3.8
			RATIOS						
3.5	3.8	3.9		5.5	4.6	1.7	6.3	4.3	1.8
1.6	1.7	1.5	Current	1.9	1.2	.9	2.0	2.3	1.4
1.0	1.1	.8		.9	.4	.4	1.1	.9	1.1
1.1	1.2	1.1		1.6	.8	1.0	1.1	1.5	.8
(104) .6	.5	.4	Quick	.3	.3	.5	.5	.8	.4
.2	.2	.2		.1	.2	.1	.2	.3	.3
2 173.2	4 102.2	2 157.8		0 UND	0 UND	6 61.7	2 173.3	10 37.3	23 16.2
25 14.9	22 16.5	19 19.5	Sales/Receivables	4 102.0	5 68.4	24 15.4	26 14.1	31 12.0	41 8.9
44 8.2	44 8.2	43 8.4		22 16.7	25 14.8	43 8.4	47 7.8	44 8.2	68 5.4
10 38.3	1 571.2	13 28.9		77 4.8	0 UND	0 UND	13 28.3	0 UND	59 6.2
123 3.0	97 3.8	83 4.4	Cost of Sales/Inventory	110 3.3	32 11.3	20 18.3	113 3.2	45 8.1	144 2.5
241 1.5	194 1.9	176 2.1		601 .6	156 2.3	117 3.1	231 1.6	204 1.8	173 2.1
3 134.7	2 222.2	1 332.6		0 UND	0 UND	11 31.9	1 265.6	2 156.9	15 25.0
19 19.6	16 22.8	21 17.2	Cost of Sales/Payables	40 9.2	8 44.7	39 9.4	10 38.1	8 45.1	33 11.2
47 7.8	48 7.6	51 7.1		105 3.5	36 10.1	58 6.3	30 12.1	61 6.0	63 5.8
2.9	2.9	4.1		1.9	5.5	7.0	2.3	3.2	4.9
9.7	8.2	11.5	Sales/Working Capital	9.2	28.5	−53.5	7.6	10.9	9.8
419.2	61.0	−44.3		−27.8	−12.8	−7.2	39.4	NM	30.0
5.6	6.9	6.3		5.3	6.0	1.3	8.6	25.8	6.0
(97) 2.5	(124) 2.4	(141) 2.5	EBIT/Interest	(18) 3.4	(32) 1.7	(12) .1	(32) 2.7	(18) 4.7	3.5
1.0	.2	.6		.6	−2.9	−2.1	1.3	.6	1.2
4.3	4.5	7.6	Net Profit + Depr., Dep.,				2.3		12.7
(24) 3.0	(33) 1.7	(34) 2.5	Amort./Cur. Mat. L/T/D			(12) 1.5		(10) 4.8	
1.0	.5	1.3					.9		2.2
.4	.4	.4		.8	1.0	.9	.2	.2	.4
.8	.9	1.1	Fixed/Worth	6.8	1.6	4.0	.9	.6	1.1
2.3	3.4	3.9		−2.0	47.4	NM	1.5	1.1	2.4
.7	.7	.6		.8	.6	1.9	.5	.2	1.1
1.4	1.5	2.2	Debt/Worth	17.0	2.1	4.7	1.2	.5	3.8
4.1	6.0	12.6		−5.9	104.1	NM	4.2	1.7	5.2
23.1	28.5	29.4	% Profit Before Taxes/Tangible	35.3	28.6	112.6	23.1	25.2	34.0
(90) 12.6	(105) 12.4	(130) 11.8	Net Worth	(17) 11.4	(26) 7.3	(10) −4.2	(33) 10.2	(18) 9.2	(26) 22.0
1.7	1.0	.4		−2.0	−18.0	−12.0	4.1	2.1	7.5
10.9	9.8	8.6	% Profit Before Taxes/Total	8.0	9.8	6.9	7.6	17.0	9.3
5.1	4.1	3.6	Assets	3.7	1.4	−1.7	4.1	5.2	5.1
−.3	−1.3	−1.3		−1.9	−7.7	−4.7	.7	.0	.7
9.2	10.1	11.9		15.3	15.3	11.1	12.2	13.4	10.8
5.9	5.3	5.9	Sales/Net Fixed Assets	3.1	6.1	4.7	5.3	7.0	5.9
3.3	3.1	2.9		1.7	3.2	1.3	3.1	3.4	3.3
2.8	2.8	2.8		2.0	3.6	3.7	2.7	3.3	2.1
1.5	1.5	1.7	Sales/Total Assets	1.2	2.5	2.2	1.6	2.0	1.6
.8	.9	.9		.8	1.2	.8	.7	1.2	1.2
2.3	2.1	1.9		1.9	1.3	1.9	2.0	1.6	2.0
(95) 3.5	(116) 3.3	(135) 3.3	% Depr., Dep., Amort./Sales	(19) 4.5	(30) 3.3	(12) 5.8	(31) 3.3	(17) 2.7	(26) 3.0
5.1	4.7	5.7		12.5	5.8	14.6	8.1	4.2	4.9
2.4	1.3	1.3	% Officers', Directors',	7.1	2.1		.8		
(47) 4.4	(51) 2.9	(63) 3.1	Owners' Comp/Sales	(12) 13.4	(17) 4.8		(17) 1.9		
8.8	6.2	9.8		18.1	10.5		5.7		
1139476M	2341667M	3155457M	Net Sales ($)	14764M	63394M	51258M	244583M	315396M	2466062M
920089M	1946643M	2023805M	Total Assets ($)	17101M	39265M	53146M	222617M	227719M	1463957M

© RMA 2005   M = $ thousand   MM = $ million
See Pages 11 through 21 for Explanation of Ratios and Data

Current Data Sorted By Assets | Comparative Historical Data

Type of Statement

Type of Statement	0-500M	500M-2MM	2-10MM	10-50MM	50-100MM	100-250MM	4/1/00-3/31/01 ALL	4/1/01-3/31/02 ALL
Unqualified	1							1
Reviewed	2	9	4				6	2
Compiled	5	5	6				9	13
Tax Returns	3	9	2	3	1		1	3
Other			4	2	1	1	10	10
	7 (4/1-9/30/04)		51 (10/1/04-3/31/05)					
NUMBER OF STATEMENTS	11	23	16	6	2		26	29

(Columns 10-50MM, 50-100MM and 100-250MM: DATA NOT AVAILABLE for the Assets, Liabilities, Income and Ratio sections.)

	0-500M %	500M-2MM %	2-10MM %	10-50MM %	50-100MM %	100-250MM %		ALL %	ALL %
ASSETS									
Cash & Equivalents	29.9	11.0	7.6					2.7	3.5
Trade Receivables (net)	7.7	12.7	14.7					19.5	12.1
Inventory	4.1	19.9	9.0					10.5	18.2
All Other Current	.6	7.9	4.4					9.6	4.0
Total Current	42.3	51.5	35.7					42.3	37.8
Fixed Assets (net)	37.3	41.4	53.3					37.7	48.7
Intangibles (net)	4.4	2.0	.1					.0	.4
All Other Non-Current	15.9	5.1	10.9					19.9	13.2
Total	100.0	100.0	100.0					100.0	100.0
LIABILITIES									
Notes Payable-Short Term	50.7	23.4	14.0					39.9	33.7
Cur. Mat.-L/T/D	3.1	5.3	3.9					6.0	3.2
Trade Payables	4.1	5.6	6.4					4.2	24.4
Income Taxes Payable	.0	.0	.1					.1	.2
All Other Current	8.8	5.2	7.7					3.2	7.7
Total Current	66.8	39.5	32.2					53.4	69.2
Long-Term Debt	36.1	22.7	23.6					24.9	52.0
Deferred Taxes	.1	.0	.0					.0	.0
All Other Non-Current	6.4	3.4	2.1					2.4	2.0
Net Worth	-9.3	34.5	42.1					19.3	-23.3
Total Liabilities & Net Worth	100.0	100.0	100.0					100.0	100.0
INCOME DATA									
Net Sales	100.0	100.0	100.0					100.0	100.0
Gross Profit									
Operating Expenses	97.0	90.6	82.3					86.9	93.6
Operating Profit	3.0	9.4	17.7					13.1	6.4
All Other Expenses (net)	1.3	2.2	3.3					2.0	4.7
Profit Before Taxes	1.7	7.2	14.4					11.1	1.7

RATIOS

Ratio	0-500M	500M-2MM	2-10MM					ALL	ALL
Current	1.6	2.2	3.8					1.5	1.4
	1.1	1.5	1.2					.9	1.0
	.3	.7	.7					.6	.3
Quick	1.5	1.1	1.5					1.1	.8
	1.0	.3	.6				(25)	.6	.3
	.3	.0	.1					.1	.1
Sales/Receivables	0 UND	0 UND	0 UND					0 UND	0 UND
	0 UND	0 UND	48 7.6					41 8.8	35 10.5
	30 12.2	45 8.0	94 3.9					192 1.9	100 3.7
Cost of Sales/Inventory									
Cost of Sales/Payables									
Sales/Working Capital	88.3	2.9	3.8					8.1	5.7
	216.0	12.0	15.9					-74.5	-113.9
	-2.0	-4.9	-20.0					-6.2	-5.0
EBIT/Interest	8.5	23.6	17.1					8.0	2.9
	(10) 2.9	3.3	5.4				(25)	1.9	1.5
	.8	1.4	2.5					.6	.2
Net Profit + Depr., Dep., Amort./Cur. Mat. L/T/D									
Fixed/Worth	.2	.4	.8					.5	.8
	1.3	.7	1.0					1.4	1.4
	-.5	6.6	4.7					-16.5	25.0
Debt/Worth	1.2	.6	.3					.7	.7
	2.3	1.9	2.3					4.0	3.7
	-2.4	5.9	6.0					-29.7	41.3
% Profit Before Taxes/Tangible Net Worth		70.0	45.9					59.8	16.5
	(20) 18.0	(15) 19.4				(17)	10.5	(23) 5.4	
		4.7	4.4					-11.1	-6.8
% Profit Before Taxes/Total Assets	15.6	23.2	17.3					21.4	7.2
	5.7	7.9	10.3					5.7	2.0
	1.8	1.4	2.0					-3.4	-2.0
Sales/Net Fixed Assets	37.2	10.9	5.0					15.3	3.9
	15.2	3.9	1.5					4.6	1.6
	2.4	1.3	.9					1.2	.8
Sales/Total Assets	4.9	2.0	1.4					2.1	1.3
	2.2	1.1	1.1					.9	.7
	1.6	.8	.4					.6	.5
% Depr., Dep., Amort./Sales		3.5	2.8					1.9	1.9
	(17) 5.8	(15) 3.5				(21)	3.0	(27) 3.9	
		15.1	16.8					8.7	7.5
% Officers', Directors', Owners' Comp/Sales									
Net Sales ($)	9867M	37017M	94865M	159810M	230190M			97135M	187669M
Total Assets ($)	3048M	26208M	66995M	96414M	109168M			146792M	153597M

M = $ thousand   MM = $ million
See Pages 11 through 21 for Explanation of Ratios and Data

Comparative Historical Data / Current Data Sorted By Sales

			Type of Statement						
	3	5	Unqualified	1					4
	4	4	Reviewed			2	1	1	
27	20	18	Compiled	4	10	3		1	
13	9	12	Tax Returns	5	7				
19	15	19	Other	6		4	1		2
4/1/02-3/31/03	4/1/03-3/31/04	4/1/04-3/31/05		7 (4/1-9/30/04)		51 (10/1/04-3/31/05)			
ALL	ALL	ALL		0-1MM	1-3MM	3-5MM	5-10MM	10-25MM	25MM & OVER
59	51	58	**NUMBER OF STATEMENTS**	16	23	9	2	2	6
%	%	%	**ASSETS**	%	%	%	%	%	%
9.2	9.8	12.7	Cash & Equivalents	15.2	16.3				
15.3	15.0	14.0	Trade Receivables (net)	10.9	12.8				
10.1	12.7	14.3	Inventory	13.8	5.9				
6.7	8.8	5.6	All Other Current	7.0	2.7				
41.4	46.4	46.5	Total Current	46.9	37.7				
47.9	35.3	42.0	Fixed Assets (net)	37.1	55.4				
3.1	3.3	1.7	Intangibles (net)	2.5	2.3				
7.6	14.9	9.8	All Other Non-Current	13.4	4.6				
100.0	100.0	100.0	Total	100.0	100.0				
			LIABILITIES						
45.4	32.6	27.0	Notes Payable-Short Term	49.0	14.2				
5.1	4.7	4.0	Cur. Mat.-L/T/D	2.4	7.2				
5.6	6.9	5.1	Trade Payables	2.2	4.4				
.1	.1	.1	Income Taxes Payable	.1	.1				
8.4	8.0	7.5	All Other Current	11.7	3.6				
64.6	52.3	43.7	Total Current	65.3	29.5				
18.2	24.8	24.0	Long-Term Debt	10.7	46.1				
.3	.0	.0	Deferred Taxes	.0	.0				
4.8	1.4	3.8	All Other Non-Current	6.0	2.1				
12.1	21.5	28.5	Net Worth	17.9	22.3				
100.0	100.0	100.0	Total Liabilities & Net Worth	100.0	100.0				
			INCOME DATA						
100.0	100.0	100.0	Net Sales	100.0	100.0				
			Gross Profit						
84.7	88.0	89.5	Operating Expenses	91.5	88.1				
15.3	12.0	10.5	Operating Profit	8.5	11.9				
4.3	2.4	2.4	All Other Expenses (net)	2.5	2.9				
10.9	9.6	8.0	Profit Before Taxes	6.0	8.9				
			RATIOS						
2.3	1.9	1.9		1.8	3.7				
1.3	1.2	1.2	Current	1.3	1.2				
.5	.4	.7		.1	.7				
1.6	1.2	1.3		1.0	2.1				
.7	.4	.5	Quick	.3	1.1				
.2	.2	.1		.1	.2				
0 UND	0 UND	0 UND		0 UND	0 UND				
23 15.7	10 35.0	9 41.2	Sales/Receivables	4 87.9	8 43.2				
108 3.4	44 8.3	56 6.5		42 8.7	72 5.1				
			Cost of Sales/Inventory						
			Cost of Sales/Payables						
4.0	4.8	4.2		3.6	3.3				
18.7	40.5	19.0	Sales/Working Capital	194.9	18.1				
−5.9	−7.9	−17.2		−2.1	−16.7				
(54) 9.0	(40) 8.0	(56) 11.5		(15) 6.7	11.6				
4.2	5.3	3.7	EBIT/Interest	2.8	3.3				
1.6	1.5	1.5		−1.0	1.4				
			Net Profit + Depr., Dep., Amort./Cur. Mat. L/T/D						
.6	.2	.4		.4	.7				
1.5	.8	1.0	Fixed/Worth	.9	1.8				
5.5	2.8	4.3		NM	15.1				
.6	1.0	.7		1.4	.8				
1.8	2.4	2.0	Debt/Worth	2.1	3.8				
12.8	53.8	15.9		NM	359.9				
(46) 57.5	(41) 89.4	(48) 49.3	% Profit Before Taxes/Tangible	(12) 72.1	(18) 63.9				
25.3	28.5	16.9	Net Worth	6.6	18.9				
9.4	10.6	5.0		−2.1	9.1				
17.7	19.2	15.7	% Profit Before Taxes/Total	14.1	15.8				
9.0	10.6	6.0	Assets	3.3	8.4				
1.4	1.7	1.9		−1.2	3.6				
13.9	159.7	12.0		13.2	8.9				
2.0	7.3	3.8	Sales/Net Fixed Assets	6.6	1.7				
.9	1.7	1.4		1.7	.9				
1.8	2.6	2.1		1.9	2.0				
.9	1.5	1.4	Sales/Total Assets	1.2	1.1				
.5	.7	.8		.8	.7				
(50) 2.1	(34) .6	(41) 2.8	% Depr., Dep., Amort./Sales	(11) 1.4	(18) 4.0				
4.8	4.5	4.5		3.4	7.7				
9.5	8.4	10.3		6.7	18.5				
	1.5		% Officers', Directors',						
	(10) 6.8		Owners' Comp/Sales						
	13.3								
474573M	757917M	531749M	Net Sales ($)	9705M	42201M	31766M	18416M	20656M	409005M
496748M	321031M	301833M	Total Assets ($)	12381M	44762M	38636M	22174M	18691M	165189M

M = $ thousand   MM = $ million
See Pages 11 through 21 for Explanation of Ratios and Data

Current Data Sorted By Assets　　　　　　　　Comparative Historical Data

						Type of Statement		
	1	4	4	2	3	Unqualified	10	1
1	4	20	15	1		Reviewed	35	34
9	21	41	14	1		Compiled	73	57
25	59	15	2	1		Tax Returns	46	28
5	24	29	4	1	1	Other	60	59
	40 (4/1-9/30/04)		273 (10/1/04-3/31/05)				4/1/00-3/31/01	4/1/01-3/31/02
0-500M	500M-2MM	2-10MM	10-50MM	50-100MM	100-250MM		ALL	ALL
40	109	109	44	7	4	NUMBER OF STATEMENTS	224	179
%	%	%	%	%	%	ASSETS	%	%
14.6	7.1	3.8	7.5			Cash & Equivalents	5.9	5.9
2.3	5.7	8.3	9.9			Trade Receivables (net)	9.8	10.0
5.5	12.1	16.3	17.6			Inventory	13.9	14.5
2.7	2.4	5.7	6.3			All Other Current	4.3	5.0
25.2	27.1	34.1	41.4			Total Current	33.9	35.3
64.8	61.7	53.9	46.3			Fixed Assets (net)	52.3	52.2
.3	1.6	1.5	2.6			Intangibles (net)	1.5	1.5
9.7	9.6	10.5	9.7			All Other Non-Current	12.3	10.9
100.0	100.0	100.0	100.0			Total	100.0	100.0
						LIABILITIES		
28.2	21.3	20.6	14.3			Notes Payable-Short Term	28.2	28.1
4.3	3.0	3.7	3.4			Cur. Mat.-L/T/D	4.6	4.8
4.1	4.3	5.7	8.0			Trade Payables	5.3	4.3
.0	.1	.0	1.2			Income Taxes Payable	.1	.4
2.1	4.9	4.7	2.3			All Other Current	6.8	10.0
38.6	33.5	34.6	29.2			Total Current	45.1	47.5
42.4	29.7	28.0	27.2			Long-Term Debt	31.1	29.2
.0	.1	.9	.7			Deferred Taxes	.9	.9
3.4	4.6	4.5	5.2			All Other Non-Current	7.6	4.7
15.5	32.1	32.1	37.7			Net Worth	15.3	17.6
100.0	100.0	100.0	100.0			Total Liabilities & Net Worth	100.0	100.0
						INCOME DATA		
100.0	100.0	100.0	100.0			Net Sales	100.0	100.0
						Gross Profit		
91.6	89.3	87.3	88.6			Operating Expenses	99.0	92.3
8.4	10.7	12.7	11.4			Operating Profit	1.0	7.7
4.1	5.3	3.4	1.2			All Other Expenses (net)	−4.4	4.5
4.3	5.4	9.2	10.3			Profit Before Taxes	5.4	3.2
						RATIOS		
2.5	3.2	1.9	1.9				1.6	1.7
.9	1.1	1.1	1.3			Current	1.0	1.0
.3	.3	.6	1.0				.5	.4
1.9	1.0	.6	.9				.9	.7
.4	(108) .3	.3	.5			Quick	(223) .4	.3
.1	.1	.1	.2				.1	.1
0 UND	0 UND	0 UND	23 15.7				0 UND	0 UND
0 UND	0 UND	16 23.0	39 9.4			Sales/Receivables	11 33.8	12 30.2
0 UND	5 73.2	42 8.6	60 6.1				47 7.8	46 8.0
						Cost of Sales/Inventory		
						Cost of Sales/Payables		
15.3	3.6	4.4	3.3				5.0	6.2
−55.7	101.0	31.7	10.9			Sales/Working Capital	64.8	−236.3
−3.7	−5.0	−6.2	−202.2				−5.2	−5.2
16.2	8.1	6.8	6.9				4.3	4.3
(35) 2.0	(101) 2.4	(100) 2.8	(41) 3.0			EBIT/Interest	(197) 1.8	(160) 1.7
−.6	.5	1.4	1.4				.7	.5
		4.7	4.2				5.0	5.0
	(14) 2.4	2.4	(12) 1.7			Net Profit + Depr., Dep., Amort./Cur. Mat. L /T/D	(47) 2.6	(29) 1.2
		1.7	.8				.9	.2
1.1	.9	.8	.6				.8	.9
2.0	1.4	1.4	1.1			Fixed/Worth	1.5	1.5
21.8	5.6	3.3	4.7				6.9	8.3
.7	.3	.7	.8				.8	.7
2.1	1.0	1.7	1.5			Debt/Worth	2.2	1.9
21.8	17.5	7.2	4.5				10.0	12.2
65.2	24.1	26.5	26.7			% Profit Before Taxes/Tangible Net Worth	23.3	29.9
(31) 13.4	(89) 5.6	(89) 11.1	(39) 10.6				(185) 7.6	(142) 7.6
−3.2	.0	4.2	4.2				−.1	.1
47.6	9.9	9.1	8.2			% Profit Before Taxes/Total Assets	7.5	8.2
4.3	1.7	3.9	4.4				3.0	2.2
−1.9	−1.6	1.5	1.3				−1.1	−3.8
8.5	5.1	3.8	4.3				5.0	6.4
2.0	1.2	1.4	1.5			Sales/Net Fixed Assets	1.8	2.2
.4	.3	.6	.6				.7	.8
4.1	1.9	1.3	1.4				1.6	1.8
1.4	.7	.8	.7			Sales/Total Assets	.8	1.0
.3	.2	.4	.4				.4	.5
3.5	4.6	2.9	2.3				2.4	2.5
(33) 7.1	(95) 10.0	(96) 6.3	(40) 4.9			% Depr., Dep., Amort./Sales	(201) 5.3	(159) 5.4
17.0	16.1	11.9	10.7				8.7	8.8
1.3	2.0	1.2					1.2	1.7
(14) 3.2	(38) 4.1	(31) 2.8				% Officers', Directors', Owners' Comp/Sales	(49) 3.6	(58) 4.2
10.6	7.0	5.1					9.1	8.2
23145M	149585M	484953M	698171M	318741M	1241553M	Net Sales ($)	1990111M	2612002M
12824M	121558M	512908M	786502M	555063M	433696M	Total Assets ($)	2080186M	1745138M

© RMA 2005　　　　　M = $ thousand　　MM = $ million
See Pages 11 through 21 for Explanation of Ratios and Data

Comparative Historical Data / Current Data Sorted By Sales

			Type of Statement						
18	21	14	Unqualified		1	2	3	1	7
49	47	41	Reviewed	3	6	10	9	8	5
73	87	86	Compiled	21	26	15	15	7	2
69	84	102	Tax Returns	70	22	6	2	1	1
74	67	70	Other	23	18	6	11	7	5
4/1/02-3/31/03 ALL	4/1/03-3/31/04 ALL	4/1/04-3/31/05 ALL		0-1MM	40 (4/1-9/30/04) 1-3MM	3-5MM	273 (10/1/04-3/31/05) 5-10MM	10-25MM	25MM & OVER
283	306	313	**NUMBER OF STATEMENTS**	117	73	39	40	24	20
%	%	%	**ASSETS**	%	%	%	%	%	%
7.2	7.3	7.0	Cash & Equivalents	6.0	10.4	6.1	5.6	4.1	9.4
11.3	10.6	7.1	Trade Receivables (net)	2.4	4.8	13.0	10.2	14.1	16.4
14.6	13.2	13.7	Inventory	8.6	12.7	14.2	20.2	24.9	20.0
6.2	6.7	4.1	All Other Current	1.9	3.4	5.4	9.2	5.2	5.8
39.2	37.8	32.0	Total Current	18.9	31.3	38.6	45.2	48.3	51.6
51.3	50.8	56.6	Fixed Assets (net)	69.8	56.8	50.9	44.2	37.2	38.4
.8	1.3	1.5	Intangibles (net)	.4	2.0	2.1	2.5	1.7	2.5
8.7	10.0	9.9	All Other Non-Current	10.9	9.8	8.5	8.1	12.7	7.5
100.0	100.0	100.0	Total	100.0	100.0	100.0	100.0	100.0	100.0
			LIABILITIES						
23.3	23.3	20.5	Notes Payable-Short Term	13.0	32.1	21.9	25.1	20.9	9.0
4.6	3.6	3.6	Cur. Mat.-L/T/D	1.9	4.8	6.3	3.1	3.9	4.1
5.5	5.2	5.3	Trade Payables	2.3	3.6	3.9	9.9	14.1	12.1
.2	.2	.2	Income Taxes Payable	.1	.0	.0	.0	2.1	.4
11.0	8.9	4.5	All Other Current	1.8	5.1	4.3	8.2	4.3	11.0
44.7	41.2	34.1	Total Current	19.1	45.7	36.4	46.3	45.4	36.7
28.5	29.7	30.1	Long-Term Debt	30.4	40.1	29.4	23.3	24.2	14.4
.5	.4	.5	Deferred Taxes	.3	.2	.7	.8	1.0	1.3
2.9	4.5	4.4	All Other Non-Current	3.6	7.0	5.4	1.9	1.5	5.7
23.4	24.3	31.0	Net Worth	46.8	7.0	28.1	27.7	28.0	41.9
100.0	100.0	100.0	Total Liabilities & Net Worth	100.0	100.0	100.0	100.0	100.0	100.0
			INCOME DATA						
100.0	100.0	100.0	Net Sales	100.0	100.0	100.0	100.0	100.0	100.0
			Gross Profit						
91.2	90.9	88.9	Operating Expenses	83.4	89.6	91.4	94.3	95.8	93.9
8.8	9.1	11.1	Operating Profit	16.6	10.4	8.6	5.7	4.2	6.1
3.7	3.7	3.8	All Other Expenses (net)	7.5	2.8	1.6	.7	-.1	.8
5.2	5.4	7.3	Profit Before Taxes	9.1	7.6	6.9	5.0	4.4	5.3
			RATIOS						
1.9	2.1	2.1	Current	3.1	1.5	2.5	1.8	1.6	2.1
1.2	1.1	1.1		1.2	.8	1.4	1.0	1.0	1.5
.6	.5	.6		.4	.3	.7	.7	.8	1.1
1.0	.9	.8	Quick	1.0	.7	1.2	.8	.8	1.0
.4 (304)	.4 (312)	.4		(116) .3	.3	.5	.3	.5	.8
.1	.1	.1		.1	.0	.3	.1	.2	.6
0 UND	0 UND	0 UND	Sales/Receivables	0 UND	0 UND	0 UND	1 456.6	24 14.9	19 19.1
12 29.2	10 37.7	0 UND		0 UND	0 UND	28 13.1	25 14.8	43 8.4	30 12.2
49 7.4	37 10.0	35 10.3		0 UND	34 10.9	70 5.2	37 9.8	53 6.9	70 5.2
			Cost of Sales/Inventory						
			Cost of Sales/Payables						
5.9	5.4	4.0	Sales/Working Capital	3.1	6.3	3.7	5.9	7.0	3.5
31.2	38.1	27.5		15.4	-27.0	10.4	119.0	UND	11.4
-6.7	-6.7	-7.7		-4.9	-4.2	-16.7	-7.2	-16.8	39.2
5.6	5.0	7.5	EBIT/Interest	4.8	11.0	12.0	6.1	6.8	10.8
(254) 2.2	(272) 2.5	(286) 2.5		(98) 1.5	(71) 3.1	(38) 2.9	(38) 2.9	(23) 3.0	(18) 4.1
.9	.9	1.1		.6	1.0	1.5	1.0	1.7	1.6
5.2	4.2	4.4	Net Profit + Depr., Dep., Amort./Cur. Mat. L/T/D						
(47) 2.6	(35) 2.2	(38) 1.9							
1.2	.9	1.1							
.7	.7	.8	Fixed/Worth	.9	.9	.7	.5	.8	.4
1.4	1.4	1.4		1.4	2.2	1.5	1.3	1.3	1.1
5.7	4.2	4.6		2.4	-8.3	4.0	4.6	4.7	2.0
.7	.7	.5	Debt/Worth	.3	.9	.7	1.1	1.2	.6
1.8	1.6	1.5		.8	2.4	2.3	2.0	2.4	1.5
12.6	6.4	7.5		2.6	-12.3	6.2	80.2	9.0	3.1
29.9	27.8	27.4	% Profit Before Taxes/Tangible Net Worth	15.7	46.7	28.1	29.4	31.4	20.6
(236) 10.0	(255) 9.2	(258) 8.8		(105) 3.9	(52) 17.5	(31) 11.4	(31) 11.6	(21) 16.9	(18) 11.6
.5	.9	1.6		.0	4.8	4.3	5.2	6.9	4.6
11.2	8.7	10.2	% Profit Before Taxes/Total Assets	5.8	13.1	15.0	9.9	10.7	7.2
3.5	3.3	3.7		1.7	5.3	6.0	4.3	3.9	4.6
-.4	-.3	.3		-.4	-.2	1.4	.5	1.3	1.1
7.0	7.2	4.9	Sales/Net Fixed Assets	1.3	6.1	3.6	7.2	9.0	10.6
2.4	2.6	1.5		.4	1.8	2.0	4.1	5.1	5.0
.8	.8	.5		.2	.7	1.0	1.2	1.5	1.5
2.0	2.1	1.7	Sales/Total Assets	.6	2.0	1.9	2.3	1.8	2.2
1.1	1.0	.7		.3	1.0	1.2	1.2	1.4	1.4
.5	.5	.3		.2	.5	.5	.7	.7	.8
2.3	2.5	3.5	% Depr., Dep., Amort./Sales	6.2	3.4	4.3	2.7	1.5	1.6
(246) 5.2	(271) 5.9	(273) 7.1		(102) 11.6	(65) 7.1	(34) 7.0	(34) 4.8	(20) 3.4	(18) 2.8
10.2	11.1	13.2		17.8	11.0	11.7	7.7	5.7	4.7
1.9	1.3	1.6	% Officers', Directors', Owners' Comp/Sales	1.4	2.7	1.8			
(80) 3.7	(97) 3.8	(89) 3.6		(39) 4.1	(21) 4.9	(12) 2.6			
6.9	9.4	6.6		7.8	10.3	5.1			
3789698M	4313280M	2916148M	Net Sales ($)	43649M	141887M	154029M	291186M	362180M	1923217M
3017050M	3237260M	2422551M	Total Assets ($)	138497M	219892M	217645M	333222M	417856M	1095439M

© RMA 2005

M = $ thousand   MM = $ million

See Pages 11 through 21 for Explanation of Ratios and Data

Current Data Sorted By Assets   Comparative Historical Data

0-500M	500M-2MM	2-10MM	10-50MM	50-100MM	100-250MM	Type of Statement		4/1/00-3/31/01 ALL		4/1/01-3/31/02 ALL
		4	3		1	Unqualified		6		5
	3	8	5	1		Reviewed		14		10
1	4	19	5	1		Compiled		25		27
6	12	9	2			Tax Returns		17		17
	10	15	8	3	1	Other		31		37
	24 (4/1-9/30/04)		97 (10/1/04-3/31/05)							
7	29	55	23	5	2	**NUMBER OF STATEMENTS**		93		96
%	%	%	%	%	%	**ASSETS**		%		%
	7.7	6.3	1.8			Cash & Equivalents		5.0		5.8
	2.4	4.7	10.2			Trade Receivables (net)		6.1		4.5
	27.0	38.0	38.1			Inventory		32.5		37.8
	2.9	4.7	3.9			All Other Current		5.7		5.4
	40.0	53.7	54.0			Total Current		49.4		53.5
	51.4	37.0	38.2			Fixed Assets (net)		38.1		33.8
	.1	.3	.6			Intangibles (net)		1.0		.8
	8.6	9.0	7.2			All Other Non-Current		11.5		12.0
	100.0	100.0	100.0			Total		100.0		100.0
						LIABILITIES				
	28.2	22.7	37.4			Notes Payable-Short Term		33.9		35.8
	6.9	4.8	1.9			Cur. Mat.-L/T/D		1.4		2.0
	1.0	2.1	3.9			Trade Payables		3.3		2.6
	.0	1.4	.1			Income Taxes Payable		.2		.3
	8.6	8.8	3.7			All Other Current		7.7		5.4
	44.7	39.8	47.0			Total Current		46.4		46.2
	28.0	21.4	23.5			Long-Term Debt		19.3		14.1
	.4	.6	.0			Deferred Taxes		1.2		.5
	7.7	6.7	.8			All Other Non-Current		6.2		5.4
	19.1	31.5	28.7			Net Worth		26.9		33.8
	100.0	100.0	100.0			Total Liabilities & Net Worth		100.0		100.0
						INCOME DATA				
	100.0	100.0	100.0			Net Sales		100.0		100.0
						Gross Profit				
	85.8	94.1	91.6			Operating Expenses		95.4		94.9
	14.2	5.9	8.4			Operating Profit		4.6		5.1
	4.1	2.5	1.1			All Other Expenses (net)		−.1		3.2
	10.0	3.4	7.4			Profit Before Taxes		4.7		1.9
						RATIOS				
	3.4	2.0	1.5					1.8		2.1
	1.0	1.4	1.1			Current		1.2		1.2
	.2	.8	1.0					.8		.8
	.8	.8	.5					.5		.4
(28)	.2	.1	.2			Quick	(90)	.1	(92)	.1
	.0	.0	.1					.0		.0
0 UND	0 UND	0 UND					0 UND	0 UND
0 UND	0 999.8	15 24.0			Sales/Receivables		0 UND	0 UND
1 305.7	17 21.6	43 8.4				17 21.4	11 32.9
						Cost of Sales/Inventory				
						Cost of Sales/Payables				
	4.5	2.8	5.4					3.7		3.8
	−225.5	8.8	17.4			Sales/Working Capital		21.2		20.2
	−3.7	−13.5	−91.3					−10.9		−11.3
	6.7	16.7	8.3					2.7		3.2
(18)	2.3	(46) 2.8	(20) 3.6			EBIT/Interest	(83)	1.3	(90)	1.4
	.4	1.2	1.6					.6		.0
		16.6				Net Profit + Depr., Dep.,		5.7		
		(11) 6.6				Amort./Cur. Mat. L /T/D	(12)	1.9		
		5.1						1.4		
	.3	.3	.4					.4		.3
	1.9	.7	1.2			Fixed/Worth		1.1		.8
	−4.4	2.3	2.7					3.1		3.0
	.5	.6	1.3					1.1		.7
	3.6	1.3	2.7			Debt/Worth		2.7		1.9
	−6.3	10.6	5.0					8.2		7.3
	21.8	25.9	46.9			% Profit Before Taxes/Tangible		16.2		18.5
(17)	9.6	(44) 12.5	(21) 21.9			Net Worth	(81)	5.3	(86)	3.8
	.6	.9	9.9					−2.5		−12.8
	9.9	11.1	12.3			% Profit Before Taxes/Total		4.2		6.5
	3.8	3.7	4.9			Assets		1.1		1.1
	−.9	−.2	1.9					−1.4		−4.1
	13.9	13.9	8.9					7.0		17.9
	2.8	4.3	3.3			Sales/Net Fixed Assets		2.9		2.9
	.4	1.1	1.7					.9		1.2
	1.8	1.8	1.5					1.5		1.8
	1.0	1.1	1.2			Sales/Total Assets		.7		1.1
	.3	.5	.7					.4		.5
	1.4	1.7	.7					1.3		1.1
(22)	7.8	(47) 3.3	(20) 2.0			% Depr., Dep., Amort./Sales	(77)	3.5	(78)	3.7
	15.2	6.9	5.4					8.6		7.6
		1.0				% Officers', Directors',		.8		.7
	(13)	2.5				Owners' Comp/Sales	(27)	1.8	(24)	1.2
		10.0						5.4		3.3
6899M	34912M	376127M	732509M	694061M	499223M	Net Sales ($)		1418205M		998243M
2161M	32127M	267966M	589640M	352161M	271681M	Total Assets ($)		1113443M		702747M

© RMA 2005   M = $ thousand   MM = $ million
See Pages 11 through 21 for Explanation of Ratios and Data

Comparative Historical Data | Current Data Sorted By Sales

			Type of Statement						
6	8	8	Unqualified			1	1	1	5
14	23	17	Reviewed		3	3	5	4	2
14	22	30	Compiled	6	4	7	3	6	4
20	24	29	Tax Returns	16	7	1	3	1	1
40	32	37	Other	6	12	3	2	8	6
4/1/02-3/31/03	4/1/03-3/31/04	4/1/04-3/31/05		24 (4/1-9/30/04)			97 (10/1/04-3/31/05)		
ALL	ALL	ALL		0-1MM	1-3MM	3-5MM	5-10MM	10-25MM	25MM & OVER
94	109	121	**NUMBER OF STATEMENTS**	28	26	15	14	20	18
%	%	%	**ASSETS**	%	%	%	%	%	%
5.4	4.1	5.4	Cash & Equivalents	5.5	4.9	9.8	9.2	3.2	2.0
4.1	5.4	6.1	Trade Receivables (net)	5.2	2.0	1.6	7.5	7.6	14.4
37.7	36.7	34.3	Inventory	15.1	36.3	40.6	35.7	46.8	41.4
4.6	4.8	3.7	All Other Current	.7	6.2	6.7	2.3	4.5	2.4
51.8	51.0	49.6	Total Current	26.5	49.4	58.7	54.6	62.0	60.3
36.0	39.4	42.5	Fixed Assets (net)	66.0	44.5	34.8	31.5	30.1	31.8
.4	.2	.3	Intangibles (net)	.2	.0	.1	1.0	.5	.3
11.8	9.4	7.6	All Other Non-Current	7.3	6.1	6.4	12.9	7.4	7.6
100.0	100.0	100.0	Total	100.0	100.0	100.0	100.0	100.0	100.0
			LIABILITIES						
41.3	35.7	26.4	Notes Payable-Short Term	10.5	34.8	30.9	23.7	28.0	35.8
3.7	4.2	4.9	Cur. Mat.-L/T/D	7.0	6.9	1.1	6.1	4.2	2.0
2.7	6.8	2.8	Trade Payables	1.5	.5	1.7	4.7	1.2	9.1
.4	.3	.6	Income Taxes Payable	.0	.8	2.0	.6	.9	.0
5.0	5.5	7.7	All Other Current	9.4	9.2	10.5	7.1	5.8	3.3
53.1	52.5	42.5	Total Current	28.4	52.2	46.2	42.2	40.1	50.3
14.0	18.4	23.3	Long-Term Debt	38.8	23.5	21.3	23.3	9.1	16.2
.1	.1	.4	Deferred Taxes	.4	.8	.7	.0	.1	.0
5.0	8.8	6.2	All Other Non-Current	9.0	6.9	4.8	4.6	4.6	5.2
27.9	20.3	27.6	Net Worth	23.5	16.6	27.1	29.8	46.1	28.3
100.0	100.0	100.0	Total Liabilities & Net Worth	100.0	100.0	100.0	100.0	100.0	100.0
			INCOME DATA						
100.0	100.0	100.0	Net Sales	100.0	100.0	100.0	100.0	100.0	100.0
			Gross Profit						
99.7	94.7	91.7	Operating Expenses	85.0	95.5	89.1	97.0	90.9	95.9
.3	5.3	8.3	Operating Profit	15.0	4.5	10.9	3.0	9.1	4.1
3.1	4.9	2.4	All Other Expenses (net)	6.6	2.8	2.2	-1.9	.8	-1.0
-2.8	.4	5.8	Profit Before Taxes	8.4	1.7	8.7	4.9	8.3	3.1
			RATIOS						
1.7	1.7	1.9	Current	2.6	2.0	2.1	2.6	3.6	1.4
1.2	1.1	1.2		.9	1.1	1.4	1.4	1.5	1.1
.8	.6	.8		.2	.4	.9	.7	1.1	1.0
.4	.4	.8	Quick	.8	.2	.9	1.5	.7	.7
.1	.1	(120) .2		(27) .2	.1	.1	.3	.2	.3
.0	.0	.0		.2	.1	.0	.0	.1	.1
0 UND	0 UND	0 UND	Sales/Receivables	0 UND	0 UND	0 UND	0 UND	0 UND	7 53.3
0 UND	0 999.8	0 999.8		0 UND	0 UND	0 UND	1 533.6	8 43.3	17 21.7
10 35.8	15 24.9	17 20.9		3 110.9	4 95.1	5 79.0	33 11.2	24 15.4	38 9.6
			Cost of Sales/Inventory						
			Cost of Sales/Payables						
5.0	5.7	3.5	Sales/Working Capital	2.9	2.2	4.4	2.0	4.0	7.8
18.0	19.5	16.3		-17.6	75.4	8.5	8.7	8.2	27.9
-12.0	-6.2	-13.1		-2.8	-3.9	-19.8	-49.7	25.7	-118.5
1.9	5.8	8.6	EBIT/Interest	4.6	6.0	11.7	10.4	20.0	11.4
(92) .6	(92) 2.8	(96) 2.8		(14) .6	(23) 2.6	(13) 4.6	(13) 2.7	(17) 6.2	(16) 2.9
-2.5	.4	1.0		-.8	1.0	1.9	-.8	2.4	.3
2.5	3.8	12.9	Net Profit + Depr., Dep., Amort./Cur. Mat. L/T/D						
(11) .9	(12) 2.4	(13) 5.7							
-1.7	1.3	1.3							
.4	.4	.3	Fixed/Worth	.9	.4	.3	.3	.3	.2
.8	.9	1.1		2.2	1.4	.6	.7	.5	1.0
1.8	3.1	6.1		10.2	-2.7	-43.5	4.5	1.2	5.8
.5	1.0	.8	Debt/Worth	.9	.4	1.2	.8	.4	1.8
1.8	2.7	2.4		3.5	2.6	2.3	2.8	1.3	2.6
9.7	12.5	15.5		-93.6	-5.3	-48.0	31.2	3.8	10.1
8.8	32.4	26.7	% Profit Before Taxes/Tangible Net Worth	17.9	14.3	48.2	25.9	36.9	49.2
(77) -.5	(86) 11.7	(93) 12.4		(20) 4.4	(16) 3.9	(10) 14.5	(12) 21.2	(19) 13.7	(16) 24.0
-22.8	-2.2	1.8		-15.9	-.1	3.8	5.3	10.1	3.1
2.7	8.6	10.2	% Profit Before Taxes/Total Assets	6.7	8.1	17.0	10.0	12.2	13.7
-.9	2.6	3.9		2.1	2.6	6.5	3.8	6.7	4.4
-10.4	-3.3	-.2		-2.4	-.5	1.3	-5.1	3.7	-.1
15.5	26.7	12.0	Sales/Net Fixed Assets	2.2	9.7	11.7	15.6	17.5	18.4
3.7	4.0	3.3		.4	2.7	4.3	6.2	9.5	7.0
1.0	1.0	.9		.1	.9	1.9	2.2	2.6	2.9
1.9	2.2	1.8	Sales/Total Assets	.8	1.7	1.6	2.6	2.1	4.0
1.0	1.1	1.1		.3	1.0	1.1	1.3	1.5	1.4
.5	.5	.5		.1	.5	1.0	.8	.9	1.1
1.6	1.0	1.4	% Depr., Dep., Amort./Sales	7.6	1.9	1.4	1.4	.7	.4
(77) 3.4	(86) 3.3	(102) 3.3		(22) 20.6	(22) 5.3	(13) 3.6	(13) 1.9	(17) 1.9	(15) .9
9.5	16.7	10.6		31.9	11.2	7.2	3.6	5.0	2.2
1.2	.8	.6	% Officers', Directors', Owners' Comp/Sales						
(24) 2.4	(18) 1.5	(21) 2.3							
7.1	2.8	10.0							
1007960M	2567628M	2343731M	Net Sales ($)	12757M	51621M	58805M	97452M	308678M	1814418M
773756M	1364535M	1515736M	Total Assets ($)	65738M	69853M	63977M	95010M	309644M	911514M

M = $ thousand   MM = $ million
See Pages 11 through 21 for Explanation of Ratios and Data

Current Data Sorted By Assets   **Comparative Historical Data**

0-500M	500M-2MM	2-10MM	10-50MM	50-100MM	100-250MM	Type of Statement	4/1/00-3/31/01 ALL	4/1/01-3/31/02 ALL
	1	13	23	8	9	Unqualified	28	43
	1	15	22	2		Reviewed	35	41
3	6	19	12			Compiled	42	38
4	6	6				Tax Returns	12	10
3	8	15	19	4	3	Other	74	79
\<58 (4/1-9/30/04)\>			\<144 (10/1/04-3/31/05)\>					
10	22	68	76	14	12	**NUMBER OF STATEMENTS**	191	211
%	%	%	%	%	%	**ASSETS**	%	%
13.1	3.1	4.9	4.6	1.4	.3	Cash & Equivalents	6.4	3.5
11.3	23.1	16.3	16.9	5.3	33.5	Trade Receivables (net)	16.2	19.1
35.8	35.2	34.5	41.1	62.3	43.7	Inventory	36.1	37.6
.4	5.2	9.7	12.5	9.7	3.0	All Other Current	7.7	9.4
60.6	66.6	65.3	75.1	78.8	80.4	Total Current	66.4	69.7
33.7	24.4	23.7	19.0	13.5	13.0	Fixed Assets (net)	24.9	22.4
.0	.0	.3	.1	.3	1.8	Intangibles (net)	2.5	1.5
5.7	9.0	10.8	5.9	7.4	4.7	All Other Non-Current	6.2	6.4
100.0	100.0	100.0	100.0	100.0	100.0	Total	100.0	100.0
						LIABILITIES		
78.5	24.0	31.5	37.2	39.0	49.1	Notes Payable-Short Term	32.7	36.5
1.1	3.9	4.0	.9	1.8	.6	Cur. Mat.-L/T/D	1.4	2.7
7.0	12.4	5.5	6.4	5.8	8.2	Trade Payables	7.3	7.3
.0	.0	.3	.4	.8	.0	Income Taxes Payable	.2	.4
3.9	2.8	7.2	8.1	5.3	4.6	All Other Current	9.0	7.8
90.5	43.1	48.5	53.0	52.7	62.4	Total Current	50.7	54.7
17.6	15.9	13.3	8.6	7.1	10.2	Long-Term Debt	11.8	11.9
.0	.0	.1	.7	1.2	.0	Deferred Taxes	.8	.7
16.8	4.6	4.4	1.1	3.0	4.4	All Other Non-Current	1.6	2.3
-24.9	36.4	33.7	36.5	36.1	22.9	Net Worth	35.1	30.4
100.0	100.0	100.0	100.0	100.0	100.0	Total Liabilities & Net Worth	100.0	100.0
						INCOME DATA		
100.0	100.0	100.0	100.0	100.0	100.0	Net Sales	100.0	100.0
						Gross Profit		
105.4	91.8	93.6	94.4	93.9	95.9	Operating Expenses	91.9	96.2
-5.4	8.2	6.4	5.6	6.1	4.1	Operating Profit	8.1	3.8
1.3	3.3	.2	-.4	1.2	.4	All Other Expenses (net)	1.9	1.1
-6.7	4.9	6.2	6.0	4.9	3.7	Profit Before Taxes	6.2	2.7
						RATIOS		
1.7	3.7	2.0	1.8	1.7	1.3		1.7	1.5
1.2	1.6	1.2	1.4	1.6	1.2	Current	1.2	1.2
.1	.9	1.0	1.1	1.4	1.1		1.1	1.1
.9	3.0	.8	.7	.2	1.0		.8	.7
.1	(21) .7	.3	(75) .4	.1	.4	Quick	.3	.4
.0	.2	.1	.1	.1	.3		.1	.1
0 UND	0 UND	0 UND	3 112.8	3 134.1	31 11.9		0 999.8	7 55.7
0 UND	11 33.2	17 21.6	29 12.8	9 42.1	48 7.6	Sales/Receivables	17 21.1	29 12.8
9 39.2	41 9.0	50 7.3	67 5.4	18 20.6	241 1.5		53 6.9	77 4.7
						Cost of Sales/Inventory		
						Cost of Sales/Payables		
9.8	2.4	4.7	4.4	4.5	6.9		4.3	5.9
24.2	16.1	17.1	7.6	5.5	8.7	Sales/Working Capital	10.8	11.8
-6.2	-94.7	107.4	14.0	6.3	12.3		61.8	44.6
2.0	8.0	9.4	13.0	10.9	4.4		4.2	3.1
-.1	(15) 5.1	(60) 3.3	(70) 4.4	3.8	(11) 3.6	EBIT/Interest	(167) 2.2	(192) 1.8
-6.6	.4	1.3	2.5	2.2	2.3		1.4	.9
			10.5				12.2	6.5
		(10)	6.2			Net Profit + Depr., Dep., Amort./Cur. Mat. L/T/D	(37) 3.9	(41) 3.0
			2.4				1.9	1.4
.1	.3	.2	.2	.1	.5		.2	.3
NM	.6	.6	.5	.3	.6	Fixed/Worth	.7	.6
-.6	NM	1.4	1.0	.8	.7		1.3	1.3
2.9	.4	.9	.8	1.0	2.7		1.0	1.3
NM	1.7	2.1	2.1	1.7	3.1	Debt/Worth	2.2	2.6
-2.0	NM	5.3	4.2	3.3	5.6		4.6	5.5
	44.2	34.8	32.3	32.9	40.7		29.4	22.7
(17)	12.4	(61) 17.9	(74) 20.1	20.7	21.4	% Profit Before Taxes/Tangible Net Worth	(178) 13.9	(198) 8.7
	.8	5.4	10.4	10.2	2.2		5.3	-1.2
3.7	12.0	9.4	9.6	13.2	6.4		9.2	6.5
-3.3	5.6	4.1	6.2	7.1	5.2	% Profit Before Taxes/Total Assets	4.8	2.3
-29.9	-1.7	1.1	3.0	3.1	.0		1.4	-.6
UND	70.3	50.6	21.8	28.7	15.1		22.5	21.4
25.0	22.2	9.9	8.2	13.4	10.6	Sales/Net Fixed Assets	8.7	9.3
3.5	3.2	3.7	4.5	7.8	7.9		3.5	4.4
7.7	4.9	2.5	1.7	1.7	2.0		2.1	2.2
3.0	2.3	1.7	1.3	1.6	1.5	Sales/Total Assets	1.5	1.5
1.6	.6	.9	1.0	1.3	.8		.8	1.1
	.3	1.0	.9	.7			.8	.8
(18)	1.2	(53) 2.2	(64) 1.6	1.1		% Depr., Dep., Amort./Sales	(165) 2.0	(184) 1.7
	2.5	3.8	2.4	1.7			3.4	2.7
		.5	.7				.7	.7
	(15)	1.6	(18) 2.8			% Officers', Directors', Owners' Comp/Sales	(35) 2.4	(40) 1.4
		3.7	4.1				5.4	4.2
13846M	110617M	989779M	2496928M	1640012M	2430827M	Net Sales ($)	5570311M	8148865M
3290M	28560M	358878M	1708022M	1085364M	1604125M	Total Assets ($)	3646601M	5104929M

M = $ thousand   MM = $ million
See Pages 11 through 21 for Explanation of Ratios and Data

Comparative Historical Data				Current Data Sorted By Sales					
			Type of Statement						
39	52	54	Unqualified	1		4	7	7	35
26	45	40	Reviewed		2	1	8	21	8
40	36	40	Compiled	2	6	3	13	11	5
14	10	16	Tax Returns	4	2	5	2	2	1
76	58	52	Other	7	7	5		14	19
4/1/02-3/31/03 ALL	4/1/03-3/31/04 ALL	4/1/04-3/31/05 ALL		58 (4/1-9/30/04) 0-1MM	1-3MM	3-5MM	144 (10/1/04-3/31/05) 5-10MM	10-25MM	25MM & OVER
195	201	202	**NUMBER OF STATEMENTS**	14	17	18	30	55	68
%	%	%	**ASSETS**	%	%	%	%	%	%
3.8	4.9	4.5	Cash & Equivalents	5.5	4.0	9.1	4.6	4.5	3.0
17.6	15.9	17.3	Trade Receivables (net)	14.6	6.6	21.3	17.4	18.8	18.1
36.6	37.7	39.6	Inventory	33.3	30.0	30.8	30.8	45.4	44.8
10.1	8.2	9.4	All Other Current	1.4	5.3	3.6	18.0	7.9	11.0
68.2	66.7	70.7	Total Current	54.8	46.0	64.8	70.8	76.7	76.9
25.4	22.4	21.1	Fixed Assets (net)	38.9	35.1	18.9	21.1	17.2	17.8
.2	.5	.3	Intangibles (net)	.0	.0	.7	.2	.1	.4
6.3	10.4	7.9	All Other Non-Current	6.3	18.9	15.7	7.9	6.0	4.9
100.0	100.0	100.0	Total	100.0	100.0	100.0	100.0	100.0	100.0
			LIABILITIES						
41.0	32.8	36.7	Notes Payable-Short Term	52.6	35.3	17.4	34.8	39.6	37.4
1.9	2.5	2.3	Cur. Mat.-L/T/D	.2	7.0	5.9	3.7	1.0	1.1
7.2	8.5	6.8	Trade Payables	.8	1.2	19.0	3.2	7.9	7.0
.2	.4	.3	Income Taxes Payable	.1	.9	.0	.1	.4	.3
7.1	6.3	6.6	All Other Current	1.1	5.0	5.4	8.5	7.2	7.2
57.4	50.5	52.8	Total Current	54.8	49.4	47.6	50.3	56.1	53.1
12.7	13.0	11.4	Long-Term Debt	19.5	18.5	13.2	9.6	7.9	11.2
.6	.6	.4	Deferred Taxes	.0	.0	.1	.2	.1	.9
5.5	4.6	3.7	All Other Non-Current	15.5	1.5	7.0	.8	2.8	3.0
23.9	31.3	31.7	Net Worth	10.2	30.6	32.0	39.3	33.1	31.8
100.0	100.0	100.0	Total Liabilities & Net Worth	100.0	100.0	100.0	100.0	100.0	100.0
			INCOME DATA						
100.0	100.0	100.0	Net Sales	100.0	100.0	100.0	100.0	100.0	100.0
			Gross Profit						
98.1	93.3	94.5	Operating Expenses	94.2	83.5	97.6	97.2	94.3	95.3
1.9	6.7	5.5	Operating Profit	5.8	16.5	2.4	2.8	5.7	4.7
1.0	1.1	.5	All Other Expenses (net)	5.1	.6	.4	-.8	-.3	.6
.8	5.7	5.1	Profit Before Taxes	.7	15.9	2.0	3.5	6.0	4.1
			RATIOS						
1.7	1.9	1.8	Current	2.0	1.9	1.9	1.9	1.8	1.7
1.2	1.4	1.3		1.3	1.0	1.5	1.3	1.3	1.4
1.0	1.1	1.1		.9	.6	.8	1.1	1.1	1.2
.7	.6	.7	Quick	1.1	1.0	1.3	.8	.7	.6
.3	.3	(200) .3		.3	(16) .1	.6	.3	(54) .3	.3
.1	.1	.1		.0	.0	.0	.1	.1	.1
6 58.7	3 140.5	1 249.1	Sales/Receivables	0 UND	0 UND	3 137.8	8 44.2	1 413.0	5 75.0
23 15.6	22 16.8	20 18.4		0 UND	0 UND	28 13.1	23 15.8	21 17.6	27 13.7
63 5.8	50 7.3	53 6.9		30 12.0	16 23.3	51 7.2	68 5.3	66 5.6	51 7.1
			Cost of Sales/Inventory						
			Cost of Sales/Payables						
5.4	4.8	4.7	Sales/Working Capital	1.4	9.8	2.9	3.9	4.7	5.5
12.2	8.7	9.8		3.9	UND	16.5	11.4	7.7	8.9
60.1	33.9	29.8		NM	-5.2	-28.5	35.8	29.2	15.2
2.9	8.6	8.6	EBIT/Interest	2.9	8.6	9.2	8.5	14.7	8.2
(182) 1.4	(187) 3.7	(180) 3.7		(13) .4	(14) 2.7	(16) 3.5	(24) 2.9	(49) 5.8	(64) 3.7
-.2	1.5	1.9		-1.9	-2.1	1.2	1.3	3.0	2.4
2.2	7.6	9.3	Net Profit + Depr., Dep., Amort./Cur. Mat. L/T/D						9.8
(36) 1.3	(34) 2.4	(25) 4.8						(11) 3.8	
.0	1.1	2.2							1.9
.3	.2	.2	Fixed/Worth	.1	.4	.1	.1	.2	.3
.8	.6	.6		.7	1.0	.4	.4	.5	.6
1.7	1.5	1.1		-6.4	9.3	NM	1.2	.8	.9
1.3	1.0	.9	Debt/Worth	.4	.5	.8	.8	1.1	1.3
2.7	2.3	2.2		6.5	2.0	1.7	1.7	2.1	2.6
7.2	5.3	5.4		-9.1	29.2	NM	4.0	5.9	4.2
21.0	34.4	33.2	% Profit Before Taxes/Tangible Net Worth		65.9	25.0	20.3	38.2	32.3
(177) 5.0	(185) 18.0	(183) 18.5			(14) 15.6	(14) 13.3	(27) 10.0	(52) 24.5	(67) 20.4
-9.7	5.9	7.0			.5	6.7	3.4	14.4	10.9
6.2	12.2	9.8	% Profit Before Taxes/Total Assets	.9	20.4	7.6	7.8	13.3	9.6
.9	5.6	5.2		-1.8	4.2	3.6	2.9	7.8	5.4
-3.5	1.3	1.6		-3.2	-.1	-1.6	1.2	2.9	3.1
23.2	30.1	31.6	Sales/Net Fixed Assets	UND	25.0	48.6	63.2	43.3	23.5
8.6	10.9	10.2		3.2	3.7	15.2	9.0	10.4	12.1
4.2	3.8	4.5		.6	.9	5.0	4.2	6.5	6.0
2.5	2.3	2.2	Sales/Total Assets	2.0	1.4	3.3	2.5	2.0	2.2
1.6	1.6	1.5		.3	.9	1.6	1.8	1.4	1.6
1.1	1.0	1.0		.2	.4	1.1	.9	1.2	1.2
.9	.8	.8	% Depr., Dep., Amort./Sales	2.3	.9	1.7	.9	.8	.8
(166) 1.8	(173) 1.6	(165) 1.7		(11) 7.2	(15) 3.0	(13) 2.2	(25) 2.3	(42) 1.5	(59) 1.1
3.1	3.3	2.8		15.6	4.9	3.5	3.7	2.1	2.1
.9	.9	.9	% Officers', Directors', Owners' Comp/Sales				1.0	.7	.3
(56) 2.3	(43) 1.7	(51) 1.5				(10) 1.4	(16) 2.7	(13) 1.0	
4.3	3.8	3.6				2.7	4.6	2.9	
5994028M	8149332M	7682009M	Net Sales ($)	5362M	35111M	70971M	223389M	936506M	6410670M
3679008M	4847434M	4788239M	Total Assets ($)	19169M	69288M	71191M	164486M	682823M	3781282M

Current Data Sorted By Assets   Comparative Historical Data

	0-500M	500M-2MM	2-10MM	10-50MM	50-100MM	100-250MM	Type of Statement	4/1/00-3/31/01 ALL	4/1/01-3/31/02 ALL
							Unqualified	1	10
		13	151	103	6	1	Reviewed	279	265
	1	12	58	14	1		Compiled	70	80
	7	10	12	1			Tax Returns	9	19
		3	23	15	1		Other	61	49
		32 (4/1-9/30/04)			406 (10/1/04-3/31/05)				
NUMBER OF STATEMENTS	8	38	245	135	11	1		420	423
	%	%	%	%	%	%	**ASSETS**	%	%
		4.5	1.9	.8	1.0		Cash & Equivalents	1.6	1.6
		8.5	8.8	10.0	16.4		Trade Receivables (net)	7.4	9.0
		13.1	12.0	11.7	16.3		Inventory	16.0	15.5
		2.6	2.3	2.3	1.6		All Other Current	2.2	2.3
		28.7	25.1	24.8	35.3		Total Current	27.2	28.4
		56.6	64.9	65.3	56.3		Fixed Assets (net)	60.7	60.4
		4.6	1.1	.8	.2		Intangibles (net)	.5	.8
		10.1	8.9	9.1	8.1		All Other Non-Current	11.7	10.4
		100.0	100.0	100.0	100.0		Total	100.0	100.0
							LIABILITIES		
		19.1	15.7	17.1	11.4		Notes Payable-Short Term	18.3	18.9
		4.4	6.6	4.6	3.6		Cur. Mat.-L/T/D	5.4	4.9
		5.2	3.1	2.2	7.1		Trade Payables	2.4	2.5
		.0	.1	.1	.2		Income Taxes Payable	.1	.1
		3.1	3.0	1.4	2.0		All Other Current	3.4	3.8
		31.9	28.5	25.4	24.4		Total Current	29.6	30.1
		48.1	37.3	36.2	31.4		Long-Term Debt	31.9	33.4
		.0	.1	.1	.3		Deferred Taxes	.2	.1
		5.1	3.2	1.3	.4		All Other Non-Current	3.3	2.8
		14.8	30.8	37.1	43.5		Net Worth	34.9	33.5
		100.0	100.0	100.0	100.0		Total Liabilities & Net Worth	100.0	100.0
							INCOME DATA		
		100.0	100.0	100.0	100.0		Net Sales	100.0	100.0
							Gross Profit		
		92.6	84.4	82.0	85.0		Operating Expenses	88.6	84.2
		7.4	15.6	18.0	15.0		Operating Profit	11.4	15.8
		2.0	5.0	4.8	.9		All Other Expenses (net)	6.5	5.6
		5.4	10.7	13.2	14.0		Profit Before Taxes	4.9	10.1
							RATIOS		
		1.4	1.3	1.3	1.8			1.2	1.4
		1.0	.9	1.0	1.5		Current	.9	1.0
		.3	.6	.7	1.0			.7	.7
		.6	.6	.6	1.0			.4	.6
		.4	(244) .4	.4	.6		Quick	(419) .3	.3
		.2	.2	.2	.4			.2	.2
	0 UND	16 22.9	22 16.2	25 14.7				19 19.4	18 20.5
	14 26.6	28 12.9	32 11.3	54 6.8			Sales/Receivables	33 11.1	30 12.1
	26 13.9	47 7.7	79 4.6	84 4.4				59 6.2	58 6.3
							Cost of Sales/Inventory		
							Cost of Sales/Payables		
		13.5	14.2	10.7	3.6			13.6	9.9
		NM	-46.9	-138.4	11.6		Sales/Working Capital	-17.5	-105.2
		-10.4	-8.2	-7.8	-943.7			-6.6	-10.3
		9.7	6.7	7.6	9.1			3.3	5.3
	(33) 4.1	(236) 3.9	4.9	(10) 4.8			EBIT/Interest	(398) 1.7	(412) 3.2
		.5	2.2	3.0	4.0			.8	1.7
			3.5					3.7	5.8
		(10) 1.4					Net Profit + Depr., Dep., Amort./Cur. Mat. L/T/D	(29) 1.9	(25) 1.7
		1.0						.9	1.1
		1.3	1.3	1.4	.9			1.0	1.1
		2.7	2.2	1.8	1.5		Fixed/Worth	1.8	1.8
		-4.0	3.9	2.9	2.1			3.1	3.3
		1.3	1.1	1.0	1.1			1.0	1.1
		3.7	2.1	1.9	1.3		Debt/Worth	1.9	1.9
		-5.9	4.7	3.1	2.2			3.6	3.9
		60.5	44.4	34.9	29.8			16.3	32.9
	(26) 36.4	(220) 27.1	(133) 24.3	21.0			% Profit Before Taxes/Tangible Net Worth	(392) 7.7	(393) 21.1
		15.7	13.8	15.1	13.8			-2.3	10.3
		18.3	13.6	12.1	10.5			7.2	11.9
		8.0	8.4	8.4	8.9		% Profit Before Taxes/Total Assets	2.4	7.5
		-1.4	4.2	4.3	5.0			-1.1	3.1
		6.9	1.8	1.3	2.3			1.6	1.8
		2.2	1.3	.9	1.1		Sales/Net Fixed Assets	1.1	1.3
		1.3	.9	.8	.7			.8	.9
		2.0	1.1	.8	1.0			.9	1.0
		1.4	.8	.6	.7		Sales/Total Assets	.7	.7
		.9	.6	.5	.4			.5	.6
		2.3	7.0	8.0	6.7			7.6	6.7
	(37) 6.0	(233) 9.4	(130) 9.8	(10) 11.0			% Depr., Dep., Amort./Sales	(401) 9.9	(407) 9.3
		9.4	12.4	12.6	12.9			12.4	11.6
		.8	.8	.5				1.0	.9
	(13) 2.9	(77) 1.4	(41) .7				% Officers', Directors', Owners' Comp/Sales	(128) 1.6	(138) 1.6
		9.0	2.7	1.0				3.9	3.0
Net Sales ($)	7930M	112557M	1253564M	1637381M	1008013M	70236M		2208436M	3300139M
Total Assets ($)	1734M	51963M	1374293M	2490091M	688329M	167431M		3663263M	4452046M

M = $ thousand   MM = $ million
See Pages 11 through 21 for Explanation of Ratios and Data

Comparative Historical Data   ## Current Data Sorted By Sales

			Type of Statement						
4	9	6	Unqualified					1	5
256	300	274	Reviewed	4	37	69	95	61	8
64	85	86	Compiled	6	21	30	16	12	1
19	22	30	Tax Returns	6	13	6	3	2	
36	31	42	Other	1	9	6	11	13	2
4/1/02-3/31/03	4/1/03-3/31/04	4/1/04-3/31/05			32 (4/1-9/30/04)			406 (10/1/04-3/31/05)	
ALL	ALL	ALL		0-1MM	1-3MM	3-5MM	5-10MM	10-25MM	25MM & OVER
379	447	438	**NUMBER OF STATEMENTS**	17	80	111	125	89	16
%	%	%	**ASSETS**	%	%	%	%	%	%
1.4	1.5	1.8	Cash & Equivalents	3.2	2.7	1.2	1.1	1.8	6.7
7.5	8.3	9.2	Trade Receivables (net)	1.0	6.6	8.3	10.2	11.5	16.2
13.2	11.6	12.2	Inventory	9.9	10.4	12.9	10.7	14.8	15.5
3.6	2.3	2.4	All Other Current	5.6	2.5	1.4	2.1	3.4	1.1
25.7	23.8	25.6	Total Current	19.7	22.2	23.8	24.0	31.5	39.6
62.6	65.8	64.0	Fixed Assets (net)	74.5	63.2	64.4	66.1	60.8	55.2
.6	.9	1.3	Intangibles (net)	.3	2.2	1.3	1.3	.8	.2
11.2	9.5	9.2	All Other Non-Current	5.6	12.4	10.5	8.5	6.9	5.0
100.0	100.0	100.0	Total	100.0	100.0	100.0	100.0	100.0	100.0
			LIABILITIES						
19.3	17.8	16.4	Notes Payable-Short Term	7.1	15.6	15.4	16.5	20.9	11.9
5.9	6.3	5.6	Cur. Mat.-L/T/D	5.6	4.3	6.6	6.9	4.2	3.3
3.1	4.5	3.1	Trade Payables	2.4	2.6	3.2	2.6	3.4	8.5
.0	.1	.1	Income Taxes Payable	.0	.3	.0	.0	.1	.2
3.3	2.4	2.6	All Other Current	3.9	3.1	1.5	2.0	2.4	11.3
31.6	31.0	27.8	Total Current	19.0	25.9	26.7	28.1	31.0	35.2
36.1	40.0	39.0	Long-Term Debt	87.2	40.6	39.1	36.8	33.6	26.7
.2	.1	.1	Deferred Taxes	.0	.3	.1	.0	.0	.3
2.3	2.3	3.1	All Other Non-Current	13.7	4.0	2.9	2.3	2.2	1.3
29.8	26.5	29.9	Net Worth	−19.9	29.2	31.2	32.8	33.2	36.6
100.0	100.0	100.0	Total Liabilities & Net Worth	100.0	100.0	100.0	100.0	100.0	100.0
			INCOME DATA						
100.0	100.0	100.0	Net Sales	100.0	100.0	100.0	100.0	100.0	100.0
			Gross Profit						
95.7	95.3	84.6	Operating Expenses	92.3	87.8	83.8	82.9	83.5	86.2
4.3	4.7	15.4	Operating Profit	7.7	12.2	16.2	17.1	16.5	13.8
6.1	5.8	4.5	All Other Expenses (net)	9.6	4.0	4.7	4.6	3.7	3.4
−1.7	−1.1	10.9	Profit Before Taxes	−1.9	8.2	11.5	12.5	12.8	10.3
			RATIOS						
1.1	1.1	1.3		2.1	1.5	1.3	1.2	1.3	1.5
.8	.8	.9	Current	.8	1.0	.9	1.0	1.0	1.1
.6	.5	.7		.3	.5	.6	.7	.7	.8
.4	.5	.6		.8	.6	.6	.7	.6	1.0
.2 (446)	.3 (437)	.4	Quick	(16) .2	.3	.3	.4	.4	.6
.1	.1	.2		.2	.2	.3			
16 23.0	17 21.4	16 23.0		0 UND	2 174.6	17 21.7	21 17.4	16 22.2	20 18.0
28 12.8	29 12.4	30 12.2	Sales/Receivables	0 UND	20 18.5	30 12.1	32 11.4	31 11.9	28 13.2
56 6.5	49 7.5	53 6.8		1 287.8	33 11.1	51 7.1	63 5.8	73 5.0	48 7.6
			Cost of Sales/Inventory						
			Cost of Sales/Payables						
20.0	29.1	12.1		4.7	11.7	11.1	17.9	11.6	7.2
−11.9	−15.1	−74.6	Sales/Working Capital	−35.3	NM	−34.9	−63.9	−177.1	61.8
−5.3	−5.5	−8.8		−2.7	−7.1	−8.1	−10.6	−8.6	−21.3
2.1	2.4	7.4		3.8	8.5	5.8	7.7	7.5	14.0
(368) .7	(429) .8	(422) 4.3	EBIT/Interest	(10) .6	(78) 3.8	(123) 3.6	(86) 4.5	(14) 5.1	5.2
−.7	−.7	2.2		−1.8	1.2	2.2	2.7	3.2	4.0
2.5	2.3	7.0	Net Profit + Depr., Dep.,						
(16) 1.4	(20) 1.4	(14) 1.9	Amort./Cur. Mat. L/T/D						
.0	.0	1.0							
1.2	1.4	1.3		1.9	1.2	1.2	1.4	1.4	.8
2.3	2.6	2.1	Fixed/Worth	18.4	1.7	2.1	2.5	1.7	1.5
3.9	5.0	3.7		−2.4	4.7	3.8	3.4	2.9	2.9
1.3	1.3	1.1		1.2	1.1	1.3	1.4	1.3	1.2
2.5	2.7	2.0	Debt/Worth	22.3	1.9	2.0	2.4	1.9	2.4
4.6	6.2	4.2		−4.4	5.0	4.4	4.0	3.7	3.3
7.4	10.1	41.4	% Profit Before Taxes/Tangible		38.2	40.5	44.4	51.0	36.6
(350) −1.2	(398) −1.2	(394) 26.0	Net Worth	(68) 20.4	(103) 27.0	(114) 28.3	(84) 28.2	22.9	
−16.7	−16.1	14.6		7.4	14.5	19.1	16.3	7.6	
2.5	3.1	13.7	% Profit Before Taxes/Total	5.1	13.9	12.7	14.5	14.4	11.2
−.6	−.7	8.4	Assets	−.1	6.4	8.1	9.5	9.6	8.6
−5.0	−5.0	4.0		−7.5	.8	4.4	5.5	5.8	2.2
1.5	1.5	1.8		2.2	2.2	1.7	1.7	1.8	11.1
1.0	1.0	1.2	Sales/Net Fixed Assets	1.0	1.4	1.2	1.2	1.2	1.5
.7	.7	.9		.2	.9	.9	.9	.8	.9
.8	.9	1.0		1.1	1.2	1.0	1.0	1.0	3.9
.6	.6	.8	Sales/Total Assets	.6	.8	.8	.8	.8	.9
.5	.5	.6		.2	.5	.6	.6	.6	.7
8.3	8.2	6.8		4.0	6.5	6.8	6.4	8.1	1.6
(364) 11.7	(427) 11.2	(418) 9.3	% Depr., Dep., Amort./Sales	(16) 10.1	(77) 9.5	(106) 8.9	(120) 8.8	(85) 10.1	(14) 8.2
14.8	14.5	12.1		20.3	13.2	11.6	11.6	13.2	11.3
1.0	1.0	.7	% Officers', Directors',		1.5	1.2	.5	.5	
(109) 2.2	(120) 1.9	(138) 1.2	Owners' Comp/Sales	(19) 2.6	(37) 1.9	(42) .7	(27) .8		
6.9	4.0	3.0		5.8	3.3	1.4	1.0		
2502644M	3035797M	4089681M	Net Sales ($)	9429M	170005M	451186M	890462M	1315232M	1253367M
3461909M	4388319M	4773841M	Total Assets ($)	30502M	231006M	685957M	1224552M	1782381M	819443M

Current Data Sorted By Assets   Comparative Historical Data

						Type of Statement		
	3	2	10		1	Unqualified	12	10
2	2	6	2			Reviewed	8	8
	2	7	1		1	Compiled	12	11
4	3	1				Tax Returns	8	8
2	4	7	2			Other	21	30
	7 (4/1-9/30/04)		55 (10/1/04-3/31/05)				4/1/00- 3/31/01	4/1/01- 3/31/02
0-500M	500M-2MM	2-10MM	10-50MM	50-100MM	100-250MM		ALL	ALL
8	14	23	15		2	NUMBER OF STATEMENTS	61	67
%	%	%	%	%	%	ASSETS	%	%
	2.5	1.7	1.9	D		Cash & Equivalents	4.8	3.0
	2.4	4.7	13.9	A		Trade Receivables (net)	5.4	4.9
	29.0	29.5	34.0	T		Inventory	31.9	28.4
	2.3	4.2	6.0	A		All Other Current	2.6	4.2
	36.1	40.0	55.7			Total Current	44.7	40.6
	59.9	51.0	28.9	N		Fixed Assets (net)	45.6	48.0
	.0	.8	.3	O		Intangibles (net)	4.1	3.7
	3.9	8.1	15.1	T		All Other Non-Current	5.6	7.7
	100.0	100.0	100.0			Total	100.0	100.0
				A		LIABILITIES		
	29.9	12.4	18.6	V		Notes Payable-Short Term	20.7	19.6
	3.2	4.1	4.5	A		Cur. Mat.-L/T/D	5.0	5.8
	2.1	5.1	3.9	I		Trade Payables	6.2	4.0
	.1	.0	.8	L		Income Taxes Payable	.0	.3
	6.1	2.9	6.6	A		All Other Current	7.7	6.7
	41.3	24.4	34.3	B		Total Current	39.5	36.4
	15.7	28.4	18.0	L		Long-Term Debt	32.7	36.3
	.0	.2	.8	E		Deferred Taxes	.2	.1
	6.7	1.7	8.0			All Other Non-Current	6.3	6.5
	36.3	45.2	38.9			Net Worth	21.3	20.7
	100.0	100.0	100.0			Total Liabilities & Net Worth	100.0	100.0
						INCOME DATA		
	100.0	100.0	100.0			Net Sales	100.0	100.0
						Gross Profit		
	84.0	89.0	88.4			Operating Expenses	86.2	88.2
	16.0	11.0	11.6			Operating Profit	13.8	11.8
	4.6	2.5	1.9			All Other Expenses (net)	5.0	4.8
	11.4	8.5	9.7			Profit Before Taxes	8.8	7.1
						RATIOS		
	1.5	2.6	3.7				2.1	2.1
	.9	1.6	1.3			Current	1.2	1.3
	.5	1.0	1.1				.8	.7
	.3	.3	1.9				.7	.3
	.0	.2	.1			Quick	.2	.1
	.0	.1	.1				.0	.0
0 UND	0 UND	2 171.6					0 UND	0 999.8
0 UND	6 58.2	11 33.2				Sales/Receivables	6 62.5	6 56.6
0 UND	17 21.3	72 5.1					15 24.2	19 18.7
						Cost of Sales/Inventory		
						Cost of Sales/Payables		
	12.0	3.7	2.8				5.9	4.9
	−24.4	10.1	10.6			Sales/Working Capital	25.8	16.7
	−9.8	210.6	48.8				−16.3	−6.4
	8.4	12.1	55.6				4.1	5.0
	4.7	(22) 4.2	(14) 7.2			EBIT/Interest	(54) 2.9	(63) 2.6
	2.2	2.9	.9				1.6	1.5
						Net Profit + Depr., Dep., Amort./Cur. Mat. L /T/D		
	1.0	.6	.0				1.0	.7
	1.7	1.3	.8			Fixed/Worth	2.8	1.8
	NM	1.9	1.6				−26.6	−10.4
	.5	.8	.4				1.3	1.0
	2.1	1.2	1.4			Debt/Worth	6.1	2.5
	NM	2.9	4.6				−30.1	−17.3
	36.7	40.2	52.2				66.4	43.9
(11)	15.3	(22) 15.3	(14) 30.9			% Profit Before Taxes/Tangible Net Worth	(43) 27.6	(50) 20.3
	5.3	8.1	.5				14.2	8.5
	16.7	13.7	35.0				13.2	15.2
	9.8	5.9	15.1			% Profit Before Taxes/Total Assets	7.7	6.5
	4.0	3.6	.0				1.6	2.4
	4.8	4.6	792.9				7.7	5.1
	1.8	2.2	6.1			Sales/Net Fixed Assets	3.0	2.3
	1.1	.8	2.3				1.3	1.2
	1.6	1.7	2.2				1.8	1.5
	1.1	.9	1.7			Sales/Total Assets	1.2	1.1
	1.0	.7	.7				.7	.7
	3.1	2.2	.1				2.0	1.4
	7.6	(21) 6.4	(13) 1.4			% Depr., Dep., Amort./Sales	(52) 5.0	(56) 3.9
	19.2	10.3	6.2				7.1	7.1
						% Officers', Directors', Owners' Comp/Sales	.8	1.0
							(15) 2.7	(17) 3.3
							5.0	8.9
8747M	22744M	128985M	606364M		297486M	Net Sales ($)	1366144M	1529708M
1947M	17993M	110492M	407180M		242063M	Total Assets ($)	1042419M	1575541M

M = $ thousand   MM = $ million
See Pages 11 through 21 for Explanation of Ratios and Data

Comparative Historical Data | | **Current Data Sorted By Sales**

				Type of Statement	0-1MM	1-3MM	3-5MM	5-10MM	10-25MM	25MM & OVER
	15	14	16	Unqualified	1	2	2	1	3	7
	4	6	12	Reviewed	1	3	2	2	2	2
	16	10	11	Compiled	2	3	2	3		1
	9	11	8	Tax Returns	4	4				
	23	19	15	Other	4	5		3	1	2
	4/1/02-3/31/03 ALL	4/1/03-3/31/04 ALL	4/1/04-3/31/05 ALL		7 (4/1-9/30/04)			55 (10/1/04-3/31/05)		
	67	60	62	**NUMBER OF STATEMENTS**	12	17	6	9	6	12
	%	%	%	**ASSETS**	%	%	%	%	%	%
	3.4	4.0	6.1	Cash & Equivalents	17.9	5.0				2.7
	4.4	5.7	5.9	Trade Receivables (net)	.3	3.1				16.2
	30.3	25.4	27.5	Inventory	9.8	21.7				39.8
	2.8	5.5	6.1	All Other Current	5.0	5.2				7.1
	41.0	40.5	45.6	Total Current	33.1	35.0				65.8
	51.2	49.8	44.0	Fixed Assets (net)	59.2	57.7				19.0
	.8	.8	.4	Intangibles (net)	.1	.3				.3
	7.0	8.8	10.0	All Other Non-Current	7.6	7.0				15.0
	100.0	100.0	100.0	Total	100.0	100.0				100.0
				LIABILITIES						
	25.6	19.6	20.6	Notes Payable-Short Term	16.4	30.4				16.7
	6.6	4.5	4.7	Cur. Mat.-L/T/D	6.4	5.0				3.9
	5.4	4.8	4.3	Trade Payables	1.1	4.3				4.5
	.0	.2	.2	Income Taxes Payable	.0	.1				.5
	5.5	7.8	5.0	All Other Current	5.0	5.3				7.4
	43.0	36.8	34.7	Total Current	29.0	45.1				33.0
	35.6	33.9	24.0	Long-Term Debt	29.0	28.9				12.7
	.3	.1	.3	Deferred Taxes	.0	.3				.5
	6.3	10.6	8.8	All Other Non-Current	13.0	11.3				3.6
	14.8	18.6	32.3	Net Worth	29.0	14.5				50.2
	100.0	100.0	100.0	Total Liabilities & Net Worth	100.0	100.0				100.0
				INCOME DATA						
	100.0	100.0	100.0	Net Sales	100.0	100.0				100.0
				Gross Profit						
	97.5	96.5	86.9	Operating Expenses	77.4	89.6				84.7
	2.5	3.5	13.1	Operating Profit	22.6	10.4				15.3
	5.4	3.3	2.5	All Other Expenses (net)	9.5	.6				.4
	-2.9	.2	10.6	Profit Before Taxes	13.1	9.8				14.9
				RATIOS						
	1.9	2.1	2.6		4.7	1.5				4.8
	1.2	1.3	1.3	Current	.9	.9				1.9
	.7	.8	.8		.2	.4				1.1
	.3	.5	.5		2.8	.3				1.9
	(66) .1	(59) .1	.2	Quick	.2	.1				.7
	.0	.0	.1		.0	.0				.1
	0 UND	0 UND	0 UND		0 UND	0 UND				3 140.4
	4 95.5	7 53.8	2 146.9	Sales/Receivables	0 UND	0 999.8				12 29.9
	11 33.5	26 14.3	15 25.1		0 UND	12 31.5				66 5.6
				Cost of Sales/Inventory						
				Cost of Sales/Payables						
	6.6	4.6	4.0		5.1	8.1				2.6
	22.3	14.3	12.5	Sales/Working Capital	-26.1	-20.7				7.8
	-8.5	-22.3	-18.1		-7.3	-9.6				40.5
	2.6	2.9	12.8							68.1
	(63) 1.1	(55) 1.3	(58) 5.3	EBIT/Interest	10.7					10.7
	-1.5	-.8	2.8		6.0					6.9
					2.4					
				Net Profit + Depr., Dep., Amort./Cur. Mat. L/T/D						
	.9	.8	.3		.7	.8				.0
	1.9	1.7	1.1	Fixed/Worth	1.7	1.7				.2
	-45.1	9.0	2.1		NM	10.1				.8
	.9	1.0	.7		.4	.4				.4
	2.5	2.1	1.3	Debt/Worth	1.9	.9				.9
	-92.5	NM	5.0		NM	19.7				1.4
	15.1	16.6	49.7			41.8				69.0
	(49) .6	(45) 3.2	(55) 21.1	% Profit Before Taxes/Tangible Net Worth		(14) 12.2			(11)	48.8
	-17.3	-7.9	7.7			2.9				27.7
	6.2	5.6	21.6		28.8	16.8				36.5
	.0	1.5	9.9	% Profit Before Taxes/Total Assets	9.5	8.8				18.3
	-8.6	-4.1	4.3		2.2	4.9				14.3
	4.3	4.7	15.7		6.0	4.4				753.5
	2.0	2.3	3.3	Sales/Net Fixed Assets	2.3	1.6				16.2
	1.0	.9	1.2		.5	1.1				3.5
	1.5	1.7	2.2		2.0	1.7				2.3
	1.0	1.0	1.1	Sales/Total Assets	1.1	1.0				2.1
	.7	.6	.7		.4	.7				1.3
	2.5	1.9	1.4		2.0	2.3				.0
	(57) 6.4	(52) 6.6	(55) 4.5	% Depr., Dep., Amort./Sales	(11) 8.5	(16) 7.3			(10)	.9
	10.9	18.0	11.2		18.7	17.9				3.6
	1.1	1.2	1.2							
	(19) 2.5	(12) 2.5	(10) 2.8	% Officers', Directors', Owners' Comp/Sales						
	8.1	11.3	5.1							
	1530656M	1377349M	1064326M	Net Sales ($)	7795M	32633M	22832M	70347M	83303M	847416M
	1463311M	1145587M	779675M	Total Assets ($)	13965M	32749M	65475M	60492M	96487M	510507M

M = $ thousand   MM = $ million
See Pages 11 through 21 for Explanation of Ratios and Data

AGRICULTURE—Chicken Egg Production NAICS 112310 (SIC 0252)

Current Data Sorted By Assets | **Comparative Historical Data**

0-500M	500M-2MM	2-10MM	10-50MM	50-100MM	100-250MM	Type of Statement	4/1/00-3/31/01 ALL	4/1/01-3/31/02 ALL
		2	6	4	1	Unqualified	10	9
		3	3		1	Reviewed	2	4
	1	2	2		1	Compiled	6	9
	3	2				Tax Returns		4
1	2	5	4	5	1	Other	9	10
		17 (4/1-9/30/04)		30 (10/1/04-3/31/05)				
1	6	12	15	9	4	NUMBER OF STATEMENTS	27	36
%	%	%	%	%	%	**ASSETS**	%	%
		8.0	13.3			Cash & Equivalents	2.6	6.1
		27.0	11.8			Trade Receivables (net)	9.9	13.3
		13.4	15.1			Inventory	22.5	18.4
		9.7	6.0			All Other Current	4.7	6.6
		58.1	46.2			Total Current	39.7	44.5
		30.5	48.9			Fixed Assets (net)	46.3	46.9
		4.5	.1			Intangibles (net)	.9	1.8
		6.9	4.9			All Other Non-Current	13.1	6.8
		100.0	100.0			Total	100.0	100.0
						LIABILITIES		
		19.5	3.2			Notes Payable-Short Term	14.3	14.0
		1.7	2.5			Cur. Mat.-L/T/D	5.0	3.5
		17.2	8.3			Trade Payables	6.3	10.4
		.5	.8			Income Taxes Payable	.7	.1
		8.6	6.1			All Other Current	9.8	5.8
		47.5	20.9			Total Current	36.1	33.8
		18.5	22.1			Long-Term Debt	19.7	24.5
		.0	.8			Deferred Taxes	2.3	1.3
		3.3	2.8			All Other Non-Current	1.7	4.2
		30.8	53.4			Net Worth	40.2	36.2
		100.0	100.0			Total Liabilities & Net Worth	100.0	100.0
						INCOME DATA		
		100.0	100.0			Net Sales	100.0	100.0
						Gross Profit		
		93.4	91.0			Operating Expenses	98.2	90.4
		6.6	9.0			Operating Profit	1.8	9.6
		–.4	.1			All Other Expenses (net)	.6	3.2
		7.0	8.9			Profit Before Taxes	1.2	6.4
						RATIOS		
		2.1	2.7			Current	1.9	3.7
		1.3	2.1				1.1	1.5
		.9	1.3				.7	.9
		1.3	2.1			Quick	.7	1.5
		.8	1.4				.3	.5
		.5	.5				.2	.2
		17 21.5	16 22.8			Sales/Receivables	12 30.8	16 22.9
		24 15.0	19 19.0				21 17.7	21 17.5
		36 10.2	24 15.1				34 10.7	28 13.2
						Cost of Sales/Inventory		
						Cost of Sales/Payables		
		6.6	6.0			Sales/Working Capital	7.8	5.6
		91.1	10.5				23.2	15.3
		–92.8	16.6				–10.3	–33.1
		54.0	26.7			EBIT/Interest	6.9	4.9
		4.4	(13) 11.8				(23) 1.5	(32) 1.6
		1.3	2.7				–.2	–.3
						Net Profit + Depr., Dep., Amort./Cur. Mat. L /T/D		
		.6	.5			Fixed/Worth	.5	.6
		1.0	1.1				1.1	1.1
		3.1	1.9				2.5	3.9
		1.6	.3			Debt/Worth	.5	.6
		3.4	1.0				1.7	.9
		9.1	2.1				3.2	23.8
		35.8	59.2			% Profit Before Taxes/Tangible Net Worth	14.3	20.5
		(11) 12.3	20.2				(23) .7	(30) 5.1
		4.3	8.1				–14.3	–13.5
		28.8	32.0			% Profit Before Taxes/Total Assets	8.0	10.5
		4.6	11.4				.4	2.5
		.5	6.4				–6.9	–3.0
		133.6	6.1			Sales/Net Fixed Assets	6.2	6.7
		9.7	3.3				3.2	3.6
		4.7	2.5				1.9	1.5
		4.2	2.8			Sales/Total Assets	1.8	2.0
		2.3	1.7				1.4	1.6
		1.9	1.0				1.0	.9
		.8	1.8			% Depr., Dep., Amort./Sales	1.5	1.3
		(10) 1.4	3.1				(20) 5.7	(29) 4.7
		6.2	5.5				11.3	9.8
						% Officers', Directors', Owners' Comp/Sales		
4713M	16830M	181273M	705385M	938816M	904340M	Net Sales ($)	1869821M	1124693M
456M	7266M	55519M	356641M	624985M	594452M	Total Assets ($)	1216302M	878710M

© RMA 2005

M = $ thousand   MM = $ million
See Pages 11 through 21 for Explanation of Ratios and Data

Comparative Historical Data · **Current Data Sorted By Sales**

	4/1/02-3/31/03 ALL	4/1/03-3/31/04 ALL	4/1/04-3/31/05 ALL		0-1MM	1-3MM	3-5MM	5-10MM	10-25MM	25MM & OVER
				Type of Statement						
Unqualified	18	19	13					1	1	11
Reviewed	3	3	7						2	5
Compiled	5	6	6				1	1	3	1
Tax Returns	5	7	4			2		1		
Other	13	12	17		2		2	2	3	9
					17 (4/1-9/30/04)			30 (10/1/04-3/31/05)		
NUMBER OF STATEMENTS	44	47	47		2	2	3	5	9	26
	%	%	%		%	%	%	%	%	%
				ASSETS						
Cash & Equivalents	4.3	6.9	10.5							13.5
Trade Receivables (net)	14.1	13.1	17.6							15.5
Inventory	17.5	16.2	14.7							15.5
All Other Current	5.9	3.8	4.9							2.5
Total Current	41.8	40.1	47.8							47.0
Fixed Assets (net)	44.6	51.0	43.2							43.8
Intangibles (net)	4.1	3.0	3.8							4.6
All Other Non-Current	9.6	6.0	5.2							4.6
Total	100.0	100.0	100.0							100.0
				LIABILITIES						
Notes Payable-Short Term	12.5	14.1	12.6							6.7
Cur. Mat.-L/T/D	4.5	4.4	2.3							3.0
Trade Payables	9.3	8.4	10.4							10.6
Income Taxes Payable	.6	.9	.6							.8
All Other Current	7.5	5.7	7.6							9.3
Total Current	34.6	33.5	33.6							30.4
Long-Term Debt	23.3	27.5	23.1							18.0
Deferred Taxes	1.6	1.3	.6							1.1
All Other Non-Current	3.0	6.4	2.3							1.9
Net Worth	37.6	31.3	40.4							48.5
Total Liabilities & Net Worth	100.0	100.0	100.0							100.0
				INCOME DATA						
Net Sales	100.0	100.0	100.0							100.0
Gross Profit										
Operating Expenses	97.3	92.9	90.1							89.3
Operating Profit	2.7	7.1	9.9							10.7
All Other Expenses (net)	1.6	2.5	1.4							.5
Profit Before Taxes	1.1	4.6	8.5							10.2
				RATIOS						
Current	2.1	2.4	2.2							2.4
	1.3	1.5	1.6							2.0
	.7	.8	1.0							1.1
Quick	1.1	1.2	1.5							1.7
	.5	.5	.8							1.0
	.3	.3	.5							.5
Sales/Receivables	20 18.1	16 22.3	17 21.2							17 21.1
	25 14.8	24 15.3	22 16.3							21 17.0
	33 10.9	31 11.7	34 10.6							25 14.7
Cost of Sales/Inventory										
Cost of Sales/Payables										
Sales/Working Capital	7.9	7.0	7.3							7.1
	23.5	14.9	15.0							13.1
	-20.7	-28.7	999.8							77.4
EBIT/Interest	3.8	7.0	31.2							30.6
	(41) 1.3	(44) 3.2	(42) 8.3						(24)	9.2
	-1.7	1.0	2.1							2.9
Net Profit + Depr., Dep., Amort./Cur. Mat. L/T/D	6.5	9.9	7.9							
	(12) 2.7	(12) 3.8	(10) 5.7							
	-.7	1.5	2.6							
Fixed/Worth	.6	.7	.6							.6
	1.2	1.4	1.2							.9
	2.7	6.3	1.9							1.8
Debt/Worth	.8	.9	.6							.5
	1.7	1.6	1.7							1.0
	4.4	8.0	3.7							2.9
% Profit Before Taxes/Tangible Net Worth	17.6	34.8	57.6							68.2
	(38) -3.7	(38) 16.0	(44) 31.6							38.7
	-20.4	1.6	8.0							12.2
% Profit Before Taxes/Total Assets	10.7	9.2	30.3							33.8
	1.5	5.5	9.8							12.0
	-6.0	.3	1.9							7.0
Sales/Net Fixed Assets	8.4	6.6	10.9							6.8
	4.0	3.1	4.2							4.0
	1.9	1.9	2.6							2.7
Sales/Total Assets	2.7	2.6	2.8							2.8
	1.7	1.7	1.9							1.8
	1.1	.9	1.0							1.2
% Depr., Dep., Amort./Sales	1.9	2.3	1.6							1.6
	(39) 3.7	(38) 4.3	(38) 3.5							(22) 3.1
	10.1	9.3	5.5							4.8
% Officers', Directors', Owners' Comp/Sales	1.1									
	(10) 4.4									
	10.0									
Net Sales ($)	1780762M	2203739M	2751357M		508M	5628M	13119M	41170M	127468M	2563464M
Total Assets ($)	1127485M	1387792M	1639319M		1544M	4664M	3560M	38553M	62107M	1528891M

© RMA 2005

M = $ thousand   MM = $ million
See Pages 11 through 21 for Explanation of Ratios and Data

Current Data Sorted By Assets							Comparative Historical Data	
			1			Type of Statement		
1	1	1	1			Unqualified		
	1	4	1			Reviewed		
9	3					Compiled		
2	3	4	2	1		Tax Returns		
	7 (4/1-9/30/04)		28 (10/1/04-3/31/05)			Other	4/1/00-3/31/01	4/1/01-3/31/02
0-500M	500M-2MM	2-10MM	10-50MM	50-100MM	100-250MM		ALL	ALL
12	8	9	5	1		NUMBER OF STATEMENTS		
%	%	%	%	%	%	ASSETS	%	%
27.0					D	Cash & Equivalents	D	D
1.8					A	Trade Receivables (net)	A	A
17.8					T	Inventory	T	T
9.2					A	All Other Current	A	A
55.9						Total Current		
41.8					N	Fixed Assets (net)	N	N
.0					O	Intangibles (net)	O	O
2.3					T	All Other Non-Current	T	T
100.0						Total		
					A	LIABILITIES	A	A
61.3					V	Notes Payable-Short Term	V	V
2.5					A	Cur. Mat.-L/T/D	A	A
6.2					I	Trade Payables	I	I
.0					L	Income Taxes Payable	L	L
31.7					A	All Other Current	A	A
101.6					B	Total Current	B	B
16.6					L	Long-Term Debt	L	L
.0					E	Deferred Taxes	E	E
.5						All Other Non-Current		
–18.7						Net Worth		
100.0						Total Liabilities & Net Worth		
						INCOME DATA		
100.0						Net Sales		
						Gross Profit		
93.1						Operating Expenses		
6.9						Operating Profit		
1.6						All Other Expenses (net)		
5.3						Profit Before Taxes		
						RATIOS		
1.5								
.7						Current		
.5								
1.4								
.2						Quick		
.1								
0 UND								
0 UND						Sales/Receivables		
1 610.9								
						Cost of Sales/Inventory		
						Cost of Sales/Payables		
NM								
–19.9						Sales/Working Capital		
–7.1								
						EBIT/Interest		
						Net Profit + Depr., Dep., Amort./Cur. Mat. L /T/D		
1.2								
–3.5						Fixed/Worth		
–1.3								
1.1								
–45.9						Debt/Worth		
–3.9								
						% Profit Before Taxes/Tangible Net Worth		
43.3								
–2.1						% Profit Before Taxes/Total Assets		
–46.2								
89.5								
12.2						Sales/Net Fixed Assets		
5.3								
10.1								
4.0						Sales/Total Assets		
1.9								
						% Depr., Dep., Amort./Sales		
						% Officers', Directors', Owners' Comp/Sales		
13162M	5802M	27312M	77229M	13382M		Net Sales ($)		
3111M	6868M	40826M	148369M	53461M		Total Assets ($)		

© RMA 2005

M = $ thousand   MM = $ million
See Pages 11 through 21 for Explanation of Ratios and Data

Comparative Historical Data   Current Data Sorted By Sales

			Type of Statement						
		1	Unqualified				1		
2	2	4	Reviewed	2	1		1	1	
3	2	6	Compiled	1	1	2	2		
7	12	12	Tax Returns	9	3				
6	6	12	Other	4	4	1	1	1	1
4/1/02-	4/1/03-	4/1/04-			7 (4/1-9/30/04)		28 (10/1/04-3/31/05)		
3/31/03	3/31/04	3/31/05							
ALL	ALL	ALL		0-1MM	1-3MM	3-5MM	5-10MM	10-25MM	25MM & OVER
18	22	35	**NUMBER OF STATEMENTS**	16	8	4	3	3	1
%	%	%	**ASSETS**	%	%	%	%	%	%
14.9	17.9	18.8	Cash & Equivalents	17.5					
6.4	4.1	4.2	Trade Receivables (net)	6.0					
23.6	16.7	15.1	Inventory	20.5					
2.9	4.0	5.7	All Other Current	6.3					
47.8	42.7	43.8	Total Current	50.2					
44.5	52.8	52.1	Fixed Assets (net)	49.0					
.0	.0	.1	Intangibles (net)	.0					
7.7	4.4	4.1	All Other Non-Current	.7					
100.0	100.0	100.0	Total	100.0					
			LIABILITIES						
10.1	27.3	34.8	Notes Payable-Short Term	53.2					
6.3	7.8	1.6	Cur. Mat.-L/T/D	2.5					
10.4	7.2	6.2	Trade Payables	5.2					
.0	.0	.0	Income Taxes Payable	.0					
23.9	44.1	19.1	All Other Current	28.5					
50.7	86.5	61.7	Total Current	89.4					
28.0	20.1	20.4	Long-Term Debt	25.6					
.0	.0	.0	Deferred Taxes	.0					
2.1	14.6	5.2	All Other Non-Current	6.0					
19.1	−21.5	12.7	Net Worth	−21.0					
100.0	100.0	100.0	Total Liabilities & Net Worth	100.0					
			INCOME DATA						
100.0	100.0	100.0	Net Sales	100.0					
			Gross Profit						
101.0	95.6	99.3	Operating Expenses	95.4					
−1.0	4.4	.7	Operating Profit	4.6					
3.9	1.6	2.8	All Other Expenses (net)	8.0					
−4.9	2.8	−2.0	Profit Before Taxes	−3.4					
			RATIOS						
1.4	1.4	1.6		1.4					
.9	1.0	.8	Current	.8					
.3	.4	.3		.3					
1.0	1.2	1.6		1.3					
.2	.5	.3	Quick	.2					
.0	.1	.1		.0					
0 UND	0 UND	0 UND		0 UND					
10 36.5	0 UND	1 712.7	Sales/Receivables	0 UND					
18 19.9	23 15.7	29 12.5		45 8.2					
			Cost of Sales/Inventory						
			Cost of Sales/Payables						
13.6	26.8	8.8		20.1					
−18.2	UND	−18.0	Sales/Working Capital	−14.7					
−4.8	−4.9	−2.7		−2.5					
2.0	4.6	4.3		1.2					
(15) .6	(17) .1	(29) .5	EBIT/Interest	(12) −1.1					
−2.9	−3.4	−5.8		−18.4					
			Net Profit + Depr., Dep., Amort./Cur. Mat. L/T/D						
.7	1.0	1.0		1.2					
2.2	9.0	1.9	Fixed/Worth	NM					
−3.7	−1.0	−2.9		−1.2					
.5	1.9	.6		2.1					
3.9	17.7	4.1	Debt/Worth	−44.5					
−37.1	−3.5	−6.3		−4.9					
59.9	41.0	21.4	% Profit Before Taxes/Tangible						
(12) 2.8	(12) 17.7	(22) 2.6	Net Worth						
−24.2	−11.9	−13.5							
3.1	9.1	4.6		1.1					
−2.8	−1.4	−.6	% Profit Before Taxes/Total Assets	−5.2					
−16.9	−8.3	−14.3		−25.6					
19.1	9.5	22.9		47.7					
4.0	4.6	2.5	Sales/Net Fixed Assets	5.8					
.6	1.6	.7		1.3					
3.0	3.8	2.0		2.2					
1.0	1.8	.9	Sales/Total Assets	1.4					
.5	.7	.5		.5					
1.3	1.8	2.9		3.2					
(13) 4.2	(20) 4.6	(28) 7.9	% Depr., Dep., Amort./Sales	(13) 7.9					
15.2	9.2	22.8		24.4					
			% Officers', Directors', Owners' Comp/Sales						
92271M	29255M	136887M	Net Sales ($)	10025M	14614M	15080M	16368M	45586M	35214M
134652M	51889M	252635M	Total Assets ($)	13055M	10965M	39926M	20944M	127514M	40231M

M = $ thousand   MM = $ million
See Pages 11 through 21 for Explanation of Ratios and Data

Current Data Sorted By Assets | Comparative Historical Data

0-500M	500M-2MM	2-10MM	10-50MM	50-100MM	100-250MM	Type of Statement	4/1/00-3/31/01	4/1/01-3/31/02
	1	5	2	2	2	Unqualified	5	6
	1	8	3	1	2	Reviewed	7	6
1	9	14	3		2	Compiled	14	18
7	16	7	2			Tax Returns	7	6
2	8	8	5		1	Other	23	31
	16 (4/1-9/30/04)		94 (10/1/04-3/31/05)				ALL	ALL
10	35	42	15	3	5	**NUMBER OF STATEMENTS**	56	67

0-500M %	500M-2MM %	2-10MM %	10-50MM %	50-100MM %	100-250MM %	ASSETS	%	%
26.7	12.7	5.9	4.6			Cash & Equivalents	9.3	10.8
1.4	10.2	13.5	1.8			Trade Receivables (net)	9.4	9.0
16.5	30.1	31.0	20.7			Inventory	17.5	22.5
1.9	1.5	4.6	5.7			All Other Current	6.4	7.0
46.5	54.5	54.9	32.8			Total Current	42.6	49.3
48.2	36.1	31.9	43.4			Fixed Assets (net)	40.9	38.4
4.1	.2	.8	.0			Intangibles (net)	.9	1.5
1.2	9.2	12.3	23.8			All Other Non-Current	15.6	10.8
100.0	100.0	100.0	100.0			Total	100.0	100.0
						LIABILITIES		
50.7	15.8	19.9	6.8			Notes Payable-Short Term	18.6	16.4
1.2	9.8	10.1	3.3			Cur. Mat.-L/T/D	5.3	5.3
1.3	4.4	8.6	2.5			Trade Payables	8.2	4.1
.0	.9	.1	.0			Income Taxes Payable	.8	.0
2.4	6.3	6.0	3.4			All Other Current	7.9	8.4
55.6	37.2	44.6	15.9			Total Current	40.8	34.2
37.1	39.6	23.3	43.2			Long-Term Debt	23.9	25.6
.0	.0	.5	.0			Deferred Taxes	.2	1.0
.5	4.9	5.7	1.1			All Other Non-Current	2.2	3.9
6.9	18.4	25.9	39.8			Net Worth	32.8	35.4
100.0	100.0	100.0	100.0			Total Liabilities & Net Worth	100.0	100.0
						INCOME DATA		
100.0	100.0	100.0	100.0			Net Sales	100.0	100.0
						Gross Profit		
79.8	97.2	92.8	70.1			Operating Expenses	87.1	88.6
20.2	2.8	7.2	29.9			Operating Profit	12.9	11.4
1.8	.8	3.2	6.3			All Other Expenses (net)	−.5	5.4
18.5	2.0	4.0	23.7			Profit Before Taxes	13.5	6.0
						RATIOS		
3.5	9.2	2.5	3.9			Current	1.9	3.3
1.1	1.7	1.2	1.2				1.2	1.3
.3	.8	.9	.6				.4	.8
3.5	2.6	1.2	.5			Quick	1.2	1.6
.5	.9	.5	.3				.3	.5
.1	.2	.2	.1				.1	.1
0 UND	0 UND	6 66.2	0 UND			Sales/Receivables	0 UND	0 UND
0 UND	5 76.9	12 31.6	3 107.7				8 46.5	10 36.8
0 UND	17 21.1	37 9.7	14 26.3				19 18.9	31 11.9
						Cost of Sales/Inventory		
						Cost of Sales/Payables		
5.9	7.6	5.3	3.0			Sales/Working Capital	10.8	2.7
83.4	28.8	31.8	36.7				40.1	15.1
−43.4	−26.7	−64.3	−4.1				−8.0	−32.1
	5.5	5.7	35.2			EBIT/Interest	8.1	3.5
(33)	1.5	(40) 2.5	(12) 9.0				(48) 3.0	(53) 1.4
	.6	1.0	1.6				1.3	.7
		2.5				Net Profit + Depr., Dep.,		
	(10)	1.4				Amort./Cur. Mat. L /T/D		
		.2						
.0	.4	.3	.0			Fixed/Worth	.3	.2
3.9	1.2	.8	.5				1.2	1.1
−1.0	4.8	2.2	2.6				3.3	2.7
1.0	1.2	1.1	.3			Debt/Worth	.6	.7
8.5	3.7	2.7	2.3				1.8	1.7
−2.5	13.1	13.3	8.8				5.3	5.7
	85.3	55.0	95.0			% Profit Before Taxes/Tangible	42.4	42.8
(29)	8.0	(38) 15.1	11.3			Net Worth	(49) 21.0	(60) 5.9
	−4.6	1.5	7.5				5.0	−5.3
67.4	14.8	9.1	9.8			% Profit Before Taxes/Total	15.1	8.0
38.1	2.4	3.3	7.2			Assets	8.7	1.9
4.4	−3.5	−.5	1.9				1.1	−1.3
UND	30.8	25.6	20.2			Sales/Net Fixed Assets	34.7	12.4
21.1	12.1	6.1	6.1				4.7	5.3
7.6	6.5	2.3	.5				1.6	1.4
12.2	5.4	3.4	1.9			Sales/Total Assets	3.7	2.3
3.5	4.2	2.3	.4				1.7	1.2
1.8	2.4	.6	.1				.7	.6
	1.0	.9	.7			% Depr., Dep., Amort./Sales	.9	.6
(25)	4.0	(35) 1.6	(14) 1.7				(47) 2.9	(55) 3.9
	5.6	8.2	9.3				6.0	9.3
	1.4	.8				% Officers', Directors',	1.7	1.4
(19)	2.4	(17) 1.4				Owners' Comp/Sales	(16) 2.7	(19) 3.5
	5.7	2.6					9.2	5.0
16703M	198926M	388547M	369912M	163205M	825648M	Net Sales ($)	1127277M	1269749M
2250M	44484M	197230M	322844M	242974M	788511M	Total Assets ($)	1058695M	1225997M

© RMA 2005

M = $ thousand   MM = $ million
See Pages 11 through 21 for Explanation of Ratios and Data

Comparative Historical Data | | | | **Current Data Sorted By Sales** | | | | |

			Type of Statement						
9	15	12	Unqualified	1		1	2	2	6
14	21	15	Reviewed	2	3	2	2	3	3
28	23	27	Compiled	4	4	3	10	5	1
13	19	32	Tax Returns	7	5	2	12	4	2
20	17	24	Other	3	6	4	4	3	4
4/1/02-3/31/03 ALL	4/1/03-3/31/04 ALL	4/1/04-3/31/05 ALL		16 (4/1-9/30/04)			94 (10/1/04-3/31/05)		
				0-1MM	1-3MM	3-5MM	5-10MM	10-25MM	25MM & OVER
84	95	110	NUMBER OF STATEMENTS	17	18	12	30	17	16
%	%	%	**ASSETS**	%	%	%	%	%	%
7.2	7.3	9.5	Cash & Equivalents	19.2	10.6	7.9	8.4	8.1	2.6
8.4	7.6	9.2	Trade Receivables (net)	1.8	7.9	8.5	9.1	14.9	13.4
25.1	20.2	26.6	Inventory	32.2	13.2	19.2	31.5	41.5	16.4
2.6	4.8	3.4	All Other Current	1.9	1.3	3.0	4.7	2.9	5.7
43.2	39.8	48.7	Total Current	55.0	33.0	38.6	53.6	67.3	38.1
39.1	41.8	39.2	Fixed Assets (net)	35.1	48.2	49.5	37.8	21.4	47.4
2.1	.4	.8	Intangibles (net)	2.4	.9	.0	.2	.2	1.1
15.7	18.0	11.3	All Other Non-Current	7.5	17.9	11.8	8.3	11.0	13.4
100.0	100.0	100.0	Total	100.0	100.0	100.0	100.0	100.0	100.0
			LIABILITIES						
17.2	16.3	18.4	Notes Payable-Short Term	25.6	18.0	16.7	10.4	32.2	12.9
3.7	7.1	7.7	Cur. Mat.-L/T/D	1.8	18.1	2.2	9.0	9.2	2.4
4.9	3.9	5.5	Trade Payables	1.1	4.7	5.2	4.9	11.4	6.0
.1	.2	.3	Income Taxes Payable	.0	.0	.0	1.1	.1	.1
7.1	9.2	5.1	All Other Current	3.0	6.4	.4	5.5	7.1	6.6
33.1	36.6	37.1	Total Current	31.5	47.2	24.6	31.0	60.0	28.0
29.9	29.7	33.5	Long-Term Debt	35.9	40.9	44.9	35.7	14.9	29.7
.2	.5	.2	Deferred Taxes	.5	.2	.0	.0	.6	.3
2.5	2.6	4.1	All Other Non-Current	4.2	4.3	9.4	4.5	1.6	2.0
34.4	30.7	25.0	Net Worth	27.9	7.4	21.2	28.8	22.9	40.0
100.0	100.0	100.0	Total Liabilities & Net Worth	100.0	100.0	100.0	100.0	100.0	100.0
			INCOME DATA						
100.0	100.0	100.0	Net Sales	100.0	100.0	100.0	100.0	100.0	100.0
			Gross Profit						
85.8	90.5	89.4	Operating Expenses	78.9	84.2	97.5	89.3	98.0	91.5
14.2	9.5	10.6	Operating Profit	21.1	15.8	2.5	10.7	2.0	8.5
3.7	2.5	2.7	All Other Expenses (net)	8.7	4.9	2.4	.3	.1	1.3
10.5	7.0	7.8	Profit Before Taxes	12.4	10.8	.0	10.4	1.8	7.2
			RATIOS						
3.5	2.7	3.2		8.2	2.2	5.9	8.6	1.2	1.8
1.5	1.2	1.3	Current	2.1	.7	1.1	1.9	1.0	1.2
.7	.6	.8		.9	.2	.7	.9	.9	1.0
1.8	.9	1.4		2.4	1.6	1.6	2.8	.7	.8
(83) .6	(94) .4	.5	Quick	.8	.2	.7	.6	.3	.4
.2	.1	.2		.4	.1	.1	.2	.1	.4
0 UND	1 477.5	0 UND		0 UND	0 UND	0 UND	0 UND	5 67.2	8 44.0
9 41.8	11 31.8	8 48.1	Sales/Receivables	0 UND	7 54.3	9 41.4	6 65.9	11 32.6	16 22.7
22 16.4	25 14.3	19 19.6		17 21.8	40 9.2	18 20.4	12 30.1	19 19.2	26 14.3
			Cost of Sales/Inventory						
			Cost of Sales/Payables						
4.1	5.4	6.0		.9	4.7	6.9	5.3	19.9	11.1
21.0	26.6	34.3	Sales/Working Capital	3.5	-18.3	34.3	12.0	58.0	62.4
-16.7	-12.1	-49.0		NM	-1.7	-31.1	-82.5	-157.9	207.4
8.5	9.3	8.0		12.9	5.2	10.2	19.2	4.7	7.9
(74) 3.2	(84) 2.5	(102) 2.8	EBIT/Interest	(12) 3.7	(16) 1.6	(11) .8	4.8	2.9	4.6
1.3	1.2	1.1		-.2	.9	-2.1	1.3	1.7	1.7
	6.2	7.4	Net Profit + Depr., Dep.,						
	(15) 3.2	(16) 2.0	Amort./Cur. Mat. L/T/D						
	1.1	1.0							
.2	.4	.3		.0	.4	.4	.4	.3	.4
1.1	.9	1.0	Fixed/Worth	1.0	3.0	1.7	1.1	.8	1.1
3.2	3.0	3.8		3.7	-1.4	NM	3.9	1.5	2.0
.5	.8	1.1		.9	1.0	.4	1.2	2.3	.8
1.6	2.7	2.6	Debt/Worth	2.1	3.3	2.6	2.4	3.5	1.5
8.6	7.7	12.6		41.3	-3.1	NM	9.8	12.4	4.7
51.5	48.2	65.0	% Profit Before Taxes/Tangible	100.0	50.3		87.8	78.2	36.1
(74) 12.0	(84) 14.9	(96) 17.3	Net Worth	(14) 11.8	(11) 11.3		(29) 36.2	46.2	17.3
3.7	2.6	2.7		-3.3	2.9		5.1	3.4	7.6
12.4	12.1	13.6	% Profit Before Taxes/Total	30.0	9.6	8.1	23.4	9.9	13.9
5.4	4.4	4.0	Assets	3.4	4.4	-.4	7.7	5.5	7.5
1.0	.5	.1		-3.1	-.6	-12.1	1.5	1.4	2.3
27.5	18.9	24.6		UND	12.9	21.3	26.0	92.0	18.0
8.1	4.3	9.0	Sales/Net Fixed Assets	3.1	3.6	5.3	13.1	25.0	3.9
.9	1.0	2.4		.7	1.8	2.6	5.6	13.4	1.5
3.9	3.1	4.2		1.8	3.3	3.8	4.7	5.6	3.7
1.4	1.4	2.4	Sales/Total Assets	.5	1.7	2.2	3.5	3.8	1.3
.4	.5	.9		.1	.4	.9	1.8	2.7	1.0
.8	1.3	1.0		4.1	1.7		.5	.3	1.0
(67) 3.2	(77) 4.3	(85) 3.4	% Depr., Dep., Amort./Sales	(11) 12.2	(14) 5.0		(24) 1.5	(14) .8	(14) 3.0
6.9	13.1	7.9		18.8	21.8		4.6	2.8	5.5
1.3	1.0	1.3	% Officers', Directors',				1.4	.5	
(22) 2.3	(32) 1.9	(45) 2.2	Owners' Comp/Sales				(14) 1.7	(11) 1.1	
3.9	6.4	8.7					3.0	2.8	
1115072M	1970782M	1962941M	Net Sales ($)	9596M	40772M	48023M	204169M	268639M	1391742M
1054879M	1993402M	1598293M	Total Assets ($)	62842M	98418M	50392M	119111M	106758M	1160772M

© RMA 2005

M = $ thousand   MM = $ million
See Pages 11 through 21 for Explanation of Ratios and Data

Current Data Sorted By Assets

Comparative Historical Data

						Type of Statement		
	1	2	5	2	1	Unqualified	14	10
	3	8	5			Reviewed	17	17
7	18	16	2		1	Compiled	28	32
10	20	7		1	2	Tax Returns	29	19
2	5	8	3			Other	24	21
	24 (4/1-9/30/04)		105 (10/1/04-3/31/05)				4/1/00-3/31/01 ALL	4/1/01-3/31/02 ALL
0-500M	500M-2MM	2-10MM	10-50MM	50-100MM	100-250MM			
19	47	41	15	3	4	**NUMBER OF STATEMENTS**	112	99
%	%	%	%	%	%	**ASSETS**	%	%
15.5	9.3	7.7	3.2			Cash & Equivalents	10.1	9.4
6.6	8.8	9.7	6.8			Trade Receivables (net)	8.2	9.6
9.4	14.5	28.4	12.4			Inventory	13.2	13.3
2.8	4.2	1.9	2.5			All Other Current	4.0	3.1
34.3	36.9	47.7	24.8			Total Current	35.5	35.4
52.5	56.0	38.8	58.8			Fixed Assets (net)	54.1	53.4
.0	.6	.2	.3			Intangibles (net)	.5	.7
13.2	6.5	13.3	16.1			All Other Non-Current	9.9	10.4
100.0	100.0	100.0	100.0			Total	100.0	100.0
						LIABILITIES		
16.4	12.0	18.9	10.7			Notes Payable-Short Term	8.7	13.9
10.8	14.7	5.9	5.8			Cur. Mat.-L/T/D	9.5	11.4
14.1	6.6	6.0	2.9			Trade Payables	4.9	5.4
.0	.1	.5	.0			Income Taxes Payable	.6	.3
4.1	2.1	4.8	5.3			All Other Current	5.2	6.5
45.4	35.5	36.0	24.8			Total Current	28.9	37.4
39.5	44.4	29.2	23.2			Long-Term Debt	27.3	29.8
.0	1.1	1.0	1.0			Deferred Taxes	.5	.6
15.5	4.5	1.0	.7			All Other Non-Current	2.5	2.1
−.4	14.5	32.8	50.3			Net Worth	40.8	30.1
100.0	100.0	100.0	100.0			Total Liabilities & Net Worth	100.0	100.0
						INCOME DATA		
100.0	100.0	100.0	100.0			Net Sales	100.0	100.0
41.2	40.6	27.1	33.6			Gross Profit	33.8	30.7
40.1	36.9	22.7	22.8			Operating Expenses	30.9	28.1
1.1	3.7	4.4	10.8			Operating Profit	2.9	2.5
.0	.8	1.0	.6			All Other Expenses (net)	.0	1.9
1.1	2.9	3.4	10.2			Profit Before Taxes	2.9	.6
						RATIOS		
2.5	1.6	2.8	1.6				2.9	1.6
.9	1.0	1.3	1.2			Current	1.2	1.0
.2	.5	.8	.6				.6	.5
1.2	.7	1.4	.9				1.3	.9
.3	(46) .5	.5	.4			Quick	.5	.5
.0	.2	.2	.3				.2	.2
0 UND	0 UND	5 74.8	11 33.1				0 999.8	4 102.3
0 UND	9 39.0	9 39.5	16 23.1			Sales/Receivables	9 39.1	11 34.4
4 86.8	19 19.4	22 16.4	26 13.8				20 17.9	24 15.5
0 UND	0 UND	8 47.8	0 UND				0 UND	0 UND
0 UND	9 41.5	36 10.0	7 53.1			Cost of Sales/Inventory	6 63.9	14 26.0
16 22.2	45 8.1	90 4.1	208 1.8				43 8.5	44 8.3
0 UND	0 UND	1 513.6	8 48.3				0 UND	0 999.8
5 68.2	6 62.7	9 40.0	13 27.1			Cost of Sales/Payables	8 46.3	10 36.6
25 14.6	30 12.3	20 18.2	24 15.4				20 18.6	19 18.7
24.9	22.3	6.6	7.4				8.5	13.1
−55.0	−999.8	76.3	16.2			Sales/Working Capital	52.4	−779.1
−4.0	−15.3	−18.0	−10.5				−15.8	−11.6
5.1	4.2	6.4	11.7				5.5	2.8
(15) 1.4	(46) 1.6	(39) 3.4	(13) 6.7			EBIT/Interest	(108) 1.9	(97) 1.4
−.2	1.0	1.5	2.6				.6	.5
						Net Profit + Depr., Dep.,	3.5	1.8
						Amort./Cur. Mat. L /T/D	(26) 1.4	(19) 1.5
							.9	1.1
.7	.9	.3	.7				.6	.8
3.6	5.6	1.2	1.3			Fixed/Worth	1.2	1.9
−2.8	−8.3	3.8	1.8				3.5	4.9
1.7	1.6	.9	.3				.6	1.1
8.0	6.1	2.5	1.2			Debt/Worth	1.3	2.2
−20.4	−15.9	8.0	2.5				3.6	14.0
45.3	83.4	46.3	37.5				27.3	29.1
(13) 18.7	(32) 20.6	(40) 17.8	(14) 12.8			% Profit Before Taxes/Tangible Net Worth	(100) 10.9	(81) 6.7
−21.4	4.0	9.0	6.0				−.2	−.8
13.9	11.7	10.7	10.9				11.7	8.9
1.6	2.3	5.3	8.5			% Profit Before Taxes/Total Assets	3.6	1.9
−5.7	−.1	1.0	2.6				−1.2	−1.9
21.4	15.8	30.9	6.0				7.5	8.2
6.8	5.1	8.9	1.6			Sales/Net Fixed Assets	3.7	3.4
1.5	3.1	2.8	.7				2.2	2.3
7.3	4.4	3.6	2.0				3.2	3.2
2.9	3.0	2.4	1.2			Sales/Total Assets	2.1	2.0
1.4	1.9	1.4	.5				1.4	1.4
3.4	2.3	1.9	2.3				3.9	3.7
(13) 14.1	(40) 8.5	(36) 5.1	6.8			% Depr., Dep., Amort./Sales	(105) 6.6	(90) 7.5
26.5	13.6	10.1	12.9				11.3	10.7
	1.3	.6					2.0	1.7
	(24) 2.4	(19) 2.3				% Officers', Directors', Owners' Comp/Sales	(52) 3.4	(35) 3.4
	4.8	4.2					7.4	6.1
20964M	198104M	444367M	543518M	652235M	1733153M	Net Sales ($)	1515766M	1788266M
5778M	58304M	166344M	304627M	187550M	646967M	Total Assets ($)	956380M	823322M

M = $ thousand   MM = $ million
See Pages 11 through 21 for Explanation of Ratios and Data

Comparative Historical Data | | | Current Data Sorted By Sales

			Type of Statement						
9	18	11	Unqualified		1	1	2	1	6
25	29	16	Reviewed		2	2	4	7	1
25	42	44	Compiled	4	11	11	10	6	2
36	31	40	Tax Returns	8	11	6	7	5	3
14	24	18	Other	2	5	3	3	2	3
4/1/02-3/31/03	4/1/03-3/31/04	4/1/04-3/31/05		24 (4/1-9/30/04)		105 (10/1/04-3/31/05)			
ALL	ALL	ALL		0-1MM	1-3MM	3-5MM	5-10MM	10-25MM	25MM & OVER
109	144	129	**NUMBER OF STATEMENTS**	14	30	23	26	21	15
%	%	%	**ASSETS**	%	%	%	%	%	%
7.9	8.3	8.9	Cash & Equivalents	11.6	10.1	9.2	9.7	6.5	5.2
10.2	10.8	8.4	Trade Receivables (net)	4.5	5.6	7.9	13.4	9.1	8.9
15.1	16.5	17.5	Inventory	19.8	10.1	25.8	16.2	20.5	15.3
3.3	3.5	3.1	All Other Current	.8	1.4	5.0	5.1	2.1	3.4
36.5	39.1	37.8	Total Current	36.7	27.2	48.0	44.4	38.2	32.8
51.3	49.0	50.7	Fixed Assets (net)	52.8	63.9	44.1	49.3	39.3	51.0
1.2	1.2	.4	Intangibles (net)	.0	.9	.4	.1	.2	.4
11.0	10.7	11.1	All Other Non-Current	10.5	8.0	7.6	6.2	22.3	15.8
100.0	100.0	100.0	Total	100.0	100.0	100.0	100.0	100.0	100.0
			LIABILITIES						
13.8	17.0	15.8	Notes Payable-Short Term	9.6	9.3	15.3	14.5	19.0	33.1
10.2	10.3	9.6	Cur. Mat.-L/T/D	12.3	11.2	12.1	11.6	5.0	2.8
6.4	5.4	7.0	Trade Payables	12.8	4.1	5.6	10.6	6.0	4.3
.2	.1	.2	Income Taxes Payable	.0	.1	.0	.5	.2	.2
4.9	4.4	3.8	All Other Current	1.7	4.3	2.4	3.3	5.8	4.7
35.6	37.3	36.3	Total Current	36.5	29.0	35.4	40.6	36.0	45.0
32.5	26.6	37.6	Long-Term Debt	56.0	48.6	34.0	26.4	28.4	36.5
.6	.8	.9	Deferred Taxes	.0	.3	2.2	.2	1.5	1.0
5.9	4.2	5.2	All Other Non-Current	13.4	6.5	1.4	4.5	.8	8.5
25.5	31.1	20.0	Net Worth	-5.8	15.6	27.0	28.3	33.3	9.1
100.0	100.0	100.0	Total Liabilities & Net Worth	100.0	100.0	100.0	100.0	100.0	100.0
			INCOME DATA						
100.0	100.0	100.0	Net Sales	100.0	100.0	100.0	100.0	100.0	100.0
31.6	30.3	35.5	Gross Profit	45.0	48.5	35.9	32.5	20.4	26.3
29.1	27.0	31.1	Operating Expenses	41.4	42.3	30.4	28.3	18.1	23.1
2.5	3.2	4.4	Operating Profit	3.6	6.2	5.5	4.2	2.3	3.2
1.6	1.5	.8	All Other Expenses (net)	2.0	1.3	.7	.1	.0	1.6
.9	1.7	3.6	Profit Before Taxes	1.6	4.9	4.8	4.1	2.2	1.7
			RATIOS						
1.9	1.9	2.1	Current	4.8	2.5	2.2	1.7	1.8	1.6
1.1	1.1	1.1		.8	1.2	1.4	1.1	1.2	.9
.5	.5	.5		.2	.5	.8	.4	.7	.6
1.1	1.0	1.0	Quick	1.4	1.2	1.5	.9	.9	.8
.4	.4	(128) .5		.3	(29) .5	.5	.5	.4	.4
.2	.2	.2		.1	.2	.2	.3	.2	.2
0 UND	2 161.6	0 UND	Sales/Receivables	0 UND	0 UND	2 210.3	3 128.0	1 533.0	0 UND
11 34.7	12 29.9	9 41.8		0 UND	8 44.7	10 35.7	12 30.1	9 41.1	12 30.1
21 17.2	25 14.5	19 19.1		5 73.4	14 26.5	22 16.4	29 12.8	18 20.3	20 18.6
0 UND	0 UND	0 UND	Cost of Sales/Inventory	0 UND	0 UND	9 41.5	0 UND	4 89.4	0 UND
14 25.5	13 28.5	13 28.1		0 UND	11 34.3	42 8.6	4 83.6	17 21.4	20 18.4
57 6.4	53 6.9	55 6.7		31 11.8	70 5.2	90 4.1	33 11.0	36 10.1	39 9.3
1 243.7	0 999.8	0 UND	Cost of Sales/Payables	0 UND	0 UND	0 UND	3 107.2	1 558.4	0 UND
9 41.9	9 40.6	8 43.9		0 UND	6 58.0	8 46.1	13 27.9	8 46.4	7 49.3
19 19.1	19 19.3	25 14.7		27 13.6	34 10.7	33 10.9	28 13.0	19 18.8	14 26.1
13.3	9.4	12.9	Sales/Working Capital	5.9	16.6	7.3	14.5	30.8	12.6
69.2	123.3	101.5		-39.2	32.5	13.9	NM	79.6	-219.2
-13.2	-12.6	-14.1		-3.9	-15.3	-15.9	-11.9	-22.4	-10.9
4.3	5.7	5.9	EBIT/Interest	5.2	4.1	4.8	7.1	6.1	6.9
(103) 1.6	(135) 2.2	(120) 2.3		(11) 1.4	(27) 1.8	(22) 2.0	(25) 4.1	(20) 2.6	1.8
.6	.5	1.0		-.2	.6	.7	1.4	1.3	1.2
1.9	2.3	3.0	Net Profit + Depr., Dep., Amort./Cur. Mat. L/T/D						
(19) 1.2	(25) 1.7	(18) 1.5							
.6	1.0	.9							
.8	.5	.7	Fixed/Worth	.2	1.3	.8	.7	.8	.7
1.7	1.4	2.3		2.4	5.3	3.2	1.7	1.3	1.7
7.2	5.0	13.7		NM	-11.2	6.9	5.8	3.5	-3.0
1.0	.8	1.2	Debt/Worth	1.7	1.3	1.4	1.1	1.0	1.2
2.7	2.3	2.8		18.2	6.2	3.8	2.3	2.8	2.3
13.5	7.9	42.9		-64.9	-18.2	10.8	15.9	9.0	-7.3
22.7	35.2	48.6	% Profit Before Taxes/Tangible Net Worth	120.7	94.4	43.8	60.3	52.6	28.2
(86) 6.4	(122) 10.4	(102) 17.7		(10) 27.2	(21) 14.9	(19) 18.3	(21) 23.1	(20) 20.3	(11) 6.1
-3.4	-2.0	4.7		.2	-9.4	.3	5.8	6.4	3.2
8.6	9.3	11.4	% Profit Before Taxes/Total Assets	13.7	12.9	11.6	14.9	9.8	8.5
1.4	3.1	4.8		1.7	4.3	6.1	7.5	5.4	2.6
-2.2	-2.3	-.1		-2.2	-1.9	-1.0	.5	1.3	.5
10.9	14.1	15.6	Sales/Net Fixed Assets	19.9	6.6	14.1	21.1	35.4	10.9
4.3	5.0	5.2		3.2	3.2	4.6	5.8	13.7	6.1
2.0	2.1	2.1		1.4	1.6	2.0	3.8	2.8	3.7
3.6	3.6	4.1	Sales/Total Assets	2.4	3.8	2.8	4.4	5.9	5.3
2.3	2.1	2.5		1.5	2.1	1.9	3.4	3.1	4.0
1.2	1.2	1.3		.8	1.3	1.0	2.5	1.6	1.3
2.6	2.1	2.2	% Depr., Dep., Amort./Sales	4.7	5.1	3.2	2.9	1.3	1.0
(98) 6.8	(131) 6.6	(106) 6.5		(10) 15.4	(26) 10.8	(21) 7.9	(20) 8.4	(19) 2.6	(10) 2.3
11.8	10.9	13.0		29.7	15.1	15.0	12.2	7.3	2.9
1.2	1.3	1.0	% Officers', Directors', Owners' Comp/Sales		2.2	2.1	1.0	.3	
(51) 2.6	(55) 2.5	(59) 2.6			(16) 4.3	(12) 3.2	(12) 1.8	(10) .8	
5.6	6.6	5.1			6.6	6.6	2.7	1.3	
2208381M	2575934M	3592341M	Net Sales ($)	8672M	58629M	91017M	178911M	330543M	2924569M
1059410M	1544913M	1369570M	Total Assets ($)	10030M	62318M	77792M	75672M	138379M	1005379M

© RMA 2005

M = $ thousand   MM = $ million
See Pages 11 through 21 for Explanation of Ratios and Data

Current Data Sorted By Assets

Comparative Historical Data

	0-500M	500M-2MM	2-10MM	10-50MM	50-100MM	100-250MM	Type of Statement	4/1/00-3/31/01 ALL	4/1/01-3/31/02 ALL
				5			Unqualified	6	4
			1	1			Reviewed	2	1
		1	1				Compiled	6	7
	1	2	2			1	Tax Returns	1	5
	4	1	1		5		Other	18	20
		4	7						
		8 (4/1-9/30/04)		31 (10/1/04-3/31/05)					
NUMBER OF STATEMENTS	5	8	13	11	2			33	37
ASSETS	%	%	%	%	%	%		%	%
Cash & Equivalents			17.1	10.3				9.6	16.0
Trade Receivables (net)			8.6	11.4				5.4	8.9
Inventory			4.1	12.4				7.6	6.6
All Other Current			13.2	5.4				9.4	4.6
Total Current			43.0	39.5				32.0	36.1
Fixed Assets (net)			47.4	45.3				53.7	46.7
Intangibles (net)			1.9	.8				1.6	2.4
All Other Non-Current			7.7	14.4				12.7	14.7
Total			100.0	100.0				100.0	100.0
LIABILITIES									
Notes Payable-Short Term			7.6	5.5				3.0	4.9
Cur. Mat.-L/T/D			5.5	4.3				11.7	9.6
Trade Payables			13.7	5.1				7.0	5.7
Income Taxes Payable			.6	.9				.1	.4
All Other Current			7.5	8.4				16.1	10.2
Total Current			34.8	24.2				37.9	30.8
Long-Term Debt			28.7	32.4				61.5	61.5
Deferred Taxes			.5	1.7				.6	.4
All Other Non-Current			3.5	2.8				5.1	6.6
Net Worth			32.4	38.8				-5.1	.7
Total Liabilities & Net Worth			100.0	100.0				100.0	100.0
INCOME DATA									
Net Sales			100.0	100.0				100.0	100.0
Gross Profit									
Operating Expenses			93.9	89.1				88.7	87.4
Operating Profit			6.1	10.9				11.3	12.6
All Other Expenses (net)			3.6	2.5				-.7	2.2
Profit Before Taxes			2.5	8.4				11.9	10.4
RATIOS									
Current			1.8	3.5				1.6	2.9
			1.1	1.8				1.0	1.4
			.5	.8				.4	.6
Quick			1.3	2.0				.9	2.3
			.6	.9				.4	.6
			.2	.5				.2	.3
Sales/Receivables			1 715.8	16 22.5				0 UND	0 UND
			5 71.0	29 12.5				7 54.0	5 78.6
			29 12.8	50 7.2				18 20.6	31 11.8
Cost of Sales/Inventory									
Cost of Sales/Payables									
Sales/Working Capital			7.6	3.3				12.1	6.8
			35.4	5.9				999.8	18.1
			-10.1	-11.2				-7.0	-16.9
EBIT/Interest			24.9	13.8				11.1	9.4
			3.3	5.1				(35) 5.5	4.3
			-.2	1.2				1.5	2.0
Net Profit + Depr., Dep., Amort./Cur. Mat. L /T/D									
Fixed/Worth			.8	.5				1.1	.7
			1.7	1.1				2.7	2.8
			37.6	9.6				NM	-5.3
Debt/Worth			.8	.6				1.4	1.2
			2.6	1.4				3.3	3.6
			46.1	14.0				NM	-20.9
% Profit Before Taxes/Tangible Net Worth			(11) 64.4	26.7				(25) 67.8	(24) 57.0
			21.6	20.1				33.4	39.6
			-1.7	5.6				8.9	12.5
% Profit Before Taxes/Total Assets			13.4	12.9				31.8	32.2
			7.5	7.4				15.3	17.3
			-3.7	.7				3.9	4.5
Sales/Net Fixed Assets			7.3	4.1				6.9	8.0
			2.7	2.8				3.2	4.5
			2.0	1.5				1.2	1.7
Sales/Total Assets			3.0	1.6				2.7	2.5
			1.5	1.3				1.6	1.7
			.8	.5				.9	1.0
% Depr., Dep., Amort./Sales			3.7	1.5				4.3	3.1
			(11) 5.2	5.5				(30) 6.2	(31) 6.7
			6.3	9.1				12.0	10.0
% Officers', Directors', Owners' Comp/Sales									
Net Sales ($)	1460M	19569M	107140M	272130M	126495M			1084294M	547514M
Total Assets ($)	1184M	10615M	63073M	241715M	120353M			465685M	361103M

(Columns 50-100MM and 100-250MM marked: DATA NOT AVAILABLE)

M = $ thousand   MM = $ million
See Pages 11 through 21 for Explanation of Ratios and Data

Comparative Historical Data / Current Data Sorted By Sales

	6 / 2 / 8 / 17 / 15	8 / 2 / 8 / 14 / 10	8 / 3 / 5 / 7 / 16	Type of Statement	0-1MM	1-3MM	3-5MM	5-10MM	10-25MM	25MM & OVER
Unqualified	6	8	8			1	1	1	2	4
Reviewed	2	2	3						2	
Compiled	8	8	5		2	2	1			
Tax Returns	17	14	7		5	1				1
Other	15	10	16			2	4	2	6	2
	4/1/02-3/31/03 ALL	4/1/03-3/31/04 ALL	4/1/04-3/31/05 ALL		8 (4/1-9/30/04)			31 (10/1/04-3/31/05)		
NUMBER OF STATEMENTS	48	42	39		7	6	6	3	10	7
	%	%	%		%	%	%	%	%	%
				ASSETS						
Cash & Equivalents	14.0	12.1	13.6						15.8	
Trade Receivables (net)	7.5	2.7	8.1						11.5	
Inventory	6.4	5.0	7.3						6.0	
All Other Current	3.7	3.1	7.7						9.1	
Total Current	31.5	23.0	36.8						42.4	
Fixed Assets (net)	52.3	60.6	48.8						48.5	
Intangibles (net)	3.1	4.6	2.8						.8	
All Other Non-Current	13.0	11.9	11.6						8.2	
Total	100.0	100.0	100.0						100.0	
				LIABILITIES						
Notes Payable-Short Term	8.0	5.9	4.5						1.4	
Cur. Mat.-L/T/D	11.6	10.7	7.5						4.2	
Trade Payables	4.5	6.6	7.7						10.2	
Income Taxes Payable	.5	.2	.4						.0	
All Other Current	17.8	11.1	14.4						11.3	
Total Current	42.4	34.5	34.4						27.1	
Long-Term Debt	48.3	51.3	38.9						31.1	
Deferred Taxes	.1	.4	.7						1.6	
All Other Non-Current	7.1	12.6	4.0						5.7	
Net Worth	2.1	1.2	22.0						34.4	
Total Liabilities & Net Worth	100.0	100.0	100.0						100.0	
				INCOME DATA						
Net Sales	100.0	100.0	100.0						100.0	
Gross Profit										
Operating Expenses	90.1	91.9	91.4						92.1	
Operating Profit	9.9	8.1	8.6						7.9	
All Other Expenses (net)	2.8	4.7	5.0						1.6	
Profit Before Taxes	7.1	3.4	3.7						6.3	
				RATIOS						
Current	2.1	1.7	2.9						3.2	
	.8	.7	1.2						1.5	
	.2	.3	.6						.9	
Quick	1.7	1.0	1.5						2.4	
	.5	.4	.8						1.0	
	.2	.2	.2						.5	
Sales/Receivables	0 UND	0 UND	0 UND						0 934.7	
	0 UND	0 UND	6 58.1						25 14.5	
	19 19.0	20 18.1	31 11.9						50 7.3	
Cost of Sales/Inventory										
Cost of Sales/Payables										
Sales/Working Capital	7.3	19.8	5.7						6.7	
	-86.8	-50.7	35.4						22.0	
	-8.2	-7.0	-10.6						-28.2	
EBIT/Interest	10.3	6.6	12.6						12.5	
	(44) 2.6	(39) 1.9	(37) 5.1						4.8	
	.5	.2	.6						.9	
Net Profit + Depr., Dep., Amort./Cur. Mat. L/T/D										
Fixed/Worth	1.1	1.3	.7						.9	
	4.1	3.2	2.0						2.2	
	-3.7	-2.1	-12.6						4.6	
Debt/Worth	1.0	1.3	.9						.8	
	5.6	4.6	3.1						3.2	
	-5.0	-3.4	-17.3						7.7	
% Profit Before Taxes/Tangible Net Worth	53.9	32.8	38.7						43.0	
	(27) 20.5	(24) 13.8	(29) 25.9						22.4	
	9.8	3.8	6.4						3.7	
% Profit Before Taxes/Total Assets	22.4	16.9	15.6						12.3	
	4.4	4.0	7.5						9.2	
	-2.0	-4.1	-1.4						.2	
Sales/Net Fixed Assets	8.2	5.3	6.5						4.7	
	3.2	3.0	2.8						2.7	
	1.6	1.6	1.6						2.3	
Sales/Total Assets	3.6	2.6	1.9						2.3	
	1.4	1.6	1.4						1.5	
	.9	.9	.8						1.1	
% Depr., Dep., Amort./Sales	3.9	5.4	3.1							
	(42) 6.7	7.1	(37) 5.2							
	12.8	11.5	7.0							
% Officers', Directors', Owners' Comp/Sales	3.8									
	(12) 5.9									
	7.9									
Net Sales ($)	682671M	331408M	526794M		3146M	12198M	23485M	21678M	148146M	318141M
Total Assets ($)	550981M	319516M	436940M		5190M	9190M	33234M	13961M	124729M	250636M

M = $ thousand   MM = $ million
See Pages 11 through 21 for Explanation of Ratios and Data

Current Data Sorted By Assets   **Comparative Historical Data**

	0-500M	500M-2MM	2-10MM	10-50MM	50-100MM	100-250MM	Type of Statement	4/1/00-3/31/01 ALL	4/1/01-3/31/02 ALL
		1					Unqualified	3	1
		1	1	3			Reviewed	2	2
	2	1	4				Compiled	7	5
	12	3	3	1			Tax Returns	15	10
	2	5	3	3			Other	8	8
		8 (4/1-9/30/04)			34 (10/1/04-3/31/05)				
	16	11	11	4			**NUMBER OF STATEMENTS**	35	26
	%	%	%	%	%	%	**ASSETS**	%	%
	10.6	12.2	9.7		D	D	Cash & Equivalents	15.1	13.3
	3.9	17.2	9.2		A	A	Trade Receivables (net)	10.8	14.1
	.5	11.5	12.1		T	T	Inventory	11.0	17.1
	7.2	3.8	1.7		A	A	All Other Current	5.5	3.5
	22.2	44.7	32.6				Total Current	42.3	48.1
	57.7	43.6	57.0		N	N	Fixed Assets (net)	42.0	34.5
	1.6	.9	8.0		O	O	Intangibles (net)	3.3	1.7
	18.5	10.9	2.3		T	T	All Other Non-Current	12.3	15.8
	100.0	100.0	100.0				Total	100.0	100.0
					A	A	**LIABILITIES**		
	17.5	6.8	7.6		V	V	Notes Payable-Short Term	56.8	13.4
	3.0	1.0	4.6		A	A	Cur. Mat.-L/T/D	8.0	4.1
	5.1	4.0	4.6		I	I	Trade Payables	12.4	8.4
	.0	.0	.4		L	L	Income Taxes Payable	.2	.1
	28.8	11.5	1.6		A	A	All Other Current	95.7	4.1
	54.4	23.2	18.9		B	B	Total Current	173.1	30.1
	33.3	32.8	30.7		L	L	Long-Term Debt	57.8	31.8
	.0	.0	.0		E	E	Deferred Taxes	.1	.2
	1.1	5.2	2.5				All Other Non-Current	12.6	5.9
	11.1	38.8	47.9				Net Worth	−143.6	32.0
	100.0	100.0	100.0				Total Liabilities & Net Worth	100.0	100.0
							INCOME DATA		
	100.0	100.0	100.0				Net Sales	100.0	100.0
							Gross Profit		
	88.2	85.7	96.6				Operating Expenses	91.9	93.7
	11.8	14.3	3.4				Operating Profit	8.1	6.3
	1.3	1.6	2.1				All Other Expenses (net)	1.9	1.6
	10.5	12.6	1.3				Profit Before Taxes	6.2	4.7
							RATIOS		
	3.7	3.2	2.4					3.8	4.2
	.2	1.5	1.8				Current	1.1	1.5
	.0	.2	.8					.1	.8
	.9	3.2	2.4					2.9	2.8
	.2	.7	1.4				Quick	.7	.7
	.0	.1	.3					.1	.2
	0 UND	1 381.0	0 UND					0 UND	0 UND
	1 246.8	13 28.9	29 12.8				Sales/Receivables	0 UND	12 31.1
	5 80.9	19 19.3	34 10.8					28 13.0	29 12.5
							Cost of Sales/Inventory		
							Cost of Sales/Payables		
	NM	7.1	3.7					10.7	5.2
	−8.4	25.8	9.6				Sales/Working Capital	109.0	16.3
	−3.8	−14.6	−10.4					−9.6	−40.1
	14.2	28.7	4.2					8.5	4.5
(15)	4.0	8.9	2.4				EBIT/Interest	(25) 3.7	2.3
	1.1	1.6	−1.6					1.2	1.3
							Net Profit + Depr., Dep., Amort./Cur. Mat. L /T/D		
	.8	.0	.8					.4	.5
	14.6	.8	1.1				Fixed/Worth	2.1	1.0
	−4.5	1.2	1.7					34.1	1.7
	1.3	.3	.3					1.2	1.2
	18.2	1.1	1.0				Debt/Worth	7.3	2.3
	−6.9	153.2	20.5					−4.5	5.6
	223.6							(25) 113.9	(24) 74.7
(10)	107.2						% Profit Before Taxes/Tangible Net Worth	38.2	23.9
	21.6							2.3	7.0
	79.9	42.1	8.7					40.0	15.2
	11.8	20.8	3.2				% Profit Before Taxes/Total Assets	12.5	7.4
	.9	2.2	−5.0					.6	.9
	17.4	165.7	5.0					56.5	60.1
	5.1	7.3	.8				Sales/Net Fixed Assets	6.0	7.8
	3.6	1.2	.4					2.7	3.4
	4.7	5.2	1.8					4.6	3.4
	2.7	2.2	.7				Sales/Total Assets	2.8	2.0
	2.0	1.0	.4					1.7	1.4
	3.8							(26) .6	(21) 1.4
(14)	6.9						% Depr., Dep., Amort./Sales	5.0	4.8
	11.3							9.7	7.6
							% Officers', Directors', Owners' Comp/Sales	(13) 2.3 / 3.8 / 24.1	
	13242M	36646M	46726M	57638M			Net Sales ($)	945311M	397453M
	3588M	11897M	52590M	73242M			Total Assets ($)	373009M	176798M

© RMA 2005

M = $ thousand   MM = $ million
See Pages 11 through 21 for Explanation of Ratios and Data

Comparative Historical Data			Type of Statement	Current Data Sorted By Sales					
2	1	1	Unqualified			1			
5	3	5	Reviewed			1		2	2
10	11	7	Compiled	1	5		2	1	
16	9	19	Tax Returns	10	6	2	1	1	
6	5	10	Other	3	2	1	3	1	
4/1/02-3/31/03 ALL	4/1/03-3/31/04 ALL	4/1/04-3/31/05 ALL		8 (4/1-9/30/04) 0-1MM	1-3MM	34 (10/1/04-3/31/05) 3-5MM	5-10MM	10-25MM	25MM & OVER
39	29	42	NUMBER OF STATEMENTS	14	13	5	7	3	
%	%	%	ASSETS	%	%	%	%	%	%
10.9	11.9	10.0	Cash & Equivalents	6.8	10.1				D
12.6	11.6	8.9	Trade Receivables (net)	2.6	5.6				A
14.1	9.4	8.5	Inventory	.2	.7				T
6.7	11.1	4.3	All Other Current	4.7	5.4				A
44.4	44.0	31.6	Total Current	14.3	21.7				
38.4	39.8	51.8	Fixed Assets (net)	66.6	64.4				N
8.2	6.4	5.6	Intangibles (net)	1.9	.6				O
9.1	9.8	11.0	All Other Non-Current	17.2	13.3				T
100.0	100.0	100.0	Total	100.0	100.0				
			LIABILITIES						A
13.2	18.9	10.8	Notes Payable-Short Term	5.9	17.8				V
8.7	5.7	3.3	Cur. Mat.-L/T/D	3.8	1.3				A
10.4	10.1	4.4	Trade Payables	1.4	5.8				I
.0	.8	.6	Income Taxes Payable	.0	.0				L
27.6	18.1	14.6	All Other Current	29.3	11.0				A
60.0	53.5	33.7	Total Current	40.4	35.9				B
19.8	33.5	31.3	Long-Term Debt	29.9	45.4				L
.7	.0	.2	Deferred Taxes	.0	.0				E
3.5	3.7	2.6	All Other Non-Current	2.5	1.2				
16.0	9.2	32.2	Net Worth	27.3	17.5				
100.0	100.0	100.0	Total Liabilities & Net Worth	100.0	100.0				
			INCOME DATA						
100.0	100.0	100.0	Net Sales	100.0	100.0				
			Gross Profit						
91.9	91.5	90.6	Operating Expenses	89.1	88.0				
8.1	8.5	9.4	Operating Profit	10.9	12.0				
.8	2.5	1.5	All Other Expenses (net)	2.0	1.7				
7.3	6.0	7.9	Profit Before Taxes	8.9	10.3				
			RATIOS						
2.4	2.7	2.4		.6	3.7				
1.3	1.3	1.0	Current	.2	.9				
.5	.4	.2		.1	.2				
1.5	1.3	1.8		.2	2.0				
.5	.6	.3	Quick	.2	.8				
.2	.3	.1		.0	.2				
0 UND	0 UND	0 UND		0 UND	0 UND				
7 53.1	16 22.9	4 91.7	Sales/Receivables	1 375.3	1 385.3				
27 13.4	31 11.9	25 14.7		5 69.9	10 37.1				
			Cost of Sales/Inventory						
			Cost of Sales/Payables						
12.2	9.3	8.6		NM	13.4				
61.7	28.0	NM	Sales/Working Capital	-6.5	-194.5				
-16.0	-17.0	-8.1		-3.4	-12.5				
15.3	8.2	14.5		9.9	19.8				
(35) 3.2	(26) 3.0	(41) 3.8	EBIT/Interest	(13) 3.6	7.8				
1.0	1.1	1.1		1.0	1.0				
			Net Profit + Depr., Dep., Amort./Cur. Mat. L/T/D						
.0	.7	.7		.7	1.0				
1.0	1.4	1.2	Fixed/Worth	2.6	1.7				
6.9	-1.9	-16.6		-9.2	-4.2				
.7	1.2	.7		.6	.5				
2.8	7.6	1.8	Debt/Worth	2.7	1.4				
-9.9	-5.5	-18.8		-11.3	-7.2				
92.9	95.0	112.3	% Profit Before Taxes/Tangible Net Worth						
(28) 39.2	(19) 30.6	(31) 19.7							
9.0	8.1	9.4							
25.2	26.1	28.8	% Profit Before Taxes/Total Assets	23.4	73.9				
7.3	8.0	6.6		5.9	11.1				
1.0	.2	.6		.2	.3				
111.8	20.6	15.4		5.4	17.2				
20.6	4.8	3.9	Sales/Net Fixed Assets	3.7	4.9				
2.6	2.5	1.6		1.3	.7				
3.7	3.4	3.1		2.3	6.3				
2.7	2.1	1.9	Sales/Total Assets	1.8	2.2				
1.4	1.1	.9		1.2	.6				
.6	.9	2.5		6.8	1.5				
(27) 2.9	(24) 4.3	(35) 5.5	% Depr., Dep., Amort./Sales	(12) 8.4	(12) 3.4				
12.0	7.7	8.9		14.1	6.4				
1.9		3.1	% Officers', Directors', Owners' Comp/Sales						
(16) 2.5		(15) 6.9							
9.3		11.7							
469849M	271697M	154252M	Net Sales ($)	6975M	21411M	19069M	52056M	54741M	
203870M	145882M	141317M	Total Assets ($)	6457M	24159M	16650M	43960M	50091M	

© RMA 2005

M = $ thousand   MM = $ million
See Pages 11 through 21 for Explanation of Ratios and Data

Current Data Sorted By Assets

Comparative Historical Data

	0-500M	500M-2MM	2-10MM	10-50MM	50-100MM	100-250MM	Type of Statement	4/1/00-3/31/01 ALL	4/1/01-3/31/02 ALL
	1	5	20				Unqualified	12	32
		3	6				Reviewed	5	3
	1	3	6	1			Compiled	7	7
	1	2					Tax Returns	2	3
		1	3				Other	13	12
		35 (4/1-9/30/04)			18 (10/1/04-3/31/05)				
NUMBER OF STATEMENTS	3	14	35	1				39	57
	%	%	%	%	%	%	**ASSETS**	%	%
Cash & Equivalents		13.9	10.6		DATA	DATA		8.6	10.0
Trade Receivables (net)		9.7	13.7					13.7	20.4
Inventory		7.3	8.8		A	A		4.5	7.1
All Other Current		9.7	7.5		T	T		10.4	7.5
Total Current		40.6	40.6		A	A		37.2	45.0
Fixed Assets (net)		51.6	50.9					51.1	43.4
Intangibles (net)		.1	.2		N	N		1.3	.4
All Other Non-Current		7.7	8.3		O	O		10.4	11.2
Total		100.0	100.0		T	T		100.0	100.0
							LIABILITIES		
Notes Payable-Short Term		11.9	4.4		A	A		10.7	12.4
Cur. Mat.-L/T/D		4.6	3.8		V	V		6.0	2.6
Trade Payables		6.4	7.5		A	A		5.9	7.1
Income Taxes Payable		.2	.1		I	I		.3	.2
All Other Current		14.1	11.9		L	L		10.1	11.7
Total Current		37.1	27.7		A	A		33.0	33.9
Long-Term Debt		15.6	16.7		B	B		26.0	13.6
Deferred Taxes		.0	.3		L	L		.6	.2
All Other Non-Current		.0	1.1		E	E		1.2	1.2
Net Worth		47.2	54.3					39.2	51.1
Total Liabilities & Net Worth		100.0	100.0					100.0	100.0
							INCOME DATA		
Net Sales		100.0	100.0					100.0	100.0
Gross Profit									
Operating Expenses		85.3	81.5					88.2	87.2
Operating Profit		14.7	18.5					11.8	12.8
All Other Expenses (net)		1.3	.8					4.2	.4
Profit Before Taxes		13.4	17.7					7.6	12.5
							RATIOS		
		2.3	3.1					1.9	1.7
Current		1.1	1.2					1.2	1.3
		.7	.9					.6	1.0
		1.8	1.4					1.2	1.6
Quick		.6	.8					.6	.9
		.3	.5					.2	.4
	0 UND		8 44.6					6 64.2	10 37.5
Sales/Receivables	12 31.7		24 15.4					23 16.0	39 9.5
	39 9.2		77 4.7					101 3.6	90 4.0
							Cost of Sales/Inventory		
							Cost of Sales/Payables		
		6.2	7.4					3.6	5.6
Sales/Working Capital		NM	16.1					15.0	11.9
		-14.3	-41.2					-12.0	476.0
		40.8	50.1					12.7	25.5
EBIT/Interest		7.8	(34) 16.4					(33) 2.5	(51) 7.1
		2.7	5.0					1.2	1.7
			12.3					7.1	148.4
Net Profit + Depr., Dep., Amort./Cur. Mat. L /T/D		(12)	6.5					(10) 3.4	(10) 13.1
			2.5					2.0	2.1
		.5	.6					.7	.5
Fixed/Worth		1.0	.9					1.0	.8
		25.4	1.3					4.3	1.3
		.3	.4					.6	.4
Debt/Worth		.7	.7					1.5	.8
		175.1	1.8					4.3	2.5
		62.8	59.9					33.0	45.4
% Profit Before Taxes/Tangible Net Worth		(12) 36.3	28.8					(34) 11.1	(56) 21.0
		6.9	16.2					5.5	7.7
		30.6	22.9					10.1	24.2
% Profit Before Taxes/Total Assets		7.3	17.2					4.4	9.2
		3.1	7.5					1.1	2.1
		7.0	5.6					4.0	6.0
Sales/Net Fixed Assets		2.4	2.2					1.9	3.3
		1.8	1.3					1.2	1.8
		2.1	1.5					1.5	1.8
Sales/Total Assets		1.6	1.0					.9	1.2
		1.0	.8					.5	.7
		2.5	3.4					3.4	2.3
% Depr., Dep., Amort./Sales		(13) 6.0	(33) 5.2					(36) 5.8	(53) 4.3
		8.6	9.5					13.3	8.2
							% Officers', Directors', Owners' Comp/Sales		
Net Sales ($)	1857M	30284M	178519M	4966M				406677M	389834M
Total Assets ($)	1150M	19138M	144993M	22795M				365962M	416440M

© RMA 2005

M = $ thousand   MM = $ million

See Pages 11 through 21 for Explanation of Ratios and Data

Comparative Historical Data   **Current Data Sorted By Sales**

			Type of Statement						
.36	27	26	Unqualified	1	7	10	7	1	1
6	7	9	Reviewed		4	2	2		1
8	15	11	Compiled	1	4	4			2
4	4	3	Tax Returns	1	3	1			
7	4	4	Other		3				
4/1/02- 3/31/03 ALL	4/1/03- 3/31/04 ALL	4/1/04- 3/31/05 ALL			35 (4/1-9/30/04)		18 (10/1/04-3/31/05)		
				0-1MM	1-3MM	3-5MM	5-10MM	10-25MM	25MM & OVER
61	53	53	NUMBER OF STATEMENTS	3	20	17	9	4	
%	%	%	ASSETS	%	%	%	%	%	%
10.9	10.3	11.2	Cash & Equivalents		13.4	9.8			D
15.2	11.6	12.9	Trade Receivables (net)		11.5	10.6			A
7.7	5.9	7.8	Inventory		4.9	9.3			T
3.8	10.2	7.7	All Other Current		11.4	7.7			A
37.5	38.1	39.6	Total Current		41.1	37.4			
51.8	51.2	51.0	Fixed Assets (net)		56.2	49.2			N
.2	.7	.2	Intangibles (net)		.2	.3			O
10.5	9.9	9.2	All Other Non-Current		2.5	13.2			T
100.0	100.0	100.0	Total		100.0	100.0			
			LIABILITIES						A
7.0	7.3	7.9	Notes Payable-Short Term		6.6	5.6			V
4.3	9.5	6.2	Cur. Mat.-L/T/D		5.0	5.2			A
6.4	7.3	7.0	Trade Payables		7.0	7.6			I
.2	.2	.1	Income Taxes Payable		.1	.2			L
11.1	10.8	11.6	All Other Current		14.2	10.0			A
28.9	34.9	32.8	Total Current		32.9	28.6			B
17.5	31.8	16.8	Long-Term Debt		16.8	18.2			L
.0	.0	.2	Deferred Taxes		.3	.0			E
1.3	.9	.7	All Other Non-Current		.7	.4			
52.3	32.3	49.5	Net Worth		49.3	52.8			
100.0	100.0	100.0	Total Liabilities & Net Worth		100.0	100.0			
			INCOME DATA						
100.0	100.0	100.0	Net Sales		100.0	100.0			
			Gross Profit						
90.5	88.5	83.6	Operating Expenses		77.3	86.8			
9.5	11.5	16.4	Operating Profit		22.7	13.2			
.3	2.9	1.3	All Other Expenses (net)		2.1	1.1			
9.2	8.6	15.1	Profit Before Taxes		20.5	12.0			
			RATIOS						
2.0	2.0	2.5			2.2	3.3			
1.3	1.2	1.2	Current		1.2	1.2			
1.0	.7	.8			.8	.7			
1.4	1.4	1.5			2.0	1.2			
1.0	.6	.8	Quick		.8	.7			
.5	.2	.4			.3	.4			
7 52.4	2 164.4	9 42.7		0 UND	9 38.6				
37 9.9	13 27.0	19 19.2	Sales/Receivables	41 8.8	15 24.0				
91 4.0	78 4.7	73 5.0		77 4.7	77 4.7				
			Cost of Sales/Inventory						
			Cost of Sales/Payables						
6.9	4.0	6.5			5.9	3.6			
15.8	17.3	16.1	Sales/Working Capital		13.9	34.5			
−117.8	−9.2	−25.6			−33.5	−12.7			
21.0	13.1	47.4			62.6	20.6			
(55) 5.4	(49) 4.7	(52) 10.5	EBIT/Interest		22.6 (16)	7.1			
1.1	1.7	2.9			4.5	2.1			
38.2	4.7	9.4	Net Profit + Depr., Dep.,						
(13) 7.5	(13) 2.4	(15) 4.4	Amort./Cur. Mat. L/T/D						
2.0	.6	2.3							
.6	.6	.6			.6	.6			
.9	1.1	.9	Fixed/Worth		1.1	1.0			
1.6	3.8	1.6			1.8	1.5			
.4	.5	.4			.4	.5			
.7	.9	.8	Debt/Worth		.7	1.0			
1.7	4.7	2.3			4.0	1.4			
47.4	43.4	61.0	% Profit Before Taxes/Tangible		69.7	59.2			
(60) 18.5	(48) 10.0	(50) 29.4	Net Worth	(18)	39.8	24.2			
2.6	4.4	13.9			22.3	3.3			
21.1	12.4	24.3	% Profit Before Taxes/Total		28.1	22.6			
6.6	5.4	12.4	Assets		19.3	9.4			
1.5	1.1	3.4			6.8	2.1			
4.9	5.0	5.7			4.6	5.3			
2.7	2.1	2.3	Sales/Net Fixed Assets		1.8	2.4			
1.1	1.0	1.3			1.0	1.5			
1.7	1.5	1.7			1.5	1.6			
1.2	.8	1.1	Sales/Total Assets		1.0	1.0			
.7	.6	.8			.7	.8			
3.5	3.9	3.4			3.0	4.6			
(60) 5.4	(51) 6.1	(49) 5.8	% Depr., Dep., Amort./Sales	(18)	7.2	6.0			
10.5	11.1	9.4			9.7	8.6			
			% Officers', Directors', Owners' Comp/Sales						
238442M	242137M	215626M	Net Sales ($)	1857M	39210M	66033M	61861M	46665M	
217958M	295007M	188076M	Total Assets ($)	1150M	40172M	77670M	50491M	18593M	

M = $ thousand   MM = $ million
See Pages 11 through 21 for Explanation of Ratios and Data

Current Data Sorted By Assets | **Comparative Historical Data**

0-500M	500M-2MM	2-10MM	10-50MM	50-100MM	100-250MM	Type of Statement	4/1/00-3/31/01 ALL	4/1/01-3/31/02 ALL
	1	1	5			Unqualified	4	6
		2		1		Reviewed	7	4
6	8	1	2			Compiled	10	10
5	5	4				Tax Returns	8	11
3	3	1	1			Other	13	12
	16 (4/1-9/30/04)		33 (10/1/04-3/31/05)					
14	17	9	8	1		NUMBER OF STATEMENTS	42	43
%	%	%	%	%	%	**ASSETS**	%	%
20.7	15.7				DATA NOT AVAILABLE	Cash & Equivalents	10.3	10.1
9.0	16.2					Trade Receivables (net)	18.3	16.5
7.0	8.1					Inventory	12.6	15.9
4.2	2.1					All Other Current	4.4	4.6
41.0	42.1					Total Current	45.6	47.1
50.9	50.7					Fixed Assets (net)	46.1	44.3
1.6	4.3					Intangibles (net)	2.1	2.3
6.6	2.9					All Other Non-Current	6.2	6.4
100.0	100.0					Total	100.0	100.0
						LIABILITIES		
34.3	3.9					Notes Payable-Short Term	8.6	9.8
9.9	7.6					Cur. Mat.-L/T/D	6.6	5.2
3.3	6.0					Trade Payables	9.8	7.4
.0	.6					Income Taxes Payable	.7	1.3
5.6	7.3					All Other Current	5.4	9.7
53.2	25.3					Total Current	31.1	33.5
63.8	29.2					Long-Term Debt	19.5	27.2
.0	.5					Deferred Taxes	1.3	1.0
7.3	6.6					All Other Non-Current	4.9	2.3
-24.3	38.4					Net Worth	43.1	36.0
100.0	100.0					Total Liabilities & Net Worth	100.0	100.0
						INCOME DATA		
100.0	100.0					Net Sales	100.0	100.0
						Gross Profit		
98.5	96.8					Operating Expenses	92.9	93.0
1.5	3.2					Operating Profit	7.1	7.0
2.0	-1.9					All Other Expenses (net)	1.2	2.1
-.4	5.1					Profit Before Taxes	5.9	4.8
						RATIOS		
4.8	5.0						2.6	3.1
.9	1.6					Current	1.3	1.4
.5	.8						1.0	1.1
4.0	4.1						1.8	2.3
.7	1.6					Quick	.9	1.1
.4	.4						.5	.4
0 UND	0 UND						15 24.4	0 UND
0 UND	21 17.7					Sales/Receivables	35 10.3	29 12.5
13 27.4	54 6.7						60 6.1	63 5.8
						Cost of Sales/Inventory		
						Cost of Sales/Payables		
4.7	4.7						5.4	5.5
NM	11.8					Sales/Working Capital	20.5	10.9
-8.6	-31.7						-233.0	43.5
7.7	12.2						5.6	5.6
(12) 1.9	(16) 1.8					EBIT/Interest	(40) 2.1	(38) 1.9
-.7	-.1						.7	.6
								3.4
						Net Profit + Depr., Dep., Amort./Cur. Mat. L/T/D		(11) 3.0
								1.8
.7	.5						.5	.4
2.4	1.3					Fixed/Worth	1.2	1.2
-1.2	8.9						2.1	3.0
.7	.5						.7	.6
2.8	2.1					Debt/Worth	1.5	1.3
-2.4	9.5						3.4	5.0
	26.1						41.0	32.8
	(14) 4.3					% Profit Before Taxes/Tangible Net Worth	(39) 14.5	(38) 12.5
	-11.8						-.6	-1.0
15.3	6.0						16.1	13.8
.6	1.7					% Profit Before Taxes/Total Assets	5.0	5.8
-7.2	-3.3						-.8	-1.5
18.0	9.1						9.9	10.9
6.2	5.7					Sales/Net Fixed Assets	4.1	4.5
2.4	1.3						2.0	2.0
5.1	3.6						2.3	2.2
2.4	2.1					Sales/Total Assets	1.7	1.5
1.5	1.0						1.1	1.1
	3.3						2.2	2.0
	(15) 6.9					% Depr., Dep., Amort./Sales	(37) 6.4	(36) 5.2
	14.8						7.8	9.1
							3.0	2.9
						% Officers', Directors', Owners' Comp/Sales	(17) 6.6	(13) 9.3
							14.4	19.0
10918M	43379M	71869M	246635M	55168M		Net Sales ($)	700827M	530551M
3706M	17807M	37589M	194464M	51578M		Total Assets ($)	497600M	414651M

M = $ thousand MM = $ million

See Pages 11 through 21 for Explanation of Ratios and Data

Comparative Historical Data — **Current Data Sorted By Sales**

			Type of Statement						
7	8	7	Unqualified		1		1	3	2
6	6	3	Reviewed				1	1	1
7	17	17	Compiled	7	4	1	4		1
5	13	14	Tax Returns	6	3	1	3	1	
13	16	8	Other	3	2	1	1		1
4/1/02-3/31/03	4/1/03-3/31/04	4/1/04-3/31/05		16 (4/1-9/30/04)			33 (10/1/04-3/31/05)		
ALL	ALL	ALL		0-1MM	1-3MM	3-5MM	5-10MM	10-25MM	25MM & OVER
38	60	49	**NUMBER OF STATEMENTS**	16	10	3	10	5	5
%	%	%	**ASSETS**	%	%	%	%	%	%
6.6	7.4	14.7	Cash & Equivalents	20.5	11.9		15.2		
21.5	17.2	13.0	Trade Receivables (net)	9.5	17.7		9.2		
11.8	15.3	13.5	Inventory	2.9	14.7		17.3		
5.0	5.4	4.9	All Other Current	2.5	4.3		4.9		
45.0	45.2	46.1	Total Current	35.4	48.6		46.5		
43.7	44.5	44.3	Fixed Assets (net)	53.5	47.2		40.8		
1.4	4.3	3.2	Intangibles (net)	4.4	2.5		4.1		
9.9	6.0	6.4	All Other Non-Current	6.7	1.7		8.6		
100.0	100.0	100.0	Total	100.0	100.0		100.0		
			LIABILITIES						
14.2	21.0	15.8	Notes Payable-Short Term	21.4	19.5		5.1		
3.6	6.1	6.6	Cur. Mat.-L/T/D	5.9	11.2		9.0		
8.5	8.0	8.0	Trade Payables	3.8	7.9		6.8		
.3	.5	.3	Income Taxes Payable	.0	.9		.3		
8.3	6.5	8.9	All Other Current	4.0	9.8		11.0		
34.8	42.0	39.7	Total Current	35.2	49.4		32.2		
24.7	34.6	34.2	Long-Term Debt	67.7	20.3		21.3		
1.1	.5	.4	Deferred Taxes	.4	.0		1.0		
2.0	1.7	5.0	All Other Non-Current	5.5	12.7		.7		
37.4	21.2	20.7	Net Worth	-8.8	17.6		44.8		
100.0	100.0	100.0	Total Liabilities & Net Worth	100.0	100.0		100.0		
			INCOME DATA						
100.0	100.0	100.0	Net Sales	100.0	100.0		100.0		
			Gross Profit						
94.7	95.4	97.8	Operating Expenses	94.4	100.2		98.4		
5.3	4.6	2.2	Operating Profit	5.6	-.2		1.6		
1.5	1.0	-.3	All Other Expenses (net)	1.4	-1.2		-1.0		
3.8	3.6	2.5	Profit Before Taxes	4.3	1.0		2.6		
			RATIOS						
2.0	2.0	3.2		8.3	1.8		3.8		
1.2	1.4	1.3	Current	1.6	1.0		1.3		
.8	.9	.7		.6	.7		.5		
1.2	1.4	1.7		8.1	1.6		3.2		
.8	.8	.8	Quick	1.5	.6		.3		
.5	.4	.3		.5	.3		.1		
8 47.3	9 41.1	0 UND		0 UND	0 UND		0 UND		
41 8.9	30 12.1	17 21.4	Sales/Receivables	0 UND	19 19.6		4 92.9		
80 4.5	61 6.0	52 7.0		40 9.0	47 7.8		35 10.4		
			Cost of Sales/Inventory						
			Cost of Sales/Payables						
7.1	6.9	4.9		4.3	9.0		4.6		
24.0	20.0	18.2	Sales/Working Capital	16.0	NM		14.1		
-41.4	-38.3	-24.8		-14.8	-20.6		-18.9		
(35) 10.5	(56) 5.5	(43) 7.1		(14) 8.5					
2.3	2.6	2.1	EBIT/Interest	1.4					
1.3	1.1	.5		-1.1					
	(16) 6.8	(12) 6.2	Net Profit + Depr., Dep.,						
	2.6	3.1	Amort./Cur. Mat. L/T/D						
	1.8	1.4							
.5	.5	.5		.8	.8		.3		
1.0	1.8	1.4	Fixed/Worth	5.0	1.7		.8		
2.0	21.2	8.9		-1.7	NM		5.2		
.7	.8	.7		.7	1.0		.5		
1.5	2.5	1.7	Debt/Worth	5.5	2.6		1.4		
2.9	49.0	14.3		-3.1	NM		5.5		
(32) 25.8	(46) 37.7	(40) 22.4	% Profit Before Taxes/Tangible				16.5		
6.8	14.4	5.5	Net Worth				6.3		
2.4	2.7	-1.4					-.4		
10.4	9.5	5.6	% Profit Before Taxes/Total	9.4	14.8		5.8		
4.8	5.1	2.5	Assets	.6	2.1		3.1		
.6	.3	-.6		-6.6	-4.2		.3		
11.1	11.4	12.1		7.0	17.6		16.2		
4.4	4.6	5.7	Sales/Net Fixed Assets	2.8	7.5		8.8		
1.9	2.4	2.2		1.2	5.7		3.7		
2.2	2.7	2.9		2.5	5.1		3.8		
1.6	1.9	1.8	Sales/Total Assets	1.5	3.4		2.5		
1.2	1.3	1.3		.9	2.0		1.5		
(34) 1.9	(50) 2.3	(41) 2.7		(11) 9.1					
4.2	4.9	5.3	% Depr., Dep., Amort./Sales	14.8					
8.2	11.0	12.5		21.0					
(10) 4.6	(18) 2.9	(20) 1.6	% Officers', Directors',						
7.1	5.0	5.9	Owners' Comp/Sales						
13.9	17.0	18.8							
435590M	813749M	427969M	Net Sales ($)	8338M	18234M	10626M	69622M	70397M	250752M
307145M	607512M	305144M	Total Assets ($)	8080M	6037M	7664M	53275M	46933M	183155M

M = $ thousand   MM = $ million
See Pages 11 through 21 for Explanation of Ratios and Data

Current Data Sorted By Assets   **Comparative Historical Data**

0-500M	500M-2MM	2-10MM	10-50MM	50-100MM	100-250MM	Type of Statement	4/1/00-3/31/01 ALL	4/1/01-3/31/02 ALL
1	4	17	22	7	5	Unqualified	34	26
2	4	34	11	1		Reviewed	39	37
2	19	20	7		1	Compiled	41	45
5	11	4	2			Tax Returns	20	13
	7	16	21	1	3	Other	53	51
	103 (4/1-9/30/04)		124 (10/1/04-3/31/05)					
10	45	91	63	9	9	**NUMBER OF STATEMENTS**	187	172
%	%	%	%	%	%	**ASSETS**	%	%
23.5	11.5	7.5	5.5			Cash & Equivalents	8.2	9.1
7.3	26.4	20.0	19.3			Trade Receivables (net)	20.9	20.4
8.1	11.2	19.5	20.5			Inventory	14.0	15.8
2.2	8.7	5.6	8.7			All Other Current	6.9	4.8
41.2	57.9	52.6	54.0			Total Current	50.0	50.2
50.6	34.1	38.3	39.4			Fixed Assets (net)	38.3	39.1
.0	1.5	1.0	1.0			Intangibles (net)	1.7	1.0
8.3	6.5	8.1	5.6			All Other Non-Current	10.0	9.7
100.0	100.0	100.0	100.0			Total	100.0	100.0
						LIABILITIES		
6.2	10.6	17.3	16.0			Notes Payable-Short Term	14.4	12.8
1.6	6.7	4.0	3.7			Cur. Mat.-L/T/D	4.0	4.2
14.7	14.5	15.8	11.7			Trade Payables	12.7	13.6
.0	.2	.2	.2			Income Taxes Payable	.6	.3
5.8	11.8	13.6	8.6			All Other Current	10.9	11.0
28.3	43.8	50.9	40.2			Total Current	42.7	41.8
28.7	22.6	20.2	17.9			Long-Term Debt	22.5	18.2
.4	.3	.5	.8			Deferred Taxes	.9	.6
22.1	7.6	2.6	3.7			All Other Non-Current	4.4	4.6
20.5	25.6	25.9	37.4			Net Worth	29.4	34.8
100.0	100.0	100.0	100.0			Total Liabilities & Net Worth	100.0	100.0
						INCOME DATA		
100.0	100.0	100.0	100.0			Net Sales	100.0	100.0
						Gross Profit		
97.3	95.3	94.4	92.1			Operating Expenses	93.6	93.6
2.7	4.7	5.6	7.9			Operating Profit	6.4	6.4
1.8	.6	1.9	1.4			All Other Expenses (net)	1.2	1.9
.9	4.1	3.7	6.5			Profit Before Taxes	5.2	4.5
						RATIOS		
6.3	3.0	1.5	1.8			Current	1.7	1.7
1.1	1.3	1.2	1.2				1.2	1.2
.5	.8	.9	1.1				.9	1.0
5.0	1.9	1.1	1.0			Quick	1.2	1.2
1.1	.8	.6	.6				.7	.8
.3	.6	.3	.4				.3	.4
0 UND	7 52.4	8 47.9	28 13.2			Sales/Receivables	15 24.9	14 26.9
0 UND	28 13.0	27 13.8	36 10.3				31 11.8	31 11.7
33 11.0	44 8.3	42 8.7	54 6.8				58 6.3	52 7.0
						Cost of Sales/Inventory		
						Cost of Sales/Payables		
9.6	6.5	11.7	8.1			Sales/Working Capital	7.5	8.1
81.0	29.9	32.1	14.6				27.5	20.9
-38.8	-20.0	-42.8	40.1				-55.2	-188.3
	8.1	6.9	10.9			EBIT/Interest	5.4	5.6
	(41) 3.4	(84) 3.0	(57) 3.4				(166) 2.2	(147) 2.6
	1.1	1.1	1.3				1.0	.9
	3.7	6.6	3.5			Net Profit + Depr., Dep., Amort./Cur. Mat. L /T/D	5.6	6.6
	(10) 2.5	(22) 2.5	(16) 1.8				(56) 2.0	(45) 2.2
	.8	1.0	1.2				.9	.7
.6	.3	.6	.5			Fixed/Worth	.5	.5
1.1	1.2	1.1	.9				1.0	1.1
-13.3	8.5	2.7	1.6				2.5	2.1
.3	.6	1.1	.9			Debt/Worth	.9	1.1
1.0	3.5	2.4	2.2				2.0	2.0
-15.4	57.4	8.8	3.8				5.4	4.8
	59.6	42.8	35.3			% Profit Before Taxes/Tangible Net Worth	29.8	31.5
	(36) 14.2	(81) 14.0	(61) 16.7				(165) 10.7	(156) 14.6
	.0	3.5	4.0				.8	1.4
16.0	13.0	9.6	12.5			% Profit Before Taxes/Total Assets	9.6	10.5
.8	5.4	4.0	5.1				3.0	4.0
-12.5	.1	.4	.8				-.2	.0
15.2	37.0	14.9	11.4			Sales/Net Fixed Assets	13.9	12.7
5.5	9.5	7.3	5.0				5.3	5.1
2.8	4.6	2.0	2.2				2.1	2.0
6.1	4.2	3.1	2.7			Sales/Total Assets	2.9	2.9
3.0	2.6	1.9	1.8				1.7	1.7
1.2	1.4	.9	1.2				1.0	.9
	.7	1.0	.9			% Depr., Dep., Amort./Sales	1.1	1.2
	(37) 1.7	(85) 2.1	(59) 3.0				(172) 2.3	(161) 2.8
	5.1	5.0	4.4				6.8	6.1
	.9	.8	.9			% Officers', Directors', Owners' Comp/Sales	1.9	1.7
	(16) 2.6	(20) 1.6	(12) 1.7				(47) 3.9	(41) 3.4
	4.4	4.4	4.2				6.4	4.9
3641M	206791M	1147391M	2491277M	773632M	2346109M	Net Sales ($)	4258723M	3918141M
1957M	53846M	445902M	1246318M	670507M	1333971M	Total Assets ($)	2643617M	2329785M

M = $ thousand   MM = $ million
See Pages 11 through 21 for Explanation of Ratios and Data

Comparative Historical Data   **Current Data Sorted By Sales**

				Type of Statement	1	6		8	9	32
35	50	56		Unqualified	1	6		8	9	32
58	52	52		Reviewed	3	5	5	14	16	9
45	57	49		Compiled	4	11	7	15	7	5
19	24	22		Tax Returns	7	5	3	3	3	1
36	39	48		Other	3	6	3	7	9	20
4/1/02-3/31/03 ALL	4/1/03-3/31/04 ALL	4/1/04-3/31/05 ALL			103 (4/1-9/30/04)			124 (10/1/04-3/31/05)		
					0-1MM	1-3MM	3-5MM	5-10MM	10-25MM	25MM & OVER
193	222	227		**NUMBER OF STATEMENTS**	18	33	18	47	44	67
%	%	%		**ASSETS**	%	%	%	%	%	%
8.3	9.1	8.4		Cash & Equivalents	14.5	8.7	7.1	7.5	8.9	7.2
21.4	19.5	20.4		Trade Receivables (net)	5.8	12.2	27.4	25.2	17.3	25.0
13.8	15.5	17.6		Inventory	7.9	10.7	10.7	18.8	24.3	20.0
6.1	6.4	6.8		All Other Current	1.7	9.3	6.9	5.4	8.6	6.8
49.5	50.5	53.1		Total Current	29.9	40.9	52.1	57.0	59.1	59.0
41.9	39.4	38.4		Fixed Assets (net)	56.4	48.0	41.2	36.3	34.3	32.1
.8	1.1	1.7		Intangibles (net)	3.7	.5	.5	.6	.7	3.5
7.8	9.0	6.8		All Other Non-Current	9.9	10.5	6.2	6.1	5.9	5.4
100.0	100.0	100.0		Total	100.0	100.0	100.0	100.0	100.0	100.0
				LIABILITIES						
15.7	14.4	14.4		Notes Payable-Short Term	4.7	9.6	10.8	16.3	22.3	13.6
4.3	3.2	4.3		Cur. Mat.-L/T/D	8.9	4.0	2.0	6.3	2.9	3.3
13.3	11.9	14.5		Trade Payables	10.4	7.4	11.0	19.9	12.3	17.7
.2	.3	.2		Income Taxes Payable	.0	.1	.8	.0	.0	.3
9.2	12.7	11.0		All Other Current	9.0	8.8	26.5	11.5	8.8	9.6
42.7	42.5	44.4		Total Current	33.0	30.0	51.1	54.1	46.4	44.5
21.4	21.5	20.1		Long-Term Debt	34.5	31.0	19.6	20.0	14.7	14.7
.6	.4	.6		Deferred Taxes	.2	.4	.4	.1	1.1	1.0
4.0	6.1	4.9		All Other Non-Current	19.9	1.3	11.5	3.6	.7	4.4
31.3	29.5	30.0		Net Worth	12.4	37.3	17.5	22.1	37.1	35.5
100.0	100.0	100.0		Total Liabilities & Net Worth	100.0	100.0	100.0	100.0	100.0	100.0
				INCOME DATA						
100.0	100.0	100.0		Net Sales	100.0	100.0	100.0	100.0	100.0	100.0
				Gross Profit						
92.8	93.5	93.7		Operating Expenses	89.6	87.4	90.7	97.7	95.7	94.5
7.2	6.5	6.3		Operating Profit	10.4	12.6	9.3	2.3	4.3	5.5
1.2	1.5	1.4		All Other Expenses (net)	9.4	1.8	1.3	.4	.3	.7
6.0	5.0	4.9		Profit Before Taxes	1.0	10.8	8.0	1.9	4.0	4.8
				RATIOS						
1.9	2.0	1.8		Current	1.7	3.0	2.0	1.5	1.6	1.8
1.2	1.2	1.2			1.0	1.3	1.2	1.0	1.2	1.3
.9	1.0	1.0			.3	.9	.9	.8	1.1	1.1
1.2	1.2	1.1		Quick	1.4	2.0	1.6	1.0	.8	1.0
.7	.7	.7			.7	.9	.8	.7	.5	.7
.4	.3	.4			.2	.3	.4	.3	.3	.5
13 28.4	9 38.5	12 30.0		Sales/Receivables	0 UND	1 555.3	10 37.4	20 18.5	11 31.9	22 16.3
33 11.2	30 12.0	31 11.7			0 UND	15 24.2	38 9.6	33 11.1	31 11.9	34 10.7
53 6.8	52 7.0	48 7.6			33 11.0	55 6.6	108 3.4	44 8.2	42 8.8	51 7.2
				Cost of Sales/Inventory						
				Cost of Sales/Payables						
7.6	6.8	9.4		Sales/Working Capital	9.6	5.6	5.2	10.4	9.4	10.0
20.3	19.5	21.9			UND	13.5	21.3	33.9	23.2	19.7
-63.0	-141.2	-156.8			-1.9	-18.0	-44.2	-27.4	108.9	71.8
8.3	7.5	9.0		EBIT/Interest		7.7	12.1	4.3	12.0	13.3
(181) 3.2	(197) 3.1	(204) 3.2				(28) 3.3	(17) 3.3	(43) 2.3	(43) 4.3	(64) 4.1
1.1	1.0	1.3				-.1	.8	.7	2.0	1.9
4.4	4.3	5.3		Net Profit + Depr., Dep.,					10.6	6.6
(55) 2.5	(55) 2.1	(59) 2.5		Amort./Cur. Mat. L/T/D				(14) 3.3	(25) 2.2	
1.2	1.0	1.0							1.0	1.1
.6	.5	.5		Fixed/Worth	1.2	.4	.5	.6	.6	.5
1.1	1.1	1.1			2.6	1.3	.9	1.5	.9	.9
2.3	2.5	2.4			-7.0	2.5	29.6	8.5	1.4	1.9
.8	.8	.9		Debt/Worth	.9	.5	.7	1.2	.9	1.2
1.8	1.9	2.3			2.9	1.7	3.6	3.1	2.0	2.2
4.0	6.1	5.7			-10.7	5.9	49.2	20.9	4.4	4.4
39.9	28.6	41.2		% Profit Before Taxes/Tangible	40.6	28.9	46.6	26.6	42.9	42.1
(169) 16.2	(193) 15.0	(202) 14.7		Net Worth	(12) 14.8	(29) 13.0	(15) 14.5	(40) 8.9	(43) 18.4	(63) 23.2
4.9	3.0	3.3			.2	-11.0	.2	2.1	3.7	6.2
13.1	10.6	11.0		% Profit Before Taxes/Total	8.6	10.2	17.4	7.9	12.6	14.1
5.3	4.2	4.7		Assets	2.6	5.4	5.6	1.9	5.9	5.5
.4	.1	.6			-5.9	-1.3	-.9	.5	1.3	2.0
12.7	11.8	14.0		Sales/Net Fixed Assets	14.6	8.9	15.4	14.0	15.6	18.1
4.6	5.7	6.6			2.0	4.5	3.7	7.6	7.1	8.8
2.0	2.1	2.3			.4	1.2	2.1	2.0	3.7	3.3
2.8	2.9	3.1		Sales/Total Assets	3.0	2.0	2.8	3.3	3.1	3.9
1.7	1.7	1.9			.7	1.1	1.6	2.4	2.0	2.1
.9	1.0	1.1			.3	.7	1.1	1.2	1.5	1.4
1.3	1.2	1.1		% Depr., Dep., Amort./Sales	2.8	2.0	.8	1.1	1.1	.7
(181) 2.8	(202) 3.1	(204) 2.3			(13) 9.1	(30) 5.4	(17) 3.0	(43) 2.8	(39) 1.7	(62) 1.4
6.5	6.0	5.2			49.1	11.0	5.2	5.5	3.7	3.4
1.5	1.0	.9		% Officers', Directors',					.8	1.1
(48) 3.6	(54) 3.0	(51) 1.9		Owners' Comp/Sales				(10) 1.0	(14) 2.4	
7.0	6.1	4.6							1.4	3.4
6886829M	6118768M	6968841M		Net Sales ($)	8016M	60566M	71014M	336091M	750990M	5742164M
3857984M	3193478M	3752501M		Total Assets ($)	22080M	88461M	50329M	203197M	422761M	2965673M

M = $ thousand   MM = $ million
See Pages 11 through 21 for Explanation of Ratios and Data

Current Data Sorted By Assets   **Comparative Historical Data**

						Type of Statement	4/1/00-3/31/01 ALL	4/1/01-3/31/02 ALL
1	3	5	6	1	1	Unqualified		11
	7	2	1			Reviewed		3
5	10	4				Compiled		6
9	4	5			1	Tax Returns		5
2		2				Other		11
13 (4/1-9/30/04)	**500M-2MM**			**56 (10/1/04-3/31/05)**				
0-500M	500M-2MM	**2-10MM**	**10-50MM**	**50-100MM**	**100-250MM**			**36**
17	24	18	7	2	1	**NUMBER OF STATEMENTS**		
%	%	%	%	%	%	**ASSETS**	%	%
8.6	11.8	11.2				Cash & Equivalents		8.9
12.1	29.3	23.3				Trade Receivables (net)	D	24.5
11.0	9.9	8.1				Inventory	A	18.6
5.5	3.2	2.6				All Other Current	T	1.4
37.2	54.2	45.2				Total Current	A	53.4
41.4	37.3	40.1				Fixed Assets (net)		31.0
.5	3.8	4.5				Intangibles (net)	N	3.3
20.9	4.7	10.2				All Other Non-Current	O	12.3
100.0	100.0	100.0				Total	T	100.0
						LIABILITIES	A	
13.8	10.3	3.6				Notes Payable-Short Term	V	17.0
2.7	2.1	4.6				Cur. Mat.-L/T/D	A	3.1
3.8	11.5	10.4				Trade Payables	I	11.3
.8	.0	.3				Income Taxes Payable	L	.2
34.0	6.0	17.3				All Other Current	A	7.6
55.1	30.0	36.3				Total Current	B	39.2
54.5	32.8	27.1				Long-Term Debt	L	16.2
.0	.3	.4				Deferred Taxes	E	.5
6.0	.2	.5				All Other Non-Current		1.3
−15.6	36.8	35.7				Net Worth		42.8
100.0	100.0	100.0				Total Liabilities & Net Worth		100.0
						INCOME DATA		
100.0	100.0	100.0				Net Sales		100.0
						Gross Profit		
94.6	93.4	92.6				Operating Expenses		96.7
5.4	6.6	7.4				Operating Profit		3.3
.5	1.1	1.9				All Other Expenses (net)		1.8
5.0	5.5	5.4				Profit Before Taxes		1.5
						RATIOS		
1.4	3.1	1.8						2.1
1.2	1.7	1.3				Current		1.5
.3	1.0	.9						1.0
1.3	2.5	1.4						1.5
.6	1.5	1.1				Quick		1.0
.1	.8	.5						.4
0 UND	19 19.0	16 22.7					13 28.2	
0 UND	37 9.8	38 9.5				Sales/Receivables	27 13.4	
13 29.0	61 6.0	57 6.5					44 8.4	
						Cost of Sales/Inventory		
						Cost of Sales/Payables		
23.3	6.0	7.2						7.9
648.2	15.7	19.2				Sales/Working Capital		17.2
−11.1	NM	−662.1						155.9
(13) 10.3	(22) 12.7	(14) 12.2					(30) 12.5	
3.5	3.5	2.2				EBIT/Interest	3.5	
−.3	1.7	.9					1.3	
						Net Profit + Depr., Dep., Amort./Cur. Mat. L /T/D		
.2	.3	.5						.3
1.5	.8	1.1				Fixed/Worth		.6
−3.2	68.7	2.5						1.3
1.5	.8	.8						.5
5.1	1.6	2.0				Debt/Worth		1.1
−25.8	83.4	5.2						4.6
(12) 90.0	(19) 57.5	(16) 36.6				% Profit Before Taxes/Tangible Net Worth	(33) 28.6	
43.2	27.2	13.9					11.4	
5.7	2.9	1.4					1.2	
27.7	22.1	12.1						10.8
7.6	9.3	3.7				% Profit Before Taxes/Total Assets		3.4
−4.5	1.0	.3						.2
104.8	52.1	8.7						31.0
18.0	10.7	4.7				Sales/Net Fixed Assets		9.8
8.0	4.1	2.5						4.1
12.2	4.0	2.4						4.0
4.9	2.6	1.7				Sales/Total Assets		2.3
2.8	1.4	.7						1.6
(11) 1.7	(20) 1.3	2.8				% Depr., Dep., Amort./Sales	(31) .7	
2.3	3.3	5.4					1.8	
4.0	6.4	8.3					4.8	
	(11) 2.0					% Officers', Directors', Owners' Comp/Sales	(11) 3.7	
	4.6						4.8	
	7.3						7.7	
29464M	92316M	142395M	185522M	189710M	246321M	Net Sales ($)		828772M
4436M	28077M	78969M	183259M	158666M	185698M	Total Assets ($)		501172M

M = $ thousand   MM = $ million
See Pages 11 through 21 for Explanation of Ratios and Data

Comparative Historical Data   **Current Data Sorted By Sales**

Type of Statement	4/1/02-3/31/03	4/1/03-3/31/04	4/1/04-3/31/05	0-1MM	1-3MM	3-5MM	5-10MM	10-25MM	25MM & OVER
Unqualified	10	10	14		2		2	6	4
Reviewed	12	3	6		2	1	1	1	1
Compiled	10	14	16	4	5	4	1	2	
Tax Returns	14	15	24	6	8	6	3	1	1
Other	10	10	9		4	2	1	1	
	ALL	ALL	ALL	13 (4/1-9/30/04)			56 (10/1/04-3/31/05)		
NUMBER OF STATEMENTS	56	52	69	10	21	13	8	11	6

	%	%	%	ASSETS	%	%	%	%	%	%
	11.7	8.9	9.8	Cash & Equivalents	8.0	10.1	7.0		16.1	
	18.0	20.8	21.3	Trade Receivables (net)	12.9	20.1	26.0		26.5	
	21.7	18.6	10.0	Inventory	4.9	11.7	10.9		12.1	
	4.5	4.6	3.9	All Other Current	3.9	4.5	.7		3.9	
	55.9	52.9	44.9	Total Current	29.6	46.5	44.7		58.5	
	32.5	38.0	40.0	Fixed Assets (net)	41.8	43.5	36.6		28.5	
	3.0	2.3	3.6	Intangibles (net)	6.4	2.4	.6		5.1	
	8.5	6.8	11.5	All Other Non-Current	22.1	7.6	18.0		7.8	
	100.0	100.0	100.0	Total	100.0	100.0	100.0		100.0	
				LIABILITIES						
	15.4	11.9	9.4	Notes Payable-Short Term	7.9	10.0	16.1		4.9	
	3.4	3.2	3.3	Cur. Mat.-L/T/D	.0	3.6	3.1		4.5	
	15.1	12.7	8.8	Trade Payables	3.5	8.7	9.4		14.6	
	.0	.3	.3	Income Taxes Payable	.0	.7	.1		.3	
	9.1	13.9	16.1	All Other Current	23.2	14.3	17.2		12.2	
	43.0	42.1	38.0	Total Current	34.6	37.3	45.9		36.4	
	24.8	27.3	34.2	Long-Term Debt	44.0	34.2	31.3		9.0	
	.5	.2	.6	Deferred Taxes	.0	.0	.5		.6	
	5.2	2.3	2.0	All Other Non-Current	.0	5.0	.1		.4	
	26.6	28.1	25.2	Net Worth	21.4	23.5	22.3		53.6	
	100.0	100.0	100.0	Total Liabilities & Net Worth	100.0	100.0	100.0		100.0	
				INCOME DATA						
	100.0	100.0	100.0	Net Sales	100.0	100.0	100.0		100.0	
				Gross Profit						
	95.1	95.1	93.7	Operating Expenses	91.1	91.4	97.2		95.0	
	4.9	4.9	6.3	Operating Profit	8.9	8.6	2.8		5.0	
	2.0	1.5	1.2	All Other Expenses (net)	1.3	2.0	1.2		.6	
	2.9	3.5	5.1	Profit Before Taxes	7.6	6.7	1.7		4.4	
				RATIOS						
	3.2	2.7	2.0	Current	14.3	1.5	2.1		1.9	
	1.6	1.4	1.3		1.0	1.2	1.4		1.7	
	1.0	.9	.8		.3	.9	.6		1.1	
	1.5	1.7	1.5	Quick	11.8	1.4	1.7		1.4	
	.8	.9	1.1		.6	1.0	1.2		1.3	
	.3	.2	.4		.3	.5	.2		.5	
	3 106.4	4 82.1	7 55.2	Sales/Receivables	0 UND	0 UND	7 51.0		16 23.0	
	27 13.5	26 14.2	30 12.1		10 37.4	36 10.2	22 16.9		40 9.0	
	47 7.8	63 5.8	57 6.4		51 7.2	61 6.0	45 8.1		92 4.0	
				Cost of Sales/Inventory						
				Cost of Sales/Payables						
	5.3	5.4	6.9	Sales/Working Capital	5.2	10.3	7.9		6.1	
	12.1	16.6	23.4		NM	23.4	37.8		11.2	
	186.7	-25.0	-37.6		-9.5	-78.7	-7.1		25.9	
	7.0	5.5	10.4	EBIT/Interest		12.7	9.3			
	(45) 2.4	(41) 2.5	(58) 3.7			(18) 3.3	(12) 1.8			
	.5	.7	1.3			1.5	.4			
		5.5	6.6	Net Profit + Depr., Dep., Amort./Cur. Mat. L/T/D						
		(10) 2.7	(13) 2.5							
		.3	1.8							
	.4	.5	.4	Fixed/Worth	.9	.4	.3		.3	
	.9	1.1	1.2		5.1	1.2	1.1		.5	
	3.5	6.7	8.6		-3.9	9.9	NM		1.8	
	.7	.8	.8	Debt/Worth	1.2	1.4	.7		.4	
	1.4	2.0	2.0		10.2	2.5	2.1		.9	
	10.0	11.8	10.2		-37.2	16.9	NM		2.4	
	41.0	48.1	50.6	% Profit Before Taxes/Tangible Net Worth		66.2	48.3		26.7	
	(49) 9.4	(43) 8.7	(56) 18.3		(17) 35.7	(10) 17.7			8.7	
	-5.8	.0	4.5		5.2	-7.1			2.9	
	11.2	16.8	14.6	% Profit Before Taxes/Total Assets	36.5	15.9	15.9		11.2	
	4.5	2.6	7.6		3.3	8.5	3.5		4.6	
	-2.0	-.4	.8		-1.3	.9	-3.0		.9	
	20.6	15.9	22.7	Sales/Net Fixed Assets	68.0	26.0	41.6		45.8	
	10.5	6.2	6.8		6.4	5.5	11.4		6.8	
	3.0	2.3	2.8		3.2	1.1	5.9		2.6	
	3.2	3.3	4.1	Sales/Total Assets	3.5	4.5	5.4		4.7	
	2.1	2.0	2.4		2.2	2.3	3.3		1.8	
	1.3	1.1	1.3		.8	.7	1.8		1.5	
	1.4	1.6	1.9	% Depr., Dep., Amort./Sales		1.9	1.7		.5	
	(50) 2.7	(41) 2.9	(58) 4.2			(19) 4.8	(10) 4.1		2.9	
	6.2	9.1	6.9			6.1	7.7		6.0	
	4.0	2.9	2.9	% Officers', Directors', Owners' Comp/Sales						
	(19) 6.2	(18) 5.0	(27) 4.7							
	17.1	9.7	7.9							
	565441M	605596M	885728M	Net Sales ($)	6806M	36362M	49305M	57138M	152856M	583261M
	355361M	394772M	639105M	Total Assets ($)	3807M	43684M	17921M	31133M	107196M	435364M

M = $ thousand   MM = $ million
See Pages 11 through 21 for Explanation of Ratios and Data

MINING

Current Data Sorted By Assets
Comparative Historical Data

0-500M	500M-2MM	2-10MM	10-50MM	50-100MM	100-250MM	Type of Statement	4/1/00-3/31/01 ALL	4/1/01-3/31/02 ALL
	1	7	18	8	16	Unqualified	42	65
2	3	1	5			Reviewed	9	9
1	3	2	3		1	Compiled	12	15
						Tax Returns	5	4
2	14	16	25	9	8	Other	75	56
	20 (4/1-9/30/04)		128 (10/1/04-3/31/05)					
5	21	29	51	17	25	**NUMBER OF STATEMENTS**	143	149
%	%	%	%	%	%	**ASSETS**	%	%
	16.6	14.2	11.1	7.4	3.6	Cash & Equivalents	9.0	9.3
	22.8	12.5	12.9	11.2	12.6	Trade Receivables (net)	13.5	12.1
	3.0	.6	1.9	1.1	1.8	Inventory	1.4	1.7
	2.2	2.9	2.6	2.6	2.0	All Other Current	4.2	4.0
	44.6	30.2	28.5	22.3	20.0	Total Current	28.1	27.2
	44.9	52.7	60.2	72.9	72.9	Fixed Assets (net)	60.6	61.2
	.4	.1	.3	2.1	2.5	Intangibles (net)	.6	1.5
	10.1	17.0	11.0	2.6	4.5	All Other Non-Current	10.8	10.0
	100.0	100.0	100.0	100.0	100.0	Total	100.0	100.0
						LIABILITIES		
	46.7	7.0	4.3	.9	1.6	Notes Payable-Short Term	2.9	4.7
	6.6	2.3	1.5	.2	1.5	Cur. Mat.-L/T/D	3.2	4.2
	10.3	9.1	11.3	9.7	12.4	Trade Payables	9.7	11.3
	.4	.0	.1	.1	.2	Income Taxes Payable	.2	.4
	4.2	25.6	6.7	3.7	6.0	All Other Current	5.4	5.2
	68.2	44.0	23.8	14.5	21.6	Total Current	21.5	25.8
	17.2	17.7	24.6	25.6	25.7	Long-Term Debt	23.9	27.8
	.0	.5	.8	1.4	2.6	Deferred Taxes	1.4	1.6
	.1	5.3	4.5	4.6	6.7	All Other Non-Current	8.7	5.8
	14.5	32.6	46.2	54.0	43.4	Net Worth	44.6	39.0
	100.0	100.0	100.0	100.0	100.0	Total Liabilities & Net Worth	100.0	100.0
						INCOME DATA		
	100.0	100.0	100.0	100.0	100.0	Net Sales	100.0	100.0
	56.2	62.7	56.0	60.3	55.3	Gross Profit	60.0	56.6
	29.7	42.1	35.0	30.0	25.8	Operating Expenses	30.2	32.1
	26.4	20.6	21.0	30.4	29.4	Operating Profit	29.8	24.5
	19.6	6.4	1.8	2.3	6.7	All Other Expenses (net)	1.7	4.6
	6.9	14.2	19.2	28.0	22.8	Profit Before Taxes	28.0	19.9
						RATIOS		
	1.7	1.8	2.8	2.3	1.4	Current	3.0	1.9
	1.0	.9	1.3	1.3	.8		1.3	1.1
	.2	.3	.7	1.0	.7		.8	.6
	1.7	1.4	2.4	2.2	1.2	Quick	2.7	1.5
	.8	.9	1.0	1.1	.8		1.1	.9
	.2	.3	.5	.7	.5		.6	.5
	0 UND	2 163.8	7 51.0	18 20.0	37 9.9	Sales/Receivables	22 16.3	17 20.9
	27 13.3	42 8.6	33 10.9	60 6.1	70 5.2		61 6.0	35 10.5
	53 6.9	81 4.5	72 5.0	79 4.6	94 3.9		86 4.3	60 6.1
	0 UND	0 UND	0 UND	0 UND	0 UND	Cost of Sales/Inventory	0 UND	0 UND
	0 UND	0 UND	0 UND	0 UND	0 UND		0 UND	0 UND
	0 UND	0 UND	4 81.9	7 51.5	8 45.3		1 331.3	3 125.5
	0 UND	0 UND	17 22.0	34 10.7	28 13.0	Cost of Sales/Payables	20 17.8	22 16.8
	9 40.6	37 10.0	73 5.0	112 3.3	142 2.6		72 5.1	67 5.5
	61 6.0	238 1.5	245 1.5	374 1.0	450 .8		208 1.8	208 1.8
	14.8	9.3	6.5	8.3	13.0	Sales/Working Capital	4.4	6.9
	-269.0	-64.1	30.8	19.7	-17.0		14.3	84.7
	-2.7	-1.8	-7.1	-109.8	-5.5		-14.6	-9.6
	13.6	41.6	24.4	23.4	25.9	EBIT/Interest	12.0	14.0
	(17) 4.1	(23) 9.3	(43) 5.7	(15) 6.2	(23) 11.0		(113) 5.7	(123) 4.9
	-2.3	5.5	2.8	4.8	5.7		2.9	2.3
						Net Profit + Depr., Dep., Amort./Cur. Mat. L /T/D	4.5	57.9
							(14) 2.5	(21) 8.0
							1.4	3.1
	.6	.6	.6	1.2	1.2	Fixed/Worth	.9	1.0
	1.6	1.3	1.2	1.4	1.7		1.4	1.6
	-2.4	3.3	3.2	1.9	2.3		2.7	3.3
	.6	.6	.3	.5	.8	Debt/Worth	.4	.6
	3.4	1.2	1.2	.7	1.2		1.4	1.6
	-7.4	6.7	3.7	2.0	2.8		2.9	5.2
	86.0	47.2	40.3	40.7	43.2	% Profit Before Taxes/Tangible Net Worth	55.0	56.5
	(13) 39.7	(24) 27.0	(49) 16.9	(16) 18.9	(24) 36.1		(136) 31.6	(136) 30.6
	6.1	13.0	6.6	15.8	11.2		16.8	12.1
	45.8	20.7	14.6	23.0	21.2	% Profit Before Taxes/Total Assets	25.5	20.0
	5.7	11.4	6.7	11.2	11.1		15.0	10.8
	-8.4	2.2	3.5	4.1	3.0		6.7	4.0
	13.9	4.5	2.2	1.6	1.5	Sales/Net Fixed Assets	2.3	3.4
	3.7	1.6	.7	.7	.7		.9	.9
	2.1	.7	.4	.4	.4		.5	.6
	2.3	1.0	.5	.8	.7	Sales/Total Assets	.9	1.3
	1.9	.7	.5	.6	.5		.6	.6
	1.2	.4	.3	.3	.3		.4	.4
	3.8	4.3	2.0	5.8	2.8	% Depr., Dep., Amort./Sales	5.1	5.6
	(12) 5.7	(25) 11.1	(40) 11.4	(13) 12.8	(10) 6.8		(107) 12.2	(112) 12.7
	11.8	15.2	20.5	24.4	18.1		16.6	18.9
						% Officers', Directors', Owners' Comp/Sales	.7	1.9
							(15) 3.3	(10) 4.4
							7.8	6.9
4143M	48015M	149026M	1731396M	1202478M	3146398M	Net Sales ($)	4772866M	5347906M
1458M	23551M	158978M	1348024M	1196962M	4285323M	Total Assets ($)	6722098M	7143831M

M = $ thousand   MM = $ million
See Pages 11 through 21 for Explanation of Ratios and Data

Comparative Historical Data   Current Data Sorted By Sales

			Type of Statement	0-1MM	1-3MM	3-5MM	5-10MM	10-25MM	25MM & OVER
73	59	49	Unqualified		3	4	5	9	28
11	12	7	Reviewed		1	1	1	2	2
13	16	11	Compiled	1	3	1	3	1	2
5	9	7	Tax Returns	2	4			1	
86	83	74	Other	6	18	5	13	14	18
					20 (4/1-9/30/04)		128 (10/1/04-3/31/05)		
4/1/02-3/31/03 ALL	4/1/03-3/31/04 ALL	4/1/04-3/31/05 ALL							
188	179	148	**NUMBER OF STATEMENTS**	9	29	11	22	27	50
%	%	%	**ASSETS**	%	%	%	%	%	%
7.9	11.2	11.0	Cash & Equivalents		19.7	5.9	11.3	8.8	7.8
11.3	12.6	14.1	Trade Receivables (net)		9.8	14.1	12.3	8.2	18.3
2.1	2.5	1.7	Inventory		1.0	1.1	.3	.5	3.2
3.6	3.6	2.4	All Other Current		1.7	3.3	2.1	5.0	1.8
24.9	29.8	29.2	Total Current		32.1	24.3	25.9	22.4	31.0
64.9	60.8	59.5	Fixed Assets (net)		47.8	64.0	62.0	70.9	60.5
1.6	1.2	1.4	Intangibles (net)		.5	.0	.4	.1	2.0
8.5	8.2	9.9	All Other Non-Current		19.6	11.7	11.7	6.6	6.5
100.0	100.0	100.0	Total		100.0	100.0	100.0	100.0	100.0
			LIABILITIES						
4.1	7.7	11.2	Notes Payable-Short Term		29.8	14.6	4.4	3.9	3.0
3.7	3.0	2.3	Cur. Mat.-L/T/D		5.0	2.8	1.4	1.6	1.3
9.8	12.5	10.8	Trade Payables		12.4	5.0	6.8	9.1	14.5
.3	.3	.1	Income Taxes Payable		.0	.8	.0	.0	.1
8.0	7.4	9.5	All Other Current		18.5	7.8	14.1	4.2	6.3
25.9	30.8	34.0	Total Current		65.7	31.0	26.8	18.8	25.2
31.0	21.7	22.6	Long-Term Debt		22.0	20.9	16.2	26.7	24.4
1.7	1.7	1.0	Deferred Taxes		.2	.5	.8	.6	1.9
4.6	6.1	4.4	All Other Non-Current		3.1	3.2	4.5	5.8	5.0
36.8	39.7	37.9	Net Worth		9.0	44.4	51.8	48.1	43.5
100.0	100.0	100.0	Total Liabilities & Net Worth		100.0	100.0	100.0	100.0	100.0
			INCOME DATA						
100.0	100.0	100.0	Net Sales		100.0	100.0	100.0	100.0	100.0
52.2	55.0	57.3	Gross Profit		64.6	55.0	59.7	63.0	48.3
36.4	30.3	33.6	Operating Expenses		36.3	33.8	38.5	33.4	26.8
15.7	24.7	23.7	Operating Profit		28.3	21.2	21.3	29.6	21.5
5.5	4.1	6.0	All Other Expenses (net)		18.1	1.4	4.6	4.2	2.4
10.2	20.6	17.7	Profit Before Taxes		10.2	19.9	16.7	25.4	19.2
			RATIOS						
2.0	2.0	1.9	Current		1.2	1.8	3.4	2.0	2.1
1.1	1.1	1.0			.5	1.0	1.0	1.3	1.2
.7	.6	.6			.2	.7	.5	.5	.8
1.7	1.8	1.7	Quick		1.0	1.8	2.5	1.8	1.6
.9	.8	.9			.5	.9	1.0	1.0	1.0
.5	.5	.5			.2	.6	.5	.5	.6
18 20.8	12 30.2	7 50.4	Sales/Receivables	0 UND	0 999.8	1 261.9	3 126.4		25 14.5
51 7.1	42 8.8	44 8.3		9 41.2	49 7.4	43 8.4	34 10.8		51 7.1
84 4.4	65 5.6	76 4.8		73 5.0	97 3.8	73 5.0	80 4.6		84 4.3
0 UND	0 UND	0 UND	Cost of Sales/Inventory	0 UND	0 UND	0 UND	0 UND	0 UND	0 UND
0 UND	0 UND	0 UND		0 UND	0 UND	0 UND	0 UND	0 UND	1 523.2
6 65.6	4 81.7	4 92.8		0 UND	0 UND	0 UND	1 535.9	0 999.8	14 26.3
17 21.8	18 20.3	10 37.2	Cost of Sales/Payables	0 UND	5 77.7	7 50.2	47 7.8		21 17.5
78 4.7	60 6.0	65 5.6		24 15.0	43 8.5	58 6.3	127 2.9		71 5.2
213 1.7	206 1.8	266 1.4		247 1.5	259 1.4	136 2.7	336 1.1		213 1.7
7.7	7.1	8.7	Sales/Working Capital		44.9	18.4	7.0	6.5	8.1
35.8	50.2	-999.8			-5.3	-256.0	-271.3	25.9	33.3
-9.5	-7.2	-6.4			-1.7	-16.2	-4.6	-8.8	-17.7
9.6	23.7	23.8	EBIT/Interest		15.1	107.1	34.0	21.2	26.5
(159) 3.1	(144) 6.7	(124) 7.8			(25) 7.6	(10) 6.5	(16) 6.4	(23) 6.2	(45) 10.4
1.0	2.5	3.0			.8	-1.0	3.0	3.2	3.3
22.2	10.9	12.0	Net Profit + Depr., Dep.,						
(21) 2.9	(27) 3.2	(18) 3.4	Amort./Cur. Mat. L/T/D						
1.4	1.3	2.2							
1.0	.8	1.0	Fixed/Worth		.7	.9	.6	1.0	1.0
1.7	1.4	1.5			2.2	1.2	1.2	1.5	1.6
3.4	2.8	3.2			-4.2	2.7	3.4	4.2	2.0
.5	.5	.6	Debt/Worth		.6	.4	.2	.5	.7
1.6	1.4	1.2			5.4	1.3	.9	.8	1.1
4.9	3.9	5.4			-6.5	4.9	3.2	3.7	2.6
30.9	51.6	44.2	% Profit Before Taxes/Tangible		85.5	34.3	33.0	62.5	43.7
(172) 14.6	(164) 26.8	(128) 21.8	Net Worth		(18) 25.5	(10) 17.4	(21) 13.0	(26) 23.7	(47) 34.5
.9	9.2	9.0			15.5	.8	4.8	15.0	10.8
11.6	21.6	20.7	% Profit Before Taxes/Total		27.7	23.0	16.7	16.4	21.2
4.4	9.4	8.9	Assets		10.9	7.0	5.8	11.9	10.9
.0	2.7	3.2			-.5	-3.7	3.5	6.4	3.6
2.1	2.9	3.7	Sales/Net Fixed Assets		4.8	2.6	1.9	1.8	5.6
.7	1.1	1.1			2.8	1.6	.6	.6	1.1
.4	.5	.5			1.0	.3	.3	.4	.6
1.1	1.4	1.6	Sales/Total Assets		2.0	1.9	1.0	.9	1.9
.5	.6	.7			.8	.6	.3	.5	.7
.3	.4	.3			.5	.3	.2	.3	.5
6.5	3.9	3.9	% Depr., Dep., Amort./Sales		4.2		7.0	9.8	.9
(151) 17.2	(138) 10.7	(103) 9.8			(22) 10.3		(17) 11.6	(23) 17.1	(29) 3.8
26.3	19.3	17.2			15.7		18.3	24.6	8.7
1.2	.9	.3	% Officers', Directors',						
(12) 3.5	(18) 2.4	(15) 2.2	Owners' Comp/Sales						
8.3	7.0	5.3							
7001634M	5460435M	6281456M	Net Sales ($)	6346M	49862M	43314M	151653M	444649M	5585632M
8699912M	7410580M	7014296M	Total Assets ($)	10433M	84564M	94370M	422201M	1056846M	5345882M

M = $ thousand   MM = $ million
See Pages 11 through 21 for Explanation of Ratios and Data

Current Data Sorted By Assets | Comparative Historical Data

Type of Statement

	0-500M	500M-2MM	2-10MM	10-50MM	50-100MM	100-250MM	Type of Statement	4/1/00-3/31/01	4/1/01-3/31/02
Unqualified		1	2	8	5	4	Unqualified	8	13
Reviewed		1	6	5			Reviewed	10	7
Compiled	2	1	4	2			Compiled	7	9
Tax Returns	1		3				Tax Returns	3	1
Other	1		4	7	5	2	Other	5	12
	13 (4/1-9/30/04)			51 (10/1/04-3/31/05)				ALL	ALL
NUMBER OF STATEMENTS	4	3	19	22	10	6	NUMBER OF STATEMENTS	33	42

ASSETS

0-500M	500M-2MM	2-10MM	10-50MM	50-100MM	100-250MM		4/1/00-3/31/01 ALL	4/1/01-3/31/02 ALL
%	%	%	%	%	%	ASSETS	%	%
		7.4	11.7	14.0		Cash & Equivalents	10.0	11.1
		14.3	17.7	9.2		Trade Receivables (net)	13.9	21.1
		7.5	4.8	4.8		Inventory	4.6	4.5
		.9	5.3	1.7		All Other Current	8.2	6.2
		30.1	39.5	29.7		Total Current	36.8	42.9
		47.6	44.4	46.6		Fixed Assets (net)	45.7	40.7
		11.3	4.7	6.6		Intangibles (net)	2.3	4.6
		11.1	11.4	17.0		All Other Non-Current	15.2	11.8
		100.0	100.0	100.0		Total	100.0	100.0

LIABILITIES

0-500M	500M-2MM	2-10MM	10-50MM	50-100MM	100-250MM		ALL	ALL
		7.1	6.1	1.6		Notes Payable-Short Term	5.5	5.3
		8.7	12.5	5.1		Cur. Mat.-L/T/D	6.8	7.6
		17.8	13.6	7.0		Trade Payables	13.4	16.2
		.0	.8	.0		Income Taxes Payable	.0	.2
		8.1	8.4	4.4		All Other Current	9.6	7.0
		41.7	41.3	18.1		Total Current	35.3	36.3
		41.3	20.9	23.4		Long-Term Debt	23.1	19.7
		.0	.5	.0		Deferred Taxes	.6	.3
		5.7	8.2	15.6		All Other Non-Current	10.2	5.8
		11.2	29.1	42.9		Net Worth	30.8	37.9
		100.0	100.0	100.0		Total Liabilities & Net Worth	100.0	100.0

INCOME DATA

0-500M	500M-2MM	2-10MM	10-50MM	50-100MM	100-250MM		ALL	ALL
		100.0	100.0	100.0		Net Sales	100.0	100.0
		25.3	24.1	21.5		Gross Profit	23.5	22.5
		21.7	15.5	12.6		Operating Expenses	18.4	15.3
		3.6	8.6	8.9		Operating Profit	5.2	7.2
		1.2	1.2	.5		All Other Expenses (net)	-2.8	.2
		2.4	7.4	8.5		Profit Before Taxes	8.0	7.0

RATIOS

0-500M	500M-2MM	2-10MM	10-50MM	50-100MM	100-250MM		ALL	ALL
		1.2	2.2	3.1		Current	2.1	1.8
		.8	1.2	1.8			1.1	1.2
		.4	.9	.7			.7	.5
		.8	1.4	2.7		Quick	1.3	1.4
		.5	.9	.9			.8	1.0
		.3	.6	.3			.3	.5
		12 29.4	25 14.5	5 71.5		Sales/Receivables	13 27.8	21 17.2
		25 14.7	30 12.0	21 17.0			32 11.5	33 10.9
		33 10.9	48 7.6	35 10.5			43 8.5	48 7.6
		0 UND	1 597.6	0 UND		Cost of Sales/Inventory	0 UND	0 UND
		7 54.5	5 67.9	15 24.7			9 41.5	6 58.4
		34 10.8	18 20.2	39 9.3			31 11.6	17 21.2
		18 19.9	21 17.7	13 27.3		Cost of Sales/Payables	15 24.6	18 20.7
		33 11.1	27 13.6	25 14.4			24 15.5	25 14.6
		66 5.6	38 9.7	36 10.1			50 7.4	46 8.0
		84.9	7.5	2.9		Sales/Working Capital	5.5	6.5
		-20.0	32.1	21.2			48.0	26.7
		-6.4	-26.9	-16.2			-14.3	-10.1
		8.6	19.8			EBIT/Interest	11.8	16.5
		2.9	(21) 6.4				(31) 3.5	(38) 4.0
		-.1	4.3				1.1	1.7
						Net Profit + Depr., Dep., Amort./Cur. Mat. L/T/D		
		1.7	.9	.6		Fixed/Worth	.5	.4
		3.9	1.2	1.3			1.6	1.0
		-2.2	3.0	NM			55.6	4.9
		2.2	1.1	.6		Debt/Worth	.5	.6
		5.6	1.7	1.6			1.6	2.2
		-4.0	5.8	NM			79.2	7.8
		98.3	73.0			% Profit Before Taxes/Tangible Net Worth	37.3	49.3
		(11) 58.0	(19) 30.4				(26) 26.1	(34) 19.7
		10.9	16.3				8.7	4.6
		22.3	21.5	24.2		% Profit Before Taxes/Total Assets	13.5	16.6
		3.5	11.7	12.8			9.0	5.1
		-2.9	4.3	-3.2			1.8	1.3
		9.6	4.9	5.2		Sales/Net Fixed Assets	7.0	10.1
		2.9	3.7	2.5			3.4	4.6
		1.7	2.7	1.4			1.8	1.7
		3.0	2.3	1.8		Sales/Total Assets	2.8	3.0
		1.6	1.7	1.2			1.2	1.3
		.9	1.1	.7			.7	1.0
		1.0	2.2			% Depr., Dep., Amort./Sales	.6	.9
		7.0	5.1				(28) 5.6	(37) 5.1
		8.8	7.9				11.0	9.6
						% Officers', Directors', Owners' Comp/Sales		1.0
							(14)	2.0
								3.2
9432M	42138M	211732M	909953M	1043090M	1015818M	Net Sales ($)	1069295M	2529014M
883M	4468M	99029M	506950M	711556M	1094786M	Total Assets ($)	1001437M	1562710M

M = $ thousand   MM = $ million
See Pages 11 through 21 for Explanation of Ratios and Data

Comparative Historical Data   ## Current Data Sorted By Sales

			Type of Statement	0-1MM	1-3MM	3-5MM	5-10MM	10-25MM	25MM & OVER
10	15	20	Unqualified	1			1	3	15
10	7	12	Reviewed	2	1		1	5	3
4	6	9	Compiled	1	1		4		3
2	5	4	Tax Returns	2	1		1		
14	18	19	Other	1			2	3	13
4/1/02-	4/1/03-	4/1/04-			13 (4/1-9/30/04)			51 (10/1/04-3/31/05)	
3/31/03	3/31/04	3/31/05							
ALL	ALL	ALL							
40	51	64	NUMBER OF STATEMENTS	7	3	9	11	34	

%	%	%	ASSETS	%	%	%	%	%	%
8.7	10.2	11.2	Cash & Equivalents					10.4	11.7
15.5	15.7	15.3	Trade Receivables (net)	D				12.6	17.2
5.1	5.9	5.2	Inventory	A				5.9	6.1
3.9	3.8	4.5	All Other Current	T				5.1	3.4
33.1	35.6	36.1	Total Current	A				33.9	38.3
52.5	48.8	44.5	Fixed Assets (net)					48.5	44.4
3.7	4.6	6.6	Intangibles (net)	N				8.6	6.2
10.7	11.0	12.8	All Other Non-Current	O				9.0	11.2
100.0	100.0	100.0	Total	T				100.0	100.0
			LIABILITIES	A					
4.1	3.9	7.5	Notes Payable-Short Term	V				10.3	3.6
9.6	7.6	8.3	Cur. Mat.-L/T/D	A				8.6	9.5
10.8	13.4	15.1	Trade Payables	I				13.2	14.8
.1	.1	.3	Income Taxes Payable	L				.2	.4
7.1	6.8	10.3	All Other Current	A				4.7	7.2
31.8	31.8	41.4	Total Current	B				37.0	35.6
30.5	21.7	24.8	Long-Term Debt	L				24.3	20.4
1.5	.5	.3	Deferred Taxes	E				.2	.4
3.8	8.5	13.8	All Other Non-Current					10.6	12.4
32.4	37.5	19.6	Net Worth					27.9	31.2
100.0	100.0	100.0	Total Liabilities & Net Worth					100.0	100.0
			INCOME DATA						
100.0	100.0	100.0	Net Sales					100.0	100.0
22.1	21.6	23.5	Gross Profit					19.2	21.2
14.9	19.0	16.8	Operating Expenses					18.2	12.1
7.1	2.6	6.8	Operating Profit					1.0	9.1
.7	.4	.7	All Other Expenses (net)					1.4	.6
6.4	2.2	6.1	Profit Before Taxes					−.4	8.5
			RATIOS						
2.2	2.2	2.0						2.1	2.1
1.2	1.1	1.0	Current					1.0	1.2
.6	.6	.7						.4	.9
1.3	1.6	1.3						1.0	1.4
.8	.7	.7	Quick					.5	.9
.3	.4	.4						.3	.5
26 14.1	25 14.5	15 23.9						15 24.6	19 −18.9
36 10.0	33 11.1	28 13.2	Sales/Receivables					29 12.8	28 12.9
48 7.6	45 8.0	40 9.1						35 10.5	42 8.7
0 UND	0 UND	0 UND						3 141.9	1 451.7
11 33.5	8 47.9	8 48.5	Cost of Sales/Inventory					11 33.4	10 36.1
31 11.7	29 12.8	27 13.4						46 7.9	24 15.4
14 26.0	20 17.9	19 19.2						28 12.9	17 20.9
25 14.4	32 11.4	28 13.2	Cost of Sales/Payables					37 9.9	24 15.1
46 7.9	49 7.4	42 8.6						57 6.4	31 11.8
5.7	8.0	9.8						3.9	10.1
31.9	36.9	235.9	Sales/Working Capital					−105.5	38.2
−13.4	−8.7	−15.4						−8.3	−354.7
24.8	12.4	17.3						13.3	51.2
(36) 3.8	(48) 3.6	(58) 5.3	EBIT/Interest					5.4	(31) 8.6
1.7	.6	.5						−6.6	3.9
2.3		3.5	Net Profit + Depr., Dep.,						
(10) 1.4		(13) 1.7	Amort./Cur. Mat. L/T/D						
.4		1.2							
.8	.7	.8						1.0	.7
1.6	1.5	1.8	Fixed/Worth					1.8	1.3
25.2	4.4	44.5						3.9	4.0
.5	.6	1.2						1.4	.7
1.9	2.2	2.2	Debt/Worth					1.9	1.8
36.5	7.4	NM						6.8	48.5
41.2	31.1	82.9	% Profit Before Taxes/Tangible					62.4	82.3
(32) 15.6	(44) 12.1	(48) 34.5	Net Worth					(10) 34.8	(28) 30.2
.8	.1	15.5						−21.2	17.0
16.6	10.0	23.6	% Profit Before Taxes/Total					15.0	24.6
8.4	5.8	9.4	Assets					8.1	12.5
1.0	−1.5	−.4						−8.2	5.5
6.1	4.9	7.9						3.8	10.2
2.3	2.4	3.5	Sales/Net Fixed Assets					3.2	3.8
1.1	1.4	1.9						2.8	1.8
1.9	2.2	2.9						1.9	3.2
1.1	1.3	1.5	Sales/Total Assets					1.4	1.5
.8	.8	1.0						1.2	1.0
3.8	3.7	1.4						3.2	1.4
(35) 6.8	(47) 7.5	(57) 5.2	% Depr., Dep., Amort./Sales					5.4	(28) 4.6
12.0	10.1	8.1						11.1	7.7
	1.6	2.7	% Officers', Directors',						
	(10) 2.1	(11) 5.2	Owners' Comp/Sales						
	5.4	10.0							
1865928M	2047972M	3232163M	Net Sales ($)	14962M	10809M	67690M	197211M	2941491M	
1707096M	1832869M	2417672M	Total Assets ($)	13507M	6707M	54194M	174473M	2168791M	

M = $ thousand   MM = $ million
See Pages 11 through 21 for Explanation of Ratios and Data

Current Data Sorted By Assets   **Comparative Historical Data**

Type of Statement									
						Unqualified		17	16
						Reviewed		4	8
						Compiled		9	12
						Tax Returns			1
						Other		13	20

	1	2	3/1/6/1/7	6/5/3/1/7	5/1	2/1/1			
		9 (4/1-9/30/04)		**44 (10/1/04-3/31/05)**				4/1/00-3/31/01	4/1/01-3/31/02
	0-500M	500M-2MM	2-10MM	10-50MM	50-100MM	100-250MM		ALL	ALL
NUMBER OF STATEMENTS	1	4	18	21	7	2		43	57
	%	%	%	%	%	%	**ASSETS**	%	%
			12.0	14.4			Cash & Equivalents	8.7	10.0
			12.8	13.4			Trade Receivables (net)	12.4	12.3
			8.8	11.0			Inventory	11.3	10.5
			5.4	3.1			All Other Current	1.8	3.7
			39.0	42.0			Total Current	34.3	36.5
			50.6	48.0			Fixed Assets (net)	52.9	51.7
			2.4	.7			Intangibles (net)	3.3	3.3
			8.0	9.3			All Other Non-Current	9.5	8.4
			100.0	100.0			Total	100.0	100.0
							LIABILITIES		
			2.6	4.9			Notes Payable-Short Term	5.3	3.1
			6.0	3.5			Cur. Mat.-L/T/D	4.0	5.6
			8.2	5.6			Trade Payables	4.8	6.5
			.1	.5			Income Taxes Payable	.4	.3
			5.6	4.2			All Other Current	5.0	3.3
			22.5	18.6			Total Current	19.5	18.7
			32.2	18.7			Long-Term Debt	18.3	23.4
			.1	1.2			Deferred Taxes	.8	.9
			.2	2.8			All Other Non-Current	4.2	4.4
			45.0	58.6			Net Worth	57.3	52.6
			100.0	100.0			Total Liabilities & Net Worth	100.0	100.0
							INCOME DATA		
			100.0	100.0			Net Sales	100.0	100.0
			40.5	32.0			Gross Profit	30.6	32.6
			29.2	17.0			Operating Expenses	19.5	21.9
			11.3	15.0			Operating Profit	11.1	10.7
			.5	.8			All Other Expenses (net)	1.0	1.5
			10.8	14.2			Profit Before Taxes	10.1	9.2
							RATIOS		
			2.5	4.2				3.9	5.1
			1.7	2.0			Current	2.2	2.1
			1.1	1.4				1.1	1.4
			1.9	2.8				2.8	2.4
			.7	1.3			Quick	1.2	1.2
			.3	.7				.5	.6
		15	24.0	34	10.9		Sales/Receivables	32	11.5	30	12.1
		33	11.0	51	7.2			41	8.8	38	9.5
		45	8.2	74	4.9			57	6.4	48	7.6

	2-10MM	10-50MM		Historical ALL	Historical ALL
Sales/Receivables	15 24.0 / 33 11.0 / 45 8.2	34 10.9 / 51 7.2 / 74 4.9		32 11.5 / 41 8.8 / 57 6.4	30 12.1 / 38 9.5 / 48 7.6
Cost of Sales/Inventory	0 UND / 24 15.4 / 66 5.5	23 16.0 / 38 9.7 / 101 3.6		26 13.8 / 54 6.7 / 95 3.8	23 15.9 / 52 7.1 / 76 4.8
Cost of Sales/Payables	15 24.1 / 29 12.6 / 57 6.4	20 18.1 / 30 12.2 / 43 8.4		12 30.6 / 24 15.2 / 34 10.7	17 21.3 / 24 15.5 / 44 8.3
Sales/Working Capital	4.0 / 8.1 / 138.7	2.4 / 4.5 / 15.7		4.1 / 6.3 / 37.2	3.5 / 6.3 / 13.7
EBIT/Interest	14.0 / (15) 3.0 / 1.1	31.4 / (17) 10.4 / 2.4		13.4 / (36) 3.6 / .9	15.3 / (54) 3.7 / 1.4
Net Profit + Depr., Dep., Amort./Cur. Mat. L/T/D				15.9 / (12) 5.4 / 1.5	6.0 / (14) 2.4 / 1.5
Fixed/Worth	.5 / 1.4 / 2.2	.5 / .8 / 1.5		.6 / .8 / 2.0	.6 / 1.1 / 2.1
Debt/Worth	.6 / 1.5 / 2.3	.3 / .6 / 1.5		.3 / .5 / 2.5	.3 / .7 / 2.8
% Profit Before Taxes/Tangible Net Worth	27.6 / (16) 10.1 / 1.0	32.8 / (20) 19.1 / 6.9		26.3 / (41) 15.2 / 3.8	28.9 / (54) 14.3 / 5.5
% Profit Before Taxes/Total Assets	13.3 / 4.7 / -.7	17.1 / 11.2 / 2.9		16.7 / 8.2 / 1.2	12.4 / 6.8 / 1.9
Sales/Net Fixed Assets	4.2 / 2.3 / 1.1	3.1 / 2.2 / 1.3		3.2 / 1.9 / 1.2	3.3 / 2.2 / 1.2
Sales/Total Assets	2.0 / 1.0 / .6	1.2 / .9 / .7		1.3 / .9 / .7	1.4 / 1.0 / .7
% Depr., Dep., Amort./Sales	4.1 / 7.1 / 14.5	3.7 / (19) 6.4 / 8.9		5.1 / (39) 8.1 / 11.7	5.0 / (53) 7.7 / 11.8
% Officers', Directors', Owners' Comp/Sales					

	0-500M	500M-2MM	2-10MM	10-50MM	50-100MM	100-250MM		ALL	ALL
Net Sales ($)	3276M	9088M	95876M	354866M	326209M	152181M		1171572M	1173097M
Total Assets ($)	427M	4460M	84277M	385793M	520397M	219774M		1321897M	1445457M

M = $ thousand   MM = $ million
See Pages 11 through 21 for Explanation of Ratios and Data

Comparative Historical Data   ### Current Data Sorted By Sales

			Type of Statement						
10	16	16	Unqualified				2	6	7
11	9	7	Reviewed		1			5	
10	17	12	Compiled		2	2	5	2	1
6	6	2	Tax Returns		2		1		
16	17	16	Other	1	1		2	7	1
					5				
4/1/02-	4/1/03-	4/1/04-			9 (4/1-9/30/04)		44 (10/1/04-3/31/05)		
3/31/03	3/31/04	3/31/05		0-1MM	1-3MM	3-5MM	5-10MM	10-25MM	25MM & OVER
ALL	ALL	ALL							
53	65	53	NUMBER OF STATEMENTS	1	8	5	10	20	9
%	%	%		%	%	%	%	%	%
			ASSETS						
10.6	11.8	11.5	Cash & Equivalents				5.0	17.9	
13.3	13.5	13.7	Trade Receivables (net)				15.2	13.4	
11.0	10.4	9.1	Inventory				9.3	9.9	
2.8	3.4	4.3	All Other Current				5.9	4.6	
37.8	39.2	38.6	Total Current				35.4	45.8	
49.3	49.6	49.3	Fixed Assets (net)				56.0	42.9	
1.9	3.7	3.0	Intangibles (net)				.2	.8	
11.0	7.6	9.1	All Other Non-Current				8.5	10.5	
100.0	100.0	100.0	Total				100.0	100.0	
			LIABILITIES						
5.9	5.7	3.8	Notes Payable-Short Term				2.6	5.4	
5.8	6.4	4.5	Cur. Mat.-L/T/D				7.6	2.4	
7.7	7.8	7.9	Trade Payables				9.8	6.2	
.1	.3	.2	Income Taxes Payable				.5	.2	
6.4	4.7	5.3	All Other Current				3.4	6.1	
25.9	24.9	21.6	Total Current				24.0	20.4	
21.0	20.2	27.2	Long-Term Debt				31.4	12.5	
.4	.5	.8	Deferred Taxes				.8	1.0	
3.6	8.2	1.8	All Other Non-Current				.4	3.1	
49.1	46.3	48.5	Net Worth				43.3	63.0	
100.0	100.0	100.0	Total Liabilities & Net Worth				100.0	100.0	
			INCOME DATA						
100.0	100.0	100.0	Net Sales				100.0	100.0	
29.5	29.5	34.2	Gross Profit				38.6	28.7	
19.8	19.4	22.4	Operating Expenses				30.8	16.2	
9.8	10.1	11.8	Operating Profit				7.8	12.5	
1.2	1.2	1.0	All Other Expenses (net)				2.4	−.4	
8.5	8.9	10.7	Profit Before Taxes				5.4	12.9	
			RATIOS						
3.2	2.7	2.7					2.3	4.2	
1.6	1.9	1.6	Current				1.5	2.0	
1.0	1.0	1.2					1.0	1.4	
2.0	2.1	2.0					1.2	2.9	
.8	1.0	1.1	Quick				.7	1.3	
.5	.5	.5					.3	1.1	
30	12.2	32	11.4	30	12.1	Sales/Receivables	22	16.8	33	11.0
40	9.1	43	8.4	38	9.5		42	8.8	44	8.3
51	7.2	55	6.6	60	6.0		68	5.4	58	6.3
11	33.6	18	20.1	12	29.7	Cost of Sales/Inventory	12	30.1	21	17.3
52	7.0	43	8.6	33	11.1		32	11.3	36	10.1
78	4.7	71	5.1	73	5.0		75	4.9	91	4.0
15	23.7	18	19.9	20	18.7	Cost of Sales/Payables	22	16.5	20	18.7
26	13.8	29	12.6	30	12.2		36	10.2	30	12.3
39	9.4	51	7.2	48	7.6		60	6.0	43	8.4
4.0	3.7	3.1	Sales/Working Capital				5.1	2.0	
8.1	6.9	6.9					16.8	5.0	
465.9	−304.9	44.1					NM	13.9	
9.9	11.4	21.0	EBIT/Interest					31.4	
(46) 3.3	(58) 3.9	(46) 4.7					(17)	11.9	
1.9	2.0	1.7						1.7	
5.7	3.4	7.1	Net Profit + Depr., Dep.,						
(12) 3.1	(18) 1.8	(11) 2.9	Amort./Cur. Mat. L/T/D						
1.8	1.4	1.3							
.5	.6	.5	Fixed/Worth				.9	.4	
1.2	1.2	1.2					1.7	.6	
2.8	2.5	2.0					2.0	1.1	
.2	.4	.3	Debt/Worth				.7	.2	
.9	1.4	.9					2.0	.5	
4.5	3.2	2.4					2.2	1.0	
41.6	31.8	29.1	% Profit Before Taxes/Tangible				21.9	29.1	
(48) 13.3	(59) 16.6	(46) 16.1	Net Worth				3.4	(19) 16.7	
4.0	8.7	3.9					−2.2	6.2	
12.0	10.9	13.0	% Profit Before Taxes/Total				8.4	17.9	
6.4	6.9	7.5	Assets				2.4	11.1	
2.4	3.2	1.3					−.7	1.7	
3.9	3.2	3.2	Sales/Net Fixed Assets				4.0	3.3	
2.3	2.1	2.2					2.1	2.5	
1.5	1.3	1.2					1.0	1.2	
1.4	1.3	1.3	Sales/Total Assets				2.3	1.3	
1.0	.9	.9					1.2	1.0	
.8	.7	.6					.6	.7	
5.0	4.9	4.1	% Depr., Dep., Amort./Sales				3.4	2.8	
(48) 7.7	(56) 7.8	(49) 7.0					5.4	(17) 6.4	
10.8	11.9	13.6					12.6	8.8	
1.3	1.5		% Officers', Directors',						
(13) 2.7	(10) 2.9		Owners' Comp/Sales						
7.2	4.8								
855842M	1205958M	941496M	Net Sales ($)	613M	17150M	18915M	69812M	317208M	517798M
1011095M	1611924M	1215128M	Total Assets ($)	2136M	24806M	16064M	72309M	412649M	687164M

© RMA 2005

M = $ thousand   MM = $ million
See Pages 11 through 21 for Explanation of Ratios and Data

Current Data Sorted By Assets   **Comparative Historical Data**

0-500M	500M-2MM	2-10MM	10-50MM	50-100MM	100-250MM	Type of Statement	4/1/00-3/31/01 ALL	4/1/01-3/31/02 ALL
		2	3	1	3	Unqualified		6
		3				Reviewed		2
	3	1				Compiled		8
1	1	6	2			Tax Returns		1
						Other		1
	3 (4/1-9/30/04)		23 (10/1/04-3/31/05)					
1	4	12	5	1	3	**NUMBER OF STATEMENTS**		18
%	%	%	%	%	%		%	%
						ASSETS		
		8.1				Cash & Equivalents		10.8
		14.5				Trade Receivables (net)		14.6
		11.8				Inventory	D A T A	8.5
		3.6				All Other Current		8.6
		38.0				Total Current		42.5
		51.9				Fixed Assets (net)		43.0
		.8				Intangibles (net)	N O T	5.6
		9.3				All Other Non-Current		9.0
		100.0				Total		100.0
						LIABILITIES	A V A	
		7.1				Notes Payable-Short Term		4.2
		7.8				Cur. Mat.-L/T/D		4.3
		7.5				Trade Payables	I L	6.1
		.0				Income Taxes Payable		.2
		3.0				All Other Current		5.4
		25.3				Total Current	B	20.1
		32.0				Long-Term Debt	L	14.2
		.6				Deferred Taxes	E	1.8
		5.1				All Other Non-Current		2.6
		36.9				Net Worth		61.3
		100.0				Total Liabilities & Net Worth		100.0
						INCOME DATA		
		100.0				Net Sales		100.0
		24.0				Gross Profit		32.7
		18.2				Operating Expenses		20.0
		5.8				Operating Profit		12.7
		1.9				All Other Expenses (net)		.5
		4.0				Profit Before Taxes		12.2
						RATIOS		
		2.5						4.4
		1.3				Current		2.3
		.9						1.1
		1.7						2.3
		.7				Quick		1.1
		.5						.7
		32 11.3						34 10.7
		37 10.0				Sales/Receivables		48 7.6
		43 8.5						61 6.0
		0 UND						20 18.3
		20 18.3				Cost of Sales/Inventory		38 9.5
		29 12.6						64 5.7
		9 39.1						11 33.3
		18 19.7				Cost of Sales/Payables		28 12.9
		64 5.7						38 9.7
		5.5						2.7
		19.9				Sales/Working Capital		6.0
		NM						28.5
		11.3						14.3
		(10) 5.0				EBIT/Interest		(17) 7.0
		2.0						2.7
						Net Profit + Depr., Dep., Amort./Cur. Mat. L /T/D		
		.7						.5
		1.3				Fixed/Worth		.7
		2.9						1.8
		1.0						.4
		1.5				Debt/Worth		.6
		3.3						1.8
		29.8						35.7
		(11) 14.2				% Profit Before Taxes/Tangible Net Worth		16.0
		7.2						9.0
		11.5						18.1
		5.8				% Profit Before Taxes/Total Assets		9.3
		.8						5.9
		7.6						4.6
		2.1				Sales/Net Fixed Assets		2.8
		1.4						1.5
		2.1						1.4
		1.1				Sales/Total Assets		1.0
		.6						.8
		2.9						.0
		4.1				% Depr., Dep., Amort./Sales		(17) 4.6
		15.4						10.2
						% Officers', Directors', Owners' Comp/Sales		
578M	5383M	97143M	101425M	48141M	297473M	Net Sales ($)		362265M
175M	3163M	66717M	79871M	73612M	328053M	Total Assets ($)		427447M

© RMA 2005

M = $ thousand   MM = $ million
See Pages 11 through 21 for Explanation of Ratios and Data

Comparative Historical Data | Current Data Sorted By Sales

			Type of Statement						
15	8	9	Unqualified			1	1	3	4
7	3	3	Reviewed				2	1	
2	10	1	Compiled			1			
1	1	4	Tax Returns	2	2				
11	7	9	Other	1	1	1	3	1	2
4/1/02-3/31/03 ALL	4/1/03-3/31/04 ALL	4/1/04-3/31/05 ALL		0-1MM	1-3MM	3 (4/1-9/30/04) 3-5MM	5-10MM	23 (10/1/04-3/31/05) 10-25MM	25MM & OVER
36	29	26	NUMBER OF STATEMENTS	3	3	3	6	5	6
%	%	%	ASSETS	%	%	%	%	%	%
9.8	9.7	7.8	Cash & Equivalents						
14.9	10.4	15.0	Trade Receivables (net)						
15.8	12.7	14.8	Inventory						
4.7	11.4	2.7	All Other Current						
45.2	44.1	40.4	Total Current						
44.8	43.4	49.6	Fixed Assets (net)						
.9	3.0	2.6	Intangibles (net)						
9.2	9.5	7.4	All Other Non-Current						
100.0	100.0	100.0	Total						
			LIABILITIES						
5.6	8.4	6.2	Notes Payable-Short Term						
5.3	3.7	7.6	Cur. Mat.-L/T/D						
8.9	4.9	6.8	Trade Payables						
.1	.1	.1	Income Taxes Payable						
9.6	5.1	4.0	All Other Current						
29.6	22.1	24.8	Total Current						
21.0	23.9	30.9	Long-Term Debt						
.5	.6	1.5	Deferred Taxes						
4.3	6.5	10.3	All Other Non-Current						
44.6	46.9	32.5	Net Worth						
100.0	100.0	100.0	Total Liabilities & Net Worth						
			INCOME DATA						
100.0	100.0	100.0	Net Sales						
29.3	28.2	28.3	Gross Profit						
22.3	22.9	19.4	Operating Expenses						
7.1	5.3	8.9	Operating Profit						
1.7	1.6	2.1	All Other Expenses (net)						
5.3	3.7	6.7	Profit Before Taxes						
			RATIOS						
3.0	5.7	3.0	Current						
1.8	1.7	1.6							
1.2	1.1	.9							
1.8	2.1	1.6	Quick						
1.0	.8	.7							
.4	.4	.4							
28 13.0	25 14.6	14 25.5	Sales/Receivables						
37 9.7	44 8.2	38 9.7							
58 6.3	58 6.3	59 6.2							
16 23.0	17 21.6	0 UND	Cost of Sales/Inventory						
44 8.3	52 7.0	26 13.8							
103 3.5	86 4.2	61 6.0							
14 26.3	11 32.4	14 26.7	Cost of Sales/Payables						
24 15.3	18 19.7	18 19.9							
51 7.2	32 11.4	42 8.7							
3.4	1.9	5.2	Sales/Working Capital						
6.6	6.0	11.7							
28.6	44.8	-27.8							
7.7	9.2	12.3	EBIT/Interest						
(31) 3.2	(25) 2.4	(21) 3.1							
1.4	.1	1.6							
3.2			Net Profit + Depr., Dep., Amort./Cur. Mat. L/T/D						
(15) 2.4									
1.8									
.6	.4	.7	Fixed/Worth						
.9	.8	1.6							
1.9	1.8	4.6							
.6	.3	.9	Debt/Worth						
.9	.9	1.9							
2.0	3.1	11.1							
30.3	21.5	39.3	% Profit Before Taxes/Tangible Net Worth						
(33) 10.6	(26) 10.5	(22) 19.5							
2.2	1.5	10.6							
11.5	11.1	16.1	% Profit Before Taxes/Total Assets						
4.3	4.5	7.2							
.1	-1.6	.7							
5.3	5.1	6.3	Sales/Net Fixed Assets						
2.5	2.3	2.8							
1.7	1.6	1.4							
1.6	1.5	2.1	Sales/Total Assets						
1.2	.9	1.2							
.8	.7	.8							
4.5	4.1	3.3	% Depr., Dep., Amort./Sales						
(33) 7.1	(23) 6.3	(25) 4.8							
11.9	10.4	9.3							
1.7			% Officers', Directors', Owners' Comp/Sales						
(10) 2.7									
6.0									
623186M	609696M	550143M	Net Sales ($)	2395M	4997M	11978M	41288M	86096M	403389M
643916M	809489M	551591M	Total Assets ($)	1671M	4284M	14595M	34990M	52665M	443386M

M = $ thousand   MM = $ million
See Pages 11 through 21 for Explanation of Ratios and Data

Current Data Sorted By Assets   Comparative Historical Data

Type of Statement

0-500M	500M-2MM	2-10MM	10-50MM	50-100MM	100-250MM	Type of Statement	4/1/00-3/31/01	4/1/01-3/31/02
2	6	8	16	5	4	Unqualified	18	14
		23	9	2		Reviewed	20	20
1	14	15	5	1		Compiled	19	24
4	10	1				Tax Returns	11	10
1	9	15	6	2	2	Other	25	39
24 (4/1-9/30/04)			137 (10/1/04-3/31/05)				ALL	ALL
8	39	62	36	10	6	NUMBER OF STATEMENTS	93	107

Data (%)

0-500M	500M-2MM	2-10MM	10-50MM	50-100MM	100-250MM		4/1/00-3/31/01	4/1/01-3/31/02
%	%	%	%	%	%	**ASSETS**	%	%
	10.2	8.5	12.5	3.8		Cash & Equivalents	9.0	9.7
	18.3	18.5	18.9	15.9		Trade Receivables (net)	16.2	16.3
	6.7	7.6	9.4	7.6		Inventory	6.9	8.7
	1.5	3.5	2.7	4.4		All Other Current	3.5	2.1
	36.7	38.1	43.5	31.8		Total Current	35.7	36.8
	54.1	52.3	46.1	45.1		Fixed Assets (net)	53.9	54.2
	1.9	2.0	1.8	1.8		Intangibles (net)	2.1	2.0
	7.3	7.6	8.5	21.3		All Other Non-Current	8.3	6.9
	100.0	100.0	100.0	100.0		Total	100.0	100.0
						LIABILITIES		
	6.2	5.3	2.8	7.9		Notes Payable-Short Term	7.1	6.0
	7.0	7.2	3.4	4.3		Cur. Mat.-L/T/D	8.1	7.1
	8.4	9.3	8.8	6.2		Trade Payables	7.4	7.0
	.0	.3	.3	.1		Income Taxes Payable	.1	.2
	7.9	3.9	7.2	5.5		All Other Current	4.9	3.6
	29.5	26.0	22.6	24.0		Total Current	27.7	23.9
	42.8	30.5	12.7	16.0		Long-Term Debt	28.6	30.5
	.4	.6	.8	3.4		Deferred Taxes	1.0	.9
	3.6	3.5	.9	3.0		All Other Non-Current	5.4	6.6
	23.6	39.4	63.0	53.6		Net Worth	37.3	38.1
	100.0	100.0	100.0	100.0		Total Liabilities & Net Worth	100.0	100.0
						INCOME DATA		
	100.0	100.0	100.0	100.0		Net Sales	100.0	100.0
	47.6	32.1	24.4	20.7		Gross Profit	32.1	38.8
	39.8	22.7	16.3	16.6		Operating Expenses	23.6	30.0
	7.7	9.4	8.1	4.1		Operating Profit	8.5	8.9
	2.9	1.7	-.6	-2.4		All Other Expenses (net)	1.8	3.5
	4.8	7.7	8.7	6.5		Profit Before Taxes	6.6	5.4
						RATIOS		
	3.1	2.2	3.9	1.9			2.6	2.5
	1.8	1.4	2.2	1.1		Current	1.3	1.6
	.9	1.0	1.4	.9			.8	.8
	2.5	1.7	2.9	1.3			1.9	1.9
	1.5	1.0	1.5	.7		Quick	.9	1.0
	.9	.4	.8	.5			.4	.5
21	17.1 (28)	13.2 (33)	11.2 (36)	10.1			25 14.4 (26)	13.8
35	10.4 (39)	9.4 (50)	7.3 (46)	7.9		Sales/Receivables	40 9.0 (37)	9.7
63	5.8 (54)	6.8 (71)	5.1 (66)	5.5			59 6.1 (60)	6.1
0	UND (1)	264.3 (5)	80.2 (8)	43.1			1 309.9 (0)	999.8
6	64.5 (21)	17.2 (31)	11.7 (19)	19.6		Cost of Sales/Inventory	16 22.8 (32)	11.5
69	5.3 (46)	8.0 (61)	6.0 (48)	7.6			61 6.0 (69)	5.3
3	140.5 (16)	22.3 (16)	22.2 (20)	18.7			14 25.8 (13)	27.6
20	18.6 (28)	13.0 (27)	13.6 (30)	12.3		Cost of Sales/Payables	24 15.1 (23)	15.7
57	6.4 (40)	9.1 (41)	8.9 (32)	11.5			46 7.9 (41)	8.9
	5.9	5.8	3.8	7.2			4.8	4.3
	13.5	14.6	6.1	NM		Sales/Working Capital	12.7	9.8
	-33.3	-223.2	13.6	-41.5			-23.5	-33.7
	7.0	10.1	31.0	29.2			5.5	5.6
	(35) 2.7	(56) 3.7	(28) 12.7	4.3		EBIT/Interest	(83) 2.6	(99) 2.5
	.8	2.0	1.8	3.1			1.1	1.2
		2.5	13.2				4.2	4.0
		(18) 1.6	(11) 4.9			Net Profit + Depr., Dep., Amort./Cur. Mat. L/T/D	(20) 1.5	(18) 1.9
		1.3	3.0				.7	1.0
	1.1	.9	.5	.5			.8	.7
	1.9	1.5	.7	1.1		Fixed/Worth	1.5	1.4
	86.9	2.6	1.0	1.4			3.6	3.9
	.9	.8	.2	.3			.6	.6
	2.3	1.7	.6	1.3		Debt/Worth	1.7	1.5
	119.3	3.8	1.3	1.9			4.3	6.3
	39.1	40.0	25.3	19.9			27.5	31.4
	(30) 15.1	(58) 17.2	13.8	12.0		% Profit Before Taxes/Tangible Net Worth	(82) 13.8	(91) 14.9
	-5.6	6.7	2.8	6.6			1.4	4.8
	12.7	12.3	16.8	7.8			13.0	13.5
	4.2	5.9	6.5	5.7		% Profit Before Taxes/Total Assets	5.9	4.9
	-2.0	1.7	1.1	4.0			.3	1.0
	3.8	5.4	5.4	3.5			3.9	4.6
	2.9	2.3	2.8	2.2		Sales/Net Fixed Assets	1.9	2.1
	1.6	1.3	1.6	1.6			1.2	1.3
	2.1	2.1	2.0	1.4			1.6	1.7
	1.3	1.3	1.2	1.0		Sales/Total Assets	1.0	1.1
	.9	.8	.7	.7			.7	.7
	6.8	5.9	3.9				5.6	5.3
	(36) 9.5	(60) 9.1	(33) 7.5			% Depr., Dep., Amort./Sales	(84) 9.2	(96) 8.8
	16.4	12.2	12.5				13.0	13.1
	1.8	1.3					2.9	1.6
	(13) 3.1	(16) 2.4				% Officers', Directors', Owners' Comp/Sales	(29) 4.4	(41) 3.6
	7.8	3.9					9.2	7.6
4992M	74585M	398558M	876428M	710234M	1069384M	Net Sales ($)	1153199M	1330787M
2129M	45617M	281543M	700949M	686787M	1004407M	Total Assets ($)	1316651M	1177704M

M = $ thousand   MM = $ million
See Pages 11 through 21 for Explanation of Ratios and Data

Comparative Historical Data   Current Data Sorted By Sales

Type of Statement

				0-1MM	1-3MM	3-5MM	5-10MM	10-25MM	25MM & OVER
29	27	33	Unqualified	2	8	1	9	6	17
31	42	42	Reviewed	3	12	9	11	4	8
24	33	36	Compiled	6	8	8	7	3	3
17	13	15	Tax Returns			1			
33	39	35	Other	6	6	6	5	6	6
4/1/02-3/31/03 ALL	4/1/03-3/31/04 ALL	4/1/04-3/31/05 ALL		24 (4/1-9/30/04)			137 (10/1/04-3/31/05)		
134	**154**	**161**	**NUMBER OF STATEMENTS**	**17**	**34**	**25**	**32**	**19**	**34**

%	%	%	ASSETS	%	%	%	%	%	%
9.4	9.6	9.5	Cash & Equivalents	10.0	9.4	6.7	8.9	14.4	9.2
15.4	16.3	17.9	Trade Receivables (net)	14.5	15.0	13.1	17.2	25.7	22.3
7.6	9.1	7.6	Inventory	2.8	7.8	9.0	6.7	7.1	9.9
3.0	3.0	2.8	All Other Current	3.2	1.1	2.5	3.4	3.6	3.7
35.4	38.1	37.8	Total Current	30.4	33.3	31.3	36.1	50.8	45.1
53.2	51.5	51.0	Fixed Assets (net)	60.4	55.2	59.8	50.5	40.8	41.8
3.0	2.6	2.3	Intangibles (net)	2.1	2.2	1.5	3.1	1.3	2.7
8.4	7.8	8.9	All Other Non-Current	7.0	9.4	7.4	10.3	7.1	10.4
100.0	100.0	100.0	Total	100.0	100.0	100.0	100.0	100.0	100.0

			LIABILITIES						
6.5	5.2	4.8	Notes Payable-Short Term	2.3	7.3	5.1	4.1	4.5	4.2
5.6	6.0	6.3	Cur. Mat.-L/T/D	8.6	6.8	9.7	5.7	4.8	3.7
6.4	8.5	8.5	Trade Payables	4.9	7.0	6.9	10.0	11.4	10.0
.3	.2	.2	Income Taxes Payable	.0	.3	.2	.1	.2	.4
6.2	7.0	6.8	All Other Current	2.1	13.0	5.3	5.6	4.7	6.4
24.9	27.0	26.7	Total Current	17.9	34.5	27.1	25.6	25.6	24.6
27.5	26.6	29.0	Long-Term Debt	46.8	39.8	29.4	27.8	15.3	17.8
1.1	.9	.9	Deferred Taxes	.2	.5	.5	.5	.5	2.8
4.3	3.1	3.7	All Other Non-Current	11.1	3.7	1.5	2.5	4.0	2.6
42.2	42.4	39.7	Net Worth	24.1	21.6	41.4	43.6	54.6	52.2
100.0	100.0	100.0	Total Liabilities & Net Worth	100.0	100.0	100.0	100.0	100.0	100.0

			INCOME DATA						
100.0	100.0	100.0	Net Sales	100.0	100.0	100.0	100.0	100.0	100.0
36.2	35.6	34.1	Gross Profit	55.4	45.7	35.5	30.0	21.4	22.0
28.4	28.3	26.1	Operating Expenses	45.3	37.3	25.8	24.3	13.9	13.9
7.8	7.3	8.1	Operating Profit	10.0	8.5	9.8	5.7	7.5	8.1
2.3	1.6	1.4	All Other Expenses (net)	7.3	2.3	.8	.0	.0	-.1
5.5	5.7	6.7	Profit Before Taxes	2.8	6.1	8.9	5.7	7.5	8.2

			RATIOS						
3.1	2.6	2.8	Current	3.4	2.6	1.8	2.5	2.9	3.1
1.5	1.5	1.6		2.0	1.5	1.2	1.3	2.2	1.6
.9	.9	1.0		.9	.9	.9	.9	1.5	1.1
2.3	2.0	2.1	Quick	2.8	2.2	1.3	1.9	2.3	2.7
1.0	1.0	1.1		1.5	1.1	.6	1.0	1.6	1.1
.5	.5	.5		.4	.4	.3	.5	1.0	.7
25 14.4	28 13.1	29 12.7	Sales/Receivables	21 17.6	28 13.1	23 16.1	26 14.0	34 10.8	36 10.1
40 9.2	41 9.0	41 8.9		32 11.6	40 9.0	32 11.4	37 9.9	49 7.5	51 7.2
54 6.8	58 6.3	62 5.9		101 3.6	63 5.8	47 7.7	58 6.3	75 4.8	69 5.3
0 UND	0 999.8	0 UND	Cost of Sales/Inventory	0 UND	0 UND	0 UND	0 UND	2 152.5	6 64.7
23 15.8	32 11.4	20 18.1		0 UND	27 13.4	20 18.1	27 13.7	20 18.7	26 13.9
61 5.9	70 5.2	54 6.7		10 36.6	74 4.9	64 5.7	40 9.2	31 11.7	55 6.7
10 35.5	13 28.6	15 24.2	Cost of Sales/Payables	0 UND	5 70.8	15 23.9	17 21.9	14 25.2	20 18.7
20 18.1	27 13.6	24 15.0		15 25.1	19 18.9	32 11.3	28 13.2	28 13.1	28 13.1
42 8.7	53 6.9	41 8.9		56 6.5	50 7.3	55 6.7	48 7.5	36 10.2	40 9.2
4.0	5.1	5.4	Sales/Working Capital	2.2	6.5	8.9	4.7	4.8	5.2
12.3	11.0	11.8		11.7	12.5	35.7	14.6	6.7	9.0
-75.8	-157.8	-114.0		-26.3	-30.8	-73.6	-180.6	15.5	50.9
9.5	9.6	11.9	EBIT/Interest	7.8	4.9	8.3	9.5	26.7	29.9
(121) 3.1	(134) 3.4	(143) 4.0		(13) 5.1	2.6	(21) 4.2	(26) 2.6	13.5	(30) 4.9
1.0	1.5	1.7		1.4	.3	2.3	.0	4.6	3.1
14.6	3.4	5.3	Net Profit + Depr., Dep., Amort./Cur. Mat. L/T/D						13.0
(32) 2.6	(33) 2.2	(40) 2.0						(12)	3.2
1.5	1.1	1.4							1.8
.6	.8	.7	Fixed/Worth	1.4	1.1	1.1	.7	.5	.5
1.2	1.2	1.3		4.8	2.0	1.7	1.3	.7	.8
4.0	2.9	2.5		NM	NM	2.2	2.9	1.2	1.2
.5	.5	.5	Debt/Worth	1.3	.9	.7	.4	.4	.2
1.3	1.4	1.4		6.4	2.2	1.5	1.2	.8	.9
5.5	3.8	3.6		NM	NM	2.8	5.8	2.5	1.7
29.0	27.9	30.9	% Profit Before Taxes/Tangible Net Worth	34.1	37.6	36.9	34.4	20.5	26.8
(117) 13.4	(135) 16.0	(142) 15.1		(13) 11.1	(26) 19.0	(23) 15.8	(30) 10.8	17.6	(31) 13.6
3.6	3.3	5.0		-24.7	-4.6	12.2	-2.0	8.6	6.6
11.4	10.7	13.2	% Profit Before Taxes/Total Assets	13.7	12.3	13.1	8.8	16.3	17.0
5.7	5.8	5.8		3.2	4.1	8.1	3.4	9.3	7.0
.0	1.0	.9		-3.2	-2.1	4.3	-1.8	4.3	4.5
4.2	4.1	4.8	Sales/Net Fixed Assets	3.3	3.8	2.9	5.5	8.0	5.5
2.3	2.6	2.7		1.2	2.3	2.0	2.8	3.9	3.1
1.4	1.4	1.4		.5	1.5	1.3	1.3	1.8	1.9
1.7	1.8	2.0	Sales/Total Assets	1.6	1.9	1.6	2.3	2.5	2.1
1.2	1.3	1.3		.7	1.2	1.1	1.4	1.5	1.4
.8	.8	.8		.3	.9	.8	.7	1.0	1.0
5.3	5.4	5.4	% Depr., Dep., Amort./Sales	6.5	6.6	7.3	5.6	2.7	3.3
(122) 8.5	(133) 8.3	(146) 8.4		(14) 16.1	(33) 9.3	(30) 11.4	(17) 7.6	7.5	(27) 5.1
13.2	12.1	12.4		27.2	13.6	13.4	9.6	12.3	8.0
1.9	1.0	1.5	% Officers', Directors', Owners' Comp/Sales		2.8			1.2	
(51) 3.6	(43) 2.8	(42) 3.2			(10) 4.8			(11) 2.5	
6.5	7.7	6.7			13.6			3.8	
1896569M	2577285M	3134181M	Net Sales ($)	8055M	65604M	96679M	210233M	310709M	2442901M
1779656M	2456683M	2721432M	Total Assets ($)	12763M	64331M	90299M	262200M	236773M	2055066M

M = $ thousand   MM = $ million
See Pages 11 through 21 for Explanation of Ratios and Data

MINING—Drilling Oil and Gas Wells NAICS 213111 (SIC 1381)

Current Data Sorted By Assets | **Comparative Historical Data**

	0-500M	500M-2MM	2-10MM	10-50MM	50-100MM	100-250MM	Type of Statement	4/1/00-3/31/01 ALL	4/1/01-3/31/02 ALL
				8	2	3	Unqualified	2	3
		1	3				Reviewed	4	5
	3	6	3	2		1	Compiled	9	7
		1	1		1		Tax Returns	7	5
	2	4	10	5			Other	17	20
	5 (4/1-9/30/04)			51 (10/1/04-3/31/05)					
NUMBER OF STATEMENTS	5	12	17	15	3	4		39	40
	%	%	%	%	%	%	**ASSETS**	%	%
		13.6	12.4	8.8			Cash & Equivalents	11.4	12.0
		21.7	20.5	27.8			Trade Receivables (net)	22.8	24.4
		1.3	.9	.5			Inventory	3.5	4.8
		3.5	6.8	1.8			All Other Current	3.1	4.0
		40.1	40.7	38.9			Total Current	40.9	45.2
		45.5	47.8	48.2			Fixed Assets (net)	44.1	43.0
		.0	2.1	8.3			Intangibles (net)	5.6	3.7
		14.4	9.4	4.6			All Other Non-Current	9.4	8.1
		100.0	100.0	100.0			Total	100.0	100.0
							LIABILITIES		
		7.5	10.0	5.7			Notes Payable-Short Term	6.1	6.6
		7.7	3.7	4.4			Cur. Mat.-L/T/D	6.8	5.5
		5.6	14.3	10.2			Trade Payables	13.9	11.8
		.4	.0	.9			Income Taxes Payable	.1	.7
		4.0	13.8	11.8			All Other Current	11.1	9.7
		25.2	41.8	33.0			Total Current	37.9	34.3
		20.2	24.2	17.3			Long-Term Debt	19.4	15.1
		.6	.2	1.9			Deferred Taxes	.4	1.2
		6.5	2.2	3.1			All Other Non-Current	3.8	2.5
		47.4	31.6	44.6			Net Worth	38.5	46.9
		100.0	100.0	100.0			Total Liabilities & Net Worth	100.0	100.0
							INCOME DATA		
		100.0	100.0	100.0			Net Sales	100.0	100.0
							Gross Profit		
		90.3	87.9	84.4			Operating Expenses	94.7	86.2
		9.7	12.1	15.6			Operating Profit	5.3	13.8
		2.4	2.4	1.2			All Other Expenses (net)	-4.7	.9
		7.3	9.7	14.4			Profit Before Taxes	10.0	12.9
							RATIOS		
		6.0	1.7	2.0				2.1	2.3
		1.9	1.1	1.1			Current	1.2	1.6
		.6	.4	.9				.7	1.0
		6.0	1.4	1.9				1.5	1.7
		1.8	1.0	1.0			Quick	1.0	1.2
		.5	.3	.8				.6	.8
		0 UND	20 18.4	52 7.0				22 16.8	34 10.8
		47 7.7	47 7.8	81 4.5			Sales/Receivables	46 7.9	50 7.3
		77 4.8	88 4.2	107 3.4				78 4.7	72 5.1
							Cost of Sales/Inventory		
							Cost of Sales/Payables		
		4.5	7.3	9.0				7.1	6.8
		8.6	37.1	19.2			Sales/Working Capital	27.1	16.2
		-23.5	-3.8	-18.9				-20.3	-236.2
		9.9	13.8	58.9				8.2	31.9
		(11) 6.2	(15) 3.4	10.8			EBIT/Interest	(31) 3.5	(39) 7.8
		1.9	2.2	2.6				1.6	1.4
							Net Profit + Depr., Dep., Amort./Cur. Mat. L /T/D		4.5
									(11) 3.1
									2.1
		.3	.7	.7				.6	.5
		.7	1.1	1.5			Fixed/Worth	1.5	1.0
		2.8	26.0	2.2				4.5	2.1
		.2	.7	1.0				.5	.6
		1.0	2.0	2.0			Debt/Worth	2.1	1.1
		2.6	27.8	3.5				11.8	3.0
		36.0	88.9	101.5				52.8	69.6
		(10) 19.5	(14) 21.0	53.2			% Profit Before Taxes/Tangible Net Worth	(31) 30.3	(37) 27.8
		5.0	5.9	10.2				12.7	6.2
		18.8	18.0	24.8				22.3	24.9
		8.7	7.3	13.2			% Profit Before Taxes/Total Assets	12.5	12.3
		2.1	1.8	5.0				3.4	1.7
		11.8	6.7	3.8				4.8	6.4
		5.5	2.8	2.0			Sales/Net Fixed Assets	2.8	4.8
		2.3	1.4	1.5				2.1	2.2
		2.5	1.8	1.6				2.3	2.4
		1.6	.9	1.1			Sales/Total Assets	1.4	1.8
		1.1	.7	.5				.7	.8
			4.0	5.6				2.8	2.8
			(16) 7.2	(14) 9.0			% Depr., Dep., Amort./Sales	(34) 6.0	(35) 4.6
			11.5	14.5				11.1	10.0
								2.1	2.0
							% Officers', Directors', Owners' Comp/Sales	(14) 5.1	(17) 3.2
								9.6	6.3
	18368M	21550M	106780M	371945M	138656M	429480M	Net Sales ($)	320339M	696815M
	1338M	12670M	89433M	268971M	171520M	704887M	Total Assets ($)	360622M	621390M

© RMA 2005

M = $ thousand   MM = $ million
See Pages 11 through 21 for Explanation of Ratios and Data

Comparative Historical Data | Current Data Sorted By Sales

			Type of Statement	0-1MM	1-3MM	3-5MM	5-10MM	10-25MM	25MM & OVER
11	9	13	Unqualified				1	5	7
2	5	7	Reviewed		1	1	1	2	1
7	6	12	Compiled	1	6		1	1	
6	7	4	Tax Returns	2		4		1	
19	13	20	Other	2	5	3	4	5	1
4/1/02-3/31/03 ALL	4/1/03-3/31/04 ALL	4/1/04-3/31/05 ALL		5 (4/1-9/30/04)			51 (10/1/04-3/31/05)		
45	40	56	**NUMBER OF STATEMENTS**	5	12	9	7	14	9
%	%	%	**ASSETS**	%	%	%	%	%	%
13.4	8.6	11.4	Cash & Equivalents		19.6			8.8	
18.3	26.0	22.3	Trade Receivables (net)		20.6			30.7	
1.9	1.1	.8	Inventory		.7			.3	
3.4	3.2	4.5	All Other Current		4.6			5.7	
37.0	38.8	39.0	Total Current		45.5			45.5	
49.7	48.3	49.1	Fixed Assets (net)		41.9			45.1	
1.8	2.1	2.9	Intangibles (net)		.0			2.2	
11.5	10.9	9.0	All Other Non-Current		12.5			7.3	
100.0	100.0	100.0	Total		100.0			100.0	
			LIABILITIES						
5.1	6.3	8.8	Notes Payable-Short Term		6.7			10.1	
5.3	5.1	7.7	Cur. Mat.-L/T/D		5.3			17.8	
10.7	10.5	9.8	Trade Payables		2.5			12.0	
.4	.4	.3	Income Taxes Payable		.4			.8	
7.5	8.6	9.8	All Other Current		6.4			8.4	
28.9	30.9	36.5	Total Current		21.3			49.1	
21.5	24.0	20.8	Long-Term Debt		24.5			13.2	
1.0	.9	1.0	Deferred Taxes		.6			1.7	
3.9	2.3	3.9	All Other Non-Current		.6			2.3	
44.7	41.9	37.8	Net Worth		53.0			33.6	
100.0	100.0	100.0	Total Liabilities & Net Worth		100.0			100.0	
			INCOME DATA						
100.0	100.0	100.0	Net Sales		100.0			100.0	
			Gross Profit						
87.9	90.4	87.2	Operating Expenses		93.2			90.0	
12.1	9.6	12.8	Operating Profit		6.8			10.0	
1.2	–.2	1.6	All Other Expenses (net)		–1.5			.1	
11.0	9.8	11.2	Profit Before Taxes		8.3			9.8	
			RATIOS						
2.4	2.7	2.5	Current		7.2			1.2	
1.2	1.2	1.3			2.7			1.0	
.8	.8	.6			1.5			.9	
2.3	2.6	2.1	Quick		7.2			1.1	
1.1	1.0	1.1			2.1			.9	
.7	.7	.5			1.2			.7	
19 19.1	33 11.1	28 13.2	Sales/Receivables	0 UND				27 13.5	
48 7.6	55 6.6	54 6.7		46 7.9				65 5.6	
67 5.4	91 4.0	81 4.5		70 5.2				108 3.4	
			Cost of Sales/Inventory						
			Cost of Sales/Payables						
7.2	5.0	5.6	Sales/Working Capital		3.6			18.3	
18.8	28.8	17.5			5.6			128.1	
–20.7	–24.1	–15.4			9.5			–29.1	
11.9	16.4	26.2	EBIT/Interest		15.9			26.2	
(38) 3.6	(34) 6.2	(53) 7.3		(10) 7.7				(13) 11.3	
.9	2.3	2.3			2.0			5.6	
		3.8	Net Profit + Depr., Dep., Amort./Cur. Mat. L/T/D						
	(10)	1.7							
		1.0							
.5	.6	.7	Fixed/Worth		.3			.4	
1.1	1.1	1.2			.7			1.3	
2.4	2.0	3.0			2.5			2.0	
.5	.4	.6	Debt/Worth		.2			.7	
1.5	1.3	1.4			1.0			1.9	
4.0	3.3	4.1			2.5			3.4	
45.3	47.0	75.1	% Profit Before Taxes/Tangible Net Worth		31.1			75.1	
(42) 18.2	(35) 21.2	(49) 23.7			16.2			(13) 44.7	
4.4	6.8	7.5			4.9			12.0	
20.4	21.5	19.8	% Profit Before Taxes/Total Assets		18.8			25.1	
6.2	7.4	11.1			9.4			13.3	
1.1	2.3	2.3			2.2			8.7	
5.7	6.9	8.3	Sales/Net Fixed Assets		12.3			15.0	
2.8	2.5	2.6			5.5			3.4	
1.2	.9	1.6			2.3			1.9	
2.2	2.0	1.9	Sales/Total Assets		2.5			2.1	
1.1	1.3	1.2			1.6			1.3	
.7	.4	.7			1.0			1.1	
3.3	3.3	4.0	% Depr., Dep., Amort./Sales		3.2			3.1	
(37) 8.0	(35) 6.6	(44) 7.1		(10) 6.3				(12) 6.4	
12.2	11.6	12.2			16.0			12.4	
1.3	1.1	1.1	% Officers', Directors', Owners' Comp/Sales						
(14) 4.7	(11) 4.2	(15) 7.0							
8.2	14.2	17.3							
805149M	960550M	1086779M	Net Sales ($)	2987M	20893M	34474M	45287M	227429M	755709M
1010534M	929821M	1248819M	Total Assets ($)	5852M	19293M	41628M	68851M	204921M	908274M

© RMA 2005

M = $ thousand   MM = $ million
See Pages 11 through 21 for Explanation of Ratios and Data

Current Data Sorted By Assets   Comparative Historical Data

	Type of Statement	4/1/00-3/31/01 ALL	4/1/01-3/31/02 ALL
1 6 13 23 10 12	Unqualified	28	41
6 2 21 6	Reviewed	14	16
10 15 18 5	Compiled	20	33
8 6 7 1	Tax Returns	9	12
35 43 18 6 2	Other	42	43

Periods: 50 (4/1-9/30/04) — columns 0-500M, 500M-2MM, 2-10MM; 224 (10/1/04-3/31/05) — columns 10-50MM, 50-100MM, 100-250MM

	0-500M	500M-2MM	2-10MM	10-50MM	50-100MM	100-250MM		4/1/00-3/31/01 ALL	4/1/01-3/31/02 ALL
NUMBER OF STATEMENTS	25	64	102	53	16	14		113	145
ASSETS	%	%	%	%	%	%		%	%
Cash & Equivalents	23.8	13.6	9.6	6.4	10.0	14.7		7.9	11.5
Trade Receivables (net)	17.2	37.1	30.3	27.5	17.9	17.7		29.0	27.2
Inventory	4.8	7.3	5.7	10.1	6.9	7.6		7.4	6.9
All Other Current	3.0	5.1	4.7	4.9	1.1	2.6		3.6	3.4
Total Current	48.9	63.1	50.3	49.0	36.0	42.6		47.8	49.1
Fixed Assets (net)	44.0	31.3	39.0	39.2	50.7	42.7		41.6	38.5
Intangibles (net)	2.6	.6	2.3	5.3	10.3	8.7		2.7	5.0
All Other Non-Current	4.5	5.0	8.4	6.6	3.0	6.0		7.8	7.3
Total	100.0	100.0	100.0	100.0	100.0	100.0		100.0	100.0
LIABILITIES									
Notes Payable-Short Term	10.0	8.6	9.0	9.3	4.6	1.7		12.7	11.1
Cur. Mat.-L/T/D	10.7	6.8	5.2	6.9	5.5	2.0		4.9	5.2
Trade Payables	10.6	13.4	12.3	10.0	7.0	8.7		12.0	12.8
Income Taxes Payable	.0	.7	.9	.4	.3	.8		.8	.6
All Other Current	12.3	8.3	8.7	10.7	4.9	13.6		6.9	7.5
Total Current	43.6	37.7	36.1	37.3	22.2	26.7		37.3	37.3
Long-Term Debt	35.5	25.2	14.6	18.0	17.6	17.3		21.5	22.3
Deferred Taxes	.0	.5	.8	1.4	3.5	2.7		1.7	1.4
All Other Non-Current	4.8	5.1	3.0	2.6	3.8	5.4		6.0	3.2
Net Worth	16.1	31.6	45.5	40.7	52.9	47.9		33.5	35.8
Total Liabilities & Net Worth	100.0	100.0	100.0	100.0	100.0	100.0		100.0	100.0
INCOME DATA									
Net Sales	100.0	100.0	100.0	100.0	100.0	100.0		100.0	100.0
Gross Profit									
Operating Expenses	93.5	92.0	89.1	86.1	87.7	81.9		91.4	89.0
Operating Profit	6.5	8.0	10.9	13.9	12.3	18.1		8.6	11.0
All Other Expenses (net)	1.1	.7	1.1	2.5	2.7	1.6		1.4	2.9
Profit Before Taxes	5.4	7.3	9.8	11.4	9.5	16.5		7.2	8.1
RATIOS									
Current	3.2	2.8	2.3	2.2	3.4	2.7		2.4	2.4
	1.9	1.7	1.3	1.3	1.6	1.8		1.6	1.5
	.5	1.1	1.0	.9	.9	1.0		1.0	.9
Quick	2.6	2.5	1.8	1.5	2.9	2.0		1.6	2.0
	1.5	1.2	1.0	.9	1.3	1.2		1.2	1.1
	.4	.8	.7	.6	.8	.8		.7	.7
Sales/Receivables	0 UND	28 13.1	30 12.0	52 7.0	47 7.8	40 9.2		31 11.7	31 11.8
	4 101.2	44 8.2	51 7.1	63 5.8	72 5.1	64 5.7		54 6.8	51 7.1
	41 9.0	71 5.2	76 4.8	87 4.2	100 3.6	88 4.1		78 4.7	72 5.1
Cost of Sales/Inventory									
Cost of Sales/Payables									
Sales/Working Capital	7.7	5.5	6.8	4.2	2.9	3.5		5.3	5.6
	20.2	14.1	18.4	16.9	4.8	7.6		11.9	13.3
	-27.2	70.9	-999.8	-40.1	NM	63.1		126.9	-100.8
EBIT/Interest	(21) 15.4	(56) 24.2	(88) 16.5	(49) 27.1	(14) 34.7	(13) 46.9		(101) 9.2	(134) 19.9
	6.7	7.9	8.0	8.1	2.2	5.7		3.8	4.3
	-1.6	2.1	2.5	3.0	.9	2.9		1.3	2.0
Net Profit + Depr., Dep., Amort./Cur. Mat. L /T/D			(22) 11.7	(15) 5.8				(23) 4.1	(39) 5.8
			2.7	3.0				1.9	2.8
			1.5	1.8				1.5	1.2
Fixed/Worth	.6	.2	.4	.5	.6	.3		.4	.4
	1.7	.8	.8	1.0	1.5	1.0		1.2	1.1
	-3.6	3.3	1.8	1.9	3.5	2.6		2.6	2.8
Debt/Worth	1.2	.8	.5	.7	.4	.6		.7	.7
	5.3	1.8	1.2	1.5	1.0	1.4		1.9	1.7
	-6.8	5.1	3.1	3.1	3.3	4.3		4.4	5.0
% Profit Before Taxes/Tangible Net Worth	(16) 324.6	(56) 70.6	(95) 55.4	(48) 63.3	(14) 30.6	(13) 50.1		(104) 49.1	(129) 62.5
	83.7	39.3	26.6	36.0	13.9	28.2		23.3	30.8
	11.8	19.0	5.1	15.5	6.9	17.0		7.9	10.1
% Profit Before Taxes/Total Assets	50.8	24.7	19.2	20.9	16.3	20.6		15.6	21.8
	18.8	15.2	10.8	9.8	6.5	7.7		8.5	8.9
	-7.7	4.3	1.5	4.4	.5	4.1		1.2	3.6
Sales/Net Fixed Assets	40.3	40.9	15.7	11.4	4.1	19.8		10.8	10.7
	6.9	14.4	6.9	3.5	2.1	1.7		4.5	5.1
	2.6	4.6	2.3	1.9	.6	.6		1.8	2.5
Sales/Total Assets	5.6	4.0	3.1	1.9	1.5	1.4		2.9	3.1
	3.6	2.6	2.0	1.4	.9	.7		1.6	1.9
	1.5	1.9	1.1	.9	.4	.5		.8	1.0
% Depr., Dep., Amort./Sales	(19) 1.6	(46) .7	(88) 2.0	(46) 1.6	(14) 5.2	(10) .3		(98) 2.1	(133) 1.5
	6.0	2.2	3.9	5.2	7.4	3.7		4.4	3.6
	11.1	7.8	7.3	9.1	18.8	8.6		7.6	7.1
% Officers', Directors', Owners' Comp/Sales	(11) 2.3	(26) 2.6	(38) 1.1					(28) 2.9	(44) 1.7
	4.3	4.9	2.8					4.3	3.3
	16.4	9.3	6.4					10.1	7.2
Net Sales ($)	29600M	270921M	1256053M	2111924M	1083946M	3115642M		3463005M	4269678M
Total Assets ($)	7313M	72690M	487292M	1215809M	1076108M	2571436M		2781985M	3157990M

M = $ thousand   MM = $ million
See Pages 11 through 21 for Explanation of Ratios and Data

Comparative Historical Data / Current Data Sorted By Sales

			Type of Statement						
42	41	65	Unqualified	1	3	4	9	14	34
25	31	29	Reviewed		1	1	10	10	7
37	59	44	Compiled	4	9	8	9	9	5
12	23	24	Tax Returns	11	2	1	5	4	1
86	105	112	Other	12	19	24	26	13	18
4/1/02-3/31/03 ALL	4/1/03-3/31/04 ALL	4/1/04-3/31/05 ALL				50 (4/1-9/30/04)		224 (10/1/04-3/31/05)	
				0-1MM	1-3MM	3-5MM	5-10MM	10-25MM	25MM & OVER
202	259	274	**NUMBER OF STATEMENTS**	28	34	38	59	50	65
%	%	%	**ASSETS**	%	%	%	%	%	%
10.2	10.8	11.5	Cash & Equivalents	15.9	16.0	11.5	10.7	7.6	11.0
25.3	27.5	28.8	Trade Receivables (net)	11.8	29.5	35.2	34.0	30.4	26.0
8.2	7.8	7.0	Inventory	2.2	7.7	5.5	4.5	6.1	12.5
4.7	4.5	4.4	All Other Current	1.9	5.5	2.6	6.0	5.3	3.8
48.4	50.6	51.7	Total Current	31.9	58.7	54.9	55.3	49.4	53.2
41.9	39.1	38.6	Fixed Assets (net)	60.4	36.1	37.5	34.1	36.0	37.1
2.9	3.1	3.3	Intangibles (net)	1.5	.5	1.6	1.5	7.5	4.9
6.8	7.2	6.5	All Other Non-Current	6.2	4.8	6.0	9.2	7.1	4.8
100.0	100.0	100.0	Total	100.0	100.0	100.0	100.0	100.0	100.0
			LIABILITIES						
10.3	8.5	8.4	Notes Payable-Short Term	6.0	13.1	8.2	8.2	8.1	7.6
8.2	4.9	6.3	Cur. Mat.-L/T/D	8.1	8.8	6.5	5.8	5.7	4.9
10.3	11.1	11.5	Trade Payables	4.5	10.6	11.6	13.1	10.7	13.9
.9	.7	.6	Income Taxes Payable	.4	.3	1.0	.5	1.2	.3
9.3	9.0	9.3	All Other Current	8.0	7.3	6.7	10.9	8.2	12.0
39.0	34.1	36.1	Total Current	27.0	40.1	34.0	38.6	33.8	38.7
17.4	18.9	20.0	Long-Term Debt	36.3	26.9	22.8	17.5	16.6	12.5
1.1	1.0	1.0	Deferred Taxes	.0	.2	1.3	.6	1.5	1.9
2.6	5.7	3.7	All Other Non-Current	6.0	1.2	2.7	6.4	2.3	3.3
39.9	40.3	39.2	Net Worth	30.7	31.6	39.2	37.0	45.9	43.7
100.0	100.0	100.0	Total Liabilities & Net Worth	100.0	100.0	100.0	100.0	100.0	100.0
			INCOME DATA						
100.0	100.0	100.0	Net Sales	100.0	100.0	100.0	100.0	100.0	100.0
			Gross Profit						
92.9	90.7	89.2	Operating Expenses	85.4	86.8	88.3	91.9	88.3	90.7
7.1	9.3	10.8	Operating Profit	14.6	13.2	11.7	8.1	11.7	9.3
1.9	1.5	1.4	All Other Expenses (net)	3.1	2.1	.7	1.0	1.3	1.2
5.2	7.8	9.4	Profit Before Taxes	11.5	11.2	11.0	7.1	10.4	8.1
			RATIOS						
2.4	2.9	2.6	Current	3.1	3.4	3.0	2.4	1.9	2.3
1.3	1.6	1.4		1.1	2.0	1.5	1.4	1.4	1.3
.9	1.0	1.0		.3	.8	1.0	1.0	1.1	1.0
1.7	2.3	2.0	Quick	2.6	2.5	2.7	1.7	1.7	1.8
.9	1.2	1.1		.8	1.4	1.3	1.1	1.1	1.0
.6	.7	.7		.2	.6	1.0	.8	.8	.7
29 12.5	30 12.4	28 12.8	Sales/Receivables	0 UND	27 13.4	37 9.8	38 9.6	37 9.9	23 16.0
50 7.4	51 7.1	53 6.9		9 40.8	55 6.6	57 6.4	60 6.1	56 6.5	53 6.9
67 5.5	71 5.2	76 4.8		55 6.7	76 4.8	94 3.9	80 4.6	83 4.4	73 5.0
			Cost of Sales/Inventory						
			Cost of Sales/Payables						
5.9	5.3	5.3	Sales/Working Capital	5.4	5.2	4.5	7.0	7.5	4.2
18.9	11.4	15.9		NM	8.2	8.6	16.0	18.8	19.0
-32.9	219.0	-999.8		-3.2	-66.7	NM	174.9	161.2	585.4
(174) 9.3	(216) 14.4	(241) 19.7	EBIT/Interest	(20) 15.4	(30) 20.0	(33) 18.4	(52) 15.9	(46) 15.1	(60) 38.8
3.2	4.3	7.7		3.3	8.0	10.2	5.5	8.1	9.1
1.0	1.4	2.3		.6	2.1	2.4	2.2	2.3	2.8
(38) 5.8	(47) 8.6	(54) 7.1	Net Profit + Depr., Dep., Amort./Cur. Mat. L/T/D					(16) 13.0	(21) 5.7
3.1	3.5	2.5						3.1	2.5
1.4	1.5	1.4						2.1	1.5
.4	.4	.4	Fixed/Worth	.8	.2	.4	.2	.5	.3
1.0	.9	1.0		1.5	.9	.9	.7	1.0	1.0
2.1	1.9	2.4		21.1	4.2	2.1	2.1	2.1	1.9
.6	.7	.6	Debt/Worth	.5	.5	.5	.6	.7	.7
1.4	1.5	1.6		1.8	1.7	1.5	1.7	1.4	1.4
3.5	3.8	4.5		21.8	16.3	3.9	3.7	3.5	3.0
(184) 38.5	(237) 47.7	(242) 64.5	% Profit Before Taxes/Tangible Net Worth	(23) 135.1	(27) 85.0	(35) 56.7	(51) 59.9	(46) 81.2	(60) 49.6
15.0	21.9	31.4		48.2	34.2	31.4	28.9	40.4	25.3
2.4	3.9	12.8		1.0	17.9	10.6	15.1	15.1	10.3
13.7	19.0	22.4	% Profit Before Taxes/Total Assets	39.9	24.4	25.0	19.0	24.2	20.8
5.2	7.8	11.4		8.9	16.0	13.0	9.3	12.3	10.0
.2	.9	3.0		-.3	4.0	4.3	2.0	2.5	3.8
13.4	17.1	19.4	Sales/Net Fixed Assets	4.5	18.8	24.5	25.1	12.4	30.1
5.1	5.1	6.1		1.9	8.1	5.3	8.7	6.6	5.7
1.8	2.0	2.2		.4	3.6	2.3	3.0	2.3	2.3
2.9	2.9	3.2	Sales/Total Assets	2.0	3.5	3.1	3.3	2.8	3.5
1.8	1.7	1.9		1.1	2.4	2.0	2.2	1.8	1.6
.9	1.0	1.0		.3	1.1	1.0	1.2	1.2	1.0
(173) 1.9	(214) 1.9	(223) 1.6	% Depr., Dep., Amort./Sales	(24) 4.4	(24) 1.8	(27) 2.3	(51) 1.4	(44) 2.2	(53) .8
4.8	4.7	4.6		10.8	3.2	5.5	4.0	4.0	2.9
10.4	9.3	8.9		20.2	7.8	10.7	6.6	10.1	6.9
(59) 3.0	(60) 2.3	(80) 1.6	% Officers', Directors', Owners' Comp/Sales		(13) 2.7	(13) 1.9	(24) -1.2	(12) 1.7	(10) .2
4.8	4.0	3.6			4.8	5.0	2.8	2.9	.7
9.3	9.4	7.6			7.9	7.5	5.6	1.7	1.7
6624019M	8123355M	7868086M	Net Sales ($)	15184M	63751M	145757M	429968M	814759M	6398667M
4401068M	5651535M	5430648M	Total Assets ($)	29373M	49409M	141322M	264144M	687032M	4259368M

© RMA 2005

M = $ thousand   MM = $ million
See Pages 11 through 21 for Explanation of Ratios and Data

UTILITIES

Current Data Sorted By Assets   Comparative Historical Data

						Type of Statement		
2	5	19	84	70	67	Unqualified	57	58
1	6	8	2		1	Reviewed	14	11
1	4	2				Compiled	14	15
3	4	1				Tax Returns	7	7
1	8	10	10	9	10	Other	33	49
	92 (4/1-9/30/04)		236 (10/1/04-3/31/05)				4/1/00-3/31/01	4/1/01-3/31/02
0-500M	500M-2MM	2-10MM	10-50MM	50-100MM	100-250MM		ALL	ALL
8	27	40	96	80	77	**NUMBER OF STATEMENTS**	125	140
%	%	%	%	%	%	**ASSETS**	%	%
	12.7	12.0	8.0	4.6	4.7	Cash & Equivalents	10.7	11.6
	32.9	20.8	8.4	9.4	5.4	Trade Receivables (net)	20.8	18.9
	5.4	3.8	2.6	2.6	1.4	Inventory	4.7	3.9
	5.7	7.0	2.0	2.3	2.2	All Other Current	3.8	4.3
	56.7	43.6	21.1	19.0	13.8	Total Current	40.0	38.7
	29.2	43.9	64.6	68.2	72.2	Fixed Assets (net)	45.5	46.3
	2.9	2.9	1.9	1.7	1.6	Intangibles (net)	4.0	4.2
	11.2	9.6	12.4	11.1	12.5	All Other Non-Current	10.5	10.8
	100.0	100.0	100.0	100.0	100.0	Total	100.0	100.0
						LIABILITIES		
	12.8	1.9	2.1	2.4	2.1	Notes Payable-Short Term	5.2	4.5
	4.1	3.9	2.4	1.9	2.8	Cur. Mat.-L/T/D	4.2	4.4
	12.8	15.7	5.8	6.4	4.9	Trade Payables	11.1	14.1
	.3	.5	.3	.3	.3	Income Taxes Payable		.3
	15.7	7.6	4.5	6.0	5.3	All Other Current	16.8	8.8
	45.8	29.7	15.1	16.9	15.4	Total Current	38.0	32.2
	26.8	31.0	32.6	36.1	45.5	Long-Term Debt	30.6	36.9
	.7	.5	.8	.4	1.1	Deferred Taxes	2.1	1.1
	1.6	5.2	6.6	4.8	3.2	All Other Non-Current	5.1	4.4
	25.2	33.6	44.9	41.9	34.8	Net Worth	24.2	25.4
	100.0	100.0	100.0	100.0	100.0	Total Liabilities & Net Worth	100.0	100.0
						INCOME DATA		
	100.0	100.0	100.0	100.0	100.0	Net Sales	100.0	100.0
						Gross Profit		
	88.4	89.2	91.4	91.3	90.2	Operating Expenses	85.6	87.3
	11.6	10.8	8.6	8.7	9.8	Operating Profit	14.4	12.7
	2.2	3.5	2.9	3.1	4.3	All Other Expenses (net)	4.0	4.9
	9.4	7.3	5.7	5.7	5.6	Profit Before Taxes	10.4	7.8
						RATIOS		
	1.8	2.4	1.8	1.4	1.3		1.8	2.2
	1.3	1.6	1.2	1.1	.9	Current	1.3	1.3
	1.1	1.1	.8	.8	.7		.8	.8
	1.6	2.0	1.4	1.1	1.0		1.6	1.8
	1.1	1.2	.9	.8	.7	Quick	.9	1.0
	.7	.8	.5	.5	.4		.5	.5
31 11.7	27 13.3	28 12.9	24 15.0	24 15.2			27 13.6	23 16.1
51 7.2	47 7.8	36 10.0	33 10.9	28 13.3		Sales/Receivables	39 9.4	35 10.4
69 5.3	77 4.8	47 7.8	46 8.0	38 9.7			62 5.9	59 6.2
						Cost of Sales/Inventory		
						Cost of Sales/Payables		
	7.3	5.2	6.4	12.6	19.0		7.5	6.6
	9.9	8.6	26.3	67.3	−75.0	Sales/Working Capital	23.4	18.1
	57.1	27.5	−25.8	−21.5	−12.7		−19.4	−24.3
	19.7	37.6	4.7	3.5	2.8		7.0	6.2
(24) 5.9	(32) 4.1	(93) 2.7	(78) 2.4	(75) 2.0		EBIT/Interest	(106) 3.4	(114) 2.5
2.4	1.7	1.8	1.8	1.6			1.6	1.5
			4.1		4.8	Net Profit + Depr., Dep.,	4.0	2.6
	(17) 3.2			(11) 2.8	Amort./Cur. Mat. L /T/D	(30) 2.7	(24) 2.0
		2.0		1.7			1.3	.3
	.4	.3	1.0	1.3	1.6		.6	.6
	.8	1.0	1.5	1.8	2.2	Fixed/Worth	1.5	1.2
	2.8	2.4	2.4	2.5	2.9		3.4	2.9
	1.0	.9	.6	.9	1.5		1.0	.8
	2.0	1.6	1.1	1.5	1.8	Debt/Worth	1.8	1.7
	7.9	5.6	2.1	2.3	2.8		5.7	6.6
	62.2	26.2	11.9	9.4	12.4	% Profit Before Taxes/Tangible	37.0	31.0
(21) 24.8	(37) 10.7	(90) 5.8	(78) 6.4	6.4	Net Worth	(112) 14.7	(127) 10.2
9.9	1.4	3.4	3.8	3.7		4.1	3.4
	22.1	12.1	5.3	4.1	3.8	% Profit Before Taxes/Total	15.6	9.9
	8.5	3.7	2.8	2.8	2.0	Assets	4.9	3.9
	1.0	1.1	1.6	1.7	1.2		1.3	1.1
	27.6	26.9	1.1	.9	.9		18.4	18.8
	10.9	3.6	.7	.7	.6	Sales/Net Fixed Assets	2.2	1.4
	2.5	.6	.5	.5	.5		.6	.6
	2.7	2.1	.8	.7	.6		2.7	2.2
	1.8	1.3	.5	.5	.5	Sales/Total Assets	.8	.7
	1.0	.4	.4	.4	.4		.4	.4
	1.1	1.0	5.3	5.2	5.2		1.7	1.4
(23) 2.1	(37) 3.0	(94) 7.3	(75) 6.7	(73) 7.0	% Depr., Dep., Amort./Sales	(110) 4.8	(125) 4.7
6.7	10.9	9.8	8.1	8.3		7.9	8.0
						% Officers', Directors',	3.8	3.5
						Owners' Comp/Sales	(22) 7.4	(22) 6.1
							12.3	8.8
6847M	56285M	305021M	1981412M	5063506M	7788473M	Net Sales ($)	3952882M	4340820M
2166M	27816M	215655M	2574794M	5525458M	12043292M	Total Assets ($)	5974037M	6005087M

M = $ thousand   MM = $ million
See Pages 11 through 21 for Explanation of Ratios and Data

Comparative Historical Data | **Current Data Sorted By Sales**

Comparative Historical Data				Current Data Sorted By Sales					
			Type of Statement						
59	69	247	Unqualified	5	12	4	28	59	139
15	17	18	Reviewed	1	6	3	5	2	1
9	12	7	Compiled	1	4	2			
5	4	8	Tax Returns	3	3	1		1	
36	43	48	Other	2	8	3	7	6	22
4/1/02-3/31/03 ALL	4/1/03-3/31/04 ALL	4/1/04-3/31/05 ALL		**92 (4/1-9/30/04)** 0-1MM	1-3MM	3-5MM	**236 (10/1/04-3/31/05)** 5-10MM	10-25MM	25MM & OVER
124	145	328	**NUMBER OF STATEMENTS**	12	33	11	42	68	162
%	%	%	**ASSETS**	%	%	%	%	%	%
12.4	11.6	8.2	Cash & Equivalents	18.4	17.5	9.5	9.2	8.3	5.3
15.9	20.5	11.7	Trade Receivables (net)	8.1	22.9	23.8	12.6	8.2	10.1
3.8	5.2	2.6	Inventory	1.3	3.6	5.8	3.9	1.4	2.5
4.2	5.8	3.1	All Other Current	2.4	3.9	2.0	2.8	4.4	2.5
36.2	43.0	25.7	Total Current	30.2	47.9	41.0	28.5	22.2	20.4
49.1	45.4	60.7	Fixed Assets (net)	48.7	41.1	49.2	53.3	64.1	66.9
3.9	2.5	1.9	Intangibles (net)	1.2	2.1	.7	5.1	1.0	1.6
10.8	9.0	11.7	All Other Non-Current	19.9	8.8	9.1	13.1	12.7	11.1
100.0	100.0	100.0	Total	100.0	100.0	100.0	100.0	100.0	100.0
			LIABILITIES						
4.4	5.7	3.0	Notes Payable-Short Term	1.4	7.0	11.3	2.3	1.6	2.4
6.2	3.5	2.7	Cur. Mat.-L/T/D	2.0	4.3	2.3	3.5	2.1	2.4
12.3	11.9	7.6	Trade Payables	1.8	9.5	11.1	10.5	5.5	7.6
.1	.3	.3	Income Taxes Payable	.0	.4	.2	.3	.4	.3
8.7	10.6	6.6	All Other Current	5.7	11.9	5.2	7.9	4.3	6.4
31.6	32.0	20.2	Total Current	10.9	33.1	30.0	24.5	14.0	19.1
35.7	24.6	35.6	Long-Term Debt	55.3	37.6	20.2	27.2	32.9	38.2
1.0	1.7	.7	Deferred Taxes	2.3	.3	1.0	1.3	.4	.7
7.6	6.4	4.6	All Other Non-Current	2.3	3.7	2.7	10.5	3.3	4.1
24.0	35.4	38.9	Net Worth	29.1	25.3	46.1	36.5	49.4	38.0
100.0	100.0	100.0	Total Liabilities & Net Worth	100.0	100.0	100.0	100.0	100.0	100.0
			INCOME DATA						
100.0	100.0	100.0	Net Sales	100.0	100.0	100.0	100.0	100.0	100.0
			Gross Profit						
86.1	89.3	90.3	Operating Expenses	68.1	88.5	91.6	90.7	91.2	91.7
13.9	10.7	9.7	Operating Profit	31.9	11.5	8.4	9.3	8.8	8.3
4.7	3.3	3.3	All Other Expenses (net)	11.0	3.4	2.6	3.7	2.2	3.2
9.3	7.4	6.4	Profit Before Taxes	20.9	8.0	5.8	5.6	6.6	5.1
			RATIOS						
1.8	1.9	1.7	Current	7.6	2.3	1.8	2.0	2.0	1.4
1.3	1.2	1.1		2.8	1.6	1.6	1.2	1.3	1.0
.9	.9	.8		1.3	1.2	1.0	.7	1.0	.7
1.7	1.5	1.4	Quick	6.5	1.7	1.6	1.5	1.7	1.1
1.0	.9	.9		2.7	1.2	1.1	.8	.9	.8
.4	.6	.5		.9	1.0	.7	.5	.5	.5
25 14.4	27 13.5	25 14.7	Sales/Receivables	23 15.9	18 20.6	34 10.6	30 12.3	30 12.3	24 15.3
37 10.0	40 9.1	35 10.3		46 8.0	43 8.4	47 7.8	38 9.6	36 10.0	31 12.0
56 6.5	61 6.0	49 7.5		76 4.8	66 5.5	78 4.7	64 5.7	47 7.8	42 8.6
			Cost of Sales/Inventory						
			Cost of Sales/Payables						
6.6	7.3	7.8	Sales/Working Capital	3.3	4.8	7.0	5.9	6.6	13.3
20.1	27.8	33.2		5.4	8.3	11.0	19.6	21.5	343.4
-43.9	-25.4	-24.5		15.0	45.5	-999.8	-9.9	-128.9	-18.3
7.7	6.3	4.7	EBIT/Interest		14.3	7.5	3.9	5.3	3.5
(107) 2.9	(131) 3.3	(307) 2.5			(29) 3.9	2.8	(36) 2.6	(65) 2.5	(159) 2.4
1.5	1.3	1.7			1.7	1.9	1.5	1.9	1.7
4.1	9.1	4.9	Net Profit + Depr., Dep., Amort./Cur. Mat. L/T/D					5.4	4.9
(16) 2.0	(31) 4.1	(46) 2.9						(10) 3.7	(22) 3.0
.8	1.5	1.7						2.6	1.9
.6	.5	1.0	Fixed/Worth	.1	.4	.5	.7	.9	1.4
1.4	1.5	1.7		1.9	1.0	1.0	1.7	1.4	1.9
3.4	3.0	2.5		5.6	2.6	2.3	2.7	2.0	2.6
.7	.7	.9	Debt/Worth	1.2	.8	.4	.8	.6	1.1
2.2	1.9	1.6		4.4	1.6	1.9	1.7	1.0	1.6
7.5	5.3	2.6		24.0	3.5	2.6	5.7	1.6	2.6
31.9	35.7	15.0	% Profit Before Taxes/Tangible Net Worth	74.6	30.0	72.8	18.5	10.8	11.6
(104) 13.4	(130) 11.3	(310) 6.8		(10) 17.4	(27) 15.5	13.1	(36) 7.1	(67) 5.6	(159) 6.6
3.0	2.4	3.6		5.7	3.9	6.3	2.2	3.1	3.8
11.1	10.7	5.2	% Profit Before Taxes/Total Assets	13.0	16.8	26.6	5.2	5.3	4.5
4.2	3.9	2.9		6.2	4.7	3.4	2.8	2.8	2.5
1.4	.8	1.5		2.5	1.3	2.2	.6	1.5	1.5
11.8	30.0	2.6	Sales/Net Fixed Assets	UND	15.2	44.7	17.3	1.0	1.1
1.2	2.1	.8		1.0	3.9	.8	.8	.7	.7
.6	.6	.5		.4	.6	.4	.4	.5	.6
1.6	2.3	1.0	Sales/Total Assets	.6	2.3	3.3	1.3	.7	.8
.6	.9	.5		.4	1.5	.6	.5	.5	.6
.4	.5	.4		.2	.4	.3	.3	.4	.4
2.1	1.4	4.6	% Depr., Dep., Amort./Sales		1.3	1.4	1.7	5.5	4.7
(105) 5.9	(118) 5.5	(307) 6.7			(29) 6.2	(10) 7.8	(39) 8.1	(67) 7.2	(153) 6.3
11.5	8.1	8.8			14.2	13.3	12.5	9.0	7.7
1.7	1.4	2.0	% Officers', Directors', Owners' Comp/Sales						
(20) 3.5	(27) 3.0	(23) 3.3							
6.9	5.9	6.4							
3973897M	5791509M	15201544M	Net Sales ($)	5977M	61564M	43720M	310550M	1115101M	13664632M
5984585M	5899612M	20389181M	Total Assets ($)	19793M	83019M	112742M	727684M	2257188M	17188755M

© RMA 2005

M = $ thousand   MM = $ million

See Pages 11 through 21 for Explanation of Ratios and Data

Current Data Sorted By Assets   Comparative Historical Data

						Type of Statement		
	1	11	15	10	22	Unqualified	35	34
	2	13	5		1	Reviewed	13	12
2	2	3	2			Compiled	14	13
2		1				Tax Returns	5	3
	4	12	11	3	6	Other	18	20
	51 (4/1-9/30/04)		77 (10/1/04-3/31/05)				4/1/00-3/31/01	4/1/01-3/31/02
0-500M	500M-2MM	2-10MM	10-50MM	50-100MM	100-250MM		ALL	ALL
4	9	40	33	13	29	NUMBER OF STATEMENTS	85	82
%	%	%	%	%	%	ASSETS	%	%
		13.4	7.4	6.2	7.5	Cash & Equivalents	8.2	6.5
		31.5	20.9	24.1	13.6	Trade Receivables (net)	18.8	20.6
		8.0	6.1	17.0	4.3	Inventory	7.7	9.7
		3.7	2.5	4.9	8.5	All Other Current	3.0	5.6
		56.6	36.8	52.1	33.9	Total Current	37.6	42.3
		35.4	50.8	33.0	50.2	Fixed Assets (net)	46.5	43.9
		1.4	4.6	4.2	3.9	Intangibles (net)	6.7	4.7
		6.6	7.8	10.6	12.0	All Other Non-Current	9.2	9.1
		100.0	100.0	100.0	100.0	Total	100.0	100.0
						LIABILITIES		
		8.4	6.1	14.1	2.5	Notes Payable-Short Term	9.1	11.4
		2.7	3.1	1.8	2.3	Cur. Mat.-L/T/D	3.0	4.2
		27.8	16.8	23.0	13.0	Trade Payables	16.3	15.9
		.2	.5	.2	.7	Income Taxes Payable	.4	.4
		8.6	6.9	3.8	7.0	All Other Current	8.6	11.0
		47.8	33.4	42.9	25.5	Total Current	37.5	42.9
		15.3	15.5	20.8	27.6	Long-Term Debt	19.9	22.0
		.8	1.4	2.2	5.0	Deferred Taxes	2.4	2.5
		2.2	3.2	6.8	6.8	All Other Non-Current	4.3	4.2
		33.9	46.5	27.3	35.1	Net Worth	35.8	28.4
		100.0	100.0	100.0	100.0	Total Liabilities & Net Worth	100.0	100.0
						INCOME DATA		
		100.0	100.0	100.0	100.0	Net Sales	100.0	100.0
						Gross Profit		
		94.7	96.3	88.6	88.1	Operating Expenses	92.3	93.8
		5.3	3.7	11.4	12.0	Operating Profit	7.7	6.2
		.7	.5	5.7	1.9	All Other Expenses (net)	1.7	1.5
		4.6	3.2	5.7	10.0	Profit Before Taxes	6.1	4.7
						RATIOS		
		1.6	2.0	1.9	1.7		1.6	1.3
		1.1	1.1	1.3	1.2	Current	1.1	1.0
		.9	.7	1.0	1.0		.7	.7
		1.4	1.4	1.3	1.1		1.1	1.1
		.9	.9	.7	.8	Quick	.8	.5
		.5	.4	.3	.4		.3	.3
	17	21.3	18 20.3	23 16.0	26 14.1		16 22.6	16 22.2
	28	13.0	33 10.9	37 9.8	34 10.9	Sales/Receivables	32 11.4	28 13.0
	50	7.3	55 6.6	67 5.4	62 5.9		50 7.3	39 9.4
						Cost of Sales/Inventory		
						Cost of Sales/Payables		
		14.7	7.4	5.9	8.4		11.2	21.9
		43.0	47.6	51.6	27.7	Sales/Working Capital	121.9	712.0
		−46.8	−11.8	UND	NM		−11.8	−10.5
		19.5	12.1	41.5	9.3		5.1	5.1
	(33)	5.6	(27) 4.7	(11) 5.4	3.9	EBIT/Interest	(73) 2.7	(72) 2.9
		2.1	2.0	1.0	2.6		1.6	1.7
					6.0		24.5	5.6
				(11) 5.2		Net Profit + Depr., Dep., Amort./Cur. Mat. L/T/D	(27) 6.6	(23) 2.9
				1.8			2.6	.8
		.2	.8	.0	.8		.7	.7
		.8	1.1	.9	2.1	Fixed/Worth	1.6	1.8
		2.3	3.2	UND	2.5		3.0	3.0
		.9	.4	1.4	1.1		1.0	1.6
		2.6	1.1	3.0	2.0	Debt/Worth	2.2	2.8
		4.4	8.0	UND	5.3		6.6	6.5
		49.5	39.1	55.2	37.0		21.6	55.8
	(36)	20.1	(30) 10.5	(11) 17.5	(28) 19.2	% Profit Before Taxes/Tangible Net Worth	(70) 13.6	(72) 17.8
		7.1	2.7	6.3	12.7		6.9	8.1
		11.4	6.6	6.8	8.8		7.0	9.3
		6.3	2.8	4.8	5.5	% Profit Before Taxes/Total Assets	4.6	5.3
		1.9	1.4	1.0	2.8		1.7	2.2
		97.5	5.9	999.8	10.5		13.0	37.3
		9.1	1.8	6.9	1.1	Sales/Net Fixed Assets	2.6	2.5
		2.5	1.0	.6	.7		1.1	1.5
		4.9	2.2	3.8	1.4		2.8	3.8
		2.7	1.0	1.1	.7	Sales/Total Assets	1.1	1.5
		1.4	.7	.4	.5		.7	.9
		.4	2.8		2.4		1.5	.6
	(37)	2.0	(28) 5.1		(25) 5.2	% Depr., Dep., Amort./Sales	(77) 4.5	(72) 2.8
		4.4	7.8		8.1		6.4	5.4
		.3					.8	.7
	(10)	1.2				% Officers', Directors', Owners' Comp/Sales	(24) 4.5	(17) 2.1
		2.4					7.4	9.9
4746M	45437M	756354M	1162125M	2576407M	5850565M	Net Sales ($)	4126664M	7835570M
990M	12096M	218023M	744423M	908302M	5135768M	Total Assets ($)	3365165M	4740440M

M = $ thousand   MM = $ million
See Pages 11 through 21 for Explanation of Ratios and Data

Comparative Historical Data / Current Data Sorted By Sales

	4/1/02-3/31/03 ALL	4/1/03-3/31/04 ALL	4/1/04-3/31/05 ALL	0-1MM	1-3MM	3-5MM	5-10MM	10-25MM	25MM & OVER
					51 (4/1-9/30/04)			77 (10/1/04-3/31/05)	
Type of Statement									
Unqualified	50	47	59	1	1	1	7	12	37
Reviewed	15	14	21	1	2	1	3	8	6
Compiled	11	14	9	2	1		1	1	4
Tax Returns	6	6	3	1	1		1		
Other	36	29	36	1	3	3	2	8	19
NUMBER OF STATEMENTS	118	110	128	6	8	5	14	29	66
	%	%	%	%	%	%	%	%	%
ASSETS									
Cash & Equivalents	10.2	9.6	9.5				7.9	7.9	9.7
Trade Receivables (net)	18.5	21.9	22.5				14.4	20.1	29.3
Inventory	6.7	8.6	7.4				6.5	12.0	6.3
All Other Current	4.2	4.8	4.4				3.2	3.6	5.7
Total Current	39.7	44.8	43.8				32.0	43.6	51.1
Fixed Assets (net)	48.1	43.5	44.6				56.6	46.9	36.7
Intangibles (net)	5.2	4.3	3.1				1.5	3.9	3.3
All Other Non-Current	7.0	7.4	8.6				10.0	5.6	9.0
Total	100.0	100.0	100.0				100.0	100.0	100.0
LIABILITIES									
Notes Payable-Short Term	9.1	6.6	7.2				5.6	10.9	5.3
Cur. Mat.-L/T/D	3.0	3.4	2.6				3.0	2.7	2.3
Trade Payables	14.1	18.1	19.8				13.0	19.1	25.7
Income Taxes Payable	.4	.3	.4				.2	.2	.6
All Other Current	9.1	8.4	7.1				8.6	7.2	7.4
Total Current	35.7	36.7	37.1				30.3	40.1	41.3
Long-Term Debt	24.3	24.4	21.7				17.0	18.3	18.1
Deferred Taxes	2.0	1.9	2.1				2.0	1.4	2.8
All Other Non-Current	4.5	5.1	4.1				.9	2.2	5.6
Net Worth	33.5	32.0	35.1				49.9	38.0	32.2
Total Liabilities & Net Worth	100.0	100.0	100.0				100.0	100.0	100.0
INCOME DATA									
Net Sales	100.0	100.0	100.0				100.0	100.0	100.0
Gross Profit									
Operating Expenses	93.7	94.0	92.8				90.8	94.7	93.0
Operating Profit	6.3	6.0	7.2				9.2	5.3	7.0
All Other Expenses (net)	1.8	1.8	1.6				1.2	2.0	1.1
Profit Before Taxes	4.5	4.2	5.6				7.9	3.3	5.8
RATIOS									
Current	1.7	1.7	1.8				1.6	1.9	1.6
	1.2	1.2	1.2				1.0	1.3	1.2
	.8	.9	.9				.6	.8	1.0
Quick	1.3	1.3	1.2				1.4	1.2	1.2
	.8	.9	.9				.7	.7	.9
	.4	.4	.4				.4	.4	.5
Sales/Receivables	17 21.3	13 28.0	19 19.7				15 24.1	19 19.3	22 16.7
	31 11.8	28 13.1	33 11.0				30 12.3	33 11.1	35 10.6
	49 7.4	48 7.6	51 7.1				44 8.4	70 5.2	54 6.8
Cost of Sales/Inventory									
Cost of Sales/Payables									
Sales/Working Capital	7.7	11.8	11.8				12.4	7.7	15.2
	30.7	36.8	37.8				NM	26.7	36.7
	-34.2	-62.0	-54.1				-10.7	-27.7	NM
EBIT/Interest	6.3	10.0	11.4				22.4	6.0	18.2
	(104) 2.7	(95) 4.2	(110) 4.3				(11) 5.9	(22) 3.2	(60) 5.0
	1.6	1.5	1.9				2.0	1.1	2.5
Net Profit + Depr., Dep., Amort./Cur. Mat. L/T/D	6.6	5.6	6.0						9.3
	(32) 2.9	(32) 2.7	(30) 3.2					(20)	4.3
	1.4	1.2	1.4						1.7
Fixed/Worth	.7	.5	.4				.8	.7	.0
	1.6	1.4	1.4				1.3	1.1	1.2
	2.8	3.1	2.9				2.1	16.8	2.5
Debt/Worth	1.0	1.0	.8				.5	.7	1.2
	2.2	2.1	2.1				1.0	2.3	2.6
	4.6	10.8	7.7				1.7	41.5	6.8
% Profit Before Taxes/Tangible Net Worth	31.6	33.8	40.6				23.6	32.3	51.8
	(100) 13.9	(93) 17.2	(113) 17.5				(13) 11.1	(24) 8.1	(63) 20.8
	4.8	6.3	6.2				7.0	1.4	11.1
% Profit Before Taxes/Total Assets	9.4	9.9	9.2				9.3	6.1	9.4
	4.3	4.9	4.9				5.2	2.3	5.5
	1.2	1.2	1.6				2.6	.1	2.8
Sales/Net Fixed Assets	19.4	30.3	36.9				13.4	24.0	320.9
	2.7	4.6	3.3				1.6	1.9	5.7
	1.0	1.1	1.0				1.0	1.0	1.1
Sales/Total Assets	2.7	4.4	3.4				2.2	3.0	4.8
	1.3	1.9	1.3				1.1	1.1	1.6
	.6	.7	.7				.7	.7	.7
% Depr., Dep., Amort./Sales	1.7	.9	1.5				2.4	.8	.2
	(100) 4.8	(97) 3.2	(108) 4.2				3.6	(26) 4.4	(51) 3.2
	7.1	5.8	6.2				6.6	6.3	5.9
% Officers', Directors', Owners' Comp/Sales	2.0	.4	.8						
	(21) 4.3	(22) 2.4	(17) 1.8						
	8.5	9.8	5.0						
Net Sales ($)	8160243M	8537650M	10395634M	3761M	19461M	20826M	109972M	485640M	9755974M
Total Assets ($)	5423885M	5173420M	7019602M	7663M	26678M	24790M	168347M	593534M	6198590M

M = $ thousand   MM = $ million
See Pages 11 through 21 for Explanation of Ratios and Data

Current Data Sorted By Assets   **Comparative Historical Data**

		49 (4/1-9/30/04)		134 (10/1/04-3/31/05)				4/1/00-3/31/01	4/1/01-3/31/02
0-500M	500M-2MM	2-10MM	10-50MM	50-100MM	100-250MM	Type of Statement		ALL	ALL
2	14	27	46	9	10	Unqualified		38	58
1	7	4	2			Reviewed		3	17
2	5	5				Compiled		11	10
7	4	4		4		Tax Returns		4	7
1	6	12	7	4	4	Other		25	26
13	36	52	55	13	14	**NUMBER OF STATEMENTS**		81	118
%	%	%	%	%	%	**ASSETS**		%	%
13.6	10.2	10.3	8.2	3.4	4.2	Cash & Equivalents		7.8	7.7
6.5	14.4	6.0	3.4	1.2	1.4	Trade Receivables (net)		7.6	7.2
6.7	5.2	2.2	1.5	.6	.3	Inventory		3.1	3.3
1.6	1.4	3.0	1.0	1.1	4.1	All Other Current		2.3	2.3
28.4	31.3	21.5	14.0	6.3	10.0	Total Current		20.8	20.4
66.5	62.1	72.4	77.8	87.5	77.9	Fixed Assets (net)		72.1	71.8
1.1	.7	.7	1.8	.5	2.1	Intangibles (net)		1.4	2.1
4.1	5.9	5.3	6.5	5.7	10.0	All Other Non-Current		5.8	5.6
100.0	100.0	100.0	100.0	100.0	100.0	Total		100.0	100.0
						LIABILITIES			
40.4	5.1	2.1	1.4	1.4	.9	Notes Payable-Short Term		4.5	1.9
1.8	8.0	2.1	2.3	2.1	3.3	Cur. Mat.-L/T/D		4.2	2.2
11.2	7.7	3.0	1.9	.9	1.2	Trade Payables		5.2	3.8
.0	.1	.2	.1	.0	.0	Income Taxes Payable		.1	.1
3.9	3.3	2.2	2.0	1.4	2.3	All Other Current		4.0	4.3
57.3	24.3	9.6	7.8	5.8	7.7	Total Current		18.0	12.3
19.9	30.8	33.0	36.2	43.7	43.7	Long-Term Debt		32.9	30.6
.0	.2	.5	1.0	.2	2.6	Deferred Taxes		1.3	1.2
14.2	4.3	10.4	12.5	2.1	12.4	All Other Non-Current		7.8	7.9
8.6	40.4	46.5	42.5	48.2	33.5	Net Worth		40.1	47.9
100.0	100.0	100.0	100.0	100.0	100.0	Total Liabilities & Net Worth		100.0	100.0
						INCOME DATA			
100.0	100.0	100.0	100.0	100.0	100.0	Net Sales		100.0	100.0
						Gross Profit			
90.4	86.4	83.3	78.4	77.5	71.0	Operating Expenses		92.5	81.9
9.6	13.6	16.7	21.6	22.5	29.0	Operating Profit		7.5	18.1
1.6	4.5	7.8	7.9	10.8	15.4	All Other Expenses (net)		−4.9	6.0
8.0	9.1	9.0	13.6	11.6	13.7	Profit Before Taxes		12.5	12.1
						RATIOS			
6.0	4.0	5.4	3.2	2.4	2.2			2.8	3.9
.7	1.6	2.0	1.6	1.4	1.1	Current		1.3	1.7
.4	.7	1.1	.8	.6	.5			.6	.8
6.0	3.1	4.2	3.0	2.0	1.4			2.3	3.5
.5	1.3	1.5	1.4	1.2	.7	Quick		(80) .9	1.3
.2	.4	.7	.7	.5	.3			.4	.6
0 UND	22 16.4	27 13.6	26 14.2	19 18.9	28 13.0			25 14.5	25 14.7
5 80.3	36 10.3	36 10.3	33 11.2	29 12.8	35 10.5	Sales/Receivables		32 11.3	33 11.0
20 18.5	81 4.5	57 6.4	39 9.3	45 8.1	40 9.1			49 7.5	48 7.7
						Cost of Sales/Inventory			
						Cost of Sales/Payables			
14.0	2.3	1.3	1.7	3.9	3.4			2.8	2.3
−28.8	9.2	4.2	8.4	10.4	44.5	Sales/Working Capital		18.9	8.4
−5.2	−13.5	43.2	−15.4	−6.4	−3.8			−7.6	−23.8
	13.6	7.7	3.6	5.1		4.0		4.2	4.1
(10) 1.5	3.0	(45) 2.2	(45) 2.6		(10) 2.8	EBIT/Interest	(65) 2.8	(105) 2.6
	−2.7	1.0	1.2	1.9		2.0		1.6	1.4
		3.6	14.6			Net Profit + Depr., Dep.,		32.1	20.6
	(13) 2.0	(10) 4.3			Amort./Cur. Mat. L /T/D	(15) 8.2	(26) 3.2
		1.0	2.9					1.8	1.5
.9	.8	1.0	1.3	1.4	1.7			1.2	1.1
4.1	1.5	1.4	2.0	1.7	3.2	Fixed/Worth		1.7	1.7
−4.5	3.0	4.2	3.0	3.0	4.1			3.1	2.8
.7	.4	.5	.7	.6	2.0			.6	.5
3.3	1.9	.8	1.4	.9	2.9	Debt/Worth		1.6	1.3
−6.9	4.0	3.8	2.8	2.4	3.3			3.3	2.6
	21.6	7.8	12.3	7.6	15.1	% Profit Before Taxes/Tangible		16.8	15.6
(33) 10.4	(49) 3.5	(51) 4.6	2.1	9.1	Net Worth	(75) 10.4	(113) 8.3
	2.9	.6	1.8	1.5	.9			2.1	2.6
28.4	10.2	3.3	4.6	2.9	4.3	% Profit Before Taxes/Total		6.1	5.5
3.0	4.9	1.9	2.3	1.4	3.1	Assets		3.6	3.5
−4.2	.0	.3	.8	.7	.3			1.0	.9
12.0	2.9	.5	.3	.2	.3			.7	.6
2.0	.6	.3	.2	.2	.2	Sales/Net Fixed Assets		.3	.3
.8	.3	.2	.2	.1	.2			.2	.2
7.2	1.7	.3	.3	.2	.2			.5	.4
1.7	.4	.2	.2	.2	.2	Sales/Total Assets		.2	.2
.5	.2	.2	.2	.1	.1			.2	.2
1.6	6.9	8.6	11.8	18.3	10.2			8.2	7.9
4.8	(35) 12.3	(50) 12.1	(54) 17.6	23.1	13.1	% Depr., Dep., Amort./Sales	(77) 12.9	(113) 14.3
11.6	18.6	17.8	23.4	27.3	15.9			17.0	19.2
		4.4				% Officers', Directors',		2.3	.9
	(10) 6.7				Owners' Comp/Sales	(13) 6.2	(15) 4.7
		15.5						20.5	11.9
11116M	42229M	110547M	404030M	118594M	343136M	Net Sales ($)		732870M	1214665M
3297M	40422M	268058M	1301779M	890873M	2277826M	Total Assets ($)		2458069M	3159703M

M = $ thousand   MM = $ million
See Pages 11 through 21 for Explanation of Ratios and Data

Comparative Historical Data			Type of Statement	Current Data Sorted By Sales					
65	67	108	Unqualified	31	35	6	16	13	7
12	13	14	Reviewed	5	3	3	2	1	
11	20	12	Compiled	5	6		1		
7	23	15	Tax Returns	9	3	1	1	1	
34	36	34	Other	8	9	3	9	4	1
4/1/02- 3/31/03 ALL	4/1/03- 3/31/04 ALL	4/1/04- 3/31/05 ALL		49 (4/1-9/30/04)			134 (10/1/04-3/31/05)		
				0-1MM	1-3MM	3-5MM	5-10MM	10-25MM	25MM & OVER
129	159	183	**NUMBER OF STATEMENTS**	58	56	13	29	19	8
%	%	%	**ASSETS**	%	%	%	%	%	%
10.1	8.9	8.9	Cash & Equivalents	11.2	7.6	11.2	7.6	7.4	
6.0	8.0	6.2	Trade Receivables (net)	3.9	5.4	12.5	8.8	5.9	
1.6	2.6	2.6	Inventory	1.2	3.7	2.4	3.5	1.1	
1.7	2.0	1.9	All Other Current	1.3	2.7	.9	.8	3.1	
19.4	21.5	19.7	Total Current	17.6	19.4	27.0	20.7	17.5	
71.7	69.6	73.0	Fixed Assets (net)	76.9	73.7	66.4	72.0	72.0	
1.8	1.5	1.2	Intangibles (net)	.9	.7	1.8	.8	2.1	
7.1	7.4	6.1	All Other Non-Current	4.7	6.2	4.8	6.5	8.4	
100.0	100.0	100.0	Total	100.0	100.0	100.0	100.0	100.0	
			LIABILITIES						
3.4	4.0	5.1	Notes Payable-Short Term	7.4	5.4	2.7	2.1	2.9	
3.6	3.8	3.4	Cur. Mat.-L/T/D	4.8	3.0	1.2	2.0	2.8	
2.8	4.1	3.9	Trade Payables	2.9	3.3	8.6	4.8	3.2	
.1	.1	.1	Income Taxes Payable	.2	.1	.1	.0	.2	
2.7	5.5	2.4	All Other Current	2.3	2.0	3.4	2.5	1.7	
12.6	17.4	14.9	Total Current	17.6	13.8	15.9	11.3	10.7	
32.6	33.7	34.2	Long-Term Debt	29.4	34.4	29.6	35.9	52.2	
.9	1.1	.7	Deferred Taxes	.1	.8	.9	1.1	1.0	
6.2	9.8	9.7	All Other Non-Current	10.1	9.0	15.4	8.7	6.5	
47.7	38.0	40.5	Net Worth	42.8	42.1	38.2	43.0	29.6	
100.0	100.0	100.0	Total Liabilities & Net Worth	100.0	100.0	100.0	100.0	100.0	
			INCOME DATA						
100.0	100.0	100.0	Net Sales	100.0	100.0	100.0	100.0	100.0	
			Gross Profit						
82.8	84.5	81.6	Operating Expenses	82.8	82.2	78.2	82.4	79.8	
17.2	15.5	18.4	Operating Profit	17.2	17.8	21.8	17.6	20.2	
7.5	5.6	7.5	All Other Expenses (net)	6.3	7.6	8.4	7.1	11.4	
9.7	9.9	10.9	Profit Before Taxes	10.9	10.1	13.5	10.6	8.7	
			RATIOS						
4.3	2.7	3.9		5.2	3.4	3.0	3.7	2.6	
1.9	1.4	1.5	Current	2.0	1.4	1.4	1.4	1.5	
.7	.6	.8		.6	.8	.9	.8	.6	
3.3	2.3	3.1		5.1	3.3	2.7	2.1	1.9	
1.6	1.0	1.2	Quick	1.7	1.0	1.3	1.2	1.2	
.5	.4	.5		.5	.4	.6	.5	.5	
25 14.6	21 17.2	25 14.6		26 14.0	17 22.1	32 11.5	26 14.1	26 13.9	
34 10.8	34 10.8	33 11.2	Sales/Receivables	34 10.8	30 12.1	40 9.1	34 10.8	34 10.6	
47 7.8	46 8.0	47 7.8		54 6.7	38 9.5	65 5.6	42 8.6	47 7.8	
			Cost of Sales/Inventory						
			Cost of Sales/Payables						
1.5	3.0	1.9		1.3	1.9	2.4	3.3	3.2	
7.1	11.9	8.8	Sales/Working Capital	4.2	8.5	11.1	20.0	8.4	
−25.9	−11.3	−15.4		−11.7	−25.4	NM	−12.9	−12.4	
4.0	5.9	4.8		5.5	3.9		4.4	3.7	
(118) 2.6	(127) 2.7	(155) 2.4	EBIT/Interest	(52) 2.5	(46) 2.3		(24) 2.6	(16) 2.5	
1.5	1.0	1.3		.9	1.2		1.3	1.5	
8.6	5.3	6.2	Net Profit + Depr., Dep.,	4.3	4.5				
(28) 3.7	(24) 2.3	(41) 3.0	Amort./Cur. Mat. L/T/D	(12) 2.7	(14) 2.5				
1.6	2.0	1.4		1.2	1.4				
1.1	1.1	1.1		1.0	1.3	1.0	1.0	1.5	
1.6	1.7	1.7	Fixed/Worth	1.6	1.7	2.0	1.6	2.1	
2.6	3.8	3.6		3.9	4.2	4.1	2.8	3.5	
.5	.6	.6		.4	.7	1.1	.5	.9	
1.1	1.3	1.4	Debt/Worth	1.0	1.0	1.9	1.5	2.4	
2.5	4.0	3.3		3.3	4.0	3.9	2.3	3.2	
16.1	14.6	13.4	% Profit Before Taxes/Tangible	12.4	12.3	10.0	18.4	11.7	
(122) 6.3	(139) 5.6	(169) 5.1	Net Worth	(54) 4.8	(52) 4.6	(12) 6.1	(27) 4.4	(17) 5.6	
1.6	.3	1.3		1.2	.8	.6	1.3	1.4	
5.1	5.4	4.8	% Profit Before Taxes/Total	5.1	3.6	4.3	5.5	4.8	
3.3	2.5	2.4	Assets	2.5	2.3	2.0	1.6	2.2	
.5	−.1	.4		−.2	.5	.3	.4	.3	
.7	1.5	.6		.6	1.0	1.5	.5	.5	
.3	.3	.3	Sales/Net Fixed Assets	.3	.2	.2	.3	.2	
.2	.2	.2		.2	.2	.2	.2	.2	
.4	.8	.4		.4	.5	.7	.4	.3	
.2	.2	.2	Sales/Total Assets	.2	.2	.2	.2	.2	
.2	.2	.1		.2	.1	.1	.1	.1	
8.2	7.9	9.2		10.0	9.2	2.3	10.3	11.4	
(124) 12.9	(149) 13.6	(179) 14.6	% Depr., Dep., Amort./Sales	(57) 15.6	(55) 14.9	12.7	(27) 15.3	13.8	
19.6	19.4	20.9		18.8	24.8	17.4	22.4	23.1	
1.4	2.0	2.2		5.8					
(16) 3.2	(26) 4.6	(26) 5.0	% Officers', Directors', Owners' Comp/Sales	(10) 12.7					
9.7	9.4	12.9		17.8					
944238M	884131M	1029652M	Net Sales ($)	29672M	97815M	53468M	202903M	306215M	339579M
3225802M	3660118M	4782255M	Total Assets ($)	141536M	493231M	396546M	967627M	1766813M	1016502M

M = $ thousand   MM = $ million
See Pages 11 through 21 for Explanation of Ratios and Data

CONSTRUCTION—GENERAL INDUSTRIES FORMAT*

Current Data Sorted By Assets   **Comparative Historical Data**

						Type of Statement		
5	15	37	63	29	14	Unqualified	77	103
9	67	109	87	13	5	Reviewed	175	177
48	167	194	66	5	1	Compiled	234	287
278	498	362	70	4	8	Tax Returns	321	321
74	182	329	135	14	13	Other	270	434
	333 (4/1-9/30/04)			2568 (10/1/04-3/31/05)			4/1/00-3/31/01	4/1/01-3/31/02
0-500M	500M-2MM	2-10MM	10-50MM	50-100MM	100-250MM		ALL	ALL
414	929	1031	421	65	41	NUMBER OF STATEMENTS	1077	1322
%	%	%	%	%	%	**ASSETS**	%	%
21.8	11.4	8.7	9.3	7.9	10.3	Cash & Equivalents	9.0	8.6
10.1	7.8	6.4	4.6	6.6	1.4	Trade Receivables (net)	10.2	9.1
29.9	54.9	60.7	66.0	65.0	59.9	Inventory	52.3	54.6
7.2	5.2	6.2	5.0	1.6	4.3	All Other Current	5.9	6.2
69.1	79.3	82.1	84.8	81.1	76.0	Total Current	77.3	78.5
19.8	13.3	10.9	8.0	10.7	12.1	Fixed Assets (net)	13.1	12.6
.9	.5	.4	.4	.4	.1	Intangibles (net)	1.1	.5
10.2	7.0	6.6	6.8	7.8	11.8	All Other Non-Current	8.5	8.4
100.0	100.0	100.0	100.0	100.0	100.0	Total	100.0	100.0
						LIABILITIES		
30.5	40.5	42.3	44.5	40+	37.0	Notes Payable-Short Term	35.1	38.3
3.4	2.8	2.9	2.7	1.7	1.9	Cur. Mat.-L/T/D	3.3	3.8
10.3	8.3	8.3	7.8	7.6	6.3	Trade Payables	10.3	10.6
.4	.2	.2	.1	.1	.2	Income Taxes Payable	.2	.2
17.8	11.8	13.3	11.3	10.7	10.5	All Other Current	14.1	13.7
62.4	63.6	67.0	66.3	60.5	55.9	Total Current	63.0	66.7
19.6	12.9	10.9	11.4	8.5	21.8	Long-Term Debt	10.0	10.8
.2	.1	.1	.0	.1	.1	Deferred Taxes	.2	.2
8.3	3.4	2.9	2.4	5.3	5.9	All Other Non-Current	4.3	3.9
9.5	20.0	19.2	19.8	25.6	16.3	Net Worth	22.4	18.5
100.0	100.0	100.0	100.0	100.0	100.0	Total Liabilities & Net Worth	100.0	100.0
						INCOME DATA		
100.0	100.0	100.0	100.0	100.0	100.0	Net Sales	100.0	100.0
23.0	17.5	16.9	17.7	20.2	23.4	Gross Profit	18.6	18.0
18.7	13.4	11.6	11.5	11.4	13.8	Operating Expenses	14.2	13.0
4.4	4.1	5.2	6.2	8.7	9.6	Operating Profit	4.4	5.0
.6	.4	.3	.4	.3	1.0	All Other Expenses (net)	.3	.7
3.8	3.7	4.9	5.8	8.4	8.6	Profit Before Taxes	4.0	4.2
						RATIOS		
2.5	1.8	1.5	1.6	1.8	2.4		1.7	1.6
1.2	1.2	1.1	1.2	1.3	1.3	Current	1.2	1.2
.8	1.0	1.0	1.1	1.1	1.1		1.0	1.0
1.5	.7	.3	.3	.4	.3		.6	.5
(412) .5	(918) .2	(1027) .1	(420) .1	.1	.1	Quick	(1068) .1	(1312) .1
.1	.0	.0	.0	.0	.0		.0	.0
0 UND	0 UND	0 UND	0 UND	0 UND	0 UND		0 UND	0 UND
0 UND	0 UND	0 UND	0 999.8	1 543.4	0 904.0	Sales/Receivables	1 622.0	0 774.9
7 55.7	7 53.6	6 61.5	3 110.5	8 47.3	2 151.8		12 29.7	10 37.4
0 UND	6 57.0	66 5.5	111 3.3	151 2.4	68 5.4		2 238.7	4 87.2
0 UND	110 3.3	173 2.1	209 1.8	240 1.5	208 1.8	Cost of Sales/Inventory	119 3.1	134 2.7
75 4.9	219 1.7	306 1.2	337 1.1	378 1.0	308 1.2		235 1.6	248 1.5
0 UND	0 UND	1 394.6	5 69.5	9 41.9	7 55.3		1 255.4	1 374.4
0 UND	3 118.0	12 30.8	15 24.5	20 18.4	23 16.0	Cost of Sales/Payables	13 28.1	12 29.5
10 36.9	20 17.9	28 13.2	29 12.6	30 12.1	31 11.8		29 12.7	28 13.1
11.9	6.4	5.7	5.1	4.0	3.9		6.6	6.5
44.0	20.7	15.9	11.1	7.0	7.2	Sales/Working Capital	18.6	19.5
-46.7	-126.2	241.4	29.8	17.7	25.6		-742.0	-378.9
16.8	19.1	23.2	27.7	31.3	13.4		12.5	14.0
(291) 4.9	(670) 5.2	(771) 5.6	(322) 7.8	(50) 7.8	(33) 7.3	EBIT/Interest	(847) 3.7	(1041) 4.2
.6	1.3	1.9	3.1	3.6	3.0		1.6	1.6
	8.3	6.1	23.9			Net Profit + Depr., Dep.,	6.6	6.0
	(45) 3.2	(74) 2.5	(31) 3.4			Amort./Cur. Mat. L/T/D	(98) 2.0	(93) 1.7
	.0	.7	1.2				.4	.3
.0	.0	.0	.0	.0	.0		.1	.1
.5	.3	.2	.1	.1	.1	Fixed/Worth	.3	.2
UND	2.5	1.1	.4	.3	1.1		1.2	1.1
1.0	1.9	2.5	2.6	2.3	2.4		1.7	2.0
6.1	5.6	6.5	5.3	3.2	3.4	Debt/Worth	4.8	5.1
-34.0	74.7	20.4	11.3	5.0	10.5		17.0	18.4
188.3	100.0	79.4	77.0	57.8	64.5	% Profit Before Taxes/Tangible	75.0	82.9
(297) 87.0	(770) 39.2	(931) 36.1	(407) 43.1	(62) 39.3	(34) 43.8	Net Worth	(953) 35.8	(1171) 37.1
14.2	8.1	12.0	20.7	22.4	33.0		11.2	11.3
40.1	14.0	12.0	12.1	14.8	16.6	% Profit Before Taxes/Total	13.6	13.7
13.4	5.0	4.7	6.9	9.2	9.9	Assets	5.7	5.8
.0	.5	1.0	2.2	4.8	5.2		1.4	1.4
999.8	415.4	487.3	360.0	167.8	278.0		223.4	218.0
71.3	69.3	82.1	99.1	55.6	74.7	Sales/Net Fixed Assets	57.7	66.5
20.5	17.2	20.8	30.4	18.8	22.0		17.0	17.3
9.4	3.3	2.4	2.1	1.9	2.3		3.5	3.2
4.9	2.1	1.5	1.5	1.3	1.5	Sales/Total Assets	2.1	1.9
2.6	1.3	1.0	1.0	.9	1.1		1.3	1.2
.4	.3	.2	.1	.1	.2		.2	.2
(207) .9	(528) .6	(578) .4	(258) .3	(45) .3	(25) .3	% Depr., Dep., Amort./Sales	(783) .5	(940) .5
2.0	1.4	.9	.6	.7	.7		1.1	1.1
2.3	1.7	1.2	.7	.2	.7	% Officers', Directors',	1.3	1.4
(218) 4.2	(487) 3.3	(472) 2.3	(150) 1.4	(15) .7	(10) 1.9	Owners' Comp/Sales	(540) 3.0	(615) 2.7
8.6	5.7	4.6	3.8	4.0	7.9		5.8	5.2
564913M	2739133M	8512370M	13670540M	7819375M	13657231M	Net Sales ($)	21584023M	28279066M
105928M	1063460M	4806478M	8778523M	4586993M	6383619M	Total Assets ($)	10182578M	14033297M

© RMA 2005

M = $ thousand   MM = $ million
See Pages 11 through 21 for Explanation of Ratios and Data

Comparative Historical Data				Current Data Sorted By Sales					
			Type of Statement						
118	178	163	Unqualified	8	7	11	12	22	103
199	343	290	Reviewed	6	37	38	61	60	88
334	510	481	Compiled	47	126	95	103	69	41
422	1072	1220	Tax Returns	244	433	211	188	96	48
450	736	747	Other	87	157	108	165	118	112
4/1/02-3/31/03	4/1/03-3/31/04	4/1/04-3/31/05		333 (4/1-9/30/04)		2568 (10/1/04-3/31/05)			
				0-1MM	1-3MM	3-5MM	5-10MM	10-25MM	25MM & OVER
ALL	ALL	ALL	**NUMBER OF STATEMENTS**						
1523	2839	2901		392	760	463	529	365	392
%	%	%	**ASSETS**	%	%	%	%	%	%
9.7	9.9	11.6	Cash & Equivalents	14.6	12.2	11.5	10.9	10.2	9.5
7.7	7.5	7.1	Trade Receivables (net)	5.6	5.9	7.8	8.1	7.0	8.4
56.2	56.4	55.3	Inventory	45.6	53.1	54.3	57.0	62.4	61.3
6.8	5.6	5.7	All Other Current	4.6	5.1	6.9	6.9	5.8	5.1
80.3	79.5	79.6	Total Current	70.5	76.4	80.5	82.9	85.4	84.3
11.0	12.2	12.5	Fixed Assets (net)	17.8	16.5	12.0	10.0	7.9	8.0
1.0	.9	.5	Intangibles (net)	.8	.4	.5	.4	.5	.4
7.6	7.4	7.4	All Other Non-Current	10.9	6.7	7.0	6.8	6.2	7.3
100.0	100.0	100.0	Total	100.0	100.0	100.0	100.0	100.0	100.0
			LIABILITIES						
40.3	38.7	40.2	Notes Payable-Short Term	38.1	42.3	35.9	41.5	42.0	40.0
3.3	3.8	2.9	Cur. Mat.-L/T/D	3.2	3.4	3.0	2.7	2.9	1.8
8.8	8.8	8.5	Trade Payables	5.5	6.3	9.9	10.6	9.4	10.4
.2	.2	.2	Income Taxes Payable	.1	.2	.3	.2	.2	.1
13.1	12.3	13.0	All Other Current	15.0	12.6	13.7	12.3	12.9	12.4
65.7	63.8	64.8	Total Current	61.9	64.8	62.8	67.3	67.3	64.8
9.9	11.7	12.9	Long-Term Debt	21.5	14.4	13.9	8.5	10.1	9.1
.2	.1	.1	Deferred Taxes	.0	.1	.0	.2	.1	.0
4.1	4.3	3.9	All Other Non-Current	7.0	3.9	2.9	3.6	2.5	3.3
20.1	20.1	18.3	Net Worth	9.6	16.8	20.4	20.5	20.0	22.8
100.0	100.0	100.0	Total Liabilities & Net Worth	100.0	100.0	100.0	100.0	100.0	100.0
			INCOME DATA						
100.0	100.0	100.0	Net Sales	100.0	100.0	100.0	100.0	100.0	100.0
18.3	18.9	18.3	Gross Profit	26.7	17.9	17.2	15.7	15.7	17.5
13.5	13.6	13.2	Operating Expenses	21.9	13.4	12.3	11.0	10.5	10.8
4.8	5.2	5.0	Operating Profit	4.8	4.6	4.9	4.7	5.1	6.6
.7	.5	.4	All Other Expenses (net)	1.1	.5	.3	.1	.1	.4
4.1	4.7	4.6	Profit Before Taxes	3.8	4.1	4.6	4.6	5.0	6.3
			RATIOS						
1.7	1.7	1.7		2.5	1.8	1.8	1.6	1.5	1.6
1.2	1.2	1.2	Current	1.2	1.1	1.2	1.1	1.2	1.2
1.0	1.0	1.0		.9	.9	1.0	1.0	1.0	1.1
.5	.5	.6		1.0	.6	.6	.6	.4	.4
(1515) .1	(2819) .1	(2883) .1	Quick	(389) .2	(752) .1	(459) .2	(526) .1	.1	.1
.0	.0	.0		.0	.0	.0	.0	.0	.0
0 UND	0 UND	0 UND		0 UND	0 UND	0 UND	0 UND	0 UND	0 UND
0 999.8	0 UND	0 UND	Sales/Receivables	0 UND	0 UND	0 UND	0 999.8	0 999.8	0 801.3
8 46.0	7 53.1	6 65.9		6 63.9	4 88.5	7 54.3	8 47.0	5 73.3	6 64.2
15 24.2	16 22.8	3 104.7		0 UND	0 UND	13 27.6	17 21.5	55 6.7	51 7.2
140 2.6	139 2.6	135 2.7	Cost of Sales/Inventory	123 3.0	123 3.0	111 3.3	134 2.7	158 2.3	162 2.2
271 1.3	264 1.4	269 1.4		433 .8	267 1.4	226 1.6	266 1.4	257 1.4	257 1.4
0 999.8	0 UND	0 UND		0 UND	0 UND	0 UND	1 253.1	2 156.2	6 60.7
11 34.4	10 35.2	8 44.4	Cost of Sales/Payables	0 UND	2 212.3	10 35.9	11 32.1	14 25.5	16 23.2
25 14.6	27 13.6	24 15.3		17 21.0	17 21.4	26 14.3	26 13.9	28 12.8	26 13.8
6.4	5.9	6.2		3.5	6.2	6.3	8.0	6.7	6.0
16.1	15.7	17.0	Sales/Working Capital	21.7	24.5	17.0	19.0	15.2	11.7
476.7	707.3	-999.8		-23.5	-57.2	-593.6	207.0	73.4	30.1
17.1	20.4	21.2		9.0	14.5	25.7	27.8	28.8	29.7
(1173) 5.4	(2117) 5.8	(2137) 5.9	EBIT/Interest	(255) 2.4	(550) 4.6	(345) 5.5	(401) 6.1	(277) 8.0	(309) 9.4
1.7	1.7	1.7		-.3	1.1	1.5	2.0	2.7	4.3
8.7	7.7	7.4			8.6	5.6	6.4	6.3	17.8
(127) 3.2	(171) 2.9	(161) 2.8	Net Profit + Depr., Dep., Amort./Cur. Mat. L/T/D		(25) 1.3	(27) 2.4	(39) 2.4	(28) 3.2	(34) 4.4
.9	1.1	.5			.2	.1	.6	1.2	.9
.0	.0	.0		.0	.0	.0	.0	.0	.0
.2	.2	.2	Fixed/Worth	.3	.4	.2	.2	.1	.1
1.0	1.4	1.5		23.3	6.5	1.4	1.0	.6	.4
2.0	2.0	2.1		2.1	2.0	1.9		2.6	2.2
4.7	5.2	5.7	Debt/Worth	7.9	7.3	5.0	5.9	6.4	3.9
19.0	22.6	23.8		-81.1	198.4	27.0	17.2	15.1	7.2
85.4	92.4	93.7		99.1	107.5	96.0	85.6	95.1	72.8
(1335) 37.9	(2453) 39.8	(2501) 41.3	% Profit Before Taxes/Tangible Net Worth	(289) 29.5	(600) 45.4	(401) 37.2	(485) 36.5	(349) 44.7	(377) 45.0
11.0	11.9	13.0		.0	9.3	12.4	11.6	18.4	25.6
14.9	14.9	14.8		14.4	14.7	15.6	14.0	12.5	16.2
6.3	6.1	5.8	% Profit Before Taxes/Total Assets	2.6	4.8	5.6	5.6	6.1	9.4
1.1	1.1	1.2		-1.9	.5	1.3	1.3	2.1	4.6
254.5	289.9	433.3		UND	425.8	341.7	491.8	557.8	269.2
72.5	71.6	79.2	Sales/Net Fixed Assets	45.4	59.7	72.0	87.0	124.9	101.6
21.9	20.1	20.0		9.6	14.3	19.3	25.7	37.4	37.2
3.1	3.1	3.1		2.6	3.2	3.4	3.3	2.7	2.9
1.9	1.9	1.8	Sales/Total Assets	1.1	1.9	2.0	2.0	1.8	1.9
1.2	1.2	1.1		.6	1.1	1.3	1.3	1.3	1.3
.2	.2	.2		.6	.3	.2	.2	.1	.1
(1032) .4	(1701) .5	(1641) .5	% Depr., Dep., Amort./Sales	(173) 1.6	(415) .6	(268) .5	(305) .4	(221) .3	(259) .3
1.1	1.2	1.1		3.5	1.4	1.3	1.2	.7	.5
1.4	1.5	1.4		3.3	2.0	1.5	1.2		.5
(703) 3.0	(1400) 3.0	(1352) 2.9	% Officers', Directors', Owners' Comp/Sales	(164) 6.4	(381) 3.5	(242) 2.6	(264) 2.4	(159) 1.9	(142) 1.1
5.8	5.8	5.4		12.4	5.6	4.7	4.6	3.9	3.2
30597518M	59995076M	46963562M	Net Sales ($)	228003M	1451118M	1812327M	3705568M	5659935M	34106611M
17867000M	27828950M	25725001M	Total Assets ($)	313262M	1151525M	1182165M	2342027M	3663839M	17072183M

M = $ thousand   MM = $ million
See Pages 11 through 21 for Explanation of Ratios and Data

Current Data Sorted By Assets | Comparative Historical Data

	0-500M	500M-2MM	2-10MM	10-50MM	50-100MM	100-250MM	Type of Statement	4/1/00-3/31/01	4/1/01-3/31/02
		3	14	15	3	6	Unqualified	32	43
	3	13	26	9			Reviewed	56	36
	7	11	11	4		1	Compiled	34	41
	23	53	24	4	1	2	Tax Returns	54	34
	5	22	24	11		3	Other	46	62
		35 (4/1-9/30/04)		266 (10/1/04-3/31/05)				ALL	ALL
	38	102	99	43	7	12	NUMBER OF STATEMENTS	222	216

	0-500M	500M-2MM	2-10MM	10-50MM	50-100MM	100-250MM		4/1/00-3/31/01 ALL	4/1/01-3/31/02 ALL
	%	%	%	%	%	%	**ASSETS**	%	%
	21.0	10.7	10.7	12.7		8.9	Cash & Equivalents	15.5	15.3
	13.1	19.5	24.2	19.9		16.4	Trade Receivables (net)	27.9	32.3
	30.3	33.6	28.9	35.1		36.7	Inventory	20.5	16.1
	6.2	8.7	9.1	4.9		4.2	All Other Current	10.6	11.0
	70.7	72.5	72.9	72.5		66.1	Total Current	74.5	74.7
	18.5	18.9	18.3	14.1		20.3	Fixed Assets (net)	17.0	16.4
	1.3	1.7	1.4	1.9		2.1	Intangibles (net)	1.1	1.4
	9.5	6.9	7.5	11.5		11.6	All Other Non-Current	7.4	7.5
	100.0	100.0	100.0	100.0		100.0	Total	100.0	100.0
							LIABILITIES		
	29.7	21.7	20.9	18.9		20.9	Notes Payable-Short Term	22.1	16.4
	3.3	8.7	6.1	2.0		7.5	Cur. Mat.-L/T/D	3.7	3.8
	9.3	13.5	17.1	20.3		10.9	Trade Payables	20.6	23.8
	.1	.3	.5	.1		.1	Income Taxes Payable	.5	.5
	19.0	12.9	13.8	12.5		12.9	All Other Current	19.2	14.6
	61.5	57.0	58.3	53.8		52.3	Total Current	66.0	59.0
	15.6	14.9	11.7	11.5		18.2	Long-Term Debt	10.7	13.9
	.0	.1	.1	.1		.0	Deferred Taxes	.3	.4
	16.4	3.6	1.9	3.9		1.4	All Other Non-Current	2.4	4.4
	6.3	24.5	28.0	30.7		28.2	Net Worth	20.7	22.4
	100.0	100.0	100.0	100.0		100.0	Total Liabilities & Net Worth	100.0	100.0
							INCOME DATA		
	100.0	100.0	100.0	100.0		100.0	Net Sales	100.0	100.0
	26.5	20.6	17.1	18.4		28.8	Gross Profit	19.0	17.9
	21.1	16.2	11.8	9.9		19.3	Operating Expenses	14.5	14.4
	5.4	4.5	5.3	8.4		9.5	Operating Profit	4.5	3.5
	1.4	.3	.5	-.7		-1.1	All Other Expenses (net)	.3	.4
	4.0	4.2	4.8	9.1		10.6	Profit Before Taxes	4.2	3.1
							RATIOS		
	2.9	2.4	2.0	2.5		2.8		1.8	1.7
	1.3	1.3	1.2	1.3		1.3	Current	1.2	1.3
	.7	1.0	1.0	1.1		.4		1.0	1.1
	2.1	1.5	1.3	1.1		1.1		1.3	1.4
	.6	(99) .5	.6	.6		.3	Quick	(221) .8	(215) 1.0
	.1	.1	.1	.1		.1		.2	.2
	0 UND	0 UND	0 UND	0 999.8		0 UND		0 999.8	2 232.0
	0 UND	3 145.8	25 14.7	10 36.4		4 89.4	Sales/Receivables	31 11.9	39 9.4
	11 33.5	40 9.1	61 5.9	50 7.3		61 6.0		59 6.2	64 5.7
	0 UND	0 UND	0 UND	0 UND		0 UND		0 UND	0 UND
	2 166.0	3 142.9	1 639.5	32 11.5		6 57.7	Cost of Sales/Inventory	0 UND	0 UND
	84 4.3	150 2.4	145 2.5	317 1.2		290 1.3		76 4.8	18 20.0
	0 UND	0 UND	4 82.7	16 22.9		0 UND		3 114.6	9 42.7
	1 636.5	10 36.6	24 15.5	28 12.9		15 24.4	Cost of Sales/Payables	23 16.1	28 12.9
	7 49.3	33 11.0	43 8.6	54 6.7		29 12.6		47 7.7	50 7.3
	8.9	7.0	6.6	2.8		2.5		8.0	7.6
	28.5	17.7	16.4	13.4		5.2	Sales/Working Capital	21.2	17.8
	-66.6	NM	-84.2	25.6		NM		275.6	82.4
	20.5	12.8	36.2	62.9				15.3	23.6
	(31) 8.4	(81) 4.6	(77) 7.3	(35) 14.8			EBIT/Interest	(171) 4.5	(177) 6.3
	2.3	1.3	2.0	4.6				1.4	1.7
			9.7				Net Profit + Depr., Dep.,	12.1	10.4
		(15) 3.0					Amort./Cur. Mat. L./T/D	(29) 2.7	(31) 2.9
			.2					.1	1.0
	.0	.1	.1	.1		.1		.1	.1
	.8	.5	.3	.1		.2	Fixed/Worth	.3	.3
	UND	3.6	1.1	.7		1.7		1.2	1.0
	1.0	1.3	1.3	1.3		1.5		1.2	1.4
	3.8	4.7	2.9	4.0		2.5	Debt/Worth	3.2	3.3
	-7.9	53.2	10.8	9.4		4.2		13.3	10.7
	189.9	54.8	52.8	75.9		72.2	% Profit Before Taxes/Tangible	69.7	51.5
	(28) 78.8	(83) 30.4	(91) 26.5	34.1		(11) 53.5	Net Worth	(199) 22.1	(196) 26.8
	30.0	10.4	7.2	14.6		14.2		5.5	8.3
	44.6	18.2	10.9	12.6		21.2	% Profit Before Taxes/Total	13.3	12.6
	16.0	5.4	5.3	7.4		10.1	Assets	5.7	5.5
	.7	.2	1.8	2.6		3.8		1.1	1.4
	593.1	243.5	208.3	304.1		147.1		151.2	134.3
	63.3	48.7	47.3	119.1		33.0	Sales/Net Fixed Assets	54.1	45.2
	16.4	8.3	7.0	11.4		4.1		11.4	14.7
	11.1	4.0	3.2	3.2		3.2		4.2	4.3
	4.4	2.6	1.8	1.2		1.4	Sales/Total Assets	2.7	2.8
	2.0	1.8	1.1	.8		.8		1.6	1.7
	.1	.2	.3	.1		.1		.3	.2
	(22) 1.2	(70) .6	(71) .6	(27) .3			% Depr., Dep., Amort./Sales	(166) .5	(178) .5
	2.6	1.9	1.3	.8				1.6	1.3
	2.1	1.8	1.3	.9				1.7	1.5
	(21) 4.0	(54) 3.9	(39) 2.2	(10) 1.4			% Officers', Directors',	(104) 3.5	(100) 3.1
	6.8	6.7	3.4	2.6			Owners' Comp/Sales	6.0	5.3
	58050M	401778M	980478M	1740219M	425622M	5012183M	Net Sales ($)	5853460M	6801194M
	10391M	114832M	440382M	845994M	407849M	1854212M	Total Assets ($)	2525657M	2582290M

M = $ thousand   MM = $ million
See Pages 11 through 21 for Explanation of Ratios and Data

Comparative Historical Data | Current Data Sorted By Sales

			Type of Statement						
29	37	41	Unqualified		1	1	4	10	25
33	48	51	Reviewed	1	7	7	16	14	6
21	40	34	Compiled	2	8	9	7	6	2
47	78	107	Tax Returns	21	34	21	20	8	3
35	70	68	Other	5	20	12	8	15	8
4/1/02-3/31/03	4/1/03-3/31/04	4/1/04-3/31/05		35 (4/1-9/30/04)			266 (10/1/04-3/31/05)		
ALL	ALL	ALL		0-1MM	1-3MM	3-5MM	5-10MM	10-25MM	25MM & OVER
165	273	301	NUMBER OF STATEMENTS	29	70	50	55	53	44
%	%	%	ASSETS	%	%	%	%	%	%
13.2	14.5	12.5	Cash & Equivalents	15.5	9.4	9.2	14.4	15.3	13.2
23.5	19.3	19.9	Trade Receivables (net)	4.8	14.0	18.9	18.2	31.7	28.5
24.6	28.6	31.5	Inventory	41.4	37.5	33.3	31.4	21.2	26.2
8.6	9.1	7.6	All Other Current	1.4	6.4	7.7	9.3	11.4	6.9
70.0	71.5	71.5	Total Current	63.1	67.2	69.1	73.3	79.6	74.8
20.8	18.2	17.9	Fixed Assets (net)	21.7	23.5	20.0	20.1	11.2	9.3
1.2	.7	1.6	Intangibles (net)	3.2	.8	1.0	2.0	.5	3.1
8.0	9.6	9.0	All Other Non-Current	11.9	8.5	9.8	4.6	8.8	12.9
100.0	100.0	100.0	Total	100.0	100.0	100.0	100.0	100.0	100.0
			LIABILITIES						
19.1	22.0	21.7	Notes Payable-Short Term	39.0	22.7	28.4	21.8	12.4	12.2
7.1	5.1	5.9	Cur. Mat.-L/T/D	1.1	9.0	6.3	6.3	6.6	2.5
18.3	16.9	14.9	Trade Payables	2.0	9.1	13.8	14.2	24.0	23.9
.5	.3	.3	Income Taxes Payable	.0	.3	.3	.5	.6	.5
15.1	15.4	13.8	All Other Current	11.6	14.2	13.7	12.6	15.3	14.6
60.1	59.7	56.7	Total Current	53.7	55.3	62.2	55.4	58.8	53.7
12.6	12.3	13.7	Long-Term Debt	21.2	17.0	12.7	13.3	9.1	10.5
.2	.2	.1	Deferred Taxes	.0	.1	.0	.1	.2	.0
3.5	3.8	4.7	All Other Non-Current	6.2	10.2	2.8	2.2	2.3	3.0
23.5	23.9	24.9	Net Worth	19.0	17.4	22.3	28.9	29.6	32.7
100.0	100.0	100.0	Total Liabilities & Net Worth	100.0	100.0	100.0	100.0	100.0	100.0
			INCOME DATA						
100.0	100.0	100.0	Net Sales	100.0	100.0	100.0	100.0	100.0	100.0
19.1	19.5	20.5	Gross Profit	33.6	24.4	20.8	16.0	14.5	18.3
15.0	14.8	14.7	Operating Expenses	21.3	19.2	14.3	12.3	11.0	11.1
4.1	4.8	5.8	Operating Profit	12.2	5.2	6.5	3.7	3.5	7.2
.4	.4	.3	All Other Expenses (net)	3.8	.3	–.1	–.1	–.6	–.2
3.6	4.3	5.6	Profit Before Taxes	8.4	4.9	6.6	3.8	4.1	7.4
			RATIOS						
1.8	1.7	2.1	Current	4.9	2.5	2.3	2.3	1.9	1.9
1.2	1.3	1.3		1.4	1.3	1.2	1.3	1.3	1.3
1.0	1.0	1.0		1.0	.8	.9	1.0	1.1	1.2
1.2	1.2	1.3	Quick	1.8	1.5	1.3	1.4	1.3	1.1
(164) .7	(271) .6	(298) .6		.1	(68) .4	.4	(54) .5	.9	.9
.1	.1	.1		.1	.1	.0	.1	.2	.1
0 UND	0 UND	0 UND	Sales/Receivables	0 UND	0 UND	0 UND	0 UND	1 424.1	0 846.9
10 37.3	6 62.7	4 82.9		0 UND	1 666.3	1 636.7	5 69.7	29 12.5	25 14.7
51 7.2	43 8.5	46 7.9		0 UND	22 16.3	44 8.3	46 8.0	68 5.4	57 6.4
0 UND	0 UND	0 UND	Cost of Sales/Inventory	0 UND	0 UND	0 UND	0 UND	0 UND	0 UND
0 UND	1 443.1	2 230.5		205 1.8	11 33.6	0 UND	7 55.4	0 UND	0 UND
121 3.0	155 2.4	154 2.4		330 1.1	187 2.0	117 3.1	135 2.7	68 5.4	129 2.8
1 308.7	2 171.0	1 614.7	Cost of Sales/Payables	0 UND	0 UND	0 UND	1 544.5	17 21.0	11 33.5
17 21.6	17 21.0	16 23.4		1 497.0	8 48.6	12 30.7	14 26.1	32 11.4	22 16.2
40 9.0	41 8.8	37 9.9		22 16.7	24 15.4	33 11.1	33 11.0	46 8.0	49 7.4
7.3	8.1	5.6	Sales/Working Capital	2.6	4.9	7.4	8.4	8.4	4.8
23.5	18.0	16.7		9.7	19.8	18.3	16.8	16.4	14.1
–503.6	–297.2	–432.7		NM	–27.0	–24.8	188.0	66.6	28.8
27.3	24.5	26.9	EBIT/Interest	14.8	15.3	32.5	15.8	18.0	191.8
(131) 5.3	(214) 7.3	(237) 6.8		(22) 5.5	(55) 4.2	(43) 8.5	(45) 4.3	(39) 6.7	(33) 28.3
1.2	2.1	2.2		1.5	1.3	3.6	.9	2.0	6.2
7.2	5.9	9.7	Net Profit + Depr., Dep., Amort./Cur. Mat. L/T/D					9.8	
(26) 2.0	(30) 2.1	(31) 3.6						(11) 2.5	
.7	.2	1.5						.1	
.1	.1	.1	Fixed/Worth	.0	.1	.1	.1	.1	.0
.4	.3	.3		.9	.6	.5	.3	.2	.1
2.0	1.6	1.7		3.7	3.6	3.7	1.7	.6	.4
1.4	1.3	1.3	Debt/Worth	2.0	1.2	1.3	1.1	1.4	1.5
3.1	3.2	3.4		4.4	5.1	5.7	3.4	2.3	2.7
10.0	9.5	17.9		UND	66.8	25.8	15.4	9.4	4.8
73.2	78.4	71.7	% Profit Before Taxes/Tangible Net Worth	109.5	58.7	81.1	74.0	52.2	71.7
(142) 29.6	(243) 38.3	(263) 32.4		(22) 37.8	(57) 32.6	(42) 41.3	(49) 28.0	(50) 23.5	(43) 45.9
8.6	9.8	11.9		12.7	6.8	21.1	5.5	6.0	18.3
15.3	17.1	17.0	% Profit Before Taxes/Total Assets	18.9	19.1	18.7	11.2	12.5	22.6
6.4	8.2	6.6		5.4	6.5	7.7	5.3	5.1	9.3
1.0	2.0	1.7		1.3	.1	2.6	1.7	1.7	5.7
126.2	174.1	251.6	Sales/Net Fixed Assets	UND	412.5	203.4	177.1	225.3	300.5
38.1	48.6	51.4		25.7	30.5	51.4	52.2	51.8	139.8
10.5	10.8	9.4		3.6	5.2	6.4	10.4	15.5	35.7
4.3	4.1	3.8	Sales/Total Assets	2.0	3.8	3.3	4.0	4.2	4.4
2.6	2.3	2.4		1.1	2.0	2.3	2.7	2.7	2.8
1.5	1.5	1.2		.4	.9	1.4	1.6	1.2	1.1
.2	.2	.2	% Depr., Dep., Amort./Sales	.8	.2	.3	.4	.2	.1
(127) .6	(187) .6	(202) .6		(14) 2.0	(45) 1.1	(30) 1.0	(42) .7	(42) .4	(29) .2
1.6	1.5	1.7		5.4	2.5	2.1	1.7	.8	.5
1.6	1.4	1.5	% Officers', Directors', Owners' Comp/Sales	3.4	2.7	1.3	1.1	1.6	
(70) 3.5	(106) 2.8	(127) 2.7		(10) 6.5	(35) 5.1	(28) 2.6	(27) 2.1	(18) 2.1	
5.9	6.0	6.0		9.0	8.2	4.2	3.4	2.8	
8314765M	6208714M	8618330M	Net Sales ($)	15147M	128491M	197299M	385597M	804267M	7087529M
2166283M	3213264M	3673660M	Total Assets ($)	27797M	104179M	135336M	216315M	511596M	2678437M

© RMA 2005   M = $ thousand   MM = $ million
See Pages 11 through 21 for Explanation of Ratios and Data

Current Data Sorted By Assets   **Comparative Historical Data**

	0-500M	500M-2MM	2-10MM	10-50MM	50-100MM	100-250MM	Type of Statement	4/1/00-3/31/01 ALL	4/1/01-3/31/02 ALL
		2	2	9	5	5	Unqualified	11	21
	2	7	10	6	2	3	Reviewed	15	17
	4	7	16	2	1		Compiled	12	20
	9	30	14	8			Tax Returns	8	7
	4	13	13	20	6	1	Other	15	28
	_ 26 (4/1-9/30/04) _			_ 175 (10/1/04-3/31/05) _					
NUMBER OF STATEMENTS	19	59	55	45	14	9		61	93
	%	%	%	%	%	%	**ASSETS**	%	%
	16.6	14.2	11.7	8.1	8.9		Cash & Equivalents	10.7	13.8
	11.2	11.5	17.8	13.4	9.2		Trade Receivables (net)	29.4	34.1
	25.8	40.7	39.6	54.4	50.7		Inventory	30.9	19.5
	9.2	4.7	7.9	7.0	4.9		All Other Current	5.1	9.3
	62.8	71.1	77.0	82.8	73.7		Total Current	76.1	76.6
	19.1	19.6	14.4	8.0	11.2		Fixed Assets (net)	16.4	15.1
	6.4	1.7	.6	.3	2.1		Intangibles (net)	1.5	.8
	11.6	7.6	8.0	8.8	13.1		All Other Non-Current	6.0	7.6
	100.0	100.0	100.0	100.0	100.0		Total	100.0	100.0
							LIABILITIES		
	33.0	33.9	28.3	32.3	36.0		Notes Payable-Short Term	19.6	17.3
	9.0	5.2	2.6	1.9	.4		Cur. Mat.-L/T/D	3.3	2.7
	6.8	12.9	15.5	13.4	8.8		Trade Payables	21.3	23.7
	.0	.3	.1	.1	.1		Income Taxes Payable	1.0	.7
	20.6	10.3	15.0	17.4	5.4		All Other Current	13.5	17.4
	69.3	62.6	61.4	65.0	50.8		Total Current	58.6	61.9
	27.1	14.4	8.8	10.4	12.7		Long-Term Debt	10.0	11.3
	.0	.0	.0	.1	.1		Deferred Taxes	.2	.1
	15.5	4.3	3.2	2.9	4.9		All Other Non-Current	4.3	1.9
	−11.9	18.7	26.6	21.6	31.5		Net Worth	26.9	24.8
	100.0	100.0	100.0	100.0	100.0		Total Liabilities & Net Worth	100.0	100.0
							INCOME DATA		
	100.0	100.0	100.0	100.0	100.0		Net Sales	100.0	100.0
	17.8	22.2	18.5	17.0	27.6		Gross Profit	19.2	19.5
	14.5	16.8	13.6	12.4	15.9		Operating Expenses	16.8	13.4
	3.3	5.4	4.9	4.6	11.8		Operating Profit	2.4	6.1
	.6	.6	.5	.0	2.1		All Other Expenses (net)	−.3	1.5
	2.7	4.8	4.3	4.6	9.7		Profit Before Taxes	2.6	4.6
							RATIOS		
	1.7	1.7	2.0	1.5	2.1		Current	1.7	1.6
	.9	1.1	1.2	1.2	1.4			1.3	1.2
	.5	.9	1.0	1.1	1.1			1.1	1.1
	.8	1.0	1.2	.8	.9		Quick	1.3	1.3
	.3	.2	.1	.1	.2			.8	.9
	.1	.0	.0	.0	.1			.1	.3
	0 UND	0 UND	0 UND	0 999.8	0 UND		Sales/Receivables	2 222.3	1 301.6
	0 UND	0 UND	2 146.1	3 113.5	2 195.1			24 15.1	39 9.4
	8 45.3	22 16.8	39 9.3	37 9.9	22 16.8			64 5.7	70 5.2
	0 UND	0 UND	0 UND	1 450.1	0 UND		Cost of Sales/Inventory	0 UND	0 UND
	0 UND	51 7.2	98 3.7	198 1.8	225 1.6			2 172.0	0 UND
	47 7.8	248 1.5	229 1.6	329 1.1	342 1.1			177 2.1	91 4.0
	0 UND	0 UND	1 458.0	10 36.0	18 20.8		Cost of Sales/Payables	10 35.8	14 25.3
	6 64.3	12 30.4	19 19.3	26 14.1	42 8.8			25 14.8	30 12.3
	18 20.0	40 9.1	45 8.1	45 8.2	57 6.4			48 7.6	57 6.5
	21.7	4.8	4.6	5.5	2.7		Sales/Working Capital	5.7	7.6
	−321.1	23.1	13.5	12.8	4.9			15.0	18.2
	−15.0	−25.8	−83.9	30.9	52.4			62.8	66.0
	12.1	11.6	19.8	24.4			EBIT/Interest	15.6	23.9
	(12) 3.8	(36) 2.7	(38) 6.4	(37) 6.8				(50) 6.2	(67) 5.9
	1.8	.1	2.1	1.9				1.8	1.5
							Net Profit + Depr., Dep., Amort./Cur. Mat. L /T/D		8.4
								(16)	2.3
									1.1
	.0	.0	.0	.0	.0		Fixed/Worth	.1	.1
	.2	.4	.2	.2	.1			.5	.3
	−1.8	8.9	1.5	.5	.4			.9	.9
	3.8	1.8	1.7	2.2	1.4		Debt/Worth	1.4	1.4
	22.6	6.9	4.7	5.7	2.3			3.0	3.4
	−5.0	−826.0	10.2	13.1	4.2			10.5	8.5
	54.8	98.7	63.0	64.6	52.2		% Profit Before Taxes/Tangible Net Worth	52.9	48.8
	(11) 36.0	(44) 27.3	(52) 32.9	(44) 32.2	37.6			(57) 27.0	(83) 21.6
	23.9	5.1	7.5	14.5	10.8			6.9	5.8
	53.0	19.0	13.0	8.4	14.9		% Profit Before Taxes/Total Assets	11.6	12.9
	5.3	5.1	6.1	3.9	10.0			4.3	5.0
	1.6	−.1	.8	2.2	3.7			1.6	1.1
	UND	834.0	204.9	208.7	800.9		Sales/Net Fixed Assets	104.7	137.8
	105.9	41.8	76.7	64.3	162.6			23.2	40.5
	15.5	6.8	12.5	18.9	9.9			9.6	13.4
	6.5	3.2	3.0	2.1	1.5		Sales/Total Assets	3.7	3.6
	5.1	1.7	2.1	1.5	1.0			2.2	2.7
	2.2	.9	.9	1.1	.7			1.2	1.3
		.2	.2	.2			% Depr., Dep., Amort./Sales	.4	.2
	(28)	1.0	(35) .5	(29) .5				(49) 1.4	(73) .5
		2.2	1.1	1.6				2.0	1.5
		2.4	1.7	.5			% Officers', Directors', Owners' Comp/Sales	1.6	1.3
	(26)	3.5	(26) 2.2	(13) 1.6				(25) 3.3	(34) 3.0
		6.4	5.1	2.9				7.5	6.6
	23816M	169079M	585267M	1724736M	986370M	1341961M	Net Sales ($)	1229232M	3093365M
	5372M	68125M	262957M	1005892M	955873M	1368689M	Total Assets ($)	695331M	1682443M

M = $ thousand   MM = $ million
See Pages 11 through 21 for Explanation of Ratios and Data

Comparative Historical Data | Current Data Sorted By Sales

16		21		23	Type of Statement	2	1	1	3	16
7		30		30	Unqualified	2	3	2	6	7	10
18		26		30	Reviewed	5	10	4	4	5	2
15		44		61	Compiled	16	20	6	9	7	3
34		30		57	Tax Returns	7	10	2	3	16	19
					Other						

4/1/02-3/31/03 ALL	4/1/03-3/31/04 ALL	4/1/04-3/31/05 ALL		26 (4/1-9/30/04)			175 (10/1/04-3/31/05)		
				0-1MM	1-3MM	3-5MM	5-10MM	10-25MM	25MM & OVER
90	151	201	NUMBER OF STATEMENTS	32	43	15	23	38	50

%	%	%	ASSETS	%	%	%	%	%	%
12.3	13.8	11.8	Cash & Equivalents	13.6	10.7	10.0	16.0	11.9	9.9
21.4	15.5	13.1	Trade Receivables (net)	.7	12.5	18.9	18.0	10.5	19.6
32.0	38.8	42.6	Inventory	41.5	40.8	37.4	42.2	47.3	43.1
10.1	6.1	6.4	All Other Current	3.1	7.5	2.5	4.6	9.0	7.5
75.8	74.2	73.9	Total Current	59.0	71.5	68.8	80.8	78.7	80.2
17.8	15.9	15.9	Fixed Assets (net)	28.8	17.5	19.3	12.9	10.4	11.0
.8	1.3	1.5	Intangibles (net)	3.6	2.6	.5	.0	.6	.8
5.6	8.6	8.6	All Other Non-Current	8.5	8.4	11.4	6.3	10.3	8.0
100.0	100.0	100.0	Total	100.0	100.0	100.0	100.0	100.0	100.0

			LIABILITIES						
34.3	23.1	31.1	Notes Payable-Short Term	41.4	35.2	23.5	30.5	30.3	24.3
4.4	3.9	3.6	Cur. Mat.-L/T/D	11.5	3.6	6.8	.8	1.1	.5
13.3	14.4	12.6	Trade Payables	5.2	11.7	10.6	16.1	15.1	15.3
.3	.3	.2	Income Taxes Payable	.1	.4	.0	.0	.1	.2
11.0	15.6	13.5	All Other Current	18.3	9.9	5.0	11.2	14.7	16.1
63.4	57.4	60.9	Total Current	76.4	60.8	46.1	58.6	61.2	56.5
8.8	10.3	13.4	Long-Term Debt	21.5	13.9	15.8	13.6	11.3	8.7
.3	.2	.0	Deferred Taxes	.0	.0	.0	.1	.0	.1
5.2	6.3	5.0	All Other Non-Current	8.3	5.8	7.3	1.9	1.9	5.3
22.2	25.7	20.6	Net Worth	−6.3	19.6	30.9	25.8	25.5	29.4
100.0	100.0	100.0	Total Liabilities & Net Worth	100.0	100.0	100.0	100.0	100.0	100.0

			INCOME DATA						
100.0	100.0	100.0	Net Sales	100.0	100.0	100.0	100.0	100.0	100.0
20.5	19.6	21.0	Gross Profit	22.5	21.4	21.0	22.3	20.8	19.4
16.1	14.4	15.0	Operating Expenses	17.1	16.3	15.0	17.4	14.7	11.9
4.4	5.2	6.0	Operating Profit	5.4	5.2	6.0	4.9	6.1	7.5
.5	.9	.8	All Other Expenses (net)	1.4	.4	.3	.6	1.6	.4
3.9	4.3	5.2	Profit Before Taxes	4.1	4.8	5.7	4.3	4.6	7.1

			RATIOS						
1.9	1.8	1.9		1.2	1.9	4.2	2.0	2.3	1.9
1.2	1.3	1.2	Current	.9	1.2	1.6	1.3	1.2	1.3
1.0	1.0	1.0		.2	.9	.9	.9	1.0	1.1
1.3	1.1	1.0		.2	1.0	1.6	1.2	1.3	1.1
.4	.3	.2	Quick	.1	.1	.6	.5	.1	.4
.1	.1	.0		.0	.0	.1	.1	.0	.1
0 UND	0 UND	0 UND		0 UND	0 UND	0 UND	0 UND	0 UND	0 UND
10 36.9	2 234.5	1 469.8	Sales/Receivables	0 UND	0 UND	6 61.3	4 99.0	1 538.0	7 51.4
45 8.2	30 12.0	21 17.1		0 UND	30 12.2	82 4.4	39 9.3	19 19.4	60 6.1
0 UND	0 UND	0 UND		0 UND	0 UND	0 UND	0 UND	0 UND	0 999.8
4 85.5	36 10.2	99 3.7	Cost of Sales/Inventory	166 2.2	98 3.7	8 47.2	23 15.6	149 2.5	109 3.3
199 1.8	259 1.4	285 1.3		372 1.0	246 1.5	417 .9	192 1.9	317 1.2	250 1.5
3 118.3	4 94.9	2 204.1		0 UND	1 515.3	2 212.3	1 312.6	5 75.5	19 18.9
22 16.8	22 16.9	20 18.6	Cost of Sales/Payables	0 UND	16 22.3	15 23.9	17 21.4	18 20.8	38 9.5
36 10.1	39 9.4	43 8.5		20 18.3	44 8.4	59 6.2	36 10.3	50 7.3	50 7.4
6.1	5.8	4.7		5.2	5.8	1.5	6.1	4.7	4.3
16.5	14.4	15.6	Sales/Working Capital	−38.0	15.6	4.6	13.6	14.7	10.9
128.5	306.3	−93.4		−2.1	−83.9	−48.7	−75.2	−506.8	30.9
25.8	19.0	16.3		11.5	11.7	7.5	11.0	24.9	27.1
(68) 5.9	(114) 6.0	(138) 5.0	EBIT/Interest	(18) 1.9	(28) 4.4	(11) 2.6	(16) 3.8	(28) 7.5	(37) 9.3
1.3	2.0	1.6		−.2	1.1	1.3	2.5	1.5	2.6
	3.8	17.4	Net Profit + Depr., Dep.,						
(18) 2.6	(13) 4.5		Amort./Cur. Mat. L/T/D						
1.4	1.8								
.1	.0	.0		.0	.0	.0	.0	.0	.0
.3	.2	.2	Fixed/Worth	2.3	.3	.1	.3	.2	.2
1.4	.9	1.6		NM	9.1	1.5	.9	1.5	.4
1.2	1.6	1.8		6.2	1.4	1.0	1.8	1.6	1.2
3.9	3.7	4.8	Debt/Worth	35.1	4.9	3.3	3.1	5.7	3.2
12.7	8.4	19.4		−6.2	108.8	6.1	8.4	19.6	6.8
78.7	68.8	64.1		88.7	85.1	67.7	58.2	76.1	55.9
(80) 24.6	(135) 25.9	(174) 33.6	% Profit Before Taxes/Tangible Net Worth	(20) 21.9	(34) 28.0	(14) 11.0	(21) 33.5	(36) 56.4	(49) 33.9
3.2	7.0	10.1		−68.7	7.3	3.1	12.9	19.8	12.6
13.6	13.8	14.6		9.3	19.0	12.4	14.9	17.6	13.9
5.6	5.4	5.3	% Profit Before Taxes/Total Assets	3.0	5.5	2.2	6.2	7.5	7.3
.5	1.2	1.7		−3.0	1.0	.5	2.0	1.8	3.1
156.4	246.0	309.6		UND	UND	200.5	277.9	366.6	199.3
31.1	51.2	63.1	Sales/Net Fixed Assets	20.0	41.8	63.1	53.3	99.1	79.3
9.6	15.1	12.4		1.2	9.7	7.5	12.5	18.1	19.1
3.1	4.0	3.0		1.6	4.3	2.4	4.4	3.0	2.8
2.0	2.1	1.7	Sales/Total Assets	.9	1.8	1.2	2.8	1.7	1.6
1.3	1.1	.9		.4	1.1	.5	1.6	1.2	1.1
.2	.3	.2		2.0	.2	.2	.2	.2	.2
(56) .6	(100) .6	(115) .6	% Depr., Dep., Amort./Sales	(10) 2.4	(26) .6	(10) .9	(16) .6	(20) .6	(33) .4
1.6	1.5	2.0		6.6	2.1	1.9	2.3	1.9	.9
1.8	1.1	1.5			2.9		1.5	.8	
(34) 3.2	(61) 2.4	(72) 2.8	% Officers', Directors', Owners' Comp/Sales	(22) 4.4		(12) 2.7	(15) 1.6		
6.4	5.9	5.6			8.2		6.2	2.5	
4031977M	4529103M	4831229M	Net Sales ($)	19274M	87126M	61469M	155304M	615519M	3892537M
2311103M	2579921M	3666908M	Total Assets ($)	31770M	58428M	72256M	105036M	574207M	2825211M

M = $ thousand   MM = $ million
See Pages 11 through 21 for Explanation of Ratios and Data

Current Data Sorted By Assets **Comparative Historical Data**

Type of Statement	0-500M	500M-2MM	2-10MM	10-50MM	50-100MM	100-250MM		4/1/00-3/31/01 ALL	4/1/01-3/31/02 ALL
Unqualified	9	10	96	85	19	9		159	156
Reviewed	7	66	118	22	1			168	141
Compiled	16	26	14	3		1		43	60
Tax Returns	7	23	13	3		1		12	14
Other		19	35	17	4	1		96	108
		128 (4/1-9/30/04)		497 (10/1/04-3/31/05)					
NUMBER OF STATEMENTS	39	144	276	130	24	12		478	479

	0-500M %	500M-2MM %	2-10MM %	10-50MM %	50-100MM %	100-250MM %	ASSETS	%	%
	20.4	18.4	18.7	19.0	16.5	23.8	Cash & Equivalents	19.5	20.1
	33.5	40.3	48.4	45.8	52.5	50.9	Trade Receivables (net)	49.8	48.2
	3.3	5.5	3.4	3.6	.7	2.4	Inventory	2.3	2.7
	5.8	11.7	9.4	11.9	9.8	9.1	All Other Current	8.0	8.5
	62.9	76.0	79.9	80.3	79.4	86.2	Total Current	79.6	79.5
	25.5	15.9	12.5	12.5	10.6	8.8	Fixed Assets (net)	13.3	13.0
	.7	1.1	.6	.8	2.9	1.2	Intangibles (net)	.7	1.2
	10.6	7.0	7.0	6.4	7.0	3.7	All Other Non-Current	6.4	6.3
	100.0	100.0	100.0	100.0	100.0	100.0	Total	100.0	100.0
							LIABILITIES		
	25.3	9.3	4.9	4.5	.7	.1	Notes Payable-Short Term	4.4	6.8
	3.8	3.7	2.5	1.3	.9	1.2	Cur. Mat.-L/T/D	1.7	2.3
	20.3	26.3	34.9	36.1	43.2	45.6	Trade Payables	35.3	35.9
	.2	.6	.5	.2	.3	.1	Income Taxes Payable	.6	.5
	15.3	15.9	16.4	18.1	19.5	24.4	All Other Current	16.2	15.4
	64.9	55.8	59.2	60.1	64.5	71.5	Total Current	58.3	61.0
	29.5	9.4	6.8	7.8	7.1	7.1	Long-Term Debt	5.6	7.6
	.0	.3	.3	.3	.3	.1	Deferred Taxes	.5	.5
	3.4	2.7	2.0	1.3	2.7	1.2	All Other Non-Current	1.4	1.5
	2.1	31.8	31.7	30.5	25.5	20.1	Net Worth	34.1	29.4
	100.0	100.0	100.0	100.0	100.0	100.0	Total Liabilities & Net Worth	100.0	100.0
							INCOME DATA		
	100.0	100.0	100.0	100.0	100.0	100.0	Net Sales	100.0	100.0
	25.2	18.3	13.7	11.1	7.5	15.4	Gross Profit	13.0	13.1
	24.0	16.0	11.7	8.8	6.5	12.5	Operating Expenses	11.0	11.6
	1.2	2.2	2.0	2.3	.9	3.0	Operating Profit	2.0	1.5
	.5	.3	.1	.0	.4	.0	All Other Expenses (net)	−.2	.1
	.8	2.0	1.9	2.3	.6	3.0	Profit Before Taxes	2.3	1.4

RATIOS

	0-500M	500M-2MM	2-10MM	10-50MM	50-100MM	100-250MM		Hist 4/1/00-3/31/01	Hist 4/1/01-3/31/02
	2.8	2.1	1.8	1.6	1.4	1.3	Current	1.7	1.7
	1.4	1.4	1.3	1.3	1.2	1.2		1.3	1.3
	.9	1.1	1.1	1.1	1.1	1.1		1.1	1.1
	2.8	1.8	1.5	1.4	1.2	1.2	Quick	1.5	1.5
	1.3	1.2	1.2	1.1	1.1	1.1		1.2	1.2
	.6	.8	.9	1.0	1.0	1.0		1.0	1.0
	0 UND	23 15.7	39 9.3	43 8.4	53 6.9	53 6.9	Sales/Receivables	39 9.3	36 10.0
	24 15.4	39 9.3	56 6.6	61 5.9	66 5.5	61 6.0		54 6.8	54 6.8
	45 8.1	61 6.0	75 4.9	82 4.5	79 4.6	74 4.9		72 5.1	70 5.2
	0 UND	0 UND	0 UND	0 UND	0 UND	0 UND	Cost of Sales/Inventory	0 UND	0 UND
	0 UND	0 UND	0 UND	0 UND	0 UND	0 UND		0 UND	0 UND
	2 195.4	2 227.9	0 999.8	1 491.9	1 282.0	0 UND		0 999.8	0 999.8
	1 247.7	12 30.0	28 12.8	31 11.9	28 13.0	47 7.7	Cost of Sales/Payables	26 14.3	27 13.8
	9 39.5	28 13.2	43 8.4	49 7.5	58 6.3	59 6.2		42 8.7	43 8.5
	29 12.8	50 7.3	60 6.1	70 5.2	68 5.3	67 5.5		58 6.3	60 6.0
	15.0	8.6	7.8	9.0	11.9	14.4	Sales/Working Capital	10.1	9.6
	35.6	16.9	16.4	18.0	20.2	25.2		18.6	19.3
	−86.5	49.7	37.5	38.6	42.2	39.5		42.4	43.1
	26.1	15.4	30.3	57.9	24.8	166.2	EBIT/Interest	34.7	28.7
	(26) 2.9	(110) 4.5	(207) 6.6	(99) 12.1	(18) 12.3	(11) 16.8		(379) 8.9	(371) 7.3
	.1	.4	1.7	1.6	2.4	8.1		2.5	1.4
		5.8	6.9	9.6			Net Profit + Depr., Dep., Amort./Cur. Mat. L/T/D	9.1	10.9
	(30)	2.4 (76)	2.8 (33)	2.8				(127) 3.5	(113) 3.2
		1.0	.6	1.0				1.4	1.0
	.2	.1	.1	.1	.1	.2	Fixed/Worth	.1	.1
	.6	.4	.2	.3	.2	.3		.3	.3
	39.4	1.1	.7	.5	.5	1.6		.5	.6
	.4	.8	1.1	1.4	2.4	2.9	Debt/Worth	1.2	1.2
	2.6	2.2	2.3	2.7	3.5	3.8		2.4	2.4
	81.6	6.7	4.5	5.3	5.3	5.8		4.3	4.5
	68.4	45.0	36.8	32.4	32.5	41.2	% Profit Before Taxes/Tangible Net Worth	43.7	37.8
	(30) 7.4	(126) 13.9	(252) 13.2	(127) 16.5	(23) 13.0	(11) 21.8		(470) 19.1	(451) 14.4
	−2.9	−1.4	2.5	2.7	1.9	17.6		6.3	3.4
	28.4	12.7	11.1	9.0	7.2	11.9	% Profit Before Taxes/Total Assets	11.9	9.9
	2.9	5.2	3.6	3.7	3.0	5.1		5.6	4.0
	−3.1	−1.4	.6	.9	.6	3.9		1.5	.7
	134.8	94.0	94.3	125.1	135.7	140.6	Sales/Net Fixed Assets	106.2	112.1
	44.8	35.0	45.4	46.7	79.8	93.4		48.8	45.4
	12.0	15.2	18.0	14.7	35.0	26.5		19.6	18.6
	8.9	4.8	3.8	3.6	3.6	3.8	Sales/Total Assets	4.3	4.4
	5.0	3.5	3.1	2.9	2.9	3.5		3.4	3.3
	2.5	2.4	2.3	2.1	2.4	2.8		2.6	2.6
	.5	.4	.3	.2	.2		% Depr., Dep., Amort./Sales	.2	.2
	(24) 1.4	(121) .9	(245) .6	(115) .5	(22) .3			(430) .5	(425) .6
	2.6	1.8	1.2	1.4	.9			1.2	1.3
	2.9	1.9	.9	.7			% Officers', Directors', Owners' Comp/Sales	1.0	1.2
	(22) 4.7	(78) 3.0	(110) 1.8	(30) 1.0				(209) 2.3	(211) 2.4
	7.7	5.0	2.8	2.3				4.4	4.6
	71573M	616370M	4043136M	7721054M	5257349M	5960435M	Net Sales ($)	20500024M	16037820M
	10779M	166311M	1284851M	2760537M	1732968M	1534613M	Total Assets ($)	6516409M	5036669M

M = $thousand   MM = $ million
See Pages 11 through 21 for Explanation of Ratios and Data

Comparative Historical Data | **Current Data Sorted By Sales**

213 / 204 / 219 etc.			Type of Statement						
213	204	219	Unqualified		4	10	22	65	118
218	234	216	Reviewed	6	25	27	63	63	32
44	70	51	Compiled	4	17	7	13	8	2
27	59	56	Tax Returns	6	23	9	11	4	3
83	89	83	Other	5	12	8	15	20	23
4/1/02-3/31/03	4/1/03-3/31/04	4/1/04-3/31/05		128 (4/1-9/30/04)			497 (10/1/04-3/31/05)		
ALL	ALL	ALL		0-1MM	1-3MM	3-5MM	5-10MM	10-25MM	25MM & OVER
585	656	625	**NUMBER OF STATEMENTS**	21	81	61	124	160	178

ASSETS (%)

Hist 1	Hist 2	Hist 3		0-1MM	1-3MM	3-5MM	5-10MM	10-25MM	25MM&OVER
21.1	21.2	18.8	Cash & Equivalents	13.9	18.1	26.2	17.5	18.2	18.7
45.3	43.2	45.3	Trade Receivables (net)	25.6	36.6	31.9	44.0	51.2	51.7
2.6	2.8	3.8	Inventory	3.5	7.1	5.9	6.3	2.1	1.2
9.1	9.0	10.2	All Other Current	10.6	7.7	10.2	9.9	10.3	11.6
78.1	76.3	78.1	Total Current	53.5	69.5	74.2	77.7	81.8	83.3
14.0	15.4	14.0	Fixed Assets (net)	30.6	20.6	16.4	13.9	12.2	9.8
.7	1.0	.9	Intangibles (net)	2.7	.4	.7	.9	.7	1.0
7.2	7.4	7.0	All Other Non-Current	12.8	9.5	8.6	7.5	5.3	5.9
100.0	100.0	100.0	Total	100.0	100.0	100.0	100.0	100.0	100.0

LIABILITIES

Hist 1	Hist 2	Hist 3		0-1MM	1-3MM	3-5MM	5-10MM	10-25MM	25MM&OVER
5.5	6.5	6.8	Notes Payable-Short Term	5.3	18.0	7.4	8.3	4.8	2.5
2.3	2.5	2.5	Cur. Mat.-L/T/D	3.3	4.3	3.6	3.5	2.0	.9
32.7	31.1	32.8	Trade Payables	15.4	19.8	21.1	31.6	37.1	41.7
.5	.5	.4	Income Taxes Payable	.2	.2	.6	.9	.4	.2
16.2	15.4	16.8	All Other Current	18.4	13.1	16.6	16.2	15.8	19.8
57.1	56.0	59.4	Total Current	42.7	55.4	49.3	60.5	60.1	65.2
6.3	8.3	9.0	Long-Term Debt	32.8	18.2	7.9	8.7	6.3	5.1
.3	.4	.3	Deferred Taxes	.0	.3	.1	.3	.5	.2
1.7	2.5	2.1	All Other Non-Current	2.2	3.6	3.2	3.0	1.0	1.4
34.6	32.9	29.2	Net Worth	22.3	22.4	39.5	27.5	32.0	28.2
100.0	100.0	100.0	Total Liabilities & Net Worth	100.0	100.0	100.0	100.0	100.0	100.0

INCOME DATA

Hist 1	Hist 2	Hist 3		0-1MM	1-3MM	3-5MM	5-10MM	10-25MM	25MM&OVER
100.0	100.0	100.0	Net Sales	100.0	100.0	100.0	100.0	100.0	100.0
14.4	16.1	14.7	Gross Profit	30.2	24.4	19.3	15.2	11.9	9.2
12.7	13.9	12.7	Operating Expenses	26.0	21.4	17.5	13.0	10.3	7.5
1.6	2.2	2.1	Operating Profit	4.2	3.0	1.8	2.2	1.7	1.7
–.1	.3	.1	All Other Expenses (net)	3.0	.4	–.3	.1	–.1	.1
1.7	1.9	1.9	Profit Before Taxes	1.1	2.6	2.1	2.1	1.7	1.6

RATIOS

Hist 1	Hist 2	Hist 3		0-1MM	1-3MM	3-5MM	5-10MM	10-25MM	25MM&OVER
1.8	1.8	1.8	Current	2.5	2.9	2.7	1.9	1.7	1.5
1.3	1.3	1.3		1.4	1.4	1.6	1.4	1.3	1.2
1.1	1.1	1.1		1.0	1.0	1.1	1.1	1.1	1.1
1.5	1.6	1.5	Quick	2.3	2.4	2.3	1.7	1.4	1.3
1.2	1.2	1.1		1.3	1.2	1.2	1.2	1.2	1.1
1.0	.9	.9		.5	.7	.7	.7	.9	1.0
35 · 10.6	35 · 10.6	34 · 10.8	Sales/Receivables	0 · UND	17 · 21.0	20 · 17.8	33 · 11.2	40 · 9.2	45 · 8.0
52 · 7.1	51 · 7.1	53 · 6.9		44 · 8.3	38 · 9.7	37 · 9.9	53 · 6.9	54 · 6.8	60 · 6.1
66 · 5.5	67 · 5.4	73 · 5.0		73 · 5.0	68 · 5.3	62 · 5.9	75 · 4.9	75 · 4.9	76 · 4.8
0 · UND	0 · UND	0 · UND	Cost of Sales/Inventory	0 · UND	0 · UND	0 · UND	0 · UND	0 · UND	0 · UND
0 · UND	0 · UND	0 · UND		0 · UND	0 · UND	0 · UND	0 · UND	0 · UND	0 · UND
0 · 888.6	0 · 937.5	1 · 659.4		0 · UND	5 · 76.7	2 · 159.3	2 · 197.0	0 · 999.8	0 · 903.4
24 · 15.3	22 · 16.9	22 · 16.2	Cost of Sales/Payables	5 · 75.6	5 · 71.0	12 · 29.8	24 · 15.0	29 · 12.6	31 · 11.8
39 · 9.3	41 · 8.9	41 · 8.9		13 · 27.2	19 · 18.8	28 · 13.1	44 · 8.3	42 · 8.7	49 · 7.5
59 · 6.2	58 · 6.3	61 · 6.0		50 · 7.3	47 · 7.7	56 · 6.5	60 · 6.1	59 · 6.2	65 · 5.6
9.1	8.5	8.9	Sales/Working Capital	4.4	6.0	5.0	7.6	9.5	11.6
17.4	16.2	17.7		20.6	16.7	11.6	12.7	17.7	20.0
40.7	41.0	42.2		UND	110.3	42.0	60.3	39.2	38.6
26.6	25.8	30.3	EBIT/Interest	8.0	14.6	24.3	26.6	26.4	54.0
(452) 5.9	(511) 5.8	(471) 6.9		(12) 1.1	(67) 3.7	(44) 8.0	(95) 3.9	(119) 7.2	(134) 14.3
1.2	.9	1.4		–12.4	1.1	.7	–1.0	2.3	2.4
7.1	6.6	8.2	Net Profit + Depr., Dep., Amort./Cur. Mat. L/T/D		7.4	4.6	6.3	8.2	11.6
(149) 2.6	(172) 2.3	(151) 2.8			(10) 2.2	(10) 2.6	(38) 1.7	(43) 3.9	(49) 3.2
.8	.4	.9			1.0	1.0	.3	1.4	1.0
.1	.1	.1	Fixed/Worth	.1	.1	.1	.1	.1	.1
.3	.3	.3		.6	.6	.3	.3	.2	.2
.5	.7	.8		NM	1.6	1.0	1.6	.6	.5
1.1	1.0	1.1	Debt/Worth	.4	.5	.5	.9	1.2	1.6
2.3	2.2	2.5		1.2	2.3	1.4	2.4	2.3	3.1
4.4	4.3	5.3		NM	9.9	5.5	7.9	4.2	5.2
33.9	35.0	38.2	% Profit Before Taxes/Tangible Net Worth	10.3	49.9	46.5	40.0	37.8	35.2
(555) 14.2	(612) 12.3	(569) 14.0		(16) .0	(68) 13.6	(56) 12.6	(103) 15.3	(153) 13.9	(173) 17.7
2.2	1.7	1.2		–5.2	.6	–1.3	–4.3	3.7	3.7
10.2	10.4	10.9	% Profit Before Taxes/Total Assets	6.5	13.8	12.2	13.6	10.6	9.1
3.9	3.4	3.8		.0	6.1	3.9	3.6	3.9	3.9
.5	.3	.4		–2.2	–.1	–.8	–2.9	.9	1.1
106.2	90.8	105.0	Sales/Net Fixed Assets	45.3	74.4	46.1	96.4	100.0	142.2
46.5	38.4	44.1		11.1	23.5	26.4	46.5	45.6	64.8
17.8	15.0	17.0		2.0	9.5	12.6	14.5	21.7	25.7
4.2	4.1	4.0	Sales/Total Assets	2.5	4.2	4.2	4.2	4.4	3.9
3.2	3.2	3.2		1.5	2.8	2.7	3.2	3.2	3.4
2.4	2.2	2.3		.8	2.0	1.8	2.2	2.7	2.6
.3	.3	.3	% Depr., Dep., Amort./Sales	1.6	.6	.6	.3	.3	.2
(524) .6	(580) .6	(536) .6		(13) 2.4	(68) 1.0	(46) 1.1	(110) .7	(141) .6	(158) .3
1.4	1.6	1.4		6.8	2.4	2.9	1.3	1.2	.9
1.1	1.3	1.1	% Officers', Directors', Owners' Comp/Sales		2.6	1.4	1.2	.8	.7
(248) 2.1	(265) 2.5	(246) 2.2			(41) 4.4	(27) 2.7	(63) 2.2	(67) 1.8	(41) 1.1
4.3	4.2	4.2			8.0	4.7	3.9	2.7	1.9
21145869M	21005794M	23669917M	Net Sales ($)	11323M	170413M	243003M	932770M	2597823M	19714585M
6778047M	6901728M	7490059M	Total Assets ($)	13597M	73718M	129899M	426517M	887381M	5958947M

Current Data Sorted By Assets   **Comparative Historical Data**

							Type of Statement		
3		19	129	143	30	16	Unqualified	153	160
13		108	225	35	2		Reviewed	177	175
16		24	26	2	1		Compiled	76	79
34		55	24	2		2	Tax Returns	28	24
14		42	83	34	6	7	Other	82	113
		223 (4/1-9/30/04)			**872 (10/1/04-3/31/05)**			4/1/00-3/31/01	4/1/01-3/31/02
0-500M		500M-2MM	2-10MM	10-50MM	50-100MM	100-250MM		ALL	ALL
80		248	487	216	39	25	NUMBER OF STATEMENTS	516	551
%		%	%	%	%	%	ASSETS	%	%
23.9		15.5	18.5	19.6	22.7	20.4	Cash & Equivalents	18.6	18.9
31.4		45.7	49.1	51.2	50.1	48.2	Trade Receivables (net)	47.1	47.7
5.3		5.0	3.9	4.2	1.5	1.7	Inventory	3.4	3.9
5.0		7.9	10.2	8.6	8.2	8.1	All Other Current	9.5	9.7
65.6		74.0	81.7	83.6	82.4	78.4	Total Current	78.6	80.2
22.2		17.0	10.9	10.2	9.5	13.6	Fixed Assets (net)	13.5	12.3
2.8		1.1	.9	.9	1.4	.9	Intangibles (net)	1.5	1.2
9.5		7.9	6.5	5.3	6.7	7.1	All Other Non-Current	6.3	6.3
100.0		100.0	100.0	100.0	100.0	100.0	Total	100.0	100.0
							LIABILITIES		
20.5		10.6	5.9	4.0	4.6	.1	Notes Payable-Short Term	5.6	6.2
6.3		2.8	1.8	1.0	1.8	5.6	Cur. Mat.-L/T/D	2.4	2.4
22.7		29.5	36.4	42.2	49.1	42.1	Trade Payables	35.7	37.4
.2		.7	.7	.2	.0	.2	Income Taxes Payable	.6	.4
16.7		13.2	15.6	19.6	16.3	20.1	All Other Current	15.8	16.8
66.4		56.8	60.3	67.0	71.7	68.1	Total Current	60.1	63.1
19.3		7.7	5.5	4.6	7.3	8.5	Long-Term Debt	5.8	5.9
.2		.3	.3	.3	.0	.2	Deferred Taxes	.6	.6
8.8		3.1	1.8	1.6	2.7	3.5	All Other Non-Current	2.3	1.6
5.4		32.2	32.0	26.5	18.3	19.7	Net Worth	31.1	28.8
100.0		100.0	100.0	100.0	100.0	100.0	Total Liabilities & Net Worth	100.0	100.0
							INCOME DATA		
100.0		100.0	100.0	100.0	100.0	100.0	Net Sales	100.0	100.0
26.2		21.1	13.6	9.6	8.4	12.0	Gross Profit	15.2	14.0
23.9		18.2	11.0	7.2	6.5	8.6	Operating Expenses	13.0	11.7
2.2		2.9	2.6	2.4	2.0	3.4	Operating Profit	2.2	2.3
.1		.3	.0	.1	.2	1.5	All Other Expenses (net)	.3	.2
2.1		2.6	2.6	2.3	1.8	1.9	Profit Before Taxes	2.0	2.1
							RATIOS		
2.3		1.9	1.7	1.4	1.3	1.3		1.7	1.6
1.2		1.4	1.3	1.2	1.2	1.2	Current	1.3	1.2
.7		1.0	1.1	1.1	1.1	1.1		1.1	1.1
2.0		1.7	1.4	1.3	1.2	1.2		1.4	1.3
.9		1.1	1.1	1.1	1.0	1.1	Quick	1.1 (550)	1.1
.5		.8	.9	.9	.9			.9	.9
1	322.5	27	13.7	40	9.1	50	7.3	47	7.8	49	7.5		32	11.3	34	10.6

1 322.5	27 13.7	40 9.1	50 7.3	47 7.8	49 7.5		32 11.3	34 10.6
14 25.5	50 7.3	58 6.3	65 5.6	64 5.7	60 6.1	Sales/Receivables	51 7.2	52 7.0
33 11.0	70 5.2	79 4.6	78 4.7	77 4.8	69 5.3		72 5.1	69 5.3
0 UND	0 UND	0 UND	0 UND	0 UND	0 UND		0 UND	0 UND
0 UND	0 UND	0 UND	0 UND	0 UND	0 UND	Cost of Sales/Inventory	0 UND	0 UND
1 440.8	1 371.4	0 999.8	0 952.5	0 UND	0 UND		0 999.8	0 999.8
0 UND	19 19.7	31 11.8	41 9.0	45 8.2	37 9.8		24 15.1	26 14.2
13 27.7	33 11.1	48 7.7	56 6.5	66 5.5	56 6.5	Cost of Sales/Payables	41 8.9	44 8.4
28 13.0	52 7.0	67 5.4	74 5.0	81 4.5	71 5.2		61 6.0	63 5.8
14.8	8.8	8.1	10.5	15.2	13.7		9.8	11.1
72.6	18.5	16.4	19.2	20.6	19.4	Sales/Working Capital	21.5	23.3
–33.0	–933.4	35.1	34.0	68.1	36.6		56.5	68.5
21.0	24.0	32.8	72.7	56.3	83.0		29.3	32.0
(58) 3.4	(207) 7.0	(387) 7.6	(166) 14.1	(26) 9.6	(18) 20.1	EBIT/Interest	(400) 7.2	(434) 6.6
–2.3	1.3	1.7	3.0	2.9	8.8		1.8	1.6
	6.5	12.5	15.2			Net Profit + Depr., Dep.,	12.0	11.4
	(56) 3.0	(110) 3.6	(56) 4.7			Amort./Cur. Mat. L /T/D	(127) 4.3	(110) 4.4
	1.1	.8	1.6				1.7	1.4
.3	.1	.1	.1	.1	.1		.1	.1
1.2	.4	.2	.2	.3	.3	Fixed/Worth	.3	.3
–.9	1.3	.6	.5	.5	1.3		.7	.7
.9	1.0	1.3	1.4	3.0	3.0		1.2	1.4
7.8	2.3	2.6	3.1	4.9	3.9	Debt/Worth	2.6	3.0
–4.7	6.0	4.7	5.8	9.9	5.6		5.6	5.6
132.5	60.9	38.2	32.7	34.2	26.5	% Profit Before Taxes/Tangible	41.7	48.3
(49) 34.8	(221) 25.9	(464) 15.4	(212) 15.6	(36) 16.9	(23) 16.8	Net Worth	(482) 19.4	(520) 20.4
5.1	4.7	3.0	5.5	8.2	8.4		5.7	6.3
34.0	16.2	11.4	8.1	5.7	5.8		11.9	11.7
9.3	6.5	4.3	4.0	2.8	3.5	% Profit Before Taxes/Total Assets	5.0	5.2
–8.5	.8	.7	1.2	1.2	1.9		1.2	1.4
133.0	81.9	110.9	157.8	179.0	142.7		121.6	133.6
42.1	36.8	50.4	70.4	93.1	69.4	Sales/Net Fixed Assets	51.5	50.2
19.0	15.1	21.1	22.0	36.9	26.2		20.0	22.0
9.0	4.6	3.9	3.6	3.5	3.6		4.5	4.5
6.0	3.4	3.1	3.0	3.2	3.1	Sales/Total Assets	3.4	3.4
3.8	2.4	2.3	2.3	2.3	2.3		2.5	2.6
.5	.4	.3	.2	.1	.1		.2	.2
(58) 1.1	(193) .9	(427) .5	(198) .3	(32) .2	(20) .4	% Depr., Dep., Amort./Sales	(438) .5	(461) .5
2.2	1.9	1.1	.8	.3	.6		1.1	1.0
3.0	2.0	.8	.6			% Officers', Directors',	1.1	1.2
(44) 5.3	(108) 3.2	(203) 1.8	(54) 1.2			Owners' Comp/Sales	(204) 2.5	(218) 2.7
6.7	5.7	3.0	1.8				4.8	4.7
145255M	1098171M	7127219M	13985400M	7968423M	12190606M	Net Sales ($)	17244172M	21481319M
21346M	300025M	2272566M	4792448M	2670567M	4226632M	Total Assets ($)	5383686M	6728957M

Comparative Historical Data | **Current Data Sorted By Sales**

			Type of Statement						
260	333	340	Unqualified	2	10	7	36	87	198
259	456	383	Reviewed	7	41	49	101	129	56
54	137	69	Compiled	4	22	11	16	13	3
56	102	117	Tax Returns	18	37	22	26	10	4
133	181	186	Other	9	26	22	38	42	49
4/1/02-3/31/03	4/1/03-3/31/04	4/1/04-3/31/05		223 (4/1-9/30/04)			872 (10/1/04-3/31/05)		
ALL	ALL	ALL		0-1MM	1-3MM	3-5MM	5-10MM	10-25MM	25MM & OVER
762	1209	1095	**NUMBER OF STATEMENTS**	40	136	111	217	281	310
%	%	%	**ASSETS**	%	%	%	%	%	%
19.6	18.9	18.6	Cash & Equivalents	17.2	17.4	17.7	17.1	18.8	20.6
46.6	44.5	47.4	Trade Receivables (net)	24.2	36.3	43.0	45.0	51.7	54.8
3.2	4.2	4.2	Inventory	6.3	10.3	5.8	5.4	2.5	1.3
9.7	10.8	8.9	All Other Current	6.3	5.6	8.1	9.8	9.8	9.4
79.2	78.4	79.1	Total Current	54.0	69.6	74.7	77.2	82.8	86.0
12.9	13.9	13.0	Fixed Assets (net)	32.9	19.4	15.9	14.1	10.6	7.8
1.0	.9	1.1	Intangibles (net)	2.8	1.6	1.7	.9	.8	1.0
6.9	6.8	6.8	All Other Non-Current	10.5	9.3	7.7	7.8	5.8	5.2
100.0	100.0	100.0	Total	100.0	100.0	100.0	100.0	100.0	100.0
			LIABILITIES						
6.4	6.9	7.5	Notes Payable-Short Term	18.0	17.5	11.7	7.3	5.1	2.5
2.0	1.9	2.3	Cur. Mat.-L/T/D	7.1	4.1	2.5	2.4	1.5	1.4
36.3	33.6	35.5	Trade Payables	12.4	22.0	28.6	31.9	38.8	46.6
.6	.6	.5	Income Taxes Payable	.4	.3	1.1	.9	.5	.2
16.7	16.2	16.1	All Other Current	11.8	14.8	11.1	14.9	16.2	19.6
62.0	59.1	61.9	Total Current	49.8	58.8	55.1	57.3	62.0	70.2
6.1	7.0	7.0	Long-Term Debt	17.0	14.4	8.5	7.5	4.6	3.7
.4	.3	.3	Deferred Taxes	.3	.3	.2	.5	.4	.1
3.2	2.5	2.6	All Other Non-Current	10.4	6.5	2.6	1.8	1.6	1.5
28.3	31.2	28.2	Net Worth	22.6	20.1	33.7	32.9	31.5	24.4
100.0	100.0	100.0	Total Liabilities & Net Worth	100.0	100.0	100.0	100.0	100.0	100.0
			INCOME DATA						
100.0	100.0	100.0	Net Sales	100.0	100.0	100.0	100.0	100.0	100.0
13.8	15.4	15.2	Gross Profit	29.6	27.3	21.0	16.9	11.8	7.9
11.7	13.6	12.6	Operating Expenses	25.3	22.8	18.4	13.8	9.5	6.3
2.0	1.9	2.6	Operating Profit	4.3	4.5	2.7	3.0	2.3	1.6
.3	.1	.1	All Other Expenses (net)	1.5	.6	.0	.1	.1	.0
1.7	1.8	2.5	Profit Before Taxes	2.8	3.9	2.7	3.0	2.2	1.6
			RATIOS						
1.6	1.7	1.7		2.6	2.1	2.0	1.8	1.6	1.4
1.3	1.3	1.3	Current	1.2	1.4	1.4	1.3	1.3	1.2
1.1	1.1	1.1		.6	.9	1.1	1.1	1.1	1.1
1.4	1.4	1.4		2.0	1.5	1.9	1.6	1.4	1.3
(761) 1.1	(1208) 1.1	1.1	Quick	.9	1.0	1.1	1.2	1.1	1.1
.9	.9	.9		.5	.6	.8	.9	1.0	.9
36 10.1	32 11.3	35 10.5		0 UND	8 47.9	26 13.9	31 11.7	41 8.8	48 7.6
53 6.8	51 7.2	56 6.5	Sales/Receivables	19 18.8	39 9.5	51 7.2	55 6.7	56 6.5	61 5.9
70 5.2	70 5.2	77 4.8		56 6.5	82 4.4	77 4.7	79 4.6	76 4.8	77 4.8
0 UND	0 UND	0 UND		0 UND	0 UND	0 UND	0 UND	0 UND	0 UND
0 UND	0 UND	0 UND	Cost of Sales/Inventory	0 UND	0 UND	0 UND	0 UND	0 UND	0 UND
0 999.8	0 819.9	0 999.8		0 UND	6 64.9	3 113.5	1 699.5	0 999.8	0 999.8
27 13.5	23 15.8	26 14.2		0 UND	6 59.4	19 18.9	23 16.0	31 11.7	40 9.1
44 8.2	43 8.4	45 8.1	Cost of Sales/Payables	16 23.5	27 13.6	37 9.7	39 9.4	48 7.7	55 6.7
63 5.8	61 5.9	67 5.5		37 9.9	56 5.7	64 5.7	60 6.1	67 5.5	73 5.0
10.0	9.5	9.4		5.4	6.2	6.8	7.7	9.0	13.7
20.7	18.1	18.9	Sales/Working Capital	34.4	19.2	15.2	14.7	18.4	21.6
50.4	45.6	51.6		-30.0	-48.5	66.8	49.0	36.0	37.1
25.7	28.4	35.0		11.5	13.9	23.7	32.4	33.5	66.5
(592) 6.4	(937) 6.9	(862) 8.4	EBIT/Interest	(25) 4.0	(110) 3.5	(94) 5.5	(181) 6.8	(223) 9.0	(229) 17.0
1.5	1.2	1.7		-1.4	-.4	1.4	1.7	1.7	4.0
10.9	9.5	14.4	Net Profit + Depr., Dep.,	5.4	7.5	5.9	10.6	8.7	23.7
(194) 4.0	(284) 3.2	(243) 3.8	Amort./Cur. Mat. L/T/D		(21) 2.8	(20) 3.2	(56) 4.1	(71) 3.6	(69) 10.7
.3	.6	1.1			.4	1.2	.7	.7	1.9
.1	.1	.1		.3	.1	.1	.1	.1	.1
.3	.3	.3	Fixed/Worth	1.2	.5	.3	.3	.2	.2
.7	.7	.7		NM	4.0	1.0	.8	.6	.4
1.3	1.3	1.4		.9	1.1	.9	.9	1.3	2.1
2.7	2.5	2.9	Debt/Worth	4.6	3.6	1.9	2.1	2.6	3.5
5.5	4.8	5.7		-10.5	32.2	5.1	4.9	4.3	6.1
40.3	37.5	41.4	% Profit Before Taxes/Tangible	61.1	58.3	51.0	46.8	37.9	36.1
(717) 16.5	(1140) 16.2	(1005) 18.2	Net Worth	(29) 26.8	(105) 26.3	(101) 18.4	(198) 16.3	(270) 15.4	(302) 17.8
3.4	2.0	4.4		6.3	3.5	1.7	1.8	3.5	6.5
10.6	10.6	11.3	% Profit Before Taxes/Total	18.3	17.3	14.6	13.1	11.7	8.1
4.0	4.3	4.5	Assets	5.6	5.8	5.5	5.9	4.5	3.7
.5	.2	.8		.8	-1.5	.2	.8	.9	1.3
118.3	113.3	121.1		58.7	89.5	69.0	93.3	105.6	174.8
48.3	47.8	50.2	Sales/Net Fixed Assets	18.4	27.9	32.8	41.2	53.8	89.1
19.2	17.6	19.7		2.3	11.2	13.1	16.1	24.2	35.2
4.3	4.2	4.1		4.5	5.0	4.1	4.0	4.1	4.0
3.3	3.2	3.2	Sales/Total Assets	2.3	2.9	3.0	3.1	3.3	3.3
2.5	2.4	2.4		.8	1.8	2.1	2.3	2.4	2.7
.2	.3	.2		1.1	.6	.4	.4	.3	.1
(678) .6	(1039) .6	(928) .5	% Depr., Dep., Amort./Sales	(25) 2.2	(95) 1.5	(94) 1.0	(185) .7	(249) .5	(280) .3
1.2	1.3	1.2		4.4	2.7	2.0	1.5	.9	.6
1.1	1.2	1.1	% Officers', Directors',	5.1	2.8	1.7	1.1	.9	.5
(298) 2.2	(493) 2.2	(417) 2.1	Owners' Comp/Sales	(19) 6.4	(65) 4.6	(47) 2.9	(101) 2.2	(112) 1.6	(73) 1.1
4.5	4.5	3.9		12.5	6.1	4.3	3.8	2.4	1.8
35095042M	49600506M	42515074M	Net Sales ($)	23556M	282292M	440975M	1587812M	4566306M	35614133M
9983838M	14189112M	14283584M	Total Assets ($)	28166M	154701M	171795M	733681M	1811612M	11383629M

M = $ thousand   MM = $ million
See Pages 11 through 21 for Explanation of Ratios and Data

Current Data Sorted By Assets   Comparative Historical Data

Type of Statement	0-500M	500M-2MM	2-10MM	10-50MM	50-100MM	100-250MM	4/1/00-3/31/01 ALL	4/1/01-3/31/02 ALL
Unqualified	1	5	56	60	9	5	81	81
Reviewed	3	35	69	11	1		84	94
Compiled	3	16	7	7	1		41	44
Tax Returns	9	11	4	1	1		13	18
Other	4	17	25	10	3	1	63	75
	87 (4/1-9/30/04)			281 (10/1/04-3/31/05)				
NUMBER OF STATEMENTS	20	84	161	82	15	6	282	312
	%	%	%	%	%	%	%	%
ASSETS								
Cash & Equivalents	17.6	11.3	13.7	16.2	11.5		13.4	12.5
Trade Receivables (net)	19.3	39.3	36.9	37.5	31.2		35.4	35.5
Inventory	4.5	2.5	2.1	4.0	4.7		2.8	2.0
All Other Current	2.7	5.4	8.6	10.7	11.2		6.7	7.1
Total Current	44.1	58.5	61.3	68.5	58.6		58.2	57.2
Fixed Assets (net)	42.3	37.1	30.7	25.9	30.6		33.7	34.9
Intangibles (net)	3.8	.8	.5	.8	6.5		1.6	1.1
All Other Non-Current	9.8	3.6	7.5	4.8	4.3		6.6	6.8
Total	100.0	100.0	100.0	100.0	100.0		100.0	100.0
LIABILITIES								
Notes Payable-Short Term	22.3	6.3	6.4	5.0	16.0		8.0	9.7
Cur. Mat.-L/T/D	4.8	7.1	5.8	4.8	6.0		7.1	7.2
Trade Payables	10.0	16.5	19.7	22.0	10.0		16.9	16.7
Income Taxes Payable	.0	.6	1.4	.1	.2		.7	.8
All Other Current	20.0	9.7	9.2	13.6	14.4		10.3	11.1
Total Current	57.1	40.2	42.5	45.5	46.8		43.0	45.6
Long-Term Debt	30.9	20.3	11.5	13.1	18.9		13.9	13.4
Deferred Taxes	.0	.5	1.3	1.1	1.3		1.3	1.8
All Other Non-Current	3.6	4.8	2.6	2.2	1.3		1.7	4.0
Net Worth	8.4	34.2	42.2	38.2	31.8		40.0	35.3
Total Liabilities & Net Worth	100.0	100.0	100.0	100.0	100.0		100.0	100.0
INCOME DATA								
Net Sales	100.0	100.0	100.0	100.0	100.0		100.0	100.0
Gross Profit	48.0	30.4	19.2	15.4	21.9		24.1	23.2
Operating Expenses	45.1	27.7	16.0	11.4	15.1		20.6	19.5
Operating Profit	3.0	2.6	3.2	4.1	6.8		3.5	3.7
All Other Expenses (net)	1.3	.5	.0	-.1	.0		.1	.9
Profit Before Taxes	1.7	2.1	3.2	4.2	6.8		3.3	2.8
RATIOS								
Current	1.6	2.4	1.9	1.9	1.9		2.1	2.0
	.9	1.5	1.4	1.4	1.6		1.4	1.4
	.4	1.1	1.1	1.2	1.2		1.1	1.1
Quick	1.5	1.9	1.6	1.7	1.5		1.8	1.8
	.7	1.3	1.2	1.1	1.1		1.2	1.2
	.4	.9	.9	.9	.9		.9	.9
Sales/Receivables	0 UND	36 10.1	46 8.0	51 7.2	36 10.2		41 9.0	38 9.6
	8 45.3	53 6.9	60 6.0	65 5.6	50 7.3		57 6.4	56 6.5
	29 12.6	75 4.8	78 4.7	75 4.9	62 5.9		77 4.7	81 4.5
Cost of Sales/Inventory	0 UND	0 UND	0 UND	0 UND	0 UND		0 UND	0 UND
	0 UND	0 UND	0 UND	0 999.8	1 316.0		0 UND	0 UND
	9 40.2	6 65.0	3 136.3	4 90.5	5 66.9		3 104.6	4 98.5
Cost of Sales/Payables	0 UND	9 40.8	21 17.2	25 14.7	7 49.8		16 22.4	16 23.5
	2 163.2	29 12.6	37 9.8	41 9.0	19 19.6		32 11.4	31 11.6
	26 14.3	49 7.4	52 7.0	60 6.1	31 11.7		47 7.8	48 7.5
Sales/Working Capital	20.8	7.3	6.5	5.7	8.3		7.2	7.3
	NM	15.0	14.1	10.8	9.7		15.6	16.2
	-12.2	88.1	46.6	20.1	17.9		47.2	72.1
EBIT/Interest	8.6	12.4	17.2	27.5	36.1		10.4	10.7
	(17) 2.4	(77) 3.3	(147) 6.4	(75) 6.9	8.5		(258) 3.6	(287) 3.6
	.5	-2.4	2.0	2.2	3.7		1.3	.9
Net Profit + Depr., Dep., Amort./Cur. Mat. L/T/D		3.9	4.4	9.4			3.4	4.2
		(18) 1.6	(61) 2.2	(32) 2.8			(97) 1.7	(98) 2.2
		.7	1.3	1.2			.9	1.1
Fixed/Worth	.9	.4	.4	.4	.3		.4	.5
	2.3	.9	.8	.7	.5		.8	.8
	NM	2.5	1.3	1.2	3.3		1.5	1.6
Debt/Worth	1.5	.8	.8	.9	1.3		.8	.9
	3.9	1.6	1.5	2.0	1.8		1.7	1.6
	NM	4.6	2.6	3.0	5.1		3.0	2.9
% Profit Before Taxes/Tangible Net Worth	110.1	38.0	29.9	37.8	64.6		33.2	37.6
	(15) 30.3	(72) 18.9	(159) 16.6	(81) 16.6	(13) 34.9		(266) 16.8	(291) 16.8
	4.6	2.0	5.1	5.7	22.1		3.2	2.3
% Profit Before Taxes/Total Assets	23.8	13.1	12.7	12.9	18.1		14.7	13.5
	6.2	4.9	5.9	6.4	10.0		6.0	5.9
	-3.8	-6.5	1.8	2.1	6.7		.7	.0
Sales/Net Fixed Assets	95.5	12.6	14.2	16.7	20.0		13.1	12.3
	6.9	7.3	7.8	7.9	10.5		7.4	6.6
	4.2	4.4	4.8	5.7	4.2		4.4	4.2
Sales/Total Assets	6.1	3.3	2.8	2.7	2.7		2.9	2.8
	3.3	2.4	2.2	2.1	2.3		2.2	2.2
	2.3	2.0	1.7	1.7	1.9		1.7	1.6
% Depr., Dep., Amort./Sales	1.5	2.1	2.2	1.2	1.4		1.8	1.9
	(15) 6.8	(71) 3.7	(153) 3.4	(80) 3.0	(10) 2.5		(262) 3.5	(297) 3.5
	11.1	7.1	5.2	4.4	3.8		5.8	5.7
% Officers', Directors', Owners' Comp/Sales	3.2	3.4	1.3	.6			1.4	1.8
	(14) 7.9	(43) 6.2	(80) 2.8	(22) 1.3			(132) 3.5	(139) 4.0
	9.4	9.4	4.5	2.0			6.5	7.5
Net Sales ($)	19433M	258044M	1763875M	3534965M	2645669M	2084545M	5571972M	6854762M
Total Assets ($)	4975M	98094M	788862M	1627206M	1078136M	1130693M	2814113M	3535463M

© RMA 2005

M = $ thousand   MM = $ million
See Pages 11 through 21 for Explanation of Ratios and Data

Comparative Historical Data | Current Data Sorted By Sales

				Type of Statement						
	103	110	136	Unqualified	1	3	10	17	43	62
	128	158	119	Reviewed	4	17	30	25	33	10
	31	48	27	Compiled	5	11	3	5	2	1
	21	34	26	Tax Returns	5	11	4	2	3	1
	57	79	60	Other	2	13	5	13	15	12
	4/1/02-3/31/03 ALL	4/1/03-3/31/04 ALL	4/1/04-3/31/05 ALL		87 (4/1-9/30/04)			281 (10/1/04-3/31/05)		
					0-1MM	1-3MM	3-5MM	5-10MM	10-25MM	25MM & OVER
	340	429	368	**NUMBER OF STATEMENTS**	17	55	52	62	96	86
	%	%	%	**ASSETS**	%	%	%	%	%	%
	13.9	13.2	13.8	Cash & Equivalents	16.1	12.3	13.9	13.3	13.9	14.6
	35.8	34.9	36.4	Trade Receivables (net)	24.5	30.9	35.3	37.9	39.0	39.0
	2.0	2.5	2.9	Inventory	5.2	2.7	3.5	1.2	2.5	3.8
	8.5	9.1	8.1	All Other Current	2.5	4.0	9.0	6.8	9.4	10.5
	60.3	59.7	61.2	Total Current	48.4	49.9	61.7	59.2	64.9	67.9
	31.6	32.6	31.6	Fixed Assets (net)	41.6	42.1	31.9	33.4	27.8	25.6
	1.2	1.5	1.3	Intangibles (net)	1.8	1.7	.7	.4	.8	2.3
	6.9	6.2	6.0	All Other Non-Current	8.2	6.2	5.7	7.0	6.5	4.2
	100.0	100.0	100.0	Total	100.0	100.0	100.0	100.0	100.0	100.0
				LIABILITIES						
	6.7	7.4	7.2	Notes Payable-Short Term	20.2	7.3	6.7	6.6	6.8	5.9
	5.8	6.5	5.8	Cur. Mat.-L/T/D	4.5	7.7	5.7	6.3	5.4	4.8
	17.4	17.2	18.4	Trade Payables	11.9	12.2	17.2	19.4	20.9	21.0
	1.0	.8	.8	Income Taxes Payable	.3	.1	1.0	2.3	.7	.2
	10.7	9.4	11.2	All Other Current	21.8	8.6	10.6	7.5	10.8	14.4
	41.5	41.2	43.4	Total Current	58.8	35.8	41.1	42.0	44.6	46.3
	13.2	14.2	15.2	Long-Term Debt	26.8	27.4	11.2	13.5	11.6	12.5
	1.0	1.1	1.0	Deferred Taxes	.2	.3	.9	1.4	1.2	1.1
	2.3	3.5	3.0	All Other Non-Current	2.0	3.5	4.0	3.8	2.2	2.5
	41.9	40.0	37.4	Net Worth	12.2	32.9	42.8	39.3	40.3	37.6
	100.0	100.0	100.0	Total Liabilities & Net Worth	100.0	100.0	100.0	100.0	100.0	100.0
				INCOME DATA						
	100.0	100.0	100.0	Net Sales	100.0	100.0	100.0	100.0	100.0	100.0
	23.3	24.4	22.5	Gross Profit	47.1	37.5	22.2	23.2	15.4	15.8
	20.0	21.7	19.1	Operating Expenses	42.1	35.6	18.9	18.9	13.0	11.1
	3.3	2.7	3.4	Operating Profit	5.0	2.0	3.3	4.3	2.4	4.7
	.4	.5	.2	All Other Expenses (net)	1.5	.7	.0	.2	–.3	.1
	2.9	2.2	3.3	Profit Before Taxes	3.5	1.3	3.3	4.1	2.6	4.6
				RATIOS						
	2.1	2.1	2.0		1.5	2.7	2.1	2.0	1.9	1.9
	1.5	1.4	1.4	Current	1.1	1.4	1.5	1.3	1.4	1.4
	1.1	1.1	1.1		.4	.8	1.1	1.1	1.2	1.2
	1.8	1.7	1.7		1.4	2.2	1.6	1.7	1.6	1.5
	1.2	1.1	1.2	Quick	.9	1.3	1.2	1.2	1.2	1.1
	.9	.8	.9		.8	.8	.8	.9	.9	.9
	37 9.9	40 9.2	44 8.3		7 51.8	12 29.7	42 8.8	43 8.4	50 7.2	49 7.5
	57 6.4	58 6.3	59 6.2	Sales/Receivables	28 13.0	50 7.4	59 6.2	56 6.5	63 5.8	63 5.8
	76 4.8	77 4.7	76 4.8		78 4.7	75 4.8	78 4.6	76 4.8	77 4.8	74 4.9
	0 UND	0 UND	0 UND		0 UND	0 UND	0 UND	0 UND	0 UND	0 UND
	0 UND	0 UND	0 UND	Cost of Sales/Inventory	0 UND	0 UND	0 UND	0 UND	0 UND	0 UND
	2 159.8	5 78.3	4 99.5		29 12.7	6 61.4	5 76.2	3 140.7	3 133.7	4 93.8
	15 25.2	17 21.2	17 21.1		0 UND	5 67.8	17 21.7	17 21.6	23 16.1	21 17.7
	29 12.4	32 11.5	33 11.0	Cost of Sales/Payables	13 28.7	21 17.1	35 10.3	38 9.5	37 9.9	32 11.5
	48 7.5	50 7.2	52 7.1		64 5.7	43 8.5	53 7.2	50 7.2	53 6.9	52 7.0
	7.0	6.7	7.1		12.3	6.9	6.2	6.2	6.6	7.5
	12.9	12.7	14.0	Sales/Working Capital	91.0	19.0	12.7	16.7	12.1	11.7
	47.0	65.8	46.4		–9.3	–35.4	60.7	68.2	33.2	19.7
	12.9	12.7	18.0		8.8	16.0	16.0	13.8	18.7	24.7
	(312) 4.1	(395) 4.2	(336) 5.1	EBIT/Interest	(15) 2.8	(49) 2.5	(48) 4.6	(56) 4.2	(87) 7.3	(81) 8.0
	1.0	1.0	1.7		1.3	–2.4	1.7	1.5	2.0	3.1
	5.0	3.4	5.4				4.2	3.9	4.8	9.4
	(112) 2.3	(137) 1.6	(115) 2.2	Net Profit + Depr., Dep., Amort./Cur. Mat. L/T/D			(18) 2.3	(20) 2.3	(38) 2.2	(32) 2.5
	1.3	.8	1.2				1.4	1.5	.9	1.2
	.4	.4	.4		.7	.5	.4	.5	.3	.3
	.7	.7	.8	Fixed/Worth	1.3	1.0	.8	.9	.7	.7
	1.4	1.5	1.5		5.8	4.1	1.5	1.7	1.1	1.3
	.7	.8	.9		1.1	.6	.8	.8	.9	1.0
	1.6	1.6	1.7	Debt/Worth	3.0	1.8	1.4	1.7	1.4	1.9
	2.9	2.8	3.3		7.3	11.3	2.3	3.7	2.7	3.0
	33.9	28.4	34.9		52.9	48.0	27.2	38.7	29.9	39.2
	(325) 13.9	(410) 13.0	(346) 17.5	% Profit Before Taxes/Tangible Net Worth	(14) 26.0	(45) 18.7	(49) 14.6	(60) 17.9	(95) 16.7	(83) 21.5
	1.2	1.1	5.1		6.9	–6.5	4.7	5.2	4.8	8.0
	13.3	10.8	13.1		14.3	15.3	10.1	13.6	12.8	13.9
	5.1	5.0	6.1	% Profit Before Taxes/Total Assets	6.3	4.0	6.1	5.6	6.0	7.5
	.2	.0	1.4		.7	–5.2	1.5	2.0	1.4	2.4
	14.1	14.2	14.4		20.0	10.5	16.8	11.0	17.0	21.8
	7.4	7.2	7.8	Sales/Net Fixed Assets	5.3	6.4	6.5	7.8	8.4	9.6
	4.9	4.4	4.9		2.9	4.0	4.6	4.6	5.5	6.0
	3.0	2.8	2.8		3.3	3.0	2.7	3.1	3.0	2.8
	2.3	2.2	2.2	Sales/Total Assets	2.3	2.3	2.0	2.3	2.3	2.2
	1.7	1.7	1.7		1.4	1.9	1.6	1.7	1.8	1.9
	1.9	2.1	2.0		5.5	2.9	1.9	2.2	2.1	1.2
	(318) 3.6	(392) 3.8	(331) 3.4	% Depr., Dep., Amort./Sales	(12) 6.8	(46) 6.1	(46) 3.5	(61) 3.2	(90) 3.5	(76) 2.4
	5.8	6.4	5.3		10.6	9.4	5.9	5.3	4.4	3.7
	1.9	1.6	1.6		5.1	4.3	2.0	1.6	1.0	.8
	(145) 3.6	(212) 3.5	(163) 3.4	% Officers', Directors', Owners' Comp/Sales	(10) 8.5	(30) 6.8	(32) 3.6	(32) 3.3	(39) 2.4	(20) 1.4
	6.8	6.7	6.8		12.7	9.4	6.4	5.2	3.9	3.7
	7652515M	8232363M	10306531M	Net Sales ($)	9636M	111796M	212677M	452979M	1556301M	7963142M
	3563400M	3967675M	4727966M	Total Assets ($)	6011M	59492M	112852M	219369M	763468M	3566774M

M = $ thousand   MM = $ million
See Pages 11 through 21 for Explanation of Ratios and Data

Current Data Sorted By Assets   Comparative Historical Data

0-500M	500M-2MM	2-10MM	10-50MM	50-100MM	100-250MM	Type of Statement	4/1/00-3/31/01 ALL	4/1/01-3/31/02 ALL
	1	4	4	2	3	Unqualified		
	2	10	1			Reviewed		
1	1	1				Compiled		
1	2					Tax Returns		
2	4	1	2			Other		
	9 (4/1-9/30/04)			33 (10/1/04-3/31/05)				
4	10	16	7	2	3	NUMBER OF STATEMENTS		
%	%	%	%	%	%		%	%
	15.1	9.0				**ASSETS** Cash & Equivalents		
	37.6	35.1				Trade Receivables (net)	D	D
	1.6	6.0				Inventory	A	A
	5.7	5.2				All Other Current	T	T
	59.9	55.4				Total Current	A	A
	33.8	34.9				Fixed Assets (net)		
	3.7	4.1				Intangibles (net)	N	N
	2.5	5.6				All Other Non-Current	O	O
	100.0	100.0				Total	T	T
	8.6	7.5				**LIABILITIES** Notes Payable-Short Term	A	A
	8.9	7.0				Cur. Mat.-L/T/D	V	V
	17.8	16.3				Trade Payables	A	A
	.1	.2				Income Taxes Payable	I	I
	9.3	15.3				All Other Current	L	L
	44.6	46.3				Total Current	A	A
	21.9	18.1				Long-Term Debt	B	B
	.3	1.1				Deferred Taxes	L	L
	.4	2.5				All Other Non-Current	E	E
	32.7	32.0				Net Worth		
	100.0	100.0				Total Liabilities & Net Worth		
	100.0	100.0				**INCOME DATA** Net Sales		
						Gross Profit		
	102.6	91.8				Operating Expenses		
	-2.6	8.2				Operating Profit		
	.5	3.7				All Other Expenses (net)		
	-3.0	4.5				Profit Before Taxes		
	2.3	1.5				**RATIOS** Current		
	1.4	1.2				Current		
	1.0	.9						
	2.2	1.2				Quick		
	1.3	.9				Quick		
	.7	.6						
	22 16.4	42 8.7				Sales/Receivables		
	54 6.7	52 7.0				Sales/Receivables		
	79 4.6	63 5.8						
						Cost of Sales/Inventory		
						Cost of Sales/Payables		
	10.0	12.6				Sales/Working Capital		
	14.7	54.3				Sales/Working Capital		
	NM	-59.4						
	4.4	7.4				EBIT/Interest		
	2.3	(14) 3.8				EBIT/Interest		
	-.2	2.1						
						Net Profit + Depr., Dep., Amort./Cur. Mat. L /T/D		
	.2	.5				Fixed/Worth		
	1.1	1.4				Fixed/Worth		
	NM	3.5						
	.8	1.3				Debt/Worth		
	1.8	2.4				Debt/Worth		
	NM	12.4						
		90.7				% Profit Before Taxes/Tangible Net Worth		
		30.6				% Profit Before Taxes/Tangible Net Worth		
		4.6						
	6.3	10.6				% Profit Before Taxes/Total Assets		
	2.1	5.0				% Profit Before Taxes/Total Assets		
	-4.0	1.8						
	44.5	23.7				Sales/Net Fixed Assets		
	10.9	9.0				Sales/Net Fixed Assets		
	4.4	4.8						
	4.6	3.5				Sales/Total Assets		
	2.4	2.4				Sales/Total Assets		
	2.0	1.4						
	1.7	1.4				% Depr., Dep., Amort./Sales		
	2.8	3.4				% Depr., Dep., Amort./Sales		
	4.6	10.6						
						% Officers', Directors', Owners' Comp/Sales		
3789M	45801M	183575M	356840M	272388M	646630M	Net Sales ($)		
1470M	14354M	75329M	176633M	127943M	432473M	Total Assets ($)		

© RMA 2005

M = $ thousand   MM = $ million
See Pages 11 through 21 for Explanation of Ratios and Data

Comparative Historical Data | Current Data Sorted By Sales

			Type of Statement						
11	26	14	Unqualified			1	2	3	8
5	11	14	Reviewed	2	1	2	4	4	1
	1	3	Compiled		1	1	1		
	6	4	Tax Returns	1	1		1	1	
6	11	7	Other	1	1	2	2	1	1
4/1/02- 3/31/03 ALL	4/1/03- 3/31/04 ALL	4/1/04- 3/31/05 ALL		9 (4/1-9/30/04)			33 (10/1/04-3/31/05)		
				0-1MM	1-3MM	3-5MM	5-10MM	10-25MM	25MM & OVER
22	55	42	**NUMBER OF STATEMENTS**	3	5	6	9	9	10
%	%	%	**ASSETS**	%	%	%	%	%	%
14.5	11.9	12.4	Cash & Equivalents						11.6
32.1	33.3	35.7	Trade Receivables (net)						38.2
3.9	3.8	4.3	Inventory						6.2
7.9	7.9	5.5	All Other Current						8.3
58.4	56.9	57.9	Total Current						64.2
32.9	35.7	34.0	Fixed Assets (net)						29.8
2.1	2.5	3.1	Intangibles (net)						.4
6.6	5.0	5.1	All Other Non-Current						5.5
100.0	100.0	100.0	Total						100.0
			LIABILITIES						
15.7	9.5	8.7	Notes Payable-Short Term						7.4
4.3	4.5	6.7	Cur. Mat.-L/T/D						2.6
17.4	15.7	16.2	Trade Payables						19.1
.0	.5	.2	Income Taxes Payable						.4
14.0	14.0	15.1	All Other Current						24.4
51.5	44.2	46.9	Total Current						53.8
15.4	17.6	18.1	Long-Term Debt						12.5
1.5	1.7	.8	Deferred Taxes						1.1
4.4	4.5	2.4	All Other Non-Current						1.1
27.3	32.0	31.9	Net Worth						31.4
100.0	100.0	100.0	Total Liabilities & Net Worth						100.0
			INCOME DATA						
100.0	100.0	100.0	Net Sales						100.0
			Gross Profit						
98.0	95.3	95.3	Operating Expenses						95.0
2.0	4.7	4.7	Operating Profit						5.0
1.3	1.0	1.3	All Other Expenses (net)						.3
.6	3.7	3.4	Profit Before Taxes						4.7
			RATIOS						
2.0	1.8	1.5	Current						1.4
1.2	1.3	1.2							1.2
.9	.9	.9							1.1
1.7	1.6	1.3	Quick						1.2
1.1	1.1	1.0							1.0
.5	.7	.7							.7
25 14.7	27 13.7	40 9.1	Sales/Receivables						48 7.6
54 6.7	48 7.7	54 6.7							56 6.5
64 5.7	66 5.5	74 5.0							67 5.5
			Cost of Sales/Inventory						
			Cost of Sales/Payables						
8.5	10.9	12.3	Sales/Working Capital						16.3
14.5	15.8	19.9							20.8
−48.8	−54.7	−129.9							30.8
17.9	15.0	7.1	EBIT/Interest						
(21) 3.5	(51) 6.3	(37) 3.8							
.6	2.9	1.6							
	4.8	5.2	Net Profit + Depr., Dep.,						
	(17) 1.9	(15) 2.4	Amort./Cur. Mat. L/T/D						
	.8	1.2							
.3	.5	.4	Fixed/Worth						.4
.8	.8	1.2							.7
5.6	4.7	2.4							1.6
.8	.9	1.3	Debt/Worth						1.6
3.0	1.9	2.4							2.5
9.4	10.4	5.2							4.3
24.8	41.8	54.2	% Profit Before Taxes/Tangible						30.1
(20) 10.9	(49) 25.4	(40) 17.7	Net Worth						16.1
−5.6	8.6	7.7							8.0
8.7	14.5	9.2	% Profit Before Taxes/Total						6.1
3.0	8.7	5.0	Assets						4.5
−3.9	2.4	1.6							2.2
22.0	15.9	21.7	Sales/Net Fixed Assets						41.7
8.5	9.0	7.6							11.9
3.2	4.0	4.3							2.6
3.2	3.1	3.5	Sales/Total Assets						3.6
2.1	2.3	2.3							2.4
1.2	1.8	1.8							1.2
1.1	1.3	1.4	% Depr., Dep., Amort./Sales						
2.9	(47) 2.7	(41) 3.1							
7.2	4.2	5.1							
	2.4	1.8	% Officers', Directors',						
	(18) 4.8	(14) 2.9	Owners' Comp/Sales						
	7.4	4.1							
564291M	2276112M	1509023M	Net Sales ($)	1351M	9749M	23678M	66475M	164370M	1243400M
459677M	996615M	828202M	Total Assets ($)	2792M	4248M	11954M	35302M	101654M	672252M

M = $ thousand   MM = $ million
See Pages 11 through 21 for Explanation of Ratios and Data

Current Data Sorted By Assets   **Comparative Historical Data**

						Type of Statement		
1	4	15	36	17	26	Unqualified	102	108
1	13	41	31	3	7	Reviewed	94	83
8	37	59	26	4	2	Compiled	191	196
48	147	170	31	4	12	Tax Returns	242	238
30	68	146	99	21	12	Other	321	323
	86 (4/1-9/30/04)		1021 (10/1/04-3/31/05)				4/1/00-3/31/01	4/1/01-3/31/02
0-500M	500M-2MM	2-10MM	10-50MM	50-100MM	100-250MM		ALL	ALL
88	269	431	223	49	47	NUMBER OF STATEMENTS	950	948
%	%	%	%	%	%	ASSETS	%	%
16.6	7.8	7.0	7.5	8.3	7.3	Cash & Equivalents	6.9	6.8
4.8	6.3	4.0	3.9	3.2	10.2	Trade Receivables (net)	5.0	5.2
30.8	30.8	41.0	40.3	39.1	30.3	Inventory	31.2	30.9
5.2	4.7	4.3	4.5	2.6	2.8	All Other Current	6.7	6.9
57.4	49.6	56.4	56.2	53.2	50.6	Total Current	49.9	49.9
24.4	38.0	30.7	25.8	26.3	37.2	Fixed Assets (net)	33.5	33.7
1.1	1.7	.9	1.3	1.8	1.1	Intangibles (net)	1.5	1.3
17.1	10.7	12.1	16.7	18.7	11.1	All Other Non-Current	15.1	15.1
100.0	100.0	100.0	100.0	100.0	100.0	Total	100.0	100.0
						LIABILITIES		
20.8	20.5	21.6	22.1	15.5	14.5	Notes Payable-Short Term	20.7	18.5
3.6	2.1	2.3	2.4	3.1	2.9	Cur. Mat.-L/T/D	4.2	4.6
6.2	3.9	3.9	4.4	5.1	6.6	Trade Payables	6.1	5.0
.0	.2	.1	.2	.8	.1	Income Taxes Payable	.2	.2
21.3	10.1	10.2	9.4	8.9	7.2	All Other Current	10.3	11.6
51.9	36.8	38.2	38.5	33.4	31.3	Total Current	41.5	39.9
15.1	30.9	32.5	27.4	34.1	29.0	Long-Term Debt	30.7	31.9
.0	.1	.1	.4	.5	.6	Deferred Taxes	.1	.1
13.1	4.6	3.8	5.1	4.2	4.1	All Other Non-Current	6.7	5.9
19.9	27.6	25.4	28.7	27.8	35.0	Net Worth	21.0	22.2
100.0	100.0	100.0	100.0	100.0	100.0	Total Liabilities & Net Worth	100.0	100.0
						INCOME DATA		
100.0	100.0	100.0	100.0	100.0	100.0	Net Sales	100.0	100.0
						Gross Profit		
78.4	76.4	78.8	80.5	78.4	77.8	Operating Expenses	80.4	80.0
21.6	23.6	21.2	19.5	21.6	22.2	Operating Profit	19.6	20.0
2.9	6.9	5.3	4.5	2.6	4.7	All Other Expenses (net)	6.2	8.6
18.7	16.7	15.9	14.9	18.9	17.5	Profit Before Taxes	13.5	11.5
						RATIOS		
5.2	3.6	3.9	2.8	4.4	4.2		2.8	3.0
1.5	1.4	1.3	1.3	1.4	1.3	Current	1.2	1.3
.7	.5	.7	1.0	.7	.9		.6	.7
1.5	1.5	.9	.9	1.0	1.0		.9	1.1
.4	.2	.2	(221) .2	.4	.5	Quick	(944) .2	(946) .2
.0	.0	.0	.0	.1	.1		.0	.0
0 UND	0 UND	0 UND	0 UND	0 UND	0 999.8		0 UND	0 UND
0 UND	0 UND	0 UND	2 206.6	1 330.5	8 48.2	Sales/Receivables	0 999.8	0 UND
0 UND	4 96.5	6 64.9	16 23.2	18 19.9	32 11.4		15 24.5	12 31.0
						Cost of Sales/Inventory		
						Cost of Sales/Payables		
3.1	2.3	1.5	1.5	1.1	2.5		2.1	2.2
45.4	13.9	7.6	6.0	6.3	9.8	Sales/Working Capital	12.8	10.8
-37.0	-5.0	-9.4	-50.2	-8.4	-61.4		-6.8	-9.9
(45) 19.0	(182) 10.7	(275) 18.3	(160) 20.5	(34) 40.8	(38) 22.2		(575) 9.0	(590) 10.5
5.5	4.4	5.7	5.2	9.7	8.0	EBIT/Interest	3.2	3.4
1.7	1.6	2.0	1.8	2.4	2.8		1.3	1.3
		7.7	7.8				2.7	5.9
		(13) 1.7	(16) 1.4			Net Profit + Depr., Dep., Amort./Cur. Mat. L /T/D	(59) 1.2	(50) 2.0
		.5	.5				.5	.5
.0	.0	.0	.0	.0	.1		.0	.0
.2	.9	.5	.2	.4	.7	Fixed/Worth	.7	.6
4.0	6.2	4.1	2.9	3.1	1.8		5.3	5.1
.2	1.1	1.4	1.4	1.4	.9		1.3	1.3
1.5	3.3	3.6	3.6	3.3	2.8	Debt/Worth	4.0	4.1
UND	15.8	14.3	9.6	7.3	4.8		25.2	16.3
283.1	100.0	87.1	67.9	47.1	52.6		57.3	64.9
(67) 92.2	(232) 34.7	(376) 34.7	(201) 29.4	(43) 35.0	(44) 23.1	% Profit Before Taxes/Tangible Net Worth	(787) 23.1	(812) 22.3
15.8	8.3	11.2	7.5	16.3	10.9		5.4	4.2
100.8	20.0	19.0	13.7	14.8	10.8		11.5	11.9
20.3	7.7	6.9	5.3	8.1	6.5	% Profit Before Taxes/Total Assets	4.2	4.2
1.3	.9	1.6	1.0	1.9	3.6		.6	.3
UND	783.1	999.8	211.6	209.7	71.2		297.0	297.3
73.2	7.2	14.9	17.2	28.6	3.6	Sales/Net Fixed Assets	7.2	9.0
4.2	.5	.9	1.1	1.2	.6		.5	.5
8.4	1.9	1.3	1.1	1.0	1.3		1.2	1.3
2.2	.8	.6	.5	.7	.6	Sales/Total Assets	.5	.6
.6	.3	.3	.2	.3	.4		.2	.2
.6	.5	.4	.3	.2	.5		.6	.4
(28) 1.9	(136) 3.7	(216) 1.8	(136) 1.3	(29) .7	(32) 1.8	% Depr., Dep., Amort./Sales	(589) 2.4	(573) 2.1
10.3	15.4	11.8	7.6	3.6	8.0		11.7	10.3
1.8	2.1	1.1	1.3				2.1	1.8
(20) 3.7	(48) 3.8	(79) 2.5	(33) 3.3			% Officers', Directors', Owners' Comp/Sales	(189) 4.6	(198) 4.4
9.2	8.2	5.5	8.6				9.8	10.1
118072M	455503M	2624583M	3939255M	2763388M	7356635M	Net Sales ($)	10538615M	14917650M
25934M	322669M	2023529M	5008048M	3415170M	7550373M	Total Assets ($)	14816284M	16547225M

M = $ thousand   MM = $ million
See Pages 11 through 21 for Explanation of Ratios and Data

Comparative Historical Data | | | **Current Data Sorted By Sales**

		Comparative Historical Data		Type of Statement			Current Data Sorted By Sales		
	104	141	99	Unqualified	7	12	4	8	17	51
	82	103	96	Reviewed	11	21	10	19	17	18
	128	234	136	Compiled	35	43	16	19	15	8
	228	397	400	Tax Returns	169	116	47	39	20	9
	243	369	376	Other	82	90	43	50	61	50
	4/1/02-3/31/03 ALL	4/1/03-3/31/04 ALL	4/1/04-3/31/05 ALL		86 (4/1-9/30/04) 0-1MM	1-3MM	3-5MM	1021 (10/1/04-3/31/05) 5-10MM	10-25MM	25MM & OVER
	785	1244	1107	NUMBER OF STATEMENTS	304	282	120	135	130	136
	%	%	%	ASSETS	%	%	%	%	%	%
	7.4	8.2	8.1	Cash & Equivalents	6.0	7.7	7.6	9.0	11.6	10.3
	4.9	5.3	4.8	Trade Receivables (net)	2.4	5.1	4.0	5.3	7.8	7.2
	33.5	34.6	37.0	Inventory	27.7	37.4	40.4	45.1	39.8	43.4
	5.9	6.3	4.4	All Other Current	4.1	3.6	6.1	4.7	5.2	4.0
	51.7	54.3	54.4	Total Current	40.2	53.8	58.0	64.2	64.5	64.8
	32.5	31.5	31.1	Fixed Assets (net)	47.2	30.2	28.0	19.4	19.0	22.6
	1.4	1.0	1.2	Intangibles (net)	1.3	1.3	1.7	1.1	.7	1.1
	14.4	13.2	13.3	All Other Non-Current	11.3	14.8	12.4	15.3	15.8	11.4
	100.0	100.0	100.0	Total	100.0	100.0	100.0	100.0	100.0	100.0
				LIABILITIES						
	19.3	19.6	20.8	Notes Payable-Short Term	19.1	19.5	23.3	23.6	20.5	22.4
	3.8	3.3	2.4	Cur. Mat.-L/T/D	2.6	2.4	2.8	3.1	1.0	2.6
	4.8	5.4	4.4	Trade Payables	1.2	3.8	3.3	5.8	7.7	9.1
	.2	.1	.2	Income Taxes Payable	.0	.2	.3	.3	.2	.2
	10.4	11.4	10.7	All Other Current	10.8	10.8	10.8	11.8	10.3	9.7
	38.5	39.8	38.5	Total Current	33.8	36.6	40.6	44.7	39.7	43.9
	29.9	28.8	29.6	Long-Term Debt	37.6	35.0	23.4	20.9	22.1	22.0
	.2	.2	.2	Deferred Taxes	.0	.1	.2	.3	.3	.5
	6.6	5.2	5.0	All Other Non-Current	6.3	4.3	8.6	4.8	3.2	2.6
	24.8	26.0	26.7	Net Worth	22.3	24.1	27.2	29.3	34.8	30.9
	100.0	100.0	100.0	Total Liabilities & Net Worth	100.0	100.0	100.0	100.0	100.0	100.0
				INCOME DATA						
	100.0	100.0	100.0	Net Sales	100.0	100.0	100.0	100.0	100.0	100.0
				Gross Profit						
	80.6	80.5	78.5	Operating Expenses	70.2	78.6	81.0	84.0	81.6	85.9
	19.4	19.5	21.5	Operating Profit	29.8	21.4	19.0	16.0	18.4	14.1
	6.6	6.0	5.2	All Other Expenses (net)	11.4	4.9	3.8	1.1	1.0	1.2
	12.8	13.5	16.3	Profit Before Taxes	18.4	16.5	15.2	14.9	17.4	13.0
				RATIOS						
	3.3	3.2	3.8		3.7	5.4	3.4	2.7	4.0	2.7
	1.3	1.3	1.4	Current	1.2	1.4	1.3	1.3	1.4	1.4
	.7	.8	.7		.2	.7	.8	1.0	1.0	1.0
	1.0	1.0	1.1		1.1	1.7	.9	.7	1.2	1.0
	(782) .2	(1237) .2	(1105) .2	Quick	(303) .2	.2	(119) .2	.2	.5	.3
	.0	.0	.0		.0	.0	.0	.0	.1	.1
	0 UND	0 UND	0 UND		0 UND	0 UND	0 UND	0 UND	0 UND	0 999.8
	0 UND	0 UND	0 UND	Sales/Receivables	0 UND	0 UND	0 UND	0 868.7	1 371.8	2 169.9
	10 38.0	10 35.6	8 45.7		1 487.3	9 42.9	8 43.1	12 29.5	12 31.1	26 14.1
				Cost of Sales/Inventory						
				Cost of Sales/Payables						
	2.3	2.0	1.8		1.0	1.5	2.0	2.3	3.1	3.0
	10.3	7.4	9.8	Sales/Working Capital	19.5	8.1	8.8	6.6	10.8	9.8
	-12.2	-14.3	-11.6		-2.4	-10.8	-14.8	-137.1	94.1	-236.7
	12.7	16.4	17.5		7.7	11.7	12.2	21.7	94.8	35.1
	(506) 4.1	(841) 4.5	(734) 5.3	EBIT/Interest	(166) 3.8	(197) 4.4	(83) 4.7	(94) 5.2	(83) 16.6	(111) 10.5
	1.5	1.6	2.0		1.6	1.6	1.6	1.4	4.1	3.4
	4.9	7.1	8.1	Net Profit + Depr., Dep.,						11.6
	(50) 2.7	(58) 1.9	(43) 1.7	Amort./Cur. Mat. L/T/D					(13)	4.1
	.7	.6	.8							1.1
	.0	.0	.0		.0	.0	.0	.0	.0	.0
	.5	.4	.5	Fixed/Worth	1.4	.6	.5	.1	.1	.2
	4.4	3.4	4.1		11.2	4.5	1.0	1.5	1.1	1.7
	1.0	1.1	1.1		1.1	1.1	1.0	1.2	.8	1.4
	3.2	3.2	3.4	Debt/Worth	3.9	3.6	3.3	3.0	2.5	3.1
	15.6	12.5	12.5		29.4	15.5	19.5	10.7	7.8	6.2
	57.3	64.9	85.1	% Profit Before Taxes/Tangible	52.4	97.7	76.1	100.1	116.3	72.8
	(661) 21.3	(1066) 26.2	(963) 34.5	Net Worth	(247) 21.1	(240) 30.3	(104) 34.3	(124) 40.9	(121) 56.0	(127) 39.5
	4.9	7.3	10.0		3.5	7.1	12.0	10.0	27.8	18.5
	13.0	15.4	19.2	% Profit Before Taxes/Total	10.8	19.1	21.9	26.0	31.7	20.2
	4.8	5.7	7.1	Assets	4.5	7.0	7.7	7.9	15.9	9.1
	.4	.9	1.4		.2	1.2	1.4	1.4	5.2	4.0
	299.2	354.6	682.2		UND	999.8	590.8	UND	999.8	169.5
	10.7	12.5	14.4	Sales/Net Fixed Assets	.7	17.3	25.7	44.5	78.7	25.5
	.6	.7	.9		.2	1.0	1.5	4.4	7.3	2.8
	1.3	1.4	1.5		.5	1.4	1.7	1.9	2.6	2.0
	.5	.6	.7	Sales/Total Assets	.2	.6	.9	1.1	1.3	1.2
	.2	.3	.3		.1	.3	.3	.4	.6	.7
	.6	.5	.4		2.6	.6	.3	.3	.2	.2
	(478) 3.1	(739) 2.6	(577) 1.8	% Depr., Dep., Amort./Sales	(158) 11.4	(134) 2.6	(65) .9	(69) .8	(63) .4	(88) .6
	13.2	12.1	10.8		20.1	12.1	6.8	2.7	1.5	2.1
	2.1	1.4	1.4		2.6	2.6	1.4	1.3	.9	.6
	(128) 5.1	(240) 3.3	(188) 3.0	% Officers', Directors', Owners' Comp/Sales	(24) 7.7	(55) 4.1	(30) 3.6	(32) 2.4	(33) 1.5	(14) 1.4
	11.9	9.4	7.6		19.6	8.4	8.2	5.1	3.2	3.6
	10519392M	18330375M	17257436M	Net Sales ($)	138281M	533067M	460320M	971084M	1973331M	13181353M
	14370913M	21306879M	18345723M	Total Assets ($)	594543M	1342019M	1175462M	1729812M	2632296M	10871591M

M = $ thousand   MM = $ million
See Pages 11 through 21 for Explanation of Ratios and Data

Current Data Sorted By Assets   **Comparative Historical Data**

						Type of Statement		
1	23	123	166	41	31	Unqualified	219	249
8	38	102	21			Reviewed	83	103
9	16	11	4			Compiled	47	65
15	18	7	1			Tax Returns	15	15
7	21	53	42	13	7	Other	96	121
137 (4/1-9/30/04)			641 (10/1/04-3/31/05)				4/1/00-3/31/01	4/1/01-3/31/02
0-500M	500M-2MM	2-10MM	10-50MM	50-100MM	100-250MM		ALL	ALL
40	116	296	234	54	38	NUMBER OF STATEMENTS	460	553
%	%	%	%	%	%	ASSETS	%	%
16.1	13.7	14.7	16.0	12.6	8.5	Cash & Equivalents	15.5	15.0
27.1	31.6	34.8	31.0	27.5	24.8	Trade Receivables (net)	31.6	32.2
2.0	4.7	3.3	3.9	6.1	5.0	Inventory	3.5	3.3
7.4	6.1	7.1	7.2	10.7	12.6	All Other Current	7.0	7.1
52.7	56.2	59.8	58.0	56.9	50.9	Total Current	57.6	57.6
41.3	35.5	32.7	33.3	31.2	35.4	Fixed Assets (net)	34.1	34.6
.4	.8	1.0	1.2	1.5	4.1	Intangibles (net)	1.3	1.3
5.6	7.5	6.5	7.5	10.3	9.7	All Other Non-Current	7.0	6.5
100.0	100.0	100.0	100.0	100.0	100.0	Total	100.0	100.0
						LIABILITIES		
12.4	8.3	5.4	3.7	3.0	2.2	Notes Payable-Short Term	6.2	5.4
5.4	6.0	6.1	4.9	4.4	3.7	Cur. Mat.-L/T/D	5.4	5.2
12.8	17.9	18.4	17.0	17.8	14.3	Trade Payables	16.9	18.2
.1	.5	1.0	.4	.8	.2	Income Taxes Payable	.8	.6
17.4	10.2	8.4	11.6	13.9	12.9	All Other Current	8.7	9.8
48.0	42.8	39.3	37.6	40.0	33.3	Total Current	38.0	39.2
24.2	18.5	13.5	13.3	19.3	17.6	Long-Term Debt	14.8	15.2
.3	.7	1.7	1.3	2.2	1.9	Deferred Taxes	1.3	1.2
2.1	5.1	3.3	2.4	2.2	3.1	All Other Non-Current	2.7	1.8
25.5	32.8	42.2	45.4	36.4	44.1	Net Worth	43.2	42.6
100.0	100.0	100.0	100.0	100.0	100.0	Total Liabilities & Net Worth	100.0	100.0
						INCOME DATA		
100.0	100.0	100.0	100.0	100.0	100.0	Net Sales	100.0	100.0
40.4	26.9	17.9	12.8	12.7	12.9	Gross Profit	16.4	17.0
36.9	24.4	14.2	9.1	9.9	9.5	Operating Expenses	13.5	13.6
3.6	2.5	3.7	3.6	2.7	3.4	Operating Profit	3.0	3.4
.1	.7	.3	-.2	.2	.1	All Other Expenses (net)	.0	.3
3.5	1.8	3.4	3.9	2.6	3.4	Profit Before Taxes	3.0	3.0
						RATIOS		
3.3	2.0	2.2	2.1	1.9	2.0	Current	2.2	2.1
1.8	1.5	1.5	1.5	1.5	1.5		1.5	1.4
.9	.9	1.2	1.2	1.1	1.2		1.1	1.1
2.8	1.8	1.8	1.7	1.3	1.3	Quick	1.9	1.7
1.4	1.1	1.3	1.3	1.0	1.0		1.2	1.2
.7	.7	.9	.9	.7			.8	.9
0 UND	22 16.4	36 10.2	37 9.8	36 10.1	40 9.2	Sales/Receivables	33 11.2	32 11.2
17 21.5	40 9.2	53 6.8	53 6.9	53 6.9	50 7.3		51 7.1	52 7.0
61 6.0	60 6.0	73 5.0	77 4.7	70 5.2	73 5.0		69 5.3	73 5.0
0 UND	0 UND	0 UND	0 UND	1 382.9	2 212.6	Cost of Sales/Inventory	0 UND	0 UND
0 UND	0 UND	0 UND	2 210.5	8 43.0	9 42.7		1 384.2	1 699.2
0 UND	6 63.4	5 67.0	9 40.4	18 20.2	21 17.2		9 38.8	9 47.1
0 UND	11 33.1	16 22.5	21 17.1	25 14.9	24 15.1	Cost of Sales/Payables	17 21.5	17 21.4
16 23.5	24 15.0	31 11.9	32 11.5	37 9.8	35 10.3		30 12.2	31 11.6
45 8.1	43 8.4	51 7.1	46 7.9	51 7.1	47 7.8		46 8.0	47 7.7
10.3	8.5	6.2	6.3	5.7	6.8	Sales/Working Capital	6.4	6.7
30.6	18.5	11.5	10.8	11.8	10.2		12.4	13.1
-29.6	-90.3	32.8	19.4	36.4	21.2		41.9	35.6
16.0	12.0	17.0	18.7	15.4	14.1	EBIT/Interest	9.8	9.7
(31) 3.6	(99) 3.4	(280) 5.8	(213) 7.3	(49) 4.5	(35) 7.6		(418) 3.2	(500) 3.6
.3	-.2	1.9	2.6	2.0	3.4		1.0	1.5
	6.3	3.9	4.3	5.0		Net Profit + Depr., Dep.,	3.9	3.4
	(20) 2.0	(117) 2.2	(79) 1.9	(23) 1.8		Amort./Cur. Mat. L /T/D	(154) 1.8	(172) 1.9
	1.1	1.3	1.1	1.2			1.0	1.0
.4	.5	.4	.5	.4	.6	Fixed/Worth	.4	.4
1.1	1.0	.8	.8	1.1	.9		.8	.8
10.2	2.6	1.3	1.2	1.8	1.1		1.4	1.4
.6	.8	.7	.7	.9	.9	Debt/Worth	.7	.7
1.9	1.7	1.5	1.3	2.3	1.5		1.4	1.4
16.0	5.2	2.8	2.3	3.7	2.3		2.9	2.9
62.5	38.6	31.1	26.5	23.4	20.7	% Profit Before Taxes/Tangible	27.6	32.0
(31) 31.7	(100) 15.3	(285) 18.3	14.9	(37) 14.4	12.6	Net Worth	(441) 12.2	(535) 14.6
4.8	2.1	4.1	5.4	2.3	8.3		.9	4.0
29.2	15.6	12.3	11.8	7.5	8.2	% Profit Before Taxes/Total	11.2	11.9
10.0	4.9	6.2	5.8	4.5	5.1	Assets	4.7	5.4
.3	-.5	1.6	2.2	1.2	3.3		.1	1.4
34.4	15.6	12.7	9.8	10.9	9.2	Sales/Net Fixed Assets	12.3	11.6
9.5	9.8	7.6	6.5	5.7	5.4		6.9	6.8
5.0	4.6	4.6	4.0	3.3	3.2		4.2	4.1
5.6	3.7	2.9	2.5	2.3	2.1	Sales/Total Assets	2.9	2.8
3.2	2.6	2.3	2.0	1.8	1.5		2.2	2.2
2.3	1.8	1.6	1.6	1.2	1.3		1.6	1.6
2.2	1.8	2.1	2.4	1.9	1.7	% Depr., Dep., Amort./Sales	2.0	1.9
(27) 3.5	(97) 3.8	(275) 3.5	(220) 3.5	(45) 4.1	(25) 2.9		(414) 3.3	(504) 3.5
9.5	6.6	5.4	4.8	4.9	4.5		5.0	5.2
5.5	2.6	1.4	.6			% Officers', Directors',	1.2	1.3
(15) 7.0	(52) 3.4	(127) 2.3	(64) 1.4			Owners' Comp/Sales	(168) 2.5	(180) 2.8
13.6	5.7	4.1	2.2				4.1	5.0
50241M	390916M	3517167M	10322056M	7077209M	9423574M	Net Sales ($)	18603770M	23486068M
11547M	138914M	1500217M	5100441M	3814223M	5580862M	Total Assets ($)	8636240M	11446375M

M = $ thousand   MM = $ million
See Pages 11 through 21 for Explanation of Ratios and Data

Comparative Historical Data | Current Data Sorted By Sales

			Type of Statement						
334	346	385	Unqualified	1	15	14	45	95	215
124	164	169	Reviewed	9	26	23	41	50	20
33	87	40	Compiled	8	12	6	7	5	2
21	37	41	Tax Returns	7	16	10	4	3	1
117	138	143	Other	4	12	13	23	35	56
4/1/02-3/31/03	4/1/03-3/31/04	4/1/04-3/31/05		137 (4/1-9/30/04)			641 (10/1/04-3/31/05)		
ALL	ALL	ALL		0-1MM	1-3MM	3-5MM	5-10MM	10-25MM	25MM & OVER
629	772	778	**NUMBER OF STATEMENTS**	29	81	66	120	188	294
%	%	%	**ASSETS**	%	%	%	%	%	%
16.2	14.3	14.6	Cash & Equivalents	14.6	12.9	16.1	16.1	13.9	14.5
29.4	30.9	31.8	Trade Receivables (net)	27.4	26.8	29.2	34.8	35.3	30.7
3.2	3.8	3.9	Inventory	5.3	4.6	4.0	2.3	3.4	4.4
7.7	8.3	7.5	All Other Current	1.5	7.1	6.7	7.8	6.8	8.7
56.5	57.4	57.7	Total Current	48.8	51.4	56.1	60.9	59.5	58.3
35.5	34.7	33.7	Fixed Assets (net)	44.0	39.0	34.5	32.5	32.7	32.3
1.2	1.2	1.2	Intangibles (net)	.3	.8	1.1	.8	1.3	1.4
6.8	6.7	7.4	All Other Non-Current	6.9	8.8	8.4	5.7	6.5	8.0
100.0	100.0	100.0	Total	100.0	100.0	100.0	100.0	100.0	100.0
			LIABILITIES						
4.5	5.2	5.4	Notes Payable-Short Term	9.2	9.0	9.0	5.5	4.9	3.4
5.6	5.3	5.4	Cur. Mat.-L/T/D	4.6	7.4	5.9	6.3	5.5	4.5
17.1	17.6	17.4	Trade Payables	10.4	11.7	18.4	18.5	18.6	18.1
.5	.5	.6	Income Taxes Payable	.1	.5	.6	.9	1.0	.4
10.3	10.6	10.7	All Other Current	21.3	9.7	7.2	8.1	9.8	12.3
38.0	39.2	39.5	Total Current	45.6	38.3	41.1	39.3	39.9	38.7
16.0	15.1	15.3	Long-Term Debt	21.2	22.2	17.6	14.4	12.9	14.4
1.3	1.3	1.4	Deferred Taxes	.7	.9	1.3	1.5	1.6	1.4
2.5	3.2	3.2	All Other Non-Current	8.1	4.2	3.6	3.3	2.7	2.5
42.2	41.3	40.6	Net Worth	24.4	34.4	36.4	41.6	43.0	43.0
100.0	100.0	100.0	Total Liabilities & Net Worth	100.0	100.0	100.0	100.0	100.0	100.0
			INCOME DATA						
100.0	100.0	100.0	Net Sales	100.0	100.0	100.0	100.0	100.0	100.0
17.1	17.7	18.3	Gross Profit	42.8	31.2	22.9	19.9	15.6	12.3
13.8	15.0	14.8	Operating Expenses	41.7	28.1	19.2	15.9	11.9	9.0
3.3	2.7	3.4	Operating Profit	1.1	3.0	3.7	3.9	3.7	3.3
.3	.2	.1	All Other Expenses (net)	.8	.7	.3	.1	.1	-.1
2.9	2.5	3.3	Profit Before Taxes	.3	2.4	3.5	3.9	3.5	3.4
			RATIOS						
2.2	2.1	2.1		3.6	2.5	2.0	2.3	2.2	2.0
1.5	1.5	1.5	Current	1.5	1.7	1.4	1.6	1.5	1.5
1.1	1.2	1.2		.8	1.0	1.0	1.2	1.2	1.2
1.8	1.7	1.7		3.6	2.2	1.7	2.0	1.8	1.5
1.2	(771) 1.2	1.2	Quick	.9	1.4	1.1	1.4	1.2	1.2
.8	.8	.8		.6	.7	.8	.8	.9	.9
30 12.2	31 11.7	33 11.0		9 42.7	12 30.8	26 14.2	34 10.6	38 9.7	36 10.2
47 7.7	49 7.4	51 7.1	Sales/Receivables	59 6.2	41 8.9	43 8.6	55 6.7	53 6.9	50 7.3
64 5.7	72 5.1	71 5.1		92 4.0	66 5.5	68 5.3	77 4.8	73 5.0	70 5.2
0 UND	0 UND	0 UND		0 UND	0 UND	0 UND	0 UND	0 UND	0 UND
0 918.5	0 839.5	1 631.1	Cost of Sales/Inventory	0 UND	0 UND	0 UND	0 UND	1 509.8	2 175.4
8 48.5	9 40.9	9 41.2		9 42.5	4 85.4	11 33.9	3 106.1	8 45.5	12 29.7
17 21.1	16 23.5	18 20.5		5 70.2	5 74.2	14 26.6	16 23.5	17 21.7	23 16.0
29 12.4	31 11.8	31 11.9	Cost of Sales/Payables	27 13.8	22 16.8	25 14.4	33 11.0	30 12.0	33 11.1
45 8.2	48 7.7	47 7.7		63 5.8	47 7.8	52 7.1	53 6.9	45 8.1	46 7.9
6.4	6.9	6.7		6.5	7.0	6.8	5.8	7.1	6.8
12.8	12.9	12.1	Sales/Working Capital	19.7	13.5	17.6	11.2	11.8	11.4
38.1	32.4	33.0		−16.1	NM	NM	24.2	34.7	23.5
13.6	10.6	16.5		5.5	8.7	12.9	20.8	18.8	17.8
(576) 4.1	(699) 4.1	(707) 5.5	EBIT/Interest	(23) 1.8	(68) 2.7	(57) 5.3	(115) 6.2	(176) 5.7	(268) 6.9
1.5	1.2	2.1		−1.2	.1	2.0	1.7	2.1	3.1
3.7	3.4	4.1			2.0	3.3	4.3	4.0	4.5
(202) 2.0	(247) 1.9	(243) 2.0	Net Profit + Depr., Dep., Amort./Cur. Mat. L/T/D		(16) 1.4	(16) 2.1	(44) 2.3	(77) 2.1	(89) 2.1
1.2	1.2	1.2			.7	1.4	1.3	1.1	1.3
.5	.4	.4		.5	.5	.3	.4	.5	.5
.8	.8	.8	Fixed/Worth	1.2	.9	.9	.7	.8	.8
1.4	1.4	1.4		9.4	2.6	2.3	1.4	1.2	1.3
.7	.8	.7		.6	.7	.6	.7	.7	.8
1.4	1.5	1.5	Debt/Worth	2.0	1.4	1.9	1.5	1.5	1.5
2.7	2.9	2.9		15.7	3.7	6.5	3.0	2.7	2.6
28.8	26.6	30.2		50.6	25.1	37.8	35.6	32.4	26.2
(604) 13.9	(733) 12.2	(741) 15.7	% Profit Before Taxes/Tangible Net Worth	(25) 14.0	(69) 8.3	(57) 20.7	(115) 19.4	(183) 17.3	(292) 15.1
3.6	1.6	4.9		−9.0	.1	6.0	3.4	4.8	6.3
12.0	11.4	12.3		14.3	11.9	16.0	15.7	13.4	10.5
5.3	4.4	5.8	% Profit Before Taxes/Total Assets	2.1	3.3	7.9	6.6	6.1	5.7
1.1	.3	1.6		−9.4	−1.3	2.3	.8	1.8	2.4
12.0	12.1	12.2		9.5	13.0	14.4	13.4	12.0	11.3
6.8	7.0	7.1	Sales/Net Fixed Assets	4.2	5.9	8.7	8.0	7.5	6.8
4.2	4.1	4.1		2.3	3.3	4.7	4.3	4.6	4.2
2.8	2.8	2.9		2.7	3.3	3.6	3.0	2.9	2.7
2.2	2.2	2.2	Sales/Total Assets	1.8	2.2	2.3	2.4	2.2	2.1
1.6	1.6	1.6		.8	1.4	1.4	1.6	1.7	1.5
2.2	2.1	2.2		4.4	2.2	2.1	2.1	2.2	2.0
(573) 3.6	(695) 3.7	(689) 3.6	% Depr., Dep., Amort./Sales	(23) 10.1	(65) 4.3	(56) 4.5	(109) 3.6	(174) 3.5	(262) 3.2
5.5	5.4	5.2		18.5	7.6	6.2	5.4	4.9	4.5
1.1	1.2	1.3			2.6	1.8	1.8	1.2	.6
(209) 2.4	(263) 2.4	(264) 2.3	% Officers', Directors', Owners' Comp/Sales	(35) 3.6	(29) 3.4	(57) 3.2	(77) 1.9		(60) 1.3
4.5	4.3	4.1		6.9	6.9	4.5	3.5		2.0
26195663M	28364203M	30781163M	Net Sales ($)	16294M	160330M	266694M	873156M	3086522M	26378167M
12808966M	14343310M	16146204M	Total Assets ($)	15547M	93770M	130035M	431031M	1521738M	13954083M

M = $ thousand   MM = $ million
See Pages 11 through 21 for Explanation of Ratios and Data

Current Data Sorted By Assets   Comparative Historical Data

Type of Statement	0-500M	500M-2MM	2-10MM	10-50MM	50-100MM	100-250MM	4/1/00-3/31/01 ALL	4/1/01-3/31/02 ALL
Unqualified		5	33	32	5	13	43	56
Reviewed	2	24	49	14	1	1	43	40
Compiled	5	14	14	1			16	24
Tax Returns	5	11	7		1		8	5
Other	5	13	18	12	4	5	45	54
	68 (4/1-9/30/04)			226 (10/1/04-3/31/05)				
NUMBER OF STATEMENTS	17	67	121	59	11	19	155	179
	%	%	%	%	%	%	%	%
ASSETS								
Cash & Equivalents	12.7	10.0	12.3	12.1	20.4	13.0	12.6	13.3
Trade Receivables (net)	26.5	40.1	35.7	39.3	25.2	27.7	32.9	36.2
Inventory	5.2	9.9	4.5	3.8	1.5	3.5	6.8	3.4
All Other Current	4.0	5.4	9.2	10.4	10.0	9.9	7.0	7.5
Total Current	48.4	65.5	61.7	65.6	57.1	54.1	59.3	60.5
Fixed Assets (net)	36.4	27.9	31.8	26.6	32.1	37.2	31.4	30.6
Intangibles (net)	3.5	1.7	.4	1.4	2.5	3.6	1.7	2.2
All Other Non-Current	11.7	5.0	6.1	6.4	8.3	5.1	7.6	6.8
Total	100.0	100.0	100.0	100.0	100.0	100.0	100.0	100.0
LIABILITIES								
Notes Payable-Short Term	15.3	13.6	9.2	4.5	4.4	3.7	7.1	5.4
Cur. Mat.-L/T/D	2.2	5.4	5.4	4.6	3.8	4.0	5.4	5.2
Trade Payables	11.8	16.9	15.9	20.3	13.8	16.6	16.4	16.9
Income Taxes Payable	.2	.5	.6	.8	.7	.3	.6	1.0
All Other Current	10.7	9.4	12.2	13.2	17.6	14.5	11.8	14.0
Total Current	40.3	45.8	43.3	43.4	40.3	39.1	41.3	42.5
Long-Term Debt	20.8	18.7	13.0	11.8	10.5	22.0	14.2	14.2
Deferred Taxes	.7	1.3	1.3	1.3	3.8	2.1	1.5	1.3
All Other Non-Current	5.6	3.3	2.2	2.3	11.4	1.6	2.4	2.7
Net Worth	32.5	30.8	40.2	41.2	34.0	35.1	40.5	39.2
Total Liabilities & Net Worth	100.0	100.0	100.0	100.0	100.0	100.0	100.0	100.0
INCOME DATA								
Net Sales	100.0	100.0	100.0	100.0	100.0	100.0	100.0	100.0
Gross Profit	44.2	32.5	21.6	17.9	19.2	15.7	22.6	21.4
Operating Expenses	39.0	26.9	17.4	14.1	15.6	9.6	18.0	16.9
Operating Profit	5.3	5.6	4.2	3.8	3.5	6.1	4.6	4.5
All Other Expenses (net)	.9	.8	.2	-.4	.1	.9	.3	.6
Profit Before Taxes	4.4	4.9	4.0	4.2	3.5	5.2	4.2	3.9
RATIOS								
Current	2.5	2.3	2.0	2.0	1.9	1.6	1.9	1.9
	1.3	1.4	1.4	1.6	1.5	1.4	1.4	1.4
	.7	1.0	1.1	1.2	1.2	1.3	1.1	1.1
Quick	2.5	1.9	1.6	1.5	1.6	1.3	1.5	1.5
	1.1	1.2	1.2	1.2	1.1	1.1	1.1	1.1
	.3	.7	.8	1.0	.6	.8	.7	.9
Sales/Receivables	0 UND	31 11.9	39 9.4	49 7.5	47 7.8	49 7.4	35 10.3	44 8.2
	34 10.6	57 6.4	59 6.2	66 5.6	58 6.3	55 6.6	55 6.6	59 6.1
	86 4.2	75 4.9	83 4.4	92 4.0	82 4.4	69 5.3	70 5.2	78 4.7
Cost of Sales/Inventory	0 UND	0 UND	0 UND	0 UND	0 UND	0 UND	0 UND	0 UND
	0 UND	0 UND	0 UND	0 999.8	0 UND	2 200.6	0 UND	0 UND
	13 28.2	14 25.6	9 41.3	10 37.6	7 53.0	5 70.2	12 31.3	6 57.1
Cost of Sales/Payables	0 UND	14 26.1	15 25.1	24 15.1	20 18.3	26 14.0	15 24.6	14 26.5
	25 14.7	27 13.6	27 13.8	37 9.9	42 8.6	35 10.5	30 12.3	29 12.4
	62 5.9	42 8.7	46 7.9	58 6.3	51 7.2	50 7.3	49 7.5	48 7.6
Sales/Working Capital	7.0	6.6	7.2	5.8	4.8	6.1	6.9	7.5
	38.3	13.5	12.1	9.1	8.7	11.6	14.2	14.1
	-59.4	132.7	40.6	22.6	25.9	18.4	80.3	41.2
EBIT/Interest	14.0	21.2	16.2	23.2		15.5	8.7	17.7
	(13) 1.7	(61) 5.7	(111) 7.7	(55) 7.2		(17) 6.5	(142) 2.9	(163) 5.1
	-5.1	1.4	1.6	2.9		3.8	1.5	2.0
Net Profit + Depr., Dep., Amort./Cur. Mat. L./T/D		4.2	3.7	3.1		3.7	4.4	6.7
	(14) 1.9	(42) 2.3	(27) 1.9			(10) 3.4	(49) 2.6	(56) 3.4
	1.5	1.1	1.2			2.0	1.2	1.5
Fixed/Worth	.4	.2	.3	.4	.3	.6	.4	.3
	1.3	.7	.8	.7	1.6	1.3	.8	.8
	9.4	3.1	1.4	1.2	3.0	1.8	1.4	1.4
Debt/Worth	.4	1.1	.9	.9	1.0	1.4	.9	.8
	2.0	2.3	1.6	1.4	1.9	2.0	1.7	1.6
	14.3	6.7	3.1	3.1	4.6	4.1	3.0	3.0
% Profit Before Taxes/Tangible Net Worth	49.0	78.8	44.7	27.8	34.1	42.4	31.2	40.0
	(14) 14.6	(59) 36.1	(119) 17.4	(58) 14.6	(10) 20.3	16.3	(150) 14.5	(170) 20.6
	-14.8	15.0	3.6	7.7	-1.9	11.0	4.9	7.4
% Profit Before Taxes/Total Assets	17.1	19.3	15.8	10.9	13.1	8.3	11.3	14.9
	10.0	9.1	7.6	5.6	6.9	6.1	5.2	7.1
	-9.5	1.8	1.1	2.1	.5	2.8	1.3	2.5
Sales/Net Fixed Assets	32.3	45.8	25.8	16.9	32.4	8.9	16.5	21.3
	7.2	16.6	7.7	8.8	8.1	5.1	8.3	8.6
	4.7	5.9	3.3	4.4	2.5	2.1	3.5	4.2
Sales/Total Assets	4.4	3.6	2.6	2.6	2.1	2.2	2.8	3.1
	2.3	2.7	2.1	2.0	1.9	1.7	2.1	2.3
	1.7	2.0	1.5	1.4	1.1	1.1	1.5	1.6
% Depr., Dep., Amort./Sales	2.3	.8	1.2	1.3		1.6	1.0	1.3
	(12) 7.4	(51) 2.5	(108) 3.3	(56) 2.7		(13) 3.6	(143) 2.8	(160) 2.8
	11.2	4.0	6.4	5.4		4.7	6.1	5.6
% Officers', Directors', Owners' Comp/Sales		2.2	1.1	.7			1.9	1.6
		(31) 3.7	(43) 1.8	(12) 1.2			(50) 3.2	(49) 3.1
		6.4	2.7	1.7			6.1	6.4
Net Sales ($)	13135M	232832M	1267603M	2907819M	1851746M	5395926M	4462097M	5789441M
Total Assets ($)	4788M	78466M	592496M	1316653M	777489M	2979586M	2412704M	2842349M

M = $ thousand   MM = $ million
See Pages 11 through 21 for Explanation of Ratios and Data

Comparative Historical Data				Type of Statement	Current Data Sorted By Sales					
83		88	88	Unqualified		3	7	8	21	49
70		90	91	Reviewed	3	9	20	24	21	14
17		41	34	Compiled	3	11	6	13	1	
13		20	24	Tax Returns	5	6	4	4	4	1
39		70	57	Other	3	9	8	11	13	13
4/1/02-3/31/03 ALL		4/1/03-3/31/04 ALL	4/1/04-3/31/05 ALL		68 (4/1-9/30/04)			226 (10/1/04-3/31/05)		
					0-1MM	1-3MM	3-5MM	5-10MM	10-25MM	25MM & OVER
222		309	294	NUMBER OF STATEMENTS	14	38	45	60	60	77
%		%	%	ASSETS	%	%	%	%	%	%
12.3		12.2	12.1	Cash & Equivalents	11.5	10.0	11.7	13.5	12.5	12.3
33.4		36.0	36.0	Trade Receivables (net)	24.3	24.8	42.5	34.1	40.2	37.9
4.2		3.5	5.5	Inventory	11.0	11.1	3.0	7.3	3.5	3.2
8.3		8.3	8.4	All Other Current	1.5	5.7	6.0	8.5	9.7	11.2
58.1		60.0	61.9	Total Current	48.3	51.6	63.2	63.4	65.8	64.5
33.4		31.9	30.5	Fixed Assets (net)	41.2	37.7	26.7	31.4	28.0	28.4
1.7		1.6	1.3	Intangibles (net)	.3	2.8	1.5	.3	.5	2.2
6.8		6.4	6.2	All Other Non-Current	10.2	7.9	8.6	5.0	5.7	4.8
100.0		100.0	100.0	Total	100.0	100.0	100.0	100.0	100.0	100.0
				LIABILITIES						
6.9		6.8	9.1	Notes Payable-Short Term	16.6	9.4	12.3	11.7	7.5	4.8
4.9		5.5	4.9	Cur. Mat.-L/T/D	1.9	6.2	6.3	5.2	3.9	4.5
16.9		19.1	16.7	Trade Payables	7.5	10.7	18.7	13.5	20.3	19.9
.7		.7	.6	Income Taxes Payable	.3	.4	.4	.8	.6	.7
12.0		13.1	12.0	All Other Current	8.3	7.4	10.4	11.7	13.8	14.8
41.4		45.2	43.3	Total Current	34.7	34.1	48.2	42.9	46.2	44.7
14.2		14.3	15.0	Long-Term Debt	20.8	24.1	15.2	14.2	10.9	13.2
1.3		1.2	1.4	Deferred Taxes	1.2	1.2	.9	1.1	2.0	1.7
3.6		3.0	3.0	All Other Non-Current	5.2	3.8	3.2	1.9	1.4	4.1
39.6		36.3	37.3	Net Worth	38.2	36.7	32.5	39.9	39.5	36.3
100.0		100.0	100.0	Total Liabilities & Net Worth	100.0	100.0	100.0	100.0	100.0	100.0
				INCOME DATA						
100.0		100.0	100.0	Net Sales	100.0	100.0	100.0	100.0	100.0	100.0
22.9		22.6	24.2	Gross Profit	44.2	34.4	27.7	24.7	21.4	15.3
18.7		19.2	19.6	Operating Expenses	35.5	27.7	24.6	19.8	17.0	11.5
4.2		3.4	4.6	Operating Profit	8.7	6.6	3.1	4.8	4.3	3.8
.7		.4	.3	All Other Expenses (net)	.8	1.3	.5	−.2	.1	.2
3.4		3.0	4.3	Profit Before Taxes	7.9	5.3	2.5	5.0	4.3	3.6
				RATIOS						
1.9		1.8	2.0		2.4	2.5	2.3	2.0	2.1	1.8
1.4		1.3	1.4	Current	1.3	1.8	1.3	1.5	1.4	1.5
1.1		1.0	1.1		.6	1.1	.9	1.2	1.1	1.2
1.5		1.5	1.6		2.4	2.2	2.1	1.7	1.8	1.4
1.1		1.1	1.2	Quick	.9	1.1	1.1	1.2	1.2	1.2
.8		.7	.8		.7	.7	.7	.7	.8	1.0

37	9.9	38	9.6	40	9.0		0	UND	13	29.1	49	7.4	34	10.9	46	7.9	47	7.7
55	6.7	57	6.4	59	6.2	Sales/Receivables	42	8.7	42	8.6	62	5.9	59	6.1	70	5.2	58	6.3
75	4.8	82	4.5	80	4.5		100	3.7	68	5.4	87	4.2	79	4.6	94	3.9	80	4.6
0	UND	0	UND	0	UND		0	UND	0	UND	0	UND	0	UND	0	UND	0	UND
0	966.0	0	UND	0	UND	Cost of Sales/Inventory	0	UND	3	145.6	0	UND	0	UND	0	UND	0	999.8
9	41.3	6	60.0	9	39.6		78	4.7	58	6.3	7	55.9	14	25.9	5	67.1	6	61.6
18	20.1	16	23.1	16	22.8		0	UND	13	29.1	18	20.2	6	64.3	21	17.7	22	16.8
33	11.2	33	11.0	32	11.5	Cost of Sales/Payables	19	19.1	22	16.8	32	11.3	24	15.3	35	10.6	36	10.3
50	7.3	54	6.8	48	7.7		40	9.2	49	7.4	42	8.6	46	7.9	59	6.2	50	7.2
	7.4		7.8		6.2			4.6		5.2		6.0		7.7		6.9		6.3
	15.0		15.8		11.7	Sales/Working Capital		24.8		10.6		16.6		10.2		11.9		11.6
	47.8		231.5		40.4			−127.1		59.3		−46.7		26.5		40.9		23.9
	12.6		12.1		16.2			16.8		10.7		14.4		20.6		21.6		18.6
(197)	4.4	(282)	4.7	(266)	6.8	EBIT/Interest	(10)	1.4	(33)	5.7	(42)	4.8	(55)	8.2	(56)	10.6	(70)	6.5
	1.4		1.2		1.8			−4.6		1.3		1.7		1.6		2.3		2.8
	3.7		4.6		3.6							3.0		7.7		4.3		4.0
(78)	2.2	(108)	1.9	(99)	2.3	Net Profit + Depr., Dep., Amort./Cur. Mat. L/T/D			(10)	1.8	(15)	2.7	(22)	2.4	(42)	2.3
	1.3		1.0		1.2							−1.2		1.1		1.2		1.4
	.4		.3		.3			.2		.4		.2		.3		.3		.4
	.8		.8		.8	Fixed/Worth		1.1		1.2		.7		.6		.8		.7
	1.6		1.9		1.6			5.4		2.6		3.0		1.3		1.3		1.6
	.8		1.0		1.0			.4		.8		.9		.8		.9		1.1
	1.6		1.8		1.7	Debt/Worth		1.9		1.6		2.3		1.4		1.8		1.6
	3.0		4.0		3.7			10.4		4.6		5.7		2.8		3.1		3.8
	29.1		34.1		44.4			40.6		62.7		57.7		50.4		42.4		31.0
(208)	16.2	(291)	16.3	(279)	18.7	% Profit Before Taxes/Tangible Net Worth	(12)	9.7	(34)	24.2	(41)	21.6	(57)	18.9	(75)	16.2	(75)	16.3
	2.5		1.4		6.8			.0		10.9		6.5		4.8		7.4		
	10.8		12.1		13.5			14.5		16.7		15.5		18.7		13.8		11.6
	4.6		5.4		7.2	% Profit Before Taxes/Total Assets		1.6		10.3		7.3		8.4		6.8		6.1
	.8		.1		1.3			−4.7		1.0		2.4		1.3		1.9		2.1
	13.9		23.4		29.3			19.6		21.9		46.0		28.3		30.9		30.4
	7.2		7.7		8.1	Sales/Net Fixed Assets		4.7		6.1		12.7		7.9		9.2		9.0
	3.4		3.7		3.8			1.4		2.1		5.5		3.5		4.5		4.4
	2.9		2.9		2.8			2.2		3.1		3.4		2.6		2.7		2.8
	2.0		2.2		2.2	Sales/Total Assets		1.7		2.6		2.6		2.1		2.2		2.2
	1.4		1.5		1.5			.9		1.3		1.5		1.5		1.6		1.6
	1.7		1.2		1.2					2.2		1.0		1.2		.8		1.1
(202)	3.9	(281)	2.9	(249)	3.1	% Depr., Dep., Amort./Sales			(31)	3.9	(38)	2.9	(49)	3.4	(55)	2.7	(67)	2.2
	6.9		6.2		5.6					7.7		4.3		7.4		4.9		4.2
	1.9		1.4		1.3					2.2		1.3		1.5		.8		1.0
(76)	3.0	(92)	2.4	(97)	2.3	% Officers', Directors', Owners' Comp/Sales			(18)	3.5	(16)	2.7	(19)	2.4	(24)	1.3	(13)	1.5
	5.7		4.3		4.7					5.5		4.6		4.6		2.0		3.5
7499383M		11445548M	11669061M	Net Sales ($)	7835M	71464M	177373M	434645M	941232M	10036512M
3407641M		5429380M	5749478M	Total Assets ($)	6220M	66092M	87632M	235778M	493693M	4860063M

© RMA 2005

M = $ thousand   MM = $ million
See Pages 11 through 21 for Explanation of Ratios and Data

Current Data Sorted By Assets **Comparative Historical Data**

	0-500M	500M-2MM	2-10MM	10-50MM	50-100MM	100-250MM		4/1/00-3/31/01 ALL	4/1/01-3/31/02 ALL
Type of Statement									
Unqualified		7	29	28	5	3		43	36
Reviewed	3	39	58	14				79	69
Compiled	9	31	17	5				58	43
Tax Returns	35	26	9		2	1		19	21
Other	9	28	45	10	3			51	72
	72 (4/1-9/30/04)			344 (10/1/04-3/31/05)					
NUMBER OF STATEMENTS	56	131	158	57	10	4		250	241
ASSETS	%	%	%	%	%	%		%	%
Cash & Equivalents	15.8	11.6	8.1	8.3	12.4			10.6	10.5
Trade Receivables (net)	23.6	40.9	43.8	39.5	30.1			40.1	40.0
Inventory	2.6	3.6	3.8	5.6	10.9			3.2	3.2
All Other Current	2.3	3.1	8.0	7.7	8.2			5.0	4.9
Total Current	44.2	59.2	63.7	61.1	61.6			58.9	58.6
Fixed Assets (net)	40.5	34.7	30.8	30.0	34.9			33.3	33.9
Intangibles (net)	2.6	.8	.8	2.0	1.2			1.6	2.1
All Other Non-Current	12.6	5.3	4.8	6.9	2.3			6.3	5.4
Total	100.0	100.0	100.0	100.0	100.0			100.0	100.0
LIABILITIES									
Notes Payable-Short Term	22.5	10.2	6.9	4.9	1.3			9.6	8.8
Cur. Mat.-L/T/D	7.1	5.8	5.6	4.3	4.5			4.7	5.7
Trade Payables	16.6	18.5	19.8	22.6	17.8			18.5	18.7
Income Taxes Payable	.5	1.2	.4	.3	.5			.5	.6
All Other Current	11.7	6.4	10.9	12.8	26.0			26.9	10.5
Total Current	58.4	42.0	43.7	45.0	50.0			60.2	44.2
Long-Term Debt	44.1	22.8	14.5	15.3	27.2			16.6	19.0
Deferred Taxes	.1	1.0	.9	.9	5.3			1.0	.7
All Other Non-Current	5.1	5.5	3.4	3.0	.7			3.6	3.7
Net Worth	-7.6	28.7	37.4	35.8	16.7			18.6	32.4
Total Liabilities & Net Worth	100.0	100.0	100.0	100.0	100.0			100.0	100.0
INCOME DATA									
Net Sales	100.0	100.0	100.0	100.0	100.0			100.0	100.0
Gross Profit	38.9	30.2	23.5	17.6	26.4			24.7	26.6
Operating Expenses	35.6	26.6	19.4	12.8	23.0			20.6	22.2
Operating Profit	3.3	3.6	4.0	4.9	3.4			4.1	4.5
All Other Expenses (net)	.8	.4	.6	.4	1.6			.6	.9
Profit Before Taxes	2.5	3.2	3.4	4.5	1.9			3.5	3.6
RATIOS									
Current	2.0	2.3	2.1	1.7	1.5			2.0	2.1
	.9	1.5	1.4	1.4	1.2			1.3	1.3
	.4	1.0	1.1	1.0	1.1			1.0	1.0
Quick	1.8	2.1	1.7	1.4	1.1			1.7	1.8
	.8	1.3	(157) 1.2	1.1	.9			1.2	1.2
	.4	.9	.8	.8	.7			.8	.8
Sales/Receivables	0 UND	36 10.2	41 8.9	44 8.3	32 11.3			33 10.9	35 10.5
	7 51.2	48 7.6	59 6.2	59 6.2	54 6.8			52 7.0	58 6.2
	33 10.9	68 5.4	84 4.4	81 4.5	75 4.9			72 5.1	83 4.4
Cost of Sales/Inventory	0 UND	0 UND	0 UND	0 UND	1 335.8			0 UND	0 UND
	0 UND	0 UND	0 UND	1 321.4	14 26.6			0 UND	0 UND
	0 UND	6 57.9	8 47.0	13 29.1	28 12.8			5 72.2	5 71.1
Cost of Sales/Payables	0 UND	12 31.5	17 21.8	25 14.7	17 20.9			14 26.7	11 34.6
	3 107.0	26 14.2	34 10.7	39 9.3	31 11.7			29 12.5	28 13.2
	34 10.8	47 7.8	53 6.9	57 6.4	53 6.9			47 7.7	51 7.2
Sales/Working Capital	25.6	7.8	7.1	8.2	10.1			7.9	7.7
	-81.4	18.6	12.8	16.8	21.9			18.1	17.4
	-11.8	119.9	91.8	259.8	41.1			-282.5	-380.3
EBIT/Interest	8.6	11.2	14.5	16.7				10.4	12.7
	(47) 2.6	(116) 3.8	(148) 5.6	(52) 7.2				(227) 3.9	(222) 3.7
	-.1	.4	2.3	2.3				1.4	1.4
Net Profit + Depr., Dep., Amort./Cur. Mat. L/T/D		2.6	3.6	3.9				3.8	4.6
		(30) 1.4	(47) 1.9	(15) 2.3				(60) 2.1	(57) 2.2
		.8	.9	1.4				1.4	1.2
Fixed/Worth	.8	.4	.4	.3	.4			.3	.5
	16.7	1.2	.6	.7	1.4			.9	.9
	-1.2	4.0	1.6	1.7	2.5			2.0	2.2
Debt/Worth	2.4	.8	.9	1.4	1.9			1.0	.9
	31.0	2.6	1.8	2.1	2.6			1.8	2.0
	-3.6	9.8	3.8	3.6	3.3			4.0	5.0
% Profit Before Taxes/Tangible Net Worth	500.0	56.1	41.3	44.7				42.9	51.0
	(31) 54.5	(113) 25.4	(148) 18.9	(55) 26.9				(224) 21.9	(217) 24.2
	11.9	4.7	9.7	8.6				6.7	6.3
% Profit Before Taxes/Total Assets	29.9	17.2	12.8	16.1	7.9			16.0	20.1
	7.6	5.2	7.2	6.9	5.4			7.3	7.0
	-6.7	.0	2.7	2.2	-.2			1.2	1.1
Sales/Net Fixed Assets	35.7	17.1	22.2	21.1	41.6			23.8	18.7
	18.8	9.6	10.9	9.5	12.6			9.8	9.4
	7.4	6.1	4.7	4.3	3.4			5.4	5.0
Sales/Total Assets	8.6	3.8	3.2	2.8	3.3			3.5	3.5
	5.0	2.9	2.5	2.2	2.1			2.8	2.5
	3.2	2.1	1.9	1.8	1.5			2.0	2.0
% Depr., Dep., Amort./Sales	1.8	1.4	1.2	1.2				1.0	1.4
	(37) 3.0	(111) 2.6	(142) 2.7	(53) 2.4				(227) 2.6	(221) 2.9
	4.5	5.1	5.3	4.1				4.5	5.5
% Officers', Directors', Owners' Comp/Sales	3.1	2.8	1.7	.7				2.2	2.0
	(38) 5.8	(70) 4.5	(66) 2.9	(14) .9				(137) 3.9	(117) 4.0
	7.7	8.2	5.0	2.1				7.2	7.4
Net Sales ($)	75007M	475446M	1911893M	2418023M	2258482M	4164950M		5009229M	3282950M
Total Assets ($)	12561M	151580M	759503M	1088005M	655232M	644729M		1776116M	1588105M

M = $ thousand   MM = $ million
See Pages 11 through 21 for Explanation of Ratios and Data

Comparative Historical Data | | | | Current Data Sorted By Sales

			Type of Statement						
48	57	72	Unqualified	1	3	3	8	17	40
85	120	114	Reviewed	1	17	22	26	38	10
52	98	62	Compiled	5	20	11	16	7	3
25	54	73	Tax Returns	16	30	11	9	4	3
64	56	95	Other	6	23	7	18	28	13
4/1/02-3/31/03	4/1/03-3/31/04	4/1/04-3/31/05		72 (4/1-9/30/04)			344 (10/1/04-3/31/05)		
ALL	ALL	ALL		0-1MM	1-3MM	3-5MM	5-10MM	10-25MM	25MM & OVER
274	385	416	**NUMBER OF STATEMENTS**	29	93	54	77	94	69
%	%	%	**ASSETS**	%	%	%	%	%	%
11.7	10.4	10.4	Cash & Equivalents	23.5	10.9	9.8	8.7	8.3	9.6
38.2	39.4	39.1	Trade Receivables (net)	15.1	34.9	37.6	40.8	47.5	42.6
3.0	3.3	4.0	Inventory	4.4	2.2	3.6	5.3	4.0	5.1
5.9	6.2	5.6	All Other Current	3.1	2.1	4.6	4.6	9.1	8.5
58.8	59.3	59.1	Total Current	46.2	50.2	55.6	59.4	68.8	65.8
33.1	33.0	33.4	Fixed Assets (net)	41.9	39.7	36.9	35.8	25.7	26.2
1.4	1.6	1.2	Intangibles (net)	.8	2.2	1.3	.5	.4	1.8
6.6	6.1	6.3	All Other Non-Current	11.1	7.9	6.2	4.4	5.1	6.2
100.0	100.0	100.0	Total	100.0	100.0	100.0	100.0	100.0	100.0
			LIABILITIES						
9.8	10.2	9.5	Notes Payable-Short Term	20.0	14.9	10.4	6.9	6.4	4.5
6.8	5.8	5.7	Cur. Mat.-L/T/D	3.4	7.0	7.1	6.5	5.1	3.6
16.1	17.7	19.2	Trade Payables	13.9	15.1	14.6	23.9	20.0	24.3
.6	.5	.6	Income Taxes Payable	1.1	1.3	.2	.7	.3	.4
9.6	10.3	10.2	All Other Current	12.3	7.4	5.4	8.0	13.5	15.0
43.0	44.5	45.3	Total Current	50.7	45.7	37.7	46.0	45.2	47.8
18.4	19.6	21.5	Long-Term Debt	39.7	31.4	20.9	20.5	11.9	15.5
.6	.8	.9	Deferred Taxes	.2	.4	1.2	1.4	.7	1.6
3.0	4.9	4.2	All Other Non-Current	1.8	7.3	4.9	3.3	3.1	3.1
34.9	30.2	28.0	Net Worth	7.5	15.2	35.3	28.8	39.1	31.9
100.0	100.0	100.0	Total Liabilities & Net Worth	100.0	100.0	100.0	100.0	100.0	100.0
			INCOME DATA						
100.0	100.0	100.0	Net Sales	100.0	100.0	100.0	100.0	100.0	100.0
26.1	26.2	26.8	Gross Profit	37.6	36.0	31.7	25.0	20.3	17.0
22.1	23.3	22.9	Operating Expenses	34.2	32.1	27.4	21.7	15.8	13.5
4.0	2.9	3.9	Operating Profit	3.4	3.9	4.3	3.3	4.5	3.6
.7	.7	.6	All Other Expenses (net)	.5	1.1	.6	.2	.4	.4
3.3	2.1	3.3	Profit Before Taxes	2.9	2.8	3.7	3.1	4.1	3.2
			RATIOS						
2.3	2.1	2.0		3.3	2.4	2.0	1.8	2.1	1.7
1.4	1.4	1.4	Current	.9	1.4	1.4	1.4	1.5	1.4
1.0	1.0	1.0		.5	.7	1.1	1.0	1.2	1.1
1.9	1.8	1.7		3.3	2.1	1.7	1.5	1.8	1.4
(273) 1.2	1.2	(415) 1.1	Quick	.8	1.2	1.1	1.2	(93) 1.2	1.1
.8	.8	.8		.2	.5	.9	.7	.9	.8
35 10.4	32 11.2	35 10.3		0 UND	18 20.6	39 9.4	36 10.1	41 8.9	42 8.8
51 7.1	54 6.8	51 7.1	Sales/Receivables	0 UND	45 8.1	53 6.9	49 7.5	62 5.9	59 6.2
73 5.0	73 5.0	75 4.9		35 10.4	70 5.2	74 5.0	65 5.6	84 4.3	81 4.5
0 UND	0 UND	0 UND		0 UND	0 UND	0 UND	0 UND	0 UND	0 UND
0 UND	0 UND	0 UND	Cost of Sales/Inventory	0 UND	0 UND	0 UND	0 854.0	0 UND	2 162.1
5 67.7	6 66.3	8 47.7		0 UND	2 162.4	9 39.1	12 29.8	7 54.0	12 30.9
11 33.6	12 31.3	14 26.9		0 UND	6 66.0	14 25.6	18 20.7	14 26.4	24 15.4
25 14.3	27 13.4	29 12.7	Cost of Sales/Payables	9 41.5	22 16.5	24 15.1	38 9.6	29 12.8	36 10.2
44 8.3	46 8.0	48 7.6		28 12.9	42 8.6	50 7.3	54 6.7	49 7.5	53 6.9
7.9	8.0	8.3		6.8	8.6	9.9	8.7	6.9	8.4
16.7	17.1	19.2	Sales/Working Capital	-108.0	28.8	18.6	19.2	12.6	19.6
-800.0	216.7	-590.4		-8.0	-16.8	347.8	-128.2	32.9	39.1
11.5	10.1	13.1		4.9	10.9	9.9	11.3	18.9	19.0
(242) 4.0	(354) 4.0	(376) 4.6	EBIT/Interest	(22) 1.8	(84) 3.5	(52) 3.8	(70) 3.5	(84) 7.3	(64) 8.5
1.3	1.0	1.7		-3.3	-.1	1.7	1.7	2.8	2.5
3.9	3.2	3.5	Net Profit + Depr., Dep.,		2.6	3.1	3.1	5.1	3.9
(65) 1.9	(92) 1.4	(103) 1.9	Amort./Cur. Mat. L/T/D		(15) 1.3	(17) 1.8	(27) 1.9	(20) 2.0	(22) 2.3
1.1	.8	1.0			.8	.9	.9	.7	1.4
.4	.4	.4		.2	.5	.6	.5	.3	.3
.8	.9	.9	Fixed/Worth	3.5	2.2	1.1	1.0	.6	.7
2.6	2.5	2.7		-10.6	-2.5	2.6	2.8	1.1	1.6
.7	.8	1.0		.8	1.0	.8	1.1	.8	1.3
1.7	2.1	2.3	Debt/Worth	4.6	5.0	1.8	2.9	1.6	2.2
5.3	6.2	7.1		-13.6	-8.6	5.2	7.9	3.2	3.6
41.6	44.4	47.8	% Profit Before Taxes/Tangible	73.3	60.6	58.0	35.2	46.4	42.1
(242) 18.2	(341) 15.9	(360) 24.1	Net Worth	(20) 20.3	(61) 25.0	(52) 22.1	(71) 22.0	(89) 24.9	(67) 24.5
4.1	2.3	8.3		-2.4	3.3	5.8	8.0	12.6	9.3
17.2	15.0	15.2	% Profit Before Taxes/Total	11.8	22.8	14.5	11.6	18.5	14.1
6.4	4.4	6.5	Assets	4.8	5.2	7.3	5.1	8.7	6.9
1.2	.0	1.3		-7.0	-3.2	1.2	1.7	3.1	2.0
21.4	21.9	23.2		29.6	21.8	14.9	17.5	32.2	30.6
10.4	10.6	10.7	Sales/Net Fixed Assets	6.5	9.2	8.1	10.3	13.8	12.2
5.2	5.4	5.2		2.5	5.2	4.5	5.6	6.5	5.4
3.6	3.6	3.7		5.1	4.2	3.5	3.9	3.6	3.1
2.6	2.6	2.7	Sales/Total Assets	2.4	3.0	2.4	2.8	2.7	2.5
1.9	2.0	2.0		1.0	1.9	2.0	2.1	2.1	1.9
1.4	1.6	1.4		2.7	1.8	2.0	1.5	.9	1.0
(248) 2.9	(332) 3.1	(350) 2.6	% Depr., Dep., Amort./Sales	(23) 3.5	(69) 3.0	(48) 3.8	(71) 2.8	(82) 2.1	(57) 1.6
5.1	5.5	4.9		4.9	5.7	7.6	5.0	4.2	2.9
2.2	1.9	1.9	% Officers', Directors',	5.4	3.5	2.4	1.7	1.5	.6
(148) 3.9	(191) 3.6	(191) 3.7	Owners' Comp/Sales	(17) 6.4	(50) 5.0	(31) 4.7	(38) 2.8	(39) 2.3	(16) .9
6.6	5.6	6.4		10.0	8.4	6.9	4.3	4.2	3.9
8226719M	6884049M	11303801M	Net Sales ($)	16064M	187125M	212176M	527092M	1459151M	8902193M
2473726M	2318159M	3311610M	Total Assets ($)	7975M	86404M	91779M	230566M	594044M	2300842M

M = $ thousand   MM = $ million
See Pages 11 through 21 for Explanation of Ratios and Data

Current Data Sorted By Assets

Comparative Historical Data

Type of Statement	0-500M	500M-2MM	2-10MM	10-50MM	50-100MM	100-250MM		4/1/00-3/31/01 ALL	4/1/01-3/31/02 ALL
Unqualified		1	15	13	3	2		14	13
Reviewed	1	18	26	5				35	27
Compiled	5	11	5					29	24
Tax Returns	5	6	3	1				2	8
Other	1	10	6	6				22	28
		33 (4/1-9/30/04)		110 (10/1/04-3/31/05)					
NUMBER OF STATEMENTS	12	46	55	25	3	2		102	100
	%	%	%	%	%	%		%	%
ASSETS									
Cash & Equivalents	17.1	7.6	9.9	7.4				10.5	11.1
Trade Receivables (net)	46.3	52.0	49.7	45.7				47.0	47.5
Inventory	.8	7.3	6.1	7.3				5.5	4.7
All Other Current	2.9	5.7	7.5	11.3				6.8	8.3
Total Current	67.1	72.6	73.2	71.8				69.8	71.7
Fixed Assets (net)	30.1	20.2	21.6	22.1				22.1	21.7
Intangibles (net)	2.7	.0	1.0	2.3				3.3	1.7
All Other Non-Current	.1	7.2	4.2	3.9				4.9	4.9
Total	100.0	100.0	100.0	100.0				100.0	100.0
LIABILITIES									
Notes Payable-Short Term	17.9	14.0	10.4	13.5				13.6	13.2
Cur. Mat.-L/T/D	8.9	8.8	4.4	3.8				2.9	3.9
Trade Payables	13.2	18.4	18.3	17.4				16.6	20.4
Income Taxes Payable	2.9	.6	.4	.4				.5	.4
All Other Current	16.5	11.0	11.7	16.1				15.3	13.0
Total Current	59.3	52.8	45.3	51.2				48.8	50.9
Long-Term Debt	5.8	13.1	10.2	11.4				13.1	13.1
Deferred Taxes	.0	.8	.8	.2				.7	.6
All Other Non-Current	7.2	4.2	4.5	3.5				1.6	2.4
Net Worth	27.6	29.1	39.2	33.7				35.7	33.0
Total Liabilities & Net Worth	100.0	100.0	100.0	100.0				100.0	100.0
INCOME DATA									
Net Sales	100.0	100.0	100.0	100.0				100.0	100.0
Gross Profit	33.4	24.1	19.5	15.6				24.2	26.8
Operating Expenses	29.8	21.4	17.5	13.5				20.4	22.9
Operating Profit	3.7	2.7	2.0	2.1				3.9	3.9
All Other Expenses (net)	.4	.3	.0	.5				.7	.8
Profit Before Taxes	3.3	2.3	2.0	1.6				3.2	3.0
RATIOS									
Current	3.4	2.6	2.1	2.1				2.3	2.1
	1.7	1.4	1.5	1.3				1.5	1.5
	1.0	1.1	1.3	1.0				1.2	1.1
Quick	3.3	2.3	1.6	1.6				2.0	1.9
	1.6	1.1	1.3	1.0				1.2	1.2
	.9	.7	1.0	.7				1.0	.8
Sales/Receivables	16 22.9	47 7.8	53 6.8	55 6.6				45 8.2	45 8.2
	47 7.7	66 5.5	77 4.7	89 4.1				71 5.2	70 5.2
	95 3.9	102 3.6	111 3.3	106 3.4				91 4.0	89 4.1
Cost of Sales/Inventory	0 UND	0 UND	0 UND	0 UND				0 UND	0 UND
	0 UND	0 UND	2 162.8	7 50.9				1 371.0	0 UND
	0 UND	9 40.2	18 20.4	34 10.7				16 22.2	8 45.0
Cost of Sales/Payables	2 164.7	11 34.5	15 25.1	20 18.6				12 30.9	16 23.3
	13 29.2	27 13.6	34 10.8	39 9.4				26 14.3	33 10.9
	19 19.0	53 6.9	47 7.7	51 7.1				47 7.8	55 6.7
Sales/Working Capital	7.5	6.0	6.5	4.3				5.8	5.8
	25.7	14.4	9.6	14.9				11.7	13.6
	NM	44.1	15.0	277.4				27.0	40.2
EBIT/Interest	40.2	12.7	11.6	8.4				12.5	9.6
	(10) 6.5	(40) 5.6	(51) 4.7	(21) 3.9				(94) 3.8	(94) 3.8
	−1.5	1.9	.6	.1				1.5	1.6
Net Profit + Depr., Dep., Amort./Cur. Mat. L/T/D		3.9	6.1					4.8	6.6
		(11) 3.0	(25) 1.9					(29) 2.5	(29) 3.2
		1.7	.4					1.4	1.7
Fixed/Worth	.2	.2	.2	.2				.3	.3
	.8	.7	.5	.6				.6	.6
	1.3	2.6	1.1	1.5				1.1	1.1
Debt/Worth	.3	.7	1.0	1.1				.8	1.0
	.8	2.3	1.9	2.1				1.7	1.8
	3.7	12.9	3.3	5.8				4.5	4.3
% Profit Before Taxes/Tangible Net Worth	65.3	71.2	28.2	30.1				50.5	46.1
	(10) 20.3	(39) 31.5	(53) 18.4	(23) 13.1				(94) 27.7	(91) 19.9
	−.1	8.0	1.0	.3				6.8	6.7
% Profit Before Taxes/Total Assets	44.9	19.7	12.2	9.7				18.2	14.2
	12.5	7.5	5.2	5.4				7.0	5.2
	−1.2	2.1	.2	.2				1.5	1.4
Sales/Net Fixed Assets	30.9	39.0	45.0	34.8				31.8	29.4
	16.9	16.0	11.3	11.3				14.5	15.1
	11.8	9.6	7.1	5.7				7.8	7.8
Sales/Total Assets	5.0	3.7	2.9	2.7				3.5	3.3
	3.4	2.8	2.4	1.9				2.6	2.6
	2.6	2.2	1.6	1.4				2.0	2.0
% Depr., Dep., Amort./Sales	1.3	.8	.8	1.1				.8	.7
	(10) 2.4	(38) 1.7	(54) 1.8	(23) 1.5				(88) 1.5	(92) 1.7
	3.5	3.4	2.9	3.3				2.9	3.2
% Officers', Directors', Owners' Comp/Sales		1.9	1.1					2.3	2.3
		(24) 3.2	(25) 3.1					(39) 5.0	(49) 5.0
		5.9	4.6					10.8	7.6
Net Sales ($)	13088M	167952M	637697M	998366M	465425M	872302M		1625665M	1579733M
Total Assets ($)	3458M	57438M	291078M	526160M	215057M	368454M		816866M	828014M

© RMA 2005

M = $ thousand   MM = $ million
See Pages 11 through 21 for Explanation of Ratios and Data

Comparative Historical Data | | | | Current Data Sorted By Sales

25	28	34	Type of Statement						
25	28	34	Unqualified			3	5	10	16
45	57	50	Reviewed		6	10	14	14	6
19	29	21	Compiled	2	10	3	5	1	
6	18	15	Tax Returns	1	7	3	2	2	
17	47	23	Other	1	3	5	5	4	5
4/1/02-3/31/03	4/1/03-3/31/04	4/1/04-3/31/05			33 (4/1-9/30/04)		110 (10/1/04-3/31/05)		
ALL	ALL	ALL		0-1MM	1-3MM	3-5MM	5-10MM	10-25MM	25MM & OVER
112	179	143	**NUMBER OF STATEMENTS**	4	26	24	31	31	27
%	%	%	**ASSETS**	%	%	%	%	%	%
8.9	9.9	9.0	Cash & Equivalents		12.7	8.4	8.0	10.0	6.8
44.8	44.7	49.4	Trade Receivables (net)		46.8	47.8	52.9	47.8	50.4
3.2	4.6	6.4	Inventory		7.8	3.3	7.9	7.2	6.0
10.9	8.6	7.3	All Other Current		3.6	8.6	5.3	8.3	11.9
67.8	67.9	72.1	Total Current		71.0	68.0	74.0	73.2	75.0
22.7	23.3	21.9	Fixed Assets (net)		23.9	23.6	21.3	21.5	19.0
1.7	1.1	1.3	Intangibles (net)		1.2	.0	.2	2.3	2.7
7.9	7.8	4.6	All Other Non-Current		3.9	8.4	4.5	3.0	3.3
100.0	100.0	100.0	Total		100.0	100.0	100.0	100.0	100.0
			LIABILITIES						
11.8	13.3	12.7	Notes Payable-Short Term		13.8	11.9	15.7	14.0	9.1
4.4	3.2	6.0	Cur. Mat.-L/T/D		11.7	3.5	5.9	4.5	3.5
16.1	17.0	17.7	Trade Payables		16.9	18.8	13.6	20.6	18.2
.8	.5	.7	Income Taxes Payable		.1	1.1	.3	.5	.4
15.1	14.6	13.0	All Other Current		12.9	7.7	11.9	11.4	18.0
48.1	48.6	50.0	Total Current		55.3	43.1	47.5	51.0	49.2
13.6	14.2	11.3	Long-Term Debt		7.0	19.6	11.9	8.4	11.5
.7	1.0	.6	Deferred Taxes		.0	.6	1.6	.6	.3
2.5	3.8	4.3	All Other Non-Current		7.5	1.7	3.5	4.3	3.7
35.0	32.5	33.7	Net Worth		30.1	35.0	35.6	35.8	35.4
100.0	100.0	100.0	Total Liabilities & Net Worth		100.0	100.0	100.0	100.0	100.0
			INCOME DATA						
100.0	100.0	100.0	Net Sales		100.0	100.0	100.0	100.0	100.0
22.9	23.3	21.2	Gross Profit		29.0	23.0	20.4	18.3	15.3
20.8	22.1	18.8	Operating Expenses		27.5	20.1	18.4	14.7	12.6
2.2	1.2	2.5	Operating Profit		1.4	2.9	2.0	3.6	2.7
.8	.5	.2	All Other Expenses (net)		.3	.2	.3	.2	.2
1.4	.6	2.2	Profit Before Taxes		1.2	2.7	1.7	3.4	2.5
			RATIOS						
2.1	2.1	2.2			2.8	3.1	2.1	2.1	2.1
1.5	1.5	1.5	Current		1.7	1.4	1.6	1.4	1.5
1.1	1.1	1.1			1.0	1.2	1.3	1.0	1.1
1.6	1.7	1.7			2.5	2.4	1.7	1.5	1.6
1.2	1.2	1.2	Quick		1.3	1.2	1.4	1.2	1.1
.9	.8	.8			.7	.9	.9	.8	.8
43 8.5	46 7.9	51 7.2			39 9.4	44 8.3	47 7.7	52 7.0	61 5.9
61 5.9	68 5.4	76 4.8	Sales/Receivables		58 6.2	65 5.6	71 5.1	84 4.4	89 4.1
93 3.9	96 3.8	104 3.5			104 3.5	96 3.8	104 3.5	118 3.1	96 3.8
0 UND	0 UND	0 UND			0 UND	0 UND	0 UND	0 UND	0 UND
0 UND	0 868.5	1 297.8	Cost of Sales/Inventory		0 UND	0 UND	0 999.8	3 116.6	7 53.7
7 52.4	10 36.8	13 28.7			7 51.3	10 35.0	18 19.9	19 18.8	16 22.4
11 32.3	14 26.5	14 25.8			9 42.7	13 29.0	9 42.7	16 22.3	20 17.9
22 16.3	28 13.2	27 13.5	Cost of Sales/Payables		18 20.3	31 11.7	18 20.1	36 10.0	36 10.1
47 7.7	47 7.7	48 7.5			45 8.1	51 7.1	41 9.0	53 6.8	49 7.5
6.4	6.0	6.2			6.1	5.4	6.5	6.3	4.7
12.9	12.3	11.0	Sales/Working Capital		15.2	12.8	8.7	10.0	11.1
40.8	52.9	42.4			-122.9	37.0	15.0	68.3	30.9
6.9	8.2	11.3			15.6	7.5	10.7	13.9	9.3
(99) 2.3	(157) 1.9	(127) 5.4	EBIT/Interest	(22) 6.5	(21) 5.6	(28) 4.0	(29) 6.0	(24) 7.1
-1.3	-2.6	1.5			-2.2	2.0	-.7	2.1	1.8
5.0	4.2	4.4					4.1	6.5	
(31) 1.8	(50) 1.4	(45) 2.3	Net Profit + Depr., Dep., Amort./Cur. Mat. L/T/D				(12) 2.1	(14) 1.4	
.3	.2	1.1					1.3	-.1	
.2	.3	.2			.2	.2	.2	.2	.2
.5	.5	.7	Fixed/Worth		.7	.8	.5	.5	.6
1.0	1.5	1.3			1.4	3.4	1.1	1.5	1.0
.8	.9	.8			.5	.7	.8	1.1	1.2
1.6	1.8	2.0	Debt/Worth		1.5	2.1	1.9	2.5	1.8
3.5	4.6	4.7			8.7	12.0	4.7	4.2	3.5
26.8	27.7	44.8			80.8	52.5	36.7	53.5	34.5
(100) 10.5	(160) 7.0	(129) 20.6	% Profit Before Taxes/Tangible Net Worth	(23) 20.6	(20) 20.3	(29) 16.0	(29) 23.7	(25) 18.1
-1.8	-12.2	1.7			-24.4	3.0	-.2	2.3	2.8
11.4	8.0	15.1			23.6	18.3	13.7	14.5	8.6
2.5	2.2	6.3	% Profit Before Taxes/Total Assets		8.6	7.4	4.5	6.8	6.4
-2.7	-7.4	.5			-7.5	1.1	-.8	.7	1.5
48.5	30.7	38.6			32.7	34.8	59.4	52.1	33.1
15.3	12.8	13.6	Sales/Net Fixed Assets		15.2	12.5	18.3	14.7	11.9
7.9	6.7	7.5			9.4	7.4	7.8	5.4	6.9
3.6	3.1	3.1			3.9	3.6	3.4	2.8	2.9
2.6	2.3	2.5	Sales/Total Assets		2.9	2.5	2.9	2.2	2.2
1.9	1.7	1.8			2.0	2.0	2.2	1.5	1.8
.7	.8	.9			1.2	1.1	.7	.8	1.1
(101) 1.7	(156) 1.7	(130) 1.7	% Depr., Dep., Amort./Sales	(21) 2.3	(20) 1.8	(29) 2.0	(29) 1.5	1.4
3.4	3.3	3.1			3.3	3.4	3.3	2.5	2.3
1.4	1.6	1.6			2.5	1.6	1.7	.5	
(49) 4.4	(76) 3.4	(61) 3.2	% Officers', Directors', Owners' Comp/Sales	(15) 4.9	(12) 2.9	(15) 4.2	(10) 2.7	
7.2	5.9	5.2			6.6	4.6	4.7	3.9	
1548513M	3598920M	3154830M	Net Sales ($)	2234M	50137M	91812M	220457M	496986M	2293204M
785998M	1650075M	1461645M	Total Assets ($)	1371M	21382M	38602M	91782M	250800M	1057708M

M = $ thousand   MM = $ million
See Pages 11 through 21 for Explanation of Ratios and Data

Current Data Sorted By Assets **Comparative Historical Data**

						Type of Statement		
		1				Unqualified		
1		6	1			Reviewed		
2	4	2				Compiled		
2	1	2				Tax Returns		
1	3	4	1			Other		
	8 (4/1-9/30/04)		23 (10/1/04-3/31/05)				4/1/00-3/31/01	4/1/01-3/31/02
0-500M	500M-2MM	2-10MM	10-50MM	50-100MM	100-250MM		ALL	ALL
6	8	15	2			NUMBER OF STATEMENTS		
%	%	%	%	%	%	ASSETS	%	%
		13.3				Cash & Equivalents		
		43.3		D	D	Trade Receivables (net)	D	D
		10.7		A	A	Inventory	A	A
		15.6		T	T	All Other Current	T	T
		82.9		A	A	Total Current	A	A
		10.7				Fixed Assets (net)		
		.8		N	N	Intangibles (net)	N	N
		5.6		O	O	All Other Non-Current	O	O
		100.0		T	T	Total	T	T
				A	A	LIABILITIES	A	A
		13.0		V	V	Notes Payable-Short Term	V	V
		1.2		A	A	Cur. Mat.-L/T/D	A	A
		21.2		I	I	Trade Payables	I	I
		1.0		L	L	Income Taxes Payable	L	L
		30.2		A	A	All Other Current	A	A
		66.5		B	B	Total Current	B	B
		3.9		L	L	Long-Term Debt	L	L
		.0		E	E	Deferred Taxes	E	E
		2.8				All Other Non-Current		
		26.9				Net Worth		
		100.0				Total Liabilities & Net Worth		
						INCOME DATA		
		100.0				Net Sales		
		12.9				Gross Profit		
		10.6				Operating Expenses		
		2.4				Operating Profit		
		.1				All Other Expenses (net)		
		2.3				Profit Before Taxes		
						RATIOS		
		1.7						
		1.2				Current		
		1.0						
		1.7						
		.9				Quick		
		.5						
	24	15.5						
	34	10.7				Sales/Receivables		
	47	7.8						
	0	UND						
	0	990.8				Cost of Sales/Inventory		
	21	17.4						
	10	38.0						
	15	23.7				Cost of Sales/Payables		
	33	11.2						
		12.7						
		41.8				Sales/Working Capital		
		−258.4						
		12.9						
	(11)	6.2				EBIT/Interest		
		−5.8						
						Net Profit + Depr., Dep., Amort./Cur. Mat. L /T/D		
		.1						
		.2				Fixed/Worth		
		1.8						
		1.6						
		3.6				Debt/Worth		
		9.1						
		132.2				% Profit Before Taxes/Tangible		
	(13)	31.4				Net Worth		
		6.1						
		20.1				% Profit Before Taxes/Total		
		10.0				Assets		
		−.8						
		410.8						
		61.4				Sales/Net Fixed Assets		
		20.2						
		6.0						
		4.0				Sales/Total Assets		
		3.3						
		.2						
	(12)	.8				% Depr., Dep., Amort./Sales		
		1.4						
						% Officers', Directors', Owners' Comp/Sales		
10239M	28847M	293671M	230755M			Net Sales ($)		
2059M	7401M	63197M	29939M			Total Assets ($)		

M = $ thousand   MM = $ million
See Pages 11 through 21 for Explanation of Ratios and Data

Comparative Historical Data | Current Data Sorted By Sales

			Type of Statement	0-1MM	1-3MM	3-5MM	5-10MM	10-25MM	25MM & OVER
1	3	1	Unqualified					1	
9	6	8	Reviewed		1			5	2
6	11	8	Compiled		4	2		1	1
4	5	5	Tax Returns	1	1	1	1	1	
4	8	9	Other		3		2		3
4/1/02-3/31/03 ALL	4/1/03-3/31/04 ALL	4/1/04-3/31/05 ALL			8 (4/1-9/30/04)			23 (10/1/04-3/31/05)	
24	33	31	NUMBER OF STATEMENTS	1	9	3	4	8	6
%	%	%	**ASSETS**	%	%	%	%	%	%
11.9	13.4	14.6	Cash & Equivalents						
51.3	38.5	42.6	Trade Receivables (net)						
10.6	13.1	12.1	Inventory						
7.6	3.1	10.1	All Other Current						
81.5	68.1	79.5	Total Current						
14.0	25.3	14.5	Fixed Assets (net)						
.5	1.3	1.4	Intangibles (net)						
4.0	5.4	4.6	All Other Non-Current						
100.0	100.0	100.0	Total						
			LIABILITIES						
22.0	9.7	14.3	Notes Payable-Short Term						
3.7	12.3	3.1	Cur. Mat.-L/T/D						
24.9	16.2	20.5	Trade Payables						
.5	.3	.5	Income Taxes Payable						
9.7	23.5	27.1	All Other Current						
60.9	62.1	65.5	Total Current						
9.3	18.9	11.1	Long-Term Debt						
.1	2.0	.0	Deferred Taxes						
6.8	3.3	2.2	All Other Non-Current						
23.0	13.7	21.1	Net Worth						
100.0	100.0	100.0	Total Liabilities & Net Worth						
			INCOME DATA						
100.0	100.0	100.0	Net Sales						
20.6	24.5	18.9	Gross Profit						
16.6	22.9	16.1	Operating Expenses						
3.9	1.6	2.8	Operating Profit						
.4	.5	.5	All Other Expenses (net)						
3.5	1.1	2.3	Profit Before Taxes						
			RATIOS						
2.0	2.1	1.8							
1.4	1.4	1.4	Current						
1.1	.8	1.0							
1.8	1.7	1.7							
1.1	1.1	1.1	Quick						
.8	.6	.5							
25 14.6	10 35.2	16 22.2	Sales/Receivables						
53 6.9	37 9.8	34 10.8							
74 4.9	70 5.2	59 6.2							
0 UND	0 UND	0 UND	Cost of Sales/Inventory						
0 UND	2 203.2	1 575.4							
16 23.2	35 10.3	25 14.6							
10 35.4	8 46.6	10 38.0	Cost of Sales/Payables						
24 14.9	17 21.9	17 22.1							
42 8.6	36 10.2	28 13.0							
7.4	9.0	12.7	Sales/Working Capital						
23.8	18.9	20.5							
44.0	−46.2	−258.4							
29.0	24.2	12.9	EBIT/Interest						
(19) 11.4	(30) 3.5	(23) 7.7							
.4	−1.1	2.2							
	23.4		Net Profit + Depr., Dep., Amort./Cur. Mat. L/T/D						
	(10) 1.0								
	−1.5								
.1	.2	.1	Fixed/Worth						
.5	.5	.3							
2.1	NM	2.2							
1.1	1.2	.9	Debt/Worth						
3.2	2.8	3.2							
13.8	NM	9.7							
112.8	55.7	84.1	% Profit Before Taxes/Tangible Net Worth						
(19) 47.5	(25) 12.1	(25) 29.3							
17.3	−5.7	15.5							
18.9	14.5	20.1	% Profit Before Taxes/Total Assets						
10.9	3.3	12.8							
.2	−6.1	2.0							
126.8	55.3	166.6	Sales/Net Fixed Assets						
42.9	33.3	40.3							
17.7	12.5	16.7							
4.6	5.4	6.0	Sales/Total Assets						
4.0	2.7	4.2							
3.1	2.2	3.3							
.3	.4	.1	% Depr., Dep., Amort./Sales						
(20) 1.0	(29) 1.0	(25) .9							
1.7	2.2	2.2							
1.6	.8	.8	% Officers', Directors', Owners' Comp/Sales						
(12) 1.8	(14) 3.6	(12) 1.6							
4.0	6.0	3.5							
279115M	367604M	563512M	Net Sales ($)	524M	18986M	11416M	35542M	127626M	369418M
70032M	161555M	102596M	Total Assets ($)	100M	5485M	2956M	10192M	28997M	54866M

© RMA 2005

M = $ thousand   MM = $ million

See Pages 11 through 21 for Explanation of Ratios and Data

Current Data Sorted By Assets   **Comparative Historical Data**

0-500M	500M-2MM	2-10MM	10-50MM	50-100MM	100-250MM	Type of Statement	ALL	ALL
	2	15	11	2		Unqualified	14	15
4	28	68	3			Reviewed	48	58
6	11	5				Compiled	27	30
17	12	1	1		1	Tax Returns	17	13
2	18	13	4		1	Other	23	25
41 (4/1-9/30/04)			184 (10/1/04-3/31/05)				4/1/00-3/31/01	4/1/01-3/31/02
29	71	102	19	2	2	**NUMBER OF STATEMENTS**	129	141
%	%	%	%	%	%	**ASSETS**	%	%
18.8	13.0	11.8	10.1			Cash & Equivalents	12.3	12.5
24.3	49.6	56.0	47.6			Trade Receivables (net)	45.7	47.5
7.3	3.1	3.5	3.9			Inventory	2.7	5.0
6.8	6.3	8.2	10.4			All Other Current	8.2	7.0
57.1	72.0	79.4	72.1			Total Current	69.0	72.0
33.0	21.8	15.3	16.5			Fixed Assets (net)	23.8	21.3
.5	1.0	.7	3.2			Intangibles (net)	1.3	1.9
9.4	5.2	4.6	8.2			All Other Non-Current	5.8	4.8
100.0	100.0	100.0	100.0			Total	100.0	100.0
						LIABILITIES		
17.8	14.2	9.2	13.5			Notes Payable-Short Term	10.9	10.3
6.6	4.1	3.1	2.0			Cur. Mat.-L/T/D	4.8	3.7
9.2	19.6	18.2	14.7			Trade Payables	14.6	15.8
.1	.9	1.0	.5			Income Taxes Payable	1.4	.6
14.4	12.1	14.1	14.8			All Other Current	16.5	17.9
48.2	50.9	45.6	45.5			Total Current	48.1	48.2
30.2	13.6	6.6	4.4			Long-Term Debt	9.9	9.1
.0	.4	.7	.2			Deferred Taxes	1.1	.7
4.9	5.8	3.8	2.2			All Other Non-Current	2.5	2.0
16.8	29.3	43.3	47.6			Net Worth	38.3	39.9
100.0	100.0	100.0	100.0			Total Liabilities & Net Worth	100.0	100.0
						INCOME DATA		
100.0	100.0	100.0	100.0			Net Sales	100.0	100.0
37.4	27.8	17.1	21.9			Gross Profit	26.1	24.6
32.7	25.8	13.9	15.5			Operating Expenses	21.0	21.2
4.7	2.0	3.1	6.5			Operating Profit	5.1	3.3
.9	.3	.1	−.4			All Other Expenses (net)	.0	.4
3.8	1.6	3.0	6.9			Profit Before Taxes	5.1	2.9
						RATIOS		
2.8	2.5	2.6	2.3				2.3	2.2
1.5	1.6	1.8	1.5			Current	1.6	1.5
.5	1.0	1.4	1.2				1.2	1.2
2.3	2.2	2.3	2.0				2.0	2.1
.7	1.3	1.5	1.1			Quick	1.3	1.3
.2	.9	1.2	.8				.9	.9
0 UND	39 9.5	55 6.6	59 6.2				42 8.7	39 9.3
0 824.0	56 6.5	73 5.0	75 4.8			Sales/Receivables	58 6.3	66 5.5
40 9.2	80 4.6	93 3.9	87 4.2			83 4.4	83 4.4
0 UND	0 UND	0 UND	0 UND				0 UND	0 UND
0 UND	0 UND	0 UND	3 127.7			Cost of Sales/Inventory	0 UND	0 UND
3 131.2	2 148.2	3 108.5	13 28.0				1 369.9	5 79.6
0 UND	12 29.9	16 22.6	12 30.2				9 39.7	11 31.9
5 69.0	26 13.8	23 15.6	26 14.1			Cost of Sales/Payables	18 19.7	21 17.6
27 13.5	42 8.7	34 10.6	36 10.2				32 11.3	33 11.2
12.0	7.3	5.2	4.9				6.4	6.8
23.8	12.2	8.4	11.9			Sales/Working Capital	11.6	13.0
−35.7	177.4	12.9	18.6				40.7	27.5
17.8	15.9	17.3	35.4				15.9	14.9
(25) 3.5	(63) 4.1	(94) 4.6	(17) 8.9			EBIT/Interest	(114) 6.7	(125) 5.1
.9	1.1	1.4	2.4				3.0	1.9
	3.6	7.9				Net Profit + Depr., Dep.,	20.3	6.7
	(14) 1.5	(31) 3.6				Amort./Cur. Mat. L /T/D	(27) 5.9	(37) 3.8
	.9	1.2					3.1	1.3
.3	.2	.2	.2				.2	.2
1.7	.5	.3	.3			Fixed/Worth	.4	.4
−2.4	7.0	.6	.4				1.2	.9
.9	.9	.7	.5				.7	.7
4.6	1.9	1.4	1.4			Debt/Worth	1.5	1.6
−5.1	22.1	2.9	2.5				3.6	3.6
118.5	48.6	34.1	69.6			% Profit Before Taxes/Tangible	51.0	43.0
(21) 22.9	(56) 19.9	(100) 12.9	(18) 16.6			Net Worth	(117) 25.3	(131) 21.8
2.7	1.9	1.5	1.9				14.6	9.3
46.2	14.9	12.8	27.7			% Profit Before Taxes/Total	20.1	16.4
10.4	5.6	5.1	7.7			Assets	10.2	7.4
−.3	−1.6	.9	1.0				4.8	2.4
92.8	58.1	41.8	30.3				31.0	33.1
18.7	20.0	23.3	17.5			Sales/Net Fixed Assets	19.2	17.4
12.3	10.4	12.5	14.3				10.2	10.4
8.4	4.2	3.2	3.3				3.8	3.6
6.4	3.1	2.6	2.4			Sales/Total Assets	3.0	2.9
3.1	2.2	2.2	2.2				2.3	2.3
1.1	.8	.7	.6				.9	.9
(19) 2.1	(57) 1.6	(96) 1.4	(17) 1.5			% Depr., Dep., Amort./Sales	(114) 1.5	(127) 1.6
4.2	3.3	2.4	2.2				2.5	2.9
5.9	2.5	1.3					2.4	2.1
(19) 8.2	(41) 4.2	(55) 2.5				% Officers', Directors', Owners' Comp/Sales	(78) 4.9	(81) 4.5
14.6	6.4	4.2					8.2	8.6
41617M	291547M	1232052M	787173M	223422M	1137466M	Net Sales ($)	1187189M	1618725M
7423M	87236M	435090M	308953M	119953M	389901M	Total Assets ($)	409264M	504125M

© RMA 2005

M = $ thousand   MM = $ million
See Pages 11 through 21 for Explanation of Ratios and Data

Comparative Historical Data			Type of Statement	Current Data Sorted By Sales					
21	21	30	Unqualified			4	3	11	12
62	103	103	Reviewed	2	10	18	43	26	4
26	50	22	Compiled		9	7	2	1	3
15	32	32	Tax Returns	9	12	3	5	1	2
23	45	38	Other	3	8	5	8	10	4
4/1/02-3/31/03 ALL	4/1/03-3/31/04 ALL	4/1/04-3/31/05 ALL		41 (4/1-9/30/04)			184 (10/1/04-3/31/05)		
				0-1MM	1-3MM	3-5MM	5-10MM	10-25MM	25MM & OVER
147	251	225	**NUMBER OF STATEMENTS**	14	39	37	61	49	25
%	%	%	**ASSETS**	%	%	%	%	%	%
12.5	11.8	12.9	Cash & Equivalents	10.5	16.2	14.9	12.1	13.3	7.5
45.8	44.5	48.9	Trade Receivables (net)	27.8	33.7	53.3	54.0	57.0	49.4
3.6	4.5	4.1	Inventory	2.9	4.7	3.8	4.0	3.9	4.5
8.6	8.1	7.6	All Other Current	5.2	7.0	4.7	8.2	8.5	10.3
70.5	69.0	73.4	Total Current	46.4	61.7	76.7	78.2	82.8	71.8
22.4	22.9	19.9	Fixed Assets (net)	46.1	28.6	16.0	16.6	13.7	17.8
1.5	1.5	1.0	Intangibles (net)	.9	1.2	.9	.4	.5	3.3
5.6	6.6	5.7	All Other Non-Current	6.4	8.5	6.4	4.8	3.0	7.1
100.0	100.0	100.0	Total	100.0	100.0	100.0	100.0	100.0	100.0
			LIABILITIES						
10.5	13.0	12.1	Notes Payable-Short Term	13.7	13.6	12.4	12.2	10.9	10.5
3.6	3.8	3.8	Cur. Mat.-L/T/D	7.5	4.2	4.0	3.9	2.8	2.2
17.7	15.9	17.1	Trade Payables	8.6	11.7	18.1	18.9	20.5	17.5
.8	.9	.8	Income Taxes Payable	.0	1.1	.3	1.5	.7	.0
15.5	14.7	13.8	All Other Current	18.0	11.1	13.0	13.6	14.3	16.6
48.1	48.2	47.6	Total Current	47.8	41.7	47.8	50.1	49.3	46.8
13.1	10.9	12.1	Long-Term Debt	38.6	17.4	9.3	11.8	3.8	10.0
.5	.5	.5	Deferred Taxes	.0	.4	.7	.4	.7	.4
3.9	2.8	4.6	All Other Non-Current	7.8	6.2	4.0	4.5	3.2	3.7
34.5	37.5	35.3	Net Worth	5.8	34.3	38.2	33.2	43.0	39.1
100.0	100.0	100.0	Total Liabilities & Net Worth	100.0	100.0	100.0	100.0	100.0	100.0
			INCOME DATA						
100.0	100.0	100.0	Net Sales	100.0	100.0	100.0	100.0	100.0	100.0
24.0	24.6	23.7	Gross Profit	45.8	33.5	24.6	19.2	16.2	20.6
21.8	22.2	20.5	Operating Expenses	39.5	31.6	21.5	17.1	11.9	15.9
2.1	2.4	3.2	Operating Profit	6.3	1.8	3.1	2.1	4.3	4.7
.2	.4	.2	All Other Expenses (net)	1.6	.4	.1	.1	.1	-.1
1.9	1.9	3.0	Profit Before Taxes	4.7	1.4	3.0	2.0	4.1	4.8
			RATIOS						
2.3	2.5	2.5	Current	3.1	2.7	2.4	2.5	2.7	2.1
1.5	1.5	1.6		1.1	1.7	1.6	1.7	1.8	1.5
1.2	1.1	1.2		.2	1.0	1.2	1.3	1.3	1.2
1.8	2.1	2.2	Quick	2.2	2.6	1.9	2.2	2.4	1.8
1.3	1.3	1.3		.7	1.2	1.5	1.4	1.5	1.1
.9	.8	.9		.2	.6	1.0	1.0	1.1	.9
41 8.8	37 9.8	40 9.1	Sales/Receivables	0 UND	0 UND	48 7.6	48 7.7	49 7.5	47 7.7
63 5.8	59 6.2	65 5.6		38 9.7	40 9.1	72 5.1	70 5.2	69 5.3	75 4.8
79 4.6	82 4.4	85 4.3		42 8.8	71 5.2	91 4.0	85 4.3	88 4.1	85 4.3
0 UND	0 UND	0 UND	Cost of Sales/Inventory	0 UND	0 UND	0 UND	0 UND	0 UND	0 UND
0 UND	0 UND	0 UND		0 UND	0 UND	0 UND	0 UND	0 UND	1 402.3
2 172.9	4 89.0	3 104.8		0 UND	1 250.3	4 91.5	4 102.3	4 98.4	15 24.8
10 36.8	10 36.6	12 30.1	Cost of Sales/Payables	0 UND	0 UND	15 23.8	14 26.5	17 21.1	17 21.3
21 17.1	21 17.0	23 16.1		7 49.1	10 35.0	25 14.4	21 17.1	24 14.9	31 11.6
42 8.6	37 9.9	38 9.7		49 7.5	38 9.5	44 8.2	36 10.0	31 11.7	41 9.0
6.6	5.9	6.1	Sales/Working Capital	10.6	7.6	5.1	5.1	5.0	8.5
13.9	12.3	11.0		NM	13.9	8.8	9.2	9.1	11.9
38.2	125.0	28.3		-20.9	-61.9	25.8	18.5	14.8	19.6
14.2	17.8	16.8	EBIT/Interest	35.3	11.1	8.0	13.1	32.4	34.8
(133) 5.2	(218) 5.1	(202) 4.6		(12) 2.8	(33) 2.5	(35) 3.5	(56) 3.6	(43) 5.8	(23) 8.9
1.3	1.7	1.3		1.5	-.7	1.4	.4	2.0	2.6
12.4	8.9	6.0	Net Profit + Depr., Dep., Amort./Cur. Mat. L/T/D			4.0	9.0	7.9	
(35) 4.2	(60) 3.1	(54) 2.8				(10) 1.7	(15) 3.2	(15) 4.1	
1.9	1.5	1.0				.9	.9	1.2	
.3	.2	.2	Fixed/Worth	.2	.3	.2	.2	.1	.2
.5	.4	.4		22.5	.6	.4	.4	.3	.3
1.2	1.2	1.0		-1.8	4.9	.9	1.0	.5	.9
.7	.6	.8	Debt/Worth	.7	.6	1.0	.8	.7	.8
1.5	1.5	1.6		29.8	1.6	1.9	1.5	1.1	1.7
4.6	4.6	4.2		-4.1	10.5	3.5	3.8	3.0	3.6
42.9	38.8	38.6	% Profit Before Taxes/Tangible Net Worth		49.3	60.9	26.5	41.2	74.5
(134) 15.8	(228) 16.9	(198) 16.0			(33) 21.6	(33) 18.4	(54) 11.2	(48) 16.9	(22) 19.3
3.2	4.0	2.1			1.8	1.0	-.7	6.5	7.3
17.5	15.3	17.1	% Profit Before Taxes/Total Assets	36.5	18.3	15.6	10.9	20.0	25.6
4.5	5.4	5.7		4.2	5.1	5.5	5.2	7.5	6.0
.1	1.3	.7		.9	-3.3	.8	-1.2	1.7	1.5
29.2	35.6	43.0	Sales/Net Fixed Assets	21.3	31.8	49.6	48.9	58.9	57.4
16.2	18.6	20.0		12.3	15.1	22.5	23.1	27.4	28.7
10.0	10.3	12.1		3.9	6.9	12.1	12.5	14.7	13.8
3.7	4.0	3.9	Sales/Total Assets	8.0	5.0	3.5	3.9	3.5	3.5
2.9	2.8	2.8		3.1	3.1	2.6	3.0	2.8	2.9
2.2	2.0	2.2		1.4	2.2	2.1	2.4	2.4	2.1
.9	1.1	.8	% Depr., Dep., Amort./Sales		1.1	.8	1.2	.5	.5
(137) 1.8	(215) 1.7	(191) 1.6			(31) 2.1	(32) 1.5	(52) 1.9	(47) 1.0	(20) .9
3.3	3.0	2.4			3.8	3.2	2.4	2.1	1.8
2.2	2.1	1.8	% Officers', Directors', Owners' Comp/Sales	5.9	3.6	3.4	1.6	1.1	1.0
(81) 4.0	(130) 3.6	(124) 3.9		(10) 7.7	(24) 4.9	(22) 4.5	(35) 3.1	(21) 1.7	(12) 1.9
6.9	7.7	6.5		13.5	9.7	6.7	5.3	2.5	5.5
2592492M	3874119M	3713277M	Net Sales ($)	8486M	79474M	150024M	428813M	798042M	2248438M
549885M	1153690M	1348556M	Total Assets ($)	3905M	28231M	60889M	146621M	286464M	822446M

Current Data Sorted By Assets

Comparative Historical Data

Type of Statement

Type of Statement	0-500M	500M-2MM	2-10MM	10-50MM	50-100MM	100-250MM		4/1/00-3/31/01	4/1/01-3/31/02
Unqualified			6	3	1			3	5
Reviewed		18	29	2				18	20
Compiled	5	9	5		1			17	17
Tax Returns	8	5	1			1		6	12
Other	3	9	8	1				17	18
		31 (4/1-9/30/04)		84 (10/1/04-3/31/05)				4/1/00-3/31/01 ALL	4/1/01-3/31/02 ALL
NUMBER OF STATEMENTS	16	41	49	6	2	1		61	72

Financial Data (%)

0-500M	500M-2MM	2-10MM	10-50MM	50-100MM	100-250MM	Item	4/1/00-3/31/01 ALL	4/1/01-3/31/02 ALL
%	%	%	%	%	%	**ASSETS**	%	%
14.5	11.7	8.7				Cash & Equivalents	8.6	10.7
38.7	53.8	53.6				Trade Receivables (net)	55.4	52.0
17.3	8.4	10.4				Inventory	9.1	8.6
.9	6.3	8.0				All Other Current	4.7	7.1
71.4	80.1	80.7				Total Current	77.8	78.4
18.7	13.7	12.2				Fixed Assets (net)	14.4	17.1
4.1	3.3	.6				Intangibles (net)	2.8	1.9
5.9	3.0	6.4				All Other Non-Current	4.6	2.6
100.0	100.0	100.0				Total	100.0	100.0
						LIABILITIES		
9.2	11.3	16.7				Notes Payable-Short Term	12.0	11.3
3.7	4.1	2.2				Cur. Mat.-L/T/D	3.2	2.8
24.0	22.8	20.1				Trade Payables	23.0	29.3
.3	.8	1.8				Income Taxes Payable	.5	.7
10.5	10.8	17.3				All Other Current	15.7	16.3
47.6	49.9	58.2				Total Current	54.4	60.5
33.6	7.6	8.1				Long-Term Debt	10.1	10.1
.0	.2	.3				Deferred Taxes	.5	.6
1.4	3.2	2.8				All Other Non-Current	1.7	3.2
17.4	39.1	30.6				Net Worth	33.0	25.6
100.0	100.0	100.0				Total Liabilities & Net Worth	100.0	100.0
						INCOME DATA		
100.0	100.0	100.0				Net Sales	100.0	100.0
48.3	29.1	25.9				Gross Profit	28.6	28.3
46.5	27.1	24.4				Operating Expenses	24.0	23.3
1.8	2.0	1.6				Operating Profit	4.6	4.9
.4	.3	.3				All Other Expenses (net)	.7	.8
1.3	1.7	1.3				Profit Before Taxes	3.9	4.1
						RATIOS		
2.9	2.6	1.9					2.1	2.2
1.5	1.6	1.4				Current	1.4	1.4
.9	1.2	1.2					1.1	1.1
1.9	2.2	1.6					1.7	1.9
1.0	1.4	1.2				Quick	1.2	1.2
.6	1.0	.9					1.0	.8
12 30.8	48 7.6	48 7.6					50 7.4	38 9.5
25 14.7	63 5.8	72 5.1				Sales/Receivables	67 5.5	62 5.9
40 9.1	80 4.5	100 3.7					87 4.2	86 4.2
16 22.5	0 UND	1 414.4					1 320.8	0 999.8
24 15.4	8 46.2	6 62.5				Cost of Sales/Inventory	7 50.5	5 69.9
31 11.9	27 13.6	32 11.3					30 12.3	20 17.8
7 56.1	20 18.3	14 25.4					22 16.9	21 17.7
32 11.3	36 10.3	29 12.6				Cost of Sales/Payables	39 9.4	34 10.6
52 7.0	53 6.8	53 6.9					57 6.4	48 7.6
11.7	6.1	6.5					7.6	7.2
20.9	10.9	10.3				Sales/Working Capital	13.6	14.7
NM	29.2	21.3					38.0	48.6
13.8	26.4	10.4					17.1	17.8
(12) 3.3	(34) 4.0	(43) 3.4				EBIT/Interest	(50) 6.6	(65) 8.7
-8.2	-2.1	.1					2.0	2.4
	9.9	6.3					6.1	9.4
	(13) 2.8	(21) 3.6				Net Profit + Depr., Dep., Amort./Cur. Mat. L /T/D	(11) 4.7	(14) 4.3
	.1	.0					2.9	1.0
.2	.2	.2					.2	.2
.5	.4	.3				Fixed/Worth	.3	.3
1.4	1.1	.6					1.5	1.3
.7	.6	.9					1.0	.9
2.6	1.9	1.8				Debt/Worth	2.8	2.4
7.2	5.9	3.9					6.6	10.4
111.1	47.3	31.7					75.4	66.7
(13) 26.8	(33) 13.8	(44) 14.0				% Profit Before Taxes/Tangible Net Worth	(53) 37.0	(58) 37.0
-32.7	-11.0	.4					13.3	14.4
30.1	17.0	12.4					19.4	23.7
10.8	6.3	3.2				% Profit Before Taxes/Total Assets	9.3	9.7
-21.9	-5.3	-.6					2.9	2.7
79.5	65.7	59.6					62.8	52.1
39.5	26.9	31.6				Sales/Net Fixed Assets	26.1	28.5
21.4	16.5	14.9					15.5	16.4
6.7	3.8	3.3					3.9	4.1
5.0	3.1	2.7				Sales/Total Assets	2.8	3.2
4.5	2.5	2.1					2.4	2.4
.8	.6	.6					.5	.4
(10) 1.5	(32) .8	(46) .8				% Depr., Dep., Amort./Sales	(51) .9	(68) .8
2.2	2.0	1.6					1.9	1.5
4.7	3.9	1.9					2.2	1.5
(13) 5.6	(24) 5.8	(23) 4.3				% Officers', Directors', Owners' Comp/Sales	(40) 4.3	(39) 4.5
11.1	10.1	6.8					6.1	8.9
20836M	142952M	574302M	205301M	2731744M	213317M	Net Sales ($)	519059M	562376M
4304M	43910M	207015M	81527M	138145M	155963M	Total Assets ($)	187779M	190171M

© RMA 2005

M = $ thousand   MM = $ million
See Pages 11 through 21 for Explanation of Ratios and Data

Comparative Historical Data | Current Data Sorted By Sales

			Type of Statement						
5	6	10	Unqualified				2	5	3
25	43	49	Reviewed		8	8	16	14	3
11	27	19	Compiled	4	5	4	5	1	
19	22	15	Tax Returns	2	9	2	1		1
16	21	22	Other		10	5	1		3
4/1/02-3/31/03	4/1/03-3/31/04	4/1/04-3/31/05			31 (4/1-9/30/04)		84 (10/1/04-3/31/05)		
ALL	ALL	ALL		0-1MM	1-3MM	3-5MM	5-10MM	10-25MM	25MM & OVER
76	119	115	**NUMBER OF STATEMENTS**	6	32	19	25	23	10
%	%	%	**ASSETS**	%	%	%	%	%	%
12.3	11.5	10.4	Cash & Equivalents		10.6	11.3	8.4	9.3	8.1
46.3	48.1	50.9	Trade Receivables (net)		47.9	49.1	53.6	57.7	51.4
9.7	11.2	10.7	Inventory		12.6	7.0	10.8	10.4	8.6
5.0	6.8	6.1	All Other Current		4.8	8.9	8.5	5.5	3.3
73.3	77.6	78.0	Total Current		75.9	76.3	81.3	82.8	71.5
19.3	14.4	14.6	Fixed Assets (net)		16.4	14.3	11.3	12.1	22.7
2.6	2.8	2.5	Intangibles (net)		4.2	3.1	.9	1.5	3.4
4.7	5.2	4.9	All Other Non-Current		3.5	6.4	6.4	3.6	2.4
100.0	100.0	100.0	Total		100.0	100.0	100.0	100.0	100.0
			LIABILITIES						
12.3	13.7	15.4	Notes Payable-Short Term		11.2	12.3	15.8	14.4	31.8
3.2	2.5	3.1	Cur. Mat.-L/T/D		3.7	3.7	2.3	3.4	.2
21.5	20.7	21.3	Trade Payables		22.2	24.1	19.4	19.4	16.7
.4	1.0	1.1	Income Taxes Payable		1.0	.7	1.3	1.1	2.4
15.0	15.1	14.0	All Other Current		10.6	12.9	14.8	15.8	22.1
52.5	53.1	55.0	Total Current		48.7	53.8	53.6	54.1	73.2
13.3	6.7	12.6	Long-Term Debt		15.8	7.1	9.8	6.4	20.0
.4	.2	.2	Deferred Taxes		.2	.1	.2	.3	.8
3.0	5.4	3.0	All Other Non-Current		2.2	5.0	2.3	3.2	4.5
30.9	34.6	29.2	Net Worth		33.1	34.0	34.1	36.0	1.4
100.0	100.0	100.0	Total Liabilities & Net Worth		100.0	100.0	100.0	100.0	100.0
			INCOME DATA						
100.0	100.0	100.0	Net Sales		100.0	100.0	100.0	100.0	100.0
32.4	30.9	30.4	Gross Profit		36.0	26.2	25.9	26.4	27.5
29.1	28.5	28.6	Operating Expenses		34.8	25.5	24.2	23.0	25.5
3.2	2.5	1.8	Operating Profit		1.2	.7	1.7	3.4	2.0
.3	.4	.4	All Other Expenses (net)		.6	.6	.2	.1	.4
2.9	2.1	1.4	Profit Before Taxes		.6	.1	1.6	3.2	1.6
			RATIOS						
2.0	2.4	2.4			2.7	2.4	2.0	1.9	2.1
1.3	1.5	1.5	Current		1.5	1.6	1.6	1.4	1.3
1.1	1.1	1.2			1.1	1.3	1.2	1.3	.9
1.6	1.8	1.8			1.9	2.3	1.8	1.7	1.7
1.1	1.2	1.2	Quick		1.3	1.2	1.2	1.2	1.2
.7	.8	.8			.8	.8	.8	1.0	.8
32 11.2	42 8.6	41 8.9		39 9.3	46 8.0	54 6.8	40 9.2	52 7.0	
56 6.5	60 6.0	62 5.9	Sales/Receivables	59 6.2	63 5.8	69 5.3	68 5.3	60 6.1	
84 4.3	81 4.5	83 4.4		79 4.6	85 4.3	98 3.7	88 4.1	70 5.2	
0 UND	1 678.4	1 424.2		7 55.2	0 UND	1 346.5	1 261.9	0 UND	
7 52.8	10 36.0	10 37.5	Cost of Sales/Inventory	22 16.3	6 64.0	4 88.7	6 62.5	1 553.4	
27 13.6	28 13.2	32 11.6		32 11.5	11 33.0	30 12.1	32 11.6	42 8.7	
17 21.0	17 21.9	17 21.0		18 20.6	27 13.4	11 32.0	18 19.8	12 30.7	
33 11.1	35 10.4	33 11.1	Cost of Sales/Payables	45 8.2	35 10.5	24 14.9	27 13.5	22 16.5	
53 6.9	53 6.8	53 6.9		60 6.1	51 7.1	52 7.0	47 7.8	47 7.8	
7.6	5.9	6.8			7.3	5.4	6.1	6.9	6.8
15.9	11.5	11.4	Sales/Working Capital		11.9	10.9	8.7	10.9	18.4
57.5	46.5	29.3			36.1	24.7	24.3	21.4	−219.0
19.5	16.5	14.1			18.6	20.0	13.8	13.1	
(67) 6.4	(101) 3.8	(98) 3.7	EBIT/Interest		(25) 3.0	(17) 3.5	(22) 2.3	(21) 5.7	
1.7	1.2	−.4			−4.8	−.5	−2.1	1.2	
19.4	7.9	8.5	Net Profit + Depr., Dep.,				4.0		
(20) 4.0	(25) 4.5	(40) 3.7	Amort./Cur. Mat. L/T/D				(12) 2.8		
2.8	1.4	.8					−1.2		
.2	.1	.2			.2	.2	.2	.2	.3
.4	.4	.4	Fixed/Worth		.5	.4	.2	.4	.4
1.1	.8	.8			1.8	.7	.5	.5	NM
1.0	.8	.9			.7	.6	.8	.9	.9
2.2	1.7	1.9	Debt/Worth		2.1	1.5	1.3	1.9	3.6
4.8	4.8	5.3			10.7	3.4	3.0	4.7	NM
52.8	35.0	38.0	% Profit Before Taxes/Tangible		44.0	38.7	25.3	39.2	
(65) 22.0	(101) 16.4	(96) 14.2	Net Worth		(25) 13.6	(16) 16.1	(22) 10.4	(21) 22.9	
4.7	4.1	−1.3			−18.6	1.8	−4.8	8.0	
16.0	12.5	15.3	% Profit Before Taxes/Total		13.6	16.5	11.6	19.0	13.1
6.5	5.0	5.9	Assets		6.2	6.3	1.8	7.4	5.6
1.6	.7	−1.0			−7.4	.8	−2.3	2.0	−1.3
45.6	50.4	60.1			56.0	56.1	67.4	74.5	46.9
25.5	28.9	29.4	Sales/Net Fixed Assets		25.7	25.0	35.3	28.1	29.8
14.3	16.1	17.0			14.9	15.8	19.3	15.3	17.8
4.3	3.7	4.1			4.4	4.1	3.2	4.4	4.8
3.1	2.8	3.0	Sales/Total Assets		3.5	3.0	2.7	3.3	2.9
2.3	2.2	2.3			2.4	2.3	2.2	2.3	2.3
.6	.6	.6			.7	.6	.6	.5	
(69) 1.2	(104) 1.0	(95) 1.0	% Depr., Dep., Amort./Sales		(23) 1.4	(15) .9	(23) .8	(21) .8	
2.4	1.9	1.8			2.2	2.0	1.7	1.3	
2.7	3.0	3.0			3.7	4.6	2.1	1.9	
(50) 4.5	(64) 5.0	(63) 5.4	% Officers', Directors', Owners' Comp/Sales		(18) 5.1	(12) 6.0	(12) 4.9	(12) 3.7	
8.7	9.6	8.6			10.8	7.3	6.6	6.7	
517218M	2650843M	3888452M	Net Sales ($)	3506M	66616M	75045M	195756M	350173M	3197356M
180366M	509882M	630864M	Total Assets ($)	675M	23349M	32232M	80520M	119941M	374147M

M = $ thousand   MM = $ million
See Pages 11 through 21 for Explanation of Ratios and Data

Current Data Sorted By Assets | Comparative Historical Data

0-500M	500M-2MM	2-10MM	10-50MM	50-100MM	100-250MM		4/1/00-3/31/01 ALL	4/1/01-3/31/02 ALL
						Type of Statement		
1	7	19	6			Unqualified	19	27
10	68	73	5			Reviewed	95	104
10	18	8	1			Compiled	42	48
14	26	3	1		2	Tax Returns	22	13
13	34	19	6		1	Other	44	50
	74 (4/1-9/30/04)		271 (10/1/04-3/31/05)					
48	153	122	19		3	**NUMBER OF STATEMENTS**	222	242
%	%	%	%	%	%	**ASSETS**	%	%
17.8	10.5	10.1	12.5	DATA NOT AVAILABLE		Cash & Equivalents	11.7	10.6
32.1	46.7	50.4	44.2			Trade Receivables (net)	43.1	46.1
7.7	7.4	7.8	7.0			Inventory	8.2	6.8
4.0	7.4	8.9	16.2			All Other Current	7.0	7.9
61.6	72.0	77.2	79.9			Total Current	70.0	71.4
25.7	17.4	14.2	11.2			Fixed Assets (net)	20.1	18.1
1.8	1.9	1.1	3.1			Intangibles (net)	2.2	3.0
11.0	8.7	7.5	5.7			All Other Non-Current	7.6	7.5
100.0	100.0	100.0	100.0			Total	100.0	100.0
						LIABILITIES		
17.3	10.0	12.0	10.2			Notes Payable-Short Term	11.7	9.7
6.6	3.1	1.8	2.1			Cur. Mat.-L/T/D	3.3	3.8
21.0	23.1	21.7	23.7			Trade Payables	20.9	20.2
.0	1.1	.5	1.7			Income Taxes Payable	.5	.5
16.2	12.9	15.0	19.8			All Other Current	12.9	14.4
61.1	50.2	51.1	57.4			Total Current	49.3	48.6
15.2	11.2	5.8	5.3			Long-Term Debt	10.7	9.8
.2	.6	.3	.3			Deferred Taxes	1.0	.7
5.2	2.3	2.8	6.6			All Other Non-Current	2.6	2.6
18.3	35.6	40.0	30.4			Net Worth	36.6	38.3
100.0	100.0	100.0	100.0			Total Liabilities & Net Worth	100.0	100.0
						INCOME DATA		
100.0	100.0	100.0	100.0			Net Sales	100.0	100.0
39.0	27.7	21.9	23.6			Gross Profit	25.0	25.5
35.3	24.9	18.6	17.8			Operating Expenses	22.7	23.1
3.7	2.8	3.3	5.8			Operating Profit	2.3	2.5
.7	.2	.4	1.6			All Other Expenses (net)	.1	.3
3.0	2.6	2.8	4.2			Profit Before Taxes	2.1	2.2
						RATIOS		
4.4	2.1	2.2	1.7				2.0	2.2
1.3	1.5	1.4	1.4			Current	1.5	1.4
.7	1.1	1.2	1.2				1.1	1.1
3.8	1.7	1.7	1.4				1.6	1.8
1.2	1.2	1.1	.9			Quick	1.1	1.2
.5	.8	.9	.8				.8	.8
4 99.6	**36** 10.1	**52** 7.1	**36** 10.3				**32** 11.4	**39** 9.3
21 17.3	**50** 7.4	**70** 5.2	**63** 5.8			Sales/Receivables	**54** 6.7	**57** 6.4
43 8.4	**71** 5.1	**95** 3.8	**83** 4.4				**73** 5.0	**81** 4.5
0 UND	**0** UND	**3** 134.8	**0** UND				**2** 224.3	**1** 367.5
0 UND	**5** 76.2	**7** 52.2	**4** 85.8			Cost of Sales/Inventory	**7** 54.9	**6** 60.6
12 29.5	**18** 20.5	**17** 21.9	**18** 20.7				**15** 24.2	**13** 28.8
4 85.0	**15** 24.6	**19** 19.0	**25** 14.4				**17** 21.6	**16** 22.4
19 19.5	**31** 11.8	**32** 11.4	**38** 9.7			Cost of Sales/Payables	**30** 12.1	**29** 12.8
36 10.1	**49** 7.5	**53** 6.9	**50** 7.2				**49** 7.4	**45** 8.1
7.8	8.8	6.6	9.2				8.3	6.8
41.6	16.1	10.6	13.4			Sales/Working Capital	13.4	13.0
-32.1	46.8	25.9	22.9				52.9	50.6
20.9	13.5	23.4	39.7				9.1	11.4
(32) 4.0	(142) 6.1	(115) 6.0	(18) 14.9			EBIT/Interest	(208) 3.1	(216) 4.0
-1.7	1.7	2.0	6.3				1.0	1.4
	6.9	6.2					4.4	4.7
	(36) 2.9	(38) 3.1				Net Profit + Depr., Dep., Amort./Cur. Mat. L /T/D	(66) 2.1	(61) 2.2
	.8	1.5					.6	.6
.2	.2	.2	.2				.2	.2
.8	.5	.3	.4			Fixed/Worth	.5	.4
-20.9	1.1	.6	1.3				1.1	1.1
.3	1.0	.7	1.1				1.0	.8
2.1	1.8	1.8	2.5			Debt/Worth	1.8	1.7
-20.4	4.1	3.5	6.7				3.4	3.9
132.8	58.9	35.1	84.6				40.5	38.0
(33) 27.3	(139) 22.8	(119) 18.2	(17) 34.0			% Profit Before Taxes/Tangible Net Worth	(203) 17.9	(219) 17.7
3.6	2.3	4.9	15.3				2.5	3.8
37.0	16.7	12.8	17.0				13.1	15.0
7.5	7.9	5.3	9.7			% Profit Before Taxes/Total Assets	5.0	5.7
-15.3	.8	1.8	4.4				.3	.8
64.2	47.0	38.7	35.1				37.4	35.1
33.4	23.9	23.2	28.5			Sales/Net Fixed Assets	19.3	20.1
15.8	13.0	13.9	18.1				11.4	12.8
8.8	4.3	3.2	3.9				3.8	3.7
4.7	3.3	2.6	3.0			Sales/Total Assets	2.9	2.9
3.6	2.5	2.0	2.3				2.3	2.2
.8	.7	.8	.6				.8	.9
(32) 1.3	(134) 1.3	(113) 1.1	(14) 1.0			% Depr., Dep., Amort./Sales	(203) 1.5	(215) 1.5
2.2	2.1	1.8	1.3				2.4	2.4
2.9	2.0	2.0					2.0	2.3
(28) 6.9	(91) 3.5	(55) 2.7				% Officers', Directors', Owners' Comp/Sales	(113) 3.4	(112) 3.9
9.3	6.2	4.7					6.7	6.9
70084M	**607180M**	**1399974M**	**1090416M**		**2812620M**	Net Sales ($)	**3647025M**	**3638337M**
11608M	**178633M**	**529297M**	**357412M**		**587699M**	Total Assets ($)	**1544392M**	**1775353M**

M = $ thousand MM = $ million

See Pages 11 through 21 for Explanation of Ratios and Data

Comparative Historical Data | Current Data Sorted By Sales

34	49	33	Type of Statement Unqualified	1	1	6	8	10	7
133	168	156	Reviewed	9	25	32	54	29	7
35	63	37	Compiled	6	14	7	4	5	1
25	44	46	Tax Returns	6	16	7	11	3	3
55	67	73	Other	3	19	21	11	13	6
4/1/02- 3/31/03 ALL	4/1/03- 3/31/04 ALL	4/1/04- 3/31/05 ALL		74 (4/1-9/30/04)		271 (10/1/04-3/31/05)			
				0-1MM	1-3MM	3-5MM	5-10MM	10-25MM	25MM & OVER
282	391	345	**NUMBER OF STATEMENTS**	25	75	73	88	60	24
%	%	%	**ASSETS**	%	%	%	%	%	%
12.4	10.2	11.6	Cash & Equivalents	18.4	12.1	9.7	13.4	8.2	10.7
45.8	47.4	45.7	Trade Receivables (net)	34.7	39.7	46.7	48.0	52.7	47.4
7.6	7.8	7.5	Inventory	4.2	9.8	7.4	6.2	8.7	5.6
8.2	7.2	8.0	All Other Current	2.4	6.2	6.9	10.0	8.5	14.0
74.0	72.7	72.8	Total Current	59.8	67.9	70.7	77.6	78.1	77.7
17.5	17.9	17.0	Fixed Assets (net)	20.1	22.2	18.2	14.4	13.7	12.1
2.0	1.9	1.6	Intangibles (net)	2.3	.7	2.8	.7	1.7	3.6
6.5	7.4	8.5	All Other Non-Current	17.9	9.1	8.3	7.3	6.5	6.6
100.0	100.0	100.0	Total	100.0	100.0	100.0	100.0	100.0	100.0
			LIABILITIES						
12.6	13.3	11.6	Notes Payable-Short Term	16.3	13.8	9.4	10.3	12.9	8.7
3.5	3.3	3.1	Cur. Mat.-L/T/D	3.9	3.7	3.2	2.0	3.7	2.6
21.1	21.4	22.3	Trade Payables	18.8	22.4	24.6	20.8	23.4	21.7
.6	.7	.7	Income Taxes Payable	.0	1.3	.8	.8	.3	1.2
14.3	13.6	14.5	All Other Current	15.8	13.7	12.7	13.8	17.6	15.7
52.2	52.3	52.4	Total Current	54.8	54.9	50.7	47.8	57.9	49.9
8.1	11.7	9.6	Long-Term Debt	17.2	14.6	10.1	7.2	4.4	6.5
.3	.4	.4	Deferred Taxes	.0	.2	.9	.5	.2	.2
2.4	3.0	3.2	All Other Non-Current	8.7	2.2	1.6	3.1	3.2	5.5
37.0	32.7	34.5	Net Worth	19.4	28.0	36.8	41.5	34.3	37.9
100.0	100.0	100.0	Total Liabilities & Net Worth	100.0	100.0	100.0	100.0	100.0	100.0
			INCOME DATA						
100.0	100.0	100.0	Net Sales	100.0	100.0	100.0	100.0	100.0	100.0
26.5	26.9	27.1	Gross Profit	40.7	32.0	26.8	24.0	20.6	26.0
24.2	24.4	23.8	Operating Expenses	40.2	28.1	24.6	20.5	17.1	19.6
2.3	2.5	3.3	Operating Profit	.5	3.9	2.3	3.4	3.5	6.3
.2	.4	.5	All Other Expenses (net)	.4	.5	.2	.4	.7	1.0
2.1	2.1	2.8	Profit Before Taxes	.1	3.4	2.1	3.0	2.9	5.3
			RATIOS						
2.0	2.1	2.2		5.8	2.2	2.1	2.4	1.8	2.1
1.4	1.4	1.4	Current	1.2	1.4	1.5	1.6	1.3	1.6
1.1	1.1	1.1		.6	.9	1.2	1.2	1.1	1.2
1.6	1.6	1.7		5.8	1.7	1.7	2.1	1.4	1.7
1.1	1.2	1.2	Quick	1.0	1.2	1.2	1.3	1.0	1.1
.8	.8	.8		.5	.7	.8	.9	.8	.9
33 11.0	38 9.6	36 10.1		11 33.0	24 15.4	36 10.0	42 8.8	45 8.1	31 11.7
54 6.7	57 6.4	54 6.7	Sales/Receivables	24 15.3	50 7.3	51 7.1	56 6.5	73 5.0	54 6.8
78 4.7	81 4.5	78 4.7		66 5.5	71 5.1	74 5.0	82 4.4	90 4.0	75 4.9
1 377.4	1 683.0	0 UND		0 UND	0 UND	0 UND	0 UND	4 96.5	0 UND
6 61.2	6 65.0	5 73.1	Cost of Sales/Inventory	0 UND	7 54.2	5 73.1	4 90.0	7 48.8	4 92.2
16 23.5	18 20.1	16 22.2		8 43.7	25 14.7	16 22.8	14 25.5	16 22.5	12 31.3
16 23.5	16 23.4	16 22.9		6 57.9	13 27.8	17 21.8	17 21.6	19 18.8	16 22.8
28 12.9	29 12.7	30 12.0	Cost of Sales/Payables	24 15.3	31 11.8	37 9.8	29 12.7	32 11.4	33 11.1
44 8.2	47 7.8	49 7.4		46 6.6	56 6.6	49 7.4	48 7.6	55 6.6	43 8.5
7.8	7.8	7.8		5.1	8.4	8.7	6.1	8.1	8.0
13.9	13.7	14.0	Sales/Working Capital	35.6	15.9	16.3	10.9	15.5	11.1
59.6	49.7	48.1		−16.1	−159.0	37.9	32.9	32.7	23.7
14.2	14.6	18.8		6.2	17.8	12.9	26.5	15.4	41.2
(247) 3.8	(344) 4.4	(309) 6.3	EBIT/Interest	(16) 1.6	(67) 6.9	(64) 4.9	(85) 6.3	(56) 5.2	(21) 18.9
.7	1.1	1.8		−6.8	−.3	1.9	2.2	2.1	7.7
5.4	5.4	6.9	Net Profit + Depr., Dep.,		3.7	7.4	9.9	4.8	
(81) 2.3	(95) 3.0	(83) 3.2	Amort./Cur. Mat. L/T/D	(14) 1.6	(15) 4.3	(27) 4.2	(18) 1.8		
.8	1.3	1.4			−.1	1.7	2.2	.0	
.2	.2	.2		.0	.2	.2	.1	.2	.2
.4	.4	.4	Fixed/Worth	.3	.5	.5	.3	.4	.3
.8	1.0	1.0		−30.9	2.9	1.0	.7	.7	.5
.8	.9	.9		.2	.9	1.0	.7	1.2	.9
1.6	1.8	1.9	Debt/Worth	3.6	1.7	1.8	1.6	2.3	2.2
3.5	4.0	4.4		−4.6	6.8	4.3	3.5	3.9	3.8
42.8	41.2	53.5	% Profit Before Taxes/Tangible	71.0	84.1	47.4	50.9	44.6	93.0
(257) 17.3	(349) 16.7	(311) 20.6	Net Worth	(16) 12.6	(64) 19.7	(65) 19.0	(86) 20.9	(58) 17.7	(22) 34.4
1.6	2.8	4.4		−10.6	−4.5	3.8	4.2	7.0	25.2
14.7	16.2	16.1	% Profit Before Taxes/Total	34.3	23.5	14.6	14.0	14.0	27.1
6.0	5.2	6.9	Assets	1.6	9.1	5.7	7.2	5.4	12.8
−.6	.4	1.2		−17.7	−3.3	1.2	1.6	2.3	7.6
45.0	41.8	43.7		117.0	43.7	42.1	43.5	42.1	40.8
23.6	22.5	24.4	Sales/Net Fixed Assets	39.2	22.5	22.3	25.2	26.3	28.2
14.0	14.1	14.5		8.4	11.8	13.3	14.2	18.8	20.3
4.0	4.1	4.1		6.0	4.3	4.3	4.0	3.5	4.0
3.1	3.1	3.1	Sales/Total Assets	3.6	3.4	3.0	3.1	2.8	3.5
2.5	2.4	2.4		1.7	2.3	2.4	2.2	2.4	2.6
1.0	.8	.8		.7	.7	.9	.7	.8	.8
(248) 1.5	(328) 1.4	(294) 1.2	% Depr., Dep., Amort./Sales	(17) 1.3	(65) 1.3	(62) 1.5	(81) 1.2	(51) 1.1	(18) 1.1
2.3	2.1	2.0		3.4	2.1	2.1	1.6	1.7	1.3
2.3	2.3	2.1	% Officers', Directors',	3.3	3.0	1.9	1.9	2.1	
(151) 4.1	(209) 4.4	(182) 3.5	Owners' Comp/Sales	(11) 6.9	(46) 5.6	(41) 3.5	(49) 2.8	(27) 2.7	
7.0	6.8	6.2		11.9	7.8	4.5	4.3	5.7	
6182290M	6848714M	5980274M	Net Sales ($)	15997M	152624M	294147M	608787M	894966M	4013753M
1450807M	1862930M	1664649M	Total Assets ($)	6302M	53859M	97153M	228625M	326815M	951895M

© RMA 2005

M = $ thousand   MM = $ million

See Pages 11 through 21 for Explanation of Ratios and Data

Current Data Sorted By Assets   Comparative Historical Data

						Type of Statement		
1	17	86	53	4	2	Unqualified	105	95
11	169	205	10	1	1	Reviewed	212	209
33	52	13	1			Compiled	132	136
44	40	14	1	4	1	Tax Returns	46	42
20	68	73	32	1	2	Other	121	141
223 (4/1-9/30/04)			736 (10/1/04-3/31/05)				4/1/00-3/31/01	4/1/01-3/31/02
0-500M	500M-2MM	2-10MM	10-50MM	50-100MM	100-250MM		ALL	ALL
109	346	391	97	10	6	**NUMBER OF STATEMENTS**	616	623
%	%	%	%	%	%	**ASSETS**	%	%
13.0	12.3	10.6	8.5	3.9		Cash & Equivalents	11.4	12.7
40.0	49.9	56.2	58.4	42.2		Trade Receivables (net)	51.1	49.4
9.7	7.9	4.2	2.6	7.2		Inventory	6.2	5.3
3.2	7.3	9.4	12.1	8.8		All Other Current	8.2	9.2
65.9	77.5	80.3	81.6	62.1		Total Current	76.9	76.7
25.7	16.1	12.2	11.3	23.9		Fixed Assets (net)	16.5	16.4
2.0	.8	1.7	1.6	3.3		Intangibles (net)	1.5	1.4
6.5	5.6	5.8	5.6	10.7		All Other Non-Current	5.1	5.5
100.0	100.0	100.0	100.0	100.0		Total	100.0	100.0
						LIABILITIES		
23.6	12.3	10.2	10.1	42.3		Notes Payable-Short Term	11.7	10.8
5.8	3.7	2.5	1.6	4.3		Cur. Mat.-L/T/D	2.8	3.2
17.6	19.7	21.4	19.2	15.4		Trade Payables	19.3	18.6
.2	.8	.9	.3	.0		Income Taxes Payable	.8	.8
14.5	12.1	16.6	19.7	21.4		All Other Current	16.3	17.5
61.6	48.6	51.5	50.9	83.4		Total Current	50.9	50.9
21.3	8.9	6.6	8.6	52.3		Long-Term Debt	8.3	8.1
.2	.5	.5	.2	.0		Deferred Taxes	.9	.7
12.3	3.2	3.0	4.9	22.7		All Other Non-Current	3.0	2.1
4.7	38.8	38.3	35.4	-58.3		Net Worth	36.8	38.2
100.0	100.0	100.0	100.0	100.0		Total Liabilities & Net Worth	100.0	100.0
						INCOME DATA		
100.0	100.0	100.0	100.0	100.0		Net Sales	100.0	100.0
38.2	25.7	19.6	16.1	27.5		Gross Profit	25.5	24.8
35.3	23.4	17.0	13.7	26.2		Operating Expenses	21.9	21.8
2.9	2.3	2.6	2.4	1.2		Operating Profit	3.6	3.0
.7	.2	.2	.1	2.0		All Other Expenses (net)	.4	.4
2.2	2.1	2.5	2.4	-.7		Profit Before Taxes	3.1	2.5
						RATIOS		
2.4	2.7	2.1	2.1	1.5		Current	2.2	2.2
1.2	1.6	1.5	1.5	1.3			1.5	1.5
.8	1.2	1.2	1.3	.2			1.2	1.2
1.9	2.2	1.8	1.6	1.2		Quick	1.8	1.8
1.0	1.3	1.3	1.3	.9			(615) 1.3	(622) 1.2
.5	.9	1.0	1.1	.1			.9	.9
10 36.2	44 8.4	57 6.4	70 5.2	0 UND		Sales/Receivables	44 8.4	44 8.3
37 9.7	59 6.2	73 5.0	81 4.5	61 6.0			64 5.7	61 6.0
57 6.4	78 4.7	91 4.0	94 3.9	85 4.3			81 4.5	78 4.7
0 UND	0 UND	0 UND	0 UND	0 UND		Cost of Sales/Inventory	0 UND	0 UND
3 135.8	4 95.7	2 154.5	1 364.3	2 196.1			3 137.1	3 133.8
18 20.6	16 23.0	9 39.8	6 62.9	5 79.0			14 26.6	10 35.5
3 145.5	16 22.5	19 19.4	19 18.8	0 UND		Cost of Sales/Payables	16 23.4	15 24.4
17 21.9	27 13.5	30 12.0	30 12.4	25 14.5			27 13.8	25 14.3
43 8.5	42 8.7	46 7.9	44 8.3	34 10.9			43 8.4	40 9.0
10.4	6.3	6.6	5.8	9.1		Sales/Working Capital	6.7	7.0
31.0	10.9	10.8	8.9	18.8			12.1	11.4
-37.4	26.9	20.1	14.3	-11.2			25.2	26.7
8.6	15.8	20.1	17.6			EBIT/Interest	16.1	15.7
(89) 2.4	(309) 3.9	(335) 6.2	(80) 6.3				(561) 5.2	(545) 5.2
-.6	.4	1.5	2.1				1.7	1.4
	4.7	7.3	16.9			Net Profit + Depr., Dep.,	7.6	7.7
	(77) 2.0	(122) 2.3	(33) 3.7			Amort./Cur. Mat. L /T/D	(182) 3.2	(177) 3.1
	1.0	1.1	1.6				1.5	1.1
.4	.2	.1	.1	.2		Fixed/Worth	.2	.2
1.2	.3	.3	.2	18.5			.4	.3
-1.8	.9	.6	.4	-.3			.7	.8
1.3	.8	.9	1.0	2.2		Debt/Worth	.8	.8
4.2	1.6	1.7	1.8	43.2			1.6	1.5
-5.6	3.4	3.2	2.9	-1.4			3.2	3.6
100.7	35.6	35.8	24.7			% Profit Before Taxes/Tangible	45.0	45.3
(70) 27.2	(318) 11.0	(369) 14.5	(93) 12.4			Net Worth	(577) 20.5	(587) 17.4
-.3	-.4	3.2	3.2				6.3	4.7
27.4	12.9	12.8	9.9	15.9		% Profit Before Taxes/Total	14.7	16.0
7.1	4.3	4.7	4.7	2.1		Assets	7.5	6.3
-3.3	-1.1	.8	1.2	-16.4			1.8	1.5
66.7	47.6	61.8	84.9	53.5		Sales/Net Fixed Assets	46.4	47.3
25.8	24.2	31.5	38.2	35.4			25.3	26.9
13.2	14.4	17.2	19.4	12.4			14.4	14.8
6.2	3.9	3.4	3.2	6.0		Sales/Total Assets	3.8	3.7
4.3	3.1	2.8	2.8	3.8			3.0	3.1
3.0	2.4	2.3	2.2	2.4			2.4	2.5
1.0	.7	.5	.4			% Depr., Dep., Amort./Sales	.5	.5
(75) 1.8	(299) 1.4	(352) .9	(82) .6				(557) 1.1	(559) 1.0
2.7	2.2	1.5	1.2				1.9	1.8
3.7	2.4	1.5	.8			% Officers', Directors',	2.4	2.5
(61) 5.9	(181) 3.9	(186) 2.5	(34) 1.4			Owners' Comp/Sales	(329) 4.4	(309) 4.7
9.2	6.7	4.6	2.1				7.8	8.4
138208M	1321723M	5048214M	6176892M	3962993M	2042136M	Net Sales ($)	9687957M	10672797M
29244M	420257M	1762973M	1793449M	711057M	912112M	Total Assets ($)	3501170M	3944160M

M = $ thousand   MM = $ million
See Pages 11 through 21 for Explanation of Ratios and Data

Comparative Historical Data | Current Data Sorted By Sales

4/1/02-3/31/03	4/1/03-3/31/04	4/1/04-3/31/05	Type of Statement	0-1MM	1-3MM	3-5MM	5-10MM	10-25MM	25MM & OVER
133	153	163	Unqualified		5	13	26	52	67
285	388	397	Reviewed	7	52	90	126	96	26
88	160	99	Compiled	19	46	18	11	4	1
60	96	104	Tax Returns	20	34	21	19	4	6
100	152	196	Other	10	37	30	45	45	29
ALL	ALL	ALL		223 (4/1-9/30/04)			736 (10/1/04-3/31/05)		
666	949	959	NUMBER OF STATEMENTS	56	174	172	227	201	129
%	%	%	**ASSETS**	%	%	%	%	%	%
12.4	12.0	11.2	Cash & Equivalents	14.8	12.7	12.5	11.6	9.5	7.5
49.9	48.7	52.1	Trade Receivables (net)	33.8	44.1	49.7	54.8	59.2	58.1
5.2	6.1	6.0	Inventory	13.7	8.9	6.8	5.0	3.8	3.1
9.2	9.6	8.2	All Other Current	3.5	5.0	8.6	8.7	9.1	11.7
76.7	76.4	77.5	Total Current	65.9	70.8	77.5	80.1	81.6	80.5
16.5	16.3	15.2	Fixed Assets (net)	24.4	21.3	15.7	12.6	11.6	12.6
1.5	1.6	1.5	Intangibles (net)	1.2	1.9	1.3	1.1	1.4	1.8
5.3	5.7	5.8	All Other Non-Current	8.6	6.0	5.4	6.2	5.4	5.1
100.0	100.0	100.0	Total	100.0	100.0	100.0	100.0	100.0	100.0
			LIABILITIES						
12.4	12.8	12.8	Notes Payable-Short Term	15.2	18.7	12.3	10.5	10.3	12.9
4.1	3.0	3.2	Cur. Mat.-L/T/D	7.6	3.3	3.5	3.1	2.4	2.2
18.5	18.6	20.0	Trade Payables	14.6	16.5	20.4	21.6	22.3	20.2
1.1	.7	.7	Income Taxes Payable	.6	.3	1.2	1.0	.5	.3
15.7	14.5	15.1	All Other Current	13.6	12.0	12.6	13.7	18.4	20.3
51.8	49.6	51.8	Total Current	51.6	50.9	50.0	50.0	53.9	55.9
9.8	9.3	9.9	Long-Term Debt	20.5	14.3	9.1	6.2	6.6	11.8
.4	.5	.4	Deferred Taxes	.0	.4	.6	.5	.4	.2
2.8	4.1	4.6	All Other Non-Current	18.0	4.5	3.0	3.0	2.8	6.5
35.2	36.4	33.3	Net Worth	9.9	30.0	37.4	40.3	36.3	25.6
100.0	100.0	100.0	Total Liabilities & Net Worth	100.0	100.0	100.0	100.0	100.0	100.0
			INCOME DATA						
100.0	100.0	100.0	Net Sales	100.0	100.0	100.0	100.0	100.0	100.0
24.7	24.6	23.7	Gross Profit	40.1	32.4	24.2	21.6	18.5	16.3
22.4	22.9	21.2	Operating Expenses	36.8	29.3	21.7	19.2	16.2	14.3
2.3	1.7	2.5	Operating Profit	3.3	3.2	2.5	2.4	2.3	2.0
.5	.4	.3	All Other Expenses (net)	1.4	.3	.2	.0	.2	.4
1.8	1.3	2.3	Profit Before Taxes	1.9	2.9	2.3	2.4	2.1	1.6
			RATIOS						
2.2	2.3	2.3	Current	3.2	2.7	2.5	2.3	2.0	1.8
1.6	1.5	1.5		1.4	1.5	1.5	1.6	1.4	1.5
1.2	1.2	1.2		.8	1.0	1.2	1.2	1.2	1.3
1.9	1.9	1.9	Quick	2.3	2.3	1.9	1.9	1.7	1.5
1.3	1.2	1.3		1.0	1.2	1.3	1.3	1.3	1.2
.9	.9	.9		.5	.8	.9	1.0	1.0	1.0
46 8.0	44 8.3	48 7.6	Sales/Receivables	16 22.4	36 10.1	44 8.3	51 7.2	58 6.3	58 6.3
63 5.8	63 5.8	66 5.5		44 8.4	55 6.6	62 5.9	66 5.5	74 5.0	74 4.9
83 4.4	81 4.5	86 4.3		83 4.4	77 4.7	80 4.6	87 4.2	92 4.0	86 4.3
0 UND	0 UND	0 UND	Cost of Sales/Inventory	0 UND	0 UND	0 UND	0 UND	0 UND	0 UND
2 173.4	3 134.4	3 143.3		7 53.6	4 94.7	5 78.1	2 150.7	2 171.6	1 296.1
10 36.2	13 28.3	12 31.1		48 7.6	26 14.0	15 25.0	11 33.8	8 45.4	4 86.1
15 24.6	15 24.4	17 21.6	Cost of Sales/Payables	6 56.4	12 31.0	16 22.4	19 19.3	18 20.4	18 20.4
26 14.3	27 13.6	28 12.9		24 15.5	26 13.8	29 12.5	29 12.8	31 11.7	26 14.2
43 8.5	41 8.8	44 8.3		43 8.4	44 8.3	47 7.7	44 8.3	47 7.7	36 10.2
6.6	6.2	6.6	Sales/Working Capital	5.9	6.2	6.4	6.2	7.0	7.7
10.8	11.3	11.2		14.9	11.9	11.1	10.5	11.7	11.4
23.9	27.0	24.2		−49.0	181.5	27.8	21.0	21.3	17.4
15.9	12.8	15.9	EBIT/Interest	6.8	13.2	17.3	17.4	19.6	17.5
(582) 3.9	(827) 3.7	(827) 4.6		(40) 2.2	(155) 4.0	(156) 3.7	(187) 4.4	(172) 6.6	(117) 6.4
1.0	.7	1.0		−3.6	.5	.5	1.3	1.6	2.1
6.1	3.5	6.8	Net Profit + Depr., Dep., Amort./Cur. Mat. L/T/D		3.4	6.5	7.2	10.6	9.5
(194) 2.2	(242) 1.7	(243) 2.5			(29) 1.8	(42) 2.2	(67) 2.4	(58) 3.0	(44) 3.3
.6	.5	1.1			.2	1.0	.9	1.3	1.3
.2	.2	.1	Fixed/Worth	.2	.2	.2	.1	.1	.1
.3	.4	.3		.9	.6	.4	.2	.3	.2
.9	.9	.9		−12.8	2.0	1.0	.6	.6	.6
.8	.8	.9	Debt/Worth	1.0	.8	.8	.8	1.0	1.2
1.6	1.8	1.8		3.5	2.1	1.8	1.5	1.9	2.1
3.5	3.9	3.7		−41.6	6.4	4.1	3.1	3.4	3.4
36.6	32.1	36.0	% Profit Before Taxes/Tangible Net Worth	90.1	47.9	34.5	31.0	36.8	26.4
(618) 14.1	(867) 10.3	(861) 13.7		(40) 14.1	(143) 15.2	(157) 10.5	(213) 11.8	(188) 15.6	(120) 14.6
2.3	.4	1.9		−1.2	.7	−1.3	2.4	3.3	4.5
12.4	11.6	13.0	% Profit Before Taxes/Total Assets	17.7	15.8	14.1	12.6	12.6	10.4
4.7	3.5	4.6		3.6	5.8	3.8	4.4	4.9	4.7
.5	−.9	.1		−5.3	−.9	−1.2	.6	.8	1.5
49.5	49.5	58.4	Sales/Net Fixed Assets	41.3	43.4	44.6	61.2	66.6	83.9
25.2	25.3	28.4		19.3	18.7		32.7	31.5	40.0
14.0	13.7	15.7		9.3	10.3	15.5	18.1	17.8	24.7
3.6	3.7	3.8	Sales/Total Assets	5.1	4.0	3.9	3.8	3.5	3.5
2.9	3.0	3.0		2.9	3.0	3.0	2.9	3.0	3.1
2.3	2.2	2.4		1.6	2.2	2.3	2.4	2.4	2.6
.7	.6	.6	% Depr., Dep., Amort./Sales	1.5	.9	.8	.5	.5	.4
(612) 1.2	(824) 1.2	(819) 1.1		(45) 2.4	(133) 1.7	(152) 1.4	(194) 1.1	(182) .8	(113) .7
2.1	2.1	1.9		3.7	2.6	2.1	1.6	1.4	1.2
2.5	2.3	1.8	% Officers', Directors', Owners' Comp/Sales	4.2	3.1	2.3	1.9	1.2	.8
(309) 4.7	(502) 4.0	(466) 3.4		(27) 8.6	(89) 4.5	(101) 3.8	(113) 3.2	(88) 2.0	(48) 1.5
8.0	7.0	5.9		12.4	7.4	6.0	5.4	4.3	3.1
13458024M	17816474M	18690166M	Net Sales ($)	33881M	343334M	671072M	1634486M	3133681M	12873712M
4381238M	5385119M	5629092M	Total Assets ($)	15969M	145234M	242067M	630698M	1179896M	3415228M

M = $ thousand   MM = $ million
See Pages 11 through 21 for Explanation of Ratios and Data

Current Data Sorted By Assets   Comparative Historical Data

0-500M	500M-2MM	2-10MM	10-50MM	50-100MM	100-250MM	Type of Statement	4/1/00-3/31/01 ALL	4/1/01-3/31/02 ALL
3	12	63	41	1	4	Unqualified	112	109
17	127	200	25	2		Reviewed	229	227
27	77	30	4		2	Compiled	155	137
64	55	26				Tax Returns	71	42
23	64	70	19	4	2	Other	139	197
	240 (4/1-9/30/04)		722 (10/1/04-3/31/05)					
134	335	389	89	7	8	NUMBER OF STATEMENTS	706	712
%	%	%	%	%	%	**ASSETS**	%	%
15.4	10.6	11.0	12.3			Cash & Equivalents	11.1	12.0
33.3	49.3	53.9	54.0			Trade Receivables (net)	49.3	49.1
10.2	8.9	6.2	3.6			Inventory	8.5	7.9
3.4	5.7	8.8	11.2			All Other Current	6.6	7.0
62.4	74.4	79.9	81.1			Total Current	75.5	75.9
29.0	17.1	13.3	9.5			Fixed Assets (net)	17.8	16.9
2.0	2.2	1.6	1.5			Intangibles (net)	1.9	1.9
6.7	6.2	5.2	7.9			All Other Non-Current	4.7	5.4
100.0	100.0	100.0	100.0			Total	100.0	100.0
						LIABILITIES		
16.5	10.9	8.9	5.7			Notes Payable-Short Term	8.7	9.0
5.4	3.6	2.3	1.3			Cur. Mat.-L/T/D	3.5	3.2
20.4	23.7	23.6	24.0			Trade Payables	23.1	22.8
1.0	.6	.9	.6			Income Taxes Payable	.7	.7
18.9	12.4	17.1	22.4			All Other Current	16.5	16.6
62.2	51.2	52.7	54.0			Total Current	52.4	52.3
32.9	11.9	7.1	6.2			Long-Term Debt	8.9	9.2
.1	.2	.4	.1			Deferred Taxes	.7	.6
3.1	2.8	2.6	2.6			All Other Non-Current	2.3	3.1
1.6	33.9	37.2	37.0			Net Worth	35.7	34.8
100.0	100.0	100.0	100.0			Total Liabilities & Net Worth	100.0	100.0
						INCOME DATA		
100.0	100.0	100.0	100.0			Net Sales	100.0	100.0
40.8	26.8	21.3	15.8			Gross Profit	26.2	25.5
38.7	24.6	19.0	13.0			Operating Expenses	22.8	22.6
2.2	2.2	2.3	2.8			Operating Profit	3.3	3.0
.8	.3	.2	.0			All Other Expenses (net)	.3	.4
1.4	1.9	2.2	2.8			Profit Before Taxes	3.1	2.6
						RATIOS		
2.2	2.1	2.0	1.8				2.0	2.0
1.4	1.5	1.4	1.4			Current	1.5	1.4
.8	1.1	1.2	1.3				1.2	1.2
1.9	1.7	1.6	1.5				1.6	1.7
(133) 1.1	1.2	1.2	1.2			Quick (704)	1.2	1.2
.5	.9	1.0	1.0				.9	.9
7 53.4	36 10.2	50 7.3	58 6.3				39 9.5	38 9.5
24 15.2	51 7.2	67 5.5	73 5.0			Sales/Receivables	58 6.3	59 6.2
45 8.1	69 5.3	85 4.3	86 4.2				80 4.5	78 4.7
0 UND	0 999.8	0 999.8	0 999.8				0 999.8	0 741.1
5 67.2	6 60.2	4 94.6	2 166.0			Cost of Sales/Inventory	5 76.9	4 96.1
19 19.1	20 18.3	13 27.8	7 54.7				16 22.7	15 23.8
1 250.9	17 21.5	22 17.0	24 15.4				18 19.8	18 19.7
19 18.9	30 12.0	32 11.3	35 10.5			Cost of Sales/Payables	31 11.9	32 11.5
45 8.0	47 7.8	49 7.4	51 7.2				48 7.7	48 7.6
11.2	8.2	7.1	7.4				7.8	7.5
25.9	14.4	12.2	11.0			Sales/Working Capital	13.4	13.1
−45.3	44.0	24.2	17.3				33.8	32.0
8.4	15.9	21.5	36.0				13.4	15.1
(101) 2.2	(300) 4.8	(352) 4.9	(76) 7.6			EBIT/Interest (625)	5.1	(629) 4.2
−.4	1.1	1.3	2.3				1.8	1.7
9.5	4.7	7.1	14.4				6.5	4.6
(11) 2.0	(78) 2.3	(137) 2.5	(20) 6.3			Net Profit + Depr., Dep., Amort./Cur. Mat. L /T/D (222)	2.3	(201) 2.5
1.0	.6	.8	2.9				1.2	1.4
.3	.2	.2	.1				.2	.2
.9	.4	.3	.2			Fixed/Worth	.4	.4
−4.9	1.0	.7	.5				.9	.9
1.0	.9	1.0	1.2				1.0	.9
2.3	1.9	1.9	1.9			Debt/Worth	1.8	1.9
−11.3	5.5	3.8	3.0				3.7	4.0
78.2	48.8	31.3	29.3				44.7	42.4
(92) 18.1	(296) 18.9	(373) 13.7	(84) 14.7			% Profit Before Taxes/Tangible Net Worth (645)	21.7	(656) 18.7
−1.2	2.6	2.6	5.8				5.8	5.2
22.4	15.2	11.5	9.3				16.6	15.1
4.6	6.0	4.3	5.3			% Profit Before Taxes/Total Assets	6.9	6.1
−6.1	.3	.6	1.7				1.8	1.3
60.4	50.6	50.4	76.9				45.8	47.2
25.7	25.3	29.0	36.3			Sales/Net Fixed Assets	25.0	24.3
13.2	14.3	17.8	21.2				13.9	14.6
8.7	4.5	3.6	3.2				3.9	3.9
4.7	3.5	2.9	2.9			Sales/Total Assets	3.1	3.2
3.5	2.7	2.3	2.3				2.5	2.5
.8	.7	.6	.4				.6	.6
(97) 1.6	(277) 1.3	(365) 1.0	(80) .7			% Depr., Dep., Amort./Sales (627)	1.1	(644) 1.2
2.6	2.0	1.7	1.2				1.9	2.0
3.6	2.5	1.4	.7				2.6	2.2
(95) 6.5	(198) 4.2	(192) 2.6	(22) 2.1			% Officers', Directors', Owners' Comp/Sales (367)	4.5	(362) 4.2
11.1	6.5	4.3	4.2				7.8	7.5
184185M	1398309M	5263374M	5125705M	1264506M	3335353M	Net Sales ($)	12159409M	12167621M
33579M	387417M	1752136M	1818257M	502826M	1232732M	Total Assets ($)	3910758M	3820718M

M = $ thousand   MM = $ million
See Pages 11 through 21 for Explanation of Ratios and Data

Comparative Historical Data				Current Data Sorted By Sales					
			Type of Statement						
128	148	124	Unqualified	1	6	7	15	39	56
316	370	371	Reviewed	4	46	58	116	111	36
130	210	140	Compiled	13	39	39	29	10	10
93	141	145	Tax Returns	33	38	33	26	14	1
144	215	182	Other	7	43	26	42	33	31
4/1/02-3/31/03	4/1/03-3/31/04	4/1/04-3/31/05		240 (4/1-9/30/04)			722 (10/1/04-3/31/05)		
ALL	ALL	ALL		0-1MM	1-3MM	3-5MM	5-10MM	10-25MM	25MM & OVER
811	1084	962	**NUMBER OF STATEMENTS**	58	172	163	228	207	134
%	%	%	**ASSETS**	%	%	%	%	%	%
12.5	12.4	11.5	Cash & Equivalents	12.8	12.2	12.5	12.1	10.6	9.0
48.7	46.6	49.4	Trade Receivables (net)	29.4	41.7	46.6	51.4	55.2	58.8
7.6	7.7	7.5	Inventory	10.6	9.1	9.8	6.8	6.5	4.0
6.6	7.8	7.2	All Other Current	4.1	4.7	5.6	8.4	7.8	10.9
75.5	74.5	75.6	Total Current	56.9	67.7	74.5	78.7	80.2	82.8
17.3	17.9	16.4	Fixed Assets (net)	30.7	23.1	17.8	14.3	12.4	9.7
1.5	1.5	1.9	Intangibles (net)	4.4	2.5	1.6	1.7	1.3	1.9
5.7	6.0	6.0	All Other Non-Current	8.1	6.6	6.1	5.3	6.1	5.5
100.0	100.0	100.0	Total	100.0	100.0	100.0	100.0	100.0	100.0
			LIABILITIES						
10.3	10.7	10.3	Notes Payable-Short Term	12.3	15.2	10.0	9.8	9.1	5.9
3.2	3.8	3.1	Cur. Mat.-L/T/D	5.9	4.4	3.4	3.0	2.1	1.6
23.7	22.4	23.3	Trade Payables	15.3	21.4	23.2	22.4	25.4	27.2
.7	.6	.8	Income Taxes Payable	.2	1.0	.6	1.0	.7	.6
16.1	15.9	16.2	All Other Current	20.3	13.9	11.6	15.1	17.1	23.5
54.0	53.4	53.6	Total Current	54.0	55.9	48.8	51.3	54.4	59.0
9.7	11.1	12.5	Long-Term Debt	42.7	17.6	15.0	7.7	6.5	7.0
.4	.5	.3	Deferred Taxes	.0	.1	.2	.4	.5	.2
3.0	3.5	2.7	All Other Non-Current	4.4	2.7	2.7	2.6	2.5	2.5
32.8	31.5	30.9	Net Worth	−1.2	23.6	33.3	38.0	36.1	31.3
100.0	100.0	100.0	Total Liabilities & Net Worth	100.0	100.0	100.0	100.0	100.0	100.0
			INCOME DATA						
100.0	100.0	100.0	Net Sales	100.0	100.0	100.0	100.0	100.0	100.0
25.8	26.9	25.4	Gross Profit	44.2	32.7	28.3	23.5	19.8	16.2
23.5	24.7	23.1	Operating Expenses	43.3	30.5	26.0	20.6	17.6	13.8
2.3	2.1	2.3	Operating Profit	.9	2.2	2.3	2.9	2.1	2.4
.3	.3	.3	All Other Expenses (net)	.7	.7	.1	.2	.2	.1
2.0	1.8	2.0	Profit Before Taxes	.2	1.5	2.2	2.7	1.9	2.4
			RATIOS						
2.1	2.0	2.1		2.3	2.3	2.3	2.2	2.0	1.6
1.4	1.4	1.5	Current	1.3	1.5	1.5	1.6	1.4	1.4
1.1	1.1	1.2		.7	1.0	1.2	1.2	1.2	1.2
1.7	1.7	1.7		1.8	2.1	1.8	1.7	1.6	1.3
1.2	1.1 (961)	1.2	Quick	(57) 1.0	1.2	1.2	1.3	1.2	1.1
.9	.8	.9		.4	.7	1.0	1.0	1.0	1.0
37 9.8	33 11.0	38 9.6		9 41.5	25 14.7	33 11.2	42 8.7	48 7.6	54 6.7
58 6.3	54 6.8	57 6.4	Sales/Receivables	29 12.7	48 7.6	49 7.5	59 6.2	63 5.8	71 5.1
78 4.7	76 4.8	78 4.7		55 6.6	64 5.7	69 5.3	81 4.5	81 4.5	85 4.3
0 UND	0 UND	0 UND		0 UND	0 UND	1 579.0	0 UND	0 999.8	0 UND
4 87.6	4 83.6	4 88.6	Cost of Sales/Inventory	9 42.0	7 53.2	6 56.6	4 88.2	4 87.1	2 185.5
15 24.5	15 23.7	15 23.9		25 14.8	22 16.5	20 18.0	13 29.0	13 27.8	5 68.5
20 18.6	18 20.5	18 20.2		0 UND	13 27.3	18 20.6	17 21.5	23 16.1	24 15.3
32 11.4	30 12.2	31 11.8	Cost of Sales/Payables	21 17.1	30 12.0	30 12.3	31 11.7	31 11.6	35 10.3
48 7.6	45 8.0	48 7.7		59 6.2	46 8.0	47 7.8	46 7.9	48 7.6	50 7.2
7.9	7.9	7.8		8.7	7.9	7.5	7.3	7.7	8.8
13.7	15.3	13.5	Sales/Working Capital	35.7	15.4	13.2	11.5	13.5	14.6
39.6	48.8	33.3		−22.9	UND	40.5	24.5	28.1	21.8
15.8	14.0	18.4		9.2	7.4	14.2	22.2	23.8	29.2
(701) 4.7	(938) 4.0	(842) 4.8	EBIT/Interest	(40) 2.8	(145) 2.8	(143) 5.3	(199) 6.1	(193) 4.8	(122) 8.7
1.4	.2	1.1		−1.7	.1	.6	1.9	.7	2.8
5.9	5.5	7.3			9.5	3.9	4.8	7.6	12.5
(217) 2.4	(264) 2.2	(252) 2.5	Net Profit + Depr., Dep., Amort./Cur. Mat. L/T/D		(27) 3.0	(39) 1.4	(73) 2.3	(73) 2.5	(36) 5.5
.9	.7	.8			1.2	−.6	.9	.8	2.6
.2	.2	.2		.3	.3	.2	.2	.2	.1
.4	.4	.4	Fixed/Worth	1.3	.6	.4	.3	.3	.3
1.0	1.0	1.0		−21.8	4.7	1.0	.6	.7	.6
.9	.9	1.0		1.4	.7	.8	.9	1.0	1.5
1.9	2.0	2.0	Debt/Worth	2.4	2.0	1.8	1.7	2.0	2.5
4.2	4.4	4.6		−16.6	17.2	4.2	3.9	3.7	4.1
37.3	36.9	39.0	% Profit Before Taxes/Tangible Net Worth	61.5	42.8	43.4	37.2	34.8	35.2
(737) 15.9	(966) 13.3	(858) 16.1		(41) 15.5	(134) 17.6	(146) 16.4	(212) 15.6	(201) 14.1	(124) 16.6
4.0	.4	2.6		−12.0	.7	−.7	5.3	−.3	7.5
11.9	12.7	13.5		18.9	13.3	16.9	13.6	13.9	9.8
4.8	4.1	5.0	% Profit Before Taxes/Total Assets	2.7	4.2	5.7	6.1	4.2	5.4
.8	−.9	.1		−9.3	−2.5	−.9	1.5	−.1	1.9
46.5	46.7	53.6		43.5	40.5	50.6	53.4	49.7	94.1
26.4	25.6	28.2	Sales/Net Fixed Assets	17.1	20.3	25.3	30.7	29.5	43.4
15.0	14.9	15.8		7.0	11.7	14.4	17.0	20.1	23.4
4.0	4.2	4.2		5.4	4.7	4.5	4.2	3.9	3.7
3.1	3.3	3.2	Sales/Total Assets	3.6	3.4	3.4	3.2	3.2	3.1
2.6	2.6	2.5		1.8	2.5	2.6	2.4	2.5	2.5
.7	.7	.6		1.1	.8	.7	.7	.6	.3
(732) 1.3	(914) 1.2	(833) 1.1	% Depr., Dep., Amort./Sales	(40) 2.1	(138) 1.5	(137) 1.3	(206) 1.1	(192) .9	(120) .6
2.1	2.1	1.8		4.2	2.4	2.1	1.8	1.5	1.0
2.2	2.4	2.0		5.3	3.0	2.6	2.0	1.2	.8
(441) 3.9	(589) 4.3	(508) 3.6	% Officers', Directors', Owners' Comp/Sales	(38) 9.8	(102) 4.8	(98) 4.3	(132) 3.4	(104) 2.3	(34) 1.6
7.4	7.3	6.5		15.9	7.6	7.2	5.0	4.6	2.9
12086690M	23658090M	16571432M	Net Sales ($)	31243M	338229M	640110M	1657608M	3165970M	10738272M
4066949M	6186611M	5726947M	Total Assets ($)	12972M	114464M	202773M	569603M	1098046M	3729089M

Current Data Sorted By Assets   **Comparative Historical Data**

0-500M	500M-2MM	2-10MM	10-50MM	50-100MM	100-250MM	Type of Statement	4/1/00-3/31/01 ALL	4/1/01-3/31/02 ALL
1	2	5	3	1		Unqualified	5	3
6	11	11	2		1	Reviewed	21	21
9	6	3	1			Compiled	14	15
8	8	2				Tax Returns	1	2
	4	13	4			Other	14	12
	19 (4/1-9/30/04)		82 (10/1/04-3/31/05)					
24	31	34	10	1	1	**NUMBER OF STATEMENTS**	55	53
%	%	%	%	%	%	**ASSETS**	%	%
23.5	6.7	9.6	14.8			Cash & Equivalents	13.2	13.2
27.2	51.6	48.9	43.5			Trade Receivables (net)	40.5	44.5
6.0	8.1	8.6	11.4			Inventory	8.5	9.7
6.5	5.5	8.6	8.7			All Other Current	8.5	3.2
63.3	71.9	75.8	78.3			Total Current	70.7	70.6
26.1	18.0	17.7	14.1			Fixed Assets (net)	21.5	22.4
2.4	3.5	1.3	.0			Intangibles (net)	2.4	2.9
8.3	6.6	5.2	7.6			All Other Non-Current	5.3	4.2
100.0	100.0	100.0	100.0			Total	100.0	100.0
						LIABILITIES		
18.8	10.3	12.8	7.4			Notes Payable-Short Term	7.5	8.8
1.5	4.2	3.6	3.6			Cur. Mat.-L/T/D	3.2	4.0
22.4	19.3	18.2	24.5			Trade Payables	14.5	20.2
.2	.7	.5	.2			Income Taxes Payable	.5	.8
20.9	14.9	16.4	8.2			All Other Current	13.1	13.3
63.8	49.4	51.4	43.9			Total Current	38.7	47.2
31.3	11.9	10.5	5.9			Long-Term Debt	11.6	12.5
.0	.2	.8	.1			Deferred Taxes	.9	.4
5.5	6.5	2.9	4.8			All Other Non-Current	4.4	2.7
-.5	32.0	34.5	45.1			Net Worth	44.4	37.2
100.0	100.0	100.0	100.0			Total Liabilities & Net Worth	100.0	100.0
						INCOME DATA		
100.0	100.0	100.0	100.0			Net Sales	100.0	100.0
42.2	32.5	27.9	23.3			Gross Profit	29.3	30.8
39.5	31.2	24.0	20.6			Operating Expenses	25.2	27.7
2.7	1.3	3.9	2.7			Operating Profit	4.2	3.1
.3	.5	.3	-.3			All Other Expenses (net)	.3	.6
2.4	.8	3.6	3.1			Profit Before Taxes	3.9	2.5
						RATIOS		
2.4	2.0	1.8	4.1			Current	3.3	2.1
1.3	1.6	1.5	1.8				1.8	1.5
.6	1.1	1.2	1.2				1.4	1.1
2.4	1.9	1.5	3.0			Quick	2.3	1.9
1.1	1.1	1.2	1.6				1.3	1.2
.4	.7	.9	.8				.9	.9
0 UND	41 9.0	41 8.8	50 7.2			Sales/Receivables	38 9.5	44 8.3
25 14.4	59 6.2	64 5.7	65 5.6				57 6.4	56 6.5
51 7.2	78 4.7	91 4.0	90 4.1				70 5.2	73 5.0
0 UND	0 UND	0 753.9	0 UND			Cost of Sales/Inventory	0 UND	0 UND
0 UND	1 447.6	9 42.3	6 57.2				2 215.0	2 177.8
12 29.7	32 11.5	24 15.0	44 8.3				24 15.2	26 13.8
0 UND	11 33.6	11 32.3	17 21.0			Cost of Sales/Payables	13 27.9	17 21.7
17 21.7	32 11.3	33 11.2	34 10.6				22 16.3	30 12.2
100 3.7	46 7.9	46 8.0	72 5.1				36 10.0	50 7.4
10.1	6.7	8.5	3.5			Sales/Working Capital	5.2	8.0
140.4	13.1	11.2	9.8				8.2	13.5
-13.5	51.7	24.3	14.4				20.0	40.7
41.8	13.0	31.7				EBIT/Interest	16.5	10.4
(18) 6.5	(28) 3.9	(33) 4.3					(51) 5.1	(48) 4.2
.4	.8	2.6					1.5	1.8
						Net Profit + Depr., Dep., Amort./Cur. Mat. L./T/D	5.9	8.3
							(14) 2.6	(12) 2.6
							1.5	2.2
.2	.1	.2	.1			Fixed/Worth	.2	.2
1.6	.4	.4	.4				.5	.6
-.7	1.3	1.5	3.2				.9	1.2
.8	1.2	.9	.4			Debt/Worth	.6	1.0
2.4	1.7	2.0	1.0				1.5	1.7
-5.3	4.9	7.0	11.4				2.8	4.0
108.1	32.4	42.5				% Profit Before Taxes/Tangible Net Worth	52.7	30.5
(13) 29.2	(28) 17.3	(31) 19.1					(53) 20.5	(47) 17.1
2.7	3.7	3.6					7.4	4.9
41.1	11.5	14.6	12.3			% Profit Before Taxes/Total Assets	18.5	12.0
4.9	5.1	5.5	7.3				8.0	5.7
-2.5	-.6	1.7	1.2				1.6	.9
78.0	80.4	56.3	59.0			Sales/Net Fixed Assets	32.2	34.4
24.2	26.8	24.6	21.6				17.2	15.4
5.6	12.6	10.6	8.8				8.2	8.1
5.9	3.8	3.7	2.9			Sales/Total Assets	3.5	3.6
4.3	3.2	2.8	2.2				2.7	3.0
2.6	2.5	2.3	1.5				2.2	2.2
.5	.3	.9				% Depr., Dep., Amort./Sales	.9	.8
(13) 1.2	(23) 1.1	(30) 1.4					(51) 1.8	(48) 1.7
3.8	2.9	2.9					3.4	3.5
5.0	3.8	2.4				% Officers', Directors', Owners' Comp/Sales	2.6	2.7
(14) 7.5	(12) 5.4	(11) 5.1					(24) 5.3	(24) 4.9
10.3	7.8	7.4					8.6	10.4
25522M	127792M	386407M	398173M	127486M	243935M	Net Sales ($)	474661M	712359M
5346M	39401M	141635M	169497M	55097M	147896M	Total Assets ($)	223555M	332733M

© RMA 2005

M = $ thousand   MM = $ million
See Pages 11 through 21 for Explanation of Ratios and Data

Comparative Historical Data | Current Data Sorted By Sales

4/1/02-3/31/03 ALL 63	4/1/03-3/31/04 ALL 99	4/1/04-3/31/05 ALL 101	Type of Statement	0-1MM	1-3MM	3-5MM	5-10MM	10-25MM	25MM & OVER
9	12	11	Unqualified			1	3	3	4
25	30	25	Reviewed		6	4	6	7	2
12	23	15	Compiled	4	3	3	5		
5	13	16	Tax Returns	3	6	3	1	2	1
12	21	34	Other	6	6	5	5	8	4
				19 (4/1-9/30/04)			82 (10/1/04-3/31/05)		
63	99	101	**NUMBER OF STATEMENTS**	13	21	16	20	20	11
%	%	%	**ASSETS**	%	%	%	%	%	%
13.9	12.5	12.3	Cash & Equivalents	14.7	17.6	12.1	6.4	12.4	10.5
43.2	41.4	43.8	Trade Receivables (net)	30.1	35.1	45.7	54.0	46.7	50.2
7.3	8.2	8.4	Inventory	9.9	5.9	6.1	7.7	9.3	14.4
8.0	8.9	7.1	All Other Current	1.7	8.8	5.6	7.9	9.1	7.9
72.3	71.0	71.7	Total Current	56.5	67.4	69.6	75.9	77.5	83.0
20.4	20.0	19.5	Fixed Assets (net)	28.8	22.3	21.9	17.1	15.4	11.8
1.0	2.1	2.2	Intangibles (net)	2.4	1.7	5.6	2.1	.7	1.1
6.2	6.9	6.5	All Other Non-Current	12.4	8.7	2.9	4.9	6.4	4.0
100.0	100.0	100.0	Total	100.0	100.0	100.0	100.0	100.0	100.0
			LIABILITIES						
11.5	15.8	13.0	Notes Payable-Short Term	4.1	25.0	10.7	11.0	12.3	8.8
3.1	3.5	3.2	Cur. Mat.-L/T/D	2.1	1.5	4.2	3.7	4.9	2.5
15.4	20.9	20.2	Trade Payables	33.1	9.0	19.9	19.6	19.8	28.8
.4	.4	.4	Income Taxes Payable	.0	.5	.9	.7	.2	.2
15.7	16.2	16.0	All Other Current	25.1	13.5	11.8	17.0	18.3	10.4
46.0	56.8	52.9	Total Current	64.5	49.6	47.5	51.9	55.5	50.7
11.8	12.3	15.6	Long-Term Debt	46.2	12.0	16.6	12.6	7.6	5.2
.6	.3	.4	Deferred Taxes	.0	.3	.7	.2	.5	.4
1.8	5.5	4.9	All Other Non-Current	10.1	6.7	3.8	1.3	3.6	5.3
39.9	25.0	26.3	Net Worth	-20.7	31.4	31.5	33.9	32.8	38.4
100.0	100.0	100.0	Total Liabilities & Net Worth	100.0	100.0	100.0	100.0	100.0	100.0
			INCOME DATA						
100.0	100.0	100.0	Net Sales	100.0	100.0	100.0	100.0	100.0	100.0
28.3	27.4	32.1	Gross Profit	48.4	38.9	35.5	24.0	25.3	21.7
27.3	25.4	29.4	Operating Expenses	46.1	36.7	31.4	22.3	21.8	19.4
1.0	2.0	2.7	Operating Profit	2.3	2.2	4.1	1.8	3.5	2.4
.1	.9	.3	All Other Expenses (net)	.8	.3	.8	-.1	.2	.2
.9	1.1	2.4	Profit Before Taxes	1.5	1.9	3.3	1.9	3.3	2.1
			RATIOS						
2.5	2.0	2.1	Current	1.7	3.3	2.2	1.9	1.7	2.8
1.6	1.3	1.5		.8	1.8	1.4	1.5	1.4	1.5
1.2	1.0	1.1		.5	1.2	1.0	1.2	1.2	1.2
1.8	1.6	1.9	Quick	1.3	2.7	1.9	1.6	1.4	2.3
1.3	(98) 1.0	1.1		.5	1.5	1.2	1.1	1.1	1.0
.9	.7	.7		.3	.7	.7	.9	.8	.8
44 8.3	33 11.0	38 9.7	Sales/Receivables	13 27.6	0 UND	40 9.0	41 9.0	41 8.8	54 6.8
71 5.1	56 6.5	56 6.5		37 9.9	47 7.7	62 5.9	63 5.8	59 6.2	69 5.3
86 4.2	75 4.9	81 4.5		65 5.6	62 5.9	91 4.0	89 4.1	84 4.4	87 4.2
0 UND	0 UND	0 UND	Cost of Sales/Inventory	0 UND	0 UND	0 UND	0 UND	0 UND	0 999.8
4 83.2	1 273.5	4 98.2		0 UND	0 UND	1 549.0	4 96.0	9 42.3	6 59.8
31 11.9	24 15.5	28 12.9		38 9.6	12 31.4	35 10.3	24 15.4	21 17.2	62 5.9
12 29.5	14 26.2	10 35.3	Cost of Sales/Payables	14 26.2	0 UND	18 20.6	11 33.2	15 25.1	23 16.0
25 14.6	32 11.5	32 11.4		95 3.9	10 37.3	42 8.6	30 12.2	33 11.0	35 10.5
46 7.9	52 7.0	53 6.9		159 2.3	20 17.9	65 5.6	44 8.3	46 7.9	66 5.5
5.9	7.8	8.4	Sales/Working Capital	9.8	7.2	7.4	9.5	7.4	4.3
11.0	13.2	12.3		-17.8	10.8	22.0	11.4	11.4	9.9
24.3	770.0	52.4		-8.4	187.8	NM	23.1	28.0	13.5
12.4	9.5	21.9	EBIT/Interest		36.3	14.1	22.6	33.0	
(56) 3.7	(90) 2.1	(89) 4.4		(16) 5.9		5.8	(19) 4.1	6.3	
.3		-1.1		1.1	2.4	-.3	1.1	3.3	
3.7	3.3	7.5	Net Profit + Depr., Dep.,						
(17) 1.4	(16) 1.6	(18) 2.4	Amort./Cur. Mat. L/T/D						
.8	-.5	1.3							
.2	.2	.2	Fixed/Worth	.4	.1	.2	.1	.2	.1
.3	.7	.4		-2.9	.4	.8	.3	.4	.2
1.0	5.6	3.2		-.8	1.9	5.0	1.1	2.4	.7
.7	1.2	1.0	Debt/Worth	1.6	.5	.7	1.2	1.0	.5
1.6	2.4	2.1		-11.1	1.5	2.0	2.0	2.6	2.9
3.2	21.9	7.2		-2.8	4.2	9.8	6.3	6.9	6.5
28.1	32.5	41.7	% Profit Before Taxes/Tangible Net Worth		27.9	50.9	42.1	46.4	26.6
(59) 9.0	(78) 7.7	(83) 19.1		(18) 13.7	(13) 21.8	(18) 18.0	(19) 30.5	(10) 17.1	
-.8	-12.5	3.6		-12.9	10.2	5.5	5.5	-6.9	
9.7	12.2	14.2	% Profit Before Taxes/Total Assets	14.2	24.2	16.1	14.7	14.3	11.8
3.3	1.6	5.6		.3	7.7	7.6	5.0	7.3	7.7
-3.1	-3.6	.2		-5.0	.6	-3.8	.6	2.8	-.1
39.2	44.4	68.7	Sales/Net Fixed Assets	30.5	191.8	71.9	109.1	45.0	135.7
20.6	22.1	24.9		13.9	24.6	25.5	32.4	32.7	28.7
8.0	10.0	9.7		4.4	8.3	4.8	15.4	10.9	12.5
3.3	3.9	4.1	Sales/Total Assets	4.8	5.1	3.9	3.7	4.0	3.0
2.6	2.7	2.9		2.7	3.6	2.6	3.0	2.9	2.4
1.9	2.1	2.3		1.8	2.2	1.7	2.6	2.4	2.0
.9	.6	.6	% Depr., Dep., Amort./Sales		.5	.6	.4	.9	.2
(60) 1.7	(84) 1.4	(77) 1.4		(14) 1.3	(13) 1.3	(14) 1.1	(19) 1.4	(10) .8	
4.1	2.3	2.9			2.9	5.2	2.4	2.1	1.8
2.8	2.2	4.1	% Officers', Directors', Owners' Comp/Sales		5.9				
(32) 4.6	(43) 4.1	(38) 5.9		(12) 7.9					
7.3	8.4	8.8			10.1				
3962584M	1506092M	1309315M	Net Sales ($)	7079M	39254M	61043M	150772M	275786M	775381M
566980M	652416M	558872M	Total Assets ($)	2650M	12242M	29037M	49176M	107543M	358224M

© RMA 2005

M = $ thousand   MM = $ million

See Pages 11 through 21 for Explanation of Ratios and Data

Current Data Sorted By Assets   Comparative Historical Data

	0-500M	500M-2MM	2-10MM	10-50MM	50-100MM	100-250MM	Type of Statement	4/1/00-3/31/01 ALL	4/1/01-3/31/02 ALL
	1	4	11	19	2	2	Unqualified	22	27
	4	40	67	6			Reviewed	71	71
	9	23	14			1	Compiled	48	49
	22	14	6	1			Tax Returns	20	20
	9	23	31	9	1		Other	49	46
	78 (4/1-9/30/04)			241 (10/1/04-3/31/05)					
NUMBER OF STATEMENTS	45	104	129	35	3	3		210	213
	%	%	%	%	%	%	**ASSETS**	%	%
	15.5	9.8	7.6	7.2			Cash & Equivalents	11.5	10.1
	39.4	52.1	54.1	60.4			Trade Receivables (net)	54.2	53.2
	7.0	5.5	6.4	3.8			Inventory	5.5	5.3
	5.4	5.9	10.3	14.0			All Other Current	7.2	8.5
	67.2	73.2	78.4	85.4			Total Current	78.4	77.1
	22.0	17.4	13.5	10.1			Fixed Assets (net)	14.8	14.2
	2.2	1.9	2.0	.5			Intangibles (net)	1.3	1.6
	8.6	7.5	6.2	4.0			All Other Non-Current	5.6	7.0
	100.0	100.0	100.0	100.0			Total	100.0	100.0
							LIABILITIES		
	22.5	14.0	15.4	10.1			Notes Payable-Short Term	14.1	12.6
	4.4	3.0	1.8	2.1			Cur. Mat.-L/T/D	2.1	2.3
	15.7	17.7	16.6	17.9			Trade Payables	16.1	16.3
	.1	.5	.9	.2			Income Taxes Payable	.9	.5
	23.8	11.6	14.4	24.3			All Other Current	16.7	16.8
	66.5	46.7	49.1	54.5			Total Current	49.8	48.5
	20.5	10.7	6.3	4.9			Long-Term Debt	7.4	8.7
	.1	.8	.5	.3			Deferred Taxes	.6	.8
	1.5	3.7	4.2	1.5			All Other Non-Current	2.0	2.9
	11.3	38.2	39.9	38.8			Net Worth	40.1	39.2
	100.0	100.0	100.0	100.0			Total Liabilities & Net Worth	100.0	100.0
							INCOME DATA		
	100.0	100.0	100.0	100.0			Net Sales	100.0	100.0
	38.0	22.7	18.6	16.1			Gross Profit	23.4	23.5
	34.9	20.6	15.5	13.9			Operating Expenses	19.1	19.7
	3.2	2.1	3.1	2.2			Operating Profit	4.3	3.8
	.1	.4	.3	.1			All Other Expenses (net)	.4	.4
	3.1	1.7	2.8	2.1			Profit Before Taxes	3.9	3.4
							RATIOS		
	2.6	2.8	2.1	2.3				2.5	2.4
	1.6	1.6	1.5	1.6			Current	1.6	1.6
	.9	1.2	1.2	1.2				1.3	1.2
	2.6	2.3	1.8	1.7				2.1	2.1
	1.5	1.4	1.2	1.2			Quick	1.3	1.3
	.6	.9	.9	.9				1.0	1.0
	0 UND	42 8.8	46 7.9	57 6.4				44 8.4	42 8.6
	26 14.0	64 5.7	65 5.6	78 4.7			Sales/Receivables	61 6.0	62 5.9
	63 5.8	84 4.4	82 4.5	91 4.0				82 4.5	81 4.5
	0 UND	0 UND	0 999.8	0 UND				0 UND	0 UND
	0 UND	1 288.0	4 81.9	2 153.6			Cost of Sales/Inventory	2 178.0	1 253.3
	10 36.8	14 25.2	13 27.6	7 52.7				9 39.9	10 37.9
	0 UND	11 32.4	12 31.0	13 27.7				12 31.4	11 32.2
	13 28.2	21 17.6	19 19.7	19 18.8			Cost of Sales/Payables	17 21.0	18 20.6
	31 11.6	32 11.3	33 11.1	30 12.1				29 12.4	27 13.5
	10.6	6.4	7.6	5.9				6.6	6.3
	27.1	11.5	10.9	9.6			Sales/Working Capital	11.4	10.5
	−107.4	35.9	26.9	19.2				27.3	27.7
	15.2	13.3	19.2	55.6				25.5	19.2
	(29) 5.0	(91) 4.1	(119) 7.3	(32) 12.5			EBIT/Interest	(186) 6.2	(192) 5.4
	1.3	1.0	1.9	2.2				1.7	1.7
		5.5	8.0	23.8			Net Profit + Depr., Dep.,	14.1	12.3
		(14) 2.1	(39) 2.9	(11) 6.1			Amort./Cur. Mat. L./T/D	(46) 3.5	(46) 4.4
		.2	1.4	1.0				1.1	1.7
	.2	.1	.1	.1				.1	.1
	.5	.4	.3	.2			Fixed/Worth	.3	.3
	−23.3	1.2	.7	.5				.7	.7
	.8	.7	.8	.8				.7	.7
	2.9	1.5	1.7	1.7			Debt/Worth	1.4	1.5
	−25.1	5.4	3.5	3.2				3.3	3.5
	104.4	52.0	34.9	38.5			% Profit Before Taxes/Tangible	58.3	47.3
	(30) 16.1	(92) 16.5	(122) 18.1	16.9			Net Worth	(200) 26.4	(194) 17.7
	.0	1.4	3.1	6.7				7.1	4.4
	51.1	13.8	16.0	14.2			% Profit Before Taxes/Total	22.8	17.7
	8.7	4.7	6.1	4.7			Assets	9.2	7.4
	−.8	−.2	1.2	1.3				2.3	1.5
	123.4	62.6	72.4	132.9				67.1	65.8
	41.6	26.8	35.0	66.0			Sales/Net Fixed Assets	34.3	33.8
	15.2	14.6	18.3	26.1				18.4	17.2
	10.0	4.5	4.0	3.4				4.3	4.0
	4.9	3.2	3.1	3.1			Sales/Total Assets	3.3	3.1
	3.1	2.2	2.5	2.7				2.6	2.5
	.5	.6	.4	.2				.5	.4
	(22) 1.3	(83) 1.0	(114) .8	(31) .5			% Depr., Dep., Amort./Sales	(183) .8	(190) .9
	2.5	2.0	1.3	1.0				1.5	1.5
	3.0	3.5	1.4	.7				2.2	2.3
	(32) 4.9	(55) 5.4	(73) 2.3	(12) 2.4			% Officers', Directors',	(119) 4.6	(126) 4.1
	10.3	7.6	4.2	4.1			Owners' Comp/Sales	7.2	7.3
	66325M	423260M	1825007M	2083570M	568174M	3873703M	Net Sales ($)	3435895M	3507584M
	11518M	122107M	556879M	714053M	202425M	535528M	Total Assets ($)	1185333M	1198869M

© RMA 2005

M = $ thousand   MM = $ million
See Pages 11 through 21 for Explanation of Ratios and Data

Comparative Historical Data | Current Data Sorted By Sales

			Type of Statement						
36	41	39	Unqualified	1	2	20	2	9	25
92	134	117	Reviewed	19			32	35	11
40	78	47	Compiled	5	13	8	8	10	3
25	55	43	Tax Returns	12	11	7	8	3	2
38	73	73	Other	3	17	5	20	17	11
4/1/02-3/31/03	4/1/03-3/31/04	4/1/04-3/31/05		78 (4/1-9/30/04)			241 (10/1/04-3/31/05)		
ALL	ALL	ALL		0-1MM	1-3MM	3-5MM	5-10MM	10-25MM	25MM & OVER
231	381	319	**NUMBER OF STATEMENTS**	21	62	40	70	74	52
%	%	%	**ASSETS**	%	%	%	%	%	%
10.3	10.8	9.5	Cash & Equivalents	21.8	9.0	11.2	9.0	6.7	8.4
52.7	51.4	51.8	Trade Receivables (net)	32.0	46.9	51.5	52.3	55.1	60.4
5.8	5.0	6.0	Inventory	8.6	6.5	3.7	6.7	6.7	4.3
9.1	8.5	8.6	All Other Current	4.1	6.9	4.6	9.5	9.3	13.4
77.9	75.6	75.9	Total Current	66.5	69.3	71.0	77.6	77.8	86.5
12.7	15.6	15.5	Fixed Assets (net)	28.8	19.2	15.4	15.4	14.0	7.8
3.2	2.1	2.0	Intangibles (net)	.1	4.1	2.6	.7	1.7	2.0
6.1	6.7	6.6	All Other Non-Current	4.5	7.4	11.0	6.3	6.5	3.7
100.0	100.0	100.0	Total	100.0	100.0	100.0	100.0	100.0	100.0
			LIABILITIES						
12.8	14.3	15.3	Notes Payable-Short Term	34.3	14.8	11.5	14.7	15.5	11.6
2.4	2.9	2.6	Cur. Mat.-L/T/D	5.0	3.7	1.9	2.3	2.5	1.4
14.8	16.7	16.9	Trade Payables	6.7	16.5	16.9	17.4	18.4	18.5
.8	.3	.6	Income Taxes Payable	.1	.3	.5	1.1	.7	.2
17.3	15.1	16.0	All Other Current	8.8	20.5	13.2	12.5	14.2	22.9
48.1	49.3	51.3	Total Current	54.8	55.8	43.9	47.9	51.4	54.5
8.4	10.2	9.8	Long-Term Debt	24.5	12.2	11.1	9.6	6.3	5.5
.6	.5	.5	Deferred Taxes	.0	.9	.6	.7	.4	.1
3.4	3.7	3.4	All Other Non-Current	3.0	3.3	4.7	3.0	3.6	2.8
39.6	36.4	35.0	Net Worth	17.4	27.9	39.7	38.7	38.2	37.2
100.0	100.0	100.0	Total Liabilities & Net Worth	100.0	100.0	100.0	100.0	100.0	100.0
			INCOME DATA						
100.0	100.0	100.0	Net Sales	100.0	100.0	100.0	100.0	100.0	100.0
23.3	23.0	22.4	Gross Profit	46.3	28.9	22.8	18.8	18.0	16.0
20.2	20.5	19.8	Operating Expenses	44.7	27.1	19.0	15.6	15.5	13.1
3.1	2.4	2.7	Operating Profit	1.6	1.8	3.8	3.2	2.4	2.9
.1	.2	.3	All Other Expenses (net)	-.3	.3	.5	.4	.2	.2
2.9	2.2	2.4	Profit Before Taxes	1.9	1.5	3.3	2.8	2.2	2.8
			RATIOS						
2.5	2.5	2.4		3.4	2.9	2.3	2.4	2.0	2.3
1.7	1.6	1.5	Current	1.8	1.6	1.7	1.6	1.4	1.5
1.2	1.2	1.2		.7	1.1	1.2	1.2	1.2	1.3
1.9	2.0	2.0		2.9	2.4	2.3	2.1	1.7	1.7
1.4	1.3	1.3	Quick	1.5	1.3	1.4	1.3	1.1	1.3
1.0	.9	.9		.5	.7	1.0	.9	.9	1.0
42 8.8	40 9.1	40 9.1		0 UND	36 10.1	40 9.1	36 10.3	43 8.5	49 7.5
64 5.7	60 6.0	62 5.9	Sales/Receivables	30 12.0	62 5.8	66 5.6	63 5.8	58 6.3	65 5.6
81 4.5	83 4.4	83 4.4		99 3.7	85 4.3	91 4.0	80 4.6	77 4.7	87 4.2
0 UND	0 UND	0 UND		0 UND	0 UND	0 UND	0 UND	0 UND	0 UND
2 147.0	1 374.1	3 143.5	Cost of Sales/Inventory	6 56.3	3 113.8	1 544.1	2 182.9	5 79.8	2 173.0
12 31.4	9 42.4	13 27.9		25 14.4	22 17.0	9 40.4	15 23.6	13 29.0	5 77.1
10 35.1	10 36.1	11 32.8		0 UND	11 34.3	8 46.9	12 31.6	12 30.9	13 28.6
17 21.5	20 18.4	19 18.8	Cost of Sales/Payables	12 29.7	22 16.6	16 22.5	19 19.4	21 17.4	19 18.7
26 13.9	34 10.7	32 11.5		25 14.8	37 9.8	28 13.2	33 11.0	34 10.7	27 13.7
6.3	6.2	7.1		5.6	5.5	6.7	6.4	8.9	6.9
11.7	11.8	11.8	Sales/Working Capital	17.0	12.2	12.3	10.8	13.9	10.7
30.9	36.6	33.6		-26.6	257.3	29.4	25.3	34.1	19.9
19.3	15.2	18.4		11.8	14.7	11.8	18.3	19.6	24.9
(203) 4.7	(329) 5.0	(276) 6.1	EBIT/Interest	(14) 4.7	(50) 3.4	(34) 4.8	(61) 6.6	(72) 7.0	(45) 11.2
2.0	1.0	1.6		.6	.4	1.2	2.2	1.7	3.1
8.5	9.1	8.0	Net Profit + Depr., Dep.,				6.8	5.5	24.7
(57) 2.6	(78) 2.8	(67) 2.9	Amort./Cur. Mat. L/T/D			(15) 3.7	(29) 2.3	(14) 8.5
1.1	.9	1.0					.9	1.2	2.3
.1	.1	.1		.2	.1	.1	.1	.2	.1
.2	.3	.3	Fixed/Worth	1.2	.3	.3	.3	.4	.2
.7	.9	.9		-15.3	1.7	1.2	.8	.6	.4
.8	.7	.8		1.1	.6	.7	.6	.9	1.0
1.5	1.6	1.7	Debt/Worth	4.8	1.4	1.6	1.6	1.8	1.8
3.5	4.4	4.6		-64.5	16.3	4.4	5.3	3.5	3.5
39.8	36.6	45.4	% Profit Before Taxes/Tangible	111.1	33.5	57.3	52.1	35.5	40.6
(211) 16.7	(338) 14.4	(284) 17.5	Net Worth	(15) 24.3	(48) 8.2	(36) 15.2	(62) 24.9	(72) 17.8	(51) 20.3
4.6	.3	1.9		.0	-2.5	1.4	5.9	3.8	8.6
16.8	14.6	16.2	% Profit Before Taxes/Total	45.8	13.3	23.7	18.4	14.1	14.9
6.5	4.9	5.6	Assets	3.5	2.4	7.4	8.3	5.3	8.5
1.7	-.1	.6		-5.8	-2.4	.4	1.8	.7	3.1
73.0	74.3	83.4		61.6	60.5	91.3	65.5	73.9	140.4
39.2	35.7	34.3	Sales/Net Fixed Assets	17.0	22.2	34.2	34.5	32.2	71.6
19.3	19.2	17.3		11.9	9.4	19.6	18.2	19.8	30.4
4.1	4.3	4.3		10.6	3.8	4.7	4.2	4.3	3.9
3.2	3.3	3.2	Sales/Total Assets	2.9	2.8	3.3	3.2	3.5	3.2
2.6	2.5	2.5		2.0	2.0	2.3	2.7	2.8	2.8
.5	.4	.5		.8	.8	.6	.6	.5	.2
(207) .9	(320) .9	(254) .8	% Depr., Dep., Amort./Sales	(10) 2.6	(41) 1.4	(31) .9	(60) .9	(68) .7	(44) .4
1.4	1.7	1.6		3.3	2.4	1.8	1.6	1.2	.8
2.4	2.0	1.9	% Officers', Directors',	2.8	3.6	3.0	1.9	1.3	1.2
(138) 4.1	(217) 3.6	(174) 3.7	Owners' Comp/Sales	(14) 8.2	(35) 6.3	(25) 4.1	(35) 3.5	(45) 2.3	(20) 2.3
6.7	6.3	6.3		13.7	9.3	6.6	4.9	4.3	3.7
6802635M	11675681M	8840039M	Net Sales ($)	12978M	117856M	156133M	502917M	1137235M	6912920M
2014541M	2519499M	2142510M	Total Assets ($)	4193M	48950M	51120M	180524M	356562M	1501161M

© RMA 2005

M = $ thousand   MM = $ million
See Pages 11 through 21 for Explanation of Ratios and Data

Current Data Sorted By Assets   **Comparative Historical Data**

						Type of Statement		
1	2	6	6			Unqualified	17	11
1	22	27	1			Reviewed	37	44
14	17	3	1			Compiled	35	33
17	11	2	1			Tax Returns	15	14
9	20	12	3			Other	21	29
	43 (4/1-9/30/04)		133 (10/1/04-3/31/05)				4/1/00-3/31/01	4/1/01-3/31/02
0-500M	500M-2MM	2-10MM	10-50MM	50-100MM	100-250MM		ALL	ALL
42	72	50	12			NUMBER OF STATEMENTS	125	131
%	%	%	%	%	%	**ASSETS**	%	%
16.6	9.1	8.3	12.3	D	D	Cash & Equivalents	10.9	12.0
28.7	53.8	56.2	51.9	A	A	Trade Receivables (net)	45.1	45.4
4.5	4.2	2.0	2.1	T	T	Inventory	4.0	3.3
5.9	5.6	10.7	13.8	A	A	All Other Current	5.6	7.2
55.7	72.6	77.2	80.1			Total Current	65.5	67.9
31.8	19.6	14.7	12.1	N	N	Fixed Assets (net)	24.2	21.2
1.1	1.1	1.8	4.3	O	O	Intangibles (net)	1.8	2.2
11.4	6.7	6.3	3.4	T	T	All Other Non-Current	8.5	8.6
100.0	100.0	100.0	100.0			Total	100.0	100.0
				A	A	**LIABILITIES**		
29.4	16.7	8.5	6.8	V	V	Notes Payable-Short Term	13.8	13.5
5.9	3.2	3.2	4.8	A	A	Cur. Mat.-L/T/D	3.8	3.5
18.3	14.5	13.8	18.8	I	I	Trade Payables	14.3	13.3
.0	.9	1.8	.2	L	L	Income Taxes Payable	.7	.7
14.6	9.9	13.8	13.8	A	A	All Other Current	14.2	15.0
68.2	45.1	41.1	44.5	B	B	Total Current	46.7	46.0
32.3	10.6	6.0	7.7	L	L	Long-Term Debt	10.1	10.2
.1	.5	.7	.1	E	E	Deferred Taxes	.8	.8
1.4	3.4	2.9	1.2			All Other Non-Current	1.8	2.4
-2.1	40.3	49.3	46.6			Net Worth	40.6	40.6
100.0	100.0	100.0	100.0			Total Liabilities & Net Worth	100.0	100.0
						INCOME DATA		
100.0	100.0	100.0	100.0			Net Sales	100.0	100.0
46.7	31.0	24.1	19.1			Gross Profit	34.0	30.3
42.3	27.6	21.5	15.2			Operating Expenses	31.5	25.8
4.4	3.4	2.6	4.0			Operating Profit	2.5	4.5
1.3	.3	.0	.2			All Other Expenses (net)	-.7	.6
3.1	3.1	2.7	3.8			Profit Before Taxes	3.2	3.9
						RATIOS		
2.2	2.5	2.8	2.4				2.3	2.5
1.1	1.8	1.8	1.7			Current	1.6	1.6
.5	1.2	1.5	1.3				1.1	1.0
2.0	2.2	2.3	2.1				2.0	2.3
.8	1.3	1.5	1.5			Quick	1.3 (130)	1.4
.4	1.0	1.1	1.1				.8	.9
0 UND	38 9.5	60 6.1	74 5.0				41 9.0	38 9.7
23 15.7	67 5.4	77 4.8	79 4.6			Sales/Receivables	61 5.9	67 5.5
40 9.0	93 3.9	106 3.4	101 3.6				88 4.1	91 4.0
0 UND	0 UND	0 UND	0 UND				0 UND	0 UND
0 UND	0 UND	0 999.8	2 240.5			Cost of Sales/Inventory	0 999.8	0 UND
0 UND	7 49.6	2 234.6	5 69.4				9 40.7	6 61.0
0 UND	8 45.8	13 27.2	20 18.3				11 33.4	8 44.7
14 25.9	20 18.5	23 15.8	31 11.6			Cost of Sales/Payables	23 16.1	19 19.3
40 9.2	35 10.4	35 10.5	47 7.8				42 8.6	38 9.7
7.6	6.2	5.6	5.5				6.0	6.0
95.5	12.9	7.4	8.8			Sales/Working Capital	11.3	12.7
-18.5	34.4	14.3	12.4				45.5	580.5
9.0	19.3	35.7	19.6				8.8	13.3
(31) 4.3	(66) 5.6	(47) 5.7	(10) 9.8			EBIT/Interest	(107) 3.9	(111) 4.1
1.1	1.8	2.4	5.0				1.5	1.2
		30.3					8.7	12.5
	(15) 6.6					Net Profit + Depr., Dep., Amort./Cur. Mat. L /T/D	(33) 3.8	(30) 3.0
	.9						1.2	1.7
.3	.2	.1	.1				.2	.2
.9	.4	.2	.2			Fixed/Worth	.5	.4
-2.1	.9	.6	1.2				1.1	1.2
.7	.7	.5	.6				.6	.7
3.9	1.4	1.2	1.4			Debt/Worth	1.3	1.2
-4.1	4.4	2.4	2.7				3.3	4.3
140.9	49.6	32.8	28.9				40.9	56.0
(28) 39.6	(67) 13.7	(49) 12.6	17.6			% Profit Before Taxes/Tangible Net Worth	(112) 16.2	(116) 20.9
2.4	3.6	6.2	11.6				5.7	6.8
59.2	14.0	17.8	10.6				16.8	17.0
9.7	5.3	5.1	8.8			% Profit Before Taxes/Total Assets	6.0	8.0
-1.4	1.3	1.8	4.3				1.5	.8
72.6	55.3	55.1	115.9				28.0	42.7
25.6	20.6	22.3	17.7			Sales/Net Fixed Assets	15.1	19.5
10.9	11.1	12.8	14.6				8.3	9.1
13.0	3.9	3.4	2.8				3.5	3.8
5.0	3.2	2.6	2.5			Sales/Total Assets	2.6	2.7
2.8	2.2	2.0	1.8				2.0	2.0
.6	.8	.6	.4				.9	.7
(30) 1.5	(60) 1.2	(45) 1.4	.8			% Depr., Dep., Amort./Sales	(113) 1.6	(112) 1.5
2.7	1.9	2.1	2.2				2.9	2.9
6.7	2.8	2.0					3.3	2.6
(28) 8.4	(42) 4.7	(26) 3.1				% Officers', Directors', Owners' Comp/Sales	(67) 6.8	(67) 5.0
16.1	7.9	6.1					11.1	7.7
51030M	235282M	481528M	520052M			Net Sales ($)	742274M	804277M
8588M	76193M	183497M	223720M			Total Assets ($)	312085M	324905M

M = $ thousand   MM = $ million
See Pages 11 through 21 for Explanation of Ratios and Data

Comparative Historical Data | Current Data Sorted By Sales

			Type of Statement						
15	27	15	Unqualified		1	2	2	5	5
54	78	51	Reviewed	1	12	11	15	11	1
26	54	35	Compiled	8	12	9	5		1
22	38	31	Tax Returns	13	11	3	3	1	
14	57	44	Other	2	15	12	8	4	3
4/1/02-3/31/03 ALL	4/1/03-3/31/04 ALL	4/1/04-3/31/05 ALL		43 (4/1-9/30/04)			133 (10/1/04-3/31/05)		
				0-1MM	1-3MM	3-5MM	5-10MM	10-25MM	25MM & OVER
131	254	176	NUMBER OF STATEMENTS	24	51	37	33	21	10
%	%	%	ASSETS	%	%	%	%	%	%
12.8	12.3	10.9	Cash & Equivalents	16.9	12.6	7.2	10.3	6.5	11.7
42.5	43.0	48.4	Trade Receivables (net)	26.7	47.6	49.0	56.2	58.2	55.6
4.6	3.4	3.5	Inventory	3.1	4.8	3.3	4.0	1.0	2.2
6.8	9.1	7.7	All Other Current	8.3	5.0	6.4	6.7	14.7	12.6
66.7	67.8	70.4	Total Current	55.0	70.0	65.9	77.3	80.3	82.1
23.3	23.6	20.6	Fixed Assets (net)	31.6	22.9	22.8	15.1	11.0	12.9
2.1	1.4	1.5	Intangibles (net)	1.1	1.5	1.8	.7	2.2	2.4
7.9	7.2	7.5	All Other Non-Current	12.2	5.6	9.4	6.9	6.5	2.6
100.0	100.0	100.0	Total	100.0	100.0	100.0	100.0	100.0	100.0
			LIABILITIES						
11.7	16.0	16.7	Notes Payable-Short Term	35.1	16.4	16.5	12.3	8.6	6.6
4.1	3.8	3.9	Cur. Mat.-L/T/D	1.6	6.0	4.9	2.2	3.1	3.2
13.7	14.6	15.5	Trade Payables	15.9	14.3	14.5	18.5	12.4	21.0
.5	.5	.9	Income Taxes Payable	.0	.6	2.3	1.1	.3	.2
14.9	15.9	12.4	All Other Current	20.8	8.0	10.0	11.9	17.3	14.6
44.8	50.8	49.5	Total Current	73.4	45.3	48.2	46.1	41.7	45.6
13.0	12.3	14.3	Long-Term Debt	27.7	16.6	15.7	6.2	6.7	7.5
.3	.7	.4	Deferred Taxes	.0	.6	.8	.4	.2	.1
5.3	6.7	2.7	All Other Non-Current	2.3	4.4	1.1	3.6	.6	1.4
36.5	29.5	33.1	Net Worth	-3.4	33.1	34.2	43.7	50.7	45.3
100.0	100.0	100.0	Total Liabilities & Net Worth	100.0	100.0	100.0	100.0	100.0	100.0
			INCOME DATA						
100.0	100.0	100.0	Net Sales	100.0	100.0	100.0	100.0	100.0	100.0
29.9	32.2	32.0	Gross Profit	55.1	35.2	29.8	23.9	21.4	16.8
27.6	29.3	28.5	Operating Expenses	49.8	31.6	26.9	21.9	17.1	13.3
2.2	3.0	3.5	Operating Profit	5.3	3.6	2.9	2.0	4.3	3.4
.8	.7	.4	All Other Expenses (net)	1.6	.4	.4	.0	.1	.2
1.4	2.3	3.0	Profit Before Taxes	3.7	3.2	2.5	2.0	4.2	3.3
			RATIOS						
2.7	2.4	2.5		2.4	2.8	2.2	3.0	2.7	2.4
1.6	1.5	1.6	Current	1.5	1.5	1.6	1.8	1.9	1.7
1.1	1.0	1.1		.5	1.0	1.2	1.2	1.5	1.5
2.3	2.0	2.2		2.0	2.4	1.9	2.5	2.2	2.1
1.3	1.2	1.4	Quick	.8	1.3	1.3	1.6	1.4	1.5
.9	.8	.9		.4	.9	.9	1.0	1.2	1.2
36 10.3	33 11.2	33 10.9		0 UND	34 10.8	33 11.0	40 9.2	55 6.6	67 5.5
59 6.2	58 6.3	65 5.6	Sales/Receivables	5 69.4	55 6.6	75 4.9	69 5.3	68 5.4	76 4.8
82 4.5	82 4.4	93 3.9		89 4.1	86 4.2	111 3.3	93 3.9	95 3.8	97 3.8
0 UND	0 UND	0 UND		0 UND	0 UND	0 UND	0 UND	0 UND	0 UND
0 UND	0 UND	0 UND	Cost of Sales/Inventory	0 UND	0 UND	0 UND	1 660.7	0 UND	2 240.5
10 36.0	6 64.5	3 126.0		0 UND	6 60.8	3 106.5	5 71.0	1 250.0	3 128.1
8 45.3	9 39.9	9 41.5		0 UND	6 58.0	11 33.7	11 34.4	9 38.5	19 19.1
19 19.6	20 17.8	21 17.1	Cost of Sales/Payables	21 17.7	22 17.0	18 20.0	23 16.1	21 17.1	31 11.6
34 10.7	42 8.6	36 10.1		35 10.5	48 7.6	32 11.4	37 9.8	29 12.7	52 7.1
6.2	6.2	6.3		6.7	6.4	7.0	5.6	5.8	5.7
11.6	13.9	11.3	Sales/Working Capital	69.5	13.9	12.4	8.9	7.9	8.8
79.9	122.5	38.1		-16.8	222.4	21.8	35.4	14.8	10.6
10.0	11.0	18.4		7.9	14.4	23.2	15.7	69.0	
(119) 3.9	(223) 3.4	(154) 5.7	EBIT/Interest	(16) 3.9	(45) 5.7	(34) 4.5	(31) 4.7	(20) 9.1	
.5	.2	1.8		1.1	1.8	1.7	1.7	3.5	
10.1	5.5	14.9	Net Profit + Depr., Dep.,						
(29) 3.1	(58) 2.3	(27) 4.7	Amort./Cur. Mat. L/T/D						
1.4	.9	2.2							
.2	.2	.1		.1	.2	.2	.2	.1	.1
.5	.6	.4	Fixed/Worth	.6	.7	.4	.3	.2	.2
1.3	1.5	1.3		-1.4	2.1	.9	.8	.4	.7
.6	.7	.6		.5	.7	.7	.5	.5	.7
1.5	1.6	1.5	Debt/Worth	3.1	2.2	1.4	1.3	.8	1.4
4.4	4.8	4.4		-2.9	8.5	2.7	3.9	2.1	2.2
27.1	39.6	48.5		164.3	73.0	41.7	24.3	55.0	25.8
(114) 10.1	(222) 12.2	(156) 14.4	% Profit Before Taxes/Tangible Net Worth	(15) 14.7	(44) 15.6	(34) 17.9	(32) 9.9	20.4	17.6
1.2	.1	4.4		.0	3.7	3.6	4.6	7.2	11.7
12.9	14.8	17.2		67.6	16.4	17.6	9.7	22.3	10.3
4.5	4.2	5.4	% Profit Before Taxes/Total Assets	9.7	6.2	5.3	3.7	10.9	8.8
-1.5	-1.7	1.5		-6.2	1.7	1.0	1.0	3.0	3.7
34.3	35.9	60.0		144.3	61.6	40.7	60.9	92.9	130.9
16.4	16.2	21.1	Sales/Net Fixed Assets	21.6	17.6	19.2	33.0	35.6	26.5
9.0	8.8	11.8		10.9	8.5	10.7	16.0	16.3	15.4
3.9	3.7	4.2		11.6	4.5	3.9	3.9	3.9	3.1
2.7	2.8	3.0	Sales/Total Assets	5.6	3.4	2.5	2.8	3.4	2.5
2.0	2.0	2.2		2.5	2.1	2.0	2.3	2.4	2.4
.8	.9	.6		.6	.9	.8	.6	.4	.3
(119) 1.7	(217) 1.8	(147) 1.3	% Depr., Dep., Amort./Sales	(15) 1.1	(44) 1.5	(33) 1.3	(25) .9	(20) 1.2	.6
3.1	3.4	2.2		3.4	2.3	2.5	1.9	1.8	1.9
2.4	3.0	2.8		7.8	2.8	3.1	2.8	.9	
(70) 5.4	(140) 6.5	(98) 5.3	% Officers', Directors', Owners' Comp/Sales	(16) 11.5	(29) 5.9	(23) 4.4	(19) 3.7	(10) 2.3	
8.7	10.2	8.2		18.2	10.2	6.4	6.1	5.0	
1701834M	3597976M	1287892M	Net Sales ($)	13697M	98398M	143532M	242039M	302592M	487634M
422281M	1033318M	491998M	Total Assets ($)	3258M	34727M	60379M	81468M	116699M	195467M

M = $ thousand   MM = $ million
See Pages 11 through 21 for Explanation of Ratios and Data

Current Data Sorted By Assets   Comparative Historical Data

Type of Statement

	0-500M	500M-2MM	2-10MM	10-50MM	50-100MM	100-250MM	Type of Statement	4/1/00-3/31/01 ALL	4/1/01-3/31/02 ALL
Unqualified		1	3	2				3	3
Reviewed		11	23	4				19	23
Compiled	9	15	3					19	31
Tax Returns	12	15	3					6	11
Other	7	21	17	4	1			14	17
		14 (4/1-9/30/04)		137 (10/1/04-3/31/05)					
NUMBER OF STATEMENTS	28	63	49	10	1			61	85

0-500M %	500M-2MM %	2-10MM %	10-50MM %	50-100MM %	100-250MM %		4/1/00-3/31/01 ALL %	4/1/01-3/31/02 ALL %
						ASSETS		
20.5	10.0	6.2	4.6			Cash & Equivalents	7.3	9.3
28.1	51.9	57.9	54.4			Trade Receivables (net)	55.4	53.8
13.1	13.9	14.4	14.7			Inventory	11.9	11.5
5.1	4.4	6.4	6.8			All Other Current	6.6	4.8
66.8	80.3	84.9	80.6			Total Current	81.1	79.4
21.4	12.6	12.6	11.4			Fixed Assets (net)	14.1	14.3
1.4	2.0	.5	.8			Intangibles (net)	.8	1.9
10.3	5.1	1.9	7.1			All Other Non-Current	4.0	4.3
100.0	100.0	100.0	100.0			Total	100.0	100.0
						LIABILITIES		
19.9	14.5	19.0	20.2			Notes Payable-Short Term	11.3	18.5
2.1	2.2	1.5	2.1			Cur. Mat.-L/T/D	4.5	3.7
22.8	17.2	21.5	13.5			Trade Payables	20.1	20.6
.1	.4	.3	.3			Income Taxes Payable	.7	.2
11.9	11.2	10.9	22.4			All Other Current	14.2	12.2
57.0	45.4	53.1	58.5			Total Current	50.8	55.1
16.9	9.1	7.9	8.3			Long-Term Debt	7.0	8.1
.0	.2	.1	.3			Deferred Taxes	.5	.4
22.7	3.4	4.4	3.8			All Other Non-Current	3.6	3.1
3.4	41.9	34.5	29.0			Net Worth	38.2	33.3
100.0	100.0	100.0	100.0			Total Liabilities & Net Worth	100.0	100.0
						INCOME DATA		
100.0	100.0	100.0	100.0			Net Sales	100.0	100.0
36.9	27.3	25.2	26.5			Gross Profit	26.9	27.1
32.8	22.5	22.2	24.3			Operating Expenses	21.1	23.3
4.1	4.7	3.0	2.2			Operating Profit	5.8	3.9
.0	.3	-.4	.3			All Other Expenses (net)	.2	.5
4.1	4.4	3.3	2.0			Profit Before Taxes	5.6	3.4
						RATIOS		
3.0	3.0	2.1	1.6			Current	2.2	2.3
1.8	1.8	1.4	1.4				1.5	1.5
.5	1.3	1.2	1.2				1.2	1.1
2.4	2.3	1.6	1.3			Quick	1.8	1.7
1.0	1.4	1.1	1.0				1.2	1.2
.3	1.0	.9	.8				.9	.9
0 UND	36 10.3	49 7.5	36 10.3			Sales/Receivables	41 9.0	38 9.5
18 20.0	49 7.5	69 5.3	64 5.7				63 5.8	51 7.2
38 9.7	63 5.8	93 3.9	90 4.1				78 4.7	75 4.9
0 UND	2 188.1	9 42.1	4 101.8			Cost of Sales/Inventory	2 168.7	2 178.6
4 91.1	12 29.8	17 21.6	12 29.7				9 39.1	11 33.6
42 8.8	35 10.5	32 11.6	25 14.7				23 16.0	23 15.9
0 UND	8 45.5	19 18.7	13 28.0			Cost of Sales/Payables	14 25.4	14 26.6
14 25.2	19 19.2	31 11.9	18 20.6				23 15.9	25 14.7
38 9.6	33 10.9	52 7.0	33 11.2				36 10.2	38 9.5
8.5	7.5	7.1	6.9			Sales/Working Capital	7.9	8.2
40.2	11.1	11.1	16.1				13.2	14.6
-29.2	33.5	19.1	21.7				25.2	53.9
27.5	18.1	12.9				EBIT/Interest	16.6	14.3
(22) 7.0	(55) 7.0	(45) 4.1					(58) 6.6	(71) 3.9
-3.0	3.9	2.0					2.6	1.6
			12.3			Net Profit + Depr., Dep.,		20.8
			(10) 4.5			Amort./Cur. Mat. L/T/D		(18) 3.0
			.5					1.2
.1	.1	.1	.2			Fixed/Worth	.1	.1
.6	.2	.3	.4				.3	.4
NM	.6	.8	.7				.7	1.2
.6	.7	.9	1.4			Debt/Worth	.8	.9
1.7	1.3	2.9	3.1				1.8	1.6
NM	4.6	5.7	5.3				3.9	5.5
100.0	65.8	58.0	42.8			% Profit Before Taxes/Tangible	83.1	66.3
(21) 63.3	(58) 37.5	(47) 29.5	28.4			Net Worth	(60) 42.1	(75) 24.1
13.1	24.6	8.3	8.7				14.6	6.6
49.8	24.6	17.2	10.6			% Profit Before Taxes/Total	27.7	23.3
16.4	14.9	6.3	5.2			Assets	10.4	9.7
-3.1	5.8	2.0	3.2				4.8	1.4
311.2	165.5	123.4	94.0			Sales/Net Fixed Assets	85.0	80.1
56.4	65.4	50.6	34.6				33.8	34.2
18.9	20.9	19.1	23.6				15.2	19.0
9.2	4.7	3.6	4.3			Sales/Total Assets	4.3	4.6
5.2	3.8	3.0	3.1				3.4	3.6
2.9	3.2	2.3	2.2				2.8	3.0
.5	.2	.3				% Depr., Dep., Amort./Sales	.5	.4
(14) 1.1	(45) .5	(46) .5					(48) .9	(70) .9
3.0	1.5	.9					1.5	1.5
6.5	1.8	1.8				% Officers', Directors',	2.3	2.5
(14) 8.7	(36) 3.6	(22) 3.4				Owners' Comp/Sales	(32) 4.5	(47) 4.3
12.2	4.5	5.8					7.2	7.0
42429M	279185M	704405M	583464M	171891M		Net Sales ($)	1104599M	1000366M
7097M	67909M	220223M	181728M	62820M		Total Assets ($)	297029M	304653M

Note: Columns 50-100MM and 100-250MM for the Assets, Liabilities, Income Data, and Ratios sections are marked "DATA NOT AVAILABLE."

M = $ thousand   MM = $ million
See Pages 11 through 21 for Explanation of Ratios and Data

Comparative Historical Data | Current Data Sorted By Sales

				Type of Statement						
	2	3	6	Unqualified		1			3	2
	38	36	38	Reviewed		2	5	13	11	7
	19	32	27	Compiled	5	6	9	6		1
	19	31	30	Tax Returns	4	10	9	4	2	1
	26	41	50	Other	6	10	9	11	8	6
	4/1/02-3/31/03	4/1/03-3/31/04	4/1/04-3/31/05		14 (4/1-9/30/04)		137 (10/1/04-3/31/05)				
	ALL	ALL	ALL		0-1MM	1-3MM	3-5MM	5-10MM	10-25MM	25MM & OVER
	104	143	151	NUMBER OF STATEMENTS	15	29	32	34	24	17
	%	%	%	ASSETS	%	%	%	%	%	%
	10.7	10.1	10.3	Cash & Equivalents	21.2	16.7	7.7	7.6	8.5	3.1
	48.6	49.3	49.6	Trade Receivables (net)	25.3	40.1	49.9	57.3	59.9	56.8
	14.9	13.1	13.9	Inventory	15.1	12.6	12.3	15.7	12.6	16.0
	5.2	4.9	5.4	All Other Current	4.0	4.4	5.1	4.7	8.3	5.9
	79.3	77.4	79.2	Total Current	65.6	73.8	75.0	85.3	89.2	81.7
	14.8	14.1	14.2	Fixed Assets (net)	20.5	19.5	17.0	9.6	8.9	10.6
	.8	2.2	1.3	Intangibles (net)	2.0	1.7	3.2	.0	.5	.5
	5.0	6.3	5.3	All Other Non-Current	11.8	5.0	4.9	5.0	1.4	7.2
	100.0	100.0	100.0	Total	100.0	100.0	100.0	100.0	100.0	100.0
				LIABILITIES						
	17.8	17.7	17.2	Notes Payable-Short Term	16.0	16.8	16.9	15.8	20.4	18.3
	4.0	3.3	1.9	Cur. Mat.-L/T/D	2.5	3.4	1.8	1.3	1.4	1.3
	17.9	20.1	19.3	Trade Payables	10.9	22.3	18.1	20.3	23.3	16.6
	.4	.5	.3	Income Taxes Payable	.2	.2	.4	.3	.4	.2
	12.6	10.1	12.0	All Other Current	7.8	11.9	12.5	11.1	11.6	17.1
	52.7	51.6	50.7	Total Current	37.3	54.6	49.6	48.7	57.1	53.4
	7.1	8.4	10.0	Long-Term Debt	8.6	18.4	12.8	5.8	6.1	5.7
	.1	.1	.1	Deferred Taxes	.0	.0	.4	.0	.2	.2
	3.4	6.3	7.5	All Other Non-Current	3.3	18.4	6.2	4.4	5.6	3.6
	36.6	33.6	31.6	Net Worth	50.8	8.6	30.9	41.1	31.0	37.1
	100.0	100.0	100.0	Total Liabilities & Net Worth	100.0	100.0	100.0	100.0	100.0	100.0
				INCOME DATA						
	100.0	100.0	100.0	Net Sales	100.0	100.0	100.0	100.0	100.0	100.0
	30.6	28.3	28.3	Gross Profit	43.7	32.4	24.6	25.0	25.3	25.4
	27.5	25.6	24.4	Operating Expenses	33.5	29.7	22.0	20.8	22.1	22.1
	3.2	2.7	3.9	Operating Profit	10.2	2.7	2.5	4.2	3.2	3.3
	.4	.3	.1	All Other Expenses (net)	.3	-.4	.5	.3	-.6	.2
	2.7	2.4	3.8	Profit Before Taxes	9.9	3.2	2.0	3.8	3.8	3.1
				RATIOS						
	2.3	2.2	2.5	Current	4.4	3.7	2.3	3.0	2.0	2.0
	1.5	1.5	1.6		1.9	1.7	1.5	1.7	1.5	1.5
	1.2	1.2	1.2		1.2	.9	1.1	1.3	1.2	1.3
	1.7	1.7	1.9	Quick	3.4	2.7	1.6	2.0	1.7	1.6
	1.1	1.2	1.1		1.2	1.3	1.1	1.4	1.1	1.0
	.8	.8	.9		.4	.5	.9	.9	.9	.9
	31 11.8	32 11.5	33 11.0	Sales/Receivables	0 UND	20 18.0	38 9.7	41 8.8	41 9.0	46 7.9
	53 6.9	57 6.4	53 6.9		34 10.9	40 9.1	50 7.3	62 5.9	66 5.5	52 7.0
	71 5.1	74 5.0	75 4.9		53 6.8	58 6.3	68 5.4	82 4.5	92 4.0	65 5.6
	2 232.7	3 130.4	3 118.6	Cost of Sales/Inventory	0 UND	0 UND	2 239.8	4 101.2	6 64.0	9 42.0
	11 33.2	12 30.8	13 27.0		31 11.6	12 31.3	6 56.7	15 24.4	13 28.3	13 28.3
	35 10.3	27 13.4	34 10.6		61 6.0	37 9.8	18 20.0	34 10.8	31 11.8	24 15.4
	13 29.1	12 29.3	11 32.3	Cost of Sales/Payables	0 UND	3 124.4	8 45.1	11 33.6	18 20.1	13 28.1
	21 17.5	25 14.7	23 15.8		18 20.1	23 16.1	19 19.0	25 14.6	31 11.8	17 21.4
	37 9.8	39 9.4	38 9.5		38 9.6	54 6.8	38 9.6	46 8.0	40 9.2	31 11.7
	7.4	8.5	7.3	Sales/Working Capital	4.3	5.4	7.8	6.6	7.8	7.0
	12.4	12.7	12.6		15.0	18.8	18.2	9.5	12.6	14.7
	29.0	47.3	36.9		51.8	-49.8	43.4	15.8	20.7	23.4
	12.6	14.9	16.7	EBIT/Interest	44.4	17.8	13.2	23.5	12.1	24.0
(92)	4.3	(123) 4.0	(131) 5.7		(10) 28.0	(23) 6.3	(30) 5.0	(31) 5.5	(23) 4.1	(14) 8.3
	2.0	1.2	2.9		6.9	.7	2.7	2.2	3.3	4.2
	9.3	5.1	10.5	Net Profit + Depr., Dep., Amort./Cur. Mat. L/T/D						
(18)	4.5	(24) 1.4	(23) 3.9							
	1.3	.2	1.5							
	.1	.1	.1	Fixed/Worth	.0	.1	.1	.1	.1	.1
	.3	.3	.3		.4	.6	.5	.2	.2	.4
	.8	1.0	.8		.8	NM	1.0	.5	.4	.5
	.8	.8	.7	Debt/Worth	.4	.6	.6	.6	1.1	.8
	1.7	2.0	1.9		.7	1.8	2.2	1.5	3.0	1.7
	3.3	5.3	5.9		2.0	NM	6.8	4.4	4.7	4.3
	50.6	51.2	66.5	% Profit Before Taxes/Tangible Net Worth	91.0	84.0	48.0	64.3	66.1	67.6
(95)	21.7	(126) 19.2	(137) 35.6		(14) 62.8	(22) 42.4	(27) 35.9	(33) 31.6	34.7	35.6
	5.4	4.6	11.3		23.2	6.7	6.3	13.3	11.0	12.5
	24.9	18.3	21.9	% Profit Before Taxes/Total Assets	50.6	28.9	16.4	21.7	17.2	14.1
	7.0	5.6	10.4		18.4	15.0	10.6	8.8	5.9	9.3
	1.5	.5	2.9		6.3	.7	1.6	2.4	2.9	4.4
	93.2	88.1	144.8	Sales/Net Fixed Assets	UND	179.3	105.5	187.8	113.7	106.9
	40.7	39.9	55.1		32.2	62.8	34.9	76.7	66.5	36.4
	18.4	21.3	21.3		10.2	14.9	14.6	35.1	43.2	24.1
	4.8	4.6	4.7	Sales/Total Assets	5.2	5.8	4.8	4.4	3.6	4.9
	3.6	3.5	3.5		3.3	3.5	3.7	3.7	3.0	3.9
	2.9	2.8	2.7		1.9	2.6	3.1	2.6	2.7	2.9
	.4	.3	.3	% Depr., Dep., Amort./Sales		.4	.4	.2	.2	.4
(96)	.7	(116) .6	(115) .5			(18) 1.1	(25) .7	(31) .4	(21) .4	(16) .6
	1.4	1.4	1.1			1.9	1.9	.8	.6	.8
	2.8	2.5	2.1	% Officers', Directors', Owners' Comp/Sales		3.9	1.8	1.6	1.5	
(65)	4.7	(85) 4.3	(74) 3.7			(16) 5.6	(19) 3.7	(21) 2.4	(10) 2.4	
	7.4	6.8	6.5			10.7	5.8	4.5	4.6	
	1999633M	1659716M	1781374M	Net Sales ($)	8938M	60295M	126584M	249147M	357978M	978432M
	552589M	496552M	539777M	Total Assets ($)	3511M	21905M	36438M	75609M	114356M	287958M

M = $ thousand   MM = $ million
See Pages 11 through 21 for Explanation of Ratios and Data

Current Data Sorted By Assets   Comparative Historical Data

0-500M	500M-2MM	2-10MM	10-50MM	50-100MM	100-250MM	Type of Statement	4/1/00-3/31/01 ALL	4/1/01-3/31/02 ALL
			1			Unqualified	2	3
1	5	5	1			Reviewed	6	5
9	3	7	3			Compiled	7	7
3	5	3	5			Tax Returns	1	
	9	5				Other	3	8
	8 (4/1-9/30/04)		49 (10/1/04-3/31/05)					
13	22	20	2			**NUMBER OF STATEMENTS**	19	23
%	%	%	%	%	%	**ASSETS**	%	%
20.6	10.2	7.6		D	D	Cash & Equivalents	8.4	10.2
34.8	36.6	52.1		A	A	Trade Receivables (net)	43.9	48.0
5.2	17.6	9.4		T	T	Inventory	13.5	10.7
1.4	4.0	4.9		A	A	All Other Current	4.5	4.5
62.1	68.5	74.0				Total Current	70.3	73.4
30.4	19.7	14.2		N	N	Fixed Assets (net)	19.7	18.0
.0	.1	1.8		O	O	Intangibles (net)	2.7	2.4
7.4	11.6	10.1		T	T	All Other Non-Current	7.3	6.3
100.0	100.0	100.0				Total	100.0	100.0
				A	A	**LIABILITIES**		
17.1	8.3	12.0		V	V	Notes Payable-Short Term	10.6	10.7
6.1	1.3	1.4		A	A	Cur. Mat.-L/T/D	3.0	3.4
19.0	12.4	20.5		I	I	Trade Payables	17.0	17.1
.0	.9	.3		L	L	Income Taxes Payable	.0	1.3
12.9	10.9	15.5		A	A	All Other Current	20.8	12.5
55.2	33.9	49.8		B	B	Total Current	51.5	44.9
29.1	15.4	6.9		L	L	Long-Term Debt	9.8	9.3
.0	.2	.0		E	E	Deferred Taxes	.8	.5
13.6	6.4	1.4				All Other Non-Current	6.0	8.9
2.1	44.1	41.9				Net Worth	32.0	36.3
100.0	100.0	100.0				Total Liabilities & Net Worth	100.0	100.0
						INCOME DATA		
100.0	100.0	100.0				Net Sales	100.0	100.0
40.1	41.0	25.6				Gross Profit	29.0	30.7
37.7	38.3	18.1				Operating Expenses	21.5	24.7
2.5	2.7	7.5				Operating Profit	7.5	5.9
.8	.4	.4				All Other Expenses (net)	.7	.7
1.7	2.4	7.1				Profit Before Taxes	6.7	5.2
						RATIOS		
4.1	4.1	1.8					1.8	2.0
1.2	2.7	1.4				Current	1.4	1.8
.6	1.2	1.2					.9	1.3
3.1	3.7	1.6					1.6	1.8
1.2	1.4	1.2				Quick	1.2	1.3
.6	.9	.9					.7	.9
0 UND	24 15.1	56 6.5					28 12.9	36 10.2
29 12.6	35 10.5	81 4.5				Sales/Receivables	50 7.3	47 7.8
42 8.7	59 6.2	88 4.1					91 4.0	78 4.7
0 UND	0 UND	0 877.6					1 376.6	2 197.4
0 UND	25 14.4	7 49.2				Cost of Sales/Inventory	8 44.9	11 33.9
1 285.3	58 6.3	16 22.5					33 11.1	21 17.4
0 UND	0 UND	20 18.6					17 21.9	14 26.2
11 32.0	18 19.8	28 12.8				Cost of Sales/Payables	31 11.8	25 14.4
35 10.6	40 9.2	63 5.8					43 8.4	44 8.3
12.8	6.2	7.5					7.4	8.0
41.1	10.4	10.1				Sales/Working Capital	12.1	11.1
−40.5	53.5	30.1					−342.3	24.3
35.3	25.9	107.0					15.7	17.7
(11) 7.4	(19) 6.6	(17) 6.4				EBIT/Interest	(16) 4.2	(21) 4.5
−5.2	1.2	2.3					1.8	1.6
						Net Profit + Depr., Dep., Amort./Cur. Mat. L /T/D		
.2	.1	.2					.2	.2
2.1	.4	.3				Fixed/Worth	.5	.4
−.6	1.0	.7					2.8	.8
1.0	.6	1.1					1.3	.8
5.2	1.4	1.4				Debt/Worth	1.6	1.4
−3.2	2.9	3.4					6.5	5.5
	82.5	63.6				% Profit Before Taxes/Tangible Net Worth	71.0	101.8
	(21) 5.8	37.2					(17) 34.7	(21) 39.8
	.8	7.2					9.8	5.9
46.6	28.2	27.4				% Profit Before Taxes/Total Assets	39.7	24.5
21.1	2.7	16.8					11.0	8.0
−18.4	.0	2.8					4.0	2.3
240.4	99.9	37.5					41.6	34.0
18.6	28.5	22.4				Sales/Net Fixed Assets	22.6	22.1
8.5	12.3	12.6					10.7	13.2
9.6	4.4	2.9					3.6	4.4
6.6	3.2	2.6				Sales/Total Assets	2.9	3.7
3.2	2.2	2.3					2.2	2.4
	.7	.6				% Depr., Dep., Amort./Sales	.5	.6
	(14) 1.7	(14) .9					(16) .9	(21) 1.3
	3.1	1.5					2.5	1.7
	1.9					% Officers', Directors', Owners' Comp/Sales		
	(13) 5.3							
	5.9							
24210M	89385M	255284M	60943M			Net Sales ($)	188567M	253607M
3868M	25948M	103709M	25731M			Total Assets ($)	76954M	101788M

Data columns 50-100MM and 100-250MM contain: "DATA NOT AVAILABLE"

Comparative Historical Data   Current Data Sorted By Sales

4/1/02-3/31/03 ALL	4/1/03-3/31/04 ALL	4/1/04-3/31/05 ALL	Type of Statement	0-1MM	1-3MM	3-5MM	5-10MM	10-25MM	25MM & OVER
6	5	6	Unqualified				1	3	2
9	14	13	Reviewed		2	2	6	1	2
2	6	4	Compiled		4				
4	10	17	Tax Returns	3	7	1	5	1	
7	10	17	Other	2	3	2	5	5	
					8 (4/1-9/30/04)		49 (10/1/04-3/31/05)		
28	45	57	NUMBER OF STATEMENTS	5	16	5	17	10	4
%	%	%	**ASSETS**	%	%	%	%	%	%
11.2	12.4	12.4	Cash & Equivalents		12.5		13.5	7.9	
38.8	38.0	41.7	Trade Receivables (net)		37.2		52.6	40.9	
16.0	15.0	11.4	Inventory		12.7		12.0	8.3	
6.8	3.7	3.8	All Other Current		2.3		3.7	6.8	
72.9	69.2	69.3	Total Current		64.7		81.8	63.8	
18.5	21.3	20.2	Fixed Assets (net)		23.9		11.8	19.4	
1.2	1.0	.7	Intangibles (net)		.0		.5	2.9	
7.5	8.5	9.8	All Other Non-Current		11.3		6.0	13.9	
100.0	100.0	100.0	Total		100.0		100.0	100.0	
			LIABILITIES						
8.6	18.4	11.4	Notes Payable-Short Term		7.1		10.0	16.3	
3.2	3.4	2.4	Cur. Mat.-L/T/D		6.4		.6	1.9	
14.9	17.8	16.5	Trade Payables		13.4		25.8	13.5	
.3	.3	.4	Income Taxes Payable		.2		.7	.0	
19.7	14.8	13.5	All Other Current		11.8		10.6	11.8	
46.7	54.8	44.3	Total Current		38.9		47.7	43.5	
12.1	14.0	15.0	Long-Term Debt		27.8		8.2	9.6	
.1	.3	.1	Deferred Taxes		.1		.2	.0	
4.9	6.7	6.1	All Other Non-Current		5.5		9.6	.8	
36.2	24.2	34.6	Net Worth		27.7		34.4	46.1	
100.0	100.0	100.0	Total Liabilities & Net Worth		100.0		100.0	100.0	
			INCOME DATA						
100.0	100.0	100.0	Net Sales		100.0		100.0	100.0	
33.3	33.0	34.9	Gross Profit		38.3		30.1	27.8	
27.9	26.8	30.3	Operating Expenses		37.1		24.6	21.5	
5.4	6.3	4.6	Operating Profit		1.2		5.5	6.4	
.7	.5	.5	All Other Expenses (net)		.5		.8	.3	
4.6	5.8	4.1	Profit Before Taxes		.7		4.7	6.1	
			RATIOS						
2.1	2.0	3.5	Current		4.6		3.9	1.9	
1.6	1.6	1.7			2.2		1.7	1.4	
1.1	1.2	1.1			1.0		1.2	1.2	
2.0	1.5	2.9	Quick		4.1		3.7	1.6	
1.0	1.2	1.2			1.4		1.3	1.2	
.7	.7	.9			.9		.9	.9	
31 11.8	18 20.7	29 12.6	Sales/Receivables		25 14.5		29 12.5	41 8.9	
59 6.2	40 9.0	48 7.6			42 8.7		57 6.4	68 5.4	
79 4.6	73 5.0	79 4.6			69 5.3		86 4.2	82 4.4	
3 121.1	4 100.1	0 UND	Cost of Sales/Inventory		0 UND		0 UND	1 295.2	
12 29.7	16 22.7	7 51.1			1 285.3		7 49.9	6 61.9	
55 6.7	36 10.0	38 9.7			38 9.6		34 10.8	21 17.0	
12 31.0	9 38.6	7 54.3	Cost of Sales/Payables		1 633.8		12 29.6	18 20.5	
27 13.4	30 12.3	22 16.3			18 20.0		26 14.1	28 13.0	
51 7.2	49 7.5	40 9.2			36 10.0		68 5.3	34 10.7	
6.0	8.3	7.1	Sales/Working Capital		5.2		7.0	7.9	
9.5	14.2	11.2			16.0		9.8	10.8	
36.1	36.8	49.6			NM		45.5	35.2	
14.2	28.4	28.0	EBIT/Interest		27.6		50.9		
(23) 4.9	(38) 7.8	(48) 6.9			(14) 6.1		(14) 14.4		
-.4	3.0	1.6			-.2		1.7		
		4.6	Net Profit + Depr., Dep., Amort./Cur. Mat. L/T/D						
	(11) 1.6								
		1.1							
.1	.2	.1	Fixed/Worth		.1		.1	.2	
.6	.5	.4			.6		.3	.5	
1.8	.9	1.0			NM		.8	.8	
.8	1.0	.6	Debt/Worth		.5		.8	.9	
1.9	1.4	1.6			1.6		2.9	1.3	
4.7	3.4	3.5			NM		4.1	2.2	
79.2	91.7	82.9	% Profit Before Taxes/Tangible Net Worth		86.3		96.7	52.7	
(25) 15.4	(40) 36.3	(50) 37.2			(12) 4.6		(16) 39.5	32.2	
.5	10.2	4.9			1.5		7.0	7.1	
17.5	26.3	29.4	% Profit Before Taxes/Total Assets		26.0		40.2	23.0	
6.1	14.8	13.1			2.3		17.4	12.0	
-.4	3.7	1.0			-12.8		1.6	3.4	
58.2	52.0	58.9	Sales/Net Fixed Assets		58.9		446.4	22.8	
14.6	24.7	25.7			28.1		28.7	13.4	
8.0	10.0	12.1			8.7		17.6	9.6	
3.4	4.3	4.1	Sales/Total Assets		4.7		4.7	2.9	
2.7	3.1	2.9			3.3		3.1	2.4	
2.2	2.3	2.3			2.0		2.7	1.8	
.9	.7	.7	% Depr., Dep., Amort./Sales		.7				
(24) 1.1	(35) 1.3	(36) 1.0			(10) .9				
1.8	1.8	2.4			2.4				
2.6	2.3	2.5	% Officers', Directors', Owners' Comp/Sales						
(15) 7.7	(26) 3.6	(27) 5.0							
9.3	7.1	7.1							
351477M	354305M	429822M	Net Sales ($)	2306M	32447M	19758M	116111M	147374M	111826M
161279M	128646M	159256M	Total Assets ($)	1739M	10669M	5380M	34342M	64801M	42325M

M = $ thousand   MM = $ million
See Pages 11 through 21 for Explanation of Ratios and Data

Current Data Sorted By Assets   **Comparative Historical Data**

Type of Statement

	0-500M	500M-2MM	2-10MM	10-50MM	50-100MM	100-250MM		4/1/00-3/31/01 ALL	4/1/01-3/31/02 ALL
Unqualified		1	2	1	1			4	7
Reviewed	2	7	24	2				28	27
Compiled	4	14	4					24	28
Tax Returns	23	9	4	1				10	15
Other	6	11	6	3	1	1		22	25
	17 (4/1-9/30/04)			110 (10/1/04-3/31/05)				4/1/00-3/31/01 ALL	4/1/01-3/31/02 ALL
NUMBER OF STATEMENTS	35	42	40	7	2	1		88	102

Financial Data

	0-500M	500M-2MM	2-10MM	10-50MM	50-100MM	100-250MM		4/1/00-3/31/01 ALL	4/1/01-3/31/02 ALL
	%	%	%	%	%	%	**ASSETS**	%	%
Cash & Equivalents	18.4	10.1	8.0					12.3	11.9
Trade Receivables (net)	32.3	35.9	50.5					40.9	43.8
Inventory	4.2	17.8	13.6					12.7	12.1
All Other Current	1.6	8.5	6.2					6.5	3.5
Total Current	56.4	72.3	78.3					72.3	71.4
Fixed Assets (net)	30.0	18.9	15.4					21.7	20.2
Intangibles (net)	.5	1.5	.1					1.4	1.1
All Other Non-Current	13.0	7.3	6.3					4.6	7.3
Total	100.0	100.0	100.0					100.0	100.0
							LIABILITIES		
Notes Payable-Short Term	16.5	7.8	12.4					11.3	9.4
Cur. Mat.-LT/D	3.8	4.8	2.3					3.6	4.2
Trade Payables	17.3	18.5	19.3					16.7	19.0
Income Taxes Payable	.8	.5	.8					.6	.4
All Other Current	20.3	17.4	12.7					11.2	17.4
Total Current	58.8	49.0	47.4					43.4	50.4
Long-Term Debt	19.4	12.3	5.9					12.3	14.0
Deferred Taxes	.0	.4	.2					.4	.3
All Other Non-Current	17.0	2.2	2.5					3.0	3.5
Net Worth	4.8	36.1	43.9					40.9	31.9
Total Liabilities & Net Worth	100.0	100.0	100.0					100.0	100.0
							INCOME DATA		
Net Sales	100.0	100.0	100.0					100.0	100.0
Gross Profit	44.5	29.6	21.5					30.4	31.6
Operating Expenses	39.6	24.9	17.1					25.9	26.6
Operating Profit	4.9	4.8	4.4					4.5	5.0
All Other Expenses (net)	.0	.4	.4					.2	.5
Profit Before Taxes	4.9	4.4	4.0					4.2	4.5
							RATIOS		
Current	2.0	2.9	2.3					2.9	2.5
	1.2	1.5	1.6					1.6	1.5
	.5	1.0	1.3					1.3	1.0
Quick	2.0	1.7	1.8					2.5	2.0
	1.1	1.0	1.3					(87) 1.2	1.1
	.4	.6	.9					.8	.7
Sales/Receivables	1 334.3	18 20.8	39 9.3					29 12.5	26 13.8
	28 13.1	32 11.5	53 7.0					43 8.4	41 9.0
	44 8.4	61 6.0	76 4.8					57 6.5	64 5.7
Cost of Sales/Inventory	0 UND	0 UND	0 UND					0 UND	0 UND
	0 UND	17 21.2	9 40.1					8 45.7	8 43.7
	9 40.4	38 9.7	41 8.9					36 10.1	32 11.4
Cost of Sales/Payables	0 UND	13 28.4	10 35.2					9 40.4	9 40.5
	16 22.4	22 16.5	25 14.9					20 18.5	20 18.5
	37 9.8	32 11.4	40 9.1					35 10.4	44 8.4
Sales/Working Capital	13.0	8.5	7.2					6.9	8.1
	86.6	16.8	10.4					12.3	15.4
	−19.4	−152.7	20.7					33.2	101.6
EBIT/Interest	8.9	18.6	25.7					16.9	16.6
	(27) 6.0	(39) 7.9	(38) 6.2					(68) 6.9	(88) 4.7
	1.8	2.3	1.1					2.1	1.9
Net Profit + Depr., Dep., Amort./Cur. Mat. L /T/D			8.1					10.4	15.9
		(12)	1.8					(24) 3.8	(23) 4.0
			.4					1.6	1.6
Fixed/Worth	.1	.2	.2					.2	.1
	1.4	.7	.3					.4	.4
	−4.9	2.9	.6					.8	1.8
Debt/Worth	.6	.7	.7					.5	.7
	3.5	1.3	1.3					1.3	1.8
	−8.7	12.0	2.7					3.9	8.6
% Profit Before Taxes/Tangible Net Worth	102.8	86.0	40.2					55.1	92.1
	(22) 67.0	(35) 35.9	(39) 22.9					(79) 29.8	(90) 33.7
	19.3	8.9	2.9					12.2	15.2
% Profit Before Taxes/Total Assets	33.1	23.1	20.3					25.1	24.0
	11.8	10.7	7.6					11.7	11.9
	.0	3.4	.6					3.7	3.5
Sales/Net Fixed Assets	171.0	76.4	52.1					49.6	73.5
	26.0	26.1	26.2					26.6	30.7
	9.3	10.5	11.5					10.8	14.0
Sales/Total Assets	6.6	4.7	4.0					4.6	5.0
	4.5	3.5	3.0					3.5	3.4
	2.7	2.7	2.2					2.7	2.8
% Depr., Dep., Amort./Sales	.8	.5	.3					.5	.5
	(23) 2.0	(31) 1.5	(34) .7					(80) 1.1	(97) 1.0
	4.0	3.1	1.4					2.1	1.8
% Officers', Directors', Owners' Comp/Sales	6.1	3.2	1.2					2.6	3.1
	(29) 9.4	(23) 4.8	(23) 2.6					(45) 4.1	(60) 5.4
	12.3	7.3	5.5					6.3	9.2
Net Sales ($)	33776M	186091M	520736M	390085M	441125M	529793M		1096557M	960820M
Total Assets ($)	7848M	49288M	163536M	100513M	191591M	116643M		299451M	281956M

M = $ thousand   MM = $ million
See Pages 11 through 21 for Explanation of Ratios and Data

Comparative Historical Data | Current Data Sorted By Sales

			Type of Statement						
5	9	5	Unqualified				2		3
24	35	35	Reviewed	1	4	3	17	5	5
19	27	22	Compiled	1	8	4	4	5	
14	16	38	Tax Returns	16	13	1	3	2	3
28	32	27	Other	2	7	3	5	6	4
4/1/02-3/31/03 ALL	4/1/03-3/31/04 ALL	4/1/04-3/31/05 ALL		17 (4/1-9/30/04) 0-1MM	1-3MM	3-5MM	110 (10/1/04-3/31/05) 5-10MM	10-25MM	25MM & OVER
90	119	127	NUMBER OF STATEMENTS	20	32	11	31	18	15
%	%	%	ASSETS	%	%	%	%	%	%
11.5	11.2	11.3	Cash & Equivalents	20.5	13.4	3.4	10.9	6.2	7.6
39.4	36.4	39.8	Trade Receivables (net)	25.8	37.5	41.7	43.2	47.8	45.5
12.2	14.5	12.4	Inventory	2.5	11.0	16.2	16.8	18.2	9.6
4.9	6.4	6.2	All Other Current	.6	5.5	11.7	7.6	3.5	11.4
67.9	68.5	69.7	Total Current	49.4	67.4	72.9	78.4	75.6	74.1
19.5	19.6	20.7	Fixed Assets (net)	33.0	24.1	12.2	16.5	19.6	13.3
2.9	1.8	1.3	Intangibles (net)	.6	1.7	1.1	.2	.0	5.7
9.7	10.1	8.3	All Other Non-Current	17.1	6.7	13.8	4.9	4.8	6.9
100.0	100.0	100.0	Total	100.0	100.0	100.0	100.0	100.0	100.0
			LIABILITIES						
13.6	15.9	12.2	Notes Payable-Short Term	14.3	14.2	10.6	10.3	9.7	13.2
3.6	3.5	3.4	Cur. Mat.-L/T/D	5.1	2.8	2.6	5.0	2.6	.9
16.5	17.7	18.7	Trade Payables	7.9	20.4	20.1	21.1	21.7	20.4
.3	.4	.6	Income Taxes Payable	1.1	.5	.4	.5	1.1	.1
13.0	13.0	16.2	All Other Current	25.0	12.5	28.1	16.0	10.8	10.6
47.0	50.5	51.2	Total Current	53.4	50.3	61.9	52.8	45.9	45.3
10.3	13.6	12.5	Long-Term Debt	21.1	17.3	3.9	7.3	10.0	10.8
.2	.3	.2	Deferred Taxes	.0	.5	.2	.1	.1	.1
5.8	3.9	6.3	All Other Non-Current	19.1	8.4	2.5	1.4	3.5	1.1
36.7	31.7	29.8	Net Worth	6.4	23.5	31.4	38.5	40.5	42.7
100.0	100.0	100.0	Total Liabilities & Net Worth	100.0	100.0	100.0	100.0	100.0	100.0
			INCOME DATA						
100.0	100.0	100.0	Net Sales	100.0	100.0	100.0	100.0	100.0	100.0
30.7	28.3	30.4	Gross Profit	47.9	36.4	23.3	25.6	22.5	18.4
27.4	25.5	25.7	Operating Expenses	41.3	32.1	20.1	20.8	19.3	12.8
3.3	2.8	4.7	Operating Profit	6.6	4.3	3.2	4.8	3.2	5.6
1.1	.6	.3	All Other Expenses (net)	.2	.2	.1	.4	.4	.2
2.2	2.2	4.4	Profit Before Taxes	6.4	4.1	3.1	4.4	2.8	5.4
			RATIOS						
2.5	2.1	2.3		2.1	3.1	1.5	2.8	2.1	2.4
1.4	1.4	1.4	Current	1.0	1.5	1.2	1.5	1.5	1.5
1.0	1.1	1.1		.5	1.0	1.1	1.1	1.3	1.3
1.8	1.6	1.6		2.1	2.7	1.2	1.5	1.8	1.5
1.1	1.1	1.1	Quick	1.0	1.2	.9	1.0	1.2	1.2
.7	.6	.7		.3	.8	.8	.9	.9	.8
21 17.2	21 17.7	21 17.2		0 UND	21 17.7	17 21.2	34 10.7	34 10.8	29 12.4
40 9.2	43 8.5	37 9.7	Sales/Receivables	12 30.3	40 9.1	44 8.2	53 6.9	44 8.3	34 10.8
66 5.5	60 6.1	61 5.9		33 11.2	63 5.8	61 6.0	76 4.8	50 7.2	68 5.4
0 UND	0 UND	0 UND		0 UND	0 UND	0 UND	0 UND	3 130.2	0 UND
14 25.6	7 54.8	8 43.8	Cost of Sales/Inventory	0 UND	11 34.6	15 24.3	13 27.8	19 19.2	9 42.4
29 12.6	37 9.9	30 12.3		0 UND	31 11.7	23 15.9	51 7.2	46 8.0	23 15.9
8 47.1	6 63.4	8 43.4		0 UND	7 50.4	20 18.1	15 25.0	12 30.6	11 32.4
20 18.2	20 18.4	21 17.0	Cost of Sales/Payables	1 394.3	19 19.4	28 12.9	26 14.3	25 14.9	19 18.8
37 10.0	40 9.1	37 9.9		21 17.1	37 9.9	32 11.5	56 6.6	33 11.1	38 9.7
7.9	7.8	8.5		9.3	6.7	13.0	7.6	9.0	6.8
16.3	15.8	17.0	Sales/Working Capital	NM	20.4	39.0	12.0	14.1	12.7
83.6	111.7	109.4		-14.5	NM	61.2	28.0	37.9	21.0
10.8	15.2	18.8		8.1	15.9	18.6	26.3	23.6	22.7
(77) 3.7	(100) 3.5	(113) 6.8	EBIT/Interest	(13) 6.0	(30) 6.7	(10) 4.9	(29) 7.7	(17) 5.8	(14) 11.9
1.2	-.6	2.1		.6	2.5	-.8	1.6	1.0	3.6
7.1	7.7	3.7	Net Profit + Depr., Dep.,						
(18) 1.7	(22) 2.5	(19) 1.8	Amort./Cur. Mat. L/T/D						
.4	.3	.7							
.2	.2	.2		.0	.3	.1	.2	.2	.1
.4	.5	.5	Fixed/Worth	3.4	.9	.6	.4	.3	.4
1.1	1.8	2.2		-4.0	-2.9	.8	1.2	.8	.9
1.0	1.0	.7		.3	.8	.8	.7	.6	.7
2.3	2.1	1.8	Debt/Worth	5.1	2.3	1.5	1.6	1.4	1.8
4.6	8.1	7.6		-6.5	-15.7	18.5	5.1	4.6	3.6
56.1	63.4	73.7	% Profit Before Taxes/Tangible	177.8	67.5	127.8	83.0	36.0	71.3
(83) 21.0	(100) 22.5	(104) 28.9	Net Worth	(12) 77.3	(22) 26.9	(10) 45.9	(29) 36.7	25.3	(13) 28.0
2.7	3.2	8.8		16.5	8.7	-4.1	9.4	1.5	10.1
15.9	18.5	23.0	% Profit Before Taxes/Total	48.4	19.7	44.0	28.1	18.9	27.7
7.3	7.1	10.6	Assets	15.9	9.4	4.5	10.7	7.2	9.0
.6	-.6	2.1		-1.9	3.7	-2.0	2.1	.9	4.0
64.5	58.3	68.6		UND	29.7	280.5	39.6	51.9	67.4
22.8	22.7	25.9	Sales/Net Fixed Assets	44.2	16.3	62.3	23.5	29.6	28.6
11.8	11.4	11.3		7.4	9.4	14.4	10.4	14.4	15.4
4.5	4.6	4.9		7.6	4.6	5.7	4.3	5.8	5.5
3.3	3.0	3.4	Sales/Total Assets	4.2	3.5	3.5	3.0	4.0	3.4
2.4	2.3	2.5		2.1	2.5	2.6	2.2	2.9	2.6
.5	.5	.5		.4	1.2		.5	.3	.2
(80) 1.3	(94) 1.2	(97) 1.2	% Depr., Dep., Amort./Sales	(13) 1.6	(24) 2.1		(25) 1.1	(15) .8	(13) .6
2.5	2.2	2.3		4.4	3.2		2.0	1.6	1.3
2.2	1.8	2.6		9.4	5.0		1.3	2.5	.7
(51) 3.8	(63) 3.6	(81) 5.5	% Officers', Directors',	(15) 11.5	(23) 6.5		(19) 2.3	(10) 4.8	(10) 1.8
8.0	8.4	9.2	Owners' Comp/Sales	14.3	7.5		4.4	7.3	4.5
974653M	1630228M	2101606M	Net Sales ($)	9954M	64086M	44272M	219652M	254543M	1509099M
293220M	624457M	629419M	Total Assets ($)	2603M	20399M	13272M	78352M	69018M	445775M

M = $ thousand   MM = $ million
See Pages 11 through 21 for Explanation of Ratios and Data

Current Data Sorted By Assets   **Comparative Historical Data**

Type of Statement	0-500M	500M-2MM	2-10MM	10-50MM	50-100MM	100-250MM		4/1/00-3/31/01 ALL	4/1/01-3/31/02 ALL
Unqualified		9	52	44	3	4		71	75
Reviewed	6	67	124	11		1		120	114
Compiled	14	36	20	1				50	64
Tax Returns	39	31	11	1		2		23	31
Other	12	21	54	12	2			74	77
	98 (4/1-9/30/04)			479 (10/1/04-3/31/05)					
NUMBER OF STATEMENTS	71	164	261	69	5	7		338	361

	0-500M %	500M-2MM %	2-10MM %	10-50MM %	50-100MM %	100-250MM %		ALL %	ALL %
ASSETS									
Cash & Equivalents	15.1	13.5	9.9	10.8				10.0	9.6
Trade Receivables (net)	20.2	30.1	35.6	38.7				31.1	30.6
Inventory	3.0	1.4	2.3	3.3				3.2	2.8
All Other Current	3.8	3.3	8.0	8.2				5.4	5.9
Total Current	42.1	48.3	55.9	61.1				49.8	48.9
Fixed Assets (net)	50.1	44.1	37.5	32.1				43.2	43.3
Intangibles (net)	1.1	1.2	.7	.6				1.2	1.0
All Other Non-Current	6.7	6.4	5.9	6.3				5.7	6.8
Total	100.0	100.0	100.0	100.0				100.0	100.0
LIABILITIES									
Notes Payable-Short Term	19.7	7.2	6.1	6.7				7.4	8.3
Cur. Mat.-L/T/D	6.0	7.6	7.0	5.5				8.0	8.0
Trade Payables	10.4	10.7	16.6	17.3				13.7	13.8
Income Taxes Payable	.5	.8	1.1	.5				.6	.8
All Other Current	11.7	7.6	9.0	12.8				8.6	8.8
Total Current	48.3	33.9	39.8	42.7				38.3	39.6
Long-Term Debt	47.1	26.8	16.5	15.0				20.1	20.5
Deferred Taxes	.1	.5	1.5	1.3				1.4	1.4
All Other Non-Current	14.4	4.6	1.7	1.0				2.2	2.7
Net Worth	-9.9	34.2	40.6	40.0				38.0	35.8
Total Liabilities & Net Worth	100.0	100.0	100.0	100.0				100.0	100.0
INCOME DATA									
Net Sales	100.0	100.0	100.0	100.0				100.0	100.0
Gross Profit	48.2	34.3	23.2	16.7				29.5	28.7
Operating Expenses	45.5	28.7	17.8	11.1				25.3	25.0
Operating Profit	2.7	5.5	5.4	5.6				4.2	3.8
All Other Expenses (net)	1.4	.8	.7	.5				.5	.9
Profit Before Taxes	1.3	4.8	4.7	5.1				3.7	2.8

RATIOS

Ratio	0-500M	500M-2MM	2-10MM	10-50MM		ALL	ALL
Current	2.5	2.6	2.0	1.8		1.9	2.0
	1.0	1.4	1.4	1.4		1.3	1.2
	.4	.9	1.1	1.1		1.0	.9
Quick	2.2	2.3	1.7	1.6		1.6	1.6
	.7	1.2	1.1	1.1		1.1	1.0
	.3	.8	.8	.9		.8	.7
Sales/Receivables	0 UND	28 13.0	43 8.6	53 6.8		34 10.7	32 11.3
	16 22.5	50 7.3	63 5.8	75 4.9		56 6.6	56 6.5
	44 8.3	76 4.8	89 4.1	90 4.1		78 4.7	79 4.6
Cost of Sales/Inventory	0 UND	0 UND	0 UND	0 UND		0 UND	0 UND
	0 UND	0 UND	0 UND	0 UND		0 UND	0 UND
	0 UND	0 UND	2 195.6	3 106.4		4 97.0	5 80.2
Cost of Sales/Payables	0 UND	8 43.2	19 19.5	25 14.5		12 30.0	12 29.5
	3 105.7	19 19.5	35 10.4	33 11.2		26 14.0	27 13.6
	44 8.2	39 9.4	52 7.0	49 7.5		46 7.9	47 7.8
Sales/Working Capital	13.4	7.1	6.3	6.0		7.4	7.9
	-93.0	16.2	14.2	11.9		19.9	25.2
	-14.7	-86.0	53.6	24.6		-169.5	-66.6
EBIT/Interest	7.6	10.7	12.1	15.7		7.4	6.2
	(61) 2.3	(155) 4.5	(239) 5.2	(67) 6.2		(315) 3.0	(343) 2.6
	-1.0	1.2	2.1	2.5		1.1	.8
Net Profit + Depr., Dep., Amort./Cur. Mat. L./T/D		3.8	2.9	2.5		3.5	2.6
		(33) 2.5	(82) 1.8	(25) 1.6		(120) 1.8	(123) 1.6
		1.7	1.1	.9		1.1	1.0
Fixed/Worth	1.1	.6	.5	.4		.6	.6
	4.9	1.1	.9	.8		1.1	1.2
	-1.9	2.6	1.7	1.2		2.0	2.1
Debt/Worth	1.4	.7	.8	.8		.8	.9
	9.2	1.6	1.6	1.5		1.7	1.8
	-4.4	5.7	2.9	3.1		3.4	3.7
% Profit Before Taxes/Tangible Net Worth	63.1	52.6	36.0	44.1		39.0	34.2
	(40) 27.3	(146) 20.5	(252) 19.7	22.1		(314) 12.1	(336) 12.9
	-2.9	3.3	4.8	8.3		1.7	1.3
% Profit Before Taxes/Total Assets	19.8	18.7	13.6	13.4		13.5	11.1
	5.4	7.2	6.3	6.2		4.8	4.4
	-11.1	.4	1.6	2.6		.4	-.1
Sales/Net Fixed Assets	18.6	8.6	10.4	10.1		9.3	8.9
	7.0	5.3	5.2	6.6		4.9	4.6
	3.7	3.1	3.3	4.0		2.9	2.9
Sales/Total Assets	5.4	2.8	2.4	2.4		2.6	2.6
	3.1	2.1	1.9	2.0		2.0	1.9
	2.0	1.5	1.5	1.4		1.4	1.4
% Depr., Dep., Amort./Sales	4.4	4.1	3.1	1.4		3.0	2.9
	(53) 6.7	(143) 6.5	(244) 4.9	(66) 3.8		(306) 5.6	(338) 5.4
	14.3	10.6	7.3	5.2		8.6	8.8
% Officers', Directors', Owners' Comp/Sales	4.4	2.4	1.4	.7		1.9	1.8
	(40) 5.8	(79) 4.7	(114) 2.5	(24) 1.7		(158) 4.5	(169) 3.8
	11.8	7.3	3.8	3.2		8.7	7.8
Net Sales ($)	74668M	427285M	2426275M	2774162M	516513M	2735710M		3484979M	3894976M
Total Assets ($)	18950M	187415M	1243982M	1503918M	362243M	1030225M		1999106M	2214714M

M = $ thousand   MM = $ million
See Pages 11 through 21 for Explanation of Ratios and Data

Comparative Historical Data				Current Data Sorted By Sales					
			Type of Statement	2	5	8	17	40	40
81	116	112	Unqualified	5	41	46	66	41	10
140	236	209	Reviewed	22	28	8	8	5	
53	106	71	Compiled	31	29	11	8	2	3
42	78	84	Tax Returns	12	20	13	21	23	12
69	74	101	Other						
4/1/02- 3/31/03	4/1/03- 3/31/04	4/1/04- 3/31/05			98 (4/1-9/30/04)		479 (10/1/04-3/31/05)		
ALL	ALL	ALL		0-1MM	1-3MM	3-5MM	5-10MM	10-25MM	25MM & OVER
385	610	577	**NUMBER OF STATEMENTS**	72	123	86	120	111	65
%	%	%	**ASSETS**	%	%	%	%	%	%
10.8	10.0	11.6	Cash & Equivalents	12.4	13.5	12.1	11.0	10.9	9.1
31.2	31.5	32.2	Trade Receivables (net)	18.2	27.2	29.2	38.2	39.3	38.0
2.7	2.1	2.3	Inventory	3.2	3.5	1.3	1.4	2.5	1.5
6.2	6.8	6.3	All Other Current	3.2	3.6	4.5	7.8	9.4	9.1
50.9	50.3	52.4	Total Current	37.0	47.9	47.1	58.4	62.0	57.7
42.2	42.8	40.5	Fixed Assets (net)	50.9	45.9	43.7	36.9	32.2	35.4
1.2	1.0	.9	Intangibles (net)	1.0	1.1	1.4	.5	.5	.7
5.8	5.8	6.2	All Other Non-Current	11.0	5.1	7.9	4.3	5.3	6.1
100.0	100.0	100.0	Total	100.0	100.0	100.0	100.0	100.0	100.0
			LIABILITIES						
7.1	7.3	8.2	Notes Payable-Short Term	16.4	7.8	7.2	7.9	5.7	5.8
7.6	8.5	6.8	Cur. Mat.-L/T/D	5.4	7.6	6.8	7.5	6.8	5.8
13.5	14.6	14.2	Trade Payables	7.3	9.5	11.4	16.9	20.6	18.3
.9	.7	.8	Income Taxes Payable	.4	.8	.9	1.3	.9	.3
8.5	8.8	9.3	All Other Current	11.2	6.9	9.2	8.6	9.7	12.7
37.6	39.9	39.3	Total Current	40.7	32.6	35.6	42.3	43.6	42.9
20.4	21.3	23.3	Long-Term Debt	40.0	31.8	25.4	14.8	13.9	17.9
1.5	1.2	1.0	Deferred Taxes	.3	.6	1.0	1.4	1.2	1.9
2.6	3.0	4.0	All Other Non-Current	15.6	3.9	1.7	2.1	1.7	1.9
37.9	34.5	32.3	Net Worth	3.4	31.0	36.4	39.4	39.6	35.5
100.0	100.0	100.0	Total Liabilities & Net Worth	100.0	100.0	100.0	100.0	100.0	100.0
			INCOME DATA						
100.0	100.0	100.0	Net Sales	100.0	100.0	100.0	100.0	100.0	100.0
28.5	27.7	28.7	Gross Profit	50.9	36.6	28.8	24.3	17.0	16.7
24.4	24.1	23.5	Operating Expenses	45.9	30.8	23.2	19.6	12.3	11.6
4.1	3.6	5.2	Operating Profit	5.0	5.8	5.6	4.7	4.8	5.0
.7	.8	.8	All Other Expenses (net)	1.9	1.0	.8	.3	.5	.4
3.4	2.8	4.4	Profit Before Taxes	3.1	4.8	4.8	4.3	4.3	4.6
			RATIOS						
2.0	2.0	2.2	Current	2.7	2.8	2.6	2.0	1.9	1.7
1.3	1.3	1.4		1.1	1.5	1.3	1.4	1.4	1.3
1.0	.9	1.0		.4	1.0	1.0	1.0	1.1	1.1
1.7	1.7	1.9	Quick	2.4	2.2	2.1	1.8	1.6	1.4
1.1	(609) 1.1	1.1		.8	1.2	1.1	1.2	1.1	1.1
.8	.7	.8		.4	.7	.8	.8	.8	.9
35 10.5	32 11.3	32 11.3	Sales/Receivables	0 UND	24 15.2	29 12.5	42 8.7	43 8.4	53 6.9
55 6.7	57 6.4	56 6.5		28 13.0	48 7.6	56 6.5	62 5.9	60 6.1	72 5.1
78 4.7	79 4.6	82 4.5		63 5.7	79 4.6	77 4.8	85 4.3	88 4.2	89 4.1
0 UND	0 UND	0 UND	Cost of Sales/Inventory	0 UND	0 UND	0 UND	0 UND	0 UND	0 UND
0 UND	0 UND	0 UND		0 UND	0 UND	0 UND	0 UND	0 UND	0 UND
4 102.8	2 211.3	1 249.9		0 UND	0 953.5	1 343.4	1 290.9	1 274.0	3 108.7
11 32.1	13 27.2	12 30.2	Cost of Sales/Payables	0 UND	2 235.7	12 30.7	17 21.3	20 18.4	25 14.4
27 13.7	29 12.8	28 13.2		13 28.8	18 20.6	24 15.0	33 10.9	36 10.3	35 10.5
46 7.9	48 7.7	48 7.6		65 5.6	42 8.6	42 8.8	49 7.5	53 6.8	50 7.3
8.1	7.6	6.8	Sales/Working Capital	6.2	6.3	7.0	6.8	6.1	9.0
19.6	19.7	15.1		NM	14.5	15.9	14.2	14.3	14.8
NM	−77.7	549.7		−10.8	−177.0	−143.9	137.9	34.7	41.4
9.1	9.4	11.9	EBIT/Interest	7.8	8.9	14.0	11.9	16.6	12.7
(351) 3.3	(570) 3.7	(533) 4.7		(61) 2.3	(115) 4.0	(79) 4.7	(115) 5.8	(100) 5.3	(63) 5.7
1.0	.8	1.7		−1.0	1.1	1.3	3.0	2.0	2.6
2.9	3.0	3.3	Net Profit + Depr., Dep., Amort./Cur. Mat. L/T/D		3.7	3.6	2.8	2.9	3.3
(133) 1.8	(178) 1.7	(152) 2.0		(24) 2.4	(17) 2.7	(40) 2.0	(36) 1.8	(27) 1.6	
1.1	1.0	1.2			1.7	1.5	1.0	1.0	.8
.6	.6	.6	Fixed/Worth	.9	.6	.7	.4	.4	.5
1.1	1.1	1.1		3.2	1.2	1.0	.9	.8	1.1
2.0	2.3	2.1		−2.7	3.5	1.8	1.8	1.5	1.6
.8	.8	.8	Debt/Worth	.8	.7	.7	.7	.9	1.2
1.6	1.7	1.8		5.9	1.8	1.3	1.6	1.6	1.9
3.6	4.2	4.1		−5.6	6.8	3.1	3.1	2.9	4.0
32.5	35.3	41.7	% Profit Before Taxes/Tangible Net Worth	44.6	55.5	46.9	34.0	39.4	39.8
(354) 14.8	(549) 14.5	(519) 20.6		(47) 20.9	(106) 18.5	(78) 19.4	(114) 21.5	(109) 20.8	21.0
3.0	1.4	4.9		−5.0	3.3	3.8	6.7	3.5	8.9
12.1	13.4	15.8	% Profit Before Taxes/Total Assets	18.3	17.9	16.4	14.2	15.6	12.2
5.0	4.5	6.3		3.8	6.6	6.9	6.4	7.5	6.1
.0	−.3	1.1		−8.1	.6	.7	2.7	1.4	2.6
9.2	9.9	10.2	Sales/Net Fixed Assets	8.0	9.4	8.2	11.4	12.7	10.1
4.9	4.9	5.5		3.9	5.0	4.5	5.6	7.3	6.5
2.9	2.9	3.3		2.3	2.9	2.8	3.8	4.5	3.9
2.5	2.7	2.6	Sales/Total Assets	3.0	2.8	2.8	2.6	2.6	2.5
2.0	2.1	2.1		1.8	2.1	1.9	2.1	2.2	2.1
1.5	1.4	1.5		1.1	1.4	1.3	1.7	1.7	1.6
3.2	3.1	3.2	% Depr., Dep., Amort./Sales	5.7	4.1	3.9	2.9	2.6	1.2
(355) 5.7	(551) 5.6	(514) 5.1		(60) 9.8	(103) 7.3	(76) 6.0	(109) 4.9	(108) 3.8	(58) 3.6
9.3	9.2	8.1		15.8	11.2	9.6	6.8	5.3	5.3
1.8	1.9	1.7	% Officers', Directors', Owners' Comp/Sales	5.5	2.9	1.8	1.6	1.2	.7
(175) 3.4	(282) 3.5	(259) 3.3		(33) 9.4	(64) 4.2	(37) 3.2	(53) 2.6	(53) 2.4	(19) 1.4
6.3	6.0	6.1		14.8	6.3	6.0	5.1	3.7	2.3
5375492M	6647157M	8954613M	Net Sales ($)	43048M	249075M	339481M	879280M	1716208M	5727521M
2699590M	3577696M	4346733M	Total Assets ($)	33354M	145419M	211432M	447420M	857733M	2651375M

M = $ thousand   MM = $ million
See Pages 11 through 21 for Explanation of Ratios and Data

Current Data Sorted By Assets | Comparative Historical Data

Type of Statement								
	3	13	51	31	5	2		
	10	88	119	15		2		
	32	61	37	1				
	84	39	12	2	2	2		
	40	72	65	16	1	1		

Unqualified	67	50
Reviewed	113	119
Compiled	94	99
Tax Returns	58	41
Other	109	108

	0-500M	500M-2MM	2-10MM	10-50MM	50-100MM	100-250MM	4/1/00-3/31/01 ALL	4/1/01-3/31/02 ALL
	155 (4/1-9/30/04)			649 (10/1/04-3/31/05)				
NUMBER OF STATEMENTS	169	273	284	65	8	5	441	417
ASSETS	%	%	%	%	%	%	%	%
Cash & Equivalents	13.1	11.1	11.2	10.3			10.3	11.1
Trade Receivables (net)	28.6	41.7	44.5	36.0			42.8	39.9
Inventory	13.2	9.5	7.4	9.6			7.4	8.9
All Other Current	3.3	5.5	8.2	8.2			7.0	6.4
Total Current	58.1	67.7	71.3	64.0			67.5	66.3
Fixed Assets (net)	31.6	25.1	21.0	26.8			24.4	24.9
Intangibles (net)	2.0	1.4	1.7	4.8			2.3	2.3
All Other Non-Current	8.3	5.8	6.0	4.4			5.8	6.4
Total	100.0	100.0	100.0	100.0			100.0	100.0
LIABILITIES								
Notes Payable-Short Term	20.3	11.6	9.9	7.3			10.9	10.1
Cur. Mat.-L/T/D	6.3	4.8	3.9	3.9			4.5	4.6
Trade Payables	16.4	17.8	18.6	18.0			19.7	16.8
Income Taxes Payable	.2	.8	1.0	.5			.6	.7
All Other Current	22.5	11.3	11.7	11.8			13.8	16.8
Total Current	65.7	46.3	45.1	41.5			49.4	48.9
Long-Term Debt	30.5	17.1	10.4	14.8			12.9	13.0
Deferred Taxes	.0	.5	1.0	.6			.7	.7
All Other Non-Current	4.9	4.4	3.1	3.3			2.9	2.9
Net Worth	-1.1	31.7	40.4	39.9			34.2	34.6
Total Liabilities & Net Worth	100.0	100.0	100.0	100.0			100.0	100.0
INCOME DATA								
Net Sales	100.0	100.0	100.0	100.0			100.0	100.0
Gross Profit	42.6	32.3	23.9	23.0			29.5	30.3
Operating Expenses	38.5	28.3	20.5	17.4			25.5	25.3
Operating Profit	4.2	4.1	3.4	5.6			4.0	5.0
All Other Expenses (net)	1.3	.6	.1	.1			.7	1.1
Profit Before Taxes	2.8	3.4	3.3	5.6			3.4	3.9
RATIOS								
Current	2.4	2.4	2.4	2.0			2.0	2.3
	1.1	1.6	1.5	1.5			1.3	1.4
	.6	1.1	1.2	1.1			1.1	1.1
Quick	1.6	1.9	1.9	1.4			1.6	1.8
	(168) .9	(272) 1.2	1.2	1.1			1.1	1.1
	.3	.8	.8	.8			.8	.8
Sales/Receivables	0 UND	30 12.3	43 8.4	41 8.9			35 10.3	32 11.4
	18 20.2	50 7.3	62 5.9	58 6.3			55 6.6	54 6.7
	36 10.1	80 4.6	86 4.2	86 4.3			79 4.6	76 4.8
Cost of Sales/Inventory	0 UND	0 UND	0 UND	0 UND			0 UND	0 UND
	0 UND	3 129.8	2 154.2	9 38.8			3 129.8	5 72.5
	23 16.2	21 17.0	21 17.8	30 12.1			19 19.2	25 14.5
Cost of Sales/Payables	0 UND	12 31.2	17 22.0	21 17.4			14 26.0	13 28.6
	13 29.0	27 13.3	29 12.8	34 10.6			29 12.5	26 14.1
	36 10.2	48 7.7	48 7.7	56 6.5			50 7.3	47 7.8
Sales/Working Capital	13.6	6.5	6.0	6.0			7.8	6.7
	78.0	12.9	11.3	11.4			17.5	13.8
	-19.9	52.8	26.0	25.8			92.3	80.3
EBIT/Interest	11.9	14.1	18.2	30.1			10.9	10.8
	(140) 3.6	(244) 5.3	(255) 5.7	(58) 9.8			(395) 4.0	(373) 4.3
	-.3	1.7	1.7	2.4			1.3	1.2
Net Profit + Depr., Dep., Amort./Cur. Mat. L /T/D		5.5	8.4	6.4			5.8	9.2
		(60) 2.2	(105) 2.8	(23) 3.5			(110) 2.6	(99) 3.2
		.9	1.3	1.3			1.3	1.5
Fixed/Worth	.4	.2	.2	.3			.2	.2
	2.2	.6	.4	.5			.6	.6
	-2.0	1.9	1.0	1.6			1.7	1.6
Debt/Worth	1.4	.8	.8	.9			1.0	.8
	6.0	1.8	1.7	1.6			2.1	1.7
	-6.1	5.6	3.5	4.0			5.1	4.8
% Profit Before Taxes/Tangible Net Worth	205.8	53.2	42.4	44.6			54.2	53.4
	(108) 55.0	(238) 26.2	(273) 17.3	(61) 27.9			(401) 22.8	(384) 24.7
	9.6	6.2	4.7	10.2			6.9	5.5
% Profit Before Taxes/Total Assets	32.4	18.8	15.3	18.1			17.2	16.9
	10.1	8.1	6.2	7.9			6.6	7.3
	-4.1	1.7	1.3	2.3			1.4	1.1
Sales/Net Fixed Assets	49.5	39.3	39.1	29.2			34.6	35.8
	19.7	16.4	16.6	10.6			16.2	16.1
	9.7	7.1	7.1	4.6			7.4	7.2
Sales/Total Assets	8.0	3.9	3.4	2.8			3.8	3.7
	5.0	2.9	2.5	2.0			2.7	2.7
	3.1	2.1	1.8	1.5			2.1	1.9
% Depr., Dep., Amort./Sales	1.0	.7	.8	.8			.6	.7
	(115) 2.3	(230) 1.5	(254) 1.6	(58) 2.0			(397) 1.6	(370) 1.7
	4.0	3.5	3.6	4.1			3.3	3.2
% Officers', Directors', Owners' Comp/Sales	3.7	2.6	1.8	1.2			2.4	2.4
	(102) 7.8	(149) 4.3	(114) 3.0	(14) 1.8			(224) 4.7	(201) 4.0
	13.8	6.7	5.3	3.8			8.5	7.6
Net Sales ($)	220862M	999711M	3222963M	2900842M	2215818M	2816641M	7561275M	5637188M
Total Assets ($)	42651M	313732M	1246897M	1336869M	538264M	878709M	3100310M	2125206M

© RMA 2005

M = $ thousand   MM = $ million
See Pages 11 through 21 for Explanation of Ratios and Data

Comparative Historical Data / Current Data Sorted By Sales

82	85	105	Type of Statement	3	6	7	18	34	37
158	223	232	Unqualified	8	38	48	69	54	15
78	127	131	Reviewed	17	52	14	33	13	2
65	124	141	Compiled	35	59	20	16	7	4
111	175	195	Tax Returns	23	49	31	43	34	15
4/1/02-	4/1/03-	4/1/04-	Other						
3/31/03	3/31/04	3/31/05		155 (4/1-9/30/04)			649 (10/1/04-3/31/05)		
ALL	ALL	ALL		0-1MM	1-3MM	3-5MM	5-10MM	10-25MM	25MM & OVER
494	734	804	**NUMBER OF STATEMENTS**	86	204	120	179	142	73
%	%	%	**ASSETS**	%	%	%	%	%	%
11.9	11.1	11.5	Cash & Equivalents	11.1	11.6	12.9	10.9	10.9	11.8
41.2	38.8	39.4	Trade Receivables (net)	31.6	33.7	42.1	43.3	43.7	41.8
8.4	9.0	9.4	Inventory	12.1	10.8	8.5	8.3	9.2	6.8
7.4	6.5	6.2	All Other Current	2.8	3.9	6.7	8.4	7.4	7.9
68.8	65.4	66.5	Total Current	57.6	60.1	70.2	71.0	71.3	68.3
22.7	25.1	25.1	Fixed Assets (net)	32.5	30.6	22.7	21.6	21.2	21.1
2.5	3.0	2.1	Intangibles (net)	1.2	2.2	1.5	1.5	2.1	5.8
5.9	6.5	6.3	All Other Non-Current	8.7	7.1	5.5	6.0	5.4	4.8
100.0	100.0	100.0	Total	100.0	100.0	100.0	100.0	100.0	100.0
			LIABILITIES						
10.3	12.3	12.5	Notes Payable-Short Term	24.1	14.9	9.1	10.5	10.0	7.2
4.6	4.3	4.7	Cur. Mat.-L/T/D	3.4	6.5	5.1	4.1	3.7	3.6
18.1	17.8	17.8	Trade Payables	15.1	16.3	16.3	17.0	21.6	22.8
.7	.7	.7	Income Taxes Payable	.1	.6	1.0	.9	.7	.7
13.8	12.9	13.9	All Other Current	25.1	12.9	11.3	12.1	12.5	14.8
47.6	47.9	49.6	Total Current	67.9	51.2	42.7	44.7	48.5	49.1
14.3	15.6	17.5	Long-Term Debt	31.0	22.3	18.4	10.8	12.0	13.5
.6	.6	.6	Deferred Taxes	.1	.5	.5	.8	.8	.7
2.3	4.2	3.9	All Other Non-Current	5.4	4.7	3.8	4.1	2.9	2.2
35.2	31.7	28.4	Net Worth	-4.3	21.3	34.5	39.7	35.8	34.5
100.0	100.0	100.0	Total Liabilities & Net Worth	100.0	100.0	100.0	100.0	100.0	100.0
			INCOME DATA						
100.0	100.0	100.0	Net Sales	100.0	100.0	100.0	100.0	100.0	100.0
30.5	31.3	30.7	Gross Profit	45.4	36.7	30.3	27.2	22.9	21.4
26.9	27.7	26.7	Operating Expenses	41.1	33.0	26.3	23.6	18.3	16.5
3.6	3.6	4.1	Operating Profit	4.4	3.7	4.0	3.7	4.6	4.9
.6	.8	.6	All Other Expenses (net)	2.5	.4	.5	.2	.5	.0
2.9	2.8	3.5	Profit Before Taxes	1.9	3.4	3.5	3.5	4.1	4.9
			RATIOS						
2.2	2.3	2.4		2.4	2.6	2.9	2.4	2.2	1.8
1.5	1.5	1.5	Current	1.1	1.4	1.7	1.6	1.4	1.5
1.1	1.0	1.1		.7	.9	1.2	1.2	1.1	1.1
1.8	1.8	1.8		1.6	2.0	2.4	1.9	1.7	1.4
1.2 (733)	1.1 (802)	1.1	Quick	.9 (203)	1.1	1.2	1.3 (141)	1.1	1.1
.8	.7	.8		.3	.6	.8	.9	.8	.9
31 11.7	28 12.8	26 13.9		0 UND	16 23.2	30 12.0	35 10.3	40 9.2	34 10.8
54 6.8	51 7.2	50 7.3	Sales/Receivables	23 15.9	40 9.2	51 7.1	54 6.8	60 6.1	54 6.7
79 4.6	75 4.9	78 4.7		64 5.7	75 4.9	81 4.5	83 4.4	80 4.6	80 4.6
0 UND	0 UND	0 UND		0 UND	0 UND	0 UND	0 UND	0 UND	0 UND
3 108.5	3 125.0	3 139.6	Cost of Sales/Inventory	0 UND	1 325.0	3 119.4	2 150.3	5 73.6	3 109.1
25 14.8	23 15.9	21 17.1		35 10.5	22 16.7	21 17.0	20 18.0	23 16.2	16 22.8
12 29.9	12 31.6	11 33.5		0 UND	8 44.9	10 37.4	13 28.8	17 22.0	20 18.6
27 13.6	27 13.6	25 14.6	Cost of Sales/Payables	18 19.9	22 16.5	22 16.5	27 13.7	28 13.2	31 11.8
48 7.6	48 7.6	46 8.0		47 7.8	48 7.6	43 8.5	45 8.2	48 7.6	47 7.8
6.7	6.8	6.7		6.8	7.7	5.5	6.3	7.0	8.9
13.1	14.1	13.9	Sales/Working Capital	37.5	21.9	12.6	11.0	13.6	12.6
51.3	209.8	102.0		-17.5	-66.1	63.4	29.0	37.5	31.5
13.7	14.0	15.1		10.1	10.4	19.7	19.2	17.9	31.1
(433) 4.8	(644) 4.2	(708) 5.5	EBIT/Interest	(67) 2.7	(183) 4.1	(108) 6.3	(157) 5.8	(128) 6.1	(65) 10.1
1.1	1.2	1.6		-1.7	1.2	2.0	1.5	2.4	2.7
5.4	5.9	7.3			3.5	10.6	9.0	8.2	6.8
(125) 2.7	(169) 2.7	(199) 2.7	Net Profit + Depr., Dep., Amort./Cur. Mat. L/T/D	(30) 1.7	(31) 2.4	(56) 2.6	(48) 3.6	(29) 3.3	
1.3	1.2	1.2			.5	.8	.9	1.6	2.3
.2	.2	.2		.3	.3	.2	.2	.2	.3
.5	.6	.6	Fixed/Worth	1.3	1.3	.5	.4	.5	.5
1.5	2.0	2.1		-13.0	13.8	1.8	1.1	1.2	1.4
.8	.9	.9		1.2	.9	.8	.7	.9	1.2
1.7	2.0	2.1	Debt/Worth	5.9	2.3	1.9	1.6	1.9	1.9
4.1	7.0	6.0		-10.3	36.2	5.1	3.3	4.1	4.6
46.3	47.3	55.2		184.2	71.0	57.5	44.3	48.2	48.3
(437) 19.8	(628) 18.4	(690) 25.7	% Profit Before Taxes/Tangible Net Worth	(58) 38.0	(157) 28.7	(108) 30.6	(166) 18.0	(134) 25.0	(67) 26.8
2.8	3.6	6.1		-5.9	6.3	6.0	4.8	10.2	9.7
16.6	17.0	18.8		25.1	20.5	20.6	16.1	17.4	17.7
6.5	5.8	7.7	% Profit Before Taxes/Total Assets	6.8	8.3	9.7	7.3	7.1	7.2
.4	.5	1.2		-11.3	.7	1.8	1.4	2.6	2.0
35.8	36.8	40.6		41.4	35.2	48.3	36.2	44.5	41.2
18.7	16.1	17.1	Sales/Net Fixed Assets	11.3	13.9	21.3	17.8	20.9	20.9
8.6	7.7	7.3		5.2	5.8	9.7	9.5	8.0	7.6
3.9	4.0	4.0		5.6	4.8	3.9	3.8	3.7	3.7
2.9	2.8	2.9	Sales/Total Assets	3.0	2.9	3.0	2.9	2.8	2.7
2.1	2.0	2.0		1.7	1.9	2.3	2.0	2.0	1.9
.9	.9	.8		1.4	1.1	.7	.7	.5	.5
(444) 1.7	(630) 1.7	(665) 1.7	% Depr., Dep., Amort./Sales	(58) 2.8	(160) 2.2	(99) 1.5	(163) 1.5	(120) 1.4	(65) 1.6
3.2	3.7	3.7		5.8	4.5	4.1	3.1	3.1	3.0
2.6	2.3	2.3		5.3	2.7	2.3	2.4	1.5	1.1
(253) 4.8	(357) 4.3	(383) 4.4	% Officers', Directors', Owners' Comp/Sales	(45) 10.3	(117) 4.6	(66) 4.3	(84) 3.8	(54) 2.2	(17) 1.7
8.6	7.5	7.6		15.2	8.0	7.7	6.0	5.2	4.9
7677416M	9651731M	12376837M	Net Sales ($)	48460M	378913M	468800M	1295242M	2175211M	8010211M
2740534M	4209845M	4357122M	Total Assets ($)	21253M	152443M	180517M	527331M	874496M	2601082M

M = $ thousand   MM = $ million
See Pages 11 through 21 for Explanation of Ratios and Data

MANUFACTURING

Current Data Sorted By Assets   Comparative Historical Data

0-500M	500M-2MM	2-10MM	10-50MM	50-100MM	100-250MM	Type of Statement	4/1/00-3/31/01 ALL	4/1/01-3/31/02 ALL
1	1	12	19	3	2	Unqualified	24	28
2	2	3	2			Reviewed	15	11
	9	8	1			Compiled	26	18
1	4	1				Tax Returns		2
	2	5	8	3	5	Other	33	26
			60 (10/1/04-3/31/05)				4/1/00-3/31/01 ALL	4/1/01-3/31/02 ALL
4	18	29	30	6	7	NUMBER OF STATEMENTS	98	85
%	%	%	%	%	%	**ASSETS**	%	%
	12.5	10.0	8.9			Cash & Equivalents	9.1	8.0
	19.8	23.3	19.1			Trade Receivables (net)	24.8	22.0
	26.6	20.9	19.2			Inventory	22.3	22.5
	1.8	3.5	3.9			All Other Current	2.7	3.5
	60.7	57.6	51.1			Total Current	58.9	56.1
	33.6	36.6	37.3			Fixed Assets (net)	32.3	34.9
	2.2	.9	3.3			Intangibles (net)	3.1	3.4
	3.4	4.9	8.3			All Other Non-Current	5.7	5.7
	100.0	100.0	100.0			Total	100.0	100.0
						LIABILITIES		
	9.4	9.6	6.5			Notes Payable-Short Term	10.0	9.5
	3.9	3.3	3.1			Cur. Mat.-L/T/D	2.6	2.5
	16.2	18.3	14.3			Trade Payables	15.0	15.6
	.4	.3	.0			Income Taxes Payable	.4	.5
	6.1	7.0	8.1			All Other Current	10.9	8.6
	36.1	38.5	32.0			Total Current	39.0	36.7
	25.4	17.6	17.5			Long-Term Debt	14.8	17.0
	.0	.4	.4			Deferred Taxes	.7	.6
	3.6	.6	4.0			All Other Non-Current	11.6	4.6
	34.9	43.0	46.2			Net Worth	33.9	41.1
	100.0	100.0	100.0			Total Liabilities & Net Worth	100.0	100.0
						INCOME DATA		
	100.0	100.0	100.0			Net Sales	100.0	100.0
	33.0	20.7	24.2			Gross Profit	24.1	24.5
	31.7	18.4	16.1			Operating Expenses	20.3	20.8
	1.3	2.3	8.1			Operating Profit	3.8	3.7
	.0	.5	3.7			All Other Expenses (net)	.3	.6
	1.3	1.8	4.4			Profit Before Taxes	3.5	3.1
						RATIOS		
	3.9	2.4	2.2			Current	2.3	2.1
	1.7	1.6	1.6				1.5	1.5
	1.1	1.1	1.1				1.1	1.1
	1.6	1.2	1.4			Quick	1.5	1.2
	.8	.9	.9				.9	.8
	.5	.5	.6				.6	.6
13 27.3	21 17.3	17 20.9				Sales/Receivables	19 19.2	18 20.8
19 18.9	30 12.1	25 14.9					33 11.2	28 13.2
29 12.6	36 10.2	38 9.5					43 8.5	37 10.0
22 16.6	13 27.8	16 23.0				Cost of Sales/Inventory	19 19.0	19 19.2
53 6.9	32 11.6	29 12.6					32 11.5	30 12.3
73 5.0	53 6.9	53 6.9					52 7.0	48 7.7
8 44.6	21 17.7	16 23.3				Cost of Sales/Payables	16 22.4	13 27.2
20 18.0	28 12.9	24 15.1					25 14.4	24 15.3
29 12.5	36 10.0	30 12.0					37 9.9	33 11.1
	7.6	7.5	6.0			Sales/Working Capital	8.8	11.1
	18.6	12.1	15.0				14.1	16.7
	51.3	43.8	82.2				51.8	52.6
	7.1	13.5	31.1			EBIT/Interest	8.3	8.2
(15)	3.5	(26) 3.8	(27) 5.0				(87) 3.3	(80) 4.0
	1.0	1.3	2.5				1.5	1.6
						Net Profit + Depr., Dep., Amort./Cur. Mat. L/T/D	3.6	12.5
							(22) 1.9	(27) 3.5
							1.1	2.1
	.3	.5	.4			Fixed/Worth	.4	.5
	1.4	.7	.8				.9	1.0
	5.1	1.5	1.7				1.7	1.9
	.8	.8	.7			Debt/Worth	.7	.8
	2.4	1.3	1.5				1.8	1.6
	12.3	3.0	2.6				4.0	2.9
	24.9	32.8	33.3			% Profit Before Taxes/Tangible Net Worth	54.3	38.0
(15)	16.0	12.2	(29) 18.0				(92) 18.4	(80) 17.0
	5.6	4.9	4.5				4.5	4.9
	12.2	13.8	12.8			% Profit Before Taxes/Total Assets	15.7	14.2
	8.3	5.1	7.7				6.0	6.5
	.0	1.9	1.8				1.7	1.9
	20.3	17.7	10.4			Sales/Net Fixed Assets	19.4	17.4
	13.4	9.5	6.1				10.0	9.0
	4.5	3.9	4.8				4.9	5.1
	4.4	3.4	3.4			Sales/Total Assets	3.7	4.1
	3.6	2.7	2.5				2.5	2.9
	2.4	1.7	1.8				1.9	2.0
	1.7	1.0	1.1			% Depr., Dep., Amort./Sales	1.1	.7
(13)	2.7	(27) 2.2	(29) 1.6				(86) 1.8	(78) 1.5
	3.6	3.7	3.1				3.2	3.0
						% Officers', Directors', Owners' Comp/Sales	1.1	.9
							(22) 2.0	(17) 1.4
							3.8	3.8
3636M	73931M	360357M	1536571M	776844M	1843420M	Net Sales ($)	4121131M	5118814M
992M	19961M	135399M	624969M	415306M	1119618M	Total Assets ($)	1656298M	1848971M

34 (4/1-9/30/04)

© RMA 2005

M = $ thousand   MM = $ million
See Pages 11 through 21 for Explanation of Ratios and Data

Comparative Historical Data   Current Data Sorted By Sales

Hist 1	Hist 2	Hist 3	Type of Statement	0-1MM	1-3MM	3-5MM	5-10MM	10-25MM	25MM & OVER
39	34	38	Unqualified	1		1	5	9	23
14	12	7	Reviewed			2	2	3	1
9	31	20	Compiled	1	5		6	4	2
1	5	6	Tax Returns		3	1	1	1	
27	31	23	Other		1	1	4	2	15
4/1/02-3/31/03 ALL	4/1/03-3/31/04 ALL	4/1/04-3/31/05 ALL			34 (4/1-9/30/04)			60 (10/1/04-3/31/05)	
90	113	94	NUMBER OF STATEMENTS	2	9	5	18	19	41
%	%	%	**ASSETS**	%	%	%	%	%	%
9.7	6.9	9.4	Cash & Equivalents				11.6	9.1	9.4
22.7	23.1	20.2	Trade Receivables (net)				24.4	22.6	17.5
20.2	20.3	21.8	Inventory				21.8	21.3	19.7
4.1	4.4	3.7	All Other Current				5.4	1.6	4.6
56.6	54.8	55.1	Total Current				63.1	54.7	51.2
35.5	34.5	34.7	Fixed Assets (net)				29.2	38.8	34.0
1.3	2.5	4.2	Intangibles (net)				.9	1.5	7.7
6.6	8.1	6.0	All Other Non-Current				6.8	5.0	7.1
100.0	100.0	100.0	Total				100.0	100.0	100.0
			LIABILITIES						
11.0	7.9	8.3	Notes Payable-Short Term				8.6	7.3	6.1
2.6	4.5	3.5	Cur. Mat.-L/T/D				2.7	3.9	3.5
13.1	15.0	15.7	Trade Payables				19.0	16.9	14.5
.4	.3	.2	Income Taxes Payable				.0	.4	.2
9.4	6.4	7.3	All Other Current				9.7	5.1	8.1
36.6	34.1	35.1	Total Current				40.1	33.6	32.3
15.3	18.7	20.3	Long-Term Debt				16.4	19.2	19.3
.6	.6	.7	Deferred Taxes				.2	.4	1.3
3.1	5.2	2.5	All Other Non-Current				3.4	.6	3.8
44.5	41.4	41.3	Net Worth				40.0	46.2	43.3
100.0	100.0	100.0	Total Liabilities & Net Worth				100.0	100.0	100.0
			INCOME DATA						
100.0	100.0	100.0	Net Sales				100.0	100.0	100.0
26.2	22.0	25.4	Gross Profit				19.3	22.4	25.0
20.8	18.4	20.7	Operating Expenses				17.0	18.3	17.3
5.4	3.6	4.7	Operating Profit				2.3	4.1	7.7
.4	-.2	1.8	All Other Expenses (net)				.3	.9	3.4
5.0	3.9	2.9	Profit Before Taxes				2.0	3.2	4.3
			RATIOS						
2.4	2.5	2.3	Current				2.3	2.6	2.2
1.6	1.5	1.6					1.6	1.6	1.5
1.2	1.1	1.1					1.2	1.1	1.2
1.4	1.4	1.2	Quick				1.4	1.2	1.2
.8	(112) .8	.8					.9	.9	.8
.6	.6	.5					.5	.5	.6
20 18.0	20 18.7	17 21.2	Sales/Receivables				14 26.9	22 16.5	17 22.0
29 12.7	28 12.8	25 14.5					29 12.5	28 13.1	24 15.0
40 9.0	39 9.3	35 10.3					43 8.4	34 10.9	38 9.7
22 16.7	15 23.6	20 18.6	Cost of Sales/Inventory				17 20.9	11 34.6	17 21.6
36 10.3	29 12.6	35 10.5					28 12.9	29 12.4	33 11.1
67 5.4	53 6.9	66 5.5					51 7.2	56 6.6	67 5.4
14 25.6	15 24.9	16 22.3	Cost of Sales/Payables				17 21.7	11 21.9	16 22.4
25 14.3	21 17.6	24 15.5					33 11.1	23 16.2	24 15.3
34 10.8	36 10.1	36 10.2					44 8.4	33 11.0	36 10.1
7.0	7.7	7.7	Sales/Working Capital				7.2	7.2	7.9
12.9	16.0	14.3					13.7	12.1	14.9
42.3	60.0	45.6					31.7	85.2	39.2
15.8	14.3	12.2	EBIT/Interest				9.1	22.2	17.3
(82) 4.2	(103) 3.8	(81) 4.4				(17) 3.6	(17) 8.1	(36) 4.8
1.7	1.3	1.6					1.6	2.0	2.4
8.7	14.6	3.6	Net Profit + Depr., Dep., Amort./Cur. Mat. L/T/D						3.7
(17) 2.5	(25) 3.5	(20) 2.5							(11) 2.1
1.9	.9	1.3							.7
.4	.4	.5	Fixed/Worth				.3	.5	.5
.7	.8	.9					.7	.8	.9
1.9	1.7	2.2					2.1	1.4	1.9
.6	.6	.8	Debt/Worth				.9	.8	.9
1.2	1.6	1.6					1.3	1.2	1.6
3.1	3.1	3.3					3.7	2.9	3.0
41.9	30.8	32.0	% Profit Before Taxes/Tangible Net Worth				18.8	35.2	36.3
(87) 19.5	(106) 20.5	(87) 17.3					10.4	21.7	(38) 22.4
3.6	2.4	5.0					4.7	5.7	7.3
18.2	15.5	12.2	% Profit Before Taxes/Total Assets				8.9	17.1	13.3
7.6	7.1	6.2					4.4	8.7	7.1
1.4	.8	1.7					1.6	2.2	2.6
15.9	14.7	17.0	Sales/Net Fixed Assets				21.3	16.9	12.0
8.0	8.3	8.4					12.1	8.5	6.4
4.6	4.8	4.6					5.6	4.5	5.0
3.5	3.6	3.5	Sales/Total Assets				4.4	3.4	3.2
2.5	2.6	2.5					3.2	2.6	2.3
2.0	1.8	1.8					1.6	1.8	1.8
.9	1.0	1.1	% Depr., Dep., Amort./Sales				1.5	.7	1.1
(84) 2.0	(103) 1.8	(81) 1.9					(15) 2.7	2.2	(35) 1.7
3.1	3.1	3.2					4.5	3.0	2.9
.7	1.3	1.1	% Officers', Directors', Owners' Comp/Sales						
(26) 1.9	(28) 1.8	(21) 2.0							
3.4	3.7	3.6							
4367055M	4712778M	4594759M	Net Sales ($)	1034M	15972M	18816M	124623M	283098M	4151216M
1908618M	2215346M	2316245M	Total Assets ($)	647M	6418M	7058M	85542M	119781M	2096799M

M = $ thousand   MM = $ million
See Pages 11 through 21 for Explanation of Ratios and Data

Current Data Sorted By Assets   Comparative Historical Data

0-500M	500M-2MM	2-10MM	10-50MM	50-100MM	100-250MM		15	16
1	1	4	7	8	6	**Type of Statement**		
	2	2	1			Unqualified	15	16
	2	2				Reviewed	5	6
	1					Compiled	7	7
1	1	3	4	1	1	Tax Returns	1	2
						Other	16	16
	27 (4/1-9/30/04)		20 (10/1/04-3/31/05)				4/1/00-3/31/01 ALL	4/1/01-3/31/02 ALL
1	7	11	12	9	7	**NUMBER OF STATEMENTS**	44	47
%	%	%	%	%	%	**ASSETS**	%	%
		3.6	4.9			Cash & Equivalents	7.5	6.7
		20.1	18.7			Trade Receivables (net)	20.1	17.8
		22.1	21.0			Inventory	17.1	17.7
		3.0	2.6			All Other Current	1.2	1.9
		48.8	47.2			Total Current	45.9	44.2
		39.5	44.9			Fixed Assets (net)	44.3	47.2
		3.9	3.6			Intangibles (net)	3.7	2.1
		7.7	4.4			All Other Non-Current	6.1	6.6
		100.0	100.0			Total	100.0	100.0
						LIABILITIES		
		6.7	8.8			Notes Payable-Short Term	7.2	8.1
		3.4	3.8			Cur. Mat.-L/T/D	3.3	3.6
		8.2	9.9			Trade Payables	12.9	10.6
		.1	.2			Income Taxes Payable	.3	.4
		8.5	6.3			All Other Current	4.9	6.4
		26.9	29.0			Total Current	28.5	29.1
		15.9	24.6			Long-Term Debt	24.9	22.3
		.5	2.5			Deferred Taxes	1.1	1.5
		1.1	4.2			All Other Non-Current	3.9	4.8
		55.7	39.7			Net Worth	41.6	42.3
		100.0	100.0			Total Liabilities & Net Worth	100.0	100.0
						INCOME DATA		
		100.0	100.0			Net Sales	100.0	100.0
		29.8	19.5			Gross Profit	22.7	23.0
		26.3	16.7			Operating Expenses	22.0	19.8
		3.4	2.7			Operating Profit	.7	3.2
		.5	1.1			All Other Expenses (net)	−.7	1.5
		3.0	1.6			Profit Before Taxes	1.3	1.8
						RATIOS		
		2.8	2.1				2.7	2.2
		1.7	1.9			Current	1.6	1.6
		1.4	1.4				1.0	1.1
		1.7	1.1				1.9	1.3
		.7	.9			Quick	1.0	.9
		.6	.7				.4	.5
		18 20.7	26 14.2				25 14.5	23 15.8
		31 12.0	30 12.1			Sales/Receivables	32 11.4	31 11.7
		45 8.2	43 8.4				41 8.9	38 9.5
		40 9.0	32 11.3				19 19.2	26 14.1
		44 8.3	47 7.8			Cost of Sales/Inventory	35 10.4	35 10.4
		54 6.7	65 5.7				57 6.4	62 5.9
		12 30.6	13 29.0				15 24.0	13 28.6
		15 24.7	16 22.2			Cost of Sales/Payables	23 16.1	18 20.3
		24 14.9	32 11.4				35 10.4	35 10.6
		6.7	7.2				6.2	6.1
		11.9	9.8			Sales/Working Capital	13.8	11.8
		29.6	15.6				218.0	121.3
			5.5				6.0	4.3
			3.4			EBIT/Interest	(42) 2.6	(44) 2.3
			1.2				1.1	.8
						Net Profit + Depr., Dep.,	5.9	5.8
						Amort./Cur. Mat. L /T/D	(14) 3.1	(15) 2.5
							1.8	1.7
		.3	.6				.6	.7
		.6	1.4			Fixed/Worth	1.1	1.4
		1.3	1.9				2.1	3.1
		.5	.7				.8	.7
		.8	1.6			Debt/Worth	1.3	1.4
		1.2	3.3				2.9	3.7
		32.2	19.3			% Profit Before Taxes/Tangible	19.4	16.8
		4.8	(10) 11.0			Net Worth	(40) 9.3	(44) 7.9
		−4.5	−.9				1.0	−1.9
		13.8	6.9			% Profit Before Taxes/Total	7.8	8.1
		3.1	3.7			Assets	3.6	2.5
		−1.0	.2				.1	−.5
		13.7	8.0				8.7	7.0
		6.8	5.9			Sales/Net Fixed Assets	4.4	4.5
		4.4	2.7				2.2	3.2
		2.9	3.0				2.6	2.7
		2.4	2.2			Sales/Total Assets	1.9	2.2
		1.9	1.3				1.2	1.5
		1.4	2.1				2.1	1.6
		(10) 2.0	2.8			% Depr., Dep., Amort./Sales	(39) 3.2	(43) 2.8
		3.5	5.1				4.4	4.5
						% Officers', Directors',		1.4
						Owners' Comp/Sales		(10) 3.9
								10.2
588M	23478M	151149M	632146M	974880M	2013397M	Net Sales ($)	2145928M	2295264M
401M	9361M	68269M	309376M	603615M	933217M	Total Assets ($)	1189207M	1336802M

M = $ thousand   MM = $ million
See Pages 11 through 21 for Explanation of Ratios and Data

Comparative Historical Data | Current Data Sorted By Sales

18	25	26	Type of Statement						
18	25	26	Unqualified				1	5	20
1	2	5	Reviewed	1	1			3	
4	10	5	Compiled	1		2	2		
2	2	1	Tax Returns		1				
13	15	10	Other				2	3	5
4/1/02-3/31/03	4/1/03-3/31/04	4/1/04-3/31/05			27 (4/1-9/30/04)			20 (10/1/04-3/31/05)	
ALL	ALL	ALL		0-1MM	1-3MM	3-5MM	5-10MM	10-25MM	25MM & OVER
38	54	47	**NUMBER OF STATEMENTS**	2	2	2	5	11	25
%	%	%	**ASSETS**	%	%	%	%	%	%
4.7	3.8	5.2	Cash & Equivalents					2.0	4.3
19.9	18.5	18.0	Trade Receivables (net)					18.2	18.4
19.2	20.0	19.8	Inventory					22.0	21.4
2.3	3.7	3.4	All Other Current					3.2	3.5
46.1	45.9	46.4	Total Current					45.4	47.6
45.4	44.4	45.2	Fixed Assets (net)					47.5	45.2
3.5	3.3	3.3	Intangibles (net)					2.2	3.7
5.0	6.3	5.1	All Other Non-Current					4.9	3.5
100.0	100.0	100.0	Total					100.0	100.0
			LIABILITIES						
11.3	10.5	8.2	Notes Payable-Short Term					9.1	7.9
2.8	3.5	3.5	Cur. Mat.-L/T/D					3.6	3.0
11.1	11.8	9.7	Trade Payables					6.2	10.5
.4	.2	.3	Income Taxes Payable					.1	.3
5.4	7.0	7.1	All Other Current					11.0	6.9
31.0	33.1	28.7	Total Current					30.0	28.6
26.1	22.9	24.1	Long-Term Debt					23.0	23.6
1.7	1.4	2.1	Deferred Taxes					.0	3.2
3.2	5.0	2.5	All Other Non-Current					1.8	3.9
38.0	37.5	42.7	Net Worth					45.2	40.7
100.0	100.0	100.0	Total Liabilities & Net Worth					100.0	100.0
			INCOME DATA						
100.0	100.0	100.0	Net Sales					100.0	100.0
21.8	24.0	21.9	Gross Profit					24.5	15.2
17.7	20.8	19.1	Operating Expenses					21.0	12.2
4.1	3.2	2.9	Operating Profit					3.5	3.0
.9	1.3	1.0	All Other Expenses (net)					1.1	1.0
3.2	1.8	1.9	Profit Before Taxes					2.4	2.0
			RATIOS						
2.3	1.9	2.1	Current					1.8	2.1
1.4	1.4	1.7						1.6	1.7
1.1	1.1	1.4						1.4	1.3
1.3	1.0	1.1	Quick					.9	1.1
.7	.7	.8						.7	.9
.5	.4	.5						.5	.5
25 14.5	25 14.7	23 15.9	Sales/Receivables					23 15.9	28 13.2
34 10.8	34 10.7	31 11.9						31 11.6	31 11.7
41 9.0	42 8.8	39 9.3						48 7.6	38 9.6
16 23.1	27 13.6	31 11.7	Cost of Sales/Inventory					32 11.3	32 11.3
43 8.4	45 8.2	46 7.9						47 7.8	47 7.8
64 5.7	59 6.2	57 6.4						63 5.8	61 6.0
16 23.3	14 26.1	14 26.6	Cost of Sales/Payables					12 30.6	14 26.0
21 17.6	27 13.5	17 21.1						15 24.7	17 21.5
29 12.6	46 8.0	30 12.4						19 19.4	34 10.9
6.7	7.8	7.0	Sales/Working Capital					5.5	7.6
14.1	16.9	11.7						13.8	10.3
51.2	74.0	25.6						29.6	20.7
6.1	5.9	12.8	EBIT/Interest						7.9
(37) 2.4	(53) 2.1	(45) 4.0							2.9
1.2	.6	1.1							1.1
5.9	4.1	3.1	Net Profit + Depr., Dep.,						3.3
(14) 3.2	(20) 2.0	(21) 1.9	Amort./Cur. Mat. L/T/D					(15)	1.9
2.8	.4	1.1							1.2
.7	.8	.6	Fixed/Worth					.5	.8
1.3	1.4	1.2						.7	1.4
2.8	2.2	1.8						1.6	1.9
.9	.9	.7	Debt/Worth					.8	.7
1.7	1.8	1.2						1.0	1.9
3.6	3.6	2.9						1.2	3.5
30.6	19.8	17.8	% Profit Before Taxes/Tangible					19.5	17.8
(35) 13.6	(49) 10.6	(43) 12.8	Net Worth					(10) 5.5	(23) 13.2
2.6	-6.3	.9						-5.0	.9
9.2	7.4	9.8	% Profit Before Taxes/Total					10.6	8.2
4.3	3.9	3.4	Assets					1.1	3.4
1.0	-1.4	.2						-1.0	.3
6.7	7.0	8.8	Sales/Net Fixed Assets					11.2	7.8
5.1	4.6	5.3						4.8	5.3
2.5	2.6	2.3						1.9	2.3
2.5	2.7	2.8	Sales/Total Assets					2.9	2.7
2.0	2.0	2.1						2.1	2.2
1.4	1.4	1.3						1.3	1.3
2.2	1.6	1.8	% Depr., Dep., Amort./Sales					1.3	2.1
(31) 2.8	(48) 2.4	(42) 3.0						(10) 2.0	(22) 2.7
4.9	3.8	4.4						4.5	4.4
1.6	1.7		% Officers', Directors',						
(12) 3.3	(10) 2.9		Owners' Comp/Sales						
6.3	6.8								
3096560M	3542131M	3795638M	Net Sales ($)	1543M	3824M	6296M	35323M	189715M	3558937M
1646673M	1969694M	1924239M	Total Assets ($)	1727M	1553M	2881M	13362M	119560M	1785156M

© RMA 2005

M = $ thousand   MM = $ million
See Pages 11 through 21 for Explanation of Ratios and Data

Current Data Sorted By Assets | Comparative Historical Data

0-500M	500M-2MM	2-10MM	10-50MM	50-100MM	100-250MM	Type of Statement	4/1/00-3/31/01 ALL	4/1/01-3/31/02 ALL
1	4	4	7	3	2	Unqualified	25	17
3	4	5	3			Reviewed	12	8
4	6					Compiled	12	15
						Tax Returns	3	4
1	4	9	6	4	3	Other	22	23
	37 (4/1-9/30/04)		41 (10/1/04-3/31/05)					
9	18	23	16	7	5	NUMBER OF STATEMENTS	74	67
%	%	%	%	%	%	**ASSETS**	%	%
	6.5	9.4	3.9			Cash & Equivalents	7.3	8.0
	17.5	19.5	19.0			Trade Receivables (net)	15.4	16.9
	39.2	25.9	33.4			Inventory	30.0	29.7
	.4	.7	4.5			All Other Current	2.2	1.3
	63.6	55.6	60.8			Total Current	55.0	56.0
	23.0	33.1	34.0			Fixed Assets (net)	36.2	36.2
	7.4	5.0	.8			Intangibles (net)	4.3	2.8
	6.0	6.3	4.4			All Other Non-Current	4.5	5.0
	100.0	100.0	100.0			Total	100.0	100.0
						LIABILITIES		
	19.7	8.5	15.2			Notes Payable-Short Term	12.2	12.2
	4.2	3.2	3.9			Cur. Mat.-L/T/D	3.4	3.7
	13.1	13.1	15.7			Trade Payables	10.9	12.8
	1.1	.2	.1			Income Taxes Payable	.1	.6
	8.2	8.1	6.0			All Other Current	6.4	6.8
	46.3	33.0	40.9			Total Current	33.0	36.1
	15.4	18.1	8.8			Long-Term Debt	19.4	16.4
	1.5	.6	1.3			Deferred Taxes	.7	.6
	18.3	6.8	3.1			All Other Non-Current	9.0	6.9
	18.5	41.4	46.0			Net Worth	37.8	39.8
	100.0	100.0	100.0			Total Liabilities & Net Worth	100.0	100.0
						INCOME DATA		
	100.0	100.0	100.0			Net Sales	100.0	100.0
	38.8	35.8	20.1			Gross Profit	33.6	34.7
	38.7	30.9	17.1			Operating Expenses	26.7	28.0
	.1	4.9	3.0			Operating Profit	6.9	6.8
	1.6	.8	.2			All Other Expenses (net)	2.3	1.1
	−1.4	4.0	2.7			Profit Before Taxes	4.5	5.7
						RATIOS		
	2.5	3.8	2.6			Current	3.2	2.6
	1.3	2.1	1.4				1.8	1.6
	.8	1.1	1.1				1.2	1.2
	.9	1.5	.9			Quick	1.3	1.4
	.4	.9	.5				.6	.6
	.2	.6	.4				.3	.4
	10 37.9	13 28.0	15 24.5			Sales/Receivables	16 23.3	12 29.9
	15 25.1	20 18.5	23 16.0				25 14.5	24 15.0
	44 8.3	45 8.1	48 7.6				38 9.5	40 9.2
	60 6.1	35 10.4	33 11.0			Cost of Sales/Inventory	50 7.4	47 7.8
	78 4.7	63 5.8	73 5.0				74 4.9	70 5.2
	113 3.2	96 3.8	95 3.8				114 3.2	100 3.6
	8 46.1	17 21.8	14 26.2			Cost of Sales/Payables	14 25.8	13 28.6
	13 28.5	24 15.0	27 13.5				22 17.0	22 16.2
	35 10.4	46 8.0	51 7.2				41 9.0	40 9.1
	6.3	4.0	5.0			Sales/Working Capital	4.7	5.6
	20.9	9.6	15.8				8.9	12.6
	−27.7	61.7	32.7				21.8	26.8
	2.7	14.5	25.0			EBIT/Interest	5.1	8.6
	(16) .4	(22) 3.3	(15) 7.0				(70) 2.0	(60) 4.2
	−4.0	1.6	1.3				1.0	1.4
						Net Profit + Depr., Dep., Amort./Cur. Mat. L/T/D	4.8	6.7
							(22) 2.8	(26) 3.4
							1.1	1.3
	.3	.4	.4			Fixed/Worth	.5	.4
	1.1	.8	.7				1.0	.9
	−2.3	1.9	1.9				2.1	1.7
	1.0	.6	.4			Debt/Worth	.5	.7
	3.3	1.5	1.1				1.8	1.5
	−15.2	3.4	5.1				3.2	2.6
	12.5	31.7	32.5			% Profit Before Taxes/Tangible Net Worth	32.6	39.4
	(13) −2.8	(19) 10.2	(14) 17.8				(67) 12.8	(61) 15.5
	−24.3	5.2	3.1				2.8	6.3
	5.4	15.1	16.0			% Profit Before Taxes/Total Assets	11.5	17.8
	−1.1	5.4	7.6				5.1	7.9
	−6.5	1.4	1.0				.1	2.0
	29.0	12.9	9.8			Sales/Net Fixed Assets	12.1	12.1
	17.8	7.3	7.3				5.9	7.3
	8.8	4.3	4.9				2.8	3.6
	3.9	3.3	2.6			Sales/Total Assets	2.6	3.1
	2.4	2.3	2.2				1.8	2.1
	1.9	1.5	1.6				1.3	1.5
	1.2	1.7	1.3			% Depr., Dep., Amort./Sales	1.4	1.2
	(15) 2.2	(22) 2.5	(14) 2.4				(64) 2.4	(60) 2.3
	3.3	3.2	3.0				4.0	3.2
	2.7					% Officers', Directors', Owners' Comp/Sales	1.4	1.6
	(10) 3.9						(24) 3.3	(22) 5.1
	6.8						7.3	9.2
8004M	65629M	240207M	793413M	746228M	1955504M	Net Sales ($)	2162390M	1699403M
2339M	20934M	105552M	378494M	480804M	927757M	Total Assets ($)	1217357M	981542M

M = $ thousand   MM = $ million
See Pages 11 through 21 for Explanation of Ratios and Data

Comparative Historical Data | **Current Data Sorted By Sales**

			Type of Statement	0-1MM	1-3MM	3-5MM	5-10MM	10-25MM	25MM & OVER
28	25	16	Unqualified		4	1	1	3	12
16	12	13	Reviewed		1	4	5	2	3
16	23	12	Compiled	2	4		3	1	
8	9	10	Tax Returns	5			1	5	
20	29	27	Other	1	2		6		13
4/1/02-3/31/03 ALL	4/1/03-3/31/04 ALL	4/1/04-3/31/05 ALL		___ 37 (4/1-9/30/04) ___			___ 41 (10/1/04-3/31/05) ___		
88	98	78	**NUMBER OF STATEMENTS**	8	11	5	16	10	28
%	%	%	**ASSETS**	%	%	%	%	%	%
8.9	8.2	7.6	Cash & Equivalents		8.5		6.3	9.9	5.0
15.5	14.7	16.1	Trade Receivables (net)		12.0		18.9	20.4	17.5
28.7	28.4	31.3	Inventory		34.8		33.7	25.2	32.0
1.8	1.9	2.4	All Other Current		3.7		.7	.5	3.9
55.0	53.2	57.4	Total Current		58.9		59.7	56.0	58.4
33.7	33.7	30.1	Fixed Assets (net)		26.4		29.1	36.7	28.8
3.1	5.0	6.2	Intangibles (net)		10.8		3.8	2.5	7.9
8.2	8.1	6.4	All Other Non-Current		3.9		7.5	4.8	5.0
100.0	100.0	100.0	Total		100.0		100.0	100.0	100.0
			LIABILITIES						
12.7	11.0	14.6	Notes Payable-Short Term		22.3		13.4	11.4	10.8
3.7	3.8	3.2	Cur. Mat.-L/T/D		1.6		4.6	2.9	2.8
11.5	10.0	13.4	Trade Payables		13.2		12.2	14.3	14.2
.2	.4	.5	Income Taxes Payable		1.5		.2	.2	.5
7.7	9.1	8.3	All Other Current		6.9		8.7	9.5	9.4
35.8	34.3	40.0	Total Current		45.4		39.2	38.2	37.6
16.8	14.8	17.4	Long-Term Debt		16.6		13.9	17.3	12.2
.5	1.1	1.2	Deferred Taxes		.0		2.2	.1	1.9
8.7	8.9	10.4	All Other Non-Current		10.0		18.1	12.1	4.4
38.3	41.0	31.0	Net Worth		28.0		26.7	32.3	43.9
100.0	100.0	100.0	Total Liabilities & Net Worth		100.0		100.0	100.0	100.0
			INCOME DATA						
100.0	100.0	100.0	Net Sales		100.0		100.0	100.0	100.0
34.3	37.7	34.0	Gross Profit		42.0		33.1	34.4	21.2
31.1	32.8	30.9	Operating Expenses		40.5		29.4	29.4	16.9
3.2	4.9	3.0	Operating Profit		1.5		3.7	5.0	4.3
1.6	1.6	1.1	All Other Expenses (net)		1.8		.4	1.2	.9
1.6	3.3	1.9	Profit Before Taxes		-.3		3.3	3.8	3.4
			RATIOS						
2.9	3.0	2.8	Current		4.2		3.5	2.7	2.6
1.5	1.6	1.5			1.2		2.0	1.2	1.4
1.0	1.0	1.0			.8		.9	.9	1.2
1.2	1.3	1.1	Quick		2.6		1.4	1.3	.9
.6 (97)	.6 (77)	.6		(10) .4		.6	.8	.6
.3	.4	.3			.2		.4	.4	.4
13 28.2	12 29.7	8 44.3	Sales/Receivables	1 517.0		12 31.5	13 27.8	16 22.8
24 15.0	24 15.5	20 18.3		7 53.8		17 21.7	19 19.3	25 14.7
40 9.2	38 9.7	41 8.9		24 15.5		45 8.1	44 8.4	41 8.8
43 8.4	45 8.1	38 9.6	Cost of Sales/Inventory	25 14.4		42 8.6	31 11.6	50 7.4
76 4.8	71 5.2	68 5.3		85 4.3		66 5.5	65 5.6	64 5.7
102 3.6	117 3.1	104 3.5		132 2.8		94 3.9	91 4.0	107 3.4
13 28.8	11 33.3	14 26.8	Cost of Sales/Payables	6 59.2		13 27.8	20 18.7	15 23.7
23 15.8	24 15.5	25 14.8		14 25.9		20 17.8	25 14.4	26 14.0
40 9.2	41 8.9	44 8.3		28 13.1		45 8.2	48 7.6	44 8.3
5.3	5.4	5.7	Sales/Working Capital		5.6		4.4	8.7	5.0
14.1	12.2	15.3			25.0		6.8	24.6	14.7
129.8	135.3	UND			-42.2		NM	-109.0	45.1
9.0	8.5	10.9	EBIT/Interest				11.9	41.6	17.5
(79) 2.8	(89) 2.8	(69) 2.7			(15) 2.0		3.3	(25) 5.5
1.1	1.1	.4					.8	1.3	1.8
9.5	3.9	6.6	Net Profit + Depr., Dep.,						
(28) 2.7	(30) 2.1	(16) 2.5	Amort./Cur. Mat. L/T/D						
1.4	1.2	1.2							
.3	.4	.4	Fixed/Worth		.8		.4	.4	.5
1.0	.8	.9			1.6		.8	1.4	.8
2.4	2.0	5.5			2.3		NM	-26.9	1.9
.6	.6	.7	Debt/Worth		1.3		.6	1.0	.6
1.5	1.7	2.0			3.5		1.4	2.2	1.5
4.5	4.6	NM			7.8		NM	-41.1	5.9
30.2	29.3	32.4	% Profit Before Taxes/Tangible				37.4		32.9
(80) 11.1	(88) 9.6	(59) 14.9	Net Worth				(12) 18.9	(23) 18.2
3.0	3.0	.8					1.3		10.3
11.2	11.0	12.1	% Profit Before Taxes/Total		4.8		16.3	7.8	14.4
4.2	3.7	4.7	Assets		2.1		6.0	4.0	7.6
.7	.4	-1.8			-4.3		.0	.5	2.7
12.6	11.3	14.1	Sales/Net Fixed Assets		46.7		14.6	23.8	11.7
6.4	6.0	9.0			23.8		9.4	5.9	7.5
3.6	4.0	5.0			7.2		6.0	4.1	5.2
2.7	2.7	3.3	Sales/Total Assets		6.2		3.6	3.4	2.6
2.0	2.0	2.2			2.3		2.3	2.5	2.1
1.4	1.5	1.6			1.8		1.9	1.7	1.3
1.6	1.7	1.3	% Depr., Dep., Amort./Sales				1.7	.8	1.3
(80) 3.1	(83) 2.8	(63) 2.4			(14) 2.3		2.9	(19) 1.8
4.3	4.1	3.2					3.1	3.6	2.8
2.1	2.2	2.7	% Officers', Directors',						
(34) 4.9	(34) 5.6	(25) 4.9	Owners' Comp/Sales						
7.9	7.7	7.0							
2527743M	3113814M	3808985M	Net Sales ($)	4022M	22001M	19748M	118507M	139817M	3504890M
1512379M	1766109M	1915880M	Total Assets ($)	2868M	12132M	6527M	52034M	63253M	1779066M

© RMA 2005

M = $ thousand   MM = $ million
See Pages 11 through 21 for Explanation of Ratios and Data

Current Data Sorted By Assets   Comparative Historical Data

0-500M	500M-2MM	2-10MM	10-50MM	50-100MM	100-250MM		4/1/00-3/31/01 ALL	4/1/01-3/31/02 ALL
1	1	1 / 3 / 1	7 / 6	4	4 / 1	Type of Statement		
						Unqualified	13	16
						Reviewed	5	7
1	2					Compiled	7	5
						Tax Returns		
1		6	8	2	2	Other	19	15
2	3	11	21	6	7	**NUMBER OF STATEMENTS**	44	43
%	%	%	%	%	%	**ASSETS**	%	%
		7.6	.8			Cash & Equivalents	5.0	5.0
		24.9	16.3			Trade Receivables (net)	18.2	17.3
		32.8	36.7			Inventory	32.9	29.2
		1.0	3.8			All Other Current	3.3	2.4
		66.3	57.5			Total Current	59.3	53.9
		21.9	33.5			Fixed Assets (net)	33.9	40.2
		.7	5.1			Intangibles (net)	2.1	2.5
		11.1	3.9			All Other Non-Current	4.6	3.4
		100.0	100.0			Total	100.0	100.0
						LIABILITIES		
		12.6	20.1			Notes Payable-Short Term	16.7	16.0
		2.5	3.2			Cur. Mat.-L/T/D	3.6	4.4
		20.0	10.0			Trade Payables	14.7	15.4
		.7	.3			Income Taxes Payable	.3	.2
		3.8	10.2			All Other Current	7.1	9.3
		39.6	43.8			Total Current	42.4	45.3
		15.0	17.7			Long-Term Debt	21.9	19.2
		.2	1.0			Deferred Taxes	1.6	.9
		6.7	5.2			All Other Non-Current	3.0	4.0
		38.5	32.3			Net Worth	31.1	30.6
		100.0	100.0			Total Liabilities & Net Worth	100.0	100.0
						INCOME DATA		
		100.0	100.0			Net Sales	100.0	100.0
		16.6	23.3			Gross Profit	18.4	21.5
		13.3	19.7			Operating Expenses	14.1	18.6
		3.3	3.6			Operating Profit	4.3	3.0
		.1	2.2			All Other Expenses (net)	1.6	2.6
		3.2	1.4			Profit Before Taxes	2.7	.4
						RATIOS		
		2.4	1.6			Current	2.4	1.9
		1.6	1.3				1.3	1.2
		1.1	1.1				1.1	1.0
		1.6	.6			Quick	1.0	.7
		.7	.4				.5	.4
		.4	.3				.3	.3
		22 16.8	25 14.5			Sales/Receivables	27 13.4	24 15.5
		31 11.6	47 7.8				34 10.9	35 10.5
		65 5.6	55 6.6				43 8.4	51 7.2
		35 10.4	73 5.0			Cost of Sales/Inventory	41 9.0	35 10.6
		51 7.1	150 2.4				99 3.7	100 3.6
		158 2.3	174 2.1				163 2.2	170 2.2
		15 24.4	16 22.6			Cost of Sales/Payables	16 22.5	18 20.2
		45 8.2	30 12.2				34 10.6	31 11.8
		69 5.3	50 7.3				45 8.1	59 6.1
		3.0	6.1			Sales/Working Capital	4.5	5.8
		10.5	12.0				10.9	17.4
		34.7	40.0				31.1	635.8
			2.8			EBIT/Interest	5.0	3.5
			2.1				(42) 1.8	(40) 1.6
			1.4				1.2	.8
						Net Profit + Depr., Dep., Amort./Cur. Mat. L /T/D	5.6	2.7
							(17) 2.4	(16) 1.4
							1.5	.8
		.1	.8			Fixed/Worth	.6	.7
		.5	.9				1.0	1.3
		1.4	2.0				2.4	3.2
		.5	1.3			Debt/Worth	1.1	1.1
		2.2	2.3				2.7	2.4
		6.0	4.8				5.4	8.0
		68.5	17.8			% Profit Before Taxes/Tangible Net Worth	28.3	16.1
		17.9	(19) 9.7				(40) 12.9	(39) 6.8
		5.1	5.1				3.4	.0
		8.3	4.0			% Profit Before Taxes/Total Assets	8.6	4.6
		5.4	2.7				3.2	2.1
		2.8	1.1				.9	-.9
		119.0	6.7			Sales/Net Fixed Assets	8.7	6.9
		9.5	3.8				4.3	3.8
		6.1	2.5				3.0	2.3
		2.6	1.7			Sales/Total Assets	1.9	2.4
		1.6	1.2				1.4	1.4
		1.2	1.0				1.1	1.1
			1.4			% Depr., Dep., Amort./Sales	.5	2.0
			3.4				(37) 2.9	(38) 3.3
			5.0				3.9	4.4
						% Officers', Directors', Owners' Comp/Sales		
279M	14851M	154249M	790805M	1015069M	1934384M	Net Sales ($)	3079261M	2492387M
212M	2914M	75809M	522691M	440320M	1425368M	Total Assets ($)	2282009M	1846835M

M = $ thousand   MM = $ million
See Pages 11 through 21 for Explanation of Ratios and Data

Comparative Historical Data   **Current Data Sorted By Sales**

Current Data columns: 24 (4/1-9/30/04) covers 0-1MM, 1-3MM, 3-5MM; 26 (10/1/04-3/31/05) covers 5-10MM, 10-25MM, 25MM & OVER

4/1/02-3/31/03 ALL	4/1/03-3/31/04 ALL	4/1/04-3/31/05 ALL	Type of Statement	0-1MM	1-3MM	3-5MM	5-10MM	10-25MM	25MM & OVER
13	24	17	Unqualified	1				1	15
9	10	10	Reviewed					5	5
1	2	2	Compiled			1		1	
1	1	2	Tax Returns			1	1		
15	11	19	Other	1		1	2	7	8
39	48	50	**NUMBER OF STATEMENTS**	2		3	3	14	28
%	%	%	**ASSETS**	%	%	%	%	%	%
2.4	5.2	4.0	Cash & Equivalents					1.8	2.8
19.8	20.0	18.4	Trade Receivables (net)					19.8	18.5
27.8	30.5	33.0	Inventory					34.0	35.1
4.0	3.3	3.9	All Other Current					.9	3.7
54.0	59.0	59.4	Total Current					56.6	60.2
38.4	34.2	31.5	Fixed Assets (net)					30.5	34.0
2.8	1.4	3.1	Intangibles (net)					7.2	1.7
4.8	5.3	6.0	All Other Non-Current					5.8	4.1
100.0	100.0	100.0	Total					100.0	100.0
			LIABILITIES						
12.7	11.6	16.4	Notes Payable-Short Term					15.3	16.3
3.0	3.2	2.6	Cur. Mat.-L/T/D					3.0	2.7
18.4	13.3	13.0	Trade Payables					12.0	13.7
.4	.2	.4	Income Taxes Payable					.6	.4
13.8	17.1	9.5	All Other Current					3.9	13.3
48.3	45.4	41.8	Total Current					34.8	46.4
17.5	19.0	17.0	Long-Term Debt					20.5	14.1
1.2	1.0	.6	Deferred Taxes					.0	.9
4.7	5.8	5.7	All Other Non-Current					11.3	1.5
28.4	28.8	34.8	Net Worth					33.4	37.1
100.0	100.0	100.0	Total Liabilities & Net Worth					100.0	100.0
			INCOME DATA						
100.0	100.0	100.0	Net Sales					100.0	100.0
17.9	18.0	20.4	Gross Profit					20.7	20.3
14.7	13.8	16.4	Operating Expenses					17.5	15.9
3.2	4.2	3.9	Operating Profit					3.2	4.3
1.8	1.4	1.5	All Other Expenses (net)					2.9	.9
1.4	2.8	2.4	Profit Before Taxes					.3	3.4
			RATIOS						
1.8	2.0	1.9	Current					2.1	1.6
1.2	1.4	1.4						1.6	1.3
.9	1.1	1.1						1.1	1.1
.7	.9	.7	Quick					.7	.6
.4	.5	.5						.6	.4
.3	.3	.3						.3	.3
24 15.0	23 15.7	25 14.4	Sales/Receivables					22 16.6	26 13.8
35 10.4	31 11.7	35 10.4						48 7.5	37 9.8
46 7.9	48 7.6	53 6.9						81 4.5	52 7.1
31 11.9	38 9.7	50 7.3	Cost of Sales/Inventory					46 8.0	76 4.8
72 5.1	82 4.4	97 3.8						119 3.1	97 3.8
131 2.8	125 2.9	168 2.2						173 2.1	163 2.2
17 21.5	13 28.5	18 20.8	Cost of Sales/Payables					13 27.9	16 22.7
31 11.7	26 13.8	29 12.4						33 11.0	27 13.4
56 6.5	42 8.8	47 7.8						70 5.2	46 8.0
10.1	6.0	6.3	Sales/Working Capital					3.0	7.1
24.1	11.7	11.9						11.3	11.9
-41.9	29.7	36.3						46.7	47.1
5.6	4.7	6.7	EBIT/Interest					4.9	10.7
(37) 2.8	(42) 2.5	(47) 2.5						2.0	3.2
.4	1.0	1.4						.6	1.9
5.7	2.8	4.9	Net Profit + Depr., Dep., Amort./Cur. Mat. L/T/D						4.9
(14) 2.4	(14) 1.6	(14) 2.0						(10)	2.7
1.4	1.2	1.2							1.3
.8	.8	.6	Fixed/Worth					.4	.7
1.3	1.2	.9						.9	.9
2.4	2.4	2.0						6.7	1.4
1.5	1.0	1.1	Debt/Worth					1.3	1.1
2.9	2.4	2.1						2.9	1.8
8.2	6.6	4.1						10.9	3.7
45.3	42.6	33.5	% Profit Before Taxes/Tangible Net Worth					18.2	37.6
(34) 19.8	(45) 15.2	(47) 11.1						(12) 10.2	13.9
.0	1.0	4.4						3.2	5.2
11.4	10.9	7.7	% Profit Before Taxes/Total Assets					5.1	10.0
2.5	4.2	3.5						2.7	4.4
-1.6	.2	1.2						-1.0	2.4
7.6	12.1	9.5	Sales/Net Fixed Assets					9.9	7.8
4.1	5.3	4.7						3.7	4.7
2.8	2.6	2.4						2.2	2.8
2.4	2.4	2.2	Sales/Total Assets					1.6	2.2
1.6	1.5	1.4						1.2	1.5
.9	1.1	1.1						1.0	1.2
1.6	1.5	1.1	% Depr., Dep., Amort./Sales					1.7	1.1
(35) 3.3	(39) 2.9	(45) 2.9						2.9	(26) 3.0
4.7	4.1	4.4						5.4	4.3
			% Officers', Directors', Owners' Comp/Sales						
1969905M	3493103M	3909637M	Net Sales ($)	279M		12148M	23562M	190554M	3683094M
1285990M	2213412M	2467314M	Total Assets ($)	212M		7000M	14922M	162568M	2282612M

M = $ thousand   MM = $ million
See Pages 11 through 21 for Explanation of Ratios and Data

Current Data Sorted By Assets   Comparative Historical Data

0-500M	500M-2MM	2-10MM	10-50MM	50-100MM	100-250MM	Type of Statement	4/1/00-3/31/01	4/1/01-3/31/02
1	7	12	3	1		Unqualified	9	10
4	4	4	1			Reviewed	5	10
3	3					Compiled	3	8
2						Tax Returns	2	2
3	4	8	3	1		Other	9	19
	17 (4/1-9/30/04)		47 (10/1/04-3/31/05)				ALL	ALL
	13	18	24	7	2	NUMBER OF STATEMENTS	28	49
%	%	%	%	%	%	**ASSETS**	%	%
D	6.3	4.9	4.6			Cash & Equivalents	7.5	8.7
A	23.9	19.6	20.7			Trade Receivables (net)	19.2	21.4
T	15.8	15.4	18.1			Inventory	21.1	19.5
A	2.8	1.2	2.5			All Other Current	2.8	.4
	48.7	41.2	46.0			Total Current	50.5	50.0
N	44.0	42.5	40.0			Fixed Assets (net)	37.0	39.5
O	1.9	9.6	4.8			Intangibles (net)	8.7	6.2
T	5.4	6.7	9.2			All Other Non-Current	3.7	4.2
	100.0	100.0	100.0			Total	100.0	100.0
A						**LIABILITIES**		
V	8.1	8.7	6.0			Notes Payable-Short Term	8.4	8.8
A	7.5	8.1	4.2			Cur. Mat.-L/T/D	2.6	6.6
I	16.8	14.5	11.1			Trade Payables	16.5	13.1
L	.2	.1	.5			Income Taxes Payable	.1	.3
A	14.2	5.9	13.2			All Other Current	10.7	12.3
B	46.8	37.2	35.0			Total Current	38.7	41.1
L	26.6	15.9	16.2			Long-Term Debt	19.2	22.0
E	.0	1.2	1.4			Deferred Taxes	.1	.4
	2.7	3.5	7.1			All Other Non-Current	10.5	6.4
	23.9	42.2	40.3			Net Worth	31.4	30.1
	100.0	100.0	100.0			Total Liabilities & Net Worth	100.0	100.0
						INCOME DATA		
	100.0	100.0	100.0			Net Sales	100.0	100.0
	44.0	33.1	25.0			Gross Profit	35.7	32.2
	40.7	30.4	21.5			Operating Expenses	30.5	28.5
	3.3	2.7	3.5			Operating Profit	5.1	3.7
	.1	1.3	.7			All Other Expenses (net)	1.9	1.5
	3.1	1.4	2.8			Profit Before Taxes	3.3	2.2
						RATIOS		
	2.6	1.6	2.4				1.8	2.0
	1.2	1.1	1.5			Current	1.6	1.2
	.6	.7	.9				.9	.9
	1.4	.9	1.2				1.0	1.2
	.7	.7	.8			Quick	.7	.8
	.5	.4	.4				.5	.5
	18 19.9	18 20.3	22 16.5				21 17.5	19 18.8
	31 11.9	28 13.1	28 12.9			Sales/Receivables	27 13.3	27 13.6
	46 7.9	35 10.4	37 9.9				34 10.7	35 10.5
	22 16.5	24 15.3	23 16.2				28 13.0	24 15.2
	39 9.3	31 11.9	33 10.9			Cost of Sales/Inventory	46 7.9	36 10.1
	69 5.3	38 9.6	52 7.1				58 6.3	55 6.6
	17 22.1	18 20.0	15 24.7				19 18.8	15 23.7
	26 14.3	29 12.5	20 18.7			Cost of Sales/Payables	32 11.6	22 16.6
	51 7.2	40 9.1	27 13.5				44 8.4	37 9.9
	7.2	16.7	8.3				9.6	13.1
	23.5	44.2	17.3			Sales/Working Capital	19.3	36.7
	−16.7	−39.0	−102.9				NM	−78.5
	6.8	7.7	13.4				6.5	4.3
	3.8 (16)	.7 (21)	8.8			EBIT/Interest	(27) 2.2	(43) 2.6
	2.0	−2.7	1.2				1.0	.4
						Net Profit + Depr., Dep., Amort./Cur. Mat. L /T/D		
	.4	.7	.8				.8	.7
	1.6	.9	1.1			Fixed/Worth	1.5	1.4
	3.4	2.3	2.8				NM	NM
	.9	.8	.8				1.3	1.1
	2.6	2.0	1.5			Debt/Worth	2.6	2.2
	6.2	3.7	4.2				NM	NM
	45.7	45.6	37.7				65.4	47.3
	(11) 26.8	(16) 8.4	(22) 21.3			% Profit Before Taxes/Tangible Net Worth	(21) 31.3	(37) 16.4
	5.4	−17.3	4.6				12.3	−5.0
	12.7	11.0	16.0				17.3	13.2
	8.9	−.8	8.4			% Profit Before Taxes/Total Assets	5.1	5.2
	2.3	−4.6	.6				.3	−3.0
	13.6	15.9	10.9				13.5	11.4
	5.4	6.1	5.5			Sales/Net Fixed Assets	8.2	5.8
	2.9	2.7	3.4				4.4	4.0
	3.6	3.5	3.3				3.4	3.5
	2.1	2.6	2.6			Sales/Total Assets	2.6	2.5
	1.4	1.5	1.4				1.9	1.9
	1.3	1.1	1.2				.6	1.2
	2.7 (15)	2.1 (20)	2.8			% Depr., Dep., Amort./Sales	(24) 2.4	(42) 2.9
	6.2	3.9	3.7				3.5	4.8
								1.2
						% Officers', Directors', Owners' Comp/Sales		(20) 3.7
								6.8
	49469M	239635M	1547443M	863524M	578168M	Net Sales ($)	1739254M	2561503M
	19558M	94119M	616922M	415743M	351804M	Total Assets ($)	835426M	1093996M

M = $ thousand   MM = $ million
See Pages 11 through 21 for Explanation of Ratios and Data

Comparative Historical Data   ## Current Data Sorted By Sales

			Type of Statement		0-1MM	1-3MM	3-5MM	5-10MM	10-25MM	25MM & OVER
12	18	24	Unqualified			2	1	4	17	
16	14	13	Reviewed		2	2	1	4	4	
5	9	6	Compiled		2	2	1	1		
	2	2	Tax Returns			2				
15	19	19	Other		1	3		4	11	
4/1/02-	4/1/03-	4/1/04-				17 (4/1-9/30/04)			47 (10/1/04-3/31/05)	
3/31/03	3/31/04	3/31/05								
ALL	ALL	ALL								
48	62	64	**NUMBER OF STATEMENTS**		5	11	3	13	32	
%	%	%	**ASSETS**	%	%	%	%	%	%	
7.0	8.6	5.7	Cash & Equivalents			4.2		5.4	6.1	
17.3	18.6	20.9	Trade Receivables (net)	D		16.8		17.2	23.3	
18.1	19.2	17.4	Inventory	A		12.6		20.0	18.4	
1.2	2.4	2.0	All Other Current	T		2.7		1.0	2.1	
43.6	48.8	45.9	Total Current	A		36.4		43.6	49.9	
40.6	36.8	39.9	Fixed Assets (net)			47.2		41.4	35.5	
10.4	4.8	7.0	Intangibles (net)	N		13.2		7.0	6.3	
5.4	9.5	7.2	All Other Non-Current	O		3.1		8.0	8.3	
100.0	100.0	100.0	Total	T		100.0		100.0	100.0	
			LIABILITIES	A						
8.4	7.8	8.1	Notes Payable-Short Term	V		4.8		6.9	8.9	
5.5	4.9	5.9	Cur. Mat.-L/T/D	A		13.6		3.7	4.0	
13.7	15.9	13.0	Trade Payables	I		15.6		12.6	11.8	
.5	.5	.3	Income Taxes Payable	L		.1		.0	.4	
7.0	8.4	10.8	All Other Current	A		7.2		6.1	12.3	
35.0	37.6	38.1	Total Current	B		41.2		29.5	37.5	
22.6	20.6	18.5	Long-Term Debt	L		29.2		21.4	13.3	
.7	.5	.9	Deferred Taxes	E		.4		1.3	1.2	
7.0	10.6	5.1	All Other Non-Current			4.9		9.6	4.1	
34.8	30.8	37.3	Net Worth			24.3		38.2	44.0	
100.0	100.0	100.0	Total Liabilities & Net Worth			100.0		100.0	100.0	
			INCOME DATA							
100.0	100.0	100.0	Net Sales			100.0		100.0	100.0	
29.4	34.8	30.4	Gross Profit			43.1		34.6	22.5	
24.5	30.3	26.3	Operating Expenses			43.1		32.1	16.7	
4.9	4.5	4.0	Operating Profit			−.1		2.5	5.7	
1.5	1.3	1.0	All Other Expenses (net)			1.0		1.2	.9	
3.3	3.1	3.1	Profit Before Taxes			−1.0		1.3	4.8	
			RATIOS							
1.8	2.0	1.9				1.9		2.3	2.2	
1.3	1.3	1.2	Current			1.2		1.2	1.4	
.8	1.0	.8				.4		1.0	.9	
1.1	1.3	1.1				1.3		1.1	1.2	
.6	.7	.7	Quick			.5		.7	.8	
.4	.5	.4				.2		.5	.4	
16 22.4	20 18.4	20 18.0	Sales/Receivables	17 20.9		19 18.9	21 17.2			
24 15.0	25 14.8	28 12.9		23 16.0		29 12.4	27 13.3			
32 11.5	33 10.9	37 9.9		32 11.4		35 10.5	42 8.6			
26 14.3	26 13.8	23 16.2	Cost of Sales/Inventory	22 16.5		30 12.2	18 20.1			
37 9.8	36 10.2	34 10.7		37 9.9		34 10.6	27 13.5			
50 7.2	59 6.1	49 7.4		50 7.3		65 5.7	44 8.4			
13 28.4	17 21.4	15 23.8	Cost of Sales/Payables	22 16.7		18 20.6	14 25.8			
28 13.1	29 12.7	24 15.3		39 9.3		28 13.0	21 17.6			
42 8.6	44 8.3	37 9.9		63 5.8		36 10.2	29 12.7			
11.7	8.6	9.3	Sales/Working Capital	13.3		10.6	8.3			
27.6	20.6	25.4		23.5		41.0	19.1			
−43.6	−88.6	−50.5		−5.3		−657.4	−92.8			
9.3	13.2	10.6	EBIT/Interest	3.5		7.4	22.3			
(43) 3.8	(57) 4.1	(58) 3.9		(10) 2.2		(12) 1.2	(28) 9.6			
1.1	1.0	.9		.1		−.8	1.8			
4.2	6.4	3.6	Net Profit + Depr., Dep.,				3.6			
(15) 2.0	(13) 2.8	(23) 2.2	Amort./Cur. Mat. L/T/D			(11)	2.2			
1.1	2.2	.7					.7			
.8	.5	.6	Fixed/Worth	1.4		.6	.4			
1.8	1.2	1.1		1.8		1.0	.9			
NM	3.0	2.8		−10.2		2.9	1.9			
.9	.9	.7	Debt/Worth	1.2		.8	.6			
3.8	1.9	1.9		2.0		1.9	1.3			
NM	6.3	5.1		−15.8		3.9	3.7			
57.1	51.3	47.4	% Profit Before Taxes/Tangible			45.4	53.4			
(36) 36.2	(52) 21.7	(56) 26.1	Net Worth			(11) 2.2	(30) 27.6			
6.3	7.9	3.9				−2.6	9.5			
12.3	13.3	17.2	% Profit Before Taxes/Total	8.9		9.9	24.0			
7.0	7.6	8.4	Assets	1.4		.6	11.9			
.6	.3	.1		−3.1		−3.9	2.7			
11.6	17.3	13.9	Sales/Net Fixed Assets	13.0		12.2	15.8			
4.8	5.9	5.7		4.2		5.8	6.3			
3.2	3.5	3.2		2.2		3.0	4.9			
3.0	3.5	3.3	Sales/Total Assets	2.8		3.4	3.3			
2.3	2.4	2.3		2.0		2.6	2.6			
1.5	1.4	1.4		1.4		1.3	1.9			
1.5	1.4	1.2	% Depr., Dep., Amort./Sales			1.6	1.1			
(44) 2.6	(51) 2.4	(56) 2.7				(12) 2.7	(27) 2.8			
4.5	4.0	3.9				3.7	3.8			
	1.8	.6	% Officers', Directors',							
	(17) 2.9	(11) 2.9	Owners' Comp/Sales							
	7.1	3.7								
2112537M	1954420M	3278239M	Net Sales ($)	10169M	42599M	24658M	206554M	2994259M	
1175898M	1018157M	1498146M	Total Assets ($)	7497M	23326M	8830M	110928M	1347565M	

M = $ thousand   MM = $ million
See Pages 11 through 21 for Explanation of Ratios and Data

Current Data Sorted By Assets   Comparative Historical Data

Type of Statement

0-500M	500M-2MM	2-10MM	10-50MM	50-100MM	100-250MM	Type of Statement	4/1/00-3/31/01 ALL	4/1/01-3/31/02 ALL
		1	13	7	11	Unqualified	23	17
	2	10	2	1		Reviewed	14	13
	2	1	1	1	1	Compiled	8	10
1	2					Tax Returns	1	
1	4	6	9	1	3	Other	23	21
	37 (4/1-9/30/04)		42 (10/1/04-3/31/05)					
2	10	18	25	9	15	NUMBER OF STATEMENTS	69	61
%	%	%	%	%	%	**ASSETS**	%	%
	8.1	5.5	1.7		1.2	Cash & Equivalents	5.2	4.9
	24.0	22.1	16.4		11.8	Trade Receivables (net)	15.0	15.5
	26.3	31.8	34.9		44.5	Inventory	34.0	35.4
	1.8	1.2	4.2		4.6	All Other Current	3.3	2.1
	60.1	60.7	57.2		62.1	Total Current	57.5	57.8
	22.9	34.2	32.9		29.9	Fixed Assets (net)	33.4	34.0
	5.4	1.0	3.1		3.8	Intangibles (net)	2.4	2.4
	11.6	4.1	6.8		4.1	All Other Non-Current	6.8	5.9
	100.0	100.0	100.0		100.0	Total	100.0	100.0
						LIABILITIES		
	12.1	14.3	18.6		13.9	Notes Payable-Short Term	17.3	15.0
	2.9	3.1	3.3		1.9	Cur. Mat.-L/T/D	2.2	2.8
	11.0	20.1	13.6		12.1	Trade Payables	12.9	13.6
	.0	.1	.5		.0	Income Taxes Payable	.1	.2
	4.0	5.0	7.0		12.5	All Other Current	6.1	5.7
	29.9	42.6	43.0		40.4	Total Current	38.7	37.3
	30.7	19.7	17.7		16.7	Long-Term Debt	21.3	18.2
	.0	.5	.5		.5	Deferred Taxes	.7	.7
	9.4	3.6	7.4		4.6	All Other Non-Current	5.2	5.4
	29.9	33.6	31.3		37.9	Net Worth	34.1	38.5
	100.0	100.0	100.0		100.0	Total Liabilities & Net Worth	100.0	100.0
						INCOME DATA		
	100.0	100.0	100.0		100.0	Net Sales	100.0	100.0
	29.0	23.5	20.7		24.2	Gross Profit	20.8	23.6
	24.9	20.8	15.4		15.8	Operating Expenses	16.2	18.1
	4.1	2.6	5.3		8.4	Operating Profit	4.6	5.4
	1.2	1.3	1.1		1.8	All Other Expenses (net)	1.7	1.7
	2.9	1.4	4.1		6.7	Profit Before Taxes	2.9	3.7
						RATIOS		
	15.4	2.5	1.9		2.3		2.4	2.5
	2.0	1.4	1.3		1.5	Current	1.5	1.7
	1.2	1.1	1.1		1.1		1.1	1.1
	6.5	1.0	.6		.4		.9	1.2
	1.3	.6	.4		.3	Quick	.5	.5
	.7	.4	.2		.3		.3	.3
	13 29.0	23 16.2	26 14.3		26 14.1		22 16.5	22 16.8
	23 16.1	28 13.3	34 10.9		30 12.1	Sales/Receivables	28 13.1	29 12.8
	32 11.5	32 11.4	49 7.5		34 10.7		35 10.3	37 9.8
	6 60.0	33 11.0	56 6.5		109 3.4		43 8.4	49 7.5
	43 8.6	49 7.4	102 3.6		135 2.7	Cost of Sales/Inventory	86 4.2	90 4.1
	75 4.9	73 5.0	154 2.4		229 1.6		147 2.5	145 2.5
	1 628.7	18 20.0	16 23.0		21 17.2		15 24.6	17 20.9
	23 15.6	31 11.6	34 10.9		34 10.7	Cost of Sales/Payables	29 12.7	28 13.2
	30 12.2	40 9.1	58 6.3		59 6.2		46 7.9	52 7.0
	6.1	6.7	5.8		4.4		5.3	4.3
	11.3	19.0	11.1		7.1	Sales/Working Capital	10.6	10.0
	21.1	153.6	45.9		16.4		44.0	39.3
	16.9	19.0	5.2		9.0		5.0	4.1
	6.3	(17) 2.6	2.1		3.2	EBIT/Interest	(67) 2.3	(57) 2.5
	1.5	1.5	1.2		1.2		1.1	1.3
			6.3				15.0	3.3
		(18)	2.0			Net Profit + Depr., Dep., Amort./Cur. Mat. L /T/D	(24) 2.8	(21) 2.4
			1.4				1.1	1.2
	.4	.5	.7		.6		.5	.5
	.7	1.0	1.1		1.0	Fixed/Worth	1.1	1.1
	−3.0	2.6	2.0		1.5		2.2	2.2
	.6		1.4		1.1		1.0	.9
	2.0	2.7	2.2		1.8	Debt/Worth	2.2	1.9
	−9.4	8.0	3.6		2.7		4.9	5.0
		32.3	27.6		31.0		35.7	27.2
		28.6 (23)	12.8	(14)	18.3	% Profit Before Taxes/Tangible Net Worth	(62) 16.6	(56) 15.1
		11.6	1.1		1.1		6.3	4.7
	13.9	12.8	10.2		8.8		11.3	10.4
	5.7	4.6	2.7		5.2	% Profit Before Taxes/Total Assets	4.1	5.0
	1.1	1.6	.3		.5		.3	1.1
	18.6	16.7	7.4		7.2		9.3	8.1
	11.3	8.5	5.1		4.4	Sales/Net Fixed Assets	5.9	6.1
	9.9	5.3	3.9		3.1		3.3	3.3
	3.8	3.4	1.9		1.7		2.4	2.1
	2.8	2.9	1.7		1.4	Sales/Total Assets	1.6	1.7
	2.1	1.8	1.2		1.0		1.3	1.3
		.8	1.3				1.1	1.6
		(16) 1.9	2.6			% Depr., Dep., Amort./Sales	(65) 2.5	(54) 2.5
		3.0	3.3				3.5	3.3
							.9	1.4
						% Officers', Directors', Owners' Comp/Sales	(13) 1.7	(11) 4.4
							2.9	6.8
2819M	39261M	291600M	1234539M	899850M	3530101M	Net Sales ($)	5021362M	4408263M
773M	13020M	107037M	722257M	608424M	2465001M	Total Assets ($)	3214604M	2727747M

M = $ thousand   MM = $ million
See Pages 11 through 21 for Explanation of Ratios and Data

Comparative Historical Data   **Current Data Sorted By Sales**

			Type of Statement						
28	27	32	Unqualified				1	1	30
12	12	15	Reviewed		1		2	8	4
4	14	5	Compiled		1	1	1	1	1
1	1	3	Tax Returns			3			
24	29	24	Other	1	1	1	4	5	12
4/1/02-3/31/03	4/1/03-3/31/04	4/1/04-3/31/05		37 (4/1-9/30/04)			42 (10/1/04-3/31/05)		
ALL	ALL	ALL		0-1MM	1-3MM	3-5MM	5-10MM	10-25MM	25MM & OVER
69	83	79	**NUMBER OF STATEMENTS**	1	3	5	8	15	47
%	%	%	**ASSETS**	%	%	%	%	%	%
3.7	4.4	3.3	Cash & Equivalents					3.9	1.3
16.7	15.9	17.2	Trade Receivables (net)					19.4	15.6
34.8	34.8	37.0	Inventory					30.1	43.1
2.4	3.9	3.2	All Other Current					.9	4.4
57.6	59.0	60.6	Total Current					54.4	64.4
33.5	32.7	29.9	Fixed Assets (net)					36.5	28.7
2.7	3.0	3.0	Intangibles (net)					3.8	2.1
6.2	5.2	6.4	All Other Non-Current					5.3	4.8
100.0	100.0	100.0	Total					100.0	100.0
			LIABILITIES						
11.4	11.9	15.1	Notes Payable-Short Term					13.3	16.9
3.3	3.9	3.0	Cur. Mat.-L/T/D					3.1	3.1
13.9	13.8	14.8	Trade Payables					17.2	15.5
.2	.2	.2	Income Taxes Payable					.2	.3
7.9	7.7	7.5	All Other Current					3.6	9.2
36.7	37.6	40.6	Total Current					37.3	45.0
18.7	18.0	19.2	Long-Term Debt					17.1	14.8
.8	.8	.4	Deferred Taxes					.4	.4
3.7	3.9	6.0	All Other Non-Current					6.3	5.8
40.2	39.7	33.8	Net Worth					38.8	34.0
100.0	100.0	100.0	Total Liabilities & Net Worth					100.0	100.0
			INCOME DATA						
100.0	100.0	100.0	Net Sales					100.0	100.0
21.8	22.0	23.1	Gross Profit					23.7	20.1
16.9	17.6	18.0	Operating Expenses					21.0	15.1
5.0	4.3	5.0	Operating Profit					2.7	5.0
1.6	1.0	1.3	All Other Expenses (net)					1.1	1.2
3.3	3.3	3.7	Profit Before Taxes					1.5	3.8
			RATIOS						
2.6	2.7	2.2	Current					3.4	1.9
1.6	1.7	1.5						1.5	1.5
1.2	1.2	1.1						1.1	1.1
.9	1.0	.8	Quick					1.4	.5
.5	.5	.5						.7	.4
.3	.3	.3						.3	.3
24 15.4	22 16.5	23 16.1	Sales/Receivables					22 16.2	26 14.2
30 12.3	28 13.1	30 12.3						27 13.5	31 11.9
40 9.2	35 10.5	37 9.9						31 11.7	45 8.0
49 7.4	40 9.2	46 7.9	Cost of Sales/Inventory					35 10.3	80 4.6
95 3.8	92 4.0	97 3.8						46 7.9	130 2.8
137 2.7	135 2.7	161 2.3						69 5.3	189 1.9
14 25.7	18 20.6	16 23.1	Cost of Sales/Payables					16 23.4	20 17.9
27 13.3	27 13.5	30 12.2						26 14.1	34 10.7
57 6.4	42 8.8	47 7.8						36 10.0	59 6.2
5.1	4.8	5.1	Sales/Working Capital					6.1	4.5
9.0	8.7	9.2						15.4	8.6
21.7	24.5	23.7						119.3	16.6
5.1	8.7	8.1	EBIT/Interest					31.9	8.0
(63) 2.7	(76) 3.4	(77) 2.8					(14) 3.4		2.8
1.4	1.5	1.5						1.6	1.2
5.3	4.8	5.6	Net Profit + Depr., Dep.,						3.2
(29) 2.7	(35) 2.3	(32) 2.2	Amort./Cur. Mat. L/T/D					(22)	2.1
1.0	1.0	1.5							1.4
.5	.4	.5	Fixed/Worth					.5	.6
.9	.9	1.0						1.0	1.0
1.8	1.9	1.8						1.8	1.3
.8	.7	1.1	Debt/Worth					.4	1.2
1.6	1.8	2.2						2.8	2.0
3.9	3.6	4.3						7.0	3.0
24.5	30.9	31.8	% Profit Before Taxes/Tangible					32.3	27.0
(64) 16.1	(78) 17.1	(72) 17.5	Net Worth					26.6	(44) 14.7
10.3	5.6	2.9						6.9	1.1
10.6	10.7	10.5	% Profit Before Taxes/Total					18.2	10.0
6.2	6.2	4.2	Assets					5.1	4.2
2.0	1.7	.9						1.8	.5
9.8	11.0	11.9	Sales/Net Fixed Assets					16.0	11.4
6.1	6.0	6.3						6.9	5.3
3.6	3.7	4.0						2.5	4.0
2.0	2.2	2.7	Sales/Total Assets					3.3	1.9
1.7	1.7	1.8						2.8	1.6
1.5	1.5	1.2						1.4	1.2
1.6	1.5	1.3	% Depr., Dep., Amort./Sales					1.2	1.3
(65) 2.4	(72) 2.3	(66) 2.3					(14) 2.4		(39) 2.2
3.3	3.3	3.3						5.8	3.3
1.2	1.3	1.2	% Officers', Directors',						
(12) 2.8	(12) 2.0	(17) 3.1	Owners' Comp/Sales						
8.2	8.5	7.3							
5705201M	6381700M	5998170M	Net Sales ($)	844M	5322M	17719M	57941M	253041M	5663303M
3467093M	3839265M	3916512M	Total Assets ($)	944M	1609M	7027M	43064M	121104M	3742764M

© RMA 2005

M = $ thousand   MM = $ million
See Pages 11 through 21 for Explanation of Ratios and Data

Current Data Sorted By Assets   Comparative Historical Data

0-500M	500M-2MM	2-10MM	10-50MM	50-100MM	100-250MM	Type of Statement	4/1/00-3/31/01 ALL	4/1/01-3/31/02 ALL
	1	4	3		3	Unqualified	11	12
	2	3	3			Reviewed	2	2
1	1	2				Compiled	5	6
	1					Tax Returns	1	1
	1	5	4	4		Other	9	18
		24 (4/1-9/30/04)		14 (10/1/04-3/31/05)				
1	6	14	10	4	3	**NUMBER OF STATEMENTS**	28	39
%	%	%	%	%	%	**ASSETS**	%	%
		5.2	7.7			Cash & Equivalents	2.6	5.0
		18.1	17.8			Trade Receivables (net)	21.3	21.1
		29.7	40.5			Inventory	41.6	34.2
		3.3	4.0			All Other Current	2.6	1.3
		56.3	70.0			Total Current	68.2	61.6
		32.1	22.8			Fixed Assets (net)	22.6	23.9
		8.3	.2			Intangibles (net)	5.2	7.5
		3.2	7.0			All Other Non-Current	4.0	7.0
		100.0	100.0			Total	100.0	100.0
						LIABILITIES		
		13.4	22.2			Notes Payable-Short Term	22.5	17.5
		2.2	1.5			Cur. Mat.-L/T/D	2.0	3.2
		13.1	12.5			Trade Payables	16.6	13.5
		.6	.2			Income Taxes Payable	.3	.2
		7.7	6.4			All Other Current	5.1	7.2
		37.0	42.8			Total Current	46.5	41.6
		17.2	14.4			Long-Term Debt	8.9	15.8
		.2	1.1			Deferred Taxes	.7	.7
		6.6	3.7			All Other Non-Current	12.0	9.1
		39.0	38.0			Net Worth	31.8	32.9
		100.0	100.0			Total Liabilities & Net Worth	100.0	100.0
						INCOME DATA		
		100.0	100.0			Net Sales	100.0	100.0
		34.4	23.4			Gross Profit	26.9	28.5
		31.1	16.7			Operating Expenses	24.7	24.1
		3.3	6.7			Operating Profit	2.3	4.4
		1.5	.8			All Other Expenses (net)	1.8	1.9
		1.8	5.9			Profit Before Taxes	.5	2.5
						RATIOS		
		3.2	2.6			Current	1.8	2.0
		1.6	1.5				1.5	1.5
		1.4	1.2				1.1	1.2
		1.8	1.1			Quick	1.0	1.0
		.8	.5				.5	.6
		.3	.3				.3	.4
		19 19.0	28 13.2			Sales/Receivables	31 11.7	24 14.9
		38 9.7	33 11.1				40 9.1	41 8.9
		45 8.0	38 9.7				50 7.3	51 7.1
		54 6.7	67 5.5			Cost of Sales/Inventory	56 6.6	46 8.0
		74 4.9	74 4.9				94 3.9	93 3.9
		111 3.3	151 2.4				237 1.5	166 2.2
		14 25.5	13 27.6			Cost of Sales/Payables	14 25.3	14 25.6
		31 11.8	26 14.1				31 11.9	24 15.3
		49 7.4	38 9.6				79 4.6	46 7.9
		5.1	6.1			Sales/Working Capital	5.1	6.2
		10.8	9.5				9.5	8.3
		32.8	13.5				17.3	41.6
		12.3	44.1			EBIT/Interest	15.7	6.0
		2.8	2.2				(27) 1.4	(37) 1.7
		-.2	.5				.2	1.0
						Net Profit + Depr., Dep., Amort./Cur. Mat. L/T/D		3.9
							(11)	1.6
								1.0
		.5	.3			Fixed/Worth	.3	.3
		1.0	.7				.5	.9
		NM	.9				2.7	1.9
		.7	.8			Debt/Worth	.8	1.1
		1.4	2.1				3.5	2.6
		NM	4.9				9.5	7.3
		67.4	48.9			% Profit Before Taxes/Tangible Net Worth	33.1	46.5
		(11) 17.0	17.0				(24) 14.1	(33) 11.0
		-1.6	-.1				1.1	-2.1
		17.0	22.6			% Profit Before Taxes/Total Assets	12.2	10.5
		3.9	4.1				1.9	3.0
		-1.4	-.3				-3.5	.0
		52.2	19.7			Sales/Net Fixed Assets	21.3	22.4
		7.3	9.1				8.5	7.2
		2.7	5.5				5.1	3.8
		3.0	2.4			Sales/Total Assets	2.8	2.7
		1.7	2.0				1.9	1.7
		1.3	1.5				1.1	1.1
		.8				% Depr., Dep., Amort./Sales	1.1	1.1
		(13) 2.7					(26) 2.0	(36) 1.9
		4.2					3.3	3.5
						% Officers', Directors', Owners' Comp/Sales		.7
							(10)	1.0
								3.9
1097M	24876M	143887M	534639M	286700M	682184M	Net Sales ($)	1236480M	1611899M
220M	7477M	75663M	255382M	273237M	536305M	Total Assets ($)	830068M	1058587M

© RMA 2005

M = $ thousand   MM = $ million
See Pages 11 through 21 for Explanation of Ratios and Data

Comparative Historical Data				Current Data Sorted By Sales					
			Type of Statement						
15	13	11	Unqualified			1	2	2	6
2	5	8	Reviewed			1	2	4	1
5	4	2	Compiled		2				
1	1	3	Tax Returns		1		2		
13	14	14	Other			1	3	3	7
4/1/02-3/31/03 ALL	**4/1/03-3/31/04 ALL**	**4/1/04-3/31/05 ALL**			24 (4/1-9/30/04)		14 (10/1/04-3/31/05)		
				0-1MM	**1-3MM**	**3-5MM**	**5-10MM**	**10-25MM**	**25MM & OVER**
36	37	38	**NUMBER OF STATEMENTS**		3	3	9	9	14
%	%	%	**ASSETS**	%	%	%	%	%	%
5.6	8.8	7.3	Cash & Equivalents	DATA NOT AVAILABLE					7.4
17.2	21.7	19.6	Trade Receivables (net)						17.4
35.8	33.9	35.1	Inventory						39.6
3.3	1.9	3.5	All Other Current						4.9
61.8	66.3	65.5	Total Current						69.3
25.6	22.3	26.0	Fixed Assets (net)						25.2
5.7	5.7	3.7	Intangibles (net)						1.1
6.9	5.7	4.8	All Other Non-Current						4.4
100.0	100.0	100.0	Total						100.0
			LIABILITIES						
16.7	17.2	15.9	Notes Payable-Short Term						17.8
4.7	1.6	2.2	Cur. Mat.-L/T/D						1.7
13.8	16.2	14.7	Trade Payables						15.3
.1	.3	.5	Income Taxes Payable						.2
6.6	7.5	8.2	All Other Current						6.7
42.0	42.8	41.4	Total Current						41.7
15.9	12.8	13.9	Long-Term Debt						12.3
.8	.6	.7	Deferred Taxes						1.6
11.0	7.6	4.5	All Other Non-Current						4.6
30.2	36.2	39.5	Net Worth						39.8
100.0	100.0	100.0	Total Liabilities & Net Worth						100.0
			INCOME DATA						
100.0	100.0	100.0	Net Sales						100.0
32.4	28.1	33.3	Gross Profit						32.5
26.9	22.3	27.7	Operating Expenses						25.2
5.6	5.8	5.6	Operating Profit						7.3
2.0	1.7	2.1	All Other Expenses (net)						2.1
3.6	4.2	3.5	Profit Before Taxes						5.3
			RATIOS						
2.1	2.4	2.4							2.1
1.6	1.6	1.5	Current						1.5
1.2	1.2	1.2							1.4
.9	1.5	1.3							.8
.5	.7	.7	Quick						.5
.3	.3	.3							.3
27 13.5	**31** 11.9	**24** 15.0							**33** 11.2
37 9.8	**37** 9.9	**36** 10.0	Sales/Receivables						**37** 9.9
50 7.3	**44** 8.3	**43** 8.4							**49** 7.5
64 5.7	**50** 7.3	**60** 6.0							**70** 5.2
131 2.8	**80** 4.5	**79** 4.6	Cost of Sales/Inventory						**142** 2.6
197 1.9	**159** 2.3	**175** 2.1							**219** 1.7
16 22.6	**18** 20.8	**13** 27.6							**19** 19.2
32 11.3	**31** 11.8	**29** 12.6	Cost of Sales/Payables						**38** 9.6
73 5.0	**55** 6.6	**51** 7.1							**78** 4.7
4.8	5.3	5.1							5.0
7.9	8.1	9.4	Sales/Working Capital						6.0
16.0	14.2	15.3							9.2
5.5	13.4	14.0							44.1
(34) 2.0	(33) 3.0	2.6	EBIT/Interest						2.6
1.1	1.2	1.0							1.3
9.7	7.6	8.0							
(15) 2.1	(16) 2.0	(14) 2.5	Net Profit + Depr., Dep., Amort./Cur. Mat. L/T/D						
.3	.6	1.2							
.4	.3	.4							.4
.9	.7	.7	Fixed/Worth						.7
4.1	1.3	1.2							.9
1.1	.8	.8							.8
3.0	2.4	1.9	Debt/Worth						2.1
7.4	4.5	4.4							3.0
56.3	41.9	47.1							27.3
(31) 14.8	(33) 13.8	(35) 15.7	% Profit Before Taxes/Tangible Net Worth						14.1
5.1	2.6	2.0							4.6
10.7	11.4	14.8							12.0
2.5	4.4	3.3	% Profit Before Taxes/Total Assets						4.4
.5	-.2	.1							.7
19.7	23.5	26.0							8.7
5.9	7.7	8.6	Sales/Net Fixed Assets						5.9
3.5	4.5	4.7							5.1
2.3	3.2	3.0							2.1
1.5	1.9	1.9	Sales/Total Assets						1.7
1.1	1.2	1.3							1.1
1.2	1.0	.9							1.6
(33) 2.3	(33) 1.8	(34) 1.8	% Depr., Dep., Amort./Sales						(13) 1.8
3.2	2.7	3.2							3.2
			% Officers', Directors', Owners' Comp/Sales						
1851804M	1722903M	1673383M	Net Sales ($)		5082M	12957M	57708M	157567M	1440069M
1400218M	1262660M	1148284M	Total Assets ($)		1678M	6895M	37413M	74200M	1028098M

M = $ thousand MM = $ million

See Pages 11 through 21 for Explanation of Ratios and Data

Current Data Sorted By Assets   **Comparative Historical Data**

0-500M	500M-2MM	2-10MM	10-50MM	50-100MM	100-250MM	Type of Statement	4/1/00-3/31/01 ALL	4/1/01-3/31/02 ALL
1	1	4	14	8	4	Unqualified	14	28
			4			Reviewed	10	4
			1			Compiled	1	6
						Tax Returns		
			12	4	1	Other	13	23
			14 (4/1-9/30/04)	40 (10/1/04-3/31/05)			13	23
1	1	4	31	12	5	**NUMBER OF STATEMENTS**	38	61
%	%	%	%	%	%	**ASSETS**	%	%
			10.5	4.5		Cash & Equivalents	8.7	7.5
			26.9	24.0		Trade Receivables (net)	26.8	31.8
			10.5	13.3		Inventory	10.5	11.9
			4.4	.6		All Other Current	1.7	3.8
			52.2	42.4		Total Current	47.6	55.1
			40.0	45.3		Fixed Assets (net)	41.8	37.7
			1.8	4.0		Intangibles (net)	2.2	1.3
			6.0	8.3		All Other Non-Current	8.3	6.0
			100.0	100.0		Total	100.0	100.0
						LIABILITIES		
			5.3	5.1		Notes Payable-Short Term	3.7	6.2
			2.0	4.0		Cur. Mat.-L/T/D	3.2	2.7
			18.9	22.2		Trade Payables	16.6	24.1
			.1	.0		Income Taxes Payable	.4	.1
			10.6	7.8		All Other Current	13.4	11.2
			37.0	39.1		Total Current	37.3	44.3
			12.1	21.3		Long-Term Debt	17.1	15.1
			.7	.0		Deferred Taxes	1.0	.4
			8.7	.7		All Other Non-Current	1.2	2.7
			41.6	38.9		Net Worth	43.3	37.6
			100.0	100.0		Total Liabilities & Net Worth	100.0	100.0
						INCOME DATA		
			100.0	100.0		Net Sales	100.0	100.0
			19.6	12.3		Gross Profit	22.9	19.1
			17.3	12.9		Operating Expenses	18.9	16.8
			2.3	-.6		Operating Profit	4.0	2.3
			1.1	.9		All Other Expenses (net)	.4	.1
			1.2	-1.6		Profit Before Taxes	3.6	2.2
						RATIOS		
			2.4	1.5			1.6	1.5
			1.3	1.2		Current	1.3	1.2
			1.1	.9			1.0	1.0
			1.8	1.2			1.3	1.1
			.9	.8		Quick	1.0	.9
			.6	.4			.8	.6
			23 15.5	21 17.7			22 16.9	22 16.3
			26 13.8	25 14.6		Sales/Receivables	28 13.0	27 13.6
			32 11.3	33 11.2			38 9.6	33 11.0
			7 53.7	8 44.9			8 47.5	5 68.7
			11 33.0	10 36.3		Cost of Sales/Inventory	15 25.2	10 36.0
			25 14.9	24 15.3			20 18.6	26 14.3
			11 31.9	18 19.9			16 23.1	18 20.2
			26 14.2	25 14.7		Cost of Sales/Payables	23 15.8	24 15.0
			32 11.2	32 11.3			30 12.0	33 11.0
			10.9	31.7			15.3	21.5
			30.2	57.4		Sales/Working Capital	33.0	52.8
			110.2	NM			NM	445.7
			24.0	12.2			10.0	11.3
		(27)	9.0	5.1		EBIT/Interest	(35) 5.7	(56) 3.8
			.4	1.6			3.5	1.9
			8.9			Net Profit + Depr., Dep.,	5.0	5.1
		(10)	6.6			Amort./Cur. Mat. L /T/D	(19) 2.7	(28) 3.5
			1.2				1.8	1.8
			.5	.9			.6	.6
			.9	1.1		Fixed/Worth	1.0	1.0
			1.1	4.1			1.6	1.8
			.7	1.0			.8	1.0
			1.3	1.4		Debt/Worth	1.4	1.9
			2.0	7.4			2.5	3.5
			24.9	27.2		% Profit Before Taxes/Tangible	36.9	28.4
		(30)	12.4	14.0		Net Worth	20.3	(59) 17.4
			-.4	5.3			12.0	9.3
			12.9	6.7		% Profit Before Taxes/Total	15.0	11.2
			5.5	5.1		Assets	8.8	5.9
			-.6	1.5			4.8	2.9
			23.0	14.8			11.5	19.7
			6.9	8.4		Sales/Net Fixed Assets	8.0	9.6
			4.7	5.0			5.5	5.7
			4.3	5.8			4.4	5.4
			3.3	3.4		Sales/Total Assets	3.5	3.9
			2.3	2.4			2.2	2.8
			.6	.7			1.0	.6
		(30)	1.8	1.5		% Depr., Dep., Amort./Sales	(36) 2.3	(56) 1.5
			3.1	2.0			3.2	2.5
						% Officers', Directors', Owners' Comp/Sales		
566M	8374M	44657M	3334432M	2975831M	3065276M	Net Sales ($)	3049054M	10837299M
60M	927M	19648M	895116M	760926M	891013M	Total Assets ($)	958408M	2419786M

M = $ thousand   MM = $ million
See Pages 11 through 21 for Explanation of Ratios and Data

Comparative Historical Data

Current Data Sorted By Sales

			Type of Statement						26
31	29	27	Unqualified	1					4
11	12	9	Reviewed			3	2		1
5	3	1	Compiled						
	3		Tax Returns				3		14
9	18	17	Other						
4/1/02-3/31/03	4/1/03-3/31/04	4/1/04-3/31/05			14 (4/1-9/30/04)		40 (10/1/04-3/31/05)		
ALL	ALL	ALL		0-1MM	1-3MM	3-5MM	5-10MM	10-25MM	25MM & OVER
56	65	54	**NUMBER OF STATEMENTS**	1			3	5	45
%	%	%	**ASSETS**	%	%	%	%	%	%
7.3	7.6	8.0	Cash & Equivalents						7.1
28.1	25.0	27.4	Trade Receivables (net)	D	D				28.3
10.8	12.1	11.3	Inventory	A	A				11.5
2.6	5.1	2.8	All Other Current	T	T				3.2
48.8	49.7	49.6	Total Current	A	A				50.1
39.1	38.6	40.0	Fixed Assets (net)						38.8
1.7	4.2	2.7	Intangibles (net)	N	N				3.2
10.4	7.5	7.7	All Other Non-Current	O	O				7.9
100.0	100.0	100.0	Total	T	T				100.0
			LIABILITIES	A	A				
5.2	9.8	5.2	Notes Payable-Short Term	V	V				5.2
2.2	2.7	2.8	Cur. Mat.-L/T/D	A	A				2.4
20.6	21.0	20.4	Trade Payables	I	I				21.5
.1	.1	.1	Income Taxes Payable	L	L				.1
13.7	11.7	9.5	All Other Current	A	A				10.1
41.9	45.3	38.1	Total Current	B	B				39.3
12.5	16.0	14.6	Long-Term Debt	L	L				15.0
.5	.5	.6	Deferred Taxes	E	E				.5
2.5	3.9	7.1	All Other Non-Current						6.6
42.7	34.4	39.7	Net Worth						38.6
100.0	100.0	100.0	Total Liabilities & Net Worth						100.0
			INCOME DATA						
100.0	100.0	100.0	Net Sales						100.0
20.6	21.1	17.6	Gross Profit						16.5
17.6	18.9	16.0	Operating Expenses						14.6
3.1	2.2	1.6	Operating Profit						1.9
.1	.7	.9	All Other Expenses (net)						1.1
2.9	1.5	.7	Profit Before Taxes						.8
			RATIOS						
1.6	1.6	1.7							1.6
1.2	1.2	1.2	Current						1.2
1.0	1.0	1.0							1.1
1.1	1.2	1.4							1.2
.9	.8	.9	Quick						.9
.6	.5	.6							.6
21 17.2	23 16.1	23 15.6							23 16.0
25 14.8	27 13.4	26 14.0	Sales/Receivables						26 14.0
31 11.6	34 10.7	32 11.3							32 11.4
6 63.0	8 44.1	6 56.3							6 59.0
12 30.4	15 23.9	11 32.9	Cost of Sales/Inventory						10 35.7
18 20.5	23 15.7	23 15.7							20 18.0
17 21.7	20 18.7	17 21.6							17 21.4
23 15.7	27 13.8	25 14.3	Cost of Sales/Payables						26 14.2
30 12.3	34 10.8	32 11.4							32 11.4
19.6	18.6	16.8							18.9
48.3	46.1	50.3	Sales/Working Capital						49.7
−287.9	NM	205.4							117.0
21.1	12.2	22.5							15.9
(52) 7.6	(59) 3.7	(48) 7.0	EBIT/Interest					(41) 7.2	
3.0	.8	1.5							1.5
10.8	6.8	6.6	Net Profit + Depr., Dep.,						6.6
(17) 4.7	(22) 3.4	(19) 3.6	Amort./Cur. Mat. L/T/D					(17) 3.6	
3.0	1.6	1.2							1.2
.6	.7	.6							.6
.9	1.1	.9	Fixed/Worth						.9
1.6	2.0	1.4							1.3
.7	.8	.8							.8
1.3	1.8	1.4	Debt/Worth						1.5
3.5	5.0	2.9							3.4
34.4	31.4	25.9	% Profit Before Taxes/Tangible						28.7
(55) 18.7	(61) 12.2	(52) 14.0	Net Worth					(44) 12.8	
8.6	2.5	3.7							3.7
14.1	12.1	11.3	% Profit Before Taxes/Total						11.1
8.4	4.2	5.2	Assets						5.4
2.5	.2	.2							.8
18.5	13.8	21.2							21.7
9.3	8.7	7.6	Sales/Net Fixed Assets						8.3
5.8	5.2	4.8							5.7
5.5	4.7	5.1							5.2
3.5	3.1	3.3	Sales/Total Assets						3.5
2.6	2.4	2.3							2.4
.7	.9	.6							.6
(52) 1.6	(60) 1.8	(53) 1.7	% Depr., Dep., Amort./Sales					(44) 1.6	
2.4	2.6	2.8							2.1
			% Officers', Directors', Owners' Comp/Sales						
9017587M	10558643M	9429136M	Net Sales ($)	566M			24259M	85548M	9318763M
2071222M	2893392M	2567690M	Total Assets ($)	60M			5801M	113199M	2448630M

M = $ thousand   MM = $ million
See Pages 11 through 21 for Explanation of Ratios and Data

Current Data Sorted By Assets   Comparative Historical Data

	0-500M	500M-2MM	2-10MM	10-50MM	50-100MM	100-250MM	Type of Statement	4/1/00-3/31/01 ALL	4/1/01-3/31/02 ALL
	1		8	14	7	5	Unqualified	17	24
		1	7	3			Reviewed	10	8
		3	2	1			Compiled	5	11
		2			1		Tax Returns		2
		2	2	9	2	2	Other	6	13
			21 (4/1-9/30/04)		51 (10/1/04-3/31/05)				
NUMBER OF STATEMENTS	1	8	19	27	10	7		38	58
	%	%	%	%	%	%	**ASSETS**	%	%
			2.6	6.1	2.1		Cash & Equivalents	5.5	4.5
			25.5	22.3	17.4		Trade Receivables (net)	25.9	26.6
			24.8	22.3	41.5		Inventory	29.1	28.6
			1.8	2.7	4.2		All Other Current	2.1	1.7
			54.7	53.4	65.3		Total Current	62.5	61.4
			37.2	38.2	26.2		Fixed Assets (net)	31.3	33.2
			1.5	2.9	6.7		Intangibles (net)	2.2	1.1
			6.6	5.6	1.8		All Other Non-Current	4.0	4.3
			100.0	100.0	100.0		Total	100.0	100.0
							LIABILITIES		
			15.0	10.3	13.7		Notes Payable-Short Term	13.4	10.9
			2.8	3.7	3.5		Cur. Mat.-L/T/D	3.0	4.5
			19.4	16.6	16.5		Trade Payables	18.2	18.7
			.1	.2	.5		Income Taxes Payable	.5	.3
			5.8	7.2	10.6		All Other Current	5.8	8.3
			43.1	38.0	44.7		Total Current	40.9	42.6
			15.2	21.0	13.4		Long-Term Debt	14.8	16.3
			1.0	1.1	1.6		Deferred Taxes	.8	.4
			10.6	5.3	1.6		All Other Non-Current	2.4	5.8
			30.1	34.7	38.7		Net Worth	41.0	34.9
			100.0	100.0	100.0		Total Liabilities & Net Worth	100.0	100.0
							INCOME DATA		
			100.0	100.0	100.0		Net Sales	100.0	100.0
			13.4	17.3	17.7		Gross Profit	16.2	15.2
			12.3	12.9	12.7		Operating Expenses	11.8	12.1
			1.1	4.4	5.0		Operating Profit	4.4	3.0
			.8	.4	.8		All Other Expenses (net)	.9	1.4
			.3	4.0	4.2		Profit Before Taxes	3.6	1.6
							RATIOS		
			1.5	2.0	2.9		Current	2.1	2.3
			1.2	1.4	1.3			1.4	1.4
			1.0	1.0	1.1			1.1	1.1
			.8	1.2	1.0		Quick	1.3	1.2
			.6	.7	.7			.6	.7
			.5	.4	.1			.4	.4
			20 18.2	19 19.3	25 14.7		Sales/Receivables	24 15.4	25 14.8
			31 11.9	26 14.0	31 11.6			34 10.6	32 11.5
			38 9.5	36 10.1	40 9.1			45 8.1	42 8.8
			17 20.9	16 22.3	32 11.3		Cost of Sales/Inventory	20 18.5	17 21.6
			33 11.1	27 13.7	89 4.1			39 9.3	34 10.7
			46 8.0	73 5.0	257 1.4			77 4.7	72 5.1
			15 24.2	18 19.9	10 37.6		Cost of Sales/Payables	16 22.6	16 23.1
			21 17.4	26 14.1	22 16.5			25 14.5	24 15.4
			30 12.3	35 10.3	46 7.9			42 8.7	34 10.9
			20.2	10.1	5.2		Sales/Working Capital	5.8	7.1
			39.8	22.8	7.0			15.2	20.3
			−519.8	−138.4	30.2			40.7	63.4
			5.8	19.9	119.5		EBIT/Interest	10.4	5.8
			4.0	(26) 4.2	15.3			(36) 3.5	(53) 2.7
			1.2	1.2	2.2			2.1	1.0
			(10) 5.0	3.4			Net Profit + Depr., Dep.,		9.5
			3.1	(10) 1.9			Amort./Cur. Mat. L /T/D	(15) 3.4	
			1.9	.9					1.6
			.7	.8	.5		Fixed/Worth	.4	.5
			1.3	1.4	.9			.7	1.0
			2.3	2.6	1.3			1.4	1.7
			1.1	1.0	.5		Debt/Worth	.7	.8
			3.1	2.6	1.9			1.7	1.9
			6.2	5.7	11.0			3.9	3.5
			34.7	36.3			% Profit Before Taxes/Tangible	34.6	28.4
			(17) 22.1	(25) 21.9			Net Worth	(35) 21.2	(54) 15.5
			5.2	7.0				12.2	3.8
			9.5	15.0	16.5		% Profit Before Taxes/Total	11.7	10.3
			5.1	5.4	11.2		Assets	7.5	5.2
			.6	.7	1.6			3.4	.4
			11.7	10.5	12.0		Sales/Net Fixed Assets	15.9	13.9
			9.3	7.5	11.2			9.4	10.6
			5.3	4.0	6.3			6.4	5.9
			4.1	3.4	3.6		Sales/Total Assets	3.4	3.9
			3.3	2.3	1.7			2.5	3.0
			2.4	1.5	.9			2.0	1.9
			1.1	1.2	1.1		% Depr., Dep., Amort./Sales	.8	.8
			(17) 1.6	1.9	1.5			(36) 1.4	(55) 1.4
			2.3	2.7	1.6			2.3	2.2
							% Officers', Directors',	1.4	.8
							Owners' Comp/Sales	(12) 2.6	(12) 2.8
								4.5	4.1
	379M	29340M	340633M	1832597M	1732491M	3114642M	Net Sales ($)	2725389M	4649900M
	120M	8799M	102582M	646633M	707413M	1044609M	Total Assets ($)	1077892M	1747768M

M = $ thousand   MM = $ million
See Pages 11 through 21 for Explanation of Ratios and Data

Comparative Historical Data

Current Data Sorted By Sales

			Type of Statement	0-1MM	1-3MM	3-5MM	5-10MM	10-25MM	25MM & OVER
21	27	35	Unqualified	1				8	26
7	12	11	Reviewed			1	2	4	4
11	10	6	Compiled		1	2		3	
3	2	3	Tax Returns		2		2		1
17	21	17	Other	1				1	13
4/1/02-3/31/03 ALL	4/1/03-3/31/04 ALL	4/1/04-3/31/05 ALL		21 (4/1-9/30/04)			51 (10/1/04-3/31/05)		
59	72	72	NUMBER OF STATEMENTS	2	3	3	4	16	44
%	%	%	ASSETS	%	%	%	%	%	%
7.0	5.9	5.6	Cash & Equivalents					5.9	4.3
21.6	20.8	21.8	Trade Receivables (net)					21.2	22.5
25.4	25.6	26.5	Inventory					24.3	28.5
2.1	2.0	2.5	All Other Current					4.1	2.3
56.0	54.3	56.4	Total Current					55.5	57.6
37.9	37.7	36.3	Fixed Assets (net)					38.1	35.4
1.9	3.2	2.7	Intangibles (net)					3.7	2.5
4.1	4.8	4.6	All Other Non-Current					2.7	4.6
100.0	100.0	100.0	Total					100.0	100.0
			LIABILITIES						
10.4	10.5	11.0	Notes Payable-Short Term					13.3	11.1
4.1	3.6	3.2	Cur. Mat.-L/T/D					2.3	3.3
14.9	16.4	17.1	Trade Payables					16.1	18.2
.1	.3	.2	Income Taxes Payable					.1	.2
7.3	7.5	7.3	All Other Current					5.5	8.7
36.8	38.3	38.7	Total Current					37.2	41.5
19.3	18.8	16.3	Long-Term Debt					14.2	18.1
.5	1.0	.9	Deferred Taxes					1.5	.9
5.3	3.9	10.7	All Other Non-Current					7.1	4.4
38.1	38.0	33.4	Net Worth					40.0	35.0
100.0	100.0	100.0	Total Liabilities & Net Worth					100.0	100.0
			INCOME DATA						
100.0	100.0	100.0	Net Sales					100.0	100.0
16.4	18.9	16.3	Gross Profit					15.3	15.3
12.6	14.0	13.0	Operating Expenses					10.9	11.7
3.9	5.0	3.3	Operating Profit					4.4	3.6
1.1	1.1	.6	All Other Expenses (net)					.9	.5
2.7	3.9	2.6	Profit Before Taxes					3.5	3.1
			RATIOS						
2.3	2.3	2.3						2.3	1.9
1.6	1.3	1.4	Current					1.5	1.4
1.1	1.0	1.1						1.1	1.0
1.4	1.3	1.2						1.3	1.0
.8	.6	.7	Quick					.6	.7
.3	.3	.4						.5	.4
20 17.8	20 18.3	19 19.5						20 18.7	19 19.4
27 13.4	30 12.3	25 14.3	Sales/Receivables					29 12.7	25 14.3
33 11.2	38 9.6	36 10.2						39 9.4	33 11.0
15 23.6	19 18.8	18 20.4						16 22.2	18 20.4
34 10.8	37 10.0	30 12.3	Cost of Sales/Inventory					34 10.6	27 13.6
70 5.2	72 5.1	71 5.1						45 8.2	90 4.0
13 28.2	13 27.8	15 24.3						18 20.0	17 21.6
20 17.8	26 14.2	22 16.6	Cost of Sales/Payables					25 14.4	22 16.6
29 12.4	36 10.2	32 11.4						29 12.5	34 10.8
8.3	7.9	8.6						7.0	9.7
16.4	20.2	18.5	Sales/Working Capital					19.5	19.6
72.0	198.2	72.8						65.5	176.1
8.7	14.7	19.2						8.8	23.9
(54) 3.6	(67) 3.5	(68) 4.4	EBIT/Interest					4.0	(43) 5.1
1.9	1.3	1.3						1.1	2.0
8.4	6.8	5.6	Net Profit + Depr., Dep.,					4.7	7.0
(18) 3.6	(23) 2.9	(26) 2.5	Amort./Cur. Mat. L/T/D				(10) 2.5	(16) 3.1
2.5	1.2	1.8						1.7	1.8
.6	.6	.6						.7	.7
1.1	1.0	1.2	Fixed/Worth					1.4	1.0
1.4	2.6	2.3						2.2	1.8
.7	.7	.7						.6	.9
1.7	1.7	2.4	Debt/Worth					2.8	2.2
3.5	5.2	6.4						6.0	5.9
37.8	30.9	35.1	% Profit Before Taxes/Tangible					27.1	36.7
(55) 13.3	(64) 19.4	(63) 20.9	Net Worth				(15) 10.0	(41) 22.0
3.3	5.9	7.3						4.5	9.6
10.8	16.3	11.7	% Profit Before Taxes/Total					6.6	14.5
4.7	5.9	6.1	Assets					4.1	7.3
2.0	.8	1.0						.2	3.2
12.2	12.4	12.0						11.1	12.0
8.0	6.9	8.2	Sales/Net Fixed Assets					8.7	7.9
4.2	3.8	4.9						4.5	5.0
3.7	3.5	3.6						3.8	3.6
2.6	2.5	2.6	Sales/Total Assets					2.6	2.7
1.9	1.6	1.9						1.7	1.8
1.3	1.2	1.2						1.3	1.1
(55) 2.0	(64) 2.0	(69) 1.7	% Depr., Dep., Amort./Sales					1.8	(42) 1.6
2.6	2.9	2.3						2.2	2.3
.5	1.4	.6	% Officers', Directors',						
(16) 1.1	(19) 2.3	(18) 1.2	Owners' Comp/Sales						
3.0	5.6	2.6							
4502938M	5983105M	7050082M	Net Sales ($)	1319M	8034M	10970M	25351M	271115M	6733293M
1812598M	2629482M	2510156M	Total Assets ($)	792M	4195M	3531M	8293M	117231M	2376114M

© RMA 2005

M = $ thousand   MM = $ million
See Pages 11 through 21 for Explanation of Ratios and Data

Current Data Sorted By Assets   **Comparative Historical Data**

Type of Statement

0-500M	500M-2MM	2-10MM	10-50MM	50-100MM	100-250MM	Type of Statement	4/1/00-3/31/01 ALL	4/1/01-3/31/02 ALL
1	2	8	16	4	5	Unqualified	23	20
1	10	8	8			Reviewed	13	13
	2	6	3			Compiled	18	15
	2	1				Tax Returns	3	7
	2	12	9			Other	24	23

31 (4/1-9/30/04)   67 (10/1/04-3/31/05)

0-500M	500M-2MM	2-10MM	10-50MM	50-100MM	100-250MM		4/1/00-3/31/01 ALL	4/1/01-3/31/02 ALL
2	16	35	36	4	5	**NUMBER OF STATEMENTS**	81	78
%	%	%	%	%	%		%	%

ASSETS

0-500M	500M-2MM	2-10MM	10-50MM	50-100MM	100-250MM		Hist 1	Hist 2
	2.8	6.7	7.3			Cash & Equivalents	6.0	6.0
	29.8	25.3	26.7			Trade Receivables (net)	25.8	25.8
	20.8	23.1	22.1			Inventory	19.8	24.2
	.6	1.8	2.2			All Other Current	3.2	2.5
	54.0	56.9	58.3			Total Current	54.8	58.4
	38.3	29.7	34.0			Fixed Assets (net)	37.2	32.6
	1.5	2.5	1.4			Intangibles (net)	1.9	2.7
	6.2	11.0	6.3			All Other Non-Current	6.1	6.3
	100.0	100.0	100.0			Total	100.0	100.0

LIABILITIES

0-500M	500M-2MM	2-10MM	10-50MM	50-100MM	100-250MM		Hist 1	Hist 2
	13.6	10.9	14.9			Notes Payable-Short Term	10.4	13.7
	3.9	2.9	1.6			Cur. Mat.-L/T/D	4.5	5.1
	13.0	14.1	14.1			Trade Payables	13.3	13.6
	.0	.1	.1			Income Taxes Payable	.2	.2
	11.8	7.7	9.8			All Other Current	8.4	8.3
	42.3	35.6	40.5			Total Current	36.7	40.9
	14.0	17.9	16.3			Long-Term Debt	16.3	17.1
	.2	.6	.9			Deferred Taxes	.3	.6
	2.4	6.8	3.1			All Other Non-Current	5.2	5.9
	41.1	39.1	39.1			Net Worth	41.5	35.5
	100.0	100.0	100.0			Total Liabilities & Net Worth	100.0	100.0

INCOME DATA

0-500M	500M-2MM	2-10MM	10-50MM	50-100MM	100-250MM		Hist 1	Hist 2
	100.0	100.0	100.0			Net Sales	100.0	100.0
	23.2	21.1	15.6			Gross Profit	18.0	17.8
	23.2	17.9	12.4			Operating Expenses	14.4	15.1
	.1	3.1	3.2			Operating Profit	3.7	2.7
	.6	1.0	.2			All Other Expenses (net)	.8	.4
	-.5	2.1	3.0			Profit Before Taxes	2.9	2.3

RATIOS

0-500M	500M-2MM	2-10MM	10-50MM	50-100MM	100-250MM		Hist 1	Hist 2
	1.9	2.3	2.1			Current	2.3	1.9
	1.5	1.6	1.4				1.4	1.4
	.9	1.0	1.1				1.2	1.1
	1.3	1.2	1.1			Quick	1.3	1.2
	.7	.7	.8				.8	.7
	.5	.5	.6				.5	.5
	14 26.8	15 24.6	16 22.7			Sales/Receivables	16 22.9	14 25.2
	28 13.1	21 17.3	21 17.2				20 18.0	20 18.5
	31 11.8	25 14.8	32 11.3				29 12.5	27 13.3
	11 34.6	14 25.9	12 31.5			Cost of Sales/Inventory	10 36.7	10 35.6
	21 17.7	22 17.0	17 21.4				19 18.9	21 17.3
	41 9.0	30 12.3	36 10.3				39 9.5	38 9.7
	6 61.2	7 50.5	8 48.6			Cost of Sales/Payables	6 62.8	7 54.4
	15 25.0	12 29.9	13 28.7				11 34.6	12 30.4
	29 12.6	19 19.1	21 17.1				19 19.1	19 19.1
	17.2	18.0	13.4			Sales/Working Capital	13.3	13.8
	28.4	32.3	32.7				22.9	29.3
	-86.2	-999.8	113.3				75.8	71.6
	5.4	10.9	18.9			EBIT/Interest	5.8	8.2
	(15) 3.0	(33) 3.1	(33) 3.0				(72) 2.7	(73) 2.9
	-2.7	.6	1.1				1.0	1.0
			29.1			Net Profit + Depr., Dep., Amort./Cur. Mat. L/T/D	(18) 5.1	(21) 5.5
		(12)	3.2				3.2	2.9
			2.0				2.1	.6
	.5	.3	.5			Fixed/Worth	.5	.5
	.6	.7	1.0				1.0	.9
	2.5	3.4	1.7				1.8	2.0
	.5	.8	1.0			Debt/Worth	.8	.9
	1.7	2.5	2.0				1.3	1.9
	4.0	5.1	3.6				3.9	4.9
	24.6	63.1	35.3			% Profit Before Taxes/Tangible Net Worth	32.3	52.6
	(14) 14.2	15.1	18.2				(73) 12.6	(70) 13.8
	-17.8	-5.5	1.3				.7	2.1
	9.5	12.5	13.6			% Profit Before Taxes/Total Assets	11.5	15.4
	3.8	4.4	4.4				5.2	5.2
	-14.3	-.8	.2				.1	.1
	45.2	62.3	25.3			Sales/Net Fixed Assets	23.5	30.4
	13.1	14.7	12.4				10.7	13.3
	3.3	8.6	6.6				5.0	6.5
	7.3	6.8	6.9			Sales/Total Assets	5.6	7.2
	3.8	4.4	3.4				3.7	4.2
	2.2	2.3	2.4				2.3	2.3
	.7	.4	.5			% Depr., Dep., Amort./Sales	.6	.6
	(13) 1.7	(32) 1.0	(32) .8				(71) .9	(72) 1.0
	5.1	2.0	1.9				2.4	2.1
		.9				% Officers', Directors', Owners' Comp/Sales	(17) .2	(27) .5
		(15) 1.9					1.2	1.7
		2.4					2.9	3.9
70M	107003M	939453M	4012284M	1923058M	2431293M	Net Sales ($)	7953455M	6984215M
246M	19911M	167549M	926541M	325144M	846580M	Total Assets ($)	2260341M	1655583M

M = $ thousand   MM = $ million
See Pages 11 through 21 for Explanation of Ratios and Data

Comparative Historical Data   Current Data Sorted By Sales

			Type of Statement	31 (4/1-9/30/04)			67 (10/1/04-3/31/05)		
35	29	33	Unqualified				1	3	29
16	26	19	Reviewed	1			3	5	10
16	18	20	Compiled	2	2	3	5	2	6
3	7	3	Tax Returns	1			1	1	
26	26	23	Other	1	1	1	3	5	12
4/1/02-3/31/03 ALL	4/1/03-3/31/04 ALL	4/1/04-3/31/05 ALL		0-1MM	1-3MM	3-5MM	5-10MM	10-25MM	25MM & OVER
96	106	98	**NUMBER OF STATEMENTS**	5	3	4	13	16	57
%	%	%	**ASSETS**	%	%	%	%	%	%
8.2	9.4	6.1	Cash & Equivalents				3.6	7.8	6.0
24.3	27.0	25.7	Trade Receivables (net)				23.7	31.3	27.8
21.7	19.6	22.5	Inventory				19.4	22.4	24.1
4.4	2.6	1.7	All Other Current				2.1	1.2	2.1
58.6	58.6	56.1	Total Current				48.8	62.6	60.0
33.0	33.0	34.3	Fixed Assets (net)				30.2	29.3	33.9
2.3	1.7	1.7	Intangibles (net)				2.5	1.5	1.5
6.1	6.7	7.9	All Other Non-Current				18.5	6.6	4.6
100.0	100.0	100.0	Total				100.0	100.0	100.0
			LIABILITIES						
11.6	9.7	12.8	Notes Payable-Short Term				10.2	11.1	13.9
4.1	4.9	2.4	Cur. Mat.-L/T/D				2.4	3.5	1.5
11.9	12.8	13.4	Trade Payables				16.1	14.9	13.5
.2	.2	.1	Income Taxes Payable				.0	.0	.2
8.5	7.9	9.0	All Other Current				9.9	6.9	8.9
36.4	35.5	37.7	Total Current				38.6	36.4	37.9
14.2	14.5	16.6	Long-Term Debt				18.7	17.3	14.5
.5	.5	.7	Deferred Taxes				.0	.2	1.1
5.9	6.6	4.5	All Other Non-Current				4.6	7.4	3.6
43.1	43.0	40.5	Net Worth				38.2	38.7	42.9
100.0	100.0	100.0	Total Liabilities & Net Worth				100.0	100.0	100.0
			INCOME DATA						
100.0	100.0	100.0	Net Sales				100.0	100.0	100.0
18.1	18.7	19.1	Gross Profit				21.3	19.9	13.6
14.6	15.8	16.6	Operating Expenses				20.6	16.5	10.9
3.6	2.9	2.5	Operating Profit				.7	3.4	2.7
.2	.3	.5	All Other Expenses (net)				-.2	.3	.6
3.4	2.6	2.0	Profit Before Taxes				.8	3.1	2.2
			RATIOS						
2.8	2.9	2.3	Current				2.2	3.4	2.4
1.7	1.7	1.5					1.6	1.6	1.5
1.3	1.2	1.1					.7	1.1	1.1
1.6	2.1	1.2	Quick				1.2	2.2	1.2
.9	1.0	.8					.7	.8	.8
.6	.6	.5					.4	.6	.6
14 25.4	15 24.0	15 24.1	Sales/Receivables				14 26.6	17 21.1	15 24.2
19 19.0	21 17.5	20 17.9					20 18.5	21 17.0	19 19.5
31 11.9	28 12.9	30 12.1					30 12.3	25 14.8	30 12.3
11 32.0	9 42.1	12 31.1	Cost of Sales/Inventory				11 32.4	15 25.2	9 39.5
22 16.5	21 17.3	21 17.0					20 18.1	22 16.4	17 21.5
35 10.5	33 11.1	37 9.8					31 11.7	31 11.6	31 11.8
6 64.4	6 57.9	7 52.9	Cost of Sales/Payables				7 49.3	7 49.9	6 62.2
10 36.3	12 30.9	13 29.0					15 24.5	11 32.8	12 30.0
17 21.0	18 19.9	22 16.4					27 13.4	20 18.1	19 19.1
10.6	10.2	14.8	Sales/Working Capital				13.6	13.2	15.9
19.2	21.8	28.8					27.7	35.7	25.6
45.8	67.4	159.8					-74.8	NM	93.7
14.3	14.1	13.9	EBIT/Interest				6.9	12.2	20.2
(88) 5.1	(96) 4.0	(91) 3.2					3.2	(14) 2.4	(54) 5.2
1.8	1.4	1.1					-4.5	1.7	1.1
7.5	7.1	13.1	Net Profit + Depr., Dep., Amort./Cur. Mat. L/T/D						23.8
(30) 3.0	(32) 3.4	(19) 3.6							(17) 3.6
1.0	1.2	1.9							2.1
.4	.4	.4	Fixed/Worth				.4	.3	.5
.9	.8	.8					.6	.7	.8
1.6	1.5	2.0					6.8	3.1	1.6
.6	.6	.7	Debt/Worth				.5	.8	.7
1.8	1.5	1.9					2.0	2.2	1.8
3.8	3.6	3.5					22.4	4.7	3.2
36.7	37.6	33.1	% Profit Before Taxes/Tangible Net Worth				25.8	76.2	34.4
(89) 16.8	(100) 18.5	(96) 18.2					(12) 4.5	22.2	20.0
6.5	6.1	.8					-26.1	6.2	1.9
16.1	13.1	12.5	% Profit Before Taxes/Total Assets				9.1	25.2	14.9
8.3	6.2	5.0					4.0	5.0	5.5
2.1	1.4	.1					-8.1	3.0	.4
27.3	33.0	27.3	Sales/Net Fixed Assets				32.7	43.6	26.4
11.8	14.4	12.4					16.6	24.3	13.2
6.4	6.0	6.4					7.1	8.9	8.4
5.6	6.5	6.6	Sales/Total Assets				5.4	6.8	7.6
3.9	3.9	4.2					4.0	4.6	4.9
2.5	2.5	2.4					2.2	3.5	2.7
.6	.5	.5	% Depr., Dep., Amort./Sales				.7	.4	.5
(85) 1.0	(95) .9	(87) 1.0					(10) 1.3	(15) .7	(52) .8
1.9	2.2	2.1					2.6	2.1	1.4
1.1	.8	.7	% Officers', Directors', Owners' Comp/Sales						
(26) 2.4	(37) 2.3	(28) 1.9							
4.3	3.6	2.9							
9111829M	8899949M	9413161M	Net Sales ($)	2034M	5920M	14971M	93013M	241683M	9055540M
2414886M	2342329M	2285971M	Total Assets ($)	5048M	2998M	29180M	30229M	54642M	2163874M

© RMA 2005

M = $ thousand   MM = $ million
See Pages 11 through 21 for Explanation of Ratios and Data

Current Data Sorted By Assets   Comparative Historical Data

0-500M	500M-2MM	2-10MM	10-50MM	50-100MM	100-250MM	Type of Statement	ALL 4/1/00-3/31/01	ALL 4/1/01-3/31/02
1	8	8	16	5	7	Unqualified	20	26
	7	12	4			Reviewed	20	19
2	9	14	6			Compiled	25	27
1		1				Tax Returns	4	4
	6	15	20	1	2	Other	28	37
	28 (4/1-9/30/04)			117 (10/1/04-3/31/05)			4/1/00-3/31/01	4/1/01-3/31/02
4	30	50	46	6	9	**NUMBER OF STATEMENTS**	97	113
%	%	%	%	%	%	**ASSETS**	%	%
	7.5	8.1	5.7			Cash & Equivalents	7.7	7.1
	28.6	26.2	23.7			Trade Receivables (net)	22.4	20.3
	26.0	17.7	22.7			Inventory	18.2	20.6
	1.8	5.2	3.0			All Other Current	2.5	1.7
	63.9	57.3	55.1			Total Current	50.8	49.8
	29.5	32.0	39.1			Fixed Assets (net)	41.0	42.9
	3.2	2.7	3.6			Intangibles (net)	2.1	2.1
	3.4	8.0	2.3			All Other Non-Current	6.0	5.1
	100.0	100.0	100.0			Total	100.0	100.0
						LIABILITIES		
	8.5	12.4	10.2			Notes Payable-Short Term	9.2	9.5
	3.7	1.9	3.2			Cur. Mat.-L/T/D	4.1	4.7
	19.3	16.6	15.6			Trade Payables	15.5	13.9
	.1	.4	.1			Income Taxes Payable	.3	.3
	6.9	8.9	7.9			All Other Current	8.5	8.3
	38.6	40.2	37.0			Total Current	37.6	36.7
	17.6	12.1	19.4			Long-Term Debt	20.7	21.3
	.2	.5	.3			Deferred Taxes	.4	.4
	3.9	5.3	4.2			All Other Non-Current	3.7	3.2
	39.7	41.9	39.2			Net Worth	37.6	38.3
	100.0	100.0	100.0			Total Liabilities & Net Worth	100.0	100.0
						INCOME DATA		
	100.0	100.0	100.0			Net Sales	100.0	100.0
	23.1	25.0	20.4			Gross Profit	24.1	24.8
	20.7	21.0	17.3			Operating Expenses	20.7	20.8
	2.4	4.0	3.2			Operating Profit	3.4	4.0
	.8	.3	.7			All Other Expenses (net)	.9	.9
	1.6	3.8	2.5			Profit Before Taxes	2.5	3.1
						RATIOS		
	3.5	2.6	2.4			Current	2.1	2.1
	1.6	1.3	1.5				1.3	1.4
	1.2	1.0	1.1				1.0	1.1
	1.9	1.8	1.3			Quick	1.1	1.2
	.8	.9	.8				.7	.8
	.6	.5	.5				.5	.5
14	25.4	13 28.3	21 17.8			Sales/Receivables	18 20.8	14 26.0
19	18.8	17 21.0	26 14.3				24 15.3	21 17.2
26	13.9	26 13.8	34 10.9				29 12.7	29 12.8
9	41.4	7 50.6	16 22.3			Cost of Sales/Inventory	15 23.8	18 20.7
23	15.8	16 23.2	29 12.8				24 15.5	24 15.4
42	8.7	37 10.0	47 7.7				39 9.2	44 8.3
4	81.9	7 55.8	10 35.5			Cost of Sales/Payables	11 34.3	10 36.7
16	22.2	15 24.1	19 19.5				16 22.6	16 22.6
24	15.4	28 13.1	32 11.3				30 12.4	27 13.4
	11.2	10.6	8.3			Sales/Working Capital	11.6	12.6
	20.6	41.9	18.6				30.8	27.2
	80.1	NM	160.6				629.8	73.9
	5.8	16.5	14.1			EBIT/Interest	7.6	8.5
(25)	2.2	(43) 2.8	(41) 8.4				(90) 3.1	(106) 3.4
	.7	1.4	1.2				1.4	1.7
		7.8	8.7			Net Profit + Depr., Dep., Amort./Cur. Mat. L/T/D	4.4	4.2
		(11) 2.8	(14) 4.0				(29) 3.1	(29) 2.7
		1.0	1.0				1.1	1.3
	.4	.4	.6			Fixed/Worth	.6	.6
	.8	.7	.9				1.1	1.1
	1.8	1.6	1.8				2.4	2.4
	.7		1.0			Debt/Worth	.8	.8
	1.9	1.4	1.4				1.5	1.6
	4.2	4.6	5.4				4.1	4.2
	26.7	30.0	46.3			% Profit Before Taxes/Tangible Net Worth	37.9	33.1
(29)	13.4	(48) 14.3	(43) 26.1				(89) 17.7	(101) 18.1
	-1.1	2.4	1.4				5.5	8.1
	9.8	15.0	19.3			% Profit Before Taxes/Total Assets	13.0	13.8
	4.5	5.0	8.9				5.6	5.9
	-.9	.8	.1				1.8	2.9
	63.8	62.0	21.0			Sales/Net Fixed Assets	14.6	13.4
	20.9	13.1	9.0				6.3	7.2
	11.6	5.9	3.4				4.6	4.5
	7.9	6.4	4.4			Sales/Total Assets	4.5	4.3
	4.8	4.0	2.9				3.0	3.0
	3.8	2.7	1.9				2.0	2.1
	.4	.3	.7			% Depr., Dep., Amort./Sales	.8	.9
(29)	1.0	(47) 1.0	(41) 1.7				(87) 1.7	(98) 1.8
	2.0	2.0	2.3				2.9	2.5
	2.3	1.2	.6			% Officers', Directors', Owners' Comp/Sales	1.6	1.4
(14)	4.7	(20) 3.4	(12) 1.2				(36) 2.8	(36) 2.6
	9.1	5.7	2.1				4.8	4.3
10280M	204531M	1317168M	3284071M	1474587M	3654519M	Net Sales ($)	6006421M	6615842M
1063M	36278M	268809M	1051591M	405294M	1296710M	Total Assets ($)	2279645M	2238273M

© RMA 2005

M = $ thousand   MM = $ million

See Pages 11 through 21 for Explanation of Ratios and Data

Comparative Historical Data | | | | **Current Data Sorted By Sales**

			Type of Statement						
39	39	36	Unqualified	1	2	1	7	4 / 6	32 / 8
35	30	25	Reviewed				7	7	10
21	38	27	Compiled		2	1	7	3	
6	13	12	Tax Returns		2	2	5		
30	47	45	Other	1		4	5	9	26

4/1/02-3/31/03 ALL	4/1/03-3/31/04 ALL	4/1/04-3/31/05 ALL		28 (4/1-9/30/04) 0-1MM	1-3MM	3-5MM	117 (10/1/04-3/31/05) 5-10MM	10-25MM	25MM & OVER
131	167	145	NUMBER OF STATEMENTS	2	6	8	24	29	76
%	%	%	ASSETS	%	%	%	%	%	%
8.1	7.1	6.8	Cash & Equivalents				8.5	9.4	4.7
24.2	25.6	25.2	Trade Receivables (net)				24.2	24.3	26.6
20.4	20.1	22.1	Inventory				21.5	21.4	22.7
2.3	3.4	3.3	All Other Current				4.6	2.3	3.9
55.1	56.1	57.5	Total Current				58.9	57.5	57.9
36.7	34.6	34.4	Fixed Assets (net)				31.1	34.0	33.5
2.7	3.8	3.5	Intangibles (net)				6.7	1.1	4.1
5.6	5.5	4.6	All Other Non-Current				3.3	7.4	4.5
100.0	100.0	100.0	Total				100.0	100.0	100.0
			LIABILITIES						
11.0	11.0	10.7	Notes Payable-Short Term				8.0	10.7	11.7
6.0	3.9	2.9	Cur. Mat.-L/T/D				3.1	1.5	2.7
14.9	17.4	16.6	Trade Payables				16.9	18.0	17.4
.2	.2	.2	Income Taxes Payable				.4	.1	.1
7.7	8.1	8.1	All Other Current				8.2	7.8	9.0
39.7	40.4	38.5	Total Current				36.7	38.2	40.9
20.4	16.2	15.6	Long-Term Debt				14.9	18.0	13.9
.3	.3	.3	Deferred Taxes				.1	.5	.4
6.2	5.7	4.8	All Other Non-Current				6.7	4.4	4.5
33.4	37.3	40.9	Net Worth				41.7	38.8	40.2
100.0	100.0	100.0	Total Liabilities & Net Worth				100.0	100.0	100.0
			INCOME DATA						
100.0	100.0	100.0	Net Sales				100.0	100.0	100.0
24.1	20.9	22.3	Gross Profit				29.0	20.9	18.1
19.0	17.3	18.9	Operating Expenses				26.6	20.3	14.5
5.2	3.6	3.4	Operating Profit				2.4	.6	3.6
1.1	.7	.5	All Other Expenses (net)				.1	.4	.4
4.1	2.9	2.9	Profit Before Taxes				2.3	.2	3.2
			RATIOS						
2.1	2.1	2.5					3.4	2.9	2.2
1.5	1.4	1.5	Current				1.8	1.9	1.5
1.1	1.1	1.1					1.1	1.1	1.1
1.4	1.3	1.4					1.9	1.9	1.2
.8	.8	.8	Quick				.7	.9	.8
.5	.5	.5					.5	.6	.5
16 22.5	16 22.6	15 23.8		14 25.4	15 24.5	17 21.8			
22 17.0	20 18.1	22 16.9	Sales/Receivables	19 19.5	21 17.1	22 16.7			
28 13.0	28 13.1	29 12.7		22 16.2	32 11.5	29 12.6			
14 25.7	12 29.7	11 31.9		9 39.8	11 31.9	12 30.6			
22 16.5	22 16.5	24 15.3	Cost of Sales/Inventory	23 15.8	20 18.4	27 13.6			
38 9.6	38 9.7	44 8.4		45 8.0	43 8.4	45 8.2			
9 41.2	9 40.5	8 44.1		13 27.7	8 45.9	10 37.4			
15 23.9	17 21.7	17 21.5	Cost of Sales/Payables	19 19.0	16 22.9	16 23.0			
23 15.6	25 14.6	26 13.8		30 12.3	29 12.4	24 15.5			
10.2	12.6	10.8					8.9	9.1	13.3
25.5	31.9	27.2	Sales/Working Capital				17.2	20.6	29.1
100.4	157.1	222.2					238.6	140.9	281.3
	10.2	14.0	14.0						
(121) 5.5	(147) 4.5	(125) 5.2	EBIT/Interest	(19) 8.3 / 2.5 / .8	(25) 9.4 / 2.5 / 1.0	(68) 17.6 / 8.5 / 2.1			
2.2	1.3	1.2							
9.4	6.9	8.3							9.3
(40) 2.9	(40) 3.2	(35) 3.1	Net Profit + Depr., Dep., Amort./Cur. Mat. L/T/D						(18) 4.0
1.4	1.5	1.1							1.2
.5	.4	.5					.6	.4	.5
1.0	.9	.8	Fixed/Worth				.8	.7	.8
2.0	2.3	1.7					2.1	1.7	1.5
.8	.9	.8					.7	.7	1.0
1.8	1.7	1.5	Debt/Worth				2.3	1.5	1.5
4.4	5.0	4.3					5.8	5.4	4.3
50.2	52.7	38.4					27.3	25.2	49.2
(120) 27.2	(152) 24.2	(138) 19.1	% Profit Before Taxes/Tangible Net Worth	(23) 9.4	(27) 12.1	(72) 28.5			
13.3	7.5	1.6		-3.9	1.0	6.3			
18.0	17.3	16.2					9.0	10.2	20.6
9.6	8.0	7.0	% Profit Before Taxes/Total Assets				3.4	3.1	10.4
3.9	1.5	.6					-1.0	.5	1.0
19.7	26.5	30.0					32.9	68.3	26.8
8.7	10.4	11.5	Sales/Net Fixed Assets				16.3	10.3	11.4
5.5	5.2	5.7					5.0	5.3	6.1
5.1	6.1	6.0					6.5	6.7	5.9
3.5	3.4	3.6	Sales/Total Assets				4.1	3.7	3.6
2.4	2.4	2.4					2.5	1.9	2.7
.9	.6	.6					.6	.3	.6
(113) 1.6	(145) 1.4	(132) 1.2	% Depr., Dep., Amort./Sales		(27) 1.0	(67) 1.2	1.1		
2.7	2.7	2.2					3.2	2.3	2.1
1.4	1.2	1.1					2.0	.9	.7
(41) 2.3	(50) 2.1	(49) 3.2	% Officers', Directors', Owners' Comp/Sales	(12) 4.1	(11) 1.9	(17) 1.3			
4.4	4.8	6.0		5.7	4.5	4.5			
12284332M	14030134M	9945156M	Net Sales ($)	847M	13001M	33263M	177492M	486045M	9234508M
3314075M	4309265M	3059745M	Total Assets ($)	237M	10144M	8690M	56999M	194184M	2789491M

Current Data Sorted By Assets   Comparative Historical Data

			7		5	Type of Statement		
	1	2	1	1		Unqualified		2
		1	1			Reviewed		3
1		1				Compiled		2
	1		1	1	1	Tax Returns		3
	6 (4/1-9/30/04)		17 (10/1/04-3/31/05)			Other	4/1/00-3/31/01 ALL	4/1/01-3/31/02 ALL
0-500M	500M-2MM	2-10MM	10-50MM	50-100MM	100-250MM			16
1	2	4	8	2	6	NUMBER OF STATEMENTS		26
%	%	%	%	%	%	ASSETS	%	%
						Cash & Equivalents		5.9
						Trade Receivables (net)	D	18.1
						Inventory	A	25.4
						All Other Current	T	1.9
						Total Current	A	51.3
						Fixed Assets (net)		31.9
						Intangibles (net)	N	4.5
						All Other Non-Current	O	12.2
						Total	T	100.0
						LIABILITIES	A	
						Notes Payable-Short Term	V	21.9
						Cur. Mat.-L/T/D	A	2.5
						Trade Payables	I	10.1
						Income Taxes Payable	L	.2
						All Other Current	A	11.6
						Total Current	B	46.3
						Long-Term Debt	L	14.0
						Deferred Taxes	E	.1
						All Other Non-Current		2.5
						Net Worth		37.0
						Total Liabilities & Net Worth		100.0
						INCOME DATA		
						Net Sales		100.0
						Gross Profit		24.5
						Operating Expenses		21.9
						Operating Profit		2.6
						All Other Expenses (net)		.7
						Profit Before Taxes		1.9
						RATIOS		
								1.8
						Current		1.2
								.7
								.8
						Quick		.6
								.3
							17	21.8
						Sales/Receivables	29	12.5
							36	10.0
							22	16.9
						Cost of Sales/Inventory	49	7.5
							72	5.0
							3	106.1
						Cost of Sales/Payables	14	26.5
							24	15.3
								8.0
						Sales/Working Capital		26.5
								-14.4
								4.5
						EBIT/Interest		2.1
								.9
						Net Profit + Depr., Dep., Amort./Cur. Mat. L /T/D		
								.5
						Fixed/Worth		.9
								1.8
								1.1
						Debt/Worth		2.6
								5.8
						% Profit Before Taxes/Tangible Net Worth		22.8
							(21)	10.9
								.3
						% Profit Before Taxes/Total Assets		8.2
								5.4
								-.4
								16.0
						Sales/Net Fixed Assets		7.8
								4.6
								3.2
						Sales/Total Assets		2.3
								1.4
								1.2
						% Depr., Dep., Amort./Sales	(23)	1.9
								3.2
						% Officers', Directors', Owners' Comp/Sales		
521M	9932M	66207M	321685M	411164M	1614737M	Net Sales ($)		1622049M
256M	2297M	20786M	169769M	127960M	927667M	Total Assets ($)		813716M

© RMA 2005

M = $ thousand MM = $ million
See Pages 11 through 21 for Explanation of Ratios and Data

Comparative Historical Data | Current Data Sorted By Sales

4/1/02-3/31/03 ALL	4/1/03-3/31/04 ALL	4/1/04-3/31/05 ALL	Type of Statement	0-1MM	6 (4/1-9/30/04) 1-3MM	3-5MM	17 (10/1/04-3/31/05) 5-10MM	10-25MM	25MM & OVER
8	14	12	Unqualified				1	1	10
3	6	4	Reviewed				2	1	1
3	2	1	Compiled						1
		2	Tax Returns	1					
8	8	4	Other		1		1		3
22	**30**	**23**	**NUMBER OF STATEMENTS**	**1**		**1**	**4**	**2**	**15**
%	%	%	**ASSETS**	%	%	%	%	%	%
10.1	6.2	8.7	Cash & Equivalents						8.1
20.1	22.3	17.1	Trade Receivables (net)						15.4
12.7	12.4	16.2	Inventory						16.4
2.2	2.5	1.5	All Other Current						2.3
45.1	43.5	43.5	Total Current						42.1
42.9	46.8	46.5	Fixed Assets (net)						51.0
3.6	2.8	5.6	Intangibles (net)						4.2
8.4	6.9	4.4	All Other Non-Current						2.8
100.0	100.0	100.0	Total						100.0
			LIABILITIES						
7.2	5.0	4.1	Notes Payable-Short Term						4.0
2.3	7.1	2.8	Cur. Mat.-L/T/D						1.9
7.3	10.9	7.3	Trade Payables						7.4
.1	.1	.2	Income Taxes Payable						.1
15.4	8.6	7.4	All Other Current						8.3
32.3	31.7	21.8	Total Current						21.7
16.7	21.2	30.6	Long-Term Debt						22.7
1.1	.7	.6	Deferred Taxes						.9
6.4	6.2	5.9	All Other Non-Current						5.6
43.4	40.3	41.1	Net Worth						49.2
100.0	100.0	100.0	Total Liabilities & Net Worth						100.0
			INCOME DATA						
100.0	100.0	100.0	Net Sales						100.0
38.8	24.1	27.9	Gross Profit						21.5
31.5	16.9	20.9	Operating Expenses						15.2
7.3	7.2	7.0	Operating Profit						6.3
1.2	.8	1.1	All Other Expenses (net)						.9
6.1	6.3	6.0	Profit Before Taxes						5.3
			RATIOS						
2.7	2.5	2.7	Current						2.7
1.9	1.4	2.0							1.9
1.2	1.1	1.3							1.5
1.9	1.4	2.0	Quick						2.2
1.0	.9	1.1							1.0
.7	.6	.6							.6
18 20.6	18 20.3	20 18.4	Sales/Receivables						20 18.4
27 13.5	27 13.4	29 12.6							22 16.7
35 10.5	34 10.6	32 11.4							31 11.7
21 17.6	9 39.6	21 17.3	Cost of Sales/Inventory						18 20.3
28 13.1	26 14.2	30 12.0							28 13.1
40 9.1	36 10.2	41 8.9							47 7.8
9 41.5	10 36.3	9 39.5	Cost of Sales/Payables						9 39.5
15 24.2	17 22.1	15 23.9							14 25.9
28 13.3	26 14.0	22 16.5							19 19.6
8.3	13.6	7.3	Sales/Working Capital						6.6
14.3	20.4	12.6							12.6
44.3	124.2	37.3							23.5
25.5	20.9	32.8	EBIT/Interest						30.6
10.0	(29) 7.5	(22) 4.5							4.5
3.4	2.2	1.8							1.9
		15.1	Net Profit + Depr., Dep., Amort./Cur. Mat. L/T/D						
	(10)	6.0							
		.9							
.7	.6	.7	Fixed/Worth						.8
1.1	1.2	1.0							1.0
2.2	2.4	1.6							1.8
.6	.7	.5	Debt/Worth						.4
1.2	1.6	1.2							1.1
2.1	4.2	2.8							2.5
32.0	61.3	46.7	% Profit Before Taxes/Tangible Net Worth						48.1
(19) 23.8	(29) 33.4	(21) 23.9						(14)	22.0
14.7	10.0	4.9							.8
20.1	23.2	17.3	% Profit Before Taxes/Total Assets						15.7
12.0	10.7	8.1							9.1
6.3	2.9	1.8							2.0
8.8	10.6	7.9	Sales/Net Fixed Assets						5.4
5.4	4.4	5.1							4.8
3.7	2.4	2.5							2.5
3.0	3.7	3.2	Sales/Total Assets						3.2
2.5	2.3	2.5							2.5
1.6	1.6	1.3							1.3
2.2	2.0	2.0	% Depr., Dep., Amort./Sales						2.1
(19) 3.0	(24) 3.0	(17) 2.7						(10)	3.1
4.5	4.1	5.0							4.9
			% Officers', Directors', Owners' Comp/Sales						
1712429M	2818355M	2424246M	Net Sales ($)	521M		4744M	26848M	32964M	2359169M
745386M	1497275M	1248735M	Total Assets ($)	256M		879M	21877M	20302M	1205421M

(Right-side columns 0-1MM through 10-25MM: **DATA NOT AVAILABLE** for Assets, Liabilities, Income Data, and Ratios.)

M = $ thousand   MM = $ million

See Pages 11 through 21 for Explanation of Ratios and Data

Current Data Sorted By Assets   Comparative Historical Data

Current Data date spans: **12 (4/1-9/30/04)** and **38 (10/1/04-3/31/05)**
Comparative date spans: **4/1/00-3/31/01 ALL** and **4/1/01-3/31/02 ALL**

Type of Statement

	0-500M	500M-2MM	2-10MM	10-50MM	50-100MM	100-250MM		4/1/00-3/31/01 ALL	4/1/01-3/31/02 ALL
Unqualified		1	1	7	5	4		20	27
Reviewed			5	2	1			7	6
Compiled			4					6	5
Tax Returns			2					3	3
Other	1	2	5	3	5	2		21	15
NUMBER OF STATEMENTS	1	3	17	12	11	6		57	56

Main Data

0-500M %	500M-2MM %	2-10MM %	10-50MM %	50-100MM %	100-250MM %		ALL %	ALL %
						ASSETS		
		8.8	7.5	4.1		Cash & Equivalents	5.7	5.0
		29.6	17.6	17.3		Trade Receivables (net)	20.3	19.1
		16.8	24.7	23.0		Inventory	22.9	23.2
		1.3	.5	.9		All Other Current	3.3	4.6
		56.5	50.3	45.3		Total Current	52.2	52.0
		34.5	43.1	48.3		Fixed Assets (net)	39.1	39.7
		4.5	2.2	3.9		Intangibles (net)	3.2	2.4
		4.5	4.4	2.6		All Other Non-Current	5.5	5.9
		100.0	100.0	100.0		Total	100.0	100.0
						LIABILITIES		
		11.8	5.9	5.5		Notes Payable-Short Term	10.5	5.7
		1.7	2.5	4.3		Cur. Mat.-L/T/D	4.2	4.8
		28.4	15.0	11.5		Trade Payables	12.8	15.6
		.1	.3	.5		Income Taxes Payable	.2	.6
		5.2	6.3	11.9		All Other Current	11.9	13.4
		47.1	29.9	33.7		Total Current	39.5	40.1
		8.7	16.0	18.3		Long-Term Debt	19.5	22.7
		.8	1.5	1.3		Deferred Taxes	1.7	1.9
		8.4	6.1	5.4		All Other Non-Current	1.8	1.5
		35.0	46.5	41.3		Net Worth	37.5	33.8
		100.0	100.0	100.0		Total Liabilities & Net Worth	100.0	100.0
						INCOME DATA		
		100.0	100.0	100.0		Net Sales	100.0	100.0
		22.0	17.3	17.2		Gross Profit	16.7	14.8
		17.9	12.3	10.7		Operating Expenses	13.7	11.6
		4.1	4.9	6.5		Operating Profit	3.0	3.2
		.3	.2	.7		All Other Expenses (net)	.4	.9
		3.8	4.7	5.9		Profit Before Taxes	2.6	2.3
						RATIOS		
		2.5	2.3	2.1		Current	2.3	2.3
		1.4	1.4	1.3			1.7	1.8
		.8	1.3	1.1			1.1	1.2
		1.9	1.0	.9		Quick	1.1	1.2
		.8	.8	.6			.7	.8
		.5	.6	.5			.5	.4
		18 19.9	14 25.4	21 17.7		Sales/Receivables	19 19.5	17 21.1
		23 15.8	18 20.2	26 13.8			23 15.8	21 17.4
		37 10.0	23 15.7	30 12.1			36 10.2	31 11.7
		7 56.1	15 23.9	27 13.6		Cost of Sales/Inventory	23 15.8	25 14.7
		19 18.8	36 10.2	35 10.3			39 9.5	39 9.3
		33 11.1	52 7.0	43 8.5			49 7.5	60 6.1
		15 24.0	13 27.3	14 26.6		Cost of Sales/Payables	10 34.9	11 32.2
		23 16.0	17 21.7	15 24.7			14 25.6	16 22.9
		45 8.2	24 15.3	20 18.3			23 16.0	23 15.9
		10.1	13.6	9.5		Sales/Working Capital	8.1	9.9
		29.1	25.0	27.6			16.9	16.3
		-48.1	41.6	142.4			47.9	35.7
		23.5	27.6	16.3		EBIT/Interest	7.1	9.0
		(13) 10.4	10.2	10.7			(53) 3.1	(50) 3.4
		1.7	3.5	2.1			-.5	1.2
						Net Profit + Depr., Dep., Amort./Cur. Mat. L/T/D	8.9	7.7
							(11) 1.7	(15) 3.4
							.8	1.4
		.5	.8	.9		Fixed/Worth	.6	.6
		.8	1.1	1.5			1.0	1.2
		6.9	1.7	2.7			1.7	1.9
		.5	.7	.8		Debt/Worth	.8	.9
		1.1	1.3	1.4			1.3	1.7
		23.6	1.7	4.5			3.0	2.8
		59.6	38.5	48.2		% Profit Before Taxes/Tangible Net Worth	36.9	41.5
		(15) 15.8	26.3	(10) 31.3			(52) 14.0	(51) 16.8
		7.9	19.7	18.4			-11.0	3.6
		17.2	17.2	18.5		% Profit Before Taxes/Total Assets	14.7	14.7
		5.4	11.4	11.9			4.6	4.3
		.8	5.0	4.9			-2.8	.4
		29.3	13.7	7.0		Sales/Net Fixed Assets	13.3	10.7
		10.6	7.6	5.4			6.9	6.0
		5.9	4.6	3.2			3.8	4.0
		5.3	4.1	3.2		Sales/Total Assets	3.7	3.9
		3.4	3.1	2.6			2.2	2.4
		2.6	2.5	2.0			1.9	1.7
		.6	1.1	1.6		% Depr., Dep., Amort./Sales	.8	1.0
		(16) 1.8	(11) 1.5	2.0			(43) 1.8	(40) 1.6
		2.9	1.9	3.7			2.9	2.7
						% Officers', Directors', Owners' Comp/Sales	.3	
							(10) .8	
							2.9	
1510M	6355M	291390M	1086178M	1879006M	2898477M	Net Sales ($)	6978163M	8262227M
344M	2613M	74981M	320305M	773785M	1117037M	Total Assets ($)	3516281M	3945270M

M = $ thousand   MM = $ million
See Pages 11 through 21 for Explanation of Ratios and Data

	Comparative Historical Data			Type of Statement	Current Data Sorted By Sales					
	23	29	18	Unqualified	1				1	16
	7	7	7	Reviewed		2		2	3
	1	8	5	Compiled		1		3	1
	2	1	2	Tax Returns				1	1
	16	7	18	Other	3				4	11
	4/1/02- 3/31/03 ALL	4/1/03- 3/31/04 ALL	4/1/04- 3/31/05 ALL		12 (4/1-9/30/04)			38 (10/1/04-3/31/05)		
					0-1MM	1-3MM	3-5MM	5-10MM	10-25MM	25MM & OVER
	49	52	50	NUMBER OF STATEMENTS	4		3		11	32
	%	%	%	ASSETS	%	%	%	%	%	%
	5.1	6.0	6.9	Cash & Equivalents	D	D			9.1	5.4
	18.5	16.3	21.4	Trade Receivables (net)	A	A			27.4	18.6
	21.7	23.4	20.5	Inventory	T	T			15.7	23.7
	4.7	5.4	1.0	All Other Current	A	A			.7	.7
	50.0	51.1	49.8	Total Current					52.9	48.4
	41.3	39.2	42.7	Fixed Assets (net)	N	N			35.6	45.2
	4.3	4.1	3.2	Intangibles (net)	O	O			6.9	2.4
	4.4	5.6	4.3	All Other Non-Current	T	T			4.6	4.0
	100.0	100.0	100.0	Total					100.0	100.0
				LIABILITIES	A	A				
	7.7	7.8	7.0	Notes Payable-Short Term	V	V			11.8	6.0
	4.0	4.5	3.3	Cur. Mat.-L/T/D	A	A			2.0	3.2
	14.2	12.3	17.7	Trade Payables	I	I			26.7	16.1
	.2	.4	.4	Income Taxes Payable	L	L			.1	.5
	8.6	9.0	6.8	All Other Current	A	A			4.6	7.9
	34.6	33.9	35.0	Total Current	B	B			45.1	33.7
	18.3	17.1	16.1	Long-Term Debt	L	L			11.2	17.0
	1.2	1.5	1.2	Deferred Taxes	E	E			.3	1.5
	2.9	3.6	5.8	All Other Non-Current					10.8	4.8
	43.1	43.9	41.9	Net Worth					32.5	43.1
	100.0	100.0	100.0	Total Liabilities & Net Worth					100.0	100.0
				INCOME DATA						
	100.0	100.0	100.0	Net Sales					100.0	100.0
	17.2	16.4	19.3	Gross Profit					19.6	16.8
	14.6	13.2	14.2	Operating Expenses					15.2	11.5
	2.6	3.2	5.1	Operating Profit					4.4	5.3
	.4	.4	.4	All Other Expenses (net)					.5	.4
	2.1	2.9	4.6	Profit Before Taxes					3.9	4.9
				RATIOS						
	2.7	2.6	2.4						2.9	2.3
	1.5	1.5	1.5	Current					1.4	1.4
	1.0	1.0	1.1						.8	1.1
	.9	1.2	1.3						1.8	1.0
	.6	.5	.8	Quick					.9	.7
	.4	.4	.6						.5	.5
15	23.7	15	23.6	18	20.0	Sales/Receivables	14	25.3	18	20.1
21	17.1	20	18.3	21	17.5		20	18.4	21	17.7
30	12.3	26	14.1	30	12.0		31	11.9	29	12.8
21	17.1	23	15.9	17	21.2	Cost of Sales/Inventory	6	57.3	24	15.0
37	9.9	35	10.5	30	12.3		19	19.3	36	10.1
70	5.2	47	7.7	43	8.4		26	14.2	44	8.2
10	37.4	10	35.0	14	26.7	Cost of Sales/Payables	12	29.7	14	26.1
16	22.7	15	24.2	18	20.1		22	16.7	17	21.6
27	13.4	24	15.0	23	15.8		39	9.3	22	16.3
	8.9	8.3	10.3	Sales/Working Capital					10.8	10.7
	19.1	16.0	22.3						29.1	25.0
	NM	NM	66.0						-53.3	79.6
	12.1	12.2	21.3	EBIT/Interest						21.0
(44)	4.8	(48)	4.4	(45)	10.4		(30)	11.3
	1.5	1.7	2.7							3.3
	7.0	4.3	8.1	Net Profit + Depr., Dep.,						
(14)	4.2	(19)	2.3	(14)	4.9	Amort./Cur. Mat. L/T/D				
	1.2	1.3	2.8							
	.7	.6	.7	Fixed/Worth					.6	.8
	1.1	1.0	1.1						.7	1.2
	2.0	2.0	1.7						50.4	1.7
	.7	.6	.7	Debt/Worth					.5	.8
	1.4	1.5	1.3						1.1	1.4
	4.9	2.8	3.7						74.1	1.9
	35.5	40.4	40.8	% Profit Before Taxes/Tangible						39.6
(47)	15.5	(49)	15.9	(47)	29.7	Net Worth				(31)	30.7
	5.5	8.1	10.2							19.4
	12.4	12.0	17.9	% Profit Before Taxes/Total					23.5	18.3
	5.7	6.0	9.6	Assets					2.5	11.8
	1.1	1.3	2.8						.4	4.7
	12.6	10.0	11.0	Sales/Net Fixed Assets					31.1	8.3
	6.4	6.3	6.7						7.8	6.7
	3.7	4.5	4.8						4.8	4.4
	3.5	3.1	4.0	Sales/Total Assets					5.0	3.4
	2.3	2.6	2.9						3.4	2.7
	1.9	2.1	2.5						2.8	2.5
	1.2	1.3	1.1	% Depr., Dep., Amort./Sales					.5	1.3
(43)	2.3	(43)	2.0	(42)	1.8		(10)	2.2	(25)	1.6
	3.6	3.3	2.9						3.2	2.5
				.5	% Officers', Directors',						
			(10)	2.8	Owners' Comp/Sales						
				3.7							
	5170629M	7048256M	6162916M	Net Sales ($)	7865M		18286M	177926M	5958839M
	2381990M	2820574M	2289065M	Total Assets ($)	2957M		7459M	49601M	2229048M

© RMA 2005

M = $ thousand   MM = $ million
See Pages 11 through 21 for Explanation of Ratios and Data

Current Data Sorted By Assets   Comparative Historical Data

0-500M	500M-2MM	2-10MM	10-50MM	50-100MM	100-250MM	Type of Statement	4/1/00-3/31/01 ALL	4/1/01-3/31/02 ALL
		4	7		4	Unqualified	11	10
	3	6	5			Reviewed	8	6
	1	3	1			Compiled	4	5
2	3					Tax Returns	1	
	2	5	6	2	2	Other	12	17
2	**9**	**18**	**19**	**2**	**6**	**NUMBER OF STATEMENTS**	**36**	**38**
%	%	%	%	%	%		%	%
						ASSETS		
		5.1	2.7			Cash & Equivalents	5.1	4.6
		26.3	24.9			Trade Receivables (net)	21.2	20.9
		35.5	29.7			Inventory	34.9	28.4
		5.0	2.5			All Other Current	3.7	4.0
		71.9	59.8			Total Current	64.8	57.8
		20.8	28.1			Fixed Assets (net)	23.0	32.6
		.4	4.4			Intangibles (net)	7.3	5.2
		6.8	7.8			All Other Non-Current	4.8	4.3
		100.0	100.0			Total	100.0	100.0
						LIABILITIES		
		28.3	23.8			Notes Payable-Short Term	29.9	19.5
		1.7	7.0			Cur. Mat.-L/T/D	3.9	7.3
		24.7	11.2			Trade Payables	16.8	16.2
		.9	.0			Income Taxes Payable	.8	.3
		7.9	7.8			All Other Current	8.7	13.3
		63.5	49.9			Total Current	60.0	56.5
		7.3	17.8			Long-Term Debt	10.5	20.3
		.7	.2			Deferred Taxes	1.1	.6
		4.1	4.1			All Other Non-Current	4.8	9.0
		24.4	28.0			Net Worth	23.6	13.5
		100.0	100.0			Total Liabilities & Net Worth	100.0	100.0
						INCOME DATA		
		100.0	100.0			Net Sales	100.0	100.0
		18.0	19.8			Gross Profit	15.8	17.5
		13.8	15.0			Operating Expenses	13.7	15.1
		4.2	4.8			Operating Profit	2.2	2.4
		.9	1.1			All Other Expenses (net)	1.5	1.0
		3.3	3.6			Profit Before Taxes	.7	1.4
						RATIOS		
		1.3	1.9			Current	1.6	1.3
		1.1	1.2				1.2	1.1
		1.0	1.0				.8	.9
		.7	.9			Quick	.6	.7
		.6	.5				.5	.4
		.3	.3				.2	.3
		19 18.8	26 13.9			Sales/Receivables	14 25.7	17 21.2
		32 11.5	32 11.3				25 14.5	26 13.8
		39 9.4	41 8.9				34 10.8	33 11.2
		24 15.4	30 12.4			Cost of Sales/Inventory	20 18.5	18 20.0
		38 9.6	46 7.9				46 7.9	34 10.7
		84 4.4	79 4.6				86 4.3	78 4.7
		11 31.9	9 42.7			Cost of Sales/Payables	8 47.8	12 29.6
		29 12.5	19 19.5				18 20.0	21 17.0
		38 9.7	25 14.7				33 11.1	33 11.0
		19.7	11.5			Sales/Working Capital	14.9	18.4
		59.7	17.7				41.3	83.5
		NM	999.8				-20.9	-59.4
		7.9	13.9			EBIT/Interest	3.0	3.2
		4.0	5.3				(35) 1.5	1.8
		1.9	.2				.7	.4
						Net Profit + Depr., Dep., Amort./Cur. Mat. L /T/D	6.0	1.9
							(16) 2.7	(14) 1.0
							1.6	.3
		.2	.4			Fixed/Worth	.5	.9
		.6	.9				1.3	1.5
		2.0	2.1				NM	3.6
		1.5	1.2			Debt/Worth	2.3	1.9
		3.2	2.3				4.5	4.4
		6.9	8.6				NM	11.1
		67.5	45.5			% Profit Before Taxes/Tangible Net Worth	52.4	54.0
		(17) 35.1	(16) 26.3				(27) 20.8	(31) 8.2
		13.6	11.2				5.0	-5.0
		14.9	15.0			% Profit Before Taxes/Total Assets	9.1	8.5
		6.6	8.2				2.3	1.7
		3.1	-3.4				-1.2	-2.5
		64.9	20.1			Sales/Net Fixed Assets	41.4	23.6
		26.4	9.4				15.4	12.0
		10.4	4.7				8.1	4.4
		4.6	3.5			Sales/Total Assets	4.7	4.1
		3.1	2.3				3.5	3.2
		2.8	1.7				1.6	2.0
		.4	.8			% Depr., Dep., Amort./Sales	.6	.5
		(17) .9	1.4				(34) 1.1	(36) 1.2
		1.8	3.0				2.2	3.2
						% Officers', Directors', Owners' Comp/Sales	.7	
							(11) 1.8	
							4.4	
1970M	43426M	273830M	992318M	221797M	1791546M	Net Sales ($)	1839436M	1457104M
706M	11769M	79980M	394958M	169908M	806189M	Total Assets ($)	934714M	772849M

M = $ thousand   MM = $ million
See Pages 11 through 21 for Explanation of Ratios and Data

Comparative Historical Data | Current Data Sorted By Sales

4/1/02- 3/31/03 ALL	4/1/03- 3/31/04 ALL	4/1/04- 3/31/05 ALL	Type of Statement	0-1MM	1-3MM	3-5MM	5-10MM	10-25MM	25MM & OVER
22	16	15	Unqualified				1	4	10
11	11	14	Reviewed			1	4	6	3
2	5	5	Compiled			1	1	1	2
7	7	5	Tax Returns	2	1		1	1	1
20	18	17	Other		1	2	1	3	10
					8 (4/1-9/30/04)			48 (10/1/04-3/31/05)	
62	57	56	**NUMBER OF STATEMENTS**	2	2	4	8	15	25
%	%	%	**ASSETS**	%	%	%	.%	%	%
5.1	7.4	5.6	Cash & Equivalents					5.4	4.7
22.9	27.2	25.3	Trade Receivables (net)					28.7	24.1
29.5	27.9	30.9	Inventory					35.7	32.0
2.6	3.8	3.4	All Other Current					7.7	2.2
60.1	66.4	65.3	Total Current					77.5	63.0
30.5	25.1	23.9	Fixed Assets (net)					15.9	28.5
3.2	2.4	3.1	Intangibles (net)					.5	3.3
6.2	6.1	7.8	All Other Non-Current					6.0	5.3
100.0	100.0	100.0	Total					100.0	100.0
			LIABILITIES						
21.9	22.6	23.4	Notes Payable-Short Term					24.2	22.6
4.7	3.2	4.3	Cur. Mat.-L/T/D					1.4	5.9
16.4	17.3	16.7	Trade Payables					22.1	12.2
.0	.8	1.0	Income Taxes Payable					1.0	.3
7.7	7.3	7.9	All Other Current					8.8	8.8
50.8	51.3	53.2	Total Current					57.6	49.8
17.4	12.1	13.5	Long-Term Debt					6.0	15.7
.4	.3	.4	Deferred Taxes					.8	.5
5.7	3.9	4.0	All Other Non-Current					3.5	5.3
25.7	32.4	28.9	Net Worth					32.0	28.7
100.0	100.0	100.0	Total Liabilities & Net Worth					100.0	100.0
			INCOME DATA						
100.0	100.0	100.0	Net Sales					100.0	100.0
18.1	16.9	19.9	Gross Profit					20.7	16.4
13.6	14.4	15.4	Operating Expenses					16.3	12.0
4.5	2.6	4.4	Operating Profit					4.4	4.4
.9	.3	.9	All Other Expenses (net)					1.0	1.2
3.5	2.3	3.6	Profit Before Taxes					3.5	3.2
			RATIOS						
1.7	1.9	1.8						1.8	1.8
1.3	1.4	1.2	Current					1.1	1.3
.9	1.1	1.0						1.1	1.1
.8	1.1	.9						.9	.8
.5	.6	.6	Quick					.6	.5
.4	.4	.3						.4	.3
22 16.3	19 19.2	24 15.5						21 17.2	27 13.7
27 13.4	31 11.9	31 11.6	Sales/Receivables					34 10.7	32 11.3
37 9.8	39 9.3	39 9.4						42 8.8	40 9.1
22 16.6	16 22.6	27 13.3						35 10.4	33 11.0
40 9.1	35 10.4	42 8.6	Cost of Sales/Inventory					43 8.4	46 7.9
63 5.8	72 5.1	80 4.5						93 3.9	71 5.1
8 44.0	7 51.2	8 44.9						16 22.3	8 44.1
24 15.4	19 19.0	18 20.0	Cost of Sales/Payables					28 12.9	15 24.6
32 11.4	30 12.3	35 10.4						35 10.3	24 15.0
12.0	8.7	10.7						9.8	9.9
27.4	22.8	25.8	Sales/Working Capital					26.2	17.7
−71.7	66.3	129.9						111.2	51.7
6.9	9.7	10.1						10.9	10.6
(61) 2.5	(55) 2.7	(54) 3.3	EBIT/Interest				(14) 4.4		3.8
1.1	.5	1.0						2.3	1.3
3.1	5.1	9.4	Net Profit + Depr., Dep.,						
(20) 1.7	(12) 2.6	(12) 3.7	Amort./Cur. Mat. L/T/D						
.6	1.6	1.8							
.6	.4	.3						.2	.4
1.1	.7	.8	Fixed/Worth					.5	.9
2.4	2.2	1.9						.9	1.7
1.3	1.2	1.3						1.1	1.3
2.6	2.3	2.6	Debt/Worth					2.4	2.3
6.0	8.6	6.5						5.6	5.9
40.4	60.7	50.1	% Profit Before Taxes/Tangible					65.5	33.2
(56) 14.9	(50) 15.8	(49) 28.7	Net Worth					38.9	(22) 24.2
.9	2.2	11.4						12.0	9.5
12.3	18.3	15.4	% Profit Before Taxes/Total					18.2	10.6
4.4	4.4	6.6	Assets					7.9	6.6
.4	−.4	.6						3.5	1.1
27.5	45.5	36.8						107.4	25.1
10.8	16.0	15.7	Sales/Net Fixed Assets					20.5	9.4
6.6	6.3	7.8						10.2	4.5
4.4	4.6	3.6						4.9	3.5
2.7	2.8	2.8	Sales/Total Assets					3.2	2.8
2.1	1.9	1.9						2.8	1.9
.8	.4	.8						.5	.8
(60) 1.4	(45) 1.1	(49) 1.1	% Depr., Dep., Amort./Sales				(14) .9		(23) 1.0
2.5	2.0	2.5						1.8	3.3
.8	.7	.7							
(21) 1.3	(16) 2.0	(17) 1.4	% Officers', Directors',						
3.3	2.4	3.1	Owners' Comp/Sales						
2770420M	3148747M	3324887M	Net Sales ($)	1680M	3673M	15081M	56753M	245823M	3001877M
1319204M	1525527M	1463510M	Total Assets ($)	1120M	1789M	13438M	21705M	84426M	1341032M

M = $ thousand   MM = $ million
See Pages 11 through 21 for Explanation of Ratios and Data

Current Data Sorted By Assets   Comparative Historical Data

0-500M	500M-2MM	2-10MM	10-50MM	50-100MM	100-250MM	Type of Statement	4/1/00-3/31/01 ALL	4/1/01-3/31/02 ALL
		2	2	1		Unqualified	12	7
	3	11	4			Reviewed	21	12
9	28	17	7			Compiled	45	37
25	19	5	1			Tax Returns	40	30
7	9	6	3	1	2	Other	21	28
	23 (4/1-9/30/04)		139 (10/1/04-3/31/05)					
41	59	41	17	2	2	**NUMBER OF STATEMENTS**	139	114
%	%	%	%	%	%	**ASSETS**	%	%
12.7	9.5	9.3	7.4			Cash & Equivalents	12.5	14.1
4.1	4.0	5.8	4.5			Trade Receivables (net)	6.3	6.7
5.6	3.2	3.2	2.1			Inventory	5.9	5.4
.9	2.5	1.9	1.8			All Other Current	2.6	2.4
23.4	19.2	20.2	15.8			Total Current	27.3	28.5
45.9	46.3	53.9	44.8			Fixed Assets (net)	51.4	49.0
18.7	22.4	11.3	28.7			Intangibles (net)	10.8	12.8
12.0	12.1	14.5	10.7			All Other Non-Current	10.4	9.7
100.0	100.0	100.0	100.0			Total	100.0	100.0
						LIABILITIES		
5.6	2.2	3.5	.8			Notes Payable-Short Term	3.2	4.9
5.3	5.2	9.8	8.0			Cur. Mat.-L/T/D	7.4	6.7
8.4	7.0	7.1	4.4			Trade Payables	11.0	9.8
.4	.0	.1	.0			Income Taxes Payable	.2	.2
18.9	15.4	5.3	7.4			All Other Current	12.0	12.8
38.7	30.0	25.7	20.6			Total Current	33.8	34.3
37.6	36.6	36.9	43.5			Long-Term Debt	35.8	34.2
.0	.0	.2	.6			Deferred Taxes	.1	.2
17.5	6.9	13.1	7.0			All Other Non-Current	8.1	8.8
6.3	26.5	24.1	28.2			Net Worth	22.2	22.5
100.0	100.0	100.0	100.0			Total Liabilities & Net Worth	100.0	100.0
						INCOME DATA		
100.0	100.0	100.0	100.0			Net Sales	100.0	100.0
48.1	44.5	41.2	45.7			Gross Profit	49.3	53.9
46.5	38.3	33.4	38.2			Operating Expenses	43.9	47.8
1.5	6.2	7.8	7.6			Operating Profit	5.4	6.1
.1	.9	1.0	1.9			All Other Expenses (net)	1.3	2.1
1.5	5.3	6.9	5.6			Profit Before Taxes	4.2	4.0
						RATIOS		
2.9	1.7	1.3	1.5			Current	1.4	1.9
.7	.6	.6	.5				.8	.9
.2	.2	.4	.3				.4	.4
1.7	1.2	1.2	1.2			Quick	1.0	1.5
.4	.4	.5	.3				.5	.7
.1	.1	.3	.2				.2	.2
0 UND	0 UND	0 UND	0 785.3			Sales/Receivables	0 UND	0 UND
1 690.0	0 UND	1 681.3	2 176.6				1 477.0	0 849.5
3 119.5	3 139.9	11 33.3	8 44.4				11 34.2	8 46.8
2 194.5	2 196.5	2 147.3	3 140.2			Cost of Sales/Inventory	3 128.4	3 130.8
4 94.3	3 117.9	4 88.7	6 59.9				6 65.5	7 50.4
11 33.5	7 51.6	11 32.6	11 34.7				20 18.0	19 19.3
0 UND	2 156.2	3 134.8	7 53.8			Cost of Sales/Payables	5 69.8	5 73.8
8 43.5	11 34.6	8 43.4	14 25.6				15 24.1	12 29.9
22 16.6	20 18.2	26 14.1	25 14.6				31 11.9	35 10.4
25.8	30.5	36.0	18.8			Sales/Working Capital	45.1	22.5
−63.2	−43.4	−37.9	−21.0				−68.0	−145.1
−11.0	−17.2	−15.3	−11.6				−16.1	−16.8
6.9	16.5	14.3	6.2			EBIT/Interest	11.5	6.8
(33) 1.4	(56) 5.9	5.1	(16) 4.1				(120) 2.8	(95) 1.9
−.4	2.2	1.7	1.8				1.0	.3
						Net Profit + Depr., Dep., Amort./Cur. Mat. L./T/D	2.5	2.0
							(17) 1.4	(19) 1.3
							1.0	.2
1.2	1.2	1.5	1.8			Fixed/Worth	.9	.9
−5.6	3.1	3.3	24.1				2.8	3.1
−1.1	−1.5	−13.8	−.7				−4.9	−2.2
3.1	1.1	1.3	2.6			Debt/Worth	1.1	1.1
−7.7	4.0	5.4	31.8				3.6	4.4
−2.6	−3.5	−18.9	−2.2				−7.8	−4.2
219.1	166.2	168.7	241.8			% Profit Before Taxes/Tangible Net Worth	109.7	88.6
(17) 59.0	(35) 81.3	(29) 67.1	(10) 84.9				(95) 55.7	(72) 36.8
9.3	21.2	12.2	21.0				9.0	6.4
28.3	22.1	27.5	14.7			% Profit Before Taxes/Total Assets	29.7	24.2
4.2	12.5	14.2	9.7				11.2	5.8
−7.0	3.6	2.6	3.8				−.3	−1.4
14.7	10.3	6.3	5.8			Sales/Net Fixed Assets	13.9	13.2
8.8	5.7	4.8	5.2				5.9	5.2
4.9	3.9	2.7	3.3				3.2	3.7
5.8	4.1	2.9	2.5			Sales/Total Assets	4.8	4.3
3.7	2.4	2.2	1.7				2.9	3.0
2.0	1.8	1.8	1.3				1.9	1.9
1.6	2.5	2.7	2.8			% Depr., Dep., Amort./Sales	1.9	1.7
(35) 2.9	(54) 3.6	(39) 3.6	4.2				(130) 3.0	(106) 3.1
6.3	4.9	5.4	6.1				4.7	5.1
4.5	1.7	1.6				% Officers', Directors', Owners' Comp/Sales	2.3	3.4
(22) 7.4	(38) 4.1	(26) 2.9					(67) 4.2	(52) 7.4
11.0	7.8	4.4					9.4	16.4
38999M	197636M	428178M	589458M	229026M	450023M	Net Sales ($)	1113911M	1075723M
11015M	63588M	169572M	306476M	139299M	273769M	Total Assets ($)	626238M	508122M

© RMA 2005

M = $ thousand   MM = $ million
See Pages 11 through 21 for Explanation of Ratios and Data

Comparative Historical Data | | | | **Current Data Sorted By Sales** | | | | | |

4/1/02-3/31/03 ALL	4/1/03-3/31/04 ALL	4/1/04-3/31/05 ALL	Type of Statement	0-1MM	1-3MM	3-5MM	5-10MM	10-25MM	25MM & OVER
7	9	5	Unqualified					2	3
11	14	18	Reviewed		2	2	4	8	2
41	83	61	Compiled	8	16	12	12	7	6
27	43	50	Tax Returns	13	23	9	4		1
15	30	28	Other	7	4	2	6	4	5
				23 (4/1-9/30/04)		139 (10/1/04-3/31/05)			
101	179	162	**NUMBER OF STATEMENTS**	28	45	25	26	21	17
%	%	%	**ASSETS**	%	%	%	%	%	%
10.1	10.4	10.0	Cash & Equivalents	11.2	9.3	13.0	9.5	8.3	8.0
4.8	3.2	4.6	Trade Receivables (net)	4.6	2.2	3.4	6.1	8.6	5.3
5.0	3.4	3.7	Inventory	6.2	2.8	1.6	4.3	4.5	2.8
2.2	2.4	1.8	All Other Current	1.1	1.2	3.2	3.2	.8	2.0
22.2	19.5	20.1	Total Current	23.2	15.6	21.3	23.0	22.2	18.0
53.0	53.8	47.6	Fixed Assets (net)	46.2	47.6	51.3	47.0	49.2	43.2
12.3	15.9	20.0	Intangibles (net)	19.4	24.3	16.7	14.1	15.9	28.6
12.5	10.8	12.3	All Other Non-Current	11.3	12.5	10.7	15.9	12.7	10.2
100.0	100.0	100.0	Total	100.0	100.0	100.0	100.0	100.0	100.0
			LIABILITIES						
6.3	4.1	3.2	Notes Payable-Short Term	5.3	2.9	2.6	1.0	5.1	2.6
6.3	6.9	6.7	Cur. Mat.-L/T/D	4.9	5.4	6.9	6.4	12.1	6.9
10.1	5.4	7.0	Trade Payables	8.6	5.9	5.0	7.1	11.0	5.4
.2	.1	.1	Income Taxes Payable	.1	.3	.0	.1	.1	.1
16.1	11.8	12.9	All Other Current	15.3	17.7	15.6	6.8	5.6	10.2
39.0	28.3	30.0	Total Current	34.2	32.3	30.2	21.3	33.8	25.3
44.1	40.4	38.1	Long-Term Debt	40.7	35.3	47.7	32.6	34.5	39.8
.2	.0	.2	Deferred Taxes	.0	.0	.0	.0	.4	1.0
4.9	8.0	11.6	All Other Non-Current	21.1	9.3	6.7	12.0	8.4	12.7
11.8	23.2	20.1	Net Worth	4.0	23.0	15.4	34.2	22.9	21.2
100.0	100.0	100.0	Total Liabilities & Net Worth	100.0	100.0	100.0	100.0	100.0	100.0
			INCOME DATA						
100.0	100.0	100.0	Net Sales	100.0	100.0	100.0	100.0	100.0	100.0
54.5	46.4	44.7	Gross Profit	48.2	45.8	41.6	44.3	40.8	46.3
48.6	39.5	39.2	Operating Expenses	46.4	40.4	36.1	37.6	31.9	40.0
5.9	6.9	5.6	Operating Profit	1.8	5.4	5.6	6.7	8.9	6.3
2.4	1.1	.9	All Other Expenses (net)	.4	.9	.7	.5	1.0	2.7
3.5	5.8	4.6	Profit Before Taxes	1.4	4.5	4.9	6.2	8.0	3.6
			RATIOS						
1.4	1.5	1.7	Current	3.0	1.5	1.7	1.4	1.6	1.0
.7	.7	.6		.9	.6	.6	1.0	.6	.5
.2	.3	.3		.2	.2	.2	.4	.3	.4
1.0	1.2	1.2	Quick	2.0	1.0	1.1	1.2	1.1	.7
.5	(176) .4	.4		.5	.3	.5	.7	.4	.4
.1	.2	.1		.0	.1	.1	.2	.3	.2
0 UND	0 UND	0 UND	Sales/Receivables	0 UND	0 UND	0 UND	0 UND	0 UND	0 785.3
1 519.7	0 UND	0 887.2		0 UND	0 999.8	0 UND	1 470.9	2 188.8	3 106.5
5 67.0	3 140.8	4 86.3		5 68.7	2 229.9	5 999.8	9 38.8	20 18.3	15 25.1
2 172.4	2 175.8	2 161.7	Cost of Sales/Inventory	1 399.0	2 176.0	2 219.1	2 166.2	3 136.0	3 140.2
5 67.5	4 101.9	4 98.8		6 63.5	4 104.1	3 135.4	4 102.7	6 57.8	8 47.1
19 19.7	10 37.7	10 36.0		11 33.1	10 35.6	4 81.8	9 40.8	16 23.4	19 19.5
2 147.0	2 233.4	3 120.8	Cost of Sales/Payables	4 100.5	1 350.7	1 674.5	3 142.4	6 56.3	5 71.0
10 35.3	7 50.7	10 36.3		8 43.7	10 38.0	6 61.7	8 44.6	17 22.0	14 25.6
37 9.8	19 19.5	22 16.4		34 10.7	19 18.8	16 23.4	26 14.1	29 12.8	27 13.4
39.9	31.2	29.0	Sales/Working Capital	18.4	48.3	30.8	26.0	28.2	NM
−75.8	−33.9	−37.0		NM	−38.6	−33.2	UND	−29.3	−21.0
−11.6	−14.0	−14.7		−10.2	−14.3	−14.2	−24.7	−10.1	−15.3
9.6	10.4	11.2	EBIT/Interest	5.9	13.3	8.3	17.3	18.3	6.2
(89) 2.9	(158) 5.2	(150) 4.2		(22) 1.2	(42) 4.5	(24) 5.3	(25) 7.9	4.1	(16) 2.5
.8	2.0	1.4		−.4	1.2	1.9	2.1	2.6	1.0
		2.1	Net Profit + Depr., Dep., Amort./Cur. Mat. L/T/D						
	(15)	1.7							
		1.3							
1.1	1.2	1.4	Fixed/Worth	4.6	1.2	2.3	.9	1.2	2.7
5.7	6.5	10.2		−4.3	8.3	7.3	2.0	4.0	11.4
−2.1	−4.3	−1.5		−1.0	−.8	−5.7	−14.3	−5.8	−.4
1.1	1.4	1.6	Debt/Worth	36.9	1.0	2.6	.8	1.3	4.0
7.4	6.8	17.7		−4.3	7.7	7.7	2.9	6.1	11.6
−4.8	−6.9	−3.1		−2.4	−2.1	−9.1	−20.4	−8.5	−1.8
89.0	133.3	153.6	% Profit Before Taxes/Tangible Net Worth		112.1	316.9	155.2	147.1	163.3
(58) 42.3	(113) 66.7	(92) 68.6		(24) 52.3	(17) 81.3	(19) 54.3	(13) 67.1		(10) 64.0
7.4	26.6	16.8			10.1	29.6	16.7	11.3	21.0
27.9	24.4	22.5	% Profit Before Taxes/Total Assets	31.8	22.3	20.3	21.2	37.6	14.6
7.7	13.4	9.9		2.3	7.7	14.2	13.0	13.1	4.2
−1.6	3.9	1.2		−7.2	.7	3.8	4.4	3.0	1.0
13.3	6.9	9.7	Sales/Net Fixed Assets	12.1	10.3	10.4	7.6	6.6	8.0
6.2	4.7	5.6		6.4	5.8	5.7	5.1	5.4	5.7
4.0	3.2	3.7		2.8	4.5	2.6	3.6	3.9	4.0
5.2	3.4	4.0	Sales/Total Assets	4.8	3.6	4.3	4.1	4.2	2.8
3.2	2.4	2.4		2.3	2.5	2.7	2.5	2.3	2.0
2.1	1.7	1.7		1.4	1.7	2.0	1.8	1.7	1.4
2.1	2.7	2.4	% Depr., Dep., Amort./Sales	1.9	2.1	2.2	2.4	2.7	2.5
(95) 3.4	(167) 3.7	(148) 3.6		(22) 5.7	(43) 3.2	(24) 3.7	(24) 3.4	(19) 3.6	(16) 3.6
5.7	5.3	5.5		8.0	4.9	5.1	4.5	5.6	6.2
2.9	1.2	1.9	% Officers', Directors', Owners' Comp/Sales	3.3	2.6	1.1	1.7	1.3	
(48) 7.1	(109) 3.1	(94) 3.7		(14) 7.4	(24) 5.5	(19) 3.6	(19) 3.6	(12) 4.8	
10.7	5.5	7.5		13.1	9.6	8.8	6.7	4.8	
2233230M	2632498M	1933320M	Net Sales ($)	15680M	79506M	97941M	177241M	369083M	1193869M
584439M	824334M	963719M	Total Assets ($)	7192M	35336M	38884M	72675M	165951M	643681M

© RMA 2005

M = $ thousand   MM = $ million

See Pages 11 through 21 for Explanation of Ratios and Data

Current Data Sorted By Assets | **Comparative Historical Data**

	0-500M	500M-2MM	2-10MM	10-50MM	50-100MM	100-250MM	Type of Statement	4/1/00-3/31/01 ALL	4/1/01-3/31/02 ALL
		2	5	19	6	5	Unqualified	29	36
		11	18	9			Reviewed	30	32
	1	7	9	2			Compiled	30	39
	9	11	3				Tax Returns	8	16
	2	10	16	11		1	Other	47	60
		32 (4/1-9/30/04)		125 (10/1/04-3/31/05)					
NUMBER OF STATEMENTS	12	41	51	41	6	6		144	183

0-500M %	500M-2MM %	2-10MM %	10-50MM %	50-100MM %	100-250MM %	ASSETS	%	%
12.0	8.4	9.8	9.4			Cash & Equivalents	9.2	8.9
21.0	24.6	20.6	15.2			Trade Receivables (net)	18.0	16.0
9.3	11.2	10.1	9.1			Inventory	9.3	8.8
.1	2.6	1.6	2.1			All Other Current	1.8	2.1
42.3	46.8	42.2	35.7			Total Current	38.4	35.8
42.3	45.2	47.6	48.9			Fixed Assets (net)	48.5	50.6
2.2	2.7	3.5	6.4			Intangibles (net)	5.8	6.7
13.2	5.3	6.7	9.0			All Other Non-Current	7.4	6.9
100.0	100.0	100.0	100.0			Total	100.0	100.0
						LIABILITIES		
8.7	7.3	6.7	2.0			Notes Payable-Short Term	6.0	4.3
2.6	4.2	6.0	5.5			Cur. Mat.-L/T/D	5.3	5.2
16.3	16.1	17.7	11.2			Trade Payables	14.8	11.9
.1	.5	.3	.3			Income Taxes Payable	.1	.2
10.2	7.7	8.6	9.1			All Other Current	8.4	8.7
37.8	35.7	39.4	28.1			Total Current	34.6	30.4
33.5	27.1	21.1	22.8			Long-Term Debt	27.8	30.9
.0	.6	.9	1.5			Deferred Taxes	.7	.7
17.0	4.9	8.1	5.4			All Other Non-Current	5.5	11.5
11.6	31.7	30.6	42.2			Net Worth	31.3	26.4
100.0	100.0	100.0	100.0			Total Liabilities & Net Worth	100.0	100.0
						INCOME DATA		
100.0	100.0	100.0	100.0			Net Sales	100.0	100.0
51.7	38.2	32.7	31.3			Gross Profit	38.7	38.0
51.2	35.5	27.0	27.9			Operating Expenses	33.7	32.6
.6	2.7	5.8	3.4			Operating Profit	5.0	5.3
.3	1.0	1.3	1.0			All Other Expenses (net)	1.3	1.7
.2	1.7	4.4	2.4			Profit Before Taxes	3.7	3.6
						RATIOS		
2.1	2.2	2.2	2.1			Current	1.8	1.9
1.3	1.5	1.3	1.4				1.2	1.1
.8	1.0	.8	.9				.7	.8
1.5	1.8	1.5	1.7			Quick	1.4	1.3
.9	.9	.9	.9				(143) .8	.8
.4	.6	.6	.5				.5	.5
0 UND	19 19.1	19 18.9	19 18.8			Sales/Receivables	19 18.9	15 24.0
12 30.2	26 14.2	27 13.5	15.3				25 14.4	24 15.0
20 18.6	35 10.5	35 10.4	31 11.8				32 11.6	33 11.2
5 70.4	8 47.3	8 43.8	12 31.3			Cost of Sales/Inventory	9 39.7	8 45.3
10 37.1	16 23.2	17 21.3	21 17.2				16 23.0	15 25.0
19 18.8	26 14.0	27 13.5	30 12.0				29 12.6	29 12.5
0 UND	11 32.3	22 16.4	16 23.0			Cost of Sales/Payables	19 19.4	15 24.6
27 13.7	24 15.2	35 10.5	23 15.8				29 12.6	24 15.1
41 9.0	34 10.9	46 7.9	35 10.3				44 8.2	40 9.2
28.4	10.9	11.3	9.9			Sales/Working Capital	12.7	13.5
133.8	21.4	25.3	33.2				52.9	69.5
−67.0	NM	−32.0	−101.4				−22.9	−32.0
25.8	8.4	19.1	13.1			EBIT/Interest	6.8	7.7
(10) .4	(39) 3.0	(44) 2.4	(39) 4.0				(139) 3.2	(165) 2.6
−10.8	.5	.3	1.3				1.5	1.2
	8.0	5.2	3.4			Net Profit + Depr., Dep., Amort./Cur. Mat. L/T/D	5.4	6.1
	(11) 1.9	(15) 2.8	(18) 2.2				(45) 2.2	(46) 2.9
	.1	1.1	.6				1.6	1.2
.7	.8	.6	.8			Fixed/Worth	.9	1.0
4.8	1.6	1.4	1.4				1.6	1.9
−2.0	5.2	4.6	4.2				6.3	7.6
.8	1.1	.7	.7			Debt/Worth	1.0	1.1
10.7	3.0	1.9	1.6				2.0	2.6
−4.3	6.6	6.2	5.9				9.7	13.9
	43.1	59.0	28.6			% Profit Before Taxes/Tangible Net Worth	41.1	51.3
	(36) 15.3	(41) 24.8	(34) 9.8				(119) 24.0	(148) 23.2
	2.0	2.7	1.9				7.8	6.7
31.3	12.7	20.5	10.9			% Profit Before Taxes/Total Assets	13.1	15.1
−.2	4.6	6.2	5.1				6.3	7.0
−19.3	−1.2	−1.4	.5				1.5	1.2
45.4	13.7	8.8	6.6			Sales/Net Fixed Assets	9.6	8.9
14.4	8.1	6.3	4.4				5.1	4.6
6.0	4.6	3.6	3.2				3.0	2.9
7.3	4.9	3.4	2.8			Sales/Total Assets	3.2	3.3
5.1	3.4	2.7	2.1				2.3	2.2
3.8	2.3	2.1	1.6				1.7	1.5
1.1	1.3	2.0	2.2			% Depr., Dep., Amort./Sales	2.0	2.0
(10) 1.6	(38) 2.1	(49) 2.8	(39) 3.1				(135) 3.0	(168) 3.2
2.1	3.9	4.4	5.0				4.3	4.8
	2.6	2.1				% Officers', Directors', Owners' Comp/Sales	2.5	2.2
	(26) 4.8	(20) 3.2					(56) 4.0	(60) 3.6
	6.9	4.6					8.3	7.0
19656M	190580M	712857M	2401693M	718123M	990434M	Net Sales ($)	4334974M	5666052M
3236M	53736M	264181M	1011845M	383031M	718480M	Total Assets ($)	2305911M	3046846M

© RMA 2005
M = $ thousand   MM = $ million
See Pages 11 through 21 for Explanation of Ratios and Data

Comparative Historical Data			Type of Statement	Current Data Sorted By Sales					
38	23	37	Unqualified		1		1	8	27
39	50	38	Reviewed		3	2	10	11	12
29	33	19	Compiled		3	5	5	4	2
10	26	23	Tax Returns	6	5	6	3	3	
34	53	40	Other	1	7	3	6	15	8
4/1/02-3/31/03 ALL	4/1/03-3/31/04 ALL	4/1/04-3/31/05 ALL		0-1MM	32 (4/1-9/30/04) 1-3MM	3-5MM	125 (10/1/04-3/31/05) 5-10MM	10-25MM	25MM & OVER
150	185	157	NUMBER OF STATEMENTS	7	19	16	25	41	49
%	%	%	ASSETS	%	%	%	%	%	%
8.6	8.5	9.0	Cash & Equivalents		10.3	8.2	8.6	11.4	7.1
18.8	17.3	19.8	Trade Receivables (net)		18.4	19.9	26.8	21.0	16.7
11.1	9.8	9.7	Inventory		5.9	9.5	12.3	10.5	9.1
2.2	2.1	2.0	All Other Current		1.2	2.1	2.5	1.6	2.7
40.7	37.7	40.5	Total Current		35.8	39.7	50.0	44.5	35.6
46.4	48.4	47.5	Fixed Assets (net)		52.1	48.7	39.4	45.1	49.9
4.9	5.3	4.2	Intangibles (net)		.6	5.6	3.4	5.9	4.5
7.9	8.6	7.8	All Other Non-Current		11.5	6.1	7.2	4.6	10.0
100.0	100.0	100.0	Total		100.0	100.0	100.0	100.0	100.0
			LIABILITIES						
8.1	6.6	5.5	Notes Payable-Short Term		3.0	5.9	9.8	5.8	2.8
5.1	5.7	5.0	Cur. Mat.-L/T/D		4.7	4.4	4.3	6.5	2.5
14.9	13.7	14.8	Trade Payables		15.3	12.0	18.7	16.6	12.7
.2	.2	.3	Income Taxes Payable		.6	.2	.2	.5	.3
9.1	10.0	8.8	All Other Current		3.8	8.2	15.7	6.2	9.9
37.4	36.3	34.5	Total Current		27.5	30.7	48.8	35.7	30.9
26.0	24.3	24.3	Long-Term Debt		36.6	27.2	15.1	22.7	19.8
.9	.8	1.1	Deferred Taxes		.2	.0	.9	.9	2.1
5.5	9.5	7.2	All Other Non-Current		14.5	2.9	2.3	9.4	6.1
30.1	29.1	32.9	Net Worth		21.2	39.2	32.9	31.3	41.0
100.0	100.0	100.0	Total Liabilities & Net Worth		100.0	100.0	100.0	100.0	100.0
			INCOME DATA						
100.0	100.0	100.0	Net Sales		100.0	100.0	100.0	100.0	100.0
35.5	36.1	35.3	Gross Profit		39.4	41.5	35.6	31.0	31.2
30.4	32.9	31.4	Operating Expenses		37.5	38.1	30.7	25.4	28.0
5.2	3.2	3.8	Operating Profit		1.9	3.4	5.0	5.6	3.2
1.3	1.4	1.1	All Other Expenses (net)		1.2	.9	.8	1.1	.9
3.8	1.9	2.8	Profit Before Taxes		.8	2.5	4.1	4.5	2.3
			RATIOS						
1.8	1.9	2.1	Current		2.1	2.3	2.2	2.5	1.7
1.1	1.2	1.3			1.4	1.4	1.3	1.3	1.1
.7	.8	.9			.6	.9	.9	.9	.8
1.2	1.3	1.6	Quick		1.8	1.7	1.7	1.7	1.2
.8	.8	.9			1.0	.8	.9	.9	.7
.4	.4	.6			.4	.6	.5	.6	.5
18 20.1	17 21.0	18 19.9	Sales/Receivables		4 83.7	16 22.6	20 18.5	19 18.9	20 17.8
25 14.3	27 13.5	25 14.5			25 14.6	28 13.0	26 14.3	27 13.6	24 15.0
34 10.7	33 10.9	32 11.4			47 7.8	33 11.0	30 12.2	36 10.1	31 11.8
10 37.3	9 40.4	9 39.4	Cost of Sales/Inventory		5 71.1	11 34.0	8 47.3	7 49.8	12 31.3
18 20.3	18 20.4	17 21.0			10 35.3	17 21.7	21 17.7	17 21.0	19 19.3
31 11.6	31 11.8	27 13.4			14 25.7	24 15.1	27 13.7	30 12.1	29 12.6
17 21.5	15 24.7	17 22.0	Cost of Sales/Payables		16 22.9	10 37.5	8 48.1	20 18.3	17 21.7
25 14.3	29 12.5	26 14.2			32 11.4	24 15.1	14 14.4	31 11.8	24 15.1
38 9.5	44 8.3	40 9.2			36 10.1	35 10.5	41 8.9	40 9.2	41 8.9
15.0	13.1	12.2	Sales/Working Capital		10.5	15.4	13.1	9.5	16.3
68.4	47.4	32.6			21.2	28.2	37.7	23.3	52.2
-24.4	-22.0	-57.2			-42.4	NM	-87.9	-62.1	-37.4
8.9	6.2	11.8	EBIT/Interest		8.4	10.1	19.8	16.4	10.8
(138) 3.6	(172) 2.8	(144) 2.8			1.8	2.2	(18) 4.2	(38) 4.2	(47) 2.6
1.6	.2	.6			-4.0	.4	1.3	1.2	1.1
5.2	2.6	4.1	Net Profit + Depr., Dep., Amort./Cur. Mat. L/T/D				8.0	4.8	3.5
(52) 2.4	(51) 1.8	(52) 2.2					(11) 1.7	(15) 2.8	(23) 2.4
1.5	1.1	.9					.6	1.3	.9
.8	1.0	.8	Fixed/Worth		.8	.9	.5	.7	.9
1.7	1.8	1.6			2.3	1.7	1.5	1.2	1.5
4.5	4.6	4.7			-6.0	5.0	3.9	5.2	3.3
.9	1.2	.8	Debt/Worth		.7	.7	.5	.9	.8
2.7	2.5	2.3			3.6	2.5	2.1	2.5	1.7
6.9	7.4	6.3			-8.3	5.7	6.9	7.0	4.1
46.8	45.9	41.9	% Profit Before Taxes/Tangible Net Worth		38.3	40.0	59.4	58.5	27.6
(126) 20.5	(153) 16.4	(130) 16.9			(13) 15.3	(15) 15.2	(21) 18.9	(32) 28.6	(44) 11.1
7.3	1.9	2.3			2.4	-15.6	6.1	8.5	1.6
15.6	11.2	14.5	% Profit Before Taxes/Total Assets		18.5	12.3	15.2	19.6	11.8
6.5	5.0	5.0			2.5	3.8	7.6	6.2	4.3
1.4	-2.8	-1.2			-11.5	-2.0	.9	.7	-.7
10.6	9.2	10.7	Sales/Net Fixed Assets		10.7	13.0	15.0	8.4	7.0
5.9	5.1	5.7			5.9	7.5	9.7	6.2	4.4
3.3	2.9	3.2			2.5	3.6	5.1	3.6	2.8
3.5	3.1	3.8	Sales/Total Assets		3.9	4.3	4.9	3.2	3.2
2.5	2.3	2.7			3.3	2.8	3.7	2.5	2.3
1.8	1.7	1.8			1.5	2.2	2.7	2.0	1.6
2.0	2.2	1.7	% Depr., Dep., Amort./Sales		1.2	2.2	1.5	1.7	2.3
(142) 3.0	(170) 3.4	(146) 2.8			(16) 2.8	3.1	(23) 2.0	(40) 2.8	(45) 3.4
4.6	5.1	4.6			5.8	4.1	3.9	4.1	6.0
1.8	2.1	2.6	% Officers', Directors', Owners' Comp/Sales		2.1	3.1	1.6	2.7	2.5
(60) 3.3	(64) 3.7	(60) 4.4			(10) 4.8	(11) 2.9	(11) 2.9	(12) 3.5	(11) 3.9
6.3	6.0	6.1			6.3	6.7	7.4	4.5	8.4
6137464M	5657776M	5033343M	Net Sales ($)	2237M	42414M	60656M	175264M	684150M	4068622M
2562443M	2881730M	2434509M	Total Assets ($)	2363M	20050M	23750M	58266M	305441M	2024639M

© RMA 2005   M = $ thousand   MM = $ million
See Pages 11 through 21 for Explanation of Ratios and Data

Current Data Sorted By Assets   Comparative Historical Data

	0-500M	500M-2MM 5 (4/1-9/30/04)	2-10MM	10-50MM 23 (10/1/04-3/31/05)	50-100MM	100-250MM		4/1/00-3/31/01 ALL	4/1/01-3/31/02 ALL
Type of Statement									
Unqualified			3	4	1	1		9	9
Reviewed		1	2	2				7	4
Compiled			4					5	5
Tax Returns	4	1						3	3
Other		2	1	2				12	9
NUMBER OF STATEMENTS	4	4	10	8	1	1		36	30
	%	%	%	%	%	%		%	%
ASSETS									
Cash & Equivalents			13.5					7.4	9.5
Trade Receivables (net)			20.9					22.9	20.3
Inventory			10.8					17.8	13.1
All Other Current			.6					2.0	.9
Total Current			45.8					50.2	43.7
Fixed Assets (net)			36.2					39.4	45.2
Intangibles (net)			3.2					6.2	6.7
All Other Non-Current			14.7					4.2	4.4
Total			100.0					100.0	100.0
LIABILITIES									
Notes Payable-Short Term			7.0					7.8	8.0
Cur. Mat.-L/T/D			5.7					4.5	5.3
Trade Payables			16.3					14.8	10.9
Income Taxes Payable			.8					.2	.1
All Other Current			7.1					6.5	7.2
Total Current			36.8					33.8	31.7
Long-Term Debt			19.8					18.9	25.8
Deferred Taxes			.0					1.2	1.0
All Other Non-Current			8.6					3.9	6.8
Net Worth			34.8					42.2	34.6
Total Liabilities & Net Worth			100.0					100.0	100.0
INCOME DATA									
Net Sales			100.0					100.0	100.0
Gross Profit			32.4					37.3	38.0
Operating Expenses			25.1					32.2	31.4
Operating Profit			7.4					5.1	6.6
All Other Expenses (net)			–.7					1.3	1.9
Profit Before Taxes			8.1					3.8	4.7
RATIOS									
Current			3.6					2.6	2.1
			1.7					1.4	1.4
			.9					1.0	1.0
Quick			3.1					1.8	1.4
			1.3					1.0	1.0
			.7					.6	.6
Sales/Receivables			23 15.7					26 13.8	20 18.7
			29 12.6					34 10.7	27 13.5
			49 7.4					42 8.7	36 10.0
Cost of Sales/Inventory			12 31.3					23 15.9	21 17.0
			31 12.0					35 10.4	27 13.6
			45 8.1					62 5.9	49 7.5
Cost of Sales/Payables			16 22.9					23 15.7	14 26.6
			31 11.6					31 11.8	23 16.0
			60 6.1					44 8.3	35 10.5
Sales/Working Capital			5.5					9.0	9.7
			13.7					15.7	15.3
			NM					NM	NM
EBIT/Interest								8.7	13.0
							(33)	3.3	(29) 3.3
								1.2	1.2
Net Profit + Depr., Dep., Amort./Cur. Mat. L /T/D									
Fixed/Worth			.5					.5	.7
			.7					1.2	1.2
			2.7					2.6	NM
Debt/Worth			.7					.5	.8
			1.1					1.2	1.5
			10.7					4.1	NM
% Profit Before Taxes/Tangible Net Worth								32.7	41.3
							(32)	19.2	(23) 19.2
								2.8	5.5
% Profit Before Taxes/Total Assets			28.3					13.3	17.7
			12.8					6.9	7.9
			1.0					.4	1.2
Sales/Net Fixed Assets			12.5					13.0	8.9
			7.2					6.1	5.1
			4.4					3.4	3.2
Sales/Total Assets			2.9					2.9	3.2
			2.5					2.2	2.2
			1.6					1.8	1.7
% Depr., Dep., Amort./Sales								1.5	1.9
							(31)	2.9	(26) 3.1
								4.8	4.4
% Officers', Directors', Owners' Comp/Sales								2.0	
							(13)	4.1	
								5.9	
Net Sales ($)	8170M	10219M	133616M	240262M	131378M	293356M		1433947M	1294581M
Total Assets ($)	1355M	3108M	62397M	151033M	71469M	125055M		759160M	617190M

Comparative Historical Data | Current Data Sorted By Sales

			Type of Statement						
8	6	9	Unqualified				1	5	3
4	6	5	Reviewed		1		2	2	2
5	5	4	Compiled				2	2	
5	2	5	Tax Returns	2	2		1		
7	13	5	Other		1	1	1	1	1
4/1/02-3/31/03 ALL	4/1/03-3/31/04 ALL	4/1/04-3/31/05 ALL		0-1MM	1-3MM	3-5MM	5-10MM	10-25MM	25MM & OVER
				5 (4/1-9/30/04)			23 (10/1/04-3/31/05)		
29	32	28	**NUMBER OF STATEMENTS**	2	4	1	7	8	6
%	%	%	**ASSETS**	%	%	%	%	%	%
16.3	8.9	9.5	Cash & Equivalents						
18.9	22.6	22.1	Trade Receivables (net)						
13.9	16.3	13.1	Inventory						
.9	1.1	.6	All Other Current						
50.0	48.9	45.3	Total Current						
41.2	40.8	38.2	Fixed Assets (net)						
5.2	4.2	5.2	Intangibles (net)						
3.5	6.2	11.3	All Other Non-Current						
100.0	100.0	100.0	Total						
			LIABILITIES						
6.7	9.3	8.3	Notes Payable-Short Term						
3.1	2.4	3.6	Cur. Mat.-L/T/D						
10.6	14.5	15.5	Trade Payables						
.4	.0	.4	Income Taxes Payable						
7.9	7.4	5.6	All Other Current						
28.7	33.5	33.3	Total Current						
21.0	12.7	20.5	Long-Term Debt						
.5	.4	.7	Deferred Taxes						
5.6	11.6	6.0	All Other Non-Current						
44.1	41.8	39.5	Net Worth						
100.0	100.0	100.0	Total Liabilities & Net Worth						
			INCOME DATA						
100.0	100.0	100.0	Net Sales						
40.0	32.3	33.0	Gross Profit						
30.3	26.5	27.8	Operating Expenses						
9.6	5.8	5.2	Operating Profit						
1.0	.4	.4	All Other Expenses (net)						
8.7	5.4	4.8	Profit Before Taxes						
			RATIOS						
4.6	2.8	3.0	Current						
1.7	1.4	1.3							
1.0	1.1	.9							
2.8	1.9	2.2	Quick						
1.1	.9	1.0							
.6	.5	.5							
17 21.6	19 19.0	24 15.2	Sales/Receivables						
28 13.1	29 12.8	29 12.4							
36 10.2	40 9.2	35 10.3							
21 17.7	21 17.5	16 23.4	Cost of Sales/Inventory						
35 10.5	36 10.1	33 11.0							
47 7.8	54 6.7	44 8.2							
10 37.4	14 26.6	15 23.9	Cost of Sales/Payables						
23 15.9	22 16.4	33 11.0							
38 9.5	41 8.9	48 7.6							
5.6	8.7	7.5	Sales/Working Capital						
10.7	22.3	25.7							
NM	176.8	NM							
16.9	29.3	18.2	EBIT/Interest						
(28) 7.6	(28) 7.7	(25) 3.1							
3.2	-.3	-.7							
19.6			Net Profit + Depr., Dep.,						
(10) 4.5			Amort./Cur. Mat. L/T/D						
1.8									
.6	.6	.5	Fixed/Worth						
.9	.9	1.1							
2.0	1.6	1.8							
.8	.4	.7	Debt/Worth						
1.3	1.0	1.5							
3.4	2.5	3.8							
76.9	43.0	36.7	% Profit Before Taxes/Tangible						
(27) 32.6	(29) 23.0	(25) 23.9	Net Worth						
18.6	4.3	-4.5							
22.8	24.9	19.1	% Profit Before Taxes/Total						
15.8	8.3	5.5	Assets						
6.2	-3.6	-1.9							
13.1	12.2	11.1	Sales/Net Fixed Assets						
6.7	6.1	4.9							
3.7	3.5	3.5							
3.1	3.4	2.9	Sales/Total Assets						
2.6	2.1	1.9							
1.6	1.6	1.6							
2.3	2.4	2.0	% Depr., Dep., Amort./Sales						
(26) 3.1	(28) 3.0	(26) 3.4							
4.2	4.0	4.8							
2.1	1.6		% Officers', Directors',						
(16) 4.3	(11) 2.9		Owners' Comp/Sales						
7.0	4.4								
1083210M	1447545M	817001M	Net Sales ($)	1140M	7895M	3823M	58103M	155366M	590674M
549656M	780786M	414417M	Total Assets ($)	660M	2720M	747M	38230M	74374M	297686M

M = $ thousand   MM = $ million
See Pages 11 through 21 for Explanation of Ratios and Data

Current Data Sorted By Assets | Comparative Historical Data

						Type of Statement		
		4	8		1	Unqualified	10	9
	1	1	4			Reviewed		2
	2	2				Compiled	12	10
		4				Tax Returns		
1	2	4	9	2	1	Other	7	12
		12 (4/1-9/30/04)	33 (10/1/04-3/31/05)				4/1/00-3/31/01	4/1/01-3/31/02
0-500M	500M-2MM	2-10MM	10-50MM	50-100MM	100-250MM		ALL	ALL
1	5	15	21	2	1	NUMBER OF STATEMENTS	29	33
%	%	%	%	%	%	**ASSETS**	%	%
		9.9	6.9			Cash & Equivalents	5.4	3.3
		21.0	18.8			Trade Receivables (net)	23.3	21.4
		15.6	13.1			Inventory	13.0	13.8
		1.0	4.3			All Other Current	2.5	2.7
		47.5	43.0			Total Current	44.2	41.3
		43.2	43.4			Fixed Assets (net)	46.6	43.2
		2.6	5.3			Intangibles (net)	3.5	9.2
		6.8	8.3			All Other Non-Current	5.7	6.3
		100.0	100.0			Total	100.0	100.0
						LIABILITIES		
		6.6	8.2			Notes Payable-Short Term	8.4	8.0
		4.2	4.9			Cur. Mat.-L/T/D	4.4	6.1
		15.9	12.7			Trade Payables	15.1	17.0
		.3	.2			Income Taxes Payable	.2	.5
		7.3	9.9			All Other Current	8.5	10.4
		34.3	35.8			Total Current	36.7	42.1
		18.8	17.9			Long-Term Debt	18.7	26.7
		.9	1.1			Deferred Taxes	1.2	1.7
		1.0	7.5			All Other Non-Current	7.4	11.6
		44.9	37.8			Net Worth	36.1	18.0
		100.0	100.0			Total Liabilities & Net Worth	100.0	100.0
						INCOME DATA		
		100.0	100.0			Net Sales	100.0	100.0
		31.4	26.2			Gross Profit	33.3	36.9
		29.1	23.2			Operating Expenses	29.4	31.9
		2.3	3.0			Operating Profit	3.9	4.9
		.5	.5			All Other Expenses (net)	.0	3.5
		1.8	2.5			Profit Before Taxes	3.9	1.4
						RATIOS		
		5.9	1.9				2.0	1.8
		1.6	1.2			Current	1.2	1.1
		.8	.8				.9	.7
		3.8	1.1				1.2	1.1
		.8	.6			Quick	.7	.6
		.3	.5				.5	.5
		18 20.4	27 13.8				26 14.2	24 15.2
		31 11.6	31 12.0			Sales/Receivables	33 11.2	32 11.3
		33 11.0	37 9.9				39 9.5	39 9.3
		14 26.4	15 23.6				19 19.3	19 19.4
		30 12.3	26 13.8			Cost of Sales/Inventory	26 14.1	32 11.4
		51 7.2	39 9.4				33 11.2	43 8.5
		16 22.2	18 20.4				22 16.7	20 17.8
		30 12.0	28 12.9			Cost of Sales/Payables	30 12.2	27 13.6
		52 7.0	39 9.4				43 8.5	41 9.0
		6.1	8.1				11.4	12.6
		13.8	33.9			Sales/Working Capital	41.4	117.0
		−24.0	−24.5				−55.0	−28.9
		18.9	17.4				6.3	4.3
		(13) 1.7	(18) 3.9			EBIT/Interest	(27) 3.5	2.7
		−1.7	1.4				2.4	2.0
						Net Profit + Depr., Dep.,	4.8	9.3
						Amort./Cur. Mat. L /T/D	(11) 3.5	(15) 3.1
							1.6	1.6
		.5	.6				.7	1.1
		1.2	1.9			Fixed/Worth	1.5	2.5
		2.2	3.8				4.2	NM
		.4	.8				.9	1.2
		1.6	1.6			Debt/Worth	1.8	3.2
		7.5	5.8				6.4	NM
		44.4	39.9			% Profit Before Taxes/Tangible	41.8	48.0
		17.0	(19) 24.8			Net Worth	(24) 23.4	(25) 25.2
		−13.5	.2				11.2	12.8
		14.0	9.6			% Profit Before Taxes/Total	14.1	10.5
		5.2	5.5			Assets	8.0	6.5
		−4.9	.9				3.9	3.0
		11.7	7.5				8.0	9.7
		4.6	6.0			Sales/Net Fixed Assets	5.5	5.7
		4.0	3.1				3.9	4.4
		3.7	2.5				3.1	3.0
		2.5	2.0			Sales/Total Assets	2.5	2.4
		1.5	1.5				2.0	1.7
		1.7	1.8				1.6	1.3
		2.0	(18) 2.9			% Depr., Dep., Amort./Sales	(27) 2.8	(29) 2.1
		5.0	3.9				3.9	3.6
						% Officers', Directors',		1.9
						Owners' Comp/Sales		(10) 3.7
								13.6
1826M	24196M	174744M	1263304M	288283M	52521M	Net Sales ($)	1563876M	2018408M
499M	7468M	69330M	626103M	137474M	131215M	Total Assets ($)	760047M	954167M

M = $ thousand   MM = $ million
See Pages 11 through 21 for Explanation of Ratios and Data

Comparative Historical Data				Current Data Sorted By Sales					

			Type of Statement						
14	14	13	Unqualified			1		2	10
4	6	6	Reviewed		1			2	3
3	6	4	Compiled	1		2	1		
5	2	4	Tax Returns		1	1	1	1	1
11	18	18	Other	2		3	3	3	10
4/1/02-3/31/03	4/1/03-3/31/04	4/1/04-3/31/05			12 (4/1-9/30/04)		33 (10/1/04-3/31/05)		
ALL	ALL	ALL		0-1MM	1-3MM	3-5MM	5-10MM	10-25MM	25MM & OVER
37	46	45	**NUMBER OF STATEMENTS**	3	3	2	7	9	24
%	%	%	**ASSETS**	%	%	%	%	%	%
6.3	6.0	7.4	Cash & Equivalents						4.1
20.3	18.5	20.4	Trade Receivables (net)						20.7
12.4	13.4	14.6	Inventory						13.2
1.8	3.5	2.7	All Other Current						4.1
40.9	41.3	45.1	Total Current						42.1
43.7	41.4	40.3	Fixed Assets (net)						43.9
7.2	9.4	7.8	Intangibles (net)						8.0
8.3	7.9	6.7	All Other Non-Current						6.1
100.0	100.0	100.0	Total						100.0
			LIABILITIES						
7.2	10.8	8.4	Notes Payable-Short Term						9.1
3.0	3.1	4.4	Cur. Mat.-L/T/D						4.9
13.8	12.4	14.0	Trade Payables						14.6
.2	.6	.2	Income Taxes Payable						.2
10.9	9.7	7.9	All Other Current						10.3
35.1	36.6	34.9	Total Current						39.0
20.2	16.6	22.3	Long-Term Debt						20.3
1.2	1.0	1.2	Deferred Taxes						1.7
2.8	4.5	6.4	All Other Non-Current						6.6
40.6	41.2	35.1	Net Worth						32.4
100.0	100.0	100.0	Total Liabilities & Net Worth						100.0
			INCOME DATA						
100.0	100.0	100.0	Net Sales						100.0
35.7	33.2	29.9	Gross Profit						27.5
31.2	30.4	26.3	Operating Expenses						24.2
4.4	2.9	3.6	Operating Profit						3.2
.9	.7	.8	All Other Expenses (net)						.8
3.5	2.1	2.7	Profit Before Taxes						2.4
			RATIOS						
2.1	2.4	2.8							1.4
1.2	1.1	1.2	Current						1.0
.8	.8	.8							.8
1.6	1.5	1.8							.9
.8	.6	.7	Quick						.6
.5	.4	.5							.5
24 15.2	22 16.4	25 14.8						28	12.9
31 11.8	29 12.6	31 11.8	Sales/Receivables					32	11.5
36 10.1	35 10.5	35 10.3						36	10.2
16 23.3	19 19.2	15 23.6						15	24.0
26 14.2	27 13.5	27 13.4	Cost of Sales/Inventory					28	13.0
35 10.5	38 9.6	46 8.0						39	9.3
15 24.4	15 24.2	17 21.8						19	18.9
22 16.5	25 14.7	28 12.9	Cost of Sales/Payables					30	12.2
43 8.6	40 9.1	43 8.5						39	9.4
10.4	8.3	7.5							16.0
71.8	51.8	33.9	Sales/Working Capital						NM
-30.0	-23.5	-25.0							-27.3
14.1	8.8	17.0							17.0
(32) 4.5	(42) 3.6	(39) 3.4	EBIT/Interest					(23)	3.9
.1	-1.5	.6							.6
5.5	6.0	6.0	Net Profit + Depr., Dep.,						5.6
(10) 2.4	(16) 2.8	(16) 3.8	Amort./Cur. Mat. L/T/D					(11)	3.7
2.2	2.1	1.8							1.4
.6	.6	.6							1.1
1.3	1.4	1.9	Fixed/Worth						2.1
3.5	4.8	4.0							3.9
.4	.7	.8							1.0
1.2	1.6	2.9	Debt/Worth						3.3
7.5	8.2	7.5							5.8
60.8	35.3	40.3	% Profit Before Taxes/Tangible						40.1
(31) 26.4	(38) 9.0	(39) 18.2	Net Worth					(21)	24.8
7.3	-3.5	.1							-1.6
19.3	12.7	12.3	% Profit Before Taxes/Total						10.0
7.5	3.4	5.4	Assets						5.6
.0	-5.9	.1							-.8
10.9	9.0	10.0							7.8
6.1	6.0	6.0	Sales/Net Fixed Assets						6.2
4.1	3.8	3.5							3.2
3.3	2.9	3.1							2.6
2.4	2.3	2.2	Sales/Total Assets						2.1
1.9	1.8	1.5							1.7
1.9	1.8	1.7							1.7
(33) 3.1	(36) 2.6	(40) 2.5	% Depr., Dep., Amort./Sales					(20)	2.6
4.9	4.7	4.2							3.7
.9	.9	1.8	% Officers', Directors',						
(11) 2.4	(10) 2.8	(13) 3.5	Owners' Comp/Sales						
11.3	6.0	9.0							
2212966M	2831937M	1804874M	Net Sales ($)		5765M	8177M	48218M	130146M	1612568M
1019740M	1321470M	972089M	Total Assets ($)		4214M	3698M	18309M	73889M	871979M

© RMA 2005

M = $ thousand   MM = $ million
See Pages 11 through 21 for Explanation of Ratios and Data

Current Data Sorted By Assets | **Comparative Historical Data**

0-500M	500M-2MM	2-10MM	10-50MM	50-100MM	100-250MM		4/1/00-3/31/01 ALL	4/1/01-3/31/02 ALL
						Type of Statement		
		3	4	1		Unqualified	5	4
1		8	2			Reviewed	2	5
1	1	2				Compiled	4	7
2	2					Tax Returns	1	1
1	4	6	2	2		Other	4	1
10 (4/1-9/30/04)			32 (10/1/04-3/31/05)					
5	7	19	8	3		**NUMBER OF STATEMENTS**	16	18
%	%	%	%	%	%	**ASSETS**	%	%
		7.5			D	Cash & Equivalents	7.0	10.6
		16.4			A	Trade Receivables (net)	22.6	20.0
		22.2			T	Inventory	21.0	20.7
		1.6			A	All Other Current	2.0	3.7
		47.7				Total Current	52.6	55.0
		41.9			N	Fixed Assets (net)	33.0	29.8
		5.5			O	Intangibles (net)	6.8	1.6
		4.9			T	All Other Non-Current	7.6	13.6
		100.0				Total	100.0	100.0
					A	**LIABILITIES**		
		14.2			V	Notes Payable-Short Term	5.7	8.5
		4.9			A	Cur. Mat.-L/T/D	4.0	3.5
		17.7			I	Trade Payables	14.7	10.4
		.4			L	Income Taxes Payable	1.2	1.2
		6.5			A	All Other Current	5.7	6.6
		43.6			B	Total Current	31.5	30.2
		25.0			L	Long-Term Debt	16.4	14.3
		2.2			E	Deferred Taxes	.4	.3
		5.2				All Other Non-Current	2.4	4.7
		24.0				Net Worth	49.4	50.5
		100.0				Total Liabilities & Net Worth	100.0	100.0
						INCOME DATA		
		100.0				Net Sales	100.0	100.0
		41.9				Gross Profit	43.3	49.2
		37.0				Operating Expenses	37.4	41.5
		4.9				Operating Profit	5.9	7.6
		1.2				All Other Expenses (net)	.8	1.1
		3.7				Profit Before Taxes	5.1	6.5
						RATIOS		
		1.7					2.1	3.9
		1.3				Current	1.7	1.8
		1.0					1.4	1.3
		1.3					1.3	2.2
		.7				Quick	1.0	1.1
		.4					.7	.6
		26 13.9					**22** 16.4	**24** 15.1
		32 11.3				Sales/Receivables	**31** 11.9	**30** 12.4
		43 8.4					**50** 7.3	**38** 9.7
		45 8.2					**39** 9.5	**50** 7.3
		61 6.0				Cost of Sales/Inventory	**53** 6.8	**70** 5.2
		98 3.7					**73** 5.0	**94** 3.9
		25 14.4					**21** 17.1	**19** 18.9
		40 9.0				Cost of Sales/Payables	**32** 11.4	**32** 11.4
		68 5.3					**56** 6.5	**49** 7.4
		8.1					7.7	5.9
		13.4				Sales/Working Capital	11.9	9.3
		-88.5					21.1	21.5
		4.9					18.3	16.7
		3.0				EBIT/Interest	(13) 3.1	(16) 4.6
		1.7					1.5	2.2
		2.7						
		(10) 1.9				Net Profit + Depr., Dep., Amort./Cur. Mat. L /T/D		
		1.6						
		1.0					.4	.4
		1.7				Fixed/Worth	.7	.6
		2.8					1.4	1.0
		1.9					.5	.4
		2.6				Debt/Worth	1.0	1.0
		7.3					1.8	2.1
		54.6					39.5	38.7
		(17) 27.3				% Profit Before Taxes/Tangible Net Worth	(14) 10.5	(17) 20.4
		10.0					3.3	9.8
		9.7					21.1	21.4
		6.7				% Profit Before Taxes/Total Assets	5.7	9.4
		1.9					1.7	3.0
		9.0					14.6	15.1
		5.3				Sales/Net Fixed Assets	8.5	9.0
		2.7					5.0	4.2
		2.5					3.3	2.8
		1.8				Sales/Total Assets	2.5	2.2
		1.6					1.9	1.7
		2.7					2.4	1.5
		3.9				% Depr., Dep., Amort./Sales	(15) 2.8	2.9
		6.0					4.7	4.7
								2.3
						% Officers', Directors', Owners' Comp/Sales		(10) 6.3
								8.2
4114M	20741M	219223M	406260M	324400M		Net Sales ($)	639552M	770617M
1102M	8190M	108653M	201433M	200633M		Total Assets ($)	317996M	405220M

M = $ thousand MM = $ million

See Pages 11 through 21 for Explanation of Ratios and Data

Comparative Historical Data | **Current Data Sorted By Sales**

Type of Statement	ALL	ALL	ALL		0-1MM	1-3MM	3-5MM	5-10MM	10-25MM	25MM & OVER
Unqualified	9	9	8					2	1	5
Reviewed	4	10	11			1	1	4	3	2
Compiled	9	4	4		1	1			1	1
Tax Returns	2	3	4		2	1	1			
Other	13	8	15		1	2	3	1	6	2
	4/1/02-3/31/03	4/1/03-3/31/04	4/1/04-3/31/05		10 (4/1-9/30/04)			32 (10/1/04-3/31/05)		
NUMBER OF STATEMENTS	37	34	42		4	5	5	7	11	10

	%	%	%	ASSETS	%	%	%	%	%	%
	8.2	7.0	5.5	Cash & Equivalents					5.9	5.3
	20.0	19.5	18.8	Trade Receivables (net)					16.4	18.6
	23.4	22.9	23.3	Inventory					28.4	23.3
	3.2	1.1	1.3	All Other Current					1.3	1.8
	54.7	50.5	48.8	Total Current					51.9	49.0
	29.5	36.6	36.3	Fixed Assets (net)					32.0	30.1
	5.5	4.0	7.4	Intangibles (net)					12.3	11.8
	10.3	8.8	7.4	All Other Non-Current					3.9	9.2
	100.0	100.0	100.0	Total					100.0	100.0

				LIABILITIES						
	8.7	9.9	11.6	Notes Payable-Short Term					21.1	9.4
	4.2	3.1	4.9	Cur. Mat.-L/T/D					4.1	4.5
	13.7	13.0	18.6	Trade Payables					19.5	13.9
	.1	.3	.3	Income Taxes Payable					.2	1.1
	8.5	8.7	5.8	All Other Current					5.9	5.8
	35.3	35.1	41.3	Total Current					50.8	34.7
	17.3	27.9	31.8	Long-Term Debt					20.3	18.8
	.4	.5	1.4	Deferred Taxes					1.4	1.7
	9.6	7.6	7.7	All Other Non-Current					6.1	2.5
	37.4	28.9	17.8	Net Worth					21.3	42.3
	100.0	100.0	100.0	Total Liabilities & Net Worth					100.0	100.0

				INCOME DATA						
	100.0	100.0	100.0	Net Sales					100.0	100.0
	42.9	44.5	41.8	Gross Profit					39.8	39.6
	38.4	39.7	36.3	Operating Expenses					35.9	32.8
	4.5	4.8	5.4	Operating Profit					3.9	6.8
	1.1	1.1	1.6	All Other Expenses (net)					2.0	1.0
	3.5	3.7	3.8	Profit Before Taxes					1.9	5.8

				RATIOS						
	3.0	2.5	2.1	Current					2.7	1.8
	1.3	1.4	1.4						1.2	1.5
	1.1	1.0	1.0						1.0	1.2
	1.9	1.3	1.1	Quick					1.3	1.0
	.8	.7	.6						.6	.7
	.4	.5	.4						.4	.4
	23 15.6	24 15.4	21 17.2	Sales/Receivables					16 22.4	21 17.2
	31 11.7	31 11.6	32 11.4						32 11.3	33 11.2
	39 9.4	40 9.1	43 8.5						43 8.5	41 9.0
	38 9.6	40 9.1	40 9.1	Cost of Sales/Inventory					64 5.7	39 9.3
	61 6.0	56 6.6	59 6.2						79 4.6	64 5.7
	95 3.9	96 3.8	91 4.0						104 3.5	95 3.8
	21 17.4	26 13.8	27 13.8	Cost of Sales/Payables					22 16.5	27 13.3
	38 9.6	34 10.7	41 8.8						51 7.2	34 10.6
	51 7.1	46 7.9	61 6.0						67 5.5	45 8.2
	5.5	7.0	9.0	Sales/Working Capital					7.5	9.8
	15.8	17.3	15.8						13.4	14.7
	64.0	NM	−83.9						−88.5	89.7
	9.6	11.1	8.6	EBIT/Interest					4.7	31.9
(32)	3.6	(29) 3.2	(41) 3.5						3.4	8.4
	1.2	.9	1.2						1.2	4.2
	10.1	10.7	5.2	Net Profit + Depr., Dep.,						
(12)	2.1	(12) 3.6	(18) 2.0	Amort./Cur. Mat. L/T/D						
	1.8	2.6	1.7							
	.3	.4	.7	Fixed/Worth					.7	.4
	.9	1.0	1.8						1.1	.9
	2.3	2.9	UND						−.7	NM
	.7	.7	1.1	Debt/Worth					1.2	.7
	1.9	1.9	2.6						2.9	1.0
	4.3	7.0	UND						−4.7	NM
	33.4	38.6	50.6	% Profit Before Taxes/Tangible						
(33)	16.7	(30) 21.7	(33) 25.1	Net Worth						
	7.5	7.8	8.6							
	13.7	14.4	12.8	% Profit Before Taxes/Total					8.7	16.8
	5.9	8.6	7.1	Assets					3.7	11.3
	1.3	1.0	1.2						1.5	8.4
	15.3	13.8	11.2	Sales/Net Fixed Assets					9.0	12.7
	9.1	7.5	7.7						8.1	9.4
	4.7	3.8	3.8						5.8	4.0
	2.6	3.0	3.0	Sales/Total Assets					2.4	2.8
	2.5	2.2	2.0						1.8	2.1
	1.6	1.6	1.6						1.6	1.7
	1.7	1.6	2.5	% Depr., Dep., Amort./Sales					2.1	2.0
(35)	2.6	(31) 3.3	(38) 3.5						4.5	3.0
	4.0	5.7	5.6						6.0	4.1
	1.6	2.1	2.4	% Officers', Directors',						
(15)	5.9	(14) 4.2	(18) 4.7	Owners' Comp/Sales						
	14.5	11.1	7.4							
	1624406M	1265290M	974738M	Net Sales ($)	1923M	11953M	18633M	46803M	173752M	721674M
	906314M	680878M	520011M	Total Assets ($)	618M	5298M	11787M	29967M	101894M	370447M

M = $ thousand   MM = $ million
See Pages 11 through 21 for Explanation of Ratios and Data

Current Data Sorted By Assets							Comparative Historical Data	
						Type of Statement		
		4	5	3	1	Unqualified	9	10
	1	6	2			Reviewed	14	13
			1			Compiled	5	10
	2					Tax Returns	2	
	4	3	3			Other	16	11
	9 (4/1-9/30/04)		26 (10/1/04-3/31/05)				**4/1/00-3/31/01**	**4/1/01-3/31/02**
0-500M	**500M-2MM**	**2-10MM**	**10-50MM**	**50-100MM**	**100-250MM**		**ALL**	**ALL**
	7	13	11	3	1	**NUMBER OF STATEMENTS**	46	44
%	%	%	%	%	%	**ASSETS**	%	%
DATA NOT AVAILABLE		11.9	13.2			Cash & Equivalents	8.4	6.3
		21.2	16.3			Trade Receivables (net)	16.3	19.0
		21.2	17.8			Inventory	29.3	26.9
		4.9	2.0			All Other Current	1.6	2.3
		59.1	49.2			Total Current	55.7	54.6
		29.6	35.5			Fixed Assets (net)	30.9	31.2
		4.7	5.2			Intangibles (net)	5.6	5.0
		6.7	10.1			All Other Non-Current	7.9	9.2
		100.0	100.0			Total	100.0	100.0
						LIABILITIES		
		10.6	5.3			Notes Payable-Short Term	10.0	12.0
		2.9	4.3			Cur. Mat.-L/T/D	6.7	3.3
		9.8	9.0			Trade Payables	13.1	11.7
		.9	.6			Income Taxes Payable	.2	.1
		6.0	6.8			All Other Current	8.1	6.3
		30.2	26.0			Total Current	38.1	33.5
		11.1	23.8			Long-Term Debt	20.3	19.8
		.5	.1			Deferred Taxes	.4	.3
		3.0	8.1			All Other Non-Current	7.6	7.1
		55.1	41.9			Net Worth	33.6	39.3
		100.0	100.0			Total Liabilities & Net Worth	100.0	100.0
						INCOME DATA		
		100.0	100.0			Net Sales	100.0	100.0
		26.8	40.7			Gross Profit	35.6	35.3
		19.2	32.4			Operating Expenses	29.6	28.8
		7.7	8.3			Operating Profit	6.0	6.4
		.8	1.8			All Other Expenses (net)	2.0	1.7
		6.8	6.5			Profit Before Taxes	4.0	4.7
						RATIOS		
		3.5	3.3				2.4	3.1
		2.2	1.8			Current	1.4	1.7
		1.1	1.1				.9	1.1
		2.6	2.4				1.3	1.2
		1.2	1.2			Quick	.7	.8
		.4	.6				.4	.4
		26 14.3	**28** 13.0				**21** 17.1	**30** 12.0
		29 12.6	**36** 10.1			Sales/Receivables	**35** 10.3	**40** 9.1
		39 9.3	**41** 8.8				**42** 8.6	**48** 7.6
		29 12.5	**49** 7.4				**36** 10.1	**49** 7.5
		46 8.0	**59** 6.2			Cost of Sales/Inventory	**67** 5.5	**70** 5.2
		88 4.1	**83** 4.4				**136** 2.7	**114** 3.2
		14 26.8	**16** 23.3				**20** 18.6	**24** 15.5
		17 21.8	**30** 12.1			Cost of Sales/Payables	**33** 11.1	**36** 10.3
		29 12.5	**56** 6.6				**59** 6.2	**44** 8.4
		4.7	3.7				4.1	3.5
		10.3	9.1			Sales/Working Capital	13.3	9.1
		NM	32.0				−56.7	109.6
			11.7				5.5	6.7
			(10) 4.3			EBIT/Interest	(42) 2.7	(39) 2.7
			2.5				1.6	1.2
							15.0	7.2
						Net Profit + Depr., Dep., Amort./Cur. Mat. L /T/D	(11) 5.4	(14) 2.8
							2.3	2.2
		.2	.7				.5	.3
		.5	.9			Fixed/Worth	.9	.8
		1.3	2.4				2.0	2.4
		.4	.5				.9	.7
		.9	.9			Debt/Worth	1.9	1.3
		2.1	8.9				6.1	4.0
		48.9	30.6				39.9	28.3
		28.1	(10) 21.6			% Profit Before Taxes/Tangible Net Worth	(40) 16.2	(38) 14.1
		−1.7	13.0				6.9	2.9
		31.6	14.3				14.3	13.3
		16.3	9.9			% Profit Before Taxes/Total Assets	7.2	4.9
		−.7	3.5				2.4	1.2
		22.8	9.1				11.9	9.7
		10.3	4.7			Sales/Net Fixed Assets	5.9	4.9
		3.7	4.2				3.4	3.4
		3.3	1.8				2.5	2.2
		2.1	1.7			Sales/Total Assets	1.8	1.7
		1.3	1.5				1.2	1.0
		.8	2.0				.6	1.4
		(11) 3.3	2.7			% Depr., Dep., Amort./Sales	(40) 1.9	(39) 2.2
		5.0	2.9				2.8	4.5
							1.7	2.5
						% Officers', Directors', Owners' Comp/Sales	(13) 4.0	(11) 3.6
							5.5	8.8
	32751M	**204572M**	**344743M**	**223565M**	**123565M**	Net Sales ($)	**1318488M**	**1131462M**
	6914M	**84443M**	**213297M**	**195324M**	**133842M**	Total Assets ($)	**1014342M**	**837504M**

M = $ thousand MM = $ million

See Pages 11 through 21 for Explanation of Ratios and Data

Comparative Historical Data | **Current Data Sorted By Sales**

4/1/02-3/31/03 ALL	4/1/03-3/31/04 ALL	4/1/04-3/31/05 ALL		0-1MM	1-3MM	3-5MM	5-10MM	10-25MM	25MM & OVER
			Type of Statement						
6	9	13	Unqualified			1		4	8
12	9	9	Reviewed			1		6	2
5	6	1	Compiled					1	
2	1	2	Tax Returns		1		1		
15	17	10	Other			2	5	1	2
					9 (4/1-9/30/04)		26 (10/1/04-3/31/05)		
40	42	35	**NUMBER OF STATEMENTS**		1	4	6	12	12
%	%	%	**ASSETS**	%	%	%	%	%	%
8.8	8.0	11.2	Cash & Equivalents	D				12.2	10.8
19.7	19.0	18.8	Trade Receivables (net)	A				20.6	16.3
27.5	25.0	22.7	Inventory	T				23.3	16.2
1.8	4.4	3.3	All Other Current	A				.9	3.6
57.6	56.4	56.0	Total Current					57.1	46.8
27.6	32.6	29.9	Fixed Assets (net)	N				36.4	28.7
5.8	2.9	6.3	Intangibles (net)	O				.5	12.5
8.9	8.0	7.9	All Other Non-Current	T				6.0	11.9
100.0	100.0	100.0	Total					100.0	100.0
			LIABILITIES	A					
8.1	7.7	7.5	Notes Payable-Short Term	V				8.3	5.4
2.6	2.3	4.3	Cur. Mat.-L/T/D	A				2.9	4.7
11.8	12.3	9.0	Trade Payables	I				7.8	11.6
.7	.5	.6	Income Taxes Payable	L				.1	.5
8.0	7.1	6.9	All Other Current	A				6.4	9.1
31.2	30.0	28.3	Total Current	B				25.5	31.3
18.4	15.7	16.7	Long-Term Debt	L				14.4	21.8
.3	.4	.4	Deferred Taxes	E				.6	.4
4.0	6.4	8.3	All Other Non-Current					3.2	8.7
46.1	47.4	46.4	Net Worth					56.3	37.8
100.0	100.0	100.0	Total Liabilities & Net Worth					100.0	100.0
			INCOME DATA						
100.0	100.0	100.0	Net Sales					100.0	100.0
31.6	31.6	36.1	Gross Profit					30.9	37.1
27.2	26.1	25.0	Operating Expenses					24.4	27.7
4.4	5.5	11.1	Operating Profit					6.5	9.4
1.4	1.2	1.3	All Other Expenses (net)					1.3	1.8
3.0	4.3	9.8	Profit Before Taxes					5.2	7.6
			RATIOS						
3.0	3.1	3.5						5.5	2.3
2.1	1.8	2.0	Current					2.5	1.2
1.3	1.2	1.1						1.7	1.1
1.7	1.7	2.4						3.1	1.2
.9	.8	1.1	Quick					1.7	.7
.6	.5	.5						.9	.6
20 18.4	**23** 15.6	**25** 14.8						**25** 14.5	**27** 13.4
32 11.3	**35** 10.5	**29** 12.5	Sales/Receivables					**33** 11.1	**32** 11.3
43 8.4	**42** 8.6	**39** 9.4						**41** 8.8	**41** 9.0
39 9.4	**47** 7.8	**37** 9.8						**34** 10.8	**41** 9.0
54 6.7	**57** 6.4	**57** 6.4	Cost of Sales/Inventory					**51** 7.2	**57** 6.4
88 4.2	**93** 3.9	**85** 4.3						**95** 3.8	**73** 5.0
16 22.8	**21** 17.4	**12** 30.2						**14** 26.7	**18** 20.2
25 14.8	**31** 11.8	**23** 16.1	Cost of Sales/Payables					**16** 22.7	**32** 11.3
38 9.7	**38** 9.5	**33** 11.2						**28** 13.2	**63** 5.8
5.2	4.8	5.4						4.7	6.5
9.8	9.6	10.3	Sales/Working Capital					5.9	21.8
19.5	21.3	39.9						11.3	92.3
6.7	8.6	15.0						14.3	8.8
(33) 3.7	(36) 4.1	(30) 4.5	EBIT/Interest					(10) 7.7	(10) 3.9
2.1	1.1	1.2						1.1	2.5
8.8	4.4	6.2							
(11) 4.2	(13) 3.0	(12) 3.1	Net Profit + Depr., Dep., Amort./Cur. Mat. L/T/D						
1.9	1.6	2.0							
.2	.3	.4						.4	.6
.7	.8	.7	Fixed/Worth					.9	.9
1.5	1.3	1.4						1.1	5.2
.7	.4	.6						.3	.7
1.3	1.2	1.3	Debt/Worth					.8	2.2
2.5	2.4	3.5						1.3	12.3
37.1	52.7	61.8						39.9	46.1
(37) 18.6	(41) 26.4	(32) 28.6	% Profit Before Taxes/Tangible Net Worth					22.7	(10) 28.1
7.6	.0	2.4						2.4	13.0
15.9	22.7	30.6						28.2	20.4
7.0	8.8	13.9	% Profit Before Taxes/Total Assets					14.1	9.4
3.3	.0	2.9						1.2	3.7
24.3	15.7	20.2						13.6	9.2
9.1	6.6	8.1	Sales/Net Fixed Assets					5.6	6.9
4.2	3.5	4.2						2.9	3.2
2.9	2.8	3.2						3.1	1.7
2.1	1.9	1.8	Sales/Total Assets					2.1	1.5
1.4	1.5	1.4						1.4	1.2
1.3	1.4	1.3						1.2	2.0
(31) 2.0	(36) 2.6	(31) 2.5	% Depr., Dep., Amort./Sales					2.6	2.6
3.0	4.2	3.3						3.5	2.8
1.8	1.3								
(11) 5.1	(11) 2.2		% Officers', Directors', Owners' Comp/Sales						
7.7	5.7								
1168251M	**1384369M**	**929196M**	Net Sales ($)		**2239M**	**14294M**	**44510M**	**198712M**	**669441M**
738911M	**874826M**	**633820M**	Total Assets ($)		**508M**	**6166M**	**20485M**	**100129M**	**506532M**

M = $ thousand MM = $ million

See Pages 11 through 21 for Explanation of Ratios and Data

Current Data Sorted By Assets   Comparative Historical Data

0-500M	500M-2MM	2-10MM	10-50MM	50-100MM	100-250MM		4/1/00-3/31/01 ALL	4/1/01-3/31/02 ALL
						Type of Statement		
		1	2		2	Unqualified	5	5
	1	4	2			Reviewed	2	1
	2	4				Compiled	5	7
1	3	1	4			Tax Returns	2	2
	5 (4/1-9/30/04)		22 (10/1/04-3/31/05)			Other	5	13
1	6	10	8		2	**NUMBER OF STATEMENTS**	19	28
%	%	%	%	%	%		%	%
		13.9				Cash & Equivalents	7.1	7.9
		17.9				Trade Receivables (net)	22.7	20.3
		20.8				Inventory	33.3	29.7
		2.8				All Other Current	2.4	2.1
		55.4				Total Current	65.5	60.0
		41.7				Fixed Assets (net)	29.2	28.3
		.4				Intangibles (net)	1.3	5.3
		2.6				All Other Non-Current	4.0	6.3
		100.0				Total	100.0	100.0
						LIABILITIES		
		10.2				Notes Payable-Short Term	16.9	10.9
		3.8				Cur. Mat.-L/T/D	2.8	4.8
		10.4				Trade Payables	15.4	12.7
		1.2				Income Taxes Payable	.1	.7
		5.4				All Other Current	5.5	7.2
		30.8				Total Current	40.7	36.2
		11.8				Long-Term Debt	12.9	12.5
		.7				Deferred Taxes	.8	1.1
		4.2				All Other Non-Current	6.9	5.3
		52.4				Net Worth	38.7	44.8
		100.0				Total Liabilities & Net Worth	100.0	100.0
						INCOME DATA		
		100.0				Net Sales	100.0	100.0
		29.6				Gross Profit	33.1	31.4
		26.8				Operating Expenses	30.1	26.7
		2.8				Operating Profit	3.0	4.7
		.7				All Other Expenses (net)	1.0	2.3
		2.1				Profit Before Taxes	1.9	2.4
						RATIOS		
		2.4					2.4	2.2
		1.8				Current	1.5	1.7
		1.3					1.2	1.2
		1.4					1.0	1.2
		1.0				Quick	.6	.7
		.5					.4	.4
		18 20.1					22 16.9	24 15.0
		30 12.3				Sales/Receivables	27 13.7	30 12.3
		38 9.5					37 9.8	39 9.4
		29 12.4					33 10.9	35 10.6
		39 9.3				Cost of Sales/Inventory	85 4.3	67 5.4
		73 5.0					98 3.7	98 3.7
		4 82.5					19 19.1	13 28.9
		17 21.8				Cost of Sales/Payables	29 12.4	24 15.2
		34 10.8					49 7.5	36 10.2
		6.8					7.4	7.3
		11.2				Sales/Working Capital	10.2	10.4
		NM					21.7	28.3
							5.0	10.2
						EBIT/Interest	2.0	(25) 3.0
							1.2	1.5
						Net Profit + Depr., Dep., Amort./Cur. Mat. L /T/D		
		.6					.4	.5
		.8				Fixed/Worth	.7	.7
		1.4					3.5	1.1
		.6					.6	.7
		.8				Debt/Worth	1.3	1.3
		1.9					4.6	3.1
		20.2					17.8	35.7
		4.7				% Profit Before Taxes/Tangible Net Worth	(17) 12.2	(26) 20.2
		3.1					2.6	1.5
		7.7					9.0	15.9
		3.1				% Profit Before Taxes/Total Assets	3.0	5.1
		1.6					1.0	.7
		10.8					35.2	15.5
		5.7				Sales/Net Fixed Assets	14.6	9.6
		3.5					6.5	5.1
		3.0					3.4	3.1
		2.0				Sales/Total Assets	2.8	2.0
		1.6					1.8	1.4
		1.5					1.4	1.3
		2.3				% Depr., Dep., Amort./Sales	(18) 2.0	2.1
		3.4					2.7	3.1
						% Officers', Directors', Owners' Comp/Sales		
1157M	28887M	129973M	279123M		583686M	Net Sales ($)	651833M	1686221M
206M	7655M	54896M	160336M		311772M	Total Assets ($)	260436M	970846M

(Columns 10-50MM and 50-100MM: DATA NOT AVAILABLE)

M = $ thousand   MM = $ million
See Pages 11 through 21 for Explanation of Ratios and Data

Comparative Historical Data | Current Data Sorted By Sales

			Type of Statement	0-1MM	1-3MM	3-5MM	5-10MM	10-25MM	25MM & OVER
7	7	5	Unqualified					1	4
8	4	7	Reviewed		1	2	1	1	2
5	9	6	Compiled			2	2	1	1
2	1	1	Tax Returns		1				
7	6	8	Other			1	3	2	2
4/1/02-3/31/03	4/1/03-3/31/04	4/1/04-3/31/05			5 (4/1-9/30/04)		22 (10/1/04-3/31/05)		
ALL	ALL	ALL							
29	27	27	**NUMBER OF STATEMENTS**		2	5	6	5	9
%	%	%	**ASSETS**	%	%	%	%	%	%
6.2	9.5	10.8	Cash & Equivalents						
21.1	17.9	18.1	Trade Receivables (net)						
24.1	22.5	26.1	Inventory						
3.5	3.8	1.5	All Other Current						
54.9	53.7	56.5	Total Current						
34.9	35.8	35.0	Fixed Assets (net)						
3.8	7.4	3.6	Intangibles (net)						
6.4	3.1	4.9	All Other Non-Current						
100.0	100.0	100.0	Total						
			LIABILITIES						
9.4	7.7	10.4	Notes Payable-Short Term						
3.2	3.6	3.5	Cur. Mat.-L/T/D						
15.7	13.5	12.8	Trade Payables						
.0	.4	.6	Income Taxes Payable						
16.3	6.8	7.1	All Other Current						
44.6	32.0	34.4	Total Current						
15.6	17.2	12.1	Long-Term Debt						
.7	1.2	.5	Deferred Taxes						
2.6	8.7	3.3	All Other Non-Current						
36.4	40.9	49.7	Net Worth						
100.0	100.0	100.0	Total Liabilities & Net Worth						
			INCOME DATA						
100.0	100.0	100.0	Net Sales						
32.6	29.6	28.1	Gross Profit						
28.0	25.0	23.2	Operating Expenses						
4.6	4.6	5.0	Operating Profit						
1.6	.9	.7	All Other Expenses (net)						
3.0	3.6	4.2	Profit Before Taxes						

(Right-side columns for ASSETS, LIABILITIES, INCOME DATA and RATIOS are marked "DATA NOT AVAILABLE.")

RATIOS

			Ratio						
1.8	2.9	2.2	Current						
1.2	1.6	1.7							
.9	1.0	1.3							
.9	1.4	1.2	Quick						
.6	.9	.9							
.4	.5	.4							
20 18.5	22 16.5	19 18.8	Sales/Receivables						
30 12.2	27 13.4	24 15.0							
37 9.8	34 10.8	35 10.5							
26 14.2	33 11.0	32 11.3	Cost of Sales/Inventory						
41 8.8	49 7.5	46 7.9							
77 4.7	64 5.7	68 5.3							
18 20.1	14 25.5	14 25.6	Cost of Sales/Payables						
27 13.5	26 13.9	18 19.8							
40 9.1	40 9.1	45 8.2							
9.4	5.2	5.7	Sales/Working Capital						
20.5	12.6	11.7							
−131.4	136.2	24.3							
7.1	8.8	10.2	EBIT/Interest						
(26) 4.3	(24) 4.3	(23) 4.8							
1.3	1.9	2.3							
11.6	4.6	4.7	Net Profit + Depr., Dep.,						
(12) 3.0	(12) 2.8	(11) 2.5	Amort./Cur. Mat. L/T/D						
1.4	1.1	1.8							
.5	.7	.5	Fixed/Worth						
1.0	1.2	.8							
3.4	2.9	1.3							
.7	.7	.7	Debt/Worth						
1.9	2.1	.9							
7.4	6.7	2.3							
44.8	37.2	25.9	% Profit Before Taxes/Tangible						
(26) 16.5	(24) 22.2	(25) 13.5	Net Worth						
2.2	6.6	5.1							
11.0	12.3	11.6	% Profit Before Taxes/Total						
5.6	7.3	6.9	Assets						
1.7	2.9	2.0							
16.4	11.4	14.1	Sales/Net Fixed Assets						
6.8	6.0	7.1							
3.8	3.3	4.3							
3.5	3.3	3.2	Sales/Total Assets						
2.3	2.1	2.3							
2.0	1.7	1.6							
1.7	2.0	1.6	% Depr., Dep., Amort./Sales						
(28) 2.5	(25) 2.6	(25) 2.3							
3.2	3.7	3.2							
6.6			% Officers', Directors',						
(11) 8.6			Owners' Comp/Sales						
10.1									
1019043M	774692M	1022826M	Net Sales ($)		3735M	18759M	45922M	83919M	870491M
589193M	426663M	534865M	Total Assets ($)		1346M	12412M	26998M	41305M	452804M

© RMA 2005   M = $ thousand   MM = $ million
See Pages 11 through 21 for Explanation of Ratios and Data

Current Data Sorted By Assets   **Comparative Historical Data**

						Type of Statement		
1		17	20	7	6	Unqualified	32	32
	7	19	6			Reviewed	18	22
	7	8	4			Compiled	23	30
5	7	4				Tax Returns	14	9
1	10	17	22	6	2	Other	45	62
	50 (4/1-9/30/04)		126 (10/1/04-3/31/05)				4/1/00-3/31/01	4/1/01-3/31/02
0-500M	500M-2MM	2-10MM	10-50MM	50-100MM	100-250MM		ALL	ALL
7	31	65	52	13	8	NUMBER OF STATEMENTS	132	155
%	%	%	%	%	%	ASSETS	%	%
	4.6	7.3	7.4	5.1		Cash & Equivalents	6.9	7.3
	24.8	21.1	17.5	16.8		Trade Receivables (net)	22.1	20.1
	25.0	22.5	24.9	24.1		Inventory	22.4	20.4
	4.4	3.2	2.3	6.4		All Other Current	2.6	3.0
	58.8	54.1	52.1	52.5		Total Current	54.1	50.7
	27.8	34.8	33.6	33.3		Fixed Assets (net)	33.7	37.3
	3.1	4.0	7.1	7.8		Intangibles (net)	6.1	4.3
	10.4	7.1	7.2	6.5		All Other Non-Current	6.1	7.6
	100.0	100.0	100.0	100.0		Total	100.0	100.0
						LIABILITIES		
	14.5	10.0	9.7	8.5		Notes Payable-Short Term	11.1	11.7
	3.7	4.9	3.6	3.3		Cur. Mat.-L/T/D	5.3	5.4
	18.1	20.1	14.2	15.6		Trade Payables	18.3	14.4
	.3	.3	.2	.6		Income Taxes Payable	.2	.2
	10.8	7.0	7.8	10.7		All Other Current	13.2	23.4
	47.3	42.2	35.4	38.8		Total Current	48.1	55.2
	15.6	20.3	21.0	12.4		Long-Term Debt	18.3	19.1
	.3	.5	.4	1.5		Deferred Taxes	.4	.6
	9.5	7.4	4.5	15.3		All Other Non-Current	5.8	8.8
	27.3	29.6	38.7	32.0		Net Worth	27.4	16.3
	100.0	100.0	100.0	100.0		Total Liabilities & Net Worth	100.0	100.0
						INCOME DATA		
	100.0	100.0	100.0	100.0		Net Sales	100.0	100.0
	31.6	28.9	27.9	31.9		Gross Profit	33.6	33.8
	29.0	24.9	22.1	19.4		Operating Expenses	29.3	28.9
	2.6	4.0	5.8	12.5		Operating Profit	4.3	5.0
	1.0	.9	1.2	1.4		All Other Expenses (net)	1.2	1.7
	1.6	3.1	4.6	11.1		Profit Before Taxes	3.1	3.3
						RATIOS		
	2.3	2.0	2.1	2.3			2.0	2.2
	1.5	1.4	1.4	1.1	Current	1.3	1.3
	1.0	.9	1.0	.8		.9	.9
	1.3	1.0	1.0	.8			1.0	1.2
	.7	.6	.6	.7	Quick	.6	.6
	.3	.5	.5	.4		.4	.4
	9 40.0	19 18.9	21 17.1	22 16.6			21 17.6	21 17.4
	25 14.4	27 13.8	29 12.5	35 10.3	Sales/Receivables	31 11.9	30 12.1
	39 9.3	39 9.4	39 9.3	46 7.9		38 9.7	39 9.4
	17 21.2	17 20.9	27 13.5	21 17.0			24 15.5	19 18.9
	29 12.4	34 10.7	52 7.0	58 6.3	Cost of Sales/Inventory	44 8.3	41 8.8
	73 5.0	68 5.4	93 3.9	102 3.6		84 4.3	85 4.3
	10 35.3	18 19.8	18 20.6	23 15.6			17 21.0	16 22.4
	26 13.9	34 10.6	26 14.1	35 10.6	Cost of Sales/Payables	31 12.0	25 14.6
	37 9.8	50 7.3	38 9.5	66 5.5		51 7.2	48 7.6
	11.3	8.5	6.8	5.4			9.6	7.7
	21.4	26.2	14.4	25.4	Sales/Working Capital	24.2	23.6
	-108.5	-62.6	NM	-102.7		-50.6	-32.8
	9.4	8.8	10.4	12.8			9.6	7.6
	(30) 5.7	(60) 3.0	(48) 3.7	(12) 4.8	EBIT/Interest	(121) 3.4	(142) 2.8
	1.0	1.0	1.3	1.9		1.3	1.0
		5.3	6.3				7.9	7.3
		(19) 3.3	(19) 2.6			Net Profit + Depr., Dep., Amort./Cur. Mat. L /T/D	(37) 2.6	(40) 3.4
		1.0	1.1				1.1	1.1
	.1	.6	.5	.6			.5	.5
	.9	1.2	1.0	1.1	Fixed/Worth	1.3	1.1
	2.3	3.1	2.6	18.3		3.6	3.5
	.8	1.4	.8	1.6			1.1	.9
	2.4	2.5	1.8	2.7	Debt/Worth	2.6	2.1
	10.0	6.5	5.1	30.5		7.5	7.8
	49.7	51.6	35.1	81.0			51.3	51.4
	(25) 27.3	(54) 24.0	(46) 17.1	(11) 42.1	% Profit Before Taxes/Tangible Net Worth	(108) 24.5	(129) 19.9
	8.9	7.1	4.7	23.2		10.9	3.2
	19.7	12.1	13.2	25.4			18.0	17.0
	7.7	5.9	5.8	10.0	% Profit Before Taxes/Total Assets	6.5	5.5
	.0	.3	.8	3.5		1.1	.0
	80.8	19.8	12.3	10.7			18.2	14.6
	19.8	8.0	7.2	6.0	Sales/Net Fixed Assets	8.1	6.7
	5.2	4.3	4.0	3.3		3.9	3.3
	5.6	3.8	2.9	2.4			3.7	3.2
	4.1	2.7	2.0	1.6	Sales/Total Assets	2.5	2.2
	1.9	1.8	1.3	1.4		1.6	1.5
	.5	1.2	1.0				1.0	1.6
	(20) 1.9	(60) 2.1	(46) 1.9			% Depr., Dep., Amort./Sales	(106) 2.2	(134) 2.4
	3.8	3.3	3.7				3.8	4.4
	1.4	2.0					2.0	1.9
	(19) 2.3	(21) 2.7				% Officers', Directors', Owners' Comp/Sales	(49) 4.1	(47) 3.6
	7.9	4.3					6.8	7.9
7488M	157706M	959361M	2624605M	2274928M	2212488M	Net Sales ($)	3603683M	4666410M
1871M	39131M	315768M	1185962M	875665M	1100001M	Total Assets ($)	1803632M	2478852M

M = $ thousand   MM = $ million
See Pages 11 through 21 for Explanation of Ratios and Data

Comparative Historical Data | **Current Data Sorted By Sales**

4/1/02-3/31/03 ALL	4/1/03-3/31/04 ALL	4/1/04-3/31/05 ALL	Type of Statement	0-1MM	1-3MM	3-5MM	5-10MM	10-25MM	25MM & OVER
					50 (4/1-9/30/04)		126 (10/1/04-3/31/05)		
38	47	51	Unqualified		2		2	15	32
22	36	32	Reviewed		3	4	8	11	6
18	28	19	Compiled		2	4	6	5	2
8	20	16	Tax Returns	2	4	4	4	2	
55	51	58	Other	1	6	3	7	14	27
141	182	176	**NUMBER OF STATEMENTS**	3	17	15	27	47	67
%	%	%	**ASSETS**	%	%	%	%	%	%
8.0	6.9	6.6	Cash & Equivalents		3.2	7.0	6.2	7.6	6.9
21.7	22.3	20.1	Trade Receivables (net)		22.9	21.5	21.8	20.3	18.9
21.9	24.2	23.9	Inventory		20.9	22.3	21.6	25.7	25.3
2.4	3.1	3.5	All Other Current		4.5	.8	1.9	4.7	3.4
54.0	56.5	54.2	Total Current		51.4	51.7	51.6	58.3	54.5
34.7	32.3	33.3	Fixed Assets (net)		33.6	38.0	34.9	29.4	33.0
4.7	5.2	4.9	Intangibles (net)		4.2	6.4	4.6	5.0	5.0
6.6	5.9	7.6	All Other Non-Current		10.7	4.0	8.9	7.3	7.5
100.0	100.0	100.0	Total		100.0	100.0	100.0	100.0	100.0
			LIABILITIES						
9.8	10.3	10.6	Notes Payable-Short Term		19.3	9.7	10.6	11.8	8.1
4.3	4.0	4.0	Cur. Mat.-L/T/D		2.4	4.9	6.2	3.7	3.3
14.7	17.0	17.2	Trade Payables		18.3	16.5	16.6	19.5	16.0
.5	.3	.2	Income Taxes Payable		.5	.1	.5	.0	.2
8.6	8.7	8.4	All Other Current		12.9	4.9	7.4	9.0	8.2
37.9	40.4	40.5	Total Current		53.4	36.1	41.3	44.1	35.8
18.0	16.4	21.0	Long-Term Debt		26.3	21.1	22.8	15.9	20.6
.4	.6	.5	Deferred Taxes		.5	.4	.4	.5	.6
6.5	9.3	7.3	All Other Non-Current		15.1	11.3	2.0	7.0	7.1
37.2	33.4	30.6	Net Worth		4.7	31.1	33.5	32.5	35.9
100.0	100.0	100.0	Total Liabilities & Net Worth		100.0	100.0	100.0	100.0	100.0
			INCOME DATA						
100.0	100.0	100.0	Net Sales		100.0	100.0	100.0	100.0	100.0
31.5	31.8	30.0	Gross Profit		34.3	31.5	24.7	30.4	29.0
26.9	26.2	25.4	Operating Expenses		33.8	31.1	20.7	24.7	22.3
4.6	5.6	4.7	Operating Profit		.5	.4	4.0	5.7	6.6
1.2	1.6	1.1	All Other Expenses (net)		1.5	1.0	.9	1.0	1.1
3.4	4.1	3.6	Profit Before Taxes		-1.0	-.7	3.0	4.7	5.6
			RATIOS						
2.2	2.1	2.1	Current		1.5	2.3	2.1	2.2	2.1
1.4	1.3	1.4			1.0	1.6	1.4	1.3	1.4
1.0	1.1	1.0			.7	1.0	.9	1.0	1.0
1.2	1.1	1.0	Quick		.8	1.5	1.3	1.0	1.0
.8	.7	.6			.5	.8	.7	.6	.7
.5	.5	.4			.3	.6	.4	.4	.5
20 18.0	22 16.4	19 18.8	Sales/Receivables		19 19.6	22 16.8	15 23.6	21 17.5	20 18.4
30 12.3	30 12.3	27 13.4			33 11.1	26 14.3	26 14.1	28 13.2	28 12.9
39 9.4	39 9.4	40 9.2			62 5.9	51 7.1	37 9.8	38 9.5	39 9.3
20 18.5	18 20.0	19 18.9	Cost of Sales/Inventory		18 20.5	17 21.2	18 20.6	18 20.0	26 14.2
43 8.4	44 8.4	41 8.9			38 9.6	41 8.9	29 12.4	39 9.3	54 6.7
79 4.6	82 4.5	81 4.5			92 4.0	86 4.2	41 9.0	94 3.9	78 4.7
13 28.2	17 20.9	17 21.0	Cost of Sales/Payables		14 25.7	18 20.1	8 45.0	15 23.6	18 19.9
25 14.4	29 12.5	28 13.1			31 11.8	26 13.8	24 15.0	32 11.6	27 13.6
39 9.5	47 7.8	45 8.1			67 5.4	50 7.3	38 9.6	50 7.3	39 9.4
6.9	7.4	8.1	Sales/Working Capital		10.5	6.1	9.4	8.9	5.9
18.0	21.4	20.2			-108.5	13.7	27.5	17.8	17.1
218.2	136.9	-109.7			-18.1	-445.6	-72.6	-75.2	194.6
13.5	13.2	9.7	EBIT/Interest		7.7	8.3	6.5	11.5	12.9
(134) 3.3	(164) 4.3	(165) 3.8			1.6	2.3	4.0	(41) 3.1	(62) 4.8
1.4	1.6	1.0			-1.5	.9	1.2	1.1	1.4
7.1	11.4	7.8	Net Profit + Depr., Dep., Amort./Cur. Mat. L/T/D					4.3	18.1
(45) 4.9	(64) 3.2	(50) 3.4						(12) 2.1	(26) 4.1
2.3	1.8	1.4						.5	1.4
.4	.5	.5	Fixed/Worth		.4	.5	.5	.5	.5
.9	1.0	1.2			3.0	2.3	1.2	1.2	.9
2.5	3.4	3.4			-1.5	4.1	1.8	3.3	2.4
1.0	.9	1.1	Debt/Worth		1.2	1.1	1.2	1.4	.9
1.9	2.1	2.5			7.6	4.3	2.2	2.5	2.1
4.5	8.6	9.9			-4.1	22.0	7.7	13.7	4.1
45.6	53.8	49.1	% Profit Before Taxes/Tangible Net Worth		76.1		47.2	54.3	49.2
(125) 21.1	(148) 24.6	(143) 22.4			(13) 15.1		(22) 21.5	(39) 26.3	(59) 21.2
5.0	6.8	8.7			-9.3		6.9	5.3	11.6
15.4	16.5	13.3	% Profit Before Taxes/Total Assets		15.9	12.8	12.3	14.5	15.2
6.0	7.4	6.1			1.7	3.5	6.1	6.4	8.2
1.5	1.9	.3			-13.1	-.3	.4	.5	2.6
20.6	20.5	21.3	Sales/Net Fixed Assets		24.9	13.9	44.7	32.1	14.0
7.9	8.8	8.5			11.0	6.0	9.2	9.0	7.9
3.7	4.9	4.3			3.2	3.5	4.0	5.2	4.4
3.8	3.6	3.8	Sales/Total Assets		4.1	4.1	4.4	4.0	3.2
2.3	2.5	2.5			2.1	2.1	2.6	2.9	2.4
1.6	1.7	1.6			1.2	1.5	1.9	1.6	1.6
1.2	1.2	1.1	% Depr., Dep., Amort./Sales		1.0	1.9	1.0	1.2	1.0
(121) 2.1	(150) 2.1	(148) 2.0			(12) 2.3	(13) 2.9	(23) 2.3	(39) 1.7	(59) 1.7
4.3	3.4	3.5			3.9	6.4	3.4	3.6	3.0
1.5	1.6	1.3	% Officers', Directors', Owners' Comp/Sales		2.2		1.3	1.5	.6
(44) 3.8	(64) 3.3	(54) 2.5			(10) 3.5		(13) 2.3	(13) 2.7	(10) 1.0
7.5	5.5	4.7			9.0		3.6	5.1	2.6
6657276M	8440117M	8236576M	Net Sales ($)	2283M	31900M	56566M	201805M	785016M	7159006M
2894652M	3792325M	3518398M	Total Assets ($)	1158M	19221M	28532M	81771M	357341M	3030375M

M = $ thousand   MM = $ million
See Pages 11 through 21 for Explanation of Ratios and Data

Current Data Sorted By Assets / Comparative Historical Data

0-500M	500M-2MM	2-10MM	10-50MM	50-100MM	100-250MM	Type of Statement	4/1/00-3/31/01 ALL	4/1/01-3/31/02 ALL
		4	21	6	7	Unqualified	30	36
	2	4	1			Reviewed	7	11
		2	1			Compiled	15	16
2	3	2				Tax Returns	2	1
	2	10	11	2	4	Other	30	40
0-500M	500M-2MM	2-10MM	10-50MM	50-100MM	100-250MM			
| 17 (4/1-9/30/04)			67 (10/1/04-3/31/05)					
2	7	22	34	8	11	**NUMBER OF STATEMENTS**	84	104
%	%	%	%	%	%	**ASSETS**	%	%
		5.0	9.2		4.5	Cash & Equivalents	7.6	7.4
		18.8	18.3		12.3	Trade Receivables (net)	18.1	17.3
		16.8	16.2		11.4	Inventory	15.5	13.9
		3.5	3.5		2.0	All Other Current	2.7	2.9
		44.2	47.2		30.2	Total Current	43.9	41.5
		38.8	36.0		42.9	Fixed Assets (net)	36.1	35.9
		8.1	9.0		20.1	Intangibles (net)	13.8	14.8
		9.0	7.8		6.8	All Other Non-Current	6.2	7.8
		100.0	100.0		100.0	Total	100.0	100.0
						LIABILITIES		
		8.0	5.5		2.0	Notes Payable-Short Term	5.9	7.0
		6.1	3.9		2.2	Cur. Mat.-L/T/D	4.6	4.2
		13.5	13.5		11.0	Trade Payables	13.0	12.3
		.4	.1		.4	Income Taxes Payable	.2	.4
		10.9	7.2		8.7	All Other Current	6.5	7.9
		38.9	30.2		24.3	Total Current	30.3	31.8
		20.4	20.3		15.1	Long-Term Debt	22.7	21.4
		.9	1.4		3.0	Deferred Taxes	1.5	1.4
		7.8	4.4		8.0	All Other Non-Current	5.4	6.7
		32.1	43.6		49.6	Net Worth	40.1	38.7
		100.0	100.0		100.0	Total Liabilities & Net Worth	100.0	100.0
						INCOME DATA		
		100.0	100.0		100.0	Net Sales	100.0	100.0
		37.1	31.6		35.6	Gross Profit	32.2	36.1
		36.0	27.1		27.4	Operating Expenses	29.0	30.4
		1.1	4.5		8.2	Operating Profit	3.2	5.8
		−.2	.3		1.9	All Other Expenses (net)	.9	1.1
		1.3	4.3		6.4	Profit Before Taxes	2.2	4.7
						RATIOS		
		2.4	2.8		1.7		1.9	1.9
		1.3	1.9		1.4	Current	1.4	1.3
		.9	1.1		.9		1.1	.9
		1.9	1.9		.9		1.3	1.3
		.7	1.0		.9	Quick	.9	.8
		.4	.5		.2		.6	.5
		21 17.7	21 17.4		26 13.9		21 17.4	22 16.8
		30 12.3	27 13.5		33 11.2	Sales/Receivables	32 11.3	27 13.4
		41 8.8	33 11.1		38 9.7		40 9.1	34 10.6
		18 20.0	22 16.9		17 21.7		18 20.8	20 18.6
		31 11.8	29 12.4		21 17.1	Cost of Sales/Inventory	28 12.9	28 13.2
		61 6.0	38 9.7		32 11.5		43 8.6	39 9.5
		16 23.4	14 26.0		20 17.9		15 23.7	14 25.2
		34 10.7	24 15.2		40 9.2	Cost of Sales/Payables	24 15.0	25 14.6
		48 7.6	43 8.5		46 7.9		40 9.1	42 8.6
		11.3	8.0		10.8		8.7	10.7
		25.1	12.6		39.0	Sales/Working Capital	19.2	25.0
		−107.7	NM		−62.5		124.4	−141.8
		22.8	47.5		76.4		8.4	9.8
		(20) 2.5	(29) 3.4		(10) 5.2	EBIT/Interest	(78) 2.0	(100) 3.1
		.7	1.0		2.3		1.0	1.0
			(10) 5.8			Net Profit + Depr., Dep.,	2.6	4.3
			2.1			Amort./Cur. Mat. L /T/D	(24) 1.1	(28) 1.9
			1.1				.6	.9
		.5	.4		.6		.6	.7
		1.3	1.0		1.8	Fixed/Worth	1.4	1.2
		3.1	2.7		3.1		10.5	−17.6
		.5	.5		.7		.8	.8
		2.5	1.2		2.3	Debt/Worth	1.5	1.8
		5.1	4.8		6.3		17.3	−28.2
		34.6	29.7			% Profit Before Taxes/Tangible	32.3	40.2
		(19) 23.7	(30) 15.9			Net Worth	(64) 17.4	(77) 22.0
		−7.9	.4				1.2	6.3
		17.1	17.7		15.1	% Profit Before Taxes/Total	12.4	14.1
		4.0	6.0		9.4	Assets	5.1	5.2
		−2.1	.0		5.3		.3	.3
		17.3	14.2		8.5		11.6	12.5
		6.1	7.7		4.2	Sales/Net Fixed Assets	6.2	6.4
		4.4	4.4		3.2		3.8	3.7
		3.5	3.4		2.6		3.0	3.1
		2.6	2.4		1.9	Sales/Total Assets	2.3	2.3
		1.5	1.7		1.2		1.4	1.4
		1.6	1.9				2.2	1.7
		(21) 3.3	(32) 3.0			% Depr., Dep., Amort./Sales	(69) 3.4	(86) 3.3
		6.0	4.5				5.1	5.0
							1.4	2.3
						% Officers', Directors',	(17) 3.9	(16) 4.3
						Owners' Comp/Sales	9.9	8.8
374M	24135M	326130M	1928642M	1276655M	3721426M	Net Sales ($)	6188955M	6958379M
354M	7872M	121755M	790822M	603026M	1873525M	Total Assets ($)	3119371M	3723808M

M = $ thousand   MM = $ million
See Pages 11 through 21 for Explanation of Ratios and Data

Comparative Historical Data — Current Data Sorted By Sales

			Type of Statement	0-1MM	1-3MM	3-5MM	5-10MM	10-25MM	25MM & OVER
45	39	38	Unqualified				1	3	34
11	11	7	Reviewed		1	1	1	3	1
2	18	3	Compiled			1	1	1	1
4	1	7	Tax Returns	5	1				1
39	27	29	Other				6	5	17
4/1/02-3/31/03 ALL	4/1/03-3/31/04 ALL	4/1/04-3/31/05 ALL		17 (4/1-9/30/04)			67 (10/1/04-3/31/05)		
101	96	84	**NUMBER OF STATEMENTS**	5	2	3	8	12	54
%	%	%	**ASSETS**	%	%	%	%	%	%
6.7	7.8	6.9	Cash & Equivalents					4.6	8.3
18.5	19.1	17.3	Trade Receivables (net)					17.0	17.9
14.6	17.8	15.2	Inventory					13.6	16.2
2.5	4.4	2.8	All Other Current					3.8	3.2
42.2	49.0	42.3	Total Current					39.1	45.6
36.6	34.4	36.9	Fixed Assets (net)					47.5	32.8
13.7	10.3	12.2	Intangibles (net)					4.9	13.4
7.5	6.2	8.7	All Other Non-Current					8.5	8.2
100.0	100.0	100.0	Total					100.0	100.0
			LIABILITIES						
8.0	11.7	6.8	Notes Payable-Short Term					13.0	4.6
4.2	4.6	5.3	Cur. Mat.-L/T/D					7.9	2.9
14.6	15.2	12.6	Trade Payables					10.5	14.2
.3	.1	.3	Income Taxes Payable					.3	.2
8.6	7.7	9.6	All Other Current					6.0	8.0
35.6	39.3	34.5	Total Current					37.6	29.9
21.2	18.2	22.7	Long-Term Debt					22.7	20.4
1.1	1.0	1.3	Deferred Taxes					2.3	1.5
8.8	10.7	7.3	All Other Non-Current					3.8	6.7
33.3	30.8	34.1	Net Worth					33.6	41.4
100.0	100.0	100.0	Total Liabilities & Net Worth					100.0	100.0
			INCOME DATA						
100.0	100.0	100.0	Net Sales					100.0	100.0
34.0	31.3	36.2	Gross Profit					39.0	31.0
29.3	27.7	33.1	Operating Expenses					35.7	25.9
4.6	3.6	3.2	Operating Profit					3.2	5.1
1.1	.7	.4	All Other Expenses (net)					–.6	.6
3.5	2.9	2.7	Profit Before Taxes					3.8	4.5
			RATIOS						
1.8	2.1	2.3						1.5	2.3
1.2	1.3	1.4	Current					1.1	1.6
.9	.9	.9						.9	1.0
1.2	1.2	1.4						.9	1.4
.7	.7	.9	Quick					.6	.9
.4	.4	.4						.2	.5
18 19.9	21 17.5	21 17.0						16 23.5	22 16.9
27 13.5	29 12.6	29 12.5	Sales/Receivables					28 13.2	28 13.0
35 10.4	38 9.7	35 10.4						37 9.9	33 11.0
19 19.3	22 16.4	20 18.4						19 19.0	19 19.1
27 13.6	29 12.5	29 12.4	Cost of Sales/Inventory					28 13.1	28 13.1
39 9.4	45 8.2	42 8.6						39 9.3	38 9.7
17 21.4	18 20.3	15 23.7						9 42.3	16 22.8
27 13.4	28 13.3	33 11.0	Cost of Sales/Payables					30 12.0	31 12.0
44 8.4	44 8.2	45 8.1						48 7.5	43 8.6
11.9	9.7	10.0						20.9	9.7
34.8	30.0	20.0	Sales/Working Capital					NM	15.8
–72.7	–81.5	–94.6						–43.7	NM
14.5	10.0	25.0						22.3	43.5
(92) 3.3	(88) 2.5	(75) 2.9	EBIT/Interest					3.3	(48) 4.2
1.0	1.1	.7						1.3	1.1
8.5	2.8	3.6	Net Profit + Depr., Dep.,						3.6
(21) 2.2	(26) 1.4	(22) 2.2	Amort./Cur. Mat. L/T/D						(16) 2.2
1.1	.7	1.1							1.2
.6	.6	.5						.8	.4
1.2	1.2	1.5	Fixed/Worth					1.9	1.1
6.1	13.9	7.4						5.2	2.8
.8	.7	.6						1.0	.6
1.8	1.9	2.4	Debt/Worth					4.5	1.4
10.2	24.9	12.8						5.4	7.4
55.8	33.2	39.2	% Profit Before Taxes/Tangible					55.8	43.0
(80) 22.3	(74) 16.9	(66) 23.8	Net Worth					25.7	(44) 26.5
5.5	3.3	.4						2.7	9.7
14.3	12.1	14.6	% Profit Before Taxes/Total					16.1	17.0
6.1	3.7	5.6	Assets					5.0	9.1
.0	.3	–1.5						1.0	.2
14.4	17.5	12.7						14.4	18.2
6.6	7.0	6.9	Sales/Net Fixed Assets					4.7	7.8
4.1	4.0	4.2						2.9	4.5
3.4	3.3	3.3						3.2	3.4
2.4	2.4	2.3	Sales/Total Assets					2.5	2.4
1.5	1.5	1.6						1.6	1.8
2.3	1.5	1.9						1.6	1.6
(80) 3.1	(76) 3.4	(70) 3.3	% Depr., Dep., Amort./Sales					(11) 5.4	(43) 2.5
4.5	4.8	4.8						7.8	3.9
.9	1.0	1.2							
(17) 2.0	(20) 2.8	(10) 2.3	% Officers', Directors', Owners' Comp/Sales						
6.0	6.3	7.2							
8236077M	7049167M	7277362M	Net Sales ($)	2998M	3707M	11416M	60979M	196365M	7001897M
4237811M	3178964M	3397354M	Total Assets ($)	5216M	1556M	6759M	33050M	100418M	3250355M

© RMA 2005

M = $ thousand   MM = $ million

See Pages 11 through 21 for Explanation of Ratios and Data

Current Data Sorted By Assets   **Comparative Historical Data**

0-500M	500M-2MM	2-10MM	10-50MM	50-100MM	100-250MM	Type of Statement	4/1/00-3/31/01 ALL	4/1/01-3/31/02 ALL
			5	1	1	Unqualified		
	6	7	5			Reviewed		
1	3	3	1			Compiled		
5	2					Tax Returns		
1	4	9	3	1	2	Other		
	11 (4/1-9/30/04)		49 (10/1/04-3/31/05)					
7	15	19	14	2	3	**NUMBER OF STATEMENTS**		
%	%	%	%	%	%	**ASSETS**	%	%
	13.1	4.2	6.1			Cash & Equivalents		
	25.6	20.8	20.8			Trade Receivables (net)	D	D
	25.3	29.3	21.2			Inventory	A	A
	.5	2.0	6.4			All Other Current	T	T
	64.5	56.4	54.5			Total Current	A	A
	27.6	28.2	34.4			Fixed Assets (net)		
	1.2	9.1	6.7			Intangibles (net)	N	N
	6.7	6.2	4.3			All Other Non-Current	O	O
	100.0	100.0	100.0			Total	T	T
						LIABILITIES	A	A
	10.2	12.0	7.4			Notes Payable-Short Term	V	V
	6.5	4.3	5.0			Cur. Mat.-L/T/D	A	A
	17.1	15.9	19.1			Trade Payables	I	I
	.1	.0	.1			Income Taxes Payable	L	L
	7.5	8.7	5.8			All Other Current	A	A
	41.4	40.9	37.4			Total Current	B	B
	19.4	16.7	19.0			Long-Term Debt	L	L
	.1	.3	1.0			Deferred Taxes	E	E
	3.4	4.5	6.6			All Other Non-Current		
	35.8	37.5	35.9			Net Worth		
	100.0	100.0	100.0			Total Liabilities & Net Worth		
						INCOME DATA		
	100.0	100.0	100.0			Net Sales		
	40.5	33.3	36.8			Gross Profit		
	40.1	32.3	31.8			Operating Expenses		
	.4	1.0	5.1			Operating Profit		
	.0	.8	.9			All Other Expenses (net)		
	.4	.2	4.1			Profit Before Taxes		
						RATIOS		
	2.8	2.1	2.3					
	1.6	1.3	1.6			Current		
	1.3	.9	1.1					
	1.6	.9	1.3					
	.8	.5	.7			Quick		
	.7	.4	.5					
	17 22.1	21 17.6	24 14.9					
	27 13.3	32 11.5	29 12.5			Sales/Receivables		
	35 10.5	44 8.2	35 10.4					
	27 13.7	13 27.4	26 13.9					
	57 6.4	41 8.9	41 9.0			Cost of Sales/Inventory		
	116 3.2	88 4.1	56 6.5					
	5 79.2	19 18.9	21 17.4					
	24 15.1	23 15.7	41 8.9			Cost of Sales/Payables		
	44 8.2	33 10.9	85 4.3					
	4.7	7.9	6.5					
	11.5	26.8	12.4			Sales/Working Capital		
	45.6	-27.5	80.1					
	6.2	7.4	29.5					
	(14) 1.9	(16) 2.4	(13) 6.7			EBIT/Interest		
	-2.8	-1.0	2.8					
						Net Profit + Depr., Dep., Amort./Cur. Mat. L /T/D		
	.1	.1	.2					
	.8	.9	1.4			Fixed/Worth		
	2.5	2.8	6.6					
	1.0	1.1	.6					
	1.7	1.9	2.0			Debt/Worth		
	3.9	4.8	10.4					
	35.0	30.8	56.3			% Profit Before Taxes/Tangible		
	(13) 2.5	(15) 17.8	(12) 30.5			Net Worth		
	-16.9	-9.1	16.1					
	12.0	11.9	14.2			% Profit Before Taxes/Total		
	1.1	2.6	9.3			Assets		
	-9.0	-4.4	6.1					
	128.7	97.0	37.5					
	15.6	8.0	8.0			Sales/Net Fixed Assets		
	6.5	3.3	3.9					
	4.8	3.5	3.4					
	3.1	2.3	2.6			Sales/Total Assets		
	2.1	1.5	1.4					
	.7	.1	.5					
	(13) 4.2	(18) 1.2	2.9			% Depr., Dep., Amort./Sales		
	6.4	7.5	4.7					
	4.1							
	(10) 4.7					% Officers', Directors', Owners' Comp/Sales		
	6.5							
12480M	60124M	313879M	528830M	142451M	949816M	Net Sales ($)		
1560M	18572M	105408M	210407M	135500M	342156M	Total Assets ($)		

M = $ thousand   MM = $ million
See Pages 11 through 21 for Explanation of Ratios and Data

Comparative Historical Data | | | | Current Data Sorted By Sales

Hist 4/1/02-3/31/03 ALL	Hist 4/1/03-3/31/04 ALL	Hist 4/1/04-3/31/05 ALL	Type of Statement	0-1MM	1-3MM	3-5MM	5-10MM	10-25MM	25MM & OVER
6	9	7	Unqualified					2	5
12	7	18	Reviewed		3	3	3	3	6
10	10	8	Compiled		2	1	3	1	1
7	7	7	Tax Returns	2	4	1	2		
11	20	20	Other		3	2	1	6	6
					11 (4/1-9/30/04)		49 (10/1/04-3/31/05)		
46	53	60	**NUMBER OF STATEMENTS**	2	12	7	9	12	18
%	%	%	**ASSETS**	%	%	%	%	%	%
7.5	6.5	7.2	Cash & Equivalents		10.7			2.6	4.8
29.1	20.9	22.8	Trade Receivables (net)		28.7			17.7	21.9
22.8	18.8	23.6	Inventory		24.6			26.8	24.1
2.1	1.9	3.7	All Other Current		.6			7.0	2.2
61.5	48.0	57.3	Total Current		64.5			54.2	53.0
27.3	36.8	29.7	Fixed Assets (net)		28.7			29.0	32.0
4.1	9.5	7.3	Intangibles (net)		.6			11.7	8.4
7.2	5.7	5.6	All Other Non-Current		6.2			5.1	6.6
100.0	100.0	100.0	Total		100.0			100.0	100.0
			LIABILITIES						
15.5	8.5	11.8	Notes Payable-Short Term		6.0			15.7	6.4
3.1	5.1	5.7	Cur. Mat.-L/T/D		6.0			6.7	2.2
20.8	12.7	19.4	Trade Payables		19.4			11.8	22.9
.2	.0	.1	Income Taxes Payable		.3			.2	.9
6.0	10.8	7.6	All Other Current		7.1			8.5	5.8
45.6	37.0	44.6	Total Current		38.9			43.0	37.4
20.0	29.6	21.7	Long-Term Debt		20.2			23.6	13.6
.5	.4	.4	Deferred Taxes		.1			.9	.5
2.5	7.8	4.7	All Other Non-Current		2.4			8.9	5.5
31.5	25.1	28.6	Net Worth		38.5			23.7	42.9
100.0	100.0	100.0	Total Liabilities & Net Worth		100.0			100.0	100.0
			INCOME DATA						
100.0	100.0	100.0	Net Sales		100.0			100.0	100.0
31.6	41.6	36.3	Gross Profit		41.9			42.9	25.7
28.3	38.6	33.6	Operating Expenses		41.3			41.2	20.7
3.3	3.0	2.7	Operating Profit		.5			1.7	5.0
1.1	1.1	.9	All Other Expenses (net)		.0			1.0	.9
2.2	1.9	1.8	Profit Before Taxes		.6			.6	4.1
			RATIOS						
2.2	2.4	2.1	Current		2.7			2.1	1.8
1.3	1.4	1.3			2.1			1.4	1.3
.9	.8	.9			1.0			.6	.9
1.2	1.5	.9	Quick		2.2			.8	1.1
.8	(52) .7	.7			.8			.4	.7
.4	.5	.4			.5			.2	.4
20 18.0	20 18.6	21 17.8	Sales/Receivables		20 17.9			22 16.8	20 18.0
32 11.3	27 13.5	28 12.9			27 13.3			30 12.3	27 13.7
43 8.5	35 10.4	35 10.3			43 8.6			35 10.5	36 10.2
14 26.8	25 14.6	19 19.7	Cost of Sales/Inventory		8 44.7			16 23.5	23 15.7
30 12.0	44 8.3	41 8.9			51 7.2			43 8.5	32 11.4
80 4.6	75 4.9	62 5.9			156 2.3			85 4.3	54 6.8
15 24.2	14 25.6	19 19.6	Cost of Sales/Payables		6 63.6			16 23.4	21 17.6
28 13.0	27 13.4	27 13.6			27 13.3			37 9.9	29 12.7
60 6.1	41 9.0	44 8.3			41 9.0			88 4.2	40 9.2
7.8	9.4	7.9	Sales/Working Capital		4.4			6.6	10.8
30.4	18.2	19.8			12.7			19.0	29.7
-51.2	-24.9	-78.7			NM			-12.1	-155.1
5.3	7.9	10.0	EBIT/Interest		14.5			4.4	47.7
(39) 1.8	(48) 2.3	(54) 3.2			2.0			(10) 2.7	(17) 7.1
-.4	.6	.9			-1.5			.0	2.2
		2.3	Net Profit + Depr., Dep.,						
	(12)	.7	Amort./Cur. Mat. L/T/D						
		.2							
.2	.5	.2	Fixed/Worth		.2			.1	.2
.7	1.4	1.2			.8			5.8	1.0
2.8	7.7	7.3			2.4			-2.2	3.1
1.0	.9	1.0	Debt/Worth		.7			1.8	.6
2.0	2.1	2.5			2.0			7.0	1.7
6.3	21.4	12.9			5.9			-6.7	8.3
32.7	59.0	40.9	% Profit Before Taxes/Tangible		35.0				37.0
(40) 5.1	(41) 13.8	(47) 23.8	Net Worth		(11) 7.0				(15) 26.7
-7.2	2.1	1.1			-9.1				17.6
11.0	12.9	13.9	% Profit Before Taxes/Total		13.8			7.8	15.2
1.5	4.3	6.7	Assets		4.1			6.0	10.3
-2.5	-2.3	-.4			-3.0			.2	3.4
164.5	14.2	54.3	Sales/Net Fixed Assets		33.4			86.5	46.1
12.2	6.7	9.8			23.0			9.6	7.8
5.0	3.5	4.2			6.3			2.7	3.9
4.1	3.5	4.4	Sales/Total Assets		5.3			3.3	4.2
2.6	2.5	2.7			3.2			1.9	3.1
1.7	1.4	1.6			1.6			1.3	1.6
.3	1.4	.5	% Depr., Dep., Amort./Sales		.8			.1	.3
(41) 1.7	(49) 4.7	(53) 2.7			(10) 3.8			(11) 3.3	(17) 1.3
5.0	8.5	6.4			6.8			10.3	4.7
1.4	2.3	.9	% Officers', Directors',						
(18) 2.7	(19) 5.0	(27) 2.0	Owners' Comp/Sales						
5.0	9.3	5.4							
1220282M	1084500M	2007580M	Net Sales ($)	1063M	24571M	27985M	67380M	206253M	1680328M
549141M	468054M	813603M	Total Assets ($)	318M	10661M	11840M	29508M	109037M	652239M

M = $ thousand   MM = $ million
See Pages 11 through 21 for Explanation of Ratios and Data

Current Data Sorted By Assets   Comparative Historical Data

0-500M	500M-2MM	2-10MM	10-50MM	50-100MM	100-250MM	Type of Statement	4/1/00-3/31/01 ALL	4/1/01-3/31/02 ALL
			4	6	3	Unqualified	9	11
1		8	2	1		Reviewed	1	3
	1	2	1			Compiled	4	4
1	1	1				Tax Returns	3	6
1	1	4	3	1	2	Other	12	13
	6 (4/1-9/30/04)		35 (10/1/04-3/31/05)					
2	4	19	10	4	2	**NUMBER OF STATEMENTS**	29	37
%	%	%	%	%	%	**ASSETS**	%	%
		11.5	4.1			Cash & Equivalents	10.0	11.0
		12.3	6.8			Trade Receivables (net)	8.8	7.7
		15.4	6.8			Inventory	11.5	13.3
		1.0	.9			All Other Current	3.5	2.2
		40.2	18.5			Total Current	33.8	34.3
		47.6	74.2			Fixed Assets (net)	49.4	52.8
		8.2	3.8			Intangibles (net)	8.0	8.0
		4.0	3.5			All Other Non-Current	8.8	5.0
		100.0	100.0			Total	100.0	100.0
						LIABILITIES		
		3.5	.9			Notes Payable-Short Term	3.3	3.4
		6.0	2.9			Cur. Mat.-L/T/D	3.9	4.5
		10.8	7.2			Trade Payables	8.6	10.4
		.6	.2			Income Taxes Payable	.0	.2
		5.6	6.1			All Other Current	7.1	6.5
		26.6	17.3			Total Current	22.8	25.1
		32.9	33.5			Long-Term Debt	27.1	30.8
		.9	3.0			Deferred Taxes	.5	.4
		3.9	5.1			All Other Non-Current	5.9	6.6
		35.8	41.2			Net Worth	43.6	37.0
		100.0	100.0			Total Liabilities & Net Worth	100.0	100.0
						INCOME DATA		
		100.0	100.0			Net Sales	100.0	100.0
		39.2	36.1			Gross Profit	38.4	36.7
		31.6	27.1			Operating Expenses	32.1	32.5
		7.6	9.0			Operating Profit	6.2	4.2
		.9	2.2			All Other Expenses (net)	2.1	1.6
		6.7	6.8			Profit Before Taxes	4.1	2.6
						RATIOS		
		2.5	1.4				2.8	2.3
		1.6	1.0			Current	1.6	1.2
		.9	.6				.7	.8
		1.3	.8				1.6	1.4
		.9	.6			Quick	.7	.6
		.4	.3				.3	.3
		7 54.8	17 21.6				3 105.7	5 70.5
		23 15.6	22 16.3			Sales/Receivables	23 15.9	17 21.3
		30 12.3	31 11.9				35 10.5	32 11.5
		23 15.7	23 15.9				23 15.9	27 13.3
		35 10.5	38 9.5			Cost of Sales/Inventory	32 11.3	41 9.0
		66 5.5	53 6.9				58 6.3	62 5.9
		13 28.6	32 11.5				16 23.0	23 15.6
		23 15.6	42 8.7			Cost of Sales/Payables	28 12.9	29 12.6
		41 8.9	51 7.1				45 8.1	50 7.4
		7.3	15.4				6.5	6.7
		28.9	NM			Sales/Working Capital	32.6	46.2
		-24.3	-16.5				-18.7	-24.5
		14.4	8.6				6.2	7.8
		6.2	4.3			EBIT/Interest	(24) 3.3	(35) 1.9
		2.4	1.4				.6	.7
		7.1				Net Profit + Depr., Dep.,		
	(10)	2.3				Amort./Cur. Mat. L /T/D		
		-.6						
		.8	1.5				.7	.8
		1.4	2.0			Fixed/Worth	1.6	2.1
		-6.8	3.3				3.3	6.9
		.6	1.0				.6	.7
		1.2	1.3			Debt/Worth	2.0	2.3
		-16.0	3.4				5.3	8.9
		58.6				% Profit Before Taxes/Tangible	45.1	33.9
	(14)	36.0				Net Worth	(26) 22.4	(32) 18.1
		10.3					-5.2	-3.9
		26.7	16.5			% Profit Before Taxes/Total	17.5	10.5
		11.6	8.7			Assets	5.9	4.8
		.9	1.2				-2.0	-2.0
		21.1	1.8				8.8	6.0
		4.3	1.2			Sales/Net Fixed Assets	2.2	3.0
		1.6	.8				1.4	1.4
		3.5	1.3				2.4	2.3
		1.9	.9			Sales/Total Assets	1.5	1.4
		1.1	.7				.9	1.0
		1.5					1.8	2.0
	(17)	3.9				% Depr., Dep., Amort./Sales	(25) 4.1	4.4
		7.7					8.1	7.2
						% Officers', Directors', Owners' Comp/Sales		
1066M	7209M	250256M	273101M	342804M	237590M	Net Sales ($)	786033M	805582M
211M	4021M	102162M	264747M	242479M	291319M	Total Assets ($)	634589M	570553M

Comparative Historical Data | Current Data Sorted By Sales

			Type of Statement						
9	12	14	Unqualified	1			3	3	7
7	8	9	Reviewed	1	1	1	4	2	
4	3	4	Compiled		2			2	
1	4	3	Tax Returns	1		1		1	
9	9	11	Other	1	1	1	1	1	7
4/1/02-3/31/03 ALL	4/1/03-3/31/04 ALL	4/1/04-3/31/05 ALL		0-1MM	6 (4/1-9/30/04) 1-3MM	3-5MM	5-10MM	35 (10/1/04-3/31/05) 10-25MM	25MM & OVER
30	36	41	**NUMBER OF STATEMENTS**	3	4	3	8	9	14
%	%	%	**ASSETS**	%	%	%	%	%	%
11.2	8.9	9.2	Cash & Equivalents						8.3
7.0	9.8	10.1	Trade Receivables (net)						10.5
10.0	15.7	14.6	Inventory						13.4
1.1	1.4	1.5	All Other Current						3.2
29.3	35.9	35.3	Total Current						35.4
58.9	52.0	50.9	Fixed Assets (net)						51.6
8.8	6.9	8.7	Intangibles (net)						11.0
2.9	5.3	5.0	All Other Non-Current						2.0
100.0	100.0	100.0	Total						100.0
			LIABILITIES						
2.4	4.4	3.3	Notes Payable-Short Term						3.6
4.1	3.9	5.1	Cur. Mat.-L/T/D						2.8
7.5	9.2	9.3	Trade Payables						9.0
.5	.1	.4	Income Taxes Payable						.5
10.7	10.4	7.3	All Other Current						7.7
25.2	28.0	25.4	Total Current						23.6
26.6	22.9	36.2	Long-Term Debt						27.8
.6	1.1	1.3	Deferred Taxes						1.2
5.0	5.5	3.6	All Other Non-Current						6.8
42.6	42.5	33.5	Net Worth						40.7
100.0	100.0	100.0	Total Liabilities & Net Worth						100.0
			INCOME DATA						
100.0	100.0	100.0	Net Sales						100.0
40.3	37.3	36.9	Gross Profit						29.0
35.1	31.7	29.8	Operating Expenses						21.7
5.1	5.6	7.1	Operating Profit						7.3
2.0	1.7	1.1	All Other Expenses (net)						1.0
3.1	3.8	6.0	Profit Before Taxes						6.3
			RATIOS						
2.3	2.5	2.4							1.9
1.5	1.3	1.4	Current						1.3
.6	1.0	.8							.8
1.5	1.5	1.3							1.0
.9	.6	.7	Quick						.7
.3	.4	.3							.3
5 76.1	10 36.3	7 52.9							13 27.5
21 17.3	23 16.1	22 16.4	Sales/Receivables						23 15.7
28 12.9	30 12.4	30 12.3							37 9.8
22 16.2	26 13.8	22 16.9							16 23.1
39 9.2	42 8.6	40 9.2	Cost of Sales/Inventory						38 9.6
57 6.4	74 4.9	72 5.1							62 5.8
17 21.5	17 21.3	16 23.3							20 17.9
28 13.1	29 12.6	31 11.6	Cost of Sales/Payables						30 12.2
44 8.3	38 9.7	45 8.1							41 9.0
7.7	6.5	7.4							7.7
15.9	25.3	25.5	Sales/Working Capital						29.7
-17.6	-177.7	-31.2							-46.4
9.8	9.9	9.5							8.8
(29) 2.2	2.9	3.8	EBIT/Interest						3.6
.7	.7	.9							.7
	3.1	5.7	Net Profit + Depr., Dep.,						
	(13) 2.3	(15) 2.8	Amort./Cur. Mat. L/T/D						
	.2	.0							
1.2	.9	.9							.8
1.8	1.3	1.6	Fixed/Worth						1.6
3.9	2.6	NM							NM
.9	.7	.9							.7
1.8	1.4	1.4	Debt/Worth						1.3
4.5	5.3	NM							NM
40.1	43.3	49.4	% Profit Before Taxes/Tangible						37.0
(26) 8.6	(32) 19.5	(31) 24.2	Net Worth						(11) 22.1
.9	4.2	8.2							13.5
13.6	14.8	17.4	% Profit Before Taxes/Total						12.6
3.1	5.9	7.4	Assets						7.5
-.2	-.6	-.3							3.5
3.8	9.2	11.0							13.4
1.6	2.4	2.1	Sales/Net Fixed Assets						1.8
1.2	1.6	1.4							1.0
1.9	2.4	3.0							2.3
1.1	1.5	1.4	Sales/Total Assets						1.1
.9	1.0	.8							.7
2.9	2.2	2.8							2.2
(28) 6.0	(32) 3.7	(33) 5.8	% Depr., Dep., Amort./Sales						(10) 6.0
8.4	6.7	8.2							10.1
			% Officers', Directors', Owners' Comp/Sales						
853511M	1155588M	1112026M	Net Sales ($)	1534M	7662M	12357M	63366M	161765M	865342M
663911M	825060M	904939M	Total Assets ($)	1189M	7018M	17654M	51971M	69531M	757576M

M = $ thousand   MM = $ million
See Pages 11 through 21 for Explanation of Ratios and Data

Current Data Sorted By Assets | Comparative Historical Data

Type of Statement	0-500M	500M-2MM	2-10MM	10-50MM	50-100MM	100-250MM	4/1/00-3/31/01 ALL	4/1/01-3/31/02 ALL
Unqualified		1	5	13	4	2	15	9
Reviewed		2	7	7	2		18	13
Compiled	1	1	4				8	12
Tax Returns	1	6	6				2	3
Other	2	5	9	7	5	1	35	31
		18 (4/1-9/30/04)		73 (10/1/04-3/31/05)				
NUMBER OF STATEMENTS	4	15	31	27	11	3	78	68
ASSETS	%	%	%	%	%	%	%	%
Cash & Equivalents		4.5	5.3	1.6	3.6		3.6	3.3
Trade Receivables (net)		12.5	8.2	13.2	13.5		9.5	8.3
Inventory		44.1	48.7	27.6	36.4		46.4	47.6
All Other Current		1.0	.6	1.9	2.6		2.0	1.9
Total Current		62.1	62.7	44.2	56.1		61.6	61.0
Fixed Assets (net)		23.9	34.3	46.2	31.5		32.4	33.1
Intangibles (net)		5.8	1.0	6.2	6.4		2.3	2.9
All Other Non-Current		8.2	2.0	3.4	6.0		3.7	3.0
Total		100.0	100.0	100.0	100.0		100.0	100.0
LIABILITIES								
Notes Payable-Short Term		13.5	7.8	11.7	12.7		17.1	13.6
Cur. Mat.-L/T/D		2.3	2.1	2.4	3.2		2.1	2.4
Trade Payables		15.1	11.8	4.5	13.1		7.6	6.5
Income Taxes Payable		.1	.1	.3	.7		.3	.2
All Other Current		5.0	9.8	7.3	4.9		5.5	6.9
Total Current		36.1	31.6	26.2	34.6		32.6	29.7
Long-Term Debt		27.9	28.6	23.0	21.2		18.9	21.8
Deferred Taxes		.0	.3	1.2	1.6		.5	.5
All Other Non-Current		13.4	10.2	2.6	3.2		3.8	5.3
Net Worth		22.6	29.3	47.1	39.4		44.1	42.6
Total Liabilities & Net Worth		100.0	100.0	100.0	100.0		100.0	100.0
INCOME DATA								
Net Sales		100.0	100.0	100.0	100.0		100.0	100.0
Gross Profit		57.0	51.9	44.3	32.3		47.7	47.7
Operating Expenses		51.0	44.9	30.6	26.0		31.4	33.2
Operating Profit		6.1	7.0	13.7	6.3		16.2	14.6
All Other Expenses (net)		2.5	3.7	5.6	.7		3.3	5.7
Profit Before Taxes		3.6	3.3	8.1	5.6		13.0	8.9
RATIOS								
Current		4.2	4.2	3.6	2.5		3.2	3.7
		1.4	2.4	1.8	1.8		2.1	2.2
		1.0	1.6	1.1	1.1		1.4	1.4
Quick		.9	1.0	1.2	.9		.6	.7
		.5	.4	.5	.4		.4	.3
		.3	.2	.3	.1		.2	.2
Sales/Receivables		21 17.2	6 60.6	33 11.2	24 15.3		25 14.7	23 15.8
		31 11.9	32 11.5	41 8.9	55 6.6		43 8.5	36 10.1
		74 4.9	48 7.7	57 6.4	72 5.1		60 6.0	51 7.1
Cost of Sales/Inventory		175 2.1	271 1.3	85 4.3	125 2.9		295 1.2	301 1.2
		375 1.0	532 .7	255 1.4	248 1.5		467 .8	515 .7
		1047 .3	761 .5	547 .7	440 .8		670 .5	813 .4
Cost of Sales/Payables		31 11.7	21 17.8	13 27.4	30 12.2		24 14.9	19 19.0
		121 3.0	74 4.9	31 11.6	69 5.3		49 7.4	46 8.0
		219 1.7	149 2.4	67 5.5	93 3.9		117 3.1	81 4.5
Sales/Working Capital		1.6	1.3	1.6	2.3		1.5	1.4
		4.6	2.3	4.6	3.4		2.6	2.4
		39.3	6.7	28.2	12.2		5.0	5.4
EBIT/Interest		5.3	7.5	26.7	8.3		8.4	4.5
		2.6	(30) 2.7	(26) 4.0	2.4		(75) 2.9	(66) 2.9
		1.2	1.4	1.3	1.6		1.7	1.1
Net Profit + Depr., Dep., Amort./Cur. Mat. L/T/D							8.1	5.3
							(32) 3.8	(20) 3.4
							1.8	2.5
Fixed/Worth		.2	.4	.7	.6		.5	.4
		1.2	1.2	1.1	.7		.7	.8
		−1.8	2.8	2.0	1.8		1.6	1.6
Debt/Worth		.7	.7	.8	1.1		.5	.6
		2.2	2.1	1.2	1.6		1.2	1.3
		−10.8	5.6	2.4	2.7		2.7	2.5
% Profit Before Taxes/Tangible Net Worth			38.3	39.3	29.7		32.8	27.0
		(27)	14.2	(25) 18.8	(10) 11.6		(71) 16.1	(61) 12.7
			8.1	1.5	3.1		7.9	2.1
% Profit Before Taxes/Total Assets		9.6	8.0	13.8	12.2		15.6	10.4
		4.4	4.1	6.9	2.5		6.8	5.4
		.8	1.2	.6	1.8		2.6	.5
Sales/Net Fixed Assets		9.4	6.5	4.6	4.7		5.9	5.3
		6.5	2.8	1.5	2.4		2.7	2.5
		2.4	1.3	.6	1.3		1.4	1.3
Sales/Total Assets		1.2	1.0	1.1	1.3		1.0	1.0
		.9	.7	.7	.8		.7	.7
		.5	.6	.3	.6		.6	.5
% Depr., Dep., Amort./Sales		3.3	2.0	1.3	2.5		2.4	3.4
		(12) 4.3	(25) 4.6	(26) 5.6	(10) 6.2		(70) 4.6	(62) 5.3
		6.7	7.4	11.0	7.5		6.6	8.9
% Officers', Directors', Owners' Comp/Sales			2.1					2.0
		(10)	4.4					(12) 5.6
			14.4					8.0
Net Sales ($)	2576M	20130M	144047M	680336M	738262M	637564M	2143629M	1276105M
Total Assets ($)	1364M	21302M	140992M	596050M	804111M	576932M	1897871M	1613096M

M = $ thousand   MM = $ million
See Pages 11 through 21 for Explanation of Ratios and Data

Comparative Historical Data				Current Data Sorted By Sales					
21	29	25	**Type of Statement** — Unqualified	1	2	1	7	2	12
13	23	18	Reviewed	1	4	3	5	3	2
6	13	6	Compiled	1	3		1	1	
5	16	13	Tax Returns	5	7		1		
42	26	29	Other	4	9	4	1	2	9
4/1/02-3/31/03 ALL	4/1/03-3/31/04 ALL	4/1/04-3/31/05 ALL		0-1MM	18 (4/1-9/30/04) 1-3MM	3-5MM	73 (10/1/04-3/31/05) 5-10MM	10-25MM	25MM & OVER
87	107	91	**NUMBER OF STATEMENTS**	12	25	8	15	8	23
%	%	%	**ASSETS**	%	%	%	%	%	%
3.6	3.7	4.0	Cash & Equivalents	5.1	4.4		2.1		3.1
8.3	9.8	10.7	Trade Receivables (net)	5.3	8.0		7.9		19.6
43.2	39.8	40.1	Inventory	37.4	49.1		33.7		36.5
2.0	2.0	1.2	All Other Current	.3	.8		1.3		2.0
57.1	55.2	56.0	Total Current	48.1	62.3		45.0		61.2
35.7	36.7	35.9	Fixed Assets (net)	37.0	33.1		51.8		28.9
1.5	3.9	4.1	Intangibles (net)	6.7	2.1		1.0		5.3
5.7	4.1	4.0	All Other Non-Current	8.2	2.5		2.2		4.6
100.0	100.0	100.0	Total	100.0	100.0		100.0		100.0
			LIABILITIES						
13.4	13.8	11.1	Notes Payable-Short Term	6.4	14.0		16.9		11.2
2.2	2.3	2.4	Cur. Mat.-L/T/D	2.0	2.6		3.0		2.6
8.2	7.9	9.7	Trade Payables	6.5	13.3		6.6		11.5
.2	.2	.3	Income Taxes Payable	.0	.3		.2		.5
6.1	9.4	7.3	All Other Current	9.4	3.8		5.1		9.3
30.1	33.6	30.8	Total Current	24.2	34.0		31.8		35.0
23.9	25.4	25.4	Long-Term Debt	25.8	31.2		33.8		16.6
.6	.4	.7	Deferred Taxes	.0	.3		1.0		1.2
6.2	4.5	8.0	All Other Non-Current	22.0	10.9		2.3		3.3
39.2	36.0	35.3	Net Worth	28.0	23.7		31.0		43.9
100.0	100.0	100.0	Total Liabilities & Net Worth	100.0	100.0		100.0		100.0
			INCOME DATA						
100.0	100.0	100.0	Net Sales	100.0	100.0		100.0		100.0
44.9	46.6	47.5	Gross Profit	59.8	53.5		46.3		34.9
36.7	36.9	38.8	Operating Expenses	65.3	42.5		35.6		25.1
8.2	9.7	8.7	Operating Profit	−5.5	11.0		10.8		9.8
4.2	3.8	3.6	All Other Expenses (net)	7.0	3.5		4.9		2.9
4.0	5.8	5.1	Profit Before Taxes	−12.4	7.5		5.8		6.8
			RATIOS						
3.2	3.1	3.8	Current	6.0	4.2		2.2		2.8
2.0	1.8	2.0		2.9	2.4		1.2		1.8
1.3	1.2	1.2		1.1	1.5		1.0		1.1
.7	.8	1.1	Quick	1.4	.7		.6		1.3
.4	.4	.5		.7	.4		.4		.5
.2	.2	.2		.3	.2		.1		.4
27 13.3	18 20.7	18 20.2	Sales/Receivables	4 81.9	12 30.0		20 18.4		32 11.4
38 9.5	38 9.5	35 10.5		30 12.3	22 16.4		35 10.4		41 8.9
54 6.7	63 5.8	56 6.5		79 4.6	51 7.2		56 6.5		61 6.0
230 1.6	185 2.0	175 2.1	Cost of Sales/Inventory	196 1.9	253 1.4		236 1.5		79 4.6
443 .8	335 1.1	325 1.1		390 .9	555 .7		274 1.3		174 2.1
761 .5	734 .5	587 .6		1679 .2	839 .4		439 .8		440 .8
26 14.1	21 17.4	17 21.9	Cost of Sales/Payables	0 UND	24 15.2		17 21.9		16 22.7
51 7.1	46 7.9	47 7.7		15 25.1	85 4.3		49 7.4		38 9.6
108 3.4	99 3.7	97 3.8		277 1.3	155 2.4		74 4.9		86 4.2
1.3	1.5	1.7	Sales/Working Capital	.7	1.4		2.9		2.5
2.5	3.5	3.3		3.2	2.2		7.2		3.7
6.1	11.7	11.9		26.5	5.3		166.9		12.2
6.8	6.1	8.3	EBIT/Interest	1.8	7.1		4.2		11.6
(81) 2.3	(97) 2.5	(87) 2.8		.1	(24) 2.8		1.8		(21) 7.8
1.0	.7	1.4		−1.8	1.4		1.0		2.3
4.0	8.3	3.5	Net Profit + Depr., Dep., Amort./Cur. Mat. L/T/D						4.7
(34) 2.7	(35) 2.2	(27) 2.5						(12)	2.0
1.1	1.5	1.1							1.3
.4	.4	.5	Fixed/Worth	.3	.4		1.3		.5
.9	1.1	1.1		1.6	1.2		2.0		.7
1.6	2.3	2.3		NM	NM		3.0		1.2
.7	.8	.8	Debt/Worth	1.0	1.1		1.6		.9
1.3	1.8	1.9		3.1	2.1		2.6		1.4
2.9	3.8	4.3		−187.7	NM		6.1		2.7
24.9	26.3	37.3	% Profit Before Taxes/Tangible Net Worth		35.3		57.7		39.5
(79) 10.5	(93) 12.3	(77) 14.2			(19) 14.5		(14) 9.5		(21) 20.0
.7	.8	3.8			7.7		2.4		6.3
8.9	9.5	11.1	% Profit Before Taxes/Total Assets	3.7	9.1		11.7		14.9
3.0	4.2	4.4		−1.1	4.1		2.4		9.0
−1.0	−.7	1.1		−8.8	1.8		.1		2.5
5.8	7.6	7.1	Sales/Net Fixed Assets	6.9	6.7		4.0		18.7
2.2	2.2	2.4		1.9	3.0		1.3		4.5
1.1	1.0	1.3		.5	1.5		.8		1.9
.9	1.0	1.2	Sales/Total Assets	.9	1.0		1.0		2.3
.6	.7	.7		.5	.7		.7		1.2
.4	.4	.6		.3	.6		.4		.7
2.5	2.2	2.5	% Depr., Dep., Amort./Sales		3.1		4.1		1.1
(76) 5.8	(97) 4.9	(79) 4.6			(22) 4.5		(13) 6.5		(21) 2.5
10.1	9.1	8.0			8.7		9.9		6.6
2.5	4.5	2.0	% Officers', Directors', Owners' Comp/Sales						
(12) 4.7	(18) 6.5	(20) 4.4							
6.5	11.5	11.5							
1970630M	1881440M	2222915M	Net Sales ($)	7112M	50619M	31494M	100898M	120952M	1911840M
2818962M	2643448M	2140751M	Total Assets ($)	16871M	86345M	73418M	167647M	178960M	1617510M

© RMA 2005

M = $ thousand   MM = $ million
See Pages 11 through 21 for Explanation of Ratios and Data

Current Data Sorted By Assets   Comparative Historical Data

						Type of Statement		
	1		4			Unqualified		
	3	1				Reviewed		
1	5	1	1			Compiled		
7	3	1	1			Tax Returns		
3	6	3	4	1		Other		
	14 (4/1-9/30/04)		32 (10/1/04-3/31/05)				4/1/00-3/31/01	4/1/01-3/31/02
0-500M	500M-2MM	2-10MM	10-50MM	50-100MM	100-250MM		ALL	ALL
11	18	7	9	1		NUMBER OF STATEMENTS		
%	%	%	%	%	%	**ASSETS**	%	%
9.0	16.3					Cash & Equivalents		
24.6	34.8				D	Trade Receivables (net)	D	D
22.9	9.6				A	Inventory	A	A
1.8	7.3				T	All Other Current	T	T
58.3	68.0				A	Total Current	A	A
20.8	20.8					Fixed Assets (net)		
4.8	2.5				N	Intangibles (net)	N	N
16.1	8.7				O	All Other Non-Current	O	O
100.0	100.0				T	Total	T	T
						LIABILITIES		
29.6	7.9				A	Notes Payable-Short Term	A	A
6.6	3.7				V	Cur. Mat.-L/T/D	V	V
31.3	23.4				A	Trade Payables	A	A
1.1	1.4				I	Income Taxes Payable	I	I
16.1	14.2				L	All Other Current	L	L
84.7	50.6				A	Total Current	A	A
33.6	16.6				B	Long-Term Debt	B	B
.0	2.0				L	Deferred Taxes	L	L
16.6	5.6				E	All Other Non-Current	E	E
-34.9	25.2					Net Worth		
100.0	100.0					Total Liabilities & Net Worth		
						INCOME DATA		
100.0	100.0					Net Sales		
49.7	38.9					Gross Profit		
48.0	34.7					Operating Expenses		
1.8	4.2					Operating Profit		
.3	1.6					All Other Expenses (net)		
1.5	2.6					Profit Before Taxes		
						RATIOS		
2.2	1.8							
1.1	1.2					Current		
.2	1.0							
.9	1.6							
.6	1.0					Quick		
.0	.7							
0 UND	10 35.8							
21 17.5	42 8.7					Sales/Receivables		
25 14.4	56 6.6							
0 UND	0 UND							
1 247.3	1 255.9					Cost of Sales/Inventory		
114 3.2	29 12.7							
0 UND	10 37.9							
39 9.3	37 10.0					Cost of Sales/Payables		
53 6.9	64 5.7							
7.8	8.8							
68.5	26.8					Sales/Working Capital		
-13.3	-416.5							
5.4	8.0							
.9	(17) 3.9					EBIT/Interest		
-.2	-1.6							
						Net Profit + Depr., Dep., Amort./Cur. Mat. L./T/D		
.1	.3							
2.5	.7					Fixed/Worth		
-.3	2.5							
2.6	1.9							
7.3	4.0					Debt/Worth		
-2.4	31.9							
	65.9							
(16)	7.0					% Profit Before Taxes/Tangible Net Worth		
	-27.6							
25.9	9.9							
-.5	2.0					% Profit Before Taxes/Total Assets		
-11.7	-.7							
130.6	72.6							
44.7	19.9					Sales/Net Fixed Assets		
19.5	6.2							
7.5	4.4							
4.7	3.7					Sales/Total Assets		
3.7	1.9							
	.7							
(16)	1.2					% Depr., Dep., Amort./Sales		
	2.6							
	1.5							
(10)	7.4					% Officers', Directors', Owners' Comp/Sales		
	11.3							
16614M	89602M	114607M	413478M	107825M		Net Sales ($)		
2865M	19792M	33043M	217595M	98080M		Total Assets ($)		

M = $ thousand   MM = $ million
See Pages 11 through 21 for Explanation of Ratios and Data

Comparative Historical Data			Type of Statement	Current Data Sorted By Sales					
6	2	6	Unqualified		1			1	4
2	1	4	Reviewed		1		2	1	
2	4	8	Compiled		3	1	2	1	1
1	2	11	Tax Returns	3	4	2	2		
3	6	17	Other	1	5	3		4	4
4/1/02-3/31/03	4/1/03-3/31/04	4/1/04-3/31/05		0-1MM	1-3MM	3-5MM	5-10MM	10-25MM	25MM & OVER
				14 (4/1-9/30/04)		32 (10/1/04-3/31/05)			
ALL	ALL	ALL		0-1MM	1-3MM	3-5MM	5-10MM	10-25MM	25MM & OVER
14	15	46	NUMBER OF STATEMENTS	4	14	6	6	7	9
%	%	%	ASSETS	%	%	%	%	%	%
4.4	16.4	15.3	Cash & Equivalents		14.7				
18.8	20.3	30.4	Trade Receivables (net)		25.4				
43.5	30.6	16.6	Inventory		10.1				
3.0	2.9	4.5	All Other Current		3.1				
69.7	70.2	66.7	Total Current		53.3				
14.0	14.3	19.0	Fixed Assets (net)		23.8				
4.7	.2	3.3	Intangibles (net)		7.0				
11.6	15.3	11.0	All Other Non-Current		15.9				
100.0	100.0	100.0	Total		100.0				
			LIABILITIES						
8.9	7.8	12.6	Notes Payable-Short Term		27.2				
2.4	5.3	4.4	Cur. Mat.-L/T/D		2.9				
22.4	19.5	23.0	Trade Payables		27.8				
.5	.0	.9	Income Taxes Payable		2.6				
4.4	18.6	13.5	All Other Current		13.9				
38.6	51.2	54.4	Total Current		74.4				
11.8	9.7	19.0	Long-Term Debt		27.8				
.9	.1	1.1	Deferred Taxes		1.1				
8.5	15.7	8.7	All Other Non-Current		9.0				
40.2	23.2	16.8	Net Worth		-12.4				
100.0	100.0	100.0	Total Liabilities & Net Worth		100.0				
			INCOME DATA						
100.0	100.0	100.0	Net Sales		100.0				
30.5	31.1	37.1	Gross Profit		49.8				
22.4	27.1	32.6	Operating Expenses		45.5				
8.1	4.0	4.6	Operating Profit		4.4				
2.1	-1.1	.8	All Other Expenses (net)		1.8				
6.0	5.1	3.8	Profit Before Taxes		2.6				
			RATIOS						
3.6	2.5	2.2			1.9				
2.1	1.4	1.4	Current		.9				
1.3	.9	1.0			.2				
2.1	1.4	1.5			1.3				
.7	.7	1.0	Quick		.8				
.2	.2	.6			.2				
14 25.6	13 27.8	15 23.7		0 UND					
32 11.4	25 14.4	37 9.9	Sales/Receivables	23 15.8					
44 8.3	40 9.2	53 6.8		46 7.9					
30 12.3	0 UND	0 UND		0 UND					
119 3.1	41 8.9	6 62.8	Cost of Sales/Inventory	0 UND					
242 1.5	192 1.9	58 6.2		29 12.7					
24 14.9	10 37.6	8 44.7		6 56.5					
40 9.1	31 11.7	31 11.6	Cost of Sales/Payables	55 6.6					
89 4.1	54 6.8	60 6.1		101 3.6					
2.1	2.9	6.8			6.7				
5.7	10.6	18.4	Sales/Working Capital		-76.8				
14.0	-60.7	-427.7			-20.2				
13.4	9.2	11.9			8.2				
(12) 5.8	(14) 1.7	(44) 4.7	EBIT/Interest		.7				
2.8	-1.9	.9			-5.7				
			Net Profit + Depr., Dep., Amort./Cur. Mat. L/T/D						
.1	.1	.2			.5				
.3	.6	.7	Fixed/Worth		2.3				
1.8	31.3	3.4			-.7				
.6	.4	1.6			2.5				
2.6	4.1	3.3	Debt/Worth		5.7				
4.1	47.5	31.9			-2.5				
48.5	30.1	73.7	% Profit Before Taxes/Tangible		128.1				
(13) 24.4	(12) 5.6	(37) 15.4	Net Worth	(10) .7					
16.1	-5.0	-.4			-66.5				
14.1	6.4	19.3	% Profit Before Taxes/Total		17.6				
6.8	.6	5.9	Assets		-.5				
4.1	-.9	-.5			-13.0				
55.4	84.9	68.5			47.9				
17.2	18.7	23.7	Sales/Net Fixed Assets		19.4				
8.9	11.6	11.6			11.5				
2.8	4.2	4.7			6.2				
2.2	2.2	3.5	Sales/Total Assets		3.5				
.5	1.5	2.0			1.9				
.7	.7	.6			.7				
(11) 1.8	(12) 1.3	(34) 1.1	% Depr., Dep., Amort./Sales	(11) 1.4					
3.2	3.5	2.2			2.4				
		2.1	% Officers', Directors',						
	(25)	6.3	Owners' Comp/Sales						
		8.7							
436516M	230038M	742126M	Net Sales ($)	2719M	25957M	23068M	40221M	129322M	520839M
522046M	234317M	371375M	Total Assets ($)	1353M	8891M	5831M	32434M	42813M	280053M

M = $ thousand   MM = $ million
See Pages 11 through 21 for Explanation of Ratios and Data

Current Data Sorted By Assets / Comparative Historical Data

0-500M	500M-2MM	2-10MM	10-50MM	50-100MM	100-250MM		4/1/00-3/31/01 ALL	4/1/01-3/31/02 ALL
						Type of Statement		
	1	6	7	2	1	Unqualified	14	3
	4	6	1			Reviewed	2	1
	2	1	1			Compiled	6	5
						Tax Returns	1	1
	1	1	6	2	2	Other	13	10
	10 (4/1-9/30/04)		34 (10/1/04-3/31/05)					
	8	14	15	4	3	NUMBER OF STATEMENTS	36	20
%	%	%	%	%	%	**ASSETS**	%	%
DATA NOT AVAILABLE		4.9	5.4			Cash & Equivalents	4.1	5.5
		13.8	17.4			Trade Receivables (net)	19.5	17.9
		26.5	16.8			Inventory	20.9	30.3
		1.9	1.8			All Other Current	2.6	2.0
		47.1	41.4			Total Current	47.0	55.7
		40.6	46.1			Fixed Assets (net)	46.3	38.1
		.2	4.3			Intangibles (net)	.7	.4
		12.1	8.3			All Other Non-Current	6.0	5.8
		100.0	100.0			Total	100.0	100.0
						LIABILITIES		
		5.6	7.3			Notes Payable-Short Term	9.4	16.6
		4.7	2.1			Cur. Mat.-L/T/D	5.3	4.2
		14.8	9.2			Trade Payables	11.4	12.2
		.1	.3			Income Taxes Payable	.7	1.0
		4.5	4.7			All Other Current	4.3	7.6
		29.7	23.6			Total Current	31.1	41.6
		33.0	13.2			Long-Term Debt	24.7	22.6
		.4	.3			Deferred Taxes	1.4	1.5
		3.4	8.4			All Other Non-Current	5.6	1.4
		33.5	54.5			Net Worth	37.3	32.9
		100.0	100.0			Total Liabilities & Net Worth	100.0	100.0
						INCOME DATA		
		100.0	100.0			Net Sales	100.0	100.0
		20.7	11.5			Gross Profit	16.0	10.5
		18.3	8.0			Operating Expenses	14.0	11.0
		2.4	3.6			Operating Profit	2.0	-.5
		-.3	1.3			All Other Expenses (net)	1.8	3.7
		2.7	2.3			Profit Before Taxes	.2	-4.2
						RATIOS		
		2.5	4.0				3.1	3.0
		1.5	1.7			Current	1.7	1.7
		.8	1.2				1.2	1.0
		1.0	2.2				1.5	1.4
		.6	1.1			Quick	.7	.6
		.2	.5				.4	.3
		10 35.9	22 16.7				29 12.4	27 13.6
		29 12.6	36 10.3			Sales/Receivables	37 10.0	37 9.8
		38 9.5	50 7.2				49 7.5	54 6.7
		21 17.7	18 20.7				23 16.0	42 8.7
		79 4.6	38 9.5			Cost of Sales/Inventory	52 7.0	53 6.9
		104 3.5	70 5.2				64 5.7	92 4.0
		11 34.2	8 45.9				16 22.4	14 27.0
		37 9.9	18 20.6			Cost of Sales/Payables	24 15.1	21 17.1
		53 6.9	42 8.8				37 9.9	34 10.7
		4.6	4.9				5.4	4.5
		11.2	10.2			Sales/Working Capital	10.6	10.4
		-24.8	24.1				21.8	NM
		9.4	8.4				3.1	2.6
		1.7	(14) 2.2			EBIT/Interest	(32) 1.2	(17) .2
		.2	.0				-.9	-3.1
							2.1	
						Net Profit + Depr., Dep., Amort./Cur. Mat. L /T/D	(11) 1.3	
							.8	
		.4	.5				.7	.5
		1.2	.8			Fixed/Worth	1.1	.9
		3.0	1.3				1.9	2.2
		1.0	.4				.7	.6
		1.7	.9			Debt/Worth	1.3	2.0
		4.9	1.8				3.6	4.7
		23.7	17.4				17.8	23.0
		(12) 8.8	(14) 7.3			% Profit Before Taxes/Tangible Net Worth	(33) 4.0	(18) -6.5
		-.4	-1.2				-8.8	-31.9
		8.7	10.9				5.0	7.9
		2.2	3.4			% Profit Before Taxes/Total Assets	1.4	-4.7
		-2.6	.1				-4.9	-10.9
		11.6	7.3				6.3	14.3
		3.7	4.3			Sales/Net Fixed Assets	3.7	3.3
		2.6	2.5				2.4	2.2
		2.1	2.5				2.4	2.0
		1.6	1.8			Sales/Total Assets	1.7	1.5
		1.3	1.5				1.3	1.2
		2.5	2.5				2.1	.1
		5.2	3.5			% Depr., Dep., Amort./Sales	(34) 3.7	(18) 4.5
		6.6	5.5				5.8	5.8
						% Officers', Directors', Owners' Comp/Sales		
	25398M	126316M	724532M	467978M	762217M	Net Sales ($)	1555657M	1176923M
	9633M	76266M	388988M	235039M	469389M	Total Assets ($)	1104182M	786133M

M = $ thousand MM = $ million

See Pages 11 through 21 for Explanation of Ratios and Data

Comparative Historical Data | Current Data Sorted By Sales

9 4 3 2 10	15 9 10 1 11	17 11 4 · 12	Type of Statement / Unqualified / Reviewed / Compiled / Tax Returns / Other					
4/1/02-3/31/03 ALL	4/1/03-3/31/04 ALL	4/1/04-3/31/05 ALL		10 (4/1-9/30/04)		34 (10/1/04-3/31/05)		

Type of Statement (current data):
- Unqualified: 1, 2, 4, 10
- Reviewed: 2, 3, 4, 1, 1
- Compiled: 1, 1, 1
- Tax Returns: —
- Other: 1, 3, 8

Hist. 4/1/02-3/31/03 ALL	Hist. 4/1/03-3/31/04 ALL	Hist. 4/1/04-3/31/05 ALL		0-1MM	1-3MM	3-5MM	5-10MM	10-25MM	25MM & OVER
28	46	44	**NUMBER OF STATEMENTS**		4	5	7	8	20
%	%	%	**ASSETS**	%	%	%	%	%	%
8.0	5.4	4.7	Cash & Equivalents						2.7
20.6	16.7	18.4	Trade Receivables (net)						17.4
20.1	26.0	24.9	Inventory						17.9
3.7	5.6	1.7	All Other Current						2.1
52.3	53.7	49.7	Total Current						40.1
39.0	37.1	38.0	Fixed Assets (net)						43.6
.2	.9	3.4	Intangibles (net)						7.1
8.4	8.4	8.8	All Other Non-Current						9.3
100.0	100.0	100.0	Total						100.0
			LIABILITIES						
9.2	8.1	8.7	Notes Payable-Short Term						7.7
4.1	6.0	3.4	Cur. Mat.-L/T/D						3.5
18.3	13.4	13.2	Trade Payables						10.4
.5	.5	.1	Income Taxes Payable						.2
4.1	3.1	4.1	All Other Current						4.6
36.2	31.1	29.6	Total Current						26.5
16.8	16.6	19.9	Long-Term Debt						16.1
.9	1.4	1.1	Deferred Taxes						1.8
4.4	7.8	7.0	All Other Non-Current						7.8
41.7	43.1	42.4	Net Worth						47.9
100.0	100.0	100.0	Total Liabilities & Net Worth						100.0
			INCOME DATA						
100.0	100.0	100.0	Net Sales						100.0
13.2	18.2	18.0	Gross Profit						11.1
11.9	16.5	14.6	Operating Expenses						7.9
1.4	1.6	3.4	Operating Profit						3.2
.0	1.5	.9	All Other Expenses (net)						1.7
1.4	.2	2.5	Profit Before Taxes						1.5
			RATIOS						
2.4 / 1.4 / 1.1	3.0 / 1.6 / 1.1	2.4 / 1.6 / 1.2	Current						2.9 / 1.6 / 1.0
1.3 / .6 / .4	1.4 / .6 / .3	1.3 / .8 / .4	Quick						1.3 / .7 / .5
27 13.7 / 36 10.2 / 49 7.4	20 18.4 / 42 8.7 / 54 6.7	19 19.6 / 36 10.0 / 47 7.7	Sales/Receivables						23 15.7 / 38 9.7 / 49 7.5
24 15.1 / 39 9.4 / 65 5.7	39 9.3 / 54 6.8 / 79 4.6	20 18.7 / 56 6.5 / 86 4.2	Cost of Sales/Inventory						19 19.5 / 39 9.4 / 64 5.7
13 29.1 / 25 14.5 / 49 7.4	17 21.2 / 27 13.3 / 47 7.7	10 35.0 / 21 17.2 / 46 8.0	Cost of Sales/Payables						10 35.0 / 19 18.9 / 44 8.4
6.7 / 13.8 / 29.8	4.2 / 8.5 / 124.1	5.4 / 9.8 / 28.3	Sales/Working Capital						5.7 / 13.1 / NM
10.1 / (27) 1.8 / -2.6	4.8 / (41) 1.7 / -.3	8.6 / (43) 2.3 / .9	EBIT/Interest						7.3 / 2.2 / .9
	(13) 1.1	1.4 / 1.1 / -.1	Net Profit + Depr., Dep., Amort./Cur. Mat. L/T/D	11.4 / (12) 5.7 / 1.7					
.4 / .8 / 1.4	.3 / .9 / 2.0	.4 / .9 / 1.7	Fixed/Worth						.6 / 1.0 / 1.7
.6 / 2.0 / 2.9	.5 / 1.4 / 2.3	.6 / 1.4 / 2.2	Debt/Worth						.5 / 1.0 / 2.0
35.9 / (26) 11.9 / -2.6	21.2 / (41) 6.3 / -3.5	22.9 / (38) 11.9 / .3	% Profit Before Taxes/Tangible Net Worth						16.7 / (17) 7.0 / -1.1
10.5 / 4.3 / -2.8	9.0 / 1.8 / -4.2	10.1 / 3.9 / -.2	% Profit Before Taxes/Total Assets						8.5 / 3.2 / -.6
9.1 / 4.0 / 2.3	10.5 / 4.6 / 2.6	10.2 / 5.2 / 2.6	Sales/Net Fixed Assets						8.9 / 4.6 / 2.5
2.2 / 1.7 / 1.2	2.3 / 1.7 / 1.2	2.6 / 1.8 / 1.4	Sales/Total Assets						2.5 / 1.8 / 1.4
1.6 / (26) 4.4 / 6.9	1.6 / (35) 4.0 / 7.2	1.6 / (40) 3.6 / 5.8	% Depr., Dep., Amort./Sales						2.3 / (17) 3.5 / 5.6
	1.3 / (13) 2.6 / 3.9	1.6 / (12) 3.3 / 3.6	% Officers', Directors', Owners' Comp/Sales						
1156827M	1770160M	2106441M	Net Sales ($)		6706M	19014M	53209M	120136M	1907376M
765033M	1077676M	1179315M	Total Assets ($)		3387M	11785M	23641M	73807M	1066695M

Note: For the current-data size categories 0-1MM, 1-3MM, 3-5MM, 5-10MM and 10-25MM, the statement indicates "DATA NOT AVAILABLE."

MANUFACTURING—Broadwoven Fabric Mills NAICS 313210 (SIC 2211, 2221, 2231)

Current Data Sorted By Assets

Comparative Historical Data

		5	5	3	4	Type of Statement		
1	1	12	4			Unqualified	32	17
	2	4	1			Reviewed	18	11
	4					Compiled	11	22
						Tax Returns	4	1
1	5	4	14	3	1	Other	29	28
	14 (4/1-9/30/04)		60 (10/1/04-3/31/05)				4/1/00-3/31/01	4/1/01-3/31/02
0-500M	500M-2MM	2-10MM	10-50MM	50-100MM	100-250MM		ALL	ALL
2	12	25	24	6	5	NUMBER OF STATEMENTS	94	79
%	%	%	%	%	%	ASSETS	%	%
	15.8	6.3	3.4			Cash & Equivalents	4.7	5.1
	35.2	25.9	22.6			Trade Receivables (net)	26.4	21.9
	25.2	31.1	29.4			Inventory	25.7	26.2
	2.6	1.8	.9			All Other Current	2.8	3.0
	78.8	65.1	56.3			Total Current	59.5	56.2
	18.1	26.4	32.1			Fixed Assets (net)	32.4	37.3
	.2	3.1	4.4			Intangibles (net)	2.4	1.6
	2.9	5.4	7.2			All Other Non-Current	5.7	4.8
	100.0	100.0	100.0			Total	100.0	100.0
						LIABILITIES		
	8.5	13.5	15.4			Notes Payable-Short Term	9.5	10.0
	.9	2.8	3.9			Cur. Mat.-L/T/D	3.4	4.2
	18.0	17.1	12.5			Trade Payables	14.0	13.9
	.0	.2	.0			Income Taxes Payable	.2	.2
	5.0	5.1	3.8			All Other Current	7.7	6.9
	32.4	38.6	35.6			Total Current	34.8	35.1
	13.7	14.8	22.6			Long-Term Debt	17.9	17.8
	.0	.9	.6			Deferred Taxes	1.0	1.0
	5.2	3.3	12.9			All Other Non-Current	4.7	4.2
	48.7	42.4	28.2			Net Worth	41.7	41.8
	100.0	100.0	100.0			Total Liabilities & Net Worth	100.0	100.0
						INCOME DATA		
	100.0	100.0	100.0			Net Sales	100.0	100.0
	32.3	25.6	23.7			Gross Profit	24.5	22.3
	28.6	24.2	17.8			Operating Expenses	19.6	20.6
	3.8	1.4	5.9			Operating Profit	4.9	1.7
	1.2	.9	1.9			All Other Expenses (net)	2.2	2.1
	2.6	.5	4.0			Profit Before Taxes	2.6	-.5
						RATIOS		
	7.7	2.3	2.5				3.0	2.9
	3.6	1.6	1.6			Current	2.0	1.8
	1.5	1.2	1.1				1.3	1.2
	3.3	1.2	1.1				1.6	1.5
	2.0	.7	.7			Quick	1.0	.8
	1.0	.5	.5				.6	.4
	26 13.9	23 15.6	44 8.3				37 9.8	32 11.4
	38 9.5	37 9.8	48 7.6			Sales/Receivables	46 7.9	45 8.1
	51 7.1	60 6.0	61 6.0				60 6.1	54 6.7
	17 21.4	46 8.0	52 7.0				37 9.9	48 7.7
	34 10.6	67 5.4	81 4.5			Cost of Sales/Inventory	69 5.3	65 5.6
	87 4.2	86 4.3	141 2.6				100 3.7	103 3.6
	3 114.2	19 19.5	19 19.1				16 22.6	17 21.9
	21 17.3	35 10.4	33 11.0			Cost of Sales/Payables	25 14.6	28 13.1
	42 8.6	47 7.7	54 6.7				41 8.8	44 8.4
	4.6	6.2	4.0				4.5	4.5
	7.2	8.8	8.7			Sales/Working Capital	7.3	7.2
	15.2	24.8	56.9				16.7	23.2
		6.8	7.9				5.3	6.6
		2.6	3.3			EBIT/Interest	(89) 2.1	(75) 1.7
		-1.5	1.2				1.1	-.9
							4.5	2.1
						Net Profit + Depr., Dep., Amort./Cur. Mat. L /T/D	(35) 2.9	(24) 1.2
							1.0	-.5
	.0	.2	.5				.5	.4
	.3	.6	1.6			Fixed/Worth	.9	.8
	1.9	1.5	7.0				1.5	2.0
	.2	.8	1.2				.6	.4
	1.4	1.7	2.0			Debt/Worth	1.4	1.3
	2.4	3.4	22.5				3.8	3.5
	31.2	22.5	38.2			% Profit Before Taxes/Tangible Net Worth	28.4	28.6
	(11) 17.6	(23) 4.2	(19) 17.9				(84) 11.9	(73) 6.2
	-7.4	-14.4	3.0				1.9	-6.7
	18.7	9.6	11.1			% Profit Before Taxes/Total Assets	11.8	7.6
	9.1	3.3	5.2				5.2	2.2
	-3.7	-4.5	.9				.5	-4.6
	769.6	34.2	9.7				13.7	11.1
	33.6	12.3	5.5			Sales/Net Fixed Assets	4.7	4.0
	10.4	4.3	3.6				3.3	2.4
	5.2	2.9	2.1				2.4	2.3
	3.3	2.1	1.7			Sales/Total Assets	1.8	1.6
	2.0	1.8	1.1				1.2	1.1
		.6	1.2				1.2	.6
		(20) 1.7	(23) 2.1			% Depr., Dep., Amort./Sales	(79) 3.3	(70) 3.0
		3.8	4.5				5.5	5.6
							2.2	1.2
						% Officers', Directors', Owners' Comp/Sales	(29) 3.8	(20) 3.2
							7.5	4.3
1207M	41532M	278318M	822142M	608273M	1619812M	Net Sales ($)	5014873M	2601098M
492M	12679M	118878M	494205M	451115M	752197M	Total Assets ($)	3228664M	1924035M

M = $ thousand   MM = $ million
See Pages 11 through 21 for Explanation of Ratios and Data

Comparative Historical Data				Current Data Sorted By Sales					
			Type of Statement						
35	22	17	Unqualified			2	1	3	11
17	23	18	Reviewed	1		1	6	8	2
11	27	7	Compiled	1	1	1	3		1
1	5	4	Tax Returns		1	3			
19	25	28	Other		3	2	4	5	14
4/1/02-3/31/03 ALL	4/1/03-3/31/04 ALL	4/1/04-3/31/05 ALL		0-1MM	1-3MM	3-5MM	5-10MM	10-25MM	25MM & OVER
					14 (4/1-9/30/04)		60 (10/1/04-3/31/05)		
83	102	74	**NUMBER OF STATEMENTS**	2	5	9	14	16	28
%	%	%	**ASSETS**	%	%	%	%	%	%
6.7	6.2	6.6	Cash & Equivalents				5.5	6.7	2.3
26.8	25.8	25.9	Trade Receivables (net)				25.3	26.1	23.3
26.3	25.4	28.5	Inventory				28.6	34.9	28.3
2.5	3.7	1.5	All Other Current				2.5	2.2	1.0
62.3	61.2	62.5	Total Current				61.8	69.9	54.9
30.9	29.4	27.7	Fixed Assets (net)				28.3	20.7	31.5
.6	3.3	3.7	Intangibles (net)				2.6	5.0	5.4
6.2	6.1	6.2	All Other Non-Current				7.2	4.4	8.2
100.0	100.0	100.0	Total				100.0	100.0	100.0
			LIABILITIES						
10.9	10.1	13.4	Notes Payable-Short Term				16.7	9.0	15.3
3.4	2.9	2.5	Cur. Mat.-L/T/D				2.9	2.8	2.8
16.4	16.4	14.4	Trade Payables				13.1	19.8	11.8
.1	.2	.2	Income Taxes Payable				.0	.2	.4
6.2	10.9	4.7	All Other Current				2.3	6.3	4.9
36.9	40.6	35.2	Total Current				35.0	38.2	35.2
13.9	13.0	16.6	Long-Term Debt				16.1	14.4	19.2
1.1	.9	.7	Deferred Taxes				1.2	.4	.7
4.9	8.0	7.6	All Other Non-Current				2.3	5.0	12.3
43.2	37.5	39.9	Net Worth				45.5	42.1	32.5
100.0	100.0	100.0	Total Liabilities & Net Worth				100.0	100.0	100.0
			INCOME DATA						
100.0	100.0	100.0	Net Sales				100.0	100.0	100.0
23.5	28.5	25.0	Gross Profit				26.4	28.6	20.0
19.3	25.1	21.5	Operating Expenses				26.4	21.9	16.1
4.2	3.5	3.4	Operating Profit				.0	6.8	3.9
1.4	1.2	1.5	All Other Expenses (net)				.3	1.4	2.3
2.8	2.3	2.0	Profit Before Taxes				−.2	5.4	1.6
			RATIOS						
2.5	2.8	2.6	Current				2.7	4.0	2.4
1.8	1.8	1.7					1.9	2.0	1.4
1.2	1.2	1.2					1.2	1.4	1.2
1.4	1.4	1.3	Quick				1.2	1.2	1.2
.9	.9	.8					.7	.8	.7
.6	.6	.5					.5	.5	.5
30 12.1	31 12.0	30 12.0	Sales/Receivables				28 13.2	31 11.9	39 9.3
44 8.2	45 8.1	46 7.9					47 7.7	42 8.8	48 7.6
64 5.7	61 6.0	60 6.1					68 5.4	58 6.3	61 6.0
38 9.7	39 9.3	43 8.4	Cost of Sales/Inventory				47 7.8	47 7.7	44 8.3
63 5.8	67 5.4	62 5.8					67 5.5	79 4.6	64 5.7
85 4.3	93 3.9	87 4.2					96 3.8	111 3.3	85 4.3
16 23.3	16 23.0	19 19.7	Cost of Sales/Payables				19 19.3	24 15.2	19 19.5
28 12.9	30 12.3	29 12.7					37 9.8	39 9.3	31 11.9
51 7.2	52 7.0	50 7.4					48 7.5	59 6.2	49 7.5
4.8	4.5	5.6	Sales/Working Capital				4.2	5.0	5.5
7.7	7.2	8.6					6.5	8.1	10.5
27.3	23.9	23.6					22.7	16.8	39.7
11.0	9.3	7.9	EBIT/Interest				4.4	13.4	7.5
(68) 3.2	(87) 4.4	(68) 3.1					2.1	5.9	(26) 3.1
1.0	.7	.3					−1.1	2.1	.0
2.8	6.0	7.1	Net Profit + Depr., Dep.,						
(23) 2.1	(24) 2.1	(21) 1.4	Amort./Cur. Mat. L/T/D						
1.3	.8	.7							
.2	.3	.3	Fixed/Worth				.2	.2	.5
.6	.6	.8					.7	.5	1.0
1.3	1.3	2.0					1.5	1.5	2.8
.5	.7	.7	Debt/Worth				.4	.7	.9
1.3	1.4	1.6					1.2	1.5	1.9
2.4	4.0	3.7					3.7	4.4	8.1
38.7	35.6	30.1	% Profit Before Taxes/Tangible				15.7	61.4	32.7
(79) 14.9	(91) 16.2	(65) 11.1	Net Worth	(13) 1.4	(14) 19.5	(23) 12.3			
.9	−.5	−8.0					−15.7	9.0	−14.4
14.4	12.8	11.0	% Profit Before Taxes/Total				8.3	14.6	10.7
5.8	5.4	3.3	Assets				1.2	6.8	2.1
.0	−1.1	−3.0					−3.3	3.3	−4.1
27.7	19.0	23.4	Sales/Net Fixed Assets				46.1	30.1	13.0
5.6	7.5	8.9					9.0	10.8	6.4
3.6	3.6	3.8					3.9	6.0	3.6
2.8	2.7	2.5	Sales/Total Assets				2.4	3.5	2.2
1.9	2.0	2.0					2.1	2.1	1.7
1.4	1.4	1.4					1.3	1.4	1.3
1.3	.7	1.0	% Depr., Dep., Amort./Sales				.9	.9	1.0
(73) 2.8	(84) 2.1	(59) 1.9		(12) 3.2	(13) 1.8	(23) 1.8			
5.3	4.8	4.0					4.8	3.7	3.6
2.2	2.1	1.9	% Officers', Directors',						
(24) 4.0	(32) 3.8	(20) 3.5	Owners' Comp/Sales						
6.0	6.7	7.5							
3004143M	4560394M	3371284M	Net Sales ($)	954M	9414M	37527M	100724M	272141M	2950524M
1720581M	2763246M	1829566M	Total Assets ($)	525M	4291M	17376M	65249M	137874M	1604251M

© RMA 2005
M = $ thousand   MM = $ million
See Pages 11 through 21 for Explanation of Ratios and Data

Current Data Sorted By Assets   Comparative Historical Data

		1	6			Type of Statement	5	3
	3	3	2			Unqualified		
1		5	1			Reviewed	4	7
	2	1				Compiled	13	11
1	1	3	5			Tax Returns	1	2
						Other	5	5

0-500M	500M-2MM	2-10MM	10-50MM	50-100MM	100-250MM		4/1/00-3/31/01 ALL	4/1/01-3/31/02 ALL
		9 (4/1-9/30/04)		25 (10/1/04-3/31/05)				
2	6	13	13			NUMBER OF STATEMENTS	28	28
%	%	%	%	%	%	ASSETS	%	%
		6.2	5.1	D	D	Cash & Equivalents	4.2	7.6
		27.0	23.2	A	A	Trade Receivables (net)	24.0	20.3
		31.0	32.7	T	T	Inventory	27.1	27.5
		.4	1.7	A	A	All Other Current	3.5	4.0
		64.5	62.7			Total Current	58.8	59.4
		24.9	27.3	N	N	Fixed Assets (net)	29.0	30.8
		7.0	1.3	O	O	Intangibles (net)	4.5	5.0
		3.7	8.7	T	T	All Other Non-Current	7.7	4.8
		100.0	100.0			Total	100.0	100.0
				A	A	LIABILITIES		
		10.5	22.7	V	V	Notes Payable-Short Term	7.9	9.8
		2.8	1.9	A	A	Cur. Mat.-L/T/D	3.1	5.5
		16.0	10.8	I	I	Trade Payables	12.2	9.9
		.8	.1	L	L	Income Taxes Payable	.3	.4
		7.3	10.8	A	A	All Other Current	8.5	6.9
		37.5	46.3	B	B	Total Current	32.0	32.6
		14.3	13.0	L	L	Long-Term Debt	18.6	17.9
		.9	.2	E	E	Deferred Taxes	.9	.7
		6.2	4.7			All Other Non-Current	11.5	5.2
		41.1	35.8			Net Worth	37.0	43.6
		100.0	100.0			Total Liabilities & Net Worth	100.0	100.0
						INCOME DATA		
		100.0	100.0			Net Sales	100.0	100.0
		23.6	19.5			Gross Profit	25.3	24.2
		20.3	17.8			Operating Expenses	20.1	21.9
		3.3	1.7			Operating Profit	5.2	2.4
		1.0	1.7			All Other Expenses (net)	1.4	1.5
		2.3	.0			Profit Before Taxes	3.7	.9
						RATIOS		
		2.8	2.8				2.9	3.4
		1.7	1.4			Current	1.8	2.0
		1.2	.9				1.2	1.3
		1.4	1.2				1.3	1.4
		.8	.6			Quick	.9	.8
		.6	.3				.6	.6
		34 10.6	37 9.8				33 11.0	28 12.9
		42 8.7	49 7.5			Sales/Receivables	43 8.4	37 9.9
		61 6.0	67 5.5				53 6.9	46 8.0
		32 11.6	75 4.9				41 8.8	39 9.3
		55 6.7	88 4.1			Cost of Sales/Inventory	72 5.1	76 4.8
		121 3.0	113 3.2				96 3.8	97 3.8
		20 18.0	11 33.2				14 26.4	9 38.8
		29 12.4	31 11.8			Cost of Sales/Payables	21 17.5	20 18.4
		52 7.1	41 8.8				37 9.8	38 9.6
		4.9	4.7				4.7	4.2
		7.9	9.4			Sales/Working Capital	7.5	8.0
		22.3	−22.9				24.5	12.9
		10.6	4.7				16.8	7.3
		5.2	1.2			EBIT/Interest	3.3	2.1
		−.3	−1.8				1.9	.2
						Net Profit + Depr., Dep.,	4.5	
						Amort./Cur. Mat. L /T/D	(12) 2.2	
							.4	
		.2	.2				.4	.5
		.5	.8			Fixed/Worth	.9	1.0
		6.3	2.0				5.2	2.9
		.5	1.3				.9	.4
		1.7	2.6			Debt/Worth	1.6	1.3
		16.9	4.1				9.1	6.9
		29.4	10.1			% Profit Before Taxes/Tangible	46.7	22.7
	(11) 9.1	(12) 1.7			Net Worth	(23) 12.5	(25) 3.3
		−11.9	−18.1				5.1	−6.2
		12.0	5.8			% Profit Before Taxes/Total	12.0	9.8
		5.1	.1			Assets	5.4	2.9
		−3.9	−5.0				2.2	−3.4
		43.2	32.4				20.3	11.6
		9.2	6.6			Sales/Net Fixed Assets	6.2	5.7
		4.3	2.7				3.9	4.2
		3.2	2.0				2.7	2.3
		1.9	1.7			Sales/Total Assets	1.8	1.7
		1.4	1.2				1.5	1.5
		.7	1.7				.0	.1
		2.4	(11) 4.1			% Depr., Dep., Amort./Sales	(26) .9	(27) 1.6
		3.9	4.7				4.2	4.3
						% Officers', Directors',	2.3	2.4
						Owners' Comp/Sales	(12) 3.8	(14) 4.5
							7.9	6.9
1586M	21000M	132915M	484084M			Net Sales ($)	937226M	554835M
842M	6585M	60141M	310839M			Total Assets ($)	651712M	361073M

(Columns 50-100MM and 100-250MM: "DATA NOT AVAILABLE" for ASSETS and LIABILITIES sections.)

© RMA 2005

M = $ thousand   MM = $ million
See Pages 11 through 21 for Explanation of Ratios and Data

Comparative Historical Data | Current Data Sorted By Sales

9 13 5 1 9	6 9 12 1 16	7 8 6 3 10	Type of Statement	0-1MM	1-3MM	3-5MM	5-10MM	10-25MM	25MM & OVER
9	6	7	Unqualified			2	3	1	5
13	9	8	Reviewed		2			2	2
5	12	6	Compiled		1		1	2	1
1	1	3	Tax Returns	1			2		
9	16	10	Other	1	1	1		1	3
4/1/02-3/31/03 ALL	4/1/03-3/31/04 ALL	4/1/04-3/31/05 ALL			9 (4/1-9/30/04)			25 (10/1/04-3/31/05)	
37	44	34	NUMBER OF STATEMENTS	2	4	3	3	6	11
%	%	%		%	%	%	%	%	%
			ASSETS						
8.5	4.3	6.6	Cash & Equivalents						2.5
21.8	21.7	28.1	Trade Receivables (net)						26.6
31.7	25.2	29.9	Inventory						34.7
1.5	4.9	1.2	All Other Current						1.9
63.6	56.2	65.8	Total Current						65.7
23.7	30.9	25.3	Fixed Assets (net)						27.1
6.5	4.5	3.5	Intangibles (net)						1.2
6.2	8.5	5.4	All Other Non-Current						6.0
100.0	100.0	100.0	Total						100.0
			LIABILITIES						
9.6	10.0	14.1	Notes Payable-Short Term						17.0
3.2	3.2	2.4	Cur. Mat.-L/T/D						1.8
12.1	15.2	16.5	Trade Payables						12.8
.3	.3	.4	Income Taxes Payable						.1
11.4	12.7	8.7	All Other Current						12.3
36.7	41.4	41.9	Total Current						44.0
11.3	13.2	13.6	Long-Term Debt						13.5
.6	.7	.4	Deferred Taxes						.1
4.9	3.9	6.3	All Other Non-Current						5.6
46.6	40.8	37.8	Net Worth						36.7
100.0	100.0	100.0	Total Liabilities & Net Worth						100.0
			INCOME DATA						
100.0	100.0	100.0	Net Sales						100.0
26.1	24.2	22.2	Gross Profit						16.3
22.2	21.0	19.2	Operating Expenses						16.4
3.9	3.3	3.1	Operating Profit						-.1
.8	1.1	1.1	All Other Expenses (net)						1.7
3.1	2.2	2.0	Profit Before Taxes						-1.8
			RATIOS						
3.0	3.0	2.9							3.0
1.7	1.4	1.6	Current						1.5
1.4	.9	1.0							1.0
1.3	1.1	1.5							1.5
.8	.6	.8	Quick						.7
.6	.4	.4							.3
33 11.1	33 11.1	35 10.5							36 10.1
41 8.8	40 9.2	46 8.0	Sales/Receivables						49 7.5
49 7.5	53 6.9	64 5.7							66 5.5
53 6.9	40 9.1	42 8.7							75 4.9
72 5.1	65 5.6	76 4.8	Cost of Sales/Inventory						88 4.2
119 3.1	97 3.8	109 3.3							108 3.4
14 26.7	20 18.6	18 20.3							13 27.9
26 13.9	29 12.8	35 10.3	Cost of Sales/Payables						31 11.8
36 10.1	42 8.6	49 7.5							43 8.5
4.8	5.1	5.0							6.1
7.5	15.9	8.4	Sales/Working Capital						8.2
16.2	-34.3	-93.5							-104.0
10.4	9.9	9.1							7.1
(32) 4.4	(42) 4.0	(31) 1.8	EBIT/Interest						.4
1.2	.1	-.4							-2.8
3.9	3.1	6.5	Net Profit + Depr., Dep.,						.2
(18) 2.7	(14) 2.0	(12) 2.4	Amort./Cur. Mat. L/T/D						.8
1.7	.1	1.4							2.2
.2	.3	.2							.7
.5	.7	.6	Fixed/Worth						2.6
1.0	2.5	1.8							4.2
.6	.6	.7							7.0
1.2	1.8	2.1	Debt/Worth						(10) -2.8
6.0	4.7	5.5							-20.3
36.9	43.2	29.4	% Profit Before Taxes/Tangible						2.0
(33) 12.0	(39) 6.0	(30) 8.6	Net Worth						-1.6
.9	-4.4	-7.3							-5.7
13.7	9.3	11.6	% Profit Before Taxes/Total						36.7
5.4	4.3	2.7	Assets						6.6
.5	-4.6	-2.7							2.9
32.7	22.5	37.4							2.3
8.3	6.6	8.8	Sales/Net Fixed Assets						1.9
5.2	3.3	4.3							1.2
2.3	2.0	2.4							.9
1.9	1.8	1.9	Sales/Total Assets						(10) 3.7
1.5	1.4	1.3							4.4
1.2	1.0	.9							2.7
(34) 2.2	(36) 3.3	(30) 2.4	% Depr., Dep., Amort./Sales						4.3
4.1	5.0	4.1							6.6
1.8	1.4	2.7	% Officers', Directors',						
(16) 3.8	(16) 3.0	(13) 4.3	Owners' Comp/Sales						
8.5	6.0	6.6							
708851M	892657M	639585M	Net Sales ($)	1392M	8927M	11503M	56697M	103043M	458023M
420451M	588256M	378407M	Total Assets ($)	1062M	6814M	3009M	36633M	50789M	280100M

© RMA 2005

M = $ thousand   MM = $ million
See Pages 11 through 21 for Explanation of Ratios and Data

Current Data Sorted By Assets   **Comparative Historical Data**

	0-500M	500M-2MM	2-10MM	10-50MM	50-100MM	100-250MM		4/1/00-3/31/01 ALL	4/1/01-3/31/02 ALL
	4 / 3 / 1	2 / 5 / 4 / 1 / 4	7 / 11 / 7 / 3	10 / 5 / 3	1	3	**Type of Statement**	10 / 10 / 9 / 2 / 4	7 / 8 / 7 / 1 / 7
							Unqualified	10	7
							Reviewed	10	8
							Compiled	9	7
							Tax Returns	2	1
							Other	4	7
		11 (4/1-9/30/04)		62 (10/1/04-3/31/05)					
	8	15	28	18	1	3	**NUMBER OF STATEMENTS**	35	30
	%	%	%	%	%	%	**ASSETS**	%	%
		14.6	7.6	3.9			Cash & Equivalents	6.2	5.5
		26.1	25.9	24.2			Trade Receivables (net)	26.5	26.9
		20.2	41.1	37.7			Inventory	24.0	24.0
		1.9	1.7	2.0			All Other Current	2.7	1.5
		62.8	76.2	67.7			Total Current	59.4	57.8
		27.0	16.7	22.3			Fixed Assets (net)	28.3	32.3
		5.5	2.6	.7			Intangibles (net)	3.7	4.6
		4.7	4.5	9.2			All Other Non-Current	8.7	5.3
		100.0	100.0	100.0			Total	100.0	100.0
							LIABILITIES		
		10.5	18.9	12.2			Notes Payable-Short Term	11.3	14.2
		6.0	2.3	3.3			Cur. Mat.-L/T/D	4.5	4.7
		22.3	19.8	14.9			Trade Payables	15.3	15.7
		.0	.5	.3			Income Taxes Payable	.2	.1
		10.5	8.8	11.7			All Other Current	14.4	6.8
		49.4	50.2	42.4			Total Current	45.7	41.5
		18.1	8.4	12.5			Long-Term Debt	19.7	24.6
		.0	.2	1.0			Deferred Taxes	.4	.6
		6.9	5.1	1.2			All Other Non-Current	2.9	4.4
		25.6	36.1	42.9			Net Worth	31.3	28.8
		100.0	100.0	100.0			Total Liabilities & Net Worth	100.0	100.0
							INCOME DATA		
		100.0	100.0	100.0			Net Sales	100.0	100.0
		41.1	28.9	21.8			Gross Profit	28.8	23.6
		32.9	25.6	17.9			Operating Expenses	26.7	21.9
		8.2	3.3	3.8			Operating Profit	2.0	1.7
		1.3	1.1	1.3			All Other Expenses (net)	1.8	1.8
		6.9	2.3	2.5			Profit Before Taxes	.2	-.1
							RATIOS		
		2.7	2.0	2.7				2.2	2.9
		1.3	1.6	1.5			Current	1.4	1.6
		.8	1.3	1.2				1.1	1.1
		1.6	1.0	1.3				1.1	1.5
		.9	.7	.7			Quick	.7	1.0
		.3	.4	.3				.4	.5
	18 20.7		33 11.1	32 11.5				30 12.3	33 11.2
	38 9.7		38 9.7	49 7.5			Sales/Receivables	43 8.5	40 9.1
	42 8.6		50 7.4	70 5.2				54 6.8	49 7.5
	1 266.2		56 6.6	51 7.2				23 15.7	22 16.4
	15 24.1		79 4.6	74 5.0			Cost of Sales/Inventory	50 7.3	46 7.9
	71 5.2		124 2.9	131 2.8				72 5.0	73 5.0
	10 36.6		25 14.4	13 27.2				15 24.4	16 22.1
	19 18.8		41 8.9	24 15.0			Cost of Sales/Payables	29 12.4	28 13.0
	70 5.2		50 7.4	50 7.3				53 6.9	39 9.3
	7.1		4.6	4.5				6.5	6.6
	28.9		8.4	8.0			Sales/Working Capital	14.1	13.2
	-13.3		26.8	15.5				80.4	142.1
	24.0		12.1	8.2				6.0	3.1
	(13) 2.5		3.9	5.5			EBIT/Interest	(33) 2.2	1.9
	-1.4		1.5	1.3				.2	.6
							Net Profit + Depr., Dep.,	6.4	
							Amort./Cur. Mat. L /T/D	(10) 2.3	
								1.4	
	.3		.1	.2				.3	.5
	.6		.3	.5			Fixed/Worth	.8	1.6
	-4.5		.8	1.0				5.2	NM
	.5		1.0	.8				.7	.7
	1.7		1.4	1.4			Debt/Worth	2.1	3.5
	-10.1		3.4	3.2				8.1	NM
	134.7		34.7	20.2				36.3	26.5
	(11) 49.2		(26) 17.8	7.4			% Profit Before Taxes/Tangible	(29) 10.6	(23) 6.2
	-6.7		2.7	.6			Net Worth	-.3	.6
	33.9		14.2	8.4				7.5	9.1
	6.3		5.2	3.5			% Profit Before Taxes/Total	4.2	2.2
	-8.7		1.0	.4			Assets	-3.0	-2.0
	67.8		85.4	43.9				28.8	21.6
	25.7		39.8	10.6			Sales/Net Fixed Assets	10.7	9.2
	7.1		10.0	5.1				4.7	3.7
	4.0		3.2	2.7				3.2	3.5
	3.0		2.5	2.0			Sales/Total Assets	2.5	2.3
	2.5		1.6	1.7				1.6	1.6
	1.7		.5	.4				.7	.3
	(12) 1.9		(23) .9	(16) 1.2			% Depr., Dep., Amort./Sales	(33) 2.0	(28) 1.8
	3.4		1.8	4.4				3.4	3.6
			2.8					1.5	2.9
			(12) 5.2				% Officers', Directors',	(13) 3.4	(10) 4.3
			8.5				Owners' Comp/Sales	6.0	6.1
	7281M	55288M	372776M	694345M	97191M	711692M	Net Sales ($)	502588M	744869M
	2422M	16571M	147550M	340355M	53164M	360428M	Total Assets ($)	261769M	372686M

© RMA 2005

M = $ thousand   MM = $ million
See Pages 11 through 21 for Explanation of Ratios and Data

Comparative Historical Data   Current Data Sorted By Sales

Type of Statement	4/1/02-3/31/03 ALL	4/1/03-3/31/04 ALL	4/1/04-3/31/05 ALL	0-1MM	1-3MM	3-5MM	5-10MM	10-25MM	25MM & OVER
Unqualified	14	18	20		1	1	3	6	10
Reviewed	15	16	19		3	3	2	7	6
Compiled	5	17	16			5	2	2	
Tax Returns	9	8	7	3	2	2	1		1
Other	21	22	11	3	2	1	2	4	1
					11 (4/1-9/30/04)		62 (10/1/04-3/31/05)		
NUMBER OF STATEMENTS	**64**	**81**	**73**	**6**	**8**	**12**	**10**	**19**	**18**
	%	%	%	%	%	%	%	%	%
ASSETS									
Cash & Equivalents	8.3	6.6	8.5			11.2	14.4	4.2	4.1
Trade Receivables (net)	28.0	26.4	25.6			26.0	20.4	29.0	25.2
Inventory	25.3	27.5	34.6			31.8	37.5	35.8	42.4
All Other Current	1.9	5.7	1.8			2.5	.6	2.3	2.3
Total Current	63.4	66.2	70.4			71.5	73.0	71.2	74.0
Fixed Assets (net)	27.3	21.7	21.6			21.2	19.0	22.6	17.2
Intangibles (net)	3.8	5.4	2.4			5.0	1.7	1.0	1.1
All Other Non-Current	5.5	6.6	5.6			2.2	6.3	5.2	7.8
Total	100.0	100.0	100.0			100.0	100.0	100.0	100.0
LIABILITIES									
Notes Payable-Short Term	12.6	11.9	16.4			31.4	5.6	15.7	8.8
Cur. Mat.-L/T/D	4.4	7.0	3.4			3.0	2.1	2.9	3.1
Trade Payables	17.6	18.1	19.8			17.7	26.4	15.5	21.6
Income Taxes Payable	.2	.2	.3			.1	1.3	.1	.1
All Other Current	7.3	8.7	9.3			10.0	8.4	12.3	7.2
Total Current	42.0	45.7	49.2			62.1	43.7	46.5	40.7
Long-Term Debt	17.5	11.7	12.3			7.6	13.3	10.1	8.8
Deferred Taxes	.3	.5	.3			.0	.0	.6	.8
All Other Non-Current	2.8	6.7	6.3			10.3	1.4	5.5	1.6
Net Worth	37.4	35.4	31.9			20.0	41.5	37.4	48.1
Total Liabilities & Net Worth	100.0	100.0	100.0			100.0	100.0	100.0	100.0
INCOME DATA									
Net Sales	100.0	100.0	100.0			100.0	100.0	100.0	100.0
Gross Profit	30.4	29.9	29.7			37.4	36.7	23.8	18.9
Operating Expenses	25.8	26.0	26.1			34.8	27.0	20.3	15.9
Operating Profit	4.6	4.0	3.6			2.6	9.6	3.5	3.0
All Other Expenses (net)	1.6	1.4	1.1			.9	1.2	1.1	1.0
Profit Before Taxes	3.0	2.6	2.5			1.7	8.5	2.3	2.1
RATIOS									
Current	2.5	2.6	2.5			2.7	2.8	2.0	2.7
	1.6	1.4	1.6			1.7	1.7	1.5	1.8
	1.0	1.0	1.1			.8	1.4	1.1	1.3
Quick	1.4	1.3	1.3			1.6	1.6	1.0	1.3
	.9	.7	.7			.9	.8	.7	.8
	.5	.4	.4			.1	.4	.4	.5
Sales/Receivables	24 15.0	23 16.0	28 12.9			9 39.3	9 39.7	33 10.9	32 11.3
	40 9.2	39 9.3	40 9.2			36 10.2	34 10.8	42 8.7	42 8.8
	52 7.0	54 6.7	52 7.0			68 5.4	48 7.6	62 5.9	52 7.1
Cost of Sales/Inventory	4 104.1	11 32.4	33 11.2			17 21.0	55 6.6	34 10.8	57 6.4
	42 8.6	52 7.1	63 5.8			76 4.8	82 4.5	62 5.9	67 5.4
	93 3.9	93 3.9	105 3.5			184 2.0	109 3.4	107 3.4	100 3.7
Cost of Sales/Payables	14 26.2	16 22.9	15 24.4			10 36.2	20 18.5	20 18.2	25 14.4
	25 14.5	28 12.9	28 13.0			48 7.6	46 8.0	25 14.4	39 9.4
	47 7.7	56 6.5	50 7.3			72 5.1	74 5.0	44 8.4	50 7.3
Sales/Working Capital	5.3	5.5	4.6			4.1	3.9	4.7	5.0
	12.7	11.4	10.9			7.4	10.5	10.9	7.2
	UND	-242.7	46.8			NM	41.1	27.5	16.0
EBIT/Interest	9.8	12.3	8.0			15.7	21.7	8.1	12.3
	(57) 3.1	(73) 3.0	(68) 3.5			(11) 3.3	7.7	5.1	(16) 4.7
	1.3	.5	1.0			-2.1	2.4	1.4	1.7
Net Profit + Depr., Dep., Amort./Cur. Mat. L/T/D	12.9	3.7	7.3						
	(12) 3.7	(26) 1.7	(19) 2.7						
	1.6	.6	1.0						
Fixed/Worth	.2	.2	.2			.1	.1	.2	.2
	.5	.5	.5			.3	.5	.5	.3
	1.9	2.0	1.6			-1.2	.9	1.4	.6
Debt/Worth	.8	.8	.9			.5	.8	1.0	.5
	1.8	2.3	1.7			1.4	1.2	1.8	1.1
	3.9	4.9	4.8			-10.6	3.5	4.4	3.2
% Profit Before Taxes/Tangible Net Worth	35.6	25.9	41.8				77.1	31.4	18.6
	(55) 11.7	(69) 8.3	(63) 11.3				36.1	9.6	6.1
	4.0	1.0	1.2				21.0	4.5	.7
% Profit Before Taxes/Total Assets	13.6	11.8	12.3			8.7	25.8	11.0	6.9
	4.1	2.4	3.7			5.1	14.1	5.2	3.6
	.5	-1.6	.1			-7.6	3.5	1.2	.5
Sales/Net Fixed Assets	40.6	54.6	49.9			58.3	93.8	47.9	51.1
	13.5	18.7	20.7			25.9	41.8	13.4	26.5
	6.7	7.3	7.1			11.4	7.4	5.2	7.3
Sales/Total Assets	3.7	3.3	3.2			3.6	3.3	2.7	3.2
	2.7	2.3	2.4			2.3	2.6	2.0	2.3
	1.6	1.8	1.7			1.2	1.7	1.6	2.0
% Depr., Dep., Amort./Sales	.6	.5	.5					.8	.4
	(59) 1.5	(63) 1.4	(62) 1.3					(16) 1.5	(17) .8
	3.7	3.4	2.6					2.4	2.4
% Officers', Directors', Owners' Comp/Sales	2.5	2.1	2.7						
	(26) 3.8	(34) 3.9	(32) 5.2						
	7.0	9.3	8.6						
Net Sales ($)	1535025M	2543021M	1938573M	3846M	14027M	46555M	77992M	335546M	1460607M
Total Assets ($)	724483M	1173283M	920490M	2083M	5132M	23841M	38456M	165996M	684982M

M = $ thousand   MM = $ million
See Pages 11 through 21 for Explanation of Ratios and Data

Current Data Sorted By Assets

Comparative Historical Data

Type of Statement		4/1/00-3/31/01 ALL	4/1/01-3/31/02 ALL
Unqualified		5	4
Reviewed		6	7
Compiled		4	4
Tax Returns		1	
Other		4	7

0-500M	500M-2MM	2-10MM	10-50MM	50-100MM	100-250MM		4/1/00-3/31/01 ALL	4/1/01-3/31/02 ALL
		1	6	2				
	1	2	1					
	2	10					5	4
		3					6	7
1		3					4	4
1		5	3				1	
	7 (4/1-9/30/04)		33 (10/1/04-3/31/05)				4	7
2	5	21	10	2		NUMBER OF STATEMENTS	20	22
%	%	%	%	%	%		%	%
						ASSETS		
		9.6	8.1		D	Cash & Equivalents	8.9	5.4
		25.9	28.0		A	Trade Receivables (net)	28.2	26.1
		31.6	28.5		T	Inventory	24.9	24.7
		.2	1.3		A	All Other Current	1.0	2.4
		67.4	65.9			Total Current	62.9	58.7
		23.3	24.7		N	Fixed Assets (net)	28.9	29.3
		4.1	1.9		O	Intangibles (net)	2.3	3.9
		5.2	7.5		T	All Other Non-Current	5.9	8.2
		100.0	100.0			Total	100.0	100.0
					A	**LIABILITIES**		
		13.4	11.3		V	Notes Payable-Short Term	13.4	9.5
		3.1	2.4		A	Cur. Mat.-L/T/D	2.3	3.8
		15.6	19.5		I	Trade Payables	13.6	14.3
		.1	.4		L	Income Taxes Payable	.8	.3
		7.6	5.6		A	All Other Current	8.2	6.1
		39.9	39.3		B	Total Current	38.3	34.0
		10.6	8.8		L	Long-Term Debt	16.2	17.6
		.3	.4		E	Deferred Taxes	1.7	.5
		2.5	8.1			All Other Non-Current	2.1	4.1
		46.6	43.5			Net Worth	41.6	43.7
		100.0	100.0			Total Liabilities & Net Worth	100.0	100.0
						INCOME DATA		
		100.0	100.0			Net Sales	100.0	100.0
		27.8	22.4			Gross Profit	23.6	23.3
		22.8	13.6			Operating Expenses	20.1	22.6
		5.0	8.9			Operating Profit	3.5	.7
		.7	1.1			All Other Expenses (net)	.1	1.1
		4.2	7.7			Profit Before Taxes	3.4	-.4
						RATIOS		
		2.5	3.0				3.1	2.3
		1.6	1.8			Current	1.8	1.6
		1.2	1.2				1.2	1.2
		1.4	2.1				1.5	1.4
		.9	.9			Quick	.9	.9
		.6	.5				.7	.6
		33 11.0	42 8.7				37 9.9	37 9.7
		48 7.5	48 7.6			Sales/Receivables	45 8.1	48 7.6
		53 6.9	55 6.6				52 7.0	60 6.1
		37 9.7	43 8.4				32 11.5	34 10.6
		66 5.5	67 5.4			Cost of Sales/Inventory	50 7.3	58 6.3
		96 3.8	80 4.6				78 4.7	77 4.7
		22 16.7	18 20.2				12 30.3	18 20.7
		38 9.5	38 9.6			Cost of Sales/Payables	20 18.3	33 11.0
		42 8.6	54 6.8				48 7.7	46 6.8
		5.8	4.8				4.2	5.9
		8.0	7.3			Sales/Working Capital	8.3	9.8
		18.2	23.0				29.7	21.0
		16.9					23.6	3.7
		5.2				EBIT/Interest	(19) 4.9	(20) 1.9
		1.7					2.0	-.6
						Net Profit + Depr., Dep., Amort./Cur. Mat. L /T/D		
		.2	.3				.2	.4
		.5	.6			Fixed/Worth	.5	.6
		.8	1.3				1.9	1.6
		.6	.7				.4	.6
		1.3	1.2			Debt/Worth	1.5	1.5
		2.9	5.4				4.8	2.9
		36.4					47.5	18.1
		(19) 15.9				% Profit Before Taxes/Tangible Net Worth	(19) 28.0	(20) 5.9
		11.4					15.0	-11.1
		15.5	14.4				22.3	7.2
		6.8	11.2			% Profit Before Taxes/Total Assets	10.1	2.7
		1.9	4.8				3.6	-3.5
		23.0	14.6				45.5	16.0
		11.8	10.7			Sales/Net Fixed Assets	6.3	7.8
		4.4	4.6				3.4	3.5
		2.9	2.5				3.1	2.5
		2.2	2.2			Sales/Total Assets	2.4	2.2
		1.4	1.5				1.6	1.3
		1.3					.4	.6
		(19) 1.8				% Depr., Dep., Amort./Sales	(13) 1.8	(20) 2.2
		3.5					3.7	3.4
		2.4						
		(10) 3.2				% Officers', Directors', Owners' Comp/Sales		
		5.0						
2251M	18373M	238772M	424493M	195359M		Net Sales ($)	946163M	809393M
425M	5830M	112802M	198429M	142155M		Total Assets ($)	561994M	443664M

© RMA 2005

M = $ thousand   MM = $ million
See Pages 11 through 21 for Explanation of Ratios and Data

Comparative Historical Data | **Current Data Sorted By Sales**

4/1/02-3/31/03 ALL	4/1/03-3/31/04 ALL	4/1/04-3/31/05 ALL	Type of Statement	0-1MM	1-3MM	3-5MM	5-10MM	10-25MM	25MM & OVER
7	8	12	Unqualified					4	7
16	7	13	Reviewed		1	1	5	6	1
1	10	5	Compiled		2	2	2		
5	1	1	Tax Returns	1		1	1		
9	12	9	Other			1		2	3
				7 (4/1-9/30/04)			33 (10/1/04-3/31/05)		
38	37	40	NUMBER OF STATEMENTS	1	3	5	8	12	11
%	%	%		%	%	%	%	%	%
			ASSETS						
10.0	6.5	8.4	Cash & Equivalents					8.2	7.4
27.4	30.3	27.9	Trade Receivables (net)					28.0	27.7
20.4	24.8	29.1	Inventory					37.4	31.1
1.7	2.1	.9	All Other Current					.4	1.4
59.4	63.6	66.4	Total Current					74.0	67.6
26.5	24.8	23.6	Fixed Assets (net)					19.9	24.9
5.5	3.4	3.5	Intangibles (net)					.7	2.2
8.6	8.2	6.5	All Other Non-Current					5.4	5.3
100.0	100.0	100.0	Total					100.0	100.0
			LIABILITIES						
8.6	11.1	15.8	Notes Payable-Short Term					13.0	10.7
3.3	4.9	5.9	Cur. Mat.-L/T/D					2.5	1.8
16.0	16.8	17.2	Trade Payables					17.2	18.5
.2	.3	.2	Income Taxes Payable					.0	.4
7.4	9.0	7.5	All Other Current					7.2	7.6
35.5	42.0	46.5	Total Current					40.0	39.1
18.9	17.5	9.2	Long-Term Debt					10.3	5.2
.5	.4	.4	Deferred Taxes					.0	.7
15.8	13.1	14.3	All Other Non-Current					2.3	8.6
29.4	27.0	29.6	Net Worth					47.4	46.4
100.0	100.0	100.0	Total Liabilities & Net Worth					100.0	100.0
			INCOME DATA						
100.0	100.0	100.0	Net Sales					100.0	100.0
27.6	26.4	28.8	Gross Profit					20.3	26.6
25.9	22.6	23.0	Operating Expenses					15.3	17.4
1.7	3.8	5.8	Operating Profit					5.0	9.2
1.3	.6	1.0	All Other Expenses (net)					.9	.5
.4	3.2	4.8	Profit Before Taxes					4.1	8.7
			RATIOS						
2.7	2.1	2.4	Current					2.6	2.7
1.5	1.5	1.5						2.1	1.8
1.2	1.2	1.2						1.4	1.2
2.0	1.3	1.4	Quick					1.8	1.5
1.0	.8	.9						.9	.8
.6	.6	.6						.6	.6
38 9.7	42 8.6	35 10.4	Sales/Receivables					33 11.0	39 9.5
49 7.5	51 7.2	48 7.6						43 8.5	49 7.5
54 6.8	60 6.1	54 6.7						51 7.1	58 6.3
25 14.5	33 11.2	29 12.4	Cost of Sales/Inventory					38 9.6	58 6.3
45 8.1	52 7.0	65 5.7						66 5.5	78 4.7
72 5.0	82 4.5	90 4.1						90 4.1	106 3.5
19 19.4	18 19.9	22 16.4	Cost of Sales/Payables					19 19.6	24 15.2
31 11.7	37 9.9	36 10.1						30 12.0	33 11.0
47 7.7	46 7.9	45 8.2						39 9.4	54 6.8
5.3	7.4	5.8	Sales/Working Capital					5.2	4.0
11.6	12.0	9.3						7.5	7.5
26.6	20.5	25.4						12.2	21.7
(31) 2.6	(33) 5.4	(38) 15.1	EBIT/Interest					14.6	
1.5	2.3	6.3						7.3	
−1.4	1.1	2.2						2.8	
(13) 1.9	(12) 9.5	(17) 5.0	Net Profit + Depr., Dep., Amort./Cur. Mat. L/T/D						
1.2	1.3	3.7							
−.3	.4	2.4							
.4	.4	.3	Fixed/Worth					.2	.3
.8	.8	.6						.4	.5
1.9	2.1	.8						.7	.9
.5	.8	.7	Debt/Worth					.6	.5
2.0	2.1	1.3						1.1	1.1
4.5	9.4	2.9						2.6	4.5
(32) 14.6	(30) 41.2	(35) 39.1	% Profit Before Taxes/Tangible Net Worth					23.9	(10) 44.1
3.1	15.5	20.6						20.0	31.3
−6.0	1.4	12.7						15.8	15.8
6.8	13.4	15.6	% Profit Before Taxes/Total Assets					15.1	20.5
1.5	4.2	9.2						10.5	12.2
−2.2	.3	3.5						4.1	4.8
19.3	19.0	22.0	Sales/Net Fixed Assets					31.4	15.1
9.3	9.5	11.0						11.4	11.0
3.4	5.5	4.8						7.3	4.1
2.9	2.5	2.9	Sales/Total Assets					3.3	2.6
1.9	2.1	2.3						2.4	2.4
1.2	1.6	1.5						1.9	1.5
(35) 1.4	(33) 1.6	(36) 1.2	% Depr., Dep., Amort./Sales					(11) 1.3	(10) .9
2.3	2.5	1.9						1.6	1.9
4.2	3.3	3.3						2.8	2.8
(16) 3.1	(10) 2.0	(15) 2.2	% Officers', Directors', Owners' Comp/Sales						
4.7	3.1	3.1							
6.6	10.7	8.2							
865802M	1038569M	879248M	Net Sales ($)	289M	5357M	19922M	62709M	182466M	608505M
482045M	515444M	459641M	Total Assets ($)	32M	3047M	10064M	39507M	82482M	324509M

M = $ thousand   MM = $ million
See Pages 11 through 21 for Explanation of Ratios and Data

Current Data Sorted By Assets　　　　　　　　　　　**Comparative Historical Data**

0-500M	500M-2MM	2-10MM	10-50MM	50-100MM	100-250MM	Type of Statement	4/1/00-3/31/01	4/1/01-3/31/02
						Unqualified	11	10
						Reviewed	3	9
						Compiled	10	7
						Tax Returns	4	3
						Other	12	15
	17 (4/1-9/30/04)		58 (10/1/04-3/31/05)					
4	13	35	15	5	3	NUMBER OF STATEMENTS	40 ALL	44 ALL
%	%	%	%	%	%	**ASSETS**	%	%
8.9	8.2	8.1				Cash & Equivalents	5.8	6.1
21.7	28.4	17.5				Trade Receivables (net)	19.6	20.7
33.8	31.4	33.6				Inventory	32.6	30.9
1.7	2.1	2.5				All Other Current	2.3	3.6
66.2	70.1	61.5				Total Current	60.4	61.3
29.4	26.0	29.9				Fixed Assets (net)	29.2	30.8
1.0	.7	1.1				Intangibles (net)	5.7	1.2
3.3	3.2	7.4				All Other Non-Current	4.7	6.7
100.0	100.0	100.0				Total	100.0	100.0
						LIABILITIES		
10.8	9.0	5.3				Notes Payable-Short Term	7.8	11.8
3.4	4.3	6.6				Cur. Mat.-L/T/D	6.2	3.3
23.7	26.8	16.9				Trade Payables	14.2	15.7
.0	.1	.7				Income Taxes Payable	.3	.1
8.8	11.7	13.1				All Other Current	7.3	9.0
46.8	51.9	42.7				Total Current	35.7	39.8
20.9	16.2	12.3				Long-Term Debt	22.4	21.3
.0	.6	1.2				Deferred Taxes	.6	.8
6.5	6.1	2.5				All Other Non-Current	3.5	2.0
25.8	25.2	41.3				Net Worth	37.7	36.1
100.0	100.0	100.0				Total Liabilities & Net Worth	100.0	100.0
						INCOME DATA		
100.0	100.0	100.0				Net Sales	100.0	100.0
36.5	27.1	29.2				Gross Profit	33.5	30.5
34.3	22.6	23.7				Operating Expenses	28.0	24.8
2.2	4.5	5.5				Operating Profit	5.5	5.6
2.0	1.1	.7				All Other Expenses (net)	.8	1.4
.2	3.5	4.8				Profit Before Taxes	4.7	4.3
						RATIOS		
1.9	2.8	3.0				Current	2.8	2.5
1.4	1.4	1.6					1.8	1.8
1.1	1.0	1.1					1.2	1.1
1.3	1.6	1.5				Quick	1.1	1.3
.8	.7	.5					.7 (43)	.8
.2	.3	.2					.4	.5
8　44.2	20　18.3	24　15.0				Sales/Receivables	16　23.4	16　23.4
37　9.8	32　11.3	39　9.4					33　10.9	34　10.9
51　7.2	45　8.1	55　6.7					54　6.8	55　6.6
19　19.4	21　17.1	47　7.7				Cost of Sales/Inventory	24　15.2	38　9.7
45　8.2	69　5.3	70　5.2					76　4.8	71　5.1
128　2.8	109　3.4	134　2.7					139　2.6	119　3.1
28　12.9	15　23.7	26　14.0				Cost of Sales/Payables	17　21.8	20　18.3
47　7.8	46　7.9	37　10.0					39　9.3	33　11.0
73　5.0	64　5.7	58　6.3					63　5.8	52　7.0
6.1	6.2	4.2				Sales/Working Capital	4.5	4.7
19.5	11.0	7.4					7.9	8.6
62.3	-999.8	41.0					27.3	57.4
3.6	14.1	24.7				EBIT/Interest	8.7	9.3
(11)　1.7	(32)　3.7	6.8					(36)　3.5	(41)　3.8
-4.5	1.4	3.0					1.7	1.7
						Net Profit + Depr., Dep., Amort./Cur. Mat. L./T/D		
.2	.3	.3				Fixed/Worth	.4	.4
1.6	.7	.5					.9	.8
5.5	2.6	1.4					2.6	1.6
1.0	.8	.6				Debt/Worth	.8	.9
4.6	2.5	1.0					1.9	1.9
14.2	5.3	4.8					5.2	4.3
55.3	57.8	36.5				% Profit Before Taxes/Tangible Net Worth	55.3	48.8
(12)　4.9	(28)　17.9	(14)　24.1					(36)　25.3	(41)　22.0
-19.9	7.8	14.1					14.0	9.6
9.0	12.8	15.9				% Profit Before Taxes/Total Assets	17.6	20.0
3.6	5.1	7.9					9.1	7.6
-9.5	1.7	5.8					3.6	1.1
37.6	33.6	14.1				Sales/Net Fixed Assets	20.7	15.1
9.8	10.6	6.3					8.8	7.5
5.5	6.5	3.7					5.0	4.8
3.3	3.8	2.2				Sales/Total Assets	3.4	2.6
2.2	2.6	1.7					2.0	2.1
1.6	1.9	1.3					1.6	1.6
.5	.6	1.5				% Depr., Dep., Amort./Sales	.7	1.1
(12)　2.4	(32)　2.0	(13)　2.4					(34)　1.6	(41)　2.3
5.2	2.8	3.5					2.6	3.3
		1.1				% Officers', Directors', Owners' Comp/Sales	1.6	1.6
	(15)　1.6						(14)　5.1	(11)　3.9
	7.0						7.2	5.6
3492M	35485M	444903M	607463M	647835M	1833078M	Net Sales ($)	1959415M	1680979M
640M	14023M	171418M	366407M	399471M	542956M	Total Assets ($)	984211M	967645M

M = $ thousand　　MM = $ million
See Pages 11 through 21 for Explanation of Ratios and Data

Comparative Historical Data   **Current Data Sorted By Sales**

			Type of Statement						
15	15	16	Unqualified			1	1	5	9
12	14	13	Reviewed		1	1	4	4	3
7	21	13	Compiled	2	3		2	6	
1	5	13	Tax Returns	2	3	1	1	3	1
18	29	20	Other		2	2	4	6	8
4/1/02-3/31/03 ALL	4/1/03-3/31/04 ALL	4/1/04-3/31/05 ALL		0-1MM	1-3MM	3-5MM	5-10MM	10-25MM	25MM & OVER
				17 (4/1-9/30/04)			58 (10/1/04-3/31/05)		
53	84	75	NUMBER OF STATEMENTS	4	9	5	12	24	21
%	%	%	**ASSETS**	%	%	%	%	%	%
9.1	7.6	8.8	Cash & Equivalents				12.1	5.7	9.6
20.4	20.5	24.6	Trade Receivables (net)				21.7	28.2	20.8
28.5	33.5	30.8	Inventory				38.9	29.7	29.7
5.0	5.5	2.0	All Other Current				1.4	2.8	1.6
63.0	67.1	66.3	Total Current				74.0	66.4	61.7
26.4	24.7	27.1	Fixed Assets (net)				21.9	29.0	29.0
3.4	1.9	1.4	Intangibles (net)				1.2	.4	2.4
7.2	6.3	5.3	All Other Non-Current				2.8	4.2	6.9
100.0	100.0	100.0	Total				100.0	100.0	100.0
			LIABILITIES						
9.6	11.4	8.9	Notes Payable-Short Term				5.2	10.0	4.9
2.9	3.5	4.2	Cur. Mat.-L/T/D				2.8	5.2	5.4
17.8	19.7	22.0	Trade Payables				20.7	29.9	17.3
.2	.2	.2	Income Taxes Payable				.0	.1	.5
12.6	11.5	10.6	All Other Current				6.1	12.2	11.1
43.2	46.2	45.9	Total Current				34.8	57.4	39.2
16.7	14.0	15.8	Long-Term Debt				11.0	19.1	13.9
.7	.5	.6	Deferred Taxes				.3	.8	1.2
4.3	4.8	5.4	All Other Non-Current				4.3	6.4	4.1
35.1	34.4	32.2	Net Worth				49.6	16.4	41.6
100.0	100.0	100.0	Total Liabilities & Net Worth				100.0	100.0	100.0
			INCOME DATA						
100.0	100.0	100.0	Net Sales				100.0	100.0	100.0
31.7	29.2	29.0	Gross Profit				28.2	26.3	26.6
25.7	25.9	24.9	Operating Expenses				24.0	20.9	21.9
6.0	3.3	4.1	Operating Profit				4.2	5.4	4.7
1.4	.7	1.1	All Other Expenses (net)				.8	1.4	.4
4.6	2.6	3.0	Profit Before Taxes				3.5	4.0	4.2
			RATIOS						
2.4	2.4	2.6	Current				3.9	2.4	2.9
1.7	1.5	1.6					2.5	1.2	1.7
1.0	1.1	1.1					1.4	1.0	1.3
1.2	1.1	1.5	Quick				1.7	1.4	1.5
.6	.6	.8					.8	.5	.8
.5	.3	.3					.5	.2	.4
13 27.2	8 44.1	20 18.5	Sales/Receivables			15 23.7	18 20.2	26 14.0
34 10.9	28 13.2	37 9.8				30 12.4	34 10.8	40 9.2
49 7.5	44 8.4	51 7.1				39 9.3	50 7.3	55 6.7
37 9.8	34 10.7	24 15.3	Cost of Sales/Inventory			69 5.3	13 27.6	43 8.5
61 6.0	72 5.1	69 5.3				98 3.7	68 5.4	69 5.3
115 3.2	134 2.7	110 3.3				114 3.2	88 4.2	115 3.2
24 15.0	25 14.5	19 19.6	Cost of Sales/Payables			15 25.1	19 19.4	23 15.8
41 8.8	39 9.4	37 10.0				31 11.9	49 7.4	35 10.5
64 5.7	59 6.1	61 5.9				71 5.2	63 5.8	51 7.2
4.5	5.4	5.4	Sales/Working Capital				3.6	7.6	4.3
9.8	10.6	9.7					6.1	25.7	7.4
136.1	59.8	59.4					12.7	-289.0	23.1
10.5	7.7	15.2	EBIT/Interest				23.4	10.0	22.9
(44) 3.6	(76) 3.0	(68) 3.7				(11) 4.2	(23) 3.1	(20) 6.0
1.4	.8	1.4					-1.6	1.5	3.3
4.6	7.3	5.3	Net Profit + Depr., Dep.,						
(15) 2.3	(21) 1.9	(17) 3.2	Amort./Cur. Mat. L/T/D						
1.0	.8	.7							
.3	.3	.3	Fixed/Worth				.1	.4	.3
.8	.8	.7					.4	1.1	.7
1.4	1.6	1.8					1.3	NM	1.4
.8	1.0	.8	Debt/Worth				.4	1.0	.7
2.2	2.1	2.0					.8	2.9	1.2
6.3	4.7	5.3					2.5	NM	4.2
49.2	31.9	44.2	% Profit Before Taxes/Tangible			59.0	60.5	38.6
(48) 27.7	(76) 13.2	(66) 17.9	Net Worth			(11) 13.7	(18) 23.6	(20) 24.6
10.7	2.5	5.2					4.3	9.2	13.4
13.9	12.5	12.4	% Profit Before Taxes/Total				26.8	13.9	14.8
8.0	4.4	6.9	Assets				6.0	5.5	8.8
1.7	.1	1.4					-.7	2.3	3.3
19.0	29.7	29.1	Sales/Net Fixed Assets				40.0	17.5	14.6
8.4	12.3	9.0					15.6	8.5	6.3
4.9	4.4	5.7					5.9	6.5	3.8
2.4	3.3	3.8	Sales/Total Assets				3.7	4.2	2.5
2.1	2.0	2.2					2.5	2.6	1.7
1.6	1.7	1.6					1.4	2.0	1.4
1.3	.6	.9	% Depr., Dep., Amort./Sales				.7	.9	1.3
(46) 2.7	(75) 1.7	(67) 2.0				(11) 1.9	(22) 2.1	(19) 2.4
3.6	3.1	3.0					2.7	2.9	3.1
2.1	1.3	1.6	% Officers', Directors',						
(13) 5.4	(23) 3.6	(27) 2.9	Owners' Comp/Sales						
11.8	6.6	7.0							
1875257M	2049345M	3572256M	Net Sales ($)	3262M	17119M	21684M	90531M	383883M	3055777M
1080627M	1205164M	1494915M	Total Assets ($)	1058M	7960M	10352M	46971M	164969M	1263605M

© RMA 2005

M = $ thousand   MM = $ million
See Pages 11 through 21 for Explanation of Ratios and Data

Current Data Sorted By Assets   Comparative Historical Data

Type of Statement

Type	0-500M	500M-2MM	2-10MM	10-50MM	50-100MM	100-250MM		12	11
Unqualified		1	4		1	3		12	11
Reviewed		4	9	2		1		14	7
Compiled	1	3		1	3			7	13
Tax Returns	3	4	2						2
Other	2	2	5	6				7	13

Current data periods: 8 (4/1-9/30/04)   49 (10/1/04-3/31/05)
Historical periods: 4/1/00-3/31/01 ALL ; 4/1/01-3/31/02 ALL

0-500M	500M-2MM	2-10MM	10-50MM	50-100MM	100-250MM		4/1/00-3/31/01 ALL 40	4/1/01-3/31/02 ALL 46
6	14	20	9	4	4	**NUMBER OF STATEMENTS**	40	46
%	%	%	%	%	%	**ASSETS**	%	%
	16.1	6.7				Cash & Equivalents	6.5	6.0
	29.6	29.8				Trade Receivables (net)	26.4	25.9
	44.4	41.6				Inventory	36.0	38.9
	.0	1.3				All Other Current	1.7	1.7
	90.1	79.4				Total Current	70.5	72.5
	5.4	14.4				Fixed Assets (net)	23.5	21.3
	2.0	.1				Intangibles (net)	1.3	1.3
	2.5	6.0				All Other Non-Current	4.7	5.0
	100.0	100.0				Total	100.0	100.0
						LIABILITIES		
	16.3	16.3				Notes Payable-Short Term	15.1	17.3
	1.9	1.8				Cur. Mat.-L/T/D	3.6	2.9
	30.4	22.4				Trade Payables	13.8	13.8
	.0	.2				Income Taxes Payable	.0	.0
	8.6	10.7				All Other Current	12.2	8.9
	57.2	51.5				Total Current	44.7	42.9
	3.1	5.3				Long-Term Debt	10.1	11.5
	.0	.0				Deferred Taxes	.3	.4
	4.1	1.2				All Other Non-Current	5.9	2.5
	35.6	42.0				Net Worth	39.0	42.6
	100.0	100.0				Total Liabilities & Net Worth	100.0	100.0
						INCOME DATA		
	100.0	100.0				Net Sales	100.0	100.0
	38.3	32.4				Gross Profit	26.9	28.6
	31.8	28.5				Operating Expenses	21.7	24.2
	6.5	4.0				Operating Profit	5.1	4.4
	.6	.0				All Other Expenses (net)	1.2	1.1
	5.9	3.9				Profit Before Taxes	3.9	3.3
						RATIOS		
	2.4	2.9					2.6	2.9
	1.8	1.9				Current	1.6	2.0
	1.0	1.2					1.2	1.3
	1.1	1.6					1.1	1.8
	.8	.8				Quick	.7	.9
	.5	.4					.5	.5
	33 / 11.1	37 / 9.9					31 / 11.6	33 / 11.1
	37 / 9.9	49 / 7.4				Sales/Receivables	47 / 7.7	42 / 8.7
	74 / 4.9	57 / 6.4					57 / 6.4	59 / 6.2
	75 / 4.9	56 / 6.6					65 / 5.6	57 / 6.4
	96 / 3.8	92 / 4.0				Cost of Sales/Inventory	86 / 4.2	93 / 3.9
	160 / 2.3	125 / 2.9					112 / 3.3	127 / 2.9
	5 / 67.1	18 / 20.6					17 / 21.3	16 / 22.4
	56 / 6.5	33 / 11.1				Cost of Sales/Payables	28 / 13.0	29 / 12.6
	85 / 4.3	47 / 7.8					42 / 8.8	40 / 9.2
	3.1	4.9					6.3	4.2
	6.8	7.3				Sales/Working Capital	8.9	7.2
	NM	23.3					14.2	14.1
		22.8					7.7	7.9
		(17) 4.4				EBIT/Interest	(37) 3.0	(40) 2.7
		2.6					1.1	.5
						Net Profit + Depr., Dep.,	9.5	5.2
						Amort./Cur. Mat. L /T/D	(10) 3.4	(12) 2.8
							.4	.6
	.0	.1					.2	.2
	.1	.3				Fixed/Worth	.5	.5
	.5	.5					1.0	1.1
	.7	.5					.9	.5
	2.0	1.3				Debt/Worth	2.0	1.4
	21.0	4.2					4.2	5.5
	138.1	39.0				% Profit Before Taxes/Tangible	43.3	29.2
	(12) 27.5	(19) 21.7				Net Worth	(38) 15.2	(45) 15.6
	3.8	10.4						-2.5
	27.9	14.6				% Profit Before Taxes/Total	17.6	13.2
	14.6	7.9				Assets	7.4	4.2
	2.5	1.6					.8	-1.7
	288.4	59.0					24.6	23.4
	66.8	23.4				Sales/Net Fixed Assets	15.4	12.2
	42.5	11.3					5.3	6.0
	2.9	2.9					2.6	2.8
	2.4	2.2				Sales/Total Assets	2.0	2.1
	1.7	1.8					1.7	1.6
		.5					.8	.7
		(19) 1.1				% Depr., Dep., Amort./Sales	(35) 1.4	(41) 1.4
		2.8					2.2	2.4
						% Officers', Directors',	1.5	1.6
						Owners' Comp/Sales	(13) 2.2	(17) 3.4
							6.2	5.5
5600M	33807M	252068M	307439M	437546M	947852M	Net Sales ($)	1360135M	1607115M
1685M	15259M	98544M	153145M	304815M	629291M	Total Assets ($)	806076M	932311M

M = $ thousand   MM = $ million
See Pages 11 through 21 for Explanation of Ratios and Data

Comparative Historical Data

Current Data Sorted By Sales

4/1/02-3/31/03 ALL	4/1/03-3/31/04 ALL	4/1/04-3/31/05 ALL	Type of Statement	0-1MM	1-3MM	3-5MM	5-10MM	10-25MM	25MM & OVER
20	20	11	Unqualified		1		2	1	7
15	18	15	Reviewed		2	2	4	4	3
8	8	4	Compiled	2	2				
3	6	9	Tax Returns	2	4	1	1	1	
15	18	18	Other	1	3		2	6	5
				8 (4/1-9/30/04)			49 (10/1/04-3/31/05)		
61	70	57	**NUMBER OF STATEMENTS**	5	12	4	9	12	15
%	%	%	**ASSETS**	%	%	%	%	%	%
9.0	5.9	8.6	Cash & Equivalents		8.9			4.4	6.8
28.1	26.6	27.2	Trade Receivables (net)		36.8			34.8	22.1
35.5	37.1	39.4	Inventory		42.0			35.6	33.7
3.9	4.2	2.2	All Other Current		.1			5.6	3.1
76.5	73.8	77.4	Total Current		87.9			80.4	65.6
16.5	17.7	14.2	Fixed Assets (net)		7.0			13.7	17.1
2.4	2.5	3.7	Intangibles (net)		2.9			.2	11.6
4.7	5.9	4.6	All Other Non-Current		2.3			5.7	5.7
100.0	100.0	100.0	Total		100.0			100.0	100.0
			LIABILITIES						
12.1	14.8	14.0	Notes Payable-Short Term		17.2			15.8	9.9
3.7	2.0	2.2	Cur. Mat.-L/T/D		.7			1.2	3.4
19.8	18.0	19.5	Trade Payables		27.2			25.9	11.8
.1	.1	.1	Income Taxes Payable		.0			.1	.2
9.9	11.6	8.7	All Other Current		6.2			10.3	7.9
45.7	46.5	44.5	Total Current		51.3			53.2	33.2
10.8	8.5	9.8	Long-Term Debt		4.8			5.1	12.2
.2	.3	.6	Deferred Taxes		.0			.2	2.0
2.6	5.1	4.3	All Other Non-Current		4.7			1.7	3.3
40.8	39.6	40.7	Net Worth		39.2			39.7	49.3
100.0	100.0	100.0	Total Liabilities & Net Worth		100.0			100.0	100.0
			INCOME DATA						
100.0	100.0	100.0	Net Sales		100.0			100.0	100.0
29.8	29.5	33.8	Gross Profit		40.0			31.0	23.3
24.5	25.9	28.2	Operating Expenses		30.3			27.4	17.4
5.4	3.6	5.6	Operating Profit		9.7			3.6	5.9
.8	.7	.5	All Other Expenses (net)		.7			–.3	1.2
4.6	2.9	5.1	Profit Before Taxes		9.0			3.9	4.7
			RATIOS						
2.6	2.7	2.9	Current		2.9			3.5	2.8
1.8	1.6	2.0			1.9			1.8	1.9
1.3	1.2	1.2			1.1			1.2	1.3
1.5	1.4	1.5	Quick		1.9			1.8	1.4
.8	.8	.8			.8			.9	.7
.5	.4	.5			.5			.5	.5
25 14.7	26 14.3	33 11.2	Sales/Receivables		33 11.0			45 8.1	26 14.1
42 8.7	41 9.0	45 8.2			43 8.5			56 6.5	42 8.7
59 6.2	53 6.9	57 6.4			74 4.9			63 5.8	50 7.3
41 8.8	49 7.5	61 6.0	Cost of Sales/Inventory		73 5.0			59 6.2	49 7.5
75 4.9	83 4.4	94 3.9			81 4.5			95 3.8	89 4.1
113 3.2	113 3.2	125 2.9			130 2.8			107 3.4	116 3.2
20 17.9	15 24.1	18 20.3	Cost of Sales/Payables		25 14.7			29 12.7	17 22.0
31 11.9	32 11.4	30 12.0			40 9.0			40 9.0	24 15.3
53 6.9	51 7.2	46 8.0			84 4.4			47 7.8	33 11.1
4.3	4.9	3.7	Sales/Working Capital		3.9			3.1	3.8
8.0	8.5	6.4			6.8			7.3	6.4
15.6	18.7	21.2			NM			23.3	16.9
8.1	12.4	17.9	EBIT/Interest						11.4
(51) 3.9	(64) 4.4	(46) 5.0						(14) 4.4	4.4
2.0	1.4	2.2							1.8
11.0	11.1	8.4	Net Profit + Depr., Dep., Amort./Cur. Mat. L/T/D						
(20) 4.0	(21) 2.3	(13) 2.0							
1.4	1.2	1.3							
.1	.1	.1	Fixed/Worth		.0			.1	.2
.4	.4	.3			.1			.4	.2
.7	.8	.5			.6			.5	1.2
.8	.7	.5	Debt/Worth		.6			.6	.5
1.9	1.5	1.5			2.0			1.2	1.5
3.3	3.3	4.6			4.3			4.2	3.1
48.4	41.8	55.8	% Profit Before Taxes/Tangible Net Worth		100.4			52.7	39.5
(58) 22.5	(63) 17.6	(51) 23.7			(10) 15.2			(11) 28.4	(13) 17.7
6.5	4.5	9.1			7.0			5.7	3.2
14.1	13.6	19.3	% Profit Before Taxes/Total Assets		37.3			18.5	18.8
7.0	6.0	7.5			11.5			9.4	6.1
2.3	.5	2.9			3.0			.8	3.0
41.1	44.6	62.1	Sales/Net Fixed Assets		334.1			60.7	32.8
17.3	17.1	25.3			63.1			19.7	10.4
9.4	8.9	9.2			31.7			8.3	6.8
3.1	3.2	2.8	Sales/Total Assets		3.5			2.8	2.5
2.3	2.4	2.2			2.6			2.0	1.9
1.8	1.8	1.7			1.9			1.5	1.3
.8	.8	.6	% Depr., Dep., Amort./Sales					.9	.9
(52) 1.3	(56) 1.5	(47) 1.4						(11) 1.4	1.4
1.7	2.4	2.1						2.8	3.3
2.4	2.2	3.0	% Officers', Directors', Owners' Comp/Sales						
(21) 4.0	(30) 2.9	(20) 4.0							
8.9	5.6	7.0							
4509940M	3452805M	1984312M	Net Sales ($)	2877M	24912M	15749M	71338M	198827M	1670609M
1215845M	1815821M	1202739M	Total Assets ($)	2115M	10459M	6642M	35300M	99228M	1048995M

M = $ thousand   MM = $ million
See Pages 11 through 21 for Explanation of Ratios and Data

Current Data Sorted By Assets | Comparative Historical Data

0-500M	500M-2MM	2-10MM	10-50MM	50-100MM	100-250MM		4/1/00-3/31/01 ALL	4/1/01-3/31/02 ALL
						Type of Statement		
		1	3			Unqualified	1	5
	7	8	1	1		Reviewed	7	12
6	4	2				Compiled	20	13
3	4	1				Tax Returns	5	5
2	4	7	2			Other	12	15
12 (4/1-9/30/04)			44 (10/1/04-3/31/05)					
11	19	19	6	1		**NUMBER OF STATEMENTS**	45	50
%	%	%	%	%	%	**ASSETS**	%	%
12.5	4.2	15.9			DATA NOT AVAILABLE	Cash & Equivalents	11.1	7.9
29.7	26.7	24.7				Trade Receivables (net)	26.9	25.5
20.6	34.2	34.7				Inventory	29.2	35.6
1.8	.7	2.7				All Other Current	2.1	1.1
64.7	65.9	78.0				Total Current	69.3	70.1
23.5	21.0	12.5				Fixed Assets (net)	22.5	22.1
7.0	3.8	4.3				Intangibles (net)	3.4	2.2
4.8	9.3	5.1				All Other Non-Current	4.8	5.6
100.0	100.0	100.0				Total	100.0	100.0
						LIABILITIES		
16.6	19.6	15.1				Notes Payable-Short Term	10.6	15.0
4.9	3.1	1.5				Cur. Mat.-L/T/D	3.7	4.4
14.6	16.3	19.3				Trade Payables	12.5	14.1
.0	.1	.0				Income Taxes Payable	.2	.1
19.0	7.1	4.1				All Other Current	14.0	17.0
55.0	46.2	40.0				Total Current	41.1	50.7
42.2	14.0	8.7				Long-Term Debt	15.5	16.2
.0	.3	.0				Deferred Taxes	.1	.0
38.6	4.8	11.6				All Other Non-Current	3.5	4.5
-35.9	34.7	39.7				Net Worth	39.8	28.6
100.0	100.0	100.0				Total Liabilities & Net Worth	100.0	100.0
						INCOME DATA		
100.0	100.0	100.0				Net Sales	100.0	100.0
50.3	35.9	29.7				Gross Profit	36.2	36.8
50.9	33.3	23.1				Operating Expenses	31.1	32.8
-.6	2.6	6.7				Operating Profit	5.1	4.0
-.2	1.3	1.0				All Other Expenses (net)	.6	1.1
-.4	1.3	5.7				Profit Before Taxes	4.5	2.9
						RATIOS		
2.2	2.1	4.5					3.6	2.8
1.0	1.7	1.8				Current	2.1	1.5
.7	1.0	1.3					1.5	1.1
1.2	1.2	2.1					2.3	1.3
.6	.9	1.0				Quick	1.2	.7
.4	.4	.5					.6	.5
15 24.1	22 16.7	25 14.4					23 16.0	23 15.7
33 11.2	34 10.6	36 10.0				Sales/Receivables	33 11.2	35 10.3
49 7.5	51 7.2	50 7.3					53 6.9	50 7.2
5 74.5	29 12.4	54 6.8					30 12.1	52 7.1
48 7.6	87 4.2	80 4.6				Cost of Sales/Inventory	62 5.9	89 4.1
69 5.3	116 3.2	98 3.7					94 3.9	125 2.9
8 43.7	17 21.1	25 14.4					6 56.8	10 37.0
32 11.4	26 14.2	36 10.2				Cost of Sales/Payables	21 17.1	22 16.4
63 5.8	45 8.1	51 7.2					38 9.5	48 7.6
12.6	6.7	4.4					4.5	4.9
-224.6	11.7	6.5				Sales/Working Capital	8.1	9.8
-20.7	77.6	22.0					14.9	101.5
	12.1	108.7					11.1	7.3
	2.5	(18) 6.9				EBIT/Interest	(41) 3.1	(45) 2.6
	.9	2.4					1.3	.2
							4.0	
						Net Profit + Depr., Dep., Amort./Cur. Mat. L /T/D	(10) 2.6	
							1.7	
.2	.3	.0					.2	.2
-2.0	.4	.4				Fixed/Worth	.4	.6
-.1	1.7	.9					1.2	2.4
1.2	.8	.6					.4	.6
-7.4	1.2	1.3				Debt/Worth	1.2	1.8
-1.9	5.4	4.2					2.8	18.5
	26.4	66.0					40.7	35.4
	(16) 9.7	(17) 16.2				% Profit Before Taxes/Tangible Net Worth	(38) 15.7	(42) 13.8
	1.0	5.7					3.8	-1.9
18.9	10.0	20.8					21.1	15.7
6.3	4.4	7.9				% Profit Before Taxes/Total Assets	5.8	5.6
-7.3	-.3	2.7					.7	-4.9
33.9	41.9	66.9					30.3	26.3
15.7	19.2	40.2				Sales/Net Fixed Assets	18.3	16.7
9.8	7.7	11.0					7.7	8.0
5.4	3.5	3.3					3.3	3.3
4.2	2.8	2.4				Sales/Total Assets	2.4	2.4
2.7	1.7	1.6					2.0	1.7
	.6	.5					.7	.9
	(17) 1.3	(18) .9				% Depr., Dep., Amort./Sales	(43) 1.3	(46) 1.2
	2.7	2.2					2.3	2.4
	3.0						3.8	2.8
	(12) 5.3					% Officers', Directors', Owners' Comp/Sales	(25) 6.6	(27) 5.3
	8.4						10.9	12.0
11279M	64492M	214290M	245993M	105181M		Net Sales ($)	948266M	587542M
2917M	25013M	76382M	126859M	68375M		Total Assets ($)	412737M	317340M

M = $ thousand MM = $ million

See Pages 11 through 21 for Explanation of Ratios and Data

Comparative Historical Data / Current Data Sorted By Sales

			Type of Statement						
5	5	4	Unqualified		1	6	1 5	2	3 3
12	14	17	Reviewed		6	1	5	1	3
11	17	12	Compiled	3	3	1	2	1	
6	9	8	Tax Returns	2	1	1	2	2	
19	20	15	Other		6	2	3	2	2
4/1/02- 3/31/03	4/1/03- 3/31/04	4/1/04- 3/31/05			12 (4/1-9/30/04)		44 (10/1/04-3/31/05)		
ALL	ALL	ALL		0-1MM	1-3MM	3-5MM	5-10MM	10-25MM	25MM & OVER
53	65	56	**NUMBER OF STATEMENTS**	5	16	10	12	5	8
%	%	%		%	%	%	%	%	%
			ASSETS						
6.9	5.4	10.4	Cash & Equivalents		6.8	9.9	11.8		
25.5	25.5	26.1	Trade Receivables (net)		24.9	19.7	31.0		
32.3	31.8	31.5	Inventory		33.2	32.9	33.9		
3.3	2.3	1.6	All Other Current		1.5	.2	3.7		
68.0	65.0	69.6	Total Current		66.4	62.8	80.5		
21.9	24.8	19.0	Fixed Assets (net)		20.4	23.0	11.0		
3.7	2.5	5.0	Intangibles (net)		6.3	4.2	2.6		
6.3	7.6	6.4	All Other Non-Current		6.9	10.0	5.9		
100.0	100.0	100.0	Total		100.0	100.0	100.0		
			LIABILITIES						
18.4	11.8	15.8	Notes Payable-Short Term		22.6	14.0	20.3		
4.2	3.9	2.8	Cur. Mat.-L/T/D		2.6	3.3	.7		
14.3	14.5	16.1	Trade Payables		17.0	13.2	18.4		
.0	.4	.2	Income Taxes Payable		.0	.0	.1		
13.8	9.9	8.6	All Other Current		9.5	8.4	4.0		
50.7	40.6	43.4	Total Current		51.8	38.9	43.5		
11.9	13.6	18.0	Long-Term Debt		34.7	14.9	5.4		
.1	.2	.1	Deferred Taxes		.0	.4	.2		
4.1	6.0	13.5	All Other Non-Current		21.8	2.6	12.1		
33.2	39.7	25.0	Net Worth		-8.3	43.2	39.0		
100.0	100.0	100.0	Total Liabilities & Net Worth		100.0	100.0	100.0		
			INCOME DATA						
100.0	100.0	100.0	Net Sales		100.0	100.0	100.0		
36.3	37.0	35.8	Gross Profit		43.9	35.0	31.5		
33.3	33.9	31.9	Operating Expenses		41.5	31.0	26.7		
3.0	3.0	3.9	Operating Profit		2.4	4.0	4.8		
.6	.0	.8	All Other Expenses (net)		1.1	1.3	1.0		
2.4	3.1	3.1	Profit Before Taxes		1.3	2.6	3.8		
			RATIOS						
2.6	2.6	3.0	Current		2.1	2.7	4.1		
1.7	1.8	1.7			1.1	1.7	1.7		
1.1	1.1	1.1			.9	1.3	1.3		
1.2	1.3	1.8	Quick		1.1	1.8	1.9		
.7	.8	.9			.6	.5	1.1		
.5	.5	.4			.4	.3	.5		
22 16.7	22 16.9	22 16.6	Sales/Receivables		21 17.6	18 20.5	27 13.7		
36 10.0	33 11.1	35 10.4			26 14.3	34 10.8	45 8.2		
48 7.6	50 7.2	49 7.5			41 8.9	52 7.0	51 7.2		
45 8.2	51 7.2	44 8.4	Cost of Sales/Inventory		44 8.2	45 8.2	52 7.0		
70 5.2	77 4.7	70 5.2			92 4.0	75 4.9	80 4.5		
108 3.4	105 3.5	113 3.2			115 3.2	151 2.4	91 4.0		
16 23.2	16 22.2	15 25.1	Cost of Sales/Payables		18 19.8	17 21.6	20 18.0		
26 13.8	27 13.3	32 11.3			33 10.9	31 11.7	34 10.6		
47 7.8	49 7.5	45 8.1			84 4.4	48 7.7	47 7.8		
6.3	5.7	5.0	Sales/Working Capital		8.2	5.4	4.5		
11.3	10.0	10.5			56.0	7.7	9.5		
146.8	40.0	56.9			-92.7	36.7	19.4		
8.7	14.1	14.4	EBIT/Interest		16.0	9.2	56.7		
(51) 3.0	(60) 4.1	(50) 4.8		(14) 3.8	2.7	(11) 4.2			
.6	1.4	1.4			-.3	1.1	-2.2		
5.0	7.4	7.3	Net Profit + Depr., Dep., Amort./Cur. Mat. L/T/D						
(12) 2.2	(18) 3.1	(12) 2.0							
.1	1.7	.8							
.3	.3	.2	Fixed/Worth		.4	.2	.0		
.6	.5	.5			2.7	.5	.4		
1.4	1.4	3.6			-.2	1.5	.8		
.7	.7	.7	Debt/Worth		.9	.7	.7		
1.5	1.3	1.4			6.4	1.2	1.5		
3.7	3.1	11.4			-2.6	4.2	3.6		
26.2	41.4	30.4	% Profit Before Taxes/Tangible Net Worth				83.9		
(43) 12.2	(59) 13.3	(43) 11.8					(11) 11.1		
-3.6	2.6	3.6					3.3		
11.0	13.8	15.7	% Profit Before Taxes/Total Assets		16.4	8.5	24.2		
6.0	5.5	6.8			3.5	5.4	6.3		
-1.0	.9	.4			-7.0	.1	-2.5		
25.3	27.7	43.9	Sales/Net Fixed Assets		63.8	29.2	147.4		
14.9	12.5	19.2			18.4	15.4	41.0		
7.9	7.5	8.7			8.2	3.5	14.0		
3.5	3.2	3.4	Sales/Total Assets		4.3	2.9	3.3		
2.4	2.6	2.6			3.0	2.2	2.5		
1.9	1.8	1.8			1.7	1.6	2.1		
1.0	1.0	.6	% Depr., Dep., Amort./Sales		.8	.8	.4		
(49) 1.7	(57) 1.5	(50) 1.2		(14) 1.9	1.7	(10) .9			
2.9	2.6	2.3			3.2	3.3	1.3		
3.8	3.2	2.6	% Officers', Directors', Owners' Comp/Sales						
(29) 7.2	(36) 6.4	(27) 5.0							
12.1	13.7	9.8							
636220M	583310M	641235M	Net Sales ($)	2216M	32370M	38036M	89116M	81875M	397622M
348149M	275592M	299546M	Total Assets ($)	731M	15625M	20043M	38580M	24914M	199653M

M = $ thousand   MM = $ million
See Pages 11 through 21 for Explanation of Ratios and Data

Current Data Sorted By Assets   **Comparative Historical Data**

	0-500M	500M-2MM	2-10MM	10-50MM	50-100MM	100-250MM	Type of Statement	4/1/00-3/31/01 ALL	4/1/01-3/31/02 ALL
		3	10	14	5	10	Unqualified	32	20
		8	20	3	1		Reviewed	28	20
	5	13	11	2	1		Compiled	40	27
	2	8	1				Tax Returns	4	6
	7	10	16	11	2	2	Other	29	39
	45 (4/1-9/30/04)			120 (10/1/04-3/31/05)					
Number of Statements	14	42	58	30	9	12		133	112
ASSETS	%	%	%	%	%	%		%	%
Cash & Equivalents	13.4	10.6	6.0	5.6		7.1		5.8	5.8
Trade Receivables (net)	28.1	28.2	24.2	24.5		19.2		25.9	24.3
Inventory	25.5	23.8	32.6	30.6		26.6		30.3	29.6
All Other Current	3.2	4.4	2.8	1.0		2.9		2.2	3.7
Total Current	70.2	67.0	65.6	61.8		55.8		64.2	63.4
Fixed Assets (net)	26.2	23.1	24.5	27.0		28.4		26.8	27.2
Intangibles (net)	.7	2.8	3.3	5.8		9.3		4.4	3.1
All Other Non-Current	3.0	7.1	6.5	5.5		6.5		4.6	6.3
Total	100.0	100.0	100.0	100.0		100.0		100.0	100.0
LIABILITIES									
Notes Payable-Short Term	21.6	10.8	14.8	14.0		4.6		12.5	13.8
Cur. Mat.-L/T/D	6.1	3.7	3.0	4.2		2.9		5.1	5.2
Trade Payables	17.4	16.4	15.4	13.4		12.9		14.7	14.0
Income Taxes Payable	.2	.3	.8	.4		1.5		.4	.2
All Other Current	13.6	18.8	7.6	7.0		8.8		9.8	6.5
Total Current	58.9	49.9	41.6	39.1		30.7		42.4	39.8
Long-Term Debt	34.8	16.3	12.3	13.1		24.3		16.4	14.6
Deferred Taxes	.0	.1	.4	.2		3.4		.4	.6
All Other Non-Current	27.9	6.3	8.2	4.0		7.0		8.3	3.2
Net Worth	-21.7	27.4	37.5	43.6		34.6		32.6	41.9
Total Liabilities & Net Worth	100.0	100.0	100.0	100.0		100.0		100.0	100.0
INCOME DATA									
Net Sales	100.0	100.0	100.0	100.0		100.0		100.0	100.0
Gross Profit	45.7	39.3	26.3	27.3		21.3		27.4	31.3
Operating Expenses	44.0	34.8	23.7	22.6		13.8		23.7	27.8
Operating Profit	1.6	4.6	2.6	4.6		7.5		3.7	3.5
All Other Expenses (net)	2.8	1.2	.8	1.0		1.3		1.4	1.0
Profit Before Taxes	-1.1	3.4	1.8	3.6		6.3		2.3	2.5
RATIOS									
Current	2.3	3.7	2.5	2.3		2.9		2.6	2.7
	1.5	1.9	1.5	1.6		2.0		1.8	1.7
	.9	1.2	1.2	1.1		1.0		1.2	1.1
Quick	1.2	1.8	1.2	1.2		1.2		1.3	1.3
	.8	.9	.7	.8		.8		.8	.8
	.7	.6	.5	.4		.3		.6	.4
Sales/Receivables	23 15.8	27 13.4	33 11.2	37 9.9		36 10.2		30 12.0	30 12.4
	32 11.4	35 10.3	40 9.0	50 7.4		44 8.3		41 9.0	41 8.8
	35 10.4	44 8.4	53 6.9	60 6.0		50 7.4		52 7.0	53 6.9
Cost of Sales/Inventory	0 UND	13 27.5	39 9.3	50 7.2		30 12.3		38 9.6	31 11.8
	41 9.0	40 9.0	65 5.6	76 4.8		69 5.3		65 5.7	71 5.1
	71 5.2	91 4.0	112 3.3	110 3.3		108 3.4		106 3.4	118 3.1
Cost of Sales/Payables	7 51.0	15 24.4	21 17.8	21 17.2		17 21.6		16 23.0	14 25.5
	27 13.4	27 13.4	29 12.4	33 11.1		32 11.5		28 13.1	26 14.2
	55 6.6	44 8.2	52 7.0	44 8.2		49 7.5		43 8.5	53 6.9
Sales/Working Capital	8.7	5.4	5.1	4.3		3.7		5.3	4.8
	14.3	9.7	8.5	8.5		6.5		8.8	8.4
	-33.0	31.5	23.0	26.7		NM		28.2	29.2
EBIT/Interest	(12) 4.2	5.7	9.3	9.7		21.1		(123) 5.9	(99) 6.3
	.4	(34) 2.0	(50) 3.5	(29) 5.7		3.7		2.1	2.2
	-1.8	1.0	1.0	1.2		2.9		1.0	.1
Net Profit + Depr., Dep., Amort./Cur. Mat. L/T/D			(17) 4.6					(38) 4.5	(31) 6.5
			3.0					1.8	1.3
			1.4					.8	.4
Fixed/Worth	.2	.3	.2	.3		.4		.3	.2
	2.1	.6	.6	.7		1.0		.8	.6
	-.8	1.4	2.2	1.4		NM		2.6	1.7
Debt/Worth	1.0	.6	.7	.9		1.1		.9	.6
	4.3	2.0	1.8	1.5		1.9		2.0	1.4
	-5.8	4.9	4.6	2.3		NM		6.2	4.6
% Profit Before Taxes/Tangible Net Worth	(10) 41.9	60.8	33.7	30.8				(113) 34.7	(102) 32.9
	26.8	(36) 12.8	(50) 13.1	(28) 13.2				16.1	10.7
	-41.3	.7	2.6	.4				.8	-.7
% Profit Before Taxes/Total Assets	15.9	15.4	13.1	11.7		12.9		13.0	13.0
	.0	4.2	4.9	5.6		6.5		4.5	2.9
	-13.6	.0	-.9	.7		4.5		.0	-2.4
Sales/Net Fixed Assets	67.8	31.3	47.6	28.8		14.0		27.0	24.5
	14.3	15.5	11.6	9.1		8.2		9.7	9.0
	6.2	7.7	4.3	4.8		4.2		4.7	4.3
Sales/Total Assets	4.8	3.6	2.9	2.5		2.2		3.0	2.9
	2.8	2.8	2.1	2.0		1.7		2.2	2.1
	2.3	2.2	1.4	1.3		1.3		1.5	1.4
% Depr., Dep., Amort./Sales	(11) .9	.8	.6	.9				(114) .7	(94) .6
	2.5	(35) 1.5	(49) 1.4	(26) 2.3				1.8	1.6
	8.5	3.2	4.4	3.3				3.9	3.4
% Officers', Directors', Owners' Comp/Sales		(26) 2.2	(19) 1.9					(52) 2.3	(45) 1.8
		5.4	5.1					4.5	3.2
		11.4	7.3					6.9	6.2
Net Sales ($)	11650M	141662M	615580M	1255831M	1585490M	3585304M		4577547M	2153511M
Total Assets ($)	3458M	49955M	283478M	658168M	683426M	1936496M		2526185M	1281000M

Comparative Historical Data | Current Data Sorted By Sales

Type of Statement									
							4	4	7	27

	4/1/02-3/31/03 ALL	4/1/03-3/31/04 ALL	4/1/04-3/31/05 ALL	0-1MM	1-3MM	3-5MM	5-10MM	10-25MM	25MM & OVER
Type of Statement				45 (4/1-9/30/04)			120 (10/1/04-3/31/05)		
Unqualified	43	52	42			4	4	7	27
Reviewed	38	39	32	1	2	7	11	8	3
Compiled	19	54	32	4	12	6	5	3	2
Tax Returns	12	13	11	1	5	2	5		
Other	43	48	48	4	8	5	11	6	14
NUMBER OF STATEMENTS	155	206	165	10	27	24	34	24	46
ASSETS	%	%	%	%	%	%	%	%	%
Cash & Equivalents	7.4	8.0	7.8	14.7	10.0	7.3	8.5	7.2	5.0
Trade Receivables (net)	23.7	24.6	25.2	18.8	26.0	30.7	24.1	23.6	24.7
Inventory	32.5	28.2	28.4	24.7	21.7	27.0	30.8	31.1	30.6
All Other Current	4.6	4.5	2.9	3.7	6.4	2.8	1.4	3.0	1.9
Total Current	68.2	65.2	64.2	62.0	64.2	67.9	64.7	64.9	62.1
Fixed Assets (net)	20.6	23.7	25.1	34.2	22.5	26.2	24.8	23.7	24.9
Intangibles (net)	4.4	5.2	4.2	.4	4.8	.6	4.1	5.7	5.8
All Other Non-Current	6.8	6.0	6.5	3.5	8.5	5.3	6.4	5.7	7.2
Total	100.0	100.0	100.0	100.0	100.0	100.0	100.0	100.0	100.0
LIABILITIES									
Notes Payable-Short Term	11.7	11.0	13.4	9.1	14.4	14.4	11.4	16.6	13.1
Cur. Mat.-L/T/D	4.0	3.9	3.6	6.0	4.7	3.7	2.5	4.0	3.0
Trade Payables	15.3	14.8	15.3	10.7	16.5	15.1	16.5	14.2	15.5
Income Taxes Payable	.3	.3	.6	.1	.5	.3	.6	1.0	.7
All Other Current	12.9	12.6	10.9	17.1	25.2	9.7	5.4	6.9	7.9
Total Current	44.2	42.6	43.8	43.0	61.2	43.2	36.4	42.6	40.2
Long-Term Debt	14.8	18.0	16.2	41.8	22.5	10.4	13.7	11.6	14.2
Deferred Taxes	.4	.6	.5	.1	.1	.2	.3	.4	1.1
All Other Non-Current	6.5	6.9	8.7	3.9	20.5	5.1	10.3	3.7	6.2
Net Worth	34.2	32.0	30.8	11.1	-4.3	41.1	39.3	41.7	38.2
Total Liabilities & Net Worth	100.0	100.0	100.0	100.0	100.0	100.0	100.0	100.0	100.0
INCOME DATA									
Net Sales	100.0	100.0	100.0	100.0	100.0	100.0	100.0	100.0	100.0
Gross Profit	26.1	31.1	30.8	49.9	43.6	30.6	27.0	29.1	23.0
Operating Expenses	24.7	27.3	26.9	43.6	42.3	27.5	22.7	24.5	18.1
Operating Profit	3.4	3.7	4.0	6.3	1.3	3.1	4.3	4.6	4.9
All Other Expenses (net)	1.4	1.3	1.2	3.1	2.0	.8	.6	.7	1.3
Profit Before Taxes	2.0	2.5	2.8	3.3	-.7	2.3	3.7	3.8	3.6
RATIOS									
Current	2.8	2.8	2.5	3.7	2.8	2.1	2.5	2.7	2.4
	1.7	1.8	1.7	1.5	1.9	1.5	1.8	1.5	1.7
	1.1	1.2	1.2	.9	1.0	1.1	1.4	1.0	1.1
Quick	1.3	1.3	1.3	1.4	1.6	1.4	1.6	1.4	1.2
	.8	.8	.8	.8	.9	.8	.8	.6	.8
	.4	.5	.5	.7	.4	.5	.6	.4	.4
Sales/Receivables	21 17.6	26 14.2	30 12.2	26 13.8	29 12.8	34 10.7	27 13.3	34 10.7	32 11.3
	37 9.9	40 9.1	39 9.2	34 10.8	34 10.8	39 9.3	40 9.1	40 9.2	43 8.4
	53 6.9	58 6.3	54 6.8	46 8.0	45 8.1	58 6.3	53 6.9	59 6.2	55 6.7
Cost of Sales/Inventory	35 10.6	36 10.2	29 12.6	0 UND	7 50.7	20 17.9	34 10.7	46 8.0	45 8.1
	70 5.2	63 5.8	61 6.0	58 6.3	39 9.4	61 5.9	63 5.8	71 5.2	68 5.3
	108 3.4	104 3.5	99 3.7	213 1.7	102 3.6	98 3.7	102 3.6	113 3.2	87 4.2
Cost of Sales/Payables	14 26.4	19 19.6	18 20.7	0 UND	15 25.0	14 26.8	20 18.6	23 15.6	21 17.4
	27 13.5	30 12.0	29 12.4	21 17.3	26 13.8	31 11.8	28 12.9	31 11.9	31 11.7
	48 7.6	49 7.5	48 7.6	68 5.3	53 6.9	51 7.2	54 6.8	52 7.0	41 8.9
Sales/Working Capital	4.5	4.5	5.2	3.3	4.5	6.4	4.7	5.3	5.2
	9.3	8.8	9.3	11.5	10.3	9.7	8.5	9.6	9.3
	41.5	29.1	28.5	-33.0	999.8	44.4	13.2	NM	45.6
EBIT/Interest	6.8	8.1	8.5		5.0	5.8	9.4	10.7	9.2
	(133) 2.7	(184) 2.6	(145) 3.4	(25) 1.5	(18) 2.1	(31) 4.2	(20) 4.1	(44) 4.2	
	1.0	1.0	1.0		-2.3	.8	1.1	1.6	1.8
Net Profit + Depr., Dep., Amort./Cur. Mat. L/T/D	5.9	5.5	4.9						9.4
	(37) 2.1	(53) 1.3	(35) 3.0					(13)	2.8
	.8	.6	1.4						1.5
Fixed/Worth	.2	.2	.3	.3	.3	.1	.2	.2	.3
	.5	.7	.7	1.0	.9	.6	.5	.8	.7
	2.1	2.5	2.2	NM	-1.1	1.3	1.4	2.4	2.3
Debt/Worth	.8	.8	.8	.5	.8	.7	.7	.6	.9
	2.0	2.1	1.9	3.4	3.1	1.5	1.8	1.7	1.7
	8.3	6.4	5.6	NM	-6.3	3.9	4.2	8.2	10.9
% Profit Before Taxes/Tangible Net Worth	41.3	37.5	35.9		37.9	62.6	41.9	37.9	30.0
	(131) 17.9	(173) 16.8	(139) 15.8	(19) 6.2	(22) 12.6	(30) 16.5	(21) 20.2	(39) 16.5	
	2.0	.8	1.6		-3.9	-2.0	2.9	3.7	6.1
% Profit Before Taxes/Total Assets	13.1	13.3	13.3	20.0	13.6	13.0	18.0	13.0	11.7
	4.7	4.8	5.6	4.0	.9	3.2	6.7	8.0	5.8
	.2	.0	.0	-5.7	-8.7	-2.2	.2	1.3	2.6
Sales/Net Fixed Assets	45.0	42.0	32.0	13.2	33.1	56.7	47.6	37.0	28.5
	15.2	11.3	10.8	5.8	14.5	17.9	17.7	9.4	9.8
	6.8	5.3	5.5	3.3	7.6	5.8	4.7	4.5	6.1
Sales/Total Assets	3.2	3.0	2.9	2.7	3.8	3.2	3.1	2.8	2.7
	2.2	2.1	2.3	2.3	2.4	2.7	2.3	1.9	2.2
	1.6	1.5	1.6	1.3	1.7	1.7	1.6	1.4	1.6
% Depr., Dep., Amort./Sales	.5	.8	.8		.9	.8	.7	.7	1.0
	(123) 1.5	(172) 1.9	(137) 1.7	(23) 2.3	(19) 1.1	(28) 1.6	(20) 1.0	(38) 1.8	
	3.2	3.3	3.3		5.9	3.4	4.5	2.5	2.7
% Officers', Directors', Owners' Comp/Sales	2.5	2.6	2.2		4.0	3.1	1.9		
	(44) 5.4	(74) 5.0	(58) 4.8		(18) 7.5	(10) 5.4	(13) 3.2		
	9.2	8.9	8.9		11.8	14.3	5.7		
Net Sales ($)	4929255M	6540195M	7195517M	5269M	58150M	96699M	257538M	401077M	6376784M
Total Assets ($)	2722860M	3616699M	3614981M	3415M	29592M	47049M	131074M	244512M	3159339M

M = $ thousand   MM = $ million
See Pages 11 through 21 for Explanation of Ratios and Data

Current Data Sorted By Assets / Comparative Historical Data

						Type of Statement		
1	1	3	1	2	3	Unqualified	4	4
1	1	3	2			Reviewed	1	3
		3				Compiled	10	6
	2		2	1		Tax Returns		
	8 (4/1-9/30/04)		14 (10/1/04-3/31/05)			Other	8	8
0-500M	500M-2MM	2-10MM	10-50MM	50-100MM	100-250MM		4/1/00-3/31/01 ALL	4/1/01-3/31/02 ALL
2	3	6	5	3	3	NUMBER OF STATEMENTS	23	21
%	%	%	%	%	%	ASSETS	%	%
						Cash & Equivalents	4.2	3.2
						Trade Receivables (net)	19.1	17.2
						Inventory	29.6	33.7
						All Other Current	3.6	2.0
						Total Current	56.5	56.1
						Fixed Assets (net)	35.2	34.4
						Intangibles (net)	1.5	3.5
						All Other Non-Current	6.8	6.0
						Total	100.0	100.0
						LIABILITIES		
						Notes Payable-Short Term	11.4	9.8
						Cur. Mat.-L/T/D	7.7	3.9
						Trade Payables	11.4	13.1
						Income Taxes Payable	.3	.0
						All Other Current	9.3	8.9
						Total Current	40.1	35.7
						Long-Term Debt	28.1	25.8
						Deferred Taxes	.5	1.5
						All Other Non-Current	27.5	1.8
						Net Worth	3.8	35.2
						Total Liabilities & Net Worth	100.0	100.0
						INCOME DATA		
						Net Sales	100.0	100.0
						Gross Profit	23.4	25.0
						Operating Expenses	20.7	21.6
						Operating Profit	2.7	3.4
						All Other Expenses (net)	3.4	1.5
						Profit Before Taxes	-.7	1.9

RATIOS

						Ratio	Hist 4/1/00-3/31/01	Hist 4/1/01-3/31/02
						Current	2.8 / 2.0 / 1.0	3.0 / 1.5 / 1.0
						Quick	1.2 / .7 / .4	1.5 / .6 / .2
						Sales/Receivables	28 13.0 / 44 8.2 / 57 6.5	11 33.2 / 37 9.8 / 53 6.8
						Cost of Sales/Inventory	53 6.9 / 86 4.2 / 111 3.3	57 6.4 / 70 5.2 / 103 3.5
						Cost of Sales/Payables	15 24.5 / 28 12.9 / 37 9.7	15 24.1 / 21 17.4 / 34 10.8
						Sales/Working Capital	3.5 / 9.7 / 177.6	4.4 / 14.7 / NM
						EBIT/Interest	3.1 / 1.2 / .3 (20)	2.5 / 1.6 / .2
						Net Profit + Depr., Dep., Amort./Cur. Mat. L/T/D	1.2 / .9 (10)	2.4 / 1.2 / .9
						Fixed/Worth	.4 / 1.4 / 6.9	.4 / 1.1 / 2.1
						Debt/Worth	.9 / 1.9 / 11.7	.8 / 2.3 / 4.4
						% Profit Before Taxes/Tangible Net Worth	22.2 / 6.1 / -6.4 (19)	20.1 / 7.8 / -15.7 (19)
						% Profit Before Taxes/Total Assets	5.3 / 1.7 / -10.0	9.4 / 2.3 / -4.3
						Sales/Net Fixed Assets	9.5 / 6.3 / 3.6	10.3 / 6.7 / 4.1
						Sales/Total Assets	2.3 / 1.7 / 1.3	2.7 / 1.9 / 1.4
						% Depr., Dep., Amort./Sales	1.6 / 3.4 / 4.3 (20)	1.3 / 2.7 / 4.5 (19)
						% Officers', Directors', Owners' Comp/Sales		
1007M	8398M	88391M	298466M	331683M	566251M	Net Sales ($)	552152M	953828M
239M	3169M	27171M	162255M	215800M	476085M	Total Assets ($)	335519M	523704M

© RMA 2005

M = $ thousand   MM = $ million
See Pages 11 through 21 for Explanation of Ratios and Data

Comparative Historical Data   **Current Data Sorted By Sales**

6 5 3 5	5 4 8 3	7 6 4 5	Type of Statement	0-1MM	1-3MM	3-5MM	5-10MM	10-25MM	25MM & OVER
			Unqualified	1	1		1	1	6
			Reviewed	1		2			3
			Compiled	1					1
			Tax Returns						
			Other		1	1			3
5 4/1/02- 3/31/03 ALL	3 4/1/03- 3/31/04 ALL	5 4/1/04- 3/31/05 ALL			8 (4/1-9/30/04)			14 (10/1/04-3/31/05)	
19	20	22	**NUMBER OF STATEMENTS**	2	2	1	3	1	13
%	%	%	**ASSETS**	%	%	%	%	%	%
3.9	4.5	4.0	Cash & Equivalents						5.2
24.2	22.5	27.9	Trade Receivables (net)						24.9
28.8	33.9	34.8	Inventory						34.0
1.1	6.5	.9	All Other Current						1.1
58.0	67.3	67.6	Total Current						65.3
27.5	23.1	19.5	Fixed Assets (net)						17.6
7.6	7.1	8.6	Intangibles (net)						13.6
6.8	2.5	4.2	All Other Non-Current						3.5
100.0	100.0	100.0	Total						100.0
			LIABILITIES						
6.6	11.8	11.9	Notes Payable-Short Term						11.4
6.0	3.2	3.7	Cur. Mat.-L/T/D						4.6
14.0	9.5	12.6	Trade Payables						11.3
.5	.1	.2	Income Taxes Payable						.3
10.7	9.7	6.8	All Other Current						6.2
37.9	34.3	35.2	Total Current						33.8
21.7	18.1	17.5	Long-Term Debt						13.2
.7	.5	.7	Deferred Taxes						1.0
53.6	6.2	6.2	All Other Non-Current						9.4
-14.0	40.8	40.4	Net Worth						42.5
100.0	100.0	100.0	Total Liabilities & Net Worth						100.0
			INCOME DATA						
100.0	100.0	100.0	Net Sales						100.0
26.9	27.7	21.2	Gross Profit						21.2
20.7	23.1	16.5	Operating Expenses						15.3
6.1	4.6	4.7	Operating Profit						5.8
1.6	1.3	1.7	All Other Expenses (net)						2.2
4.5	3.4	3.0	Profit Before Taxes						3.6
			RATIOS						
3.6	4.0	3.3							3.9
1.6	2.1	1.8	Current						1.6
1.3	1.3	1.4							1.4
1.9	1.6	1.2							1.2
.9	.8	1.0	Quick						1.0
.5	.5	.6							.6
34 10.9	29 12.6	37 9.8							40 9.2
51 7.2	43 8.4	48 7.7	Sales/Receivables						51 7.1
60 6.1	64 5.7	59 6.2							69 5.3
40 9.2	56 6.5	42 8.7							44 8.3
74 5.0	87 4.2	96 3.8	Cost of Sales/Inventory						96 3.8
92 4.0	107 3.4	120 3.0							116 3.1
20 18.4	10 34.9	15 23.7							19 19.7
26 14.2	19 18.9	24 15.4	Cost of Sales/Payables						25 14.8
36 10.2	28 13.0	39 9.4							35 10.5
4.2	3.7	3.9							3.0
10.8	5.3	8.1	Sales/Working Capital						10.1
40.3	23.7	14.7							15.1
6.8	5.2	6.0							7.3
(17) 3.3	(19) 2.1	2.5	EBIT/Interest						3.0
1.5	1.4	1.2							1.4
	6.3	1.7	Net Profit + Depr., Dep.,						
(12) 2.1	(11) 1.3		Amort./Cur. Mat. L/T/D						
.6	.9								
.3	.2	.3							.3
.6	.7	.5	Fixed/Worth						.5
-14.9	1.9	1.8							NM
.5	.9	1.0							.8
1.4	2.0	1.6	Debt/Worth						1.3
-20.0	3.8	5.0							NM
33.7	19.3	25.5	% Profit Before Taxes/Tangible						25.7
(14) 22.9	(17) 11.1	(19) 10.4	Net Worth					(10) 14.0
5.1	2.0	2.9							2.8
14.1	11.3	10.1	% Profit Before Taxes/Total						10.1
9.2	4.8	2.8	Assets						2.8
1.8	1.4	.9							1.1
14.2	18.9	31.1							17.8
8.8	9.0	10.4	Sales/Net Fixed Assets						10.2
5.2	4.8	6.6							7.1
2.5	2.3	2.8							2.2
2.0	1.9	1.9	Sales/Total Assets						1.7
1.7	1.5	1.6							1.2
1.5	1.0	1.4	% Depr., Dep., Amort./Sales						1.4
(17) 2.6	(19) 2.0	(20) 1.8						(12) 1.8
4.4	3.3	2.8							2.7
			% Officers', Directors', Owners' Comp/Sales						
1212419M	1070470M	1294196M	Net Sales ($)	1007M	4308M	4090M	18153M	11625M	1255013M
790115M	756343M	884719M	Total Assets ($)	239M	1983M	1186M	8336M	6104M	866871M

© RMA 2005

M = $ thousand   MM = $ million
See Pages 11 through 21 for Explanation of Ratios and Data

Current Data Sorted By Assets

Comparative Historical Data

Type of Statement	0-500M	500M-2MM	2-10MM	10-50MM	50-100MM	100-250MM		4/1/00-3/31/01 ALL	4/1/01-3/31/02 ALL
Unqualified	1	1	3	2		4		3	2
Reviewed			1	1				9	7
Compiled	1	1	3			1		3	3
Tax Returns			1					2	
Other		1	2	1	2			5	3
	7 (4/1-9/30/04)			19 (10/1/04-3/31/05)					
NUMBER OF STATEMENTS	2	3	10	4	2	5		22	15
	%	%	%	%	%	%	ASSETS	%	%
			9.9				Cash & Equivalents	6.9	8.9
			34.5				Trade Receivables (net)	28.1	28.6
			23.0				Inventory	29.7	34.4
			1.8				All Other Current	2.9	2.5
			69.2				Total Current	67.5	74.3
			25.1				Fixed Assets (net)	21.4	15.1
			.1				Intangibles (net)	3.5	.3
			5.6				All Other Non-Current	6.5	8.6
			100.0				Total	100.0	100.0
							LIABILITIES		
			14.5				Notes Payable-Short Term	15.9	18.5
			1.3				Cur. Mat.-L/T/D	3.2	4.5
			15.5				Trade Payables	12.1	12.9
			.0				Income Taxes Payable	.1	.1
			9.8				All Other Current	6.3	5.8
			41.1				Total Current	37.6	41.7
			9.7				Long-Term Debt	17.0	4.7
			.2				Deferred Taxes	.1	.0
			3.6				All Other Non-Current	10.1	13.1
			45.4				Net Worth	35.2	40.4
			100.0				Total Liabilities & Net Worth	100.0	100.0
							INCOME DATA		
			100.0				Net Sales	100.0	100.0
			32.5				Gross Profit	26.5	24.5
			24.2				Operating Expenses	22.6	25.2
			8.3				Operating Profit	3.9	-.7
			.6				All Other Expenses (net)	2.3	1.6
			7.7				Profit Before Taxes	1.6	-2.4
							RATIOS		
			2.6				Current	3.2	3.0
			1.6					2.1	1.8
			1.1					1.1	1.2
			2.2				Quick	1.6	1.2
			1.1					.9	.9
			.4					.6	.6
		31	11.9				Sales/Receivables	24 15.4	31 11.8
		46	7.9					55 6.7	45 8.2
		87	4.2					66 5.5	85 4.3
		11	33.6				Cost of Sales/Inventory	32 11.5	20 18.6
		27	13.5					75 4.8	69 5.3
		120	3.0					153 2.4	166 2.2
		19	19.5				Cost of Sales/Payables	13 27.5	12 29.6
		37	10.0					25 14.9	25 14.4
		69	5.3					42 8.7	33 11.0
			3.0				Sales/Working Capital	3.6	3.3
			8.8					5.7	6.8
			NM					21.7	13.2
							EBIT/Interest	(18) 4.4	(13) 5.1
								2.1	1.5
								1.0	-1.4
							Net Profit + Depr., Dep., Amort./Cur. Mat. L /T/D		
			.0				Fixed/Worth	.2	.1
			.2					.5	.5
			1.4					3.4	1.0
			.6				Debt/Worth	.7	.5
			1.3					1.8	1.5
			2.6					5.5	3.7
			63.1				% Profit Before Taxes/Tangible Net Worth	(18) 24.2	(14) 16.0
			25.8					6.2	3.9
			4.2					-2.8	-55.9
			21.5				% Profit Before Taxes/Total Assets	9.1	7.3
			8.6					2.2	.0
			1.4					-.6	-14.6
			358.9				Sales/Net Fixed Assets	38.7	86.9
			17.2					11.5	17.9
			3.1					4.2	6.2
			2.9				Sales/Total Assets	2.4	2.9
			1.8					1.7	2.2
			1.2					1.3	1.4
							% Depr., Dep., Amort./Sales	(18) .7	(14) .3
								1.4	1.6
								4.5	4.9
							% Officers', Directors', Owners' Comp/Sales		
	1464M	12425M	106251M	255849M	245367M	1761714M	Net Sales ($)	1345397M	185916M
	670M	2441M	41344M	117882M	155179M	914861M	Total Assets ($)	824362M	86563M

M = $ thousand   MM = $ million
See Pages 11 through 21 for Explanation of Ratios and Data

Comparative Historical Data | **Current Data Sorted By Sales**

	4/1/02-3/31/03 ALL	4/1/03-3/31/04 ALL	4/1/04-3/31/05 ALL	Type of Statement	0-1MM	1-3MM	3-5MM	5-10MM	10-25MM	25MM & OVER
	14	12	10	Unqualified			1	2	1	6
	7	1	3	Reviewed		1			1	1
	6	3	5	Compiled		1	1	2		1
			2	Tax Returns	1	1				
	5	8	6	Other	1			2		3
					7 (4/1-9/30/04)			19 (10/1/04-3/31/05)		
	32	24	26	**NUMBER OF STATEMENTS**	2	3	4	4	2	11
	%	%	%	**ASSETS**	%	%	%	%	%	%
	11.1	7.0	10.3	Cash & Equivalents						11.3
	27.6	29.9	29.6	Trade Receivables (net)						27.5
	31.5	34.1	29.7	Inventory						36.4
	2.9	3.6	1.9	All Other Current						2.7
	73.1	74.6	71.4	Total Current						78.0
	18.6	17.4	18.5	Fixed Assets (net)						13.9
	.7	5.0	4.0	Intangibles (net)						2.6
	7.7	3.0	6.0	All Other Non-Current						5.5
	100.0	100.0	100.0	Total						100.0
				LIABILITIES						
	9.9	10.3	13.7	Notes Payable-Short Term						9.1
	4.8	4.4	2.1	Cur. Mat.-L/T/D						3.0
	14.8	19.7	15.6	Trade Payables						12.9
	.2	.9	.1	Income Taxes Payable						.3
	4.8	11.2	8.5	All Other Current						8.8
	34.6	46.5	40.0	Total Current						34.1
	11.6	12.9	9.0	Long-Term Debt						9.0
	.4	.3	.2	Deferred Taxes						.2
	7.8	2.3	4.4	All Other Non-Current						3.8
	45.6	38.1	46.3	Net Worth						52.7
	100.0	100.0	100.0	Total Liabilities & Net Worth						100.0
				INCOME DATA						
	100.0	100.0	100.0	Net Sales						100.0
	26.0	31.1	29.0	Gross Profit						26.4
	22.7	26.4	23.1	Operating Expenses						19.2
	3.2	4.7	6.0	Operating Profit						7.2
	.8	1.4	1.1	All Other Expenses (net)						.7
	2.5	3.3	4.8	Profit Before Taxes						6.4
				RATIOS						
	4.6	3.9	3.3							4.3
	2.5	2.1	1.9	Current						3.0
	1.5	1.1	1.1							1.2
	2.7	1.6	2.2							2.9
	1.5	1.0	1.1	Quick						1.5
	.7	.3	.5							.4
	26 13.8	35 10.6	32 11.4							34 10.7
	41 8.8	44 8.3	48 7.6	Sales/Receivables						53 6.9
	74 4.9	70 5.2	64 5.7							64 5.7
	29 12.8	40 9.2	26 14.1							27 13.3
	72 5.1	100 3.6	75 4.9	Cost of Sales/Inventory						79 4.6
	124 2.9	146 2.5	155 2.4							178 2.1
	12 30.7	23 15.6	21 17.1							17 21.1
	28 13.1	29 12.4	27 13.5	Cost of Sales/Payables						24 15.2
	43 8.6	53 6.9	53 6.9							50 7.2
	2.5	3.1	2.9							2.4
	5.0	7.7	7.0	Sales/Working Capital						4.3
	14.5	34.9	35.8							10.2
	5.0	14.9	12.9							75.4
	(29) 2.3	(23) 2.5	(24) 4.5	EBIT/Interest						11.1
	1.3	1.5	2.2							4.4
	7.0			Net Profit + Depr., Dep.,						
	(10) 1.7			Amort./Cur. Mat. L/T/D						
	.5									
	.1	.1	.0							.0
	.3	.3	.3	Fixed/Worth						.2
	.6	11.4	1.2							.9
	.3	.5	.5							.4
	1.2	.9	1.2	Debt/Worth						.8
	3.0	18.9	4.0							5.0
	19.3	35.6	56.9	% Profit Before Taxes/Tangible						68.4
	(30) 7.6	(19) 13.8	(24) 18.0	Net Worth						24.0
	-.1	9.6	1.2							17.6
	9.2	11.4	12.3	% Profit Before Taxes/Total						16.4
	2.6	7.2	7.7	Assets						9.2
	.1	2.5	1.3							6.0
	94.9	82.8	141.0							145.3
	13.0	12.9	13.0	Sales/Net Fixed Assets						11.2
	6.0	7.5	5.9							8.1
	2.9	2.6	2.7							2.9
	1.9	2.0	2.0	Sales/Total Assets						1.8
	1.3	1.5	1.3							1.5
	.8	.6	.3							
	(28) 1.7	(19) 1.6	(19) 1.5	% Depr., Dep., Amort./Sales						
	3.4	4.2	2.8							
	.8			% Officers', Directors',						
	(10) 3.5			Owners' Comp/Sales						
	5.9									
	1371173M	1695146M	2383070M	Net Sales ($)	1464M	6707M	16561M	28292M	33406M	2296640M
	749120M	926338M	1232377M	Total Assets ($)	670M	18871M	11450M	12519M	10261M	1178606M

M = $ thousand   MM = $ million

See Pages 11 through 21 for Explanation of Ratios and Data

Current Data Sorted By Assets   Comparative Historical Data

0-500M	500M-2MM	2-10MM	10-50MM	50-100MM	100-250MM	Type of Statement	4/1/00-3/31/01 ALL	4/1/01-3/31/02 ALL
		4	8	1		Unqualified		
	1	7	1			Reviewed		
3	5		2			Compiled		
3	3	2	2			Tax Returns		
2		1	3		1	Other		
	13 (4/1-9/30/04)		34 (10/1/04-3/31/05)					
8	9	14	14	1	1	**NUMBER OF STATEMENTS**		
%	%	%	%	%	%	**ASSETS**	%	%
		15.5	6.6			Cash & Equivalents		
		26.7	41.5			Trade Receivables (net)		
		34.4	33.9			Inventory		
		5.2	3.4			All Other Current	D	D
		81.8	85.4			Total Current	A	A
		9.7	4.4			Fixed Assets (net)	T	T
		.9	5.6			Intangibles (net)	A	A
		7.6	4.6			All Other Non-Current		
		100.0	100.0			Total	N	N
						LIABILITIES	O	O
		15.3	20.1			Notes Payable-Short Term	T	T
		1.2	3.2			Cur. Mat.-L/T/D		
		11.6	15.2			Trade Payables	A	A
		.0	.0			Income Taxes Payable	V	V
		5.2	8.4			All Other Current	A	A
		33.5	47.0			Total Current	I	I
		4.4	1.9			Long-Term Debt	L	L
		.0	.1			Deferred Taxes	A	A
		2.9	1.3			All Other Non-Current	B	B
		59.2	49.8			Net Worth	L	L
		100.0	100.0			Total Liabilities & Net Worth	E	E
						INCOME DATA		
		100.0	100.0			Net Sales		
		33.3	30.0			Gross Profit		
		30.3	26.0			Operating Expenses		
		3.0	4.0			Operating Profit		
		-.2	.5			All Other Expenses (net)		
		3.1	3.5			Profit Before Taxes		
						RATIOS		
		5.7	2.8					
		3.0	1.7			Current		
		1.5	1.5					
		3.6	1.3					
		1.2	1.1			Quick		
		.7	.7					
		19 / 19.3	42 / 8.6					
		38 / 9.7	58 / 6.2			Sales/Receivables		
		71 / 5.1	73 / 5.0					
		65 / 5.6	38 / 9.7					
		84 / 4.3	78 / 4.7			Cost of Sales/Inventory		
		118 / 3.1	168 / 2.2					
		25 / 14.8	17 / 22.1					
		30 / 12.0	27 / 13.3			Cost of Sales/Payables		
		38 / 9.6	49 / 7.4					
		2.8	3.0					
		4.0	6.6			Sales/Working Capital		
		10.6	10.9					
		6.7	17.1					
		(10) 2.4	(13) 7.3			EBIT/Interest		
		1.6	4.1					
						Net Profit + Depr., Dep., Amort./Cur. Mat. L./T/D		
		.0	.0					
		.1	.1			Fixed/Worth		
		.5	.1					
		.3	.6					
		.6	1.2			Debt/Worth		
		1.5	2.3					
		23.1	26.5					
		8.3	15.8			% Profit Before Taxes/Tangible Net Worth		
		3.6	10.6					
		8.3	9.1					
		3.7	7.9			% Profit Before Taxes/Total Assets		
		1.9	4.7					
		347.5	423.2					
		57.5	75.6			Sales/Net Fixed Assets		
		10.0	19.8					
		2.4	3.3					
		1.8	2.1			Sales/Total Assets		
		1.6	1.3					
		.2	.2					
		.6	(11) .3			% Depr., Dep., Amort./Sales		
		1.2	1.0					
						% Officers', Directors', Owners' Comp/Sales		
8440M	28826M	147007M	678407M	118658M	480698M	Net Sales ($)		
2464M	10273M	75238M	305739M	89039M	243853M	Total Assets ($)		

© RMA 2005

Comparative Historical Data | **Current Data Sorted By Sales**

4/1/02-3/31/03 ALL	4/1/03-3/31/04 ALL	4/1/04-3/31/05 ALL	Type of Statement	0-1MM	1-3MM	3-5MM	5-10MM	10-25MM	25MM & OVER
6	4	13	Unqualified		1	1	5	4	8
11	11	9	Reviewed		3	1	1	1	1
6	13	10	Compiled		2	5		1	1
3	2	8	Tax Returns	3	1	1	1	1	
5	7	7	Other	1				1	3
					13 (4/1-9/30/04)		34 (10/1/04-3/31/05)		
31	37	47	**NUMBER OF STATEMENTS**	4	7	8	7	8	13
%	%	%	**ASSETS**	%	%	%	%	%	%
11.3	10.4	8.6	Cash & Equivalents						4.6
25.4	23.9	28.2	Trade Receivables (net)						42.5
37.3	38.1	37.7	Inventory						37.7
5.6	6.2	4.6	All Other Current						3.9
79.6	78.6	79.1	Total Current						88.7
14.2	14.6	12.1	Fixed Assets (net)						5.8
1.5	1.4	4.0	Intangibles (net)						1.6
4.7	5.5	4.8	All Other Non-Current						3.9
100.0	100.0	100.0	Total						100.0
			LIABILITIES						
12.7	11.4	17.4	Notes Payable-Short Term						17.7
4.4	6.3	4.6	Cur. Mat.-L/T/D						4.0
13.4	17.7	14.2	Trade Payables						18.2
.3	.4	.0	Income Taxes Payable						.0
11.4	8.5	6.4	All Other Current						11.2
42.3	44.3	42.7	Total Current						51.2
10.4	10.3	7.3	Long-Term Debt						4.7
.3	.2	.1	Deferred Taxes						.0
6.8	8.2	7.2	All Other Non-Current						1.4
40.2	37.0	42.6	Net Worth						42.6
100.0	100.0	100.0	Total Liabilities & Net Worth						100.0
			INCOME DATA						
100.0	100.0	100.0	Net Sales						100.0
32.4	32.7	33.9	Gross Profit						29.5
29.3	30.1	30.9	Operating Expenses						26.6
3.1	2.5	3.1	Operating Profit						2.9
.9	.8	.2	All Other Expenses (net)						.1
2.2	1.7	2.9	Profit Before Taxes						2.9
			RATIOS						
2.8	3.3	3.8	Current						2.0
2.0	1.7	1.8							1.6
1.3	1.3	1.4							1.5
1.6	1.6	1.4	Quick						1.2
.9	.8	.8							1.0
.5	.4	.5							.7
24 15.1	20 17.9	23 16.0	Sales/Receivables						41 8.8
43 8.6	41 8.9	42 8.7							57 6.4
61 6.0	63 5.8	60 6.1							72 5.1
49 7.5	61 5.9	53 6.9	Cost of Sales/Inventory						39 9.4
110 3.3	93 3.9	93 3.9							87 4.2
148 2.5	174 2.1	149 2.4							138 2.7
13 27.4	17 22.0	18 20.8	Cost of Sales/Payables						21 17.3
24 15.2	44 8.3	29 12.5							29 12.5
39 9.5	89 4.1	48 7.6							45 8.1
3.3	3.2	3.6	Sales/Working Capital						4.6
6.5	4.3	6.4							6.8
14.3	26.6	12.2							11.1
10.0	8.9	9.8	EBIT/Interest						14.3
(28) 2.7	(35) 3.5	(40) 3.9						(12)	6.2
1.5	-.6	1.2							3.9
			Net Profit + Depr., Dep., Amort./Cur. Mat. L/T/D						
.0	.1	.0	Fixed/Worth						.0
.2	.3	.1							.1
.7	.8	.5							.2
.5	.5	.5	Debt/Worth						.9
1.3	1.5	1.4							1.6
3.4	6.6	2.6							2.5
24.9	33.9	25.6	% Profit Before Taxes/Tangible Net Worth						24.8
(27) 11.9	(31) 10.8	(42) 11.5							16.0
1.4	-.1	3.8							8.3
13.0	10.8	9.5	% Profit Before Taxes/Total Assets						9.1
5.7	5.5	6.1							7.7
.6	-4.3	.9							3.8
106.3	86.4	150.5	Sales/Net Fixed Assets						655.8
33.8	23.1	37.3							87.0
8.3	8.1	10.4							17.1
3.1	3.4	3.3	Sales/Total Assets						3.3
2.2	2.0	2.1							2.8
1.3	1.1	1.6							1.9
.3	.2	.2	% Depr., Dep., Amort./Sales						.2
(28) .7	(34) .7	(40) .7						(11)	.3
1.2	1.9	1.5							1.0
2.9	1.3	2.2	% Officers', Directors', Owners' Comp/Sales						
(18) 5.3	(17) 3.9	(28) 4.1							
7.5	6.7	6.6							
605487M	953864M	1462036M	Net Sales ($)	2137M	11521M	32522M	55449M	125862M	1234545M
335253M	532686M	726606M	Total Assets ($)	1118M	4902M	11761M	33237M	107137M	568451M

© RMA 2005

M = $ thousand   MM = $ million

See Pages 11 through 21 for Explanation of Ratios and Data

Current Data Sorted By Assets   **Comparative Historical Data**

0-500M	500M-2MM	2-10MM	10-50MM	50-100MM	100-250MM	Type of Statement	4/1/00-3/31/01 ALL	4/1/01-3/31/02 ALL
		1	8	1	1	Unqualified		
	2	5	4		1	Reviewed		
1	2	2				Compiled		
1	2	1				Tax Returns		
		2				Other		
2	5	10	12	1	2	**NUMBER OF STATEMENTS**		
%	%	%	%	%	%		%	%
						ASSETS		
		14.5	6.4			Cash & Equivalents	D	D
		28.2	37.1			Trade Receivables (net)	A	A
		33.1	37.7			Inventory	T	T
		11.4	7.1			All Other Current	A	A
		87.2	88.3			Total Current		
		6.5	5.7			Fixed Assets (net)	N	N
		1.1	.6			Intangibles (net)	O	O
		5.2	5.4			All Other Non-Current	T	T
		100.0	100.0			Total		
						LIABILITIES	A	A
		15.0	34.4			Notes Payable-Short Term	V	V
		.2	.7			Cur. Mat.-L/T/D	A	A
		17.7	18.6			Trade Payables	I	I
		.1	.0			Income Taxes Payable	L	L
		10.2	6.9			All Other Current	A	A
		43.2	60.6			Total Current	B	B
		1.7	.1			Long-Term Debt	L	L
		1.1	.6			Deferred Taxes	E	E
		5.9	8.6			All Other Non-Current		
		48.0	30.0			Net Worth		
		100.0	100.0			Total Liabilities & Net Worth		
						INCOME DATA		
		100.0	100.0			Net Sales		
		32.3	27.6			Gross Profit		
		30.6	25.3			Operating Expenses		
		1.7	2.4			Operating Profit		
		1.5	1.3			All Other Expenses (net)		
		.2	1.1			Profit Before Taxes		
						RATIOS		
		4.6	4.9			Current		
		2.0	1.4					
		1.4	1.1					
		1.8	2.0			Quick		
		.9	.8					
		.6	.4					
		1 487.7	33 11.0			Sales/Receivables		
		29 12.4	53 6.9					
		69 5.3	70 5.2					
		17 21.8	42 8.7			Cost of Sales/Inventory		
		43 8.4	56 6.5					
		106 3.4	116 3.2					
		17 21.1	15 23.8			Cost of Sales/Payables		
		26 14.1	29 12.5					
		44 8.2	49 7.5					
		3.0	4.0			Sales/Working Capital		
		10.2	11.4					
		21.7	94.3					
		10.4	3.5			EBIT/Interest		
		5.7	(11) 2.7					
		2.0	.6					
						Net Profit + Depr., Dep., Amort./Cur. Mat. L /T/D		
		.1	.0			Fixed/Worth		
		.1	.1					
		.3	.4					
		.5	.6			Debt/Worth		
		.8	2.3					
		2.6	9.0					
			35.8			% Profit Before Taxes/Tangible Net Worth		
		(11)	23.9					
			−1.1					
		21.9	7.8			% Profit Before Taxes/Total Assets		
		8.9	3.8					
		3.4	−1.7					
		257.7	204.5			Sales/Net Fixed Assets		
		47.8	121.5					
		23.3	66.8					
		5.0	4.0			Sales/Total Assets		
		3.4	3.2					
		1.7	1.2					
						% Depr., Dep., Amort./Sales		
						% Officers', Directors', Owners' Comp/Sales		
3356M	20063M	134258M	783245M	77006M	553042M	Net Sales ($)		
160M	4575M	37485M	261357M	64117M	306929M	Total Assets ($)		

M = $ thousand   MM = $ million
See Pages 11 through 21 for Explanation of Ratios and Data

Comparative Historical Data | **Current Data Sorted By Sales**

Type of Statement

4/1/02-3/31/03 ALL	4/1/03-3/31/04 ALL	4/1/04-3/31/05 ALL	Type of Statement	0-1MM	1-3MM	3-5MM	5-10MM	10-25MM	25MM & OVER
9	11	11	Unqualified		2	1		2	9
9	10	12	Reviewed		1	3		4	4
3	5	5	Compiled			2	3	1	
1		1	Tax Returns						
5	4	3	Other						
				2 (4/1-9/30/04)			30 (10/1/04-3/31/05)		
27	30	32	NUMBER OF STATEMENTS		3	6	3	7	13

ASSETS

4/1/02-3/31/03 ALL	4/1/03-3/31/04 ALL	4/1/04-3/31/05 ALL		0-1MM	1-3MM	3-5MM	5-10MM	10-25MM	25MM & OVER
%	%	%	ASSETS	%	%	%	%	%	%
14.2	8.3	14.1	Cash & Equivalents						14.1
26.1	31.5	28.7	Trade Receivables (net)						34.4
34.5	35.3	30.6	Inventory						29.0
2.4	5.5	8.9	All Other Current						8.6
77.2	80.6	82.3	Total Current						86.1
13.5	8.7	9.6	Fixed Assets (net)						6.2
.2	3.3	.7	Intangibles (net)						.9
9.0	7.4	7.4	All Other Non-Current						6.8
100.0	100.0	100.0	Total						100.0

(Current data columns 0-1MM through 10-25MM: DATA NOT AVAILABLE)

LIABILITIES

4/1/02-3/31/03	4/1/03-3/31/04	4/1/04-3/31/05		25MM & OVER
12.8	8.4	31.0	Notes Payable-Short Term	20.2
1.9	.7	.4	Cur. Mat.-L/T/D	.8
12.0	22.5	14.8	Trade Payables	16.5
.5	.6	1.2	Income Taxes Payable	.0
12.2	13.6	8.2	All Other Current	9.6
39.4	45.7	55.6	Total Current	47.1
8.8	1.4	1.1	Long-Term Debt	.5
.2	.4	.6	Deferred Taxes	.6
10.7	7.9	6.0	All Other Non-Current	8.1
40.9	44.6	36.8	Net Worth	43.7
100.0	100.0	100.0	Total Liabilities & Net Worth	100.0

INCOME DATA

4/1/02-3/31/03	4/1/03-3/31/04	4/1/04-3/31/05		25MM & OVER
100.0	100.0	100.0	Net Sales	100.0
29.5	33.0	32.5	Gross Profit	29.1
25.5	30.1	30.0	Operating Expenses	24.8
4.0	2.8	2.4	Operating Profit	4.3
1.2	.2	1.1	All Other Expenses (net)	.8
2.8	2.7	1.3	Profit Before Taxes	3.5

RATIOS

4/1/02-3/31/03	4/1/03-3/31/04	4/1/04-3/31/05		25MM & OVER
3.8	3.7	4.8	Current	5.5
2.0	1.9	1.7		1.8
1.3	1.3	1.3		1.2
2.4	2.7	2.2	Quick	4.0
1.1	(29) .9	.9		1.0
.6	.5	.5		.7
18 19.9	18 20.5	5 70.9	Sales/Receivables	34 10.6
35 10.4	31 11.9	41 8.8		47 7.8
46 7.9	47 7.8	57 6.4		59 6.2
40 9.1	32 11.5	19 19.4	Cost of Sales/Inventory	29 12.6
52 7.0	44 8.2	46 7.9		46 7.9
90 4.1	67 5.5	102 3.6		71 5.1
9 39.3	16 22.9	11 32.6	Cost of Sales/Payables	13 27.1
17 21.3	25 14.6	22 16.3		16 22.7
25 14.9	37 9.9	42 8.8		41 9.0
4.2	4.9	3.3	Sales/Working Capital	2.9
7.7	13.1	10.7		8.4
18.7	31.5	42.1		30.9
15.8	15.3	6.3	EBIT/Interest	8.8
(21) 6.8	(26) 7.8	(28) 2.7		(10) 3.2
2.4	1.3	.9		1.8
			Net Profit + Depr., Dep., Amort./Cur. Mat. L/T/D	
.1	.1	.0	Fixed/Worth	.0
.1	.1	.2		.1
.5	.5	.3		.3
.4	.5	.4	Debt/Worth	.3
1.1	1.4	.9		.9
2.3	2.7	2.7		3.7
31.3	56.4	31.9	% Profit Before Taxes/Tangible Net Worth	35.5
(24) 18.2	(28) 20.1	(29) 13.5		(12) 24.0
-5.9	3.7	1.9		9.0
19.5	18.6	17.6	% Profit Before Taxes/Total Assets	17.2
9.8	9.5	5.8		7.1
-3.0	-.9	.7		3.0
126.5	346.6	214.3	Sales/Net Fixed Assets	222.1
33.3	83.5	78.0		115.0
11.4	39.1	24.2		47.9
3.9	5.4	4.8	Sales/Total Assets	4.2
3.1	3.8	3.5		3.4
2.2	2.3	1.6		1.8
.2	.1	.2	% Depr., Dep., Amort./Sales	.1
(21) .8	(24) .3	(25) .4		(11) .4
1.8	.9	1.1		1.0
1.5	2.1	1.6	% Officers', Directors', Owners' Comp/Sales	
(13) 3.6	(11) 3.2	(16) 3.0		
5.5	6.9	8.6		

Net Sales / Total Assets

4/1/02-3/31/03	4/1/03-3/31/04	4/1/04-3/31/05		0-1MM	1-3MM	3-5MM	5-10MM	10-25MM	25MM & OVER
1956292M	1850675M	1570970M	Net Sales ($)		6169M	25112M	21586M	107267M	1410836M
933927M	577026M	674623M	Total Assets ($)		690M	13247M	18321M	48289M	594076M

M = $ thousand   MM = $ million
See Pages 11 through 21 for Explanation of Ratios and Data

Current Data Sorted By Assets   Comparative Historical Data

0-500M	500M-2MM	2-10MM	10-50MM	50-100MM	100-250MM	Type of Statement	4/1/00-3/31/01 ALL	4/1/01-3/31/02 ALL
1	1	4	5	1	2	Unqualified	6	7
		4	1			Reviewed	8	3
	2					Compiled	4	6
3	2					Tax Returns	1	2
	1	2	1			Other	4	8
		6 (4/1-9/30/04)		24 (10/1/04-3/31/05)				
4	6	10	7	1	2	NUMBER OF STATEMENTS	23	26
%	%	%	%	%	%		%	%
						ASSETS		
		7.9				Cash & Equivalents	6.2	6.0
		24.8				Trade Receivables (net)	31.1	25.7
		48.7				Inventory	42.2	43.1
		1.9				All Other Current	1.3	2.8
		83.4				Total Current	80.9	77.5
		7.8				Fixed Assets (net)	14.9	13.8
		5.2				Intangibles (net)	1.5	1.0
		3.5				All Other Non-Current	2.8	7.7
		100.0				Total	100.0	100.0
						LIABILITIES		
		19.3				Notes Payable-Short Term	18.4	18.6
		1.4				Cur. Mat.-L/T/D	1.1	6.7
		21.0				Trade Payables	16.5	17.5
		1.7				Income Taxes Payable	.4	.6
		8.6				All Other Current	7.5	13.7
		51.9				Total Current	43.9	57.2
		5.6				Long-Term Debt	11.6	12.2
		.3				Deferred Taxes	.4	.4
		1.9				All Other Non-Current	1.5	9.5
		40.4				Net Worth	42.6	20.8
		100.0				Total Liabilities & Net Worth	100.0	100.0
						INCOME DATA		
		100.0				Net Sales	100.0	100.0
		34.8				Gross Profit	25.9	28.9
		33.3				Operating Expenses	22.6	28.2
		1.5				Operating Profit	3.3	.7
		.8				All Other Expenses (net)	1.4	2.6
		.7				Profit Before Taxes	1.9	−1.9
						RATIOS		
		2.2					2.8	2.3
		1.7				Current	1.7	1.7
		1.3					1.4	1.1
		.9					1.5	.8
		.7				Quick	.7	.6
		.2					.5	.3
		1 332.6					32 11.3	25 14.6
		27 13.3				Sales/Receivables	54 6.7	46 8.0
		59 6.2					68 5.3	61 6.0
		45 8.1					77 4.8	74 4.9
		100 3.6				Cost of Sales/Inventory	95 3.8	116 3.2
		199 1.8					146 2.5	170 2.1
		27 13.4					24 15.5	23 15.7
		39 9.3				Cost of Sales/Payables	39 9.3	34 10.6
		57 6.4					63 5.8	58 6.3
		5.1					3.9	4.4
		7.2				Sales/Working Capital	6.1	5.6
		NM					9.5	50.3
		14.5					(21) 5.8	(25) 3.9
		2.9				EBIT/Interest	2.3	2.0
		−.3					1.3	−1.4
						Net Profit + Depr., Dep., Amort./Cur. Mat. L /T/D		
		.1					.1	.1
		.1				Fixed/Worth	.3	.3
		.5					.6	3.2
		1.1					1.0	1.0
		1.8				Debt/Worth	1.6	1.6
		3.5					2.5	NM
		37.4					24.1	22.9
		9.6				% Profit Before Taxes/Tangible Net Worth	7.8	(20) 8.9
		−14.9					1.0	−7.4
		17.3					9.0	8.9
		4.8				% Profit Before Taxes/Total Assets	3.8	3.0
		−3.3					.3	−10.3
		112.6					54.4	68.8
		54.6				Sales/Net Fixed Assets	24.4	33.8
		22.0					6.8	9.9
		3.1					2.4	2.5
		2.8				Sales/Total Assets	1.9	2.0
		1.8					1.4	1.6
		.3					.2	.4
		.7				% Depr., Dep., Amort./Sales	(22) .7	(23) .8
		1.4					1.5	1.7
						% Officers', Directors', Owners' Comp/Sales		
3715M	13637M	178784M	307981M	197801M	519492M	Net Sales ($)	878816M	1098697M
900M	5270M	67203M	138109M	78964M	291174M	Total Assets ($)	450357M	599434M

M = $ thousand   MM = $ million
See Pages 11 through 21 for Explanation of Ratios and Data

Comparative Historical Data / Current Data Sorted By Sales

4/1/02-3/31/03 ALL	4/1/03-3/31/04 ALL	4/1/04-3/31/05 ALL		0-1MM	1-3MM	3-5MM	5-10MM	10-25MM	25MM & OVER
				6 (4/1-9/30/04)			24 (10/1/04-3/31/05)		
			Type of Statement						
14	14	12	Unqualified				1	3	8
5	2	7	Reviewed		1		3	3	
4	5	2	Compiled		2				
1	2	5	Tax Returns	2	3				
4	9	4	Other		1			1	2
28	32	30	**NUMBER OF STATEMENTS**	2	7		4	7	10
%	%	%	**ASSETS**	%	%	%	%	%	%
6.9	11.1	12.1	Cash & Equivalents			D			3.6
25.0	25.0	26.4	Trade Receivables (net)			A			38.6
45.6	40.3	40.4	Inventory			T			32.7
2.0	1.8	2.0	All Other Current			A			2.8
79.5	78.1	80.9	Total Current						77.8
13.3	13.0	10.6	Fixed Assets (net)			N			9.7
.5	1.0	2.6	Intangibles (net)			O			4.7
6.7	7.9	5.9	All Other Non-Current			T			7.8
100.0	100.0	100.0	Total						100.0
			LIABILITIES			A			
15.2	16.2	18.3	Notes Payable-Short Term			V			27.4
2.8	1.8	3.5	Cur. Mat.-L/T/D			A			2.2
15.2	13.8	18.2	Trade Payables			I			12.8
.6	.9	.9	Income Taxes Payable			L			.8
10.9	13.4	7.0	All Other Current			A			6.5
44.7	46.1	47.8	Total Current			B			49.7
18.1	11.4	27.5	Long-Term Debt			L			6.0
.3	.3	.1	Deferred Taxes			E			.1
20.8	2.6	1.8	All Other Non-Current						.3
16.0	39.6	22.8	Net Worth						43.9
100.0	100.0	100.0	Total Liabilities & Net Worth						100.0
			INCOME DATA						
100.0	100.0	100.0	Net Sales						100.0
28.8	33.0	38.2	Gross Profit						30.9
26.8	30.9	33.3	Operating Expenses						26.6
2.0	2.1	4.9	Operating Profit						4.3
1.7	1.1	.7	All Other Expenses (net)						-.6
.4	1.0	4.2	Profit Before Taxes						4.9
			RATIOS						
2.7	2.7	3.3							1.9
1.9	1.8	1.8	Current						1.7
1.4	1.4	1.3							1.3
1.4	1.7	1.8							1.3
.7	.7	.8	Quick						.9
.3	.3	.5							.5
22 16.3	**22** 16.9	**1** 363.4							**20** 18.5
37 10.0	**38** 9.7	**39** 9.3	Sales/Receivables						**55** 6.6
62 5.9	**55** 6.7	**64** 5.7							**87** 4.2
54 6.8	**47** 7.8	**46** 8.0							**34** 10.9
115 3.2	**95** 3.8	**83** 4.4	Cost of Sales/Inventory						**57** 6.4
160 2.3	**155** 2.4	**165** 2.2							**134** 2.7
14 25.8	**12** 30.5	**10** 34.9							**8** 46.0
35 10.5	**29** 12.4	**33** 11.2	Cost of Sales/Payables						**23** 16.1
45 8.2	**43** 8.4	**78** 4.7							**41** 8.9
5.0	3.3	4.5							4.9
6.4	6.7	6.7	Sales/Working Capital						8.5
9.6	15.1	15.3							29.2
7.1	8.0	9.6							12.9
(25) 2.2	(28) 2.9	(28) 3.2	EBIT/Interest						4.5
1.3	1.5	.1							2.8
			Net Profit + Depr., Dep., Amort./Cur. Mat. L/T/D						
.1	.1	.1							.1
.3	.4	.2	Fixed/Worth						.1
.6	.8	.7							.5
.6	.7	.8							1.1
1.1	1.4	1.5	Debt/Worth						1.3
3.2	2.7	4.7							2.3
23.1	21.5	36.1							59.9
(24) 6.2	(28) 7.4	(27) 8.0	% Profit Before Taxes/Tangible Net Worth						20.9
2.3	3.6	-6.5							8.0
11.5	9.8	15.3							16.1
2.6	4.0	4.0	% Profit Before Taxes/Total Assets						9.2
.9	1.7	-2.5							3.6
63.3	92.2	64.3							115.1
23.6	20.0	36.9	Sales/Net Fixed Assets						35.8
11.7	10.7	19.7							20.3
3.2	3.2	3.1							3.5
2.1	2.4	2.5	Sales/Total Assets						2.7
1.7	1.7	1.8							1.8
.4	.4	.4							
(26) .8	(28) 1.2	(25) .7	% Depr., Dep., Amort./Sales						
1.7	1.6	1.4							
	2.3								
	(10) 3.9		% Officers', Directors', Owners' Comp/Sales						
	6.3								
1736622M	2674120M	1221410M	Net Sales ($)	1175M	11150M		32286M	123886M	1052913M
824559M	1321560M	581620M	Total Assets ($)	135M	4285M		13835M	81769M	481596M

M = $ thousand MM = $ million

See Pages 11 through 21 for Explanation of Ratios and Data

Current Data Sorted By Assets   Comparative Historical Data

Type of Statement distribution (current period):

```
         1        2        6        3        2        1
                           4        3
 1       2                 4
 1       2                 4
 5                         1
         3                 6        4        1        1
```

0-500M	500M-2MM	2-10MM	10-50MM	50-100MM	100-250MM	Type of Statement	4/1/00-3/31/01 ALL	4/1/01-3/31/02 ALL
						Unqualified	18	12
						Reviewed	10	10
						Compiled	16	10
						Tax Returns	2	1
						Other	12	15
	11 (4/1-9/30/04)		39 (10/1/04-3/31/05)					
7	7	21	10	3	2	**NUMBER OF STATEMENTS**	58	48
%	%	%	%	%	%		%	%
						ASSETS		
		6.5	12.5			Cash & Equivalents	11.3	13.1
		27.9	29.3			Trade Receivables (net)	25.2	22.6
		36.9	36.3			Inventory	35.7	37.9
		3.9	1.0			All Other Current	2.9	2.4
		75.2	79.1			Total Current	75.0	76.0
		12.6	13.0			Fixed Assets (net)	17.5	14.9
		5.8	.6			Intangibles (net)	2.3	2.5
		6.3	7.3			All Other Non-Current	5.2	6.6
		100.0	100.0			Total	100.0	100.0
						LIABILITIES		
		24.2	20.3			Notes Payable-Short Term	13.4	13.4
		1.9	1.7			Cur. Mat.-L/T/D	2.6	2.5
		17.0	15.0			Trade Payables	13.3	12.3
		.0	.1			Income Taxes Payable	.2	.4
		5.8	10.8			All Other Current	9.0	8.9
		48.9	48.0			Total Current	38.6	37.6
		6.1	8.9			Long-Term Debt	9.1	12.1
		.1	.5			Deferred Taxes	.4	.5
		6.8	4.5			All Other Non-Current	7.3	9.0
		38.1	38.1			Net Worth	44.6	40.9
		100.0	100.0			Total Liabilities & Net Worth	100.0	100.0
						INCOME DATA		
		100.0	100.0			Net Sales	100.0	100.0
		29.9	28.8			Gross Profit	28.2	31.4
		29.9	30.0			Operating Expenses	25.9	27.0
		.0	-1.2			Operating Profit	2.3	4.5
		1.0	1.0			All Other Expenses (net)	1.1	1.6
		-1.0	-2.2			Profit Before Taxes	1.2	2.9
						RATIOS		
		2.1	6.1				4.3	3.2
		1.6	1.8			Current	1.8	2.3
		1.0	1.1				1.3	1.5
		1.0	2.9				1.8	2.0
		.6	.9			Quick	.9	1.0
		.4	.7				.5	.5
		29 12.5	36 10.1				28 13.3	24 15.0
		44 8.3	50 7.3			Sales/Receivables	43 8.4	43 8.5
		59 6.2	56 6.5				62 5.9	57 6.4
		48 7.6	54 6.8				58 6.3	55 6.7
		99 3.7	68 5.4			Cost of Sales/Inventory	83 4.4	112 3.2
		156 2.3	142 2.6				140 2.6	155 2.4
		17 21.7	13 28.2				14 26.2	11 34.1
		36 10.3	27 13.5			Cost of Sales/Payables	23 15.6	20 18.1
		49 7.5	58 6.3				42 8.6	42 8.7
		4.1	2.7				3.6	2.9
		7.5	8.8			Sales/Working Capital	6.3	4.7
		NM	27.8				13.4	10.3
		2.9					7.3	7.6
		(20) 1.1				EBIT/Interest	(51) 2.2	(42) 2.5
		-1.2					1.1	1.2
						Net Profit + Depr., Dep.,	4.6	7.1
						Amort./Cur. Mat. L./T/D	(13) 2.2	(13) 1.6
							1.0	1.0
		.1	.1				.2	.1
		.4	.5			Fixed/Worth	.4	.2
		1.5	NM				.7	.6
		1.1	.2				.3	.5
		2.1	2.4			Debt/Worth	1.3	1.1
		6.0	NM				3.3	2.5
		25.6				% Profit Before Taxes/Tangible	28.4	24.7
		(18) 2.4				Net Worth	(52) 8.2	(42) 13.0
		-10.2					.7	1.4
		5.7	10.4			% Profit Before Taxes/Total	11.6	12.8
		.4	-.6			Assets	3.6	4.2
		-3.4	-9.5				-.3	.0
		91.9	37.9				33.7	58.3
		30.9	21.2			Sales/Net Fixed Assets	13.7	17.3
		11.9	11.8				8.6	8.2
		2.5	2.5				2.9	2.6
		2.0	2.1			Sales/Total Assets	2.0	1.8
		1.7	1.8				1.5	1.4
		.4	.8				.7	.6
		(19) .7	1.2			% Depr., Dep., Amort./Sales	(48) 1.4	(36) 1.4
		2.0	1.6				2.5	2.3
		2.3				% Officers', Directors',	1.3	1.3
		(12) 3.9				Owners' Comp/Sales	(23) 2.2	(14) 2.1
		7.9					6.7	4.9
9587M	29200M	200308M	412096M	391422M	459687M	Net Sales ($)	1795372M	2273722M
1683M	7905M	92795M	196868M	232855M	264771M	Total Assets ($)	1017529M	1384919M

© RMA 2005

M = $ thousand   MM = $ million
See Pages 11 through 21 for Explanation of Ratios and Data

Comparative Historical Data   Current Data Sorted By Sales

4/1/02-3/31/03 ALL	4/1/03-3/31/04 ALL	4/1/04-3/31/05 ALL	Type of Statement	0-1MM	1-3MM	3-5MM	5-10MM	10-25MM	25MM & OVER
19	15	12	Unqualified				1	2	4
20	13	10	Reviewed				2	3	3
5	13	7	Compiled		3		2	2	
4	2	6	Tax Returns	3	2	1	1	1	
9	13	15	Other		3	3	5	3	6
					11 (4/1-9/30/04)			39 (10/1/04-3/31/05)	
57	56	50	NUMBER OF STATEMENTS	3	8	4	11	11	13
%	%	%	ASSETS	%	%	%	%	%	%
11.1	10.1	7.4	Cash & Equivalents				4.3	9.7	10.5
24.0	27.8	25.4	Trade Receivables (net)				41.8	21.2	30.9
42.6	37.0	38.6	Inventory				33.7	39.4	38.0
2.5	2.3	3.7	All Other Current				1.1	2.5	1.5
80.2	77.2	75.1	Total Current				80.9	72.9	80.9
13.5	11.6	14.9	Fixed Assets (net)				6.5	17.6	10.9
1.1	6.0	2.9	Intangibles (net)				7.3	.6	1.6
5.2	5.1	7.1	All Other Non-Current				5.2	8.9	6.6
100.0	100.0	100.0	Total				100.0	100.0	100.0
			LIABILITIES						
16.3	12.7	21.1	Notes Payable-Short Term				31.2	18.9	20.2
4.2	2.2	3.2	Cur. Mat.-L/T/D				1.5	1.6	3.0
11.5	17.7	14.2	Trade Payables				18.6	15.6	13.9
.2	.1	.2	Income Taxes Payable				.0	.4	.4
6.1	9.1	8.8	All Other Current				4.8	8.3	9.0
38.2	41.8	47.6	Total Current				56.1	44.8	46.5
9.7	8.5	9.3	Long-Term Debt				4.0	10.1	7.2
.3	.2	.2	Deferred Taxes				.2	.0	.5
8.2	9.8	9.4	All Other Non-Current				5.6	6.6	3.1
43.5	39.7	33.5	Net Worth				34.2	38.6	42.7
100.0	100.0	100.0	Total Liabilities & Net Worth				100.0	100.0	100.0
			INCOME DATA						
100.0	100.0	100.0	Net Sales				100.0	100.0	100.0
32.4	31.3	32.5	Gross Profit				34.6	28.8	30.6
30.4	27.7	30.9	Operating Expenses				31.9	30.0	27.2
2.0	3.6	1.5	Operating Profit				2.7	-1.2	3.4
.6	1.8	.9	All Other Expenses (net)				1.2	.9	.7
1.3	1.8	.6	Profit Before Taxes				1.4	-2.1	2.7
			RATIOS						
5.6	4.6	3.8	Current				2.1	2.3	4.7
2.6	1.9	1.6					1.2	1.8	3.5
1.3	1.2	1.0					1.1	1.0	1.1
2.5	1.9	1.4	Quick				1.4	1.3	2.5
1.0	1.1	.7					.7	.6	.9
.5	.5	.3					.4	.3	.6
25 14.4	30 12.1	9 38.9	Sales/Receivables				46 7.9	10 37.5	41 8.9
43 8.6	46 7.9	44 8.3					59 6.2	42 8.7	49 7.4
68 5.4	71 5.1	59 6.2					82 4.5	56 6.5	72 5.1
79 4.6	51 7.1	43 8.4	Cost of Sales/Inventory				38 9.6	34 10.6	62 5.9
129 2.8	86 4.3	99 3.7					81 4.5	83 4.4	88 4.2
172 2.1	146 2.5	155 2.4					151 2.4	171 2.1	166 2.2
13 29.0	16 23.5	13 28.9	Cost of Sales/Payables				24 15.2	12 29.5	14 25.3
24 15.3	32 11.4	29 12.7					32 11.3	36 10.3	30 12.1
42 8.6	58 6.3	46 7.9					46 8.0	51 7.1	52 7.0
2.6	3.4	3.5	Sales/Working Capital				6.7	3.9	2.6
4.6	6.4	8.3					12.0	6.8	4.0
10.4	19.7	NM					48.9	-84.7	28.5
7.1	13.5	6.5	EBIT/Interest				3.3	2.8	58.7
(50) 2.7	(51) 2.5	(46) 1.6					(10) 2.2	(10) 1.1	3.2
.8	1.5	-.2					-.2	-1.6	.1
18.7			Net Profit + Depr., Dep.,						
(22) 3.3			Amort./Cur. Mat. L/T/D						
1.8									
.1	.1	.1	Fixed/Worth				.0	.0	.1
.2	.3	.4					.2	.1	.4
.5	1.1	3.2					.7	1.7	1.0
.4	.6	.7	Debt/Worth				1.5	1.1	.3
1.1	2.2	2.0					3.1	1.4	1.7
2.8	7.1	9.6					4.8	7.3	5.4
33.4	71.2	34.3	% Profit Before Taxes/Tangible					30.3	27.6
(51) 7.2	(49) 14.4	(41) 16.7	Net Worth					(10) 1.3	(11) 17.9
-1.9	2.9	-1.0						-5.1	.6
10.1	12.4	9.4	% Profit Before Taxes/Total				7.9	7.4	15.4
3.1	5.9	1.8	Assets				5.1	.2	8.6
-2.6	.8	-3.2					-2.7	-6.7	-2.3
50.4	72.5	87.8	Sales/Net Fixed Assets				188.8	190.3	64.5
20.9	24.5	21.3					72.7	22.2	20.4
8.4	13.5	10.1					19.7	8.4	12.3
2.5	2.9	2.8	Sales/Total Assets				2.4	2.9	2.6
1.9	2.1	2.1					1.9	2.1	2.1
1.5	1.5	1.8					1.7	2.0	1.6
.6	.4	.4	% Depr., Dep., Amort./Sales					.4	.4
(53) 1.4	(49) .9	(43) .9						(10) .6	1.1
2.4	1.8	2.0						1.9	1.9
2.2	2.2	2.6	% Officers', Directors',						
(20) 3.7	(20) 3.5	(24) 4.6	Owners' Comp/Sales						
7.0	5.5	7.5							
1721038M	1571532M	1502300M	Net Sales ($)	1722M	14145M	15836M	82785M	169137M	1218675M
1058466M	819441M	796877M	Total Assets ($)	489M	7395M	7236M	40254M	74908M	666595M

M = $ thousand   MM = $ million
See Pages 11 through 21 for Explanation of Ratios and Data

Current Data Sorted By Assets   **Comparative Historical Data**

0-500M	500M-2MM	2-10MM	10-50MM	50-100MM	100-250MM	Type of Statement	4/1/00-3/31/01 ALL	4/1/01-3/31/02 ALL
	1	8	3		1	Unqualified	4	6
		1	3			Reviewed	9	7
	1					Compiled	7	3
						Tax Returns	1	
	1		3			Other	2	4
	7 (4/1-9/30/04)		15 (10/1/04-3/31/05)					
	3	9	9		1	NUMBER OF STATEMENTS	23	20
%	%	%	%	%	%	ASSETS	%	%
D				D		Cash & Equivalents	15.7	10.5
A				A		Trade Receivables (net)	28.6	26.3
T				T		Inventory	37.5	39.1
A				A		All Other Current	5.7	4.5
						Total Current	87.5	80.4
N				N		Fixed Assets (net)	5.0	12.2
O				O		Intangibles (net)	.7	2.2
T				T		All Other Non-Current	6.9	5.3
						Total	100.0	100.0
A				A		LIABILITIES		
V				V		Notes Payable-Short Term	13.3	23.0
A				A		Cur. Mat.-L/T/D	1.1	1.5
I				I		Trade Payables	19.9	23.4
L				L		Income Taxes Payable	.2	.3
A				A		All Other Current	11.5	10.9
B				B		Total Current	46.0	59.1
L				L		Long-Term Debt	5.0	8.4
E				E		Deferred Taxes	.0	.0
						All Other Non-Current	2.8	1.1
						Net Worth	46.5	31.4
						Total Liabilities & Net Worth	100.0	100.0
						INCOME DATA		
						Net Sales	100.0	100.0
						Gross Profit	38.1	35.5
						Operating Expenses	31.0	34.7
						Operating Profit	7.1	.8
						All Other Expenses (net)	.2	1.6
						Profit Before Taxes	6.9	-.8

RATIOS

						Ratio	Hist 1	Hist 2
						Current	2.7	2.5
							1.9	1.6
							1.3	1.3
						Quick	1.2	1.1
							1.0	.7
							.6	.5
						Sales/Receivables	19 / 18.8	5 / 79.9
							42 / 8.6	39 / 9.3
							58 / 6.3	53 / 6.9
						Cost of Sales/Inventory	43 / 8.4	40 / 9.2
							64 / 5.7	61 / 6.0
							166 / 2.2	127 / 2.9
						Cost of Sales/Payables	28 / 13.0	13 / 27.7
							43 / 8.6	37 / 10.0
							47 / 7.8	50 / 7.4
						Sales/Working Capital	3.7	4.8
							7.0	9.4
							15.3	20.5
						EBIT/Interest	7.8	5.3
							(15) 2.4	(15) 1.6
							.0	-.3
						Net Profit + Depr., Dep., Amort./Cur. Mat. L /T/D		
						Fixed/Worth	.0	.1
							.1	.2
							.2	.5
						Debt/Worth	.6	1.0
							1.1	1.4
							2.5	3.8
						% Profit Before Taxes/Tangible Net Worth	60.9	25.9
							(22) 24.1	(18) 6.6
							5.5	-12.2
						% Profit Before Taxes/Total Assets	23.6	8.7
							12.9	2.2
							.3	-12.1
						Sales/Net Fixed Assets	231.2	94.0
							99.4	32.9
							22.7	20.0
						Sales/Total Assets	3.8	3.8
							2.8	3.0
							2.0	2.0
						% Depr., Dep., Amort./Sales	.1	.2
							(18) .3	(16) .7
							.6	1.2
						% Officers', Directors', Owners' Comp/Sales		3.2
								(10) 6.8
								9.8
11280M	236473M	515875M		63463M		Net Sales ($)	713332M	338403M
4093M	55415M	192608M		117792M		Total Assets ($)	325176M	113880M

M = $ thousand   MM = $ million
See Pages 11 through 21 for Explanation of Ratios and Data

Comparative Historical Data | **Current Data Sorted By Sales**

Type of Statement	4/1/02-3/31/03 ALL	4/1/03-3/31/04 ALL	4/1/04-3/31/05 ALL	0-1MM	1-3MM	3-5MM	5-10MM	10-25MM	25MM & OVER
						7 (4/1-9/30/04)		15 (10/1/04-3/31/05)	
Unqualified	13	9	3						3
Reviewed	19	17	13		1		1	6	6
Compiled	4	6	1		1				
Tax Returns		1	1						
Other	2	7	4	1	1		1	1	2
NUMBER OF STATEMENTS	38	40	22	1	3			7	11
ASSETS	%	%	%	%	%	%	%	%	%
Cash & Equivalents	10.8	9.4	7.6						9.7
Trade Receivables (net)	25.2	30.1	32.6						22.2
Inventory	43.9	39.9	43.8	D			D		47.7
All Other Current	4.2	4.9	3.8	A			A		4.4
Total Current	84.2	84.4	87.9	T			T		84.0
Fixed Assets (net)	7.1	8.4	6.0	A			A		7.1
Intangibles (net)	2.9	1.5	2.8						5.4
All Other Non-Current	5.6	5.7	3.4	N			N		3.5
Total	100.0	100.0	100.0	O			O		100.0
LIABILITIES				T			T		
Notes Payable-Short Term	14.2	10.1	17.2						15.9
Cur. Mat.-L/T/D	1.5	1.4	2.9	A			A		3.5
Trade Payables	28.9	23.2	25.9	V			V		22.4
Income Taxes Payable	.6	.3	.1	A			A		.2
All Other Current	11.5	14.8	10.3	I			I		8.9
Total Current	56.7	49.7	56.3	L			L		50.9
Long-Term Debt	5.3	3.8	2.4	A			A		1.2
Deferred Taxes	.2	.3	.3	B			B		.0
All Other Non-Current	3.5	5.0	1.5	L			L		2.5
Net Worth	34.0	41.1	39.5	E			E		45.4
Total Liabilities & Net Worth	100.0	100.0	100.0						100.0
INCOME DATA									
Net Sales	100.0	100.0	100.0						100.0
Gross Profit	31.8	33.0	32.4						32.0
Operating Expenses	28.0	31.2	30.2						28.8
Operating Profit	3.8	1.8	2.2						3.2
All Other Expenses (net)	.7	.4	.2						.2
Profit Before Taxes	3.1	1.4	2.0						3.1
RATIOS									
Current	2.0	2.8	2.3						2.3
	1.5	1.7	1.4						1.4
	1.2	1.3	1.2						1.2
Quick	1.0	1.2	.9						.7
	.6	.7	.6						.6
	.2	.4	.5						.2
Sales/Receivables	1 328.1	19 19.5	18 19.9						3 123.7
	25 14.8	36 10.2	43 8.4						20 18.2
	46 7.9	54 6.8	53 6.9						51 7.1
Cost of Sales/Inventory	38 9.5	39 9.4	49 7.4						52 7.0
	56 6.5	57 6.4	80 4.6						90 4.0
	113 3.2	125 2.9	135 2.7						133 2.7
Cost of Sales/Payables	25 14.7	19 19.1	20 18.2						21 17.4
	32 11.4	31 11.6	29 12.6						29 12.4
	46 7.9	52 7.0	60 6.1						64 5.7
Sales/Working Capital	8.0	5.1	5.8						6.3
	14.0	11.2	13.7						18.0
	38.9	27.0	21.1						20.0
EBIT/Interest	(32) 8.2	(33) 12.2	(19) 7.6						(10) 5.1
	4.2	4.0	3.1						2.9
	1.2	1.2	1.4						.5
Net Profit + Depr., Dep., Amort./Cur. Mat. L/T/D									
Fixed/Worth	.0	.1	.1						.1
	.2	.2	.2						.2
	.8	.4	.2						.5
Debt/Worth	.8	.5	.7						.5
	1.9	1.4	2.2						2.2
	8.7	2.9	3.5						3.2
% Profit Before Taxes/Tangible Net Worth	69.3	58.6	35.2						32.2
	(35) 27.1	(38) 17.3	(21) 15.3						15.3
	3.8	1.8	4.1						-3.2
% Profit Before Taxes/Total Assets	20.1	17.5	13.4						15.7
	11.3	6.7	5.8						6.7
	.6	.6	.7						-.4
Sales/Net Fixed Assets	367.7	227.3	140.2						134.2
	85.5	69.4	64.3						35.1
	28.3	21.7	28.4						18.4
Sales/Total Assets	5.4	4.8	4.6						4.7
	4.0	3.3	3.1						3.5
	2.5	2.1	2.3						1.7
% Depr., Dep., Amort./Sales	(31) .2	(31) .2	(17) .2						
	.3	.5	.4						
	.9	1.4	.5						
% Officers', Directors', Owners' Comp/Sales	(14) 2.2	(18) 2.2							
	5.0	3.6							
	9.0	7.3							
Net Sales ($)	1560678M	1425451M	827091M	2941M	12919M			141430M	669801M
Total Assets ($)	554506M	503439M	369908M	1250M	4893M			46999M	316766M

© RMA 2005

M = $ thousand   MM = $ million

See Pages 11 through 21 for Explanation of Ratios and Data

Current Data Sorted By Assets   **Comparative Historical Data**

						Type of Statement		10	10
	1	3	5	1	1	Unqualified		10	10
1	4	12	2			Reviewed		20	19
1	3	1				Compiled		15	14
1	3					Tax Returns			
1	1		2	1		Other		10	12
	14 (4/1-9/30/04)		29 (10/1/04-3/31/05)					4/1/00-3/31/01	4/1/01-3/31/02
0-500M	500M-2MM	2-10MM	10-50MM	50-100MM	100-250MM			ALL	ALL
3	12	16	9	2	1	NUMBER OF STATEMENTS		55	55
%	%	%	%	%	%	**ASSETS**		%	%
	13.8	7.0				Cash & Equivalents		6.1	4.6
	27.3	37.1				Trade Receivables (net)		31.6	29.4
	48.4	39.2				Inventory		35.2	39.0
	1.7	.1				All Other Current		3.7	3.5
	91.3	83.4				Total Current		76.6	76.4
	7.1	8.8				Fixed Assets (net)		14.0	14.6
	.3	1.3				Intangibles (net)		1.8	3.3
	1.3	6.6				All Other Non-Current		7.6	5.7
	100.0	100.0				Total		100.0	100.0
						LIABILITIES			
	15.7	15.7				Notes Payable-Short Term		18.5	15.4
	9.0	3.8				Cur. Mat.-L/T/D		3.0	1.8
	15.4	19.0				Trade Payables		15.6	16.1
	.1	.1				Income Taxes Payable		.2	.3
	21.7	5.1				All Other Current		9.8	10.5
	62.0	43.7				Total Current		47.0	44.1
	5.9	1.3				Long-Term Debt		8.4	14.6
	.0	.0				Deferred Taxes		.2	.3
	5.0	5.3				All Other Non-Current		4.2	5.0
	27.2	49.7				Net Worth		40.2	35.9
	100.0	100.0				Total Liabilities & Net Worth		100.0	100.0
						INCOME DATA			
	100.0	100.0				Net Sales		100.0	100.0
	34.5	31.0				Gross Profit		33.4	32.4
	31.8	26.3				Operating Expenses		29.5	27.5
	2.7	4.7				Operating Profit		3.8	4.9
	.8	.6				All Other Expenses (net)		1.0	1.8
	1.9	4.0				Profit Before Taxes		2.8	3.1
						RATIOS			
	1.8	2.9						2.8	2.7
	1.4	2.0				Current		1.6	1.8
	1.2	1.3						1.2	1.3
	1.2	1.5						1.5	1.4
	.6	1.2				Quick		.7 (54)	.8
	.2	.5						.4	.4
	17 21.3	24 15.3						18 20.3	12 30.9
	29 12.8	46 7.9				Sales/Receivables		49 7.5	36 10.3
	60 6.1	61 6.0						60 6.1	61 6.0
	30 12.2	42 8.8						35 10.5	35 10.4
	113 3.2	98 3.7				Cost of Sales/Inventory		72 5.1	75 4.9
	217 1.7	129 2.8						122 3.0	108 3.4
	8 46.0	9 40.9						18 19.8	15 24.6
	33 11.0	32 11.3				Cost of Sales/Payables		28 13.3	22 16.7
	67 5.4	50 7.4						40 9.0	41 8.9
	7.4	4.2						5.3	5.0
	10.7	7.5				Sales/Working Capital		9.4	9.4
	14.9	16.9						22.9	19.6
	11.8	35.6						6.7	7.5
	2.8 (15)	5.7				EBIT/Interest		(50) 2.8	(51) 2.6
	1.2	2.6						1.7	1.4
						Net Profit + Depr., Dep.,			21.4
						Amort./Cur. Mat. L /T/D		(12)	8.2
									1.2
	.1	.0						.1	.1
	.3	.2				Fixed/Worth		.2	.3
	.7	.6						.7	.9
	1.9	.5						.6	.8
	3.8	1.0				Debt/Worth		1.7	1.5
	4.7	2.3						3.5	3.0
	53.5	56.4						40.8	45.4
	13.0	28.2				% Profit Before Taxes/Tangible Net Worth		(48) 15.6	(50) 14.3
	1.6	12.7						5.0	4.0
	11.4	20.9						13.1	17.2
	5.9	7.5				% Profit Before Taxes/Total Assets		5.3	6.4
	.4	4.2						1.7	2.0
	128.4	116.1						73.7	67.9
	42.7	37.2				Sales/Net Fixed Assets		29.8	36.1
	30.8	17.9						13.2	14.8
	3.3	4.0						3.7	4.2
	2.6	2.9				Sales/Total Assets		2.6	2.8
	2.3	2.0						1.9	1.9
	.4	.2						.2	.2
	.7 (15)	.4				% Depr., Dep., Amort./Sales		(43) .7	(47) .8
	1.2	1.1						1.7	1.3
								1.1	1.3
						% Officers', Directors', Owners' Comp/Sales		(22) 3.1	(24) 2.9
								4.6	5.5
3093M	43960M	263188M	630926M	441624M	398740M	Net Sales ($)		2539897M	2782580M
855M	15441M	82614M	205885M	124208M	161028M	Total Assets ($)		1164474M	1047037M

M = $ thousand   MM = $ million
See Pages 11 through 21 for Explanation of Ratios and Data

Comparative Historical Data   **Current Data Sorted By Sales**

4/1/02-3/31/03 ALL	4/1/03-3/31/04 ALL	4/1/04-3/31/05 ALL		0-1MM	1-3MM	3-5MM	5-10MM	10-25MM	25MM & OVER
			Type of Statement						
20	13	11	Unqualified			2	1	1	7
39	23	18	Reviewed			3	5	5	5
4	5	5	Compiled	1	1	3			
1	2	4	Tax Returns		3	1			
5	9	5	Other	1	1				3
				14 (4/1-9/30/04)			**29 (10/1/04-3/31/05)**		
69	52	43	**NUMBER OF STATEMENTS**	2	5	9	6	6	15
%	%	%	**ASSETS**	%	%	%	%	%	%
7.4	7.4	10.1	Cash & Equivalents						10.6
30.2	30.6	31.2	Trade Receivables (net)						27.7
42.1	41.1	43.0	Inventory						47.1
3.2	2.6	1.1	All Other Current						1.6
82.9	81.7	85.4	Total Current						87.0
9.7	8.9	8.4	Fixed Assets (net)						7.4
1.6	2.2	.9	Intangibles (net)						.8
5.8	7.2	5.4	All Other Non-Current						4.8
100.0	100.0	100.0	Total						100.0
			LIABILITIES						
12.4	12.7	15.2	Notes Payable-Short Term						13.9
1.2	1.1	5.5	Cur. Mat.-L/T/D						5.2
21.0	19.8	16.9	Trade Payables						18.1
.4	.5	.1	Income Taxes Payable						.2
11.8	14.0	12.3	All Other Current						11.7
46.8	48.0	50.2	Total Current						49.2
5.4	2.5	3.7	Long-Term Debt						3.8
.1	.3	.0	Deferred Taxes						.0
5.5	9.9	5.6	All Other Non-Current						4.8
42.2	39.3	40.6	Net Worth						42.2
100.0	100.0	100.0	Total Liabilities & Net Worth						100.0
			INCOME DATA						
100.0	100.0	100.0	Net Sales						100.0
29.9	29.6	33.1	Gross Profit						30.4
26.6	26.1	30.1	Operating Expenses						24.4
3.3	3.6	3.1	Operating Profit						6.0
.4	1.4	.9	All Other Expenses (net)						1.6
2.9	2.2	2.1	Profit Before Taxes						4.3
			RATIOS						
2.6	2.4	2.9	Current						3.2
1.8	1.7	1.7							1.9
1.4	1.4	1.3							1.4
1.4	1.4	1.4	Quick						1.5
.8	.8	.9							.9
.5	.4	.5							.5
12 31.1	15 24.1	18 20.2	Sales/Receivables						14 25.7
35 10.6	34 10.7	35 10.5							23 15.9
59 6.2	63 5.8	57 6.4							48 7.6
36 10.1	39 9.3	43 8.5	Cost of Sales/Inventory						43 8.5
68 5.4	68 5.4	94 3.9							73 5.0
112 3.2	105 3.5	133 2.7							111 3.3
18 20.5	19 19.1	15 24.5	Cost of Sales/Payables						16 23.2
31 11.9	29 12.6	28 13.2							23 15.6
46 8.0	41 8.8	39 9.2							33 11.0
4.7	5.2	5.6	Sales/Working Capital						5.6
9.6	9.4	8.0							7.8
17.6	15.2	15.1							13.7
12.8	12.1	29.1	EBIT/Interest						30.2
(64) 3.1	(48) 4.7	(40) 5.1						(14)	7.9
1.6	1.1	1.5							2.1
29.3			Net Profit + Depr., Dep.,						
(16) 3.5			Amort./Cur. Mat. L/T/D						
1.0									
.1	.1	.1	Fixed/Worth						.1
.2	.2	.2							.1
.5	.4	.6							.9
.8	.8	.6	Debt/Worth						.4
1.4	1.7	1.4							1.0
2.8	3.5	4.3							4.6
35.3	41.1	49.8	% Profit Before Taxes/Tangible						42.4
(64) 14.7	(49) 24.8	(39) 22.1	Net Worth						(12) 28.2
6.3	6.8	9.5							21.2
16.0	16.0	18.5	% Profit Before Taxes/Total						28.6
6.5	7.9	7.6	Assets						17.3
1.8	1.1	.7							7.3
131.3	81.4	129.7	Sales/Net Fixed Assets						143.6
53.8	43.3	43.3							65.1
18.7	19.8	19.2							29.8
4.1	4.0	3.9	Sales/Total Assets						4.5
2.8	2.8	2.7							3.5
2.2	2.0	2.1							2.5
.3	.2	.3	% Depr., Dep., Amort./Sales						.2
(63) .6	(42) .6	(38) .7						(11)	.3
1.1	1.3	1.3							.7
1.1	1.1	1.2	% Officers', Directors',						
(27) 2.6	(20) 2.3	(21) 3.0	Owners' Comp/Sales						
4.5	3.9	6.8							
3244161M	3298351M	1781531M	Net Sales ($)	883M	10136M	37096M	42931M	99359M	1591126M
1286839M	1512271M	590031M	Total Assets ($)	472M	3788M	18986M	26302M	30296M	510187M

© RMA 2005

M = $ thousand   MM = $ million
See Pages 11 through 21 for Explanation of Ratios and Data

Current Data Sorted By Assets   Comparative Historical Data

						Type of Statement		
	1		3			Unqualified		
	1	3				Reviewed		
3	4	3	3			Compiled		
1	3					Tax Returns		
	1	4		1		Other		
	9 (4/1-9/30/04)		19 (10/1/04-3/31/05)				4/1/00-3/31/01	4/1/01-3/31/02
0-500M	500M-2MM	2-10MM	10-50MM	50-100MM	100-250MM		ALL	ALL
4	10	10	4			NUMBER OF STATEMENTS		
%	%	%	%	%	%	ASSETS	%	%
	19.1	12.4		D	D	Cash & Equivalents		D
	22.4	25.0		A	A	Trade Receivables (net)	D	A
	36.6	44.8		T	T	Inventory	A	T
	.8	2.0		A	A	All Other Current	T	A
	78.9	84.2				Total Current	A	
	15.1	11.2		N	N	Fixed Assets (net)		N
	.1	.8		O	O	Intangibles (net)	N	O
	5.8	3.8		T	T	All Other Non-Current	O	T
	100.0	100.0				Total	T	
				A	A	LIABILITIES		A
	11.3	6.5		V	V	Notes Payable-Short Term	A	V
	2.6	1.2		A	A	Cur. Mat.-L/T/D	V	A
	16.7	23.1		I	I	Trade Payables	A	I
	.0	.8		L	L	Income Taxes Payable	I	L
	6.1	12.0		A	A	All Other Current	L	A
	36.8	43.6		B	B	Total Current	A	B
	8.9	3.2		L	L	Long-Term Debt	B	L
	.0	.4		E	E	Deferred Taxes	L	E
	11.2	2.5				All Other Non-Current	E	
	43.1	50.3				Net Worth		
	100.0	100.0				Total Liabilities & Net Worth		
						INCOME DATA		
	100.0	100.0				Net Sales		
	43.5	29.4				Gross Profit		
	39.2	24.7				Operating Expenses		
	4.4	4.7				Operating Profit		
	.3	.0				All Other Expenses (net)		
	4.1	4.7				Profit Before Taxes		
						RATIOS		
	5.8	3.0						
	2.4	1.9				Current		
	1.5	1.6						
	3.2	1.8						
	1.4	.9				Quick		
	.6	.4						
	5 75.8	24 15.3						
	38 9.6	31 11.8				Sales/Receivables		
	49 7.5	45 8.1						
	34 10.6	36 10.1						
	85 4.3	90 4.1				Cost of Sales/Inventory		
	145 2.5	136 2.7						
	19 19.0	20 18.4						
	44 8.3	27 13.3				Cost of Sales/Payables		
	67 5.5	45 8.1						
	3.9	4.1						
	6.4	8.8				Sales/Working Capital		
	11.9	12.9						
						EBIT/Interest		
						Net Profit + Depr., Dep., Amort./Cur. Mat. L /T/D		
	.2	.2						
	.4	.2				Fixed/Worth		
	1.3	.3						
	.3	.6						
	2.7	.9				Debt/Worth		
	6.5	2.2						
	32.5	49.8						
	8.0	24.8				% Profit Before Taxes/Tangible Net Worth		
	-15.3	9.4						
	21.5	27.9						
	2.5	11.7				% Profit Before Taxes/Total Assets		
	-2.0	4.7						
	38.1	59.5						
	17.6	24.3				Sales/Net Fixed Assets		
	9.9	16.6						
	2.9	3.6						
	2.5	2.8				Sales/Total Assets		
	1.6	1.7						
		.5						
		1.3				% Depr., Dep., Amort./Sales		
		1.9						
						% Officers', Directors', Owners' Comp/Sales		
4589M	22377M	151424M	128069M			Net Sales ($)		
1426M	9944M	52053M	83442M			Total Assets ($)		

© RMA 2005

M = $ thousand   MM = $ million
See Pages 11 through 21 for Explanation of Ratios and Data

Comparative Historical Data / Current Data Sorted By Sales

			Type of Statement	0-1MM	1-3MM	3-5MM	5-10MM	10-25MM	25MM & OVER
4	11	4	Unqualified		1			2	1
2	2	4	Reviewed		1		2		1
4	10	10	Compiled	2	4	1	2		
	1	4	Tax Returns		4				
10	7	6	Other		1				
10	7	6	*(dates)* 4/1/02-3/31/03 ALL / 4/1/03-3/31/04 ALL / 4/1/04-3/31/05 ALL — 9 (4/1-9/30/04) — 19 (10/1/04-3/31/05)						
20	31	28	**NUMBER OF STATEMENTS**	2	11	1	5	5	4
%	%	%	**ASSETS**	%	%	%	%	%	%
11.1	10.4	15.7	Cash & Equivalents		18.0				
23.9	28.7	23.4	Trade Receivables (net)		26.0				
42.9	36.1	37.8	Inventory		33.6				
2.3	3.9	1.8	All Other Current		.8				
80.2	79.1	78.8	Total Current		78.3				
14.8	14.3	15.1	Fixed Assets (net)		15.8				
1.3	2.6	.4	Intangibles (net)		.1				
3.7	4.0	5.7	All Other Non-Current		5.8				
100.0	100.0	100.0	Total		100.0				
			LIABILITIES						
23.4	17.4	11.7	Notes Payable-Short Term		10.3				
2.7	2.6	3.6	Cur. Mat.-L/T/D		7.0				
16.6	17.8	18.8	Trade Payables		15.8				
.5	.2	.3	Income Taxes Payable		.0				
6.0	9.7	7.5	All Other Current		3.9				
49.2	47.6	41.9	Total Current		37.0				
10.8	6.1	8.9	Long-Term Debt		13.5				
.0	.6	.2	Deferred Taxes		.0				
1.1	3.1	8.5	All Other Non-Current		17.4				
38.9	42.6	40.5	Net Worth		32.1				
100.0	100.0	100.0	Total Liabilities & Net Worth		100.0				
			INCOME DATA						
100.0	100.0	100.0	Net Sales		100.0				
33.9	36.3	35.2	Gross Profit		40.4				
29.7	30.3	31.0	Operating Expenses		36.0				
4.2	6.0	4.2	Operating Profit		4.4				
1.1	.8	.2	All Other Expenses (net)		.4				
3.2	5.2	4.0	Profit Before Taxes		4.0				
			RATIOS						
4.6	2.5	4.0	Current		5.0				
1.6	1.6	1.9			1.7				
1.1	1.2	1.5			1.5				
1.9	1.9	2.0	Quick		3.0				
.8	.9	.9			1.3				
.4	.4	.5			.8				
31 11.6	29 12.7	18 20.1	Sales/Receivables		14 26.2				
41 8.9	46 7.9	36 10.1			37 9.7				
68 5.4	60 6.0	48 7.7			48 7.6				
68 5.4	41 9.0	27 13.4	Cost of Sales/Inventory		24 15.2				
121 3.0	105 3.5	89 4.1			53 6.9				
197 1.9	145 2.5	133 2.8			116 3.1				
16 23.2	22 16.9	21 17.6	Cost of Sales/Payables		14 26.7				
35 10.3	39 9.4	34 10.8			28 12.9				
59 6.2	53 6.9	67 5.5			67 5.5				
2.6	3.8	4.5	Sales/Working Capital		4.5				
7.8	7.6	7.5			6.9				
27.0	21.7	13.3			13.5				
8.8	16.0	22.3	EBIT/Interest						
(19) 3.8	(30) 6.4	(24) 2.7							
.6	2.6	.7							
			Net Profit + Depr., Dep., Amort./Cur. Mat. L/T/D						
.1	.1	.2	Fixed/Worth		.3				
.3	.3	.3			.4				
1.2	.6	1.1			2.0				
.3	.7	.4	Debt/Worth		.4				
2.1	1.5	1.1			3.4				
5.8	3.6	6.2			14.0				
35.5	58.2	36.3	% Profit Before Taxes/Tangible Net Worth						
(18) 22.2	(30) 30.0	(25) 18.0							
7.8	12.1	-.3							
13.9	22.2	22.8	% Profit Before Taxes/Total Assets		23.9				
5.5	8.6	5.8			1.4				
-.4	5.0	-1.3			-3.0				
53.3	52.3	38.7	Sales/Net Fixed Assets		39.0				
24.7	21.9	20.4			20.9				
9.0	13.0	11.1			10.7				
2.9	3.1	3.5	Sales/Total Assets		3.5				
1.7	2.3	2.5			2.7				
1.5	1.6	1.6			1.6				
.7	.7	.7	% Depr., Dep., Amort./Sales		.6				
(17) 1.8	(27) 1.5	(26) 1.4			(10) 1.3				
3.1	2.2	2.4			2.5				
2.0	3.1	3.3	% Officers', Directors', Owners' Comp/Sales						
(10) 5.0	(10) 6.5	(13) 5.7							
12.7	14.8	11.6							
540028M	1454112M	306459M	Net Sales ($)	1380M	22263M	3323M	41567M	92270M	145656M
346125M	868383M	146865M	Total Assets ($)	703M	9139M	1528M	17666M	45452M	72377M

M = $ thousand   MM = $ million
See Pages 11 through 21 for Explanation of Ratios and Data

Current Data Sorted By Assets | **Comparative Historical Data**

Type of Statement	0-500M	500M-2MM	2-10MM	10-50MM	50-100MM	100-250MM		4/1/00-3/31/01 ALL	4/1/01-3/31/02 ALL
Unqualified	1	7	9	15	4	4		18	11
Reviewed	2	8	18	6				18	11
Compiled	3	9	6					15	19
Tax Returns			2					4	9
Other	5	4	9	11	4	4		26	30
	32 (4/1-9/30/04)			99 (10/1/04-3/31/05)					
NUMBER OF STATEMENTS	11	28	44	32	8	8		81	80
	%	%	%	%	%	%	**ASSETS**	%	%
Cash & Equivalents	12.2	7.5	9.9	7.2				8.2	7.7
Trade Receivables (net)	30.6	30.4	24.0	30.2				25.4	23.1
Inventory	27.9	30.4	39.9	37.3				36.4	38.6
All Other Current	2.4	2.4	2.6	1.6				3.0	2.4
Total Current	73.1	70.7	76.4	76.4				72.9	71.9
Fixed Assets (net)	16.3	24.7	15.4	12.3				14.5	19.9
Intangibles (net)	3.8	.6	2.4	3.6				4.9	3.6
All Other Non-Current	6.8	3.9	5.8	7.7				7.7	4.7
Total	100.0	100.0	100.0	100.0				100.0	100.0
							LIABILITIES		
Notes Payable-Short Term	10.3	17.2	12.5	19.7				18.8	17.1
Cur. Mat.-L/T/D	1.7	1.6	1.9	1.1				3.1	4.7
Trade Payables	33.3	15.3	13.7	14.6				15.8	14.3
Income Taxes Payable	.1	.0	.2	.2				.4	.1
All Other Current	17.6	3.5	10.7	9.9				8.6	12.5
Total Current	62.9	37.6	39.0	45.6				46.7	48.7
Long-Term Debt	43.7	10.8	10.1	8.5				9.1	12.0
Deferred Taxes	.0	.2	.4	.4				.3	.1
All Other Non-Current	6.9	9.2	3.4	3.0				4.8	5.3
Net Worth	-13.6	42.3	47.0	42.5				39.3	33.9
Total Liabilities & Net Worth	100.0	100.0	100.0	100.0				100.0	100.0
							INCOME DATA		
Net Sales	100.0	100.0	100.0	100.0				100.0	100.0
Gross Profit	48.7	37.8	31.5	34.1				31.7	33.6
Operating Expenses	49.5	34.9	26.9	27.4				26.2	29.8
Operating Profit	-.8	2.9	4.6	6.7				5.6	3.8
All Other Expenses (net)	.4	.6	.9	1.0				1.4	1.4
Profit Before Taxes	-1.2	2.3	3.7	5.7				4.1	2.4
							RATIOS		
Current	4.2	4.3	3.2	3.3				2.5	2.6
	1.4	1.9	1.9	1.8				1.7	1.7
	.6	1.3	1.5	1.3				1.1	1.0
Quick	2.4	1.7	1.8	1.4				1.1	1.2
	1.2	.9	.9	.9				.7	.6
	.3	.6	.4	.5				.4	.3
Sales/Receivables	17 21.7	12 29.7	17 21.1	36 10.0				22 16.9	17 21.6
	21 17.3	38 9.7	36 10.0	48 7.6				39 9.3	37 9.8
	71 5.1	60 6.1	58 6.3	60 6.1				54 6.7	53 6.9
Cost of Sales/Inventory	27 13.5	24 14.9	39 9.5	60 6.1				55 6.6	45 8.2
	43 8.4	52 7.1	105 3.5	99 3.7				82 4.5	92 4.0
	111 3.3	125 2.9	145 2.5	157 2.3				138 2.7	149 2.4
Cost of Sales/Payables	10 37.6	16 22.3	16 23.3	18 20.3				17 21.7	14 26.0
	29 12.8	27 13.4	28 13.2	31 11.6				27 13.6	26 13.8
	72 5.1	42 8.8	41 8.9	57 6.4				42 8.7	40 9.2
Sales/Working Capital	3.5	4.9	3.8	4.2				5.0	5.0
	20.2	8.8	5.9	7.5				9.1	8.2
	-14.2	22.8	11.1	12.9				36.8	185.7
EBIT/Interest		17.3	15.1	12.2				10.0	6.8
		(26) 3.0	(42) 4.0	(26) 4.5				(75) 3.6	(73) 2.2
		1.0	1.2	1.6				1.4	1.2
Net Profit + Depr., Dep., Amort./Cur. Mat. L/T/D			5.9	25.2				6.4	9.1
			(11) 4.4	(11) 4.0				(21) 3.7	(15) 1.5
			1.7	.9				1.8	.7
Fixed/Worth	.1	.2	.1	.1				.1	.2
	.5	.6	.2	.2				.3	.5
	-12.6	.9	.6	.6				1.0	2.1
Debt/Worth	1.2	.8	.6	.4				.8	.9
	3.2	1.8	1.1	1.3				1.6	2.1
	-40.7	3.0	2.5	3.5				5.1	5.2
% Profit Before Taxes/Tangible Net Worth		32.9	45.4	40.5				40.4	34.4
		(42) 14.6	(42) 12.8	(29) 22.1				(72) 20.3	(67) 12.7
		-.1	.8	11.0				4.9	1.9
% Profit Before Taxes/Total Assets	7.3	11.8	17.4	19.6				16.4	13.2
	1.5	6.1	4.4	10.6				7.7	4.5
	-10.0	-.1	.6	2.9				1.3	.2
Sales/Net Fixed Assets	63.9	36.5	63.8	101.5				62.9	37.9
	42.0	16.6	22.9	18.9				17.7	18.7
	11.2	5.3	12.2	11.0				11.2	9.2
Sales/Total Assets	5.1	3.7	3.3	2.8				3.0	3.5
	3.9	2.5	2.2	2.1				2.3	2.4
	2.3	1.9	1.7	1.6				1.6	1.7
% Depr., Dep., Amort./Sales		1.0	.6	.5				.4	.7
		(22) 1.5	(38) .9	(28) 1.3				(67) 1.3	(69) 1.3
		2.6	1.8	1.9				1.9	2.6
% Officers', Directors', Owners' Comp/Sales		2.6	1.7					1.7	2.9
		(12) 4.6	(16) 2.7					(34) 3.2	(38) 5.1
		8.9	6.2					6.6	8.6
Net Sales ($)	13400M	89357M	558135M	1746411M	1000488M	2358325M		3074997M	2205997M
Total Assets ($)	3455M	32537M	217044M	718489M	563325M	1317782M		1629230M	1185733M

M = $ thousand   MM = $ million
See Pages 11 through 21 for Explanation of Ratios and Data

Comparative Historical Data				Current Data Sorted By Sales					
			Type of Statement						
33	36	32	Unqualified				2	9	21
28	41	32	Reviewed		5	5	7	9	6
21	26	16	Compiled		6	4	4	2	
12	17	14	Tax Returns	1	7	3	1	1	1
34	41	37	Other	4	5	3	4	5	16
4/1/02-3/31/03	4/1/03-3/31/04	4/1/04-3/31/05			32 (4/1-9/30/04)		99 (10/1/04-3/31/05)		
ALL	ALL	ALL		0-1MM	1-3MM	3-5MM	5-10MM	10-25MM	25MM & OVER
128	161	131	**NUMBER OF STATEMENTS**	5	23	15	18	26	44
%	%	%	**ASSETS**	%	%	%	%	%	%
8.5	10.3	8.1	Cash & Equivalents		7.9	9.6	13.9	8.8	5.4
25.6	23.0	27.4	Trade Receivables (net)		24.1	29.5	32.3	19.1	31.3
34.0	36.7	36.5	Inventory		29.8	29.7	38.4	40.6	38.8
3.4	3.0	2.5	All Other Current		2.0	1.5	1.8	4.2	2.5
71.6	73.1	74.4	Total Current		63.8	70.3	86.3	72.6	78.0
18.7	16.6	16.4	Fixed Assets (net)		26.0	22.2	11.0	15.4	11.3
3.2	4.3	3.0	Intangibles (net)		4.8	.8	.2	2.9	4.3
6.6	6.0	6.1	All Other Non-Current		5.4	6.6	2.5	9.1	6.4
100.0	100.0	100.0	Total		100.0	100.0	100.0	100.0	100.0
			LIABILITIES						
13.1	14.2	15.8	Notes Payable-Short Term		15.3	12.2	14.0	11.4	20.8
3.5	2.6	1.6	Cur. Mat.-L/T/D		2.0	3.0	.6	2.1	1.2
16.4	14.4	15.6	Trade Payables		11.6	18.6	11.9	14.4	15.4
.2	.5	.2	Income Taxes Payable		.0	.0	.1	.1	.5
10.2	12.7	9.4	All Other Current		9.0	4.1	9.8	10.2	10.5
43.5	44.5	42.5	Total Current		38.0	37.9	36.3	38.3	48.5
11.0	12.8	12.4	Long-Term Debt		15.5	10.6	5.3	7.4	7.5
.5	.4	.3	Deferred Taxes		.1	.4	.5	.5	.3
5.9	5.4	5.8	All Other Non-Current		9.5	7.3	3.2	2.6	6.8
39.1	36.8	38.9	Net Worth		37.0	43.8	54.8	51.2	36.9
100.0	100.0	100.0	Total Liabilities & Net Worth		100.0	100.0	100.0	100.0	100.0
			INCOME DATA						
100.0	100.0	100.0	Net Sales		100.0	100.0	100.0	100.0	100.0
34.4	34.2	35.4	Gross Profit		46.8	31.1	29.8	32.3	32.7
31.0	30.8	30.7	Operating Expenses		44.7	27.5	25.2	28.4	25.4
3.4	3.3	4.7	Operating Profit		2.1	3.6	4.6	3.9	7.3
.8	1.0	.9	All Other Expenses (net)		.1	1.1	.8	.7	1.1
2.6	2.4	3.8	Profit Before Taxes		2.0	2.5	3.8	3.2	6.2
			RATIOS						
3.1	3.1	3.2			4.4	5.2	3.6	3.6	2.6
1.8	1.7	1.9	Current		1.8	1.8	2.4	2.2	1.6
1.3	1.2	1.3			1.1	1.1	1.8	1.4	1.3
1.4	1.4	1.5			1.4	1.8	2.3	1.8	1.3
.8	.7	.9	Quick		.9	.8	1.1	.9	.7
.5	.4	.5			.3	.5	.8	.3	.5
26 14.2	16 22.4	22 16.4		11 34.5	21 17.3	25 14.4	12 30.6	36 10.2	
39 9.4	36 10.1	41 9.0	Sales/Receivables	31 11.7	38 9.6	48 7.6	35 10.3	45 8.2	
60 6.1	54 6.7	60 6.1		56 6.6	59 6.1	67 5.5	60 6.1	59 6.1	
31 11.6	44 8.3	41 9.0		34 10.8	22 16.3	34 10.9	65 5.6	60 6.1	
85 4.3	91 4.0	96 3.8	Cost of Sales/Inventory	61 6.0	71 5.2	116 3.2	109 3.3	101 3.6	
148 2.5	156 2.3	153 2.4		125 2.9	113 3.2	155 2.4	160 2.3	152 2.4	
19 18.7	16 22.6	17 21.3		15 23.6	20 18.2	11 33.8	17 21.4	19 18.8	
30 12.4	29 12.5	30 12.2	Cost of Sales/Payables	31 11.9	30 12.0	19 19.1	35 10.6	33 11.2	
46 7.9	50 7.3	46 8.0		52 7.0	38 9.5	33 11.0	45 8.0	52 7.1	
4.3	4.3	4.2			4.8	4.2	3.7	2.9	5.2
7.8	7.8	6.7	Sales/Working Capital		6.7	10.3	5.3	6.0	8.7
16.4	22.7	14.0			35.0	38.1	7.4	12.2	13.1
10.0	10.1	18.1			6.3	29.8	22.3	18.5	19.9
(109) 4.0	(143) 3.6	(119) 3.9	EBIT/Interest		(21) 2.1	(14) 2.6	4.4	(24) 3.9	(38) 5.7
1.3	1.0	1.3			.3	-.2	1.5	.3	2.6
8.9	4.6	11.5	Net Profit + Depr., Dep.,						19.0
(28) 2.8	(27) 1.4	(28) 4.6	Amort./Cur. Mat. L/T/D						(13) 6.8
1.2	.5	1.8							2.7
.1	.1	.1			.2	.1	.1	.1	.1
.3	.3	.3	Fixed/Worth		.8	.3	.1	.2	.2
1.0	1.2	.9			2.2	.9	.5	.6	.5
.6	.7	.6			.9	.5	.3	.4	.7
1.2	1.6	1.3	Debt/Worth		2.5	2.0	.8	1.1	1.7
3.5	5.0	3.5			5.5	3.0	1.8	2.3	3.8
40.0	30.4	42.0	% Profit Before Taxes/Tangible		41.3	57.1	31.2	33.3	53.2
(112) 15.4	(141) 13.1	(121) 15.5	Net Worth		(21) 12.1	9.7	(17) 13.3	13.4	(39) 27.6
3.5	1.7	2.4			-18.8	-10.2	2.6	-1.5	10.9
12.6	13.6	17.1	% Profit Before Taxes/Total		10.5	19.3	17.3	18.7	21.1
6.2	4.7	7.1	Assets		5.0	3.0	5.6	3.2	9.7
.7	.1	.8			-3.1	-.6	1.0	-.4	3.5
41.4	62.6	59.4			37.1	43.3	82.4	52.8	69.7
19.4	25.9	19.5	Sales/Net Fixed Assets		16.3	17.3	33.9	16.4	24.2
8.2	8.7	10.5			4.7	8.5	16.8	10.4	13.1
3.3	3.0	3.3			3.6	4.0	3.2	3.0	3.3
2.2	2.3	2.2	Sales/Total Assets		2.5	2.4	2.3	2.0	2.1
1.6	1.6	1.7			1.8	1.9	1.7	1.6	1.7
.8	.6	.6			.8	.7	.6	.7	.5
(111) 1.5	(127) 1.1	(105) 1.2	% Depr., Dep., Amort./Sales		(18) 1.4	(11) 1.5	(15) .9	(24) 1.3	(36) 1.0
2.6	1.9	1.9			2.3	2.2	1.7	2.4	1.7
3.4	2.3	2.2			6.8				
(44) 5.0	(49) 6.4	(39) 3.7	% Officers', Directors',		(10) 9.5				
9.4	9.6	9.5	Owners' Comp/Sales		11.8				
5323777M	8102481M	5766116M	Net Sales ($)	2986M	44806M	60329M	135534M	452692M	5069769M
2926588M	4254696M	2852632M	Total Assets ($)	1775M	21866M	26392M	62319M	243232M	2497048M

M = $ thousand   MM = $ million
See Pages 11 through 21 for Explanation of Ratios and Data

Current Data Sorted By Assets   Comparative Historical Data

0-500M	500M-2MM	2-10MM	10-50MM	50-100MM	100-250MM	Type of Statement	4/1/00-3/31/01 ALL	4/1/01-3/31/02 ALL
	1	3	3	2	2	Unqualified	3	8
1	2	9	3			Reviewed	8	6
1	1					Compiled	6	7
1	1	2				Tax Returns	2	
1	6	7	3			Other	6	6
	12 (4/1-9/30/04)		36 (10/1/04-3/31/05)					
2	11	22	9	2	2	**NUMBER OF STATEMENTS**	25	27
%	%	%	%	%	%	**ASSETS**	%	%
	3.1	12.0				Cash & Equivalents	7.6	7.0
	29.2	23.9				Trade Receivables (net)	34.4	25.0
	32.0	24.6				Inventory	31.6	31.1
	3.5	3.8				All Other Current	2.0	6.7
	67.8	64.2				Total Current	75.5	69.8
	25.1	26.6				Fixed Assets (net)	15.0	19.2
	2.3	5.3				Intangibles (net)	2.6	3.0
	4.8	3.9				All Other Non-Current	6.8	8.0
	100.0	100.0				Total	100.0	100.0
						LIABILITIES		
	16.0	8.2				Notes Payable-Short Term	16.4	17.5
	1.3	4.7				Cur. Mat.-L/T/D	3.1	1.7
	19.0	17.0				Trade Payables	22.8	15.6
	.1	.5				Income Taxes Payable	.1	.1
	9.4	9.1				All Other Current	4.4	7.3
	45.7	39.6				Total Current	46.7	42.3
	15.8	7.9				Long-Term Debt	10.2	12.6
	.0	.2				Deferred Taxes	.0	.1
	2.9	5.0				All Other Non-Current	3.7	3.9
	35.6	47.3				Net Worth	39.3	41.1
	100.0	100.0				Total Liabilities & Net Worth	100.0	100.0
						INCOME DATA		
	100.0	100.0				Net Sales	100.0	100.0
	34.1	32.3				Gross Profit	20.0	19.8
	27.3	29.3				Operating Expenses	16.6	16.9
	6.8	3.1				Operating Profit	3.4	2.9
	1.1	1.6				All Other Expenses (net)	1.0	1.5
	5.6	1.5				Profit Before Taxes	2.4	1.5
						RATIOS		
	2.1	2.3					2.4	2.6
	1.5	1.7				Current	1.6	1.8
	1.2	1.1					1.2	1.2
	1.3	1.5					1.4	1.1
	.8	.8				Quick	.8	.9
	.5	.6					.6	.4
	18 19.7	34 10.6					29 12.6	31 12.0
	44 8.2	43 8.5				Sales/Receivables	48 7.5	36 10.0
	53 6.8	62 5.9					56 6.5	46 8.0
	25 14.7	29 12.8					16 22.8	22 16.9
	70 5.2	56 6.5				Cost of Sales/Inventory	45 8.1	51 7.1
	99 3.7	122 3.0					126 2.9	116 3.1
	18 20.3	19 19.1					16 23.2	9 42.7
	34 10.6	27 13.7				Cost of Sales/Payables	21 17.8	19 19.2
	63 5.8	59 6.1					42 8.8	34 10.8
	6.7	5.5					5.8	4.9
	13.6	8.5				Sales/Working Capital	9.2	7.5
	28.3	NM					31.1	37.4
	27.1	13.3					6.6	6.0
	4.0	(21) 3.9				EBIT/Interest	(21) 2.1	(25) 1.9
	2.2	−2.5					.2	1.1
						Net Profit + Depr., Dep., Amort./Cur. Mat. L /T/D		
	.0	.2					.1	.1
	.6	.8				Fixed/Worth	.2	.3
	1.1	1.4					.7	1.4
	.9	.7					.7	.6
	1.7	1.0				Debt/Worth	1.9	1.3
	5.2	4.8					3.6	4.2
	70.1	38.7				% Profit Before Taxes/Tangible	40.2	35.3
	(10) 27.2	(20) 14.3				Net Worth	(24) 11.7	(25) 21.7
	6.6	.6					−6.7	2.0
	35.3	11.3				% Profit Before Taxes/Total	15.1	12.2
	6.4	6.3				Assets	3.4	2.9
	4.0	−2.4					−1.2	.5
	138.5	31.8					347.5	87.5
	24.9	8.1				Sales/Net Fixed Assets	39.1	17.7
	6.8	4.1					9.0	10.2
	4.3	3.0					3.9	3.6
	2.9	2.2				Sales/Total Assets	2.4	2.4
	2.5	1.2					1.6	1.4
		1.2					.5	.2
	(21)	2.1				% Depr., Dep., Amort./Sales	(21) 1.0	(22) .8
		3.8					3.0	2.7
		3.5					1.1	
	(11)	5.7				% Officers', Directors', Owners' Comp/Sales	(13) 2.0	
		7.0					6.7	
969M	44365M	217786M	404052M	263200M	564506M	Net Sales ($)	1258456M	1645218M
127M	14384M	97430M	148175M	117536M	342517M	Total Assets ($)	527912M	702744M

M = $ thousand   MM = $ million
See Pages 11 through 21 for Explanation of Ratios and Data

Comparative Historical Data | Current Data Sorted By Sales

			Type of Statement						
13	13	11	Unqualified		1			2	8
10	10	15	Reviewed	1	3	1	2	7	1
7	10	2	Compiled		1	1			
2	2	4	Tax Returns		1	1	1		
9	13	16	Other	1		7	4	4	1
4/1/02-3/31/03 ALL	4/1/03-3/31/04 ALL	4/1/04-3/31/05 ALL		12 (4/1-9/30/04)			36 (10/1/04-3/31/05)		
				0-1MM	1-3MM	3-5MM	5-10MM	10-25MM	25MM & OVER
41	48	48	**NUMBER OF STATEMENTS**	2	6	10	7	13	10
%	%	%	**ASSETS**	%	%	%	%	%	%
7.9	8.1	9.7	Cash & Equivalents			8.3		15.0	3.7
25.8	29.7	24.9	Trade Receivables (net)			28.3		24.8	28.6
25.5	26.9	29.6	Inventory			21.7		27.5	33.1
5.5	3.3	2.9	All Other Current			2.1		5.8	1.2
64.7	68.0	67.0	Total Current			60.4		73.0	66.7
21.9	22.2	22.5	Fixed Assets (net)			28.9		19.6	14.8
5.5	6.2	5.0	Intangibles (net)			6.5		2.9	7.6
8.0	3.7	5.5	All Other Non-Current			4.2		4.5	10.9
100.0	100.0	100.0	Total			100.0		100.0	100.0
			LIABILITIES						
16.2	15.6	13.6	Notes Payable-Short Term			8.0		7.6	16.4
2.3	1.7	3.1	Cur. Mat.-L/T/D			2.2		2.3	2.4
17.2	17.1	16.0	Trade Payables			16.8		20.6	16.9
.3	.2	.3	Income Taxes Payable			.0		.2	.0
10.3	12.6	8.2	All Other Current			6.8		11.0	5.2
46.3	47.2	41.3	Total Current			33.7		41.6	40.9
13.5	11.5	10.2	Long-Term Debt			20.1		7.6	8.9
.1	.2	.3	Deferred Taxes			.0		.7	.2
2.8	2.5	4.7	All Other Non-Current			2.8		8.6	3.4
37.4	38.6	43.5	Net Worth			43.4		41.5	46.7
100.0	100.0	100.0	Total Liabilities & Net Worth			100.0		100.0	100.0
			INCOME DATA						
100.0	100.0	100.0	Net Sales			100.0		100.0	100.0
27.8	25.6	30.6	Gross Profit			36.6		30.3	19.3
24.9	20.9	26.2	Operating Expenses			33.9		22.9	16.8
2.9	4.8	4.5	Operating Profit			2.7		7.4	2.5
1.1	1.2	1.3	All Other Expenses (net)			1.8		1.4	1.1
1.9	3.6	3.1	Profit Before Taxes			.8		6.1	1.3
			RATIOS						
2.6	2.5	2.9	Current			2.2		3.5	3.4
1.6	1.5	1.7				1.5		1.9	1.9
1.0	1.0	1.2				1.4		1.2	1.0
1.7	1.7	1.6	Quick			1.4		2.0	1.8
.7	.7	.8				.8		.8	1.0
.4	.4	.5				.6		.6	.4
28 13.3	35 10.5	28 12.9	Sales/Receivables			34 10.8		34 10.7	26 13.9
38 9.7	43 8.4	44 8.3				48 7.6		46 8.0	42 8.7
56 6.5	63 5.8	59 6.1				64 5.7		64 5.7	58 6.3
20 17.9	23 16.1	30 12.2	Cost of Sales/Inventory			28 13.0		23 15.6	32 11.4
44 8.3	43 8.5	67 5.4				48 7.7		65 5.6	60 6.1
113 3.2	123 3.0	113 3.2				90 4.1		100 3.6	97 3.7
13 27.3	15 24.1	19 19.2	Cost of Sales/Payables			24 15.2		22 16.4	21 17.3
23 15.8	28 13.0	31 11.9				37 10.0		33 11.2	31 11.9
40 9.2	46 8.0	46 8.0				61 6.0		38 9.6	45 8.0
5.6	5.8	5.6	Sales/Working Capital			5.6		3.7	7.4
11.4	11.5	9.4				10.3		6.4	10.4
UND	818.3	26.7				22.5		NM	NM
6.7	11.3	11.5	EBIT/Interest			27.2		14.9	7.2
(35) 2.1	(45) 5.5	(44) 4.0				5.8		(11) 3.1	4.1
.8	1.3	1.3				1.8			-1.1
		5.2	Net Profit + Depr., Dep.,						
		(13) 2.2	Amort./Cur. Mat. L/T/D						
		.7							
.2	.2	.1	Fixed/Worth			.1		.1	.1
.4	.6	.6				1.0		.4	.3
5.3	1.2	1.1				NM		1.3	1.0
.6	.9	.8	Debt/Worth			.8		.7	.7
1.5	1.6	1.4				1.2		1.1	1.5
17.8	6.0	5.0				NM		11.1	2.9
57.2	43.2	43.3	% Profit Before Taxes/Tangible					46.0	21.3
(33) 16.5	(44) 26.2	(44) 14.7	Net Worth					(12) 19.4	13.9
7.0	4.0	4.3						4.3	-9.2
14.1	16.2	11.5	% Profit Before Taxes/Total			25.5		19.6	8.7
6.0	6.6	6.2	Assets			6.8		6.2	4.4
1.0	.5	.6				1.5		.9	-3.7
44.8	52.9	64.2	Sales/Net Fixed Assets			71.1		67.6	62.6
13.7	18.3	14.4				7.6		16.7	14.5
6.1	7.5	6.5				2.7		6.2	10.4
3.4	3.2	3.3	Sales/Total Assets			3.4		3.1	3.3
2.4	2.2	2.4				2.7		2.2	2.6
1.5	1.4	1.5				1.2		1.5	1.7
.6	.8	.7	% Depr., Dep., Amort./Sales					.5	.4
(35) 1.7	(40) 2.2	(44) 1.6						1.5	1.3
2.7	3.7	3.1						2.8	2.0
1.9	3.2	3.7	% Officers', Directors',						
(12) 4.4	(14) 5.6	(19) 5.7	Owners' Comp/Sales						
10.0	9.7	7.0							
2403259M	1936071M	1494878M	Net Sales ($)	969M	13439M	41811M	48960M	190049M	1199650M
1160535M	990165M	720169M	Total Assets ($)	127M	10620M	23886M	18647M	93234M	573655M

© RMA 2005

M = $ thousand   MM = $ million
See Pages 11 through 21 for Explanation of Ratios and Data

Current Data Sorted By Assets   Comparative Historical Data

						Type of Statement		
1	2	7	37	13	8	Unqualified	58	79
1	14	35	21		2	Reviewed	65	61
3	20	21	3	1	2	Compiled	63	79
7	14	3	2			Tax Returns	18	22
2	6	14	27	4	3	Other	64	86
	58 (4/1-9/30/04)		215 (10/1/04-3/31/05)				4/1/00-3/31/01	4/1/01-3/31/02
0-500M	500M-2MM	2-10MM	10-50MM	50-100MM	100-250MM		ALL	ALL
14	56	80	90	18	15	NUMBER OF STATEMENTS	268	327
%	%	%	%	%	%	ASSETS	%	%
6.5	7.0	5.0	4.4	7.8	4.7	Cash & Equivalents	5.7	5.3
9.8	14.8	14.5	10.4	8.8	6.6	Trade Receivables (net)	11.7	11.8
17.4	24.2	27.9	30.4	24.7	14.2	Inventory	27.9	26.8
1.6	4.9	3.2	4.0	6.9	5.3	All Other Current	3.9	4.8
35.4	50.9	50.7	49.2	48.3	30.8	Total Current	49.3	48.7
51.2	44.5	40.3	42.5	36.4	46.9	Fixed Assets (net)	40.6	41.0
.4	.8	.7	.5	2.8	.2	Intangibles (net)	1.0	.8
12.9	3.8	8.3	7.8	12.4	22.2	All Other Non-Current	9.1	9.5
100.0	100.0	100.0	100.0	100.0	100.0	Total	100.0	100.0
						LIABILITIES		
24.5	14.5	14.8	16.6	4.8	4.2	Notes Payable-Short Term	15.4	13.1
10.0	9.4	6.4	5.6	5.0	3.9	Cur. Mat.-L/T/D	5.4	5.4
9.9	9.5	6.3	6.4	6.1	4.3	Trade Payables	6.5	7.0
.0	.1	.1	.2	1.0	1.1	Income Taxes Payable	.2	.1
1.1	4.9	7.7	5.9	6.4	4.0	All Other Current	6.7	5.5
45.5	38.3	35.4	34.7	23.3	17.5	Total Current	34.2	31.0
36.4	22.6	18.8	20.3	28.3	34.6	Long-Term Debt	22.2	25.0
.0	.4	.5	.8	1.6	.8	Deferred Taxes	.5	.6
3.2	8.7	3.0	5.9	1.8	3.8	All Other Non-Current	3.3	3.6
15.0	30.0	42.3	38.4	45.0	43.2	Net Worth	39.8	39.8
100.0	100.0	100.0	100.0	100.0	100.0	Total Liabilities & Net Worth	100.0	100.0
						INCOME DATA		
100.0	100.0	100.0	100.0	100.0	100.0	Net Sales	100.0	100.0
30.5	31.5	23.4	18.9	20.9	23.1	Gross Profit	19.5	20.3
29.1	27.1	17.9	11.7	9.9	11.1	Operating Expenses	16.0	17.4
1.5	4.4	5.5	7.3	11.0	12.0	Operating Profit	3.5	2.9
1.1	.9	1.0	.9	1.0	1.6	All Other Expenses (net)	1.5	1.4
.3	3.5	4.5	6.4	10.1	10.4	Profit Before Taxes	2.0	1.5
						RATIOS		
3.6	2.7	2.5	2.7	2.8	2.2		2.7	2.9
.7	1.6	1.5	1.6	2.2	1.8	Current	1.5	1.7
.3	.9	1.1	1.1	1.4	1.2		1.0	1.1
2.9	1.6	1.1	.8	1.5	.9		1.0	1.0
.3	.6	.5	.4	.6	.6	Quick	.5	.5
.1	.2	.2	.3	.3	.3		.2	.2
0 UND	7 53.3	11 32.6	12 29.5	13 29.0	14 26.5		11 33.0	11 34.4
7 55.6	15 24.1	18 20.3	17 21.1	15 24.2	23 16.2	Sales/Receivables	16 22.8	18 20.7
27 13.7	28 12.9	27 13.5	24 14.9	20 18.0	29 12.8		25 14.4	26 14.0
0 UND	18 19.8	30 12.4	42 8.6	44 8.4	28 13.3		32 11.4	32 11.5
29 12.7	46 7.9	56 6.6	61 5.9	61 6.0	55 6.6	Cost of Sales/Inventory	56 6.6	56 6.5
59 6.1	71 5.1	97 3.8	104 3.5	112 3.2	105 3.5		94 3.9	95 3.8
0 UND	3 145.5	5 76.1	8 43.3	10 35.5	12 31.1		4 86.3	4 84.7
3 131.8	12 30.7	8 48.4	13 27.2	14 26.6	15 24.5	Cost of Sales/Payables	9 38.5	11 31.9
30 12.2	29 12.6	19 19.4	20 18.6	20 18.1	24 14.9		17 21.4	20 18.1
9.0	7.5	7.5	5.9	5.2	5.3		6.3	5.5
−33.3	16.3	14.3	10.5	7.5	10.4	Sales/Working Capital	12.7	11.3
−6.9	−72.5	49.8	43.8	16.0	15.8		180.6	61.2
	8.2	11.3	17.2	20.0	13.0		5.1	3.6
(53) 4.2	(77) 4.5	(88) 5.5	(17) 10.9	5.7	EBIT/Interest	(252) 1.8	(302) 1.5
	1.2	2.2	2.4	6.3	2.3		.6	.3
		3.8	3.6			Net Profit + Depr., Dep.,	3.0	3.3
		(23) 2.4	(24) 2.4			Amort./Cur. Mat. L /T/D	(66) 1.4	(81) 1.5
		1.4	1.4				.7	.2
.9	.5	.5	.6	.4	.5		.5	.5
2.4	1.1	.9	1.0	1.0	.7	Fixed/Worth	1.0	.9
UND	2.9	1.8	2.0	1.3	2.4		2.1	2.2
1.6	.7	.5	.7	.7	.9		.7	.6
2.1	1.5	1.7	1.4	1.4	1.5	Debt/Worth	1.5	1.5
UND	6.2	2.7	3.1	2.2	3.0		3.4	4.5
97.1	45.4	34.0	43.5	35.0	40.8	% Profit Before Taxes/Tangible	22.6	21.0
(11) 53.2	(46) 12.4	(76) 18.4	(85) 28.3	(17) 30.5	29.5	Net Worth	(243) 9.6	(300) 6.5
.9	2.5	7.9	13.1	17.9	8.9		−1.6	−5.1
25.7	18.4	16.0	19.6	19.1	19.0	% Profit Before Taxes/Total	9.7	8.5
8.4	5.8	7.5	10.2	11.9	7.4	Assets	3.3	2.1
−1.8	.5	2.8	3.3	9.1	3.5		−2.2	−2.9
13.3	10.8	9.4	8.5	8.1	3.9		9.8	9.5
9.2	6.1	5.6	4.4	5.3	2.4	Sales/Net Fixed Assets	5.4	4.9
3.7	3.7	3.3	2.9	2.7	.8		3.2	2.9
5.7	3.3	2.8	2.3	2.1	1.4		2.8	2.6
3.6	2.4	2.1	1.7	1.5	1.0	Sales/Total Assets	2.0	1.8
1.9	2.0	1.5	1.4	1.1	.6		1.4	1.3
1.9	1.7	2.2	2.1	1.3	2.7		2.1	1.7
(12) 2.6	(52) 2.7	(77) 3.0	(84) 4.0	2.3	(10) 3.8	% Depr., Dep., Amort./Sales	(248) 3.3	(306) 3.3
5.0	5.1	5.5	5.1	4.5	10.0		5.5	5.5
	1.3	1.3	1.2			% Officers', Directors',	1.2	1.3
(25) 3.5	(31) 2.2	(19) 1.8			Owners' Comp/Sales	(92) 1.9	(100) 1.9
	7.6	3.1	2.7				4.6	4.0
10208M	194328M	807533M	3569923M	2341113M	2565650M	Net Sales ($)	9489578M	7802169M
3486M	69009M	379941M	1913051M	1324314M	2320578M	Total Assets ($)	5023073M	5260892M

© RMA 2005   M = $ thousand   MM = $ million
See Pages 11 through 21 for Explanation of Ratios and Data

Comparative Historical Data | Current Data Sorted By Sales

Hist 1	Hist 2	Hist 3	Type of Statement	0-1MM	1-3MM	3-5MM	5-10MM	10-25MM	25MM & OVER
69	69	68	Unqualified	1	1	3	3	10	50
63	58	73	Reviewed	2	8	13	9	23	18
52	68	50	Compiled	2	12	10	14	9	3
25	32	26	Tax Returns	6	7	6	5	1	1
60	60	56	Other	2	5	4	5	13	27
4/1/02-3/31/03 ALL	4/1/03-3/31/04 ALL	4/1/04-3/31/05 ALL		58 (4/1-9/30/04)			215 (10/1/04-3/31/05)		
269	287	273	NUMBER OF STATEMENTS	13	33	36	36	56	99
%	%	%	ASSETS	%	%	%	%	%	%
5.1	6.0	5.5	Cash & Equivalents	4.5	6.1	6.6	5.3	4.1	5.8
10.3	11.5	12.2	Trade Receivables (net)	7.7	12.1	11.9	17.5	13.5	10.2
26.2	26.0	26.5	Inventory	14.9	17.5	24.3	31.8	33.3	26.0
4.8	4.8	4.1	All Other Current	7.7	4.3	2.2	2.8	3.0	5.4
46.3	48.2	48.2	Total Current	34.8	40.0	45.0	57.5	53.8	47.3
44.3	43.0	42.5	Fixed Assets (net)	48.4	54.9	46.4	34.8	38.1	41.6
1.0	1.2	.8	Intangibles (net)	.4	.2	1.6	1.2	.5	.7
8.4	7.6	8.5	All Other Non-Current	16.3	5.0	7.0	6.5	7.7	10.4
100.0	100.0	100.0	Total	100.0	100.0	100.0	100.0	100.0	100.0
			LIABILITIES						
13.3	13.1	14.6	Notes Payable-Short Term	19.2	19.7	12.1	13.9	19.6	10.6
7.0	6.2	6.7	Cur. Mat.-L/T/D	13.3	9.3	9.2	5.7	5.1	5.4
6.0	6.3	7.0	Trade Payables	10.5	6.6	8.3	6.4	7.1	6.5
.1	.2	.2	Income Taxes Payable	.0	.0	.1	.1	.2	.5
4.8	5.4	5.9	All Other Current	1.9	3.5	3.0	11.0	5.6	6.5
31.2	31.3	34.5	Total Current	45.0	39.2	32.7	37.1	37.6	29.5
25.1	26.1	22.5	Long-Term Debt	33.7	25.4	26.6	16.6	17.1	23.7
.6	.6	.7	Deferred Taxes	.0	.3	.6	.5	.8	.8
6.1	5.4	5.1	All Other Non-Current	3.1	11.6	4.8	1.8	4.0	5.0
37.0	36.6	37.3	Net Worth	18.2	23.5	35.3	44.0	40.5	40.9
100.0	100.0	100.0	Total Liabilities & Net Worth	100.0	100.0	100.0	100.0	100.0	100.0
			INCOME DATA						
100.0	100.0	100.0	Net Sales	100.0	100.0	100.0	100.0	100.0	100.0
19.0	21.5	23.8	Gross Profit	35.5	37.5	23.3	23.1	20.7	19.8
17.0	17.8	17.4	Operating Expenses	32.7	33.4	18.5	18.1	15.1	10.7
1.9	3.7	6.4	Operating Profit	2.8	4.2	4.8	4.9	5.6	9.1
1.2	1.0	1.0	All Other Expenses (net)	1.7	1.2	1.1	.7	1.0	.9
.8	2.7	5.4	Profit Before Taxes	1.1	2.9	3.7	4.2	4.6	8.2
			RATIOS						
2.5	2.9	2.6	Current	7.0	2.4	2.5	3.0	2.6	2.6
1.6	1.6	1.6		.6	1.4	1.2	1.7	1.6	1.7
1.1	1.1	1.1		.3	.7	.9	1.1	1.1	1.2
.9	1.1	1.0	Quick	3.5	1.4	.8	1.5	1.0	1.0
.4	.5	.5		.2	.5	.5	.5	.4	.6
.2	.2	.3		.2	.2	.2	.3	.3	.3
10 35.4	10 34.8	11 33.0	Sales/Receivables	0 UND	7 50.9	6 65.5	12 31.0	12 30.3	13 28.7
17 21.9	17 21.2	17 22.1		10 37.7	16 23.3	14 26.4	20 18.4	17 21.5	17 21.7
24 15.3	26 14.0	26 14.1		20 17.8	32 11.3	23 15.9	31 11.8	27 13.6	23 16.0
27 13.6	31 11.9	30 12.3	Cost of Sales/Inventory	0 UND	11 33.8	23 16.1	32 11.2	43 8.5	36 10.1
56 6.5	56 6.6	55 6.6		24 15.0	43 8.4	50 7.3	61 6.0	73 5.0	54 6.7
91 4.0	95 3.8	98 3.7		91 4.0	72 5.1	79 4.6	95 3.9	126 2.9	95 3.8
5 80.6	6 65.4	6 59.1	Cost of Sales/Payables	0 UND	4 84.8	5 74.1	1 254.4	6 62.6	9 40.8
10 36.1	12 30.4	12 30.2		2 148.5	11 33.1	10 36.2	7 50.6	12 31.0	13 27.1
20 17.9	18 20.2	22 16.8		47 7.7	35 10.5	27 13.7	17 21.6	22 16.3	20 18.4
6.5	5.7	6.5	Sales/Working Capital	6.0	7.4	7.9	7.6	6.2	5.9
13.0	11.4	13.1		-34.7	30.3	26.4	13.8	11.4	9.7
89.8	56.5	96.8		-4.3	-19.9	-30.3	39.2	39.5	33.3
4.1	7.4	12.9	EBIT/Interest		5.4	10.5	8.9	19.3	17.8
(253) 1.7	(272) 2.6	(259) 5.4			(29) 3.0	3.4	(33) 4.9	7.5	(96) 7.0
.1	1.1	2.2			1.1	1.2	2.5	2.3	3.0
3.4	3.1	3.8	Net Profit + Depr., Dep.,				6.9	2.9	4.1
(66) 1.6	(72) 2.0	(67) 2.4	Amort./Cur. Mat. L/T/D				(12) 3.1	(15) 2.3	(28) 2.5
.4	1.0	1.3					1.0	1.8	1.2
.6	.5	.6	Fixed/Worth	.5	.7	.9	.5	.5	.6
1.1	1.1	1.0		2.1	1.5	1.5	1.0	.9	.9
2.7	2.3	2.1		UND	34.7	2.8	1.2	1.8	1.8
.7	.6	.7	Debt/Worth	1.1	.6	1.0	.5	.5	.7
1.8	1.8	1.5		1.8	1.7	2.3	1.5	1.8	1.4
3.9	4.0	3.1		UND	37.6	6.0	2.4	3.5	2.5
19.0	26.3	41.8	% Profit Before Taxes/Tangible	81.1	34.1	41.2	39.0	33.4	45.0
(245) 7.1	(265) 10.5	(250) 24.2	Net Worth	(10) 23.2	(26) 6.8	(32) 20.2	(34) 23.4	(52) 17.2	(96) 31.6
-4.4	1.4	9.6		-1.8	-1.3	4.9	6.3	11.1	16.4
7.1	10.3	18.5	% Profit Before Taxes/Total	22.8	13.0	12.8	15.7	16.7	20.9
1.9	3.8	8.1	Assets	.6	5.0	5.0	8.2	7.2	12.2
-2.1	.3	2.6		-5.8	-.9	.4	3.4	3.4	5.7
8.2	9.2	9.2	Sales/Net Fixed Assets	14.5	6.8	9.5	13.2	9.8	8.7
4.7	4.6	5.3		5.6	3.9	4.8	6.4	4.9	5.0
2.9	2.8	3.0		1.3	1.7	3.0	5.1	3.3	2.8
2.7	2.7	2.7	Sales/Total Assets	5.3	2.7	2.9	3.2	2.7	2.4
1.8	1.8	2.0		2.0	2.0	2.1	2.4	1.8	1.9
1.2	1.2	1.4		.6	1.0	1.5	1.9	1.4	1.3
2.2	2.0	2.0	% Depr., Dep., Amort./Sales	1.9	2.2	1.9	1.4	2.4	1.9
(249) 3.7	(264) 3.8	(253) 3.2		(12) 3.0	(30) 4.4	(33) 3.2	(35) 2.6	(52) 3.0	(91) 3.5
5.5	6.1	5.1		9.9	9.0	6.8	3.8	5.0	4.9
1.1	1.3	1.4	% Officers', Directors',		1.9	1.4	.9	1.1	1.2
(86) 2.3	(90) 2.5	(84) 2.2	Owners' Comp/Sales		(14) 4.7	(11) 2.6	(17) 1.7	(20) 1.7	(15) 2.0
3.7	4.7	4.4			7.3	4.2	4.2	2.7	2.9
7727374M	8387657M	9488755M	Net Sales ($)	7235M	64429M	141464M	267772M	910243M	8097612M
4961739M	5294992M	6010379M	Total Assets ($)	4340M	47587M	81424M	122796M	618418M	5135814M

© RMA 2005

M = $ thousand   MM = $ million

See Pages 11 through 21 for Explanation of Ratios and Data

Current Data Sorted By Assets   **Comparative Historical Data**

						Type of Statement		
		5	10		1	Unqualified	6	9
	1	7	1			Reviewed	10	6
2	1	2				Compiled	6	8
2	1					Tax Returns	3	
1	2	4	4		1	Other	19	16
	15 (4/1-9/30/04)		30 (10/1/04-3/31/05)				4/1/00-3/31/01 ALL	4/1/01-3/31/02 ALL
0-500M	500M-2MM	2-10MM	10-50MM	50-100MM	100-250MM			
5	5	18	15		2	**NUMBER OF STATEMENTS**	44	39
%	%	%	%	%	%	**ASSETS**	%	%
		3.5	2.8	D		Cash & Equivalents	4.1	3.7
		26.7	22.5	A		Trade Receivables (net)	17.0	21.8
		37.7	37.3	T		Inventory	36.7	31.3
		1.0	1.6	A		All Other Current	2.4	2.5
		69.0	64.3			Total Current	60.1	59.3
		24.9	26.3	N		Fixed Assets (net)	32.0	31.0
		.1	.6	O		Intangibles (net)	.5	.9
		6.0	8.8	T		All Other Non-Current	7.4	8.7
		100.0	100.0			Total	100.0	100.0
				A		**LIABILITIES**		
		24.9	14.4	V		Notes Payable-Short Term	19.8	13.1
		3.4	4.1	A		Cur. Mat.-L/T/D	6.0	2.8
		8.9	16.1	I		Trade Payables	7.2	8.6
		.5	.0	L		Income Taxes Payable	.1	.2
		8.1	6.6	A		All Other Current	9.5	3.7
		45.8	41.2	B		Total Current	42.5	28.4
		7.2	18.4	L		Long-Term Debt	18.2	21.2
		.6	.3	E		Deferred Taxes	.2	.4
		5.0	3.7			All Other Non-Current	2.0	3.5
		41.4	36.4			Net Worth	37.1	46.6
		100.0	100.0			Total Liabilities & Net Worth	100.0	100.0
						INCOME DATA		
		100.0	100.0			Net Sales	100.0	100.0
		15.6	13.9			Gross Profit	18.2	19.0
		11.9	10.0			Operating Expenses	13.3	13.0
		3.7	3.8			Operating Profit	4.9	6.0
		.0	.4			All Other Expenses (net)	1.3	.8
		3.7	3.4			Profit Before Taxes	3.6	5.2
						RATIOS		
		2.4	2.0				2.4	3.5
		1.7	1.6			Current	1.6	2.1
		1.1	1.3				1.1	1.4
		.9	1.0				.8	1.6
		.6	.6			Quick	.4	.8
		.4	.3				.2	.5
		15 23.9	17 21.8				8 47.6	14 26.5
		26 14.0	23 16.0			Sales/Receivables	14 26.1	26 14.3
		33 11.0	36 10.3				26 14.1	33 11.0
		22 16.5	38 9.7				26 14.3	21 17.8
		46 7.9	53 6.9			Cost of Sales/Inventory	46 7.9	45 8.1
		64 5.7	70 5.2				89 4.1	67 5.4
		5 68.4	8 47.3				5 79.5	6 59.7
		9 38.8	17 22.1			Cost of Sales/Payables	9 41.2	9 39.8
		13 27.1	38 9.6				17 21.6	16 23.2
		10.2	7.9				7.4	6.6
		17.6	10.3			Sales/Working Capital	17.4	10.4
		85.4	22.9				90.2	21.1
		32.6	15.6				(41) 5.4	(38) 7.4
	(17)	9.7	(14) 8.3			EBIT/Interest	2.6	4.2
		4.2	2.3				1.1	1.7
						Net Profit + Depr., Dep., Amort./Cur. Mat. L/T/D		
		.3	.3				.4	.3
		.5	.7			Fixed/Worth	.8	.7
		1.4	2.1				1.7	1.2
		.8	.8				.6	.5
		1.4	1.7			Debt/Worth	1.7	1.0
		2.5	5.7				3.8	2.3
		68.5	52.9			% Profit Before Taxes/Tangible	(42) 34.1	(35) 38.3
		38.3	(14) 39.8			Net Worth	14.2	26.1
		19.1	9.0				4.2	10.7
		24.6	22.8			% Profit Before Taxes/Total	13.7	17.8
		16.3	8.9			Assets	4.1	10.1
		3.5	3.6				.4	2.9
		42.6	45.0				27.8	42.3
		15.6	16.3			Sales/Net Fixed Assets	12.8	12.9
		8.5	5.5				5.3	6.2
		5.1	4.8				5.4	4.4
		4.0	3.1			Sales/Total Assets	3.3	3.1
		2.6	2.1				1.9	1.8
		.6	.5				(41) .8	(36) .4
	(17)	.9	(13) .7			% Depr., Dep., Amort./Sales	1.2	1.3
		1.8	2.2				2.9	2.6
						% Officers', Directors',	(11) .4	(10) .4
						Owners' Comp/Sales	1.5	.8
							3.5	2.2
7148M	17803M	368238M	1174484M		626791M	Net Sales ($)	2164589M	1854996M
1565M	5243M	91317M	361974M		309851M	Total Assets ($)	806719M	677553M

M = $ thousand   MM = $ million
See Pages 11 through 21 for Explanation of Ratios and Data

Comparative Historical Data / Current Data Sorted By Sales

Hist 1	Hist 2	Hist 3	Type of Statement	0-1MM	1-3MM	3-5MM	5-10MM	10-25MM	25MM & OVER
13	17	16	Unqualified				1	3	12
9	8	9	Reviewed				2	3	4
7	8	5	Compiled	1		2		2	
2	1	3	Tax Returns	1	2	1			
16	9	12	Other	1	1	1	2	2	5
4/1/02-3/31/03 ALL	4/1/03-3/31/04 ALL	4/1/04-3/31/05 ALL		15 (4/1-9/30/04)			30 (10/1/04-3/31/05)		
47	43	45	**NUMBER OF STATEMENTS**	3	3	3	5	10	21
%	%	%	**ASSETS**	%	%	%	%	%	%
5.1	3.6	6.5	Cash & Equivalents					4.6	3.1
20.7	22.1	23.7	Trade Receivables (net)					20.9	25.4
32.5	35.6	32.8	Inventory					33.5	38.0
1.8	2.2	2.3	All Other Current					1.2	1.3
60.1	63.6	65.3	Total Current					60.3	67.9
30.0	27.9	28.0	Fixed Assets (net)					34.0	22.9
1.3	1.3	.4	Intangibles (net)					.0	.6
8.5	7.2	6.3	All Other Non-Current					5.7	8.6
100.0	100.0	100.0	Total					100.0	100.0
			LIABILITIES						
15.2	16.2	19.4	Notes Payable-Short Term					19.8	19.9
3.4	3.3	3.8	Cur. Mat.-L/T/D					4.3	3.1
9.3	11.6	12.3	Trade Payables					8.0	14.8
.1	1.1	.2	Income Taxes Payable					.5	.1
7.7	6.7	7.4	All Other Current					10.1	6.1
35.7	38.9	43.1	Total Current					42.8	44.1
17.8	19.4	13.7	Long-Term Debt					10.7	14.1
.4	1.1	.5	Deferred Taxes					.6	.7
1.5	4.2	3.5	All Other Non-Current					7.6	2.6
44.6	36.4	39.3	Net Worth					38.2	38.6
100.0	100.0	100.0	Total Liabilities & Net Worth					100.0	100.0
			INCOME DATA						
100.0	100.0	100.0	Net Sales					100.0	100.0
19.2	15.2	21.3	Gross Profit					16.3	13.4
16.1	12.2	15.2	Operating Expenses					12.4	9.3
3.2	2.9	6.2	Operating Profit					3.9	4.0
.5	.5	.3	All Other Expenses (net)					.3	.2
2.6	2.4	5.9	Profit Before Taxes					3.5	3.9
			RATIOS						
3.0	2.7	2.5	Current					2.4	2.0
1.7	1.8	1.7						1.8	1.6
1.3	1.2	1.3						1.0	1.3
1.3	1.0	1.0	Quick					.9	.9
.8	.6	.7						.6	.6
.4	.5	.4						.4	.3
12 30.8	19 19.6	16 22.1	Sales/Receivables					16 22.4	14 25.2
21 17.0	26 13.9	26 14.2						26 14.0	23 16.1
30 12.0	34 10.6	35 10.5						34 10.6	32 11.5
20 18.7	22 16.7	21 17.5	Cost of Sales/Inventory					23 15.9	25 14.7
45 8.2	44 8.2	47 7.8						46 8.0	47 7.7
73 5.0	79 4.6	65 5.6						55 6.6	66 5.5
5 72.2	7 51.4	6 58.6	Cost of Sales/Payables					6 62.8	7 52.2
10 35.6	13 27.8	12 30.4						12 30.9	9 38.5
18 20.0	19 19.6	26 13.8						17 21.7	20 18.0
6.8	5.6	7.6	Sales/Working Capital					8.3	8.6
15.7	13.7	14.5						11.6	18.9
29.5	40.9	30.9						NM	24.2
11.1	9.2	18.8	EBIT/Interest					14.7	19.0
(44) 5.3	(41) 3.7	(38) 8.6						8.1	(20) 9.3
2.0	1.1	2.7						2.5	4.6
4.2	2.8	7.6	Net Profit + Depr., Dep., Amort./Cur. Mat. L/T/D						
(14) 2.4	(17) 1.9	(16) 3.2							
1.1	.7	1.7							
.4	.4	.3	Fixed/Worth					.4	.3
.7	.7	.5						1.0	.5
1.1	1.4	1.4						1.9	1.0
.7	.9	.7	Debt/Worth					.7	.8
1.1	1.9	1.5						2.4	1.6
2.2	3.8	2.5						2.6	2.4
33.6	33.2	65.4	% Profit Before Taxes/Tangible Net Worth					96.6	55.4
(44) 20.1	(39) 20.5	(42) 40.7						29.3	(20) 44.5
7.8	3.7	13.1						7.2	27.6
14.2	16.6	23.4	% Profit Before Taxes/Total Assets					21.5	23.4
6.8	6.6	14.6						13.4	18.6
1.9	.4	4.2						2.5	5.2
33.2	28.9	42.9	Sales/Net Fixed Assets					28.1	42.4
10.3	12.4	14.7						8.4	17.8
6.1	7.6	7.5						6.9	10.3
4.7	4.4	4.6	Sales/Total Assets					4.3	4.8
3.2	3.3	3.3						3.2	4.4
2.3	1.9	2.2						2.1	2.5
.7	.7	.6	% Depr., Dep., Amort./Sales						.5
(42) 1.2	(40) 1.1	(40) 1.1						(19)	.7
2.5	1.7	2.3							1.1
.6	.5	1.0	% Officers', Directors', Owners' Comp/Sales						
(17) 1.2	(17) 1.2	(13) 2.2							
2.7	2.4	4.3							
3054074M	2235006M	2194464M	Net Sales ($)	2045M	4152M	11941M	34528M	175370M	1966428M
1071037M	791797M	769950M	Total Assets ($)	820M	1302M	2990M	14709M	63701M	686428M

M = $ thousand   MM = $ million
See Pages 11 through 21 for Explanation of Ratios and Data

Current Data Sorted By Assets   Comparative Historical Data

						Type of Statement		
		2	10	3	1	Unqualified	20	19
	1	11	3		1	Reviewed	16	16
1	5	8	3			Compiled	11	5
1	3	3				Tax Returns	1	2
1	4	5	7	3	3	Other	19	13
	16 (4/1-9/30/04)		63 (10/1/04-3/31/05)				4/1/00-3/31/01	4/1/01-3/31/02
0-500M	500M-2MM	2-10MM	10-50MM	50-100MM	100-250MM		ALL	ALL
3	13	29	23	6	5	**NUMBER OF STATEMENTS**	67	55
%	%	%	%	%	%	**ASSETS**	%	%
	9.6	6.8	4.7			Cash & Equivalents	7.5	5.5
	27.2	23.7	18.8			Trade Receivables (net)	18.1	14.6
	22.7	33.2	40.2			Inventory	29.5	32.5
	2.1	1.5	3.0			All Other Current	3.2	5.3
	61.6	65.2	66.8			Total Current	58.2	58.0
	31.9	27.6	28.9			Fixed Assets (net)	31.5	32.4
	.6	3.1	.7			Intangibles (net)	1.7	.8
	5.9	4.1	3.7			All Other Non-Current	8.5	8.8
	100.0	100.0	100.0			Total	100.0	100.0
						LIABILITIES		
	12.8	13.7	21.2			Notes Payable-Short Term	14.7	15.6
	6.1	4.1	2.9			Cur. Mat.-L/T/D	3.5	5.2
	27.1	15.2	9.4			Trade Payables	8.7	10.2
	.2	.2	.2			Income Taxes Payable	.4	.4
	11.5	7.1	7.1			All Other Current	7.0	4.1
	57.6	40.2	40.7			Total Current	34.3	35.4
	21.4	14.7	13.4			Long-Term Debt	18.8	17.2
	.2	.5	1.2			Deferred Taxes	.7	.7
	9.0	6.3	3.3			All Other Non-Current	2.1	2.1
	11.8	38.4	41.3			Net Worth	44.0	44.6
	100.0	100.0	100.0			Total Liabilities & Net Worth	100.0	100.0
						INCOME DATA		
	100.0	100.0	100.0			Net Sales	100.0	100.0
	27.4	20.2	19.5			Gross Profit	19.2	18.1
	31.7	17.0	14.2			Operating Expenses	14.6	14.6
	-4.3	3.1	5.3			Operating Profit	4.6	3.5
	.1	1.2	1.4			All Other Expenses (net)	1.1	1.2
	-4.4	1.9	3.9			Profit Before Taxes	3.5	2.3
						RATIOS		
	2.6	3.4	3.1				2.8	3.1
	1.2	1.7	1.6			Current	1.8	1.7
	.5	1.1	1.1				1.2	1.2
	1.3	1.5	1.4				1.4	1.3
	.7	.7	.6			Quick	.8	.5
	.2	.5	.3				.4	.3
24	15.4 24	15.2 26	14.0				21 17.5	17 21.8
32	11.3 38	9.5 41	8.9			Sales/Receivables	30 12.0	28 13.1
49	7.5 53	6.8 52	7.0				45 8.1	39 9.5
14	26.3 30	12.3 62	5.9				32 11.6	46 8.0
24	15.4 71	5.1 111	3.3			Cost of Sales/Inventory	67 5.4	80 4.6
64	5.7 108	3.4 158	2.3				115 3.2	125 2.9
13	28.6 16	23.5 13	28.7				9 41.9	10 38.2
29	12.7 28	13.2 18	20.2			Cost of Sales/Payables	14 26.2	16 22.6
71	5.2 37	10.0 32	11.3				27 13.7	28 12.9
	8.0	4.7	3.1				4.1	4.7
	46.0	8.0	6.8			Sales/Working Capital	9.5	8.3
	-7.7	38.3	36.1				22.6	26.1
	5.1	7.0	17.5				7.0	3.8
	(12) 1.8	(27) 4.2	5.2			EBIT/Interest	(63) 2.6	(54) 2.3
	-11.5	1.1	1.7				1.1	1.1
			5.3			Net Profit + Depr., Dep.,	7.8	6.8
		(10)	2.4			Amort./Cur. Mat. L/T/D	(21) 2.6	(20) 3.3
			1.1				.9	1.6
	.4	.4	.4				.3	.4
	1.0	.7	.7			Fixed/Worth	.8	.8
	-2.8	1.5	1.7				1.4	1.2
	1.3	1.0	.5				.7	.7
	2.4	2.1	1.9			Debt/Worth	1.1	1.2
	-8.0	3.8	4.4				3.1	2.8
		50.5	35.8			% Profit Before Taxes/Tangible	33.0	17.4
		(25) 10.4	12.8			Net Worth	(62) 14.4	(54) 8.1
		3.6	6.5				3.9	1.2
	11.5	12.6	13.1			% Profit Before Taxes/Total	14.5	6.7
	2.8	4.0	6.3			Assets	5.9	3.4
	-31.6	1.0	2.3				.7	.6
	31.0	30.5	10.2				12.5	11.5
	10.5	8.0	5.8			Sales/Net Fixed Assets	7.4	6.1
	4.1	4.4	3.7				3.9	3.6
	4.2	3.0	2.1				2.5	2.2
	2.5	2.0	1.6			Sales/Total Assets	2.0	1.8
	1.7	1.6	1.1				1.2	1.2
	1.1	1.4	1.5				1.3	1.1
	(11) 2.1	(27) 2.1	(21) 2.9			% Depr., Dep., Amort./Sales	(59) 2.3	(49) 2.6
	3.7	3.8	3.7				4.1	4.9
		1.0				% Officers', Directors',	1.4	
	(11)	1.8				Owners' Comp/Sales	(14) 3.8	
		3.2					5.8	
2511M	45173M	338257M	1027751M	839979M	1579354M	Net Sales ($)	2330461M	1758879M
1129M	15599M	144638M	578371M	421340M	778736M	Total Assets ($)	1295142M	1063646M

M = $ thousand   MM = $ million
See Pages 11 through 21 for Explanation of Ratios and Data

Comparative Historical Data | Current Data Sorted By Sales

				Type of Statement						
	18	23	16	Unqualified					4	12
	12	16	16	Reviewed			2	5	6	3
	7	11	17	Compiled	1	2	2	6	4	2
	3	10	7	Tax Returns	1	2		3	1	
	24	19	23	Other	1	2	2	3	7	8
	4/1/02-3/31/03 ALL	4/1/03-3/31/04 ALL	4/1/04-3/31/05 ALL		16 (4/1-9/30/04)			63 (10/1/04-3/31/05)		
					0-1MM	1-3MM	3-5MM	5-10MM	10-25MM	25MM & OVER
	64	79	79	NUMBER OF STATEMENTS	3	6	6	17	22	25
	%	%	%	**ASSETS**	%	%	%	%	%	%
	5.5	5.7	6.4	Cash & Equivalents				3.4	10.4	4.3
	18.0	19.7	20.9	Trade Receivables (net)				23.8	22.3	16.9
	32.7	31.7	33.1	Inventory				25.5	41.3	35.3
	3.2	3.7	2.9	All Other Current				2.8	1.9	2.4
	59.4	60.8	63.3	Total Current				55.5	75.9	58.9
	29.3	29.6	28.3	Fixed Assets (net)				37.0	18.4	29.6
	3.7	3.1	3.5	Intangibles (net)				4.3	.9	6.9
	7.6	6.5	4.9	All Other Non-Current				3.3	4.9	4.5
	100.0	100.0	100.0	Total				100.0	100.0	100.0
				LIABILITIES						
	14.7	13.2	14.8	Notes Payable-Short Term				17.0	13.7	17.6
	4.9	4.7	4.2	Cur. Mat.-L/T/D				5.9	2.0	3.1
	12.2	9.8	14.7	Trade Payables				12.7	16.7	8.0
	.2	.1	.1	Income Taxes Payable				.1	.3	.0
	5.8	7.7	7.3	All Other Current				6.6	6.6	6.4
	37.9	35.6	41.1	Total Current				42.3	39.3	35.0
	16.1	15.4	15.2	Long-Term Debt				20.3	8.8	12.8
	1.1	1.0	.6	Deferred Taxes				.6	.3	1.3
	2.5	5.0	6.4	All Other Non-Current				4.5	6.8	5.0
	42.4	43.1	36.7	Net Worth				32.3	44.8	45.8
	100.0	100.0	100.0	Total Liabilities & Net Worth				100.0	100.0	100.0
				INCOME DATA						
	100.0	100.0	100.0	Net Sales				100.0	100.0	100.0
	18.9	20.1	21.9	Gross Profit				20.0	19.7	17.4
	16.5	17.8	18.7	Operating Expenses				18.3	14.8	10.8
	2.4	2.3	3.2	Operating Profit				1.6	4.9	6.6
	.8	.5	1.0	All Other Expenses (net)				1.4	.8	1.0
	1.6	1.8	2.2	Profit Before Taxes				.2	4.2	5.6
				RATIOS						
	2.7	2.9	3.1	Current				2.9	4.5	2.9
	1.6	1.9	1.6					1.6	1.8	1.6
	1.2	1.2	1.1					.7	1.3	1.1
	1.1	1.4	1.4	Quick				1.3	3.3	1.4
	.6	.7	.7					.7	.8	.6
	.4	.4	.3					.4	.5	.3
17	21.0	18 19.7	24 15.5	Sales/Receivables				31 11.9	24 15.2	19 19.1
30	12.2	31 11.8	37 10.0					38 9.5	37 9.7	34 10.9
50	7.3	48 7.6	47 7.8					56 6.5	45 8.2	44 8.3
33	11.0	36 10.0	33 10.9	Cost of Sales/Inventory				25 14.5	30 12.2	50 7.3
68	5.4	87 4.2	79 4.6					71 5.1	82 4.4	90 4.1
115	3.2	131 2.8	127 2.9					103 3.5	147 2.5	135 2.7
12	29.6	10 37.8	13 28.0	Cost of Sales/Payables				17 22.1	14 26.8	13 29.2
18	19.9	17 20.9	22 16.4					29 12.7	22 17.0	17 21.6
36	10.2	23 16.1	36 10.1					37 9.8	36 10.0	23 15.8
	4.9	4.5	4.4	Sales/Working Capital				4.8	2.8	4.6
	11.7	9.7	8.4					19.3	6.5	9.6
	25.2	24.8	50.2					-7.9	20.1	43.1
	4.5	6.0	9.1	EBIT/Interest				5.5	20.1	22.0
(61)	1.9	(77) 2.7	(75) 4.1					(15) 1.5	5.6	(24) 4.6
	1.1	.7	1.4					-.9	3.0	1.8
	3.5	6.6	4.9	Net Profit + Depr., Dep., Amort./Cur. Mat. L/T/D						5.3
(19)	1.9	(30) 1.8	(26) 1.7						(12)	1.9
	.9	.8	.8							.5
	.4	.4	.4	Fixed/Worth				.5	.1	.5
	.7	.7	.7					1.3	.5	.7
	1.4	1.2	1.7					-14.7	.8	1.7
	.7	.7	.9	Debt/Worth				1.0	.3	.6
	1.4	1.5	1.9					1.5	2.2	1.6
	3.6	3.1	4.4					-29.1	3.2	4.1
	14.2	20.9	40.1	% Profit Before Taxes/Tangible Net Worth				29.2	41.3	39.6
(59)	7.5	(73) 7.9	(68) 12.8					(12) 10.2	11.6	(23) 13.3
	1.0	-.9	4.4					.9	5.8	5.1
	5.7	7.9	14.2	% Profit Before Taxes/Total Assets				7.9	15.7	15.8
	2.5	3.6	5.3					1.9	6.2	7.6
	.0	-.5	1.3					-6.7	2.4	2.1
	15.5	16.2	20.3	Sales/Net Fixed Assets				16.7	34.4	9.9
	7.0	7.2	7.8					5.1	12.7	7.1
	3.9	3.8	4.5					2.6	6.2	3.7
	2.6	2.5	2.8	Sales/Total Assets				2.7	3.4	2.5
	1.8	1.8	1.9					1.9	2.0	1.8
	1.4	1.3	1.5					1.4	1.6	1.3
	1.3	1.1	1.4	% Depr., Dep., Amort./Sales				1.5	.8	1.7
(52)	2.6	(65) 2.6	(69) 2.2					2.3	(19) 1.9	(22) 2.7
	4.2	3.5	3.7					3.9	3.0	3.6
	1.3	1.5	1.1	% Officers', Directors', Owners' Comp/Sales						
(11)	3.2	(14) 2.7	(21) 3.2							
	5.1	7.2	4.9							
	2252865M	3584615M	3833025M	Net Sales ($)	2511M	12319M	22438M	121307M	398549M	3275901M
	1385344M	1937453M	1939813M	Total Assets ($)	1129M	7077M	10117M	74822M	219914M	1626754M

M = $ thousand   MM = $ million
See Pages 11 through 21 for Explanation of Ratios and Data

Current Data Sorted By Assets							Comparative Historical Data	
	1	7	6	1	2	Type of Statement		
		14	3	1		Unqualified	7	3
	8	6	1			Reviewed	13	11
3	8	4	1			Compiled	16	21
	11	11	4		1	Tax Returns	7	6
						Other	14	22
	8 (4/1-9/30/04)		85 (10/1/04-3/31/05)				4/1/00-3/31/01	4/1/01-3/31/02
0-500M	500M-2MM	2-10MM	10-50MM	50-100MM	100-250MM		ALL	ALL
3	28	42	15	3	2	NUMBER OF STATEMENTS	57	63
%	%	%	%	%	%	ASSETS	%	%
	7.7	4.6	5.6			Cash & Equivalents	5.5	8.0
	28.9	31.1	33.1			Trade Receivables (net)	26.2	27.2
	23.9	21.5	23.9			Inventory	19.8	21.0
	1.3	1.9	2.8			All Other Current	2.0	3.0
	61.8	59.1	65.5			Total Current	53.5	59.2
	31.4	32.2	22.0			Fixed Assets (net)	34.5	30.7
	4.0	3.3	5.8			Intangibles (net)	3.0	5.0
	2.7	5.4	6.7			All Other Non-Current	9.0	5.2
	100.0	100.0	100.0			Total	100.0	100.0
						LIABILITIES		
	4.7	10.5	15.9			Notes Payable-Short Term	11.6	13.6
	5.8	4.4	3.6			Cur. Mat.-L/T/D	6.0	4.4
	15.4	12.7	13.3			Trade Payables	10.6	10.8
	.0	.5	.3			Income Taxes Payable	.3	.6
	6.5	9.3	8.6			All Other Current	8.7	10.8
	32.3	37.3	41.7			Total Current	37.3	40.2
	19.5	18.9	11.8			Long-Term Debt	20.1	19.9
	.2	.8	.5			Deferred Taxes	.4	.3
	3.5	6.9	8.9			All Other Non-Current	4.2	3.5
	44.5	36.1	37.1			Net Worth	38.1	36.2
	100.0	100.0	100.0			Total Liabilities & Net Worth	100.0	100.0
						INCOME DATA		
	100.0	100.0	100.0			Net Sales	100.0	100.0
	30.8	24.7	21.8			Gross Profit	30.1	30.1
	25.3	21.6	15.4			Operating Expenses	24.6	26.2
	5.6	3.1	6.4			Operating Profit	5.5	3.9
	.5	.5	.2			All Other Expenses (net)	1.6	1.1
	5.1	2.6	6.2			Profit Before Taxes	3.9	2.7
						RATIOS		
	3.8	3.6	4.0				2.4	2.3
	2.5	1.8	1.7			Current	1.4	1.5
	1.4	1.0	1.1				1.1	1.2
	2.5	2.0	2.5				1.3	1.3
	1.6	1.1	.9			Quick	.9	.9
	.7	.6	.4				.6	.6
	24 15.1	29 12.8	35 10.5				22 16.6	21 17.8
	30 12.3	39 9.5	46 8.0			Sales/Receivables	30 12.0	30 12.3
	41 8.8	51 7.2	71 5.1				40 9.2	40 9.1
	24 15.1	21 17.6	31 11.7				19 19.5	22 16.9
	36 10.3	33 10.9	36 10.2			Cost of Sales/Inventory	32 11.5	36 10.3
	56 6.6	52 7.0	53 6.9				45 8.2	49 7.5
	5 69.4	9 39.1	12 30.9				6 58.4	8 47.4
	12 30.1	16 23.2	18 20.6			Cost of Sales/Payables	16 23.5	14 26.6
	25 14.4	27 13.5	33 11.1				30 12.3	27 13.4
	6.5	6.9	4.7				9.4	8.4
	10.1	11.8	10.2			Sales/Working Capital	21.5	17.1
	18.4	164.7	49.0				102.3	50.7
	24.2	12.3	24.3				7.7	6.9
	(25) 9.6	(38) 5.1	6.8			EBIT/Interest	(51) 3.8	(61) 2.9
	1.9	.5	2.4				1.4	.9
		3.5				Net Profit + Depr., Dep.,	4.3	4.0
		(10) 2.1				Amort./Cur. Mat. L/T/D	(14) 1.8	(13) 2.7
		-.6					.3	1.2
	.5	.3	.3				.6	.5
	.6	1.0	.6			Fixed/Worth	.9	.9
	1.6	3.6	30.0				2.6	2.2
	.6	.4	.4				.9	.8
	1.0	2.5	1.6			Debt/Worth	2.0	1.9
	6.0	8.0	49.8				3.9	6.3
	78.7	67.2	55.3			% Profit Before Taxes/Tangible	70.0	52.8
	(26) 36.9	(36) 28.2	(12) 29.6			Net Worth	(53) 33.2	(55) 21.7
	3.5	8.2	23.2				7.9	-.6
	34.3	17.7	21.1			% Profit Before Taxes/Total	21.5	17.0
	14.1	8.6	10.7			Assets	10.0	6.4
	.7	-.1	5.7				2.7	-.5
	25.6	18.8	19.2				20.3	19.9
	8.5	8.4	11.8			Sales/Net Fixed Assets	10.0	12.3
	6.6	4.7	7.9				5.5	6.2
	3.9	3.4	2.7				4.0	4.1
	3.1	2.5	2.4			Sales/Total Assets	2.9	2.9
	2.4	2.0	2.2				2.2	2.3
	1.0	1.4	.7				1.3	1.4
	(25) 2.6	(39) 2.2	1.6			% Depr., Dep., Amort./Sales	(51) 2.3	(58) 1.9
	4.0	3.2	2.6				3.2	3.5
	2.1	1.0				% Officers', Directors',	1.7	2.7
	(12) 4.8	(16) 3.2				Owners' Comp/Sales	(20) 2.6	(21) 4.0
	7.0	5.2					5.9	6.2
6354M	121774M	549953M	578140M	614183M	329567M	Net Sales ($)	835248M	729735M
1158M	34770M	191531M	222931M	240240M	319319M	Total Assets ($)	329287M	291776M

© RMA 2005

M = $ thousand   MM = $ million
See Pages 11 through 21 for Explanation of Ratios and Data

Comparative Historical Data				Current Data Sorted By Sales					
			Type of Statement						
11	9	17	Unqualified		1	1	5	2	8
23	19	18	Reviewed			2	3	10	3
18	23	15	Compiled		4	3	3	3	2
5	8	16	Tax Returns		5	4	1	5	1
17	32	27	Other		2	6	7	6	6
4/1/02-3/31/03	**4/1/03-3/31/04**	**4/1/04-3/31/05**			**8 (4/1-9/30/04)**		**85 (10/1/04-3/31/05)**		
ALL	**ALL**	**ALL**		**0-1MM**	**1-3MM**	**3-5MM**	**5-10MM**	**10-25MM**	**25MM & OVER**
74	91	93	**NUMBER OF STATEMENTS**		12	16	19	26	20
%	%	%	**ASSETS**	%	%	%	%	%	%
6.7	8.9	5.7	Cash & Equivalents	DATA NOT AVAILABLE	7.9	9.0	4.9	3.6	5.3
27.0	28.3	30.5	Trade Receivables (net)		23.0	27.4	31.7	32.2	34.3
19.7	22.6	22.3	Inventory		22.9	21.9	20.9	25.1	20.2
2.9	3.1	2.9	All Other Current		3.7	1.7	2.1	1.7	5.5
56.3	62.9	61.5	Total Current		57.5	60.0	59.6	62.6	65.3
32.7	29.4	30.1	Fixed Assets (net)		38.2	34.0	30.4	28.1	24.6
2.5	1.7	3.7	Intangibles (net)		2.7	4.8	4.8	2.8	3.6
8.5	6.1	4.7	All Other Non-Current		1.7	1.2	5.3	6.5	6.5
100.0	100.0	100.0	Total		100.0	100.0	100.0	100.0	100.0
			LIABILITIES						
13.8	9.8	9.9	Notes Payable-Short Term		5.8	8.9	5.9	12.6	13.4
4.5	3.9	4.8	Cur. Mat.-L/T/D		7.6	6.9	5.2	3.6	2.6
9.0	11.1	13.3	Trade Payables		16.4	14.1	14.7	11.0	12.4
.2	.3	.3	Income Taxes Payable		1.0	.0	.0	.3	.2
11.1	10.8	8.5	All Other Current		8.4	9.5	8.6	7.6	8.8
38.6	35.9	36.7	Total Current		39.1	39.4	34.4	35.1	37.5
22.7	16.4	17.6	Long-Term Debt		16.1	20.6	19.7	17.9	13.7
.4	.4	.5	Deferred Taxes		.5	.0	.9	.6	.7
2.8	4.5	6.2	All Other Non-Current		3.2	3.3	9.0	4.0	10.6
35.5	42.7	38.9	Net Worth		41.0	36.8	36.0	42.5	37.6
100.0	100.0	100.0	Total Liabilities & Net Worth		100.0	100.0	100.0	100.0	100.0
			INCOME DATA						
100.0	100.0	100.0	Net Sales		100.0	100.0	100.0	100.0	100.0
30.4	26.7	26.2	Gross Profit		28.6	26.8	28.0	26.1	22.5
25.9	22.1	21.7	Operating Expenses		29.2	22.5	23.2	20.5	16.7
4.5	4.5	4.5	Operating Profit		–.5	4.3	4.8	5.6	5.8
.7	.6	.5	All Other Expenses (net)		.2	1.1	.3	.4	.3
3.8	4.0	4.0	Profit Before Taxes		–.8	3.2	4.5	5.2	5.5
			RATIOS						
2.5	3.3	3.6			3.2	3.9	3.5	4.2	3.6
1.6	1.8	2.0	Current		2.0	2.3	2.1	1.8	1.8
1.1	1.3	1.1			.9	1.0	.9	1.1	1.3
1.6	1.8	2.2			2.3	2.7	1.7	2.2	2.4
1.0	1.0	1.1	Quick		.8	1.5	1.3	.9	1.1
.6	.7	.6			.4	.5	.7	.6	.5
23 16.1	**24** 15.1	**27** 13.6			**15** 24.5	**26** 13.8	**27** 13.5	**28** 12.9	**31** 11.7
34 10.8	**36** 10.1	**38** 9.5	Sales/Receivables		**23** 15.8	**34** 10.7	**39** 9.5	**38** 9.6	**45** 8.1
45 8.1	**46** 8.0	**49** 7.4			**45** 8.1	**43** 8.4	**48** 7.7	**50** 7.3	**70** 5.2
23 15.7	**26** 14.2	**24** 15.1			**27** 13.3	**20** 18.3	**19** 19.1	**31** 11.8	**28** 13.2
33 11.0	**36** 10.2	**34** 10.7	Cost of Sales/Inventory		**40** 9.1	**41** 8.8	**26** 13.9	**36** 10.0	**32** 11.4
49 7.5	**52** 7.0	**53** 6.9			**74** 5.0	**54** 6.8	**39** 9.4	**56** 6.5	**45** 8.2
6 56.5	**6** 56.7	**8** 43.7			**3** 132.8	**6** 61.3	**7** 52.9	**9** 39.8	**12** 30.6
15 24.7	**15** 24.5	**15** 24.1	Cost of Sales/Payables		**13** 29.2	**13** 27.5	**15** 24.9	**16** 23.2	**15** 23.6
23 16.1	**25** 14.6	**26** 14.2			**36** 10.2	**35** 10.5	**30** 12.2	**25** 14.9	**23** 16.0
7.9	6.4	6.3			7.4	6.1	6.9	6.2	5.9
16.0	11.4	11.5	Sales/Working Capital		13.5	11.9	10.1	12.3	8.8
124.7	29.3	54.5			NM	370.1	–119.4	60.5	26.7
9.1	12.2	15.6				16.3	42.0	15.8	19.6
(69) 4.1	(81) 4.1	(85) 5.3	EBIT/Interest			4.2	(16) 5.7	(24) 7.9	5.8
1.5	1.6	1.6				.2	.4	2.8	2.7
5.2	3.6	4.7							
(19) 3.4	(17) 2.0	(23) 2.1	Net Profit + Depr., Dep., Amort./Cur. Mat. L/T/D						
1.5	–.7	1.7							
.5	.4	.4			.5	.5	.3	.3	.3
.8	.8	.7	Fixed/Worth		1.1	.8	.5	.8	.6
2.3	1.3	2.9			6.1	40.5	4.0	2.6	1.4
.7	.6	.5			.5	.4	.5	.5	.6
1.9	1.4	1.5	Debt/Worth		1.0	1.3	2.2	1.8	1.6
4.2	3.3	7.2			9.6	100.8	10.1	5.1	3.9
53.7	55.4	60.4			33.4	63.6	100.5	68.7	48.4
(65) 18.6	(87) 24.1	(81) 28.7	% Profit Before Taxes/Tangible Net Worth		(10) 9.0	(13) 28.6	(16) 55.4	(25) 30.5	(17) 25.4
6.1	5.5	13.9			–16.3	–1.1	19.4	13.9	18.3
15.9	20.6	23.5			15.4	29.3	34.7	22.7	19.3
6.7	7.3	9.8	% Profit Before Taxes/Total Assets		.2	10.4	10.2	11.1	8.6
1.7	1.5	1.9			–9.0	–1.5	2.2	7.0	5.7
16.2	19.1	21.3			20.6	24.4	26.3	18.9	36.8
9.1	11.0	9.0	Sales/Net Fixed Assets		7.7	7.3	9.3	11.2	10.7
5.5	5.9	6.2			2.6	4.8	6.7	6.1	7.4
3.7	3.7	3.5			4.9	3.7	3.9	3.5	3.3
2.6	2.7	2.5	Sales/Total Assets		2.4	2.7	3.1	2.5	2.5
2.0	2.1	2.2			1.5	2.0	2.2	2.2	2.2
1.5	1.2	1.1			1.3	1.0	1.2	1.3	1.0
(66) 2.1	(84) 1.9	(86) 2.1	% Depr., Dep., Amort./Sales		(10) 3.0	(15) 3.0	(16) 2.1	(25) 2.4	1.6
3.2	2.8	3.2			4.5	4.0	2.4	3.4	2.3
1.7	1.7	1.6						.8	
(23) 4.5	(34) 3.5	(32) 3.7	% Officers', Directors', Owners' Comp/Sales					(10) 2.4	
7.4	6.4	6.1						5.4	
1967760M	**1641506M**	**2199971M**	Net Sales ($)		**21663M**	**66080M**	**141583M**	**400138M**	**1570507M**
974638M	**573765M**	**1009949M**	Total Assets ($)		**10405M**	**26011M**	**49691M**	**151839M**	**772003M**

M = $ thousand MM = $ million

See Pages 11 through 21 for Explanation of Ratios and Data

Current Data Sorted By Assets   Comparative Historical Data

			7	16	6		Type of Statement		
	1	17	38	6	1		Unqualified	28	34
	9	20	20				Reviewed	60	47
	4	9	4				Compiled	45	43
	4	13	13	10	2	5	Tax Returns	9	13
							Other	55	69
	36 (4/1-9/30/04)			169 (10/1/04-3/31/05)				4/1/00- 3/31/01	4/1/01- 3/31/02
	0-500M	500M-2MM	2-10MM	10-50MM	50-100MM	100-250MM		ALL	ALL
	18	59	82	32	9	5	NUMBER OF STATEMENTS	197	206
	%	%	%	%	%	%	ASSETS	%	%
	11.3	6.6	5.4	5.0			Cash & Equivalents	6.3	5.9
	34.5	38.4	32.6	20.4			Trade Receivables (net)	30.2	30.5
	24.1	20.4	26.2	30.0			Inventory	25.1	23.7
	1.8	2.3	2.3	5.0			All Other Current	2.3	3.6
	71.7	67.8	66.5	60.4			Total Current	63.9	63.6
	20.9	28.1	28.5	27.2			Fixed Assets (net)	28.7	28.5
	3.5	.6	1.3	4.9			Intangibles (net)	1.8	1.7
	4.0	3.6	3.7	7.6			All Other Non-Current	5.5	6.0
	100.0	100.0	100.0	100.0			Total	100.0	100.0
							LIABILITIES		
	34.2	11.7	17.3	14.2			Notes Payable-Short Term	13.1	12.8
	4.4	5.3	3.5	3.3			Cur. Mat.-L/T/D	3.7	3.6
	21.6	18.2	13.0	8.8			Trade Payables	12.4	13.0
	.0	.4	.3	.1			Income Taxes Payable	.3	.2
	13.4	10.6	8.6	10.1			All Other Current	10.2	9.4
	73.6	46.2	42.8	36.6			Total Current	39.7	39.0
	13.9	18.7	17.2	12.5			Long-Term Debt	17.9	17.9
	.0	.6	.2	.6			Deferred Taxes	.5	.4
	8.5	7.0	5.3	4.6			All Other Non-Current	4.1	4.0
	3.9	27.6	34.5	45.8			Net Worth	37.9	38.5
	100.0	100.0	100.0	100.0			Total Liabilities & Net Worth	100.0	100.0
							INCOME DATA		
	100.0	100.0	100.0	100.0			Net Sales	100.0	100.0
	39.4	29.5	25.0	22.9			Gross Profit	29.0	25.8
	34.8	27.3	21.5	16.9			Operating Expenses	24.3	22.3
	4.5	2.2	3.4	6.0			Operating Profit	4.7	3.5
	.0	.8	.8	.6			All Other Expenses (net)	1.1	1.2
	4.5	1.4	2.6	5.4			Profit Before Taxes	3.6	2.3
							RATIOS		
	2.3	3.0	2.7	2.9				2.5	2.8
	1.3	1.6	1.6	2.0			Current	1.7	1.7
	.8	1.1	1.1	1.3				1.2	1.2
	1.8	2.2	1.5	1.2				1.5	1.7
	.8	1.0	.9	.8			Quick	1.0	1.0
	.2	.6	.6	.4				.5	.5

13	28.8	32	11.5	30	12.2	19	19.7			Sales/Receivables	25	14.8	24	14.9
27	13.5	45	8.1	40	9.2	26	14.2				38	9.6	38	9.7
45	8.1	64	5.7	59	6.2	45	8.1				56	6.6	54	6.7
10	37.9	15	24.9	23	15.6	44	8.2			Cost of Sales/Inventory	22	16.8	15	24.3
26	14.1	31	11.7	43	8.6	65	5.6				48	7.6	43	8.5
57	6.4	47	7.7	71	5.2	84	4.4				70	5.2	67	5.4
8	44.4	15	23.9	10	35.7	10	35.1			Cost of Sales/Payables	10	35.4	10	36.2
18	20.1	28	12.9	21	17.0	16	23.5				19	19.1	19	19.4
42	8.7	44	8.3	38	9.7	25	14.7				34	10.8	33	11.1

	9.5	5.8	6.3	5.0			Sales/Working Capital	6.1	6.2
	27.0	11.3	13.2	8.2				11.7	11.1
	-19.2	90.1	64.9	20.2				33.3	32.4

	19.5		6.7		9.1		14.9			EBIT/Interest		10.6		7.2
(15)	5.0	(52)	2.5	(79)	3.1	(29)	5.3				(185)	3.2	(186)	2.4
	1.2		-.6		1.4		2.7					1.4		1.0
			4.6		8.7		6.5			Net Profit + Depr., Dep.,		4.4		5.1
		(13)	2.1	(16)	3.9	(15)	2.4			Amort./Cur. Mat. L /T/D	(49)	2.3	(62)	2.5
			1.1		2.2		1.2					1.4		1.2

	.3	.3	.5	.4			Fixed/Worth	.3	.3
	.6	.9	1.0	.6				.7	.7
	-.5	6.8	1.8	1.3				1.5	1.7
	1.0	1.1	1.0	.6			Debt/Worth	.8	.7
	3.3	2.6	2.3	1.2				1.8	1.5
	-3.8	8.5	5.2	3.5				3.5	4.7

	125.0		40.4		41.6		49.9			% Profit Before Taxes/Tangible		45.9		31.9
(11)	56.5	(47)	11.4	(77)	22.5	(31)	18.4			Net Worth	(175)	23.4	(186)	15.5
	28.0		.3		3.6		13.6					8.7		3.6

	28.6	8.8	13.5	14.3			% Profit Before Taxes/Total	18.1	14.2
	11.0	3.8	6.4	9.6			Assets	8.5	5.5
	-1.5	-4.8	1.4	3.0				1.5	.3
	114.9	31.5	21.1	15.9			Sales/Net Fixed Assets	22.0	20.2
	25.7	11.6	12.3	9.2				10.1	10.6
	14.1	6.6	5.6	6.4				5.2	6.0
	5.1	3.7	3.3	2.8			Sales/Total Assets	3.6	3.5
	3.9	3.0	2.6	2.2				2.6	2.6
	3.4	2.0	2.0	1.7				1.9	2.0

			.9		1.1		1.2			% Depr., Dep., Amort./Sales		.9		1.1
(13)	1.4	(57)	1.7	(77)	1.6	(31)	1.9				(174)	1.7	(191)	2.0
	3.0		3.3		2.8		2.7					2.9		3.0
			2.0		1.9					% Officers', Directors',		2.0		1.9
		(32)	4.4	(33)	3.3					Owners' Comp/Sales	(82)	4.4	(71)	4.0
			5.5		4.5							7.0		8.0

23991M	214155M	941476M	1691250M	1754741M	1572625M	Net Sales ($)	3762896M	5667132M
5111M	70075M	357188M	729434M	650791M	823694M	Total Assets ($)	1676850M	2339345M

M = $ thousand   MM = $ million
See Pages 11 through 21 for Explanation of Ratios and Data

Comparative Historical Data / Current Data Sorted By Sales

			Type of Statement						
29	36	29	Unqualified				4	5	20
73	71	63	Reviewed	1	5	8	26	13	10
47	59	49	Compiled	7	14	6	13	9	
14	25	17	Tax Returns	2	8	2	4	1	
56	57	47	Other	1	10	4	7	7	18
4/1/02-3/31/03	4/1/03-3/31/04	4/1/04-3/31/05			36 (4/1-9/30/04)		169 (10/1/04-3/31/05)		
ALL	ALL	ALL		0-1MM	1-3MM	3-5MM	5-10MM	10-25MM	25MM & OVER
219	248	205	NUMBER OF STATEMENTS	11	37	20	54	35	48
%	%	%	ASSETS	%	%	%	%	%	%
7.5	7.3	6.5	Cash & Equivalents	10.7	7.1	6.4	5.5	7.3	5.6
30.0	30.6	31.8	Trade Receivables (net)	22.2	38.7	40.2	36.0	27.8	23.4
23.2	22.8	25.1	Inventory	17.9	19.9	20.5	23.3	30.6	30.8
3.1	3.5	2.8	All Other Current	2.8	2.0	3.0	2.0	2.5	4.2
63.8	64.1	66.2	Total Current	53.6	67.6	70.1	66.8	68.2	64.0
27.4	28.8	27.7	Fixed Assets (net)	39.0	27.7	26.9	27.6	25.5	27.0
2.4	2.5	1.8	Intangibles (net)	4.7	.6	.2	1.0	2.6	3.2
6.4	4.5	4.3	All Other Non-Current	2.6	4.0	2.9	4.6	3.6	5.8
100.0	100.0	100.0	Total	100.0	100.0	100.0	100.0	100.0	100.0
			LIABILITIES						
12.3	15.3	16.0	Notes Payable-Short Term	37.5	12.2	11.4	18.0	12.7	16.1
4.4	4.0	4.0	Cur. Mat.-L/T/D	4.7	4.5	5.1	4.8	3.2	2.5
13.6	14.3	14.4	Trade Payables	16.9	17.2	18.0	15.5	12.2	10.3
.4	.3	.3	Income Taxes Payable	.0	.3	.2	.3	.4	.2
9.8	8.8	10.0	All Other Current	9.4	8.7	11.8	10.9	9.4	10.0
40.5	42.6	44.6	Total Current	68.5	42.9	46.5	49.6	37.8	39.1
18.1	17.0	16.2	Long-Term Debt	24.4	21.2	13.3	16.8	15.3	11.6
.3	.3	.5	Deferred Taxes	.0	.5	.8	.2	.4	.8
5.2	5.9	5.8	All Other Non-Current	11.6	5.3	7.8	6.0	6.2	3.5
36.0	34.3	32.9	Net Worth	-4.5	30.1	31.5	27.4	40.3	45.0
100.0	100.0	100.0	Total Liabilities & Net Worth	100.0	100.0	100.0	100.0	100.0	100.0
			INCOME DATA						
100.0	100.0	100.0	Net Sales	100.0	100.0	100.0	100.0	100.0	100.0
29.3	27.2	27.1	Gross Profit	45.6	31.9	27.4	25.7	23.7	23.1
25.6	24.6	23.4	Operating Expenses	39.3	29.0	24.8	23.4	19.4	17.7
3.8	2.5	3.7	Operating Profit	6.3	2.9	2.6	2.3	4.3	5.3
.9	.8	.6	All Other Expenses (net)	.2	1.0	1.1	.7	.6	.2
2.9	1.7	3.1	Profit Before Taxes	6.2	1.8	1.5	1.5	3.7	5.2
			RATIOS						
2.7	2.6	2.8		2.6	3.3	2.0	2.1	3.4	3.1
1.6	1.7	1.7	Current	1.2	1.9	1.8	1.4	1.9	1.7
1.1	1.1	1.1		.4	1.2	1.2	1.0	1.1	1.2
1.6	1.5	1.5		1.1	2.8	1.6	1.4	1.9	1.2
.9	.9	.9	Quick	.7	1.2	1.2	.9	.9	.8
.5	.5	.5		.2	.6	.8	.6	.5	.6

23	16.0	24	15.3	25	14.4	Sales/Receivables	0	UND	32	11.3	34	10.8	28	12.9	22	16.3	21	17.8
35	10.3	38	9.7	38	9.6		24	15.5	50	7.3	49	7.5	40	9.0	34	10.6	29	12.7
53	6.9	53	6.8	57	6.4		36	10.1	68	5.4	92	4.0	57	6.4	50	7.3	47	7.8
17	21.0	15	24.3	22	16.6	Cost of Sales/Inventory	0	UND	13	28.7	11	32.6	19	19.2	26	14.1	44	8.2
39	9.4	41	9.0	44	8.3		22	16.4	35	10.5	29	12.5	35	10.4	58	6.3	60	6.1
68	5.4	66	5.5	68	5.4		77	4.7	56	6.5	64	5.7	51	7.1	72	5.1	79	4.6
12	31.6	11	32.4	10	35.1	Cost of Sales/Payables	0	UND	15	24.0	18	20.5	10	36.1	9	39.4	12	30.7
20	18.0	19	18.8	20	18.4		18	20.8	28	12.9	32	11.3	22	16.4	16	22.5	16	22.7
36	10.2	34	10.9	35	10.5		27	13.7	50	7.2	43	8.5	33	11.2	33	11.2	25	14.3
	6.2		6.0		5.8	Sales/Working Capital		18.6		4.8		5.1		7.4		4.8		4.9
	11.4		10.8		11.3			30.7		8.1		10.0		19.4		8.7		10.1
	49.1		54.4		48.4			-4.5		71.2		18.2		UND		44.1		25.3
	10.1		9.6		9.2	EBIT/Interest				6.8		13.6		9.0		9.1		13.4
(201)	3.6	(224)	3.1	(186)	3.7		(32)		(32)	3.2	(19)	2.2	(52)	2.8	(33)	6.1	(42)	5.7
	1.5		.1		1.4					-.4		-1.6		.9		2.4		2.3
	6.0		4.8		5.8	Net Profit + Depr., Dep., Amort./Cur. Mat. L/T/D								5.7				6.2
(58)	2.7	(61)	2.7	(47)	3.2								(11)	3.9			(16)	3.0
	1.4		.9		1.7									2.7				2.2
	.3		.3		.3	Fixed/Worth		.5		.3		.3		.5		.3		.3
	.8		.8		.8			3.1		1.2		.7		1.0		.8		.6
	2.1		2.0		2.0			-.4		2.8		2.1		2.2		1.7		1.1
	.7		.7		.8	Debt/Worth		2.2		.9		.7		1.2		.6		.6
	1.8		2.0		2.1			3.7		2.1		2.3		2.8		1.7		1.2
	5.4		5.3		5.2			-3.0		6.6		7.6		7.0		5.1		3.1
	44.9		31.4		42.4	% Profit Before Taxes/Tangible Net Worth				48.3		38.5		39.8		46.6		43.6
(191)	17.3	(218)	14.3	(180)	20.4				(31)	13.3	(17)	7.7	(47)	14.4	(33)	25.6	(46)	22.4
	6.5		.0		5.1					-10.0		-1.2		.4		6.4		12.4
	14.4		12.2		13.4	% Profit Before Taxes/Total Assets		27.6		12.2		8.8		11.7		13.6		17.6
	6.2		4.4		6.4			7.6		5.3		3.2		4.6		7.0		10.0
	1.6		-2.3		1.0			.9		-6.1		-4.3		-.9		2.9		2.8
	20.5		20.8		22.8	Sales/Net Fixed Assets		27.7		19.7		30.0		26.6		32.0		16.1
	11.3		11.1		11.6			15.5		12.9		9.3		12.7		13.7		11.1
	6.6		6.1		6.4			3.0		5.2		6.7		7.0		7.2		6.7
	3.6		3.4		3.5	Sales/Total Assets		4.2		3.6		3.1		3.7		3.2		3.1
	2.6		2.6		2.8			3.6		2.5		2.6		3.1		2.6		2.4
	2.0		1.9		2.0			1.6		1.7		1.9		2.2		2.2		1.9
	1.0		1.1		1.1	% Depr., Dep., Amort./Sales				1.0		1.3		1.0		1.1		1.1
(207)	1.8	(224)	1.9	(190)	1.7				(33)	2.0		2.0	(50)	1.8	(33)	1.4	(45)	1.8
	3.0		3.3		2.8					3.4		3.3		2.7		2.0		2.6
	2.0		1.7		1.7	% Officers', Directors', Owners' Comp/Sales				2.7		2.7		1.8		1.4		
(94)	4.7	(101)	4.0	(81)	3.3				(22)	4.4	(11)	4.7	(27)	3.3	(10)	2.9		
	8.5		6.3		5.3					6.2		9.5		5.1		4.2		
6887912M		5566939M		6198238M		Net Sales ($)	7185M		71730M		77260M		413017M		519117M		5109929M
2745665M		2572804M		2636293M		Total Assets ($)	3377M		33730M		31439M		149539M		205465M		2212743M

Current Data Sorted By Assets   Comparative Historical Data

0-500M	500M-2MM	2-10MM	10-50MM	50-100MM	100-250MM	Type of Statement	4/1/00-3/31/01 ALL	4/1/01-3/31/02 ALL
	1	3	15	5	1	Unqualified	15	15
1	2	12	6			Reviewed	14	18
	3	7				Compiled	18	18
1	3	5	3			Tax Returns	2	4
1	4	5	5		1	Other	17	17
	13 (4/1-9/30/04)		71 (10/1/04-3/31/05)					
3	13	32	29	6	1	**NUMBER OF STATEMENTS**	66	72
%	%	%	%	%	%	**ASSETS**	%	%
	5.1	5.0	6.4			Cash & Equivalents	8.2	6.4
	20.7	18.7	12.9			Trade Receivables (net)	17.5	16.8
	28.0	37.0	35.5			Inventory	30.6	30.7
	.3	.8	2.2			All Other Current	2.6	2.2
	54.1	61.5	57.1			Total Current	58.8	56.2
	39.2	33.7	34.1			Fixed Assets (net)	33.1	35.4
	.1	.1	1.0			Intangibles (net)	2.8	2.2
	6.7	4.7	7.8			All Other Non-Current	5.2	6.2
	100.0	100.0	100.0			Total	100.0	100.0
						LIABILITIES		
	20.2	18.1	20.1			Notes Payable-Short Term	15.0	17.8
	5.9	3.3	3.5			Cur. Mat.-L/T/D	4.9	5.2
	14.0	10.2	7.1			Trade Payables	8.8	8.3
	.0	.1	.0			Income Taxes Payable	.3	.0
	6.3	7.8	3.8			All Other Current	9.4	8.2
	46.4	39.4	34.5			Total Current	38.4	39.6
	24.2	22.6	15.5			Long-Term Debt	21.1	23.0
	.0	.0	.5			Deferred Taxes	.4	.3
	14.2	11.8	1.0			All Other Non-Current	3.3	3.0
	15.2	26.1	48.5			Net Worth	36.8	34.2
	100.0	100.0	100.0			Total Liabilities & Net Worth	100.0	100.0
						INCOME DATA		
	100.0	100.0	100.0			Net Sales	100.0	100.0
	23.7	22.3	20.7			Gross Profit	21.0	23.2
	20.2	15.1	14.8			Operating Expenses	16.2	20.9
	3.5	7.3	5.9			Operating Profit	4.8	2.2
	−.1	2.2	.5			All Other Expenses (net)	1.2	2.1
	3.6	5.0	5.4			Profit Before Taxes	3.6	.1
						RATIOS		
	2.2	3.1	2.7				2.8	2.5
	1.2	1.5	1.5			Current	1.7	1.5
	.9	1.0	1.1				1.1	1.1
	1.3	1.3	1.4				1.3	1.2
	.5	.4	.4			Quick	.6	.6
	.3	.3	.2				.4	.4
	14 25.6	15 24.8	12 30.6				17 22.1	19 19.7
	25 14.6	24 15.4	19 19.7			Sales/Receivables	24 15.4	24 15.0
	38 9.6	28 12.9	32 11.3				40 9.0	35 10.3
	19 19.5	38 9.5	37 10.0				21 17.3	33 10.9
	30 12.3	63 5.8	77 4.7			Cost of Sales/Inventory	60 6.0	64 5.7
	65 5.6	98 3.7	117 3.1				101 3.6	114 3.2
	4 87.8	7 50.5	7 51.0				6 56.6	8 48.4
	15 24.3	11 34.3	12 29.5			Cost of Sales/Payables	13 27.3	14 25.6
	48 7.6	17 21.1	21 17.8				21 17.3	27 13.7
	10.3	5.9	5.7				5.2	5.8
	33.8	13.5	10.4			Sales/Working Capital	13.1	9.4
	−71.8	NM	33.0				76.7	69.7
	8.3	8.5	18.3				5.8	4.0
	(31) 1.7	3.9	(27) 4.4			EBIT/Interest	(61) 2.1	(64) 1.5
	.9	2.4	1.7				.7	−.4
							5.9	1.3
						Net Profit + Depr., Dep., Amort./Cur. Mat. L /T/D	(13) 2.0	(16) .9
							1.6	.1
	.4	.5	.3				.4	.4
	2.1	1.1	.7			Fixed/Worth	1.0	1.0
	−5.3	2.9	1.3				4.0	3.2
	2.1	1.1	.5				.6	.6
	4.5	2.0	1.4			Debt/Worth	1.9	1.9
	−10.4	7.5	2.3				7.6	5.3
		66.3	34.3			% Profit Before Taxes/Tangible Net Worth	50.9	27.9
	(28)	28.6	22.3				(61) 12.0	(66) 6.8
		11.2	7.9				−.8	−8.3
	14.0	15.7	17.2			% Profit Before Taxes/Total Assets	17.3	10.2
	6.2	4.8	8.9				5.5	1.6
	−.2	2.1	2.8				−1.0	−7.2
	22.3	13.9	12.4			Sales/Net Fixed Assets	17.2	14.0
	6.8	7.3	6.3				6.5	5.7
	3.9	4.9	4.7				3.9	3.0
	3.8	3.2	2.4			Sales/Total Assets	3.4	2.6
	2.4	2.3	2.1				2.1	1.8
	1.9	1.9	1.8				1.4	1.4
	.1	1.0	1.4			% Depr., Dep., Amort./Sales	1.6	1.2
	(11) 1.8	(31) 2.0	(25) 2.5				(57) 2.8	(67) 2.9
	3.9	4.4	3.0				3.8	4.8
		.9				% Officers', Directors', Owners' Comp/Sales	1.7	1.5
	(12)	1.3					(30) 2.2	(27) 2.4
		2.9					4.0	8.5
4739M	44445M	442782M	1226458M	496505M	94488M	Net Sales ($)	1371894M	1502117M
1127M	15108M	163631M	574467M	386839M	140569M	Total Assets ($)	865558M	828332M

Comparative Historical Data   **Current Data Sorted By Sales**

4/1/02-3/31/03 ALL	4/1/03-3/31/04 ALL	4/1/04-3/31/05 ALL	Type of Statement	0-1MM	1-3MM	3-5MM	5-10MM	10-25MM	25MM & OVER
14	20	25	Unqualified				1	5	19
15	17	21	Reviewed		1	3	4	9	4
10	17	10	Compiled	1	1		4	4	
10	14	12	Tax Returns	1	3		3	2	3
11	25	16	Other		4	1	1	5	5
				13 (4/1-9/30/04)			71 (10/1/04-3/31/05)		
60	**93**	**84**	**NUMBER OF STATEMENTS**	**2**	**9**	**4**	**13**	**25**	**31**
%	%	%	**ASSETS**	%	%	%	%	%	%
5.1	6.8	5.6	Cash & Equivalents				6.4	5.9	5.9
16.4	15.6	15.9	Trade Receivables (net)				21.7	19.3	12.5
33.3	31.7	34.9	Inventory				31.3	37.3	35.0
1.2	2.5	1.3	All Other Current				.4	1.6	2.0
55.9	56.7	57.8	Total Current				59.9	64.1	55.4
37.6	34.6	32.6	Fixed Assets (net)				33.8	30.5	28.8
.9	1.9	1.4	Intangibles (net)				.3	.2	3.4
5.6	6.8	8.3	All Other Non-Current				6.0	5.2	12.4
100.0	100.0	100.0	Total				100.0	100.0	100.0
			LIABILITIES						
12.2	19.7	17.7	Notes Payable-Short Term				15.5	17.2	18.4
7.4	4.0	3.8	Cur. Mat.-L/T/D				3.2	3.4	4.0
10.3	12.6	9.4	Trade Payables				13.6	9.5	6.6
.2	.1	.0	Income Taxes Payable				.1	.1	.0
4.5	10.8	6.3	All Other Current				7.8	6.8	3.9
34.6	47.2	37.3	Total Current				40.1	37.0	32.9
25.7	21.8	21.9	Long-Term Debt				18.8	21.2	19.4
.4	.2	.3	Deferred Taxes				.0	.3	.7
.9	5.2	7.2	All Other Non-Current				6.0	11.8	1.4
38.4	25.7	33.3	Net Worth				35.1	29.7	45.6
100.0	100.0	100.0	Total Liabilities & Net Worth				100.0	100.0	100.0
			INCOME DATA						
100.0	100.0	100.0	Net Sales				100.0	100.0	100.0
20.7	22.2	22.6	Gross Profit				20.8	19.4	21.5
17.6	19.1	16.2	Operating Expenses				15.7	14.5	14.8
3.1	3.1	6.4	Operating Profit				5.1	4.9	6.7
1.0	.9	1.2	All Other Expenses (net)				.5	.5	1.0
2.1	2.1	5.2	Profit Before Taxes				4.6	4.4	5.7
			RATIOS						
2.7	3.1	2.6	Current				2.3	4.0	2.8
1.7	1.5	1.5					1.3	1.7	1.6
1.1	1.0	1.1					1.0	1.1	1.2
1.2	1.3	1.3	Quick				1.3	2.4	1.4
.6	(92) .5	.5					.6	.6	.4
.3	.3	.2					.2	.3	.3
16 22.6	13 27.4	14 25.2	Sales/Receivables				15 23.8	14 25.8	14 25.2
23 15.7	24 15.1	21 17.5					21 17.4	27 13.5	19 19.7
37 9.9	34 10.8	29 12.6					37 10.0	31 11.7	27 13.3
35 10.5	36 10.1	33 10.9	Cost of Sales/Inventory				26 14.3	39 9.3	34 10.6
62 5.9	73 5.0	64 5.7					72 5.1	61 6.0	68 5.4
119 3.1	110 3.3	107 3.4					117 3.1	89 4.1	103 3.5
7 50.4	7 51.7	7 48.8	Cost of Sales/Payables				6 64.0	8 46.8	7 52.2
13 27.8	15 25.1	12 30.7					11 31.9	11 31.9	12 29.9
28 13.2	31 11.7	21 17.7					29 12.8	25 -14.4	18 20.0
5.5	5.1	6.0	Sales/Working Capital				5.7	5.5	5.9
8.1	10.9	12.1					17.5	8.5	10.0
212.3	226.9	70.1					NM	71.5	31.4
6.4	7.3	9.4	EBIT/Interest				8.1	11.9	15.3
(58) 1.9	(87) 2.4	(79) 3.6					5.6	3.4	(29) 3.6
1.0	.8	1.5					1.4	1.6	1.8
3.3	2.2	4.9	Net Profit + Depr., Dep., Amort./Cur. Mat. L/T/D						11.3
(17) 1.4	(20) .9	(21) 2.0							(10) 2.1
1.1	.4	.3							.3
.3	.4	.3	Fixed/Worth				.7	.3	.3
.9	1.1	.9					1.1	.9	.7
2.1	4.0	2.2					2.1	2.6	1.6
.5	1.2	1.0	Debt/Worth				1.0	1.0	.6
1.5	2.3	1.7					2.3	1.5	1.4
4.7	7.3	4.6					4.0	6.1	2.7
24.9	39.7	42.7	% Profit Before Taxes/Tangible Net Worth				60.4	42.7	34.3
(52) 11.7	(81) 11.7	(73) 24.9					28.2	(21) 21.7	(29) 22.5
1.9	1.8	9.1					6.5	7.0	10.2
10.4	12.7	16.0	% Profit Before Taxes/Total Assets				17.2	17.3	16.2
3.4	3.4	6.4					8.6	4.7	8.7
.1	-.1	2.0					1.7	1.8	3.9
12.4	13.6	14.5	Sales/Net Fixed Assets				31.7	13.8	15.4
5.2	6.0	7.9					5.4	8.3	8.5
3.4	4.1	4.9					4.0	5.0	5.1
2.8	2.8	3.0	Sales/Total Assets				3.8	3.3	2.5
2.0	2.1	2.2					2.1	2.4	2.2
1.3	1.4	1.8					1.5	2.1	1.2
1.8	1.5	1.1	% Depr., Dep., Amort./Sales				.3	.9	1.4
(55) 3.4	(86) 2.6	(76) 2.1					2.2	2.0	(26) 2.4
5.1	5.0	3.7					5.1	3.4	3.2
1.0	1.1	.9	% Officers', Directors', Owners' Comp/Sales						
(20) 1.7	(33) 3.0	(24) 1.5							
2.8	5.5	3.5							
1396166M	1956022M	2309417M	Net Sales ($)	1336M	16103M	15001M	92703M	428979M	1755295M
874446M	1191589M	1281741M	Total Assets ($)	4485M	6044M	8512M	47183M	187909M	1027608M

M = $ thousand   MM = $ million
See Pages 11 through 21 for Explanation of Ratios and Data

Current Data Sorted By Assets   **Comparative Historical Data**

Type of Statement	0-500M	500M-2MM	2-10MM	10-50MM	50-100MM	100-250MM
Unqualified			11	5	2	
Reviewed		6	8	2		
Compiled	1	8	4	1		
Tax Returns	5	4	1	2		
Other	3	7	9	2		
	17 (4/1-9/30/04)			62 (10/1/04-3/31/05)		

0-500M	500M-2MM	2-10MM	10-50MM	50-100MM	100-250MM		4/1/00-3/31/01 ALL	4/1/01-3/31/02 ALL
9	25	33	10	2		**NUMBER OF STATEMENTS**		
%	%	%	%	%	%	**ASSETS**	%	%
	6.3	3.4	3.3		D	Cash & Equivalents	D	D
	37.3	24.8	23.1		A	Trade Receivables (net)	A	A
	20.1	29.5	37.1		T	Inventory	T	T
	2.6	1.6	1.3		A	All Other Current	A	A
	66.3	59.3	64.7			Total Current		
	29.3	34.8	25.5		N	Fixed Assets (net)	N	N
	.2	1.3	3.5		O	Intangibles (net)	O	O
	4.2	4.6	6.3		T	All Other Non-Current	T	T
	100.0	100.0	100.0			Total		
					A	**LIABILITIES**	A	A
	15.0	15.9	10.3		V	Notes Payable-Short Term	V	V
	7.8	4.6	9.4		A	Cur. Mat.-L/T/D	A	A
	12.8	13.4	9.0		I	Trade Payables	I	I
	.2	.3	.1		L	Income Taxes Payable	L	L
	10.1	10.9	6.4		A	All Other Current	A	A
	45.8	45.1	35.0		B	Total Current	B	B
	22.2	24.3	24.6		L	Long-Term Debt	L	L
	.2	.2	.6		E	Deferred Taxes	E	E
	3.3	3.1	1.9			All Other Non-Current		
	28.5	27.4	37.8			Net Worth		
	100.0	100.0	100.0			Total Liabilities & Net Worth		
						INCOME DATA		
	100.0	100.0	100.0			Net Sales		
	31.0	21.2	23.1			Gross Profit		
	28.9	17.0	18.3			Operating Expenses		
	2.0	4.3	4.8			Operating Profit		
	.5	.8	.3			All Other Expenses (net)		
	1.6	3.5	4.5			Profit Before Taxes		
						RATIOS		
	2.6	1.8	4.3					
	1.6	1.3	2.2			Current		
	1.3	1.1	1.3					
	1.5	1.0	1.3					
	1.1	.6	.8			Quick		
	.5	.3	.6					
	21 17.0	17 22.0	24 15.0					
	47 7.7	33 10.9	35 10.5			Sales/Receivables		
	66 5.5	46 7.9	51 7.2					
	3 111.9	28 13.1	58 6.3					
	19 19.5	46 8.0	82 4.4			Cost of Sales/Inventory		
	50 7.3	87 4.2	131 2.8					
	8 44.6	12 29.7	10 34.9					
	21 17.0	19 19.0	18 20.5			Cost of Sales/Payables		
	38 9.5	37 10.0	35 10.4					
	7.1	7.7	2.9					
	10.6	22.5	7.2			Sales/Working Capital		
	20.4	138.4	28.1					
	16.3	9.4	27.6					
	(23) 5.3	3.8	7.1			EBIT/Interest		
	.8	1.8	1.6					
		4.4				Net Profit + Depr., Dep.,		
		(10) 2.1				Amort./Cur. Mat. L/T/D		
		1.1						
	.3	.6	.1					
	.9	1.1	1.2			Fixed/Worth		
	2.2	4.6	NM					
	1.0	1.2	.4					
	2.5	2.5	2.9			Debt/Worth		
	3.8	9.5	NM					
	35.8	46.8				% Profit Before Taxes/Tangible		
	(21) 19.1	(28) 21.6				Net Worth		
	2.9	5.6						
	12.2	13.3	23.0			% Profit Before Taxes/Total		
	6.4	8.0	7.5			Assets		
	-.3	2.9	3.0					
	31.3	14.5	21.3					
	14.5	7.3	12.7			Sales/Net Fixed Assets		
	6.7	4.7	3.4					
	3.5	3.0	2.4					
	3.0	2.4	1.8			Sales/Total Assets		
	2.3	2.0	1.4					
	1.2	1.1	1.1					
	(22) 2.1	(32) 2.4	2.2			% Depr., Dep., Amort./Sales		
	4.3	3.5	4.9					
	2.3	1.1				% Officers', Directors',		
	(17) 3.1	(15) 1.7				Owners' Comp/Sales		
	5.0	5.1						
11203M	77412M	444840M	436809M	218481M		Net Sales ($)		
2524M	26895M	173707M	202329M	112554M		Total Assets ($)		

M = $ thousand   MM = $ million
See Pages 11 through 21 for Explanation of Ratios and Data

Comparative Historical Data | Current Data Sorted By Sales

	4/1/02-3/31/03 ALL	4/1/03-3/31/04 ALL	4/1/04-3/31/05 ALL		0-1MM	1-3MM	3-5MM	5-10MM	10-25MM	25MM & OVER
Type of Statement						17 (4/1-9/30/04)		62 (10/1/04-3/31/05)		
Unqualified	4	6	18			1	1	7	8	9
Reviewed	5	10	16			2	2		4	2
Compiled	11	12	13		1	7	1	1	2	1
Tax Returns	4	9	11		4	4	2		1	
Other	10	20	21		1	2	6	5	4	1
NUMBER OF STATEMENTS	34	57	79		6	16	12	13	19	13
ASSETS	%	%	%		%	%	%	%	%	%
Cash & Equivalents	6.8	8.7	5.0			9.4	3.2	3.4	3.8	3.4
Trade Receivables (net)	23.1	27.4	30.0			35.6	38.3	32.9	24.5	23.3
Inventory	24.3	23.5	25.7			18.9	22.0	21.7	24.8	44.8
All Other Current	4.9	1.1	2.7			1.5	.1	3.7	2.1	1.5
Total Current	59.1	60.7	63.4			65.5	63.6	61.6	55.2	72.9
Fixed Assets (net)	32.1	32.0	30.2			31.9	29.5	32.4	38.5	19.7
Intangibles (net)	.7	1.0	1.3			.4	1.6	.5	1.2	2.5
All Other Non-Current	8.1	6.3	5.1			2.3	5.3	5.5	5.1	4.9
Total	100.0	100.0	100.0			100.0	100.0	100.0	100.0	100.0
LIABILITIES										
Notes Payable-Short Term	10.7	12.9	14.8			12.6	11.5	14.3	15.1	16.6
Cur. Mat.-L/T/D	4.6	4.3	5.7			9.0	4.0	3.7	5.6	8.1
Trade Payables	13.9	10.1	13.8			13.2	17.2	13.7	14.7	8.3
Income Taxes Payable	.2	.2	.2			.1	.2	.6	.1	.0
All Other Current	7.9	7.8	9.0			10.2	7.1	13.4	7.6	10.7
Total Current	37.3	35.4	43.6			45.1	40.0	45.8	43.1	43.6
Long-Term Debt	20.6	19.0	22.9			23.4	37.3	15.1	21.3	17.6
Deferred Taxes	.3	.2	.2			.0	.3	.4	.2	.3
All Other Non-Current	5.3	3.7	4.1			10.1	1.5	2.9	2.2	3.8
Net Worth	36.5	41.7	29.2			21.4	20.9	35.8	33.2	34.6
Total Liabilities & Net Worth	100.0	100.0	100.0			100.0	100.0	100.0	100.0	100.0
INCOME DATA										
Net Sales	100.0	100.0	100.0			100.0	100.0	100.0	100.0	100.0
Gross Profit	24.5	30.0	26.6			32.5	29.3	27.2	17.6	22.5
Operating Expenses	20.4	24.3	22.8			30.4	24.5	22.8	13.9	18.0
Operating Profit	4.0	5.6	3.8			2.1	4.7	4.4	3.7	4.5
All Other Expenses (net)	.4	.8	.6			.6	1.7	1.2	.6	-.5
Profit Before Taxes	3.6	4.9	3.2			1.5	3.1	3.2	3.2	5.0
RATIOS										
Current	3.3	4.2	2.2			3.5	2.1	1.8	1.7	3.3
	1.6	1.7	1.5			1.8	1.9	1.3	1.3	2.5
	1.2	1.2	1.2			1.0	1.3	1.0	1.1	1.1
Quick	1.8	2.1	1.4			2.3	1.4	1.2	1.1	1.2
	.7	1.1	.8			1.3	1.0	.7	.7	.7
	.5	.5	.4			.4	.6	.5	.3	.4
Sales/Receivables	17 21.8	20 18.2	21 17.5		24 15.5	25 14.8	16 22.7	19 19.4	23 15.9	
	25 14.8	37 9.8	37 10.0		47 7.8	44 8.3	38 9.5	34 10.6	33 11.0	
	41 8.8	52 7.1	52 7.0		63 5.8	65 5.6	63 5.8	42 8.7	46 8.0	
Cost of Sales/Inventory	17 21.8	19 19.0	14 26.6		3 119.9	12 29.7	14 25.7	20 18.0	62 5.9	
	39 9.4	41 9.0	38 9.5		15 24.5	44 8.3	31 11.8	38 9.5	81 4.5	
	68 5.4	82 4.5	86 4.2		38 9.5	93 3.9	101 3.6	73 5.0	126 2.9	
Cost of Sales/Payables	8 46.6	8 45.2	11 33.5		15 24.4	11 33.0	12 29.6	11 32.0	9 38.5	
	18 19.9	16 23.1	19 18.8		22 16.3	25 14.7	19 19.2	19 19.0	12 29.5	
	34 10.9	28 12.9	37 9.9		35 10.3	40 9.1	41 8.9	33 11.1	20 18.3	
Sales/Working Capital	7.0	5.4	7.1			4.3	7.1	7.8	12.4	3.4
	12.5	8.6	14.8			11.8	10.0	20.6	23.4	6.6
	37.8	34.0	33.2			NM	18.4	NM	61.2	NM
EBIT/Interest	8.3	12.7	11.9			21.0	16.3	9.0	9.9	21.2
	(28) 3.6	(50) 3.7	(75) 4.7			(15) 6.2	(11) 3.4	4.7	5.4	8.1
	1.1	1.1	1.5			.6	1.4	1.0	2.8	2.2
Net Profit + Depr., Dep., Amort./Cur. Mat. L/T/D		4.7	4.3							
		(14) 1.5	(21) 1.6							
		.9	.9							
Fixed/Worth	.5	.3	.3			.4	.4	.4	.7	.2
	.8	.9	1.0			1.0	1.0	.9	1.1	.6
	2.3	1.8	3.0			NM	5.0	2.5	4.5	NM
Debt/Worth	.6	.6	1.0			.8	1.4	1.0	1.0	.6
	2.2	1.4	2.5			2.3	2.6	2.2	3.0	2.0
	7.3	3.6	8.5			NM	15.7	4.0	8.2	NM
% Profit Before Taxes/Tangible Net Worth	55.9	64.4	57.2			56.2	74.8	38.1	73.9	68.8
	(30) 27.0	(52) 16.7	(66) 24.5			(12) 18.2	(10) 19.4	(12) 20.1	(18) 21.6	(10) 47.8
	1.1	5.3	5.7			.0	11.9	.4	5.4	17.4
% Profit Before Taxes/Total Assets	20.9	19.3	14.6			22.4	10.7	20.3	12.1	23.9
	10.8	8.1	8.0			5.1	8.1	6.5	8.9	7.3
	.2	1.4	1.9			-1.7	2.2	.1	3.3	3.8
Sales/Net Fixed Assets	20.8	18.4	22.3			35.3	29.2	20.5	9.6	23.3
	7.6	8.5	9.8			13.2	8.7	9.8	5.8	15.7
	4.6	4.8	5.2			5.8	4.8	6.5	4.5	10.0
Sales/Total Assets	4.2	3.1	3.4			3.6	3.3	3.8	2.8	3.7
	2.7	2.3	2.6			2.8	2.7	3.3	2.4	2.0
	1.8	1.7	2.0			2.1	1.7	1.9	2.2	1.6
% Depr., Dep., Amort./Sales	1.6	1.3	1.1			1.2	1.2	1.2	1.1	.9
	(30) 2.8	(49) 2.6	(72) 2.2			(13) 4.3	(11) 2.4	2.1	(18) 2.5	1.2
	4.4	4.5	3.8			7.7	6.2	2.7	3.7	2.9
% Officers', Directors', Owners' Comp/Sales	1.3	1.7	1.5			2.3				
	(18) 3.1	(25) 3.5	(38) 3.2			(12) 3.1				
	4.3	7.9	7.0			7.6				
Net Sales ($)	281565M	603785M	1188745M		3986M	32051M	46570M	90282M	300037M	715819M
Total Assets ($)	123091M	295348M	518009M		1526M	12754M	21810M	41684M	123562M	316673M

M = $ thousand   MM = $ million
See Pages 11 through 21 for Explanation of Ratios and Data

Current Data Sorted By Assets   Comparative Historical Data

Type of Statement						
					Unqualified	7	2

	0-500M	500M-2MM	2-10MM	10-50MM	50-100MM	100-250MM		ALL 4/1/00-3/31/01	ALL 4/1/01-3/31/02
Type of Statement									
Unqualified			3	5				7	2
Reviewed		15	22	5				22	15
Compiled	4	21	17	1				38	42
Tax Returns	13	15	8					10	11
Other	11	12	15		1			31	25
	28 (4/1-9/30/04)		140 (10/1/04-3/31/05)						
NUMBER OF STATEMENTS	28	63	65	11	1			108	95
	%	%	%	%	%	%	**ASSETS**	%	%
Cash & Equivalents	4.1	5.5	4.2	4.6				4.6	4.6
Trade Receivables (net)	31.8	36.1	26.2	18.0				30.3	29.8
Inventory	18.6	23.3	22.7	29.1				21.1	19.8
All Other Current	3.9	2.0	1.7	1.6				1.4	4.1
Total Current	58.4	66.8	54.9	53.3	DATA			57.4	58.3
Fixed Assets (net)	33.0	25.9	37.5	40.1	NOT			33.6	33.5
Intangibles (net)	2.5	2.7	1.5	2.2	AVAILABLE			2.8	2.7
All Other Non-Current	6.1	4.7	6.1	4.4				6.2	5.4
Total	100.0	100.0	100.0	100.0				100.0	100.0
							LIABILITIES		
Notes Payable-Short Term	20.9	14.7	14.8	18.4				17.8	15.1
Cur. Mat.-L/T/D	8.5	4.0	6.0	6.4				3.9	5.3
Trade Payables	23.2	15.1	14.4	11.4				12.8	13.8
Income Taxes Payable	.1	.1	.1	.1				.2	.1
All Other Current	11.1	7.1	9.1	4.7				11.8	7.8
Total Current	63.8	41.0	44.3	41.0				46.4	42.1
Long-Term Debt	29.8	21.0	17.9	18.1				18.4	19.1
Deferred Taxes	.0	.1	.6	.1				.2	.2
All Other Non-Current	7.3	5.0	7.2	1.7				3.4	3.9
Net Worth	−.9	33.0	30.1	39.1				31.5	34.6
Total Liabilities & Net Worth	100.0	100.0	100.0	100.0				100.0	100.0
							INCOME DATA		
Net Sales	100.0	100.0	100.0	100.0				100.0	100.0
Gross Profit	36.5	27.6	22.0	20.8				22.5	22.8
Operating Expenses	33.4	25.4	18.7	16.4				19.7	20.8
Operating Profit	3.1	2.3	3.2	4.5				2.7	2.0
All Other Expenses (net)	1.2	.6	.7	1.3				.6	.8
Profit Before Taxes	1.9	1.7	2.6	3.2				2.1	1.2
							RATIOS		
Current	2.3 / 1.0 / .6	3.4 / 1.4 / 1.0	2.0 / 1.3 / .9	1.7 / 1.0 / .9				2.2 / 1.3 / 1.0	2.4 / 1.4 / 1.0
Quick	1.4 / .6 / .4	2.1 / .9 / .6	1.2 / .7 / .5	1.2 / .3 / .2				1.3 / .8 / .5	1.4 / .9 / .5
Sales/Receivables	19 19.0 / 29 12.6 / 46 7.9	33 11.0 / 39 9.3 / 44 8.4	23 15.7 / 32 11.6 / 40 9.2	19 19.6 / 29 12.7 / 42 8.6				23 15.9 / 32 11.3 / 40 9.1	25 14.5 / 35 10.5 / 42 8.7
Cost of Sales/Inventory	14 25.9 / 25 14.7 / 44 8.2	17 20.9 / 32 11.3 / 58 6.3	21 17.1 / 33 11.0 / 54 6.8	20 18.4 / 50 7.3 / 131 2.8				16 23.0 / 29 12.8 / 46 8.0	12 29.2 / 31 11.8 / 48 7.6
Cost of Sales/Payables	14 26.7 / 29 12.4 / 48 7.6	7 55.6 / 15 24.6 / 31 11.7	12 30.4 / 19 19.7 / 31 11.9	12 29.8 / 29 12.7 / 35 10.4				7 51.1 / 14 26.0 / 25 12.4	10 38.1 / 16 23.1 / 30 12.4
Sales/Working Capital	10.8 / −135.4 / −14.5	7.1 / 18.1 / 355.6	10.8 / 22.7 / −71.8	9.0 / 85.8 / −91.8				10.4 / 22.4 / −224.4	7.6 / 21.7 / −205.0
EBIT/Interest	(24) 4.1 / 1.2 / .0	(58) 10.0 / 3.0 / .8	(64) 7.4 / 3.3 / 1.4	(10) 10.5 / 2.8 / 1.4				(106) 5.9 / 2.3 / 1.2	(92) 3.7 / 1.6 / .4
Net Profit + Depr., Dep., Amort./Cur. Mat. L /T/D		(10) 2.6 / 1.5 / .8	(14) 3.2 / 2.3 / 1.3					(23) 3.3 / 2.2 / 1.2	(23) 2.6 / 1.1 / .6
Fixed/Worth	1.1 / 9.1 / −1.8	.2 / .8 / 4.1	.6 / 1.1 / 2.4	.8 / 1.4 / 2.1				.5 / 1.2 / 2.8	.5 / 1.2 / 2.8
Debt/Worth	2.2 / 30.6 / −5.8	.7 / 1.8 / 9.8	1.0 / 2.2 / 4.4	.7 / 1.8 / 2.9				.8 / 1.8 / 6.5	1.0 / 1.8 / 5.6
% Profit Before Taxes/Tangible Net Worth	(16) 95.9 / 25.0 / −22.4	(53) 37.2 / 13.9 / 1.1	(58) 51.7 / 14.4 / 2.1	(10) 36.7 / 14.4 / 5.9				(91) 40.9 / 11.9 / 2.1	(86) 26.3 / 7.9 / −4.4
% Profit Before Taxes/Total Assets	13.1 / 1.8 / −10.3	14.2 / 4.0 / −1.1	12.1 / 4.8 / .7	8.6 / 3.6 / 1.8				12.7 / 4.8 / .9	8.0 / 2.1 / −2.2
Sales/Net Fixed Assets	30.5 / 9.9 / 7.7	46.9 / 12.7 / 7.2	15.6 / 10.1 / 5.6	8.8 / 6.1 / 3.4				20.8 / 9.9 / 5.7	19.7 / 8.6 / 5.1
Sales/Total Assets	7.2 / 3.6 / 2.7	4.7 / 3.1 / 2.3	3.8 / 3.0 / 2.2	2.5 / 2.1 / 1.7				4.5 / 3.4 / 2.3	3.9 / 3.0 / 2.2
% Depr., Dep., Amort./Sales	(20) 1.6 / 2.1 / 2.7	(53) 1.0 / 2.4 / 3.6	(62) 1.5 / 2.0 / 3.5	1.5 / 2.5 / 2.7				(98) 1.1 / 2.0 / 2.9	(87) .6 / 2.1 / 3.1
% Officers', Directors', Owners' Comp/Sales	(15) 2.8 / 3.8 / 8.6	(37) 1.7 / 2.8 / 3.9	(27) .8 / 1.6 / 2.1					(56) 1.3 / 2.4 / 3.9	(52) 2.0 / 2.9 / 4.3
Net Sales ($)	46748M	262496M	863120M	512004M	163951M			2218493M	815665M
Total Assets ($)	9665M	75900M	265136M	216681M	61817M			921040M	368996M

M = $ thousand   MM = $ million
See Pages 11 through 21 for Explanation of Ratios and Data

Comparative Historical Data — **Current Data Sorted By Sales**

			Type of Statement						
7	4	8	Unqualified				1	1	6
32	35	42	Reviewed	1	8	4	11	13	5
39	39	43	Compiled	2	4	11	15	10	1
22	25	36	Tax Returns	5	9	10	8	4	
35	52	39	Other	6	12	4	9	5	3
4/1/02- 3/31/03	4/1/03- 3/31/04	4/1/04- 3/31/05		28 (4/1-9/30/04)			140 (10/1/04-3/31/05)		
ALL	ALL	ALL		0-1MM	1-3MM	3-5MM	5-10MM	10-25MM	25MM & OVER
135	155	168	**NUMBER OF STATEMENTS**	14	33	29	44	33	15
%	%	%	**ASSETS**	%	%	%	%	%	%
5.5	7.5	4.7	Cash & Equivalents	10.7	2.4	5.7	4.6	3.0	5.8
27.1	28.8	30.3	Trade Receivables (net)	30.1	30.8	30.5	31.8	30.2	24.7
21.0	22.1	22.7	Inventory	11.7	25.3	17.1	26.0	25.2	22.5
3.1	2.3	2.2	All Other Current	.1	1.9	3.6	2.9	1.6	1.0
56.7	60.8	59.8	Total Current	52.8	60.5	57.0	65.3	60.0	54.0
36.8	31.2	32.6	Fixed Assets (net)	33.5	32.1	36.1	28.6	33.3	36.4
2.0	2.1	2.1	Intangibles (net)	4.9	3.6	1.7	1.2	.8	2.9
4.5	5.9	5.4	All Other Non-Current	8.8	3.8	5.3	4.8	5.9	6.7
100.0	100.0	100.0	Total	100.0	100.0	100.0	100.0	100.0	100.0
			LIABILITIES						
14.0	16.6	16.1	Notes Payable-Short Term	9.1	22.5	10.1	15.3	18.4	16.9
5.1	4.7	5.7	Cur. Mat.-L/T/D	6.6	4.6	8.8	4.0	5.4	6.9
13.2	15.5	15.9	Trade Payables	16.7	13.3	19.4	16.8	15.5	12.4
.1	.1	.1	Income Taxes Payable	.0	.1	.0	.1	.2	.0
8.3	9.1	8.4	All Other Current	11.4	6.7	5.4	8.6	10.0	10.7
40.8	46.1	46.1	Total Current	43.7	47.1	43.7	44.6	49.6	47.0
22.1	21.2	21.0	Long-Term Debt	42.6	25.2	21.0	17.9	12.7	19.2
.2	.3	.3	Deferred Taxes	.0	.1	.0	.0	1.2	.2
4.9	9.3	6.1	All Other Non-Current	12.8	2.7	7.9	2.6	11.2	2.5
32.1	23.1	26.6	Net Worth	.9	24.8	27.4	34.8	25.4	31.2
100.0	100.0	100.0	Total Liabilities & Net Worth	100.0	100.0	100.0	100.0	100.0	100.0
			INCOME DATA						
100.0	100.0	100.0	Net Sales	100.0	100.0	100.0	100.0	100.0	100.0
25.7	25.3	26.4	Gross Profit	41.7	30.2	32.6	23.7	18.2	17.3
23.9	23.1	23.4	Operating Expenses	36.4	29.3	28.4	20.9	15.8	12.9
1.8	2.2	2.9	Operating Profit	5.3	.9	4.2	2.8	2.4	4.4
.8	.8	.8	All Other Expenses (net)	1.8	1.0	.8	.4	.6	.9
1.0	1.4	2.2	Profit Before Taxes	3.5	-.1	3.4	2.4	1.8	3.6
			RATIOS						
2.4	2.2	2.1		3.4	2.6	3.3	2.0	1.9	1.7
1.4	1.3	1.3	Current	1.4	1.4	1.3	1.3	1.5	1.0
1.0	1.0	.9		.7	.9	.9	1.1	1.0	.9
1.6	1.4	1.4		2.6	1.3	1.9	1.4	1.1	1.0
.8	.7	.8	Quick	1.0	.8	.9	.8	.9	.6
.4	.5	.5		.5	.5	.5	.5	.5	.3
23 15.7	25 14.6	24 15.2		29 12.5	27 13.7	28 12.9	24 15.3	22 16.4	15 23.9
34 10.8	34 10.7	35 10.5	Sales/Receivables	43 8.5	40 9.0	35 10.3	34 10.6	29 12.4	29 12.5
42 8.6	43 8.4	43 8.5		55 6.7	47 7.8	40 9.1	43 8.4	38 9.7	38 9.5
18 20.8	17 21.7	18 20.4		19 18.9	23 16.0	12 31.2	17 21.1	22 17.0	13 27.2
32 11.5	32 11.4	32 11.4	Cost of Sales/Inventory	27 13.5	50 7.3	30 12.3	32 11.4	27 13.3	34 10.9
56 6.5	51 7.2	54 6.8		55 6.6	73 5.0	48 7.5	53 6.8	52 7.1	50 7.3
9 42.8	10 38.0	10 36.1		11 32.0	7 55.9	10 38.0	11 32.2	11 32.9	8 45.7
17 20.9	19 19.6	19 19.5	Cost of Sales/Payables	26 14.1	15 24.6	21 17.7	22 16.7	16 23.1	15 24.7
29 12.6	34 10.7	33 11.0		58 6.3	34 10.7	42 8.7	32 11.3	25 14.6	34 10.8
7.5	8.4	9.8		6.2	7.8	6.9	9.3	10.8	10.0
16.7	22.1	23.3	Sales/Working Capital	NM	25.5	31.2	19.6	22.9	148.1
999.8	-127.4	-86.1		-14.7	-109.5	-67.5	51.4	-116.9	-47.0
	3.4	5.1	8.1		4.1	4.1	11.4	9.7	4.7	22.5
(122) 1.7	(141) 2.1	(157) 2.7	EBIT/Interest	(12) .9	(30) 1.4	(26) 3.0	(43) 4.3	(31) 2.6	6.6
-.3	-.1	1.0		-.2	-.9	.4	1.3	1.4	2.4
2.6	2.9	3.4	Net Profit + Depr., Dep.,						
(24) 1.3	(28) 1.9	(25) 1.9	Amort./Cur. Mat. L/T/D						
.4	1.1	.9							
.5	.5	.5		1.2	.5	.6	.4	.5	.8
1.3	1.2	1.2	Fixed/Worth	9.1	1.6	1.6	.8	.9	1.4
3.9	3.5	4.1		-.7	NM	NM	1.8	2.3	2.0
1.0	1.1	.9		1.8	.9	.6	.9	1.0	1.8
2.1	2.5	2.4	Debt/Worth	29.9	2.8	3.0	1.7	2.2	2.7
8.8	8.7	9.3		-3.4	NM	NM	3.2	4.8	4.4
34.1	35.7	42.9	% Profit Before Taxes/Tangible		28.4	47.5	38.8	49.2	92.0
(114) 8.9	(125) 13.7	(138) 15.6	Net Worth	(25) 13.9	(22) 25.9	(39) 14.4	(31) 12.0	(13) 44.8
-6.2	-3.9	2.6		-4.0	-1.1	2.7	4.1	14.2
9.5	11.1	13.3	% Profit Before Taxes/Total	12.1	10.5	20.0	12.9	9.8	27.1
2.4	4.1	3.7	Assets	1.6	1.8	4.9	4.9	3.6	8.9
-3.8	-3.0	.0		-6.6	-5.0	-2.1	.9	.5	2.6
13.1	17.5	21.9		11.9	18.9	44.7	32.4	21.4	16.2
7.7	10.0	10.6	Sales/Net Fixed Assets	8.0	8.7	10.1	13.6	9.5	9.8
4.6	6.0	6.3		5.6	4.7	4.0	9.1	6.8	6.1
4.0	4.1	4.2		4.2	4.0	5.0	4.4	4.1	4.2
2.8	3.0	3.0	Sales/Total Assets	2.7	2.7	3.1	3.2	3.0	3.5
2.1	2.0	2.2		1.6	1.8	2.2	2.6	2.7	2.5
1.6	1.2	1.3		2.2	1.5	1.7	1.0	1.0	1.7
(125) 2.4	(146) 2.2	(146) 2.2	% Depr., Dep., Amort./Sales	(10) 2.7	(29) 3.0	(21) 2.6	(41) 1.8	(31) 2.0	(14) 2.5
3.8	3.8	3.4		3.8	4.4	4.5	2.8	2.8	3.6
2.2	1.5	1.3	% Officers', Directors',		1.1	1.9	1.3		
(70) 3.6	(70) 2.9	(83) 2.2	Owners' Comp/Sales	(16) 3.5	(22) 3.0	(23) 2.1			
5.6	4.7	3.9		5.6	4.0	2.9			
1192753M	1313923M	1848319M	Net Sales ($)	9673M	66423M	114704M	303411M	466183M	887925M
517280M	498760M	629199M	Total Assets ($)	4262M	27769M	44487M	102036M	160798M	289847M

© RMA 2005

M = $ thousand   MM = $ million
See Pages 11 through 21 for Explanation of Ratios and Data

Current Data Sorted By Assets | **Comparative Historical Data**

0-500M	500M-2MM	2-10MM	10-50MM	50-100MM	100-250MM		4/1/00-3/31/01 ALL	4/1/01-3/31/02 ALL
						Type of Statement		
		6	7	6	1	Unqualified	15	9
		2				Reviewed	1	3
	3	3				Compiled	6	8
	1	1				Tax Returns	1	1
	4	5	2		2	Other	10	18
	9 (4/1-9/30/04)		34 (10/1/04-3/31/05)					
	8	17	9	6	3	**NUMBER OF STATEMENTS**	33	39
%	%	%	%	%	%	**ASSETS**	%	%
DATA NOT AVAILABLE		7.2				Cash & Equivalents	10.3	12.3
		16.9				Trade Receivables (net)	17.2	15.3
		32.1				Inventory	27.8	23.9
		6.1				All Other Current	8.8	3.9
		62.3				Total Current	64.1	55.4
		27.7				Fixed Assets (net)	21.8	29.6
		1.3				Intangibles (net)	3.1	6.3
		8.7				All Other Non-Current	11.1	8.7
		100.0				Total	100.0	100.0
						LIABILITIES		
		13.1				Notes Payable-Short Term	12.6	9.3
		1.8				Cur. Mat.-L/T/D	3.4	2.5
		14.9				Trade Payables	9.2	6.6
		.4				Income Taxes Payable	.2	.3
		14.6				All Other Current	20.6	18.0
		44.8				Total Current	46.1	36.7
		15.1				Long-Term Debt	9.2	15.9
		.2				Deferred Taxes	.9	.7
		4.7				All Other Non-Current	2.9	5.0
		35.2				Net Worth	40.9	41.8
		100.0				Total Liabilities & Net Worth	100.0	100.0
						INCOME DATA		
		100.0				Net Sales	100.0	100.0
		17.9				Gross Profit	19.1	24.3
		15.3				Operating Expenses	15.1	21.7
		2.6				Operating Profit	4.1	2.6
		.5				All Other Expenses (net)	.9	.9
		2.1				Profit Before Taxes	3.2	1.7
						RATIOS		
		2.0					2.1	2.4
		1.3				Current	1.4	1.5
		1.0					1.0	1.0
		.7					1.4	1.3
		.5				Quick	.6	.7
		.3					.2	.4
		8 45.2					**13** 28.9	**13** 27.7
		14 26.8				Sales/Receivables	**21** 17.2	**22** 16.7
		20 18.4					**32** 11.3	**39** 9.4
		26 14.3					**17** 20.9	**27** 13.6
		50 7.3				Cost of Sales/Inventory	**30** 12.3	**39** 9.5
		56 6.6					**67** 5.5	**74** 4.9
		8 43.5					**7** 55.3	**7** 52.2
		11 32.9				Cost of Sales/Payables	**12** 31.2	**12** 29.6
		23 15.9					**20** 17.8	**17** 21.3
		8.2					7.3	5.8
		26.1				Sales/Working Capital	13.0	17.5
		NM					-55.9	158.2
		6.1					14.2	7.4
		(14) 2.8				EBIT/Interest	(30) 6.6	(33) 2.0
		.9					1.8	1.0
						Net Profit + Depr., Dep., Amort./Cur. Mat. L /T/D		
		.3					.2	.4
		.8				Fixed/Worth	.4	.8
		2.0					1.6	1.6
		.9					.6	.7
		2.9				Debt/Worth	1.2	1.8
		4.9					4.1	2.7
		43.2					29.5	24.1
		(16) 22.9				% Profit Before Taxes/Tangible Net Worth	(27) 23.3	(35) 10.0
		-2.5					11.6	.5
		9.9					13.3	9.0
		4.2				% Profit Before Taxes/Total Assets	7.0	3.7
		-2.3					2.8	-.1
		37.1					38.8	14.9
		12.7				Sales/Net Fixed Assets	13.2	7.8
		5.5					7.2	5.0
		4.5					3.2	2.7
		3.0				Sales/Total Assets	2.2	2.1
		2.3					1.3	1.2
		.6					.6	.7
		(13) .9				% Depr., Dep., Amort./Sales	(27) 1.0	(36) 1.1
		2.7					1.5	1.6
								.9
						% Officers', Directors', Owners' Comp/Sales		(10) 2.9
								10.6
	47574M	319576M	487551M	860336M	438768M	Net Sales ($)	3105737M	2292838M
	10340M	97784M	231121M	401664M	379998M	Total Assets ($)	1677515M	1368428M

M = $ thousand MM = $ million

See Pages 11 through 21 for Explanation of Ratios and Data

Comparative Historical Data   Current Data Sorted By Sales

4/1/02-3/31/03 ALL	4/1/03-3/31/04 ALL	4/1/04-3/31/05 ALL	Type of Statement	0-1MM	1-3MM	3-5MM	5-10MM	10-25MM	25MM & OVER
11	11	20	Unqualified		1			4	15
4	7	2	Reviewed					2	
8	9	6	Compiled				2	3	1
2	4	2	Tax Returns		1			1	
16	10	13	Other		1	2	2	4	4
					9 (4/1-9/30/04)			34 (10/1/04-3/31/05)	
41	41	43	**NUMBER OF STATEMENTS**		3	2	4	14	20

ASSETS (%) — data not available for 0-1MM through 5-10MM columns

4/1/02-3/31/03 ALL	4/1/03-3/31/04 ALL	4/1/04-3/31/05 ALL	ASSETS	10-25MM	25MM & OVER
10.6	11.3	11.8	Cash & Equivalents	8.7	16.1
15.0	13.8	16.4	Trade Receivables (net)	17.3	18.5
25.3	27.3	30.9	Inventory	33.4	22.3
8.2	6.1	3.3	All Other Current	4.7	3.8
59.1	58.6	62.4	Total Current	64.1	60.6
26.5	27.6	24.8	Fixed Assets (net)	30.1	20.8
5.4	5.7	5.2	Intangibles (net)	1.3	10.2
8.9	8.1	7.6	All Other Non-Current	4.5	8.4
100.0	100.0	100.0	Total	100.0	100.0

LIABILITIES

4/1/02-3/31/03 ALL	4/1/03-3/31/04 ALL	4/1/04-3/31/05 ALL	LIABILITIES	10-25MM	25MM & OVER
13.2	10.0	14.3	Notes Payable-Short Term	14.6	6.2
3.3	1.4	1.2	Cur. Mat.-L/T/D	1.6	1.3
8.6	9.5	12.0	Trade Payables	15.2	9.9
.1	.1	.2	Income Taxes Payable	.0	.2
14.3	18.6	14.6	All Other Current	12.5	19.0
39.6	39.7	42.3	Total Current	43.9	36.6
10.3	12.4	11.9	Long-Term Debt	19.0	6.5
1.0	.8	.9	Deferred Taxes	1.3	.9
4.2	9.1	4.3	All Other Non-Current	5.3	4.5
44.9	38.0	40.7	Net Worth	30.5	51.5
100.0	100.0	100.0	Total Liabilities & Net Worth	100.0	100.0

INCOME DATA

4/1/02-3/31/03 ALL	4/1/03-3/31/04 ALL	4/1/04-3/31/05 ALL	INCOME DATA	10-25MM	25MM & OVER
100.0	100.0	100.0	Net Sales	100.0	100.0
21.6	22.6	19.7	Gross Profit	19.1	18.1
19.3	19.9	16.4	Operating Expenses	14.7	13.7
2.3	2.7	3.3	Operating Profit	4.4	4.4
.2	.8	.2	All Other Expenses (net)	−.1	.3
2.1	1.8	3.1	Profit Before Taxes	4.5	4.2

RATIOS

4/1/02-3/31/03 ALL	4/1/03-3/31/04 ALL	4/1/04-3/31/05 ALL	RATIOS	10-25MM	25MM & OVER
1.9 / 1.5 / 1.0	2.0 / 1.4 / 1.1	2.1 / 1.6 / 1.1	Current	2.3 / 1.3 / 1.0	2.1 / 1.7 / 1.4
1.1 / .6 / .3	1.0 / .6 / .3	1.1 / .7 / .3	Quick	.9 / .5 / .3	1.5 / 1.0 / .5
13 27.8 / 18 20.6 / 25 14.9	9 39.3 / 18 19.9 / 23 15.9	11 33.2 / 16 22.5 / 27 13.6	Sales/Receivables	5 80.4 / 14 25.8 / 22 16.7	14 26.0 / 21 17.5 / 34 10.7
23 15.9 / 32 11.5 / 54 6.7	25 14.4 / 38 9.5 / 59 6.2	26 14.1 / 49 7.5 / 61 5.9	Cost of Sales/Inventory	30 12.3 / 50 7.3 / 55 6.7	23 16.2 / 44 8.3 / 59 6.2
7 50.8 / 12 29.3 / 20 18.3	8 43.3 / 12 29.4 / 22 17.0	9 39.0 / 14 25.8 / 22 16.5	Cost of Sales/Payables	8 48.6 / 14 26.7 / 23 16.1	10 37.3 / 14 26.0 / 21 17.7
7.6 / 14.7 / 111.8	8.5 / 16.2 / 61.0	8.1 / 13.8 / 127.7	Sales/Working Capital	7.7 / 23.8 / −463.7	5.8 / 10.7 / 16.0
9.7 / (39) 2.5 / −1.6	5.8 / (37) 1.8 / −.3	5.7 / (33) 2.7 / .3	EBIT/Interest	5.7 / (13) 3.3 / 2.0	13.9 / (14) 2.8 / −2.7
			Net Profit + Depr., Dep., Amort./Cur. Mat. L/T/D		
.3 / .6 / 1.4	.2 / .6 / 2.2	.3 / .6 / 2.0	Fixed/Worth	.3 / .7 / 2.7	.2 / .4 / 1.6
.7 / 1.3 / 2.7	.7 / 1.9 / 5.5	.7 / 1.6 / 4.6	Debt/Worth	1.6 / 2.4 / 6.1	.5 / 1.0 / 3.8
31.5 / (38) 8.6 / −13.0	41.2 / (38) 12.1 / −4.0	31.1 / (39) 16.2 / 1.2	% Profit Before Taxes/Tangible Net Worth	44.5 / (13) 27.1 / 13.0	33.3 / (18) 17.0 / −.7
11.5 / 4.1 / −4.4	10.7 / 3.0 / −3.2	9.2 / 4.7 / .5	% Profit Before Taxes/Total Assets	14.0 / 5.9 / 3.6	10.7 / 5.4 / −1.1
16.5 / 10.0 / 6.9	26.3 / 12.5 / 7.4	34.3 / 13.9 / 6.2	Sales/Net Fixed Assets	44.8 / 10.9 / 4.9	30.5 / 14.3 / 9.1
3.6 / 2.6 / 1.5	4.0 / 2.6 / 1.5	4.2 / 2.8 / 1.5	Sales/Total Assets	4.5 / 2.9 / 2.0	3.9 / 2.5 / 1.3
.9 / (35) 1.1 / 1.6	.8 / (37) 1.0 / 2.1	.6 / (37) .9 / 1.8	% Depr., Dep., Amort./Sales	.6 / (11) .9 / 2.3	.6 / (19) .9 / 1.6
			% Officers', Directors', Owners' Comp/Sales		

4/1/02-3/31/03 ALL	4/1/03-3/31/04 ALL	4/1/04-3/31/05 ALL		0-1MM	1-3MM	3-5MM	5-10MM	10-25MM	25MM & OVER
2644418M	1964454M	2153805M	Net Sales ($)		6156M	7839M	25548M	240243M	1874019M
1410715M	1083342M	1120907M	Total Assets ($)		5951M	2298M	5169M	115259M	992230M

© RMA 2005   M = $ thousand   MM = $ million
See Pages 11 through 21 for Explanation of Ratios and Data

Current Data Sorted By Assets   Comparative Historical Data

0-500M	500M-2MM	2-10MM	10-50MM	50-100MM	100-250MM	Type of Statement	4/1/00-3/31/01 ALL	4/1/01-3/31/02 ALL
		3	11			Unqualified	10	8
	4	14	2			Reviewed	13	12
2	8	7				Compiled	17	14
2	6	2	1			Tax Returns	6	8
2	4	14	3	1		Other	35	28
	14 (4/1-9/30/04)		72 (10/1/04-3/31/05)					
6	22	40	17	1		**NUMBER OF STATEMENTS**	81	70
%	%	%	%	%	%	**ASSETS**	%	%
	12.2	11.6	12.5			Cash & Equivalents	10.5	11.9
	26.2	23.1	15.0	D		Trade Receivables (net)	21.7	18.7
	28.5	20.0	21.6	A		Inventory	26.1	24.7
	1.5	5.2	3.1	T		All Other Current	4.3	3.8
	68.5	59.8	52.3	A		Total Current	62.6	59.2
	24.2	31.5	28.3			Fixed Assets (net)	26.8	31.0
	4.7	2.1	7.3	N		Intangibles (net)	3.4	2.2
	2.6	6.6	12.1	O		All Other Non-Current	7.2	7.6
	100.0	100.0	100.0	T		Total	100.0	100.0
				A		**LIABILITIES**		
	13.9	9.1	11.6	V		Notes Payable-Short Term	13.2	8.4
	5.3	3.3	3.4	A		Cur. Mat.-L/T/D	3.7	2.5
	17.5	16.5	13.3	I		Trade Payables	11.2	11.4
	.1	.7	.1	L		Income Taxes Payable	.4	.0
	12.0	13.8	17.3	A		All Other Current	18.9	15.0
	48.7	43.4	45.6	B		Total Current	47.5	37.3
	12.7	15.0	10.5	L		Long-Term Debt	12.5	17.5
	.0	.3	.3	E		Deferred Taxes	.2	.3
	2.7	3.9	8.0			All Other Non-Current	4.4	5.2
	35.8	37.5	35.6			Net Worth	35.4	39.6
	100.0	100.0	100.0			Total Liabilities & Net Worth	100.0	100.0
						INCOME DATA		
	100.0	100.0	100.0			Net Sales	100.0	100.0
	29.9	27.0	27.6			Gross Profit	25.0	29.3
	26.8	21.9	21.6			Operating Expenses	21.0	23.2
	3.1	5.2	6.0			Operating Profit	4.0	6.1
	.6	.4	.5			All Other Expenses (net)	−.1	1.7
	2.6	4.7	5.5			Profit Before Taxes	4.1	4.4
						RATIOS		
	2.4	2.1	1.6				2.2	2.8
	1.5	1.3	1.0			Current	1.4	1.5
	1.0	1.1	.6				.9	1.0
	1.7	1.1	.8				1.3	1.7
	.8	.7	.5			Quick	.7	.7
	.4	.4	.2				.3	.4
	16 22.2	13 27.7	9 39.5				12 29.6	12 31.1
	27 13.5	31 11.7	17 21.6			Sales/Receivables	23 16.1	21 17.2
	48 7.6	47 7.8	51 7.2				44 8.3	41 8.9
	23 15.7	18 20.2	30 12.1				28 12.9	31 11.8
	43 8.5	36 10.2	46 8.0			Cost of Sales/Inventory	41 9.0	39 9.3
	72 5.1	68 5.3	74 4.9				68 5.4	53 6.8
	6 57.0	14 26.3	15 24.3				10 35.7	7 51.9
	21 17.8	22 16.9	22 16.2			Cost of Sales/Payables	17 21.4	16 22.5
	53 6.8	42 8.7	46 7.9				31 11.8	26 13.9
	7.8	9.3	10.7				8.0	8.0
	16.0	17.4	−90.4			Sales/Working Capital	17.5	15.1
	−753.9	54.2	−9.2				−134.3	213.4
	11.9	22.3	7.2				14.0	13.9
	(21) 4.4	(38) 4.3	(15) 4.7			EBIT/Interest	(78) 5.1	(66) 5.6
	1.3	2.3	1.9				1.1	1.1
		7.1				Net Profit + Depr., Dep.,	15.9	18.6
		(11) 3.4				Amort./Cur. Mat. L /T/D	(25) 2.5	(20) 7.5
		1.2					1.4	2.6
	.3	.4	.4				.3	.3
	.8	1.0	1.3			Fixed/Worth	.9	.6
	2.4	2.1	3.2				1.9	1.8
	.6	.7	1.2				.7	.5
	2.3	1.9	2.4			Debt/Worth	1.9	1.8
	9.7	5.3	6.9				5.9	3.2
	42.4	53.7	65.8			% Profit Before Taxes/Tangible	51.0	52.0
	(19) 21.2	(38) 38.6	(16) 35.7			Net Worth	(72) 30.6	(63) 30.8
	6.6	15.6	10.9				10.4	6.4
	15.1	18.1	12.2			% Profit Before Taxes/Total	21.5	22.9
	7.2	7.4	8.6			Assets	6.8	9.6
	1.9	3.7	1.1				1.0	.9
	37.9	19.1	19.8				26.8	22.0
	11.3	8.0	6.5			Sales/Net Fixed Assets	11.6	10.2
	8.0	4.9	4.3				5.9	5.0
	3.5	2.9	2.9				3.4	3.7
	2.8	2.4	1.9			Sales/Total Assets	2.6	2.7
	2.2	2.1	1.4				2.0	1.8
	.9	1.0	.8				1.3	1.4
	(19) 1.5	(37) 1.9	(16) 1.4			% Depr., Dep., Amort./Sales	(69) 1.9	(65) 1.7
	3.0	3.1	2.0				2.8	2.8
		.7	.8			% Officers', Directors',	.9	1.2
	(12) 2.4	(11) 2.3				Owners' Comp/Sales	(22) 1.9	(22) 2.7
	11.1	6.3					5.6	4.4
5780M	84599M	597489M	754623M	183846M		Net Sales ($)	1730443M	1244676M
1957M	27749M	228718M	343066M	70505M		Total Assets ($)	866373M	716858M

M = $ thousand   MM = $ million
See Pages 11 through 21 for Explanation of Ratios and Data

Comparative Historical Data / Current Data Sorted By Sales

			Type of Statement	0-1MM	1-3MM	3-5MM	5-10MM	10-25MM	25MM & OVER
12	20	14	Unqualified					7	7
18	25	20	Reviewed		1	1	5	9	4
13	15	17	Compiled	1	3	6	5	2	
6	7	11	Tax Returns	2	2	3	2	2	
18	25	24	Other	1	3	1	6	9	4
4/1/02-3/31/03 ALL	4/1/03-3/31/04 ALL	4/1/04-3/31/05 ALL		14 (4/1-9/30/04)		72 (10/1/04-3/31/05)			
67	92	86	**NUMBER OF STATEMENTS**	4	9	11	18	29	15
%	%	%	**ASSETS**	%	%	%	%	%	%
12.1	10.4	11.8	Cash & Equivalents			15.0	9.0	10.3	19.0
20.2	21.2	23.0	Trade Receivables (net)			27.8	20.6	23.1	17.9
26.6	25.8	22.9	Inventory			24.7	22.6	18.5	24.0
1.6	2.6	4.2	All Other Current			.9	7.3	2.5	3.9
60.5	59.9	61.9	Total Current			68.4	59.5	54.4	64.8
28.8	30.2	28.0	Fixed Assets (net)			25.2	31.1	32.5	23.9
4.9	3.3	3.7	Intangibles (net)			4.7	3.6	2.8	4.0
5.7	6.7	6.4	All Other Non-Current			1.6	5.8	10.4	7.3
100.0	100.0	100.0	Total			100.0	100.0	100.0	100.0
			LIABILITIES						
13.2	12.8	14.4	Notes Payable-Short Term			8.0	15.7	8.6	10.6
2.4	3.1	3.6	Cur. Mat.-L/T/D			4.8	3.5	3.7	1.7
11.2	12.5	16.3	Trade Payables			10.7	16.3	16.7	12.6
.2	.2	.4	Income Taxes Payable			.1	.2	.8	.1
16.5	15.3	14.3	All Other Current			11.9	16.9	11.6	17.8
43.4	43.8	48.9	Total Current			35.4	52.6	41.5	42.8
15.1	16.8	12.6	Long-Term Debt			15.0	13.7	17.2	6.6
.1	.2	.2	Deferred Taxes			.1	.4	.2	.2
3.9	5.4	4.6	All Other Non-Current			4.1	1.1	6.5	6.5
37.5	33.8	33.7	Net Worth			45.4	32.3	34.6	43.9
100.0	100.0	100.0	Total Liabilities & Net Worth			100.0	100.0	100.0	100.0
			INCOME DATA						
100.0	100.0	100.0	Net Sales			100.0	100.0	100.0	100.0
30.4	28.9	27.7	Gross Profit			30.6	27.6	26.4	25.3
25.4	25.5	23.1	Operating Expenses			26.2	24.6	20.5	18.6
5.0	3.4	4.6	Operating Profit			4.4	3.0	5.9	6.7
.7	.6	.5	All Other Expenses (net)			.3	.0	1.0	.0
4.3	2.9	4.1	Profit Before Taxes			4.1	3.0	4.8	6.7
			RATIOS						
2.5	2.2	2.0				7.0	1.4	1.9	2.6
1.6	1.4	1.3	Current			1.8	1.1	1.3	1.2
1.1	.9	.9				1.3	1.0	.9	.9
1.8	1.2	1.3				2.7	.9	1.1	1.9
.8	.8	.6	Quick			.9	.4	.7	.5
.4	.4	.4				.5	.2	.5	.4
9 40.4	9 39.4	13 28.5				17 21.7	6 57.3	17 22.0	11 33.5
24 15.3	24 15.4	28 13.0	Sales/Receivables			31 11.8	23 16.2	36 10.1	14 27.0
37 9.8	47 7.7	47 7.8				57 6.4	39 9.3	54 6.7	35 10.6
27 13.6	26 14.1	23 15.9				30 12.2	16 22.7	24 15.2	23 15.8
46 8.0	51 7.2	40 9.0	Cost of Sales/Inventory			45 8.2	36 10.1	36 10.0	41 9.0
67 5.5	69 5.3	71 5.2				53 6.8	94 3.9	59 6.1	71 5.1
9 39.0	10 35.0	13 28.9				6 66.0	11 32.3	16 23.2	14 26.9
16 22.6	21 17.3	21 17.3	Cost of Sales/Payables			15 24.4	21 17.6	22 16.3	16 23.0
34 10.8	33 11.0	48 7.5				52 7.0	53 6.9	47 7.8	23 15.6
6.3	7.9	9.0				4.8	15.1	8.9	5.0
14.0	19.6	20.1	Sales/Working Capital			10.2	29.1	20.6	22.5
71.0	−69.5	−44.0				28.0	−792.0	−54.1	−90.4
20.5	11.9	16.7				48.1	13.6	17.4	19.5
(62) 7.0	(85) 4.1	(80) 4.5	EBIT/Interest			9.7	(17) 4.4	(27) 3.9	(14) 5.9
1.8	1.1	2.0				3.7	1.9	2.4	2.9
20.4	16.3	8.9	Net Profit + Depr., Dep.,						
(21) 6.3	(21) 4.2	(20) 2.1	Amort./Cur. Mat. L/T/D						
2.4	1.2	.7							
.4	.4	.3				.3	.6	.4	.3
.7	.9	1.0	Fixed/Worth			.6	.8	1.0	.6
2.0	2.1	2.4				2.3	2.1	3.8	1.4
.6	1.0	.9				.5	1.2	1.1	.7
1.7	2.2	2.2	Debt/Worth			2.0	2.2	2.9	1.3
4.6	4.9	6.6				5.0	7.2	7.2	4.2
62.6	52.2	49.0	% Profit Before Taxes/Tangible			65.3	44.4	51.1	71.4
(58) 42.6	(83) 17.2	(76) 30.1	Net Worth	(10) 24.2	(17) 24.4	(27) 40.4	46.1		
10.0	3.3	11.4				13.1	9.5	20.1	16.4
24.4	16.6	15.4	% Profit Before Taxes/Total			16.5	12.9	16.1	21.8
10.1	5.3	7.7	Assets			8.5	6.3	7.3	9.4
1.7	.6	2.2				3.9	2.2	3.5	4.8
24.0	18.2	24.6				36.3	31.5	15.6	29.4
10.6	9.8	9.2	Sales/Net Fixed Assets			11.5	7.0	7.0	12.2
6.3	5.0	5.4				6.2	4.7	4.7	6.5
3.6	3.5	3.1				4.7	3.3	2.7	3.8
2.7	2.7	2.5	Sales/Total Assets			2.8	2.4	2.3	2.8
1.8	1.8	2.0				2.1	1.8	2.0	2.3
1.3	1.0	.9				1.0	2.3	.8	.6
(63) 1.9	(82) 1.6	(76) 1.6	% Depr., Dep., Amort./Sales	(10) 1.4	(15) 2.9	(28) 1.5	(14) 1.2		
2.8	2.5	2.9				3.1	4.3	2.1	1.7
1.3	1.2	.8	% Officers', Directors',						
(20) 2.7	(22) 3.9	(27) 2.4	Owners' Comp/Sales						
5.6	7.6	6.3							
1201951M	1363789M	1626337M	Net Sales ($)	2778M	17657M	43329M	134206M	511675M	916692M
686549M	578996M	671995M	Total Assets ($)	1006M	6691M	16186M	58346M	249957M	339809M

© RMA 2005   M = $ thousand   MM = $ million
See Pages 11 through 21 for Explanation of Ratios and Data

Current Data Sorted By Assets   Comparative Historical Data

0-500M	500M-2MM	2-10MM	10-50MM	50-100MM	100-250MM	Type of Statement	4/1/00-3/31/01 ALL	4/1/01-3/31/02 ALL
	2	10	17	4	1	Unqualified	33	30
	8	24	12	1		Reviewed	41	41
5	15	7	2			Compiled	35	34
10	16	4	1			Tax Returns	13	19
4	14	21	12	2	3	Other	48	73
	47 (4/1-9/30/04)		148 (10/1/04-3/31/05)					
19	55	66	44	7	4	**NUMBER OF STATEMENTS**	170	197
%	%	%	%	%	%	**ASSETS**	%	%
9.2	7.9	5.9	7.1			Cash & Equivalents	4.3	6.5
24.0	26.8	27.1	21.7			Trade Receivables (net)	22.9	24.6
25.7	27.9	32.7	29.0			Inventory	27.5	26.4
2.0	1.4	2.3	1.0			All Other Current	1.9	2.2
60.9	64.0	67.9	58.7			Total Current	56.6	59.7
34.2	26.8	23.9	28.8			Fixed Assets (net)	31.8	29.8
.3	4.0	2.5	6.1			Intangibles (net)	4.4	3.0
4.6	5.3	5.7	6.4			All Other Non-Current	7.2	7.4
100.0	100.0	100.0	100.0			Total	100.0	100.0
						LIABILITIES		
27.8	17.1	16.4	10.9			Notes Payable-Short Term	14.5	13.4
4.5	6.3	3.5	5.0			Cur. Mat.-L/T/D	4.0	4.3
16.4	15.5	13.8	9.8			Trade Payables	12.6	12.0
.0	.1	.2	.2			Income Taxes Payable	.3	.2
12.1	11.6	5.7	7.4			All Other Current	9.2	9.3
60.8	50.5	39.7	33.4			Total Current	40.6	39.2
35.7	18.6	13.1	17.2			Long-Term Debt	24.0	19.4
.0	.1	.3	.4			Deferred Taxes	.7	.4
21.5	6.8	4.1	2.4			All Other Non-Current	5.4	4.9
-18.0	24.0	42.9	46.6			Net Worth	29.3	36.1
100.0	100.0	100.0	100.0			Total Liabilities & Net Worth	100.0	100.0
						INCOME DATA		
100.0	100.0	100.0	100.0			Net Sales	100.0	100.0
40.9	30.9	23.9	22.2			Gross Profit	27.0	28.4
37.0	26.0	19.7	16.4			Operating Expenses	22.4	23.7
3.9	4.9	4.2	5.9			Operating Profit	4.6	4.7
1.7	1.0	.8	.7			All Other Expenses (net)	1.7	1.4
2.2	4.0	3.4	5.2			Profit Before Taxes	2.8	3.2
						RATIOS		
2.8	1.9	2.5	3.3				2.3	2.4
1.2	1.4	1.5	1.8			Current	1.5	1.5
.6	.9	1.2	1.2				1.1	1.2
2.2	1.3	1.3	1.7				1.2	1.4
.4	.7	.8	.8			Quick (169)	.7	.8
.1	.3	.4	.4				.4	.4
11 34.0	20 18.2	23 15.5	19 18.9				23 16.0	25 14.6
26 14.1	30 12.0	34 10.8	33 11.1			Sales/Receivables	35 10.5	36 10.2
33 11.1	42 8.6	46 8.0	47 7.8				47 7.7	48 7.6
13 28.3	16 22.7	34 10.8	36 10.0				31 11.6	30 12.2
40 9.2	45 8.2	58 6.3	57 6.4			Cost of Sales/Inventory	57 6.4	56 6.6
72 5.1	99 3.7	99 3.7	112 3.3				89 4.1	95 3.8
3 110.5	10 35.8	12 30.4	9 40.3				11 33.2	11 34.3
10 35.7	26 14.2	22 16.3	17 21.5			Cost of Sales/Payables	21 17.2	21 17.6
25 14.8	46 8.0	40 9.1	25 14.5				36 10.0	37 10.0
9.6	6.4	5.3	5.2				6.7	6.6
30.0	17.8	10.4	10.7			Sales/Working Capital	11.3	12.0
-16.8	-29.4	27.5	26.9				65.7	39.2
9.4	10.5	10.6	10.9				6.7	7.4
2.0	(48) 3.3	(59) 4.8	(42) 4.6			EBIT/Interest (160)	2.2 (185)	2.8
-2.3	1.3	2.1	1.9				.9	1.1
	10.2	4.5	12.5			Net Profit + Depr., Dep.,	3.9	3.8
	(11) 1.7	(22) 2.4	(13) 4.7			Amort./Cur. Mat. L /T/D (49)	2.0 (57)	2.0
	.4	1.6	2.1				.8	1.2
1.0	.4	.2	.4				.5	.4
3.9	1.1	.6	.8			Fixed/Worth	1.1	.9
-.4	19.7	1.2	1.4				4.2	2.1
2.8	1.2	.8	.7				1.1	.8
12.8	3.3	1.8	1.3			Debt/Worth	2.4	1.7
-2.7	455.3	3.3	3.3				10.3	4.4
129.9	69.8	39.9	36.1			% Profit Before Taxes/Tangible	45.5	46.8
(10) 54.6	(42) 31.4	(63) 19.2	(42) 20.9			Net Worth (138)	20.8 (174)	21.7
-18.4	5.5	6.0	7.0				2.2	5.7
30.4	14.2	14.5	15.5			% Profit Before Taxes/Total	13.9	16.4
6.8	7.0	7.8	6.7			Assets	5.3	7.3
-11.2	.6	2.9	2.9				-.4	1.2
31.7	44.0	34.1	11.2				16.0	25.9
19.8	9.8	13.7	7.5			Sales/Net Fixed Assets	7.7	7.7
7.8	5.1	5.4	5.0				4.8	4.7
5.7	3.8	3.4	3.0				3.2	3.2
4.0	2.8	2.5	2.2			Sales/Total Assets	2.2	2.1
2.1	1.6	1.8	1.6				1.6	1.6
1.4	.9	.6	1.5				1.2	1.2
(14) 3.4	(48) 2.0	(63) 1.9	(39) 2.2			% Depr., Dep., Amort./Sales (150)	2.1 (177)	2.1
4.2	4.3	2.8	3.6				3.7	3.4
	2.2	1.7					1.6	1.9
	(28) 4.3	(25) 2.2				% Officers', Directors', Owners' Comp/Sales (72)	3.6 (70)	3.9
	6.3	3.0					6.9	6.7
18073M	187702M	864706M	2764095M	778488M	786948M	Net Sales ($)	4299068M	5161938M
5091M	66902M	317342M	962842M	522855M	553816M	Total Assets ($)	2627764M	2526579M

M = $ thousand   MM = $ million
See Pages 11 through 21 for Explanation of Ratios and Data

Comparative Historical Data · Current Data Sorted By Sales

			Type of Statement						
31	32	34	Unqualified		1	1	2	10	20
42	51	45	Reviewed		3	8	7	16	11
32	34	29	Compiled	5	10	5	5	1	3
19	32	31	Tax Returns	8	7	6	7	2	1
50	54	56	Other	3	9	3	14	9	18
4/1/02-3/31/03 ALL	4/1/03-3/31/04 ALL	4/1/04-3/31/05 ALL		\<--- 47 (4/1-9/30/04) ---\>		\<--- 148 (10/1/04-3/31/05) ---\>			
				0-1MM	1-3MM	3-5MM	5-10MM	10-25MM	25MM & OVER
174	203	195	NUMBER OF STATEMENTS	16	30	23	35	38	53
%	%	%	**ASSETS**	%	%	%	%	%	%
6.8	6.5	6.8	Cash & Equivalents	5.6	8.1	11.1	6.0	6.0	5.8
21.5	22.7	25.2	Trade Receivables (net)	19.2	21.2	26.8	30.8	24.8	25.3
26.2	27.9	29.2	Inventory	29.3	26.1	28.4	28.1	36.0	27.1
2.8	1.9	1.9	All Other Current	1.7	1.5	2.3	1.6	1.5	2.4
57.3	59.1	63.1	Total Current	55.7	56.8	68.6	66.5	68.4	60.5
31.3	30.2	26.7	Fixed Assets (net)	35.7	31.7	25.8	24.1	21.4	26.9
4.0	4.3	4.5	Intangibles (net)	3.3	5.3	.6	4.4	2.3	7.7
7.3	6.5	5.7	All Other Non-Current	5.2	6.2	4.9	4.9	7.9	4.8
100.0	100.0	100.0	Total	100.0	100.0	100.0	100.0	100.0	100.0
			LIABILITIES						
14.1	13.9	16.0	Notes Payable-Short Term	25.8	22.1	12.0	16.3	14.6	12.0
4.7	4.3	4.8	Cur. Mat.-L/T/D	4.3	5.1	8.3	3.8	4.9	3.8
12.7	12.6	13.5	Trade Payables	9.9	16.2	12.6	17.9	11.2	12.0
.4	.2	.2	Income Taxes Payable	.0	.1	.1	.1	.3	.3
8.5	8.8	8.4	All Other Current	12.3	6.5	13.9	7.3	6.5	7.9
40.4	39.7	42.7	Total Current	52.2	50.0	46.8	45.4	37.5	35.9
21.1	18.5	18.2	Long-Term Debt	43.4	20.5	13.0	13.7	14.4	17.3
.4	.3	.3	Deferred Taxes	.0	.0	.2	.2	.3	.5
3.5	6.9	6.3	All Other Non-Current	33.9	1.5	3.1	6.8	3.9	3.2
34.5	34.6	32.5	Net Worth	-29.5	28.0	36.8	33.8	43.9	43.0
100.0	100.0	100.0	Total Liabilities & Net Worth	100.0	100.0	100.0	100.0	100.0	100.0
			INCOME DATA						
100.0	100.0	100.0	Net Sales	100.0	100.0	100.0	100.0	100.0	100.0
27.4	28.2	27.5	Gross Profit	36.1	39.2	27.0	26.6	22.7	22.7
22.9	24.3	22.8	Operating Expenses	30.9	32.8	24.7	22.5	17.6	17.6
4.5	3.9	4.8	Operating Profit	5.1	6.5	2.3	4.1	5.1	5.1
1.3	1.1	1.0	All Other Expenses (net)	3.0	1.3	.5	.2	1.1	.9
3.2	2.8	3.8	Profit Before Taxes	2.2	5.1	1.8	3.9	4.0	4.2
			RATIOS						
2.3	2.4	2.4	Current	2.3	2.0	2.0	2.1	4.1	2.4
1.5	1.5	1.5		1.4	1.2	1.4	1.4	1.7	1.7
1.1	1.1	1.1		.7	.8	1.0	1.0	1.2	1.3
1.3	1.3	1.3	Quick	1.3	1.4	1.5	1.3	1.9	1.2
(172) .7	.7	.7		.5	.4	.9	.8	.7	.8
.4	.4	.4		.1	.3	.4	.4	.4	.6
18 20.7	20 18.2	22 16.6	Sales/Receivables	13 29.0	16 22.8	20 18.2	24 15.5	22 16.5	23 15.6
29 12.4	33 11.0	32 11.3		31 11.7	27 13.5	30 12.0	34 10.6	32 11.5	35 10.4
42 8.8	46 7.9	44 8.3		43 8.5	40 9.2	43 8.4	48 7.7	47 7.8	47 7.7
27 13.4	33 11.1	27 13.6	Cost of Sales/Inventory	3 143.4	13 28.1	15 24.0	26 14.0	47 7.7	26 13.9
52 7.0	56 6.5	51 7.1		58 6.3	48 7.6	50 7.3	49 7.4	83 4.4	45 8.1
84 4.4	86 4.2	103 3.5		135 2.7	106 3.5	99 3.7	87 4.2	111 3.3	84 4.4
9 41.1	10 37.6	10 36.3	Cost of Sales/Payables	3 109.3	12 30.1	6 57.6	15 24.9	10 35.7	9 40.0
18 20.1	20 18.1	20 18.0		16 23.1	27 13.3	22 16.8	31 11.8	17 22.1	18 20.7
36 10.2	38 9.7	37 9.9		44 8.4	52 7.0	33 11.1	41 8.9	33 11.0	30 12.3
7.2	6.2	5.8	Sales/Working Capital	5.3	6.1	5.3	7.0	4.7	5.5
13.1	12.4	11.5		17.8	20.4	16.4	12.6	9.2	10.7
63.3	92.1	51.0		-34.5	-21.4	-815.5	438.3	19.1	29.5
9.2	7.6	10.1	EBIT/Interest	7.2	15.0	12.0	9.9	9.3	12.6
(163) 3.1	(191) 2.7	(179) 4.4		1.8	(27) 3.2	(18) 4.0	(32) 3.3	(34) 5.2	(52) 4.8
1.1	1.1	1.7		-.7	.9	1.6	1.7	2.0	2.7
3.8	3.7	5.7	Net Profit + Depr., Dep., Amort./Cur. Mat. L/T/D				3.1	7.2	7.0
(44) 1.9	(48) 2.0	(54) 2.4					(12) 1.7	(13) 2.9	(22) 2.7
1.0	1.0	1.4					.8	1.6	1.6
.4	.4	.4	Fixed/Worth	1.5	.6	.2	.3	.2	.4
1.1	.9	.9		-8.1	1.5	.7	.7	.6	.8
2.8	2.5	1.9		-.4	4.0	2.0	1.8	1.1	1.4
.9	.8	.9	Debt/Worth	3.6	1.2	.8	.8	.8	.9
2.1	2.0	2.2		-12.0	3.2	1.7	3.3	1.7	1.8
7.7	5.6	5.4		-2.7	14.9	3.8	5.0	3.0	3.6
50.4	38.8	45.6	% Profit Before Taxes/Tangible Net Worth		76.7	38.0	41.2	42.5	39.6
(149) 20.6	(175) 14.8	(166) 21.4			(24) 30.3	(19) 11.4	(31) 21.8	(37) 19.5	(49) 28.2
5.5	2.6	6.6			2.0	3.6	5.8	5.4	11.9
16.7	12.4	14.5	% Profit Before Taxes/Total Assets	22.9	16.8	11.2	12.7	15.9	15.2
6.3	4.7	7.0		4.7	8.4	5.7	7.0	8.5	6.7
.8	.1	1.7		-7.5	-.1	.8	1.0	1.6	3.6
19.9	23.8	24.7	Sales/Net Fixed Assets	21.8	17.8	47.9	39.7	35.2	20.1
7.9	8.1	9.5		8.3	8.8	9.8	14.2	9.8	8.8
4.7	4.3	5.3		3.5	4.5	4.9	6.8	5.5	5.7
3.5	3.3	3.5	Sales/Total Assets	4.1	3.6	4.0	3.6	3.1	3.4
2.4	2.3	2.5		1.9	2.5	2.7	2.6	2.3	2.5
1.6	1.6	1.7		1.2	1.5	1.8	1.9	1.6	1.7
1.4	1.2	.9	% Depr., Dep., Amort./Sales	2.7	1.1	1.1	.7	.5	.8
(160) 2.4	(177) 2.3	(173) 2.1		(14) 4.0	(27) 2.8	(18) 2.0	(30) 2.1	(37) 1.4	(47) 2.0
4.0	3.9	3.7		5.1	4.5	4.4	3.8	2.4	3.1
1.5	1.9	1.8	% Officers', Directors', Owners' Comp/Sales		2.1		2.1		.8
(61) 3.5	(77) 3.9	(70) 3.0			(18) 5.5		(16) 3.0		(12) 2.3
6.7	7.0	5.5			9.8		3.7		3.0
3404158M	4281048M	5400012M	Net Sales ($)	8936M	58417M	89844M	246558M	609665M	4386592M
1763696M	1862370M	2428848M	Total Assets ($)	6408M	28917M	38049M	117868M	282583M	1955023M

© RMA 2005

M = $ thousand   MM = $ million

See Pages 11 through 21 for Explanation of Ratios and Data

Current Data Sorted By Assets   Comparative Historical Data

0-500M	500M-2MM	2-10MM	10-50MM	50-100MM	100-250MM	Type of Statement	4/1/00-3/31/01 ALL	4/1/01-3/31/02 ALL
		1	9	2	9	Unqualified	26	17
	1	6	2			Reviewed	10	4
	2	1				Compiled	2	7
1	1	2	1			Tax Returns		2
2	4	7	3	2		Other	16	27
							4/1/00-3/31/01	4/1/01-3/31/02
1	6	14	19	5	11	**NUMBER OF STATEMENTS**	54	57
%	%	%	%	%	%	**ASSETS**	%	%
		6.9	.9		3.8	Cash & Equivalents	2.7	4.0
		30.6	18.9		14.7	Trade Receivables (net)	23.1	22.8
		30.2	22.2		16.6	Inventory	21.2	15.2
		1.2	3.1		2.2	All Other Current	.9	2.5
		69.0	45.0		37.3	Total Current	47.9	44.5
		26.3	49.6		55.8	Fixed Assets (net)	44.0	46.9
		1.1	1.8		2.6	Intangibles (net)	3.9	4.1
		3.6	3.6		4.3	All Other Non-Current	3.6	4.5
		100.0	100.0		100.0	Total	100.0	100.0
						LIABILITIES		
		15.6	8.8		4.9	Notes Payable-Short Term	9.1	8.8
		2.6	6.1		2.4	Cur. Mat.-L/T/D	7.2	7.0
		18.2	14.0		11.9	Trade Payables	15.1	12.8
		.0	.0		.1	Income Taxes Payable	.1	.2
		3.4	9.5		8.3	All Other Current	8.2	8.8
		39.9	38.4		27.7	Total Current	39.7	37.5
		14.0	23.2		31.8	Long-Term Debt	25.2	25.1
		.3	1.0		1.9	Deferred Taxes	1.6	1.1
		.1	4.3		2.3	All Other Non-Current	5.1	4.3
		45.7	33.0		36.3	Net Worth	28.4	31.9
		100.0	100.0		100.0	Total Liabilities & Net Worth	100.0	100.0
						INCOME DATA		
		100.0	100.0		100.0	Net Sales	100.0	100.0
		21.6	26.2		18.8	Gross Profit	21.7	24.9
		19.6	22.3		15.1	Operating Expenses	16.6	19.6
		2.0	3.9		3.7	Operating Profit	5.1	5.3
		.6	1.4		.7	All Other Expenses (net)	2.1	2.6
		1.4	2.5		3.0	Profit Before Taxes	3.0	2.7
						RATIOS		
		2.6	2.3		1.9		1.6	2.0
		1.5	1.0		1.5	Current	1.3	1.2
		1.3	.7		1.2		.9	.8
		1.2	.7		1.1		.9	1.3
		1.0	.5		.8	Quick	.6	.7
		.5	.4		.5		.5	.4
		20 18.7	31 11.9		28 12.8		30 12.1	31 11.7
		37 9.8	35 10.3		38 9.7	Sales/Receivables	39 9.4	38 9.5
		61 6.0	47 7.7		50 7.3		48 7.6	52 7.1
		8 43.4	22 16.2		38 9.7		31 11.7	17 21.5
		42 8.7	45 8.1		46 7.9	Cost of Sales/Inventory	46 8.0	35 10.3
		72 5.1	64 5.7		55 6.7		66 5.5	68 5.4
		12 31.0	26 14.1		22 16.7		22 16.8	18 20.5
		24 15.4	37 9.9		37 9.8	Cost of Sales/Payables	32 11.4	29 12.7
		41 9.0	59 6.2		56 6.5		39 9.4	51 7.1
		5.3	6.2		7.4		10.1	9.9
		14.9	-211.5		11.7	Sales/Working Capital	22.3	19.1
		30.9	-14.3		26.5		-113.2	-23.0
		12.7	5.4		12.0		5.3	5.9
		(13) 2.6	(18) 3.1		3.8	EBIT/Interest	(53) 3.1	(49) 2.1
		.2	-.8		.5		.1	.7
						Net Profit + Depr., Dep.,	3.5	2.8
						Amort./Cur. Mat. L./T/D	(21) 1.5	(15) 1.8
							.2	.9
		.2	.9		1.0		.7	.8
		.5	1.8		1.8	Fixed/Worth	1.5	1.3
		.8	3.0		6.4		3.5	3.3
		.7	1.1		.7		1.0	.9
		1.3	2.5		1.4	Debt/Worth	2.3	2.1
		2.9	4.9		6.6		8.8	7.1
		30.6	40.3			% Profit Before Taxes/Tangible	50.2	33.2
		4.5	(18) 13.0			Net Worth	(45) 21.2	(48) 14.0
		-1.4	-25.2				-8.0	-1.0
		12.3	10.3		8.8	% Profit Before Taxes/Total	13.6	12.1
		1.7	4.8		7.6	Assets	8.0	5.3
		-.5	-3.6		-3.4		-3.6	-.8
		52.7	5.3		5.0		8.8	6.9
		17.2	4.0		2.8	Sales/Net Fixed Assets	4.2	3.4
		6.4	2.2		1.2		2.6	2.5
		4.7	2.3		2.0		2.6	2.2
		2.6	1.7		1.3	Sales/Total Assets	1.8	1.7
		1.5	1.6		.8		1.4	1.3
		.3	2.4				1.4	1.7
		(13) 1.0	(17) 4.5			% Depr., Dep., Amort./Sales	(47) 2.9	(43) 3.8
		4.9	6.0				4.5	6.6
						% Officers', Directors',		1.5
						Owners' Comp/Sales		(11) 2.8
								6.3
1409M	20878M	221721M	793762M	422500M	2498027M	Net Sales ($)	2906514M	2699066M
310M	6849M	69056M	477981M	324700M	1814427M	Total Assets ($)	2066267M	1967051M

Comparative Historical Data / Current Data Sorted By Sales

Type of Statement

Item	'02-'03	'03-'04	'04-'05	0-1MM	1-3MM	3-5MM	5-10MM	10-25MM	25MM & OVER
Unqualified	19	23	21				1	1	19
Reviewed	14	11	9		1		1	5	2
Compiled	4	4	3			2	1		
Tax Returns	3	3	5		2	1		1	1
Other	25	22	18	1			1	6	10
	4/1/02-3/31/03 ALL	4/1/03-3/31/04 ALL	4/1/04-3/31/05 ALL	\<-- 9 (4/1-9/30/04) -->			\<-- 47 (10/1/04-3/31/05) -->		
NUMBER OF STATEMENTS	65	63	56	1	3	3	4	13	32

Historical columns and current columns are percentages (%).

ASSETS

Item	'02-'03	'03-'04	'04-'05	0-1MM	1-3MM	3-5MM	5-10MM	10-25MM	25MM & OVER
Cash & Equivalents	5.2	4.1	4.6					2.3	3.6
Trade Receivables (net)	24.1	22.9	23.5					24.6	19.5
Inventory	18.2	17.8	21.1					25.7	20.5
All Other Current	2.3	1.5	2.0					2.0	2.3
Total Current	49.8	46.2	51.1					54.7	45.8
Fixed Assets (net)	38.8	41.7	42.1					38.3	48.5
Intangibles (net)	4.4	4.8	1.9					1.7	2.5
All Other Non-Current	7.0	7.2	4.9					5.3	3.2
Total	100.0	100.0	100.0					100.0	100.0

LIABILITIES

Item	'02-'03	'03-'04	'04-'05	0-1MM	1-3MM	3-5MM	5-10MM	10-25MM	25MM & OVER
Notes Payable-Short Term	10.5	6.2	10.4					12.4	6.8
Cur. Mat.-L/T/D	4.2	3.2	3.6					3.9	4.1
Trade Payables	15.0	14.8	14.7					20.3	13.2
Income Taxes Payable	.1	.1	.0					.0	.1
All Other Current	6.6	8.8	8.8					2.8	9.8
Total Current	36.4	33.0	37.6					39.4	34.0
Long-Term Debt	19.2	21.1	27.8					20.3	31.5
Deferred Taxes	1.4	1.7	.8					.9	1.0
All Other Non-Current	4.5	7.9	2.5					1.3	3.4
Net Worth	38.6	36.2	31.3					38.1	30.0
Total Liabilities & Net Worth	100.0	100.0	100.0					100.0	100.0

INCOME DATA

Item	'02-'03	'03-'04	'04-'05	0-1MM	1-3MM	3-5MM	5-10MM	10-25MM	25MM & OVER
Net Sales	100.0	100.0	100.0					100.0	100.0
Gross Profit	24.6	25.9	23.5					22.7	21.3
Operating Expenses	21.5	21.1	20.2					20.1	17.4
Operating Profit	3.2	4.8	3.3					2.6	4.0
All Other Expenses (net)	1.5	1.3	1.5					1.0	1.8
Profit Before Taxes	1.6	3.5	1.9					1.7	2.2

RATIOS

Item	'02-'03	'03-'04	'04-'05	0-1MM	1-3MM	3-5MM	5-10MM	10-25MM	25MM & OVER
Current	2.2	2.0	2.2					2.4	2.2
	1.4	1.5	1.4					1.3	1.5
	1.0	1.1	.9					.9	1.0
Quick	1.4	1.2	1.1					1.0	1.1
	1.0	.9	.7					.7	.7
	.5	.6	.4					.4	.4

Turnover ratios below are shown as "days / times":

Item	'02-'03	'03-'04	'04-'05	0-1MM	1-3MM	3-5MM	5-10MM	10-25MM	25MM & OVER
Sales/Receivables	34 / 10.7	32 / 11.3	29 / 12.6					34 / 10.9	29 / 12.8
	44 / 8.3	38 / 9.5	36 / 10.0					45 / 8.2	33 / 11.0
	59 / 6.2	48 / 7.6	47 / 7.7					61 / 5.9	43 / 8.4
Cost of Sales/Inventory	29 / 12.6	18 / 20.8	21 / 17.1					20 / 17.9	26 / 14.3
	48 / 7.7	38 / 9.7	42 / 8.7					35 / 10.4	45 / 8.1
	71 / 5.1	65 / 5.6	62 / 5.8					69 / 5.3	62 / 5.9
Cost of Sales/Payables	21 / 17.4	24 / 15.4	18 / 19.9					24 / 15.4	20 / 18.3
	34 / 10.7	33 / 11.0	32 / 11.6					59 / 6.2	30 / 12.0
	54 / 6.8	44 / 8.3	46 / 8.0					65 / 5.6	43 / 8.6
Sales/Working Capital	6.5	7.9	6.9					9.5	6.9
	12.8	16.3	14.7					18.8	12.5
	NM	78.6	-34.6					-34.9	NM
EBIT/Interest	7.8	7.7	10.1					8.6	7.2
	(60) 3.3	(57) 3.9	(49) 3.4					2.6	(30) 3.6
	.8	1.6	.6					-.5	1.2
Net Profit + Depr., Dep., Amort./Cur. Mat. L/T/D	4.1	5.5	3.6						
	(18) 2.6	(20) 3.2	(15) 2.2						
	1.4	1.7	1.6						
Fixed/Worth	.4	.7	.6					.5	.8
	1.2	1.2	1.5					.8	1.7
	2.7	3.9	2.9					2.0	3.3
Debt/Worth	.7	.9	1.0					1.0	.8
	2.0	1.9	2.1					1.8	2.0
	5.9	5.3	4.8					3.8	6.7
% Profit Before Taxes/Tangible Net Worth	29.3	31.4	28.7					25.4	27.3
	(54) 15.7	(54) 19.0	(48) 9.3					5.7	(27) 12.7
	1.2	3.9	-.4					-12.3	1.2
% Profit Before Taxes/Total Assets	10.2	10.6	9.0					9.8	9.0
	4.7	5.4	4.4					2.2	5.5
	-.8	1.5	-.8					-2.4	.5
Sales/Net Fixed Assets	15.3	9.4	14.0					34.3	5.8
	4.3	4.3	4.3					6.5	3.9
	2.3	2.1	2.3					2.5	2.2
Sales/Total Assets	2.2	2.4	2.5					3.5	2.3
	1.6	1.8	1.8					2.4	1.7
	1.1	1.1	1.1					1.3	1.1
% Depr., Dep., Amort./Sales	1.4	1.7	1.2					.7	1.7
	(50) 3.3	(50) 3.5	(43) 3.6					(12) 4.0	(24) 3.4
	5.6	5.1	6.0					5.8	4.9
% Officers', Directors', Owners' Comp/Sales	1.3	1.7	.7						
	(18) 3.3	(17) 3.9	(14) 2.7						
	5.9	5.3	4.5						
Net Sales ($)	3337911M	3847893M	3958297M	829M	5950M	11082M	26590M	209556M	3704290M
Total Assets ($)	2718305M	3011050M	2693323M	1480M	3152M	7072M	13695M	149833M	2518091M

Current Data Sorted By Assets   Comparative Historical Data

0-500M	500M-2MM	2-10MM	10-50MM	50-100MM	100-250MM	Type of Statement	ALL 4/1/00-3/31/01	ALL 4/1/01-3/31/02
		11	21	2	2	Unqualified	34	34
	6	48	14		2	Reviewed	59	46
3	15	22	3			Compiled	43	36
4	4	3				Tax Returns	8	4
2	8	32	26			Other	56	68
	43 (4/1-9/30/04)		185 (10/1/04-3/31/05)					
9	33	116	64	4	2	**NUMBER OF STATEMENTS**	200	188
%	%	%	%	%	%	**ASSETS**	%	%
	7.8	7.0	5.4			Cash & Equivalents	5.7	7.2
	37.5	27.3	25.1			Trade Receivables (net)	29.4	26.7
	16.8	15.3	17.4			Inventory	15.3	15.1
	.3	1.6	2.6			All Other Current	2.9	1.7
	62.4	51.2	50.5			Total Current	53.3	50.6
	23.9	38.7	39.4			Fixed Assets (net)	37.1	38.3
	1.4	3.1	3.9			Intangibles (net)	2.1	3.1
	12.3	6.9	6.1			All Other Non-Current	7.5	7.9
	100.0	100.0	100.0			Total	100.0	100.0
						LIABILITIES		
	11.5	9.2	11.9			Notes Payable-Short Term	9.4	7.5
	4.6	6.2	5.0			Cur. Mat.-L/T/D	4.8	5.1
	25.0	16.7	15.4			Trade Payables	17.3	15.3
	.1	.1	.2			Income Taxes Payable	.1	.1
	7.7	5.8	6.7			All Other Current	8.0	6.9
	48.9	38.1	39.4			Total Current	39.6	34.9
	15.8	21.0	21.1			Long-Term Debt	20.9	21.0
	.2	1.2	.9			Deferred Taxes	.9	1.3
	3.7	3.7	4.6			All Other Non-Current	3.7	3.5
	31.4	35.9	34.0			Net Worth	34.8	39.4
	100.0	100.0	100.0			Total Liabilities & Net Worth	100.0	100.0
						INCOME DATA		
	100.0	100.0	100.0			Net Sales	100.0	100.0
	27.4	27.0	20.9			Gross Profit	24.1	24.8
	27.3	24.0	17.4			Operating Expenses	20.3	21.8
	.1	3.0	3.5			Operating Profit	3.8	3.0
	.5	.7	.5			All Other Expenses (net)	1.0	1.1
	-.4	2.3	3.0			Profit Before Taxes	2.8	1.9
						RATIOS		
	2.6	2.2	1.9			Current	2.2	2.6
	1.4	1.3	1.3				1.3	1.4
	.9	.9	.9				1.0	1.0
	1.8	1.5	1.1			Quick	1.4	1.7
	1.0	.8	.7				.9	1.0
	.6	.6	.5				.6	.6
35	10.5 35	10.5 31	11.8			Sales/Receivables	33 11.1	31 11.9
41	8.8 40	9.2 37	9.8				40 9.2	37 9.9
54	6.8 47	7.8 49	7.4				46 7.9	43 8.5
11	32.2 20	17.9 21	17.3			Cost of Sales/Inventory	18 20.7	18 20.1
28	13.2 30	12.3 31	11.6				28 13.3	25 14.5
40	9.1 48	7.7 44	8.2				39 9.4	39 9.3
22	16.5 17	21.5 14	25.6			Cost of Sales/Payables	16 22.2	16 23.2
35	10.4 27	13.6 27	13.3				28 12.9	26 14.3
54	6.8 51	7.1 41	8.8				42 8.7	38 9.6
	7.4	8.9	7.6			Sales/Working Capital	9.0	7.4
	19.0	21.9	24.3				20.9	17.2
	-127.5	-61.1	-33.6				-495.6	-158.5
	6.8	8.0	9.1			EBIT/Interest	5.9	6.4
(31)	2.5	(110) 2.6	(58) 3.6				(182) 2.4	(175) 2.4
	-.8	1.3	1.5				1.4	.8
		1.8	5.0			Net Profit + Depr., Dep., Amort./Cur. Mat. L /T/D	3.4	3.3
	(36)	1.2	(28) 2.2				(69) 2.0	(62) 1.7
		.9	1.1				1.3	.8
	.3	.6	.7			Fixed/Worth	.6	.5
	.6	1.3	1.6				1.2	1.2
	3.2	3.1	3.3				2.7	2.5
	.7	.8	.8			Debt/Worth	.8	.6
	2.4	2.0	2.2				2.0	1.6
	6.7	4.7	7.1				6.3	5.7
	48.0	27.1	33.7			% Profit Before Taxes/Tangible Net Worth	33.0	25.1
(27)	6.6	(101) 11.8	(55) 18.3				(174) 16.3	(167) 9.4
	-5.4	2.7	4.5				5.7	-.1
	10.9	10.7	12.4			% Profit Before Taxes/Total Assets	10.9	10.0
	2.7	3.8	4.9				5.3	3.5
	-7.4	.9	1.3				1.4	-.4
	55.8	12.9	9.3			Sales/Net Fixed Assets	12.6	12.0
	15.0	6.2	5.1				7.2	6.0
	6.2	3.9	4.1				4.0	3.6
	4.1	2.9	2.6			Sales/Total Assets	3.3	3.2
	3.5	2.3	2.3				2.4	2.3
	2.3	1.9	1.8				1.8	1.7
	.7	1.9	1.9			% Depr., Dep., Amort./Sales	1.5	1.4
(31)	2.0	(109) 2.8	(62) 2.7				(185) 2.6	(172) 2.8
	3.6	4.1	3.7				3.6	4.1
	2.9	1.7	1.0			% Officers', Directors', Owners' Comp/Sales	1.7	1.9
(17)	5.7	(47) 4.0	(16) 1.6				(70) 3.7	(72) 3.5
	7.5	6.3	2.7				6.0	5.6
10794M	133999M	1854064M	2875830M	329085M	380348M	Net Sales ($)	5258800M	5350003M
2610M	42542M	611796M	1326314M	228904M	364775M	Total Assets ($)	2710940M	2678763M

M = $ thousand   MM = $ million
See Pages 11 through 21 for Explanation of Ratios and Data

Comparative Historical Data / Current Data Sorted By Sales

Comparative Historical Data			Type of Statement	Current Data Sorted By Sales					
			Unqualified				3	11	22
44	34	36	Reviewed		3	2	23	25	17
72	67	70	Compiled	1	10	7	11	11	3
34	55	43	Tax Returns	3	3	1	2	2	
8	6	11	Other	1	2	6	18	15	26
74	62	68			43 (4/1-9/30/04)		185 (10/1/04-3/31/05)		
4/1/02-3/31/03 ALL	4/1/03-3/31/04 ALL	4/1/04-3/31/05 ALL		0-1MM	1-3MM	3-5MM	5-10MM	10-25MM	25MM & OVER
232	224	228	**NUMBER OF STATEMENTS**	5	18	16	57	64	68
%	%	%	**ASSETS**	%	%	%	%	%	%
7.8	8.4	7.1	Cash & Equivalents		9.3	6.6	7.2	5.9	6.9
25.8	26.7	28.1	Trade Receivables (net)		29.9	36.7	29.2	27.2	25.9
15.5	15.2	16.3	Inventory		19.4	13.8	16.1	16.0	16.5
1.9	2.5	1.7	All Other Current		1.3	1.6	1.3	1.8	2.3
51.0	52.8	53.2	Total Current		60.0	58.8	53.7	50.9	51.7
39.4	38.0	35.9	Fixed Assets (net)		28.2	29.2	37.1	39.0	37.3
2.4	2.2	3.5	Intangibles (net)		.4	2.4	3.5	2.6	4.3
7.2	7.1	7.4	All Other Non-Current		11.5	9.5	5.7	7.4	6.8
100.0	100.0	100.0	Total		100.0	100.0	100.0	100.0	100.0
			LIABILITIES						
8.7	9.8	10.9	Notes Payable-Short Term		12.9	11.9	8.9	8.3	11.7
5.4	4.6	5.4	Cur. Mat.-L/T/D		3.3	6.4	6.4	5.2	5.4
14.9	14.6	18.1	Trade Payables		20.0	26.4	18.0	16.7	16.4
.1	.2	.1	Income Taxes Payable		.2	.0	.1	.1	.2
7.4	6.8	6.3	All Other Current		2.8	9.3	5.9	7.1	6.4
36.5	36.0	40.8	Total Current		39.1	54.0	39.4	37.4	40.0
21.1	21.9	20.8	Long-Term Debt		18.8	33.3	19.8	19.8	20.5
1.0	.8	1.0	Deferred Taxes		.0	.4	1.3	1.1	1.0
5.9	4.8	3.9	All Other Non-Current		5.6	4.6	3.8	4.0	3.5
35.6	36.5	33.5	Net Worth		36.5	7.6	35.7	37.7	34.8
100.0	100.0	100.0	Total Liabilities & Net Worth		100.0	100.0	100.0	100.0	100.0
			INCOME DATA						
100.0	100.0	100.0	Net Sales		100.0	100.0	100.0	100.0	100.0
25.6	26.3	25.5	Gross Profit		30.9	27.2	26.1	25.6	21.7
22.7	23.8	23.0	Operating Expenses		31.1	25.8	23.0	22.9	17.9
2.8	2.5	2.5	Operating Profit		−.3	1.4	3.1	2.7	3.8
.8	.8	.5	All Other Expenses (net)		.8	.9	.8	.3	.6
2.0	1.7	1.9	Profit Before Taxes		−1.1	.5	2.3	2.4	3.2
			RATIOS						
2.5	2.6	2.2	Current		2.5	1.8	2.3	2.4	1.9
1.5	1.5	1.3			1.6	1.0	1.4	1.4	1.3
1.0	1.0	.9			1.0	.8	.9	.9	.9
1.6	1.7	1.4	Quick		1.6	1.5	1.8	1.5	1.2
.9	.9	.8			1.1	.7	.8	.8	.7
.6	.6	.6			.7	.6	.6	.6	.5
30 12.3	31 11.6	33 11.0	Sales/Receivables	34 10.7	34 10.6	37 9.9	31 11.7	32 11.5	
39 9.5	40 9.2	40 9.2		46 7.9	39 9.5	41 9.0	39 9.4	37 9.9	
47 7.8	47 7.7	48 7.7		58 6.3	47 7.8	48 7.7	47 7.8	48 7.7	
19 18.9	19 19.5	20 18.2	Cost of Sales/Inventory	24 15.3	9 42.1	20 18.1	21 17.2	20 18.4	
28 13.1	28 13.0	30 12.3		40 9.1	23 15.8	30 12.1	29 12.5	30 12.1	
40 9.1	40 9.1	45 8.0		60 6.1	44 8.2	50 7.3	44 8.2	44 8.3	
16 23.0	13 27.6	17 20.9	Cost of Sales/Payables	22 16.5	20 18.3	21 17.7	15 24.8	15 23.8	
25 14.4	24 15.3	30 12.1		42 8.6	34 10.7	27 13.6	27 13.5	28 13.0	
42 8.6	41 8.9	49 7.5		57 6.4	46 7.9	49 7.4	52 7.0	41 8.8	
7.7	7.9	8.5	Sales/Working Capital		6.8	12.5	8.0	7.8	9.0
15.7	16.0	21.9			12.6	−435.1	19.5	18.8	26.8
−173.6	−208.2	−58.5			NM	−14.9	−61.3	−113.2	−43.1
6.1	6.6	8.1	EBIT/Interest		13.4	6.6	11.6	7.5	9.9
(223) 2.9	(208) 2.0	(211) 2.9		(17) 2.1	(15) 2.5	(55) 3.1	(60) 2.4	(60) 3.6	
1.2	.4	1.1			−2.7	.0	1.4	1.0	1.6
2.9	2.6	2.4	Net Profit + Depr., Dep., Amort./Cur. Mat. L/T/D				1.8	2.0	4.7
(85) 2.0	(74) 1.4	(72) 1.5				(14) 1.5	(24) 1.2	(26) 2.2	
1.0	.6	.9					.9	.7	1.1
.6	.5	.5	Fixed/Worth		.2	.5	.5	.6	.6
1.2	1.2	1.3			.6	3.2	1.2	1.3	1.4
3.0	2.6	3.2			2.7	−1.0	6.6	2.4	2.6
.7	.7	.8	Debt/Worth		.7	1.0	.8	.8	.8
1.9	1.9	2.2			2.1	4.6	1.5	1.8	2.2
5.5	4.6	6.3			4.7	−4.6	15.2	4.4	6.7
29.8	27.6	33.0	% Profit Before Taxes/Tangible Net Worth		46.4	41.5	25.4	33.6	34.1
(204) 11.7	(197) 7.7	(194) 11.8		(17) 6.6	(11) 7.3	(47) 13.2	(59) 9.2	(57) 21.4	
1.9	−1.6	2.4			−29.7	−13.7	7.1	.7	4.7
10.3	8.4	12.0	% Profit Before Taxes/Total Assets		18.0	14.1	9.8	10.4	15.3
4.2	2.8	4.1			3.7	1.4	5.0	3.3	5.6
.2	−1.1	.3			−8.3	−8.4	1.4	.0	1.5
11.5	13.1	15.4	Sales/Net Fixed Assets		50.1	34.3	13.6	11.0	15.3
6.0	5.9	6.6			10.1	15.6	6.8	5.3	5.8
3.6	3.7	4.0			3.7	3.7	3.9	4.0	4.2
3.0	2.9	3.0	Sales/Total Assets		3.9	4.4	3.0	2.9	2.8
2.3	2.3	2.3			2.5	3.2	2.3	2.3	2.4
1.8	1.8	1.8			1.4	1.8	1.9	1.8	1.9
1.9	1.8	1.7	% Depr., Dep., Amort./Sales		.8	1.3	1.5	2.0	1.6
(217) 3.0	(206) 3.0	(211) 2.7		(16) 3.7	(14) 2.2	(54) 2.7	(62) 2.8	(63) 2.6	
4.2	4.5	3.8			4.8	2.9	3.9	4.2	3.6
1.6	1.9	1.7	% Officers', Directors', Owners' Comp/Sales			2.2	2.1	1.9	.8
(92) 3.2	(94) 3.3	(86) 3.4			(11) 5.9	(29) 4.0	(22) 4.1	(18) 1.6	
5.4	5.6	6.6				7.6	7.3	6.6	3.0
5955353M	5659081M	5584120M	Net Sales ($)	2977M	39090M	65874M	428660M	1023742M	4023777M
3239665M	2882358M	2576941M	Total Assets ($)	1094M	22978M	26336M	207068M	476140M	1843325M

M = $ thousand   MM = $ million
See Pages 11 through 21 for Explanation of Ratios and Data

Current Data Sorted By Assets | Comparative Historical Data

Type of Statement	0-500M	500M-2MM	2-10MM	10-50MM	50-100MM	100-250MM		4/1/00-3/31/01 ALL	4/1/01-3/31/02 ALL
Unqualified			2	5	1	1		1	6
Reviewed		1	8	6				7	6
Compiled		1	2					10	6
Tax Returns		1	2					2	3
Other		2	6	12	2	1		11	10
	10 (4/1-9/30/04)			43 (10/1/04-3/31/05)					
NUMBER OF STATEMENTS		5	20	23	3	2		31	31

	0-500M %	500M-2MM %	2-10MM %	10-50MM %	50-100MM %	100-250MM %		ALL %	ALL %
ASSETS									
Cash & Equivalents			4.2	3.8				4.3	2.5
Trade Receivables (net)			25.4	17.3				24.8	20.3
Inventory			24.9	20.9				24.8	21.6
All Other Current			1.7	1.4				1.7	2.0
Total Current			56.3	43.3				55.6	46.4
Fixed Assets (net)			36.2	48.7				32.5	44.8
Intangibles (net)			1.8	1.4				4.5	2.9
All Other Non-Current			5.7	6.6				7.4	5.9
Total			100.0	100.0				100.0	100.0
LIABILITIES									
Notes Payable-Short Term			13.9	10.7				13.4	11.4
Cur. Mat.-L/T/D			5.5	3.9				5.1	5.1
Trade Payables			13.9	10.2				13.3	12.0
Income Taxes Payable			.1	.1				.3	.2
All Other Current			5.2	6.9				6.3	7.7
Total Current			38.6	31.8				38.4	36.3
Long-Term Debt			19.2	24.1				24.8	25.2
Deferred Taxes			.6	1.8				1.5	1.6
All Other Non-Current			1.5	2.5				8.0	2.7
Net Worth			40.1	39.9				27.3	34.2
Total Liabilities & Net Worth			100.0	100.0				100.0	100.0
INCOME DATA									
Net Sales			100.0	100.0				100.0	100.0
Gross Profit			22.8	20.4				23.4	23.5
Operating Expenses			19.4	15.9				20.8	20.6
Operating Profit			3.4	4.5				2.6	3.0
All Other Expenses (net)			.9	1.2				2.2	1.8
Profit Before Taxes			2.5	3.3				.4	1.2

RATIOS

	0-500M	500M-2MM	2-10MM	10-50MM	50-100MM	100-250MM		ALL	ALL
Current			2.1	1.9				1.8	2.4
			1.4	1.4				1.5	1.3
			1.1	1.0				1.2	.9
Quick			1.1	1.3				1.0	1.3
			.7	.6				.7	.7
			.5	.4				.6	.5
Sales/Receivables			35 10.4	29 12.4				32 11.4	27 13.5
			42 8.7	33 11.0				39 9.2	36 10.2
			53 6.9	43 8.5				47 7.7	43 8.5
Cost of Sales/Inventory			35 10.3	37 9.9				32 11.3	29 12.6
			52 7.0	55 6.7				48 7.6	54 6.8
			86 4.2	73 5.0				85 4.3	76 4.8
Cost of Sales/Payables			21 17.6	17 21.1				16 23.0	14 25.6
			30 12.3	24 15.4				28 13.0	26 14.3
			45 8.1	32 11.2				38 9.5	40 9.2
Sales/Working Capital			8.3	8.8				7.7	7.0
			16.4	13.9				14.2	23.2
			85.8	60.0				21.8	-43.5
EBIT/Interest			5.7	5.8				3.7	4.3
			(18) 2.5	3.3				(30) 1.8	2.1
			1.1	1.8				.7	.4
Net Profit + Depr., Dep., Amort./Cur. Mat. L/T/D				4.7					3.3
			(10)	2.6				(16)	1.9
				1.5					.8
Fixed/Worth			.5	1.1				.6	.7
			1.1	1.4				1.3	1.3
			2.1	2.0				5.5	3.4
Debt/Worth			.7	1.1				1.3	.9
			1.8	1.7				2.6	2.0
			3.9	3.1				27.3	6.8
% Profit Before Taxes/Tangible Net Worth			28.2	31.3				38.3	23.6
			(18) 9.4	10.8				(26) 12.8	(27) 12.9
			1.8	5.0				-5.8	-18.6
% Profit Before Taxes/Total Assets			8.6	9.8				7.8	9.3
			2.9	4.0				3.8	3.7
			.7	1.2				-2.2	-4.5
Sales/Net Fixed Assets			9.8	4.3				8.6	7.0
			5.7	3.6				5.9	4.5
			3.5	2.5				4.4	3.0
Sales/Total Assets			2.5	1.9				2.9	2.5
			1.7	1.8				2.0	1.8
			1.6	1.5				1.5	1.6
% Depr., Dep., Amort./Sales			2.6	3.7				.5	2.0
			3.2	(20) 4.8				(27) 2.5	(29) 3.4
			5.3	6.0				4.0	4.8
% Officers', Directors', Owners' Comp/Sales								2.9	
								(11) 4.2	
								6.1	
Net Sales ($)		14412M	194713M	1041119M	309122M	484619M		1170884M	1160625M
Total Assets ($)		5794M	103514M	599631M	200139M	420148M		642061M	615805M

© RMA 2005

M = $ thousand   MM = $ million

See Pages 11 through 21 for Explanation of Ratios and Data

Comparative Historical Data | Current Data Sorted By Sales

Type of Statement	4/1/02-3/31/03 ALL	4/1/03-3/31/04 ALL	4/1/04-3/31/05 ALL	0-1MM	1-3MM	3-5MM	5-10MM	10-25MM	25MM & OVER
Unqualified	12	10	9					2	7
Reviewed	16	13	15		2		5	5	3
Compiled	2	13	3	1			2		
Tax Returns	1	1	3		1		2		
Other	12	13	23		1	1	2	7	12
					10 (4/1-9/30/04)		43 (10/1/04-3/31/05)		
NUMBER OF STATEMENTS	43	50	53	1	1	4	11	14	22
ASSETS	%	%	%	%	%	%	%	%	%
Cash & Equivalents	3.8	5.5	3.9				5.3	4.5	3.0
Trade Receivables (net)	20.3	20.4	21.5				22.6	24.3	16.9
Inventory	22.9	22.5	22.3				29.4	22.0	18.8
All Other Current	1.5	2.7	1.7				2.3	.8	2.3
Total Current	48.4	51.0	49.3				59.7	51.6	41.0
Fixed Assets (net)	43.9	39.9	41.5				36.5	37.8	48.6
Intangibles (net)	1.3	3.2	1.5				2.5	.7	1.4
All Other Non-Current	6.3	5.9	7.7				1.2	9.9	9.0
Total	100.0	100.0	100.0				100.0	100.0	100.0
LIABILITIES									
Notes Payable-Short Term	8.5	10.5	12.1				13.2	14.6	9.5
Cur. Mat.-L/T/D	4.7	5.0	4.1				5.1	4.2	3.8
Trade Payables	12.5	12.9	12.2				17.1	11.2	10.2
Income Taxes Payable	.2	.1	.1				.0	.2	.1
All Other Current	8.1	6.7	5.9				4.2	6.2	7.3
Total Current	34.0	35.1	34.3				39.5	36.4	30.9
Long-Term Debt	22.7	18.9	22.1				19.9	19.5	22.6
Deferred Taxes	2.0	1.4	1.1				.5	1.0	1.8
All Other Non-Current	4.8	5.5	2.3				1.7	1.5	2.6
Net Worth	36.5	39.1	40.1				38.3	41.7	42.2
Total Liabilities & Net Worth	100.0	100.0	100.0				100.0	100.0	100.0
INCOME DATA									
Net Sales	100.0	100.0	100.0				100.0	100.0	100.0
Gross Profit	24.7	22.1	21.9				25.8	18.3	18.3
Operating Expenses	20.4	18.8	18.0				23.8	12.5	15.7
Operating Profit	4.3	3.3	3.9				2.1	5.8	2.6
All Other Expenses (net)	2.0	1.2	1.5				.5	1.4	.7
Profit Before Taxes	2.3	2.1	2.4				1.6	4.4	2.0
RATIOS									
Current	2.0	2.1	1.9				2.3	2.9	1.7
	1.3	1.3	1.4				1.2	1.6	1.4
	1.1	1.0	1.1				1.1	1.0	1.1
Quick	1.0	1.0	1.1				.9	1.7	1.1
	.7	.6	.7				.6	.8	.6
	.5	.5	.5					.4	
Sales/Receivables	29 12.5	28 12.9	30 12.2				30 12.1	32 11.5	29 12.5
	34 10.6	38 9.5	37 9.9				38 9.5	43 8.4	33 11.1
	47 7.8	48 7.7	52 7.1				51 7.1	59 6.2	45 8.2
Cost of Sales/Inventory	37 9.9	36 10.2	37 9.8				33 11.2	34 10.8	37 9.8
	56 6.5	53 6.9	54 6.7				75 4.8	43 8.6	48 7.6
	79 4.6	73 5.0	76 4.8				106 3.4	81 4.5	59 6.2
Cost of Sales/Payables	17 21.9	16 23.1	18 20.0				25 14.6	13 27.4	20 18.3
	28 12.8	25 14.5	29 12.7				38 9.6	30 12.3	25 14.4
	40 9.1	42 8.6	38 9.6				65 5.6	40 9.2	35 10.2
Sales/Working Capital	7.5	5.6	9.0				5.7	4.8	10.2
	18.4	14.4	13.9				20.7	12.1	14.0
	30.8	-597.5	57.8				48.8	-330.3	78.1
EBIT/Interest	4.9	5.9	6.0				3.3	15.3	5.0
	(42) 2.8	(47) 2.9	(50) 2.7				(10) 2.1	(13) 3.0	3.2
	.8	1.2	1.4				1.0	1.2	1.5
Net Profit + Depr., Dep., Amort./Cur. Mat. L/T/D	2.2	2.4	4.7						
	(15) 1.7	(15) 1.5	(18) 2.3						
	1.1	1.0	1.4						
Fixed/Worth	.8	.6	.6				.4	.5	1.1
	1.3	1.1	1.2				1.2	1.2	1.4
	2.2	2.2	2.1				2.2	2.1	1.9
Debt/Worth	1.1	1.0	.9				1.1	.3	1.0
	1.9	1.7	1.7				2.0	2.0	1.6
	4.1	3.6	3.2				7.1	3.4	2.9
% Profit Before Taxes/Tangible Net Worth	21.2	25.8	27.8				17.1	29.0	25.6
	(42) 8.9	(46) 8.6	(50) 10.1				(10) 5.4	(13) 19.6	9.3
	-1.7	1.9	1.9				-.5	4.6	1.2
% Profit Before Taxes/Total Assets	7.5	8.8	9.8				4.9	20.2	7.2
	3.3	3.9	3.6				2.9	7.1	3.7
	-.4	.4	.6				.4	.7	.6
Sales/Net Fixed Assets	7.6	7.7	8.3				9.7	10.3	4.1
	4.0	4.7	4.0				6.7	4.1	3.5
	2.6	2.8	3.0				3.4	3.3	2.6
Sales/Total Assets	2.5	2.4	2.1				2.5	2.0	1.9
	1.7	1.8	1.8				1.8	1.7	1.8
	1.4	1.3	1.4				1.5	1.4	1.4
% Depr., Dep., Amort./Sales	2.7	2.1	2.7				1.6	2.9	3.6
	(39) 3.7	(42) 3.1	(48) 4.2				3.0	(13) 5.3	(18) 4.6
	5.4	5.6	5.5				4.5	6.0	5.8
% Officers', Directors', Owners' Comp/Sales	1.2	2.0	1.7						
	(10) 2.2	(17) 3.7	(10) 3.0						
	7.2	6.3	5.0						
Net Sales ($)	1346874M	1839062M	2043985M	177M	2626M	16166M	78789M	242057M	1704170M
Total Assets ($)	792457M	1000659M	1329226M	1258M	693M	6707M	42696M	147155M	1130717M

M = $ thousand   MM = $ million
See Pages 11 through 21 for Explanation of Ratios and Data

Current Data Sorted By Assets   Comparative Historical Data

						Type of Statement		
1		4	10	1		Unqualified	17	14
	2	12	5			Reviewed	24	20
1	3	2	1			Compiled	16	8
	3	1				Tax Returns	1	
1	4	11	7	1	1	Other	21	18
	8 (4/1-9/30/04)			**63 (10/1/04-3/31/05)**			4/1/00-3/31/01	4/1/01-3/31/02
0-500M	500M-2MM	2-10MM	10-50MM	50-100MM	100-250MM		ALL	ALL
3	12	30	23	2	1	**NUMBER OF STATEMENTS**	79	60
%	%	%	%	%	%	**ASSETS**	%	%
	5.0	7.2	2.9			Cash & Equivalents	5.8	5.0
	40.6	27.5	23.0			Trade Receivables (net)	25.3	22.2
	19.1	20.1	19.2			Inventory	20.1	18.3
	.5	.9	1.8			All Other Current	1.8	2.6
	65.1	55.7	46.9			Total Current	53.1	48.0
	29.9	34.7	39.8			Fixed Assets (net)	39.0	44.2
	.2	2.4	6.6			Intangibles (net)	2.4	2.2
	4.8	7.3	6.7			All Other Non-Current	5.6	5.5
	100.0	100.0	100.0			Total	100.0	100.0
						LIABILITIES		
	25.0	8.7	8.2			Notes Payable-Short Term	9.8	11.0
	3.7	4.3	4.4			Cur. Mat.-L/T/D	6.3	4.6
	24.9	16.0	14.0			Trade Payables	14.7	12.7
	.1	.1	.2			Income Taxes Payable	.2	.0
	7.8	6.0	6.7			All Other Current	6.7	6.6
	61.5	35.0	33.5			Total Current	37.7	35.0
	20.2	22.8	21.8			Long-Term Debt	19.2	24.9
	.1	.9	1.6			Deferred Taxes	.8	1.1
	11.6	4.9	3.1			All Other Non-Current	3.6	5.0
	6.6	36.3	40.0			Net Worth	38.7	34.1
	100.0	100.0	100.0			Total Liabilities & Net Worth	100.0	100.0
						INCOME DATA		
	100.0	100.0	100.0			Net Sales	100.0	100.0
	26.5	23.7	22.7			Gross Profit	26.0	23.5
	27.1	20.3	18.6			Operating Expenses	20.6	20.7
	-.6	3.4	4.2			Operating Profit	5.4	2.8
	.6	.6	.4			All Other Expenses (net)	1.1	1.4
	-1.2	2.8	3.8			Profit Before Taxes	4.3	1.5
						RATIOS		
	1.5	2.3	1.9				2.0	2.1
	1.1	1.8	1.4			Current	1.4	1.4
	.8	1.0	.9				1.1	1.1
	1.2	1.6	1.2				1.2	1.2
	.7	.9	.7			Quick	.8	.7
	.5	.6	.5				.5	.5
	28 12.9	36 10.2	33 11.1				33 11.2	27 13.4
	42 8.8	44 8.2	42 8.7			Sales/Receivables	40 9.0	38 9.6
	58 6.3	55 6.7	51 7.2				47 7.8	49 7.4
	14 26.2	25 14.6	26 13.9				27 13.3	26 14.1
	33 10.9	37 9.8	39 9.3			Cost of Sales/Inventory	40 9.1	37 10.0
	45 8.1	65 5.6	56 6.5				62 5.9	71 5.1
	15 24.5	18 20.8	21 17.1				15 24.9	15 23.7
	32 11.4	28 13.0	31 12.0			Cost of Sales/Payables	28 13.0	25 14.4
	57 6.5	50 7.3	51 7.2				42 8.7	45 8.2
	15.3	4.4	7.1				8.5	6.8
	53.6	13.1	13.6			Sales/Working Capital	16.2	14.1
	-44.6	166.6	-45.2				77.9	82.9
	10.1	7.6	13.0				6.3	4.0
	(10) 3.2	(26) 3.5	(22) 4.1			EBIT/Interest	(72) 2.6	(58) 1.8
	-2.2	1.8	1.8				1.3	.5
						Net Profit + Depr., Dep.,	4.3	3.5
						Amort./Cur. Mat. L /T/D	(30) 1.6	(22) 2.3
							1.1	1.0
	.5	.5	.8				.6	.9
	3.4	1.3	1.3			Fixed/Worth	1.2	1.4
	-1.0	2.0	2.9				2.3	3.4
	1.8	.8	.9				.8	1.0
	11.3	2.0	2.2			Debt/Worth	1.7	1.9
	-5.1	3.6	7.7				3.5	6.3
		37.0	35.6			% Profit Before Taxes/Tangible	40.1	21.5
		(29) 18.3	(21) 23.9			Net Worth	(72) 21.0	(55) 9.0
		8.8	8.1				5.3	-3.1
	17.4	10.0	12.9			% Profit Before Taxes/Total	16.3	6.8
	6.0	6.3	5.5			Assets	6.1	2.8
	-3.4	2.5	2.2				1.4	-2.9
	38.0	11.6	9.8				10.9	9.2
	14.1	6.3	4.6			Sales/Net Fixed Assets	5.3	3.7
	5.1	3.6	3.1				3.2	2.8
	4.1	2.7	2.3				2.9	2.9
	3.5	2.1	1.8			Sales/Total Assets	2.0	1.9
	2.4	1.7	1.5				1.6	1.5
	1.7	1.9	1.8				1.6	2.3
	(10) 2.7	(27) 3.4	(21) 3.2			% Depr., Dep., Amort./Sales	(76) 2.6	(56) 3.4
	4.1	4.8	4.4				4.0	4.7
		1.8				% Officers', Directors',	1.8	1.1
		(15) 3.4				Owners' Comp/Sales	(32) 3.4	(19) 2.2
		7.3					5.8	4.1
1396M	40022M	372364M	939273M	254432M	438961M	Net Sales ($)	2518235M	2169118M
495M	11961M	174559M	507157M	122978M	132511M	Total Assets ($)	1359178M	1291259M

M = $ thousand   MM = $ million
See Pages 11 through 21 for Explanation of Ratios and Data

Comparative Historical Data | Current Data Sorted By Sales

			Type of Statement						
14	17	16	Unqualified	1			3	5	10
30	18	19	Reviewed		1		1	12	3
10	18	7	Compiled	1	2	1	1	1	1
2	2	4	Tax Returns		2	1			
11	14	25	Other	1		5	5	5	9
4/1/02-3/31/03	4/1/03-3/31/04	4/1/04-3/31/05			8 (4/1-9/30/04)			63 (10/1/04-3/31/05)	
ALL	ALL	ALL		0-1MM	1-3MM	3-5MM	5-10MM	10-25MM	25MM & OVER
67	69	71	**NUMBER OF STATEMENTS**	3	5	7	10	23	23
%	%	%	**ASSETS**	%	%	%	%	%	%
6.7	6.2	5.0	Cash & Equivalents				4.8	5.8	2.4
25.3	25.6	29.3	Trade Receivables (net)				31.1	25.3	25.3
17.2	18.6	19.8	Inventory				16.2	20.2	20.9
1.6	2.1	1.5	All Other Current				.9	1.0	1.8
50.9	52.5	55.5	Total Current				53.1	52.2	50.4
40.0	39.2	34.8	Fixed Assets (net)				35.9	35.9	38.6
4.2	2.5	3.4	Intangibles (net)				2.5	4.3	4.9
4.9	5.8	6.2	All Other Non-Current				8.5	7.6	6.1
100.0	100.0	100.0	Total				100.0	100.0	100.0
			LIABILITIES						
9.4	10.7	11.6	Notes Payable-Short Term				11.1	8.4	8.3
6.5	4.2	4.1	Cur. Mat.-L/T/D				7.9	3.9	4.3
12.3	13.9	17.9	Trade Payables				16.1	14.6	15.7
.1	.4	.1	Income Taxes Payable				.2	.1	.2
6.0	5.6	6.4	All Other Current				6.6	5.0	7.0
34.3	34.9	40.2	Total Current				41.8	32.0	35.5
23.7	22.6	22.2	Long-Term Debt				20.4	27.4	20.5
.8	1.0	1.0	Deferred Taxes				.9	1.0	1.7
5.6	4.8	5.4	All Other Non-Current				6.2	5.2	3.4
35.7	36.7	31.1	Net Worth				30.7	34.4	38.9
100.0	100.0	100.0	Total Liabilities & Net Worth				100.0	100.0	100.0
			INCOME DATA						
100.0	100.0	100.0	Net Sales				100.0	100.0	100.0
27.2	26.9	24.5	Gross Profit				26.0	22.1	22.6
23.8	24.3	21.5	Operating Expenses				22.3	18.7	18.7
3.4	2.6	3.0	Operating Profit				3.8	3.4	3.9
1.2	.9	.5	All Other Expenses (net)				.1	.9	.4
2.2	1.7	2.5	Profit Before Taxes				3.7	2.6	3.5
			RATIOS						
2.4 / 1.6 / 1.1	2.5 / 1.6 / 1.1	2.0 / 1.3 / 1.0	Current				2.2 / 1.2 / .9	2.4 / 1.8 / 1.0	1.9 / 1.4 / .9
1.6 / 1.0 / .6	1.4 / .8 / .6	1.3 / .8 / .6	Quick				1.1 / .8 / .6	1.6 / .9 / .6	1.2 / .6 / .5
31 11.9 / 35 10.3 / 44 8.3	31 11.9 / 37 9.8 / 51 7.2	35 10.3 / 43 8.5 / 54 6.7	Sales/Receivables				25 14.3 / 50 7.3 / 70 5.2	35 10.3 / 42 8.7 / 51 7.2	33 11.1 / 42 8.7 / 51 7.1
24 15.3 / 34 10.9 / 53 6.9	23 15.6 / 35 10.4 / 66 5.6	25 14.4 / 38 9.6 / 55 6.6	Cost of Sales/Inventory				12 30.8 / 38 9.7 / 45 8.2	26 14.2 / 36 10.0 / 64 5.7	26 13.9 / 39 9.3 / 57 6.4
14 25.8 / 25 14.7 / 33 10.9	15 23.6 / 29 12.8 / 47 7.8	21 17.3 / 31 12.0 / 51 7.1	Cost of Sales/Payables				11 34.0 / 26 14.0 / 62 5.9	18 20.7 / 29 12.7 / 45 8.2	21 17.3 / 32 11.6 / 51 7.1
7.3 / 15.2 / 50.2	6.1 / 11.1 / 93.9	7.1 / 15.0 / 332.5	Sales/Working Capital				3.5 / 42.4 / -92.8	6.7 / 13.5 / 165.8	7.1 / 13.6 / -95.5
4.6 / (66) 2.5 / .8	5.7 / (66) 2.4 / .9	8.7 / (63) 3.4 / 1.6	EBIT/Interest					7.1 / (21) 3.7 / 1.8	13.0 / (22) 3.2 / 1.8
3.5 / (24) 2.5 / 1.0	3.6 / (21) 2.5 / 1.6	4.4 / (20) 2.4 / 1.1	Net Profit + Depr., Dep., Amort./Cur. Mat. L/T/D						3.9 / (11) 1.6 / .9
.7 / 1.1 / 2.1	.7 / 1.2 / 2.0	.6 / 1.3 / 2.8	Fixed/Worth				.4 / 1.0 / 2.3	.6 / 1.4 / 2.4	.7 / 1.1 / 2.9
1.0 / 1.7 / 4.4	.8 / 1.8 / 3.4	1.1 / 2.7 / 5.5	Debt/Worth				.9 / 1.7 / 4.9	1.2 / 2.9 / 4.0	.9 / 2.2 / 3.8
21.7 / (60) 9.8 / -2.0	17.7 / (63) 9.6 / -1.0	31.4 / (63) 17.1 / 6.3	% Profit Before Taxes/Tangible Net Worth					30.9 / (22) 18.8 / 9.0	35.6 / (21) 23.3 / 8.1
10.0 / 2.4 / -1.0	7.6 / 3.6 / -.1	10.6 / 5.9 / 1.4	% Profit Before Taxes/Total Assets				13.0 / 8.0 / 3.7	9.4 / 6.6 / 2.7	12.9 / 5.0 / 2.2
11.5 / 5.0 / 3.5	10.8 / 4.7 / 3.3	12.4 / 6.4 / 3.7	Sales/Net Fixed Assets				21.1 / 9.0 / 3.3	9.0 / 6.1 / 3.7	9.8 / 4.7 / 3.4
2.7 / 2.1 / 1.6	2.9 / 2.1 / 1.5	2.9 / 2.2 / 1.6	Sales/Total Assets				3.9 / 2.5 / 1.5	2.7 / 2.1 / 1.6	2.3 / 2.0 / 1.0
2.3 / (64) 3.6 / 5.3	2.0 / (66) 3.4 / 4.5	1.9 / (64) 3.2 / 4.2	% Depr., Dep., Amort./Sales					1.9 / (20) 3.3 / 4.0	1.9 / (22) 3.5 / 4.5
2.1 / (28) 4.6 / 9.3	1.6 / (30) 3.9 / 6.9	1.9 / (26) 3.5 / 7.3	% Officers', Directors', Owners' Comp/Sales						
1728201M	2102513M	2046448M	Net Sales ($)	1396M	10361M	27017M	73534M	354498M	1579642M
871930M	1140277M	949661M	Total Assets ($)	495M	4195M	10295M	33857M	177385M	723434M

© RMA 2005

M = $ thousand   MM = $ million
See Pages 11 through 21 for Explanation of Ratios and Data

Current Data Sorted By Assets   Comparative Historical Data

0-500M	500M-2MM	2-10MM	10-50MM	50-100MM	100-250MM	Type of Statement	4/1/00-3/31/01 ALL	4/1/01-3/31/02 ALL
1	1	7	15	2	4	Unqualified	12	15
3	3	15	4	1		Reviewed	16	12
4	4	5				Compiled	16	19
1	1					Tax Returns	2	2
3	2	7	11	1	3	Other	24	33
	16 (4/1-9/30/04)		74 (10/1/04-3/31/05)					
0-500M	500M-2MM	2-10MM	10-50MM	50-100MM	100-250MM	NUMBER OF STATEMENTS	ALL	ALL
4	11	34	30	4	7		70	81
%	%	%	%	%	%	ASSETS	%	%
	6.9	6.3	4.1			Cash & Equivalents	6.2	5.3
	34.8	28.7	23.8			Trade Receivables (net)	29.3	26.3
	24.0	26.4	20.8			Inventory	21.7	21.6
	.3	1.5	1.1			All Other Current	2.2	1.5
	65.9	62.8	49.8			Total Current	59.3	54.7
	27.6	29.1	38.3			Fixed Assets (net)	29.1	35.3
	3.1	3.6	3.2			Intangibles (net)	5.0	5.3
	3.3	4.5	8.7			All Other Non-Current	6.6	4.7
	100.0	100.0	100.0			Total	100.0	100.0
						LIABILITIES		
	15.9	14.8	11.3			Notes Payable-Short Term	10.9	12.0
	6.9	3.5	4.5			Cur. Mat.-L/T/D	5.2	5.2
	22.0	15.5	13.9			Trade Payables	22.8	16.2
	.0	.5	.4			Income Taxes Payable	.2	.1
	6.9	8.4	8.0			All Other Current	6.9	6.4
	51.7	42.8	38.3			Total Current	45.9	39.9
	14.8	21.3	17.7			Long-Term Debt	17.7	21.3
	.0	.9	.5			Deferred Taxes	.4	.7
	3.8	3.7	7.7			All Other Non-Current	3.1	3.9
	29.8	31.3	35.8			Net Worth	32.8	34.3
	100.0	100.0	100.0			Total Liabilities & Net Worth	100.0	100.0
						INCOME DATA		
	100.0	100.0	100.0			Net Sales	100.0	100.0
	31.8	27.5	22.4			Gross Profit	27.6	27.8
	26.6	20.5	18.7			Operating Expenses	23.5	22.4
	5.1	7.1	3.8			Operating Profit	4.1	5.4
	1.2	1.7	.3			All Other Expenses (net)	1.0	2.2
	3.9	5.3	3.5			Profit Before Taxes	3.1	3.3
						RATIOS		
	2.4	3.0	2.1			Current	2.2	2.4
	1.5	1.6	1.3				1.3	1.3
	1.0	1.1	.9				1.0	1.1
	1.2	1.5	1.0			Quick	1.3	1.3
	.9	(29) .9	.8				.8	.7
	.8	.6	.6				.5	.5
40 9.2	28 12.8	30 12.0				Sales/Receivables	31 11.9	31 11.8
43 8.5	39 9.4	41 8.9					40 9.2	40 9.2
78 4.7	48 7.5	49 7.5					52 7.0	49 7.4
48 7.6	26 14.0	28 12.8				Cost of Sales/Inventory	25 14.7	32 11.3
64 5.7	42 8.8	43 8.5					47 7.7	46 7.9
71 5.1	66 5.5	64 5.7					74 5.0	66 5.6
15 23.6	16 22.7	17 21.5				Cost of Sales/Payables	23 15.8	16 22.6
48 7.5	23 15.8	31 11.8					35 10.3	32 11.5
75 4.9	36 10.2	44 8.3					62 5.9	44 8.3
	5.4	6.5	8.5			Sales/Working Capital	6.8	7.3
	9.9	12.2	23.5				25.0	18.4
	432.4	109.4	-46.9				181.8	150.2
	15.5	21.5	8.2			EBIT/Interest	7.9	7.3
	3.5	(31) 5.8	(26) 3.3				(67) 3.2	(78) 2.9
	.3	2.5	1.7				.7	1.0
			4.0			Net Profit + Depr., Dep.,	4.6	4.0
		(14)	2.4			Amort./Cur. Mat. L/T/D	(24) 3.1	(21) 1.8
			1.7				.8	.7
	.4	.4	.5			Fixed/Worth	.5	.6
	.6	.7	1.2				.8	1.3
	1.6	2.3	4.0				2.3	2.8
	1.6	.5	.8			Debt/Worth	1.1	1.0
	2.4	1.6	2.2				3.2	2.4
	4.7	8.5	6.3				8.9	8.5
	74.8	51.0	37.0			% Profit Before Taxes/Tangible	72.6	55.5
(10)	28.7	(29) 28.3	(28) 24.6			Net Worth	(62) 24.3	(73) 28.2
	1.2	10.9	6.9				2.8	7.4
	19.6	20.9	12.8			% Profit Before Taxes/Total	14.9	14.3
	4.4	8.8	6.3			Assets	4.4	7.1
	-2.2	4.6	1.1				-1.5	.0
	13.9	19.4	10.0			Sales/Net Fixed Assets	19.1	13.5
	9.8	9.7	5.9				8.8	6.3
	7.3	5.8	3.4				4.1	3.5
	3.4	3.6	2.4			Sales/Total Assets	3.5	3.3
	2.4	2.7	1.8				2.2	2.1
	1.3	2.0	1.6				1.6	1.6
	.6	.9	1.9			% Depr., Dep., Amort./Sales	1.4	1.4
	1.9	(32) 1.5	(27) 3.0				(63) 2.6	(74) 3.0
	2.7	3.3	3.6				3.9	4.7
		1.5				% Officers', Directors',	2.4	2.4
	(12)	2.4				Owners' Comp/Sales	(27) 3.6	(25) 4.0
		6.9					6.3	5.8
2866M	36259M	525734M	1311764M	266235M	1995386M	Net Sales ($)	1435604M	2351093M
682M	14668M	189900M	639700M	222272M	1099169M	Total Assets ($)	901348M	1363849M

M = $ thousand   MM = $ million
See Pages 11 through 21 for Explanation of Ratios and Data

Comparative Historical Data | Current Data Sorted By Sales

4/1/02-3/31/03 ALL	4/1/03-3/31/04 ALL	4/1/04-3/31/05 ALL	Type of Statement	0-1MM	1-3MM	3-5MM	5-10MM	10-25MM	25MM & OVER
23	19	29	Unqualified	1			1	9	18
12	23	24	Reviewed	1		3	4	11	5
10	15	9	Compiled		1	2	1	4	1
3	8	1	Tax Returns		1				
20	24	27	Other	3	2	1	2	6	13
				16 (4/1-9/30/04)			74 (10/1/04-3/31/05)		
68	89	90	**NUMBER OF STATEMENTS**	5	4	6	8	30	37
%	%	%		%	%	%	%	%	%
			ASSETS						
5.8	6.8	5.3	Cash & Equivalents					5.1	3.3
24.6	26.0	27.3	Trade Receivables (net)					26.7	25.3
21.0	22.7	23.3	Inventory					26.2	23.8
1.0	2.2	1.1	All Other Current					1.3	1.0
52.4	57.7	57.0	Total Current					59.2	53.4
35.5	31.0	31.2	Fixed Assets (net)					30.4	31.8
6.8	5.2	5.6	Intangibles (net)					3.3	7.6
5.3	6.1	6.3	All Other Non-Current					7.1	7.2
100.0	100.0	100.0	Total					100.0	100.0
			LIABILITIES						
8.7	10.4	12.9	Notes Payable-Short Term					11.6	11.7
5.3	4.8	4.1	Cur. Mat.-L/T/D					4.7	3.6
14.7	16.6	15.3	Trade Payables					15.1	14.3
.1	.1	.4	Income Taxes Payable					.4	.4
7.6	10.6	8.0	All Other Current					7.4	8.9
36.5	42.5	40.6	Total Current					39.1	39.0
21.6	19.4	18.9	Long-Term Debt					22.6	19.2
.6	.4	.8	Deferred Taxes					1.4	.9
5.1	6.4	5.2	All Other Non-Current					5.6	5.1
36.2	31.3	34.4	Net Worth					31.3	35.8
100.0	100.0	100.0	Total Liabilities & Net Worth					100.0	100.0
			INCOME DATA						
100.0	100.0	100.0	Net Sales					100.0	100.0
28.7	26.3	25.8	Gross Profit					25.7	20.7
23.2	22.2	19.9	Operating Expenses					21.2	15.9
5.5	4.0	6.0	Operating Profit					4.6	4.8
2.1	.9	1.1	All Other Expenses (net)					.3	.5
3.4	3.1	4.9	Profit Before Taxes					4.3	4.3
			RATIOS						
2.1	2.2	2.4						2.9	1.8
1.4	1.4	1.5	Current					1.8	1.5
1.1	1.0	1.0						1.0	1.1
1.2	1.2	1.2						1.3	1.0
.8	(89) .9	.8	Quick					.9	.8
.6	.5	.6						.6	.6
30 12.3	30 12.2	31 11.7						30 12.3	31 11.6
39 9.4	38 9.6	40 9.0	Sales/Receivables					36 10.1	41 8.9
48 7.6	47 7.8	50 7.3						47 7.8	49 7.4
29 12.5	31 11.7	29 12.5						33 11.1	31 11.7
50 7.2	48 7.6	48 7.6	Cost of Sales/Inventory					51 7.2	45 8.0
71 5.1	67 5.5	69 5.3						70 5.2	60 6.1
16 22.4	16 22.5	16 22.3						16 22.3	17 21.7
30 12.1	33 10.9	30 12.0	Cost of Sales/Payables					30 12.3	29 12.6
44 8.3	45 8.1	43 8.4						37 9.8	43 8.4
8.8	7.4	6.8						6.5	9.1
14.3	14.8	13.0	Sales/Working Capital					9.3	13.6
37.0	NM	82.3						NM	72.6
7.8	9.1	13.9						19.4	9.8
(66) 3.6	(81) 3.4	(80) 4.4	EBIT/Interest					(27) 4.8	(34) 3.9
1.2	1.1	2.0						1.9	2.3
5.6	2.9	4.9	Net Profit + Depr., Dep.,						3.1
(21) 1.9	(23) 1.7	(27) 2.5	Amort./Cur. Mat. L/T/D						(18) 2.2
1.1	1.1	1.6							1.6
.5	.5	.4						.4	.6
1.2	1.0	.9	Fixed/Worth					.7	1.3
2.6	4.0	2.4						2.9	2.4
1.1	1.0	.8						.7	1.1
2.1	2.8	2.1	Debt/Worth					1.6	2.9
5.3	8.6	5.3						7.6	4.8
49.1	41.7	48.1	% Profit Before Taxes/Tangible					48.1	38.2
(60) 18.9	(74) 21.3	(79) 25.5	Net Worth					(27) 25.5	(32) 24.7
2.1	4.3	10.1						10.6	12.5
13.2	13.3	15.9	% Profit Before Taxes/Total					14.7	11.2
6.2	5.8	7.8	Assets					8.1	8.4
.4	.2	2.4						3.7	4.7
11.0	13.9	14.1						18.3	10.5
6.9	7.7	7.5	Sales/Net Fixed Assets					8.6	6.6
3.6	4.6	4.3						4.2	4.4
2.9	3.2	3.2						3.5	2.9
2.1	2.2	2.1	Sales/Total Assets					2.3	1.8
1.4	1.5	1.6						1.9	1.6
1.3	1.2	1.2						1.1	1.2
(61) 3.0	(81) 2.7	(78) 2.4	% Depr., Dep., Amort./Sales					(27) 1.9	(32) 2.5
5.1	4.0	3.5						3.3	3.5
1.6	2.0	1.5	% Officers', Directors',						
(17) 4.1	(28) 3.7	(20) 2.6	Owners' Comp/Sales						
5.4	9.5	7.3							
2578553M	3213099M	4138244M	Net Sales ($)	1990M	6233M	23467M	58717M	493058M	3554779M
1582601M	1796995M	2166391M	Total Assets ($)	3774M	3199M	9880M	38393M	218068M	1893077M

© RMA 2005

M = $ thousand   MM = $ million

See Pages 11 through 21 for Explanation of Ratios and Data

MANUFACTURING—Coated and Laminated Paper Manufacturing   NAICS 322222   (SIC 2672, 2679)

Current Data Sorted By Assets							Comparative Historical Data	
2	9	3	12	4	1	Type of Statement — Unqualified	15	21
	3	12	4			Reviewed	21	17
2	3	4				Compiled	12	10
1		1				Tax Returns	2	3
	4	10	11	2	2	Other	23	21
0-500M	19 (4/1-9/30/04) 500M-2MM	2-10MM	71 (10/1/04-3/31/05) 10-50MM	50-100MM	100-250MM		4/1/00-3/31/01 ALL	4/1/01-3/31/02 ALL
5	19	30	27	6	3	NUMBER OF STATEMENTS	73	72
%	%	%	%	%	%	ASSETS	%	%
	6.7	5.3	8.7			Cash & Equivalents	8.1	5.4
	35.1	28.0	24.1			Trade Receivables (net)	25.8	27.7
	21.6	28.2	26.1			Inventory	19.6	21.3
	.8	.8	1.3			All Other Current	2.2	2.1
	64.3	62.3	60.2			Total Current	55.7	56.5
	27.8	29.3	30.5			Fixed Assets (net)	31.3	32.6
	2.8	2.1	2.2			Intangibles (net)	5.2	3.9
	5.2	6.3	7.1			All Other Non-Current	7.7	7.1
	100.0	100.0	100.0			Total	100.0	100.0
						LIABILITIES		
	14.9	10.2	9.5			Notes Payable-Short Term	7.0	10.7
	5.2	2.8	3.4			Cur. Mat.-L/T/D	5.1	5.4
	20.4	15.6	12.4			Trade Payables	15.5	17.6
	.0	.0	.3			Income Taxes Payable	.1	.0
	3.6	5.6	8.8			All Other Current	6.7	6.6
	44.1	34.2	34.4			Total Current	34.3	40.4
	17.1	18.3	15.0			Long-Term Debt	17.7	17.6
	.2	.5	1.3			Deferred Taxes	.5	.6
	5.7	10.5	4.2			All Other Non-Current	3.7	4.4
	33.0	36.5	45.0			Net Worth	43.9	37.0
	100.0	100.0	100.0			Total Liabilities & Net Worth	100.0	100.0
						INCOME DATA		
	100.0	100.0	100.0			Net Sales	100.0	100.0
	35.7	29.1	26.1			Gross Profit	31.1	28.0
	30.9	25.2	20.6			Operating Expenses	25.0	25.3
	4.8	3.9	5.4			Operating Profit	6.1	2.7
	.9	.4	1.8			All Other Expenses (net)	1.4	1.5
	3.9	3.5	3.6			Profit Before Taxes	4.7	1.3
						RATIOS		
	2.6	3.4	2.9			Current	2.8	2.4
	1.4	1.9	1.5				1.7	1.4
	1.2	1.1	1.3				1.0	1.0
	1.3	1.8	1.8			Quick	1.8	1.4
	.9	1.1	.9				1.0	.8
	.7	.6	.5				.6	.5
36	10.0 35	10.4 38	9.6			Sales/Receivables	32 11.6 38	9.7
43	8.5 42	8.8 45	8.1				41 8.9 43	8.4
62	5.9 53	6.9 54	6.8				52 7.1 53	6.8
19	19.1 27	13.3 46	8.0			Cost of Sales/Inventory	27 13.8 29	12.6
30	12.1 58	6.3 61	6.0				45 8.2 49	7.4
53	6.8 89	4.1 100	3.6				67 5.5 71	5.2
22	16.3 19	19.1 12	30.4			Cost of Sales/Payables	18 19.9 23	16.2
43	8.5 30	12.3 32	11.3				34 10.8 35	10.5
72	5.1 47	7.7 44	8.2				52 7.0 55	6.6
	7.5	4.4	4.2			Sales/Working Capital	6.2	7.0
	17.5	9.3	10.2				11.5	14.5
	36.4	51.2	20.1				254.7	125.3
	7.3	7.9	10.9			EBIT/Interest	6.5	3.4
(18)	2.5 (28)	3.1 (24)	3.1				(66) 2.3 (65)	1.5
	-.1	.9	1.5				1.0	.7
			4.1			Net Profit + Depr., Dep., Amort./Cur. Mat. L/T/D	3.4	2.1
		(14)	2.2				(23) 1.9 (27)	1.4
			1.1				.9	.7
	.3	.4	.4			Fixed/Worth	.4	.5
	.8	.7	.7				.8	1.0
	3.3	1.5	1.2				1.5	2.3
	1.1	.8	.6			Debt/Worth	.8	.9
	2.0	1.5	1.2				1.4	2.4
	5.6	3.9	2.7				2.6	6.0
	40.8	26.6	26.8			% Profit Before Taxes/Tangible Net Worth	36.3	21.6
(17)	10.4 (27)	8.8 (25)	15.0				(67) 13.8 (66)	9.1
	-5.6	1.0	7.1				.4	-.7
	14.1	9.7	13.1			% Profit Before Taxes/Total Assets	14.4	7.5
	5.0	4.9	4.8				5.6	1.7
	-2.6	.1	1.9				.1	-.7
	37.0	15.7	9.4			Sales/Net Fixed Assets	16.9	15.1
	13.7	8.9	5.7				7.5	6.6
	4.4	5.0	3.7				4.1	3.9
	3.6	3.1	2.5			Sales/Total Assets	3.1	3.0
	2.7	2.3	1.7				2.2	2.1
	1.8	1.8	1.5				1.5	1.5
	.8	1.7	2.1			% Depr., Dep., Amort./Sales	.8	1.4
	1.4	2.5 (25)	2.9				(65) 2.6 (64)	2.4
	3.9	3.2	4.2				4.2	4.0
	2.8	1.8				% Officers', Directors', Owners' Comp/Sales	1.6	1.8
(12)	6.2 (13)	3.8					(26) 2.8 (32)	3.6
	8.7	5.8					6.0	5.5
5398M	66926M	326878M	963893M	815292M	598651M	Net Sales ($)	2188129M	2758349M
768M	24655M	133246M	536462M	435676M	405748M	Total Assets ($)	1340947M	1765464M

M = $ thousand   MM = $ million
See Pages 11 through 21 for Explanation of Ratios and Data

Comparative Historical Data · **Current Data Sorted By Sales**

	4/1/02-3/31/03 ALL	4/1/03-3/31/04 ALL	4/1/04-3/31/05 ALL	Type of Statement	0-1MM	1-3MM	3-5MM	5-10MM	10-25MM	25MM & OVER
	16	18	20	Unqualified	2	2	7	8	7	13
	31	31	27	Reviewed	1	1	3	2	4	4
	7	16	7	Compiled		3	1	1		
	2	9	6	Tax Returns					1	
	19	22	30	Other	1	3	1	5	5	15
							19 (4/1-9/30/04)		71 (10/1/04-3/31/05)	
NUMBER OF STATEMENTS	75	96	90		4	9	12	16	17	32
	%	%	%	**ASSETS**	%	%	%	%	%	%
Cash & Equivalents	5.2	6.3	6.7				11.2	4.8	7.1	5.7
Trade Receivables (net)	26.6	25.7	26.6				27.1	29.6	28.1	24.6
Inventory	22.0	23.3	26.4				26.3	25.4	23.3	24.9
All Other Current	1.5	2.0	1.1				.0	1.8	.5	1.7
Total Current	55.3	57.3	60.8				64.6	61.6	59.0	57.0
Fixed Assets (net)	33.9	31.2	29.7				22.8	30.6	30.4	32.2
Intangibles (net)	4.5	5.0	3.3				4.7	1.6	3.6	4.7
All Other Non-Current	6.3	6.6	6.2				7.9	6.2	7.0	6.1
Total	100.0	100.0	100.0				100.0	100.0	100.0	100.0
				LIABILITIES						
Notes Payable-Short Term	9.6	12.8	10.9				19.6	9.1	9.0	9.4
Cur. Mat.-L/T/D	6.1	4.3	3.5				4.6	3.1	3.1	3.7
Trade Payables	15.5	14.3	15.1				13.6	17.1	16.5	13.0
Income Taxes Payable	.2	.1	.1				.0	.0	.5	.0
All Other Current	8.4	6.7	7.0				2.3	6.4	5.7	9.8
Total Current	39.9	38.3	36.7				40.1	35.8	34.8	35.9
Long-Term Debt	17.1	14.5	17.9				18.8	14.0	22.0	19.2
Deferred Taxes	.9	.8	.7				.4	.0	1.1	1.1
All Other Non-Current	6.5	8.5	7.9				12.2	5.3	7.7	9.6
Net Worth	35.5	37.9	36.9				28.4	44.9	34.4	34.1
Total Liabilities & Net Worth	100.0	100.0	100.0				100.0	100.0	100.0	100.0
				INCOME DATA						
Net Sales	100.0	100.0	100.0				100.0	100.0	100.0	100.0
Gross Profit	31.8	32.1	29.1				33.3	30.5	30.3	23.0
Operating Expenses	28.1	28.1	24.6				27.0	26.4	26.1	17.9
Operating Profit	3.7	4.0	4.5				6.3	4.1	4.2	5.1
All Other Expenses (net)	1.8	1.1	1.1				1.6	.3	.5	1.9
Profit Before Taxes	1.9	2.9	3.4				4.6	3.8	3.7	3.2
				RATIOS						
Current	2.1	2.7	2.7				3.9	2.5	3.1	2.2
	1.5	1.6	1.7				1.9	1.7	1.9	1.5
	1.1	1.1	1.2				1.1	1.2	1.2	1.1
Quick	1.1	1.5	1.6				2.0	1.3	1.8	1.3
	.8	.9	.9				1.0	.9	1.2	.7
	.6	.6	.5				.5	.6	.7	.5
Sales/Receivables	37 9.7	33 11.0	36 10.2				34 10.8	36 10.2	36 10.0	37 9.9
	43 8.4	43 8.4	43 8.6				36 10.0	42 8.7	42 8.6	44 8.4
	50 7.4	51 7.1	53 6.8				57 6.4	53 6.9	53 6.8	52 7.0
Cost of Sales/Inventory	27 13.3	31 11.9	30 12.1				14 25.2	26 14.0	34 10.8	39 9.2
	43 8.5	49 7.4	53 6.9				25 14.8	50 7.2	57 6.4	54 6.8
	67 5.4	76 4.8	81 4.5				99 3.7	88 4.2	73 5.0	72 5.1
Cost of Sales/Payables	21 17.1	15 24.4	17 20.9				16 23.0	19 19.3	20 18.7	14 26.3
	32 11.4	33 11.0	32 11.4				30 12.4	32 11.3	32 11.3	32 11.3
	45 8.2	44 8.2	48 7.6				47 7.8	60 6.1	48 7.6	44 8.3
Sales/Working Capital	6.7	5.9	5.1				4.4	5.1	4.2	6.2
	17.4	12.2	10.4				9.3	11.3	10.8	11.0
	95.3	107.8	27.5				58.1	26.6	28.6	28.9
EBIT/Interest	6.1	6.9	8.7				7.4	8.7	9.2	9.2
	(69) 2.7	(87) 3.1	(79) 3.0			(11)	2.5	(15) 2.6	(16) 4.0	(28) 3.9
	1.3	1.0	1.1				.1	1.7	1.7	1.2
Net Profit + Depr., Dep., Amort./Cur. Mat. L/T/D	3.6	3.0	3.5							3.1
	(27) 1.6	(32) 1.8	(32) 2.4							(16) 2.3
	1.1	.8	1.6							1.1
Fixed/Worth	.5	.5	.4				.2	.4	.6	.4
	1.0	.9	.8				.9	.7	1.0	.8
	2.4	2.2	1.8				NM	1.0	1.6	2.9
Debt/Worth	1.0	.7	.8				.8	.8	.8	1.0
	2.0	1.8	1.7				2.0	1.2	2.0	1.9
	5.0	4.8	4.6				NM	3.4	3.9	10.6
% Profit Before Taxes/Tangible Net Worth	28.6	23.9	31.0					38.4	24.0	31.0
	(66) 14.6	(83) 14.2	(78) 14.5				(15)	8.5	(16) 14.2	(26) 18.0
	2.3	2.2	1.3					2.8	7.0	2.0
% Profit Before Taxes/Total Assets	11.4	11.7	12.3				10.9	14.5	8.1	13.4
	4.2	3.4	5.2				5.2	2.7	6.3	5.3
	.7	.2	.4				−.9	.9	2.1	.6
Sales/Net Fixed Assets	11.4	12.8	15.7				39.7	17.5	12.5	10.0
	7.0	7.6	7.5				14.7	8.5	8.5	6.9
	4.3	4.4	4.3				4.8	4.0	4.4	3.6
Sales/Total Assets	2.8	2.8	2.9				3.1	3.4	3.1	2.6
	2.3	2.0	2.0				1.9	2.5	2.0	1.9
	1.7	1.6	1.6				1.7	1.6	1.5	1.5
% Depr., Dep., Amort./Sales	2.0	1.6	1.7				2.2	2.2	1.6	1.9
	(69) 3.1	(86) 2.8	(81) 2.8			(11)	3.2	2.9	2.3	(28) 2.8
	4.9	4.3	3.6				3.6	4.0	3.2	3.7
% Officers', Directors', Owners' Comp/Sales	2.4	3.9	2.3							
	(33) 4.4	(34) 6.3	(32) 4.4							
	6.8	9.1	7.0							
Net Sales ($)	2006729M	1646080M	2777038M		1112M	19744M	46191M	112266M	271971M	2325754M
Total Assets ($)	1182330M	1023308M	1536555M		1071M	8883M	20501M	50462M	145539M	1310099M

M = $ thousand   MM = $ million

See Pages 11 through 21 for Explanation of Ratios and Data

Current Data Sorted By Assets   Comparative Historical Data

0-500M	500M-2MM	2-10MM	10-50MM	50-100MM	100-250MM	Type of Statement	4/1/00-3/31/01 ALL	4/1/01-3/31/02 ALL
	1	7	8	1	3	Unqualified	15	21
		9				Reviewed	11	15
	1	6	3			Compiled	13	11
3	3	1				Tax Returns	4	1
1	3	4	6	1	2	Other	11	17
		24 (4/1-9/30/04)		40 (10/1/04-3/31/05)				
4	8	27	18	2	5	NUMBER OF STATEMENTS	54	65
%	%	%	%	%	%	**ASSETS**	%	%
		5.6	5.6			Cash & Equivalents	5.8	3.2
		28.8	21.9			Trade Receivables (net)	25.6	24.2
		23.5	20.1			Inventory	19.8	23.2
		1.3	2.6			All Other Current	1.3	1.0
		59.2	50.2			Total Current	52.6	51.6
		32.4	40.5			Fixed Assets (net)	36.1	37.7
		1.7	4.5			Intangibles (net)	4.2	4.0
		6.7	4.8			All Other Non-Current	7.1	6.7
		100.0	100.0			Total	100.0	100.0
						LIABILITIES		
		12.6	11.6			Notes Payable-Short Term	10.9	11.7
		4.3	4.4			Cur. Mat.-L/T/D	5.3	6.9
		17.5	14.5			Trade Payables	14.5	17.2
		.5	.0			Income Taxes Payable	.2	.3
		7.4	5.5			All Other Current	6.7	6.4
		42.3	35.9			Total Current	37.5	42.5
		14.0	23.6			Long-Term Debt	20.1	22.1
		.6	1.5			Deferred Taxes	.9	1.1
		14.8	4.1			All Other Non-Current	8.2	11.4
		28.3	34.9			Net Worth	33.3	22.9
		100.0	100.0			Total Liabilities & Net Worth	100.0	100.0
						INCOME DATA		
		100.0	100.0			Net Sales	100.0	100.0
		19.8	24.5			Gross Profit	26.2	26.5
		17.9	20.6			Operating Expenses	21.7	23.4
		1.9	3.9			Operating Profit	4.5	3.1
		.6	1.0			All Other Expenses (net)	2.1	2.6
		1.3	2.9			Profit Before Taxes	2.4	.6
						RATIOS		
		2.7	2.5			Current	2.3	1.6
		1.4	1.6				1.4	1.2
		1.0	.9				1.0	.9
		1.6	1.3			Quick	1.3	.9
		.8	.8				.8	.6
		.5	.5				.5	.5
		35 10.4	39 9.4			Sales/Receivables	36 10.2	32 11.4
		43 8.4	47 7.7				42 8.6	40 9.0
		50 7.3	49 7.4				52 7.1	47 7.8
		30 12.3	35 10.5			Cost of Sales/Inventory	32 11.4	36 10.3
		43 8.4	55 6.6				43 8.5	52 7.1
		56 6.5	79 4.6				59 6.1	65 5.7
		21 17.4	30 12.1			Cost of Sales/Payables	18 20.3	23 16.0
		30 12.2	43 8.5				34 10.8	39 9.5
		46 7.9	52 7.1				48 7.5	50 7.3
		6.4	5.6			Sales/Working Capital	7.2	11.6
		19.4	14.0				15.2	33.5
		-987.4	-27.5				-548.6	-56.3
		5.3	9.7			EBIT/Interest	4.8	5.0
		(26) 2.5	(16) 2.5				(49) 2.7	(62) 1.8
		.8	-1.1				1.0	.7
		8.3				Net Profit + Depr., Dep., Amort./Cur. Mat. L /T/D	2.6	1.8
		(10) 2.0					(16) 1.5	(18) 1.2
		1.4					.6	.6
		.5	.6			Fixed/Worth	.6	.8
		.9	2.1				1.0	1.7
		1.8	7.1				3.3	-16.2
		.8	.4			Debt/Worth	.8	1.5
		1.7	3.5				1.7	2.4
		4.9	13.4				4.7	-43.5
		24.5	77.1			% Profit Before Taxes/Tangible Net Worth	36.2	24.9
		(25) 10.6	(17) 25.0				(44) 15.4	(48) 11.5
		-.5	-7.0				6.4	1.7
		6.5	12.4			% Profit Before Taxes/Total Assets	13.5	10.2
		2.5	7.1				6.4	3.0
		-.5	-3.7				.1	-.7
		13.2	8.0			Sales/Net Fixed Assets	9.7	11.1
		7.8	4.2				5.8	6.4
		4.8	2.9				3.6	3.1
		2.7	2.1			Sales/Total Assets	2.6	2.9
		2.4	1.8				2.1	2.0
		1.9	1.3				1.6	1.5
		1.5	2.3			% Depr., Dep., Amort./Sales	1.0	2.1
		(25) 2.5	(16) 3.1				(52) 3.0	(56) 3.0
		5.7	5.1				4.7	4.8
		2.2				% Officers', Directors', Owners' Comp/Sales	2.0	2.0
		(16) 3.6					(23) 3.6	(23) 2.7
		4.9					5.8	3.4
3685M	20778M	309360M	727748M	181893M	990969M	Net Sales ($)	1396404M	2959276M
1081M	9983M	136089M	389768M	109752M	632607M	Total Assets ($)	796877M	1257733M

© RMA 2005

M = $ thousand   MM = $ million
See Pages 11 through 21 for Explanation of Ratios and Data

Comparative Historical Data | **Current Data Sorted By Sales**

			Type of Statement						
15	21	19	Unqualified		1	1	1	8	10
17	15	11	Reviewed				2	5	2
10	8	10	Compiled		4	1	3	4	2
1	3	7	Tax Returns		1	1	4		
15	17	17	Other	1 2	1	1	3	3	6
4/1/02-3/31/03	4/1/03-3/31/04	4/1/04-3/31/05		24 (4/1-9/30/04)			40 (10/1/04-3/31/05)		
ALL	ALL	ALL		0-1MM	1-3MM	3-5MM	5-10MM	10-25MM	25MM & OVER
58	64	64	**NUMBER OF STATEMENTS**	3	6	4	11	20	20
%	%	%	**ASSETS**	%	%	%	%	%	%
5.3	3.7	5.4	Cash & Equivalents				4.2	5.5	3.2
21.7	24.8	25.2	Trade Receivables (net)				28.2	27.0	22.6
22.6	21.5	22.2	Inventory				21.3	21.5	21.1
1.2	2.0	1.8	All Other Current				.6	2.0	3.1
50.8	52.0	54.5	Total Current				54.4	55.9	50.0
38.7	39.2	34.1	Fixed Assets (net)				36.1	33.3	38.8
3.4	3.0	5.2	Intangibles (net)				1.4	4.6	6.8
7.1	5.7	6.2	All Other Non-Current				8.1	6.2	4.4
100.0	100.0	100.0	Total				100.0	100.0	100.0
			LIABILITIES						
10.6	10.7	13.7	Notes Payable-Short Term				12.2	16.8	9.6
5.9	5.3	4.8	Cur. Mat.-L/T/D				2.9	5.5	4.2
16.7	18.4	18.6	Trade Payables				14.6	19.9	15.3
.5	.2	.3	Income Taxes Payable				.2	.5	.3
6.9	8.2	6.4	All Other Current				5.8	7.0	5.6
40.6	42.7	43.8	Total Current				35.7	49.8	35.0
18.5	20.4	18.7	Long-Term Debt				13.7	15.0	25.1
1.5	1.4	1.1	Deferred Taxes				1.1	.7	2.2
12.0	12.1	9.4	All Other Non-Current				7.9	17.6	3.8
27.5	23.3	26.9	Net Worth				41.7	16.9	33.9
100.0	100.0	100.0	Total Liabilities & Net Worth				100.0	100.0	100.0
			INCOME DATA						
100.0	100.0	100.0	Net Sales				100.0	100.0	100.0
27.4	25.2	21.6	Gross Profit				22.8	19.5	20.3
23.7	21.6	19.8	Operating Expenses				22.5	18.1	15.6
3.7	3.7	1.8	Operating Profit				.4	1.3	4.7
1.8	1.7	.7	All Other Expenses (net)				.1	1.0	1.1
1.9	2.0	1.1	Profit Before Taxes				.2	.3	3.6
			RATIOS						
1.8	1.9	2.3					2.9	1.7	2.1
1.2	1.2	1.1	Current				1.7	1.0	1.3
.8	.9	.9					.9	.8	1.0
1.0	1.0	1.3					1.8	1.1	1.2
.6	.6	.6	Quick				.9	.6	.6
.4	.4	.4					.5	.4	.5
29 12.5	34 10.6	35 10.4					40 9.2	37 9.9	35 10.5
41 8.9	43 8.5	42 8.6	Sales/Receivables				43 8.4	44 8.3	41 8.8
50 7.3	53 6.9	51 7.2					71 5.1	56 6.6	48 7.5
37 9.9	41 9.0	30 12.3					28 13.0	30 12.2	34 10.7
53 6.9	52 7.0	44 8.4	Cost of Sales/Inventory				54 6.8	43 8.6	45 8.1
78 4.7	62 5.9	70 5.2					57 6.4	79 4.6	64 5.7
27 13.7	29 12.6	26 14.0					16 22.5	28 12.8	26 14.3
42 8.7	40 9.2	37 9.8	Cost of Sales/Payables				25 14.4	46 7.9	35 10.3
60 6.1	52 7.0	51 7.2					57 6.4	62 5.9	43 8.5
8.1	7.7	6.6					5.3	8.5	6.8
20.5	27.2	46.4	Sales/Working Capital				10.1	89.3	19.6
-30.6	-41.8	-30.4					-29.8	-17.3	NM
4.6	5.1	6.1					6.1	2.5	10.1
(56) 2.3	(62) 2.3	(59) 2.2	EBIT/Interest				2.7	(19) 1.5	(18) 3.4
1.2	1.0	-.8					-1.5	-.8	1.8
4.3	4.0	8.3	Net Profit + Depr., Dep.,						
(25) 1.6	(26) 1.9	(21) 1.9	Amort./Cur. Mat. L/T/D						
1.3	1.2	.9							
.7	.8	.6					.5	.7	1.0
1.4	1.5	1.5	Fixed/Worth				.9	1.7	1.6
2.7	5.4	6.3					2.1	7.1	6.3
1.1	1.4	1.0					.5	1.0	1.4
2.2	2.5	2.9	Debt/Worth				1.6	3.8	3.4
6.1	10.4	16.4					13.2	12.3	12.1
33.3	24.3	32.9	% Profit Before Taxes/Tangible				11.5	27.3	66.2
(50) 11.7	(53) 12.2	(55) 12.9	Net Worth				3.8	(17) 2.6	(18) 29.0
3.2	3.7	-6.1					-61.2	-13.1	4.9
8.9	7.4	7.9	% Profit Before Taxes/Total				6.5	3.6	12.7
4.0	3.3	3.3	Assets				2.2	1.1	7.1
.4	.0	-3.4					-4.0	-3.4	3.0
10.3	9.9	10.2					14.7	12.0	7.8
5.0	4.6	5.7	Sales/Net Fixed Assets				8.1	5.6	4.5
2.7	3.3	3.9					2.8	4.0	3.4
2.5	2.6	2.6					2.8	2.5	2.3
1.9	2.0	2.0	Sales/Total Assets				2.5	2.0	1.9
1.5	1.6	1.5					1.5	1.4	1.6
2.5	2.4	2.0					2.0	1.6	2.3
(57) 3.6	(58) 3.6	(53) 3.1	% Depr., Dep., Amort./Sales				3.6	(18) 2.7	(15) 3.1
5.5	5.0	5.1					6.7	6.2	4.8
1.9	1.7	2.3	% Officers', Directors',						
(24) 3.3	(21) 2.4	(24) 4.1	Owners' Comp/Sales						
6.8	6.9	5.0							
1497456M	1629232M	2234433M	Net Sales ($)	1582M	8960M	17336M	79886M	288093M	1838576M
878849M	934743M	1279280M	Total Assets ($)	1091M	5253M	7825M	43054M	155086M	1066971M

M = $ thousand   MM = $ million
See Pages 11 through 21 for Explanation of Ratios and Data

Current Data Sorted By Assets   Comparative Historical Data

						Type of Statement		
0-500M	500M-2MM	2-10MM	10-50MM	50-100MM	100-250MM			
	1	5	8	1	1	Unqualified	12	8
		7	3			Reviewed	11	8
		1				Compiled	6	3
	1					Tax Returns		
	1	5	3			Other	7	9
	8 (4/1-9/30/04)		29 (10/1/04-3/31/05)				7 4/1/00- 3/31/01 ALL	9 4/1/01- 3/31/02 ALL
	3	18	14	1	1	**NUMBER OF STATEMENTS**	36	28
%	%	%	%	%	%	**ASSETS**	%	%
		5.4	3.9			Cash & Equivalents	6.7	7.0
		32.9	26.8			Trade Receivables (net)	31.0	24.7
		14.5	22.2			Inventory	17.0	16.5
		1.1	.7			All Other Current	1.0	.6
		53.9	53.6			Total Current	55.8	48.8
		41.3	41.2			Fixed Assets (net)	36.4	41.7
		.5	.8			Intangibles (net)	4.3	4.4
		4.2	4.3			All Other Non-Current	4.5	5.2
		100.0	100.0			Total	100.0	100.0
						LIABILITIES		
		13.6	9.5			Notes Payable-Short Term	12.5	14.8
		6.4	6.2			Cur. Mat.-L/T/D	7.6	8.2
		13.7	9.0			Trade Payables	15.5	17.1
		.1	.1			Income Taxes Payable	.1	.0
		7.0	6.0			All Other Current	5.6	5.7
		40.8	30.8			Total Current	41.4	45.7
		26.8	28.7			Long-Term Debt	24.3	24.3
		1.0	.6			Deferred Taxes	.5	.7
		3.4	6.0			All Other Non-Current	3.4	3.7
		28.0	34.0			Net Worth	30.4	25.6
		100.0	100.0			Total Liabilities & Net Worth	100.0	100.0
						INCOME DATA		
		100.0	100.0			Net Sales	100.0	100.0
		24.7	19.4			Gross Profit	21.0	27.2
		22.5	17.0			Operating Expenses	19.4	25.6
		2.2	2.4			Operating Profit	1.6	1.6
		.4	.9			All Other Expenses (net)	1.3	1.6
		1.8	1.6			Profit Before Taxes	.3	-.1
						RATIOS		
		2.1	3.2			Current	2.3	1.5
		1.3	1.8				1.2	1.1
		.9	1.2				.9	.8
		1.4	1.6			Quick	1.8	.9
		.9	.8				.8	.7
		.6	.7				.6	.5
		39 9.4	40 9.1			Sales/Receivables	38 9.7	38 9.7
		47 7.7	47 7.8				49 7.5	45 8.2
		59 6.2	50 7.3				55 6.6	52 7.0
		19 19.2	33 11.1			Cost of Sales/Inventory	21 17.4	24 15.3
		29 12.6	42 8.8				29 12.5	32 11.4
		39 9.4	88 4.2				42 8.7	43 8.5
		20 18.5	17 21.5			Cost of Sales/Payables	16 23.2	18 20.2
		27 13.3	20 18.2				24 15.0	31 11.7
		34 10.6	24 15.1				39 9.4	52 7.0
		8.7	4.2			Sales/Working Capital	5.6	10.4
		22.8	10.6				33.3	48.8
		-88.0	29.0				-151.2	-17.6
		5.5	7.5			EBIT/Interest	1.9	1.9
		2.3	2.7				(31) 1.2	(27) 1.0
		1.0	-.9				.3	-.2
						Net Profit + Depr., Dep.,	2.4	1.7
						Amort./Cur. Mat. L /T/D	(13) 1.2	(10) 1.2
							.4	.7
		1.0	.7			Fixed/Worth	.8	1.1
		1.4	1.4				1.4	1.9
		2.4	2.9				3.3	3.9
		1.4	.8			Debt/Worth	.9	2.1
		2.6	2.1				2.1	3.5
		4.8	4.3				5.7	8.1
		31.9	18.2			% Profit Before Taxes/Tangible	30.8	10.1
	(16) 17.1		(13) 3.6			Net Worth	(31) 3.5	(26) 1.7
		2.5	-6.7				-2.5	-9.3
		10.1	9.4			% Profit Before Taxes/Total	4.8	2.1
		2.9	2.8			Assets	1.5	.2
		.2	-2.5				-2.4	-4.9
		10.2	5.3			Sales/Net Fixed Assets	11.2	8.1
		6.1	4.8				5.8	4.7
		3.7	3.2				3.8	2.7
		2.9	2.3			Sales/Total Assets	2.8	2.8
		2.6	1.9				2.0	2.0
		1.8	1.6				1.7	1.3
		2.4	2.6			% Depr., Dep., Amort./Sales	1.6	2.2
		3.3	(13) 3.1				(33) 2.8	(27) 3.3
		4.5	4.2				3.7	4.9
						% Officers', Directors',	1.5	2.3
						Owners' Comp/Sales	(10) 2.5	(10) 3.4
							8.6	11.0
	8187M	213930M	685006M	81838M	174137M	Net Sales ($)	1216321M	479611M
	3394M	94693M	356038M	66193M	100513M	Total Assets ($)	598550M	264226M

(Left columns 0-500M and 500M-2MM: DATA NOT AVAILABLE)

M = $ thousand   MM = $ million
See Pages 11 through 21 for Explanation of Ratios and Data

Comparative Historical Data | Current Data Sorted By Sales

4/1/02-3/31/03 ALL	4/1/03-3/31/04 ALL	4/1/04-3/31/05 ALL	Type of Statement	0-1MM	8 (4/1-9/30/04) 1-3MM	3-5MM	29 (10/1/04-3/31/05) 5-10MM	10-25MM	25MM & OVER
11	10	15	Unqualified				2	3	10
9	10	11	Reviewed		1		2	6	2
2	2	2	Compiled					1	
		1	Tax Returns		1	1			
8	7	9	Other				2	3	3
30	29	37	NUMBER OF STATEMENTS		2	1	6	13	15
%	%	%	ASSETS	%	%	%	%	%	%
5.1	7.5	5.2	Cash & Equivalents					2.8	5.4
27.0	28.2	29.5	Trade Receivables (net)					33.9	27.0
18.2	16.3	18.3	Inventory					16.3	21.0
1.7	1.0	.9	All Other Current					.9	.7
52.0	53.0	53.9	Total Current					53.9	54.1
41.2	38.2	41.3	Fixed Assets (net)					43.1	40.6
1.1	3.0	.6	Intangibles (net)					.2	.7
5.6	5.8	4.1	All Other Non-Current					2.8	4.5
100.0	100.0	100.0	Total					100.0	100.0
			LIABILITIES						
13.2	12.7	11.5	Notes Payable-Short Term					12.2	9.8
5.8	5.4	5.7	Cur. Mat.-L/T/D					6.0	5.9
11.2	11.3	12.6	Trade Payables					15.2	10.0
.2	.1	.1	Income Taxes Payable					.2	.1
6.5	6.2	7.4	All Other Current					7.6	7.5
36.9	35.8	37.3	Total Current					41.2	33.4
22.0	20.0	27.4	Long-Term Debt					26.0	27.0
.7	1.3	.7	Deferred Taxes					.9	.5
9.5	5.6	6.1	All Other Non-Current					4.7	6.0
30.8	37.3	28.6	Net Worth					27.2	33.1
100.0	100.0	100.0	Total Liabilities & Net Worth					100.0	100.0
			INCOME DATA						
100.0	100.0	100.0	Net Sales					100.0	100.0
24.8	27.3	23.4	Gross Profit					26.6	18.4
22.3	23.7	20.9	Operating Expenses					24.2	16.0
2.5	3.6	2.6	Operating Profit					2.4	2.4
1.6	.8	.7	All Other Expenses (net)					.8	.7
.9	2.8	1.9	Profit Before Taxes					1.6	1.6
			RATIOS						
2.2	2.1	2.0	Current					1.8	1.9
1.4	1.4	1.3						1.3	1.4
1.1	1.1	1.1						1.0	1.2
1.2	1.4	1.4	Quick					1.3	1.4
.8	.9	.8						.9	.8
.6	.7	.6						.7	.6
38 9.6	38 9.6	39 9.4	Sales/Receivables					38 9.5	42 8.8
47 7.8	46 8.0	47 7.8						46 7.9	47 7.8
59 6.2	55 6.6	54 6.7						56 6.5	52 7.1
24 15.5	20 18.0	24 15.4	Cost of Sales/Inventory					21 17.6	27 13.4
39 9.4	32 11.4	37 10.0						28 12.8	39 9.3
58 6.3	69 5.3	48 7.6						39 9.4	73 5.0
17 22.0	16 22.1	18 20.0	Cost of Sales/Payables					22 16.5	17 21.5
21 17.8	22 16.4	23 16.1						31 11.8	20 17.9
31 12.0	33 11.2	33 10.9						35 10.4	30 12.3
7.0	6.3	7.5	Sales/Working Capital					9.4	6.3
14.2	12.3	16.7						18.8	11.3
56.0	61.3	51.4						197.1	28.7
5.2	5.0	6.0	EBIT/Interest					7.7	7.3
2.0	2.5	2.4						2.4	2.9
.4	1.3	.8						1.0	-.7
3.0	2.8	3.6	Net Profit + Depr., Dep.,						
(11) 1.8	(14) 2.2	(17) 1.8	Amort./Cur. Mat. L/T/D						
1.3	1.4	.9							
.9	.7	.9	Fixed/Worth					.8	.7
1.3	1.0	1.4						1.1	1.3
2.5	2.0	2.5						3.5	1.9
1.2	1.0	1.2	Debt/Worth					1.3	1.0
2.2	1.9	2.2						2.3	2.1
4.7	4.1	5.0						5.5	3.0
29.0	25.3	27.4	% Profit Before Taxes/Tangible					31.9	17.3
(28) 10.1	(28) 8.4	(33) 14.2	Net Worth					(11) 17.8	(14) 5.5
-3.8	3.1	2.1						7.9	-6.0
11.1	10.1	9.2	% Profit Before Taxes/Total					11.1	8.4
2.7	3.5	2.2	Assets					3.1	2.2
-1.1	.9	-.7						-.2	-2.3
6.9	8.7	7.7	Sales/Net Fixed Assets					10.7	5.2
4.7	5.2	5.1						6.7	4.7
3.4	3.6	3.4						3.6	3.7
2.4	2.7	2.8	Sales/Total Assets					3.1	2.3
2.0	1.9	2.0						2.8	1.9
1.7	1.4	1.6						1.9	1.6
2.4	2.6	2.5	% Depr., Dep., Amort./Sales					2.4	2.6
(28) 3.3	3.4	(36) 3.2						2.9	(14) 3.2
5.1	4.6	4.3						4.8	4.2
		2.2	% Officers', Directors',						
	(11)	3.1	Owners' Comp/Sales						
		5.4							
1010739M	1193326M	1163098M	Net Sales ($)		4005M	4182M	47163M	182678M	925070M
553508M	734488M	620831M	Total Assets ($)		2474M	920M	27413M	77964M	512060M

(For the ASSETS, LIABILITIES, INCOME DATA sections the columns 0-1MM, 1-3MM, 3-5MM and 5-10MM are marked "DATA NOT AVAILABLE.")

M = $ thousand   MM = $ million
See Pages 11 through 21 for Explanation of Ratios and Data

Current Data Sorted By Assets   Comparative Historical Data

0-500M	500M-2MM	2-10MM	10-50MM	50-100MM	100-250MM	Type of Statement	4/1/00- 3/31/01	4/1/01- 3/31/02
		2	3	1	3	Unqualified	7	6
	1	4	1		1	Reviewed	4	2
1	1		1			Compiled	2	2
1						Tax Returns		
1	2	1	2	2	1	Other	6	6
	6 (4/1-9/30/04)		20 (10/1/04-3/31/05)				ALL	ALL
2	4	7	6	3	4	**NUMBER OF STATEMENTS**	19	16
%	%	%	%	%	%	**ASSETS**	%	%
						Cash & Equivalents	4.5	2.7
						Trade Receivables (net)	27.8	23.9
						Inventory	17.5	18.7
						All Other Current	1.4	1.2
						Total Current	51.2	46.5
						Fixed Assets (net)	43.2	40.5
						Intangibles (net)	1.8	5.4
						All Other Non-Current	3.8	7.6
						Total	100.0	100.0
						LIABILITIES		
						Notes Payable-Short Term	6.9	7.1
						Cur. Mat.-L/T/D	4.4	2.8
						Trade Payables	17.3	18.6
						Income Taxes Payable	.0	.0
						All Other Current	3.9	3.2
						Total Current	32.5	31.6
						Long-Term Debt	33.5	26.7
						Deferred Taxes	1.2	.7
						All Other Non-Current	.5	3.0
						Net Worth	32.2	38.0
						Total Liabilities & Net Worth	100.0	100.0
						INCOME DATA		
						Net Sales	100.0	100.0
						Gross Profit	26.8	28.9
						Operating Expenses	20.1	19.6
						Operating Profit	6.8	9.3
						All Other Expenses (net)	2.4	2.4
						Profit Before Taxes	4.4	6.9
						RATIOS		
						Current	2.3 / 1.4 / 1.1	2.4 / 1.9 / 1.2
						Quick	1.7 / .9 / .5	1.5 / 1.0 / .7
						Sales/Receivables	37 9.7 / 44 8.4 / 60 6.1	30 12.0 / 49 7.5 / 54 6.8
						Cost of Sales/Inventory	37 9.8 / 49 7.4 / 55 6.6	43 8.4 / 49 7.5 / 68 5.4
						Cost of Sales/Payables	30 12.0 / 52 7.1 / 74 4.9	31 11.6 / 49 7.5 / 57 6.4
						Sales/Working Capital	5.8 / 14.3 / 31.4	6.2 / 9.1 / 29.2
						EBIT/Interest	5.4 / (17) 3.1 / 1.3	13.6 / (15) 3.2 / 1.5
						Net Profit + Depr., Dep., Amort./Cur. Mat. L /T/D		
						Fixed/Worth	.8 / 1.5 / 2.9	.6 / 1.2 / 1.7
						Debt/Worth	1.7 / 2.3 / 3.3	.8 / 1.6 / 2.6
						% Profit Before Taxes/Tangible Net Worth	58.2 / (18) 21.2 / 14.9	67.2 / (15) 37.0 / 7.5
						% Profit Before Taxes/Total Assets	15.5 / 7.6 / 3.1	33.4 / 10.6 / 1.7
						Sales/Net Fixed Assets	9.7 / 3.5 / 1.9	10.4 / 5.4 / 2.8
						Sales/Total Assets	2.4 / 1.6 / 1.0	2.1 / 1.8 / 1.3
						% Depr., Dep., Amort./Sales	1.1 / (17) 1.9 / 4.4	2.1 / (15) 4.0 / 5.0
						% Officers', Directors', Owners' Comp/Sales		
2478M	14242M	75206M	340953M	379746M	1022990M	Net Sales ($)	1164002M	792829M
482M	5870M	39914M	169055M	179189M	602653M	Total Assets ($)	886748M	607615M

© RMA 2005

M = $ thousand   MM = $ million
See Pages 11 through 21 for Explanation of Ratios and Data

Comparative Historical Data				Current Data Sorted By Sales					
			Type of Statement						
12	15	9	Unqualified					2	7
2	8	5	Reviewed				3	2	
3	5	2	Compiled		1			1	
2	2	2	Tax Returns	1	1				
8	10	8	Other		1		2		5
				6 (4/1-9/30/04)			20 (10/1/04-3/31/05)		
4/1/02-3/31/03 ALL	4/1/03-3/31/04 ALL	4/1/04-3/31/05 ALL		0-1MM	1-3MM	3-5MM	5-10MM	10-25MM	25MM & OVER
27	40	26	**NUMBER OF STATEMENTS**	1	3		5	5	12
%	%	%	**ASSETS**	%	%	%	%	%	%
7.1	6.8	4.4	Cash & Equivalents			DATA NOT AVAILABLE			3.1
23.6	22.2	23.6	Trade Receivables (net)						22.4
25.9	24.8	27.4	Inventory						20.8
1.3	1.8	4.3	All Other Current						2.9
57.8	55.6	59.7	Total Current						49.2
34.5	35.8	33.1	Fixed Assets (net)						40.8
3.7	4.6	3.7	Intangibles (net)						7.3
3.9	4.0	3.5	All Other Non-Current						2.8
100.0	100.0	100.0	Total						100.0
			LIABILITIES						
5.7	5.8	14.1	Notes Payable-Short Term						8.0
6.1	2.9	4.0	Cur. Mat.-L/T/D						3.8
12.0	14.4	17.1	Trade Payables						16.5
.1	.2	.0	Income Taxes Payable						.0
7.2	12.3	5.7	All Other Current						5.2
31.2	35.6	40.9	Total Current						33.5
21.3	23.2	22.1	Long-Term Debt						30.8
.8	.9	.8	Deferred Taxes						1.4
5.5	4.0	7.1	All Other Non-Current						8.6
41.3	36.3	29.1	Net Worth						25.7
100.0	100.0	100.0	Total Liabilities & Net Worth						100.0
			INCOME DATA						
100.0	100.0	100.0	Net Sales						100.0
33.8	29.1	30.0	Gross Profit						25.6
26.2	22.7	21.6	Operating Expenses						18.5
7.6	6.4	8.4	Operating Profit						7.1
1.7	2.0	1.3	All Other Expenses (net)						1.9
5.9	4.4	7.1	Profit Before Taxes						5.2
			RATIOS						
2.9	2.8	2.6							2.4
2.1	1.9	1.6	Current						1.5
1.4	1.1	1.2							1.1
2.1	1.5	1.4							1.3
1.1	.8	.6	Quick						.9
.5	.4	.4							.5
34 10.8	**29** 12.4	**30** 12.4							**34** 10.7
42 8.8	**40** 9.0	**43** 8.6	Sales/Receivables						**45** 8.2
51 7.2	**50** 7.2	**49** 7.4							**49** 7.4
29 12.4	**35** 10.3	**44** 8.3							**42** 8.6
60 6.1	**51** 7.2	**61** 5.9	Cost of Sales/Inventory						**46** 7.9
94 3.9	**89** 4.1	**94** 3.9							**71** 5.1
20 18.5	**17** 21.6	**23** 15.9							**24** 15.2
33 11.2	**33** 11.2	**37** 9.9	Cost of Sales/Payables						**38** 9.5
45 8.2	**47** 7.7	**61** 5.9							**64** 5.7
5.3	6.0	5.7							7.2
7.4	9.2	9.9	Sales/Working Capital						12.8
22.2	57.4	30.7							50.5
26.9	19.6	17.3							17.9
(23) 5.2	(38) 5.7	(21) 4.4	EBIT/Interest						(10) 3.9
.6	1.2	2.8							1.8
	3.0								
	(13) 2.1		Net Profit + Depr., Dep., Amort./Cur. Mat. L/T/D						
	1.2								
.3	.5	.4							1.5
1.1	1.4	1.7	Fixed/Worth						2.1
1.7	3.4	7.0							-3.9
.7	.8	1.0							1.6
1.3	1.8	2.7	Debt/Worth						3.1
2.0	11.7	14.9							-12.1
60.6	73.4	66.1							
(23) 40.3	(35) 27.6	(21) 19.3	% Profit Before Taxes/Tangible Net Worth						
3.2	8.0	8.4							
29.2	17.6	20.2							15.9
7.4	9.4	9.0	% Profit Before Taxes/Total Assets						3.5
-.7	1.1	2.4							-.4
17.3	11.4	24.2							11.2
6.0	7.0	5.7	Sales/Net Fixed Assets						4.1
3.1	3.2	3.3							3.4
2.8	2.7	2.7							2.3
1.9	1.9	1.9	Sales/Total Assets						1.9
1.4	1.5	1.4							1.5
1.7	2.0	.8							
(24) 2.9	(35) 3.0	(18) 2.4	% Depr., Dep., Amort./Sales						
5.7	3.7	5.0							
			% Officers', Directors', Owners' Comp/Sales						
1605234M	3608372M	1835615M	Net Sales ($)	910M	5501M		32699M	76490M	1720015M
1078313M	2024170M	997163M	Total Assets ($)	259M	2911M		22135M	39216M	932642M

M = $ thousand MM = $ million

See Pages 11 through 21 for Explanation of Ratios and Data

Current Data Sorted By Assets | Comparative Historical Data

Type of Statement	0-500M	500M-2MM	2-10MM	10-50MM	50-100MM	100-250MM		4/1/00-3/31/01 ALL	4/1/01-3/31/02 ALL
Unqualified		1	6	9	2	1		20	25
Reviewed	2	8	14	5				10	18
Compiled	2	4	6	3				14	20
Tax Returns	1	9	2	13	1			5	4
Other			6					17	27
		16 (4/1-9/30/04)		79 (10/1/04-3/31/05)					
NUMBER OF STATEMENTS	5	22	34	30	3	1		66	94

0-500M %	500M-2MM %	2-10MM %	10-50MM %	50-100MM %	100-250MM %	ITEM	4/1/00-3/31/01 ALL %	4/1/01-3/31/02 ALL %
						ASSETS		
	8.2	7.8	6.6			Cash & Equivalents	4.1	6.1
	36.8	27.2	24.5			Trade Receivables (net)	25.4	26.6
	21.0	28.7	23.7			Inventory	26.8	23.6
	2.4	1.7	2.6			All Other Current	1.5	1.9
	68.3	65.4	57.4			Total Current	57.8	58.1
	27.3	25.2	31.4			Fixed Assets (net)	32.0	32.1
	.7	2.6	5.8			Intangibles (net)	3.6	3.5
	3.6	6.8	5.4			All Other Non-Current	6.6	6.3
	100.0	100.0	100.0			Total	100.0	100.0
						LIABILITIES		
	15.3	10.8	14.5			Notes Payable-Short Term	14.5	12.9
	4.5	3.2	3.1			Cur. Mat.-L/T/D	4.1	5.4
	21.6	16.7	13.3			Trade Payables	16.4	15.2
	.5	.1	.1			Income Taxes Payable	.5	.4
	14.6	8.2	5.3			All Other Current	8.1	7.4
	56.5	39.0	36.3			Total Current	43.6	41.3
	12.9	11.0	16.3			Long-Term Debt	19.7	17.2
	.0	.6	.5			Deferred Taxes	.5	.5
	3.0	4.4	6.8			All Other Non-Current	3.9	5.8
	27.5	45.0	40.2			Net Worth	32.3	35.2
	100.0	100.0	100.0			Total Liabilities & Net Worth	100.0	100.0
						INCOME DATA		
	100.0	100.0	100.0			Net Sales	100.0	100.0
	29.8	30.4	24.0			Gross Profit	29.0	25.6
	23.7	25.1	16.8			Operating Expenses	25.1	21.5
	6.1	5.3	7.3			Operating Profit	3.9	4.0
	1.2	1.3	2.3			All Other Expenses (net)	-.4	1.2
	4.9	4.0	4.9			Profit Before Taxes	4.3	2.8
						RATIOS		
	2.0	2.5	2.9			Current	2.0	2.1
	1.2	1.7	1.5				1.3	1.4
	.9	1.1	1.1				.9	1.0
	1.5	1.7	1.5			Quick	1.0	1.2
	.9	.8	.8				.7	.9
	.6	.5	.5				.5	.5
	28 13.0	31 11.8	35 10.5			Sales/Receivables	32 11.3	34 10.7
	38 9.7	36 10.1	44 8.2				40 9.1	42 8.6
	46 8.0	51 7.2	57 6.4				53 6.9	50 7.3
	16 23.3	38 9.5	36 10.1			Cost of Sales/Inventory	34 10.8	29 12.5
	29 12.6	53 6.9	49 7.4				51 7.1	45 8.2
	51 7.1	74 4.9	82 4.5				92 4.0	78 4.7
	17 21.7	19 19.6	18 20.4			Cost of Sales/Payables	23 16.2	17 20.9
	33 11.1	38 9.6	27 13.3				32 11.5	30 12.4
	45 8.2	50 7.3	46 7.9				48 7.6	44 8.3
	8.1	6.9	4.9			Sales/Working Capital	6.8	6.4
	29.0	10.8	10.4				15.8	14.6
	-71.3	23.8	42.8				-74.5	UND
	(21) 12.8	(29) 17.7	(27) 6.5			EBIT/Interest	(63) 5.3	(89) 5.1
	4.8	4.6	2.9				2.3	2.0
	1.3	1.7	1.6				1.3	.8
						Net Profit + Depr., Dep., Amort./Cur. Mat. L/T/D	(20) 5.4	(22) 5.9
							2.5	2.1
							1.7	.7
	.3	.3	.3			Fixed/Worth	.5	.5
	.7	.5	.9				1.0	1.0
	3.2	1.0	1.8				2.2	2.3
	.9	.5	.9			Debt/Worth	1.1	.8
	2.3	1.4	2.0				2.1	2.2
	3.9	2.8	3.6				6.6	4.5
	(18) 52.1	(32) 38.8	(27) 25.6			% Profit Before Taxes/Tangible Net Worth	(59) 37.1	(82) 28.0
	22.3	14.0	18.7				16.3	10.0
	4.7	4.0	5.4				5.3	.1
	22.8	17.0	12.7			% Profit Before Taxes/Total Assets	11.7	12.6
	6.4	7.3	4.5				4.2	3.6
	-.4	2.0	1.3				.9	-.7
	37.5	34.4	13.9			Sales/Net Fixed Assets	16.2	19.3
	9.1	13.9	6.4				7.6	7.6
	7.0	4.9	2.8				4.0	3.8
	3.9	3.3	2.2			Sales/Total Assets	2.9	3.0
	3.0	2.6	1.8				2.0	2.1
	2.2	1.6	1.3				1.5	1.6
	(19) .8	(32) 1.2	(26) 1.4			% Depr., Dep., Amort./Sales	(61) 1.0	(82) .9
	2.5	1.7	2.3				2.6	2.4
	3.7	3.8	4.5				4.6	4.4
	(11) 3.2	(13) 2.0				% Officers', Directors', Owners' Comp/Sales	(26) 1.7	(28) 1.6
	4.7	3.2					4.3	4.3
	6.6	4.3					6.8	5.5
3025M	90670M	462773M	1394891M	206220M	215574M	Net Sales ($)	1988404M	2827354M
1621M	27660M	179986M	790120M	208797M	127317M	Total Assets ($)	991789M	1494352M

M = $ thousand   MM = $ million
See Pages 11 through 21 for Explanation of Ratios and Data

Comparative Historical Data | Current Data Sorted By Sales

			Type of Statement						
19	29	18	Unqualified			1		3	14
17	25	20	Reviewed		1		6	8	5
19	18	19	Compiled	1	5	2	5	5	1
4	8	8	Tax Returns	2	2		2	2	
26	36	30	Other	2	1	5	5	3	14
4/1/02-	4/1/03-	4/1/04-			16 (4/1-9/30/04)		79 (10/1/04-3/31/05)		
3/31/03	3/31/04	3/31/05		0-1MM	1-3MM	3-5MM	5-10MM	10-25MM	25MM & OVER
ALL	ALL	ALL							
85	116	95	NUMBER OF STATEMENTS	5	9	8	18	21	34
%	%	%	ASSETS	%	%	%	%	%	%
8.9	6.9	8.1	Cash & Equivalents				10.7	6.9	6.4
27.6	25.4	27.3	Trade Receivables (net)				35.1	26.6	24.2
22.2	24.0	24.6	Inventory				23.2	29.9	24.3
1.6	2.2	2.1	All Other Current				2.3	2.7	1.6
60.2	58.6	62.1	Total Current				71.3	66.0	56.4
27.7	29.5	28.2	Fixed Assets (net)				21.1	26.1	29.8
5.5	4.6	4.2	Intangibles (net)				1.1	.6	7.6
6.6	7.2	5.5	All Other Non-Current				6.5	7.3	6.1
100.0	100.0	100.0	Total				100.0	100.0	100.0
			LIABILITIES						
13.9	9.8	12.3	Notes Payable-Short Term				10.4	12.0	13.2
4.0	3.5	3.5	Cur. Mat.-L/T/D				4.1	2.8	3.1
15.0	14.6	15.7	Trade Payables				22.9	16.4	12.8
.3	.3	.2	Income Taxes Payable				.6	.0	.1
7.5	8.2	8.4	All Other Current				7.8	6.3	6.5
40.8	36.5	40.2	Total Current				45.9	37.5	35.7
14.3	15.3	15.7	Long-Term Debt				10.8	10.8	15.8
.4	.8	.4	Deferred Taxes				.2	.0	1.0
6.2	5.3	5.2	All Other Non-Current				.9	3.3	7.7
38.3	42.1	38.5	Net Worth				42.3	48.4	39.8
100.0	100.0	100.0	Total Liabilities & Net Worth				100.0	100.0	100.0
			INCOME DATA						
100.0	100.0	100.0	Net Sales				100.0	100.0	100.0
25.8	25.8	29.7	Gross Profit				30.0	25.4	24.8
21.2	20.7	23.1	Operating Expenses				26.0	19.3	18.4
4.6	5.0	6.6	Operating Profit				4.0	6.1	6.4
1.2	.7	1.6	All Other Expenses (net)				.3	1.0	2.7
3.4	4.3	5.0	Profit Before Taxes				3.7	5.1	3.7
			RATIOS						
2.5	2.5	2.7					2.2	2.9	2.7
1.6	1.7	1.5	Current				1.3	1.6	1.5
1.0	1.2	1.1					1.1	1.2	1.2
1.7	1.6	1.5					1.7	1.6	1.5
1.0	.8	.8	Quick				.9	.8	.8
.6	.6	.5					.7	.5	.5
33 11.1	29 12.4	32 11.3					28 12.8	30 12.0	33 11.0
42 8.6	40 9.1	41 8.8	Sales/Receivables				36 10.3	41 8.9	43 8.4
51 7.1	50 7.3	50 7.3					51 7.2	49 7.5	55 6.6
26 14.1	31 11.9	29 12.4					20 18.6	41 8.9	36 10.3
45 8.1	51 7.2	47 7.8	Cost of Sales/Inventory				31 11.6	55 6.7	49 7.4
66 5.5	79 4.6	73 5.0					67 5.5	88 4.1	73 5.0
16 23.0	16 22.3	18 20.3					21 17.3	17 21.2	18 20.4
27 13.4	29 12.5	31 11.8	Cost of Sales/Payables				41 9.0	34 10.7	24 15.3
44 8.3	43 8.4	45 8.0					47 7.7	42 8.6	46 7.9
4.8	5.4	5.0					8.4	5.2	5.1
11.4	11.0	12.0	Sales/Working Capital				21.9	10.5	10.4
215.2	30.3	36.9					45.5	21.2	37.8
6.7	10.3	10.5					19.8	15.8	6.2
(78) 2.5	(107) 3.9	(85) 3.8	EBIT/Interest		(15) 4.6			(17) 7.2	(32) 3.0
.9	1.5	1.8					.8	2.7	1.6
5.3	4.5	6.2	Net Profit + Depr., Dep.,						10.8
(22) 2.3	(28) 2.2	(22) 2.4	Amort./Cur. Mat. L/T/D						(11) 5.0
.4	1.4	1.5							1.6
.3	.3	.3					.1	.2	.3
.7	.8	.6	Fixed/Worth				.4	.5	.9
1.6	1.6	1.7					1.0	1.0	2.3
.8	.7	.7					.7	.5	.9
1.7	1.8	1.8	Debt/Worth				1.9	1.5	2.5
4.9	4.1	3.5					2.7	2.1	3.9
29.4	34.1	39.8	% Profit Before Taxes/Tangible				37.3	47.9	27.0
(77) 13.1	(108) 16.3	(84) 17.1	Net Worth				9.9	(20) 18.6	(30) 18.9
-1.0	3.0	5.1					-2.3	4.7	5.4
11.3	14.1	16.0	% Profit Before Taxes/Total				14.4	21.7	9.0
4.5	7.1	5.8	Assets				4.6	8.8	4.5
.2	1.1	1.5					-.8	3.1	1.3
23.8	26.4	29.1					40.8	27.7	22.7
8.1	8.0	8.5	Sales/Net Fixed Assets				27.7	9.5	7.1
4.0	4.0	4.7					6.2	4.3	4.2
3.3	2.9	3.0					4.3	3.2	2.6
2.0	2.1	2.2	Sales/Total Assets				3.0	2.5	2.0
1.4	1.5	1.6					1.8	1.7	1.3
1.3	1.3	1.3					.9	.9	1.4
(68) 2.8	(102) 2.6	(84) 2.0	% Depr., Dep., Amort./Sales		(15) 1.4			(20) 1.6	(30) 2.6
4.5	4.2	3.9					3.5	3.1	4.6
1.1	1.3	1.5	% Officers', Directors',						
(33) 3.0	(45) 3.1	(32) 3.2	Owners' Comp/Sales						
4.4	5.3	4.6							
2856781M	4059490M	2373153M	Net Sales ($)	2063M	16901M	34327M	131882M	309201M	1878779M
1529879M	2449116M	1335501M	Total Assets ($)	2562M	8723M	18199M	52829M	145061M	1108127M

M = $ thousand   MM = $ million
See Pages 11 through 21 for Explanation of Ratios and Data

Current Data Sorted By Assets

Comparative Historical Data

1	4	34	54	10	3	Type of Statement		
4	28	129	30		1	Unqualified	103	99
10	53	60	2	1		Reviewed	200	182
25	35	18				Compiled	186	182
17	52	85	38	9	1	Tax Returns	41	39
						Other	203	252

	176 (4/1-9/30/04)			528 (10/1/04-3/31/05)			4/1/00-3/31/01	4/1/01-3/31/02
0-500M	500M-2MM	2-10MM	10-50MM	50-100MM	100-250MM		ALL	ALL
57	172	326	124	20	5	**NUMBER OF STATEMENTS**	733	754
%	%	%	%	%	%	**ASSETS**	%	%
12.6	8.5	8.0	6.5	3.6		Cash & Equivalents	7.0	6.8
37.7	33.4	28.2	27.5	23.6		Trade Receivables (net)	29.0	27.5
9.3	9.3	9.9	13.1	8.4		Inventory	9.7	9.4
3.1	1.1	1.5	1.6	1.0		All Other Current	1.3	1.8
62.7	52.4	47.7	48.7	36.7		Total Current	47.0	45.6
28.0	36.3	44.5	44.5	46.6		Fixed Assets (net)	43.4	44.6
3.8	3.5	2.9	1.9	12.3		Intangibles (net)	3.3	3.5
5.5	7.8	4.9	4.9	4.4		All Other Non-Current	6.3	6.3
100.0	100.0	100.0	100.0	100.0		Total	100.0	100.0
						LIABILITIES		
14.1	8.6	7.9	8.5	7.5		Notes Payable-Short Term	8.3	8.8
9.1	8.1	7.5	6.5	6.1		Cur. Mat.-L/T/D	7.4	7.7
16.8	16.1	13.8	13.2	12.8		Trade Payables	14.2	13.5
.8	.4	.2	.2	.1		Income Taxes Payable	.2	.2
12.0	7.5	6.5	9.7	9.7		All Other Current	7.6	7.7
52.9	40.6	35.9	38.1	36.3		Total Current	37.8	37.8
31.1	31.5	26.8	21.9	27.7		Long-Term Debt	29.5	32.8
.3	.5	1.0	1.2	2.5		Deferred Taxes	.8	.8
5.0	7.5	3.8	4.1	5.9		All Other Non-Current	3.1	4.5
10.7	19.8	32.5	34.8	27.6		Net Worth	28.9	24.1
100.0	100.0	100.0	100.0	100.0		Total Liabilities & Net Worth	100.0	100.0
						INCOME DATA		
100.0	100.0	100.0	100.0	100.0		Net Sales	100.0	100.0
51.7	42.0	32.7	26.4	25.8		Gross Profit	33.6	33.9
48.7	38.7	29.0	21.5	20.3		Operating Expenses	29.7	31.3
3.0	3.3	3.7	4.9	5.4		Operating Profit	3.9	2.7
.7	1.1	1.2	1.0	2.3		All Other Expenses (net)	1.7	1.9
2.2	2.1	2.5	3.9	3.2		Profit Before Taxes	2.2	.8
						RATIOS		
2.3	2.3	1.9	1.8	1.5			1.9	1.9
1.3	1.3	1.3	1.3	1.0		Current	1.3	1.3
.9	.9	1.0	1.0	.7			.9	.9
1.8	1.9	1.4	1.2	1.3			1.5	1.4
1.0	1.1	1.0	.9	.7		Quick	1.0	.9
.6	.7	.7	.6	.5			.7	.6
24 15.0	34 10.7	41 9.0	43 8.4	51 7.2			38 9.6	36 10.2
35 10.4	44 8.2	51 7.2	51 7.1	54 6.7		Sales/Receivables	49 7.4	47 7.8
45 8.1	56 6.5	60 6.1	63 5.8	73 5.0			60 6.1	57 6.4
7 50.6	6 65.0	12 29.4	19 18.8	16 22.3			12 31.2	11 32.9
15 23.9	16 23.5	22 16.8	27 13.7	25 14.6		Cost of Sales/Inventory	21 17.8	21 17.6
30 12.4	32 11.5	34 10.8	44 8.3	39 9.4			33 11.0	32 11.3
9 38.9	20 18.1	20 18.0	21 17.7	21 17.2			20 18.2	19 19.4
23 16.0	31 11.7	32 11.3	29 12.7	35 10.5		Cost of Sales/Payables	31 11.9	30 12.0
49 7.5	54 6.8	51 7.1	44 8.3	65 5.6			47 7.7	47 7.7
10.9	8.5	8.2	9.1	10.5			9.2	9.9
32.7	23.1	19.3	18.4	NM		Sales/Working Capital	22.2	21.7
-88.4	-70.6	-170.0	514.2	-11.5			-60.1	-51.8
9.0	5.8	5.8	8.6	6.2			4.3	3.4
(52) 1.6	(159) 2.0	(310) 2.4	(120) 3.1	2.9		EBIT/Interest	(699) 1.9	(721) 1.5
-1.6	.5	1.1	1.6	1.5			.7	.1
	2.8	2.4	3.3	3.5			2.5	2.4
	(37) 1.4	(118) 1.5	(54) 1.6	(12) 1.4		Net Profit + Depr., Dep., Amort./Cur. Mat. L /T/D	(239) 1.5	(244) 1.3
	.9	1.0	1.2	.9			.8	.7
.5	.6	.8	.9	1.8			.9	.9
1.7	1.5	1.8	1.4	3.4		Fixed/Worth	1.8	1.8
-1.8	62.3	3.3	2.5	NM			4.1	5.0
.9	1.3	1.2	1.1	2.2			1.3	1.2
11.2	3.6	2.4	2.3	5.5		Debt/Worth	2.7	2.7
-5.2	103.4	5.6	4.3	NM			7.8	8.5
98.1	55.6	34.3	34.7	45.1			35.8	26.1
(31) 12.3	(130) 13.3	(294) 15.3	(116) 18.7	(15) 23.1		% Profit Before Taxes/Tangible Net Worth	(636) 13.6	(630) 9.1
-18.2	.0	1.2	7.6	12.5			1.2	-7.6
23.4	14.2	10.2	11.0	7.8			10.3	8.2
3.0	3.9	4.0	4.6	6.3		% Profit Before Taxes/Total Assets	3.5	2.2
-9.6	-1.9	.2	1.8	1.6			-1.0	-3.4
34.1	13.3	7.1	6.2	5.4			8.3	8.3
16.3	7.9	4.5	3.8	2.8		Sales/Net Fixed Assets	4.6	4.5
7.7	4.7	2.9	2.8	2.1			3.1	2.8
5.8	3.4	2.4	2.2	1.7			2.6	2.7
3.6	2.6	1.9	1.8	1.4		Sales/Total Assets	2.1	2.0
2.8	2.1	1.6	1.4	1.1			1.6	1.5
1.6	2.4	3.2	3.2	4.3			2.8	2.9
(42) 3.2	(154) 4.6	(312) 4.6	(118) 4.4	4.9		% Depr., Dep., Amort./Sales	(676) 4.3	(709) 4.5
4.8	7.1	6.5	6.0	6.8			6.1	6.5
5.9	3.4	2.3	1.8				2.5	2.8
(43) 7.5	(100) 5.3	(163) 3.5	(31) 3.1			% Officers', Directors', Owners' Comp/Sales	(330) 4.2	(350) 4.7
13.4	7.9	5.1					7.4	8.7
73134M	512746M	3053013M	4657795M	1907656M	799648M	Net Sales ($)	10180949M	11004918M
16127M	190387M	1539272M	2518625M	1326418M	694488M	Total Assets ($)	5750166M	6543164M

M = $ thousand   MM = $ million
See Pages 11 through 21 for Explanation of Ratios and Data

Comparative Historical Data / Current Data Sorted By Sales

			Type of Statement	176 (4/1-9/30/04)		528 (10/1/04-3/31/05)			
				0-1MM	1-3MM	3-5MM	5-10MM	10-25MM	25MM & OVER
109	100	106	Unqualified	1	4	5	13	30	54
207	195	192	Reviewed		21	20	74	56	20
144	187	126	Compiled	7	36	29	34	16	4
56	62	78	Tax Returns	12	36	12	14	4	
180	210	202	Other	10	44	30	32	45	41
4/1/02-3/31/03 ALL	4/1/03-3/31/04 ALL	4/1/04-3/31/05 ALL							
696	754	704	NUMBER OF STATEMENTS	30	141	96	167	151	119
%	%	%	**ASSETS**	%	%	%	%	%	%
7.4	7.5	8.1	Cash & Equivalents	9.6	9.0	9.9	8.1	7.8	5.6
27.8	27.9	30.0	Trade Receivables (net)	32.3	32.0	30.4	29.4	27.9	30.1
9.8	10.1	10.2	Inventory	9.3	8.8	8.8	9.9	11.3	12.5
1.7	2.6	1.6	All Other Current	4.3	1.1	1.5	1.4	1.5	1.7
46.8	48.1	49.9	Total Current	55.5	50.9	50.6	48.9	48.5	49.8
44.6	42.8	41.1	Fixed Assets (net)	33.1	37.0	40.9	43.7	43.2	42.0
3.2	3.6	3.4	Intangibles (net)	4.1	4.4	2.8	2.0	3.3	4.4
5.5	5.5	5.6	All Other Non-Current	7.3	7.6	5.7	5.5	5.0	3.8
100.0	100.0	100.0	Total	100.0	100.0	100.0	100.0	100.0	100.0
			LIABILITIES						
7.7	8.9	8.6	Notes Payable-Short Term	13.4	8.9	9.0	8.0	7.7	8.6
8.2	7.1	7.5	Cur. Mat.-L/T/D	7.6	8.9	7.7	7.6	7.3	5.9
13.7	14.0	14.5	Trade Payables	15.3	14.2	14.2	14.5	14.2	15.0
.2	.2	.3	Income Taxes Payable	.6	.4	.4	.4	.2	.1
8.4	10.2	7.9	All Other Current	6.9	7.7	5.8	7.9	7.1	10.9
38.3	40.3	38.8	Total Current	43.8	40.1	37.1	38.4	36.5	40.6
30.8	27.1	27.5	Long-Term Debt	31.3	36.4	27.1	25.1	25.7	21.6
.7	.8	.9	Deferred Taxes	.6	.6	.6	1.3	.9	1.1
4.3	5.8	4.9	All Other Non-Current	5.5	8.7	3.8	3.4	4.0	4.6
25.8	26.0	27.9	Net Worth	18.9	14.2	31.3	31.8	32.9	32.1
100.0	100.0	100.0	Total Liabilities & Net Worth	100.0	100.0	100.0	100.0	100.0	100.0
			INCOME DATA						
100.0	100.0	100.0	Net Sales	100.0	100.0	100.0	100.0	100.0	100.0
34.6	34.0	35.1	Gross Profit	55.0	43.8	39.6	33.0	30.2	25.4
32.0	31.1	31.3	Operating Expenses	51.9	41.3	35.1	29.2	26.5	20.2
2.5	2.9	3.8	Operating Profit	3.1	2.5	4.4	3.8	3.8	5.2
1.8	1.4	1.1	All Other Expenses (net)	1.1	1.3	1.2	1.1	1.0	1.2
.8	1.5	2.7	Profit Before Taxes	2.0	1.2	3.2	2.7	2.8	4.0
			RATIOS						
2.0	1.8	1.9	Current	2.8	2.4	2.3	2.0	1.9	1.7
1.3	1.2	1.3		1.5	1.3	1.2	1.3	1.3	1.2
.9	.9	1.0		.9	.9	1.0	1.0	1.0	.9
1.5	1.4	1.5	Quick	2.4	1.9	1.7	1.5	1.4	1.2
.9	.9	1.0		1.1	1.1	1.0	1.0	1.0	.8
.6	.6	.7		.5	.6	.7	.7	.7	.6
37 9.9	36 10.2	38 9.5	Sales/Receivables	26 13.9	33 11.2	37 10.0	40 9.1	41 8.9	45 8.2
47 7.7	46 7.9	49 7.5		37 10.0	44 8.3	47 7.7	49 7.4	50 7.3	52 7.0
59 6.2	58 6.3	60 6.1		52 7.0	56 6.5	57 6.4	58 6.3	61 6.0	67 5.4
11 32.4	11 33.4	12 30.8	Cost of Sales/Inventory	7 55.0	7 49.7	8 46.0	12 30.1	14 25.9	18 19.9
21 17.5	21 17.4	22 16.8		19 18.8	16 22.5	18 20.5	19 19.2	25 14.4	25 14.4
34 10.7	36 10.2	36 10.2		32 11.3	36 10.1	32 11.4	30 12.3	43 8.5	41 8.8
18 20.1	19 19.0	20 18.5	Cost of Sales/Payables	15 24.1	16 22.9	19 19.4	21 17.0	21 17.8	21 17.0
31 11.9	30 12.2	31 11.7		36 10.3	30 12.3	35 10.5	30 12.2	31 11.8	32 11.4
47 7.7	47 7.8	50 7.3		66 5.6	55 6.7	54 6.8	46 7.9	51 7.1	44 8.3
8.5	9.9	8.7	Sales/Working Capital	6.8	7.2	7.4	9.0	8.6	10.4
24.5	26.3	21.2		20.5	22.7	23.8	21.0	19.3	19.5
-64.6	-45.8	-120.2		-108.4	-45.4	-314.4	-83.1	584.3	-64.1
3.7	4.3	6.5	EBIT/Interest	6.7	5.4	5.7	6.0	6.1	10.8
(665) 1.6	(714) 1.8	(666) 2.4		(27) .9	(131) 1.8	(88) 2.4	(161) 2.4	(144) 2.4	(115) 4.4
.3	.2	.9		-2.2	.2	1.3	.9	1.1	1.7
2.6	2.5	2.5	Net Profit + Depr., Dep., Amort./Cur. Mat. L/T/D		2.6	2.7	2.4	2.4	3.7
(233) 1.6	(231) 1.5	(227) 1.5		(29) 1.3	(22) 1.2	(66) 1.6	(58) 1.5	(49) 1.6	
.9	.7	1.0		.8	.9	.9	1.2	1.1	
.9	.8	.8	Fixed/Worth	.6	.7	.6	.7	.9	.9
1.9	1.8	1.7		2.5	2.4	1.3	1.5	1.7	1.7
4.7	5.6	4.1		-2.8	-3.3	3.0	3.2	3.0	3.2
1.3	1.3	1.2	Debt/Worth	.8	1.2	1.1	1.1	1.4	1.3
2.9	2.8	2.7		10.9	4.8	2.5	2.3	2.4	2.8
8.4	11.1	7.5		-7.6	-11.3	5.5	5.4	5.1	5.5
25.6	30.8	37.3	% Profit Before Taxes/Tangible Net Worth	62.9	45.3	47.1	36.0	31.6	40.7
(583) 7.8	(624) 10.9	(589) 15.9		(17) 7.2	(93) 11.3	(87) 18.3	(152) 13.6	(134) 13.6	(106) 23.8
-6.9	-5.1	2.2		-25.5	-5.6	6.1	-3.2	2.1	13.2
7.5	8.6	11.4	% Profit Before Taxes/Total Assets	14.2	13.1	13.8	10.4	10.0	11.5
2.1	2.7	4.2		-.3	2.5	4.2	4.4	3.6	6.7
-2.7	-2.6	-.1		-11.8	-2.8	1.8	-.1	.2	2.4
7.9	9.0	9.8	Sales/Net Fixed Assets	20.8	12.7	12.8	7.8	7.4	7.2
4.5	4.9	5.0		11.1	7.1	5.9	4.5	4.7	4.6
3.0	3.1	3.2		5.3	3.8	3.0	2.9	2.9	3.3
2.6	2.8	2.8	Sales/Total Assets	4.3	3.2	3.2	2.5	2.5	2.3
2.0	2.0	2.1		3.2	2.4	2.3	2.0	2.0	2.0
1.5	1.5	1.6		2.2	1.6	1.6	1.6	1.5	1.5
3.5	2.9	3.0	% Depr., Dep., Amort./Sales	1.8	2.9	2.3	3.4	3.1	2.9
(661) 5.1	(698) 4.7	(649) 4.5		(26) 3.9	(121) 5.0	(88) 3.8	(157) 4.8	(145) 4.5	(112) 4.2
7.0	6.7	6.3		5.3	7.7	5.9	6.8	6.2	5.1
2.8	2.7	2.6	% Officers', Directors', Owners' Comp/Sales	5.0	4.8	3.4	2.4	1.8	1.1
(334) 4.7	(344) 4.5	(340) 4.3		(17) 7.5	(83) 6.9	(55) 4.6	(103) 3.5	(61) 2.9	(21) 2.8
7.6	8.6	7.4		22.3	9.7	6.9	5.5	5.5	6.9
10468077M	11900788M	11003992M	Net Sales ($)	20287M	282277M	382478M	1214100M	2186472M	6918378M
6234194M	7317599M	6285317M	Total Assets ($)	7536M	138903M	185425M	641323M	1250455M	4061675M

© RMA 2005

M = $ thousand   MM = $ million
See Pages 11 through 21 for Explanation of Ratios and Data

Current Data Sorted By Assets   **Comparative Historical Data**

						Type of Statement		
3	4	5 6	6 1	1		Unqualified		
2	3	3				Reviewed		
5	5		1			Compiled		
2	3	5	3		1	Tax Returns		
						Other		
	14 (4/1-9/30/04)		**45 (10/1/04-3/31/05)**				**4/1/00-3/31/01**	**4/1/01-3/31/02**
0-500M	**500M-2MM**	**2-10MM**	**10-50MM**	**50-100MM**	**100-250MM**		**ALL**	**ALL**
12	15	19	11	1	1	NUMBER OF STATEMENTS		
%	%	%	%	%	%	ASSETS	%	%
11.7	7.3	8.3	3.8			Cash & Equivalents	D	D
23.7	35.6	28.3	29.3			Trade Receivables (net)	A	A
10.8	9.9	10.6	15.1			Inventory	T	T
.0	.3	1.9	1.3			All Other Current	A	A
46.2	53.1	49.1	49.6			Total Current		
29.5	36.9	42.1	44.7			Fixed Assets (net)	N	N
1.6	3.6	4.3	2.5			Intangibles (net)	O	O
22.8	6.5	4.4	3.2			All Other Non-Current	T	T
100.0	100.0	100.0	100.0			Total		
						LIABILITIES	A	A
7.2	11.3	16.4	7.6			Notes Payable-Short Term	V	V
7.5	5.9	6.3	4.3			Cur. Mat.-L/T/D	A	A
29.9	15.6	14.3	24.7			Trade Payables	I	I
.0	.2	.1	.1			Income Taxes Payable	L	L
8.7	2.7	5.4	7.9			All Other Current	A	A
53.3	35.7	42.5	44.7			Total Current	B	B
37.6	29.5	28.8	19.4			Long-Term Debt	L	L
.0	.4	.3	1.2			Deferred Taxes	E	E
6.3	4.3	6.7	9.8			All Other Non-Current		
2.8	30.2	21.7	25.0			Net Worth		
100.0	100.0	100.0	100.0			Total Liabilities & Net Worth		
						INCOME DATA		
100.0	100.0	100.0	100.0			Net Sales		
43.8	46.8	33.3	28.1			Gross Profit		
40.6	43.0	28.5	25.3			Operating Expenses		
3.1	3.8	4.7	2.8			Operating Profit		
.7	1.0	1.0	1.0			All Other Expenses (net)		
2.5	2.8	3.7	1.8			Profit Before Taxes		
						RATIOS		
3.7	1.7	2.0	2.1					
.9	1.5	1.6	1.3			Current		
.6	1.3	.8	1.0					
3.6	1.4	1.8	1.5					
.7	1.2	1.1	.9			Quick		
.3	1.1	.4	.7					
4 94.3	34 10.6	40 9.1	42 8.6					
22 16.7	46 8.0	46 8.0	50 7.3			Sales/Receivables		
32 11.5	59 6.2	58 6.3	72 5.1					
0 UND	15 24.8	2 222.1	22 16.6					
5 69.5	19 19.2	21 17.4	33 11.0			Cost of Sales/Inventory		
28 13.1	31 11.9	43 8.6	53 6.9					
11 32.4	17 21.0	18 20.0	23 15.9					
44 8.3	46 7.9	23 15.7	32 11.6			Cost of Sales/Payables		
74 4.9	62 5.9	58 6.3	37 10.0					
25.6	11.9	7.2	6.1					
-68.0	16.5	13.5	13.4			Sales/Working Capital		
-15.0	31.0	-16.5	256.8					
4.6	6.1	4.9	8.5					
(10) 2.3	1.2	2.2	3.7			EBIT/Interest		
-.4	-1.3	1.6	1.0					
						Net Profit + Depr., Dep., Amort./Cur. Mat. L /T/D		
.6	.6	1.2	.7					
7.4	1.3	1.7	1.0			Fixed/Worth		
-1.7	4.1	-41.1	2.7					
4.0	1.4	1.5	1.0					
NM	2.7	2.2	1.9			Debt/Worth		
-4.7	7.7	-93.3	4.4					
	49.1	54.3	24.7					
(12) 8.1	(14) 22.6	(10) 13.1				% Profit Before Taxes/Tangible Net Worth		
	-15.6	3.4	1.3					
16.8	13.4	9.1	9.0					
6.1	1.0	5.4	2.6			% Profit Before Taxes/Total Assets		
-3.2	-3.4	1.8	-.3					
48.8	15.4	7.5	6.6					
20.6	9.4	4.2	4.5			Sales/Net Fixed Assets		
13.5	5.0	3.3	3.7					
5.7	3.2	2.1	2.3					
3.8	2.6	2.0	2.0			Sales/Total Assets		
2.6	2.1	1.5	1.5					
	1.6	3.7	2.7					
(13) 3.5	(18) 5.1	4.1				% Depr., Dep., Amort./Sales		
	6.1	7.7	5.5					
	3.6							
(11) 4.9						% Officers', Directors', Owners' Comp/Sales		
	6.6							
15370M	45355M	205282M	557395M	56158M	242000M	Net Sales ($)		
3205M	16640M	101211M	226814M	64668M	178100M	Total Assets ($)		

M = $ thousand   MM = $ million
See Pages 11 through 21 for Explanation of Ratios and Data

Comparative Historical Data | Current Data Sorted By Sales

Type of Statement	4/1/02-3/31/03 ALL	4/1/03-3/31/04 ALL	4/1/04-3/31/05 ALL	0-1MM	1-3MM	3-5MM	5-10MM	10-25MM	25MM & OVER
Unqualified	4	6	12	1	4	2	1	4	7
Reviewed	4	7	14	1	2	4	4	2	1
Compiled	3	7	8	1	3	3	1		1
Tax Returns	4	5	11	3	3		1	4	1
Other	4	6	14	2	2		2	4	3
				\multicolumn{3}	14 (4/1-9/30/04)			45 (10/1/04-3/31/05)	
NUMBER OF STATEMENTS	19	31	59	7	12	9	9	10	12
ASSETS	%	%	%	%	%	%	%	%	%
Cash & Equivalents	6.1	9.5	7.6		6.6			5.6	1.5
Trade Receivables (net)	32.6	35.1	29.2		31.3			27.8	30.4
Inventory	10.8	9.9	11.2		12.6			15.1	15.0
All Other Current	1.4	.4	.9		.3			1.8	1.1
Total Current	50.9	55.0	48.9		50.8			50.3	48.0
Fixed Assets (net)	34.7	35.8	38.7		35.3			39.4	43.0
Intangibles (net)	8.8	2.2	4.0		4.5			4.4	6.1
All Other Non-Current	5.7	7.0	8.3		9.3			5.9	2.9
Total	100.0	100.0	100.0		100.0			100.0	100.0
LIABILITIES									
Notes Payable-Short Term	7.8	7.1	11.0		11.0			12.0	9.5
Cur. Mat.-L/T/D	8.0	10.7	6.0		7.6			6.0	3.8
Trade Payables	11.9	18.7	19.4		20.4			13.9	26.8
Income Taxes Payable	.0	.0	.1		.3			.2	.0
All Other Current	7.8	7.0	6.0		4.7			7.6	8.1
Total Current	35.6	43.6	42.5		43.9			39.7	48.2
Long-Term Debt	22.8	20.6	29.0		26.5			21.4	21.0
Deferred Taxes	.5	.2	.5		.4			1.0	.7
All Other Non-Current	1.7	7.4	6.6		3.9			10.0	10.1
Net Worth	39.5	28.2	21.4		25.1			27.8	20.0
Total Liabilities & Net Worth	100.0	100.0	100.0		100.0			100.0	100.0
INCOME DATA									
Net Sales	100.0	100.0	100.0		100.0			100.0	100.0
Gross Profit	40.3	38.6	37.7		50.2			27.7	26.3
Operating Expenses	37.2	35.7	33.6		45.9			23.5	21.9
Operating Profit	3.1	2.9	4.1		4.3			4.2	4.4
All Other Expenses (net)	1.3	1.4	1.0		.9			1.8	1.5
Profit Before Taxes	1.9	1.4	3.0		3.4			2.4	2.9
RATIOS									
Current	2.9 1.4 1.0	2.1 1.5 .9	2.0 1.4 .9		1.6 1.3 .9			2.1 1.4 .7	1.8 1.4 1.0
Quick	2.4 1.1 .6	2.0 1.2 .7	1.5 1.1 .5		1.4 1.1 .5			1.6 .9 .4	1.3 .9 .5
Sales/Receivables	36 10.0 41 8.9 63 5.7	40 9.2 48 7.6 66 5.5	31 11.8 44 8.3 55 6.6		28 13.2 39 9.3 58 6.3			42 8.7 52 7.0 65 5.6	43 8.5 50 7.3 71 5.1
Cost of Sales/Inventory	15 24.0 21 17.4 36 10.3	7 49.3 20 18.2 38 9.7	7 51.7 22 16.6 35 10.5		2 208.9 18 20.0 30 12.1			33 11.2 38 9.7 45 8.1	20 17.9 31 11.9 49 7.5
Cost of Sales/Payables	9 39.8 23 16.0 44 8.3	17 21.1 31 11.7 48 7.6	17 21.0 31 11.8 53 6.8		16 23.1 52 7.0 69 5.3			11 32.3 30 12.0 58 6.3	22 16.7 33 10.9 52 7.0
Sales/Working Capital	7.0 26.0 999.8	8.7 15.5 -76.3	10.5 19.6 -76.9		13.2 23.7 -65.6			5.4 20.2 -15.2	10.1 13.1 NM
EBIT/Interest	5.4 (17) 1.7 -.5	4.1 (29) 2.3 -.2	4.8 (57) 2.4 .9		8.7 2.0 .4			4.8 2.4 1.5	7.5 3.3 1.2
Net Profit + Depr., Dep., Amort./Cur. Mat. L/T/D		3.5 (10) 2.3 1.3	3.8 (16) 2.3 1.5						
Fixed/Worth	.5 1.1 -4.4	.5 1.4 2.4	.7 1.7 40.1		.6 3.0 -12.0			.5 2.2 NM	.8 1.7 30.8
Debt/Worth	.3 2.2 -14.9	.8 2.2 4.1	1.4 2.8 -93.3		1.1 4.9 -28.5			1.3 3.1 NM	1.2 2.1 57.6
% Profit Before Taxes/Tangible Net Worth	53.8 (14) 11.5 -.5	29.8 (26) 15.1 1.0	51.0 (44) 22.0 -3.3						30.1 (10) 22.8 2.7
% Profit Before Taxes/Total Assets	12.0 5.4 -3.8	9.5 5.3 -1.1	12.1 5.0 -.3		14.4 5.3 -.7			6.9 5.3 1.8	10.6 5.2 .4
Sales/Net Fixed Assets	12.2 7.8 5.5	14.4 8.1 3.5	13.8 6.5 3.6		15.3 10.0 5.4			6.9 5.0 3.8	7.9 4.3 3.6
Sales/Total Assets	3.2 2.3 1.6	3.3 2.4 1.6	3.0 2.1 1.8		5.1 2.5 1.9			2.2 2.0 1.4	2.5 2.0 1.6
% Depr., Dep., Amort./Sales	2.4 4.4 7.0	2.0 (29) 3.9 5.7	2.3 (52) 4.3 5.8		1.9 (11) 2.9 6.1			3.7 4.8 7.5	2.5 (10) 3.8 4.5
% Officers', Directors', Owners' Comp/Sales		2.1 (15) 4.8 9.8	2.8 (24) 4.4 7.5						
Net Sales ($)	215193M	926767M	1121560M	4381M	21999M	35584M	61063M	148324M	850209M
Total Assets ($)	119330M	418004M	590638M	1710M	8807M	13966M	33038M	80114M	453003M

© RMA 2005

M = $ thousand   MM = $ million
See Pages 11 through 21 for Explanation of Ratios and Data

Current Data Sorted By Assets   Comparative Historical Data

						Type of Statement		
	1	1	1	2		Unqualified		
1	10	13	5			Reviewed		
4	8	1				Compiled		
5	4	1				Tax Returns		
5	6	6	3		1	Other		
	17 (4/1-9/30/04)		60 (10/1/04-3/31/05)				4/1/00-3/31/01 ALL	4/1/01-3/31/02 ALL
0-500M	500M-2MM	2-10MM	10-50MM	50-100MM	100-250MM			
15	29	22	10		1	NUMBER OF STATEMENTS		
%	%	%	%	%	%	ASSETS	%	%
8.9	10.3	12.0	6.7	D		Cash & Equivalents		
32.8	28.3	25.0	33.3	A		Trade Receivables (net)	D	D
9.4	21.8	18.0	18.8	T		Inventory	A	A
3.0	2.1	1.8	3.2	A		All Other Current	T	T
54.0	62.5	56.8	62.0			Total Current	A	A
35.9	29.7	34.3	20.8	N		Fixed Assets (net)		
2.3	1.4	2.7	8.9	O		Intangibles (net)	N	N
7.8	6.4	6.2	8.2	T		All Other Non-Current	O	O
100.0	100.0	100.0	100.0			Total	T	T
				A		LIABILITIES		
16.1	6.9	13.8	13.6	V		Notes Payable-Short Term	A	A
13.4	4.8	7.2	3.1	A		Cur. Mat.-L/T/D	V	V
21.8	14.8	13.5	15.1	I		Trade Payables	A	A
.1	.0	.3	.1	L		Income Taxes Payable	I	I
12.6	7.7	9.9	10.0	A		All Other Current	L	L
64.1	34.2	44.7	41.9	B		Total Current	A	A
39.1	21.8	26.2	10.0	L		Long-Term Debt	B	B
.5	.5	.5	1.4	E		Deferred Taxes	L	L
11.3	3.4	7.5	3.7			All Other Non-Current	E	E
-15.0	40.1	21.1	43.1			Net Worth		
100.0	100.0	100.0	100.0			Total Liabilities & Net Worth		
						INCOME DATA		
100.0	100.0	100.0	100.0			Net Sales		
48.6	40.2	35.2	31.3			Gross Profit		
42.9	37.0	28.7	26.4			Operating Expenses		
5.7	3.2	6.5	4.9			Operating Profit		
.7	1.0	1.7	1.6			All Other Expenses (net)		
5.0	2.3	4.7	3.3			Profit Before Taxes		
						RATIOS		
2.4	2.5	2.3	2.0					
1.0	1.6	1.1	1.5			Current		
.3	1.3	.7	1.2					
1.7	1.5	1.6	1.4					
.9	1.0	.6	1.1			Quick		
.3	.7	.5	.7					
24 15.2	33 11.1	28 13.2	42 8.7					
30 12.0	40 9.1	44 8.4	55 6.6			Sales/Receivables		
43 8.4	47 7.8	60 6.1	77 4.7					
3 132.5	16 23.2	18 20.7	11 33.0					
15 23.9	35 10.5	41 8.9	43 8.4			Cost of Sales/Inventory		
29 12.5	91 4.0	63 5.8	76 4.8					
14 26.0	19 19.5	19 18.9	20 17.9					
35 10.5	25 14.4	34 10.6	32 11.5			Cost of Sales/Payables		
57 6.5	46 8.0	48 7.5	51 7.1					
7.8	5.6	6.4	6.1					
265.3	11.1	536.8	10.6			Sales/Working Capital		
-9.3	25.5	-13.2	39.9					
7.7	4.3	10.7	18.1					
2.9	(25) 2.6	(20) 1.8	3.6			EBIT/Interest		
1.9	.8	1.1	2.2					
						Net Profit + Depr., Dep., Amort./Cur. Mat. L /T/D		
.4	.4	.4	.2					
7.8	.8	1.4	.4			Fixed/Worth		
-.6	1.6	2.9	4.0					
1.7	.8	.8	.8					
17.6	1.8	2.3	1.4			Debt/Worth		
-2.6	5.0	6.0	10.1					
196.8	42.4	43.7						
(10) 65.9	(28) 9.8	(21) 9.7				% Profit Before Taxes/Tangible Net Worth		
1.2	-1.0	1.7						
24.8	11.3	14.7	13.5					
7.9	4.0	2.1	5.4			% Profit Before Taxes/Total Assets		
.9	-.4	.7	2.2					
41.6	22.1	13.0	37.2					
12.5	9.7	9.3	16.1			Sales/Net Fixed Assets		
7.3	6.2	4.1	5.6					
6.7	3.0	3.0	2.8					
3.4	2.6	2.4	1.9			Sales/Total Assets		
2.6	2.2	1.7	1.4					
.8	1.4	1.9	.6					
(10) 2.0	(28) 2.1	(21) 3.2	1.9			% Depr., Dep., Amort./Sales		
3.8	3.4	6.4	4.0					
4.0	6.7							
(12) 7.4	(15) 8.9					% Officers', Directors', Owners' Comp/Sales		
12.4	13.9							
15753M	92242M	237406M	421551M		1281443M	Net Sales ($)		
4293M	36555M	97932M	178873M		188118M	Total Assets ($)		

M = $ thousand   MM = $ million
See Pages 11 through 21 for Explanation of Ratios and Data

Comparative Historical Data   **Current Data Sorted By Sales**

			Type of Statement						
6	4	4	Unqualified		1		2	1	
12	20	29	Reviewed		7	4	9	3	
7	13	13	Compiled	2	7	1	3		
3	8	10	Tax Returns	2	5	3			
10	25	21	Other	3	6	3	3	2	4
					17 (4/1-9/30/04)		60 (10/1/04-3/31/05)		
4/1/02-	4/1/03-	4/1/04-		0-1MM	1-3MM	3-5MM	5-10MM	10-25MM	25MM & OVER
3/31/03	3/31/04	3/31/05							
ALL	ALL	ALL							
38	70	77	**NUMBER OF STATEMENTS**	7	24	15	10	13	8
%	%	%	**ASSETS**	%	%	%	%	%	%
9.9	8.6	10.1	Cash & Equivalents		6.7	13.0	11.1	8.9	
28.1	26.8	29.1	Trade Receivables (net)		27.9	30.7	31.4	28.9	
11.3	15.3	17.9	Inventory		15.8	23.2	19.1	17.0	
1.2	1.6	2.3	All Other Current		.5	3.3	1.2	4.2	
50.6	52.3	59.5	Total Current		51.0	70.3	62.8	58.9	
39.8	37.8	30.8	Fixed Assets (net)		42.4	21.5	25.9	26.3	
4.6	3.0	2.9	Intangibles (net)		2.0	.5	3.0	7.3	
5.1	6.9	6.8	All Other Non-Current		4.6	7.8	8.3	7.5	
100.0	100.0	100.0	Total		100.0	100.0	100.0	100.0	
			LIABILITIES						
11.3	11.4	11.7	Notes Payable-Short Term		9.2	7.4	10.5	15.0	
6.9	5.3	6.9	Cur. Mat.-L/T/D		8.6	3.1	5.1	8.1	
14.3	15.1	15.8	Trade Payables		17.1	13.3	18.1	14.6	
.3	.2	.1	Income Taxes Payable		.1	.1	.1	.3	
7.0	7.4	10.5	All Other Current		5.3	10.2	14.0	9.5	
39.7	39.4	44.9	Total Current		40.2	34.2	47.7	47.6	
24.9	24.6	24.9	Long-Term Debt		29.9	22.2	14.0	27.3	
.6	.8	.6	Deferred Taxes		.6	.7	.0	.7	
4.2	4.1	6.1	All Other Non-Current		2.1	4.5	.3	13.7	
30.7	31.2	23.5	Net Worth		27.2	38.5	38.1	10.7	
100.0	100.0	100.0	Total Liabilities & Net Worth		100.0	100.0	100.0	100.0	
			INCOME DATA						
100.0	100.0	100.0	Net Sales		100.0	100.0	100.0	100.0	
41.0	38.9	39.3	Gross Profit		46.9	35.8	35.3	33.8	
36.3	35.4	34.4	Operating Expenses		42.4	32.0	31.0	26.4	
4.7	3.5	4.9	Operating Profit		4.5	3.7	4.3	7.4	
2.3	1.0	1.2	All Other Expenses (net)		1.1	.9	.6	2.7	
2.4	2.4	3.7	Profit Before Taxes		3.4	2.9	3.7	4.7	
			RATIOS						
2.2	2.2	2.3			2.2	3.5	2.0	1.7	
1.4	1.4	1.4	Current		1.5	2.1	1.3	1.0	
.9	.9	.9			1.0	1.2	.9	.9	
1.6	1.7	1.5			1.5	1.7	1.7	1.2	
1.0	.9	.9	Quick		.9	1.1	.9	.6	
.6	.6	.6			.6	.9	.5	.5	
34 10.7	31 11.9	30 12.2		29 12.7	35 10.4	23 15.7	23 16.0		
45 8.1	41 8.9	41 8.8	Sales/Receivables	37 9.7	42 8.8	42 8.7	51 7.2		
53 6.8	51 7.2	52 7.0		46 7.9	55 6.6	52 7.0	68 5.4		
12 30.4	12 31.2	14 25.9		8 45.2	19 19.2	7 55.7	22 16.8		
30 12.1	27 13.8	31 11.9	Cost of Sales/Inventory	21 17.3	45 8.0	43 8.5	39 9.3		
48 7.6	53 6.9	63 5.8		65 5.6	91 4.0	61 6.0	58 6.3		
24 15.0	18 20.8	19 19.5		18 20.8	19 19.1	19 18.9	19 19.3		
31 11.6	30 12.3	27 13.6	Cost of Sales/Payables	29 12.5	23 15.7	42 8.6	37 9.8		
53 6.9	47 7.8	49 7.4		51 7.1	40 9.2	45 8.1	58 6.3		
7.4	8.0	6.7			7.8	4.0	9.7	7.2	
22.2	16.9	14.4	Sales/Working Capital		21.3	8.9	19.8	86.7	
−25.7	−51.1	−85.7			−322.1	15.2	NM	−44.0	
7.8	6.7	7.9			5.0	4.2	50.7	12.0	
(36) 2.4	(67) 1.9	(70) 2.6	EBIT/Interest	(23) 2.5	(12) 2.6	2.2	(12) 2.4		
.1	.2	1.3			1.3	1.1	1.3	.7	
14.0	5.9	5.2	Net Profit + Depr., Dep.,						
(18) 2.0	(18) 2.6	(21) 2.0	Amort./Cur. Mat. L/T/D						
.8	1.4	1.2							
.7	.6	.4			.5	.2	.4	.4	
1.4	1.1	1.0	Fixed/Worth		1.4	.9	.8	1.0	
NM	7.4	3.6			6.4	1.4	2.0	66.2	
.9	.8	1.0			1.0	.5	.9	1.1	
2.1	1.8	2.3	Debt/Worth		2.1	2.4	2.3	1.6	
NM	17.2	8.1			9.5	5.0	4.4	151.3	
32.1	36.7	52.9	% Profit Before Taxes/Tangible		122.6	51.3	37.3	44.4	
(29) 14.3	(56) 9.7	(68) 11.4	Net Worth	(22) 9.0	(14) 18.1	12.1	(11) 9.7		
.7	−4.1	1.3			.7	8.3	2.8	−16.5	
12.6	14.3	14.1	% Profit Before Taxes/Total		13.8	11.0	16.7	21.5	
4.2	3.2	4.8	Assets		4.4	7.5	4.7	1.5	
−2.5	−3.1	.7			.6	2.3	.8	−.5	
11.4	13.3	23.6			11.6	23.9	23.2	23.5	
4.6	7.0	9.9	Sales/Net Fixed Assets		6.7	14.9	12.2	11.0	
3.1	4.0	5.7			4.1	8.1	7.6	5.1	
3.0	3.1	3.3			3.5	3.1	3.2	3.4	
1.9	2.3	2.5	Sales/Total Assets		2.5	2.6	2.5	2.4	
1.5	1.8	1.9			1.8	1.9	2.4	1.7	
2.3	1.8	1.4			1.7	1.4		1.3	
(36) 4.7	(66) 3.3	(69) 2.2	% Depr., Dep., Amort./Sales	(21) 2.8	1.9	(12) 2.6			
6.3	5.4	4.6			5.9	3.4	4.3		
3.2	4.9	2.6			6.5				
(18) 5.7	(32) 6.9	(38) 7.4	% Officers', Directors',	(17) 10.4					
8.5	12.9	12.3	Owners' Comp/Sales		14.4				
368072M	1242423M	2048395M	Net Sales ($)	4720M	43459M	59635M	67624M	227922M	1645035M
213121M	407521M	505771M	Total Assets ($)	2576M	20517M	26775M	25317M	104137M	326449M

M = $ thousand   MM = $ million
See Pages 11 through 21 for Explanation of Ratios and Data

Current Data Sorted By Assets | Comparative Historical Data

	0-500M	500M-2MM	2-10MM	10-50MM	50-100MM	100-250MM	Type of Statement	4/1/00-3/31/01 ALL	4/1/01-3/31/02 ALL
			2	8	2		Unqualified		
		7	12	7			Reviewed		
	6	16	6	2			Compiled		
	6	7	1				Tax Returns		
	8	8	10	1			Other		
	29 (4/1-9/30/04)			80 (10/1/04-3/31/05)					
NUMBER OF STATEMENTS	20	38	31	18	2				
	%	%	%	%	%	%	**ASSETS**	%	%
Cash & Equivalents	6.6	6.1	5.0	6.6					
Trade Receivables (net)	33.0	31.4	28.7	24.9		D		D	D
Inventory	5.0	10.6	9.5	12.4		A		A	A
All Other Current	1.4	.9	1.1	.5		T		T	T
Total Current	46.1	49.0	44.3	44.3		A		A	A
Fixed Assets (net)	42.3	42.8	44.5	47.8					
Intangibles (net)	7.8	2.0	2.2	1.0		N		N	N
All Other Non-Current	3.8	6.1	9.1	6.9		O		O	O
Total	100.0	100.0	100.0	100.0		T		T	T
						A	**LIABILITIES**	A	A
Notes Payable-Short Term	4.7	8.8	14.6	10.8		V		V	V
Cur. Mat.-L/T/D	4.9	10.2	7.1	6.4		A		A	A
Trade Payables	19.4	14.6	13.1	12.3		I		I	I
Income Taxes Payable	.1	.0	.0	.1		L		L	L
All Other Current	6.1	7.3	8.8	6.3		A		A	A
Total Current	35.1	40.8	43.7	35.9		B		B	B
Long-Term Debt	46.7	31.3	22.0	24.5		L		L	L
Deferred Taxes	.1	.3	1.8	1.9		E		E	E
All Other Non-Current	2.9	2.0	7.2	7.0					
Net Worth	15.3	25.6	25.3	30.7					
Total Liabilities & Net Worth	100.0	100.0	100.0	100.0					
							INCOME DATA		
Net Sales	100.0	100.0	100.0	100.0					
Gross Profit									
Operating Expenses	96.8	96.4	96.0	92.5					
Operating Profit	3.2	3.6	4.0	7.5					
All Other Expenses (net)	1.0	1.6	1.9	2.1					
Profit Before Taxes	2.2	2.0	2.1	5.4					
							RATIOS		
Current	5.3	1.5	1.6	1.6					
	1.5	1.2	1.1	1.1					
	.8	.8	.7	.9					
Quick	4.8	1.3	1.3	1.1					
	(19) 1.6	.9	.8	.8					
	.8	.6	.5	.6					
Sales/Receivables	25 14.9	33 11.2	41 8.9	42 8.6					
	31 11.7	39 9.4	53 6.8	46 7.9					
	41 9.0	47 7.7	64 5.7	59 6.2					
Cost of Sales/Inventory									
Cost of Sales/Payables									
Sales/Working Capital	8.8	12.2	10.5	11.0					
	39.6	52.5	58.3	59.3					
	-37.6	-20.9	-9.4	-64.1					
EBIT/Interest	10.5	2.7	2.9	10.2					
	(16) 1.7	(37) 1.8	1.4	(17) 3.7					
	-2.3	-.1	-.4	.8					
Net Profit + Depr., Dep., Amort./Cur. Mat. L /T/D			(15) 2.4						
			1.0						
			.8						
Fixed/Worth	.6	1.0	.8	.8					
	3.3	1.8	2.0	2.0					
	-1.6	3.1	3.6	3.5					
Debt/Worth	.7	1.8	1.4	1.2					
	10.3	3.1	3.2	2.5					
	-5.1	5.4	7.7	5.3					
% Profit Before Taxes/Tangible Net Worth	(13) 99.3	(34) 28.9	(26) 16.8	(17) 26.4					
	19.0	8.3	5.5	14.3					
	-19.7	-.9	-14.8	-3.7					
% Profit Before Taxes/Total Assets	25.6	6.7	6.1	9.5					
	6.8	2.1	1.1	6.9					
	-6.3	-2.3	-5.0	.3					
Sales/Net Fixed Assets	14.6	14.4	9.1	5.4					
	8.7	5.5	3.9	3.4					
	5.1	4.0	3.0	2.8					
Sales/Total Assets	4.4	3.0	2.5	2.2					
	3.9	2.5	1.9	1.9					
	2.6	1.8	1.4	1.3					
% Depr., Dep., Amort./Sales	(16) 1.1	(36) 4.1	(30) 3.4	3.4					
	3.5	5.0	4.6	4.3					
	4.8	7.6	8.3	6.0					
% Officers', Directors', Owners' Comp/Sales	(13) 6.3	(24) 2.9	(18) 2.6						
	10.1	6.0	3.0						
	11.9	8.7	5.5						
Net Sales ($)	22792M	108207M	252149M	632007M	125324M				
Total Assets ($)	5972M	42635M	131545M	331591M	120039M				

© RMA 2005

M = $ thousand   MM = $ million
See Pages 11 through 21 for Explanation of Ratios and Data

Comparative Historical Data | | | Current Data Sorted By Sales

15	16	12	Type of Statement					3	9
			Unqualified					7	3
31	40	26	Reviewed		4	4	8	1	
35	39	30	Compiled	3	12	10	4	1	
11	15	14	Tax Returns	5	5	3	4	1	1
31	32	27	Other	3	13	1	6	3	1
4/1/02-3/31/03 ALL	4/1/03-3/31/04 ALL	4/1/04-3/31/05 ALL		29 (4/1-9/30/04)			80 (10/1/04-3/31/05)		
				0-1MM	1-3MM	3-5MM	5-10MM	10-25MM	25MM & OVER
123	142	109	**NUMBER OF STATEMENTS**	11	34	18	18	15	13
%	%	%	**ASSETS**	%	%	%	%	%	%
6.9	6.9	6.0	Cash & Equivalents	8.5	5.9	6.3	5.1	8.3	2.6
28.0	28.0	29.7	Trade Receivables (net)	23.2	29.8	29.2	35.5	29.9	27.1
9.4	8.9	9.4	Inventory	4.0	8.2	11.5	8.3	11.2	13.7
1.8	.9	1.0	All Other Current	.6	1.6	.6	.8	.9	.5
46.0	44.7	46.1	Total Current	36.2	45.5	47.6	49.6	50.3	44.0
43.5	43.6	43.9	Fixed Assets (net)	51.3	45.8	43.0	40.9	37.6	44.9
2.8	4.7	3.4	Intangibles (net)	9.9	3.7	2.1	.2	2.2	5.0
7.6	7.0	6.7	All Other Non-Current	2.6	5.0	7.3	9.3	9.9	6.2
100.0	100.0	100.0	Total	100.0	100.0	100.0	100.0	100.0	100.0
			LIABILITIES						
9.6	9.5	9.9	Notes Payable-Short Term	1.3	8.8	12.5	11.0	13.1	11.1
7.8	7.2	7.6	Cur. Mat.-L/T/D	3.1	9.4	8.5	6.3	8.2	6.5
16.1	14.2	14.5	Trade Payables	12.8	15.9	12.7	15.7	13.6	14.1
.1	.2	.0	Income Taxes Payable	.0	.1	.1	.0	.1	.0
6.8	6.9	7.4	All Other Current	5.9	6.5	5.2	12.8	6.1	7.9
40.4	38.0	39.4	Total Current	23.0	40.6	39.0	45.9	41.1	39.6
31.7	33.5	30.2	Long-Term Debt	52.4	39.2	28.6	16.9	14.9	25.8
.9	.8	1.0	Deferred Taxes	.0	.3	.6	1.8	2.0	1.7
5.1	5.7	4.6	All Other Non-Current	4.7	1.7	5.9	6.1	3.1	9.7
22.0	22.0	24.9	Net Worth	20.0	18.1	26.0	29.2	38.9	23.2
100.0	100.0	100.0	Total Liabilities & Net Worth	100.0	100.0	100.0	100.0	100.0	100.0
			INCOME DATA						
100.0	100.0	100.0	Net Sales	100.0	100.0	100.0	100.0	100.0	100.0
			Gross Profit						
97.1	96.3	95.6	Operating Expenses	83.5	96.3	97.5	99.0	97.0	95.2
2.9	3.7	4.4	Operating Profit	16.5	3.7	2.5	1.0	3.0	4.8
1.7	2.1	1.7	All Other Expenses (net)	5.1	1.0	1.2	1.1	1.1	2.5
1.3	1.6	2.7	Profit Before Taxes	11.4	2.7	1.3	-.1	1.9	2.3
			RATIOS						
1.8	2.0	1.7	Current	4.8	2.3	1.4	1.8	1.9	1.5
1.2	1.1	1.2		1.6	.9	1.3	1.0	1.1	1.2
.8	.8	.8		.5	.8	1.1	.7	.9	.9
1.4	1.5	1.5	Quick	4.5	1.8	1.2	1.4	1.5	1.1
.9	.9 (108)	.9		(10) 1.9	.8	1.1	.8	.9	.7
.6	.6	.6		1.0	.5	.7	.6	.5	.6
34 10.7	33 10.9	33 11.2	Sales/Receivables	0 UND	29 12.5	36 10.2	40 9.1	44 8.4	42 8.7
45 8.1	44 8.4	44 8.3		26 14.2	34 10.9	44 8.3	49 7.5	48 7.6	50 7.3
56 6.5	57 6.4	59 6.2		74 5.0	54 6.7	57 6.5	64 5.7	58 6.3	66 5.5
			Cost of Sales/Inventory						
			Cost of Sales/Payables						
10.8	9.7	11.4	Sales/Working Capital	4.4	11.1	17.7	11.7	9.7	12.3
37.8	43.6	49.2		14.3	-66.7	27.1	NM	51.5	34.0
-23.8	-27.1	-24.5		-16.9	-18.4	84.7	-12.6	-19.6	-83.0
4.1	3.9	4.3	EBIT/Interest	3.5	4.9	3.8	3.3	5.8	
(114) 1.5	(131) 1.5	(103) 2.0		(31) 1.8	2.2	1.0	(14) 2.3	2.9	
.4	.0	-.3		.6	.4	-1.2	-.3	.3	
2.2	2.6	2.9	Net Profit + Depr., Dep., Amort./Cur. Mat. L/T/D						
(42) 1.5	(37) 1.3	(25) 1.2							
.8	.8	.8							
.9	.9	.8	Fixed/Worth	.7	1.0	.7	.7	.5	1.3
1.7	1.9	1.8		3.5	2.0	1.7	1.1	1.2	2.7
208.0	9.8	4.6		-.9	9.9	7.2	3.4	2.5	7.2
1.4	1.3	1.5	Debt/Worth	.6	1.9	1.6	.7	1.4	1.5
3.1	3.1	3.2		3.1	4.0	3.2	2.3	2.4	4.2
-98.4	27.6	10.6		-2.2	NM	10.8	6.2	3.5	13.0
29.1	24.1	27.3	% Profit Before Taxes/Tangible Net Worth	45.1	37.8	13.2	19.5	34.4	
(92) 11.3	(113) 8.1	(92) 10.6		(26) 10.2	(15) 12.2	(16) 4.0	10.3	(12) 19.8	
-3.3	-4.3	-10.9		-2.4	4.0	-13.9	-13.4	-16.6	
9.0	7.8	8.6	% Profit Before Taxes/Total Assets	25.8	11.3	9.6	5.7	7.1	10.7
1.9	1.9	3.0		6.3	2.3	3.2	-.1	5.6	7.6
-3.1	-4.3	-2.9		-8.0	-2.3	-2.3	-4.1	-3.8	-2.5
8.2	9.7	10.2	Sales/Net Fixed Assets	9.4	12.8	13.3	11.8	10.7	6.7
4.8	5.1	5.1		5.1	5.3	5.3	5.8	3.4	3.8
2.8	2.7	3.3		1.6	4.0	3.2	3.5	3.1	2.9
2.9	2.9	3.0	Sales/Total Assets	4.1	3.7	3.2	3.0	2.6	2.3
2.1	2.1	2.2		1.9	2.5	2.5	2.4	1.7	2.1
1.5	1.5	1.6		1.4	1.7	1.5	1.9	1.4	1.4
2.9	3.0	3.3	% Depr., Dep., Amort./Sales	1.2	3.8	3.1	3.8	3.2	3.2
(116) 4.7	(129) 4.7	(102) 4.6		(10) 4.2	(31) 5.4	4.4	(15) 4.9	3.9	4.2
6.9	7.1	6.7		9.7	7.8	5.1	5.7	6.8	5.0
2.7	2.6	2.8	% Officers', Directors', Owners' Comp/Sales	3.9	2.8	2.4			
(63) 5.2	(71) 5.4	(60) 5.4		(20) 6.2	(15) 6.0	(11) 2.8			
8.8	10.6	8.2		9.4	6.7	3.6			
1736154M	1826634M	1140479M	Net Sales ($)	4685M	65305M	67891M	111997M	248321M	642280M
968276M	951034M	631782M	Total Assets ($)	4823M	37399M	33507M	53079M	141865M	361109M

M = $ thousand   MM = $ million
See Pages 11 through 21 for Explanation of Ratios and Data

Current Data Sorted By Assets   Comparative Historical Data

Type of Statement								
	4	4	7			Unqualified	8	8
	7	7	4			Reviewed	8	16
	1	1				Compiled	10	6
						Tax Returns	3	2
	2	6	8	1		Other	16	21
	20 (4/1-9/30/04)		**32** (10/1/04-3/31/05)				4/1/00-3/31/01	4/1/01-3/31/02
0-500M	500M-2MM	2-10MM	10-50MM	50-100MM	100-250MM		ALL	ALL
	14	18	19	1		**NUMBER OF STATEMENTS**	45	53
%	%	%	%	%	%	**ASSETS**	%	%
	5.3	5.8	7.8			Cash & Equivalents	5.1	7.3
	46.3	33.3	30.0			Trade Receivables (net)	33.7	34.2
	17.5	15.7	16.3			Inventory	16.6	16.0
	.9	1.8	4.0			All Other Current	1.5	1.4
	69.9	56.6	58.0			Total Current	56.9	58.9
	23.9	33.4	32.0			Fixed Assets (net)	33.5	30.5
	.7	3.7	3.1			Intangibles (net)	5.4	5.5
	5.4	6.2	6.9			All Other Non-Current	4.1	5.1
	100.0	100.0	100.0			Total	100.0	100.0
						LIABILITIES		
	14.5	10.1	10.9			Notes Payable-Short Term	9.2	12.5
	4.0	6.7	5.1			Cur. Mat.-L/T/D	5.7	5.4
	23.7	18.7	15.7			Trade Payables	15.8	17.6
	.0	.4	.1			Income Taxes Payable	.4	.4
	8.5	6.6	14.9			All Other Current	9.2	12.5
	50.7	42.5	46.7			Total Current	40.4	48.3
	17.4	24.6	7.3			Long-Term Debt	17.9	17.5
	.4	.1	.9			Deferred Taxes	.9	.7
	1.0	.8	5.5			All Other Non-Current	4.5	3.6
	30.5	31.9	39.7			Net Worth	36.4	29.8
	100.0	100.0	100.0			Total Liabilities & Net Worth	100.0	100.0
						INCOME DATA		
	100.0	100.0	100.0			Net Sales	100.0	100.0
	29.0	27.8	32.7			Gross Profit	29.3	29.1
	30.6	24.5	30.3			Operating Expenses	25.8	26.6
	-1.6	3.2	2.4			Operating Profit	3.5	2.5
	.3	.7	-.3			All Other Expenses (net)	1.4	.5
	-1.9	2.5	2.7			Profit Before Taxes	2.1	2.0
						RATIOS		
	2.7	2.3	1.8				1.8	1.9
	1.4	1.3	1.1			Current	1.5	1.4
	1.0	.8	1.0				.9	.9
	1.6	1.6	1.3				1.3	1.3
	1.0	.8	.7			Quick	.9	1.0
	.7	.5	.6				.6	.6
	31 11.7	35 10.3	35 10.5				32 11.5	33 11.1
	39 9.4	41 8.9	50 7.3			Sales/Receivables	46 8.0	39 9.3
	55 6.7	57 6.4	66 5.5				56 6.5	51 7.1
	6 58.0	14 26.2	20 18.3				21 17.3	18 19.9
	22 16.5	23 15.6	31 11.8			Cost of Sales/Inventory	27 13.3	24 14.9
	43 8.5	44 8.2	51 7.1				49 7.5	51 7.1
	22 16.6	25 14.8	25 14.7				17 20.9	16 22.8
	27 13.3	34 10.6	36 10.1			Cost of Sales/Payables	27 13.6	26 14.0
	41 8.9	57 6.4	47 7.8				44 8.2	43 8.4
	9.7	8.2	9.5				10.3	10.5
	21.6	28.9	43.7			Sales/Working Capital	16.0	18.0
	NM	-41.7	-93.6				-70.0	-44.1
	12.6	6.6	25.6				6.3	5.2
	(12) 2.5	2.6	6.1			EBIT/Interest	(42) 2.1	(48) 2.6
	-4.7	1.3	-5.3				.8	.3
							5.9	10.1
						Net Profit + Depr., Dep., Amort./Cur. Mat. L /T/D	(10) 1.2	(19) 2.6
							.3	.6
	.2	.2	.7				.5	.3
	.7	.9	1.0			Fixed/Worth	1.2	.8
	1.6	36.9	1.7				4.0	2.3
	.8	.9	.8				1.0	.8
	2.1	1.9	1.4			Debt/Worth	1.9	1.6
	7.0	47.4	3.6				9.4	4.8
	34.9	28.5	43.3				32.6	45.2
	(12) 15.8	(15) 11.0	(18) 17.6			% Profit Before Taxes/Tangible Net Worth	(41) 17.2	(46) 16.7
	-4.9	.7	-6.2				3.9	2.4
	14.8	9.6	14.1				12.2	11.3
	3.2	3.5	6.6			% Profit Before Taxes/Total Assets	5.4	5.3
	-9.5	.6	-9.5				-.1	-2.5
	60.8	28.7	10.7				14.3	22.4
	20.3	9.7	6.3			Sales/Net Fixed Assets	7.3	8.9
	8.2	4.3	4.9				4.2	4.5
	4.8	3.5	2.5				3.4	3.4
	3.8	2.4	2.3			Sales/Total Assets	2.6	2.8
	3.1	1.8	1.7				1.8	2.0
		1.2	2.1				1.0	.9
		2.8	(18) 3.1			% Depr., Dep., Amort./Sales	(41) 2.7	(48) 2.6
		4.0	4.6				4.1	4.4
	5.4						1.8	1.6
	(10) 6.8					% Officers', Directors', Owners' Comp/Sales	(10) 4.2	(18) 5.2
	8.5						6.6	8.1
	60146M	215361M	737754M	103989M		Net Sales ($)	964415M	1019125M
	15423M	85873M	333152M	52072M		Total Assets ($)	463968M	428057M

Note: Columns 0-500M, 50-100MM, and 100-250MM are marked "DATA NOT AVAILABLE."

© RMA 2005

M = $ thousand   MM = $ million
See Pages 11 through 21 for Explanation of Ratios and Data

Comparative Historical Data | Current Data Sorted By Sales

Current Data periods: **20 (4/1-9/30/04)** spans columns 0-1MM, 1-3MM, 3-5MM. **32 (10/1/04-3/31/05)** spans columns 5-10MM, 10-25MM, 25MM & OVER.

For the ASSETS, LIABILITIES, INCOME DATA and RATIOS percentage figures, columns 0-1MM through 5-10MM are marked **DATA NOT AVAILABLE**.

4/1/02-3/31/03 ALL	4/1/03-3/31/04 ALL	4/1/04-3/31/05 ALL	Type of Statement	0-1MM	1-3MM	3-5MM	5-10MM	10-25MM	25MM & OVER
7	9	11	Unqualified			1	1	4	5
14	11	15	Reviewed			2	6	4	3
6	13	8	Compiled		4	2	1	1	
2	3	1	Tax Returns		1				
23	14	17	Other				1	8	8
52	50	52	**NUMBER OF STATEMENTS**		5	5	9	17	16
%	%	%	**ASSETS**					%	%
7.5	9.0	6.3	Cash & Equivalents					5.6	7.0
34.4	35.9	35.4	Trade Receivables (net)					39.9	29.1
16.9	14.4	16.9	Inventory					18.7	17.3
2.6	2.5	2.4	All Other Current					2.8	3.5
61.4	61.7	61.0	Total Current					66.9	56.9
28.2	28.7	30.3	Fixed Assets (net)					23.9	31.9
6.0	5.4	2.6	Intangibles (net)					3.3	3.6
4.5	4.2	6.2	All Other Non-Current					5.9	7.5
100.0	100.0	100.0	Total					100.0	100.0
			LIABILITIES						
9.4	10.4	11.4	Notes Payable-Short Term					11.9	8.4
4.6	4.1	5.3	Cur. Mat.-L/T/D					5.4	5.0
18.7	18.1	19.1	Trade Payables					20.8	16.8
.4	.1	.2	Income Taxes Payable					.4	.1
9.6	9.4	10.1	All Other Current					8.2	15.3
42.7	42.1	46.0	Total Current					46.7	45.5
15.1	15.3	16.4	Long-Term Debt					14.2	9.0
.8	1.0	.5	Deferred Taxes					.0	1.1
1.9	4.6	2.6	All Other Non-Current					.3	6.6
39.4	37.1	34.4	Net Worth					38.8	37.7
100.0	100.0	100.0	Total Liabilities & Net Worth					100.0	100.0
			INCOME DATA						
100.0	100.0	100.0	Net Sales					100.0	100.0
31.4	29.9	29.6	Gross Profit					30.0	32.5
27.6	27.0	28.0	Operating Expenses					25.7	31.1
3.8	2.9	1.6	Operating Profit					4.3	1.4
.8	.4	.2	All Other Expenses (net)					.6	-.7
3.0	2.6	1.4	Profit Before Taxes					3.7	2.1
			RATIOS						
2.2	2.2	2.0	Current					2.5	1.8
1.6	1.5	1.3						1.6	1.2
1.1	1.0	.9						1.0	1.0
1.5	1.5	1.4	Quick					1.6	1.1
1.0	1.1	.8						1.0	.8
.7	.7	.6						.6	.6
33 11.1	32 11.3	34 10.6	Sales/Receivables					36 10.2	34 10.8
39 9.4	40 9.1	43 8.6						42 8.7	47 7.7
48 7.6	54 6.8	58 6.3						68 5.4	63 5.8
19 19.4	12 31.3	14 25.3	Cost of Sales/Inventory					13 27.7	22 16.7
25 14.3	23 16.0	28 12.9						23 16.0	33 11.1
46 8.0	34 10.9	48 7.6						58 6.3	51 7.1
20 18.5	18 20.8	24 15.0	Cost of Sales/Payables					27 13.5	24 15.4
31 11.8	26 14.1	33 11.0						35 10.6	35 10.3
47 7.7	40 9.2	50 7.3						43 8.4	56 6.5
8.5	8.7	9.2	Sales/Working Capital					8.1	9.7
14.1	15.9	21.6						11.5	31.4
63.9	218.2	-76.1						-124.9	NM
13.6	8.8	12.6	EBIT/Interest					27.2	21.9
(45) 2.6	(46) 2.5	(50) 2.7						(16) 3.5	4.3
.4	.5	.8						2.0	-6.0
4.2	5.5	8.0	Net Profit + Depr., Dep., Amort./Cur. Mat. L/T/D						
(17) 1.4	(16) 1.8	(19) 2.0							
.9	1.0	.9							
.3	.4	.3	Fixed/Worth					.2	.8
.8	.7	.9						.5	1.0
2.4	2.1	1.7						1.4	1.7
.7	.8	.9	Debt/Worth					.8	.9
1.3	1.6	1.9						1.9	1.6
5.2	5.4	4.5						3.1	3.5
40.1	38.7	33.3	% Profit Before Taxes/Tangible Net Worth					34.3	45.6
(46) 17.8	(44) 16.2	(46) 15.3						(16) 19.5	(15) 13.2
-2.1	.1	.7						11.3	-29.6
18.9	12.6	13.5	% Profit Before Taxes/Total Assets					14.0	16.7
4.2	3.0	4.0						7.3	4.9
-2.4	-.8	-.1						2.7	-11.6
24.5	26.1	25.8	Sales/Net Fixed Assets					43.1	12.6
8.7	9.5	9.1						10.7	6.4
4.9	5.7	5.6						7.8	5.0
3.6	4.2	3.6	Sales/Total Assets					3.7	2.7
2.6	3.1	2.5						2.9	2.4
2.0	2.2	2.0						2.1	2.0
1.4	1.2	1.4	% Depr., Dep., Amort./Sales					1.0	1.8
(47) 2.8	(42) 2.5	(46) 2.6						(16) 2.4	(15) 2.7
3.9	3.6	4.1						4.2	4.2
2.8	2.4	3.1	% Officers', Directors', Owners' Comp/Sales						
(16) 5.1	(19) 4.4	(17) 6.7							
8.0	6.6	8.3							
1266550M	1116919M	1117250M	Net Sales ($)		11694M	17620M	59824M	271390M	756722M
641993M	485294M	486520M	Total Assets ($)		4028M	8165M	27978M	106113M	340236M

M = $ thousand   MM = $ million
See Pages 11 through 21 for Explanation of Ratios and Data

Current Data Sorted By Assets   Comparative Historical Data

0-500M	500M-2MM	2-10MM	10-50MM	50-100MM	100-250MM	Type of Statement	4/1/00-3/31/01 ALL	4/1/01-3/31/02 ALL
			4	1	1	Unqualified	11	7
		3	6			Reviewed	4	5
		1	1			Compiled	5	4
1	2	1				Tax Returns		
4	3		3		1	Other	4	7
4 (4/1-9/30/04)			28 (10/1/04-3/31/05)					
1	6	8	14	1	2	**NUMBER OF STATEMENTS**	24	23
%	%	%	%	%	%	**ASSETS**	%	%
			7.3			Cash & Equivalents	5.0	6.1
			27.3			Trade Receivables (net)	30.4	30.5
			16.5			Inventory	12.0	12.9
			3.9			All Other Current	1.7	1.8
			55.1			Total Current	49.0	51.2
			31.8			Fixed Assets (net)	38.2	36.5
			3.4			Intangibles (net)	5.8	4.7
			9.8			All Other Non-Current	7.1	7.6
			100.0			Total	100.0	100.0
						LIABILITIES		
			7.1			Notes Payable-Short Term	4.6	9.8
			2.8			Cur. Mat.-L/T/D	2.8	4.9
			11.9			Trade Payables	16.0	14.6
			.1			Income Taxes Payable	.4	1.6
			8.9			All Other Current	8.4	9.7
			30.7			Total Current	32.2	40.6
			12.6			Long-Term Debt	29.0	24.4
			.6			Deferred Taxes	1.9	3.1
			9.4			All Other Non-Current	2.0	1.6
			46.7			Net Worth	34.9	30.4
			100.0			Total Liabilities & Net Worth	100.0	100.0
						INCOME DATA		
			100.0			Net Sales	100.0	100.0
			29.7			Gross Profit	25.6	29.7
			23.2			Operating Expenses	21.0	23.9
			6.4			Operating Profit	4.6	5.9
			1.3			All Other Expenses (net)	1.1	1.1
			5.2			Profit Before Taxes	3.5	4.8
						RATIOS		
			3.4			Current	2.1	2.1
			1.9				1.6	1.4
			1.5				1.1	1.0
			2.4			Quick	1.5	1.5
			1.2				1.0	1.0
			.7				.8	.6
			41 8.9			Sales/Receivables	39 9.4	45 8.1
			53 6.8				53 6.9	58 6.3
			79 4.6				68 5.4	63 5.8
			19 19.6			Cost of Sales/Inventory	16 23.5	17 21.4
			36 10.1				23 16.1	25 14.8
			81 4.5				37 9.8	54 6.8
			19 18.9			Cost of Sales/Payables	27 13.3	23 16.0
			26 14.3				33 10.9	35 10.5
			58 6.3				50 7.2	53 6.9
			4.5			Sales/Working Capital	6.6	6.4
			5.6				16.7	12.8
			13.8				41.2	88.6
			17.4			EBIT/Interest	6.5	9.0
			(13) 3.2				(22) 2.7	3.8
			1.9				1.9	1.6
						Net Profit + Depr., Dep., Amort./Cur. Mat. L /T/D		
			.5			Fixed/Worth	.6	.6
			.7				1.3	1.0
			1.4				4.1	2.4
			.6			Debt/Worth	1.0	.9
			.9				1.6	1.4
			2.3				10.2	4.4
			33.7			% Profit Before Taxes/Tangible Net Worth	40.9	31.4
			(12) 5.7				(21) 18.4	(20) 19.2
			2.9				10.3	5.5
			11.7			% Profit Before Taxes/Total Assets	10.9	11.1
			3.2				6.6	8.9
			1.3				3.0	2.4
			14.2			Sales/Net Fixed Assets	10.1	6.4
			5.6				5.0	5.4
			3.1				3.4	3.4
			2.0			Sales/Total Assets	2.7	2.4
			1.7				1.9	1.9
			1.4				1.4	1.4
			1.6			% Depr., Dep., Amort./Sales	2.1	2.0
			4.0				(20) 3.8	(18) 3.9
			5.5				4.3	4.4
						% Officers', Directors', Owners' Comp/Sales		
647M	17209M	79950M	541371M	98577M	309756M	Net Sales ($)	1083854M	744058M
404M	6871M	35143M	315602M	91665M	279584M	Total Assets ($)	788498M	460788M

M = $ thousand   MM = $ million
See Pages 11 through 21 for Explanation of Ratios and Data

Comparative Historical Data				Current Data Sorted By Sales					
Type of Statement									
	8	7	6	Unqualified				1	5
	7	9	9	Reviewed	1		1	4	3
	2	2	2	Compiled				1	1
	1	1	4	Tax Returns	1	2		1	
	7	10	11	Other	1	1	1	1	4	3
	4/1/02-3/31/03	4/1/03-3/31/04	4/1/04-3/31/05	4 (4/1-9/30/04)			28 (10/1/04-3/31/05)		
	ALL	ALL	ALL	0-1MM	1-3MM	3-5MM	5-10MM	10-25MM	25MM & OVER
NUMBER OF STATEMENTS	24	29	32	2	4	1	3	10	12
ASSETS	%	%	%	%	%	%	%	%	%
Cash & Equivalents	3.4	8.2	7.6					10.3	6.0
Trade Receivables (net)	27.8	34.0	29.0					27.9	25.0
Inventory	13.5	13.1	14.8					15.5	14.0
All Other Current	4.0	2.5	3.2					3.5	4.3
Total Current	48.8	57.7	54.5					57.3	49.2
Fixed Assets (net)	40.0	31.9	34.4					30.4	37.6
Intangibles (net)	3.1	2.9	4.4					1.6	7.3
All Other Non-Current	8.2	7.5	6.7					10.7	5.9
Total	100.0	100.0	100.0					100.0	100.0
LIABILITIES									
Notes Payable-Short Term	9.4	11.7	8.2					11.3	4.4
Cur. Mat.-L/T/D	3.4	4.8	2.6					3.2	2.6
Trade Payables	11.0	17.8	13.8					11.7	10.3
Income Taxes Payable	.2	.0	.1					.1	.0
All Other Current	8.2	9.3	8.2					7.8	9.5
Total Current	32.3	43.7	32.9					34.0	26.9
Long-Term Debt	20.9	14.7	18.1					19.2	8.1
Deferred Taxes	1.3	.6	.7					.1	1.0
All Other Non-Current	4.8	6.8	14.2					5.9	24.4
Net Worth	40.7	34.1	34.1					40.8	39.7
Total Liabilities & Net Worth	100.0	100.0	100.0					100.0	100.0
INCOME DATA									
Net Sales	100.0	100.0	100.0					100.0	100.0
Gross Profit	28.7	34.0	32.4					33.7	26.1
Operating Expenses	25.3	30.8	26.9					24.6	20.8
Operating Profit	3.4	3.3	5.5					9.0	5.3
All Other Expenses (net)	1.3	1.0	2.2					1.6	3.5
Profit Before Taxes	2.1	2.2	3.3					7.4	1.7
RATIOS									
Current	2.6 / 1.6 / 1.0	2.7 / 1.4 / .9	2.9 / 1.8 / 1.3					3.6 / 1.6 / 1.2	2.9 / 2.0 / 1.4
Quick	1.9 / 1.0 / .6	2.0 / 1.1 / .7	2.1 / 1.3 / .6					2.8 / 1.2 / .6	2.1 / 1.3 / .7
Sales/Receivables	56 6.5 / 60 6.1 / 76 4.8	52 7.0 / 61 6.1 / 73 5.0	42 8.8 / 52 7.0 / 68 5.4					39 9.4 / 53 6.8 / 79 4.6	37 9.8 / 55 6.6 / 68 5.4
Cost of Sales/Inventory	21 17.6 / 30 12.2 / 52 7.0	12 29.4 / 24 15.0 / 68 5.4	11 32.7 / 30 12.2 / 56 6.5					18 19.9 / 33 11.1 / 81 4.5	13 28.1 / 31 11.8 / 41 9.0
Cost of Sales/Payables	18 20.0 / 26 13.9 / 54 6.8	21 17.5 / 32 11.3 / 77 4.7	20 18.3 / 29 12.4 / 46 7.9					18 20.5 / 28 13.2 / 68 5.4	19 19.5 / 24 15.4 / 34 10.6
Sales/Working Capital	4.7 / 10.1 / -383.9	4.8 / 12.1 / -77.7	4.9 / 7.2 / 25.0					4.0 / 9.5 / 24.4	4.6 / 5.3 / 23.1
EBIT/Interest	8.5 / 2.4 / .1	6.0 / (27) 2.1 / 1.1	12.6 / (28) 3.0 / .1						8.3 / (10) 2.2 / -1.4
Net Profit + Depr., Dep., Amort./Cur. Mat. L/T/D	4.3 / (10) 3.2 / 1.3								
Fixed/Worth	.6 / 1.1 / 1.8	.4 / .9 / 2.6	.5 / .9 / 3.0					.3 / .8 / 4.1	.5 / .8 / NM
Debt/Worth	.6 / 1.3 / 3.6	1.1 / 2.2 / 4.9	.7 / 1.7 / 12.2					.6 / 1.4 / 14.4	.5 / .8 / NM
% Profit Before Taxes/Tangible Net Worth	24.4 / (21) 6.1 / .0	31.7 / (25) 9.1 / .8	33.7 / (27) 9.5 / 2.8						
% Profit Before Taxes/Total Assets	8.2 / 2.4 / -2.3	6.5 / 2.3 / .4	13.2 / 2.8 / -.6					17.2 / 11.4 / 1.2	5.0 / 1.8 / -3.9
Sales/Net Fixed Assets	6.7 / 3.7 / 2.5	41.5 / 5.4 / 3.7	13.3 / 6.4 / 3.2					14.9 / 8.3 / 2.9	11.0 / 4.3 / 2.5
Sales/Total Assets	1.9 / 1.6 / 1.0	2.3 / 1.9 / 1.4	2.6 / 1.9 / 1.4					2.6 / 1.9 / 1.2	2.1 / 1.6 / 1.2
% Depr., Dep., Amort./Sales	3.0 / (21) 4.5 / 5.6	1.0 / (24) 3.4 / 5.5	1.9 / (27) 4.2 / 5.7					1.7 / 3.3 / 5.0	
% Officers', Directors', Owners' Comp/Sales									
Net Sales ($)	887837M	937751M	1047510M	1544M	9520M	3664M	23844M	154138M	854800M
Total Assets ($)	580166M	629317M	729269M	938M	6356M	1802M	8316M	106468M	605389M

M = $ thousand   MM = $ million
See Pages 11 through 21 for Explanation of Ratios and Data

Current Data Sorted By Assets   **Comparative Historical Data**

	0-500M	500M-2MM	2-10MM	10-50MM	50-100MM	100-250MM	Type of Statement	4/1/00-3/31/01 ALL	4/1/01-3/31/02 ALL
		1	19	19	8	3	Unqualified	39	30
	2	23	63	14			Reviewed	80	61
	15	33	26	1			Compiled	129	112
	13	19	9				Tax Returns	33	39
	10	31	42	23	5	2	Other	117	133
	84 (4/1-9/30/04)			297 (10/1/04-3/31/05)					
NUMBER OF STATEMENTS	40	107	159	57	13	5		398	375
	%	%	%	%	%	%	**ASSETS**	%	%
	17.0	8.2	6.2	9.0	6.0		Cash & Equivalents	8.7	7.8
	34.5	32.2	30.2	25.0	25.0		Trade Receivables (net)	29.4	28.3
	9.1	12.2	12.8	14.4	14.5		Inventory	12.3	11.2
	1.6	1.8	2.0	1.6	1.7		All Other Current	1.7	1.4
	62.3	54.4	51.2	50.0	47.2		Total Current	52.0	48.8
	31.5	36.4	40.0	40.1	34.0		Fixed Assets (net)	39.8	41.5
	2.5	2.7	3.7	2.7	13.9		Intangibles (net)	3.8	4.4
	3.7	6.6	5.2	7.2	4.8		All Other Non-Current	4.5	5.3
	100.0	100.0	100.0	100.0	100.0		Total	100.0	100.0
							LIABILITIES		
	22.5	11.4	10.5	7.4	4.6		Notes Payable-Short Term	8.5	8.6
	4.1	7.1	6.9	5.5	3.7		Cur. Mat.-L/T/D	6.3	7.4
	24.2	17.4	14.6	12.9	11.1		Trade Payables	14.8	13.9
	.0	.3	.3	.4	.2		Income Taxes Payable	.2	.2
	6.0	8.1	7.4	7.2	7.7		All Other Current	7.9	7.3
	56.7	44.3	39.7	33.5	27.2		Total Current	37.6	37.5
	34.0	26.2	24.0	19.1	23.1		Long-Term Debt	25.3	27.5
	.0	.4	1.1	1.1	2.6		Deferred Taxes	.7	.5
	8.6	5.4	7.9	5.0	4.9		All Other Non-Current	4.4	4.9
	.4	23.8	27.4	41.3	42.1		Net Worth	31.9	29.6
	100.0	100.0	100.0	100.0	100.0		Total Liabilities & Net Worth	100.0	100.0
							INCOME DATA		
	100.0	100.0	100.0	100.0	100.0		Net Sales	100.0	100.0
	41.5	38.3	32.4	28.9	26.1		Gross Profit	35.5	36.8
	37.2	36.6	28.5	23.1	16.9		Operating Expenses	31.4	33.5
	4.3	1.8	3.9	5.8	9.2		Operating Profit	4.1	3.4
	1.5	1.1	1.4	1.7	1.5		All Other Expenses (net)	1.4	2.0
	2.9	.7	2.5	4.2	7.6		Profit Before Taxes	2.7	1.4
							RATIOS		
	2.1	2.0	2.1	2.5	3.2		Current	2.3	2.1
	1.5	1.3	1.3	1.3	1.9			1.4	1.3
	.8	.9	1.0	1.1	1.3			1.0	1.0
	1.9	1.7	1.5	1.5	2.1		Quick	1.8	1.6
	1.2	1.0	.9	1.0	1.2			1.0	.9
	.6	.6	.6	.7	.7			.6	.6
	14 25.3	33 11.0	39 9.4	37 9.8	49 7.5		Sales/Receivables	34 10.6	33 11.0
	29 12.5	41 8.9	50 7.3	45 8.1	56 6.5			46 7.9	45 8.1
	42 8.7	53 6.9	61 5.9	61 6.0	65 5.6			57 6.4	58 6.3
	3 112.6	7 51.8	14 25.6	19 19.5	21 17.1		Cost of Sales/Inventory	10 34.9	10 34.9
	10 37.7	20 18.1	27 13.8	31 11.7	40 9.1			23 16.1	22 16.7
	25 14.8	41 8.8	43 8.4	54 6.8	61 6.0			41 9.0	43 8.5
	17 21.7	21 17.1	17 21.2	21 17.4	18 19.8		Cost of Sales/Payables	18 20.1	19 19.6
	24 15.0	37 9.7	31 11.6	30 12.3	32 11.4			31 11.7	31 11.9
	48 7.6	52 7.1	50 7.3	40 9.1	40 9.1			49 7.5	48 7.6
	14.9	10.2	8.0	5.6	4.7		Sales/Working Capital	7.5	8.4
	22.9	23.9	21.1	16.8	8.2			17.4	18.6
	-26.3	-39.0	-117.1	32.2	15.5			UND	-116.9
	20.8	6.0	5.2	12.9	9.3		EBIT/Interest	5.2	4.6
	(33) 3.8	(98) 1.9	(154) 2.8	(55) 4.0	(12) 4.5			(370) 2.2	(356) 1.6
	.6	.3	1.2	2.1	2.9			.8	.6
		3.0	3.2	3.8			Net Profit + Depr., Dep., Amort./Cur. Mat. L /T/D	3.6	3.0
		(26) 2.1	(52) 2.0	(23) 1.8				(100) 1.9	(95) 1.3
		.6	1.3	1.1				1.0	.7
	.4	.6	.9	.5	.5		Fixed/Worth	.6	.7
	1.8	1.7	1.6	1.0	1.6			1.4	1.7
	-1.8	16.6	3.4	2.2	5.8			4.0	4.9
	1.0	1.2	1.2	.7	.8		Debt/Worth	.9	1.0
	4.1	3.2	2.6	1.8	5.5			2.5	2.7
	-3.6	32.8	7.5	3.5	10.9			7.7	8.9
	146.5	52.6	42.3	35.3	67.1		% Profit Before Taxes/Tangible Net Worth	38.0	32.0
	(26) 49.8	(85) 18.8	(134) 19.0	(55) 20.5	(12) 30.4			(337) 18.5	(316) 9.9
	14.5	-.4	4.8	10.1	10.8			.6	-.3
	41.9	14.5	9.8	13.9	16.0		% Profit Before Taxes/Total Assets	13.7	10.2
	14.9	2.9	4.4	7.9	7.6			4.9	2.5
	-4.3	-3.0	.8	3.5	3.5			-.9	-1.6
	46.1	14.3	9.6	8.9	8.2		Sales/Net Fixed Assets	10.5	10.3
	19.2	8.0	5.3	4.4	4.5			6.2	5.5
	7.6	4.9	3.2	3.0	2.8			3.7	3.1
	6.6	3.4	2.7	2.3	2.0		Sales/Total Assets	3.0	2.9
	4.1	2.8	2.1	1.9	1.4			2.2	2.1
	3.1	2.1	1.6	1.2	1.1			1.7	1.6
	1.1	2.4	2.5	2.6	3.0		% Depr., Dep., Amort./Sales	2.0	1.9
	(31) 2.3	(95) 4.1	(151) 4.2	(54) 3.4	4.2			(372) 3.6	(350) 4.0
	4.6	6.5	6.3	5.3	5.8			5.4	6.0
	4.8	3.3	2.1				% Officers', Directors', Owners' Comp/Sales	3.1	2.9
	(22) 6.6	(64) 5.1	(66) 3.4					(188) 5.1	(185) 5.0
	8.5	7.7	6.8					9.4	5.2
	45273M	349457M	1505453M	1928061M	1404632M	1173816M	Net Sales ($)	5244548M	5522774M
	10717M	128839M	717437M	1069842M	855611M	772838M	Total Assets ($)	2733624M	2973728M

© RMA 2005

M = $ thousand   MM = $ million
See Pages 11 through 21 for Explanation of Ratios and Data

Comparative Historical Data

Current Data Sorted By Sales

Hist 1	Hist 2	Hist 3	Type of Statement	0-1MM	1-3MM	3-5MM	5-10MM	10-25MM	25MM & OVER
49	61	50	Unqualified			2	6	16	26
83	74	102	Reviewed	2	11	11	39	32	7
88	104	75	Compiled	9	23	20	14	8	1
49	45	41	Tax Returns	6	18	10	5	2	
104	107	113	Other	6	23	16	26	23	19
4/1/02-3/31/03 ALL	4/1/03-3/31/04 ALL	4/1/04-3/31/05 ALL		84 (4/1-9/30/04)			297 (10/1/04-3/31/05)		
373	391	381	**NUMBER OF STATEMENTS**	23	75	59	90	81	53
%	%	%	**ASSETS**	%	%	%	%	%	%
8.5	8.8	8.3	Cash & Equivalents	19.6	9.4	6.6	6.8	7.5	7.3
28.6	28.5	30.1	Trade Receivables (net)	24.7	29.7	32.0	30.3	32.3	27.2
11.4	11.7	12.6	Inventory	7.0	11.0	12.1	13.5	12.9	15.5
1.9	2.4	1.8	All Other Current	1.4	2.1	1.6	2.4	1.3	1.8
50.4	51.5	52.8	Total Current	52.7	52.2	52.3	53.0	54.0	51.8
40.1	37.9	37.9	Fixed Assets (net)	34.9	38.7	40.4	36.2	39.4	36.0
3.5	4.0	3.6	Intangibles (net)	5.6	2.5	2.8	4.4	1.7	6.5
6.0	6.5	5.7	All Other Non-Current	6.8	6.6	4.5	6.4	4.8	5.7
100.0	100.0	100.0	Total	100.0	100.0	100.0	100.0	100.0	100.0
			LIABILITIES						
7.9	9.4	11.2	Notes Payable-Short Term	10.9	17.8	10.2	10.4	9.9	6.6
7.7	7.8	6.3	Cur. Mat.-L/T/D	4.7	5.2	8.3	7.1	6.5	4.6
16.1	15.8	15.9	Trade Payables	12.5	18.7	17.2	16.1	14.8	13.6
.3	.3	.3	Income Taxes Payable	.0	.2	.7	.2	.2	.1
8.6	9.4	7.5	All Other Current	8.7	5.9	7.4	8.1	7.4	8.3
40.6	42.6	41.1	Total Current	36.9	47.7	43.9	41.8	38.7	33.2
26.7	24.8	24.9	Long-Term Debt	28.8	32.8	27.5	23.3	20.7	18.4
.6	.8	.9	Deferred Taxes	.3	.3	.6	1.2	.8	1.7
3.3	5.8	6.6	All Other Non-Current	7.2	7.4	3.5	10.2	4.8	5.5
28.8	26.0	26.4	Net Worth	26.5	11.8	24.5	23.4	35.0	41.1
100.0	100.0	100.0	Total Liabilities & Net Worth	100.0	100.0	100.0	100.0	100.0	100.0
			INCOME DATA						
100.0	100.0	100.0	Net Sales	100.0	100.0	100.0	100.0	100.0	100.0
36.6	35.7	34.2	Gross Profit	38.4	39.4	38.9	34.1	29.1	27.7
32.9	32.0	30.3	Operating Expenses	36.5	37.9	35.0	30.7	24.0	20.6
3.7	3.7	3.9	Operating Profit	1.8	1.6	3.9	3.4	5.0	7.1
1.5	1.3	1.4	All Other Expenses (net)	1.2	1.2	1.7	1.3	1.5	1.2
2.2	2.4	2.5	Profit Before Taxes	.6	.4	2.2	2.1	3.6	5.9
			RATIOS						
2.0	2.1	2.1	Current	2.6	2.1	2.2	2.0	2.1	2.6
1.3	1.3	1.3		1.5	1.2	1.2	1.3	1.4	1.5
.9	.9	1.0		1.1	.8	.9	.9	1.0	1.2
1.5	1.6	1.6	Quick	1.9	1.7	1.7	1.5	1.6	1.5
.9	(390) .9	1.0		1.3	.9	1.0	.9	.9	1.0
.6	.6	.6		.9	.5	.6	.6	.7	.7
35 10.5	34 10.8	35 10.4	Sales/Receivables	16 22.5	25 14.7	36 10.0	36 10.2	41 8.9	37 9.8
43 8.4	44 8.2	45 8.1		38 9.5	39 9.4	48 7.6	44 8.2	51 7.1	50 7.3
56 6.5	55 6.6	57 6.4		55 6.6	48 7.7	58 6.3	58 6.3	63 5.8	61 6.0
11 33.4	12 31.2	11 31.9	Cost of Sales/Inventory	6 59.9	6 60.4	13 27.7	12 31.0	15 24.6	19 19.3
23 15.7	22 16.7	24 15.1		15 24.7	18 20.1	24 15.1	23 15.9	28 12.8	36 10.3
40 9.0	41 8.9	43 8.5		38 9.5	39 9.4	43 8.5	42 8.6	42 8.7	60 6.1
20 18.6	19 18.9	19 19.5	Cost of Sales/Payables	11 33.7	19 19.4	24 15.5	18 20.4	17 21.3	22 16.7
34 10.6	33 10.9	32 11.6		28 13.1	33 11.0	41 9.0	33 11.2	29 12.7	30 12.3
51 7.1	50 7.3	49 7.4		55 6.6	50 7.4	54 6.8	52 7.1	47 7.7	37 9.8
8.7	7.1	8.4	Sales/Working Capital	8.9	11.1	9.0	9.5	7.4	5.6
21.3	20.4	19.2		20.1	24.0	29.6	21.6	17.2	11.3
-49.9	-44.6	-111.8		62.8	-34.7	-33.0	-59.9	164.4	26.9
5.1	7.0	7.3	EBIT/Interest	16.6	5.2	5.4	7.0	7.1	15.1
(351) 2.2	(362) 2.5	(356) 2.9		(19) 2.6	(69) 2.1	(54) 2.4	(87) 2.7	(77) 3.2	(50) 5.9
.4	.9	1.1		-.9	.6	.7	1.2	1.5	2.9
2.3	2.7	3.3	Net Profit + Depr., Dep., Amort./Cur. Mat. L/T/D		6.0	4.0	3.1	3.2	4.1
(98) 1.2	(90) 1.5	(111) 2.0			(11) 1.0	(18) 2.2	(29) 2.4	(32) 1.7	(20) 1.9
.6	1.0	1.0			.7	.8	1.1	1.3	1.2
.6	.6	.6	Fixed/Worth	.5	.5	.7	.8	.6	.5
1.5	1.5	1.4		1.9	1.8	2.0	1.6	1.3	1.3
4.5	6.9	4.1		-5.0	-6.8	4.6	6.6	2.5	2.6
1.0	1.0	1.0	Debt/Worth	.7	1.1	1.2	1.0	1.0	.6
2.6	2.7	2.5		5.4	2.6	3.5	2.6	2.2	2.0
10.3	13.9	9.1		-7.6	-21.7	7.9	17.0	4.1	4.6
40.8	41.0	48.0	% Profit Before Taxes/Tangible Net Worth	456.9	48.6	42.4	55.5	35.1	56.8
(310) 13.2	(309) 15.3	(317) 20.5		(16) 52.2	(54) 17.2	(50) 10.9	(72) 19.8	(74) 19.1	(51) 29.8
-.1	3.8	4.8		19.3	.1	.3	2.1	8.2	10.6
11.7	11.3	12.9	% Profit Before Taxes/Total Assets	48.8	14.5	12.6	11.3	10.6	16.3
3.6	4.6	5.2		15.0	3.7	3.5	4.6	6.0	9.0
-1.8	-.2	.3		-6.2	-3.0	-.7	.7	2.1	4.1
11.8	14.0	12.4	Sales/Net Fixed Assets	33.0	18.0	9.8	11.5	9.9	9.4
5.6	6.1	6.6		8.6	8.4	6.2	7.4	5.1	5.1
3.2	3.4	3.6		3.5	3.9	3.3	4.4	3.3	3.5
3.1	3.1	3.2	Sales/Total Assets	4.5	3.5	3.1	3.2	2.8	2.5
2.2	2.2	2.3		3.4	2.8	2.3	2.4	2.1	1.9
1.6	1.6	1.7		1.3	1.9	1.7	1.8	1.7	1.4
2.6	2.2	2.4	% Depr., Dep., Amort./Sales	1.9	2.3	3.2	2.1	2.5	2.6
(346) 4.4	(352) 4.0	(345) 3.9		(17) 3.5	(65) 4.6	(55) 4.1	(81) 3.5	(78) 3.9	(49) 3.5
6.4	6.1	6.2		6.5	7.4	6.0	5.7	5.9	5.0
3.2	2.8	2.9	% Officers', Directors', Owners' Comp/Sales	5.3	3.2	3.2	1.9	1.9	
(175) 5.2	(175) 4.6	(159) 4.6		(13) 7.3	(45) 5.3	(35) 5.3	(39) 3.4	(23) 2.9	
8.8	8.9	7.2		9.1	7.6	7.9	6.0	4.4	
6398156M	6331846M	6406692M	Net Sales ($)	15807M	145164M	232801M	648493M	1248996M	4115431M
3495185M	3404971M	3555284M	Total Assets ($)	29643M	62393M	121340M	308049M	647051M	2386808M

M = $ thousand   MM = $ million
See Pages 11 through 21 for Explanation of Ratios and Data

Current Data Sorted By Assets **Comparative Historical Data**

						Type of Statement		
			4			Unqualified	3	1
	7	3				Reviewed	16	18
2	6	9				Compiled	19	14
2	2	4				Tax Returns	2	2
	5	7	1			Other	16	20
	13 (4/1-9/30/04)		39 (10/1/04-3/31/05)				4/1/00-3/31/01	4/1/01-3/31/02
0-500M	500M-2MM	2-10MM	10-50MM	50-100MM	100-250MM		ALL	ALL
4	20	23	5			NUMBER OF STATEMENTS	56	55
%	%	%	%	%	%	**ASSETS**	%	%
	6.8	9.7				Cash & Equivalents	8.9	9.2
	33.1	28.8				Trade Receivables (net)	29.8	27.6
	11.9	6.4	D	D		Inventory	7.0	4.7
	.6	.5	A	A		All Other Current	1.8	2.1
	52.4	45.5	T	T		Total Current	47.5	43.7
	36.8	42.7	A	A		Fixed Assets (net)	45.6	47.2
	4.5	5.5	N	N		Intangibles (net)	1.6	2.8
	6.2	6.4	O	O		All Other Non-Current	5.3	6.3
	100.0	100.0	T	T		Total	100.0	100.0
						LIABILITIES		
	15.5	7.2	A	A		Notes Payable-Short Term	10.2	8.6
	7.8	6.5	V	V		Cur. Mat.-L/T/D	7.3	7.2
	9.1	8.1	A	A		Trade Payables	10.8	7.6
	.2	1.0	I	I		Income Taxes Payable	.2	.3
	7.1	7.4	L	L		All Other Current	6.2	6.5
	39.6	30.3	A	A		Total Current	34.7	30.1
	21.4	26.3	B	B		Long-Term Debt	23.9	26.0
	.4	1.2	L	L		Deferred Taxes	.8	.7
	5.4	12.8	E	E		All Other Non-Current	3.4	4.2
	33.2	29.3				Net Worth	37.1	38.8
	100.0	100.0				Total Liabilities & Net Worth	100.0	100.0
						INCOME DATA		
	100.0	100.0				Net Sales	100.0	100.0
	40.5	27.9				Gross Profit	37.1	39.1
	35.3	24.0				Operating Expenses	32.8	35.6
	5.2	3.9				Operating Profit	4.3	3.5
	1.1	1.6				All Other Expenses (net)	1.0	1.3
	4.1	2.3				Profit Before Taxes	3.3	2.2
						RATIOS		
	2.3	2.3					2.0	2.8
	1.3	1.4				Current	1.4	1.3
	.8	1.0					.9	.9
	1.8	1.5					1.7	2.7
	.9	1.2				Quick	1.1	1.1
	.5	.8					.8	.8
41	9.0	46 8.0					36 10.3	36 10.2
46	8.0	52 7.0				Sales/Receivables	48 7.6	43 8.5
62	5.8	59 6.2					61 5.9	57 6.4
0	UND	5 79.4					0 UND	0 UND
10	35.7	9 39.6				Cost of Sales/Inventory	7 53.1	6 58.7
57	6.5	23 15.6					26 14.3	13 29.0
9	42.8	10 37.0					11 33.9	4 93.7
16	23.3	16 22.2				Cost of Sales/Payables	21 17.3	16 22.4
35	10.4	29 12.5					36 10.2	30 12.3
	7.3	6.9					8.5	8.0
	22.7	21.1				Sales/Working Capital	18.7	21.9
	-23.0	-999.8					-77.6	-55.8
	8.1	3.9					5.2	5.4
	3.5	(22) 1.7				EBIT/Interest	(54) 2.5	(53) 1.7
	1.0	1.1					1.0	-.5
		2.7					2.3	3.3
	(10)	1.4				Net Profit + Depr., Dep., Amort./Cur. Mat. L /T/D	(15) 1.6	(18) 1.5
		1.0					1.0	.8
	.5	.8					.7	.6
	1.1	1.2				Fixed/Worth	1.5	1.3
	4.1	3.2					2.6	3.8
	.9	.9					.9	.7
	2.1	2.8				Debt/Worth	2.3	1.8
	7.3	5.6					3.5	5.5
	56.7	27.6					42.8	33.5
	(17) 9.9	(20) 10.7				% Profit Before Taxes/Tangible Net Worth	(54) 21.4	(50) 11.0
	1.6	1.6					3.1	-13.7
	19.4	7.8					10.8	13.0
	3.5	1.9				% Profit Before Taxes/Total Assets	5.6	3.0
	.2	.4					.1	-5.6
	13.6	7.0					10.5	7.5
	7.2	4.6				Sales/Net Fixed Assets	4.8	4.4
	4.5	3.0					2.5	2.6
	2.8	2.2					3.1	2.9
	2.3	1.7				Sales/Total Assets	2.0	1.9
	1.9	1.4					1.6	1.5
	3.0	3.1					2.6	2.9
	(18) 3.9	4.7				% Depr., Dep., Amort./Sales	(55) 4.9	(54) 5.6
	7.7	7.3					7.1	8.0
	2.4	2.2					3.4	4.6
	(11) 5.5	(13) 3.3				% Officers', Directors', Owners' Comp/Sales	(30) 6.3	(30) 7.5
	9.8	7.5					10.3	10.7
3552M	55809M	195212M	174915M			Net Sales ($)	294802M	465159M
1352M	24064M	106912M	87605M			Total Assets ($)	163364M	284658M

© RMA 2005

M = $ thousand   MM = $ million
See Pages 11 through 21 for Explanation of Ratios and Data

Comparative Historical Data | Current Data Sorted By Sales

			Type of Statement		13.(4/1-9/30/04)		39 (10/1/04-3/31/05)		
				0-1MM	1-3MM	3-5MM	5-10MM	10-25MM	25MM & OVER
3	5	7	Unqualified			1	1	2	3
15	20	16	Reviewed		3	6	3	4	
15	14	12	Compiled	2	6	3		1	
5	5	4	Tax Returns	1	3				
15	17	13	Other		4	3	3	3	
4/1/02-3/31/03	4/1/03-3/31/04	4/1/04-3/31/05							
ALL	ALL	ALL							
53	61	52	NUMBER OF STATEMENTS	3	16	13	7	10	3
%	%	%	ASSETS	%	%	%	%	%	%
5.7	9.2	8.2	Cash & Equivalents		7.9	7.6		6.7	
27.1	26.6	31.9	Trade Receivables (net)		35.1	28.7		33.4	
4.5	7.2	8.7	Inventory		8.0	9.2		12.2	
.7	1.8	.5	All Other Current		.2	1.0		.8	
38.0	44.8	49.3	Total Current		51.2	46.5		53.1	
51.6	43.3	40.2	Fixed Assets (net)		41.1	40.2		35.5	
4.1	4.5	4.4	Intangibles (net)		5.5	4.5		3.7	
6.3	7.4	6.2	All Other Non-Current		2.2	8.8		7.6	
100.0	100.0	100.0	Total		100.0	100.0		100.0	
			LIABILITIES						
9.2	10.1	12.2	Notes Payable-Short Term		17.7	9.3		11.6	
6.8	8.7	6.9	Cur. Mat.-L/T/D		9.1	3.8		7.0	
8.3	8.3	9.1	Trade Payables		7.6	7.7		12.5	
.4	.4	.5	Income Taxes Payable		.0	1.6		.1	
7.4	7.4	8.1	All Other Current		6.8	7.2		9.3	
32.1	34.9	36.8	Total Current		41.2	29.7		40.5	
31.3	25.4	24.7	Long-Term Debt		26.7	18.3		23.3	
1.9	.8	.7	Deferred Taxes		.4	.1		1.8	
4.4	6.8	8.6	All Other Non-Current		5.1	17.4		4.6	
30.2	32.0	29.3	Net Worth		26.6	34.5		29.7	
100.0	100.0	100.0	Total Liabilities & Net Worth		100.0	100.0		100.0	
			INCOME DATA						
100.0	100.0	100.0	Net Sales		100.0	100.0		100.0	
37.8	35.1	35.0	Gross Profit		45.2	33.9		28.9	
34.5	31.8	30.2	Operating Expenses		38.3	31.8		25.2	
3.3	3.3	4.8	Operating Profit		6.9	2.2		3.7	
1.5	1.4	1.4	All-Other Expenses (net)		1.5	1.3		1.0	
1.9	1.9	3.5	Profit Before Taxes		5.5	.9		2.7	
			RATIOS						
2.0	2.4	2.3			2.2	2.4		1.6	
1.3	1.4	1.3	Current		1.3	1.3		1.2	
.8	.8	.9			.7	1.0		1.0	
1.7	1.9	1.8			2.2	1.6		1.5	
1.2	1.1	1.0	Quick		1.0	1.0		.9	
.8	.7	.7			.5	.8		.7	
38 9.6	36 10.0	43 8.5			41 9.0	43 8.4		44 8.3	
51 7.1	48 7.7	51 7.2	Sales/Receivables		50 7.3	51 7.1		54 6.8	
67 5.5	58 6.3	62 5.8			72 5.1	62 5.9		65 5.6	
0 UND	0 UND	0 UND			0 UND	0 UND		0 UND	
6 59.3	8 48.4	9 41.8	Cost of Sales/Inventory		5 79.4	7 50.4		12 29.2	
15 24.8	25 14.4	29 12.5			29 12.5	50 7.3		63 5.8	
11 34.7	12 29.5	11 32.8			6 57.0	12 30.6		19 19.3	
21 17.7	18 20.3	22 16.9	Cost of Sales/Payables		16 23.3	16 23.0		27 13.4	
30 12.3	27 13.4	32 11.5			41 8.9	28 12.9		38 9.7	
9.3	6.6	7.1			7.4	6.1		9.5	
30.0	19.7	22.7	Sales/Working Capital		26.2	23.2		42.1	
-29.5	-37.1	-100.1			-14.8	NM		-770.3	
4.4	4.1	6.3			10.6	4.6		3.9	
(49) 2.0	(59) 1.6	(51) 1.9	EBIT/Interest		3.5	(12) 1.0		1.8	
.6	.5	1.0			1.1	-2.3		1.6	
11.4	2.1	2.5	Net Profit + Depr., Dep.,						
(11) 2.5	(20) 1.3	(16) 1.4	Amort./Cur. Mat. L/T/D						
.8	.9	1.0							
1.0	.7	.7			.7	.5		.5	
2.1	1.4	1.3	Fixed/Worth		2.4	1.1		1.4	
5.8	4.0	3.7			NM	2.7		3.1	
1.1	.9	.9			1.0	.6		1.7	
3.3	2.2	2.3	Debt/Worth		4.0	1.6		3.1	
9.1	9.8	6.4			NM	5.7		6.2	
43.6	17.5	33.2	% Profit Before Taxes/Tangible		66.6	12.8		34.7	
(46) 9.3	(51) 4.7	(44) 11.1	Net Worth		(12) 21.9	(11) 2.7		24.6	
-4.2	-2.2	1.6			5.1	-19.1		2.7	
12.0	6.6	12.2	% Profit Before Taxes/Total		22.1	6.5		8.0	
3.2	1.5	3.2	Assets		8.7	1.0		5.2	
-1.7	-1.1	.2			.6	-5.5		.9	
6.7	8.2	9.1			13.6	10.4		10.9	
3.6	5.9	6.1	Sales/Net Fixed Assets		6.7	3.9		7.6	
2.1	2.8	3.5			4.0	2.7		4.6	
2.4	2.6	2.6			2.8	2.5		3.2	
1.8	1.9	2.1	Sales/Total Assets		2.3	1.8		2.0	
1.3	1.4	1.5			1.7	1.3		1.6	
3.8	3.3	3.1			3.0	3.7		2.6	
(51) 5.8	(59) 5.4	(50) 4.2	% Depr., Dep., Amort./Sales		(14) 3.8	5.9		3.0	
9.0	7.4	7.4			8.5	9.8		5.8	
3.1	3.5	2.3	% Officers', Directors',		3.2				
(27) 4.4	(30) 6.3	(27) 5.0	Owners' Comp/Sales		(10) 8.6				
6.2	11.9	8.1			11.7				
387964M	459236M	429488M	Net Sales ($)	2035M	34768M	53856M	53430M	144351M	141048M
223507M	261112M	219933M	Total Assets ($)	920M	16804M	34437M	30731M	74796M	62245M

© RMA 2005   M = $ thousand   MM = $ million
See Pages 11 through 21 for Explanation of Ratios and Data

Current Data Sorted By Assets

Comparative Historical Data

0-500M	500M-2MM	2-10MM	10-50MM	50-100MM	100-250MM	Type of Statement	4/1/00-3/31/01 ALL	4/1/01-3/31/02 ALL
1	3	2	5	1		Unqualified	8	6
1	8	8	1	2		Reviewed	11	12
		3				Compiled	14	15
2		1				Tax Returns	4	1
4	4	4	1	1	3	Other	21	11
	6 (4/1-9/30/04)		49 (10/1/04-3/31/05)				4/1/00-3/31/01	4/1/01-3/31/02
8	15	18	9	2	3	NUMBER OF STATEMENTS	58 (ALL)	45 (ALL)
%	%	%	%	%	%	ASSETS	%	%
	7.7	15.9				Cash & Equivalents	8.1	10.8
	36.9	26.2				Trade Receivables (net)	30.9	32.3
	8.3	7.6				Inventory	7.2	7.3
	2.8	2.3				All Other Current	2.2	3.4
	55.6	52.0				Total Current	48.4	53.8
	35.2	34.0				Fixed Assets (net)	39.2	32.0
	5.0	4.7				Intangibles (net)	6.1	9.0
	4.2	9.3				All Other Non-Current	6.4	4.6
	100.0	100.0				Total	100.0	100.0
						LIABILITIES		
	4.8	7.5				Notes Payable-Short Term	11.2	7.9
	10.5	5.0				Cur. Mat.-L/T/D	8.6	7.0
	15.8	10.7				Trade Payables	12.8	12.3
	.0	.3				Income Taxes Payable	.1	.2
	6.3	8.9				All Other Current	8.2	8.0
	37.4	32.3				Total Current	41.0	35.5
	36.4	21.0				Long-Term Debt	28.5	21.4
	.0	.4				Deferred Taxes	.4	.4
	15.8	1.2				All Other Non-Current	4.5	3.0
	10.4	45.0				Net Worth	25.6	39.7
	100.0	100.0				Total Liabilities & Net Worth	100.0	100.0
						INCOME DATA		
	100.0	100.0				Net Sales	100.0	100.0
	38.7	35.1				Gross Profit	39.1	36.8
	33.5	32.1				Operating Expenses	34.2	31.1
	5.2	3.1				Operating Profit	4.9	5.6
	1.5	.3				All Other Expenses (net)	1.7	1.7
	3.7	2.7				Profit Before Taxes	3.2	3.9
						RATIOS		
	2.6	4.0					2.3	3.2
	2.0	1.5				Current	1.5	1.8
	.9	.9					.8	1.0
	2.0	3.5					1.8	2.3
	1.3	1.4				Quick	1.3	1.4
	.5	.5					.6	.8
	37 9.9	38 9.7					37 9.9	41 8.9
	44 8.2	58 6.3				Sales/Receivables	52 7.0	55 6.6
	65 5.7	87 4.2					71 5.1	69 5.3
	12 30.5	15 23.8					6 56.2	7 54.0
	16 23.5	26 13.9				Cost of Sales/Inventory	19 19.0	14 26.4
	39 9.5	57 6.4					30 12.1	30 12.2
	9 39.2	10 34.8					13 28.6	12 31.1
	27 13.7	29 12.4				Cost of Sales/Payables	27 13.5	23 16.2
	44 8.3	66 5.6					49 7.4	45 8.1
	5.0	3.7					7.5	4.7
	14.5	11.3				Sales/Working Capital	15.3	11.1
	-31.2	-30.5					-19.5	UND
	11.0	18.1					6.9	6.3
	(13) 3.6	(15) .7				EBIT/Interest	(54) 2.1	(40) 2.0
	1.2	-3.7					.7	.1
						Net Profit + Depr., Dep., Amort./Cur. Mat. L/T/D		
	.5	.3					.6	.4
	1.6	.5				Fixed/Worth	1.3	.9
	-4.3	8.2					7.7	4.7
	.8	.5					.7	.5
	3.1	.9				Debt/Worth	2.0	2.7
	-9.0	16.8					12.2	8.5
	61.0	26.0					48.0	55.9
	(10) 44.3	(15) 13.0				% Profit Before Taxes/Tangible Net Worth	(45) 20.0	(36) 16.8
	18.1	-14.7					2.4	-3.9
	16.3	12.8					15.2	17.4
	6.0	6.6				% Profit Before Taxes/Total Assets	4.6	3.7
	.7	-5.0					.0	-1.8
	13.7	10.1					11.4	11.7
	8.1	6.3				Sales/Net Fixed Assets	6.9	7.4
	4.2	1.8					3.5	4.2
	3.9	2.1					2.8	2.6
	2.4	1.7				Sales/Total Assets	2.2	2.3
	1.8	.9					1.6	1.6
	2.5	3.2					3.3	1.7
	(14) 3.7	4.7				% Depr., Dep., Amort./Sales	(53) 5.1	(41) 4.1
	8.8	7.5					7.0	6.9
							4.4	2.1
						% Officers', Directors', Owners' Comp/Sales	(29) 7.7	(22) 5.9
							13.8	8.1
7881M	43224M	112677M	324254M	235197M	731992M	Net Sales ($)	540316M	769987M
1869M	15301M	77958M	166178M	130408M	541006M	Total Assets ($)	429547M	580919M

M = $ thousand   MM = $ million

See Pages 11 through 21 for Explanation of Ratios and Data

Comparative Historical Data   Current Data Sorted By Sales

			Type of Statement						
6	5	8	Unqualified				2	2	4
10	15	13	Reviewed	2	1	2	5	2	1
11	15	14	Compiled	1	7	2	1	2	1
5	3	3	Tax Returns		2	1			
16	18	17	Other	1	7	1	2	1	5
4/1/02-3/31/03 ALL	4/1/03-3/31/04 ALL	4/1/04-3/31/05 ALL		0-1MM	6 (4/1-9/30/04) 1-3MM	3-5MM	49 (10/1/04-3/31/05) 5-10MM	10-25MM	25MM & OVER
48	56	55	NUMBER OF STATEMENTS	4	17	6	10	7	11
%	%	%	ASSETS	%	%	%	%	%	%
10.5	13.0	11.6	Cash & Equivalents		8.3		18.3		5.1
29.5	31.4	30.9	Trade Receivables (net)		33.3		31.7		26.1
9.2	9.7	10.9	Inventory		8.3		6.2		20.1
3.3	2.1	1.9	All Other Current		4.2		.8		1.3
52.6	56.3	55.3	Total Current		54.1		57.0		52.6
35.1	31.8	32.7	Fixed Assets (net)		33.6		30.6		31.7
6.0	5.5	6.1	Intangibles (net)		5.1		4.3		10.0
6.4	6.5	6.0	All Other Non-Current		7.2		8.0		5.7
100.0	100.0	100.0	Total		100.0		100.0		100.0
			LIABILITIES						
7.5	7.2	9.1	Notes Payable-Short Term		6.1		6.8		8.6
4.9	10.2	15.1	Cur. Mat.-L/T/D		35.8		3.5		5.5
11.1	11.4	14.2	Trade Payables		20.4		8.3		9.8
.1	.2	.2	Income Taxes Payable		.0		.5		.2
7.7	8.7	9.9	All Other Current		5.7		9.5		15.4
31.3	37.7	48.4	Total Current		67.9		28.6		39.5
24.0	16.5	22.7	Long-Term Debt		34.9		9.2		19.8
.6	.6	.4	Deferred Taxes		.0		.1		1.1
2.9	6.7	8.2	All Other Non-Current		14.0		2.8		3.9
41.3	38.6	20.4	Net Worth		−16.9		59.3		35.6
100.0	100.0	100.0	Total Liabilities & Net Worth		100.0		100.0		100.0
			INCOME DATA						
100.0	100.0	100.0	Net Sales		100.0		100.0		100.0
39.6	40.1	38.4	Gross Profit		40.5		37.9		33.1
36.1	35.1	33.8	Operating Expenses		35.2		34.3		25.3
3.5	5.0	4.6	Operating Profit		5.3		3.5		7.8
1.2	.4	1.1	All Other Expenses (net)		1.6		−.9		2.2
2.2	4.6	3.5	Profit Before Taxes		3.7		4.4		5.6
			RATIOS						
2.7	3.3	2.4	Current		2.5		5.2		2.0
1.8	1.9	1.5			1.3		3.0		1.5
1.1	1.0	1.0			.7		1.3		1.0
2.0	3.0	2.1	Quick		1.9		4.3		1.5
1.4	1.5	1.1			.7		2.8		.9
.8	.8	.5			.4		1.1		.5
41 8.9	36 10.2	35 10.4	Sales/Receivables	30 12.3		34 10.9		35 10.3	
53 6.9	50 7.3	52 7.0		55 6.7		52 7.0		54 6.7	
64 5.7	66 5.5	69 5.3		69 5.3		82 4.4		86 4.2	
10 34.8	10 36.7	14 25.5	Cost of Sales/Inventory	13 27.8		6 58.3		25 14.3	
19 19.0	17 21.2	25 14.3		22 16.8		20 18.6		62 5.9	
42 8.7	29 12.6	46 8.0		39 9.2		27 13.7		91 4.0	
16 22.9	14 27.0	10 37.9	Cost of Sales/Payables	8 46.0		10 35.0		8 48.6	
24 15.0	25 14.5	28 13.3		42 8.6		23 15.7		28 13.3	
43 8.4	36 10.2	63 5.8		93 3.9		43 8.6		57 6.4	
4.4	5.2	5.4	Sales/Working Capital		5.5		2.9		5.8
11.1	10.4	17.2			22.1		6.2		22.5
63.3	168.6	−65.4			−6.6		NM		−86.5
7.6	11.8	8.0	EBIT/Interest		4.9				8.4
(44) 2.1	(50) 4.1	(49) 3.6			(15) 1.3				6.4
.6	1.6	−.3			−.1				3.9
2.7	9.3	4.9	Net Profit + Depr., Dep., Amort./Cur. Mat. L/T/D						
(11) 2.0	(10) 1.9	(14) 2.3							
1.4	1.1	1.0							
.5	.4	.4	Fixed/Worth		.4		.2		.6
1.1	.7	.9			5.8		.5		1.0
2.1	1.7	16.1			−.7		.9		1.9
.7	.5	.7	Debt/Worth		.5		.2		1.2
2.0	1.4	2.3			8.7		.8		1.9
4.2	5.0	37.1			−2.6		1.7		2.5
42.0	46.1	48.7	% Profit Before Taxes/Tangible Net Worth				39.7		
(43) 19.2	(49) 19.7	(42) 18.7					17.6		
−4.8	4.3	1.2					−20.2		
13.0	19.1	14.2	% Profit Before Taxes/Total Assets		16.5		24.2		18.4
3.3	7.2	6.0			3.7		9.9		10.3
−2.4	1.4	−.5			−6.0		−4.5		2.4
10.2	19.5	13.7	Sales/Net Fixed Assets		22.1		12.3		11.1
5.8	7.0	7.4			7.4		8.8		5.1
3.9	4.1	4.6			4.1		4.7		4.6
2.4	3.1	3.3	Sales/Total Assets		4.1		2.3		2.4
2.0	2.0	2.1			2.2		1.8		2.0
1.5	1.6	1.4			1.5		1.4		1.6
2.7	2.3	2.9	% Depr., Dep., Amort./Sales		2.2		3.2		
(42) 4.1	(47) 4.4	(49) 3.9			(16) 4.5		3.5		
6.6	7.1	6.7			8.0		6.5		
3.6	3.9	2.3	% Officers', Directors', Owners' Comp/Sales		3.2				
(18) 6.2	(18) 7.4	(20) 4.8			(11) 5.3				
12.5	11.5	11.0			11.3				
656375M	812309M	1455225M	Net Sales ($)	1168M	30304M	24495M	63943M	107040M	1228275M
466265M	540531M	932720M	Total Assets ($)	2784M	17057M	12312M	38043M	69289M	793235M

© RMA 2005   M = $ thousand   MM = $ million
See Pages 11 through 21 for Explanation of Ratios and Data

Current Data Sorted By Assets   Comparative Historical Data

Type of Statement	0-500M	500M-2MM	2-10MM	10-50MM	50-100MM	100-250MM	4/1/00-3/31/01 ALL	4/1/01-3/31/02 ALL
Unqualified				9	3	10	19	16
Reviewed		1	3	1			6	2
Compiled	5	7	3	1			7	5
Tax Returns		1						
Other		2		6	4	2	15	15

11 (4/1-9/30/04)   48 (10/1/04-3/31/05)

0-500M	500M-2MM	2-10MM	10-50MM	50-100MM	100-250MM		4/1/00-3/31/01 ALL	4/1/01-3/31/02 ALL
5	9	9	17	7	12	**NUMBER OF STATEMENTS**	47	38
%	%	%	%	%	%	**ASSETS**	%	%
			8.5		9.8	Cash & Equivalents	7.7	9.7
			19.3		20.8	Trade Receivables (net)	23.2	22.3
			10.2		19.0	Inventory	14.9	16.7
			3.1		1.5	All Other Current	4.3	4.0
			41.0		51.0	Total Current	50.1	52.7
			45.8		33.6	Fixed Assets (net)	39.4	34.8
			4.0		.6	Intangibles (net)	2.0	3.2
			9.2		14.8	All Other Non-Current	8.5	9.3
			100.0		100.0	Total	100.0	100.0
						LIABILITIES		
			3.8		.2	Notes Payable-Short Term	6.1	7.9
			2.5		.6	Cur. Mat.-L/T/D	2.6	3.3
			16.8		24.4	Trade Payables	18.8	18.9
			.2		.5	Income Taxes Payable	.4	.2
			7.6		8.3	All Other Current	7.0	7.7
			31.0		34.1	Total Current	34.8	38.0
			21.9		9.9	Long-Term Debt	20.5	17.2
			1.3		1.9	Deferred Taxes	1.9	1.6
			4.8		4.2	All Other Non-Current	2.9	3.7
			41.1		49.9	Net Worth	39.8	39.5
			100.0		100.0	Total Liabilities & Net Worth	100.0	100.0
						INCOME DATA		
			100.0		100.0	Net Sales	100.0	100.0
			15.4		9.3	Gross Profit	28.6	24.2
			10.1		4.0	Operating Expenses	19.2	15.7
			5.3		5.4	Operating Profit	9.4	8.5
			1.0		-.1	All Other Expenses (net)	.1	.8
			4.3		5.5	Profit Before Taxes	9.3	7.7
						RATIOS		
			1.7		1.7		2.1	2.0
			1.4		1.5	Current	1.3	1.4
			.8		1.3		1.1	.9
			1.2		1.4		1.3	1.2
			.8		.9	Quick	.8	.8
			.6		.6		.6	.6
			16 23.2		13 27.4		18 20.7	14 26.5
			23 15.8		20 18.6	Sales/Receivables	32 11.4	28 13.0
			33 11.0		29 12.5		55 6.6	52 7.0
			8 47.1		8 46.2		9 39.2	9 39.4
			10 35.0		25 14.6	Cost of Sales/Inventory	20 18.0	24 15.2
			18 20.8		28 13.2		58 6.3	48 7.6
			12 30.8		16 22.5		22 16.4	15 23.8
			20 18.3		25 14.8	Cost of Sales/Payables	37 10.0	24 15.1
			32 11.5		30 12.1		57 6.4	54 6.7
			14.1		15.7		8.9	9.2
			42.1		22.2	Sales/Working Capital	24.9	20.8
			-37.6		74.0		185.5	-269.5
			16.9		119.7		11.2	14.5
			(14) 5.8		(10) 65.5	EBIT/Interest	(42) 4.1	(36) 8.0
			2.8		4.8		1.8	2.3
						Net Profit + Depr., Dep.,	12.1	12.8
						Amort./Cur. Mat. L./T/D	(15) 2.6	(12) 2.8
							.4	1.3
			.7		.3		.4	.3
			1.2		.6	Fixed/Worth	1.0	.9
			2.0		1.1		2.0	1.9
			1.0		.7		.9	.8
			1.6		1.2	Debt/Worth	1.6	1.7
			2.9		1.4		2.9	2.9
			40.0		66.2	% Profit Before Taxes/Tangible	51.1	60.3
			31.8		43.3	Net Worth	(46) 27.4	(34) 34.1
			7.6		16.3		5.3	10.9
			14.4		28.1	% Profit Before Taxes/Total	17.1	25.4
			8.8		18.7	Assets	8.0	12.1
			2.7		8.9		2.3	5.1
			14.2		25.9		19.5	35.3
			7.5		13.2	Sales/Net Fixed Assets	7.5	9.4
			2.1		7.4		2.9	3.9
			4.5		5.3		3.7	3.8
			2.1		4.5	Sales/Total Assets	2.2	2.5
			1.2		1.7		1.4	1.6
			.7		.3		.9	.6
			1.4		(11) .9	% Depr., Dep., Amort./Sales	(38) 1.5	(34) 1.4
			3.8		1.1		4.0	3.5
						% Officers', Directors',	2.3	
						Owners' Comp/Sales	(10) 4.5	
							9.8	
6439M	19585M	218496M	1546265M	2085446M	8463518M	Net Sales ($)	6167750M	5260492M
1016M	10529M	44280M	397629M	514048M	2160993M	Total Assets ($)	2773021M	1994066M

© RMA 2005

M = $ thousand   MM = $ million

See Pages 11 through 21 for Explanation of Ratios and Data

Comparative Historical Data | | | | **Current Data Sorted By Sales**

			Type of Statement						
15	26	23	Unqualified			2	1	20	
5	7	5	Reviewed		1	1	1	3	
1	4	16	Compiled	9	3	2	2		
3	4	1	Tax Returns		1				
15	16	14	Other		1	1	1	11	
4/1/02-3/31/03	4/1/03-3/31/04	4/1/04-3/31/05		11 (4/1-9/30/04)		48 (10/1/04-3/31/05)			
ALL	ALL	ALL		0-1MM	1-3MM	3-5MM	5-10MM	10-25MM	25MM & OVER
39	57	59	**NUMBER OF STATEMENTS**	9	3	3	5	3	36
%	%	%	**ASSETS**	%	%	%	%	%	%
10.9	12.4	10.2	Cash & Equivalents						9.0
21.3	20.7	18.4	Trade Receivables (net)						23.8
15.9	14.0	17.6	Inventory						17.2
6.5	1.9	1.7	All Other Current						2.3
54.6	49.1	47.8	Total Current						52.3
34.3	36.7	40.6	Fixed Assets (net)						35.6
3.0	3.7	3.3	Intangibles (net)						1.6
8.2	10.5	8.3	All Other Non-Current						10.5
100.0	100.0	100.0	Total						100.0
			LIABILITIES						
6.2	6.2	3.1	Notes Payable-Short Term						3.6
3.0	3.4	2.5	Cur. Mat.-L/T/D						1.9
20.6	18.2	21.5	Trade Payables						23.7
.3	.3	.3	Income Taxes Payable						.3
9.8	6.5	9.6	All Other Current						8.9
39.9	34.6	37.0	Total Current						38.5
9.4	13.5	23.9	Long-Term Debt						13.4
1.8	1.2	1.1	Deferred Taxes						1.7
5.7	3.0	9.7	All Other Non-Current						8.6
43.2	47.7	28.4	Net Worth						37.9
100.0	100.0	100.0	Total Liabilities & Net Worth						100.0
			INCOME DATA						
100.0	100.0	100.0	Net Sales						100.0
20.3	21.5	14.5	Gross Profit						10.6
14.9	15.9	11.2	Operating Expenses						6.4
5.3	5.6	3.2	Operating Profit						4.2
.3	1.0	.5	All Other Expenses (net)						-.3
5.1	4.6	2.7	Profit Before Taxes						4.5
			RATIOS						
1.8	2.1	1.7							1.7
1.4	1.5	1.3	Current						1.5
1.0	1.1	.8							1.1
1.1	1.4	1.2							1.2
.8	.9	.8	Quick						.8
.5	.6	.3							.5
17 21.1	18 20.2	4 96.9							10 35.0
28 13.1	25 14.8	19 18.9	Sales/Receivables						20 17.8
37 9.7	43 8.5	31 11.8							31 11.8
10 36.3	10 37.4	10 35.1							8 43.3
21 17.6	20 18.1	18 19.8	Cost of Sales/Inventory						15 24.7
38 9.7	31 11.6	40 9.1							26 13.9
19 19.5	15 24.2	15 23.6							15 23.6
31 11.6	27 13.4	24 15.2	Cost of Sales/Payables						23 16.0
45 8.1	44 8.3	38 9.6							28 12.9
8.7	9.7	14.4							14.6
22.8	16.5	48.4	Sales/Working Capital						38.6
999.8	74.2	-41.8							144.0
31.7	16.1	24.5							27.7
(35) 7.4	(50) 5.6	(48) 4.4	EBIT/Interest						(31) 10.5
2.5	1.9	2.0							3.1
	6.7	33.4	Net Profit + Depr., Dep.,						
	(14) 2.5	(12) 10.5	Amort./Cur. Mat. L/T/D						
	.6	2.2							
.2	.4	.4							.5
.8	.8	1.0	Fixed/Worth						.9
1.5	1.6	2.3							1.5
.8	.7	1.1							.8
1.6	1.2	1.7	Debt/Worth						1.4
2.6	2.2	11.3							2.5
36.1	33.0	44.5	% Profit Before Taxes/Tangible						49.4
(37) 12.6	(53) 15.9	(47) 26.3	Net Worth						(35) 31.8
6.0	2.4	8.3							12.6
16.0	18.0	15.7	% Profit Before Taxes/Total						20.0
6.8	7.1	5.0	Assets						11.3
1.7	.4	.8							4.1
29.0	18.5	33.3							31.2
8.1	7.0	9.2	Sales/Net Fixed Assets						12.6
3.9	3.4	2.3							6.0
3.7	3.8	5.2							5.3
2.4	2.3	2.8	Sales/Total Assets						4.0
1.8	1.3	1.2							2.1
.5	.8	.7							.4
(37) 1.7	(53) 1.4	(54) 1.3	% Depr., Dep., Amort./Sales						(35) 1.0
3.7	4.4	3.1							1.4
	.5		% Officers', Directors',						
	(10) 1.5		Owners' Comp/Sales						
	2.8								
6786976M	8588491M	12339749M	Net Sales ($)	4460M	5224M	10084M	40003M	46600M	12233378M
2265149M	2923010M	3128495M	Total Assets ($)	9220M	484M	16748M	24394M	29844M	3047805M

© RMA 2005

M = $ thousand   MM = $ million
See Pages 11 through 21 for Explanation of Ratios and Data

Current Data Sorted By Assets   Comparative Historical Data

Type of Statement	0-500M	500M-2MM	2-10MM	10-50MM	50-100MM	100-250MM	4/1/00-3/31/01 ALL	4/1/01-3/31/02 ALL
Unqualified		4	7	10	4	1	13	15
Reviewed		12	8	5			13	17
Compiled	2	2	5	1			8	13
Tax Returns	3	4					6	5
Other		3	7	7		1	11	23
		15 (4/1-9/30/04)		71 (10/1/04-3/31/05)				
NUMBER OF STATEMENTS	5	25	27	23	4	2	51	73

	0-500M %	500M-2MM %	2-10MM %	10-50MM %	50-100MM %	100-250MM %	ALL %	ALL %
ASSETS								
Cash & Equivalents		20.8	10.5	12.5			8.1	9.1
Trade Receivables (net)		23.5	23.5	21.9			25.8	25.6
Inventory		7.3	9.3	13.5			6.5	8.4
All Other Current		4.6	5.6	3.2			8.6	5.8
Total Current		56.3	49.0	51.0			49.0	48.9
Fixed Assets (net)		31.4	39.6	38.4			41.8	40.6
Intangibles (net)		1.2	1.7	1.1			2.5	1.5
All Other Non-Current		11.2	9.7	9.5			6.7	9.1
Total		100.0	100.0	100.0			100.0	100.0
LIABILITIES								
Notes Payable-Short Term		8.4	5.9	4.6			6.4	7.7
Cur. Mat.-L/T/D		3.7	6.0	3.8			15.7	5.8
Trade Payables		13.5	15.0	14.4			16.1	14.7
Income Taxes Payable		.6	.6	.2			.5	.2
All Other Current		7.5	9.6	6.2			9.0	8.2
Total Current		33.7	37.0	29.1			47.6	36.7
Long-Term Debt		15.5	21.3	17.0			15.5	17.9
Deferred Taxes		.8	.4	.8			.9	.7
All Other Non-Current		6.7	2.1	1.7			9.7	5.8
Net Worth		43.2	39.3	51.3			26.3	38.9
Total Liabilities & Net Worth		100.0	100.0	100.0			100.0	100.0
INCOME DATA								
Net Sales		100.0	100.0	100.0			100.0	100.0
Gross Profit		26.8	22.4	23.4			20.9	23.7
Operating Expenses		20.9	16.8	19.0			17.0	16.8
Operating Profit		5.9	5.6	4.4			3.8	7.0
All Other Expenses (net)		.3	.9	.4			.3	1.3
Profit Before Taxes		5.5	4.7	4.0			3.6	5.6
RATIOS								
Current		5.1	2.1	3.1			2.5	2.0
		1.6	1.3	1.6			1.4	1.3
		1.0	.9	1.1			.9	1.1
Quick		3.8	1.2	2.4			1.8	1.4
		1.3	.9	1.1			1.1	1.1
		.7	.4	.8			.6	.7
Sales/Receivables	(9)	38.7	(12) 30.1	(21) 17.6			(22) 16.5	(23) 15.6
	(27)	13.7	(43) 8.6	(41) 8.9			(42) 8.6	(40) 9.2
	(44)	8.3	(63) 5.8	(58) 6.3			(65) 5.6	(68) 5.4
Cost of Sales/Inventory	(0)	UND	(2) 162.6	(13) 29.1			(0) UND	(2) 185.6
	(6)	58.1	(14) 27.0	(30) 12.1			(9) 42.9	(10) 35.8
	(19)	19.6	(33) 11.1	(43) 8.5			(20) 18.1	(27) 13.7
Cost of Sales/Payables	(5)	77.5	(14) 26.2	(19) 19.2			(16) 22.3	(10) 35.4
	(23)	15.6	(27) 13.6	(33) 11.1			(25) 14.7	(26) 14.0
	(38)	9.7	(55) 6.7	(47) 7.7			(42) 8.6	(37) 9.8
Sales/Working Capital		7.1	5.5	4.3			6.6	8.7
		12.9	16.9	9.4			18.1	17.4
		UND	-53.2	45.5			-70.2	62.7
EBIT/Interest		33.9	21.1	18.2			12.4	12.5
	(23)	4.8	(23) 3.3	7.4			(49) 3.2	(66) 4.7
		1.7	1.2	1.5			1.5	2.0
Net Profit + Depr., Dep., Amort./Cur. Mat. L/T/D			4.7				5.1	4.5
			(10) 3.2				(15) 2.2	(30) 2.2
			1.2				1.2	1.6
Fixed/Worth		.4	.4	.5			.5	.5
		.8	.8	.8			1.0	1.0
		1.8	4.6	1.2			1.9	2.0
Debt/Worth		.7	.7	.4			.5	.8
		1.2	2.0	1.0			1.4	1.5
		4.5	6.1	2.0			4.3	3.4
% Profit Before Taxes/Tangible Net Worth		61.2	39.5	28.4			30.1	38.5
	(23)	44.6	(24) 14.0	18.8			(46) 15.6	(68) 20.1
		8.4	4.7	5.7			6.5	7.3
% Profit Before Taxes/Total Assets		24.0	16.2	12.1			12.6	14.2
		9.9	4.0	8.1			5.3	8.2
		5.8	.6	1.4			1.9	2.9
Sales/Net Fixed Assets		24.0	9.3	8.0			10.0	9.2
		10.6	4.3	5.2			6.3	5.8
		5.8	3.6	2.8			2.5	2.9
Sales/Total Assets		3.4	2.5	2.6			3.2	3.0
		2.9	2.3	1.9			2.0	2.1
		2.4	1.3	1.2			1.5	1.4
% Depr., Dep., Amort./Sales		1.5	2.2	2.0			2.0	1.2
	(24)	3.6	3.3	(22) 2.9			(47) 3.7	(69) 3.2
		4.6	5.2	5.9			7.0	6.0
% Officers', Directors', Owners' Comp/Sales		.8	2.0				1.4	1.6
	(11)	2.4	(10) 2.4				(18) 2.7	(21) 2.2
		5.6	2.7				5.1	3.6
Net Sales ($)	9977M	96428M	295149M	849995M	514411M	467879M	1375202M	5144906M
Total Assets ($)	1184M	33634M	149845M	434216M	292658M	312839M	781389M	2080926M

M = $ thousand   MM = $ million
See Pages 11 through 21 for Explanation of Ratios and Data

Comparative Historical Data | | | | **Current Data Sorted By Sales**

		Comparative Historical Data		Type of Statement				Current Data Sorted By Sales		
	21	22	26	Unqualified			3	5	6	12
	23	17	25	Reviewed		4	6	5	7	3
	5	10	10	Compiled		3	3	1	2	1
	3	7	7	Tax Returns		3	4			
	10	19	18	Other		2	2	3	4	7
	4/1/02-3/31/03 ALL	4/1/03-3/31/04 ALL	4/1/04-3/31/05 ALL			15 (4/1-9/30/04)		71 (10/1/04-3/31/05)		
					0-1MM	1-3MM	3-5MM	5-10MM	10-25MM	25MM & OVER
NUMBER OF STATEMENTS	62	75	86			12	18	14	19	23
	%	%	%	**ASSETS**	%	%	%	%	%	%
Cash & Equivalents	11.7	11.8	14.2		20.8	18.0	13.2	11.3	11.0	
Trade Receivables (net)	22.6	21.6	22.8		14.2	21.2	23.5	25.8	25.7	
Inventory	8.8	8.4	10.1		7.3	7.7	9.7	9.7	14.0	
All Other Current	5.2	5.9	4.5		5.8	6.3	.8	5.8	3.5	
Total Current	48.3	47.6	51.6		48.1	53.1	47.3	52.6	54.1	
Fixed Assets (net)	39.7	42.4	36.6		37.3	34.2	39.6	36.9	36.1	
Intangibles (net)	2.2	2.5	1.6		1.4	.4	1.7	3.0	1.3	
All Other Non-Current	9.8	7.5	10.2		13.2	12.3	11.4	7.5	8.5	
Total	100.0	100.0	100.0		100.0	100.0	100.0	100.0	100.0	

(0-1MM column: DATA NOT AVAILABLE)

	4/1/02-3/31/03	4/1/03-3/31/04	4/1/04-3/31/05	LIABILITIES	0-1MM	1-3MM	3-5MM	5-10MM	10-25MM	25MM & OVER
Notes Payable-Short Term	9.4	7.1	9.2			29.2	8.1	4.4	6.2	5.0
Cur. Mat.-L/T/D	6.1	5.2	5.2			6.1	5.8	4.8	4.9	4.9
Trade Payables	13.7	11.9	13.9			5.2	16.6	9.1	17.5	16.3
Income Taxes Payable	.7	.5	.5			.1	.7	.9	.1	.6
All Other Current	5.7	8.5	7.5			6.1	5.1	12.6	7.1	7.4
Total Current	35.7	33.3	36.3			46.7	36.3	31.8	35.8	34.2
Long-Term Debt	14.8	25.2	21.4			42.3	21.4	18.7	17.3	15.4
Deferred Taxes	1.4	1.5	.8			.2	1.1	.2	.6	1.3
All Other Non-Current	2.6	2.9	3.3			3.0	3.3	6.9	3.0	1.8
Net Worth	45.5	37.1	38.2			7.9	37.9	42.4	43.3	47.4
Total Liabilities & Net Worth	100.0	100.0	100.0			100.0	100.0	100.0	100.0	100.0
				INCOME DATA						
Net Sales	100.0	100.0	100.0			100.0	100.0	100.0	100.0	100.0
Gross Profit	21.3	26.2	24.7			33.4	23.6	28.0	22.8	20.7
Operating Expenses	17.6	23.4	19.3			27.0	18.8	22.0	17.2	15.6
Operating Profit	3.6	2.8	5.4			6.4	4.7	5.9	5.6	5.1
All Other Expenses (net)	.7	.9	.7			1.6	.5	.6	1.2	.1
Profit Before Taxes	2.9	1.9	4.7			4.8	4.3	5.3	4.4	5.0

RATIOS

	4/1/02-3/31/03	4/1/03-3/31/04	4/1/04-3/31/05	Ratio	0-1MM	1-3MM	3-5MM	5-10MM	10-25MM	25MM & OVER
	2.1	2.5	2.8	Current		6.9	1.9	6.0	3.2	2.3
	1.5	1.5	1.5			2.0	1.5	1.5	1.3	1.5
	.9	1.0	1.0			1.0	.9	.9	.9	1.2
	1.5	1.9	1.8	Quick		5.6	1.6	4.6	1.4	1.3
	1.0	1.1	1.0			1.5	1.1	1.2	.9	1.0
	.5	.6	.7			.6	.7	.7	.6	.8
	13 27.8	14 27.0	14 25.2	Sales/Receivables	0 759.8	6 65.3	9 40.5	12 30.1	21 17.3	
	36 10.2	44 8.2	35 10.4		16 22.2	26 14.3	45 8.0	43 8.6	47 7.7	
	58 6.3	64 5.7	58 6.2		32 11.4	55 6.6	60 6.1	68 5.3	59 6.2	
	1 282.3	0 UND	2 166.3	Cost of Sales/Inventory	0 UND	0 UND	0 UND	4 95.9	13 29.1	
	10 35.7	10 35.2	14 25.9		4 82.8	8 44.6	9 38.9	19 18.9	25 14.5	
	30 12.2	31 11.7	32 11.5		26 14.1	21 17.2	25 14.4	39 9.3	43 8.5	
	11 32.1	11 33.8	10 37.7	Cost of Sales/Payables	1 445.6	16 23.1	3 113.6	21 17.8	23 16.2	
	24 15.3	24 14.9	28 13.0		6 65.1	28 12.8	20 18.2	36 10.2	33 11.1	
	52 7.0	41 9.0	46 7.9		18 19.7	55 6.7	40 9.1	59 6.2	43 8.4	
	7.5	5.7	5.5	Sales/Working Capital		6.0	6.2	3.4	5.5	6.0
	13.9	15.7	13.9			12.7	15.2	14.3	18.1	11.9
	-65.7	-208.8	133.6			NM	-296.2	-47.7	-81.6	34.8
	8.6	12.7	20.5	EBIT/Interest		25.5	30.8	32.6	14.7	20.5
	(54) 4.5	(69) 3.7	(79) 5.1			(10) 8.6	(17) 4.2	(12) 4.2	(17) 2.1	12.7
	1.3	1.1	1.5			.1	1.7	1.1	1.1	3.8
	3.2	6.6	4.5	Net Profit + Depr., Dep., Amort./Cur. Mat. L/T/D						3.7
	(19) 1.5	(27) 2.0	(32) 3.2						(11)	3.3
	1.0	.9	1.5							1.3
	.4	.5	.5	Fixed/Worth		.4	.4	.6	.4	.5
	.9	.9	.8			.9	.8	1.4	.6	.9
	1.6	2.9	1.8			NM	2.0	3.9	4.6	1.2
	.5	.6	.7	Debt/Worth		.4	.9	.6	.4	.4
	1.2	1.3	1.3			.8	1.3	2.0	1.5	1.4
	2.7	3.9	3.3			NM	4.1	5.8	6.2	2.0
	31.1	30.0	41.2	% Profit Before Taxes/Tangible Net Worth			64.9	60.3	26.6	34.3
	(59) 17.1	(70) 17.1	(78) 22.4			(16)	37.4	(13) 21.3	(17) 13.4	23.2
	4.9	3.4	7.7				7.9	1.8	8.0	13.5
	12.1	13.1	19.3	% Profit Before Taxes/Total Assets		33.3	25.7	16.9	14.3	16.2
	5.8	6.2	9.1			11.9	8.9	8.9	4.7	9.9
	1.1	.5	1.3			-.5	3.4	.8	.9	6.3
	10.0	9.9	11.1	Sales/Net Fixed Assets		24.0	16.8	12.3	10.8	8.0
	5.8	5.1	6.3			12.4	8.5	5.2	4.3	5.9
	2.9	2.8	4.1			3.4	5.0	2.2	3.6	4.2
	2.8	2.9	3.0	Sales/Total Assets		5.6	3.3	3.0	2.5	2.6
	1.9	1.8	2.4			3.4	2.6	2.3	2.3	2.2
	1.3	1.3	1.5			1.4	2.2	1.1	1.3	1.5
	2.8	2.4	2.0	% Depr., Dep., Amort./Sales		2.6	1.5	2.6	1.6	1.9
	(56) 3.7	(67) 3.5	(82) 3.2			(10) 3.8	3.6	(13) 4.7	3.3	(22) 2.6
	6.1	6.5	4.8			6.0	5.6	7.8	4.8	3.3
	1.6	2.8	1.3	% Officers', Directors', Owners' Comp/Sales						
	(19) 2.8	(21) 5.3	(31) 2.5							
	4.3	7.9	4.8							
	1955895M	1768526M	2233839M	Net Sales ($)		21393M	70747M	105179M	290419M	1746101M
	973660M	1090776M	1224376M	Total Assets ($)		10054M	29838M	74278M	158279M	951927M

© RMA 2005   M = $ thousand   MM = $ million
See Pages 11 through 21 for Explanation of Ratios and Data

Current Data Sorted By Assets   Comparative Historical Data

0-500M	500M-2MM	2-10MM	10-50MM	50-100MM	100-250MM	Type of Statement	4/1/00-3/31/01 ALL	4/1/01-3/31/02 ALL
	1	2	7		3	Unqualified	10	11
	5	6	7			Reviewed	14	10
	2	3				Compiled	7	5
1		2				Tax Returns	3	3
		7	6	3	1	Other	6	17
1	8	20	20	3	4	**NUMBER OF STATEMENTS**	40	46
%	%	%	%	%	%	**ASSETS**	%	%
		9.8	6.0			Cash & Equivalents	10.6	7.2
		29.4	22.8			Trade Receivables (net)	29.2	27.6
		29.2	24.7			Inventory	21.1	24.1
		.9	1.8			All Other Current	.9	3.3
		69.3	55.2			Total Current	61.8	62.2
		22.8	34.7			Fixed Assets (net)	24.1	27.3
		1.1	2.2			Intangibles (net)	3.4	6.6
		6.8	7.9			All Other Non-Current	10.7	3.9
		100.0	100.0			Total	100.0	100.0
						LIABILITIES		
		15.0	11.0			Notes Payable-Short Term	11.0	11.4
		2.4	3.4			Cur. Mat.-L/T/D	3.4	3.1
		20.2	16.8			Trade Payables	21.0	17.5
		.4	.2			Income Taxes Payable	.1	.1
		6.1	5.2			All Other Current	9.1	6.0
		44.2	36.5			Total Current	44.6	38.0
		11.8	14.3			Long-Term Debt	12.9	15.6
		.2	1.8			Deferred Taxes	.4	.7
		1.5	11.1			All Other Non-Current	4.4	3.5
		42.3	36.3			Net Worth	37.6	42.2
		100.0	100.0			Total Liabilities & Net Worth	100.0	100.0
						INCOME DATA		
		100.0	100.0			Net Sales	100.0	100.0
		31.5	26.6			Gross Profit	29.2	33.7
		27.4	22.0			Operating Expenses	25.2	29.8
		4.1	4.6			Operating Profit	4.0	3.9
		.1	1.0			All Other Expenses (net)	.4	.9
		4.0	3.6			Profit Before Taxes	3.7	3.1
						RATIOS		
		2.8	3.3				2.6	2.6
		1.4	1.4			Current	1.3	1.6
		1.2	1.0				.9	1.2
		1.5	1.5				1.5	1.6
		1.0	.7			Quick	.8	.8
		.5	.4				.6	.7
		31 11.8	32 11.5				37 10.0	35 10.4
		42 8.8	40 9.1			Sales/Receivables	46 8.0	42 8.7
		57 6.4	47 7.8				56 6.6	51 7.2
		27 13.6	23 15.8				29 12.4	42 8.7
		69 5.3	57 6.4			Cost of Sales/Inventory	55 6.7	59 6.2
		124 3.0	80 4.6				74 4.9	82 4.5
		25 14.7	19 19.6				25 14.4	24 15.4
		37 9.9	26 14.0			Cost of Sales/Payables	40 9.2	31 11.6
		60 6.0	49 7.4				60 6.1	56 6.5
		5.0	4.5				5.1	5.5
		8.7	12.3			Sales/Working Capital	19.5	9.8
		34.6	NM				-96.9	30.0
		24.3	10.0				8.5	9.0
		5.4	(19) 2.9			EBIT/Interest	(39) 3.5	(40) 3.4
		.9	.8				1.6	1.0
						Net Profit + Depr., Dep.,	4.3	3.9
						Amort./Cur. Mat. L /T/D	(17) 3.4	(11) 2.8
							1.2	1.3
		.3	.5				.3	.3
		.5	1.1			Fixed/Worth	.5	.6
		1.3	1.9				1.9	1.5
		.6	.9				.7	.7
		1.5	2.5			Debt/Worth	2.1	1.7
		3.2	4.6				4.2	5.4
		44.0	35.8			% Profit Before Taxes/Tangible	37.1	50.8
		(19) 20.3	(19) 21.7			Net Worth	(38) 17.5	(44) 14.9
		6.4	-4.6				8.5	1.2
		23.2	11.2			% Profit Before Taxes/Total	12.2	15.8
		8.2	5.8			Assets	6.8	5.2
		.1	-.1				1.2	.1
		30.3	10.5				27.4	20.9
		14.1	6.7			Sales/Net Fixed Assets	12.3	9.9
		5.0	4.6				5.0	4.3
		3.4	3.0				3.2	3.0
		2.8	2.2			Sales/Total Assets	2.3	2.1
		1.7	1.6				1.6	1.7
		.7	1.6				.3	.9
		1.5	(19) 1.9			% Depr., Dep., Amort./Sales	1.2	(41) 1.8
		2.8	3.0				2.3	3.2
							1.9	1.9
						% Officers', Directors',	(17) 3.6	(11) 3.2
						Owners' Comp/Sales	6.4	5.3
1343M	30616M	261063M	805340M	275543M	1223136M	Net Sales ($)	1747752M	1264670M
207M	9933M	96712M	344205M	225803M	613746M	Total Assets ($)	716754M	687201M

M = $ thousand   MM = $ million
See Pages 11 through 21 for Explanation of Ratios and Data

Comparative Historical Data | Current Data Sorted By Sales

			Type of Statement						
19	12	13	Unqualified		1		1	2	9
17	12	18	Reviewed		1	2	2	5	8
7	7	5	Compiled	1	1	1		2	
1	3	3	Tax Returns		1	1		1	
11	14	17	Other			2	3	4	8
4/1/02-3/31/03	4/1/03-3/31/04	4/1/04-3/31/05			9 (4/1-9/30/04)		47 (10/1/04-3/31/05)		
ALL	ALL	ALL		0-1MM	1-3MM	3-5MM	5-10MM	10-25MM	25MM & OVER
55	48	56	**NUMBER OF STATEMENTS**	1	4	6	6	14	25
%	%	%	**ASSETS**	%	%	%	%	%	%
7.9	6.6	7.9	Cash & Equivalents					11.1	5.7
26.2	29.6	29.1	Trade Receivables (net)					23.9	26.2
24.4	22.9	24.3	Inventory					24.8	25.0
1.9	2.3	1.2	All Other Current					2.2	1.1
60.3	61.4	62.6	Total Current					62.0	58.0
27.5	30.8	26.6	Fixed Assets (net)					29.7	27.8
3.9	2.2	3.3	Intangibles (net)					2.6	5.2
8.3	5.5	7.5	All Other Non-Current					5.6	9.0
100.0	100.0	100.0	Total					100.0	100.0
			LIABILITIES						
9.4	9.3	12.8	Notes Payable-Short Term					8.9	11.3
3.2	4.0	3.5	Cur. Mat.-L/T/D					2.9	3.5
15.9	21.1	17.4	Trade Payables					18.8	18.4
.4	.1	.2	Income Taxes Payable					.4	.2
10.4	6.7	5.9	All Other Current					5.8	5.8
39.3	41.2	39.9	Total Current					36.8	39.3
12.2	17.2	14.1	Long-Term Debt					11.9	17.2
1.0	.7	1.2	Deferred Taxes					.5	2.1
4.8	10.8	8.7	All Other Non-Current					5.4	7.4
42.7	30.1	36.1	Net Worth					45.4	34.0
100.0	100.0	100.0	Total Liabilities & Net Worth					100.0	100.0
			INCOME DATA						
100.0	100.0	100.0	Net Sales					100.0	100.0
34.3	36.7	31.1	Gross Profit					28.1	26.0
28.3	33.6	26.0	Operating Expenses					22.4	20.3
5.9	3.1	5.1	Operating Profit					5.7	5.7
.7	.6	.8	All Other Expenses (net)					.5	1.2
5.2	2.5	4.3	Profit Before Taxes					5.2	4.5
			RATIOS						
2.7	2.7	2.6						3.2	2.5
1.5	1.5	1.6	Current					1.7	1.5
1.1	1.1	1.1						1.1	1.1
1.4	1.5	1.5						1.6	1.3
.9	.8	.9	Quick					.9	.7
.5	.5	.5						.5	.5
31 12.0	32 11.3	34 10.7						29 12.6	34 10.9
45 8.1	45 8.0	42 8.6	Sales/Receivables					41 9.0	41 9.0
59 6.2	55 6.6	53 6.8						49 7.5	49 7.4
34 10.7	32 11.2	25 14.8						23 15.8	33 11.2
62 5.9	50 7.3	54 6.7	Cost of Sales/Inventory					45 8.1	55 6.6
73 5.0	75 4.9	85 4.3						72 5.1	83 4.4
23 16.2	24 15.1	19 19.6						15 23.8	22 16.9
35 10.5	35 10.4	29 12.5	Cost of Sales/Payables					29 12.5	27 13.3
53 6.9	56 6.5	49 7.4						60 6.1	48 7.5
6.1	6.2	4.9						4.6	5.9
12.2	12.1	11.5	Sales/Working Capital					8.7	12.4
62.7	73.3	35.6						106.2	45.3
17.8	13.4	20.0						31.6	20.3
(49) 6.8	(45) 4.0	(54) 4.5	EBIT/Interest					(13) 3.0	4.9
2.0	.1	1.5						.6	2.6
8.1	6.0	7.7	Net Profit + Depr., Dep.,						9.1
(17) 5.7	(14) 2.2	(17) 2.2	Amort./Cur. Mat. L/T/D					(10) 2.3	2.3
1.3	1.0	1.1							1.0
.3	.4	.4						.3	.6
.6	1.0	.9	Fixed/Worth					.6	1.1
1.7	2.0	1.8						1.6	1.9
.6	.9	.8						.5	1.2
1.5	1.8	2.5	Debt/Worth					1.6	2.9
3.9	6.3	4.6						3.4	5.0
43.1	48.4	51.1	% Profit Before Taxes/Tangible					50.9	57.1
(52) 19.8	(42) 16.2	(51) 23.4	Net Worth					26.1	(23) 31.0
4.7	−1.2	7.3						−4.7	12.7
19.8	14.4	17.5	% Profit Before Taxes/Total					28.7	14.9
9.1	5.3	6.7	Assets					5.4	7.7
2.2	−1.3	1.8						−1.5	3.6
18.4	17.6	23.0						24.5	14.5
10.6	8.5	10.1	Sales/Net Fixed Assets					9.3	7.8
4.5	4.8	5.0						4.0	5.4
3.1	3.4	3.3						3.7	3.2
2.2	2.6	2.4	Sales/Total Assets					2.7	2.3
1.5	1.8	1.7						1.5	1.8
.9	.8	.9						1.2	1.4
(52) 1.9	(39) 1.8	(53) 1.6	% Depr., Dep., Amort./Sales					1.7	(22) 1.8
2.8	2.9	2.7						3.7	2.3
2.0	2.6	1.6	% Officers', Directors',						
(17) 3.2	(13) 7.9	(16) 3.1	Owners' Comp/Sales						
4.9	12.9	7.3							
1609820M	1140462M	2597041M	Net Sales ($)	971M	7325M	22860M	43340M	228643M	2293902M
929386M	536392M	1290606M	Total Assets ($)	3737M	3201M	12930M	16023M	108162M	1146553M

M = $ thousand   MM = $ million
See Pages 11 through 21 for Explanation of Ratios and Data

Current Data Sorted By Assets

Comparative Historical Data

0-500M	500M-2MM	2-10MM	10-50MM	50-100MM	100-250MM	Type of Statement	4/1/00-3/31/01 ALL	4/1/01-3/31/02 ALL
	3	2	4 2	1	2	Unqualified		
						Reviewed		
						Compiled		
1	4 (4/1-9/30/04)	2	2	1	2	Tax Returns		
			18 (10/1/04-3/31/05)			Other		
4	4	4	8	2	4	NUMBER OF STATEMENTS		
%	%	%	%	%	%	**ASSETS**	%	%
D						Cash & Equivalents	D	D
A						Trade Receivables (net)	A	A
T						Inventory	T	T
A						All Other Current	A	A
						Total Current		
N						Fixed Assets (net)	N	N
O						Intangibles (net)	O	O
T						All Other Non-Current	T	T
						Total		
A						**LIABILITIES**	A	A
V						Notes Payable-Short Term	V	V
A						Cur. Mat.-L/T/D	A	A
I						Trade Payables	I	I
L						Income Taxes Payable	L	L
A						All Other Current	A	A
B						Total Current	B	B
L						Long-Term Debt	L	L
E						Deferred Taxes	E	E
						All Other Non-Current		
						Net Worth		
						Total Liabilities & Net Worth		
						INCOME DATA		
						Net Sales		
						Gross Profit		
						Operating Expenses		
						Operating Profit		
						All Other Expenses (net)		
						Profit Before Taxes		
						RATIOS		
						Current		
						Quick		
						Sales/Receivables		
						Cost of Sales/Inventory		
						Cost of Sales/Payables		
						Sales/Working Capital		
						EBIT/Interest		
						Net Profit + Depr., Dep., Amort./Cur. Mat. L /T/D		
						Fixed/Worth		
						Debt/Worth		
						% Profit Before Taxes/Tangible Net Worth		
						% Profit Before Taxes/Total Assets		
						Sales/Net Fixed Assets		
						Sales/Total Assets		
						% Depr., Dep., Amort./Sales		
						% Officers', Directors', Owners' Comp/Sales		
	9539M	125401M	885318M	144323M	941762M	Net Sales ($)		
	5255M	20389M	167465M	133663M	622934M	Total Assets ($)		

M = $ thousand　　MM = $ million
See Pages 11 through 21 for Explanation of Ratios and Data

Comparative Historical Data | Current Data Sorted By Sales

					Type of Statement							
	6		8	7	Unqualified							7
	4		2	2	Reviewed						1	1
	2		12	5	Compiled		3				1	1
	1				Tax Returns							
	6		8	8	Other			1	1	2		4
	4/1/02-3/31/03 ALL		4/1/03-3/31/04 ALL	4/1/04-3/31/05 ALL				4 (4/1-9/30/04)		18 (10/1/04-3/31/05)		
						0-1MM	1-3MM	3-5MM	5-10MM	10-25MM	25MM & OVER	
	19		30	22	NUMBER OF STATEMENTS		3	1	1	4	13	
	%		%	%	ASSETS	%	%	%	%	%	%	
	12.3		10.7	8.5	Cash & Equivalents	D					5.6	
	19.7		32.5	29.0	Trade Receivables (net)	A					29.4	
	17.1		17.9	21.4	Inventory	T					15.7	
	3.2		2.2	.7	All Other Current	A					1.0	
	52.3		63.4	59.7	Total Current						51.6	
	33.6		27.6	30.6	Fixed Assets (net)	N					36.7	
	2.3		3.0	3.2	Intangibles (net)	O					4.8	
	11.8		6.1	6.5	All Other Non-Current	T					6.9	
	100.0		100.0	100.0	Total						100.0	
					LIABILITIES	A						
	11.0		12.4	9.4	Notes Payable-Short Term	V					4.0	
	4.4		4.9	3.9	Cur. Mat.-L/T/D	A					5.0	
	12.5		21.2	19.6	Trade Payables	I					21.6	
	.1		.2	.2	Income Taxes Payable	L					.2	
	10.0		7.0	8.4	All Other Current	A					7.1	
	37.9		45.6	41.5	Total Current	B					37.9	
	18.8		16.2	13.7	Long-Term Debt	L					17.7	
	.8		.6	1.8	Deferred Taxes	E					3.0	
	5.4		10.8	10.3	All Other Non-Current						7.5	
	37.2		26.9	32.8	Net Worth						34.0	
	100.0		100.0	100.0	Total Liabilities & Net Worth						100.0	
					INCOME DATA							
	100.0		100.0	100.0	Net Sales						100.0	
	21.4		27.2	18.1	Gross Profit						12.2	
	17.4		25.3	13.2	Operating Expenses						8.3	
	4.0		1.9	4.9	Operating Profit						3.9	
	2.7		.6	.2	All Other Expenses (net)						.6	
	1.3		1.3	4.8	Profit Before Taxes						3.3	
					RATIOS							
	2.4		2.5	2.2							2.0	
	1.3		1.7	1.4	Current						1.4	
	.8		1.0	.9							.9	
	1.8		1.8	1.7							1.4	
	.8		1.1	.8	Quick						.9	
	.3		.5	.5							.6	
23	15.7	28	13.1	28 13.0							17 22.1	
40	9.2	46	7.9	40 9.2	Sales/Receivables						32 11.5	
53	6.8	63	5.8	56 6.5							48 7.7	
15	25.0	9	39.6	22 16.3							7 49.7	
46	7.9	34	10.6	41 9.0	Cost of Sales/Inventory						35 10.5	
74	4.9	62	5.9	62 5.9							48 7.6	
13	27.4	16	22.8	15 25.1							13 27.1	
38	9.7	41	8.9	30 12.0	Cost of Sales/Payables						27 13.6	
49	7.5	54	6.8	63 5.8							40 9.1	
	5.9		6.7	5.5							11.1	
	23.3		14.1	20.1	Sales/Working Capital						21.7	
	−24.1		NM	−111.4							−132.5	
	6.5		12.4	23.0							18.8	
(13)	1.9	(23)	4.1	(19) 8.5	EBIT/Interest						8.5	
	.7		.9	2.7							3.4	
					Net Profit + Depr., Dep., Amort./Cur. Mat. L/T/D							
	.2		.2	.2							.7	
	1.0		.9	1.0	Fixed/Worth						1.1	
	3.1		2.8	1.9							1.6	
	.4		.8	1.0							1.6	
	1.6		1.9	2.6	Debt/Worth						1.9	
	5.8		5.8	4.1							3.8	
	20.4		56.5	79.6							72.0	
(15)	11.6	(25)	14.2	(20) 21.2	% Profit Before Taxes/Tangible Net Worth						(12) 27.0	
	1.4		−3.3	8.1							9.5	
	14.5		13.2	18.1							16.4	
	3.2		3.9	6.9	% Profit Before Taxes/Total Assets						6.7	
	−1.4		−2.9	2.1							4.3	
	16.2		32.6	40.5							40.5	
	6.7		11.6	6.8	Sales/Net Fixed Assets						6.1	
	2.4		5.2	3.1							2.8	
	2.8		3.3	3.8							7.4	
	1.9		2.6	2.2	Sales/Total Assets						2.4	
	1.1		1.8	1.2							1.4	
	1.1		.8	.7							.5	
(16)	3.5	(25)	1.5	(20) 1.1	% Depr., Dep., Amort./Sales						(12) 1.7	
	6.4		4.1	3.7							2.5	
					% Officers', Directors', Owners' Comp/Sales							
	784244M		1268522M	2106343M	Net Sales ($)		6324M	3215M	8294M	61461M	2027049M	
	619015M		723693M	949706M	Total Assets ($)		4307M	948M	2547M	53858M	888046M	

M = $ thousand   MM = $ million
See Pages 11 through 21 for Explanation of Ratios and Data

Current Data Sorted By Assets   **Comparative Historical Data**

						Type of Statement		
		5	18	4	6	Unqualified	17	15
	5	11	5			Reviewed	12	14
1	4	2				Compiled	10	15
2	5	1				Tax Returns	4	2
1	1	4	5	2	4	Other	29	33
0-500M	500M-2MM	2-10MM	10-50MM	50-100MM	100-250MM		4/1/00-3/31/01 ALL	4/1/01-3/31/02 ALL
	16 (4/1-9/30/04)			70 (10/1/04-3/31/05)				
4	15	23	28	6	10	**NUMBER OF STATEMENTS**	72	79
%	%	%	%	%	%	**ASSETS**	%	%
	5.7	7.0	4.4		2.6	Cash & Equivalents	6.9	6.5
	35.2	31.0	22.4		16.7	Trade Receivables (net)	24.5	24.5
	19.5	24.7	14.2		17.5	Inventory	19.5	18.2
	2.8	.7	1.0		1.8	All Other Current	3.4	2.7
	63.1	63.4	42.0		38.6	Total Current	54.3	51.8
	33.2	25.7	48.5		40.0	Fixed Assets (net)	30.3	36.6
	.7	.5	2.8		12.8	Intangibles (net)	6.5	4.7
	2.9	10.4	6.6		8.7	All Other Non-Current	8.2	6.9
	100.0	100.0	100.0		100.0	Total	100.0	100.0
						LIABILITIES		
	15.2	15.8	6.4		5.8	Notes Payable-Short Term	8.4	9.0
	3.9	4.1	4.5		6.4	Cur. Mat.-L/T/D	3.4	4.9
	22.8	20.5	13.9		11.1	Trade Payables	14.6	14.5
	.0	.2	.2		.1	Income Taxes Payable	.4	.4
	8.9	7.2	6.4		6.3	All Other Current	8.0	8.1
	50.9	47.7	31.4		29.7	Total Current	34.8	37.0
	11.3	16.1	26.7		35.3	Long-Term Debt	18.1	20.9
	.7	.5	2.0		2.3	Deferred Taxes	.9	.8
	4.9	4.2	2.6		7.3	All Other Non-Current	7.7	8.5
	32.2	31.4	37.4		25.4	Net Worth	38.5	32.2
	100.0	100.0	100.0		100.0	Total Liabilities & Net Worth	100.0	100.0
						INCOME DATA		
	100.0	100.0	100.0		100.0	Net Sales	100.0	100.0
	40.0	35.4	32.1		29.6	Gross Profit	34.0	34.9
	35.4	30.4	25.4		19.7	Operating Expenses	27.3	31.1
	4.5	5.0	6.7		9.9	Operating Profit	6.7	3.8
	.8	.7	1.5		3.8	All Other Expenses (net)	2.2	1.9
	3.7	4.4	5.2		6.1	Profit Before Taxes	4.5	1.9
						RATIOS		
	1.9	1.8	2.2		1.7		2.5	2.2
	1.2	1.3	1.4		1.4	Current	1.6	1.6
	.9	.9	.8		1.0		1.0	1.0
	1.1	1.1	1.2		1.0		1.4	1.5
	.8	.8	.9		.7	Quick	1.0	.7
	.5	.6	.5		.3		.5	.5
	31 11.8	33 11.2	39 9.5		31 11.6		35 10.5	32 11.4
	42 8.7	45 8.2	47 7.7		48 7.6	Sales/Receivables	46 8.0	42 8.7
	62 5.9	61 6.0	60 6.0		74 5.0		59 6.2	52 7.0
	22 16.9	31 11.8	20 18.6		41 9.0		38 9.7	25 14.4
	26 13.9	48 7.7	37 9.9		63 5.8	Cost of Sales/Inventory	54 6.8	46 8.0
	52 7.1	79 4.6	70 5.3		119 3.1		89 4.1	77 4.7
	30 12.2	30 12.2	25 14.8		29 12.7		23 15.8	23 15.9
	43 8.5	49 7.4	40 9.2		44 8.3	Cost of Sales/Payables	34 10.6	34 10.9
	60 6.1	64 5.7	55 6.6		64 5.7		58 6.3	59 6.2
	8.8	8.8	7.6		7.0		4.9	5.7
	26.9	12.8	12.5		9.8	Sales/Working Capital	8.4	13.1
	−59.2	−81.7	−22.3		NM		775.6	−189.6
	16.9	13.2	12.4				8.7	7.2
	3.7	(21) 2.9	(25) 5.8			EBIT/Interest	(62) 3.6	(75) 2.6
	1.1	1.7	1.9				1.2	1.0
			3.1			Net Profit + Depr., Dep.,	10.7	7.0
		(10) 1.8				Amort./Cur. Mat. L/T/D	(19) 1.8	(16) 2.4
			.8				1.1	1.3
	.2	.2	.7		.9		.4	.5
	1.1	.7	1.3		1.8	Fixed/Worth	1.0	1.4
	2.4	2.8	2.8		NM		2.6	5.2
	1.3	1.2	.7		1.5		.8	.8
	2.5	2.2	1.5		2.2	Debt/Worth	1.9	2.3
	5.5	5.5	3.2		NM		12.8	9.7
	32.5	65.5	32.9		43.5	% Profit Before Taxes/Tangible	43.5	32.3
	(14) 15.2	(21) 12.8	(25) 21.0			Net Worth	(60) 20.1	(66) 15.3
	−1.5	7.6	10.2				5.4	3.2
	21.7	25.3	16.2		9.5	% Profit Before Taxes/Total	15.2	13.3
	5.8	5.3	7.7		8.0	Assets	6.8	4.9
	.4	2.0	3.0		2.3		.4	.4
	35.8	39.1	5.7		4.4		16.1	14.7
	11.4	16.1	3.0		2.3	Sales/Net Fixed Assets	5.7	4.7
	5.2	5.0	1.9		2.1		3.3	2.7
	4.4	3.5	2.1		1.5		2.7	3.1
	3.3	2.6	1.6		1.0	Sales/Total Assets	1.7	1.9
	2.0	1.5	.9		.8		1.1	1.1
	1.1	1.0	2.6				1.0	1.2
	(13) 2.7	(20) 2.8	4.3			% Depr., Dep., Amort./Sales	(57) 2.9	(69) 2.9
	4.7	4.2	6.4				4.9	4.9
		1.6				% Officers', Directors',	2.2	2.3
		(10) 7.2				Owners' Comp/Sales	(18) 3.7	(22) 5.1
		10.1					9.7	12.1
4361M	63216M	238844M	878349M	564234M	1813196M	Net Sales ($)	3277314M	2446249M
1036M	19581M	105431M	511735M	365421M	1568236M	Total Assets ($)	2732900M	1667479M

M = $ thousand   MM = $ million
See Pages 11 through 21 for Explanation of Ratios and Data

Comparative Historical Data | Current Data Sorted By Sales

Hist 1	Hist 2	Hist 3	Type of Statement	0-1MM	1-3MM	3-5MM	5-10MM	10-25MM	25MM & OVER
27	34	33	Unqualified			1	3	7	22
12	15	21	Reviewed		2	2	7	9	1
4	17	7	Compiled		2	3	2		
5	7	8	Tax Returns		3	2	3		
27	20	17	Other	1	2	3	2		9
4/1/02-3/31/03 ALL	4/1/03-3/31/04 ALL	4/1/04-3/31/05 ALL			16 (4/1-9/30/04)		70 (10/1/04-3/31/05)		
75	93	86	**NUMBER OF STATEMENTS**	1	7	10	18	18	32
%	%	%	**ASSETS**	%	%	%	%	%	%
8.5	5.9	5.6	Cash & Equivalents			2.9	7.1	6.2	4.7
23.5	26.7	27.6	Trade Receivables (net)			27.0	30.6	24.4	24.1
18.5	21.6	18.9	Inventory			10.3	25.9	17.1	17.7
2.2	3.2	1.3	All Other Current			3.8	.6	.8	1.4
52.8	57.4	53.4	Total Current			44.1	64.2	48.5	47.9
35.1	30.9	36.9	Fixed Assets (net)			52.7	25.7	42.0	38.9
5.9	2.9	2.8	Intangibles (net)			.8	1.1	1.0	6.1
6.2	8.8	6.8	All Other Non-Current			2.4	8.9	8.6	7.1
100.0	100.0	100.0	Total			100.0	100.0	100.0	100.0
			LIABILITIES						
6.5	11.8	11.7	Notes Payable-Short Term			11.6	17.6	10.3	5.9
4.5	4.5	4.3	Cur. Mat.-L/T/D			10.9	1.3	4.2	4.6
15.7	18.9	17.0	Trade Payables			21.9	20.3	14.7	14.2
.2	.2	.1	Income Taxes Payable			.0	.3	.0	.1
10.2	12.4	7.0	All Other Current			7.8	8.0	7.7	6.0
37.2	47.7	40.1	Total Current			52.3	47.5	37.0	30.8
18.7	14.3	20.5	Long-Term Debt			28.6	15.6	21.4	23.8
.8	.8	1.3	Deferred Taxes			1.1	.2	1.5	2.0
5.3	8.2	5.1	All Other Non-Current			4.9	5.4	1.3	6.5
38.0	29.0	33.1	Net Worth			13.2	31.2	38.9	36.9
100.0	100.0	100.0	Total Liabilities & Net Worth			100.0	100.0	100.0	100.0
			INCOME DATA						
100.0	100.0	100.0	Net Sales			100.0	100.0	100.0	100.0
35.1	34.5	34.9	Gross Profit			40.6	38.8	34.1	28.4
28.8	30.2	28.5	Operating Expenses			39.1	35.9	25.1	20.3
6.3	4.2	6.4	Operating Profit			1.5	3.0	9.0	8.1
1.5	1.2	1.4	All Other Expenses (net)			2.1	.8	1.5	1.6
4.7	3.0	5.1	Profit Before Taxes			-.6	2.2	7.5	6.5
			RATIOS						
2.2	2.0	1.9	Current			1.3	2.0	1.8	2.2
1.5	1.3	1.4				.9	1.3	1.3	1.6
1.0	.8	.9				.3	1.0	.9	1.1
1.4	1.1	1.1	Quick			.9	1.3	1.1	1.5
.9	.7	.8				.5	.8	.7	.9
.5	.5	.5				.2	.6	.5	.6
33 11.2	34 10.7	34 10.8	Sales/Receivables	23 16.1		32 11.3	34 10.7		36 10.0
44 8.3	45 8.1	45 8.1		39 9.3		42 8.8	47 7.8		50 7.2
54 6.8	56 6.5	62 5.9		61 6.0		62 5.9	58 6.3		64 5.7
29 12.7	27 13.3	23 16.2	Cost of Sales/Inventory	0 UND		30 12.1	30 12.2		27 13.8
53 6.8	45 8.1	42 8.7		22 16.4		49 7.4	48 7.6		42 8.7
93 3.9	85 4.3	80 4.6		30 12.4		163 2.2	87 4.2		77 4.7
27 13.5	29 12.7	28 13.1	Cost of Sales/Payables	34 10.7		25 14.4	21 17.3		29 12.6
43 8.6	38 9.5	42 8.6		49 7.4		53 6.9	41 8.8		37 9.8
64 5.7	60 6.1	61 6.0		98 3.7		66 5.5	56 6.5		62 5.9
6.0	6.8	7.5	Sales/Working Capital			22.4	8.8	8.7	6.6
11.2	17.1	13.4				-65.7	20.6	17.8	9.3
165.9	-24.6	-62.0				-5.8	-754.5	-40.3	72.8
10.9	9.4	12.8	EBIT/Interest			7.2	3.7	34.3	12.7
(72) 4.5	(85) 3.2	(80) 3.8				1.4	(17) 2.6	7.7	(27) 5.2
1.3	1.3	1.5				.1	1.7	2.2	2.1
5.8	3.1	3.4	Net Profit + Depr., Dep., Amort./Cur. Mat. L/T/D						4.0
(30) 1.8	(27) 2.1	(29) 2.2						(13) 2.1	
.8	1.5	1.2							.7
.5	.3	.5	Fixed/Worth			.7	.3	.5	.6
.9	.8	1.1				3.4	.9	1.3	1.3
2.5	3.0	2.8				NM	1.5	3.0	2.0
.7	.9	1.1	Debt/Worth			1.7	1.2	.7	1.0
1.5	2.2	1.9				3.7	2.2	1.7	1.7
3.9	6.9	4.1				NM	5.6	3.4	2.5
34.1	32.4	39.9	% Profit Before Taxes/Tangible Net Worth				39.3	44.6	43.1
(65) 20.7	(82) 11.4	(76) 20.5					(17) 11.1	(17) 29.5	(28) 22.4
3.0	2.8	7.6					4.6	10.2	9.2
14.1	10.2	16.7	% Profit Before Taxes/Total Assets			11.8	9.8	26.7	17.2
7.4	4.8	6.7				2.0	3.5	8.8	9.3
.5	.6	1.9				-3.1	1.3	3.7	2.6
11.2	27.6	17.7	Sales/Net Fixed Assets			41.2	23.0	16.1	8.3
4.8	7.6	5.4				5.5	15.5	4.0	3.7
2.7	3.2	2.3				1.0	6.0	1.7	2.2
2.6	2.8	3.3	Sales/Total Assets			3.6	3.7	2.6	2.1
1.6	1.9	1.9				2.4	2.9	1.8	1.6
1.1	1.3	1.1				.9	1.4	.9	1.1
1.6	1.2	1.6	% Depr., Dep., Amort./Sales				1.0	1.4	1.8
(67) 3.1	(80) 2.5	(74) 3.5					(16) 3.3	3.7	(26) 3.5
4.8	4.5	5.2					4.8	5.6	4.8
2.6	2.1	1.7	% Officers', Directors', Owners' Comp/Sales						
(18) 7.5	(25) 6.0	(23) 4.4							
19.2	14.2	10.0							
2663219M	2889584M	3562200M	Net Sales ($)	430M	13110M	39686M	133467M	283998M	3091509M
1906124M	1973033M	2571440M	Total Assets ($)	113M	5301M	31828M	65825M	190504M	2277869M

M = $ thousand   MM = $ million
See Pages 11 through 21 for Explanation of Ratios and Data

Current Data Sorted By Assets   Comparative Historical Data

						Type of Statement		
1	4	6	13	6	2	Unqualified	23	28
		8	6			Reviewed	10	8
	2		1			Compiled	7	10
1	1		1			Tax Returns		2
1	1	8	10	3	7	Other	19	19
							4/1/00-3/31/01	4/1/01-3/31/02
	23 (4/1-9/30/04)		59 (10/1/04-3/31/05)				ALL	ALL
0-500M	500M-2MM	2-10MM	10-50MM	50-100MM	100-250MM			
3	8	22	31	9	9	NUMBER OF STATEMENTS	59	67
%	%	%	%	%	%	ASSETS	%	%
		5.2	4.6			Cash & Equivalents	8.2	6.8
		28.1	19.7			Trade Receivables (net)	20.9	19.5
		19.7	19.0			Inventory	18.8	17.5
		1.1	4.6			All Other Current	2.4	4.5
		54.0	47.9			Total Current	50.3	48.4
		39.1	43.4			Fixed Assets (net)	35.7	37.9
		1.2	2.0			Intangibles (net)	6.5	5.3
		5.8	6.7			All Other Non-Current	7.5	8.4
		100.0	100.0			Total	100.0	100.0
						LIABILITIES		
		15.9	7.5			Notes Payable-Short Term	6.3	6.4
		5.9	4.0			Cur. Mat.-L/T/D	3.2	4.5
		17.6	13.2			Trade Payables	12.6	12.0
		.4	.1			Income Taxes Payable	.3	.3
		6.4	6.1			All Other Current	6.9	7.4
		46.1	30.9			Total Current	29.3	30.6
		22.2	19.5			Long-Term Debt	21.0	20.7
		1.0	1.1			Deferred Taxes	1.3	1.0
		1.6	5.2			All Other Non-Current	3.7	5.3
		29.0	43.3			Net Worth	44.6	42.4
		100.0	100.0			Total Liabilities & Net Worth	100.0	100.0
						INCOME DATA		
		100.0	100.0			Net Sales	100.0	100.0
		32.6	24.9			Gross Profit	32.2	33.5
		27.0	17.5			Operating Expenses	24.0	25.9
		5.7	7.4			Operating Profit	8.2	7.7
		1.3	.6			All Other Expenses (net)	.4	1.2
		4.3	6.8			Profit Before Taxes	7.9	6.4
						RATIOS		
		1.9	2.7			Current	2.5	2.6
		1.2	1.7				1.8	1.8
		1.0	1.1				1.2	1.1
		1.1	1.3			Quick	1.4	1.6
		.8	1.0				1.0	.8
		.5	.4				.7	.5
		41 8.9	26 14.3			Sales/Receivables	32 11.3	32 11.4
		45 8.1	42 8.6				47 7.7	43 8.5
		52 7.0	51 7.2				57 6.4	56 6.5
		21 17.0	17 21.4			Cost of Sales/Inventory	26 14.1	24 15.5
		47 7.7	46 7.9				57 6.4	58 6.3
		81 4.5	82 4.5				87 4.2	80 4.6
		23 16.0	18 20.3			Cost of Sales/Payables	21 17.1	22 16.3
		43 8.5	30 12.2				40 9.1	32 11.3
		61 6.0	45 8.0				54 6.7	67 5.5
		7.7	4.4			Sales/Working Capital	4.4	4.3
		26.3	14.2				8.2	9.0
		-86.6	47.1				25.6	81.2
		8.6	15.8			EBIT/Interest	9.9	9.1
		(21) 4.1	8.5				(56) 3.8	(63) 3.1
		1.2	2.6				1.6	1.2
		21.6	10.8			Net Profit + Depr., Dep.,	12.0	5.8
		(10) 2.4	(14) 2.1			Amort./Cur. Mat. L/T/D	(20) 2.3	(21) 1.4
		1.3	.7				1.3	1.0
		.7	.6			Fixed/Worth	.4	.3
		1.7	1.0				1.1	1.0
		3.4	1.6				1.9	1.8
		.8	.5			Debt/Worth	.6	.7
		2.9	.9				1.3	1.6
		7.4	3.7				4.2	3.4
		58.1	52.0			% Profit Before Taxes/Tangible	51.4	47.9
		(19) 28.4	(30) 31.1			Net Worth	(53) 21.5	(62) 17.9
		9.0	13.2				10.4	1.8
		15.8	19.6			% Profit Before Taxes/Total	17.0	14.8
		7.1	9.7			Assets	8.4	5.5
		1.4	3.9				1.6	.6
		13.8	14.1			Sales/Net Fixed Assets	15.1	12.5
		5.5	4.4				4.8	4.8
		3.4	2.2				2.3	1.9
		2.8	2.3			Sales/Total Assets	2.2	2.1
		1.9	1.7				1.4	1.4
		1.6	1.3				1.0	.9
		1.2	2.2			% Depr., Dep., Amort./Sales	1.3	1.0
		2.8	(28) 3.9				(49) 2.7	(58) 3.1
		4.4	5.0				5.1	5.7
						% Officers', Directors',	2.2	1.6
						Owners' Comp/Sales	(11) 4.3	(19) 2.9
							8.4	10.4
4568M	28408M	226380M	1330040M	784586M	1569030M	Net Sales ($)	2573668M	2728520M
582M	9169M	109664M	747070M	569855M	1221459M	Total Assets ($)	1869397M	2184806M

M = $ thousand   MM = $ million
See Pages 11 through 21 for Explanation of Ratios and Data

Comparative Historical Data | **Current Data Sorted By Sales**

Type of Statement										
26	28	27	Unqualified				3	4	20
9	15	19	Reviewed		3	3	4	6	3
8	6	3	Compiled			1	1	1	
2	2	3	Tax Returns		2			1	
23	30	30	Other	1		3	5	3	18
4/1/02-3/31/03 ALL	4/1/03-3/31/04 ALL	4/1/04-3/31/05 ALL		23 (4/1-9/30/04)			59 (10/1/04-3/31/05)		
				0-1MM	1-3MM	3-5MM	5-10MM	10-25MM	25MM & OVER
68	81	82	**NUMBER OF STATEMENTS**	1	5	7	13	15	41
%	%	%	**ASSETS**	%	%	%	%	%	%
7.7	6.5	6.6	Cash & Equivalents				6.4	4.2	6.2
23.4	21.7	23.2	Trade Receivables (net)				24.0	25.3	20.3
19.6	17.0	18.8	Inventory				17.9	23.7	16.6
4.1	3.4	2.7	All Other Current				1.5	7.4	2.0
54.8	48.7	51.3	Total Current				49.9	60.5	45.2
34.7	40.1	38.9	Fixed Assets (net)				40.9	26.7	43.9
3.5	5.1	3.3	Intangibles (net)				1.0	.9	5.8
7.1	6.1	6.5	All Other Non-Current				8.2	11.9	5.2
100.0	100.0	100.0	Total				100.0	100.0	100.0
			LIABILITIES						
6.2	9.5	10.4	Notes Payable-Short Term				9.9	12.1	7.3
3.2	4.8	4.1	Cur. Mat.-L/T/D				5.9	3.6	4.0
12.3	14.0	16.0	Trade Payables				12.5	21.1	12.1
.2	.3	.2	Income Taxes Payable				.5	.2	.1
10.9	9.1	7.0	All Other Current				4.8	8.5	5.9
32.8	37.7	37.7	Total Current				33.7	45.5	29.4
16.7	18.7	20.8	Long-Term Debt				25.4	14.1	19.3
1.2	.7	1.1	Deferred Taxes				.3	1.6	1.3
4.8	9.0	7.6	All Other Non-Current				2.5	5.2	3.3
44.6	33.9	32.8	Net Worth				38.1	33.6	46.6
100.0	100.0	100.0	Total Liabilities & Net Worth				100.0	100.0	100.0
			INCOME DATA						
100.0	100.0	100.0	Net Sales				100.0	100.0	100.0
30.0	28.1	29.2	Gross Profit				41.8	23.0	23.0
23.3	21.9	22.9	Operating Expenses				34.3	18.6	14.6
6.7	6.2	6.3	Operating Profit				7.5	4.4	8.4
.9	1.4	.8	All Other Expenses (net)				1.2	.5	.6
5.8	4.8	5.5	Profit Before Taxes				6.4	3.9	7.9
			RATIOS						
2.8	2.1	2.2					1.9	3.7	2.5
1.7	1.3	1.5	Current				1.3	1.7	1.6
1.3	.9	1.1					1.0	1.1	1.2
1.3	1.2	1.3					1.2	2.0	1.4
1.0	.7	.9	Quick				1.1	.8	1.0
.6	.5	.6					.6	.4	.6
36 10.0	23 15.6	29 12.5					35 10.3	37 10.0	22 16.6
47 7.8	42 8.8	45 8.1	Sales/Receivables				44 8.2	46 7.9	46 7.9
62 5.9	52 7.0	53 6.9					52 7.0	52 7.0	56 6.5
22 16.8	18 20.8	20 18.3					20 18.7	24 15.0	20 18.3
51 7.2	35 10.5	44 8.3	Cost of Sales/Inventory				53 6.9	61 6.0	35 10.4
90 4.1	72 5.0	75 4.9					96 3.8	86 4.2	63 5.8
19 19.0	19 19.5	20 18.7					22 16.3	28 13.0	15 24.8
32 11.5	34 10.6	37 9.9	Cost of Sales/Payables				41 8.9	50 7.2	30 12.2
51 7.2	57 6.4	56 6.5					57 6.4	63 5.8	45 8.0
4.3	5.7	6.6					7.3	3.4	5.8
8.8	20.2	13.4	Sales/Working Capital				13.9	7.6	12.1
16.4	-53.7	81.5					NM	27.8	44.9
11.3	12.5	10.6					12.4	8.7	13.3
(61) 5.9	(74) 3.6	(77) 4.3	EBIT/Interest				(12) 5.2	4.1	(39) 7.8
1.6	1.1	1.4					2.0	.4	2.9
13.6	10.6	6.8	Net Profit + Depr., Dep.,						4.4
(20) 2.2	(21) 1.7	(33) 2.1	Amort./Cur. Mat. L/T/D						(19) 2.2
.4	1.2	1.1							1.0
.2	.4	.6					.7	.3	.6
.6	1.2	1.4	Fixed/Worth				1.4	.7	1.4
1.6	2.9	3.1					3.1	1.8	2.4
.6	.7	.6					.7	.4	.5
1.3	1.5	1.9	Debt/Worth				1.9	2.6	1.0
2.9	5.1	7.4					6.5	4.2	3.8
37.0	33.3	47.1	% Profit Before Taxes/Tangible				61.0	35.3	44.8
(64) 19.0	(69) 18.5	(69) 26.1	Net Worth				(12) 40.2	(13) 15.6	(38) 29.6
4.8	1.6	9.9					6.6	4.5	13.2
17.8	14.5	17.8	% Profit Before Taxes/Total				17.9	9.7	19.3
6.7	7.0	7.4	Assets				10.1	6.4	9.3
2.0	.3	1.9					4.0	-1.0	3.9
23.4	11.6	14.0					11.0	30.4	13.0
5.1	5.5	5.5	Sales/Net Fixed Assets				4.4	8.5	4.1
2.3	1.7	2.5					3.0	4.4	2.1
2.0	2.5	2.3					2.2	3.0	2.3
1.4	1.5	1.8	Sales/Total Assets				1.7	1.8	1.6
1.1	1.1	1.3					1.5	1.3	1.1
1.3	1.4	1.4					1.5	.6	1.9
(58) 2.4	(67) 3.3	(75) 2.8	% Depr., Dep., Amort./Sales				2.6	(14) 3.0	(36) 3.5
5.0	5.9	4.7					4.7	4.0	5.0
1.7	1.4	2.1	% Officers', Directors',						
(16) 2.3	(12) 2.1	(19) 3.4	Owners' Comp/Sales						
7.5	9.6	8.1							
2486877M	4242406M	3943012M	Net Sales ($)	429M	9441M	28570M	100084M	241052M	3563436M
1908228M	2743150M	2657799M	Total Assets ($)	215M	3003M	25303M	57411M	144386M	2427481M

M = $ thousand   MM = $ million
See Pages 11 through 21 for Explanation of Ratios and Data

Current Data Sorted By Assets							Comparative Historical Data	
						Type of Statement		
1	1	12	22	8	9	Unqualified	36	32
1	7	23	14	1		Reviewed	30	21
5	14	13	1			Compiled	32	32
7	6	4	2			Tax Returns	6	6
5	7	28	20	2	2	Other	40	58
	46 (4/1-9/30/04)		169 (10/1/04-3/31/05)				4/1/00-3/31/01	4/1/01-3/31/02
0-500M	500M-2MM	2-10MM	10-50MM	50-100MM	100-250MM		ALL	ALL
19	35	80	59	11	11	**NUMBER OF STATEMENTS**	144	149
%	%	%	%	%	%	**ASSETS**	%	%
14.4	8.9	6.4	2.6	4.3	3.3	Cash & Equivalents	4.5	6.5
28.9	31.8	26.6	28.8	27.1	19.1	Trade Receivables (net)	29.6	24.9
16.8	20.0	23.9	22.5	17.8	18.5	Inventory	22.3	21.4
1.3	.7	3.3	2.0	1.6	1.2	All Other Current	2.6	3.1
61.4	61.5	60.2	55.9	50.8	42.1	Total Current	58.9	56.0
28.0	32.9	31.4	32.8	35.2	42.7	Fixed Assets (net)	34.2	36.0
1.4	1.1	2.9	6.8	5.3	11.1	Intangibles (net)	2.6	3.8
8.9	4.5	5.4	4.5	8.7	4.1	All Other Non-Current	4.3	4.2
100.0	100.0	100.0	100.0	100.0	100.0	Total	100.0	100.0
						LIABILITIES		
16.0	11.7	10.1	14.8	8.7	4.3	Notes Payable-Short Term	13.3	11.8
10.2	4.7	3.9	5.0	2.9	3.0	Cur. Mat.-L/T/D	5.3	5.1
17.9	18.3	20.0	19.1	11.7	12.3	Trade Payables	17.7	14.4
.1	.3	.3	.1	.6	.6	Income Taxes Payable	.5	.2
16.7	9.0	7.3	5.4	9.0	8.0	All Other Current	11.6	10.9
60.9	44.0	41.6	44.3	32.9	28.1	Total Current	48.3	42.4
32.1	15.9	16.7	18.2	13.4	29.4	Long-Term Debt	20.2	21.0
.1	.4	.7	1.1	3.1	.9	Deferred Taxes	.7	.6
3.3	7.3	6.9	2.7	12.1	5.5	All Other Non-Current	7.7	5.2
3.5	32.4	34.0	33.8	38.5	36.1	Net Worth	23.0	30.8
100.0	100.0	100.0	100.0	100.0	100.0	Total Liabilities & Net Worth	100.0	100.0
						INCOME DATA		
100.0	100.0	100.0	100.0	100.0	100.0	Net Sales	100.0	100.0
44.9	31.3	27.6	18.5	19.7	22.7	Gross Profit	27.6	26.1
39.7	27.8	23.0	13.5	16.0	16.9	Operating Expenses	22.6	22.5
5.2	3.5	4.5	5.0	3.7	5.8	Operating Profit	5.0	3.5
.7	1.4	.8	.9	.8	1.1	All Other Expenses (net)	1.9	1.8
4.5	2.1	3.7	4.0	3.0	4.6	Profit Before Taxes	3.1	1.7
						RATIOS		
2.1	2.4	2.1	1.7	2.3	2.0		2.0	2.4
1.1	1.4	1.5	1.2	1.8	1.5	Current	1.4	1.4
.6	.8	1.0	1.0	1.2	1.2		1.0	1.0
1.6	1.6	1.3	1.0	1.4	1.0		1.2	1.3
.8	1.0	.8	.6	1.0	.8	Quick	.8	.8
.3	.4	.6	.5	.7	.6		.5	.5
16 23.0	34 10.9	30 12.2	44 8.3	50 7.3	35 10.5		38 9.6	35 10.5
42 8.7	40 9.2	42 8.6	54 6.8	53 6.8	52 7.0	Sales/Receivables	48 7.6	45 8.2
46 7.9	52 7.0	55 6.7	64 5.7	56 6.5	56 6.5		59 6.1	54 6.7
0 UND	19 19.3	28 12.8	35 10.5	38 9.7	40 9.1		32 11.3	30 12.2
30 12.0	30 12.3	52 7.0	48 7.6	44 8.4	71 5.2	Cost of Sales/Inventory	49 7.5	44 8.2
61 6.0	65 5.6	81 4.5	69 5.3	60 6.1	87 4.2		73 5.0	70 5.2
11 32.4	13 27.6	25 14.3	28 13.0	18 19.9	25 14.6		21 17.0	18 20.1
35 10.6	30 12.0	41 9.0	45 8.2	27 13.3	41 8.9	Cost of Sales/Payables	34 10.6	30 12.1
49 7.5	55 6.7	52 7.0	56 6.5	40 9.2	52 7.1		54 6.8	49 7.4
7.1	6.0	5.9	9.2	5.5	6.8		7.0	5.7
37.2	21.1	13.6	22.9	8.5	9.6	Sales/Working Capital	15.4	14.0
-28.1	-26.2	NM	-186.8	23.2	21.8		NM	-88.3
11.9	8.9	16.0	8.5	14.0	9.1		4.8	4.7
(13) 6.2	4.1	(77) 5.2	(55) 4.1	(10) 4.0	4.9	EBIT/Interest	(131) 2.4	(134) 2.2
-2.3	.8	1.7	2.0	.4	1.7		1.0	.4
		6.7	4.6			Net Profit + Depr., Dep.,	6.0	2.7
		(21) 2.2	(21) 2.5			Amort./Cur. Mat. L /T/D	(41) 2.7	(46) 1.6
		1.2	.8				1.4	.9
.5	.2	.3	.4	.6	1.0		.5	.5
2.1	.8	.9	1.3	.9	1.9	Fixed/Worth	1.2	1.4
-10.5	3.3	2.2	2.6	1.3	-38.0		3.6	3.1
1.6	.9	.8	1.2	.9	1.3		1.0	.9
7.0	1.7	1.8	2.9	1.4	2.2	Debt/Worth	2.3	2.3
-72.7	7.4	4.0	7.5	2.8	-74.3		7.0	7.9
301.7	65.7	43.2	34.7	28.1		% Profit Before Taxes/Tangible	42.5	27.5
(14) 28.5	(31) 25.0	(73) 23.7	(54) 21.1	(10) 12.2		Net Worth	(122) 26.2	(126) 11.5
2.9	4.0	8.6	7.6	-2.2			3.8	-.3
32.3	16.2	16.3	11.4	12.0	10.7	% Profit Before Taxes/Total	13.9	11.2
13.9	7.9	7.7	5.4	5.3	4.7	Assets	5.5	4.2
1.2	-.4	1.6	2.4	-.1	3.2		.4	-2.0
50.3	32.2	18.1	9.1	7.2	4.3		14.3	13.0
15.9	11.1	7.5	5.6	5.0	2.4	Sales/Net Fixed Assets	6.1	5.3
6.3	4.6	4.2	3.5	3.0	1.9		3.6	3.1
5.0	3.7	2.9	2.3	2.1	1.4		2.9	2.6
3.3	2.9	2.3	1.9	1.6	1.3	Sales/Total Assets	2.1	1.9
1.8	1.8	1.6	1.3	1.2	1.0		1.4	1.4
1.5	.9	1.4	1.5	2.6			1.1	1.3
(14) 2.5	(33) 3.0	(77) 2.7	(53) 3.3	4.3		% Depr., Dep., Amort./Sales	(123) 2.2	(130) 2.7
4.3	5.3	4.7	4.7	7.3			4.2	4.7
	3.8	1.5				% Officers', Directors',	1.6	2.7
	(19) 7.1	(39) 3.2				Owners' Comp/Sales	(47) 4.0	(42) 6.8
	8.8	5.8					8.6	10.3
17207M	125442M	926347M	2494229M	1298860M	2512037M	Net Sales ($)	4510836M	5275774M
5313M	44558M	413615M	1330578M	747147M	1801475M	Total Assets ($)	2917156M	3734934M

Comparative Historical Data						Type of Statement	Current Data Sorted By Sales					
61		46		53		Unqualified	1	1		6	9	36
42		39		46		Reviewed	1	5	4	11	16	9
21		43		33		Compiled	4	8	4	11	6	
12		13		19		Tax Returns	5	5	3	1	4	1
61		64		64		Other	3	4	5	10	18	24
4/1/02-3/31/03 ALL		4/1/03-3/31/04 ALL		4/1/04-3/31/05 ALL			46 (4/1-9/30/04)			169 (10/1/04-3/31/05)		
							0-1MM	1-3MM	3-5MM	5-10MM	10-25MM	25MM & OVER
197		205		215		NUMBER OF STATEMENTS	14	23	16	39	53	70
%		%		%		ASSETS	%	%	%	%	%	%
5.5		5.9		6.2		Cash & Equivalents	14.2	11.0	6.3	9.2	4.6	2.5
25.6		28.3		27.9		Trade Receivables (net)	22.0	28.4	30.0	24.6	30.4	28.4
22.3		21.4		21.7		Inventory	11.7	20.1	20.7	22.9	24.2	21.8
2.8		2.5		2.2		All Other Current	.4	1.2	.6	3.8	1.8	2.5
56.2		57.9		57.9		Total Current	48.4	60.8	57.6	60.6	60.9	55.3
35.9		32.8		32.5		Fixed Assets (net)	40.2	32.2	30.9	33.1	30.9	32.4
3.3		4.2		4.1		Intangibles (net)	1.8	1.7	3.0	2.8	2.9	7.2
4.6		5.1		5.4		All Other Non-Current	9.3	5.4	8.5	3.6	5.3	5.1
100.0		100.0		100.0		Total	100.0	100.0	100.0	100.0	100.0	100.0
						LIABILITIES						
9.9		12.7		11.8		Notes Payable-Short Term	12.6	12.9	13.9	6.8	13.2	12.6
6.3		4.7		4.8		Cur. Mat.-L/T/D	12.6	5.4	4.4	4.2	3.6	4.3
16.4		18.1		18.4		Trade Payables	14.0	16.8	15.1	17.6	21.0	19.1
.3		.2		.3		Income Taxes Payable	.0	.4	.3	.5	.1	.3
9.9		12.1		8.0		All Other Current	15.3	9.4	13.0	7.6	6.0	6.7
42.7		47.7		43.3		Total Current	54.6	44.9	46.7	36.6	43.9	43.0
21.6		18.3		18.8		Long-Term Debt	38.7	21.2	11.3	20.2	14.6	18.2
1.0		1.2		.8		Deferred Taxes	.1	.4	.3	1.1	.4	1.4
7.2		8.2		5.7		All Other Non-Current	5.2	6.5	21.8	3.2	3.8	4.7
27.4		24.5		31.3		Net Worth	1.2	27.0	19.8	38.9	37.2	32.7
100.0		100.0		100.0		Total Liabilities & Net Worth	100.0	100.0	100.0	100.0	100.0	100.0
						INCOME DATA						
100.0		100.0		100.0		Net Sales	100.0	100.0	100.0	100.0	100.0	100.0
26.8		27.0		26.6		Gross Profit	48.8	33.6	26.9	30.3	25.3	18.6
22.1		21.6		22.0		Operating Expenses	40.1	32.7	23.3	25.4	20.1	14.0
4.6		5.4		4.6		Operating Profit	8.6	.8	3.6	4.9	5.2	4.6
1.5		1.6		.9		All Other Expenses (net)	1.8	1.3	1.7	.5	.6	.9
3.1		3.8		3.6		Profit Before Taxes	6.8	-.4	1.9	4.4	4.6	3.6
						RATIOS						
2.2		2.0		2.0		Current	2.1	2.5	2.3	2.5	2.0	1.7
1.4		1.4		1.4			1.0	1.3	1.3	1.6	1.4	1.3
1.0		1.0		1.0			.4	.9	.7	1.2	1.0	1.1
1.2		1.2		1.2		Quick	1.5	1.8	1.3	1.6	1.2	1.0
.7		.7		.8			.9	.9	.8	.9	.8	.8
.5		.5		.5			.3	.3	.3	.6	.6	.5
34	10.7	34	10.6	34	10.9	Sales/Receivables	0 UND	26 13.9	30 12.2	27 13.6	34 10.6	44 8.3
45	8.1	46	7.9	47	7.7		43 8.4	39 9.5	36 10.0	44 8.3	47 7.7	52 7.0
54	6.7	55	6.6	56	6.5		58 6.3	48 7.5	60 6.1	58 6.3	62 5.9	57 6.5
33	11.1	31	11.9	28	13.1	Cost of Sales/Inventory	0 UND	24 15.4	9 42.1	27 13.6	31 11.6	34 10.6
49	7.5	48	7.6	47	7.7		35 10.4	38 9.7	39 9.3	47 7.7	53 6.9	46 7.9
65	5.6	68	5.4	70	5.2		65 5.6	59 6.2	87 4.2	81 4.5	71 5.1	68 5.4
21	17.0	24	15.4	22	16.4	Cost of Sales/Payables	0 UND	21 17.1	7 53.9	22 16.5	29 12.6	26 13.9
36	10.1	38	9.7	39	9.3		17 21.4	36 10.1	31 11.7	36 10.2	43 8.5	41 9.0
48	7.6	51	7.1	52	7.0		63 5.8	51 7.1	48 7.6	52 7.0	58 6.2	49 7.4
	6.6		7.3		7.8	Sales/Working Capital	5.3	5.5	5.9	5.4	7.3	8.8
	12.5		15.0		15.0		NM	14.5	39.7	10.2	14.2	16.4
	584.7		-140.2		-999.8		-7.9	-48.4	-17.8	38.9	-106.3	62.9
	7.4		8.4		11.9	EBIT/Interest	11.8	7.9	15.9	14.7	20.7	8.7
(185)	3.0	(188)	3.1	(201)	4.4		(11) 3.6	(20) 2.7	4.5	(37) 5.2	(51) 6.1	(66) 4.0
	.8		1.1		1.7		-6.3	.5	.4	3.1	1.5	1.9
	4.5		4.8		6.0	Net Profit + Depr., Dep., Amort./Cur. Mat. L/T/D				4.6	6.0	
(55)	2.1	(59)	2.1	(62)	2.3					(18) 1.7	(25) 2.2	
	.8		1.1		1.2					.8	1.0	
	.6		.5		.4	Fixed/Worth	.9	.5	.2	.2	.4	.5
	1.3		1.3		1.1		4.4	1.3	.8	.9	1.0	1.3
	3.1		3.2		2.9		-8.0	2.8	3.5	2.2	2.2	2.6
	1.1		1.2		1.0	Debt/Worth	1.0	.9	.9	.8	.8	1.3
	2.2		2.5		2.4		8.6	2.7	2.1	1.6	1.8	2.8
	7.5		10.0		6.9		-55.3	14.0	7.8	4.3	4.1	9.2
	41.7		50.6		41.1	% Profit Before Taxes/Tangible Net Worth	226.2	29.6	51.5	45.5	40.3	36.2
(171)	18.4	(174)	20.9	(190)	21.8		(10) 24.6	(19) 14.9	(14) 22.4	(37) 27.3	(49) 23.1	(61) 18.5
	4.1		4.9		7.8		-1.8	2.1	7.3	9.0	10.5	7.4
	12.8		16.8		13.9	% Profit Before Taxes/Total Assets	34.8	13.9	19.5	16.3	15.9	11.0
	5.9		4.7		6.9		7.7	7.9	6.8	9.7	7.7	4.9
	-.2		.6		1.7		-1.7	-3.3	-1.1	3.7	1.3	2.3
	12.7		16.2		17.5	Sales/Net Fixed Assets	27.9	18.1	18.1	28.4	12.6	10.0
	5.5		6.1		6.6		5.9	9.6	13.3	7.4	6.4	5.7
	3.3		3.8		4.0		2.4	4.4	5.0	3.7	4.2	3.6
	2.8		2.8		3.0	Sales/Total Assets	3.9	3.7	3.2	2.9	2.9	2.5
	2.1		2.1		2.1		1.7	3.1	2.7	2.3	2.2	1.9
	1.4		1.5		1.5		.9	1.6	1.6	1.7	1.6	1.3
	1.6		1.3		1.5	% Depr., Dep., Amort./Sales	1.9	2.2	.8	1.1	1.6	1.4
(174)	3.2	(184)	3.0	(195)	3.0		(13) 3.9	(18) 3.5	2.9	(37) 3.1	(49) 2.5	(62) 3.1
	5.3		5.3		4.9		11.2	5.7	5.1	5.4	4.1	5.0
	2.6		2.4		1.7	% Officers', Directors', Owners' Comp/Sales				1.8	1.3	
(54)	4.6	(54)	5.1	(70)	4.5				(20) 3.6	(21) 1.9	
	7.8		7.2		7.1					6.6	4.7	
9187583M		6849523M		7374122M		Net Sales ($)	7325M	43685M	64860M	277977M	841544M	6138731M
4808785M		3943602M		4342686M		Total Assets ($)	7157M	20108M	30244M	162673M	439642M	3682862M

M = $ thousand   MM = $ million
See Pages 11 through 21 for Explanation of Ratios and Data

Current Data Sorted By Assets   Comparative Historical Data

Type of Statement

	0-500M	500M-2MM	2-10MM	10-50MM	50-100MM	100-250MM	Type of Statement	4/1/00-3/31/01 ALL	4/1/01-3/31/02 ALL
							Unqualified	10	10
	1	2	7			1			
							Reviewed	7	6
	2	5	1						
							Compiled	6	5
	2	2							
							Tax Returns	1	2
	2	2							
							Other	18	10
1	1		1						

Date spans (left): **11 (4/1-9/30/04)** covers 0-500M / 500M-2MM / 2-10MM; **19 (10/1/04-3/31/05)** covers 10-50MM / 50-100MM / 100-250MM.

	0-500M	500M-2MM	2-10MM	10-50MM	50-100MM	100-250MM		4/1/00-3/31/01 ALL	4/1/01-3/31/02 ALL
NUMBER OF STATEMENTS	1	8	11	9		1		42	33

ASSETS (%)

(Left columns 0-500M, 500M-2MM, 10-50MM, 50-100MM, 100-250MM: "DATA NOT AVAILABLE")

	2-10MM		4/1/00-3/31/01	4/1/01-3/31/02
Cash & Equivalents	8.3		4.7	6.8
Trade Receivables (net)	21.9		23.1	21.6
Inventory	25.9		27.5	25.4
All Other Current	1.7		1.8	2.5
Total Current	57.8		57.1	56.3
Fixed Assets (net)	32.2		31.5	30.1
Intangibles (net)	.7		4.9	7.0
All Other Non-Current	9.4		6.5	6.6
Total	100.0		100.0	100.0

LIABILITIES

	2-10MM		4/1/00-3/31/01	4/1/01-3/31/02
Notes Payable-Short Term	24.1		17.2	14.5
Cur. Mat.-L/T/D	7.0		3.3	3.2
Trade Payables	7.6		14.9	12.5
Income Taxes Payable	.3		.4	.5
All Other Current	10.3		12.5	10.4
Total Current	49.4		48.3	41.1
Long-Term Debt	7.3		10.4	14.7
Deferred Taxes	.6		.5	.5
All Other Non-Current	.5		4.7	5.1
Net Worth	42.2		36.0	38.6
Total Liabilities & Net Worth	100.0		100.0	100.0

INCOME DATA

	2-10MM		4/1/00-3/31/01	4/1/01-3/31/02
Net Sales	100.0		100.0	100.0
Gross Profit	27.9		31.4	33.0
Operating Expenses	22.0		28.5	29.4
Operating Profit	5.9		3.0	3.6
All Other Expenses (net)	.1		.5	1.0
Profit Before Taxes	5.8		2.5	2.6

RATIOS

Ratio	2-10MM		4/1/00-3/31/01	4/1/01-3/31/02
Current	1.9		2.1	2.4
	1.2		1.3	1.3
	.8		.9	1.1
Quick	1.1		1.2	1.2
	.6		.6	.7
	.4		.3	.4
Sales/Receivables	(19) 19.6		(28) 13.0	(25) 14.6
	(26) 13.8		(36) 10.2	(40) 9.0
	(83) 4.4		(56) 6.5	(60) 6.1
Cost of Sales/Inventory	(36) 10.1		(39) 9.4	(53) 6.9
	(53) 6.8		(60) 6.1	(72) 5.1
	(118) 3.1		(125) 2.9	(105) 3.5
Cost of Sales/Payables	(7) 54.6		(20) 18.3	(23) 16.2
	(16) 22.4		(32) 11.3	(33) 11.0
	(27) 13.4		(50) 7.3	(47) 7.8
Sales/Working Capital	10.0		8.2	7.6
	26.6		18.0	15.1
	-27.6		-50.9	47.4
EBIT/Interest	6.4		8.1	17.6
	4.8		(40) 2.0	(30) 3.0
	1.2		1.3	1.2
Net Profit + Depr., Dep., Amort./Cur. Mat. L/T/D			5.5	
			(13) 1.8	
			1.2	
Fixed/Worth	.5		.5	.4
	.9		.9	.7
	1.2		2.9	1.9
Debt/Worth	.9		.6	.6
	1.8		1.7	1.5
	2.7		5.2	3.9
% Profit Before Taxes/Tangible Net Worth	28.7		30.1	38.8
	24.3		(36) 18.2	(30) 15.1
	1.1		8.8	6.0
% Profit Before Taxes/Total Assets	10.9		11.4	10.8
	6.5		4.0	5.6
	.6		1.2	1.5
Sales/Net Fixed Assets	11.0		13.3	16.1
	6.2		6.7	6.5
	3.2		4.3	4.1
Sales/Total Assets	2.9		2.5	2.1
	1.7		1.9	1.9
	1.3		1.7	1.4
% Depr., Dep., Amort./Sales	1.5		1.7	1.4
	3.1		(39) 2.4	(30) 2.1
	5.6		4.1	4.1
% Officers', Directors', Owners' Comp/Sales			1.6	1.7
			(14) 3.8	(13) 4.5
			8.6	9.2

Dollar Totals

	0-500M	500M-2MM	2-10MM	10-50MM	50-100MM	100-250MM		4/1/00-3/31/01	4/1/01-3/31/02
Net Sales ($)	1231M	29926M	106225M	602233M		561041M		1550978M	806334M
Total Assets ($)	194M	10249M	56347M	244979M		155993M		870549M	512544M

© RMA 2005

M = $ thousand   MM = $ million
See Pages 11 through 21 for Explanation of Ratios and Data

Comparative Historical Data | Current Data Sorted By Sales

4/1/02-3/31/03 ALL	4/1/03-3/31/04 ALL	4/1/04-3/31/05 ALL	Type of Statement	0-1MM	1-3MM	3-5MM	5-10MM	10-25MM	25MM & OVER
12	21	11	Unqualified		1		1	1	8
11	6	8	Reviewed		2	1	1	3	1
2	6	4	Compiled			2	2		
2	3	4	Tax Returns		1		3		
10	9	3	Other		1		1		1
				11 (4/1-9/30/04)			19 (10/1/04-3/31/05)		
37	45	30	NUMBER OF STATEMENTS		5	3	8	4	10
%	%	%	ASSETS	%	%	%	%	%	%
7.9	9.0	10.3	Cash & Equivalents	DATA NOT AVAILABLE					10.0
22.0	22.0	21.5	Trade Receivables (net)						26.0
25.0	23.3	31.3	Inventory						32.7
1.1	3.3	1.4	All Other Current						1.2
56.0	57.6	64.5	Total Current						70.0
32.8	32.9	26.3	Fixed Assets (net)						24.9
2.7	3.8	1.7	Intangibles (net)						3.0
8.5	5.7	7.5	All Other Non-Current						2.2
100.0	100.0	100.0	Total						100.0
			LIABILITIES						
12.1	10.2	17.1	Notes Payable-Short Term						17.4
3.1	4.6	4.2	Cur. Mat.-L/T/D						2.6
15.8	15.6	13.8	Trade Payables						20.2
.6	.5	.3	Income Taxes Payable						.4
9.5	9.1	13.2	All Other Current						14.6
41.1	40.1	48.5	Total Current						55.2
13.8	18.3	11.9	Long-Term Debt						5.8
.8	.9	.7	Deferred Taxes						1.3
3.6	5.4	2.5	All Other Non-Current						1.3
40.6	35.4	36.4	Net Worth						36.4
100.0	100.0	100.0	Total Liabilities & Net Worth						100.0
			INCOME DATA						
100.0	100.0	100.0	Net Sales						100.0
32.3	27.9	25.5	Gross Profit						19.1
29.1	23.7	21.5	Operating Expenses						17.7
3.2	4.2	4.1	Operating Profit						1.5
.2	.9	.1	All Other Expenses (net)						-.3
3.0	3.3	4.0	Profit Before Taxes						1.8
			RATIOS						
2.1	2.3	1.9							1.4
1.4	1.3	1.2	Current						1.2
1.0	1.1	1.0							1.1
1.3	1.3	.9							.8
.7	.8	.6	Quick						.6
.4	.5	.5							.4
21 17.7	**26** 14.0	**15** 24.6							**22** 16.2
36 10.2	**38** 9.7	**30** 12.3	Sales/Receivables						**37** 9.8
60 6.1	**57** 6.4	**52** 7.0							**56** 6.5
46 8.0	**37** 9.8	**36** 10.3							**29** 12.5
60 6.1	**61** 6.0	**65** 5.6	Cost of Sales/Inventory						**66** 5.5
89 4.1	**89** 4.1	**92** 4.0							**84** 4.3
22 16.3	**21** 17.3	**11** 33.7							**23** 16.1
35 10.5	**40** 9.1	**24** 15.1	Cost of Sales/Payables						**32** 11.3
60 6.0	**54** 6.8	**45** 8.1							**49** 7.5
7.7	6.7	9.7							13.8
19.2	14.4	18.2	Sales/Working Capital						24.3
-84.1	47.1	NM							80.4
5.6	6.3	6.8							
(36) 3.7	(44) 3.4	(28) 3.4	EBIT/Interest						
1.1	.8	1.5							
6.5	10.6	8.4							
(13) 2.4	(16) 3.2	(13) 2.7	Net Profit + Depr., Dep., Amort./Cur. Mat. L/T/D						
1.0	2.2	1.2							
.5	.5	.5							.5
.8	.9	.9	Fixed/Worth						.8
1.5	1.7	1.2							1.3
.6	.8	.9							1.1
1.4	2.0	1.9	Debt/Worth						1.9
2.6	4.1	4.3							4.3
31.1	27.7	28.5							17.3
(35) 17.5	(42) 19.0	(29) 15.8	% Profit Before Taxes/Tangible Net Worth						5.4
1.1	5.2	4.6							3.8
10.6	11.3	10.1							7.3
6.5	5.4	6.4	% Profit Before Taxes/Total Assets						2.6
.4	.0	1.5							.6
15.1	14.8	20.2							25.5
7.0	5.8	10.0	Sales/Net Fixed Assets						11.7
3.7	2.8	4.2							4.4
2.8	2.5	3.4							3.6
2.1	1.9	2.4	Sales/Total Assets						2.4
1.5	1.3	1.5							1.8
1.9	1.5	1.0							.9
(35) 2.6	(39) 2.5	(27) 2.1	% Depr., Dep., Amort./Sales						1.4
5.1	4.6	3.6							3.3
1.8	1.9								
(13) 3.9	(10) 5.0		% Officers', Directors', Owners' Comp/Sales						
7.7	6.5								
1223942M	**1413326M**	**1300656M**	Net Sales ($)		**8860M**	**13608M**	**58519M**	**56395M**	**1163274M**
596216M	**784428M**	**467762M**	Total Assets ($)		**4819M**	**8352M**	**26471M**	**27148M**	**400972M**

M = $ thousand MM = $ million

See Pages 11 through 21 for Explanation of Ratios and Data

Current Data Sorted By Assets   **Comparative Historical Data**

0-500M	500M-2MM	2-10MM	10-50MM	50-100MM	100-250MM	Type of Statement	4/1/00-3/31/01 ALL	4/1/01-3/31/02 ALL
		3	3	2	1	Unqualified	7	5
	1	1				Reviewed	2	2
		6				Compiled	5	4
						Tax Returns	1	
	1	1	3		1	Other	5	11
	9 (4/1-9/30/04)		**16 (10/1/04-3/31/05)**					
2	11	8	2	2		**NUMBER OF STATEMENTS**	20	22
%	%	%	%	%	%	**ASSETS**	%	%
		13.3				Cash & Equivalents	11.4	4.3
		27.3				Trade Receivables (net)	21.4	21.3
		21.5				Inventory	31.6	28.7
		1.7				All Other Current	1.0	3.7
		63.8				Total Current	65.4	58.0
		30.4				Fixed Assets (net)	25.6	34.5
		.1				Intangibles (net)	2.5	2.2
		5.6				All Other Non-Current	6.6	5.3
		100.0				Total	100.0	100.0
						LIABILITIES		
		8.9				Notes Payable-Short Term	14.4	15.1
		2.0				Cur. Mat.-L/T/D	4.9	7.8
		17.5				Trade Payables	12.7	29.5
		.5				Income Taxes Payable	.3	.6
		7.5				All Other Current	5.3	5.7
		36.4				Total Current	37.6	58.8
		8.3				Long-Term Debt	13.1	13.9
		2.3				Deferred Taxes	.3	1.0
		1.4				All Other Non-Current	6.5	.3
		51.7				Net Worth	42.4	26.0
		100.0				Total Liabilities & Net Worth	100.0	100.0
						INCOME DATA		
		100.0				Net Sales	100.0	100.0
		38.8				Gross Profit	30.2	25.3
		30.3				Operating Expenses	24.8	23.4
		8.6				Operating Profit	5.4	2.0
		1.1				All Other Expenses (net)	-2.1	1.3
		7.4				Profit Before Taxes	7.5	.6
						RATIOS		
		2.8				Current	4.2	2.1
		1.6					1.3	1.2
		1.3					1.2	.8
		2.0				Quick	1.7	.9
		.9					.7	.6
		.6					.5	.3
	18	20.0				Sales/Receivables	23 16.0	28 13.0
	40	9.1					35 10.4	38 9.5
	79	4.6					45 8.1	43 8.6
	47	7.8				Cost of Sales/Inventory	47 7.8	36 10.3
	91	4.0					84 4.3	57 6.4
	107	3.4					128 2.9	92 4.0
	20	18.1				Cost of Sales/Payables	19 19.3	25 14.7
	32	11.3					33 11.0	39 9.4
	59	6.2					39 9.3	70 5.2
		5.4				Sales/Working Capital	4.4	9.0
		9.4					10.1	16.7
		11.0					26.2	-13.7
						EBIT/Interest	9.9	4.3
							(18) 3.9	(18) 1.9
							1.9	1.3
						Net Profit + Depr., Dep., Amort./Cur. Mat. L./T/D		
		.0				Fixed/Worth	.3	.5
		.7					.9	1.2
		1.0					1.8	2.4
		.3				Debt/Worth	.8	.9
		1.0					1.4	3.2
		2.7					4.6	5.3
		37.9				% Profit Before Taxes/Tangible Net Worth	54.9	26.0
		25.2					(19) 27.8	(20) 11.6
		12.8					16.4	2.5
		17.8				% Profit Before Taxes/Total Assets	18.4	11.1
		12.6					10.7	2.6
		6.5					7.7	-.5
		65.6				Sales/Net Fixed Assets	14.6	10.1
		5.9					7.9	7.2
		3.3					6.2	4.4
		2.4				Sales/Total Assets	2.6	2.6
		1.8					2.0	2.0
		1.4					1.6	1.6
						% Depr., Dep., Amort./Sales	1.4	.9
							1.8 (20)	1.8
							3.3	3.0
						% Officers', Directors', Owners' Comp/Sales		
	4701M	120612M	426875M	204985M	737288M	Net Sales ($)	501982M	632971M
	2622M	52645M	197813M	119072M	267451M	Total Assets ($)	264335M	328190M

(In the 0-500M and 500M-2MM current-data columns the body reads vertically: DATA NOT AVAILABLE)

M = $ thousand   MM = $ million
See Pages 11 through 21 for Explanation of Ratios and Data

Comparative Historical Data | Current Data Sorted By Sales

	3/4/5/8	7/2/10/6	9/3/7/6	Type of Statement						
	3	7	9	Unqualified			1	1	1	7
	4	2	3	Reviewed		1			1	
	5	10	7	Compiled		3	2	2		
				Tax Returns						
	8	6	6	Other	1				1	4

	4/1/02-3/31/03 ALL	4/1/03-3/31/04 ALL	4/1/04-3/31/05 ALL		0-1MM	9 (4/1-9/30/04) 1-3MM	3-5MM	16 (10/1/04-3/31/05) 5-10MM	10-25MM	25MM & OVER
NUMBER OF STATEMENTS	20	25	25		1		4	3	5	12
	%	%	%	ASSETS	%	%	%	%	%	%
Cash & Equivalents	5.3	8.8	9.4							7.8
Trade Receivables (net)	20.0	21.4	24.4							28.0
Inventory	28.8	25.4	28.6							30.0
All Other Current	4.4	2.7	3.2			DATA NOT AVAILABLE				4.5
Total Current	58.6	58.4	65.6							70.5
Fixed Assets (net)	36.6	35.0	28.1							20.4
Intangibles (net)	1.0	1.1	.4							.8
All Other Non-Current	3.8	5.6	5.9							8.4
Total	100.0	100.0	100.0							100.0
				LIABILITIES						
Notes Payable-Short Term	11.1	12.7	12.8							14.2
Cur. Mat.-L/T/D	10.8	5.3	2.3							2.5
Trade Payables	13.5	15.2	17.2							22.0
Income Taxes Payable	.2	.6	.2							.0
All Other Current	6.8	6.6	9.1							14.0
Total Current	42.3	40.5	41.6							52.8
Long-Term Debt	10.1	16.4	9.6							6.1
Deferred Taxes	1.1	1.4	1.7							1.3
All Other Non-Current	6.8	2.0	1.7							2.3
Net Worth	39.7	39.7	45.4							37.4
Total Liabilities & Net Worth	100.0	100.0	100.0							100.0
				INCOME DATA						
Net Sales	100.0	100.0	100.0							100.0
Gross Profit	33.0	31.1	31.1							20.8
Operating Expenses	27.1	26.8	24.3							16.6
Operating Profit	5.9	4.4	6.7							4.2
All Other Expenses (net)	1.4	.6	.8							.6
Profit Before Taxes	4.4	3.8	5.9							3.6
				RATIOS						
Current	2.4	2.6	2.4							2.0
	1.5	1.3	1.5							1.3
	1.1	1.1	1.2							1.1
Quick	.9	1.3	1.2							1.1
	.6	.6	.8							.7
	.3	.5	.5							.4
Sales/Receivables	17 21.5	18 19.8	19 19.7							21 17.2
	34 10.8	38 9.6	40 9.1							39 9.4
	57 6.4	47 7.8	63 5.8							58 6.3
Cost of Sales/Inventory	40 9.1	40 9.0	49 7.5							37 9.8
	74 4.9	66 5.5	82 4.5							71 5.2
	103 3.6	83 4.4	105 3.5							96 3.8
Cost of Sales/Payables	18 20.4	10 38.2	22 16.9							29 12.8
	26 14.2	29 12.5	32 11.3							33 11.0
	47 7.7	43 8.5	54 6.8							46 7.9
Sales/Working Capital	4.8	5.4	5.1							6.6
	13.0	17.4	11.0							13.0
	35.5	52.7	19.2							62.8
EBIT/Interest	7.0	11.4	9.3							9.0
	3.3	(23) 5.9	(22) 5.0							(10) 4.6
	1.5	.5	1.3							1.1
Net Profit + Depr., Dep., Amort./Cur. Mat. L/T/D		7.6								
		(10) 3.7								
		1.8								
Fixed/Worth	.4	.3	.3							.3
	.8	.6	.6							.5
	2.3	1.4	.9							.8
Debt/Worth	.7	.6	.6							.9
	1.3	1.5	1.3							2.0
	4.2	4.7	2.8							3.0
% Profit Before Taxes/Tangible Net Worth	35.6	37.8	37.7							28.1
	(19) 24.0	(22) 18.3	23.1							11.1
	6.3	1.9	1.4							.3
% Profit Before Taxes/Total Assets	16.0	16.2	16.5							15.0
	5.1	7.3	7.2							2.9
	1.1	-2.8	.6							.1
Sales/Net Fixed Assets	14.1	18.5	18.0							20.8
	7.6	7.3	9.5							11.4
	3.9	4.6	3.5							8.0
Sales/Total Assets	2.7	3.0	2.6							3.5
	2.1	2.2	1.8							2.4
	1.5	1.5	1.4							1.6
% Depr., Dep., Amort./Sales	1.5	1.6	1.4							1.3
	(17) 2.2	(23) 2.5	(20) 2.2							(10) 2.0
	4.1	4.9	3.5							2.6
% Officers', Directors', Owners' Comp/Sales										
Net Sales ($)	936237M	530645M	1494461M		727M		16283M	21673M	76716M	1379062M
Total Assets ($)	430530M	273128M	639603M		936M		9897M	13117M	39688M	575965M

© RMA 2005

M = $ thousand   MM = $ million
See Pages 11 through 21 for Explanation of Ratios and Data

Current Data Sorted By Assets　　　　　　　　　　Comparative Historical Data

0-500M	500M-2MM	2-10MM	10-50MM	50-100MM	100-250MM	Type of Statement	4/1/00-3/31/01 ALL	4/1/01-3/31/02 ALL
	2	4	5	5	4	Unqualified	7	12
		4	3			Reviewed	1	1
		2				Compiled	10	7
						Tax Returns	1	
4	2	6	3		2	Other	6	7
		14 (4/1-9/30/04)		32 (10/1/04-3/31/05)				
4	4	16	11	5	6	NUMBER OF STATEMENTS	25	27
%	%	%	%	%	%	ASSETS	%	%
		13.9	7.1			Cash & Equivalents	6.0	8.7
		25.2	17.8			Trade Receivables (net)	19.8	21.5
		26.8	31.8			Inventory	33.7	27.4
		1.9	2.4			All Other Current	1.8	2.7
		67.9	59.1			Total Current	61.3	60.2
		23.8	25.9			Fixed Assets (net)	22.3	25.2
		1.9	4.4			Intangibles (net)	6.1	3.4
		6.4	10.7			All Other Non-Current	10.3	11.2
		100.0	100.0			Total	100.0	100.0
						LIABILITIES		
		5.7	7.2			Notes Payable-Short Term	10.0	15.4
		3.5	2.5			Cur. Mat.-L/T/D	1.8	2.5
		13.8	12.0			Trade Payables	12.7	12.0
		.9	.3			Income Taxes Payable	.1	.4
		11.3	13.5			All Other Current	8.8	5.9
		35.1	35.5			Total Current	33.4	36.3
		12.9	11.4			Long-Term Debt	16.3	13.1
		1.7	1.0			Deferred Taxes	.2	.4
		6.7	7.3			All Other Non-Current	7.6	1.6
		43.6	44.8			Net Worth	42.4	48.7
		100.0	100.0			Total Liabilities & Net Worth	100.0	100.0
						INCOME DATA		
		100.0	100.0			Net Sales	100.0	100.0
		39.6	34.9			Gross Profit	30.3	30.0
		35.2	29.2			Operating Expenses	25.5	26.1
		4.4	5.7			Operating Profit	4.8	4.0
		1.5	1.4			All Other Expenses (net)	2.9	1.5
		3.0	4.3			Profit Before Taxes	1.9	2.4
						RATIOS		
		3.0	3.4			Current	3.7	3.5
		2.0	2.1				1.9	1.8
		1.2	1.1				1.2	1.0
		1.5	1.1			Quick	1.7	2.1
		1.0	.8				.8	.7
		.7	.4				.3	.5
		29　12.8	31　11.7			Sales/Receivables	20　18.3	34　10.8
		43　8.5	42　8.7				36　10.2	42　8.7
		60　6.1	71　5.1				53　6.9	65　5.6
		40　9.2	81　4.5			Cost of Sales/Inventory	53　6.9	37　9.9
		76　4.8	127　2.9				94　3.9	84　4.3
		114　3.2	163　2.2				177　2.1	164　2.2
		14　26.0	20　18.4			Cost of Sales/Payables	17　22.0	17　21.2
		41　9.0	37　9.8				31　11.9	37　10.0
		60　6.1	67　5.5				62　5.9	51　7.2
		3.5	3.4			Sales/Working Capital	3.8	3.8
		4.8	6.2				6.4	5.3
		32.2	33.7				31.9	89.1
		16.4	24.7			EBIT/Interest	6.7	3.5
		(13)　5.4	4.4				(23)　1.7	(21)　1.7
		-.1	1.8				.9	1.0
						Net Profit + Depr., Dep., Amort./Cur. Mat. L /T/D		
		.1	.3			Fixed/Worth	.2	.2
		.4	.6				.3	.4
		1.4	1.0				1.5	1.2
		.6	.6			Debt/Worth	.3	.3
		1.3	1.6				1.0	1.2
		3.4	3.3				4.2	2.8
		34.2	42.1			% Profit Before Taxes/Tangible Net Worth	29.5	17.4
		(14)　12.5	18.7				(21)　16.0	(25)　10.1
		6.3	1.5				2.1	2.1
		19.4	10.6			% Profit Before Taxes/Total Assets	13.3	10.9
		4.2	8.5				2.8	3.0
		-1.1	1.0				-.1	.9
		30.0	10.1			Sales/Net Fixed Assets	39.9	17.2
		12.7	5.6				11.7	11.7
		3.3	3.8				6.0	3.7
		2.7	1.7			Sales/Total Assets	2.7	2.1
		2.0	1.4				1.7	1.5
		1.7	1.1				1.1	1.1
		.8	1.6			% Depr., Dep., Amort./Sales	.3	1.3
		(13)　2.2	(10)　2.3				(24)　1.4	(24)　1.7
		3.4	3.5				3.3	3.1
						% Officers', Directors', Owners' Comp/Sales		
7235M	23327M	152238M	361216M	538513M	1805640M	Net Sales ($)	1498201M	1479118M
1675M	5859M	75190M	268212M	337254M	1114166M	Total Assets ($)	1040981M	876403M

© RMA 2005

M = $ thousand　　MM = $ million
See Pages 11 through 21 for Explanation of Ratios and Data

Comparative Historical Data				Current Data Sorted By Sales					

Type of Statement

15		18		20	Unqualified		1				2	6	11
5		5		7	Reviewed						3	2	2
4		8		2	Compiled			2					
4				4	Tax Returns		4						
7		6		13	Other			3		3	3	3	4
4/1/02- 3/31/03 ALL		4/1/03- 3/31/04 ALL		4/1/04- 3/31/05 ALL			0-1MM	14 (4/1-9/30/04) 1-3MM	3-5MM	5-10MM	32 (10/1/04-3/31/05) 10-25MM		25MM & OVER
31		41		46	**NUMBER OF STATEMENTS**		5	5	5	8	11		17
%		%		%	**ASSETS**	%	%	%	%	%	%		%
5.4		9.8		9.9	Cash & Equivalents						17.8		5.2
23.1		24.8		22.7	Trade Receivables (net)	D					22.3		20.6
32.1		25.3		29.4	Inventory	A					24.0		31.7
4.3		3.8		3.4	All Other Current	T					3.4		3.4
64.9		63.7		65.4	Total Current	A					67.4		60.9
23.1		24.2		21.4	Fixed Assets (net)						23.2		16.6
5.1		6.8		4.7	Intangibles (net)	N					2.7		9.4
7.0		5.3		8.5	All Other Non-Current	O					6.6		13.1
100.0		100.0		100.0	Total	T					100.0		100.0
					LIABILITIES	A							
13.3		8.8		7.9	Notes Payable-Short Term	V					2.2		7.2
2.9		1.8		2.4	Cur. Mat.-L/T/D	A					2.3		2.2
15.6		13.0		12.8	Trade Payables	I					10.6		15.6
.4		.4		.5	Income Taxes Payable	L					.9		.7
9.4		8.9		11.5	All Other Current	A					8.6		14.3
41.6		33.0		35.2	Total Current	B					24.6		40.1
11.4		15.7		16.4	Long-Term Debt	L					12.9		11.9
1.4		1.1		1.2	Deferred Taxes	E					.5		1.5
4.2		6.8		5.6	All Other Non-Current						7.3		2.1
41.4		43.4		41.6	Net Worth						54.7		44.5
100.0		100.0		100.0	Total Liabilities & Net Worth						100.0		100.0
					INCOME DATA								
100.0		100.0		100.0	Net Sales						100.0		100.0
29.8		36.1		36.2	Gross Profit						42.3		30.8
23.6		29.9		30.1	Operating Expenses						35.7		22.1
6.2		6.2		6.1	Operating Profit						6.6		8.7
1.4		.8		.9	All Other Expenses (net)						.7		.6
4.7		5.4		5.1	Profit Before Taxes						5.9		8.0
					RATIOS								
2.1		3.6		3.2							4.0		2.8
1.6		2.2		2.0	Current						3.0		1.5
1.1		1.4		1.2							1.9		1.1
1.1		1.8		1.5							3.2		1.3
.8		1.0		.9	Quick						1.4		.7
.4		.8		.5							.8		.4

31	11.7	28	13.0	27	13.4				28	12.8	33	11.2
37	9.8	38	9.6	35	10.5	Sales/Receivables			37	9.9	42	8.6
58	6.3	73	5.0	60	6.1				54	6.8	70	5.2
48	7.7	39	9.3	58	6.3				41	9.0	88	4.2
95	3.9	81	4.5	95	3.8	Cost of Sales/Inventory			80	4.5	143	2.6
131	2.8	114	3.2	143	2.5				122	3.0	174	2.1
23	15.6	10	37.9	18	20.8				11	32.1	32	11.6
37	9.8	31	11.7	39	9.4	Cost of Sales/Payables			20	18.4	53	6.9
61	6.0	51	7.1	67	5.5				67	5.5	77	4.8
	5.1		4.0		3.6					3.5		3.5
	6.9		5.6		6.1	Sales/Working Capital				4.3		6.9
	25.5		14.7		30.7					5.1		35.7
	6.9		17.9		12.3								18.8
(27)	3.2	(35)	5.0	(41)	5.4	EBIT/Interest						7.9
	1.8		2.0		1.7								4.0
	11.9		11.1		15.9	Net Profit + Depr., Dep.,						
(13)	3.3	(12)	4.0	(11)	3.6	Amort./Cur. Mat. L/T/D						
	1.7		1.8		2.9								
	.2		.2		.2					.1		.2
	.4		.4		.5	Fixed/Worth				.3		.4
	1.0		1.0		1.2					1.2		.7
	.8		.5		.7					.3		.8
	1.7		1.6		1.7	Debt/Worth				.9		1.8
	3.4		3.7		3.5					1.7		3.1
	33.9		54.2		40.3	% Profit Before Taxes/Tangible				48.5		40.7
(29)	17.1	(37)	19.4	(42)	23.3	Net Worth				27.4	(16)	34.1
	5.2		9.8		8.5					7.4		19.1
	12.4		13.9		12.5	% Profit Before Taxes/Total				21.7		12.5
	6.1		7.9		6.1	Assets				10.2		10.6
	2.3		3.3		1.8					3.6		5.8
	37.8		19.7		26.6					30.6		20.6
	11.1		10.9		12.3	Sales/Net Fixed Assets				8.4		10.1
	3.2		4.7		4.5					4.7		4.3
	2.5		3.0		2.7					3.2		1.8
	1.7		1.7		1.7	Sales/Total Assets				1.7		1.4
	1.2		1.3		1.2					1.3		.8
	1.1		.8		1.0							1.0
(26)	1.9	(37)	1.8	(36)	2.2	% Depr., Dep., Amort./Sales					(14)	1.5
	4.0		3.3		3.0								3.1
			2.2		2.3	% Officers', Directors',						
		(10)	3.5	(12)	3.9	Owners' Comp/Sales						
			7.5		8.3								
1974867M		1324691M		2888169M	Net Sales ($)		9189M	22209M	65832M	180164M		2610775M
1204994M		961214M		1802356M	Total Assets ($)		2548M	13795M	33495M	106582M		1645936M

© RMA 2005

M = $ thousand   MM = $ million
See Pages 11 through 21 for Explanation of Ratios and Data

Current Data Sorted By Assets   Comparative Historical Data

0-500M	500M-2MM	2-10MM	10-50MM	50-100MM	100-250MM		4/1/00-3/31/01 ALL	4/1/01-3/31/02 ALL
						Type of Statement		
1		7	8	5	2	Unqualified	18	15
		2	1		1	Reviewed	8	6
	2	3				Compiled	10	5
1	3	2				Tax Returns	2	2
2	4	7	7	6	2	Other	19	22
	14 (4/1-9/30/04)		52 (10/1/04-3/31/05)					
4	9	21	16	11	5	**NUMBER OF STATEMENTS**	57	50
%	%	%	%	%	%	**ASSETS**	%	%
		5.6	8.0	14.1		Cash & Equivalents	8.7	7.7
		19.1	15.9	14.0		Trade Receivables (net)	17.8	21.4
		25.2	23.6	21.1		Inventory	26.2	25.9
		1.8	4.5	1.2		All Other Current	5.7	2.1
		51.7	52.1	50.4		Total Current	58.4	57.2
		36.7	19.0	28.6		Fixed Assets (net)	29.7	29.0
		6.3	26.1	9.6		Intangibles (net)	5.6	8.1
		5.3	2.9	11.4		All Other Non-Current	6.3	5.7
		100.0	100.0	100.0		Total	100.0	100.0
						LIABILITIES		
		8.4	11.3	4.3		Notes Payable-Short Term	6.2	7.0
		3.1	3.6	5.1		Cur. Mat.-L/T/D	3.2	4.9
		10.2	11.5	8.0		Trade Payables	13.2	14.2
		.3	.1	.3		Income Taxes Payable	.2	.3
		12.5	11.0	15.9		All Other Current	8.4	10.7
		34.6	37.6	33.7		Total Current	31.2	37.1
		10.1	18.4	6.4		Long-Term Debt	21.8	15.0
		.7	.5	.4		Deferred Taxes	.5	.4
		15.0	5.6	13.5		All Other Non-Current	4.5	4.8
		39.7	38.0	45.9		Net Worth	42.1	42.8
		100.0	100.0	100.0		Total Liabilities & Net Worth	100.0	100.0
						INCOME DATA		
		100.0	100.0	100.0		Net Sales	100.0	100.0
		47.3	49.2	46.7		Gross Profit	44.1	44.1
		44.8	32.6	36.8		Operating Expenses	38.4	39.3
		2.5	16.7	9.9		Operating Profit	5.7	4.9
		1.4	.2	1.7		All Other Expenses (net)	.7	1.2
		1.1	16.4	8.2		Profit Before Taxes	5.0	3.7
						RATIOS		
		2.6	2.3	3.4			2.7	2.4
		1.6	1.2	1.8		Current	2.2	1.6
		1.0	.9	1.1			1.4	1.2
		1.2	1.2	1.2			1.3	1.3
		.7	.5	.9		Quick	.8	.8
		.5	.3	.5			.5	.6
		30 12.4	4 98.3	27 13.3			27 13.6	31 11.9
		39 9.4	33 11.1	42 8.7		Sales/Receivables	40 9.0	40 9.1
		49 7.5	54 6.8	56 6.5			53 6.9	54 6.8
		45 8.1	62 5.8	70 5.2			69 5.3	69 5.3
		107 3.4	108 3.4	97 3.8		Cost of Sales/Inventory	104 3.5	91 4.0
		137 2.7	137 2.7	200 1.8			135 2.7	139 2.6
		25 14.4	20 18.4	23 16.1			27 13.5	28 13.1
		29 12.8	45 8.2	34 10.6		Cost of Sales/Payables	43 8.4	36 10.1
		50 7.3	59 6.2	65 5.6			67 5.4	71 5.1
		5.2	5.5	3.0			4.1	4.6
		11.9	16.6	9.1		Sales/Working Capital	6.3	10.2
		NM	−100.4	34.0			13.2	24.8
		5.8	48.3				11.9	8.8
	(18)	4.4	(13) 20.3			EBIT/Interest	(52) 2.9	(45) 2.6
		.9	8.9				1.2	.6
						Net Profit + Depr., Dep.,	7.0	3.5
						Amort./Cur. Mat. L/T/D	(23) 2.5	(18) 1.5
							.5	.7
		.3	.3	.3			.4	.4
		.9	.6	.6		Fixed/Worth	.7	.7
		2.5	1.9	1.7			1.4	2.1
		.7	.8	.4			.7	.8
		1.5	2.2	.7		Debt/Worth	1.5	1.9
		5.3	NM	2.1			3.7	3.4
		50.2	117.2	46.6		% Profit Before Taxes/Tangible	31.1	38.9
	(18)	20.6	(12) 42.9	(10) 32.6		Net Worth	(52) 14.0	(45) 19.2
		3.0	11.3	7.3			4.7	.6
		15.4	28.9	27.5		% Profit Before Taxes/Total	13.5	13.2
		7.2	20.8	7.4		Assets	5.4	4.7
		−.5	7.8	1.3			1.1	−1.5
		16.9	21.7	11.8			13.0	13.9
		7.1	11.7	6.0		Sales/Net Fixed Assets	7.7	7.2
		1.9	7.0	1.8			3.5	4.0
		2.8	2.0	1.8			2.5	2.7
		1.7	1.6	1.5		Sales/Total Assets	1.9	1.8
		1.0	1.2	.8			1.1	1.1
		1.3	1.0				1.5	2.0
	(19)	2.8	(13) 2.2			% Depr., Dep., Amort./Sales	(53) 2.8	(43) 2.8
		4.0	3.3				5.0	4.2
							2.4	.8
						% Officers', Directors',	(10) 5.7	(11) 3.2
						Owners' Comp/Sales	9.2	12.3
6641M	35261M	211708M	799037M	1333646M	1175885M	Net Sales ($)	3198151M	2482459M
1600M	12351M	118876M	428279M	818510M	642921M	Total Assets ($)	1834223M	1773070M

M = $ thousand   MM = $ million
See Pages 11 through 21 for Explanation of Ratios and Data

Comparative Historical Data | Current Data Sorted By Sales

			Type of Statement						
20	16	23	Unqualified	1			1	8	13
4	7	4	Reviewed				2	1	1
4	7	5	Compiled			2	3		
3	4	6	Tax Returns		4	2			
27	21	28	Other		5	1	6	2	14
4/1/02-3/31/03	4/1/03-3/31/04	4/1/04-3/31/05		14 (4/1-9/30/04)			52 (10/1/04-3/31/05)		
ALL	ALL	ALL		0-1MM	1-3MM	3-5MM	5-10MM	10-25MM	25MM & OVER
58	55	66	**NUMBER OF STATEMENTS**	1	9	5	12	11	28
%	%	%	**ASSETS**	%	%	%	%	%	%
7.8	9.2	9.9	Cash & Equivalents				3.5	7.1	12.5
23.2	20.3	20.5	Trade Receivables (net)				15.7	24.2	15.9
27.7	27.8	24.3	Inventory				29.3	28.0	24.1
2.4	4.4	2.5	All Other Current				1.0	1.6	3.8
61.2	61.7	57.2	Total Current				49.5	60.8	56.3
26.6	24.6	25.8	Fixed Assets (net)				24.9	18.6	24.8
4.0	5.1	10.9	Intangibles (net)				16.5	18.1	11.4
8.2	8.5	6.0	All Other Non-Current				9.1	2.4	7.5
100.0	100.0	100.0	Total				100.0	100.0	100.0
			LIABILITIES						
7.8	7.1	8.4	Notes Payable-Short Term				5.6	10.2	7.7
5.3	2.6	3.2	Cur. Mat.-L/T/D				3.9	3.9	3.8
13.9	14.4	11.7	Trade Payables				14.3	10.5	11.1
.6	.8	.3	Income Taxes Payable				.1	.6	.4
13.0	12.7	11.7	All Other Current				6.5	9.5	14.6
40.7	37.6	35.3	Total Current				30.4	34.8	37.5
10.7	7.5	13.4	Long-Term Debt				17.6	10.3	9.5
.4	.8	.5	Deferred Taxes				.5	.8	.7
5.5	10.8	8.7	All Other Non-Current				17.7	12.8	7.2
42.8	43.3	42.1	Net Worth				33.9	41.3	45.1
100.0	100.0	100.0	Total Liabilities & Net Worth				100.0	100.0	100.0
			INCOME DATA						
100.0	100.0	100.0	Net Sales				100.0	100.0	100.0
43.4	45.9	48.5	Gross Profit				48.7	51.8	48.6
37.1	38.8	40.1	Operating Expenses				35.6	41.4	37.9
6.3	7.1	8.4	Operating Profit				13.1	10.5	10.7
1.8	1.0	.9	All Other Expenses (net)				.6	2.0	.7
4.5	6.2	7.5	Profit Before Taxes				12.5	8.4	9.9
			RATIOS						
2.1	2.6	2.6					2.4	2.8	2.7
1.5	1.7	1.7	Current				1.6	1.6	1.6
1.0	1.3	1.1					1.0	1.2	1.1
1.3	1.4	1.3					1.1	1.4	1.2
.7	.8	.8	Quick				.6	.8	.8
.5	.4	.5					.4	.5	.5
31 11.6	27 13.6	26 14.2					7 51.4	39 9.5	25 14.4
39 9.4	38 9.6	39 9.4	Sales/Receivables				30 12.4	43 8.4	38 9.7
60 6.1	56 6.5	53 6.9					43 8.5	55 6.6	57 6.4
63 5.8	68 5.4	55 6.6					70 5.2	79 4.6	70 5.2
90 4.0	99 3.7	97 3.7	Cost of Sales/Inventory				98 3.7	135 2.7	120 3.1
144 2.5	158 2.3	138 2.7					134 2.7	146 2.5	153 2.4
28 13.2	26 14.3	23 15.7					16 23.4	19 18.9	27 13.7
41 9.0	43 8.5	39 9.4	Cost of Sales/Payables				38 9.6	36 10.1	45 8.2
64 5.7	68 5.4	59 6.2					56 6.5	56 6.5	64 5.7
5.6	4.4	5.1					6.1	4.1	4.6
11.1	7.9	9.4	Sales/Working Capital				12.0	9.1	9.4
100.7	17.8	36.3					NM	24.2	68.1
13.5	24.5	24.0							52.7
(51) 3.4	(47) 5.6	(55) 5.8	EBIT/Interest					(24)	22.0
1.0	1.7	2.2							5.8
3.9	13.9	9.3	Net Profit + Depr., Dep.,						
(20) 1.8	(22) 3.8	(18) 4.8	Amort./Cur. Mat. L/T/D						
.6	1.6	2.6							
.2	.3	.2					.0	.2	.4
.7	.5	.5	Fixed/Worth				.3	.3	.6
1.3	1.4	1.8					1.9	1.1	1.9
.8	.5	.6					.9	.5	.5
1.4	1.1	1.5	Debt/Worth				3.4	1.5	.8
3.2	2.8	4.3					NM	52.5	3.5
44.4	42.3	52.7	% Profit Before Taxes/Tangible						48.7
(56) 22.7	(49) 21.0	(57) 26.2	Net Worth					(25)	27.1
.6	5.8	9.2							11.7
16.4	18.4	24.1	% Profit Before Taxes/Total				23.5	27.5	27.1
6.4	6.6	11.9	Assets				13.7	8.5	16.1
.1	2.7	1.9					2.8	4.2	6.8
22.5	16.9	22.2					796.8	20.3	17.1
9.2	9.5	10.2	Sales/Net Fixed Assets				15.9	12.6	9.5
4.5	5.2	4.8					3.4	7.1	4.9
2.7	2.6	2.9					3.1	2.2	2.8
2.0	1.8	1.8	Sales/Total Assets				2.1	1.7	1.6
1.3	1.3	1.3					1.0	1.6	1.0
1.2	1.5	1.3						2.0	1.1
(48) 2.5	(46) 2.5	(53) 2.4	% Depr., Dep., Amort./Sales				(10) 3.0	(25) 2.2	
4.4	3.5	3.7						3.4	4.7
2.4	1.7	3.3	% Officers', Directors',						
(14) 5.7	(18) 4.7	(11) 5.3	Owners' Comp/Sales						
15.4	12.9	10.0							
2451263M	2963094M	3562178M	Net Sales ($)	534M	19700M	21151M	88437M	175737M	3256619M
1425039M	1963423M	2022537M	Total Assets ($)	190M	14629M	12603M	66977M	95897M	1832241M

M = $ thousand   MM = $ million
See Pages 11 through 21 for Explanation of Ratios and Data

Current Data Sorted By Assets / Comparative Historical Data

0-500M	500M-2MM	2-10MM	10-50MM	50-100MM	100-250MM	Type of Statement	4/1/00-3/31/01 ALL	4/1/01-3/31/02 ALL
1	2	9	18	6	7	Unqualified	25	26
	3	15	4		1	Reviewed	9	7
2	5	9	2			Compiled	16	23
2	3	1				Tax Returns	2	4
2	7	12	18	8	5	Other	22	21

Periods: 21 (4/1-9/30/04) [0-500M, 500M-2MM, 2-10MM] — 121 (10/1/04-3/31/05) [10-50MM, 50-100MM, 100-250MM]

0-500M	500M-2MM	2-10MM	10-50MM	50-100MM	100-250MM		4/1/00-3/31/01 ALL	4/1/01-3/31/02 ALL
7	20	46	42	14	13	NUMBER OF STATEMENTS	74	81
%	%	%	%	%	%	**ASSETS**	%	%
	14.6	12.7	8.1	15.4	15.2	Cash & Equivalents	8.7	10.3
	25.7	30.0	21.6	17.7	20.4	Trade Receivables (net)	24.6	25.3
	24.5	22.6	24.9	14.3	16.8	Inventory	22.7	21.3
	2.9	3.0	2.3	2.1	3.2	All Other Current	2.6	3.7
	67.7	68.2	57.0	49.5	55.6	Total Current	58.7	60.6
	18.5	21.9	27.8	21.9	21.8	Fixed Assets (net)	28.6	23.3
	4.2	3.4	9.9	18.6	18.5	Intangibles (net)	7.4	7.5
	9.5	6.5	5.4	10.1	4.1	All Other Non-Current	5.3	8.6
	100.0	100.0	100.0	100.0	100.0	Total	100.0	100.0
						LIABILITIES		
	11.2	6.1	8.4	5.6	4.4	Notes Payable-Short Term	8.0	5.0
	4.0	3.5	3.0	4.2	.7	Cur. Mat.-L/T/D	4.6	3.1
	23.1	21.7	13.9	9.5	8.7	Trade Payables	17.1	18.3
	.0	.4	.5	.1	.2	Income Taxes Payable	.4	1.0
	6.9	9.7	7.2	15.7	13.2	All Other Current	9.1	10.0
	45.2	41.3	33.0	35.1	27.2	Total Current	39.2	37.3
	9.5	11.9	17.1	11.5	15.1	Long-Term Debt	18.8	17.3
	.3	.8	.6	.6	.3	Deferred Taxes	.4	.4
	8.3	6.2	8.5	7.7	2.7	All Other Non-Current	5.8	4.6
	36.8	39.8	40.9	45.1	54.7	Net Worth	35.8	40.3
	100.0	100.0	100.0	100.0	100.0	Total Liabilities & Net Worth	100.0	100.0
						INCOME DATA		
	100.0	100.0	100.0	100.0	100.0	Net Sales	100.0	100.0
	46.3	43.4	33.8	52.2	47.7	Gross Profit	42.1	46.5
	45.5	38.9	26.2	45.1	34.7	Operating Expenses	33.7	37.3
	.7	4.5	7.6	7.1	13.0	Operating Profit	8.4	9.2
	-.1	.5	1.9	.9	-.5	All Other Expenses (net)	1.3	.6
	.8	4.0	5.7	6.2	13.5	Profit Before Taxes	7.1	8.6
						RATIOS		
	2.6	2.6	2.4	2.3	3.1	Current	2.7	2.9
	1.9	1.8	1.7	1.6	2.4		1.6	1.8
	1.0	1.3	1.3	.8	1.7		1.2	1.3
	1.7	1.6	1.2	1.7	2.2	Quick	1.5	1.9
	1.1	1.1	.9	.9	1.5		.8	1.0
	.4	.7	.6	.5	1.1		.5	.7
	18 20.7	30 12.0	36 10.1	41 8.9	54 6.8	Sales/Receivables	35 10.3	34 10.7
	35 10.6	39 9.4	44 8.2	57 6.4	63 5.8		47 7.8	50 7.3
	60 6.0	58 6.3	56 6.5	66 5.5	67 5.5		68 5.3	68 5.4
	33 10.9	30 12.3	53 6.9	60 6.0	65 5.6	Cost of Sales/Inventory	46 7.9	44 8.3
	72 5.1	66 5.5	93 3.9	89 4.1	102 3.6		94 3.9	85 4.3
	99 3.7	126 2.9	124 2.9	146 2.5	140 2.6		135 2.7	137 2.7
	27 13.6	34 10.7	25 14.6	34 10.7	28 13.0	Cost of Sales/Payables	31 11.7	27 13.4
	47 7.8	46 7.9	39 9.3	69 5.3	42 8.6		49 7.4	45 8.1
	71 5.2	85 4.3	59 6.2	94 3.9	61 6.0		81 4.5	88 4.1
	5.1	4.2	4.4	4.3	2.6	Sales/Working Capital	4.1	4.1
	6.7	7.2	6.9	9.4	3.5		8.2	7.4
	NM	18.8	13.5	-15.8	6.2		21.1	18.4
	13.8	26.8	10.0	50.7	142.0	EBIT/Interest	13.2	20.8
	(17) 3.4	(39) 5.2	(39) 4.1	6.7	14.9		(68) 4.2	(67) 8.4
	-6.2	2.2	2.2	.9	9.4		1.7	3.0
		5.0	9.3			Net Profit + Depr., Dep., Amort./Cur. Mat. L/T/D	7.4	10.7
		(11) 3.0	(15) 4.2				(29) 2.9	(25) 4.5
		.2	1.3				1.4	1.8
	.2	.3	.4	.2	.3	Fixed/Worth	.3	.3
	.5	.6	.8	.9	.5		.7	.5
	1.7	1.1	1.6	-20.3	1.9		1.7	1.0
	.6	.5	.8	.5	.5	Debt/Worth	.9	.6
	1.8	1.9	1.7	1.3	1.2		1.9	1.2
	6.4	4.5	4.4	-42.0	4.1		6.6	4.1
	42.5	60.8	54.7	35.1	57.0	% Profit Before Taxes/Tangible Net Worth	65.0	52.2
	(16) 14.6	(42) 26.9	(36) 17.1	(10) 13.0	(11) 24.8		(66) 30.9	(72) 29.0
	-42.4	9.0	5.3	-10.9	18.3		12.0	11.5
	19.1	20.5	12.5	15.7	18.0	% Profit Before Taxes/Total Assets	16.7	22.7
	8.5	7.4	5.2	7.6	11.7		8.0	10.5
	-10.8	2.3	1.3	-1.0	8.5		2.1	3.3
	52.8	31.5	17.0	51.8	17.1	Sales/Net Fixed Assets	14.6	25.8
	15.2	10.7	6.1	6.4	4.5		5.2	9.2
	8.6	5.4	2.9	3.2	2.9		2.8	3.6
	3.6	2.8	2.2	1.6	1.7	Sales/Total Assets	2.5	2.6
	2.6	2.3	1.5	.9	1.3		1.4	1.8
	1.6	1.5	1.1	.7	.7		1.1	1.1
	.9	.9	1.0	2.0	2.7	% Depr., Dep., Amort./Sales	.9	.2
	(15) 1.4	(42) 2.0	(38) 2.3	(11) 2.6	(10) 3.5		(64) 2.4	(66) 1.5
	4.4	3.6	3.5	10.6	4.3		4.5	3.5
	2.8	2.2				% Officers', Directors', Owners' Comp/Sales	1.3	2.3
	(10) 9.5	(20) 3.1					(20) 5.2	(24) 5.2
	17.8	7.7					10.1	14.2
13391M	85348M	560976M	1735693M	1228097M	2285883M	Net Sales ($)	3058663M	2641317M
2100M	28976M	244160M	1063006M	993866M	1838131M	Total Assets ($)	2702597M	2005562M

M = $ thousand   MM = $ million
See Pages 11 through 21 for Explanation of Ratios and Data

Comparative Historical Data | Current Data Sorted By Sales

	4/1/02-3/31/03 ALL	4/1/03-3/31/04 ALL	4/1/04-3/31/05 ALL	Type of Statement	0-1MM	1-3MM	3-5MM	5-10MM	10-25MM	25MM & OVER
	50	49	43	Unqualified	2	1	2	2	10	26
	16	21	23	Reviewed		1	1	6	9	6
	11	41	18	Compiled		3	5	7	1	2
	6	5	6	Tax Returns		3	1		2	
	43	45	52	Other		6	2	9	7	28
						21 (4/1-9/30/04)		121 (10/1/04-3/31/05)		
NUMBER OF STATEMENTS	126	161	142		2	14	11	24	29	62
	%	%	%	**ASSETS**	%	%	%	%	%	%
Cash & Equivalents	13.8	14.5	11.9			12.9	7.8	11.7	11.3	12.4
Trade Receivables (net)	25.3	25.6	24.3			25.6	13.7	24.4	35.6	21.1
Inventory	18.9	21.2	22.3			18.3	37.5	21.3	22.4	21.2
All Other Current	4.0	4.4	2.9			2.1	8.2	3.4	1.7	2.5
Total Current	62.0	65.7	61.5			59.0	67.1	60.7	70.9	57.2
Fixed Assets (net)	25.0	22.8	23.3			28.3	21.1	24.9	19.2	23.9
Intangibles (net)	6.9	6.0	8.5			5.6	1.9	5.3	4.3	13.3
All Other Non-Current	6.2	5.5	6.7			7.1	9.9	9.2	5.6	5.6
Total	100.0	100.0	100.0			100.0	100.0	100.0	100.0	100.0
				LIABILITIES						
Notes Payable-Short Term	6.5	6.0	7.9			11.5	6.7	10.4	7.2	6.7
Cur. Mat.-L/T/D	3.4	2.9	3.0			4.9	2.3	3.1	3.5	2.6
Trade Payables	15.3	15.8	16.6			13.7	14.4	21.6	21.7	13.6
Income Taxes Payable	.7	.5	.3			.0	.0	.7	.2	.3
All Other Current	10.5	10.9	9.6			6.5	7.4	7.2	11.7	10.6
Total Current	36.4	36.2	37.5			36.7	30.8	42.9	44.3	33.9
Long-Term Debt	16.1	14.2	14.5			24.8	17.0	13.5	9.8	14.2
Deferred Taxes	.4	.6	.5			.2	.4	.5	.7	.5
All Other Non-Current	6.4	5.2	7.7			19.2	10.7	6.4	7.1	5.5
Net Worth	40.7	43.9	39.7			19.1	41.0	36.6	38.0	45.8
Total Liabilities & Net Worth	100.0	100.0	100.0			100.0	100.0	100.0	100.0	100.0
				INCOME DATA						
Net Sales	100.0	100.0	100.0			100.0	100.0	100.0	100.0	100.0
Gross Profit	45.9	44.8	42.5			53.1	38.2	44.1	41.3	40.6
Operating Expenses	35.1	37.6	36.3			48.5	35.3	42.2	35.8	31.8
Operating Profit	10.8	7.2	6.2			4.6	2.9	1.9	5.5	8.9
All Other Expenses (net)	1.1	.5	.8			.9	-.2	.5	.7	1.2
Profit Before Taxes	9.6	6.7	5.4			3.6	3.1	1.4	4.8	7.7
				RATIOS						
Current	3.0	3.5	2.5			2.6	5.6	3.2	2.5	2.5
	1.9	1.8	1.8			2.0	2.1	1.5	1.9	1.8
	1.3	1.3	1.3			1.3	1.4	1.1	1.2	1.3
Quick	2.2	2.0	1.6			2.0	3.9	1.8	1.5	1.6
	1.0	1.1	(141) 1.0			1.3	(10) .9	.9	1.1	1.0
	.6	.6	.6							
Sales/Receivables	32 11.3	32 11.4	32 11.4			12 31.2	0 UND	29 12.6	33 11.2	39 9.3
	46 7.9	45 8.2	44 8.2			45 8.0	24 15.5	37 9.9	49 7.5	47 7.8
	59 6.2	57 6.4	62 5.9			65 5.6	39 9.5	64 5.7	64 5.7	61 6.0
Cost of Sales/Inventory	33 11.1	50 7.2	42 8.7			13 28.6	34 10.7	33 11.1	25 14.4	53 6.9
	77 4.7	82 4.4	82 4.4			70 5.2	85 4.3	56 6.6	85 4.3	87 4.2
	129 2.8	125 2.9	122 3.0			105 3.5	158 2.3	127 2.9	116 3.1	121 3.0
Cost of Sales/Payables	25 14.5	27 13.5	27 13.4			12 31.3	8 43.8	25 14.8	34 10.8	31 11.6
	40 9.2	44 8.3	43 8.4			49 7.5	24 15.5	56 6.5	44 8.2	43 8.6
	62 5.8	70 5.2	77 4.8			98 3.7	42 8.7	91 4.0	87 4.2	70 5.2
Sales/Working Capital	3.8	3.6	4.2			2.9	3.3	3.9	4.8	4.1
	7.5	7.6	6.7			6.0	7.2	8.1	6.7	6.5
	16.3	19.2	20.2			95.8	19.9	31.9	17.9	20.3
EBIT/Interest	27.8	26.9	15.9			15.2		10.1	23.6	23.2
	(115) 7.5	(141) 8.7	(126) 5.1			(12) 2.9		(22) 3.7	(24) 6.7	(60) 6.7
	2.8	2.4	2.1			-5.2		-1.4	2.8	2.6
Net Profit + Depr., Dep., Amort./Cur. Mat. L/T/D	19.6	12.9	8.5							9.3
	(31) 3.5	(41) 2.7	(40) 2.9							(23) 2.5
	1.8	1.2	.9							1.0
Fixed/Worth	.2	.2	.3			.5	.3	.3	.2	.3
	.7	.5	.7			1.6	.4	.7	.8	.7
	1.4	1.3	1.7			-2.5	1.2	1.4	1.1	1.8
Debt/Worth	.5	.6	.6			1.7	.2	.5	.7	.6
	1.4	1.5	1.8			5.6	2.1	1.6	1.9	1.4
	4.7	3.1	6.2			-11.5	5.0	5.6	5.9	4.5
% Profit Before Taxes/Tangible Net Worth	68.7	56.6	53.0				28.0	40.4	89.2	47.1
	(110) 29.3	(142) 23.4	(119) 21.2				(10) 13.4	(20) 13.1	(26) 29.9	(53) 23.9
	13.6	9.8	6.0				-30.4	-10.9	8.1	9.4
% Profit Before Taxes/Total Assets	25.3	20.7	18.0			26.5	11.9	15.6	22.0	17.8
	13.0	9.8	7.3			7.3	6.6	3.6	8.2	8.0
	3.5	3.8	1.4			-5.3	-4.9	-2.4	2.5	2.6
Sales/Net Fixed Assets	30.7	27.6	30.1			24.4	60.5	20.5	37.3	26.8
	7.1	8.5	8.4			11.1	13.7	9.3	18.5	6.1
	3.8	3.9	4.2			3.3	5.4	5.4	6.6	3.6
Sales/Total Assets	2.6	2.7	2.7			3.3	3.8	2.8	3.2	2.2
	1.8	1.8	1.8			2.0	2.3	2.0	2.4	1.5
	1.1	1.1	1.2			1.3	1.8	1.2	1.3	1.0
% Depr., Dep., Amort./Sales	1.2	1.1	1.1					1.1	.6	1.6
	(96) 2.1	(137) 2.3	(118) 2.3					(19) 2.3	(27) 1.2	(53) 2.4
	3.7	3.7	3.8					4.6	3.0	3.8
% Officers', Directors', Owners' Comp/Sales	1.4	2.2	2.2							1.8
	(30) 4.9	(46) 3.7	(38) 3.7							(16) 2.6
	14.1	8.9	9.3							6.4
Net Sales ($)	5116983M	6827835M	5909388M		917M	27712M	47454M	176497M	463766M	5193042M
Total Assets ($)	4018632M	5491642M	4170239M		789M	26979M	20404M	108360M	260761M	3752946M

M = $ thousand   MM = $ million
See Pages 11 through 21 for Explanation of Ratios and Data

Current Data Sorted By Assets   **Comparative Historical Data**

						Type of Statement		
		7	13	2	1	Unqualified	21	21
	4	14	4			Reviewed	26	21
2	8	10	2			Compiled	21	29
5	7	2				Tax Returns	3	4
3	8	15	5		2	Other	27	36
	19 (4/1-9/30/04)		95 (10/1/04-3/31/05)				4/1/00-3/31/01	4/1/01-3/31/02
0-500M	500M-2MM	2-10MM	10-50MM	50-100MM	100-250MM		ALL	ALL
10	27	48	24	2	3	**NUMBER OF STATEMENTS**	98	111
%	%	%	%	%	%	**ASSETS**	%	%
5.5	9.6	6.9	9.9			Cash & Equivalents	6.2	8.7
35.5	33.2	27.8	25.5			Trade Receivables (net)	28.1	26.0
25.0	21.1	29.2	27.8			Inventory	29.2	25.2
11.4	3.5	1.2	2.1			All Other Current	2.1	2.4
77.4	67.4	65.2	65.3			Total Current	65.6	62.3
12.3	19.9	25.0	24.4			Fixed Assets (net)	23.6	25.0
1.7	4.4	3.9	4.4			Intangibles (net)	4.9	3.9
8.5	8.3	6.0	5.9			All Other Non-Current	5.9	8.9
100.0	100.0	100.0	100.0			Total	100.0	100.0
						LIABILITIES		
36.6	10.4	12.3	8.6			Notes Payable-Short Term	10.9	7.7
1.3	6.6	3.0	2.5			Cur. Mat.-L/T/D	2.9	3.8
11.0	18.4	18.2	18.5			Trade Payables	19.0	16.3
.0	.1	.2	.2			Income Taxes Payable	.3	.2
18.5	5.9	6.4	7.6			All Other Current	8.7	10.0
67.4	41.3	40.0	37.5			Total Current	41.7	38.0
14.2	17.0	15.0	14.4			Long-Term Debt	14.1	13.4
.0	.2	.4	.3			Deferred Taxes	.4	.2
67.9	3.9	6.5	4.6			All Other Non-Current	5.5	5.0
-49.5	37.7	38.1	43.3			Net Worth	38.3	43.4
100.0	100.0	100.0	100.0			Total Liabilities & Net Worth	100.0	100.0
						INCOME DATA		
100.0	100.0	100.0	100.0			Net Sales	100.0	100.0
47.8	33.6	32.2	32.2			Gross Profit	32.7	34.8
45.1	30.8	27.4	28.4			Operating Expenses	29.3	32.3
2.8	2.8	4.8	3.8			Operating Profit	3.4	2.5
.7	.9	.4	-.1			All Other Expenses (net)	1.1	1.2
2.1	2.0	4.3	4.0			Profit Before Taxes	2.2	1.3
						RATIOS		
4.1	2.6	3.2	2.3			Current	2.7	3.4
2.0	1.5	1.6	2.1				1.5	1.8
1.1	1.2	1.1	1.4				1.1	1.2
2.9	1.6	1.8	1.4			Quick	1.4	1.7
1.2	1.0	.8	1.0				.8	1.0
.3	.6	.6	.6				.5	.6
27 13.4	36 10.2	38 9.6	38 9.5			Sales/Receivables	33 11.2	34 10.7
42 8.7	49 7.5	46 8.0	50 7.3				41 8.9	43 8.5
54 6.8	71 5.1	58 6.2	54 6.7				54 6.8	54 6.8
0 UND	9 42.8	46 7.9	63 5.8			Cost of Sales/Inventory	46 7.9	48 7.6
44 8.4	49 7.4	68 5.3	75 4.9				70 5.2	71 5.2
68 5.3	90 4.0	93 3.9	100 3.6				94 3.9	91 4.0
0 UND	19 18.9	26 13.9	40 9.2			Cost of Sales/Payables	25 14.6	21 17.6
20 18.0	42 8.6	40 9.0	44 8.3				37 10.0	35 10.5
29 12.4	59 6.2	55 6.6	64 5.7				55 6.7	51 7.1
5.8	6.9	6.0	3.5			Sales/Working Capital	5.1	4.5
11.7	13.3	9.3	6.5				10.8	7.8
NM	26.9	46.0	11.1				36.3	27.3
	5.0	12.7	21.1			EBIT/Interest	7.5	6.9
	(24) 1.3	(46) 5.3	(23) 7.5				(93) 2.2	(93) 1.6
	.1	1.5	1.0				1.0	-.1
		17.5				Net Profit + Depr., Dep.,	14.3	6.5
		(11) 3.1				Amort./Cur. Mat. L /T/D	(37) 2.7	(28) 1.4
		.7					.9	-.2
.1	.2	.2	.4			Fixed/Worth	.3	.3
.5	.5	.8	.6				.8	.7
-.2	8.9	3.1	1.4				2.9	1.7
.6	.4	.5	.6			Debt/Worth	.7	.5
NM	1.8	1.8	1.7				1.8	1.4
-1.9	13.6	8.2	3.2				7.0	4.4
	37.4	56.0	25.5			% Profit Before Taxes/Tangible	35.0	22.6
	(24) 6.5	(41) 15.0	(23) 12.3			Net Worth	(87) 11.4	(98) 8.1
	-2.3	4.6	3.6				1.3	-3.3
25.7	9.4	16.6	11.2			% Profit Before Taxes/Total	10.7	8.8
9.4	1.8	6.1	7.0			Assets	3.9	2.2
-6.5	-1.5	.5	.1				.4	-2.9
244.0	37.9	23.6	14.6			Sales/Net Fixed Assets	23.6	17.9
56.7	16.9	9.2	9.4				11.4	9.0
10.6	7.7	5.4	4.9				5.9	5.4
5.9	3.4	2.9	2.4			Sales/Total Assets	3.1	2.9
3.2	2.4	2.1	2.0				2.4	2.0
2.1	1.9	1.6	1.4				1.8	1.5
	1.0	1.0	1.2			% Depr., Dep., Amort./Sales	1.0	.8
	(20) 1.5	(44) 1.6	(21) 1.4				(92) 1.6	(101) 1.6
	3.0	2.6	2.4				2.6	2.8
	3.1	.8				% Officers', Directors',	3.6	2.4
	(14) 5.0	(15) 3.3				Owners' Comp/Sales	(27) 4.7	(37) 4.5
	9.3	6.2					8.7	7.2
8852M	84107M	514468M	1143031M	255118M	832983M	Net Sales ($)	2394571M	3150182M
2514M	32483M	229886M	581521M	138939M	472018M	Total Assets ($)	1247408M	1682686M

Comparative Historical Data						Type of Statement	Current Data Sorted By Sales					
	22		21		23	Unqualified		1		3	4	15
	32		29		22	Reviewed		1	5	8	5	3
	15		26		22	Compiled	2	3	5	8	2	2
	6		8		14	Tax Returns	3	6	3	1	1	
	31		30		33	Other	1	6	4	7	8	7
	4/1/02- 3/31/03 ALL		4/1/03- 3/31/04 ALL		4/1/04- 3/31/05 ALL		0-1MM	19 (4/1-9/30/04) 1-3MM	3-5MM	95 (10/1/04-3/31/05) 5-10MM	10-25MM	25MM & OVER
	106		114		114	NUMBER OF STATEMENTS	6	17	17	27	20	27
	%		%		%	ASSETS	%	%	%	%	%	%
	8.4		8.3		7.8	Cash & Equivalents		8.3	5.9	9.2	9.5	6.3
	25.3		25.5		29.0	Trade Receivables (net)		35.3	28.6	28.4	28.7	26.5
	26.6		27.5		26.2	Inventory		20.6	29.0	24.4	30.0	29.1
	2.1		3.7		3.1	All Other Current		3.3	1.8	1.0	2.2	3.1
	62.4		64.9		66.0	Total Current		67.6	65.3	63.1	70.5	65.0
	25.8		23.0		22.4	Fixed Assets (net)		17.9	24.4	24.6	23.4	22.2
	4.2		4.5		4.7	Intangibles (net)		7.3	3.0	3.7	3.5	6.6
	7.6		7.6		6.9	All Other Non-Current		7.2	7.2	8.6	2.6	6.2
	100.0		100.0		100.0	Total		100.0	100.0	100.0	100.0	100.0
						LIABILITIES						
	7.1		12.6		12.9	Notes Payable-Short Term		9.2	13.9	12.3	11.9	7.9
	6.4		3.1		3.6	Cur. Mat.-L/T/D		7.9	2.3	4.0	2.7	2.3
	14.8		16.2		17.5	Trade Payables		15.6	17.6	15.6	22.5	18.6
	.2		.1		.2	Income Taxes Payable		.1	.2	.1	.2	.3
	8.5		10.7		7.7	All Other Current		15.6	3.7	6.6	7.7	7.7
	37.0		42.7		41.7	Total Current		48.4	37.7	38.5	45.0	36.7
	16.6		15.9		15.1	Long-Term Debt		19.2	19.6	13.9	11.1	13.0
	.3		.3		.3	Deferred Taxes		.6	.1	.0	.6	.5
	3.6		6.0		11.3	All Other Non-Current		5.3	9.2	7.4	1.5	6.8
	42.5		35.0		31.5	Net Worth		26.5	33.3	40.1	41.9	43.0
	100.0		100.0		100.0	Total Liabilities & Net Worth		100.0	100.0	100.0	100.0	100.0
						INCOME DATA						
	100.0		100.0		100.0	Net Sales		100.0	100.0	100.0	100.0	100.0
	34.5		33.4		33.9	Gross Profit		37.9	33.2	29.5	31.9	33.9
	30.9		30.4		29.9	Operating Expenses		32.4	32.0	26.4	25.7	29.3
	3.6		3.0		4.0	Operating Profit		5.5	1.2	3.1	6.2	4.6
	.9		.7		.5	All Other Expenses (net)		1.0	1.0	.2	.0	.2
	2.8		2.2		3.5	Profit Before Taxes		4.5	.2	2.9	6.2	4.4
						RATIOS						
	3.2		3.1		2.7			2.9	3.0	3.3	2.2	2.2
	1.9		1.8		1.6	Current		1.3	2.0	1.7	1.6	2.1
	1.3		1.2		1.2			1.1	1.2	1.1	1.1	1.5
	1.6		1.7		1.6			1.9	1.6	2.1	1.3	1.2
	.9		.8		.9	Quick		.8	1.0	.8	.7	.9
	.6		.5		.6			.5	.6	.6	.6	.6
34	10.8	33	11.0	37	9.8		44	8.3	33	11.1	36	10.1	36	10.0	31	11.9
42	8.7	45	8.2	47	7.7	Sales/Receivables	53	6.9	55	6.7	45	8.1	41	8.8	50	7.3
52	7.0	56	6.6	56	6.5		69	5.3	76	4.8	54	6.7	52	7.0	55	6.7
51	7.2	53	6.9	42	8.6		28	13.1	42	8.8	43	8.5	42	8.7	60	6.0
70	5.2	70	5.2	67	5.5	Cost of Sales/Inventory	49	7.4	88	4.1	54	6.8	77	4.7	76	4.8
89	4.1	97	3.7	90	4.1		71	5.1	103	3.5	88	4.2	92	4.0	90	4.1
21	17.0	24	15.5	25	14.5		20	18.6	23	15.6	19	19.5	40	9.0	34	10.9
32	11.5	35	10.3	41	8.8	Cost of Sales/Payables	43	8.5	38	9.7	34	10.8	46	7.9	43	8.5
48	7.6	53	6.8	54	6.8		62	5.9	75	4.9	45	8.1	56	6.6	61	6.0
	4.7		4.5		6.0			6.8	5.5	6.6	5.3	4.9
	7.7		7.4		9.2	Sales/Working Capital		15.0	8.0	9.1	10.0	6.8
	18.3		24.4		27.5			107.5	17.6	33.3	46.0	11.2
	9.9		9.2		12.9			7.1	7.5	12.2	19.7	24.5
(95)	3.9	(103)	2.1	(106)	4.4	EBIT/Interest	(15)	2.8	1.1	(25) 5.1	(19) 7.9	(26) 8.7
	1.1		−.1		1.1			1.0	.3	1.7	1.6	1.5
	7.5		8.6		11.9	Net Profit + Depr., Dep.,						15.0
(27)	2.9	(28)	2.5	(28)	2.9	Amort./Cur. Mat. L/T/D					(12)	7.9
	1.7		1.2		1.0							1.3
	.3		.3		.3			.1	.3	.3	.2	.3
	.7		.5		.6	Fixed/Worth		4.6	.5	.6	.7	.6
	1.5		1.7		3.1			NM	NM	3.2	1.7	1.8
	.5		.6		.6			.5	.6	.3	.9	.5
	1.3		1.8		1.9	Debt/Worth		12.3	1.9	1.6	1.7	2.2
	4.3		5.7		11.3			NM	NM	19.1	3.5	3.6
	29.0		25.0		37.6	% Profit Before Taxes/Tangible		56.5	11.5	27.0	62.5	27.7
(96)	11.4	(99)	6.7	(96)	12.0	Net Worth	(13)	8.9	(13) 1.1	(23) 15.0	31.6	(24) 12.8
	2.4		−2.7		1.2			−7.8	−5.8	7.4	5.8	5.9
	12.4		9.5		13.1	% Profit Before Taxes/Total		13.1	6.5	14.2	19.8	13.6
	3.6		2.8		6.0	Assets		5.1	.2	6.1	8.4	7.2
	.2		−2.9		.2			.2	−1.6	.5	1.7	1.4
	15.4		20.0		24.0			56.7	30.9	23.4	34.1	15.2
	9.3		10.9		10.4	Sales/Net Fixed Assets		16.9	10.2	9.5	10.4	10.2
	5.4		5.5		6.0			6.0	5.1	5.3	6.4	5.7
	2.6		2.9		2.9			3.2	2.6	3.1	3.1	2.7
	2.1		2.2		2.2	Sales/Total Assets		2.3	2.1	2.1	2.3	2.1
	1.6		1.6		1.6			1.5	1.6	1.6	1.8	1.6
	1.3		1.1		1.0			.3	1.3	1.3	.7	.9
(88)	1.9	(100)	1.7	(97)	1.6	% Depr., Dep., Amort./Sales	(13)	1.0	(14) 1.7	(26) 1.8	(17) 1.6	(23) 1.4
	3.4		2.8		2.6			2.8	3.4	2.7	1.8	2.1
	2.2		1.4		1.1	% Officers', Directors',				1.0		
(24)	3.8	(31)	4.5	(39)	4.0	Owners' Comp/Sales				(12) 3.8		
	6.7		10.4		6.3					6.5		
	3109220M		3012578M		2838559M	Net Sales ($)	2944M	29616M	63758M	209185M	318542M	2214514M
	1624223M		1682079M		1457361M	Total Assets ($)	853M	14951M	33829M	101033M	150882M	1155813M

M = $ thousand   MM = $ million
See Pages 11 through 21 for Explanation of Ratios and Data

Current Data Sorted By Assets   Comparative Historical Data

0-500M	500M-2MM	2-10MM	10-50MM	50-100MM	100-250MM	Type of Statement	4/1/00-3/31/01 ALL	4/1/01-3/31/02 ALL
		8	12	2	4	Unqualified	18	12
	5	11	5			Reviewed	13	15
	6	2	1			Compiled	18	12
1	4	2				Tax Returns	3	4
2	2	11	4	2	2	Other	32	25
	24 (4/1-9/30/04)		62 (10/1/04-3/31/05)					
3	17	34	22	4	6	**NUMBER OF STATEMENTS**	84	68
%	%	%	%	%	%	**ASSETS**	%	%
	8.5	7.6	6.9			Cash & Equivalents	5.7	5.6
	28.3	30.5	25.7			Trade Receivables (net)	26.0	28.8
	22.7	23.2	22.5			Inventory	24.8	24.3
	.3	3.4	2.1			All Other Current	1.9	2.1
	59.8	64.7	57.2			Total Current	58.3	60.9
	28.0	22.6	22.9			Fixed Assets (net)	24.3	24.1
	.5	4.2	8.1			Intangibles (net)	9.9	9.0
	11.7	8.5	11.8			All Other Non-Current	7.4	6.0
	100.0	100.0	100.0			Total	100.0	100.0
						LIABILITIES		
	16.0	13.0	6.6			Notes Payable-Short Term	9.2	10.0
	2.3	2.5	4.1			Cur. Mat.-L/T/D	5.6	4.4
	19.8	19.0	14.1			Trade Payables	15.9	15.2
	.1	.3	.6			Income Taxes Payable	.4	.3
	8.9	8.8	9.1			All Other Current	7.1	7.5
	47.1	43.5	34.5			Total Current	38.3	37.3
	14.8	11.2	14.6			Long-Term Debt	13.0	13.6
	.5	.7	2.0			Deferred Taxes	.7	.7
	3.4	4.3	5.8			All Other Non-Current	6.3	4.2
	34.3	40.3	43.0			Net Worth	41.8	44.2
	100.0	100.0	100.0			Total Liabilities & Net Worth	100.0	100.0
						INCOME DATA		
	100.0	100.0	100.0			Net Sales	100.0	100.0
	38.9	32.1	34.2			Gross Profit	36.4	35.3
	34.2	27.2	25.4			Operating Expenses	31.2	31.2
	4.7	5.0	8.9			Operating Profit	5.2	4.2
	1.4	.6	.3			All Other Expenses (net)	−.4	1.6
	3.3	4.4	8.5			Profit Before Taxes	5.6	2.5
						RATIOS		
	3.5	2.7	2.7				2.2	2.2
	1.6	1.6	1.7			Current	1.6	1.7
	.9	1.2	1.2				1.2	1.2
	2.1	1.8	1.5				1.2	1.4
	1.1	.8	.9			Quick	.8	.9
	.5	.6	.6				.6	.6
23 16.2	33 11.0	38 9.6					38 9.6	37 9.9
34 10.8	45 8.2	49 7.4				Sales/Receivables	48 7.5	48 7.5
40 9.1	55 6.6	64 5.7					59 6.2	60 6.1
30 12.1	38 9.7	48 7.6					43 8.5	43 8.6
42 8.6	54 6.7	62 5.9				Cost of Sales/Inventory	67 5.4	59 6.1
56 6.5	75 4.9	72 5.1					102 3.6	85 4.3
16 22.2	24 15.1	28 13.1					29 12.5	25 14.7
36 10.2	35 10.3	35 10.3				Cost of Sales/Payables	39 9.3	37 10.0
60 6.1	60 6.0	49 7.4					58 6.3	50 7.3
	7.2	6.1	5.6				6.0	5.9
	17.7	10.5	9.2			Sales/Working Capital	9.9	8.3
	−56.6	62.6	21.4				23.1	19.4
	27.0	11.9	19.2				6.2	5.9
	(15) 2.7	(31) 4.7	(20) 10.5			EBIT/Interest	(82) 2.9	(65) 2.5
	1.0	1.2	5.4				1.3	.9
		6.6	7.6				3.5	4.3
	(13) 2.4		(18) 3.5			Net Profit + Depr., Dep., Amort./Cur. Mat. L /T/D	(24) 1.7	(27) 1.5
	1.5		1.8				.7	.6
	.2	.2	.3				.3	.3
	.7	.5	.7			Fixed/Worth	.8	.7
	NM	1.4	1.4				2.3	1.2
	.6	.7	.7				.8	1.0
	1.4	1.5	1.7			Debt/Worth	1.6	1.5
	NM	3.2	4.4				4.3	3.8
	76.2	38.6	76.9				42.0	43.9
	(13) 15.4	(32) 12.1	(20) 29.0			% Profit Before Taxes/Tangible Net Worth	(73) 15.7	(64) 10.1
	4.6	3.3	17.7				4.8	−4.7
	34.7	16.3	18.3				12.1	15.8
	4.8	6.4	12.2			% Profit Before Taxes/Total Assets	4.8	4.0
	−3.6	.7	6.4				1.3	−.3
	58.2	43.9	16.8				19.3	21.1
	12.0	12.6	9.3			Sales/Net Fixed Assets	9.9	9.7
	6.0	5.8	6.2				4.9	5.1
	4.1	3.2	2.4				2.6	2.8
	3.0	2.3	2.0			Sales/Total Assets	2.0	2.1
	2.3	1.8	1.5				1.6	1.5
	.9	.7	1.5				1.4	1.2
	(16) 1.8	(29) 1.6	2.0			% Depr., Dep., Amort./Sales	(74) 2.3	(63) 2.2
	2.7	2.4	2.6				3.5	3.4
		3.2					2.8	2.7
	(14)	6.8				% Officers', Directors', Owners' Comp/Sales	(27) 6.2	(16) 5.8
		9.9					9.0	10.7
3620M	67156M	374374M	902646M	361996M	1123884M	Net Sales ($)	2122580M	2390942M
849M	20398M	158461M	465154M	268857M	808559M	Total Assets ($)	1926287M	1555604M

M = $ thousand   MM = $ million
See Pages 11 through 21 for Explanation of Ratios and Data

Comparative Historical Data   Current Data Sorted By Sales

			Type of Statement	0-1MM	1-3MM	3-5MM	5-10MM	10-25MM	25MM & OVER
19	31	26	Unqualified		1		3	7	15
20	19	21	Reviewed		1	4	7	5	4
8	16	9	Compiled	1	1	2	3	2	
5	6	7	Tax Returns	1	1	3	1	1	
22	26	23	Other		4	2	3	8	6
4/1/02-3/31/03	4/1/03-3/31/04	4/1/04-3/31/05		24 (4/1-9/30/04)		62 (10/1/04-3/31/05)			
ALL	ALL	ALL							
74	98	86	NUMBER OF STATEMENTS	2	8	11	17	23	25
%	%	%	ASSETS	%	%	%	%	%	%
7.3	7.2	7.4	Cash & Equivalents			10.9	7.5	7.7	5.7
26.5	29.3	28.6	Trade Receivables (net)			25.1	31.5	31.8	26.7
23.7	24.4	22.2	Inventory			22.6	24.5	22.7	22.7
3.0	3.4	2.1	All Other Current			.4	3.7	2.5	1.9
60.5	64.4	60.3	Total Current			59.0	67.2	64.7	57.0
22.2	23.7	24.2	Fixed Assets (net)			27.3	22.5	23.0	25.2
8.3	3.7	5.9	Intangibles (net)			.2	1.9	4.3	11.7
9.1	8.3	9.6	All Other Non-Current			13.6	8.4	8.0	6.1
100.0	100.0	100.0	Total			100.0	100.0	100.0	100.0
			LIABILITIES						
10.8	12.0	11.6	Notes Payable-Short Term			13.7	13.4	11.3	5.8
4.4	3.3	2.7	Cur. Mat.-L/T/D			3.2	2.2	2.6	3.4
16.4	18.5	18.4	Trade Payables			18.8	18.5	18.1	15.8
.2	.5	.3	Income Taxes Payable			.1	.4	.5	.4
7.0	8.3	8.6	All Other Current			6.6	9.9	10.5	7.5
38.9	42.5	41.6	Total Current			42.4	44.4	43.0	32.9
10.6	13.3	13.6	Long-Term Debt			6.6	8.6	13.2	16.4
.6	.9	1.2	Deferred Taxes			.1	.6	1.7	1.5
5.3	4.1	5.8	All Other Non-Current			4.1	4.9	3.0	9.8
44.6	39.2	37.8	Net Worth			46.9	41.6	39.2	39.4
100.0	100.0	100.0	Total Liabilities & Net Worth			100.0	100.0	100.0	100.0
			INCOME DATA						
100.0	100.0	100.0	Net Sales			100.0	100.0	100.0	100.0
35.3	33.7	34.4	Gross Profit			45.0	33.2	35.8	29.2
29.4	29.6	28.0	Operating Expenses			35.3	29.0	29.8	21.8
5.9	4.0	6.4	Operating Profit			9.7	4.2	6.0	7.5
1.2	.7	.9	All Other Expenses (net)			.5	1.2	.1	1.3
4.8	3.3	5.5	Profit Before Taxes			9.2	3.0	5.9	6.2
			RATIOS						
2.4	2.2	2.7				3.7	2.7	2.5	2.8
1.5	1.5	1.6	Current			1.6	1.6	1.7	1.8
1.2	1.2	1.1				.8	1.0	1.0	1.3
1.3	1.4	1.7				2.4	1.8	1.9	1.5
.7	.8	.9	Quick			1.2	.8	1.0	1.0
.5	.6	.6				.6	.5	.6	.7
33 11.0	36 10.1	33 10.9				18 20.4	32 11.5	35 10.5	39 9.5
40 9.0	48 7.6	44 8.3	Sales/Receivables			39 9.3	39 9.3	47 7.7	48 7.6
50 7.3	58 6.2	55 6.6				46 7.9	50 7.3	57 6.4	65 5.6
41 8.8	43 8.5	38 9.5				35 10.4	39 9.2	38 9.5	47 7.8
57 6.4	62 5.9	55 6.6	Cost of Sales/Inventory			50 7.2	55 6.6	53 6.8	59 6.1
86 4.2	80 4.5	70 5.2				82 4.4	67 5.4	75 4.9	75 4.9
24 15.5	25 14.8	26 13.9				20 17.8	24 15.5	31 11.9	28 13.3
37 9.8	38 9.6	36 10.0	Cost of Sales/Payables			39 9.5	27 13.4	38 9.6	34 10.6
54 6.8	60 6.1	58 6.3				54 6.7	62 5.9	48 7.7	59 6.2
5.8	5.6	6.0				6.1	6.5	4.4	5.6
11.2	9.5	11.2	Sales/Working Capital			11.9	11.5	9.9	8.6
31.1	31.0	44.3				−12.2	−548.2	185.4	13.9
6.4	10.5	14.7					7.0	19.9	16.3
(66) 3.4	(86) 4.1	(78) 6.2	EBIT/Interest				(15) 4.1	(21) 10.0	(24) 9.7
1.0	1.2	1.6					.3	2.8	3.7
3.7	6.4	8.6	Net Profit + Depr., Dep.,					11.1	7.8
(27) 1.9	(35) 1.9	(40) 2.8	Amort./Cur. Mat. L/T/D					(12) 3.6	(17) 2.6
1.0	1.1	1.8						2.2	1.8
.2	.2	.3				.3	.1	.2	.4
.6	.5	.7	Fixed/Worth			.4	.5	.5	.9
1.3	1.4	2.1				.7	1.5	1.8	2.9
.7	.9	.7				.4	.9	.6	.8
1.7	1.6	1.7	Debt/Worth			.8	1.3	1.4	2.5
3.5	2.9	5.3				2.5	2.9	3.7	21.9
37.5	36.2	55.4	% Profit Before Taxes/Tangible			83.0	27.0	52.5	73.1
(65) 15.4	(91) 13.8	(72) 20.9	Net Worth			(10) 44.6	(16) 15.1	(21) 18.3	(20) 26.0
.5	2.6	7.8				11.0	−.1	6.3	17.7
14.8	14.1	16.5	% Profit Before Taxes/Total			37.5	13.0	23.1	15.0
6.4	5.4	8.1	Assets			15.5	6.5	7.5	10.7
.1	.5	2.9				.7	−.6	4.1	6.2
24.7	23.0	24.2				23.3	79.0	26.9	14.4
10.3	10.3	10.5	Sales/Net Fixed Assets			12.0	11.8	11.8	6.9
5.2	5.1	6.0				6.1	5.1	6.0	5.1
2.7	2.8	3.1				3.7	3.1	3.4	2.5
2.1	2.1	2.2	Sales/Total Assets			2.8	2.7	2.2	2.0
1.5	1.6	1.7				1.8	1.9	1.7	1.5
1.1	.9	.9				1.0	.5	.8	1.6
(66) 2.2	(83) 1.9	(78) 1.9	% Depr., Dep., Amort./Sales			1.9	(15) 1.3	(20) 1.7	(23) 2.5
3.0	3.1	2.7				2.8	2.3	2.5	2.8
4.2	2.3	2.8	% Officers', Directors',						
(22) 7.2	(29) 4.1	(27) 5.6	Owners' Comp/Sales						
10.0	10.2	9.3							
2023294M	2527039M	2833676M	Net Sales ($)	1657M	15594M	42628M	122287M	389940M	2261570M
1345912M	1439752M	1722278M	Total Assets ($)	852M	12457M	24314M	52197M	205884M	1426574M

M = $ thousand   MM = $ million
See Pages 11 through 21 for Explanation of Ratios and Data

Current Data Sorted By Assets

Comparative Historical Data

Type of Statement

	0-500M	500M-2MM	2-10MM	10-50MM	50-100MM	100-250MM		4/1/00-3/31/01 ALL	4/1/01-3/31/02 ALL
Unqualified		1	2	9	2	2		13	7
Reviewed		2	8					8	4
Compiled	5	2	3					6	11
Tax Returns	4	4	1					3	2
Other	1	5	9	7				14	16

	0-500M	500M-2MM	2-10MM	10-50MM	50-100MM	100-250MM		4/1/00- 3/31/01 ALL	4/1/01- 3/31/02 ALL
		14 (4/1-9/30/04)		53 (10/1/04-3/31/05)					
NUMBER OF STATEMENTS	10	14	23	16	2	2		44	40
	%	%	%	%	%	%	ASSETS	%	%
Cash & Equivalents	18.9	3.4	5.8	4.3				7.6	6.3
Trade Receivables (net)	20.8	35.2	31.2	21.3				23.7	26.6
Inventory	25.6	30.7	28.0	26.0				25.9	25.6
All Other Current	2.7	2.0	1.1	4.4				3.7	2.6
Total Current	68.1	71.3	66.2	56.0				60.9	61.1
Fixed Assets (net)	27.1	16.4	24.7	30.3				26.6	28.0
Intangibles (net)	.0	1.1	1.7	6.7				4.9	6.3
All Other Non-Current	4.8	11.2	7.4	6.9				7.6	4.6
Total	100.0	100.0	100.0	100.0				100.0	100.0
							LIABILITIES		
Notes Payable-Short Term	4.3	13.9	16.3	16.4				11.0	12.8
Cur. Mat.-L/T/D	7.9	1.2	2.1	3.2				3.7	5.2
Trade Payables	24.7	18.9	21.4	19.6				16.0	16.8
Income Taxes Payable	.5	.7	1.5	.2				.4	.3
All Other Current	9.9	8.4	8.0	7.8				8.7	19.2
Total Current	47.3	43.1	49.2	47.2				39.9	54.3
Long-Term Debt	15.4	11.4	11.3	12.8				14.1	16.4
Deferred Taxes	.6	.0	.0	.3				.4	.6
All Other Non-Current	5.6	10.1	4.6	7.0				4.6	5.6
Net Worth	31.1	35.5	34.9	32.7				40.9	23.0
Total Liabilities & Net Worth	100.0	100.0	100.0	100.0				100.0	100.0
							INCOME DATA		
Net Sales	100.0	100.0	100.0	100.0				100.0	100.0
Gross Profit	34.3	47.6	34.6	27.8				40.5	41.3
Operating Expenses	33.3	43.5	29.7	26.1				34.5	35.6
Operating Profit	1.0	4.2	5.0	1.7				6.0	5.7
All Other Expenses (net)	.2	.8	.6	1.5				1.3	1.8
Profit Before Taxes	.8	3.3	4.4	.2				4.8	3.9
							RATIOS		
Current	3.9	2.2	2.1	1.7				2.7	1.8
	1.4	1.6	1.4	1.1				1.4	1.3
	.8	1.0	1.0	.8				1.0	.9
Quick	1.6	1.3	1.2	.8				1.5	1.0
	.9	.8	.9	.5				.6	.6
	.4	.7	.4	.4				.5	.5
Sales/Receivables	0 UND	32 11.4	27 13.3	33 11.1				26 14.0	32 11.4
	24 15.2	37 9.9	46 7.9	46 8.0				41 9.0	41 8.8
	42 8.7	44 8.3	59 6.2	59 6.2				54 6.8	50 7.2
Cost of Sales/Inventory	0 UND	38 9.5	43 8.6	32 11.5				46 8.0	42 8.7
	52 7.1	71 5.1	65 5.7	58 6.3				63 5.8	58 6.3
	102 3.6	111 3.3	87 4.2	78 4.7				92 4.0	81 4.5
Cost of Sales/Payables	14 25.2	22 16.5	28 13.1	32 11.5				16 23.1	18 20.7
	36 10.1	31 11.9	45 8.1	38 9.5				34 10.7	38 9.7
	76 4.8	76 4.8	70 5.2	84 4.3				58 6.2	70 5.2
Sales/Working Capital	8.5	8.7	7.3	7.4				7.0	8.4
	14.6	13.6	18.2	36.0				14.3	18.3
	−24.5	NM	347.7	−19.7				NM	−53.3
EBIT/Interest		108.5	22.9	9.8				15.3	8.1
		(13) 16.6	(22) 5.7	1.8				(38) 4.1	(37) 2.6
		.7	1.7	−.1				1.5	1.2
Net Profit + Depr., Dep., Amort./Cur. Mat. L./T/D									
Fixed/Worth	.2	.1	.3	.6				.3	.4
	.7	.3	.8	.8				.8	.9
	NM	NM	1.5	3.8				2.1	2.7
Debt/Worth	.3	.6	.9	.9				.8	1.1
	.8	1.1	1.9	2.0				2.0	2.6
	NM	NM	4.8	7.4				3.7	6.5
% Profit Before Taxes/Tangible Net Worth		49.0	57.3	36.6				44.9	37.8
	(11) 30.3	(21) 28.4	(13) 24.8					(41) 23.0	(33) 15.8
		−.7	5.1	−3.0				6.0	2.6
% Profit Before Taxes/Total Assets	7.4	22.0	22.4	9.3				17.9	12.0
	1.4	11.1	5.8	1.8				9.0	5.4
	−2.4	−1.0	1.9	−2.1				.9	.8
Sales/Net Fixed Assets	75.3	130.2	25.9	9.3				25.9	30.5
	9.5	44.8	11.3	5.6				10.1	8.5
	6.5	15.1	4.5	4.4				5.7	5.2
Sales/Total Assets	4.6	4.2	3.4	2.5				2.9	3.1
	2.3	3.5	2.6	1.9				2.2	2.3
	1.3	2.0	1.9	1.4				1.9	1.9
% Depr., Dep., Amort./Sales			.8	1.1				.8	1.1
		(22) 1.5	(14) 2.4					(36) 1.8	(34) 2.2
		3.0	5.5					3.2	3.9
% Officers', Directors', Owners' Comp/Sales								2.5	2.9
								(13) 5.2	(17) 5.4
								11.1	12.9
Net Sales ($)	8300M	47576M	293604M	706444M	80116M	641263M		2179955M	1019067M
Total Assets ($)	2835M	15453M	113563M	357455M	127734M	256170M		1085276M	600592M

M = $ thousand   MM = $ million
See Pages 11 through 21 for Explanation of Ratios and Data

Comparative Historical Data | Current Data Sorted By Sales

	4/1/02-3/31/03 ALL	4/1/03-3/31/04 ALL	4/1/04-3/31/05 ALL	Type of Statement	0-1MM	1-3MM	3-5MM	5-10MM	10-25MM	25MM & OVER
	14	13	16	Unqualified			2		5	9
	7	13	10	Reviewed		2	1	3	4	
	6	13	10	Compiled		1	2		2	
	4	3	9	Tax Returns	4	2	2	2		
	11	10	22	Other	3	2	5	1	6	6
						14 (4/1-9/30/04)		53 (10/1/04-3/31/05)		
NUMBER OF STATEMENTS	42	52	67		9	7	12	7	17	15

ASSETS (%)

	4/1/02-3/31/03 ALL	4/1/03-3/31/04 ALL	4/1/04-3/31/05 ALL		0-1MM	1-3MM	3-5MM	5-10MM	10-25MM	25MM & OVER
Cash & Equivalents	6.5	7.5	7.0				5.8		5.2	3.0
Trade Receivables (net)	28.5	29.1	26.7				33.7		28.1	20.9
Inventory	26.6	24.9	27.3				28.7		29.0	29.5
All Other Current	4.0	3.2	2.6				4.4		3.7	2.8
Total Current	65.7	64.7	63.7				72.6		66.1	56.3
Fixed Assets (net)	26.1	22.9	24.1				13.3		23.7	25.5
Intangibles (net)	3.2	4.9	4.8				1.0		6.9	10.7
All Other Non-Current	4.9	7.4	7.4				13.1		3.3	7.5
Total	100.0	100.0	100.0				100.0		100.0	100.0

LIABILITIES

	4/1/02-3/31/03 ALL	4/1/03-3/31/04 ALL	4/1/04-3/31/05 ALL		3-5MM	10-25MM	25MM & OVER
Notes Payable-Short Term	15.1	12.5	13.5		9.9	16.9	18.4
Cur. Mat.-L/T/D	4.0	5.3	3.4		.9	2.4	3.7
Trade Payables	18.4	19.9	20.4		17.3	20.0	22.4
Income Taxes Payable	.2	.3	1.0		.5	1.3	1.2
All Other Current	9.5	8.0	8.2		7.9	5.9	7.0
Total Current	47.1	46.0	46.5		36.5	46.5	52.7
Long-Term Debt	13.0	14.0	13.3		7.5	12.8	12.5
Deferred Taxes	.4	.1	.3		.0	.5	.3
All Other Non-Current	5.4	2.9	6.6		12.8	7.6	5.9
Net Worth	34.0	36.9	33.4		43.1	32.6	28.6
Total Liabilities & Net Worth	100.0	100.0	100.0		100.0	100.0	100.0

INCOME DATA

	4/1/02-3/31/03 ALL	4/1/03-3/31/04 ALL	4/1/04-3/31/05 ALL		3-5MM	10-25MM	25MM & OVER
Net Sales	100.0	100.0	100.0		100.0	100.0	100.0
Gross Profit	35.3	37.3	36.1		44.9	31.5	29.1
Operating Expenses	30.9	32.9	32.1		40.9	25.2	25.1
Operating Profit	4.3	4.3	4.0		4.0	6.2	4.1
All Other Expenses (net)	.8	1.2	1.1		.5	2.0	1.4
Profit Before Taxes	3.6	3.2	2.9		3.5	4.2	2.7

RATIOS

	4/1/02-3/31/03 ALL	4/1/03-3/31/04 ALL	4/1/04-3/31/05 ALL		3-5MM	10-25MM	25MM & OVER
Current	2.4	2.0	1.9		3.1	1.9	1.3
	1.6	1.5	1.3		2.0	1.4	1.0
	1.1	1.1	.9		1.4	1.1	.9
Quick	1.4	1.3	1.2		1.6	1.1	.5
	.8	.7	.7		1.1	.7	.4
	.5	.5	.4		.8	.4	.3
Sales/Receivables	31 11.8	33 11.0	27 13.5		28 12.8	23 15.8	24 14.9
	40 9.1	45 8.1	41 8.9		37 9.9	46 7.9	40 9.1
	52 7.0	57 6.4	52 7.0		94 3.9	53 6.9	49 7.5
Cost of Sales/Inventory	38 9.6	40 9.2	37 9.9		39 9.3	40 9.1	38 9.5
	60 6.1	55 6.7	63 5.8		71 5.1	63 5.8	59 6.1
	78 4.7	78 4.7	93 3.9		91 4.0	76 4.8	99 3.7
Cost of Sales/Payables	23 15.8	30 12.1	26 14.3		21 17.0	27 13.4	34 10.8
	44 8.3	42 8.7	39 9.4		38 9.7	37 9.8	39 9.4
	63 5.8	71 5.2	70 5.2		86 4.2	65 5.6	82 4.5
Sales/Working Capital	6.3	5.8	9.1		5.0	7.2	13.7
	11.3	12.0	17.2		10.4	18.2	347.7
	34.0	36.2	-105.8		18.4	76.3	-31.3
EBIT/Interest	11.4	16.2	20.4		55.0	23.6	18.1
	(37) 4.4	(50) 3.6	(60) 3.0		(10) 5.5	7.7	2.7
	1.4	.7	.6		2.1	.3	.5
Net Profit + Depr., Dep., Amort./Cur. Mat. L/T/D	4.4	2.1	21.4				
	(10) 1.8	(15) 1.4	(14) 2.3				
	-.6	.8	.7				
Fixed/Worth	.3	.3	.3		.1	.3	.6
	.8	.6	.8		.2	.8	1.7
	1.8	1.3	2.3		.7	1.4	-6.6
Debt/Worth	.7	1.1	.8		.7	1.3	1.1
	1.9	1.9	1.8		.9	2.2	3.4
	3.7	4.0	5.7		1.5	5.0	-14.8
% Profit Before Taxes/Tangible Net Worth	35.5	48.8	39.8		49.0	79.4	40.7
	(37) 18.3	(47) 12.4	(55) 16.2		(11) 12.4	(15) 28.5	(11) 36.4
	1.7	-1.3	1.5		2.9	-3.6	7.2
% Profit Before Taxes/Total Assets	14.1	20.3	17.2		25.6	26.8	11.4
	6.2	4.4	5.3		5.0	8.0	3.9
	.5	-1.0	-1.0		2.0	-1.6	-2.5
Sales/Net Fixed Assets	23.0	24.2	47.5		117.5	23.2	22.4
	9.7	10.2	10.6		44.1	11.3	6.0
	6.0	6.8	5.1		9.0	7.5	4.8
Sales/Total Assets	3.0	3.0	3.4		5.1	3.3	3.1
	2.3	2.3	2.4		2.5	2.7	2.3
	1.8	1.6	1.6		1.5	1.7	1.5
% Depr., Dep., Amort./Sales	1.4	1.0	.7			.8	.9
	(38) 2.0	(49) 2.0	(56) 1.8			(16) 1.5	(14) 2.1
	3.0	2.9	4.1			3.0	5.5
% Officers', Directors', Owners' Comp/Sales	2.6	2.2	1.6				
	(13) 4.3	(15) 4.2	(22)				
	11.8	7.7	6.4				

	4/1/02-3/31/03 ALL	4/1/03-3/31/04 ALL	4/1/04-3/31/05 ALL		0-1MM	1-3MM	3-5MM	5-10MM	10-25MM	25MM & OVER
Net Sales ($)	1398233M	1639564M	1777303M		5106M	15613M	46332M	52297M	303490M	1354465M
Total Assets ($)	705114M	903796M	873210M		2383M	13972M	30474M	22450M	187494M	616437M

© RMA 2005

M = $ thousand   MM = $ million

See Pages 11 through 21 for Explanation of Ratios and Data

Current Data Sorted By Assets | Comparative Historical Data

Note: Columns 50-100MM and 100-250MM are marked **DATA NOT AVAILABLE**.

	0-500M	500M-2MM	2-10MM	10-50MM	50-100MM	100-250MM	Type of Statement	4/1/00-3/31/01 ALL	4/1/01-3/31/02 ALL
		2	7	10			Unqualified	14	13
	1	1	12	4	1		Reviewed	17	14
	1	1	7				Compiled	14	16
	1	2					Tax Returns	2	4
	3	7	5	5			Other	21	27
		19 (4/1-9/30/04)			50 (10/1/04-3/31/05)				
NUMBER OF STATEMENTS	5	13	31	19	1			68	74
	%	%	%	%	%	%	**ASSETS**	%	%
Cash & Equivalents		8.0	5.9	7.1				4.8	7.5
Trade Receivables (net)		39.3	30.5	27.9				33.0	32.6
Inventory		23.2	27.9	24.1				24.7	23.7
All Other Current		3.1	2.1	1.1				1.2	1.3
Total Current		73.6	66.4	60.2				63.7	65.1
Fixed Assets (net)		14.1	22.2	22.8				22.5	20.0
Intangibles (net)		5.1	7.1	7.2				5.3	7.2
All Other Non-Current		7.2	4.3	9.8				8.5	7.7
Total		100.0	100.0	100.0				100.0	100.0
							LIABILITIES		
Notes Payable-Short Term		19.0	11.1	12.4				14.6	13.2
Cur. Mat.-L/T/D		2.4	2.3	2.7				4.8	3.3
Trade Payables		19.6	21.0	17.6				17.9	19.1
Income Taxes Payable		.0	.3	.1				.2	.2
All Other Current		7.2	8.7	8.2				10.1	9.3
Total Current		48.4	43.3	40.9				47.6	45.0
Long-Term Debt		13.8	10.2	12.4				11.1	13.2
Deferred Taxes		.2	.5	.3				.2	.3
All Other Non-Current		1.5	4.4	7.0				4.1	3.3
Net Worth		36.1	41.6	39.3				36.9	38.2
Total Liabilities & Net Worth		100.0	100.0	100.0				100.0	100.0
							INCOME DATA		
Net Sales		100.0	100.0	100.0				100.0	100.0
Gross Profit		38.3	38.2	34.9				39.3	41.0
Operating Expenses		37.5	32.8	27.0				35.2	36.6
Operating Profit		.8	5.3	7.9				4.1	4.4
All Other Expenses (net)		.2	1.6	1.3				.7	1.1
Profit Before Taxes		.5	3.8	6.6				3.4	3.3
							RATIOS		
Current		2.9	2.1	2.0				1.9	2.3
		1.2	1.6	1.5				1.3	1.4
		1.1	1.1	1.1				1.0	1.1
Quick		1.9	1.1	1.1				1.1	1.4
		.9	.9	.7				.8	.8
		.6	.5	.5				.6	.6
Sales/Receivables	35 10.5	35 10.4	42 8.8					38 9.6	36 10.1
	43 8.5	43 8.4	49 7.5					48 7.7	44 8.2
	82 4.5	59 6.2	60 6.1					55 6.6	54 6.7
Cost of Sales/Inventory	29 12.4	49 7.4	38 9.7					42 8.7	46 7.9
	60 6.1	71 5.1	71 5.1					58 6.3	62 5.9
	84 4.3	92 4.0	99 3.7					87 4.2	82 4.4
Cost of Sales/Payables	23 15.7	36 10.1	23 15.9					25 14.7	21 17.4
	44 8.4	46 8.0	49 7.4					41 9.0	42 8.7
	69 5.3	66 5.5	55 6.6					54 6.7	58 6.3
Sales/Working Capital		5.5	6.6	7.6				7.6	6.0
		21.5	10.2	12.6				18.9	16.2
		33.8	42.5	29.8				123.4	75.2
EBIT/Interest		6.3	29.0	10.7				7.3	6.7
		(12) 1.5	(29) 3.0	(17) 4.7				(63) 2.5	(65) 2.5
		−3.3	1.5	1.7				1.0	1.1
Net Profit + Depr., Dep., Amort./Cur. Mat. L /T/D			9.6					7.3	3.2
			(14) 2.8					(27) 1.8	(16) 1.3
			1.3					1.3	.6
Fixed/Worth		.3	.3	.3				.3	.2
		.6	.5	.9				.6	.6
		1.8	1.3	4.1				1.4	1.8
Debt/Worth		.5	.8	.9				1.1	.7
		3.2	2.1	1.9				1.8	1.9
		18.6	3.8	9.2				4.4	6.3
% Profit Before Taxes/Tangible Net Worth		17.3	35.8	28.1				35.7	32.4
		(12) 3.4	(30) 14.2	(15) 19.2				(62) 13.8	(61) 13.6
		−38.5	1.0	5.5				1.8	2.5
% Profit Before Taxes/Total Assets		4.3	12.5	18.9				11.6	11.5
		1.5	6.1	6.4				3.8	4.1
		−4.1	.7	1.6				.0	.4
Sales/Net Fixed Assets		31.7	28.5	18.8				25.4	28.5
		16.7	14.8	11.2				15.1	16.1
		11.7	6.3	4.5				7.3	7.2
Sales/Total Assets		3.1	2.7	2.6				3.3	3.3
		2.6	2.4	2.2				2.5	2.5
		2.0	1.9	1.4				1.9	1.8
% Depr., Dep., Amort./Sales		.7	1.0	.6				.9	1.0
		(12) 1.5	(29) 1.3	1.1				(59) 1.5	(64) 1.6
		1.8	1.9	2.2				3.0	2.7
% Officers', Directors', Owners' Comp/Sales			1.7					2.9	3.1
			(12) 3.9					(22) 3.6	(27) 4.1
			8.0					6.5	8.4
Net Sales ($)	3471M	35546M	357807M	1020631M	71266M			1832843M	1826510M
Total Assets ($)	1360M	14656M	147413M	463200M	68205M			951397M	912929M

© RMA 2005

M = $ thousand   MM = $ million
See Pages 11 through 21 for Explanation of Ratios and Data

Comparative Historical Data / Current Data Sorted By Sales

			Type of Statement	0-1MM	1-3MM	3-5MM	5-10MM	10-25MM	25MM & OVER
15	16	19	Unqualified		1	1	2	7	8
17	12	18	Reviewed		1	1	6	5	5
4	10	9	Compiled	1		1	1	5	1
4	5	3	Tax Returns	1	2				
29	29	20	Other	2	6	1	5	3	3
4/1/02-3/31/03 ALL	4/1/03-3/31/04 ALL	4/1/04-3/31/05 ALL			19 (4/1-9/30/04)			50 (10/1/04-3/31/05)	
73	72	69	**NUMBER OF STATEMENTS**	4	10	4	14	20	17
%	%	%	**ASSETS**	%	%	%	%	%	%
7.0	7.4	6.7	Cash & Equivalents		11.0		6.1	5.0	8.6
27.7	30.5	31.9	Trade Receivables (net)		35.1		28.9	29.8	30.2
23.7	25.3	26.2	Inventory		15.7		25.9	28.4	27.2
3.5	2.3	1.9	All Other Current		3.7		3.2	1.3	.9
62.0	65.4	66.7	Total Current		65.6		64.1	64.5	66.9
26.0	22.3	20.3	Fixed Assets (net)		14.2		23.5	24.6	19.8
5.1	5.3	6.8	Intangibles (net)		13.5		8.5	6.5	2.2
6.9	7.0	6.1	All Other Non-Current		6.7		3.9	4.5	11.1
100.0	100.0	100.0	Total		100.0		100.0	100.0	100.0
			LIABILITIES						
9.7	12.5	12.4	Notes Payable-Short Term		10.4		12.3	11.4	12.1
4.1	3.3	3.2	Cur. Mat.-L/T/D		3.7		2.5	2.1	2.2
18.0	17.8	19.9	Trade Payables		17.8		20.9	20.0	19.2
.5	.4	.1	Income Taxes Payable		.0		.3	.2	.1
12.1	9.5	8.2	All Other Current		6.7		8.7	8.2	8.6
44.4	43.5	43.9	Total Current		38.6		44.7	41.9	42.2
16.2	12.5	11.7	Long-Term Debt		15.2		8.7	14.5	9.3
.3	.2	.4	Deferred Taxes		.0		.4	.6	.4
3.9	5.7	6.1	All Other Non-Current		.1		8.5	4.3	3.7
35.2	38.1	37.9	Net Worth		46.2		37.6	38.7	44.5
100.0	100.0	100.0	Total Liabilities & Net Worth		100.0		100.0	100.0	100.0
			INCOME DATA						
100.0	100.0	100.0	Net Sales		100.0		100.0	100.0	100.0
38.9	38.3	37.1	Gross Profit		39.2		40.9	37.2	32.0
34.6	33.3	32.2	Operating Expenses		34.9		34.5	32.5	25.5
4.3	5.0	4.8	Operating Profit		4.3		6.4	4.7	6.5
1.0	1.0	1.2	All Other Expenses (net)		.5		2.7	1.2	.4
3.2	4.0	3.6	Profit Before Taxes		3.8		3.7	3.5	6.0
			RATIOS						
2.2	2.3	2.2			2.9		2.0	2.2	3.4
1.4	1.5	1.5	Current		1.7		1.2	1.6	1.5
1.1	1.2	1.1			1.2		1.0	1.1	1.1
1.2	1.4	1.2			2.2		1.1	1.1	2.5
.8	.9	.8	Quick		1.1		.6	.9	.7
.5	.6	.5			.7		.5	.7	.7
32 11.4	38 9.7	36 10.0		32 11.3			37 9.7	35 10.3	38 9.6
43 8.5	45 8.2	45 8.1	Sales/Receivables	44 8.4			55 6.6	43 8.4	45 8.1
53 6.9	54 6.8	61 6.0		81 4.5			66 5.5	58 6.3	55 6.6
43 8.5	39 9.4	43 8.5		0 UND			56 6.5	51 7.2	39 9.3
55 6.6	62 5.9	71 5.1	Cost of Sales/Inventory	35 10.6			76 4.8	69 5.3	66 5.5
79 4.6	88 4.1	96 3.8		83 4.4			92 4.0	104 3.5	97 3.8
30 12.4	24 14.9	29 12.5		20 18.2			40 9.1	36 10.1	21 17.5
43 8.6	39 9.3	44 8.2	Cost of Sales/Payables	40 9.0			63 5.8	46 8.0	35 10.6
55 6.6	58 6.3	66 5.6		75 4.8			88 4.1	59 6.2	54 6.7
7.1	6.8	6.6			5.3		5.7	6.9	5.8
12.9	11.4	11.8	Sales/Working Capital		7.8		16.7	9.7	12.6
46.0	34.4	30.8			27.6		−280.8	21.7	25.7
12.4	13.1	7.8					6.3	7.3	14.6
(66) 4.6	(62) 5.4	(63) 3.0	EBIT/Interest				(12) 2.5	2.6	(14) 5.5
1.5	1.5	1.3					1.2	1.7	1.8
10.6	4.2	4.6	Net Profit + Depr., Dep.,					13.7	
(27) 2.5	(25) 2.1	(24) 1.8	Amort./Cur. Mat. L/T/D					(10) 3.4	
1.3	.6	1.2						1.1	
.4	.3	.3			.3		.2	.3	.2
.9	.8	.7	Fixed/Worth		.6		.8	.9	.5
1.8	1.9	1.4			1.2		1.8	1.3	2.5
.9	.7	.8			.5		.9	1.1	.5
2.4	1.8	2.2	Debt/Worth		2.3		2.2	2.3	1.2
5.7	6.1	6.4			11.1		4.3	3.7	7.3
47.0	39.0	28.4	% Profit Before Taxes/Tangible				41.5	46.7	27.6
(68) 18.8	(64) 20.0	(61) 11.1	Net Worth				(13) 22.3	(19) 8.8	(14) 21.3
3.0	6.9	1.0					1.3	1.0	10.0
12.4	14.2	11.9	% Profit Before Taxes/Total		8.7		10.5	12.0	17.2
7.1	8.4	5.1	Assets		1.7		7.2	2.8	8.1
1.3	1.0	.6			−3.8		.5	.7	4.1
16.0	21.4	26.9			29.9		30.9	17.2	40.3
10.3	13.8	14.3	Sales/Net Fixed Assets		16.6		10.3	12.8	13.7
5.8	6.3	7.1			10.6		4.0	6.0	5.7
2.8	2.9	2.9			3.3		2.5	3.5	2.9
2.4	2.3	2.3	Sales/Total Assets		2.5		2.1	2.4	2.3
1.6	1.8	1.7			1.3		1.8	1.6	1.7
1.2	.8	.8					1.0	1.0	.7
(65) 1.9	(62) 1.3	(64) 1.3	% Depr., Dep., Amort./Sales				(19) 1.4	(16) 1.2	1.1
2.6	1.9	1.9					2.4	1.5	1.8
3.2	2.1	2.3	% Officers', Directors',						
(24) 4.1	(23) 5.2	(21) 5.2	Owners' Comp/Sales						
9.9	12.3	9.2							
2201019M	1905876M	1488721M	Net Sales ($)	2148M	19227M	14898M	97018M	314768M	1040662M
1128267M	927275M	694834M	Total Assets ($)	1030M	10435M	5608M	54650M	153159M	469952M

© RMA 2005

M = $ thousand   MM = $ million

See Pages 11 through 21 for Explanation of Ratios and Data

Current Data Sorted By Assets | Comparative Historical Data

	0-500M	500M-2MM	2-10MM	10-50MM	50-100MM	100-250MM	Type of Statement	ALL 4/1/00-3/31/01	ALL 4/1/01-3/31/02
			8	12	3		Unqualified	22	23
		2	7	2			Reviewed	7	7
	1	3	2				Compiled	20	19
		3	3				Tax Returns	4	2
	1	6	9	6	2	3	Other	27	29
		13 (4/1-9/30/04)		60 (10/1/04-3/31/05)					
NUMBER OF STATEMENTS	2	14	29	20	5	3		80	80
	%	%	%	%	%	%	**ASSETS**	%	%
		2.1	4.7	9.1			Cash & Equivalents	6.3	7.7
		32.0	32.9	26.8			Trade Receivables (net)	29.2	26.3
		38.6	38.3	30.9			Inventory	32.5	31.2
		1.9	1.2	5.2			All Other Current	1.8	1.8
		74.6	77.1	71.9			Total Current	69.8	67.0
		15.8	14.8	15.5			Fixed Assets (net)	21.2	19.9
		3.5	2.8	7.9			Intangibles (net)	4.8	6.8
		6.1	5.3	4.7			All Other Non-Current	4.2	6.4
		100.0	100.0	100.0			Total	100.0	100.0
							LIABILITIES		
		30.4	17.9	15.6			Notes Payable-Short Term	10.9	13.1
		2.5	2.8	4.6			Cur. Mat.-L/T/D	2.6	4.7
		38.8	22.3	16.1			Trade Payables	19.4	17.5
		.1	.1	.2			Income Taxes Payable	.3	.6
		6.1	10.8	8.6			All Other Current	10.3	7.9
		77.9	54.0	45.1			Total Current	43.6	43.8
		17.0	10.4	11.2			Long-Term Debt	15.7	11.4
		.0	.2	.0			Deferred Taxes	.3	.3
		2.2	5.8	2.2			All Other Non-Current	7.0	8.9
		2.9	29.7	41.5			Net Worth	33.4	35.6
		100.0	100.0	100.0			Total Liabilities & Net Worth	100.0	100.0
							INCOME DATA		
		100.0	100.0	100.0			Net Sales	100.0	100.0
		41.0	38.0	39.5			Gross Profit	40.5	42.8
		39.4	31.8	32.4			Operating Expenses	34.3	38.9
		1.6	6.2	7.1			Operating Profit	6.2	3.9
		1.4	1.1	.9			All Other Expenses (net)	1.6	1.4
		.2	5.2	6.3			Profit Before Taxes	4.7	2.5
							RATIOS		
		1.9	2.2	2.5				2.5	2.5
		1.2	1.5	1.5			Current	1.7	1.7
		.7	1.1	1.2				1.2	1.2
		1.0	1.0	1.2				1.3	1.2
		.6	.6	.8			Quick	.8	.8
		.2	.5	.5				.5	.5
	18	20.2	37 9.9	45 8.0				38 9.6	33 10.9
	41	9.0	46 7.9	54 6.7			Sales/Receivables	48 7.6	46 8.0
	62	5.8	61 5.9	59 6.2				64 5.7	62 5.9
	33	11.1	56 6.5	70 5.2				58 6.3	72 5.1
	74	4.9	82 4.5	104 3.5			Cost of Sales/Inventory	97 3.8	99 3.7
	154	2.4	158 2.3	149 2.5				156 2.3	163 2.2
	24	15.5	17 21.7	36 10.1				32 11.5	25 14.8
	72	5.0	51 7.2	56 6.6			Cost of Sales/Payables	50 7.3	43 8.4
	125	2.9	70 5.2	64 5.7				66 5.5	70 5.2
		10.9	6.0	4.4				4.8	4.5
		17.2	8.7	7.3			Sales/Working Capital	7.8	7.2
		−19.2	44.0	21.4				23.2	32.5
		15.1	15.0	16.5				6.4	9.5
		(13) 1.9	(26) 3.9	(19) 8.5			EBIT/Interest	(75) 2.8	(69) 2.6
		.9	1.5	2.4				1.3	1.1
							Net Profit + Depr., Dep., Amort./Cur. Mat. L /T/D	6.7	8.3
								(29) 3.1	(23) 2.5
								1.0	.3
		.1	.2	.2				.3	.3
		.6	.4	.5			Fixed/Worth	.6	.5
		NM	1.8	1.0				1.5	1.6
		1.8	1.0	.8				1.0	.8
		5.2	2.6	2.0			Debt/Worth	2.3	2.1
		NM	13.5	2.6				5.1	6.5
		73.8	117.9	65.3			% Profit Before Taxes/Tangible Net Worth	54.3	46.3
		(11) 31.2	(27) 38.6	(18) 35.6				(72) 24.6	(68) 17.0
		5.3	10.6	9.8				7.8	2.2
		10.2	21.3	21.8			% Profit Before Taxes/Total Assets	17.1	15.7
		3.7	10.5	9.7				7.0	4.8
		−5.2	1.5	3.2				1.8	.4
		166.8	47.2	31.3				24.1	24.6
		21.6	25.0	15.5			Sales/Net Fixed Assets	12.6	12.1
		8.1	10.0	9.4				5.8	6.2
		3.2	3.2	2.2				2.6	2.6
		2.8	2.4	1.7			Sales/Total Assets	2.1	2.0
		2.3	1.9	1.6				1.7	1.3
		.4	.6	.9				.9	.9
		(12) 1.1	(28) 1.4	(17) 1.5			% Depr., Dep., Amort./Sales	(70) 1.7	(69) 1.7
		3.1	1.9	1.9				2.8	2.8
			1.9				% Officers', Directors', Owners' Comp/Sales	1.7	3.0
			(13) 2.3					(28) 3.9	(30) 5.4
			4.5					7.0	11.8
	1096M	42660M	373788M	883267M	452964M	442761M	Net Sales ($)	2966858M	2888523M
	812M	15596M	146526M	462371M	380882M	324923M	Total Assets ($)	1701416M	1909431M

M = $ thousand   MM = $ million
See Pages 11 through 21 for Explanation of Ratios and Data

Comparative Historical Data / Current Data Sorted By Sales

			Type of Statement	0-1MM	1-3MM	3-5MM	5-10MM	10-25MM	25MM & OVER
28	34	23	Unqualified				1	10	12
12	15	11	Reviewed			2		3	3
11	21	6	Compiled	2	1	2	3	1	
5	1	6	Tax Returns	1	1	1	1	2	
31	25	27	Other	1	3	3	2	8	10
4/1/02-3/31/03 ALL	4/1/03-3/31/04 ALL	4/1/04-3/31/05 ALL		13 (4/1-9/30/04)			60 (10/1/04-3/31/05)		
87	96	73	**NUMBER OF STATEMENTS**	4	5	9	7	23	25
%	%	%	**ASSETS**	%	%	%	%	%	%
8.2	8.7	6.6	Cash & Equivalents					6.1	10.9
26.5	27.2	29.1	Trade Receivables (net)					33.7	26.5
31.3	29.6	35.0	Inventory					36.8	25.6
2.3	3.3	2.5	All Other Current					1.7	4.5
68.3	68.7	73.2	Total Current					78.4	67.5
20.2	18.5	15.4	Fixed Assets (net)					13.8	17.6
6.8	7.6	5.9	Intangibles (net)					3.4	10.3
4.7	5.1	5.4	All Other Non-Current					4.4	4.7
100.0	100.0	100.0	Total					100.0	100.0
			LIABILITIES						
15.1	13.1	19.1	Notes Payable-Short Term					18.1	10.5
4.1	2.5	3.1	Cur. Mat.-L/T/D					3.0	4.1
19.0	17.7	22.8	Trade Payables					23.2	14.2
.7	.6	.1	Income Taxes Payable					.1	.2
10.7	9.3	9.7	All Other Current					10.0	8.3
49.6	43.3	54.8	Total Current					54.4	37.3
13.6	10.9	11.6	Long-Term Debt					9.2	10.1
.3	.4	.1	Deferred Taxes					.1	.1
7.7	9.7	4.2	All Other Non-Current					3.7	4.9
28.7	35.6	29.3	Net Worth					32.6	47.7
100.0	100.0	100.0	Total Liabilities & Net Worth					100.0	100.0
			INCOME DATA						
100.0	100.0	100.0	Net Sales					100.0	100.0
39.4	40.2	40.7	Gross Profit					37.3	42.0
35.1	33.1	34.1	Operating Expenses					30.3	33.0
4.3	7.1	6.6	Operating Profit					7.0	9.1
1.0	1.1	1.2	All Other Expenses (net)					.9	1.0
3.3	6.0	5.4	Profit Before Taxes					6.1	8.1
			RATIOS						
2.7	2.2	2.3						2.9	2.8
1.5	1.6	1.5	Current					1.5	1.7
1.1	1.2	1.2						1.1	1.3
1.3	1.3	1.2						1.2	1.6
.8	.8	.7	Quick					.7	1.0
.5	.5	.5						.5	.7
33 11.1	35 10.3	37 9.9						34 10.8	45 8.1
46 7.9	45 8.2	47 7.7	Sales/Receivables					46 7.9	54 6.7
62 5.9	55 6.7	61 6.0						62 5.9	62 5.9
54 6.7	52 7.0	59 6.2						53 6.8	66 5.5
82 4.4	84 4.3	93 3.9	Cost of Sales/Inventory					82 4.5	95 3.8
143 2.6	133 2.7	149 2.4						133 2.7	117 3.1
24 15.0	28 13.0	22 16.5						16 22.7	31 11.8
41 8.8	50 7.3	51 7.2	Cost of Sales/Payables					54 6.8	45 8.2
74 5.0	69 5.3	76 4.8						72 5.1	61 6.0
4.6	4.9	4.9						4.8	3.4
10.7	8.9	8.7	Sales/Working Capital					7.0	6.7
25.2	21.4	23.4						51.7	10.7
9.2	19.7	16.2						25.4	20.0
(80) 3.5	(85) 6.2	(67) 5.7	EBIT/Interest					(20) 5.5	(23) 8.5
1.2	2.1	1.7						1.7	2.4
10.1	10.5	7.7	Net Profit + Depr., Dep.,						
(33) 3.2	(27) 4.1	(18) 1.6	Amort./Cur. Mat. L/T/D						
.6	1.7	.9							
.2	.2	.2						.2	.2
.7	.6	.5	Fixed/Worth					.4	.5
3.4	1.8	1.4						2.1	1.0
1.1	.8	1.0						.8	.6
2.5	1.9	2.5	Debt/Worth					1.6	2.0
15.2	6.2	7.9						13.2	2.6
45.9	63.4	74.2	% Profit Before Taxes/Tangible					112.5	67.9
(70) 23.6	(84) 30.4	(64) 35.1	Net Worth					(20) 47.0	(23) 24.4
3.8	13.7	10.4						22.6	10.0
14.9	20.5	19.3	% Profit Before Taxes/Total					26.2	20.3
7.2	10.2	9.2	Assets					12.3	11.0
.6	2.9	2.0						2.0	3.2
38.7	28.7	55.4						62.0	28.8
11.2	14.2	18.7	Sales/Net Fixed Assets					25.8	13.8
6.4	7.3	8.2						10.2	5.4
2.8	2.8	3.0						3.2	2.3
2.1	2.1	2.2	Sales/Total Assets					2.6	1.8
1.5	1.5	1.5						2.1	1.2
1.2	1.0	.7						.5	1.0
(71) 2.1	(78) 1.6	(64) 1.5	% Depr., Dep., Amort./Sales					1.1	(21) 1.6
2.9	3.0	2.1						1.6	2.5
1.9	1.8	2.2	% Officers', Directors',						
(26) 4.3	(20) 4.3	(22) 4.0	Owners' Comp/Sales						
9.5	8.4	8.2							
3851542M	3242981M	2196536M	Net Sales ($)	2733M	10947M	36987M	44091M	368159M	1733619M
2264998M	1966404M	1331110M	Total Assets ($)	2231M	4353M	18815M	21027M	153409M	1131275M

M = $ thousand   MM = $ million
See Pages 11 through 21 for Explanation of Ratios and Data

Current Data Sorted By Assets | Comparative Historical Data

0-500M	500M-2MM	2-10MM	10-50MM	50-100MM	100-250MM	Type of Statement	4/1/00-3/31/01 ALL	4/1/01-3/31/02 ALL
	1	2				Unqualified	4	3
	2	6				Reviewed	5	2
	1	1	1			Compiled	4	3
	1	1	1			Tax Returns	1	
2		1		4		Other	6	5
	4 (4/1-9/30/04)			20 (10/1/04-3/31/05)				
2	5	11	6			NUMBER OF STATEMENTS	20	13
%	%	%	%	%	%	ASSETS	%	%
		1.2		D	D	Cash & Equivalents	4.8	6.7
		36.8		A	A	Trade Receivables (net)	29.1	28.1
		36.7		T	T	Inventory	31.0	28.6
		2.0		A	A	All Other Current	1.7	1.6
		76.7				Total Current	66.7	65.0
		15.4		N	N	Fixed Assets (net)	24.6	26.2
		5.2		O	O	Intangibles (net)	5.9	6.1
		2.8		T	T	All Other Non-Current	2.9	2.7
		100.0				Total	100.0	100.0
				A	A	LIABILITIES		
		27.6		V	V	Notes Payable-Short Term	13.8	19.6
		4.5		A	A	Cur. Mat.-L/T/D	5.0	3.2
		24.3		I	I	Trade Payables	18.8	16.5
		.1		L	L	Income Taxes Payable	.6	.3
		7.6		A	A	All Other Current	11.5	12.6
		64.2		B	B	Total Current	49.8	52.2
		7.9		L	L	Long-Term Debt	11.2	10.6
		.4		E	E	Deferred Taxes	.7	.2
		14.5				All Other Non-Current	8.8	12.2
		13.1				Net Worth	29.6	24.8
		100.0				Total Liabilities & Net Worth	100.0	100.0
						INCOME DATA		
		100.0				Net Sales	100.0	100.0
		31.1				Gross Profit	35.2	30.1
		28.5				Operating Expenses	31.3	27.2
		2.7				Operating Profit	3.9	2.9
		.5				All Other Expenses (net)	1.7	1.8
		2.2				Profit Before Taxes	2.1	1.1
						RATIOS		
		1.9					2.4	1.7
		1.7				Current	1.5	1.3
		.9					1.1	.9
		.9					1.3	.8
		.6				Quick	.7	.7
		.6					.5	.4
		34 10.8					33 11.1	33 11.2
		47 7.8				Sales/Receivables	41 8.8	47 7.8
		59 6.1					51 7.1	53 6.9
		47 7.7					39 9.4	46 8.0
		78 4.7				Cost of Sales/Inventory	76 4.8	64 5.7
		86 4.2					89 4.1	83 4.4
		27 13.3					24 15.3	22 16.9
		40 9.1				Cost of Sales/Payables	37 9.9	30 12.1
		60 6.1					61 6.0	40 9.1
		8.0					6.8	10.8
		8.6				Sales/Working Capital	10.8	16.5
		-29.7					75.3	NM
		8.4					9.5	3.7
		3.7				EBIT/Interest	(18) 2.1	(12) 1.6
		2.1					.3	-.7
						Net Profit + Depr., Dep., Amort./Cur. Mat. L /T/D		
		.3					.4	.5
		.6				Fixed/Worth	.7	1.2
		-1.7					3.4	4.8
		1.4					.9	1.4
		6.1				Debt/Worth	2.7	3.3
		-8.5					9.2	16.8
							62.3	58.8
						% Profit Before Taxes/Tangible Net Worth	(17) 15.0	(11) 9.3
							-11.0	-13.4
		11.4					10.1	10.7
		4.8				% Profit Before Taxes/Total Assets	3.8	4.0
		.5					-1.9	-5.4
		29.2					27.6	23.1
		18.1				Sales/Net Fixed Assets	10.6	9.2
		12.6					6.1	6.1
		3.4					3.1	3.2
		2.6				Sales/Total Assets	2.5	2.2
		2.5					1.9	2.0
		.9					1.2	.6
		(10) 1.3				% Depr., Dep., Amort./Sales	(18) 1.6	1.8
		2.2					2.2	2.4
						% Officers', Directors', Owners' Comp/Sales		
750M	26764M	126863M	251301M			Net Sales ($)	326764M	281952M
468M	7177M	46342M	131151M			Total Assets ($)	152020M	133043M

M = $ thousand   MM = $ million
See Pages 11 through 21 for Explanation of Ratios and Data

Comparative Historical Data — Current Data Sorted By Sales

			Type of Statement	0-1MM	1-3MM	3-5MM	5-10MM	10-25MM	25MM & OVER
5	2	3	Unqualified				1	2	1
6	9	9	Reviewed				5	3	1
1	5	3	Compiled		1			1	
		2	Tax Returns		1		1		1
5	5	7	Other	2	1		1		4
4/1/02-3/31/03	4/1/03-3/31/04	4/1/04-3/31/05			**4 (4/1-9/30/04)**			**20 (10/1/04-3/31/05)**	
ALL	ALL	ALL							
17	21	24	**NUMBER OF STATEMENTS**	2		2	8	6	6
%	%	%	**ASSETS**	%	%	%	%	%	%
3.7	5.7	3.3	Cash & Equivalents						
27.5	31.1	32.2	Trade Receivables (net)						
34.5	30.8	34.0	Inventory						
2.6	4.0	3.2	All Other Current						
68.3	71.6	72.6	Total Current						
25.5	18.3	17.6	Fixed Assets (net)			DATA			
3.8	3.4	4.3	Intangibles (net)			NOT			
2.5	6.7	5.5	All Other Non-Current			AVAILABLE			
100.0	100.0	100.0	Total						
			LIABILITIES						
18.0	14.5	24.1	Notes Payable-Short Term						
2.5	2.8	2.8	Cur. Mat.-L/T/D						
21.9	22.2	22.0	Trade Payables						
.7	.1	.3	Income Taxes Payable						
13.0	11.2	7.9	All Other Current						
56.1	50.7	57.1	Total Current						
11.1	11.0	4.7	Long-Term Debt						
.2	.3	.2	Deferred Taxes						
6.8	11.2	10.2	All Other Non-Current						
25.9	26.8	27.8	Net Worth						
100.0	100.0	100.0	Total Liabilities & Net Worth						
			INCOME DATA						
100.0	100.0	100.0	Net Sales						
31.2	32.7	30.5	Gross Profit						
28.0	27.9	28.6	Operating Expenses						
3.3	4.7	1.9	Operating Profit						
.6	.9	.8	All Other Expenses (net)						
2.6	3.9	1.1	Profit Before Taxes						
			RATIOS						
1.6	2.9	2.0							
1.3	1.4	1.5	Current						
.9	1.1	1.0							
.8	1.6	1.0							
.6	.8	.7	Quick						
.4	.5	.5							
25 14.5	35 10.3	35 10.5							
47 7.7	46 7.9	43 8.4	Sales/Receivables						
53 6.9	51 7.1	51 7.1							
48 7.5	49 7.5	49 7.5							
77 4.7	63 5.7	70 5.2	Cost of Sales/Inventory						
95 3.8	96 3.8	89 4.1							
23 16.2	22 16.7	24 15.4							
39 9.4	35 10.4	30 12.0	Cost of Sales/Payables						
53 6.8	55 6.7	60 6.1							
7.0	5.4	7.5							
15.4	10.5	11.3	Sales/Working Capital						
-35.4	124.1	145.4							
17.0	11.3	16.1							
(16) 4.6	(19) 3.7	(23) 3.7	EBIT/Interest						
2.5	.8	2.1							
			Net Profit + Depr., Dep., Amort./Cur. Mat. L/T/D						
.6	.4	.3							
1.0	.9	.6	Fixed/Worth						
2.6	-4.8	-12.5							
1.6	1.2	.9							
1.9	2.8	1.8	Debt/Worth						
12.1	-24.9	-73.0							
60.3	50.4	42.3							
(14) 27.2	(15) 21.9	(17) 22.8	% Profit Before Taxes/Tangible Net Worth						
8.1	3.6	6.1							
18.1	18.7	13.7							
7.2	5.5	6.3	% Profit Before Taxes/Total Assets						
3.5	.3	.5							
25.3	28.0	29.4							
9.0	12.4	16.1	Sales/Net Fixed Assets						
5.9	8.6	11.7							
3.1	3.1	3.5							
2.4	2.4	2.6	Sales/Total Assets						
1.9	2.0	1.9							
1.3	1.0	1.1							
1.8	(19) 1.6	(20) 1.5	% Depr., Dep., Amort./Sales						
2.9	2.8	2.4							
			% Officers', Directors', Owners' Comp/Sales						
388886M	383985M	405678M	Net Sales ($)	750M		9266M	58534M	85827M	251301M
236981M	172994M	185138M	Total Assets ($)	468M		2460M	19597M	31462M	131151M

M = $ thousand   MM = $ million
See Pages 11 through 21 for Explanation of Ratios and Data

Current Data Sorted By Assets   Comparative Historical Data

0-500M	500M-2MM	2-10MM	10-50MM	50-100MM	100-250MM	Type of Statement	4/1/00-3/31/01 ALL	4/1/01-3/31/02 ALL
		1	2	1	1	Unqualified	7	6
	1	1	2			Reviewed	3	2
	1	1				Compiled	2	4
						Tax Returns	1	
		7	3			Other	9	13
	3 (4/1-9/30/04)		18 (10/1/04-3/31/05)					
	2	10	7	1	1	NUMBER OF STATEMENTS	22	25
%	%	%	%	%	%	**ASSETS**	%	%
		4.7				Cash & Equivalents	4.6	5.8
		29.5				Trade Receivables (net)	28.1	24.3
		31.5				Inventory	21.2	19.6
		.3				All Other Current	2.2	2.9
		66.0				Total Current	56.0	52.6
		28.5				Fixed Assets (net)	32.4	33.2
		4.0				Intangibles (net)	8.3	10.4
		1.5				All Other Non-Current	3.3	3.9
		100.0				Total	100.0	100.0
						LIABILITIES		
		17.5				Notes Payable-Short Term	9.8	7.2
		3.2				Cur. Mat.-L/T/D	5.5	4.7
		16.0				Trade Payables	16.5	14.7
		.0				Income Taxes Payable	.2	.2
		8.1				All Other Current	5.0	7.5
		44.8				Total Current	37.1	34.3
		8.4				Long-Term Debt	29.3	21.9
		.0				Deferred Taxes	1.4	2.0
		29.3				All Other Non-Current	5.2	10.1
		17.5				Net Worth	27.0	31.7
		100.0				Total Liabilities & Net Worth	100.0	100.0
						INCOME DATA		
		100.0				Net Sales	100.0	100.0
		30.7				Gross Profit	27.6	22.3
		24.5				Operating Expenses	21.8	18.3
		6.1				Operating Profit	5.8	4.0
		1.3				All Other Expenses (net)	3.0	2.4
		4.8				Profit Before Taxes	2.8	1.6
						RATIOS		
		4.1				Current	2.0	2.4
		1.4					1.5	1.4
		1.0					1.2	1.1
		2.5				Quick	1.2	1.1
		.7					.9	.7
		.5					.6	.6
		38 9.7				Sales/Receivables	41 8.9	30 12.0
		41 8.9					49 7.5	42 8.7
		49 7.4					56 6.5	52 7.1
		45 8.1				Cost of Sales/Inventory	33 11.0	28 13.2
		68 5.4					57 6.4	43 8.5
		93 3.9					67 5.5	58 6.3
		17 21.6				Cost of Sales/Payables	27 13.3	20 17.9
		36 10.2					37 9.9	30 12.2
		50 7.4					48 7.5	41 8.9
		5.0				Sales/Working Capital	6.2	6.9
		14.1					12.1	13.8
		NM					65.4	NM
						EBIT/Interest	5.0	9.4
							(21) 1.5	2.3
							.5	.9
						Net Profit + Depr., Dep., Amort./Cur. Mat. L /T/D		
		.4				Fixed/Worth	.7	.7
		.8					3.4	1.5
		NM					NM	12.1
		.2				Debt/Worth	1.1	.9
		2.3					8.2	3.1
		NM					NM	21.1
						% Profit Before Taxes/Tangible Net Worth	34.8	50.4
							(17) 27.7	(20) 18.9
							7.4	5.2
		18.7				% Profit Before Taxes/Total Assets	11.8	10.3
		14.1					2.8	4.3
		.7					-2.1	.4
		16.1				Sales/Net Fixed Assets	9.8	10.6
		9.3					5.0	5.7
		5.7					3.4	3.5
		3.2				Sales/Total Assets	2.5	2.7
		2.4					1.7	2.1
		2.0					1.2	1.3
		1.7				% Depr., Dep., Amort./Sales	.6	1.8
		2.6					(20) 2.1	(22) 3.5
		4.2					4.5	5.4
						% Officers', Directors', Owners' Comp/Sales		
	8943M	117937M	367538M	71655M	328986M	Net Sales ($)	805264M	793707M
	3691M	46310M	174700M	60090M	143986M	Total Assets ($)	618465M	533042M

M = $ thousand   MM = $ million
See Pages 11 through 21 for Explanation of Ratios and Data

The left-most column (0-500M) and the "DATA NOT AVAILABLE" notation appear along the left margin indicating data not available for that size category.

Comparative Historical Data   Current Data Sorted By Sales

			Type of Statement	0-1MM	1-3MM	3-5MM	5-10MM	10-25MM	25MM & OVER
3	5	5	Unqualified					1	4
3	3	4	Reviewed				2	1	1
	5	2	Compiled		1		1		
1			Tax Returns	1					
10	8	10	Other	1			4	3	2
4/1/02-3/31/03	4/1/03-3/31/04	4/1/04-3/31/05		3 (4/1-9/30/04)		18 (10/1/04-3/31/05)			
ALL	ALL	ALL							
20	22	21	**NUMBER OF STATEMENTS**			2	7	5	7
%	%	%	**ASSETS**	%	%	%	%	%	%
5.2	5.9	3.5	Cash & Equivalents						
28.4	21.7	26.7	Trade Receivables (net)	D	D				
21.3	27.7	26.9	Inventory	A	A				
1.7	3.5	1.3	All Other Current	T	T				
56.7	58.9	58.4	Total Current	A	A				
34.8	34.6	27.6	Fixed Assets (net)						
5.1	2.5	8.3	Intangibles (net)	N	N				
3.4	3.9	5.7	All Other Non-Current	O	O				
100.0	100.0	100.0	Total	T	T				
			LIABILITIES	A	A				
13.3	12.4	17.2	Notes Payable-Short Term	V	V				
6.9	5.4	5.7	Cur. Mat.-L/T/D	A	A				
14.3	13.3	14.6	Trade Payables	I	I				
.0	.1	.0	Income Taxes Payable	L	L				
6.9	5.7	10.0	All Other Current	A	A				
41.3	36.9	47.5	Total Current	B	B				
20.7	23.0	11.2	Long-Term Debt	L	L				
1.1	1.2	.7	Deferred Taxes	E	E				
11.1	6.2	15.6	All Other Non-Current						
25.8	32.8	25.0	Net Worth						
100.0	100.0	100.0	Total Liabilities & Net Worth						
			INCOME DATA						
100.0	100.0	100.0	Net Sales						
31.9	35.2	28.5	Gross Profit						
25.6	28.2	22.4	Operating Expenses						
6.3	7.1	6.1	Operating Profit						
2.3	1.8	1.6	All Other Expenses (net)						
4.0	5.3	4.5	Profit Before Taxes						
			RATIOS						
2.3	3.5	1.5							
1.5	1.6	1.1	Current						
.8	1.0	1.0							
1.7	2.2	.9							
.9	.7	.6	Quick						
.4	.4	.4							
34 10.7	31 11.7	39 9.4							
42 8.7	40 9.1	42 8.7	Sales/Receivables						
59 6.2	49 7.4	56 6.6							
36 10.1	48 7.7	44 8.4							
51 7.2	64 5.7	70 5.2	Cost of Sales/Inventory						
67 5.4	119 3.1	96 3.8							
16 23.5	22 16.6	27 13.7							
33 11.1	40 9.2	38 9.5	Cost of Sales/Payables						
48 7.7	53 6.8	48 7.6							
6.4	4.7	9.0							
16.3	9.1	32.3	Sales/Working Capital						
NM	NM	NM							
13.4	12.4	17.8							
4.0	(21) 2.7	(20) 5.7	EBIT/Interest						
1.4	2.0	2.2							
			Net Profit + Depr., Dep., Amort./Cur. Mat. L/T/D						
.7	.6	.5							
1.9	.9	1.0	Fixed/Worth						
11.0	5.6	5.1							
1.1	.7	1.0							
4.5	2.7	2.5	Debt/Worth						
20.8	12.6	10.7							
121.1	54.9	56.7							
(17) 39.4	(20) 32.1	(17) 25.8	% Profit Before Taxes/Tangible Net Worth						
17.6	10.1	8.5							
20.7	15.4	14.7							
5.9	10.0	10.5	% Profit Before Taxes/Total Assets						
2.0	3.3	2.8							
11.5	15.2	14.4							
7.0	5.6	7.8	Sales/Net Fixed Assets						
3.6	2.6	5.4							
3.1	3.0	2.9							
2.2	1.9	2.2	Sales/Total Assets						
1.5	1.3	1.7							
1.6	1.7	1.6							
3.1	(19) 3.4	(19) 2.5	% Depr., Dep., Amort./Sales						
4.9	4.6	4.5							
1.4									
(10) 3.8			% Officers', Directors', Owners' Comp/Sales						
12.8									
605235M	628793M	895059M	Net Sales ($)			8088M	49635M	92303M	745033M
360992M	361265M	428777M	Total Assets ($)			12210M	22239M	36730M	357598M

© RMA 2005

M = $ thousand   MM = $ million

See Pages 11 through 21 for Explanation of Ratios and Data

Current Data Sorted By Assets | **Comparative Historical Data**

						Type of Statement		
1	1	14	14	6	3	Unqualified	20	20
	8	20	7	1		Reviewed	19	15
1	5	11	1			Compiled	30	25
1	5	5				Tax Returns	9	2
3	9	15	22	2	6	Other	42	28
	36 (4/1-9/30/04)			125 (10/1/04-3/31/05)			4/1/00-3/31/01	4/1/01-3/31/02
0-500M	500M-2MM	2-10MM	10-50MM	50-100MM	100-250MM		ALL	ALL
6	28	65	44	9	9	NUMBER OF STATEMENTS	120	90
%	%	%	%	%	%	ASSETS	%	%
	8.5	8.4	6.9			Cash & Equivalents	6.0	8.9
	30.9	31.4	25.9			Trade Receivables (net)	27.1	26.7
	21.7	24.7	22.0			Inventory	22.2	23.5
	5.1	2.9	2.3			All Other Current	4.0	2.7
	66.2	67.4	57.1			Total Current	59.2	61.8
	25.6	24.7	29.3			Fixed Assets (net)	27.2	26.9
	3.2	3.6	8.2			Intangibles (net)	6.3	5.5
	5.0	4.2	5.4			All Other Non-Current	7.3	5.8
	100.0	100.0	100.0			Total	100.0	100.0
						LIABILITIES		
	19.5	11.4	8.2			Notes Payable-Short Term	11.0	9.5
	2.4	3.6	3.8			Cur. Mat.-L/T/D	4.2	3.7
	24.0	20.6	15.9			Trade Payables	16.5	15.9
	.3	.3	.5			Income Taxes Payable	.2	.2
	9.7	8.7	8.3			All Other Current	10.0	9.3
	55.8	44.7	36.8			Total Current	41.9	38.6
	17.6	9.7	18.4			Long-Term Debt	16.2	12.9
	.1	.3	.6			Deferred Taxes	.5	.4
	7.0	4.3	4.1			All Other Non-Current	3.4	2.9
	19.5	41.0	40.1			Net Worth	37.9	45.2
	100.0	100.0	100.0			Total Liabilities & Net Worth	100.0	100.0
						INCOME DATA		
	100.0	100.0	100.0			Net Sales	100.0	100.0
	37.6	35.1	29.3			Gross Profit	34.8	37.0
	33.5	29.2	22.8			Operating Expenses	29.7	31.6
	4.1	5.9	6.4			Operating Profit	5.1	5.4
	1.4	.4	1.1			All Other Expenses (net)	1.2	1.1
	2.7	5.4	5.4			Profit Before Taxes	3.9	4.4
						RATIOS		
	1.6	2.5	2.5			Current	2.4	2.8
	1.2	1.5	1.5				1.5	1.6
	.8	1.0	1.2				1.0	1.1
	1.0	1.4	1.3			Quick	1.5	1.6
	.6	.8	.9				.8	.9
	.4	.6	.6				.5	.6
30	12.1	33 11.1	35 10.3			Sales/Receivables	36 10.2	35 10.4
42	8.7	45 8.1	49 7.4				47 7.8	43 8.5
52	7.1	60 6.1	56 6.5				56 6.5	54 6.7
18	19.9	32 11.3	37 10.0			Cost of Sales/Inventory	35 10.3	39 9.3
55	6.7	51 7.1	62 5.9				58 6.3	59 6.2
73	5.0	84 4.4	88 4.1				85 4.3	95 3.8
14	26.8	28 13.2	23 15.6			Cost of Sales/Payables	26 13.8	24 15.2
43	8.5	46 7.9	39 9.4				41 9.0	36 10.2
86	4.2	61 6.0	56 6.6				60 6.0	61 6.0
	10.3	5.2	5.7			Sales/Working Capital	5.5	4.8
	24.1	14.6	9.4				11.9	9.0
	-25.8	605.6	29.1				NM	43.5
	11.1	17.3	11.5			EBIT/Interest	10.5	14.1
(27)	2.6	(59) 6.4	(39) 3.9				(107) 2.6	(78) 2.8
	1.0	2.3	2.1				1.1	1.3
		4.9	4.2			Net Profit + Depr., Dep., Amort./Cur. Mat. L./T/D	6.2	10.2
	(16)	3.8	(13) 2.4				(44) 1.9	(30) 2.8
		1.8	1.3				.5	.8
	.6	.2	.4			Fixed/Worth	.3	.3
	2.8	.6	.8				.7	.6
	137.4	1.3	2.1				2.8	1.5
	1.5	.7	.7			Debt/Worth	.7	.6
	12.3	1.8	2.0				1.9	1.5
	199.8	3.2	4.2				7.4	4.5
	137.9	47.8	37.0			% Profit Before Taxes/Tangible Net Worth	43.9	39.3
(23)	46.2	(61) 24.9	(40) 21.3				(108) 17.7	(82) 18.3
	1.3	11.3	9.6				2.1	4.5
	11.5	18.7	15.3			% Profit Before Taxes/Total Assets	13.8	15.1
	3.9	9.3	5.8				5.1	4.9
	.1	3.1	2.4				.4	1.1
	33.9	30.3	12.8			Sales/Net Fixed Assets	23.1	16.4
	10.7	14.1	7.1				9.3	8.3
	4.8	6.2	4.1				4.3	4.9
	3.5	3.2	2.1			Sales/Total Assets	2.9	2.8
	2.6	2.5	1.7				2.0	2.1
	1.5	2.0	1.3				1.4	1.3
	1.0	.9	1.1			% Depr., Dep., Amort./Sales	.6	.6
(21)	2.3	(63) 1.6	(39) 3.2				(104) 1.6	(78) 1.4
	4.2	3.0	4.3				3.6	3.2
	4.8	2.8				% Officers', Directors', Owners' Comp/Sales	2.4	3.0
(12)	5.7	(27) 4.7					(38) 5.9	(32) 5.1
	11.4	7.0					9.5	8.7
3688M	86896M	1235474M	2317807M	1405681M	1619461M	Net Sales ($)	3912471M	3688980M
1380M	32793M	322338M	1023451M	607283M	1473777M	Total Assets ($)	2898928M	2421379M

M = $ thousand   MM = $ million
See Pages 11 through 21 for Explanation of Ratios and Data

Comparative Historical Data | Current Data Sorted By Sales

					Type of Statement						
	36		33		39	Unqualified	1	1		1	14	22
	20		31		36	Reviewed	2	2	9	7	12	6
	11		32		18	Compiled	3	4	3	8	8	
	2		7		11	Tax Returns	2	4	2	1	2	
	33		51		57	Other	3	5	3	8	13	25
	4/1/02-		4/1/03-		4/1/04-			36 (4/1-9/30/04)		125 (10/1/04-3/31/05)		
	3/31/03		3/31/04		3/31/05		0-1MM	1-3MM	3-5MM	5-10MM	10-25MM	25MM & OVER
	ALL		ALL		ALL							
	102		154		161	NUMBER OF STATEMENTS	6	15	18	20	49	53
	%		%		%	ASSETS	%	%	%	%	%	%
	10.3		6.8		7.7	Cash & Equivalents		4.1	12.9	6.4	9.6	6.2
	25.9		28.5		28.8	Trade Receivables (net)		22.2	31.4	32.8	29.4	27.3
	23.1		23.8		22.7	Inventory		19.0	23.5	24.6	22.3	23.8
	2.9		3.6		3.3	All Other Current		6.4	2.0	5.8	1.9	3.0
	62.2		62.7		62.5	Total Current		51.8	69.8	69.6	63.3	60.4
	28.0		26.5		26.8	Fixed Assets (net)		37.4	24.9	21.6	26.1	25.7
	5.3		5.1		6.1	Intangibles (net)		4.9	1.3	4.5	5.1	9.6
	4.5		5.7		4.7	All Other Non-Current		6.0	4.0	4.3	5.5	4.3
	100.0		100.0		100.0	Total		100.0	100.0	100.0	100.0	100.0
					LIABILITIES						
	9.4		10.8		11.3	Notes Payable-Short Term		19.0	17.0	10.5	9.2	9.2
	4.1		3.9		3.5	Cur. Mat.-L/T/D		2.4	4.5	3.9	2.9	4.3
	18.5		18.9		19.1	Trade Payables		23.8	20.0	20.5	19.3	16.7
	.2		.4		.3	Income Taxes Payable		.2	.3	.6	.5	.3
	9.8		9.8		9.5	All Other Current		7.6	8.1	10.8	7.6	9.0
	42.0		43.8		43.8	Total Current		53.1	49.9	46.3	39.5	39.5
	15.5		12.3		14.0	Long-Term Debt		24.5	7.7	12.2	11.6	15.5
	.5		.6		.6	Deferred Taxes		.2	.0	.3	.4	1.3
	6.0		5.9		5.0	All Other Non-Current		5.7	11.9	4.6	2.7	4.2
	36.0		37.5		36.7	Net Worth		16.6	30.4	36.6	45.9	39.5
	100.0		100.0		100.0	Total Liabilities & Net Worth		100.0	100.0	100.0	100.0	100.0
					INCOME DATA						
	100.0		100.0		100.0	Net Sales		100.0	100.0	100.0	100.0	100.0
	34.2		34.9		33.1	Gross Profit		40.1	38.9	34.8	38.7	23.6
	28.3		30.6		27.4	Operating Expenses		36.7	34.7	30.9	30.8	17.8
	5.8		4.3		5.7	Operating Profit		3.4	4.2	4.0	7.9	5.8
	1.1		.8		.8	All Other Expenses (net)		2.3	.5	.7	.4	1.3
	4.8		3.5		4.8	Profit Before Taxes		1.1	3.7	3.2	7.5	4.5
					RATIOS						
	2.7		2.3		2.2			1.2	3.4	2.5	2.6	2.5
	1.5		1.4		1.5	Current		.9	1.3	1.5	1.5	1.6
	1.1		1.1		1.0			.7	.9	1.1	1.1	1.2
	1.3		1.2		1.3			.7	2.3	1.4	1.4	1.3
	.8		.8		.8	Quick		.4	1.0	.8	.8	.9
	.5		.5		.5			.3	.4	.6	.7	.6
35	10.5	34	10.7	32	11.2		31	12.0	32	11.5	37	9.9	32	11.3	35	10.5
46	8.0	44	8.2	47	7.8	Sales/Receivables	44	8.4	43	8.5	44	8.4	45	8.1	49	7.5
58	6.3	57	6.4	57	6.5		55	6.6	61	6.0	61	5.9	57	6.4	55	6.6
32	11.3	35	10.4	35	10.3		35	10.3	39	9.3	40	9.2	26	14.0	36	10.1
56	6.5	59	6.2	57	6.4	Cost of Sales/Inventory	63	5.8	53	6.8	49	7.5	56	6.5	61	6.0
90	4.1	87	4.2	83	4.4		94	3.9	92	4.0	95	3.9	78	4.7	87	4.2
22	16.4	23	15.6	25	14.8		33	11.0	13	28.6	24	15.4	28	13.0	24	15.1
39	9.3	38	9.6	40	9.1	Cost of Sales/Payables	80	4.5	40	9.2	46	7.9	46	7.9	35	10.5
59	6.2	66	5.5	61	6.0		99	3.7	66	5.5	64	5.7	61	6.0	51	7.1
	4.3		5.7		5.6			24.3	5.6	5.5	5.3	5.4
	9.5		13.1		12.6	Sales/Working Capital		-64.6	17.5	13.8	10.1	10.3
	126.6		82.7		170.8			-12.3	-38.4	54.2	51.8	27.0
	10.5		10.4		11.7			3.2	23.2	10.7	31.1	9.6
(94)	3.5	(137)	5.3	(146)	4.6	EBIT/Interest	(14)	2.0	5.0	(18)	5.0	(42)	8.0	(49)	4.0
	1.4		1.4		1.8			.4	.3	1.5	3.8	2.2
	9.6		5.6		5.7	Net Profit + Depr., Dep.,					7.1	5.4
(36)	2.7	(47)	2.2	(42)	3.0	Amort./Cur. Mat. L/T/D				(14)	3.1	(20)	2.5
	.8		1.0		1.6						2.0	1.1
	.4		.3		.3			2.4	.3	.2	.2	.4
	.8		.7		.8	Fixed/Worth		7.8	1.0	.6	.6	.7
	2.2		1.9		2.3			15.8	4.1	2.2	1.2	1.4
	.7		.8		.8			4.0	.5	.7	.6	1.0
	1.9		2.3		2.1	Debt/Worth		13.0	1.7	1.8	1.6	2.1
	6.9		5.9		6.5			49.6	33.4	3.1	2.8	4.9
	49.7		47.3		52.5	% Profit Before Taxes/Tangible		139.6	56.5	47.4	60.4	37.1
(89)	16.9	(139)	18.1	(144)	24.7	Net Worth	(13)	22.7	(15)	15.6	(18)	24.4	(46)	31.6	(48)	19.0
	4.9		3.8		8.1			-17.7	-3.3	11.8	15.2	5.2
	16.2		14.0		16.6	% Profit Before Taxes/Total		4.5	26.7	13.9	24.5	12.9
	7.1		6.0		6.1	Assets		3.6	4.6	9.1	13.9	5.4
	1.2		1.4		2.2			-1.5	-1.3	2.0	4.0	1.7
	20.4		28.3		25.3			10.8	29.1	22.3	32.1	16.5
	7.7		8.9		9.4	Sales/Net Fixed Assets		5.3	11.0	14.5	12.3	7.9
	4.8		4.5		4.6			3.1	4.9	6.8	4.4	4.6
	2.6		2.9		3.0			2.8	3.4	3.3	3.1	2.5
	1.9		2.2		2.1	Sales/Total Assets		1.6	2.5	2.4	2.3	1.9
	1.5		1.4		1.4			1.2	1.9	2.0	1.5	1.4
	1.0		.8		1.0			.8	1.1	1.0	1.0	.5
(93)	2.3	(134)	2.0	(143)	2.1	% Depr., Dep., Amort./Sales	(11)	3.2	(16)	2.5	(18)	1.6	(47)	1.7	(46)	2.8
	3.7		3.5		4.0			5.7	7.5	3.3	3.3	4.6
	2.0		2.1		3.0	% Officers', Directors',					2.2	
(29)	3.7	(43)	5.5	(47)	4.8	Owners' Comp/Sales				(18)	3.6	
	7.2		7.8		7.0						7.0	
	4017244M		5224499M		6669007M	Net Sales ($)	2734M	28853M	71505M	146853M	748691M	5670371M
	2332718M		2884974M		3461022M	Total Assets ($)	1600M	21404M	33741M	73291M	377174M	2953812M

Current Data Sorted By Assets   **Comparative Historical Data**

	0-500M	500M-2MM	2-10MM	10-50MM	50-100MM	100-250MM	Type of Statement	4/1/00-3/31/01 ALL	4/1/01-3/31/02 ALL
			10	8	3		Unqualified	12	10
		3	15	3	1		Reviewed	12	13
		3	4	1			Compiled	10	13
	1	2	1	1			Tax Returns	3	1
	1	1	8	6	3	1	Other	19	20
			15 (4/1-9/30/04)	59 (10/1/04-3/31/05)					
NUMBER OF STATEMENTS	2	9	38	18	6	1		56	57
	%	%	%	%	%	%	**ASSETS**	%	%
			6.6	4.3			Cash & Equivalents	3.9	5.5
			31.0	26.1			Trade Receivables (net)	26.3	24.8
			25.6	26.4			Inventory	24.2	21.6
			.5	1.9			All Other Current	1.5	2.2
			63.6	58.7			Total Current	55.9	54.0
			27.5	35.9			Fixed Assets (net)	35.8	39.0
			2.6	.4			Intangibles (net)	2.1	1.6
			6.3	5.0			All Other Non-Current	6.2	5.4
			100.0	100.0			Total	100.0	100.0
							LIABILITIES		
			12.3	13.8			Notes Payable-Short Term	9.5	10.4
			2.6	3.8			Cur. Mat.-L/T/D	6.1	4.9
			21.9	15.7			Trade Payables	19.3	16.3
			.4	1.1			Income Taxes Payable	.0	.7
			6.6	8.3			All Other Current	7.3	9.4
			43.9	42.7			Total Current	42.3	41.7
			10.7	14.5			Long-Term Debt	16.9	16.6
			.2	1.5			Deferred Taxes	.3	.8
			10.2	9.7			All Other Non-Current	4.6	5.4
			35.0	31.6			Net Worth	35.8	35.4
			100.0	100.0			Total Liabilities & Net Worth	100.0	100.0
							INCOME DATA		
			100.0	100.0			Net Sales	100.0	100.0
			23.8	23.0			Gross Profit	26.9	26.1
			18.3	17.5			Operating Expenses	21.3	21.7
			5.5	5.5			Operating Profit	5.5	4.4
			.7	1.3			All Other Expenses (net)	1.2	1.3
			4.8	4.2			Profit Before Taxes	4.3	3.1
							RATIOS		
			2.5	1.9			Current	1.8	2.2
			1.6	1.4				1.3	1.3
			1.0	1.0				1.1	.9
			1.7	1.2			Quick	1.0	1.3
			.8	.7				.7	.7
			.5	.4				.5	.6
			36 10.0	38 9.7			Sales/Receivables	33 11.0	37 9.8
			48 7.6	46 7.9				44 8.2	42 8.6
			58 6.3	56 6.5				55 6.7	52 7.0
			40 9.2	48 7.5			Cost of Sales/Inventory	34 10.9	34 10.7
			52 7.1	56 6.6				51 7.2	48 7.6
			66 5.5	67 5.5				79 4.6	71 5.2
			34 10.6	15 23.6			Cost of Sales/Payables	24 15.5	21 17.1
			40 9.2	33 10.9				38 9.6	32 11.4
			53 6.9	52 7.0				56 6.5	51 7.1
			6.1	5.7			Sales/Working Capital	8.3	6.4
			10.7	12.6				17.1	18.2
			−779.2	NM				109.4	−98.2
			25.0	10.4			EBIT/Interest	7.7	5.3
			(36) 5.3	(17) 5.0				(52) 2.8	(53) 2.4
			1.8	2.2				1.2	.5
				.8			Net Profit + Depr., Dep., Amort./Cur. Mat. L/T/D	5.5	3.1
				1.3				(16) 2.9	(24) 2.3
				1.8				.6	1.2
			.2	.8			Fixed/Worth	.5	.6
			.8	1.3				1.1	1.1
			2.6	1.8				1.8	2.6
			.8	1.3			Debt/Worth	.9	.9
			1.5	2.0				2.0	1.8
			5.5	3.6				4.4	4.2
			42.6	39.3			% Profit Before Taxes/Tangible Net Worth	36.6	25.0
			(34) 24.8	(17) 18.8				(52) 13.2	(50) 13.6
			6.3	11.2				2.3	1.0
			18.4	12.5			% Profit Before Taxes/Total Assets	11.0	10.6
			8.0	7.3				6.1	5.3
			1.9	2.2				1.0	−1.0
			30.1	13.0			Sales/Net Fixed Assets	17.0	9.7
			12.2	5.0				5.2	4.7
			5.3	3.6				3.0	2.8
			3.0	2.6			Sales/Total Assets	3.1	2.7
			2.5	1.9				2.0	1.8
			1.6	1.6				1.5	1.3
			1.0	1.1			% Depr., Dep., Amort./Sales	1.1	1.1
			(35) 2.3	(17) 2.9				(53) 2.6	(53) 3.2
			3.1	4.4				4.7	5.3
			2.0				% Officers', Directors', Owners' Comp/Sales	2.0	1.8
			(14) 3.1					(21) 4.7	(17) 3.1
			5.1					5.4	7.9
	741M	36262M	484615M	780436M	651879M	185800M	Net Sales ($)	1573718M	2153750M
	227M	12509M	209203M	399421M	410892M	137400M	Total Assets ($)	869958M	1475534M

M = $ thousand   MM = $ million
See Pages 11 through 21 for Explanation of Ratios and Data

Comparative Historical Data | **Current Data Sorted By Sales**

			Type of Statement						
16	22	21	Unqualified				6	5	10
19	19	21	Reviewed			3	6	9	3
5	8	8	Compiled		2	2	1	2	1
1	4	4	Tax Returns	1	2		1		
30	24	20	Other	1	1		2	6	10
4/1/02-3/31/03 ALL	4/1/03-3/31/04 ALL	4/1/04-3/31/05 ALL			15 (4/1-9/30/04)			59 (10/1/04-3/31/05)	
				0-1MM	1-3MM	3-5MM	5-10MM	10-25MM	25MM & OVER
71	77	74	**NUMBER OF STATEMENTS**	2	5	5	16	22	24
%	%	%	**ASSETS**	%	%	%	%	%	%
4.4	5.2	6.0	Cash & Equivalents				6.8	4.4	5.2
25.1	28.3	30.6	Trade Receivables (net)				27.7	33.2	26.5
25.4	25.6	26.4	Inventory				23.6	29.8	25.2
1.6	1.3	1.3	All Other Current				.6	.7	2.1
56.5	60.4	64.3	Total Current				58.8	68.0	59.0
32.7	33.4	28.4	Fixed Assets (net)				29.7	25.5	34.9
3.5	1.8	1.8	Intangibles (net)				4.5	1.3	1.0
7.2	4.4	5.5	All Other Non-Current				7.0	5.2	5.1
100.0	100.0	100.0	Total				100.0	100.0	100.0
			LIABILITIES						
10.3	12.8	12.4	Notes Payable-Short Term				11.8	15.1	10.3
4.0	3.3	3.0	Cur. Mat.-L/T/D				4.0	2.3	3.3
17.7	17.4	19.9	Trade Payables				18.3	21.8	18.7
.5	.6	.5	Income Taxes Payable				.8	.0	1.0
9.0	5.9	7.4	All Other Current				5.8	4.6	11.2
41.5	40.0	43.4	Total Current				40.6	43.8	44.6
15.3	18.4	12.0	Long-Term Debt				11.5	11.2	13.9
.7	.5	.6	Deferred Taxes				.2	.3	1.1
8.9	7.8	9.7	All Other Non-Current				16.1	7.1	10.2
33.5	33.3	34.4	Net Worth				31.5	37.6	30.2
100.0	100.0	100.0	Total Liabilities & Net Worth				100.0	100.0	100.0
			INCOME DATA						
100.0	100.0	100.0	Net Sales				100.0	100.0	100.0
27.1	24.9	25.2	Gross Profit				26.0	24.3	20.7
22.7	21.1	20.2	Operating Expenses				20.4	19.6	16.4
4.3	3.8	4.9	Operating Profit				5.6	4.7	4.3
.8	.9	.9	All Other Expenses (net)				1.4	.4	1.4
3.5	3.0	4.1	Profit Before Taxes				4.2	4.3	3.0
			RATIOS						
2.5	2.3	2.5	Current				2.7	2.6	1.9
1.4	1.5	1.5					1.3	1.6	1.4
1.0	1.0	1.0					.9	1.1	.9
1.4	1.4	1.5	Quick				1.9	1.6	1.2
.7	.8	.8					.7	.9	.7
.5	.5	.5					.4	.6	.5
34 10.8	38 9.6	38 9.6	Sales/Receivables				36 10.3	38 9.5	38 9.6
43 8.5	46 7.9	50 7.3					47 7.7	46 8.0	47 7.7
50 7.2	56 6.6	58 6.3					60 6.1	54 6.8	57 6.4
40 9.2	36 10.1	43 8.4	Cost of Sales/Inventory				39 9.4	39 9.3	48 7.5
58 6.3	54 6.7	56 6.5					58 6.3	52 7.0	56 6.5
81 4.5	75 4.8	73 5.0					72 5.1	68 5.4	64 5.7
22 16.7	26 14.2	28 13.1	Cost of Sales/Payables				36 10.2	32 11.4	19 18.8
36 10.1	38 9.7	39 9.5					43 8.4	38 9.7	37 9.9
62 5.9	51 7.1	53 6.9					54 6.8	42 8.7	59 6.2
6.2	5.8	5.5	Sales/Working Capital				5.3	6.3	5.7
14.4	11.5	10.3					22.3	8.3	14.0
140.9	123.5	190.3					−32.2	42.7	−121.8
10.8	11.4	15.4	EBIT/Interest				10.1	37.5	10.4
(67) 3.3	(74) 4.2	(67) 5.0					(14) 4.2	5.1	(23) 4.1
1.1	1.3	2.0					1.1	2.2	1.4
8.3	5.6	8.0	Net Profit + Depr., Dep., Amort./Cur. Mat. L/T/D						
(27) 3.9	(19) 3.2	(19) 3.0							
1.6	2.1	1.8							
.3	.4	.3	Fixed/Worth				.2	.3	.8
1.0	.9	.8					1.0	.7	1.4
3.1	2.4	1.9					25.8	1.4	2.0
.8	.9	.9	Debt/Worth				.7	.8	1.3
2.0	1.8	1.9					1.9	1.6	2.3
4.4	5.9	4.1					46.7	3.6	4.1
46.2	36.8	34.6	% Profit Before Taxes/Tangible Net Worth				41.3	50.8	35.7
(61) 16.7	(67) 15.3	(66) 17.8					(13) 16.1	(21) 23.0	(22) 16.6
4.1	2.9	6.3					7.6	5.4	
14.9	12.7	16.1	% Profit Before Taxes/Total Assets				19.4	18.4	8.6
6.0	4.9	6.0					4.3	7.5	5.3
.3	.5	1.6					1.2	2.2	1.1
20.4	18.1	23.0	Sales/Net Fixed Assets				29.4	30.1	11.1
6.1	7.4	8.8					8.3	12.5	5.3
3.1	3.4	4.2					2.6	5.7	3.7
2.6	2.9	2.9	Sales/Total Assets				2.7	3.5	2.7
1.9	2.2	2.1					1.9	2.6	1.9
1.5	1.5	1.6					1.3	2.0	1.4
1.1	1.2	1.0	% Depr., Dep., Amort./Sales				1.0	1.1	1.4
(68) 2.5	(68) 2.8	(67) 2.3					2.4	(21) 1.9	(21) 2.9
5.0	4.1	3.2					3.2	2.6	4.3
2.5	1.6	2.0	% Officers', Directors', Owners' Comp/Sales						
(19) 4.4	(18) 4.2	(23) 3.3							
6.2	8.2	7.4							
2656157M	2624408M	2139733M	Net Sales ($)	741M	12399M	21893M	115277M	373123M	1616300M
1683095M	1526659M	1169652M	Total Assets ($)	227M	7116M	10132M	70153M	151907M	930117M

M = $ thousand   MM = $ million
See Pages 11 through 21 for Explanation of Ratios and Data

Current Data Sorted By Assets   **Comparative Historical Data**

Type of Statement	0-500M	500M-2MM	2-10MM	10-50MM	50-100MM	100-250MM	4/1/00-3/31/01 ALL	4/1/01-3/31/02 ALL
Unqualified		1	7	9	4		5	1
Reviewed	1	9	18	7			2	4
Compiled	4	6	4	4	1		1	6
Tax Returns	5	5	4				1	1
Other	2	9	12			2	7	8
		21 (4/1-9/30/04)		93 (10/1/04-3/31/05)				
NUMBER OF STATEMENTS	12	30	45	20	5	2	16	20

	0-500M %	500M-2MM %	2-10MM %	10-50MM %	50-100MM %	100-250MM %	4/1/00-3/31/01 ALL %	4/1/01-3/31/02 ALL %
ASSETS								
Cash & Equivalents	13.0	4.5	6.3	5.5			8.7	8.1
Trade Receivables (net)	34.6	30.3	25.0	24.6			23.4	25.2
Inventory	19.5	24.1	20.2	21.8			15.6	18.0
All Other Current	1.8	.3	1.2	.9			1.0	2.3
Total Current	68.8	59.3	52.6	52.8			48.7	53.7
Fixed Assets (net)	24.6	34.1	34.7	38.4			47.4	33.7
Intangibles (net)	1.6	1.5	5.5	3.6			.1	6.6
All Other Non-Current	5.0	5.1	7.2	5.2			3.7	6.0
Total	100.0	100.0	100.0	100.0			100.0	100.0
LIABILITIES								
Notes Payable-Short Term	31.6	13.6	9.1	11.3			5.7	9.9
Cur. Mat.-L/T/D	7.7	5.3	5.0	3.9			4.5	6.7
Trade Payables	29.8	19.4	14.3	14.0			10.9	14.3
Income Taxes Payable	.0	.0	.1	.0			.1	.3
All Other Current	5.7	10.3	6.4	7.3			10.3	6.4
Total Current	74.7	48.7	34.9	36.6			31.5	37.7
Long-Term Debt	22.1	26.0	16.9	11.8			24.1	27.5
Deferred Taxes	.0	.2	.6	.7			.1	.1
All Other Non-Current	5.3	14.0	4.3	3.0			2.2	6.3
Net Worth	-2.1	11.1	43.4	47.9			42.1	28.5
Total Liabilities & Net Worth	100.0	100.0	100.0	100.0			100.0	100.0
INCOME DATA								
Net Sales	100.0	100.0	100.0	100.0			100.0	100.0
Gross Profit	35.7	31.2	27.6	19.7			28.7	26.2
Operating Expenses	31.5	29.0	22.0	16.1			19.4	22.5
Operating Profit	4.2	2.2	5.6	3.6			9.2	3.7
All Other Expenses (net)	.7	2.0	1.2	1.1			1.7	2.0
Profit Before Taxes	3.5	.2	4.4	2.5			7.6	1.7
RATIOS								
Current	2.1	2.0	2.6	3.6			3.4	3.2
	1.3	1.4	1.5	1.3			1.8	1.7
	.8	1.0	1.0	.9			1.6	1.1
Quick	1.4	1.3	1.5	1.8			2.3	2.2
	.9	.8	.7	.7			1.1	.8
	.5	.5	.6	.5			.7	.5
Sales/Receivables	18 20.8	36 10.0	34 10.8	35 10.5			29 12.6	30 12.0
	34 10.6	42 8.7	47 7.8	46 8.0			37 9.9	36 10.2
	49 7.4	52 7.1	53 6.8	57 6.4			44 8.3	52 7.1
Cost of Sales/Inventory	0 UND	23 15.8	36 10.0	35 10.3			25 14.4	24 15.1
	38 9.7	37 9.9	47 7.7	50 7.4			38 9.7	38 9.5
	65 5.6	81 4.5	69 5.3	65 5.6			64 5.7	64 5.7
Cost of Sales/Payables	13 28.0	21 17.7	20 18.1	18 19.9			12 29.2	16 22.8
	30 12.2	32 11.5	31 11.7	31 11.9			23 15.8	27 13.4
	56 6.5	54 6.8	47 7.7	44 8.2			41 8.9	37 9.7
Sales/Working Capital	11.1	7.8	6.5	5.3			5.5	5.5
	17.6	13.4	13.6	18.0			9.5	12.1
	UND	NM	NM	NM			12.8	60.0
EBIT/Interest		4.7	14.4	33.1			19.2	11.4
		(29) 2.2	(42) 3.9	(18) 4.8			(14) 5.7	(18) 2.9
		-.7	1.6	.9			2.6	-.3
Net Profit + Depr., Dep., Amort./Cur. Mat. L/T/D		4.3						
		(13) 1.4						
		.5						
Fixed/Worth	.2	.5	.4	.5			.6	.4
	.9	1.2	1.1	.8			.9	1.2
	NM	-3.1	2.9	2.7			1.8	-4.1
Debt/Worth	.9	.9	.6	.3			.4	.6
	2.8	4.3	1.7	.7			1.1	1.8
	NM	-6.9	5.0	3.8			2.1	-13.7
% Profit Before Taxes/Tangible Net Worth		54.3	41.7	21.7			48.0	27.5
	(20)	21.1	(40) 23.1	(18) 12.7			(15) 30.5	(13) 15.1
		-1.5	5.6	3.6			14.4	2.0
% Profit Before Taxes/Total Assets	51.6	11.5	13.9	12.6			21.5	20.5
	7.0	2.8	6.2	5.7			11.1	4.6
	-13.3	-3.7	1.8	-.2			5.8	-5.6
Sales/Net Fixed Assets	58.9	18.3	13.2	8.2			8.3	16.1
	13.7	7.2	5.1	5.3			3.7	8.0
	6.5	4.4	3.6	3.1			2.4	3.0
Sales/Total Assets	4.6	3.3	2.5	2.3			2.6	2.7
	2.7	2.7	2.0	1.9			1.8	2.2
	2.1	1.9	1.4	1.4			1.5	1.5
% Depr., Dep., Amort./Sales		1.8	2.4	2.1			2.0	1.6
	(29)	2.8	(41) 3.6	3.0			(14) 3.9	(18) 3.2
		5.0	5.3	4.7			5.2	4.6
% Officers', Directors', Owners' Comp/Sales		2.2	2.3					
	(18)	3.8	(15) 3.6					
		5.2	8.7					
Net Sales ($)	14492M	95240M	419530M	694623M	525867M	374982M	413917M	536051M
Total Assets ($)	3604M	35128M	215608M	347056M	330704M	282027M	239226M	468651M

© RMA 2005

M = $ thousand   MM = $ million
See Pages 11 through 21 for Explanation of Ratios and Data

Comparative Historical Data

Current Data Sorted By Sales

Hist 1	Hist 2	Hist 3	Type of Statement	0-1MM	1-3MM	3-5MM	5-10MM	10-25MM	25MM & OVER
8	14	21	Unqualified		1	1	2	7	10
10	15	35	Reviewed	1	4	5	14	9	2
9	10	15	Compiled	2	5	3	4		1
6	9	14	Tax Returns	5	3	3	2	1	
8	15	29	Other	1	6	4	7	6	5
4/1/02-3/31/03 ALL	4/1/03-3/31/04 ALL	4/1/04-3/31/05 ALL		21 (4/1-9/30/04)			93 (10/1/04-3/31/05)		
41	63	114	NUMBER OF STATEMENTS	9	19	16	29	23	18
%	%	%	**ASSETS**	%	%	%	%	%	%
8.2	7.3	6.0	Cash & Equivalents		8.0	8.3	7.0	3.4	3.0
24.1	22.2	27.1	Trade Receivables (net)		30.4	26.7	24.2	30.0	25.5
18.1	20.6	21.3	Inventory		19.7	21.5	20.6	22.5	20.8
3.5	1.4	1.1	All Other Current		.5	.9	.7	1.7	1.7
53.9	51.4	55.5	Total Current		58.6	57.4	52.5	57.6	50.9
36.0	36.4	34.7	Fixed Assets (net)		37.0	32.3	34.1	32.2	40.3
3.0	4.2	3.8	Intangibles (net)		.2	5.3	4.7	5.3	3.5
7.1	8.0	6.0	All Other Non-Current		4.1	4.9	8.7	5.0	5.4
100.0	100.0	100.0	Total		100.0	100.0	100.0	100.0	100.0
			LIABILITIES						
7.7	10.2	12.9	Notes Payable-Short Term		14.6	15.8	10.9	10.2	10.9
5.4	5.4	5.1	Cur. Mat.-L/T/D		6.0	4.2	5.0	5.4	3.3
13.5	12.8	17.2	Trade Payables		12.5	27.1	15.4	17.2	15.7
.4	.1	.1	Income Taxes Payable		.0	.0	.1	.2	.0
6.0	5.9	7.8	All Other Current		6.3	13.6	7.9	6.4	8.5
33.1	34.4	43.1	Total Current		39.4	60.7	39.3	39.4	38.5
23.7	29.6	20.2	Long-Term Debt		26.5	26.2	16.0	13.3	21.7
.7	.5	.5	Deferred Taxes		.0	.4	.6	.8	1.0
2.8	3.0	6.6	All Other Non-Current		19.4	3.6	3.5	4.3	2.2
39.7	32.5	29.6	Net Worth		14.6	9.1	40.6	42.2	36.7
100.0	100.0	100.0	Total Liabilities & Net Worth		100.0	100.0	100.0	100.0	100.0
			INCOME DATA						
100.0	100.0	100.0	Net Sales		100.0	100.0	100.0	100.0	100.0
33.3	29.1	27.7	Gross Profit		33.3	28.6	28.2	23.4	20.2
29.6	25.0	23.6	Operating Expenses		26.8	25.7	23.2	18.7	16.9
3.7	4.1	4.1	Operating Profit		6.5	2.9	5.0	4.7	3.3
1.0	1.3	1.4	All Other Expenses (net)		1.7	1.6	1.3	1.1	1.2
2.7	2.8	2.7	Profit Before Taxes		4.8	1.3	3.7	3.6	2.1
			RATIOS						
3.7	2.6	2.1	Current		2.2	2.5	2.1	2.6	2.0
1.8	1.5	1.4			1.5	1.5	1.3	1.3	1.4
1.1	1.0	1.0			1.3	.7	1.0	.9	.9
2.2	1.5	1.3	Quick		1.4	1.4	1.7	1.4	1.1
.9	.8	.7			1.0	.7	.7	.7	.7
.6	.5	.5			.7	.4	.5	.6	.5
31 11.7	29 12.4	34 10.7	Sales/Receivables		33 11.0	29 12.7	32 11.2	38 9.7	39 9.4
37 9.9	40 9.2	44 8.2			42 8.8	41 8.8	40 9.0	50 7.3	50 7.3
58 6.3	50 7.3	54 6.8			55 6.6	50 7.4	48 7.5	66 5.5	55 6.6
21 17.4	33 11.2	30 12.3	Cost of Sales/Inventory		18 19.8	36 10.2	28 13.1	37 10.0	25 14.5
42 8.7	45 8.1	46 7.9			33 11.1	44 8.3	44 8.2	45 8.1	55 6.7
70 5.2	69 5.3	72 5.1			59 6.2	77 4.7	66 5.5	65 5.6	90 4.1
13 27.8	18 20.1	20 18.3	Cost of Sales/Payables		14 26.6	22 16.6	20 18.1	19 19.6	22 16.4
30 12.1	27 13.3	32 11.5			27 13.8	38 9.6	30 12.0	36 10.2	35 10.5
49 7.5	44 8.4	50 7.2			35 10.5	53 6.9	41 8.9	54 6.8	53 6.9
5.2	5.3	7.8	Sales/Working Capital		9.3	6.6	8.9	5.7	6.5
9.2	13.7	15.1			11.8	13.7	14.7	19.7	15.0
100.3	−356.8	UND			23.8	−12.0	NM	−42.7	−48.3
9.8	7.0	14.0	EBIT/Interest		24.4	6.3	12.9	12.6	34.9
(37) 2.9	(56) 2.5	(104) 3.0			3.8	(14) 2.9	(27) 2.3	(21) 4.0	(17) 3.7
.0	.6	.8			.8	−1.1	.9	1.7	.0
	4.2	4.2	Net Profit + Depr., Dep., Amort./Cur. Mat. L/T/D				1.5		
(14)	2.4	(27) 2.6					(11) .9		
	1.4	.9					.2		
.4	.4	.5	Fixed/Worth		.4	.7	.4	.4	.6
.9	1.0	1.1			1.0	1.9	.9	1.0	1.9
2.1	2.7	6.1			−4.4	−3.8	3.5	2.9	5.6
.4	.6	.6	Debt/Worth		.6	1.1	.5	.6	.6
1.1	1.5	2.1			2.1	2.6	1.9	1.2	2.4
4.4	8.8	13.0			−37.0	−7.6	8.6	5.0	11.6
24.9	27.5	41.5	% Profit Before Taxes/Tangible Net Worth		70.1	39.7	49.9	41.2	32.9
(33) 10.9	(51) 9.2	(93) 17.0		(14) 21.1	(10) 18.3	(26) 23.1	(19) 13.7	(16) 17.5	
.3	−5.8	.4			−4.2	6.2	4.7	5.4	−1.6
12.0	9.7	13.5	% Profit Before Taxes/Total Assets		42.8	10.2	13.9	12.4	14.1
3.9	3.6	5.2			8.2	3.8	5.3	5.1	6.9
−2.7	.0	−.4			−.4	−3.5	.0	2.8	−.9
10.9	12.3	14.2	Sales/Net Fixed Assets		22.3	19.9	12.0	19.4	8.0
6.7	6.5	6.5			6.5	5.9	6.8	8.4	4.6
3.6	3.3	3.4			3.1	3.6	4.4	3.3	3.0
2.7	2.8	2.8	Sales/Total Assets		4.0	3.0	2.8	2.7	2.5
2.1	2.0	2.2			2.7	2.2	2.3	2.0	2.0
1.4	1.4	1.6			1.8	1.6	1.5	1.5	1.4
2.4	2.4	2.1	% Depr., Dep., Amort./Sales		1.5	1.8	2.6	1.5	1.5
(37) 3.7	(58) 3.6	(102) 3.5		(15) 3.3	(14) 3.1	(27) 3.6	(22) 2.8	(17) 3.5	
6.1	6.1	5.3			5.7	5.1	5.6	4.2	5.2
3.0	2.7	2.4	% Officers', Directors', Owners' Comp/Sales		2.5		2.1		
(12) 4.3	(29) 4.7	(44) 4.1		(15) 4.2		(13) 3.1			
8.4	8.4	8.3			5.8		6.9		
661416M	1170000M	2124734M	Net Sales ($)	5283M	38900M	63017M	199736M	389390M	1428408M
395657M	677452M	1214127M	Total Assets ($)	3460M	16185M	38879M	101035M	201510M	853058M

© RMA 2005   M = $ thousand   MM = $ million
See Pages 11 through 21 for Explanation of Ratios and Data

Current Data Sorted By Assets | Comparative Historical Data

	0-500M	500M-2MM	2-10MM	10-50MM	50-100MM	100-250MM		4/1/00-3/31/01 ALL	4/1/01-3/31/02 ALL
Type of Statement									
Unqualified			10	14	3	2		6	10
Reviewed		4	34	6	1			5	5
Compiled	3	14	5	2				4	7
Tax Returns		1	1					3	1
Other	2	13	24	12	3	6		11	10
		41 (4/1-9/30/04)		119 (10/1/04-3/31/05)					
NUMBER OF STATEMENTS	5	32	74	34	7	8		29	33
	%	%	%	%	%	%	**ASSETS**	%	%
		8.8	3.8	5.3			Cash & Equivalents	4.5	4.9
		32.5	25.7	24.9			Trade Receivables (net)	21.7	22.6
		20.6	24.1	19.9			Inventory	22.5	21.5
		1.9	.9	1.2			All Other Current	.9	2.3
		63.7	54.6	51.3			Total Current	49.6	51.3
		29.2	35.8	38.7			Fixed Assets (net)	42.7	44.4
		.0	4.2	2.9			Intangibles (net)	2.1	1.5
		7.0	5.4	7.0			All Other Non-Current	5.7	2.7
		100.0	100.0	100.0			Total	100.0	100.0
							LIABILITIES		
		15.1	14.5	13.3			Notes Payable-Short Term	9.4	10.9
		5.0	4.4	4.3			Cur. Mat.-L/T/D	7.2	6.4
		14.0	16.2	16.7			Trade Payables	14.3	12.7
		.0	.4	.1			Income Taxes Payable	.7	.1
		6.4	7.9	6.8			All Other Current	8.2	12.8
		40.5	43.5	41.2			Total Current	39.9	42.9
		12.4	17.0	17.2			Long-Term Debt	25.7	18.0
		.4	1.0	.9			Deferred Taxes	1.0	1.6
		7.8	6.7	3.6			All Other Non-Current	2.4	6.8
		38.8	31.8	37.1			Net Worth	31.1	30.6
		100.0	100.0	100.0			Total Liabilities & Net Worth	100.0	100.0
							INCOME DATA		
		100.0	100.0	100.0			Net Sales	100.0	100.0
		26.6	24.9	23.7			Gross Profit	29.5	25.8
		24.5	21.5	18.4			Operating Expenses	22.2	23.7
		2.1	3.4	5.3			Operating Profit	7.4	2.1
		-.2	1.8	.8			All Other Expenses (net)	2.1	2.1
		2.3	1.6	4.5			Profit Before Taxes	5.3	.0
							RATIOS		
		3.1	2.0	1.8				1.7	2.1
		1.5	1.2	1.3			Current	1.1	1.2
		1.1	.9	.8				.9	.9
		1.6	1.3	1.0				.8	1.0
		.9	.6	.8			Quick	.6	.6
		.6	.4	.5				.5	.4
	30 12.2	34 10.9	36 10.1					30 12.1	29 12.5
	46 8.0	44 8.3	47 7.8				Sales/Receivables	38 9.6	40 9.1
	51 7.1	59 6.2	63 5.8					52 7.1	48 7.7
	21 17.1	39 9.3	34 10.6					41 8.9	43 8.5
	35 10.6	57 6.5	44 8.3				Cost of Sales/Inventory	60 6.1	49 7.5
	54 6.8	94 3.9	69 5.3					85 4.7	77 4.7
	12 29.7	25 14.6	26 13.8					23 15.9	15 23.6
	21 17.0	39 9.4	39 9.4				Cost of Sales/Payables	37 10.0	25 14.4
	36 10.0	60 6.1	64 5.7					51 7.2	44 8.3
		7.2	6.4	8.9				7.3	7.2
		13.7	19.0	16.1			Sales/Working Capital	27.9	22.4
		74.2	-36.6	-31.5				-71.3	-75.1
		9.6	6.1	17.6				6.1	4.6
		(28) 2.6	(67) 2.3	(31) 4.5			EBIT/Interest	2.7	(32) 1.5
		.1	.2	2.0				1.5	-1.2
			3.2	5.5			Net Profit + Depr., Dep.,	7.5	2.2
		(22) 1.3	(12) 2.9				Amort./Cur. Mat. L /T/D	(11) 4.7	(10) 1.7
			.6	1.3				1.6	.5
		.4	.7	.5				.9	.9
		.7	1.3	.9			Fixed/Worth	1.2	1.5
		2.1	3.0	2.4				2.9	2.9
		.6	1.1	.9				1.1	1.1
		1.3	2.5	1.5			Debt/Worth	2.9	2.0
		5.1	7.7	4.2				4.0	5.9
		29.3	39.4	40.6			% Profit Before Taxes/Tangible	50.0	19.6
		(27) 8.1	(63) 15.6	(30) 19.3			Net Worth	(27) 26.9	(28) 10.9
		-1.9	.5	10.8				4.5	-.5
		11.8	8.8	12.4			% Profit Before Taxes/Total	19.7	6.7
		4.0	4.0	6.3			Assets	7.0	2.3
		-.9	-1.8	2.7				1.2	-5.5
		15.5	10.1	7.2				7.0	6.7
		9.5	5.7	4.5			Sales/Net Fixed Assets	4.7	5.3
		6.9	3.1	3.1				2.3	2.7
		3.3	2.2	2.3				2.3	2.4
		2.7	1.8	1.7			Sales/Total Assets	1.9	2.0
		2.1	1.4	1.2				1.2	1.5
		1.9	2.1	2.7				2.4	2.0
		(30) 3.0	(71) 3.5	(27) 4.2			% Depr., Dep., Amort./Sales	(27) 3.0	(31) 2.9
		4.1	5.4	5.9				5.3	5.0
		2.5	1.3					3.9	3.0
		(23) 4.2	(33) 2.4				% Officers', Directors', Owners' Comp/Sales	(10) 5.8	(11) 5.2
		8.0	4.1					9.3	7.2
	7416M	111087M	718141M	1454489M	790038M	2004725M	Net Sales ($)	986822M	1511989M
	1936M	40710M	396884M	785215M	488069M	1173599M	Total Assets ($)	528792M	861600M

© RMA 2005

M = $ thousand   MM = $ million
See Pages 11 through 21 for Explanation of Ratios and Data

Comparative Historical Data				Current Data Sorted By Sales					
			Type of Statement		**41 (4/1-9/30/04)**		**119 (10/1/04-3/31/05)**		
28	33	29	Unqualified			1	6	4	18
35	37	45	Reviewed	1	3	4	16	17	4
17	38	24	Compiled	2	9	2	9		2
4	5	2	Tax Returns				2		
61	61	60	Other	2	9	7	8	16	18
4/1/02-3/31/03	4/1/03-3/31/04	4/1/04-3/31/05		0-1MM	1-3MM	3-5MM	5-10MM	10-25MM	25MM & OVER
ALL	ALL	ALL							
145	174	160	**NUMBER OF STATEMENTS**	5	21	14	41	37	42
%	%	%	**ASSETS**	%	%	%	%	%	%
4.8	4.3	4.9	Cash & Equivalents		5.5	5.0	3.5	3.3	4.4
26.3	26.8	27.0	Trade Receivables (net)		29.7	33.0	30.3	23.2	26.0
18.4	20.1	22.2	Inventory		18.3	26.7	21.4	26.9	18.8
1.9	1.2	1.6	All Other Current		.4	.8	1.1	.7	2.6
51.4	52.4	55.7	Total Current		53.9	65.5	56.3	54.0	51.8
35.0	36.9	34.5	Fixed Assets (net)		35.9	28.9	32.9	38.7	35.0
5.6	3.7	3.0	Intangibles (net)		.6	.1	5.0	3.0	3.5
7.9	6.9	6.8	All Other Non-Current		9.6	5.5	5.8	4.3	9.7
100.0	100.0	100.0	Total		100.0	100.0	100.0	100.0	100.0
			LIABILITIES						
12.4	13.2	13.7	Notes Payable-Short Term		9.7	21.8	15.0	12.8	12.6
5.3	6.4	4.7	Cur. Mat.-L/T/D		4.3	6.6	4.4	4.5	4.5
16.3	16.5	15.9	Trade Payables		11.0	16.8	14.3	19.2	17.4
.3	.1	.2	Income Taxes Payable		.2	.0	.3	.3	.1
8.9	8.3	7.9	All Other Current		5.8	10.5	7.7	7.3	7.7
43.2	44.4	42.4	Total Current		31.0	55.7	41.6	44.1	42.2
19.6	18.7	15.6	Long-Term Debt		15.9	11.1	15.6	20.1	12.4
1.1	.9	1.0	Deferred Taxes		.8	.6	.6	1.4	1.5
5.3	5.3	6.1	All Other Non-Current		6.4	13.8	8.3	3.1	4.6
30.9	30.7	34.9	Net Worth		45.9	18.5	33.9	31.3	39.3
100.0	100.0	100.0	Total Liabilities & Net Worth		100.0	100.0	100.0	100.0	100.0
			INCOME DATA						
100.0	100.0	100.0	Net Sales		100.0	100.0	100.0	100.0	100.0
26.0	27.1	24.7	Gross Profit		30.3	25.2	25.2	23.1	21.6
21.9	24.4	21.3	Operating Expenses		25.8	27.4	22.1	18.5	17.7
4.1	2.7	3.4	Operating Profit		4.5	−2.1	3.1	4.6	3.9
1.8	1.3	1.1	All Other Expenses (net)		1.0	1.4	1.5	1.3	1.0
2.4	1.4	2.3	Profit Before Taxes		3.5	−3.5	1.7	3.3	3.0
			RATIOS						
1.7	1.9	1.9	Current		3.6	2.2	2.5	1.7	1.6
1.2	1.2	1.3			1.9	1.1	1.4	1.2	1.3
.9	.9	.9			1.2	.8	1.0	.9	.9
1.0	1.1	1.2	Quick		2.3	1.7	1.4	.8	1.0
.7	.7	.7			1.0	.7	.9	.5	.8
.5	.4	.5			.7	.5	.5	.5	.5
36 10.2	36 10.2	35 10.4	Sales/Receivables		34 10.9	42 8.6	34 10.8	29 12.6	40 9.1
48 7.7	47 7.8	45 8.0			45 8.1	48 7.5	49 7.5	41 9.0	47 7.7
58 6.3	61 6.0	57 6.4			50 7.3	65 5.7	60 6.1	54 6.8	65 5.6
27 13.7	30 12.2	33 11.2	Cost of Sales/Inventory		21 17.7	41 9.0	30 12.0	41 8.9	32 11.6
48 7.6	45 8.1	49 7.5			36 10.1	57 6.4	49 7.5	59 6.2	41 8.9
66 5.5	66 5.5	79 4.6			71 5.2	97 3.8	67 5.5	97 3.7	59 6.2
26 14.0	22 16.7	21 17.2	Cost of Sales/Payables		12 30.9	13 27.5	16 22.3	29 12.4	27 13.4
36 10.1	35 10.5	34 10.6			27 13.6	29 12.4	33 11.0	39 9.4	40 9.0
53 6.9	56 6.5	56 6.5			39 9.4	52 7.1	58 6.3	69 5.3	58 6.3
9.3	8.4	7.3	Sales/Working Capital		6.8	6.1	6.3	7.2	9.5
18.3	22.9	16.9			11.9	42.9	16.7	21.7	17.7
−42.3	−24.8	−44.6			54.7	−15.0	NM	−36.2	−66.0
8.7	9.0	7.1	EBIT/Interest		6.6	4.7	11.0	6.3	12.0
(137) 2.3	(166) 2.0	(145) 3.2			(20) 3.3	(13) −.1	(37) 2.0	(34) 3.1	(39) 4.2
.6	.4	.7			1.8	−7.5	.6	1.2	1.1
4.1	4.1	4.1	Net Profit + Depr., Dep.,				3.6	1.9	4.7
(46) 2.5	(49) 1.9	(48) 1.9	Amort./Cur. Mat. L/T/D				(12) 1.1	(10) 1.3	(17) 2.0
1.1	1.0	.9					.6	.8	.6
.6	.6	.5	Fixed/Worth		.4	.6	.7	.7	.5
1.2	1.3	1.1			.7	1.1	1.7	1.3	.9
4.6	3.5	2.4			1.2	−4.8	2.9	5.3	1.7
1.0	1.0	.8	Debt/Worth		.7	.7	.9	1.4	.8
2.5	2.4	2.0			1.0	4.8	2.2	2.5	1.5
13.8	10.2	6.1			2.8	−10.8	10.1	7.3	3.6
45.3	33.0	38.3	% Profit Before Taxes/Tangible		39.1		36.2	44.4	37.0
(117) 18.9	(147) 11.6	(138) 14.5	Net Worth		(20) 10.5		(34) 13.1	(33) 24.4	(38) 15.2
.8	−1.0	2.4			6.3		−7.7	7.9	6.7
12.0	9.0	10.6	% Profit Before Taxes/Total		17.4	9.6	9.5	9.3	11.8
4.2	2.9	4.4	Assets		4.6	−1.1	1.3	6.4	4.9
−.9	−1.5	−.7			1.5	−11.4	−2.1	1.8	−.3
8.8	10.1	11.2	Sales/Net Fixed Assets		15.2	12.4	14.0	9.1	7.2
5.6	5.9	6.6			7.3	9.0	7.0	5.8	5.6
3.5	3.6	3.6			3.9	4.3	3.1	3.1	3.9
2.4	2.5	2.6	Sales/Total Assets		3.0	2.6	2.6	2.5	2.3
1.8	1.9	1.9			2.6	2.1	1.8	1.9	1.8
1.3	1.4	1.5			1.7	1.7	1.4	1.5	1.3
2.5	2.4	2.0	% Depr., Dep., Amort./Sales		1.4	1.8	2.4	1.9	2.4
(127) 3.9	(158) 3.8	(143) 3.5			3.6	3.3	(39) 3.9	(35) 2.8	(31) 4.0
5.0	5.4	4.9			5.5	4.2	6.2	4.2	5.2
2.0	1.7	1.4	% Officers', Directors',		3.1		1.4	1.0	
(51) 3.5	(68) 3.3	(66) 2.7	Owners' Comp/Sales		(13) 6.1		(24) 3.3	(14) 2.1	
5.8	6.0	6.0			8.3		4.6	2.4	
4717603M	4655230M	5085896M	Net Sales ($)	3102M	48820M	54321M	293498M	549954M	4136201M
2995444M	2773993M	2886413M	Total Assets ($)	4036M	24798M	28160M	174760M	400642M	2254017M

M = $ thousand   MM = $ million
See Pages 11 through 21 for Explanation of Ratios and Data

Current Data Sorted By Assets **Comparative Historical Data**

0-500M	500M-2MM	2-10MM	10-50MM	50-100MM	100-250MM	Type of Statement	ALL	ALL
		1	8	2	4	Unqualified	5	5
		5				Reviewed	6	8
2	5	1				Compiled	7	7
	2	2				Tax Returns	1	1
	3	5	3		1	Other	16	11
	10 (4/1-9/30/04)		34 (10/1/04-3/31/05)				4/1/00-3/31/01	4/1/01-3/31/02
0-500M	500M-2MM	2-10MM	10-50MM	50-100MM	100-250MM		ALL	ALL
2	10	14	11	2	5	NUMBER OF STATEMENTS	35	32
%	%	%	%	%	%	**ASSETS**	%	%
	8.1	5.3	3.2			Cash & Equivalents	6.3	6.5
	26.5	36.3	25.4			Trade Receivables (net)	24.8	27.1
	14.4	26.2	23.8			Inventory	22.7	23.0
	.6	1.1	1.3			All Other Current	2.3	.9
	49.6	69.0	53.8			Total Current	56.1	57.4
	36.4	26.1	31.2			Fixed Assets (net)	31.0	28.7
	3.2	.4	9.0			Intangibles (net)	6.0	6.6
	10.8	4.5	6.0			All Other Non-Current	6.8	7.3
	100.0	100.0	100.0			Total	100.0	100.0
						LIABILITIES		
	8.3	16.2	11.3			Notes Payable-Short Term	13.1	10.3
	6.3	2.9	4.6			Cur. Mat.-L/T/D	4.3	3.3
	11.4	20.5	15.8			Trade Payables	15.1	15.9
	.3	.0	.0			Income Taxes Payable	.1	.2
	5.9	3.5	7.9			All Other Current	7.3	6.6
	32.1	43.1	39.6			Total Current	39.9	36.4
	17.6	12.8	16.5			Long-Term Debt	15.8	14.9
	.2	.5	1.3			Deferred Taxes	.8	.6
	9.2	1.2	11.2			All Other Non-Current	5.9	2.8
	41.0	42.3	31.4			Net Worth	37.7	45.3
	100.0	100.0	100.0			Total Liabilities & Net Worth	100.0	100.0
						INCOME DATA		
	100.0	100.0	100.0			Net Sales	100.0	100.0
	34.8	24.7	27.0			Gross Profit	28.4	28.3
	28.6	20.4	19.3			Operating Expenses	22.8	24.7
	6.2	4.3	7.7			Operating Profit	5.5	3.5
	1.2	1.4	1.5			All Other Expenses (net)	1.4	1.0
	5.0	2.9	6.2			Profit Before Taxes	4.1	2.6
						RATIOS		
	2.6	2.3	2.7			Current	2.7	3.6
	1.5	1.6	1.2				1.7	1.8
	.9	1.2	1.0				1.1	1.2
	2.0	1.8	1.1			Quick	1.7	2.2
	.9	.9	.7				.9	1.0
	.6	.6	.5				.5	.6
	31 12.0	41 9.0	40 9.0			Sales/Receivables	40 9.2	39 9.3
	39 9.3	49 7.5	48 7.6				46 8.0	47 7.7
	56 6.5	54 6.7	51 7.1				54 6.8	60 6.1
	12 31.3	25 14.8	46 7.9			Cost of Sales/Inventory	40 9.1	34 10.9
	29 12.6	52 7.0	53 6.8				57 6.4	52 7.0
	67 5.4	83 4.4	80 4.6				69 4.6	79 4.6
	20 18.5	26 14.2	26 14.0			Cost of Sales/Payables	25 14.6	22 16.4
	30 12.4	35 10.5	37 9.9				38 9.5	28 12.9
	37 9.9	53 6.9	51 7.2				53 6.9	48 7.6
	7.1	7.8	5.6			Sales/Working Capital	5.6	4.7
	19.3	12.1	23.6				9.8	7.5
	−86.3	19.0	−262.9				46.8	32.6
	17.0	13.1	11.1			EBIT/Interest	7.1	10.9
	4.4	(12) 3.8	5.6				(30) 3.0	(30) 2.4
	1.2	.5	2.7				1.4	.9
						Net Profit + Depr., Dep., Amort./Cur. Mat. L /T/D	10.7	
							(10) 4.3	
							1.6	
	.4	.4	.7			Fixed/Worth	.5	.3
	1.1	.5	1.6				.8	.7
	9.2	1.6	2.9				2.2	1.9
	.6	.5	1.4			Debt/Worth	.6	.4
	1.9	1.6	3.6				1.8	1.6
	18.0	3.8	4.1				5.7	4.4
		34.9				% Profit Before Taxes/Tangible Net Worth	39.8	23.6
	(13)	17.0					(32) 20.5	(29) 6.5
		−1.5					6.1	.5
	22.5	13.2	14.9			% Profit Before Taxes/Total Assets	14.7	10.2
	5.0	7.0	9.7				6.2	2.7
	.4	.4	4.8				1.3	.1
	14.4	19.3	46.6			Sales/Net Fixed Assets	11.6	14.6
	5.9	12.4	5.6				6.4	5.9
	2.9	5.2	3.6				3.6	3.6
	2.8	3.3	2.1			Sales/Total Assets	2.6	2.8
	2.1	2.2	1.7				1.9	1.8
	1.7	1.8	1.4				1.4	1.3
		.7	2.1			% Depr., Dep., Amort./Sales	2.0	.6
	(13)	2.1	(10) 3.5				(28) 3.3	(25) 2.3
		3.9	5.6				4.8	4.1
						% Officers', Directors', Owners' Comp/Sales		
2260M	27709M	151997M	410762M	194883M	1092209M	Net Sales ($)	1256313M	858180M
617M	11961M	60128M	229895M	150877M	660506M	Total Assets ($)	804515M	644504M

© RMA 2005

M = $ thousand   MM = $ million

See Pages 11 through 21 for Explanation of Ratios and Data

Comparative Historical Data | Current Data Sorted By Sales

4/1/02-3/31/03 ALL	4/1/03-3/31/04 ALL	4/1/04-3/31/05 ALL	Type of Statement	0-1MM	1-3MM	3-5MM	5-10MM	10-25MM	25MM & OVER
10	11	15	Unqualified					3	12
4	5	5	Reviewed	3	2	1	1	3	
7	9	8	Compiled		1	1	1	1	
2		4	Tax Returns		1	1	1	1	
11	12	12	Other		1	2	3	1	4
				← 10 (4/1-9/30/04)			34 (10/1/04-3/31/05) →		
34	37	44	NUMBER OF STATEMENTS	3	5	5	6	9	16
%	%	%	**ASSETS**	%	%	%	%	%	%
6.2	5.4	5.6	Cash & Equivalents						4.9
23.6	26.3	29.7	Trade Receivables (net)						24.7
22.6	23.4	20.8	Inventory						18.9
.8	1.7	1.0	All Other Current						1.5
53.2	56.8	57.1	Total Current						50.0
37.2	33.1	30.6	Fixed Assets (net)						31.2
6.1	5.5	5.1	Intangibles (net)						10.5
3.5	4.7	7.2	All Other Non-Current						8.3
100.0	100.0	100.0	Total						100.0
			LIABILITIES						
13.6	15.1	11.4	Notes Payable-Short Term						7.1
2.8	3.5	4.2	Cur. Mat.-L/T/D						4.2
12.1	15.4	15.8	Trade Payables						15.0
.0	.1	.1	Income Taxes Payable						.1
7.4	9.5	9.5	All Other Current						9.5
36.0	43.6	40.9	Total Current						35.8
17.8	19.1	16.7	Long-Term Debt						17.7
1.2	1.0	1.2	Deferred Taxes						2.8
7.6	7.5	6.3	All Other Non-Current						10.1
37.4	28.7	34.8	Net Worth						33.6
100.0	100.0	100.0	Total Liabilities & Net Worth						100.0
			INCOME DATA						
100.0	100.0	100.0	Net Sales						100.0
27.4	28.2	27.3	Gross Profit						23.4
23.3	23.8	21.5	Operating Expenses						16.0
4.1	4.4	5.8	Operating Profit						7.4
1.9	1.6	1.4	All Other Expenses (net)						1.5
2.2	2.7	4.4	Profit Before Taxes						5.9
			RATIOS						
2.3 / 1.8 / 1.2	2.5 / 1.5 / 1.0	2.5 / 1.5 / 1.1	Current						2.4 / 1.2 / 1.0
1.5 / .9 / .7	1.2 / .9 / .6	1.5 / .9 / .6	Quick						1.3 / .9 / .6
34 10.8 / 41 9.0 / 50 7.3	40 9.2 / 46 8.0 / 53 6.9	40 9.2 / 47 7.7 / 54 6.7	Sales/Receivables						41 9.0 / 49 7.5 / 55 6.6
38 9.7 / 48 7.6 / 65 5.6	41 8.9 / 54 6.8 / 78 4.7	30 12.2 / 49 7.5 / 69 5.3	Cost of Sales/Inventory						39 9.3 / 50 7.4 / 60 6.1
21 17.5 / 29 12.4 / 42 8.8	29 12.7 / 36 10.3 / 59 6.2	24 15.3 / 33 11.0 / 49 7.5	Cost of Sales/Payables						24 15.0 / 34 10.6 / 50 7.3
4.9 / 9.1 / 26.4	5.9 / 12.6 / 255.9	6.7 / 14.1 / 54.8	Sales/Working Capital						5.8 / 19.3 / 239.8
7.1 / (29) 1.6 / .4	9.1 / (34) 2.4 / .2	12.0 / (41) 4.5 / 1.8	EBIT/Interest						12.9 / (15) 5.6 / 2.5
	2.8 / (15) 2.1 / 1.5	6.3 / (10) 2.2 / 1.2	Net Profit + Depr., Dep., Amort./Cur. Mat. L/T/D						
.6 / .9 / 2.2	.5 / .9 / 3.7	.5 / .9 / 2.4	Fixed/Worth						.5 / 1.8 / 7.6
.6 / 1.7 / 4.9	.9 / 2.3 / 6.7	.7 / 2.2 / 4.1	Debt/Worth						1.2 / 3.7 / 17.3
27.9 / (31) 16.1 / -6.4	38.0 / (31) 13.4 / -.9	37.3 / (38) 21.3 / 3.6	% Profit Before Taxes/Tangible Net Worth						56.4 / (13) 34.6 / 16.7
12.2 / 3.2 / -1.4	12.6 / 3.7 / -1.5	11.9 / 7.2 / 3.0	% Profit Before Taxes/Total Assets						12.5 / 8.4 / 4.6
10.1 / 4.9 / 3.6	11.3 / 5.6 / 3.8	15.6 / 6.1 / 4.4	Sales/Net Fixed Assets						8.3 / 4.9 / 4.1
2.4 / 1.9 / 1.6	2.6 / 1.8 / 1.4	2.7 / 2.0 / 1.6	Sales/Total Assets						2.0 / 1.6 / 1.4
2.3 / (31) 3.7 / 5.6	1.2 / (31) 2.8 / 5.1	2.0 / (39) 3.1 / 4.4	% Depr., Dep., Amort./Sales						2.8 / (13) 4.0 / 5.1
1.8 / (11) 3.3 / 4.5	2.6 / (17) 4.3 / 6.0	1.7 / (13) 4.0 / 5.2	% Officers', Directors', Owners' Comp/Sales						
1413727M	1145906M	1879820M	Net Sales ($)	2573M	11413M	19670M	45148M	146411M	1654605M
936019M	840672M	1113984M	Total Assets ($)	1289M	6131M	9059M	17513M	66146M	1013846M

M = $ thousand   MM = $ million

See Pages 11 through 21 for Explanation of Ratios and Data

Current Data Sorted By Assets   Comparative Historical Data

0-500M	500M-2MM	2-10MM	10-50MM	50-100MM	100-250MM	Type of Statement	4/1/00-3/31/01 ALL	4/1/01-3/31/02 ALL
		9	7	1	2	Unqualified	13	16
	2	11	3		2	Reviewed	22	18
3	11	5	1			Compiled	12	15
1	3	1	1			Tax Returns	2	2
6		10	3		1	Other	26	25
		18 (4/1-9/30/04)		62 (10/1/04-3/31/05)				
4	22	36	14	1	3	**NUMBER OF STATEMENTS**	75	76
%	%	%	%	%	%	**ASSETS**	%	%
	7.5	5.2	5.0			Cash & Equivalents	3.9	5.4
	33.7	29.0	29.0			Trade Receivables (net)	28.6	27.9
	19.1	21.4	19.5			Inventory	21.2	19.1
	2.2	1.7	2.0			All Other Current	1.8	1.8
	62.4	57.3	55.5			Total Current	55.4	54.2
	27.2	35.1	38.9			Fixed Assets (net)	33.0	35.8
	2.0	3.1	2.0			Intangibles (net)	3.7	3.2
	8.4	4.5	3.7			All Other Non-Current	7.9	6.7
	100.0	100.0	100.0			Total	100.0	100.0
						LIABILITIES		
	6.1	10.1	13.2			Notes Payable-Short Term	12.6	13.2
	7.7	4.4	4.1			Cur. Mat.-L/T/D	6.6	3.4
	22.8	16.3	14.7			Trade Payables	18.2	16.0
	.1	.2	.1			Income Taxes Payable	.3	.1
	4.9	9.3	6.2			All Other Current	11.5	12.1
	41.7	40.3	38.3			Total Current	49.2	44.9
	20.3	16.7	23.6			Long-Term Debt	22.6	19.9
	.4	.8	1.1			Deferred Taxes	.6	.4
	5.3	.8	4.3			All Other Non-Current	7.2	3.9
	32.3	41.5	32.8			Net Worth	20.4	30.9
	100.0	100.0	100.0			Total Liabilities & Net Worth	100.0	100.0
						INCOME DATA		
	100.0	100.0	100.0			Net Sales	100.0	100.0
	31.6	30.4	18.9			Gross Profit	28.0	26.2
	29.0	24.8	14.6			Operating Expenses	23.4	22.8
	2.5	5.6	4.3			Operating Profit	4.6	3.5
	1.5	.7	.6			All Other Expenses (net)	2.2	1.9
	1.1	4.9	3.7			Profit Before Taxes	2.5	1.6
						RATIOS		
	2.9	2.3	2.1				1.7	2.1
	1.5	1.3	1.2			Current	1.2	1.3
	1.2	1.0	1.0				.9	1.0
	2.0	1.2	1.4				1.0	1.3
	.9	.8	.7			Quick	.7	.7
	.7	.5	.6				.5	.6
31	11.6 / 38 9.5	38 9.7	38 9.7			Sales/Receivables	31 11.8 / 32 11.5	
38	9.5 / 45 8.1	47 7.8	47 7.8				42 8.8 / 42 8.6	
57	6.4 / 63 5.8	58 6.3	58 6.3				53 6.9 / 51 7.2	
17	20.9 / 31 11.7	27 13.6				Cost of Sales/Inventory	24 15.3 / 26 13.9	
33	11.1 / 45 8.1	38 9.7					38 9.6 / 37 9.9	
53	6.9 / 67 5.4	50 7.3					63 5.8 / 57 6.4	
25	14.8 / 20 18.0	23 15.8				Cost of Sales/Payables	24 15.2 / 17 21.5	
41	9.0 / 37 9.7	25 14.5					34 10.6 / 24 14.9	
59	6.2 / 54 6.8	35 10.4					50 7.3 / 45 8.1	
	6.6	6.2	8.3			Sales/Working Capital	10.4	8.4
	11.3	21.0	33.3				24.6	21.7
	51.0	NM	NM				-30.6	-254.2
	8.9	13.2	11.6			EBIT/Interest	5.9	4.9
	(17) 3.2	(31) 6.3	6.1				(73) 3.3 / (74) 2.8	
	.2	2.1	2.7				1.2	1.0
		3.0				Net Profit + Depr., Dep., Amort./Cur. Mat. L/T/D	5.3	6.6
		(14) 2.5					(20) 3.4 / (21) 2.3	
		1.8					1.1	1.4
	.3	.5	.8			Fixed/Worth	.6	.6
	1.0	.8	1.6				1.4	1.0
	4.3	2.2	2.7				3.0	3.0
	.7	.8	1.3			Debt/Worth	1.3	1.0
	2.5	1.4	2.8				2.4	2.1
	32.5	3.7	4.3				8.4	7.7
	70.8	42.4	38.2			% Profit Before Taxes/Tangible Net Worth	57.1	41.1
	(18) 34.0	(33) 27.7	22.6				(63) 21.1 / (68) 15.1	
	2.6	6.5	14.5				5.8	2.6
	15.2	17.9	11.2			% Profit Before Taxes/Total Assets	13.2	11.5
	5.3	9.3	6.6				7.0	5.1
	-.7	2.3	4.0				1.1	.0
	26.4	13.2	9.1			Sales/Net Fixed Assets	18.0	15.3
	14.4	6.2	6.0				8.2	6.1
	7.0	3.8	3.8				4.3	4.4
	3.7	2.7	2.7			Sales/Total Assets	3.3	3.3
	2.9	2.2	2.1				2.5	2.3
	1.8	1.5	1.8				1.7	1.7
	1.4	1.9	1.5			% Depr., Dep., Amort./Sales	1.2	1.3
	(18) 2.8	(34) 2.9	3.5				(72) 2.0 / (72) 2.5	
	4.7	3.9	3.9				3.4	4.4
	1.6	2.5				% Officers', Directors', Owners' Comp/Sales	2.6	1.4
	(12) 2.3	(12) 3.9					(24) 5.0 / (26) 3.3	
	4.8	6.5					7.6	7.2
4153M	80189M	439720M	796956M	92973M	578503M	Net Sales ($)	2988317M	2133729M
1138M	26656M	195746M	346678M	81368M	462335M	Total Assets ($)	1360338M	1158113M

M = $ thousand   MM = $ million
See Pages 11 through 21 for Explanation of Ratios and Data

Comparative Historical Data				Current Data Sorted By Sales					

Type of Statement

			Type of Statement	0-1MM	1-3MM	3-5MM	5-10MM	10-25MM	25MM & OVER
18	17	19	Unqualified				2	5	12
27	18	16	Reviewed		1	4	5	4	2
9	13	20	Compiled	1	7	4	3	4	1
5	6	5	Tax Returns	1	1	1	2		
22	21	20	Other	1	2	2	7	5	3
4/1/02-3/31/03 ALL	4/1/03-3/31/04 ALL	4/1/04-3/31/05 ALL		18 (4/1-9/30/04)			62 (10/1/04-3/31/05)		
81	75	80	**NUMBER OF STATEMENTS**	3	11	11	19	18	18

ASSETS

%	%	%		%	%	%	%	%	%
6.5	6.0	6.0	Cash & Equivalents		4.0	6.3	8.6	4.2	4.9
28.7	29.8	30.4	Trade Receivables (net)		32.1	31.4	33.8	25.3	31.4
19.4	17.5	20.2	Inventory		21.1	19.4	16.6	22.9	20.8
1.9	2.8	1.8	All Other Current		2.4	3.0	1.6	1.3	1.9
56.4	56.0	58.5	Total Current		59.6	60.1	60.7	53.7	58.9
35.4	36.2	32.7	Fixed Assets (net)		30.7	26.7	31.1	41.4	30.9
2.7	1.5	3.3	Intangibles (net)		.8	3.8	3.2	2.1	6.2
5.5	6.2	5.5	All Other Non-Current		8.9	9.4	5.0	2.8	4.0
100.0	100.0	100.0	Total		100.0	100.0	100.0	100.0	100.0

LIABILITIES

				0-1MM	1-3MM	3-5MM	5-10MM	10-25MM	25MM & OVER
8.5	8.9	9.2	Notes Payable-Short Term		5.2	10.1	7.2	11.7	11.0
4.6	4.1	5.0	Cur. Mat.-L/T/D		4.9	3.3	4.6	3.3	3.9
17.1	18.8	18.2	Trade Payables		24.1	17.9	20.1	15.4	15.7
.1	.2	.1	Income Taxes Payable		.2	.1	.2	.0	.1
18.6	7.5	8.1	All Other Current		4.9	5.1	9.2	7.0	8.6
48.9	39.5	40.6	Total Current		39.3	36.5	41.3	37.3	39.4
19.2	18.7	18.6	Long-Term Debt		15.5	24.8	14.6	23.3	18.4
.5	.8	.7	Deferred Taxes		.2	.9	.3	1.1	.9
3.4	3.4	2.9	All Other Non-Current		8.8	2.9	.9	.4	4.4
28.0	37.6	37.2	Net Worth		36.2	35.0	42.9	37.7	37.0
100.0	100.0	100.0	Total Liabilities & Net Worth		100.0	100.0	100.0	100.0	100.0

INCOME DATA

				0-1MM	1-3MM	3-5MM	5-10MM	10-25MM	25MM & OVER
100.0	100.0	100.0	Net Sales		100.0	100.0	100.0	100.0	100.0
27.2	27.2	28.6	Gross Profit		29.7	31.7	34.8	26.6	20.6
23.9	23.3	24.3	Operating Expenses		28.7	26.6	26.7	23.1	16.2
3.2	3.9	4.3	Operating Profit		1.0	5.1	8.0	3.5	4.4
1.1	.8	1.0	All Other Expenses (net)		1.0	2.2	.8	.4	1.0
2.2	3.1	3.4	Profit Before Taxes		.1	2.9	7.2	3.1	3.4

RATIOS

				0-1MM	1-3MM	3-5MM	5-10MM	10-25MM	25MM & OVER
2.2	2.4	2.4			2.7	4.3	2.1	2.8	2.1
1.4	1.4	1.3	Current		1.7	1.3	1.4	1.3	1.3
1.0	1.1	1.0			1.0	1.2	1.0	.9	1.1
1.6	1.4	1.3			1.7	2.3	2.0	1.4	1.2
.8	(74) .9	.8	Quick		.9	1.0	.8	.7	.8
.6	.6	.6			.6	.7	.7	.4	.7
31 11.7	36 10.2	34 10.9			34 10.7	32 11.4	24 15.3	28 13.2	42 8.7
44 8.3	44 8.3	43 8.4	Sales/Receivables		49 7.5	40 9.2	40 9.2	42 8.8	45 8.1
53 6.9	57 6.4	59 6.1			60 6.1	69 5.3	76 4.8	55 6.6	59 6.2
26 14.1	21 17.5	25 14.7			20 18.2	30 12.3	11 34.7	27 13.3	30 12.1
39 9.4	33 10.9	39 9.5	Cost of Sales/Inventory		34 10.7	36 10.2	38 9.7	42 8.7	37 9.7
59 6.2	51 7.1	60 6.1			74 4.9	51 7.1	71 5.1	60 6.1	61 6.0
21 17.5	24 15.2	21 17.1			35 10.4	25 14.6	21 17.5	19 19.1	22 16.7
33 10.9	31 11.7	35 10.3	Cost of Sales/Payables		45 8.2	38 9.5	37 9.8	29 12.6	26 13.8
47 7.8	45 8.0	50 7.3			80 4.6	61 6.0	49 7.5	53 6.9	46 7.9
6.9	7.0	6.7			5.1	6.2	8.6	5.9	8.3
13.9	14.2	21.1	Sales/Working Capital		9.9	10.8	30.2	23.8	20.7
99.5	57.2	99.6			98.8	39.2	107.6	−29.8	66.6
7.5	8.1	9.5					3.5	18.2	7.6	10.8
(74) 4.0	(66) 4.0	(69) 4.8	EBIT/Interest				(10) 2.7	(16) 7.3	(14) 3.8	5.5
.9	1.4	2.2					1.8	4.6	1.0	2.9
5.3	3.7	3.2								
(23) 2.1	(21) 1.9	(26) 2.5	Net Profit + Depr., Dep., Amort./Cur. Mat. L/T/D							
.9	1.1	1.7								
.5	.5	.4			.4	.5	.4	.5	.6
1.0	1.0	1.0	Fixed/Worth		.6	1.6	1.0	1.5	1.1
2.2	2.5	2.5			2.7	5.2	2.2	3.3	2.0
.7	.7	.8			.4	.8	.8	1.1	1.0
1.6	1.8	1.8	Debt/Worth		2.2	4.6	1.3	2.3	2.2
5.2	4.6	7.0			10.5	65.2	3.8	4.9	4.3
35.0	56.5	43.0	% Profit Before Taxes/Tangible				204.0	62.7	35.2	35.8
(70) 13.9	(67) 22.8	(71) 26.2	Net Worth				(10) 40.5	(18) 33.5	(16) 26.7	(17) 19.8
5.6	6.1	9.5					2.8	18.3	−.5	10.9
16.6	12.9	16.0	% Profit Before Taxes/Total			13.7	10.1	21.6	11.0	15.9
6.3	6.8	6.4	Assets			2.7	6.5	12.5	8.2	6.1
−.2	.8	2.2				−2.7	1.8	5.1	.0	3.6
14.8	15.0	14.8				14.3	16.8	24.2	14.2	10.0
6.5	6.7	7.0	Sales/Net Fixed Assets			7.0	12.9	8.5	5.1	6.2
4.1	3.5	4.5				5.4	4.5	4.4	3.4	5.2
3.2	3.2	3.0				2.9	3.8	3.5	2.6	2.9
2.4	2.4	2.4	Sales/Total Assets			2.6	2.9	2.4	2.2	2.3
1.6	1.6	1.6				1.5	1.3	1.5	1.9	1.7
1.5	1.6	1.6				1.4		1.5	1.9	1.4
(74) 2.8	(68) 2.7	(70) 3.0	% Depr., Dep., Amort./Sales		(10) 2.9		(18) 2.5	(17) 3.2	(16) 2.5
4.5	4.3	4.5				6.0		3.6	4.0	3.7
2.4	2.7	2.3	% Officers', Directors',				2.2			
(28) 3.7	(26) 4.3	(29) 3.5	Owners' Comp/Sales			(10) 2.9				
6.2	8.1	7.2					4.9			
2596671M	2479185M	1992494M	Net Sales ($)	2038M	20997M	41436M	140064M	288395M	1499564M
1419085M	1186512M	1113921M	Total Assets ($)	897M	10977M	20192M	64497M	133645M	883713M

© RMA 2005

M = $ thousand   MM = $ million
See Pages 11 through 21 for Explanation of Ratios and Data

Current Data Sorted By Assets							Comparative Historical Data	
						Type of Statement		
		1	3	1	3	Unqualified	6	6
		2	1			Reviewed	1	
						Compiled	4	4
						Tax Returns	1	
	1	4	4	2	1	Other	10	11
	4 (4/1-9/30/04)		19 (10/1/04-3/31/05)				**4/1/00-3/31/01**	**4/1/01-3/31/02**
0-500M	**500M-2MM**	**2-10MM**	**10-50MM**	**50-100MM**	**100-250MM**		**ALL**	**ALL**
	1	7	8	3	4	**NUMBER OF STATEMENTS**	22	21
%	%	%	%	%	%	**ASSETS**	%	%
D A T A N O T A V A I L A B L E						Cash & Equivalents	5.4	2.7
						Trade Receivables (net)	19.1	15.8
						Inventory	14.6	13.5
						All Other Current	1.6	2.0
						Total Current	40.7	34.0
						Fixed Assets (net)	48.7	60.2
						Intangibles (net)	6.2	2.3
						All Other Non-Current	4.5	3.5
						Total	100.0	100.0
						LIABILITIES		
						Notes Payable-Short Term	9.7	7.6
						Cur. Mat.-L/T/D	5.9	9.0
						Trade Payables	12.7	9.6
						Income Taxes Payable	.1	.1
						All Other Current	5.2	5.9
						Total Current	33.7	32.2
						Long-Term Debt	25.1	32.2
						Deferred Taxes	.5	.6
						All Other Non-Current	9.4	7.0
						Net Worth	31.3	28.0
						Total Liabilities & Net Worth	100.0	100.0
						INCOME DATA		
						Net Sales	100.0	100.0
						Gross Profit	23.6	24.7
						Operating Expenses	15.3	18.8
						Operating Profit	8.3	6.0
						All Other Expenses (net)	2.5	3.3
						Profit Before Taxes	5.8	2.7
						RATIOS		
							1.9	1.7
						Current	1.2	1.4
							.8	.8
							1.1	1.0
						Quick	.7	.6
							.5	.5
							33 11.0	**31** 11.9
						Sales/Receivables	**41** 8.9	**41** 9.0
							55 6.6	**45** 8.2
							26 14.1	**31** 11.6
						Cost of Sales/Inventory	**40** 9.1	**42** 8.7
							63 5.8	**58** 6.3
							23 15.7	**18** 20.4
						Cost of Sales/Payables	**36** 10.3	**32** 11.6
							44 8.3	**41** 9.0
							5.8	10.4
						Sales/Working Capital	26.7	20.7
							-16.1	-20.8
							6.1	3.4
						EBIT/Interest	(20) 2.3	2.0
							1.5	1.0
						Net Profit + Depr., Dep., Amort./Cur. Mat. L /T/D		
							1.2	1.6
						Fixed/Worth	2.0	2.4
							18.7	3.9
							1.3	1.9
						Debt/Worth	2.3	2.8
							43.8	4.4
							37.3	41.1
						% Profit Before Taxes/Tangible Net Worth	(18) 26.6	(20) 8.6
							5.4	2.2
							14.9	10.7
						% Profit Before Taxes/Total Assets	6.1	3.1
							1.3	.1
							4.8	3.6
						Sales/Net Fixed Assets	2.4	2.3
							1.9	1.8
							1.9	1.9
						Sales/Total Assets	1.4	1.3
							1.2	1.2
							2.7	4.0
						% Depr., Dep., Amort./Sales	(20) 5.0	(15) 7.5
							8.0	8.7
						% Officers', Directors', Owners' Comp/Sales		
	2201M	**65817M**	**270278M**	**302374M**	**854250M**	Net Sales ($)	**929001M**	**1309830M**
	565M	**38697M**	**166754M**	**203796M**	**666011M**	Total Assets ($)	**822142M**	**921789M**

M = $ thousand MM = $ million

See Pages 11 through 21 for Explanation of Ratios and Data

Comparative Historical Data / Current Data Sorted By Sales

4/1/02-3/31/03 ALL	4/1/03-3/31/04 ALL	4/1/04-3/31/05 ALL		0-1MM	1-3MM	3-5MM	5-10MM	10-25MM	25MM & OVER
			Type of Statement						
8	6	8	Unqualified					3	5
2	5	3	Reviewed					3	
	5		Compiled						
			Tax Returns						
9	8	12	Other		1	1	3	2	5
					4 (4/1-9/30/04)		19 (10/1/04-3/31/05)		
19	24	23	**NUMBER OF STATEMENTS**		1	1	3	8	10
%	%	%	**ASSETS**	%	%	%	%	%	%
3.4	5.1	7.9	Cash & Equivalents	DATA NOT AVAILABLE					5.0
15.1	16.5	18.2	Trade Receivables (net)						18.4
15.9	13.5	14.8	Inventory						13.9
2.0	2.6	1.8	All Other Current						3.4
36.4	37.7	42.7	Total Current						40.6
55.5	53.5	49.1	Fixed Assets (net)						46.6
4.0	5.7	4.1	Intangibles (net)						7.3
4.2	3.1	4.1	All Other Non-Current						5.5
100.0	100.0	100.0	Total						100.0
			LIABILITIES						
5.6	6.3	2.6	Notes Payable-Short Term						1.2
6.0	7.1	6.1	Cur. Mat.-L/T/D						8.2
11.4	10.8	8.9	Trade Payables						10.8
.7	.8	.1	Income Taxes Payable						.2
6.6	11.6	5.9	All Other Current						7.7
30.2	36.5	23.6	Total Current						28.0
29.5	23.7	21.7	Long-Term Debt						20.6
.5	1.1	1.0	Deferred Taxes						1.5
4.7	8.4	8.4	All Other Non-Current						7.8
35.0	30.3	45.3	Net Worth						42.1
100.0	100.0	100.0	Total Liabilities & Net Worth						100.0
			INCOME DATA						
100.0	100.0	100.0	Net Sales						100.0
30.9	20.8	24.8	Gross Profit						22.9
21.7	15.7	17.1	Operating Expenses						16.5
9.3	5.1	7.7	Operating Profit						6.4
2.2	1.8	1.6	All Other Expenses (net)						.6
7.1	3.3	6.1	Profit Before Taxes						5.8
			RATIOS						
1.6	2.4	2.9							2.0
1.1	1.0	1.8	Current						1.7
.7	.7	1.2							1.3
.7	1.3	2.2							1.1
.5	.6	1.0	Quick						.9
.4	.4	.6							.4
28 12.8	**27** 13.3	**29** 12.5							**26** 14.3
39 9.4	**34** 10.7	**39** 9.4	Sales/Receivables						**42** 8.6
41 9.0	**42** 8.7	**52** 7.0							**57** 6.4
30 12.3	**26** 14.2	**32** 11.2							**26** 14.1
44 8.2	**34** 10.6	**46** 7.9	Cost of Sales/Inventory						**47** 7.8
81 4.5	**46** 8.0	**68** 5.4							**63** 5.8
30 12.2	**19** 19.7	**14** 26.4							**26** 14.2
42 8.6	**29** 12.7	**22** 16.3	Cost of Sales/Payables						**30** 12.1
55 6.7	**41** 8.9	**44** 8.3							**48** 7.6
9.5	9.6	6.4							6.9
29.0	NM	9.6	Sales/Working Capital						10.2
−20.5	−20.3	17.7							140.5
6.8	7.1	12.3							12.5
(18) 4.1	3.9	3.6	EBIT/Interest						5.4
1.8	1.3	2.5							2.1
			Net Profit + Depr., Dep., Amort./Cur. Mat. L/T/D						
1.5	1.1	.8							1.0
2.1	2.0	1.3	Fixed/Worth						1.5
2.5	2.9	2.1							2.8
1.7	1.0	.7							.8
2.1	1.9	1.5	Debt/Worth						1.7
3.1	3.8	2.2							3.6
59.7	39.3	30.8							
38.3	(20) 27.6	(22) 17.9	% Profit Before Taxes/Tangible Net Worth						
12.8	16.2	8.9							
18.8	12.6	16.5							11.9
10.7	6.3	5.8	% Profit Before Taxes/Total Assets						6.7
3.1	1.4	3.3							2.5
3.5	6.1	4.3							4.2
2.6	2.7	2.9	Sales/Net Fixed Assets						3.4
1.9	1.9	1.9							2.2
2.0	2.0	1.9							1.9
1.5	1.5	1.5	Sales/Total Assets						1.6
1.1	1.1	1.2							1.1
3.5	1.2	3.6							
(14) 6.1	(18) 3.7	(18) 6.4	% Depr., Dep., Amort./Sales						
7.8	7.5	8.5							
			% Officers', Directors', Owners' Comp/Sales						
1573589M	1550330M	1494920M	Net Sales ($)		2201M	4028M	21704M	118364M	1348623M
1195280M	973329M	1075823M	Total Assets ($)		565M	2538M	17891M	80997M	973832M

M = $ thousand MM = $ million

See Pages 11 through 21 for Explanation of Ratios and Data

Current Data Sorted By Assets   Comparative Historical Data

						Type of Statement		
	1	59	84	30	18	Unqualified	185	159
4	41	138	31	1		Reviewed	233	208
10	54	49	4			Compiled	186	172
11	17	19				Tax Returns	37	30
7	43	95	91	15	15	Other	271	334
	181 (4/1-9/30/04)		656 (10/1/04-3/31/05)				4/1/00-3/31/01	4/1/01-3/31/02
0-500M	500M-2MM	2-10MM	10-50MM	50-100MM	100-250MM		ALL	ALL
32	156	360	210	46	33	NUMBER OF STATEMENTS	912	903
%	%	%	%	%	%	ASSETS	%	%
13.1	7.3	5.9	4.5	4.0	2.3	Cash & Equivalents	6.1	5.9
31.2	30.6	28.4	24.4	21.9	21.3	Trade Receivables (net)	26.7	25.5
23.5	22.8	21.2	20.5	19.4	16.3	Inventory	19.5	19.6
1.9	2.4	1.7	2.2	3.5	3.1	All Other Current	1.9	1.6
69.8	63.0	57.2	51.6	48.8	43.0	Total Current	54.2	52.5
20.5	28.8	35.7	37.9	37.4	34.1	Fixed Assets (net)	36.3	37.7
1.3	2.8	2.7	5.0	7.1	14.3	Intangibles (net)	4.0	4.4
8.2	5.4	4.5	5.5	6.6	8.6	All Other Non-Current	5.5	5.5
100.0	100.0	100.0	100.0	100.0	100.0	Total	100.0	100.0
						LIABILITIES		
19.1	10.9	10.7	11.8	8.8	5.2	Notes Payable-Short Term	10.6	10.5
4.8	6.2	5.4	4.7	4.2	6.0	Cur. Mat.-L/T/D	5.3	6.6
20.5	20.3	17.9	15.6	14.5	13.6	Trade Payables	15.6	14.9
.0	.3	.2	.2	.2	.1	Income Taxes Payable	.2	.2
12.8	9.3	7.6	7.6	7.8	7.8	All Other Current	7.8	7.4
57.3	47.0	41.9	39.9	35.5	32.6	Total Current	39.4	39.6
18.6	19.6	17.7	18.8	21.2	21.7	Long-Term Debt	19.7	20.8
.0	.2	.7	1.0	1.6	2.7	Deferred Taxes	.6	.7
20.9	8.5	5.0	5.3	8.1	6.2	All Other Non-Current	4.8	5.5
3.2	24.7	34.7	34.9	33.5	36.8	Net Worth	35.4	33.4
100.0	100.0	100.0	100.0	100.0	100.0	Total Liabilities & Net Worth	100.0	100.0
						INCOME DATA		
100.0	100.0	100.0	100.0	100.0	100.0	Net Sales	100.0	100.0
41.3	32.6	24.6	22.1	21.9	23.9	Gross Profit	27.1	26.6
35.8	28.6	20.2	17.4	16.3	17.0	Operating Expenses	21.9	23.0
5.5	4.0	4.4	4.7	5.7	6.9	Operating Profit	5.2	3.6
1.0	.9	1.1	1.4	1.6	2.4	All Other Expenses (net)	1.7	2.0
4.6	3.1	3.3	3.3	4.1	4.5	Profit Before Taxes	3.5	1.6
						RATIOS		
3.2	2.2	2.2	2.0	1.6	2.0		2.2	2.2
1.2	1.4	1.3	1.3	1.4	1.6	Current	1.4	1.3
.8	1.0	1.0	1.0	1.1	1.0		1.0	1.0
1.7	1.3	1.4	1.1	1.0	1.0		1.4	1.3
.8	(155) .9	.8	.7	.7	.8	Quick	.8	.8
.3	.5	.5	.5	.5	.6		.5	.5

15	23.6	29	12.5	37	9.8	41	8.9	44	8.4	41	8.9	Sales/Receivables	36 10.1	35 10.5
36	10.1	40	9.1	47	7.7	50	7.3	51	7.2	46	7.9		47 7.7	45 8.1
45	8.1	57	6.4	60	6.1	60	6.0	57	6.4	58	6.3		59 6.2	57 6.4
6	61.1	25	14.4	30	12.0	36	10.1	38	9.5	33	10.9	Cost of Sales/Inventory	29 12.7	27 13.3
31	11.9	40	9.0	46	8.0	53	6.9	61	5.9	53	6.9		45 8.1	46 8.0
81	4.5	61	6.0	65	5.6	73	5.0	78	4.7	74	5.0		67 5.5	66 5.6
10	37.8	17	21.9	23	16.0	26	14.0	33	11.1	26	14.2	Cost of Sales/Payables	20 17.8	20 18.5
26	14.0	34	10.9	35	10.5	38	9.5	40	9.2	40	9.1		34 10.9	31 11.6
59	6.2	61	6.0	53	6.9	54	6.8	54	6.8	54	6.7		49 7.4	48 7.7

6.1	8.0	6.4	7.1	5.9	6.6	Sales/Working Capital	6.5	6.8
20.5	13.6	14.3	13.8	13.4	10.3		14.0	15.7
−22.0	295.4	−85.9	NM	33.6	145.2		−608.8	−88.4
8.3	8.0	10.0	8.7	8.2	17.0	EBIT/Interest	7.2	5.3
(22) 2.9	(135) 3.5	(335) 3.6	(202) 3.3	(44) 3.9	(32) 4.2		(845) 2.6	(847) 1.9
.7	1.0	1.3	1.3	1.3	1.3		1.1	.3
	6.4	4.2	3.4	3.6	3.5	Net Profit + Depr., Dep., Amort./Cur. Mat. L /T/D	4.2	3.2
	(24) 1.6	(110) 2.1	(89) 1.9	(28) 2.3	(16) 2.1		(261) 1.9	(250) 1.5
	.5	1.3	1.0	1.8	.4		1.0	.6
.2	.4	.5	.7	.7	.8	Fixed/Worth	.5	.6
1.6	1.0	1.3	1.4	1.2	1.1		1.2	1.2
−1.3	5.0	2.9	3.4	2.6	3.6		2.4	2.9
1.4	1.1	.9	.9	1.2	.9	Debt/Worth	.9	1.0
5.7	2.3	2.2	2.4	2.0	2.9		2.0	2.0
−6.8	10.9	6.2	6.2	4.1	6.9		5.0	5.7
129.9	61.5	41.1	29.9	31.1	34.2	% Profit Before Taxes/Tangible Net Worth	41.7	33.7
(20) 60.6	(123) 25.1	(313) 21.7	(180) 14.0	(41) 14.9	(26) 14.3		(806) 18.8	(780) 12.1
11.5	4.2	6.7	2.9	6.7	7.8		4.5	−2.5
24.4	16.4	14.5	9.9	8.7	7.6	% Profit Before Taxes/Total Assets	14.2	10.7
10.1	6.5	6.4	4.1	5.6	5.3		5.6	3.3
.2	−.1	.8	.6	.7	1.6		.4	−2.7
39.0	24.2	10.8	7.3	6.1	5.9	Sales/Net Fixed Assets	9.7	9.6
24.3	10.8	6.1	4.5	4.5	4.8		5.7	5.4
9.8	5.7	3.5	3.0	2.9	3.5		3.6	3.2
4.4	3.6	2.6	2.1	1.9	1.7	Sales/Total Assets	2.6	2.6
3.0	2.5	2.1	1.7	1.5	1.4		2.0	1.9
2.3	2.0	1.6	1.3	1.2	1.2		1.5	1.4
1.0	1.7	2.1	2.4	2.5	2.8	% Depr., Dep., Amort./Sales	2.0	2.1
(25) 2.1	(128) 2.8	(334) 3.4	(195) 3.5	(40) 4.2	(20) 3.5		(818) 3.5	(809) 3.7
3.5	4.3	5.2	5.2	5.8	4.8		5.2	5.4
5.1	2.3	1.8	1.0			% Officers', Directors', Owners' Comp/Sales	2.1	1.8
(13) 9.4	(75) 3.9	(126) 3.3	(36) 1.3				(318) 3.7	(301) 3.3
12.9	4.3	5.2	3.2				6.1	6.0
33316M	538143M	3795334M	7854109M	5051146M	7145856M	Net Sales ($)	21899571M	21677401M
10027M	194468M	1803878M	4621942M	3206817M	4601996M	Total Assets ($)	13811470M	13915511M

M = $ thousand   MM = $ million
See Pages 11 through 21 for Explanation of Ratios and Data

Comparative Historical Data   Current Data Sorted By Sales

			Type of Statement						
165	188	192	Unqualified		1	3	19	59	110
207	213	215	Reviewed	4	22	27	71	67	24
114	137	117	Compiled	9	34	29	26	16	3
45	55	47	Tax Returns	8	13	6	11	9	
307	266	266	Other	11	18	24	54	71	88
4/1/02-3/31/03 ALL	4/1/03-3/31/04 ALL	4/1/04-3/31/05 ALL		181 (4/1-9/30/04)		656 (10/1/04-3/31/05)			
				0-1MM	1-3MM	3-5MM	5-10MM	10-25MM	25MM & OVER
838	859	837	**NUMBER OF STATEMENTS**	32	88	89	181	222	225
%	%	%	**ASSETS**	%	%	%	%	%	%
6.4	6.4	5.8	Cash & Equivalents	13.7	7.7	7.3	6.1	5.2	3.8
24.7	26.2	27.3	Trade Receivables (net)	20.7	29.1	30.5	28.5	27.0	25.4
20.8	20.7	21.1	Inventory	19.8	19.8	23.5	21.2	21.8	20.2
2.0	2.3	2.1	All Other Current	.9	2.6	.9	2.2	1.7	2.9
53.9	55.6	56.3	Total Current	55.2	59.2	62.3	58.1	55.6	52.3
36.3	34.8	34.4	Fixed Assets (net)	30.5	33.0	29.7	34.3	36.0	35.8
4.2	4.1	3.9	Intangibles (net)	4.5	2.3	3.1	2.4	3.6	6.4
5.5	5.4	5.3	All Other Non-Current	9.6	5.4	4.9	5.2	4.8	5.5
100.0	100.0	100.0	Total	100.0	100.0	100.0	100.0	100.0	100.0
			LIABILITIES						
10.4	9.4	11.0	Notes Payable-Short Term	15.8	13.3	10.0	10.3	11.1	10.3
5.7	5.5	5.3	Cur. Mat.-L/T/D	7.2	5.6	4.7	6.2	5.0	4.7
14.6	14.8	17.5	Trade Payables	15.7	18.9	17.7	18.1	17.5	16.7
.2	.2	.2	Income Taxes Payable	.0	.2	.3	.2	.2	.2
8.7	9.5	8.2	All Other Current	7.6	10.9	8.3	7.4	8.1	7.8
39.6	39.5	42.2	Total Current	46.4	49.0	41.0	42.3	41.8	39.7
19.8	18.6	18.7	Long-Term Debt	27.1	20.6	19.0	17.0	18.3	18.6
.7	.7	.8	Deferred Taxes	.0	.3	.4	.7	.7	1.5
5.6	7.0	6.6	All Other Non-Current	19.0	6.5	6.5	6.3	5.5	6.1
34.3	34.2	31.7	Net Worth	7.5	23.6	33.0	33.7	33.7	34.2
100.0	100.0	100.0	Total Liabilities & Net Worth	100.0	100.0	100.0	100.0	100.0	100.0
			INCOME DATA						
100.0	100.0	100.0	Net Sales	100.0	100.0	100.0	100.0	100.0	100.0
27.9	26.9	25.9	Gross Profit	45.9	33.4	31.7	25.2	22.5	21.8
23.3	22.3	21.3	Operating Expenses	37.7	31.2	27.8	21.0	17.4	16.7
4.6	4.6	4.6	Operating Profit	8.2	2.2	3.9	4.2	5.1	5.2
1.6	1.4	1.2	All Other Expenses (net)	2.1	.8	.8	.9	1.4	1.5
3.0	3.1	3.4	Profit Before Taxes	6.2	1.4	3.1	3.3	3.7	3.6
			RATIOS						
2.2	2.3	2.1		3.2	1.9	2.4	2.4	2.1	1.8
1.4	1.5	1.4	Current	1.2	1.4	1.6	1.4	1.3	1.3
1.0	1.1	1.0		.7	.9	1.1	1.0	.9	1.1
1.4	1.4	1.2		2.4	1.3	1.5	1.4	1.3	1.0
(837) .8	.8	(836) .8	Quick	.7	.8	.9	(180) .8	.7	.7
.5	.5	.5		.2	.5	.6	.5	.5	.5
34 10.8	36 10.2	37 10.0		12 31.3	33 11.2	35 10.4	36 10.2	38 9.7	41 9.0
45 8.1	47 7.8	47 7.7	Sales/Receivables	36 10.2	41 8.9	49 7.4	47 7.8	47 7.7	49 7.4
56 6.5	58 6.3	59 6.2		77 4.7	60 6.1	59 6.2	59 6.2	60 6.1	58 6.2
32 11.3	31 11.8	31 11.9		0 UND	27 13.5	27 13.4	33 11.0	30 12.0	33 11.0
49 7.5	49 7.5	47 7.7	Cost of Sales/Inventory	42 8.6	43 8.4	51 7.1	45 8.2	46 7.9	51 7.1
72 5.1	74 5.0	70 5.2		128 2.8	67 5.5	78 4.7	63 5.8	70 5.2	72 5.1
21 17.7	21 17.7	23 16.1		9 39.9	16 22.7	21 17.5	23 15.6	21 17.6	28 13.1
34 10.8	33 11.2	36 10.1	Cost of Sales/Payables	32 11.2	33 11.1	37 9.9	34 10.7	35 10.4	39 9.4
47 7.7	48 7.6	54 6.8		124 2.9	65 5.7	50 7.2	51 7.1	54 6.8	53 6.9
6.2	6.0	6.8		5.4	8.4	5.9	6.4	7.0	7.3
13.2	11.9	13.9	Sales/Working Capital	14.5	19.2	11.1	13.8	15.2	13.9
-324.6	86.1	-406.2		-9.5	-64.2	37.3	-95.2	-73.5	71.5
8.1	8.3	8.8		5.2	6.1	6.7	9.9	9.7	10.0
(783) 2.9	(804) 3.1	(770) 3.4	EBIT/Interest	(22) 2.2	(78) 2.6	(78) 3.0	(164) 3.9	(209) 3.4	(219) 3.8
1.1	1.2	1.2		.5	-.2	.4	1.5	1.4	1.3
3.9	3.7	3.7			3.7	6.2	4.2	4.3	3.3
(248) 2.1	(238) 1.9	(270) 2.0	Net Profit + Depr., Dep., Amort./Cur. Mat. L/T/D		(11) 1.3	(25) 1.8	(60) 2.0	(67) 2.4	(105) 1.9
1.1	1.1	1.2			.7	1.1	1.0	1.4	1.0
.6	.6	.6		.4	.5	.3	.5	.6	.7
1.1	1.2	1.3	Fixed/Worth	4.2	1.3	.9	1.1	1.4	1.2
2.8	2.9	3.5		-1.6	4.3	4.4	2.2	3.9	3.0
.9	.9	1.0		1.6	1.0	.9	.8	.9	1.0
1.9	2.0	2.3	Debt/Worth	8.3	2.1	2.1	2.1	2.6	2.3
5.5	6.1	7.5		-6.8	24.0	10.2	4.3	7.5	5.9
40.3	38.0	41.6		96.2	59.3	46.0	41.1	49.7	31.9
(722) 16.7	(744) 15.3	(703) 19.6	% Profit Before Taxes/Tangible Net Worth	(19) 46.5	(70) 23.2	(72) 18.8	(155) 21.1	(197) 22.8	(190) 15.0
2.9	2.5	4.8		4.6	-2.2	3.8	6.0	5.7	5.0
12.7	11.8	12.8		14.6	14.6	12.7	15.1	12.5	10.3
5.2	5.0	5.8	% Profit Before Taxes/Total Assets	6.8	5.5	5.2	6.9	6.2	5.4
.2	.4	.5		-1.6	-2.1	-1.4	1.3	1.0	.8
10.2	10.4	12.0		21.0	19.7	16.1	13.3	10.5	7.5
5.6	5.7	6.1	Sales/Net Fixed Assets	8.2	7.5	7.6	6.6	5.3	5.3
3.4	3.4	3.6		3.0	4.2	3.9	3.5	3.3	3.6
2.5	2.5	2.6		2.5	3.1	2.8	2.8	2.5	2.2
1.9	1.9	2.0	Sales/Total Assets	1.9	2.3	2.2	2.2	1.9	1.8
1.4	1.4	1.5		.7	1.7	1.6	1.6	1.5	1.4
2.4	2.3	2.1		2.4	2.0	1.9	2.3	2.0	2.3
(769) 3.9	(755) 3.7	(742) 3.3	% Depr., Dep., Amort./Sales	(22) 3.8	(79) 3.3	(70) 3.3	(165) 3.3	(211) 3.2	(195) 3.2
5.6	5.3	5.0		8.5	6.6	5.1	5.0	4.9	4.8
2.0	1.8	1.7			3.3	2.3	1.9	1.3	.9
(262) 3.7	(247) 3.5	(251) 3.3	% Officers', Directors', Owners' Comp/Sales	(42) 5.3	(40) 3.8	(77) 3.1	(57) 2.6	(26) 1.3	
6.8	6.3	5.6		9.0	6.6	4.4	3.9	2.1	
21309130M	23318369M	24417904M	Net Sales ($)	21673M	190247M	347226M	1314064M	3542194M	19002500M
13401841M	14714196M	14439128M	Total Assets ($)	17490M	102736M	192406M	663990M	2037246M	11425260M

© RMA 2005

M = $ thousand   MM = $ million
See Pages 11 through 21 for Explanation of Ratios and Data

Current Data Sorted By Assets / Comparative Historical Data

0-500M	500M-2MM	2-10MM	10-50MM	50-100MM	100-250MM		4/1/00-3/31/01 ALL	4/1/01-3/31/02 ALL
						Type of Statement		
			1			Unqualified	2	2
	1	5	1			Reviewed	10	4
	3	6				Compiled	14	17
3	4	1				Tax Returns	6	5
1	2	4	2			Other	10	10
6 (4/1-9/30/04)			28 (10/1/04-3/31/05)					
4	10	16	4			**NUMBER OF STATEMENTS**	42	38
%	%	%	%	%	%	**ASSETS**	%	%
	2.9	3.2		DATA NOT AVAILABLE	DATA NOT AVAILABLE	Cash & Equivalents	4.3	5.8
	17.6	26.7				Trade Receivables (net)	25.9	23.5
	26.1	35.7				Inventory	30.1	32.8
	6.9	3.6				All Other Current	.9	2.3
	53.5	69.3				Total Current	61.3	64.4
	32.8	20.3				Fixed Assets (net)	31.6	28.8
	9.1	4.6				Intangibles (net)	3.4	2.5
	4.6	5.8				All Other Non-Current	3.7	4.3
	100.0	100.0				Total	100.0	100.0
						LIABILITIES		
	5.2	8.1				Notes Payable-Short Term	10.1	16.0
	5.7	2.9				Cur. Mat.-L/T/D	3.0	3.7
	19.2	37.3				Trade Payables	33.1	37.0
	.0	.2				Income Taxes Payable	.0	.1
	6.3	6.4				All Other Current	14.7	8.8
	36.5	54.9				Total Current	60.8	65.6
	41.9	18.7				Long-Term Debt	26.7	19.6
	.8	.3				Deferred Taxes	.1	.1
	4.7	1.6				All Other Non-Current	6.7	5.4
	16.1	24.6				Net Worth	5.7	9.3
	100.0	100.0				Total Liabilities & Net Worth	100.0	100.0
						INCOME DATA		
	100.0	100.0				Net Sales	100.0	100.0
	40.1	39.8				Gross Profit	33.6	34.3
	40.2	38.4				Operating Expenses	32.7	31.7
	-.1	1.3				Operating Profit	1.0	2.6
	1.1	1.0				All Other Expenses (net)	.6	.6
	-1.3	.4				Profit Before Taxes	.4	2.0
						RATIOS		
	2.1	1.8				Current	1.4	1.5
	1.4	1.2					1.1	1.2
	.7	1.0					.9	.9
	.9	.8				Quick	.8	.8
	.4	.4					.5	.5
	.2	.4					.3	.3
	3 127.9	**22** 16.6				Sales/Receivables	**15** 24.0	**12** 30.1
	21 17.5	**35** 10.4					**34** 10.8	**26** 13.8
	51 7.2	**52** 7.0					**44** 8.2	**39** 9.4
	25 14.9	**50** 7.2				Cost of Sales/Inventory	**31** 11.6	**33** 11.0
	56 6.5	**63** 5.8					**55** 6.7	**58** 6.3
	102 3.6	**93** 3.9					**88** 4.1	**84** 4.4
	40 9.1	**47** 7.8				Cost of Sales/Payables	**24** 15.1	**30** 12.0
	52 7.1	**80** 4.6					**51** 7.2	**56** 6.6
	70 5.2	**88** 4.2					**89** 4.1	**91** 4.0
	5.7	9.6				Sales/Working Capital	17.5	12.0
	13.1	22.4					66.1	28.3
	-39.3	NM					-34.3	-60.9
	5.1	6.3				EBIT/Interest	7.1	5.1
	.6	3.2					(39) 2.0	(36) 2.3
	-2.3	1.5					.9	.9
						Net Profit + Depr., Dep., Amort./Cur. Mat. L/T/D		
	.5	.3				Fixed/Worth	.7	.6
	1.6	.9					1.4	1.5
	-322.6	3.4					10.7	4.2
	1.6	1.9				Debt/Worth	2.1	2.0
	5.4	3.8					4.0	4.4
	-442.0	20.8					38.5	10.7
		38.0				% Profit Before Taxes/Tangible Net Worth	30.1	47.8
		(14) 16.2					(33) 13.5	(30) 21.1
		5.2					2.6	1.1
	1.3	6.5				% Profit Before Taxes/Total Assets	9.9	12.0
	-2.7	2.5					1.8	3.9
	-6.3	1.0					-.3	-.5
	30.5	34.7				Sales/Net Fixed Assets	20.8	26.2
	7.5	17.3					15.0	13.2
	4.2	8.8					4.8	6.8
	2.6	3.6				Sales/Total Assets	4.1	4.3
	2.0	2.5					2.8	3.1
	1.3	1.4					2.0	2.2
		.6				% Depr., Dep., Amort./Sales	.9	1.0
		(15) 1.7					(39) 1.9	(36) 1.6
		2.2					2.5	2.5
						% Officers', Directors', Owners' Comp/Sales	1.3	.7
							(18) 3.5	(22) 1.3
							6.1	5.5
3638M	20413M	202405M	297177M			Net Sales ($)	487797M	785280M
720M	11093M	80201M	95191M			Total Assets ($)	174263M	305475M

M = $ thousand MM = $ million

See Pages 11 through 21 for Explanation of Ratios and Data

Comparative Historical Data   Current Data Sorted By Sales

				Type of Statement						
7	5	1		Unqualified						1
10	10	7		Reviewed		1	1	1	3	1
17	24	9		Compiled		2	1	1	3	2
3	6	8		Tax Returns	3	5				
8	7	9		Other	1	2	2		2	2
4/1/02-3/31/03	4/1/03-3/31/04	4/1/04-3/31/05				6 (4/1-9/30/04)			28 (10/1/04-3/31/05)	
ALL	ALL	ALL			0-1MM	1-3MM	3-5MM	5-10MM	10-25MM	25MM & OVER
45	52	34		NUMBER OF STATEMENTS	4	10	4	2	8	6
%	%	%			%	%	%	%	%	%
				ASSETS						
5.2	6.6	3.6		Cash & Equivalents		3.0				
23.9	24.9	23.7		Trade Receivables (net)		16.6				
29.1	33.7	33.0		Inventory		32.0				
3.3	2.1	4.2		All Other Current		7.2				
61.5	67.2	64.5		Total Current		58.9				
28.7	25.2	25.2		Fixed Assets (net)		31.3				
4.5	3.6	5.4		Intangibles (net)		6.8				
5.3	3.9	4.8		All Other Non-Current		3.1				
100.0	100.0	100.0		Total		100.0				
				LIABILITIES						
8.7	8.6	9.4		Notes Payable-Short Term		3.7				
5.0	4.9	3.7		Cur. Mat.-L/T/D		6.9				
28.1	30.0	30.3		Trade Payables		23.2				
.0	.1	.1		Income Taxes Payable		.0				
12.7	8.1	6.4		All Other Current		5.9				
54.6	51.7	49.9		Total Current		39.8				
18.4	20.5	28.2		Long-Term Debt		42.5				
.4	.3	.5		Deferred Taxes		.0				
1.8	4.9	2.5		All Other Non-Current		1.9				
24.8	22.7	18.9		Net Worth		15.8				
100.0	100.0	100.0		Total Liabilities & Net Worth		100.0				
				INCOME DATA						
100.0	100.0	100.0		Net Sales		100.0				
35.8	37.0	38.5		Gross Profit		43.0				
33.2	34.4	37.8		Operating Expenses		42.4				
2.6	2.6	.7		Operating Profit		.6				
.3	.1	.7		All Other Expenses (net)		1.2				
2.3	2.4	.1		Profit Before Taxes		-.6				
				RATIOS						
1.5	1.9	1.8				2.1				
1.1	1.4	1.2		Current		1.4				
1.0	1.1	1.0				1.0				
.9	1.0	.8				.8				
.5	.6	.5		Quick		.4				
.3	.4	.3				.2				
11 32.8	17 20.9	13 28.6				9 40.9				
36 10.0	31 11.7	34 10.7		Sales/Receivables		14 26.5				
46 8.0	45 8.1	49 7.4				48 7.6				
34 10.9	43 8.6	39 9.4				48 7.6				
60 6.1	61 6.0	56 6.5		Cost of Sales/Inventory		72 5.1				
88 4.1	94 3.9	81 4.5				102 3.6				
30 12.3	31 11.8	40 9.1				40 9.1				
50 7.3	61 6.0	60 6.1		Cost of Sales/Payables		53 6.9				
69 5.3	85 4.3	84 4.3				76 4.8				
12.4	8.0	8.9				5.7				
42.8	20.9	18.3		Sales/Working Capital		18.3				
-88.0	111.5	NM				NM				
7.3	7.2	5.8				1.5				
(43) 3.0	(48) 3.3	2.2		EBIT/Interest		.6				
1.5	1.7	.5				-4.8				
2.6	2.6	3.8		Net Profit + Depr., Dep.,						
(14) 1.7	(15) 2.1	(12) 1.8		Amort./Cur. Mat. L/T/D						
1.2	.6	1.0								
.6	.4	.4				.7				
1.3	.8	1.4		Fixed/Worth		3.1				
2.8	2.6	NM				-1.8				
1.8	1.6	1.8				3.1				
3.9	3.4	3.8		Debt/Worth		7.5				
6.5	7.5	NM				-5.2				
61.4	39.8	33.2		% Profit Before Taxes/Tangible						
(39) 18.6	(45) 20.2	(26) 12.7		Net Worth						
5.2	10.3	-4.6								
10.3	10.0	7.4		% Profit Before Taxes/Total		2.6				
3.9	4.7	2.2		Assets		-1.9				
1.2	1.7	-2.6				-10.7				
20.3	29.2	30.0				30.5				
11.3	16.7	16.0		Sales/Net Fixed Assets		7.9				
6.3	7.8	6.8				4.2				
3.5	4.1	3.7				3.4				
2.7	2.8	2.6		Sales/Total Assets		2.2				
2.1	2.1	1.6				1.5				
1.4	1.2	.9				1.6				
(41) 2.1	(45) 2.0	(32) 1.8		% Depr., Dep., Amort./Sales		3.6				
2.7	2.4	2.5				4.6				
.7	.8	1.3		% Officers', Directors',						
(21) 2.3	(31) 2.3	(18) 2.8		Owners' Comp/Sales						
4.2	3.8	5.6								
620107M	743837M	523633M		Net Sales ($)	2926M	19403M	16457M	15572M	119266M	350009M
255758M	251903M	187205M		Total Assets ($)	2082M	13348M	14816M	6541M	40249M	110169M

© RMA 2005

M = $ thousand   MM = $ million
See Pages 11 through 21 for Explanation of Ratios and Data

Current Data Sorted By Assets   Comparative Historical Data

0-500M	500M-2MM	2-10MM	10-50MM	50-100MM	100-250MM		4/1/00-3/31/01 ALL	4/1/01-3/31/02 ALL
						Type of Statement		
	2	6			2	Unqualified	3	5
		7	1			Reviewed	3	5
	2	3				Compiled	6	6
						Tax Returns	1	
	2	4	3	1		Other	17	6
	7 (4/1-9/30/04)		26 (10/1/04-3/31/05)					
	6	20	6	1		**NUMBER OF STATEMENTS**	30	22
%	%	%	%	%	%	**ASSETS**	%	%
		8.4				Cash & Equivalents	7.9	6.3
		27.7				Trade Receivables (net)	31.7	28.5
		27.4				Inventory	27.4	31.0
		2.2				All Other Current	2.3	.9
		65.7				Total Current	69.1	66.6
		24.0				Fixed Assets (net)	23.7	24.5
		3.8				Intangibles (net)	.4	1.5
		6.5				All Other Non-Current	6.8	7.5
		100.0				Total	100.0	100.0
						LIABILITIES		
		6.8				Notes Payable-Short Term	10.6	13.5
		2.3				Cur. Mat.-L/T/D	3.2	5.0
		11.5				Trade Payables	17.7	13.8
		.4				Income Taxes Payable	.6	.2
		9.3				All Other Current	10.2	14.4
		30.3				Total Current	42.4	46.8
		16.4				Long-Term Debt	14.5	25.1
		.5				Deferred Taxes	.5	.8
		7.1				All Other Non-Current	.7	1.2
		45.7				Net Worth	42.0	26.0
		100.0				Total Liabilities & Net Worth	100.0	100.0
						INCOME DATA		
		100.0				Net Sales	100.0	100.0
		30.9				Gross Profit	30.5	29.9
		24.1				Operating Expenses	25.0	26.6
		6.7				Operating Profit	5.4	3.3
		1.7				All Other Expenses (net)	1.0	2.2
		5.0				Profit Before Taxes	4.4	1.1
						RATIOS		
		3.0				Current	2.8	2.4
		2.3					1.8	1.6
		1.7					1.1	1.3
		1.7				Quick	1.6	1.2
		1.3					1.0	1.0
		1.0					.6	.6
		47 7.8				Sales/Receivables	43 8.5	35 10.4
		50 7.2					49 7.4	45 8.1
		63 5.8					56 6.5	50 7.4
		44 8.2				Cost of Sales/Inventory	37 9.9	42 8.7
		67 5.5					64 5.7	61 6.0
		91 4.0					101 3.6	105 3.5
		22 16.8				Cost of Sales/Payables	23 15.9	15 25.0
		30 12.1					32 11.3	25 14.8
		41 9.0					51 7.1	38 9.5
		3.9				Sales/Working Capital	4.2	5.2
		5.9					7.4	9.2
		8.3					46.7	20.6
		19.3				EBIT/Interest	19.2	6.3
	(18)	5.9					(29) 4.0	(19) 2.5
		2.8					1.8	1.0
						Net Profit + Depr., Dep., Amort./Cur. Mat. L /T/D		
		.2				Fixed/Worth	.2	.1
		.6					.5	.5
		1.1					1.3	2.3
		.6				Debt/Worth	.7	.6
		1.2					1.4	1.2
		2.5					3.1	3.0
		41.4				% Profit Before Taxes/Tangible Net Worth	35.6	36.2
	(18)	23.2					25.3	(20) 9.7
		4.1					8.4	.5
		16.0				% Profit Before Taxes/Total Assets	18.8	11.3
		6.1					7.3	4.4
		1.3					3.2	-.5
		14.1				Sales/Net Fixed Assets	34.2	37.1
		7.5					11.2	17.9
		5.0					5.0	4.1
		2.2				Sales/Total Assets	2.8	3.0
		1.7					2.3	2.4
		1.5					1.7	1.5
		1.9				% Depr., Dep., Amort./Sales	.9	.5
	(18)	3.0					(28) 1.6	(21) 1.2
		4.0					3.3	2.9
						% Officers', Directors', Owners' Comp/Sales	2.4	
							(13) 4.0	
							8.0	
	20104M	188320M	187360M	27788M		Net Sales ($)	736549M	412017M
	8074M	100100M	131972M	53063M		Total Assets ($)	335566M	200074M

M = $ thousand   MM = $ million
See Pages 11 through 21 for Explanation of Ratios and Data

Comparative Historical Data					Current Data Sorted By Sales					
9	11	10	Type of Statement Unqualified				3	3	3	1
3	6	8	Reviewed				3	2	2	1
7	11	5	Compiled			1	1	3		
1	1		Tax Returns							
11	9	10	Other		1	1	1	1	4	3
4/1/02- 3/31/03 ALL	4/1/03- 3/31/04 ALL	4/1/04- 3/31/05 ALL				7 (4/1-9/30/04)		26 (10/1/04-3/31/05)		
					0-1MM	1-3MM	3-5MM	5-10MM	10-25MM	25MM & OVER
31	38	33	NUMBER OF STATEMENTS		1	1	8	9	9	5
%	%	%	ASSETS		%	%	%	%	%	%
9.3	8.9	8.5	Cash & Equivalents							
24.0	24.5	26.0	Trade Receivables (net)							
26.3	31.5	28.4	Inventory							
1.0	3.8	3.1	All Other Current							
60.5	68.7	66.0	Total Current							
28.9	22.2	21.5	Fixed Assets (net)							
4.9	5.0	4.5	Intangibles (net)							
5.7	4.1	8.0	All Other Non-Current							
100.0	100.0	100.0	Total							
			LIABILITIES							
5.7	9.4	8.7	Notes Payable-Short Term							
3.9	3.2	2.3	Cur. Mat.-L/T/D							
12.9	13.4	13.6	Trade Payables							
.4	.5	.4	Income Taxes Payable							
18.1	20.4	8.9	All Other Current							
41.0	46.9	33.9	Total Current							
21.9	14.8	15.8	Long-Term Debt							
.3	.8	.8	Deferred Taxes							
7.1	3.7	4.7	All Other Non-Current							
29.7	33.8	44.8	Net Worth							
100.0	100.0	100.0	Total Liabilities & Net Worth							
			INCOME DATA							
100.0	100.0	100.0	Net Sales							
32.8	30.3	30.8	Gross Profit							
26.6	24.8	26.3	Operating Expenses							
6.2	5.5	4.5	Operating Profit							
1.9	.9	1.4	All Other Expenses (net)							
4.3	4.5	3.0	Profit Before Taxes							
			RATIOS							
5.1	3.3	3.0								
2.1	1.8	2.1	Current							
1.2	1.3	1.5								
2.5	1.7	1.7								
1.4	.9	1.2	Quick							
.7	.5	.6								
38 9.7	35 10.5	40 9.1								
46 7.9	43 8.6	49 7.5	Sales/Receivables							
51 7.1	55 6.7	62 5.9								
36 10.1	51 7.1	54 6.7								
56 6.5	72 5.1	65 5.6	Cost of Sales/Inventory							
85 4.3	112 3.3	95 3.8								
16 22.1	18 19.8	26 13.8								
27 13.3	30 12.2	33 11.0	Cost of Sales/Payables							
44 8.3	43 8.4	48 7.7								
3.6	3.8	3.7								
7.9	7.0	6.0	Sales/Working Capital							
29.1	16.7	11.6								
9.1	22.3	14.8								
(28) 4.4	(34) 6.0	(29) 5.2	EBIT/Interest							
2.3	.9	1.9								
	13.9		Net Profit + Depr., Dep.,							
	(13) 1.5		Amort./Cur. Mat. L/T/D							
	.8									
.3	.3	.2								
.7	.5	.6	Fixed/Worth							
2.8	1.2	1.1								
.3	.4	.6								
1.0	1.5	1.2	Debt/Worth							
5.2	3.0	4.3								
43.2	50.6	40.7	% Profit Before Taxes/Tangible							
(25) 12.1	(35) 13.9	(29) 18.5	Net Worth							
4.3	2.1	3.2								
17.4	13.3	13.0	% Profit Before Taxes/Total							
6.6	7.8	6.3	Assets							
2.0	.1	.8								
17.0	31.3	16.4								
6.5	8.0	8.0	Sales/Net Fixed Assets							
4.1	5.3	5.2								
2.7	2.7	2.2								
1.9	1.9	1.7	Sales/Total Assets							
1.3	1.4	1.4								
1.1	1.2	1.5								
(30) 2.6	(33) 2.6	(29) 2.5	% Depr., Dep., Amort./Sales							
5.1	4.2	3.9								
	1.7	1.5	% Officers', Directors',							
	(10) 2.8	(11) 3.2	Owners' Comp/Sales							
	5.7	5.5								
717991M	892662M	423572M	Net Sales ($)		832M	2120M	33467M	59463M	147015M	180675M
436229M	496997M	293209M	Total Assets ($)		905M	1159M	20049M	31692M	86513M	152891M

M = $ thousand   MM = $ million
See Pages 11 through 21 for Explanation of Ratios and Data

Current Data Sorted By Assets   Comparative Historical Data

		3	2	1		Type of Statement	7	2
	1	5				Unqualified		
	5	1				Reviewed	5	6
1		1				Compiled	7	6
	3	1				Tax Returns	2	1
		1				Other	11	10

0-500M	500M-2MM	3 (4/1-9/30/04) 2-10MM	10-50MM	21 (10/1/04-3/31/05) 50-100MM	100-250MM		4/1/00-3/31/01 ALL	4/1/01-3/31/02 ALL
1	9	11	2	1		**NUMBER OF STATEMENTS**	32	25
%	%	%	%	%	%	**ASSETS**	%	%
		4.8			D	Cash & Equivalents	10.1	8.4
		32.0			A	Trade Receivables (net)	28.3	27.3
		18.3			T	Inventory	17.4	16.7
		3.6			A	All Other Current	2.8	4.5
		58.7				Total Current	58.6	56.9
		31.6			N	Fixed Assets (net)	30.8	32.9
		4.0			O	Intangibles (net)	5.8	3.0
		5.7			T	All Other Non-Current	4.8	7.2
		100.0				Total	100.0	100.0
					A	**LIABILITIES**		
		14.3			V	Notes Payable-Short Term	9.3	9.5
		4.8			A	Cur. Mat.-L/T/D	2.8	4.9
		15.5			I	Trade Payables	14.1	16.6
		.2			L	Income Taxes Payable	.2	.4
		3.8			A	All Other Current	8.8	10.1
		38.6			B	Total Current	35.1	41.5
		25.2			L	Long-Term Debt	13.9	26.8
		.2			E	Deferred Taxes	.5	.9
		3.3				All Other Non-Current	4.4	4.9
		32.6				Net Worth	46.1	26.0
		100.0				Total Liabilities & Net Worth	100.0	100.0
						INCOME DATA		
		100.0				Net Sales	100.0	100.0
		27.2				Gross Profit	30.0	37.0
		21.0				Operating Expenses	25.0	34.1
		6.2				Operating Profit	5.0	2.9
		2.0				All Other Expenses (net)	.6	2.2
		4.1				Profit Before Taxes	4.3	.7
						RATIOS		
		2.3					3.0	2.8
		1.6				Current	2.0	1.4
		1.1					1.1	.8
		1.6					2.0	2.1
		1.0				Quick	1.4	.9
		.6					.7	.5
		45 8.1					30 12.3	34 10.7
		56 6.6				Sales/Receivables	41 9.0	49 7.4
		63 5.8					51 7.1	56 6.5
		26 13.8					22 16.8	22 16.2
		39 9.3				Cost of Sales/Inventory	32 11.4	39 9.4
		63 5.8					61 5.9	64 5.7
		20 18.3					17 21.0	27 13.3
		38 9.7				Cost of Sales/Payables	26 13.8	35 10.5
		46 7.9					33 10.9	59 6.2
		5.3					5.7	7.9
		11.3				Sales/Working Capital	9.7	15.4
		46.3					56.9	-38.8
		21.6					13.2	9.9
		3.4				EBIT/Interest	(27) 3.4	(24) 2.5
		2.7					1.5	-2.4
						Net Profit + Depr., Dep., Amort./Cur. Mat. L /T/D		
		.4					.3	.4
		1.1				Fixed/Worth	.7	1.2
		4.2					2.5	NM
		.9					.4	1.7
		2.4				Debt/Worth	1.1	2.7
		7.0					6.2	NM
		95.1					28.2	72.7
	(10)	33.0				% Profit Before Taxes/Tangible Net Worth	(27) 12.4	(19) 26.0
		.0					3.4	-36.2
		16.8					19.2	22.3
		8.8				% Profit Before Taxes/Total Assets	5.3	7.6
		2.6					1.4	-13.2
		12.5					16.2	14.4
		8.2				Sales/Net Fixed Assets	8.4	7.9
		4.4					4.9	3.1
		3.0					3.2	2.9
		2.0				Sales/Total Assets	2.2	1.9
		1.5					1.7	1.5
		1.7					1.2	.9
		2.9				% Depr., Dep., Amort./Sales	(30) 2.2	(23) 2.5
		3.3					4.6	4.1
							2.7	3.7
						% Officers', Directors', Owners' Comp/Sales	(15) 5.3	(12) 5.0
							9.7	10.1
558M	26444M	104249M	114736M	84950M		Net Sales ($)	752951M	194380M
169M	8423M	47667M	63221M	56071M		Total Assets ($)	407029M	126145M

M = $ thousand   MM = $ million
See Pages 11 through 21 for Explanation of Ratios and Data

Comparative Historical Data | Current Data Sorted By Sales

			Type of Statement						
3	3	6	Unqualified				1	1	4
2	6	6	Reviewed		1		3	2	
8	13	6	Compiled	1	2	1	2		
3	5	2	Tax Returns	1	1				
14	16	4	Other		1	2	1		
4/1/02-3/31/03	4/1/03-3/31/04	4/1/04-3/31/05		3 (4/1-9/30/04)			21 (10/1/04-3/31/05)		
ALL	ALL	ALL		0-1MM	1-3MM	3-5MM	5-10MM	10-25MM	25MM & OVER
30	43	24	**NUMBER OF STATEMENTS**	2	5	3	7	3	4
%	%	%	**ASSETS**	%	%	%	%	%	%
8.2	4.9	5.3	Cash & Equivalents						
34.2	31.9	33.7	Trade Receivables (net)						
19.0	19.6	20.1	Inventory						
3.0	1.4	2.8	All Other Current						
64.3	57.8	62.0	Total Current						
30.3	34.6	30.0	Fixed Assets (net)						
.5	4.1	2.6	Intangibles (net)						
5.0	3.5	5.4	All Other Non-Current						
100.0	100.0	100.0	Total						
			LIABILITIES						
9.1	11.9	11.8	Notes Payable-Short Term						
6.5	6.6	4.5	Cur. Mat.-L/T/D						
17.5	19.3	16.4	Trade Payables						
.1	.7	.4	Income Taxes Payable						
8.9	9.8	6.5	All Other Current						
42.0	48.3	39.5	Total Current						
18.1	25.9	21.6	Long-Term Debt						
.3	.7	.3	Deferred Taxes						
6.8	9.7	4.8	All Other Non-Current						
32.8	15.5	33.8	Net Worth						
100.0	100.0	100.0	Total Liabilities & Net Worth						
			INCOME DATA						
100.0	100.0	100.0	Net Sales						
32.3	28.6	32.0	Gross Profit						
27.9	25.2	26.2	Operating Expenses						
4.4	3.4	5.8	Operating Profit						
1.2	1.6	1.4	All Other Expenses (net)						
3.2	1.9	4.4	Profit Before Taxes						
			RATIOS						
2.6	2.0	2.0							
1.6	1.2	1.7	Current						
1.0	.9	1.2							
1.5	1.3	1.4							
1.0	.8	1.0	Quick						
.8	.4	.7							
36 10.3	39 9.3	42 8.6							
47 7.7	49 7.5	55 6.7	Sales/Receivables						
65 5.6	57 6.5	61 6.0							
26 14.0	25 14.8	28 12.9							
36 10.0	33 11.1	41 8.8	Cost of Sales/Inventory						
49 7.5	66 5.6	62 5.9							
20 18.5	20 18.2	21 17.7							
37 9.9	40 9.2	38 9.5	Cost of Sales/Payables						
50 7.3	55 6.7	46 7.9							
6.0	7.9	6.4							
12.4	19.3	11.7	Sales/Working Capital						
−810.1	−111.2	38.1							
7.8	6.3	16.4							
(26) 2.4	(42) 2.8	6.1	EBIT/Interest						
.7	.8	2.8							
	2.1		Net Profit + Depr., Dep.,						
	(12) 1.5		Amort./Cur. Mat. L/T/D						
	.6								
.4	.5	.4							
1.2	1.8	1.1	Fixed/Worth						
2.4	−3.2	3.3							
.7	1.5	1.0							
3.0	5.3	2.0	Debt/Worth						
5.9	−6.6	6.1							
69.2	51.7	67.4	% Profit Before Taxes/Tangible						
(27) 14.5	(29) 20.0	(22) 38.5	Net Worth						
6.2	1.5	8.4							
13.3	14.0	19.8	% Profit Before Taxes/Total						
5.9	7.3	9.6	Assets						
1.6	−.8	2.4							
22.4	12.9	14.0							
10.0	8.4	9.3	Sales/Net Fixed Assets						
3.7	4.8	4.6							
3.4	3.5	3.2							
2.7	2.4	2.6	Sales/Total Assets						
1.9	1.8	1.6							
1.1	1.6	1.3							
(28) 2.5	(39) 2.9	(22) 2.6	% Depr., Dep., Amort./Sales						
5.7	5.1	3.8							
2.6	2.4	4.1	% Officers', Directors',						
(17) 5.2	(16) 4.3	(10) 8.6	Owners' Comp/Sales						
6.8	9.7	11.2							
353218M	650769M	330937M	Net Sales ($)	1545M	9719M	11547M	47532M	31990M	228604M
210478M	441414M	175551M	Total Assets ($)	815M	5065M	3643M	21861M	15935M	128232M

M = $ thousand   MM = $ million
See Pages 11 through 21 for Explanation of Ratios and Data

Current Data Sorted By Assets Comparative Historical Data

0-500M	500M-2MM	2-10MM	10-50MM	50-100MM	100-250MM	Type of Statement	4/1/00-3/31/01 ALL	4/1/01-3/31/02 ALL
		9	16	4	1	Unqualified	27	32
	2	18	6			Reviewed	40	28
1	2	11				Compiled	26	24
1		1				Tax Returns	2	5
1	7	10	11	2	2	Other	41	63
	23 (4/1-9/30/04)		82 (10/1/04-3/31/05)					
3	11	49	33	6	3	**NUMBER OF STATEMENTS**	136	152
%	%	%	%	%	%	**ASSETS**	%	%
	4.9	7.4	7.0			Cash & Equivalents	7.8	8.4
	29.4	29.4	24.1			Trade Receivables (net)	24.3	26.6
	30.6	22.8	21.5			Inventory	24.2	23.4
	5.1	2.7	1.5			All Other Current	1.8	1.7
	70.1	62.4	54.2			Total Current	58.2	60.0
	22.9	28.8	32.4			Fixed Assets (net)	29.9	29.0
	.4	1.6	4.8			Intangibles (net)	5.5	3.9
	6.6	7.2	8.7			All Other Non-Current	6.5	7.0
	100.0	100.0	100.0			Total	100.0	100.0
						LIABILITIES		
	10.4	12.1	8.3			Notes Payable-Short Term	11.1	11.9
	3.4	2.9	3.2			Cur. Mat.-L/T/D	4.2	5.0
	10.6	17.0	13.1			Trade Payables	11.5	13.9
	.5	.1	.2			Income Taxes Payable	.2	.2
	12.5	10.4	9.4			All Other Current	10.0	7.0
	37.4	42.5	34.1			Total Current	37.1	38.0
	11.4	12.4	12.5			Long-Term Debt	17.1	16.2
	.2	.8	.2			Deferred Taxes	.7	.5
	39.2	2.5	13.7			All Other Non-Current	4.0	4.5
	11.7	41.7	39.5			Net Worth	41.1	40.8
	100.0	100.0	100.0			Total Liabilities & Net Worth	100.0	100.0
						INCOME DATA		
	100.0	100.0	100.0			Net Sales	100.0	100.0
	36.0	28.0	24.8			Gross Profit	28.9	31.7
	34.2	25.7	19.3			Operating Expenses	23.7	26.7
	1.9	2.3	5.5			Operating Profit	5.2	5.1
	-.1	.9	.7			All Other Expenses (net)	1.9	1.6
	1.9	1.4	4.8			Profit Before Taxes	3.3	3.5
						RATIOS		
	3.0	2.5	3.1			Current	2.8	2.9
	2.2	1.6	1.5				1.5	1.6
	1.0	1.0	1.0				1.1	1.1
	1.6	1.5	1.9			Quick	1.5	1.8
	1.1	1.0	.8				.7	.9
	.6	.6	.5				.5	.6
	24 15.5	36 10.1	46 7.9			Sales/Receivables	34 10.6	36 10.1
	37 9.8	49 7.4	52 7.0				44 8.4	45 8.1
	55 6.6	63 5.8	60 6.1				53 6.9	59 6.2
	42 8.7	32 11.6	34 10.8			Cost of Sales/Inventory	30 12.0	31 11.9
	59 6.1	43 8.6	48 7.6				55 6.6	50 7.3
	104 3.5	81 4.5	97 3.8				90 4.1	93 3.9
	8 48.3	18 20.1	25 14.7			Cost of Sales/Payables	15 24.1	18 19.8
	23 16.1	33 11.2	34 10.7				28 13.1	29 12.6
	47 7.7	48 7.6	49 7.4				39 9.3	43 8.5
	3.8	4.8	4.5			Sales/Working Capital	5.4	4.4
	7.6	9.6	10.2				9.3	9.8
	-343.9	129.4	NM				44.4	132.0
		9.2	35.1			EBIT/Interest	6.0	5.8
		(47) 3.4	(29) 5.3				(116) 2.7	(134) 2.3
		1.3	1.6				.9	1.1
		6.4	7.9			Net Profit + Depr., Dep.,	9.8	4.8
		(17) 4.0	(12) 4.6			Amort./Cur. Mat. L/T/D	(43) 2.7	(50) 2.5
		2.3	1.4				1.2	1.0
	.1	.3	.5			Fixed/Worth	.5	.4
	.4	.5	1.0				.8	.8
	6.6	1.5	3.3				2.0	2.1
	.6	.6	.5			Debt/Worth	.6	.6
	2.0	1.2	2.2				1.5	1.4
	12.7	3.8	6.1				4.4	4.3
		20.8	30.2			% Profit Before Taxes/Tangible	43.6	36.2
		(45) 6.2	(27) 14.1			Net Worth	(118) 12.6	(134) 12.9
		2.4	3.5				2.3	1.5
	11.7	9.9	20.8			% Profit Before Taxes/Total	15.9	12.4
	5.4	3.0	4.1			Assets	4.7	4.4
	1.3	.4	1.4				-.7	.3
	39.0	16.3	9.2			Sales/Net Fixed Assets	14.2	16.2
	10.4	9.3	6.1				7.5	8.2
	7.1	4.1	3.7				4.3	4.7
	3.0	2.7	2.0			Sales/Total Assets	2.6	2.9
	2.3	2.0	1.7				2.2	2.1
	2.1	1.4	1.4				1.5	1.4
		1.4	2.4			% Depr., Dep., Amort./Sales	1.5	1.6
		(47) 1.8	(30) 3.3				(122) 2.8	(145) 3.0
		3.9	4.3				4.2	4.1
		2.0				% Officers', Directors',	1.9	2.4
		(18) 3.0				Owners' Comp/Sales	(32) 3.7	(43) 4.7
		5.0					7.9	8.3
4516M	50595M	460033M	1237609M	654701M	524105M	Net Sales ($)	2637949M	4014413M
1156M	15806M	214588M	741709M	369794M	329971M	Total Assets ($)	1689788M	2523090M

M = $ thousand MM = $ million
See Pages 11 through 21 for Explanation of Ratios and Data

Comparative Historical Data							Current Data Sorted By Sales					

						Type of Statement						
	27		30		30	Unqualified			1	4	7	18
	32		31		26	Reviewed		1	4	6	12	3
	13		22		14	Compiled		2	4	5	3	
	6		8		2	Tax Returns	1			1		
	37		31		33	Other		6	6	2	9	10
	4/1/02- 3/31/03 ALL		4/1/03- 3/31/04 ALL		4/1/04- 3/31/05 ALL			23 (4/1-9/30/04)			82 (10/1/04-3/31/05)	
							0-1MM	1-3MM	3-5MM	5-10MM	10-25MM	25MM & OVER
	115		122		105	NUMBER OF STATEMENTS	1	9	15	18	31	31
	%		%		%	ASSETS	%	%	%	%	%	%
	7.6		6.5		6.6	Cash & Equivalents			3.3	11.5	6.2	4.7
	23.3		24.6		27.2	Trade Receivables (net)			20.0	28.3	32.0	25.4
	21.6		21.1		23.1	Inventory			17.1	24.6	25.4	22.5
	2.7		2.7		2.5	All Other Current			4.8	.6	3.7	1.5
	55.2		55.0		59.4	Total Current			45.2	65.1	67.2	54.1
	36.5		34.0		29.7	Fixed Assets (net)			38.3	31.2	23.1	31.4
	3.7		5.3		3.7	Intangibles (net)			2.7	.8	3.7	6.5
	4.5		5.7		7.2	All Other Non-Current			13.7	2.9	6.0	8.0
	100.0		100.0		100.0	Total			100.0	100.0	100.0	100.0
						LIABILITIES						
	9.4		10.1		10.0	Notes Payable-Short Term			7.7	12.7	12.8	7.9
	4.8		4.2		3.6	Cur. Mat.-L/T/D			4.0	2.5	3.1	4.8
	12.7		15.5		14.9	Trade Payables			8.9	14.3	18.0	13.0
	.3		.2		.2	Income Taxes Payable			.3	.1	.2	.3
	9.9		10.3		10.1	All Other Current			10.3	12.1	10.3	10.3
	37.0		40.3		38.7	Total Current			31.2	41.6	44.4	36.3
	18.2		17.4		13.1	Long-Term Debt			19.4	15.2	10.2	12.5
	.9		.6		.6	Deferred Taxes			1.0	.5	.6	.7
	5.3		11.7		10.7	All Other Non-Current			.6	4.1	8.2	12.3
	38.6		30.0		36.9	Net Worth			47.8	38.6	36.6	38.3
	100.0		100.0		100.0	Total Liabilities & Net Worth			100.0	100.0	100.0	100.0
						INCOME DATA						
	100.0		100.0		100.0	Net Sales			100.0	100.0	100.0	100.0
	29.5		28.1		28.3	Gross Profit			34.8	28.5	23.6	23.4
	25.5		23.9		24.5	Operating Expenses			31.3	28.1	19.2	17.4
	4.1		4.2		3.8	Operating Profit			3.5	.3	4.5	6.0
	1.2		1.4		.9	All Other Expenses (net)			.5	1.3	1.0	.9
	2.9		2.8		2.9	Profit Before Taxes			3.0	−1.0	3.4	5.1
						RATIOS						
	3.1		2.7		2.6				2.5	2.7	3.0	2.1
	1.7		1.5		1.6	Current			1.4	2.0	1.5	1.5
	1.0		.9		1.0				.8	.9	1.0	1.1
	1.8		1.4		1.6				1.2	2.1	1.7	1.3
	.9		.9		.9	Quick			1.0	1.1	.9	.7
	.5		.5		.6				.5	.4	.6	.6
33	10.9	34	10.7	37	9.8				33 11.1	34 10.9	41 8.9	44 8.2
43	8.4	43	8.4	49	7.4	Sales/Receivables			45 8.1	38 9.5	51 7.2	50 7.3
58	6.3	55	6.6	60	6.1				66 5.6	61 5.9	63 5.8	58 6.3
32	11.5	26	13.8	33	11.0				36 10.1	28 13.1	22 16.8	36 10.1
56	6.5	45	8.1	46	7.9	Cost of Sales/Inventory			46 8.0	49 7.4	41 9.0	49 7.4
83	4.4	72	5.1	86	4.2				79 4.6	80 4.6	106 3.5	78 4.7
18	19.8	17	21.8	23	16.0				17 21.9	9 38.6	24 15.2	24 14.9
28	12.9	29	12.6	33	10.9	Cost of Sales/Payables			34 10.7	25 14.9	37 10.0	31 11.8
40	9.0	42	8.7	46	7.9				43 8.5	49 7.4	50 7.4	41 8.8
	5.1		5.8		4.8				7.3	4.6	3.8	5.3
	9.8		13.8		9.6	Sales/Working Capital			10.8	7.0	12.0	10.2
	−211.8		−42.9		98.7				−10.7	−172.8	160.9	69.2
	8.1		8.8		11.5				8.6	8.1	13.4	18.8
(103)	2.9	(113)	2.5	(92)	3.0	EBIT/Interest		(13) 2.8	(17) 3.4	(28) 3.3	(28) 4.6
	1.2		.0		1.3				1.3	.7	1.5	1.7
	4.3		2.4		6.3							7.9
(44)	2.2	(35)	1.2	(35)	4.0	Net Profit + Depr., Dep., Amort./Cur. Mat. L/T/D					(12) 4.6
	1.3		.8		1.4							1.4
	.5		.4		.4				.4	.4	.2	.5
	.9		1.0		.8	Fixed/Worth			.8	.5	.8	1.0
	2.4		7.8		2.1				1.6	3.2	1.5	3.5
	.6		.7		.6				.6	.6	.8	.5
	1.6		2.1		1.4	Debt/Worth			1.1	1.5	1.5	1.8
	5.9		13.6		4.9				2.0	6.4	5.3	4.9
	36.4		30.1		28.9				28.9	21.5	24.3	40.6
(99)	17.1	(97)	11.2	(90)	13.0	% Profit Before Taxes/Tangible Net Worth	(14) 7.0	(16) 7.8	(28) 10.2	(24) 17.2
	3.4		−1.1		2.9				1.9	2.2	3.1	4.3
	12.6		10.5		11.9				11.7	8.2	10.0	20.9
	4.3		3.7		3.2	% Profit Before Taxes/Total Assets			3.0	4.6	2.7	3.6
	.2		−2.6		.9				.5	−.1	1.3	1.9
	11.1		14.9		13.7				10.4	14.0	26.7	8.2
	5.3		7.2		8.2	Sales/Net Fixed Assets			3.5	10.1	13.4	6.1
	3.0		3.5		4.2				2.4	4.8	6.1	4.3
	2.5		2.7		2.5				2.0	2.9	2.8	2.0
	1.8		2.0		1.9	Sales/Total Assets			1.4	2.3	2.1	1.8
	1.3		1.5		1.5				1.3	1.6	1.4	1.6
	1.8		1.6		1.5				1.5	1.4	.8	2.6
(105)	3.4	(103)	2.8	(95)	2.6	% Depr., Dep., Amort./Sales		(12) 2.4	1.8	(29) 1.6	(28) 3.4
	4.8		4.5		4.1				4.1	4.0	2.8	4.3
	1.9		2.6		2.0						2.1	
(40)	4.8	(37)	5.4	(31)	3.5	% Officers', Directors', Owners' Comp/Sales				(11) 3.3	
	8.0		7.7		7.8						8.7	
	3098244M		3192372M		2931559M	Net Sales ($)	884M	17826M	60750M	139852M	477261M	2234986M
	2087943M		1761633M		1673024M	Total Assets ($)	204M	11328M	40145M	87223M	251750M	1282374M

M = $ thousand   MM = $ million
See Pages 11 through 21 for Explanation of Ratios and Data

Current Data Sorted By Assets | **Comparative Historical Data**

Type of Statement	0-500M	500M-2MM	2-10MM	10-50MM	50-100MM	100-250MM		4/1/00-3/31/01 ALL	4/1/01-3/31/02 ALL
Unqualified			3	9	1	3		16	14
Reviewed		2	4	3		1		4	5
Compiled			1					7	10
Tax Returns		1	1						
Other	3	3	3	8	1			11	14
		9 (4/1-9/30/04)		38 (10/1/04-3/31/05)					
NUMBER OF STATEMENTS	3	6	12	20	2	4		38	43
	%	%	%	%	%	%		%	%
ASSETS									
Cash & Equivalents			5.0	11.6				11.8	8.6
Trade Receivables (net)			20.6	11.8				15.3	15.6
Inventory			32.6	14.2				17.0	17.5
All Other Current			1.2	1.9				2.8	2.9
Total Current			59.4	39.4				46.9	44.6
Fixed Assets (net)			29.9	50.0				41.8	44.0
Intangibles (net)			3.7	2.8				1.5	2.6
All Other Non-Current			7.0	7.8				9.8	8.9
Total			100.0	100.0				100.0	100.0
LIABILITIES									
Notes Payable-Short Term			7.5	5.6				7.1	8.3
Cur. Mat.-L/T/D			3.9	3.6				5.0	3.4
Trade Payables			10.3	4.8				7.6	7.5
Income Taxes Payable			.0	.1				.2	.1
All Other Current			8.0	2.6				5.8	5.5
Total Current			29.6	16.7				25.7	24.9
Long-Term Debt			24.5	33.4				19.8	22.4
Deferred Taxes			1.9	3.3				1.1	2.0
All Other Non-Current			5.6	8.2				1.5	4.2
Net Worth			38.4	38.4				51.9	46.6
Total Liabilities & Net Worth			100.0	100.0				100.0	100.0
INCOME DATA									
Net Sales			100.0	100.0				100.0	100.0
Gross Profit			30.2	35.0				33.1	29.6
Operating Expenses			25.7	22.9				20.4	21.8
Operating Profit			4.5	12.1				12.7	7.8
All Other Expenses (net)			1.0	3.8				1.3	2.3
Profit Before Taxes			3.5	8.3				11.4	5.5
RATIOS									
Current			2.7 / 2.1 / 1.5	4.8 / 2.6 / 1.6				4.5 / 2.3 / 1.4	3.2 / 1.9 / 1.2
Quick			2.1 / .6 / .5	2.6 / 1.6 / .7				2.8 / 1.2 / .5	2.1 / .8 / .5
Sales/Receivables			25 14.7 / 34 10.6 / 59 6.2	34 10.8 / 39 9.3 / 51 7.1				32 11.6 / 39 9.5 / 47 7.8	29 12.4 / 38 9.7 / 48 7.6
Cost of Sales/Inventory			42 8.7 / 90 4.0 / 161 2.3	44 8.3 / 81 4.5 / 101 3.6				33 11.0 / 75 4.9 / 109 3.4	39 9.3 / 64 5.7 / 105 3.5
Cost of Sales/Payables			23 16.2 / 35 10.5 / 41 8.9	12 29.2 / 24 15.4 / 33 11.1				16 22.6 / 25 14.8 / 35 10.4	17 21.2 / 25 14.5 / 34 10.8
Sales/Working Capital			4.1 / 5.6 / 8.3	2.9 / 3.9 / 7.5				2.9 / 5.8 / 13.2	3.6 / 8.1 / 30.4
EBIT/Interest			10.2 / 2.5 / 1.0	13.0 / (19) 5.2 / 2.4				15.8 / (35) 3.9 / 2.3	12.3 / (40) 2.7 / 1.4
Net Profit + Depr., Dep., Amort./Cur. Mat. L /T/D								180.0 / (10) 6.8 / 2.0	6.2 / (12) 3.0 / 1.3
Fixed/Worth			.3 / .5 / 4.2	.8 / 1.4 / 2.9				.5 / .7 / 1.1	.5 / .8 / 1.6
Debt/Worth			1.0 / 1.7 / 5.5	.9 / 1.7 / 3.6				.4 / .7 / 2.4	.4 / 1.3 / 2.8
% Profit Before Taxes/Tangible Net Worth			43.3 / (11) 5.8 / −1.3	42.9 / (18) 22.3 / 7.7				36.9 / (36) 25.1 / 11.3	26.3 / (39) 15.4 / 5.8
% Profit Before Taxes/Total Assets			12.6 / 3.6 / −.1	12.9 / 7.5 / 3.0				19.3 / 13.0 / 4.6	12.0 / 5.8 / 1.1
Sales/Net Fixed Assets			10.4 / 8.6 / 3.2	2.7 / 2.1 / 1.2				4.6 / 3.0 / 1.5	5.3 / 3.2 / 1.6
Sales/Total Assets			2.2 / 1.6 / 1.2	1.4 / 1.0 / .6				1.5 / 1.2 / .7	1.9 / 1.2 / .8
% Depr., Dep., Amort./Sales			.9 / (10) 3.9 / 6.5	4.9 / 6.9 / 10.1				2.9 / (37) 4.1 / 7.9	2.0 / (39) 4.0 / 5.2
% Officers', Directors', Owners' Comp/Sales								1.1 / (11) 2.2 / 3.2	2.5 / (15) 3.7 / 5.7
Net Sales ($)	3837M	16591M	79605M	372464M	234103M	572367M		902608M	1065160M
Total Assets ($)	789M	7031M	51436M	387692M	157905M	682770M		975820M	1035056M

M = $ thousand   MM = $ million
See Pages 11 through 21 for Explanation of Ratios and Data

Comparative Historical Data | Current Data Sorted By Sales

			Type of Statement						
14	11	16	Unqualified			2	3	6	5
6	11	10	Reviewed			3	3	2	2
2	9	1	Compiled			1			
1	2	2	Tax Returns		1	1			
10	11	18	Other	1	4	1	5	5	2
4/1/02-3/31/03 ALL	4/1/03-3/31/04 ALL	4/1/04-3/31/05 ALL		0-1MM	1-3MM	3-5MM	5-10MM	10-25MM	25MM & OVER
					9 (4/1-9/30/04)		38 (10/1/04-3/31/05)		
33	44	47	**NUMBER OF STATEMENTS**	1	5	8	11	13	9
%	%	%	**ASSETS**	%	%	%	%	%	%
7.3	8.5	9.4	Cash & Equivalents				6.6	12.0	
11.8	19.3	18.0	Trade Receivables (net)				15.6	13.5	
21.3	19.4	22.7	Inventory				23.4	16.4	
1.6	3.5	1.5	All Other Current				1.1	.9	
42.1	50.7	51.5	Total Current				46.8	42.9	
49.2	40.9	37.4	Fixed Assets (net)				37.9	48.8	
1.7	1.9	3.3	Intangibles (net)				4.7	1.3	
7.0	6.6	7.8	All Other Non-Current				10.6	7.0	
100.0	100.0	100.0	Total				100.0	100.0	
			LIABILITIES						
4.1	5.3	4.9	Notes Payable-Short Term				7.8	5.5	
3.6	3.5	6.2	Cur. Mat.-L/T/D				3.0	3.4	
5.4	7.8	8.8	Trade Payables				7.0	6.6	
.2	.3	.1	Income Taxes Payable				.0	.1	
7.3	6.8	9.5	All Other Current				5.5	2.5	
20.5	23.7	29.4	Total Current				23.3	18.1	
30.2	24.9	25.2	Long-Term Debt				28.6	30.4	
1.8	1.1	2.3	Deferred Taxes				3.6	2.6	
1.8	1.7	6.2	All Other Non-Current				16.0	3.0	
45.7	48.6	36.9	Net Worth				28.5	45.8	
100.0	100.0	100.0	Total Liabilities & Net Worth				100.0	100.0	
			INCOME DATA						
100.0	100.0	100.0	Net Sales				100.0	100.0	
34.5	32.3	32.8	Gross Profit				31.6	33.4	
24.6	23.1	24.4	Operating Expenses				23.4	23.8	
9.9	9.2	8.4	Operating Profit				8.1	9.7	
1.7	.9	2.5	All Other Expenses (net)				5.3	1.4	
8.2	8.3	5.9	Profit Before Taxes				2.8	8.3	
			RATIOS						
3.4	3.9	3.3	Current				2.7	5.6	
2.5	2.1	2.1					1.9	3.2	
1.6	1.5	1.4					1.4	1.5	
1.8	2.0	2.0	Quick				1.9	3.6	
1.1	1.1	1.0					.6	1.8	
.5	.6	.5					.5	.7	
25 14.5	33 11.1	29 12.5	Sales/Receivables				27 13.3	31 11.6	
35 10.4	41 8.9	39 9.3					39 9.3	38 9.6	
54 6.8	54 6.7	52 7.0					70 5.2	52 7.1	
51 7.1	40 9.1	41 9.0	Cost of Sales/Inventory				40 9.1	69 5.3	
91 4.0	64 5.7	81 4.5					86 4.2	85 4.3	
160 2.3	115 3.2	131 2.8					194 1.9	95 3.8	
16 23.3	19 19.7	18 19.8	Cost of Sales/Payables				14 25.6	14 26.9	
25 14.8	26 13.9	27 13.6					32 11.4	25 14.6	
35 10.3	36 10.2	40 9.0					41 8.9	39 9.4	
3.0	3.5	3.5	Sales/Working Capital				3.5	2.8	
4.2	5.2	4.6					4.1	3.9	
9.2	10.7	9.9					7.7	8.2	
9.4	16.9	13.1	EBIT/Interest				6.7	24.8	
(31) 5.2	(41) 8.1	(45) 3.7					3.2	(12) 5.5	
2.3	3.7	1.8					.9	2.4	
	4.7	11.9	Net Profit + Depr., Dep., Amort./Cur. Mat. L/T/D						
(13) 2.5		(13) 3.4							
1.3	2.1								
.6	.4	.4	Fixed/Worth				.4	.7	
1.0	.9	1.0					.8	1.4	
1.9	1.6	3.0					26.6	2.5	
.4	.5	.9	Debt/Worth				1.3	.4	
1.5	1.1	1.7					1.7	1.8	
2.2	2.1	4.3					36.2	3.2	
27.8	43.0	43.3	% Profit Before Taxes/Tangible Net Worth					40.5	
(32) 17.0	(42) 18.3	(40) 15.4						24.1	
7.3	9.0	5.9						9.0	
14.5	17.7	13.0	% Profit Before Taxes/Total Assets				8.2	14.5	
6.6	10.3	6.6					2.8	10.9	
3.2	4.0	2.0					-.2	4.4	
4.5	11.0	10.3	Sales/Net Fixed Assets				10.3	3.9	
2.2	3.8	3.0					2.3	2.3	
1.3	1.7	1.8					1.2	1.4	
1.4	2.4	2.1	Sales/Total Assets				1.6	1.4	
1.0	1.2	1.3					.9	1.1	
.8	.8	.8					.6	.9	
3.8	1.5	2.5	% Depr., Dep., Amort./Sales				1.5	4.1	
(31) 4.8	(37) 3.9	(39) 5.3					(10) 4.9	7.8	
9.2	6.8	8.1					11.1	9.9	
		1.8	% Officers', Directors', Owners' Comp/Sales						
	(15)	3.1							
		4.7							
877196M	1156283M	1278967M	Net Sales ($)	313M	7622M	35851M	88875M	220351M	925955M
863241M	1006418M	1287623M	Total Assets ($)	106M	3553M	19959M	104179M	227069M	932757M

M = $ thousand   MM = $ million
See Pages 11 through 21 for Explanation of Ratios and Data

Current Data Sorted By Assets   Comparative Historical Data

						Type of Statement		
1		3	5			Unqualified	12	11
	8	13	5			Reviewed	23	17
3	7	6				Compiled	17	15
4	4	4				Tax Returns	6	2
4	5	10	6	2	2	Other	31	29
	19 (4/1-9/30/04)		73 (10/1/04-3/31/05)				4/1/00-3/31/01	4/1/01-3/31/02
0-500M	500M-2MM	2-10MM	10-50MM	50-100MM	100-250MM		ALL	ALL
12	24	36	16	2	2	NUMBER OF STATEMENTS	89	74
%	%	%	%	%	%	**ASSETS**	%	%
12.2	8.3	5.0	7.7			Cash & Equivalents	8.4	6.5
22.8	30.5	31.6	23.0			Trade Receivables (net)	25.5	26.1
35.9	26.1	23.5	17.0			Inventory	20.0	19.9
1.1	2.6	2.5	2.7			All Other Current	2.3	2.1
72.0	67.5	62.6	50.4			Total Current	56.1	54.6
24.2	26.5	25.3	35.9			Fixed Assets (net)	31.6	33.8
.5	.8	4.6	7.3			Intangibles (net)	6.0	5.8
3.3	5.2	7.5	6.3			All Other Non-Current	6.3	5.8
100.0	100.0	100.0	100.0			Total	100.0	100.0
						LIABILITIES		
25.2	9.2	10.2	9.6			Notes Payable-Short Term	8.6	9.2
3.6	3.2	5.1	3.9			Cur. Mat.-L/T/D	5.0	4.2
20.5	13.4	15.8	9.0			Trade Payables	12.7	13.2
.1	.2	.6	.5			Income Taxes Payable	.4	.7
26.8	6.6	9.2	8.4			All Other Current	7.3	8.6
76.2	32.6	40.9	31.4			Total Current	34.0	35.9
15.8	12.2	13.8	19.7			Long-Term Debt	20.3	17.9
.0	.2	.8	1.6			Deferred Taxes	.5	.4
12.1	5.4	4.5	5.3			All Other Non-Current	9.6	6.3
−4.1	49.6	40.0	42.0			Net Worth	35.7	39.5
100.0	100.0	100.0	100.0			Total Liabilities & Net Worth	100.0	100.0
						INCOME DATA		
100.0	100.0	100.0	100.0			Net Sales	100.0	100.0
42.7	36.1	30.0	23.1			Gross Profit	30.6	28.0
47.0	31.7	25.4	20.4			Operating Expenses	25.4	25.3
−4.3	4.3	4.6	2.7			Operating Profit	5.1	2.7
.2	.0	.8	1.3			All Other Expenses (net)	1.3	1.4
−4.5	4.3	3.8	1.3			Profit Before Taxes	3.8	1.3
						RATIOS		
1.8	4.1	2.7	3.0				2.8	3.1
1.2	2.3	1.6	1.7			Current	1.8	1.5
.6	1.3	1.1	1.2				1.2	1.0
1.0	2.2	1.5	1.8				1.7	1.6
.5	1.1	.9	.9			Quick	1.0	.9
.3	.7	.6	.6				.6	.6
9 40.3	30 12.3	37 9.9	28 13.1				32 11.3	35 10.5
25 14.8	35 10.4	42 8.6	44 8.3			Sales/Receivables	44 8.3	42 8.7
40 9.2	47 7.7	60 6.1	59 6.2				52 7.1	52 7.0
38 9.6	23 15.7	26 13.9	22 16.5				21 17.4	25 14.6
90 4.1	55 6.6	41 8.8	39 9.4			Cost of Sales/Inventory	41 8.8	42 8.8
132 2.8	82 4.4	81 4.5	84 4.3				67 5.4	78 4.7
20 18.5	12 29.5	19 19.4	11 33.0				18 20.5	16 22.5
33 10.9	19 18.8	30 12.1	20 18.2			Cost of Sales/Payables	27 13.8	24 15.0
72 5.1	40 9.2	50 7.3	30 12.2				41 8.8	40 9.1
10.5	4.4	5.0	3.9				5.3	5.9
43.8	7.4	10.9	9.7			Sales/Working Capital	8.9	10.0
−9.1	21.6	77.6	22.0				27.2	NM
4.3	7.0	15.6	6.7				6.1	5.7
(10) .0	(20) 1.9	(34) 4.7	3.6			EBIT/Interest	(82) 2.9	(67) 2.6
−4.1	.5	2.5	.4				1.3	.0
						Net Profit + Depr., Dep.,	4.2	3.7
						Amort./Cur. Mat. L /T/D	(25) 2.2	(21) 2.3
							1.1	.8
.5	.3	.3	.7				.4	.5
NM	.6	.6	1.0			Fixed/Worth	1.0	.9
−.8	1.0	1.4	2.4				3.5	3.7
1.4	.3	.6	1.0				.8	.8
NM	.8	1.9	1.4			Debt/Worth	2.7	2.2
−4.2	2.5	3.1	2.6				6.9	7.0
	18.9	35.9	22.9			% Profit Before Taxes/Tangible	41.2	29.8
	(22) 4.1	(32) 16.4	(13) 9.4			Net Worth	(74) 19.2	(63) 15.4
	−.6	4.4	−1.2				5.8	1.0
12.2	9.5	16.9	9.6			% Profit Before Taxes/Total	14.0	12.1
−6.3	1.4	6.9	4.5			Assets	5.3	4.4
−34.3	−1.8	1.1	−.9				1.6	−4.0
24.4	17.6	23.9	10.4				15.9	13.5
14.6	12.3	10.5	5.3			Sales/Net Fixed Assets	7.6	6.8
8.9	7.8	5.8	2.8				4.2	3.7
3.9	3.4	3.0	2.5				2.8	2.7
3.0	2.7	2.2	1.7			Sales/Total Assets	2.1	2.2
1.9	2.1	1.8	1.0				1.5	1.3
.7	1.0	1.1	2.0				1.4	1.2
(10) 1.3	(21) 1.7	(31) 2.2	(14) 3.5			% Depr., Dep., Amort./Sales	(80) 2.4	(63) 2.7
3.9	2.9	3.3	5.7				3.8	4.4
	2.8	1.6				% Officers', Directors',	2.0	1.9
	(14) 5.3	(15) 2.3				Owners' Comp/Sales	(32) 4.9	(28) 3.1
	10.5						9.5	6.0
9859M	82968M	407525M	608606M	267928M	356596M	Net Sales ($)	2098095M	1893841M
3346M	30710M	175513M	358821M	107477M	255364M	Total Assets ($)	1186134M	1280045M

Comparative Historical Data / Current Data Sorted By Sales

			Type of Statement	0-1MM	1-3MM	3-5MM	5-10MM	10-25MM	25MM & OVER
19	12	9	Unqualified	1			1	3	4
21	30	26	Reviewed		3	4	10	6	3
17	19	16	Compiled	3	2	6	2	2	1
13	13	12	Tax Returns	3	2	2	4	1	
35	34	29	Other	2	5	4	3	7	8
4/1/02-3/31/03	4/1/03-3/31/04	4/1/04-3/31/05		19 (4/1-9/30/04)		73 (10/1/04-3/31/05)			
ALL	ALL	ALL							
105	108	92	NUMBER OF STATEMENTS	9	12	16	20	19	16
%	%	%	ASSETS	%	%	%	%	%	%
6.9	7.2	7.2	Cash & Equivalents	8.3	5.8	10.9	3.9		3.1
26.0	26.9	28.4	Trade Receivables (net)	30.1	27.1	31.1	31.3		26.4
21.9	22.3	24.3	Inventory	25.4	30.3	19.2	21.9		19.4
2.7	2.7	2.4	All Other Current	.6	4.1	1.7	2.8		2.7
57.5	59.2	62.2	Total Current	64.4	67.4	63.0	59.8		51.6
32.4	30.9	27.0	Fixed Assets (net)	29.5	27.4	26.9	26.2		28.2
4.6	4.1	4.4	Intangibles (net)	.3	.8	5.0	4.1		12.5
5.5	5.8	6.3	All Other Non-Current	5.8	4.4	5.1	9.8		7.6
100.0	100.0	100.0	Total	100.0	100.0	100.0	100.0	100.0	100.0
			LIABILITIES						
10.6	10.7	11.6	Notes Payable-Short Term	7.5	13.2	7.8	9.8		11.0
4.7	4.8	4.0	Cur. Mat.-L/T/D	1.9	4.2	5.8	3.6		3.4
13.8	13.8	14.7	Trade Payables	17.7	14.8	14.3	13.3		13.6
.3	.2	.4	Income Taxes Payable	.0	.1	1.4	.2		.2
11.0	7.9	10.5	All Other Current	2.9	10.0	6.3	10.2		9.3
40.4	37.4	41.2	Total Current	30.0	42.2	35.6	37.1		37.6
20.1	18.3	15.2	Long-Term Debt	13.9	12.8	14.6	13.8		19.8
.6	.7	.7	Deferred Taxes	.0	.3	.4	1.1		1.8
5.0	5.2	6.0	All Other Non-Current	5.3	2.1	3.8	6.4		7.1
33.9	38.4	36.8	Net Worth	50.8	42.6	45.5	41.6		33.7
100.0	100.0	100.0	Total Liabilities & Net Worth	100.0	100.0	100.0	100.0	100.0	100.0
			INCOME DATA						
100.0	100.0	100.0	Net Sales	100.0	100.0	100.0	100.0	100.0	100.0
32.1	31.2	31.5	Gross Profit	41.9	31.3	29.2	30.2		21.2
28.2	29.0	28.6	Operating Expenses	35.4	31.6	24.2	24.5		18.4
3.9	2.2	2.9	Operating Profit	6.5	-.3	5.1	5.6		2.8
1.4	1.0	.6	All Other Expenses (net)	-.5	.5	.6	.6		1.5
2.6	1.2	2.3	Profit Before Taxes	7.1	-.8	4.5	5.1		1.4
			RATIOS						
2.6	2.7	3.0	Current	7.1	3.4	4.3	3.1		1.8
1.5	1.6	1.6		2.7	1.7	1.6	1.9		1.5
1.0	1.0	1.2		1.4	1.3	1.1	1.1		1.0
1.4	1.7	1.7	Quick	3.5	1.4	2.2	1.7		1.1
.9	.8	.9		1.2	.9	1.2	.9		.6
.6	.5	.6		.6	.5	.9	.6		.5
30 12.1	32 11.6	33 11.2	Sales/Receivables	26 14.1	30 12.3	36 10.3	37 10.0		37 9.8
43 8.6	40 9.2	40 9.1		35 10.4	33 11.1	45 8.2	41 8.9		43 8.5
54 6.8	52 7.1	52 7.1		50 7.2	56 6.5	50 7.3	68 5.3		53 6.8
27 13.7	28 13.0	26 14.3	Cost of Sales/Inventory	37 9.9	32 11.4	16 23.5	25 14.4		24 15.2
50 7.3	48 7.6	43 8.5		56 6.5	59 6.2	27 13.7	38 9.7		39 9.4
81 4.5	86 4.2	87 4.2		82 4.4	102 3.6	46 7.9	86 4.3		58 6.3
18 20.3	17 21.4	16 22.4	Cost of Sales/Payables	13 27.8	14 25.6	16 22.6	13 28.0		19 19.0
29 12.8	30 12.4	27 13.5		35 10.3	23 16.0	22 16.6	28 13.1		31 11.6
48 7.6	42 8.7	48 7.7		51 7.1	52 7.1	44 8.3	36 10.0		41 9.0
6.1	5.0	5.1	Sales/Working Capital	4.2	4.6	4.0	4.9		8.6
11.3	9.2	10.8		8.2	7.4	12.3	8.5		13.2
UND	132.4	34.5		19.1	26.8	64.8	35.7		NM
(97) 6.3	(98) 7.8	(83) 9.4	EBIT/Interest		(10) 7.2	(13) 5.1	(19) 15.3	16.3	(15) 7.9
2.8	2.4	3.9			4.4	1.6	5.3	6.8	4.0
1.1	.0	.6			.4	-1.3	2.4	2.6	.6
(25) 3.6	(28) 3.9	(19) 3.5	Net Profit + Depr., Dep., Amort./Cur. Mat. L/T/D						
2.1	2.0	1.5							
1.0	.9	.9							
.4	.5	.3	Fixed/Worth	.2	.4	.3	.3		.4
1.0	1.0	.8		.7	.7	.5	.7		1.3
2.9	2.2	1.9		1.6	1.0	1.1	1.3		-4.4
1.0	.8	.6	Debt/Worth	.2	.4	.8	.6		1.2
1.9	1.8	1.7		.8	1.7	1.9	1.0		2.5
8.2	4.8	4.3		5.0	3.0	2.3	2.7		-14.9
(90) 33.3	(96) 28.8	(75) 25.9	% Profit Before Taxes/Tangible Net Worth		(10) 36.4	(14) 12.1	35.8	(16) 40.8	(11) 30.9
14.6	12.8	10.7			10.2	1.8		20.9	12.8
2.2	-2.6	.0			-.5	-10.2	4.2	7.2	-2.1
11.3	12.5	11.4	% Profit Before Taxes/Total Assets	14.2	3.8	17.7	17.3		9.6
4.7	3.3	4.5		6.2	.7	6.0	8.7		4.2
.5	-1.8	-1.9		-1.6	-5.7	1.5	3.3		-1.2
14.4	15.2	18.1	Sales/Net Fixed Assets	20.2	13.4	24.2	23.6		12.9
8.0	8.5	10.3		13.9	10.3	9.9	9.7		8.0
4.1	4.1	5.3		4.3	7.7	6.0	4.4		5.0
2.7	3.1	3.1	Sales/Total Assets	3.9	3.3	3.1	3.0		2.8
2.2	2.1	2.3		2.8	2.4	2.4	2.2		1.8
1.6	1.6	1.8		2.0	1.9	1.8	1.5		1.4
(96) 1.6	(97) 1.7	(80) 1.1	% Depr., Dep., Amort./Sales		(10) .7	(14) 1.8	(18) 1.3	(16) 1.2	(14) 1.0
2.8	2.9	2.3			1.5	2.9	2.7	2.2	2.7
4.8	4.7	3.9			2.2	3.7	4.8	3.9	4.0
(43) 3.3	(46) 1.3	(39) 1.8	% Officers', Directors', Owners' Comp/Sales		(10) 2.2				
4.8	3.6	3.5			3.3				
7.4	7.9	7.0			7.2				
2045399M	2978163M	1733482M	Net Sales ($)	5425M	23763M	62066M	151027M	319092M	1172109M
1191460M	1625564M	931231M	Total Assets ($)	2120M	9906M	27798M	71630M	155981M	663796M

M = $ thousand   MM = $ million
See Pages 11 through 21 for Explanation of Ratios and Data

Current Data Sorted By Assets   **Comparative Historical Data**

	0-500M	500M-2MM	2-10MM	10-50MM	50-100MM	100-250MM		4/1/00-3/31/01 ALL	4/1/01-3/31/02 ALL
Type of Statement									
Unqualified		1	6	24	7	11		37	31
Reviewed		7	21	23	1			47	34
Compiled	2	18	22	3		1		39	43
Tax Returns	3	7	10	1				7	4
Other		5	29	18	2	3		56	59
		33 (4/1-9/30/04)		192 (10/1/04-3/31/05)					
NUMBER OF STATEMENTS	5	38	88	69	10	15		186	171
	%	%	%	%	%	%		%	%
ASSETS									
Cash & Equivalents		12.5	8.9	6.2	4.3	5.4		8.0	9.2
Trade Receivables (net)		32.0	27.9	23.0	21.8	17.4		23.4	23.1
Inventory		6.2	5.6	7.3	11.8	5.7		7.0	7.0
All Other Current		2.1	2.1	2.0	4.4	3.0		2.1	3.0
Total Current		52.7	44.6	38.6	42.3	31.5		40.4	42.3
Fixed Assets (net)		38.1	48.8	50.1	48.9	56.4		48.5	47.6
Intangibles (net)		2.5	2.2	2.7	2.1	4.8		2.5	3.1
All Other Non-Current		6.6	4.4	8.6	6.7	7.3		8.6	7.0
Total		100.0	100.0	100.0	100.0	100.0		100.0	100.0
LIABILITIES									
Notes Payable-Short Term		3.8	4.1	4.9	6.7	1.7		5.4	5.3
Cur. Mat.-L/T/D		6.6	6.2	5.5	4.1	3.1		5.9	6.0
Trade Payables		20.2	15.3	13.1	11.9	7.6		13.5	12.2
Income Taxes Payable		.3	.2	.2	.6	.0		.2	.2
All Other Current		7.8	4.5	7.7	6.8	4.0		6.5	6.6
Total Current		38.8	30.3	31.4	30.2	16.4		31.6	30.2
Long-Term Debt		21.7	25.0	19.5	18.3	20.9		20.8	20.7
Deferred Taxes		.5	.8	2.0	4.3	1.7		1.3	1.3
All Other Non-Current		5.6	3.4	2.1	1.6	2.0		3.7	4.1
Net Worth		33.5	40.5	45.0	45.6	59.0		42.6	43.6
Total Liabilities & Net Worth		100.0	100.0	100.0	100.0	100.0		100.0	100.0
INCOME DATA									
Net Sales		100.0	100.0	100.0	100.0	100.0		100.0	100.0
Gross Profit		30.8	29.2	25.4	17.1	21.7		26.9	27.9
Operating Expenses		27.1	26.2	20.9	14.2	12.2		22.6	23.5
Operating Profit		3.6	2.9	4.5	2.9	9.5		4.3	4.4
All Other Expenses (net)		1.2	.4	.1	−.4	.4		.4	.7
Profit Before Taxes		2.4	2.6	4.3	3.4	9.2		3.9	3.7
RATIOS									
Current		2.9	2.5	1.9	2.4	3.3		2.0	2.2
		1.7	1.7	1.4	1.2	2.1		1.3	1.5
		.8	1.1	.9	.9	1.2		.9	1.1
Quick		2.4	2.1	1.5	1.5	2.0		1.6	1.8
		1.4	1.4	1.0	.8	1.4		.9	1.1
		.6	.9	.6	.5	.9		.7	.7
Sales/Receivables	23 15.8	36 10.1	37 9.8	37 9.9	39 9.3		32 11.3	34 10.8
	43 8.6	43 8.5	46 8.0	52 7.0	50 7.3		42 8.6	43 8.5
	55 6.7	57 6.4	56 6.5	68 5.4	66 5.5		53 6.9	51 7.1
Cost of Sales/Inventory	1 381.2	4 87.4	6 63.3	7 49.3	17 22.1		6 60.2	5 67.8
	6 60.0	9 39.7	16 23.4	21 17.1	21 17.2		15 25.0	12 29.7
	17 21.1	18 20.3	34 10.9	31 11.6	54 6.7		30 12.2	29 12.8
Cost of Sales/Payables	11 32.0	23 15.9	23 16.0	19 19.5	18 20.8		18 20.4	18 20.7
	34 10.9	34 10.7	29 12.4	25 14.4	26 14.0		29 12.4	26 14.0
	59 6.2	45 8.0	47 7.8	50 7.3	47 7.8		45 8.0	40 9.1
Sales/Working Capital		7.1	8.0	8.6	5.1	4.3		8.5	7.7
		17.9	13.9	15.7	25.8	9.6		21.0	16.6
		−96.3	66.2	−65.2	−151.9	27.7		−42.2	145.1
EBIT/Interest		17.5	10.4	11.0	10.7	431.0		7.5	9.9
	(33) 5.6	(86) 3.4	(62) 5.3	3.9	(10) 6.3		(176) 2.9	(162) 3.0
		2.0	1.5	2.5	2.6	2.6		1.3	1.4
Net Profit + Depr., Dep., Amort./Cur. Mat. L /T/D			3.8	3.6				3.7	4.7
		(26) 2.2	(28) 2.1				(59) 2.1	(57) 1.9
			1.4	1.7				1.3	.9
Fixed/Worth		.5	.7	.7	.6	.7		.7	.7
		1.1	1.2	1.2	1.4	1.0		1.3	1.1
		6.4	2.5	1.8	1.7	1.8		2.4	2.1
Debt/Worth		.5	.7	.7	.9	.3		.6	.6
		1.7	1.2	1.2	1.7	.6		1.4	1.5
		13.4	3.6	2.2	2.2	2.0		3.3	2.8
% Profit Before Taxes/Tangible Net Worth		54.0	34.4	28.9	24.1	38.0		34.2	31.1
	(30) 18.3	(80) 14.7	(67) 18.6	14.0	(14) 17.0		(174) 16.5	(160) 15.4
		7.9	5.8	6.0	8.1	7.9		4.8	4.8
% Profit Before Taxes/Total Assets		21.1	11.5	13.1	8.8	11.6		12.4	12.3
		8.3	5.4	6.5	5.8	9.8		6.3	5.8
		−.1	.7	3.3	3.7	5.7		1.4	1.7
Sales/Net Fixed Assets		13.4	6.1	5.5	5.1	2.9		6.4	6.8
		7.0	4.6	3.4	3.6	2.2		3.8	4.1
		5.0	3.0	2.4	1.9	1.8		2.7	2.7
Sales/Total Assets		3.4	2.7	2.0	2.3	1.4		2.5	2.5
		2.8	2.2	1.7	1.9	1.2		1.9	1.9
		1.9	1.8	1.5	.9	.9		1.4	1.5
% Depr., Dep., Amort./Sales		2.5	3.0	3.3	2.4	4.8		3.2	3.5
	(36) 3.8	(85) 4.8	(65) 4.7	4.9	(10) 5.2		(176) 4.8	(157) 5.1
		5.5	6.9	5.8	7.0	8.8		6.9	6.7
% Officers', Directors', Owners' Comp/Sales		2.2	1.1	.8				1.6	1.1
	(18) 4.4	(29) 2.3	(10) 1.2				(71) 2.4	(53) 2.0
		6.6	3.3	1.8				4.9	3.5
Net Sales ($)	4510M	139709M	911662M	2701319M	1189643M	2437607M		5158821M	5293258M
Total Assets ($)	1460M	50153M	406870M	1583704M	719981M	2342239M		3400893M	3396428M

M = $ thousand   MM = $ million
See Pages 11 through 21 for Explanation of Ratios and Data

Comparative Historical Data				Current Data Sorted By Sales					
			Type of Statement						
50	49	49	Unqualified				2	10	37
54	46	52	Reviewed		6	4	9	14	19
38	57	46	Compiled		8	12	14	7	4
13	22	21	Tax Returns	1	3	3	7	5	4
51	61	57	Other	3	3	3	15	15	21
4/1/02-3/31/03	4/1/03-3/31/04	4/1/04-3/31/05			33 (4/1-9/30/04)		192 (10/1/04-3/31/05)		
ALL	ALL	ALL		0-1MM	1-3MM	3-5MM	5-10MM	10-25MM	25MM & OVER
206	235	225	**NUMBER OF STATEMENTS**	4	20	22	47	51	81
%	%	%	**ASSETS**	%	%	%	%	%	%
9.0	9.6	8.3	Cash & Equivalents		13.2	11.2	9.3	7.1	6.4
23.6	24.6	26.0	Trade Receivables (net)		21.6	32.7	28.3	30.3	21.7
6.9	7.5	6.6	Inventory		8.4	3.8	4.9	6.7	7.7
2.5	3.0	2.2	All Other Current		1.4	2.2	1.7	2.5	2.5
42.0	44.6	43.1	Total Current		44.6	49.9	44.2	46.6	38.4
48.8	46.6	47.9	Fixed Assets (net)		43.0	43.6	48.8	45.9	50.8
2.1	2.2	2.6	Intangibles (net)		5.3	.5	2.5	1.8	3.0
7.1	6.5	6.4	All Other Non-Current		7.2	6.0	4.5	5.7	7.8
100.0	100.0	100.0	Total		100.0	100.0	100.0	100.0	100.0
			LIABILITIES						
5.5	5.3	4.3	Notes Payable-Short Term		4.7	6.4	2.7	4.0	4.4
6.0	5.6	5.9	Cur. Mat.-L/T/D		5.6	7.0	6.0	6.0	5.4
13.8	13.2	14.7	Trade Payables		13.5	16.8	17.3	16.8	11.9
.2	.2	.2	Income Taxes Payable		.0	.4	.2	.3	.2
6.8	6.9	6.0	All Other Current		10.2	3.9	4.6	6.2	6.5
32.4	31.3	31.2	Total Current		34.1	34.5	30.9	33.3	28.6
20.0	22.0	22.4	Long-Term Debt		24.0	28.7	27.1	18.1	19.3
1.5	1.2	1.3	Deferred Taxes		.8	.4	.7	1.0	2.3
4.5	4.7	4.0	All Other Non-Current		6.1	3.8	4.4	3.3	1.8
41.7	40.9	41.1	Net Worth		35.0	32.7	36.9	44.4	48.0
100.0	100.0	100.0	Total Liabilities & Net Worth		100.0	100.0	100.0	100.0	100.0
			INCOME DATA						
100.0	100.0	100.0	Net Sales		100.0	100.0	100.0	100.0	100.0
29.0	28.9	27.6	Gross Profit		33.3	31.7	29.9	28.5	22.3
25.7	25.5	23.7	Operating Expenses		32.1	28.9	27.1	24.2	17.0
3.3	3.4	3.9	Operating Profit		1.2	2.8	2.8	4.2	5.3
.3	.5	.4	All Other Expenses (net)		.5	.1	.5	.4	.0
2.9	2.8	3.5	Profit Before Taxes		.6	2.7	2.3	3.8	5.3
			RATIOS						
2.3	2.6	2.3			2.9	3.2	2.7	2.2	2.1
1.5	1.5	1.6	Current		2.0	1.7	1.6	1.5	1.5
.9	.9	1.0			1.0	.9	1.0	1.0	1.0
1.8	1.9	1.9			2.3	3.1	2.1	1.9	1.6
1.2	1.1	1.1	Quick		1.6	1.5	1.4	1.2	1.0
.6	.7	.7			.5	.7	.9	.7	.7
31　11.6	31　11.7	36　10.1		22　16.5	42　8.7	30　12.3	37　9.7	37　9.9	
40　9.1	41　8.8	43　8.4	Sales/Receivables	39　9.2	48　7.7	43　8.6	46　8.0	43　8.4	
51　7.2	53　6.9	57　6.4		55　6.7	69　5.3	59　6.2	58　6.3	55　6.7	
5　72.9	4　90.7	5　74.3		1　727.0	2　184.8	2　234.0	5　78.3	7　50.8	
13　27.1	11　32.6	11　33.9	Cost of Sales/Inventory	8　45.4	7　65.6	7　54.0	11　32.4	19　19.6	
31　11.9	28　13.0	23　15.9		47　7.7	12　29.3	17　21.9	22　16.9	32　11.4	
19　19.2	18　20.0	21　17.7		5　71.1	18　19.9	18　20.1	24　15.0	20　18.1	
27　13.3	28　13.0	32　11.6	Cost of Sales/Payables	32　11.2	35　10.4	30　12.2	36　10.2	27　13.5	
43　8.5	40　9.0	47　7.8		54　6.8	65　5.6	46　8.0	45　8.1	45　8.1	
7.5	6.8	7.9			6.5	6.1	8.8	7.9	6.7
15.7	15.9	15.6	Sales/Working Capital		19.4	12.8	13.7	15.2	15.6
-68.5	-156.3	NM			NM	-224.0	999.8	241.2	NM
7.6	8.5	10.5			8.5	9.7	8.2	15.7	11.8
(188)　3.6	(214)　3.8	(205)　4.5	EBIT/Interest	(16)　5.5	(21)　3.8	(46)　3.4	(49)　4.5	(70)　5.6	
1.4	.9	1.8			-1.0	.4	.5	1.9	3.0
3.4	3.3	3.9	Net Profit + Depr., Dep.,				5.7	3.1	3.9
(63)　2.0	(65)　2.0	(69)　2.2	Amort./Cur. Mat. L/T/D			(13)　2.1	(18)　1.8	(33)　2.4	
1.3	1.3	1.4					1.4	1.2	1.5
.6	.6	.7			.4	.6	.8	.7	.7
1.2	1.2	1.2	Fixed/Worth		1.6	1.3	1.2	1.0	1.2
2.4	2.3	2.1			NM	NM	3.1	1.9	1.8
.6	.6	.7			.3	.6	.7	.7	.7
1.3	1.4	1.3	Debt/Worth		1.5	2.2	1.4	1.2	1.2
3.1	3.3	3.1			NM	NM	9.9	2.2	2.0
28.8	29.0	32.3	% Profit Before Taxes/Tangible		48.0	26.5	35.1	35.6	30.1
(189)　13.0	(209)　14.9	(203)　16.0	Net Worth	(15)　18.8	(17)　12.4	(41)　14.0	(50)　17.1	(79)　18.6	
2.7	3.2	7.4			7.4	-4.7	4.8	5.8	9.3
11.1	11.9	12.6	% Profit Before Taxes/Total		18.9	13.8	10.8	17.8	12.6
4.9	5.4	6.2	Assets		6.2	5.2	4.8	5.3	8.2
.7	-.2	2.3			-11.0	-3.2	-.8	2.4	4.1
6.7	7.4	6.9			10.8	6.9	7.2	8.0	4.8
4.0	4.3	4.3	Sales/Net Fixed Assets		4.2	5.7	4.6	4.7	3.3
2.5	2.8	2.6			2.3	3.5	3.1	3.0	2.3
2.6	2.7	2.7			2.8	2.9	3.0	2.8	2.1
1.9	2.0	2.0	Sales/Total Assets		2.1	2.1	2.2	2.3	1.6
1.5	1.5	1.5			1.0	1.8	1.8	1.9	1.3
3.5	3.1	3.1			2.7	4.4	2.5	2.4	3.3
(188)　5.3	(213)　4.9	(210)　4.7	% Depr., Dep., Amort./Sales	(19)　4.0	(21)　5.2	(44)　4.4	(49)　4.7	(74)　4.8	
7.4	7.1	6.6			6.2	7.0	7.3	6.9	5.7
1.5	1.3	1.2	% Officers', Directors',				2.0	1.2	.9
(80)　2.5	(79)　2.6	(60)　2.3	Owners' Comp/Sales			(10)　2.8	(19)　2.3	(14)　1.7	
4.2	4.6	4.1					5.9	3.4	2.9
6320909M	6465259M	7384450M	Net Sales ($)	2344M	37681M	86925M	354480M	793627M	6109393M
4484821M	4230076M	5104407M	Total Assets ($)	1638M	23926M	43018M	189745M	384019M	4462061M

M = $ thousand　　MM = $ million
See Pages 11 through 21 for Explanation of Ratios and Data

Current Data Sorted By Assets   **Comparative Historical Data**

Type of Statement	0-500M	500M-2MM	2-10MM	10-50MM	50-100MM	100-250MM	4/1/00-3/31/01 ALL	4/1/01-3/31/02 ALL
Unqualified		2	8	13	2	5	16	24
Reviewed		8	23	9	1		26	29
Compiled		4	6	1			24	20
Tax Returns		1	3				11	10
Other	1	10	11	9	3	1	29	27
		14 (4/1-9/30/04)		107 (10/1/04-3/31/05)				
NUMBER OF STATEMENTS	1	25	51	32	6	6	106	110
	%	%	%	%	%	%	%	%
ASSETS								
Cash & Equivalents		6.6	5.6	10.5			8.0	7.2
Trade Receivables (net)		23.3	22.9	20.8			20.2	20.7
Inventory		28.5	20.6	15.9			19.0	18.7
All Other Current		.9	1.1	2.4			2.4	3.3
Total Current		59.3	50.2	49.7			49.6	50.0
Fixed Assets (net)		33.7	41.1	41.0			42.2	43.1
Intangibles (net)		2.2	1.5	3.7			2.5	1.0
All Other Non-Current		4.8	7.1	5.6			5.7	6.0
Total		100.0	100.0	100.0			100.0	100.0
LIABILITIES								
Notes Payable-Short Term		18.8	7.6	5.7			8.9	8.9
Cur. Mat.-L/T/D		5.7	6.1	3.8			4.8	5.8
Trade Payables		12.6	12.9	11.4			10.9	12.3
Income Taxes Payable		.2	1.0	.4			.3	.5
All Other Current		6.1	5.8	7.8			6.4	6.5
Total Current		43.3	33.4	29.1			31.3	33.9
Long-Term Debt		22.2	21.0	21.7			22.3	26.9
Deferred Taxes		.4	.6	.9			.7	.5
All Other Non-Current		2.0	5.5	3.8			6.8	4.0
Net Worth		32.1	39.5	44.5			38.9	34.8
Total Liabilities & Net Worth		100.0	100.0	100.0			100.0	100.0
INCOME DATA								
Net Sales		100.0	100.0	100.0			100.0	100.0
Gross Profit		27.0	31.1	30.6			31.1	32.0
Operating Expenses		21.6	27.3	20.8			25.2	26.2
Operating Profit		5.4	3.8	9.8			5.9	5.8
All Other Expenses (net)		.8	.7	.6			1.0	1.3
Profit Before Taxes		4.6	3.1	9.1			4.9	4.5
RATIOS								
Current		3.0	2.3	2.7			3.1	2.3
		1.6	1.7	1.9			1.7	1.5
		.9	1.0	1.3			1.1	1.0
Quick		1.9	1.4	2.0			1.9	1.5
		.8	.8	1.1			.8	.8
		.4	.5	.7			.5	.5
Sales/Receivables		18 20.3	30 12.2	32 11.4			24 15.3	27 13.6
		32 11.3	41 9.0	39 9.4			39 9.4	38 9.5
		54 6.8	54 6.7	49 7.4			52 7.0	51 7.2
Cost of Sales/Inventory		34 10.8	36 10.2	26 13.9			27 13.5	35 10.5
		54 6.8	63 5.7	57 6.4			55 6.6	57 6.4
		100 3.7	99 3.7	81 4.5			79 4.6	82 4.4
Cost of Sales/Payables		10 37.3	24 15.0	24 14.9			17 21.1	18 20.4
		34 10.8	33 11.0	34 10.8			29 12.6	27 13.7
		44 8.3	45 8.0	45 8.2			42 8.7	43 8.4
Sales/Working Capital		5.8	6.4	5.0			5.4	6.2
		14.9	9.2	8.0			9.4	10.8
		-33.6	-472.6	14.2			60.2	96.2
EBIT/Interest		9.1	10.8	16.3			7.4	7.4
		(22) 3.7	(49) 2.5	(29) 7.7			(99) 2.7	(100) 3.4
		1.4	1.1	3.6			1.4	1.3
Net Profit + Depr., Dep., Amort./Cur. Mat. L/T/D			2.1	8.1			6.8	5.8
			(14) 1.4	(12) 5.6			(32) 2.2	(36) 2.1
			.8	2.1			1.3	1.0
Fixed/Worth		.5	.5	.7			.6	.6
		.7	1.2	.9			1.2	1.2
		NM	2.4	1.7			2.4	2.1
Debt/Worth		.6	.7	.8			.7	.7
		1.1	1.2	1.5			1.7	1.7
		NM	5.4	3.0			3.8	3.7
% Profit Before Taxes/Tangible Net Worth		37.5	40.0	47.8			33.3	36.5
		(19) 28.0	(46) 16.5	30.6			(93) 18.8	(101) 22.9
		8.7	1.3	21.4			7.3	8.7
% Profit Before Taxes/Total Assets		18.0	13.0	19.8			15.2	16.3
		8.4	3.6	11.0			6.7	6.9
		1.5	.5	7.2			2.4	2.2
Sales/Net Fixed Assets		15.9	8.4	7.9			6.9	7.3
		5.7	4.2	4.1			4.3	4.0
		3.8	2.7	2.8			2.9	2.6
Sales/Total Assets		3.0	2.4	2.1			2.3	2.3
		2.3	1.9	1.7			1.8	1.8
		1.4	1.4	1.3			1.5	1.4
% Depr., Dep., Amort./Sales		1.1	2.6	1.8			2.1	2.3
		(22) 3.0	(47) 4.7	(27) 3.2			(103) 3.3	(104) 3.7
		5.5	6.6	6.0			5.9	6.0
% Officers', Directors', Owners' Comp/Sales		2.5	1.6				1.9	2.1
		(11) 3.9	(19) 2.3				(45) 3.8	(44) 3.2
		5.8	4.6				6.5	5.0
Net Sales ($)	11M	83121M	436825M	1228412M	629257M	1352382M	1534042M	2194082M
Total Assets ($)	6M	32385M	245698M	693846M	440121M	908596M	949047M	1268220M

© RMA 2005

M = $ thousand   MM = $ million

See Pages 11 through 21 for Explanation of Ratios and Data

Comparative Historical Data — **Current Data Sorted By Sales**

Current data period groupings: 14 (4/1-9/30/04); 107 (10/1/04-3/31/05)

4/1/02-3/31/03 ALL	4/1/03-3/31/04 ALL	4/1/04-3/31/05 ALL	Type of Statement	0-1MM	1-3MM	3-5MM	5-10MM	10-25MM	25MM & OVER
24	17	30	Unqualified		2	2	5	2	19
30	29	41	Reviewed		5	7	12	10	7
11	14	11	Compiled	1	1	3	4	1	1
7	7	4	Tax Returns		1		3		
26	43	35	Other	1	4	6	5	11	8
98	110	121	**NUMBER OF STATEMENTS**	2	13	18	29	24	35
%	%	%	**ASSETS**	%	%	%	%	%	%
7.4	8.0	7.1	Cash & Equivalents		4.6	5.6	5.5	12.0	6.7
19.9	19.4	22.2	Trade Receivables (net)		18.8	20.2	24.8	21.8	23.2
17.9	17.7	20.5	Inventory		27.2	28.7	17.9	20.1	16.7
1.7	2.8	1.4	All Other Current		1.3	.5	1.2	1.4	2.3
46.9	47.9	51.2	Total Current		51.9	55.0	49.4	55.3	48.9
44.2	43.9	40.4	Fixed Assets (net)		39.7	35.3	44.5	34.3	42.7
2.3	1.9	2.5	Intangibles (net)		4.0	1.0	1.1	3.2	3.4
6.6	6.3	6.0	All Other Non-Current		4.5	8.7	4.9	7.1	5.0
100.0	100.0	100.0	Total		100.0	100.0	100.0	100.0	100.0
			LIABILITIES						
7.2	6.3	9.0	Notes Payable-Short Term		25.0	8.7	8.6	5.0	6.6
6.7	5.2	5.3	Cur. Mat.-L/T/D		8.5	5.1	6.1	3.8	4.3
11.1	11.6	12.2	Trade Payables		12.5	11.0	12.3	12.4	12.2
.5	.2	.6	Income Taxes Payable		.3	.0	.9	1.0	.5
5.8	7.9	6.7	All Other Current		3.4	9.2	5.7	6.0	8.4
31.4	31.3	33.8	Total Current		49.7	34.1	33.6	28.2	31.9
24.1	25.0	21.1	Long-Term Debt		34.1	24.0	18.9	14.1	21.0
1.0	1.0	.8	Deferred Taxes		.4	.6	.3	1.4	.8
4.0	6.6	4.0	All Other Non-Current		2.7	3.7	4.5	7.0	2.4
39.4	36.1	40.3	Net Worth		13.1	37.6	42.7	49.3	43.9
100.0	100.0	100.0	Total Liabilities & Net Worth		100.0	100.0	100.0	100.0	100.0
			INCOME DATA						
100.0	100.0	100.0	Net Sales		100.0	100.0	100.0	100.0	100.0
32.7	34.4	29.9	Gross Profit		24.4	30.4	30.4	34.5	28.3
27.4	28.9	23.2	Operating Expenses		18.8	27.1	26.4	24.8	19.4
5.4	5.5	6.7	Operating Profit		5.7	3.3	4.0	9.7	8.9
1.2	1.1	.7	All Other Expenses (net)		1.3	1.1	.9	.3	.5
4.2	4.4	6.0	Profit Before Taxes		4.4	2.2	3.1	9.4	8.4
			RATIOS						
2.7	2.7	2.4	Current		2.4	2.3	2.4	3.8	2.0
1.6	1.6	1.7			1.2	1.6	1.7	2.3	1.7
1.0	1.0	1.1			.9	.9	1.0	1.4	1.3
1.7	1.4	1.5	Quick		1.4	1.2	1.5	2.4	1.5
.8	.8	.9			.5	.8	.9	1.4	.9
.5	.5	.5			.2	.4	.4	.7	.6
29 12.6	28 13.0	29 12.6	Sales/Receivables		17 21.6	27 13.4	27 13.7	28 13.0	34 10.7
39 9.3	39 9.4	39 9.4			38 9.6	42 8.7	34 10.6	37 9.9	41 8.9
52 7.0	54 6.8	54 6.8			61 6.0	53 6.9	55 6.6	49 7.5	56 6.6
28 13.1	31 11.6	35 10.4	Cost of Sales/Inventory		38 9.6	67 5.4	16 22.1	32 11.5	26 14.3
56 6.5	58 6.3	58 6.3			76 4.8	95 3.9	49 7.4	64 5.7	56 6.5
89 4.1	92 4.0	91 4.0			132 2.8	106 3.4	82 4.5	83 4.4	70 5.2
17 21.3	18 20.0	23 15.9	Cost of Sales/Payables		7 49.5	21 17.5	21 17.3	21 17.5	24 15.1
28 13.0	30 12.2	33 11.0			37 9.9	35 10.4	32 11.5	32 11.5	33 11.0
43 8.6	46 7.9	45 8.0			44 8.3	49 7.4	37 10.0	46 7.9	46 8.0
5.7	5.3	6.1	Sales/Working Capital		5.9	4.9	6.4	4.3	6.7
10.1	10.7	8.8			18.9	7.8	9.9		8.4
−264.8	112.2	38.7			−23.2	−31.1	−278.4	16.6	19.0
9.2	8.3	13.6	EBIT/Interest		8.0	4.5	10.2	31.7	27.8
(93) 3.1	(96) 3.4	(111) 4.7			2.5	(16) 2.0	(28) 2.8	(20) 11.3	(33) 7.7
1.6	1.3	1.9			1.3	.8	1.3	3.1	3.6
4.8	10.7	5.7	Net Profit + Depr., Dep., Amort./Cur. Mat. L/T/D						8.1
(38) 2.3	(33) 2.6	(40) 2.8							(20) 4.9
1.4	1.3	1.5							1.9
.6	.7	.6	Fixed/Worth		.7	.4	.6	.5	.8
1.2	1.4	.9			.9	.7	1.2	.7	1.0
2.2	3.1	2.0			−1.2	−11.9	1.9	1.6	1.7
.7	.8	.7	Debt/Worth		.8	.7	.7	.4	.8
1.6	1.8	1.3			1.3	1.3	1.7	.7	1.3
4.4	5.1	3.3			−4.2	−16.7	2.7	3.8	2.9
32.8	45.6	43.3	% Profit Before Taxes/Tangible Net Worth		21.4		31.9	76.9	43.5
(89) 14.7	(96) 18.9	(109) 27.6			(13) 7.8		(28) 12.1	31.8	(34) 33.9
4.3	5.5	8.6			1.9		1.3	26.2	20.0
13.2	13.7	17.8	% Profit Before Taxes/Total Assets		15.8	9.2	11.0	26.8	20.4
5.6	6.2	9.0			3.6	1.6	3.8	16.9	10.9
1.7	.7	2.7			.8	−.3	.6	10.2	7.1
6.4	5.8	8.6	Sales/Net Fixed Assets		7.8	13.6	7.4	15.0	6.3
3.8	3.8	4.2			4.3	4.0	4.1	7.5	3.8
2.6	2.3	2.8			3.2	2.4	2.9	2.4	3.8
2.2	2.2	2.3	Sales/Total Assets		2.4	2.4	2.5	2.5	2.1
1.7	1.7	1.7			1.6	1.6	2.0	2.1	1.7
1.3	1.2	1.3			1.3	1.2	1.5	1.2	1.3
3.0	2.9	2.4	% Depr., Dep., Amort./Sales		2.7	2.0	3.2	1.6	2.3
(96) 4.2	(93) 4.7	(109) 3.6			(12) 4.1	(17) 4.2	(25) 5.6	(21) 2.7	(32) 3.0
7.1	7.4	6.3			6.6	6.5	7.0	5.5	4.4
1.7	2.0	1.8	% Officers', Directors', Owners' Comp/Sales				1.8		
(33) 3.2	(30) 3.5	3.0					(13) 3.0		
6.2	5.9	5.3					5.6		
2500364M	3165747M	3730008M	Net Sales ($)	935M	24459M	70450M	213395M	356201M	3064568M
1665301M	1987542M	2320652M	Total Assets ($)	722M	14325M	50020M	125289M	209476M	1920820M

M = $ thousand   MM = $ million
See Pages 11 through 21 for Explanation of Ratios and Data

Current Data Sorted By Assets   **Comparative Historical Data**

0-500M	500M-2MM	2-10MM	10-50MM	50-100MM	100-250MM		ALL 4/1/00-3/31/01	ALL 4/1/01-3/31/02
						Type of Statement		
		9	19	6	5	Unqualified	25	32
	3	31	5			Reviewed	34	37
1	11	13				Compiled	32	40
7	2	3	1			Tax Returns	9	8
2	5	18	11	4	2	Other	36	45
	27 (4/1-9/30/04)		131 (10/1/04-3/31/05)					
10	21	74	36	10	7	**NUMBER OF STATEMENTS**	136	162
%	%	%	%	%	%	**ASSETS**	%	%
6.7	11.1	7.8	5.1	2.6		Cash & Equivalents	9.1	6.8
15.7	30.1	29.8	31.0	36.2		Trade Receivables (net)	29.6	30.0
19.4	11.5	15.3	16.5	9.4		Inventory	13.3	13.8
1.5	.7	1.8	3.9	4.8		All Other Current	3.6	3.4
43.2	53.4	54.7	56.5	53.1		Total Current	55.6	54.0
53.4	31.2	35.9	36.3	40.1		Fixed Assets (net)	37.4	36.8
2.3	5.0	3.1	2.4	3.4		Intangibles (net)	3.0	2.7
1.1	10.4	6.3	4.7	3.5		All Other Non-Current	4.0	6.4
100.0	100.0	100.0	100.0	100.0		Total	100.0	100.0
						LIABILITIES		
37.4	9.6	7.1	7.6	1.1		Notes Payable-Short Term	7.9	9.1
11.3	4.0	5.1	4.7	3.3		Cur. Mat.-L/T/D	4.3	4.7
8.8	15.1	13.4	15.8	14.3		Trade Payables	14.2	15.3
.0	.2	.4	.4	.8		Income Taxes Payable	.3	.2
4.8	9.0	7.6	7.2	11.9		All Other Current	10.5	10.5
62.3	37.9	33.7	35.7	31.5		Total Current	37.3	39.8
54.9	16.8	18.6	18.1	16.3		Long-Term Debt	22.4	21.0
.0	.3	.5	1.4	1.1		Deferred Taxes	.5	.6
29.4	4.1	5.7	5.6	9.2		All Other Non-Current	3.6	4.1
−46.6	40.9	41.5	39.2	41.8		Net Worth	36.3	34.4
100.0	100.0	100.0	100.0	100.0		Total Liabilities & Net Worth	100.0	100.0
						INCOME DATA		
100.0	100.0	100.0	100.0	100.0		Net Sales	100.0	100.0
57.1	38.8	31.1	20.2	16.7		Gross Profit	30.4	28.6
47.9	34.9	25.1	17.4	12.2		Operating Expenses	23.9	24.1
9.2	3.9	6.1	2.9	4.5		Operating Profit	6.5	4.6
1.3	.5	1.2	.7	1.2		All Other Expenses (net)	1.2	1.5
7.9	3.4	4.9	2.2	3.4		Profit Before Taxes	5.3	3.1
						RATIOS		
2.8	2.1	2.6	2.5	2.5			2.2	2.2
.8	1.6	1.7	1.7	2.0		Current	1.6	1.4
.3	1.2	1.2	1.2	1.3			1.1	1.0
1.2	1.9	1.7	1.5	2.0			1.6	1.4
.6	1.3	1.1	1.0	1.3		Quick	1.1	1.0
.1	.7	.7	.6	1.0			.7	.6
0 UND	26 14.2	42 8.7	56 6.5	48 7.7			32 11.3	34 10.7
19 19.2	35 10.5	57 6.4	62 5.9	65 5.6		Sales/Receivables	47 7.8	50 7.3
48 7.6	58 6.3	82 4.5	80 4.6	96 3.8			72 5.1	70 5.2
0 UND	14 26.7	19 19.6	20 18.4	7 51.2			11 34.5	10 38.2
39 9.4	23 15.8	43 8.5	51 7.2	11 34.5		Cost of Sales/Inventory	28 12.9	33 11.0
79 4.6	60 6.1	78 4.7	67 5.5	41 8.9			59 6.2	63 5.8
0 UND	15 23.9	22 16.8	23 15.6	24 15.4			19 19.0	22 16.9
21 17.5	28 12.8	36 10.2	39 9.3	32 11.4		Cost of Sales/Payables	31 11.7	33 11.1
31 11.7	57 6.4	53 6.9	57 6.4	39 9.4			46 8.0	49 7.4
6.6	7.2	4.3	4.3	5.4			6.0	6.8
−34.6	12.5	7.9	7.9	6.1		Sales/Working Capital	9.5	14.6
−14.1	381.0	21.7	18.1	18.0			57.6	−421.6
	12.1	22.9	9.1				9.1	7.1
	(20) 4.6	(70) 4.5	(32) 5.7			EBIT/Interest	(119) 2.9	(149) 3.0
	2.2	1.3	.7				1.5	1.4
		2.5	4.0				4.7	5.0
		(21) 1.9	(17) 1.9			Net Profit + Depr., Dep., Amort./Cur. Mat. L /T/D	(41) 2.1	(56) 2.4
		1.3	1.2				1.3	1.4
2.0	.3	.4	.7	.7			.5	.6
−1.5	.7	.9	1.0	1.0		Fixed/Worth	1.0	1.2
−.3	1.9	1.9	1.5	2.0			2.1	3.2
1.6	.7	.7	.8	.4			.8	1.0
−5.0	2.1	1.3	1.8	2.0		Debt/Worth	1.6	2.3
−1.8	3.1	3.7	3.4	3.5			3.9	5.4
	42.0	37.6	22.1				44.9	40.3
	(18) 11.7	(67) 16.1	(31) 14.7			% Profit Before Taxes/Tangible Net Worth	(121) 24.6	(144) 19.8
	7.1	4.0	6.5				9.4	8.3
16.0	11.0	17.4	8.3	16.0			17.8	12.4
6.6	5.1	6.7	4.9	6.1		% Profit Before Taxes/Total Assets	7.4	6.2
−20.1	2.5	1.4	−.4	1.6			2.2	1.4
21.8	27.3	10.5	7.1	6.9			12.5	10.1
9.6	9.7	5.2	5.2	4.7		Sales/Net Fixed Assets	5.7	6.0
1.8	5.6	3.3	2.7	3.4			3.5	3.8
5.3	3.3	2.4	2.1	2.1			2.6	2.6
2.6	2.7	1.8	1.6	1.8		Sales/Total Assets	2.0	2.0
1.3	1.7	1.3	1.2	1.3			1.5	1.5
	1.7	2.1	2.3				1.5	1.7
	(17) 2.3	(69) 4.2	(34) 3.2			% Depr., Dep., Amort./Sales	(129) 3.2	(146) 3.3
	5.5	6.1	4.1				4.9	4.8
	2.0	1.4					2.4	1.9
	(13) 5.9	(36) 2.9				% Officers', Directors', Owners' Comp/Sales	(43) 4.0	(60) 3.7
	10.4	4.2					6.3	8.1
6327M	63114M	691717M	1470471M	1293500M	2328333M	Net Sales ($)	2862304M	3283755M
2151M	25058M	366652M	886020M	691182M	1205734M	Total Assets ($)	1555730M	1945310M

Comparative Historical Data | Current Data Sorted By Sales

			Type of Statement	0-1MM	1-3MM	3-5MM	5-10MM	10-25MM	25MM & OVER
32	37	39	Unqualified			2	4	7	26
49	40	39	Reviewed		3	6	15	12	3
18	40	25	Compiled	2	10	4	7	2	
11	14	13	Tax Returns	5	3	2	1	2	
41	34	42	Other	2	3	4	8	12	13
4/1/02-3/31/03 ALL	4/1/03-3/31/04 ALL	4/1/04-3/31/05 ALL			27 (4/1-9/30/04)		131 (10/1/04-3/31/05)		
151	165	158	**NUMBER OF STATEMENTS**	9	19	18	35	35	42
%	%	%	**ASSETS**	%	%	%	%	%	%
7.2	8.1	6.8	Cash & Equivalents		8.1	7.0	9.7	8.2	2.3
28.9	29.2	29.0	Trade Receivables (net)		25.8	25.9	27.6	33.2	32.3
13.3	14.5	15.0	Inventory		15.3	14.1	15.1	12.6	17.5
3.8	3.3	3.0	All Other Current		1.1	1.6	1.5	4.4	5.0
53.2	55.2	53.9	Total Current		50.3	48.5	53.8	58.4	57.1
38.8	36.4	36.9	Fixed Assets (net)		36.2	32.8	40.4	31.4	35.7
2.0	1.8	3.2	Intangibles (net)		2.6	13.2	1.4	1.5	2.5
6.0	6.6	6.1	All Other Non-Current		10.9	5.4	4.4	8.7	4.7
100.0	100.0	100.0	Total		100.0	100.0	100.0	100.0	100.0
			LIABILITIES						
7.3	6.7	8.9	Notes Payable-Short Term		14.5	6.9	5.9	7.9	6.1
4.8	4.6	5.0	Cur. Mat.-L/T/D		5.4	6.7	4.0	6.3	3.4
14.2	14.1	13.8	Trade Payables		9.8	9.1	15.8	16.9	14.9
.3	.3	.4	Income Taxes Payable		.0	.3	.3	.6	.5
9.5	8.0	7.7	All Other Current		8.0	5.9	8.7	6.2	10.1
36.0	33.5	35.8	Total Current		37.7	29.0	34.7	37.8	35.1
22.4	19.6	21.1	Long-Term Debt		20.2	28.4	15.4	15.0	20.9
.3	.7	.7	Deferred Taxes		.3	.6	.4	1.5	.6
3.8	4.3	7.2	All Other Non-Current		9.6	9.6	4.9	5.7	4.5
37.4	41.9	35.1	Net Worth		32.2	32.5	44.6	39.9	38.8
100.0	100.0	100.0	Total Liabilities & Net Worth		100.0	100.0	100.0	100.0	100.0
			INCOME DATA						
100.0	100.0	100.0	Net Sales		100.0	100.0	100.0	100.0	100.0
31.0	31.5	30.2	Gross Profit		38.0	38.1	29.3	25.9	21.4
25.9	26.6	24.9	Operating Expenses		34.5	30.5	22.9	23.2	16.4
5.2	4.9	5.3	Operating Profit		3.5	7.6	6.4	2.7	5.0
.9	1.1	1.0	All Other Expenses (net)		1.2	1.9	1.3	.2	.9
4.2	3.8	4.3	Profit Before Taxes		2.3	5.7	5.1	2.5	4.1
			RATIOS						
2.6	2.6	2.5	Current		2.1	2.1	3.1	2.7	2.4
1.7	1.7	1.7			1.7	1.6	1.8	1.7	1.8
1.1	1.2	1.2			1.3	1.3	1.2	1.1	1.3
1.7	1.8	1.6	Quick		1.8	1.5	2.3	1.7	1.5
1.1	1.2 (157)	1.1			1.2	1.1	1.1	1.0 (41)	1.1
.6	.7	.7			.6	.6	.7	.8	.7
33 11.0	39 9.3	39 9.3	Sales/Receivables	30 12.1	25 14.4	35 10.5	44 8.3	49 7.5	
52 7.1	56 6.6	56 6.5		56 6.5	65 5.6	48 7.5	61 6.0	59 6.2	
76 4.8	74 4.9	72 5.1		64 5.7	86 4.2	64 5.7	83 4.4	69 5.3	
12 29.9	15 25.1	15 24.2	Cost of Sales/Inventory	23 15.7	20 17.9	19 19.5	8 44.7	16 22.8	
33 11.2	37 9.9	39 9.5		48 7.6	57 6.4	43 8.6	24 15.1	40 9.0	
68 5.3	69 5.3	67 5.5		88 4.2	87 4.2	67 5.4	48 7.5	65 5.6	
17 20.9	19 19.5	20 18.5	Cost of Sales/Payables	16 23.3	15 23.7	20 18.6	34 10.7	23 16.2	
29 12.4	32 11.3	33 11.0		24 15.4	30 12.3	33 11.0	42 8.6	29 12.5	
49 7.5	50 7.3	50 7.3		36 10.1	46 7.9	56 6.5	54 6.8	43 8.5	
5.3	5.3	5.2	Sales/Working Capital		4.4	4.4	4.0	4.3	5.5
9.5	8.1	8.6			9.2	8.9	8.2	9.3	8.1
46.1	21.3	24.0			25.7	20.3	25.2	45.9	16.5
10.0	13.1	10.4	EBIT/Interest		7.1	7.6	39.1	25.5	10.2
(133) 3.5	(155) 4.2	(145) 4.5		(17) 2.2	3.7	(33) 5.7	(33) 2.6	(37) 6.1	
1.4	1.0	1.5			1.2	2.4	1.4	.9	2.4
4.7	4.2	3.8	Net Profit + Depr., Dep., Amort./Cur. Mat. L/T/D					2.0	4.2
(52) 2.5	(50) 1.8	(48) 2.0					(12) 1.6	(18) 3.1	
1.4	.8	1.3						.7	1.7
.5	.4	.5	Fixed/Worth		.3	.7	.4	.4	.6
.9	.9	1.0			.7	1.4	1.0	.8	1.0
1.8	2.1	2.2			2.7	NM	1.6	1.7	1.4
.6	.6	.8	Debt/Worth		.6	1.3	.4	.7	.9
1.4	1.4	1.6			1.7	2.1	1.2	1.4	1.7
3.0	3.3	3.7			3.1	NM	3.2	3.7	2.8
38.8	37.1	34.9	% Profit Before Taxes/Tangible Net Worth		23.6	53.7	44.5	26.3	30.6
(140) 20.2	(149) 17.5	(135) 15.5		(16) 6.9	(14) 19.9	(32) 18.7	(30) 12.2	(38) 15.1	
7.2	4.1	4.7			1.8	7.9	4.5	4.8	5.4
14.6	14.3	13.7	% Profit Before Taxes/Total Assets		8.4	17.3	21.2	11.9	12.8
7.3	5.8	6.0			4.6	11.5	9.2	4.4	6.5
1.5	.1	1.7			.6	4.0	1.6	.2	2.2
8.5	11.0	9.9	Sales/Net Fixed Assets		13.5	25.1	8.8	11.8	7.3
4.9	5.4	5.5			6.3	5.3	5.1	7.9	5.5
3.0	3.2	3.2			3.0	2.4	3.0	3.7	4.3
2.4	2.4	2.4	Sales/Total Assets		3.3	2.4	2.5	2.6	2.2
1.9	1.9	1.8			1.7	1.5	1.8	2.0	1.9
1.4	1.3	1.3			1.2	1.1	1.4	1.4	1.6
2.1	2.2	2.1	% Depr., Dep., Amort./Sales		2.2	1.2	2.1	2.2	2.0
(139) 3.5	(148) 3.5	(138) 3.4		(17) 4.1	(17) 3.0	(33) 4.6	(32) 3.3	(33) 2.6	
5.4	5.4	5.4			6.2	5.6	6.7	5.4	3.4
1.6	2.0	1.5	% Officers', Directors', Owners' Comp/Sales		1.7		2.0	.6	
(56) 3.2	(60) 3.5	(60) 2.9			(14) 3.1	(14)	3.1	(15) 1.5	
7.0	6.9	5.4			8.2		4.4	2.1	
3074844M	4649120M	5853462M	Net Sales ($)	4813M	39925M	68381M	246561M	568298M	4925484M
1817536M	2826868M	3176797M	Total Assets ($)	2740M	27340M	50590M	156690M	341503M	2597934M

M = $ thousand   MM = $ million
See Pages 11 through 21 for Explanation of Ratios and Data

Current Data Sorted By Assets | Comparative Historical Data

0-500M	500M-2MM	2-10MM	10-50MM	50-100MM	100-250MM	Type of Statement	4/1/00-3/31/01 ALL	4/1/01-3/31/02 ALL
	3	5	4	3	1	Unqualified	12	9
1	5	9	2			Reviewed	7	13
	1	3				Compiled	14	26
						Tax Returns	1	6
	4	6	4	1		Other	7	30
	8 (4/1-9/30/04)		44 (10/1/04-3/31/05)					
1	13	23	10	4	1	**NUMBER OF STATEMENTS**	41	84
%	%	%	%	%	%	**ASSETS**	%	%
	9.9	4.5	6.3			Cash & Equivalents	4.6	7.1
	29.8	29.0	18.4			Trade Receivables (net)	24.9	25.4
	21.0	29.3	28.2			Inventory	25.2	25.1
	2.2	1.3	3.3			All Other Current	3.1	3.8
	62.9	64.1	56.1			Total Current	57.8	61.5
	30.4	31.2	25.9			Fixed Assets (net)	33.0	29.2
	1.8	1.2	6.5			Intangibles (net)	4.0	2.5
	4.9	3.5	11.5			All Other Non-Current	5.2	6.8
	100.0	100.0	100.0			Total	100.0	100.0
						LIABILITIES		
	15.1	10.6	3.3			Notes Payable-Short Term	12.0	12.1
	4.7	4.7	9.0			Cur. Mat.-L/T/D	3.9	5.2
	14.2	15.8	11.0			Trade Payables	14.0	12.2
	2.8	.8	.1			Income Taxes Payable	.3	.2
	4.0	8.1	9.9			All Other Current	8.3	6.4
	40.8	40.0	33.2			Total Current	38.5	36.1
	24.8	23.6	7.3			Long-Term Debt	24.1	15.3
	.1	.3	.7			Deferred Taxes	.4	.7
	1.2	3.7	9.3			All Other Non-Current	4.1	5.8
	33.0	32.4	49.4			Net Worth	32.8	42.2
	100.0	100.0	100.0			Total Liabilities & Net Worth	100.0	100.0
						INCOME DATA		
	100.0	100.0	100.0			Net Sales	100.0	100.0
	37.4	29.2	29.6			Gross Profit	30.1	29.0
	25.7	24.3	21.3			Operating Expenses	25.5	26.0
	11.7	4.9	8.3			Operating Profit	4.6	3.0
	1.8	.9	.9			All Other Expenses (net)	1.9	1.2
	9.9	4.0	7.5			Profit Before Taxes	2.7	1.8
						RATIOS		
	2.8	2.5	3.7				2.7	3.5
	2.2	1.6	2.0			Current	1.5	1.8
	.9	1.2	1.0				1.1	1.1
	1.5	1.3	1.4				1.8	1.8
	1.1	.8	1.0			Quick	.8	.9
	.6	.5	.4				.4	.5
	26 14.0	39 9.4	32 11.4				35 10.3	37 9.9
	50 7.3	48 7.6	35 10.3			Sales/Receivables	44 8.4	47 7.8
	68 5.3	58 6.3	50 7.3				60 6.1	60 6.1
	16 22.4	34 10.7	65 5.6				36 10.0	36 10.1
	87 4.2	72 5.1	80 4.6			Cost of Sales/Inventory	60 6.1	57 6.4
	117 3.1	98 3.7	115 3.2				89 4.1	102 3.6
	19 18.9	19 19.6	15 25.1				18 20.0	15 24.7
	35 10.6	38 9.6	26 13.9			Cost of Sales/Payables	31 11.8	24 14.9
	58 6.3	48 7.5	44 8.4				42 8.8	41 9.0
	4.4	4.8	3.7				6.0	4.2
	7.0	9.4	6.6			Sales/Working Capital	9.9	7.7
	−30.3	18.9	NM				42.8	38.4
	26.4	11.1	37.4				8.7	6.4
	(12) 6.2	(21) 5.2	13.7			EBIT/Interest	(40) 3.3	(74) 2.9
	2.7	2.4	5.0				.8	.4
						Net Profit + Depr., Dep., Amort./Cur. Mat. L /T/D		4.6
							(28) 1.6	
								.5
	.3	.3	.3				.6	.3
	1.1	.8	.6			Fixed/Worth	1.1	.7
	5.1	2.1	NM				2.5	2.1
	1.1	.7	.4				.8	.5
	3.3	2.9	1.0			Debt/Worth	2.2	1.4
	8.1	5.9	NM				7.8	4.8
	143.6	43.0					43.8	30.9
	(12) 97.0	(22) 25.1				% Profit Before Taxes/Tangible Net Worth	(37) 25.5	(77) 14.2
	33.8	9.5					2.8	−3.0
	31.5	13.6	18.1				11.8	12.3
	16.0	7.2	11.5			% Profit Before Taxes/Total Assets	6.7	4.4
	5.6	4.9	7.0				−1.2	−2.4
	20.3	12.2	11.1				11.0	12.9
	10.8	7.2	7.5			Sales/Net Fixed Assets	6.1	7.2
	2.8	3.9	4.4				3.7	3.6
	4.1	2.7	2.0				2.3	2.5
	2.5	1.9	1.9			Sales/Total Assets	1.8	1.9
	1.3	1.5	1.4				1.4	1.4
	1.3	1.2					2.1	1.6
	(11) 2.3	(21) 2.0				% Depr., Dep., Amort./Sales	(37) 3.1	(75) 2.5
	2.9	3.8					4.9	4.1
							3.6	3.5
						% Officers', Directors', Owners' Comp/Sales	(12) 6.8	(33) 5.4
							13.0	9.0
709M	35646M	236293M	476686M	276938M	133812M	Net Sales ($)	992258M	1596588M
246M	14427M	108993M	288168M	248039M	151865M	Total Assets ($)	710007M	996330M

M = $ thousand   MM = $ million
See Pages 11 through 21 for Explanation of Ratios and Data

Comparative Historical Data / Current Data Sorted By Sales

				Type of Statement	0-1MM	1-3MM	3-5MM	5-10MM	10-25MM	25MM & OVER
	8	11	13	Unqualified				1	5	7
	16	15	14	Reviewed		4	2	4	2	2
	3	5	9	Compiled	1	3		4	1	
	1	2	1	Tax Returns			1			
	7	9	15	Other	2	2	2	1	3	5
	4/1/02-3/31/03	4/1/03-3/31/04	4/1/04-3/31/05		8 (4/1-9/30/04)			44 (10/1/04-3/31/05)		
	ALL	ALL	ALL							
	35	42	52	**NUMBER OF STATEMENTS**	3	9	5	10	11	14
	%	%	%	**ASSETS**	%	%	%	%	%	%
	5.9	7.0	7.5	Cash & Equivalents				13.0	7.6	7.4
	24.7	28.5	25.5	Trade Receivables (net)				28.1	27.5	17.9
	24.7	27.2	25.7	Inventory				30.2	24.1	24.4
	4.7	1.9	2.6	All Other Current				1.6	1.1	5.2
	60.1	64.6	61.3	Total Current				72.8	60.4	54.9
	27.9	25.2	28.9	Fixed Assets (net)				18.8	34.4	25.0
	4.6	4.0	2.7	Intangibles (net)				1.2	1.0	6.4
	7.4	6.2	7.1	All Other Non-Current				7.1	4.2	13.7
	100.0	100.0	100.0	Total				100.0	100.0	100.0
				LIABILITIES						
	11.2	12.9	9.6	Notes Payable-Short Term				9.1	9.5	2.6
	7.4	5.6	5.6	Cur. Mat.-L/T/D				2.2	6.6	8.5
	14.2	17.6	13.8	Trade Payables				12.8	18.1	10.6
	.3	.5	1.1	Income Taxes Payable				3.2	1.3	.0
	6.0	7.2	6.9	All Other Current				9.9	7.0	8.4
	39.1	43.7	37.0	Total Current				37.2	42.4	30.2
	15.6	10.5	18.8	Long-Term Debt				21.0	16.5	7.8
	.4	.5	.4	Deferred Taxes				.0	.7	.7
	2.4	6.3	4.4	All Other Non-Current				4.6	3.8	7.7
	42.4	39.0	39.5	Net Worth				37.2	36.6	53.6
	100.0	100.0	100.0	Total Liabilities & Net Worth				100.0	100.0	100.0
				INCOME DATA						
	100.0	100.0	100.0	Net Sales				100.0	100.0	100.0
	30.5	28.8	30.9	Gross Profit				32.1	19.1	29.5
	24.9	24.1	23.6	Operating Expenses				28.6	15.0	20.8
	5.6	4.7	7.3	Operating Profit				3.5	4.1	8.8
	1.6	.9	.9	All Other Expenses (net)				.6	.7	.2
	4.0	3.7	6.4	Profit Before Taxes				2.9	3.4	8.5
				RATIOS						
	2.9	3.2	2.6	Current				3.5	2.6	3.7
	1.6	1.5	1.9					2.1	1.6	2.2
	1.0	1.1	1.2					1.4	1.1	1.2
	1.7	1.6	1.5	Quick				2.4	1.5	1.7
	.9	.9	.9					1.0	.8	1.1
	.5	.5	.6					.6	.6	.4
	35 10.5	38 9.7	34 10.7	Sales/Receivables	29 12.8			37 9.9		32 11.3
	46 7.9	50 7.3	47 7.7		46 8.0			45 8.2		42 8.6
	59 6.2	59 6.2	58 6.3		58 6.2			55 6.6		52 7.1
	39 9.4	49 7.4	48 7.6	Cost of Sales/Inventory	0 UND			26 14.0		56 6.6
	68 5.3	70 5.2	71 5.2		80 4.6			50 7.3		74 4.9
	84 4.4	92 4.0	105 3.5		110 3.3			62 5.9		115 3.2
	15 24.0	20 18.6	18 19.9	Cost of Sales/Payables	15 24.1			19 19.6		15 25.1
	27 13.6	36 10.2	35 10.5		22 16.4			38 9.6		28 13.2
	46 8.0	53 6.9	48 7.6		40 9.1			50 7.3		49 7.5
	4.4	4.6	4.7	Sales/Working Capital				4.6	5.0	3.7
	7.8	10.2	6.8					5.5	9.8	6.4
	148.9	42.0	20.7					12.7	88.5	191.9
	10.1	13.4	19.3	EBIT/Interest					8.8	77.2
	2.9 (41)	6.1 (49)	7.0						4.5	14.3
	1.3	1.5	2.7						2.2	5.7
	5.5	4.5	8.0	Net Profit + Depr., Dep.,						
	(11) 2.2	(16) 1.3	(15) 4.7	Amort./Cur. Mat. L/T/D						
	1.3	.4	.8							
	.4	.3	.3	Fixed/Worth				.1	.5	.3
	.8	.6	.7					.4	1.1	.4
	2.0	1.8	2.1					1.2	2.2	1.0
	.6	.5	.6	Debt/Worth				.5	.8	.4
	1.3	1.8	1.7					1.0	3.7	.8
	5.0	8.2	5.2					4.2	4.7	2.1
	32.3	35.5	63.9	% Profit Before Taxes/Tangible					55.3	43.8
	(33) 20.9	(38) 21.5	(48) 28.6	Net Worth					27.1	(12) 28.7
	1.7	4.7	13.2						9.8	12.6
	10.6	14.1	17.1	% Profit Before Taxes/Total				25.8	15.9	18.1
	6.3	4.9	9.2	Assets				6.7	6.7	11.5
	.8	1.0	5.9					−1.7	2.7	7.3
	9.7	12.6	12.1	Sales/Net Fixed Assets				UND	11.3	11.9
	6.8	7.5	8.4					12.6	7.1	7.5
	4.5	5.4	3.7					7.8	3.9	3.8
	2.3	2.3	2.6	Sales/Total Assets				3.3	2.8	2.0
	1.8	1.9	1.9					2.2	2.0	1.6
	1.4	1.4	1.4					1.7	1.7	1.2
	2.0	1.6	1.5	% Depr., Dep., Amort./Sales					1.4	2.1
	(33) 2.9	(41) 2.4	(46) 2.5						(10) 2.8	(12) 2.6
	4.2	3.6	4.0						5.5	4.0
	2.0	2.6	1.6	% Officers', Directors',						
	(12) 3.6	(10) 4.6	(12) 3.6	Owners' Comp/Sales						
	4.9	8.7	6.6							
	635832M	847687M	1160084M	Net Sales ($)	2339M	19139M	17001M	69472M	186439M	865694M
	492525M	589385M	811738M	Total Assets ($)	2053M	14300M	7556M	31373M	125217M	631239M

M = $ thousand   MM = $ million
See Pages 11 through 21 for Explanation of Ratios and Data

Current Data Sorted By Assets   Comparative Historical Data

						Type of Statement		
	2	7	2		1	Unqualified	6	9
1	4	15				Reviewed	10	16
5	13	9				Compiled	16	24
9	7	2	1			Tax Returns	14	7
3	16	16	5	1		Other	12	19
	17 (4/1-9/30/04)		102 (10/1/04-3/31/05)				4/1/00-3/31/01	4/1/01-3/31/02
0-500M	500M-2MM	2-10MM	10-50MM	50-100MM	100-250MM		ALL	ALL
18	42	49	8	1	1	NUMBER OF STATEMENTS	58	75
%	%	%	%	%	%	ASSETS	%	%
9.4	6.7	4.1				Cash & Equivalents	8.1	11.0
25.3	28.2	26.4				Trade Receivables (net)	22.3	22.2
25.3	22.9	26.8				Inventory	20.9	17.8
4.6	1.9	4.2				All Other Current	1.9	2.2
64.6	59.7	61.5				Total Current	53.2	53.2
28.7	31.2	32.6				Fixed Assets (net)	39.9	37.7
1.5	3.2	2.7				Intangibles (net)	1.8	3.1
5.1	5.8	3.2				All Other Non-Current	5.1	6.1
100.0	100.0	100.0				Total	100.0	100.0
						LIABILITIES		
10.4	12.3	13.2				Notes Payable-Short Term	10.0	6.8
5.1	7.2	4.0				Cur. Mat.-L/T/D	4.1	7.7
20.5	20.2	15.4				Trade Payables	14.5	12.3
.4	.3	.3				Income Taxes Payable	.3	.1
19.3	5.2	6.0				All Other Current	6.8	9.3
55.6	45.2	38.8				Total Current	35.8	36.2
22.5	21.1	19.0				Long-Term Debt	19.0	21.3
.0	.2	.5				Deferred Taxes	.3	.4
2.9	4.0	4.9				All Other Non-Current	4.0	5.6
19.0	29.6	36.8				Net Worth	40.9	36.5
100.0	100.0	100.0				Total Liabilities & Net Worth	100.0	100.0
						INCOME DATA		
100.0	100.0	100.0				Net Sales	100.0	100.0
43.5	36.6	30.7				Gross Profit	34.4	35.2
39.8	31.0	25.9				Operating Expenses	27.2	27.7
3.7	5.6	4.8				Operating Profit	7.2	7.5
.2	1.2	1.0				All Other Expenses (net)	.3	1.7
3.5	4.4	3.7				Profit Before Taxes	6.9	5.8
						RATIOS		
1.9	2.1	2.5					2.2	2.5
1.4	1.7	1.8				Current	1.6	1.4
.9	1.0	1.1					1.1	1.0
1.3	1.5	1.3					1.3	1.5
.7	.9	.8				Quick	.8	.8
.3	.4	.5					.5	.5
12 31.5	17 21.0	34 10.7					20 17.8	21 17.3
26 13.9	31 11.7	41 8.9				Sales/Receivables	35 10.5	34 10.8
58 6.3	45 8.2	57 6.4					47 7.8	42 8.7
12 31.2	19 19.5	28 13.0					20 18.3	13 27.0
51 7.2	44 8.3	52 7.0				Cost of Sales/Inventory	53 6.9	33 11.0
99 3.7	75 4.8	122 3.0					99 3.7	91 4.0
15 25.2	15 24.1	17 21.5					16 23.0	13 27.1
39 9.4	32 11.5	34 10.7				Cost of Sales/Payables	27 13.4	23 15.8
78 4.7	59 6.2	47 7.7					45 8.1	46 7.9
7.8	7.1	6.3					5.8	6.8
17.0	15.8	9.9				Sales/Working Capital	10.7	14.0
−84.1	−599.5	31.6					44.0	747.6
11.8	12.4	13.1					12.3	12.6
(12) 5.3	(37) 3.5	(48) 3.9				EBIT/Interest	(56) 4.1	(68) 2.8
2.2	.7	1.8					1.7	1.2
		8.1				Net Profit + Depr., Dep.,	9.8	4.1
	(14) 2.6					Amort./Cur. Mat. L /T/D	(17) 2.7	(19) 2.1
		.8					1.3	1.3
.4	.5	.4					.4	.5
.9	1.1	1.0				Fixed/Worth	.9	.9
NM	3.3	2.4					2.1	4.0
1.6	.9	.9					.6	.7
6.6	2.4	2.4				Debt/Worth	1.4	1.8
NM	7.8	4.1					3.5	6.4
183.7	59.7	49.1				% Profit Before Taxes/Tangible	54.1	56.2
(14) 93.4	(34) 20.2	(46) 26.3				Net Worth	(54) 24.3	(67) 28.8
20.3	1.0	7.9					8.9	10.5
26.7	17.0	20.5				% Profit Before Taxes/Total	22.9	22.8
8.9	6.5	5.6				Assets	8.6	7.6
.2	−1.0	1.9					2.4	1.4
40.5	17.0	17.3					13.5	12.8
17.8	11.5	7.8				Sales/Net Fixed Assets	6.6	6.2
3.9	5.7	4.3					2.6	3.4
4.4	3.9	2.8					3.0	3.0
2.6	2.9	2.1				Sales/Total Assets	2.2	2.3
1.8	1.9	1.5					1.4	1.4
.9	1.2	1.2					1.6	1.3
(11) 1.4	(33) 2.4	(44) 2.1				% Depr., Dep., Amort./Sales	(51) 2.7	(68) 2.7
3.8	4.0	3.5					5.1	4.8
2.9	3.3	1.2				% Officers', Directors',	1.9	2.6
(10) 6.8	(21) 4.4	(25) 2.4				Owners' Comp/Sales	(37) 4.4	(42) 4.1
13.8	5.6	4.3					6.9	6.2
17310M	140507M	439088M	391867M	237036M	147471M	Net Sales ($)	598417M	976144M
5743M	46159M	195279M	175772M	99693M	122451M	Total Assets ($)	496361M	610669M

M = $ thousand   MM = $ million
See Pages 11 through 21 for Explanation of Ratios and Data

Comparative Historical Data | Current Data Sorted By Sales

			Type of Statement	0-1MM	1-3MM	3-5MM	5-10MM	10-25MM	25MM & OVER
10	17	12	Unqualified		1	2	4	1	4
12	14	20	Reviewed	1	3	2	9	5	
12	18	27	Compiled	3	9	6	7	2	
16	21	19	Tax Returns	4	10	1	3		1
24	27	41	Other	5	7	11	8	7	3
4/1/02-3/31/03 ALL	4/1/03-3/31/04 ALL	4/1/04-3/31/05 ALL		17 (4/1-9/30/04)			102 (10/1/04-3/31/05)		
74	97	119	**NUMBER OF STATEMENTS**	13	30	22	31	15	8
%	%	%	**ASSETS**	%	%	%	%	%	%
5.4	10.3	5.9	Cash & Equivalents	3.0	7.8	8.3	5.2	2.2	
24.7	24.0	26.8	Trade Receivables (net)	21.1	23.8	29.9	27.4	28.6	
22.2	22.4	25.2	Inventory	20.2	26.5	24.9	25.1	31.4	
3.1	5.5	3.3	All Other Current	4.7	4.7	3.8	1.8	2.3	
55.5	62.2	61.1	Total Current	49.0	62.7	67.0	59.5	64.5	
36.3	32.1	31.3	Fixed Assets (net)	41.4	28.0	29.3	32.8	30.6	
2.0	2.1	3.1	Intangibles (net)	1.4	3.3	2.1	3.9	.7	
6.2	3.7	4.5	All Other Non-Current	8.1	6.1	1.6	3.7	4.1	
100.0	100.0	100.0	Total	100.0	100.0	100.0	100.0	100.0	
			LIABILITIES						
8.4	11.0	12.4	Notes Payable-Short Term	16.9	9.5	17.5	10.5	12.5	
4.8	4.2	5.1	Cur. Mat.-L/T/D	4.4	5.8	7.8	4.8	2.9	
20.0	12.9	18.4	Trade Payables	13.6	17.8	17.5	17.8	24.7	
.1	.3	.3	Income Taxes Payable	.5	.3	.2	.0	1.1	
9.4	8.7	7.8	All Other Current	18.2	8.4	6.2	5.3	5.6	
42.8	37.2	44.1	Total Current	53.6	41.7	49.1	38.4	46.9	
19.9	23.4	19.9	Long-Term Debt	22.6	27.2	15.6	19.4	14.7	
.3	.5	.3	Deferred Taxes	.0	.2	.1	.6	.4	
5.4	4.5	4.4	All Other Non-Current	2.4	5.7	2.0	5.4	4.7	
31.6	34.4	31.4	Net Worth	21.4	25.2	33.3	36.3	33.4	
100.0	100.0	100.0	Total Liabilities & Net Worth	100.0	100.0	100.0	100.0	100.0	
			INCOME DATA						
100.0	100.0	100.0	Net Sales	100.0	100.0	100.0	100.0	100.0	
36.5	38.3	34.7	Gross Profit	52.1	36.6	36.4	28.8	30.7	
32.2	31.4	29.7	Operating Expenses	47.2	32.1	30.3	24.6	24.6	
4.3	6.9	4.9	Operating Profit	4.9	4.5	6.1	4.2	6.1	
1.2	1.1	1.0	All Other Expenses (net)	2.0	1.0	.8	.8	.8	
3.0	5.9	3.9	Profit Before Taxes	2.9	3.5	5.3	3.4	5.3	
			RATIOS						
2.2	3.2	2.2		1.6	2.2	2.6	2.4	2.2	
1.6	2.0	1.6	Current	1.2	1.6	1.8	1.7	1.4	
1.0	1.4	1.1		.1	1.0	1.0	1.1	1.2	
1.2	1.8	1.3		.9	1.5	1.7	1.4	1.1	
.7	.9	.8	Quick	.3	.9	.8	.9	.9	
.4	.6	.5		.1	.4	.5	.5	.5	
23 16.1	21 17.5	25 14.6		3 113.5	17 21.7	26 13.8	23 16.0	32 11.5	
35 10.5	35 10.3	37 9.9	Sales/Receivables	28 13.1	36 10.0	43 8.6	36 10.1	36 10.0	
45 8.1	55 6.7	55 6.7		79 4.6	53 6.9	58 6.3	53 6.9	60 6.1	
17 21.8	26 13.8	23 15.8		0 UND	30 12.1	18 20.3	26 13.8	36 10.1	
44 8.2	49 7.5	52 7.0	Cost of Sales/Inventory	56 6.5	56 6.6	33 11.2	48 7.6	99 3.7	
95 3.8	87 4.2	97 3.8		199 1.8	74 4.9	144 2.5	73 5.0	142 2.6	
14 25.6	14 26.8	17 21.4		6 65.2	17 21.7	15 24.0	17 21.4	21 17.6	
27 13.8	24 15.0	34 10.6	Cost of Sales/Payables	63 5.8	40 9.1	30 12.0	33 10.9	36 10.1	
52 7.0	39 9.4	57 6.4		144 2.5	63 5.8	59 6.2	47 7.8	69 5.3	
7.0	4.8	7.0		6.5	6.2	4.4	7.2	8.3	
13.1	9.0	12.0	Sales/Working Capital	12.4	11.3	11.5	12.5	10.0	
UND	16.5	59.2		-4.9	118.1	UND	34.5	22.8	
11.6	12.6	11.0			7.9	47.4	10.2	18.1	
(70) 4.5	(86) 5.3	(107) 3.9	EBIT/Interest		(29) 2.9	(20) 2.3	(30) 4.0	(14) 6.1	
1.2	1.4	1.7			1.3	-.3	1.7	2.0	
5.8	5.4	6.7					8.1		
(17) 2.7	(23) 3.0	(23) 2.5	Net Profit + Depr., Dep., Amort./Cur. Mat. L/T/D				(10) 2.7		
1.0	1.1	1.4					.3		
.5	.3	.4		.7	.4	.2	.7	.3	
.9	.9	1.1	Fixed/Worth	3.1	.9	.9	1.5	1.3	
3.1	2.2	2.7		31.9	NM	2.5	2.4	1.9	
.9	.7	1.0		1.7	1.0	.7	.9	1.2	
2.1	1.4	2.4	Debt/Worth	6.1	3.3	2.0	2.6	2.0	
7.1	4.1	7.4		90.4	NM	5.6	4.1	4.5	
68.7	51.4	59.2		171.4	68.7	60.5	51.7	62.9	
(61) 24.2	(84) 19.0	(103) 22.6	% Profit Before Taxes/Tangible Net Worth	(11) 92.6	(23) 19.2	(20) 35.7	(28) 23.6	(14) 30.7	
7.9	10.0	5.7		1.6	5.0	.4	5.1	15.6	
19.7	23.6	20.2		13.2	15.4	23.5	16.8	21.8	
5.7	8.2	6.0	% Profit Before Taxes/Total Assets	8.5	4.5	5.9	6.5	10.5	
.7	2.1	.9		-4.8	.5	-3.5	1.6	2.2	
21.3	20.8	18.6		16.7	25.0	24.9	15.8	22.4	
7.0	8.4	10.0	Sales/Net Fixed Assets	3.8	13.1	11.4	9.9	7.8	
2.9	3.6	4.4		1.8	5.7	5.4	4.6	4.3	
3.7	3.2	3.5		2.0	3.7	3.7	3.8	2.8	
2.3	2.3	2.3	Sales/Total Assets	1.8	2.7	2.6	2.5	1.7	
1.4	1.4	1.6		.8	1.8	1.6	1.8	1.6	
1.9	1.4	2.2			1.2	.9	1.2	1.2	
(64) 3.1	(85) 3.1	(97) 2.2	% Depr., Dep., Amort./Sales		(25) 2.1	(17) 3.0	(28) 2.0	(12) 1.5	
6.8	5.0	3.8			4.0	4.1	3.9	2.9	
2.0	2.5	2.2				3.2	1.4		
(43) 4.2	(53) 4.3	(58) 3.8	% Officers', Directors', Owners' Comp/Sales			(21) 4.6	(17) 2.4		
6.9	7.6	5.7				9.7	4.6		
1120953M	1068163M	1373279M	Net Sales ($)	6479M	61524M	82275M	228961M	224005M	770035M
493389M	597199M	645097M	Total Assets ($)	6464M	29912M	39392M	99672M	120866M	348791M

M = $ thousand   MM = $ million
See Pages 11 through 21 for Explanation of Ratios and Data

Current Data Sorted By Assets   **Comparative Historical Data**

						Type of Statement		
		2	2	1	1	Unqualified		
	2	4	5			Reviewed		
1	1	2				Compiled		
	1	2				Tax Returns		
						Other	4/1/00-3/31/01 ALL	4/1/01-3/31/02 ALL
0-500M	3 (4/1-9/30/04) 500M-2MM	2-10MM	21 (10/1/04-3/31/05) 10-50MM	50-100MM	100-250MM			
1	4	10	7	1	1	NUMBER OF STATEMENTS		
%	%	%	%	%	%		%	%
		17.2				Cash & Equivalents	D	D
		24.9				Trade Receivables (net)	A	A
		17.0				Inventory	T	T
		.5				All Other Current	A	A
		59.5				Total Current		
		31.1				Fixed Assets (net)	N	N
		4.9				Intangibles (net)	O	O
		4.4				All Other Non-Current	T	T
		100.0				Total		
						LIABILITIES	A	A
		5.7				Notes Payable-Short Term	V	V
		3.2				Cur. Mat.-L/T/D	A	A
		9.4				Trade Payables	I	I
		.3				Income Taxes Payable	L	L
		6.1				All Other Current	A	A
		24.7				Total Current	B	B
		13.5				Long-Term Debt	L	L
		.0				Deferred Taxes	E	E
		4.8				All Other Non-Current		
		57.0				Net Worth		
		100.0				Total Liabilities & Net Worth		
						INCOME DATA		
		100.0				Net Sales		
		37.3				Gross Profit		
		30.8				Operating Expenses		
		6.5				Operating Profit		
		.4				All Other Expenses (net)		
		6.2				Profit Before Taxes		
						RATIOS		
		5.4						
		2.5				Current		
		1.6						
		3.5						
		2.3				Quick		
		1.2						
	30	12.3						
	41	9.0				Sales/Receivables		
	49	7.5						
	17	21.7						
	39	9.4				Cost of Sales/Inventory		
	106	3.5						
	17	21.2						
	23	15.8				Cost of Sales/Payables		
	30	12.1						
		2.9						
		7.2				Sales/Working Capital		
		18.0						
						EBIT/Interest		
						Net Profit + Depr., Dep., Amort./Cur. Mat. L /T/D		
		.3						
		.7				Fixed/Worth		
		1.5						
		.3						
		.8				Debt/Worth		
		3.5						
		44.0				% Profit Before Taxes/Tangible		
		22.4				Net Worth		
		11.3						
		18.0				% Profit Before Taxes/Total		
		10.5				Assets		
		5.5						
		12.4						
		7.3				Sales/Net Fixed Assets		
		3.0						
		2.8						
		2.2				Sales/Total Assets		
		1.3						
		1.8						
		3.9				% Depr., Dep., Amort./Sales		
		6.7						
						% Officers', Directors', Owners' Comp/Sales		
736M	9930M	98638M	241060M	130634M	211354M	Net Sales ($)		
446M	4029M	48330M	116183M	63513M	184150M	Total Assets ($)		

M = $ thousand   MM = $ million
See Pages 11 through 21 for Explanation of Ratios and Data

Comparative Historical Data / Current Data Sorted By Sales

				Type of Statement						
3		5	6	Unqualified		2	2	2	2	4
11		15	11	Reviewed					3	2
3		3	4	Compiled	1		2	2	1	
1		3	3	Tax Returns		1	1	1		
11		6		Other				2		
4/1/02- 3/31/03 ALL		4/1/03- 3/31/04 ALL	4/1/04- 3/31/05 ALL		0-1MM	3 (4/1-9/30/04) 1-3MM	3-5MM	21 (10/1/04-3/31/05) 5-10MM	10-25MM	25MM & OVER
29		32	24	**NUMBER OF STATEMENTS**	1	3	3	5	6	6
%		%	%	**ASSETS**	%	%	%	%	%	%
9.3		10.0	10.7	Cash & Equivalents						
25.8		23.1	26.7	Trade Receivables (net)						
17.8		13.8	16.8	Inventory						
3.3		2.4	.9	All Other Current						
56.3		49.4	55.1	Total Current						
33.1		39.3	34.4	Fixed Assets (net)						
3.5		2.9	3.6	Intangibles (net)						
7.1		8.4	6.9	All Other Non-Current						
100.0		100.0	100.0	Total						
				LIABILITIES						
8.9		5.8	5.2	Notes Payable-Short Term						
6.0		3.9	5.8	Cur. Mat.-L/T/D						
13.8		10.1	11.0	Trade Payables						
.1		.3	.5	Income Taxes Payable						
8.0		6.8	5.8	All Other Current						
36.9		26.9	28.3	Total Current						
12.5		19.2	20.5	Long-Term Debt						
1.8		1.9	1.2	Deferred Taxes						
3.3		5.8	4.8	All Other Non-Current						
45.5		46.1	45.2	Net Worth						
100.0		100.0	100.0	Total Liabilities & Net Worth						
				INCOME DATA						
100.0		100.0	100.0	Net Sales						
36.8		34.1	36.7	Gross Profit						
28.8		31.1	27.1	Operating Expenses						
7.9		3.0	9.6	Operating Profit						
.6		.8	.9	All Other Expenses (net)						
7.3		2.1	8.7	Profit Before Taxes						
				RATIOS						
2.7		3.0	3.2							
1.6		1.6	1.7	Current						
1.2		1.2	1.3							
1.8		2.5	2.3							
1.1		1.1	1.2	Quick						
.6		.7	.7							
30 12.2	36	10.0	32 11.4							
45 8.0	47	7.8	42 8.7	Sales/Receivables						
71 5.2	73	5.0	58 6.3							
26 14.2	17	21.9	16 23.0							
48 7.6	34	10.7	35 10.5	Cost of Sales/Inventory						
78 4.7	79	4.6	98 3.7							
20 18.6	12	29.5	18 20.0							
33 11.0	33	11.2	27 13.8	Cost of Sales/Payables						
50 7.3	41	9.0	43 8.5							
5.0		5.0	5.0							
10.4		8.6	12.2	Sales/Working Capital						
41.2		29.8	24.1							
12.2		8.9	23.0							
(28) 5.1	(28)	4.1	(23) 7.8	EBIT/Interest						
2.8		1.1	3.0							
		6.1	7.4	Net Profit + Depr., Dep.,						
	(10)	3.2	(10) 3.6	Amort./Cur. Mat. L/T/D						
		2.4	1.8							
.4		.5	.5							
.7		.9	1.0	Fixed/Worth						
1.5		1.7	1.6							
.6		.6	.6							
1.1		1.2	1.5	Debt/Worth						
3.5		3.0	3.5							
36.7		34.5	41.8	% Profit Before Taxes/Tangible						
(26) 21.0	(30)	15.0	(23) 25.4	Net Worth						
8.2		-2.5	14.9							
14.7		13.4	20.7	% Profit Before Taxes/Total						
8.4		3.9	10.2	Assets						
3.9		-2.8	6.4							
16.0		6.9	9.6							
6.1		4.8	6.5	Sales/Net Fixed Assets						
3.5		2.3	4.1							
3.0		2.1	2.7							
2.0		1.5	2.1	Sales/Total Assets						
1.2		1.2	1.5							
1.2		2.3	2.2							
(26) 3.2	(30)	4.0	(22) 3.2	% Depr., Dep., Amort./Sales						
5.5		6.1	5.2							
2.0		2.7	2.8							
(10) 2.8	(12)	4.3	(10) 5.2	% Officers', Directors', Owners' Comp/Sales						
8.9		9.0	14.2							
767456M		394483M	692352M	Net Sales ($)	736M	6779M	10986M	41605M	114507M	517739M
607594M		323775M	416651M	Total Assets ($)	446M	2735M	7959M	18754M	55333M	331424M

M = $ thousand   MM = $ million
See Pages 11 through 21 for Explanation of Ratios and Data

Current Data Sorted By Assets

Comparative Historical Data

0-500M	500M-2MM	2-10MM	10-50MM	50-100MM	100-250MM	Type of Statement	4/1/00-3/31/01	4/1/01-3/31/02
		5	10	3	2	Unqualified	23	26
	5	22	5	1		Reviewed	15	12
1	10	6				Compiled	8	19
6	4	1				Tax Returns	6	1
1	9	13	6	3	3	Other	28	33
	24 (4/1-9/30/04)		92 (10/1/04-3/31/05)				ALL	ALL
8	28	47	21	7	5	NUMBER OF STATEMENTS	80	91
%	%	%	%	%	%	ASSETS	%	%
	9.6	4.4	1.5			Cash & Equivalents	5.2	4.5
	43.9	34.9	25.1			Trade Receivables (net)	25.2	26.1
	17.0	24.1	29.4			Inventory	20.4	22.0
	1.7	3.6	.9			All Other Current	2.7	3.1
	72.1	67.0	56.9			Total Current	53.4	55.6
	21.3	26.2	29.8			Fixed Assets (net)	35.5	33.4
	.4	2.1	4.6			Intangibles (net)	3.5	2.6
	6.2	4.7	8.7			All Other Non-Current	7.7	8.4
	100.0	100.0	100.0			Total	100.0	100.0
						LIABILITIES		
	10.8	16.6	12.3			Notes Payable-Short Term	9.3	11.7
	4.9	3.2	2.5			Cur. Mat.-L/T/D	4.5	4.0
	25.2	22.1	16.0			Trade Payables	14.6	14.5
	.3	.2	.7			Income Taxes Payable	.5	.4
	5.6	9.7	7.5			All Other Current	8.3	9.6
	46.8	51.8	39.1			Total Current	37.2	40.2
	15.0	12.3	13.0			Long-Term Debt	21.6	17.4
	.5	.6	.5			Deferred Taxes	.9	.7
	2.2	7.1	14.5			All Other Non-Current	6.0	3.5
	35.5	28.2	32.9			Net Worth	34.4	38.2
	100.0	100.0	100.0			Total Liabilities & Net Worth	100.0	100.0
						INCOME DATA		
	100.0	100.0	100.0			Net Sales	100.0	100.0
	27.8	24.6	18.4			Gross Profit	22.1	22.1
	23.9	21.0	11.2			Operating Expenses	17.6	18.4
	3.9	3.6	7.2			Operating Profit	4.5	3.7
	1.1	1.0	.8			All Other Expenses (net)	2.5	1.7
	2.8	2.6	6.4			Profit Before Taxes	2.0	2.0
						RATIOS		
	3.6	1.8	2.1			Current	2.1	2.3
	1.5	1.3	1.5				1.4	1.4
	1.1	1.1	1.1				1.0	1.0
	2.1	1.1	.9			Quick	1.3	1.2
	1.2	.7	.7				.8	.8
	.7	.6	.6				.5	.4
	(39) 9.3	(42) 8.7	(34) 10.9			Sales/Receivables	(36) 10.0	(35) 10.4
	(51) 7.2	(53) 6.9	(45) 8.1				(49) 7.4	(47) 7.7
	(85) 4.3	(63) 5.8	(54) 6.7				(59) 6.1	(59) 6.2
	(2) 152.0	(28) 12.8	(43) 8.6			Cost of Sales/Inventory	(22) 16.6	(24) 15.2
	(23) 15.6	(54) 6.8	(61) 6.0				(57) 6.4	(55) 6.6
	(71) 5.1	(70) 5.2	(75) 4.9				(82) 4.5	(91) 4.0
	(19) 19.1	(23) 15.7	(18) 20.5			Cost of Sales/Payables	(23) 15.6	(14) 25.3
	(42) 8.6	(43) 8.4	(29) 12.7				(37) 9.8	(33) 11.0
	(59) 6.2	(61) 5.9	(49) 7.4				(53) 6.9	(46) 7.9
	4.8	8.6	6.5			Sales/Working Capital	5.7	5.2
	12.5	17.0	11.4				12.3	11.7
	68.1	48.5	51.6				93.0	999.8
	19.6	7.5	23.2			EBIT/Interest	5.0	4.8
	(26) 4.8	(45) 3.5	(20) 8.6				(71) 2.3	(81) 2.1
	1.5	1.3	3.7				.9	.6
		16.7	55.7			Net Profit + Depr., Dep., Amort./Cur. Mat. L/T/D	3.4	7.9
		(12) 2.4	(10) 4.5				(21) 1.7	(18) 2.0
		.9	1.8				.9	1.0
	.1	.5	.4			Fixed/Worth	.6	.4
	.4	.9	1.1				1.2	.8
	3.3	1.5	2.0				3.5	1.6
	.4	1.4	1.2			Debt/Worth	.9	.9
	2.2	2.6	2.2				2.2	1.9
	8.1	7.0	5.0				7.8	4.5
	68.3	46.9	77.9			% Profit Before Taxes/Tangible Net Worth	27.7	28.2
	(25) 28.0	(42) 20.2	(18) 40.0				(69) 9.2	(83) 13.3
	8.9	4.3	25.5				.0	-2.3
	17.5	11.9	20.5			% Profit Before Taxes/Total Assets	8.9	10.4
	9.5	3.8	12.2				3.9	3.9
	2.0	.3	5.2				-.7	-1.3
	46.1	17.9	17.5			Sales/Net Fixed Assets	9.6	15.8
	15.1	10.2	6.4				5.3	6.2
	9.7	4.2	4.6				2.9	3.1
	3.9	2.9	3.0			Sales/Total Assets	2.4	2.5
	3.0	2.4	2.0				1.7	1.9
	1.7	1.4	1.5				1.2	1.2
	.5	1.1	1.0			% Depr., Dep., Amort./Sales	1.6	1.0
	(23) 2.6	(44) 2.0	1.9				(65) 3.0	(77) 2.6
	5.3	3.0	2.7				5.4	4.5
	2.7	1.0				% Officers', Directors', Owners' Comp/Sales	1.9	2.3
	(13) 3.5	(22) 3.1					(17) 4.9	(25) 3.3
	9.6	4.2					7.3	7.8
9331M	91742M	532202M	1033943M	1387487M	1611243M	Net Sales ($)	3626800M	4549108M
2263M	32805M	241759M	471224M	522173M	692343M	Total Assets ($)	2874293M	3244067M

M = $ thousand MM = $ million
See Pages 11 through 21 for Explanation of Ratios and Data

Comparative Historical Data | Current Data Sorted By Sales

				Type of Statement						
17		19	20	Unqualified				2	2	16
14		24	33	Reviewed		1	6	8	11	7
11		13	17	Compiled		6	6	2	2	
4		12	11	Tax Returns	1	6	6	2	2	
25		37	35	Other	3	5	1	1	1	
					1	7	1	4	12	10
4/1/02- 3/31/03		4/1/03- 3/31/04	4/1/04- 3/31/05			24 (4/1-9/30/04)			92 (10/1/04-3/31/05)	
ALL		ALL	ALL		0-1MM	1-3MM	3-5MM	5-10MM	10-25MM	25MM & OVER
71		105	116	**NUMBER OF STATEMENTS**	5	19	14	17	28	33
%		%	%	**ASSETS**	%	%	%	%	%	%
5.7		8.0	5.2	Cash & Equivalents		12.2	5.6	7.1	3.2	1.5
27.0		28.3	33.0	Trade Receivables (net)		35.1	38.8	35.8	38.1	25.6
20.3		20.0	24.9	Inventory		18.1	18.6	21.9	24.6	35.6
3.8		2.4	2.3	All Other Current		.7	1.9	4.3	3.5	1.5
56.8		58.7	65.4	Total Current		66.1	64.9	69.2	69.3	64.2
32.5		29.4	26.1	Fixed Assets (net)		24.6	24.7	25.5	24.3	25.6
2.6		3.4	2.5	Intangibles (net)		4.4	.3	.1	3.2	2.8
8.0		8.6	6.0	All Other Non-Current		4.9	10.0	5.2	3.3	7.4
100.0		100.0	100.0	Total		100.0	100.0	100.0	100.0	100.0
				LIABILITIES						
11.2		10.2	14.4	Notes Payable-Short Term		11.8	14.4	14.1	16.7	13.7
4.0		2.6	3.8	Cur. Mat.-L/T/D		2.8	3.1	5.3	2.9	2.0
15.6		17.7	20.8	Trade Payables		16.3	23.3	24.5	23.1	18.7
.3		.6	.3	Income Taxes Payable		.3	.0	.0	.3	.6
8.8		11.3	8.1	All Other Current		8.5	7.5	7.7	9.9	7.5
39.9		42.4	47.3	Total Current		39.5	48.4	51.5	52.9	42.6
16.5		15.2	13.8	Long-Term Debt		22.2	10.7	16.6	10.5	9.5
.4		.7	.7	Deferred Taxes		.7	.0	1.1	.4	1.0
6.1		9.5	6.7	All Other Non-Current		2.1	2.8	9.0	6.3	10.7
37.1		32.2	31.6	Net Worth		35.4	38.1	21.8	29.9	36.3
100.0		100.0	100.0	Total Liabilities & Net Worth		100.0	100.0	100.0	100.0	100.0
				INCOME DATA						
100.0		100.0	100.0	Net Sales		100.0	100.0	100.0	100.0	100.0
24.9		23.0	24.3	Gross Profit		36.5	24.0	22.0	24.7	17.2
20.3		21.3	19.4	Operating Expenses		32.6	21.4	17.9	20.5	9.2
4.7		1.7	4.8	Operating Profit		3.9	2.6	4.1	4.3	7.9
.8		.6	.9	All Other Expenses (net)		.9	1.1	.6	.8	.6
3.8		1.1	3.9	Profit Before Taxes		3.0	1.5	3.4	3.5	7.3
				RATIOS						
2.4		2.5	2.1			3.4	2.3	2.4	1.8	2.0
1.6		1.4	1.4	Current		1.6	1.3	1.1	1.3	1.6
1.0		1.0	1.1			1.2	.7	1.0	1.1	1.2
1.4		1.3	1.2			2.9	1.7	1.4	1.2	.9
.9		.8	.7	Quick		1.0	.8	.7	.8	.7
.5		.6	.6			.7	.6	.6	.5	.5
37 9.9	34	10.6	34 10.6		34 10.9	35 10.5	40 9.1	41 8.9	30 12.3	
47 7.7	48	7.6	49 7.5	Sales/Receivables	47 7.7	53 6.9	49 7.4	53 6.9	42 8.7	
57 6.5	63	5.8	62 5.9		83 4.4	75 4.8	63 5.8	60 6.1	52 7.0	
16 23.5	15	23.7	21 17.1		8 43.0	0 UND	17 21.0	25 14.9	46 7.9	
50 7.4	43	8.4	53 6.9	Cost of Sales/Inventory	30 12.3	31 11.8	48 7.6	53 6.9	64 5.7	
92 4.0	80	4.5	74 4.9		82 4.4	96 3.8	69 5.3	66 5.5	79 4.6	
20 18.0	18	20.2	20 18.2		13 29.0	18 20.8	17 21.9	23 15.7	23 15.8	
33 11.2	35	10.3	37 9.9	Cost of Sales/Payables	40 9.0	38 9.7	41 8.8	40 9.0	31 11.6	
50 7.3	52	7.1	56 6.5		52 7.1	55 6.6	68 5.4	60 6.0	48 7.6	
4.5		4.9	6.8			4.0	5.4	4.6	8.8	6.7
11.3		12.6	15.5	Sales/Working Capital		12.0	14.4	26.6	16.0	10.1
-154.9		-238.3	52.5			43.9	-36.8	NM	48.4	24.7
10.4		9.0	12.8			5.6	27.6	11.0	9.9	38.0
(65) 3.6	(91)	2.9	(109) 5.0	EBIT/Interest	(16) 3.8	1.8	(16) 3.0	(27) 5.3	(31) 9.5	
.7		-.6	1.8			1.0	.3	1.2	2.5	4.3
		9.3	15.5							27.9
	(22)	4.5	(27) 3.9	Net Profit + Depr., Dep., Amort./Cur. Mat. L/T/D					(12) 5.3	
		1.7	1.7							2.0
.4		.4	.3			.2	.3	.4	.5	.2
.9		.8	.8	Fixed/Worth		.5	.6	.9	.8	.7
2.1		2.6	2.1			2.8	2.7	14.9	1.7	1.5
.6		.8	1.0			.4	.7	1.6	1.5	1.0
2.2		2.4	2.5	Debt/Worth		2.0	1.8	5.0	2.8	1.7
4.6		9.4	7.5			7.9	8.8	39.6	5.8	4.3
51.6		36.3	65.6	% Profit Before Taxes/Tangible Net Worth		29.5	41.6	116.0	52.9	83.0
(65) 24.3	(91)	6.9	(101) 30.3		(17) 12.7	(12) 9.7	(14) 38.3	(26) 32.8	(29) 40.2	
3.7		-5.0	12.6			2.8	-4.1	5.4	13.9	25.1
16.4		8.1	18.1	% Profit Before Taxes/Total Assets		11.3	11.8	17.7	12.9	27.0
6.3		2.7	8.9			3.6	3.2	9.6	7.1	12.7
-.6		-3.6	1.5			.5	-2.0	.5	1.7	6.1
14.4		18.5	24.4	Sales/Net Fixed Assets		27.0	29.9	42.4	19.9	23.1
6.6		8.3	10.9			15.5	11.9	12.6	12.1	9.8
3.0		3.6	5.4			6.5	3.4	4.3	8.6	5.3
2.7		3.0	3.2	Sales/Total Assets		3.9	4.0	3.2	2.9	3.1
1.9		2.1	2.5			2.9	2.3	2.5	2.5	2.2
1.3		1.3	1.6			1.6	1.3	1.3	2.1	1.6
1.5		1.1	1.1	% Depr., Dep., Amort./Sales		1.4	.7	.5	1.1	1.0
(63) 2.9	(89)	2.5	(107) 2.2		(16) 3.1	(12) 2.6	(15) 2.3	(27) 1.5	(32) 1.9	
5.0		4.4	3.3			5.4	3.1	4.5	2.7	2.6
1.0		1.5	1.2	% Officers', Directors', Owners' Comp/Sales		2.7			.7	
(22) 1.9	(36)	2.4	(43) 3.3		(10) 7.9			(13) 3.4		
4.0		4.3	6.3			12.2			5.6	
2363486M 1576547M		3117697M 1875985M	4665948M 1962567M	Net Sales ($) Total Assets ($)	4205M 2964M	36716M 16511M	54152M 26167M	119555M 65398M	395707M 176451M	4055613M 1675076M

M = $ thousand   MM = $ million
See Pages 11 through 21 for Explanation of Ratios and Data

Current Data Sorted By Assets   Comparative Historical Data

0-500M	500M-2MM	2-10MM	10-50MM	50-100MM	100-250MM		ALL 55 4/1/00-3/31/01	ALL 65 4/1/01-3/31/02
						Type of Statement		
		4	10	4	4	Unqualified	11	13
1	2	8	6			Reviewed	8	9
	3	3	3			Compiled	8	7
4	1	1				Tax Returns	1	2
	3	10	9	2	1	Other	27	34
	14 (4/1-9/30/04)		65 (10/1/04-3/31/05)					
5	9	26	28	6	5	**NUMBER OF STATEMENTS**	55	65
%	%	%	%	%	%		%	%
						ASSETS		
		3.3	2.2			Cash & Equivalents	4.1	4.0
		37.1	31.5			Trade Receivables (net)	28.6	26.1
		31.6	37.9			Inventory	28.9	27.3
		2.9	2.3			All Other Current	1.8	2.1
		74.9	73.9			Total Current	63.4	59.4
		20.6	19.0			Fixed Assets (net)	29.1	31.7
		1.2	.9			Intangibles (net)	1.9	1.8
		3.4	6.2			All Other Non-Current	5.5	7.1
		100.0	100.0			Total	100.0	100.0
						LIABILITIES		
		18.6	17.7			Notes Payable-Short Term	12.9	13.0
		1.3	4.0			Cur. Mat.-L/T/D	3.1	3.5
		18.5	15.8			Trade Payables	18.0	13.7
		.3	.3			Income Taxes Payable	.3	.6
		8.2	8.5			All Other Current	9.5	8.8
		46.9	46.3			Total Current	43.9	39.6
		9.6	9.4			Long-Term Debt	17.2	15.5
		.5	.7			Deferred Taxes	.8	.8
		3.9	4.4			All Other Non-Current	6.4	7.0
		39.2	39.1			Net Worth	31.7	36.4
		100.0	100.0			Total Liabilities & Net Worth	100.0	100.0
						INCOME DATA		
		100.0	100.0			Net Sales	100.0	100.0
		21.3	22.6			Gross Profit	19.4	21.2
		15.9	13.4			Operating Expenses	15.0	17.1
		5.4	9.3			Operating Profit	4.4	4.0
		.7	.8			All Other Expenses (net)	1.2	1.2
		4.7	8.5			Profit Before Taxes	3.2	2.8
						RATIOS		
		2.6	2.3				2.3	2.4
		1.5	1.6			Current	1.6	1.5
		1.1	1.2				1.0	1.1
		1.3	1.0				1.1	1.2
		.9	.7			Quick	.7	.8
		.6	.5				.5	.5
		41 9.0	46 7.9				37 10.0	33 11.0
		50 7.2	57 6.4			Sales/Receivables	47 7.8	46 7.9
		68 5.4	82 4.4				61 6.0	56 6.5
		39 9.3	62 5.9				41 8.9	32 11.3
		71 5.1	83 4.4			Cost of Sales/Inventory	64 5.7	59 6.2
		104 3.5	123 3.0				101 3.6	92 4.0
		22 16.3	11 32.6				17 21.2	18 20.1
		40 9.1	25 14.4			Cost of Sales/Payables	29 12.4	29 12.6
		55 6.6	50 7.3				58 6.3	46 8.0
		4.6	4.0				5.2	5.0
		7.8	7.1			Sales/Working Capital	10.6	10.5
		33.8	13.9				197.4	115.3
		10.5	29.4				8.1	9.3
		(23) 5.2	(25) 7.1			EBIT/Interest	(54) 3.9	(64) 2.5
		2.3	4.0				1.1	.5
							6.7	4.4
						Net Profit + Depr., Dep., Amort./Cur. Mat. L./T/D	(14) 4.3	(21) 2.4
							1.9	1.2
		.2	.1				.3	.4
		.5	.4			Fixed/Worth	.9	1.0
		1.0	.7				2.2	2.0
		1.0	.8				.9	.8
		1.8	1.6			Debt/Worth	1.9	1.9
		2.9	5.2				5.8	4.3
		42.3	60.0				47.2	41.0
		(25) 20.2	(27) 37.3			% Profit Before Taxes/Tangible Net Worth	(51) 21.2	(60) 19.8
		7.6	18.5				5.1	1.1
		15.8	21.8				14.2	14.2
		7.9	10.3			% Profit Before Taxes/Total Assets	6.9	4.8
		2.9	5.9				.6	−1.6
		31.5	46.9				19.2	13.3
		15.8	14.3			Sales/Net Fixed Assets	7.0	5.8
		5.5	4.8				4.2	3.8
		2.8	2.4				2.5	2.5
		2.4	1.9			Sales/Total Assets	2.1	2.0
		1.5	1.4				1.6	1.5
		.7	.5				.7	1.2
		(22) 1.6	(27) 1.8			% Depr., Dep., Amort./Sales	(49) 1.9	(57) 2.9
		3.8	3.0				3.2	4.3
		2.0					1.1	1.8
		(11) 3.8				% Officers', Directors', Owners' Comp/Sales	(17) 2.8	(13) 3.9
		7.6					7.4	8.7
5624M	27496M	338503M	1149101M	674058M	1304159M	Net Sales ($)	2535239M	3540742M
1096M	10066M	132436M	616687M	396124M	702835M	Total Assets ($)	1563464M	2159538M

Comparative Historical Data | Current Data Sorted By Sales

20	27	22	Type of Statement				3	4	15
13	29	17	Unqualified			5	2	8	2
9	19	9	Reviewed		1	1	2	3	2
7	4	6	Compiled	3	2		1		
24	25	25	Tax Returns		2		4	10	9
4/1/02-	4/1/03-	4/1/04-	Other						
3/31/03	3/31/04	3/31/05		14 (4/1-9/30/04)			65 (10/1/04-3/31/05)		
ALL	ALL	ALL		0-1MM	1-3MM	3-5MM	5-10MM	10-25MM	25MM & OVER
73	104	79	NUMBER OF STATEMENTS	3	5	6	12	25	28

%	%	%	ASSETS	%	%	%	%	%	%
6.2	5.2	4.6	Cash & Equivalents				2.6	3.7	2.7
30.4	31.5	31.3	Trade Receivables (net)				39.7	28.6	33.6
26.1	25.2	31.2	Inventory				26.4	38.9	33.8
1.8	2.5	4.1	All Other Current				5.2	.8	2.7
64.4	64.4	71.2	Total Current				73.9	72.1	72.8
28.7	28.9	23.3	Fixed Assets (net)				21.6	20.1	22.0
2.4	2.0	1.2	Intangibles (net)				.4	.3	2.3
4.4	4.7	4.3	All Other Non-Current				4.0	7.6	2.9
100.0	100.0	100.0	Total				100.0	100.0	100.0
			LIABILITIES						
14.1	16.2	15.8	Notes Payable-Short Term				14.7	17.8	18.0
3.9	3.1	3.6	Cur. Mat.-L/T/D				1.2	4.3	2.2
17.2	18.6	17.5	Trade Payables				23.0	16.4	15.0
.3	.2	.2	Income Taxes Payable				.0	.5	.2
7.6	7.7	8.1	All Other Current				7.8	8.7	8.3
43.0	45.8	45.3	Total Current				46.7	47.6	43.6
17.0	16.9	12.1	Long-Term Debt				9.5	12.3	9.1
.7	.8	.6	Deferred Taxes				.7	.5	1.1
6.2	8.4	5.5	All Other Non-Current				.9	5.2	6.0
33.0	28.0	36.5	Net Worth				42.2	34.3	40.2
100.0	100.0	100.0	Total Liabilities & Net Worth				100.0	100.0	100.0
			INCOME DATA						
100.0	100.0	100.0	Net Sales				100.0	100.0	100.0
23.5	23.8	24.4	Gross Profit				15.5	26.3	18.2
20.7	20.6	17.2	Operating Expenses				12.0	16.4	10.9
2.8	3.2	7.1	Operating Profit				3.6	9.8	7.3
.9	1.0	.7	All Other Expenses (net)				.6	1.3	.3
1.9	2.2	6.4	Profit Before Taxes				2.9	8.6	7.0
			RATIOS						
2.3	2.5	2.4					2.5	2.1	2.7
1.7	1.5	1.5	Current				1.5	1.5	1.6
1.1	1.0	1.2					1.2	1.1	1.3
1.4	1.4	1.2					1.4	1.0	1.4
.8	.7	.8	Quick				.9	.7	.8
.5	.5	.6					.6	.4	.6
36 10.1	38 9.5	38 9.6					43 8.6	42 8.8	45 8.2
46 7.9	50 7.4	49 7.4	Sales/Receivables				54 6.8	49 7.4	52 7.0
60 6.1	69 5.3	65 5.6					69 5.3	72 5.1	65 5.6
32 11.5	30 12.3	40 9.1					15 24.2	69 5.3	48 7.6
58 6.3	56 6.6	71 5.2	Cost of Sales/Inventory				50 7.4	95 3.9	70 5.2
91 4.0	89 4.1	110 3.3					71 5.2	131 2.8	109 3.3
15 23.6	15 24.0	17 21.6					19 18.7	9 40.2	13 28.4
32 11.2	33 10.9	32 11.2	Cost of Sales/Payables				42 8.6	32 11.4	27 13.5
49 7.5	56 6.5	51 7.2					50 7.3	56 6.5	43 8.4
5.1	4.6	4.3					4.4	4.5	4.6
9.9	11.5	7.9	Sales/Working Capital				9.5	6.3	7.9
67.6	−155.6	22.0					32.0	34.5	12.3
6.2	7.7	17.1					11.0	14.2	32.0
(68) 2.0	(90) 2.4	(69) 6.4	EBIT/Interest		(11) 2.7	(22) 6.9	(25) 9.6
.7	.3	3.6					1.2	3.9	4.8
6.4	4.9	39.6	Net Profit + Depr., Dep.,						
(15) 3.1	(28) 1.4	(17) 5.3	Amort./Cur. Mat. L/T/D						
1.3	.8	2.0							
.4	.3	.2					.1	.2	.2
1.1	1.1	.6	Fixed/Worth				.5	.4	.5
3.4	3.7	1.3					.8	1.2	1.0
.9	1.0	.9					.6	.9	1.1
1.9	2.4	1.8	Debt/Worth				2.1	1.8	1.5
9.7	8.6	4.9					2.8	7.4	3.0
38.9	40.8	57.6	% Profit Before Taxes/Tangible				44.2	69.5	65.2
(62) 12.4	(88) 12.1	(73) 29.2	Net Worth				19.7	(23) 33.1	(27) 35.6
−.4	−7.1	15.6					2.0	19.2	18.9
10.3	11.9	18.6	% Profit Before Taxes/Total				13.9	21.5	21.5
3.8	3.3	9.4	Assets				4.7	10.5	11.4
−.5	−2.6	5.8					.6	7.3	7.1
19.2	19.8	35.0					37.6	36.9	36.9
7.9	8.0	11.0	Sales/Net Fixed Assets				14.5	19.9	10.2
4.2	4.0	4.8					3.9	5.5	5.0
3.0	2.8	2.7					3.0	2.6	2.7
2.2	2.0	2.0	Sales/Total Assets				2.1	2.0	1.9
1.5	1.6	1.5					1.3	1.4	1.6
1.1	1.1	.9					.7	.9	.8
(70) 2.2	(90) 2.6	(67) 1.9	% Depr., Dep., Amort./Sales		(10) 1.7	(21) 1.9	(26) 1.6
4.2	4.0	3.4					5.5	3.4	3.1
2.3	2.7	1.6	% Officers', Directors',						
(22) 6.6	(34) 5.1	(22) 6.8	Owners' Comp/Sales						
11.7	9.1	9.8							
2789981M	3855320M	3498941M	Net Sales ($)	1150M	6206M	20833M	80569M	420084M	2970099M
1694595M	2166942M	1859244M	Total Assets ($)	406M	3927M	10748M	41976M	270538M	1531649M

© RMA 2005

M = $ thousand   MM = $ million
See Pages 11 through 21 for Explanation of Ratios and Data

Current Data Sorted By Assets   Comparative Historical Data

0-500M	500M-2MM	2-10MM	10-50MM	50-100MM	100-250MM	Type of Statement	4/1/00-3/31/01 ALL	4/1/01-3/31/02 ALL
		1	9	2	4	Unqualified	12	10
	1	13	4	2		Reviewed	12	7
2	4	13	1			Compiled	8	8
5	1	1				Tax Returns	1	1
		7	7	1	3	Other	12	13
	17 (4/1-9/30/04)		64 (10/1/04-3/31/05)				45	39
7	6	35	21	5	7	NUMBER OF STATEMENTS	45	39
%	%	%	%	%	%	ASSETS	%	%
		4.8	4.8			Cash & Equivalents	5.8	9.0
		32.2	27.4			Trade Receivables (net)	28.8	24.8
		26.4	33.6			Inventory	24.0	22.0
		2.1	1.2			All Other Current	1.1	4.1
		65.5	66.9			Total Current	59.7	59.9
		30.2	28.6			Fixed Assets (net)	31.9	31.2
		.5	.2			Intangibles (net)	1.6	2.9
		3.8	4.2			All Other Non-Current	6.8	6.0
		100.0	100.0			Total	100.0	100.0
						LIABILITIES		
		16.7	14.3			Notes Payable-Short Term	15.0	9.8
		4.4	2.3			Cur. Mat.-L/T/D	5.5	3.8
		18.1	16.8			Trade Payables	16.8	13.3
		.3	.0			Income Taxes Payable	.1	.0
		5.7	4.2			All Other Current	7.2	9.9
		45.3	37.7			Total Current	44.7	37.0
		16.2	15.0			Long-Term Debt	23.9	15.4
		.4	1.0			Deferred Taxes	.8	.2
		3.7	1.3			All Other Non-Current	5.6	7.4
		34.5	45.1			Net Worth	24.8	39.8
		100.0	100.0			Total Liabilities & Net Worth	100.0	100.0
						INCOME DATA		
		100.0	100.0			Net Sales	100.0	100.0
		25.7	23.7			Gross Profit	23.6	23.7
		23.0	15.3			Operating Expenses	19.1	20.2
		2.7	8.4			Operating Profit	4.5	3.5
		.6	2.0			All Other Expenses (net)	.4	1.1
		2.1	6.4			Profit Before Taxes	4.1	2.4
						RATIOS		
		2.1	3.2				3.0	3.4
		1.4	1.6			Current	1.6	1.8
		1.1	1.2				.9	1.1
		1.3	1.2				1.7	2.1
		.9	.8			Quick	.8	1.0
		.5	.5				.5	.6
		34 10.6	41 8.9				29 12.4	33 11.0
		49 7.4	47 7.7			Sales/Receivables	44 8.2	47 7.8
		63 5.8	61 6.0				55 6.7	55 6.6
		11 32.1	42 8.8				19 19.5	26 13.8
		48 7.6	85 4.3			Cost of Sales/Inventory	48 7.5	46 8.0
		83 4.4	108 3.4				91 4.0	89 4.1
		16 23.4	22 16.6				17 20.9	13 27.2
		32 11.2	38 9.7			Cost of Sales/Payables	27 13.3	26 13.9
		52 7.0	48 7.7				47 7.8	46 8.0
		6.3	4.1				4.6	4.4
		11.5	11.1			Sales/Working Capital	10.1	8.4
		26.1	21.1				-88.2	44.2
		18.7	26.1				4.4	4.3
	(33)	4.8	(19) 5.3			EBIT/Interest	(40) 2.5	(32) .9
		1.3	2.8				1.3	-1.6
		8.8				Net Profit + Depr., Dep.,	7.4	4.3
	(10)	4.4				Amort./Cur. Mat. L/T/D	(13) 2.2	(10) .5
		1.2					1.7	-.2
		.4	.2				.5	.3
		.7	.6			Fixed/Worth	1.2	.9
		1.9	1.9				10.8	1.8
		.8	.5				.6	.6
		1.7	1.8			Debt/Worth	2.6	1.3
		4.1	3.2				25.8	5.5
		40.1	54.8			% Profit Before Taxes/Tangible	30.7	28.0
	(32)	18.4	26.0			Net Worth	(35) 14.4	(36) 6.1
		4.1	10.2				7.7	-10.3
		15.7	19.6			% Profit Before Taxes/Total	16.6	10.8
		4.6	8.3			Assets	6.1	.3
		.3	2.2				1.4	-6.0
		18.1	20.3				19.1	12.7
		10.0	9.1			Sales/Net Fixed Assets	8.6	6.9
		5.4	4.4				3.9	3.5
		2.8	2.6				3.0	2.5
		2.3	2.0			Sales/Total Assets	2.2	1.8
		1.7	1.6				1.6	1.5
		1.1	1.0				1.3	.9
	(33)	1.6	2.0			% Depr., Dep., Amort./Sales	(41) 2.1	(35) 2.5
		3.9	2.7				4.3	4.5
		.7				% Officers', Directors',		
	(12)	1.5				Owners' Comp/Sales		
		3.5						
10433M	15694M	493650M	867440M	603345M	2153463M	Net Sales ($)	2209475M	1179435M
1918M	5569M	192671M	412994M	322310M	1262117M	Total Assets ($)	1097863M	726460M

© RMA 2005

M = $ thousand   MM = $ million
See Pages 11 through 21 for Explanation of Ratios and Data

Comparative Historical Data | | | Current Data Sorted By Sales

						Type of Statement	0-1MM	1-3MM	3-5MM	5-10MM	10-25MM	25MM & OVER
	13		17		16	Unqualified					2	14
	21		16		20	Reviewed			3	5	5	7
	10		11		20	Compiled		5	3	3	8	1
	3		6		7	Tax Returns	4	1		2		
	14		23		18	Other				4	3	11
	4/1/02-3/31/03 ALL		4/1/03-3/31/04 ALL		4/1/04-3/31/05 ALL		17 (4/1-9/30/04)			64 (10/1/04-3/31/05)		
	61		73		81	NUMBER OF STATEMENTS	4	6	6	14	18	33
	%		%		%	ASSETS	%	%	%	%	%	%
	5.9		5.3		5.7	Cash & Equivalents				7.6	6.6	5.4
	24.7		25.0		28.4	Trade Receivables (net)				29.4	32.8	28.0
	29.5		28.1		28.3	Inventory				27.1	31.7	30.2
	2.4		1.9		2.3	All Other Current				1.9	2.7	1.3
	62.5		60.3		64.8	Total Current				66.0	73.8	65.0
	29.1		32.9		30.5	Fixed Assets (net)				28.1	23.0	30.0
	1.6		.8		.6	Intangibles (net)				.1	.6	.7
	6.7		6.0		4.2	All Other Non-Current				5.8	2.7	4.3
	100.0		100.0		100.0	Total				100.0	100.0	100.0
						LIABILITIES						
	14.4		15.7		22.5	Notes Payable-Short Term				25.4	16.9	11.0
	4.3		3.7		3.6	Cur. Mat.-L/T/D				5.2	2.1	2.2
	15.9		16.0		18.0	Trade Payables				17.6	19.5	16.1
	.1		.2		.2	Income Taxes Payable				.1	.6	.2
	6.8		7.2		4.8	All Other Current				6.4	4.9	4.7
	41.5		42.8		49.1	Total Current				54.7	44.0	34.2
	17.4		18.0		16.8	Long-Term Debt				14.0	12.4	14.7
	.8		.7		.9	Deferred Taxes				.7	.2	1.7
	6.6		7.7		7.0	All Other Non-Current				4.3	3.5	4.6
	33.7		30.8		26.2	Net Worth				26.3	39.9	44.7
	100.0		100.0		100.0	Total Liabilities & Net Worth				100.0	100.0	100.0
						INCOME DATA						
	100.0		100.0		100.0	Net Sales				100.0	100.0	100.0
	21.9		22.3		27.6	Gross Profit				28.9	22.6	20.3
	18.7		21.1		22.9	Operating Expenses				28.5	18.2	11.8
	3.2		1.2		4.8	Operating Profit				.4	4.4	8.6
	1.2		1.1		1.1	All Other Expenses (net)				.5	.6	1.4
	2.0		.1		3.6	Profit Before Taxes				-.1	3.9	7.2
						RATIOS						
	2.5		2.6		2.3	Current				2.2	2.2	3.1
	1.6		1.5		1.5					1.5	1.5	2.2
	1.1		1.1		1.1					.8	1.3	1.4
	1.2		1.3		1.3	Quick				1.5	1.3	1.8
	.8		.6		.9					.7	1.0	.9
	.4		.5		.5					.4	.5	.7
36	10.2	37	9.9	37	10.0	Sales/Receivables				38 9.7	39 9.2	38 9.5
46	7.9	46	7.9	47	7.7					54 6.8	51 7.2	46 7.9
55	6.7	58	6.3	60	6.1					64 5.7	69 5.3	55 6.7
40	9.1	37	9.9	23	15.8	Cost of Sales/Inventory				12 30.9	27 13.4	41 8.8
71	5.1	62	5.9	60	6.0					39 9.3	74 4.9	62 5.9
102	3.6	98	3.7	100	3.6					113 3.2	107 3.4	88 4.2
19	18.9	17	22.0	21	17.0	Cost of Sales/Payables				9 38.4	29 12.6	21 17.0
33	11.2	35	10.5	33	11.2					40 9.1	38 9.6	30 12.0
52	7.1	49	7.5	50	7.3					57 6.4	49 7.5	45 8.1
	4.9		5.6		5.3	Sales/Working Capital				5.5	5.1	4.4
	9.2		11.1		10.8					11.0	10.4	8.6
	27.5		70.2		24.4					-21.6	22.0	12.3
	8.8		4.9		16.2	EBIT/Interest				15.0	36.0	25.3
(56)	2.2	(68)	2.3	(76)	4.6				(13)	3.2	(16) 5.2	(32) 8.2
	-.2		-.2		1.3					1.2	1.5	3.7
	7.3		5.4		7.7	Net Profit + Depr., Dep.,						
(17)	2.0	(25)	2.6	(20)	3.5	Amort./Cur. Mat. L/T/D						
	.6		.4		1.7							
	.4		.5		.4	Fixed/Worth				.4	.2	.5
	.7		.9		.7					.6	.6	.6
	2.0		2.1		2.5					3.1	1.7	1.1
	.7		.7		.8	Debt/Worth				1.2	.7	.7
	1.7		2.0		1.9					1.8	1.7	1.5
	5.5		4.2		4.5					9.0	5.2	2.6
	30.5		18.4		48.0	% Profit Before Taxes/Tangible				19.5	42.6	62.1
(54)	7.3	(64)	6.6	(69)	21.3	Net Worth			(12)	9.9	(17) 24.2	(32) 41.5
	-4.4		-2.3		6.0					4.1	7.4	13.2
	8.9		7.5		16.2	% Profit Before Taxes/Total				6.6	14.5	25.3
	3.3		2.4		6.2	Assets				4.0	5.9	14.4
	-2.2		-3.0		.5					-.8	1.5	5.9
	13.7		14.6		19.3	Sales/Net Fixed Assets				30.7	26.9	17.5
	7.5		5.9		8.6					7.2	10.9	8.8
	3.8		3.0		4.6					5.2	6.7	4.1
	2.5		2.4		2.8	Sales/Total Assets				2.7	2.8	2.8
	1.9		1.9		2.2					1.8	2.3	2.4
	1.2		1.4		1.6					1.6	1.7	1.6
	1.4		1.4		1.0	% Depr., Dep., Amort./Sales				1.1	.8	1.1
(57)	2.3	(70)	2.4	(77)	1.9				(12)	1.4	1.6	(31) 1.9
	4.0		4.4		3.5					4.4	3.2	2.7
	1.1		1.6		.8	% Officers', Directors',						
(18)	2.6	(19)	3.0	(30)	2.5	Owners' Comp/Sales						
	4.3		5.4		6.3							
	2442961M		3339373M		4144025M	Net Sales ($)	2002M	8854M	22597M	103402M	305573M	3701597M
	1624952M		1775113M		2197579M	Total Assets ($)	1000M	3630M	13225M	55350M	143149M	1981225M

Current Data Sorted By Assets | **Comparative Historical Data**

0-500M	500M-2MM	2-10MM	10-50MM	50-100MM	100-250MM		4/1/00-3/31/01 ALL	4/1/01-3/31/02 ALL
						Type of Statement		
			12			Unqualified	13	15
	5	9	3			Reviewed	12	9
1	1	7	2			Compiled	3	3
1	3					Tax Returns	2	4
1	2	6	4	2		Other	18	17
	16 (4/1-9/30/04)		43 (10/1/04-3/31/05)					
3	11	22	21	2		**NUMBER OF STATEMENTS**	48	48
%	%	%	%	%	%	**ASSETS**	%	%
	3.4	9.2	4.6		DATA NOT AVAILABLE	Cash & Equivalents	5.7	5.7
	37.9	28.6	28.7			Trade Receivables (net)	25.1	27.3
	24.4	31.2	31.2			Inventory	27.4	24.3
	.9	1.1	.9			All Other Current	2.1	1.1
	66.6	70.1	65.3			Total Current	60.2	58.4
	19.3	20.1	25.3			Fixed Assets (net)	29.9	33.8
	.2	5.6	4.6			Intangibles (net)	2.2	2.9
	13.9	4.2	4.8			All Other Non-Current	7.7	4.9
	100.0	100.0	100.0			Total	100.0	100.0
						LIABILITIES		
	18.0	11.6	15.8			Notes Payable-Short Term	12.5	11.8
	1.0	3.4	2.2			Cur. Mat.-L/T/D	2.7	4.1
	19.4	17.7	15.6			Trade Payables	15.8	17.1
	.1	.2	.3			Income Taxes Payable	.2	.3
	3.1	4.1	8.9			All Other Current	6.5	8.3
	41.5	36.9	42.8			Total Current	37.8	41.7
	17.3	10.2	13.5			Long-Term Debt	12.9	13.4
	.0	.7	1.1			Deferred Taxes	.3	.6
	9.3	3.8	7.9			All Other Non-Current	5.3	6.3
	31.9	48.3	34.6			Net Worth	43.7	38.1
	100.0	100.0	100.0			Total Liabilities & Net Worth	100.0	100.0
						INCOME DATA		
	100.0	100.0	100.0			Net Sales	100.0	100.0
	30.8	27.6	16.9			Gross Profit	23.3	22.3
	31.0	21.9	11.3			Operating Expenses	18.1	19.0
	-.2	5.7	5.7			Operating Profit	5.2	3.4
	1.2	1.1	1.2			All Other Expenses (net)	1.3	1.3
	-1.4	4.6	4.5			Profit Before Taxes	3.9	2.0
						RATIOS		
	2.7	4.9	2.0				2.6	2.1
	1.8	1.7	1.4			Current	1.4	1.4
	1.4	1.1	1.2				1.1	1.1
	1.9	2.5	1.2				1.2	1.3
	.9	1.2	.7			Quick	.7	.7
	.3	.5	.4				.5	.5
	26 14.0	34 10.7	36 10.1				34 10.8	33 10.9
	47 7.7	46 8.0	50 7.2			Sales/Receivables	44 8.2	41 8.8
	75 4.8	59 6.2	67 5.5				54 6.8	50 7.4
	25 14.8	46 7.9	41 8.8				33 10.9	25 14.5
	41 8.9	81 4.5	62 5.8			Cost of Sales/Inventory	58 6.3	49 7.4
	97 3.8	105 3.5	83 4.4				87 4.2	78 4.7
	9 42.1	14 25.2	14 25.8				21 17.3	17 21.1
	46 8.0	36 10.0	27 13.5			Cost of Sales/Payables	32 11.6	31 11.6
	78 4.7	52 7.0	46 7.9				46 7.9	46 7.9
	3.8	4.0	7.3				5.0	8.1
	7.7	7.4	13.5			Sales/Working Capital	13.1	16.5
	25.8	19.0	25.7				24.9	77.8
	4.0	18.2	22.6				9.1	7.0
	2.9	(16) 5.5	(18) 6.9			EBIT/Interest	(42) 3.0	(44) 1.8
	.7	1.8	2.0				1.5	.1
			13.1				9.3	
			(11) 3.7			Net Profit + Depr., Dep., Amort./Cur. Mat. L /T/D	(12) 1.6	
			2.3				.7	
	.1	.1	.3				.2	.3
	.5	.4	1.0			Fixed/Worth	.6	1.0
	3.3	1.4	1.8				1.7	3.3
	.8	.2	1.2				.5	.7
	1.6	1.7	2.5			Debt/Worth	1.5	1.7
	6.8	4.1	4.4				3.6	6.5
		47.3	50.5				28.3	24.5
		(21) 16.9	(19) 28.3			% Profit Before Taxes/Tangible Net Worth	(44) 16.1	(42) 9.5
		6.9	19.1				4.7	-3.1
	7.0	15.8	15.2				13.0	10.0
	4.2	7.1	8.7			% Profit Before Taxes/Total Assets	5.0	3.6
	-.5	2.4	4.6				1.2	-2.7
	76.4	70.4	15.8				22.5	14.8
	19.3	18.8	8.6			Sales/Net Fixed Assets	7.2	6.6
	8.9	7.3	5.3				3.6	3.9
	2.9	2.7	2.6				2.3	2.6
	2.3	2.3	2.0			Sales/Total Assets	2.0	2.1
	1.3	1.6	1.6				1.4	1.6
		1.1	1.2				1.0	1.1
		(18) 1.7	(18) 2.4			% Depr., Dep., Amort./Sales	(41) 2.2	(41) 2.9
		2.7	3.8				3.3	4.4
							1.7	2.4
						% Officers', Directors', Owners' Comp/Sales	(17) 4.1	(19) 5.5
							6.5	8.3
2379M	39092M	226946M	1084554M	279088M		Net Sales ($)	2058063M	1457735M
771M	15729M	96598M	466515M	122937M		Total Assets ($)	1175347M	877749M

M = $ thousand MM = $ million

See Pages 11 through 21 for Explanation of Ratios and Data

Comparative Historical Data   **Current Data Sorted By Sales**

4/1/02-3/31/03 ALL	4/1/03-3/31/04 ALL	4/1/04-3/31/05 ALL	Type of Statement	0-1MM	1-3MM	3-5MM	5-10MM	10-25MM	25MM & OVER
11	12	12	Unqualified					2	10
12	18	17	Reviewed		3	5	3	4	2
5	4	11	Compiled	1	1	1	4	1	3
6	5	4	Tax Returns	1	2	1		1	
18	19	15	Other	1	1	1	1	6	5
				16 (4/1-9/30/04)			43 (10/1/04-3/31/05)		
52	58	59	**NUMBER OF STATEMENTS**	3	7	8	8	13	20
%	%	%	**ASSETS**	%	%	%	%	%	%
5.9	6.3	6.1	Cash & Equivalents					9.4	3.4
25.2	27.0	30.7	Trade Receivables (net)					29.6	29.5
33.2	28.2	29.8	Inventory					33.3	34.5
1.5	1.4	.9	All Other Current					2.0	.8
65.8	62.9	67.6	Total Current					74.3	68.2
25.1	28.4	21.8	Fixed Assets (net)					21.6	22.2
2.5	1.9	4.2	Intangibles (net)					2.8	3.9
6.6	6.7	6.5	All Other Non-Current					1.3	5.7
100.0	100.0	100.0	Total					100.0	100.0
			LIABILITIES						
20.0	15.6	14.4	Notes Payable-Short Term					15.6	17.8
3.2	3.4	2.3	Cur. Mat.-L/T/D					3.2	1.8
16.8	17.2	18.4	Trade Payables					19.8	16.6
.3	.2	.3	Income Taxes Payable					.2	.4
5.5	7.6	5.8	All Other Current					4.6	8.2
45.7	44.0	41.2	Total Current					43.4	44.9
10.9	11.0	13.2	Long-Term Debt					9.8	10.5
.8	.6	.8	Deferred Taxes					.6	1.0
5.7	7.4	6.9	All Other Non-Current					6.0	7.1
36.9	37.1	37.9	Net Worth					40.1	36.6
100.0	100.0	100.0	Total Liabilities & Net Worth					100.0	100.0
			INCOME DATA						
100.0	100.0	100.0	Net Sales					100.0	100.0
21.9	17.3	24.5	Gross Profit					23.4	16.3
19.9	16.2	19.7	Operating Expenses					18.4	10.3
2.0	1.1	4.8	Operating Profit					5.0	6.0
.4	.9	1.2	All Other Expenses (net)					.8	1.3
1.5	.1	3.6	Profit Before Taxes					4.2	4.7
			RATIOS						
1.9	2.9	2.7	Current					4.0	2.1
1.3	1.4	1.5						1.5	1.3
1.1	1.1	1.1						1.2	1.2
1.0	1.4	1.7	Quick					1.9	1.2
.6	.8	.8						.8	.7
.4	.4	.5						.4	.7
35 10.4	38 9.7	34 10.7	Sales/Receivables					33 11.0	33 11.1
46 7.9	45 8.1	49 7.5						37 9.8	47 7.8
55 6.6	55 6.7	62 5.9						57 6.4	56 6.5
50 7.3	31 11.8	38 9.7	Cost of Sales/Inventory					21 17.0	46 7.9
74 4.9	56 6.5	67 5.4						92 4.0	60 6.0
121 3.0	84 4.4	93 3.9						117 3.1	82 4.5
22 16.2	14 26.1	14 25.4	Cost of Sales/Payables					14 26.1	16 22.5
38 9.6	27 13.3	31 11.6						37 9.7	27 13.6
52 7.0	50 7.3	51 7.2						50 7.3	45 8.1
5.1	5.4	5.7	Sales/Working Capital					5.3	7.2
12.0	15.6	10.1						10.4	14.1
62.3	72.8	22.9						19.7	26.9
3.0	3.9	11.5	EBIT/Interest						23.0
(45) 1.5	(52) 1.3	(50) 5.1						(18)	10.7
-1.7	-.9	2.0							5.9
49.0	3.9	6.6	Net Profit + Depr., Dep., Amort./Cur. Mat. L/T/D						
(15) 2.6	(17) 1.6	(19) 3.4							
1.3	.7	2.3							
.2	.3	.2	Fixed/Worth					.1	.3
.7	.8	.5						.3	.8
1.5	2.2	1.9						1.7	1.5
1.0	.9	.8	Debt/Worth					.3	1.2
1.9	1.9	1.8						2.9	2.0
3.6	6.7	5.0						5.0	4.0
17.5	19.6	47.8	% Profit Before Taxes/Tangible Net Worth					48.3	50.6
(47) 8.2	(52) 1.0	(52) 22.5						(12) 27.2	(19) 31.8
-5.3	-14.1	12.1						4.3	19.1
5.3	5.8	14.3	% Profit Before Taxes/Total Assets					20.9	15.8
2.0	.6	7.3						5.9	9.2
-3.7	-3.5	3.2						.8	6.7
25.1	23.6	33.4	Sales/Net Fixed Assets					51.3	18.9
8.9	8.4	11.5						22.1	9.5
4.5	4.6	6.5						4.5	6.6
2.3	2.6	2.8	Sales/Total Assets					3.1	2.7
2.0	2.2	2.2						2.5	2.3
1.3	1.6	1.6						1.6	1.9
.7	1.2	.9	% Depr., Dep., Amort./Sales					.6	1.2
(47) 2.0	(54) 2.4	(48) 1.9						(10) 2.4	(17) 2.0
4.0	4.1	3.2						4.0	3.0
2.1	1.7	1.3	% Officers', Directors', Owners' Comp/Sales						
(18) 3.9	(19) 3.9	(19) 4.0							
8.1	7.3	8.9							
1318766M	1619493M	1632059M	Net Sales ($)	2379M	12801M	32942M	63944M	208745M	1311248M
1088433M	829139M	702550M	Total Assets ($)	771M	10656M	17151M	28801M	103297M	541874M

© RMA 2005

M = $ thousand   MM = $ million
See Pages 11 through 21 for Explanation of Ratios and Data

Current Data Sorted By Assets   **Comparative Historical Data**

						Type of Statement		
		6	12	5	3	Unqualified	6	7
	1	13	5			Reviewed	8	9
1	4	3	1			Compiled	7	7
			1			Tax Returns	3	2
1	1	7	7	1		Other	13	12
	4 (4/1-9/30/04)		68 (10/1/04-3/31/05)				4/1/00-3/31/01	4/1/01-3/31/02
0-500M	500M-2MM	2-10MM	10-50MM	50-100MM	100-250MM		ALL	ALL
2	6	29	26	6	3	NUMBER OF STATEMENTS	37	37
%	%	%	%	%	%	**ASSETS**	%	%
		3.2	4.4			Cash & Equivalents	4.3	7.0
		31.4	27.2			Trade Receivables (net)	26.2	24.0
		29.7	23.7			Inventory	25.1	22.2
		2.6	2.9			All Other Current	1.0	2.7
		66.9	58.2			Total Current	56.6	55.9
		22.8	32.2			Fixed Assets (net)	33.3	34.2
		3.5	3.8			Intangibles (net)	4.6	6.5
		6.9	5.8			All Other Non-Current	5.4	3.4
		100.0	100.0			Total	100.0	100.0
						LIABILITIES		
		16.5	16.2			Notes Payable-Short Term	10.2	9.1
		3.8	3.3			Cur. Mat.-L/T/D	3.7	3.0
		23.0	14.6			Trade Payables	14.9	13.4
		.2	.4			Income Taxes Payable	.3	.3
		7.4	8.8			All Other Current	7.7	6.0
		50.9	43.3			Total Current	36.8	31.8
		10.6	16.7			Long-Term Debt	19.4	22.7
		.6	.9			Deferred Taxes	.5	1.0
		7.2	4.6			All Other Non-Current	2.8	6.9
		30.7	34.6			Net Worth	40.5	37.7
		100.0	100.0			Total Liabilities & Net Worth	100.0	100.0
						INCOME DATA		
		100.0	100.0			Net Sales	100.0	100.0
		24.3	19.6			Gross Profit	20.7	22.1
		18.6	13.2			Operating Expenses	14.5	17.5
		5.7	6.4			Operating Profit	6.1	4.6
		.7	1.4			All Other Expenses (net)	1.0	1.3
		5.0	5.0			Profit Before Taxes	5.2	3.2
						RATIOS		
		1.6	1.8				2.5	4.2
		1.3	1.4			Current	1.5	1.6
		1.2	1.0				1.1	1.1
		.9	.9				1.3	1.5
		.6	.7			Quick	.8	.9
		.5	.5				.5	.6
		30 12.4	35 10.5				33 10.9	33 11.2
		41 8.8	50 7.3			Sales/Receivables	41 8.8	39 9.3
		59 6.2	57 6.4				53 6.9	55 6.7
		31 11.7	30 12.0				33 11.0	29 12.6
		50 7.2	57 6.4			Cost of Sales/Inventory	50 7.4	48 7.7
		79 4.6	82 4.5				77 4.7	78 4.7
		22 17.0	18 20.1				17 22.1	19 19.1
		36 10.1	29 12.4			Cost of Sales/Payables	27 13.3	27 13.7
		57 6.4	44 8.3				36 10.2	37 9.8
		7.4	8.7				6.6	3.4
		18.8	15.5			Sales/Working Capital	15.3	11.1
		48.0	−170.4				35.5	45.2
		13.3	18.8				11.6	7.8
		(27) 7.4	(24) 4.1			EBIT/Interest	(34) 4.0	(34) 3.4
		3.3	1.7				2.2	.2
						Net Profit + Depr., Dep.,	19.7	14.4
						Amort./Cur. Mat. L./T/D	(12) 4.9 (12) 3.6	
							1.5	.6
		.3	.5				.5	.4
		.8	1.2			Fixed/Worth	1.0	1.1
		1.4	2.7				2.0	3.1
		1.6	1.2				.8	.9
		2.4	2.4			Debt/Worth	1.7	2.1
		6.2	9.1				3.0	7.0
		70.4	31.0			% Profit Before Taxes/Tangible	57.6	40.5
		(26) 25.3	(23) 19.0			Net Worth	(34) 26.3	(33) 13.6
		7.1	1.3				10.5	−4.3
		19.7	14.1			% Profit Before Taxes/Total	17.8	15.6
		9.3	7.4			Assets	9.4	6.0
		3.2	1.6				4.2	−2.0
		30.7	13.9				12.2	9.8
		13.2	5.7			Sales/Net Fixed Assets	7.7	6.7
		6.2	3.7				4.3	3.1
		3.5	2.6				2.9	2.7
		2.5	1.8			Sales/Total Assets	2.1	1.6
		1.6	1.6				1.6	1.4
		.7	1.1				1.4	.9
		(27) 1.7	(24) 2.2			% Depr., Dep., Amort./Sales	(34) 1.8	(35) 2.1
		2.7	3.7				3.3	3.4
		1.3				% Officers', Directors',	1.3	
		(10) 1.6				Owners' Comp/Sales	(15) 4.0	
		2.1					7.2	
3167M	18865M	450157M	1224094M	904875M	520275M	Net Sales ($)	1714174M	1651548M
935M	8673M	164358M	587542M	396336M	389533M	Total Assets ($)	906300M	1061044M

Comparative Historical Data | Current Data Sorted By Sales

					Type of Statement						
	13		12		26	Unqualified					5	21
	7		13		19	Reviewed		1	3	3	6	6
	3		8		9	Compiled	1	2	2		4	
	3		6		1	Tax Returns						1
	10		14		17	Other		3		3	4	7

	4/1/02-3/31/03 ALL		4/1/03-3/31/04 ALL		4/1/04-3/31/05 ALL		4 (4/1-9/30/04)			68 (10/1/04-3/31/05)		
							0-1MM	1-3MM	3-5MM	5-10MM	10-25MM	25MM & OVER
	36		53		72	NUMBER OF STATEMENTS	1	6	5	6	19	35
	%		%		%	ASSETS	%	%	%	%	%	%
	4.0		4.3		4.0	Cash & Equivalents					4.2	3.3
	28.2		31.7		29.0	Trade Receivables (net)					30.0	31.4
	24.2		23.6		25.1	Inventory					29.3	23.1
	2.1		1.8		2.5	All Other Current					1.9	2.8
	58.5		61.4		60.5	Total Current					65.4	60.6
	34.2		32.7		30.2	Fixed Assets (net)					28.5	31.2
	3.2		2.2		3.5	Intangibles (net)					.6	4.1
	4.2		3.6		5.8	All Other Non-Current					5.5	4.0
	100.0		100.0		100.0	Total					100.0	100.0
						LIABILITIES						
	11.1		11.0		14.2	Notes Payable-Short Term					16.9	14.7
	4.2		5.1		3.9	Cur. Mat.-L/T/D					3.0	4.0
	16.3		18.3		19.0	Trade Payables					25.0	17.7
	.1		.1		.2	Income Taxes Payable					.2	.3
	8.8		9.5		7.7	All Other Current					8.3	8.9
	40.3		44.0		45.1	Total Current					53.4	45.5
	15.5		17.9		17.7	Long-Term Debt					11.5	17.8
	1.1		.7		.9	Deferred Taxes					.3	1.3
	15.0		10.7		5.9	All Other Non-Current					3.0	5.5
	28.1		26.7		30.4	Net Worth					31.8	29.9
	100.0		100.0		100.0	Total Liabilities & Net Worth					100.0	100.0
						INCOME DATA						
	100.0		100.0		100.0	Net Sales					100.0	100.0
	20.0		23.5		22.0	Gross Profit					18.2	17.9
	16.0		20.2		16.2	Operating Expenses					14.5	11.5
	3.9		3.4		5.8	Operating Profit					3.7	6.4
	1.5		1.0		1.1	All Other Expenses (net)					.6	1.4
	2.4		2.3		4.7	Profit Before Taxes					3.1	5.0
						RATIOS						
	2.9		2.3		1.7	Current					1.7	1.7
	1.4		1.3		1.3						1.2	1.3
	1.2		1.0		1.0						1.0	1.0
	1.3		1.3		1.0	Quick					.8	1.0
	.9		.8		.7						.6	.7
	.6		.5		.5						.5	.5
34	10.7	35	10.4	32	11.4	Sales/Receivables				32	11.4	35	10.4
45	8.2	48	7.6	43	8.6					41	8.9	49	7.4
61	6.0	63	5.8	56	6.5					64	5.7	57	6.5
27	13.6	28	13.2	31	11.7	Cost of Sales/Inventory				33	11.1	27	13.5
40	9.2	43	8.5	50	7.4					54	6.7	45	8.1
78	4.7	72	5.1	76	4.8					73	5.0	64	5.7
18	20.1	25	14.8	24	15.2	Cost of Sales/Payables				27	13.6	24	15.2
30	12.2	34	10.9	34	10.7					38	9.7	31	11.7
37	9.9	47	7.7	47	7.7					59	6.2	43	8.5
	5.1		7.4		8.5	Sales/Working Capital					9.5	8.8
	16.1		19.1		16.3						21.2	23.9
	42.2		−828.9		76.9						−72.9	158.9
	8.5		8.3		11.1	EBIT/Interest					13.0	11.5
(33)	3.4	(46)	3.4	(66)	4.2				(17)	5.2	(33)	4.1
	1.2		.7		1.9						2.5	1.7
	4.3		8.4		6.0	Net Profit + Depr., Dep., Amort./Cur. Mat. L/T/D						7.3
(11)	2.8	(15)	2.2	(23)	3.0						(12)	2.8
	1.7		1.2		1.3							1.4
	.5		.6		.4	Fixed/Worth					.4	.5
	1.0		1.5		1.2						1.0	1.6
	3.3		4.3		2.7						1.4	2.8
	.9		1.7		1.5	Debt/Worth					1.2	1.8
	2.1		3.1		2.5						2.2	2.9
	9.4		8.9		8.7						3.7	8.7
	53.9		52.9		64.0	% Profit Before Taxes/Tangible Net Worth					40.8	86.5
(29)	11.3	(45)	19.2	(63)	21.7				(17)	19.0	(31)	21.7
	4.5		.1		6.2						6.8	4.6
	17.1		12.5		14.2	% Profit Before Taxes/Total Assets					14.1	14.2
	5.0		6.3		7.3						7.5	6.7
	.8		.4		1.8						2.6	1.8
	15.4		15.1		16.9	Sales/Net Fixed Assets					16.9	17.2
	7.0		8.2		7.4						12.9	6.1
	3.4		4.1		4.6						5.7	3.9
	3.0		2.8		3.0	Sales/Total Assets					3.2	3.0
	2.1		2.3		2.1						2.3	2.1
	1.5		1.8		1.6						1.6	1.7
	1.7		1.2		1.0	% Depr., Dep., Amort./Sales					1.4	.9
(31)	2.5	(48)	2.3	(66)	2.0				(18)	1.9	(32)	2.1
	4.6		3.9		3.3						2.3	3.7
	1.0		1.6		1.2	% Officers', Directors', Owners' Comp/Sales						1.1
(14)	1.9	(14)	2.6	(24)	1.8						(12)	1.4
	3.4		4.0		3.4							3.6
	1190099M		1615423M		3121433M	Net Sales ($)	698M	13961M	20708M	46178M	320239M	2719649M
	631192M		826312M		1547377M	Total Assets ($)	1439M	12140M	11934M	24287M	150780M	1346797M

M = $ thousand   MM = $ million
See Pages 11 through 21 for Explanation of Ratios and Data

Current Data Sorted By Assets							Comparative Historical Data	

Type of Statement

0-500M	500M-2MM	2-10MM	10-50MM	50-100MM	100-250MM	Type of Statement	4/1/00-3/31/01 ALL	4/1/01-3/31/02 ALL
		2	4	2		Unqualified	10	9
		9	1			Reviewed	7	9
	1	1				Compiled	6	3
	1					Tax Returns		
	2	2	1	2	4	Other	10	6
	9 (4/1-9/30/04)	23 (10/1/04-3/31/05)						
4	14	6	4	4		**NUMBER OF STATEMENTS**	33	27

%	%	%	%	%	%	ASSETS	%	%
		3.8				Cash & Equivalents	3.6	2.8
		27.6				Trade Receivables (net)	32.4	28.3
		30.9				Inventory	28.2	26.8
		.7				All Other Current	2.9	2.2
		63.0				Total Current	67.0	60.2
		31.9				Fixed Assets (net)	25.5	30.5
		2.4				Intangibles (net)	3.9	4.8
		2.8				All Other Non-Current	3.6	4.5
		100.0				Total	100.0	100.0

(DATA NOT AVAILABLE for other asset size categories)

0-500M	500M-2MM	2-10MM	10-50MM	50-100MM	100-250MM	LIABILITIES	33	27
		18.3				Notes Payable-Short Term	15.9	12.6
		8.3				Cur. Mat.-L/T/D	3.4	3.2
		19.8				Trade Payables	22.5	16.7
		.1				Income Taxes Payable	.3	.2
		7.8				All Other Current	4.8	4.3
		54.4				Total Current	46.8	37.0
		9.8				Long-Term Debt	18.0	17.6
		1.3				Deferred Taxes	1.0	.7
		4.4				All Other Non-Current	2.3	1.3
		30.1				Net Worth	32.0	43.4
		100.0				Total Liabilities & Net Worth	100.0	100.0

0-500M	500M-2MM	2-10MM	10-50MM	50-100MM	100-250MM	INCOME DATA	33	27
		100.0				Net Sales	100.0	100.0
		22.9				Gross Profit	27.4	25.8
		24.1				Operating Expenses	21.1	23.2
		-1.2				Operating Profit	6.3	2.6
		.6				All Other Expenses (net)	1.1	2.5
		-1.8				Profit Before Taxes	5.2	.2

RATIOS

0-500M	500M-2MM	2-10MM	10-50MM	50-100MM	100-250MM	RATIOS	33	27
		1.9				Current	1.8	3.0
		1.2					1.5	1.8
		1.0					1.1	1.1
		1.0				Quick	1.2	1.6
		.6					.7	.9
		.5					.5	.7
		40 9.2				Sales/Receivables	43 8.6	38 9.7
		47 7.8					54 6.8	45 8.1
		56 6.5					65 5.7	59 6.2
		53 6.8				Cost of Sales/Inventory	42 8.7	35 10.4
		72 5.1					64 5.7	61 6.0
		83 4.4					87 4.2	113 3.2
		22 16.8				Cost of Sales/Payables	32 11.3	23 15.6
		44 8.3					47 7.8	38 9.6
		53 6.8					60 6.1	50 7.3
		8.4				Sales/Working Capital	5.6	4.7
		27.1					10.3	9.4
		NM					97.9	32.9
		3.7				EBIT/Interest	7.2	2.4
		2.3					(32) 2.9	(24) 1.2
		-1.2					1.7	-.9
						Net Profit + Depr., Dep., Amort./Cur. Mat. L/T/D	7.0	
							(13) 2.1	
							.6	
		.6				Fixed/Worth	.4	.4
		1.0					1.0	.8
		2.5					2.5	2.2
		1.4				Debt/Worth	1.5	.5
		2.6					2.8	1.5
		9.5					6.7	5.1
		23.4				% Profit Before Taxes/Tangible Net Worth	50.3	14.9
	(12)	9.8					(29) 28.3	(26) 4.4
		-1.1					14.0	-5.2
		3.8				% Profit Before Taxes/Total Assets	14.8	5.1
		2.6					6.9	1.3
		-8.7					2.2	-2.2
		15.4				Sales/Net Fixed Assets	20.1	15.8
		8.7					8.3	6.6
		3.0					6.0	2.9
		2.7				Sales/Total Assets	2.7	3.0
		2.4					2.3	2.1
		1.5					1.6	1.4
		1.3				% Depr., Dep., Amort./Sales	.8	.7
		2.8					1.6	(26) 1.9
		4.8					2.8	3.1
						% Officers', Directors', Owners' Comp/Sales		
10284M	161005M	450407M	652174M	1167698M		Net Sales ($)	1568105M	877538M
4530M	73757M	192646M	268967M	715973M		Total Assets ($)	936525M	559050M

M = $ thousand   MM = $ million
See Pages 11 through 21 for Explanation of Ratios and Data

Comparative Historical Data				Current Data Sorted By Sales					
			Type of Statement						
10	6	8	Unqualified					2	6
12	11	10	Reviewed				5	3	2
5	3	2	Compiled			2			
1	1	1	Tax Returns		1				
11	13	11	Other		2	1		1	7
4/1/02-3/31/03 ALL	**4/1/03-3/31/04 ALL**	**4/1/04-3/31/05 ALL**			**9 (4/1-9/30/04)**		**23 (10/1/04-3/31/05)**		
				0-1MM	**1-3MM**	**3-5MM**	**5-10MM**	**10-25MM**	**25MM & OVER**
39	34	32	**NUMBER OF STATEMENTS**		3	3	5	6	15
%	%	%	**ASSETS**	%	%	%	%	%	%
6.5	2.8	4.2	Cash & Equivalents	**DATA NOT AVAILABLE**					2.7
25.8	27.5	28.4	Trade Receivables (net)						27.7
29.1	28.1	29.1	Inventory						31.0
1.5	3.7	2.3	All Other Current						3.9
62.9	62.1	64.1	Total Current						65.4
27.3	26.9	27.6	Fixed Assets (net)						22.8
5.5	5.9	3.4	Intangibles (net)						5.1
4.3	5.0	4.9	All Other Non-Current						6.8
100.0	100.0	100.0	Total						100.0
			LIABILITIES						
12.1	12.6	13.6	Notes Payable-Short Term						11.2
3.8	4.2	5.8	Cur. Mat.-L/T/D						3.5
13.8	18.2	18.2	Trade Payables						16.7
.3	.2	.2	Income Taxes Payable						.3
5.4	5.9	7.1	All Other Current						7.0
35.4	41.2	44.8	Total Current						38.7
13.4	9.8	10.8	Long-Term Debt						8.2
.9	1.1	1.4	Deferred Taxes						1.1
4.6	8.5	5.3	All Other Non-Current						6.9
45.8	39.4	37.7	Net Worth						45.2
100.0	100.0	100.0	Total Liabilities & Net Worth						100.0
			INCOME DATA						
100.0	100.0	100.0	Net Sales						100.0
28.9	23.5	24.5	Gross Profit						19.7
24.3	19.6	21.1	Operating Expenses						12.4
4.6	3.9	3.4	Operating Profit						7.2
1.9	1.0	.5	All Other Expenses (net)						.3
2.8	2.8	2.9	Profit Before Taxes						7.0
			RATIOS						
3.0	2.4	2.6							2.8
2.0	1.4	1.5	Current						2.1
1.1	1.1	1.1							1.1
1.9	1.0	1.1							1.2
.8	.7	.7	Quick						.9
.6	.5	.6							.6
37 9.7	**41** 8.9	**41** 8.9							**42** 8.8
42 8.6	**45** 8.1	**47** 7.8	Sales/Receivables						**44** 8.3
51 7.1	**62** 5.9	**53** 6.9							**50** 7.3
52 7.0	**46** 8.0	**42** 8.7							**39** 9.3
74 4.9	**65** 5.6	**68** 5.3	Cost of Sales/Inventory						**63** 5.8
116 3.1	**93** 3.9	**91** 4.0							**102** 3.6
20 18.5	**29** 12.5	**25** 14.4							**25** 14.6
33 11.2	**41** 9.0	**38** 9.6	Cost of Sales/Payables						**35** 10.4
43 8.5	**57** 6.4	**50** 7.3							**43** 8.6
4.2	4.2	4.7							4.2
8.0	12.4	9.9	Sales/Working Capital						5.8
28.9	49.5	39.5							29.2
5.5	12.3	11.3							70.9
(35) 2.1	2.9	(30) 3.6	EBIT/Interest						(14) 8.5
.6	-.3	1.1							4.2
12.1	3.7	13.9							
(13) 1.7	(14) 1.3	(13) 5.6	Net Profit + Depr., Dep., Amort./Cur. Mat. L/T/D						
.4	.2	1.7							
.3	.4	.4							.3
.7	.8	.8	Fixed/Worth						.5
1.5	1.4	1.6							1.1
.5	.9	.7							.6
1.7	1.7	1.9	Debt/Worth						1.5
3.1	4.4	4.0							3.8
42.2	42.8	37.9							61.2
(35) 12.2	(31) 15.4	(30) 21.5	% Profit Before Taxes/Tangible Net Worth						33.4
.4	-3.1	5.7							26.1
9.2	10.2	12.5							18.1
3.1	4.6	4.4	% Profit Before Taxes/Total Assets						12.4
.0	-2.8	1.1							9.5
17.9	14.1	15.6							18.7
8.5	7.8	9.7	Sales/Net Fixed Assets						10.7
3.6	4.9	5.1							5.7
2.8	2.7	2.8							2.7
2.0	2.0	2.1	Sales/Total Assets						1.9
1.4	1.6	1.5							1.6
.8	1.3	1.2							1.0
(38) 2.2	(29) 2.5	(31) 2.9	% Depr., Dep., Amort./Sales						(14) 2.4
3.7	3.6	4.5							3.5
2.5									
(10) 7.1			% Officers', Directors', Owners' Comp/Sales						
9.8									
1975633M	**2512083M**	**2441568M**	Net Sales ($)		**7014M**	**9857M**	**39359M**	**88077M**	**2297261M**
1209453M	**1473122M**	**1255873M**	Total Assets ($)		**3427M**	**5515M**	**21904M**	**37539M**	**1187488M**

M = $ thousand MM = $ million

See Pages 11 through 21 for Explanation of Ratios and Data

Current Data Sorted By Assets   Comparative Historical Data

						Type of Statement		
		2	5		2	Unqualified	8	10
	1	4	2			Reviewed	5	3
1	3	3				Compiled	6	7
	1					Tax Returns		1
		2	4	2		Other	12	8
	9 (4/1-9/30/04)		23 (10/1/04-3/31/05)				4/1/00-3/31/01	4/1/01-3/31/02
0-500M	500M-2MM	2-10MM	10-50MM	50-100MM	100-250MM		ALL	ALL
1	5	11	11	2	2	NUMBER OF STATEMENTS	31	29
%	%	%	%	%	%	ASSETS	%	%
		6.3	10.2			Cash & Equivalents	6.5	5.5
		28.4	26.0			Trade Receivables (net)	22.5	25.7
		34.4	22.5			Inventory	32.1	30.4
		.8	1.3			All Other Current	1.7	4.6
		69.9	60.0			Total Current	62.9	66.1
		22.6	30.3			Fixed Assets (net)	26.8	26.9
		2.6	3.3			Intangibles (net)	2.7	1.5
		4.9	6.5			All Other Non-Current	7.7	5.5
		100.0	100.0			Total	100.0	100.0
						LIABILITIES		
		13.2	11.0			Notes Payable-Short Term	14.5	15.2
		8.4	1.8			Cur. Mat.-L/T/D	2.2	1.7
		19.6	15.3			Trade Payables	12.8	15.6
		.4	.2			Income Taxes Payable	.8	1.0
		6.1	5.9			All Other Current	6.6	6.9
		47.6	34.3			Total Current	36.8	40.4
		12.9	10.8			Long-Term Debt	11.0	9.7
		.2	.7			Deferred Taxes	1.1	.7
		9.1	5.3			All Other Non-Current	7.4	4.8
		30.2	48.9			Net Worth	43.7	44.4
		100.0	100.0			Total Liabilities & Net Worth	100.0	100.0
						INCOME DATA		
		100.0	100.0			Net Sales	100.0	100.0
		19.1	19.9			Gross Profit	22.6	21.4
		14.7	11.8			Operating Expenses	17.0	18.3
		4.4	8.1			Operating Profit	5.6	3.2
		1.2	1.1			All Other Expenses (net)	2.6	1.1
		3.2	7.0			Profit Before Taxes	3.0	2.0
						RATIOS		
		3.1	3.0				2.8	2.7
		1.3	1.7			Current	1.7	1.5
		1.0	1.4				1.2	1.3
		1.2	1.5				1.4	1.3
		.6	.8			Quick	.7	.8
		.5	.7				.5	.5
	33	11.1	38 9.6				35 10.4	34 10.7
	43	8.4	41 8.8			Sales/Receivables	44 8.2	43 8.4
	61	6.0	61 6.0				50 7.4	55 6.7
	32	11.3	35 10.3				40 9.1	31 11.8
	95	3.9	48 7.6			Cost of Sales/Inventory	64 5.7	68 5.3
	155	2.4	83 4.4				119 3.1	118 3.1
	30	12.0	9 40.6				14 26.8	16 23.4
	42	8.7	29 12.7			Cost of Sales/Payables	26 14.2	24 15.0
	53	6.9	43 8.5				40 9.1	51 7.2
		2.3	3.7				4.4	3.8
		9.9	9.5			Sales/Working Capital	6.3	7.6
		174.5	15.0				22.2	22.0
		8.2	54.4				8.4	4.6
	(10)	4.1	(10) 17.2			EBIT/Interest	(28) 2.7	(25) 2.2
		.7	2.4				1.3	1.2
						Net Profit + Depr., Dep., Amort./Cur. Mat. L /T/D		
		.5	.3				.4	.3
		1.3	.4			Fixed/Worth	.6	.5
		2.1	1.4				.9	1.2
		1.1	.7				.7	.6
		3.7	1.1			Debt/Worth	1.2	1.1
		7.2	2.1				4.4	3.4
		77.6	56.0			% Profit Before Taxes/Tangible	24.4	18.9
	(10)	27.5	25.4			Net Worth	(28) 11.0	(28) 7.4
		11.7	8.0				2.5	−.6
		18.3	26.0			% Profit Before Taxes/Total	10.4	7.4
		5.8	5.6			Assets	4.3	2.6
		2.8	3.5				.7	−.1
		25.3	20.4				18.6	29.4
		7.5	8.8			Sales/Net Fixed Assets	6.8	8.4
		4.3	2.3				3.8	5.2
		4.3	3.1				2.4	2.4
		1.8	1.3			Sales/Total Assets	1.7	1.9
		1.5	1.1				1.2	1.3
		.9	.8				.9	.6
	(10)	2.0	1.3			% Depr., Dep., Amort./Sales	(24) 2.3	(25) 2.1
		3.1	4.4				4.0	3.6
						% Officers', Directors', Owners' Comp/Sales		
1390M	11036M	141726M	451517M	244838M	421017M	Net Sales ($)	1415191M	1047565M
327M	5688M	63913M	239009M	149487M	252264M	Total Assets ($)	894304M	682555M

M = $ thousand   MM = $ million
See Pages 11 through 21 for Explanation of Ratios and Data

Comparative Historical Data | Current Data Sorted By Sales

			Type of Statement	0-1MM	1-3MM	3-5MM	5-10MM	10-25MM	25MM & OVER
5	7	9	Unqualified		1		1	5	4
4	7	7	Reviewed					3	2
3	5	7	Compiled		4		2	1	
2	1	1	Tax Returns						
10	10	8	Other		1		1	1	5
4/1/02-3/31/03 ALL	4/1/03-3/31/04 ALL	4/1/04-3/31/05 ALL			9 (4/1-9/30/04)			23 (10/1/04-3/31/05)	
24	30	32	**NUMBER OF STATEMENTS**		5	2	4	10	11
%	%	%	**ASSETS**	%	%	%	%	%	%
5.7	5.3	7.1	Cash & Equivalents					9.0	5.9
24.9	28.2	27.4	Trade Receivables (net)					21.6	29.9
25.5	26.4	28.1	Inventory					28.2	22.5
.9	1.3	1.0	All Other Current					.5	2.2
56.9	61.2	63.6	Total Current					59.4	60.5
35.5	29.7	28.3	Fixed Assets (net)					26.9	31.9
3.1	2.3	2.8	Intangibles (net)					4.6	3.8
4.4	6.8	5.2	All Other Non-Current					9.1	3.9
100.0	100.0	100.0	Total					100.0	100.0
			LIABILITIES		(DATA NOT AVAILABLE)				
13.4	16.0	13.5	Notes Payable-Short Term					7.4	9.6
5.4	3.1	5.4	Cur. Mat.-L/T/D					2.2	10.1
16.5	14.1	16.9	Trade Payables					13.7	20.5
.0	1.0	.2	Income Taxes Payable					.4	.2
6.6	8.1	6.9	All Other Current					5.0	7.6
41.9	42.2	42.8	Total Current					28.7	48.0
14.7	9.5	13.6	Long-Term Debt					9.0	9.7
.2	.9	.6	Deferred Taxes					.2	1.5
7.3	8.5	10.1	All Other Non-Current					7.2	8.2
35.9	38.9	32.9	Net Worth					54.9	32.5
100.0	100.0	100.0	Total Liabilities & Net Worth					100.0	100.0
			INCOME DATA						
100.0	100.0	100.0	Net Sales					100.0	100.0
21.6	24.5	19.0	Gross Profit					22.8	14.0
19.8	22.5	14.0	Operating Expenses					16.4	8.3
1.8	2.0	5.0	Operating Profit					6.4	5.7
1.0	.7	1.1	All Other Expenses (net)					1.0	1.2
.7	1.2	3.9	Profit Before Taxes					5.4	4.5
			RATIOS						
3.1	2.6	2.9						4.9	1.7
1.3	1.6	1.4	Current					2.1	1.3
.9	1.2	1.1						1.3	1.1
1.6	1.3	1.3						3.7	1.0
.7	.7	.7	Quick					.7	.7
.5	.5	.5						.5	.5
31 11.9	43 8.5	38 9.6						34 10.7	37 9.7
45 8.0	53 6.8	46 7.9	Sales/Receivables					38 9.6	47 7.8
53 6.8	66 5.6	57 6.4						47 7.8	57 6.4
26 13.8	40 9.1	31 11.9						22 16.4	32 11.3
62 5.9	69 5.3	57 6.4	Cost of Sales/Inventory					72 5.1	40 9.2
81 4.5	107 3.4	99 3.7						135 2.7	58 6.3
17 21.5	23 15.6	22 16.4						8 44.8	26 13.9
23 15.5	34 10.7	34 10.8	Cost of Sales/Payables					15 24.3	31 11.6
44 8.3	48 7.6	44 8.4						52 7.0	43 8.5
5.2	4.3	3.9						2.5	11.7
20.6	8.0	10.8	Sales/Working Capital					8.4	15.0
NM	23.2	35.6						12.9	48.7
6.1	6.5	9.1							24.1
(22) 2.3	(25) 2.0	(30) 3.6	EBIT/Interest						3.4
1.4	.7	1.5							1.5
	4.0	3.0							
	(11) 2.4	(14) 2.1	Net Profit + Depr., Dep., Amort./Cur. Mat. L/T/D						
	1.3	.4							
.5	.2	.4						.1	.4
.8	.7	1.0	Fixed/Worth					.5	1.0
2.2	1.2	2.4						1.6	2.5
.6	.7	1.0						.3	1.1
2.0	1.5	1.8	Debt/Worth					.9	1.3
5.0	4.6	10.4						2.7	11.5
23.0	24.7	37.1						32.8	
(21) 8.9	(28) 7.2	(27) 18.8	% Profit Before Taxes/Tangible Net Worth					15.3	
-5.7	-1.6	10.6						9.6	
7.0	6.8	11.9						14.1	15.0
2.9	2.0	5.2	% Profit Before Taxes/Total Assets					5.5	4.9
-1.4	-.9	2.1						4.1	1.5
13.5	12.7	20.2						29.5	20.4
6.8	6.6	7.3	Sales/Net Fixed Assets					9.7	5.7
3.2	3.3	3.8						3.2	3.6
3.4	2.7	2.8						2.4	3.2
2.4	1.5	1.6	Sales/Total Assets					1.5	2.0
1.1	1.2	1.3						1.1	1.5
1.3	1.2	.7						.9	1.0
(21) 3.0	(26) 2.9	(30) 1.6	% Depr., Dep., Amort./Sales					1.6	(10) 2.2
4.6	4.0	3.5						3.4	3.8
		(10) 1.8	% Officers', Directors', Owners' Comp/Sales						
		2.2							
		4.6							
708836M	1033247M	1271524M	Net Sales ($)		9310M	7130M	30406M	148214M	1076464M
535169M	781337M	710688M	Total Assets ($)		4033M	8340M	20258M	98043M	580014M

M = $ thousand   MM = $ million
See Pages 11 through 21 for Explanation of Ratios and Data

Current Data Sorted By Assets   Comparative Historical Data

0-500M	500M-2MM	2-10MM	10-50MM	50-100MM	100-250MM		4/1/00-3/31/01 ALL	4/1/01-3/31/02 ALL
						Type of Statement		
	2	3	9	2	1	Unqualified	17	13
	2	4	3			Reviewed	13	12
	1	2	1			Compiled	6	5
	1					Tax Returns	3	2
1	4	4	4	4		Other	9	12
	15 (4/1-9/30/04)		33 (10/1/04-3/31/05)				4/1/00-3/31/01	4/1/01-3/31/02
1	10	13	17	6	1	**NUMBER OF STATEMENTS**	48	44
%	%	%	%	%	%	**ASSETS**	%	%
	8.2	7.7	5.0			Cash & Equivalents	5.6	6.5
	31.8	26.6	26.1			Trade Receivables (net)	24.4	24.2
	26.7	32.3	38.4			Inventory	33.4	32.4
	.6	2.4	3.1			All Other Current	1.3	2.2
	67.3	68.9	72.7			Total Current	64.6	65.3
	21.2	25.2	19.9			Fixed Assets (net)	25.6	22.8
	4.3	1.5	1.8			Intangibles (net)	2.1	2.2
	7.3	4.4	5.6			All Other Non-Current	7.7	9.6
	100.0	100.0	100.0			Total	100.0	100.0
						LIABILITIES		
	16.5	13.6	18.7			Notes Payable-Short Term	16.1	18.6
	6.1	3.0	1.2			Cur. Mat.-L/T/D	4.1	4.1
	18.8	20.2	20.6			Trade Payables	17.3	14.3
	.1	.8	.9			Income Taxes Payable	.3	.7
	8.6	9.8	9.5			All Other Current	9.6	8.0
	50.2	47.3	50.9			Total Current	47.4	45.6
	14.4	14.6	10.0			Long-Term Debt	15.9	27.5
	.2	1.0	.8			Deferred Taxes	.9	.6
	4.9	4.0	3.0			All Other Non-Current	5.9	6.1
	30.3	33.0	35.3			Net Worth	30.0	20.2
	100.0	100.0	100.0			Total Liabilities & Net Worth	100.0	100.0
						INCOME DATA		
	100.0	100.0	100.0			Net Sales	100.0	100.0
	23.0	20.0	15.7			Gross Profit	23.1	20.9
	22.9	19.1	11.5			Operating Expenses	19.7	17.3
	.1	.9	4.3			Operating Profit	3.4	3.6
	.5	.7	.3			All Other Expenses (net)	1.2	1.6
	-.4	.2	3.9			Profit Before Taxes	2.1	2.0
						RATIOS		
	1.9	1.8	2.9				2.2	2.5
	1.4	1.5	1.6			Current	1.6	1.6
	1.1	1.3	1.0				1.0	1.0
	1.2	1.1	1.3				1.1	1.2
	.8	.8	.7			Quick	.6	.7
	.6	.2	.3				.5	.3
	24 15.2	8 46.5	20 18.6				18 20.0	19 19.0
	40 9.0	29 12.7	41 9.0			Sales/Receivables	36 10.0	36 10.0
	78 4.7	63 5.8	54 6.8				49 7.5	48 7.6
	12 29.5	24 15.1	44 8.3				29 12.7	27 13.4
	53 6.9	34 10.7	58 6.3			Cost of Sales/Inventory	63 5.8	52 7.1
	63 5.8	83 4.4	119 3.1				80 4.6	86 4.2
	0 UND	4 101.7	17 21.9				16 22.2	14 25.4
	37 9.9	26 13.9	33 11.1			Cost of Sales/Payables	29 12.7	24 15.1
	89 4.1	71 5.2	51 7.1				43 8.6	34 10.8
	7.4	8.1	5.5				6.1	6.4
	11.0	14.2	12.6			Sales/Working Capital	17.7	15.7
	113.9	39.3	NM				NM	132.9
		19.7	25.4				7.8	4.9
		(12) 8.8	(15) 3.3			EBIT/Interest	(46) 3.1	(41) 1.6
		2.5	2.0				1.3	.8
						Net Profit + Depr., Dep.,	8.4	6.3
						Amort./Cur. Mat. L /T/D	(12) 4.7	(11) 2.8
							1.5	1.1
	.3	.1	.3				.3	.2
	.6	.4	.7			Fixed/Worth	.7	.7
	2.4	2.2	1.3				1.7	3.4
	1.6	.9	.8				.9	.8
	2.8	1.8	4.5			Debt/Worth	1.5	1.6
	5.6	4.6	6.5				5.4	12.1
		63.2	48.6			% Profit Before Taxes/Tangible	25.0	27.3
		(12) 23.7	(15) 22.7			Net Worth	(41) 15.0	(36) 9.0
		8.9	11.3				4.6	-.1
	17.4	15.4	21.7			% Profit Before Taxes/Total	10.0	7.2
	4.0	8.4	3.8			Assets	3.8	2.4
	.1	2.1	1.2				.7	-.2
	64.0	79.7	24.1				37.8	40.1
	12.4	16.4	19.9			Sales/Net Fixed Assets	12.3	15.2
	4.9	3.3	8.1				5.5	6.1
	3.8	6.5	3.5				4.0	3.8
	2.8	3.1	2.8			Sales/Total Assets	2.8	2.5
	1.4	1.3	1.7				1.7	1.7
		.3	.5				.5	.5
		(10) 1.0	(16) 1.0			% Depr., Dep., Amort./Sales	(44) 1.2	(39) 1.0
		2.5	1.9				2.7	3.1
						% Officers', Directors',	1.1	1.6
						Owners' Comp/Sales	(24) 2.7	(21) 2.8
							6.4	7.8
580M	43630M	269851M	1227265M	875968M	208490M	Net Sales ($)	1565928M	1655869M
228M	13100M	67173M	479150M	383174M	106833M	Total Assets ($)	633585M	792930M

M = $ thousand   MM = $ million
See Pages 11 through 21 for Explanation of Ratios and Data

Comparative Historical Data | **Current Data Sorted By Sales**

			Type of Statement						
14	16	17	Unqualified		2		2		13
8	11	9	Reviewed		1		1	3	5
5	5	4	Compiled		2		1	1	1
1	2	1	Tax Returns		1				
10	12	17	Other	1	3	1	2	3	7
4/1/02-3/31/03 ALL	4/1/03-3/31/04 ALL	4/1/04-3/31/05 ALL		0-1MM	15 (4/1-9/30/04) 1-3MM	3-5MM	5-10MM	33 (10/1/04-3/31/05) 10-25MM	25MM & OVER
38	46	48	**NUMBER OF STATEMENTS**	1	8	1	5	7	26
%	%	%	**ASSETS**	%	%	%	%	%	%
6.2	6.9	7.0	Cash & Equivalents						6.7
25.3	29.0	27.6	Trade Receivables (net)						27.7
26.5	31.9	31.0	Inventory						39.0
2.6	1.8	3.2	All Other Current						2.7
60.7	69.6	68.7	Total Current						76.1
27.8	22.5	22.8	Fixed Assets (net)						17.1
5.0	2.0	2.0	Intangibles (net)						1.2
6.6	5.9	6.6	All Other Non-Current						5.6
100.0	100.0	100.0	Total						100.0
			LIABILITIES						
11.4	19.6	14.9	Notes Payable-Short Term						17.7
6.6	2.0	3.0	Cur. Mat.-L/T/D						1.7
17.2	19.0	20.0	Trade Payables						20.9
.5	.3	.6	Income Taxes Payable						1.0
10.6	8.5	10.9	All Other Current						5.9
46.3	49.4	49.5	Total Current						47.1
10.6	8.4	12.6	Long-Term Debt						10.2
.9	.8	.7	Deferred Taxes						.7
4.9	6.6	4.7	All Other Non-Current						3.5
37.4	34.8	32.6	Net Worth						38.5
100.0	100.0	100.0	Total Liabilities & Net Worth						100.0
			INCOME DATA						
100.0	100.0	100.0	Net Sales						100.0
21.0	16.5	18.9	Gross Profit						13.9
18.1	14.4	16.2	Operating Expenses						9.3
2.8	2.2	2.7	Operating Profit						4.6
.3	.6	.5	All Other Expenses (net)						.2
2.6	1.6	2.2	Profit Before Taxes						4.4
			RATIOS						
2.2	2.3	2.2	Current						3.0
1.4	1.4	1.5							1.7
.9	1.0	1.1							1.1
1.3	1.2	1.2	Quick						1.4
.7	.8	.8							.7
.4	.5	.4							.4
26 13.9	31 11.8	20 18.2	Sales/Receivables						18 19.8
42 8.7	42 8.8	40 9.0							38 9.6
55 6.6	56 6.5	54 6.7							51 7.1
18 20.6	31 11.8	27 13.5	Cost of Sales/Inventory						29 12.4
46 7.9	47 7.7	49 7.5							50 7.3
86 4.3	92 4.0	79 4.6							77 4.8
19 19.7	19 19.4	18 19.8	Cost of Sales/Payables						15 25.1
39 9.4	34 10.7	33 10.9							30 12.2
50 7.3	45 8.1	54 6.7							48 7.6
4.7	6.8	6.7	Sales/Working Capital						5.2
17.9	15.1	12.6							13.2
-50.0	UND	87.6							52.8
8.9	3.8	18.8	EBIT/Interest						24.1
(36) 2.1	(43) 1.8	(44) 5.2						(24)	6.0
.6	.0	1.8							2.1
5.1	3.4	8.4	Net Profit + Depr., Dep., Amort./Cur. Mat. L/T/D						19.2
(10) 1.3	(16) 2.6	(16) 2.8						(10)	3.7
.6	1.1	2.0							2.1
.3	.3	.2	Fixed/Worth						.2
1.0	.9	.7							.5
2.4	1.8	2.1							1.2
.7	1.2	1.0	Debt/Worth						.7
1.7	2.8	2.8							2.2
6.8	7.9	5.5							5.1
25.1	20.2	44.7	% Profit Before Taxes/Tangible Net Worth						44.8
(35) 10.5	(45) 10.4	(43) 22.7						(25)	22.7
-1.3	-4.6	10.6							12.1
9.2	7.9	15.6	% Profit Before Taxes/Total Assets						17.5
3.5	1.7	5.3							7.5
-.8	-1.7	1.1							1.8
25.7	24.3	35.0	Sales/Net Fixed Assets						32.4
12.0	14.8	14.4							20.8
4.4	6.4	6.0							9.8
3.6	3.2	3.7	Sales/Total Assets						4.0
2.1	2.7	2.6							3.0
1.4	1.8	1.5							2.1
.8	.6	.5	% Depr., Dep., Amort./Sales						.4
(34) 1.7	(43) 1.4	(40) 1.0						(23)	.9
3.4	2.6	2.1							1.5
2.0	.8	.6	% Officers', Directors', Owners' Comp/Sales						
(19) 2.9	(16) 1.6	(15) 1.6							
4.7	2.8	5.7							
2636779M	1748078M	2625784M	Net Sales ($)	580M	16251M	4736M	31932M	134159M	2438126M
972139M	804056M	1049658M	Total Assets ($)	228M	11169M	1959M	27163M	101346M	907793M

M = $ thousand   MM = $ million
See Pages 11 through 21 for Explanation of Ratios and Data

Current Data Sorted By Assets   Comparative Historical Data

0-500M	500M-2MM	2-10MM	10-50MM	50-100MM	100-250MM	Type of Statement	4/1/00-3/31/01 ALL	4/1/01-3/31/02 ALL
		6	11	3	3	Unqualified	23	21
	5	10	4			Reviewed	19	12
1	6	5	1		1	Compiled	14	14
	2					Tax Returns		1
2	2	12	5			Other	35	21
	17 (4/1-9/30/04)		62 (10/1/04-3/31/05)					
3	15	33	21	3	4	NUMBER OF STATEMENTS	91	69
%	%	%	%	%	%	ASSETS	%	%
	10.1	6.2	5.1			Cash & Equivalents	7.4	6.9
	33.2	27.9	28.1			Trade Receivables (net)	24.6	22.5
	18.9	16.8	19.0			Inventory	14.6	17.9
	.8	1.9	2.2			All Other Current	1.8	2.9
	63.0	52.7	54.3			Total Current	48.3	50.1
	30.7	36.8	37.1			Fixed Assets (net)	42.3	39.1
	1.2	3.9	3.1			Intangibles (net)	3.3	2.7
	5.2	6.5	5.5			All Other Non-Current	6.1	8.1
	100.0	100.0	100.0			Total	100.0	100.0
						LIABILITIES		
	6.9	9.7	9.5			Notes Payable-Short Term	7.8	8.4
	3.2	6.4	6.1			Cur. Mat.-L/T/D	4.3	4.1
	16.4	14.7	14.9			Trade Payables	13.4	11.1
	.8	.6	.1			Income Taxes Payable	.3	.2
	13.0	7.4	6.4			All Other Current	9.1	7.4
	40.4	38.7	37.1			Total Current	34.9	31.2
	12.5	19.1	16.0			Long-Term Debt	21.4	18.4
	.4	1.3	2.2			Deferred Taxes	.9	.8
	18.4	8.1	3.6			All Other Non-Current	4.2	5.2
	28.2	32.8	41.1			Net Worth	38.7	44.4
	100.0	100.0	100.0			Total Liabilities & Net Worth	100.0	100.0
						INCOME DATA		
	100.0	100.0	100.0			Net Sales	100.0	100.0
	28.8	22.8	16.9			Gross Profit	19.8	21.3
	23.3	16.8	13.1			Operating Expenses	16.3	18.9
	5.5	6.0	3.8			Operating Profit	3.5	2.4
	1.2	1.2	1.0			All Other Expenses (net)	1.2	1.0
	4.3	4.9	2.8			Profit Before Taxes	2.3	1.3
						RATIOS		
	2.5	2.2	2.2				2.3	3.0
	1.4	1.4	1.8			Current	1.4	1.8
	1.0	.9	1.1				.9	1.1
	2.0	1.6	1.7				1.6	2.0
	.9	.9	1.0			Quick	.9	1.0
	.7	.6	.7				.5	.5
	36 10.1	41 9.0	47 7.8				38 9.5	36 10.2
	41 9.0	53 6.9	54 6.8			Sales/Receivables	47 7.7	44 8.3
	58 6.3	61 6.0	61 5.9				57 6.4	57 6.5
	14 25.4	20 18.2	25 14.7				19 19.0	23 16.0
	29 12.7	33 11.0	33 11.2			Cost of Sales/Inventory	31 11.7	39 9.5
	68 5.4	53 6.9	50 7.3				52 7.0	68 5.4
	16 23.3	20 18.0	21 17.4				17 21.9	14 26.1
	28 13.2	32 11.4	31 11.8			Cost of Sales/Payables	27 13.4	23 16.0
	44 8.2	43 8.6	45 8.1				41 8.9	36 10.3
	3.6	6.9	5.6				6.2	4.6
	20.6	14.5	7.2			Sales/Working Capital	14.4	9.3
	179.6	−518.9	91.3				−70.3	32.6
	32.9	9.0	9.4				5.3	4.5
	(13) 9.5	(31) 4.0	(20) 3.3			EBIT/Interest	(82) 2.0	(60) 1.8
	−1.5	1.9	.4				.5	−1.0
		4.8	3.0			Net Profit + Depr., Dep.,		4.1	3.2
		(13) 2.3	(10) 1.9			Amort./Cur. Mat. L/T/D	(27) 2.7	(16) 1.7
		1.4	1.1				1.7	.8
	.1	.4	.4				.6	.4
	1.0	1.1	1.0			Fixed/Worth	1.2	.9
	−1.6	2.9	1.5				2.5	1.8
	.4	.9	.7				.6	.5
	1.0	1.7	1.2			Debt/Worth	1.7	1.1
	−4.3	5.8	4.0				4.3	3.6
	53.3	39.2	32.0			% Profit Before Taxes/Tangible	22.6	16.2
	(11) 25.9	(28) 23.1	(19) 12.6			Net Worth	(80) 9.8	(63) 4.0
	7.2	8.5	3.9				.9	−11.1
	18.2	15.2	14.0			% Profit Before Taxes/Total	8.1	9.0
	15.1	7.9	5.3			Assets	3.4	2.0
	2.1	3.7	−1.8				−1.6	−4.2
	51.1	15.0	9.7				7.0	7.3
	6.4	5.3	5.1			Sales/Net Fixed Assets	4.0	4.5
	4.5	3.6	2.5				2.9	2.7
	3.4	2.4	2.2				2.2	2.1
	2.4	2.0	1.8			Sales/Total Assets	1.7	1.8
	1.5	1.4	1.2				1.2	1.3
	1.1	1.8	2.3				2.3	2.2
	(14) 2.3	(31) 3.0	(19) 4.1			% Depr., Dep., Amort./Sales	(87) 3.6	(63) 4.1
	5.5	4.3	5.2				5.3	6.4
						% Officers', Directors',	1.4	1.0
						Owners' Comp/Sales	(21) 3.8	(17) 2.0
							5.2	5.1
3193M	50726M	338916M	799360M	305347M	834876M	Net Sales ($)	2075006M	1420078M
755M	20572M	172324M	433366M	246258M	750784M	Total Assets ($)	1498381M	1108209M

M = $ thousand   MM = $ million
See Pages 11 through 21 for Explanation of Ratios and Data

Comparative Historical Data				Current Data Sorted By Sales					
			Type of Statement						
20	16	23	Unqualified				3	7	13
10	17	19	Reviewed		4	2	6	3	4
16	14	14	Compiled	1	4	1	4	3	1
1	1	2	Tax Returns			2			
25	30	21	Other	1	2	1	6	7	4
4/1/02-3/31/03	4/1/03-3/31/04	4/1/04-3/31/05			17 (4/1-9/30/04)		62 (10/1/04-3/31/05)		
ALL	ALL	ALL		0-1MM	1-3MM	3-5MM	5-10MM	10-25MM	25MM & OVER
72	78	79	**NUMBER OF STATEMENTS**	2	10	6	19	20	22
%	%	%	**ASSETS**	%	%	%	%	%	%
7.9	8.9	7.4	Cash & Equivalents		12.4		7.1	6.6	5.6
21.5	22.0	28.0	Trade Receivables (net)		23.3		34.6	29.1	24.3
17.4	17.2	18.1	Inventory		17.4		15.4	16.0	18.6
2.0	2.6	1.6	All Other Current		.8		2.7	1.1	1.9
48.8	50.7	55.2	Total Current		53.9		59.9	52.8	50.5
41.4	40.1	34.8	Fixed Assets (net)		31.7		31.7	41.8	34.3
1.5	3.2	3.5	Intangibles (net)		6.7		2.1	1.5	5.9
8.4	6.1	6.5	All Other Non-Current		7.7		6.3	3.9	9.4
100.0	100.0	100.0	Total		100.0		100.0	100.0	100.0
			LIABILITIES						
7.2	9.7	9.5	Notes Payable-Short Term		7.1		9.0	10.6	6.0
5.8	5.1	5.0	Cur. Mat.-L/T/D		3.3		8.4	2.9	5.6
12.9	12.4	14.2	Trade Payables		14.5		16.3	13.3	13.9
.4	.3	.5	Income Taxes Payable		1.2		.3	.7	.3
6.5	9.1	7.9	All Other Current		7.8		5.6	8.7	6.3
32.8	36.5	37.1	Total Current		34.0		39.6	36.2	32.2
19.1	18.3	16.1	Long-Term Debt		15.4		17.1	16.3	15.1
.9	1.2	1.3	Deferred Taxes		.2		.7	3.0	1.1
5.4	5.2	8.4	All Other Non-Current		13.1		7.1	2.0	8.5
41.8	38.8	37.2	Net Worth		37.3		35.5	42.6	43.2
100.0	100.0	100.0	Total Liabilities & Net Worth		100.0		100.0	100.0	100.0
			INCOME DATA						
100.0	100.0	100.0	Net Sales		100.0		100.0	100.0	100.0
23.4	23.2	22.9	Gross Profit		32.2		21.2	23.3	17.6
21.6	19.9	17.4	Operating Expenses		26.5		14.8	18.0	12.8
1.8	3.2	5.5	Operating Profit		5.6		6.4	5.3	4.9
1.2	1.3	.9	All Other Expenses (net)		2.3		.8	.8	.4
.6	1.9	4.6	Profit Before Taxes		3.4		5.6	4.5	4.5
			RATIOS						
3.2	2.6	2.2			2.7		2.3	2.2	2.6
1.6	1.5	1.5	Current		1.4		1.8	1.6	1.9
1.0	.9	1.1			.8		1.3	1.2	1.2
1.9	1.9	1.8			1.8		1.9	1.6	1.8
.9	.8	1.0	Quick		.9		1.1	.9	1.1
.5	.5	.7			.6		.8	.7	.8
39 9.4	41 8.8	40 9.1			39 9.3		41 8.9	44 8.3	39 9.3
49 7.4	47 7.8	51 7.2	Sales/Receivables		45 8.2		55 6.6	54 6.7	51 7.1
59 6.2	57 6.3	60 6.1			60 6.1		68 5.4	62 5.9	59 6.2
28 12.8	25 14.6	20 18.0			19 19.4		14 25.4	21 17.7	25 14.3
38 9.7	38 9.6	33 11.0	Cost of Sales/Inventory		33 11.1		22 16.5	36 10.2	35 10.4
66 5.6	68 5.3	60 6.0			96 3.8		47 7.8	47 7.8	62 5.9
18 20.5	18 20.8	18 20.5			13 27.5		30 12.1	20 18.2	19 19.4
31 11.7	29 12.6	31 11.8	Cost of Sales/Payables		28 13.1		33 11.0	31 11.8	28 13.1
43 8.6	43 8.5	42 8.7			65 5.7		43 8.4	41 8.8	42 8.7
4.8	4.7	5.6			3.4		5.3	7.0	4.6
10.5	12.4	11.8	Sales/Working Capital		95.3		10.8	11.2	9.6
−360.4	−54.4	82.0			−22.9		24.8	30.2	40.0
4.8	7.1	13.4					14.6	10.1	19.8
(64) 1.2	(68) 2.3	(72) 4.9	EBIT/Interest				(18) 4.1	(18) 3.9	(21) 8.7
−1.3	.5	1.9					1.8	2.2	.1
3.0	3.8	4.9	Net Profit + Depr., Dep.,						
(20) 1.8	(30) 1.6	(27) 2.3	Amort./Cur. Mat. L/T/D						
1.0	1.0	1.3							
.5	.5	.4			.3		.2	.5	.3
1.0	1.1	1.0	Fixed/Worth		.4		.9	1.1	.7
2.9	3.0	2.1			−1.5		1.7	1.6	9.5
.7	.6	.8			.4		1.0	.8	.5
1.3	1.4	1.2	Debt/Worth		.9		1.4	1.3	1.1
4.1	4.4	4.7			−3.4		5.5	3.6	17.1
17.2	17.8	40.4	% Profit Before Taxes/Tangible				46.9	33.7	64.2
(65) 5.7	(69) 8.7	(68) 20.8	Net Worth				(17) 22.5	(19) 21.7	(19) 17.8
−9.8	−1.6	8.4					6.8	8.2	8.9
8.4	10.1	15.2	% Profit Before Taxes/Total		19.0		20.6	13.5	14.3
.6	2.4	8.3	Assets		5.7		5.8	8.1	8.0
−4.4	−1.3	3.0			−9.8		3.0	3.6	−3.5
6.8	7.6	12.7			17.6		20.0	7.4	9.6
3.8	4.0	5.3	Sales/Net Fixed Assets		5.3		6.4	4.2	4.9
2.5	2.7	3.3			3.6		3.9	2.9	3.0
2.0	2.1	2.4			2.3		2.6	2.4	2.7
1.6	1.6	1.9	Sales/Total Assets		1.5		2.0	1.8	1.4
1.2	1.2	1.3			1.0		1.6	1.5	1.2
2.8	2.2	1.4			1.4		1.2	2.6	1.9
(65) 4.5	(73) 3.7	(71) 3.0	% Depr., Dep., Amort./Sales		3.0		(18) 2.7	(18) 3.4	(18) 3.9
7.4	6.3	4.7			5.6		4.3	4.6	5.5
1.6	1.3	1.2	% Officers', Directors',						
(18) 3.4	(23) 3.1	(23) 2.3	Owners' Comp/Sales						
6.0	7.8	5.3							
1475869M	1863831M	2332418M	Net Sales ($)	1218M	20554M	22853M	127354M	313434M	1847005M
1211984M	1473782M	1624059M	Total Assets ($)	343M	14800M	10410M	69638M	177919M	1350949M

M = $ thousand   MM = $ million
See Pages 11 through 21 for Explanation of Ratios and Data

Current Data Sorted By Assets   Comparative Historical Data

0-500M	500M-2MM	2-10MM	10-50MM	50-100MM	100-250MM	Type of Statement	4/1/00-3/31/01 ALL	4/1/01-3/31/02 ALL
		6	6	4	2	Unqualified	7	7
	5	6	5			Reviewed	16	8
1	4	6	1			Compiled	12	5
	1	1				Tax Returns		1
	1	11	4	2	3	Other	14	12
	24 (4/1-9/30/04)		45 (10/1/04-3/31/05)					
1	11	30	16	6	5	**NUMBER OF STATEMENTS**	49	33
%	%	%	%	%	%	**ASSETS**	%	%
	6.6	8.0	2.4			Cash & Equivalents	7.9	8.6
	38.4	32.4	27.7			Trade Receivables (net)	29.5	24.1
	24.1	22.5	40.2			Inventory	21.3	21.8
	.4	2.1	1.9			All Other Current	1.2	1.7
	69.6	64.9	72.3			Total Current	60.0	56.2
	22.4	29.6	19.5			Fixed Assets (net)	32.9	36.5
	.3	.9	.8			Intangibles (net)	1.8	1.2
	7.7	4.6	7.4			All Other Non-Current	5.3	6.1
	100.0	100.0	100.0			Total	100.0	100.0
						LIABILITIES		
	7.1	16.1	19.2			Notes Payable-Short Term	10.9	13.1
	22.1	3.5	1.8			Cur. Mat.-L/T/D	5.9	7.6
	24.8	19.9	17.6			Trade Payables	16.5	14.9
	.3	.0	.4			Income Taxes Payable	.1	.2
	15.8	6.5	12.2			All Other Current	10.2	6.4
	70.1	46.0	51.2			Total Current	43.6	42.2
	8.9	15.2	8.7			Long-Term Debt	17.3	12.4
	.3	.4	1.1			Deferred Taxes	.8	1.5
	9.0	1.6	9.0			All Other Non-Current	8.2	4.7
	11.7	36.8	30.0			Net Worth	30.1	39.3
	100.0	100.0	100.0			Total Liabilities & Net Worth	100.0	100.0
						INCOME DATA		
	100.0	100.0	100.0			Net Sales	100.0	100.0
	27.2	25.8	19.5			Gross Profit	24.2	19.5
	19.9	18.9	12.9			Operating Expenses	19.6	18.5
	7.3	6.9	6.6			Operating Profit	4.6	1.0
	2.5	2.9	-.1			All Other Expenses (net)	1.6	1.6
	4.8	3.9	6.7			Profit Before Taxes	3.0	-.6
						RATIOS		
	1.7	1.6	2.0				2.1	1.8
	1.1	1.4	1.5			Current	1.5	1.6
	.8	1.1	1.2				1.0	.9
	1.0	1.2	.7				1.2	1.2
	.8	.8	.6			Quick	.9	.8
	.5	.6	.4				.5	.5
	36 10.2	43 8.4	35 10.5				39 9.4	34 10.9
	40 9.2	58 6.3	48 7.6			Sales/Receivables	47 7.8	49 7.4
	79 4.6	69 5.3	60 6.1				66 5.6	64 5.7
	28 12.9	22 16.3	42 8.8				23 15.8	29 12.8
	48 7.6	51 7.2	83 4.4			Cost of Sales/Inventory	50 7.3	38 9.6
	64 5.7	67 5.4	129 2.8				73 5.0	83 4.4
	26 13.8	32 11.5	21 17.3				20 18.4	20 18.5
	44 8.4	44 8.4	34 10.7			Cost of Sales/Payables	30 12.3	32 11.6
	62 5.9	57 6.3	46 8.0				49 7.4	42 8.7
	17.3	7.6	5.2				6.1	6.0
	26.2	11.9	9.4			Sales/Working Capital	12.5	9.7
	-15.7	48.8	19.2				172.1	-71.2
	17.0	9.0	12.9				4.5	3.1
	(10) 5.2	(28) 4.1	6.0			EBIT/Interest	(45) 1.7	(27) 1.6
	3.0	.9	2.2				.9	-1.3
						Net Profit + Depr., Dep., Amort./Cur. Mat. L./T/D	2.4	
							(12) 1.2	
							.1	
	.2	.4	.2				.4	.5
	.4	.8	.5			Fixed/Worth	1.1	.9
	4.0	2.0	1.3				2.7	1.9
	1.8	1.2	1.1				1.0	.8
	9.0	1.7	2.2			Debt/Worth	2.3	2.0
	12.4	5.5	6.8				6.5	3.4
	192.9	57.8	74.1			% Profit Before Taxes/Tangible Net Worth	46.0	24.5
	(10) 62.3	(29) 13.2	(14) 41.6				(45) 13.5	6.5
	12.1	2.0	1.4				.2	-8.4
	24.2	16.4	28.6			% Profit Before Taxes/Total Assets	10.5	6.5
	7.9	5.0	7.8				2.8	1.6
	5.1	.4	1.2				-.6	-6.3
	152.9	15.9	29.9				9.3	10.6
	10.3	6.6	12.8			Sales/Net Fixed Assets	6.4	5.6
	8.1	4.6	4.4				3.6	2.4
	4.0	2.6	2.5				2.5	2.3
	2.6	1.9	1.9			Sales/Total Assets	1.9	1.8
	1.8	1.8	1.4				1.5	1.2
		1.4	1.0				1.4	2.2
		(27) 1.8	(13) 1.8			% Depr., Dep., Amort./Sales	(44) 2.8	(28) 3.7
		3.1	3.7				4.9	5.8
		.8					1.4	
		(11) 3.2				% Officers', Directors', Owners' Comp/Sales	(10) 2.3	
		3.9					7.4	
559M	48934M	333983M	759202M	623442M	1544752M	Net Sales ($)	1252070M	1026204M
391M	15666M	146441M	391062M	432515M	821582M	Total Assets ($)	700998M	603632M

M = $ thousand   MM = $ million
See Pages 11 through 21 for Explanation of Ratios and Data

Comparative Historical Data | Current Data Sorted By Sales

11	13	18	Type of Statement					2	5	11
14	16	16	Unqualified		3	3	4	2		4
8	10	12	Reviewed	1	2	4	1	1	3	2
4	2	2	Compiled		1	1	1			
14	17	21	Tax Returns		2	1	1		7	8
4/1/02-3/31/03	4/1/03-3/31/04	4/1/04-3/31/05	Other							
ALL	ALL	ALL		0-1MM	1-3MM	3-5MM	5-10MM	10-25MM	25MM & OVER	
					24 (4/1-9/30/04)			45 (10/1/04-3/31/05)		
51	58	69	**NUMBER OF STATEMENTS**	1	8	9	9	17	25	
%	%	%	**ASSETS**	%	%	%	%	%	%	
6.5	4.0	5.3	Cash & Equivalents					7.9	3.4	
27.2	28.0	30.7	Trade Receivables (net)					31.8	28.2	
21.9	21.9	26.8	Inventory					23.6	33.9	
2.2	2.4	2.0	All Other Current					2.9	1.8	
57.8	56.3	64.8	Total Current					66.2	67.3	
33.4	33.8	28.4	Fixed Assets (net)					30.2	24.6	
2.1	3.3	1.4	Intangibles (net)					.3	2.8	
6.7	6.5	5.4	All Other Non-Current					3.3	5.4	
100.0	100.0	100.0	Total					100.0	100.0	
			LIABILITIES							
13.2	12.7	13.7	Notes Payable-Short Term					16.8	14.2	
4.5	5.0	6.0	Cur. Mat.-L/T/D					3.4	1.8	
16.9	19.0	20.5	Trade Payables					27.1	18.7	
.2	.1	.2	Income Taxes Payable					.1	.3	
8.9	7.0	9.5	All Other Current					8.6	10.0	
43.7	43.8	49.8	Total Current					56.0	44.9	
16.4	17.7	13.9	Long-Term Debt					12.7	12.2	
1.1	1.0	.7	Deferred Taxes					.6	1.2	
5.6	8.1	6.1	All Other Non-Current					4.9	8.8	
33.2	29.4	29.5	Net Worth					25.8	32.9	
100.0	100.0	100.0	Total Liabilities & Net Worth					100.0	100.0	
			INCOME DATA							
100.0	100.0	100.0	Net Sales					100.0	100.0	
24.6	21.9	23.8	Gross Profit					20.0	19.5	
19.5	19.7	16.8	Operating Expenses					14.3	11.6	
5.0	2.2	7.0	Operating Profit					5.7	7.9	
1.3	.9	2.1	All Other Expenses (net)					.9	1.7	
3.7	1.3	5.0	Profit Before Taxes					4.9	6.2	
			RATIOS							
2.2	1.7	1.7						1.6	2.1	
1.3	1.2	1.3	Current					1.3	1.4	
.8	1.0	1.1						.8	1.2	
1.2	1.1	1.0						1.1	.9	
.8	.7	.7	Quick					.6	.6	
.5	.5	.5						.5	.5	
39 9.5	41 8.8	39 9.5						40 9.2	37 9.9	
46 7.9	52 7.0	56 6.5	Sales/Receivables					52 7.0	55 6.7	
58 6.3	61 6.0	67 5.5						65 5.7	62 5.9	
24 14.9	26 14.0	23 16.2						19 19.0	26 14.0	
54 6.8	50 7.4	53 6.9	Cost of Sales/Inventory					50 7.3	67 5.5	
99 3.7	81 4.5	81 4.5						63 5.8	113 3.2	
18 20.7	28 12.8	30 12.1						30 12.3	25 14.4	
33 10.9	45 8.1	41 8.8	Cost of Sales/Payables					44 8.4	39 9.4	
51 7.2	60 6.1	57 6.4						53 6.9	57 6.4	
6.5	7.1	6.6						8.2	5.3	
15.6	14.7	13.0	Sales/Working Capital					15.0	9.5	
-22.8	UND	48.4						-63.3	21.9	
8.5	5.1	10.1						7.3	12.4	
(44) 3.0	(52) 2.2	(66) 4.5	EBIT/Interest					(15) 4.5	5.5	
.8	-.4	1.8						.6	2.5	
	5.2	4.8								
	(16) .9	(17) 2.3	Net Profit + Depr., Dep., Amort./Cur. Mat. L/T/D							
	.3	1.1								
.5	.6	.3						.4	.2	
.9	1.2	.8	Fixed/Worth					1.3	.5	
2.8	2.9	2.2						3.5	1.7	
.7	1.4	1.3						1.0	1.2	
2.9	3.2	2.2	Debt/Worth					5.4	2.2	
6.0	7.3	7.9						101.8	5.9	
46.8	35.3	74.3	% Profit Before Taxes/Tangible Net Worth					122.1	86.1	
(47) 21.2	(54) 10.7	(64) 24.5						(14) 34.6	(24) 38.5	
-.9	-7.2	3.6						1.3	4.2	
14.2	9.0	16.8	% Profit Before Taxes/Total Assets					18.8	16.8	
4.4	2.4	7.0						7.5	7.4	
-.6	-3.2	1.1						-.3	1.3	
11.1	11.8	19.0						41.3	28.8	
6.1	6.0	8.1	Sales/Net Fixed Assets					6.3	12.4	
3.1	3.1	4.2						4.3	3.7	
2.7	2.6	2.6						3.1	2.6	
1.9	1.8	1.9	Sales/Total Assets					1.9	1.9	
1.2	1.4	1.6						1.8	1.4	
1.2	1.3	1.3						1.1	1.1	
(42) 2.4	(54) 2.8	(56) 1.8	% Depr., Dep., Amort./Sales					(14) 1.7	(19) 1.8	
4.7	4.9	3.4						3.5	4.4	
2.1	1.8	1.4	% Officers', Directors', Owners' Comp/Sales							
(14) 3.3	(20) 3.8	(20) 3.2								
5.8	6.0	4.6								
2155156M	2017924M	3310872M	Net Sales ($)	559M	19835M	39403M	62369M	286666M	2902040M	
1269219M	1087512M	1807657M	Total Assets ($)	391M	12782M	21760M	26039M	189708M	1556977M	

© RMA 2005

M = $ thousand   MM = $ million
See Pages 11 through 21 for Explanation of Ratios and Data

Current Data Sorted By Assets   **Comparative Historical Data**

0-500M	500M-2MM	2-10MM	10-50MM	50-100MM	100-250MM	Type of Statement	4/1/00-3/31/01	4/1/01-3/31/02
	1	6	8	1	1	Unqualified	15	14
	5	12	2	1		Reviewed	15	18
	2	5	2	1		Compiled	9	16
1						Tax Returns	7	3
2	3	3	8			Other	21	22
	13 (4/1-9/30/04)		52 (10/1/04-3/31/05)				ALL	ALL
3	11	26	20	4	1	NUMBER OF STATEMENTS	67	73
%	%	%	%	%	%		%	%
						ASSETS		
	11.3	5.6	3.5			Cash & Equivalents	6.0	8.3
	31.6	27.9	27.5			Trade Receivables (net)	26.1	25.3
	18.9	20.6	19.7			Inventory	17.4	19.9
	.8	1.6	1.8			All Other Current	1.3	2.3
	62.6	55.7	52.5			Total Current	50.8	55.7
	27.5	37.0	40.1			Fixed Assets (net)	41.3	36.2
	.0	1.9	1.2			Intangibles (net)	1.8	1.2
	9.9	5.5	6.2			All Other Non-Current	6.2	6.9
	100.0	100.0	100.0			Total	100.0	100.0
						LIABILITIES		
	8.9	13.2	11.9			Notes Payable-Short Term	12.7	10.6
	3.9	5.3	3.2			Cur. Mat.-L/T/D	4.2	6.2
	17.4	17.0	16.9			Trade Payables	15.6	13.3
	.0	.1	.1			Income Taxes Payable	.1	.2
	13.8	6.3	7.4			All Other Current	8.4	7.7
	44.0	41.9	39.4			Total Current	41.0	38.0
	16.8	15.2	18.1			Long-Term Debt	21.4	14.5
	.9	.8	1.2			Deferred Taxes	.8	.9
	.0	5.8	5.3			All Other Non-Current	3.6	2.8
	38.3	36.4	35.9			Net Worth	33.3	43.8
	100.0	100.0	100.0			Total Liabilities & Net Worth	100.0	100.0
						INCOME DATA		
	100.0	100.0	100.0			Net Sales	100.0	100.0
	35.3	22.1	16.6			Gross Profit	23.2	22.4
	29.3	19.0	11.7			Operating Expenses	19.4	19.4
	6.1	3.2	4.9			Operating Profit	3.8	3.0
	.5	.8	.7			All Other Expenses (net)	1.4	1.1
	5.5	2.3	4.3			Profit Before Taxes	2.4	2.0
						RATIOS		
	2.1	1.7	2.2				2.4	2.9
	1.8	1.2	1.3			Current	1.4	1.6
	1.2	1.0	1.0				.8	1.0
	1.6	1.1	1.3				1.9	1.9
	1.0	.7	.8			Quick	.9	.9
	.7	.5	.6				.4	.5
	34 10.9	46 8.0	36 10.2				40 9.0	37 9.8
	45 8.0	54 6.8	55 6.6			Sales/Receivables	47 7.7	50 7.3
	61 6.0	62 5.8	69 5.3				57 6.4	61 6.0
	22 16.3	33 11.0	22 16.8				23 16.1	24 15.4
	33 11.1	43 8.6	36 10.2			Cost of Sales/Inventory	32 11.4	41 8.8
	74 5.0	76 4.8	69 5.3				63 5.8	78 4.7
	23 16.1	25 14.6	23 15.9				17 21.0	19 19.5
	32 11.6	43 8.5	35 10.5			Cost of Sales/Payables	33 11.0	28 13.1
	64 5.7	53 6.8	53 6.9				47 7.8	44 8.3
	7.7	6.6	7.4				6.6	5.0
	12.2	24.9	20.1			Sales/Working Capital	16.8	9.8
	16.4	NM	NM				-19.4	103.0
	20.0	4.5	13.1				7.7	7.5
	(10) 5.6	(25) 2.8	6.8			EBIT/Interest	(64) 2.1	(66) 2.0
	3.2	1.6	1.2				.9	.3
			7.0			Net Profit + Depr., Dep.,	4.1	5.5
		(10) 2.2				Amort./Cur. Mat. L /T/D	(14) 2.9	(32) 1.9
		1.7					1.2	.7
	.3	.4	.8				.6	.4
	.4	1.1	1.3			Fixed/Worth	1.1	.9
	.9	2.9	1.5				4.4	1.8
	.6	1.0	1.2				.6	.5
	1.4	2.3	1.9			Debt/Worth	1.6	1.4
	4.4	5.1	5.7				8.0	3.0
		26.9	58.8			% Profit Before Taxes/Tangible	37.4	20.1
		(24) 10.8	18.4			Net Worth	(56) 17.3	(68) 6.9
		6.2	-1.6				3.6	-10.2
	17.3	6.1	13.0				13.1	9.8
	8.2	4.0	7.5			% Profit Before Taxes/Total	3.6	2.8
	4.8	2.0	-.1			Assets	-.4	-3.5
	27.4	8.6	8.3				7.0	8.2
	10.9	5.7	4.1			Sales/Net Fixed Assets	4.7	4.9
	4.6	3.2	3.0				3.3	3.2
	2.9	2.3	2.0				2.4	2.2
	2.4	1.8	1.8			Sales/Total Assets	1.9	1.7
	2.1	1.4	1.6				1.5	1.5
	1.2	1.9	2.9				2.7	1.4
	(10) 2.8	3.6	(18) 3.7			% Depr., Dep., Amort./Sales	(62) 3.9	(65) 3.4
	4.8	6.4	4.7				5.1	5.6
		.9					2.3	1.7
		(12) 1.7				% Officers', Directors',	(24) 3.2	(28) 3.7
		4.3				Owners' Comp/Sales	6.3	7.4
2405M	31744M	223181M	849096M	709301M	314245M	Net Sales ($)	1472328M	1603825M
930M	12287M	123371M	463925M	280445M	205239M	Total Assets ($)	827846M	932033M

M = $ thousand   MM = $ million
See Pages 11 through 21 for Explanation of Ratios and Data

Comparative Historical Data | Current Data Sorted By Sales

Comparative Historical Data			Type of Statement	0-1MM	1-3MM	3-5MM	5-10MM	10-25MM	25MM & OVER
12	13	16	Unqualified				3	5	8
16	22	16	Reviewed				9	4	2
10	14	14	Compiled	1	4	1	1	2	2
3	5	4	Tax Returns	1	2	1			
24	21	15	Other		3				7
4/1/02-3/31/03	4/1/03-3/31/04	4/1/04-3/31/05			13 (4/1-9/30/04)			52 (10/1/04-3/31/05)	
ALL	ALL	ALL							
65	**75**	**65**	**NUMBER OF STATEMENTS**	2	9	6	15	14	19
%	%	%	**ASSETS**	%	%	%	%	%	%
7.3	7.8	5.9	Cash & Equivalents				6.7	3.1	5.3
25.5	27.6	29.1	Trade Receivables (net)				26.5	30.6	26.4
16.3	17.3	19.1	Inventory				21.0	21.2	19.3
1.6	2.4	1.4	All Other Current				1.1	2.3	1.8
50.8	55.2	55.6	Total Current				55.3	57.2	52.8
39.6	36.5	36.3	Fixed Assets (net)				37.4	31.1	43.0
2.9	2.6	2.0	Intangibles (net)				.1	4.1	.9
6.8	5.7	6.1	All Other Non-Current				7.2	7.7	3.4
100.0	100.0	100.0	Total				100.0	100.0	100.0
			LIABILITIES						
8.8	10.1	11.2	Notes Payable-Short Term				8.8	17.4	8.4
3.9	4.5	4.2	Cur. Mat.-L/T/D				5.4	5.6	4.2
14.8	14.6	16.5	Trade Payables				18.2	20.9	14.1
.2	.2	.1	Income Taxes Payable				.1	.1	.1
11.1	8.4	7.8	All Other Current				6.0	7.0	8.1
38.8	37.8	39.8	Total Current				38.5	51.0	34.9
28.6	17.9	16.7	Long-Term Debt				20.3	9.9	19.8
1.1	.7	.9	Deferred Taxes				.8	1.0	1.0
4.8	5.5	4.6	All Other Non-Current				4.5	6.8	6.2
26.7	38.0	38.0	Net Worth				35.9	31.4	38.2
100.0	100.0	100.0	Total Liabilities & Net Worth				100.0	100.0	100.0
			INCOME DATA						
100.0	100.0	100.0	Net Sales				100.0	100.0	100.0
22.3	24.1	23.9	Gross Profit				25.5	17.2	17.0
19.1	20.7	19.3	Operating Expenses				21.8	14.5	11.2
3.2	3.4	4.6	Operating Profit				3.7	2.7	5.8
.8	.8	.7	All Other Expenses (net)				.9	.6	.7
2.4	2.7	3.9	Profit Before Taxes				2.7	2.1	5.0
			RATIOS						
2.2	2.7	2.2					2.3	1.3	2.4
1.3	1.5	1.3	Current				1.2	1.1	1.6
.9	1.0	1.0					1.0	1.1	.9
1.4	1.7	1.4					1.3	.8	1.6
.9	1.0	.8	Quick				.8	.6	.9
.5	.6	.6					.6	.5	.9
38 9.5	42 8.7	41 8.8					37 9.9	42 8.8	40 9.1
46 7.9	50 7.3	53 6.8	Sales/Receivables				50 7.3	57 6.5	58 6.3
60 6.1	60 6.0	66 5.6					60 6.1	80 4.6	68 5.3
22 16.9	24 15.4	23 16.1					33 11.1	28 12.9	20 18.4
36 10.2	37 10.0	37 10.0	Cost of Sales/Inventory				48 7.6	38 9.7	45 8.1
58 6.3	59 6.2	71 5.2					95 3.8	76 4.8	63 5.8
18 20.7	19 19.6	23 15.9					26 14.2	30 12.3	18 20.6
29 12.7	32 11.3	36 10.0	Cost of Sales/Payables				37 10.0	46 7.9	33 11.0
46 7.9	49 7.4	53 6.9					58 6.3	59 6.2	52 7.1
7.1	5.6	6.8					6.3	17.1	5.9
16.7	9.8	15.4	Sales/Working Capital				17.6	31.0	9.1
-28.8	102.4	91.6					96.4	76.7	-104.8
7.5	8.9	12.1					7.1	6.1	13.1
(61) 3.5	(70) 2.7	(63) 3.8	EBIT/Interest				3.2	3.1	8.7
.8	.1	2.2					1.4	2.3	1.9
9.8	3.3	7.9							
(23) 2.4	(26) 2.2	(20) 2.2	Net Profit + Depr., Dep., Amort./Cur. Mat. L/T/D						
.8	1.1	1.7							
.5	.5	.4					.4	.4	.8
1.4	1.1	1.0	Fixed/Worth				1.0	1.0	1.3
3.2	2.4	1.7					3.7	3.0	1.5
.6	.6	.8					.8	1.4	1.0
1.9	1.7	1.7	Debt/Worth				2.4	2.6	1.7
5.3	4.7	4.7					5.0	10.6	3.6
32.1	30.1	36.1					29.3	50.5	56.4
(56) 10.8	(68) 13.7	(60) 16.6	% Profit Before Taxes/Tangible Net Worth				(14) 9.6	(13) 15.2	19.7
1.1	-.8	7.4					6.9	4.5	7.5
10.9	10.4	12.9					6.6	6.8	15.5
4.3	4.6	5.2	% Profit Before Taxes/Total Assets				4.1	4.8	7.2
-.5	-2.5	2.8					1.2	2.5	3.6
7.2	8.3	9.8					11.7	17.0	7.0
4.9	5.1	5.2	Sales/Net Fixed Assets				4.9	6.2	4.4
3.1	3.1	3.6					2.5	4.3	3.1
2.2	2.3	2.4					2.5	2.1	2.0
1.8	1.8	1.9	Sales/Total Assets				1.5	1.8	1.8
1.5	1.5	1.5					1.4	1.6	1.6
2.1	2.0	2.0					2.0	1.3	2.9
(59) 3.8	(69) 3.7	(59) 3.3	% Depr., Dep., Amort./Sales				3.3	(13) 3.2	(15) 3.7
5.5	5.2	5.3					7.6	4.8	4.5
1.6	1.1	1.0							
(23) 3.7	(30) 2.7	(23) 1.8	% Officers', Directors', Owners' Comp/Sales						
6.3	6.8	5.8							
2055325M	2269031M	2129972M	Net Sales ($)	1161M	18446M	22973M	108188M	230385M	1748819M
1215355M	1274956M	1086197M	Total Assets ($)	702M	9179M	10795M	61071M	126632M	877818M

M = $ thousand   MM = $ million
See Pages 11 through 21 for Explanation of Ratios and Data

MANUFACTURING—Nonferrous (except Aluminum) Die-Casting Foundries NAICS 331522 (SIC 3364)

Current Data Sorted By Assets   **Comparative Historical Data**

0-500M	500M-2MM	2-10MM	10-50MM	50-100MM	100-250MM	Type of Statement	4/1/00-3/31/01 ALL	4/1/01-3/31/02 ALL
		5	2			Unqualified	3	2
2	3		4		1	Reviewed	3	6
			2			Compiled	7	9
						Tax Returns		1
1	1	2	2			Other	8	10
	3 (4/1-9/30/04)		22 (10/1/04-3/31/05)					
3	4	7	10		1	NUMBER OF STATEMENTS	21	28
%	%	%	%	%	%	**ASSETS**	%	%
			8.9			Cash & Equivalents	7.9	6.6
			23.4			Trade Receivables (net)	29.7	25.7
			15.8			Inventory	17.8	17.8
			1.6			All Other Current	1.7	2.4
			49.7			Total Current	57.1	52.5
			32.6			Fixed Assets (net)	30.6	36.7
			1.0			Intangibles (net)	3.3	4.8
			16.6			All Other Non-Current	9.0	6.1
			100.0			Total	100.0	100.0
						LIABILITIES		
			5.4			Notes Payable-Short Term	9.9	9.5
			2.0			Cur. Mat.-L/T/D	3.0	6.2
			11.9			Trade Payables	14.7	13.3
			.1			Income Taxes Payable	.2	.1
			6.3			All Other Current	6.7	9.8
			25.7			Total Current	34.4	38.9
			6.2			Long-Term Debt	15.4	22.1
			.7			Deferred Taxes	.1	.3
			4.1			All Other Non-Current	2.8	5.6
			63.3			Net Worth	47.3	33.0
			100.0			Total Liabilities & Net Worth	100.0	100.0
						INCOME DATA		
			100.0			Net Sales	100.0	100.0
			14.2			Gross Profit	28.4	24.5
			13.0			Operating Expenses	20.9	19.8
			1.2			Operating Profit	7.4	4.6
			−1.8			All Other Expenses (net)	−.6	1.6
			3.0			Profit Before Taxes	8.0	3.1
						RATIOS		
			3.2				2.5	2.5
			2.1			Current	1.8	1.5
			1.2				1.2	1.0
			2.0				1.6	1.7
			1.3			Quick	1.2	.9
			.9				.6	.5
		43	8.5				37 9.7	39 9.3
		48	7.7			Sales/Receivables	51 7.2	47 7.8
		56	6.6				65 5.6	60 6.1
		27	13.5				30 12.1	31 11.8
		33	11.0			Cost of Sales/Inventory	39 9.5	42 8.7
		53	6.9				61 6.0	73 5.0
		14	25.8				18 20.3	16 23.2
		24	15.0			Cost of Sales/Payables	30 12.2	34 10.7
		45	8.1				53 6.8	51 7.2
			4.2				6.3	6.5
			7.4			Sales/Working Capital	8.7	10.2
			22.4				30.7	NM
							18.1	6.5
						EBIT/Interest	(19) 5.4	(25) 2.2
							2.4	.6
						Net Profit + Depr., Dep., Amort./Cur. Mat. L /T/D		
			.3				.3	.9
			.6			Fixed/Worth	.7	1.4
			.7				1.4	20.2
			.4				.5	.8
			.6			Debt/Worth	1.5	2.9
			.8				2.2	51.2
			11.3				48.6	50.8
			4.4			% Profit Before Taxes/Tangible Net Worth	33.3 (22)	10.5
			2.0				10.5	−5.0
			6.7				22.6	10.7
			3.1			% Profit Before Taxes/Total Assets	15.2	4.1
			1.0				4.0	−1.6
			8.5				10.5	9.5
			6.3			Sales/Net Fixed Assets	6.8	4.7
			3.1				3.9	2.7
			2.0				2.8	2.6
			1.8			Sales/Total Assets	1.7	1.6
			1.3				1.4	1.1
							1.1	2.0
						% Depr., Dep., Amort./Sales	(19) 2.6	(24) 4.0
							3.9	6.2
								2.0
						% Officers', Directors', Owners' Comp/Sales	(11)	3.8
								6.3
1691M	16808M	76455M	293019M		195646M	Net Sales ($)	533759M	543396M
753M	5331M	34444M	174945M		137190M	Total Assets ($)	327139M	341369M

M = $ thousand   MM = $ million
See Pages 11 through 21 for Explanation of Ratios and Data

Comparative Historical Data

Current Data Sorted By Sales

4/1/02-3/31/03 ALL	4/1/03-3/31/04 ALL	4/1/04-3/31/05 ALL	Type of Statement	0-1MM	1-3MM	3-5MM	5-10MM	10-25MM	25MM & OVER
8	5	3	Unqualified				2	5	3
7	13	9	Reviewed					2	
7	9	7	Compiled	2	1	1		3	
1	1	1	Tax Returns				1	2	
3	8	6	Other	1	1		1	2	1
					3 (4/1-9/30/04)			22 (10/1/04-3/31/05)	
26	36	25	**NUMBER OF STATEMENTS**	3	2	1	3	10	6
%	%	%		%	%	%	%	%	%
			ASSETS						
8.9	8.2	8.5	Cash & Equivalents					8.6	
21.6	24.2	27.7	Trade Receivables (net)					28.4	
16.8	19.5	16.6	Inventory					19.3	
2.6	2.7	2.1	All Other Current					2.6	
49.9	54.7	54.9	Total Current					58.9	
38.4	34.6	34.8	Fixed Assets (net)					27.3	
4.5	3.4	1.8	Intangibles (net)					2.5	
7.3	7.3	8.6	All Other Non-Current					11.3	
100.0	100.0	100.0	Total					100.0	
			LIABILITIES						
5.1	7.2	7.8	Notes Payable-Short Term					11.8	
3.6	4.7	2.0	Cur. Mat.-L/T/D					1.6	
10.5	13.7	14.6	Trade Payables					14.9	
.3	.1	.0	Income Taxes Payable					.0	
7.7	9.4	8.3	All Other Current					7.4	
27.2	35.2	32.7	Total Current					35.7	
15.8	16.6	15.5	Long-Term Debt					3.1	
.7	.4	.4	Deferred Taxes					.5	
1.8	3.7	2.6	All Other Non-Current					4.8	
54.5	44.1	48.8	Net Worth					56.0	
100.0	100.0	100.0	Total Liabilities & Net Worth					100.0	
			INCOME DATA						
100.0	100.0	100.0	Net Sales					100.0	
23.1	21.8	20.3	Gross Profit					18.1	
21.1	19.8	19.4	Operating Expenses					17.6	
2.0	2.0	.9	Operating Profit					.5	
.3	.3	-.5	All Other Expenses (net)					-2.0	
1.7	1.7	1.4	Profit Before Taxes					2.5	
			RATIOS						
2.7	2.2	3.0						2.6	
1.8	1.7	1.8	Current					1.8	
1.4	1.4	1.3						1.3	
1.8	1.6	1.7						2.0	
1.0	1.1	1.1	Quick					1.0	
.8	.6	.8						.7	
38 9.7	37 9.9	42 8.6						42 8.7	
48 7.6	45 8.1	46 7.9	Sales/Receivables					44 8.3	
53 6.9	60 6.1	54 6.7						50 7.3	
28 13.2	31 12.0	23 16.0						31 11.9	
43 8.6	37 9.9	33 11.0	Cost of Sales/Inventory					36 10.2	
63 5.8	69 5.3	56 6.5						66 5.5	
15 24.3	15 24.3	13 29.0						13 27.4	
28 13.1	28 13.1	23 15.6	Cost of Sales/Payables					23 15.9	
37 10.0	46 7.9	44 8.2						27 13.3	
5.3	5.2	5.1						4.2	
8.2	9.7	9.4	Sales/Working Capital					9.5	
14.0	23.3	20.1						19.7	
5.3	6.9	12.3							
(22) 2.7	(30) 3.0	(22) 3.7	EBIT/Interest						
-1.7	-.7	-1.7							
	4.2								
	(11) 2.2		Net Profit + Depr., Dep., Amort./Cur. Mat. L/T/D						
	1.1								
.5	.5	.3						.3	
.8	.8	.7	Fixed/Worth					.6	
1.2	2.2	.9						.7	
.4	.5	.5						.5	
1.0	1.4	.8	Debt/Worth					.8	
2.0	3.2	1.8						1.4	
21.1	25.0	15.0						19.5	
8.3	(32) 12.4	(24) 5.2	% Profit Before Taxes/Tangible Net Worth					5.7	
-5.2	-5.1	-4.0						-3.3	
10.7	11.2	9.3						8.1	
3.2	5.6	3.7	% Profit Before Taxes/Total Assets					3.9	
-3.2	-3.8	-2.5						-1.6	
7.6	9.8	11.3						17.1	
5.3	6.7	6.3	Sales/Net Fixed Assets					6.4	
2.9	3.5	3.9						5.1	
2.6	2.4	2.4						2.6	
1.7	1.9	2.0	Sales/Total Assets					1.9	
1.2	1.5	1.4						1.6	
3.2	2.3	2.1							
(23) 4.2	(31) 3.5	(22) 3.9	% Depr., Dep., Amort./Sales						
7.8	4.4	4.5							
	2.3	1.5							
	(16) 3.1	(12) 2.1	% Officers', Directors', Owners' Comp/Sales						
	9.2	3.6							
1009419M	1155968M	583619M	Net Sales ($)	1691M	3046M	3372M	19182M	158197M	398131M
610532M	601578M	352663M	Total Assets ($)	753M	2001M	1725M	8568M	84543M	255073M

© RMA 2005

M = $ thousand   MM = $ million
See Pages 11 through 21 for Explanation of Ratios and Data

Current Data Sorted By Assets   **Comparative Historical Data**

0-500M	500M-2MM	2-10MM	10-50MM	50-100MM	100-250MM	Type of Statement	4/1/00-3/31/01 ALL	4/1/01-3/31/02 ALL
		5	1			Unqualified	5	4
2		8	4			Reviewed	7	10
2	5	5				Compiled	7	9
	1	1				Tax Returns		3
1		6	7			Other	17	17
		13 (4/1-9/30/04)	35 (10/1/04-3/31/05)					
5	6	25	12			**NUMBER OF STATEMENTS**	36	43
%	%	%	%	%	%	**ASSETS**	%	%
		5.9	3.7			Cash & Equivalents	6.9	4.7
		28.0	27.8			Trade Receivables (net)	26.8	25.2
		16.6	25.3			Inventory	16.1	14.3
		3.3	1.2	DATA	DATA	All Other Current	1.4	1.7
		53.7	58.1	NOT	NOT	Total Current	51.2	45.8
		41.5	36.0	AVAILABLE	AVAILABLE	Fixed Assets (net)	39.7	45.2
		.3	1.2			Intangibles (net)	2.4	2.6
		4.5	4.8			All Other Non-Current	6.7	6.3
		100.0	100.0			Total	100.0	100.0
						LIABILITIES		
		10.3	2.9			Notes Payable-Short Term	8.0	11.0
		4.2	1.9			Cur. Mat.-L/T/D	3.6	5.0
		13.8	18.1			Trade Payables	14.2	12.5
		.1	.0			Income Taxes Payable	.0	.0
		7.0	7.6			All Other Current	7.4	7.9
		35.4	30.4			Total Current	33.2	36.4
		23.9	16.4			Long-Term Debt	17.9	25.5
		.5	.2			Deferred Taxes	.3	.4
		5.0	8.3			All Other Non-Current	13.7	3.3
		35.2	44.7			Net Worth	34.9	34.4
		100.0	100.0			Total Liabilities & Net Worth	100.0	100.0
						INCOME DATA		
		100.0	100.0			Net Sales	100.0	100.0
		24.1	17.4			Gross Profit	19.3	22.2
		20.0	12.0			Operating Expenses	16.6	20.6
		4.1	5.3			Operating Profit	2.7	1.6
		1.2	.7			All Other Expenses (net)	1.6	1.9
		2.9	4.7			Profit Before Taxes	1.2	-.4
						RATIOS		
		2.3	3.4				3.0	2.0
		1.5	1.9			Current	1.7	1.2
		1.1	1.3				1.0	1.0
		1.7	1.9				1.8	1.3
		1.1	1.3			Quick	1.0	.8
		.6	.6				.7	.6
	40	9.2	38 9.6				43 8.4	41 8.9
	50	7.2	52 7.0			Sales/Receivables	51 7.2	53 6.9
	62	5.9	59 6.2				61 6.0	62 5.9
	21	17.4	25 14.4				21 17.8	19 19.7
	33	11.1	54 6.7			Cost of Sales/Inventory	33 11.0	31 11.9
	50	7.3	88 4.2				60 6.1	45 8.1
	16	22.2	17 21.3				21 17.5	23 15.8
	30	12.1	33 11.2			Cost of Sales/Payables	28 13.1	31 11.8
	44	8.3	39 9.4				40 9.2	39 9.4
		7.1	3.8				5.1	8.3
		12.8	6.9			Sales/Working Capital	11.2	22.3
		514.3	20.6				119.8	-77.7
		5.5	10.6				8.4	2.9
	(21)	2.2	(11) 6.3			EBIT/Interest	(33) 2.1	(40) 1.2
		.9	1.4				.2	-.6
						Net Profit + Depr., Dep., Amort./Cur. Mat. L./T/D		1.8
							(13)	1.3
								.4
		.5	.6				.5	.9
		1.2	1.0			Fixed/Worth	1.3	1.6
		2.7	1.2				4.3	3.4
		1.0	.5				.7	1.2
		2.2	1.8			Debt/Worth	2.2	2.5
		4.0	2.2				6.2	7.2
		40.2	41.5				45.9	26.9
	(23)	12.3	23.6			% Profit Before Taxes/Tangible Net Worth	(31) 13.8	(41) 2.9
		-.2	4.5				-5.5	-20.7
		10.1	18.9				12.0	8.1
		3.8	7.9			% Profit Before Taxes/Total Assets	3.3	3.3
		-.2	1.6				-3.9	-6.5
		10.7	9.2				8.6	7.4
		4.5	5.2			Sales/Net Fixed Assets	5.6	4.6
		2.9	3.8				2.7	2.2
		2.6	2.6				2.6	2.3
		1.8	2.1			Sales/Total Assets	1.7	1.8
		1.5	1.5				1.4	1.3
		2.7	2.1				1.4	1.9
	(24)	3.7	(10) 4.5			% Depr., Dep., Amort./Sales	(31) 2.7	(37) 3.5
		5.2	6.0				4.2	6.2
							2.6	3.3
						% Officers', Directors', Owners' Comp/Sales	(12) 3.8	(19) 5.3
							5.4	9.0
4812M	17268M	284252M	621217M			Net Sales ($)	690396M	929029M
1523M	7529M	130624M	305112M			Total Assets ($)	513565M	870270M

© RMA 2005

M = $ thousand   MM = $ million
See Pages 11 through 21 for Explanation of Ratios and Data

Comparative Historical Data				Current Data Sorted By Sales					
			Type of Statement						
6	12	6	Unqualified			1	2	2	1
8	14	14	Reviewed	1	1		3	5	4
9	8	12	Compiled		8		3	1	
	1	1	Tax Returns					1	
10	10	15	Other	1		1	4	3	6
4/1/02-3/31/03 ALL	4/1/03-3/31/04 ALL	4/1/04-3/31/05 ALL		0-1MM	13 (4/1-9/30/04) 1-3MM	3-5MM	5-10MM	35 (10/1/04-3/31/05) 10-25MM	25MM & OVER
33	45	48	**NUMBER OF STATEMENTS**	2	9	2	12	12	11
%	%	%	**ASSETS**	%	%	%	%	%	%
7.6	6.1	5.3	Cash & Equivalents				5.7	7.2	2.5
24.5	27.0	29.5	Trade Receivables (net)				29.8	28.4	30.9
12.3	18.4	19.4	Inventory				10.1	19.7	30.7
2.4	2.2	2.1	All Other Current				1.2	3.2	.6
46.7	53.6	56.2	Total Current				46.8	58.4	64.8
44.7	38.7	38.9	Fixed Assets (net)				47.9	36.7	29.3
3.2	2.2	1.0	Intangibles (net)				1.0	.6	1.3
5.3	5.5	3.8	All Other Non-Current				4.4	4.3	4.6
100.0	100.0	100.0	Total				100.0	100.0	100.0
			LIABILITIES						
8.8	11.4	8.2	Notes Payable-Short Term				8.4	8.8	7.7
4.2	4.4	4.1	Cur. Mat.-L/T/D				4.9	2.9	1.8
11.6	13.8	16.6	Trade Payables				14.3	14.5	21.2
.1	.1	.1	Income Taxes Payable				.0	.3	.0
7.1	6.5	7.4	All Other Current				5.7	10.2	6.6
31.7	36.1	36.3	Total Current				33.4	36.7	37.2
23.1	19.0	26.1	Long-Term Debt				29.5	15.1	17.2
.8	.5	.3	Deferred Taxes				.6	.5	.2
5.1	6.6	14.4	All Other Non-Current				5.7	.7	8.8
39.3	37.8	22.9	Net Worth				30.8	47.1	36.5
100.0	100.0	100.0	Total Liabilities & Net Worth				100.0	100.0	100.0
			INCOME DATA						
100.0	100.0	100.0	Net Sales				100.0	100.0	100.0
22.8	21.1	21.5	Gross Profit				22.3	21.7	15.9
21.7	17.2	17.2	Operating Expenses				18.0	15.7	12.3
1.1	3.9	4.4	Operating Profit				4.3	6.0	3.6
1.7	1.0	1.2	All Other Expenses (net)				2.2	.4	.9
-.6	2.9	3.2	Profit Before Taxes				2.1	5.6	2.8
			RATIOS						
2.6 1.6 1.0	2.7 1.5 1.0	2.8 1.6 1.1	Current				2.6 1.3 1.0	2.3 1.6 1.2	2.8 1.8 1.2
1.9 1.0 .6	1.7 .9 .6	1.7 1.2 .6	Quick				1.9 1.1 .7	1.5 1.3 .6	1.5 1.3 .6
40 9.2 48 7.6 60 6.1	42 8.7 47 7.7 59 6.2	39 9.3 51 7.2 62 5.9	Sales/Receivables				43 8.5 51 7.1 60 6.1	39 9.4 50 7.3 62 5.9	36 10.3 46 8.0 59 6.2
19 19.2 28 13.2 39 9.4	23 15.7 34 10.7 59 6.2	25 14.9 36 10.2 58 6.3	Cost of Sales/Inventory				17 21.6 22 16.7 39 9.5	24 15.3 41 9.0 52 7.0	26 14.2 58 6.3 92 4.0
17 21.9 28 13.1 36 10.0	14 26.3 22 16.2 42 8.7	16 22.4 33 11.2 49 7.4	Cost of Sales/Payables				13 28.2 29 12.7 46 7.9	21 17.3 30 12.3 42 8.6	18 20.1 33 11.1 41 8.9
6.5 14.2 458.3	5.3 11.9 -161.6	5.8 11.7 45.4	Sales/Working Capital				7.8 15.9 762.0	7.0 10.3 19.3	4.0 8.0 27.5
3.2 (29) 1.1 -3.1	3.5 (39) 2.1 .2	6.0 (41) 3.4 .9	EBIT/Interest				8.3 (11) 2.1 1.0		9.9 4.3 .6
	1.8 (13) 1.3 .5	1.8 (10) 1.4 1.0	Net Profit + Depr., Dep., Amort./Cur. Mat. L/T/D						
.6 1.5 3.0	.7 1.2 2.7	.8 1.2 3.6	Fixed/Worth				.9 1.4 4.6	.4 .9 1.7	.2 1.0 1.2
.7 2.1 4.0	.8 2.1 4.5	1.1 2.2 6.7	Debt/Worth				1.1 1.7 12.9	.4 1.8 3.2	1.7 2.0 3.4
24.9 (29) .8 -9.1	34.5 (40) 9.8 .4	44.8 (41) 18.3 4.4	% Profit Before Taxes/Tangible Net Worth				40.2 (11) 12.3 -1.8	55.5 20.5 6.4	43.3 18.3 -6.1
9.1 .2 -6.3	10.9 3.3 -.5	13.2 4.9 -.1	% Profit Before Taxes/Total Assets				8.4 2.3 -.3	20.2 7.9 4.0	10.3 5.2 -1.9
6.2 4.3 2.7	7.5 5.2 3.5	13.1 4.8 3.2	Sales/Net Fixed Assets				6.2 3.7 2.8	13.4 5.0 3.4	28.6 5.6 4.4
2.3 1.8 1.3	2.4 1.9 1.5	2.7 2.0 1.5	Sales/Total Assets				2.2 1.8 1.5	2.7 1.8 1.5	2.9 2.3 1.5
3.3 (31) 3.9 5.8	2.6 (43) 3.7 5.0	1.9 (44) 3.5 5.7	% Depr., Dep., Amort./Sales				3.6 (11) 4.4 5.2	1.3 (11) 3.1 4.5	1.4 (10) 3.5 5.4
3.4 (16) 5.8 11.3	2.4 (17) 3.3 7.4	1.9 (17) 4.1 8.5	% Officers', Directors', Owners' Comp/Sales						
473184M	815944M	927549M	Net Sales ($)	430M	16899M	7882M	81175M	201026M	620137M
346348M	439522M	444788M	Total Assets ($)	273M	9821M	5333M	44692M	101091M	283578M

© RMA 2005

M = $ thousand   MM = $ million
See Pages 11 through 21 for Explanation of Ratios and Data

Current Data Sorted By Assets							Comparative Historical Data	
		1	2			Type of Statement Unqualified	4	3
	3	6	1			Reviewed	12	8
	3	2				Compiled	8	8
	2					Tax Returns	3	1
	3	4	1	1		Other	4	8
	6 (4/1-9/30/04)		23 (10/1/04-3/31/05)				4/1/00-3/31/01	4/1/01-3/31/02
0-500M	500M-2MM	2-10MM	10-50MM	50-100MM	100-250MM		ALL	ALL
	11	13	4	1		NUMBER OF STATEMENTS	31	28
%	%	%	%	%	%	ASSETS	%	%
DATA NOT AVAILABLE	8.7	6.6			DATA NOT AVAILABLE	Cash & Equivalents	6.4	6.7
	28.6	26.0				Trade Receivables (net)	27.9	25.2
	22.3	21.2				Inventory	13.7	16.7
	3.0	1.2				All Other Current	4.5	4.3
	62.7	55.0				Total Current	52.5	52.8
	33.5	40.8				Fixed Assets (net)	41.5	35.7
	.5	.4				Intangibles (net)	1.2	5.4
	3.3	3.8				All Other Non-Current	4.7	6.1
	100.0	100.0				Total	100.0	100.0
						LIABILITIES		
	10.7	12.7				Notes Payable-Short Term	9.3	8.6
	6.5	7.5				Cur. Mat.-L/T/D	5.0	5.7
	15.2	16.1				Trade Payables	15.1	17.3
	.0	.2				Income Taxes Payable	.3	.4
	9.8	7.9				All Other Current	12.2	8.2
	42.3	44.3				Total Current	41.9	40.2
	16.7	16.9				Long-Term Debt	19.8	16.6
	.6	.6				Deferred Taxes	.5	.7
	1.5	5.1				All Other Non-Current	2.7	2.7
	38.9	33.1				Net Worth	35.0	39.8
	100.0	100.0				Total Liabilities & Net Worth	100.0	100.0
						INCOME DATA		
	100.0	100.0				Net Sales	100.0	100.0
	28.2	25.0				Gross Profit	27.4	22.9
	21.6	17.7				Operating Expenses	20.2	19.2
	6.6	7.3				Operating Profit	7.2	3.7
	1.0	1.1				All Other Expenses (net)	1.2	1.6
	5.6	6.2				Profit Before Taxes	6.0	2.1
						RATIOS		
	3.6	1.9					2.3	2.4
	1.2	1.4				Current	1.4	1.4
	1.1	1.0					1.0	1.1
	1.5	1.3					1.4	1.5
	.8	.7				Quick	.9	.9
	.6	.4					.6	.4
	32 11.3	24 15.4					32 11.3	35 10.4
	46 8.0	39 9.3				Sales/Receivables	45 8.1	46 7.9
	65 5.6	59 6.2					58 6.3	56 6.6
	26 13.8	17 21.9					11 34.4	18 20.6
	45 8.1	45 8.2				Cost of Sales/Inventory	32 11.4	42 8.8
	73 5.0	68 5.4					46 7.9	59 6.2
	22 16.7	14 26.0					18 20.4	18 20.3
	36 10.2	29 12.5				Cost of Sales/Payables	27 13.6	32 11.5
	40 9.1	52 7.1					44 8.3	47 7.8
	5.3	7.9					6.7	6.2
	31.5	10.7				Sales/Working Capital	22.9	11.7
	65.4	277.0					-83.7	70.4
	17.0	15.3					11.9	4.6
	(10) 9.4	(12) 3.7				EBIT/Interest	(28) 2.6	(24) 1.1
	3.5	1.5					1.0	.2
							5.3	2.4
						Net Profit + Depr., Dep., Amort./Cur. Mat. L/T/D	(11) 3.6	(10) 1.1
							1.2	-.6
	.4	.9					.6	.5
	1.0	1.2				Fixed/Worth	1.2	.9
	1.6	2.5					3.3	2.8
	.6	1.2					.7	.6
	1.7	1.9				Debt/Worth	2.0	1.7
	2.5	5.0					6.5	8.7
	61.1	63.1					61.4	20.2
	(10) 24.5	(12) 33.0				% Profit Before Taxes/Tangible Net Worth	(27) 22.6	(25) 4.7
	12.0	14.1					1.6	-10.1
	18.8	20.6					22.0	10.0
	10.3	10.0				% Profit Before Taxes/Total Assets	6.3	2.6
	5.0	1.9					.2	-2.1
	16.8	12.6					10.8	9.7
	7.7	5.3				Sales/Net Fixed Assets	4.8	6.0
	2.7	3.3					3.1	2.8
	3.1	2.9					2.8	2.7
	2.4	2.0				Sales/Total Assets	1.9	1.9
	1.6	1.7					1.6	1.3
	1.5	1.7					1.1	1.5
	(10) 3.0	(12) 3.5				% Depr., Dep., Amort./Sales	2.5	(26) 3.2
	4.5	4.8					3.9	5.1
							1.4	1.3
						% Officers', Directors', Owners' Comp/Sales	(11) 6.0	(10) 4.9
							6.4	9.1
	36539M	109655M	191216M	83070M		Net Sales ($)	352359M	301617M
	15984M	51923M	124067M	58322M		Total Assets ($)	195449M	197525M

M = $ thousand MM = $ million

See Pages 11 through 21 for Explanation of Ratios and Data

Comparative Historical Data | Current Data Sorted By Sales

				Type of Statement	0-1MM	1-3MM	3-5MM	5-10MM	10-25MM	25MM & OVER
	7	4	3	Unqualified			1		1	2
	9	11	10	Reviewed		5	2	2	1	1
	10	12	5	Compiled		1	2	1	1	1
	1	4	2	Tax Returns		1		1		
	8	7	9	Other	1	3		4		2
	4/1/02-3/31/03	4/1/03-3/31/04	4/1/04-3/31/05			6 (4/1-9/30/04)			23 (10/1/04-3/31/05)	
	ALL	ALL	ALL							
	35	38	29	**NUMBER OF STATEMENTS**	1	5	7	8	3	5
	%	%	%	**ASSETS**	%	%	%	%	%	%
	8.3	3.8	7.0	Cash & Equivalents	D					
	24.7	28.0	26.2	Trade Receivables (net)	A					
	18.3	17.7	22.1	Inventory	T					
	2.5	3.6	2.1	All Other Current	A					
	53.8	53.1	57.3	Total Current						
	31.6	41.1	37.2	Fixed Assets (net)	N					
	6.0	.9	.4	Intangibles (net)	O					
	8.6	4.9	5.1	All Other Non-Current	T					
	100.0	100.0	100.0	Total						
				LIABILITIES	A					
	9.1	12.4	10.2	Notes Payable-Short Term	V					
	4.8	6.8	6.2	Cur. Mat.-L/T/D	A					
	13.1	14.6	15.3	Trade Payables	I					
	.3	.5	.3	Income Taxes Payable	L					
	9.5	7.2	8.7	All Other Current	A					
	36.9	41.5	40.7	Total Current	B					
	20.5	19.7	16.4	Long-Term Debt	L					
	.4	.4	.9	Deferred Taxes	E					
	8.0	5.4	3.1	All Other Non-Current						
	34.2	33.0	38.9	Net Worth						
	100.0	100.0	100.0	Total Liabilities & Net Worth						
				INCOME DATA						
	100.0	100.0	100.0	Net Sales						
	26.2	24.4	24.8	Gross Profit						
	23.7	21.9	18.2	Operating Expenses						
	2.5	2.5	6.7	Operating Profit						
	1.8	1.3	.9	All Other Expenses (net)						
	.7	1.3	5.7	Profit Before Taxes						
				RATIOS						
	2.5	2.2	2.1	Current						
	1.7	1.5	1.4							
	1.1	.9	1.0							
	1.5	1.4	1.4	Quick						
	1.0	.8	.8							
	.6	.5	.6							
	28 13.2	38 9.6	32 11.6	Sales/Receivables						
	48 7.5	52 7.0	46 8.0							
	59 6.2	69 5.3	61 6.0							
	20 18.4	19 19.3	24 15.2	Cost of Sales/Inventory						
	34 10.7	37 9.8	46 8.0							
	61 6.0	68 5.4	70 5.2							
	14 26.0	17 21.2	17 21.5	Cost of Sales/Payables						
	24 15.4	35 10.4	30 12.1							
	41 8.8	56 6.5	44 8.2							
	7.3	6.2	7.2	Sales/Working Capital						
	14.1	11.3	10.7							
	38.1	-75.0	101.0							
	7.5	5.4	16.7	EBIT/Interest						
	(30) 1.8	(32) 1.6	(26) 6.7							
	.1	-1.2	2.4							
	3.1		3.8	Net Profit + Depr., Dep.,						
	(10) 1.3		(10) 2.3	Amort./Cur. Mat. L/T/D						
	-.6		1.5							
	.4	.6	.6	Fixed/Worth						
	1.0	1.3	1.1							
	6.3	2.4	1.8							
	.5	.7	.7	Debt/Worth						
	1.8	1.8	1.7							
	31.5	4.7	3.8							
	25.9	25.5	58.9	% Profit Before Taxes/Tangible						
	(28) 16.7	(33) 13.0	(27) 22.9	Net Worth						
	5.1	-2.7	13.7							
	9.3	8.2	15.8	% Profit Before Taxes/Total						
	3.8	2.7	9.8	Assets						
	.0	-3.8	3.6							
	14.4	8.8	13.0	Sales/Net Fixed Assets						
	8.0	4.4	5.3							
	3.5	2.6	3.4							
	2.7	2.5	2.7	Sales/Total Assets						
	2.1	1.7	2.0							
	1.4	1.4	1.5							
	1.4	2.0	1.8	% Depr., Dep., Amort./Sales						
	(31) 3.2	3.4	(27) 3.3							
	4.1	5.1	4.3							
	1.3	1.5	2.9	% Officers', Directors',						
	(10) 5.2	(16) 6.1	(12) 5.6	Owners' Comp/Sales						
	7.8	9.0	9.0							
	647485M	362669M	420480M	Net Sales ($)		10056M	28847M	60076M	47215M	274286M
	453863M	232506M	250296M	Total Assets ($)		6391M	13561M	24014M	23941M	182389M

© RMA 2005

M = $ thousand   MM = $ million

See Pages 11 through 21 for Explanation of Ratios and Data

Current Data Sorted By Assets   Comparative Historical Data

Type of Statement	0-500M	500M-2MM	2-10MM	10-50MM	50-100MM	100-250MM		4/1/00-3/31/01	4/1/01-3/31/02
Unqualified		5	6	13	2	4		23	21
Reviewed		6	11	6				16	11
Compiled	1	1	4					12	15
Tax Returns	1	1	2					2	4
Other	1	5	13	16	2	1		29	33
		22 (4/1-9/30/04)		77 (10/1/04-3/31/05)				ALL	ALL
NUMBER OF STATEMENTS	2	17	36	35	4	5		82	84

0-500M	500M-2MM	2-10MM	10-50MM	50-100MM	100-250MM		4/1/00-3/31/01	4/1/01-3/31/02
%	%	%	%	%	%	**ASSETS**	%	%
	12.3	5.1	3.9			Cash & Equivalents	5.9	4.7
	32.6	27.4	20.7			Trade Receivables (net)	25.1	22.9
	18.5	28.0	26.5			Inventory	24.8	23.9
	1.3	1.5	1.1			All Other Current	2.1	2.5
	64.7	62.0	52.3			Total Current	57.9	53.9
	27.4	29.9	34.0			Fixed Assets (net)	34.4	35.6
	2.2	2.7	5.8			Intangibles (net)	2.0	3.9
	5.7	5.4	8.0			All Other Non-Current	5.7	6.5
	100.0	100.0	100.0			Total	100.0	100.0
						LIABILITIES		
	13.6	14.3	10.9			Notes Payable-Short Term	10.7	14.6
	4.4	5.3	6.1			Cur. Mat.-L/T/D	4.6	4.8
	22.0	16.0	15.9			Trade Payables	15.0	14.7
	.4	.1	.4			Income Taxes Payable	.4	.3
	6.1	9.3	6.9			All Other Current	7.3	8.0
	46.4	45.0	40.2			Total Current	37.9	42.3
	16.4	15.2	16.0			Long-Term Debt	16.4	21.0
	.0	.8	2.2			Deferred Taxes	.7	.7
	5.6	4.7	7.9			All Other Non-Current	7.7	4.3
	31.6	34.3	33.8			Net Worth	37.3	31.8
	100.0	100.0	100.0			Total Liabilities & Net Worth	100.0	100.0
						INCOME DATA		
	100.0	100.0	100.0			Net Sales	100.0	100.0
	25.5	27.0	18.8			Gross Profit	23.1	24.7
	24.4	21.3	13.7			Operating Expenses	18.3	21.3
	1.2	5.7	5.1			Operating Profit	4.9	3.4
	.2	1.1	.7			All Other Expenses (net)	.8	1.8
	1.0	4.6	4.4			Profit Before Taxes	4.1	1.6
						RATIOS		
	2.2	2.2	2.1				2.4	2.2
	1.3	1.6	1.3			Current	1.5	1.3
	1.1	1.2	1.0				1.1	1.0
	1.7	1.5	1.1				1.3	1.1
	1.0	.8	.6			Quick	.7	.6
	.6	.4	.3				.5	.4
	28 12.8	38 9.6	35 10.5				40 9.1	38 9.7
	52 7.1	50 7.3	54 6.7			Sales/Receivables	47 7.8	48 7.6
	72 5.1	58 6.3	64 5.7				58 6.3	58 6.3
	32 11.5	28 13.2	48 7.6				28 13.3	32 11.5
	50 7.3	65 5.6	77 4.7			Cost of Sales/Inventory	58 6.3	61 5.9
	55 6.6	101 3.6	109 3.3				102 3.6	89 4.1
	18 19.8	26 14.0	31 12.0				21 17.4	25 14.7
	28 13.2	38 9.7	38 9.7			Cost of Sales/Payables	33 11.2	35 10.3
	62 5.9	48 7.5	63 5.8				52 7.1	51 7.2
	5.8	5.5	4.8				4.7	5.6
	19.8	9.5	11.1			Sales/Working Capital	9.7	13.6
	63.6	24.6	-118.1				39.9	NM
	9.0	19.0	8.7				6.4	5.1
	(13) 3.5	(34) 3.9	(32) 2.9			EBIT/Interest	(72) 2.3	(79) 1.8
	-1.7	1.8	1.8				.8	.1
			5.1			Net Profit + Depr., Dep.,	3.1	3.2
			(12) 1.4			Amort./Cur. Mat. L./T/D	(21) 1.4	(28) 1.3
			.5				.6	.7
	.2	.4	.5				.4	.5
	1.0	.7	1.2			Fixed/Worth	.9	1.2
	UND	2.2	4.8				2.0	3.6
	.8	.7	.9				.9	1.1
	1.1	2.3	2.7			Debt/Worth	1.5	1.9
	UND	4.9	6.9				3.6	6.6
	67.2	52.7	40.5			% Profit Before Taxes/Tangible	28.8	29.0
	(13) 29.2	(32) 28.4	(28) 14.7			Net Worth	(73) 15.4	(69) 15.4
	7.4	9.9	7.2				1.8	-2.9
	17.8	19.3	11.9			% Profit Before Taxes/Total	11.3	9.8
	6.4	6.3	6.0			Assets	4.3	3.1
	-4.1	3.4	2.0				-.1	-4.5
	21.3	17.6	10.6				11.8	10.6
	8.4	8.3	4.6			Sales/Net Fixed Assets	5.2	5.1
	5.1	3.9	2.9				3.5	3.1
	2.7	2.5	1.9				2.4	2.2
	2.1	1.9	1.5			Sales/Total Assets	1.6	1.6
	2.0	1.5	1.1				1.3	1.3
	1.1	1.3	2.3				1.3	1.5
	(13) 2.0	(34) 2.6	(32) 3.4			% Depr., Dep., Amort./Sales	(73) 3.0	(80) 3.2
	6.5	5.6	4.7				4.5	4.7
		3.1					2.0	1.9
		(15) 7.0				% Officers', Directors',	(20) 5.4	(19) 3.5
		8.2				Owners' Comp/Sales	9.9	8.4
1253M	47144M	398254M	1341962M	394805M	952810M	Net Sales ($)	2589364M	2453606M
425M	20412M	194736M	891083M	287683M	781553M	Total Assets ($)	1793783M	1706065M

M = $ thousand   MM = $ million
See Pages 11 through 21 for Explanation of Ratios and Data

Comparative Historical Data / Current Data Sorted By Sales

			Type of Statement	0-1MM	1-3MM	3-5MM	5-10MM	10-25MM	25MM & OVER
23	17	25	Unqualified			1	3	5	16
20	21	22	Reviewed		3	5	2	9	3
10	10	10	Compiled	1	4	1	3	1	
8	5	4	Tax Returns	1		1	2		
27	32	38	Other	1	3	4	4	10	16
4/1/02-3/31/03	4/1/03-3/31/04	4/1/04-3/31/05			22 (4/1-9/30/04)		77 (10/1/04-3/31/05)		
ALL	ALL	ALL							
88	85	99	NUMBER OF STATEMENTS	3	10	12	14	25	35
%	%	%	ASSETS	%	%	%	%	%	%
5.9	6.2	5.7	Cash & Equivalents		12.6	10.2	3.9	4.0	4.5
22.6	24.8	26.0	Trade Receivables (net)		32.0	24.5	26.8	23.6	24.3
23.3	23.1	24.9	Inventory		17.8	22.2	26.3	27.4	26.3
2.4	2.7	1.3	All Other Current		1.1	2.2	1.4	1.2	1.1
54.3	56.6	57.9	Total Current		63.5	59.1	58.4	56.1	56.2
35.9	32.1	31.7	Fixed Assets (net)		26.7	32.9	34.7	32.8	31.1
2.7	2.8	3.5	Intangibles (net)		2.8	.9	4.3	5.2	3.3
7.2	8.5	6.9	All Other Non-Current		6.9	7.0	2.6	5.9	9.4
100.0	100.0	100.0	Total		100.0	100.0	100.0	100.0	100.0
			LIABILITIES						
13.6	14.8	11.6	Notes Payable-Short Term		10.2	9.5	9.9	14.9	9.4
6.1	4.8	5.3	Cur. Mat.-L/T/D		4.7	4.0	9.0	4.3	5.5
12.5	17.4	17.1	Trade Payables		18.9	21.2	13.5	15.1	17.3
.1	.3	.2	Income Taxes Payable		.7	.0	.0	.2	.3
7.5	7.6	8.2	All Other Current		6.6	5.0	7.5	10.2	7.6
39.9	44.9	42.5	Total Current		41.1	39.7	39.8	44.8	40.0
20.7	13.8	15.4	Long-Term Debt		12.9	23.1	18.9	17.0	12.1
.8	.7	1.1	Deferred Taxes		.0	.0	.0	.9	2.3
8.6	8.6	6.3	All Other Non-Current		8.7	6.1	5.1	4.6	7.8
30.0	32.0	34.8	Net Worth		37.4	31.0	36.2	32.7	37.7
100.0	100.0	100.0	Total Liabilities & Net Worth		100.0	100.0	100.0	100.0	100.0
			INCOME DATA						
100.0	100.0	100.0	Net Sales		100.0	100.0	100.0	100.0	100.0
23.8	26.7	22.8	Gross Profit		27.7	26.9	27.0	24.5	16.3
22.4	23.9	18.3	Operating Expenses		26.1	23.4	22.0	17.8	12.2
1.4	2.8	4.5	Operating Profit		1.7	3.5	4.9	6.6	4.1
1.2	.7	.8	All Other Expenses (net)		.4	.6	.3	1.0	1.0
.2	2.1	3.7	Profit Before Taxes		1.3	2.9	4.7	5.6	3.1
			RATIOS						
2.1	2.5	2.2			2.7	2.2	2.4	2.1	2.2
1.4	1.5	1.5	Current		1.2	1.8	1.6	1.3	1.5
1.0	1.1	1.1			1.1	1.2	1.0	1.1	1.1
1.2	1.3	1.3			1.7	1.9	1.3	1.2	1.1
.7	.8	.8	Quick		1.0	.7	.7	.7	.8
.5	.5	.4			.6	.3	.4	.3	.6
36 10.0	41 8.8	37 9.7		38 9.7	21 17.5	41 9.0	37 9.8	41 9.0	
48 7.6	49 7.5	52 7.0	Sales/Receivables	52 7.0	36 10.2	48 7.5	52 7.0	58 6.3	
60 6.1	59 6.2	63 5.8		68 5.3	59 6.2	60 6.1	59 6.2	68 5.4	
34 10.8	31 11.7	42 8.7		36 10.2	3 105.2	34 10.8	46 7.9	46 8.0	
62 5.9	53 6.9	58 6.3	Cost of Sales/Inventory	50 7.2	46 7.9	79 4.6	71 5.2	69 5.3	
105 3.5	94 3.9	99 3.7		54 6.8	108 3.4	94 3.9	137 2.7	101 3.6	
19 19.6	20 17.9	27 13.5		17 21.1	14 25.7	25 14.8	30 12.2	31 12.0	
32 11.3	32 11.4	38 9.5	Cost of Sales/Payables	33 11.0	31 11.8	34 10.8	45 8.1	40 9.0	
47 7.7	49 7.5	54 6.8		51 7.1	81 4.5	49 7.4	55 6.6	58 6.3	
5.7	4.7	5.3			5.3	4.9	5.6	5.5	3.9
11.9	11.3	10.4	Sales/Working Capital		23.5	11.0	8.6	11.5	9.5
786.4	59.6	39.1			48.4	19.4	NM	40.5	39.1
4.5	8.2	9.6				19.5	8.6	10.2	8.4
(80) 1.9	(78) 2.8	(88) 3.2	EBIT/Interest		(11) 2.3	(12) 3.2	6.5	(32) 2.8	
.3	.4	1.5				.9	1.9	2.4	.0
3.3	4.1	8.1	Net Profit + Depr., Dep.,						8.1
(26) 2.0	(17) 2.4	(24) 2.2	Amort./Cur. Mat. L/T/D					(12)	2.8
.6	1.6	.8							.8
.6	.3	.5			.2	.3	.5	.4	.5
1.2	.8	.8	Fixed/Worth		.7	1.0	.9	.8	.7
3.6	2.1	2.4			UND	-10.8	3.8	14.0	1.5
1.1	.8	.9			.8	.5	1.0	.6	.9
2.2	1.9	2.3	Debt/Worth		2.0	1.8	2.0	2.9	2.2
8.6	5.1	6.6			UND	-20.9	9.2	31.5	3.7
24.3	31.5	45.8	% Profit Before Taxes/Tangible				40.3	55.7	33.7
(69) 10.0	(75) 14.1	(83) 17.9	Net Worth			(13) 28.6	(20) 19.0	(32) 9.3	
-5.0	-1.9	7.1					8.0	10.7	2.5
7.3	9.2	13.3	% Profit Before Taxes/Total		16.9	18.5	16.1	14.2	12.3
3.3	4.6	5.3	Assets		8.4	6.7	4.9	8.4	3.2
-3.2	-.9	2.0			-3.4	.4	3.0	3.9	-1.5
9.5	13.3	14.1			15.6	20.4	17.9	13.4	11.8
4.3	5.1	5.5	Sales/Net Fixed Assets		7.9	8.7	5.9	4.8	4.6
2.9	3.2	3.5			5.7	3.4	3.5	2.9	3.3
2.1	2.2	2.2			2.6	2.6	2.5	2.3	1.9
1.7	1.7	1.7	Sales/Total Assets		2.1	2.0	1.7	1.8	1.6
1.3	1.3	1.3			2.0	1.4	1.5	1.1	1.3
2.0	1.8	1.5				1.9	1.2	2.2	1.3
(82) 3.9	(80) 3.4	(86) 3.3	% Depr., Dep., Amort./Sales		(10) 4.7	(13) 4.0	(24) 3.3	(30) 3.3	
6.0	5.6	5.0				7.2	6.1	4.1	4.8
2.5	1.9	2.5	% Officers', Directors',						
(28) 6.2	(31) 4.1	(26) 5.0	Owners' Comp/Sales						
12.0	5.8	8.2							
2157727M	2089133M	3136228M	Net Sales ($)	1852M	24903M	45174M	111647M	391578M	2561074M
1637446M	1506072M	2175892M	Total Assets ($)	1242M	11459M	25616M	68139M	271080M	1798356M

© RMA 2005

M = $ thousand   MM = $ million
See Pages 11 through 21 for Explanation of Ratios and Data

Current Data Sorted By Assets   Comparative Historical Data

						Type of Statement		
2	1	11	29	7	1	Unqualified	36	35
1	16	62	19	1		Reviewed	74	77
3	24	20	6			Compiled	62	53
8	7	4	2			Tax Returns	12	13
1	16	27	19	7	2	Other	72	63

60 (4/1-9/30/04)			236 (10/1/04-3/31/05)				4/1/00-3/31/01	4/1/01-3/31/02
0-500M	500M-2MM	2-10MM	10-50MM	50-100MM	100-250MM		ALL	ALL
15	64	124	75	15	3	NUMBER OF STATEMENTS	256	241
%	%	%	%	%	%	ASSETS	%	%
7.3	7.2	6.0	5.9	2.2		Cash & Equivalents	6.2	6.8
34.4	32.2	28.4	26.7	22.5		Trade Receivables (net)	26.1	24.5
21.9	21.6	23.3	22.4	16.7		Inventory	20.7	21.0
3.4	1.3	1.6	1.8	2.8		All Other Current	1.9	1.6
67.0	62.3	59.4	56.8	44.2		Total Current	55.0	53.8
27.2	28.6	31.8	33.7	39.9		Fixed Assets (net)	36.6	37.3
3.5	3.9	3.0	2.3	7.8		Intangibles (net)	3.2	3.7
2.4	5.3	5.8	7.2	8.2		All Other Non-Current	5.2	5.2
100.0	100.0	100.0	100.0	100.0		Total	100.0	100.0
						LIABILITIES		
11.9	13.5	10.3	9.2	9.6		Notes Payable-Short Term	8.3	8.8
5.4	6.1	4.4	5.3	4.7		Cur. Mat.-L/T/D	5.9	5.5
10.6	19.7	15.4	12.9	16.1		Trade Payables	14.1	13.1
.2	.3	.1	.4	.2		Income Taxes Payable	.3	.2
19.3	8.6	6.1	8.8	11.9		All Other Current	8.7	6.7
47.5	48.1	36.3	36.6	42.5		Total Current	37.2	34.3
25.5	15.3	15.0	17.1	25.3		Long-Term Debt	18.5	19.3
.3	.6	.9	.5	.9		Deferred Taxes	.9	.8
9.7	6.6	6.8	7.4	18.9		All Other Non-Current	4.6	4.5
17.0	29.4	41.0	38.5	12.4		Net Worth	38.7	41.2
100.0	100.0	100.0	100.0	100.0		Total Liabilities & Net Worth	100.0	100.0
						INCOME DATA		
100.0	100.0	100.0	100.0	100.0		Net Sales	100.0	100.0
42.7	31.6	24.1	20.1	15.3		Gross Profit	25.6	24.4
42.8	29.5	18.9	15.2	11.2		Operating Expenses	20.7	21.7
-.1	2.1	5.2	4.8	4.1		Operating Profit	4.9	2.7
.7	1.2	.7	.7	2.3		All Other Expenses (net)	1.3	1.5
-.8	.9	4.4	4.1	1.8		Profit Before Taxes	3.6	1.1
						RATIOS		
2.6	2.3	2.7	2.3	1.6			2.3	2.9
1.4	1.4	1.7	1.6	1.1		Current	1.6	1.6
.7	1.0	1.1	1.2	.8			1.1	1.1
2.6	1.4	1.7	1.4	.9			1.4	1.7
1.0	.9	.9	.8	.6		Quick	.9	.9
.3	.5	.6	.6	.5			.6	.6

												Sales/Receivables				
27	13.8	33	10.9	38	9.6	46	7.9	47	7.7				35	10.3	34	10.9
43	8.4	47	7.8	51	7.2	55	6.6	51	7.2			Sales/Receivables	46	7.9	44	8.2
90	4.1	63	5.8	60	6.1	69	5.3	56	6.5				56	6.5	56	6.5
4	102.8	23	15.6	34	10.8	41	8.9	29	12.7				28	13.0	30	12.2
46	8.0	46	7.9	52	7.1	53	6.8	42	8.7			Cost of Sales/Inventory	45	8.1	45	8.0
134	2.7	65	5.6	76	4.8	80	4.6	52	7.0				67	5.4	73	5.0
15	25.0	25	14.7	21	17.3	17	21.4	37	9.9				19	18.8	16	22.4
30	12.0	40	9.1	31	11.7	26	13.8	40	9.1			Cost of Sales/Payables	29	12.8	26	14.1
68	5.4	55	6.6	48	7.6	44	8.3	45	8.1				41	8.9	40	9.1

									Sales/Working Capital		
	6.0		6.2		5.4		4.4	8.7		6.2	5.6
	17.4		16.4		9.6		9.0	77.2	Sales/Working Capital	11.1	10.0
	-9.0		-999.8		30.1		30.2	-14.6		62.1	46.0

														EBIT/Interest				
	5.7		6.2		12.5		16.0		6.6					7.4		4.5
(12)	1.6	(59)	2.3	(116)	4.8	(72)	5.5	(14)	1.4			EBIT/Interest	(238)	2.9	(225)	1.8
	-2.7		.1		1.6		1.5		.5					1.2		.3

													Net Profit + Depr., Dep., Amort./Cur. Mat. L /T/D				
			3.0		5.3		6.8						3.9		3.5
		(11)	1.7	(31)	3.6	(25)	3.5			Net Profit + Depr., Dep., Amort./Cur. Mat. L /T/D	(80)	2.0	(72)	1.6
			.4		1.5		2.5					1.1		.7

									Fixed/Worth		
	.2		.4		.4		.4	1.0		.5	.5
	.7		.9		.8		.8	-5.8	Fixed/Worth	1.1	1.0
	95.5		3.4		1.8		1.8	-1.5		2.1	2.0
	.9		1.1		.6		.6	1.4		.7	.7
	4.8		2.6		1.5		1.7	-14.4	Debt/Worth	1.7	1.6
	-7.6		13.0		3.6		4.1	-4.3		4.3	3.9

													% Profit Before Taxes/Tangible Net Worth		
	66.4		54.2		42.0		44.5					40.0		26.3
(10)	12.8	(52)	7.6	(112)	23.0	(67)	17.7			% Profit Before Taxes/Tangible Net Worth	(229)	18.8	(222)	9.3
	-8.9		-.6		3.9		5.3					3.6		-4.0

								% Profit Before Taxes/Total Assets		
	13.8		12.5		17.0		12.3	8.5		14.1	8.4
	.0		1.2		8.5		7.2	2.4	% Profit Before Taxes/Total Assets	6.1	2.9
	-14.8		-3.7		1.1		1.5	-3.7		.7	-1.9

								Sales/Net Fixed Assets		
	65.8		19.8		10.8		8.7	5.4		10.0	8.9
	18.1		10.2		6.8		6.0	4.3	Sales/Net Fixed Assets	5.6	5.6
	3.8		5.2		4.6		3.5	2.9		3.8	3.4

								Sales/Total Assets		
	3.8		3.0		2.5		2.2	2.2		2.7	2.5
	2.3		2.5		2.1		1.8	1.5	Sales/Total Assets	2.1	2.0
	1.5		1.9		1.7		1.4	1.1		1.5	1.5

										% Depr., Dep., Amort./Sales		
	1.5		1.5		2.1		1.7	3.3		1.9	2.2
(11)	2.3	(52)	3.1	(120)	3.0	(70)	2.8	(12)	4.5	% Depr., Dep., Amort./Sales	(236)	3.1	(219)	3.5
	6.3		5.1		4.5		4.5	5.8		4.9	5.6

								% Officers', Directors', Owners' Comp/Sales		
			3.3		1.9		1.2			2.9	2.1
		(39)	5.6	(56)	3.2	(25)	1.5		% Officers', Directors', Owners' Comp/Sales	(112)	5.9	(100)	4.9
			9.4		6.0		4.5			8.8	8.4

						Net Sales ($)		
12090M	189372M	1282903M	2573786M	1940675M	540552M	Net Sales ($)	4253687M	4556160M
4149M	77698M	619104M	1500726M	1147777M	403251M	Total Assets ($)	2461283M	2861080M

© RMA 2005   M = $ thousand   MM = $ million   See Pages 11 through 21 for Explanation of Ratios and Data

Comparative Historical Data / Current Data Sorted By Sales

4/1/02-3/31/03 ALL	4/1/03-3/31/04 ALL	4/1/04-3/31/05 ALL	Type of Statement	0-1MM	1-3MM	3-5MM	5-10MM	10-25MM	25MM & OVER
53	49	51	Unqualified	1	1		5	15	29
96	90	99	Reviewed	1	6	17	28	37	10
64	74	53	Compiled	4	12	13	11	11	2
10	16	21	Tax Returns	7	5	3	3	2	1
84	76	72	Other	2	9	10	11	19	21
				60 (4/1-9/30/04)			236 (10/1/04-3/31/05)		
307	305	296	**NUMBER OF STATEMENTS**	15	33	43	58	84	63
%	%	%	**ASSETS**	%	%	%	%	%	%
7.7	7.1	6.2	Cash & Equivalents	6.9	7.3	7.6	6.4	6.5	3.8
25.4	26.3	28.7	Trade Receivables (net)	28.2	29.3	30.9	27.8	28.2	28.5
20.5	19.9	22.2	Inventory	26.3	19.0	21.9	22.0	23.6	21.5
1.6	2.3	1.8	All Other Current	1.0	1.8	3.5	1.6	1.3	1.7
55.2	55.7	58.9	Total Current	62.4	57.4	63.8	57.9	59.6	55.5
36.4	35.6	31.8	Fixed Assets (net)	25.6	32.7	29.9	32.8	29.4	36.5
2.9	2.4	3.3	Intangibles (net)	9.7	3.6	1.2	2.6	3.8	3.2
5.5	6.3	6.0	All Other Non-Current	2.3	6.3	5.1	6.7	7.2	4.9
100.0	100.0	100.0	Total	100.0	100.0	100.0	100.0	100.0	100.0
			LIABILITIES						
10.2	9.3	10.7	Notes Payable-Short Term	20.3	11.3	12.2	8.4	10.2	9.9
6.0	5.6	5.0	Cur. Mat.-L/T/D	5.5	8.6	4.3	3.8	5.1	4.5
13.3	13.5	15.5	Trade Payables	11.9	16.1	18.6	14.5	14.3	16.4
.1	.1	.2	Income Taxes Payable	.2	.5	.0	.2	.2	.3
8.9	8.6	8.3	All Other Current	18.5	7.6	8.7	6.8	6.4	10.0
38.6	37.2	39.8	Total Current	56.4	44.1	43.8	33.7	36.2	41.1
18.8	16.8	16.6	Long-Term Debt	20.2	21.6	12.6	17.4	14.3	18.4
.6	.7	.7	Deferred Taxes	.4	.1	.8	.7	.9	.7
5.7	6.1	7.7	All Other Non-Current	10.4	1.8	8.3	6.1	9.9	8.1
36.3	39.2	35.2	Net Worth	12.5	32.3	34.5	42.1	38.7	31.7
100.0	100.0	100.0	Total Liabilities & Net Worth	100.0	100.0	100.0	100.0	100.0	100.0
			INCOME DATA						
100.0	100.0	100.0	Net Sales	100.0	100.0	100.0	100.0	100.0	100.0
25.0	25.4	25.1	Gross Profit	37.0	36.1	29.2	25.6	22.2	17.1
23.0	22.4	21.0	Operating Expenses	42.1	32.2	26.3	21.8	16.2	12.2
2.0	3.0	4.1	Operating Profit	-5.1	3.9	2.9	3.8	6.0	4.9
1.4	1.0	.9	All Other Expenses (net)	2.2	1.2	.7	1.0	.5	1.2
.6	2.0	3.2	Profit Before Taxes	-7.3	2.7	2.2	2.8	5.5	3.6
			RATIOS						
2.5	2.6	2.5	Current	2.4	2.5	2.3	3.0	2.6	2.0
1.4	1.5	1.5		1.2	1.3	1.5	1.6	1.8	1.4
1.0	1.0	1.1		.5	.9	1.1	1.1	1.2	1.0
1.6	1.5	1.5	Quick	1.3	2.0	1.6	1.8	1.7	1.2
.8	.9	.9		.5	.8	.8	1.0	1.0	.8
.5	.6	.6		.2	.5	.5	.6	.6	.6
36 10.0	39 9.4	38 9.6	Sales/Receivables	35 10.4	36 10.1	31 11.8	37 9.8	39 9.4	46 7.9
47 7.7	49 7.5	52 7.1		43 8.4	55 6.7	50 7.3	51 7.1	51 7.2	54 6.8
57 6.4	59 6.2	63 5.8		95 3.9	63 5.8	62 5.9	61 6.0	63 5.8	64 5.7
31 11.8	30 12.1	33 11.0	Cost of Sales/Inventory	38 9.6	16 23.2	25 14.5	33 11.0	37 9.8	33 11.0
46 7.9	46 7.9	50 7.4		72 5.1	42 8.6	54 6.8	52 7.0	51 7.1	46 8.0
76 4.8	71 5.1	72 5.1		157 2.3	95 3.8	65 5.6	77 4.7	77 4.7	61 6.0
19 19.7	16 22.8	21 17.6	Cost of Sales/Payables	19 19.0	16 23.2	25 14.7	20 18.0	18 19.8	20 17.8
30 12.1	31 11.8	34 10.8		40 9.1	43 8.5	41 8.9	28 13.0	29 12.7	35 10.6
43 8.5	44 8.3	49 7.5		70 5.2	61 6.0	56 6.6	48 7.7	42 8.7	47 7.7
5.8	5.5	5.6	Sales/Working Capital	5.9	5.8	5.5	5.2	5.1	6.4
11.6	10.3	11.7		49.6	19.6	11.7	10.0	8.4	12.6
-443.5	354.3	57.7		-4.2	UND	25.6	80.0	19.8	135.6
5.3	7.2	12.0	EBIT/Interest	3.7	8.2	9.7	8.4	14.4	14.9
(287) 1.7	(277) 2.2	(276) 4.2		(12) -.2	(30) 3.5	(41) 1.2	(54) 3.7	(79) 5.8	(60) 5.3
.0	.1	1.0		-5.1	.1	.2	1.5	2.3	1.0
3.1	2.7	4.5	Net Profit + Depr., Dep., Amort./Cur. Mat. L/T/D				4.2	7.8	3.6
(94) 1.6	(81) 1.4	(76) 2.9					(15) 2.0	(23) 4.4	(24) 2.7
.5	.4	1.4					1.5	3.4	1.4
.5	.5	.4	Fixed/Worth	.1	.5	.3	.4	.4	.7
1.0	1.0	.9		1.2	.7	.8	.8	.7	1.1
2.9	2.4	2.8		-1.5	3.0	2.6	1.8	1.8	3.7
.7	.6	.7	Debt/Worth	.9	.8	.9	.6	.6	.8
2.2	1.7	1.9		134.5	2.2	1.6	1.8	1.6	2.0
5.6	4.5	6.4		-4.0	8.0	6.4	3.2	4.6	10.2
26.5	28.1	42.8	% Profit Before Taxes/Tangible Net Worth		59.3	27.3	30.8	53.4	47.0
(267) 8.4	(276) 8.8	(250) 18.0		(28) 30.0	(38) 3.4	(54) 12.7	(72) 25.1	(50) 20.0	
-5.8	-1.4	2.2		-12.8	-4.6	2.7	10.4	7.9	
9.2	10.1	13.8	% Profit Before Taxes/Total Assets	1.8	18.5	11.2	12.5	16.1	12.6
2.1	3.0	6.4		-5.6	6.4	.5	4.2	9.1	7.0
-2.6	-1.0	.0		-18.1	-6.8	-2.2	1.3	2.6	-.5
9.4	10.0	12.7	Sales/Net Fixed Assets	65.8	16.6	20.4	13.0	11.8	8.2
5.3	5.5	6.9		12.4	8.3	8.3	6.8	7.2	5.4
3.5	3.6	4.3		2.1	3.8	4.3	4.2	5.1	3.8
2.5	2.4	2.6	Sales/Total Assets	2.3	2.8	2.9	2.5	2.5	2.3
1.9	1.9	2.0		1.5	2.1	2.3	2.1	2.0	2.0
1.4	1.4	1.5		.9	1.2	1.7	1.6	1.6	1.5
2.5	2.3	1.9	% Depr., Dep., Amort./Sales	1.7	1.8	1.6	1.8	2.1	2.1
(283) 3.7	(289) 3.7	(267) 3.1		(10) 4.5	(27) 5.0	(37) 3.0	(56) 3.0	(81) 3.0	(56) 3.1
5.5	5.5	4.7		10.9	6.3	4.2	4.7	4.4	3.9
2.1	2.0	1.9	% Officers', Directors', Owners' Comp/Sales		3.9	2.0	1.9	1.4	1.1
(137) 4.5	(138) 4.1	(128) 3.8			(21) 6.3	(26) 3.7	(27) 3.2	(33) 3.0	(13) 1.4
7.8	6.9				8.9	6.7	8.1	5.5	3.2
5353564M	5317909M	6539378M	Net Sales ($)	8876M	63667M	171957M	413327M	1335384M	4546167M
3372480M	3201289M	3752705M	Total Assets ($)	6325M	35959M	101671M	264083M	768369M	2576298M

M = $ thousand   MM = $ million
See Pages 11 through 21 for Explanation of Ratios and Data

Current Data Sorted By Assets   Comparative Historical Data

0-500M	500M-2MM	2-10MM	10-50MM	50-100MM	100-250MM	Type of Statement	4/1/00-3/31/01 ALL	4/1/01-3/31/02 ALL
	3	5	8	1	3	Unqualified	10	8
2	9	15	5			Reviewed	11	8
1	5	7	1			Compiled	6	8
3	5		4	2		Tax Returns	2	3
		6				Other	6	11
	18 (4/1-9/30/04)		67 (10/1/04-3/31/05)					
6	22	33	18	3	3	**NUMBER OF STATEMENTS**	35	38
%	%	%	%	%	%	**ASSETS**	%	%
	6.7	6.1	6.8			Cash & Equivalents	6.4	5.9
	27.0	23.2	27.6			Trade Receivables (net)	25.8	24.7
	29.3	35.8	27.3			Inventory	30.7	28.2
	1.4	2.3	4.5			All Other Current	1.2	3.5
	64.3	67.4	66.3			Total Current	64.2	62.3
	28.4	22.0	22.7			Fixed Assets (net)	25.6	27.9
	2.3	4.3	2.4			Intangibles (net)	6.1	3.8
	4.9	6.3	8.7			All Other Non-Current	4.2	6.0
	100.0	100.0	100.0			Total	100.0	100.0
						LIABILITIES		
	9.2	13.6	7.8			Notes Payable-Short Term	12.1	15.8
	7.5	3.7	1.6			Cur. Mat.-L/T/D	4.9	4.2
	12.2	12.2	7.8			Trade Payables	13.0	10.4
	.0	.0	.3			Income Taxes Payable	.2	.3
	5.5	9.3	7.1			All Other Current	8.2	8.1
	34.5	38.8	24.6			Total Current	38.3	38.7
	17.0	13.9	8.5			Long-Term Debt	20.2	24.5
	.4	.3	.1			Deferred Taxes	.1	.7
	5.5	4.1	5.0			All Other Non-Current	5.1	3.6
	42.6	42.9	61.9			Net Worth	36.3	32.4
	100.0	100.0	100.0			Total Liabilities & Net Worth	100.0	100.0
						INCOME DATA		
	100.0	100.0	100.0			Net Sales	100.0	100.0
	43.0	31.0	32.9			Gross Profit	35.3	36.2
	39.4	27.4	23.0			Operating Expenses	31.8	35.0
	3.6	3.5	9.9			Operating Profit	3.5	1.1
	1.1	1.3	.7			All Other Expenses (net)	2.1	2.5
	2.5	2.3	9.2			Profit Before Taxes	1.4	-1.3
						RATIOS		
	3.3	3.0	5.1			Current	3.8	3.2
	1.8	1.7	3.0				1.6	1.7
	1.2	1.2	1.8				1.1	1.1
	2.3	1.3	2.3			Quick	1.8	1.5
	1.0	.7	1.6				.9	.8
	.4	.4	.9				.6	.5
	33 11.1	38 9.5	41 8.8			Sales/Receivables	33 11.1	38 9.5
	38 9.6	47 7.7	54 6.8				42 8.6	43 8.4
	56 6.6	63 5.8	68 5.3				54 6.7	55 6.6
	17 20.9	77 4.7	65 5.6			Cost of Sales/Inventory	60 6.1	45 8.1
	64 5.7	123 3.0	82 4.4				91 4.0	92 4.0
	221 1.7	183 2.0	116 3.1				119 3.1	127 2.9
	16 23.1	19 19.3	17 21.0			Cost of Sales/Payables	19 18.9	16 23.4
	31 11.7	31 11.7	23 16.1				31 11.9	25 14.6
	47 7.7	54 6.8	32 11.4				42 8.6	44 8.3
	3.9	3.6	2.9			Sales/Working Capital	4.0	4.3
	7.6	6.2	4.1				6.4	8.5
	16.6	16.0	6.9				62.6	22.7
	9.7	4.3	34.2			EBIT/Interest	6.4	4.0
	(31) 4.2	2.0	(15) 13.9				(33) 2.4	(36) 1.4
	1.3	.0	4.0				.7	-1.8
		2.1				Net Profit + Depr., Dep.,	2.3	2.4
		(11) .7				Amort./Cur. Mat. L /T/D	(10) 1.1	(11) 1.5
		.3					.8	.1
	.3	.2	.2			Fixed/Worth	.3	.4
	.7	.6	.3				.8	.8
	1.1	1.6	.5				1.4	3.5
	.7	.4	.2			Debt/Worth	.8	.9
	1.6	1.6	.6				1.6	1.8
	3.1	6.6	1.2				7.1	11.1
	26.7	27.6	31.6			% Profit Before Taxes/Tangible	35.7	21.3
	9.3	(29) 11.8	22.5			Net Worth	(29) 14.1	(30) 9.5
	.4	-4.5	11.8				2.3	-25.0
	12.3	10.4	20.9			% Profit Before Taxes/Total	14.9	9.6
	4.0	3.0	10.5			Assets	3.6	1.6
	.2	-1.7	5.8				-.8	-10.0
	18.2	14.0	13.0			Sales/Net Fixed Assets	15.8	16.7
	9.8	8.6	7.8				7.8	6.5
	3.1	5.4	5.1				5.5	3.9
	2.7	2.0	2.2			Sales/Total Assets	2.5	2.5
	2.0	1.6	1.7				2.0	1.8
	1.2	1.3	1.2				1.5	1.3
	1.8	1.8	1.4			% Depr., Dep., Amort./Sales	1.2	1.5
	(19) 5.1	(31) 2.8	(17) 2.4				(34) 2.3	(35) 2.6
	8.3	4.0	3.8				4.1	4.4
	3.7	1.3				% Officers', Directors',	3.0	4.0
	(17) 6.7	(13) 3.4				Owners' Comp/Sales	(20) 6.7	(16) 7.6
	8.8	8.6					8.3	9.5
3456M	61328M	254268M	541847M	295257M	578075M	Net Sales ($)	788830M	627143M
1495M	28548M	149373M	318502M	185165M	511309M	Total Assets ($)	523525M	354654M

© RMA 2005

M = $ thousand   MM = $ million
See Pages 11 through 21 for Explanation of Ratios and Data

Comparative Historical Data / Current Data Sorted By Sales

			Type of Statement						
19	19	17	Unqualified				2	5	10
12	20	23	Reviewed		2		8	6	1
9	9	19	Compiled	3	4	7	2	2	1
4	7	6	Tax Returns	3	1	2			1
12	19	20	Other	4	3	2	4	3	4
4/1/02-3/31/03	4/1/03-3/31/04	4/1/04-3/31/05		18 (4/1-9/30/04)			67 (10/1/04-3/31/05)		
ALL	ALL	ALL		0-1MM	1-3MM	3-5MM	5-10MM	10-25MM	25MM & OVER
56	74	85	**NUMBER OF STATEMENTS**	10	10	17	16	16	16
%	%	%	**ASSETS**	%	%	%	%	%	%
7.8	7.4	6.4	Cash & Equivalents	5.7	6.3	5.2	7.7	7.1	6.0
24.9	25.3	25.6	Trade Receivables (net)	28.4	19.8	24.6	28.0	25.6	26.2
31.9	31.3	31.4	Inventory	29.9	26.5	35.0	35.2	32.2	27.0
1.7	1.7	2.4	All Other Current	1.0	.8	1.0	2.0	6.4	2.3
66.3	65.7	65.8	Total Current	65.0	53.3	65.8	72.9	71.4	61.5
22.4	22.6	23.3	Fixed Assets (net)	25.1	30.1	25.7	18.8	20.8	22.6
4.2	3.1	4.0	Intangibles (net)	1.9	10.2	2.9	1.4	2.2	7.0
7.1	8.7	6.8	All Other Non-Current	7.9	6.4	5.5	6.9	5.7	8.9
100.0	100.0	100.0	Total	100.0	100.0	100.0	100.0	100.0	100.0
			LIABILITIES						
8.7	15.7	14.2	Notes Payable-Short Term	41.8	10.7	13.4	8.6	11.1	8.4
4.0	3.5	3.8	Cur. Mat.-L/T/D	2.9	6.0	7.3	2.9	3.1	.9
11.5	12.2	12.2	Trade Payables	18.6	6.1	11.7	18.0	10.9	7.9
.1	.2	.1	Income Taxes Payable	.0	.0	.0	.0	.4	.1
10.4	9.1	8.5	All Other Current	15.7	3.3	8.4	10.5	6.6	7.4
34.7	40.7	38.8	Total Current	79.1	26.1	40.8	40.0	32.1	24.7
17.1	14.7	14.0	Long-Term Debt	25.8	23.6	15.9	5.4	9.6	11.6
.2	.3	.3	Deferred Taxes	.0	.0	.3	.6	.2	.3
4.5	6.0	5.1	All Other Non-Current	4.0	4.6	7.5	4.3	4.6	4.8
43.5	38.2	41.9	Net Worth	−8.9	45.7	35.4	49.6	53.5	58.6
100.0	100.0	100.0	Total Liabilities & Net Worth	100.0	100.0	100.0	100.0	100.0	100.0
			INCOME DATA						
100.0	100.0	100.0	Net Sales	100.0	100.0	100.0	100.0	100.0	100.0
36.0	34.6	35.6	Gross Profit	51.7	44.9	31.9	31.6	32.4	31.0
31.9	30.8	30.6	Operating Expenses	51.8	38.1	30.0	27.3	25.7	21.3
4.1	3.8	5.0	Operating Profit	.0	6.8	1.8	4.2	6.7	9.7
1.1	1.0	1.1	All Other Expenses (net)	1.8	1.8	1.6	.6	.6	.8
3.0	2.8	3.9	Profit Before Taxes	−1.9	5.0	.2	3.6	6.1	8.8
			RATIOS						
3.7	3.5	3.5	Current	2.7	7.0	2.6	4.1	5.0	3.9
2.3	2.1	1.9		1.2	1.6	1.8	1.7	2.5	3.0
1.4	1.2	1.3		.4	1.2	1.2	1.2	1.5	1.7
1.6	1.9	1.7	Quick	1.5	2.7	1.3	1.6	2.1	2.0
1.2	.9	.8		.5	1.0	.7	.8	1.2	1.5
.6	.5	.5		.2	.4	.4	.5	.6	.8
35 10.5	32 11.4	37 9.9	Sales/Receivables	31 11.8	30 12.1	39 9.4	34 10.7	38 9.7	41 9.0
45 8.1	46 8.0	47 7.7		42 8.7	37 9.8	46 8.0	47 7.7	51 7.2	49 7.5
59 6.2	59 6.2	59 6.2		69 5.3	57 6.4	59 6.2	65 5.6	60 6.0	58 6.3
52 7.1	56 6.6	58 6.3	Cost of Sales/Inventory	34 10.6	0 UND	37 9.9	39 9.3	79 4.6	63 5.8
99 3.7	94 3.9	96 3.8		174 2.1	91 4.0	103 3.5	113 3.2	96 3.8	79 4.6
139 2.6	128 2.9	157 2.3		348 1.0	267 1.4	198 1.8	175 2.1	135 2.7	108 3.4
15 24.4	15 24.6	18 19.8	Cost of Sales/Payables	10 36.5	11 32.0	16 23.3	23 16.0	19 19.3	15 24.5
28 13.2	24 14.9	30 12.2		41 8.9	20 18.0	30 12.1	41 8.8	29 12.5	24 15.3
47 7.8	38 9.6	45 8.1		124 2.9	63 5.8	40 9.1	70 5.2	36 10.0	36 10.1
3.4	3.5	3.6	Sales/Working Capital	2.7	3.7	4.2	2.5	2.9	3.5
5.4	6.1	5.7		14.4	8.9	6.6	7.3	4.7	4.5
13.6	16.2	13.8		−3.5	19.7	24.4	21.6	7.5	7.6
8.6	14.3	12.2	EBIT/Interest		9.7	4.9	10.7	16.3	36.8
(53) 4.2	(69) 4.2	(79) 3.8			4.2	1.6	(14) 3.8	(15) 4.0	(14) 13.1
1.0	1.0	.9			1.8	.8	−.5	2.7	7.6
9.9	6.5	9.2	Net Profit + Depr., Dep., Amort./Cur. Mat. L/T/D						
(17) 2.4	(21) 2.2	(26) 3.1							
1.0	.4	.7							
.3	.3	.3	Fixed/Worth	.5	.6	.2	.2	.2	.3
.4	.6	.6		2.5	.8	.7	.3	.4	.4
.9	1.4	1.3		−.7	1.6	2.0	.8	.7	.7
.5	.5	.4	Debt/Worth	1.5	.6	.8	.3	.4	.3
1.5	1.4	1.3		7.6	2.0	2.0	.9	1.0	.8
4.6	5.2	3.6		−6.4	3.5	4.9	2.9	1.9	1.4
37.6	34.3	30.5	% Profit Before Taxes/Tangible Net Worth			27.4	28.9	30.4	41.7
(52) 12.8	(63) 12.1	(77) 15.1			(15) 6.8	9.8	(15) 15.7	(15) 24.3	
1.8	1.5	4.6				−2.4	−5.0	8.0	13.9
11.7	12.8	12.7	% Profit Before Taxes/Total Assets	12.9	11.2	8.1	13.8	16.8	22.4
6.9	5.9	6.0		.4	4.9	.4	4.6	8.9	11.2
.6	−2.0	.1		−16.2	3.2	−.9	−2.4	3.1	5.8
21.1	21.9	16.8	Sales/Net Fixed Assets	28.6	11.1	20.9	16.4	27.8	14.5
9.3	9.9	8.6		12.9	8.5	8.1	10.1	8.3	7.8
5.1	4.7	5.1		2.2	2.7	3.6	7.2	5.6	4.9
2.5	2.6	2.3	Sales/Total Assets	3.6	2.1	2.5	2.0	2.4	2.2
1.7	1.9	1.7		1.3	1.6	1.8	1.8	1.8	1.7
1.4	1.5	1.2		.7	1.0	1.2	1.4	1.2	1.4
1.5	1.7	1.6	% Depr., Dep., Amort./Sales			1.9	1.2	1.5	1.4
(47) 2.6	(68) 2.9	(74) 2.9			(15) 3.6	(15) 1.8	(15) 2.9	(13) 1.7	
4.2	4.4	4.6				5.1	3.1	4.0	2.7
3.4	2.9	2.5	% Officers', Directors', Owners' Comp/Sales			3.2			
(19) 7.0	(26) 4.2	(37) 5.2			(12) 3.8				
9.4	8.9	7.8				8.3			
1944009M	1986201M	1734231M	Net Sales ($)	5979M	21498M	65999M	106575M	250192M	1283988M
1236281M	1104097M	1194392M	Total Assets ($)	5561M	17112M	41403M	69021M	151384M	909911M

M = $ thousand   MM = $ million
See Pages 11 through 21 for Explanation of Ratios and Data

Current Data Sorted By Assets   Comparative Historical Data

0-500M	500M-2MM	2-10MM	10-50MM	50-100MM	100-250MM	Type of Statement	4/1/00-3/31/01	4/1/01-3/31/02
		7	4	2	3	Unqualified	12	12
	6	17	7			Reviewed	10	13
1	5	6				Compiled	6	12
1	1					Tax Returns	7	4
2	1	7	9	3	4	Other	11	15
	16 (4/1-9/30/04)		70 (10/1/04-3/31/05)				ALL	ALL
4	13	37	20	5	7	**NUMBER OF STATEMENTS**	46	56
%	%	%	%	%	%	**ASSETS**	%	%
	8.3	9.2	6.6			Cash & Equivalents	8.7	11.7
	30.2	28.1	26.9			Trade Receivables (net)	26.2	26.9
	31.3	27.0	21.0			Inventory	26.8	21.4
	2.1	3.9	4.2			All Other Current	2.7	2.5
	72.0	68.1	58.7			Total Current	64.3	62.5
	21.9	25.9	33.1			Fixed Assets (net)	28.5	27.4
	2.5	.7	2.9			Intangibles (net)	3.2	3.1
	3.6	5.2	5.4			All Other Non-Current	3.9	7.0
	100.0	100.0	100.0			Total	100.0	100.0
						LIABILITIES		
	20.2	10.2	8.0			Notes Payable-Short Term	7.9	8.7
	3.6	3.9	2.9			Cur. Mat.-L/T/D	4.1	5.5
	22.5	16.9	12.7			Trade Payables	15.1	13.6
	.2	.1	.4			Income Taxes Payable	.2	.6
	11.6	19.1	10.6			All Other Current	12.6	11.3
	58.1	50.2	34.6			Total Current	40.0	39.7
	8.7	16.8	14.8			Long-Term Debt	16.7	14.5
	.1	.3	.8			Deferred Taxes	.7	.4
	4.2	3.8	1.2			All Other Non-Current	2.5	4.1
	29.0	28.8	48.8			Net Worth	40.0	41.4
	100.0	100.0	100.0			Total Liabilities & Net Worth	100.0	100.0
						INCOME DATA		
	100.0	100.0	100.0			Net Sales	100.0	100.0
	26.8	29.1	26.7			Gross Profit	27.8	28.7
	24.3	23.9	20.5			Operating Expenses	21.8	24.3
	2.5	5.2	6.2			Operating Profit	6.0	4.4
	.5	.8	1.6			All Other Expenses (net)	.8	.6
	2.0	4.4	4.6			Profit Before Taxes	5.2	3.8
						RATIOS		
	2.2	2.0	2.6				2.1	2.3
	1.1	1.4	1.8			Current	1.5	1.6
	.9	.9	1.3				1.3	1.2
	1.0	1.1	1.5				1.3	1.4
	.9	.7	.9			Quick	.9	1.0
	.3	.4	.8				.6	.7
	20 18.0	23 16.2	36 10.2				21 17.4	28 13.0
	28 13.2	36 10.3	54 6.7			Sales/Receivables	44 8.4	40 9.1
	44 8.4	65 5.6	74 5.0				60 6.1	50 7.3
	21 17.5	32 11.4	29 12.5				27 13.7	22 16.5
	47 7.8	47 7.8	48 7.6			Cost of Sales/Inventory	44 8.4	37 9.8
	91 4.0	80 4.6	76 4.8				78 4.7	65 5.6
	18 19.8	18 20.1	16 23.2				17 22.1	13 28.6
	31 11.8	29 12.8	23 15.6			Cost of Sales/Payables	29 12.5	26 14.0
	48 7.6	49 7.5	45 8.1				46 8.0	40 9.1
	9.7	6.2	4.6				7.2	6.0
	32.8	11.1	7.6			Sales/Working Capital	10.5	11.0
	-235.2	-53.9	16.8				21.9	28.9
	20.3	18.2	22.5				13.9	15.0
	4.7	(36) 7.5	6.9			EBIT/Interest	(44) 5.2	(54) 4.3
	1.8	2.5	2.0				2.0	.9
		8.3					13.0	3.6
		(16) 4.1				Net Profit + Depr., Dep., Amort./Cur. Mat. L/T/D	(20) 3.3	(20) 1.8
		1.2					1.5	.7
	.2	.4	.4				.3	.3
	.8	1.0	.7			Fixed/Worth	.8	.7
	7.1	4.1	1.4				1.4	1.6
	.7	1.0	.4				1.1	.8
	2.4	2.7	1.3			Debt/Worth	1.8	1.7
	15.9	15.0	2.3				3.5	2.9
	35.0	74.3	35.1				71.2	48.6
	(11) 14.3	(30) 32.3	23.4			% Profit Before Taxes/Tangible Net Worth	(44) 31.0	(54) 29.3
	9.7	8.0	5.1				13.4	1.6
	14.3	20.1	19.5				18.4	20.4
	5.6	9.4	13.6			% Profit Before Taxes/Total Assets	9.6	9.7
	3.8	2.0	1.4				2.4	-.2
	59.5	22.3	10.5				19.0	18.2
	20.1	8.7	6.3			Sales/Net Fixed Assets	9.1	9.6
	8.7	6.0	4.0				6.0	6.1
	3.7	3.1	2.4				3.0	3.7
	3.1	2.3	2.0			Sales/Total Assets	2.6	2.6
	2.7	1.7	1.4				1.9	2.0
	.6	.9	1.3				1.2	1.0
	(12) 2.3	(35) 2.0	1.7			% Depr., Dep., Amort./Sales	(43) 1.8	(52) 1.8
	4.0	3.5	2.6				2.5	3.0
		1.9					3.2	2.6
		(12) 3.8				% Officers', Directors', Owners' Comp/Sales	(13) 4.5	(21) 4.0
		5.4					6.3	6.4
4962M	62288M	405599M	762779M	789021M	1966619M	Net Sales ($)	1596958M	1773843M
1336M	19329M	169646M	381744M	344106M	1110809M	Total Assets ($)	756330M	1015313M

M = $ thousand   MM = $ million
See Pages 11 through 21 for Explanation of Ratios and Data

Comparative Historical Data | Current Data Sorted By Sales

			Type of Statement	0-1MM	1-3MM	3-5MM	5-10MM	10-25MM	25MM & OVER
13	14	16	Unqualified			2	2	7	7
18	21	30	Reviewed		2		11	15	1
4	10	12	Compiled		1	7	2	2	
5	2	2	Tax Returns	1					
11	23	26	Other		2	2	2	4	16
4/1/02-3/31/03 ALL	4/1/03-3/31/04 ALL	4/1/04-3/31/05 ALL		16 (4/1-9/30/04)		70 (10/1/04-3/31/05)			
51	70	86	NUMBER OF STATEMENTS	1	5	11	17	28	24

Hist 02/03	Hist 03/04	Hist 04/05		0-1MM	1-3MM	3-5MM	5-10MM	10-25MM	25MM & OVER
%	%	%	**ASSETS**	%	%	%	%	%	%
10.5	9.5	8.5	Cash & Equivalents			9.9	6.1	9.6	8.4
29.0	27.9	28.5	Trade Receivables (net)			29.2	25.6	31.4	25.9
24.4	26.0	25.2	Inventory			32.6	27.8	22.8	21.4
3.9	3.7	3.7	All Other Current			3.9	4.1	3.6	3.6
67.8	67.2	66.0	Total Current			75.7	63.6	67.5	59.3
26.6	26.3	26.1	Fixed Assets (net)			22.4	28.5	26.5	29.1
1.0	1.7	2.6	Intangibles (net)			.3	2.7	.6	6.4
4.7	4.9	5.4	All Other Non-Current			1.7	5.1	5.4	5.2
100.0	100.0	100.0	Total			100.0	100.0	100.0	100.0
			LIABILITIES						
10.6	12.1	9.7	Notes Payable-Short Term			22.8	9.4	10.9	4.0
2.9	3.7	3.5	Cur. Mat.-L/T/D			2.7	5.6	3.2	2.2
16.3	15.1	16.7	Trade Payables			21.8	19.5	14.4	15.4
.4	.2	.2	Income Taxes Payable			.1	.2	.3	.2
11.1	10.2	15.6	All Other Current			10.4	12.8	17.2	15.4
41.2	41.3	45.6	Total Current			57.9	47.5	45.9	37.2
19.9	18.5	14.9	Long-Term Debt			10.8	19.6	14.0	13.6
.6	.9	.5	Deferred Taxes			.0	.3	.4	1.0
4.7	5.5	4.2	All Other Non-Current			2.5	5.3	2.8	4.0
33.6	33.8	34.8	Net Worth			28.8	27.3	36.9	44.2
100.0	100.0	100.0	Total Liabilities & Net Worth			100.0	100.0	100.0	100.0
			INCOME DATA						
100.0	100.0	100.0	Net Sales			100.0	100.0	100.0	100.0
25.3	27.3	27.2	Gross Profit			27.7	28.3	27.6	24.5
22.9	22.9	22.6	Operating Expenses			26.2	24.2	20.8	19.7
2.3	4.4	4.6	Operating Profit			1.5	4.1	6.9	4.8
.4	.8	.8	All Other Expenses (net)			.6	.8	.5	1.6
1.9	3.6	3.8	Profit Before Taxes			.9	3.3	6.3	3.2
			RATIOS						
3.3	2.9	2.2				2.2	2.0	2.4	2.4
1.7	1.8	1.4	Current			1.4	1.5	1.5	1.6
1.3	1.2	1.1				1.1	1.0	1.1	1.2
1.4	1.6	1.1				1.0	1.2	1.3	1.2
1.0	1.0	.8	Quick			.8	.6	.8	.9
.6	.5	.5				.3	.3	.6	.7
(27) 13.5	(29) 12.4	(23) 15.8				(20) 17.9	(20) 18.4	(32) 11.5	(23) 15.8
(38) 9.6	(45) 8.0	(38) 9.5	Sales/Receivables			(29) 12.4	(30) 12.1	(44) 8.3	(42) 8.6
(60) 6.0	(58) 6.3	(64) 5.7				(70) 5.2	(61) 5.9	(76) 4.8	(59) 6.2
(29) 12.4	(30) 12.2	(29) 12.8				(23) 15.5	(27) 13.5	(25) 14.7	(30) 12.2
(43) 8.5	(52) 7.0	(47) 7.7	Cost of Sales/Inventory			(89) 4.1	(47) 7.8	(41) 8.8	(56) 6.5
(70) 5.2	(89) 4.1	(77) 4.8				(115) 3.2	(79) 4.6	(68) 5.4	(66) 5.5
(13) 27.7	(16) 22.3	(17) 21.7				(21) 17.8	(17) 21.2	(16) 23.1	(15) 23.6
(25) 14.5	(32) 11.4	(28) 13.2	Cost of Sales/Payables			(40) 9.0	(33) 11.2	(25) 14.8	(29) 12.7
(42) 8.8	(52) 7.0	(46) 8.0				(64) 5.7	(58) 6.3	(42) 8.7	(43) 8.5
5.2	4.9	6.2				5.4	5.7	7.2	6.1
10.0	8.8	11.4	Sales/Working Capital			15.6	12.8	14.9	10.4
20.1	23.9	61.2				56.7	NM	34.0	19.0
12.2	10.4	18.6				24.2	17.3	24.0	62.4
(48) 4.2	(68) 4.1	(85) 6.9	EBIT/Interest			4.7	4.1	(27) 9.3	7.0
1.2	1.5	1.9				1.1	1.5	5.7	2.2
5.7	4.9	6.9					5.7		21.7
(12) 2.0	(23) 2.8	(36) 3.9	Net Profit + Depr., Dep., Amort./Cur. Mat. L/T/D				(11) 3.0		(15) 4.0
1.0	1.5	2.0					.9		2.5
.3	.4	.4				.1	.4	.3	.4
.6	.7	.8	Fixed/Worth			.8	1.0	.9	.7
1.5	1.6	2.6				3.5	18.1	1.9	1.5
.6	1.1	.7				.7	1.0	.6	.7
1.4	2.0	2.0	Debt/Worth			2.4	3.1	1.4	1.6
3.0	4.2	9.1				9.1	28.8	5.6	2.8
38.2	40.8	41.8				37.6	86.6	49.7	37.4
(47) 20.5	(63) 21.8	(73) 24.9	% Profit Before Taxes/Tangible Net Worth			(10) 10.1	(14) 15.2	(24) 27.5	(22) 21.7
2.3	5.9	9.5				-5.9	8.0	11.0	12.8
19.4	14.3	19.0				7.7	20.4	20.3	19.5
5.2	5.7	8.1	% Profit Before Taxes/Total Assets			5.5	7.1	13.1	7.9
.5	1.0	2.1				.3	2.4	4.0	2.5
21.3	15.2	21.2				39.2	19.0	22.7	11.0
10.0	8.6	8.7	Sales/Net Fixed Assets			10.8	8.4	9.5	7.2
5.9	5.5	5.7				5.7	6.2	5.6	5.6
3.3	2.8	3.1				3.2	3.2	3.2	2.5
2.4	2.1	2.4	Sales/Total Assets			2.6	2.6	2.3	2.1
1.9	1.7	1.7				1.7	1.7	1.5	1.7
.9	1.2	1.1					.9	.9	1.4
(43) 1.8	(64) 1.9	(77) 2.0	% Depr., Dep., Amort./Sales				2.1	(27) 1.4	(22) 1.8
2.8	2.8	3.2					3.1	3.5	2.6
2.5	1.4	2.4							
(17) 4.7	(19) 4.3	(25) 5.0	% Officers', Directors', Owners' Comp/Sales						
8.5	11.1	7.0							
3209776M	2645720M	3991268M	Net Sales ($)	961M	9408M	45920M	118421M	458726M	3357832M
1434119M	1329456M	2026970M	Total Assets ($)	136M	9743M	20397M	50970M	220026M	1725698M

M = $ thousand   MM = $ million
See Pages 11 through 21 for Explanation of Ratios and Data

Current Data Sorted By Assets　　　　　　　　　　　　　　　　**Comparative Historical Data**

	0-500M	500M-2MM	2-10MM	10-50MM	50-100MM	100-250MM	Type of Statement	ALL	ALL
	1	2	35	43	3	9	Unqualified	67	67
	2	37	98	25	1		Reviewed	117	108
	11	33	21	2			Compiled	122	107
	13	33	4				Tax Returns	35	24
	6	45	43	15	9	5	Other	106	126
		105 (4/1-9/30/04)		391 (10/1/04-3/31/05)				4/1/00-3/31/01	4/1/01-3/31/02
	33	150	201	85	13	14	NUMBER OF STATEMENTS	447	432
	%	%	%	%	%	%	**ASSETS**	%	%
	14.3	9.0	6.6	9.2	1.0	3.5	Cash & Equivalents	8.2	8.9
	32.3	36.7	38.3	36.2	29.8	29.9	Trade Receivables (net)	37.1	35.1
	14.9	17.1	19.6	21.8	30.3	22.6	Inventory	15.6	15.2
	1.7	3.0	5.2	5.8	4.4	9.9	All Other Current	5.1	5.3
	63.2	65.9	69.8	73.1	65.5	65.9	Total Current	66.0	64.4
	32.4	27.7	23.7	19.9	29.9	26.0	Fixed Assets (net)	26.4	27.5
	.6	1.3	1.3	.7	1.7	3.0	Intangibles (net)	2.1	2.8
	3.8	5.2	5.2	6.3	2.9	5.1	All Other Non-Current	5.6	5.2
	100.0	100.0	100.0	100.0	100.0	100.0	Total	100.0	100.0
							LIABILITIES		
	16.3	12.9	13.3	15.1	11.9	4.4	Notes Payable-Short Term	11.1	11.5
	6.8	4.2	3.4	2.3	2.7	2.9	Cur. Mat.-L/T/D	3.7	3.7
	18.7	20.7	18.8	18.2	16.0	15.1	Trade Payables	16.7	15.6
	.0	.4	.5	.3	.3	.5	Income Taxes Payable	.3	.3
	11.5	8.3	9.4	10.1	12.1	12.3	All Other Current	11.2	9.9
	53.3	46.5	45.4	46.2	43.0	35.2	Total Current	43.0	41.1
	24.4	16.6	13.3	10.4	16.1	16.2	Long-Term Debt	15.0	15.4
	.0	.1	.3	.4	1.4	2.4	Deferred Taxes	.6	.6
	3.4	6.5	3.6	1.4	1.9	8.9	All Other Non-Current	4.3	4.9
	18.9	30.3	37.4	41.7	37.5	37.2	Net Worth	37.1	38.0
	100.0	100.0	100.0	100.0	100.0	100.0	Total Liabilities & Net Worth	100.0	100.0
							INCOME DATA		
	100.0	100.0	100.0	100.0	100.0	100.0	Net Sales	100.0	100.0
	41.3	29.8	23.1	18.7	25.0	17.9	Gross Profit	28.2	27.4
	40.2	27.5	19.4	15.1	14.8	12.3	Operating Expenses	23.0	23.3
	1.1	2.4	3.7	3.6	10.2	5.6	Operating Profit	5.2	4.1
	.8	.6	.7	.4	4.2	2.0	All Other Expenses (net)	1.1	1.1
	.3	1.7	3.0	3.2	6.0	3.6	Profit Before Taxes	4.1	3.0
							RATIOS		
	2.0	2.3	2.2	2.4	2.2	2.3		2.4	2.6
	1.3	1.5	1.6	1.6	1.6	1.8	Current	1.5	1.6
	1.0	1.1	1.1	1.2	1.0	1.6		1.1	1.1
	1.5	1.5	1.4	1.6	1.0	1.3		1.6	1.8
	1.1	1.0	1.0	1.0	.6	.9	Quick	1.1	1.0
	.7	.6	.7	.6	.4	.7		.7	.7
	20　17.9	34　10.6	45　8.1	47　7.7	38　9.5	39　9.5		39　9.4	36　10.0
	35　10.6	49　7.4	60　6.1	67　5.5	46　8.0	56　6.5	Sales/Receivables	53　6.9	53　6.9
	50　7.3	68　5.3	78　4.7	81　4.5	59　6.2	79　4.6		74　4.9	70　5.2
	2　171.0	9　40.3	13　28.1	19　19.7	24　15.1	12　31.2		8　46.4	8　46.8
	14　25.8	26　14.2	35　10.4	50　7.2	48　7.6	50　7.3	Cost of Sales/Inventory	26　14.0	27　13.6
	48　7.6	51　7.1	70　5.2	81　4.5	153　2.4	71　5.1		54　6.8	53　6.9
	7　53.0	20　17.9	21　17.2	24　15.5	24　15.4	23　16.1		18　20.5	17　22.0
	36　10.2	35　10.5	36　10.1	34　10.6	34　10.6	32　11.6	Cost of Sales/Payables	31　11.8	29　12.6
	62　5.9	59　6.2	53　6.9	54　6.8	59　6.2	52　7.1		47　7.8	46　7.9
	8.7	7.2	6.0	4.6	6.3	5.1		5.8	5.2
	31.3	13.2	9.4	8.4	9.4	6.5	Sales/Working Capital	10.8	10.4
	NM	66.6	25.1	19.4	NM	9.1		35.7	33.0
	8.5	10.2	12.6	15.2	39.6	13.9		9.9	8.5
	(27)　2.4	(139)　3.6	(190)　4.0	(79)　4.5	(12)　14.1	3.0	EBIT/Interest	(405)　3.8	(394)　2.5
	-.6	.8	1.3	1.2	5.6	.4		1.6	1.0
		5.3	5.4	7.6		13.7	Net Profit + Depr., Dep.,	7.5	6.0
	(24)　2.0	(61)　2.8	(36)　2.9		(11)　1.4		Amort./Cur. Mat. L /T/D	(122)　3.1	(103)　2.7
	1.3	1.0	.9		-.7			1.5	1.2
	.7	.3	.3	.2	.3	.5		.3	.3
	1.3	.8	.6	.4	.8	.7	Fixed/Worth	.7	.7
	-5.0	2.8	1.2	.9	1.6	1.8		1.5	1.8
	.8	.9	.9	.7	1.0	1.2		.8	.7
	3.8	2.2	2.0	1.6	1.8	2.1	Debt/Worth	1.7	1.8
	-13.9	8.5	3.8	3.3	3.8	4.4		4.4	4.5
	53.0	47.1	38.2	29.0	54.1	30.8	% Profit Before Taxes/Tangible	49.3	37.4
	(23)　9.5	(125)　14.9	(192)　14.7	(84)　16.4	35.7	13.2	Net Worth	(411)　25.3	(389)　15.0
	-32.3	1.1	2.6	.6	12.3	-13.6		7.3	1.7
	17.7	12.8	13.7	11.8	26.1	13.5	% Profit Before Taxes/Total	17.6	13.5
	5.7	5.4	4.6	4.9	13.7	4.0	Assets	8.2	5.1
	-9.1	-.8	.7	.3	2.6	-2.8		2.2	.2
	30.9	23.2	23.2	20.9	22.1	10.9		21.9	19.2
	15.2	12.2	11.0	10.9	7.4	7.1	Sales/Net Fixed Assets	10.6	9.6
	7.6	6.4	5.5	6.9	5.7	5.5		5.3	5.5
	5.2	3.2	2.7	2.6	2.7	2.2		3.2	3.0
	3.3	2.6	2.1	1.9	1.9	1.8	Sales/Total Assets	2.4	2.2
	2.7	1.9	1.7	1.5	1.6	1.5		1.8	1.7
	1.0	1.2	.8	1.0	.8	1.4		1.0	1.0
	(30)　2.2	(126)　2.1	(192)　1.5	(83)　1.7	(11)　2.1	(12)　2.2	% Depr., Dep., Amort./Sales	(411)　1.8	(403)　1.8
	4.0	3.9	2.9	2.2	3.3	2.7		3.1	3.4
	2.8	2.4	1.9	.7				2.3	2.0
	(23)　6.6	(94)　3.8	(86)　2.8	(19)　1.8			% Officers', Directors', Owners' Comp/Sales	(201)　4.9	(182)　4.1
	9.4	5.9	6.0	3.3				8.1	7.7
	36001M	506996M	2132758M	3387280M	1913583M	4119066M	Net Sales ($)	10610294M	9079120M
	9578M	181551M	973115M	1621057M	925570M	2131530M	Total Assets ($)	4964310M	5063790M

© RMA 2005　　　　　　M = $ thousand　　MM = $ million
See Pages 11 through 21 for Explanation of Ratios and Data

Comparative Historical Data — **Current Data Sorted By Sales**

			Type of Statement						
78	80	93	Unqualified	2	3	3	9	34	44
141	146	163	Reviewed		13	26	49	58	15
93	122	67	Compiled	12	21	11	14	9	
28	42	50	Tax Returns	6	23	14	3	4	
123	129	123	Other	7	26	24	20	21	25
4/1/02- 3/31/03 ALL	4/1/03- 3/31/04 ALL	4/1/04- 3/31/05 ALL		105 (4/1-9/30/04)			391 (10/1/04-3/31/05)		
				0-1MM	1-3MM	3-5MM	5-10MM	10-25MM	25MM & OVER
463	519	496	NUMBER OF STATEMENTS	27	86	78	95	126	84
%	%	%	ASSETS	%	%	%	%	%	%
9.8	8.4	8.1	Cash & Equivalents	11.9	11.0	8.1	6.2	8.9	4.6
33.4	34.6	36.6	Trade Receivables (net)	32.2	31.3	36.7	39.3	38.3	37.9
15.9	16.4	19.3	Inventory	13.6	17.0	17.0	18.2	21.7	23.1
4.5	5.3	4.5	All Other Current	2.4	2.7	2.9	5.0	5.0	7.2
63.6	64.7	68.5	Total Current	60.3	62.1	64.7	68.8	73.9	72.8
28.4	28.0	25.1	Fixed Assets (net)	36.3	30.2	27.8	24.3	21.3	20.1
2.1	2.1	1.2	Intangibles (net)	.3	1.6	1.6	1.6	.5	1.3
5.9	5.2	5.2	All Other Non-Current	3.1	6.1	5.9	5.3	4.3	5.8
100.0	100.0	100.0	Total	100.0	100.0	100.0	100.0	100.0	100.0
			LIABILITIES						
11.4	11.9	13.4	Notes Payable-Short Term	19.1	14.2	10.2	14.3	11.9	14.8
4.1	3.8	3.7	Cur. Mat.-L/T/D	7.4	4.4	4.8	3.5	2.6	2.5
15.2	16.9	19.1	Trade Payables	15.3	18.3	20.2	19.8	18.9	19.5
.5	.3	.4	Income Taxes Payable	.0	.2	.6	.2	.6	.4
9.4	9.4	9.5	All Other Current	12.5	9.2	6.3	9.2	10.1	11.2
40.5	42.3	46.0	Total Current	54.3	46.2	42.2	46.9	44.2	48.5
15.5	16.1	14.7	Long-Term Debt	19.9	23.4	13.6	14.7	10.4	11.4
.5	.4	.3	Deferred Taxes	.0	.1	.3	.3	.2	1.0
4.2	5.8	4.2	All Other Non-Current	7.4	4.9	5.8	4.2	2.9	2.9
39.3	35.3	34.8	Net Worth	18.4	25.2	38.2	33.9	42.3	36.2
100.0	100.0	100.0	Total Liabilities & Net Worth	100.0	100.0	100.0	100.0	100.0	100.0
			INCOME DATA						
100.0	100.0	100.0	Net Sales	100.0	100.0	100.0	100.0	100.0	100.0
27.6	26.5	25.5	Gross Profit	42.5	34.2	27.1	24.3	20.8	18.0
24.7	25.1	22.2	Operating Expenses	41.8	32.2	25.0	19.8	17.0	13.5
2.9	1.4	3.3	Operating Profit	.7	2.0	2.2	4.5	3.8	4.5
.9	.8	.7	All Other Expenses (net)	.8	1.0	.5	1.2	.3	.8
2.0	.6	2.6	Profit Before Taxes	-.1	1.0	1.7	3.3	3.4	3.7
			RATIOS						
2.6	2.4	2.2		1.9	2.3	2.4	2.0	2.3	2.2
1.6	1.5	1.5	Current	1.3	1.4	1.6	1.4	1.6	1.6
1.2	1.1	1.1		.8	1.0	1.1	1.1	1.2	1.2
1.8	1.6	1.4		1.6	1.5	1.6	1.4	1.5	1.3
(462) 1.1	1.0	1.0	Quick	1.0	.9	1.1	.9	1.0	.9
.7	.7	.6		.4	.6	.7	.7	.7	.6
37 10.0	39 9.4	40 9.0		30 12.1	28 13.0	35 10.4	44 8.4	46 8.0	44 8.3
51 7.1	55 6.7	56 6.6	Sales/Receivables	45 8.1	48 7.6	50 7.3	57 6.4	62 5.9	58 6.3
70 5.2	75 4.9	75 4.9		75 4.9	68 5.3	72 5.1	81 4.5	74 4.9	79 4.6
9 39.9	10 37.1	11 32.1		2 232.5	7 55.0	14 26.8	9 39.7	13 27.4	14 25.7
29 12.4	31 11.9	35 10.6	Cost of Sales/Inventory	12 30.3	32 11.5	26 14.2	27 13.4	40 9.1	47 7.7
61 6.0	61 6.0	66 5.6		53 6.8	78 4.7	59 6.1	58 6.3	71 5.1	69 5.3
17 20.9	18 19.8	21 17.7		9 39.2	18 19.9	20 17.9	20 18.6	21 17.2	24 15.4
31 11.9	32 11.3	35 10.4	Cost of Sales/Payables	35 10.4	37 10.0	35 10.3	33 11.1	36 10.0	33 11.0
48 7.7	51 7.1	54 6.7		58 6.3	62 5.9	64 5.7	58 6.3	48 7.5	53 6.9
5.4	5.4	6.2		6.5	6.2	5.8	6.7	5.6	6.3
9.9	10.4	10.2	Sales/Working Capital	29.7	18.0	10.2	11.6	8.5	9.2
28.8	38.4	36.8		-95.3	-92.0	58.5	36.6	18.0	20.0
9.3	7.1	12.5		6.2	8.9	9.5	10.0	16.9	17.9
(432) 2.7	(475) 1.9	(461) 4.0	EBIT/Interest	(22) 2.9	(78) 2.9	(74) 3.0	(89) 3.2	(116) 6.0	(82) 6.7
.5	-.7	1.1		.5	-.7	.5	1.3	1.6	1.6
3.7	4.2	5.6			3.5	8.6	4.2	6.6	7.7
(137) 1.8	(135) 1.7	(137) 2.4	Net Profit + Depr., Dep., Amort./Cur. Mat. L/T/D		(13) 1.5	(18) 2.7	(26) 1.9	(36) 3.2	(43) 2.9
.6	.9	.9			.2	.7	.9	1.6	.5
.3	.3	.3		.6	.4	.3	.3	.3	.3
.7	.7	.7	Fixed/Worth	1.7	1.0	.7	.7	.5	.5
1.6	2.0	1.5		-8.5	16.2	1.8	1.5	.9	1.0
.7	.8	.9		1.0	1.0	.7	1.2	.7	1.1
1.7	1.9	2.0	Debt/Worth	5.9	2.9	1.8	2.2	1.5	2.3
4.0	4.8	4.5		-12.5	56.3	3.7	4.8	3.2	3.5
28.3	26.4	39.4		100.0	42.8	31.4	43.6	35.6	40.3
(424) 10.1	(454) 7.8	(451) 15.3	% Profit Before Taxes/Tangible Net Worth	(19) 7.4	(66) 13.1	(72) 13.3	(87) 15.7	(124) 12.4	(83) 19.2
-.9	-6.3	1.7		-14.2	-1.8	-.2	5.1	2.9	3.2
10.6	9.4	12.9		14.6	10.8	12.0	12.8	14.4	13.5
3.4	2.4	5.2	% Profit Before Taxes/Total Assets	4.2	4.4	4.9	4.3	5.4	7.1
-1.1	-3.6	.2		-6.5	-6.5	-.9	.9	1.1	.6
18.6	18.0	22.0		19.2	19.2	23.0	21.1	26.5	23.7
8.5	9.3	11.0	Sales/Net Fixed Assets	7.5	10.5	10.6	11.6	12.6	11.5
4.6	4.9	6.2		3.3	4.7	5.0	6.8	6.6	7.5
2.9	2.8	2.9		3.7	2.9	3.2	3.0	2.8	2.8
2.1	2.1	2.3	Sales/Total Assets	2.5	2.3	2.4	2.3	2.3	2.2
1.6	1.5	1.7		1.2	1.6	1.8	1.7	1.7	1.7
1.3	1.2	1.0		1.3	1.2	1.2	.9	.9	.8
(428) 2.2	(471) 2.3	(454) 1.8	% Depr., Dep., Amort./Sales	(21) 3.7	(77) 2.4	(69) 2.3	(88) 1.5	(120) 1.5	(79) 1.5
3.7	3.8	3.1		5.6	5.0	3.9	2.6	2.4	2.3
2.3	2.5	2.0		3.5	2.6	2.8	1.6	1.8	.7
(195) 4.7	(208) 4.1	(223) 3.5	% Officers', Directors', Owners' Comp/Sales	(15) 6.6	(51) 4.5	(49) 4.1	(40) 2.4	(51) 3.0	(17) 1.6
8.3	7.6	6.0		17.3	7.8	5.6	4.3	6.0	2.2
9062637M	9337410M	12095684M	Net Sales ($)	18682M	172846M	299570M	694367M	2001274M	8908945M
4944587M	5091264M	5842401M	Total Assets ($)	10309M	90110M	144995M	415583M	969258M	4212146M

M = $ thousand   MM = $ million
See Pages 11 through 21 for Explanation of Ratios and Data

Current Data Sorted By Assets   Comparative Historical Data

0-500M	500M-2MM	2-10MM	10-50MM	50-100MM	100-250MM	Type of Statement	4/1/00-3/31/01 ALL	4/1/01-3/31/02 ALL
	1	11	11	2	2	Unqualified	34	34
2	12	31	8			Reviewed	38	34
3	10	6				Compiled	42	31
3	3	1				Tax Returns	8	6
1	15	13	9	1	3	Other	37	43
	43 (4/1-9/30/04)			105 (10/1/04-3/31/05)				
9	41	62	28	3	5	**NUMBER OF STATEMENTS**	159	148
%	%	%	%	%	%	**ASSETS**	%	%
	5.2	10.1	4.5			Cash & Equivalents	7.7	9.1
	34.9	26.4	26.1			Trade Receivables (net)	29.1	26.3
	23.2	24.0	25.6			Inventory	19.9	19.6
	3.6	3.6	7.3			All Other Current	4.1	3.5
	66.9	64.1	63.5			Total Current	60.7	58.5
	26.0	26.4	28.3			Fixed Assets (net)	31.4	31.9
	1.8	1.9	1.1			Intangibles (net)	2.1	2.3
	5.3	7.6	7.2			All Other Non-Current	5.9	7.3
	100.0	100.0	100.0			Total	100.0	100.0
						LIABILITIES		
	17.9	9.9	9.5			Notes Payable-Short Term	11.4	11.2
	3.5	2.8	2.2			Cur. Mat.-L/T/D	3.3	3.9
	21.2	14.4	13.3			Trade Payables	13.0	12.7
	.3	.5	.4			Income Taxes Payable	.3	.2
	9.2	9.7	18.1			All Other Current	12.0	9.5
	52.2	37.3	43.6			Total Current	40.0	37.5
	15.8	14.1	14.3			Long-Term Debt	17.3	17.7
	.3	.5	.2			Deferred Taxes	.6	.7
	9.2	4.2	7.3			All Other Non-Current	5.1	5.2
	22.5	43.9	34.6			Net Worth	37.1	38.9
	100.0	100.0	100.0			Total Liabilities & Net Worth	100.0	100.0
						INCOME DATA		
	100.0	100.0	100.0			Net Sales	100.0	100.0
	29.0	23.7	19.8			Gross Profit	26.5	27.3
	26.5	20.0	17.5			Operating Expenses	21.8	24.6
	2.5	3.8	2.2			Operating Profit	4.6	2.7
	.5	.3	.2			All Other Expenses (net)	1.2	1.1
	2.0	3.4	2.0			Profit Before Taxes	3.4	1.6
						RATIOS		
	2.5	3.3	2.2				2.4	2.6
	1.5	1.7	1.5			Current	1.6	1.7
	.9	1.2	1.1				1.1	1.1
	1.9	1.7	1.3				1.5	1.8
	.8	1.0	.7			Quick	.9	.9
	.4	.6	.5				.6	.6
30 12.1	38 9.6	40 9.1					36 10.0	34 10.6
47 7.8	51 7.1	51 7.2				Sales/Receivables	49 7.4	47 7.7
75 4.9	65 5.6	70 5.2					64 5.7	59 6.2
18 20.5	37 10.0	34 10.8					23 15.6	26 14.0
44 8.2	61 6.0	58 6.2				Cost of Sales/Inventory	43 8.4	47 7.7
66 5.5	97 3.7	104 3.5					68 5.4	72 5.1
20 18.6	19 18.8	23 15.5					16 23.1	17 21.1
40 9.2	28 13.0	31 11.8				Cost of Sales/Payables	26 14.1	26 14.1
59 6.2	42 8.7	49 7.4					44 8.4	41 8.8
	5.9	3.5	4.0				5.1	5.1
	17.6	7.3	9.1			Sales/Working Capital	11.2	9.0
	-29.9	16.6	25.1				54.1	37.5
	8.1	11.1	12.1				11.7	8.1
	(37) 2.2	(51) 5.5	(26) 5.8			EBIT/Interest	(143) 2.8	(139) 2.1
	.8	1.3	.0				1.4	.5
		6.4	71.9			Net Profit + Depr., Dep.,	5.8	5.0
	(20) 2.8	(13) 5.9				Amort./Cur. Mat. L /T/D	(56) 2.1	(51) 2.0
	1.4	.7					1.3	.8
	.4	.4	.4				.4	.4
	.9	.7	.8			Fixed/Worth	.9	.9
	11.1	1.2	1.8				2.2	2.2
	.9	.5	.8				.6	.6
	3.7	1.4	2.1			Debt/Worth	1.8	1.6
	24.7	3.8	5.0				4.0	4.6
	56.7	36.1	44.1			% Profit Before Taxes/Tangible	38.7	25.8
	(32) 22.0	(59) 11.0	(26) 21.7			Net Worth	(142) 18.8	(134) 9.0
	5.8	1.3	-2.6				5.8	-1.2
	13.2	14.1	12.8			% Profit Before Taxes/Total	14.1	9.9
	3.8	8.1	6.0			Assets	5.9	3.4
	-1.5	1.0	-1.0				1.5	-1.1
	20.3	17.4	12.3				15.7	13.5
	10.2	8.2	6.4			Sales/Net Fixed Assets	7.1	6.5
	5.9	4.5	3.9				4.1	3.7
	3.8	2.3	2.2				2.7	2.6
	2.3	1.8	1.6			Sales/Total Assets	2.1	2.0
	1.7	1.3	1.3				1.5	1.4
	1.1	1.1	1.6				1.4	1.3
	(38) 2.0	(56) 1.9	(27) 2.0			% Depr., Dep., Amort./Sales	(146) 2.2	(139) 2.4
	3.7	3.2	3.1				3.6	3.9
	3.3	1.8				% Officers', Directors',	2.5	3.2
	(21) 5.0	(16) 4.2				Owners' Comp/Sales	(60) 5.6	(51) 5.0
	6.9	9.7					8.4	7.2
12885M	157480M	579265M	917279M	370650M	1449867M	Net Sales ($)	3559730M	3295283M
3557M	56988M	298371M	542250M	199269M	845268M	Total Assets ($)	2003210M	1922502M

M = $ thousand   MM = $ million
See Pages 11 through 21 for Explanation of Ratios and Data

Comparative Historical Data / Current Data Sorted By Sales

Hist 1	Hist 2	Hist 3	Type of Statement	0-1MM	1-3MM	3-5MM	5-10MM	10-25MM	25MM & OVER
25	27	27	Unqualified		1	1	3	12	10
48	44	53	Reviewed	1	10	10	10	18	4
25	26	19	Compiled	1	6	7	5		
5	6	7	Tax Returns		4	2		1	
37	37	42	Other	1	7	6	12	7	9
4/1/02-3/31/03 ALL	4/1/03-3/31/04 ALL	4/1/04-3/31/05 ALL			43 (4/1-9/30/04)		105 (10/1/04-3/31/05)		
140	140	148	NUMBER OF STATEMENTS	3	28	26	30	38	23
%	%	%	**ASSETS**	%	%	%	%	%	%
8.0	10.0	7.6	Cash & Equivalents		9.3	7.7	8.5	6.6	3.9
26.9	28.5	29.5	Trade Receivables (net)		31.2	30.9	30.5	26.9	28.8
19.4	19.5	23.1	Inventory		19.6	21.4	25.0	25.8	24.4
4.6	3.2	4.3	All Other Current		3.5	3.7	2.9	6.3	4.8
58.9	61.2	64.6	Total Current		63.7	63.7	66.9	65.6	62.0
32.0	28.3	26.4	Fixed Assets (net)		27.7	29.3	22.1	27.0	25.2
2.6	2.4	2.5	Intangibles (net)		2.2	1.7	2.5	1.7	5.0
6.4	8.0	6.6	All Other Non-Current		6.5	5.3	8.5	5.7	7.7
100.0	100.0	100.0	Total		100.0	100.0	100.0	100.0	100.0
			LIABILITIES						
13.6	12.3	11.8	Notes Payable-Short Term		14.4	15.2	11.1	11.2	7.4
4.4	4.2	3.5	Cur. Mat.-L/T/D		3.3	2.7	2.9	2.8	2.3
13.7	15.2	16.5	Trade Payables		16.8	15.5	17.9	17.3	15.0
.3	.2	.5	Income Taxes Payable		.5	.1	.4	.6	.7
11.4	10.0	11.2	All Other Current		7.4	6.6	10.9	16.1	12.5
43.4	42.0	43.3	Total Current		42.3	40.1	43.3	48.0	38.0
16.5	15.0	15.3	Long-Term Debt		20.2	16.9	9.7	15.7	15.6
.4	.7	.4	Deferred Taxes		.6	.1	.4	.3	.9
5.6	5.0	6.1	All Other Non-Current		7.1	8.4	3.8	5.7	6.9
34.1	37.3	34.9	Net Worth		29.8	34.6	42.9	30.3	38.6
100.0	100.0	100.0	Total Liabilities & Net Worth		100.0	100.0	100.0	100.0	100.0
			INCOME DATA						
100.0	100.0	100.0	Net Sales		100.0	100.0	100.0	100.0	100.0
26.7	26.0	24.9	Gross Profit		30.1	26.7	24.3	21.9	20.7
24.5	23.9	21.7	Operating Expenses		29.7	24.8	19.0	18.3	15.5
2.3	2.1	3.3	Operating Profit		.4	1.9	5.3	3.6	5.2
1.2	1.0	.5	All Other Expenses (net)		.7	.6	.0	.5	.7
1.1	1.1	2.8	Profit Before Taxes		-.3	1.3	5.3	3.1	4.4
			RATIOS						
2.4	2.8	2.6	Current		4.4	3.4	3.3	1.8	2.1
1.4	1.6	1.6			2.0	1.6	1.8	1.4	1.5
1.0	1.1	1.1			1.0	1.0	1.2	1.1	1.2
1.4	2.0	1.6	Quick		2.6	2.0	1.9	1.1	1.4
.8	.9	.9			1.1	.9	.9	.7	.9
.5	.6	.5			.5	.6	.6	.5	.7
31 11.7	34 10.8	38 9.7	Sales/Receivables	35 10.3	39 9.5	37 9.8	30 12.3	40 9.2	
43 8.5	48 7.6	51 7.2		51 7.2	59 6.2	51 7.1	45 8.2	51 7.2	
61 5.9	64 5.7	64 5.7		68 5.4	70 5.2	68 5.4	56 6.5	71 5.1	
24 15.0	22 16.5	27 13.4	Cost of Sales/Inventory	17 21.2	28 12.8	39 9.3	20 18.4	28 12.8	
46 7.9	44 8.3	54 6.8		54 6.8	59 6.2	56 6.5	50 7.3	57 6.4	
72 5.0	74 4.9	85 4.3		93 3.9	85 4.3	77 4.8	75 4.9	91 4.0	
16 23.5	19 19.3	20 18.5	Cost of Sales/Payables	18 20.5	23 16.1	19 19.6	21 17.0	23 16.2	
27 13.6	30 12.2	30 12.0		32 11.5	35 10.5	28 13.1	30 12.0	30 12.3	
46 8.0	49 7.5	49 7.5		50 7.3	51 7.1	47 7.7	41 8.9	53 6.9	
5.6	4.1	4.4	Sales/Working Capital		3.9	3.6	3.8	6.7	5.1
11.2	10.1	9.2			7.8	9.5	8.0	11.9	7.8
283.1	91.5	47.5			-305.2	85.7	17.0	44.5	23.2
6.3	10.1	10.9	EBIT/Interest		5.6	5.1	17.0	9.0	14.6
(131) 2.0	(127) 2.3	(129) 3.7			(26) 2.7	(22) 2.1	(23) 9.5	(35) 3.6	(22) 8.4
.5	-.4	1.1			-1.2	.1	3.6	.3	2.4
3.8	4.3	13.8	Net Profit + Depr., Dep., Amort./Cur. Mat. L/T/D					36.8	107.4
(33) 1.8	(41) 1.7	(43) 3.0						(16) 2.9	(10) 10.3
.8	.4	1.3						.8	1.5
.5	.4	.4	Fixed/Worth		.4	.6	.3	.5	.4
1.1	.8	.8			.7	1.0	.4	1.0	.9
2.9	2.5	1.7			10.4	4.8	1.1	1.3	1.4
.8	.6	.7	Debt/Worth		.6	.8	.4	1.4	1.1
1.9	1.8	1.9			1.2	2.4	1.2	2.6	2.0
8.1	5.6	5.2			25.0	18.9	3.8	4.9	4.0
28.0	28.4	43.2	% Profit Before Taxes/Tangible Net Worth		41.6	56.7	31.6	43.2	47.2
(121) 10.1	(119) 11.3	(131) 17.2			(22) 9.6	(24) 19.1	(26) 10.9	(35) 19.6	(22) 28.3
.3	-8.3	1.3			-8.9	.0	4.9	-.6	-.8
8.3	11.5	13.6	% Profit Before Taxes/Total Assets		7.3	9.9	15.1	16.4	18.4
2.9	4.0	5.2			3.9	3.7	7.4	6.5	9.1
-1.0	-5.2	.2			-8.6	-2.9	2.7	-.5	.2
14.8	17.2	18.6	Sales/Net Fixed Assets		18.5	20.7	24.3	16.6	14.4
7.4	7.8	8.2			7.8	8.9	12.0	10.3	6.6
4.1	4.3	4.8			4.0	3.7	4.7	5.0	4.8
2.6	2.6	2.7	Sales/Total Assets		3.0	2.3	2.9	3.0	2.3
2.0	1.9	1.9			1.8	1.9	2.0	2.1	1.8
1.5	1.4	1.5			1.4	1.3	1.5	1.6	1.5
1.3	1.3	1.3	% Depr., Dep., Amort./Sales		1.6	1.5	.7	1.1	1.5
(134) 2.3	(126) 2.2	(136) 2.0			(26) 2.2	(22) 2.6	(27) 1.8	(36) 1.7	(22) 2.2
3.8	3.7	3.3			4.6	3.8	2.7	2.8	3.2
3.0	2.0	2.1	% Officers', Directors', Owners' Comp/Sales		4.0		2.3		
(55) 5.1	(53) 4.6	(49) 4.0			(15) 5.6		(11) 3.6		
9.5	7.2	7.0			14.1		7.0		
2321631M	2804369M	3487426M	Net Sales ($)	2309M	58024M	107191M	214569M	613611M	2491722M
1137665M	1670807M	1945703M	Total Assets ($)	830M	35482M	62222M	115548M	326921M	1404700M

© RMA 2005

M = $ thousand   MM = $ million

See Pages 11 through 21 for Explanation of Ratios and Data

Current Data Sorted By Assets   Comparative Historical Data

Type of Statement

	0-500M	500M-2MM	2-10MM	10-50MM	50-100MM	100-250MM		4/1/00-3/31/01 ALL	4/1/01-3/31/02 ALL
Unqualified			10	10	1	3		28	19
Reviewed		8	25	7				29	28
Compiled	2	9	7					23	20
Tax Returns	2	11	1	1				5	3
Other	2	12	14	14	2	2		40	40
	6	40	57	32	3	5	NUMBER OF STATEMENTS	125	110

Current Data columns: **30 (4/1-9/30/04)** = 0-500M, 500M-2MM, 2-10MM; **113 (10/1/04-3/31/05)** = 10-50MM, 50-100MM, 100-250MM.

0-500M	500M-2MM	2-10MM	10-50MM	50-100MM	100-250MM		4/1/00-3/31/01 ALL	4/1/01-3/31/02 ALL
%	%	%	%	%	%	**ASSETS**	%	%
	7.1	6.9	9.7			Cash & Equivalents	5.0	8.1
	36.5	35.4	27.0			Trade Receivables (net)	28.2	29.0
	28.9	28.3	23.9			Inventory	30.1	26.5
	2.0	2.7	2.4			All Other Current	1.7	2.0
	74.5	73.3	63.0			Total Current	64.9	65.6
	19.0	18.5	25.7			Fixed Assets (net)	25.2	24.3
	1.0	2.2	4.6			Intangibles (net)	3.1	3.5
	5.5	6.1	6.7			All Other Non-Current	6.8	6.5
	100.0	100.0	100.0			Total	100.0	100.0
						LIABILITIES		
	11.2	12.3	8.5			Notes Payable-Short Term	12.7	10.7
	4.4	3.1	3.5			Cur. Mat.-L/T/D	3.3	3.9
	26.9	16.7	11.3			Trade Payables	14.4	13.4
	.0	.6	.3			Income Taxes Payable	.3	.2
	11.9	12.7	9.6			All Other Current	8.5	10.2
	54.5	45.4	33.2			Total Current	39.2	38.4
	17.3	9.8	15.8			Long-Term Debt	18.4	15.3
	.1	.4	.8			Deferred Taxes	.4	.7
	10.5	3.5	5.3			All Other Non-Current	4.9	5.3
	17.5	40.9	44.9			Net Worth	37.2	40.3
	100.0	100.0	100.0			Total Liabilities & Net Worth	100.0	100.0
						INCOME DATA		
	100.0	100.0	100.0			Net Sales	100.0	100.0
	34.3	26.8	26.1			Gross Profit	28.5	29.6
	33.4	24.2	18.9			Operating Expenses	23.8	24.1
	.9	2.6	7.1			Operating Profit	4.7	5.6
	.7	.4	.8			All Other Expenses (net)	1.4	1.1
	.2	2.2	6.3			Profit Before Taxes	3.3	4.4
						RATIOS		
	2.2	2.1	3.8				3.0	2.8
	1.4	1.7	2.7			Current	1.7	1.7
	1.1	1.2	1.3				1.2	1.2
	1.4	1.3	2.6				1.5	1.5
	.8	.9	1.3			Quick	.8	.9
	.5	.7	.8				.5	.6
	24 15.0	37 9.9	30 12.3				28 12.9	29 12.6
	42 8.6	49 7.4	38 9.6			Sales/Receivables	41 8.8	41 8.9
	52 7.0	73 5.0	71 5.1				52 7.0	60 6.0
	21 17.1	36 10.0	34 10.6				41 8.8	37 9.8
	50 7.3	57 6.4	50 7.3			Cost of Sales/Inventory	59 6.2	50 7.3
	74 4.9	86 4.2	82 4.5				82 4.4	78 4.7
	24 14.9	20 18.2	14 26.2				16 22.8	13 27.9
	40 9.0	29 12.7	18 20.2			Cost of Sales/Payables	25 14.5	23 16.0
	62 5.9	43 8.4	31 11.9				40 9.0	40 9.1
	6.3	6.0	4.0				5.7	5.4
	16.3	9.1	5.7			Sales/Working Capital	10.0	9.5
	132.4	20.6	21.4				24.7	22.4
	8.2	12.6	27.0				9.4	8.8
	(34) 1.5	(51) 3.9	(30) 8.9			EBIT/Interest	(116) 2.6	(96) 2.6
	-2.4	1.1	2.8				1.1	1.4
		4.8	4.2			Net Profit + Depr., Dep.,	7.5	3.9
		(24) 1.7	(15) 3.1			Amort./Cur. Mat. L /T/D	(40) 2.4	(37) 2.0
		.7	1.1				1.0	1.3
	.3	.2	.3				.4	.3
	.8	.4	.6			Fixed/Worth	.7	.6
	-2.4	1.2	1.8				1.6	1.6
	.8	.8	.5				.8	.7
	3.4	1.4	1.2			Debt/Worth	1.9	1.5
	-12.4	3.5	4.9				5.7	4.8
	42.1	30.7	48.8			% Profit Before Taxes/Tangible	42.0	35.4
	(28) 8.9	(52) 9.3	(28) 29.7			Net Worth	(115) 18.7	(98) 19.0
	.6	2.1	15.8				2.4	3.5
	9.4	10.1	20.1			% Profit Before Taxes/Total	16.0	15.5
	2.8	4.8	12.8			Assets	6.4	5.6
	-5.9	.4	3.7				.2	1.1
	55.0	26.2	14.6				21.6	22.3
	23.7	13.2	10.4			Sales/Net Fixed Assets	11.1	12.3
	10.0	9.4	4.5				5.8	5.2
	4.2	2.9	2.5				3.1	3.0
	3.1	2.6	2.0			Sales/Total Assets	2.3	2.2
	2.4	2.0	1.6				1.9	1.8
	.7	1.0	1.1				1.0	1.2
	(32) 1.6	(53) 1.4	1.5			% Depr., Dep., Amort./Sales	(111) 1.6	(95) 1.7
	2.9	2.2	2.5				2.5	2.7
	1.9	1.3					1.2	1.5
	(24) 4.2	(24) 2.0				% Officers', Directors', Owners' Comp/Sales	(43) 3.0	(33) 2.5
	6.0	2.7					6.6	4.9
7241M	174301M	672603M	1236664M	566548M	1352759M	Net Sales ($)	5309744M	4647583M
1890M	49209M	262744M	603678M	257301M	712359M	Total Assets ($)	2667811M	2525345M

M = $ thousand   MM = $ million
See Pages 11 through 21 for Explanation of Ratios and Data

Comparative Historical Data / Current Data Sorted By Sales

4/1/02-3/31/03 ALL	4/1/03-3/31/04 ALL	4/1/04-3/31/05 ALL	Type of Statement	0-1MM	1-3MM	3-5MM	5-10MM	10-25MM	25MM & OVER
28	23	24	Unqualified	1	1	7	3	8	13
39	42	43	Reviewed				11	14	9
24	31	21	Compiled	1	3	7	5	4	1
3	9	14	Tax Returns		6	4	4		
46	36	41	Other	1	6	2	8	12	12
				30 (4/1-9/30/04)			113 (10/1/04-3/31/05)		
140	141	143	NUMBER OF STATEMENTS	3	16	20	31	38	35
%	%	%	**ASSETS**	%	%	%	%	%	%
6.6	8.6	7.3	Cash & Equivalents		6.0	12.2	5.9	6.6	7.7
30.3	32.1	33.8	Trade Receivables (net)		41.9	34.8	35.5	36.7	26.6
27.3	24.9	26.4	Inventory		28.3	25.4	32.2	24.7	23.6
3.4	2.9	2.4	All Other Current		.6	1.7	1.2	5.1	1.9
67.6	68.5	70.0	Total Current		76.8	74.1	74.8	73.0	59.9
23.4	22.8	21.6	Fixed Assets (net)		18.4	18.3	16.4	20.1	29.3
3.6	2.4	2.5	Intangibles (net)		2.4	2.4	1.7	1.3	4.1
5.3	6.3	5.9	All Other Non-Current		2.4	5.1	7.1	5.6	6.7
100.0	100.0	100.0	Total		100.0	100.0	100.0	100.0	100.0
			LIABILITIES						
11.4	9.7	11.1	Notes Payable-Short Term		9.2	11.5	12.7	14.6	5.9
3.7	3.6	3.5	Cur. Mat.-L/T/D		5.9	3.4	2.8	3.1	3.9
16.9	17.1	18.2	Trade Payables		29.7	15.9	23.7	16.5	12.3
.5	.2	.3	Income Taxes Payable		.1	.1	.2	.6	.4
10.5	12.1	11.3	All Other Current		8.9	11.8	12.9	13.3	9.5
43.0	42.8	44.4	Total Current		53.9	42.7	52.2	48.0	31.9
15.5	15.4	14.4	Long-Term Debt		33.5	9.4	10.3	8.5	18.8
.5	.5	.5	Deferred Taxes		.1	.2	.0	.7	1.2
6.7	5.6	6.3	All Other Non-Current		16.4	8.0	4.0	3.0	4.3
34.3	35.6	34.3	Net Worth		-3.9	39.6	33.4	39.8	43.8
100.0	100.0	100.0	Total Liabilities & Net Worth		100.0	100.0	100.0	100.0	100.0
			INCOME DATA						
100.0	100.0	100.0	Net Sales		100.0	100.0	100.0	100.0	100.0
31.2	30.2	29.1	Gross Profit		35.2	33.1	31.7	25.2	26.3
26.9	25.9	26.2	Operating Expenses		36.1	30.9	29.5	22.0	19.6
4.3	4.3	3.0	Operating Profit		-.9	2.2	2.2	3.2	6.7
1.2	.9	.6	All Other Expenses (net)		.8	.6	.2	.7	.8
3.1	3.4	2.3	Profit Before Taxes		-1.7	1.5	2.0	2.6	5.9
			RATIOS						
2.7	2.7	2.6	Current		2.7	2.8	1.9	2.4	3.3
1.6	1.7	1.7			1.8	1.7	1.7	1.7	2.0
1.1	1.2	1.2			.9	1.1	1.2	1.1	1.3
1.4	1.7	1.4	Quick		1.4	1.9	1.2	1.4	2.0
.9	.9	1.0			1.1	1.2	.9	.9	1.1
.6	.6	.6			.6	.6	.4	.7	.8
28 13.1	27 13.7	30 12.0	Sales/Receivables		44 8.3	25 14.4	38 9.5	31 11.8	29 12.4
41 8.9	41 8.8	46 7.9			51 7.1	41 9.0	51 7.1	45 8.1	38 9.6
60 6.1	58 6.3	63 5.8			60 6.1	62 5.9	73 5.0	67 5.5	60 6.1
30 12.2	26 13.8	33 11.1	Cost of Sales/Inventory		28 13.0	24 15.3	39 9.3	28 13.2	34 10.8
54 6.8	45 8.1	50 7.2			51 7.2	55 6.6	77 4.8	50 7.3	46 8.0
85 4.3	76 4.8	80 4.6			74 4.9	84 4.4	102 3.6	61 6.0	64 5.7
15 24.1	14 25.6	18 20.3	Cost of Sales/Payables		33 11.0	11 33.4	23 15.6	16 23.4	15 24.2
28 13.0	23 15.6	29 12.5			45 8.0	26 14.0	43 8.5	25 14.4	24 15.1
43 8.5	41 8.9	44 8.2			70 5.2	47 7.8	74 4.9	40 9.1	34 10.8
5.7	5.7	5.6	Sales/Working Capital		6.1	5.9	5.6	6.3	4.8
10.4	9.5	9.8			11.2	9.8	10.2	9.3	9.6
38.7	26.4	27.1			NM	34.1	27.1	30.9	25.4
9.6	18.0	12.5	EBIT/Interest		3.4	10.7	5.3	19.6	27.2
(128) 3.0	(127) 3.7	(128) 3.4		(15) .9	(16) 3.1	(24) 2.6	(37) 6.0	(33) 8.5	
1.3	1.8	1.1			-3.8	1.4	1.1	2.0	2.0
6.8	6.0	4.2	Net Profit + Depr., Dep., Amort./Cur. Mat. L/T/D					4.1	7.9
(50) 2.5	(43) 3.1	(51) 2.1						(20) 2.2	(18) 2.7
1.2	.9	.8						1.1	1.0
.3	.3	.3	Fixed/Worth		.3	.1	.2	.3	.4
.7	.5	.6			NM	.5	.5	.5	.7
1.6	1.3	1.6			-.5	28.5	1.3	1.2	1.6
.9	.7	.8	Debt/Worth		1.3	.5	1.3	.7	.6
2.0	1.6	1.7			NM	1.0	2.2	1.3	1.5
5.4	3.9	5.7			-3.0	638.8	8.3	3.5	4.8
40.6	35.0	37.5	% Profit Before Taxes/Tangible Net Worth			12.4	47.5	33.9	61.6
(122) 17.6	(126) 15.7	(120) 15.5			(16) 6.1	(28) 11.5	(34) 15.5	(32) 29.7	
4.1	4.3	3.5			4.5	1.6	6.2	9.1	
16.0	16.1	14.2	% Profit Before Taxes/Total Assets		11.5	6.9	11.1	11.3	20.4
5.2	5.9	5.7			.1	4.2	2.1	7.4	12.9
.8	1.3	.4			-12.6	1.9	.2	2.0	3.5
27.8	32.1	28.9	Sales/Net Fixed Assets		35.8	54.6	42.8	28.0	14.3
13.4	14.2	13.1			16.6	22.8	19.8	13.0	8.1
6.7	6.5	8.1			8.8	10.6	9.4	9.5	4.7
3.4	3.3	3.1	Sales/Total Assets		3.8	3.9	3.1	3.4	2.6
2.4	2.5	2.5			2.6	3.0	2.7	2.8	2.2
1.9	1.9	1.9			2.3	2.2	2.0	2.1	1.8
1.0	1.1	1.0	% Depr., Dep., Amort./Sales		1.1	1.0	.8	.7	1.2
(128) 1.6	(122) 1.7	(128) 1.6		(14) 2.0	(18) 1.8	(23) 1.3	(37) 1.4	(34) 1.6	
2.5	2.6	2.4			3.9	2.7	2.3	2.2	2.4
1.8	1.8	1.5	% Officers', Directors', Owners' Comp/Sales	3.8	1.8	1.6			
(54) 3.6	(58) 3.8	(56) 2.5		(10) 5.2	(11) 2.9	(19) 2.5			
6.8	7.3	5.1		8.0	5.3	5.2			
5580453M	3999891M	4010116M	Net Sales ($)	1563M	34373M	81564M	211714M	579239M	3101663M
2922846M	1946817M	1887181M	Total Assets ($)	1879M	12344M	33884M	92074M	233856M	1513144M

M = $ thousand   MM = $ million
See Pages 11 through 21 for Explanation of Ratios and Data

Current Data Sorted By Assets   Comparative Historical Data

		11	21	6	3	Type of Statement	25	28
2	22	62	14			Unqualified	97	78
6	31	25	3	1		Reviewed	84	75
14	19	10				Compiled	11	17
7	26	41	16	2		Tax Returns	62	60
						Other		

0-500M	500M-2MM	2-10MM	10-50MM	50-100MM	100-250MM		4/1/00-3/31/01 ALL	4/1/01-3/31/02 ALL
	64 (4/1-9/30/04)		278 (10/1/04-3/31/05)					
29	98	149	54	9	3	**NUMBER OF STATEMENTS**	279	258
%	%	%	%	%	%	**ASSETS**	%	%
9.0	9.4	7.2	8.3			Cash & Equivalents	10.2	9.2
28.4	37.9	32.3	24.3			Trade Receivables (net)	32.0	29.1
12.9	16.0	21.3	26.7			Inventory	16.7	18.2
3.5	3.2	2.6	3.1			All Other Current	2.5	2.5
53.9	66.4	63.4	62.4			Total Current	61.5	59.0
40.1	27.9	29.6	27.5			Fixed Assets (net)	31.4	33.2
2.5	1.3	2.3	3.9			Intangibles (net)	2.4	2.8
3.6	4.4	4.7	6.2			All Other Non-Current	4.6	4.9
100.0	100.0	100.0	100.0			Total	100.0	100.0
						LIABILITIES		
21.8	13.0	10.7	9.8			Notes Payable-Short Term	9.1	11.6
6.3	6.1	5.5	3.6			Cur. Mat.-L/T/D	4.5	4.7
17.0	17.4	15.4	13.4			Trade Payables	14.6	13.6
.0	.2	.2	.1			Income Taxes Payable	.4	.2
7.3	8.4	8.3	10.5			All Other Current	9.1	9.6
52.4	45.1	40.2	37.3			Total Current	37.7	39.8
30.1	17.5	16.1	18.2			Long-Term Debt	18.9	19.4
.6	.2	.5	.6			Deferred Taxes	.6	.5
17.5	5.7	4.8	2.8			All Other Non-Current	3.8	4.2
−.7	31.4	38.5	41.1			Net Worth	39.0	36.2
100.0	100.0	100.0	100.0			Total Liabilities & Net Worth	100.0	100.0
						INCOME DATA		
100.0	100.0	100.0	100.0			Net Sales	100.0	100.0
36.6	33.0	26.9	22.8			Gross Profit	29.8	27.8
31.9	29.2	22.1	16.1			Operating Expenses	23.9	25.1
4.7	3.8	4.7	6.8			Operating Profit	5.9	2.7
1.1	.8	.9	1.3			All Other Expenses (net)	.9	1.5
3.6	3.0	3.9	5.5			Profit Before Taxes	4.9	1.2
						RATIOS		
1.9	2.5	2.4	2.2				2.8	2.5
1.0	1.5	1.6	1.7			Current	1.7	1.5
.6	1.0	1.2	1.2				1.1	1.1
1.4	1.8	1.7	1.2				2.0	1.7
.6	1.0	1.0	.8			Quick	1.2	1.0
.4	.7	.6	.6				.7	.6
16 22.3	32 11.5	37 9.9	35 10.5				36 10.1	32 11.3
35 10.3	50 7.4	48 7.6	49 7.5			Sales/Receivables	48 7.7	45 8.1
55 6.7	59 6.2	64 5.7	63 5.8				61 6.0	60 6.1
0 UND	10 35.4	22 16.3	44 8.4				15 24.1	17 21.8
16 23.4	27 13.3	42 8.7	73 5.0			Cost of Sales/Inventory	32 11.3	35 10.5
36 10.0	46 7.9	65 5.6	95 3.8				54 6.7	65 5.6
10 38.3	19 19.4	20 18.2	18 19.9				15 24.6	12 30.5
28 13.0	34 10.8	29 12.7	35 10.4			Cost of Sales/Payables	28 12.9	25 14.9
43 8.4	45 8.1	46 7.9	48 7.5				44 8.4	41 8.9
11.5	6.6	6.0	5.1				5.8	5.8
116.0	15.0	10.2	8.0			Sales/Working Capital	10.0	11.5
−12.9	208.5	26.2	17.6				37.9	132.9
	8.8	9.0	19.6				10.7	5.3
(25) 3.6	(86) 2.7	(139) 3.8	(48) 5.4			EBIT/Interest	(253) 3.7	(238) 1.9
2.0	1.1	1.9	1.5				1.8	.3
1.0								
	4.6	4.8	8.1			Net Profit + Depr., Dep.,	3.6	2.9
	(20) 2.2	(41) 2.2	(18) 3.8			Amort./Cur. Mat. L /T/D	(95) 1.9	(80) 1.3
	1.2	1.3	1.5				1.2	.4
.6	.3	.3	.3				.4	.4
4.0	1.0	.8	.8			Fixed/Worth	.8	.9
−1.1	2.4	1.9	1.4				1.8	2.5
1.4	.8	.9	.8				.7	.8
5.0	2.2	2.0	1.6			Debt/Worth	1.7	2.0
−4.8	6.6	4.0	3.9				3.9	5.5
78.1	59.9	50.3	47.4				48.9	34.6
(18) 47.6	(86) 22.0	(136) 21.4	(50) 20.3			% Profit Before Taxes/Tangible Net Worth	(254) 24.4	(229) 9.8
9.9	.6	4.6	6.7				9.8	−1.8
13.6	17.0	14.7	15.6				17.5	10.7
5.8	7.1	6.9	5.5			% Profit Before Taxes/Total Assets	7.9	3.4
.0	.2	1.4	1.4				3.4	−3.1
32.1	23.6	15.9	14.3				13.9	14.5
10.5	9.5	8.6	6.4			Sales/Net Fixed Assets	7.9	7.0
4.9	6.6	4.8	4.1				4.6	4.0
5.2	3.5	2.8	2.2				3.0	2.9
3.3	2.8	2.3	1.7			Sales/Total Assets	2.3	2.2
2.0	2.2	1.8	1.4				1.8	1.6
1.1	1.5	1.4	1.3				1.4	1.5
(24) 2.3	(80) 2.9	(144) 2.7	(50) 2.5			% Depr., Dep., Amort./Sales	(258) 2.6	(241) 2.7
4.3	4.3	4.0	4.0				4.1	5.0
3.5	3.4	1.8					3.1	2.1
(16) 9.1	(54) 4.5	(69) 3.0				% Officers', Directors', Owners' Comp/Sales	(135) 5.8	(124) 4.3
16.9	7.4	5.4					8.5	7.6
35946M	308910M	1531625M	1824004M	965916M	793231M	Net Sales ($)	4989224M	3575184M
9834M	113169M	677427M	1051678M	605606M	442923M	Total Assets ($)	2406908M	1833729M

M = $ thousand MM = $ million
See Pages 11 through 21 for Explanation of Ratios and Data

Comparative Historical Data | Current Data Sorted By Sales

Type of Statement	4/1/02-3/31/03 ALL	4/1/03-3/31/04 ALL	4/1/04-3/31/05 ALL	0-1MM	1-3MM	3-5MM	5-10MM	10-25MM	25MM & OVER
Unqualified	46	41	41			1	2	13	25
Reviewed	87	96	100	2	12	15	32	27	12
Compiled	73	77	66		18	19	16	9	4
Tax Returns	20	21	43	6	18	12	5	2	
Other	75	86	92	4	16	15	23	23	11
				64 (4/1-9/30/04)			**278 (10/1/04-3/31/05)**		
NUMBER OF STATEMENTS	301	321	342	12	64	62	78	74	52
ASSETS	%	%	%	%	%	%	%	%	%
Cash & Equivalents	8.3	7.6	8.0	5.4	10.1	10.0	6.4	7.7	6.5
Trade Receivables (net)	28.2	32.1	32.1	23.8	33.0	35.7	33.4	30.6	28.9
Inventory	18.3	19.2	20.0	12.2	12.9	16.4	22.4	23.4	26.4
All Other Current	3.5	3.1	3.0	1.6	4.5	2.5	2.0	2.7	3.9
Total Current	58.4	62.0	63.1	43.0	60.5	64.5	64.2	64.5	65.6
Fixed Assets (net)	33.2	30.9	29.5	41.4	34.6	28.5	28.6	28.7	24.4
Intangibles (net)	3.1	2.6	2.6	6.0	2.5	.7	2.0	3.4	3.7
All Other Non-Current	5.3	4.5	4.8	9.7	2.4	6.3	5.2	3.4	6.3
Total	100.0	100.0	100.0	100.0	100.0	100.0	100.0	100.0	100.0
LIABILITIES									
Notes Payable-Short Term	10.5	11.4	12.1	20.8	15.5	10.6	10.5	11.3	11.5
Cur. Mat.-L/T/D	5.4	4.3	5.4	6.0	6.5	6.9	4.8	4.7	3.7
Trade Payables	13.3	15.9	15.7	11.8	15.6	16.2	17.3	14.7	15.3
Income Taxes Payable	.3	.3	.2	.0	.2	.4	.1	.2	.2
All Other Current	8.9	9.5	8.9	3.5	9.8	8.1	7.7	8.3	12.6
Total Current	38.5	41.5	42.3	42.1	47.6	42.2	40.5	39.1	43.2
Long-Term Debt	19.6	18.3	18.1	42.3	18.5	18.8	17.9	16.1	14.4
Deferred Taxes	.4	.5	.5	.0	.6	.5	.3	.4	.6
All Other Non-Current	4.7	6.4	5.8	12.8	8.9	5.0	5.6	4.6	2.9
Net Worth	36.7	33.3	33.4	2.5	24.4	33.5	35.7	39.7	38.8
Total Liabilities & Net Worth	100.0	100.0	100.0	100.0	100.0	100.0	100.0	100.0	100.0
INCOME DATA									
Net Sales	100.0	100.0	100.0	100.0	100.0	100.0	100.0	100.0	100.0
Gross Profit	28.2	27.4	28.9	48.6	34.7	29.7	26.4	26.8	23.3
Operating Expenses	26.2	25.3	24.0	43.9	31.0	25.0	21.6	21.4	16.9
Operating Profit	1.9	2.1	4.9	4.7	3.7	4.7	4.7	5.4	6.4
All Other Expenses (net)	1.3	1.1	.9	2.1	.8	1.0	.7	.9	.6
Profit Before Taxes	.7	1.0	4.1	2.6	2.9	3.7	4.0	4.4	5.8
RATIOS									
Current	2.5	2.6	2.4	2.2	2.3	2.9	2.4	2.1	2.2
	1.6	1.6	1.5	1.0	1.5	1.5	1.6	1.6	1.6
	1.1	1.2	1.1	.6	.8	1.1	1.1	1.3	1.1
Quick	1.7	1.7	1.6	1.7	1.6	2.0	1.6	1.5	1.2
	.9 (320)	1.0	.9	.6	1.0	1.1	1.0	.9	.9
	.6	.6	.6	.5	.5	.7	.6	.6	.6
Sales/Receivables	33 11.0	36 10.1	35 10.5	33 11.1	27 13.6	33 11.2	35 10.5	37 10.0	37 9.9
	46 7.9	50 7.3	49 7.5	53 6.9	42 8.7	50 7.4	49 7.5	47 7.7	51 7.2
	60 6.0	68 5.3	63 5.8	65 5.6	60 6.1	64 5.7	63 5.8	61 6.0	68 5.4
Cost of Sales/Inventory	20 18.0	18 19.7	18 20.3	0 UND	9 42.2	12 31.0	21 17.2	28 12.9	38 9.6
	41 8.8	41 8.9	38 9.7	32 11.3	22 16.3	29 12.7	43 8.5	51 7.1	66 5.6
	68 5.4	76 4.8	66 5.5	66 5.5	37 9.8	55 6.6	65 5.6	83 4.4	98 3.7
Cost of Sales/Payables	15 24.7	20 18.7	18 19.8	12 30.2	10 35.0	21 17.8	20 17.8	20 18.3	18 19.9
	26 13.8	29 12.5	33 11.2	38 9.7	28 13.3	33 11.1	30 12.2	28 13.0	36 10.2
	41 9.0	47 7.8	46 7.9	69 5.3	44 8.4	44 8.3	46 7.9	47 7.8	48 7.7
Sales/Working Capital	5.8	5.4	6.2	33.2	7.2	5.4	6.1	6.6	5.6
	10.6	10.1	11.0	UND	16.8	13.6	11.2	9.4	8.4
	59.5	30.2	64.5	-10.5	-21.0	74.1	37.2	15.8	34.2
EBIT/Interest	6.3	7.0	10.2	1.6	9.0	8.0	9.5	12.4	23.6
	(269) 1.8	(289) 2.2	(309) 3.7	(10) 1.0	(57) 2.9	(54) 2.6	(75) 3.7	(64) 3.6	(49) 7.5
	-1.0	-.9	1.5	-3.0	1.1	1.4	1.9	1.6	3.5
Net Profit + Depr., Dep., Amort./Cur. Mat. L/T/D	3.6	6.1	5.8		2.5	4.8	3.9	5.8	10.0
	(80) 1.4	(94) 2.4	(86) 2.5		(12) 1.6	(13) 4.2	(17) 1.5	(23) 2.3	(20) 4.5
	.1	.8	1.3		.7	1.6	1.3	1.3	1.7
Fixed/Worth	.4	.4	.3	.7	.5	.3	.3	.4	.3
	.9	.9	.9	5.8	1.3	1.0	.8	.9	.8
	2.5	2.2	2.4	-.5	8.0	2.0	2.0	1.5	1.5
Debt/Worth	.7	.7	.9	.7	.8	.8	.9	.9	.9
	1.9	1.8	2.1	5.7	2.7	2.1	2.1	2.0	1.9
	5.6	5.3	5.5	-3.0	18.6	6.0	4.8	4.0	4.6
% Profit Before Taxes/Tangible Net Worth	29.1	38.6	55.5		69.7	64.5	56.1	46.2	52.3
	(266) 7.4	(281) 11.4	(301) 22.7	(51) 20.7	(56) 23.9	(67) 23.1	(70) 20.2	(50) 24.4	
	-11.6	-5.4	5.2	.5	3.3	5.4	4.4	9.7	
% Profit Before Taxes/Total Assets	11.9	11.2	15.5	11.0	15.7	22.9	15.1	15.5	16.8
	2.6	3.4	6.8	.0	6.7	7.2	7.6	6.3	7.0
	-5.2	-4.3	1.2	-3.0	.1	.8	2.1	1.1	3.0
Sales/Net Fixed Assets	14.6	16.9	18.0	28.3	17.5	25.6	17.1	21.5	15.1
	6.7	7.5	8.6	5.3	8.6	9.3	9.5	7.5	8.6
	3.9	4.2	5.0	1.8	5.9	4.8	5.5	5.0	4.7
Sales/Total Assets	2.7	2.9	3.0	2.5	3.7	3.3	3.0	2.8	2.4
	2.1	2.2	2.3	1.7	2.8	2.4	2.4	2.2	2.0
	1.6	1.5	1.7	.9	2.1	2.0	1.9	1.6	1.6
% Depr., Dep., Amort./Sales	1.9	1.6	1.3		1.4	1.4	1.5	1.3	1.2
	(288) 3.2	(290) 2.9	(308) 2.6	(56) 2.5	(52) 3.0	(72) 3.0	(71) 2.5	(48) 1.9	
	5.3	4.6	4.1	4.6	4.7	4.2	3.8	2.9	
% Officers', Directors', Owners' Comp/Sales	2.3	2.1			3.5	2.7	2.4	1.5	
	(143) 4.6	(129) 4.4	(143) 3.8	(36) 6.2	(36) 4.0	(36) 3.6	(23) 2.0		
	7.5	6.9	6.9	9.6	5.2	6.9	3.6		
Net Sales ($)	3379011M	4809074M	5459632M	5542M	126727M	239060M	558498M	1125597M	3404208M
Total Assets ($)	1969078M	2423760M	2900637M	3767M	53858M	111463M	256128M	588222M	1887199M

Current Data Sorted By Assets   Comparative Historical Data

	0-500M	500M-2MM	2-10MM	10-50MM	50-100MM	100-250MM	Type of Statement	4/1/00-3/31/01 ALL	4/1/01-3/31/02 ALL
			2	4	2	1	Unqualified	6	9
		8	19	2			Reviewed	18	24
		6	5	1			Compiled	20	13
	5	7	3	1		1	Tax Returns	9	5
	1	6	13	3		1	Other	17	16
		14 (4/1-9/30/04)		77 (10/1/04-3/31/05)					
NUMBER OF STATEMENTS	6	27	42	11	2	3		70	67
ASSETS	%	%	%	%	%	%		%	%
Cash & Equivalents		6.1	5.7	10.2				11.8	10.2
Trade Receivables (net)		42.9	38.9	24.1				29.9	29.2
Inventory		22.6	21.9	21.2				20.2	18.9
All Other Current		3.3	5.6	3.6				3.1	3.7
Total Current		74.8	72.1	59.1				65.0	62.0
Fixed Assets (net)		17.5	17.8	23.5				26.5	27.4
Intangibles (net)		3.0	2.6	6.4				3.4	3.4
All Other Non-Current		4.7	7.5	10.9				5.1	7.3
Total		100.0	100.0	100.0				100.0	100.0
LIABILITIES									
Notes Payable-Short Term		9.3	13.0	9.1				13.1	11.6
Cur. Mat.-L/T/D		4.3	2.6	1.9				4.3	4.6
Trade Payables		19.8	19.5	7.4				13.1	14.8
Income Taxes Payable		.6	.6	.6				.5	.6
All Other Current		9.8	12.5	14.1				13.8	9.3
Total Current		43.8	48.1	33.2				44.9	40.9
Long-Term Debt		15.6	11.0	9.6				15.4	17.0
Deferred Taxes		.3	.3	1.2				.6	.4
All Other Non-Current		8.4	4.1	9.1				3.2	3.3
Net Worth		31.9	36.5	46.9				36.0	38.3
Total Liabilities & Net Worth		100.0	100.0	100.0				100.0	100.0
INCOME DATA									
Net Sales		100.0	100.0	100.0				100.0	100.0
Gross Profit		33.0	30.9	24.9				36.6	36.0
Operating Expenses		29.1	26.2	18.9				32.1	30.9
Operating Profit		3.9	4.8	6.0				4.5	5.0
All Other Expenses (net)		.4	.0	.5				.6	.8
Profit Before Taxes		3.5	4.7	5.5				3.9	4.2
RATIOS									
Current		3.3	1.9	3.1				2.2	2.1
		1.6	1.5	1.4				1.5	1.6
		1.3	1.2	1.2				1.2	1.1
Quick		1.6	1.3	1.7				1.5	1.3
		1.0	.8	.9				1.0	.9
		.8	.6	.6				.6	.6
Sales/Receivables	33	10.9	38 9.5	36 10.1				28 13.2	31 11.6
	55	6.6	58 6.3	52 7.0				44 8.4	44 8.4
	76	4.8	80 4.5	57 6.4				62 5.8	59 6.2
Cost of Sales/Inventory	5	75.6	12 31.4	43 8.4				13 28.2	10 37.8
	32	11.4	39 9.3	66 5.5				42 8.6	40 9.2
	66	5.5	94 3.9	79 4.6				81 4.5	74 4.9
Cost of Sales/Payables	16	22.7	25 14.3	8 47.6				15 24.3	16 23.3
	28	12.9	43 8.4	21 17.3				28 13.2	27 13.5
	46	7.9	55 6.7	25 14.6				43 8.6	46 7.9
Sales/Working Capital		6.5	6.2	4.7				7.1	7.0
		9.9	10.2	10.7				12.0	12.0
		21.5	21.3	23.9				31.0	48.4
EBIT/Interest	(24)	18.1	(41) 15.4	(10) 25.4				(66) 8.3	(59) 8.3
		4.3	7.1	6.4				2.9	3.9
		1.4	4.4	1.5				1.1	1.6
Net Profit + Depr., Dep., Amort./Cur. Mat. L./T/D			(10) 10.5					(22) 7.0	(19) 3.6
			4.1					2.4	2.0
			2.8					1.2	1.1
Fixed/Worth		.3	.2	.1				.3	.3
		.5	.4	.8				.8	.7
		1.3	1.0	1.0				2.0	2.2
Debt/Worth		.7	1.3	.7				.9	.9
		2.3	2.2	1.6				2.2	1.7
		11.1	3.3	2.9				4.1	4.9
% Profit Before Taxes/Tangible Net Worth	(23)	47.0	59.5	(10) 41.3				(64) 40.7	(60) 46.9
		24.3	26.4	13.4				22.0	23.9
		1.4	9.3	8.1				4.7	6.6
% Profit Before Taxes/Total Assets		17.9	14.3	19.9				14.6	17.6
		3.6	7.5	3.7				5.8	7.5
		.5	3.2	1.9				.5	1.6
Sales/Net Fixed Assets		34.3	28.7	22.6				24.1	22.9
		20.8	16.1	8.8				13.4	11.7
		10.9	7.4	4.9				6.1	5.2
Sales/Total Assets		3.5	3.0	2.4				3.0	2.9
		2.9	2.4	2.0				2.3	2.3
		2.3	1.8	1.5				1.8	1.8
% Depr., Dep., Amort./Sales	(22)	.7	(36) .8	(10) 1.4				(67) 1.1	(60) 1.1
		1.6	1.4	1.9				1.7	2.0
		2.5	2.0	2.6				2.6	3.3
% Officers', Directors', Owners' Comp/Sales	(16)	2.7	(23) 2.3					(35) 4.1	(36) 3.3
		5.9	3.8					6.2	5.2
		8.5	8.5					13.1	7.6
Net Sales ($)	5108M	101957M	479223M	470268M	177983M	1167124M		1079015M	1058583M
Total Assets ($)	1195M	33617M	206205M	253065M	141357M	356786M		618485M	623389M

M = $ thousand   MM = $ million
See Pages 11 through 21 for Explanation of Ratios and Data

Comparative Historical Data | **Current Data Sorted By Sales**

Hist 4/1/02-3/31/03 ALL	Hist 4/1/03-3/31/04 ALL	Hist 4/1/04-3/31/05 ALL		0-1MM	1-3MM	3-5MM	5-10MM	10-25MM	25MM & OVER
			Type of Statement						
9	13	9	Unqualified					3	6
26	35	29	Reviewed		2	5	10	9	3
10	17	12	Compiled		3	2	4	2	1
10	9	17	Tax Returns	3	7	1	3	1	2
14	23	24	Other		4	3	5	8	4
					14 (4/1-9/30/04)		77 (10/1/04-3/31/05)		
69	97	91	**NUMBER OF STATEMENTS**	3	16	11	22	23	16
%	%	%	**ASSETS**	%	%	%	%	%	%
7.0	8.2	6.1	Cash & Equivalents		8.4	6.9	3.5	6.1	7.7
34.9	38.6	37.1	Trade Receivables (net)		35.0	46.3	37.2	40.8	25.5
19.1	15.3	21.3	Inventory		24.4	21.0	27.8	15.7	21.2
5.4	6.1	4.2	All Other Current		2.0	4.8	4.6	6.5	2.8
66.4	68.2	68.7	Total Current		69.7	79.0	73.2	69.0	57.1
25.4	22.7	21.2	Fixed Assets (net)		24.6	15.4	13.0	20.8	31.8
3.0	2.7	3.1	Intangibles (net)		2.4	3.4	2.6	2.4	6.0
5.2	6.5	7.0	All Other Non-Current		3.2	2.2	11.3	7.8	5.0
100.0	100.0	100.0	Total		100.0	100.0	100.0	100.0	100.0
			LIABILITIES						
11.9	10.6	10.4	Notes Payable-Short Term		10.2	12.5	12.8	10.5	5.7
4.5	2.9	5.9	Cur. Mat.-L/T/D		19.7	3.0	2.3	3.0	3.7
15.8	19.2	17.7	Trade Payables		17.9	17.7	22.9	16.8	11.2
.9	.6	.5	Income Taxes Payable		.0	1.6	.6	.4	.5
10.6	11.0	14.1	All Other Current		30.0	8.4	8.8	13.8	12.1
43.7	44.3	48.7	Total Current		77.7	43.2	47.4	44.4	33.2
16.6	13.3	14.5	Long-Term Debt		23.0	8.5	10.2	11.7	13.1
.5	.6	.5	Deferred Taxes		.3	.3	.1	.5	1.3
5.0	4.8	6.5	All Other Non-Current		8.1	5.6	7.6	2.7	7.7
34.2	37.0	29.8	Net Worth		-9.2	42.5	34.7	40.7	44.7
100.0	100.0	100.0	Total Liabilities & Net Worth		100.0	100.0	100.0	100.0	100.0
			INCOME DATA						
100.0	100.0	100.0	Net Sales		100.0	100.0	100.0	100.0	100.0
34.7	32.0	31.2	Gross Profit		32.7	27.5	32.4	28.1	29.2
31.8	29.2	27.5	Operating Expenses		34.6	22.6	27.2	23.4	23.0
2.9	2.9	3.7	Operating Profit		-1.9	4.9	5.2	4.6	6.2
.9	.9	.2	All Other Expenses (net)		-.3	.6	-.3	.2	.8
2.0	2.0	3.5	Profit Before Taxes		-1.6	4.3	5.5	4.4	5.4
			RATIOS						
2.2	2.3	2.1			2.7	2.4	2.1	1.9	2.6
1.6	1.6	1.5	Current		1.4	1.8	1.5	1.5	1.6
1.1	1.2	1.2			1.1	1.6	1.2	1.2	1.2
1.5	1.8	1.5			1.4	1.6	1.3	1.4	1.5
.9	1.1	.8	Quick		.8	1.4	.8	1.0	.9
.6	.6	.7			.7	.7	.8	.7	.7
34 10.7	38 9.6	36 10.1		28 13.1	47 7.8	37 9.8	34 10.8	39 9.4	
53 6.8	53 6.9	52 7.0	Sales/Receivables	55 6.7	66 5.5	47 7.8	62 5.9	50 7.2	
68 5.3	78 4.7	72 5.0		75 4.9	80 4.5	66 5.6	87 4.2	57 6.4	
2 151.6	2 221.1	12 30.8		26 14.3	2 161.4	27 13.4	1 336.7	43 8.4	
33 11.0	25 14.4	42 8.7	Cost of Sales/Inventory	44 8.4	28 13.2	47 7.8	30 12.0	56 6.5	
80 4.6	56 6.5	69 5.3		72 5.1	89 4.1	79 4.6	80 4.6	69 5.3	
14 26.0	20 18.2	19 18.9		17 20.9	10 37.2	23 15.7	17 21.6	9 40.9	
32 11.3	41 8.9	35 10.5	Cost of Sales/Payables	36 10.2	28 12.9	39 9.4	38 9.5	24 15.4	
48 7.6	60 6.1	51 7.2		52 7.1	60 6.1	54 6.8	48 7.6	40 9.0	
6.3	5.9	6.4			5.2	6.2	6.2	6.4	5.7
9.5	9.6	10.5	Sales/Working Capital		16.2	7.8	11.9	10.3	9.5
34.2	23.5	22.7			25.4	9.9	21.7	25.9	23.2
11.1	10.6	12.2			11.2	10.2	16.8	14.0	9.8
(67) 2.5	(84) 2.7	(84) 5.3	EBIT/Interest	(13) 1.6	4.7	(21) 10.3	5.4	(13) 5.6	
1.2	-.6	1.7			-.1	1.3	4.0	4.5	1.5
5.3	5.5	11.0	Net Profit + Depr., Dep.,						
(21) 3.3	(19) 1.3	(24) 3.6	Amort./Cur. Mat. L/T/D						
1.4	-1.0	1.8							
.3	.3	.3			.4	.2	.1	.2	.6
.7	.5	.6	Fixed/Worth		1.1	.3	.4	.5	.8
2.1	1.6	1.3			NM	.5	1.0	1.0	1.3
.8	.8	1.1			2.0	.7	1.3	1.0	.8
1.9	1.8	2.1	Debt/Worth		3.9	1.4	2.3	2.0	1.6
4.8	4.6	3.9			NM	3.7	5.3	2.7	3.2
42.3	28.0	46.7	% Profit Before Taxes/Tangible		42.2	60.7	57.5	60.6	41.3
(59) 10.5	(86) 14.6	(81) 24.3	Net Worth	(12) 13.2	(10) 6.8	(21) 25.0	27.0	(14) 13.4	
2.8	-3.2	4.8			-1.0	.7	12.1	9.2	4.2
11.3	13.8	14.1	% Profit Before Taxes/Total		9.3	13.2	23.8	13.9	17.7
3.6	3.9	6.6	Assets		1.2	4.9	9.3	7.7	4.7
.6	-1.8	1.5			-5.4	.3	3.9	3.0	1.9
29.3	24.6	27.6			22.9	46.3	60.6	22.6	16.3
11.7	14.8	14.8	Sales/Net Fixed Assets		11.0	18.5	25.3	12.3	6.5
4.9	7.4	7.4			7.6	12.6	15.5	7.2	4.7
3.2	3.1	3.3			3.8	3.5	3.6	2.8	3.0
2.3	2.5	2.4	Sales/Total Assets		2.8	2.5	2.6	2.4	2.1
1.8	1.8	2.0			2.0	2.0	2.1	1.9	1.5
1.0	1.1	.8			1.3		.7	1.1	1.4
(62) 2.0	(86) 2.2	(78) 1.7	% Depr., Dep., Amort./Sales	(13) 2.2		(17) 1.0	(21) 1.7	(15) 2.2	
3.0	3.1	2.6			3.4		1.8	2.4	3.0
3.6	2.3	2.3			3.8		2.3	1.8	
(40) 5.8	(45) 4.8	(47) 5.0	% Officers', Directors', Owners' Comp/Sales	(11) 5.4		(10) 3.7	(12) 3.5		
10.4	8.8	8.8			7.9		9.5	8.0	
1587389M	1524881M	2401663M	Net Sales ($)	1111M	31589M	44150M	162746M	331615M	1830452M
680188M	796216M	992225M	Total Assets ($)	394M	15191M	18526M	63607M	154253M	740254M

M = $ thousand   MM = $ million
See Pages 11 through 21 for Explanation of Ratios and Data

Current Data Sorted By Assets   Comparative Historical Data

						Type of Statement		
		1	2	1		Unqualified		
	3	6				Reviewed		
	3	3				Compiled		
	4					Tax Returns		
	3	4	4	1		Other		
	7 (4/1-9/30/04)		28 (10/1/04-3/31/05)				4/1/00-3/31/01	4/1/01-3/31/02
0-500M	500M-2MM	2-10MM	10-50MM	50-100MM	100-250MM		ALL	ALL
	13	14	6	2		NUMBER OF STATEMENTS		
%	%	%	%	%	%	ASSETS	%	%
D	9.1	8.2			D	Cash & Equivalents	D	D
A	31.4	31.5			A	Trade Receivables (net)	A	A
T	32.5	26.5			T	Inventory	T	T
A	4.2	.3			A	All Other Current	A	A
	77.2	66.5				Total Current		
N	15.0	16.4			N	Fixed Assets (net)	N	N
O	5.6	10.1			O	Intangibles (net)	O	O
T	2.2	6.9			T	All Other Non-Current	T	T
	100.0	100.0				Total		
A					A	LIABILITIES	A	A
V	17.1	17.2			V	Notes Payable-Short Term	V	V
A	9.7	1.9			A	Cur. Mat.-L/T/D	A	A
I	17.0	14.2			I	Trade Payables	I	I
L	.4	.2			L	Income Taxes Payable	L	L
A	4.9	11.3			A	All Other Current	A	A
B	49.1	44.8			B	Total Current	B	B
L	22.9	6.4			L	Long-Term Debt	L	L
E	.2	.2			E	Deferred Taxes	E	E
	2.1	12.7				All Other Non-Current		
	25.7	35.8				Net Worth		
	100.0	100.0				Total Liabilities & Net Worth		
						INCOME DATA		
	100.0	100.0				Net Sales		
	33.5	28.1				Gross Profit		
	29.9	22.6				Operating Expenses		
	3.6	5.5				Operating Profit		
	1.0	1.2				All Other Expenses (net)		
	2.6	4.3				Profit Before Taxes		
						RATIOS		
	2.9	3.2						
	1.7	1.4				Current		
	.9	1.0						
	1.5	1.7						
	.9	.8				Quick		
	.5	.5						
23	15.9	35 10.4						
48	7.6	46 7.9				Sales/Receivables		
57	6.3	57 6.5						
29	12.7	37 9.8						
61	6.0	59 6.2				Cost of Sales/Inventory		
105	3.5	97 3.8						
15	23.7	15 24.0						
34	10.8	24 14.9				Cost of Sales/Payables		
49	7.4	35 10.4						
	4.4	4.3						
	9.1	14.6				Sales/Working Capital		
	NM	NM						
	15.2	12.3						
(11)	4.3	(13) 5.9				EBIT/Interest		
	1.4	1.5						
						Net Profit + Depr., Dep., Amort./Cur. Mat. L /T/D		
	.0	.2						
	.5	1.1				Fixed/Worth		
	2.5	NM						
	2.1	.4						
	6.3	6.9				Debt/Worth		
	NM	NM						
	44.5	65.2						
(10)	21.9	(11) 25.6				% Profit Before Taxes/Tangible Net Worth		
	13.0	8.5						
	14.9	16.8						
	5.7	8.9				% Profit Before Taxes/Total Assets		
	2.2	2.2						
	649.3	42.9						
	26.2	12.1				Sales/Net Fixed Assets		
	9.4	8.3						
	4.0	3.2						
	2.6	2.0				Sales/Total Assets		
	2.1	1.5						
		.6						
	(13)	1.2				% Depr., Dep., Amort./Sales		
		3.2						
						% Officers', Directors', Owners' Comp/Sales		
	54570M	145771M	358769M	143667M		Net Sales ($)		
	16368M	61077M	131121M	120429M		Total Assets ($)		

© RMA 2005

M = $ thousand   MM = $ million
See Pages 11 through 21 for Explanation of Ratios and Data

Comparative Historical Data | Current Data Sorted By Sales

4/1/02-3/31/03 ALL	4/1/03-3/31/04 ALL	4/1/04-3/31/05 ALL	Type of Statement	0-1MM	1-3MM	3-5MM	5-10MM	10-25MM	25MM & OVER
3	3	4	Unqualified						4
7	12	9	Reviewed		1	3	3	3	
4	3	6	Compiled		2	2	1		
3	5	4	Tax Returns		2	1	1		
4	8	12	Other		2	3	1	1	5
					7 (4/1-9/30/04)		28 (10/1/04-3/31/05)		
21	31	35	**NUMBER OF STATEMENTS**		5	9	6	6	9
%	%	%	**ASSETS**	%	%	%	%	%	%
8.2	6.8	7.0	Cash & Equivalents						
24.8	28.1	32.3	Trade Receivables (net)	D					
21.5	24.4	27.4	Inventory	A					
2.1	5.0	2.5	All Other Current	T					
56.7	64.2	69.3	Total Current	A					
36.2	29.2	18.6	Fixed Assets (net)						
3.9	3.1	7.6	Intangibles (net)	N					
3.2	3.5	4.5	All Other Non-Current	O					
100.0	100.0	100.0	Total	T					
			LIABILITIES	A					
11.0	16.0	14.5	Notes Payable-Short Term	V					
9.0	5.4	5.6	Cur. Mat.-L/T/D	A					
12.6	13.1	16.1	Trade Payables	I					
.1	.5	.6	Income Taxes Payable	L					
6.9	5.2	8.9	All Other Current	A					
39.5	40.1	45.6	Total Current	B					
19.5	17.5	15.4	Long-Term Debt	L					
.3	1.1	.4	Deferred Taxes	E					
5.4	1.6	7.5	All Other Non-Current						
35.3	39.6	31.0	Net Worth						
100.0	100.0	100.0	Total Liabilities & Net Worth						
			INCOME DATA						
100.0	100.0	100.0	Net Sales						
35.2	37.2	30.3	Gross Profit						
32.4	31.5	25.2	Operating Expenses						
2.8	5.7	5.0	Operating Profit						
1.2	.9	1.2	All Other Expenses (net)						
1.6	4.7	3.8	Profit Before Taxes						
			RATIOS						
2.6	2.8	2.6							
1.8	1.4	1.5	Current						
1.0	1.1	1.0							
1.4	1.4	1.3							
1.0	.8	.8	Quick						
.4	.5	.6							
39 9.4	32 11.3	35 10.6							
46 8.0	44 8.3	48 7.6	Sales/Receivables						
62 5.9	52 7.0	63 5.8							
34 10.9	20 17.8	32 11.6							
55 6.6	43 8.4	54 6.8	Cost of Sales/Inventory						
92 4.0	77 4.7	91 4.0							
20 18.7	12 31.3	21 17.4							
28 12.8	30 12.2	34 10.8	Cost of Sales/Payables						
50 7.3	46 8.0	38 9.7							
5.3	5.6	4.9							
9.8	12.0	11.0	Sales/Working Capital						
NM	84.8	582.1							
8.4	9.6	14.8							
2.6	(29) 4.5	(32) 4.7	EBIT/Interest						
.0	2.3	1.5							
			Net Profit + Depr., Dep., Amort./Cur. Mat. L/T/D						
.5	.3	.2							
1.0	.7	.8	Fixed/Worth						
3.2	2.0	2.9							
.7	.8	.9							
3.0	1.9	5.3	Debt/Worth						
8.5	3.4	9.7							
39.9	44.8	46.1	% Profit Before Taxes/Tangible Net Worth						
(19) 13.4	(30) 24.4	(28) 25.0							
−4.1	12.0	13.0							
12.9	16.7	15.7							
7.0	8.5	7.9	% Profit Before Taxes/Total Assets						
−2.0	2.6	2.7							
12.2	19.7	45.9							
7.0	9.9	12.8	Sales/Net Fixed Assets						
3.1	5.0	8.8							
2.9	3.3	3.2							
1.7	2.4	2.5	Sales/Total Assets						
1.3	1.9	1.7							
1.6	1.2	.9							
(20) 3.9	(24) 1.6	(28) 1.6	% Depr., Dep., Amort./Sales						
6.7	4.0	2.7							
	2.5	2.3							
	(16) 3.2	(17) 3.7	% Officers', Directors', Owners' Comp/Sales						
	7.1	6.5							
172643M	544195M	702777M	Net Sales ($)		9842M	36586M	40381M	83456M	532512M
94110M	270375M	328995M	Total Assets ($)		4771M	19172M	16863M	30248M	257941M

M = $ thousand   MM = $ million
See Pages 11 through 21 for Explanation of Ratios and Data

Current Data Sorted By Assets   Comparative Historical Data

		6	12	4	4	Type of Statement		
	3	10	4		1	Unqualified	27	31
2	9	10	1		1	Reviewed	23	18
1	8	1				Compiled	30	31
	5	14	4	1		Tax Returns	11	8
						Other	27	56
	21 (4/1-9/30/04)		78 (10/1/04-3/31/05)				4/1/00-3/31/01	4/1/01-3/31/02
0-500M	500M-2MM	2-10MM	10-50MM	50-100MM	100-250MM		ALL	ALL
3	25	41	20	6	4	NUMBER OF STATEMENTS	118	144
%	%	%	%	%	%	**ASSETS**	%	%
	13.8	5.1	8.2			Cash & Equivalents	8.2	6.8
	26.9	25.0	21.5			Trade Receivables (net)	24.9	22.4
	28.2	32.9	27.6			Inventory	26.6	29.0
	2.3	2.8	3.7			All Other Current	1.7	2.0
	71.2	65.8	61.0			Total Current	61.3	60.2
	24.3	28.5	22.3			Fixed Assets (net)	28.6	28.2
	1.7	1.8	7.8			Intangibles (net)	5.0	7.1
	2.7	3.9	8.8			All Other Non-Current	5.0	4.5
	100.0	100.0	100.0			Total	100.0	100.0
						LIABILITIES		
	13.2	12.5	11.7			Notes Payable-Short Term	9.5	11.4
	1.9	13.3	2.2			Cur. Mat.-L/T/D	3.6	3.6
	15.4	14.1	9.4			Trade Payables	12.7	12.4
	.1	.1	.3			Income Taxes Payable	.3	.2
	8.9	11.7	6.4			All Other Current	7.6	6.9
	39.5	51.7	30.0			Total Current	33.7	34.5
	17.0	17.4	9.6			Long-Term Debt	17.7	19.1
	.1	1.1	.2			Deferred Taxes	.6	.6
	12.5	5.8	7.5			All Other Non-Current	3.2	4.9
	30.9	23.9	52.7			Net Worth	44.9	41.0
	100.0	100.0	100.0			Total Liabilities & Net Worth	100.0	100.0
						INCOME DATA		
	100.0	100.0	100.0			Net Sales	100.0	100.0
	34.5	29.4	31.8			Gross Profit	32.9	31.2
	31.1	24.5	23.1			Operating Expenses	26.1	26.1
	3.4	4.9	8.6			Operating Profit	6.8	5.0
	.7	1.5	2.2			All Other Expenses (net)	1.1	1.6
	2.7	3.4	6.4			Profit Before Taxes	5.7	3.5
						RATIOS		
	7.3	2.5	7.8				3.4	3.5
	2.3	1.7	2.3			Current	2.1	1.9
	1.1	1.0	1.3				1.2	1.3
	3.1	1.1	2.9				2.0	1.8
	1.2	.6	1.3			Quick	1.0	1.0
	.7	.4	.6				.6	.5
	(27) 13.5	(31) 11.7	(38) 9.5				(36) 10.3	(33) 11.2
	(37) 9.8	(45) 8.1	(44) 8.3			Sales/Receivables	(44) 8.3	(42) 8.7
	(52) 7.0	(53) 6.9	(54) 6.8				(56) 6.6	(54) 6.8
	(14) 26.8	(46) 7.9	(50) 7.3				(37) 9.9	(46) 8.0
	(67) 5.4	(86) 4.3	(80) 4.6			Cost of Sales/Inventory	(69) 5.3	(70) 5.2
	(131) 2.8	(143) 2.5	(125) 2.9				(111) 3.3	(123) 3.0
	(20) 18.2	(22) 16.9	(11) 33.3				(19) 19.4	(16) 23.5
	(29) 12.6	(34) 10.6	(16) 23.2			Cost of Sales/Payables	(27) 13.4	(25) 14.5
	(41) 9.0	(45) 8.1	(39) 9.4				(41) 8.9	(46) 8.0
	3.4	4.4	3.2				4.1	4.3
	5.3	7.7	4.9			Sales/Working Capital	6.9	7.6
	77.1	NM	12.8				25.0	16.5
	17.6	5.8	31.5				19.6	9.6
	(20) 3.3	(39) 3.0	(17) 6.1			EBIT/Interest	(108) 4.5	(130) 2.5
	1.7	1.3	1.6				1.5	1.1
		4.3				Net Profit + Depr., Dep.,	5.7	4.3
		(16) 2.0				Amort./Cur. Mat. L/T/D	(43) 2.5	(33) 2.5
		1.1					1.4	1.2
	.2	.4	.2				.3	.3
	.6	.8	.5			Fixed/Worth	.7	.7
	NM	7.0	.9				1.3	2.0
	.4	.9	.4				.4	.5
	2.4	2.4	.7			Debt/Worth	1.2	1.3
	NM	22.6	2.8				4.0	4.9
	(19) 43.6	(34) 40.7	(18) 37.1			% Profit Before Taxes/Tangible	(103) 39.8	(120) 28.1
	23.0	14.0	17.3			Net Worth	24.7	12.3
	4.5	6.8	7.2				7.7	.8
	14.5	10.0	14.4			% Profit Before Taxes/Total	19.3	11.7
	9.3	4.7	8.8			Assets	9.1	5.3
	1.3	1.0	2.4				2.5	.3
	38.4	15.7	14.1				13.1	14.4
	20.0	6.7	7.7			Sales/Net Fixed Assets	7.1	7.7
	7.3	4.1	6.3				4.5	3.8
	3.3	2.6	2.2				2.4	2.5
	2.4	1.9	1.9			Sales/Total Assets	1.9	1.8
	1.7	1.5	1.3				1.5	1.3
	(23) .8	(39) 1.3	(18) 1.5			% Depr., Dep., Amort./Sales	(110) 1.6	(130) 1.5
	1.5	2.4	2.3				2.8	2.6
	3.2	4.8	3.1				4.3	4.6
	(15) 2.3	(17) 2.7				% Officers', Directors',	(49) 3.1	(42) 2.8
	4.8	5.1				Owners' Comp/Sales	5.6	4.5
	7.9	7.0					12.9	10.3
1743M	79214M	366087M	764652M	638050M	744140M	Net Sales ($)	3729056M	5056870M
491M	30504M	178172M	434601M	380807M	655957M	Total Assets ($)	2474253M	3432756M

M = $ thousand   MM = $ million
See Pages 11 through 21 for Explanation of Ratios and Data

Comparative Historical Data | **Current Data Sorted By Sales**

Type of Statement counts (Comparative Historical Data: 4/1/02–3/31/03 ALL, 4/1/03–3/31/04 ALL, 4/1/04–3/31/05 ALL):

4/1/02–3/31/03 ALL	4/1/03–3/31/04 ALL	4/1/04–3/31/05 ALL	Type of Statement	0-1MM	1-3MM	3-5MM	5-10MM	10-25MM	25MM & OVER
23	25	26	Unqualified				3	7	16
22	22	18	Reviewed		1	4	4	5	4
9	25	21	Compiled	1	6	6	5	5	3
4	6	10	Tax Returns	2	4	4			
24	12	24	Other	1	3	5	7	4	4
			(period)	4	21 (4/1–9/30/04) →		78 (10/1/04–3/31/05) →		
82	90	99	**NUMBER OF STATEMENTS**	4	14	19	19	19	24
%	%	%	**ASSETS**	%	%	%	%	%	%
6.0	8.1	8.8	Cash & Equivalents		9.9	11.1	8.3	5.2	10.3
21.3	23.2	24.9	Trade Receivables (net)		27.3	23.0	22.5	29.3	24.8
30.3	31.1	28.6	Inventory		25.1	33.8	30.9	31.1	26.3
2.3	2.2	2.8	All Other Current		2.2	3.4	2.5	3.4	2.5
59.8	64.6	65.1	Total Current		64.6	71.3	64.3	69.1	64.0
28.1	24.2	26.5	Fixed Assets (net)		27.2	24.9	28.8	17.9	26.0
5.3	5.9	3.3	Intangibles (net)		4.8	1.3	4.9	3.4	2.2
6.8	5.4	5.1	All Other Non-Current		3.4	2.5	2.1	9.6	7.9
100.0	100.0	100.0	Total		100.0	100.0	100.0	100.0	100.0
			LIABILITIES						
11.2	10.0	11.6	Notes Payable-Short Term		13.6	9.0	13.7	12.8	10.3
5.6	3.4	6.7	Cur. Mat.-L/T/D		2.4	3.0	24.6	2.8	2.0
11.2	13.3	13.2	Trade Payables		16.2	11.1	14.0	14.8	12.4
.3	.3	.2	Income Taxes Payable		.1	.2	.1	.3	.3
9.6	8.5	9.5	All Other Current		8.3	10.1	8.9	14.4	7.3
37.9	35.5	41.2	Total Current		40.5	33.5	61.3	45.0	32.3
15.9	18.1	15.5	Long-Term Debt		21.9	13.8	15.5	14.0	9.2
.6	.7	.6	Deferred Taxes		.0	1.6	.7	.4	.3
3.6	7.1	8.3	All Other Non-Current		22.0	2.5	8.8	4.9	7.9
41.9	38.6	34.4	Net Worth		15.5	48.7	13.7	35.8	50.3
100.0	100.0	100.0	Total Liabilities & Net Worth		100.0	100.0	100.0	100.0	100.0
			INCOME DATA						
100.0	100.0	100.0	Net Sales		100.0	100.0	100.0	100.0	100.0
30.1	32.0	32.2	Gross Profit		35.2	31.4	34.2	26.0	31.2
24.9	27.1	26.9	Operating Expenses		33.0	27.6	27.7	20.0	24.0
5.2	4.9	5.3	Operating Profit		2.2	3.8	6.5	6.0	7.2
1.3	1.0	1.4	All Other Expenses (net)		.9	.4	2.5	2.2	.6
3.8	3.9	3.9	Profit Before Taxes		1.3	3.4	4.0	3.8	6.5
			RATIOS						
2.8	4.0	3.6			6.8	5.5	2.6	3.0	3.2
1.9	2.0	1.9	Current		1.6	2.3	1.3	1.7	2.3
1.3	1.3	1.2			1.0	1.5	1.0	1.2	1.6
1.3	1.8	2.2			1.9	2.8	1.2	1.9	2.3
.9	.9	.9	Quick		.9	.8	.6	.8	1.3
.5	.6	.5			.4	.5	.5	.5	.6
29 12.6	30 12.2	31 11.7			13 28.6	26 14.1	35 10.4	31 11.7	40 9.2
38 9.6	42 8.7	45 8.2	Sales/Receivables		46 8.0	37 9.8	46 8.0	47 7.8	48 7.5
47 7.7	55 6.6	54 6.7			53 6.9	47 7.7	50 7.3	54 6.7	61 6.0
46 8.0	55 6.7	40 9.1			8 45.8	32 11.4	45 8.2	49 7.5	49 7.5
69 5.3	78 4.7	74 5.0	Cost of Sales/Inventory		68 5.3	90 4.1	70 5.2	76 4.8	73 5.0
109 3.3	117 3.1	120 3.0			192 1.9	121 3.0	160 2.3	105 3.5	115 3.2
13 27.9	13 27.6	20 18.5			21 17.1	20 18.5	19 19.0	11 33.5	21 17.8
23 15.7	26 14.2	32 11.5	Cost of Sales/Payables		36 10.1	24 15.5	34 10.6	24 15.4	36 10.0
35 10.4	39 9.4	45 8.2			49 7.4	34 10.6	45 8.1	38 9.5	50 7.2
4.7	3.8	3.6			4.8	3.0	3.8	4.0	3.4
8.0	6.5	5.9	Sales/Working Capital		11.0	4.7	12.9	7.2	5.1
16.0	14.8	24.4			NM	9.0	−982.8	30.2	9.7
13.3	12.0	16.2			12.0	17.9	7.5	21.9	29.7
(76) 3.3	(76) 3.3	(88) 3.2	EBIT/Interest		(12) 2.6	(15) 2.9	(18) 3.0	(18) 4.8	(21) 13.5
1.0	1.2	1.4			1.3	1.6	1.5	1.0	2.5
4.1	6.2	6.6	Net Profit + Depr., Dep.,						
(31) 2.4	(33) 2.3	(29) 2.7	Amort./Cur. Mat. L/T/D						
1.1	.9	1.2							
.4	.2	.3			.3	.2	.4	.2	.3
.7	.6	.6	Fixed/Worth		2.0	.5	1.0	.4	.5
1.3	1.6	2.3			−2.8	1.3	10.3	2.3	.7
.6	.4	.6			.8	.3	.9	.5	.5
1.2	1.2	1.5	Debt/Worth		6.0	.9	2.5	1.9	.8
4.2	4.6	5.8			−11.2	3.3	29.9	4.5	2.8
32.2	30.2	39.2	% Profit Before Taxes/Tangible			38.1	43.7	62.4	30.8
(68) 16.3	(75) 13.5	(82) 17.0	Net Worth			(17) 10.5	(15) 19.8	(16) 14.0	(23) 18.3
1.2	3.4	7.5				3.5	7.9	2.5	14.7
16.2	11.8	13.4	% Profit Before Taxes/Total		13.8	14.6	10.4	12.7	16.1
6.0	5.1	5.8	Assets		5.8	5.7	5.8	4.7	10.2
−.5	.4	1.4			1.3	.3	2.8	.2	3.3
17.2	19.0	20.0			43.1	25.2	20.8	27.0	10.4
7.3	9.1	8.4	Sales/Net Fixed Assets		10.0	10.9	6.3	12.9	6.6
4.4	4.6	5.2			4.9	5.4	4.0	8.0	5.4
2.6	2.5	2.6			4.2	2.7	2.3	2.9	2.2
1.9	1.9	2.0	Sales/Total Assets		2.1	2.1	1.7	2.1	1.9
1.5	1.3	1.4			1.4	1.6	1.4	1.6	1.3
1.5	1.3	1.3			1.1	.9	1.6	.8	1.6
(77) 3.0	(78) 2.2	(89) 2.2	% Depr., Dep., Amort./Sales		(13) 1.5	(17) 2.1	(18) 2.8	2.2	(19) 2.2
4.4	3.9	3.8			4.3	4.0	5.0	3.2	3.0
2.4	2.6	2.3	% Officers', Directors',		2.9	4.9			
(28) 3.9	(34) 3.9	(34) 4.7	Owners' Comp/Sales		(10) 4.5	(11) 7.0			
6.1	7.2	7.0			5.7	7.9			
2285807M	2252171M	2593886M	Net Sales ($)	1622M	31895M	74742M	121327M	304131M	2060169M
1523779M	1615711M	1680532M	Total Assets ($)	2191M	16780M	37449M	74801M	162516M	1386795M

© RMA 2005

M = $ thousand   MM = $ million
See Pages 11 through 21 for Explanation of Ratios and Data

Current Data Sorted By Assets   Comparative Historical Data

						Type of Statement		
	4	2	6	1		Unqualified	3	3
	3	6	3			Reviewed	12	13
1	1	4	1			Compiled	8	8
	2	1	1			Tax Returns	2	
		4	4	1		Other	11	6
	10 (4/1-9/30/04)		30 (10/1/04-3/31/05)				4/1/00-3/31/01	4/1/01-3/31/02
0-500M	500M-2MM	2-10MM	10-50MM	50-100MM	100-250MM		ALL	ALL
1	10	17	11	1		NUMBER OF STATEMENTS	36	30
%	%	%	%	%	%	ASSETS	%	%
	7.5	6.0	9.5			Cash & Equivalents	5.2	6.2
	28.5	27.6	19.9			Trade Receivables (net)	26.7	24.8
	21.5	26.9	21.1			Inventory	19.9	18.7
	.3	.8	2.8			All Other Current	.9	2.5
	57.8	61.2	53.3			Total Current	52.6	52.1
	22.6	32.2	38.5			Fixed Assets (net)	40.0	38.3
	7.5	2.9	1.0			Intangibles (net)	4.2	4.6
	12.2	3.7	7.1			All Other Non-Current	3.1	4.9
	100.0	100.0	100.0			Total	100.0	100.0
						LIABILITIES		
	12.0	23.1	5.5			Notes Payable-Short Term	9.8	8.3
	5.8	3.0	1.9			Cur. Mat.-L/T/D	4.8	4.7
	14.8	16.1	9.0			Trade Payables	13.4	10.3
	1.8	.1	.0			Income Taxes Payable	.2	.2
	5.2	8.8	7.7			All Other Current	9.8	11.4
	39.5	51.0	24.1			Total Current	38.1	34.8
	22.3	14.6	13.5			Long-Term Debt	19.6	17.7
	.0	.8	1.9			Deferred Taxes	.4	.9
	3.8	3.7	3.2			All Other Non-Current	8.8	10.3
	34.4	29.9	57.4			Net Worth	33.0	36.3
	100.0	100.0	100.0			Total Liabilities & Net Worth	100.0	100.0
						INCOME DATA		
	100.0	100.0	100.0			Net Sales	100.0	100.0
	34.3	21.3	22.3			Gross Profit	27.6	27.6
	26.0	19.2	18.0			Operating Expenses	22.3	25.0
	8.4	2.2	4.2			Operating Profit	5.3	2.6
	.7	1.0	.1			All Other Expenses (net)	2.3	1.5
	7.6	1.1	4.1			Profit Before Taxes	3.0	1.1
						RATIOS		
	2.4	2.3	3.0				2.2	3.6
	1.6	1.8	1.9			Current	1.6	1.5
	1.0	1.1	1.5				1.1	1.2
	1.4	1.5	2.2				1.3	1.8
	1.0	.9	1.1			Quick	.9	.9
	.6	.5	.5				.6	.6
	31 11.8	41 8.8	47 7.8				39 9.3	38 9.6
	45 8.1	48 7.6	49 7.4			Sales/Receivables	50 7.3	48 7.6
	63 5.8	52 7.0	60 6.1				59 6.2	58 6.3
	20 17.9	45 8.1	33 11.1				35 10.5	31 11.7
	41 8.8	57 6.4	59 6.2			Cost of Sales/Inventory	47 7.8	49 7.5
	71 5.2	81 4.5	108 3.4				72 5.0	61 6.0
	12 30.6	19 19.6	12 30.0				19 19.6	11 33.6
	19 18.9	30 12.2	30 12.3			Cost of Sales/Payables	36 10.2	22 16.5
	65 5.6	44 8.4	45 8.1				47 7.8	35 10.3
	6.6	6.2	4.2				7.0	5.4
	13.0	9.2	5.7			Sales/Working Capital	10.2	11.8
	NM	48.1	7.6				29.5	32.8
		12.6					5.2	4.0
		(16) 5.3				EBIT/Interest	(34) 2.0	(28) 1.3
		1.3					1.2	-.4
						Net Profit + Depr., Dep.,	4.9	
						Amort./Cur. Mat. L /T/D	(11) 2.0	
							1.6	
	.1	.4	.5				.6	.5
	.8	1.0	.7			Fixed/Worth	1.0	1.0
	2.2	3.0	1.0				1.8	1.5
	.7	.6	.3				.7	.5
	2.3	1.4	.6			Debt/Worth	1.4	1.0
	9.9	9.7	2.5				4.3	3.3
		45.6	25.7				28.8	15.1
		(15) 24.3	13.6			% Profit Before Taxes/Tangible Net Worth	(31) 10.2	(27) 4.4
		7.7	-.9				1.7	-2.8
	27.3	10.3	11.8				10.9	7.2
	15.2	6.6	4.3			% Profit Before Taxes/Total Assets	3.9	1.2
	5.5	1.3	-.7				.6	-3.3
	37.0	12.6	5.5				9.0	8.5
	16.8	6.5	4.6			Sales/Net Fixed Assets	5.2	6.4
	6.8	3.8	2.5				2.7	2.4
	2.7	2.6	1.8				2.5	2.3
	2.6	2.1	1.5			Sales/Total Assets	2.1	1.8
	1.9	1.7	.9				1.4	1.2
		2.1	3.1				2.4	2.6
		(16) 2.4	3.6			% Depr., Dep., Amort./Sales	(32) 3.8	(29) 3.9
		5.1	5.7				5.9	6.6
							2.7	2.2
						% Officers', Directors', Owners' Comp/Sales	(19) 5.9	(11) 2.8
							8.4	7.4
1292M	23945M	186082M	274748M	105395M		Net Sales ($)	464139M	251752M
375M	9853M	84616M	184155M	67631M		Total Assets ($)	319082M	153624M

(The 100-250MM column is marked "DATA NOT AVAILABLE".)

M = $ thousand   MM = $ million
See Pages 11 through 21 for Explanation of Ratios and Data

Comparative Historical Data   Current Data Sorted By Sales

				Type of Statement	0-1MM	1-3MM	3-5MM	5-10MM	10-25MM	25MM & OVER
2	3	9	Unqualified		3			4	5	
9	9	13	Reviewed						5	
9	7	9	Compiled		4	1	4			
1	1	2	Tax Returns		1			1		
8	12	7	Other		3			3		1
4/1/02-3/31/03 ALL	4/1/03-3/31/04 ALL	4/1/04-3/31/05 ALL			10 (4/1-9/30/04)			30 (10/1/04-3/31/05)		
29	32	40	**NUMBER OF STATEMENTS**		11	1	9	13	6	
%	%	%	**ASSETS**	%	%	%	%	%	%	
8.0	5.1	7.6	Cash & Equivalents		8.2			11.8		
23.7	23.7	25.9	Trade Receivables (net)		28.2			25.4		
23.5	22.7	23.4	Inventory		21.6			23.9		
3.6	2.0	1.3	All Other Current		.5			1.0		
58.8	53.5	58.2	Total Current		58.5			62.1		
32.8	38.1	31.7	Fixed Assets (net)		27.4			32.6		
3.6	4.6	3.4	Intangibles (net)		2.9			1.8		
4.8	3.8	6.7	All Other Non-Current		11.1			3.6		
100.0	100.0	100.0	Total		100.0			100.0		
			LIABILITIES							
11.6	13.6	14.8	Notes Payable-Short Term		28.1			10.6		
4.1	4.9	3.3	Cur. Mat.-L/T/D		3.1			1.9		
10.4	12.3	13.7	Trade Payables		16.5			13.1		
.1	.1	.5	Income Taxes Payable		1.6			.2		
14.9	6.6	7.6	All Other Current		6.7			7.9		
41.0	37.5	40.0	Total Current		55.9			33.7		
15.6	18.2	15.9	Long-Term Debt		14.5			8.7		
.5	.8	.9	Deferred Taxes		.0			1.4		
8.9	5.2	3.6	All Other Non-Current		2.7			1.2		
33.9	38.4	39.5	Net Worth		26.9			55.0		
100.0	100.0	100.0	Total Liabilities & Net Worth		100.0			100.0		
			INCOME DATA							
100.0	100.0	100.0	Net Sales		100.0			100.0		
34.2	26.7	24.6	Gross Profit		29.7			21.8		
27.2	22.7	20.3	Operating Expenses		24.8			18.3		
6.9	4.1	4.3	Operating Profit		4.9			3.5		
1.4	1.0	.7	All Other Expenses (net)		1.2			-.1		
5.5	3.0	3.6	Profit Before Taxes		3.7			3.6		
			RATIOS							
3.3	2.5	2.3			2.3			3.9		
1.7	1.7	1.8	Current		1.7			1.9		
1.2	1.2	1.3			1.0			1.4		
1.4	1.6	1.5			1.4			3.0		
1.0	.8	1.0	Quick		1.0			1.3		
.6	.5	.6			.6			.5		
37 9.7	**35** 10.5	**41** 8.9			**38** 9.7			**40** 9.2		
44 8.3	**46** 7.9	**48** 7.6	Sales/Receivables		**48** 7.6			**47** 7.8		
56 6.6	**59** 6.1	**57** 6.5			**63** 5.8			**49** 7.4		
45 8.1	**38** 9.6	**34** 10.8			**21** 17.3			**23** 16.1		
64 5.7	**50** 7.3	**49** 7.4	Cost of Sales/Inventory		**42** 8.7			**45** 8.1		
100 3.6	**91** 4.0	**79** 4.6			**68** 5.4			**82** 4.4		
12 30.5	**18** 19.9	**13** 27.2			**13** 28.0			**12** 29.9		
25 14.5	**29** 12.4	**29** 12.7	Cost of Sales/Payables		**21** 17.0			**28** 13.2		
44 8.3	**40** 9.2	**44** 8.4			**83** 4.4			**37** 9.8		
5.2	5.5	5.1			7.0			5.2		
7.2	8.9	8.9	Sales/Working Capital		11.9			8.1		
22.8	34.5	16.6			96.9			11.8		
8.0	8.6	13.3						41.3		
(28) 2.5	(30) 2.4	(35) 4.5	EBIT/Interest					(11) 6.2		
1.1	.7	1.5						1.7		
		10.0	Net Profit + Depr., Dep.,							
	(12)	3.0	Amort./Cur. Mat. L/T/D							
		1.6								
.4	.4	.5			.1			.4		
.8	.8	.8	Fixed/Worth		.7			.6		
1.6	2.2	1.7			1.9			1.4		
.5	.7	.5			.8			.3		
1.0	1.1	1.1	Debt/Worth		1.6			.6		
3.0	3.3	5.0			5.9			3.7		
25.0	30.5	38.0	% Profit Before Taxes/Tangible		154.3			33.6		
(24) 5.4	(28) 7.3	(37) 19.6	Net Worth		(10) 35.0			24.3		
.2	.0	4.2			9.9			4.3		
11.4	9.5	15.2	% Profit Before Taxes/Total		16.4			13.3		
3.4	4.1	7.6	Assets		14.0			9.2		
.1	.0	1.1			1.0			1.1		
13.5	11.4	13.0			36.3			12.6		
7.3	5.2	6.3	Sales/Net Fixed Assets		11.6			6.1		
2.6	3.0	3.9			6.4			3.4		
2.5	2.3	2.6			2.7			2.9		
1.9	1.8	1.9	Sales/Total Assets		2.5			2.0		
1.3	1.5	1.6			1.9			1.4		
2.3	2.2	2.0						1.3		
(27) 4.4	(28) 3.6	(35) 3.2	% Depr., Dep., Amort./Sales					2.5		
5.2	5.7	5.5						4.8		
3.0	2.7	3.4	% Officers', Directors',							
(16) 6.2	(13) 3.5	(14) 5.2	Owners' Comp/Sales							
12.7	8.1	8.7								
282075M	862891M	591462M	Net Sales ($)		22359M	4889M	67804M	201942M	294468M	
187592M	479661M	346630M	Total Assets ($)		10584M	2825M	44434M	110012M	178775M	

(Current Data columns for 0-1MM, 3-5MM, 5-10MM, and 25MM & OVER: DATA NOT AVAILABLE)

© RMA 2005   M = $ thousand   MM = $ million

See Pages 11 through 21 for Explanation of Ratios and Data

Current Data Sorted By Assets   **Comparative Historical Data**

0-500M	500M-2MM	2-10MM	10-50MM	50-100MM	100-250MM	Type of Statement	4/1/00-3/31/01 ALL	4/1/01-3/31/02 ALL
		9	21	6	5	Unqualified	40	32
	9	38	6			Reviewed	53	47
1	12	15	2			Compiled	37	48
6	14	4				Tax Returns	19	11
3	11	20	17	2	4	Other	57	72
	46 (4/1-9/30/04)			159 (10/1/04-3/31/05)				
10	46	86	46	8	9	**NUMBER OF STATEMENTS**	206	210
%	%	%	%	%	%	**ASSETS**	%	%
14.1	7.3	7.2	5.3			Cash & Equivalents	7.0	7.0
23.9	35.3	28.3	24.8			Trade Receivables (net)	27.5	25.7
28.1	24.3	26.2	27.7			Inventory	24.0	23.8
6.8	1.2	1.9	2.2			All Other Current	2.4	1.3
72.9	68.1	63.6	60.1			Total Current	60.9	57.8
19.0	26.4	28.7	30.2			Fixed Assets (net)	30.2	32.9
1.8	1.5	2.1	5.6			Intangibles (net)	2.6	3.5
6.3	4.0	5.6	4.1			All Other Non-Current	6.3	5.7
100.0	100.0	100.0	100.0			Total	100.0	100.0
						LIABILITIES		
10.5	11.1	11.3	10.4			Notes Payable-Short Term	12.7	11.9
1.1	5.4	3.8	4.1			Cur. Mat.-L/T/D	3.6	4.5
15.0	21.2	17.1	11.5			Trade Payables	16.0	14.5
.9	.2	.4	.2			Income Taxes Payable	.3	.4
41.5	7.4	6.9	10.5			All Other Current	7.1	7.7
69.0	45.3	39.3	36.7			Total Current	39.7	39.0
13.5	21.0	18.6	17.2			Long-Term Debt	17.1	17.2
.0	.0	.5	.9			Deferred Taxes	.6	.7
49.5	4.9	4.2	10.0			All Other Non-Current	4.1	5.9
-32.0	28.8	37.4	35.2			Net Worth	38.5	37.2
100.0	100.0	100.0	100.0			Total Liabilities & Net Worth	100.0	100.0
						INCOME DATA		
100.0	100.0	100.0	100.0			Net Sales	100.0	100.0
33.7	34.0	26.4	21.2			Gross Profit	28.7	26.4
38.3	29.2	22.7	16.0			Operating Expenses	23.3	23.7
-4.6	4.9	3.7	5.2			Operating Profit	5.4	2.7
-.6	.9	.5	2.3			All Other Expenses (net)	1.5	1.6
-4.0	4.0	3.2	2.9			Profit Before Taxes	3.9	1.1
						RATIOS		
2.7	2.5	2.3	2.9				2.8	2.6
1.6	1.6	1.6	1.6			Current	1.5	1.5
.7	1.1	1.2	1.2				1.1	1.1
1.9	1.7	1.4	1.5				1.5	1.5
.9	1.0	.9	.8			Quick	.9	.9
.2	.6	.6	.5				.6	.5
0 UND	32 11.5	38 9.7	39 9.4				38 9.7	36 10.3
24 15.0	47 7.8	50 7.4	49 7.5			Sales/Receivables	47 7.8	43 8.4
43 8.5	56 6.6	59 6.1	59 6.2				57 6.4	54 6.8
0 UND	17 22.0	38 9.6	37 9.9				34 10.8	32 11.5
33 11.1	42 8.7	58 6.3	66 5.5			Cost of Sales/Inventory	54 6.8	55 6.7
72 5.1	73 5.0	83 4.4	124 3.0				83 4.4	85 4.3
0 UND	17 21.3	23 15.7	18 20.6				17 21.1	16 22.2
14 25.5	40 9.2	35 10.3	26 14.3			Cost of Sales/Payables	30 12.1	29 12.5
34 10.7	57 6.4	49 7.5	38 9.7				50 7.3	48 7.7
7.5	5.7	5.5	4.6				5.6	6.0
17.2	12.3	9.2	8.9			Sales/Working Capital	10.4	10.9
-22.9	NM	19.0	18.0				34.8	49.4
	10.6	10.1	7.8				7.0	4.6
	(43) 3.3	(80) 4.3	(42) 4.2			EBIT/Interest	(177) 2.7	(190) 1.9
	1.0	1.1	1.4				1.2	-.2
		6.2	5.1			Net Profit + Depr., Dep.,	6.0	4.6
		(29) 2.5	(14) 1.7			Amort./Cur. Mat. L./T/D	(71) 2.3	(66) 1.4
		1.2	1.2				1.4	.6
.1	.2	.3	.4				.3	.4
NM	.8	.7	.9			Fixed/Worth	.8	1.0
-.3	3.6	1.4	1.7				2.0	2.3
.8	.9	.9	.8				.6	.7
NM	3.0	1.6	1.8			Debt/Worth	2.0	1.9
-3.8	18.3	3.1	4.3				4.5	4.7
	65.2	43.4	41.8			% Profit Before Taxes/Tangible	43.1	28.4
	(42) 23.8	(78) 20.3	(41) 19.7			Net Worth	(187) 16.3	(185) 8.0
	-.3	5.2	5.3				4.3	-7.0
19.6	15.5	13.5	12.9			% Profit Before Taxes/Total	15.2	9.1
.1	6.0	6.6	4.9			Assets	5.5	3.1
-58.0	-.3	.6	.7				.9	-3.3
UND	41.2	19.1	10.0				18.2	14.3
30.3	18.0	7.5	6.8			Sales/Net Fixed Assets	6.8	5.9
18.2	6.5	4.2	4.1				3.8	3.5
9.6	3.9	2.6	2.3				2.7	2.7
3.8	2.8	2.1	1.8			Sales/Total Assets	2.1	2.0
3.1	2.2	1.6	1.3				1.5	1.3
	.9	1.4	1.8				1.2	1.1
	(37) 2.0	(81) 2.2	(41) 3.0			% Depr., Dep., Amort./Sales	(190) 2.1	(189) 2.7
	3.1	3.8	4.5				3.7	4.4
	2.9	1.9				% Officers', Directors',	2.3	2.5
	(24) 5.1	(40) 3.1				Owners' Comp/Sales	(84) 4.0	(80) 4.4
	11.0	4.6					7.8	8.2
13338M	141908M	887744M	1818382M	938030M	2507379M	Net Sales ($)	5105111M	5050480M
2756M	49344M	428135M	989124M	563013M	1501163M	Total Assets ($)	3043376M	2980016M

M = $ thousand   MM = $ million
See Pages 11 through 21 for Explanation of Ratios and Data

Comparative Historical Data | Current Data Sorted By Sales

			Type of Statement						
37	41	41	Unqualified		1		4	12	24
54	56	53	Reviewed	1	4	5	17	20	6
25	39	30	Compiled		8	8	8	5	1
19	23	24	Tax Returns	6	5	10	3		
70	61	57	Other	2	9	3	11	15	17
4/1/02-3/31/03	4/1/03-3/31/04	4/1/04-3/31/05		| 46 (4/1-9/30/04) |			| 159 (10/1/04-3/31/05) |		
ALL	ALL	ALL		0-1MM	1-3MM	3-5MM	5-10MM	10-25MM	25MM & OVER
205	220	205	**NUMBER OF STATEMENTS**	9	27	26	43	52	48
%	%	%	**ASSETS**	%	%	%	%	%	%
6.9	7.8	7.0	Cash & Equivalents		10.7	8.2	6.8	5.5	4.8
25.1	26.7	28.3	Trade Receivables (net)		29.6	31.1	32.0	27.3	26.2
25.0	25.6	25.9	Inventory		25.3	22.8	24.7	28.2	27.1
2.6	2.4	2.2	All Other Current		1.4	2.5	1.8	1.5	2.8
59.6	62.6	63.3	Total Current		67.1	64.6	65.3	62.6	60.8
31.6	29.1	29.0	Fixed Assets (net)		27.8	26.6	25.5	29.9	31.4
4.0	3.2	2.7	Intangibles (net)		1.2	2.9	3.7	2.8	2.8
4.9	5.0	5.0	All Other Non-Current		3.9	5.9	5.6	4.8	5.0
100.0	100.0	100.0	Total		100.0	100.0	100.0	100.0	100.0
			LIABILITIES						
10.8	12.8	10.6	Notes Payable-Short Term		9.3	10.6	12.2	10.7	11.0
4.4	2.9	4.0	Cur. Mat.-L/T/D		3.9	4.5	3.8	4.7	3.0
14.1	14.4	16.3	Trade Payables		16.6	18.5	20.2	15.0	14.5
.3	.2	.3	Income Taxes Payable		.5	.0	.3	.4	.4
8.3	9.0	9.6	All Other Current		9.3	15.5	6.3	8.9	9.7
37.9	39.3	40.9	Total Current		39.5	49.2	42.9	39.7	38.5
18.0	14.5	18.0	Long-Term Debt		18.3	18.1	20.7	16.2	14.3
.5	.6	.5	Deferred Taxes		.4	.0	.3	.9	.7
4.3	6.1	7.7	All Other Non-Current		3.4	15.3	2.6	3.8	8.0
39.3	39.4	32.9	Net Worth		38.3	17.3	33.5	39.4	38.4
100.0	100.0	100.0	Total Liabilities & Net Worth		100.0	100.0	100.0	100.0	100.0
			INCOME DATA						
100.0	100.0	100.0	Net Sales		100.0	100.0	100.0	100.0	100.0
28.4	29.2	27.2	Gross Profit		29.3	30.2	31.7	23.7	20.3
24.6	25.4	23.0	Operating Expenses		24.8	28.9	26.9	19.0	15.2
3.9	3.8	4.2	Operating Profit		4.5	1.3	4.8	4.7	5.1
1.6	1.4	1.0	All Other Expenses (net)		.5	1.3	.7	1.1	1.0
2.2	2.4	3.2	Profit Before Taxes		4.0	-.1	4.1	3.6	4.1
			RATIOS						
2.7	2.8	2.5	Current		2.8	3.1	2.2	2.2	2.7
1.6	1.7	1.6			1.7	1.7	1.5	1.7	1.6
1.2	1.2	1.2			1.2	.8	1.1	1.2	1.2
1.6	1.7	1.5	Quick		1.9	1.8	1.4	1.3	1.2
.9	1.0	.9			1.1	1.2	.8	.8	.9
.5	.5	.6			.6	.6	.6	.6	.6
32 11.4	36 10.1	36 10.1	Sales/Receivables	28 13.0	31 11.8	39 9.3	38 9.6	38 9.5	
43 8.4	47 7.8	47 7.8		44 8.3	50 7.3	49 7.5	50 7.3	45 8.0	
55 6.6	57 6.4	57 6.4		57 6.5	59 6.2	59 6.2	59 6.2	55 6.7	
35 10.4	32 11.3	31 11.9	Cost of Sales/Inventory	11 34.4	15 23.8	24 15.3	49 7.5	34 10.8	
60 6.1	58 6.3	57 6.4		42 8.7	46 8.0	58 6.3	62 5.8	55 6.6	
93 3.9	93 3.9	88 4.2		84 4.3	102 3.6	85 4.3	95 3.9	106 3.4	
18 20.6	15 24.8	21 17.7	Cost of Sales/Payables	18 20.8	16 22.3	23 15.7	23 15.7	21 17.6	
28 12.9	27 13.4	32 11.2		32 11.4	33 11.2	39 9.3	33 11.2	31 11.7	
46 8.0	46 8.0	49 7.4		46 7.9	50 7.2	57 6.4	47 7.7	42 8.6	
4.7	5.0	5.5	Sales/Working Capital		4.5	4.3	6.7	5.6	5.4
9.2	8.4	9.3			8.9	9.7	13.7	7.8	9.1
27.8	28.3	22.2			23.1	-26.7	68.7	16.6	17.5
6.8	6.8	9.2	EBIT/Interest		12.7	3.4	11.5	9.6	9.2
(183) 2.3	(199) 2.1	(189) 4.2		(23) 3.6	(25) 1.7	(39) 5.4	(47) 4.5	(47) 6.1	
1.0	.0	1.1			1.0	-1.9	2.1	1.7	1.4
3.6	3.5	5.9	Net Profit + Depr., Dep.,			8.9	2.3	11.4	
(66) 2.3	(61) 1.9	(55) 2.0	Amort./Cur. Mat. L/T/D			(14) 4.7	(17) 1.5	(19) 3.5	
1.0	.9	1.0				2.3	.6	1.3	
.4	.3	.3	Fixed/Worth		.1	.2	.3	.4	.4
.8	.7	.8			.7	1.0	.6	.8	.8
2.1	1.7	1.9			3.7	10.9	2.8	1.4	1.1
.6	.7	.8	Debt/Worth		.4	.9	1.0	.9	.7
1.7	1.5	1.7			1.2	3.4	1.9	1.6	1.3
4.9	4.1	5.1			15.0	17.2	9.3	2.9	3.5
28.5	36.5	46.3	% Profit Before Taxes/Tangible		57.5	29.0	55.2	39.4	46.1
(182) 10.8	(200) 7.1	(183) 19.7	Net Worth	(23) 19.2	(22) 2.9	(37) 21.4	(49) 22.8	(45) 19.7	
.6	-2.2	3.4			-7.9	-15.4	10.0	5.7	5.6
11.3	11.5	14.2	% Profit Before Taxes/Total		15.4	6.9	13.0	14.0	15.3
4.1	2.9	5.6	Assets		5.1	1.5	7.2	6.7	5.4
.1	-1.7	.4			-.7	-5.3	1.1	1.5	.9
20.4	22.3	22.7	Sales/Net Fixed Assets		37.7	29.6	25.6	13.3	10.5
6.9	8.2	8.5			16.9	18.7	10.7	6.9	6.7
3.7	4.1	4.2			4.2	8.2	4.6	4.0	4.1
2.6	2.8	2.8	Sales/Total Assets		3.1	4.0	3.2	2.3	2.4
1.9	2.1	2.1			2.7	2.4	2.2	2.0	2.0
1.4	1.4	1.6			1.9	1.6	1.9	1.5	1.5
1.3	1.2	1.3	% Depr., Dep., Amort./Sales		.9	.9	1.3	1.6	1.8
(179) 2.9	(196) 2.3	(180) 2.3		(23) 1.9	(24) 2.0	(38) 2.3	(46) 2.3	(43) 3.0	
4.9	4.1	4.1			2.9	4.7	4.9	3.8	4.4
2.5	2.1	2.3	% Officers', Directors',		1.7	3.6	2.6	1.7	
(82) 4.6	(89) 4.6	(77) 3.7	Owners' Comp/Sales	(11) 4.8	(18) 6.0	(19) 3.4	(18) 2.7		
9.1	7.5	7.7			6.1	12.3	4.4	4.8	
3940919M	4898699M	6306781M	Net Sales ($)	5955M	57631M	94602M	305887M	826845M	5015861M
2587274M	3156281M	3533535M	Total Assets ($)	3758M	27609M	46176M	156616M	486576M	2812800M

© RMA 2005   M = $ thousand   MM = $ million
See Pages 11 through 21 for Explanation of Ratios and Data

Current Data Sorted By Assets **Comparative Historical Data**

						Type of Statement		
1		24	26	5	3	Unqualified	59	50
4	42	101	17	8	1	Reviewed	179	142
30	93	54	8	1		Compiled	214	223
31	43	18			1	Tax Returns	72	59
25	63	72	28	5	1	Other	184	196
	148 (4/1-9/30/04)		548 (10/1/04-3/31/05)				4/1/00-3/31/01	4/1/01-3/31/02
0-500M	500M-2MM	2-10MM	10-50MM	50-100MM	100-250MM		ALL	ALL
91	241	269	79	11	5	**NUMBER OF STATEMENTS**	708	670
%	%	%	%	%	%	**ASSETS**	%	%
9.0	8.7	7.7	6.0	3.6		Cash & Equivalents	9.1	8.0
25.8	27.3	25.4	23.4	22.9		Trade Receivables (net)	25.8	23.7
11.7	17.6	22.7	23.0	16.5		Inventory	17.1	17.7
2.3	1.4	2.5	3.4	2.7		All Other Current	2.0	1.8
48.8	55.0	58.3	55.9	45.6		Total Current	54.0	51.2
40.3	36.5	33.1	35.4	39.5		Fixed Assets (net)	38.1	39.5
2.9	1.8	2.3	4.0	10.1		Intangibles (net)	2.8	3.3
8.0	6.7	6.2	4.7	4.7		All Other Non-Current	5.1	6.0
100.0	100.0	100.0	100.0	100.0		Total	100.0	100.0
						LIABILITIES		
18.4	10.9	10.3	12.3	6.8		Notes Payable-Short Term	8.6	10.5
8.4	8.0	5.6	3.8	7.7		Cur. Mat.-L/T/D	6.7	7.2
15.6	11.8	12.8	14.3	22.0		Trade Payables	11.7	10.9
.1	.2	.3	.1	.2		Income Taxes Payable	.3	.2
14.1	7.8	8.2	10.7	9.3		All Other Current	8.5	7.5
56.6	38.7	37.1	41.2	45.9		Total Current	35.7	36.3
37.4	26.4	18.0	16.5	18.8		Long-Term Debt	21.1	24.9
.1	.3	.8	.7	.6		Deferred Taxes	.7	.6
15.8	5.3	7.8	3.2	12.9		All Other Non-Current	4.9	5.0
-9.9	29.3	36.3	38.4	21.8		Net Worth	37.6	33.2
100.0	100.0	100.0	100.0	100.0		Total Liabilities & Net Worth	100.0	100.0
						INCOME DATA		
100.0	100.0	100.0	100.0	100.0		Net Sales	100.0	100.0
47.6	38.3	27.7	21.0	20.8		Gross Profit	32.5	31.5
43.4	33.2	22.3	15.9	17.2		Operating Expenses	27.5	28.6
4.2	5.2	5.4	5.2	3.6		Operating Profit	5.0	2.9
1.5	1.3	1.2	1.0	1.6		All Other Expenses (net)	1.6	2.0
2.7	3.8	4.2	4.1	2.0		Profit Before Taxes	3.4	.9
						RATIOS		
1.8	2.7	2.5	1.8	1.7			2.6	2.4
1.1	1.5	1.6	1.3	1.2		Current	1.6	1.5
.6	1.0	1.2	1.0	.6			1.1	1.0
1.6	1.9	1.4	1.0	.8			1.7	1.5
.7	(240) 1.0	.9	.7	.6		Quick	1.0	.9
.4	.6	.6	.5	.5			.6	.6
12 29.9	33 11.0	38 9.6	39 9.4	40 9.1			33 11.0	30 12.0
34 10.9	46 8.0	50 7.3	50 7.3	50 7.3		Sales/Receivables	45 8.1	43 8.4
48 7.6	58 6.3	63 5.8	66 5.6	60 6.1			59 6.2	57 6.4
0 UND	7 50.6	27 13.7	26 13.8	19 18.9			13 27.1	15 24.2
10 35.9	31 11.7	50 7.4	57 6.4	45 8.1		Cost of Sales/Inventory	36 10.2	40 9.2
36 10.3	69 5.3	95 3.8	89 4.1	72 5.1			73 5.0	78 4.7
10 38.2	13 29.2	18 19.9	24 15.1	27 13.4			14 26.3	13 28.4
25 14.4	24 15.4	29 12.7	34 10.7	43 8.5		Cost of Sales/Payables	25 14.4	25 14.6
53 7.6	44 8.2	45 8.1	49 7.4	55 6.7			41 9.0	41 8.9
13.5	6.1	5.2	5.5	6.9			5.5	5.5
88.7	12.8	9.7	14.7	37.5		Sales/Working Capital	11.1	11.6
-11.9	212.8	31.1	-324.3	-9.4			98.1	-131.9
6.1	7.0	12.6	8.8	2.8			6.3	4.4
(80) 2.4	(219) 3.0	(250) 4.0	(74) 4.1	(10) 2.0		EBIT/Interest	(643) 2.6	(627) 1.6
.6	1.1	1.8	.5	.5			.9	-.1
	2.3	4.6	6.1			Net Profit + Depr., Dep.,	3.8	2.9
	(53) 1.3	(76) 2.2	(24) 2.8			Amort./Cur. Mat. L /T/D	(206) 2.0	(190) 1.5
	.6	1.2	1.9				1.0	1.0
1.1	.5	.4	.5	1.0			.5	.6
3.2	1.2	.9	1.1	6.2		Fixed/Worth	1.1	1.2
-1.2	4.0	2.4	1.9	-3.6			2.6	3.4
2.4	1.1	.7	1.1	1.0			.7	.9
5.8	2.3	1.7	2.4	8.0		Debt/Worth	1.7	2.0
-4.1	7.5	5.0	3.9	-6.7			4.8	6.4
102.7	47.8	40.8	44.8			% Profit Before Taxes/Tangible	45.0	31.5
(56) 35.1	(200) 20.2	(241) 19.4	(76) 20.9			Net Worth	(623) 18.3	(566) 9.4
.3	3.1	5.9	1.6				2.5	-9.3
23.8	13.6	14.4	11.7	7.2		% Profit Before Taxes/Total	15.4	10.2
6.7	6.1	6.4	6.2	2.2		Assets	5.9	2.3
-2.5	.5	1.7	-.1	-.5			.1	-4.5
14.5	13.1	11.6	10.8	6.1			10.3	9.3
6.8	6.3	6.2	4.2	3.7		Sales/Net Fixed Assets	5.4	4.8
4.0	3.5	3.3	2.9	2.4			3.4	2.9
3.8	2.7	2.3	2.0	1.8			2.6	2.4
2.8	2.1	1.8	1.5	1.5		Sales/Total Assets	2.0	1.8
1.8	1.6	1.3	1.1	1.2			1.5	1.3
2.2	2.2	1.8	1.7	2.0			2.1	2.6
(73) 5.1	(215) 4.7	(252) 3.7	(76) 3.3	(10) 4.9		% Depr., Dep., Amort./Sales	(669) 3.8	(621) 4.5
8.7	7.0	5.8	5.6	7.0			6.3	7.0
5.6	3.3	1.9	.8			% Officers', Directors',	3.0	3.1
(51) 8.3	(144) 6.1	(121) 3.2	(14) 1.9			Owners' Comp/Sales	(371) 5.7	5.4
14.4	9.8	5.8	3.3				9.3	9.5
78105M	616953M	2288421M	2752105M	1240642M	1514136M	Net Sales ($)	7183766M	7051444M
25399M	280342M	1199412M	1519305M	766579M	891187M	Total Assets ($)	3922601M	4406821M

M = $ thousand   MM = $ million
See Pages 11 through 21 for Explanation of Ratios and Data

Comparative Historical Data			Type of Statement	Current Data Sorted By Sales					
51	49	59	Unqualified		1	3	10	18	27
130	137	164	Reviewed	9	30	30	44	40	11
167	193	186	Compiled	23	83	35	32	10	3
83	76	93	Tax Returns	25	43	12	8	4	1
154	158	194	Other	24	50	33	31	30	26
4/1/02-3/31/03	4/1/03-3/31/04	4/1/04-3/31/05		148 (4/1-9/30/04)			548 (10/1/04-3/31/05)		
ALL	ALL	ALL		0-1MM	1-3MM	3-5MM	5-10MM	10-25MM	25MM & OVER
585	613	696	**NUMBER OF STATEMENTS**	81	207	113	125	102	68
%	%	%	**ASSETS**	%	%	%	%	%	%
8.0	8.5	8.0	Cash & Equivalents	8.1	9.3	8.0	7.0	8.4	5.1
23.3	25.6	25.8	Trade Receivables (net)	20.7	26.1	27.5	26.7	24.9	28.2
17.7	18.5	19.4	Inventory	12.0	15.1	21.2	24.0	24.5	21.5
2.6	2.8	2.2	All Other Current	2.2	1.4	1.8	2.2	2.4	4.6
51.5	55.4	55.4	Total Current	43.0	52.0	58.5	60.0	60.2	59.5
39.9	36.0	35.5	Fixed Assets (net)	47.8	37.4	34.1	32.1	31.9	29.3
3.0	2.4	2.7	Intangibles (net)	3.0	2.3	1.1	2.3	2.7	6.9
5.6	6.2	6.4	All Other Non-Current	6.2	8.3	6.4	5.5	5.1	4.4
100.0	100.0	100.0	Total	100.0	100.0	100.0	100.0	100.0	100.0
			LIABILITIES						
10.9	10.9	11.8	Notes Payable-Short Term	17.0	11.3	11.9	9.9	9.6	13.3
7.5	6.7	6.6	Cur. Mat.-L/T/D	9.2	7.5	7.1	6.0	4.5	4.1
11.2	11.5	13.1	Trade Payables	10.0	12.1	12.5	12.8	14.6	19.1
.3	.2	.2	Income Taxes Payable	.0	.2	.1	.3	.3	.1
7.8	8.9	9.1	All Other Current	12.5	7.3	8.6	9.7	9.3	9.9
37.7	38.2	40.8	Total Current	48.7	38.5	40.2	38.8	38.3	46.5
25.6	23.2	23.4	Long-Term Debt	42.3	26.3	23.2	18.3	14.5	15.6
.7	.6	.5	Deferred Taxes	.2	.5	.2	.6	.8	.7
5.6	8.0	7.6	All Other Non-Current	16.2	6.3	7.0	8.1	5.3	5.3
30.5	30.0	27.7	Net Worth	-7.4	28.5	29.5	34.2	41.2	31.9
100.0	100.0	100.0	Total Liabilities & Net Worth	100.0	100.0	100.0	100.0	100.0	100.0
			INCOME DATA						
100.0	100.0	100.0	Net Sales	100.0	100.0	100.0	100.0	100.0	100.0
33.2	34.0	33.2	Gross Profit	50.4	40.0	29.3	28.5	24.3	20.3
30.9	31.1	28.1	Operating Expenses	43.3	35.5	25.4	23.7	17.6	15.8
2.3	2.9	5.1	Operating Profit	7.2	4.6	4.0	4.8	6.7	4.5
2.0	1.7	1.3	All Other Expenses (net)	3.4	1.0	1.2	1.0	.8	1.1
.3	1.2	3.8	Profit Before Taxes	3.8	3.6	2.8	3.9	5.9	3.4
			RATIOS						
2.6	2.9	2.3		1.9	2.8	2.5	2.3	2.4	1.7
1.4	1.6	1.4	Current	1.1	1.4	1.5	1.6	1.5	1.3
1.0	1.0	1.0		.6	.9	1.0	1.2	1.1	1.0
1.6	1.8	1.5		1.5	2.0	1.6	1.3	1.4	1.0
.9	.9	(695) .9	Quick	.7	(206) 1.0	.9	.9	.8	.7
.5	.5	.5		.4	.6	.6	.6	.5	.5
31 11.8	36 10.0	33 11.0		15 23.8	33 11.0	36 10.0	39 9.2	30 12.3	39 9.4
45 8.1	49 7.4	46 7.9	Sales/Receivables	38 9.6	46 8.0	47 7.8	50 7.3	48 7.6	49 7.5
58 6.3	61 6.0	60 6.1		55 6.6	60 6.0	59 6.2	62 5.9	61 6.0	65 5.6
14 26.7	15 24.6	13 28.2		0 UND	7 52.8	19 19.6	31 11.8	30 12.1	20 18.6
40 9.1	39 9.2	39 9.4	Cost of Sales/Inventory	8 43.5	26 14.3	40 9.2	59 6.2	49 7.4	46 8.0
79 4.6	83 4.4	78 4.7		45 8.1	71 5.1	74 4.9	96 3.8	88 4.1	79 4.6
14 26.9	15 24.5	16 22.5		8 48.3	14 26.8	13 28.8	19 18.8	19 19.0	27 13.5
26 14.2	27 13.3	28 13.1	Cost of Sales/Payables	26 14.0	24 15.1	25 14.3	29 12.4	29 12.5	37 9.9
42 8.7	43 8.4	47 7.8		53 6.8	48 7.6	42 8.7	44 8.4	47 7.7	51 7.2
5.8	4.9	5.8		9.6	5.4	5.8	5.4	5.4	8.2
12.9	10.1	12.8	Sales/Working Capital	54.3	13.0	11.8	9.4	9.8	16.5
391.1	104.2	-678.2		-11.0	-122.8	NM	23.6	61.2	-268.8
4.3	5.9	8.7		4.3	7.1	9.2	10.9	14.0	8.8
(548) 1.7	(559) 1.8	(637) 3.2	EBIT/Interest	(69) 2.2	(189) 2.9	(104) 3.0	(120) 4.3	(94) 5.3	(61) 3.1
-.7	-.5	1.2		.2	1.1	1.2	1.9	2.4	1.1
2.9	2.4	3.5		1.8	3.2	1.7	6.1	6.5	3.0
(156) 1.5	(129) 1.5	(166) 1.8	Net Profit + Depr., Dep., Amort./Cur. Mat. L/T/D	(10) 1.1	(38) 1.5	(31) 1.1	(40) 2.2	(29) 2.9	(18) 2.0
.6	.6	1.1		.4	1.2	.3	1.1	2.2	.6
.6	.4	.5		1.6	.5	.5	.4	.4	.4
1.2	1.1	1.2	Fixed/Worth	7.7	1.2	.9	.9	.8	1.1
3.8	3.8	3.4		-1.8	3.1	4.7	2.4	1.8	2.2
.7	.7	.9		2.9	.8	.8	.8	.7	1.2
2.0	2.1	2.4	Debt/Worth	11.8	2.3	1.7	1.6	1.8	2.8
7.1	8.4	7.5		-4.3	5.6	9.6	5.8	3.8	6.0
29.6	29.3	45.9		68.9	43.3	41.9	40.6	60.8	44.3
(493) 7.5	(499) 9.0	(583) 20.5	% Profit Before Taxes/Tangible Net Worth	(46) 28.4	(176) 18.2	(95) 16.7	(109) 20.0	(98) 22.4	(59) 22.1
-8.3	-4.0	4.8		1.6	2.2	2.3	8.7	7.6	10.0
9.4	10.4	14.2		17.2	14.0	11.7	13.2	19.1	11.3
2.5	2.9	6.2	% Profit Before Taxes/Total Assets	5.5	5.2	5.9	6.8	9.2	6.1
-5.5	-4.1	.7		-.9	.3	.6	1.7	1.8	1.0
10.8	10.9	12.4		8.4	12.4	13.6	10.4	15.4	18.2
4.9	5.7	6.1	Sales/Net Fixed Assets	4.9	5.7	7.0	6.3	7.4	6.4
2.8	3.2	3.4		2.4	3.3	3.2	4.3	3.2	3.7
2.5	2.5	2.6		2.8	2.7	2.7	2.4	2.6	2.8
1.8	1.8	1.9	Sales/Total Assets	1.9	2.0	2.0	1.9	1.8	1.8
1.3	1.3	1.4		1.3	1.4	1.5	1.4	1.3	1.5
2.7	2.3	2.0		3.6	2.7	2.0	2.3	1.3	1.4
(558) 4.9	(550) 4.6	(629) 4.1	% Depr., Dep., Amort./Sales	(70) 5.9	(185) 5.1	(100) 4.3	(116) 3.6	(96) 2.8	(62) 2.6
7.8	7.1	6.5		11.4	7.7	5.9	5.5	5.4	4.7
2.9	3.0	2.5		5.4	4.1	2.5	2.1	1.5	.6
(309) 6.0	(311) 5.2	(333) 4.9	% Officers', Directors', Owners' Comp/Sales	(42) 8.0	(123) 6.3	(65) 3.8	(55) 3.3	(37) 2.6	(11) .8
10.2	8.8	8.6		16.4	10.6	7.5	6.0	3.7	1.8
5838787M	7194882M	8490362M	Net Sales ($)	48169M	414867M	448354M	868500M	1506017M	5204455M
3277596M	3920997M	4682224M	Total Assets ($)	31415M	240305M	247530M	521881M	867978M	2773115M

© RMA 2005

M = $ thousand   MM = $ million
See Pages 11 through 21 for Explanation of Ratios and Data

Current Data Sorted By Assets

Comparative Historical Data

0-500M	500M-2MM	2-10MM	10-50MM	50-100MM	100-250MM	Type of Statement	4/1/00-3/31/01 ALL	4/1/01-3/31/02 ALL
	1	11	12	1		Unqualified	20	23
1	14	49	7			Reviewed	62	49
4	14	20	1			Compiled	65	49
5	12	2				Tax Returns	7	6
1	11	18	12	2		Other	44	49
64 (4/1-9/30/04)			134 (10/1/04-3/31/05)					
11	52	100	32	3		**NUMBER OF STATEMENTS**	198	176
%	%	%	%	%	%	**ASSETS**	%	%
10.6	6.0	5.2	3.2			Cash & Equivalents	6.6	5.2
31.4	33.3	21.6	21.0			Trade Receivables (net)	23.6	22.6
19.0	25.2	24.4	19.9			Inventory	21.2	20.1
.7	.9	.7	1.9			All Other Current	1.5	1.6
61.7	65.3	52.0	45.9			Total Current	52.9	49.5
31.3	28.7	38.3	44.6			Fixed Assets (net)	37.6	41.4
.1	1.2	5.6	4.8	DATA NOT AVAILABLE		Intangibles (net)	3.5	3.2
6.8	4.8	4.1	4.6			All Other Non-Current	6.0	5.9
100.0	100.0	100.0	100.0			Total	100.0	100.0
						LIABILITIES		
10.4	9.6	10.2	8.8			Notes Payable-Short Term	8.7	10.5
4.5	6.3	6.3	4.9			Cur. Mat.-L/T/D	6.8	7.7
11.3	16.3	12.8	10.7			Trade Payables	11.4	11.7
.0	.1	.1	.1			Income Taxes Payable	.3	.2
6.6	8.2	6.5	5.8			All Other Current	7.3	5.7
32.9	40.5	35.8	30.2			Total Current	34.6	35.8
26.8	19.1	20.2	22.0			Long-Term Debt	21.6	22.5
.0	.5	1.0	.9			Deferred Taxes	1.0	.9
15.1	7.1	8.3	6.7			All Other Non-Current	5.1	4.1
25.3	32.8	34.7	40.3			Net Worth	37.8	36.6
100.0	100.0	100.0	100.0			Total Liabilities & Net Worth	100.0	100.0
						INCOME DATA		
100.0	100.0	100.0	100.0			Net Sales	100.0	100.0
35.5	32.6	24.7	19.7			Gross Profit	27.3	27.0
29.9	28.6	20.3	15.1			Operating Expenses	22.7	24.8
5.6	4.0	4.4	4.7			Operating Profit	4.6	2.2
.2	.3	1.5	1.9			All Other Expenses (net)	2.2	2.4
5.4	3.6	3.0	2.8			Profit Before Taxes	2.4	-.2
						RATIOS		
6.9	2.6	1.9	2.5				2.2	2.3
1.8	1.7	1.5	1.5			Current	1.5	1.4
.9	1.2	1.1	1.1				1.1	1.0
4.2	1.6	1.1	1.4				1.4	1.4
1.1	1.0	.7	.8			Quick	.8	.8
.7	.6	.5	.5				.6	.5
21 17.2	35 10.3	37 9.9	49 7.5				33 11.0	34 10.7
38 9.7	49 7.4	51 7.2	52 7.0			Sales/Receivables	45 8.2	44 8.3
54 6.8	61 6.0	60 6.1	63 5.8				55 6.7	52 7.0
2 223.5	28 13.2	44 8.3	38 9.5				27 13.7	31 11.9
19 18.7	47 7.8	68 5.4	65 5.6			Cost of Sales/Inventory	49 7.4	50 7.3
45 8.1	87 4.2	105 3.5	87 4.2				83 4.4	77 4.8
4 83.0	20 17.9	20 18.3	23 15.8				15 24.0	15 25.1
16 22.5	30 12.2	32 11.4	32 11.3			Cost of Sales/Payables	23 15.6	27 13.4
41 8.8	48 7.7	49 7.5	49 7.5				38 9.6	39 9.3
4.5	5.4	5.4	4.8				5.9	6.7
19.8	8.5	10.1	9.0			Sales/Working Capital	11.6	13.7
-41.8	26.5	47.4	57.3				49.8	140.8
	8.5	6.8	10.8				4.8	3.0
	(46) 2.9	(96) 2.4	(31) 4.3			EBIT/Interest	(180) 2.3	(168) 1.5
	1.0	.7	1.1				1.2	-.2
	2.3	3.1	5.4			Net Profit + Depr., Dep.,	2.7	2.5
	(12) 1.8	(36) 1.8	(12) 2.1			Amort./Cur. Mat. L/T/D	(51) 1.4	(56) 1.3
	1.5	1.2	1.4				.4	.6
.3	.4	.7	.7				.5	.6
1.0	1.0	1.3	1.3			Fixed/Worth	1.1	1.2
-4.2	3.1	2.7	3.0				2.2	2.6
1.0	.8	1.0	.7				.8	.8
2.5	2.1	2.0	1.5			Debt/Worth	1.7	1.7
-9.1	7.0	4.8	5.2				3.9	4.9
	43.6	33.5	24.7			% Profit Before Taxes/Tangible	29.3	21.6
	(44) 14.3	(84) 16.4	(28) 11.6			Net Worth	(173) 16.1	(155) 6.4
	1.1	2.3	3.4				4.0	-15.0
17.8	17.6	10.8	7.4			% Profit Before Taxes/Total	11.8	8.0
8.8	5.0	4.3	4.4			Assets	5.0	1.9
.4	.0	-.8	.2				.7	-5.5
53.0	22.2	8.4	3.9				10.0	8.1
13.9	8.4	3.8	2.9			Sales/Net Fixed Assets	5.3	4.4
4.1	5.0	2.6	2.2				3.3	2.7
4.1	2.8	2.0	1.6				2.5	2.5
3.1	2.2	1.6	1.4			Sales/Total Assets	1.9	1.8
2.1	1.8	1.2	1.1				1.4	1.3
	2.2	3.2	3.9				2.1	2.6
	(44) 4.0	(97) 5.0	(29) 5.6			% Depr., Dep., Amort./Sales	(182) 3.9	(167) 4.6
	5.9	7.8	6.6				5.9	6.8
	2.6	2.1					3.4	2.7
	(36) 4.9	(47) 3.5				% Officers', Directors', Owners' Comp/Sales	(114) 5.8	(88) 5.0
	8.6	6.9					9.1	8.5
11345M	142702M	795834M	753142M	201640M		Net Sales ($)	1840795M	1703405M
3626M	60035M	494832M	541623M	172556M		Total Assets ($)	1225276M	1098324M

M = $ thousand   MM = $ million
See Pages 11 through 21 for Explanation of Ratios and Data

Comparative Historical Data — **Current Data Sorted By Sales**

Current data groupings: **64 (4/1-9/30/04)** covers 0-1MM and 1-3MM; **134 (10/1/04-3/31/05)** covers 3-5MM, 5-10MM, 10-25MM, 25MM & OVER.

	4/1/02-3/31/03 ALL	4/1/03-3/31/04 ALL	4/1/04-3/31/05 ALL	0-1MM	1-3MM	3-5MM	5-10MM	10-25MM	25MM & OVER
Type of Statement									
Unqualified	20	30	25			4	7	6	8
Reviewed	59	68	71		9	19	23	18	2
Compiled	39	40	39	4	12	9	11	3	1
Tax Returns	7	12	19	4	11	2	1	1	
Other	45	38	44	1	9	6	9	17	2
NUMBER OF STATEMENTS	170	188	198	9	41	40	51	45	12
ASSETS	%	%	%	%	%	%	%	%	%
Cash & Equivalents	5.0	6.2	5.4		5.7	5.0	5.6	5.3	3.4
Trade Receivables (net)	22.2	22.1	25.0		31.7	22.0	22.2	23.4	23.2
Inventory	21.6	22.0	23.4		28.9	24.0	24.2	20.8	21.2
All Other Current	1.6	1.0	1.0		.5	1.3	.6	1.5	1.1
Total Current	50.3	51.2	54.8		66.8	52.3	52.6	51.1	48.9
Fixed Assets (net)	40.3	39.5	36.7		27.0	39.6	36.8	40.0	46.1
Intangibles (net)	3.0	2.9	4.0		2.0	4.6	6.5	3.5	2.3
All Other Non-Current	6.4	6.3	4.5		4.2	3.6	4.1	5.4	2.8
Total	100.0	100.0	100.0		100.0	100.0	100.0	100.0	100.0
LIABILITIES									
Notes Payable-Short Term	9.8	11.5	9.7		10.5	8.6	8.0	10.8	8.9
Cur. Mat.-L/T/D	7.1	7.0	6.0		5.1	7.6	6.2	5.3	4.8
Trade Payables	11.4	11.3	13.3		15.7	10.9	15.0	12.5	11.5
Income Taxes Payable	.2	.1	.1		.1	.1	.1	.1	.0
All Other Current	6.8	7.1	7.1		10.0	3.9	7.5	6.2	11.8
Total Current	35.3	36.9	36.1		41.4	31.1	36.9	34.9	37.1
Long-Term Debt	24.3	21.6	20.9		19.3	21.8	20.1	19.8	20.0
Deferred Taxes	.8	.9	.9		.6	.9	.7	1.2	1.8
All Other Non-Current	4.2	7.3	8.1		9.4	10.0	8.3	4.3	7.6
Net Worth	35.4	33.4	34.0		29.3	36.2	34.0	39.8	33.5
Total Liabilities & Net Worth	100.0	100.0	100.0		100.0	100.0	100.0	100.0	100.0
INCOME DATA									
Net Sales	100.0	100.0	100.0		100.0	100.0	100.0	100.0	100.0
Gross Profit	26.1	26.4	26.3		30.8	29.5	23.5	21.8	16.7
Operating Expenses	25.0	24.6	22.0		27.2	24.0	20.0	16.5	13.5
Operating Profit	1.1	1.7	4.3		3.6	5.4	3.5	5.3	3.1
All Other Expenses (net)	2.2	1.5	1.2		.3	1.6	1.4	1.6	1.2
Profit Before Taxes	-1.1	.2	3.1		3.3	3.8	2.1	3.8	1.9
RATIOS									
Current	2.4	2.3	2.3		2.8	2.5	1.9	2.0	2.5
	1.4	1.5	1.5		1.7	1.7	1.4	1.5	1.3
	1.0	1.0	1.1		1.1	1.4	1.1	1.0	1.0
Quick	1.2	1.4	1.4		1.7	1.3	1.0	1.1	.9
	.7	.8	.8		.9	.9	.7	.7	.8
	.5	.5	.5		.6	.6	.4	.5	.5
Sales/Receivables	37 9.8	40 9.2	37 9.7	38 9.7	32 11.2	42 8.7	38 9.7	46 8.0	
	43 8.4	48 7.6	50 7.2	50 7.3	45 8.0	51 7.1	52 7.0	50 7.3	
	58 6.3	57 6.5	60 6.1	68 5.3	57 6.4	58 6.3	62 5.9	64 5.7	
Cost of Sales/Inventory	29 12.6	32 11.5	35 10.5	31 11.8	39 9.3	46 7.9	36 10.1	30 12.1	
	55 6.6	57 6.4	57 6.4	54 6.7	70 5.2	69 5.3	54 6.7	39 9.4	
	89 4.1	92 4.0	94 3.9	108 3.4	111 3.3	90 4.0	78 4.7	84 4.4	
Cost of Sales/Payables	15 24.9	16 22.1	20 18.5	20 18.4	15 23.8	22 16.7	20 18.6	17 21.3	
	26 14.1	30 12.3	31 11.7	33 11.1	30 12.0	32 11.3	31 11.6	28 13.2	
	40 9.1	47 7.8	49 7.5	55 6.7	49 7.5	47 7.7	47 7.8	50 7.3	
Sales/Working Capital	5.9	5.8	5.7		5.2	5.4	6.5	5.7	5.0
	13.6	9.7	10.0		8.3	8.3	10.2	10.8	17.0
	205.4	845.0	44.8		29.1	12.4	54.1	104.2	NM
EBIT/Interest	3.7	4.5	7.6		6.8	8.9	5.7	8.4	20.7
	(161) 1.4	(171) 1.4	(184) 2.6		(37) 2.5	(37) 2.8	(48) 1.9	(43) 4.3	3.4
	-1.0	-.7	.9		.7	1.3	-.4	1.6	.7
Net Profit + Depr., Dep., Amort./Cur. Mat. L/T/D	2.4	2.7	3.0			2.2	3.2	4.2	
	(58) 1.4	(55) 1.3	(63) 1.8		(12) 1.8	(14) 1.3	(22) 2.2		
	.7	.9	1.3			1.4	.4	1.4	
Fixed/Worth	.6	.6	.7		.4	.7	.8	.6	.7
	1.2	1.3	1.2		1.2	1.2	1.2	1.3	1.4
	3.0	3.5	3.0		11.9	2.6	3.3	2.5	2.5
Debt/Worth	.8	.8	1.0		.9	1.0	1.0	1.0	.6
	1.6	1.8	2.0		2.1	1.4	2.2	1.6	2.1
	5.8	5.7	5.4		51.8	3.9	6.2	4.8	3.9
% Profit Before Taxes/Tangible Net Worth	19.9	18.9	33.1		31.9	31.2	43.0	31.2	22.2
	(143) 5.4	(158) 5.9	(166) 14.7		(32) 12.2	(34) 15.7	(41) 13.5	(42) 17.8	(10) 9.1
	-8.8	-8.3	1.8		.8	5.2	-4.7	3.9	-1.0
% Profit Before Taxes/Total Assets	6.6	7.1	12.3		13.9	13.9	13.0	11.1	8.9
	1.5	1.3	4.6		3.5	5.9	3.1	5.9	3.7
	-5.9	-4.5	.0		.0	1.9	-2.2	1.2	-.4
Sales/Net Fixed Assets	9.2	8.4	10.0		24.9	7.1	11.1	7.2	5.2
	3.7	4.1	4.3		9.4	4.3	3.9	3.6	3.1
	2.5	2.6	2.8		4.2	2.8	2.2	2.7	2.1
Sales/Total Assets	2.2	2.0	2.3		2.8	2.4	2.3	2.0	1.8
	1.6	1.6	1.7		2.1	1.6	1.6	1.6	1.6
	1.2	1.2	1.3		1.7	1.3	1.1	1.2	1.2
% Depr., Dep., Amort./Sales	2.9	3.1	2.9		1.8	3.9	2.5	2.9	4.2
	(159) 5.1	(179) 5.1	(181) 4.9		(33) 3.6	(37) 5.1	(50) 5.1	(41) 4.4	6.0
	7.6	8.3	7.6		7.6	8.3	8.3	6.0	7.1
% Officers', Directors', Owners' Comp/Sales	2.8	2.5	2.1		2.5	3.2	1.9	1.8	
	(91) 5.2	(94) 5.6	(97) 3.8		(26) 4.6	(18) 4.7	(28) 2.8	(16) 2.9	
	8.7	9.3	7.7		9.2	8.2	6.0	4.8	
Net Sales ($)	1378753M	1677630M	1904663M	5995M	88534M	161547M	365581M	744340M	538666M
Total Assets ($)	978671M	1148812M	1272672M	3031M	45270M	104828M	252462M	493572M	373509M

M = $ thousand   MM = $ million
See Pages 11 through 21 for Explanation of Ratios and Data

Current Data Sorted By Assets   Comparative Historical Data

0-500M	500M-2MM	2-10MM	10-50MM	50-100MM	100-250MM	Type of Statement	4/1/00-3/31/01 ALL	4/1/01-3/31/02 ALL
		9	18	2	2	Unqualified	18	19
	9	23	7			Reviewed	32	29
	5	5				Compiled	21	15
	5	2	1			Tax Returns	4	2
1	6	12	11	3	1	Other	24	19
	28 (4/1-9/30/04)		94 (10/1/04-3/31/05)					
1	25	51	37	5	3	**NUMBER OF STATEMENTS**	99	84
%	%	%	%	%	%	**ASSETS**	%	%
	6.8	4.0	3.9			Cash & Equivalents	5.8	6.7
	36.3	27.2	23.9			Trade Receivables (net)	25.8	22.5
	29.4	34.7	30.2			Inventory	29.6	27.1
	1.2	1.8	1.5			All Other Current	1.7	1.3
	73.8	67.7	59.5			Total Current	62.9	57.6
	19.1	26.6	30.4			Fixed Assets (net)	28.9	33.3
	2.0	1.6	5.2			Intangibles (net)	2.8	3.7
	5.1	4.1	4.9			All Other Non-Current	5.3	5.3
	100.0	100.0	100.0			Total	100.0	100.0
						LIABILITIES		
	13.8	20.5	14.2			Notes Payable-Short Term	11.2	11.2
	2.7	3.7	4.0			Cur. Mat.-L/T/D	4.3	5.6
	21.2	16.5	13.6			Trade Payables	12.5	12.2
	.0	.1	.2			Income Taxes Payable	.2	.1
	6.5	7.3	6.6			All Other Current	7.5	5.5
	44.2	48.0	38.7			Total Current	35.8	34.6
	13.8	12.1	12.4			Long-Term Debt	13.9	15.7
	.4	.5	1.0			Deferred Taxes	.7	.8
	2.7	8.3	5.8			All Other Non-Current	2.9	2.8
	38.9	31.1	42.1			Net Worth	46.7	46.1
	100.0	100.0	100.0			Total Liabilities & Net Worth	100.0	100.0
						INCOME DATA		
	100.0	100.0	100.0			Net Sales	100.0	100.0
	31.9	23.1	24.5			Gross Profit	27.9	26.1
	27.0	19.8	18.4			Operating Expenses	22.2	22.9
	4.9	3.2	6.1			Operating Profit	5.6	3.2
	.6	1.3	1.1			All Other Expenses (net)	1.1	1.9
	4.3	1.9	5.0			Profit Before Taxes	4.6	1.3
						RATIOS		
	2.3	2.2	2.6				2.8	2.6
	1.6	1.4	1.4			Current	1.7	1.6
	1.2	1.0	1.1				1.3	1.3
	1.4	1.0	1.1				1.5	1.5
	1.0	.7	.7			Quick	.9	.8
	.7	.4	.5				.5	.5
	42 8.7	42 8.6	42 8.7				39 9.4	38 9.7
	52 7.0	49 7.4	53 6.9			Sales/Receivables	45 8.2	45 8.1
	66 5.5	56 6.5	62 5.9				52 7.0	55 6.6
	42 8.6	59 6.2	57 6.4				41 8.9	48 7.7
	58 6.3	75 4.8	78 4.7			Cost of Sales/Inventory	71 5.2	70 5.2
	91 4.0	108 3.4	133 2.7				105 3.5	108 3.4
	27 13.6	27 13.6	25 14.4				17 21.6	20 18.0
	43 8.5	35 10.4	38 9.6			Cost of Sales/Payables	28 13.1	30 12.1
	61 6.0	51 7.2	47 7.8				42 8.7	41 8.8
	5.9	5.7	4.1				4.9	4.7
	8.0	12.5	12.3			Sales/Working Capital	8.2	8.9
	21.5	89.6	54.9				17.2	17.8
	18.7	5.6	8.7				9.2	4.1
	(20) 4.9	(50) 2.7	(36) 4.4			EBIT/Interest	(85) 3.4	(78) 1.9
	-.4	-.3	1.6				1.6	-.1
		3.1	36.5			Net Profit + Depr., Dep.,	6.5	3.2
		(15) 2.5	(10) 3.7			Amort./Cur. Mat. L/T/D	(35) 3.7	(28) 2.0
		1.5	1.9				1.4	.8
	.1	.3	.5				.4	.4
	.5	.7	1.0			Fixed/Worth	.6	.8
	1.3	2.9	1.6				1.1	1.6
	.8	.8	.7				.5	.5
	1.6	2.0	1.9			Debt/Worth	1.4	1.4
	6.0	5.8	3.3				2.9	3.0
	99.0	36.4	33.3			% Profit Before Taxes/Tangible	38.1	26.3
	(23) 16.4	(44) 11.2	(33) 17.0			Net Worth	(94) 16.7	(77) 7.9
	4.0	-2.9	5.1				5.5	-5.6
	18.8	9.4	14.0			% Profit Before Taxes/Total	15.3	11.0
	7.1	4.4	6.2			Assets	7.6	3.8
	1.3	-1.9	.5				1.9	-2.2
	61.0	19.1	8.1				12.8	9.2
	11.5	8.1	5.7			Sales/Net Fixed Assets	7.4	6.1
	9.2	4.9	3.3				4.1	3.0
	3.1	2.4	2.1				2.5	2.3
	2.3	2.0	1.6			Sales/Total Assets	1.9	1.7
	1.9	1.7	1.3				1.5	1.3
	.8	1.3	2.1				1.4	1.6
	(21) 1.4	(46) 2.7	(34) 2.9			% Depr., Dep., Amort./Sales	(89) 2.6	(81) 3.2
	2.3	3.7	4.7				4.0	4.8
	3.8	1.2				% Officers', Directors',	3.2	3.4
	(15) 5.3	(18) 2.4				Owners' Comp/Sales	(33) 5.4	(22) 4.6
	9.0	4.1					7.8	6.6
478M	75018M	527342M	1307584M	639509M	502533M	Net Sales ($)	2548536M	1759116M
470M	30356M	261225M	777550M	353253M	348832M	Total Assets ($)	1611471M	1208607M

M = $ thousand   MM = $ million
See Pages 11 through 21 for Explanation of Ratios and Data

Comparative Historical Data				Current Data Sorted By Sales					
Type of Statement									
24	30	31	Unqualified				5	9	17
38	35	39	Reviewed		8	4	10	12	5
18	26	10	Compiled			5	3	2	
3	6	8	Tax Returns		2	3	1	1	1
28	31	34	Other	2	3	2	3	15	9
4/1/02-3/31/03 ALL	4/1/03-3/31/04 ALL	4/1/04-3/31/05 ALL		28 (4/1-9/30/04)			94 (10/1/04-3/31/05)		
				0-1MM	1-3MM	3-5MM	5-10MM	10-25MM	25MM & OVER
111	128	122	**NUMBER OF STATEMENTS**	2	13	14	22	39	32
%	%	%	**ASSETS**	%	%	%	%	%	%
7.1	4.8	4.4	Cash & Equivalents		6.7	7.7	3.2	4.0	2.8
22.6	24.4	27.5	Trade Receivables (net)		31.5	28.3	29.7	26.5	24.9
29.1	29.8	31.5	Inventory		34.0	28.2	31.0	33.8	30.6
1.8	2.2	1.5	All Other Current		1.8	1.4	.6	1.9	1.5
60.5	61.1	64.8	Total Current		74.0	65.6	64.5	66.2	59.8
30.2	30.1	27.0	Fixed Assets (net)		17.7	26.9	29.4	25.8	29.9
4.3	4.0	3.7	Intangibles (net)		3.5	2.6	.9	4.4	5.5
5.0	4.8	4.5	All Other Non-Current		4.7	4.9	5.3	3.7	4.8
100.0	100.0	100.0	Total		100.0	100.0	100.0	100.0	100.0
			LIABILITIES						
11.6	10.7	16.9	Notes Payable-Short Term		13.3	12.6	21.4	18.6	14.8
5.1	4.2	3.5	Cur. Mat.-L/T/D		3.4	2.8	4.6	3.0	3.8
12.2	12.9	16.6	Trade Payables		16.1	16.7	21.7	14.4	15.2
.2	.2	.1	Income Taxes Payable		.0	.1	.0	.1	.2
7.0	8.8	6.7	All Other Current		8.4	9.1	4.7	7.1	6.5
36.1	36.8	43.8	Total Current		41.3	41.3	52.3	43.2	40.5
13.3	15.2	12.9	Long-Term Debt		16.3	15.6	10.4	13.5	11.9
.8	.7	.7	Deferred Taxes		.2	.0	1.1	.6	1.0
5.0	5.0	7.0	All Other Non-Current		.8	6.5	15.0	5.0	5.2
44.8	42.3	35.6	Net Worth		41.3	36.6	21.2	37.7	41.3
100.0	100.0	100.0	Total Liabilities & Net Worth		100.0	100.0	100.0	100.0	100.0
			INCOME DATA						
100.0	100.0	100.0	Net Sales		100.0	100.0	100.0	100.0	100.0
26.3	28.6	25.3	Gross Profit		31.8	30.0	19.1	25.7	22.1
23.1	24.8	21.1	Operating Expenses		26.9	25.2	18.6	20.2	16.3
3.2	3.8	4.2	Operating Profit		4.9	4.8	.5	5.5	5.8
1.2	1.3	1.2	All Other Expenses (net)		.6	1.0	1.5	1.1	1.4
2.0	2.5	3.0	Profit Before Taxes		4.3	3.8	−1.0	4.4	4.5
			RATIOS						
3.0	2.9	2.2			3.1	2.3	2.2	2.1	2.1
1.7	1.7	1.4	Current		1.5	1.6	1.3	1.4	1.5
1.3	1.2	1.1			1.2	1.0	1.0	1.1	1.0
1.4	1.5	1.1			1.6	1.5	1.2	1.0	.9
.8	.8	.8	Quick		.9	.9	.6	.7	.8
.5	.5	.5			.7	.5	.3	.4	.5
37 9.8	39 9.5	41 8.8			38 9.5	41 9.0	43 8.6	44 8.4	39 9.2
43 8.4	47 7.8	50 7.2	Sales/Receivables		51 7.1	48 7.6	53 6.8	51 7.2	47 7.7
53 6.9	56 6.5	59 6.2			62 5.9	58 6.3	60 6.1	57 6.4	60 6.1
53 6.8	51 7.2	55 6.6			44 8.3	45 8.2	53 6.9	60 6.1	55 6.6
77 4.7	75 4.9	74 4.9	Cost of Sales/Inventory		76 4.8	77 4.8	68 5.4	78 4.7	74 5.0
114 3.2	115 3.2	108 3.4			116 3.1	111 3.3	98 3.7	110 3.3	130 2.8
17 21.1	19 19.5	26 13.8			13 28.2	28 13.2	34 10.7	24 15.0	25 14.6
29 12.8	33 11.2	38 9.6	Cost of Sales/Payables		30 12.1	36 10.3	43 8.4	35 10.5	37 9.8
46 8.0	44 8.2	51 7.1			55 6.6	57 6.4	55 6.6	51 7.2	46 8.0
4.6	4.5	5.7			5.2	5.9	5.6	6.1	4.8
7.5	7.9	11.5	Sales/Working Capital		8.0	8.1	19.7	11.1	11.3
18.8	21.4	65.3			18.0	−268.2	NM	45.3	758.0
6.2	8.4	9.4			18.4	6.1		24.1	8.7
(96) 2.6	(117) 2.4	(114) 3.6	EBIT/Interest		(12) 2.9	2.2		3.4	(31) 5.3
.4	.4	.8			−.6	−2.6		1.5	1.4
3.0	2.6	6.5	Net Profit + Depr., Dep.,					11.0	
(39) 2.0	(36) 1.3	(33) 2.5	Amort./Cur. Mat. L/T/D					(13) 2.8	
1.1	.6	1.3						2.1	
.4	.3	.3			.1	.1	.3	.3	.5
.7	.7	.9	Fixed/Worth		.5	1.0	.9	.9	.9
1.9	2.1	1.7			1.5	158.5	3.0	1.6	1.5
.4	.5	.8			.4	.8	.6	.8	.8
1.3	1.3	2.0	Debt/Worth		1.6	2.3	2.1	1.9	1.9
3.7	4.6	5.4			8.9	259.2	5.9	4.3	3.4
23.5	26.7	36.8	% Profit Before Taxes/Tangible		166.8	30.4	52.4	37.3	33.8
(99) 8.5	(115) 9.1	(105) 16.4	Net Worth		(12) 8.1	(12) 11.7	(18) 8.8	(34) 21.3	(28) 17.4
−4.2	−3.2	1.8			−7.0	−41.3	−4.6	5.4	3.2
9.8	9.8	12.8	% Profit Before Taxes/Total		19.7	13.1	7.8	13.9	13.8
3.2	3.4	5.0	Assets		6.0	4.8	1.7	5.2	5.9
−3.1	−1.7	−.1			−.9	−2.7	−5.8	.8	.3
11.1	15.0	18.7			518.9	36.9	14.9	19.1	8.6
6.4	6.2	7.3	Sales/Net Fixed Assets		18.6	8.4	6.7	7.6	6.0
4.1	3.6	4.8			9.9	5.2	4.5	4.7	4.7
2.2	2.4	2.4			3.1	2.8	2.8	2.4	2.2
1.7	1.8	1.9	Sales/Total Assets		2.0	2.1	2.0	1.9	1.7
1.3	1.4	1.5			1.7	1.2	1.5	1.5	1.5
2.0	1.4	1.4			.8	.5	2.0	1.6	1.8
(101) 3.6	(112) 2.8	(110) 2.5	% Depr., Dep., Amort./Sales		(11) 1.1	(11) 2.2	(20) 3.0	(34) 2.5	2.8
5.3	5.0	4.2			3.0	9.9	4.3	4.3	4.3
2.5	1.6	1.9	% Officers', Directors',		3.2			.5	
(32) 6.1	(47) 4.1	(37) 3.7	Owners' Comp/Sales		(10) 4.7			(10) 1.3	
8.2	6.6	5.1			6.2			3.1	
2818190M	3407853M	3052464M	Net Sales ($)	1326M	27528M	55222M	153624M	613729M	2201035M
2141842M	2534176M	1771686M	Total Assets ($)	1233M	12644M	32179M	78334M	365118M	1282178M

M = $ thousand   MM = $ million
See Pages 11 through 21 for Explanation of Ratios and Data

Current Data Sorted By Assets — Comparative Historical Data

	0-500M	500M-2MM	2-10MM	10-50MM	50-100MM	100-250MM	Type of Statement	4/1/00-3/31/01 ALL	4/1/01-3/31/02 ALL
		1	5	6	1		Unqualified	10	8
		7	12	4			Reviewed	20	16
		11	4				Compiled	25	10
	2		2				Tax Returns	1	1
	1	8	13	5		1	Other	15	23
		22 (4/1-9/30/04)		61 (10/1/04-3/31/05)					
	3	27	36	15	1	1	**NUMBER OF STATEMENTS**	71	58
	%	%	%	%	%	%	**ASSETS**	%	%
		7.2	6.7	14.1			Cash & Equivalents	9.8	6.6
		31.5	23.6	18.4			Trade Receivables (net)	23.8	23.9
		3.4	8.1	6.3			Inventory	6.6	4.7
		.5	1.1	1.0			All Other Current	1.7	.8
		42.7	39.6	39.7			Total Current	41.8	36.0
		46.0	51.5	48.3			Fixed Assets (net)	48.4	52.0
		3.0	3.8	3.2			Intangibles (net)	2.2	4.2
		8.3	5.1	8.7			All Other Non-Current	7.6	7.8
		100.0	100.0	100.0			Total	100.0	100.0
							LIABILITIES		
		10.8	6.5	2.9			Notes Payable-Short Term	7.6	8.6
		4.5	6.7	10.9			Cur. Mat.-L/T/D	6.6	7.3
		12.1	9.5	11.3			Trade Payables	10.3	10.7
		.4	.0	.5			Income Taxes Payable	.4	.2
		4.9	6.4	8.9			All Other Current	7.3	6.5
		32.5	29.2	34.5			Total Current	32.3	33.2
		19.2	31.1	20.3			Long-Term Debt	21.0	27.4
		.9	2.0	.4			Deferred Taxes	1.2	.8
		21.6	1.9	6.5			All Other Non-Current	5.0	3.0
		25.7	35.8	38.3			Net Worth	40.4	35.7
		100.0	100.0	100.0			Total Liabilities & Net Worth	100.0	100.0
							INCOME DATA		
		100.0	100.0	100.0			Net Sales	100.0	100.0
		40.4	34.4	32.3			Gross Profit	29.8	31.4
		32.4	27.4	22.9			Operating Expenses	25.6	28.2
		8.0	6.9	9.4			Operating Profit	4.1	3.3
		1.8	1.8	1.8			All Other Expenses (net)	.7	2.2
		6.1	5.1	7.6			Profit Before Taxes	3.5	1.1
							RATIOS		
		2.7	1.8	2.4			Current	2.9	1.8
		1.5	1.4	1.4				1.2	1.0
		.7	1.0	.7				.8	.7
		2.7	1.7	2.2			Quick	2.9	1.8
		1.4	1.1	1.1				1.0	.9
		.6	.5	.6				.6	.6
		43 8.6	47 7.8	45 8.1			Sales/Receivables	38 9.7	42 8.7
		51 7.2	53 6.9	59 6.2				50 7.4	53 6.8
		65 5.6	66 5.6	70 5.2				56 6.5	62 5.9
		0 UND	0 UND	0 UND			Cost of Sales/Inventory	0 UND	0 UND
		0 UND	6 60.1	22 16.8				1 292.5	3 141.6
		10 38.1	34 10.6	37 9.9				11 34.7	12 31.0
		15 24.5	16 23.0	23 16.1			Cost of Sales/Payables	10 34.8	16 22.2
		23 16.2	30 12.2	57 6.4				22 16.5	24 15.0
		31 11.6	45 8.1	78 4.7				39 9.4	40 9.2
		8.3	8.7	4.0			Sales/Working Capital	6.0	8.4
		11.9	13.2	12.4				24.6	NM
		-18.8	772.1	-16.4				-27.6	-11.8
		7.5	8.3	32.7			EBIT/Interest	4.4	4.4
		(26) 4.4	(33) 4.1	(12) 8.4				(65) 2.2	(53) 1.5
		2.1	1.5	3.0				.7	.0
			3.5				Net Profit + Depr., Dep.,	2.9	2.5
			(13) 2.2				Amort./Cur. Mat. L /T/D	(23) 1.6	(26) 1.1
			.9					1.0	-.1
		.6	1.1	.8			Fixed/Worth	.6	1.0
		1.0	1.6	1.2				1.4	1.8
		4.3	2.5	5.4				3.9	6.6
		.6	1.1	1.5			Debt/Worth	.6	.9
		1.1	2.1	1.5				1.7	1.9
		8.5	3.2	6.0				5.6	10.4
		43.7	40.4	42.0			% Profit Before Taxes/Tangible	32.5	26.9
		(23) 20.4	(33) 19.4	(13) 25.8			Net Worth	(61) 11.5	(47) 7.0
		4.2	4.1	13.0				.8	-6.2
		17.6	12.9	14.0			% Profit Before Taxes/Total	10.8	7.6
		8.2	5.9	8.7			Assets	4.0	2.0
		2.4	1.8	6.0				-.7	-4.8
		8.8	5.7	4.6			Sales/Net Fixed Assets	7.6	4.9
		5.0	2.5	2.2				3.0	2.7
		2.4	1.5	1.7				1.8	1.5
		3.0	2.1	1.6			Sales/Total Assets	2.3	2.1
		2.0	1.4	1.3				1.7	1.5
		1.3	1.1	.9				1.1	1.0
		2.5	3.4	2.7			% Depr., Dep., Amort./Sales	3.1	3.6
		(26) 4.6	(34) 5.0	7.5				(70) 5.6	(55) 6.3
		6.9	7.6	9.4				8.0	8.9
		4.4	2.7				% Officers', Directors',	2.5	2.3
		(14) 7.0	(17) 5.2				Owners' Comp/Sales	(32) 4.7	(24) 5.1
		10.6	10.4					7.1	7.5
	1955M	72875M	300216M	338270M	73952M	208275M	Net Sales ($)	439762M	413665M
	724M	35263M	205714M	273071M	70006M	133497M	Total Assets ($)	297303M	377600M

M = $ thousand   MM = $ million
See Pages 11 through 21 for Explanation of Ratios and Data

Comparative Historical Data			Type of Statement	Current Data Sorted By Sales					
8	10	13	Unqualified		1		3	4	5
22	30	23	Reviewed	1	4	5	5	8	
16	21	15	Compiled	1	9	2	2	1	
5	7	4	Tax Returns	2	1		1		
16	23	28	Other		8	3	5	10	2
4/1/02-3/31/03	4/1/03-3/31/04	4/1/04-3/31/05		22 (4/1-9/30/04)			61 (10/1/04-3/31/05)		
ALL	ALL	ALL		0-1MM	1-3MM	3-5MM	5-10MM	10-25MM	25MM & OVER
67	91	83	NUMBER OF STATEMENTS	4	23	10	16	23	7
%	%	%	ASSETS	%	%	%	%	%	%
5.2	5.7	8.5	Cash & Equivalents		8.0	4.7	14.4	6.3	
22.8	26.5	25.9	Trade Receivables (net)		30.3	27.9	24.0	26.0	
5.7	6.8	7.0	Inventory		2.8	8.9	3.0	10.8	
1.2	1.9	1.2	All Other Current		.6	.2	1.7	1.0	
34.9	40.9	42.6	Total Current		41.6	41.7	43.0	44.1	
53.4	46.5	47.6	Fixed Assets (net)		45.1	44.5	48.2	49.5	
3.5	3.5	3.3	Intangibles (net)		4.7	5.8	3.3	1.5	
8.2	9.1	6.5	All Other Non-Current		8.6	8.0	5.5	4.8	
100.0	100.0	100.0	Total		100.0	100.0	100.0	100.0	
			LIABILITIES						
8.7	8.9	8.7	Notes Payable-Short Term		10.2	14.9	4.0	5.2	
8.8	6.6	6.5	Cur. Mat.-L/T/D		4.1	4.7	8.5	9.3	
10.3	9.8	10.9	Trade Payables		9.8	16.1	7.4	12.9	
.1	.2	.2	Income Taxes Payable		.4	.0	.2	.2	
5.8	8.0	6.4	All Other Current		4.4	3.7	5.9	8.7	
33.8	33.5	32.7	Total Current		28.9	39.4	26.2	36.2	
26.6	22.8	24.0	Long-Term Debt		19.0	32.5	22.1	27.9	
1.1	1.0	1.2	Deferred Taxes		1.2	.4	2.4	1.2	
3.2	9.2	9.3	All Other Non-Current		5.8	46.3	4.8	1.4	
35.3	33.5	32.7	Net Worth		45.2	−18.6	44.5	33.2	
100.0	100.0	100.0	Total Liabilities & Net Worth		100.0	100.0	100.0	100.0	
			INCOME DATA						
100.0	100.0	100.0	Net Sales		100.0	100.0	100.0	100.0	
34.8	37.6	36.1	Gross Profit		43.2	31.0	36.0	31.3	
32.4	33.4	28.6	Operating Expenses		36.8	25.5	27.9	23.8	
2.4	4.3	7.5	Operating Profit		6.4	5.6	8.1	7.5	
2.1	1.8	1.8	All Other Expenses (net)		1.0	1.4	2.4	1.4	
.3	2.5	5.7	Profit Before Taxes		5.5	4.1	5.7	6.1	
			RATIOS						
2.2	2.0	2.2	Current		2.8	2.0	3.6	1.5	
1.0	1.3	1.4			1.5	1.2	1.6	1.4	
.7	.9	.9			.8	.6	1.1	1.0	
1.9	1.8	2.1	Quick		2.8	1.8	2.7	1.3	
.8	1.0	1.1			1.5	1.0	1.4	.9	
.5	.6	.6			.6	.4	1.0	.7	
46 8.0	47 7.8	44 8.2	Sales/Receivables		44 8.4	40 9.1	45 8.1	52 7.1	
55 6.7	53 6.9	54 6.8			60 6.1	47 7.8	50 7.3	59 6.2	
63 5.8	64 5.7	66 5.6			71 5.1	55 6.7	62 5.9	66 5.5	
0 UND	0 UND	0 UND	Cost of Sales/Inventory		0 UND	0 UND	0 UND	5 76.3	
1 281.1	4 87.3	5 72.3			0 UND	5 72.1	0 UND	22 16.5	
11 33.0	21 17.0	31 11.7			11 33.8	11 33.6	11 34.0	57 6.4	
15 24.1	15 23.8	17 21.2	Cost of Sales/Payables		13 28.6	21 17.6	13 28.1	26 14.1	
24 15.4	25 14.6	29 12.6			21 17.5	31 11.7	23 16.2	35 10.3	
52 7.0	46 7.9	48 7.7			31 11.6	50 7.4	38 9.5	54 6.7	
8.1	9.3	8.3	Sales/Working Capital		6.3	10.8	7.7	9.5	
264.7	23.6	12.4			11.2	18.0	12.7	11.9	
−10.1	−29.0	−29.6			−23.9	−12.0	77.3	999.8	
2.8	5.2	9.5	EBIT/Interest		6.5	10.0	9.2	9.2	
(58) 1.6	(88) 2.1	(75) 4.3			(20) 4.3	3.3	(15) 2.9	(20) 4.8	
.1	−.8	2.0			1.5	2.0	.1	3.7	
2.6	5.3	4.1	Net Profit + Depr., Dep., Amort./Cur. Mat. L/T/D					4.6	
(24) 1.4	(26) 2.2	(22) 2.2					(10)	2.6	
.7	1.3	1.0						1.5	
.9	.7	.7	Fixed/Worth		.6	1.0	.4	1.2	
2.0	1.3	1.3			1.0	1.2	1.5	1.5	
4.5	3.6	2.8			4.3	−3.8	2.7	2.4	
.9	.7	.7	Debt/Worth		.5	1.1	.6	1.1	
1.9	1.8	2.0			1.0	2.5	1.6	2.1	
6.4	4.5	4.3			8.5	−7.6	3.4	3.2	
23.8	25.1	42.8	% Profit Before Taxes/Tangible Net Worth		41.4		39.9	39.9	
(57) 6.0	(75) 8.8	(73) 20.4			(20) 17.2	(15) 10.0	(21) 27.4		
−4.9	−6.4	5.0			3.0		2.6	11.6	
6.8	8.6	13.2	% Profit Before Taxes/Total Assets		10.8	18.6	12.9	13.7	
2.4	2.7	7.0			5.9	8.7	4.8	8.4	
−4.3	−4.6	2.2			2.3	−.9	−2.2	5.1	
5.6	7.1	7.0	Sales/Net Fixed Assets		7.6	9.5	10.4	5.5	
2.3	3.5	3.5			3.3	5.2	2.5	2.9	
1.4	1.9	1.8			1.7	3.0	1.7	1.8	
2.2	2.2	2.3	Sales/Total Assets		2.7	2.7	2.8	2.0	
1.4	1.5	1.5			1.4	1.9	1.4	1.4	
1.0	1.1	1.1			1.1	1.2	.8	1.2	
3.6	3.6	2.7	% Depr., Dep., Amort./Sales		3.7	2.1	2.7	2.5	
(62) 6.6	(85) 5.9	(79) 5.0			(21) 5.7	3.2	(15) 5.3	(22) 5.3	
9.7	8.9	7.5			8.9	4.5	9.5	8.2	
2.8	3.3	3.5	% Officers', Directors', Owners' Comp/Sales		5.9		3.9		
(28) 4.5	(43) 6.0	(36) 6.4			(13) 10.3		(10) 5.5		
8.1	9.2	10.6			11.4		9.4		
425808M	985871M	995543M	Net Sales ($)	2486M	47819M	38826M	110701M	323156M	472555M
329955M	698937M	718275M	Total Assets ($)	5287M	35424M	23485M	98650M	220944M	334485M

Current Data Sorted By Assets | Comparative Historical Data

0-500M	500M-2MM	2-10MM	10-50MM	50-100MM	100-250MM	Type of Statement	4/1/00-3/31/01 ALL	4/1/01-3/31/02 ALL
	2	7	6		2	Unqualified	16	14
1	10	15	6			Reviewed	38	29
1	10	6				Compiled	33	24
4	6					Tax Returns	10	7
2	16	13	6		4	Other	37	49
	20 (4/1-9/30/04)			97 (10/1/04-3/31/05)				
8	44	41	18		6	NUMBER OF STATEMENTS	134	123

Columns 50-100MM and 100-250MM: **DATA NOT AVAILABLE**

0-500M	500M-2MM	2-10MM	10-50MM	Item	ALL 4/1/00-3/31/01	ALL 4/1/01-3/31/02
%	%	%	%	**ASSETS**	%	%
	8.4	7.6	4.6	Cash & Equivalents	6.8	7.0
	28.1	28.0	27.8	Trade Receivables (net)	31.2	27.7
	11.6	13.6	14.5	Inventory	12.4	14.8
	2.2	2.6	1.7	All Other Current	1.1	2.9
	50.3	51.9	48.5	Total Current	51.5	52.4
	40.7	38.8	39.6	Fixed Assets (net)	38.2	37.6
	2.3	2.5	5.0	Intangibles (net)	3.6	3.5
	6.7	6.8	6.9	All Other Non-Current	6.7	6.5
	100.0	100.0	100.0	Total	100.0	100.0
				LIABILITIES		
	10.4	11.1	12.0	Notes Payable-Short Term	12.0	12.9
	4.3	4.9	4.2	Cur. Mat.-L/T/D	5.4	6.0
	10.5	11.4	15.4	Trade Payables	14.8	12.7
	.5	.2	.2	Income Taxes Payable	.4	.2
	11.3	9.8	5.5	All Other Current	8.7	8.1
	37.0	37.4	37.2	Total Current	41.3	40.0
	21.0	23.7	21.6	Long-Term Debt	26.6	24.9
	.1	.7	.5	Deferred Taxes	.5	.6
	6.9	3.4	4.3	All Other Non-Current	7.1	6.5
	35.0	34.8	36.3	Net Worth	24.6	28.0
	100.0	100.0	100.0	Total Liabilities & Net Worth	100.0	100.0
				INCOME DATA		
	100.0	100.0	100.0	Net Sales	100.0	100.0
	36.9	31.2	21.2	Gross Profit	32.5	31.4
	34.6	25.8	16.7	Operating Expenses	25.7	27.5
	2.3	5.3	4.5	Operating Profit	6.8	4.0
	.8	1.6	1.0	All Other Expenses (net)	1.7	2.1
	1.5	3.8	3.5	Profit Before Taxes	5.1	1.9
				RATIOS		
	2.7	2.8	2.0	Current	2.1	2.2
	1.4	1.4	1.2		1.3	1.3
	.9	1.0	.9		.9	.9
	2.2	1.9	1.4	Quick	1.6	1.4
	1.0	1.0	.8		1.0	.8
	.6	.6	.7		.6	.5
	39 9.4	44 8.3	44 8.2	Sales/Receivables	39 9.4	35 10.3
	49 7.5	54 6.8	58 6.3		48 7.5	46 7.9
	64 5.7	62 5.8	67 5.5		59 6.2	58 6.3
	5 73.2	7 50.4	15 25.0	Cost of Sales/Inventory	8 45.6	11 33.7
	21 17.6	25 14.8	40 9.2		20 18.6	25 14.3
	39 9.3	72 5.1	51 7.2		40 9.1	55 6.6
	14 26.0	17 20.9	18 20.3	Cost of Sales/Payables	19 19.7	13 28.0
	20 18.5	28 13.0	28 13.1		27 13.3	27 13.4
	49 7.4	48 7.6	56 6.6		40 9.0	41 8.9
	6.8	5.6	8.0	Sales/Working Capital	8.5	5.7
	10.9	12.0	17.2		17.6	24.4
	−199.3	NM	−110.3		−38.9	−56.4
	7.4	10.0	7.5	EBIT/Interest	9.6	5.7
	(41) 2.5	(38) 3.1	(17) 3.7		(126) 3.0	(116) 2.0
	.3	1.3	−.1		1.0	−.3
				Net Profit + Depr., Dep., Amort./Cur. Mat. L /T/D	7.9	5.1
					(29) 2.5	(37) 1.5
					1.3	.8
	.5	.7	.8	Fixed/Worth	.6	.5
	1.0	1.1	1.3		1.5	1.4
	3.4	2.3	1.6		6.4	5.5
	.6	.9	1.2	Debt/Worth	.7	.9
	2.1	2.1	1.8		2.3	2.2
	6.7	4.5	3.1		13.4	9.1
	40.7	48.0	45.6	% Profit Before Taxes/Tangible Net Worth	55.7	34.3
	(37) 12.7	(38) 16.0	(17) 20.5		(110) 23.5	(102) 13.5
	−1.5	−.3	2.6		6.5	−5.2
	13.7	15.2	11.9	% Profit Before Taxes/Total Assets	21.0	12.4
	4.0	5.2	5.4		8.3	3.1
	−2.4	−2.5	−.8		.0	−4.1
	10.2	10.7	11.0	Sales/Net Fixed Assets	14.1	16.0
	4.8	4.0	4.2		7.1	6.0
	2.5	2.2	2.3		3.2	2.7
	2.7	2.2	2.2	Sales/Total Assets	3.2	2.9
	2.0	1.6	1.6		2.2	1.9
	1.5	1.0	1.2		1.5	1.2
	2.1	1.8	1.5	% Depr., Dep., Amort./Sales	1.4	1.7
	(41) 3.8	(35) 3.3	(17) 4.0		(126) 2.5	(114) 3.0
	5.7	4.6	6.5		4.9	5.7
	2.9	3.3		% Officers', Directors', Owners' Comp/Sales	2.6	2.7
	(18) 5.9	(15) 5.9			(58) 4.8	(48) 4.7
	8.0	7.8			12.9	10.3

0-500M	500M-2MM	2-10MM	10-50MM	50-100MM	100-250MM		ALL	ALL
9029M	119409M	307286M	731467M		1632344M	Net Sales ($)	2719574M	2579486M
2711M	57564M	165839M	413579M		956963M	Total Assets ($)	1095523M	1432425M

M = $ thousand   MM = $ million
See Pages 11 through 21 for Explanation of Ratios and Data

	Comparative Historical Data				Current Data Sorted By Sales					

Type of Statement

	20	17	17	Unqualified		2	2	3	2	8
	33	33	32	Reviewed		11	6	4	10	1
	21	23	17	Compiled	1	5	7	3	1	
	10	13	10	Tax Returns	4	6				
	43	44	41	Other	2	13	12		5	8
	4/1/02-3/31/03	4/1/03-3/31/04	4/1/04-3/31/05			20 (4/1-9/30/04)			97 (10/1/04-3/31/05)	
	ALL	ALL	ALL		0-1MM	1-3MM	3-5MM	5-10MM	10-25MM	25MM & OVER
	127	130	117	**NUMBER OF STATEMENTS**	7	37	27	11	18	17
	%	%	%	**ASSETS**	%	%	%	%	%	%
	6.9	7.4	7.3	Cash & Equivalents	9.5	7.4	5.5	8.3	2.9	
	27.3	26.2	28.2	Trade Receivables (net)	21.7	32.6	30.4	30.4	28.7	
	12.3	11.4	12.5	Inventory	10.9	12.7	13.8	14.9	15.2	
	2.1	2.4	2.1	All Other Current	1.4	3.0	2.5	1.0	2.0	
	48.6	47.5	50.0	Total Current	43.6	55.8	52.2	54.6	48.8	
	41.3	41.9	39.7	Fixed Assets (net)	46.6	36.4	38.8	34.4	37.6	
	3.7	1.8	4.0	Intangibles (net)	3.4	1.4	2.7	3.4	9.2	
	6.4	8.8	6.4	All Other Non-Current	6.4	6.4	6.3	7.6	4.5	
	100.0	100.0	100.0	Total	100.0	100.0	100.0	100.0	100.0	
				LIABILITIES						
	11.6	11.8	11.0	Notes Payable-Short Term	9.3	10.7	11.1	12.1	9.8	
	5.8	6.1	4.1	Cur. Mat.-L/T/D	4.6	3.6	6.2	4.8	3.3	
	11.9	12.3	11.7	Trade Payables	8.3	11.0	9.6	15.4	16.6	
	.1	.1	.3	Income Taxes Payable	.0	.8	.4	.2	.2	
	8.5	8.1	10.1	All Other Current	12.9	10.2	8.9	10.3	7.0	
	38.0	38.3	37.2	Total Current	35.1	36.3	36.2	42.7	37.0	
	27.3	22.0	26.6	Long-Term Debt	36.2	17.9	16.4	15.8	27.1	
	.4	.5	.4	Deferred Taxes	.0	.3	1.5	.5	.7	
	5.7	5.6	5.5	All Other Non-Current	6.5	5.0	2.4	.7	6.6	
	28.8	33.7	30.3	Net Worth	22.2	40.6	43.5	40.3	28.7	
	100.0	100.0	100.0	Total Liabilities & Net Worth	100.0	100.0	100.0	100.0	100.0	
				INCOME DATA						
	100.0	100.0	100.0	Net Sales	100.0	100.0	100.0	100.0	100.0	
	32.3	30.1	32.5	Gross Profit	43.5	28.5	33.8	21.8	20.6	
	26.8	26.8	28.1	Operating Expenses	40.1	25.1	26.6	15.4	16.0	
	5.5	3.3	4.3	Operating Profit	3.4	3.4	7.2	6.4	4.6	
	1.9	1.1	1.2	All Other Expenses (net)	1.4	.6	.9	1.2	1.5	
	3.6	2.2	3.1	Profit Before Taxes	2.0	2.8	6.4	5.3	3.2	

RATIOS

	2.4	2.3	2.3		3.5	2.5	2.3	2.1	2.0	
	1.3	1.3	1.4	Current	1.3	1.5	1.5	1.3	1.2	
	.8	.9	1.0		.8	1.2	.9	.9	1.1	
	1.5	1.7	1.9		2.8	2.0	1.8	1.5	1.1	
	.9	1.0	1.0	Quick	1.0	1.1	1.0	.8	.9	
	.6	.6	.6		.5	.8	.6	.6	.7	
37	9.8	36 10.2	40 9.1		29 12.6	40 9.1	42 8.7	43 8.6	42 8.8	
48	7.7	48 7.6	52 7.0	Sales/Receivables	51 7.2	52 7.0	47 7.8	49 7.4	57 6.4	
61	6.0	60 6.1	63 5.8		68 5.4	59 6.2	57 6.4	65 5.6	64 5.7	
12	31.1	8 47.8	7 53.0		1 279.3	9 42.9	6 65.2	13 29.0	15 24.8	
23	15.6	24 15.2	24 15.0	Cost of Sales/Inventory	22 16.2	24 15.4	18 20.3	28 12.8	38 9.5	
47	7.8	45 8.1	49 7.5		73 5.0	46 8.0	36 10.2	52 7.1	52 7.0	
15	24.3	14 27.0	15 23.9		13 27.9	14 25.4	16 23.2	21 17.6	22 16.4	
25	14.7	26 14.3	27 13.8	Cost of Sales/Payables	26 13.8	20 18.6	22 16.5	30 12.3	35 10.4	
37	10.0	39 9.4	49 7.5		56 6.6	47 7.8	28 13.0	49 7.4	50 7.3	
	6.9	7.1	6.5		5.5	6.2	7.9	7.5	7.4	
	19.7	16.1	14.6	Sales/Working Capital	10.3	12.0	9.8	16.8	19.0	
	−28.7	−43.4	NM		−22.0	25.4	−91.6	−32.0	52.2	
	7.5	7.2	8.2		5.2	9.5	15.8	20.2	5.5	
(120)	3.1	(116) 2.4	(110) 3.1	EBIT/Interest	(33) 2.5	(26) 4.0	6.4	(16) 6.7	3.7	
	.8	.3	.9		−1.0	1.1	2.2	1.4	.2	
	2.9	1.8	2.6	Net Profit + Depr., Dep.,						
(28)	1.5	(26) 1.3	(20) 1.9	Amort./Cur. Mat. L/T/D						
	.8	.4	.6							
	.7	.6	.6		.7	.6	.3	.4	.9	
	1.6	1.1	1.2	Fixed/Worth	2.0	.9	1.0	1.0	1.5	
	9.7	4.6	3.6		10.5	1.7	1.2	1.6	9.1	
	.9	.7	.9		1.1	.6	.8	.8	1.5	
	2.2	2.0	2.2	Debt/Worth	3.2	2.0	1.2	1.4	2.6	
	11.0	7.1	6.9		14.0	4.5	2.6	2.7	20.8	
	44.9	29.0	46.4	% Profit Before Taxes/Tangible	46.8	23.4	58.0	49.5	45.8	
(104)	20.1	(108) 12.4	(98) 17.3	Net Worth	(30) 5.7	(25) 11.1	25.2	(16) 25.5	(14) 20.9	
	1.3	−.6	.9		−15.2	2.8	12.7	5.0	−2.6	
	16.9	13.0	14.3	% Profit Before Taxes/Total	13.8	13.8	29.8	23.0	9.9	
	5.0	3.7	5.2	Assets	2.5	4.8	8.6	12.7	5.2	
	−.2	−1.5	−2.0		−4.7	−.1	4.0	.6	−1.8	
	11.8	10.3	10.7		8.1	10.7	13.5	17.9	12.6	
	5.0	5.2	4.7	Sales/Net Fixed Assets	3.1	6.7	4.5	6.4	4.6	
	2.6	2.6	2.5		2.1	3.7	2.9	2.9	3.4	
	2.5	2.8	2.5		2.1	3.0	2.7	2.7	2.5	
	1.8	2.1	1.8	Sales/Total Assets	1.5	2.1	2.1	1.9	1.9	
	1.2	1.2	1.2		1.0	1.7	1.4	1.4	1.3	
	2.0	1.9	2.0		2.2	1.7	1.8	1.5	1.4	
(117)	3.5	(116) 3.7	(102) 3.6	% Depr., Dep., Amort./Sales	(32) 3.9	(24) 2.6	(10) 3.1	(17) 3.6	(12) 3.2	
	5.6	5.6	5.6		7.7	4.5	4.5	4.7	4.9	
	2.4	2.7	3.1	% Officers', Directors',	4.2	3.0				
(46)	4.8	(44) 4.8	(44) 5.7	Owners' Comp/Sales	(16) 6.4	(15) 5.9				
	8.6	9.6	7.8		7.7	9.1				
	3738587M	3334180M	2799535M	Net Sales ($)	5745M	75006M	103155M	68799M	329389M	2217441M
	1605604M	1614957M	1596656M	Total Assets ($)	3415M	54598M	52822M	38005M	188073M	1259743M

M = $ thousand   MM = $ million
See Pages 11 through 21 for Explanation of Ratios and Data

Current Data Sorted By Assets   Comparative Historical Data

0-500M	500M-2MM	2-10MM	10-50MM	50-100MM	100-250MM	Type of Statement	4/1/00-3/31/01 ALL	4/1/01-3/31/02 ALL
		8	6	1		Unqualified	21	22
1	11	28	3		1	Reviewed	44	44
4	22	13	2			Compiled	34	46
8	10					Tax Returns	10	6
10	15	23	9			Other	46	52
	32 (4/1-9/30/04)		143 (10/1/04-3/31/05)					
23	58	72	20	1	1	**NUMBER OF STATEMENTS**	155	170
%	%	%	%	%	%	**ASSETS**	%	%
17.3	8.3	7.3	4.4			Cash & Equivalents	8.2	8.8
33.5	31.7	26.8	25.1			Trade Receivables (net)	27.9	25.7
7.8	10.7	9.5	13.7			Inventory	6.7	7.6
2.5	1.6	2.3	.6			All Other Current	1.9	2.3
61.1	52.3	45.8	43.9			Total Current	44.7	44.5
28.3	39.3	44.5	44.8			Fixed Assets (net)	44.1	45.0
2.3	3.4	1.8	2.1			Intangibles (net)	4.2	3.5
8.3	5.0	7.9	9.2			All Other Non-Current	7.0	7.0
100.0	100.0	100.0	100.0			Total	100.0	100.0
						LIABILITIES		
11.5	10.8	10.2	9.9			Notes Payable-Short Term	6.6	10.4
10.1	3.4	5.2	5.4			Cur. Mat.-L/T/D	5.8	5.5
18.1	12.6	13.1	16.7			Trade Payables	11.2	11.5
.0	.1	.2	.0			Income Taxes Payable	.1	.4
16.4	5.9	11.5	10.0			All Other Current	9.6	9.1
56.1	32.8	40.4	42.1			Total Current	33.4	36.9
39.5	22.0	20.9	25.2			Long-Term Debt	25.2	22.7
.0	.7	.6	.6			Deferred Taxes	.6	.6
30.9	10.2	6.5	6.2			All Other Non-Current	5.7	7.4
-26.5	34.4	31.7	25.9			Net Worth	35.0	32.5
100.0	100.0	100.0	100.0			Total Liabilities & Net Worth	100.0	100.0
						INCOME DATA		
100.0	100.0	100.0	100.0			Net Sales	100.0	100.0
47.8	38.0	26.9	20.8			Gross Profit	31.6	30.0
46.1	33.4	23.0	14.8			Operating Expenses	25.6	27.4
1.7	4.6	3.9	6.0			Operating Profit	6.1	2.6
.8	2.6	1.4	.8			All Other Expenses (net)	1.8	2.3
.9	2.0	2.5	5.2			Profit Before Taxes	4.3	.4
						RATIOS		
3.4	2.8	2.0	1.4				2.7	2.0
1.5	1.5	1.2	.9			Current	1.5	1.4
.6	1.2	.9	.7				.9	.9
2.6	2.6	1.9	1.0				2.1	1.7
1.2	1.2	.9	.7			Quick	1.1	1.0
.5	.7	.5	.4				.7	.6
8 45.7	36 10.1	40 9.1	38 9.7				39 9.3	34 10.6
42 8.6	48 7.6	53 6.9	47 7.7			Sales/Receivables	47 7.8	45 8.0
57 6.4	61 6.0	58 6.3	52 7.0				56 6.5	57 6.4
0 UND	1 325.3	6 57.5	10 37.0				3 120.5	4 96.9
5 73.5	12 29.9	17 21.8	24 15.0			Cost of Sales/Inventory	8 45.4	10 36.1
14 25.3	28 13.2	33 11.2	44 8.3				25 14.9	27 13.4
13 28.4	12 31.7	19 19.5	23 16.1				14 25.3	14 26.0
27 13.7	24 15.0	28 13.1	30 12.0			Cost of Sales/Payables	23 15.7	24 14.9
40 9.1	49 7.4	46 7.9	47 7.8				36 10.2	40 9.1
9.1	7.6	8.5	15.1				7.5	9.8
14.5	15.2	28.1	-24.1			Sales/Working Capital	16.6	21.9
-35.9	50.6	-45.5	-11.8				-38.5	-35.7
12.9	9.7	8.4	14.0				7.0	4.2
(18) 4.9	(51) 3.3	(68) 4.4	4.2			EBIT/Interest	(141) 2.5	(155) 1.2
-1.8	1.3	.9	1.3				1.0	-1.5
		4.9					4.9	3.1
		(28) 2.3				Net Profit + Depr., Dep., Amort./Cur. Mat. L/T/D	(47) 2.4	(49) 1.5
		1.5					1.0	.4
.4	.5	.7	.9				.6	.7
1.3	1.0	1.3	1.8			Fixed/Worth	1.4	1.5
-.3	2.7	5.2	9.3				5.8	3.9
.7	.7	.9	.9				.6	.7
2.5	1.5	2.1	4.1			Debt/Worth	1.7	1.9
-2.1	5.1	6.6	18.4				16.6	8.3
95.6	39.5	46.8	71.2				42.5	28.1
(12) 21.8	(50) 15.8	(65) 18.6	(17) 32.9			% Profit Before Taxes/Tangible Net Worth	(126) 19.0	(141) 7.8
1.4	1.3	1.6	7.2				3.9	-15.0
47.2	17.7	15.1	17.4				14.1	9.7
9.7	5.4	7.2	7.2			% Profit Before Taxes/Total Assets	5.3	1.5
-15.1	-1.3	-.3	.5				.3	-7.2
24.5	13.8	8.2	7.9				8.7	9.0
14.4	7.2	4.3	3.9			Sales/Net Fixed Assets	4.9	4.6
8.9	3.7	2.4	2.7				2.8	2.3
4.9	3.2	2.5	2.2				2.8	2.7
3.7	2.5	2.0	1.7			Sales/Total Assets	2.1	1.9
2.9	1.9	1.2	1.5				1.4	1.3
1.3	1.6	2.5	2.4				2.1	2.3
(19) 2.7	(55) 3.5	(70) 3.7	4.1			% Depr., Dep., Amort./Sales	(144) 3.6	(155) 4.2
4.1	6.1	6.6	5.1				6.5	7.3
7.4	3.7	2.2					3.6	2.6
(13) 11.7	(37) 6.3	(29) 4.2				% Officers', Directors', Owners' Comp/Sales	(82) 5.8	(81) 5.3
18.9	10.2	7.1					9.9	7.9
29602M	182261M	697724M	835419M	104527M	297835M	Net Sales ($)	1694964M	2418295M
7786M	69702M	339732M	434023M	65010M	245969M	Total Assets ($)	1023064M	1212177M

© RMA 2005

M = $ thousand   MM = $ million

See Pages 11 through 21 for Explanation of Ratios and Data

Comparative Historical Data | Current Data Sorted By Sales

			Type of Statement						
16	18	15	Unqualified		1	1	4	2	7
53	48	44	Reviewed		8	9	12	11	4
35	45	41	Compiled	5	11	13	5	5	2
15	17	18	Tax Returns	5	8	3	2		
48	54	57	Other	6	15	7	13	8	8
4/1/02- 3/31/03 ALL	4/1/03- 3/31/04 ALL	4/1/04- 3/31/05 ALL			32 (4/1-9/30/04)		143 (10/1/04-3/31/05)		
				0-1MM	1-3MM	3-5MM	5-10MM	10-25MM	25MM & OVER
167	182	175	**NUMBER OF STATEMENTS**	16	43	33	36	26	21
%	%	%	**ASSETS**	%	%	%	%	%	%
8.8	8.2	8.6	Cash & Equivalents	14.8	8.4	11.0	8.9	5.1	4.4
25.1	26.6	29.0	Trade Receivables (net)	23.8	29.4	30.0	28.1	31.9	28.4
8.1	8.5	10.2	Inventory	12.6	7.3	9.2	10.5	10.1	15.2
1.4	1.8	2.0	All Other Current	2.7	2.0	1.1	1.4	4.0	1.5
43.4	45.1	49.8	Total Current	53.9	47.1	51.4	48.9	51.1	49.5
46.1	44.2	40.7	Fixed Assets (net)	29.4	44.4	39.7	42.0	41.0	41.0
2.2	3.7	2.4	Intangibles (net)	7.7	2.4	3.4	.6	.5	2.6
8.3	6.9	7.1	All Other Non-Current	8.9	6.2	5.5	8.6	7.4	6.9
100.0	100.0	100.0	Total	100.0	100.0	100.0	100.0	100.0	100.0
			LIABILITIES						
12.2	13.4	10.6	Notes Payable-Short Term	15.6	9.5	9.3	8.8	13.8	9.9
6.2	4.8	5.2	Cur. Mat.-L/T/D	10.7	3.5	4.2	6.9	4.3	4.5
11.5	11.9	14.0	Trade Payables	18.5	11.7	11.8	12.6	16.5	18.0
.1	.1	.1	Income Taxes Payable	.0	.1	.0	.4	.0	.1
8.7	7.9	10.1	All Other Current	16.3	5.7	9.0	8.7	16.5	10.4
38.6	38.0	40.0	Total Current	61.1	30.6	34.3	37.4	51.1	42.9
22.2	22.0	24.1	Long-Term Debt	46.1	29.8	13.3	20.8	20.8	22.8
.5	.6	.6	Deferred Taxes	.4	.5	.7	.6	.6	.6
4.7	8.0	11.0	All Other Non-Current	15.8	21.1	6.2	7.3	6.2	6.8
33.9	31.4	24.3	Net Worth	-23.5	18.1	45.5	33.9	21.4	26.8
100.0	100.0	100.0	Total Liabilities & Net Worth	100.0	100.0	100.0	100.0	100.0	100.0
			INCOME DATA						
100.0	100.0	100.0	Net Sales	100.0	100.0	100.0	100.0	100.0	100.0
32.6	33.9	32.5	Gross Profit	43.4	39.2	36.0	29.0	25.5	19.9
29.3	30.5	28.5	Operating Expenses	47.6	34.7	30.4	23.0	22.2	15.2
3.4	3.3	4.1	Operating Profit	-4.2	4.5	5.6	6.0	3.3	4.8
2.1	1.7	1.6	All Other Expenses (net)	3.1	2.4	1.0	1.4	1.4	.8
1.3	1.6	2.4	Profit Before Taxes	-7.3	2.1	4.6	4.6	1.9	4.0
			RATIOS						
2.1	2.1	2.5		3.2	3.1	2.6	2.2	2.4	1.6
1.3	1.3	1.3	Current	1.2	1.5	1.5	1.2	1.2	1.1
.8	.9	.9		.6	1.1	1.1	.9	.8	.8
1.6	1.7	1.9		1.9	2.8	2.4	1.9	1.8	1.1
1.0	.9	1.0	Quick	.7	1.2	1.2	.9	.8	.9
.6	.6	.5		.3	.7	.8	.5	.6	.5

35	10.4	38	9.6	36	10.0		36	10.2	36	10.2	36	10.0	36	10.1	44	8.3	36	10.1
45	8.1	48	7.6	49	7.4	Sales/Receivables	58	6.3	49	7.4	46	7.9	47	7.7	53	6.9	47	7.8
53	6.9	58	6.3	58	6.3		75	4.9	62	5.9	59	6.2	56	6.5	58	6.3	52	7.0
4	84.1	5	75.7	5	81.0		0	UND	0	UND	4	94.4	9	40.3	7	48.7	8	44.7
14	26.8	13	28.6	14	25.3	Cost of Sales/Inventory	12	30.1	9	42.9	13	29.1	16	22.7	15	25.0	25	14.7
31	11.9	38	9.5	32	11.4		54	6.8	24	15.1	32	11.2	33	11.2	35	10.3	42	8.7
15	24.8	15	23.6	16	23.5		19	18.8	13	27.3	11	32.8	13	28.1	18	19.8	23	16.0
24	15.5	26	14.0	27	13.5	Cost of Sales/Payables	34	10.8	27	13.7	26	14.2	27	13.4	30	12.1	30	12.3
44	8.2	42	8.7	44	8.3		138	2.6	37	9.9	51	7.1	44	8.4	46	7.9	40	9.2
	9.7		8.2		8.5			6.0		7.3		7.1		7.6		9.0		13.9
	22.4		21.9		18.5	Sales/Working Capital		NM		14.1		18.5		36.8		24.9		218.1
	-26.7		-43.5		-51.0			-3.6		69.7		68.2		-36.1		-41.6		-17.7
	5.3		5.5		9.7			3.7		5.8		28.1		7.5		8.2		27.1
(158)	1.7	(173)	2.1	(159)	4.0	EBIT/Interest	(12)	.2	(39)	2.8	(29)	8.3	(33)	4.6	(25)	4.5		4.3
	.0		-.3		.8			-2.4		.1		1.6		1.8		-.2		.5
	4.8		5.3		4.7	Net Profit + Depr., Dep.,								5.0		4.3		
(38)	1.9	(48)	1.9	(48)	2.4	Amort./Cur. Mat. L/T/D							(11)	3.2	(12)	2.2		
	.6		1.2		1.4									2.1		1.1		
	.7		.7		.6			.3		.7		.4		.6		.7		.7
	1.4		1.6		1.2	Fixed/Worth		NM		1.5		.8		1.2		1.3		1.7
	3.0		3.3		5.4			-.4		3.8		2.1		5.2		5.6		11.9
	.9		.8		.8			1.0		.8		.3		.9		1.0		1.1
	2.0		2.2		2.1	Debt/Worth		NM		2.0		1.1		2.3		2.2		3.1
	5.3		6.3		8.9			-1.8		7.9		4.5		8.0		10.9		25.4
	28.6		31.2		48.2	% Profit Before Taxes/Tangible				34.9		39.5		79.4		58.3		71.2
(142)	9.2	(155)	7.8	(145)	18.8	Net Worth			(33)	10.7	(30)	22.7	(34)	26.7	(22)	17.5	(18)	34.3
	-3.6		-8.0		2.2					-6.0		8.1		5.7		-5.0		9.5
	10.0		9.5		16.3	% Profit Before Taxes/Total		8.5		12.7		18.6		20.6		16.6		16.5
	2.5		2.7		7.6	Assets		-4.5		4.0		13.8		9.7		6.7		8.8
	-2.5		-3.4		-1.4			-13.1		-5.5		1.7		2.6		-3.7		-1.1
	8.5		9.1		11.6			17.5		10.5		12.7		11.3		11.4		9.2
	4.3		4.2		5.9	Sales/Net Fixed Assets		11.3		5.8		7.2		6.5		5.3		4.5
	2.5		2.7		3.3			2.5		2.9		3.0		2.9		3.3		3.7
	2.8		2.6		3.1			3.0		3.4		3.1		3.1		3.0		3.2
	2.0		1.9		2.2	Sales/Total Assets		1.9		2.2		2.5		2.0		2.3		1.9
	1.3		1.2		1.6			.5		1.5		1.5		1.4		1.6		1.6
	2.7		2.4		1.9			1.2		2.4		1.9		2.1		1.9		1.7
(154)	4.2	(172)	4.7	(165)	3.5	% Depr., Dep., Amort./Sales	(14)	3.7	(39)	4.4	(32)	3.0	(34)	3.6		2.8	(20)	3.8
	7.2		6.6		5.7			10.4		7.5		4.2		6.6		4.4		5.2
	2.9		3.3		3.4	% Officers', Directors',				3.8		3.6		3.7		1.4		
(82)	5.4	(83)	5.6	(83)	5.9	Owners' Comp/Sales			(26)	7.4	(20)	6.1	(14)	5.0	(11)	1.7		
	10.0		10.0		9.8					11.9		9.1		8.4		4.2		

1617666M	1634763M	2147368M	Net Sales ($)	11002M	86026M	131590M	265975M	361256M	1291519M
1041739M	1025803M	1162222M	Total Assets ($)	9749M	49540M	67332M	141694M	177598M	716309M

M = $ thousand   MM = $ million
See Pages 11 through 21 for Explanation of Ratios and Data

Current Data Sorted By Assets   Comparative Historical Data

	0-500M	500M-2MM	2-10MM	10-50MM	50-100MM	100-250MM		4/1/00-3/31/01 ALL	4/1/01-3/31/02 ALL
Type of Statement									
Unqualified			6	5	3	2		8	4
Reviewed		1	5	2	1			6	10
Compiled	1	3	6	1				11	8
Tax Returns	1	5	1					4	4
Other		4	11	10	1			18	21
		14 (4/1-9/30/04)		55 (10/1/04-3/31/05)					
NUMBER OF STATEMENTS	2	13	29	18	5	2		47	47
	%	%	%	%	%	%	ASSETS	%	%
Cash & Equivalents		2.8	6.0	6.4				9.1	8.5
Trade Receivables (net)		34.0	28.6	25.1				27.7	25.8
Inventory		31.2	31.1	29.8				30.6	31.8
All Other Current		.7	2.3	1.6				1.3	1.1
Total Current		68.7	68.1	62.9				68.7	67.1
Fixed Assets (net)		19.3	25.2	24.3				23.3	22.9
Intangibles (net)		3.1	1.5	4.3				1.7	3.9
All Other Non-Current		8.9	5.2	8.4				6.3	6.1
Total		100.0	100.0	100.0				100.0	100.0
							LIABILITIES		
Notes Payable-Short Term		21.4	17.3	9.7				13.5	11.5
Cur. Mat.-L/T/D		3.0	5.8	2.6				3.0	3.9
Trade Payables		18.6	12.0	8.4				16.5	12.7
Income Taxes Payable		.1	.3	.3				.1	.2
All Other Current		18.4	16.8	10.7				11.0	10.7
Total Current		61.6	52.2	31.7				44.1	39.1
Long-Term Debt		13.6	13.2	12.3				14.8	14.6
Deferred Taxes		.0	.0	.3				.5	.2
All Other Non-Current		10.3	8.6	4.5				9.0	14.6
Net Worth		14.5	25.9	51.1				31.6	31.5
Total Liabilities & Net Worth		100.0	100.0	100.0				100.0	100.0
							INCOME DATA		
Net Sales		100.0	100.0	100.0				100.0	100.0
Gross Profit		46.1	32.4	27.4				32.6	34.0
Operating Expenses		42.2	27.5	20.5				26.2	31.3
Operating Profit		3.9	4.9	6.8				6.4	2.7
All Other Expenses (net)		1.2	.8	.6				1.3	1.7
Profit Before Taxes		2.6	4.1	6.3				5.1	1.0
							RATIOS		
Current		1.9	2.7	4.2				3.0	2.9
		1.1	1.1	2.8				1.7	1.9
		.9	.9	1.3				1.2	1.3
Quick		1.4	1.3	2.3				1.6	1.3
		.7	.7	1.3				1.0	.9
		.3	.4	.6				.6	.5
Sales/Receivables	37 9.8	41 8.8	40 9.1					38 9.6	38 9.7
	45 8.0	54 6.8	54 6.7					48 7.6	49 7.5
	65 5.7	62 5.9	65 5.6					61 6.0	57 6.5
Cost of Sales/Inventory	20 17.9	46 8.0	60 6.1					37 9.8	59 6.2
	80 4.6	76 4.8	89 4.1					88 4.1	102 3.6
	160 2.3	113 3.2	127 2.9					130 2.8	157 2.3
Cost of Sales/Payables	14 25.9	16 22.4	15 24.5					14 25.5	17 21.6
	52 7.0	27 13.5	26 14.0					30 12.3	36 10.3
	64 5.7	46 8.0	34 10.8					48 7.6	51 7.2
Sales/Working Capital		10.5	4.0	3.2				4.2	3.9
		50.2	33.9	4.9				6.8	6.4
		-28.3	-60.8	12.7				23.4	13.9
EBIT/Interest		7.5	6.8	29.7				9.6	3.9
	(12) 3.8	(27) 3.5	(16) 4.2					(43) 3.1	(44) 1.7
		-1.5	1.1	1.8				1.3	.0
Net Profit + Depr., Dep., Amort./Cur. Mat. L./T/D								18.3	6.0
							(10) 3.3	(13) 2.0	
								1.9	.4
Fixed/Worth		.2	.4	.3				.2	.4
		.9	1.1	.5				.6	.9
		4.2	17.5	1.2				2.4	5.0
Debt/Worth		1.9	1.1	.4				.7	.8
		6.3	2.4	.9				1.7	2.4
		NM	240.0	2.5				5.5	23.9
% Profit Before Taxes/Tangible Net Worth		98.6	61.1	32.0				44.7	28.6
	(10) 56.3	(23) 23.3	(17) 24.2					(40) 20.7	(39) 11.7
		33.6	3.3	7.4				3.1	2.8
% Profit Before Taxes/Total Assets		21.6	17.7	20.9				17.7	9.2
		5.7	5.5	8.4				6.9	2.6
		-3.5	-1.0	1.7				.7	-4.3
Sales/Net Fixed Assets		56.5	29.6	9.9				32.8	22.9
		14.3	11.4	8.6				10.3	7.9
		8.7	4.0	5.2				4.3	4.6
Sales/Total Assets		3.6	2.6	2.0				2.8	2.4
		2.6	1.9	1.7				1.9	1.7
		2.1	1.4	1.2				1.4	1.3
% Depr., Dep., Amort./Sales		.8	1.3	1.7				.6	1.3
	(10) 1.6	(27) 2.6	2.4					(38) 1.4	(44) 2.3
		3.8	4.7	3.4				3.2	4.1
% Officers', Directors', Owners' Comp/Sales		2.2	1.8					1.6	1.7
	(11) 3.9	(12) 3.9						(15) 2.8	(19) 5.1
		5.8	5.8					4.8	8.0
Net Sales ($)	3514M	38221M	229198M	929491M	491522M	399696M		1058863M	797805M
Total Assets ($)	844M	14677M	119909M	450999M	347462M	272357M		806147M	622477M

M = $ thousand   MM = $ million
See Pages 11 through 21 for Explanation of Ratios and Data

Comparative Historical Data | **Current Data Sorted By Sales**

				Type of Statement	0-1MM	1-3MM	3-5MM	5-10MM	10-25MM	25MM & OVER
	12	12	16	Unqualified		1		3	3	9
	11	14	9	Reviewed				2	3	3
	8	11	11	Compiled	1	4	1	5	1	
	9	8	7	Tax Returns		3		3		
	23	25	26	Other	1	2	2	8	4	9
	4/1/02-3/31/03	4/1/03-3/31/04	4/1/04-3/31/05		14 (4/1-9/30/04)			55 (10/1/04-3/31/05)		
	ALL	ALL	ALL							
	63	70	69	NUMBER OF STATEMENTS	2	10	4	21	11	21
	%	%	%	**ASSETS**	%	%	%	%	%	%
	6.2	8.0	5.3	Cash & Equivalents		1.9		5.2	6.5	5.7
	25.0	27.2	28.7	Trade Receivables (net)		29.5		31.6	25.5	25.2
	31.3	26.5	30.1	Inventory		34.4		28.6	29.6	31.1
	1.5	1.9	1.9	All Other Current		.7		2.4	1.9	2.5
	63.9	63.6	66.0	Total Current		66.5		67.8	63.6	64.6
	26.6	26.9	24.4	Fixed Assets (net)		22.4		27.1	21.6	25.7
	3.8	4.1	3.2	Intangibles (net)		2.9		.2	6.8	4.7
	5.7	5.3	6.4	All Other Non-Current		8.1		4.8	8.0	5.1
	100.0	100.0	100.0	Total		100.0		100.0	100.0	100.0
				LIABILITIES						
	14.3	10.4	15.4	Notes Payable-Short Term		15.5		17.5	14.8	9.1
	7.1	4.6	3.9	Cur. Mat.-L/T/D		2.2		3.4	8.7	2.6
	15.9	12.8	12.4	Trade Payables		19.8		12.8	13.1	8.2
	.0	.1	.4	Income Taxes Payable		.1		.3	.4	.6
	8.5	10.1	14.4	All Other Current		32.7		12.7	13.1	9.5
	45.8	38.0	46.5	Total Current		70.4		46.7	50.1	30.1
	16.9	14.9	13.8	Long-Term Debt		18.6		15.8	10.4	14.9
	.3	.6	.2	Deferred Taxes		.0		.0	.0	.5
	10.9	6.5	9.8	All Other Non-Current		16.0		11.6	2.6	11.2
	26.1	39.9	29.7	Net Worth		-5.0		25.9	36.8	43.3
	100.0	100.0	100.0	Total Liabilities & Net Worth		100.0		100.0	100.0	100.0
				INCOME DATA						
	100.0	100.0	100.0	Net Sales		100.0		100.0	100.0	100.0
	35.3	36.8	34.1	Gross Profit		46.1		31.3	28.4	30.8
	32.0	31.7	28.0	Operating Expenses		45.3		26.4	20.4	21.3
	3.2	5.1	6.0	Operating Profit		.8		4.8	8.0	9.5
	1.4	1.3	1.1	All Other Expenses (net)		1.3		.5	.6	1.7
	1.8	3.8	5.0	Profit Before Taxes		-.5		4.3	7.4	7.9
				RATIOS						
	2.6	3.1	2.8			1.7		2.3	3.0	3.8
	1.6	1.9	1.7	Current		1.1		1.1	1.7	2.5
	1.1	1.1	1.0			.8		.9	1.0	1.7
	1.3	1.8	1.5			1.0		1.5	1.9	1.9
	.8	1.0	.8	Quick		.7		.8	.7	1.1
	.5	.6	.5			.2		.5	.4	.7
	32 11.3	40 9.1	41 8.9		23 15.6		43 8.5	41 9.0	42 8.8	
	49 7.5	54 6.8	54 6.8	Sales/Receivables	49 7.5		54 6.8	46 7.9	55 6.7	
	58 6.2	63 5.8	64 5.7		70 5.2		59 6.2	66 5.6	64 5.7	
	51 7.1	46 8.0	44 8.2		22 16.9		38 9.5	46 7.9	73 5.0	
	75 4.9	83 4.4	81 4.5	Cost of Sales/Inventory	89 4.1		51 7.2	76 4.8	102 3.6	
	153 2.4	130 2.8	147 2.5		183 2.0		93 3.9	116 3.1	156 2.3	
	20 18.3	19 18.9	17 21.3		43 8.4		14 26.2	22 16.6	16 22.4	
	30 12.0	31 11.7	29 12.5	Cost of Sales/Payables	51 7.1		22 16.5	27 13.5	27 13.3	
	54 6.8	49 7.4	46 8.0		64 5.7		45 8.2	40 9.2	33 11.1	
	4.3	4.2	4.0			8.6		4.2	3.6	3.8
	9.6	6.1	8.7	Sales/Working Capital		42.7		50.2	5.6	4.9
	22.5	28.3	-161.0			-18.9		-60.8	442.1	6.0
	3.9	10.9	16.9					5.4	57.5	41.8
(58)	1.7	(62) 3.2	(63) 3.8	EBIT/Interest		(18) 3.2		3.8	(19) 7.2	
	-.8	1.0	1.5					.5	1.7	1.8
	3.6	5.1	5.0	Net Profit + Depr., Dep.,						3.6
(17)	.8	(14) 1.4	(20) 1.9	Amort./Cur. Mat. L/T/D					(12) 1.9	
	.0	.8	1.2							.7
	.4	.2	.4			.6		.4	.4	.3
	.9	.7	.9	Fixed/Worth		3.6		1.2	.5	.7
	2.5	2.4	4.2			-.9		17.5	-.5	1.1
	.7	.5	.5			3.8		1.3	.3	.4
	2.2	1.7	2.4	Debt/Worth		12.4		3.2	1.2	1.4
	17.6	5.2	38.1			-3.2		240.0	-4.1	3.3
	38.0	38.7	59.1	% Profit Before Taxes/Tangible				79.7		48.6
(51)	9.2	(59) 16.1	(56) 27.0	Net Worth				(17) 37.8	(19) 24.7	
	-7.5	2.2	8.4					3.6		11.0
	9.7	12.9	19.8	% Profit Before Taxes/Total		16.8		13.0	23.9	21.5
	1.8	5.8	5.9	Assets		4.3		5.5	11.7	11.8
	-5.5	.2	1.6			-12.3		-1.0	1.6	1.8
	16.8	16.7	21.5			52.8		25.6	27.6	9.4
	8.3	8.2	9.2	Sales/Net Fixed Assets		16.6		11.4	6.6	8.3
	4.1	4.5	5.4			4.6		3.6	5.6	5.1
	2.7	2.4	2.5			3.0		3.1	2.5	1.9
	1.9	1.9	1.9	Sales/Total Assets		2.2		2.2	1.7	1.6
	1.3	1.3	1.3			1.3		1.4	1.2	1.3
	1.8	1.4	1.5					1.4	.8	2.2
(55)	2.7	(63) 2.8	(64) 2.5	% Depr., Dep., Amort./Sales			(20)	2.3	2.2	2.5
	4.9	4.6	4.2					4.7	3.7	3.8
	2.5	4.3	2.1					2.1		
(22)	6.3	(28) 6.6	(26) 3.9	% Officers', Directors', Owners' Comp/Sales			(13)	3.9		
	9.1	10.3	5.7					7.9		
	1107311M	1214180M	2091642M	Net Sales ($)	1669M	20287M	16851M	139062M	165215M	1748558M
	805742M	840919M	1206248M	Total Assets ($)	2251M	11263M	6093M	72701M	103011M	1010929M

© RMA 2005

M = $ thousand   MM = $ million
See Pages 11 through 21 for Explanation of Ratios and Data

Current Data Sorted By Assets   **Comparative Historical Data**

Current Data asset-size groups: **15 (4/1-9/30/04)** covers 0-500M, 500M-2MM; **37 (10/1/04-3/31/05)** covers 2-10MM through 100-250MM.

Comparative Historical columns: **4/1/00-3/31/01 ALL** and **4/1/01-3/31/02 ALL**.

0-500M	500M-2MM	2-10MM	10-50MM	50-100MM	100-250MM		4/1/00-3/31/01 ALL	4/1/01-3/31/02 ALL
						Type of Statement		
		3	7	1	1	Unqualified	8	5
	1	13	3			Reviewed	1	4
2	6	2	1			Compiled	5	4
1	1					Tax Returns		
	3	4		1	2	Other	8	3
3	11	22	11	2	3	**NUMBER OF STATEMENTS**	22	16
%	%	%	%	%	%	**ASSETS**	%	%
	5.0	7.7	1.5			Cash & Equivalents	8.3	4.8
	24.6	22.2	18.4			Trade Receivables (net)	25.1	24.7
	28.9	35.1	35.9			Inventory	29.9	29.9
	.5	3.4	3.6			All Other Current	1.6	2.2
	58.9	68.4	59.3			Total Current	65.0	61.6
	29.7	20.0	25.2			Fixed Assets (net)	23.2	30.7
	.5	2.6	8.1			Intangibles (net)	5.7	2.6
	10.9	9.0	7.4			All Other Non-Current	6.0	5.1
	100.0	100.0	100.0			Total	100.0	100.0
						LIABILITIES		
	7.5	14.4	12.3			Notes Payable-Short Term	25.8	9.3
	4.9	2.3	7.3			Cur. Mat.-L/T/D	3.1	3.6
	14.2	10.6	13.5			Trade Payables	15.8	15.6
	.1	.2	.1			Income Taxes Payable	.1	.0
	17.4	6.2	6.6			All Other Current	6.5	4.6
	44.2	33.7	39.8			Total Current	51.3	33.1
	18.7	11.1	20.2			Long-Term Debt	17.1	15.4
	.5	.4	.5			Deferred Taxes	.4	1.1
	2.5	3.0	3.5			All Other Non-Current	3.8	3.1
	34.2	51.8	36.0			Net Worth	27.4	47.4
	100.0	100.0	100.0			Total Liabilities & Net Worth	100.0	100.0
						INCOME DATA		
	100.0	100.0	100.0			Net Sales	100.0	100.0
	42.9	34.8	22.2			Gross Profit	31.6	34.1
	44.6	29.8	19.8			Operating Expenses	25.3	31.2
	-1.7	5.0	2.5			Operating Profit	6.3	2.8
	.2	1.0	1.4			All Other Expenses (net)	1.6	.5
	-2.0	4.0	1.1			Profit Before Taxes	4.8	2.3
						RATIOS		
	1.9	4.2	3.1				3.7	3.1
	1.4	1.9	1.4			Current	2.2	2.2
	1.2	1.4	1.2				1.3	1.3
	1.1	1.4	.8				1.7	1.8
	.8	.8	.5			Quick	1.1	1.1
	.2	.5	.4				.5	.4
	17 22.0	35 10.3	34 10.8				41 9.0	36 10.0
	49 7.5	51 7.2	43 8.4			Sales/Receivables	49 7.5	46 7.9
	59 6.2	74 4.9	55 6.6				63 5.8	56 6.5
	57 6.4	52 7.0	70 5.2				51 7.2	52 7.1
	106 3.5	117 3.1	116 3.1			Cost of Sales/Inventory	75 4.8	85 4.3
	123 3.0	199 1.8	153 2.4				118 3.1	116 3.1
	24 15.0	15 24.8	18 20.6				21 17.3	22 16.4
	26 13.9	30 12.3	33 11.0			Cost of Sales/Payables	33 11.1	34 10.6
	49 7.4	76 4.8	51 7.2				51 7.1	44 8.3
	5.5	3.1	3.6				3.4	4.4
	10.4	5.5	7.7			Sales/Working Capital	5.8	6.5
	28.1	7.8	21.6				17.1	17.1
	10.8	12.6	6.3				6.9	6.1
	(18) 2.4	5.0	(10) 1.6			EBIT/Interest	(18) 4.1	(14) 2.8
	-1.2	2.1	.1				1.8	1.1
						Net Profit + Depr., Dep., Amort./Cur. Mat. L./T/D		
	.2	.1	.4				.1	.4
	.9	.2	.7			Fixed/Worth	.6	.6
	1.8	.6	1.7				23.6	1.5
	1.0	.5	.9				.4	.4
	2.0	1.2	1.5			Debt/Worth	1.1	.9
	2.7	2.2	5.1				53.4	2.6
	28.8	40.2					46.8	29.2
	(10) 12.0	7.9				% Profit Before Taxes/Tangible Net Worth	(18) 21.8	(15) 11.0
	-24.9	2.3					10.3	1.8
	8.4	13.1	5.4				15.5	9.2
	4.5	3.9	2.3			% Profit Before Taxes/Total Assets	10.1	5.4
	-9.1	1.6	-2.3				4.3	.5
	29.4	29.8	19.1				29.4	11.5
	8.4	12.2	5.2			Sales/Net Fixed Assets	8.6	6.8
	3.9	4.2	3.9				4.3	4.3
	2.4	1.7	2.0				2.4	2.3
	2.0	1.5	1.4			Sales/Total Assets	2.1	1.9
	1.6	1.2	1.1				1.1	1.4
		1.1	2.1				.5	1.1
	(21)	2.2	(10) 3.7			% Depr., Dep., Amort./Sales	(13) 1.4	(14) 3.2
		5.3	4.8				2.7	4.1
	3.6							
	(10) 7.8					% Officers', Directors', Owners' Comp/Sales		
	10.9							
3760M	37592M	151187M	360492M	216262M	642440M	Net Sales ($)	1268270M	535180M
1223M	15399M	97927M	235650M	133034M	521402M	Total Assets ($)	1021785M	307364M

M = $ thousand   MM = $ million
See Pages 11 through 21 for Explanation of Ratios and Data

Comparative Historical Data | **Current Data Sorted By Sales**

			Type of Statement	0-1MM	1-3MM	3-5MM	5-10MM	10-25MM	25MM & OVER
14	14	12	Unqualified		1		1	6	5
11	15	17	Reviewed		7	5	7	2	2
4	12	11	Compiled		5	1	3	1	1
2	2	2	Tax Returns	1		1			
12	16	10	Other		5	1	1		3
4/1/02-	4/1/03-	4/1/04-			15 (4/1-9/30/04)		37 (10/1/04-3/31/05)		
3/31/03	3/31/04	3/31/05							
ALL	ALL	ALL							
43	59	52	**NUMBER OF STATEMENTS**	1	11	8	12	9	11
%	%	%	**ASSETS**	%	%	%	%	%	%
5.1	4.1	5.3	Cash & Equivalents		4.2		7.3		2.3
20.5	23.3	22.3	Trade Receivables (net)		22.3		26.1		19.3
32.5	35.1	33.1	Inventory		31.8		26.4		30.1
2.8	2.8	2.7	All Other Current		1.4		2.5		4.3
60.9	65.4	63.4	Total Current		59.7		62.3		56.0
29.5	24.5	25.3	Fixed Assets (net)		31.4		26.2		36.9
3.5	3.8	3.4	Intangibles (net)		.5		2.9		2.1
6.2	6.4	8.0	All Other Non-Current		8.4		8.6		4.9
100.0	100.0	100.0	Total		100.0		100.0		100.0
			LIABILITIES						
16.4	18.0	11.8	Notes Payable-Short Term		15.8		6.1		7.5
5.6	4.4	4.3	Cur. Mat.-L/T/D		3.8		3.8		6.1
13.3	13.8	12.4	Trade Payables		14.5		12.4		14.0
.0	.3	.2	Income Taxes Payable		.0		.1		.3
9.0	8.7	8.8	All Other Current		6.2		12.2		7.3
44.3	45.2	37.4	Total Current		40.4		34.5		35.2
17.8	11.9	15.2	Long-Term Debt		19.3		11.1		15.8
.5	.4	.6	Deferred Taxes		.5		.6		1.2
5.4	6.1	2.7	All Other Non-Current		1.1		1.3		3.9
32.1	36.5	44.1	Net Worth		38.7		52.5		44.0
100.0	100.0	100.0	Total Liabilities & Net Worth		100.0		100.0		100.0
			INCOME DATA						
100.0	100.0	100.0	Net Sales		100.0		100.0		100.0
30.8	31.1	33.4	Gross Profit		37.7		38.0		21.9
26.9	27.5	29.8	Operating Expenses		33.3		37.3		16.4
3.8	3.7	3.6	Operating Profit		4.4		.7		5.5
1.8	1.2	.9	All Other Expenses (net)		1.3		.7		1.3
2.1	2.4	2.7	Profit Before Taxes		3.1		.0		4.1
			RATIOS						
2.4	2.0	2.7			1.7		5.7		3.1
1.4	1.4	1.7	Current		1.4		1.9		1.7
1.0	1.1	1.3			1.2		1.1		1.3
1.1	1.0	1.1			1.0		3.1		.9
.6	.5	.8	Quick		.6		1.0		.8
.3	.4	.5			.3		.6		.5
32 11.3	37 9.9	35 10.6		36 10.2			32 11.5		33 11.0
46 7.9	47 7.8	48 7.6	Sales/Receivables	48 7.5			51 7.1		44 8.3
58 6.3	56 6.5	59 6.2		59 6.2			70 5.2		50 7.3
54 6.8	48 7.6	58 6.3		67 5.5			21 17.6		39 9.3
101 3.6	96 3.8	105 3.5	Cost of Sales/Inventory	106 3.5			69 5.3		70 5.2
139 2.6	147 2.5	163 2.2		248 1.5			147 2.5		125 2.9
20 18.6	24 14.9	18 20.3		21 17.6			13 27.5		15 23.6
38 9.5	37 9.9	31 11.8	Cost of Sales/Payables	43 8.5			28 13.1		33 10.9
54 6.7	56 6.5	50 7.3		93 3.9			50 7.3		45 8.0
4.8	5.3	3.8			5.5		3.1		3.6
11.3	11.0	6.7	Sales/Working Capital		6.8		7.3		7.4
−75.5	26.7	16.2			18.1		26.2		21.6
6.0	8.1	12.4			10.8		13.9		18.3
(40) 2.6	(55) 3.0	(47) 3.7	EBIT/Interest		1.8	(10)	5.4	(10)	4.4
.6	.6	1.5			−1.2		1.1		.1
4.3	7.5	3.6	Net Profit + Depr., Dep.,						
(17) 2.4	(12) 3.4	(11) 2.0	Amort./Cur. Mat. L/T/D						
.9	.3	.6							
.4	.3	.2			.3		.1		.5
.9	.7	.5	Fixed/Worth		.7		.3		1.0
2.4	1.4	1.2			1.6		1.8		1.6
.9	.8	.7			1.0		.3		.6
1.6	1.6	1.5	Debt/Worth		1.8		1.2		1.2
7.4	5.4	2.3			2.3		2.5		2.1
21.9	24.4	32.7	% Profit Before Taxes/Tangible		60.4		32.9		36.4
(37) 7.8	(48) 8.0	(49) 12.9	Net Worth	(10) 12.9			9.5	(10)	16.1
−1.8	−.8	3.1			−15.0		2.3		3.1
6.7	8.5	12.2	% Profit Before Taxes/Total		20.9		12.6		15.3
3.4	3.6	3.9	Assets		2.8		4.3		3.7
−1.9	−1.5	.8			−5.7		1.5		−1.6
20.0	25.4	28.4			8.7		24.7		9.6
6.2	9.6	8.3	Sales/Net Fixed Assets		4.9		11.8		3.9
3.8	3.7	3.9			3.4		3.5		2.8
2.4	2.4	2.2			2.4		3.3		2.0
1.6	1.8	1.6	Sales/Total Assets		1.6		1.6		1.6
1.0	1.3	1.2			1.0		1.4		1.2
2.2	1.1	1.3			1.0		1.6		
(37) 3.4	(46) 2.4	(44) 2.7	% Depr., Dep., Amort./Sales		2.9		(10) 3.4		
5.8	4.6	4.7			7.4		6.9		
1.9	1.1	3.4	% Officers', Directors',						
(12) 3.8	(21) 4.3	(21) 5.8	Owners' Comp/Sales						
6.2	6.6	10.6							
799962M	1387695M	1411733M	Net Sales ($)	959M	21621M	33014M	86855M	145160M	1124124M
511756M	1011960M	1004635M	Total Assets ($)	306M	18177M	22493M	47122M	115029M	801508M

M = $ thousand   MM = $ million
See Pages 11 through 21 for Explanation of Ratios and Data

Current Data Sorted By Assets							Comparative Historical Data		
		2	3	1	1	Type of Statement			
		1	2			Unqualified		7	2
	2	1	2			Reviewed		5	9
1	1	1				Compiled		4	4
	1	1	4			Tax Returns		1	2
	1	4	3	3	2	Other		8	13
	6 (4/1-9/30/04)		25 (10/1/04-3/31/05)					4/1/00-3/31/01	4/1/01-3/31/02
0-500M	500M-2MM	2-10MM	10-50MM	50-100MM	100-250MM			ALL	ALL
1	4	9	10	4	3	NUMBER OF STATEMENTS		25	30
%	%	%	%	%	%	ASSETS		%	%
			5.5			Cash & Equivalents		4.0	5.0
			25.2			Trade Receivables (net)		24.1	22.6
			28.3			Inventory		29.5	35.3
			2.3			All Other Current		3.0	2.3
			61.2			Total Current		60.6	65.3
			24.4			Fixed Assets (net)		26.3	22.5
			9.6			Intangibles (net)		3.0	5.3
			4.8			All Other Non-Current		10.1	6.9
			100.0			Total		100.0	100.0
						LIABILITIES			
			9.7			Notes Payable-Short Term		9.3	9.6
			3.5			Cur. Mat.-L/T/D		2.8	3.1
			11.7			Trade Payables		10.7	14.0
			.2			Income Taxes Payable		.1	.1
			6.8			All Other Current		12.7	11.7
			31.9			Total Current		35.6	38.5
			23.5			Long-Term Debt		16.3	16.0
			.7			Deferred Taxes		.3	.2
			2.9			All Other Non-Current		1.7	3.5
			41.0			Net Worth		46.2	41.8
			100.0			Total Liabilities & Net Worth		100.0	100.0
						INCOME DATA			
			100.0			Net Sales		100.0	100.0
			32.8			Gross Profit		31.3	32.5
			26.5			Operating Expenses		25.3	29.6
			6.3			Operating Profit		6.1	3.0
			1.0			All Other Expenses (net)		.8	1.3
			5.3			Profit Before Taxes		5.2	1.7
						RATIOS			
			2.6					2.6	2.6
			2.0			Current		1.6	1.9
			1.4					1.1	1.3
			1.5					1.3	1.3
			.8			Quick		.8	.7
			.8					.6	.6
		41	8.9				35	10.5	31 11.7
		53	6.8			Sales/Receivables	43	8.6	40 9.1
		64	5.7				51	7.1	55 6.7
		47	7.7				49	7.5	54 6.8
		100	3.7			Cost of Sales/Inventory	77	4.7	94 3.9
		136	2.7				112	3.3	138 2.6
		23	16.0				17	21.8	18 20.0
		38	9.6			Cost of Sales/Payables	23	15.7	27 13.4
		47	7.7				37	9.9	64 5.7
			4.1					5.2	4.1
			5.5			Sales/Working Capital		11.0	6.6
			9.3					25.8	17.9
								10.4	6.0
						EBIT/Interest	(19)	3.1	(27) 1.3
								1.1	.4
						Net Profit + Depr., Dep.,			9.1
						Amort./Cur. Mat. L /T/D		(10)	3.5
									1.5
			.3					.2	.2
			.9			Fixed/Worth		.6	.5
			21.8					1.0	1.0
			.8					.7	.5
			1.6			Debt/Worth		1.3	1.1
			102.6					2.5	3.1
						% Profit Before Taxes/Tangible		60.4	47.5
						Net Worth	(27)	13.8	9.5
								-1.4	-5.8
			17.5					20.6	16.3
			7.8			% Profit Before Taxes/Total		7.9	1.0
			1.5			Assets		-.1	-2.6
			13.2					22.8	24.4
			9.5			Sales/Net Fixed Assets		8.9	13.4
			4.3					4.6	5.7
			1.9					2.3	2.3
			1.8			Sales/Total Assets		1.9	1.9
			1.4					1.6	1.3
			1.6					1.2	1.0
			2.2			% Depr., Dep., Amort./Sales	(20)	2.2	(26) 2.4
			4.8					3.3	3.4
						% Officers', Directors', Owners' Comp/Sales			
928M	16367M	107444M	412189M	409199M	793428M	Net Sales ($)		1350765M	1288201M
430M	5284M	54454M	244941M	217279M	477073M	Total Assets ($)		759534M	645124M

© RMA 2005

M = $ thousand   MM = $ million
See Pages 11 through 21 for Explanation of Ratios and Data

Comparative Historical Data — **Current Data Sorted By Sales**

Current data groupings: 6 (4/1-9/30/04) covers 0-1MM and 1-3MM; 25 (10/1/04-3/31/05) covers 3-5MM through 25MM & Over.

4/1/02-3/31/03 ALL	4/1/03-3/31/04 ALL	4/1/04-3/31/05 ALL	Type of Statement	0-1MM	1-3MM	3-5MM	5-10MM	10-25MM	25MM & OVER
3	10	7	Unqualified					2	5
9	13	3	Reviewed				1		2
2	8	5	Compiled		1	1		2	1
1	3	3	Tax Returns	1			1	1	
8	7	13	Other			2	2	1	8
23	41	31	**NUMBER OF STATEMENTS**	1	1	3	4	6	16
%	%	%	**ASSETS**	%	%	%	%	%	%
6.7	5.3	6.8	Cash & Equivalents						5.5
30.5	28.1	23.9	Trade Receivables (net)						26.7
33.4	35.0	37.0	Inventory						30.1
2.4	3.7	2.0	All Other Current						2.6
73.0	72.0	69.7	Total Current						64.9
19.8	18.9	17.2	Fixed Assets (net)						20.4
2.9	2.7	7.8	Intangibles (net)						10.5
4.3	6.3	5.3	All Other Non-Current						4.3
100.0	100.0	100.0	Total						100.0
			LIABILITIES						
9.5	10.8	11.1	Notes Payable-Short Term						12.8
3.4	2.4	2.2	Cur. Mat.-L/T/D						2.3
13.6	14.8	12.0	Trade Payables						12.9
.3	.4	.1	Income Taxes Payable						.3
13.2	11.1	9.9	All Other Current						11.3
40.0	39.5	35.2	Total Current						39.6
12.7	10.5	14.7	Long-Term Debt						18.5
.1	.6	.3	Deferred Taxes						.5
5.0	9.3	5.1	All Other Non-Current						4.9
42.2	40.2	44.6	Net Worth						36.4
100.0	100.0	100.0	Total Liabilities & Net Worth						100.0
			INCOME DATA						
100.0	100.0	100.0	Net Sales						100.0
34.2	33.8	33.0	Gross Profit						31.4
29.6	30.6	27.8	Operating Expenses						26.1
4.7	3.3	5.1	Operating Profit						5.3
.5	1.0	.6	All Other Expenses (net)						1.2
4.2	2.2	4.6	Profit Before Taxes						4.1
			RATIOS						
2.3 / 1.9 / 1.4	2.6 / 2.0 / 1.4	2.9 / 2.0 / 1.4	Current						2.1 / 1.6 / 1.3
1.4 / .9 / .6	1.3 / .9 / .6	2.0 / .8 / .6	Quick						1.0 / .8 / .7
40 9.1 / 49 7.4 / 66 5.6	38 9.5 / 48 7.7 / 62 5.9	32 11.3 / 42 8.8 / 62 5.9	Sales/Receivables						38 9.6 / 52 7.1 / 65 5.6
56 6.6 / 88 4.1 / 139 2.6	72 5.1 / 96 3.8 / 131 2.8	63 5.8 / 97 3.8 / 144 2.5	Cost of Sales/Inventory						54 6.8 / 78 4.7 / 114 3.2
22 16.6 / 30 12.4 / 46 7.9	23 15.8 / 30 12.4 / 47 7.7	19 19.0 / 31 11.6 / 45 8.1	Cost of Sales/Payables						24 15.0 / 33 11.1 / 49 7.4
5.0 / 6.4 / 9.3	4.1 / 6.3 / 11.3	4.1 / 6.0 / 11.5	Sales/Working Capital						5.2 / 7.1 / 15.3
18.8 / (22) 4.4 / 2.4	12.8 / (39) 4.4 / -.2	25.7 / (28) 6.6 / 1.8	EBIT/Interest						16.9 / (14) 2.8 / 1.4
	5.1 / (12) 2.8 / 1.8	3.7 / (11) 1.9 / 1.0	Net Profit + Depr., Dep., Amort./Cur. Mat. L/T/D						
.2 / .4 / .9	.2 / .4 / 1.3	.2 / .4 / 1.4	Fixed/Worth						.3 / .5 / 7.7
.7 / 1.1 / 2.4	.7 / 1.2 / 4.0	.6 / 1.1 / 3.8	Debt/Worth						.8 / 1.6 / 29.5
37.7 / (21) 21.6 / 5.4	39.2 / (38) 9.5 / .4	47.1 / (27) 20.9 / 5.9	% Profit Before Taxes/Tangible Net Worth						53.5 / (14) 24.4 / 2.7
18.2 / 4.9 / 2.3	11.4 / 4.6 / -.1	19.7 / 8.1 / 1.6	% Profit Before Taxes/Total Assets						19.2 / 3.9 / 1.3
26.1 / 17.0 / 8.0	29.9 / 14.5 / 6.6	36.6 / 14.4 / 8.6	Sales/Net Fixed Assets						17.7 / 9.9 / 7.1
2.5 / 2.1 / 1.7	2.5 / 2.2 / 1.5	2.2 / 1.9 / 1.7	Sales/Total Assets						2.0 / 1.8 / 1.7
.7 / (22) 1.8 / 2.5	.9 / (39) 1.7 / 3.1	.6 / (25) 1.8 / 2.9	% Depr., Dep., Amort./Sales						1.1 / (13) 1.9 / 3.8
	(16) 1.9 / 5.7 / 8.9		% Officers', Directors', Owners' Comp/Sales						
1503110M	1299598M	1739555M	Net Sales ($)	928M	2058M	12389M	24465M	97577M	1602138M
715808M	745415M	999461M	Total Assets ($)	430M	537M	5293M	13457M	68698M	911046M

M = $ thousand   MM = $ million
See Pages 11 through 21 for Explanation of Ratios and Data

Current Data Sorted By Assets   Comparative Historical Data

							Type of Statement		
		1	8	13	2	4	Unqualified	30	33
		3	10	7			Reviewed	16	14
	1	5	8		1		Compiled	17	13
	2	3					Tax Returns	3	
	1	4	12	11	1	1	Other	28	32
		20 (4/1-9/30/04)		78 (10/1/04-3/31/05)				4/1/00-3/31/01	4/1/01-3/31/02
0-500M	500M-2MM	2-10MM	10-50MM	50-100MM	100-250MM			ALL	ALL
4	16	38	31	4	5	**NUMBER OF STATEMENTS**	94	92
%	%	%	%	%	%	**ASSETS**	%	%
	7.0	6.0	9.6			Cash & Equivalents	4.7	5.5
	28.4	30.2	20.3			Trade Receivables (net)	29.3	27.0
	30.0	37.3	29.1			Inventory	29.5	32.3
	4.9	1.6	1.1			All Other Current	2.0	1.4
	70.4	75.0	60.1			Total Current	65.5	66.1
	18.6	17.2	18.2			Fixed Assets (net)	22.3	22.6
	8.5	1.9	12.6			Intangibles (net)	4.0	3.7
	2.5	5.9	9.0			All Other Non-Current	8.2	7.6
	100.0	100.0	100.0			Total	100.0	100.0
						LIABILITIES		
	8.5	17.0	5.9			Notes Payable-Short Term	11.7	15.6
	5.4	2.8	3.4			Cur. Mat.-L/T/D	3.7	3.7
	20.2	16.0	8.4			Trade Payables	14.8	15.6
	.0	.3	.5			Income Taxes Payable	.3	.3
	12.0	10.6	8.2			All Other Current	8.6	6.8
	46.1	46.7	26.5			Total Current	39.2	41.9
	16.2	12.6	18.0			Long-Term Debt	15.0	14.6
	.0	.4	.9			Deferred Taxes	.3	.3
	11.2	3.2	5.0			All Other Non-Current	4.1	2.8
	26.5	37.1	49.6			Net Worth	41.5	40.3
	100.0	100.0	100.0			Total Liabilities & Net Worth	100.0	100.0
						INCOME DATA		
	100.0	100.0	100.0			Net Sales	100.0	100.0
	35.8	29.4	31.2			Gross Profit	32.2	30.6
	31.9	24.3	21.3			Operating Expenses	26.7	25.7
	3.9	5.1	9.9			Operating Profit	5.6	4.9
	1.5	.8	1.6			All Other Expenses (net)	1.3	1.9
	2.4	4.3	8.2			Profit Before Taxes	4.2	2.9
						RATIOS		
	2.9	2.6	4.9				2.8	2.6
	1.4	1.4	2.3			Current	1.7	1.8
	1.0	1.2	1.5				1.2	1.2
	1.9	1.3	2.4				1.4	1.3
	.7	.9	1.1			Quick	.9	.9
	.5	.5	.7				.6	.5
40 9.2	34 10.9	42 8.8				Sales/Receivables	42 8.8	42 8.7
46 7.9	52 7.1	50 7.3					50 7.4	46 7.9
53 6.9	64 5.7	62 5.9					61 6.0	54 6.7
17 22.1	55 6.6	67 5.4				Cost of Sales/Inventory	55 6.6	52 7.0
58 6.3	99 3.7	98 3.7					80 4.6	90 4.1
85 4.3	142 2.6	166 2.2					110 3.3	140 2.6
31 11.9	17 21.2	17 22.0				Cost of Sales/Payables	17 21.2	20 18.0
48 7.5	33 11.0	30 12.0					33 11.1	36 10.1
75 4.9	46 7.9	41 9.0					51 7.2	53 6.9
6.6	4.1	2.8				Sales/Working Capital	4.4	4.4
10.9	7.7	4.7					6.9	6.6
NM	27.8	7.5					20.6	17.2
38.3	10.5	20.7				EBIT/Interest	8.8	6.4
(13) 1.9	(33) 4.9	(25) 6.3					(88) 2.9	(87) 2.1
−1.4	2.5	2.4					1.3	.8
	7.3	6.9				Net Profit + Depr., Dep.,	5.2	4.7
(11) 4.3	(13) 4.7				Amort./Cur. Mat. L /T/D	(27) 2.3	(23) .8
	2.4	1.5					1.0	−.1
.2	.1	.2				Fixed/Worth	.2	.2
1.2	.4	.4					.5	.5
NM	1.0	.7					1.0	1.4
.6	.9	.5				Debt/Worth	.8	.6
2.9	1.8	1.5					1.5	1.7
−34.4	4.5	2.9					4.4	4.1
94.3	53.1	30.4				% Profit Before Taxes/Tangible	38.7	27.9
(11) 31.3	(34) 20.1	(26) 14.9				Net Worth	(86) 14.3	(84) 9.3
9.2	8.9	9.3					4.9	−.5
23.1	12.8	17.9				% Profit Before Taxes/Total	13.1	12.0
.9	7.5	8.5				Assets	5.5	3.7
−7.4	2.8	3.7					1.3	−.5
35.9	39.9	19.3				Sales/Net Fixed Assets	28.2	20.8
15.0	13.7	10.1					9.7	9.2
8.1	6.1	6.1					5.0	4.5
3.3	2.8	1.7				Sales/Total Assets	2.7	2.4
2.7	1.9	1.5					1.9	1.8
2.0	1.5	1.2					1.4	1.3
1.4	.7	2.2				% Depr., Dep., Amort./Sales	.8	.8
(13) 2.3	(32) 1.9	(25) 2.5					(82) 2.1	(84) 2.3
4.3	4.2	3.2					3.6	3.6
2.0						% Officers', Directors',	1.6	1.5
(10) 3.7						Owners' Comp/Sales	(33) 3.5	(29) 3.8
9.2							6.6	6.1
3625M	53125M	438646M	924252M	396134M	935505M	Net Sales ($)	2400456M	2049816M
1403M	20644M	207906M	662432M	253732M	808446M	Total Assets ($)	1707243M	1365528M

M = $ thousand   MM = $ million
See Pages 11 through 21 for Explanation of Ratios and Data

Comparative Historical Data | Current Data Sorted By Sales

			Type of Statement						
34	25	28	Unqualified			2	2	9	15
20	22	20	Reviewed		1	3	5	6	5
8	12	15	Compiled	1	2	5	2	4	1
	2	5	Tax Returns	2	2	1			
28	27	30	Other	1	1	3	8	10	7
4/1/02-	4/1/03-	4/1/04-			20 (4/1-9/30/04)		78 (10/1/04-3/31/05)		
3/31/03	3/31/04	3/31/05		0-1MM	1-3MM	3-5MM	5-10MM	10-25MM	25MM & OVER
ALL	ALL	ALL							
90	88	98	**NUMBER OF STATEMENTS**	4	6	14	17	29	28
%	%	%	**ASSETS**	%	%	%	%	%	%
6.2	6.7	7.4	Cash & Equivalents			7.3	7.6	7.9	8.4
25.5	25.6	26.3	Trade Receivables (net)			26.0	28.8	25.3	25.1
30.9	31.4	31.6	Inventory			29.1	36.7	33.3	28.2
2.0	2.4	2.1	All Other Current			4.8	3.3	1.2	1.4
64.5	66.1	67.4	Total Current			67.2	76.3	67.7	63.1
24.0	21.7	18.8	Fixed Assets (net)			26.1	15.4	14.3	19.9
4.3	6.0	6.9	Intangibles (net)			5.8	2.1	9.2	7.8
7.1	6.1	7.0	All Other Non-Current			.9	6.1	8.8	9.1
100.0	100.0	100.0	Total			100.0	100.0	100.0	100.0
			LIABILITIES						
14.2	12.3	11.1	Notes Payable-Short Term			11.9	10.6	12.7	7.7
3.2	3.2	3.4	Cur. Mat.-L/T/D			4.2	1.5	3.1	3.3
13.5	12.9	13.5	Trade Payables			17.5	12.4	13.3	8.8
.2	.3	.3	Income Taxes Payable			.0	.5	.2	.5
7.6	9.7	10.6	All Other Current			12.3	12.6	7.9	9.8
38.6	38.3	38.8	Total Current			45.9	37.6	37.2	30.1
11.5	10.1	15.5	Long-Term Debt			15.9	13.7	13.2	15.3
.5	.4	.5	Deferred Taxes			.4	.5	.2	1.1
4.0	6.5	5.1	All Other Non-Current			.6	4.0	5.3	2.0
45.4	44.7	40.1	Net Worth			37.1	44.3	44.1	51.4
100.0	100.0	100.0	Total Liabilities & Net Worth			100.0	100.0	100.0	100.0
			INCOME DATA						
100.0	100.0	100.0	Net Sales			100.0	100.0	100.0	100.0
31.1	32.3	32.5	Gross Profit			35.6	32.4	30.5	32.4
26.6	27.3	25.9	Operating Expenses			31.4	25.5	23.0	22.1
4.5	5.0	6.6	Operating Profit			4.2	6.9	7.5	10.3
.9	1.4	1.1	All Other Expenses (net)			1.0	.4	1.9	.5
3.6	3.6	5.5	Profit Before Taxes			3.3	6.5	5.6	9.8
			RATIOS						
3.2	3.3	3.3				2.7	5.3	3.4	4.8
1.7	1.9	1.8	Current			1.5	1.9	1.7	2.3
1.2	1.3	1.2				1.1	1.2	1.3	1.5
1.4	1.8	1.9				1.9	2.9	1.8	2.4
.8	1.0	.9	Quick			1.0	.9	.9	1.3
.5	.5	.6				.4	.5	.5	.8

38	9.6	42	8.7	39	9.3	Sales/Receivables			35	10.3	35	10.6	38	9.5	46	8.0
49	7.4	52	7.1	50	7.3				45	8.1	53	6.9	48	7.7	55	6.6
63	5.8	63	5.8	63	5.8				52	7.0	64	5.7	63	5.8	68	5.4
59	6.2	61	6.0	56	6.6	Cost of Sales/Inventory			42	8.7	35	10.4	65	5.6	68	5.4
88	4.1	92	4.0	91	4.0				64	5.7	123	3.0	99	3.7	92	3.9
134	2.7	139	2.6	141	2.6				133	2.8	175	2.1	150	2.4	120	3.1
20	18.2	20	18.5	18	20.2	Cost of Sales/Payables			24	15.3	10	38.2	23	15.7	16	22.8
31	11.9	31	11.8	33	11.0				37	9.9	33	11.0	37	10.0	22	16.4
47	7.8	47	7.8	47	7.8				70	5.2	46	7.9	48	7.6	35	10.3

3.5	3.7	3.6	Sales/Working Capital			6.4	3.1	3.2	3.3
6.4	5.8	6.5				9.4	4.6	5.6	5.0
18.2	14.5	18.9				NM	15.3	16.0	7.5

	15.2		12.5		14.4	EBIT/Interest			32.8		12.9		9.9	22.4
(87)	3.0	(77)	3.8	(81)	4.9		(11)	2.8	(14)	6.2	(24)	2.7	(23)	11.0
	1.2		.9		2.2			1.4		3.6		2.3		4.3

	7.1		7.0		7.3	Net Profit + Depr., Dep.,			12.2
(39)	1.8	(37)	3.2	(32)	4.5	Amort./Cur. Mat. L/T/D	(16)		5.5
	.8		.6		1.8				2.8

.3	.2	.2	Fixed/Worth			.6	.1	.1	.2
.5	.6	.5				1.1	.3	.3	.5
1.3	1.2	1.3				NM	.9	1.0	.7
.5	.5	.7	Debt/Worth			.7	.3	.7	.4
1.4	1.3	1.8				2.2	1.7	1.8	1.3
3.5	3.3	5.1				NM	4.1	4.0	2.7

	28.7		30.2		42.0	% Profit Before Taxes/Tangible		60.9	54.6	38.5	41.9
(80)	10.8	(77)	11.5	(82)	20.8	Net Worth	(11) 20.4 (15)	18.7 (26)	18.0 (26)	24.1
	1.7		4.1		9.1			3.3	9.1	8.9	12.0

11.0	11.0	15.0	% Profit Before Taxes/Total			14.8	20.1	11.9	20.1
5.0	6.2	7.5	Assets			2.4	8.3	7.1	12.7
.3	.3	2.1				.5	2.8	3.5	6.6
18.9	23.4	23.8	Sales/Net Fixed Assets			21.8	44.1	32.6	14.7
8.1	8.7	11.0				9.3	13.9	15.7	8.8
4.7	5.1	6.0				5.2	7.0	8.6	5.0
2.2	2.1	2.5	Sales/Total Assets			2.8	2.9	2.5	1.9
1.6	1.7	1.7				2.2	1.6	1.7	1.6
1.3	1.2	1.4				1.8	1.3	1.3	1.2

	1.2		1.2		1.2	% Depr., Dep., Amort./Sales			1.7		.8		.8	2.1
(83)	2.9	(77)	2.7	(81)	2.5		(12) 3.5	(14)	2.1	(23)	2.3	(24)	2.6
	4.0		4.7		4.0				5.6		4.0		3.1	3.3

	1.6		1.7		1.7	% Officers', Directors',
(33)	3.5	(22)	3.0	(28)	3.3	Owners' Comp/Sales
	7.6		6.1		6.8	

2600149M	2220917M	2751287M	Net Sales ($)	3119M	10838M	54740M	125992M	494541M	2062057M
1726429M	1584391M	1954563M	Total Assets ($)	2516M	4649M	26892M	73222M	339689M	1507595M

M = $ thousand   MM = $ million
See Pages 11 through 21 for Explanation of Ratios and Data

Current Data Sorted By Assets   Comparative Historical Data

0-500M	500M-2MM	2-10MM	10-50MM	50-100MM	100-250MM	Type of Statement	4/1/00-3/31/01 ALL	4/1/01-3/31/02 ALL
1		2	2	2	1	Unqualified	2	6
	3	4	1			Reviewed	3	5
2	4	3				Compiled	6	6
		1				Tax Returns		1
		1		2		Other	6	6
	9 (4/1-9/30/04)			20 (10/1/04-3/31/05)				
3	7	11	5	2	1	NUMBER OF STATEMENTS	17	24
%	%	%	%	%	%	**ASSETS**	%	%
		7.4				Cash & Equivalents	6.5	10.0
		25.8				Trade Receivables (net)	20.3	21.4
		31.1				Inventory	29.9	30.5
		1.3				All Other Current	3.1	1.8
		65.7				Total Current	59.7	63.8
		19.2				Fixed Assets (net)	33.7	28.1
		5.4				Intangibles (net)	2.6	3.8
		9.7				All Other Non-Current	4.0	4.4
		100.0				Total	100.0	100.0
						LIABILITIES		
		10.3				Notes Payable-Short Term	4.0	7.1
		2.8				Cur. Mat.-L/T/D	4.0	4.5
		11.0				Trade Payables	13.0	12.0
		.7				Income Taxes Payable	.2	.3
		10.9				All Other Current	6.6	7.1
		35.7				Total Current	27.7	31.1
		14.2				Long-Term Debt	27.6	22.2
		.3				Deferred Taxes	.5	.5
		18.6				All Other Non-Current	5.1	3.2
		31.1				Net Worth	39.0	43.0
		100.0				Total Liabilities & Net Worth	100.0	100.0
						INCOME DATA		
		100.0				Net Sales	100.0	100.0
		30.7				Gross Profit	26.8	26.7
		21.5				Operating Expenses	19.3	22.7
		9.3				Operating Profit	7.5	4.0
		3.2				All Other Expenses (net)	1.2	1.4
		6.0				Profit Before Taxes	6.3	2.6
						RATIOS		
		4.5				Current	3.7	4.0
		1.9					2.3	1.9
		1.4					1.6	1.2
		2.3				Quick	1.5	2.2
		1.3					.9	.8
		.5					.7	.7
		32 11.6				Sales/Receivables	41 9.0	39 9.3
		48 7.6					53 6.8	46 8.0
		73 5.0					70 5.2	59 6.2
		54 6.7				Cost of Sales/Inventory	72 5.1	51 7.2
		84 4.4					92 4.0	84 4.3
		140 2.6					165 2.2	138 2.6
		11 34.3				Cost of Sales/Payables	17 21.5	16 22.5
		28 13.2					35 10.4	25 14.4
		47 7.8					52 7.0	42 8.7
		3.6				Sales/Working Capital	2.6	2.3
		4.9					5.3	6.5
		9.8					8.2	18.3
		71.3				EBIT/Interest	10.2	5.9
		7.3					(23) 3.4	2.0
		2.0					1.4	.8
						Net Profit + Depr., Dep., Amort./Cur. Mat. L./T/D		
		.0				Fixed/Worth	.4	.3
		.4					1.0	.7
		-4.6					2.1	1.8
		1.2				Debt/Worth	.7	.5
		1.5					2.7	1.8
		-11.1					3.5	4.6
						% Profit Before Taxes/Tangible Net Worth	36.6	19.6
							(16) 22.2	(21) 10.8
							7.0	.3
		17.6				% Profit Before Taxes/Total Assets	12.0	8.2
		7.4					8.8	2.2
		3.0					1.6	-1.1
		159.8				Sales/Net Fixed Assets	7.1	24.6
		14.2					4.6	5.0
		4.6					2.9	2.7
		2.6				Sales/Total Assets	1.9	1.9
		1.7					1.4	1.3
		1.2					1.0	1.1
						% Depr., Dep., Amort./Sales	.2	.5
							(16) 3.3	(21) 1.9
							5.3	3.7
						% Officers', Directors', Owners' Comp/Sales		
2972M	24660M	103793M	111710M	177628M	257973M	Net Sales ($)	780134M	481787M
502M	10162M	60181M	60376M	156290M	214025M	Total Assets ($)	746369M	445014M

M = $ thousand   MM = $ million
See Pages 11 through 21 for Explanation of Ratios and Data

Comparative Historical Data & Current Data Sorted By Sales

			Type of Statement						
6	3	8	Unqualified	1			1	3	3
7	5	8	Reviewed		1	1	3	2	1
5	9	9	Compiled		3	4	2		
		1	Tax Returns					1	
8	8	3	Other					2	1
4/1/02- 3/31/03 ALL	4/1/03- 3/31/04 ALL	4/1/04- 3/31/05 ALL		0-1MM	1-3MM	3-5MM	5-10MM	10-25MM	25MM & OVER
					9 (4/1-9/30/04)			20 (10/1/04-3/31/05)	
26	25	29	NUMBER OF STATEMENTS	1	4	5	6	8	5
%	%	%	ASSETS	%	%	%	%	%	%
9.1	4.4	6.3	Cash & Equivalents						
20.9	27.4	29.9	Trade Receivables (net)						
26.8	30.9	32.7	Inventory						
1.8	3.5	1.1	All Other Current						
58.5	66.3	70.0	Total Current						
28.8	24.2	19.6	Fixed Assets (net)						
4.8	3.3	2.9	Intangibles (net)						
7.9	6.2	7.6	All Other Non-Current						
100.0	100.0	100.0	Total						
			LIABILITIES						
7.5	11.7	11.8	Notes Payable-Short Term						
6.0	3.7	2.7	Cur. Mat.-L/T/D						
9.8	14.4	16.8	Trade Payables						
.4	.3	.5	Income Taxes Payable						
4.9	6.9	11.1	All Other Current						
28.7	37.0	42.9	Total Current						
18.6	15.8	13.4	Long-Term Debt						
.5	.3	.3	Deferred Taxes						
4.2	9.6	11.1	All Other Non-Current						
48.0	37.4	32.3	Net Worth						
100.0	100.0	100.0	Total Liabilities & Net Worth						
			INCOME DATA						
100.0	100.0	100.0	Net Sales						
27.0	32.3	28.3	Gross Profit						
22.9	27.5	22.8	Operating Expenses						
4.1	4.8	5.5	Operating Profit						
.9	.8	1.9	All Other Expenses (net)						
3.2	4.0	3.7	Profit Before Taxes						
			RATIOS						
4.2	3.5	2.9							
2.1	1.7	1.9	Current						
1.2	1.1	1.2							
2.3	2.0	1.4							
1.1	.8	.8	Quick						
.5	.4	.6							
42 8.8	33 10.9	34 10.7							
50 7.3	51 7.2	52 7.0	Sales/Receivables						
59 6.1	61 6.0	70 5.2							
59 6.2	50 7.3	52 7.0							
88 4.2	103 3.5	84 4.4	Cost of Sales/Inventory						
131 2.8	170 2.2	134 2.7							
14 25.8	16 22.3	20 18.4							
28 12.9	36 10.2	34 10.8	Cost of Sales/Payables						
50 7.3	52 7.0	56 6.5							
2.6	2.6	3.6							
4.9	6.2	4.9	Sales/Working Capital						
11.4	246.6	25.7							
8.0	5.7	14.2							
(22) 2.5	(20) 2.0	(27) 4.2	EBIT/Interest						
.3	1.3	2.0							
7.4		9.0	Net Profit + Depr., Dep.,						
(12) 2.4		(10) 2.9	Amort./Cur. Mat. L/T/D						
.6		1.1							
.1	.1	.2							
.6	.7	.4	Fixed/Worth						
2.4	1.9	1.7							
.5	.5	.8							
1.5	2.3	2.5	Debt/Worth						
3.8	3.3	6.3							
23.0	32.7	41.6	% Profit Before Taxes/Tangible						
(25) 17.0	(22) 10.3	(24) 19.5	Net Worth						
−7.4	1.2	7.6							
11.5	9.8	12.7	% Profit Before Taxes/Total						
4.1	3.9	4.5	Assets						
−2.0	.3	1.7							
11.6	32.4	54.2							
4.9	9.5	12.7	Sales/Net Fixed Assets						
2.7	3.4	4.6							
1.9	2.5	2.7							
1.5	1.8	1.8	Sales/Total Assets						
1.0	1.1	1.4							
2.1	1.6	1.1							
(23) 3.4	(19) 3.6	(20) 2.1	% Depr., Dep., Amort./Sales						
4.6	6.6	5.3							
			% Officers', Directors', Owners' Comp/Sales						
878636M	547454M	678736M	Net Sales ($)	17M	7417M	18702M	47319M	110138M	495143M
840405M	497574M	501536M	Total Assets ($)	11M	3176M	8936M	31514M	64401M	393498M

Current Data Sorted By Assets   **Comparative Historical Data**

0-500M	500M-2MM	2-10MM	10-50MM	50-100MM	100-250MM	Type of Statement	4/1/00-3/31/01 ALL	4/1/01-3/31/02 ALL
		8	8	2	2	Unqualified	15	14
1	2	15	8	2	2	Reviewed	28	24
1	15	3	5			Compiled	24	20
2	2	2				Tax Returns	3	4
2	3	8	5	1		Other	29	33
	23 (4/1-9/30/04)		64 (10/1/04-3/31/05)					
6	22	36	18	3	2	**NUMBER OF STATEMENTS**	99	95
%	%	%	%	%	%	**ASSETS**	%	%
	9.1	6.8	3.1			Cash & Equivalents	7.2	7.3
	40.1	31.9	31.0			Trade Receivables (net)	30.6	28.9
	22.5	26.1	28.8			Inventory	24.3	23.3
	4.7	2.6	3.2			All Other Current	3.2	2.5
	76.4	67.4	66.1			Total Current	65.3	62.0
	15.7	23.7	27.1			Fixed Assets (net)	27.0	28.0
	.9	4.0	2.9			Intangibles (net)	2.3	3.1
	7.0	5.0	4.0			All Other Non-Current	5.4	6.9
	100.0	100.0	100.0			Total	100.0	100.0
						LIABILITIES		
	11.1	9.4	13.2			Notes Payable-Short Term	11.0	11.2
	1.9	3.8	2.0			Cur. Mat.-L/T/D	3.8	4.0
	20.0	17.6	16.0			Trade Payables	18.4	17.0
	.4	.4	.5			Income Taxes Payable	.6	.4
	9.9	6.0	7.8			All Other Current	9.2	7.7
	43.3	37.3	39.4			Total Current	43.0	40.3
	11.2	11.0	14.0			Long-Term Debt	11.2	15.3
	.4	.5	1.3			Deferred Taxes	.6	1.0
	3.1	3.6	4.4			All Other Non-Current	4.7	3.5
	42.1	47.6	40.9			Net Worth	40.5	39.9
	100.0	100.0	100.0			Total Liabilities & Net Worth	100.0	100.0
						INCOME DATA		
	100.0	100.0	100.0			Net Sales	100.0	100.0
	35.0	27.0	24.7			Gross Profit	24.5	26.8
	32.6	22.2	20.1			Operating Expenses	20.7	23.4
	2.4	4.7	4.6			Operating Profit	3.8	3.4
	.6	.3	.4			All Other Expenses (net)	1.1	1.4
	1.8	4.4	4.2			Profit Before Taxes	2.7	2.0
						RATIOS		
	3.2	3.6	2.8				2.4	2.2
	1.8	1.8	1.9			Current	1.5	1.5
	1.3	1.2	1.2				1.1	1.2
	1.8	2.3	1.5				1.4	1.2
	1.3	1.0	1.0			Quick	.9	.9
	.8	.7	.7				.6	.6
37 9.9	42 8.7	47 7.8					39 9.5	35 10.5
57 6.4	50 7.3	56 6.5				Sales/Receivables	51 7.2	46 7.9
65 5.6	62 5.9	90 4.1					58 6.3	61 6.0
16 23.1	31 11.9	41 8.9					23 15.7	25 14.7
40 9.1	54 6.7	60 6.1				Cost of Sales/Inventory	42 8.6	46 7.9
86 4.2	113 3.2	127 2.9					97 3.8	105 3.5
20 18.6	17 22.0	19 18.8					20 17.9	18 20.4
28 13.1	36 10.2	39 9.3				Cost of Sales/Payables	33 11.1	31 11.6
72 5.1	52 7.0	61 5.9					48 7.5	49 7.5
	4.8	3.7	3.6				4.9	5.8
	8.6	8.0	6.9			Sales/Working Capital	9.5	9.6
	15.1	18.8	14.1				54.7	27.7
	26.0	16.1	8.5				10.0	6.5
(19)	2.7	(34) 8.4	(16) 5.3			EBIT/Interest	(91) 2.8	(89) 2.4
	-1.2	1.5	1.7				1.1	.3
		5.4					7.4	9.2
	(12)	3.6				Net Profit + Depr., Dep., Amort./Cur. Mat. L /T/D	(32) 3.1	(30) 3.4
		1.9					1.0	1.0
	.1	.2	.5				.4	.4
	.3	.4	.9			Fixed/Worth	.6	.7
	1.0	1.7	1.2				1.4	1.5
	.5	.6	.7				.7	.7
	1.3	1.1	1.6			Debt/Worth	1.6	1.6
	4.6	4.2	3.1				3.2	3.2
	63.8	37.4	43.5				37.5	33.1
(20)	8.1	(33) 20.2	(17) 17.5			% Profit Before Taxes/Tangible Net Worth	(90) 11.8	(86) 11.9
	-7.5	1.9	8.4				2.2	-.8
	11.0	18.1	12.7				14.2	11.5
	2.6	9.1	5.9			% Profit Before Taxes/Total Assets	4.5	4.7
	-5.1	1.2	2.2				.4	-1.3
	53.5	35.3	12.1				18.3	15.9
	18.8	13.0	5.7			Sales/Net Fixed Assets	9.8	8.0
	9.4	5.4	3.9				4.3	4.2
	3.4	2.9	2.0				3.1	2.6
	2.9	2.4	1.6			Sales/Total Assets	2.1	2.0
	1.8	1.5	1.4				1.5	1.4
	.9	.8	.5				1.0	1.1
(18)	2.1	(33) 1.8	(17) 2.3			% Depr., Dep., Amort./Sales	(90) 2.1	(88) 2.3
	4.8	3.4	3.5				3.4	4.1
	2.6	1.8					1.7	1.7
(11)	4.8	(16) 3.1				% Officers', Directors', Owners' Comp/Sales	(38) 2.5	(39) 2.9
	8.7	4.2					8.4	5.8
6918M	75481M	444596M	692383M	463653M	270988M	Net Sales ($)	2571143M	1744741M
2217M	27679M	195062M	400716M	210427M	248640M	Total Assets ($)	1305259M	1092669M

M = $ thousand   MM = $ million
See Pages 11 through 21 for Explanation of Ratios and Data

Comparative Historical Data   **Current Data Sorted By Sales**

			Type of Statement						
16	19	20	Unqualified			1	2	6	11
22	23	23	Reviewed		3	3	5	11	1
19	23	19	Compiled	2	4	9	2	2	
7	5	6	Tax Returns			2	3	1	
22	26	19	Other	1	2	3	3	4	6
4/1/02-3/31/03 ALL	4/1/03-3/31/04 ALL	4/1/04-3/31/05 ALL		**23 (4/1-9/30/04)**		**64 (10/1/04-3/31/05)**			
				0-1MM	1-3MM	3-5MM	5-10MM	10-25MM	25MM & OVER
86	96	87	**NUMBER OF STATEMENTS**	3	11	19	12	24	18
%	%	%	**ASSETS**	%	%	%	%	%	%
6.4	5.9	6.8	Cash & Equivalents		8.5	9.2	6.5	4.2	4.6
28.6	30.9	33.8	Trade Receivables (net)		39.2	30.4	37.8	36.0	28.1
26.1	27.6	25.5	Inventory		17.5	21.7	23.7	30.3	30.8
3.1	2.8	3.4	All Other Current		8.0	1.8	6.9	1.3	3.3
64.1	67.2	69.4	Total Current		73.3	63.1	75.0	71.7	66.8
29.5	25.1	22.6	Fixed Assets (net)		17.3	26.2	16.5	21.4	27.0
1.6	2.4	2.6	Intangibles (net)		.5	5.3	1.4	2.8	1.9
4.8	5.3	5.4	All Other Non-Current		9.0	5.3	7.2	4.1	4.4
100.0	100.0	100.0	Total		100.0	100.0	100.0	100.0	100.0
			LIABILITIES						
10.5	15.1	10.4	Notes Payable-Short Term		7.1	11.5	13.8	11.8	8.1
4.2	3.1	3.4	Cur. Mat.-L/T/D		5.9	2.8	2.0	3.7	1.4
16.8	16.4	18.0	Trade Payables		23.9	15.1	17.8	19.6	17.1
.3	.3	.4	Income Taxes Payable		.2	.2	.8	.3	.6
9.0	9.6	7.4	All Other Current		11.1	7.4	5.1	6.3	7.8
40.8	44.4	39.6	Total Current		48.3	37.1	39.5	41.7	35.1
15.9	14.1	14.0	Long-Term Debt		27.1	13.6	3.4	12.3	14.2
1.3	.6	.6	Deferred Taxes		.7	.5	.3	.5	1.1
4.3	5.4	4.1	All Other Non-Current		3.0	4.2	3.8	3.4	3.3
37.7	35.5	41.6	Net Worth		20.9	44.6	53.0	42.0	46.2
100.0	100.0	100.0	Total Liabilities & Net Worth		100.0	100.0	100.0	100.0	100.0
			INCOME DATA						
100.0	100.0	100.0	Net Sales		100.0	100.0	100.0	100.0	100.0
26.1	28.0	28.7	Gross Profit		29.4	35.5	28.0	24.1	23.6
23.1	26.2	24.6	Operating Expenses		26.3	33.8	23.1	19.0	17.4
3.0	1.8	4.0	Operating Profit		3.1	1.7	4.9	5.1	6.2
1.1	1.3	.5	All Other Expenses (net)		.2	.5	.6	.4	.5
1.9	.5	3.6	Profit Before Taxes		2.9	1.2	4.4	4.7	5.6
			RATIOS						
2.3	2.5	3.1			3.6	3.1	4.4	2.6	3.1
1.6	1.7	1.8	Current		1.5	1.9	2.1	1.7	2.0
1.3	1.1	1.3			.9	1.2	1.3	1.2	1.5
1.5	1.4	1.8			1.7	2.3	2.4	1.7	1.4
.8	.9	1.0	Quick		1.5	1.1	1.1	1.0	1.0
.5	.6	.7			.6	.7	.8	.6	.7
37 9.8	39 9.5	43 8.4			35 10.5	36 10.2	49 7.4	41 8.9	45 8.1
47 7.7	52 7.0	53 6.9	Sales/Receivables		63 5.8	45 8.1	67 5.5	48 7.7	54 6.8
60 6.1	67 5.5	66 5.6			75 4.9	58 6.2	77 4.7	64 5.7	64 5.7
26 14.0	31 11.7	31 11.6			0 802.0	24 14.9	23 16.1	36 10.0	38 9.6
55 6.6	67 5.5	54 6.8	Cost of Sales/Inventory		43 8.5	66 5.5	34 10.8	48 7.6	65 5.6
117 3.1	116 3.2	92 4.0			85 4.3	90 4.0	173 2.1	113 3.2	100 3.7
17 21.0	17 21.1	19 19.1			21 17.8	19 19.1	17 21.6	17 21.6	23 15.9
33 11.1	35 10.6	34 10.7	Cost of Sales/Payables		72 5.1	26 13.8	26 14.0	38 9.6	31 11.6
51 7.1	51 7.1	54 6.8			85 4.3	49 7.5	71 5.1	57 6.4	53 6.9
4.4	4.2	3.9			3.2	6.7	2.9	4.9	3.6
9.2	8.7	8.0	Sales/Working Capital		9.8	8.8	6.8	8.6	5.7
18.7	23.9	15.1			-25.5	20.5	13.1	20.2	10.4
10.0	6.9	16.1			11.4	4.8	25.1	18.9	47.2
(80) 2.3	(86) 1.8	(79) 5.5	EBIT/Interest		(10) 3.2	(16) 2.4	10.2	(23) 9.0	(16) 5.6
.0	.3	1.4			.5	.7	.0	6.3	3.5
7.3	5.6	4.4	Net Profit + Depr., Dep.,						
(35) 2.4	(26) 2.0	(23) 3.3	Amort./Cur. Mat. L/T/D						
1.3	.7	1.7							
.3	.3	.2			.2	.2	.2	.1	.4
.6	.6	.5	Fixed/Worth		.3	.7	.3	.5	.5
1.7	1.6	1.5			-1.4	1.7	.5	.9	1.2
.8	.8	.6			.3	.5	.3	.8	.5
1.6	1.4	1.3	Debt/Worth		1.7	1.4	1.1	1.2	1.2
3.1	4.1	3.9			-5.9	5.4	4.4	3.6	2.2
31.1	20.3	38.8	% Profit Before Taxes/Tangible			35.1	41.1	52.3	38.9
(77) 11.3	(85) 7.7	(78) 14.1	Net Worth			(17) 3.6	14.5	(23) 23.2	(17) 18.5
-1.1	-2.6	1.5				-6.5	.6	6.2	11.9
12.2	11.5	13.8	% Profit Before Taxes/Total		9.9	8.6	15.5	23.8	14.0
3.8	2.2	7.0	Assets		7.0	1.9	8.8	11.0	9.5
-1.9	-2.0	.7			.9	-1.6	-.1	3.6	4.8
21.2	26.2	32.3			52.7	51.7	28.9	35.3	25.7
6.7	8.3	12.9	Sales/Net Fixed Assets		16.4	16.1	18.7	13.1	5.7
3.7	4.1	5.4			6.4	3.9	5.4	6.8	3.8
2.6	2.7	2.9			2.9	3.1	3.2	3.0	2.5
1.9	1.9	2.2	Sales/Total Assets		2.4	2.2	2.4	2.6	1.7
1.4	1.4	1.5			1.7	1.5	1.2	1.8	1.4
1.0	1.1	.8				1.2	1.0	.5	.5
(83) 2.5	(87) 2.3	(77) 2.2	% Depr., Dep., Amort./Sales			(18) 2.7	(11) 1.7	(21) 1.7	(17) 2.6
4.3	3.5	3.6				6.3	2.9	2.6	3.6
2.4	2.1	1.9	% Officers', Directors',			3.8		1.3	
(34) 3.7	(35) 3.9	(34) 3.1	Owners' Comp/Sales			(10) 4.5		(10) 2.2	
7.6	10.5	6.7				9.8		3.0	
2058050M	2185770M	1954019M	Net Sales ($)	1810M	19882M	77539M	88065M	415588M	1351135M
1123868M	1184238M	1084741M	Total Assets ($)	1222M	9543M	43370M	55139M	180328M	795139M

Current Data Sorted By Assets   **Comparative Historical Data**

0-500M	500M-2MM	2-10MM	10-50MM	50-100MM	100-250MM	Type of Statement	67	62
	3	30	31	8	4	Unqualified	67	62
	32	108	16			Reviewed	104	99
13	46	47	4		1	Compiled	141	103
30	35	16			1	Tax Returns	53	32
5	32	46	37	7	1	Other	165	160
	106 (4/1-9/30/04)		447 (10/1/04-3/31/05)				4/1/00-3/31/01 ALL	4/1/01-3/31/02 ALL
48	148	247	88	15	7	**NUMBER OF STATEMENTS**	530	456
%	%	%	%	%	%	**ASSETS**	%	%
10.2	8.5	8.1	5.5	5.9		Cash & Equivalents	7.6	7.8
25.6	32.3	28.1	26.3	22.8		Trade Receivables (net)	28.4	24.4
18.6	21.7	25.2	25.4	31.6		Inventory	20.8	21.2
.6	1.8	2.8	2.9	2.4		All Other Current	1.8	2.2
55.0	64.3	64.2	60.0	62.7		Total Current	58.6	55.5
34.2	28.0	28.4	29.2	27.6		Fixed Assets (net)	33.3	34.7
2.5	3.0	2.5	6.1	3.1		Intangibles (net)	3.5	3.8
8.2	4.7	4.9	4.6	6.6		All Other Non-Current	4.7	6.0
100.0	100.0	100.0	100.0	100.0		Total	100.0	100.0
						LIABILITIES		
22.9	13.7	11.0	11.1	8.9		Notes Payable-Short Term	13.6	9.7
7.1	4.7	3.9	3.9	2.3		Cur. Mat.-L/T/D	4.9	5.4
22.6	17.6	14.7	13.5	12.5		Trade Payables	14.8	12.5
.0	.2	.4	.3	.3		Income Taxes Payable	.4	.3
11.3	7.0	7.9	8.6	9.7		All Other Current	10.4	8.0
63.9	43.2	37.9	37.4	33.7		Total Current	44.1	35.8
47.4	18.7	15.9	16.9	18.7		Long-Term Debt	19.3	22.1
.0	.2	.5	.6	1.7		Deferred Taxes	.5	.7
10.6	10.0	4.9	7.2	4.5		All Other Non-Current	4.6	4.0
-21.9	27.8	40.9	37.8	41.5		Net Worth	31.5	37.4
100.0	100.0	100.0	100.0	100.0		Total Liabilities & Net Worth	100.0	100.0
						INCOME DATA		
100.0	100.0	100.0	100.0	100.0		Net Sales	100.0	100.0
45.0	34.0	27.5	23.5	22.4		Gross Profit	31.1	30.5
41.9	30.2	22.2	17.1	15.7		Operating Expenses	25.2	27.2
3.1	3.7	5.2	6.3	6.7		Operating Profit	5.9	3.3
1.9	1.0	.8	1.9	1.2		All Other Expenses (net)	1.5	1.5
1.1	2.7	4.5	4.4	5.5		Profit Before Taxes	4.3	1.8
						RATIOS		
1.7	2.6	2.7	2.2	3.1		Current	2.6	2.7
1.0	1.5	1.8	1.6	1.9			1.6	1.6
.5	1.0	1.2	1.2	1.4			1.1	1.1
1.2	1.6	1.6	1.3	1.6		Quick	1.7	1.6
.6	.9	.9	.9	.8			.9 (455)	.9
.2	.6	.6	.6	.6			.6	.6
11 34.2	31 11.8	36 10.1	41 8.9	35 10.4		Sales/Receivables	33 11.0	32 11.5
26 14.1	43 8.5	48 7.7	55 6.7	39 9.3			46 8.0	41 8.8
44 8.3	58 6.3	61 5.9	67 5.4	58 6.3			60 6.1	55 6.7
0 UND	11 33.1	31 11.7	44 8.3	43 8.5		Cost of Sales/Inventory	20 18.6	22 16.6
13 28.6	41 8.9	54 6.8	70 5.2	70 5.2			43 8.4	48 7.7
64 5.7	73 5.0	87 4.2	96 3.8	97 3.7			78 4.7	87 4.2
3 121.9	19 19.5	20 18.6	21 17.8	17 21.3		Cost of Sales/Payables	16 22.3	15 24.7
22 16.3	32 11.3	30 12.1	34 10.6	22 16.4			29 12.8	25 14.3
41 8.9	50 7.3	47 7.8	50 7.3	40 9.2			44 8.2	41 8.8
12.2	5.4	5.1	4.8	4.0		Sales/Working Capital	5.8	5.2
NM	12.8	8.4	8.7	5.6			10.8	10.5
-11.0	-582.8	17.0	22.0	10.5			55.7	57.5
5.7	10.0	13.1	13.3	28.1		EBIT/Interest	8.5	6.0
(39) 1.3	(131) 3.3	(229) 4.4	(82) 4.6	(14) 6.3			(489) 3.1	(421) 2.0
-1.4	.9	1.7	1.6	1.9			1.2	.4
	6.1	4.7	5.9			Net Profit + Depr., Dep., Amort./Cur. Mat. L./T/D	5.2	3.6
	(20) 2.1	(62) 2.3	(38) 2.7				(148) 2.4	(126) 1.6
	1.5	1.5	1.4				1.2	.8
.6	.3	.3	.4	.4		Fixed/Worth	.4	.4
6.0	1.1	.7	.9	.7			1.0	.9
-.9	5.5	1.8	2.2	1.6			2.6	2.4
2.2	.8	.6	.9	.7		Debt/Worth	.7	.7
UND	3.5	1.5	2.0	1.5			1.8	1.7
-2.8	15.0	3.9	4.8	4.5			5.7	5.1
93.8	66.8	40.7	36.4	44.3		% Profit Before Taxes/Tangible Net Worth	48.5	31.9
(24) 18.5	(120) 20.0	(231) 21.0	(76) 20.4	(14) 21.4			(467) 23.1	(398) 12.0
-4.1	1.0	8.3	4.9	10.4			5.8	-.3
14.7	17.5	14.7	13.1	15.4		% Profit Before Taxes/Total Assets	17.7	12.0
2.0	4.2	7.0	6.0	7.7			7.4	3.7
-8.6	-.4	1.8	1.3	4.7			.9	-2.3
41.6	22.5	17.8	12.7	10.4		Sales/Net Fixed Assets	14.5	13.0
12.0	12.3	8.1	6.3	8.3			7.2	6.2
5.7	5.8	4.4	3.7	4.9			3.9	3.4
4.8	3.2	2.7	2.2	2.3		Sales/Total Assets	2.8	2.6
3.2	2.5	2.1	1.7	2.0			2.1	1.9
2.4	1.9	1.5	1.3	1.5			1.5	1.4
1.4	1.4	1.4	1.6	1.5		% Depr., Dep., Amort./Sales	1.4	1.5
(34) 2.9	(123) 2.7	(226) 2.3	(79) 2.6	(13) 2.7			(481) 2.8	(416) 2.9
5.4	5.3	4.2	4.7	3.0			4.7	5.1
2.9	2.3	1.9	.9			% Officers', Directors', Owners' Comp/Sales	2.8	2.9
(30) 6.5	(87) 4.0	(110) 3.9	(11) 2.9				(261) 4.8	(197) 4.5
10.1	7.3	7.7					8.2	7.9
47883M	464993M	2344640M	2857472M	2066319M	1768384M	Net Sales ($)	11080584M	8383931M
13336M	179938M	1150501M	1693869M	1037769M	1247968M	Total Assets ($)	5307303M	4851500M

M = $ thousand MM = $ million
See Pages 11 through 21 for Explanation of Ratios and Data

Comparative Historical Data / Current Data Sorted By Sales

4/1/02-3/31/03 ALL	4/1/03-3/31/04 ALL	4/1/04-3/31/05 ALL	Type of Statement	0-1MM	1-3MM	3-5MM	5-10MM	10-25MM	25MM & OVER
74	65	76	Unqualified		1	4	13	26	32
127	135	156	Reviewed		14	32	51	48	11
99	128	111	Compiled	9	26	32	27	15	2
58	56	82	Tax Returns	20	32	15	11	3	1
149	161	128	Other	3	24	24	15	28	34
				106 (4/1-9/30/04)			447 (10/1/04-3/31/05)		
507	545	553	**NUMBER OF STATEMENTS**	32	97	107	117	120	80
%	%	%	**ASSETS**	%	%	%	%	%	%
9.1	8.6	7.9	Cash & Equivalents	9.0	8.6	7.6	10.6	6.4	5.6
25.1	26.9	28.4	Trade Receivables (net)	27.0	25.2	31.4	28.2	30.1	26.6
21.2	21.8	23.9	Inventory	15.9	20.1	22.8	24.2	27.1	27.9
2.8	2.6	2.4	All Other Current	.6	1.6	2.9	2.6	2.2	3.3
58.2	59.7	62.6	Total Current	52.5	55.4	64.8	65.6	65.7	63.4
34.0	31.4	29.0	Fixed Assets (net)	32.2	35.6	28.3	27.1	27.3	25.8
3.2	3.5	3.3	Intangibles (net)	5.5	2.9	2.8	2.3	3.3	4.8
4.6	5.3	5.2	All Other Non-Current	9.8	6.1	4.1	5.1	3.7	5.9
100.0	100.0	100.0	Total	100.0	100.0	100.0	100.0	100.0	100.0
			LIABILITIES						
10.4	12.2	12.7	Notes Payable-Short Term	23.2	15.5	13.2	9.0	12.2	11.0
5.4	4.9	4.4	Cur. Mat.-L/T/D	7.4	5.1	4.5	4.1	3.5	3.9
13.8	14.8	15.8	Trade Payables	23.9	11.7	18.1	14.9	17.2	14.0
.3	.3	.3	Income Taxes Payable	.0	.3	.2	.2	.4	.4
9.2	9.2	8.2	All Other Current	13.8	5.5	7.2	8.3	8.1	10.6
39.1	41.3	41.4	Total Current	68.4	38.0	43.2	36.5	41.4	39.9
20.0	18.6	19.7	Long-Term Debt	49.9	26.1	19.3	14.6	14.7	15.5
.6	.6	.4	Deferred Taxes	.0	.3	.3	.5	.4	.9
6.7	6.6	7.1	All Other Non-Current	6.3	14.5	5.6	5.4	6.7	3.8
33.7	32.8	31.3	Net Worth	-24.6	21.2	31.6	43.0	36.9	39.9
100.0	100.0	100.0	Total Liabilities & Net Worth	100.0	100.0	100.0	100.0	100.0	100.0
			INCOME DATA						
100.0	100.0	100.0	Net Sales	100.0	100.0	100.0	100.0	100.0	100.0
29.4	29.0	29.9	Gross Profit	40.5	38.9	31.9	26.8	25.7	22.9
26.3	26.1	25.1	Operating Expenses	37.9	35.0	27.6	21.7	20.4	16.6
3.1	3.0	4.8	Operating Profit	2.6	3.8	4.4	5.1	5.3	6.4
1.4	1.1	1.2	All Other Expenses (net)	2.1	1.5	1.2	.5	1.0	1.7
1.6	1.8	3.6	Profit Before Taxes	.6	2.3	3.2	4.6	4.3	4.6
			RATIOS						
2.6	2.6	2.6	Current	1.6	2.7	2.7	2.9	2.3	2.3
1.6	1.6	1.6		1.0	1.5	1.7	1.9	1.7	1.6
1.1	1.1	1.1		.5	.9	1.0	1.2	1.2	1.2
1.6	1.7	1.5	Quick	1.4	1.6	1.6	1.9	1.4	1.2
.9	.9	.9		.6	.9	.9	1.0	.9	.8
.5	.5	.6		.2	.5	.6	.6	.6	.6
32 11.6	32 11.5	32 11.4	Sales/Receivables	25 14.9	24 15.5	36 10.3	35 10.4	35 10.4	35 10.4
43 8.5	46 8.0	46 7.9		35 10.4	40 9.2	48 7.5	43 8.4	50 7.4	46 7.9
57 6.4	59 6.2	60 6.1		59 6.1	59 6.2	62 5.9	59 6.2	63 5.8	60 6.1
23 15.9	23 16.1	26 14.1	Cost of Sales/Inventory	0 UND	10 38.0	20 18.3	28 12.9	41 8.9	39 9.4
46 7.9	49 7.4	52 7.0		11 34.4	39 9.3	48 7.6	51 7.2	56 6.5	67 5.5
78 4.7	82 4.5	87 4.2		67 5.4	84 4.3	86 4.2	87 4.2	90 4.1	90 4.1
16 23.3	17 21.4	19 19.3	Cost of Sales/Payables	5 67.5	14 26.8	21 17.5	17 21.1	24 15.2	18 20.0
28 13.0	29 12.4	31 11.8		22 16.6	28 13.1	35 10.3	28 13.2	39 9.3	28 13.1
44 8.3	48 7.6	47 7.8		47 7.7	45 8.0	54 6.8	43 8.5	53 6.9	41 8.9
5.0	5.1	5.3	Sales/Working Capital	13.0	5.7	4.7	4.5	5.7	5.2
9.8	9.5	9.5		NM	13.5	9.4	7.7	9.0	9.0
93.9	53.1	38.9		-6.3	-88.0	378.8	16.9	18.1	22.2
7.2	8.2	11.8	EBIT/Interest	6.4	5.8	8.9	15.3	13.3	20.3
(464) 2.6	(496) 2.4	(501) 4.0		(25) 1.6	(86) 1.7	(98) 3.0	(106) 4.5	(112) 5.2	(74) 6.5
.1	.3	1.3		-.4	-.1	1.3	2.3	1.7	1.9
5.1	4.2	6.9	Net Profit + Depr., Dep., Amort./Cur. Mat. L/T/D		5.4	8.4	3.8	4.2	14.1
(119) 2.4	(126) 2.0	(135) 2.7			(13) 2.1	(21) 2.2	(31) 2.0	(32) 2.3	(36) 4.1
1.1	.8	1.5			1.1	1.9	1.3	1.5	1.9
.4	.4	.4	Fixed/Worth	.3	.5	.3	.2	.4	.4
1.0	.9	.8		5.7	2.2	1.0	.6	.7	.7
3.1	3.1	2.7		-.4	-8.7	3.8	1.7	1.6	1.6
.7	.7	.8	Debt/Worth	1.5	.9	.8	.5	.8	.8
1.8	1.9	2.1		UND	4.2	2.4	1.2	1.8	1.7
6.2	7.3	6.9		-2.0	-23.1	8.0	3.8	4.0	4.3
32.2	34.8	42.3	% Profit Before Taxes/Tangible Net Worth	99.1	41.9	38.7	43.8	40.8	42.3
(430) 12.2	(463) 13.4	(471) 20.5		(16) 27.6	(71) 12.9	(91) 15.7	(111) 21.0	(110) 23.1	(72) 24.5
-3.0	-1.8	5.2		-1.9	-1.4	3.8	8.6	8.5	5.5
12.6	11.9	14.4	% Profit Before Taxes/Total Assets	14.7	11.4	11.9	16.8	15.5	15.3
4.2	3.6	6.2		5.5	1.8	5.2	7.7	6.5	8.4
-2.5	-1.9	.9		-1.2	-3.5	.8	2.6	1.9	1.7
13.4	16.3	18.2	Sales/Net Fixed Assets	51.2	14.4	23.3	23.4	18.1	14.5
6.7	7.4	8.5		10.7	7.4	10.5	9.4	7.8	8.2
3.4	3.9	4.7		4.8	3.7	5.2	4.9	4.0	5.0
2.6	2.7	2.8	Sales/Total Assets	3.8	2.8	3.0	2.7	2.7	2.7
1.9	2.0	2.1		2.7	2.2	2.2	2.2	2.1	2.0
1.5	1.5	1.6		1.3	1.5	1.6	1.6	1.6	1.5
1.7	1.4	1.4	% Depr., Dep., Amort./Sales	2.3	1.9	1.3	1.5	1.3	1.3
(459) 3.2	(486) 3.0	(482) 2.5		(19) 4.5	(86) 3.6	(92) 2.7	(105) 2.3	(107) 2.3	(73) 2.1
5.7	5.3	4.4		5.9	6.4	5.5	3.6	3.9	3.2
2.4	2.7	2.2	% Officers', Directors', Owners' Comp/Sales	3.9	2.9	2.3	2.4	1.6	1.0
(211) 5.1	(226) 4.6	(239) 4.0		(13) 8.4	(62) 6.0	(61) 3.5	(57) 4.0	(34) 2.7	(12) 2.0
8.4	8.0	7.7		13.1	8.3	6.2	8.3	6.5	4.7
8389389M	9663312M	9549691M	Net Sales ($)	18902M	195225M	427545M	853365M	1891594M	6163060M
5277631M	5810475M	5323381M	Total Assets ($)	9443M	112650M	218772M	452164M	1025537M	3504815M

M = $ thousand   MM = $ million
See Pages 11 through 21 for Explanation of Ratios and Data

Current Data Sorted By Assets   Comparative Historical Data

	0-500M	500M-2MM	2-10MM	10-50MM	50-100MM	100-250MM	Type of Statement	4/1/00-3/31/01 ALL	4/1/01-3/31/02 ALL
		1	14	14	2	1	Unqualified	36	27
		6	13	11			Reviewed	22	26
	4	12	5	3			Compiled	30	28
	3	7	1				Tax Returns	5	15
	1	3	11	10		4	Other	47	38
		29 (4/1-9/30/04)		97 (10/1/04-3/31/05)					
NUMBER OF STATEMENTS	8	29	44	38	2	5		140	134
	%	%	%	%	%	%	**ASSETS**	%	%
		11.7	5.9	6.3			Cash & Equivalents	6.7	6.1
		13.5	20.5	19.1			Trade Receivables (net)	19.5	18.6
		49.8	46.2	39.7			Inventory	40.6	41.7
		1.2	3.5	2.4			All Other Current	2.3	2.4
		76.1	76.1	67.5			Total Current	69.0	68.8
		19.4	16.0	23.0			Fixed Assets (net)	22.3	20.6
		.8	2.7	3.4			Intangibles (net)	3.5	4.0
		3.6	5.2	6.1			All Other Non-Current	5.2	6.6
		100.0	100.0	100.0			Total	100.0	100.0
							LIABILITIES		
		10.7	16.6	13.6			Notes Payable-Short Term	14.9	16.8
		3.8	2.2	2.4			Cur. Mat.-L/T/D	3.0	3.3
		10.9	13.6	12.3			Trade Payables	11.3	11.0
		.1	.3	.7			Income Taxes Payable	.2	.2
		6.8	13.9	12.6			All Other Current	11.1	9.9
		32.3	46.5	41.6			Total Current	40.6	41.2
		12.0	10.9	11.8			Long-Term Debt	13.8	12.9
		.0	.1	.4			Deferred Taxes	.6	.3
		9.4	3.8	2.4			All Other Non-Current	7.8	5.7
		46.3	38.7	43.8			Net Worth	37.3	40.0
		100.0	100.0	100.0			Total Liabilities & Net Worth	100.0	100.0
							INCOME DATA		
		100.0	100.0	100.0			Net Sales	100.0	100.0
		26.6	24.0	25.3			Gross Profit	27.4	27.1
		23.2	20.6	17.5			Operating Expenses	22.7	24.2
		3.4	3.4	7.8			Operating Profit	4.7	2.9
		1.0	.1	1.3			All Other Expenses (net)	1.6	1.3
		2.4	3.3	6.6			Profit Before Taxes	3.1	1.6
							RATIOS		
		5.1	2.6	2.5				3.1	2.8
		2.7	1.7	1.7			Current	1.8	1.8
		1.5	1.4	1.2				1.2	1.2
		2.7	1.1	1.0				1.2	1.1
		.9	.6	.7			Quick	.7	.6
		.4	.2	.4				.3	.4
	10 37.9	26 14.2	19 19.1					21 17.3	19 18.9
	19 19.4	45 8.1	36 10.1				Sales/Receivables	34 10.8	32 11.5
	34 10.9	59 6.2	63 5.8					51 7.2	52 7.0
	69 5.3	72 5.0	69 5.3					61 6.0	54 6.7
	119 3.1	102 3.6	101 3.6				Cost of Sales/Inventory	103 3.5	102 3.6
	191 1.9	171 2.1	174 2.1					163 2.2	162 2.3
	6 62.1	15 24.9	15 23.9					13 27.3	12 30.1
	19 18.8	24 15.2	30 12.0				Cost of Sales/Payables	23 16.0	25 14.9
	41 8.9	39 9.3	48 7.5					36 10.1	33 11.2
		3.0	3.7	3.6				3.5	3.9
		4.3	6.8	6.7			Sales/Working Capital	6.5	7.3
		9.1	10.6	13.3				17.2	19.2
		11.3	8.1	18.9				5.3	7.6
		(22) 3.6	(39) 3.3	(37) 5.0			EBIT/Interest	(131) 2.1	(125) 1.8
		1.4	1.5	2.1				1.0	.5
				13.3				5.9	6.2
			(20) 4.3				Net Profit + Depr., Dep., Amort./Cur. Mat. L /T/D	(38) 2.6	(37) 2.0
			1.7					1.2	.8
		.1	.1	.3				.3	.2
		.3	.4	.6			Fixed/Worth	.6	.5
		1.0	.9	1.0				1.2	1.3
		.4	.7	.6				.8	.6
		1.1	1.7	1.7			Debt/Worth	1.5	1.4
		5.0	3.6	3.5				4.4	4.6
		34.0	32.4	41.1				27.0	21.7
		(27) 12.7	(40) 11.9	17.6			% Profit Before Taxes/Tangible Net Worth	(128) 9.7	(117) 6.3
		4.5	2.8	8.5				.5	-1.1
		15.8	11.7	13.0				11.0	8.9
		6.2	5.4	7.6			% Profit Before Taxes/Total Assets	4.2	1.7
		2.2	1.3	4.2				-.1	-2.1
		38.2	29.0	18.7				19.5	24.8
		17.7	12.1	8.5			Sales/Net Fixed Assets	9.3	11.2
		6.7	8.0	5.0				5.5	6.3
		3.1	2.4	2.0				2.4	2.7
		2.0	1.8	1.6			Sales/Total Assets	1.8	1.9
		1.5	1.4	1.3				1.3	1.3
		.9	.9	.9				1.0	.8
		(25) 1.5	(38) 1.5	(37) 1.6			% Depr., Dep., Amort./Sales	(123) 2.0	(121) 1.9
		3.5	2.2	2.3				3.2	2.9
		2.1	1.3					1.8	.9
		(15) 3.0	(11) 2.3				% Officers', Directors', Owners' Comp/Sales	(44) 3.5	(46) 2.5
		5.4	3.5					5.7	6.0
	8625M	80668M	422367M	1172851M	279946M	1162685M	Net Sales ($)	3332209M	3265305M
	3205M	35611M	225864M	704899M	170468M	805395M	Total Assets ($)	2236457M	2203059M

M = $ thousand   MM = $ million
See Pages 11 through 21 for Explanation of Ratios and Data

Comparative Historical Data | Current Data Sorted By Sales

			Type of Statement	0-1MM	1-3MM	3-5MM	5-10MM	10-25MM	25MM & OVER
33	38	32	Unqualified		3	2	2	12	13
24	31	30	Reviewed	1	1	3	9	8	8
21	25	24	Compiled	5	9	3	4	3	
9	20	11	Tax Returns		9	1	1		
25	32	29	Other	1	2	3	4	11	8

4/1/02-3/31/03 ALL	4/1/03-3/31/04 ALL	4/1/04-3/31/05 ALL		29 (4/1-9/30/04)			97 (10/1/04-3/31/05)		
				0-1MM	1-3MM	3-5MM	5-10MM	10-25MM	25MM & OVER
112	146	126	NUMBER OF STATEMENTS	7	24	12	20	34	29
%	%	%	ASSETS	%	%	%	%	%	%
6.1	5.8	7.5	Cash & Equivalents		11.2	12.3	6.0	5.7	5.6
19.3	19.2	18.5	Trade Receivables (net)		14.7	14.5	19.3	20.8	21.7
43.2	43.3	44.3	Inventory		48.0	45.7	49.5	44.6	36.5
1.8	2.4	2.4	All Other Current		.4	2.8	2.9	3.4	2.3
70.4	70.7	72.7	Total Current		74.3	75.3	77.8	74.5	66.1
20.8	20.3	19.0	Fixed Assets (net)		21.0	16.6	13.9	19.8	19.8
4.2	3.4	3.2	Intangibles (net)		2.3	2.5	1.4	.9	8.5
4.6	5.6	5.1	All Other Non-Current		2.5	5.7	6.8	4.8	5.6
100.0	100.0	100.0	Total		100.0	100.0	100.0	100.0	100.0
			LIABILITIES						
19.0	15.7	13.4	Notes Payable-Short Term		7.6	25.9	11.1	18.0	9.8
2.8	4.0	3.2	Cur. Mat.-L/T/D		5.9	1.8	1.4	2.8	3.9
10.4	11.9	12.2	Trade Payables		8.2	4.4	18.2	15.8	10.4
.2	.2	.4	Income Taxes Payable		.1	.0	.0	.4	.9
11.0	10.1	11.6	All Other Current		10.8	8.7	17.2	11.6	11.9
43.4	41.8	40.9	Total Current		32.5	40.8	48.0	48.6	36.8
14.0	14.6	11.9	Long-Term Debt		11.6	9.1	14.4	8.7	15.3
.3	.3	.2	Deferred Taxes		.0	.0	.2	.2	.7
7.7	7.2	5.1	All Other Non-Current		12.5	1.6	4.3	3.5	1.2
34.6	36.0	41.9	Net Worth		43.3	48.5	33.1	39.0	46.0
100.0	100.0	100.0	Total Liabilities & Net Worth		100.0	100.0	100.0	100.0	100.0
			INCOME DATA						
100.0	100.0	100.0	Net Sales		100.0	100.0	100.0	100.0	100.0
27.2	26.5	25.3	Gross Profit		31.5	25.4	23.3	23.1	25.1
24.1	22.8	20.5	Operating Expenses		24.4	20.4	19.9	20.5	17.7
3.1	3.7	4.8	Operating Profit		7.2	5.1	3.4	2.6	7.4
1.0	.9	.9	All Other Expenses (net)		.6	-.5	-.4	1.1	1.1
2.0	2.7	3.9	Profit Before Taxes		6.6	5.5	3.7	1.5	6.2
			RATIOS						
2.9	2.9	3.2			5.4	6.8	2.5	2.4	2.9
1.7	1.7	1.8	Current		2.6	1.6	1.9	1.5	1.9
1.2	1.3	1.3			1.4	1.3	1.4	1.2	1.4
1.1	1.1	1.2			2.8	3.2	1.2	.9	1.3
.6	.6	.6	Quick		.8	.7	.5	.5	.7
.3	.3	.4			.3	.5	.3	.2	.5
18 19.8	18 20.3	16 22.2		10 36.5	6 63.0	10 36.1		19 19.5	27 13.5
35 10.3	36 10.1	33 11.1	Sales/Receivables	20 18.6	39 9.4	44 8.3		37 9.8	39 9.3
55 6.6	57 6.4	59 6.2		31 11.9	55 6.6	60 6.1		62 5.8	61 6.0
73 5.0	68 5.4	71 5.1		62 5.9	93 3.9	77 4.7		71 5.1	65 5.6
105 3.5	113 3.2	107 3.4	Cost of Sales/Inventory	118 3.1	134 2.7	114 3.2		95 3.8	97 3.8
179 2.0	167 2.2	173 2.1		219 1.7	185 2.0	147 2.5		174 2.1	137 2.7
13 28.7	13 28.6	12 30.0		6 64.2	3 112.4	22 16.8		18 20.1	19 19.1
23 16.2	24 15.2	24 15.5	Cost of Sales/Payables	16 23.0	10 38.0	28 12.9		28 13.1	30 12.2
42 8.8	49 7.5	44 8.3		35 10.5	16 23.4	45 8.0		62 5.8	44 8.2
3.5	3.8	3.4			3.3	2.4	3.7	5.4	3.7
6.9	6.5	6.0	Sales/Working Capital		4.3	6.2	6.4	7.5	6.0
14.5	13.5	10.3			8.8	16.6	10.5	17.8	9.4
6.2	6.8	11.1			13.1	18.3	5.9	11.6	18.3
(103) 2.1	(135) 3.3	(112) 3.7	EBIT/Interest		(21) 4.0	(10) 3.7	(18) 3.4	(30) 3.3	(28) 8.2
.8	1.2	1.8			-.2	2.5	1.2	1.6	2.3
9.8	6.4	7.5	Net Profit + Depr., Dep.,					18.7	7.5
(32) 3.6	(33) 3.0	(39) 3.9	Amort./Cur. Mat. L/T/D				(13) 3.6	(15) 4.8	
.9	.7	1.6						.4	1.6
.3	.2	.2			.1	.2	.1	.3	.3
.5	.5	.4	Fixed/Worth		.5	.3	.3	.5	.7
2.1	1.1	.9			1.1	1.1	.8	.9	.9
.6	.8	.6			.3	.2	.9	.6	.9
1.7	1.8	1.5	Debt/Worth		1.1	1.1	1.7	2.0	1.6
5.2	4.9	3.8			4.5	5.0	4.3	5.6	2.7
25.0	27.8	34.5	% Profit Before Taxes/Tangible		32.9	42.1	32.7	21.6	45.7
(96) 8.3	(133) 12.4	(118) 15.0	Net Worth		(21) 12.7	(11) 12.8	(19) 14.5	(32) 13.2	25.3
1.3	2.6	4.7			-4.3	9.5	2.8	5.6	10.0
7.9	8.9	11.9	% Profit Before Taxes/Total		17.4	14.1	11.6	9.4	14.6
2.1	4.5	6.4	Assets		5.3	8.1	5.3	5.3	8.9
-.4	.6	1.8			-2.1	3.5	.8	1.1	5.1
22.8	21.1	25.8			37.0	20.8	37.9	22.6	11.7
9.3	10.6	11.3	Sales/Net Fixed Assets		17.4	13.5	18.8	10.7	9.4
5.7	6.3	6.9			6.5	9.6	10.4	6.7	6.8
2.2	2.4	2.4			3.1	2.4	2.6	2.4	2.2
1.6	1.8	1.8	Sales/Total Assets		1.9	1.9	1.9	1.7	1.6
1.3	1.3	1.4			1.3	1.2	1.5	1.5	1.4
1.3	1.1	.9			1.1	1.1	.5	.8	1.4
(99) 2.0	(125) 2.0	(113) 1.5	% Depr., Dep., Amort./Sales	(18) 1.4	1.5	(19) 1.1	(31) 1.5	(27) 1.7	
3.3	3.1	2.3			3.3	2.8	2.0	2.3	2.2
1.6	1.3	1.3			2.1				
(37) 2.6	(51) 2.7	(36) 2.6	% Officers', Directors', Owners' Comp/Sales	(15) 4.0					
5.2	5.1	4.4			7.7				
3241679M	4434951M	3127142M	Net Sales ($)	3956M	47933M	46454M	143427M	548494M	2336878M
2257617M	2900890M	1945442M	Total Assets ($)	4332M	46155M	28108M	74670M	325538M	1466639M

M = $ thousand   MM = $ million
See Pages 11 through 21 for Explanation of Ratios and Data

Current Data Sorted By Assets | Comparative Historical Data

0-500M	500M-2MM	2-10MM	10-50MM	50-100MM	100-250MM	Type of Statement	4/1/00-3/31/01 ALL	4/1/01-3/31/02 ALL
		1	5		2	Unqualified	8	13
		3	2		1	Reviewed	1	1
	1	2	2			Compiled	5	5
2	1	2	2			Tax Returns	4	5
	4	4	6	3	2	Other	11	13
		11 (4/1-9/30/04)		32 (10/1/04-3/31/05)				
2	7	11	15	3	5	**NUMBER OF STATEMENTS**	29	37
%	%	%	%	%	%	**ASSETS**	%	%
		6.3	1.4			Cash & Equivalents	4.0	5.1
		18.9	22.7			Trade Receivables (net)	18.1	17.4
		46.9	45.0			Inventory	43.4	42.1
		1.6	3.8			All Other Current	1.4	1.4
		73.6	72.7			Total Current	66.8	66.0
		17.6	18.0			Fixed Assets (net)	23.0	25.2
		3.9	3.2			Intangibles (net)	4.4	3.8
		4.9	6.0			All Other Non-Current	5.8	5.0
		100.0	100.0			Total	100.0	100.0
						LIABILITIES		
		19.7	25.8			Notes Payable-Short Term	13.9	18.8
		.6	1.2			Cur. Mat.-L/T/D	3.3	4.1
		9.2	15.2			Trade Payables	15.7	17.8
		.0	.1			Income Taxes Payable	.0	.0
		6.4	9.0			All Other Current	7.5	10.0
		35.9	51.2			Total Current	40.4	50.8
		8.4	7.2			Long-Term Debt	17.3	18.6
		.1	.5			Deferred Taxes	.3	.5
		6.0	8.9			All Other Non-Current	4.9	6.7
		49.5	32.2			Net Worth	37.1	23.5
		100.0	100.0			Total Liabilities & Net Worth	100.0	100.0
						INCOME DATA		
		100.0	100.0			Net Sales	100.0	100.0
		29.1	25.3			Gross Profit	28.5	29.4
		24.5	21.2			Operating Expenses	24.0	25.6
		4.5	4.2			Operating Profit	4.5	3.8
		1.2	1.8			All Other Expenses (net)	1.1	1.9
		3.4	2.4			Profit Before Taxes	3.4	1.8
						RATIOS		
		4.5	2.5			Current	2.8	2.9
		2.4	1.7				1.8	1.3
		1.3	1.0				1.1	1.0
		1.7	.9			Quick	.9	1.2
		.7	.5				.6 (36)	.5
		.3	.2				.2	.3
		19	19.4	24	15.1	Sales/Receivables	11	32.5	12	29.6
		31	11.7	41	8.8		38	9.7	34	10.9
		50	7.3	65	5.7		55	6.6	49	7.4
		67	5.5	71	5.2	Cost of Sales/Inventory	64	5.7	71	5.2
		111	3.3	114	3.2		95	3.8	86	4.2
		193	1.9	155	2.4		125	2.9	140	2.6
		8	43.3	15	24.0	Cost of Sales/Payables	11	34.5	11	32.5
		16	23.2	32	11.4		33	11.0	27	13.6
		42	8.7	43	8.5		47	7.7	55	6.6
		3.3	3.8			Sales/Working Capital	3.8	3.8
		4.3	7.7				9.2	16.3
		18.4	-58.3				27.2	NM
		16.9	7.8			EBIT/Interest	4.5	7.9
		(10) 2.6	(14) 5.1				(28) 2.3	(36) 1.6
		1.2	-.7				1.3	1.1
						Net Profit + Depr., Dep., Amort./Cur. Mat. L./T/D		
		.1	.3			Fixed/Worth	.3	.4
		.2	.5				.6	.8
		.5	-2.6				1.6	4.0
		.3	.7			Debt/Worth	.8	1.1
		1.2	1.6				1.8	3.6
		2.5	-16.9				7.0	20.6
		37.0	24.2			% Profit Before Taxes/Tangible Net Worth	33.3	36.6
		(10) 8.5	(11) 16.3				(27) 14.2	(29) 20.3
		2.1	9.1				5.7	1.3
		13.7	8.2			% Profit Before Taxes/Total Assets	9.7	11.3
		2.5	4.4				4.0	2.4
		.2	-1.3				1.1	.4
		33.8	33.3			Sales/Net Fixed Assets	29.8	15.5
		17.7	11.5				12.3	7.7
		6.2	6.5				5.2	5.8
		2.8	2.4			Sales/Total Assets	2.7	2.7
		2.2	1.9				2.1	1.8
		1.5	1.5				1.4	1.4
		1.1				% Depr., Dep., Amort./Sales	.6	1.3
		1.8					(26) 1.3	(32) 1.9
		2.6					2.2	3.2
						% Officers', Directors', Owners' Comp/Sales	2.0	1.3
							(12) 3.4	(16) 3.6
							7.0	10.7
2228M	19430M	126028M	672425M	410859M	1097903M	Net Sales ($)	911445M	1653824M
730M	8661M	57604M	326559M	260549M	720220M	Total Assets ($)	527907M	920384M

M = $ thousand   MM = $ million
See Pages 11 through 21 for Explanation of Ratios and Data

Comparative Historical Data | **Current Data Sorted By Sales**

Current Data periods: 11 (4/1-9/30/04) · 32 (10/1/04-3/31/05)
M = $ thousand   MM = $ million

	13 · 4/1/02-3/31/03 ALL	14 · 4/1/03-3/31/04 ALL	8 · 4/1/04-3/31/05 ALL	Type of Statement	0-1MM	1-3MM	3-5MM	5-10MM	10-25MM	25MM & OVER
	13	14	8	Unqualified				1	2	7
	3	2	6	Reviewed				1		3
	5	4	3	Compiled		1		1	1	
	7	7	7	Tax Returns		2	1	1	2	2
	20	13	19	Other		3	3		3	9
	48	40	43	**NUMBER OF STATEMENTS**		6	4	4	8	21
	%	%	%	**ASSETS**						%
	5.5	6.9	6.3	Cash & Equivalents						5.4
	20.2	20.6	21.9	Trade Receivables (net)						21.4
	42.5	38.6	42.3	Inventory		D A T A				38.6
	1.9	2.7	3.3	All Other Current						3.5
	70.0	68.9	73.7	Total Current		N O T				68.9
	21.5	20.5	17.5	Fixed Assets (net)						18.6
	3.1	4.0	4.4	Intangibles (net)		A V A I L A B L E				6.8
	5.4	6.6	4.4	All Other Non-Current						5.7
	100.0	100.0	100.0	Total						100.0
				LIABILITIES						
	16.7	15.9	19.0	Notes Payable-Short Term						21.0
	2.0	2.5	1.1	Cur. Mat.-L/T/D						1.1
	18.5	14.5	15.2	Trade Payables						15.4
	.4	.7	.0	Income Taxes Payable						.0
	10.4	7.5	7.6	All Other Current						10.0
	48.0	41.1	42.9	Total Current						47.5
	16.2	7.8	7.8	Long-Term Debt						8.3
	.1	.3	.4	Deferred Taxes						.6
	5.0	6.0	9.0	All Other Non-Current						8.0
	30.8	44.8	40.0	Net Worth						35.6
	100.0	100.0	100.0	Total Liabilities & Net Worth						100.0
				INCOME DATA						
	100.0	100.0	100.0	Net Sales						100.0
	28.3	29.4	28.3	Gross Profit						25.0
	25.5	25.5	22.9	Operating Expenses						20.1
	2.8	3.9	5.4	Operating Profit						5.0
	1.3	1.2	1.2	All Other Expenses (net)						1.8
	1.5	2.7	4.1	Profit Before Taxes						3.1
				RATIOS						
	2.9 / 1.6 / 1.0	2.9 / 1.7 / 1.3	3.1 / 1.7 / 1.3	Current						2.1 / 1.7 / 1.3
	1.3 / .5 / .3	1.3 / .6 / .4	1.4 / .7 / .3	Quick						.9 / .7 / .2
	18 19.9 / 41 8.9 / 58 6.2	19 19.5 / 37 10.0 / 65 5.6	23 15.9 / 41 8.8 / 58 6.2	Sales/Receivables						26 13.8 / 44 8.4 / 59 6.2
	65 5.6 / 91 4.0 / 165 2.2	57 6.4 / 88 4.2 / 155 2.4	67 5.5 / 100 3.6 / 148 2.5	Cost of Sales/Inventory						59 6.2 / 85 4.3 / 134 2.7
	15 24.4 / 28 13.1 / 47 7.8	11 32.3 / 29 12.6 / 51 7.2	15 24.0 / 32 11.4 / 45 8.2	Cost of Sales/Payables						25 14.6 / 33 11.0 / 44 8.3
	3.9 / 8.4 / 97.7	3.8 / 7.7 / 22.6	3.5 / 7.2 / 11.2	Sales/Working Capital						3.9 / 7.7 / 12.7
	(46) 11.0 / 2.3 / .3	(37) 7.8 / 3.3 / .6	(41) 13.5 / 4.2 / .9	EBIT/Interest						10.1 / 5.5 / .5
		(13) 6.1 / 1.9 / 1.7		Net Profit + Depr., Dep., Amort./Cur. Mat. L/T/D						
	.3 / .5 / 1.3	.3 / .4 / .7	.2 / .4 / .8	Fixed/Worth						.3 / .5 / 3.0
	.8 / 2.6 / 6.2	.5 / 1.4 / 2.8	.6 / 1.5 / 5.0	Debt/Worth						.6 / 1.8 / 7.7
	(44) 37.3 / 17.6 / -3.3	(38) 24.2 / 9.2 / .0	(37) 39.6 / 16.3 / 6.6	% Profit Before Taxes/Tangible Net Worth						(17) 38.8 / 17.4 / 10.3
	9.1 / 4.3 / -.8	8.8 / 3.4 / -.4	20.6 / 4.7 / .2	% Profit Before Taxes/Total Assets						10.6 / 6.5 / .2
	31.5 / 8.6 / 5.6	27.1 / 9.8 / 6.0	25.9 / 13.4 / 7.3	Sales/Net Fixed Assets						22.5 / 11.5 / 6.9
	2.9 / 1.9 / 1.4	2.5 / 1.9 / 1.4	2.6 / 1.9 / 1.5	Sales/Total Assets						2.3 / 1.9 / 1.4
	(42) 1.4 / 2.1 / 3.3	(36) 1.2 / 2.0 / 3.5	(39) .7 / 1.7 / 2.9	% Depr., Dep., Amort./Sales						(20) 1.2 / 1.7 / 2.5
	(15) 1.3 / 3.2 / 9.5	(15) 1.9 / 3.4 / 6.3	(12) 1.3 / 2.1 / 7.4	% Officers', Directors', Owners' Comp/Sales						
	1852339M	2200348M	2328873M	Net Sales ($)		10658M	14044M	31164M	123738M	2149269M
	1047645M	1242683M	1374323M	Total Assets ($)		5370M	7763M	17049M	60582M	1283559M

© RMA 2005

M = $ thousand   MM = $ million
See Pages 11 through 21 for Explanation of Ratios and Data

Current Data Sorted By Assets

Comparative Historical Data

Type of Statement	0-500M	500M-2MM	2-10MM	10-50MM	50-100MM	100-250MM	4/1/00-3/31/01 ALL	4/1/01-3/31/02 ALL
Unqualified	1	8	10	15	4	7	32	45
Reviewed	5	4	18	8			26	30
Compiled	4	3	4				21	20
Tax Returns			1				10	8
Other	1	8	21	9	4	7	40	58
		37 (4/1-9/30/04)		105 (10/1/04-3/31/05)				
NUMBER OF STATEMENTS	11	23	54	32	8	14	129	161
ASSETS	%	%	%	%	%	%	%	%
Cash & Equivalents	15.7	9.4	6.5	8.1		5.1	6.7	5.8
Trade Receivables (net)	24.8	33.2	23.1	27.5		20.5	23.0	24.5
Inventory	18.4	27.8	37.2	33.7		26.7	34.3	31.1
All Other Current	.7	5.8	4.1	2.1		4.6	2.5	3.8
Total Current	59.6	76.2	70.8	71.4		56.9	66.6	65.1
Fixed Assets (net)	28.1	14.6	23.7	20.1		25.5	22.7	23.9
Intangibles (net)	.4	1.4	1.7	3.8		10.9	3.9	4.0
All Other Non-Current	11.8	7.8	3.8	4.7		6.7	6.7	7.0
Total	100.0	100.0	100.0	100.0		100.0	100.0	100.0
LIABILITIES								
Notes Payable-Short Term	18.5	10.1	16.4	15.8		2.4	14.2	16.4
Cur. Mat.-L/T/D	1.9	2.5	4.1	2.8		2.5	3.6	4.7
Trade Payables	18.2	17.8	14.1	12.8		12.9	13.7	14.4
Income Taxes Payable	.3	.1	.8	.6		.4	.6	.5
All Other Current	7.8	16.1	11.6	11.6		12.0	9.1	9.8
Total Current	46.7	46.6	46.9	43.6		30.2	41.2	45.8
Long-Term Debt	21.9	13.7	14.0	7.6		18.1	16.0	16.0
Deferred Taxes	.3	.2	.7	.6		1.8	.4	.4
All Other Non-Current	1.2	6.2	5.9	9.1		6.6	3.5	3.8
Net Worth	29.9	33.3	32.6	39.1		43.4	38.9	34.0
Total Liabilities & Net Worth	100.0	100.0	100.0	100.0		100.0	100.0	100.0
INCOME DATA								
Net Sales	100.0	100.0	100.0	100.0		100.0	100.0	100.0
Gross Profit	48.4	30.3	29.1	24.9		25.5	26.1	27.1
Operating Expenses	39.0	28.2	22.3	19.3		20.3	22.4	23.7
Operating Profit	9.4	2.1	6.8	5.7		5.1	3.7	3.4
All Other Expenses (net)	1.6	.1	1.5	.0		.5	1.3	1.7
Profit Before Taxes	7.8	2.0	5.4	5.7		4.6	2.4	1.7
RATIOS								
Current	3.0	3.2	2.2	2.4		3.7	2.7	2.5
	2.1	1.9	1.6	1.7		1.8	1.7	1.5
	.8	1.1	1.2	1.2		1.4	1.2	1.1
Quick	2.1	2.1	1.1	1.4		1.7	1.3	1.2
	.7	.9	.6	.7		.8	.7	.7
	.3	.5	.4	.4		.6	.4	.4
Sales/Receivables	0 UND	21 17.1	29 12.4	42 8.6		41 8.8	30 12.1	31 11.8
	25 14.6	37 9.8	43 8.5	60 6.1		44 8.3	44 8.4	48 7.6
	46 7.9	65 5.7	52 7.1	75 4.9		53 6.8	56 6.5	64 5.7
Cost of Sales/Inventory	0 UND	19 19.1	53 6.9	64 5.7		12 31.4	52 7.1	37 9.9
	24 14.9	46 7.9	88 4.1	112 3.3		89 4.1	92 4.0	86 4.2
	104 3.5	93 3.9	156 2.3	139 2.6		140 2.6	136 2.7	142 2.6
Cost of Sales/Payables	0 UND	11 33.1	21 17.1	21 17.5		21 17.5	15 24.1	16 22.6
	8 46.4	28 13.1	31 11.8	32 11.4		34 10.7	26 14.2	31 12.0
	33 11.0	43 8.5	47 7.8	43 8.5		44 8.2	47 7.8	52 7.0
Sales/Working Capital	5.1	4.8	3.9	3.4		2.9	4.4	5.2
	13.3	7.9	6.9	6.9		5.4	7.2	9.5
	-28.4	64.9	28.6	13.3		12.5	27.2	29.5
EBIT/Interest		13.8	13.2	16.5		28.9	7.8	5.6
		(19) 4.2	(52) 4.7	(30) 7.3		(12) 3.3	(122) 2.8	(153) 2.0
		-1.8	2.0	3.1		1.7	1.2	.1
Net Profit + Depr., Dep., Amort./Cur. Mat. L /T/D			6.3	2.1			4.3	5.3
			(20) 2.8	(11) 1.1			(31) 2.4	(36) 2.2
			1.8	.2			1.5	1.1
Fixed/Worth	.1	.1	.4	.3		.4	.3	.3
	1.8	.3	.7	.5		.6	.5	.7
	-11.0	1.6	2.1	1.8		1.9	1.5	1.7
Debt/Worth	.3	.5	1.1	1.1		1.0	.6	.8
	2.4	2.1	2.1	1.3		2.0	1.6	2.0
	-54.7	11.4	8.8	7.2		3.4	4.2	6.0
% Profit Before Taxes/Tangible Net Worth		96.6	51.1	48.7		26.1	32.0	29.2
		(19) 20.1	(50) 26.6	(28) 16.7		(13) 12.0	(115) 17.4	(140) 11.2
		6.4	11.7	5.4		2.5	4.1	-6.7
% Profit Before Taxes/Total Assets	37.6	24.9	14.6	11.8		7.6	12.2	8.8
	7.7	4.6	7.4	7.5		2.4	5.8	2.9
	-2.3	-8.5	3.3	2.1		.9	.9	-2.9
Sales/Net Fixed Assets	68.2	53.9	20.9	38.3		7.4	21.6	20.6
	18.1	33.4	11.2	8.5		6.7	11.0	8.2
	2.9	11.9	5.2	3.4		5.1	4.7	4.7
Sales/Total Assets	4.9	3.8	2.6	2.4		2.1	2.4	2.4
	3.2	2.9	2.0	1.5		1.7	1.8	1.7
	1.9	2.4	1.5	1.0		1.1	1.3	1.2
% Depr., Dep., Amort./Sales	(10) .3	(19) .8	(50) 1.1	(29) .8		(10) 1.5	(113) 1.1	(144) 1.2
	1.3	1.1	1.8	1.7		2.7	1.7	2.1
	10.9	2.6	3.3	2.7		3.3	4.1	4.2
% Officers', Directors', Owners' Comp/Sales		(13) 2.2	(15) 2.0				(30) 2.6	(41) 2.3
		4.2	3.6				5.1	3.5
		7.3	5.4				7.4	7.6
Net Sales ($)	10091M	88288M	544861M	1108860M	777287M	3466613M	4256144M	6180935M
Total Assets ($)	2928M	28583M	266264M	677274M	564457M	2172388M	2906237M	4237544M

M = $ thousand   MM = $ million
See Pages 11 through 21 for Explanation of Ratios and Data

Comparative Historical Data | Current Data Sorted By Sales

Comparative Historical Data				Current Data Sorted By Sales					
Type of Statement									
41	39	36	Unqualified				5	12	19
31	39	35	Reviewed	1	3	4	11	11	5
19	22	13	Compiled	3	3	2	4	1	
5	8	8	Tax Returns	3	4			1	
40	44	50	Other	2	5	5	8	11	19
4/1/02-3/31/03 ALL	4/1/03-3/31/04 ALL	4/1/04-3/31/05 ALL		0-1MM	1-3MM 37 (4/1-9/30/04)	3-5MM	5-10MM	10-25MM 105 (10/1/04-3/31/05)	25MM & OVER
136	152	142	**NUMBER OF STATEMENTS**	9	15	11	28	36	43
%	%	%	**ASSETS**	%	%	%	%	%	%
6.3	7.3	8.4	Cash & Equivalents		14.6	6.9	7.4	9.5	6.8
25.3	27.1	25.5	Trade Receivables (net)		23.8	37.8	25.7	23.1	27.0
30.3	31.3	32.2	Inventory		27.7	27.3	37.0	30.7	33.4
3.7	3.8	3.7	All Other Current		4.0	2.5	3.9	5.4	2.9
65.7	69.5	69.7	Total Current		70.1	74.5	73.9	68.7	70.2
25.4	21.9	21.3	Fixed Assets (net)		23.3	19.1	19.7	23.8	17.4
3.6	2.9	3.0	Intangibles (net)		1.9	2.2	.3	2.5	6.3
5.3	5.7	6.0	All Other Non-Current		4.7	4.3	6.1	4.9	6.1
100.0	100.0	100.0	Total		100.0	100.0	100.0	100.0	100.0
			LIABILITIES						
13.3	16.6	13.7	Notes Payable-Short Term		14.4	10.7	14.7	10.9	12.7
5.5	3.1	3.0	Cur. Mat.-L/T/D		1.3	2.7	4.1	4.6	1.8
13.1	12.9	14.3	Trade Payables		15.1	19.9	18.0	11.5	14.1
.3	.4	.6	Income Taxes Payable		.0	.2	1.0	.4	.7
11.8	14.7	11.9	All Other Current		21.1	4.9	12.1	12.1	11.1
44.0	47.8	43.5	Total Current		51.9	38.4	50.0	39.5	40.3
15.9	12.0	13.8	Long-Term Debt		11.9	16.2	11.7	13.0	12.4
.5	.5	.6	Deferred Taxes		.3	1.0	.8	.5	.8
4.5	5.7	6.4	All Other Non-Current		3.7	6.8	3.4	9.2	8.0
35.0	34.0	35.6	Net Worth		32.2	37.5	34.2	37.7	38.5
100.0	100.0	100.0	Total Liabilities & Net Worth		100.0	100.0	100.0	100.0	100.0
			INCOME DATA						
100.0	100.0	100.0	Net Sales		100.0	100.0	100.0	100.0	100.0
27.3	28.9	29.2	Gross Profit		31.3	33.3	27.0	30.7	23.4
24.1	25.4	23.8	Operating Expenses		25.8	28.9	22.1	25.4	18.1
3.2	3.6	5.5	Operating Profit		5.5	4.3	4.9	5.3	5.4
1.1	.8	.8	All Other Expenses (net)		.6	.1	1.0	.3	.7
2.1	2.7	4.7	Profit Before Taxes		4.9	4.3	3.9	5.0	4.7
			RATIOS						
2.6 / 1.6 / 1.1	2.6 / 1.5 / 1.1	2.6 / 1.7 / 1.2	Current		6.7 / 1.1 / .8	2.8 / 2.1 / 1.4	2.4 / 1.5 / 1.0	2.9 / 1.7 / 1.3	2.2 / 1.8 / 1.3
1.4 / .7 / .4	1.4 / .7 / .4	1.4 / .7 / .5	Quick		2.3 / .7 / .4	1.8 / 1.1 / .8	1.1 / .6 / .4	1.4 / .8 / .5	1.4 / .8 / .5
34 10.7 / 49 7.5 / 71 5.2	33 11.1 / 48 7.6 / 70 5.2	32 11.5 / 44 8.4 / 62 5.9	Sales/Receivables		6 65.9 / 32 11.3 / 65 5.7	36 10.2 / 49 7.4 / 77 4.7	27 13.7 / 45 8.0 / 51 7.2	30 12.0 / 43 8.5 / 64 5.7	39 9.4 / 50 7.4 / 65 5.6
36 10.1 / 87 4.2 / 148 2.5	49 7.5 / 79 4.6 / 126 2.9	39 9.4 / 90 4.1 / 136 2.7	Cost of Sales/Inventory		18 20.7 / 73 5.0 / 108 3.4	35 10.4 / 86 4.3 / 95 3.8	35 10.3 / 78 4.7 / 166 2.2	57 6.4 / 90 4.1 / 126 2.9	39 9.3 / 97 3.7 / 139 2.6
17 21.8 / 30 12.2 / 47 7.8	12 30.3 / 26 14.3 / 47 7.7	20 18.5 / 28 12.9 / 44 8.2	Cost of Sales/Payables		3 115.8 / 11 33.1 / 33 11.0	26 14.2 / 42 8.8 / 68 5.3	24 15.4 / 36 10.2 / 51 7.2	21 17.2 / 29 12.7 / 44 8.3	21 17.8 / 28 12.8 / 41 8.8
3.9 / 7.7 / 33.5	4.4 / 8.0 / 30.9	3.9 / 7.1 / 23.1	Sales/Working Capital		4.8 / 46.6 / -9.8	4.1 / 5.9 / 15.3	5.6 / 7.9 / NM	3.3 / 6.0 / 15.1	3.6 / 6.4 / 19.7
(130) 6.3 / 2.3 / .7	(140) 9.3 / 2.6 / .9	(126) 13.1 / 5.3 / 1.9	EBIT/Interest		(10) 7.9 / 1.8 / -9.8	(10) 15.5 / 3.7 / .7	(26) 15.6 / 4.0 / 2.0	(34) 21.7 / 7.4 / 3.3	(39) 14.7 / 5.7 / 1.9
(35) 3.7 / 1.5 / .5	(48) 4.9 / 2.0 / .8	(47) 4.8 / 2.3 / 1.0	Net Profit + Depr., Dep., Amort./Cur. Mat. L/T/D				(11) 10.8 / 3.1 / 1.7	(15) 4.2 / 2.1 / .8	(17) 4.3 / 2.8 / .7
.3 / .8 / 2.6	.3 / .6 / 1.5	.3 / .6 / 1.9	Fixed/Worth		.1 / .8 / -9.3	.1 / .7 / 1.6	.2 / .5 / 1.4	.5 / .7 / 2.7	.2 / .5 / 1.5
1.0 / 2.3 / 7.3	.9 / 1.8 / 4.9	1.0 / 2.0 / 7.4	Debt/Worth		.2 / 5.1 / -48.2	.6 / 1.6 / 10.5	.8 / 2.1 / 7.6	1.0 / 1.6 / 8.0	1.1 / 1.9 / 4.5
(124) 24.9 / 11.8 / -1.4	(137) 36.1 / 10.8 / .4	(125) 49.8 / 19.3 / 7.1	% Profit Before Taxes/Tangible Net Worth		(10) 97.2 / 26.9 / -2.4	48.1 / 14.7 / 1.2	(26) 51.1 / 19.8 / 8.2	(32) 54.3 / 24.6 / 12.0	(38) 47.0 / 16.2 / 4.9
9.2 / 3.0 / -.7	11.7 / 3.7 / -.1	13.2 / 6.5 / 1.7	% Profit Before Taxes/Total Assets		16.1 / 8.8 / -8.5	30.8 / 3.9 / .8	16.5 / 4.5 / 1.8	14.0 / 10.1 / 3.1	11.1 / 5.0 / 1.3
20.6 / 7.9 / 4.1	23.0 / 10.9 / 5.7	31.5 / 12.0 / 5.3	Sales/Net Fixed Assets		41.2 / 18.1 / 4.3	39.3 / 12.4 / 6.9	38.5 / 14.5 / 5.5	17.6 / 6.6 / 3.7	28.8 / 11.9 / 6.8
2.6 / 1.7 / 1.2	2.7 / 1.9 / 1.3	2.8 / 2.0 / 1.3	Sales/Total Assets		3.3 / 2.7 / 1.2	3.1 / 2.6 / 1.5	3.2 / 2.2 / 1.6	2.4 / 1.7 / 1.2	2.4 / 1.9 / 1.3
(118) 1.4 / 2.1 / 3.4	(140) 1.0 / 1.7 / 3.0	(124) .9 / 1.7 / 2.9	% Depr., Dep., Amort./Sales		(14) .8 / 1.6 / 3.2	(10) .9 / 1.7 / 4.6	(26) .9 / 1.7 / 2.7	(33) 1.1 / 1.8 / 3.0	(35) .9 / 1.5 / 2.8
(33) 2.5 / 4.8 / 8.5	(41) 2.0 / 3.6 / 5.6	(40) 1.9 / 3.5 / 5.4	% Officers', Directors', Owners' Comp/Sales						
3684849M	4020817M	5996000M	Net Sales ($)	4597M	26869M	42263M	197020M	516120M	5209131M
2457737M	2397041M	3711894M	Total Assets ($)	5858M	14800M	19627M	99332M	393292M	3178985M

© RMA 2005

M = $ thousand   MM = $ million
See Pages 11 through 21 for Explanation of Ratios and Data

Current Data Sorted By Assets / Comparative Historical Data

0-500M	500M-2MM	2-10MM	10-50MM	50-100MM	100-250MM	Type of Statement	4/1/00-3/31/01 ALL	4/1/01-3/31/02 ALL
1		3	3	2	2	Unqualified	7	10
	2	8	1			Reviewed	6	6
1	1	2	1			Compiled	7	10
	1	1				Tax Returns	1	2
	5	7		2		Other	7	7
	8 (4/1-9/30/04)		33 (10/1/04-3/31/05)					
2	8	21	6	2	2	NUMBER OF STATEMENTS	28	35
%	%	%	%	%	%	ASSETS	%	%
		7.0				Cash & Equivalents	7.7	9.0
		30.9				Trade Receivables (net)	23.9	22.9
		31.4				Inventory	28.8	25.7
		1.9				All Other Current	1.7	1.1
		71.2				Total Current	62.2	58.8
		22.3				Fixed Assets (net)	30.6	30.2
		1.2				Intangibles (net)	1.2	4.2
		5.3				All Other Non-Current	6.0	6.8
		100.0				Total	100.0	100.0
						LIABILITIES		
		14.4				Notes Payable-Short Term	12.3	9.9
		3.3				Cur. Mat.-L/T/D	3.8	4.4
		20.9				Trade Payables	12.5	14.7
		.3				Income Taxes Payable	.2	.2
		6.9				All Other Current	8.9	8.4
		45.8				Total Current	37.7	37.6
		14.2				Long-Term Debt	21.0	20.2
		.3				Deferred Taxes	.3	.8
		4.7				All Other Non-Current	4.3	1.4
		35.0				Net Worth	36.6	40.1
		100.0				Total Liabilities & Net Worth	100.0	100.0
						INCOME DATA		
		100.0				Net Sales	100.0	100.0
		27.8				Gross Profit	33.5	33.0
		23.5				Operating Expenses	28.8	29.0
		4.3				Operating Profit	4.7	3.9
		.8				All Other Expenses (net)	1.6	1.7
		3.5				Profit Before Taxes	3.1	2.2
						RATIOS		
		1.8				Current	2.9	2.6
		1.5					1.9	1.9
		1.2					1.1	1.1
		1.3				Quick	1.6	1.6
		.8					.8	.9
		.6					.6	.5
	40	9.1				Sales/Receivables	27 13.6	37 9.9
	48	7.6					53 6.8	45 8.1
	65	5.6					69 5.3	67 5.5
	36	10.2				Cost of Sales/Inventory	46 8.0	41 9.0
	85	4.3					103 3.5	87 4.2
	123	3.0					144 2.5	150 2.4
	20	18.3				Cost of Sales/Payables	17 21.5	15 25.0
	45	8.1					34 10.8	34 10.8
	73	5.0					47 7.7	66 5.5
		5.5				Sales/Working Capital	3.7	3.4
		9.4					6.9	8.6
		28.1					19.4	49.7
		6.8				EBIT/Interest	7.5	9.3
		(20) 2.5					2.0	(31) 2.9
		1.6					1.2	1.8
						Net Profit + Depr., Dep., Amort./Cur. Mat. L /T/D		7.7
							(14)	2.2
								1.0
		.3				Fixed/Worth	.3	.4
		.6					.9	.8
		1.5					2.2	2.4
		1.1				Debt/Worth	.7	.6
		2.1					2.5	1.5
		3.4					5.3	5.6
		33.1				% Profit Before Taxes/Tangible Net Worth	37.5	34.6
		(20) 15.2					12.8	(32) 15.1
		4.1					2.9	7.9
		15.2				% Profit Before Taxes/Total Assets	7.1	12.2
		4.0					3.8	5.2
		1.3					.9	1.8
		27.9				Sales/Net Fixed Assets	16.0	10.0
		11.5					6.2	6.4
		5.7					3.2	3.8
		2.8				Sales/Total Assets	2.1	2.2
		2.0					1.5	1.5
		1.6					1.1	1.2
		1.1				% Depr., Dep., Amort./Sales	.8	1.0
		1.7					(26) 2.0	(32) 2.3
		3.1					3.1	3.2
						% Officers', Directors', Owners' Comp/Sales	2.4	1.7
							(10) 4.2	(10) 4.0
							6.7	5.8
1609M	20160M	228712M	218867M	346440M	423036M	Net Sales ($)	530897M	806042M
595M	8287M	105234M	125039M	150779M	321693M	Total Assets ($)	362443M	568042M

M = $ thousand   MM = $ million
See Pages 11 through 21 for Explanation of Ratios and Data

Comparative Historical Data / Current Data Sorted By Sales

			Type of Statement	0-1MM	1-3MM	3-5MM	5-10MM	10-25MM	25MM & OVER
9	10	11	Unqualified			2		1	7
7	10	9	Reviewed			1	3	5	
7	7	4	Compiled		2	1		1	
2	6	3	Tax Returns	1	1		1		
9	9	14	Other		5	1	1	5	2
4/1/02-3/31/03	4/1/03-3/31/04	4/1/04-3/31/05			8 (4/1-9/30/04)			33 (10/1/04-3/31/05)	
ALL	ALL	ALL							
34	42	41	NUMBER OF STATEMENTS	1	8	5	6	12	9
%	%	%	ASSETS	%	%	%	%	%	%
8.0	5.1	9.4	Cash & Equivalents					6.2	
23.3	25.1	26.3	Trade Receivables (net)					29.7	
30.1	32.1	32.1	Inventory					38.6	
1.8	1.5	1.4	All Other Current					.7	
63.2	63.8	69.2	Total Current					75.1	
25.3	24.4	23.1	Fixed Assets (net)					19.1	
5.1	4.4	2.8	Intangibles (net)					1.4	
6.4	7.4	4.9	All Other Non-Current					4.3	
100.0	100.0	100.0	Total					100.0	
			LIABILITIES						
8.9	11.1	10.6	Notes Payable-Short Term					12.4	
3.4	3.2	4.3	Cur. Mat.-L/T/D					3.2	
11.8	13.7	20.2	Trade Payables					19.4	
.2	.1	.3	Income Taxes Payable					.3	
8.3	12.2	7.3	All Other Current					6.8	
32.6	40.3	42.6	Total Current					42.1	
21.9	19.0	16.8	Long-Term Debt					12.1	
.3	.2	.3	Deferred Taxes					.2	
.9	4.7	5.1	All Other Non-Current					5.3	
44.3	35.8	35.1	Net Worth					40.2	
100.0	100.0	100.0	Total Liabilities & Net Worth					100.0	
			INCOME DATA						
100.0	100.0	100.0	Net Sales					100.0	
33.2	35.2	31.9	Gross Profit					33.1	
30.3	31.5	26.2	Operating Expenses					26.8	
2.9	3.7	5.6	Operating Profit					6.3	
.9	.7	.8	All Other Expenses (net)					.7	
2.0	3.0	4.9	Profit Before Taxes					5.6	
			RATIOS						
3.4	2.7	2.4	Current					2.2	
2.0	1.6	1.5						1.8	
1.4	1.1	1.1						1.4	
1.6	1.2	1.2	Quick					1.3	
1.0	(41) .8	.8						.9	
.5	.5	.6						.6	
38 9.6	37 9.9	38 9.7	Sales/Receivables					36 10.0	
44 8.3	47 7.8	45 8.1						45 8.2	
56 6.6	63 5.8	61 6.0						55 6.6	
38 9.6	36 10.1	40 9.0	Cost of Sales/Inventory					41 8.9	
90 4.1	95 3.8	75 4.8						82 4.5	
182 2.0	176 2.1	123 3.0						143 2.5	
15 24.6	18 20.6	28 13.2	Cost of Sales/Payables					17 20.9	
36 10.0	32 11.3	43 8.4						38 9.6	
56 6.5	57 6.4	62 5.9						67 5.5	
3.7	3.7	4.3	Sales/Working Capital					4.8	
5.4	7.7	9.5						6.3	
14.2	20.9	41.2						14.4	
11.3	12.1	12.5	EBIT/Interest					56.8	
(32) 2.5	(41) 2.2	(37) 3.9						6.5	
1.2	.8	1.6						1.7	
5.3	9.3	5.0	Net Profit + Depr., Dep., Amort./Cur. Mat. L/T/D						
(14) 2.2	(15) 1.3	(16) 2.6							
1.5	.5	1.4							
.3	.3	.3	Fixed/Worth					.2	
.6	.7	.6						.3	
1.5	1.5	1.7						1.2	
.4	.7	.9	Debt/Worth					.8	
1.2	2.2	2.5						1.3	
7.0	4.9	4.7						2.7	
25.7	25.1	39.1	% Profit Before Taxes/Tangible Net Worth					49.8	
(31) 15.8	(37) 13.7	(37) 20.9						(11) 29.2	
4.7	1.8	8.5						3.4	
9.2	9.6	15.1	% Profit Before Taxes/Total Assets					26.6	
3.4	4.9	5.8						12.1	
.8	.1	1.5						2.0	
13.1	15.6	21.0	Sales/Net Fixed Assets					39.7	
6.4	8.1	10.8						12.6	
4.2	4.8	5.9						10.0	
2.1	2.4	3.0	Sales/Total Assets					3.2	
1.5	1.7	2.0						2.1	
1.2	1.1	1.5						1.8	
1.4	1.8	1.1	% Depr., Dep., Amort./Sales					.8	
(30) 2.4	(39) 2.2	(39) 1.7						1.2	
3.6	3.6	2.9						3.0	
.7	2.0	.6	% Officers', Directors', Owners' Comp/Sales						
(11) 4.0	(14) 4.2	(14) 2.5							
4.4	4.8	3.9							
925876M	1038698M	1238824M	Net Sales ($)	255M	17202M	20716M	46685M	180221M	973745M
625599M	660332M	711627M	Total Assets ($)	147M	7140M	12090M	27165M	78794M	586291M

© RMA 2005

M = $ thousand   MM = $ million
See Pages 11 through 21 for Explanation of Ratios and Data

Current Data Sorted By Assets   Comparative Historical Data

0-500M	500M-2MM	2-10MM	10-50MM	50-100MM	100-250MM	Type of Statement	4/1/00-3/31/01 ALL	4/1/01-3/31/02 ALL
	1	3	5	1	3	Unqualified	12	12
	1	3	1			Reviewed	4	6
	2	12				Compiled	6	8
1	7	1		1	3	Tax Returns	3	4
3	11	10	2	1	2	Other	24	23
	17 (4/1-9/30/04)		53 (10/1/04-3/31/05)					
4	22	29	8	2	5	NUMBER OF STATEMENTS	49	53
%	%	%	%	%	%	**ASSETS**	%	%
	8.6	9.7				Cash & Equivalents	9.8	7.0
	33.4	31.8				Trade Receivables (net)	29.3	28.9
	21.6	23.5				Inventory	25.3	28.6
	2.2	1.6				All Other Current	2.3	4.3
	65.9	66.6				Total Current	66.8	68.8
	26.9	23.8				Fixed Assets (net)	22.8	20.0
	.1	3.5				Intangibles (net)	5.3	5.6
	7.1	6.0				All Other Non-Current	5.1	5.5
	100.0	100.0				Total	100.0	100.0
						LIABILITIES		
	7.8	15.8				Notes Payable-Short Term	9.9	13.9
	4.7	3.1				Cur. Mat.-L/T/D	2.9	2.5
	21.9	16.8				Trade Payables	17.7	15.4
	.0	.3				Income Taxes Payable	.5	.5
	10.1	7.4				All Other Current	8.9	9.0
	44.4	43.5				Total Current	40.0	41.2
	15.1	14.5				Long-Term Debt	15.4	12.5
	.0	.7				Deferred Taxes	1.0	1.2
	2.6	6.9				All Other Non-Current	1.8	3.3
	37.9	34.5				Net Worth	41.8	41.7
	100.0	100.0				Total Liabilities & Net Worth	100.0	100.0
						INCOME DATA		
	100.0	100.0				Net Sales	100.0	100.0
	41.7	32.5				Gross Profit	29.9	30.9
	41.4	27.3				Operating Expenses	25.0	24.5
	.3	5.2				Operating Profit	4.9	6.3
	.2	.0				All Other Expenses (net)	.7	1.6
	.1	5.2				Profit Before Taxes	4.2	4.7
						RATIOS		
	3.0	2.5				Current	3.4	2.8
	1.3	1.8					2.0	1.8
	1.1	1.2					1.3	1.2
	2.4	1.5				Quick	1.7	1.3
	.9	1.0					1.0	.8
	.5	.6					.7	.5
30	12.3	45	8.0			Sales/Receivables	46 8.0	42 8.7
47	7.7	52	7.0				58 6.3	54 6.7
81	4.5	79	4.6				86 4.2	76 4.8
2	175.9	13	28.2			Cost of Sales/Inventory	35 10.5	31 11.8
39	9.4	57	6.4				80 4.6	60 6.1
84	4.3	85	4.3				155 2.4	141 2.6
14	25.8	27	13.4			Cost of Sales/Payables	23 15.9	22 16.8
51	7.2	46	8.0				40 9.1	35 10.5
92	3.9	56	6.5				54 6.7	49 7.4
	6.0	4.4				Sales/Working Capital	3.0	4.1
	12.3	6.8					5.3	5.3
	34.9	19.2					14.4	21.0
	24.7	10.3				EBIT/Interest	9.0	8.1
(19)	1.1	(27) 3.4					(42) 2.5	(48) 4.0
	-3.6	.9					-.3	1.7
						Net Profit + Depr., Dep., Amort./Cur. Mat. L /T/D	6.3	5.2
							(13) 1.2	(13) 1.9
							.3	1.1
	.3	.2				Fixed/Worth	.2	.2
	.5	.9					.5	.6
	2.2	2.7					1.4	1.2
	.4	1.0				Debt/Worth	.4	.6
	2.5	1.9					1.3	1.5
	6.8	6.8					3.1	5.8
	49.2	58.7				% Profit Before Taxes/Tangible Net Worth	33.1	46.7
(21)	3.7	(27) 11.1					(44) 14.5	(47) 22.8
	-54.0	-3.4					-3.4	7.4
	17.7	16.9				% Profit Before Taxes/Total Assets	15.0	16.9
	3.9	4.5					4.8	6.5
	-8.9	-.7					-1.9	1.5
	29.5	39.9				Sales/Net Fixed Assets	13.0	22.0
	11.4	11.6					8.9	11.0
	5.1	3.8					4.8	5.7
	2.8	2.4				Sales/Total Assets	2.2	2.6
	2.3	2.0					1.4	1.7
	1.9	1.4					1.1	1.3
	1.5	.6				% Depr., Dep., Amort./Sales	1.7	1.4
(16)	3.2	(25) 1.5					(33) 3.2	(45) 2.9
	5.0	3.4					4.6	3.8
	2.4					% Officers', Directors', Owners' Comp/Sales	2.2	1.8
(12)	7.0						(10) 3.4	(16) 3.2
	7.6						7.9	9.8
4811M	67329M	247026M	511347M	130173M	1331685M	Net Sales ($)	1776641M	2142662M
1325M	28218M	131745M	249233M	151445M	754100M	Total Assets ($)	1607680M	1478566M

M = $ thousand   MM = $ million
See Pages 11 through 21 for Explanation of Ratios and Data

Comparative Historical Data / Current Data Sorted By Sales

		Comparative Historical Data		Type of Statement		17 (4/1-9/30/04)		53 (10/1/04-3/31/05)			
					0-1MM	1-3MM	3-5MM	5-10MM	10-25MM	25MM & OVER	
16	18	13		Unqualified		1		2	3	7	
6	8	5		Reviewed		2	1	1		1	
11	11	14		Compiled		2	3	9			
4	5	9		Tax Returns		5	3	1			
26	32	29		Other	2	5	7	5	5	5	
4/1/02-3/31/03 ALL	4/1/03-3/31/04 ALL	4/1/04-3/31/05 ALL									
63	74	70		**NUMBER OF STATEMENTS**	2	15	14	18	8	13	

Item	4/1/02-3/31/03 ALL	4/1/03-3/31/04 ALL	4/1/04-3/31/05 ALL	0-1MM	1-3MM	3-5MM	5-10MM	10-25MM	25MM & OVER
	%	%	%	%	%	%	%	%	%
ASSETS									
Cash & Equivalents	8.1	8.2	9.2		9.9	9.2	12.6		9.3
Trade Receivables (net)	27.3	27.7	31.2		31.8	35.5	33.5		23.9
Inventory	25.2	25.9	22.4		18.6	20.1	21.8		25.8
All Other Current	3.0	4.1	2.0		.7	4.5	.6		3.0
Total Current	63.7	66.0	64.8		61.1	69.2	68.6		61.9
Fixed Assets (net)	25.6	22.5	25.4		30.9	19.8	23.7		22.4
Intangibles (net)	6.5	5.6	3.3		.4	1.9	2.8		7.5
All Other Non-Current	4.2	5.9	6.5		7.7	9.0	5.0		8.2
Total	100.0	100.0	100.0		100.0	100.0	100.0		100.0
LIABILITIES									
Notes Payable-Short Term	10.2	9.7	10.7		8.9	12.8	13.0		4.9
Cur. Mat.-L/T/D	4.4	3.3	3.6		4.9	5.9	2.5		2.4
Trade Payables	11.8	12.1	19.0		18.6	22.4	18.4		12.4
Income Taxes Payable	.8	.3	.4		.1	.0	.3		1.1
All Other Current	6.8	9.8	8.2		4.1	10.0	7.7		8.4
Total Current	34.0	35.2	41.8		36.6	51.0	41.8		29.2
Long-Term Debt	10.1	9.2	18.0		21.7	15.1	14.0		16.5
Deferred Taxes	1.0	1.1	.5		.4	.0	.7		.8
All Other Non-Current	5.6	9.2	5.0		2.4	1.8	10.0		1.5
Net Worth	49.3	45.3	34.7		38.9	32.1	33.4		52.0
Total Liabilities & Net Worth	100.0	100.0	100.0		100.0	100.0	100.0		100.0
INCOME DATA									
Net Sales	100.0	100.0	100.0		100.0	100.0	100.0		100.0
Gross Profit	34.8	34.7	36.6		47.1	45.9	31.1		28.5
Operating Expenses	29.6	30.8	31.8		42.8	43.8	26.9		18.0
Operating Profit	5.2	3.9	4.7		4.2	2.1	4.2		10.5
All Other Expenses (net)	2.0	1.1	.4		1.1	-.1	-.7		.8
Profit Before Taxes	3.2	2.9	4.3		3.1	2.2	4.9		9.7
RATIOS									
Current	3.2	3.0	2.6		4.1	3.7	2.1		3.0
	1.9	1.8	1.6		2.2	1.3	1.8		2.0
	1.2	1.4	1.2		1.3	1.0	1.3		1.6
Quick	1.9	1.7	1.8		4.0	2.9	1.5		1.7
	1.0	1.0	1.0		1.3	.9	.9		1.3
	.6	.6	.6		.5	.4	.7		.8
Sales/Receivables	43 8.4	44 8.3	37 9.9		36 10.0	22 16.5	46 8.0		34 10.6
	57 6.4	58 6.3	52 7.0		43 8.5	58 6.3	52 7.1		49 7.4
	76 4.8	75 4.8	79 4.6		82 4.4	78 4.7	81 4.5		83 4.4
Cost of Sales/Inventory	23 16.2	24 14.9	22 16.6		1 655.0	0 UND	17 22.0		28 13.0
	81 4.5	78 4.7	53 6.9		57 6.4	29 12.5	50 7.3		73 5.0
	123 3.0	146 2.5	99 3.7		163 2.2	58 6.3	81 4.5		112 3.2
Cost of Sales/Payables	19 19.6	21 17.2	21 17.4		18 20.7	13 27.7	34 10.9		15 24.5
	37 9.9	35 10.6	46 7.9		43 8.6	39 9.3	46 7.9		39 9.4
	48 7.7	65 5.6	65 5.6		89 4.1	71 5.2	56 6.5		51 7.2
Sales/Working Capital	3.6	3.2	5.0		4.2	5.8	6.1		4.7
	5.9	5.4	7.6		5.5	16.2	7.1		5.5
	13.5	12.6	23.5		18.1	NM	18.1		8.0
EBIT/Interest	8.8	10.7	14.5		11.0	32.3	17.5		22.0
	(60) 4.0	(68) 3.1	(60) 3.6		(11) 7.8	(13) 2.2	(17) 3.4		(10) 5.4
	.8	1.2	.0		-1.2	-1.9	.6		2.6
Net Profit + Depr., Dep., Amort./Cur. Mat. L/T/D	6.8	4.0	4.7						
	(16) 2.6	(27) 2.3	(20) 2.5						
	1.5	1.0	1.3						
Fixed/Worth	.2	.2	.2		.1	.2	.2		.3
	.5	.5	.6		.5	.9	.4		.4
	1.6	1.3	2.0		1.5	2.3	3.8		.7
Debt/Worth	.4	.6	.9		.4	.8	1.0		.6
	1.1	1.3	1.9		1.6	2.6	2.1		1.6
	2.8	4.1	5.4		6.7	7.4	6.9		2.2
% Profit Before Taxes/Tangible Net Worth	25.6	26.4	55.5		25.5	94.4	51.8		59.9
	(58) 13.8	(69) 10.9	(65) 16.9		(14) 9.0	(12) 6.6	(17) 11.1		27.9
	2.0	2.9	-4.0		-52.5	-24.2	-5.7		17.7
% Profit Before Taxes/Total Assets	12.9	10.5	18.0		16.4	26.0	15.8		24.2
	5.4	4.4	6.4		5.9	4.6	4.7		12.7
	-.3	.9	-.7		-7.7	-5.8	-1.0		5.3
Sales/Net Fixed Assets	29.6	28.2	26.4		28.6	114.2	33.6		18.3
	6.7	8.0	9.4		6.5	18.4	9.9		7.9
	3.5	4.4	4.0		2.2	7.6	3.9		4.7
Sales/Total Assets	2.4	2.3	2.8		3.5	2.8	2.1		3.4
	1.6	1.6	2.1		2.0	2.3	2.1		1.4
	1.1	1.2	1.4		1.0	2.1	1.6		1.0
% Depr., Dep., Amort./Sales	1.4	1.7	1.0		1.1		.7		
	(53) 2.9	(63) 3.1	(55) 2.4		(12) 2.8		(16) 1.5		
	4.4	4.7	4.2		5.6		3.0		
% Officers', Directors', Owners' Comp/Sales	2.7	3.6	2.3						
	(19) 3.6	(20) 5.0	(21) 7.2						
	8.9	10.7	10.5						
Net Sales ($)	2292622M	2212382M	2292371M	1193M	29521M	54273M	133140M	131620M	1942624M
Total Assets ($)	1893606M	1832416M	1316066M	777M	22356M	22161M	73866M	96131M	1100775M

M = $ thousand   MM = $ million
See Pages 11 through 21 for Explanation of Ratios and Data

Current Data Sorted By Assets

Comparative Historical Data

	0-500M	500M-2MM	2-10MM	10-50MM	50-100MM	100-250MM		4/1/00-3/31/01 ALL	4/1/01-3/31/02 ALL
		2 2 1 2 1	1 6 3	2 1 4			**Type of Statement** Unqualified Reviewed Compiled Tax Returns Other		
		4 (4/1-9/30/04)		19 (10/1/04-3/31/05)					
			6	10	7		**NUMBER OF STATEMENTS**		
	%	%	%	%	%	%	**ASSETS**	%	%
	D		5.7	D	D	D	Cash & Equivalents	D	D
	A		29.5	A	A	A	Trade Receivables (net)	A	A
	T		16.0	T	T	T	Inventory	T	T
	A		3.5	A	A	A	All Other Current	A	A
			54.7				Total Current		
	N		32.0	N	N	N	Fixed Assets (net)	N	N
	O		.7	O	O	O	Intangibles (net)	O	O
	T		12.6	T	T	T	All Other Non-Current	T	T
			100.0				Total		
	A			A	A	A	**LIABILITIES**	A	A
	V		10.1	V	V	V	Notes Payable-Short Term	V	V
	A		6.5	A	A	A	Cur. Mat.-L/T/D	A	A
	I		20.0	I	I	I	Trade Payables	I	I
	L		.1	L	L	L	Income Taxes Payable	L	L
	A		12.5	A	A	A	All Other Current	A	A
	B		49.2	B	B	B	Total Current	B	B
	L		17.2	L	L	L	Long-Term Debt	L	L
	E		.6	E	E	E	Deferred Taxes	E	E
			4.1				All Other Non-Current		
			28.9				Net Worth		
			100.0				Total Liabilities & Net Worth		
							INCOME DATA		
			100.0				Net Sales		
			21.2				Gross Profit		
			20.4				Operating Expenses		
			.8				Operating Profit		
			.8				All Other Expenses (net)		
			.0				Profit Before Taxes		
							RATIOS		
			1.6						
			1.3				Current		
			1.0						
			1.1						
			.8				Quick		
			.7						
		43	8.4						
		52	7.1				Sales/Receivables		
		55	6.6						
		20	18.4						
		32	11.3				Cost of Sales/Inventory		
		53	6.9						
		29	12.7						
		40	9.1				Cost of Sales/Payables		
		51	7.2						
			9.1						
			21.0				Sales/Working Capital		
			NM						
			4.9						
			.7				EBIT/Interest		
			−2.9						
							Net Profit + Depr., Dep., Amort./Cur. Mat. L /T/D		
			.7						
			1.0				Fixed/Worth		
			2.0						
			1.1						
			2.1				Debt/Worth		
			7.6						
							% Profit Before Taxes/Tangible Net Worth		
			8.6						
			−1.1				% Profit Before Taxes/Total Assets		
			−8.8						
			14.4						
			5.9				Sales/Net Fixed Assets		
			4.3						
			2.6						
			2.3				Sales/Total Assets		
			1.8						
			1.8						
			3.6				% Depr., Dep., Amort./Sales		
			3.9						
							% Officers', Directors', Owners' Comp/Sales		
		19272M	110272M	279767M			Net Sales ($)		
		6974M	50564M	168280M			Total Assets ($)		

M = $ thousand   MM = $ million
See Pages 11 through 21 for Explanation of Ratios and Data

Comparative Historical Data | **Current Data Sorted By Sales**

				Type of Statement						
8	8	3		Unqualified		1		6	2 / 1	1 / 1
5	6	9		Reviewed						
4	3	1		Compiled	1					
3	5	2		Tax Returns		1	1			
13	13	8		Other		1		2	4	1
4/1/02-	4/1/03-	4/1/04-				4 (4/1-9/30/04)		19 (10/1/04-3/31/05)		
3/31/03	3/31/04	3/31/05			0-1MM	1-3MM	3-5MM	5-10MM	10-25MM	25MM & OVER
ALL	ALL	ALL								
33	35	23		**NUMBER OF STATEMENTS**	1	3	1	8	7	3
%	%	%		**ASSETS**	%	%	%	%	%	%
7.7	7.5	8.6		Cash & Equivalents						
25.5	29.2	25.3		Trade Receivables (net)						
24.0	19.3	19.5		Inventory						
2.3	1.8	2.8		All Other Current						
59.6	57.7	56.1		Total Current						
29.1	28.4	28.4		Fixed Assets (net)						
2.0	4.8	4.4		Intangibles (net)						
9.3	9.0	11.1		All Other Non-Current						
100.0	100.0	100.0		Total						
				LIABILITIES						
16.3	22.0	9.7		Notes Payable-Short Term						
4.9	6.5	7.8		Cur. Mat.-L/T/D						
17.5	15.9	17.0		Trade Payables						
.5	.2	.5		Income Taxes Payable						
15.1	13.7	14.2		All Other Current						
54.3	58.4	49.1		Total Current						
15.0	19.3	24.3		Long-Term Debt						
.3	.4	.4		Deferred Taxes						
5.6	7.8	4.9		All Other Non-Current						
24.8	14.1	21.4		Net Worth						
100.0	100.0	100.0		Total Liabilities & Net Worth						
				INCOME DATA						
100.0	100.0	100.0		Net Sales						
26.4	30.8	23.8		Gross Profit						
29.0	28.4	20.6		Operating Expenses						
-2.6	2.4	3.2		Operating Profit						
1.3	1.1	.8		All Other Expenses (net)						
-4.0	1.3	2.4		Profit Before Taxes						
				RATIOS						
1.5	1.6	1.5								
1.1	1.4	1.2		Current						
.8	.9	.9								
1.0	1.0	.9								
.6	.8	.7		Quick						
.3	.4	.4								
23 15.5	38 9.7	30 12.3								
46 7.9	48 7.7	46 7.9		Sales/Receivables						
72 5.1	69 5.3	54 6.8								
32 11.3	23 16.2	18 20.4								
59 6.2	52 7.0	40 9.2		Cost of Sales/Inventory						
116 3.2	73 5.0	63 5.8								
25 14.7	20 18.6	25 14.6								
34 10.6	31 11.9	38 9.7		Cost of Sales/Payables						
63 5.8	51 7.1	51 7.1								
8.9	7.5	10.0								
30.7	14.1	24.0		Sales/Working Capital						
-16.4	-61.5	-16.7								
4.2	6.8	5.4								
(28) 1.2	(33) 3.1	(22) 3.3		EBIT/Interest						
-2.4	-2.8	-1.2								
	6.4			Net Profit + Depr., Dep.,						
	(10) 1.1			Amort./Cur. Mat. L/T/D						
	-.6									
.5	.5	.6								
1.2	1.1	1.1		Fixed/Worth						
NM	3.5	8.4								
1.2	1.0	1.7								
3.9	3.7	3.7		Debt/Worth						
NM	9.1	12.5								
28.9	46.2	47.1		% Profit Before Taxes/Tangible						
(25) 6.3	(27) 18.2	(18) 19.6		Net Worth						
-11.5	-9.4	-21.4								
4.5	12.5	14.0		% Profit Before Taxes/Total						
.0	5.3	5.3		Assets						
-12.6	-10.8	-5.0								
18.6	21.7	26.4								
6.6	9.9	9.1		Sales/Net Fixed Assets						
3.3	4.1	4.2								
2.3	2.4	2.7								
1.8	1.9	2.2		Sales/Total Assets						
1.2	1.4	1.5								
1.2	1.7	1.9								
(32) 3.9	(32) 3.0	(19) 3.5		% Depr., Dep., Amort./Sales						
6.2	4.3	4.1								
3.9	2.9			% Officers', Directors',						
(12) 6.0	(16) 5.0			Owners' Comp/Sales						
6.5	6.7									
296460M	316179M	409311M		Net Sales ($)	915M	6898M	4635M	64625M	135872M	196366M
155411M	184606M	225818M		Total Assets ($)	1246M	2291M	1653M	29887M	75571M	115170M

© RMA 2005

M = $ thousand   MM = $ million
See Pages 11 through 21 for Explanation of Ratios and Data

Current Data Sorted By Assets   Comparative Historical Data

0-500M	500M-2MM	2-10MM	10-50MM	50-100MM	100-250MM	Type of Statement	4/1/00-3/31/01 ALL	4/1/01-3/31/02 ALL
1	3	6	2		1	Unqualified	8	7
1	6	7				Reviewed	9	10
		2				Compiled	4	5
		1				Tax Returns	2	2
2	3	4	3		1	Other	11	13
	2 (4/1-9/30/04)		41 (10/1/04-3/31/05)					
4	12	20	5		2	NUMBER OF STATEMENTS	34	37

0-500M %	500M-2MM %	2-10MM %	10-50MM %	50-100MM %	100-250MM %	ASSETS	%	%
	11.7	8.8				Cash & Equivalents	7.0	6.6
	31.5	29.0				Trade Receivables (net)	23.6	24.0
	20.7	35.1	DATA			Inventory	35.1	35.1
	1.4	2.0	NOT			All Other Current	2.8	2.5
	65.4	74.8	AVAILABLE			Total Current	68.5	68.2
	30.6	17.3				Fixed Assets (net)	22.8	21.6
	2.0	.5				Intangibles (net)	3.1	3.1
	2.0	7.4				All Other Non-Current	5.6	7.0
	100.0	100.0				Total	100.0	100.0

						LIABILITIES		
	12.8	15.7				Notes Payable-Short Term	12.0	12.9
	3.2	1.9				Cur. Mat.-L/T/D	2.5	5.1
	15.9	13.2				Trade Payables	12.1	15.0
	.0	.1				Income Taxes Payable	.5	.1
	26.6	17.4				All Other Current	17.0	16.4
	58.5	48.2				Total Current	44.1	49.5
	18.4	7.9				Long-Term Debt	11.5	9.1
	.0	.6				Deferred Taxes	.3	.3
	.9	10.6				All Other Non-Current	7.1	14.0
	22.2	32.6				Net Worth	36.9	27.2
	100.0	100.0				Total Liabilities & Net Worth	100.0	100.0

						INCOME DATA		
	100.0	100.0				Net Sales	100.0	100.0
	31.5	25.9				Gross Profit	32.1	31.9
	30.2	21.4				Operating Expenses	27.4	30.1
	1.3	4.5				Operating Profit	4.6	1.8
	1.2	.3				All Other Expenses (net)	1.2	1.4
	.1	4.2				Profit Before Taxes	3.5	.3

						RATIOS		
	1.5	2.3					2.3	2.4
	1.2	1.8				Current	1.5	1.4
	.9	1.2					1.1	1.1
	.9	1.2					1.1	1.0
	.7	.8				Quick	.6	.7
	.5	.6					.4	.5
	33 10.9	40 9.2					36 10.1	35 10.3
	47 7.8	53 6.9				Sales/Receivables	42 8.7	44 8.2
	70 5.2	59 6.2					56 6.5	57 6.4
	17 20.9	56 6.6					56 6.5	56 6.5
	41 9.0	80 4.6				Cost of Sales/Inventory	101 3.6	86 4.3
	73 5.0	127 2.9					146 2.5	166 2.2
	18 20.6	18 20.3					19 19.4	18 20.1
	35 10.3	30 12.1				Cost of Sales/Payables	31 11.7	30 12.0
	58 6.3	40 9.2					46 7.9	54 6.8
	10.4	3.5					4.3	4.1
	31.8	7.9				Sales/Working Capital	8.2	7.4
	−21.3	14.8					38.9	48.1
		14.5					9.8	3.7
		(19) 5.1				EBIT/Interest	(32) 3.7	(33) 1.0
		2.4					1.3	−2.4
						Net Profit + Depr., Dep.,	5.7	
						Amort./Cur. Mat. L/T/D	(10) 2.9	
							.3	
	.4	.2					.2	.2
	1.6	.5				Fixed/Worth	.6	.6
	75.0	2.5					2.9	2.4
	1.7	.6					.9	.6
	4.4	1.5				Debt/Worth	1.4	1.6
	115.3	6.7					6.4	9.1
	61.5	38.4					56.4	26.1
	(10) 15.3	(17) 13.5				% Profit Before Taxes/Tangible Net Worth	(31) 17.4	(31) 1.0
	−192.6	3.3					4.2	−7.0
	16.6	13.4					14.0	7.9
	.0	4.6				% Profit Before Taxes/Total Assets	5.2	.0
	−9.9	1.5					.7	−4.2
	46.6	57.5					26.2	19.1
	7.1	13.3				Sales/Net Fixed Assets	10.0	10.6
	3.4	7.2					6.3	6.9
	2.7	2.8					2.5	2.5
	2.0	1.8				Sales/Total Assets	1.8	1.7
	1.4	1.3					1.4	1.4
	1.0	.3					.7	1.4
	2.6	(19) 1.5				% Depr., Dep., Amort./Sales	(32) 1.5	(35) 2.2
	3.5	2.3					3.4	3.6
							1.8	2.1
						% Officers', Directors', Owners' Comp/Sales	(14) 4.1	(16) 2.9
							7.7	6.5
3770M	28843M	179765M	231883M		268157M	Net Sales ($)	416977M	755401M
1032M	13694M	92180M	135930M		293530M	Total Assets ($)	279967M	509055M

© RMA 2005

M = $ thousand   MM = $ million
See Pages 11 through 21 for Explanation of Ratios and Data

Comparative Historical Data / Current Data Sorted By Sales

			Type of Statement	0-1MM	1-3MM	3-5MM	5-10MM	10-25MM	25MM & OVER
8	10	8	Unqualified				3	1	3
18	18	12	Reviewed	1	2	2	3	3	1
8	4	9	Compiled	1	5	1	2		
2	2	1	Tax Returns				1		
16	14	13	Other		4	1	3	1	4
4/1/02-3/31/03	4/1/03-3/31/04	4/1/04-3/31/05			2 (4/1-9/30/04)		41 (10/1/04-3/31/05)		
ALL	ALL	ALL							
52	48	43	**NUMBER OF STATEMENTS**	2	11	5	12	5	8
%	%	%	**ASSETS**	%	%	%	%	%	%
8.7	11.4	10.4	Cash & Equivalents		10.9		10.9		
26.6	26.8	29.0	Trade Receivables (net)		35.5		28.0		
29.0	24.7	28.5	Inventory		21.9		32.1		
4.6	3.7	2.8	All Other Current		1.6		.3		
69.0	66.6	70.7	Total Current		69.8		71.2		
22.1	25.9	22.4	Fixed Assets (net)		27.0		22.6		
2.6	1.8	1.8	Intangibles (net)		1.8		.2		
6.4	5.6	5.0	All Other Non-Current		1.4		6.0		
100.0	100.0	100.0	Total		100.0		100.0		
			LIABILITIES						
16.7	12.3	11.7	Notes Payable-Short Term		12.6		12.2		
3.4	3.1	2.1	Cur. Mat.-L/T/D		2.2		2.1		
16.0	12.2	14.0	Trade Payables		15.3		8.7		
.1	.3	.3	Income Taxes Payable		.0		.2		
17.9	16.5	22.3	All Other Current		31.1		17.0		
54.0	44.4	50.5	Total Current		61.3		40.2		
11.4	13.6	12.6	Long-Term Debt		24.8		9.5		
.4	.5	.4	Deferred Taxes		.0		1.0		
10.3	6.0	10.6	All Other Non-Current		19.3		7.9		
23.9	35.6	25.9	Net Worth		-5.4		41.4		
100.0	100.0	100.0	Total Liabilities & Net Worth		100.0		100.0		
			INCOME DATA						
100.0	100.0	100.0	Net Sales		100.0		100.0		
29.8	29.6	29.3	Gross Profit		35.4		28.2		
26.8	26.4	26.3	Operating Expenses		35.7		22.1		
3.0	3.3	3.1	Operating Profit		-.3		6.2		
1.0	.6	.9	All Other Expenses (net)		1.1		1.0		
2.0	2.6	2.2	Profit Before Taxes		-1.5		5.2		
			RATIOS						
2.1	2.4	2.1			1.5		2.6		
1.5	1.8	1.4	Current		1.2		2.0		
1.1	1.0	1.2			.9		1.2		
1.0	1.2	1.2			1.0		1.5		
.8	.9	.7	Quick		.7		.9		
.5	.6	.6			.5		.7		
38 9.5	41 8.9	38 9.7		32 11.4		46 7.9			
49 7.4	51 7.2	48 7.6	Sales/Receivables	48 7.6		55 6.6			
64 5.7	69 5.3	63 5.8		71 5.1		73 5.0			
38 9.6	31 11.9	38 9.7		21 17.3		56 6.5			
76 4.8	62 5.9	62 5.9	Cost of Sales/Inventory	35 10.6		80 4.6			
153 2.4	104 3.5	122 3.0		78 4.6		120 3.0			
21 17.0	13 27.4	20 17.8		20 17.8		12 30.3			
37 9.9	29 12.7	30 12.3	Cost of Sales/Payables	47 7.7		29 12.5			
52 7.0	43 8.4	52 7.0		64 5.7		33 11.0			
5.1	3.8	4.2			8.7		3.1		
8.6	8.2	9.3	Sales/Working Capital		28.2		5.5		
34.0	80.9	32.5			-16.0		13.5		
5.3	6.9	15.3					15.3		
(48) 2.4	(44) 3.2	(35) 3.7	EBIT/Interest			(11)	5.9		
-.8	.0	.3					2.6		
4.3	3.8		Net Profit + Depr., Dep.,						
(16) 1.3	(15) 2.3		Amort./Cur. Mat. L/T/D						
-1.4	.3								
.3	.3	.3			.3		.1		
.7	.6	.7	Fixed/Worth		3.0		.5		
10.3	3.4	3.8			97.8		2.4		
1.0	.6	.7			2.3		.4		
2.2	1.5	2.0	Debt/Worth		10.6		1.2		
70.8	6.8	10.6			166.0		5.9		
43.6	24.2	39.5	% Profit Before Taxes/Tangible				36.3		
(43) 18.0	(42) 9.5	(36) 14.3	Net Worth			(11)	9.3		
-5.9	1.2	2.6					2.8		
13.7	10.8	14.5	% Profit Before Taxes/Total		19.1		12.7		
3.2	3.0	4.5	Assets		-.8		4.0		
-4.2	-.8	-2.2			-18.3		1.7		
19.2	22.2	29.0			53.5		26.6		
10.4	9.1	10.7	Sales/Net Fixed Assets		8.8		10.3		
5.3	3.6	5.0			3.1		3.5		
2.6	2.2	2.7			3.4		2.0		
1.7	1.7	1.9	Sales/Total Assets		1.8		1.6		
1.2	1.1	1.3			1.4		1.2		
1.4	1.5	.9			.9		.7		
(49) 2.1	(41) 2.1	(42) 1.7	% Depr., Dep., Amort./Sales		1.8	(11)	1.6		
3.0	3.7	3.3			3.5		3.3		
1.6	1.6	.9	% Officers', Directors',						
(18) 3.1	(14) 3.1	(15) 2.6	Owners' Comp/Sales						
6.3	6.3	4.7							
918974M	1085861M	712418M	Net Sales ($)	1019M	20560M	18912M	76496M	69097M	526334M
683649M	844644M	536366M	Total Assets ($)	569M	10596M	9777M	54194M	23123M	438107M

© RMA 2005

M = $ thousand   MM = $ million
See Pages 11 through 21 for Explanation of Ratios and Data

Current Data Sorted By Assets   Comparative Historical Data

Note: In the table below, the columns 0-500M, 500M-2MM, 50-100MM and 100-250MM show **DATA NOT AVAILABLE** for the Assets, Liabilities, Income Data and Ratios sections (printed vertically in the source across the 50-100MM column). Only the 2-10MM and 10-50MM current-data columns and the two historical columns contain values for those sections.

0-500M	500M-2MM	2-10MM	10-50MM	50-100MM	100-250MM	Type of Statement	4/1/00-3/31/01 ALL	4/1/01-3/31/02 ALL
	1	4	10		1	Unqualified	20	12
	2	8	1			Reviewed	19	8
	2	4				Compiled	25	18
2	2	2				Tax Returns	3	
	1	4	3			Other	20	24
	4 (4/1-9/30/04)		43 (10/1/04-3/31/05)					
2	8	22	14		1	NUMBER OF STATEMENTS	87	62
%	%	%	%	%	%	**ASSETS**	%	%
		6.6	8.6			Cash & Equivalents	9.3	10.9
		21.5	22.0			Trade Receivables (net)	22.2	19.3
		41.8	33.3			Inventory	27.0	30.1
		2.5	4.1			All Other Current	4.6	5.5
		72.3	68.0			Total Current	63.2	65.9
		18.3	21.0			Fixed Assets (net)	23.9	23.5
		3.0	2.7			Intangibles (net)	5.6	3.1
		6.4	8.3			All Other Non-Current	7.4	7.6
		100.0	100.0			Total	100.0	100.0
						LIABILITIES		
		12.7	8.4			Notes Payable-Short Term	13.0	7.7
		5.1	1.2			Cur. Mat.-L/T/D	3.9	2.6
		18.8	9.1			Trade Payables	10.8	11.9
		.0	.6			Income Taxes Payable	.5	.5
		12.5	16.5			All Other Current	15.5	12.9
		49.1	35.8			Total Current	43.7	35.5
		10.4	8.6			Long-Term Debt	12.6	15.6
		.1	.9			Deferred Taxes	.4	.5
		2.9	2.1			All Other Non-Current	7.6	3.5
		37.4	52.6			Net Worth	35.8	44.8
		100.0	100.0			Total Liabilities & Net Worth	100.0	100.0
						INCOME DATA		
		100.0	100.0			Net Sales	100.0	100.0
		30.0	28.8			Gross Profit	32.1	33.8
		27.4	24.0			Operating Expenses	29.1	29.7
		2.6	4.8			Operating Profit	2.9	4.1
		.9	−.6			All Other Expenses (net)	1.3	1.8
		1.8	5.3			Profit Before Taxes	1.7	2.3
						RATIOS		
		2.2	3.4			Current	2.6	3.1
		1.6	2.3				1.6	1.9
		1.2	1.5				1.1	1.3
		.9	1.8			Quick	1.5	1.4
		.6	1.2				.8	.9
		.4	.5				.4	.7
		26 14.1	35 10.3			Sales/Receivables	30 12.3	28 13.1
		36 10.1	45 8.1				42 8.7	44 8.3
		61 6.0	60 6.1				59 6.2	57 6.4
		69 5.3	63 5.8			Cost of Sales/Inventory	39 9.3	53 6.9
		125 2.9	112 3.3				78 4.7	100 3.6
		157 2.3	135 2.7				139 2.6	133 2.8
		26 14.2	12 29.9			Cost of Sales/Payables	15 23.9	13 27.5
		40 9.0	26 14.1				27 13.5	24 15.2
		57 6.5	36 10.0				46 7.9	45 8.2
		4.3	3.4			Sales/Working Capital	4.1	3.5
		7.9	4.0				7.8	5.8
		24.2	6.7				29.2	9.8
		19.4	19.9			EBIT/Interest	9.2	9.9
		3.5	(13) 6.0				(74) 3.4	(56) 3.1
		1.2	2.3				.9	.4
						Net Profit + Depr., Dep., Amort./Cur. Mat. L /T/D	5.6	2.3
							(20) 1.5	(15) 1.0
							.4	.5
		.1	.3			Fixed/Worth	.2	.2
		.3	.5				.5	.5
		1.7	.7				3.3	1.1
		.7	.4			Debt/Worth	.7	.5
		1.8	.8				1.7	1.1
		7.5	3.1				7.6	3.3
		37.9	32.3			% Profit Before Taxes/Tangible Net Worth	34.3	27.9
		(21) 14.4	(13) 11.4				(72) 14.4	(56) 12.7
		8.4	4.8				2.1	.7
		9.1	12.4			% Profit Before Taxes/Total Assets	12.6	12.0
		5.1	7.1				5.7	3.4
		.5	3.4				−1.2	−1.2
		28.8	26.8			Sales/Net Fixed Assets	16.4	23.5
		14.8	7.2				7.9	8.5
		7.8	4.0				5.3	4.2
		2.2	2.3			Sales/Total Assets	2.3	2.1
		1.9	1.4				1.7	1.6
		1.4	1.2				1.2	1.2
		.9	.8			% Depr., Dep., Amort./Sales	1.2	.6
		(19) 1.4	(13) 1.6				(76) 2.2	(52) 1.8
		4.1	3.1				3.1	4.5
						% Officers', Directors', Owners' Comp/Sales	3.8	3.6
							(30) 7.0	(18) 5.5
							10.4	8.3
4595M	19029M	192648M	548148M		150910M	Net Sales ($)	1615526M	1751998M
725M	10690M	100644M	339332M		100675M	Total Assets ($)	1232041M	1195473M

M = $ thousand   MM = $ million
See Pages 11 through 21 for Explanation of Ratios and Data

Comparative Historical Data   Current Data Sorted By Sales

Type of Statement	4/1/02-3/31/03	4/1/03-3/31/04	4/1/04-3/31/05	0-1MM	1-3MM	3-5MM	5-10MM	10-25MM	25MM & OVER
Unqualified	12	11	16		1	1	2	3	9
Reviewed	17	17	11		4	1	1	4	1
Compiled	10	15	6		2	2	2		
Tax Returns	4	3	6	1		3	2		
Other	12	15	8		1		3	2	2
	4/1/02-3/31/03 ALL	4/1/03-3/31/04 ALL	4/1/04-3/31/05 ALL	4 (4/1-9/30/04)			43 (10/1/04-3/31/05)		
NUMBER OF STATEMENTS	55	61	47	1	8	7	10	9	12
ASSETS	%	%	%	%	%	%	%	%	%
Cash & Equivalents	12.4	11.1	7.6				5.8		6.7
Trade Receivables (net)	22.1	20.3	22.0				26.7		23.5
Inventory	30.7	30.5	39.6				38.2		33.5
All Other Current	4.8	5.7	2.6				.9		4.3
Total Current	70.0	67.6	71.7				71.6		67.9
Fixed Assets (net)	21.0	22.6	18.4				16.5		19.8
Intangibles (net)	1.3	1.9	2.6				6.4		3.3
All Other Non-Current	7.7	7.9	7.3				5.5		9.0
Total	100.0	100.0	100.0				100.0		100.0
LIABILITIES									
Notes Payable-Short Term	10.5	14.3	11.2				10.4		8.5
Cur. Mat.-L/T/D	2.4	2.1	4.0				2.2		1.3
Trade Payables	12.0	14.1	13.5				15.6		9.6
Income Taxes Payable	.2	.1	.2				.0		.8
All Other Current	15.3	12.8	12.8				12.8		17.8
Total Current	40.5	43.4	41.7				40.9		38.0
Long-Term Debt	7.6	9.3	11.7				16.6		9.8
Deferred Taxes	.4	.5	.3				.0		.8
All Other Non-Current	4.1	3.8	3.7				1.2		2.6
Net Worth	47.4	42.9	42.5				41.2		48.8
Total Liabilities & Net Worth	100.0	100.0	100.0				100.0		100.0
INCOME DATA									
Net Sales	100.0	100.0	100.0				100.0		100.0
Gross Profit	30.7	30.5	32.3				34.8		28.2
Operating Expenses	28.3	27.4	29.2				33.5		21.8
Operating Profit	2.4	3.1	3.1				1.3		6.4
All Other Expenses (net)	.6	.4	.4				.7		-.5
Profit Before Taxes	1.8	2.7	2.7				.6		7.0
RATIOS									
Current	3.2	3.5	2.8				2.9		2.7
	2.1	1.8	1.8				2.0		2.0
	1.2	1.3	1.4				1.3		1.4
Quick	1.5	1.6	1.3				1.1		1.4
	.9	.9	.7				.9		.9
	.6	.5	.5				.6		.5
Sales/Receivables	28 12.9	29 12.8	32 11.3				31 11.6		36 10.1
	43 8.5	42 8.7	40 9.1				53 6.9		45 8.1
	55 6.6	51 7.1	60 6.1				64 5.7		59 6.2
Cost of Sales/Inventory	46 7.9	46 7.9	71 5.1				80 4.6		52 7.1
	86 4.3	107 3.4	122 3.0				123 3.0		94 3.9
	152 2.4	140 2.6	157 2.3				157 2.3		124 3.0
Cost of Sales/Payables	14 26.7	17 21.3	17 21.9				28 13.0		13 28.1
	27 13.7	30 12.1	32 11.5				43 8.5		29 12.6
	42 8.8	53 6.9	47 7.8				51 7.1		34 10.8
Sales/Working Capital	2.8	3.0	3.6				4.1		3.7
	4.9	5.8	6.3				6.3		4.8
	15.8	15.3	12.9				16.9		10.7
EBIT/Interest	7.8	8.6	18.5				20.1		18.4
	(47) 2.7	(54) 3.5	(46) 3.5				3.1	(11) 6.0	
	-.8	.1	1.3				-4.0		3.0
Net Profit + Depr., Dep., Amort./Cur. Mat. L/T/D	4.6	4.5							
	(16) 1.7	(14) 1.7							
	.2	-.2							
Fixed/Worth	.2	.2	.2				.3		.3
	.4	.5	.4				.5		.4
	1.0	1.1	.9				58.4		1.1
Debt/Worth	.4	.5	.6				.5		.4
	.9	1.1	1.4				1.1		.9
	2.5	3.2	5.3				264.0		5.2
% Profit Before Taxes/Tangible Net Worth	26.7	24.9	34.3						47.7
	(53) 9.0	(57) 10.6	(45) 11.7					(11) 13.6	
	-3.7	-.1	4.4						10.4
% Profit Before Taxes/Total Assets	10.1	9.9	12.4				7.7		17.8
	2.7	3.0	5.2				5.5		8.3
	-2.4	-.6	.8				-3.6		4.2
Sales/Net Fixed Assets	21.8	24.3	27.5				27.0		29.9
	9.6	10.7	12.3				11.7		8.6
	5.6	3.8	6.3				8.0		4.4
Sales/Total Assets	2.6	2.5	2.2				2.3		2.4
	1.7	1.7	1.7				2.0		1.7
	1.1	1.1	1.3				1.5		1.3
% Depr., Dep., Amort./Sales	1.0	.6	.8						.7
	(50) 2.0	(54) 1.9	(40) 1.6					(11) 1.4	
	3.7	3.4	3.0						3.1
% Officers', Directors', Owners' Comp/Sales	2.9	3.0							
	(21) 4.4	(17) 4.0							
	8.4	7.3							
Net Sales ($)	503704M	997921M	915330M	562M	16529M	28326M	75981M	145770M	648162M
Total Assets ($)	373850M	817884M	552066M	459M	13950M	14910M	41647M	83805M	397295M

M = $ thousand   MM = $ million
See Pages 11 through 21 for Explanation of Ratios and Data

Current Data Sorted By Assets   Comparative Historical Data

0-500M	500M-2MM	2-10MM	10-50MM	50-100MM	100-250MM		4/1/00-3/31/01 ALL	4/1/01-3/31/02 ALL
		2	6	1	2	Type of Statement		
						Unqualified	14	18
	3	11				Reviewed	13	12
	2	3				Compiled	11	15
1	2					Tax Returns		2
1	1	10	5	4	2	Other	18	19
	12 (4/1-9/30/04)		43 (10/1/04-3/31/05)					
1	8	26	11	5	4	**NUMBER OF STATEMENTS**	56	66
%	%	%	%	%	%	**ASSETS**	%	%
		7.0	9.6			Cash & Equivalents	9.1	8.2
		20.0	19.8			Trade Receivables (net)	24.4	24.3
		29.5	26.2			Inventory	27.8	27.5
		2.9	6.1			All Other Current	1.4	4.9
		59.5	61.8			Total Current	62.8	64.9
		30.2	19.4			Fixed Assets (net)	23.3	22.7
		4.4	7.8			Intangibles (net)	7.3	7.0
		5.9	11.1			All Other Non-Current	6.6	5.4
		100.0	100.0			Total	100.0	100.0
						LIABILITIES		
		9.8	10.0			Notes Payable-Short Term	10.5	8.3
		5.7	3.8			Cur. Mat.-L/T/D	4.2	4.8
		15.2	9.6			Trade Payables	14.2	14.0
		.6	1.1			Income Taxes Payable	.8	.3
		14.3	12.4			All Other Current	13.6	17.7
		45.6	36.9			Total Current	43.4	45.1
		18.1	9.0			Long-Term Debt	8.8	11.0
		.5	2.6			Deferred Taxes	.5	.5
		4.4	2.6			All Other Non-Current	4.8	6.7
		31.4	49.0			Net Worth	42.5	36.8
		100.0	100.0			Total Liabilities & Net Worth	100.0	100.0
						INCOME DATA		
		100.0	100.0			Net Sales	100.0	100.0
		31.3	38.6			Gross Profit	36.0	32.6
		28.9	34.4			Operating Expenses	31.1	31.6
		2.3	4.2			Operating Profit	4.8	1.0
		1.3	2.1			All Other Expenses (net)	.4	1.7
		1.0	2.1			Profit Before Taxes	4.5	−.7
						RATIOS		
		1.9	2.1				2.4	2.8
		1.4	1.9			Current	1.5	1.4
		.9	1.2				1.0	1.1
		1.0	1.2				1.4	1.4
		.6	.6			Quick	.8	.8
		.3	.6				.5	.4
		25 14.4	41 8.9				30 12.3	33 11.2
		40 9.2	56 6.6			Sales/Receivables	50 7.3	49 7.5
		49 7.4	60 6.1				67 5.4	63 5.8
		22 16.9	69 5.3				36 10.3	25 14.7
		79 4.6	93 3.9			Cost of Sales/Inventory	86 4.2	81 4.5
		153 2.4	185 2.0				144 2.5	140 2.6
		22 16.7	21 17.7				23 15.7	22 16.4
		37 9.9	33 10.9			Cost of Sales/Payables	35 10.4	38 9.6
		59 6.2	52 7.0				51 7.2	53 6.9
		4.7	3.5				4.0	4.6
		12.1	4.3			Sales/Working Capital	11.8	10.2
		−38.6	16.2				72.8	50.7
		5.7					10.9	5.4
		(22) 3.2				EBIT/Interest	(47) 3.8	(60) 1.2
		−1.1					1.1	−2.0
						Net Profit + Depr., Dep.,	21.4	5.1
						Amort./Cur. Mat. L/T/D	(23) 2.9	(19) 1.0
							1.1	−.1
		.2	.2				.3	.3
		1.1	.5			Fixed/Worth	.6	.6
		3.6	1.2				2.1	4.7
		1.1	.4				.6	.8
		1.7	1.2			Debt/Worth	1.7	2.5
		10.1	3.7				5.2	11.9
		52.0	54.7			% Profit Before Taxes/Tangible	37.2	19.2
		(23) 11.6	10.5			Net Worth	(47) 15.1	(53) 2.7
		2.0	−3.8				4.3	−15.0
		7.7	9.9			% Profit Before Taxes/Total	15.0	6.7
		3.2	5.9			Assets	6.2	1.2
		−2.7	−1.7				1.2	−7.5
		25.5	15.9				27.6	32.5
		9.1	7.7			Sales/Net Fixed Assets	9.1	9.8
		2.8	3.7				4.1	4.6
		2.3	1.6				2.6	2.4
		1.6	1.3			Sales/Total Assets	1.7	1.7
		1.0	1.1				1.2	1.3
		1.2	1.4				1.0	.9
		(22) 2.4	3.4			% Depr., Dep., Amort./Sales	(51) 1.9	(56) 2.3
		3.8	4.4				3.8	4.6
						% Officers', Directors',	3.1	3.8
						Owners' Comp/Sales	(18) 5.4	(15) 5.6
							11.0	7.8
735M	27931M	219638M	452582M	452071M	735336M	Net Sales ($)	2101584M	2440456M
33M	11478M	115829M	326518M	280537M	604607M	Total Assets ($)	1407611M	1674488M

M = $ thousand   MM = $ million
See Pages 11 through 21 for Explanation of Ratios and Data

Comparative Historical Data | **Current Data Sorted By Sales**

				0-1MM	1-3MM	3-5MM	5-10MM	10-25MM	25MM & OVER
18	11	11	Type of Statement — Unqualified				5	4	7
18	10	14	Reviewed		3	3		2	1
5	16	5	Compiled		1	1	3		
	4	3	Tax Returns	1	1	1			
18	19	22	Other		3	2	2	5	10
4/1/02-3/31/03 ALL	4/1/03-3/31/04 ALL	4/1/04-3/31/05 ALL			12 (4/1-9/30/04)			43 (10/1/04-3/31/05)	
59	60	55	NUMBER OF STATEMENTS	1	8	7	10	11	18
%	%	%	**ASSETS**	%	%	%	%	%	%
8.4	9.3	9.8	Cash & Equivalents				7.1	6.7	10.9
22.0	27.1	23.6	Trade Receivables (net)				23.0	25.6	23.6
31.8	26.3	26.2	Inventory				33.2	27.0	25.0
4.1	2.1	3.0	All Other Current				1.5	5.2	3.5
66.3	64.9	62.6	Total Current				64.8	64.5	63.0
20.9	24.7	23.0	Fixed Assets (net)				23.9	15.1	19.6
7.2	5.2	7.7	Intangibles (net)				8.9	4.4	12.0
5.6	5.2	6.7	All Other Non-Current				2.4	16.0	5.4
100.0	100.0	100.0	Total				100.0	100.0	100.0
			LIABILITIES						
7.9	15.8	13.0	Notes Payable-Short Term				11.8	10.4	5.5
4.9	3.7	4.9	Cur. Mat.-L/T/D				6.5	3.7	5.5
12.0	14.4	13.9	Trade Payables				19.5	16.7	10.2
.4	.2	.5	Income Taxes Payable				1.3	.3	.7
17.6	15.0	14.0	All Other Current				15.2	10.2	16.8
42.7	49.1	46.2	Total Current				54.2	41.3	38.7
12.3	15.0	13.7	Long-Term Debt				13.2	13.3	7.5
.4	.5	1.2	Deferred Taxes				.1	2.4	1.9
5.4	5.6	3.2	All Other Non-Current				7.7	1.0	3.2
39.1	29.7	35.7	Net Worth				24.8	42.0	48.6
100.0	100.0	100.0	Total Liabilities & Net Worth				100.0	100.0	100.0
			INCOME DATA						
100.0	100.0	100.0	Net Sales				100.0	100.0	100.0
33.7	34.2	35.0	Gross Profit				31.4	34.0	34.5
31.1	31.6	31.4	Operating Expenses				32.8	28.9	29.0
2.6	2.6	3.6	Operating Profit				-1.4	5.2	5.5
1.3	1.2	1.4	All Other Expenses (net)				1.5	1.9	1.0
1.3	1.5	2.2	Profit Before Taxes				-2.9	3.3	4.5
			RATIOS						
2.7	2.4	2.0	Current				2.1	2.0	2.2
1.6	1.6	1.7					1.3	1.7	1.8
1.2	1.1	1.1					.9	1.2	1.2
1.3	1.5	1.2	Quick				1.0	1.2	1.3
.8	.8	.8					.6	.7	.7
.4	.5	.5					.4	.4	.6
33 11.0	34 10.7	37 9.8	Sales/Receivables				27 13.5	35 10.5	52 7.1
45 8.1	43 8.4	49 7.5					41 9.0	41 8.9	57 6.3
62 5.9	62 5.9	59 6.2					46 8.0	56 6.5	67 5.5
56 6.5	21 17.6	26 14.0	Cost of Sales/Inventory				12 30.7	38 9.6	56 6.5
82 4.5	75 4.9	77 4.8					119 3.1	81 4.5	73 5.0
150 2.4	119 3.1	133 2.7					159 2.3	126 2.9	117 3.1
20 18.5	22 16.5	23 15.6	Cost of Sales/Payables				25 14.9	25 14.3	23 15.7
32 11.3	34 10.8	35 10.3					35 10.5	38 9.5	35 10.3
46 7.9	45 8.1	52 7.0					69 5.3	60 6.1	50 7.2
4.2	4.4	4.0	Sales/Working Capital				4.6	4.6	3.7
7.1	8.9	8.5					16.5	7.4	8.4
17.9	33.5	62.6					-20.1	16.2	17.2
7.0	11.3	12.4	EBIT/Interest				6.0		17.6
(54) 1.8	(52) 2.3	(45) 3.7					2.0		(13) 3.7
-.2	.4	.0					-4.5		1.5
5.5	2.1	2.4	Net Profit + Depr., Dep., Amort./Cur. Mat. L/T/D						
(23) 1.2	(15) 1.0	(14) .6							
.2	.1	-.6							
.2	.2	.2	Fixed/Worth				.2	.2	.2
.6	.6	.5					1.1	.3	.6
1.4	2.4	2.0					NM	.7	1.3
.8	.8	.9	Debt/Worth				1.4	.7	.7
1.9	1.9	1.5					2.1	1.2	1.3
3.7	7.6	4.2					NM	4.1	3.7
28.6	35.1	36.3	% Profit Before Taxes/Tangible Net Worth					69.1	35.0
(52) 9.3	(52) 13.4	(49) 14.2						(10) 12.5	18.1
-4.9	-2.6	.7						4.6	4.9
7.1	9.4	10.5	% Profit Before Taxes/Total Assets				9.4	13.2	12.1
1.9	2.8	5.1					1.9	6.1	5.4
-3.2	-1.5	-1.7					-9.5	.9	.9
31.9	30.7	26.6	Sales/Net Fixed Assets				31.0	29.0	26.7
9.0	10.8	10.9					9.1	15.9	8.1
4.9	4.0	3.9					4.6	6.9	3.2
2.0	2.6	2.1	Sales/Total Assets				2.4	2.6	1.7
1.6	1.6	1.5					1.9	1.9	1.4
1.3	1.3	1.2					1.4	1.3	1.2
1.1	1.1	1.1	% Depr., Dep., Amort./Sales				1.2		1.0
(54) 2.7	(54) 2.9	(48) 2.3					2.5		(17) 2.2
4.2	4.6	3.7					3.5		3.4
3.9	2.7	2.8	% Officers', Directors', Owners' Comp/Sales						
(19) 7.5	(17) 4.4	(12) 7.6							
12.0	10.1	9.2							
1914485M	2032417M	1888293M	Net Sales ($)	735M	17753M	27109M	62168M	163148M	1617380M
1401816M	1348934M	1339002M	Total Assets ($)	33M	17711M	15596M	35011M	103720M	1166931M

© RMA 2005

M = $ thousand   MM = $ million
See Pages 11 through 21 for Explanation of Ratios and Data

Current Data Sorted By Assets   Comparative Historical Data

0-500M	500M-2MM	2-10MM	10-50MM	50-100MM	100-250MM	Type of Statement	4/1/00-3/31/01 ALL	4/1/01-3/31/02 ALL
	1	4	12	1	2	Unqualified	12	9
1	4	18	5	1		Reviewed	15	13
	3	5				Compiled	11	9
2	5					Tax Returns	2	
2	5	7	7		2	Other	15	25
	17 (4/1-9/30/04)		68 (10/1/04-3/31/05)					
3	18	34	24	2	4	**NUMBER OF STATEMENTS**	55	56
%	%	%	%	%	%	**ASSETS**	%	%
	12.1	8.8	8.3			Cash & Equivalents	8.1	8.5
	34.1	27.8	24.2			Trade Receivables (net)	24.1	22.8
	34.1	35.2	31.5			Inventory	30.3	33.2
	1.1	2.1	4.7			All Other Current	4.1	3.8
	81.3	73.9	68.7			Total Current	66.6	68.3
	12.5	15.8	21.7			Fixed Assets (net)	20.2	21.3
	2.3	3.4	4.4			Intangibles (net)	7.2	5.9
	3.9	6.9	5.2			All Other Non-Current	6.1	4.5
	100.0	100.0	100.0			Total	100.0	100.0
						LIABILITIES		
	9.7	12.1	7.2			Notes Payable-Short Term	7.4	9.6
	2.1	3.8	2.5			Cur. Mat.-L/T/D	6.0	5.1
	25.1	15.9	13.1			Trade Payables	10.9	11.8
	.2	.3	.7			Income Taxes Payable	.2	.2
	15.6	19.1	25.8			All Other Current	15.5	14.7
	52.6	51.2	49.3			Total Current	40.3	41.3
	13.1	10.9	13.0			Long-Term Debt	13.3	14.5
	.0	.1	.4			Deferred Taxes	.4	.3
	8.0	4.1	3.9			All Other Non-Current	5.7	5.4
	26.2	33.8	33.3			Net Worth	40.3	38.5
	100.0	100.0	100.0			Total Liabilities & Net Worth	100.0	100.0
						INCOME DATA		
	100.0	100.0	100.0			Net Sales	100.0	100.0
	40.6	30.3	32.9			Gross Profit	34.3	33.7
	37.9	26.4	28.6			Operating Expenses	32.0	30.0
	2.7	3.9	4.3			Operating Profit	2.3	3.7
	.8	.5	.4			All Other Expenses (net)	.7	1.5
	1.9	3.4	3.9			Profit Before Taxes	1.6	2.2
						RATIOS		
	2.7	2.0	2.3				2.7	3.0
	1.4	1.4	1.3			Current	1.7	1.5
	1.2	1.1	1.0				1.2	1.3
	1.5	1.0	.9				1.2	1.2
	.7	.6	.6			Quick	.9	.7
	.5	.5	.4				.5	.5
34	10.6 31	11.6 38	9.5				41 8.9	32 11.2
40	9.0 41	9.0 43	8.5			Sales/Receivables	52 7.0	44 8.3
47	7.8 62	5.9 60	6.0				61 5.9	58 6.3
19	18.8 39	9.3 57	6.4				63 5.8	72 5.0
68	5.4 88	4.2 94	3.9			Cost of Sales/Inventory	102 3.6	102 3.6
164	2.2 150	2.4 122	3.0				145 2.5	153 2.4
31	11.8 23	15.8 21	17.4				18 20.6	16 23.4
48	7.5 35	10.5 36	10.1			Cost of Sales/Payables	29 12.4	27 13.3
80	4.5 55	6.6 59	6.2				52 7.0	43 8.6
	5.0	6.1	4.0				3.6	3.3
	11.5	9.2	15.2			Sales/Working Capital	6.1	8.1
	25.6	31.0	66.0				16.7	14.8
	5.9	16.7	22.4				8.3	9.1
	(16) 3.0	(32) 4.0	(22) 6.8			EBIT/Interest	(53) 2.0	(53) 2.7
	1.1	2.0	.4				.6	-.1
		9.8	14.5				3.0	3.0
		(14) 5.5	(11) 5.3			Net Profit + Depr., Dep., Amort./Cur. Mat. L /T/D	(19) 1.5	(19) 1.4
		1.6	1.3				.1	.1
	.1	.2	.4				.3	.3
	.3	.4	1.0			Fixed/Worth	.5	.6
	1.4	.8	2.1				1.4	1.4
	1.5	.8	.8				.7	1.0
	2.6	2.1	2.7			Debt/Worth	1.6	1.8
	9.5	4.2	18.9				6.4	4.3
	58.7	34.5	41.2				31.7	29.7
	(15) 18.3	(31) 12.7	(22) 15.3			% Profit Before Taxes/Tangible Net Worth	(48) 11.8	(47) 15.1
	2.6	6.6	-.4				-2.7	-9.0
	11.7	11.8	12.3				11.9	13.7
	4.8	4.5	3.5			% Profit Before Taxes/Total Assets	3.3	4.5
	.3	1.7	-1.3				-.8	-3.8
	92.7	33.0	13.7				16.3	16.1
	31.3	15.5	10.5			Sales/Net Fixed Assets	8.6	10.9
	20.1	8.5	6.3				5.2	6.6
	3.7	2.6	2.3				2.3	2.2
	2.8	2.1	1.8			Sales/Total Assets	1.7	1.8
	2.1	1.5	1.6				1.3	1.3
	.6	.8	1.2				1.4	.8
	(12) .8	(30) 1.5	(23) 1.8			% Depr., Dep., Amort./Sales	(50) 2.1	(51) 1.7
	1.3	2.3	2.2				2.8	3.5
	2.4	1.6					2.6	2.7
	(15) 3.7	(11) 4.0				% Officers', Directors', Owners' Comp/Sales	(14) 4.4	(14) 3.8
	7.1	9.5					6.6	8.2
4241M	60205M	338902M	890568M	161444M	900476M	Net Sales ($)	1219503M	1154377M
1138M	20072M	167509M	465716M	130049M	648730M	Total Assets ($)	872244M	894204M

M = $ thousand   MM = $ million
See Pages 11 through 21 for Explanation of Ratios and Data

Comparative Historical Data / Current Data Sorted By Sales

			Type of Statement						
21	11	20	Unqualified		2	1	7	10	
17	22	28	Reviewed		3	13	8	4	
12	14	9	Compiled	1	2	2	2		
6	6	5	Tax Returns		4	1			
17	23	23	Other		6	2	3	5	7
4/1/02-3/31/03	4/1/03-3/31/04	4/1/04-3/31/05			17 (4/1-9/30/04)		68 (10/1/04-3/31/05)		
ALL	ALL	ALL		0-1MM	1-3MM	3-5MM	5-10MM	10-25MM	25MM & OVER
73	76	85	NUMBER OF STATEMENTS	1	12	10	19	22	21
%	%	%	ASSETS	%	%	%	%	%	%
12.9	11.1	9.4	Cash & Equivalents		12.4	11.2	7.6	12.0	6.3
23.9	23.6	28.1	Trade Receivables (net)		30.8	33.4	29.9	26.8	24.0
26.6	33.6	32.4	Inventory		34.3	26.1	37.2	30.8	30.0
3.5	3.2	2.9	All Other Current		2.8	.4	1.0	3.1	5.4
66.8	71.4	72.8	Total Current		80.3	71.1	75.7	72.7	65.7
20.3	18.0	16.9	Fixed Assets (net)		13.4	15.6	13.5	20.0	19.9
5.9	5.3	4.9	Intangibles (net)		1.7	2.1	6.1	3.2	8.8
7.0	5.3	5.4	All Other Non-Current		4.7	11.2	4.7	4.0	5.6
100.0	100.0	100.0	Total		100.0	100.0	100.0	100.0	100.0
			LIABILITIES						
6.5	10.8	8.9	Notes Payable-Short Term		4.7	10.6	12.5	9.7	5.4
3.5	3.1	2.9	Cur. Mat.-L/T/D		1.8	3.2	4.1	2.2	3.4
10.5	12.2	17.2	Trade Payables		24.8	17.3	18.2	14.9	14.3
.3	.2	.4	Income Taxes Payable		.1	.3	.4	.4	.6
15.3	20.6	20.1	All Other Current		11.8	16.3	22.2	17.8	28.2
36.1	46.9	49.6	Total Current		43.3	47.6	57.4	44.9	51.9
13.3	12.0	13.2	Long-Term Debt		20.9	8.1	10.9	9.4	15.7
.8	.4	.3	Deferred Taxes		.0	.2	.0	.1	1.0
5.8	9.5	5.0	All Other Non-Current		6.7	7.9	3.4	5.0	2.7
44.0	31.1	31.9	Net Worth		29.0	36.1	28.3	40.5	28.8
100.0	100.0	100.0	Total Liabilities & Net Worth		100.0	100.0	100.0	100.0	100.0
			INCOME DATA						
100.0	100.0	100.0	Net Sales		100.0	100.0	100.0	100.0	100.0
36.4	34.3	33.9	Gross Profit		38.7	38.4	31.1	32.9	32.1
30.5	30.0	29.8	Operating Expenses		34.0	36.5	27.4	27.9	27.9
6.0	4.2	4.1	Operating Profit		4.6	1.9	3.8	5.0	4.2
1.1	.7	.6	All Other Expenses (net)		1.4	-.2	.6	.4	.4
4.9	3.5	3.5	Profit Before Taxes		3.3	2.1	3.1	4.6	3.3
			RATIOS						
3.0	2.2	2.2			3.4	2.6	1.6	2.5	1.7
1.8	1.4	1.4	Current		1.9	1.4	1.4	1.7	1.2
1.3	1.1	1.1			1.3	1.1	1.0	1.2	1.1
1.7	1.1	1.1			1.7	1.6	1.0	1.5	.7
.9	.7	.7	Quick		1.0	.7	.6	.7	.6
.6	.5	.5			.5	.5	.4	.5	.4
30 12.3	29 12.7	34 10.9		29 12.8	34 10.8	32 11.4	29 12.6	36 10.3	
41 8.9	42 8.8	41 8.9	Sales/Receivables	39 9.3	43 8.6	39 9.5	48 7.6	41 8.9	
54 6.8	55 6.7	56 6.5		48 7.6	60 6.1	53 6.9	57 6.4	61 6.0	
43 8.4	60 6.1	49 7.5		3 127.8	16 23.4	50 7.3	37 9.9	58 6.3	
92 4.0	98 3.7	81 4.5	Cost of Sales/Inventory	92 4.0	77 4.8	79 4.6	77 4.7	89 4.1	
125 2.9	151 2.4	131 2.8		155 2.4	165 2.2	127 2.9	145 2.5	115 3.2	
16 22.4	16 23.0	23 15.8		21 17.6	23 15.6	24 15.1	17 21.0	25 14.8	
25 14.5	31 11.8	38 9.7	Cost of Sales/Payables	48 7.6	39 9.5	38 9.7	29 12.6	37 9.8	
40 9.1	53 6.9	60 6.1		82 4.4	55 6.7	57 6.4	43 8.5	62 5.9	
3.8	4.7	5.1		4.9	5.8	6.3	4.6	7.5	
7.5	8.7	11.2	Sales/Working Capital	6.3	11.8	11.3	7.3	20.6	
17.5	24.1	31.0		14.8	NM	-291.2	21.1	64.1	
11.0	12.6	18.5		22.9		12.1	19.1	22.7	
(62) 3.1	(67) 5.0	(78) 4.8	EBIT/Interest	(10) 5.0		3.8	(19) 6.2	(20) 8.0	
1.2	1.9	1.3		1.1		.9	1.9	1.0	
5.0	4.9	9.8	Net Profit + Depr., Dep.,					11.9	
(25) 1.5	(20) 1.7	(30) 4.2	Amort./Cur. Mat. L/T/D					(10) 3.5	
1.0	1.0	1.5						1.3	
.2	.2	.2		.0	.1	.2	.2	.5	
.4	.5	.5	Fixed/Worth	.2	.3	.6	.4	1.2	
1.5	1.3	1.3		1.2	.5	1.7	1.1	6.3	
.5	1.3	1.1		.8	.9	1.8	.8	1.3	
1.5	2.2	2.3	Debt/Worth	2.4	1.5	3.3	1.5	4.5	
3.8	5.2	6.4		NM	5.1	7.3	3.8	29.4	
28.3	54.4	43.7	% Profit Before Taxes/Tangible			79.8	46.1	40.4	
(63) 11.6	(63) 16.1	(74) 14.3	Net Worth			(17) 9.2	(21) 13.1	(18) 19.6	
-.7	5.3	5.3				5.1	5.1	-2.4	
15.0	14.7	12.3	% Profit Before Taxes/Total		17.4	8.2	11.7	15.7	11.9
5.6	5.1	4.9	Assets		9.4	4.4	4.2	4.6	8.3
-.2	1.8	.4			.9	.9	-.3	2.2	-.6
20.6	34.4	31.6			182.3	UND	40.9	29.2	14.6
10.6	11.9	14.3	Sales/Net Fixed Assets		32.9	15.8	24.6	12.7	11.8
6.9	7.6	8.1			11.9	7.2	10.4	6.6	6.4
2.4	2.5	2.7			3.2	3.8	3.1	2.5	2.3
1.8	1.9	2.0	Sales/Total Assets		2.7	2.5	1.8	2.1	1.7
1.2	1.4	1.6			2.0	1.5	1.7	1.4	1.5
1.2	.9	.8				.8	.7	1.3	
(65) 2.1	(68) 1.8	(71) 1.4	% Depr., Dep., Amort./Sales			(18) 1.3	(19) 1.4	(19) 1.7	
3.1	2.7	2.1				2.3	2.2	2.0	
3.5	3.0	2.3	% Officers', Directors',		2.3				
(22) 5.1	(21) 3.7	(29) 3.8	Owners' Comp/Sales		(10) 5.6				
9.6	6.0	8.3			11.8				
1784465M	1757707M	2355836M	Net Sales ($)	841M	23310M	39755M	147596M	370544M	1773790M
1436769M	1089398M	1433214M	Total Assets ($)	542M	10167M	20457M	78920M	199437M	1123691M

M = $ thousand   MM = $ million
See Pages 11 through 21 for Explanation of Ratios and Data

Current Data Sorted By Assets   Comparative Historical Data

0-500M	500M-2MM	2-10MM	10-50MM	50-100MM	100-250MM	Type of Statement	4/1/00-3/31/01 ALL	4/1/01-3/31/02 ALL
	1	9	19	3	6	Unqualified	45	28
2	9	22	4			Reviewed	49	51
6	18	23		1	2	Compiled	54	50
2	4	2			1	Tax Returns	11	11
6	8	23	21	2	2	Other	64	74
\	43 (4/1-9/30/04)		153 (10/1/04-3/31/05)					
16	40	79	44	6	11	**NUMBER OF STATEMENTS**	223	214
%	%	%	%	%	%	**ASSETS**	%	%
13.2	11.8	7.9	10.9		15.5	Cash & Equivalents	8.7	8.3
31.8	31.0	26.8	22.6		22.3	Trade Receivables (net)	27.1	24.4
22.4	26.0	30.9	27.0		22.1	Inventory	28.1	29.6
.3	3.4	4.6	4.7		1.0	All Other Current	4.0	3.7
67.6	72.0	70.2	65.2		60.9	Total Current	68.0	66.0
27.4	18.3	19.5	20.4		23.2	Fixed Assets (net)	20.8	23.9
.3	3.0	3.5	6.9		9.7	Intangibles (net)	5.4	4.3
4.6	6.7	6.9	7.5		6.2	All Other Non-Current	5.8	5.8
100.0	100.0	100.0	100.0		100.0	Total	100.0	100.0
						LIABILITIES		
35.2	14.9	14.8	11.2		15.1	Notes Payable-Short Term	12.3	13.2
2.7	3.6	3.7	3.2		1.7	Cur. Mat.-L/T/D	2.8	5.2
15.9	18.6	15.9	12.2		10.9	Trade Payables	13.6	13.8
.1	.1	.2	.2		.1	Income Taxes Payable	.3	.3
11.4	12.0	14.6	18.0		11.4	All Other Current	16.2	13.7
65.3	49.2	49.2	44.7		39.1	Total Current	45.2	46.2
19.2	14.0	13.7	10.5		10.9	Long-Term Debt	12.4	13.6
.0	.7	.6	.8		.6	Deferred Taxes	.3	.4
7.3	6.3	4.1	3.2		5.6	All Other Non-Current	4.0	4.5
8.2	29.8	32.3	40.8		43.8	Net Worth	38.1	35.4
100.0	100.0	100.0	100.0		100.0	Total Liabilities & Net Worth	100.0	100.0
						INCOME DATA		
100.0	100.0	100.0	100.0		100.0	Net Sales	100.0	100.0
38.9	35.0	30.9	26.2		40.9	Gross Profit	31.3	32.6
35.3	31.9	26.8	21.8		34.6	Operating Expenses	26.1	30.0
3.6	3.1	4.0	4.4		6.3	Operating Profit	5.3	2.6
1.0	1.4	.9	.8		2.6	All Other Expenses (net)	.9	1.3
2.6	1.7	3.1	3.6		3.7	Profit Before Taxes	4.4	1.3
						RATIOS		
4.9	2.5	2.4	2.4		5.3	Current	2.4	2.4
2.3	1.5	1.5	1.4		1.2		1.6	1.6
.7	1.2	1.1	1.1		1.0		1.1	1.0
4.4	1.6	1.2	1.2		3.3	Quick	1.2	1.2
1.1	.9	.7	.8		.8		.8	.7
.5	.6	.5	.5		.6		.5	.4
17 21.1	35 10.5	31 11.8	38 9.5		52 7.0	Sales/Receivables	36 10.2	32 11.4
29 12.8	43 8.4	49 7.5	52 7.1		59 6.2		51 7.2	46 8.0
46 8.0	56 6.5	66 5.5	65 5.6		66 5.5		69 5.3	62 5.9
0 UND	18 20.8	40 9.0	39 9.2		42 8.6	Cost of Sales/Inventory	36 10.1	42 8.7
17 21.7	48 7.6	76 4.8	96 3.8		94 3.9		73 5.0	79 4.6
73 5.0	109 3.4	139 2.6	126 2.9		178 2.1		120 3.1	150 2.4
0 UND	22 16.5	20 18.4	18 20.4		27 13.5	Cost of Sales/Payables	19 19.0	18 20.3
16 22.6	38 9.7	32 11.4	37 9.8		40 9.2		32 11.5	31 11.7
48 7.5	71 5.1	65 5.6	62 5.9		73 5.0		50 7.2	57 6.3
4.3	5.7	4.6	4.3		1.7	Sales/Working Capital	4.4	4.2
9.7	8.1	8.0	9.2		13.5		7.9	7.7
−21.1	22.8	39.0	24.2		531.0		29.2	67.6
(13) 15.7	(35) 17.0	(69) 9.3	(35) 13.9		(10) 13.0	EBIT/Interest	(191) 11.6	(193) 6.4
9.7	3.0	3.6	3.6		4.4		3.1	2.0
−1.8	.4	.3	1.7		−5.0		1.3	−.3
		(21) 4.4	(11) 6.3			Net Profit + Depr., Dep., Amort./Cur. Mat. L /T/D	(52) 6.8	(52) 6.0
		2.3	1.5				2.2	1.6
		.0	1.2				.5	.9
.1	.3	.2	.2		.1	Fixed/Worth	.2	.2
.6	.5	.6	.5		.5		.5	.6
NM	NM	1.8	1.5		1.9		2.2	2.1
.3	.8	.8	.9		.3	Debt/Worth	.7	.8
1.8	2.0	2.3	2.1		2.5		1.9	1.8
NM	NM	6.4	4.2		32.7		6.0	6.0
(12) 153.3	(30) 36.0	(70) 45.1	(42) 46.5			% Profit Before Taxes/Tangible Net Worth	(192) 41.1	(182) 28.3
45.0	16.0	17.0	23.5				17.6	9.3
17.9	−5.4	.8	4.7				3.8	−4.8
66.0	20.4	14.3	15.3		11.3	% Profit Before Taxes/Total Assets	14.1	11.0
17.7	5.6	6.5	8.3		8.1		5.7	3.4
−10.5	−1.8	−.4	1.3		−10.6		1.0	−2.7
80.2	29.8	47.4	26.6		13.4	Sales/Net Fixed Assets	26.1	21.5
16.7	21.8	15.9	13.5		8.2		10.2	9.3
6.5	8.2	4.9	5.1		5.0		5.6	4.6
5.7	3.5	2.6	2.1		4.1	Sales/Total Assets	2.5	2.4
3.6	2.5	1.8	1.6		1.4		1.8	1.8
2.0	2.0	1.4	1.2		.8		1.3	1.3
(10) 1.1	(36) .9	(76) .8	(38) 1.0			% Depr., Dep., Amort./Sales	(191) .8	(192) 1.2
2.2	1.9	1.8	1.9				1.7	2.3
4.9	3.2	3.5	3.0				3.1	3.6
	(18) 3.0	(24) 2.5				% Officers', Directors', Owners' Comp/Sales	(69) 2.5	(72) 2.9
	5.7	4.1					5.7	5.0
	7.9	8.1					10.9	8.8
17229M	121438M	686530M	1481050M	673969M	6258739M	Net Sales ($)	4969837M	4391542M
4453M	48085M	357990M	888680M	381661M	1795884M	Total Assets ($)	3900478M	3310238M

M = $ thousand   MM = $ million
See Pages 11 through 21 for Explanation of Ratios and Data

Comparative Historical Data | Current Data Sorted By Sales

Hist 4/1/02-3/31/03 ALL	Hist 4/1/03-3/31/04 ALL	Hist 4/1/04-3/31/05 ALL	Type of Statement	0-1MM	1-3MM	3-5MM	5-10MM	10-25MM	25MM & OVER
46	37	38	Unqualified		1	1	5	9	22
23	29	37	Reviewed	1	6	8	14	7	1
35	55	50	Compiled	5	14	6	16	5	4
11	12	9	Tax Returns	2	3	2		1	1
53	49	62	Other	5	9	6	8	19	15
				43 (4/1-9/30/04)			153 (10/1/04-3/31/05)		
168	182	196	**NUMBER OF STATEMENTS**	13	33	23	43	41	43
%	%	%	**ASSETS**	%	%	%	%	%	%
10.8	9.4	10.4	Cash & Equivalents	12.4	11.7	5.9	9.6	7.9	14.4
24.8	27.8	26.8	Trade Receivables (net)	22.1	26.3	28.5	28.0	29.9	23.7
28.4	26.2	27.6	Inventory	33.4	26.9	27.2	28.7	29.0	24.2
4.4	3.7	3.8	All Other Current	.4	1.4	1.6	6.2	5.7	3.5
68.3	67.1	68.7	Total Current	68.3	66.4	63.1	72.5	72.6	65.9
21.8	23.3	20.2	Fixed Assets (net)	25.6	20.9	22.5	20.6	17.2	19.3
2.5	3.8	4.3	Intangibles (net)	.6	2.3	6.3	1.0	5.0	8.4
7.4	5.7	6.8	All Other Non-Current	5.6	10.5	8.0	5.8	5.2	6.4
100.0	100.0	100.0	Total	100.0	100.0	100.0	100.0	100.0	100.0
			LIABILITIES						
13.5	12.4	15.5	Notes Payable-Short Term	44.0	16.5	8.8	17.0	14.2	9.4
3.2	4.1	3.3	Cur. Mat.-L/T/D	3.1	2.3	4.1	4.3	3.0	3.1
12.3	14.6	15.3	Trade Payables	13.1	19.1	11.6	15.6	18.2	11.8
.2	.2	.2	Income Taxes Payable	.1	.1	.3	.1	.3	.3
14.6	17.6	14.5	All Other Current	7.8	15.0	11.1	15.0	11.9	19.8
43.9	49.0	48.8	Total Current	68.1	53.0	35.9	52.0	47.5	44.4
11.7	14.5	13.4	Long-Term Debt	27.9	9.7	22.1	10.1	14.7	9.5
.5	.6	.6	Deferred Taxes	.3	.2	.8	.9	.7	.4
3.9	6.4	4.7	All Other Non-Current	9.6	5.5	4.0	2.7	5.2	4.5
40.1	29.5	32.5	Net Worth	-5.9	31.6	37.2	34.3	31.9	41.2
100.0	100.0	100.0	Total Liabilities & Net Worth	100.0	100.0	100.0	100.0	100.0	100.0
			INCOME DATA						
100.0	100.0	100.0	Net Sales	100.0	100.0	100.0	100.0	100.0	100.0
31.7	32.6	32.1	Gross Profit	39.6	36.6	35.7	28.2	29.6	30.6
29.6	29.9	27.9	Operating Expenses	37.6	35.9	32.1	23.7	24.7	24.0
2.0	2.7	4.2	Operating Profit	2.0	.7	3.5	4.5	5.0	6.7
1.0	.7	1.1	All Other Expenses (net)	2.1	1.6	.7	.8	.8	1.1
1.0	2.0	3.1	Profit Before Taxes	-.1	-.8	2.9	3.7	4.2	5.6
			RATIOS						
2.6	2.6	2.6		7.3	2.5	2.7	2.7	2.6	2.3
1.7	1.6	1.5	Current	1.9	1.5	1.7	1.7	1.4	1.4
1.2	1.1	1.1		.8	1.0	1.3	1.0	1.2	1.1
1.4	1.3	1.4		3.9	1.2	1.5	1.6	1.3	1.4
.8	.8	.8	Quick	.8	.6	.8	.8	.8	.8
.5	.5	.5		.3	.4	.6	.4	.5	.6
34 10.8	38 9.6	31 11.7		8 45.2	30 12.1	38 9.5	32 11.3	33 11.1	31 11.7
50 7.4	53 6.9	47 7.7	Sales/Receivables	29 12.8	44 8.3	47 7.8	49 7.5	52 7.1	52 7.1
71 5.1	69 5.3	64 5.7		61 6.0	63 5.8	65 5.6	59 6.2	71 5.1	60 6.1
45 8.1	37 9.8	30 12.2		0 UND	24 15.1	36 10.2	30 12.2	27 13.7	41 8.9
78 4.7	73 5.0	74 4.9	Cost of Sales/Inventory	70 5.2	53 6.9	92 4.0	66 5.5	83 4.4	80 4.6
137 2.7	123 3.0	125 2.9		197 1.9	115 3.2	147 2.5	133 2.7	123 3.0	106 3.4
17 21.3	21 17.1	18 20.1		0 UND	34 10.8	16 22.9	16 23.4	21 17.3	16 22.9
32 11.4	37 9.8	36 10.1	Cost of Sales/Payables	17 21.8	46 8.0	31 11.8	30 12.0	38 9.6	36 10.1
49 7.5	52 7.1	64 5.7		98 3.7	82 4.4	75 4.9	54 6.8	66 5.5	61 6.0
3.5	3.8	4.6		3.9	6.6	4.2	4.4	5.0	4.9
6.6	8.0	8.6	Sales/Working Capital	4.4	9.9	7.4	7.7	8.4	11.0
20.5	28.7	28.0		-38.1	NM	14.6	83.8	20.9	33.7
(146) 10.0	(151) 10.0	(168) 12.2		(10) 6.6	(28) 15.4	(22) 8.9	(35) 20.8	(37) 7.2	(36) 17.7
2.7	2.5	3.9	EBIT/Interest	1.0	2.5	3.9	4.6	2.6	10.4
-.1	-.3	.6		-5.5	-1.6	-2.5	.4	1.3	2.3
5.4	2.7	5.4					4.1		7.2
(47) 2.5	(50) 1.2	(48) 2.1	Net Profit + Depr., Dep., Amort./Cur. Mat. L/T/D				(13) 2.0		(13) 2.5
.8	.5	.2					.2		1.2
.2	.3	.2		.2	.2	.2	.2	.2	.2
.5	.6	.5	Fixed/Worth	3.1	.4	.7	.6	.6	.4
1.2	2.5	1.8		-1.2	2.3	2.8	1.8	1.8	1.4
.5	.8	.8		.4	.9	.8	.5	1.1	.8
1.5	1.8	2.2	Debt/Worth	2.8	1.6	2.2	1.1	2.6	2.3
4.0	8.7	5.5		-7.0	6.0	4.6	7.0	6.1	4.8
(153) 29.3	(152) 35.6	(169) 53.2	% Profit Before Taxes/Tangible Net Worth		(27) 24.6	(19) 87.4	(40) 37.7	(36) 52.5	(39) 79.6
8.0	13.8	21.3			11.2	20.1	15.6	25.2	38.2
-5.7	.8	2.7			-5.8	-15.0	.0	4.8	6.9
10.5	11.2	17.0	% Profit Before Taxes/Total Assets	25.8	18.2	10.0	16.8	13.9	18.0
3.1	3.9	7.4		3.3	3.5	7.8	8.0	7.0	10.3
-3.1	-1.8	-.3		-17.1	-2.8	-6.2	-.9	.7	1.3
20.2	20.1	36.4		54.1	40.2	26.1	46.2	48.2	28.7
9.4	9.8	15.2	Sales/Net Fixed Assets	11.4	16.2	9.6	18.5	17.9	14.8
5.5	4.8	5.6		5.2	6.2	5.4	4.9	5.5	6.6
2.2	2.3	2.7		3.6	3.4	2.1	2.9	2.9	2.5
1.7	1.8	2.0	Sales/Total Assets	2.1	2.2	1.6	2.0	1.8	1.9
1.2	1.3	1.4		1.1	1.6	1.3	1.3	1.4	1.4
(152) 1.4	(164) 1.1	(170) .9	% Depr., Dep., Amort./Sales		(26) 1.0	.9	(41) .7	(39) .8	(32) .8
2.2	2.2	1.9			2.3	2.3	1.6	1.7	1.4
4.1	4.0	3.3			3.6	3.9	3.7	2.8	2.7
2.9	2.5	2.6	% Officers', Directors', Owners' Comp/Sales		(14) 5.6		(11) 2.4	(14) .8	
(52) 5.1	(54) 4.3	(59) 5.1			7.5		3.4	3.0	
8.9	8.2	8.4			11.9		8.1	6.7	
3269336M	3262391M	9238955M	Net Sales ($)	7792M	74091M	91569M	299766M	626404M	8139333M
2522589M	2111858M	3476753M	Total Assets ($)	4617M	75127M	56756M	164215M	364701M	2811337M

M = $ thousand   MM = $ million
See Pages 11 through 21 for Explanation of Ratios and Data

Current Data Sorted By Assets   Comparative Historical Data

	0-500M	500M-2MM	2-10MM	10-50MM	50-100MM	100-250MM	Type of Statement	4/1/00-3/31/01 ALL	4/1/01-3/31/02 ALL
		1	5	3	1	1	Unqualified	14	9
		3	1	2	1		Reviewed	11	14
		3	2				Compiled	9	8
	1	1	1				Tax Returns	1	3
	2	3	6	4	3	1	Other	13	15
			17 (4/1-9/30/04)		28 (10/1/04-3/31/05)				
NUMBER OF STATEMENTS	3	11	15	9	5	2		48	49
	%	%	%	%	%	%	ASSETS	%	%
		9.9	6.6				Cash & Equivalents	7.8	7.1
		34.0	22.6				Trade Receivables (net)	24.7	25.0
		18.1	27.3				Inventory	27.8	27.3
		1.1	4.1				All Other Current	5.1	2.4
		63.0	60.5				Total Current	65.3	61.8
		27.4	20.7				Fixed Assets (net)	23.9	24.7
		2.9	11.2				Intangibles (net)	4.1	4.9
		6.7	7.5				All Other Non-Current	6.6	8.6
		100.0	100.0				Total	100.0	100.0
							LIABILITIES		
		7.0	5.9				Notes Payable-Short Term	4.8	11.9
		7.4	5.1				Cur. Mat.-L/T/D	3.1	3.5
		22.3	10.6				Trade Payables	15.8	10.3
		.0	.2				Income Taxes Payable	.7	.5
		7.3	8.3				All Other Current	12.3	6.9
		44.0	30.0				Total Current	36.6	33.1
		20.4	10.9				Long-Term Debt	12.5	15.5
		.2	.2				Deferred Taxes	.7	.3
		2.1	6.5				All Other Non-Current	5.1	3.3
		33.3	52.4				Net Worth	45.2	47.7
		100.0	100.0				Total Liabilities & Net Worth	100.0	100.0
							INCOME DATA		
		100.0	100.0				Net Sales	100.0	100.0
		42.8	38.6				Gross Profit	40.4	42.2
		41.9	31.1				Operating Expenses	35.0	36.4
		1.0	7.6				Operating Profit	5.5	5.9
		.6	1.2				All Other Expenses (net)	1.9	1.5
		.3	6.3				Profit Before Taxes	3.5	4.3
							RATIOS		
		2.7	2.8					3.0	3.9
		1.7	1.9				Current	1.7	1.9
		1.1	1.6					1.3	1.4
		1.7	1.2					1.3	1.7
		1.1	.9				Quick	1.0	1.0
		.5	.8					.7	.6
	35	10.5	25 14.4					31 11.9	35 10.3
	40	9.1	43 8.6				Sales/Receivables	52 7.1	44 8.3
	56	6.5	56 6.5					66 5.5	72 5.1
	18	20.2	81 4.5					55 6.7	54 6.7
	29	12.5	96 3.8				Cost of Sales/Inventory	96 3.8	105 3.5
	76	4.8	111 3.3					143 2.6	160 2.3
	24	15.3	17 20.9					21 17.4	16 22.4
	30	12.0	33 11.2				Cost of Sales/Payables	38 9.7	34 10.9
	65	5.6	50 7.3					82 4.5	54 6.8
		8.3	5.2					3.7	3.6
		14.0	6.9				Sales/Working Capital	6.2	5.1
		31.0	10.0					14.5	16.0
		4.7	22.0					13.9	4.9
	(10)	2.0	(13) 3.8				EBIT/Interest	(44) 3.4	(44) 2.1
		-3.3	-.2					1.6	.8
							Net Profit + Depr., Dep.,	9.9	5.5
							Amort./Cur. Mat. L/T/D	(17) 3.3	(21) 2.1
								1.9	.8
		.5	.2					.2	.3
		1.0	.5				Fixed/Worth	.4	.6
		3.1	1.7					1.0	1.0
		.6	.6					.5	.5
		2.1	1.0				Debt/Worth	1.5	1.2
		8.7	1.6					3.2	3.3
			72.6				% Profit Before Taxes/Tangible	42.4	36.1
		(12)	21.9				Net Worth	(46) 14.2	(46) 12.4
			1.4					5.6	.3
		11.0	28.5				% Profit Before Taxes/Total	15.7	10.9
		4.3	8.7				Assets	6.5	3.0
		-2.9	-.2					1.7	-.2
		17.1	33.1					21.8	18.2
		13.2	15.5				Sales/Net Fixed Assets	9.5	8.4
		5.6	4.5					4.2	4.1
		4.1	2.9					2.5	2.3
		3.1	1.5				Sales/Total Assets	1.8	1.8
		2.3	1.3					1.2	1.2
		1.7	.5					1.1	1.7
	(10)	2.8	1.8				% Depr., Dep., Amort./Sales	(36) 2.0	(44) 2.7
		4.2	4.5					4.9	4.6
							% Officers', Directors',	4.6	2.1
							Owners' Comp/Sales	(14) 7.9	(12) 5.3
								11.0	12.4
3124M	40679M	161185M	322875M	380008M	251850M		Net Sales ($)	2203626M	1653073M
732M	12814M	89998M	236640M	305197M	286296M		Total Assets ($)	1505463M	1176331M

M = $ thousand   MM = $ million
See Pages 11 through 21 for Explanation of Ratios and Data

Comparative Historical Data | Current Data Sorted By Sales

4/1/02-3/31/03 ALL	4/1/03-3/31/04 ALL	4/1/04-3/31/05 ALL	Type of Statement	0-1MM	1-3MM	3-5MM	5-10MM	10-25MM	25MM & OVER
						17 (4/1-9/30/04)	28 (10/1/04-3/31/05)		
10	12	11	Unqualified			1	2	5	3
8	12	7	Reviewed		1		3	1	2
5	12	6	Compiled	1	1	2	2		
1	2	4	Tax Returns	1	1		2		
21	15	17	Other	1	1	1	3	4	7
45	53	45	NUMBER OF STATEMENTS	3	4	4	12	10	12
%	%	%	ASSETS	%	%	%	%	%	%
11.2	11.8	10.1	Cash & Equivalents				5.2	5.0	13.3
23.3	25.4	25.4	Trade Receivables (net)				24.1	24.9	25.0
26.0	29.8	24.7	Inventory				24.7	25.5	27.0
4.8	2.5	3.0	All Other Current				5.3	.9	3.2
65.3	69.5	63.3	Total Current				59.3	56.3	68.6
23.9	22.1	23.0	Fixed Assets (net)				23.2	34.0	13.4
3.8	2.6	8.4	Intangibles (net)				9.3	6.5	14.1
6.9	5.9	5.4	All Other Non-Current				8.3	3.2	3.9
100.0	100.0	100.0	Total				100.0	100.0	100.0
			LIABILITIES						
8.1	6.6	6.7	Notes Payable-Short Term				3.2	9.6	7.8
3.2	4.0	4.9	Cur. Mat.-L/T/D				5.7	7.4	.9
10.4	12.9	13.2	Trade Payables				14.0	8.0	9.8
.1	.2	.3	Income Taxes Payable				.1	.2	.7
9.3	11.4	11.4	All Other Current				7.7	9.0	12.3
31.3	35.2	36.6	Total Current				30.7	34.2	31.5
13.1	14.4	13.9	Long-Term Debt				13.5	13.7	8.3
.3	.5	.6	Deferred Taxes				.3	1.6	.6
4.3	4.3	5.9	All Other Non-Current				5.2	7.2	8.8
51.0	45.7	43.1	Net Worth				50.3	43.3	50.8
100.0	100.0	100.0	Total Liabilities & Net Worth				100.0	100.0	100.0
			INCOME DATA						
100.0	100.0	100.0	Net Sales				100.0	100.0	100.0
40.5	41.7	41.3	Gross Profit				34.7	41.7	44.4
35.9	35.3	35.2	Operating Expenses				31.8	29.1	36.4
4.7	6.4	6.1	Operating Profit				2.9	12.6	8.0
.8	1.9	1.5	All Other Expenses (net)				.8	2.9	1.6
3.8	4.5	4.7	Profit Before Taxes				2.1	9.7	6.4
			RATIOS						
4.1	2.8	2.8	Current				2.6	2.4	2.8
2.1	2.2	1.9					1.8	1.8	2.5
1.5	1.5	1.3					1.5	1.1	1.9
2.5	1.6	1.5	Quick				1.2	1.2	1.8
1.0	1.1	1.0					.9	1.0	1.2
.6	.7	.6					.6	.4	1.0
34 10.7	35 10.5	33 11.0	Sales/Receivables				25 14.8	47 7.7	38 9.6
46 7.9	47 7.8	44 8.3					36 10.0	54 6.7	62 5.9
67 5.5	62 5.9	68 5.4					50 7.4	71 5.1	81 4.5
52 7.1	58 6.3	34 10.7	Cost of Sales/Inventory				33 10.9	62 5.9	94 3.9
103 3.5	97 3.7	93 3.9					88 4.1	98 3.7	132 2.8
140 2.6	142 2.6	124 2.9					107 3.4	130 2.8	176 2.1
17 21.8	18 20.1	19 19.4	Cost of Sales/Payables				24 14.9	16 23.5	19 19.5
27 13.6	30 12.3	33 11.2					34 10.7	32 11.3	37 9.8
53 6.9	58 6.2	52 7.0					41 8.8	50 7.2	67 5.5
3.3	3.4	4.0	Sales/Working Capital				5.6	5.3	2.3
4.9	5.2	7.8					8.5	8.7	3.4
9.5	14.6	16.1					13.0	NM	5.9
8.1	19.1	13.0	EBIT/Interest				4.7	31.1	77.4
(40) 3.1	(45) 4.3	(39) 3.8				(10) 1.7	6.7	(11) 8.1
1.2	1.8	.7					-3.7	1.4	1.9
6.5	21.1	4.1	Net Profit + Depr., Dep., Amort./Cur. Mat. L/T/D						
(11) 3.2	(14) 3.7	(18) 2.7							
.7	1.5	1.0							
.2	.2	.2	Fixed/Worth				.3	.4	.1
.4	.4	.5					.6	1.0	.2
1.0	1.1	2.7					1.6	3.0	.6
.4	.6	.6	Debt/Worth				.6	1.0	.6
1.0	1.0	1.2					1.0	1.4	.9
2.3	2.4	5.2					2.8	3.4	4.9
30.7	47.7	44.7	% Profit Before Taxes/Tangible Net Worth				47.5		41.7
(43) 14.9	(50) 19.7	(37) 25.2					(10) 10.1		(11) 32.2
.5	7.3	2.2					-8.3		13.2
14.0	17.9	17.9	% Profit Before Taxes/Total Assets				12.3	34.6	15.9
4.8	8.6	7.1					4.3	16.2	10.9
.0	1.7	-.1					-6.9	2.5	4.7
18.4	27.2	26.8	Sales/Net Fixed Assets				26.3	22.6	36.5
10.0	12.1	13.2					14.8	5.2	10.9
5.1	6.5	4.9					5.9	1.5	5.6
2.4	2.8	3.1	Sales/Total Assets				3.6	2.7	2.1
1.7	1.8	1.8					1.9	1.5	1.0
1.1	1.4	1.0					1.2	.9	.9
1.7	1.4	1.5	% Depr., Dep., Amort./Sales				1.2	.7	
(40) 2.7	(42) 3.1	(39) 2.9					(11) 1.9	2.6	
5.3	4.3	5.2					5.2	7.6	
3.2	1.7	2.0	% Officers', Directors', Owners' Comp/Sales						
(15) 5.1	(19) 4.4	(16) 4.3							
9.3	8.3	5.6							
1387863M	1317640M	1159721M	Net Sales ($)	2244M	8705M	13480M	84090M	167217M	883985M
1162121M	957630M	931677M	Total Assets ($)	1210M	3187M	4480M	51028M	144619M	727153M

© RMA 2005

M = $ thousand   MM = $ million
See Pages 11 through 21 for Explanation of Ratios and Data

Current Data Sorted By Assets — Comparative Historical Data

0-500M	500M-2MM	2-10MM	10-50MM	50-100MM	100-250MM	Type of Statement	4/1/00-3/31/01 ALL	4/1/01-3/31/02 ALL
		1	2	2	1	Unqualified	9	10
	2	4	3			Reviewed	4	4
		1				Compiled	4	6
	1	1				Tax Returns	3	2
	1	6	3	1		Other	17	11
	10 (4/1-9/30/04)		19 (10/1/04-3/31/05)					
	4	13	8	3	1	NUMBER OF STATEMENTS	37	33
%	%	%	%	%	%	**ASSETS**	%	%
		6.2				Cash & Equivalents	7.4	8.7
		25.8				Trade Receivables (net)	24.9	22.8
		22.2				Inventory	28.0	29.2
		1.1				All Other Current	5.2	3.9
		55.4				Total Current	65.5	64.6
		35.5				Fixed Assets (net)	20.2	24.6
		2.1				Intangibles (net)	6.9	6.1
		7.1				All Other Non-Current	7.4	5.1
		100.0				Total	100.0	100.0
						LIABILITIES		
		17.1				Notes Payable-Short Term	7.0	10.3
		3.7				Cur. Mat.-L/T/D	8.1	7.0
		14.7				Trade Payables	14.0	14.1
		.7				Income Taxes Payable	.6	.7
		11.9				All Other Current	12.6	10.8
		48.1				Total Current	42.4	42.9
		16.8				Long-Term Debt	12.7	19.0
		.4				Deferred Taxes	.5	.6
		1.5				All Other Non-Current	3.8	3.8
		33.1				Net Worth	40.6	33.8
		100.0				Total Liabilities & Net Worth	100.0	100.0
						INCOME DATA		
		100.0				Net Sales	100.0	100.0
		39.2				Gross Profit	38.1	38.2
		33.3				Operating Expenses	33.5	37.4
		5.9				Operating Profit	4.6	.8
		2.0				All Other Expenses (net)	1.5	1.1
		3.9				Profit Before Taxes	3.2	-.3
						RATIOS		
		1.8					3.1	2.1
		1.3				Current	2.0	1.5
		.9					1.2	1.1
		1.3					1.5	1.2
		.7				Quick	.9	.8
		.3					.5	.5
		32 11.5					26 14.1	23 15.8
		46 8.0				Sales/Receivables	45 8.1	40 9.2
		58 6.3					63 5.8	54 6.8
		22 16.2					28 13.0	43 8.5
		41 9.0				Cost of Sales/Inventory	79 4.6	87 4.2
		137 2.7					135 2.7	143 2.5
		23 15.6					18 19.8	19 19.7
		39 9.4				Cost of Sales/Payables	29 12.7	29 12.4
		62 5.9					63 5.8	47 7.8
		7.1					4.0	4.1
		18.5				Sales/Working Capital	7.2	9.4
		-185.7					40.8	102.6
		11.7					13.9	4.6
		3.6				EBIT/Interest	(31) 3.6	(29) 2.0
		-.1					1.1	-.6
						Net Profit + Depr., Dep.,		2.2
						Amort./Cur. Mat. L /T/D	(10) 1.7	1.7
								-1.3
		.6					.2	.4
		1.4				Fixed/Worth	.4	1.1
		5.5					1.6	1.9
		.7					.6	1.3
		1.2				Debt/Worth	1.3	1.8
		28.1					4.4	10.8
		35.3					38.7	39.3
		(11) 9.7				% Profit Before Taxes/Tangible Net Worth	(33) 21.8	(29) 12.2
		-1.4					6.5	-7.1
		15.9					20.2	5.8
		6.1				% Profit Before Taxes/Total Assets	6.0	2.5
		-1.5					.6	-4.7
		20.7					31.8	22.5
		6.8				Sales/Net Fixed Assets	10.9	8.9
		2.5					6.7	4.9
		2.8					2.9	3.1
		2.0				Sales/Total Assets	2.0	1.9
		1.3					1.4	1.3
		1.3					1.1	1.0
		(11) 1.8				% Depr., Dep., Amort./Sales	(29) 1.9	(30) 2.5
		8.9					4.0	4.9
						% Officers', Directors', Owners' Comp/Sales	2.2	
							(10) 3.7	
							9.5	
	10125M	112636M	353100M	317686M	203132M	Net Sales ($)	1116909M	838907M
	4159M	58338M	171781M	213403M	189517M	Total Assets ($)	793489M	662074M

(Left columns 0-500M through 100-250M: DATA NOT AVAILABLE)

M = $ thousand   MM = $ million
See Pages 11 through 21 for Explanation of Ratios and Data

Comparative Historical Data				Type of Statement	Current Data Sorted By Sales					
8	8	6		Unqualified				1		5
5	10	9		Reviewed	1	2		2	3	1
3	1	1		Compiled				1		
3	2	2		Tax Returns	1				1	
13	7	11		Other	1	1		4	2	3
						10 (4/1-9/30/04)		19 (10/1/04-3/31/05)		
4/1/02-3/31/03 ALL	4/1/03-3/31/04 ALL	4/1/04-3/31/05 ALL			0-1MM	1-3MM	3-5MM	5-10MM	10-25MM	25MM & OVER
32	28	29		**NUMBER OF STATEMENTS**	1	3	2	8	6	9
%	%	%		**ASSETS**	%	%	%	%	%	%
8.2	7.7	7.5		Cash & Equivalents						
22.6	22.5	23.5		Trade Receivables (net)						
24.1	31.1	28.0		Inventory						
1.7	2.1	1.0		All Other Current						
56.6	63.4	60.0		Total Current						
33.6	25.4	29.3		Fixed Assets (net)						
4.6	5.2	4.7		Intangibles (net)						
5.2	5.9	6.0		All Other Non-Current						
100.0	100.0	100.0		Total						
				LIABILITIES						
12.6	10.1	13.0		Notes Payable-Short Term						
5.5	3.7	5.7		Cur. Mat.-L/T/D						
13.2	13.2	13.1		Trade Payables						
.5	.7	.6		Income Taxes Payable						
10.7	10.1	12.8		All Other Current						
42.6	37.9	45.1		Total Current						
15.8	13.6	17.9		Long-Term Debt						
1.6	.5	.5		Deferred Taxes						
1.9	4.2	1.4		All Other Non-Current						
38.2	43.8	35.2		Net Worth						
100.0	100.0	100.0		Total Liabilities & Net Worth						
				INCOME DATA						
100.0	100.0	100.0		Net Sales						
40.8	37.9	36.6		Gross Profit						
37.6	33.7	30.7		Operating Expenses						
3.2	4.2	5.8		Operating Profit						
1.6	.8	1.6		All Other Expenses (net)						
1.6	3.3	4.3		Profit Before Taxes						
				RATIOS						
2.0	3.0	3.0								
1.3	1.7	1.6		Current						
.8	1.1	1.0								
1.0	1.3	1.6								
.6	.8	.7		Quick						
.4	.5	.4								
28 12.8	24 14.9	31 11.7								
45 8.1	42 8.8	41 9.0		Sales/Receivables						
59 6.1	58 6.3	53 6.9								
34 10.7	44 8.2	39 9.3								
68 5.4	78 4.7	80 4.6		Cost of Sales/Inventory						
111 3.3	137 2.7	109 3.3								
21 17.7	22 16.4	17 21.1								
38 9.5	27 13.7	25 14.5		Cost of Sales/Payables						
59 6.2	51 7.1	45 8.1								
7.3	4.3	4.3								
16.0	9.1	8.4		Sales/Working Capital						
−20.5	47.3	NM								
9.6	12.2	12.0								
(31) 3.1	(26) 5.4	(27) 3.8		EBIT/Interest						
.8	2.0	.7								
4.0	3.9	6.3								
(11) 1.8	(11) 1.5	(11) 4.0		Net Profit + Depr., Dep., Amort./Cur. Mat. L/T/D						
.4	.2	1.3								
.5	.3	.3								
.9	.6	.8		Fixed/Worth						
2.6	1.5	2.3								
.9	.9	.5								
1.7	1.5	1.2		Debt/Worth						
5.5	4.4	6.0								
32.0	38.9	32.9								
(30) 11.7	(27) 10.0	(25) 11.9		% Profit Before Taxes/Tangible Net Worth						
.4	2.7	.4								
11.9	10.6	15.3								
3.1	4.2	8.8		% Profit Before Taxes/Total Assets						
−.4	1.4	.1								
19.4	23.4	21.2								
8.7	9.1	7.8		Sales/Net Fixed Assets						
2.9	3.5	3.9								
2.8	3.2	2.8								
1.9	2.0	2.0		Sales/Total Assets						
1.4	1.2	1.3								
1.4	1.3	1.4								
(27) 3.6	(27) 2.6	(25) 2.3		% Depr., Dep., Amort./Sales						
5.4	4.7	5.1								
				% Officers', Directors', Owners' Comp/Sales						
905935M	866760M	996679M		Net Sales ($)	573M	6009M	8736M	62562M	105187M	813612M
678305M	628776M	637198M		Total Assets ($)	3627M	2921M	4085M	39061M	48819M	538685M

M = $ thousand   MM = $ million
See Pages 11 through 21 for Explanation of Ratios and Data

Current Data Sorted By Assets   Comparative Historical Data

	0-500M	500M-2MM	2-10MM	10-50MM	50-100MM	100-250MM	Type of Statement	4/1/00-3/31/01 ALL	4/1/01-3/31/02 ALL
		1	14	14	3	4	Unqualified	24	31
	1	11	19	3			Reviewed	22	15
	1	8	10	1			Compiled	11	14
	3	4	4	1			Tax Returns	2	1
	3	12	25	10	5	1	Other	27	18
		27 (4/1-9/30/04)			131 (10/1/04-3/31/05)				
NUMBER OF STATEMENTS	8	36	72	29	8	5		86	79
ASSETS	%	%	%	%	%	%		%	%
Cash & Equivalents		9.5	6.9	6.3				8.5	8.1
Trade Receivables (net)		34.1	27.2	28.2				27.0	28.8
Inventory		28.9	27.3	27.8				28.5	26.6
All Other Current		1.1	4.0	3.1				3.6	3.5
Total Current		73.6	65.3	65.4				67.5	67.1
Fixed Assets (net)		17.2	23.0	19.9				19.8	19.8
Intangibles (net)		4.6	4.3	7.8				5.2	6.1
All Other Non-Current		4.6	7.5	6.9				7.5	7.0
Total		100.0	100.0	100.0				100.0	100.0
LIABILITIES									
Notes Payable-Short Term		19.3	12.9	25.5				9.7	12.3
Cur. Mat.-L/T/D		3.6	3.9	2.9				4.7	3.4
Trade Payables		22.6	14.5	12.1				15.1	13.4
Income Taxes Payable		.3	.4	.1				.3	.2
All Other Current		6.8	11.0	12.8				10.7	13.2
Total Current		52.7	42.7	53.3				40.5	42.4
Long-Term Debt		14.5	14.1	10.4				14.1	14.2
Deferred Taxes		.2	.4	.5				.3	.2
All Other Non-Current		14.4	8.5	2.0				4.8	7.7
Net Worth		18.2	34.3	33.9				40.3	35.5
Total Liabilities & Net Worth		100.0	100.0	100.0				100.0	100.0
INCOME DATA									
Net Sales		100.0	100.0	100.0				100.0	100.0
Gross Profit		35.5	36.4	33.9				33.8	34.9
Operating Expenses		35.4	30.8	28.5				29.7	33.1
Operating Profit		.1	5.5	5.4				4.0	1.8
All Other Expenses (net)		.8	1.4	.9				1.4	1.5
Profit Before Taxes		-.6	4.1	4.4				2.6	.3
RATIOS									
Current		2.5	2.1	2.7				2.8	2.6
		1.5	1.4	1.4				1.8	1.6
		1.1	1.2	1.0				1.2	1.2
Quick		1.3	1.2	1.6				1.5	1.3
		.9	.8	.8				.9	.9
		.4	.5	.5				.6	.7
Sales/Receivables	31	11.9	33 11.1	43 8.4				33 11.0	34 10.9
	49	7.4	48 7.7	51 7.2				47 7.8	51 7.1
	63	5.8	58 6.3	82 4.5				61 6.0	71 5.2
Cost of Sales/Inventory	23	16.1	33 11.0	54 6.8				36 10.3	55 6.7
	55	6.6	72 5.1	70 5.2				71 5.1	75 4.8
	109	3.3	122 3.0	111 3.3				115 3.2	126 2.9
Cost of Sales/Payables	19	19.5	20 18.0	21 17.3				19 19.3	20 18.6
	39	9.3	34 10.7	32 11.5				38 9.6	31 11.7
	69	5.3	58 6.3	49 7.5				54 6.8	49 7.5
Sales/Working Capital		5.5	5.4	4.3				4.4	4.0
		11.5	10.0	11.1				8.4	7.3
		48.7	19.2	233.6				33.1	15.5
EBIT/Interest	(34)	5.7	(64) 9.6	(27) 23.2				(77) 6.6	(73) 5.0
		3.5	4.3	6.3				3.6	2.0
		-5.6	1.8	2.0				.9	-.3
Net Profit + Depr., Dep., Amort./Cur. Mat. L/T/D			(30) 5.9	(11) 14.5				(26) 4.6	(30) 3.8
			2.6	4.4				1.4	1.9
			.9	1.5				.8	.6
Fixed/Worth		.2	.2	.1				.3	.2
		.4	.6	.6				.6	.7
		11.1	1.7	2.8				1.4	1.7
Debt/Worth		1.5	1.0	.6				.7	.7
		3.5	2.2	1.5				1.7	2.1
		36.5	4.8	6.5				6.0	5.4
% Profit Before Taxes/Tangible Net Worth	(29)	77.6	(63) 38.9	(25) 43.0				(77) 41.8	(69) 29.2
		23.1	18.2	26.5				16.2	10.4
		2.4	10.0	13.1				2.5	-3.5
% Profit Before Taxes/Total Assets		10.9	14.0	15.0				14.5	8.5
		3.4	6.9	7.9				7.1	3.1
		-12.2	1.8	3.4				.1	-2.2
Sales/Net Fixed Assets		51.4	26.8	28.1				31.4	33.3
		28.9	13.9	10.6				11.1	11.5
		11.1	5.1	5.6				6.5	5.6
Sales/Total Assets		3.2	2.8	2.3				3.0	2.4
		2.4	2.0	1.8				2.0	1.9
		1.9	1.5	1.1				1.6	1.5
% Depr., Dep., Amort./Sales	(28)	.7	(66) 1.0	(28) 1.2				(75) .9	(70) .9
		1.8	2.1	1.8				1.7	1.7
		3.1	3.4	2.8				3.0	3.1
% Officers', Directors', Owners' Comp/Sales	(20)	2.8	(26) 1.8					(27) 1.9	(18) 1.9
		4.5	4.4					4.6	4.3
		6.6	7.3					8.8	8.0
Net Sales ($)	8347M	112703M	703731M	1185338M	979717M	1449767M		2262400M	3584236M
Total Assets ($)	2191M	43720M	343352M	642987M	572794M	720124M		1408727M	2274181M

M = $ thousand   MM = $ million
See Pages 11 through 21 for Explanation of Ratios and Data

Comparative Historical Data | Current Data Sorted By Sales

H1	H2	H3	Type of Statement	0-1MM	1-3MM	3-5MM	5-10MM	10-25MM	25MM & OVER
43	32	36	Unqualified		2	2	5	9	18
24	33	34	Reviewed	1	7	7	7	10	2
18	28	20	Compiled		6	5	8	1	
7	12	12	Tax Returns	3	2	2	2	2	1
40	42	56	Other		9	9	10	16	12
4/1/02-3/31/03 ALL	4/1/03-3/31/04 ALL	4/1/04-3/31/05 ALL		27 (4/1-9/30/04)			131 (10/1/04-3/31/05)		
132	147	158	**NUMBER OF STATEMENTS**	4	26	25	32	38	33
%	%	%	**ASSETS**	%	%	%	%	%	%
6.4	8.0	7.6	Cash & Equivalents		7.7	9.0	8.3	7.1	5.6
27.6	28.3	29.6	Trade Receivables (net)		30.1	28.1	30.2	29.9	28.7
29.4	27.8	27.1	Inventory		24.8	27.5	25.4	29.1	29.2
2.9	3.2	3.3	All Other Current		2.2	3.3	4.4	3.6	3.2
66.2	67.4	67.6	Total Current		64.8	67.8	68.2	69.7	66.6
22.0	20.9	20.6	Fixed Assets (net)		25.8	16.2	22.6	18.2	20.7
5.5	5.1	5.0	Intangibles (net)		3.9	9.4	1.0	5.5	6.5
6.2	6.7	6.7	All Other Non-Current		5.5	6.6	8.1	6.7	6.2
100.0	100.0	100.0	Total		100.0	100.0	100.0	100.0	100.0
			LIABILITIES						
13.3	13.6	16.0	Notes Payable-Short Term		17.2	15.5	11.5	16.9	17.7
7.3	4.1	3.6	Cur. Mat.-L/T/D		6.0	2.6	3.9	3.3	2.7
13.4	15.5	16.4	Trade Payables		22.4	14.2	17.9	15.5	12.8
.7	.1	.3	Income Taxes Payable		.3	.1	.5	.3	.3
12.0	11.0	11.3	All Other Current		13.2	11.2	10.3	9.1	14.1
46.7	44.3	47.5	Total Current		59.2	43.6	44.3	45.0	47.7
15.6	11.9	13.8	Long-Term Debt		22.0	16.5	11.9	8.5	13.4
.2	.3	.4	Deferred Taxes		.2	.4	.5	.2	.8
10.3	9.9	8.6	All Other Non-Current		18.0	5.6	6.8	9.5	4.5
27.2	33.5	29.7	Net Worth		.5	33.9	36.5	36.9	33.6
100.0	100.0	100.0	Total Liabilities & Net Worth		100.0	100.0	100.0	100.0	100.0
			INCOME DATA						
100.0	100.0	100.0	Net Sales		100.0	100.0	100.0	100.0	100.0
35.0	33.9	36.1	Gross Profit		40.7	40.7	33.6	35.8	31.1
32.6	30.3	31.8	Operating Expenses		39.7	35.6	27.6	31.7	25.3
2.4	3.6	4.3	Operating Profit		1.0	5.1	6.0	4.1	5.9
1.5	.9	1.1	All Other Expenses (net)		2.1	.9	.9	.6	1.4
.9	2.7	3.2	Profit Before Taxes		−1.1	4.2	5.1	3.5	4.5
			RATIOS						
2.4 / 1.7 / 1.2	2.6 / 1.6 / 1.1	2.3 / 1.5 / 1.1	Current		1.8 / 1.1 / .6	2.9 / 1.4 / 1.1	2.1 / 1.5 / 1.3	2.4 / 1.7 / 1.2	2.5 / 1.8 / 1.2
1.4 / .8 / .5	1.3 / .9 / .5	1.3 / .9 / .5	Quick		1.0 / .8 / .3	1.8 / 1.0 / .4	1.3 / .9 / .5	1.4 / .8 / .5	1.5 / .9 / .7
34 10.8 / 47 7.7 / 64 5.7	32 11.6 / 45 8.1 / 61 6.0	35 10.6 / 48 7.6 / 63 5.8	Sales/Receivables		25 14.8 / 43 8.6 / 72 5.1	42 8.7 / 54 6.8 / 59 6.2	32 11.4 / 47 7.7 / 56 6.5	36 10.2 / 48 7.7 / 61 6.0	33 10.9 / 45 8.1 / 67 5.4
46 7.9 / 74 4.9 / 116 3.1	36 10.2 / 63 5.8 / 108 3.4	34 10.6 / 70 5.2 / 107 3.4	Cost of Sales/Inventory		25 14.9 / 64 5.7 / 104 3.5	23 16.0 / 75 4.9 / 127 2.9	12 29.5 / 46 8.0 / 95 3.9	43 8.5 / 72 5.1 / 116 3.2	54 6.8 / 72 5.1 / 104 3.5
19 19.1 / 34 10.7 / 56 6.6	19 19.3 / 33 11.0 / 51 7.1	21 17.7 / 34 10.7 / 61 6.0	Cost of Sales/Payables		18 20.4 / 56 6.5 / 87 4.2	25 14.9 / 39 9.3 / 70 5.2	19 19.1 / 34 10.8 / 56 6.5	20 18.3 / 34 10.8 / 63 5.8	21 17.5 / 29 12.6 / 40 9.2
4.5 / 8.1 / 20.8	4.9 / 9.0 / 32.7	5.3 / 10.5 / 25.5	Sales/Working Capital		6.9 / 38.5 / −8.1	4.5 / 9.0 / 20.1	5.6 / 11.6 / 20.4	4.4 / 10.0 / 23.5	4.6 / 7.1 / 20.8
5.4 / (120) 2.4 / .5	9.6 / (134) 3.1 / 1.0	9.9 / (144) 4.2 / 1.8	EBIT/Interest		8.2 / (23) 3.4 / −2.6	5.4 / (23) 3.8 / 1.8	18.4 / (29) 6.0 / 2.0	7.6 / (33) 3.6 / 1.4	22.9 / (32) 6.5 / 4.3
4.0 / (43) 1.8 / 1.1	4.4 / (46) 1.9 / .6	7.2 / (50) 3.0 / 1.3	Net Profit + Depr., Dep., Amort./Cur. Mat. L/T/D				3.1 / (11) 1.5 / .4	6.5 / (16) 3.8 / .5	14.0 / (13) 5.9 / 1.8
.3 / .7 / 2.6	.3 / .6 / 1.7	.2 / .6 / 2.2	Fixed/Worth		.2 / 1.1 / −4.7	.3 / .4 / 2.0	.2 / .6 / 1.5	.2 / .5 / 2.2	.2 / .6 / 2.4
.9 / 2.1 / 9.2	.8 / 1.9 / 7.3	1.0 / 2.4 / 7.3	Debt/Worth		1.9 / 7.8 / −8.0	1.3 / 2.8 / 13.2	.8 / 2.0 / 3.2	.8 / 1.6 / 7.3	.5 / 1.8 / 5.0
30.4 / (115) 12.4 / −.6	38.4 / (129) 14.1 / 2.0	46.5 / (132) 21.1 / 10.0	% Profit Before Taxes/Tangible Net Worth		64.1 / (17) 21.1 / 11.0	77.2 / (22) 21.0 / 5.4	55.7 / (29) 18.8 / 10.5	40.5 / (33) 16.4 / 8.5	36.5 / (27) 25.9 / 15.5
8.8 / 3.9 / −1.4	12.0 / 6.0 / .2	13.8 / 7.6 / 1.8	% Profit Before Taxes/Total Assets		17.0 / 7.2 / −10.3	14.4 / 5.0 / 1.7	18.6 / 7.5 / 1.7	12.4 / 6.4 / 1.6	13.0 / 9.8 / 5.5
28.8 / 12.3 / 5.5	33.6 / 14.4 / 6.9	31.5 / 16.0 / 5.7	Sales/Net Fixed Assets		38.3 / 15.8 / 2.9	38.9 / 22.5 / 11.1	37.4 / 13.0 / 5.0	27.7 / 15.5 / 7.0	26.1 / 13.3 / 6.1
2.6 / 2.0 / 1.5	3.1 / 2.2 / 1.6	2.8 / 2.1 / 1.6	Sales/Total Assets		3.2 / 2.2 / 1.5	2.4 / 1.9 / 1.3	3.5 / 2.3 / 1.8	2.3 / 2.1 / 1.4	2.3 / 2.1 / 1.7
1.0 / (117) 1.8 / 3.4	.9 / (128) 1.8 / 3.1	1.0 / (139) 1.9 / 3.1	% Depr., Dep., Amort./Sales		1.2 / (21) 1.9 / 5.6	.8 / (20) 1.9 / 3.0	1.0 / (27) 2.6 / 4.1	1.0 / (37) 1.5 / 2.8	1.0 / (30) 1.6 / 2.7
1.5 / (37) 3.1 / 3.4	3.3 / (51) 5.2 / 6.6	1.9 / (58) 3.9 / 7.0	% Officers', Directors', Owners' Comp/Sales		2.7 / (10) 5.6 / 7.6	2.8 / (14) 4.4 / 8.8	2.5 / (13) 4.9 / 8.6	1.3 / (11) 1.8 / 4.7	
4458459M	4714291M	4439603M	Net Sales ($)	2326M	52248M	96803M	227048M	611129M	3450049M
2714591M	2560812M	2325168M	Total Assets ($)	1087M	32476M	60621M	107629M	338258M	1785097M

© RMA 2005

M = $ thousand   MM = $ million
See Pages 11 through 21 for Explanation of Ratios and Data

Current Data Sorted By Assets

Comparative Historical Data

						Type of Statement		
	1	3	4	3	1	Unqualified	9	9
	1	7	4			Reviewed	18	6
	5	3				Compiled	7	13
1		3				Tax Returns	4	1
	2	3	7			Other	18	14
	10 (4/1-9/30/04)	5	40 (10/1/04-3/31/05)				4/1/00-3/31/01	4/1/01-3/31/02
0-500M	500M-2MM	2-10MM	10-50MM	50-100MM	100-250MM		ALL	ALL
1	9	21	15	3	1	**NUMBER OF STATEMENTS**	56	43
%	%	%	%	%	%	**ASSETS**	%	%
		7.8	9.1			Cash & Equivalents	9.1	9.9
		32.6	27.1			Trade Receivables (net)	30.8	25.1
		21.2	16.5			Inventory	20.7	20.8
		4.7	4.3			All Other Current	4.6	5.0
		66.2	57.0			Total Current	65.2	60.8
		22.1	26.7			Fixed Assets (net)	23.8	26.7
		4.4	6.4			Intangibles (net)	3.9	5.7
		7.2	9.8			All Other Non-Current	7.0	6.8
		100.0	100.0			Total	100.0	100.0
						LIABILITIES		
		14.7	6.7			Notes Payable-Short Term	7.7	6.9
		3.2	3.2			Cur. Mat.-L/T/D	1.8	6.2
		16.6	11.0			Trade Payables	16.8	12.6
		.5	.6			Income Taxes Payable	.1	.1
		10.7	15.4			All Other Current	15.2	12.3
		45.7	36.8			Total Current	41.6	38.0
		14.8	10.2			Long-Term Debt	11.2	12.6
		.3	1.5			Deferred Taxes	.4	.7
		6.1	4.5			All Other Non-Current	4.7	1.6
		33.1	47.0			Net Worth	42.0	47.0
		100.0	100.0			Total Liabilities & Net Worth	100.0	100.0
						INCOME DATA		
		100.0	100.0			Net Sales	100.0	100.0
		29.5	28.5			Gross Profit	31.4	28.9
		25.3	20.6			Operating Expenses	24.5	24.3
		4.2	8.0			Operating Profit	6.9	4.6
		.8	.6			All Other Expenses (net)	1.4	1.7
		3.4	7.3			Profit Before Taxes	5.5	2.9
						RATIOS		
		2.7	2.3				3.1	3.0
		1.5	1.7			Current	1.7	1.7
		1.1	1.1				1.1	1.1
		1.3	1.6				1.7	1.9
		.9	1.0			Quick	1.1	1.0
		.6	.7				.6	.5
		37 9.7	47 7.8				38 9.5	30 12.1
		59 6.2	55 6.6			Sales/Receivables	54 6.7	49 7.4
		73 5.0	60 6.0				62 5.8	58 6.3
		29 12.4	24 15.2				28 12.9	31 11.6
		53 6.9	44 8.3			Cost of Sales/Inventory	54 6.8	62 5.9
		82 4.5	75 4.9				80 4.6	77 4.8
		21 17.6	17 21.7				18 20.7	14 25.6
		28 13.2	30 12.2			Cost of Sales/Payables	29 12.4	20 17.9
		35 10.3	40 9.2				47 7.7	37 9.8
		6.4	5.0				4.3	3.6
		10.2	8.6			Sales/Working Capital	8.4	9.2
		44.1	28.4				40.0	79.1
		10.9	44.0				9.2	12.9
		(20) 4.0	(14) 10.0			EBIT/Interest	(48) 3.8	(39) 2.9
		1.6	3.1				1.9	.6
						Net Profit + Depr., Dep.,	4.9	5.2
						Amort./Cur. Mat. L /T/D	(14) 3.5	(15) 1.8
							.6	.5
		.3	.4				.3	.3
		.6	.7			Fixed/Worth	.5	.7
		3.5	1.2				1.5	1.7
		.8	.8				.5	.4
		2.9	1.3			Debt/Worth	1.5	1.2
		15.8	2.6				3.9	6.2
		41.9	59.7			% Profit Before Taxes/Tangible	34.2	21.4
		(17) 18.2	25.7			Net Worth	(50) 17.9	(38) 13.4
		5.1	8.2				4.7	-4.1
		13.2	20.7			% Profit Before Taxes/Total	16.6	9.8
		3.9	14.3			Assets	6.0	5.7
		1.3	4.4				2.2	-2.1
		26.2	13.9				19.2	16.2
		11.7	7.5			Sales/Net Fixed Assets	11.8	8.5
		5.1	6.4				5.0	4.7
		2.7	2.3				2.6	2.6
		1.8	1.8			Sales/Total Assets	2.0	1.7
		1.6	1.2				1.5	1.3
		.9	2.0				1.0	1.0
		(20) 1.5	(13) 2.6			% Depr., Dep., Amort./Sales	(54) 1.9	(41) 2.1
		2.2	4.1				3.3	3.2
							2.0	1.0
						% Officers', Directors',	(19) 4.2	(10) 5.6
						Owners' Comp/Sales	7.0	11.1
735M	31699M	164910M	650322M	273024M	199933M	Net Sales ($)	1253298M	1548733M
355M	11134M	87325M	349797M	191829M	159670M	Total Assets ($)	744218M	1082064M

M = $ thousand   MM = $ million
See Pages 11 through 21 for Explanation of Ratios and Data

Comparative Historical Data | | | Current Data Sorted By Sales

			Type of Statement	0-1MM	1-3MM	3-5MM	5-10MM	10-25MM	25MM & OVER
10	10	12	Unqualified			3		1	7
16	9	12	Reviewed		1	2	4	2	3
10	13	8	Compiled		2	2	3	1	
4	2	4	Tax Returns	1		2		1	
12	17	14	Other		1	1	4		5
4/1/02- 3/31/03 ALL	4/1/03- 3/31/04 ALL	4/1/04- 3/31/05 ALL		10 (4/1-9/30/04)			40 (10/1/04-3/31/05)		
52	51	50	NUMBER OF STATEMENTS	1	4	6	16	8	15
%	%	%	**ASSETS**	%	%	%	%	%	%
9.1	10.1	8.0	Cash & Equivalents				9.7		8.9
28.1	32.2	34.0	Trade Receivables (net)				32.2		29.1
20.9	21.5	19.1	Inventory				21.5		16.6
4.8	5.4	4.2	All Other Current				3.7		4.4
62.8	69.1	65.2	Total Current				67.2		59.0
27.2	21.6	22.0	Fixed Assets (net)				19.6		25.4
3.7	3.6	4.7	Intangibles (net)				5.0		4.4
6.3	5.7	8.0	All Other Non-Current				8.2		11.3
100.0	100.0	100.0	Total				100.0		100.0
			LIABILITIES						
11.2	10.3	11.6	Notes Payable-Short Term				13.5		5.6
4.3	2.9	3.3	Cur. Mat.-L/T/D				5.8		2.7
15.8	18.0	15.9	Trade Payables				21.3		12.0
.2	.3	.4	Income Taxes Payable				.7		.7
16.9	11.8	13.9	All Other Current				11.2		17.8
48.3	43.3	45.2	Total Current				52.4		38.9
11.0	9.2	11.4	Long-Term Debt				16.4		12.4
.3	.3	.7	Deferred Taxes				.4		1.0
5.5	9.9	4.9	All Other Non-Current				8.0		4.7
35.0	37.4	37.7	Net Worth				22.7		43.0
100.0	100.0	100.0	Total Liabilities & Net Worth				100.0		100.0
			INCOME DATA						
100.0	100.0	100.0	Net Sales				100.0		100.0
33.5	31.9	30.3	Gross Profit				27.2		27.5
29.1	27.9	24.6	Operating Expenses				23.7		19.4
4.4	3.9	5.6	Operating Profit				3.6		8.1
.8	.6	1.2	All Other Expenses (net)				.9		.7
3.6	3.3	4.4	Profit Before Taxes				2.7		7.4
			RATIOS						
2.3	2.7	2.3	Current				2.1		2.2
1.5	1.7	1.5					1.2		1.7
1.0	1.1	1.1					1.0		1.2
1.6	1.7	1.4	Quick				1.1		1.3
.9	1.1	1.0					.8		1.0
.5	.6	.7					.5		.7
37 10.0	40 9.1	44 8.3	Sales/Receivables				37 9.8		48 7.6
49 7.4	52 7.0	58 6.3					54 6.8		56 6.5
63 5.8	67 5.5	72 5.1					71 5.1		68 5.3
25 14.5	33 11.1	24 15.1	Cost of Sales/Inventory				29 12.5		24 15.3
49 7.5	56 6.5	46 7.9					50 7.4		44 8.3
90 4.1	84 4.4	77 4.8					85 4.3		75 4.9
17 21.7	17 21.1	22 16.7	Cost of Sales/Payables				24 15.2		19 19.6
30 12.2	33 11.0	31 11.7					32 11.5		35 10.4
46 7.9	51 7.1	49 7.5					52 7.0		42 8.7
5.5	4.8	5.8	Sales/Working Capital				7.7		5.0
13.7	8.8	10.5					21.9		8.6
-151.1	39.5	41.4					NM		20.9
12.4	19.8	24.2	EBIT/Interest				7.9		38.7
(45) 4.7	(45) 3.4	(46) 4.1					(15) 2.6	(13) 10.1	
1.0	.6	1.8					1.5		2.7
8.0	8.9	8.0	Net Profit + Depr., Dep.,						
(19) 4.6	(16) 2.1	(18) 4.6	Amort./Cur. Mat. L/T/D						
1.6	1.1	2.5							
.4	.3	.3	Fixed/Worth				.4		.4
.6	.7	.6					1.0		.7
1.9	1.4	1.6					NM		1.2
.6	.6	.8	Debt/Worth				1.8		.8
1.8	1.6	1.9					5.7		1.4
8.1	5.7	7.3					NM		2.4
58.4	33.5	55.4	% Profit Before Taxes/Tangible				53.5		50.5
(44) 15.3	(44) 16.3	(44) 21.3	Net Worth				(12) 18.6		25.7
2.9	1.7	9.1					9.3		15.6
13.8	15.2	15.2	% Profit Before Taxes/Total				10.2		16.7
7.8	4.4	6.6	Assets				3.7		12.9
.1	-.6	1.9					1.1		5.3
21.8	28.1	19.1	Sales/Net Fixed Assets				48.7		13.9
9.6	10.5	10.6					11.2		7.4
5.0	6.3	6.3					5.4		6.4
2.7	3.1	2.6	Sales/Total Assets				2.8		2.3
1.9	2.2	1.9					1.9		1.9
1.5	1.5	1.5					1.6		1.3
1.7	1.0	1.0	% Depr., Dep., Amort./Sales				.9		1.8
(47) 2.2	(44) 1.7	(47) 1.9					(15) 1.1	(14) 2.2	
3.1	2.7	2.5					2.1		3.2
3.2	3.1	3.1	% Officers', Directors',						
(12) 5.7	(12) 6.0	(14) 3.8	Owners' Comp/Sales						
10.4	14.6	8.0							
1288522M	1134938M	1320623M	Net Sales ($)	735M	9579M	23737M	118547M	116050M	1051975M
644608M	654587M	800110M	Total Assets ($)	355M	5314M	8423M	64616M	76014M	645388M

M = $ thousand   MM = $ million
See Pages 11 through 21 for Explanation of Ratios and Data

Current Data Sorted By Assets   Comparative Historical Data

0-500M	500M-2MM	2-10MM	10-50MM	50-100MM	100-250MM		ALL 46	ALL 45
						Type of Statement		
	1	9	7	1	3	Unqualified	12	13
	4	16	6			Reviewed	8	12
	1	5	2			Compiled	10	6
1	4	2				Tax Returns		2
1	4	6	6	1		Other	16	12
	19 (4/1-9/30/04)		61 (10/1/04-3/31/05)				16 4/1/00-3/31/01	12 4/1/01-3/31/02
2	14	38	21	2	3	**NUMBER OF STATEMENTS**	46	45
%	%	%	%	%	%	**ASSETS**	%	%
	14.4	9.1	8.7			Cash & Equivalents	6.1	6.8
	36.1	27.2	29.4			Trade Receivables (net)	31.8	28.8
	27.2	31.2	23.9			Inventory	28.1	28.3
	1.8	2.7	6.8			All Other Current	4.0	2.1
	79.5	70.2	68.8			Total Current	70.0	66.0
	9.3	21.2	22.4			Fixed Assets (net)	20.0	23.4
	2.4	2.9	3.1			Intangibles (net)	3.5	2.5
	8.9	5.7	5.8			All Other Non-Current	6.5	8.1
	100.0	100.0	100.0			Total	100.0	100.0
						LIABILITIES		
	5.7	10.6	8.2			Notes Payable-Short Term	10.8	9.6
	9.7	3.2	3.0			Cur. Mat.-L/T/D	2.7	4.6
	23.6	13.9	13.1			Trade Payables	14.6	10.9
	.0	.1	.3			Income Taxes Payable	.1	.2
	8.9	12.3	21.8			All Other Current	13.7	17.6
	47.9	40.1	46.4			Total Current	42.1	42.8
	14.0	13.8	9.1			Long-Term Debt	14.2	14.7
	.0	.3	.3			Deferred Taxes	.8	.4
	4.5	5.6	8.4			All Other Non-Current	6.1	2.2
	33.6	40.2	35.9			Net Worth	36.9	39.9
	100.0	100.0	100.0			Total Liabilities & Net Worth	100.0	100.0
						INCOME DATA		
	100.0	100.0	100.0			Net Sales	100.0	100.0
	31.3	29.6	30.9			Gross Profit	33.7	25.8
	28.6	26.5	23.2			Operating Expenses	27.4	22.8
	2.7	3.1	7.7			Operating Profit	6.4	3.1
	.0	1.2	2.2			All Other Expenses (net)	1.8	1.7
	2.7	1.9	5.5			Profit Before Taxes	4.6	1.4
						RATIOS		
	2.9	3.5	2.4				2.9	2.5
	2.0	1.7	1.7			Current	1.8	2.0
	1.2	1.2	1.0				1.2	1.2
	1.6	2.2	1.2				1.6	1.5
	1.2	.8	.9			Quick	.8	.9
	.9	.6	.5				.6	.6
24	15.3	31 11.7	35 10.4				39 9.4	36 10.1
46	8.0	45 8.2	55 6.7			Sales/Receivables	55 6.7	51 7.2
60	6.1	67 5.5	70 5.2				68 5.4	60 6.1
12	29.5	48 7.6	41 9.0				35 10.5	36 10.0
31	11.6	70 5.3	59 6.2			Cost of Sales/Inventory	77 4.8	68 5.4
87	4.2	109 3.3	103 3.5				121 3.0	107 3.4
19	19.3	14 26.0	15 24.9				24 15.4	11 31.9
38	9.6	23 15.9	28 13.3			Cost of Sales/Payables	32 11.2	19 19.2
58	6.3	48 7.6	55 6.7				54 6.8	32 11.4
	5.8	4.6	4.7				4.4	5.1
	9.1	8.1	8.1			Sales/Working Capital	6.8	7.8
	28.2	23.6	NM				18.3	16.7
	19.6	6.8	21.1				7.8	6.3
	(12) 7.6	(34) 2.3	(19) 3.7			EBIT/Interest	(44) 3.4	(44) 2.7
	.5	.2	1.1				1.9	.2
		2.7				Net Profit + Depr., Dep.,	4.5	3.6
	(14)	1.8				Amort./Cur. Mat. L /T/D	(14) 2.9	(11) 1.4
		.6					1.4	.4
	.1	.3	.2				.3	.3
	.5	.6	.7			Fixed/Worth	.5	.6
	1.0	1.0	1.3				1.3	1.3
	.7	.6	.7				.7	.6
	2.0	1.7	1.5			Debt/Worth	1.5	1.3
	7.1	3.3	5.9				4.4	2.7
	47.5	32.3	57.3			% Profit Before Taxes/Tangible	52.0	24.0
	(12) 9.3	(35) 7.9	(20) 27.9			Net Worth	(42) 16.6	(42) 8.4
	.6	.4	10.1				7.0	-8.8
	18.1	12.2	22.9			% Profit Before Taxes/Total	12.9	11.0
	4.0	3.2	7.7			Assets	7.8	4.1
	-.1	.0	.9				2.9	-3.0
	164.1	20.7	32.6				23.7	16.0
	52.6	14.5	7.8			Sales/Net Fixed Assets	14.7	9.0
	24.8	6.3	5.4				5.3	5.3
	4.3	2.8	2.5				2.5	2.5
	2.9	2.3	1.9			Sales/Total Assets	2.1	2.0
	2.6	1.7	1.4				1.6	1.6
	.7	1.1	1.4				1.0	1.3
	(10) .9	(36) 1.5	(20) 2.6			% Depr., Dep., Amort./Sales	(41) 1.6	(43) 1.9
	1.5	2.4	3.8				2.9	3.0
		1.7				% Officers', Directors',	2.1	1.6
	(16)	4.6				Owners' Comp/Sales	(10) 4.1	(10) 3.0
		10.9					8.1	5.9
3301M	53295M	436717M	1035406M	176719M	740644M	Net Sales ($)	1616389M	1098731M
793M	16998M	194355M	530281M	122803M	517238M	Total Assets ($)	962620M	650205M

M = $ thousand MM = $ million
See Pages 11 through 21 for Explanation of Ratios and Data

Comparative Historical Data   **Current Data Sorted By Sales**

	4/1/02-3/31/03 ALL	4/1/03-3/31/04 ALL	4/1/04-3/31/05 ALL	Type of Statement	0-1MM	1-3MM	3-5MM	5-10MM	10-25MM	25MM & OVER
	22	27	21	Unqualified				3	7	10
	19	33	26	Reviewed		3	4	4	9	6
	10	18	8	Compiled			1	5		2
	2	4	7	Tax Returns	1	1	1	3	1	
	18	21	18	Other	1	3	2	3	4	6
					19 (4/1-9/30/04)			61 (10/1/04-3/31/05)		
	71	103	80	**NUMBER OF STATEMENTS**	1	7	9	18	21	24
	%	%	%	**ASSETS**	%	%	%	%	%	%
	8.5	7.4	10.2	Cash & Equivalents				10.7	9.7	8.9
	26.0	27.8	29.3	Trade Receivables (net)				23.1	29.6	29.6
	30.2	29.2	28.3	Inventory				32.3	28.2	24.4
	2.7	4.0	3.6	All Other Current				2.1	3.1	6.7
	67.4	68.4	71.4	Total Current				68.1	70.6	69.6
	20.4	19.2	19.1	Fixed Assets (net)				25.7	21.8	20.3
	4.1	4.5	3.3	Intangibles (net)				1.9	2.4	4.7
	8.2	7.9	6.2	All Other Non-Current				4.3	5.1	5.4
	100.0	100.0	100.0	Total				100.0	100.0	100.0
				LIABILITIES						
	10.4	10.4	8.8	Notes Payable-Short Term				9.3	9.3	6.9
	3.2	4.2	4.2	Cur. Mat.-L/T/D				2.7	3.7	3.4
	13.0	14.7	15.3	Trade Payables				13.5	11.6	14.3
	.2	.2	.2	Income Taxes Payable				.1	.1	.4
	13.2	14.7	14.1	All Other Current				9.3	16.5	17.4
	40.0	44.2	42.6	Total Current				34.9	41.2	42.4
	13.1	12.0	12.4	Long-Term Debt				14.8	12.4	12.1
	.3	.4	.3	Deferred Taxes				.1	.3	.4
	6.4	7.3	5.8	All Other Non-Current				5.8	5.1	9.2
	40.2	36.0	39.0	Net Worth				44.4	41.0	35.9
	100.0	100.0	100.0	Total Liabilities & Net Worth				100.0	100.0	100.0
				INCOME DATA						
	100.0	100.0	100.0	Net Sales				100.0	100.0	100.0
	34.6	33.0	30.8	Gross Profit				29.6	30.8	28.2
	30.6	29.0	26.4	Operating Expenses				25.3	27.7	20.4
	4.1	4.0	4.4	Operating Profit				4.3	3.1	7.8
	1.1	.7	1.2	All Other Expenses (net)				2.3	1.1	1.3
	3.0	3.3	3.2	Profit Before Taxes				2.1	1.9	6.5
				RATIOS						
	2.7	2.7	2.9					4.2	3.9	2.4
	1.9	1.6	1.8	Current				2.1	2.0	1.8
	1.3	1.1	1.2					1.2	1.0	1.3
	1.4	1.4	1.5					2.2	2.3	1.2
	.8	.8	1.0	Quick				1.0	1.1	.9
	.6	.5	.6					.6	.6	.8
	37 10.0	35 10.4	32 11.4					24 15.2	29 12.5	35 10.5
	51 7.1	50 7.2	49 7.4	Sales/Receivables				43 8.5	52 7.0	50 7.3
	61 6.0	64 5.7	68 5.4					61 5.9	71 5.1	66 5.5
	47 7.8	47 7.8	34 10.7					33 11.1	49 7.5	26 13.9
	98 3.7	91 4.0	68 5.4	Cost of Sales/Inventory				77 4.7	65 5.6	64 5.7
	133 2.7	121 3.0	106 3.5					109 3.4	104 3.5	89 4.1
	19 19.7	21 17.6	14 25.2					15 25.1	11 33.1	15 24.8
	32 11.4	30 12.0	31 11.9	Cost of Sales/Payables				22 16.6	20 18.0	37 10.0
	57 6.4	51 7.1	50 7.3					44 8.3	40 9.0	50 7.3
	4.1	4.6	4.7					4.1	4.7	4.7
	6.7	7.3	8.2	Sales/Working Capital				8.0	6.7	7.0
	14.8	43.7	23.2					16.3	NM	20.7
	7.0	12.5	14.2					7.6	17.0	14.8
	(64) 2.8	(94) 4.9	(72) 3.6	EBIT/Interest			(14) 2.3	(20) 2.4	(22) 5.8	
	.6	1.2	1.0					-.9	.7	3.2
	5.3	4.5	4.6	Net Profit + Depr., Dep.,					4.3	27.2
	(15) 3.3	(25) 1.7	(28) 2.3	Amort./Cur. Mat. L/T/D				(10) 1.7	(10) 3.6	
	1.5	1.0	.7						.6	1.2
	.2	.2	.2					.4	.3	.3
	.6	.5	.6	Fixed/Worth				.7	.6	.5
	1.7	1.4	1.1					1.0	3.5	1.0
	.6	.7	.7					.7	.4	.7
	1.3	1.8	1.6	Debt/Worth				1.5	1.2	1.5
	4.2	5.1	5.1					3.0	8.7	6.0
	34.8	41.5	40.1	% Profit Before Taxes/Tangible				43.1	29.1	55.9
	(61) 9.3	(91) 14.7	(74) 13.5	Net Worth				10.1	(19) 10.5	(22) 29.2
	.7	2.1	1.9					-4.6	.4	17.9
	12.1	12.5	13.6	% Profit Before Taxes/Total				13.1	15.5	17.8
	4.1	6.9	5.4	Assets				4.7	2.0	8.9
	-.7	.9	.2					-2.1	-.1	5.7
	24.3	28.6	44.6					17.4	20.9	49.8
	9.1	11.4	13.8	Sales/Net Fixed Assets				8.6	13.8	8.8
	5.7	5.5	6.1					4.7	7.1	5.7
	2.3	2.7	2.9					3.0	2.8	2.7
	1.7	2.0	2.2	Sales/Total Assets				1.9	2.4	1.9
	1.4	1.4	1.6					1.5	1.4	1.7
	1.3	1.1	1.1					1.3	1.1	.9
	(62) 2.0	(86) 1.8	(70) 1.6	% Depr., Dep., Amort./Sales			(17) 2.1	(19) 1.3	(22) 2.1	
	3.3	2.7	2.9					3.5	2.6	4.0
	2.6	2.1	1.9	% Officers', Directors',						
	(20) 3.5	(33) 3.1	(27) 3.6	Owners' Comp/Sales						
	8.0	4.9	9.2							
	1653789M	2312796M	2446082M	Net Sales ($)	979M	15959M	36621M	129079M	327849M	1935595M
	992436M	1440613M	1382468M	Total Assets ($)	300M	6755M	19313M	67349M	185265M	1103486M

© RMA 2005

M = $ thousand   MM = $ million
See Pages 11 through 21 for Explanation of Ratios and Data

Current Data Sorted By Assets | Comparative Historical Data

0-500M	500M-2MM	2-10MM	10-50MM	50-100MM	100-250MM	Type of Statement	4/1/00-3/31/01 ALL	4/1/01-3/31/02 ALL
		11	12	6	5	Unqualified	20	14
1	10	16	2			Reviewed	14	11
1	4	1				Compiled	22	17
3	5					Tax Returns	4	3
1	9	15	9	1	1	Other	29	29
	21 (4/1-9/30/04)		92 (10/1/04-3/31/05)					
6	28	43	23	7	6	NUMBER OF STATEMENTS	89	74
%	%	%	%	%	%	ASSETS	%	%
	8.3	6.4	8.8			Cash & Equivalents	7.7	8.8
	42.7	35.2	30.4			Trade Receivables (net)	32.0	29.3
	18.8	25.9	28.3			Inventory	29.7	25.2
	3.5	2.9	5.4			All Other Current	3.0	3.8
	73.3	70.5	72.9			Total Current	72.4	67.1
	15.2	20.0	14.3			Fixed Assets (net)	20.1	20.9
	5.1	2.7	5.6			Intangibles (net)	2.4	4.4
	6.4	6.8	7.2			All Other Non-Current	5.2	7.6
	100.0	100.0	100.0			Total	100.0	100.0
						LIABILITIES		
	7.2	14.3	9.2			Notes Payable-Short Term	10.1	8.2
	2.6	2.7	1.9			Cur. Mat.-L/T/D	2.9	2.9
	17.4	19.0	16.3			Trade Payables	21.3	16.0
	.6	.3	.4			Income Taxes Payable	.3	.5
	19.1	13.3	15.5			All Other Current	12.4	13.6
	46.9	49.5	43.2			Total Current	47.0	41.3
	19.3	12.2	10.7			Long-Term Debt	11.1	11.2
	.3	.3	1.4			Deferred Taxes	.6	.6
	4.7	3.2	8.3			All Other Non-Current	3.0	5.1
	28.9	34.8	36.4			Net Worth	38.2	41.8
	100.0	100.0	100.0			Total Liabilities & Net Worth	100.0	100.0
						INCOME DATA		
	100.0	100.0	100.0			Net Sales	100.0	100.0
	33.0	29.3	22.5			Gross Profit	28.6	30.3
	29.2	24.5	16.4			Operating Expenses	23.5	26.5
	3.8	4.8	6.1			Operating Profit	5.1	3.8
	1.2	1.0	1.4			All Other Expenses (net)	.5	1.1
	2.6	3.8	4.7			Profit Before Taxes	4.6	2.7
						RATIOS		
	2.1	2.2	3.1			Current	2.3	3.2
	1.7	1.5	1.8				1.6	1.7
	1.2	1.2	1.2				1.2	1.1
	1.7	1.3	2.0			Quick	1.3	1.8
	1.1	.9	.8				.8	.9
	.7	.6	.5				.6	.5
	34 10.8	37 9.7	39 9.3			Sales/Receivables	31 11.8	36 10.2
	49 7.5	50 7.4	51 7.2				48 7.6	45 8.1
	57 6.4	65 5.6	62 5.9				59 6.2	61 6.0
	5 66.7	35 10.3	44 8.3			Cost of Sales/Inventory	36 10.1	34 10.8
	14 26.6	55 6.7	57 6.4				63 5.8	58 6.3
	58 6.3	73 5.0	106 3.4				97 3.8	100 3.7
	15 24.1	18 20.3	22 16.3			Cost of Sales/Payables	21 17.1	20 18.1
	24 15.5	32 11.6	34 10.6				35 10.3	26 14.0
	32 11.6	55 6.7	43 8.5				60 6.1	49 7.5
	8.6	6.6	3.5			Sales/Working Capital	5.3	4.2
	11.9	10.9	7.4				8.9	8.8
	26.4	22.9	19.9				22.2	35.2
	19.2	15.5	31.3			EBIT/Interest	13.6	10.1
	(27) 6.8	(37) 3.8	(18) 5.9				(78) 4.1	(65) 3.2
	1.5	1.8	3.7				1.6	.7
		3.0				Net Profit + Depr., Dep.,	11.0	4.8
		(10) 1.6				Amort./Cur. Mat. L/T/D	(18) 3.9	(24) 2.1
		.8					1.6	1.1
	.2	.2	.2			Fixed/Worth	.2	.2
	.6	.5	.5				.5	.6
	1.6	1.3	1.3				1.0	1.6
	1.1	1.0	.6			Debt/Worth	.9	.6
	2.3	2.0	2.9				1.7	1.5
	6.2	6.5	18.2				4.4	5.9
	57.6	61.8	47.1			% Profit Before Taxes/Tangible	55.4	41.1
	(23) 26.4	(38) 21.7	(20) 28.9			Net Worth	(80) 26.8	(65) 12.3
	4.5	8.5	15.3				4.8	.8
	22.6	19.9	11.7			% Profit Before Taxes/Total	17.4	16.0
	6.6	5.3	9.2			Assets	9.5	5.0
	1.0	1.2	3.8				1.7	-1.9
	68.2	35.7	35.1			Sales/Net Fixed Assets	31.1	29.9
	23.8	21.5	14.4				12.9	12.8
	10.8	6.9	9.1				7.2	5.0
	4.5	3.2	2.4			Sales/Total Assets	3.0	3.0
	3.5	2.5	2.0				2.1	2.1
	2.1	1.8	1.7				1.9	1.5
	1.0	.7	.8			% Depr., Dep., Amort./Sales	.7	.7
	(20) 1.8	(40) 1.3	(18) 1.1				(76) 1.3	(67) 1.4
	2.8	2.6	1.8				2.2	3.2
	2.0					% Officers', Directors',	1.9	1.8
	(14) 3.9					Owners' Comp/Sales	(25) 3.9	(22) 2.9
	7.8						7.0	5.5
4939M	132679M	528630M	1080122M	782037M	1214711M	Net Sales ($)	2070454M	1934756M
1418M	33532M	209751M	526009M	470052M	837960M	Total Assets ($)	1117756M	1163835M

M = $ thousand   MM = $ million
See Pages 11 through 21 for Explanation of Ratios and Data

Comparative Historical Data				Current Data Sorted By Sales					
			Type of Statement						
27	34	34	Unqualified			1	3	9	21
15	14	29	Reviewed	2	1	8	8	9	1
15	20	6	Compiled	1	1	2	1	1	
4	11	8	Tax Returns	4	1	1	2		
28	32	36	Other	2	3	4	5	11	11
4/1/02-	4/1/03-	4/1/04-			21 (4/1-9/30/04)		92 (10/1/04-3/31/05)		
3/31/03	3/31/04	3/31/05		0-1MM	1-3MM	3-5MM	5-10MM	10-25MM	25MM & OVER
ALL	ALL	ALL							
89	111	113	**NUMBER OF STATEMENTS**	9	6	16	19	30	33
%	%	%	**ASSETS**	%	%	%	%	%	%
9.6	8.6	7.1	Cash & Equivalents			10.0	5.5	9.2	5.4
28.4	29.0	33.5	Trade Receivables (net)			38.9	47.8	31.7	29.2
26.7	26.7	24.8	Inventory			13.8	19.7	30.3	25.3
3.1	5.4	3.6	All Other Current			4.1	3.0	4.6	3.3
67.8	69.6	69.1	Total Current			66.8	76.1	75.8	63.1
20.7	19.8	18.2	Fixed Assets (net)			23.5	15.7	15.1	18.9
4.9	4.4	5.8	Intangibles (net)			.7	3.3	3.3	11.1
6.6	6.2	7.0	All Other Non-Current			8.9	5.0	5.7	6.9
100.0	100.0	100.0	Total			100.0	100.0	100.0	100.0
			LIABILITIES						
8.1	10.3	10.3	Notes Payable-Short Term			8.4	12.2	10.7	10.7
2.9	3.3	3.7	Cur. Mat.-L/T/D			2.4	2.7	2.3	4.9
15.8	17.9	17.3	Trade Payables			16.7	22.3	14.2	17.4
.7	.4	.4	Income Taxes Payable			1.3	.0	.4	.4
18.1	13.4	14.5	All Other Current			12.8	15.4	16.7	13.6
45.5	45.3	46.2	Total Current			41.6	52.6	44.3	46.9
13.1	12.2	15.0	Long-Term Debt			8.4	15.9	12.4	14.3
.5	.7	.7	Deferred Taxes			.6	.2	.3	1.7
7.7	7.5	5.4	All Other Non-Current			2.1	2.7	4.1	9.6
33.1	34.3	32.7	Net Worth			47.3	28.6	39.0	27.5
100.0	100.0	100.0	Total Liabilities & Net Worth			100.0	100.0	100.0	100.0
			INCOME DATA						
100.0	100.0	100.0	Net Sales			100.0	100.0	100.0	100.0
30.2	30.6	29.0	Gross Profit			36.2	28.8	28.2	23.2
25.8	25.4	24.1	Operating Expenses			30.6	25.1	21.3	18.0
4.4	5.2	4.9	Operating Profit			5.6	3.7	6.9	5.2
.9	.8	1.4	All Other Expenses (net)			.8	.5	.9	2.4
3.5	4.4	3.6	Profit Before Taxes			4.8	3.2	6.1	2.8
			RATIOS						
3.2	2.5	2.2				2.9	1.9	2.5	2.3
1.8	1.6	1.5	Current			1.6	1.4	1.7	1.5
1.2	1.2	1.2				1.1	1.2	1.2	1.1
1.8	1.5	1.4				1.9	1.5	1.4	1.1
1.0	.9	.9	Quick			1.2	1.1	.9	.8
.6	.5	.6				.8	.7	.5	.5
31 11.8	30 12.1	37 9.7		31 11.7	46 8.0	32 11.5	41 8.9		
44 8.4	43 8.4	49 7.5	Sales/Receivables	52 7.1	53 6.9	45 8.2	53 6.9		
59 6.2	55 6.7	58 6.3		58 6.3	65 5.6	58 6.3	66 5.5		
42 8.7	25 14.5	18 19.9		3 122.9	6 62.0	40 9.0	46 7.9		
59 6.2	55 6.7	55 6.7	Cost of Sales/Inventory	19 19.0	20 18.2	55 6.6	65 5.6		
92 3.9	99 3.7	90 4.1		61 6.0	66 5.5	74 4.9	91 4.0		
18 20.0	20 18.4	19 19.3		19 19.5	23 16.0	15 24.1	25 14.7		
29 12.5	32 11.5	31 11.9	Cost of Sales/Payables	28 12.9	29 12.5	26 13.8	34 10.8		
43 8.5	54 6.8	46 8.0		58 6.3	50 7.3	35 10.4	46 8.0		
4.4	4.4	5.6				5.6	9.7	4.3	5.0
8.1	9.3	10.3	Sales/Working Capital			9.3	17.0	9.9	9.0
20.6	26.5	25.1				31.3	20.6	22.2	25.6
12.4	13.3	16.9				24.7	13.5	18.2	22.2
(73) 4.0	(97) 5.4	(98) 4.5	EBIT/Interest	(14) 16.4	(18) 5.3	(26) 4.7	(28) 4.6		
1.5	1.8	1.7				3.3	2.5	1.9	1.4
13.7	17.8	6.9							25.9
(30) 3.5	(30) 5.4	(35) 2.3	Net Profit + Depr., Dep., Amort./Cur. Mat. L/T/D					(17)	4.3
2.1	2.5	.9							.7
.2	.3	.2				.1	.3	.2	.3
.5	.6	.6	Fixed/Worth			.6	.6	.4	.8
2.3	3.7	1.8				1.4	1.0	.9	-1.2
.7	.6	1.0				.4	1.3	.9	.9
1.8	2.0	2.1	Debt/Worth			1.3	3.1	1.9	3.4
5.7	9.8	8.9				2.9	6.3	6.5	-5.2
52.5	51.7	47.7	% Profit Before Taxes/Tangible Net Worth			42.1	64.6	60.2	45.3
(74) 20.8	(90) 18.7	(92) 18.9				22.5 (17)	28.1 (27)	36.2 (23)	17.8
3.4	6.6	8.3				5.0	11.1	8.7	14.4
17.3	14.8	13.1	% Profit Before Taxes/Total Assets			22.6	18.6	28.4	10.9
6.6	6.5	6.0				7.1	5.9	8.7	7.0
1.1	2.1	1.5				1.8	3.2	3.2	1.1
28.5	44.5	42.6	Sales/Net Fixed Assets			36.4	54.1	61.0	23.5
12.3	15.5	17.7				19.5	28.4	22.1	12.4
6.7	7.3	7.0				6.8	16.2	10.9	6.6
2.9	3.3	3.3	Sales/Total Assets			4.1	4.5	3.2	3.0
2.1	2.3	2.4				3.0	3.1	2.5	2.0
1.7	1.5	1.7				1.4	2.4	1.8	1.5
.8	.8	.9	% Depr., Dep., Amort./Sales			1.0	.5	.8	.8
(75) 1.5	(98) 1.6	(94) 1.5		(13)	(17) 2.0	(24) 1.3	(30) 1.3		1.4
2.4	2.8	2.9				3.0	2.3	2.5	3.2
2.2	2.4	1.6	% Officers', Directors', Owners' Comp/Sales						
(22) 3.5	(34) 3.6	(28) 3.3							*
7.3	7.7	6.9							
3537965M	3135489M	3743118M	Net Sales ($)	4939M	13037M	62954M	133965M	490841M	3037382M
1968623M	1549911M	2078722M	Total Assets ($)	4823M	7037M	29058M	47167M	216915M	1773722M

© RMA 2005

M = $ thousand   MM = $ million
See Pages 11 through 21 for Explanation of Ratios and Data

Current Data Sorted By Assets

Comparative Historical Data

							Type of Statement		
	1	5	3	1	1		Unqualified		
1	16	26	2				Reviewed		
2	17	13					Compiled		
5	10	2					Tax Returns		
1	9	11	2	1			Other		
	41 (4/1-9/30/04)		88 (10/1/04-3/31/05)					4/1/00-3/31/01 ALL	4/1/01-3/31/02 ALL
0-500M	500M-2MM	2-10MM	10-50MM	50-100MM	100-250MM				
9	53	57	7	2	1	NUMBER OF STATEMENTS			
%	%	%	%	%	%	ASSETS		%	%
	10.0	5.7				Cash & Equivalents		D	D
	28.9	26.8				Trade Receivables (net)		A	A
	14.8	19.0				Inventory		T	T
	1.3	2.3				All Other Current		A	A
	54.9	53.8				Total Current			
	37.0	38.0				Fixed Assets (net)		N	N
	2.3	1.1				Intangibles (net)		O	O
	5.7	7.2				All Other Non-Current		T	T
	100.0	100.0				Total			
						LIABILITIES		A	A
	13.3	10.1				Notes Payable-Short Term		V	V
	7.6	7.0				Cur. Mat.-L/T/D		A	A
	11.9	11.2				Trade Payables		I	I
	.2	.2				Income Taxes Payable		L	L
	6.0	8.7				All Other Current		A	A
	38.9	37.1				Total Current		B	B
	25.6	19.0				Long-Term Debt		L	L
	.7	1.1				Deferred Taxes		E	E
	6.6	4.6				All Other Non-Current			
	28.1	38.1				Net Worth			
	100.0	100.0				Total Liabilities & Net Worth			
						INCOME DATA			
	100.0	100.0				Net Sales			
	32.7	25.2				Gross Profit			
	30.1	21.5				Operating Expenses			
	2.5	3.6				Operating Profit			
	1.1	1.0				All Other Expenses (net)			
	1.4	2.6				Profit Before Taxes			
						RATIOS			
	2.9	2.2							
	1.3	1.5				Current			
	1.0	1.1							
	1.9	1.3							
	.9	.9				Quick			
	.6	.6							
35	10.3	45	8.1			Sales/Receivables			
48	7.7	54	6.8						
67	5.5	74	4.9						
17	21.2	24	15.2			Cost of Sales/Inventory			
33	11.2	46	7.9						
55	6.7	68	5.3						
11	31.9	16	22.6			Cost of Sales/Payables			
28	13.1	27	13.7						
44	8.3	42	8.7						
	5.8	6.1				Sales/Working Capital			
	15.1	12.1							
	NM	29.2							
	6.2	5.2				EBIT/Interest			
(51)	2.6	(55)	2.5						
	−.1	1.1							
	3.1	6.5				Net Profit + Depr., Dep., Amort./Cur. Mat. L /T/D			
(14)	1.8	(25)	2.2						
	1.4	1.7							
	.6	.6				Fixed/Worth			
	1.6	1.0							
	109.5	2.2							
	.7	.8				Debt/Worth			
	2.7	1.6							
	266.3	3.6							
	46.0	26.4				% Profit Before Taxes/Tangible Net Worth			
(41)	18.8	(53)	12.2						
	6.2	2.0							
	13.6	10.3				% Profit Before Taxes/Total Assets			
	4.5	3.4							
	−3.8	.2							
	10.7	7.5				Sales/Net Fixed Assets			
	4.9	5.0							
	3.8	2.9							
	2.4	2.2				Sales/Total Assets			
	2.0	1.7							
	1.6	1.3							
	3.3	3.2				% Depr., Dep., Amort./Sales			
(50)	4.6	(56)	4.4						
	7.5	6.1							
	3.4	1.3				% Officers', Directors', Owners' Comp/Sales			
(36)	6.2	(32)	3.7						
	8.9	6.3							
9508M	128295M	404527M	213262M	173064M	216000M	Net Sales ($)			
2802M	65449M	242428M	154805M	139592M	208000M	Total Assets ($)			

M = $ thousand   MM = $ million
See Pages 11 through 21 for Explanation of Ratios and Data

Comparative Historical Data | | | Current Data Sorted By Sales

	4/1/02-3/31/03 ALL	4/1/03-3/31/04 ALL	4/1/04-3/31/05 ALL	Type of Statement	0-1MM	1-3MM	3-5MM	5-10MM	10-25MM	25MM & OVER
	3	4	11	Unqualified		1	1	1	3	5
	15	10	45	Reviewed	1	12	12	10	9	1
	12	15	32	Compiled	1	14	8	8	1	
	3	11	17	Tax Returns	5	8	2	2		
	11	12	24	Other	1	11	2	5	3	2
					41 (4/1-9/30/04)		**88 (10/1/04-3/31/05)**			
	44	52	129	**NUMBER OF STATEMENTS**	8	46	25	26	16	8
	%	%	%	**ASSETS**	%	%	%	%	%	%
	5.3	6.9	7.9	Cash & Equivalents		8.7	10.0	6.5	3.8	
	24.9	24.7	27.4	Trade Receivables (net)		28.2	27.5	28.1	27.6	
	11.6	11.1	16.0	Inventory		16.9	15.9	19.0	16.7	
	3.8	2.0	2.2	All Other Current		.9	1.7	2.5	2.2	
	45.7	44.8	53.6	Total Current		54.6	55.1	56.2	50.3	
	47.2	45.9	38.0	Fixed Assets (net)		36.9	37.8	37.0	39.8	
	1.1	2.0	2.3	Intangibles (net)		2.2	1.0	1.1	1.5	
	6.0	7.3	6.1	All Other Non-Current		6.3	6.1	5.8	8.4	
	100.0	100.0	100.0	Total		100.0	100.0	100.0	100.0	
				LIABILITIES						
	9.9	10.9	12.0	Notes Payable-Short Term		15.0	7.1	8.7	11.4	
	9.3	9.3	7.1	Cur. Mat.-L/T/D		8.5	7.9	3.9	4.7	
	7.1	9.1	11.6	Trade Payables		12.1	10.3	13.4	9.6	
	.1	.1	.2	Income Taxes Payable		.3	.0	.4	.0	
	7.8	6.7	7.6	All Other Current		5.5	7.9	7.9	11.0	
	34.3	36.1	38.4	Total Current		41.3	33.2	34.3	36.7	
	20.7	26.3	21.3	Long-Term Debt		24.8	22.8	14.0	23.5	
	.7	1.5	.9	Deferred Taxes		.5	1.3	1.5	.7	
	6.5	9.6	7.7	All Other Non-Current		12.6	6.4	4.5	1.5	
	37.9	26.5	31.7	Net Worth		20.7	36.4	45.6	37.6	
	100.0	100.0	100.0	Total Liabilities & Net Worth		100.0	100.0	100.0	100.0	
				INCOME DATA						
	100.0	100.0	100.0	Net Sales		100.0	100.0	100.0	100.0	
	26.9	34.1	28.9	Gross Profit		33.5	27.3	23.7	24.6	
	26.9	32.5	26.0	Operating Expenses		31.3	22.9	20.2	20.2	
	.0	1.6	2.8	Operating Profit		2.3	4.4	3.5	4.4	
	1.9	2.3	1.1	All Other Expenses (net)		1.2	1.2	.9	1.0	
	-1.9	-.7	1.8	Profit Before Taxes		1.1	3.2	2.6	3.5	
				RATIOS						
	1.8	2.1	2.3			2.7	2.9	2.5	2.0	
	1.3	1.3	1.4	Current		1.3	1.6	1.6	1.5	
	1.0	.8	1.1			1.0	1.1	1.2	1.0	
	1.4	1.3	1.5			1.9	1.9	1.6	1.3	
	.9	.9	.9	Quick		.8	1.1	.9	1.0	
	.6	.5	.6			.5	.7	.7	.6	
34 10.8	37 9.8	37 9.8		Sales/Receivables	37 9.9	34 10.6	38 9.6	47 7.8		
53 6.8	48 7.7	49 7.4			49 7.5	52 7.0	50 7.4	52 7.0		
71 5.2	58 6.3	70 5.2			70 5.2	71 5.1	70 5.2	72 5.1		
14 25.8	12 29.3	17 21.2		Cost of Sales/Inventory	20 18.1	15 24.3	19 19.5	25 14.6		
30 12.1	26 13.9	39 9.3			34 10.8	46 7.9	43 8.5	40 9.1		
56 6.5	41 8.8	60 6.1			69 5.3	63 5.8	53 6.9	71 5.2		
9 40.7	15 25.1	14 25.3		Cost of Sales/Payables	13 27.4	12 30.0	15 24.1	16 22.3		
20 18.1	25 14.3	26 13.8			30 12.3	24 15.3	26 13.9	25 14.4		
28 13.1	36 10.1	40 9.1			48 7.5	37 9.8	50 7.2	33 11.0		
	6.5	9.9	6.1	Sales/Working Capital		6.1	5.5	5.0	6.1	
	18.2	20.9	12.4			14.6	10.7	9.4	14.2	
	471.3	-28.5	76.4			-96.6	44.7	22.4	117.6	
	3.1	2.9	5.7			4.9	5.1	12.6	5.7	
(43) 1.1	(50) 1.5	(124) 2.6		EBIT/Interest	(45) 2.6	(24) 2.7	(25) 3.0	(15) 2.5		
	-.5	-.3	.7			-.3	1.6	.2	1.1	
	1.9	1.7	3.7	Net Profit + Depr., Dep.,		3.4		9.9		
(16) 1.4	(13) 1.2	(43) 2.1		Amort./Cur. Mat. L/T/D	(13) 1.6	(11) 2.2			
	.8	.7	1.4			1.4		1.1		
	.9	.9	.6			.7	.4	.5	.8	
	1.4	1.8	1.1	Fixed/Worth		1.7	1.3	.9	1.0	
	1.9	5.7	3.9			NM	3.1	1.3	2.2	
	.8	.9	.8			.9	.8	.6	1.3	
	1.8	2.8	1.8	Debt/Worth		3.0	2.6	1.2	1.7	
	3.0	11.4	7.3			NM	6.2	2.4	3.4	
	9.7	29.1	33.8	% Profit Before Taxes/Tangible		55.3	31.2	27.1	30.7	
(41) 3.7	(45) 11.9	(109) 14.3		Net Worth	(35) 20.6	(23) 16.4	(24) 10.8	13.3		
	-19.7	-8.3	3.8			5.7	4.2	3.4	.3	
	4.9	8.3	11.4	% Profit Before Taxes/Total		13.2	10.3	11.6	7.4	
	1.2	1.6	4.3	Assets		3.7	4.6	4.2	4.8	
	-4.6	-4.4	-1.2			-4.3	2.2	.4	.2	
	5.2	8.4	9.0			11.5	8.9	7.9	6.7	
	3.5	3.8	5.0	Sales/Net Fixed Assets		4.8	5.0	5.4	4.6	
	2.6	2.8	3.5			3.7	3.7	3.5	2.8	
	2.0	2.2	2.3			2.4	2.2	2.7	2.2	
	1.6	1.8	1.8	Sales/Total Assets		1.7	2.1	1.9	1.6	
	1.2	1.5	1.4			1.4	1.5	1.5	1.2	
	4.4	3.9	3.2			3.4	3.9	2.6	3.1	
(42) 6.7	(48) 5.5	(122) 4.5		% Depr., Dep., Amort./Sales	(41) 4.5	4.6	(25) 3.3	4.8		
	8.7	7.5	6.5			7.8	5.9	4.8	6.4	
	2.5	3.1	2.4	% Officers', Directors',		2.8	3.5	.8		
(25) 4.3	(35) 5.2	(76) 5.0		Owners' Comp/Sales	(29) 7.0	(18) 5.4	(15) 2.3			
	7.9	6.9	8.8			8.8	7.9			
	392543M	237918M	1144656M	Net Sales ($)	6719M	96953M	94773M	173127M	190816M	582268M
	256695M	148315M	813076M	Total Assets ($)	2815M	56346M	52694M	105615M	119807M	475799M

M = $ thousand   MM = $ million
See Pages 11 through 21 for Explanation of Ratios and Data

Current Data Sorted By Assets   Comparative Historical Data

0-500M	500M-2MM	2-10MM	10-50MM	50-100MM	100-250MM	Type of Statement	4/1/00-3/31/01 ALL	4/1/01-3/31/02 ALL
		7	17	6	2	Unqualified	33	27
	11	42	8			Reviewed	50	47
9	31	21	1		1	Compiled	56	53
8	5	4				Tax Returns	10	14
6	16	20	12	3	1	Other	57	63
	50 (4/1-9/30/04)		181 (10/1/04-3/31/05)					
23	63	94	38	9	4	**NUMBER OF STATEMENTS**	206	204
%	%	%	%	%	%	**ASSETS**	%	%
9.1	9.4	7.5	7.8			Cash & Equivalents	8.3	8.3
40.6	28.1	23.9	21.5			Trade Receivables (net)	27.3	26.4
15.2	18.2	24.1	27.1			Inventory	20.1	20.5
.8	1.4	2.2	5.8			All Other Current	2.2	3.0
65.6	57.1	57.6	62.2			Total Current	57.9	58.2
30.0	35.7	34.4	25.6			Fixed Assets (net)	33.8	34.2
.3	1.6	2.8	4.3			Intangibles (net)	2.5	2.0
4.0	5.5	5.1	7.8			All Other Non-Current	5.7	5.7
100.0	100.0	100.0	100.0			Total	100.0	100.0
						LIABILITIES		
21.2	13.0	9.3	7.7			Notes Payable-Short Term	9.9	11.7
10.5	6.0	4.9	6.1			Cur. Mat.-L/T/D	5.3	5.2
19.2	15.3	10.8	10.3			Trade Payables	11.6	13.2
.2	.1	.1	.2			Income Taxes Payable	.4	.1
4.6	9.6	10.5	13.6			All Other Current	10.2	8.6
55.8	44.0	35.5	37.9			Total Current	37.4	38.8
20.4	24.8	20.6	15.2			Long-Term Debt	18.3	21.5
.1	.7	.8	.4			Deferred Taxes	.6	.5
7.3	4.5	2.1	6.7			All Other Non-Current	4.0	5.2
16.4	26.1	40.9	39.8			Net Worth	39.6	34.1
100.0	100.0	100.0	100.0			Total Liabilities & Net Worth	100.0	100.0
						INCOME DATA		
100.0	100.0	100.0	100.0			Net Sales	100.0	100.0
46.4	34.8	31.2	26.1			Gross Profit	32.8	33.0
42.5	31.9	26.7	22.1			Operating Expenses	27.9	30.8
3.8	2.9	4.5	4.0			Operating Profit	4.9	2.3
.9	.9	.9	.7			All Other Expenses (net)	1.4	1.4
3.0	2.0	3.6	3.3			Profit Before Taxes	3.5	.8
						RATIOS		
2.0	2.1	2.7	2.7			Current	2.5	2.5
1.4	1.5	1.5	1.9				1.7	1.6
.7	1.0	1.2	1.2				1.1	1.0
1.8	1.5	1.6	1.5			Quick	1.7	1.6
1.1	.9	.9	.8				1.0 (203)	.9
.4	.6	.5	.4				.6	.6
32 11.5	33 11.0	39 9.4	48 7.6			Sales/Receivables	40 9.1	32 11.5
42 8.7	46 7.9	49 7.4	60 6.1				55 6.7	49 7.4
71 5.1	60 6.1	67 5.5	78 4.7				68 5.3	65 5.6
0 UND	12 29.2	33 11.2	40 9.0			Cost of Sales/Inventory	19 19.3	17 22.0
13 29.2	30 12.4	70 5.2	99 3.7				57 6.4	49 7.4
53 6.8	63 5.8	106 3.4	189 1.9				104 3.5	104 3.5
10 37.6	17 22.0	15 25.1	18 20.5			Cost of Sales/Payables	15 23.6	14 25.8
28 12.9	34 10.8	31 11.7	37 9.8				27 13.5	26 14.2
68 5.4	50 7.4	47 7.8	46 8.0				45 8.1	46 8.0
9.2	6.5	4.6	3.0			Sales/Working Capital	4.8	4.9
24.1	13.4	9.7	4.3				8.9	10.2
-10.8	172.1	27.4	10.2				37.7	207.5
10.7	8.5	6.6	9.7			EBIT/Interest	5.3	4.3
(21) 2.0	(61) 3.7	(87) 2.8	3.7				(193) 2.4	(185) 1.5
-2.1	1.1	1.5	-.7				1.1	-.9
	4.8	2.7	2.8			Net Profit + Depr., Dep.,	4.3	2.9
(15) 2.2	(28) 1.7	(16) 1.6				Amort./Cur. Mat. L /T/D	(72) 2.1	(56) 1.5
	2.0	.9	.3				1.0	.4
.4	.6	.4	.3			Fixed/Worth	.4	.4
1.2	1.2	1.0	.7				.9	1.1
-2.2	3.3	2.2	2.0				1.6	3.0
1.1	1.0	.8	.5			Debt/Worth	.8	.8
2.2	2.0	1.7	1.5				1.5	2.0
-6.0	8.0	3.5	3.7				3.7	5.3
77.4	48.6	26.9	37.0			% Profit Before Taxes/Tangible	33.1	31.5
(15) 42.9	(53) 14.1	(89) 12.2	(35) 12.0			Net Worth	(189) 13.9	(179) 9.5
-11.1	4.0	2.0	2.9				2.4	-12.0
24.1	12.8	8.8	10.4			% Profit Before Taxes/Total	11.8	10.3
3.8	5.6	4.1	3.5			Assets	4.6	2.2
-7.3	.3	.9	-2.6				.5	-6.3
47.0	12.0	9.8	8.4			Sales/Net Fixed Assets	10.3	12.7
14.1	6.5	5.0	6.2				5.6	5.5
5.8	3.3	2.9	3.2				3.3	3.3
4.1	2.8	2.0	1.6			Sales/Total Assets	2.2	2.3
3.1	2.1	1.6	1.1				1.7	1.9
2.5	1.6	1.2	.8				1.3	1.3
1.3	2.0	2.5	1.7			% Depr., Dep., Amort./Sales	1.7	1.9
(17) 3.4	(58) 4.3	(86) 4.3	(34) 3.1				(189) 3.6	(191) 3.6
7.3	6.6	6.8	6.1				6.4	6.0
6.4	3.8	2.0				% Officers', Directors',	3.0	3.0
(11) 11.8	(36) 7.1	(49) 3.9				Owners' Comp/Sales	(89) 5.1	(98) 5.6
17.4	14.2	5.5					9.6	10.2
20202M	164079M	759583M	1030848M	706397M	1004540M	Net Sales ($)	3625472M	2818985M
6495M	75378M	426773M	861783M	575956M	535638M	Total Assets ($)	2574749M	1995136M

M = $ thousand   MM = $ million
See Pages 11 through 21 for Explanation of Ratios and Data

Comparative Historical Data | **Current Data Sorted By Sales**

	4/1/02-3/31/03 ALL	4/1/03-3/31/04 ALL	4/1/04-3/31/05 ALL	Type of Statement	0-1MM	1-3MM	3-5MM	5-10MM	10-25MM	25MM & OVER
	21	29	32	Unqualified			2	1	12	17
	63	61	61	Reviewed		7	15	22	15	2
	47	57	63	Compiled	5	27	14	13	3	1
	16	15	17	Tax Returns	7	7	1	2		
	44	46	58	Other	5	16	6	11	4	16
					50 (4/1-9/30/04)		181 (10/1/04-3/31/05)			
	191	208	231	NUMBER OF STATEMENTS	17	57	38	49	34	36
	%	%	%	ASSETS	%	%	%	%	%	%
	7.1	7.2	8.6	Cash & Equivalents	8.8	6.7	10.5	7.9	8.7	10.3
	24.2	24.7	26.4	Trade Receivables (net)	36.3	29.8	22.8	25.3	25.3	22.7
	20.7	22.7	21.7	Inventory	16.7	18.0	21.4	22.7	24.1	26.9
	3.0	3.0	2.7	All Other Current	.5	1.7	.8	2.3	4.2	6.8
	55.0	57.5	59.4	Total Current	62.3	56.1	55.6	58.1	62.3	66.6
	37.0	34.1	32.0	Fixed Assets (net)	35.0	36.2	38.1	32.7	28.4	19.7
	1.5	1.8	2.7	Intangibles (net)	.3	2.3	1.3	3.6	3.9	3.8
	6.5	6.5	5.8	All Other Non-Current	2.4	5.3	5.0	5.6	5.5	9.8
	100.0	100.0	100.0	Total	100.0	100.0	100.0	100.0	100.0	100.0
				LIABILITIES						
	11.9	13.7	11.0	Notes Payable-Short Term	27.1	13.3	8.2	8.2	8.1	9.3
	6.2	6.1	5.9	Cur. Mat.-L/T/D	12.1	5.7	7.0	4.3	5.9	4.0
	11.9	11.5	12.6	Trade Payables	17.0	14.3	13.1	9.5	15.3	9.0
	.2	.2	.2	Income Taxes Payable	.3	.1	.1	.2	.2	.4
	9.6	12.6	10.3	All Other Current	5.6	11.1	6.6	9.4	9.6	16.9
	39.8	44.1	39.9	Total Current	62.0	44.5	34.9	31.7	39.0	39.5
	21.1	17.0	20.1	Long-Term Debt	40.8	21.3	20.6	21.5	15.2	10.4
	.4	.5	.6	Deferred Taxes	.0	.4	1.4	.7	.6	.4
	4.1	6.8	4.5	All Other Non-Current	10.4	3.1	4.3	2.2	3.6	7.8
	34.6	31.7	34.9	Net Worth	-13.2	30.6	38.7	43.9	41.5	41.9
	100.0	100.0	100.0	Total Liabilities & Net Worth	100.0	100.0	100.0	100.0	100.0	100.0
				INCOME DATA						
	100.0	100.0	100.0	Net Sales	100.0	100.0	100.0	100.0	100.0	100.0
	31.9	32.8	32.7	Gross Profit	45.5	37.3	34.6	29.4	29.0	25.6
	31.4	31.1	28.7	Operating Expenses	46.6	32.7	31.1	24.6	23.8	21.8
	.6	1.7	4.0	Operating Profit	-1.1	4.7	3.5	4.8	5.2	3.8
	1.6	1.4	.8	All Other Expenses (net)	1.7	.8	.3	1.1	.6	.7
	-1.1	.3	3.2	Profit Before Taxes	-2.8	3.8	3.2	3.7	4.5	3.1
				RATIOS						
	2.3 / 1.4 / 1.0	2.3 / 1.4 / 1.0	2.7 / 1.5 / 1.1	Current	2.4 / .8 / .6	2.0 / 1.3 / 1.0	2.1 / 1.5 / 1.1	3.0 / 1.8 / 1.2	2.7 / 1.6 / 1.2	2.9 / 1.8 / 1.3
	1.2 / .8 / .5	1.3 / .8 / .5	1.6 / .9 / .5	Quick	1.8 / .6 / .4	1.4 / 1.0 / .6	1.7 / .9 / .6	1.8 / 1.1 / .6	1.6 / 1.0 / .5	1.7 / .9 / .6
	36 10.0 / 49 7.4 / 66 5.6	38 9.6 / 51 7.2 / 67 5.5	39 9.4 / 51 7.2 / 69 5.3	Sales/Receivables	24 15.5 / 46 7.9 / 71 5.2	40 9.1 / 54 6.8 / 72 5.1	32 11.3 / 44 8.3 / 55 6.7	40 9.2 / 47 7.7 / 67 5.4	45 8.1 / 61 6.0 / 76 4.8	41 8.9 / 58 6.3 / 76 4.8
	23 15.8 / 48 7.5 / 107 3.4	23 15.5 / 60 6.1 / 115 3.2	19 19.0 / 54 6.7 / 104 3.5	Cost of Sales/Inventory	0 UND / 13 29.2 / 106 3.5	5 77.5 / 29 12.7 / 82 4.4	26 14.3 / 56 6.5 / 98 3.7	34 10.8 / 61 6.0 / 98 3.7	26 14.2 / 70 5.2 / 148 2.5	45 8.1 / 84 4.4 / 157 2.3
	17 21.6 / 31 12.0 / 51 7.2	16 23.3 / 28 13.1 / 48 7.6	16 23.0 / 32 11.4 / 48 7.6	Cost of Sales/Payables	15 23.7 / 30 12.2 / 68 5.4	16 23.0 / 34 10.8 / 60 6.1	16 22.8 / 39 9.4 / 51 7.1	14 26.8 / 24 15.3 / 40 9.2	26 14.0 / 40 9.1 / 57 6.4	16 23.1 / 26 14.1 / 40 9.2
	5.3 / 12.1 / -147.3	4.8 / 11.6 / UND	4.5 / 9.3 / 34.1	Sales/Working Capital	7.6 / -13.9 / -8.3	6.4 / 15.4 / NM	6.0 / 10.5 / 35.5	4.3 / 7.2 / 13.9	3.0 / 8.9 / 28.5	3.5 / 5.4 / 10.4
	3.1 / (170) 1.3 / -1.5	5.2 / (192) 1.8 / -1.0	9.1 / (219) 3.3 / 1.0	EBIT/Interest	9.3 / (14) .1 / -6.0	7.8 / 3.4 / 1.0	8.0 / (36) 4.0 / 1.4	6.3 / (45) 2.5 / 1.6	12.2 / (33) 4.6 / 1.6	13.9 / (34) 3.0 / .0
	2.7 / (54) 1.4 / .3	2.0 / (59) 1.1 / -.1	2.9 / (65) 1.8 / .7	Net Profit + Depr., Dep., Amort./Cur. Mat. L/T/D		4.8 / (11) 2.2 / 1.9	2.8 / (10) 1.8 / .6	3.0 / (17) 2.1 / 1.2	2.8 / (11) 1.5 / .9	2.7 / (15) 1.2 / -.2
	.5 / 1.1 / 2.4	.5 / 1.0 / 2.6	.4 / .9 / 2.2	Fixed/Worth	.5 / -8.7 / -1.1	.6 / 1.2 / 3.8	.4 / 1.1 / 2.2	.3 / .8 / 2.3	.3 / .8 / 1.7	.2 / .5 / .8
	.7 / 2.1 / 5.2	.7 / 2.1 / 5.4	.8 / 1.7 / 4.8	Debt/Worth	1.6 / -18.4 / -4.6	1.2 / 2.0 / 9.1	.7 / 2.1 / 3.3	.5 / 1.3 / 4.1	.5 / 1.8 / 3.5	.6 / 1.3 / 2.9
	22.3 / (171) 2.5 / -16.1	24.0 / (178) 6.6 / -8.9	38.1 / (204) 13.6 / 2.4	% Profit Before Taxes/Tangible Net Worth		50.1 / (49) 17.1 / 2.2	36.6 / (36) 11.5 / 2.5	23.3 / (46) 10.6 / 1.4	39.4 / (33) 14.8 / 4.5	40.7 / (32) 15.5 / 1.3
	5.9 / .7 / -7.9	7.9 / 1.4 / -5.4	12.1 / 4.1 / .2	% Profit Before Taxes/Total Assets	19.5 / -4.5 / -25.9	14.3 / 5.6 / .0	11.0 / 4.5 / 1.1	6.9 / 3.3 / .8	10.4 / 4.5 / 2.2	13.6 / 4.1 / -2.5
	10.4 / 4.7 / 2.8	11.8 / 5.0 / 3.0	12.1 / 6.0 / 3.3	Sales/Net Fixed Assets	15.4 / 8.6 / 4.9	12.6 / 5.3 / 2.9	11.3 / 5.1 / 2.8	10.3 / 5.7 / 3.2	8.0 / 5.6 / 3.7	18.2 / 7.7 / 5.0
	2.1 / 1.6 / 1.2	2.2 / 1.6 / 1.2	2.4 / 1.7 / 1.2	Sales/Total Assets	3.4 / 2.7 / 1.9	2.5 / 1.7 / 1.4	2.8 / 1.8 / 1.4	2.0 / 1.6 / 1.3	2.3 / 1.6 / .9	1.8 / 1.4 / 1.1
	2.2 / (178) 4.1 / 7.4	2.0 / (191) 4.0 / 7.1	2.0 / (208) 3.5 / 6.6	% Depr., Dep., Amort./Sales	1.4 / (12) 3.7 / 9.3	1.7 / (53) 4.2 / 8.2	3.0 / (35) 5.3 / 7.2	1.8 / (44) 3.6 / 6.8	2.9 / (31) 3.8 / 5.6	.8 / (33) 2.2 / 3.1
	3.1 / (85) 6.1 / 10.6	3.4 / (95) 5.5 / 9.5	2.6 / (105) 4.7 / 8.0	% Officers', Directors', Owners' Comp/Sales		4.5 / (31) 7.2 / 15.3	3.2 / (21) 4.6 / 7.4	2.0 / (24) 3.2 / 5.3	1.0 / (15) 2.6 / 4.1	
	2306298M	2488811M	3685649M	Net Sales ($)	10435M	112107M	147865M	354976M	533807M	2526459M
	1637054M	1998244M	2482023M	Total Assets ($)	4450M	72072M	84821M	230827M	433153M	1656700M

M = $ thousand   MM = $ million
See Pages 11 through 21 for Explanation of Ratios and Data

Current Data Sorted By Assets   **Comparative Historical Data**

0-500M	500M-2MM	2-10MM	10-50MM	50-100MM	100-250MM	Type of Statement	4/1/00-3/31/01 ALL	4/1/01-3/31/02 ALL
		5	3	1	1	Unqualified	16	11
2	7	16	3			Reviewed	29	23
2	18	6	2			Compiled	21	28
6	3	1				Tax Returns	3	4
1	7	14	12	1	1	Other	23	29
	27 (4/1-9/30/04)		85 (10/1/04-3/31/05)					
11	35	42	20	2	2	**NUMBER OF STATEMENTS**	92	95
%	%	%	%	%	%	**ASSETS**	%	%
16.8	8.1	8.2	6.6			Cash & Equivalents	7.3	7.5
29.6	30.3	22.7	23.1			Trade Receivables (net)	30.8	22.8
11.4	19.7	23.3	21.0			Inventory	23.3	22.5
2.2	2.4	3.9	6.0			All Other Current	1.4	3.8
60.1	60.5	58.1	56.8			Total Current	62.8	56.5
36.5	30.4	32.1	24.8			Fixed Assets (net)	28.7	31.4
1.3	2.7	2.8	8.2			Intangibles (net)	3.2	5.5
1.3	6.4	6.9	10.2			All Other Non-Current	5.3	6.5
100.0	100.0	100.0	100.0			Total	100.0	100.0
						LIABILITIES		
28.2	7.7	9.2	16.3			Notes Payable-Short Term	8.6	10.4
15.5	6.5	5.5	3.6			Cur. Mat.-L/T/D	4.2	6.4
18.5	13.4	13.5	12.5			Trade Payables	13.2	9.5
.1	.1	.5	.0			Income Taxes Payable	.3	.3
4.5	12.1	11.9	11.0			All Other Current	12.0	12.1
66.7	39.9	40.5	43.4			Total Current	38.2	38.7
31.4	17.8	21.8	22.5			Long-Term Debt	16.5	21.1
.0	.8	.3	.7			Deferred Taxes	.9	.4
4.3	5.7	9.1	8.5			All Other Non-Current	5.7	5.4
-2.4	35.8	28.3	25.0			Net Worth	38.8	34.4
100.0	100.0	100.0	100.0			Total Liabilities & Net Worth	100.0	100.0
						INCOME DATA		
100.0	100.0	100.0	100.0			Net Sales	100.0	100.0
48.2	32.6	27.1	18.3			Gross Profit	28.0	29.8
42.7	27.6	22.0	17.3			Operating Expenses	22.9	28.4
5.6	5.0	5.1	1.0			Operating Profit	5.1	1.5
2.1	.5	1.3	.8			All Other Expenses (net)	1.7	2.1
3.4	4.5	3.8	.2			Profit Before Taxes	3.4	-.7
						RATIOS		
3.3	2.8	2.4	2.2				2.8	2.8
1.1	1.9	1.4	1.1			Current	1.7	1.6
.7	1.1	1.0	1.0				1.1	1.0
2.1	2.4	1.3	1.6				1.7	1.8
1.0	1.2	.6	.5			Quick	1.0	.8
.4	.6	.5	.4				.6	.5
12 29.5	32 11.5	30 12.2	49 7.4				44 8.4	37 9.9
37 9.8	54 6.8	43 8.6	65 5.6			Sales/Receivables	54 6.7	49 7.4
50 7.3	73 5.0	57 6.4	87 4.2				74 4.9	62 5.9
4 83.0	16 22.2	35 10.4	43 8.5				25 14.8	25 14.7
13 27.7	38 9.7	56 6.5	76 4.8			Cost of Sales/Inventory	61 5.9	64 5.7
36 10.2	69 5.3	95 3.9	108 3.4				103 3.5	108 3.4
16 22.8	13 28.9	19 19.1	27 13.3				13 28.2	10 36.6
31 11.9	21 17.0	39 9.3	48 7.6			Cost of Sales/Payables	27 13.5	21 17.3
46 8.0	52 7.0	49 7.4	62 5.9				49 7.4	42 8.6
12.3	5.1	5.7	4.3				3.9	4.0
24.9	9.5	11.6	17.4			Sales/Working Capital	7.1	9.2
-16.1	41.4	NM	NM				28.3	-92.6
9.6	5.7	12.8	3.3				6.4	5.6
(10) 1.9	(30) 4.0	(41) 4.1	(19) 1.3			EBIT/Interest	(81) 2.8	(84) 1.8
.8	1.6	1.5	-.7				1.2	-1.0
		2.9					7.2	3.1
	(12) 1.4					Net Profit + Depr., Dep., Amort./Cur. Mat. L /T/D	(36) 3.0	(30) 1.3
		.9					1.1	-.2
.4	.3	.5	.6				.3	.4
2.8	.7	1.5	1.7			Fixed/Worth	.8	.9
-3.0	5.3	5.2	7.7				1.7	5.6
1.3	.7	1.3	2.6				.8	1.0
12.2	1.5	3.1	4.7			Debt/Worth	1.7	2.1
-5.8	4.9	7.7	21.5				4.4	17.8
	45.5	56.4	17.1				36.0	28.4
	(29) 15.9	(36) 35.0	(16) 8.0			% Profit Before Taxes/Tangible Net Worth	(84) 15.0	(79) 6.9
	1.0	5.4	-20.1				2.6	-16.3
25.3	12.3	14.6	7.4				14.2	8.1
4.7	5.8	6.8	.9			% Profit Before Taxes/Total Assets	6.0	2.6
-.3	.1	1.3	-5.4				.9	-8.3
76.6	28.7	8.7	8.7				16.6	9.9
12.1	8.9	6.1	4.5			Sales/Net Fixed Assets	6.3	6.0
4.4	3.4	4.1	3.4				3.9	3.7
6.6	3.1	2.3	1.5				2.4	2.0
4.0	1.9	1.8	1.3			Sales/Total Assets	1.7	1.6
1.8	1.2	1.5	1.0				1.3	1.2
	1.5	1.9	2.0				1.3	1.9
	(29) 3.8	(40) 3.3	(17) 3.5			% Depr., Dep., Amort./Sales	(79) 2.8	(91) 3.6
	8.5	5.5	4.9				4.7	5.7
	2.9	2.1					3.2	3.0
	(24) 4.7	(14) 3.7				% Officers', Directors', Owners' Comp/Sales	(43) 5.1	(36) 5.7
	8.9	5.9					8.2	12.6
9361M	80904M	355028M	548986M	154870M	366505M	Net Sales ($)	1858510M	1153525M
2966M	38378M	194218M	430735M	128700M	373787M	Total Assets ($)	1232670M	908915M

M = $ thousand   MM = $ million
See Pages 11 through 21 for Explanation of Ratios and Data

Comparative Historical Data			Type of Statement	Current Data Sorted By Sales					
15	11	10	Unqualified				3	4	3
29	32	28	Reviewed	4	3	4	6	10	1
20	30	28	Compiled	5	12	7	2	2	
7	15	10	Tax Returns	5	4			1	
30	28	36	Other	1	6	3	11	7	8
4/1/02- 3/31/03 ALL	4/1/03- 3/31/04 ALL	4/1/04- 3/31/05 ALL		27 (4/1-9/30/04)			85 (10/1/04-3/31/05)		
				0-1MM	1-3MM	3-5MM	5-10MM	10-25MM	25MM & OVER
101	116	112	**NUMBER OF STATEMENTS**	15	25	14	22	24	12
%	%	%	**ASSETS**	%	%	%	%	%	%
7.6	9.1	8.5	Cash & Equivalents	18.2	8.0	9.2	5.9	7.8	2.4
23.6	24.7	25.7	Trade Receivables (net)	21.1	31.3	27.4	24.1	23.3	25.3
22.9	21.2	20.7	Inventory	16.5	18.9	18.3	22.4	22.4	26.1
3.1	4.5	3.7	All Other Current	2.3	2.8	.4	6.0	4.7	5.4
57.2	59.5	58.6	Total Current	58.1	61.0	55.3	58.4	58.2	59.3
31.2	29.9	30.9	Fixed Assets (net)	34.2	33.5	27.4	30.6	29.6	28.2
5.9	3.9	3.9	Intangibles (net)	1.7	.2	5.6	5.6	4.9	6.5
5.8	6.8	6.6	All Other Non-Current	5.4	5.2	11.7	5.4	7.3	6.0
100.0	100.0	100.0	Total	100.0	100.0	100.0	100.0	100.0	100.0
			LIABILITIES						
13.2	12.3	11.9	Notes Payable-Short Term	9.0	15.6	9.1	8.9	12.2	16.0
7.2	7.5	6.3	Cur. Mat.-L/T/D	10.1	9.0	6.2	4.7	4.1	3.8
9.9	11.7	13.7	Trade Payables	9.7	15.9	11.2	17.1	12.2	13.4
.1	.2	.2	Income Taxes Payable	.1	.0	.3	.3	.5	.0
12.3	13.1	10.9	All Other Current	7.2	13.0	12.9	10.1	9.0	13.9
42.7	44.8	43.0	Total Current	36.1	53.6	39.7	41.1	38.0	47.0
22.2	17.6	22.1	Long-Term Debt	28.6	19.5	17.5	24.7	21.3	21.7
.3	.4	.5	Deferred Taxes	.1	.7	1.0	.7	.2	.0
5.9	7.7	7.6	All Other Non-Current	5.3	4.4	7.5	13.9	6.8	7.1
28.9	29.5	26.8	Net Worth	29.9	21.8	34.3	19.6	33.7	24.1
100.0	100.0	100.0	Total Liabilities & Net Worth	100.0	100.0	100.0	100.0	100.0	100.0
			INCOME DATA						
100.0	100.0	100.0	Net Sales	100.0	100.0	100.0	100.0	100.0	100.0
30.0	29.6	29.4	Gross Profit	44.7	34.0	28.7	23.9	24.8	20.6
29.6	27.8	24.5	Operating Expenses	40.5	28.4	24.6	19.8	20.2	13.7
.3	1.7	4.8	Operating Profit	4.1	5.6	4.1	4.1	4.6	6.9
1.6	1.2	1.2	All Other Expenses (net)	1.1	.9	.6	1.6	.7	2.3
−1.3	.6	3.7	Profit Before Taxes	3.0	4.6	3.5	2.4	3.9	4.6
			RATIOS						
3.3	2.4	2.5		7.1	3.1	2.3	2.0	2.4	1.7
1.4	1.6	1.4	Current	1.5	1.7	1.4	1.3	1.7	1.1
1.0	.9	1.1		1.0	1.0	.8	1.1	1.1	1.0
1.7	1.6	1.6		3.4	2.0	1.8	1.3	1.6	.7
.8	.8	.8	Quick	1.0	1.0	.7	.6	.8	.5
.5	.5	.5		.4	.6	.4	.4	.6	.4
38	9.6	35	10.5	34	10.7	Sales/Receivables	13	27.8	31	11.6	34	10.8	30	12.2	43	8.6	50	7.3

Comparative Historical Data						Type of Statement	Current Data Sorted By Sales											
38	9.6	35	10.5	34	10.7	Sales/Receivables	13	27.8	31	11.6	34	10.8	30	12.2	43	8.6	50	7.3
53	6.9	50	7.2	49	7.4		39	9.5	44	8.3	49	7.5	41	8.9	54	6.8	67	5.4
64	5.7	72	5.0	70	5.2		73	5.0	70	5.2	61	6.0	56	6.6	72	5.0	94	3.9
33	11.1	25	14.8	24	15.5	Cost of Sales/Inventory	7	53.5	15	24.9	7	51.4	29	12.5	42	8.7	56	6.5
67	5.5	61	6.0	52	7.0		27	13.4	38	9.7	44	8.3	54	6.8	57	6.4	78	4.7
108	3.4	100	3.7	92	4.0		140	2.6	69	5.3	88	4.2	84	4.4	104	3.5	124	2.9
12	29.4	15	24.3	18	20.3	Cost of Sales/Payables	9	40.2	17	21.8	13	27.4	19	19.7	23	15.9	28	13.0
25	14.6	28	13.2	31	11.7		20	18.1	22	16.5	25	14.5	47	7.8	38	9.5	46	8.0
42	8.6	52	7.1	51	7.1		34	10.7	60	6.1	37	9.9	57	6.4	49	7.5	53	6.9
	4.1		3.8		5.5	Sales/Working Capital		6.3		5.0		8.2		6.0		4.1		6.2
	9.4		9.6		11.6			16.2		10.5		10.8		12.4		8.0		24.0
	NM		−59.5		75.4			82.0		NM		−53.3		62.0		41.0		NM
	5.6		5.7		7.6	EBIT/Interest		5.1		9.7		33.4		5.8		14.0		6.6
(92)	1.4	(102)	1.4	(103)	3.3		(12)	1.9	(23)	4.1	(13)	2.3		3.4	(22)	4.0	(11)	2.8
	−1.3		−.7		1.1			1.1		1.0		1.2		1.2		1.3		.2
	2.5		4.7		3.4	Net Profit + Depr., Dep., Amort./Cur. Mat. L/T/D												
(32)	1.4	(29)	1.6	(30)	1.8													
	−.2		.3		.8													
	.5		.4		.4	Fixed/Worth		.1		.4		.3		.6		.5		.5
	1.1		.8		1.4			.8		1.0		.7		2.0		1.5		1.4
	4.4		4.4		8.3			9.4		NM		7.0		−5.8		2.9		8.3
	.7		.7		1.0	Debt/Worth		.7		.5		.9		2.3		.9		1.8
	2.5		2.0		3.1			3.4		1.5		2.9		3.6		3.0		4.0
	9.7		14.6		16.4			17.6		NM		12.9		−15.5		10.3		21.5
	25.1		21.5		49.5	% Profit Before Taxes/Tangible Net Worth		74.6		48.4		56.7		48.9		56.9		21.7
(80)	5.3	(92)	3.3	(91)	18.8		(12)	24.8	(19)	15.9	(12)	13.3	(16)	24.1	(22)	32.6	(10)	13.6
	−14.6		−6.8		1.5			.1		.2		1.6		6.8		3.3		4.9
	9.1		9.3		13.0	% Profit Before Taxes/Total Assets		8.9		15.8		17.8		14.6		13.0		10.8
	.8		1.2		5.2			4.3		6.5		5.4		6.4		6.8		2.3
	−8.1		−5.2		.0			−.3		−.2		.4		.8		.1		−1.5
	11.1		14.6		12.9	Sales/Net Fixed Assets		54.7		17.9		18.7		9.6		7.8		15.4
	5.2		5.4		6.1			5.2		7.1		10.4		5.8		6.0		4.5
	3.2		3.5		3.5			3.4		3.3		3.4		3.3		4.1		3.5
	2.1		2.1		2.3	Sales/Total Assets		2.3		3.4		3.0		2.4		1.9		1.6
	1.5		1.5		1.7			1.6		1.9		2.0		1.9		1.5		1.3
	1.1		1.1		1.3			1.2		1.3		1.6		1.4		1.3		1.0
	2.3		1.6		1.8	% Depr., Dep., Amort./Sales		2.2		1.8		1.4		1.0		2.0		
(91)	4.4	(104)	4.1	(97)	3.4		(11)	3.7	(21)	5.1		2.8	(20)	3.5	(23)	3.1		
	6.7		6.8		5.7			18.6		8.5		5.6		5.7		4.4		
	3.2		3.2		2.8	% Officers', Directors', Owners' Comp/Sales		3.8		3.1								
(46)	5.6	(46)	5.9	(51)	4.4		(10)	9.6	(17)	4.4								
	9.1		9.2		9.6			13.9		7.2								
1122927M		1130426M		1515654M		Net Sales ($)	10161M		51345M		54007M		151479M		387755M		860907M
911569M		904310M		1168784M		Total Assets ($)	6857M		27263M		28776M		98954M		268550M		738384M

M = $ thousand   MM = $ million
See Pages 11 through 21 for Explanation of Ratios and Data

Current Data Sorted By Assets **Comparative Historical Data**

	0-500M	500M-2MM	2-10MM	10-50MM	50-100MM	100-250MM	Type of Statement	4/1/00-3/31/01 ALL	4/1/01-3/31/02 ALL
		1	19	26	4	1	Unqualified	36	36
	3	39	98	20			Reviewed	186	167
	22	62	41	4		1	Compiled	200	156
	12	19	10	1			Tax Returns	35	20
	13	32	54	25	3	3	Other	147	176
		122 (4/1-9/30/04)			391 (10/1/04-3/31/05)				
	50	153	222	76	7	5	NUMBER OF STATEMENTS	604	555
	%	%	%	%	%	%	ASSETS	%	%
	8.5	7.9	7.1	4.2			Cash & Equivalents	6.7	6.8
	30.9	35.2	30.7	27.6			Trade Receivables (net)	28.2	26.3
	10.8	14.7	16.8	17.3			Inventory	14.9	14.3
	2.8	1.4	4.0	4.2			All Other Current	2.8	3.3
	53.0	59.2	58.7	53.3			Total Current	52.6	50.7
	38.7	33.2	35.0	35.5			Fixed Assets (net)	39.9	41.1
	2.9	2.2	1.5	3.6			Intangibles (net)	2.7	2.5
	5.3	5.4	4.9	7.6			All Other Non-Current	4.9	5.7
	100.0	100.0	100.0	100.0			Total	100.0	100.0
							LIABILITIES		
	18.9	14.3	13.3	13.6			Notes Payable-Short Term	12.3	13.4
	7.0	4.7	5.4	4.3			Cur. Mat.-L/T/D	6.6	7.5
	12.1	13.6	11.4	11.5			Trade Payables	11.1	9.7
	.2	.1	.2	.1			Income Taxes Payable	.2	.1
	9.7	11.5	10.7	9.0			All Other Current	10.2	8.5
	47.9	44.3	41.1	38.5			Total Current	40.4	39.2
	30.3	19.9	16.2	16.1			Long-Term Debt	22.0	24.0
	.1	.6	1.0	1.2			Deferred Taxes	.7	.6
	12.1	7.7	4.8	4.1			All Other Non-Current	4.1	4.8
	9.6	27.6	37.0	40.1			Net Worth	32.9	31.5
	100.0	100.0	100.0	100.0			Total Liabilities & Net Worth	100.0	100.0
							INCOME DATA		
	100.0	100.0	100.0	100.0			Net Sales	100.0	100.0
	42.5	31.7	26.9	22.0			Gross Profit	29.8	28.0
	38.4	28.7	21.8	16.7			Operating Expenses	25.0	25.8
	4.1	3.0	5.1	5.3			Operating Profit	4.8	2.2
	1.6	1.1	1.3	.6			All Other Expenses (net)	2.2	2.3
	2.5	1.9	3.8	4.6			Profit Before Taxes	2.7	-.1
							RATIOS		
	2.8	2.3	2.4	2.1			Current	2.0	2.2
	1.4	1.4	1.5	1.4				1.3	1.3
	.6	.9	1.0	1.0				1.0	.9
	2.3	1.8	1.5	1.2			Quick	1.4	1.5
	1.0	1.0	.9	.8				.8	.8
	.4	.6	.6	.5				.6	.6
	24 15.0	40 9.1	43 8.4	52 7.1			Sales/Receivables	38 9.5	37 9.9
	38 9.6	54 6.8	58 6.3	67 5.4				51 7.2	50 7.2
	57 6.5	71 5.1	75 4.9	89 4.1				69 5.3	69 5.3
	4 84.8	11 32.5	23 15.8	31 11.8			Cost of Sales/Inventory	13 28.5	11 32.4
	19 18.8	28 13.0	39 9.4	49 7.4				32 11.3	31 11.9
	33 11.1	56 6.6	67 5.5	77 4.8				57 6.4	56 6.5
	12 30.8	14 25.8	16 23.2	18 20.2			Cost of Sales/Payables	14 26.5	12 29.7
	21 17.3	25 14.4	27 13.6	34 10.7				23 15.6	22 16.6
	43 8.4	46 7.9	46 8.0	50 7.4				41 9.0	35 10.5
	6.4	6.7	5.0	5.5			Sales/Working Capital	7.1	6.3
	25.6	16.1	10.3	10.4				16.3	15.7
	-19.8	-75.7	77.2	347.1				-117.2	-44.3
	13.7	8.3	8.2	10.4			EBIT/Interest	5.2	3.7
	(43) 1.8	(138) 3.1	(204) 3.3	(70) 4.5				(578) 2.3	(538) 1.4
	-.8	.1	1.3	1.7				.6	-.7
		2.8	4.9	4.6			Net Profit + Depr., Dep., Amort./Cur. Mat. L./T/D	3.5	2.2
		(32) 1.6	(73) 2.3	(27) 2.2				(184) 1.6	(163) 1.1
		.5	1.6	1.6				.9	.2
	.5	.5	.5	.5			Fixed/Worth	.7	.6
	3.2	1.1	.9	1.1				1.3	1.3
	-1.4	12.2	2.0	2.5				3.0	3.5
	.9	.8	.8	.8			Debt/Worth	.9	.9
	5.0	2.4	2.0	1.9				2.0	2.2
	-3.7	30.0	3.9	4.6				5.7	6.3
	56.4	36.1	36.2	32.0			% Profit Before Taxes/Tangible Net Worth	38.2	27.6
	(31) 20.6	(118) 18.0	(204) 15.8	(71) 14.9				(527) 16.0	(480) 6.8
	-12.5	1.1	2.9	3.8				.8	-15.4
	19.4	11.9	12.6	10.6			% Profit Before Taxes/Total Assets	11.8	8.4
	4.9	5.2	4.7	4.9				4.7	1.5
	-7.6	-2.0	.7	1.3				-1.4	-6.8
	13.0	14.5	9.0	7.1			Sales/Net Fixed Assets	8.3	7.6
	6.9	7.1	5.3	3.9				4.5	4.5
	4.5	4.5	3.3	2.5				3.0	2.8
	3.3	2.7	2.2	1.8			Sales/Total Assets	2.4	2.4
	2.7	2.1	1.8	1.4				1.8	1.8
	2.0	1.8	1.3	1.0				1.4	1.3
	3.5	2.2	2.6	2.2			% Depr., Dep., Amort./Sales	2.8	3.1
	(35) 6.0	(139) 3.6	(213) 4.4	(74) 3.9				(576) 4.6	(536) 5.1
	8.0	5.3	6.2	6.4				6.8	7.6
	7.4	3.9	2.2	1.0			% Officers', Directors', Owners' Comp/Sales	3.2	3.1
	(30) 11.1	(104) 6.3	(108) 3.4	(17) 1.3				(347) 5.6	(288) 5.1
	13.6	8.9	6.1	2.9				9.8	9.5
	41752M	434671M	1751884M	2142931M	694291M	785872M	Net Sales ($)	5764631M	4896411M
	15407M	189323M	983399M	1542343M	523881M	626307M	Total Assets ($)	3728551M	3203840M

© RMA 2005

M = $ thousand   MM = $ million

See Pages 11 through 21 for Explanation of Ratios and Data

Comparative Historical Data

Current Data Sorted By Sales

			Type of Statement						
38	52	51	Unqualified		1	4	13	14	19
160	176	160	Reviewed	2	23	31	66	29	9
172	161	130	Compiled	20	45	29	25	9	2
37	32	42	Tax Returns	8	20	7	4	3	
145	129	130	Other	15	27	18	25	22	23
4/1/02-3/31/03	4/1/03-3/31/04	4/1/04-3/31/05		122 (4/1-9/30/04)			391 (10/1/04-3/31/05)		
ALL	ALL	ALL		0-1MM	1-3MM	3-5MM	5-10MM	10-25MM	25MM & OVER
552	550	513	**NUMBER OF STATEMENTS**	45	116	89	133	77	53
%	%	%	**ASSETS**	%	%	%	%	%	%
6.8	7.5	7.0	Cash & Equivalents	7.6	8.3	8.9	6.7	5.1	4.3
27.4	29.0	31.7	Trade Receivables (net)	28.3	31.8	32.8	32.3	31.1	32.0
15.5	15.6	15.6	Inventory	8.8	14.4	15.9	16.5	17.9	18.1
3.6	3.6	3.2	All Other Current	3.1	1.8	2.6	3.2	5.2	4.0
53.3	55.6	57.5	Total Current	47.8	56.3	60.3	58.7	59.3	58.4
38.3	36.1	34.9	Fixed Assets (net)	42.8	35.8	33.1	34.4	32.7	33.3
2.4	2.0	2.1	Intangibles (net)	3.1	2.4	2.3	1.2	2.4	2.5
6.0	6.3	5.5	All Other Non-Current	6.4	5.5	4.4	5.7	5.6	5.9
100.0	100.0	100.0	Total	100.0	100.0	100.0	100.0	100.0	100.0
			LIABILITIES						
14.5	13.4	14.3	Notes Payable-Short Term	19.2	14.2	15.7	11.8	14.4	14.6
7.6	5.9	5.2	Cur. Mat.-L/T/D	5.7	5.2	5.6	5.3	5.2	3.7
10.7	11.3	12.1	Trade Payables	10.9	11.7	13.5	11.4	12.2	13.6
.2	.2	.2	Income Taxes Payable	.2	.1	.2	.2	.2	.2
10.2	10.7	10.6	All Other Current	11.8	10.3	10.6	11.8	9.2	9.1
43.2	41.5	42.4	Total Current	47.8	41.4	45.6	40.4	41.3	41.1
20.6	19.6	18.6	Long-Term Debt	31.4	23.4	12.2	16.9	17.6	13.7
.6	.7	.8	Deferred Taxes	.1	.6	.6	1.1	1.0	1.5
6.4	6.4	6.2	All Other Non-Current	12.8	7.7	6.6	4.9	3.9	3.4
29.2	31.7	32.0	Net Worth	8.0	26.9	35.0	36.7	36.1	40.3
100.0	100.0	100.0	Total Liabilities & Net Worth	100.0	100.0	100.0	100.0	100.0	100.0
			INCOME DATA						
100.0	100.0	100.0	Net Sales	100.0	100.0	100.0	100.0	100.0	100.0
28.3	29.9	29.0	Gross Profit	44.9	33.4	28.5	27.2	22.5	20.8
26.9	26.7	24.6	Operating Expenses	38.2	30.9	24.5	22.0	18.1	15.1
1.4	3.2	4.4	Operating Profit	6.7	2.5	4.0	5.2	4.3	5.7
1.9	1.2	1.2	All Other Expenses (net)	2.7	1.4	.9	1.0	1.0	.5
−.5	1.9	3.2	Profit Before Taxes	4.0	1.0	3.1	4.2	3.3	5.2
			RATIOS						
2.3	2.5	2.3		3.1	2.3	2.3	2.3	2.2	2.1
1.3	1.4	1.4	Current	1.1	1.4	1.2	1.5	1.6	1.3
.9	.9	1.0		.5	1.0	.9	1.1	1.1	1.0
1.5	1.7	1.5		2.2	1.8	1.7	1.5	1.3	1.3
.8	.9	.9	Quick	.9	1.0	.9	1.0	.8	.9
.5	.6	.6		.3	.6	.6	.7	.6	.6
40	9.2	40	9.0	41	8.8	Sales/Receivables	24	15.3	36	10.0	41	8.8	43	8.4	46	8.0	53	6.9
54	6.8	55	6.7	57	6.4		43	8.5	53	6.8	56	6.6	56	6.5	62	5.9	63	5.8
73	5.0	72	5.0	74	4.9		72	5.1	71	5.1	77	4.8	73	5.0	78	4.7	88	4.1
15	25.0	14	25.5	17	21.8	Cost of Sales/Inventory	0	UND	11	34.0	20	18.0	18	19.9	26	13.9	31	11.8
35	10.5	33	11.0	34	10.7		18	19.8	30	12.2	34	10.7	34	10.7	39	9.3	54	6.8
65	5.7	68	5.4	62	5.9		40	9.1	61	6.0	66	5.5	64	5.7	65	5.6	73	5.0
13	27.8	15	24.2	15	24.1	Cost of Sales/Payables	10	36.8	13	27.8	13	27.5	16	22.8	16	22.3	24	15.5
26	14.0	27	13.6	27	13.4		23	15.8	24	15.2	28	13.1	24	15.4	30	12.4	37	9.8
44	8.3	41	8.8	47	7.8		53	6.8	44	8.4	57	6.4	38	9.7	45	8.1	51	7.2
5.8	5.3	5.5	Sales/Working Capital	5.5	5.8	4.8	5.7	5.5	5.5
14.9	12.0	12.0		76.2	14.2	16.7	10.9	9.2	10.5
−30.4	−43.4	−676.7		−6.7	−69.1	−26.3	55.2	58.4	79.2
	3.6		5.5		8.9	EBIT/Interest		3.5		7.5		8.5		9.5		8.4		12.4
(523)	1.4	(516)	2.2	(466)	3.1		(37)	1.8	(106)	3.1	(80)	3.2	(122)	2.8	(74)	4.3	(47)	4.6
	−1.1		.1		1.2			−1.0		.7		1.1		1.3		1.3		1.6
	2.5		2.3		4.4	Net Profit + Depr., Dep., Amort./Cur. Mat. L/T/D				2.8		7.5		4.9		2.9		4.5
(165)	1.4	(146)	1.5	(139)	2.0				(22)	1.3	(24)	2.6	(49)	2.0	(23)	1.9	(17)	2.3
	.3		.7		1.3					−.7		1.5		1.6		1.2		1.5
.6	.5	.5	Fixed/Worth	.5	.5	.4	.5	.5	.5
1.2	1.2	1.0		8.4	1.2	.8	.9	.9	1.0
3.8	3.0	2.9		−2.1	8.2	2.9	1.9	1.9	1.9
.8	.8	.8	Debt/Worth	1.0	.7	.6	.9	1.0	.7
2.0	2.0	2.1		13.9	2.6	1.8	1.9	2.1	2.0
8.6	6.2	5.8		−5.8	20.7	6.7	3.9	4.0	3.9
	24.5		32.5		36.2	% Profit Before Taxes/Tangible Net Worth		57.3		34.6		35.9		37.1		34.6		35.6
(464)	6.7	(469)	11.8	(436)	15.6		(27)	17.3	(92)	19.0	(75)	15.2	(120)	15.3	(71)	17.0	(51)	13.8
	−13.3		−1.5		2.9			−9.4		.2		4.2		3.5		3.3		3.8
7.2	10.1	12.1	% Profit Before Taxes/Total Assets	14.6	12.2	11.3	13.8	11.7	10.6
1.7	3.1	4.8		4.4	4.9	4.3	4.8	4.9	4.9
−7.0	−2.7	.4		−5.7	−2.2	.4	1.1	.6	1.4
9.2	9.4	10.8	Sales/Net Fixed Assets	9.8	12.3	12.3	11.2	8.4	8.2
4.8	5.1	5.7		5.1	5.6	6.1	6.0	5.4	5.9
2.8	3.3	3.5		2.4	3.7	3.6	3.6	3.8	2.7
2.2	2.4	2.4	Sales/Total Assets	2.7	2.6	2.3	2.4	2.3	2.0
1.7	1.7	1.9		2.0	1.9	1.9	1.9	1.7	1.7
1.2	1.3	1.4		1.3	1.5	1.5	1.5	1.3	1.1
	3.3		2.9		2.4	% Depr., Dep., Amort./Sales		4.3		2.8		2.3		2.6		2.3		1.8
(529)	5.0	(523)	4.7	(471)	4.2		(33)	7.1	(104)	4.0	(82)	4.5	(129)	4.2	(74)	3.7	(49)	3.3
	7.6		7.0		6.1			10.3		6.1		6.2		6.1		5.3		4.6
	2.9		3.2		2.7	% Officers', Directors', Owners' Comp/Sales		7.1		4.0		2.9		2.1		1.4		1.0
(319)	5.3	(291)	5.2	(261)	5.0		(21)	11.2	(78)	6.3	(60)	5.4	(64)	3.5	(27)	2.7	(11)	1.1
	9.8		9.4		8.3			13.2		10.4		7.9		6.8		4.3		3.3
4687907M	5333364M	5851401M	Net Sales ($)	29314M	234544M	349170M	943056M	1227586M	3067731M
3331962M	3692946M	3880660M	Total Assets ($)	21987M	131649M	200815M	573038M	786308M	2166863M

M = $ thousand   MM = $ million
See Pages 11 through 21 for Explanation of Ratios and Data

Current Data Sorted By Assets   Comparative Historical Data

						Type of Statement		
	1	8	12	2	1	Unqualified	17	10
1	10	34	6			Reviewed	53	42
9	14	7	1			Compiled	39	39
2	8	1				Tax Returns	9	7
1	10	17	11		2	Other	30	46
	40 (4/1-9/30/04)		118 (10/1/04-3/31/05)				4/1/00-3/31/01	4/1/01-3/31/02
0-500M	500M-2MM	2-10MM	10-50MM	50-100MM	100-250MM		ALL	ALL
13	43	67	30	2	3	**NUMBER OF STATEMENTS**	148	144
%	%	%	%	%	%	**ASSETS**	%	%
11.3	9.9	6.7	5.6			Cash & Equivalents	8.2	8.7
40.3	33.0	25.3	19.5			Trade Receivables (net)	27.7	25.0
17.7	17.1	27.6	26.9			Inventory	23.4	23.7
.1	2.0	2.7	1.7			All Other Current	1.0	1.6
69.3	61.9	62.3	53.7			Total Current	60.3	59.1
20.6	32.0	29.2	33.6			Fixed Assets (net)	30.2	30.2
1.4	1.1	2.0	4.8			Intangibles (net)	2.3	3.1
8.7	5.0	6.5	7.9			All Other Non-Current	7.1	7.6
100.0	100.0	100.0	100.0			Total	100.0	100.0
						LIABILITIES		
14.8	10.2	12.1	8.7			Notes Payable-Short Term	11.1	8.7
10.1	6.5	5.7	2.9			Cur. Mat.-L/T/D	6.0	6.0
9.5	14.0	10.8	9.5			Trade Payables	10.1	11.9
.0	.0	.2	.2			Income Taxes Payable	.2	.1
11.0	6.2	7.7	8.6			All Other Current	8.7	8.8
45.4	36.9	36.6	29.9			Total Current	36.1	35.5
16.3	23.8	14.9	13.5			Long-Term Debt	19.6	18.3
.6	.5	.8	.7			Deferred Taxes	.6	.6
4.4	7.9	4.9	6.8			All Other Non-Current	5.0	3.9
33.2	30.8	42.8	49.1			Net Worth	38.6	41.6
100.0	100.0	100.0	100.0			Total Liabilities & Net Worth	100.0	100.0
						INCOME DATA		
100.0	100.0	100.0	100.0			Net Sales	100.0	100.0
41.6	35.1	32.8	30.8			Gross Profit	35.2	34.3
38.1	31.5	28.4	25.5			Operating Expenses	30.9	33.0
3.5	3.6	4.4	5.3			Operating Profit	4.4	1.4
–.1	.6	.9	.8			All Other Expenses (net)	1.8	1.2
3.6	2.9	3.5	4.5			Profit Before Taxes	2.5	.1
						RATIOS		
4.1	2.5	2.8	2.8				2.9	2.8
1.6	1.8	1.7	1.7			Current	1.7	1.8
1.2	1.1	1.2	1.4				1.2	1.1
3.4	2.2	1.6	1.2				1.8	1.6
1.2	1.0	.8	.7			Quick	.9	1.0
.7	.7	.6	.6				.6	.6
28 13.2	35 10.3	43 8.5	47 7.8				40 9.2	37 10.0
57 6.5	52 7.0	54 6.8	55 6.6			Sales/Receivables	51 7.1	48 7.6
65 5.6	67 5.5	68 5.4	58 6.3				65 5.6	59 6.2
9 41.9	9 39.4	48 7.6	70 5.2				30 12.1	25 14.4
18 20.5	30 12.1	84 4.3	92 4.0			Cost of Sales/Inventory	69 5.3	72 5.1
55 6.7	72 5.1	137 2.7	163 2.2				115 3.2	108 3.4
8 48.6	19 19.5	15 23.6	15 24.7				15 25.0	16 23.4
15 24.1	28 13.1	30 12.1	28 12.9			Cost of Sales/Payables	27 13.4	26 14.3
28 12.9	37 9.8	52 7.0	50 7.4				41 8.9	41 8.9
6.3	5.3	3.9	3.2				4.0	3.9
13.0	9.4	6.8	6.0			Sales/Working Capital	7.9	7.3
UND	32.6	14.9	11.9				23.1	41.1
18.8	8.9	12.1	5.7				5.2	3.4
(10) 2.9	(40) 3.7	(65) 3.4	(28) 3.2			EBIT/Interest	(133) 1.8	(130) 1.1
–1.1	1.3	1.7	1.7				.8	–1.3
		2.9	5.9			Net Profit + Depr., Dep.,	3.0	1.5
	(27) 2.1		(16) 2.8			Amort./Cur. Mat. L/T/D	(49) 1.3	(38) .4
		1.4	1.7				.7	–.1
.3	.5	.4	.5				.3	.3
.7	.9	.7	.6			Fixed/Worth	.7	.7
NM	1.9	1.4	1.1				2.2	1.7
.7	1.0	.5	.7				.6	.6
1.2	1.8	1.5	1.1			Debt/Worth	1.3	1.3
NM	6.7	2.6	2.4				5.6	3.8
38.9	49.5	28.5	21.7			% Profit Before Taxes/Tangible	31.4	19.3
(10) 13.8	(36) 19.5	(64) 9.3	(28) 8.7			Net Worth	(132) 10.7	(130) 1.7
–2.1	4.2	2.2	2.0				–1.3	–21.3
21.8	15.4	10.8	8.5			% Profit Before Taxes/Total	10.5	6.1
10.6	5.7	4.1	4.1			Assets	3.1	.1
–1.7	.3	.9	1.1				–2.4	–7.8
28.0	13.6	11.5	5.9				11.9	12.5
15.4	7.0	5.4	4.0			Sales/Net Fixed Assets	6.7	6.3
8.3	4.9	3.3	2.5				3.8	3.6
4.4	2.8	1.9	1.6				2.3	2.6
3.0	2.2	1.6	1.3			Sales/Total Assets	1.7	1.8
2.2	1.8	1.3	1.1				1.3	1.3
1.5	2.1	1.5	2.5				1.9	1.7
(12) 3.1	(38) 3.9	(63) 3.7	(28) 3.8			% Depr., Dep., Amort./Sales	(133) 3.4	(128) 3.6
5.1	5.9	6.2	5.0				5.2	6.2
	3.6	2.2					4.4	4.2
	(26) 5.5	(35) 4.2				% Officers', Directors',	(68) 7.2	(61) 6.7
	9.7	7.7				Owners' Comp/Sales	11.1	10.9
13904M	118793M	488633M	850918M	248487M	506011M	Net Sales ($)	1857369M	1153028M
3841M	48918M	307290M	629502M	161557M	455298M	Total Assets ($)	1426715M	835585M

© RMA 2005

M = $ thousand   MM = $ million
See Pages 11 through 21 for Explanation of Ratios and Data

Comparative Historical Data

Current Data Sorted By Sales

			Type of Statement						
14	20	24	Unqualified		1	1	5	7	10
42	60	51	Reviewed		7	14	18	9	3
36	40	31	Compiled	6	16	4	2	3	
12	13	11	Tax Returns	3	4	3	1		
51	40	41	Other		5	13	5	12	6
4/1/02-3/31/03	4/1/03-3/31/04	4/1/04-3/31/05			40 (4/1-9/30/04)		118 (10/1/04-3/31/05)		
ALL	ALL	ALL		0-1MM	1-3MM	3-5MM	5-10MM	10-25MM	25MM & OVER
155	173	158	NUMBER OF STATEMENTS	9	33	35	31	31	19
%	%	%	ASSETS	%	%	%	%	%	%
7.8	7.2	7.7	Cash & Equivalents	11.2	11.6	3.7	4.5	7.2	
26.1	24.7	27.4	Trade Receivables (net)	34.6	25.3	27.1	25.5	20.6	
23.0	26.1	23.9	Inventory	16.8	21.2	28.4	27.8	27.8	
2.4	2.6	2.2	All Other Current	2.3	1.0	3.3	2.4	2.9	
59.2	60.5	61.2	Total Current	64.8	59.1	62.6	60.1	58.5	
31.6	29.5	29.9	Fixed Assets (net)	29.2	35.5	26.0	28.9	31.5	
4.2	3.5	2.4	Intangibles (net)	1.8	.5	3.7	3.8	3.8	
5.0	6.5	6.5	All Other Non-Current	4.1	4.9	7.7	7.2	6.2	
100.0	100.0	100.0	Total	100.0	100.0	100.0	100.0	100.0	
			LIABILITIES						
10.6	10.9	11.1	Notes Payable-Short Term	11.8	7.5	11.3	10.5	9.4	
6.5	6.4	5.6	Cur. Mat.-L/T/D	7.0	6.2	6.2	3.1	3.1	
10.4	11.5	11.3	Trade Payables	10.4	11.5	11.6	14.8	7.9	
.1	.2	.1	Income Taxes Payable	.0	.2	.3	.2	.1	
7.8	9.9	7.9	All Other Current	7.7	7.7	5.6	8.5	10.0	
35.4	38.9	36.0	Total Current	37.0	33.1	34.9	37.1	30.4	
16.2	18.5	16.8	Long-Term Debt	25.2	19.1	16.4	10.7	9.4	
.5	.6	.8	Deferred Taxes	.3	.7	.9	.9	1.1	
6.1	9.1	6.3	All Other Non-Current	9.7	5.0	4.3	6.2	8.9	
41.7	32.9	40.1	Net Worth	27.8	42.2	43.4	45.1	50.3	
100.0	100.0	100.0	Total Liabilities & Net Worth	100.0	100.0	100.0	100.0	100.0	
			INCOME DATA						
100.0	100.0	100.0	Net Sales	100.0	100.0	100.0	100.0	100.0	
34.5	32.7	33.6	Gross Profit	36.1	34.8	32.1	32.2	26.5	
32.5	31.1	29.4	Operating Expenses	34.8	30.8	25.6	27.2	22.8	
1.9	1.6	4.2	Operating Profit	1.4	4.1	6.5	5.1	3.7	
1.5	1.6	.7	All Other Expenses (net)	.6	.9	1.0	.5	.5	
.4	.0	3.5	Profit Before Taxes	.7	3.2	5.4	4.6	3.2	
			RATIOS						
3.0	2.8	2.8		3.1	3.1	3.1	2.2	3.1	
1.7	1.7	1.7	Current	1.8	2.1	1.8	1.6	1.9	
1.2	1.1	1.3		1.2	1.3	1.2	1.3	1.4	
1.8	1.6	1.7		2.6	2.3	1.2	1.1	1.6	
.9	.8	.9	Quick	1.2	1.2	.8	.7	.8	
.6	.5	.6		.8	.6	.6	.6	.6	

											Sales/Receivables						
41	8.9	39	9.3	42	8.7		44	8.3	35	10.4	44	8.3	46	7.9	46	7.9
49	7.4	50	7.2	54	6.8		58	6.3	48	7.7	51	7.2	55	6.6	52	7.1
66	5.6	62	5.9	65	5.7		70	5.2	61	6.0	64	5.7	70	5.3	58	6.3

											Cost of Sales/Inventory						
24	15.2	33	11.1	31	11.7		9	41.3	26	13.9	37	9.9	57	6.5	66	5.5
64	5.7	80	4.5	73	5.0		30	12.1	76	4.8	81	4.5	88	4.1	90	4.1
121	3.0	138	2.7	124	3.0		75	4.9	109	3.4	150	2.4	140	2.6	116	3.2

											Cost of Sales/Payables						
15	23.8	18	20.1	16	23.3		15	24.3	14	26.8	16	22.7	24	15.1	15	24.8
25	14.3	31	11.6	28	13.0		27	13.6	25	14.4	29	12.7	50	7.3	22	16.4
42	8.7	44	8.2	47	7.7		35	10.4	50	7.2	47	7.8	70	5.2	40	9.1

			Sales/Working Capital						
4.3	4.2	4.1		5.5	3.7	3.9	4.7	3.3	
7.7	7.6	7.5		8.0	6.7	7.6	7.6	5.6	
25.2	32.2	18.1		22.0	19.6	19.7	12.2	13.4	

						EBIT/Interest							
	4.8		4.2		9.4			8.1		8.6		13.7	7.4	9.7
(140)	1.6	(156)	1.7	(148)	3.4		(28)	2.2	(34)	4.0	(30)	3.8	(29) 3.4	3.0
	-.6		-.8		1.4			-.7		2.0		1.8	1.0	1.6

						Net Profit + Depr., Dep., Amort./Cur. Mat. L/T/D							
	2.3		2.7		5.6					7.8		2.4	8.3	
(44)	1.1	(54)	1.4	(54)	2.2				(10)	2.6	(15)	1.8	(13) 3.4	
	.1		.7		1.3					1.7		1.4	2.0	

			Fixed/Worth						
.3	.4	.4		.4	.4	.2	.4	.4	
.8	.8	.7		.9	.8	.7	.6	.6	
1.7	2.4	1.4		3.3	1.7	1.4	1.0	1.0	

			Debt/Worth						
.6	.7	.7		1.0	.5	.4	.9	.5	
1.4	1.6	1.4		2.4	1.1	1.8	1.4	.9	
4.8	4.9	3.2		11.3	3.3	2.7	2.4	1.3	

						% Profit Before Taxes/Tangible Net Worth							
	18.2		23.8		31.8			45.7		38.1		26.8	27.0	23.3
(140)	4.9	(152)	4.3	(144)	9.8		(26)	9.2	(32)	13.4	(30)	11.3	9.4	(18) 9.6
	-12.8		-8.4		2.5			-8.6		3.4		4.3	2.0	2.0

			% Profit Before Taxes/Total Assets						
6.8	8.3	12.5		11.3	15.4	11.3	14.2	8.2	
1.7	2.0	4.6		2.7	5.7	4.5	4.1	4.6	
-4.8	-4.6	.8		-3.9	1.7	1.5	.9	.9	

			Sales/Net Fixed Assets						
12.8	13.8	12.1		16.1	8.2	31.4	12.0	9.2	
5.9	6.1	5.6		7.4	5.3	9.0	5.6	4.7	
3.3	3.3	3.6		4.5	3.3	3.1	2.8	3.3	

			Sales/Total Assets						
2.3	2.3	2.3		2.9	2.3	2.2	1.9	1.7	
1.7	1.7	1.7		2.2	1.6	1.7	1.4	1.5	
1.1	1.2	1.3		1.8	1.3	1.3	1.2	1.3	

						% Depr., Dep., Amort./Sales							
	2.0		2.1		1.9			1.8		2.6		1.1	1.6	2.6
(138)	3.8	(151)	3.9	(145)	3.8		(28)	3.6	(32)	4.8	(28)	3.3	(30) 3.3	(18) 3.8
	6.3		5.7		5.6			5.8		7.9		5.5	5.0	4.9

						% Officers', Directors', Owners' Comp/Sales							
	3.6		4.1		3.0			3.9		2.7		2.2	2.2	
(70)	7.4	(80)	6.6	(72)	5.1		(20)	5.7	(23)	4.3	(11)	3.5	(12) 4.4	
	10.5		11.4		9.3			9.9		6.7		6.1	9.6	

			Net Sales ($)						
3366155M	2008849M	2226746M	Net Sales ($)	4754M	63682M	135907M	218217M	477625M	1326561M
1695137M	1602178M	1606406M	Total Assets ($)	3085M	34360M	85532M	139794M	343307M	1000328M

M = $ thousand   MM = $ million
See Pages 11 through 21 for Explanation of Ratios and Data

Current Data Sorted By Assets | **Comparative Historical Data**

Type of Statement

Type of Statement	0-500M	500M-2MM	2-10MM	10-50MM	50-100MM	100-250MM	4/1/00-3/31/01 ALL	4/1/01-3/31/02 ALL
Unqualified			3	5	2	2	11	6
Reviewed		3	12	3			14	17
Compiled	3	4	8				10	9
Tax Returns	3	1					1	2
Other	2	5	8	1	1		20	17
	13 (4/1-9/30/04)			53 (10/1/04-3/31/05)				
NUMBER OF STATEMENTS	8	13	31	9	3	2	56	51

Data

0-500M	500M-2MM	2-10MM	10-50MM	50-100MM	100-250MM	Item	4/1/00-3/31/01 ALL	4/1/01-3/31/02 ALL
%	%	%	%	%	%	**ASSETS**	%	%
	11.8	4.5				Cash & Equivalents	7.9	9.5
	27.5	36.5				Trade Receivables (net)	27.5	24.1
	26.0	24.5				Inventory	22.3	22.9
	.5	9.3				All Other Current	5.8	5.0
	65.7	74.9				Total Current	63.6	61.6
	29.3	19.9				Fixed Assets (net)	27.0	30.1
	1.8	2.1				Intangibles (net)	4.0	3.6
	3.2	3.1				All Other Non-Current	5.4	4.8
	100.0	100.0				Total	100.0	100.0
						LIABILITIES		
	6.3	13.9				Notes Payable-Short Term	15.3	14.0
	5.9	2.9				Cur. Mat.-L/T/D	3.2	4.7
	11.8	19.7				Trade Payables	12.8	11.2
	.0	.0				Income Taxes Payable	.8	.1
	15.8	14.2				All Other Current	24.1	12.0
	39.8	50.8				Total Current	56.0	41.9
	31.9	9.0				Long-Term Debt	16.3	24.8
	.1	.3				Deferred Taxes	.6	.1
	9.6	9.2				All Other Non-Current	5.8	8.2
	18.6	30.8				Net Worth	21.3	25.0
	100.0	100.0				Total Liabilities & Net Worth	100.0	100.0
						INCOME DATA		
	100.0	100.0				Net Sales	100.0	100.0
	41.3	26.9				Gross Profit	29.7	32.0
	34.6	22.0				Operating Expenses	26.3	31.0
	6.7	4.8				Operating Profit	3.4	1.0
	2.1	.8				All Other Expenses (net)	1.8	1.7
	4.5	4.0				Profit Before Taxes	1.6	-.7
						RATIOS		
	2.8	2.5				Current	1.8	3.4
	1.5	1.3					1.3	1.3
	1.2	1.1					1.0	1.0
	1.7	1.2				Quick	1.3	1.7
	.8	.9					.7	.7
	.6	.5					.4	.4
	31 11.8	47 7.8				Sales/Receivables	38 9.7	29 12.5
	50 7.3	55 6.6					49 7.5	44 8.3
	69 5.3	90 4.0					62 5.9	61 6.0
	39 9.3	17 21.9				Cost of Sales/Inventory	16 22.2	20 18.2
	61 5.9	57 6.4					64 5.7	57 6.4
	111 3.3	107 3.4					97 3.8	101 3.6
	10 35.4	18 20.3				Cost of Sales/Payables	15 24.0	14 25.6
	40 9.0	36 10.0					28 12.9	28 13.2
	61 6.0	62 5.9					48 7.7	44 8.4
	5.0	4.0				Sales/Working Capital	4.8	4.4
	10.9	11.2					15.0	14.4
	27.0	27.4					397.4	-318.0
	8.8	15.0				EBIT/Interest	3.6	4.4
	3.0	(26) 3.3					(51) 1.6	(45) 1.9
	1.5	1.3					-.2	-1.3
						Net Profit + Depr., Dep.,	5.6	
						Amort./Cur. Mat. L/T/D	(18) 1.8	
							.4	
	.1	.3				Fixed/Worth	.4	.4
	1.3	.5					1.0	1.1
	-35.0	1.7					3.5	5.7
	2.1	1.0				Debt/Worth	1.1	.6
	4.5	2.1					3.4	3.5
	-44.5	6.3					23.2	28.1
		35.3				% Profit Before Taxes/Tangible	32.5	25.8
		(26) 21.6				Net Worth	(47) 7.0	(41) 9.0
		5.6					-4.0	-28.6
	18.8	10.2				% Profit Before Taxes/Total	6.1	12.3
	5.6	8.1				Assets	2.1	3.8
	1.9	.3					-3.2	-9.5
	75.4	37.5				Sales/Net Fixed Assets	37.7	27.8
	17.0	16.0					8.8	9.9
	2.9	7.4					3.5	3.4
	3.0	2.5				Sales/Total Assets	2.5	2.5
	1.8	2.1					1.8	1.9
	1.2	1.6					1.2	1.4
	1.1	.9				% Depr., Dep., Amort./Sales	.9	1.2
	(11) 4.8	(29) 1.5					(51) 2.4	(46) 2.6
	8.9	3.6					4.2	5.5
		2.1				% Officers', Directors',	2.2	2.0
		(12) 3.6				Owners' Comp/Sales	(24) 4.4	(19) 3.4
		7.2					10.1	12.8
5698M	30011M	253221M	249362M	220532M	370008M	Net Sales ($)	745604M	523878M
1786M	14261M	124332M	204527M	235753M	296881M	Total Assets ($)	538965M	347051M

M = $ thousand   MM = $ million
See Pages 11 through 21 for Explanation of Ratios and Data

Comparative Historical Data

Current Data Sorted By Sales

			Type of Statement						
7	8	12	Unqualified				1	5	6
16	16	18	Reviewed		2	4	8	1	3
13	15	15	Compiled	3	3	4	4	1	
3	10	4	Tax Returns	3		1			
11	23	17	Other	2	5	1	4	5	
4/1/02- 3/31/03	4/1/03- 3/31/04	4/1/04- 3/31/05			13 (4/1-9/30/04)			53 (10/1/04-3/31/05)	
ALL	ALL	ALL		0-1MM	1-3MM	3-5MM	5-10MM	10-25MM	25MM & OVER
50	72	66	**NUMBER OF STATEMENTS**	8	10	10	17	12	9
%	%	%	**ASSETS**	%	%	%	%	%	%
12.5	9.2	8.0	Cash & Equivalents		12.3	6.8	3.8	6.5	
26.7	30.3	31.8	Trade Receivables (net)		31.6	35.5	35.7	31.1	
20.1	22.0	23.0	Inventory		22.0	29.7	26.0	20.1	
6.1	3.9	5.4	All Other Current		.4	10.0	9.6	3.1	
65.3	65.4	68.2	Total Current		66.3	82.0	75.1	60.8	
29.9	26.0	24.1	Fixed Assets (net)		26.6	15.1	19.7	23.6	
.8	1.9	2.9	Intangibles (net)		1.9	1.1	2.5	6.8	
4.0	6.8	4.7	All Other Non-Current		5.3	1.8	2.8	8.8	
100.0	100.0	100.0	Total		100.0	100.0	100.0	100.0	
			LIABILITIES						
16.1	14.1	14.2	Notes Payable-Short Term		4.9	13.9	14.6	6.9	
4.3	3.2	3.4	Cur. Mat.-L/T/D		6.7	3.0	2.8	3.0	
11.1	14.4	14.2	Trade Payables		9.3	14.8	20.8	16.1	
.2	.1	.1	Income Taxes Payable		.0	.1	.0	.2	
14.3	15.2	14.4	All Other Current		11.4	17.0	14.9	16.6	
46.0	47.0	46.3	Total Current		32.3	48.7	53.2	42.7	
18.6	18.4	15.7	Long-Term Debt		32.6	8.3	8.7	9.0	
.1	.3	.2	Deferred Taxes		.1	.9	.0	.0	
7.1	8.4	10.7	All Other Non-Current		23.6	1.8	14.9	9.4	
28.2	25.9	27.2	Net Worth		11.4	40.3	23.2	38.9	
100.0	100.0	100.0	Total Liabilities & Net Worth		100.0	100.0	100.0	100.0	
			INCOME DATA						
100.0	100.0	100.0	Net Sales		100.0	100.0	100.0	100.0	
32.7	33.6	31.8	Gross Profit		40.0	29.1	29.0	25.7	
30.9	30.0	26.9	Operating Expenses		32.4	25.0	24.9	20.2	
1.8	3.6	4.9	Operating Profit		7.6	4.1	4.1	5.6	
2.2	1.5	1.0	All Other Expenses (net)		2.4	.4	1.1	-.5	
-.4	2.1	4.0	Profit Before Taxes		5.2	3.7	3.0	6.1	
			RATIOS						
2.5	2.4	2.5			3.9	2.8	2.3	2.4	
1.6	1.5	1.3	Current		2.3	1.9	1.3	1.2	
1.1	1.0	1.1			1.2	1.2	1.1	1.0	
1.5	1.6	1.2			3.2	1.3	1.0	1.2	
1.0	.8	.8	Quick		1.1	.8	.6	1.0	
.6	.5	.5			.8	.5	.5	.4	
36 10.1	42 8.7	39 9.4		34 10.6	35 10.4	48 7.6	41 8.8		
48 7.6	54 6.8	54 6.7	Sales/Receivables	46 8.0	56 6.5	57 6.4	48 7.6		
70 5.2	70 5.2	76 4.8		67 5.4	99 3.7	76 4.8	102 3.6		
9 42.2	22 16.4	19 19.5		0 UND	19 19.6	24 15.4	17 21.8		
56 6.6	57 6.4	63 5.8	Cost of Sales/Inventory	58 6.3	80 4.6	56 6.5	64 5.7		
100 3.6	106 3.4	108 3.4		104 3.5	148 2.5	102 3.6	118 3.1		
14 26.6	19 19.1	15 24.3		0 UND	16 23.1	25 14.6	12 29.7		
23 15.7	33 11.1	34 10.7	Cost of Sales/Payables	27 13.6	30 12.1	36 10.0	29 12.6		
47 7.8	56 6.5	60 6.1		60 6.1	61 5.9	69 5.3	64 5.7		
3.9	4.2	4.9			4.4	3.5	4.9	6.0	
8.4	12.3	11.1	Sales/Working Capital		7.5	5.8	9.8	11.4	
41.9	-70.6	29.0			17.6	24.1	63.7	NM	
	3.5	7.6	12.4		7.6		16.2	13.6	
(45) 1.0	(64) 1.7	(60) 3.0	EBIT/Interest		3.6	(15) 2.3	(10) 2.4		
-1.6	-.7	1.1			1.4		.1	-2.8	
7.6	2.8	8.5	Net Profit + Depr., Dep.,						
(13) 1.9	(13) 1.0	(16) 5.1	Amort./Cur. Mat. L/T/D						
.1	-1.5	1.3							
.6	.4	.3			.2	.1	.3	.4	
1.0	.9	.6	Fixed/Worth		6.1	.4	.5	1.1	
2.9	11.5	3.5			-1.4	.6	4.4	NM	
.8	.9	1.0			1.6	.9	1.7	.7	
1.9	2.3	2.4	Debt/Worth		10.5	1.6	2.5	2.2	
6.5	125.3	11.2			-6.0	3.4	20.6	NM	
25.3	50.8	35.8	% Profit Before Taxes/Tangible			31.3	35.8		
(42) 3.2	(55) 13.9	(53) 18.4	Net Worth			13.2	(14) 20.3		
-9.6	-4.9	3.2				8.2	-13.9		
6.2	11.7	11.4	% Profit Before Taxes/Total		24.3	9.9	16.4	17.3	
.2	3.5	5.7	Assets		7.3	5.9	4.2	8.2	
-4.3	-4.0	.2			1.8	3.1	-4.5	-.9	
20.5	20.0	31.0			37.4	72.3	34.6	43.8	
6.7	10.1	10.7	Sales/Net Fixed Assets		17.1	10.4	17.2	11.5	
2.8	4.2	4.2			3.0	7.5	8.9	3.9	
2.2	2.3	2.5			3.6	2.5	2.6	2.5	
1.6	1.7	1.9	Sales/Total Assets		1.9	1.8	2.2	2.0	
1.3	1.3	1.3			1.5	1.5	1.7	1.2	
1.3	.9	1.1					.8	.8	
(45) 3.5	(64) 2.8	(58) 2.6	% Depr., Dep., Amort./Sales			(16) 1.3	(11) 1.4		
6.5	5.4	4.8					2.8	4.0	
1.9	2.5	2.8							
(25) 4.0	(29) 5.4	(25) 6.1	% Officers', Directors',						
9.8	8.0	8.1	Owners' Comp/Sales						
811700M	762349M	1128832M	Net Sales ($)	4692M	17881M	39873M	119717M	210503M	736166M
564662M	564156M	877540M	Total Assets ($)	2546M	9527M	21586M	62652M	208011M	573218M

© RMA 2005   M = $ thousand   MM = $ million
See Pages 11 through 21 for Explanation of Ratios and Data

Current Data Sorted By Assets   Comparative Historical Data

0-500M	500M-2MM	2-10MM	10-50MM	50-100MM	100-250MM	Type of Statement	4/1/00-3/31/01 ALL	4/1/01-3/31/02 ALL
		3	2		2	Unqualified	11	9
	1	7	2	1	2	Reviewed	9	12
	1	1				Compiled	2	5
	1		5			Tax Returns	1	1
	2	4				Other	11	8
	11 (4/1-9/30/04)		20 (10/1/04-3/31/05)					
	4	15	9	1	2	**NUMBER OF STATEMENTS**	34	35
%	%	%	%	%	%	**ASSETS**	%	%
		9.2				Cash & Equivalents	7.1	8.4
		22.5				Trade Receivables (net)	24.0	23.6
		35.7				Inventory	25.6	22.3
		1.4				All Other Current	.8	1.1
		68.8				Total Current	57.5	55.3
		23.5				Fixed Assets (net)	35.6	37.3
		.5				Intangibles (net)	1.6	3.1
		7.2				All Other Non-Current	5.4	4.3
		100.0				Total	100.0	100.0
						LIABILITIES		
		6.4				Notes Payable-Short Term	7.9	8.4
		6.2				Cur. Mat.-L/T/D	8.6	8.7
		9.0				Trade Payables	11.1	9.6
		.0				Income Taxes Payable	.1	.1
		5.8				All Other Current	7.5	7.5
		27.4				Total Current	35.2	34.3
		7.3				Long-Term Debt	15.5	15.5
		.5				Deferred Taxes	.6	.4
		.3				All Other Non-Current	3.5	3.8
		64.5				Net Worth	45.1	46.0
		100.0				Total Liabilities & Net Worth	100.0	100.0
						INCOME DATA		
		100.0				Net Sales	100.0	100.0
		33.6				Gross Profit	25.9	25.1
		27.6				Operating Expenses	22.8	25.3
		6.0				Operating Profit	3.1	-.1
		1.6				All Other Expenses (net)	.9	1.4
		4.5				Profit Before Taxes	2.2	-1.6
						RATIOS		
		6.7					2.6	3.0
		2.5				Current	1.7	1.8
		1.7					1.2	1.0
		3.6					2.1	2.1
		1.2				Quick	.9	1.1
		.6					.5	.5
	44	8.3					40 9.1	40 9.2
	56	6.5				Sales/Receivables	53 6.9	50 7.3
	58	6.3					59 6.2	57 6.4
	68	5.4					40 9.0	35 10.4
	117	3.1				Cost of Sales/Inventory	73 5.0	65 5.6
	206	1.8					117 3.1	92 4.0
	16	23.2					18 20.3	13 27.6
	20	17.9				Cost of Sales/Payables	28 13.1	24 15.0
	44	8.3					41 8.8	38 9.7
		2.3					4.1	3.6
		4.5				Sales/Working Capital	7.5	7.9
		6.8					18.1	54.1
		17.9					3.3	2.4
	(14)	2.3				EBIT/Interest	(31) 2.8	(31) 1.1
		.4					.8	-2.3
						Net Profit + Depr., Dep., Amort./Cur. Mat. L /T/D		
		.1					.5	.5
		.3				Fixed/Worth	.8	.7
		.9					1.9	2.3
		.1					.6	.4
		.6				Debt/Worth	1.2	1.1
		.8					3.2	4.1
		20.3					21.3	16.2
		3.7				% Profit Before Taxes/Tangible Net Worth	(31) 7.7	(31) 2.0
		-1.1					.3	-25.2
		13.7					6.9	6.4
		2.9				% Profit Before Taxes/Total Assets	4.2	.8
		-.7					-1.0	-12.8
		16.5					12.6	7.4
		6.8				Sales/Net Fixed Assets	4.2	4.2
		3.6					2.3	2.3
		2.0					2.2	2.1
		1.5				Sales/Total Assets	1.6	1.5
		1.1					1.1	1.2
		2.6					2.2	2.4
	(12)	4.5				% Depr., Dep., Amort./Sales	(32) 4.4	(33) 5.9
		7.8					6.4	7.6
						% Officers', Directors', Owners' Comp/Sales		
	9493M	99667M	188416M	104496M	340482M	Net Sales ($)	1045898M	732662M
	3313M	61431M	141556M	85431M	299581M	Total Assets ($)	844203M	595229M

Note: DATA NOT AVAILABLE (0-500M column).

M = $ thousand   MM = $ million
See Pages 11 through 21 for Explanation of Ratios and Data

Comparative Historical Data						Current Data Sorted By Sales					
Type of Statement											
8		11		7	Unqualified		1		1	2	3
8		13		11	Reviewed		2	4	2	1	2
7		4		1	Compiled			1			
2				1	Tax Returns		1				
12		7		11	Other		1	1	2	6	1
4/1/02- 3/31/03		4/1/03- 3/31/04		4/1/04- 3/31/05			11 (4/1-9/30/04)		20 (10/1/04-3/31/05)		
ALL		ALL		ALL		0-1MM	1-3MM	3-5MM	5-10MM	10-25MM	25MM & OVER
37		35		31	**NUMBER OF STATEMENTS**		5	6	5	9	6
%		%		%	**ASSETS**	%	%	%	%	%	%
10.1		10.0		9.1	Cash & Equivalents						
24.7		20.5		23.5	Trade Receivables (net)						
23.0		26.4		31.1	Inventory						
1.5		1.4		1.0	All Other Current						
59.3		58.4		64.6	Total Current						
33.1		33.8		28.0	Fixed Assets (net)						
2.5		1.1		1.2	Intangibles (net)						
5.1		6.8		6.2	All Other Non-Current						
100.0		100.0		100.0	Total						
					LIABILITIES						
9.7		7.9		7.4	Notes Payable-Short Term						
8.9		5.2		4.5	Cur. Mat.-L/T/D						
12.7		8.5		10.8	Trade Payables						
.1		.2		.0	Income Taxes Payable						
7.4		7.4		7.1	All Other Current						
38.8		29.2		29.9	Total Current						
14.0		12.2		10.4	Long-Term Debt						
.5		.6		1.3	Deferred Taxes						
7.7		5.9		3.3	All Other Non-Current						
39.0		52.0		55.1	Net Worth						
100.0		100.0		100.0	Total Liabilities & Net Worth						
					INCOME DATA						
100.0		100.0		100.0	Net Sales						
29.8		23.9		28.0	Gross Profit						
28.0		22.9		22.7	Operating Expenses						
1.8		1.0		5.4	Operating Profit						
1.6		.4		1.0	All Other Expenses (net)						
.1		.6		4.4	Profit Before Taxes						
					RATIOS						
3.0		4.0		6.1							
1.7		2.6		2.5	Current						
1.1		1.3		1.4							
2.3		2.8		3.5							
1.1		1.0		1.2	Quick						
.5		.5		.6							
39	9.3	47	7.8	42	8.8	Sales/Receivables					
51	7.2	55	6.6	56	6.5						
63	5.8	65	5.6	67	5.5						
35	10.3	43	8.5	59	6.2	Cost of Sales/Inventory					
52	7.0	86	4.2	79	4.6						
94	3.9	130	2.8	120	3.0						
16	23.5	17	22.0	16	23.2	Cost of Sales/Payables					
25	14.3	32	11.4	23	16.0						
50	7.2	41	9.0	42	8.7						
3.5		2.9		2.9	Sales/Working Capital						
7.1		3.9		4.6							
97.3		17.7		10.4							
4.3		4.7		16.2	EBIT/Interest						
(34)	1.3	(30)	1.1	(27)	3.0						
-1.6		-2.4		.8							
		7.4			Net Profit + Depr., Dep., Amort./Cur. Mat. L/T/D						
		(12)	1.2								
		1.0									
.5		.4		.2	Fixed/Worth						
.8		.6		.5							
2.9		1.5		1.3							
.5		.3		.2	Debt/Worth						
1.7		.8		.8							
6.7		3.0		2.1							
12.2		13.9		25.5	% Profit Before Taxes/Tangible Net Worth						
(32)	3.0		1.5	(30)	8.4						
-7.5		-7.4		-1.1							
4.4		5.7		12.3	% Profit Before Taxes/Total Assets						
1.1		.3		5.9							
-5.1		-3.9		-.3							
11.2		7.1		16.5	Sales/Net Fixed Assets						
5.0		3.9		5.8							
2.9		2.7		2.5							
2.3		1.7		2.3	Sales/Total Assets						
1.7		1.3		1.5							
1.2		1.0		1.1							
2.5		3.2		2.7	% Depr., Dep., Amort./Sales						
(36)	4.7		5.4	(27)	4.8						
7.5		8.4		7.3							
3.5		3.1		2.0	% Officers', Directors', Owners' Comp/Sales						
(13)	6.0	(14)	5.3	(11)	3.7						
9.3		9.8		10.1							
979007M		1009069M		742554M	Net Sales ($)		10035M	25816M	35947M	140116M	530640M
934573M		847928M		591312M	Total Assets ($)		6929M	15572M	23676M	118555M	426580M

In the Current Data columns under ASSETS through INCOME DATA, the 0-1MM column reads: **DATA NOT AVAILABLE**

© RMA 2005

M = $ thousand   MM = $ million
See Pages 11 through 21 for Explanation of Ratios and Data

Current Data Sorted By Assets   Comparative Historical Data

Type of Statement	0-500M	500M-2MM	2-10MM	10-50MM	50-100MM	100-250MM		7 4/1/00-3/31/01 ALL	8 4/1/01-3/31/02 ALL
Unqualified			3	2		1		9	7
Reviewed	1	2	6	1				6	5
Compiled		5						9	6
Tax Returns	1		1						
Other	1	1	5	7		1		7	8
			12 (4/1-9/30/04)	26 (10/1/04-3/31/05)					
NUMBER OF STATEMENTS	3	8	15	10		2		31	26

Data in the 50-100MM column marked "DATA NOT AVAILABLE."

	2-10MM %	10-50MM %		4/1/00-3/31/01 ALL %	4/1/01-3/31/02 ALL %
ASSETS					
Cash & Equivalents	4.2	5.4		4.5	5.0
Trade Receivables (net)	25.7	29.2		26.8	25.1
Inventory	32.9	23.8		29.7	29.2
All Other Current	1.1	1.9		1.9	3.2
Total Current	63.8	60.4		63.0	62.5
Fixed Assets (net)	22.2	32.8		26.4	27.8
Intangibles (net)	2.1	2.6		6.4	5.1
All Other Non-Current	12.0	4.1		4.2	4.7
Total	100.0	100.0		100.0	100.0
LIABILITIES					
Notes Payable-Short Term	7.9	7.5		7.6	27.5
Cur. Mat.-L/T/D	1.8	6.8		8.8	8.0
Trade Payables	15.8	16.7		14.2	13.3
Income Taxes Payable	.1	.0		.4	.1
All Other Current	11.2	12.8		6.4	7.8
Total Current	36.8	43.8		37.5	56.7
Long-Term Debt	10.4	12.8		27.1	11.5
Deferred Taxes	1.1	.5		.9	.5
All Other Non-Current	2.9	9.7		4.7	6.7
Net Worth	48.9	33.2		29.8	24.7
Total Liabilities & Net Worth	100.0	100.0		100.0	100.0
INCOME DATA					
Net Sales	100.0	100.0		100.0	100.0
Gross Profit	33.5	24.9		35.7	30.5
Operating Expenses	28.7	18.3		26.2	25.2
Operating Profit	4.8	6.6		9.4	5.2
All Other Expenses (net)	1.8	1.2		3.0	2.7
Profit Before Taxes	3.0	5.4		6.5	2.5

RATIOS

	2-10MM	10-50MM		4/1/00-3/31/01 ALL	4/1/01-3/31/02 ALL
Current	2.8	1.8		2.8	2.5
	2.0	1.4		1.7	1.4
	1.3	.9		1.2	1.0
Quick	1.1	1.2		1.1	1.2
	.9	.8		.8	.6
	.7	.6		.6	.5
Sales/Receivables	38 9.6	42 8.6		42 8.7	36 10.0
	51 7.2	52 7.0		52 7.1	47 7.8
	63 5.8	64 5.7		67 5.5	60 6.1
Cost of Sales/Inventory	46 7.9	35 10.5		58 6.3	50 7.3
	108 3.4	70 5.2		80 4.6	76 4.8
	164 2.2	85 4.3		141 2.6	125 2.9
Cost of Sales/Payables	24 15.2	27 13.3		27 13.5	20 17.9
	47 7.8	41 8.9		42 8.7	31 11.6
	87 4.2	51 7.1		56 6.5	50 7.4
Sales/Working Capital	3.9	5.9		4.0	3.5
	8.6	13.9		5.6	8.9
	12.0	−73.6		20.6	245.5
EBIT/Interest	11.3			5.1	4.5
	(13) 7.5			3.0	(24) 2.1
	2.3			2.0	.3
Net Profit + Depr., Dep., Amort./Cur. Mat. L/T/D				4.7	
				(15) 2.8	
				.9	
Fixed/Worth	.2	.6		.3	.3
	.5	1.2		.8	.7
	.7	7.1		1.7	1.8
Debt/Worth	.6	.9		.8	.6
	.8	2.4		1.8	2.0
	1.7	17.7		3.9	4.1
% Profit Before Taxes/Tangible Net Worth	25.1			37.8	17.7
	(14) 12.5			(28) 21.3	(23) 10.7
	.5			10.2	−26.9
% Profit Before Taxes/Total Assets	13.3	17.0		12.8	12.0
	6.4	6.6		8.5	4.1
	1.5	6.1		3.4	−1.6
Sales/Net Fixed Assets	20.5	8.7		12.5	9.6
	6.7	5.8		7.0	6.5
	4.9	4.5		3.7	3.9
Sales/Total Assets	2.5	2.8		2.5	2.2
	1.7	1.9		1.8	1.8
	1.2	1.3		1.3	1.4
% Depr., Dep., Amort./Sales	1.7			1.5	1.5
	(13) 3.1			(27) 2.1	(25) 2.7
	4.0			4.0	4.5
% Officers', Directors', Owners' Comp/Sales					

	0-500M	500M-2MM	2-10MM	10-50MM	50-100MM	100-250MM		4/1/00-3/31/01 ALL	4/1/01-3/31/02 ALL
Net Sales ($)	2544M	35848M	131810M	441158M		516598M		1214520M	553947M
Total Assets ($)	820M	9485M	74711M	218406M		349540M		1027894M	349349M

M = $ thousand   MM = $ million
See Pages 11 through 21 for Explanation of Ratios and Data

Comparative Historical Data   Current Data Sorted By Sales

			Type of Statement						
11	7	6	Unqualified				1	3	2
9	10	10	Reviewed		2	1	5	1	1
3	3	5	Compiled		3	1	1		
1	2	2	Tax Returns			1			
11	11	15	Other	1	3			4	7
					12 (4/1-9/30/04)		26 (10/1/04-3/31/05)		
4/1/02-3/31/03	4/1/03-3/31/04	4/1/04-3/31/05		0-1MM	1-3MM	3-5MM	5-10MM	10-25MM	25MM & OVER
ALL	ALL	ALL							
35	33	38	**NUMBER OF STATEMENTS**	2	8	3	7	8	10
%	%	%	**ASSETS**	%	%	%	%	%	%
5.1	8.6	7.3	Cash & Equivalents						5.1
28.0	27.2	30.6	Trade Receivables (net)						28.8
26.5	26.0	26.7	Inventory						23.3
3.0	1.5	2.0	All Other Current						5.1
62.6	63.4	66.6	Total Current						62.3
28.1	26.8	25.2	Fixed Assets (net)						29.7
3.9	4.3	1.6	Intangibles (net)						1.6
5.4	5.4	6.6	All Other Non-Current						6.3
100.0	100.0	100.0	Total						100.0
			LIABILITIES						
19.7	11.7	8.7	Notes Payable-Short Term						7.0
3.8	3.7	3.5	Cur. Mat.-L/T/D						6.5
11.5	14.3	14.9	Trade Payables						19.3
.7	.6	.4	Income Taxes Payable						.3
11.7	8.6	11.9	All Other Current						16.3
47.3	38.9	39.4	Total Current						49.4
26.0	16.6	11.3	Long-Term Debt						14.0
.3	.4	.7	Deferred Taxes						.5
6.0	4.3	4.9	All Other Non-Current						11.4
20.4	39.8	43.8	Net Worth						24.6
100.0	100.0	100.0	Total Liabilities & Net Worth						100.0
			INCOME DATA						
100.0	100.0	100.0	Net Sales						100.0
32.4	29.6	32.9	Gross Profit						23.4
27.3	27.2	27.3	Operating Expenses						17.3
5.2	2.4	5.6	Operating Profit						6.0
1.6	1.3	1.1	All Other Expenses (net)						1.1
3.6	1.1	4.5	Profit Before Taxes						4.9
			RATIOS						
2.9	2.5	2.9	Current						1.5
1.8	1.9	1.7							1.3
1.5	1.2	1.3							.9
1.4	1.5	1.4	Quick						.9
1.0	.9	1.0							.7
.8	.6	.7							.6
39 9.5	38 9.6	38 9.6	Sales/Receivables						42 8.6
51 7.1	53 6.9	49 7.5							49 7.4
70 5.2	65 5.6	61 5.9							63 5.8
46 8.0	44 8.2	32 11.5	Cost of Sales/Inventory						31 11.7
85 4.3	73 5.0	76 4.8							51 7.2
135 2.7	104 3.5	139 2.6							78 4.7
12 30.4	20 17.8	23 15.8	Cost of Sales/Payables						31 11.8
29 12.7	29 12.6	33 11.1							41 8.8
53 6.9	43 8.4	51 7.1							53 6.8
3.5	4.3	4.1	Sales/Working Capital						7.5
6.3	7.2	9.6							14.0
13.2	24.8	21.6							−73.6
9.3	5.2	22.1	EBIT/Interest						
(34) 3.8	(29) 1.3	(31) 7.9							
1.3	−3.1	4.6							
			Net Profit + Depr., Dep., Amort./Cur. Mat. L/T/D						
.4	.5	.3	Fixed/Worth						.6
.8	.8	.6							1.2
1.2	2.4	1.1							7.1
.8	.7	.6	Debt/Worth						1.9
1.5	1.2	1.3							3.4
2.4	5.6	2.5							17.7
38.1	18.4	59.2	% Profit Before Taxes/Tangible Net Worth						
(31) 14.3	(29) 1.0	(35) 16.2							
2.3	−10.2	4.9							
12.9	8.8	17.0	% Profit Before Taxes/Total Assets						17.0
4.9	1.1	6.7							8.7
1.2	−4.4	2.1							5.3
15.3	14.5	15.5	Sales/Net Fixed Assets						10.1
5.5	6.7	8.1							6.3
3.6	4.2	5.0							5.4
2.3	2.6	3.0	Sales/Total Assets						2.8
1.7	1.9	2.0							2.0
1.1	1.3	1.4							1.5
1.5	2.1	1.7	% Depr., Dep., Amort./Sales						
(30) 2.9	(29) 3.1	(33) 2.9							
4.5	4.4	3.3							
			% Officers', Directors', Owners' Comp/Sales						
1018324M	839739M	1127958M	Net Sales ($)	1368M	18102M	11116M	56060M	121717M	919595M
825166M	647294M	652962M	Total Assets ($)	622M	11606M	11771M	30448M	78087M	520428M

Current Data Sorted By Assets   **Comparative Historical Data**

Type of Statement

0-500M	500M-2MM	2-10MM	10-50MM	50-100MM	100-250MM	Type of Statement	4/1/00-3/31/01 ALL	4/1/01-3/31/02 ALL
		8	13	3		Unqualified	39	20
1	2	17	4			Reviewed	25	22
	7	11				Compiled	26	28
1	2	1				Tax Returns	8	1
1	10	14	8	2	1	Other	44	32

19 (4/1-9/30/04) covers 0-500M through 2-10MM; 87 (10/1/04-3/31/05) covers 10-50MM through 100-250MM.

0-500M	500M-2MM	2-10MM	10-50MM	50-100MM	100-250MM		4/1/00-3/31/01 ALL	4/1/01-3/31/02 ALL
3	21	51	25	5	1	**NUMBER OF STATEMENTS**	142	103
%	%	%	%	%	%	**ASSETS**	%	%
	7.7	6.8	8.6			Cash & Equivalents	7.2	8.2
	35.4	29.8	26.6			Trade Receivables (net)	27.5	28.9
	32.4	31.8	30.8			Inventory	30.0	28.4
	2.3	1.8	1.7			All Other Current	2.6	2.8
	77.9	70.2	67.8			Total Current	67.2	68.3
	17.6	20.1	23.7			Fixed Assets (net)	23.5	22.2
	1.3	3.9	2.5			Intangibles (net)	3.9	3.1
	3.3	5.8	6.1			All Other Non-Current	5.3	6.4
	100.0	100.0	100.0			Total	100.0	100.0
						LIABILITIES		
	7.2	15.6	8.2			Notes Payable-Short Term	11.6	9.4
	2.4	2.4	2.7			Cur. Mat.-L/T/D	3.1	2.9
	20.3	14.3	10.5			Trade Payables	12.9	13.4
	.3	.3	.4			Income Taxes Payable	.4	.4
	9.8	9.5	12.5			All Other Current	11.1	10.7
	39.9	42.2	34.2			Total Current	39.1	36.8
	13.8	9.6	8.9			Long-Term Debt	11.2	9.2
	.0	.5	1.1			Deferred Taxes	.6	.6
	17.6	4.4	3.3			All Other Non-Current	3.8	3.1
	28.7	43.3	52.4			Net Worth	45.3	50.3
	100.0	100.0	100.0			Total Liabilities & Net Worth	100.0	100.0
						INCOME DATA		
	100.0	100.0	100.0			Net Sales	100.0	100.0
	33.3	33.4	27.7			Gross Profit	33.8	33.1
	29.5	28.8	22.5			Operating Expenses	28.7	28.8
	3.8	4.6	5.2			Operating Profit	5.1	4.2
	.9	.9	.6			All Other Expenses (net)	.9	.8
	2.9	3.7	4.6			Profit Before Taxes	4.2	3.4
						RATIOS		
	3.2	2.5	3.7				2.6	3.5
	2.1	1.8	2.2			Current	1.7	1.9
	1.5	1.2	1.4				1.3	1.3
	1.3	1.5	2.0				1.4	1.8
	1.0	.9	1.2			Quick	.9	1.1
	.8	.8	.7				.6	.6
39 9.4	39 9.2	46 7.9					41 9.0	41 8.8
49 7.5	56 6.5	54 6.8				Sales/Receivables	54 6.8	51 7.2
67 5.4	72 5.1	62 5.9					68 5.4	65 5.7
60 6.1	54 6.7	63 5.8					46 7.9	48 7.7
92 4.0	76 4.8	77 4.8				Cost of Sales/Inventory	86 4.3	78 4.7
102 3.6	129 2.8	116 3.1					141 2.6	118 3.1
27 13.5	19 18.8	20 18.5					20 18.3	18 19.7
34 10.8	31 11.6	25 14.4				Cost of Sales/Payables	34 10.7	32 11.3
58 6.2	58 6.3	38 9.6					51 7.1	49 7.5
	4.9	3.8	3.6				4.3	3.5
	6.7	6.8	5.3			Sales/Working Capital	6.7	6.7
	9.9	20.0	10.0				14.9	13.7
	6.3	17.4	27.7				12.6	17.9
	(18) 3.6	(47) 4.7	(19) 7.2			EBIT/Interest	(126) 3.5	(95) 3.4
	1.2	1.4	2.4				1.3	1.0
		9.6					12.3	6.7
		(14) 3.5				Net Profit + Depr., Dep., Amort./Cur. Mat. L /T/D	(39) 3.0	(31) 1.8
		1.1					.6	1.2
	.1	.2	.3				.2	.2
	.3	.5	.5			Fixed/Worth	.5	.4
	1.3	1.0	.6				1.1	.9
	.9	.6	.5				.7	.4
	1.3	1.3	.8			Debt/Worth	1.3	1.0
	3.3	3.0	2.2				2.9	2.7
	21.2	32.7	25.0				31.5	33.4
	(19) 12.6	(47) 17.7	(24) 12.6			% Profit Before Taxes/Tangible Net Worth	(133) 15.3	(99) 10.3
	2.1	4.8	6.9				3.7	.2
	9.3	14.1	11.8				13.9	13.9
	5.6	5.1	6.3			% Profit Before Taxes/Total Assets	6.3	5.8
	.4	.8	4.1				.8	.1
	83.9	37.7	11.8				21.2	26.6
	25.1	13.7	7.0			Sales/Net Fixed Assets	9.9	10.7
	5.6	5.7	5.4				4.6	5.0
	3.1	2.6	2.1				2.3	2.4
	2.5	2.1	1.9			Sales/Total Assets	1.8	2.0
	1.8	1.5	1.4				1.4	1.4
	.8	.8	1.2				1.0	.9
	(16) 1.8	(46) 1.5	2.3			% Depr., Dep., Amort./Sales	(121) 2.1	(91) 1.9
	2.4	2.5	3.0				3.6	3.3
		2.1					2.4	1.6
		(22) 4.4				% Officers', Directors', Owners' Comp/Sales	(48) 5.7	(31) 4.2
		5.5					9.2	9.2
2353M	60563M	492159M	912847M	452046M	203554M	Net Sales ($)	3098900M	2495037M
1037M	25306M	248249M	516137M	300241M	165344M	Total Assets ($)	2032966M	1744982M

M = $ thousand   MM = $ million
See Pages 11 through 21 for Explanation of Ratios and Data

Comparative Historical Data   **Current Data Sorted By Sales**

	4/1/02-3/31/03 ALL	4/1/03-3/31/04 ALL	4/1/04-3/31/05 ALL	Type of Statement	0-1MM	1-3MM	3-5MM	5-10MM	10-25MM	25MM & OVER
						19 (4/1-9/30/04)		87 (10/1/04-3/31/05)			
	30	19	24	Unqualified		1	2	3	7	12
	21	18	24	Reviewed	1	1	4	6	11	1
	20	30	18	Compiled		5	5	5	2	
	2	7	4	Tax Returns	1		1	1		1
	39	34	36	Other	1	5	9	5	9	7
	112	108	106	**NUMBER OF STATEMENTS**	3	12	21	20	29	21
	%	%	%	**ASSETS**	%	%	%	%	%	%
	8.4	7.5	7.9	Cash & Equivalents		4.9	6.3	7.8	10.6	7.4
	28.2	28.7	30.7	Trade Receivables (net)		33.2	25.3	34.6	28.4	29.6
	30.0	31.4	31.1	Inventory		32.8	29.4	29.4	34.2	30.3
	2.5	3.2	1.9	All Other Current		3.0	1.9	1.1	1.7	2.2
	69.2	70.7	71.6	Total Current		74.0	62.9	72.9	75.0	69.5
	21.0	20.6	20.3	Fixed Assets (net)		19.1	26.6	15.3	19.6	22.9
	3.1	3.5	3.0	Intangibles (net)		2.4	3.6	5.4	.9	3.6
	6.6	5.2	5.2	All Other Non-Current		4.5	7.0	6.4	4.6	4.1
	100.0	100.0	100.0	Total		100.0	100.0	100.0	100.0	100.0
				LIABILITIES						
	11.1	13.5	12.5	Notes Payable-Short Term		10.6	7.7	18.2	12.3	7.6
	4.3	4.1	2.6	Cur. Mat.-L/T/D		2.0	2.7	2.8	2.0	3.8
	13.9	16.8	14.9	Trade Payables		19.1	15.3	15.6	11.3	13.1
	.2	.3	.3	Income Taxes Payable		.4	.0	.2	.7	.3
	10.8	8.5	10.6	All Other Current		12.4	6.8	8.6	11.5	13.7
	40.2	43.2	40.9	Total Current		44.5	32.5	45.4	37.7	38.5
	10.6	10.2	9.9	Long-Term Debt		14.8	16.6	7.9	5.8	9.2
	.4	.6	.5	Deferred Taxes		.2	.4	.4	.9	.5
	4.0	4.5	7.1	All Other Non-Current		6.0	16.6	3.0	4.1	7.3
	44.7	41.6	41.6	Net Worth		34.5	33.8	43.3	51.5	44.6
	100.0	100.0	100.0	Total Liabilities & Net Worth		100.0	100.0	100.0	100.0	100.0
				INCOME DATA						
	100.0	100.0	100.0	Net Sales		100.0	100.0	100.0	100.0	100.0
	32.5	32.2	31.6	Gross Profit		33.3	34.5	34.8	31.2	25.3
	29.2	29.5	27.1	Operating Expenses		28.9	30.4	30.8	25.9	20.3
	3.4	2.8	4.6	Operating Profit		4.4	4.1	4.0	5.3	5.0
	1.2	.6	.8	All Other Expenses (net)		.9	1.4	.6	.6	.7
	2.1	2.2	3.8	Profit Before Taxes		3.5	2.7	3.4	4.7	4.3
				RATIOS						
	3.6	3.2	3.1			2.2	2.6	3.7	5.2	3.6
	1.9	1.7	1.9	Current		1.6	1.9	1.4	2.3	1.9
	1.2	1.2	1.3			1.5	1.6	1.1	1.4	1.3
	1.8	1.4	1.5			1.1	1.4	1.6	2.9	2.0
	1.0	.9	.9	Quick		.9	.9	.8	1.3	1.1
	.6	.5	.6			.5	.6	.6	.7	.6
	41 8.9	39 9.4	41 8.8			41 9.0	32 11.4	43 8.5	33 10.9	47 7.7
	51 7.2	49 7.4	55 6.6	Sales/Receivables		52 7.1	49 7.5	54 6.7	53 6.9	58 6.3
	67 5.5	70 5.2	70 5.2			77 4.7	66 5.5	73 5.0	70 5.2	66 5.5
	52 7.0	51 7.2	58 6.3			63 5.8	62 5.9	34 10.7	63 5.8	54 6.8
	85 4.3	80 4.5	80 4.5	Cost of Sales/Inventory		92 4.0	96 3.8	59 6.2	93 3.9	76 4.8
	126 2.9	131 2.8	118 3.1			113 3.2	125 2.9	139 2.6	119 3.1	108 3.4
	19 18.8	21 17.3	21 17.5			32 11.6	21 17.3	25 14.5	15 25.0	18 19.8
	29 12.5	29 12.6	31 11.7	Cost of Sales/Payables		36 10.2	36 10.0	31 11.7	26 13.9	30 12.1
	52 7.0	49 7.5	49 7.5			79 4.6	65 5.6	52 7.0	37 9.8	42 8.7
	3.5	3.9	4.1			4.4	4.6	4.7	2.7	4.0
	6.3	7.4	6.3	Sales/Working Capital		6.1	7.6	10.7	5.3	6.1
	17.4	21.4	14.1			12.4	9.4	39.8	9.4	13.7
	9.7	14.3	15.8			7.0	8.5	12.0	22.2	23.7
	(99) 3.0	(97) 3.2	(91) 4.8	EBIT/Interest		2.7	(18) 3.8	(18) 3.5	(23) 6.9	(18) 7.3
	.4	.7	1.4			.4	-.6	1.5	2.4	2.3
	4.7	4.2	8.5	Net Profit + Depr., Dep.,						
	(31) 2.0	(32) 1.5	(26) 2.1	Amort./Cur. Mat. L/T/D						
	.3	.8	.9							
	.2	.2	.2			.2	.1	.2	.1	.4
	.4	.4	.5	Fixed/Worth		.5	.7	.4	.3	.5
	1.0	1.1	1.0			1.4	1.8	1.6	.7	1.2
	.5	.6	.6			1.2	.6	.5	.4	.6
	1.2	1.4	1.3	Debt/Worth		1.9	1.3	1.7	.9	1.7
	3.5	3.4	3.0			5.9	2.8	9.2	1.8	3.4
	26.0	20.0	30.3	% Profit Before Taxes/Tangible		31.3	21.2	34.6	29.7	33.0
	(100) 10.0	(97) 9.9	(97) 13.9	Net Worth	(11) 4.9	(19) 13.1	(19) 12.9	(27) 21.9	(20) 15.5
	1.8	.8	5.1			-1.9	3.8	6.0	4.8	9.4
	9.7	9.2	13.3	% Profit Before Taxes/Total		10.2	9.3	11.0	14.6	15.0
	3.9	3.5	5.6	Assets		4.0	5.6	4.8	8.6	7.1
	-.7	-.6	.7			-.8	-2.1	1.0	.7	4.1
	25.0	29.7	35.8			80.5	47.7	39.7	39.9	12.1
	10.8	10.3	10.9	Sales/Net Fixed Assets		20.0	6.8	19.3	7.7	7.5
	5.0	5.7	5.6			4.8	2.8	8.6	6.1	5.4
	2.4	2.5	2.5			2.8	2.3	2.8	2.5	2.2
	1.8	1.9	1.9	Sales/Total Assets		1.8	2.0	2.2	2.0	1.9
	1.3	1.4	1.5			1.5	1.2	1.5	1.5	1.5
	1.1	1.0	1.0			.9	1.0	.7	1.1	1.3
	(99) 2.2	(92) 2.2	(94) 1.7	% Depr., Dep., Amort./Sales		(10) 1.9	(17) 1.9	(19) 1.4	(26) 1.6	2.3
	3.3	3.9	2.8			3.1	2.8	2.4	2.8	3.2
	2.0	3.1	2.6							
	(29) 3.6	(36) 4.4	(34) 4.4	% Officers', Directors',						
	9.2	10.6	5.8	Owners' Comp/Sales						
	2069265M	1629986M	2123522M	Net Sales ($)	2353M	24903M	83010M	145469M	477231M	1390556M
	1368973M	1121651M	1256314M	Total Assets ($)	1037M	13811M	51377M	82053M	274371M	833665M

© RMA 2005

M = $ thousand   MM = $ million

See Pages 11 through 21 for Explanation of Ratios and Data

Current Data Sorted By Assets   **Comparative Historical Data**

0-500M	500M-2MM	2-10MM	10-50MM	50-100MM	100-250MM	Type of Statement	4/1/00-3/31/01 ALL	4/1/01-3/31/02 ALL
		2				Unqualified	5	2
	1	7	1			Reviewed	4	2
	1	1				Compiled	5	4
1						Tax Returns	1	1
		4	6			Other	10	7
	4 (4/1-9/30/04)		**20 (10/1/04-3/31/05)**					
1	2	14	7			**NUMBER OF STATEMENTS**	25	16
%	%	%	%	%	%	**ASSETS**	%	%
		4.1				Cash & Equivalents	4.0	3.2
		29.1		D	D	Trade Receivables (net)	31.0	25.3
		36.1		A	A	Inventory	36.8	42.2
		2.7		T	T	All Other Current	2.3	3.3
		72.0		A	A	Total Current	74.1	74.0
		15.9				Fixed Assets (net)	16.4	18.2
		3.4		N	N	Intangibles (net)	3.0	3.6
		8.8		O	O	All Other Non-Current	6.5	4.2
		100.0		T	T	Total	100.0	100.0
						LIABILITIES		
		20.5		A	A	Notes Payable-Short Term	12.6	20.4
		1.8		V	V	Cur. Mat.-L/T/D	4.5	1.3
		14.2		A	A	Trade Payables	18.7	11.2
		.2		I	I	Income Taxes Payable	.7	.4
		10.2		L	L	All Other Current	14.5	14.2
		46.8		A	A	Total Current	51.0	47.5
		10.7		B	B	Long-Term Debt	12.6	8.3
		.2		L	L	Deferred Taxes	.3	.5
		12.4		E	E	All Other Non-Current	5.7	2.5
		29.9				Net Worth	30.4	41.2
		100.0				Total Liabilities & Net Worth	100.0	100.0
						INCOME DATA		
		100.0				Net Sales	100.0	100.0
		27.5				Gross Profit	33.4	38.7
		24.3				Operating Expenses	28.2	35.1
		3.3				Operating Profit	5.2	3.6
		1.2				All Other Expenses (net)	.9	1.8
		2.1				Profit Before Taxes	4.3	1.8
						RATIOS		
		2.6					2.0	2.5
		1.5				Current	1.5	1.7
		1.2					1.1	1.0
		1.1					.9	1.3
		.8				Quick	.6 (15)	.6
		.5					.5	.4
	48	7.6					39 9.5	33 11.1
	65	5.7				Sales/Receivables	55 6.6	43 8.5
	82	4.5					68 5.4	65 5.6
	83	4.4					68 5.4	71 5.1
	101	3.6				Cost of Sales/Inventory	85 4.3	85 4.3
	132	2.8					146 2.5	272 1.3
	24	15.1					31 11.9	14 26.8
	42	8.6				Cost of Sales/Payables	41 8.9	36 10.0
	61	6.0					76 7.9	46 7.9
		4.4					4.9	3.2
		7.3				Sales/Working Capital	7.1	5.4
		13.2					72.1	NM
		4.6					(21) 7.5	(13) 3.1
		(13) 1.2				EBIT/Interest	3.3	1.2
		-1.6					1.4	.0
						Net Profit + Depr., Dep., Amort./Cur. Mat. L /T/D		
		.0					.2	.2
		.6				Fixed/Worth	.4	.6
		3.2					1.8	.9
		.7					1.1	.9
		2.5				Debt/Worth	1.7	1.3
		30.6					5.8	3.7
		26.4					(21) 49.2	(15) 32.4
		(12) 5.2				% Profit Before Taxes/Tangible Net Worth	24.1	1.0
		-7.3					6.6	-6.7
		6.0					16.9	6.1
		1.3				% Profit Before Taxes/Total Assets	6.7	.4
		-3.3					.5	-3.9
		63.0					34.0	25.6
		31.8				Sales/Net Fixed Assets	14.1	10.6
		6.4					8.5	5.4
		2.0					2.7	2.6
		1.7				Sales/Total Assets	2.3	1.7
		1.3					1.4	1.2
		.8					(21) 1.0	(14) .8
		(10) 1.2				% Depr., Dep., Amort./Sales	1.5	1.7
		2.6					2.4	2.4
						% Officers', Directors', Owners' Comp/Sales		
1073M	1795M	109457M	177656M			Net Sales ($)	659447M	488243M
364M	1896M	65682M	163189M			Total Assets ($)	412036M	303048M

M = $ thousand   MM = $ million
See Pages 11 through 21 for Explanation of Ratios and Data

Comparative Historical Data				Current Data Sorted By Sales					

© RMA 2005

			Type of Statement						
5	4	2	Unqualified		1		1		
7	7	9	Reviewed	1	1		5	2	
4	8	1	Compiled	1		1			
1	1	1	Tax Returns			1			
6	13	11	Other		1		3	4	3
4/1/02- 3/31/03 ALL	4/1/03- 3/31/04 ALL	4/1/04- 3/31/05 ALL		4 (4/1-9/30/04)		20 (10/1/04-3/31/05)			
				0-1MM	1-3MM	3-5MM	5-10MM	10-25MM	25MM & OVER
23	33	24	NUMBER OF STATEMENTS	2	1	3	9	6	3
%	%	%	ASSETS	%	%	%	%	%	%
7.7	5.6	4.2	Cash & Equivalents						
34.3	27.8	24.3	Trade Receivables (net)						
30.8	31.5	38.0	Inventory						
1.5	1.2	1.9	All Other Current						
74.4	66.1	68.4	Total Current						
17.2	26.6	18.7	Fixed Assets (net)						
4.8	3.1	4.1	Intangibles (net)						
3.6	4.2	8.8	All Other Non-Current						
100.0	100.0	100.0	Total						
			LIABILITIES						
11.1	16.0	18.0	Notes Payable-Short Term						
3.6	2.6	1.9	Cur. Mat.-L/T/D						
23.5	17.2	12.7	Trade Payables						
.1	.3	.2	Income Taxes Payable						
12.4	9.0	9.6	All Other Current						
50.6	45.0	42.3	Total Current						
13.6	14.7	11.6	Long-Term Debt						
.1	.2	.4	Deferred Taxes						
13.1	8.0	10.3	All Other Non-Current						
22.5	32.1	35.3	Net Worth						
100.0	100.0	100.0	Total Liabilities & Net Worth						
			INCOME DATA						
100.0	100.0	100.0	Net Sales						
33.5	36.0	32.0	Gross Profit						
30.1	32.5	27.5	Operating Expenses						
3.4	3.5	4.5	Operating Profit						
2.2	2.5	1.3	All Other Expenses (net)						
1.2	.9	3.2	Profit Before Taxes						
			RATIOS						
1.9	2.5	2.5							
1.4	1.7	1.5	Current						
1.2	1.2	1.3							
1.1	1.1	.9							
.8	.8	.7	Quick						
.6	.6	.5							
42	8.8	43	8.6	35	10.4		Sales/Receivables		
53	6.9	53	6.9	57	6.5				
76	4.8	71	5.1	79	4.6				
31	11.7	56	6.6	85	4.3		Cost of Sales/Inventory		
100	3.7	92	4.0	104	3.5				
163	2.2	201	1.8	168	2.2				
24	15.2	21	17.7	21	17.3		Cost of Sales/Payables		
35	10.3	36	10.1	44	8.3				
105	3.5	73	5.0	64	5.7				
4.4	3.7	3.5	Sales/Working Capital						
13.1	6.3	6.2							
30.1	16.7	12.7							
	12.9		9.7		4.5		EBIT/Interest		
(20)	3.8	(30)	2.4	(22)	1.4				
	1.2		-.9		-1.0				
			Net Profit + Depr., Dep., Amort./Cur. Mat. L/T/D						
.1	.1	.1	Fixed/Worth						
.4	.7	.5							
4.4	3.9	1.9							
1.1	.9	.7	Debt/Worth						
2.2	2.0	2.0							
-34.6	5.4	4.6							
	33.4		24.8		24.3		% Profit Before Taxes/Tangible Net Worth		
(17)	10.5	(27)	4.8	(22)	3.1				
	1.6		-6.6		-6.7				
12.9	8.0	9.0	% Profit Before Taxes/Total Assets						
4.4	2.2	1.0							
.7	-4.4	-2.9							
54.6	41.8	47.8	Sales/Net Fixed Assets						
14.8	12.0	11.3							
9.6	4.0	4.9							
3.3	2.3	1.9	Sales/Total Assets						
1.9	1.5	1.5							
1.1	1.0	1.2							
	.7		1.1		1.0		% Depr., Dep., Amort./Sales		
(20)	1.5	(25)	1.6	(18)	1.3				
	3.7		3.7		3.0				
	2.5						% Officers', Directors', Owners' Comp/Sales		
(10)	4.5								
	7.6								
309898M	506968M	289981M	Net Sales ($)	1795M	1073M	11589M	64941M	96721M	113862M
254450M	425253M	231131M	Total Assets ($)	1896M	364M	8540M	40062M	88487M	91782M

M = $ thousand   MM = $ million
See Pages 11 through 21 for Explanation of Ratios and Data

Current Data Sorted By Assets   **Comparative Historical Data**

0-500M	500M-2MM	2-10MM	10-50MM	50-100MM	100-250MM	Type of Statement	4/1/00-3/31/01 ALL	4/1/01-3/31/02 ALL
	1	6	11		2	Unqualified	22	20
1	9	26	7			Reviewed	32	21
1	14	6	1			Compiled	26	27
1	2	2				Tax Returns	4	5
1	2	16	4	3		Other	29	29
	38 (4/1-9/30/04)		78 (10/1/04-3/31/05)					
4	28	56	23	3	2	NUMBER OF STATEMENTS	113	102
%	%	%	%	%	%	ASSETS	%	%
	10.5	6.6	14.5			Cash & Equivalents	9.3	10.7
	41.1	34.2	35.6			Trade Receivables (net)	34.7	33.3
	24.6	24.9	18.0			Inventory	19.9	21.5
	1.2	2.4	5.1			All Other Current	6.0	5.2
	77.4	68.1	73.2			Total Current	69.9	70.7
	16.8	23.2	17.8			Fixed Assets (net)	20.6	20.1
	1.6	1.8	1.3			Intangibles (net)	4.5	3.4
	4.2	7.0	7.7			All Other Non-Current	4.9	5.7
	100.0	100.0	100.0			Total	100.0	100.0
						LIABILITIES		
	13.1	13.6	8.3			Notes Payable-Short Term	8.8	11.4
	1.8	3.6	2.2			Cur. Mat.-L/T/D	1.7	3.2
	25.2	17.1	17.5			Trade Payables	16.6	16.3
	.7	.4	.1			Income Taxes Payable	.8	.5
	11.8	16.1	16.0			All Other Current	16.8	14.4
	52.6	50.8	44.1			Total Current	44.7	45.8
	6.3	10.8	11.4			Long-Term Debt	10.2	10.8
	.3	.5	.3			Deferred Taxes	.8	.5
	8.7	4.0	4.2			All Other Non-Current	3.9	4.5
	32.1	33.9	40.0			Net Worth	40.4	38.3
	100.0	100.0	100.0			Total Liabilities & Net Worth	100.0	100.0
						INCOME DATA		
	100.0	100.0	100.0			Net Sales	100.0	100.0
	31.7	30.6	22.9			Gross Profit	28.8	28.8
	30.1	27.9	21.0			Operating Expenses	25.7	26.8
	1.6	2.7	1.9			Operating Profit	3.2	2.1
	.3	.8	.7			All Other Expenses (net)	.0	.8
	1.3	1.9	1.2			Profit Before Taxes	3.2	1.2
						RATIOS		
	2.1	2.0	2.5			Current	2.8	3.0
	1.4	1.4	1.5				1.7	1.6
	1.1	1.1	1.3				1.2	1.1
	1.5	1.3	1.8			Quick	1.6	1.9
	1.0	.9	1.0				1.0	1.0
	.7	.5	.8				.7	.6
35 10.5	43 8.5	51 7.1				Sales/Receivables	42 8.6	39 9.3
51 7.2	57 6.4	59 6.2					52 7.1	53 6.9
65 5.6	74 4.9	74 4.9					71 5.2	67 5.5
11 32.8	30 12.3	25 14.9				Cost of Sales/Inventory	18 20.0	20 18.2
47 7.7	63 5.8	53 6.9					45 8.1	48 7.5
99 3.7	101 3.6	96 3.8					75 4.9	77 4.7
26 14.1	24 15.5	18 19.9				Cost of Sales/Payables	19 19.1	16 22.3
36 10.0	38 9.5	35 10.4					29 12.7	27 13.6
72 5.1	51 7.1	61 6.0					45 8.1	39 9.3
	5.4	5.9	3.6			Sales/Working Capital	5.2	5.0
	15.0	10.8	7.9				8.4	8.3
	43.4	100.1	13.8				28.0	35.1
	21.4	8.5	11.1			EBIT/Interest	11.0	6.0
	(26) 4.8	(52) 3.5	(20) 6.6				(101) 3.4	(93) 1.7
	.6	-.5	-.6				1.4	-.3
		3.5	5.9			Net Profit + Depr., Dep., Amort./Cur. Mat. L /T/D	6.5	4.3
	(15) 1.3	(10) 3.0					(33) 2.6	(27) 1.7
		-.5	.0				1.3	.0
	.2	.2	.2			Fixed/Worth	.2	.2
	.5	.7	.4				.5	.5
	.8	1.7	.9				1.5	1.2
	.9	.8	.7			Debt/Worth	.6	.6
	2.0	2.2	2.0				1.4	1.6
	7.3	5.2	3.4				4.0	5.4
	55.4	36.9	41.6			% Profit Before Taxes/Tangible Net Worth	38.9	20.9
	(24) 12.3	(48) 13.4	13.2				(102) 15.4	(93) 5.6
	.2	-4.0	-5.8				3.9	-7.4
	11.0	11.0	10.5			% Profit Before Taxes/Total Assets	13.9	9.7
	4.8	4.1	4.9				5.7	1.8
	-2.1	-3.9	-1.6				1.0	-3.2
	49.0	21.0	19.9			Sales/Net Fixed Assets	26.0	28.7
	21.8	11.8	10.8				14.8	15.6
	7.7	5.9	5.5				6.0	6.3
	4.3	2.5	2.3			Sales/Total Assets	2.9	2.9
	2.6	2.1	1.8				2.1	2.3
	2.2	1.7	1.2				1.7	1.6
	.9	1.0	.5			% Depr., Dep., Amort./Sales	.7	.6
	(25) 1.2	(55) 1.7	1.6				(101) 1.5	(95) 1.4
	2.4	3.0	3.2				2.5	2.5
	3.4	2.0				% Officers', Directors', Owners' Comp/Sales	2.4	2.0
	(15) 4.7	(18) 4.7					(38) 5.0	(36) 3.7
	7.9	10.7					8.3	7.1
4976M	106521M	536037M	884196M	175993M	419416M	Net Sales ($)	2144365M	2053986M
1462M	34481M	263664M	496872M	183460M	364406M	Total Assets ($)	1337823M	1133427M

M = $ thousand   MM = $ million
See Pages 11 through 21 for Explanation of Ratios and Data

Comparative Historical Data — **Current Data Sorted By Sales**

			Type of Statement						
21	19	20	Unqualified			1	5	4	10
35	44	43	Reviewed	3	3	4	17	12	4
14	30	22	Compiled		7	7	6	1	1
2	4	5	Tax Returns	1	2		2		
31	26	26	Other	1		1	7	10	7
4/1/02-3/31/03 ALL	4/1/03-3/31/04 ALL	4/1/04-3/31/05 ALL			38 (4/1-9/30/04)			78 (10/1/04-3/31/05)	
				0-1MM	1-3MM	3-5MM	5-10MM	10-25MM	25MM & OVER
103	123	116	**NUMBER OF STATEMENTS**	5	12	13	37	27	22
%	%	%	**ASSETS**	%	%	%	%	%	%
9.0	10.5	9.1	Cash & Equivalents		5.8	7.7	10.2	8.1	9.0
31.8	31.4	35.8	Trade Receivables (net)		52.8	26.4	33.9	35.7	38.1
22.6	24.9	22.8	Inventory		22.1	27.3	25.7	22.1	13.9
4.4	3.5	3.1	All Other Current		1.0	2.5	1.8	2.3	8.5
67.9	70.3	70.8	Total Current		81.7	63.9	71.7	68.3	69.5
21.2	20.2	20.0	Fixed Assets (net)		16.1	23.9	19.9	21.9	18.2
4.5	2.5	2.9	Intangibles (net)		1.1	.7	1.9	1.7	8.5
6.4	6.9	6.3	All Other Non-Current		1.1	11.5	6.5	8.1	3.7
100.0	100.0	100.0	Total		100.0	100.0	100.0	100.0	100.0
			LIABILITIES						
10.4	9.6	13.3	Notes Payable-Short Term		9.6	17.9	13.9	8.8	16.3
3.9	3.5	2.9	Cur. Mat.-L/T/D		3.1	2.1	2.2	4.6	2.4
15.6	14.4	19.2	Trade Payables		34.2	16.7	19.4	14.9	19.0
.4	.3	.4	Income Taxes Payable		1.3	.1	.4	.2	.1
15.5	19.2	15.4	All Other Current		10.6	15.0	12.4	19.1	16.2
45.8	47.0	51.2	Total Current		58.8	51.8	48.3	47.6	54.0
13.0	8.6	9.5	Long-Term Debt		5.7	12.9	8.5	9.5	11.4
.5	.7	.4	Deferred Taxes		.0	.6	.3	.7	.2
8.0	6.5	5.7	All Other Non-Current		3.9	9.0	2.8	4.9	6.7
32.7	37.3	33.2	Net Worth		31.6	25.7	40.1	37.2	27.6
100.0	100.0	100.0	Total Liabilities & Net Worth		100.0	100.0	100.0	100.0	100.0
			INCOME DATA						
100.0	100.0	100.0	Net Sales		100.0	100.0	100.0	100.0	100.0
30.5	31.1	28.9	Gross Profit		33.3	33.1	30.9	26.7	21.8
27.9	27.9	26.7	Operating Expenses		32.2	33.8	28.5	23.3	18.9
2.6	3.2	2.2	Operating Profit		1.1	-.7	2.4	3.4	2.9
1.1	.6	1.0	All Other Expenses (net)		.6	1.3	.5	.6	2.1
1.4	2.6	1.2	Profit Before Taxes		.5	-2.0	1.9	2.8	.8
			RATIOS						
2.3	2.4	2.1			2.9	1.6	2.2	2.7	2.1
1.5	1.6	1.4	Current		1.2	1.4	1.6	1.4	1.4
1.1	1.1	1.1			1.0	1.0	1.1	1.0	1.2
1.4	1.6	1.4			1.4	1.0	1.5	1.5	1.2
.8	.9	.9	Quick		1.0	.8	.9	.9	.9
.6	.6	.6			.9	.5	.5	.6	.8
41 8.9	39 9.5	43 8.5			50 7.3	32 11.5	33 11.1	47 7.7	55 6.6
52 7.0	52 7.1	57 6.4	Sales/Receivables		60 6.1	47 7.8	53 6.9	57 6.4	63 5.8
75 4.9	72 5.1	70 5.2			78 4.7	65 5.6	58 6.2	84 4.3	87 4.2
27 13.4	28 12.9	24 15.0			0 UND	39 9.3	26 14.2	31 11.7	7 49.3
58 6.3	51 7.2	53 6.9	Cost of Sales/Inventory		46 7.9	78 4.7	52 7.0	62 5.9	27 13.8
92 4.0	111 3.3	99 3.7			103 3.6	107 3.4	109 3.4	86 4.3	60 6.0
21 17.2	18 20.3	26 14.2			37 9.8	22 16.5	22 16.6	19 19.7	26 14.0
33 11.1	30 12.2	38 9.6	Cost of Sales/Payables		55 6.6	28 13.1	35 10.4	36 10.2	40 9.2
54 6.8	44 8.3	55 6.7			87 4.2	78 4.7	50 7.3	48 7.6	62 5.9
5.5	5.1	5.1			4.5	7.8	5.1	4.0	5.3
8.8	9.4	10.8	Sales/Working Capital		27.7	11.7	12.4	9.4	9.4
26.9	28.7	40.5			106.2	NM	32.0	121.0	18.5
7.6	11.8	10.6			10.9	4.2	19.5	14.6	8.8
(98) 2.8	(107) 3.6	(106) 3.8	EBIT/Interest		2.1	(12) 1.6	(33) 4.9	(26) 3.8	(20) 5.2
.9	.1	-.6			-1.8	-1.5	-.5	.4	-1.8
4.2	3.6	3.4	Net Profit + Depr., Dep.,						
(42) 1.4	(38) 1.7	(32) 1.5	Amort./Cur. Mat. L/T/D						
.5	.7	-.1							
.3	.3	.2			.2	.4	.2	.2	.3
.6	.6	.6	Fixed/Worth		.4	.8	.6	.6	.6
1.7	1.3	1.5			1.3	NM	1.0	1.9	2.8
.8	.6	.8			.7	1.4	.6	.8	1.5
2.2	1.3	2.2	Debt/Worth		3.1	2.0	1.5	1.7	3.1
7.5	5.7	6.4			15.7	NM	3.4	5.1	21.7
27.3	31.4	39.3	% Profit Before Taxes/Tangible		13.1	24.1	44.7	33.8	73.4
(89) 10.3	(104) 10.2	(99) 13.3	Net Worth	(11) 4.8	(10) 13.4	(33) 9.9	(24) 15.9	(18) 21.6	
.1	1.8	-2.7			-24.1	-17.3	-3.6	2.7	1.9
8.9	9.9	10.7	% Profit Before Taxes/Total		7.4	4.9	15.2	10.7	10.8
3.9	4.1	4.7	Assets		2.7	-.1	4.8	5.1	6.1
-.1	-1.0	-3.3			-4.0	-5.6	-3.5	-1.1	-2.1
21.8	28.2	32.1			64.2	40.9	34.5	21.1	24.0
11.3	13.4	13.2	Sales/Net Fixed Assets		30.3	10.8	14.7	11.9	12.7
5.9	5.8	6.1			6.8	3.4	7.1	4.9	8.1
2.6	2.9	2.6			4.2	2.5	3.0	2.4	2.4
2.0	2.1	2.2	Sales/Total Assets		2.7	2.2	2.2	2.1	2.0
1.5	1.5	1.6			1.7	1.2	1.8	1.6	1.3
1.1	1.0	.9			.9	1.2	.8	1.0	.4
(100) 1.8	(110) 1.6	(109) 1.6	% Depr., Dep., Amort./Sales	(11) 1.2	2.7	(36) 1.6	(26) 1.6	(21) 1.1	
2.7	3.1	2.9			2.5	6.2	2.9	2.3	2.7
2.2	2.1	2.5	% Officers', Directors',				2.3		
(29) 3.3	(34) 4.4	(35) 4.3	Owners' Comp/Sales			(14) 3.8			
7.8	7.9	8.0					8.7		
2141726M	2708009M	2127139M	Net Sales ($)	3163M	27082M	49329M	268678M	400749M	1378138M
1363320M	1762421M	1344345M	Total Assets ($)	2864M	11288M	31530M	141152M	243973M	913538M

M = $ thousand   MM = $ million
See Pages 11 through 21 for Explanation of Ratios and Data

Current Data Sorted By Assets   Comparative Historical Data

0-500M	500M-2MM	2-10MM	10-50MM	50-100MM	100-250MM	Type of Statement	4/1/00-3/31/01 ALL	4/1/01-3/31/02 ALL
	1	1	3	1		Unqualified	4	5
	1	4	1		1	Reviewed	3	2
1	4	4	2			Compiled	7	7
	1	2				Tax Returns		3
	3	2				Other	5	8
		4 (4/1-9/30/04)		27 (10/1/04-3/31/05)				
1	9	13	6	1	1	NUMBER OF STATEMENTS	19	25
%	%	%	%	%	%	**ASSETS**	%	%
		2.1				Cash & Equivalents	7.0	6.9
		38.0				Trade Receivables (net)	38.5	34.1
		26.3				Inventory	19.6	22.5
		10.5				All Other Current	6.5	7.4
		76.9				Total Current	71.6	70.9
		12.9				Fixed Assets (net)	23.0	19.9
		3.5				Intangibles (net)	1.1	2.7
		6.7				All Other Non-Current	4.4	6.5
		100.0				Total	100.0	100.0
						LIABILITIES		
		21.2				Notes Payable-Short Term	11.1	9.7
		2.5				Cur. Mat.-L/T/D	2.2	1.9
		17.0				Trade Payables	16.8	16.8
		.2				Income Taxes Payable	1.1	.9
		10.9				All Other Current	18.4	11.3
		51.8				Total Current	49.7	40.6
		5.7				Long-Term Debt	10.7	11.5
		.6				Deferred Taxes	.4	.5
		2.6				All Other Non-Current	3.2	4.2
		39.4				Net Worth	35.9	43.3
		100.0				Total Liabilities & Net Worth	100.0	100.0
						INCOME DATA		
		100.0				Net Sales	100.0	100.0
		29.8				Gross Profit	30.0	29.5
		25.8				Operating Expenses	26.8	28.3
		4.0				Operating Profit	3.2	1.2
		.5				All Other Expenses (net)	.8	.6
		3.5				Profit Before Taxes	2.4	.5
						RATIOS		
		2.4				Current	2.0	2.6
		1.4					1.7	1.7
		1.1					1.1	1.5
		1.5				Quick	1.3	1.4
		.7					1.0	1.2
		.5					.6	.9
		44 8.2				Sales/Receivables	43 8.6	47 7.7
		62 5.9					54 6.8	52 7.0
		70 5.2					72 5.1	61 6.0
		16 22.4				Cost of Sales/Inventory	21 17.1	24 15.3
		50 7.2					43 8.4	48 7.6
		103 3.5					59 6.2	72 5.1
		20 18.1				Cost of Sales/Payables	23 15.7	21 17.4
		31 11.8					28 12.9	37 9.8
		50 7.2					52 7.0	56 6.5
		6.0				Sales/Working Capital	6.6	4.7
		10.6					7.8	8.3
		35.8					126.8	12.4
		17.2				EBIT/Interest	11.4	9.6
		(12) 4.1					2.7	(22) 2.7
		1.8					1.0	−5.8
						Net Profit + Depr., Dep., Amort./Cur. Mat. L /T/D		
		.1				Fixed/Worth	.3	.3
		.2					.5	.4
		1.8					1.4	.8
		.6				Debt/Worth	1.1	.7
		2.0					1.7	1.4
		31.0					4.4	3.2
		54.8				% Profit Before Taxes/Tangible Net Worth	29.3	22.1
		(11) 18.8					(18) 19.4	(24) 4.8
		6.9					−1.2	−27.0
		11.3				% Profit Before Taxes/Total Assets	11.7	9.7
		5.7					5.0	2.1
		.0					.0	−4.6
		85.9				Sales/Net Fixed Assets	29.6	30.7
		39.0					11.7	12.5
		20.1					4.9	5.1
		3.0				Sales/Total Assets	3.1	3.0
		2.3					2.3	1.9
		1.5					1.8	1.6
		.9				% Depr., Dep., Amort./Sales	1.0	.7
		(11) 1.3					1.4	(21) 1.3
		1.6					2.7	2.4
						% Officers', Directors', Owners' Comp/Sales		3.3
							(10)	5.2
								8.4
602M	28838M	132012M	240127M	133431M	147906M	Net Sales ($)	223311M	326064M
317M	10455M	56531M	132805M	87170M	110212M	Total Assets ($)	170193M	186752M

M = $ thousand   MM = $ million
See Pages 11 through 21 for Explanation of Ratios and Data

Comparative Historical Data				Current Data Sorted By Sales					

Type of Statement

Hist 1	Hist 2	Hist 3	Type of Statement	0-1MM	1-3MM	3-5MM	5-10MM	10-25MM	25MM & OVER
7	3	5	Unqualified				1	1	3
4	6	6	Reviewed			2		3	1
11	9	10	Compiled	2	1	2	3	2	
2	4	3	Tax Returns		1		1	1	
6	12	7	Other			1	2	3	1
4/1/02-3/31/03 ALL	4/1/03-3/31/04 ALL	4/1/04-3/31/05 ALL		4 (4/1-9/30/04)			27 (10/1/04-3/31/05)		
30	34	31	**NUMBER OF STATEMENTS**	2	2	5	7	10	5

ASSETS

Hist 1	Hist 2	Hist 3		0-1MM	1-3MM	3-5MM	5-10MM	10-25MM	25MM & OVER
%	%	%		%	%	%	%	%	%
5.7	7.0	4.3	Cash & Equivalents					2.2	
32.5	30.8	34.4	Trade Receivables (net)					36.3	
29.5	28.7	27.4	Inventory					33.2	
4.8	6.4	7.7	All Other Current					7.9	
72.5	72.8	73.9	Total Current					79.5	
18.8	19.3	17.4	Fixed Assets (net)					10.3	
2.3	3.2	4.4	Intangibles (net)					3.4	
6.4	4.8	4.4	All Other Non-Current					6.8	
100.0	100.0	100.0	Total					100.0	

LIABILITIES

Hist 1	Hist 2	Hist 3		0-1MM	1-3MM	3-5MM	5-10MM	10-25MM	25MM & OVER
9.7	13.2	13.2	Notes Payable-Short Term					22.9	
4.6	3.1	2.7	Cur. Mat.-L/T/D					.9	
16.0	18.3	18.5	Trade Payables					18.6	
.5	.3	.5	Income Taxes Payable					.0	
10.8	14.7	11.6	All Other Current					11.1	
41.5	49.6	46.4	Total Current					53.5	
10.6	10.8	8.2	Long-Term Debt					6.2	
.3	.3	.3	Deferred Taxes					.0	
5.1	3.3	5.2	All Other Non-Current					2.1	
42.5	36.0	39.9	Net Worth					38.3	
100.0	100.0	100.0	Total Liabilities & Net Worth					100.0	

INCOME DATA

Hist 1	Hist 2	Hist 3		0-1MM	1-3MM	3-5MM	5-10MM	10-25MM	25MM & OVER
100.0	100.0	100.0	Net Sales					100.0	
30.0	31.8	29.0	Gross Profit					27.1	
26.3	28.5	26.0	Operating Expenses					21.7	
3.7	3.3	3.0	Operating Profit					5.4	
.3	.8	.4	All Other Expenses (net)					.6	
3.4	2.5	2.6	Profit Before Taxes					4.9	

RATIOS

Hist 1	Hist 2	Hist 3		0-1MM	1-3MM	3-5MM	5-10MM	10-25MM	25MM & OVER
2.5	2.1	2.7	Current					3.3	
1.7	1.6	1.6						1.4	
1.3	1.3	1.1						1.0	
1.6	1.3	1.3	Quick					1.5	
1.0	.8	.9						.7	
.6	.6	.5						.5	
40 9.2	34 10.8	47 7.8	Sales/Receivables					35 10.5	
52 7.0	48 7.6	59 6.2						52 7.1	
69 5.3	55 6.6	67 5.4						70 5.2	
39 9.4	28 13.2	31 12.0	Cost of Sales/Inventory					22 16.2	
71 5.1	66 5.5	54 6.8						52 7.0	
134 2.7	119 3.1	107 3.4						128 2.8	
20 17.9	16 23.1	25 14.6	Cost of Sales/Payables					20 18.0	
35 10.6	35 10.5	34 10.7						29 12.5	
61 6.0	50 7.3	53 6.8						50 7.3	
5.2	5.1	4.8	Sales/Working Capital					4.8	
7.3	8.8	7.5						12.2	
9.7	12.1	47.7						NM	
14.6	11.7	9.2	EBIT/Interest						
(28) 4.5	(31) 3.2	(27) 2.3							
-.2	.3	.5							
5.6			Net Profit + Depr., Dep.,						
(12) 1.6			Amort./Cur. Mat. L/T/D						
.0									
.2	.2	.2	Fixed/Worth					.1	
.4	.5	.3						.2	
1.0	1.4	2.1						14.0	
.6	.8	.7	Debt/Worth					.6	
1.3	1.6	1.6						2.1	
2.9	3.5	4.3						88.9	
36.7	41.6	29.4	% Profit Before Taxes/Tangible						
(28) 14.4	(28) 7.2	(28) 11.3	Net Worth						
.7	-2.8	-3.9							
14.9	14.0	11.2	% Profit Before Taxes/Total					26.4	
5.5	4.9	3.2	Assets					6.9	
-.3	-1.4	-.9						.0	
29.3	35.0	51.9	Sales/Net Fixed Assets					132.1	
12.1	17.4	24.5						41.4	
7.2	6.1	6.4						14.6	
2.7	3.2	2.9	Sales/Total Assets					3.5	
2.2	2.5	2.2						2.5	
1.3	1.3	1.4						1.5	
1.3	1.2	.9	% Depr., Dep., Amort./Sales						
(28) 1.8	(30) 1.6	(27) 1.4							
2.4	3.0	2.5							
2.4	1.9	1.8	% Officers', Directors',						
(11) 4.2	(15) 3.7	(15) 3.0	Owners' Comp/Sales						
8.4	6.1	6.7							
416214M	364948M	682916M	Net Sales ($)	1142M	2914M	17472M	50259M	159587M	451542M
226874M	226665M	397490M	Total Assets ($)	918M	1793M	7784M	23034M	79625M	284336M

M = $ thousand   MM = $ million
See Pages 11 through 21 for Explanation of Ratios and Data

Current Data Sorted By Assets   **Comparative Historical Data**

Type of Statement

0-500M	500M-2MM	2-10MM	10-50MM	50-100MM	100-250MM	Type of Statement	4/1/00-3/31/01 ALL	4/1/01-3/31/02 ALL
		8	6	1	3	Unqualified	8	6
		5	1		1	Reviewed	8	6
2	1	1				Compiled	3	3
1	2	3				Tax Returns	5	2
3		8	6	1		Other	12	9
	14 (4/1-9/30/04)		39 (10/1/04-3/31/05)					
3	6	25	13	3	3	**NUMBER OF STATEMENTS**	36	26
%	%	%	%	%	%		%	%

ASSETS

0-500M	500M-2MM	2-10MM	10-50MM	50-100MM	100-250MM		Hist 1	Hist 2
		3.6	3.5			Cash & Equivalents	7.4	4.3
		30.2	21.0			Trade Receivables (net)	23.5	21.1
		34.1	28.9			Inventory	30.9	35.7
		1.5	1.9			All Other Current	2.2	1.5
		69.4	55.3			Total Current	64.0	62.7
		20.3	24.2			Fixed Assets (net)	24.2	20.0
		5.3	7.7			Intangibles (net)	5.4	5.8
		5.0	12.9			All Other Non-Current	6.3	11.5
		100.0	100.0			Total	100.0	100.0

LIABILITIES

0-500M	500M-2MM	2-10MM	10-50MM	50-100MM	100-250MM		Hist 1	Hist 2
		15.3	16.2			Notes Payable-Short Term	14.1	15.4
		2.3	3.6			Cur. Mat.-L/T/D	4.0	5.1
		18.1	17.6			Trade Payables	13.8	9.2
		.5	.1			Income Taxes Payable	.1	.5
		10.0	10.2			All Other Current	7.9	8.0
		46.1	47.7			Total Current	39.9	38.3
		16.4	12.6			Long-Term Debt	24.6	15.0
		.6	.9			Deferred Taxes	.6	.9
		9.4	1.3			All Other Non-Current	2.4	4.9
		27.5	37.4			Net Worth	32.5	40.9
		100.0	100.0			Total Liabilities & Net Worth	100.0	100.0

INCOME DATA

0-500M	500M-2MM	2-10MM	10-50MM	50-100MM	100-250MM		Hist 1	Hist 2
		100.0	100.0			Net Sales	100.0	100.0
		24.2	21.8			Gross Profit	23.4	26.0
		20.7	19.5			Operating Expenses	19.3	24.0
		3.4	2.3			Operating Profit	4.1	2.1
		1.3	.8			All Other Expenses (net)	1.3	1.7
		2.2	1.5			Profit Before Taxes	2.8	.3

RATIOS

0-500M	500M-2MM	2-10MM	10-50MM	50-100MM	100-250MM		Hist 1	Hist 2
		2.2	1.2			Current	2.3	2.6
		1.4	1.1				1.5	1.6
		1.1	.9				1.1	1.3
		1.1	.8			Quick	1.2	1.3
		.7	.5				.6	.7
		.4	.4				.4	.3
		19 19.1	14 26.5			Sales/Receivables	21 17.7	30 12.4
		47 7.7	39 9.4				42 8.7	44 8.3
		62 5.9	50 7.3				58 6.3	53 6.8
		24 15.2	33 10.9			Cost of Sales/Inventory	43 8.5	59 6.2
		76 4.8	62 5.9				69 5.3	76 4.8
		141 2.6	77 4.7				113 3.2	110 3.3
		16 22.2	17 21.3			Cost of Sales/Payables	13 28.2	10 35.2
		37 10.0	30 12.0				28 12.9	25 14.6
		64 5.7	49 7.5				41 8.9	42 8.6
		5.9	24.9			Sales/Working Capital	4.5	4.6
		10.0	49.0				9.8	6.4
		79.1	−69.8				38.7	18.1
		19.3	10.0			EBIT/Interest	5.1	2.8
		3.8	3.6				(31) 2.1	(24) .6
		.6	−.1				.7	−.2
						Net Profit + Depr., Dep., Amort./Cur. Mat. L/T/D	4.4	
							(13) 1.0	
							.1	
		.2	.5			Fixed/Worth	.3	.2
		.9	2.1				.8	.5
		3.7					3.0	1.1
		1.2	1.0			Debt/Worth	1.0	.7
		2.9	2.7				3.2	1.5
		46.5	15.2				9.2	2.7
		58.9	42.0			% Profit Before Taxes/Tangible Net Worth	48.3	16.2
		(21) 14.3	9.3				(30) 14.8	(24) −.5
		3.3	−1.8				4.7	−7.4
		19.2	11.1			% Profit Before Taxes/Total Assets	12.4	5.7
		4.3	5.0				4.2	−.4
		−.7	−1.8				−1.0	−3.5
		32.7	20.0			Sales/Net Fixed Assets	18.9	27.8
		13.4	9.3				10.8	11.4
		8.1	5.3				5.5	4.8
		3.1	3.0			Sales/Total Assets	2.6	2.5
		2.2	2.3				2.1	1.8
		1.5	1.6				1.7	1.4
		.7	.7			% Depr., Dep., Amort./Sales	.8	1.0
		(24) 1.4	(12) 1.1				(31) 2.2	(21) 1.6
		2.7	2.7				3.6	2.4
		1.4				% Officers', Directors', Owners' Comp/Sales		
		(11) 3.5						
		5.6						

0-500M	500M-2MM	2-10MM	10-50MM	50-100MM	100-250MM		Hist 1	Hist 2
2497M	22670M	364635M	630602M	232668M	687724M	Net Sales ($)	1394796M	759621M
735M	7960M	130356M	246612M	167765M	420712M	Total Assets ($)	808795M	432942M

M = $ thousand   MM = $ million
See Pages 11 through 21 for Explanation of Ratios and Data

Comparative Historical Data | Current Data Sorted By Sales

Hist 1	Hist 2	Hist 3	Type of Statement	0-1MM	1-3MM	3-5MM	5-10MM	10-25MM	25MM & OVER
22	16	18	Unqualified				1	4	13
11	9	7	Reviewed		1			2	2
4	5	4	Compiled	2			2		
3	4	6	Tax Returns		1	2	3		
17	20	18	Other	1	1	3	3	5	5
4/1/02-3/31/03 ALL	4/1/03-3/31/04 ALL	4/1/04-3/31/05 ALL		14 (4/1-9/30/04)			39 (10/1/04-3/31/05)		
57	54	53	**NUMBER OF STATEMENTS**	3	3	5	11	11	20
%	%	%	**ASSETS**	%	%	%	%	%	%
6.9	7.9	4.4	Cash & Equivalents				2.6	5.1	6.2
23.1	22.4	25.7	Trade Receivables (net)				19.6	35.4	22.2
24.4	30.6	32.0	Inventory				31.2	35.9	29.4
1.6	3.6	1.8	All Other Current				3.1	.5	1.9
56.0	64.5	63.9	Total Current				56.6	76.9	59.8
29.1	26.6	23.4	Fixed Assets (net)				28.6	16.2	25.0
6.0	3.5	5.3	Intangibles (net)				4.6	3.6	6.5
9.0	5.4	7.4	All Other Non-Current				10.3	3.3	8.7
100.0	100.0	100.0	Total				100.0	100.0	100.0
			LIABILITIES						
12.0	14.1	15.4	Notes Payable-Short Term				11.0	17.6	17.1
3.4	5.1	3.6	Cur. Mat.-L/T/D				2.1	3.1	3.7
15.1	13.7	18.3	Trade Payables				17.7	20.5	16.6
.3	.2	.2	Income Taxes Payable				.1	.9	.1
9.2	9.7	9.0	All Other Current				7.5	9.6	10.2
40.0	42.8	46.6	Total Current				38.3	51.8	47.6
28.6	23.1	15.9	Long-Term Debt				24.5	11.9	10.9
.8	.5	1.0	Deferred Taxes				.9	.4	2.0
5.4	7.4	6.1	All Other Non-Current				15.5	5.8	1.5
25.1	26.2	30.3	Net Worth				20.8	30.1	38.0
100.0	100.0	100.0	Total Liabilities & Net Worth				100.0	100.0	100.0
			INCOME DATA						
100.0	100.0	100.0	Net Sales				100.0	100.0	100.0
25.4	23.9	24.0	Gross Profit				26.6	25.3	18.8
22.7	20.6	20.3	Operating Expenses				26.3	20.0	14.6
2.7	3.3	3.6	Operating Profit				.3	5.3	4.2
1.7	1.2	.9	All Other Expenses (net)				−.2	3.1	.2
1.0	2.1	2.7	Profit Before Taxes				.5	2.1	4.0
			RATIOS						
2.5	2.6	1.7	Current				2.6	2.8	1.4
1.4	1.4	1.2					1.3	1.4	1.1
1.1	1.1	1.0					1.1	1.0	1.0
1.3	1.3	1.1	Quick				1.0	1.6	.8
.8	.7	.5					.4	.7	.5
.5	.4	.3					.3	.5	.4
33 11.0	18 20.0	15 23.7	Sales/Receivables				9 39.8	40 9.2	21 17.3
43 8.5	43 8.5	41 8.8					44 8.2	47 7.7	39 9.4
55 6.7	51 7.1	60 6.1					60 6.1	70 6.6	53 6.9
30 12.0	29 12.7	33 11.0	Cost of Sales/Inventory				34 10.7	51 7.1	24 14.9
59 6.2	55 6.6	65 5.7					76 4.8	57 6.4	59 6.2
101 3.6	89 4.1	112 3.3					158 2.3	137 2.7	73 5.0
18 19.9	14 25.3	22 16.7	Cost of Sales/Payables				24 15.5	22 16.7	12 29.5
27 13.3	22 16.4	37 10.0					44 8.2	30 12.2	29 12.8
48 7.5	36 10.1	61 6.0					67 5.5	64 5.7	46 7.9
4.5	5.5	7.3	Sales/Working Capital				6.3	4.6	15.6
14.3	15.3	18.7					13.9	10.0	47.1
59.2	54.3	153.6					49.0	−124.9	NM
6.0	7.2	14.1	EBIT/Interest				4.2	9.6	32.0
(49) 1.4	(46) 2.0	(52) 3.6					.9	2.9	7.3
−1.3	−.4	.3					−3.2	1.4	3.4
3.0	2.9	4.9	Net Profit + Depr., Dep.,						
(20) 1.4	(15) 1.6	(19) 1.4	Amort./Cur. Mat. L/T/D						
.1	.5	.5							
.4	.3	.3	Fixed/Worth				.7	.2	.4
1.0	.7	1.0					1.5	.9	.8
3.8	3.3	2.1					56.8	1.2	1.6
.6	1.2	1.2	Debt/Worth				1.2	1.0	1.2
2.4	2.6	2.8					4.1	2.9	2.1
12.2	12.1	9.3					133.2	7.7	4.9
31.9	44.7	50.6	% Profit Before Taxes/Tangible					56.9	55.4
(48) 9.4	(47) 17.2	(46) 15.4	Net Worth					(10) 11.5	17.8
−7.2	−14.8	3.5						−3.4	7.6
10.0	14.4	13.7	% Profit Before Taxes/Total				13.5	7.7	21.0
1.3	3.6	4.4	Assets				−.2	4.3	9.0
−5.0	−5.4	−1.2					−4.2	1.1	1.2
13.3	19.1	27.2	Sales/Net Fixed Assets				22.3	25.4	29.3
6.6	9.8	12.6					7.5	13.4	11.0
3.6	4.2	7.1					4.8	10.0	6.2
2.2	2.9	3.2	Sales/Total Assets				3.2	3.0	3.7
1.8	2.0	2.3					2.2	2.8	2.4
1.3	1.5	1.5					1.4	1.5	1.6
1.4	.8	.8	% Depr., Dep., Amort./Sales				.7	1.0	.6
(49) 2.8	(44) 2.1	(49) 1.3					1.7	(10) 2.3	(18) .9
4.4	3.6	2.6					3.5	2.9	2.0
	1.1	1.8	% Officers', Directors',						
	(14) 3.1	(16) 3.3	Owners' Comp/Sales						
	6.7	5.0							
1706237M	1068027M	1940796M	Net Sales ($)	1994M	4672M	21283M	72930M	178824M	1661093M
1080309M	575562M	974140M	Total Assets ($)	1839M	3216M	10689M	40842M	85017M	832537M

© RMA 2005

M = $ thousand   MM = $ million
See Pages 11 through 21 for Explanation of Ratios and Data

	Current Data Sorted By Assets						Comparative Historical Data	

0-500M	500M-2MM 13 (4/1-9/30/04)	2-10MM	10-50MM 38 (10/1/04-3/31/05)	50-100MM	100-250MM	Type of Statement	4/1/00-3/31/01 ALL	4/1/01-3/31/02 ALL
		2				Unqualified	4	4
	2	7	5	1	2	Reviewed	12	12
	4	1	4			Compiled	6	4
1	1	2				Tax Returns		3
3	3	9	4			Other	5	7
4	10	21	13	1	2	**NUMBER OF STATEMENTS**	27	30
%	%	%	%	%	%	**ASSETS**	%	%
	11.9	8.0	3.4			Cash & Equivalents	8.9	8.8
	35.3	24.9	33.9			Trade Receivables (net)	32.2	31.0
	21.1	31.3	18.3			Inventory	24.9	23.6
	.9	3.3	7.6			All Other Current	5.3	4.6
	69.2	67.5	63.2			Total Current	71.2	68.0
	22.0	22.6	25.9			Fixed Assets (net)	19.1	25.9
	1.3	1.1	.9			Intangibles (net)	2.6	1.2
	7.5	8.8	10.0			All Other Non-Current	7.0	4.8
	100.0	100.0	100.0			Total	100.0	100.0
						LIABILITIES		
	16.2	9.7	14.3			Notes Payable-Short Term	13.3	12.9
	2.1	2.3	2.4			Cur. Mat.-L/T/D	2.1	2.8
	19.4	14.1	14.4			Trade Payables	16.6	14.0
	1.3	.4	.1			Income Taxes Payable	.7	.1
	12.1	12.1	12.8			All Other Current	11.6	12.2
	51.0	38.6	44.0			Total Current	44.3	42.1
	5.9	14.8	12.9			Long-Term Debt	11.4	11.2
	.0	.4	.8			Deferred Taxes	.2	.2
	2.8	5.7	6.1			All Other Non-Current	8.8	5.3
	40.3	40.6	36.2			Net Worth	35.3	41.1
	100.0	100.0	100.0			Total Liabilities & Net Worth	100.0	100.0
						INCOME DATA		
	100.0	100.0	100.0			Net Sales	100.0	100.0
	31.8	33.3	26.5			Gross Profit	33.9	30.6
	30.0	30.2	21.2			Operating Expenses	26.7	27.5
	1.8	3.1	5.4			Operating Profit	7.2	3.1
	-.5	.2	1.8			All Other Expenses (net)	1.4	.8
	2.3	2.9	3.5			Profit Before Taxes	5.9	2.3
						RATIOS		
	3.1	3.5	1.9				2.5	2.6
	1.2	2.0	1.4			Current	1.6	1.8
	1.0	1.3	1.1				1.1	1.2
	2.2	2.1	1.0				1.5	1.5
	.8	1.0	.8			Quick	1.0	1.0
	.6	.5	.6				.5	.6
35 10.4	35 10.4	37 9.8	63 5.8				39 9.3	46 7.9
40 9.1	40 9.1	47 7.8	69 5.3			Sales/Receivables	54 6.7	59 6.2
67 5.5	67 5.5	57 6.4	80 4.5				83 4.4	82 4.5
13 27.2	13 27.2	66 5.5	5 74.8				12 30.4	23 15.6
37 10.0	37 10.0	107 3.4	34 10.7			Cost of Sales/Inventory	82 4.4	71 5.1
84 4.3	84 4.3	130 2.8	104 3.5				114 3.2	124 3.0
23 15.7	23 15.7	21 17.8	11 32.7				21 17.6	16 23.4
37 9.9	37 9.9	34 10.8	54 6.8			Cost of Sales/Payables	39 9.4	29 12.7
71 5.2	71 5.2	45 8.2	78 4.7				51 7.1	51 7.1
	6.7	3.7	5.1				4.7	3.8
	15.5	6.0	10.0			Sales/Working Capital	8.7	6.6
	-142.6	12.3	38.1				21.4	23.7
		45.9	7.1				33.2	8.2
	(17)	4.2	(11) 3.9			EBIT/Interest	(25) 3.1	(27) 2.3
		.5	1.0				1.5	.0
						Net Profit + Depr., Dep.,		8.3
						Amort./Cur. Mat. L /T/D	(10)	3.2
								1.6
	.2	.1	.2				.2	.2
	.6	.6	.5			Fixed/Worth	.7	.6
	1.4	3.9	3.5				1.8	1.3
	.4	.3	.9				.5	.5
	2.7	1.1	2.0			Debt/Worth	2.7	1.7
	5.6	24.6	5.7				7.8	6.5
	22.2	35.1	32.9				59.3	33.6
	8.6	(18) 13.8	(11) 10.3			% Profit Before Taxes/Tangible Net Worth	(23) 40.8	(28) 8.0
	4.8	-.8	.0				11.9	-11.4
	7.6	18.8	13.1				29.0	13.1
	3.2	5.1	3.8			% Profit Before Taxes/Total Assets	7.5	3.8
	1.9	-.4	.6				2.8	-2.9
	31.3	23.2	13.9				25.5	17.6
	13.0	7.9	7.4			Sales/Net Fixed Assets	12.3	8.1
	6.6	3.9	3.5				6.3	5.3
	2.9	2.2	1.9				2.4	2.5
	2.1	1.7	1.5			Sales/Total Assets	2.0	2.0
	1.7	1.4	1.2				1.8	1.4
		1.0	1.6				.8	1.3
	(19)	2.2	(12) 2.7			% Depr., Dep., Amort./Sales	(24) 1.3	2.0
		3.9	4.4				2.3	3.1
								1.2
						% Officers', Directors', Owners' Comp/Sales	(11)	3.9
								5.9
5025M	29130M	185350M	390183M	91100M	315067M	Net Sales ($)	354766M	524377M
1357M	12705M	103150M	240225M	80054M	335650M	Total Assets ($)	198793M	294807M

M = $ thousand　　MM = $ million
See Pages 11 through 21 for Explanation of Ratios and Data

Comparative Historical Data | **Current Data Sorted By Sales**

					Type of Statement							
	5		5		10	Unqualified					4	6
	10		15		13	Reviewed		1	2	3	4	3
	5		10		5	Compiled		2	3			
	1		4		4	Tax Returns		2	1	1		
	7		7		19	Other	1	5	1	7	3	2
	4/1/02-3/31/03 ALL		4/1/03-3/31/04 ALL		4/1/04-3/31/05 ALL			13 (4/1-9/30/04)			38 (10/1/04-3/31/05)	
							0-1MM	1-3MM	3-5MM	5-10MM	10-25MM	25MM & OVER
	28		41		51	NUMBER OF STATEMENTS	1	10	7	11	11	11
	%		%		%	ASSETS	%	%	%	%	%	%
	9.0		7.9		8.5	Cash & Equivalents		24.5		8.7	3.4	3.2
	30.8		28.4		30.1	Trade Receivables (net)		30.2		23.0	27.4	39.2
	27.1		24.2		22.8	Inventory		9.8		29.0	32.6	11.8
	4.2		3.4		3.5	All Other Current		.5		3.8	5.6	6.0
	71.1		63.9		65.0	Total Current		65.0		64.6	69.0	60.2
	23.5		28.2		25.4	Fixed Assets (net)		25.2		26.0	22.5	29.1
	.9		2.2		1.0	Intangibles (net)		1.3		.8	.4	1.4
	4.5		5.8		8.5	All Other Non-Current		8.5		8.6	8.1	9.4
	100.0		100.0		100.0	Total		100.0		100.0	100.0	100.0
					LIABILITIES						
	19.0		19.1		13.4	Notes Payable-Short Term		11.6		8.3	15.4	16.6
	2.2		4.2		2.1	Cur. Mat.-L/T/D		.8		3.4	1.5	2.7
	18.9		14.0		14.7	Trade Payables		12.2		12.2	14.6	16.8
	.4		.4		.4	Income Taxes Payable		1.3		.6	.1	.0
	10.9		9.2		12.1	All Other Current		12.1		16.2	11.0	10.3
	51.4		46.8		42.7	Total Current		38.0		40.7	42.6	46.4
	13.3		14.7		14.3	Long-Term Debt		14.5		11.7	13.1	17.1
	.1		.1		.8	Deferred Taxes		.0		.3	1.0	2.3
	4.5		7.1		5.0	All Other Non-Current		2.0		11.0	4.5	5.3
	30.7		31.3		37.2	Net Worth		45.6		36.4	38.8	29.0
	100.0		100.0		100.0	Total Liabilities & Net Worth		100.0		100.0	100.0	100.0
					INCOME DATA						
	100.0		100.0		100.0	Net Sales		100.0		100.0	100.0	100.0
	32.2		34.3		32.2	Gross Profit		34.5		37.8	29.8	24.3
	28.3		31.5		27.7	Operating Expenses		28.5		37.7	25.1	18.1
	3.9		2.9		4.5	Operating Profit		6.0		.1	4.7	6.3
	1.6		1.3		.4	All Other Expenses (net)		-1.1		.2	1.4	.8
	2.3		1.5		4.1	Profit Before Taxes		7.1		-.1	3.3	5.5
					RATIOS						
	2.9		2.4		2.7			5.0		3.5	2.4	1.5
	1.5		1.4		1.6	Current		1.9		2.0	1.6	1.3
	1.0		1.0		1.1			1.1		1.1	1.3	1.0
	1.3		1.8		1.7			4.3		2.3	1.0	.9
	.9		.8		.9	Quick		1.7		1.0	.7	.8
	.5		.5		.6			.8		.5	.5	.8

38	9.6	38	9.5	38	9.7		2	221.6			39	9.2	40	9.1	60	6.1
49	7.5	53	6.9	52	7.0	Sales/Receivables	39	9.3			45	8.0	59	6.2	73	5.0
71	5.2	74	4.9	69	5.3		72	5.1			54	6.7	69	5.3	87	4.2
39	9.3	22	16.8	22	16.8		3	139.7			70	5.2	65	5.6	5	76.8
77	4.8	58	6.3	65	5.6	Cost of Sales/Inventory	17	22.1			111	3.3	92	4.0	34	10.7
105	3.5	124	2.9	116	3.2		43	8.5			133	2.7	127	2.9	40	9.0
15	24.3	13	27.3	21	17.1		0	UND			26	14.1	12	30.6	31	11.7
37	9.7	35	10.5	34	10.8	Cost of Sales/Payables	24	15.3			34	10.8	34	7.9	46	7.9
71	5.1	52	7.1	54	6.7		55	6.6			40	9.2	69	5.3	56	6.6

				Sales/Working Capital					
	4.3	4.8	4.5			4.5	2.7	3.4	6.8
	8.4	9.2	9.5			10.1	6.0	8.7	16.0
	-67.8	NM	28.2			NM	34.9	21.2	-401.6

						EBIT/Interest					
	6.7		5.5		14.5					14.7	
(27)	1.8	(37)	3.2	(43)	3.9					4.0	
	.1		.0		1.5					-.2	

						Net Profit + Depr., Dep., Amort./Cur. Mat. L/T/D					
			4.1		5.0						
		(10)	1.1	(13)	3.5						
			-3.1		1.7						

					Fixed/Worth					
	.3	.3	.2			.2	.1	.2	.2
	.7	.8	.6			.5	.6	.5	.9
	NM	6.6	1.6			.8	-2.2	1.6	5.4

					Debt/Worth					
	.7	.6	.6			.3	.3	.8	2.0
	1.9	2.4	2.0			2.4	.7	1.5	2.5
	NM	15.9	4.5			5.4	-7.1	4.5	6.9

						% Profit Before Taxes/Tangible Net Worth					
	45.9		44.1		33.1					25.4	
(21)	16.1	(34)	10.5	(45)	12.9					8.3	
	4.9		-4.0		4.7					-51.7	

					% Profit Before Taxes/Total Assets					
	10.7	10.0	17.1			26.4	24.4	19.3	9.3
	3.7	3.5	4.5			7.3	2.9	3.8	4.9
	-1.8	-2.8	1.7			3.2	-.2	-4.9	2.0

					Sales/Net Fixed Assets					
	25.3	15.2	16.6			24.3	15.9	14.3	16.2
	7.8	7.2	10.0			16.5	6.2	11.2	10.2
	5.2	3.7	4.1			6.6	3.4	4.1	1.8

					Sales/Total Assets					
	2.6	2.6	2.5			3.3	2.5	2.0	3.1
	2.1	1.8	1.7			2.1	1.8	1.6	1.4
	1.4	1.3	1.3			1.7	1.0	1.2	1.0

						% Depr., Dep., Amort./Sales					
	1.3		1.0		1.3					1.4	1.0
	1.7	(36)	1.8	(43)	2.7				(10)	3.1	1.6
	2.6		2.8		3.6					3.7	4.9

						% Officers', Directors', Owners' Comp/Sales					
			4.8		2.4						
		(16)	7.1	(15)	3.7						
			10.0		7.8						

272404M		669945M		1015855M		Net Sales ($)	371M	19620M	27334M	75782M	189158M	703590M
156529M		367215M		773141M		Total Assets ($)	50M	10093M	15892M	48228M	126470M	572408M

M = $ thousand   MM = $ million
See Pages 11 through 21 for Explanation of Ratios and Data

Current Data Sorted By Assets   Comparative Historical Data

						Type of Statement		
1	1	6	4		3	Unqualified	13	12
	1	16	4			Reviewed	14	11
1	2	5				Compiled	13	11
1	2	1				Tax Returns	4	2
	5	8	4	1	1	Other	17	19
	17 (4/1-9/30/04)		50 (10/1/04-3/31/05)				4/1/00-3/31/01	4/1/01-3/31/02
0-500M	500M-2MM	2-10MM	10-50MM	50-100MM	100-250MM		ALL	ALL
3	11	36	12	1	4	NUMBER OF STATEMENTS	61	55
%	%	%	%	%	%	ASSETS	%	%
	14.7	9.4	9.8			Cash & Equivalents	6.1	6.4
	29.5	24.9	18.2			Trade Receivables (net)	26.8	29.2
	28.6	31.7	29.5			Inventory	32.0	27.3
	2.4	3.7	7.1			All Other Current	3.4	1.9
	75.2	69.8	64.6			Total Current	68.2	64.8
	17.4	13.3	18.0			Fixed Assets (net)	19.4	20.5
	.3	7.4	4.4			Intangibles (net)	6.3	8.0
	7.1	9.6	13.0			All Other Non-Current	6.0	6.4
	100.0	100.0	100.0			Total	100.0	100.0
						LIABILITIES		
	13.1	9.0	4.1			Notes Payable-Short Term	14.0	12.4
	1.1	2.3	1.4			Cur. Mat.-L/T/D	2.6	3.0
	19.6	13.2	8.5			Trade Payables	17.1	19.1
	.1	.2	.2			Income Taxes Payable	.2	1.3
	25.4	21.5	19.7			All Other Current	15.8	17.0
	59.4	46.2	33.9			Total Current	49.7	52.8
	6.5	11.5	10.9			Long-Term Debt	13.9	10.9
	.2	.3	1.1			Deferred Taxes	.2	.3
	3.9	4.3	2.1			All Other Non-Current	3.5	3.8
	30.0	37.7	52.0			Net Worth	32.9	32.0
	100.0	100.0	100.0			Total Liabilities & Net Worth	100.0	100.0
						INCOME DATA		
	100.0	100.0	100.0			Net Sales	100.0	100.0
	42.6	33.2	33.7			Gross Profit	33.1	32.0
	41.9	27.9	25.6			Operating Expenses	30.3	27.3
	.7	5.3	8.1			Operating Profit	2.8	4.7
	.9	.9	-.4			All Other Expenses (net)	1.5	1.5
	-.1	4.4	8.5			Profit Before Taxes	1.4	3.2
						RATIOS		
	1.8	2.0	3.0				2.0	1.9
	1.4	1.5	1.9			Current	1.4	1.2
	1.0	1.3	1.3				1.0	1.0
	1.3	1.0	1.1				1.0	1.0
	.6	.7	.8			Quick	.6	.6
	.5	.4	.7				.4	.4
30 12.0	31 11.7	31 11.7					33 11.2	35 10.3
52 7.0	38 9.6	44 8.3				Sales/Receivables	48 7.5	44 8.4
57 6.4	50 7.3	58 6.3					63 5.8	56 6.6
14 26.9	55 6.6	51 7.2					39 9.4	33 11.0
70 5.3	97 3.8	85 4.3				Cost of Sales/Inventory	95 3.8	78 4.7
149 2.4	138 2.7	176 2.1					149 2.5	113 3.2
39 9.3	21 17.6	12 29.2					21 17.8	18 20.2
50 7.3	36 10.2	26 14.2				Cost of Sales/Payables	36 10.2	40 9.0
71 5.1	45 8.1	54 6.7					61 6.0	48 7.6
	4.2	4.2	3.3				5.1	6.4
	12.5	8.6	6.6			Sales/Working Capital	8.7	16.9
	743.5	18.4	20.6				170.7	-64.0
	17.8	19.5	51.4				9.0	11.6
	(10) .9	(32) 5.4	(11) 17.9			EBIT/Interest	(57) 1.8	(48) 2.2
	-3.4	2.1	9.1				-.1	.1
		23.6				Net Profit + Depr., Dep.,	7.0	7.2
		(15) 2.7				Amort./Cur. Mat. L /T/D	(12) 2.6	(14) 2.5
		1.5					-.4	1.7
	.2	.2	.1				.2	.2
	.4	.5	.3			Fixed/Worth	.6	.6
	1.1	1.0	.7				2.6	2.5
	1.0	.8	.7				.9	1.2
	2.3	2.1	.9			Debt/Worth	2.7	3.1
	6.2	6.0	1.8				8.3	11.9
	13.9	61.1	55.0			% Profit Before Taxes/Tangible	56.8	47.6
	(10) 2.7	(32) 15.2	22.6			Net Worth	(51) 18.7	(44) 22.2
	-8.0	3.9	9.9				-1.7	-1.3
	3.5	14.3	22.6			% Profit Before Taxes/Total	15.0	14.3
	.3	6.0	10.5			Assets	3.1	6.1
	-3.7	2.2	5.0				-1.0	-2.4
	74.4	54.4	22.9				30.4	37.1
	21.2	24.1	12.5			Sales/Net Fixed Assets	9.8	9.1
	7.3	9.3	5.4				5.3	6.0
	2.9	2.5	1.9				2.2	2.5
	2.1	1.8	1.6			Sales/Total Assets	1.7	1.8
	1.8	1.4	1.1				1.3	1.5
	.6	.7	.6				.8	.9
	(10) 1.5	(35) 1.0	(10) 2.2			% Depr., Dep., Amort./Sales	(52) 1.6	(43) 2.1
	4.5	2.4	5.4				2.8	3.1
						% Officers', Directors',	2.2	2.2
						Owners' Comp/Sales	(21) 4.4	(15) 4.2
							8.1	10.3
1639M	27735M	367717M	288140M	98733M	827003M	Net Sales ($)	1564699M	1803848M
589M	12796M	187232M	199560M	91415M	669413M	Total Assets ($)	1250522M	1208119M

© RMA 2005

M = $ thousand   MM = $ million
See Pages 11 through 21 for Explanation of Ratios and Data

Comparative Historical Data | **Current Data Sorted By Sales**

	4/1/02-3/31/03 ALL	4/1/03-3/31/04 ALL	4/1/04-3/31/05 ALL	0-1MM	1-3MM	3-5MM	5-10MM	10-25MM	25MM & OVER
				17 (4/1-9/30/04)			50 (10/1/04-3/31/05)		
Type of Statement									
Unqualified	17	11	15	1	1		4	3	6
Reviewed	12	12	21		5		5	9	2
Compiled	14	14	8		2	2	2	2	
Tax Returns	5	6	4	1		2	1		
Other	11	26	19		3	3	4	6	3
NUMBER OF STATEMENTS	59	69	67	2	11	7	16	20	11
ASSETS	%	%	%	%	%	%	%	%	%
Cash & Equivalents	11.0	9.8	10.3		12.9		10.3	9.5	7.0
Trade Receivables (net)	27.5	25.4	24.4		26.3		21.7	24.3	26.7
Inventory	28.1	31.6	29.9		29.9		27.1	31.7	21.4
All Other Current	3.4	3.1	4.1		3.0		2.6	3.7	11.3
Total Current	70.0	70.0	68.6		72.1		61.7	69.2	66.5
Fixed Assets (net)	18.0	18.1	15.7		20.5		13.7	14.5	19.3
Intangibles (net)	5.5	6.2	6.4		.6		9.6	6.2	8.6
All Other Non-Current	6.4	5.7	9.2		6.8		15.0	10.1	5.6
Total	100.0	100.0	100.0		100.0		100.0	100.0	100.0
LIABILITIES									
Notes Payable-Short Term	6.1	8.5	9.0		15.1		7.1	8.5	6.4
Cur. Mat.-L/T/D	3.1	1.7	1.9		1.0		3.3	1.4	1.8
Trade Payables	17.2	15.8	13.2		14.6		12.1	12.2	12.4
Income Taxes Payable	.5	.5	.2		.1		.1	.3	.5
All Other Current	19.4	20.4	21.6		14.9		21.8	23.6	17.8
Total Current	46.4	46.8	45.9		45.8		44.5	45.9	39.0
Long-Term Debt	11.9	8.4	11.2		7.2		15.2	10.8	13.0
Deferred Taxes	.6	.5	.7		.2		.4	.5	.7
All Other Non-Current	4.7	6.5	4.3		6.5		6.1	2.0	4.3
Net Worth	36.4	37.8	38.0		40.3		33.8	40.7	41.9
Total Liabilities & Net Worth	100.0	100.0	100.0		100.0		100.0	100.0	100.0
INCOME DATA									
Net Sales	100.0	100.0	100.0		100.0		100.0	100.0	100.0
Gross Profit	32.7	35.6	35.7		45.9		35.0	32.6	30.2
Operating Expenses	29.1	30.9	30.8		44.5		28.7	26.1	23.7
Operating Profit	3.6	4.7	4.9		1.4		6.3	6.4	6.5
All Other Expenses (net)	1.1	.9	.8		.9		1.5	.6	.9
Profit Before Taxes	2.5	3.7	4.1		.5		4.8	5.9	5.6
RATIOS									
Current	2.4	2.1	2.3		2.4		1.9	2.5	2.3
	1.6	1.6	1.5		1.4		1.5	1.4	1.8
	1.2	1.2	1.2		1.4		1.0	1.2	1.1
Quick	1.3	1.1	1.0		1.7		1.1	1.0	1.2
	1.0	.7	.8		.8		.6	.8	.9
	.5	.5	.5		.5		.4	.5	.7
Sales/Receivables	33 11.1	28 13.2	34 10.9		37 9.8		28 13.1	34 10.8	34 10.8
	47 7.8	41 8.9	42 8.7		52 7.0		38 9.7	40 9.0	51 7.2
	59 6.2	53 6.8	56 6.5		57 6.4		49 7.4	51 7.2	67 5.4
Cost of Sales/Inventory	33 11.1	43 8.4	50 7.3		16 22.1		48 7.7	40 9.2	50 7.3
	69 5.3	82 4.5	92 4.0		99 3.7		97 3.8	80 4.5	54 6.7
	146 2.5	144 2.5	138 2.6		171 2.1		138 2.7	125 2.9	99 3.7
Cost of Sales/Payables	21 17.7	21 17.4	22 16.9		39 9.3		23 15.8	12 29.2	13 27.3
	36 10.0	30 12.0	36 10.1		47 7.8		43 8.5	28 12.8	31 11.9
	51 7.2	56 6.5	49 7.4		55 6.6		49 7.4	42 8.6	42 8.8
Sales/Working Capital	4.4	5.0	4.3		3.7		3.9	7.6	4.3
	7.9	7.7	8.6		6.1		9.0	9.2	5.6
	24.2	22.5	24.6		18.4		NM	32.0	22.1
EBIT/Interest	13.9	18.1	23.2		18.4		11.5	27.2	26.8
	(55) 3.4	(61) 5.3	(60) 5.4		(10) .9		(13) 5.3	(18) 8.6	(10) 13.2
	.2	1.6	1.2		-2.5		2.1	3.0	1.9
Net Profit + Depr., Dep., Amort./Cur. Mat. L/T/D	14.3	9.5	17.0						
	(22) 3.1	(21) 2.6	(22) 4.9						
	.8	1.1	1.7						
Fixed/Worth	.2	.3	.2		.2		.4	.1	.2
	.4	.5	.4		.6		.7	.3	.4
	1.1	1.9	1.1		1.0		1.4	1.0	.8
Debt/Worth	.7	.9	.8		.8		.9	1.0	.7
	1.9	2.1	1.9		1.1		3.9	2.0	1.5
	8.9	6.0	5.5		6.2		24.2	3.4	4.5
% Profit Before Taxes/Tangible Net Worth	66.6	48.9	37.2		11.3		98.3	57.1	31.3
	(51) 12.4	(58) 18.4	(60) 14.7		.6	(13) 32.0	(19) 15.4	(10) 17.7	
	1.4	3.1	2.9		-10.2		3.5	8.4	12.0
% Profit Before Taxes/Total Assets	18.5	16.6	11.5		5.6		14.4	21.1	10.6
	3.6	7.6	4.9		.3		8.9	5.8	9.4
	-1.3	1.0	1.3		-3.7		1.9	2.5	2.7
Sales/Net Fixed Assets	38.0	31.0	43.4		74.4		42.3	60.1	18.4
	12.4	14.1	19.9		8.8		22.4	24.3	10.9
	5.9	6.7	7.2		6.8		7.7	7.8	4.4
Sales/Total Assets	2.5	2.6	2.2		2.8		2.0	2.6	2.0
	1.9	1.9	1.8		2.1		1.6	2.0	1.6
	1.4	1.5	1.3		1.4		1.2	1.3	1.3
% Depr., Dep., Amort./Sales	.8	.8	.7				.7	.7	
	(54) 1.5	(58) 1.6	(60) 1.5			(15) 1.4	(19) .8		
	3.3	3.2	2.5				3.0	2.2	
% Officers', Directors', Owners' Comp/Sales	2.1	1.9	1.8						
	(20) 3.9	(24) 3.5	(18) 3.7						
	10.4	12.0	7.2						
Net Sales ($)	1043465M	1569537M	1610967M	592M	23847M	27457M	129057M	316453M	1113561M
Total Assets ($)	686454M	991665M	1161005M	136M	13224M	16258M	86469M	189366M	855552M

Current Data Sorted By Assets   Comparative Historical Data

Type of Statement

	0-500M	500M-2MM	2-10MM	10-50MM	50-100MM	100-250MM		4/1/00-3/31/01 ALL	4/1/01-3/31/02 ALL
Unqualified			5	8				13	9
Reviewed		2	6	2				11	9
Compiled		3	2					11	6
Tax Returns	1		1					2	
Other	1	2	10	4				12	11
		9 (4/1-9/30/04)		38 (10/1/04-3/31/05)					
NUMBER OF STATEMENTS	2	7	24	14				49	35
	%	%	%	%	%	%		%	%
ASSETS									
Cash & Equivalents			9.4	8.7				9.9	6.9
Trade Receivables (net)			33.7	33.1				28.6	29.9
Inventory			20.2	15.9	D A T A	D A T A		24.8	20.8
All Other Current			5.4	6.9				5.3	2.5
Total Current			68.7	64.7				68.6	60.2
Fixed Assets (net)			22.2	17.1	N O T	N O T		18.7	25.3
Intangibles (net)			3.6	8.7				8.6	6.5
All Other Non-Current			5.4	9.5				4.2	8.0
Total			100.0	100.0				100.0	100.0
LIABILITIES					A V A	A V A			
Notes Payable-Short Term			10.6	7.7				8.4	14.7
Cur. Mat.-L/T/D			3.5	4.4	I L A	I L A		3.1	6.2
Trade Payables			22.6	13.8				13.9	12.3
Income Taxes Payable			.0	.3	B L E	B L E		.3	.1
All Other Current			15.6	19.6				19.0	13.4
Total Current			52.3	45.7				44.7	46.8
Long-Term Debt			15.0	8.0				14.6	19.2
Deferred Taxes			.1	2.2				.3	.4
All Other Non-Current			7.8	6.7				3.2	7.6
Net Worth			24.9	37.4				37.2	26.1
Total Liabilities & Net Worth			100.0	100.0				100.0	100.0
INCOME DATA									
Net Sales			100.0	100.0				100.0	100.0
Gross Profit			34.5	25.0				33.6	32.5
Operating Expenses			28.0	20.7				27.0	28.8
Operating Profit			6.5	4.3				6.6	3.7
All Other Expenses (net)			3.7	-.6				1.9	1.5
Profit Before Taxes			2.7	4.9				4.7	2.2
RATIOS									
Current			2.3	2.0				2.4	2.3
			1.5	1.5				1.6	1.3
			.9	1.1				1.1	1.0
Quick			1.3	1.2				1.4	1.2
			.9	.9				.9	.8
			.6	.7				.6	.5
Sales/Receivables			43 8.5	33 11.0				36 10.1	36 10.1
			54 6.7	74 4.9				49 7.5	52 7.0
			88 4.1	96 3.8				67 5.5	67 5.5
Cost of Sales/Inventory			33 11.1	11 32.5				40 9.2	21 17.4
			55 6.6	27 13.4				60 6.1	58 6.3
			78 4.7	70 5.2				93 3.9	87 4.2
Cost of Sales/Payables			29 12.5	28 12.8				19 19.6	13 28.8
			39 9.4	39 9.3				29 12.8	26 14.2
			62 5.9	49 7.5				45 8.0	50 7.3
Sales/Working Capital			3.9	5.6				5.2	7.2
			7.7	8.2				8.4	12.7
			-25.4	187.2				25.3	71.2
EBIT/Interest			11.7	29.0				9.4	3.8
			(21) 1.5	(12) 8.5				(37) 2.7	(30) 1.5
			-3.2	3.0				1.1	-.8
Net Profit + Depr., Dep., Amort./Cur. Mat. L /T/D								13.2	
								(15) 1.7	
								.2	
Fixed/Worth			.3	.3				.3	.4
			.8	.5				.5	.7
			-15.9	1.1				1.6	-2.3
Debt/Worth			1.3	.9				.7	.9
			2.3	1.9				2.5	3.6
			-152.6	5.8				7.9	-15.3
% Profit Before Taxes/Tangible Net Worth			62.5	37.2				60.5	44.7
			(17) 11.4	(12) 24.3				(42) 18.8	(26) 11.2
			1.0	12.4				1.8	-22.8
% Profit Before Taxes/Total Assets			23.2	13.1				17.5	16.4
			1.1	7.3				6.7	3.4
			-10.0	2.8				.2	-7.7
Sales/Net Fixed Assets			22.1	36.0				26.2	18.6
			12.5	7.8				13.6	11.0
			6.9	5.8				6.7	5.4
Sales/Total Assets			2.4	1.9				2.8	2.9
			2.1	1.4				2.1	1.9
			1.4	1.3				1.5	1.4
% Depr., Dep., Amort./Sales			.9	.8				.8	1.1
			(20) 1.5	(10) 1.7				(39) 1.7	(26) 1.7
			2.3	2.9				2.3	3.7
% Officers', Directors', Owners' Comp/Sales								3.3	
								(12) 5.8	
								10.7	
Net Sales ($)	1859M	22998M	240371M	450345M				668016M	489104M
Total Assets ($)	601M	8203M	123830M	274637M				505847M	315233M

© RMA 2005

M = $ thousand   MM = $ million
See Pages 11 through 21 for Explanation of Ratios and Data

Comparative Historical Data | Current Data Sorted By Sales

				Type of Statement						
13	10	13		Unqualified				3	4	6
12	11	10		Reviewed		1	1	3	3	2
7	3	6		Compiled	1	1	3	1		
3	2	2		Tax Returns		1		1		
12	9	16		Other	1	1	2	4	5	3
4/1/02-3/31/03 ALL	4/1/03-3/31/04 ALL	4/1/04-3/31/05 ALL			| 9 (4/1-9/30/04)			| 38 (10/1/04-3/31/05)		
					0-1MM	1-3MM	3-5MM	5-10MM	10-25MM	25MM & OVER
47	35	47		NUMBER OF STATEMENTS	2	4	6	12	12	11
%	%	%		ASSETS	%	%	%	%	%	%
12.0	10.0	9.6		Cash & Equivalents				11.6	5.4	8.4
27.7	31.1	33.9		Trade Receivables (net)				30.7	35.9	35.5
24.0	20.7	20.0		Inventory				23.0	19.5	15.0
4.0	5.2	4.9		All Other Current				3.2	9.0	6.9
67.8	66.9	68.4		Total Current				68.5	70.0	65.7
21.3	20.4	20.8		Fixed Assets (net)				23.4	15.5	17.2
3.8	6.6	4.4		Intangibles (net)				3.1	4.1	10.4
7.1	6.0	6.4		All Other Non-Current				4.9	10.4	6.6
100.0	100.0	100.0		Total				100.0	100.0	100.0
				LIABILITIES						
10.8	7.9	10.1		Notes Payable-Short Term				11.3	9.6	8.1
6.2	4.0	3.9		Cur. Mat.-L/T/D				3.6	4.2	5.1
15.6	15.6	19.8		Trade Payables				18.7	19.3	14.9
.4	.5	.1		Income Taxes Payable				.1	.1	.3
14.5	12.7	16.7		All Other Current				11.4	24.3	19.9
47.4	40.7	50.6		Total Current				45.2	57.4	48.1
14.8	14.8	13.4		Long-Term Debt				7.8	15.0	6.1
.6	1.1	.8		Deferred Taxes				.6	1.4	1.2
6.9	7.1	6.8		All Other Non-Current				3.3	12.9	7.8
30.3	36.2	28.3		Net Worth				43.1	13.2	36.7
100.0	100.0	100.0		Total Liabilities & Net Worth				100.0	100.0	100.0
				INCOME DATA						
100.0	100.0	100.0		Net Sales				100.0	100.0	100.0
30.5	30.7	31.5		Gross Profit				28.3	28.1	23.2
28.7	26.0	25.7		Operating Expenses				25.6	29.6	19.3
1.9	4.7	5.9		Operating Profit				2.7	-1.5	3.9
1.6	.7	1.8		All Other Expenses (net)				.5	.6	.0
.3	4.1	4.0		Profit Before Taxes				2.2	-2.0	3.9
				RATIOS						
2.2	2.2	2.0						2.8	1.6	1.9
1.5	1.7	1.5		Current				1.7	1.5	1.3
1.1	1.4	1.0						1.1	1.0	1.0
1.4	1.6	1.2						1.4	1.1	1.4
.9	1.0	.9		Quick				1.0	.9	.9
.5	.6	.7						.8	.4	.7
37 9.9	36 10.1	39 9.3						40 9.1	45 8.1	42 8.7
52 7.0	55 6.6	54 6.7		Sales/Receivables				53 6.9	58 6.3	74 4.9
69 5.3	63 5.8	85 4.3						84 4.4	83 4.4	95 3.9
25 14.5	22 16.4	20 17.8						36 10.2	18 20.6	9 39.1
64 5.7	40 9.0	48 7.7		Cost of Sales/Inventory				69 5.3	43 8.5	23 16.0
95 3.8	87 4.2	79 4.6						107 3.4	71 5.1	60 6.1
16 23.2	21 17.0	26 13.8						27 13.5	32 11.4	30 12.3
31 11.7	29 12.6	38 9.6		Cost of Sales/Payables				36 10.3	43 8.5	38 9.6
61 6.0	49 7.5	61 6.0						62 5.9	61 6.0	48 7.7
5.5	5.1	5.9						3.2	6.1	6.1
9.5	7.1	8.3		Sales/Working Capital				6.5	11.7	8.3
48.3	14.3	94.8						70.9	NM	590.7
6.0	14.0	17.1						12.0	8.4	36.0
(41) 1.9	(30) 4.5	(42) 4.7		EBIT/Interest				(11) 1.5	(11) 1.6	(10) 15.2
-.8	-.5	1.1						-4.5	-3.2	1.7
2.8	4.0	6.3		Net Profit + Depr., Dep.,						
(19) 1.7	(10) 1.9	(10) 3.2		Amort./Cur. Mat. L/T/D						
.5	.0	.2								
.3	.3	.3						.3	.3	.3
.8	.6	.6		Fixed/Worth				.5	.9	.6
3.2	1.2	9.5						1.2	-1.2	1.3
1.0	.7	.9						.8	1.7	.9
2.6	1.7	2.0		Debt/Worth				1.5	3.0	2.0
9.4	4.0	48.1						2.5	-10.7	5.8
60.8	61.3	62.5		% Profit Before Taxes/Tangible				59.1		
(41) 8.4	(30) 20.3	(37) 20.1		Net Worth				(11) 10.7		
-12.3	-1.3	6.4						-31.9		
11.4	14.5	16.6		% Profit Before Taxes/Total				23.2	10.6	12.3
3.0	6.5	5.5		Assets				1.9	1.4	6.9
-7.7	-7.3	.4						-9.0	-13.9	2.2
26.1	29.6	29.0						16.1	26.5	34.5
12.8	13.7	12.2		Sales/Net Fixed Assets				11.1	15.9	6.8
5.2	5.7	6.2						4.0	10.7	5.9
3.0	3.0	2.7						2.4	2.7	2.3
1.9	2.2	2.0		Sales/Total Assets				2.0	2.1	1.5
1.3	1.3	1.4						1.2	1.4	1.4
1.5	.8	.9						1.1	.9	
(41) 2.2	(30) 2.1	(37) 1.5		% Depr., Dep., Amort./Sales				(10) 1.6	(10) 1.3	
4.5	5.0	2.5						2.6	1.7	
3.3		1.7		% Officers', Directors',						
(10) 5.0		(10) 4.1		Owners' Comp/Sales						
6.7		9.2								
559265M	395638M	715573M		Net Sales ($)	1000M	8545M	23551M	81865M	195195M	405417M
386368M	234375M	407271M		Total Assets ($)	2277M	3596M	9867M	50388M	103900M	237243M

M = $ thousand   MM = $ million
See Pages 11 through 21 for Explanation of Ratios and Data

Current Data Sorted By Assets   Comparative Historical Data

0-500M	500M-2MM	2-10MM	10-50MM	50-100MM	100-250MM	Type of Statement	4/1/00-3/31/01 ALL	4/1/01-3/31/02 ALL
1	13	17	13	4	4	Unqualified	37	39
1	15	41	9		1	Reviewed	54	40
3	7	9	4	1		Compiled	40	37
		4	1			Tax Returns	7	2
4	14	28	13	3	1	Other	46	40
	40 (4/1-9/30/04)		166 (10/1/04-3/31/05)					
9	49	99	36	8	5	**NUMBER OF STATEMENTS**	184	158
%	%	%	%	%	%	**ASSETS**	%	%
	7.1	6.9	10.6			Cash & Equivalents	6.5	7.2
	33.8	30.6	28.1			Trade Receivables (net)	30.9	28.0
	24.6	27.6	26.7			Inventory	26.9	23.5
	3.7	4.1	5.2			All Other Current	4.1	4.9
	69.1	69.3	70.6			Total Current	68.3	63.7
	23.9	21.4	20.0			Fixed Assets (net)	23.0	24.7
	2.7	3.4	2.2			Intangibles (net)	3.3	4.7
	4.3	5.9	7.2			All Other Non-Current	5.3	7.0
	100.0	100.0	100.0			Total	100.0	100.0
						LIABILITIES		
	17.3	12.2	7.3			Notes Payable-Short Term	11.2	10.4
	4.5	3.0	2.2			Cur. Mat.-L/T/D	3.0	3.7
	19.6	13.9	18.8			Trade Payables	14.3	11.7
	.2	.2	.9			Income Taxes Payable	.4	.5
	15.5	17.0	14.7			All Other Current	12.5	14.7
	57.1	46.2	43.8			Total Current	41.3	41.0
	17.3	10.2	11.6			Long-Term Debt	12.5	13.0
	.1	.6	.5			Deferred Taxes	.6	.5
	6.1	6.7	5.7			All Other Non-Current	5.3	3.5
	19.5	36.3	38.4			Net Worth	40.3	42.0
	100.0	100.0	100.0			Total Liabilities & Net Worth	100.0	100.0
						INCOME DATA		
	100.0	100.0	100.0			Net Sales	100.0	100.0
	35.2	29.7	29.3			Gross Profit	33.2	31.0
	30.2	26.5	23.1			Operating Expenses	28.0	28.3
	5.0	3.2	6.3			Operating Profit	5.2	2.7
	.8	.7	.5			All Other Expenses (net)	1.0	1.2
	4.2	2.5	5.8			Profit Before Taxes	4.3	1.5
						RATIOS		
	2.1	2.5	2.3			Current	2.4	2.5
	1.2	1.6	1.5				1.7	1.6
	1.0	1.1	1.2				1.2	1.1
	1.2	1.5	1.3			Quick	1.4	1.4
	.8	.7	.8				.8	.9
	.5	.5	.5				.6	.5
	35 10.5	40 9.1	46 7.9			Sales/Receivables	38 9.5	39 9.3
	47 7.8	53 6.9	60 6.0				55 6.6	51 7.1
	60 6.1	69 5.3	72 5.1				70 5.2	67 5.5
	21 17.8	38 9.7	37 10.0			Cost of Sales/Inventory	36 10.3	29 12.5
	49 7.4	78 4.7	78 4.7				70 5.2	67 5.5
	87 4.2	117 3.1	115 3.2				108 3.4	107 3.4
	19 19.7	20 18.0	23 16.1			Cost of Sales/Payables	21 17.3	19 18.9
	32 11.5	30 12.1	35 10.5				34 12.1	29 12.5
	54 6.7	54 6.7	70 5.2				53 6.9	45 8.2
	8.8	4.9	4.2			Sales/Working Capital	4.8	4.1
	20.2	8.2	9.1				8.2	9.1
	-93.7	25.6	24.4				19.1	53.5
	7.4	11.7	33.5			EBIT/Interest	9.8	8.5
	(42) 2.7	(94) 5.3	(34) 9.7				(167) 3.6	(145) 2.4
	.8	2.4	3.2				1.5	.4
		10.0	9.5			Net Profit + Depr., Dep.,	5.7	4.3
		(25) 2.6	(16) 2.1			Amort./Cur. Mat. L/T/D	(58) 3.3	(45) 1.9
		.8	1.4				1.5	1.5
	.3	.2	.3			Fixed/Worth	.2	.3
	1.3	.6	.6				.6	.6
	NM	1.3	.9				1.5	1.5
	1.0	.8	.9			Debt/Worth	.7	.7
	3.8	1.7	2.1				1.4	1.6
	-13.5	4.9	3.5				4.9	4.2
	81.6	35.6	54.7			% Profit Before Taxes/Tangible	39.7	28.1
	(36) 22.3	(85) 18.9	(34) 20.5			Net Worth	(165) 18.3	(141) 12.5
	4.1	6.8	6.1				8.3	-2.9
	15.8	11.9	16.1			% Profit Before Taxes/Total	13.9	11.6
	6.3	6.5	7.2			Assets	7.0	4.5
	-1.1	1.8	1.8				1.9	-2.3
	37.8	34.7	18.4			Sales/Net Fixed Assets	22.3	20.6
	15.6	12.0	10.0				9.5	7.9
	5.9	5.2	6.6				5.2	4.3
	3.5	2.7	2.2			Sales/Total Assets	2.6	2.6
	2.5	2.0	1.8				2.1	1.9
	1.9	1.4	1.4				1.5	1.2
	.9	.9	.6			% Depr., Dep., Amort./Sales	1.0	1.1
	(44) 2.0	(93) 1.9	(34) 1.6				(163) 2.0	(142) 2.3
	4.2	3.7	3.1				3.2	3.9
	3.9	2.0				% Officers', Directors',	3.0	2.6
	(21) 5.7	(39) 3.6				Owners' Comp/Sales	(49) 4.6	(38) 4.2
	9.6	5.3					8.9	6.6
5978M	154834M	909010M	1295119M	806027M	1037363M	Net Sales ($)	4366063M	4257890M
2461M	57172M	453972M	717621M	535212M	768148M	Total Assets ($)	2827990M	3091702M

M = $ thousand   MM = $ million
See Pages 11 through 21 for Explanation of Ratios and Data

Comparative Historical Data				Current Data Sorted By Sales					
			Type of Statement						
42	32	38	Unqualified		3	2	5	11	17
47	42	65	Reviewed	1	13	8	21	16	6
24	29	25	Compiled		13	6	5	1	
4	17	15	Tax Returns	2	5	4	3	1	
42	50	63	Other	5	6	10	11	15	16
4/1/02-3/31/03 ALL	4/1/03-3/31/04 ALL	4/1/04-3/31/05 ALL			40 (4/1-9/30/04)		166 (10/1/04-3/31/05)		
				0-1MM	1-3MM	3-5MM	5-10MM	10-25MM	25MM & OVER
159	170	206	**NUMBER OF STATEMENTS**	8	40	30	45	44	39
%	%	%	**ASSETS**	%	%	%	%	%	%
8.3	9.7	7.5	Cash & Equivalents		6.9	5.7	8.7	7.4	9.5
26.8	29.1	30.2	Trade Receivables (net)		25.7	31.3	35.9	30.5	29.2
24.5	23.0	25.9	Inventory		26.0	27.3	23.3	31.6	22.7
4.1	4.9	4.2	All Other Current		4.4	4.1	4.2	2.7	6.0
63.7	66.8	67.8	Total Current		63.0	68.3	72.1	72.2	67.4
24.4	23.9	23.1	Fixed Assets (net)		26.7	25.5	21.2	17.5	20.0
5.2	3.5	3.6	Intangibles (net)		4.9	1.3	3.0	3.4	5.2
6.6	5.8	5.5	All Other Non-Current		5.5	4.8	3.7	6.9	7.3
100.0	100.0	100.0	Total		100.0	100.0	100.0	100.0	100.0
			LIABILITIES						
8.8	10.6	12.2	Notes Payable-Short Term		18.9	12.4	12.8	7.1	9.9
4.3	4.0	3.5	Cur. Mat.-L/T/D		3.5	4.5	2.9	2.7	3.3
11.4	15.0	16.3	Trade Payables		15.6	18.0	14.2	17.3	17.4
.3	.3	.3	Income Taxes Payable		.0	.3	.3	.5	.6
14.2	14.0	16.3	All Other Current		14.8	15.3	15.8	17.9	17.8
39.1	43.9	48.5	Total Current		52.9	50.6	45.9	45.6	49.0
14.2	12.4	13.1	Long-Term Debt		14.7	20.1	8.0	8.4	14.3
.6	.5	.5	Deferred Taxes		.1	.6	.3	.8	.8
4.6	7.3	7.1	All Other Non-Current		9.9	6.9	5.8	4.2	8.2
41.5	36.0	30.7	Net Worth		22.4	21.8	40.0	41.0	27.7
100.0	100.0	100.0	Total Liabilities & Net Worth		100.0	100.0	100.0	100.0	100.0
			INCOME DATA						
100.0	100.0	100.0	Net Sales		100.0	100.0	100.0	100.0	100.0
31.4	32.2	31.7	Gross Profit		32.9	32.6	30.8	30.5	28.8
27.6	29.6	27.6	Operating Expenses		30.8	28.9	25.8	26.3	22.9
3.8	2.6	4.1	Operating Profit		2.0	3.7	5.1	4.3	5.9
1.2	1.0	.8	All Other Expenses (net)		1.5	.6	-.3	.6	1.2
2.7	1.6	3.3	Profit Before Taxes		.5	3.1	5.4	3.6	4.8
			RATIOS						
2.6	2.4	2.3	Current		2.2	1.9	2.6	2.6	1.8
1.7	1.6	1.5			1.2	1.4	1.5	1.7	1.5
1.2	1.1	1.1			.9	1.1	1.2	1.2	1.1
1.6	1.5	1.3	Quick		1.3	1.1	1.8	1.4	1.2
.8	.9	.8			.6	.8	1.0	.7	.7
.5	.5	.5			.3	.5	.6	.5	.5
38 9.5	36 10.2	40 9.1	Sales/Receivables	36 10.1	40 9.2	38 9.6	42 8.6	46 8.0	
51 7.2	50 7.3	52 7.0		50 7.3	63 5.8	49 7.4	49 7.4	57 6.4	
64 5.7	66 5.5	68 5.3		62 5.9	68 5.3	68 5.4	65 5.6	75 4.9	
35 10.5	24 15.5	28 13.0	Cost of Sales/Inventory	30 12.3	50 7.4	12 29.9	55 6.7	28 13.2	
74 5.0	57 6.4	70 5.2		68 5.3	81 4.5	48 7.6	78 4.7	64 5.7	
112 3.3	97 3.8	108 3.4		122 3.0	116 3.1	96 3.8	121 3.0	101 3.6	
19 18.8	20 18.5	22 16.9	Cost of Sales/Payables	17 21.4	25 14.9	17 22.0	20 18.6	25 14.4	
28 13.1	33 11.2	32 11.5		37 9.8	46 7.9	23 15.9	32 11.4	38 9.6	
43 8.5	51 7.2	57 6.4		59 6.2	74 5.0	37 9.8	49 7.4	57 6.5	
4.2	4.5	5.6	Sales/Working Capital		4.0	5.2	4.9	5.6	6.0
8.8	7.4	10.2			20.8	11.2	10.3	7.6	10.2
27.5	44.6	43.1			-26.7	40.1	27.3	14.0	37.7
13.6	13.9	12.2	EBIT/Interest		4.1	10.1	16.0	21.0	21.1
(149) 3.9	(152) 3.6	(192) 4.8		(37) 2.1	(28) 4.8	(41) 6.1	(41) 6.7	(37) 4.7	
.5	.9	1.8			.2	1.1	3.4	3.4	2.0
6.3	6.8	8.3	Net Profit + Depr., Dep., Amort./Cur. Mat. L/T/D				8.3	9.8	8.0
(46) 2.4	(52) 2.3	(55) 2.6				(10) 2.9	(15) 2.9	(17) 1.4	
.4	.8	.9					1.3	1.7	.3
.3	.2	.3	Fixed/Worth		.3	.5	.2	.1	.4
.6	.6	.7			1.3	1.0	.4	.5	.7
1.4	2.1	2.1			-21.2	5.3	1.3	.9	1.2
.7	.7	1.0	Debt/Worth		1.2	1.4	.7	.7	1.2
1.4	1.6	2.1			2.4	3.9	1.6	1.4	2.4
3.6	5.2	6.6			-12.1	21.6	3.8	3.3	6.8
26.8	35.5	44.5	% Profit Before Taxes/Tangible Net Worth		32.1	64.8	36.6	38.7	59.3
(142) 12.2	(139) 16.0	(170) 19.5		(28) 7.3	(25) 27.1	(38) 17.4	(40) 22.1	(34) 24.7	
.0	2.2	6.9			1.1	9.4	8.6	8.3	9.3
10.0	12.4	12.0	% Profit Before Taxes/Total Assets		9.3	13.0	14.9	10.7	16.4
5.4	5.4	6.2			1.7	5.9	7.3	7.3	6.1
-.6	-.1	1.2			-2.7	-.7	2.3	2.4	1.6
17.8	27.6	31.1	Sales/Net Fixed Assets		24.1	31.1	46.6	36.4	17.6
8.2	10.7	11.2			11.7	7.6	17.8	14.1	10.1
4.4	4.9	5.2			4.9	4.3	5.8	7.1	6.0
2.4	2.6	2.7	Sales/Total Assets		2.5	2.8	3.4	2.7	2.3
1.9	1.9	2.0			1.9	1.7	2.4	2.1	1.9
1.2	1.4	1.4			1.2	1.3	1.6	1.6	1.5
1.4	1.3	.9	% Depr., Dep., Amort./Sales		1.0	1.5	.6	.9	1.3
(141) 2.4	(148) 2.1	(188) 1.9		(36) 2.3	2.1	(42) 1.7	(42) 1.8	(32) 2.0	
4.2	4.2	3.5			3.8	4.3	3.9	3.1	3.4
1.8	2.5	2.2	% Officers', Directors', Owners' Comp/Sales		5.1	3.6	1.7	2.0	
(48) 3.6	(52) 4.7	(74) 4.6		(13) 6.3	(12) 5.3	(22) 4.2	(17) 3.1		
6.5	8.9	7.0			9.2	8.8	5.0	4.8	
4421384M	3457764M	4208331M	Net Sales ($)	4476M	82142M	119595M	331631M	668939M	3001548M
2872431M	2205449M	2534586M	Total Assets ($)	4908M	65277M	74451M	162778M	343819M	1883353M

© RMA 2005

M = $ thousand   MM = $ million
See Pages 11 through 21 for Explanation of Ratios and Data

Current Data Sorted By Assets   Comparative Historical Data

Type of Statement	0-500M	500M-2MM	2-10MM	10-50MM	50-100MM	100-250MM	4/1/00-3/31/01 ALL	4/1/01-3/31/02 ALL
Unqualified		4	6	6		2	19	13
Reviewed		1	6	1			6	4
Compiled		2	2				11	12
Tax Returns	1		3				2	2
Other	4	6	9	6	2	1	17	20
		17 (4/1-9/30/04)		45 (10/1/04-3/31/05)				
NUMBER OF STATEMENTS	5	13	26	13	2	3	55	51
	%	%	%	%	%	%	%	%
ASSETS								
Cash & Equivalents		7.3	15.4	17.6			12.3	16.1
Trade Receivables (net)		34.2	33.6	28.9			31.5	33.1
Inventory		31.1	26.7	28.5			23.2	23.5
All Other Current		7.3	2.6	2.6			1.7	4.5
Total Current		79.9	78.3	77.7			68.6	77.2
Fixed Assets (net)		14.5	10.8	17.3			16.3	13.6
Intangibles (net)		.1	1.8	1.1			7.0	4.1
All Other Non-Current		5.4	9.2	4.0			8.0	5.1
Total		100.0	100.0	100.0			100.0	100.0
LIABILITIES								
Notes Payable-Short Term		21.8	14.1	6.3			10.1	11.3
Cur. Mat.-L/T/D		.9	1.8	.8			2.0	1.8
Trade Payables		16.5	13.9	18.9			16.4	18.6
Income Taxes Payable		.2	.1	.9			.8	.4
All Other Current		11.2	9.2	15.8			10.1	9.7
Total Current		50.6	39.1	42.6			39.5	41.8
Long-Term Debt		14.4	10.1	5.4			10.7	8.3
Deferred Taxes		.0	.2	.2			.4	.3
All Other Non-Current		8.0	7.0	1.1			4.7	4.5
Net Worth		27.0	43.5	50.7			44.6	45.2
Total Liabilities & Net Worth		100.0	100.0	100.0			100.0	100.0
INCOME DATA								
Net Sales		100.0	100.0	100.0			100.0	100.0
Gross Profit		32.9	35.0	36.2			37.8	35.4
Operating Expenses		27.1	32.0	34.0			31.8	32.8
Operating Profit		5.9	3.0	2.2			6.1	2.7
All Other Expenses (net)		.6	.1	.5			.9	.4
Profit Before Taxes		5.3	2.9	1.7			5.2	2.2
RATIOS								
Current		3.4	3.7	4.0			3.1	4.4
		2.3	2.0	1.8			1.8	1.9
		1.1	1.4	1.4			1.2	1.2
Quick		1.2	3.0	2.7			2.3	3.2
		.8	1.2	1.2			1.2	1.0
		.6	.6	.8			.7	.7
Sales/Receivables	16 22.6	34 10.7	29 12.6				28 13.2	33 10.9
	27 13.5	50 7.3	47 7.8				54 6.7	45 8.1
	54 6.7	65 5.6	53 6.9				67 5.4	68 5.4
Cost of Sales/Inventory	7 55.1	34 10.8	39 9.4				17 21.7	17 21.3
	44 8.2	70 5.2	62 5.9				52 7.0	61 6.0
	74 4.9	133 2.7	104 3.5				134 2.7	108 3.4
Cost of Sales/Payables	4 97.2	13 28.5	31 11.8				27 13.8	18 20.5
	22 16.4	25 14.5	41 8.9				39 9.3	35 10.4
	41 8.9	55 6.7	53 6.9				68 5.3	65 5.6
Sales/Working Capital		7.1	3.2	2.6			3.8	3.4
		17.7	5.7	6.2			7.4	6.2
		223.0	16.9	20.8			23.8	16.3
EBIT/Interest		25.1	17.1				13.9	14.5
		(12) 2.6	(21) 4.9				(48) 3.4	(43) 2.7
		1.0	1.3				1.4	-1.3
Net Profit + Depr., Dep., Amort./Cur. Mat. L/T/D							18.4	
							(16) 4.6	
							2.8	
Fixed/Worth		.2	.1	.1			.1	.1
		.7	.2	.3			.4	.3
		NM	.5	.5			1.2	.8
Debt/Worth		.6	.6	.5			.4	.6
		6.6	1.4	.9			1.6	1.4
		NM	5.1	2.0			4.3	4.3
% Profit Before Taxes/Tangible Net Worth		73.5	68.9	43.6			47.4	32.9
		(10) 23.5	(25) 22.5	25.4			(50) 22.8	(47) 5.3
		.1	5.2	-19.0			6.1	-11.9
% Profit Before Taxes/Total Assets		48.2	20.6	19.8			18.8	12.5
		6.5	8.9	12.4			8.2	2.7
		.1	1.4	-10.0			1.2	-6.5
Sales/Net Fixed Assets		167.8	95.3	51.0			52.4	57.5
		41.4	36.6	35.1			15.7	24.7
		11.3	11.0	6.6			5.4	7.3
Sales/Total Assets		6.2	3.2	3.2			3.6	3.6
		3.0	2.1	2.2			1.9	2.1
		2.5	1.5	1.7			1.1	1.4
% Depr., Dep., Amort./Sales		.2	.7	.7			.3	.6
		(10) .7	(22) 1.2	(11) 1.1			(42) 1.2	(41) 1.6
		1.4	2.0	3.5			5.6	3.2
% Officers', Directors', Owners' Comp/Sales			1.4				5.3	
			(12) 4.6				(11) 6.2	
			6.6				18.0	
Net Sales ($)	7345M	60716M	350656M	653924M	157907M	449636M	2293675M	1690501M
Total Assets ($)	1823M	14381M	134472M	309098M	132716M	501304M	1778528M	1221650M

© RMA 2005

M = $ thousand   MM = $ million
See Pages 11 through 21 for Explanation of Ratios and Data

Comparative Historical Data | Current Data Sorted By Sales

4/1/02-3/31/03 ALL	4/1/03-3/31/04 ALL	4/1/04-3/31/05 ALL	Type of Statement	0-1MM	1-3MM	3-5MM	5-10MM	10-25MM	25MM & OVER
11	14	14	Unqualified				2	4	8
7	7	11	Reviewed	1		2	3	3	2
6	5	3	Compiled				2	1	
3	8	6	Tax Returns		1	2	2	1	
33	25	28	Other		7	3	3	6	8
				17 (4/1-9/30/04)			45 (10/1/04-3/31/05)		
60	59	62	NUMBER OF STATEMENTS	1	10	6	12	15	18
%	%	%	ASSETS	%	%	%	%	%	%
13.2	17.0	15.0	Cash & Equivalents		5.4		20.8	9.8	24.9
26.7	32.2	31.9	Trade Receivables (net)		33.6		36.9	37.9	26.5
26.1	24.9	27.2	Inventory		27.5		19.8	32.1	24.0
4.7	3.5	3.5	All Other Current		3.2		1.4	2.4	3.0
70.7	77.6	77.6	Total Current		69.7		79.0	82.2	78.4
17.2	16.2	13.6	Fixed Assets (net)		11.2		17.7	10.4	12.1
6.9	1.7	2.3	Intangibles (net)		.2		.5	2.9	4.9
5.3	4.6	6.5	All Other Non-Current		18.9		2.8	4.5	4.6
100.0	100.0	100.0	Total		100.0		100.0	100.0	100.0
			LIABILITIES						
12.1	9.3	13.7	Notes Payable-Short Term		24.0		17.6	14.2	5.0
2.8	2.0	1.4	Cur. Mat.-L/T/D		1.7		2.9	1.5	.6
14.7	20.1	16.7	Trade Payables		16.3		12.0	17.1	17.8
.6	.7	.4	Income Taxes Payable		.0		.0	.1	1.2
10.2	11.4	10.3	All Other Current		3.8		11.2	8.5	14.6
40.5	43.5	42.4	Total Current		45.9		43.7	41.4	39.3
12.5	8.4	10.5	Long-Term Debt		4.5		14.9	10.1	2.8
.1	.0	.1	Deferred Taxes		.1		.3	.0	.2
6.0	7.5	6.5	All Other Non-Current		12.3		4.3	8.8	1.5
40.8	40.6	40.4	Net Worth		37.3		36.8	39.7	56.2
100.0	100.0	100.0	Total Liabilities & Net Worth		100.0		100.0	100.0	100.0
			INCOME DATA						
100.0	100.0	100.0	Net Sales		100.0		100.0	100.0	100.0
38.8	39.2	37.0	Gross Profit		44.1		35.5	33.9	38.5
35.9	33.9	32.8	Operating Expenses		42.7		34.3	28.5	31.2
2.9	5.3	4.1	Operating Profit		1.4		1.2	5.4	7.4
1.0	.4	.4	All Other Expenses (net)		.7		.6	-.1	.3
1.9	4.9	3.7	Profit Before Taxes		.7		.6	5.5	7.0
			RATIOS						
3.4 / 1.6 / 1.2	3.3 / 1.8 / 1.3	3.9 / 2.0 / 1.2	Current		4.2 / 2.0 / .7		3.5 / 2.1 / 1.2	4.0 / 2.2 / 1.3	4.2 / 2.2 / 1.5
1.4 / .9 / .5	2.6 / 1.3 / .7	2.9 / 1.0 / .7	Quick		3.1 / 1.1 / .4		3.0 / 1.5 / .8	2.8 / 1.0 / .6	3.7 / 1.2 / .8
29 12.4 / 46 8.0 / 69 5.3	29 12.6 / 44 8.3 / 57 6.4	30 12.4 / 45 8.1 / 57 6.4	Sales/Receivables		35 10.5 / 47 7.8 / 53 6.8		19 19.1 / 41 8.9 / 94 3.9	34 10.9 / 45 8.2 / 62 5.9	34 10.8 / 44 8.2 / 55 6.6
29 12.7 / 75 4.9 / 108 3.4	14 25.3 / 57 6.4 / 92 4.0	32 11.4 / 61 6.0 / 101 3.6	Cost of Sales/Inventory		23 15.7 / 62 5.9 / 132 2.8		7 54.5 / 49 7.5 / 70 5.2	35 10.4 / 53 6.9 / 134 2.7	34 10.9 / 67 5.5 / 101 3.6
20 18.3 / 37 9.8 / 59 6.2	23 15.6 / 41 8.9 / 59 6.2	16 22.2 / 34 10.6 / 56 6.5	Cost of Sales/Payables		9 42.9 / 38 9.6 / 67 5.5		12 31.7 / 25 14.5 / 49 7.4	13 28.4 / 28 13.1 / 46 7.9	30 12.2 / 44 8.2 / 59 6.2
4.2 / 7.6 / 25.0	4.1 / 7.4 / 18.8	3.1 / 6.8 / 20.2	Sales/Working Capital		3.6 / 10.3 / -11.7		2.5 / 4.8 / 19.5	3.6 / 6.7 / 16.1	2.4 / 4.7 / 15.7
14.3 / (51) 2.1 / -2.5	23.5 / (48) 6.3 / 1.8	30.4 / (50) 5.7 / 1.1	EBIT/Interest					33.5 / (14) 9.1 / 2.9	109.7 / (12) 22.6 / 16.8
		26.7 / (13) 15.5 / 3.0	Net Profit + Depr., Dep., Amort./Cur. Mat. L/T/D						
.1 / .5 / 1.5	.1 / .3 / .8	.1 / .3 / .6	Fixed/Worth		.1 / .2 / -.3		.2 / .4 / 1.0	.1 / .3 / .7	.1 / .2 / .4
.6 / 1.8 / 5.6	.5 / 1.4 / 3.7	.5 / 1.4 / 6.5	Debt/Worth		.2 / .7 / -3.8		.7 / 2.1 / 6.4	.6 / 1.5 / 10.7	.3 / .9 / 1.8
67.9 / (54) 14.5 / -10.5	61.0 / (51) 20.6 / 6.2	51.7 / (55) 22.6 / 3.1	% Profit Before Taxes/Tangible Net Worth				70.6 / 11.4 / 1.0	78.5 / (14) 39.9 / 14.4	41.2 / 24.1 / 12.2
12.7 / 3.7 / -7.7	21.1 / 8.7 / 2.1	20.4 / 11.1 / .2	% Profit Before Taxes/Total Assets		17.8 / 8.5 / -7.9		17.8 / 4.1 / .3	28.2 / 15.0 / 2.2	19.1 / 12.2 / 5.2
60.9 / 13.9 / 4.9	82.0 / 37.7 / 11.5	70.3 / 32.7 / 10.5	Sales/Net Fixed Assets		126.8 / 33.5 / 10.9		61.9 / 20.5 / 11.0	177.6 / 48.4 / 12.5	48.5 / 27.8 / 6.9
3.3 / 1.9 / 1.2	4.0 / 2.5 / 1.7	3.8 / 2.4 / 1.6	Sales/Total Assets		4.4 / 2.9 / 1.3		4.0 / 2.2 / 1.3	3.5 / 2.6 / 2.0	3.1 / 1.9 / 1.0
.6 / (42) 2.4 / 4.0	.3 / (50) 1.0 / 2.0	.6 / (51) 1.2 / 2.6	% Depr., Dep., Amort./Sales				.6 / (11) 1.1 / 1.8	.4 / (12) .9 / 1.8	.4 / (16) 1.3 / 3.4
1.8 / (13) 8.2 / 11.5	1.1 / (23) 5.7 / 14.7	2.3 / (22) 4.8 / 9.8	% Officers', Directors', Owners' Comp/Sales						
2265232M	1852936M	1680184M	Net Sales ($)	628M	18268M	25108M	89390M	219283M	1327507M
1738511M	843948M	1093794M	Total Assets ($)	342M	13338M	8891M	61812M	87313M	922098M

© RMA 2005

M = $ thousand   MM = $ million
See Pages 11 through 21 for Explanation of Ratios and Data

Current Data Sorted By Assets — Comparative Historical Data

Date headers: 500M-2MM column under **16 (4/1-9/30/04)**; 2-10MM, 10-50MM, 50-100MM, 100-250MM columns under **59 (10/1/04-3/31/05)**. Historical columns: **4/1/00-3/31/01 ALL** and **4/1/01-3/31/02 ALL**.

	0-500M	500M-2MM	2-10MM	10-50MM	50-100MM	100-250MM	4/1/00-3/31/01 ALL	4/1/01-3/31/02 ALL
Type of Statement								
Unqualified			4	14	8	7	19	14
Reviewed		6	7	3			13	6
Compiled	2	1	3		1		8	8
Tax Returns	1		1	1			4	
Other		6	6	3	4	1	21	24
NUMBER OF STATEMENTS	3	13	21	18	12	8	65	52
ASSETS (%)								
Cash & Equivalents		6.8	14.0	16.9	19.7		11.0	12.8
Trade Receivables (net)		34.6	36.0	23.3	22.9		29.5	26.5
Inventory		31.7	27.5	22.0	16.7		25.6	22.3
All Other Current		1.2	.9	5.9	3.4		2.3	2.3
Total Current		74.3	78.4	68.1	62.7		68.4	63.9
Fixed Assets (net)		10.3	14.5	20.9	10.4		13.1	17.5
Intangibles (net)		9.9	1.9	5.2	17.9		11.6	12.9
All Other Non-Current		5.5	5.3	5.8	9.0		7.0	5.7
Total		100.0	100.0	100.0	100.0		100.0	100.0
LIABILITIES								
Notes Payable-Short Term		13.0	10.1	4.7	2.3		13.7	8.3
Cur. Mat.-L/T/D		2.1	1.7	2.9	2.1		3.6	4.9
Trade Payables		21.3	18.3	15.9	13.4		15.6	13.5
Income Taxes Payable		.0	1.1	.3	.5		.3	.2
All Other Current		10.7	8.6	11.0	13.5		11.2	11.9
Total Current		47.0	39.7	34.8	31.8		44.5	38.9
Long-Term Debt		26.8	6.2	20.6	10.1		13.1	11.4
Deferred Taxes		.2	.3	.5	.3		.5	.7
All Other Non-Current		3.4	4.0	4.1	3.0		19.4	4.5
Net Worth		22.6	49.9	40.0	54.7		22.5	44.5
Total Liabilities & Net Worth		100.0	100.0	100.0	100.0		100.0	100.0
INCOME DATA								
Net Sales		100.0	100.0	100.0	100.0		100.0	100.0
Gross Profit		43.5	42.9	33.5	39.2		39.0	38.8
Operating Expenses		38.9	36.6	28.1	32.0		34.8	39.8
Operating Profit		4.6	6.3	5.4	7.2		4.2	-1.0
All Other Expenses (net)		.9	.3	1.7	.5		.8	1.3
Profit Before Taxes		3.8	6.0	3.6	6.7		3.4	-2.3
RATIOS								
Current		3.3	3.7	3.0	3.9		3.1	3.2
		1.5	1.8	2.1	1.9		1.7	1.7
		1.2	1.2	1.6	1.4		1.2	1.3
Quick		1.8	2.9	2.1	3.8		1.7	2.3
		.9	1.2	1.2	1.0		.8	.9
		.6	.7	.6	.7		.6	.6
Sales/Receivables		35 10.5	39 9.3	38 9.5	47 7.7		41 8.9	35 10.4
		47 7.8	49 7.4	50 7.3	56 6.6		56 6.6	57 6.4
		59 6.2	67 5.5	56 6.5	69 5.3		75 4.9	70 5.2
Cost of Sales/Inventory		32 11.3	37 9.8	45 8.1	31 11.9		41 8.9	26 14.1
		75 4.9	68 5.3	65 5.6	54 6.7		75 4.9	58 6.3
		109 3.4	120 3.1	83 4.4	76 4.8		113 3.2	106 3.4
Cost of Sales/Payables		27 13.7	25 14.8	31 11.6	30 12.1		30 12.0	21 17.0
		42 8.8	47 7.8	40 9.1	51 7.2		41 8.9	32 11.3
		101 3.6	58 6.3	60 6.1	78 4.7		65 5.6	64 5.7
Sales/Working Capital		5.5	2.0	3.3	1.8		4.0	4.6
		9.6	8.6	4.6	5.7		7.0	7.5
		22.5	23.2	14.4	11.1		17.4	21.0
EBIT/Interest		9.3	65.5	17.2			11.4	10.1
		(11) 4.8	(17) 7.2	(16) 2.9			(55) 2.9	(42) 1.0
		.6	3.4	-1.2			.1	-1.9
Net Profit + Depr., Dep., Amort./Cur. Mat. L /T/D							37.4	
							(12) 1.7	
							.7	
Fixed/Worth		.2	.2	.2	.1		.2	.1
		.4	.3	.5	.3		.4	.4
		NM	.5	1.0	1.5		4.6	2.0
Debt/Worth		1.1	.4	.5	.3		.8	.4
		2.2	1.1	1.0	.9		2.0	1.3
		NM	3.3	3.8	8.0		27.3	10.7
% Profit Before Taxes/Tangible Net Worth		57.7	50.5	65.6	29.1		58.4	31.1
		(10) 26.9	(20) 25.6	(16) 19.7	(11) 12.6		(52) 20.6	(42) 3.7
		6.9	7.2	-3.7	3.1		2.0	-32.3
% Profit Before Taxes/Total Assets		16.1	17.3	18.3	11.5		12.9	13.1
		7.0	11.4	5.0	7.2		7.9	.0
		-.3	4.6	-5.0	3.0		-2.6	-11.7
Sales/Net Fixed Assets		58.5	44.1	21.5	18.5		37.2	30.5
		35.5	23.4	11.5	15.8		17.8	14.1
		23.6	7.4	5.6	13.2		8.1	6.9
Sales/Total Assets		3.9	3.6	2.3	1.9		2.7	2.4
		3.0	2.3	1.7	1.1		1.7	1.9
		2.0	1.3	1.2	.8		1.1	1.2
% Depr., Dep., Amort./Sales			.5	1.4			.9	1.1
			(16) 1.3	2.3			(49) 2.0	(35) 2.3
			2.1	4.5			4.0	4.2
% Officers', Directors', Owners' Comp/Sales							2.4	1.5
							(16) 6.2	(11) 3.1
							10.1	10.5
Net Sales ($)	1281M	56491M	209090M	892694M	1265729M	1586553M	3108637M	2160209M
Total Assets ($)	608M	18610M	89028M	516888M	921553M	1310316M	2223170M	1705982M

M = $ thousand   MM = $ million
See Pages 11 through 21 for Explanation of Ratios and Data

Comparative Historical Data · **Current Data Sorted By Sales**

	Comparative Historical Data			Current Data Sorted By Sales					
Type of Statement					16 (4/1-9/30/04)			59 (10/1/04-3/31/05)	
Unqualified	26	23	33			1	2	4	26
Reviewed	14	11	13		3	2	6	2	
Compiled	2	15	6	2	1	2	1		
Tax Returns	4	2	3	1		1			1
Other	27	22	20	1	1	2	5	3	8
	4/1/02-3/31/03	4/1/03-3/31/04	4/1/04-3/31/05	0-1MM	1-3MM	3-5MM	5-10MM	10-25MM	25MM & OVER
	ALL	ALL	ALL						
NUMBER OF STATEMENTS	73	73	75	4	5	8	14	9	35
	%	%	%	%	%	%	%	%	%
ASSETS									
Cash & Equivalents	13.6	15.8	14.8				10.1		19.4
Trade Receivables (net)	28.4	26.4	28.1				38.9		23.9
Inventory	23.2	21.2	22.9				27.4		19.2
All Other Current	3.8	2.8	3.5				1.5		5.9
Total Current	69.0	66.3	69.4				77.8		68.5
Fixed Assets (net)	14.7	19.1	14.9				14.5		14.8
Intangibles (net)	11.3	9.0	9.4				1.9		10.3
All Other Non-Current	5.0	5.7	6.3				5.8		6.4
Total	100.0	100.0	100.0				100.0		100.0
LIABILITIES									
Notes Payable-Short Term	6.5	11.5	7.5				7.2		3.5
Cur. Mat.-L/T/D	3.9	2.3	2.2				3.1		2.2
Trade Payables	16.3	13.1	15.6				17.4		14.2
Income Taxes Payable	.3	.7	.6				1.6		.6
All Other Current	11.6	11.0	10.8				13.1		12.9
Total Current	38.6	38.5	36.7				42.4		33.5
Long-Term Debt	15.2	19.2	18.3				4.0		16.8
Deferred Taxes	.7	.4	.3				.5		.3
All Other Non-Current	6.8	5.2	3.9				3.0		3.3
Net Worth	38.7	36.7	40.9				50.1		46.1
Total Liabilities & Net Worth	100.0	100.0	100.0				100.0		100.0
INCOME DATA									
Net Sales	100.0	100.0	100.0				100.0		100.0
Gross Profit	36.6	41.6	40.1				46.6		34.6
Operating Expenses	35.1	38.2	34.0				37.6		27.9
Operating Profit	1.4	3.4	6.2				9.0		6.7
All Other Expenses (net)	1.5	1.5	1.0				.4		.8
Profit Before Taxes	−.1	1.9	5.2				8.6		5.9
RATIOS									
Current	3.4	3.0	3.5				3.5		3.2
	1.6	2.0	1.9				1.8		2.0
	1.2	1.3	1.2				1.2		1.4
Quick	2.3	2.1	2.1				2.4		2.7
	1.0	1.1	1.1				1.0		1.3
	.7	.6	.7				.7		.8
Sales/Receivables	37 9.9	37 9.8	39 9.5				35 10.6		39 9.5
	50 7.3	50 7.3	50 7.4				45 8.1		52 7.0
	68 5.4	68 5.4	62 5.9				66 5.5		61 6.0
Cost of Sales/Inventory	20 18.0	29 12.4	35 10.4				36 10.1		35 10.4
	68 5.4	68 5.4	61 6.0				54 6.8		58 6.3
	112 3.3	102 3.6	99 3.7				80 4.6		81 4.5
Cost of Sales/Payables	26 13.8	23 15.6	29 12.6				21 17.2		27 13.4
	41 8.9	41 8.8	42 8.6				46 8.0		38 9.5
	60 6.1	60 6.0	63 5.8				68 5.3		63 5.8
Sales/Working Capital	3.9	3.2	3.0				5.1		2.8
	7.8	6.4	5.9				9.9		5.0
	28.4	23.5	17.3				29.9		12.4
EBIT/Interest	10.3	22.9	21.7				140.5		33.0
	(64) 2.4	(62) 2.2	(60) 4.8				(10) 14.0	(26)	6.0
	−.7	.3	1.4				1.1		2.4
Net Profit + Depr., Dep., Amort./Cur. Mat. L/T/D	11.7	4.5	14.0						32.1
	(16) 1.8	(15) 2.5	(24) 4.2					(13)	5.2
	−2.9	1.8	1.6						2.3
Fixed/Worth	.1	.1	.2				.2		.1
	.4	.5	.3				.3		.4
	1.1	1.2	.8				.5		.9
Debt/Worth	.5	.5	.5				.4		.4
	1.8	1.2	1.2				.8		1.0
	6.7	4.0	3.8				3.5		4.9
% Profit Before Taxes/Tangible Net Worth	43.4	33.1	43.0				49.6		37.9
	(62) 12.8	(63) 12.1	(65) 19.8				(13) 21.0	(31)	17.1
	−4.0	−3.1	7.0				5.0		7.2
% Profit Before Taxes/Total Assets	15.1	15.5	14.4				33.2		14.0
	4.6	3.4	8.4				12.1		8.4
	−3.3	−2.6	2.4				1.5		3.9
Sales/Net Fixed Assets	42.5	28.9	32.9				36.5		21.2
	15.8	14.5	17.6				24.9		14.0
	8.5	6.3	8.4				10.0		9.1
Sales/Total Assets	2.8	2.5	2.8				3.8		2.0
	1.8	1.6	1.9				2.9		1.6
	1.1	.9	1.1				1.9		1.0
% Depr., Dep., Amort./Sales	1.1	1.1	1.1						1.5
	(56) 2.1	(59) 2.2	(55) 1.7					(29)	2.2
	3.7	4.7	3.5						3.8
% Officers', Directors', Owners' Comp/Sales	2.7		1.6						
	(11) 6.5		(10) 3.1						
	10.4		8.5						
Net Sales ($)	3503991M	2363290M	4011838M	1856M	10642M	31993M	105496M	173360M	3688491M
Total Assets ($)	2309632M	2212885M	2857003M	1392M	6715M	23896M	44950M	171739M	2608311M

© RMA 2005 · M = $ thousand   MM = $ million

See Pages 11 through 21 for Explanation of Ratios and Data

Current Data Sorted By Assets **Comparative Historical Data**

0-500M	500M-2MM	2-10MM	10-50MM	50-100MM	100-250MM	Type of Statement	4/1/00-3/31/01 ALL	4/1/01-3/31/02 ALL
1		5	2	3	4	Unqualified	16	12
	2	2	1			Reviewed	2	5
1		1				Compiled	11	8
1	2					Tax Returns	4	3
	2	5	3	1	3	Other	20	10
		8 (4/1-9/30/04)		31 (10/1/04-3/31/05)				
3	6	13	6	4	7	NUMBER OF STATEMENTS	53	38
%	%	%	%	%	%	**ASSETS**	%	%
		10.0				Cash & Equivalents	11.8	15.5
		28.5				Trade Receivables (net)	25.6	22.2
		30.1				Inventory	27.7	23.6
		2.5				All Other Current	4.8	2.2
		71.2				Total Current	69.9	63.5
		14.5				Fixed Assets (net)	17.3	16.9
		8.5				Intangibles (net)	7.4	11.6
		5.9				All Other Non-Current	5.4	7.9
		100.0				Total	100.0	100.0
						LIABILITIES		
		15.0				Notes Payable-Short Term	11.3	9.2
		3.8				Cur. Mat.-L/T/D	4.7	3.6
		14.3				Trade Payables	11.7	12.2
		.3				Income Taxes Payable	.3	.3
		19.0				All Other Current	12.9	8.4
		52.4				Total Current	40.9	33.7
		18.5				Long-Term Debt	10.7	17.6
		.0				Deferred Taxes	.4	.2
		30.3				All Other Non-Current	3.9	8.4
		-1.3				Net Worth	44.1	40.1
		100.0				Total Liabilities & Net Worth	100.0	100.0
						INCOME DATA		
		100.0				Net Sales	100.0	100.0
		45.3				Gross Profit	40.7	41.7
		42.8				Operating Expenses	38.8	40.5
		2.5				Operating Profit	1.9	1.2
		1.3				All Other Expenses (net)	-1.4	1.5
		1.2				Profit Before Taxes	3.2	-.3
						RATIOS		
		2.4					3.5	5.6
		1.3				Current	1.6	1.8
		1.0					1.2	1.2
		1.2					1.7	3.2
		.6				Quick	.8	.9
		.4					.5	.4
		39 9.3					41 8.9	35 10.5
		46 8.0				Sales/Receivables	55 6.7	44 8.2
		56 6.5					71 5.2	53 6.9
		49 7.5					58 6.3	41 8.9
		89 4.1				Cost of Sales/Inventory	93 3.9	73 5.0
		165 2.2					132 2.8	145 2.5
		22 16.3					20 17.8	16 22.7
		58 6.3				Cost of Sales/Payables	37 9.8	29 12.7
		74 4.9					69 5.3	59 6.2
		5.8					3.1	3.0
		17.0				Sales/Working Capital	7.5	6.9
		NM					16.4	24.5
		8.8					4.7	3.4
		1.9				EBIT/Interest	(42) 2.3	(32) 1.7
		-.7					.8	-2.4
						Net Profit + Depr., Dep.,	19.6	10.3
						Amort./Cur. Mat. L /T/D	(12) 3.0	(11) 2.1
							.9	-.4
		.2					.2	.2
		.9				Fixed/Worth	.4	.4
		-2.6					1.0	1.8
		1.0					.4	.3
		6.4				Debt/Worth	1.4	2.0
		-7.8					3.9	9.3
							28.6	28.4
						% Profit Before Taxes/Tangible Net Worth	(46) 14.5	(31) 8.9
							-1.5	.5
		14.7					11.2	11.6
		5.0				% Profit Before Taxes/Total Assets	5.8	2.2
		-3.6					-.7	-6.8
		158.9					22.9	29.4
		43.1				Sales/Net Fixed Assets	13.7	12.9
		11.4					6.1	6.3
		3.1					2.6	2.7
		2.6				Sales/Total Assets	1.7	1.8
		1.8					1.1	1.1
		.4					.9	.9
	(10)	1.4				% Depr., Dep., Amort./Sales	(40) 2.0	(36) 2.3
		3.6					3.2	4.2
							3.9	7.1
						% Officers', Directors', Owners' Comp/Sales	(10) 6.4	(12) 17.1
							12.8	21.5
4766M	24109M	156639M	297978M	351103M	1699190M	Net Sales ($)	3184859M	1629716M
834M	8071M	63425M	148519M	290547M	1051467M	Total Assets ($)	2242775M	1240245M

M = $ thousand   MM = $ million
See Pages 11 through 21 for Explanation of Ratios and Data

Comparative Historical Data | Current Data Sorted By Sales

			Type of Statement	0-1MM	1-3MM	3-5MM	5-10MM	10-25MM	25MM & OVER
9	16	15	Unqualified		1		4	4	9
10	7	5	Reviewed		1		1		
3	6	2	Compiled			1	1		
	1	3	Tax Returns		2	1			
18	18	14	Other	1		2	1	2	8
4/1/02-3/31/03	4/1/03-3/31/04	4/1/04-3/31/05			8 (4/1-9/30/04)			31 (10/1/04-3/31/05)	
ALL	ALL	ALL							
40	48	39	**NUMBER OF STATEMENTS**	1	4	4	7	6	17
%	%	%	**ASSETS**	%	%	%	%	%	%
14.6	14.9	14.0	Cash & Equivalents						19.6
25.8	23.5	27.2	Trade Receivables (net)						27.1
25.1	22.6	23.9	Inventory						18.2
4.5	5.0	4.5	All Other Current						6.7
70.1	65.9	69.5	Total Current						71.7
15.1	18.8	13.2	Fixed Assets (net)						9.9
6.8	8.8	8.4	Intangibles (net)						11.0
7.9	6.5	8.8	All Other Non-Current						7.5
100.0	100.0	100.0	Total						100.0
			LIABILITIES						
12.0	13.7	9.8	Notes Payable-Short Term						1.7
7.2	2.4	2.5	Cur. Mat.-L/T/D						1.4
13.2	16.3	15.3	Trade Payables						10.3
.4	.9	.5	Income Taxes Payable						1.0
11.0	17.2	17.3	All Other Current						19.9
43.8	50.4	45.5	Total Current						34.2
18.1	14.3	11.6	Long-Term Debt						10.6
.2	.5	.1	Deferred Taxes						.1
6.0	10.0	14.4	All Other Non-Current						7.2
32.0	24.8	28.4	Net Worth						47.9
100.0	100.0	100.0	Total Liabilities & Net Worth						100.0
			INCOME DATA						
100.0	100.0	100.0	Net Sales						100.0
38.9	44.7	39.7	Gross Profit						36.0
36.5	39.6	36.1	Operating Expenses						30.3
2.4	5.1	3.7	Operating Profit						5.7
2.2	1.7	.8	All Other Expenses (net)						.6
.2	3.4	2.8	Profit Before Taxes						5.1
			RATIOS						
3.8	2.5	2.5							3.9
2.3	1.4	1.6	Current						2.2
1.2	.9	1.1							1.4
2.4	1.2	1.5							2.2
1.2	.8	.9	Quick						1.5
.6	.4	.5							.8
25 14.6	26 13.9	33 11.1							40 9.1
44 8.4	40 9.1	46 8.0	Sales/Receivables						60 6.1
66 5.5	54 6.7	62 5.9							69 5.3
43 8.6	38 9.5	34 10.6							30 12.2
85 4.3	63 5.8	67 5.4	Cost of Sales/Inventory						59 6.2
143 2.6	94 3.9	118 3.1							115 3.2
18 19.9	27 13.3	22 16.9							20 18.3
29 12.4	38 9.5	30 12.3	Cost of Sales/Payables						27 13.4
56 6.5	60 6.1	58 6.3							44 8.2
3.5	3.9	4.6							2.8
5.4	13.5	11.3	Sales/Working Capital						4.6
18.1	-31.6	54.4							16.4
13.1	19.3	42.0							251.0
(34) 2.3	(43) 4.3	(35) 6.4	EBIT/Interest						(13) 12.1
.1	.6	-.5							2.2
263.1	72.3		Net Profit + Depr., Dep.,						
(10) 6.3	(14) 31.3		Amort./Cur. Mat. L/T/D						
.4	2.2								
.2	.2	.2							.1
.3	.6	.3	Fixed/Worth						.2
1.2	NM	2.4							1.1
.5	.6	.5							.4
1.7	2.5	1.6	Debt/Worth						1.0
4.9	NM	93.0							14.9
39.9	49.4	65.9	% Profit Before Taxes/Tangible						53.1
(32) 14.5	(36) 16.6	(30) 24.7	Net Worth						(15) 23.7
2.4	8.2	5.1							5.3
12.7	13.2	15.4	% Profit Before Taxes/Total						15.6
6.1	5.9	7.0	Assets						7.4
-5.4	-2.6	-1.9							2.3
38.2	59.2	52.5							36.0
15.3	19.8	20.3	Sales/Net Fixed Assets						17.1
9.0	5.1	8.5							8.2
2.8	3.0	3.0							2.3
2.0	1.8	2.2	Sales/Total Assets						1.6
1.2	1.0	1.3							1.1
1.0	.8	.9							.9
(29) 1.7	(34) 2.1	(29) 1.4	% Depr., Dep., Amort./Sales						(13) 1.2
3.6	5.7	3.7							4.3
3.8			% Officers', Directors',						
(10) 7.4			Owners' Comp/Sales						
11.4									
2766984M	1728678M	2533785M	Net Sales ($)	40M	7668M	14022M	48724M	97300M	2366031M
1309144M	1391883M	1562863M	Total Assets ($)	30M	4940M	5094M	31513M	33305M	1487981M

Current Data Sorted By Assets   **Comparative Historical Data**

	0-500M	500M-2MM	2-10MM	10-50MM	50-100MM	100-250MM	Type of Statement	4/1/00-3/31/01 ALL	4/1/01-3/31/02 ALL
		1	6	9	10	2	Unqualified	27	20
		5	13	2	1		Reviewed	9	10
		4	4	4			Compiled	13	6
1		6	2				Tax Returns	2	2
1		4	6	10	1	1	Other	21	27
		27 (4/1-9/30/04)			62 (10/1/04-3/31/05)				
	2	20	31	21	12	3	**NUMBER OF STATEMENTS**	72	65
	%	%	%	%	%	%	**ASSETS**	%	%
		7.2	8.1	12.2	11.8		Cash & Equivalents	10.7	12.2
		40.4	28.2	28.4	17.9		Trade Receivables (net)	26.8	26.1
		27.0	30.8	26.6	20.8		Inventory	25.5	26.8
		4.5	1.7	5.6	6.6		All Other Current	3.7	2.9
		79.1	68.9	72.8	57.0		Total Current	66.7	68.0
		16.2	21.7	14.8	24.7		Fixed Assets (net)	23.6	20.7
		1.6	2.4	6.3	7.8		Intangibles (net)	5.2	5.3
		3.1	7.0	6.1	10.6		All Other Non-Current	4.5	6.0
		100.0	100.0	100.0	100.0		Total	100.0	100.0
							LIABILITIES		
		16.1	11.5	10.7	4.0		Notes Payable-Short Term	7.0	10.6
		4.3	5.0	1.8	2.3		Cur. Mat.-L/T/D	4.1	2.6
		24.2	14.2	14.1	10.0		Trade Payables	11.5	13.7
		.0	.8	1.0	.8		Income Taxes Payable	.2	.1
		17.9	10.1	15.2	10.6		All Other Current	11.1	11.6
		62.5	41.6	42.8	27.6		Total Current	33.9	38.6
		12.4	11.0	7.4	11.9		Long-Term Debt	12.1	10.5
		.1	.4	.2	1.1		Deferred Taxes	1.5	2.7
		6.3	5.8	4.3	1.5		All Other Non-Current	2.4	3.9
		18.7	41.1	45.2	57.8		Net Worth	50.1	44.3
		100.0	100.0	100.0	100.0		Total Liabilities & Net Worth	100.0	100.0
							INCOME DATA		
		100.0	100.0	100.0	100.0		Net Sales	100.0	100.0
		42.7	37.7	32.9	38.6		Gross Profit	39.6	38.1
		36.4	29.7	26.5	30.9		Operating Expenses	33.0	36.0
		6.3	8.0	6.4	7.7		Operating Profit	6.6	2.1
		1.0	.4	.8	2.8		All Other Expenses (net)	1.4	.7
		5.3	7.6	5.5	4.8		Profit Before Taxes	5.2	1.4
							RATIOS		
		1.7	2.8	3.5	4.0			3.4	3.4
		1.4	1.5	1.5	2.1		Current	2.2	2.1
		.9	1.2	1.2	1.1			1.3	1.3
		1.3	1.3	1.7	2.0			2.2	2.1
		.7	.9	.8	1.1		Quick	1.0	1.1
		.5	.5	.7	.5			.6	.6
		38 9.7	30 12.3	44 8.2	38 9.6			44 8.3	31 11.9
		57 6.4	50 7.3	54 6.7	50 7.4		Sales/Receivables	51 7.1	44 8.2
		79 4.6	61 5.9	63 5.8	63 5.8			68 5.4	60 6.1
		0 UND	42 8.6	52 7.0	44 8.4			41 8.8	41 8.9
		36 10.0	79 4.6	98 3.7	95 3.9		Cost of Sales/Inventory	81 4.5	76 4.8
		116 3.2	121 3.0	128 2.8	119 3.1			138 2.6	138 2.7
		21 17.6	18 20.4	25 14.9	22 16.6			20 17.9	18 19.8
		48 7.7	32 11.5	36 10.1	30 12.2		Cost of Sales/Payables	31 11.8	29 12.7
		131 2.8	57 6.4	61 6.0	77 4.7			45 8.0	52 7.0
		5.0	4.1	3.6	2.4			3.0	3.8
		10.8	9.2	6.4	6.5		Sales/Working Capital	5.6	6.2
		-30.1	23.0	19.1	47.7			11.4	22.8
		11.8	23.8	68.6	62.8			15.7	13.0
	(16)	5.3	(26) 7.7	(14) 5.5	(10) 20.8		EBIT/Interest	(59) 4.2	(54) 2.5
		1.5	1.1	3.4	2.3			1.4	.8
			7.6					8.2	12.1
			(14) 1.8				Net Profit + Depr., Dep., Amort./Cur. Mat. L /T/D	(29) 2.8	(18) 4.1
			.7					.8	1.8
		.3	.1	.2	.1			.2	.2
		.6	.7	.3	.5		Fixed/Worth	.4	.4
		-1.1	2.0	1.4	1.0			1.0	1.2
		1.3	.5	.4	.2			.4	.5
		3.2	1.7	1.1	.8		Debt/Worth	1.0	1.1
		-11.5	6.5	18.6	2.6			2.2	4.1
		68.8	45.3	36.4	20.5			49.0	38.2
	(13)	41.1	(28) 17.0	(19) 20.7	(11) 10.0		% Profit Before Taxes/Tangible Net Worth	(69) 16.6	(57) 16.2
		11.7	2.8	6.3	2.9			2.8	-.5
		29.7	23.5	15.1	12.7			23.1	14.1
		8.9	5.8	8.4	5.5		% Profit Before Taxes/Total Assets	8.3	4.0
		.9	.1	3.2	.4			1.0	-1.6
		51.3	33.8	37.3	19.0			26.6	27.2
		22.8	14.4	18.9	11.4		Sales/Net Fixed Assets	9.6	14.9
		13.5	6.3	8.6	3.9			5.1	5.6
		3.0	2.6	2.0	1.7			2.6	2.8
		2.4	2.1	1.7	1.3		Sales/Total Assets	1.7	1.9
		2.0	1.8	1.4	.9			1.1	1.5
		.3	.7	.6	1.9			.7	.9
	(15)	1.1	(29) 1.6	(17) 1.5	(11) 2.9		% Depr., Dep., Amort./Sales	(60) 2.1	(46) 1.9
		2.1	3.7	3.4	4.4			3.5	3.5
		4.2	1.8					1.6	3.5
	(11)	5.7	(11) 4.4				% Officers', Directors', Owners' Comp/Sales	(13) 4.1	(13) 6.4
		9.3	8.5					6.9	13.5
	1516M	67424M	416456M	840624M	1006134M	550074M	Net Sales ($)	2824651M	3288146M
	502M	27845M	165487M	474315M	831798M	449862M	Total Assets ($)	2114607M	1820477M

M = $ thousand   MM = $ million
See Pages 11 through 21 for Explanation of Ratios and Data

Comparative Historical Data				Current Data Sorted By Sales					

			Type of Statement						
28	38	28	Unqualified		1		4	4	19
25	24	21	Reviewed	1	3	2	2	10	3
12	12	8	Compiled		4	2	1	1	
8	4	9	Tax Returns		3	3	3		
32	26	23	Other	2	2	1	4	4	10
4/1/02- 3/31/03 ALL	4/1/03- 3/31/04 ALL	4/1/04- 3/31/05 ALL		27 (4/1-9/30/04)			62 (10/1/04-3/31/05)		
				0-1MM	1-3MM	3-5MM	5-10MM	10-25MM	25MM & OVER
105	104	89	**NUMBER OF STATEMENTS**	3	12	9	14	19	32
%	%	%	**ASSETS**	%	%	%	%	%	%
11.6	10.9	10.4	Cash & Equivalents		10.1		8.2	8.7	14.3
25.3	26.6	29.7	Trade Receivables (net)		33.2		29.3	28.5	26.0
26.9	24.8	27.1	Inventory		29.6		35.1	32.8	23.4
3.6	4.0	3.8	All Other Current		.8		3.6	.6	5.9
67.3	66.2	71.1	Total Current		73.7		76.2	70.6	69.6
21.0	21.3	18.6	Fixed Assets (net)		16.9		17.1	21.2	14.7
5.4	5.3	3.8	Intangibles (net)		2.4		1.1	3.4	6.9
6.3	7.2	6.5	All Other Non-Current		7.0		5.6	4.8	8.7
100.0	100.0	100.0	Total		100.0		100.0	100.0	100.0
			LIABILITIES						
14.9	9.8	11.8	Notes Payable-Short Term		14.3		13.9	11.6	9.5
3.1	3.8	3.4	Cur. Mat.-L/T/D		2.9		5.5	3.9	1.7
14.9	14.3	15.6	Trade Payables		22.8		19.2	10.6	13.4
.1	.2	.6	Income Taxes Payable		.9		.3	1.1	.7
12.9	11.4	13.1	All Other Current		7.4		13.7	8.8	15.2
45.9	39.6	44.6	Total Current		48.3		52.6	36.1	40.4
11.2	11.9	10.2	Long-Term Debt		7.7		12.1	10.4	7.4
.7	1.4	.4	Deferred Taxes		.1		.6	.4	.4
3.0	6.6	4.6	All Other Non-Current		9.3		6.3	5.6	2.9
39.3	40.5	40.2	Net Worth		34.5		28.4	47.6	48.8
100.0	100.0	100.0	Total Liabilities & Net Worth		100.0		100.0	100.0	100.0
			INCOME DATA						
100.0	100.0	100.0	Net Sales		100.0		100.0	100.0	100.0
39.2	34.2	37.4	Gross Profit		50.1		34.2	33.7	33.0
35.4	31.1	30.0	Operating Expenses		34.8		31.1	28.0	26.0
3.8	3.1	7.4	Operating Profit		15.3		3.1	5.7	7.1
1.7	.8	.9	All Other Expenses (net)		.5		3.0	.4	.5
2.2	2.3	6.5	Profit Before Taxes		14.7		.1	5.3	6.6
			RATIOS						
3.4	3.1	3.0	Current		2.1		3.5	3.2	3.8
1.8	1.9	1.5			1.4		1.4	2.4	1.5
1.1	1.2	1.1			1.2		1.1	1.2	1.1
2.1	1.7	1.7	Quick		1.7		1.2	1.9	2.0
1.0	1.0	.8			.7		.6	1.0	.9
.5	.6	.5			.4		.4	.6	.6
32 11.3	32 11.3	37 9.9	Sales/Receivables		36 10.0		23 15.6	30 12.3	44 8.2
48 7.7	46 8.0	52 7.0			61 6.0		50 7.3	50 7.3	54 6.8
62 5.8	58 6.3	65 5.6			83 4.4		66 5.5	59 6.2	63 5.8
36 10.0	25 14.5	40 9.0	Cost of Sales/Inventory		3 109.8		42 8.7	51 7.1	43 8.5
77 4.7	59 6.2	79 4.6			112 3.3		77 4.7	88 4.1	88 4.2
147 2.5	99 3.7	118 3.1			261 1.4		118 3.1	159 2.3	112 3.3
19 18.9	19 19.7	22 16.9	Cost of Sales/Payables		26 13.9		26 13.8	14 25.9	21 17.0
36 10.0	29 12.8	32 11.4			105 3.5		36 10.1	25 14.7	31 11.6
63 5.8	50 7.3	67 5.4			131 2.8		79 4.6	46 7.9	64 5.7
3.4	3.8	4.0	Sales/Working Capital		4.5		4.8	3.6	3.0
6.5	7.5	8.0			6.7		9.9	6.9	8.0
31.2	27.5	27.8			16.7		31.7	20.1	54.0
11.6	14.4	26.8	EBIT/Interest		25.9			17.8	75.8
(85) 3.3	(86) 3.8	(70) 6.6			(11) 5.7			(15) 6.6	(26) 8.0
−1.0	.5	1.5			1.5			1.1	3.1
3.6	9.0	14.8	Net Profit + Depr., Dep., Amort./Cur. Mat. L/T/D						42.2
(33) 1.5	(35) 4.0	(30) 3.0							(13) 6.5
−1.5	1.5	.8							1.3
.2	.1	.2	Fixed/Worth		.2		.1	.1	.1
.4	.4	.5			.4		.9	.5	.4
1.4	1.6	1.9			NM		−3.2	1.7	.8
.5	.6	.5	Debt/Worth		.4		.9	.5	.4
1.4	1.3	1.7			2.4		4.2	1.1	1.2
4.3	4.8	7.5			NM		−25.9	5.0	5.0
33.5	32.3	44.7	% Profit Before Taxes/Tangible Net Worth				46.2	43.8	35.3
(93) 11.6	(89) 15.5	(76) 18.9			(10) 10.8		10.8	19.9	(29) 16.9
−11.9	1.2	6.6					−4.9	4.3	8.0
15.0	17.5	17.9	% Profit Before Taxes/Total Assets		24.7		15.1	23.5	15.0
4.6	4.8	8.2			5.1		2.3	9.6	7.8
−5.5	−1.7	1.1			.9		−.4	1.7	2.9
25.6	34.6	34.4	Sales/Net Fixed Assets		39.9		60.3	33.8	33.2
12.2	13.6	17.0			21.3		25.5	10.6	17.4
5.4	6.4	7.4			13.5		8.1	5.9	8.5
2.5	2.7	2.5	Sales/Total Assets		2.7		2.8	2.6	2.1
1.9	2.0	1.9			2.2		2.1	2.1	1.7
1.3	1.6	1.4			1.1		1.9	1.7	1.3
1.1	.9	.7	% Depr., Dep., Amort./Sales		.9		.3	1.2	.6
(87) 2.2	(86) 2.0	(74) 1.6			(11) 1.4		(12) 1.2	2.2	(25) 1.8
3.8	4.0	3.2			2.3		4.3	3.8	3.0
2.5	2.7	3.4	% Officers', Directors', Owners' Comp/Sales						
(31) 6.5	(26) 4.1	(24) 5.4							
11.8	8.5	9.0							
2951791M	4975899M	2882228M	Net Sales ($)	1806M	28033M	36296M	105343M	306639M	2404111M
1646785M	2631130M	1949809M	Total Assets ($)	2545M	21126M	17137M	137484M	162601M	1608916M

© RMA 2005   **M = $ thousand   MM = $ million**
See Pages 11 through 21 for Explanation of Ratios and Data

Current Data Sorted By Assets   Comparative Historical Data

Type of Statement

0-500M	500M-2MM	2-10MM	10-50MM	50-100MM	100-250MM	Type of Statement	4/1/00-3/31/01 ALL	4/1/01-3/31/02 ALL
	4	3	5	2	2	Unqualified	23	24
		10	2			Reviewed	8	8
1						Compiled	10	8
	4	1				Tax Returns	4	3
3	4	8	5		3	Other	13	24
	15 (4/1-9/30/04)		46 (10/1/04-3/31/05)					
8	12	22	12	2	5	NUMBER OF STATEMENTS	58	67

ASSETS

0-500M %	500M-2MM %	2-10MM %	10-50MM %	50-100MM %	100-250MM %		ALL %	ALL %
	8.0	8.4	20.2			Cash & Equivalents	11.5	9.2
	39.3	27.8	30.1			Trade Receivables (net)	35.4	30.1
	31.2	31.3	22.5			Inventory	23.9	22.9
	2.2	3.4	4.4			All Other Current	3.1	4.2
	80.9	71.0	77.2			Total Current	73.8	66.3
	11.0	14.5	14.2			Fixed Assets (net)	13.9	18.2
	3.9	4.9	5.4			Intangibles (net)	4.4	7.3
	4.2	9.5	3.3			All Other Non-Current	7.9	8.2
	100.0	100.0	100.0			Total	100.0	100.0

LIABILITIES

0-500M	500M-2MM	2-10MM	10-50MM	50-100MM	100-250MM		ALL	ALL
	10.3	12.7	10.6			Notes Payable-Short Term	12.7	9.5
	1.7	7.3	.7			Cur. Mat.-L/T/D	2.2	4.3
	29.1	12.2	15.7			Trade Payables	14.0	13.5
	.0	.7	1.4			Income Taxes Payable	1.1	.2
	9.6	10.6	11.1			All Other Current	17.1	12.2
	50.8	43.4	39.5			Total Current	47.1	39.7
	9.3	7.3	1.2			Long-Term Debt	6.1	9.3
	.0	.3	1.2			Deferred Taxes	.0	.4
	6.5	6.0	11.5			All Other Non-Current	6.2	6.7
	33.4	43.0	46.6			Net Worth	40.6	43.9
	100.0	100.0	100.0			Total Liabilities & Net Worth	100.0	100.0

INCOME DATA

0-500M	500M-2MM	2-10MM	10-50MM	50-100MM	100-250MM		ALL	ALL
	100.0	100.0	100.0			Net Sales	100.0	100.0
	41.7	42.7	43.0			Gross Profit	40.3	38.6
	34.6	41.7	34.0			Operating Expenses	34.3	35.1
	7.1	.9	9.1			Operating Profit	6.1	3.5
	.5	1.0	.6			All Other Expenses (net)	.5	1.5
	6.6	-.1	8.5			Profit Before Taxes	5.5	2.0

RATIOS

0-500M	500M-2MM	2-10MM	10-50MM	50-100MM	100-250MM		ALL	ALL
	2.9 / 1.5 / 1.1	2.8 / 1.8 / 1.4	3.8 / 1.9 / 1.4			Current	3.3 / 1.9 / 1.3	3.8 / 1.9 / 1.2
	1.4 / .8 / .6	1.7 / .8 / .3	2.8 / 1.2 / .8			Quick	2.1 / 1.1 / .7	2.3 / 1.0 / .6
19 / 44 / 79	19.0 / 8.3 / 4.6	54 6.8 / 61 6.0 / 67 5.5	42 8.6 / 47 7.7 / 77 4.7			Sales/Receivables	47 7.7 / 60 6.1 / 80 4.6	34 10.6 / 48 7.6 / 67 5.4
9 / 20 / 111	40.2 / 17.8 / 3.3	50 7.3 / 135 2.7 / 171 2.1	59 6.1 / 79 4.6 / 94 3.9			Cost of Sales/Inventory	25 14.5 / 78 4.7 / 120 3.0	26 14.0 / 61 6.0 / 101 3.6
39 / 44 / 71	9.3 / 8.4 / 5.2	20 18.7 / 42 8.8 / 85 4.3	21 17.1 / 40 9.1 / 69 5.3			Cost of Sales/Payables	14 25.7 / 30 12.2 / 65 5.6	17 21.3 / 25 14.6 / 56 6.5
	6.2 / 15.9 / 90.2	3.0 / 4.8 / 9.1	3.3 / 5.9 / 11.5			Sales/Working Capital	3.1 / 6.1 / 15.7	4.0 / 7.4 / 23.8
	117.9 / 4.3 / 2.0	10.3 / (18) 2.2 / -2.0				EBIT/Interest	(48) 17.2 / 4.6 / 1.7	(57) 10.1 / 2.4 / .1
						Net Profit + Depr., Dep., Amort./Cur. Mat. L /T/D	(15) 9.7 / 4.9 / 1.3	(15) 12.3 / 4.9 / 1.5
	.1 / .3 / 19.1	.2 / .4 / .9	.1 / .3 / .8			Fixed/Worth	.2 / .3 / .7	.2 / .4 / 1.2
	1.0 / 2.5 / 97.5	.4 / 1.5 / 2.7	.4 / 1.8 / 3.6			Debt/Worth	.5 / 1.4 / 3.7	.4 / 1.5 / 5.6
	289.4 / (10) 57.1 / 5.5	25.5 / (19) 15.7 / -3.9	69.0 / (11) 15.3 / 7.5			% Profit Before Taxes/Tangible Net Worth	63.5 / (52) 25.2 / 5.1	42.5 / (56) 16.3 / -3.5
	32.0 / 9.2 / .9	13.1 / 6.3 / -3.6	34.7 / 8.0 / 2.9			% Profit Before Taxes/Total Assets	20.7 / 9.1 / 1.5	16.6 / 7.2 / -2.6
	111.8 / 33.3 / 14.5	22.3 / 11.8 / 7.2	39.4 / 23.2 / 12.8			Sales/Net Fixed Assets	38.9 / 14.9 / 7.6	26.0 / 14.7 / 6.5
	4.3 / 3.1 / 2.3	2.1 / 1.6 / .9	2.2 / 1.9 / 1.4			Sales/Total Assets	2.9 / 1.8 / 1.1	2.8 / 2.1 / 1.2
		.7 / (20) 1.6 / 3.1				% Depr., Dep., Amort./Sales	(51) 1.1 / 1.8 / 3.2	(58) .9 / 2.0 / 3.2
						% Officers', Directors', Owners' Comp/Sales	(18) 3.7 / 5.3 / 13.4	(18) 6.5 / 9.9 / 13.1
9423M	48883M	155746M	433384M	112962M	522713M	Net Sales ($)	1874886M	1835773M
2629M	14087M	102780M	236607M	105106M	623368M	Total Assets ($)	1431759M	1398853M

M = $ thousand   MM = $ million
See Pages 11 through 21 for Explanation of Ratios and Data

Comparative Historical Data | Current Data Sorted By Sales

4/1/02-3/31/03 ALL	4/1/03-3/31/04 ALL	4/1/04-3/31/05 ALL	Type of Statement	0-1MM	1-3MM	3-5MM	5-10MM	10-25MM	25MM & OVER
28	29	12	Unqualified				1	4	7
13	17	16	Reviewed		2	3	6	3	2
7	8	1	Compiled	1					
4	6	9	Tax Returns	2	5		2		
19	15	23	Other		8	3	3	2	7
				0-1MM	15 (4/1-9/30/04) 1-3MM	3-5MM	5-10MM	46 (10/1/04-3/31/05) 10-25MM	25MM & OVER
71	75	61	NUMBER OF STATEMENTS	3	15	6	12	9	16
%	%	%	ASSETS	%	%	%	%	%	%
10.0	10.6	11.3	Cash & Equivalents		3.0		7.8		21.0
31.2	30.2	28.8	Trade Receivables (net)		21.1		37.3		23.4
21.9	23.2	27.5	Inventory		40.5		30.8		19.2
4.8	3.5	2.8	All Other Current		1.6		1.1		3.9
67.9	67.5	70.5	Total Current		66.3		77.0		67.4
18.7	18.1	14.5	Fixed Assets (net)		14.7		12.7		12.2
6.2	8.2	7.2	Intangibles (net)		5.8		7.1		11.9
7.2	6.1	7.9	All Other Non-Current		13.2		3.2		8.4
100.0	100.0	100.0	Total		100.0		100.0		100.0
			LIABILITIES						
12.2	10.7	10.9	Notes Payable-Short Term		18.4		10.1		6.9
3.5	2.5	3.3	Cur. Mat.-L/T/D		9.5		2.0		1.2
18.2	15.5	15.9	Trade Payables		14.3		24.9		13.1
.5	.7	.6	Income Taxes Payable		.0		.4		1.3
9.1	12.0	9.4	All Other Current		7.8		6.6		10.2
43.4	41.4	40.1	Total Current		50.0		44.1		32.6
9.0	11.4	6.9	Long-Term Debt		8.4		10.0		6.0
1.0	1.0	.5	Deferred Taxes		.0		.6		1.0
4.6	6.9	7.7	All Other Non-Current		9.7		5.6		9.6
42.1	39.3	44.9	Net Worth		31.9		39.7		50.8
100.0	100.0	100.0	Total Liabilities & Net Worth		100.0		100.0		100.0
			INCOME DATA						
100.0	100.0	100.0	Net Sales		100.0		100.0		100.0
38.3	40.2	43.0	Gross Profit		48.8		35.5		45.8
37.0	36.2	37.7	Operating Expenses		49.6		28.8		35.3
1.3	4.0	5.3	Operating Profit		-.8		6.8		10.5
1.4	1.8	.9	All Other Expenses (net)		1.0		.5		1.3
-.1	2.2	4.4	Profit Before Taxes		-1.8		6.3		9.2
			RATIOS						
2.9	3.0	3.0			2.4		2.0		3.8
1.8	1.7	1.8	Current		1.7		1.8		2.1
1.2	1.3	1.4			.7		1.5		1.4
1.6	1.7	1.9			1.2		1.3		3.0
1.0	1.0	(60) 1.0	Quick	(14) .3		.9		1.2	
.6	.7	.6			.2		.7		.7
35 10.5	39 9.3	37 9.9			24 14.9		26 14.2		36 10.2
48 7.7	52 7.0	54 6.8	Sales/Receivables		48 7.6		55 6.6		47 7.7
60 6.0	63 5.8	69 5.3			59 6.2		64 5.7		71 5.2
20 17.8	23 15.9	33 11.2			12 29.8		20 18.5		60 6.1
59 6.2	71 5.1	75 4.9	Cost of Sales/Inventory		84 4.4		51 7.2		82 4.5
109 3.3	110 3.3	139 2.6			716 .5		144 2.5		97 3.8
20 18.6	17 20.9	24 15.1			25 14.7		34 10.6		28 12.9
37 10.0	39 9.3	42 8.6	Cost of Sales/Payables		50 7.3		43 8.5		47 7.8
64 5.7	53 6.9	65 5.6			87 4.2		60 6.0		62 5.9
5.0	4.2	3.1			2.9		5.1		2.3
8.0	6.7	6.9	Sales/Working Capital		9.1		7.8		4.4
23.3	28.5	14.6			-22.1		18.9		11.5
10.7	17.5	15.0			7.2		17.8		314.7
(60) 2.1	(61) 3.9	(50) 4.8	EBIT/Interest	(13) .6		(11) 6.4		(12) 12.2	
-4.4	-.5	.5			-2.6		3.2		2.5
9.9	13.5	12.6	Net Profit + Depr., Dep.,						
(22) 2.6	(24) 1.9	(15) 2.3	Amort./Cur. Mat. L/T/D						
.2	1.0	.3							
.2	.2	.1			.1		.2		.1
.4	.5	.4	Fixed/Worth		.7		.4		.3
1.3	1.1	1.0			-.2		1.0		.8
.5	.5	.4			.4		1.3		.3
1.5	1.5	1.6	Debt/Worth		1.6		1.9		1.8
3.2	7.0	3.4			-5.4		2.9		5.1
39.7	43.3	68.2	% Profit Before Taxes/Tangible		84.4		111.4		77.5
(62) 15.7	(60) 21.4	(52) 19.1	Net Worth	(10) 23.4		(11) 19.3		(14) 21.2	
-8.1	-.2	3.6			-15.8		11.4		7.3
14.5	16.4	16.9	% Profit Before Taxes/Total		12.0		23.2		17.4
3.2	5.1	7.8	Assets		.3		7.8		10.6
-7.0	-3.3	-.5			-7.3		3.3		3.2
32.4	37.7	43.9			63.5		100.7		26.9
16.9	13.8	17.1	Sales/Net Fixed Assets		21.6		19.5		18.8
7.9	6.5	10.2			5.2		11.6		7.8
3.5	3.0	2.8			3.1		4.3		2.2
2.2	1.9	1.9	Sales/Total Assets		2.1		2.7		1.4
1.2	1.2	1.0			.7		1.7		1.0
1.0	.8	.6			.4		.4		.8
(56) 1.7	(55) 2.0	(51) 1.0	% Depr., Dep., Amort./Sales	(12) .7		(11) 1.8		(14) 1.3	
3.6	3.5	2.4			1.1		2.6		2.7
2.4	2.7	2.4	% Officers', Directors',						
(20) 6.8	(21) 7.1	(19) 5.0	Owners' Comp/Sales						
9.8	10.1	9.6							
2362951M	1672593M	1283111M	Net Sales ($)	2162M	28148M	23341M	81356M	143214M	1004890M
1850816M	1287038M	1084577M	Total Assets ($)	884M	28287M	14353M	34208M	95957M	910888M

M = $ thousand   MM = $ million
See Pages 11 through 21 for Explanation of Ratios and Data

Current Data Sorted By Assets   Comparative Historical Data

0-500M	500M-2MM	2-10MM	10-50MM	50-100MM	100-250MM	Type of Statement	4/1/00-3/31/01 ALL	4/1/01-3/31/02 ALL
	1	4	9	1	5	Unqualified	8	14
	1	12	1	1		Reviewed	5	8
	2	1				Compiled	8	8
1	1					Tax Returns	3	
	4	7	4	2	2	Other	16	21
	14 (4/1-9/30/04)		45 (10/1/04-3/31/05)					
1	9	24	14	4	7	**NUMBER OF STATEMENTS**	40	51
%	%	%	%	%	%	**ASSETS**	%	%
		5.1	11.6			Cash & Equivalents	7.2	11.0
		38.8	27.7			Trade Receivables (net)	31.3	29.5
		36.8	36.3			Inventory	36.3	33.3
		1.9	1.7			All Other Current	2.4	3.1
		82.6	77.3			Total Current	77.3	76.9
		10.2	9.4			Fixed Assets (net)	16.1	15.1
		2.5	4.4			Intangibles (net)	2.3	3.6
		4.7	8.9			All Other Non-Current	4.3	4.4
		100.0	100.0			Total	100.0	100.0
						LIABILITIES		
		20.8	12.4			Notes Payable-Short Term	12.8	13.9
		4.3	1.0			Cur. Mat.-L/T/D	2.2	4.5
		19.1	12.2			Trade Payables	16.8	13.4
		.3	.7			Income Taxes Payable	.4	.4
		11.6	8.6			All Other Current	9.9	11.4
		56.1	34.8			Total Current	42.0	43.5
		7.0	3.3			Long-Term Debt	9.8	7.5
		.2	.4			Deferred Taxes	.2	.1
		5.4	4.6			All Other Non-Current	3.9	3.3
		31.2	56.8			Net Worth	44.1	45.5
		100.0	100.0			Total Liabilities & Net Worth	100.0	100.0
						INCOME DATA		
		100.0	100.0			Net Sales	100.0	100.0
		38.5	35.3			Gross Profit	37.6	37.2
		35.8	30.2			Operating Expenses	30.1	32.0
		2.7	5.1			Operating Profit	7.5	5.2
		.8	-.5			All Other Expenses (net)	1.0	.3
		1.9	5.5			Profit Before Taxes	6.5	4.9
						RATIOS		
		2.4	4.4				2.9	4.3
		1.5	2.6			Current	2.0	1.9
		1.2	1.4				1.2	1.3
		1.2	2.5				1.6	1.9
		.8	1.5			Quick	.8	1.1
		.5	.6				.6	.6
		42 8.7	40 9.1				43 8.4	32 11.3
		60 6.1	48 7.6			Sales/Receivables	50 7.2	49 7.5
		73 5.0	70 5.2				66 5.5	60 6.1
		53 6.9	73 5.0				58 6.3	53 6.9
		103 3.5	104 3.5			Cost of Sales/Inventory	94 3.9	87 4.2
		126 2.9	144 2.5				144 2.5	135 2.7
		19 18.7	15 24.8				22 16.8	19 19.0
		47 7.8	31 11.9			Cost of Sales/Payables	37 10.0	31 11.7
		59 6.1	57 6.4				60 6.1	47 7.7
		5.2	2.6				4.1	2.9
		8.6	4.8			Sales/Working Capital	5.7	6.2
		17.5	10.7				20.9	15.0
		7.1	32.0				13.4	19.7
		(23) 1.8	(11) 8.4			EBIT/Interest	(34) 4.8	(46) 4.7
		.4	3.8				1.6	1.2
		9.7				Net Profit + Depr., Dep.,	19.9	68.2
		(10) 5.3				Amort./Cur. Mat. L /T/D	(10) 5.7	(16) 9.1
		1.2					2.4	2.4
		.1	.1				.1	.1
		.4	.1			Fixed/Worth	.3	.3
		.6	.3				.8	.7
		.7	.3				.6	.3
		2.4	.7			Debt/Worth	1.2	1.3
		8.4	2.5				3.5	2.6
		37.2	42.7				64.7	52.1
		(22) 17.5	22.7			% Profit Before Taxes/Tangible Net Worth	(38) 28.9	(48) 19.2
		-2.5	8.1				10.3	3.5
		12.8	15.3				21.3	19.4
		2.4	9.7			% Profit Before Taxes/Total Assets	10.7	7.1
		-2.4	5.3				3.2	1.1
		65.3	44.8				35.2	37.1
		27.4	19.8			Sales/Net Fixed Assets	21.2	18.4
		17.0	13.8				8.5	8.8
		3.1	2.6				3.3	3.0
		2.5	1.8			Sales/Total Assets	2.2	2.0
		1.7	1.3				1.4	1.5
		.4	1.5				.4	.5
		(23) 1.2	(12) 1.9			% Depr., Dep., Amort./Sales	(38) 1.6	(41) 1.5
		1.5	2.9				2.4	2.5
							1.5	1.4
						% Officers', Directors', Owners' Comp/Sales	(14) 3.4	(12) 2.8
							7.9	5.3
586M	35101M	308576M	648632M	767099M	1359013M	Net Sales ($)	2152834M	1908999M
280M	11220M	124881M	321647M	222340M	995567M	Total Assets ($)	1158990M	1128390M

© RMA 2005

M = $ thousand   MM = $ million
See Pages 11 through 21 for Explanation of Ratios and Data

Comparative Historical Data   **Current Data Sorted By Sales**

	Hist 4/1/02-3/31/03 ALL	Hist 4/1/03-3/31/04 ALL	Hist 4/1/04-3/31/05 ALL	0-1MM	1-3MM	3-5MM	5-10MM	10-25MM	25MM & OVER
Type of Statement									
Unqualified	17	16	20				3	6	11
Reviewed	11	12	15		1	3	2	7	2
Compiled	5	9	3		1		2		
Tax Returns	2	6	2	1		1			
Other	21	19	19		2	1	2	6	8
					14 (4/1-9/30/04)			45 (10/1/04-3/31/05)	
NUMBER OF STATEMENTS	56	62	59	1	4	5	9	19	21
	%	%	%	%	%	%	%	%	%
ASSETS									
Cash & Equivalents	9.4	11.9	8.5					6.2	10.5
Trade Receivables (net)	26.8	29.5	33.3					39.2	31.9
Inventory	34.0	32.2	35.3					33.0	34.7
All Other Current	3.2	3.9	2.2					1.7	2.6
Total Current	73.4	77.5	79.2					80.1	79.7
Fixed Assets (net)	16.9	14.4	12.5					9.8	12.5
Intangibles (net)	4.3	3.5	2.4					1.4	3.3
All Other Non-Current	5.3	4.6	5.9					8.7	4.4
Total	100.0	100.0	100.0					100.0	100.0
LIABILITIES									
Notes Payable-Short Term	14.4	14.8	17.5					20.0	12.2
Cur. Mat.-L/T/D	1.7	2.7	2.7					4.4	1.1
Trade Payables	15.1	16.6	15.6					20.0	14.4
Income Taxes Payable	.5	.4	.4					.3	.6
All Other Current	10.6	9.6	12.9					12.9	12.0
Total Current	42.3	44.2	49.2					57.7	40.2
Long-Term Debt	9.2	6.6	6.1					6.0	4.3
Deferred Taxes	.3	.2	.3					.0	.3
All Other Non-Current	3.6	5.6	3.9					6.3	3.7
Net Worth	44.5	43.4	40.5					30.0	51.4
Total Liabilities & Net Worth	100.0	100.0	100.0					100.0	100.0
INCOME DATA									
Net Sales	100.0	100.0	100.0					100.0	100.0
Gross Profit	34.7	38.1	37.5					32.1	34.4
Operating Expenses	29.3	33.7	33.1					30.1	28.0
Operating Profit	5.4	4.5	4.4					1.9	6.4
All Other Expenses (net)	.7	1.1	.6					.2	.4
Profit Before Taxes	4.7	3.4	3.8					1.7	6.0
RATIOS									
Current	2.9	3.4	2.7					1.7	3.6
	1.8	1.8	1.5					1.5	2.3
	1.2	1.2	1.2					1.1	1.4
Quick	1.5	1.8	1.5					1.0	2.1
	.9	.9	.8					.7	1.4
	.5	.6	.6					.5	.6
Sales/Receivables	29 12.7	34 10.7	40 9.2					44 8.3	44 8.3
	43 8.5	50 7.3	53 6.9					52 7.0	54 6.7
	60 6.0	71 5.2	70 5.3					75 4.9	66 5.5
Cost of Sales/Inventory	49 7.4	57 6.4	58 6.3					48 7.6	65 5.6
	91 4.0	95 3.8	100 3.6					79 4.6	88 4.1
	122 3.0	139 2.6	149 2.4					111 3.3	139 2.6
Cost of Sales/Payables	19 19.1	17 22.0	16 22.9					15 24.1	16 22.8
	32 11.3	35 10.4	34 10.8					41 9.0	29 12.5
	50 7.2	60 6.1	55 6.6					55 6.7	61 6.0
Sales/Working Capital	4.4	3.2	4.2					5.2	2.6
	7.7	6.2	7.9					13.0	5.1
	19.0	18.9	17.6					37.7	12.7
EBIT/Interest	20.9	18.5	12.9					8.1	21.2
	(48) 6.3	(55) 3.1	(53) 4.8					(17) 1.8	(18) 9.8
	1.7	1.1	1.5					1.0	4.8
Net Profit + Depr., Dep., Amort./Cur. Mat. L/T/D	7.6	5.8	14.6						
	(14) 5.1	(12) 2.6	(19) 5.9						
	2.1	.9	1.6						
Fixed/Worth	.1	.1	.1					.1	.1
	.4	.3	.3					.4	.2
	1.0	1.0	.6					.6	.4
Debt/Worth	.6	.5	.5					.7	.3
	1.4	1.2	1.7					3.3	1.5
	3.8	4.9	4.1					8.6	2.6
% Profit Before Taxes/Tangible Net Worth	53.1	35.8	44.4					35.9	47.8
	(52) 21.3	(55) 18.1	(57) 17.0					(17) 16.0	29.4
	7.2	4.8	5.4					5.7	11.5
% Profit Before Taxes/Total Assets	15.5	13.0	15.0					12.3	16.1
	8.2	5.5	7.3					2.9	10.0
	2.1	.6	1.2					.9	5.2
Sales/Net Fixed Assets	39.8	41.2	53.3					45.2	89.2
	17.3	25.1	27.0					27.0	28.5
	7.0	9.7	12.5					18.1	7.7
Sales/Total Assets	2.9	2.9	3.1					3.1	3.2
	2.1	2.1	2.1					2.5	1.6
	1.4	1.5	1.6					1.9	1.3
% Depr., Dep., Amort./Sales	.7	.7	.6					.6	.5
	(49) 1.6	(53) 1.3	(52) 1.4					1.4	(17) 1.8
	2.9	2.8	2.4					1.6	3.1
% Officers', Directors', Owners' Comp/Sales	2.0	2.7	2.0						
	(15) 4.2	(19) 6.3	(14) 4.7						
	7.7	8.8	5.7						
Net Sales ($)	3369242M	2661576M	3119007M	586M	7965M	21186M	68606M	308875M	2711789M
Total Assets ($)	1785046M	1637071M	1675935M	280M	4206M	10835M	33114M	142368M	1485132M

Current Data Sorted By Assets   **Comparative Historical Data**

0-500M	500M-2MM	2-10MM	10-50MM	50-100MM	100-250MM	Type of Statement	4/1/00-3/31/01 ALL	4/1/01-3/31/02 ALL
	4	3	3	1		Unqualified	23	17
	8	2				Reviewed	14	13
2		2				Compiled	16	10
						Tax Returns	2	3
	2	3	4			Other	24	25
	8 (4/1-9/30/04)		26 (10/1/04-3/31/05)					
2	14	10	7	1		**NUMBER OF STATEMENTS**	79	68
%	%	%	%	%	%	**ASSETS**	%	%
	8.8	6.3				Cash & Equivalents	8.7	8.0
	29.5	27.0				Trade Receivables (net)	30.3	27.9
	27.4	31.2				Inventory	29.5	29.8
	1.2	.5				All Other Current	2.5	3.3
	66.8	65.0				Total Current	71.0	69.0
	28.5	16.6				Fixed Assets (net)	19.8	21.0
	.1	10.6				Intangibles (net)	3.3	3.9
	4.5	7.8				All Other Non-Current	5.9	6.1
	100.0	100.0				Total	100.0	100.0
						LIABILITIES		
	8.9	15.2				Notes Payable-Short Term	10.9	13.2
	5.4	2.6				Cur. Mat.-L/T/D	2.5	3.7
	13.4	18.0				Trade Payables	15.5	14.6
	.3	.1				Income Taxes Payable	.4	.2
	5.3	9.7				All Other Current	9.1	9.1
	33.3	45.7				Total Current	38.4	40.7
	14.2	8.5				Long-Term Debt	12.8	13.4
	.2	.0				Deferred Taxes	.4	.3
	15.3	5.1				All Other Non-Current	4.7	4.9
	36.9	40.7				Net Worth	43.8	40.7
	100.0	100.0				Total Liabilities & Net Worth	100.0	100.0
						INCOME DATA		
	100.0	100.0				Net Sales	100.0	100.0
	38.0	30.0				Gross Profit	30.3	29.4
	32.0	28.5				Operating Expenses	24.9	27.6
	6.1	1.6				Operating Profit	5.4	1.8
	.3	.6				All Other Expenses (net)	.4	1.6
	5.8	1.0				Profit Before Taxes	5.0	.2
						RATIOS		
	5.1	2.4					2.7	2.7
	2.1	1.5				Current	1.8	1.7
	1.2	1.2					1.4	1.2
	3.1	1.3					1.6	1.3
	1.1	.7				Quick	.9	.9
	.7	.5					.6	.6
37	10.0	33 11.1					43 8.4	36 10.2
44	8.2	42 8.8				Sales/Receivables	55 6.7	46 8.0
56	6.5	67 5.4					64 5.7	59 6.2
20	18.5	41 8.8					43 8.5	40 9.1
67	5.5	75 4.8				Cost of Sales/Inventory	81 4.5	79 4.6
96	3.8	141 2.6					115 3.2	126 2.9
12	30.3	26 13.9					26 14.2	19 19.0
25	14.6	43 8.5				Cost of Sales/Payables	36 10.1	34 10.9
37	9.9	57 6.5					49 7.4	49 7.4
	3.7	6.7					4.2	4.5
	6.8	9.9				Sales/Working Capital	6.2	6.8
	19.6	NM					12.2	19.5
	26.3	37.3					9.4	5.5
	(12) 7.9	3.0				EBIT/Interest	(71) 3.6	(64) 2.7
	2.3	-3.6					1.3	-3.9
						Net Profit + Depr., Dep.,	4.8	3.8
						Amort./Cur. Mat. L /T/D	(27) 1.7	(23) 2.9
							1.0	1.0
	.3	.2					.2	.3
	.6	.4				Fixed/Worth	.5	.5
	1.8	NM					1.0	1.2
	.5	1.1					.7	.8
	1.3	1.7				Debt/Worth	1.4	1.7
	6.5	NM					2.6	3.7
	37.0					% Profit Before Taxes/Tangible	49.3	28.1
	(12) 21.4					Net Worth	(76) 19.0	(63) 9.4
	7.3						3.8	-17.4
	21.8	8.4				% Profit Before Taxes/Total	18.3	12.1
	10.4	3.1				Assets	7.5	3.4
	3.8	-14.5					1.3	-8.4
	25.1	51.0					21.9	21.7
	11.9	12.9				Sales/Net Fixed Assets	13.7	10.6
	7.2	6.4					6.4	5.7
	3.1	3.5					2.5	2.7
	2.2	1.9				Sales/Total Assets	2.0	1.9
	1.8	1.5					1.6	1.4
	1.7	1.3					1.1	1.1
	(13) 2.6	1.7				% Depr., Dep., Amort./Sales	(67) 2.2	(55) 2.5
	4.5	2.1					3.7	4.3
						% Officers', Directors',	2.1	2.2
						Owners' Comp/Sales	(16) 3.9	(21) 3.2
							5.5	6.6
1907M	41997M	129854M	260942M	97587M		Net Sales ($)	3107367M	1912020M
401M	18062M	56543M	160269M	54250M		Total Assets ($)	2004571M	1268340M

The columns 10-50MM, 50-100MM, and 100-250MM are marked **DATA NOT AVAILABLE**.

© RMA 2005

M = $ thousand   MM = $ million

See Pages 11 through 21 for Explanation of Ratios and Data

Comparative Historical Data / Current Data Sorted By Sales

			Type of Statement						
16	10	7	Unqualified		2		1	2	4
12	12	6	Reviewed		5	2		2	
8	14	10	Compiled		1	3	1	1	
4	1	2	Tax Returns	1	1				
22	10	9	Other		2	1	1	3	2
4/1/02-3/31/03 ALL	4/1/03-3/31/04 ALL	4/1/04-3/31/05 ALL			8 (4/1-9/30/04)		26 (10/1/04-3/31/05)		
				0-1MM	1-3MM	3-5MM	5-10MM	10-25MM	25MM & OVER
62	47	34	NUMBER OF STATEMENTS	1	10	6	3	8	6
%	%	%	ASSETS	%	%	%	%	%	%
7.2	9.4	10.8	Cash & Equivalents		7.4				
27.7	28.8	26.6	Trade Receivables (net)		24.8				
29.4	31.2	26.7	Inventory		27.8				
3.3	1.7	2.8	All Other Current		1.5				
67.6	71.1	66.9	Total Current		61.5				
23.5	20.4	22.0	Fixed Assets (net)		28.5				
3.7	2.7	5.3	Intangibles (net)		4.5				
5.2	5.9	5.8	All Other Non-Current		5.5				
100.0	100.0	100.0	Total		100.0				
			LIABILITIES						
12.1	10.2	11.4	Notes Payable-Short Term		4.5				
3.3	3.7	3.8	Cur. Mat.-L/T/D		6.2				
14.3	16.7	15.2	Trade Payables		15.4				
.3	.3	.2	Income Taxes Payable		.3				
8.8	8.8	10.0	All Other Current		11.9				
38.8	39.7	40.7	Total Current		38.4				
14.8	10.7	11.2	Long-Term Debt		18.5				
.4	.1	.2	Deferred Taxes		.3				
6.4	10.3	9.9	All Other Non-Current		21.4				
39.6	39.2	38.0	Net Worth		21.4				
100.0	100.0	100.0	Total Liabilities & Net Worth		100.0				
			INCOME DATA						
100.0	100.0	100.0	Net Sales		100.0				
33.1	34.5	35.9	Gross Profit		41.5				
32.6	32.2	30.2	Operating Expenses		32.0				
.5	2.3	5.7	Operating Profit		9.5				
1.6	1.8	.8	All Other Expenses (net)		.3				
−1.1	.5	4.9	Profit Before Taxes		9.2				
			RATIOS						
3.6	3.6	3.1	Current		3.3				
1.9	2.0	1.8			2.1				
1.2	1.2	1.2			1.1				
1.6	2.2	1.4	Quick		1.5				
.9	.9	1.0			.9				
.6	.5	.6			.6				
42 8.8	39 9.3	35 10.4	Sales/Receivables		37 10.0				
48 7.6	49 7.4	44 8.2			46 7.9				
63 5.8	64 5.7	67 5.4			70 5.3				
39 9.3	46 8.0	20 17.8	Cost of Sales/Inventory		20 18.5				
81 4.5	91 4.0	73 5.0			89 4.1				
136 2.7	151 2.4	122 3.0			133 2.8				
22 16.8	21 17.3	16 23.3	Cost of Sales/Payables		16 23.3				
29 12.7	35 10.4	32 11.2			26 14.1				
48 7.6	46 8.0	47 7.8			59 6.1				
3.7	4.0	3.9	Sales/Working Capital		3.0				
5.5	6.0	8.9			6.4				
19.0	16.8	19.6			NM				
8.1	7.6	26.3	EBIT/Interest						
(58) 1.6	(42) 2.7	(32) 6.6							
−1.7	−.4	1.6							
5.9			Net Profit + Depr., Dep., Amort./Cur. Mat. L/T/D						
(16) 2.4									
.2									
.2	.2	.3	Fixed/Worth		.3				
.6	.5	.5			2.4				
1.6	1.4	1.2			−2.0				
.6	.5	.9	Debt/Worth		.8				
1.6	1.7	1.5			4.0				
6.2	4.7	3.9			−4.8				
36.8	36.1	28.7	% Profit Before Taxes/Tangible Net Worth						
(56) 3.8	(41) 16.1	(29) 19.4							
−21.5	−.8	5.4							
12.3	11.3	16.0	% Profit Before Taxes/Total Assets		28.6				
1.3	3.2	7.0			13.8				
−8.1	−2.7	1.9			4.3				
21.3	21.4	29.1	Sales/Net Fixed Assets		25.1				
10.6	12.6	11.3			11.4				
4.7	6.6	7.4			2.9				
2.6	2.7	3.3	Sales/Total Assets		2.4				
1.9	1.9	2.1			2.1				
1.2	1.5	1.4			1.1				
1.3	1.7	1.5	% Depr., Dep., Amort./Sales						
(51) 2.7	(45) 2.4	(30) 2.0							
4.9	3.3	3.3							
2.4	2.4		% Officers', Directors', Owners' Comp/Sales						
(21) 4.1	(12) 3.5								
11.7	5.3								
1631581M	1194796M	532287M	Net Sales ($)	391M	19472M	22740M	22899M	133258M	333527M
1024585M	643216M	289525M	Total Assets ($)	77M	12249M	9079M	10557M	75573M	181990M

M = $ thousand   MM = $ million
See Pages 11 through 21 for Explanation of Ratios and Data

Current Data Sorted By Assets   Comparative Historical Data

						Type of Statement		
	1	9	7	4	2	Unqualified	27	22
1	6	10	1			Reviewed	34	35
3	9	7				Compiled	31	28
2	7	3				Tax Returns	8	1
	10	22	8		1	Other	53	60
	25 (4/1-9/30/04)		88 (10/1/04-3/31/05)				4/1/00-3/31/01	4/1/01-3/31/02
0-500M	500M-2MM	2-10MM	10-50MM	50-100MM	100-250MM		ALL	ALL
6	33	51	16	5	2	**NUMBER OF STATEMENTS**	153	146
%	%	%	%	%	%	**ASSETS**	%	%
	12.6	10.5	12.9			Cash & Equivalents	7.1	8.2
	34.4	26.5	25.3			Trade Receivables (net)	30.9	26.7
	17.4	25.7	24.3			Inventory	23.7	22.3
	.2	1.0	1.5			All Other Current	.8	1.3
	64.6	63.7	64.0			Total Current	62.4	58.4
	26.8	26.7	23.1			Fixed Assets (net)	29.5	32.5
	3.0	4.4	7.7			Intangibles (net)	3.8	4.7
	5.5	5.2	5.2			All Other Non-Current	4.3	4.3
	100.0	100.0	100.0			Total	100.0	100.0
						LIABILITIES		
	8.1	10.0	4.2			Notes Payable-Short Term	8.1	11.0
	7.0	2.8	2.8			Cur. Mat.-L/T/D	7.0	6.2
	21.6	13.5	17.0			Trade Payables	17.8	14.8
	.2	.4	.6			Income Taxes Payable	.7	.3
	11.1	8.8	7.7			All Other Current	9.7	9.2
	48.0	35.4	32.3			Total Current	43.3	41.5
	29.5	17.6	15.2			Long-Term Debt	15.0	16.2
	.3	.3	.2			Deferred Taxes	.5	.4
	10.9	4.4	9.0			All Other Non-Current	5.0	5.1
	11.2	42.3	43.4			Net Worth	36.1	36.8
	100.0	100.0	100.0			Total Liabilities & Net Worth	100.0	100.0
						INCOME DATA		
	100.0	100.0	100.0			Net Sales	100.0	100.0
	35.7	28.4	26.0			Gross Profit	26.9	25.5
	32.1	26.6	15.8			Operating Expenses	20.6	22.8
	3.6	1.8	10.3			Operating Profit	6.3	2.7
	1.9	.6	.2			All Other Expenses (net)	1.4	1.4
	1.7	1.2	10.0			Profit Before Taxes	4.8	1.3
						RATIOS		
	1.9	3.2	2.9				2.1	2.1
	1.4	1.8	2.2			Current	1.4	1.4
	.9	1.4	1.6				1.1	1.0
	1.5	2.2	2.3				1.3	1.5
	1.1	1.1	1.1			Quick	.9	.8
	.5	.6	.7				.6	.5
	25 14.3	38 9.6	40 9.2				40 9.1	37 9.9
	43 8.5	49 7.5	45 8.0			Sales/Receivables	51 7.2	43 8.5
	56 6.6	59 6.2	54 6.7				62 5.9	53 6.9
	6 62.9	37 9.9	16 22.9				20 18.5	19 19.2
	26 14.1	53 6.9	62 5.9			Cost of Sales/Inventory	49 7.4	41 8.9
	58 6.3	93 3.9	126 2.9				77 4.7	70 5.2
	21 17.2	21 17.8	24 15.0				21 17.1	20 18.3
	38 9.5	30 12.2	36 10.1			Cost of Sales/Payables	38 9.7	28 13.3
	58 6.3	43 8.5	58 6.3				56 6.6	40 9.2
	6.8	5.0	4.1				6.9	6.2
	16.9	7.2	5.7			Sales/Working Capital	11.6	13.4
	−61.9	12.2	9.1				30.2	105.7
	6.7	7.1	53.7				11.8	6.6
	(28) 4.0	(42) 4.1	(13) 11.9			EBIT/Interest	(140) 4.0	(134) 2.1
	1.6	1.2	4.3				1.3	.0
	.	6.7					5.4	3.6
		(10) 2.7				Net Profit + Depr., Dep., Amort./Cur. Mat. L /T/D	(47) 2.3	(45) 1.7
		.9					1.1	1.1
	.3	.3	.3				.4	.5
	1.0	.5	.7			Fixed/Worth	.8	.9
	NM	1.6	1.3				2.0	2.3
	1.2	.6	.7				.9	.8
	2.6	1.3	1.6			Debt/Worth	2.0	1.8
	−7.9	4.1	2.9				4.0	4.2
	67.3	28.7	68.0				52.4	38.3
	(23) 27.5	(47) 12.4	(14) 39.2			% Profit Before Taxes/Tangible Net Worth	(140) 24.6	(123) 13.8
	4.6	2.1	15.4				7.1	−3.3
	14.9	9.4	28.6				19.2	13.8
	6.9	4.2	13.8			% Profit Before Taxes/Total Assets	8.7	4.0
	2.2	.6	4.7				1.6	−3.7
	35.1	15.9	23.1				16.3	14.9
	11.6	8.3	8.3			Sales/Net Fixed Assets	8.9	7.5
	5.4	4.1	4.5				4.6	4.3
	3.8	2.4	2.5				2.8	2.8
	2.7	2.0	2.0			Sales/Total Assets	2.2	2.3
	1.9	1.5	1.0				1.7	1.6
	2.1	1.5	1.1				1.4	1.9
	(21) 3.5	(46) 2.8	(15) 2.3			% Depr., Dep., Amort./Sales	(140) 2.6	(127) 3.4
	8.1	6.0	2.5				4.4	5.3
	1.8	2.9					2.3	1.6
	(18) 4.2	(18) 6.0				% Officers', Directors', Owners' Comp/Sales	(54) 3.4	(46) 4.6
	6.7	8.0					7.3	7.3
5504M	115800M	535916M	589409M	599184M	428251M	Net Sales ($)	4000672M	2765449M
1572M	38900M	266183M	318574M	403677M	343487M	Total Assets ($)	2343885M	1428441M

M = $ thousand   MM = $ million
See Pages 11 through 21 for Explanation of Ratios and Data

Comparative Historical Data · Current Data Sorted By Sales

				Type of Statement						
26		22	23	Unqualified		1	6	6	10	
34		31	17	Reviewed	3	2	9	2	1	
25		19	17	Compiled	2 4	6	3	2		
5		8	13	Tax Returns	2 3	5	2	1		
44		51	43	Other	2 9	4	8	12	8	
4/1/02- 3/31/03 ALL		4/1/03- 3/31/04 ALL	4/1/04- 3/31/05 ALL		25 (4/1-9/30/04)		88 (10/1/04-3/31/05)			
					0-1MM	1-3MM	3-5MM	5-10MM	10-25MM	25MM & OVER
134		131	113	NUMBER OF STATEMENTS	6	19	18	28	23	19
%		%	%	ASSETS	%	%	%	%	%	%
8.5		8.8	11.2	Cash & Equivalents	12.0	10.0	13.0	10.8	9.6	
27.5		29.2	29.3	Trade Receivables (net)	32.2	35.3	26.0	28.6	27.2	
23.6		23.0	22.6	Inventory	15.7	24.0	20.4	24.9	27.3	
1.1		1.5	.8	All Other Current	.4	.9	.5	1.2	1.2	
60.7		62.5	64.0	Total Current	60.4	70.3	59.9	65.5	65.3	
31.7		29.3	25.7	Fixed Assets (net)	29.3	23.1	27.1	26.5	21.9	
3.0		3.6	5.4	Intangibles (net)	4.3	2.8	6.3	3.4	9.0	
4.7		4.6	5.0	All Other Non-Current	6.1	3.8	6.7	4.6	3.9	
100.0		100.0	100.0	Total	100.0	100.0	100.0	100.0	100.0	
				LIABILITIES						
12.1		9.5	8.9	Notes Payable-Short Term	7.9	9.0	5.5	10.2	9.6	
6.6		5.0	4.1	Cur. Mat.-L/T/D	10.0	2.5	2.7	4.0	2.3	
16.4		16.7	16.7	Trade Payables	14.5	21.4	15.6	13.1	21.3	
.1		.1	.3	Income Taxes Payable	.0	.4	.6	.4	.2	
8.1		13.8	9.6	All Other Current	11.2	8.4	8.7	10.6	6.2	
43.4		45.2	39.6	Total Current	43.6	41.6	33.0	38.4	39.7	
15.4		14.5	20.5	Long-Term Debt	31.5	28.3	22.5	9.9	12.0	
.2		.3	.3	Deferred Taxes	.1	.2	.2	.2	.5	
6.0		5.9	7.0	All Other Non-Current	9.0	9.6	4.9	5.1	8.0	
35.0		34.1	32.6	Net Worth	15.8	20.4	39.3	46.4	39.8	
100.0		100.0	100.0	Total Liabilities & Net Worth	100.0	100.0	100.0	100.0	100.0	
				INCOME DATA						
100.0		100.0	100.0	Net Sales	100.0	100.0	100.0	100.0	100.0	
26.2		30.1	29.8	Gross Profit	34.9	35.4	29.6	27.1	21.5	
25.4		26.8	26.0	Operating Expenses	33.9	33.8	25.4	23.3	13.3	
.8		3.3	3.8	Operating Profit	1.1	1.6	4.2	3.8	8.2	
1.2		1.2	1.0	All Other Expenses (net)	1.4	.6	.9	.2	1.0	
-.4		2.1	2.8	Profit Before Taxes	-.3	1.0	3.3	3.6	7.2	
				RATIOS						
2.1		2.3	2.7		1.8	3.0	3.5	2.4	2.5	
1.5		1.5	1.7	Current	1.5	1.9	1.8	2.0	1.5	
1.0		1.1	1.3		1.1	1.3	1.4	1.2	1.3	
1.5		1.6	2.0		1.5	2.3	2.7	2.0	2.0	
.8		.8	1.1	Quick	1.3	1.3	1.2	.9	.8	
.5		.5	.6		.7	.6	.7	.6	.6	
38 9.5	40 9.1	36 10.3		Sales/Receivables	35 10.4	38 9.7	34 10.8	35 10.6	41 8.9	
48 7.7	48 7.6	46 7.9			44 8.3	56 6.5	44 8.3	43 8.5	52 7.0	
57 6.4	59 6.2	59 6.2			57 6.4	67 5.4	57 6.4	57 6.4	62 5.9	
24 15.3	26 14.1	21 17.4		Cost of Sales/Inventory	10 35.5	16 22.9	33 11.2	18 19.8	31 11.7	
45 8.1	49 7.5	48 7.5			27 13.5	45 8.1	55 6.7	47 7.7	62 5.9	
75 4.9	76 4.8	84 4.3			57 6.4	87 4.2	102 3.6	63 5.8	87 4.2	
19 19.1	23 15.9	21 17.8		Cost of Sales/Payables	8 44.5	23 15.7	21 17.5	18 20.7	29 12.7	
34 10.9	38 9.6	35 10.6			25 14.9	38 9.6	35 10.6	24 14.9	48 7.7	
50 7.3	54 6.8	53 6.9			56 6.5	71 5.2	49 7.4	35 10.4	67 5.4	
6.2		6.5	5.3	Sales/Working Capital	7.2	5.5	4.5	5.6	5.5	
12.0		11.4	8.4		16.4	8.1	6.6	8.2	9.3	
177.1		32.7	20.7		88.0	13.0	11.2	25.7	13.2	
8.0		9.3	7.7		5.9	6.4	44.2	7.4	24.1	
(123) 2.3	(118) 2.6	(95) 4.3		EBIT/Interest	(18) 2.2	(13) 4.3	(23) 5.8	(19) 4.5	(18) 6.2	
-1.2	.0	1.3			-1.3	1.6	1.3	1.3	1.5	
4.2		4.2	7.5	Net Profit + Depr., Dep.,					7.0	
(42) 1.9	(35) 2.4	(26) 3.5		Amort./Cur. Mat. L/T/D				(11)	3.7	
.3	1.1	1.1							1.5	
.5		.3	.3		.4	.3	.3	.3	.4	
.8		.7	.7	Fixed/Worth	.9	.8	.5	.5	.7	
2.8		2.3	1.7		7.9	9.3	2.1	1.6	1.2	
.7		.7	.7		1.2	.6	.5	.7	.7	
1.8		1.7	1.7	Debt/Worth	3.4	2.1	1.2	1.5	1.9	
8.4		5.0	4.7		-7.8	NM	4.6	2.1	4.4	
29.0		35.0	40.8	% Profit Before Taxes/Tangible	53.6	20.2	41.2	35.6	61.8	
(115) 12.0	(113) 11.6	(94) 16.1		Net Worth	(14) 21.7	(14) 6.7	(24) 15.9	(22) 15.9	(16) 39.2	
-8.9	.6	4.0			-20.8	-14.3	2.2	7.1	11.2	
10.8		13.5	13.8	% Profit Before Taxes/Total	11.5	13.8	17.8	10.3	22.2	
3.0		4.1	5.3	Assets	4.8	4.8	4.9	6.2	8.9	
-7.4	-2.5	1.2			-8.2	.9	.3	2.4	1.6	
15.9		19.3	22.1	Sales/Net Fixed Assets	34.2	23.0	14.5	19.7	24.2	
7.9		8.6	8.9		8.5	10.1	8.5	11.9	10.3	
4.0		4.0	4.5		3.6	7.0	3.9	5.8	4.6	
2.8		2.9	2.9	Sales/Total Assets	3.6	2.9	2.5	2.9	2.7	
2.1		2.1	2.1		2.4	2.2	2.0	2.2	2.1	
1.5		1.6	1.5		1.5	1.5	1.1	1.9	1.0	
2.0		1.8	1.5	% Depr., Dep., Amort./Sales	3.4	1.4	1.9	1.5	1.3	
(124) 3.3	(118) 3.1	(92) 2.6			(12) 4.6	(14) 2.4	(23) 3.6	(21) 2.3	(18) 2.3	
6.2	5.3	5.7			8.9	6.9	6.9	5.6	4.1	
2.6		2.5	2.4	% Officers', Directors',	2.9		2.7	2.0		
(42) 4.8	(47) 3.8	(40) 4.7		Owners' Comp/Sales	(10) 6.0		(10) 4.7	(10) 5.8		
6.8	7.5	6.8			9.3		8.9	7.0		
2312011M	2480934M	2274064M	Net Sales ($)	3771M	40421M	74507M	195872M	368262M	1591231M
1356039M	1324110M	1372393M	Total Assets ($)	2797M	20727M	38630M	125466M	167221M	1017552M

M = $ thousand   MM = $ million
See Pages 11 through 21 for Explanation of Ratios and Data

MANUFACTURING—Semiconductor and Related Device Manufacturing NAICS 334413 (SIC 3674)

Current Data Sorted By Assets							Comparative Historical Data	

0-500M	500M-2MM	2-10MM	10-50MM	50-100MM	100-250MM	Type of Statement		
1	1	6	10	3	6	Unqualified	23	32
	2	6				Reviewed	7	10
	1	4				Compiled	8	11
1	2	1	1			Tax Returns	2	1
	3	8	7	2	1	Other	18	24
	15 (4/1-9/30/04)		51 (10/1/04-3/31/05)				4/1/00-3/31/01	4/1/01-3/31/02
							ALL	ALL
2	9	25	18	5	7	NUMBER OF STATEMENTS	58	78
%	%	%	%	%	%		%	%
						ASSETS		
		8.0	14.6			Cash & Equivalents	14.8	17.6
		28.1	22.1			Trade Receivables (net)	26.5	19.8
		26.5	29.5			Inventory	24.6	21.7
		1.7	3.7			All Other Current	1.5	3.2
		64.3	69.9			Total Current	67.4	62.4
		22.8	20.1			Fixed Assets (net)	23.1	25.0
		6.1	4.2			Intangibles (net)	5.0	6.2
		6.8	5.9			All Other Non-Current	4.6	6.4
		100.0	100.0			Total	100.0	100.0
						LIABILITIES		
		10.9	17.5			Notes Payable-Short Term	5.6	9.0
		5.7	2.0			Cur. Mat.-L/T/D	2.6	3.8
		16.1	14.6			Trade Payables	12.3	9.6
		.1	1.3			Income Taxes Payable	.7	.2
		10.4	10.1			All Other Current	11.6	12.7
		43.3	45.5			Total Current	32.7	35.3
		10.6	9.1			Long-Term Debt	10.8	9.8
		.2	.8			Deferred Taxes	.2	.4
		9.3	4.5			All Other Non-Current	6.9	4.7
		36.5	40.0			Net Worth	49.4	49.7
		100.0	100.0			Total Liabilities & Net Worth	100.0	100.0
						INCOME DATA		
		100.0	100.0			Net Sales	100.0	100.0
		33.5	32.9			Gross Profit	33.1	33.1
		28.8	25.9			Operating Expenses	27.5	31.3
		4.7	7.0			Operating Profit	5.6	1.8
		1.1	1.5			All Other Expenses (net)	−1.0	1.0
		3.6	5.5			Profit Before Taxes	6.6	.8
						RATIOS		
		3.0	3.0				3.3	4.1
		1.5	1.5			Current	2.1	2.0
		1.1	1.1				1.6	1.4
		1.4	2.0				2.0	2.4
		.8	.8			Quick	1.3	1.2
		.5	.5				.8	.6
		41 8.9	32 11.5				46 7.9	34 10.8
		52 7.0	50 7.3			Sales/Receivables	57 6.4	46 7.9
		64 5.7	57 6.4				77 4.7	57 6.4
		37 9.8	56 6.5				51 7.2	41 9.0
		71 5.1	92 4.0			Cost of Sales/Inventory	86 4.2	74 4.9
		120 3.0	113 3.2				118 3.1	107 3.4
		30 12.2	20 17.9				22 16.9	14 26.2
		46 7.9	39 9.3			Cost of Sales/Payables	35 10.6	25 14.5
		64 5.7	57 6.4				57 6.4	42 8.7
		3.0	3.0				2.8	2.6
		8.7	9.5			Sales/Working Capital	5.1	5.4
		59.0	74.7				10.1	16.0
		7.6	56.9				17.2	10.6
		(22) 2.5	(15) 5.7			EBIT/Interest	(49) 6.1	(65) 1.9
		1.4	4.3				1.9	−1.3
						Net Profit + Depr., Dep.,	16.9	11.3
						Amort./Cur. Mat. L /T/D	(14) 9.4	(28) 5.3
							3.3	.8
		.2	.3				.2	.2
		.7	.4			Fixed/Worth	.4	.4
		2.4	2.5				1.0	1.1
		.6	.5				.5	.3
		2.1	2.1			Debt/Worth	1.0	1.0
		10.1	8.4				2.9	2.7
		48.7	68.8			% Profit Before Taxes/Tangible	43.6	25.0
		(20) 4.8	(15) 38.7			Net Worth	(52) 19.0	(71) 6.8
		3.1	10.1				4.0	−6.4
		13.2	21.9			% Profit Before Taxes/Total	17.6	10.7
		3.7	9.6			Assets	9.0	1.7
		.9	2.9				1.7	−6.1
		29.1	14.5				22.7	24.6
		11.3	8.3			Sales/Net Fixed Assets	6.2	7.7
		4.8	5.9				3.7	3.0
		2.3	2.3				2.2	2.4
		1.5	1.8			Sales/Total Assets	1.4	1.3
		1.2	1.2				1.0	.9
		1.6	1.4				1.3	1.3
		(24) 2.3	(16) 2.5			% Depr., Dep., Amort./Sales	(49) 2.9	(62) 2.9
		5.4	3.7				5.3	7.1
							1.6	1.7
						% Officers', Directors',	(10) 5.5	(14) 3.7
						Owners' Comp/Sales	17.8	17.9
1389M	40286M	210772M	603285M	1437910M	1091507M	Net Sales ($)	3193272M	4717305M
156M	11580M	113059M	366975M	386070M	1257146M	Total Assets ($)	2391966M	4149491M

M = $ thousand   MM = $ million
See Pages 11 through 21 for Explanation of Ratios and Data

Comparative Historical Data				Current Data Sorted By Sales					
			Type of Statement						
19	28	27	Unqualified	1		1	3	6	16
11	9	8	Reviewed		1	2	5		
3	3	5	Compiled		1	2	2		
2	5	5	Tax Returns		2		1	1	1
21	31	21	Other			2	8		8
4/1/02-	4/1/03-	4/1/04-			15 (4/1-9/30/04)		51 (10/1/04-3/31/05)		
3/31/03	3/31/04	3/31/05							
ALL	ALL	ALL		0-1MM	1-3MM	3-5MM	5-10MM	10-25MM	25MM & OVER
56	76	66	**NUMBER OF STATEMENTS**	1	4	7	19	10	25
%	%	%	**ASSETS**	%	%	%	%	%	%
15.3	14.6	15.7	Cash & Equivalents				13.5	13.5	19.8
21.2	23.3	25.8	Trade Receivables (net)				26.0	31.4	22.0
26.6	24.8	26.0	Inventory				26.0	21.2	25.1
2.8	3.5	2.7	All Other Current				1.8	2.9	4.0
65.9	66.3	70.2	Total Current				67.3	69.0	70.8
23.9	22.9	18.3	Fixed Assets (net)				24.3	20.3	16.4
5.0	5.4	4.8	Intangibles (net)				2.6	8.0	5.0
5.3	5.5	6.6	All Other Non-Current				5.8	2.7	7.8
100.0	100.0	100.0	Total				100.0	100.0	100.0
			LIABILITIES						
9.8	8.2	11.0	Notes Payable-Short Term				11.0	12.8	9.7
3.5	2.5	3.3	Cur. Mat.-L/T/D				4.7	7.2	1.3
15.3	13.0	15.6	Trade Payables				18.1	16.5	16.2
.6	.5	.6	Income Taxes Payable				.2	.1	1.3
10.8	14.5	9.6	All Other Current				9.9	7.9	10.8
40.0	38.7	40.0	Total Current				43.9	44.4	39.3
14.3	9.8	8.7	Long-Term Debt				11.3	9.4	7.0
.7	.4	.3	Deferred Taxes				.1	.7	.5
5.1	5.2	6.1	All Other Non-Current				6.4	7.4	3.6
40.0	45.9	44.8	Net Worth				38.3	38.1	49.6
100.0	100.0	100.0	Total Liabilities & Net Worth				100.0	100.0	100.0
			INCOME DATA						
100.0	100.0	100.0	Net Sales				100.0	100.0	100.0
28.5	32.2	33.9	Gross Profit				33.7	27.7	32.4
30.0	30.6	29.7	Operating Expenses				30.6	25.3	27.7
−1.4	1.6	4.2	Operating Profit				3.1	2.4	4.7
2.0	.6	.8	All Other Expenses (net)				.5	1.9	.7
−3.4	1.0	3.4	Profit Before Taxes				2.5	.5	4.0
			RATIOS						
2.6	2.8	3.4					2.7	4.1	3.6
1.9	1.9	1.8	Current				1.7	1.8	2.2
1.2	1.2	1.2					1.1	.8	1.2
1.8	1.7	2.0					1.6	3.1	2.3
.9	1.0	1.0	Quick				.8	.9	1.2
.6	.6	.6					.5	.5	.6
37 9.7	40 9.1	37 10.0					37 9.9	36 10.2	35 10.3
48 7.6	50 7.3	49 7.4	Sales/Receivables				49 7.4	56 6.5	47 7.8
64 5.7	63 5.8	63 5.8					54 6.7	94 3.9	59 6.1
41 8.8	52 7.1	42 8.7					35 10.4	38 9.7	50 7.3
76 4.8	79 4.6	75 4.8	Cost of Sales/Inventory				77 4.8	62 5.9	79 4.6
124 2.9	114 3.2	115 3.2					109 3.4	79 4.6	111 3.3
25 14.7	19 19.2	24 15.1					28 13.2	20 18.3	26 14.2
38 9.7	37 9.9	38 9.6	Cost of Sales/Payables				46 7.9	40 9.2	38 9.6
69 5.3	57 6.4	61 6.0					63 5.8	64 5.7	61 6.0
2.8	3.0	2.5					3.2	1.8	2.1
5.4	5.2	6.8	Sales/Working Capital				11.5	7.1	5.0
27.4	18.9	29.0					32.2	−29.5	25.8
10.2	6.3	16.0					11.4		32.1
(45) 1.4	(64) 2.0	(58) 4.5	EBIT/Interest				(17) 2.5	(23) 5.4	
−2.1	−1.7	1.4					1.3		.0
5.0	8.7	12.5	Net Profit + Depr., Dep.,						18.6
(19) 1.7	(21) 3.0	(24) 3.0	Amort./Cur. Mat. L/T/D					(12) 12.3	
−1.1	1.4	1.1							2.3
.2	.2	.2					.2	.3	.1
.4	.4	.4	Fixed/Worth				.5	.5	.4
1.4	1.0	1.2					1.4	−1.1	.9
.5	.5	.5					.5	.4	.3
1.2	1.0	1.2	Debt/Worth				1.3	1.5	1.2
6.8	4.0	4.2					3.9	−7.0	4.2
21.6	18.9	43.0	% Profit Before Taxes/Tangible				45.7		56.1
(47) 2.3	(70) 3.3	(58) 10.4	Net Worth				(17) 7.6	(23) 25.9	
−12.9	−6.3	1.1					.5		.6
7.7	7.7	14.4	% Profit Before Taxes/Total				16.3	10.4	19.5
.6	1.2	4.6	Assets				2.8	3.6	8.3
−11.9	−5.4	.2					−2.0	−3.7	.0
25.5	23.1	29.3					29.0	15.1	26.9
9.6	8.2	12.8	Sales/Net Fixed Assets				11.3	7.5	12.4
3.6	4.3	5.9					4.6	4.9	5.6
2.5	2.2	2.5					2.8	2.5	2.3
1.3	1.4	1.7	Sales/Total Assets				1.6	1.7	1.7
.8	1.0	1.1					1.4	1.0	1.0
1.3	1.3	1.0					1.6		.9
(43) 2.9	(54) 2.9	(54) 2.1	% Depr., Dep., Amort./Sales				2.5	(17) 2.1	
6.0	5.7	4.7					5.5		3.3
	2.0	.8	% Officers', Directors',						
	(16) 4.3	(16) 2.4	Owners' Comp/Sales						
	8.5	5.7							
2879958M	3875852M	3385149M	Net Sales ($)	19M	8565M	28767M	132555M	174544M	3040699M
2278426M	3094836M	2134986M	Total Assets ($)	17M	3603M	20481M	73385M	124354M	1913146M

© RMA 2005

M = $ thousand   MM = $ million
See Pages 11 through 21 for Explanation of Ratios and Data

Current Data Sorted By Assets   **Comparative Historical Data**

0-500M	500M-2MM	2-10MM	10-50MM	50-100MM	100-250MM	Type of Statement	4/1/00-3/31/01 ALL	4/1/01-3/31/02 ALL
	1	2	5	1		Unqualified	7	9
	1	7	1			Reviewed	6	5
	2					Compiled		4
1	1					Tax Returns		
1		6	8		1	Other	7	7
	7 (4/1-9/30/04)		30 (10/1/04-3/31/05)					
2	4	15	14	1	1	**NUMBER OF STATEMENTS**	20	25
%	%	%	%	%	%	**ASSETS**	%	%
		5.7	1.9			Cash & Equivalents	5.4	8.2
		33.5	23.9			Trade Receivables (net)	28.8	24.6
		21.8	27.8			Inventory	30.4	26.0
		1.1	1.2			All Other Current	.8	4.4
		62.1	54.8			Total Current	65.4	63.1
		19.8	24.0			Fixed Assets (net)	26.7	25.4
		.9	14.9			Intangibles (net)	4.7	7.5
		17.3	6.3			All Other Non-Current	3.2	4.0
		100.0	100.0			Total	100.0	100.0
						LIABILITIES		
		11.9	10.2			Notes Payable-Short Term	13.2	10.9
		4.2	7.0			Cur. Mat.-L/T/D	3.3	3.1
		16.6	14.6			Trade Payables	13.7	10.3
		.6	.1			Income Taxes Payable	.7	.9
		7.3	11.8			All Other Current	12.4	9.5
		40.5	43.7			Total Current	43.3	34.6
		7.8	10.7			Long-Term Debt	11.4	10.4
		.2	.3			Deferred Taxes	.5	.8
		4.6	15.7			All Other Non-Current	1.9	6.0
		46.9	29.6			Net Worth	42.8	48.1
		100.0	100.0			Total Liabilities & Net Worth	100.0	100.0
						INCOME DATA		
		100.0	100.0			Net Sales	100.0	100.0
		29.2	20.6			Gross Profit	29.3	27.2
		22.8	16.3			Operating Expenses	22.7	23.0
		6.4	4.3			Operating Profit	6.6	4.2
		–.3	1.5			All Other Expenses (net)	1.8	.9
		6.7	2.8			Profit Before Taxes	4.8	3.3
						RATIOS		
		2.1	1.7				2.1	2.6
		1.6	1.5			Current	1.5	1.7
		1.0	1.0				1.2	1.2
		1.8	.8				1.2	1.5
		1.0	.6			Quick	.7	.9
		.6	.4				.6	.5
		35 10.3	38 9.5				35 10.4	34 10.7
		48 7.6	50 7.3			Sales/Receivables	47 7.7	47 7.8
		53 6.9	67 5.5				58 6.3	55 6.7
		33 11.0	50 7.3				49 7.5	54 6.7
		51 7.2	70 5.2			Cost of Sales/Inventory	81 4.5	70 5.2
		73 5.0	114 3.2				89 4.1	83 4.4
		20 18.4	28 13.1				18 20.3	16 23.4
		25 14.7	38 9.6			Cost of Sales/Payables	30 12.1	26 13.9
		42 8.6	50 7.4				53 6.9	37 9.9
		6.4	5.7				5.3	4.4
		12.7	10.3			Sales/Working Capital	11.2	7.6
		–127.5	NM				19.7	37.6
		48.2	6.5				10.4	14.0
		(14) 15.5	2.7			EBIT/Interest	(18) 3.4	(21) 1.8
		2.4	1.6				1.5	–.6
						Net Profit + Depr., Dep., Amort./Cur. Mat. L /T/D		
		.3	.5				.4	.3
		.4	.7			Fixed/Worth	.7	.6
		1.4	–.4				2.2	2.0
		.4	1.1				.8	.4
		1.4	1.4			Debt/Worth	1.5	1.1
		3.6	–2.2				6.0	3.4
		97.5	24.4				48.2	24.9
		32.0	(10) 8.8			% Profit Before Taxes/Tangible Net Worth	(18) 31.1	(21) 7.0
		4.7	1.8				9.6	–14.8
		31.5	12.0				17.7	13.1
		14.1	4.6			% Profit Before Taxes/Total Assets	8.1	2.7
		2.0	.8				2.8	–6.5
		29.7	14.9				14.2	12.7
		12.2	7.0			Sales/Net Fixed Assets	7.5	7.3
		7.4	4.8				5.6	5.4
		3.2	2.0				2.7	2.5
		2.5	1.5			Sales/Total Assets	1.8	1.7
		2.2	1.4				1.6	1.4
		.9					.9	1.1
		(13) 1.9				% Depr., Dep., Amort./Sales	(19) 1.9	2.8
		3.2					3.3	4.5
						% Officers', Directors', Owners' Comp/Sales		
3715M	16991M	172945M	602467M	78269M	192679M	Net Sales ($)	1023010M	753185M
763M	5093M	65620M	351538M	94139M	113870M	Total Assets ($)	573752M	402146M

© RMA 2005

M = $ thousand   MM = $ million
See Pages 11 through 21 for Explanation of Ratios and Data

Comparative Historical Data / Current Data Sorted By Sales

4/1/02-3/31/03 ALL	4/1/03-3/31/04 ALL	4/1/04-3/31/05 ALL		0-1MM	1-3MM	3-5MM	5-10MM	10-25MM	25MM & OVER
			Type of Statement						
9	5	8	Unqualified			1		2	5
7	5	9	Reviewed				5	4	
3	3	3	Compiled		2	1			
	3	1	Tax Returns			1			
8	11	16	Other		1		3	5	7
				7 (4/1-9/30/04)		30 (10/1/04-3/31/05)			
27	27	37	**NUMBER OF STATEMENTS**		3	3	8	11	12
%	%	%	**ASSETS**	%	%	%	%	%	%
3.4	5.2	5.6	Cash & Equivalents	DATA NOT AVAILABLE				3.6	3.9
25.9	30.0	31.2	Trade Receivables (net)					31.1	25.9
27.6	25.7	24.2	Inventory					18.9	25.5
1.2	1.4	1.1	All Other Current					1.2	1.3
58.0	62.4	62.1	Total Current					54.9	56.7
26.5	25.9	20.7	Fixed Assets (net)					21.6	27.4
9.4	3.6	6.5	Intangibles (net)					7.6	11.5
6.1	8.2	10.8	All Other Non-Current					16.0	4.5
100.0	100.0	100.0	Total					100.0	100.0
			LIABILITIES						
10.4	16.7	11.3	Notes Payable-Short Term					8.7	10.3
6.0	5.8	4.8	Cur. Mat.-L/T/D					6.8	3.1
13.2	13.0	16.2	Trade Payables					18.5	13.7
.4	.3	.4	Income Taxes Payable					.2	.4
10.1	16.3	10.9	All Other Current					7.8	11.8
40.1	52.2	43.7	Total Current					42.0	39.2
11.4	9.1	10.0	Long-Term Debt					10.5	9.9
1.1	.6	.4	Deferred Taxes					.2	1.0
12.8	10.8	8.5	All Other Non-Current					10.3	12.5
34.6	27.1	37.4	Net Worth					36.9	37.3
100.0	100.0	100.0	Total Liabilities & Net Worth					100.0	100.0
			INCOME DATA						
100.0	100.0	100.0	Net Sales					100.0	100.0
25.2	29.3	27.5	Gross Profit					26.1	24.5
22.7	27.6	22.1	Operating Expenses					19.5	19.6
2.5	1.7	5.3	Operating Profit					6.7	4.9
1.3	1.7	.5	All Other Expenses (net)					.3	1.0
1.2	.0	4.8	Profit Before Taxes					6.4	3.8
			RATIOS						
1.9	2.0	2.0						1.8	2.0
1.6	1.4	1.5	Current					1.6	1.5
1.1	1.0	1.0						.9	1.0
1.0	1.1	1.4						1.5	1.4
.6	.7	.8	Quick					.8	.6
.5	.4	.6						.5	.4
30 12.2	**34** 10.9	**37** 9.8						**35** 10.3	**43** 8.4
41 8.9	**50** 7.2	**49** 7.4	Sales/Receivables					**49** 7.4	**53** 6.9
49 7.4	**57** 6.4	**53** 6.9						**53** 6.9	**67** 5.5
38 9.6	**34** 10.8	**33** 11.1						**24** 15.5	**33** 11.2
56 6.5	**62** 5.9	**53** 6.9	Cost of Sales/Inventory					**38** 9.7	**69** 5.3
85 4.3	**119** 3.1	**79** 4.6						**62** 5.9	**104** 3.5
16 23.4	**20** 18.1	**21** 17.7						**25** 14.7	**24** 15.3
24 15.0	**33** 11.1	**28** 12.9	Cost of Sales/Payables					**36** 10.1	**35** 10.5
36 10.1	**47** 7.7	**45** 8.1						**80** 4.6	**48** 7.6
6.2	5.8	6.2						6.6	5.5
10.8	15.0	11.4	Sales/Working Capital					17.0	10.3
75.5	UND	547.4						−51.1	764.3
3.4	10.2	16.9						47.9	6.6
(25) 1.6	(26) 2.3	(36) 5.6	EBIT/Interest					15.7	3.9
−1.4	−.8	2.0						2.2	1.8
		7.5							
		(12) 3.0	Net Profit + Depr., Dep., Amort./Cur. Mat. L/T/D						
		1.7							
.5	.4	.3						.4	.5
.7	.7	.5	Fixed/Worth					.6	.7
20.8	UND	1.5						2.7	2.7
.7	.8	.8						.5	1.0
1.3	1.3	1.7	Debt/Worth					1.4	1.4
90.3	UND	5.4						45.5	5.6
21.9	23.3	45.6							30.9
(21) 7.1	(21) 10.5	(33) 22.8	% Profit Before Taxes/Tangible Net Worth						(10) 11.4
−11.9	1.6	3.6							1.8
6.6	7.8	20.4						31.5	12.1
3.2	1.1	6.7	% Profit Before Taxes/Total Assets					14.1	6.6
−5.9	−7.1	1.7						3.0	1.1
14.1	14.1	32.3						34.9	14.4
8.3	6.8	12.2	Sales/Net Fixed Assets					15.6	7.0
6.0	4.7	6.4						5.3	5.2
2.6	2.5	3.2						3.7	2.0
2.1	1.8	2.2	Sales/Total Assets					2.3	1.6
1.6	1.4	1.5						1.2	1.5
1.3	1.6	.9							
(24) 3.0	(21) 3.9	(28) 2.6	% Depr., Dep., Amort./Sales						
4.9	5.0	3.4							
			% Officers', Directors', Owners' Comp/Sales						
829639M	714752M	1067066M	Net Sales ($)		6608M	12251M	62657M	180405M	805145M
421505M	409320M	631023M	Total Assets ($)		1392M	6253M	27682M	92177M	503519M

M = $ thousand MM = $ million

See Pages 11 through 21 for Explanation of Ratios and Data

Current Data Sorted By Assets   **Comparative Historical Data**

© RMA 2005
M = $ thousand   MM = $ million
See Pages 11 through 21 for Explanation of Ratios and Data

		2	6			Type of Statement		
1		7	1			Unqualified	14	9
	3	2				Reviewed	6	3
2		2				Compiled	6	3
2	3	5	1	1		Tax Returns		
10 (4/1-9/30/04)			28 (10/1/04-3/31/05)			Other	11	10
0-500M	500M-2MM	2-10MM	10-50MM	50-100MM	100-250MM		4/1/00-3/31/01 ALL	4/1/01-3/31/02 ALL
5	6	18	8	1		NUMBER OF STATEMENTS	37	25
%	%	%	%	%	%	**ASSETS**	%	%
		12.0				Cash & Equivalents	6.7	9.9
		18.4			D	Trade Receivables (net)	25.6	22.0
		28.1			A	Inventory	29.2	27.8
		1.8			T	All Other Current	1.3	1.6
		60.3			A	Total Current	62.8	61.4
		32.3				Fixed Assets (net)	28.2	30.5
		3.5			N	Intangibles (net)	4.4	3.9
		3.9			O	All Other Non-Current	4.6	4.2
		100.0			T	Total	100.0	100.0
					A	**LIABILITIES**		
		14.3			V	Notes Payable-Short Term	14.0	8.1
		4.1			A	Cur. Mat.-L/T/D	5.8	7.3
		11.7			I	Trade Payables	13.5	10.6
		.6			L	Income Taxes Payable	.4	.1
		7.1			A	All Other Current	10.8	8.0
		37.9			B	Total Current	44.4	34.1
		19.6			L	Long-Term Debt	14.6	12.3
		1.0			E	Deferred Taxes	.7	.5
		5.2				All Other Non-Current	9.6	4.2
		36.3				Net Worth	30.6	48.8
		100.0				Total Liabilities & Net Worth	100.0	100.0
						INCOME DATA		
		100.0				Net Sales	100.0	100.0
		31.6				Gross Profit	34.4	28.8
		27.3				Operating Expenses	25.8	23.8
		4.2				Operating Profit	8.7	5.1
		1.3				All Other Expenses (net)	2.7	1.7
		3.0				Profit Before Taxes	5.9	3.3
						RATIOS		
		3.7					2.3	3.5
		2.0				Current	1.5	2.1
		1.0					1.2	1.2
		2.6					1.2	2.3
		.9				Quick	.6	1.0
		.4					.5	.4
		26 14.2					40 9.1	31 11.9
		40 9.0				Sales/Receivables	53 6.9	46 8.0
		50 7.3					64 5.7	57 6.4
		55 6.6					65 5.6	53 6.9
		68 5.4				Cost of Sales/Inventory	97 3.8	72 5.1
		109 3.4					131 2.8	108 3.4
		17 21.8					23 15.9	15 24.2
		36 10.3				Cost of Sales/Payables	38 9.6	28 13.0
		49 7.4					52 7.0	33 11.1
		4.1					4.0	3.9
		8.2				Sales/Working Capital	10.1	5.7
		NM					22.2	26.8
		11.4					3.4	21.3
	(16)	3.9				EBIT/Interest	(32) 2.3	(23) 1.8
		1.3					1.7	-3.4
						Net Profit + Depr., Dep.,	3.2	4.6
						Amort./Cur. Mat. L /T/D	(12) 1.1	(10) .7
							.6	-.2
		.3					.4	.3
		.8				Fixed/Worth	1.0	.6
		8.4					2.3	1.7
		.6					1.0	.4
		1.0				Debt/Worth	2.2	1.4
		16.7					4.8	2.5
		59.3				% Profit Before Taxes/Tangible	49.4	43.9
	(15)	31.7				Net Worth	(32) 24.6	(24) 15.7
		3.3					6.0	-12.2
		19.7				% Profit Before Taxes/Total	17.9	25.0
		5.1				Assets	6.2	4.3
		.5					1.6	-6.9
		14.7					13.5	13.4
		6.8				Sales/Net Fixed Assets	6.7	5.8
		3.1					3.8	2.9
		2.1					2.1	2.2
		1.8				Sales/Total Assets	1.8	1.6
		1.3					1.3	1.2
		1.2					1.4	1.3
	(15)	2.9				% Depr., Dep., Amort./Sales	(33) 2.9	(22) 3.5
		6.1					4.8	5.0
						% Officers', Directors',	1.4	
						Owners' Comp/Sales	(11) 4.1	
							8.3	
4992M	20422M	217271M	303463M	260124M		Net Sales ($)	1350055M	1109653M
1319M	7354M	111543M	181109M	97190M		Total Assets ($)	954884M	942392M

Comparative Historical Data				Current Data Sorted By Sales					

				Type of Statement						
11	10	8	Unqualified					5	3
4	8	9	Reviewed		1		2	6	
4	8	5	Compiled			3	2		
2	3	4	Tax Returns	2	1			1	
11	17	12	Other		6		1	3	2

	4/1/02-	4/1/03-	4/1/04-		10 (4/1-9/30/04)			28 (10/1/04-3/31/05)		
	3/31/03	3/31/04	3/31/05		0-1MM	1-3MM	3-5MM	5-10MM	10-25MM	25MM & OVER
	ALL	ALL	ALL							
	32	46	38	**NUMBER OF STATEMENTS**	2	8	3	5	15	5
	%	%	%	**ASSETS**	%	%	%	%	%	%
	10.3	8.2	14.1	Cash & Equivalents					14.9	
	21.8	26.4	20.7	Trade Receivables (net)					22.4	
	28.9	27.6	28.8	Inventory					26.0	
	2.8	3.1	1.3	All Other Current					1.2	
	63.9	65.3	64.9	Total Current					64.5	
	28.3	21.9	25.3	Fixed Assets (net)					26.4	
	4.0	9.1	4.0	Intangibles (net)					5.0	
	3.9	3.8	5.8	All Other Non-Current					4.2	
	100.0	100.0	100.0	Total					100.0	
				LIABILITIES						
	6.1	13.1	14.6	Notes Payable-Short Term					10.2	
	4.7	4.4	4.7	Cur. Mat.-L/T/D					4.0	
	9.6	12.7	11.0	Trade Payables					10.0	
	.4	.7	.4	Income Taxes Payable					.3	
	14.1	9.2	9.6	All Other Current					10.0	
	34.8	40.2	40.3	Total Current					34.6	
	13.5	14.2	16.7	Long-Term Debt					19.2	
	.5	.4	.6	Deferred Taxes					.4	
	6.0	7.4	4.9	All Other Non-Current					6.3	
	45.2	37.7	37.5	Net Worth					39.6	
	100.0	100.0	100.0	Total Liabilities & Net Worth					100.0	
				INCOME DATA						
	100.0	100.0	100.0	Net Sales					100.0	
	35.2	33.3	35.8	Gross Profit					35.5	
	31.5	27.8	30.4	Operating Expenses					26.4	
	3.7	5.5	5.5	Operating Profit					9.2	
	1.8	1.2	1.4	All Other Expenses (net)					.9	
	1.9	4.3	4.1	Profit Before Taxes					8.2	
				RATIOS						
	3.4	2.9	3.7						3.7	
	2.0	1.8	1.9	Current					2.0	
	1.6	1.2	1.3						1.5	
	1.6	1.5	2.3						2.7	
	1.0	.8	1.1	Quick					1.1	
	.6	.5	.5						.7	
32	11.4	36 10.0	26 13.8						33 11.1	
43	8.4	48 7.6	39 9.3	Sales/Receivables					41 8.8	
58	6.3	63 5.8	50 7.3						54 6.7	
68	5.4	63 5.8	54 6.7						55 6.6	
95	3.8	75 4.9	71 5.2	Cost of Sales/Inventory					62 5.9	
119	3.1	106 3.4	109 3.4						73 5.0	
15	24.2	19 18.9	16 23.2						16 23.4	
27	13.4	31 12.0	26 13.9	Cost of Sales/Payables					24 15.2	
43	8.6	43 8.5	42 8.7						36 10.2	
	4.2	4.1	4.1						3.6	
	5.9	6.9	9.0	Sales/Working Capital					7.1	
	10.4	20.0	17.7						13.5	
	23.0	14.9	14.2						40.2	
(28)	2.6	(42) 4.4	(32) 4.9	EBIT/Interest					(13) 11.5	
	-1.7	-1.3	1.2						5.3	
	13.4	15.2		Net Profit + Depr., Dep.,						
(12)	2.6	(17) 3.5		Amort./Cur. Mat. L/T/D						
	.4	1.7								
	.3	.3	.2						.2	
	.6	.6	.5	Fixed/Worth					.7	
	1.4	2.0	6.9						4.2	
	.5	.9	.5						.5	
	1.3	1.6	1.1	Debt/Worth					1.1	
	4.5	4.8	15.8						13.1	
	39.4	44.1	61.0	% Profit Before Taxes/Tangible					67.0	
(28)	17.7	(39) 16.2	(31) 35.5	Net Worth					(12) 38.3	
	1.7	-12.4	3.3						26.6	
	15.4	18.5	23.1	% Profit Before Taxes/Total					28.9	
	2.7	7.7	8.2	Assets					20.7	
	-3.5	-2.1	.4						5.4	
	11.4	16.9	19.5						14.3	
	6.1	9.7	11.0	Sales/Net Fixed Assets					10.5	
	3.7	5.5	4.3						5.3	
	2.5	2.3	2.7						2.3	
	1.7	1.7	2.0	Sales/Total Assets					2.0	
	1.3	1.3	1.3						1.7	
	1.7	1.5	1.2						1.2	
(26)	3.5	(40) 2.6	(30) 2.5	% Depr., Dep., Amort./Sales					(13) 2.9	
	5.3	4.0	4.7						3.6	
		2.3	3.4	% Officers', Directors',						
		(11) 5.3	(12) 5.6	Owners' Comp/Sales						
		6.9	22.1							
	912468M	921081M	806272M	Net Sales ($)	316M	17098M	11300M	31449M	264930M	481179M
	603061M	604699M	398515M	Total Assets ($)	297M	9398M	6107M	20898M	133107M	228708M

© RMA 2005

M = $ thousand   MM = $ million

See Pages 11 through 21 for Explanation of Ratios and Data

Current Data Sorted By Assets   **Comparative Historical Data**

	0-500M	500M-2MM	2-10MM	10-50MM	50-100MM	100-250MM	Type of Statement	4/1/00-3/31/01 ALL	4/1/01-3/31/02 ALL
	1	3	19	25	4	10	Unqualified	65	49
	1	8	31	6			Reviewed	45	41
	6	12	14				Compiled	43	41
	10	10	1				Tax Returns	8	11
	2	8	15	19	1	3	Other	68	74
		53 (4/1-9/30/04)		156 (10/1/04-3/31/05)					
	0-500M	500M-2MM	2-10MM	10-50MM	50-100MM	100-250MM			
	20	41	80	50	5	13	NUMBER OF STATEMENTS	229	216
	%	%	%	%	%	%	**ASSETS**	%	%
	12.5	10.1	7.0	10.0		30.9	Cash & Equivalents	9.0	10.4
	31.1	33.4	30.7	25.8		18.9	Trade Receivables (net)	29.2	26.5
	24.9	26.2	32.2	33.1		14.5	Inventory	29.0	29.7
	.4	3.7	1.2	2.6		3.4	All Other Current	2.6	2.3
	68.9	73.4	71.2	71.6		67.7	Total Current	69.7	68.9
	15.4	17.2	18.5	18.7		17.2	Fixed Assets (net)	20.6	22.0
	4.9	2.3	3.9	3.1		9.9	Intangibles (net)	4.3	4.0
	10.8	7.1	6.4	6.6		5.2	All Other Non-Current	5.4	5.0
	100.0	100.0	100.0	100.0		100.0	Total	100.0	100.0
							LIABILITIES		
	34.6	11.8	14.2	9.5		.0	Notes Payable-Short Term	11.6	13.5
	4.3	3.0	3.6	2.7		.5	Cur. Mat.-L/T/D	3.2	4.9
	24.4	16.5	15.3	12.1		8.0	Trade Payables	15.0	14.3
	.0	.2	.3	.5		1.5	Income Taxes Payable	.3	.2
	8.4	9.4	9.4	10.2		12.8	All Other Current	10.0	10.4
	71.8	40.8	42.9	34.9		22.8	Total Current	40.1	43.3
	26.8	6.3	9.0	9.8		22.3	Long-Term Debt	12.8	14.7
	.0	.1	.3	.8		.9	Deferred Taxes	.3	.2
	12.3	9.9	6.1	4.0		16.3	All Other Non-Current	6.7	4.7
	−10.9	43.0	41.7	50.5		37.6	Net Worth	40.1	37.1
	100.0	100.0	100.0	100.0		100.0	Total Liabilities & Net Worth	100.0	100.0
							INCOME DATA		
	100.0	100.0	100.0	100.0		100.0	Net Sales	100.0	100.0
	41.5	39.6	30.6	26.1		43.5	Gross Profit	32.0	31.2
	41.6	33.9	25.7	19.8		33.8	Operating Expenses	28.0	27.7
	−.1	5.7	4.9	6.4		9.7	Operating Profit	4.0	3.5
	1.4	.5	.5	.1		1.9	All Other Expenses (net)	.8	1.3
	−1.4	5.2	4.4	6.2		7.8	Profit Before Taxes	3.2	2.2
							RATIOS		
	2.9	3.9	2.5	3.6		6.1		3.1	2.9
	1.7	2.4	1.7	2.0		3.7	Current	1.8	1.6
	.3	1.2	1.3	1.4		2.5		1.3	1.2
	1.8	2.4	1.4	1.7		5.3		1.7	1.5
	.9	1.2	.9	1.0		2.0	Quick	1.0	.8
	.2	.5	.6	.6		1.5		.6	.5
16	22.8	31 11.9	37 9.9	41 9.0		47 7.8		39 9.4	35 10.5
26	14.0	47 7.8	47 7.7	51 7.2		60 6.1	Sales/Receivables	53 6.9	45 8.1
49	7.5	67 5.5	59 6.2	61 6.0		71 5.2		65 5.6	57 6.4
0	UND	22 16.5	48 7.5	62 5.9		43 8.5		45 8.1	46 7.9
35	10.5	49 7.4	75 4.9	85 4.3		83 4.4	Cost of Sales/Inventory	74 4.9	75 4.9
80	4.6	117 3.1	104 3.5	121 3.0		101 3.6		112 3.3	121 3.0
6	56.3	14 26.1	19 18.8	20 18.2		30 12.0		19 18.8	18 20.1
19	19.1	33 11.1	35 10.4	32 11.6		37 9.8	Cost of Sales/Payables	33 10.9	30 12.3
78	4.7	55 6.6	46 7.9	44 8.3		57 6.4		53 6.9	49 7.4
	5.9	4.2	4.8	3.7		1.3		3.7	4.2
	11.8	6.1	8.2	6.0		2.3	Sales/Working Capital	6.8	8.3
	−5.6	26.6	16.4	10.4		4.4		15.1	24.3
	7.6	27.6	17.4	26.9				9.9	6.5
(16)	2.8	(33) 8.4	(77) 5.8	(46) 17.0			EBIT/Interest	(199) 3.0	(196) 1.9
	−.5	2.2	2.2	3.6				1.0	.3
			6.1	13.1			Net Profit + Depr., Dep.,	8.8	5.1
		(24) 3.0	(21) 5.2				Amort./Cur. Mat. L /T/D	(73) 3.0	(66) 1.6
			.8	2.0				1.2	.1
	.0	.1	.2	.2		.1		.2	.2
	.2	.3	.4	.4		.3	Fixed/Worth	.5	.7
	−.9	.8	.9	.7		NM		1.2	1.5
	1.0	.3	.6	.5		.2		.5	.7
	4.3	.9	1.7	1.1		.4	Debt/Worth	1.6	1.8
	−3.2	2.7	4.2	2.3		NM		3.9	5.3
	58.0	39.8	53.1	39.9		24.4	% Profit Before Taxes/Tangible	43.4	36.3
(12)	27.8	(36) 21.5	(74) 22.8	(48) 21.6		(10) 13.0	Net Worth	(206) 18.6	(189) 12.3
	4.2	6.8	7.4	12.8		2.8		4.5	−2.0
	21.6	17.8	16.8	16.8		13.2	% Profit Before Taxes/Total	14.6	15.6
	5.1	9.4	7.7	11.7		7.3	Assets	6.4	2.9
	−6.3	1.9	2.9	4.3		.9		.0	−1.9
	331.3	48.4	44.0	19.7		18.8		29.2	25.7
	76.4	24.8	15.6	11.2		7.0	Sales/Net Fixed Assets	11.3	10.6
	15.5	10.4	8.1	6.2		4.7		5.2	5.2
	5.3	3.8	2.6	2.3		1.4		2.6	2.7
	3.5	2.5	2.3	1.9		1.1	Sales/Total Assets	2.0	2.0
	2.0	1.7	1.6	1.3		.8		1.4	1.5
	.6	.6	.7	1.8				.7	.8
(10)	1.1	(34) 1.5	(70) 1.7	(46) 2.5			% Depr., Dep., Amort./Sales	(187) 1.9	(181) 2.2
	15.8	2.2	2.7	3.9				3.5	3.4
		2.7	1.8				% Officers', Directors',	2.4	2.5
		(24) 6.3	(20) 3.0				Owners' Comp/Sales	(62) 4.8	(67) 4.7
		8.9	6.4					8.6	8.4
	18612M	135988M	819870M	1925234M	440866M	2716406M	Net Sales ($)	6596599M	5754380M
	5219M	51253M	371790M	1021156M	350235M	2304821M	Total Assets ($)	5094821M	3682475M

M = $ thousand   MM = $ million
See Pages 11 through 21 for Explanation of Ratios and Data

	Comparative Historical Data			Type of Statement	Current Data Sorted By Sales					
				Unqualified	1	1	5	7	18	30
	49	53	62	Reviewed	1	3	7	16	16	3
	48	57	46	Compiled	6	8	3	9	6	
	30	33	32	Tax Returns	6	11	2	2		
	10	14	21	Other	1	7	3	10	13	14
	77	64	48			53 (4/1-9/30/04)		156 (10/1/04-3/31/05)			
	4/1/02- 3/31/03 ALL	4/1/03- 3/31/04 ALL	4/1/04- 3/31/05 ALL		0-1MM	1-3MM	3-5MM	5-10MM	10-25MM	25MM & OVER
	214	221	209	NUMBER OF STATEMENTS	15	30	20	44	53	47
	%	%	%	ASSETS	%	%	%	%	%	%
	10.3	9.7	10.5	Cash & Equivalents	16.0	8.6	8.5	7.9	10.5	13.4
	26.9	30.4	29.1	Trade Receivables (net)	24.5	30.7	32.4	31.9	28.8	26.0
	28.5	28.9	29.2	Inventory	18.9	27.9	23.4	31.8	32.9	29.3
	3.2	2.2	2.3	All Other Current	.3	4.6	1.4	1.0	1.9	3.4
	68.9	71.1	71.1	Total Current	59.7	71.8	65.8	72.6	74.0	72.1
	20.8	19.7	17.9	Fixed Assets (net)	17.1	19.3	22.1	16.4	17.0	18.1
	4.6	3.8	4.1	Intangibles (net)	6.6	4.0	5.0	2.7	2.9	5.5
	5.7	5.4	6.9	All Other Non-Current	16.7	4.8	7.1	8.4	6.1	4.4
	100.0	100.0	100.0	Total	100.0	100.0	100.0	100.0	100.0	100.0
				LIABILITIES						
	11.4	11.2	13.5	Notes Payable-Short Term	40.1	11.9	13.1	14.0	12.7	6.5
	4.4	4.6	3.1	Cur. Mat.-L/T/D	5.5	1.8	5.1	4.3	2.2	2.0
	15.5	15.8	15.0	Trade Payables	30.2	15.1	12.8	15.3	13.8	12.1
	.4	.3	.4	Income Taxes Payable	.0	.2	.1	.3	.4	.9
	12.1	13.0	9.8	All Other Current	6.1	10.2	9.2	10.0	9.0	11.9
	43.7	44.9	41.8	Total Current	81.9	39.2	40.2	43.9	38.1	33.4
	12.6	11.5	11.1	Long-Term Debt	30.1	8.6	7.9	9.2	8.2	13.0
	.4	.4	.4	Deferred Taxes	.0	.0	.1	.2	.5	.9
	5.4	7.6	8.2	All Other Non-Current	6.3	11.0	21.7	3.1	5.2	9.4
	37.8	35.5	38.6	Net Worth	−18.2	41.2	30.1	43.6	48.0	43.4
	100.0	100.0	100.0	Total Liabilities & Net Worth	100.0	100.0	100.0	100.0	100.0	100.0
				INCOME DATA						
	100.0	100.0	100.0	Net Sales	100.0	100.0	100.0	100.0	100.0	100.0
	31.2	31.9	33.5	Gross Profit	46.7	40.6	39.3	30.2	27.4	32.1
	28.6	27.8	28.2	Operating Expenses	48.1	35.3	33.1	26.9	20.8	25.0
	2.6	4.1	5.2	Operating Profit	−1.4	5.3	6.3	3.4	6.6	7.2
	1.7	1.0	.6	All Other Expenses (net)	1.3	.8	1.0	.0	.1	1.0
	.9	3.1	4.7	Profit Before Taxes	−2.7	4.5	5.3	3.3	6.5	6.2
				RATIOS						
	3.0	3.0	3.3		2.8	3.0	3.7	2.4	3.2	3.5
	1.6	1.7	2.0	Current	.9	2.2	2.3	1.7	2.0	2.4
	1.2	1.2	1.3		.3	1.2	1.0	1.2	1.4	1.6
	1.5	1.8	1.8		2.0	1.7	2.5	1.5	1.8	1.8
	.8	.9	1.1	Quick	.5	1.1	1.2	.9	1.0	1.2
	.5	.5	.6		.2	.5	.5	.5	.7	.8
	36 10.1	40 9.2	35 10.3		16 23.4	25 14.6	40 9.2	33 11.1	39 9.5	42 8.8
	50 7.4	52 7.0	48 7.6	Sales/Receivables	26 14.0	38 9.6	51 7.1	45 8.2	48 7.6	52 7.1
	61 6.0	66 5.6	63 5.8		63 5.8	70 5.2	62 5.9	69 5.3	58 6.3	64 5.7
	44 8.2	43 8.6	42 8.7		0 UND	11 31.8	38 9.5	39 9.3	56 6.5	55 6.7
	81 4.5	82 4.5	75 4.8	Cost of Sales/Inventory	33 11.2	52 7.0	65 5.6	75 4.9	82 4.5	83 4.4
	118 3.1	113 3.2	107 3.4		126 2.9	130 2.8	93 3.9	112 3.3	106 3.4	107 3.4
	19 19.1	22 16.2	18 20.2		11 33.2	16 23.5	15 24.6	17 20.9	18 19.8	23 16.2
	32 11.5	34 10.9	33 11.0	Cost of Sales/Payables	64 5.7	31 11.7	34 10.8	34 10.8	30 12.1	34 10.6
	54 6.7	53 6.9	49 7.4		164 2.2	52 7.0	49 7.4	50 7.4	45 8.1	50 7.4
	3.9	4.0	4.1		4.6	4.4	3.8	4.4	4.1	3.0
	7.9	7.3	6.7	Sales/Working Capital	−46.9	7.9	6.3	9.6	6.7	5.2
	21.2	18.5	14.1		−3.4	40.5	NM	24.4	10.5	9.1
	7.7	11.4	20.5		3.1	18.1	50.0	19.2	21.5	32.1
(192)	2.8	(191) 3.7	(185) 8.1	EBIT/Interest	(11) 1.8	(24) 8.0	(19) 9.6	(41) 5.8	(48) 9.1	(42) 17.9
	−.3	.9	2.4		−4.0	3.1	1.8	2.0	2.4	4.5
	4.6	6.1	8.5	Net Profit + Depr., Dep.,				5.6	7.0	15.6
(61)	1.5	(69) 2.1	(58) 4.5	Amort./Cur. Mat. L/T/D			(12) 3.2	(20) 4.8	(19) 8.2	
	.4	.7	1.8					.7	2.2	2.1
	.3	.2	.2		.0	.1	.1	.2	.2	.2
	.6	.5	.4	Fixed/Worth	.9	.3	.5	.4	.4	.4
	1.5	1.1	.8		−.8	2.3	1.3	.8	.6	.8
	.5	.7	.5		.8	.6	.3	.4	.5	.5
	1.5	1.6	1.4	Debt/Worth	36.3	.9	1.2	1.7	1.4	1.1
	5.2	4.0	3.5		−3.0	8.2	3.0	4.3	2.7	2.4
	28.3	45.7	41.5	% Profit Before Taxes/Tangible		35.9	47.5	56.1	41.4	40.1
(186)	12.3	(194) 14.8	(184) 21.6	Net Worth	(26) 18.9	(16) 26.0	(41) 20.6	(50) 19.0	(43) 20.1	
	−2.3	.8	7.4			3.6	8.7	6.9	10.6	11.2
	11.5	13.6	16.7	% Profit Before Taxes/Total	8.6	14.9	21.5	16.8	20.1	17.0
	3.5	5.2	9.2	Assets	2.3	10.8	7.3	8.5	10.3	12.1
	−3.3	−.3	2.8		−19.5	1.0	1.0	3.0	3.5	3.6
	25.5	30.7	44.3		336.0	57.2	30.3	48.8	34.6	20.8
	10.2	11.5	15.0	Sales/Net Fixed Assets	55.3	22.5	11.6	22.5	12.0	11.2
	5.0	6.2	7.7		3.3	9.8	7.9	8.3	6.5	7.0
	2.5	2.5	2.7		3.6	4.3	2.9	3.1	2.6	2.4
	1.9	2.0	2.1	Sales/Total Assets	2.2	2.3	1.9	2.4	2.2	2.0
	1.3	1.5	1.4		1.2	1.5	1.5	1.7	1.3	1.3
	1.4	1.0	1.0			.6	1.0	1.1	.8	1.3
(178)	2.5	(189) 2.0	(171) 1.9	% Depr., Dep., Amort./Sales		(23) 1.2	(16) 2.0	(37) 1.9	(49) 2.0	(38) 2.1
	4.5	3.3	3.0			2.2	3.0	3.2	2.8	3.0
	3.1	3.3	2.3			5.2		1.5	1.8	
(61)	4.8	(61) 6.2	(56) 5.0	% Officers', Directors', Owners' Comp/Sales		(15) 6.8		(14) 2.8	(12) 3.0	
	11.3	9.2	8.9			9.5		8.9	6.1	
	7214947M	5510992M	6056976M	Net Sales ($)	7774M	63651M	84258M	318314M	876065M	4706914M
	4137853M	3529886M	4104474M	Total Assets ($)	4551M	31097M	44758M	163757M	508090M	3352221M

© RMA 2005

M = $ thousand   MM = $ million
See Pages 11 through 21 for Explanation of Ratios and Data

Current Data Sorted By Assets   **Comparative Historical Data**

0-500M	500M-2MM	2-10MM	10-50MM	50-100MM	100-250MM	Type of Statement	4/1/00-3/31/01 ALL	4/1/01-3/31/02 ALL
			10		1	Unqualified	13	12
	3	3	1			Reviewed	1	2
		1	1			Compiled	4	2
1	4	2	3			Tax Returns	3	4
3		3	3	3	3	Other	9	19
	13 (4/1-9/30/04)		32 (10/1/04-3/31/05)					
4	7	9	18	3	4	**NUMBER OF STATEMENTS**	30	39
%	%	%	%	%	%	**ASSETS**	%	%
			26.2			Cash & Equivalents	10.4	12.7
			20.6			Trade Receivables (net)	26.5	24.1
			21.6			Inventory	26.4	22.3
			2.6			All Other Current	2.0	3.2
			71.1			Total Current	65.3	62.3
			16.2			Fixed Assets (net)	14.6	15.9
			8.9			Intangibles (net)	9.0	13.0
			3.8			All Other Non-Current	11.1	8.8
			100.0			Total	100.0	100.0
						LIABILITIES		
			2.4			Notes Payable-Short Term	8.6	7.9
			2.2			Cur. Mat.-L/T/D	1.1	2.1
			7.9			Trade Payables	14.0	8.5
			.3			Income Taxes Payable	.4	.5
			15.6			All Other Current	7.7	10.8
			28.5			Total Current	31.9	29.8
			5.8			Long-Term Debt	7.0	13.2
			.1			Deferred Taxes	.3	.3
			6.7			All Other Non-Current	18.1	13.5
			59.0			Net Worth	42.7	43.3
			100.0			Total Liabilities & Net Worth	100.0	100.0
						INCOME DATA		
			100.0			Net Sales	100.0	100.0
			52.2			Gross Profit	48.1	48.7
			41.4			Operating Expenses	43.1	41.8
			10.8			Operating Profit	5.0	6.8
			.1			All Other Expenses (net)	-1.7	1.9
			10.7			Profit Before Taxes	6.7	4.9
						RATIOS		
			4.1				4.3	3.4
			3.2			Current	2.7	2.4
			2.4				1.6	1.5
			3.4				2.4	1.9
			2.0			Quick	1.4	1.3
			1.1				.6	.8
		48	7.6				51 7.2	44 8.3
		56	6.5			Sales/Receivables	67 5.4	59 6.2
		64	5.7				91 4.0	94 3.9
		66	5.5				75 4.9	76 4.8
		113	3.2			Cost of Sales/Inventory	124 2.9	121 3.0
		141	2.6				232 1.6	167 2.2
		20	18.4				37 10.0	28 12.9
		36	10.1			Cost of Sales/Payables	56 6.5	40 9.2
		61	6.0				75 4.8	60 6.1
			1.9				2.4	2.6
			3.1			Sales/Working Capital	3.2	3.8
			6.1				8.9	7.0
			65.1				26.1	13.4
		(16)	13.7			EBIT/Interest	(21) 3.0	(36) 4.3
			-.9				1.1	.3
						Net Profit + Depr., Dep.,		7.4
						Amort./Cur. Mat. L /T/D	(15)	1.8
								.2
			.1				.2	.2
			.3			Fixed/Worth	.3	.4
			.6				1.0	1.9
			.5				.3	.4
			.5			Debt/Worth	1.1	1.7
			1.2				5.1	9.3
			87.8			% Profit Before Taxes/Tangible	36.1	56.5
			30.7			Net Worth	(26) 16.0	(33) 21.9
			-1.2				.7	-.9
			27.0			% Profit Before Taxes/Total	13.9	16.5
			10.8			Assets	4.5	6.5
			-.7				-.2	-1.7
			25.1				16.5	18.4
			12.1			Sales/Net Fixed Assets	10.4	9.0
			7.3				4.7	5.1
			1.7				2.1	1.7
			1.4			Sales/Total Assets	1.4	1.3
			1.1				.9	.9
			1.6				1.7	2.0
		(15)	2.2			% Depr., Dep., Amort./Sales	(23) 2.7	(34) 3.1
			4.4				3.8	5.3
						% Officers', Directors', Owners' Comp/Sales		
3601M	23946M	110612M	641441M	271522M	782841M	Net Sales ($)	866628M	1590376M
796M	9158M	37554M	414646M	246535M	628918M	Total Assets ($)	951305M	1650438M

M = $ thousand   MM = $ million
See Pages 11 through 21 for Explanation of Ratios and Data

Comparative Historical Data | | | | Current Data Sorted By Sales

					Type of Statement						
	15		13		11	Unqualified					5	6
	2		2		4	Reviewed				2	1	1
					1	Compiled				1		1
					4			1	1	1		
	4		5		7	Tax Returns	1	2	1	2	1	
	13		18		19	Other	2	1	1	1	3	11

	4/1/02-3/31/03 ALL		4/1/03-3/31/04 ALL		4/1/04-3/31/05 ALL		13 (4/1-9/30/04)			32 (10/1/04-3/31/05)		
							0-1MM	1-3MM	3-5MM	5-10MM	10-25MM	25MM & OVER
	34		39		45	NUMBER OF STATEMENTS	3	4	3	6	10	19
	%		%		%	ASSETS	%	%	%	%	%	%
	16.0		17.7		21.1	Cash & Equivalents					27.8	25.1
	24.6		25.2		24.8	Trade Receivables (net)					19.8	25.5
	20.0		22.2		24.1	Inventory					20.0	19.7
	5.1		4.9		2.3	All Other Current					1.9	3.2
	65.6		70.0		72.2	Total Current					69.5	73.4
	18.0		16.9		13.9	Fixed Assets (net)					13.5	13.6
	9.1		7.9		7.5	Intangibles (net)					15.2	5.7
	7.2		5.2		6.4	All Other Non-Current					1.8	7.2
	100.0		100.0		100.0	Total					100.0	100.0
						LIABILITIES						
	8.8		10.9		10.8	Notes Payable-Short Term					5.5	4.2
	2.8		1.1		6.8	Cur. Mat.-L/T/D					1.7	1.5
	11.0		9.6		14.5	Trade Payables					9.7	10.1
	.3		.5		.5	Income Taxes Payable					1.0	.4
	13.3		13.2		16.8	All Other Current					10.8	18.6
	36.2		35.3		49.5	Total Current					28.7	34.8
	9.2		8.8		6.6	Long-Term Debt					6.4	5.2
	.3		.4		.3	Deferred Taxes					.2	.4
	5.8		4.6		12.0	All Other Non-Current					12.3	2.4
	48.5		50.9		31.6	Net Worth					52.4	57.1
	100.0		100.0		100.0	Total Liabilities & Net Worth					100.0	100.0
						INCOME DATA						
	100.0		100.0		100.0	Net Sales					100.0	100.0
	48.3		50.8		48.1	Gross Profit					45.3	51.1
	44.5		43.1		40.2	Operating Expenses					34.7	42.6
	3.9		7.8		7.9	Operating Profit					10.6	8.4
	.1		1.0		.9	All Other Expenses (net)					1.6	-.2
	3.8		6.8		7.0	Profit Before Taxes					9.1	8.7
						RATIOS						
	4.3		4.7		3.3						4.3	3.7
	2.6		2.7		2.6	Current					2.7	3.1
	1.6		1.5		1.2						2.2	1.4
	2.5		3.2		2.5						3.5	3.0
	1.7		1.6		1.3	Quick					1.4	1.9
	.9		.8		.5						1.1	.9
43	8.4	32	11.5	37	9.9					46	7.9	48	7.6
56	6.5	53	6.9	50	7.4	Sales/Receivables				56	6.6	57	6.4
77	4.7	76	4.8	60	6.1					62	5.9	71	5.1
47	7.8	69	5.3	59	6.2					35	10.5	66	5.5
96	3.8	97	3.8	84	4.3	Cost of Sales/Inventory				87	4.2	96	3.8
143	2.6	143	2.6	131	2.8					120	3.1	158	2.3
31	11.8	17	21.0	21	17.8					19	19.2	27	13.5
41	8.9	36	10.2	44	8.3	Cost of Sales/Payables				36	10.1	44	8.3
58	6.2	46	8.0	65	5.7					65	5.6	61	5.9
	2.2		2.3		2.9						2.6	1.8
	3.6		4.1		4.8	Sales/Working Capital					3.3	3.1
	11.3		9.2		27.9						8.9	12.7
	45.8		75.8		19.8							411.8
(30)	8.4	(29)	13.9	(37)	8.2	EBIT/Interest					(17)	15.1
	-2.5		1.1		.6							2.2
	74.4		41.6		23.6	Net Profit + Depr., Dep.,						
(12)	4.2	(15)	10.8	(11)	8.3	Amort./Cur. Mat. L/T/D						
	1.2		2.0		1.8							
	.1		.2		.1						.1	.1
	.3		.4		.3	Fixed/Worth					.4	.2
	.6		.6		.9						.5	.7
	.3		.3		.5						.5	.4
	.6		.6		1.1	Debt/Worth					.9	.5
	1.4		2.1		8.2						5.0	1.6
	28.9		63.2		84.4	% Profit Before Taxes/Tangible					101.4	58.5
(28)	14.8	(36)	17.9	(39)	33.5	Net Worth					45.4	33.5
	-5.5		1.2		2.8						12.5	2.8
	16.9		19.9		23.4	% Profit Before Taxes/Total					21.1	24.7
	8.1		11.7		10.1	Assets					13.9	10.1
	-3.6		.4		.9						6.9	2.4
	16.1		19.3		39.7						54.4	21.6
	10.9		10.9		16.5	Sales/Net Fixed Assets					19.8	13.7
	6.3		6.5		9.0						6.0	8.7
	2.2		2.1		2.9						2.2	1.7
	1.4		1.7		1.7	Sales/Total Assets					1.4	1.4
	.9		1.2		1.2						.9	1.1
	1.6		1.5		1.6							1.8
(26)	2.7	(31)	2.3	(35)	2.2	% Depr., Dep., Amort./Sales					(15)	2.2
	3.8		3.9		4.4							4.4
					1.9	% Officers', Directors',						
			(10)	2.7		Owners' Comp/Sales						
					5.2							
	1175576M		1931541M		1833963M	Net Sales ($)	1587M	7095M	12003M	46644M	155737M	1610897M
	995793M		1593282M		1337607M	Total Assets ($)	359M	2916M	5608M	19344M	132767M	1176613M

M = $ thousand   MM = $ million
See Pages 11 through 21 for Explanation of Ratios and Data

Current Data Sorted By Assets

Comparative Historical Data

0-500M	500M-2MM	2-10MM	10-50MM	50-100MM	100-250MM	Type of Statement	4/1/00-3/31/01 ALL	4/1/01-3/31/02 ALL
	1	4	8	4	2	Unqualified	16	18
	2	8	1			Reviewed	6	8
	2	2				Compiled	2	5
2	1					Tax Returns	1	2
1	3	4	4		1	Other	14	22
	19 (4/1-9/30/04)		31 (10/1/04-3/31/05)					
3	9	18	13	5	2	NUMBER OF STATEMENTS	39	55
%	%	%	%	%	%	ASSETS	%	%
		11.2	14.3			Cash & Equivalents	11.5	10.8
		32.8	20.1			Trade Receivables (net)	26.5	27.4
		21.3	26.7			Inventory	29.3	26.2
		6.1	6.2			All Other Current	4.0	6.2
		71.4	67.2			Total Current	71.3	70.6
		18.1	18.2			Fixed Assets (net)	18.0	16.8
		5.5	7.2			Intangibles (net)	3.1	5.6
		5.0	7.4			All Other Non-Current	7.7	7.0
		100.0	100.0			Total	100.0	100.0
						LIABILITIES		
		4.7	5.3			Notes Payable-Short Term	8.0	10.4
		2.8	1.4			Cur. Mat.-L/T/D	4.1	4.2
		11.9	7.8			Trade Payables	12.0	12.3
		1.2	.5			Income Taxes Payable	.9	.9
		8.5	13.9			All Other Current	12.9	11.0
		29.1	28.9			Total Current	37.9	38.8
		16.1	5.9			Long-Term Debt	9.3	8.2
		.3	.3			Deferred Taxes	.4	.7
		5.9	13.2			All Other Non-Current	5.1	5.2
		48.7	51.7			Net Worth	47.3	47.0
		100.0	100.0			Total Liabilities & Net Worth	100.0	100.0
						INCOME DATA		
		100.0	100.0			Net Sales	100.0	100.0
		39.2	32.8			Gross Profit	35.3	33.6
		28.7	23.2			Operating Expenses	29.3	28.1
		10.5	9.6			Operating Profit	6.1	5.5
		.6	1.4			All Other Expenses (net)	1.6	1.5
		9.8	8.2			Profit Before Taxes	4.5	4.0
						RATIOS		
		2.9	5.5			Current	3.5	3.1
		2.5	2.6				1.7	1.9
		1.9	1.2				1.4	1.3
		2.0	3.3			Quick	2.0	1.7
		1.4	.8				.9	1.0
		.9	.3				.6	.7
		38 9.7	39 9.4			Sales/Receivables	39 9.4	43 8.5
		50 7.3	51 7.1				54 6.8	60 6.1
		68 5.3	67 5.5				83 4.4	92 4.0
		2 148.0	51 7.2			Cost of Sales/Inventory	48 7.6	43 8.5
		67 5.5	109 3.4				107 3.4	97 3.8
		124 2.9	134 2.7				158 2.3	167 2.2
		20 17.8	15 24.2			Cost of Sales/Payables	22 16.7	22 16.5
		25 14.7	32 11.3				32 11.3	36 10.1
		40 9.2	50 7.3				50 7.3	58 6.3
		3.4	1.9			Sales/Working Capital	2.8	3.1
		4.8	4.7				6.2	4.8
		10.9	16.9				8.6	9.7
		34.4	30.9			EBIT/Interest	19.0	10.3
		(14) 11.9	(10) 7.0				(34) 4.4	(46) 2.9
		6.3	1.8				1.8	.8
						Net Profit + Depr., Dep., Amort./Cur. Mat. L /T/D	15.3	11.5
							(16) 2.4	(19) 2.8
							1.2	1.4
		.1	.1			Fixed/Worth	.2	.2
		.3	.4				.4	.4
		.9	NM				.8	.8
		.4	.2			Debt/Worth	.4	.6
		.9	.8				1.3	1.6
		2.7	NM				2.8	3.5
		49.4	52.5			% Profit Before Taxes/Tangible Net Worth	32.6	39.1
		(15) 36.4	(10) 23.9				(37) 17.9	(54) 19.8
		17.1	4.2				6.5	-1.1
		29.6	19.5			% Profit Before Taxes/Total Assets	13.0	17.6
		18.1	5.4				8.6	6.7
		7.6	1.8				2.7	-.5
		34.6	19.1			Sales/Net Fixed Assets	18.9	20.9
		11.1	8.7				10.3	10.7
		5.5	4.8				6.3	5.0
		3.0	2.0			Sales/Total Assets	2.2	1.9
		1.9	1.2				1.7	1.5
		1.3	.9				1.2	1.1
		1.1	1.4			% Depr., Dep., Amort./Sales	1.7	1.2
		(15) 2.3	(12) 2.3				(34) 2.4	(47) 2.2
		2.7	2.8				4.0	3.4
						% Officers', Directors', Owners' Comp/Sales		4.3
								(11) 5.5
								9.2
5973M	30911M	161594M	496110M	414933M	325293M	Net Sales ($)	1738280M	2263454M
1023M	12443M	85824M	335229M	367367M	320672M	Total Assets ($)	1423000M	1756846M

© RMA 2005

M = $ thousand   MM = $ million
See Pages 11 through 21 for Explanation of Ratios and Data

Comparative Historical Data				Current Data Sorted By Sales					
			Type of Statement						
14	19	19	Unqualified		2		1	7	9
9	8	11	Reviewed			4	3	4	
5	8	4	Compiled		1	1	2		
2	1	3	Tax Returns	1	1	1			
22	9	13	Other		2	1	4	1	5
4/1/02-3/31/03	4/1/03-3/31/04	4/1/04-3/31/05		19 (4/1-9/30/04)			31 (10/1/04-3/31/05)		
ALL	ALL	ALL		0-1MM	1-3MM	3-5MM	5-10MM	10-25MM	25MM & OVER
52	45	50	**NUMBER OF STATEMENTS**	1	6	7	10	12	14
%	%	%	**ASSETS**	%	%	%	%	%	%
13.2	13.0	13.6	Cash & Equivalents				12.3	15.5	13.5
30.2	28.6	26.6	Trade Receivables (net)				38.8	25.7	19.5
23.1	25.6	23.6	Inventory				26.5	18.1	26.3
7.1	7.1	5.4	All Other Current				4.3	10.9	4.9
73.6	74.4	69.2	Total Current				81.9	70.1	64.2
14.0	17.7	17.5	Fixed Assets (net)				14.6	18.8	19.4
6.4	2.2	7.8	Intangibles (net)				2.0	6.5	8.3
6.0	5.7	5.6	All Other Non-Current				1.5	4.6	8.1
100.0	100.0	100.0	Total				100.0	100.0	100.0
			LIABILITIES						
8.9	5.8	5.0	Notes Payable-Short Term				5.1	3.0	5.3
1.9	2.4	2.3	Cur. Mat.-L/T/D				2.5	1.6	2.7
11.9	13.0	10.9	Trade Payables				14.5	8.9	8.3
.4	.9	.8	Income Taxes Payable				.4	1.6	.5
13.0	14.2	14.0	All Other Current				6.6	10.4	18.3
36.0	36.3	33.0	Total Current				29.0	25.5	35.0
5.6	10.8	10.3	Long-Term Debt				15.9	10.9	8.4
.6	.8	.7	Deferred Taxes				.2	.2	.6
2.9	5.2	7.4	All Other Non-Current				.3	8.0	14.6
55.0	46.8	48.6	Net Worth				54.6	55.3	41.4
100.0	100.0	100.0	Total Liabilities & Net Worth				100.0	100.0	100.0
			INCOME DATA						
100.0	100.0	100.0	Net Sales				100.0	100.0	100.0
37.3	41.3	36.8	Gross Profit				41.7	35.0	31.6
29.4	33.3	27.3	Operating Expenses				28.0	25.1	23.8
7.9	8.0	9.5	Operating Profit				13.7	9.8	7.8
.6	.7	.8	All Other Expenses (net)				.3	.8	1.0
7.3	7.4	8.7	Profit Before Taxes				13.4	9.0	6.8
			RATIOS						
4.9	3.7	3.4	Current				4.6	4.5	3.0
2.4	2.1	2.3					2.7	2.7	2.0
1.5	1.4	1.3					2.3	1.5	1.1
3.1	2.0	2.0	Quick				2.3	2.4	1.4
1.3	.9	1.3					1.7	1.6	.8
.7	.7	.7					1.0	1.5	.6
41 8.9	40 9.2	38 9.7	Sales/Receivables				41 8.9	34 10.6	44 8.2
65 5.6	50 7.3	51 7.1					54 6.8	52 7.0	53 6.9
79 4.6	82 4.5	67 5.5					73 5.0	71 5.1	75 4.9
29 12.6	18 19.8	31 11.8	Cost of Sales/Inventory				3 104.5	15 23.6	51 7.1
94 3.9	89 4.1	83 4.4					77 4.7	49 7.5	121 3.0
156 2.3	145 2.5	136 2.7					126 2.9	108 3.4	143 2.5
19 19.1	27 13.4	20 18.4	Cost of Sales/Payables				19 18.9	15 24.2	29 12.5
33 10.9	35 10.3	30 12.0					24 15.5	24 14.9	33 10.9
56 6.5	54 6.8	44 8.3					37 10.0	47 7.7	44 8.3
2.4	2.7	2.9	Sales/Working Capital				3.3	2.0	2.8
4.9	5.5	4.9					4.7	4.1	4.8
10.0	11.8	15.1					6.0	13.7	27.4
44.8	43.5	29.2	EBIT/Interest					36.9	32.5
(37) 6.7	(39) 7.7	(42) 7.2						(10) 21.4	(12) 7.0
1.3	1.5	3.9						2.1	
10.3	6.2	9.6	Net Profit + Depr., Dep., Amort./Cur. Mat. L/T/D						13.0
(18) 4.2	(15) 3.2	(22) 3.4						(10) 2.5	
2.4	.4	2.0							.3
.1	.1	.1	Fixed/Worth				.0	.1	.3
.2	.3	.4					.2	.3	.8
.6	1.1	1.1					.4	1.6	2.6
.3	.5	.4	Debt/Worth				.3	.3	.7
1.0	1.0	1.1					.6	.6	3.3
2.1	3.1	4.1					2.1	3.6	7.8
42.2	53.6	47.3	% Profit Before Taxes/Tangible Net Worth					56.6	54.2
(47) 21.5	(40) 19.4	(42) 25.5						(10) 27.7	(12) 24.3
3.9	9.3	13.5						2.5	6.6
20.0	25.0	21.3	% Profit Before Taxes/Total Assets				48.5	24.4	13.7
9.6	8.9	10.4					27.1	15.6	6.7
1.2	2.9	4.1					9.7	1.6	1.9
29.3	29.0	32.5	Sales/Net Fixed Assets				196.5	29.5	11.2
13.2	12.9	11.2					23.4	12.5	7.7
5.4	5.9	5.5					6.3	4.1	4.7
2.2	2.5	2.7	Sales/Total Assets				3.1	2.0	2.0
1.5	1.7	1.7					2.7	1.6	1.1
1.1	1.2	1.1					1.7	1.1	.9
1.1	1.0	1.3	% Depr., Dep., Amort./Sales					1.4	2.4
(43) 2.0	(41) 1.8	(41) 2.4						2.3	(12) 2.7
3.3	3.1	3.1						3.0	3.8
2.3		1.8	% Officers', Directors', Owners' Comp/Sales						
(14) 4.3		(15) 3.7							
6.6		11.0							
2824709M	1086677M	1434814M	Net Sales ($)	336M	12061M	30338M	75584M	188087M	1128408M
2113812M	812774M	1122558M	Total Assets ($)	212M	11041M	14126M	35368M	133636M	928175M

M = $ thousand   MM = $ million
See Pages 11 through 21 for Explanation of Ratios and Data

Current Data Sorted By Assets							Comparative Historical Data	
						Type of Statement		
	1	5	4		2	Unqualified	9	6
	2	4	2			Reviewed	4	3
	1	2				Compiled	9	10
1	3					Tax Returns	1	6
	1	3	1			Other	13	13
	5 (4/1-9/30/04)		27 (10/1/04-3/31/05)				4/1/00-3/31/01	4/1/01-3/31/02
0-500M	500M-2MM	2-10MM	10-50MM	50-100MM	100-250MM		ALL	ALL
1	8	14	7		2	**NUMBER OF STATEMENTS**	36	38
%	%	%	%	%	%	**ASSETS**	%	%
		5.5		DATA NOT AVAILABLE		Cash & Equivalents	9.7	10.8
		31.4				Trade Receivables (net)	33.6	29.8
		24.7				Inventory	21.8	23.3
		.7				All Other Current	5.2	5.8
		62.4				Total Current	70.3	69.6
		22.1				Fixed Assets (net)	15.5	18.8
		9.4				Intangibles (net)	7.0	6.4
		6.1				All Other Non-Current	7.2	5.2
		100.0				Total	100.0	100.0
						LIABILITIES		
		12.7				Notes Payable-Short Term	6.3	5.5
		4.4				Cur. Mat.-L/T/D	4.5	5.9
		15.2				Trade Payables	13.7	12.9
		.6				Income Taxes Payable	.4	.2
		10.6				All Other Current	12.8	14.9
		43.6				Total Current	37.7	39.4
		15.0				Long-Term Debt	13.1	11.4
		.7				Deferred Taxes	.7	.6
		6.4				All Other Non-Current	4.2	5.0
		34.4				Net Worth	44.3	43.7
		100.0				Total Liabilities & Net Worth	100.0	100.0
						INCOME DATA		
		100.0				Net Sales	100.0	100.0
		35.4				Gross Profit	42.1	35.0
		27.0				Operating Expenses	32.6	29.8
		8.4				Operating Profit	9.6	5.3
		.5				All Other Expenses (net)	.9	1.1
		7.9				Profit Before Taxes	8.7	4.2
						RATIOS		
		2.1					3.2	3.1
		1.4				Current	1.8	1.9
		1.2					1.2	1.1
		1.2					2.4	2.5
		.9				Quick	1.0	1.2
		.7					.8	.5
		44 8.3					48 7.6	30 12.1
		51 7.1				Sales/Receivables	63 5.8	50 7.3
		57 6.4					76 4.8	68 5.3
		43 8.5					31 11.6	21 17.3
		62 5.9				Cost of Sales/Inventory	79 4.6	64 5.7
		91 4.0					131 2.8	106 3.4
		19 19.5					21 17.3	18 20.1
		30 12.1				Cost of Sales/Payables	38 9.7	29 12.6
		59 6.2					53 7.0	45 8.2
		6.0					3.5	4.1
		11.1				Sales/Working Capital	6.4	7.7
		265.4					14.1	33.5
		16.5					16.4	11.9
		(12) 7.2				EBIT/Interest	(30) 6.0	(32) 2.1
		2.9					1.6	.9
							11.1	9.3
						Net Profit + Depr., Dep., Amort./Cur. Mat. L /T/D	(10) 6.2	(11) 1.2
							2.3	.6
		.3					.2	.2
		1.1				Fixed/Worth	.4	.4
		14.8					1.2	1.6
		1.3					.4	.4
		3.6				Debt/Worth	1.6	2.3
		38.8					5.6	12.5
		133.8					60.7	58.7
		(12) 50.1				% Profit Before Taxes/Tangible Net Worth	(33) 32.2	(33) 15.8
		33.4					17.0	.5
		22.5					26.9	17.7
		13.3				% Profit Before Taxes/Total Assets	10.3	5.6
		4.7					4.9	.6
		39.6					22.9	30.0
		12.5				Sales/Net Fixed Assets	12.8	11.6
		3.4					7.0	8.1
		2.5					2.5	2.9
		2.3				Sales/Total Assets	1.8	1.9
		1.4					1.3	1.5
		.5					.5	.5
		1.3				% Depr., Dep., Amort./Sales	(30) 1.4	(32) 1.9
		2.3					2.9	3.1
								1.8
						% Officers', Directors', Owners' Comp/Sales		(15) 7.7
								13.5
1177M	30932M	125429M	253207M		423574M	Net Sales ($)	619119M	815151M
133M	10411M	63815M	128437M		335072M	Total Assets ($)	304342M	436099M

M = $ thousand MM = $ million

See Pages 11 through 21 for Explanation of Ratios and Data

Comparative Historical Data

Current Data Sorted By Sales

			Type of Statement						
10	10	12	Unqualified		1		2	4	5
6	6	8	Reviewed				6	2	
5	11	3	Compiled	1			2		
4	3	4	Tax Returns	2	2				
10	8	5	Other		1		2	2	
4/1/02- 3/31/03 ALL	4/1/03- 3/31/04 ALL	4/1/04- 3/31/05 ALL			5 (4/1-9/30/04)		27 (10/1/04-3/31/05)		
				0-1MM	1-3MM	3-5MM	5-10MM	10-25MM	25MM & OVER
35	38	32	**NUMBER OF STATEMENTS**		4	3	12	8	5
%	%	%	**ASSETS**	%	%	%	%	%	%
12.2	12.2	9.4	Cash & Equivalents				7.5		
29.3	28.7	36.5	Trade Receivables (net)				37.0		
20.6	18.3	17.9	Inventory				23.8		
5.1	4.5	2.3	All Other Current				.9		
67.2	63.7	66.1	Total Current				69.1		
16.6	22.5	22.6	Fixed Assets (net)				18.5		
9.7	8.4	7.3	Intangibles (net)				8.7		
6.5	5.4	4.0	All Other Non-Current				3.7		
100.0	100.0	100.0	Total				100.0		
			LIABILITIES						
5.4	8.3	22.8	Notes Payable-Short Term				14.1		
3.2	4.4	3.9	Cur. Mat.-L/T/D				2.5		
13.9	11.5	15.5	Trade Payables				13.1		
.1	.2	.5	Income Taxes Payable				.7		
12.4	11.1	13.5	All Other Current				11.1		
35.1	35.5	56.2	Total Current				41.5		
13.6	10.3	13.9	Long-Term Debt				13.0		
.5	1.0	.6	Deferred Taxes				.8		
2.0	6.4	4.5	All Other Non-Current				5.4		
48.8	46.9	24.8	Net Worth				39.4		
100.0	100.0	100.0	Total Liabilities & Net Worth				100.0		
			INCOME DATA						
100.0	100.0	100.0	Net Sales				100.0		
38.3	42.6	36.4	Gross Profit				37.3		
33.2	36.4	29.8	Operating Expenses				28.3		
5.1	6.2	6.6	Operating Profit				9.0		
.3	.8	.8	All Other Expenses (net)				.5		
4.8	5.4	5.8	Profit Before Taxes				8.5		
			RATIOS						
3.1	3.2	2.3					2.8		
1.6	1.8	1.4	Current				1.6		
1.4	1.4	.9					1.3		
1.9	2.0	1.4					1.9		
1.3	1.2	1.0	Quick				1.0		
.8	.8	.6					.8		
40 9.1	41 9.0	44 8.3					44 8.3		
52 7.0	55 6.6	57 6.4	Sales/Receivables				45 8.0		
67 5.4	72 5.0	65 5.6					62 5.9		
34 10.7	24 15.2	6 62.6					35 10.5		
67 5.5	56 6.5	50 7.3	Cost of Sales/Inventory				53 6.8		
106 3.4	91 4.0	93 3.9					86 4.2		
18 20.0	17 21.2	18 20.0					17 21.5		
24 15.2	27 13.3	35 10.5	Cost of Sales/Payables				23 15.9		
48 7.5	48 7.7	57 6.4					50 7.2		
3.7	3.9	5.7					4.7		
7.9	6.5	10.8	Sales/Working Capital				9.6		
17.2	12.4	NM					17.4		
12.9	20.6	13.1					13.1		
(31) 3.5	(32) 5.4	(30) 6.0	EBIT/Interest				(10) 7.5		
−.7	−.7	2.4					3.8		
			Net Profit + Depr., Dep., Amort./Cur. Mat. L/T/D						
.2	.2	.3					.2		
.3	.4	1.1	Fixed/Worth				.4		
.8	1.5	38.5					37.3		
.5	.5	1.2					.9		
1.5	1.1	3.6	Debt/Worth				1.6		
3.8	4.3	60.6					54.6		
45.8	50.8	109.9	% Profit Before Taxes/Tangible				74.3		
(32) 9.6	(35) 20.0	(26) 48.6	Net Worth				(10) 42.8		
−3.2	4.5	15.6					27.8		
16.8	15.7	19.7	% Profit Before Taxes/Total				29.6		
5.2	7.0	11.2	Assets				19.5		
−.1	−.9	2.4					7.3		
40.6	23.5	50.6					46.1		
17.4	8.9	11.4	Sales/Net Fixed Assets				18.6		
6.8	5.4	5.2					8.1		
2.3	2.2	2.8					3.2		
1.7	1.7	2.3	Sales/Total Assets				2.4		
1.5	1.5	1.4					2.1		
1.4	1.0	.6					.5		
(29) 2.2	(33) 2.3	(27) 2.1	% Depr., Dep., Amort./Sales				(11) 1.2		
4.3	3.8	2.9					2.3		
2.5	3.6	2.9	% Officers', Directors',						
(19) 5.7	(14) 7.2	(13) 3.6	Owners' Comp/Sales						
9.0	13.1	8.6							
602156M	963897M	834319M	Net Sales ($)	8302M	10477M		92281M	118979M	604280M
383987M	629952M	537868M	Total Assets ($)	3730M	3461M		41969M	76580M	412128M

Current Data Sorted By Assets   Comparative Historical Data

0-500M	500M-2MM	2-10MM	10-50MM	50-100MM	100-250MM	Type of Statement	4/1/00-3/31/01 ALL	4/1/01-3/31/02 ALL
	2	9	8	3	5	Unqualified	31	25
1	5	24	3			Reviewed	38	37
2	6	9				Compiled	23	20
2	3	2				Tax Returns	6	2
2	12	16	8	4	1	Other	44	41
	25 (4/1-9/30/04)		102 (10/1/04-3/31/05)					
7	28	60	19	7	6	**NUMBER OF STATEMENTS**	142	125
%	%	%	%	%	%	**ASSETS**	%	%
	9.3	10.1	4.5			Cash & Equivalents	13.6	11.4
	42.2	32.2	30.5			Trade Receivables (net)	29.2	28.7
	26.5	29.0	29.8			Inventory	28.1	27.3
	5.1	1.9	2.1			All Other Current	3.2	3.3
	83.1	73.2	67.0			Total Current	74.1	70.7
	12.9	16.6	17.3			Fixed Assets (net)	16.4	17.6
	.4	5.6	8.1			Intangibles (net)	4.8	6.3
	3.7	4.6	7.6			All Other Non-Current	4.7	5.4
	100.0	100.0	100.0			Total	100.0	100.0
						LIABILITIES		
	26.9	11.4	9.5			Notes Payable-Short Term	10.5	9.4
	3.3	1.8	2.4			Cur. Mat.-L/T/D	3.6	4.4
	21.6	14.2	11.2			Trade Payables	12.0	12.1
	.3	.4	.7			Income Taxes Payable	.6	.5
	11.7	13.4	8.8			All Other Current	12.1	11.9
	63.9	41.1	32.7			Total Current	38.7	38.4
	10.0	8.1	17.4			Long-Term Debt	9.4	12.0
	.1	.3	.3			Deferred Taxes	.2	.2
	14.3	5.2	14.8			All Other Non-Current	7.5	6.1
	11.7	45.3	34.8			Net Worth	44.3	43.4
	100.0	100.0	100.0			Total Liabilities & Net Worth	100.0	100.0
						INCOME DATA		
	100.0	100.0	100.0			Net Sales	100.0	100.0
	42.2	42.3	38.3			Gross Profit	42.2	39.7
	38.3	36.2	30.4			Operating Expenses	36.0	35.9
	3.9	6.1	7.9			Operating Profit	6.2	3.8
	1.1	1.0	2.0			All Other Expenses (net)	1.2	1.4
	2.7	5.0	5.9			Profit Before Taxes	4.9	2.4
						RATIOS		
	2.7	2.7	3.3			Current	3.7	3.2
	1.4	1.8	2.5				2.1	2.1
	1.1	1.3	1.5				1.3	1.3
	1.6	1.5	1.8			Quick	2.2	2.0
	1.0	1.0	1.3				1.2	1.1
	.6	.7	.7				.7	.7
	41 8.8	43 8.5	53 6.9			Sales/Receivables	42 8.8	37 9.8
	51 7.1	54 6.8	62 5.9				54 6.7	50 7.3
	75 4.8	66 5.5	72 5.0				70 5.2	67 5.5
	39 9.3	57 6.4	75 4.9			Cost of Sales/Inventory	65 5.6	51 7.2
	70 5.3	87 4.2	98 3.7				106 3.5	94 3.9
	111 3.3	150 2.4	143 2.6				137 2.7	147 2.5
	26 14.1	18 19.9	27 13.4			Cost of Sales/Payables	19 19.0	18 19.9
	39 9.2	38 9.7	34 10.8				34 10.9	30 12.3
	75 4.8	68 5.3	48 7.7				50 7.3	46 8.0
	5.2	3.9	3.3			Sales/Working Capital	3.0	3.4
	11.1	6.4	5.0				5.1	5.5
	93.3	13.4	9.1				11.8	13.2
	14.4	16.1	45.0			EBIT/Interest	10.7	10.0
	(26) 2.9	(53) 5.7	(17) 4.7				(117) 3.1	(106) 2.6
	.8	1.5	1.4				1.4	.2
		8.2	18.2			Net Profit + Depr., Dep.,	7.0	7.2
		(18) 3.0	(10) 2.5			Amort./Cur. Mat. L/T/D	(41) 3.2	(47) 1.7
		.7	1.6				1.5	.1
	.1	.1	.2			Fixed/Worth	.2	.2
	.6	.4	.4				.4	.4
	2.8	.8	51.3				.9	1.0
	1.1	.6	.5			Debt/Worth	.4	.5
	3.6	1.3	1.1				1.1	1.0
	NM	3.9	341.8				3.8	3.9
	54.5	42.3	33.8			% Profit Before Taxes/Tangible	41.3	30.4
	(21) 29.3	(54) 16.0	(15) 22.9			Net Worth	(131) 15.8	(113) 9.1
	1.6	3.6	8.5				4.3	-5.7
	18.7	19.4	17.7			% Profit Before Taxes/Total	16.7	14.5
	6.2	4.8	5.4			Assets	5.9	3.4
	.2	1.6	.5				1.2	-3.8
	86.8	46.3	28.1			Sales/Net Fixed Assets	31.8	29.9
	46.6	18.1	14.4				13.1	13.6
	11.8	6.5	8.4				7.2	7.2
	3.5	2.6	2.0			Sales/Total Assets	2.5	2.5
	2.6	2.0	1.5				1.8	1.9
	1.9	1.5	1.4				1.3	1.3
	.5	.7	1.2			% Depr., Dep., Amort./Sales	1.0	1.1
	(22) .8	(53) 1.3	(17) 1.9				(120) 1.9	(106) 2.0
	2.0	2.3	2.6				2.8	3.2
	2.4	2.5				% Officers', Directors',	3.4	2.0
	(14) 5.9	(16) 4.3				Owners' Comp/Sales	(39) 6.4	(29) 4.4
	13.7	7.4					11.4	11.3
8957M	94071M	579424M	693025M	643000M	942468M	Net Sales ($)	2443394M	2307172M
2479M	33282M	280512M	384816M	526253M	986068M	Total Assets ($)	1747989M	1535466M

M = $ thousand   MM = $ million
See Pages 11 through 21 for Explanation of Ratios and Data

Comparative Historical Data | Current Data Sorted By Sales

Hist 1	Hist 2	Hist 3	Type of Statement	0-1MM	1-3MM	3-5MM	5-10MM	10-25MM	25MM & OVER
41	34	27	Unqualified		1	1	6	4	15
29	42	33	Reviewed		3	7	10	11	2
19	20	17	Compiled	1	5	4	4	3	
5	4	7	Tax Returns	2		3	2		
28	41	43	Other	2	7	6	9	7	12
4/1/02-3/31/03	4/1/03-3/31/04	4/1/04-3/31/05			25 (4/1-9/30/04)		102 (10/1/04-3/31/05)		
ALL	ALL	ALL							
122	141	127	**NUMBER OF STATEMENTS**	5	16	21	31	25	29
%	%	%	**ASSETS**	%	%	%	%	%	%
10.4	10.7	9.2	Cash & Equivalents		5.0	12.4	9.2	6.9	9.2
31.7	31.1	33.8	Trade Receivables (net)		43.3	31.7	34.7	34.4	26.7
25.7	25.4	28.0	Inventory		31.3	26.6	28.1	30.3	26.4
3.5	2.2	2.6	All Other Current		2.5	2.3	3.1	3.1	2.3
71.2	69.5	73.7	Total Current		82.1	73.0	75.1	74.7	64.6
19.9	17.0	15.6	Fixed Assets (net)		12.5	16.8	15.2	18.2	15.9
4.9	7.3	5.6	Intangibles (net)		.6	7.3	4.9	1.5	12.2
4.0	6.2	5.2	All Other Non-Current		4.8	2.8	4.9	5.6	7.3
100.0	100.0	100.0	Total		100.0	100.0	100.0	100.0	100.0
			LIABILITIES						
10.7	12.2	14.4	Notes Payable-Short Term		35.3	10.0	12.4	12.4	7.3
2.9	2.7	2.1	Cur. Mat.-L/T/D		3.3	1.3	3.0	1.2	2.1
14.7	13.6	15.5	Trade Payables		23.4	12.6	16.0	17.5	10.2
.5	.4	.4	Income Taxes Payable		.1	.5	.0	.9	.8
12.2	12.5	11.4	All Other Current		12.8	6.9	15.4	11.5	9.2
41.0	41.4	43.9	Total Current		74.9	31.2	46.8	43.6	29.7
15.7	11.7	10.0	Long-Term Debt		4.4	10.5	11.4	7.5	14.5
.3	.4	.4	Deferred Taxes		.1	.1	.0	.6	.8
5.9	6.3	9.2	All Other Non-Current		20.9	9.4	3.9	6.4	10.3
37.1	40.2	36.5	Net Worth		-.3	48.8	37.8	41.9	44.7
100.0	100.0	100.0	Total Liabilities & Net Worth		100.0	100.0	100.0	100.0	100.0
			INCOME DATA						
100.0	100.0	100.0	Net Sales		100.0	100.0	100.0	100.0	100.0
39.8	43.1	41.7	Gross Profit		39.7	47.8	43.8	35.3	40.7
36.3	36.3	35.1	Operating Expenses		37.7	41.6	38.1	29.1	30.5
3.5	6.7	6.6	Operating Profit		2.0	6.2	5.7	6.2	10.2
1.1	1.5	1.2	All Other Expenses (net)		1.3	.6	1.4	1.2	1.5
2.4	5.2	5.4	Profit Before Taxes		.8	5.6	4.3	5.0	8.7
			RATIOS						
3.2	3.1	2.9	Current		2.9	4.7	2.3	2.7	3.3
2.0	1.9	1.8			1.3	2.4	1.8	1.8	2.4
1.1	1.2	1.3			.9	1.6	1.2	1.3	1.6
1.9	1.8	1.6	Quick		1.6	3.1	1.4	1.7	2.1
1.0	1.1	1.1			.8	1.4	1.0	.8	1.2
.7	.7	.7			.5	.9	.7	.6	.8
42 8.7	45 8.2	45 8.1	Sales/Receivables		45 8.2	36 10.0	40 9.2	45 8.2	54 6.8
55 6.7	54 6.7	56 6.5			54 6.7	53 6.8	53 6.8	58 6.3	61 6.0
67 5.5	72 5.1	69 5.3			67 5.4	77 4.7	60 6.1	67 5.4	73 5.0
45 8.2	52 7.0	57 6.4	Cost of Sales/Inventory		47 7.8	59 6.1	43 8.5	49 7.5	84 4.3
94 3.9	92 4.0	91 4.0			98 3.7	89 4.1	91 4.0	75 4.8	102 3.6
133 2.7	147 2.5	123 3.0			120 3.0	156 2.3	133 2.7	114 3.2	130 2.8
20 18.3	18 19.9	22 16.4	Cost of Sales/Payables		26 14.1	18 20.5	20 18.6	21 17.1	27 13.5
31 11.8	36 10.1	37 9.8			35 10.4	40 9.1	35 10.5	39 9.3	38 9.6
52 7.0	58 6.3	57 6.4			83 4.4	57 6.4	52 7.0	73 5.0	52 7.0
3.5	3.6	3.9	Sales/Working Capital		5.9	2.9	4.9	5.0	3.0
6.0	6.5	6.3			11.4	-4.7	7.6	6.9	4.5
26.6	16.5	13.5			-43.3	10.7	18.2	12.7	6.9
13.4	16.8	16.5	EBIT/Interest		13.0	23.9	16.1	10.1	28.2
(114) 2.8	(129) 4.5	(112) 6.0		(15) 2.2	(19) 8.5	7.0	(19) 2.4	(24) 7.5	
.2	1.4	1.5			-.2	2.3	1.5	1.7	3.3
12.3	12.2	9.4	Net Profit + Depr., Dep., Amort./Cur. Mat. L/T/D					11.4	5.2
(46) 2.7	(39) 2.5	(36) 2.8					(10) 4.2	(12) 2.5	
.5	.8	1.2						1.8	1.1
.2	.2	.1	Fixed/Worth		.1	.1	.1	.1	.2
.4	.4	.4			1.0	.4	.4	.5	.4
1.2	1.1	1.1			-.2	.8	1.4	.8	.8
.5	.5	.6	Debt/Worth		.7	.3	.8	.5	.5
1.4	1.4	1.6			3.3	.9	2.1	1.6	1.1
4.8	5.3	4.8			-2.5	4.7	6.3	3.0	3.5
29.3	39.5	44.4	% Profit Before Taxes/Tangible Net Worth		37.1	43.5	46.2	32.4	45.1
(108) 9.2	(121) 16.7	(108) 20.1		(11) 15.5	(17) 18.8	(28) 26.3	(23) 12.6	(25) 22.9	
-2.6	3.9	4.6			-17.5	2.9	7.0	2.8	14.7
13.5	17.0	19.3	% Profit Before Taxes/Total Assets		9.3	21.5	21.0	19.7	16.4
3.5	6.9	5.7			4.9	5.5	5.6	4.0	10.3
-2.1	1.5	1.6			-6.5	2.1	1.6	1.3	3.7
30.6	36.6	47.6	Sales/Net Fixed Assets		65.6	67.2	47.2	41.0	24.2
12.2	14.0	14.9			48.4	15.7	23.3	13.3	13.3
5.6	7.1	7.8			9.9	5.1	9.1	8.1	5.1
2.7	2.5	2.6	Sales/Total Assets		3.2	2.5	3.3	2.7	2.0
1.9	1.8	2.0			2.5	1.7	2.2	2.2	1.4
1.4	1.4	1.4			1.9	1.4	1.7	1.7	1.1
1.0	1.1	.8	% Depr., Dep., Amort./Sales		.5	.8	.6	.8	1.4
(107) 1.8	(119) 1.9	(108) 1.5		(11) 1.0	(17) 1.0	(28) 1.4	(24) 1.4	(25) 2.2	
3.0	2.8	2.4			2.2	2.1	2.3	2.3	3.2
2.8	2.5	2.7	% Officers', Directors', Owners' Comp/Sales					2.4	
(36) 5.6	(32) 5.3	(35) 5.5					(11) 3.2		
10.6	9.1	11.6						5.7	
2930395M	2452898M	2960945M	Net Sales ($)	3817M	32580M	84030M	219749M	388093M	2232676M
1958985M	1966243M	2213410M	Total Assets ($)	1865M	13490M	48597M	105419M	187634M	1856405M

M = $ thousand   MM = $ million
See Pages 11 through 21 for Explanation of Ratios and Data

Current Data Sorted By Assets   **Comparative Historical Data**

0-500M	500M-2MM	2-10MM	10-50MM	50-100MM	100-250MM	Type of Statement	4/1/00-3/31/01 ALL	4/1/01-3/31/02 ALL
		6	1	1	2	Unqualified	2	2
3	3	8	1			Reviewed	10	7
	2	2				Compiled	3	3
	1					Tax Returns		1
1	5	6	4			Other	6	5
	8 (4/1-9/30/04)		38 (10/1/04-3/31/05)					
4	11	22	6	1	2	**NUMBER OF STATEMENTS**	21	18
%	%	%	%	%	%	**ASSETS**	%	%
	8.4	8.4				Cash & Equivalents	9.0	7.7
	23.0	26.5				Trade Receivables (net)	29.2	23.5
	43.7	36.8				Inventory	32.6	31.4
	7.7	2.8				All Other Current	2.2	2.1
	82.8	74.5				Total Current	73.0	64.6
	10.1	16.7				Fixed Assets (net)	16.1	21.4
	4.0	1.5				Intangibles (net)	3.8	4.4
	3.1	7.3				All Other Non-Current	7.1	9.5
	100.0	100.0				Total	100.0	100.0
						LIABILITIES		
	17.4	10.8				Notes Payable-Short Term	9.0	13.1
	4.6	1.9				Cur. Mat.-L/T/D	1.2	3.6
	16.9	13.7				Trade Payables	14.5	11.9
	.1	.8				Income Taxes Payable	.8	.2
	17.9	9.3				All Other Current	12.3	12.0
	56.8	36.5				Total Current	37.7	40.7
	15.4	8.3				Long-Term Debt	8.4	13.9
	.5	.3				Deferred Taxes	.3	.8
	4.8	4.8				All Other Non-Current	3.8	10.8
	22.5	50.0				Net Worth	49.7	33.7
	100.0	100.0				Total Liabilities & Net Worth	100.0	100.0
						INCOME DATA		
	100.0	100.0				Net Sales	100.0	100.0
	48.1	35.7				Gross Profit	42.9	41.9
	48.4	31.3				Operating Expenses	39.1	36.3
	-.3	4.4				Operating Profit	3.8	5.5
	1.2	.5				All Other Expenses (net)	1.0	1.6
	-1.5	3.8				Profit Before Taxes	2.8	3.9
						RATIOS		
	3.8	3.3					4.1	2.9
	1.8	2.4				Current	1.9	1.7
	1.4	1.5					1.3	1.2
	1.8	1.8					2.4	1.2
	.6	1.0				Quick	1.0	.7
	.2	.6					.6	.5
	24 15.4	33 11.0					37 9.9	31 11.9
	54 6.7	44 8.3				Sales/Receivables	52 7.0	45 8.1
	74 4.9	50 7.3					71 5.1	54 6.8
	120 3.1	66 5.6					83 4.4	78 4.7
	176 2.1	98 3.7				Cost of Sales/Inventory	110 3.3	122 3.0
	280 1.3	236 1.5					158 2.3	149 2.5
	48 7.7	12 30.6					20 18.6	14 26.3
	73 5.0	27 13.7				Cost of Sales/Payables	34 10.7	27 13.6
	93 3.9	68 5.4					94 3.9	62 5.9
	2.6	3.5					3.2	4.4
	5.0	4.5				Sales/Working Capital	6.6	6.2
	10.2	8.6					10.6	17.6
		16.5					7.8	14.0
		(20) 4.7				EBIT/Interest	(18) 2.7	2.7
		1.6					.7	1.1
							8.6	
						Net Profit + Depr., Dep., Amort./Cur. Mat. L./T/D	(10) 3.1	
							1.2	
	.1	.1					.2	.2
	.4	.3				Fixed/Worth	.3	.4
	-.6	.6					.5	.9
	1.0	.4					.6	.4
	1.4	.9				Debt/Worth	1.1	1.1
	-19.5	1.7					3.2	3.4
		25.5					21.7	18.6
		(21) 9.3				% Profit Before Taxes/Tangible Net Worth	(20) 14.3	(16) 9.1
		3.1					2.7	1.9
	11.2	14.0					11.7	13.0
	.3	4.1				% Profit Before Taxes/Total Assets	3.7	3.8
	-16.5	1.4					.7	.3
	46.9	35.0					29.3	36.2
	28.3	13.7				Sales/Net Fixed Assets	16.3	9.4
	11.3	8.2					7.6	5.6
	2.2	2.6					2.5	2.6
	1.7	2.2				Sales/Total Assets	1.9	1.8
	1.3	1.5					1.3	1.4
		.7					.5	.3
	(20)	1.5				% Depr., Dep., Amort./Sales	(20) 1.3	1.8
		2.3					2.5	3.7
						% Officers', Directors', Owners' Comp/Sales		
2289M	23548M	221898M	227148M	171288M	329950M	Net Sales ($)	446155M	281100M
1196M	13559M	101521M	148810M	74460M	272754M	Total Assets ($)	291311M	183326M

© RMA 2005   M = $ thousand   MM = $ million
See Pages 11 through 21 for Explanation of Ratios and Data

Comparative Historical Data | Current Data Sorted By Sales

			Type of Statement						
7	5	10	Unqualified				2	4	4
10	13	12	Reviewed		4	1	5	2	
5	5	7	Compiled	4	1		2		
1		1	Tax Returns		1				
10	10	16	Other	1	4	2	3	2	4
4/1/02-3/31/03	4/1/03-3/31/04	4/1/04-3/31/05			8 (4/1-9/30/04)		38 (10/1/04-3/31/05)		
ALL	ALL	ALL		0-1MM	1-3MM	3-5MM	5-10MM	10-25MM	25MM & OVER
33	33	46	**NUMBER OF STATEMENTS**	5	10	3	12	8	8
%	%	%	**ASSETS**	%	%	%	%	%	%
11.0	12.1	9.4	Cash & Equivalents		7.7		9.0		
22.9	24.6	26.2	Trade Receivables (net)		24.4		22.8		
31.9	31.1	34.3	Inventory		42.8		40.8		
8.6	3.5	4.5	All Other Current		8.4		4.1		
74.5	71.3	74.4	Total Current		83.3		76.7		
16.2	18.6	15.6	Fixed Assets (net)		8.6		14.8		
4.3	4.9	2.7	Intangibles (net)		4.4		1.1		
5.0	5.2	7.3	All Other Non-Current		3.7		7.4		
100.0	100.0	100.0	Total		100.0		100.0		
			LIABILITIES						
12.2	13.2	12.2	Notes Payable-Short Term		22.9		9.2		
3.2	2.3	3.1	Cur. Mat.-L/T/D		4.3		1.9		
10.8	13.7	14.7	Trade Payables		14.7		12.6		
.3	.3	.5	Income Taxes Payable		.1		.3		
11.8	14.2	11.4	All Other Current		19.4		9.9		
38.3	43.7	41.9	Total Current		61.4		33.9		
7.8	8.0	13.8	Long-Term Debt		14.9		8.9		
.5	.7	.4	Deferred Taxes		.6		.2		
5.6	9.5	4.8	All Other Non-Current		3.2		4.4		
47.7	38.0	39.0	Net Worth		19.9		52.6		
100.0	100.0	100.0	Total Liabilities & Net Worth		100.0		100.0		
			INCOME DATA						
100.0	100.0	100.0	Net Sales		100.0		100.0		
41.1	40.1	37.9	Gross Profit		48.1		33.9		
37.8	35.0	34.0	Operating Expenses		49.3		31.9		
3.3	5.1	3.9	Operating Profit		−1.2		2.1		
1.0	.8	.7	All Other Expenses (net)		1.6		−.1		
2.4	4.2	3.2	Profit Before Taxes		−2.8		2.2		
			RATIOS						
2.9	2.6	3.3			2.8		4.4		
2.0	2.1	2.3	Current		1.8		2.6		
1.3	1.5	1.5			1.2		1.8		
1.6	1.4	1.8			1.2		1.8		
.8	1.0	1.0	Quick		.7		1.2		
.5	.6	.6			.2		.6		
38 9.6	36 10.1	35 10.4		23 15.6		32 11.6			
48 7.6	47 7.7	47 7.7	Sales/Receivables	59 6.2		45 8.1			
60 6.1	59 6.2	62 5.9		77 4.7		49 7.4			
67 5.4	50 7.3	50 7.4		94 3.9		72 5.0			
106 3.4	81 4.5	101 3.6	Cost of Sales/Inventory	220 1.7		119 3.1			
156 2.3	136 2.7	236 1.5		298 1.2		208 1.8			
22 16.3	27 13.6	19 19.2		35 10.3		14 25.6			
36 10.1	46 8.0	39 9.4	Cost of Sales/Payables	79 4.6		27 13.7			
54 6.8	58 6.2	74 4.9		93 3.9		60 6.0			
3.3	3.5	3.3			3.5		3.5		
5.1	5.4	5.1	Sales/Working Capital		4.7		4.0		
8.5	9.5	8.6			NM		6.9		
11.7	19.2	18.2					13.6		
(31) 1.9	(29) 3.2	(39) 3.9	EBIT/Interest			(10) 6.0			
−.1	1.1	1.2					1.7		
6.8	8.3		Net Profit + Depr., Dep.,						
(11) 1.9	(10) 4.2		Amort./Cur. Mat. L/T/D						
.8	2.4								
.2	.2	.1			.1		.1		
.3	.4	.3	Fixed/Worth		.3		.2		
.8	.9	.7			NM		.4		
.5	.6	.5			1.0		.4		
1.1	1.2	1.1	Debt/Worth		1.6		.6		
3.0	1.9	2.3			NM		1.3		
26.7	44.4	28.9	% Profit Before Taxes/Tangible				21.9		
(31) 8.9	(29) 9.3	(40) 11.8	Net Worth			(11) 9.3			
−12.1	−2.6	4.0					−3.3		
10.8	16.0	14.0	% Profit Before Taxes/Total		8.2		13.0		
3.5	2.7	4.9	Assets		.5		3.9		
−1.8	−1.5	.5			−10.9		−1.0		
32.7	33.7	31.0			46.3		41.6		
12.7	13.7	13.7	Sales/Net Fixed Assets		28.0		13.7		
6.7	6.9	8.5			11.2		7.8		
2.3	2.4	2.6			2.3		2.4		
1.7	2.0	2.1	Sales/Total Assets		1.6		2.1		
1.3	1.4	1.3			1.3		1.6		
1.0	1.0	.9					.6		
(30) 1.6	(25) 1.5	(39) 1.7	% Depr., Dep., Amort./Sales				1.3		
2.6	2.6	2.4					2.3		
2.7	3.2	3.5	% Officers', Directors',						
(11) 6.3	(12) 5.2	(12) 8.1	Owners' Comp/Sales						
9.2	9.9	13.5							
670866M	758551M	976121M	Net Sales ($)	2960M	20863M	12128M	89576M	124888M	725706M
432741M	380055M	612300M	Total Assets ($)	1774M	13618M	9077M	49633M	60557M	477641M

© RMA 2005

M = $ thousand   MM = $ million

See Pages 11 through 21 for Explanation of Ratios and Data

Current Data Sorted By Assets | Comparative Historical Data

0-500M	500M-2MM	2-10MM	10-50MM	50-100MM	100-250MM	Type of Statement	4/1/00-3/31/01	4/1/01-3/31/02
		3	6	1	5	Unqualified	16	10
	2	3	1			Reviewed	5	7
2	5	6				Compiled	5	13
						Tax Returns	4	
	1	6	5	2	2	Other	11	9
	18 (4/1-9/30/04)		32 (10/1/04-3/31/05)				ALL	ALL
2	8	18	12	3	7	**NUMBER OF STATEMENTS**	41	39
%	%	%	%	%	%	**ASSETS**	%	%
		10.5	14.9			Cash & Equivalents	14.9	14.4
		30.6	20.8			Trade Receivables (net)	25.9	24.1
		37.1	26.8			Inventory	28.4	28.5
		1.8	1.4			All Other Current	4.3	5.0
		80.0	63.8			Total Current	73.5	72.0
		14.9	20.9			Fixed Assets (net)	17.2	19.0
		2.1	7.1			Intangibles (net)	5.1	4.1
		2.9	8.2			All Other Non-Current	4.2	4.9
		100.0	100.0			Total	100.0	100.0
						LIABILITIES		
		8.4	2.1			Notes Payable-Short Term	12.3	6.8
		3.1	2.3			Cur. Mat.-L/T/D	3.7	4.3
		8.6	7.2			Trade Payables	11.4	8.6
		.6	.3			Income Taxes Payable	.6	.4
		15.5	13.8			All Other Current	12.9	14.2
		36.1	25.6			Total Current	40.9	34.3
		6.1	10.3			Long-Term Debt	13.3	12.6
		.5	.0			Deferred Taxes	.3	.2
		2.2	6.6			All Other Non-Current	2.4	3.5
		55.1	57.5			Net Worth	43.2	49.3
		100.0	100.0			Total Liabilities & Net Worth	100.0	100.0
						INCOME DATA		
		100.0	100.0			Net Sales	100.0	100.0
		42.4	47.4			Gross Profit	44.4	42.3
		35.6	38.3			Operating Expenses	35.3	38.9
		6.8	9.1			Operating Profit	9.1	3.4
		.9	2.8			All Other Expenses (net)	1.5	1.5
		6.0	6.4			Profit Before Taxes	7.6	1.9
						RATIOS		
		3.8	3.9				3.2	3.9
		2.5	2.4			Current	1.9	2.3
		1.5	2.0				1.5	1.5
		1.8	2.6				1.8	2.3
		1.3	1.5			Quick	1.0	1.1
		.8	.9				.6	.7
		38 9.6	35 10.5				40 9.0	36 10.2
		45 8.1	50 7.4			Sales/Receivables	57 6.4	46 7.9
		77 4.7	66 5.5				74 5.0	72 5.1
		73 5.0	84 4.4				61 6.0	72 5.1
		120 3.0	107 3.4			Cost of Sales/Inventory	117 3.1	107 3.4
		175 2.1	177 2.1				163 2.2	144 2.5
		17 21.8	16 22.8				24 15.3	17 21.9
		21 17.0	24 15.0			Cost of Sales/Payables	34 10.7	25 14.4
		34 10.6	48 7.6				57 6.4	46 8.0
		3.8	2.6				3.4	2.9
		4.9	4.0			Sales/Working Capital	5.1	5.1
		6.4	5.2				8.6	7.6
		44.0	37.4				23.2	10.1
		(17) 10.6	(11) 6.7			EBIT/Interest	(33) 6.4	(36) 2.7
		2.9	2.2				3.0	-.8
						Net Profit + Depr., Dep.,		3.7
						Amort./Cur. Mat. L /T/D	(14)	1.7
								.2
		.1	.2				.2	.2
		.3	.4			Fixed/Worth	.4	.4
		.5	.7				.9	.9
		.3	.4				.4	.4
		.7	.7			Debt/Worth	.9	.9
		2.0	2.2				2.6	3.0
		56.1	25.2				34.1	27.4
		18.7	(11) 7.8			% Profit Before Taxes/Tangible Net Worth	(37) 20.9	(37) 10.9
		11.4	1.6				8.2	-3.9
		17.5	18.6				17.4	10.5
		9.9	6.6			% Profit Before Taxes/Total Assets	8.2	4.6
		4.7	1.7				3.5	-3.1
		41.2	16.5				21.0	20.3
		19.6	13.8			Sales/Net Fixed Assets	10.0	9.8
		6.5	5.0				5.6	5.4
		2.4	2.1				2.2	2.1
		1.9	1.4			Sales/Total Assets	1.8	1.5
		1.5	1.0				1.2	1.2
		1.0	1.6				1.3	1.4
		(17) 1.6	(11) 1.9			% Depr., Dep., Amort./Sales	(35) 2.1	(33) 2.5
		3.0	3.3				4.2	4.2
							6.6	3.9
						% Officers', Directors', Owners' Comp/Sales	(11) 8.8	(11) 9.2
							13.3	10.5
1206M	24368M	143386M	371158M	225544M	831919M	Net Sales ($)	1275404M	934478M
195M	10504M	73490M	244525M	170452M	1063007M	Total Assets ($)	1182505M	783745M

Comparative Historical Data | **Current Data Sorted By Sales**

			Type of Statement						
12	10	15	Unqualified		1		1	5	8
8	8	6	Reviewed	1	2		2		1
5	8	13	Compiled	3	2	1	5	2	
	2		Tax Returns						
10	12	16	Other			3	3	2	8
4/1/02-3/31/03	4/1/03-3/31/04	4/1/04-3/31/05			18 (4/1-9/30/04)		32 (10/1/04-3/31/05)		
ALL	ALL	ALL		0-1MM	1-3MM	3-5MM	5-10MM	10-25MM	25MM & OVER
35	40	50	**NUMBER OF STATEMENTS**	3	3	7	11	9	17
%	%	%	**ASSETS**	%	%	%	%	%	%
14.9	12.7	15.0	Cash & Equivalents				9.5		20.9
25.5	26.9	27.2	Trade Receivables (net)				35.8		20.6
28.0	27.3	29.5	Inventory				31.2		23.3
2.7	2.2	1.7	All Other Current				1.6		2.9
71.2	69.1	73.4	Total Current				78.1		67.6
18.7	17.1	14.9	Fixed Assets (net)				12.2		16.8
3.2	6.3	4.6	Intangibles (net)				6.3		7.1
6.8	7.4	7.1	All Other Non-Current				3.4		8.4
100.0	100.0	100.0	Total				100.0		100.0
			LIABILITIES						
7.9	9.3	13.4	Notes Payable-Short Term				9.2		1.5
2.8	3.0	2.3	Cur. Mat.-L/T/D				3.9		1.7
10.6	11.2	11.1	Trade Payables				7.4		8.0
.5	.3	.4	Income Taxes Payable				.3		.6
10.8	12.5	16.3	All Other Current				22.1		13.8
32.5	36.3	43.6	Total Current				42.9		25.5
9.4	10.5	8.1	Long-Term Debt				10.3		7.2
.2	.1	.3	Deferred Taxes				.6		.4
5.0	10.3	5.1	All Other Non-Current				11.9		3.7
52.8	42.8	42.8	Net Worth				34.3		63.2
100.0	100.0	100.0	Total Liabilities & Net Worth				100.0		100.0
			INCOME DATA						
100.0	100.0	100.0	Net Sales				100.0		100.0
42.6	42.0	45.1	Gross Profit				41.9		47.3
41.0	40.1	37.3	Operating Expenses				30.9		41.5
1.6	1.9	7.8	Operating Profit				10.9		5.9
.8	1.3	1.1	All Other Expenses (net)				1.7		.7
.8	.6	6.7	Profit Before Taxes				9.2		5.2
			RATIOS						
3.8	3.7	3.7					3.5		4.2
2.5	2.3	2.4	Current				2.0		2.7
1.7	1.4	1.6					1.4		2.0
2.1	2.0	2.3					1.9		2.8
1.4	1.2	1.5	Quick				1.0		1.6
1.0	.8	.8					.7		1.0
38 9.7	48 7.6	38 9.6					38 9.6		47 7.7
51 7.2	54 6.8	55 6.7	Sales/Receivables				52 7.1		59 6.2
69 5.3	71 5.2	70 5.2					60 6.1		71 5.2
74 4.9	72 5.1	76 4.8					61 6.0		88 4.2
89 4.1	98 3.7	107 3.4	Cost of Sales/Inventory				96 3.8		109 3.4
147 2.5	147 2.5	163 2.2					153 2.4		177 2.1
21 17.0	19 19.5	17 21.5					8 44.5		26 14.2
33 11.2	33 11.2	30 12.2	Cost of Sales/Payables				21 17.5		47 7.8
54 6.8	53 6.9	51 7.2					26 14.1		52 7.0
2.7	3.1	2.7					4.3		1.7
4.9	5.0	4.3	Sales/Working Capital				5.4		3.7
7.2	9.6	7.4					8.7		5.0
17.5	13.5	39.8					36.0		83.4
(29) 3.5	(36) 2.4	(42) 6.6	EBIT/Interest				10.6		(13) 8.5
-1.1	.2	2.6					2.9		2.0
6.8	12.8	33.6	Net Profit + Depr., Dep.,						
(15) 2.3	(17) 3.3	(15) 6.6	Amort./Cur. Mat. L/T/D						
.9	.6	.8							
.2	.2	.1					.1		.2
.3	.5	.2	Fixed/Worth				.3		.2
.6	.9	.5					.6		.5
.3	.5	.3					.4		.3
.9	1.4	.6	Debt/Worth				1.8		.5
1.4	6.0	2.5					4.1		1.6
23.5	24.9	47.1	% Profit Before Taxes/Tangible						46.8
(32) 4.6	(33) 9.0	(47) 17.8	Net Worth						12.4
-5.5	-3.7	4.5							1.2
12.6	10.5	17.1	% Profit Before Taxes/Total				21.0		15.9
2.5	3.3	8.5	Assets				14.5		6.2
-4.1	-1.3	3.4					5.3		.8
24.1	25.0	41.6					70.4		14.6
9.8	11.0	14.7	Sales/Net Fixed Assets				40.9		6.4
5.7	6.6	6.1					8.5		5.0
2.4	2.3	2.3					2.9		1.8
1.7	1.7	1.6	Sales/Total Assets				2.1		1.2
1.1	1.1	1.1					1.3		.9
1.3	1.1	.9					.5		1.8
(30) 2.3	(37) 2.0	(43) 1.8	% Depr., Dep., Amort./Sales				(10) 1.0		(14) 3.1
3.8	3.2	3.3					3.2		4.6
3.5	3.3	2.2	% Officers', Directors',						
(12) 4.4	(12) 4.4	(14) 7.3	Owners' Comp/Sales						
9.6	11.7	12.0							
906546M	1006055M	1597581M	Net Sales ($)	2018M	5656M	29630M	70727M	137526M	1352024M
836395M	866969M	1562173M	Total Assets ($)	1001M	3841M	16848M	41206M	102862M	1396415M

M = $ thousand   MM = $ million
See Pages 11 through 21 for Explanation of Ratios and Data

Current Data Sorted By Assets   Comparative Historical Data

	0-500M	500M-2MM	2-10MM	10-50MM	50-100MM	100-250MM	Type of Statement	4/1/00-3/31/01 ALL	4/1/01-3/31/02 ALL
		1	7	5	1	2	Unqualified	16	12
		1	7	3			Reviewed	8	6
	1	1	3				Compiled	7	8
		2	3	1			Tax Returns	2	2
	1	3	7	5	1		Other	11	17
		9 (4/1-9/30/04)		46 (10/1/04-3/31/05)					
NUMBER OF STATEMENTS	2	8	27	14	2	2		44	45
	%	%	%	%	%	%	ASSETS	%	%
Cash & Equivalents			8.5	12.7				8.3	10.4
Trade Receivables (net)			30.8	22.8				29.3	24.8
Inventory			32.3	24.3				30.0	30.8
All Other Current			3.7	4.5				2.3	2.4
Total Current			75.4	64.3				69.8	68.4
Fixed Assets (net)			12.1	14.2				16.3	15.9
Intangibles (net)			7.5	17.9				7.5	9.1
All Other Non-Current			5.0	3.5				6.4	6.6
Total			100.0	100.0				100.0	100.0
							LIABILITIES		
Notes Payable-Short Term			6.4	4.6				8.4	10.7
Cur. Mat.-L/T/D			2.7	4.3				3.4	3.4
Trade Payables			16.2	7.2				12.5	10.6
Income Taxes Payable			1.0	.1				.3	.6
All Other Current			12.7	20.7				12.6	10.9
Total Current			39.0	36.8				37.2	36.2
Long-Term Debt			6.9	10.5				13.9	11.7
Deferred Taxes			.4	.7				.7	.8
All Other Non-Current			2.9	5.9				5.2	4.7
Net Worth			50.8	46.1				43.0	46.7
Total Liabilities & Net Worth			100.0	100.0				100.0	100.0
							INCOME DATA		
Net Sales			100.0	100.0				100.0	100.0
Gross Profit			47.5	39.1				45.6	47.6
Operating Expenses			40.0	29.4				39.4	42.7
Operating Profit			7.5	9.8				6.2	4.9
All Other Expenses (net)			.2	.9				1.8	1.8
Profit Before Taxes			7.3	8.9				4.4	3.1
							RATIOS		
Current			4.5	3.8				3.3	3.8
			1.7	1.6				1.9	2.0
			1.3	1.2				1.4	1.3
Quick			2.0	2.4				1.7	2.2
			1.1	1.0				1.1	1.0
			.6	.5				.6	.6
Sales/Receivables			46 7.9	52 7.0				43 8.4	47 7.8
			61 6.0	58 6.3				60 6.1	56 6.5
			72 5.1	68 5.4				84 4.4	70 5.2
Cost of Sales/Inventory			73 5.0	79 4.6				79 4.6	82 4.5
			118 3.1	109 3.3				122 3.0	132 2.8
			193 1.9	129 2.8				157 2.3	183 2.0
Cost of Sales/Payables			31 11.7	16 22.9				27 13.7	21 17.7
			51 7.1	26 13.9				41 8.8	39 9.3
			74 4.9	41 8.8				64 5.7	60 6.0
Sales/Working Capital			3.0	2.4				3.2	2.9
			4.6	6.7				6.1	5.2
			13.3	17.8				10.9	11.7
EBIT/Interest			36.4	38.7				11.9	14.2
			11.1	(12) 12.8				(41) 4.8	(44) 2.4
			4.3	4.4				1.1	.4
Net Profit + Depr., Dep., Amort./Cur. Mat. L./T/D								7.0	4.3
								(12) 3.0	(12) .9
								1.7	−1.0
Fixed/Worth			.2	.3				.2	.2
			.3	.7				.4	.4
			.6	NM				.9	9.6
Debt/Worth			.3	.3				.5	.4
			1.6	2.4				1.3	1.0
			2.9	NM				4.6	35.4
% Profit Before Taxes/Tangible Net Worth			57.7	50.1				38.9	31.7
		(25) 26.3		(11) 24.9				(36) 22.5	(35) 9.7
			6.0	8.5				4.4	−.8
% Profit Before Taxes/Total Assets			21.0	16.6				14.0	13.0
			10.8	8.3				7.1	3.9
			3.3	4.0				1.1	−1.1
Sales/Net Fixed Assets			41.5	21.1				24.3	22.5
			21.4	11.2				13.4	13.0
			13.3	5.6				5.8	5.6
Sales/Total Assets			2.4	1.7				2.1	2.2
			1.9	1.4				1.6	1.6
			1.3	.9				1.2	1.1
% Depr., Dep., Amort./Sales			.7	.9				1.4	.9
		(21) 1.0		(12) 2.8				(37) 1.7	(37) 2.0
			2.0	4.0				2.6	3.6
% Officers', Directors', Owners' Comp/Sales									
Net Sales ($)	3806M	20187M	254796M	417131M	122383M	373795M		1223398M	1209635M
Total Assets ($)	833M	11333M	136758M	306403M	143899M	311541M		1037511M	1176401M

Comparative Historical Data | **Current Data Sorted By Sales**

4/1/02-3/31/03 ALL	4/1/03-3/31/04 ALL	4/1/04-3/31/05 ALL		0-1MM	1-3MM	3-5MM	5-10MM	10-25MM	25MM & OVER
			Type of Statement						
17	14	16	Unqualified			1	3	5	7
9	17	11	Reviewed		1	1	5	3	1
5	9	5	Compiled		2	1	2		
4	4	6	Tax Returns		1	2	1	1	1
14	12	17	Other		4	1	2	8	2
				9 (4/1-9/30/04)			46 (10/1/04-3/31/05)		
49	56	55	**NUMBER OF STATEMENTS**		8	6	13	17	11
%	%	%	**ASSETS**	%	%	%	%	%	%
9.1	10.0	8.9	Cash & Equivalents	DATA NOT AVAILABLE			6.0	13.6	7.5
26.8	27.2	27.9	Trade Receivables (net)				29.9	27.8	23.6
31.3	25.9	27.9	Inventory				31.2	27.4	26.5
2.0	4.3	3.9	All Other Current				3.9	2.9	6.0
69.1	67.4	68.7	Total Current				71.1	71.6	63.6
15.8	16.6	13.6	Fixed Assets (net)				14.4	10.3	19.9
8.6	9.4	11.2	Intangibles (net)				8.4	14.1	8.0
6.5	6.6	6.5	All Other Non-Current				6.0	4.0	8.4
100.0	100.0	100.0	Total				100.0	100.0	100.0
			LIABILITIES						
11.1	10.2	8.3	Notes Payable-Short Term				3.4	8.2	5.3
3.9	3.0	2.7	Cur. Mat.-L/T/D				3.6	1.9	4.2
11.7	12.3	13.1	Trade Payables				16.1	12.6	9.6
.6	1.1	.6	Income Taxes Payable				1.2	.6	.5
13.8	12.8	14.6	All Other Current				15.6	13.7	24.1
41.1	39.3	39.3	Total Current				39.9	37.0	43.6
14.6	9.4	8.1	Long-Term Debt				8.7	8.1	7.4
.3	.4	.6	Deferred Taxes				.7	.2	1.7
4.8	6.7	4.6	All Other Non-Current				5.0	4.6	1.8
39.1	44.2	47.5	Net Worth				45.7	50.0	45.4
100.0	100.0	100.0	Total Liabilities & Net Worth				100.0	100.0	100.0
			INCOME DATA						
100.0	100.0	100.0	Net Sales				100.0	100.0	100.0
45.3	43.5	43.8	Gross Profit				49.4	41.7	39.3
43.1	38.4	36.3	Operating Expenses				39.8	32.7	35.0
2.3	5.2	7.5	Operating Profit				9.6	9.1	4.3
1.5	.6	.6	All Other Expenses (net)				.6	.7	-.2
.8	4.6	7.0	Profit Before Taxes				9.0	8.4	4.5
			RATIOS						
2.9	3.5	3.1					4.8	4.5	1.9
1.6	1.6	1.6	Current				1.7	1.6	1.6
1.2	1.2	1.2					1.4	1.2	1.0
1.4	1.5	2.0					2.5	2.1	1.4
.9	.9	1.0	Quick				.9	1.0	.8
.6	.6	.6					.6	.7	.3
48 7.5	**46** 7.9	**46** 7.9					**52** 7.0	**41** 9.0	**54** 6.7
59 6.2	**55** 6.6	**57** 6.4	Sales/Receivables				**61** 5.9	**57** 6.4	**59** 6.2
72 5.1	**71** 5.1	**68** 5.4					**69** 5.3	**67** 5.5	**69** 5.3
87 4.2	**60** 6.1	**64** 5.7					**68** 5.4	**67** 5.4	**72** 5.0
130 2.8	**102** 3.6	**109** 3.3	Cost of Sales/Inventory				**123** 3.0	**97** 3.8	**109** 3.3
192 1.9	**162** 2.3	**159** 2.3					**206** 1.8	**148** 2.5	**203** 1.8
25 14.6	**24** 15.1	**23** 15.6					**32** 11.5	**17** 21.3	**25** 14.9
46 7.9	**38** 9.5	**43** 8.4	Cost of Sales/Payables				**48** 7.6	**38** 9.7	**45** 8.1
62 5.9	**54** 6.8	**59** 6.2					**89** 4.1	**56** 6.6	**53** 6.9
3.1	3.2	3.5					3.1	2.9	5.0
7.0	6.8	6.7	Sales/Working Capital				6.7	4.8	7.3
13.5	20.3	20.3					10.7	16.8	36.9
10.2	23.5	33.4					43.7	90.1	44.4
(46) 3.1	(49) 5.3	(50) 9.2	EBIT/Interest				9.8	(15) 4.5	(10) 25.3
.7	1.0	4.2					6.2	2.8	7.8
6.7	8.2	40.8							
(13) 2.7	(24) 3.8	(21) 10.0	Net Profit + Depr., Dep., Amort./Cur. Mat. L/T/D						
.7	1.6	1.4							
.2	.2	.2					.2	.1	.4
.5	.5	.4	Fixed/Worth				.3	.2	.7
NM	1.9	1.2					1.2	1.1	.8
.6	.4	.4					.4	.3	1.0
2.1	1.7	1.6	Debt/Worth				1.8	1.8	1.6
NM	9.1	5.5					9.6	4.3	3.4
36.6	37.3	53.7					63.1	44.8	50.1
(37) 17.9	(45) 15.9	(48) 27.3	% Profit Before Taxes/Tangible Net Worth				(11) 44.2	(14) 21.6	31.4
1.4	2.7	7.6					18.0	3.2	8.5
9.4	11.7	19.0					21.3	21.6	14.0
3.4	6.7	9.4	% Profit Before Taxes/Total Assets				16.9	7.1	9.4
-1.0	-.2	3.3					8.0	2.3	3.3
27.6	37.2	35.3					35.7	69.9	12.0
13.3	14.4	16.7	Sales/Net Fixed Assets				22.2	24.5	9.5
5.8	6.5	8.4					10.7	10.1	4.1
2.1	2.2	2.0					2.2	2.2	1.7
1.7	1.7	1.7	Sales/Total Assets				1.6	1.8	1.6
1.2	1.3	1.3					1.4	1.1	1.2
1.6	1.3	.7						.7	
(41) 2.3	(45) 1.9	(43) 1.5	% Depr., Dep., Amort./Sales					(15) .8	
4.1	3.4	3.6						3.3	
	4.0								
	(10) 5.9		% Officers', Directors', Owners' Comp/Sales						
	12.8								
1159129M	1339461M	1192098M	Net Sales ($)		17025M	23581M	92145M	259148M	800199M
1150079M	1136361M	910767M	Total Assets ($)		8730M	16194M	53092M	184307M	648444M

M = $ thousand MM = $ million

See Pages 11 through 21 for Explanation of Ratios and Data

Current Data Sorted By Assets   Comparative Historical Data

0-500M	500M-2MM	2-10MM	10-50MM	50-100MM	100-250MM	Type of Statement	4/1/00-3/31/01 ALL	4/1/01-3/31/02 ALL
	2	10	11	3	4	Unqualified	16	24
	5	7	2	2		Reviewed	17	20
	3	3	2	2		Compiled	15	15
2	3					Tax Returns		
1	4	9	12	3	5	Other	32	32
	14 (4/1-9/30/04)		76 (10/1/04-3/31/05)					
3	17	28	27	6	9	NUMBER OF STATEMENTS	80	91
%	%	%	%	%	%	ASSETS	%	%
	7.0	9.5	8.5			Cash & Equivalents	8.1	10.8
	37.8	30.5	27.8			Trade Receivables (net)	31.4	27.1
	20.9	28.4	20.9			Inventory	28.8	27.9
	3.1	3.0	3.9			All Other Current	3.8	5.0
	68.8	71.5	61.2			Total Current	72.1	70.8
	21.6	16.0	23.5			Fixed Assets (net)	16.6	15.5
	3.8	5.5	9.3			Intangibles (net)	5.5	8.1
	5.8	7.1	6.0			All Other Non-Current	5.9	5.5
	100.0	100.0	100.0			Total	100.0	100.0
						LIABILITIES		
	21.3	10.8	7.8			Notes Payable-Short Term	12.7	9.7
	2.7	1.6	3.5			Cur. Mat.-L/T/D	3.3	4.0
	17.9	13.1	10.7			Trade Payables	14.7	10.6
	.2	.2	.4			Income Taxes Payable	.4	.4
	17.1	15.2	13.4			All Other Current	14.2	11.7
	59.1	40.9	35.9			Total Current	45.3	36.4
	10.7	11.0	12.7			Long-Term Debt	10.7	14.4
	.2	.4	.4			Deferred Taxes	.5	.2
	18.6	3.5	6.0			All Other Non-Current	4.0	7.8
	11.4	44.2	45.1			Net Worth	39.5	41.2
	100.0	100.0	100.0			Total Liabilities & Net Worth	100.0	100.0
						INCOME DATA		
	100.0	100.0	100.0			Net Sales	100.0	100.0
	49.3	38.1	38.8			Gross Profit	40.0	41.7
	46.1	32.7	29.7			Operating Expenses	35.2	36.8
	3.2	5.4	9.0			Operating Profit	4.8	4.9
	.6	.5	1.2			All Other Expenses (net)	1.9	1.5
	2.6	4.9	7.8			Profit Before Taxes	3.0	3.4
						RATIOS		
	2.0	3.7	3.3				3.0	3.2
	1.1	1.9	1.6			Current	1.7	2.2
	.9	1.1	1.1				1.2	1.4
	1.3	1.8	2.1				1.5	1.9
	.8	1.3	.9			Quick	.8	1.1
	.5	.5	.6				.6	.6
	38 9.5	46 8.0	44 8.2				48 7.7	40 9.1
	52 7.0	56 6.5	51 7.1			Sales/Receivables	57 6.4	53 6.9
	59 6.2	71 5.2	68 5.4				71 5.2	68 5.4
	17 21.4	68 5.4	40 9.0				52 7.0	70 5.2
	52 7.0	100 3.6	67 5.4			Cost of Sales/Inventory	95 3.8	99 3.7
	107 3.4	141 2.6	125 2.9				147 2.5	150 2.4
	23 16.2	19 19.2	22 16.5				24 15.1	17 21.0
	51 7.2	33 11.0	27 13.3			Cost of Sales/Payables	42 8.7	30 12.2
	76 4.8	55 6.7	46 7.9				58 6.3	52 7.0
	7.7	3.3	4.2				4.1	3.3
	45.4	5.9	10.0			Sales/Working Capital	7.1	5.3
	-43.2	44.7	28.7				20.0	9.5
	12.0	17.1	19.5				7.9	8.7
	(15) 4.2	(23) 6.9	(23) 5.7			EBIT/Interest	(72) 2.1	(81) 3.1
	.0	1.5	2.5				.3	1.0
		14.0				Net Profit + Depr., Dep.,	3.5	9.4
		(10) 4.7				Amort./Cur. Mat. L/T/D	(22) 1.4	(25) 2.6
		.6					.1	.8
	.3	.2	.4				.2	.2
	.9	.3	.6			Fixed/Worth	.4	.4
	-4.1	1.0	2.0				1.1	.9
	.9	.6	.8				.6	.6
	4.0	1.2	2.0			Debt/Worth	1.8	1.4
	-20.0	4.2	3.1				5.6	5.3
	85.8	36.5	62.9			% Profit Before Taxes/Tangible	35.6	25.9
	(11) 13.5	(26) 22.5	(23) 22.1			Net Worth	(70) 15.9	(75) 14.9
	6.2	10.5	9.2				-2.0	.3
	22.7	19.5	14.7			% Profit Before Taxes/Total	14.4	14.0
	7.3	9.0	8.9			Assets	5.5	6.0
	-.7	2.3	3.1				-1.7	.1
	30.9	29.9	14.3				36.5	31.2
	14.7	14.9	8.2			Sales/Net Fixed Assets	13.5	14.4
	9.2	6.2	5.1				7.8	7.1
	3.5	2.3	2.2				2.4	2.6
	2.5	1.7	1.6			Sales/Total Assets	1.9	1.6
	2.2	1.4	1.2				1.3	1.2
	.9	1.2	1.4				.7	.9
	(14) 2.2	(24) 1.9	(25) 2.2			% Depr., Dep., Amort./Sales	(67) 1.9	(73) 2.1
	4.9	2.9	3.3				3.5	3.4
						% Officers', Directors',	2.9	3.0
						Owners' Comp/Sales	(18) 5.1	(23) 5.1
							8.4	8.7
2033M	62020M	278978M	1033151M	525849M	1475785M	Net Sales ($)	2192208M	2070025M
592M	22266M	160776M	562665M	401503M	1309393M	Total Assets ($)	1301506M	1567569M

© RMA 2005   M = $ thousand   MM = $ million
See Pages 11 through 21 for Explanation of Ratios and Data

Comparative Historical Data | **Current Data Sorted By Sales**

			Type of Statement	0-1MM	1-3MM	3-5MM	5-10MM	10-25MM	25MM & OVER
23	19	30	Unqualified		1	2	5	9	13
15	17	14	Reviewed		3	1	6	4	
12	8	7	Compiled		2	1	2	1	1
2	4	5	Tax Returns	2		2	1		
35	48	34	Other	1	3	1	6		17
4/1/02-3/31/03 ALL	4/1/03-3/31/04 ALL	4/1/04-3/31/05 ALL		14 (4/1-9/30/04)			76 (10/1/04-3/31/05)		
87	96	90	**NUMBER OF STATEMENTS**	3	9	7	20	20	31
%	%	%	**ASSETS**	%	%	%	%	%	%
10.3	12.5	10.4	Cash & Equivalents				11.9	7.2	13.3
29.7	27.6	29.9	Trade Receivables (net)				29.3	26.4	28.5
27.4	24.9	22.6	Inventory				25.5	25.4	20.3
4.4	3.9	3.2	All Other Current				2.8	2.3	4.4
71.8	68.9	66.1	Total Current				69.6	61.4	66.5
16.0	19.1	19.9	Fixed Assets (net)				14.4	25.2	18.1
7.7	6.4	7.5	Intangibles (net)				7.5	7.0	9.7
4.5	5.6	6.5	All Other Non-Current				8.4	6.5	5.7
100.0	100.0	100.0	Total				100.0	100.0	100.0
			LIABILITIES						
12.0	10.3	10.7	Notes Payable-Short Term				13.1	7.7	5.1
4.1	3.2	2.3	Cur. Mat.-L/T/D				2.1	3.6	1.6
12.5	12.5	12.8	Trade Payables				12.4	11.4	9.8
.4	.6	.5	Income Taxes Payable				.1	.2	1.0
14.9	15.5	14.4	All Other Current				13.8	16.8	12.0
43.8	42.1	40.7	Total Current				41.5	39.6	29.5
10.7	10.0	12.0	Long-Term Debt				14.5	11.2	10.4
.2	.2	.4	Deferred Taxes				.2	.4	.5
4.4	6.1	8.6	All Other Non-Current				1.3	5.4	10.0
40.9	41.6	38.4	Net Worth				42.6	43.3	49.5
100.0	100.0	100.0	Total Liabilities & Net Worth				100.0	100.0	100.0
			INCOME DATA						
100.0	100.0	100.0	Net Sales				100.0	100.0	100.0
40.9	43.9	42.7	Gross Profit				42.3	35.1	42.1
36.6	38.3	35.2	Operating Expenses				37.1	28.2	31.8
4.3	5.6	7.5	Operating Profit				5.2	6.9	10.3
1.0	1.4	.7	All Other Expenses (net)				.5	1.5	.5
3.4	4.2	6.7	Profit Before Taxes				4.7	5.4	9.9
			RATIOS						
2.9	3.2	3.0					4.2	2.7	3.6
1.8	1.8	1.8	Current				1.8	1.2	2.5
1.2	1.3	1.1					1.0	1.1	1.6
1.7	1.8	1.8					2.1	1.5	2.5
1.0	1.0	1.0	Quick				1.1	.8	1.4
.6	.6	.6					.5	.5	.9
46 7.9	42 8.8	44 8.3				38 9.7	39 9.3	49 7.5
58 6.3	55 6.6	55 6.7	Sales/Receivables			52 7.0	51 7.1	60 6.1
68 5.3	68 5.4	70 5.2				67 5.4	68 5.4	76 4.8
56 6.5	44 8.2	42 8.6				67 5.4	41 8.8	43 8.4
103 3.5	93 3.9	86 4.2	Cost of Sales/Inventory			100 3.6	90 4.0	74 4.9
148 2.5	156 2.3	131 2.8				140 2.6	137 2.7	131 2.8
21 17.5	21 17.0	22 16.4				17 21.7	20 18.3	26 14.2
35 10.3	36 10.1	37 9.9	Cost of Sales/Payables			31 11.7	28 13.2	38 9.7
57 6.4	55 6.6	53 6.9				57 6.4	49 7.5	45 8.1
3.2	3.2	3.5					3.3	3.8	2.9
5.4	5.7	7.5	Sales/Working Capital				6.8	18.8	4.2
16.2	15.0	44.8					60.2	86.5	9.3
7.4	11.7	19.9					14.9	19.5	70.3
(80) 2.8	(88) 4.5	(77) 6.9	EBIT/Interest	(16) 6.0		(19) 5.7	(26) 14.6	
-.2	1.4	1.9					1.5	1.7	
6.9	5.8	10.5	Net Profit + Depr., Dep.,						15.8
(30) 1.5	(28) 1.9	(32) 4.3	Amort./Cur. Mat. L/T/D					(15) 6.8	
.2	.5	1.2							3.5
.2	.2	.2					.2	.3	.3
.4	.5	.5	Fixed/Worth				.3	.8	.4
1.2	1.0	2.0					1.2	1.8	.8
.5	.6	.6					.7	.7	.3
2.0	1.5	1.6	Debt/Worth				1.4	1.7	1.2
5.0	3.9	7.9					4.6	3.2	2.7
39.6	37.5	48.1	% Profit Before Taxes/Tangible				41.9	34.9	62.4
(75) 10.8	(81) 13.3	(74) 22.6	Net Worth	(18) 22.5		(18) 21.1	(26) 30.4	
-6.6	2.7	10.6					10.5	4.8	11.0
10.2	14.2	19.8	% Profit Before Taxes/Total				18.6	14.3	17.9
4.2	4.7	8.7	Assets				7.5	8.7	9.9
-1.6	1.0	3.4					2.4	1.3	4.2
27.1	22.7	23.3					37.5	13.7	15.0
13.3	11.0	11.7	Sales/Net Fixed Assets				19.3	9.3	10.8
6.5	6.0	5.7					6.0	5.1	5.5
2.2	2.3	2.4					2.3	2.1	2.2
1.8	1.7	1.8	Sales/Total Assets				1.5	1.6	1.5
1.2	1.3	1.3					1.1	1.3	1.1
1.3	1.2	1.2					1.2	1.5	1.0
(72) 2.1	(81) 2.1	(76) 2.1	% Depr., Dep., Amort./Sales	(16) 1.6		(19) 2.5	(28) 1.8	
3.3	3.3	3.3					2.9	3.7	2.7
2.9	4.9	4.1	% Officers', Directors',						
(18) 6.2	(19) 8.6	(16) 7.5	Owners' Comp/Sales						
8.8	10.8	13.9							
1884905M	2082833M	3377816M	Net Sales ($)	2033M	20784M	29966M	158686M	324919M	2841428M
1387395M	1435038M	2457195M	Total Assets ($)	592M	10264M	11341M	98435M	206511M	2130052M

© RMA 2005   M = $ thousand   MM = $ million

See Pages 11 through 21 for Explanation of Ratios and Data

Current Data Sorted By Assets   Comparative Historical Data

						Type of Statement		
				1	2	Unqualified	6	11
		3	5			Reviewed	13	7
		7	4			Compiled	8	13
1	4	3				Tax Returns	2	2
3	1					Other	7	11
1	2	5			1		4/1/00-3/31/01	4/1/01-3/31/02
6 (4/1-9/30/04)			37 (10/1/04-3/31/05)				ALL	ALL
0-500M	500M-2MM	2-10MM	10-50MM	50-100MM	100-250MM	NUMBER OF STATEMENTS	36	44
5	7	18	9	1	3			
%	%	%	%	%	%	ASSETS	%	%
		6.7				Cash & Equivalents	2.9	4.4
		27.7				Trade Receivables (net)	30.5	26.8
		40.1				Inventory	37.7	36.6
		2.3				All Other Current	2.4	2.3
		76.8				Total Current	73.5	70.1
		13.1				Fixed Assets (net)	18.5	18.5
		5.3				Intangibles (net)	2.9	6.8
		4.8				All Other Non-Current	5.1	4.6
		100.0				Total	100.0	100.0
						LIABILITIES		
		16.1				Notes Payable-Short Term	17.7	14.6
		3.5				Cur. Mat.-L/T/D	1.7	2.2
		16.1				Trade Payables	13.8	17.1
		1.0				Income Taxes Payable	.1	1.3
		8.7				All Other Current	12.9	14.5
		45.4				Total Current	46.2	49.7
		18.1				Long-Term Debt	9.2	11.2
		.3				Deferred Taxes	.5	.2
		7.1				All Other Non-Current	1.9	5.7
		29.0				Net Worth	42.2	33.2
		100.0				Total Liabilities & Net Worth	100.0	100.0
						INCOME DATA		
		100.0				Net Sales	100.0	100.0
		37.9				Gross Profit	37.8	33.8
		30.8				Operating Expenses	33.5	29.1
		7.1				Operating Profit	4.4	4.7
		1.5				All Other Expenses (net)	1.2	1.5
		5.6				Profit Before Taxes	3.2	3.2
						RATIOS		
		2.9					2.2	2.7
		1.8				Current	1.6	1.5
		1.3					1.2	1.1
		1.4					1.0	1.1
		.8				Quick	.7	.6
		.4					.5	.4
34		10.8					39 9.3	33 11.0
45		8.2				Sales/Receivables	51 7.1	41 8.9
61		6.0					65 5.6	52 7.0
80		4.6					74 4.9	47 7.7
99		3.7				Cost of Sales/Inventory	104 3.5	86 4.2
133		2.7					130 2.8	125 2.9
15		25.1					17 22.0	15 24.5
27		13.6				Cost of Sales/Payables	36 10.2	32 11.6
47		7.8					48 7.5	51 7.2
		4.5					5.1	4.4
		7.1				Sales/Working Capital	8.1	10.8
		15.2					21.6	32.1
		9.0					5.5	8.8
	(16)	2.5				EBIT/Interest	(33) 2.8	(41) 2.1
		1.6					1.4	1.2
						Net Profit + Depr., Dep.,	23.3	19.9
						Amort./Cur. Mat. L./T/D	(13) 3.2	(15) 3.8
							.4	1.1
		.3					.2	.2
		.5				Fixed/Worth	.3	.6
		-3.3					.9	2.1
		1.2					.7	1.1
		1.8				Debt/Worth	1.9	2.4
		-36.6					3.1	13.2
		41.7				% Profit Before Taxes/Tangible	40.8	64.5
	(13)	20.2				Net Worth	17.9	(39) 23.5
		5.5					3.0	3.6
		18.7				% Profit Before Taxes/Total	12.6	17.6
		3.7				Assets	5.2	6.4
		1.8					1.5	.5
		40.4					35.9	48.2
		20.7				Sales/Net Fixed Assets	15.6	16.3
		11.3					8.0	8.0
		2.8					2.8	3.7
		2.4				Sales/Total Assets	2.2	2.1
		2.0					1.6	1.6
		.5					.7	.3
	(16)	1.0				% Depr., Dep., Amort./Sales	(32) 1.1	(36) 1.2
		2.0					1.8	2.2
						% Officers', Directors',	1.7	2.0
						Owners' Comp/Sales	(18) 5.1	(15) 3.0
							9.5	5.2
4184M	14451M	196244M	350760M	198124M	687306M	Net Sales ($)	897511M	1293425M
1462M	6626M	88149M	182114M	92947M	434454M	Total Assets ($)	544517M	716928M

Comparative Historical Data / Current Data Sorted By Sales

4/1/02-3/31/03 ALL	4/1/03-3/31/04 ALL	4/1/04-3/31/05 ALL	Type of Statement	0-1MM	1-3MM	3-5MM	5-10MM	10-25MM	25MM & OVER
				6 (4/1-9/30/04)			37 (10/1/04-3/31/05)		
13	10	11	Unqualified				1	2	8
8	9	11	Reviewed				4	4	3
9	12	8	Compiled		5		3		
2	3	4	Tax Returns	2	2				
14	12	9	Other	1	2		4	1	1
46	46	43	NUMBER OF STATEMENTS	3	9		12	7	12
%	%	%	ASSETS	%	%	%	%	%	%
5.8	9.1	6.9	Cash & Equivalents			DATA NOT AVAILABLE	6.7		4.7
27.8	26.8	27.8	Trade Receivables (net)				26.2		29.6
35.7	38.2	37.4	Inventory				39.9		33.7
2.0	1.5	1.7	All Other Current				3.4		1.2
71.3	75.5	73.8	Total Current				76.1		69.3
19.4	16.1	17.1	Fixed Assets (net)				11.2		21.2
3.1	2.4	5.4	Intangibles (net)				7.7		6.4
6.2	6.1	3.7	All Other Non-Current				5.0		3.2
100.0	100.0	100.0	Total				100.0		100.0
			LIABILITIES						
14.4	13.4	13.8	Notes Payable-Short Term				18.6		1.8
2.0	2.0	2.6	Cur. Mat.-L/T/D				1.4		1.7
17.4	16.1	14.8	Trade Payables				14.4		14.5
1.4	1.2	.4	Income Taxes Payable				.9		.0
11.1	11.5	8.2	All Other Current				8.6		9.9
46.3	44.3	39.8	Total Current				43.9		27.9
13.0	9.1	17.6	Long-Term Debt				16.0		18.7
.2	.1	.2	Deferred Taxes				.3		.2
5.6	9.0	7.9	All Other Non-Current				10.5		4.0
34.9	37.5	34.4	Net Worth				29.2		49.3
100.0	100.0	100.0	Total Liabilities & Net Worth				100.0		100.0
			INCOME DATA						
100.0	100.0	100.0	Net Sales				100.0		100.0
33.3	38.6	40.5	Gross Profit				40.0		40.1
28.4	33.0	34.2	Operating Expenses				32.4		31.6
4.8	5.5	6.3	Operating Profit				7.6		8.5
1.2	.8	1.1	All Other Expenses (net)				1.2		.7
3.6	4.7	5.2	Profit Before Taxes				6.4		7.8
			RATIOS						
2.8	2.8	3.1					2.8		3.8
1.5	2.0	2.0	Current				1.8		2.5
1.1	1.3	1.5					1.5		1.9
1.3	1.4	1.6					1.8		1.9
.7	.9	.9	Quick				.8		1.3
.5	.4	.5					.4		.8
28 13.0	30 12.1	35 10.4					32 11.3		42 8.6
41 8.9	40 9.1	45 8.2	Sales/Receivables				45 8.2		59 6.2
56 6.5	58 6.3	62 5.9					59 6.2		79 4.6
43 8.5	57 6.4	76 4.8					73 5.0		83 4.4
71 5.1	107 3.4	105 3.5	Cost of Sales/Inventory				109 3.3		112 3.3
120 3.0	122 3.0	132 2.8					136 2.7		122 3.0
15 24.9	17 21.2	19 19.6					11 31.8		23 16.0
28 13.3	27 13.4	29 12.6	Cost of Sales/Payables				25 14.4		26 14.0
60 6.0	50 7.4	56 6.5					44 8.2		59 6.2
5.4	4.4	4.2					4.9		3.7
9.8	6.5	6.3	Sales/Working Capital				6.5		4.9
38.8	17.1	10.5					10.5		6.6
16.4	33.0	14.1					8.1		71.5
(43) 2.8	(41) 5.0	(40) 3.3	EBIT/Interest				(10) 2.5		(11) 15.0
1.2	1.5	1.6					2.2		3.9
17.0	15.9		Net Profit + Depr., Dep.,						
(13) 5.7	(12) 5.9		Amort./Cur. Mat. L/T/D						
1.8	1.3								
.2	.2	.2					.3		.2
.5	.3	.5	Fixed/Worth				.5		.3
1.8	1.3	2.1					-2.0		.6
.8	.7	.8					1.3		.6
2.4	1.3	1.7	Debt/Worth				1.5		1.2
5.0	4.6	11.3					-27.8		2.0
51.3	49.0	42.5	% Profit Before Taxes/Tangible						50.9
(41) 34.6	(39) 33.3	(34) 19.3	Net Worth						(11) 26.7
10.6	9.1	5.3							11.9
19.5	23.4	18.2	% Profit Before Taxes/Total				15.9		25.1
7.5	8.7	5.4	Assets				4.4		15.3
.8	1.9	1.7					2.2		4.3
53.7	40.0	35.8					61.8		17.4
18.6	15.3	14.4	Sales/Net Fixed Assets				23.9		12.1
7.0	10.0	9.8					12.5		6.4
3.3	2.9	2.7					2.7		2.5
2.4	2.4	2.3	Sales/Total Assets				2.4		2.1
1.7	1.9	1.9					1.6		1.6
.7	.4	.8					.4		1.4
(41) 1.5	(44) 1.2	(39) 1.4	% Depr., Dep., Amort./Sales				(10) .8		(11) 2.0
2.4	2.0	2.1					1.7		2.7
1.4	1.4	1.6	% Officers', Directors',						
(18) 3.0	(15) 2.4	(12) 3.4	Owners' Comp/Sales						
5.0	3.8	6.8							
1346000M	1791217M	1451069M	Net Sales ($)	1576M	17059M		91260M	114471M	1226703M
627230M	898503M	805752M	Total Assets ($)	726M	7362M		46644M	53534M	697486M

M = $ thousand MM = $ million

See Pages 11 through 21 for Explanation of Ratios and Data

Current Data Sorted By Assets / Comparative Historical Data

0-500M	500M-2MM	2-10MM	10-50MM	50-100MM	100-250MM		4/1/00-3/31/01 ALL	4/1/01-3/31/02 ALL
						Type of Statement		
	1	4	3	3	2	Unqualified	8	9
	2	10	3			Reviewed	15	4
	2	1	1			Compiled	4	6
3	3	1				Tax Returns	6	4
2	3	5	3	1	1	Other	18	11
13 (4/1-9/30/04)			41 (10/1/04-3/31/05)					
5	11	21	10	4	3	**NUMBER OF STATEMENTS**	51	34
%	%	%	%	%	%	**ASSETS**	%	%
	5.2	6.3	6.0			Cash & Equivalents	6.3	4.6
	27.5	30.8	37.1			Trade Receivables (net)	32.9	26.0
	42.5	30.9	30.7			Inventory	34.1	37.0
	2.3	1.5	2.1			All Other Current	1.6	1.5
	77.5	69.5	75.9			Total Current	74.9	69.1
	15.9	22.4	16.0			Fixed Assets (net)	17.2	21.9
	3.6	4.5	2.9			Intangibles (net)	3.9	6.5
	2.9	3.6	5.3			All Other Non-Current	3.9	2.4
	100.0	100.0	100.0			Total	100.0	100.0
						LIABILITIES		
	13.1	13.2	16.6			Notes Payable-Short Term	12.4	15.3
	4.8	3.5	5.0			Cur. Mat.-L/T/D	2.3	2.5
	17.1	16.7	17.5			Trade Payables	17.5	16.4
	.9	.2	.0			Income Taxes Payable	.2	.1
	11.7	11.2	10.8			All Other Current	10.6	10.0
	47.5	44.8	50.0			Total Current	43.0	44.2
	13.4	12.9	7.1			Long-Term Debt	12.3	19.4
	.2	.7	.7			Deferred Taxes	.2	.2
	11.4	6.9	3.7			All Other Non-Current	6.3	1.9
	27.4	34.8	38.6			Net Worth	38.3	34.2
	100.0	100.0	100.0			Total Liabilities & Net Worth	100.0	100.0
						INCOME DATA		
	100.0	100.0	100.0			Net Sales	100.0	100.0
	36.6	35.8	36.1			Gross Profit	34.2	36.2
	31.5	31.1	31.6			Operating Expenses	28.5	34.1
	5.1	4.7	4.5			Operating Profit	5.7	2.1
	1.2	.6	1.4			All Other Expenses (net)	.9	1.0
	3.9	4.0	3.2			Profit Before Taxes	4.8	1.0
						RATIOS		
	2.3	2.7	2.3				2.4	2.5
	1.8	1.7	1.6			Current	1.8	1.7
	1.3	1.1	1.3				1.4	1.1
	1.2	1.6	1.8				1.4	1.2
	.6	.9	.8			Quick	1.0	.7
	.3	.7	.6				.6	.4
	30 12.1	**39** 9.4	**49** 7.5				**37** 9.8	**27** 13.3
	40 9.2	**43** 8.5	**64** 5.7			Sales/Receivables	**51** 7.2	**36** 10.1
	51 7.2	**55** 6.6	**73** 5.0				**56** 6.6	**51** 7.1
	49 7.5	**39** 9.3	**35** 10.5				**45** 8.1	**55** 6.7
	84 4.4	**77** 4.8	**86** 4.2			Cost of Sales/Inventory	**73** 5.0	**79** 4.6
	127 2.9	**102** 3.6	**114** 3.2				**120** 3.0	**135** 2.7
	26 14.0	**20** 17.8	**29** 12.8				**20** 17.9	**18** 20.0
	46 8.0	**29** 12.8	**37** 9.8			Cost of Sales/Payables	**29** 12.7	**34** 10.7
	58 6.3	**45** 8.1	**62** 5.9				**52** 7.1	**55** 6.7
	5.7	4.4	6.0				4.9	4.4
	7.5	10.1	6.6			Sales/Working Capital	7.6	9.1
	15.8	51.2	22.9				17.7	75.9
	7.7	22.3					13.2	10.8
	2.4	(20) 5.3				EBIT/Interest	(45) 4.6	(30) 4.1
	.8	1.9					2.1	.2
		4.6						
		(10) 1.7				Net Profit + Depr., Dep., Amort./Cur. Mat. L/T/D		
		.4						
	.2	.2	.2				.2	.3
	.6	.6	.6			Fixed/Worth	.4	.5
	-6.2	1.5	1.0				1.0	1.9
	1.1	1.0	.7				1.0	.7
	3.5	1.9	1.3			Debt/Worth	1.5	1.8
	-11.0	8.2	7.5				3.5	7.9
		40.3					56.8	32.8
		(19) 25.6				% Profit Before Taxes/Tangible Net Worth	(46) 26.1	(29) 20.2
		10.6					13.0	-5.5
	10.6	18.9	17.4				19.6	13.9
	3.5	10.4	7.6			% Profit Before Taxes/Total Assets	9.0	5.9
	-.5	2.6	-1.3				2.4	-3.6
	44.0	52.0	36.5				36.6	26.5
	29.2	14.2	14.3			Sales/Net Fixed Assets	17.4	12.4
	10.9	7.2	8.4				7.8	8.1
	3.3	3.0	2.6				3.0	2.9
	2.8	2.5	2.1			Sales/Total Assets	2.3	2.2
	1.8	1.8	1.9				1.8	1.6
		.7					.8	1.0
		(20) 1.9				% Depr., Dep., Amort./Sales	(43) 1.0	(25) 2.0
		2.7					2.7	3.6
		1.6					2.1	3.7
		(10) 2.9				% Officers', Directors', Owners' Comp/Sales	(20) 4.9	(11) 6.1
		4.1					9.5	9.8
4369M	35056M	224446M	416214M	475827M	648047M	Net Sales ($)	1295926M	855744M
1669M	14227M	91644M	199793M	239050M	436213M	Total Assets ($)	668703M	518880M

M = $ thousand MM = $ million

See Pages 11 through 21 for Explanation of Ratios and Data

Comparative Historical Data							Current Data Sorted By Sales					
						Type of Statement						
	7		8		13	Unqualified		1		1	4	7
	17		14		15	Reviewed		1	3	3	6	2
	6		7		4	Compiled		1		2		1
	3		2		7	Tax Returns	1	4	1		1	
	14		18		15	Other	2	2	1	3	2	5
	4/1/02-		4/1/03-		4/1/04-			13 (4/1-9/30/04)		41 (10/1/04-3/31/05)		
	3/31/03		3/31/04		3/31/05							
	ALL		ALL		ALL		0-1MM	1-3MM	3-5MM	5-10MM	10-25MM	25MM & OVER
	47		49		54	**NUMBER OF STATEMENTS**	3	9	5	9	13	15
	%		%		%	**ASSETS**	%	%	%	%	%	%
	6.3		5.9		5.2	Cash & Equivalents					6.4	4.3
	32.3		29.8		31.8	Trade Receivables (net)					32.3	38.2
	32.6		30.0		30.9	Inventory					33.8	25.4
	3.8		2.3		2.2	All Other Current					1.2	2.3
	75.1		68.0		70.1	Total Current					73.7	70.2
	17.3		22.0		19.3	Fixed Assets (net)					17.8	19.0
	3.5		5.1		6.9	Intangibles (net)					6.0	6.7
	4.2		5.0		3.8	All Other Non-Current					2.5	4.1
	100.0		100.0		100.0	Total					100.0	100.0
						LIABILITIES						
	16.4		14.7		11.6	Notes Payable-Short Term					19.9	9.9
	3.8		4.5		3.9	Cur. Mat.-L/T/D					5.8	1.2
	16.0		15.9		17.0	Trade Payables					16.4	18.6
	.5		.5		.3	Income Taxes Payable					.3	.1
	12.0		9.5		12.8	All Other Current					15.4	12.1
	48.7		45.2		45.7	Total Current					57.9	41.9
	10.7		14.9		18.9	Long-Term Debt					7.7	21.0
	.3		.3		.5	Deferred Taxes					1.0	.6
	2.9		6.6		6.4	All Other Non-Current					6.7	3.7
	37.5		33.0		28.5	Net Worth					26.8	32.8
	100.0		100.0		100.0	Total Liabilities & Net Worth					100.0	100.0
						INCOME DATA						
	100.0		100.0		100.0	Net Sales					100.0	100.0
	34.0		36.3		35.5	Gross Profit					39.5	29.7
	32.2		32.3		31.0	Operating Expenses					32.9	25.3
	1.7		4.0		4.4	Operating Profit					6.6	4.4
	1.2		1.1		1.3	All Other Expenses (net)					.8	1.8
	.5		2.8		3.1	Profit Before Taxes					5.8	2.6
						RATIOS						
	2.2		2.2		2.4						1.7	2.2
	1.5		1.6		1.7	Current					1.5	1.7
	1.2		1.1		1.1						.9	1.4
	1.3		1.3		1.4						1.1	1.6
	.8		.8		.9	Quick					.7	.9
	.6		.6		.5						.4	.7
33	11.2	40	9.1	40	9.2						37 9.8	56 6.5
45	8.1	48	7.6	51	7.2	Sales/Receivables					41 8.9	64 5.7
63	5.8	59	6.2	64	5.7						55 6.7	73 5.0
32	11.3	43	8.4	45	8.2						51 7.2	33 11.1
77	4.8	82	4.4	80	4.6	Cost of Sales/Inventory					77 4.8	79 4.6
110	3.3	118	3.1	111	3.3						93 3.9	96 3.8
18	20.0	22	16.3	26	14.1						23 15.8	29 12.6
33	11.0	41	8.8	41	8.9	Cost of Sales/Payables					38 9.5	39 9.3
45	8.1	59	6.2	55	6.7						46 7.9	60 6.1
	5.2		4.7		5.6						7.2	5.4
	9.1		8.8		7.6	Sales/Working Capital					10.9	6.5
	21.3		105.5		38.0						NM	10.1
	8.9		10.0		12.2						24.2	12.6
(42)	3.0	(47)	2.6	(51)	4.0	EBIT/Interest				(12)	9.4	(14) 3.6
	.3		-.3		.8						3.6	.3
	5.9		4.9		9.4	Net Profit + Depr., Dep.,						
(15)	1.2	(17)	1.4	(20)	3.0	Amort./Cur. Mat. L/T/D						
	.1		-1.6		1.0							
	.1		.2		.2						.2	.2
	.5		.7		.6	Fixed/Worth					.7	.7
	1.2		8.5		2.7						NM	2.2
	.6		.7		1.0						1.6	.8
	1.9		2.0		2.8	Debt/Worth					3.1	3.7
	5.0		21.2		11.5						NM	9.0
	36.0		36.5		42.3	% Profit Before Taxes/Tangible					53.3	32.7
(41)	9.8	(39)	15.4	(44)	22.3	Net Worth				(10)	39.6	(14) 14.2
	-3.4		2.4		.7						26.3	-2.7
	12.0		15.9		15.9	% Profit Before Taxes/Total					19.2	9.8
	3.1		3.8		7.0	Assets					11.9	4.0
	-1.8		-3.7		-.6						7.1	-.7
	67.2		39.2		40.1						52.0	43.7
	19.9		13.5		14.1	Sales/Net Fixed Assets					24.0	13.3
	9.8		4.9		7.8						10.4	6.0
	3.0		2.6		3.0						3.2	2.8
	2.5		2.0		2.1	Sales/Total Assets					2.7	1.8
	2.0		1.5		1.7						2.0	1.6
	.5		1.0		.8						.4	.5
(42)	1.4	(37)	1.8	(47)	2.0	% Depr., Dep., Amort./Sales				(11)	1.1	(14) 2.4
	2.8		3.7		2.7						2.6	3.3
	2.8		3.1		2.1	% Officers', Directors',						
(22)	4.6	(18)	5.1	(21)	3.8	Owners' Comp/Sales						
	7.0		7.0		5.5							
1051834M		1456692M		1803959M		Net Sales ($)	1499M	18921M	21591M	61325M	201126M	1499497M
659739M		918624M		982596M		Total Assets ($)	1014M	8651M	12490M	30805M	82233M	847403M

© RMA 2005

M = $ thousand   MM = $ million
See Pages 11 through 21 for Explanation of Ratios and Data

Current Data Sorted By Assets **Comparative Historical Data**

0-500M	500M-2MM	2-10MM	10-50MM	50-100MM	100-250MM	Type of Statement	4/1/00-3/31/01 ALL	4/1/01-3/31/02 ALL
	1	1	2		1	Unqualified	6	6
2	1	9	2			Reviewed	6	6
4	3	4				Compiled	8	6
	1					Tax Returns	2	1
1	1	3	5	1	2	Other	10	10
	5 (4/1-9/30/04)			39 (10/1/04-3/31/05)				
7	7	17	9	1	3	**NUMBER OF STATEMENTS**	32	29
%	%	%	%	%	%		%	%
						ASSETS		
		5.4				Cash & Equivalents	7.6	7.9
		29.9				Trade Receivables (net)	28.2	24.2
		23.9				Inventory	29.3	32.4
		5.6				All Other Current	2.0	1.9
		64.9				Total Current	67.1	66.4
		19.1				Fixed Assets (net)	17.4	21.9
		4.7				Intangibles (net)	9.9	7.2
		11.3				All Other Non-Current	5.6	4.5
		100.0				Total	100.0	100.0
						LIABILITIES		
		11.5				Notes Payable-Short Term	14.6	13.3
		2.7				Cur. Mat.-L/T/D	3.4	3.6
		13.2				Trade Payables	12.6	10.9
		.6				Income Taxes Payable	.5	.8
		8.0				All Other Current	7.8	7.3
		36.0				Total Current	38.9	35.9
		13.1				Long-Term Debt	10.5	14.2
		.2				Deferred Taxes	.9	.4
		2.5				All Other Non-Current	4.1	5.0
		48.2				Net Worth	45.6	44.4
		100.0				Total Liabilities & Net Worth	100.0	100.0
						INCOME DATA		
		100.0				Net Sales	100.0	100.0
		33.5				Gross Profit	37.7	36.6
		27.9				Operating Expenses	29.7	29.7
		5.6				Operating Profit	8.1	6.9
		.6				All Other Expenses (net)	1.7	1.1
		5.0				Profit Before Taxes	6.3	5.8
						RATIOS		
		2.7				Current	3.3	3.1
		1.6					1.9	1.8
		1.3					1.1	1.2
		1.3				Quick	2.2	1.5
		1.0					.9	.9
		.5					.5	.6
		34 10.8				Sales/Receivables	34 10.7	36 10.3
		51 7.1					49 7.4	41 8.9
		66 5.5					58 6.3	52 7.0
		43 8.4				Cost of Sales/Inventory	55 6.7	57 6.4
		80 4.6					80 4.6	96 3.8
		111 3.3					117 3.1	122 3.0
		16 22.9				Cost of Sales/Payables	15 24.2	13 28.9
		29 12.7					25 14.4	24 15.5
		52 7.0					52 7.0	48 7.6
		4.2				Sales/Working Capital	3.8	3.8
		6.3					6.7	9.0
		13.4					29.3	15.5
		17.6				EBIT/Interest	11.7	7.1
		(16) 7.1					(24) 4.3	(24) 2.7
		3.6					1.5	1.1
						Net Profit + Depr., Dep., Amort./Cur. Mat. L /T/D		
		.2				Fixed/Worth	.2	.2
		.4					.5	.5
		1.0					1.7	1.0
		.5				Debt/Worth	.6	.8
		1.2					1.5	1.3
		2.7					4.6	2.6
		34.3				% Profit Before Taxes/Tangible Net Worth	48.7	43.2
		(16) 24.9					(28) 27.6	(27) 12.0
		11.9					−4.8	.0
		14.9				% Profit Before Taxes/Total Assets	25.5	14.5
		9.5					13.3	6.5
		7.3					−.8	.7
		27.6				Sales/Net Fixed Assets	33.1	22.3
		11.4					12.6	9.8
		5.0					7.2	5.8
		2.8				Sales/Total Assets	2.4	2.5
		1.6					1.9	1.9
		1.1					1.5	1.5
		1.0				% Depr., Dep., Amort./Sales	.9	.9
		(16) 1.8					(26) 1.6	(25) 1.9
		4.6					3.0	4.0
						% Officers', Directors', Owners' Comp/Sales	2.9	
							(15) 5.9	
							9.4	
6645M	21499M	142501M	364890M	83949M	735074M	Net Sales ($)	909673M	1048870M
1806M	8653M	83862M	194211M	51528M	502172M	Total Assets ($)	560363M	585399M

M = $ thousand   MM = $ million
See Pages 11 through 21 for Explanation of Ratios and Data

Comparative Historical Data

Current Data Sorted By Sales

4/1/02-3/31/03 ALL	4/1/03-3/31/04 ALL	4/1/04-3/31/05 ALL	Type of Statement	0-1MM	1-3MM	3-5MM	5-10MM	10-25MM	25MM & OVER
9	10	5	Unqualified		1		1		3
7	11	14	Reviewed	2	1	1	3	6	1
4	7	11	Compiled	2	4	2	3		
2	2	1	Tax Returns		1				
19	9	13	Other	1		1	2	1	8
				5 (4/1-9/30/04)			39 (10/1/04-3/31/05)		
41	39	44	NUMBER OF STATEMENTS	5	7	4	9	7	12
%	%	%	ASSETS	%	%	%	%	%	%
5.6	11.2	7.1	Cash & Equivalents						6.5
20.7	21.2	33.5	Trade Receivables (net)						28.3
31.3	28.8	25.2	Inventory						32.0
2.2	2.1	4.5	All Other Current						5.8
59.8	63.4	70.2	Total Current						72.5
21.5	19.0	16.9	Fixed Assets (net)						17.1
9.6	7.9	6.4	Intangibles (net)						7.3
9.1	9.7	6.5	All Other Non-Current						3.1
100.0	100.0	100.0	Total						100.0
			LIABILITIES						
11.4	10.1	11.7	Notes Payable-Short Term						12.4
3.2	3.4	2.7	Cur. Mat.-L/T/D						3.0
12.4	11.7	14.1	Trade Payables						14.5
.7	1.0	.4	Income Taxes Payable						.5
9.0	8.2	10.0	All Other Current						16.9
36.7	34.5	39.0	Total Current						47.4
18.0	15.1	20.6	Long-Term Debt						24.4
.2	.1	.1	Deferred Taxes						.1
4.8	7.3	2.7	All Other Non-Current						2.1
40.3	43.1	37.6	Net Worth						26.0
100.0	100.0	100.0	Total Liabilities & Net Worth						100.0
			INCOME DATA						
100.0	100.0	100.0	Net Sales						100.0
35.1	37.0	34.7	Gross Profit						29.2
29.1	31.8	29.5	Operating Expenses						25.1
6.0	5.2	5.2	Operating Profit						4.1
2.2	1.2	2.7	All Other Expenses (net)						7.8
3.8	4.0	2.5	Profit Before Taxes						−3.7
			RATIOS						
3.1	3.9	2.9							2.7
1.5	2.0	1.8	Current						1.7
1.0	1.3	1.4							1.0
1.7	1.9	1.6							1.2
.7	.9	1.0	Quick						.7
.4	.5	.6							.4
24 15.0	27 13.7	44 8.3							52 7.1
41 8.9	45 8.1	54 6.7	Sales/Receivables						56 6.5
57 6.4	53 6.9	64 5.7							63 5.8
48 7.6	57 6.4	36 10.2							61 6.0
97 3.8	92 4.0	68 5.3	Cost of Sales/Inventory						85 4.3
138 2.6	138 2.6	99 3.7							110 3.3
19 19.6	22 16.4	17 21.4							25 14.3
30 12.3	32 11.5	31 11.8	Cost of Sales/Payables						38 9.6
49 7.4	54 6.8	47 7.7							46 8.0
3.8	3.7	4.2							4.2
7.7	6.5	6.9	Sales/Working Capital						5.0
508.6	15.2	12.2							NM
8.9	9.7	21.4							74.9
(39) 3.0	(33) 3.9	(40) 5.6	EBIT/Interest					(10)	13.4
.9	2.1	1.5							−3.8
3.9		34.6	Net Profit + Depr., Dep.,						
(12) 2.5		(12) 3.8	Amort./Cur. Mat. L/T/D						
.3		2.1							
.2	.2	.2							.3
.5	.5	.4	Fixed/Worth						.4
1.7	1.3	1.2							7.5
.7	.6	.7							.5
1.6	1.7	1.4	Debt/Worth						1.8
5.1	4.0	6.0							18.3
38.5	40.3	35.2	% Profit Before Taxes/Tangible						38.1
(36) 14.5	(36) 21.3	(38) 25.7	Net Worth					(10)	28.4
2.6	4.2	7.2							−44.5
15.1	13.8	14.9	% Profit Before Taxes/Total						21.4
5.5	5.6	9.1	Assets						4.6
−.2	.2	1.1							−24.4
25.7	29.4	33.8							27.4
10.2	12.0	13.1	Sales/Net Fixed Assets						12.4
5.8	6.0	7.1							6.3
2.3	2.3	3.0							2.2
1.8	1.7	2.2	Sales/Total Assets						1.8
1.3	1.4	1.4							1.4
.9	1.1	.7							.6
(35) 1.6	(29) 2.1	(38) 1.7	% Depr., Dep., Amort./Sales					(10)	1.8
3.8	3.4	2.9							2.5
1.2	3.8	4.2	% Officers', Directors',						
(15) 4.1	(15) 6.6	(12) 6.1	Owners' Comp/Sales						
6.6	8.2	7.7							
1548840M	1295381M	1354558M	Net Sales ($)	3376M	14041M	13885M	63679M	96471M	1163106M
1181740M	832912M	842232M	Total Assets ($)	1149M	7092M	7928M	39157M	52588M	734318M

M = $ thousand   MM = $ million
See Pages 11 through 21 for Explanation of Ratios and Data

Current Data Sorted By Assets							Comparative Historical Data		

			3	9	1	2	Type of Statement	12	11
	1		10	2			Unqualified	12	11
	2		1				Reviewed	15	10
			1				Compiled	14	11
							Tax Returns	1	2
1	3		9	8	2	1	Other	12	14
			10 (4/1-9/30/04)		46 (10/1/04-3/31/05)			4/1/00-3/31/01	4/1/01-3/31/02
0-500M	500M-2MM		2-10MM	10-50MM	50-100MM	100-250MM		ALL	ALL
1	6		24	19	3	3	NUMBER OF STATEMENTS	54	48
%	%		%	%	%	%	ASSETS	%	%
			5.5	2.7			Cash & Equivalents	5.8	7.3
			34.4	27.1			Trade Receivables (net)	30.1	27.0
			33.7	33.8			Inventory	30.4	31.9
			2.2	1.0			All Other Current	2.2	1.7
			75.8	64.6			Total Current	68.5	67.9
			17.5	23.0			Fixed Assets (net)	22.4	20.9
			.7	3.1			Intangibles (net)	4.4	7.8
			6.1	9.3			All Other Non-Current	4.8	3.4
			100.0	100.0			Total	100.0	100.0
							LIABILITIES		
			13.6	15.1			Notes Payable-Short Term	12.1	10.2
			2.3	1.6			Cur. Mat.-L/T/D	4.0	3.8
			19.7	13.2			Trade Payables	17.7	14.8
			.3	.2			Income Taxes Payable	.4	.5
			10.8	14.8			All Other Current	11.1	11.5
			46.7	44.9			Total Current	45.3	40.8
			10.4	13.0			Long-Term Debt	13.9	12.9
			.3	.3			Deferred Taxes	.4	.3
			5.3	7.1			All Other Non-Current	3.3	7.6
			37.4	34.8			Net Worth	37.1	38.5
			100.0	100.0			Total Liabilities & Net Worth	100.0	100.0
							INCOME DATA		
			100.0	100.0			Net Sales	100.0	100.0
			30.0	21.9			Gross Profit	29.2	30.8
			28.2	19.7			Operating Expenses	25.2	28.1
			1.7	2.2			Operating Profit	4.0	2.7
			.6	1.1			All Other Expenses (net)	1.3	1.2
			1.2	1.1			Profit Before Taxes	2.6	1.5
							RATIOS		
			2.0	2.1				2.5	2.6
			1.6	1.4			Current	1.7	1.5
			1.2	1.1				1.2	1.1
			1.2	1.0				1.3	1.5
			.8	.7			Quick	.9	.8
			.7	.5				.6	.5
			43 8.6	42 8.8				37 9.8	35 10.5
			55 6.7	49 7.5			Sales/Receivables	48 7.6	47 7.8
			69 5.3	60 6.1				63 5.8	58 6.3
			42 8.7	48 7.6				45 8.1	52 7.0
			84 4.3	81 4.5			Cost of Sales/Inventory	68 5.3	73 5.0
			105 3.5	144 2.5				105 3.5	116 3.2
			21 17.4	23 16.0				24 14.9	22 16.4
			40 9.0	28 13.1			Cost of Sales/Payables	32 11.5	37 10.0
			59 6.2	40 9.2				51 7.1	46 7.9
			4.4	6.1				5.4	4.5
			8.9	11.0			Sales/Working Capital	9.1	9.4
			12.4	27.0				18.8	27.1
			8.0	8.7				9.6	8.7
		(23)	3.2	5.3			EBIT/Interest	(46) 3.1	(44) 2.4
			-.9	.7				.9	1.0
							Net Profit + Depr., Dep., Amort./Cur. Mat. L/T/D	7.9	20.0
								(15) 4.3	(10) 5.3
								.4	3.2
			.3	.4				.2	.2
			.4	.8			Fixed/Worth	.5	.6
			.9	1.1				1.4	1.8
			.6	1.1				.7	1.0
			1.7	2.3			Debt/Worth	1.9	1.8
			4.8	10.4				4.0	6.4
			36.9	37.1				56.3	53.1
		(22)	16.2	(18) 20.1			% Profit Before Taxes/Tangible Net Worth	(50) 18.8	(42) 11.2
			6.1	-6.6				2.6	.7
			10.7	14.0				17.0	12.8
			6.4	6.1			% Profit Before Taxes/Total Assets	5.2	4.0
			-.7	-.3				.2	.2
			32.0	24.2				27.0	35.0
			12.0	8.8			Sales/Net Fixed Assets	13.5	16.0
			8.3	4.3				5.7	5.8
			2.9	2.8				2.9	2.5
			2.3	1.7			Sales/Total Assets	2.1	2.1
			1.8	1.3				1.6	1.6
			.8	1.1				.9	.7
			1.3	(18) 1.9			% Depr., Dep., Amort./Sales	(44) 1.7	(40) 1.5
			2.1	2.4				2.6	2.8
							% Officers', Directors', Owners' Comp/Sales	1.5	3.1
								(18) 2.7	(17) 6.6
								9.8	10.7
691M	17277M		247031M	1034588M	247056M	959753M	Net Sales ($)	1659378M	1500992M
359M	6596M		113739M	479239M	196805M	615522M	Total Assets ($)	1126403M	1008227M

© RMA 2005

M = $ thousand   MM = $ million
See Pages 11 through 21 for Explanation of Ratios and Data

Comparative Historical Data | **Current Data Sorted By Sales**

			Type of Statement						
19	16	15	Unqualified				2	3	10
12	13	13	Reviewed	1	1		5	5	1
9	8	3	Compiled	1	1			1	
3	2	1	Tax Returns					1	
21	16	24	Other	1	3	1	3	8	8
4/1/02-3/31/03	4/1/03-3/31/04	4/1/04-3/31/05			10 (4/1-9/30/04)			46 (10/1/04-3/31/05)	
ALL	ALL	ALL		0-1MM	1-3MM	3-5MM	5-10MM	10-25MM	25MM & OVER
64	55	56	NUMBER OF STATEMENTS	1	5	3	10	18	19
%	%	%	ASSETS	%	%	%	%	%	%
9.8	7.8	5.7	Cash & Equivalents				3.1	5.3	5.8
27.3	28.2	29.0	Trade Receivables (net)				31.2	34.3	25.6
29.4	23.2	32.2	Inventory				29.5	34.3	26.1
2.0	3.3	1.5	All Other Current				1.5	2.4	1.2
68.5	62.5	68.3	Total Current				65.4	76.2	58.7
21.7	24.0	21.8	Fixed Assets (net)				26.6	14.7	29.4
4.1	5.7	3.5	Intangibles (net)				1.3	1.6	5.7
5.7	7.8	6.4	All Other Non-Current				6.7	7.4	6.2
100.0	100.0	100.0	Total				100.0	100.0	100.0
			LIABILITIES						
10.1	13.1	12.7	Notes Payable-Short Term				9.5	17.1	12.7
2.7	2.5	2.2	Cur. Mat.-L/T/D				3.8	1.1	1.6
13.3	13.9	15.9	Trade Payables				12.3	20.3	13.8
.3	.3	.2	Income Taxes Payable				.2	.5	.1
11.7	13.2	11.6	All Other Current				8.4	11.8	13.5
38.0	43.0	42.6	Total Current				34.3	50.7	41.7
12.1	13.2	13.6	Long-Term Debt				14.1	5.2	17.4
.4	.5	.3	Deferred Taxes				.6	.3	.3
3.6	6.7	7.3	All Other Non-Current				2.6	4.6	6.6
45.8	36.6	36.2	Net Worth				48.5	39.2	34.0
100.0	100.0	100.0	Total Liabilities & Net Worth				100.0	100.0	100.0
			INCOME DATA						
100.0	100.0	100.0	Net Sales				100.0	100.0	100.0
29.2	30.0	27.2	Gross Profit				33.4	26.9	21.0
25.6	25.7	23.9	Operating Expenses				28.9	24.8	15.2
3.6	4.2	3.3	Operating Profit				4.5	2.1	5.8
1.3	1.1	1.2	All Other Expenses (net)				.0	1.3	1.1
2.3	3.1	2.2	Profit Before Taxes				4.6	.8	4.7
			RATIOS						
3.0	2.5	2.3					2.8	1.9	2.3
1.8	1.4	1.6	Current				1.9	1.4	1.4
1.4	1.1	1.2					1.5	1.1	1.1
1.7	1.5	1.3					1.3	1.2	1.1
.9	.8	.8	Quick				1.0	.7	.7
.6	.5	.5					.7	.5	.5
35 10.5	36 10.2	39 9.4					36 10.1	48 7.7	34 10.9
48 7.6	50 7.3	48 7.7	Sales/Receivables				48 7.7	59 6.2	46 8.0
58 6.3	62 5.9	60 6.1					68 5.4	70 5.2	52 7.1
45 8.1	32 11.3	45 8.2					48 7.6	38 9.7	44 8.2
68 5.3	54 6.7	75 4.9	Cost of Sales/Inventory				75 4.8	90 4.1	52 7.0
98 3.7	73 5.0	107 3.4					112 3.2	145 2.5	81 4.5
22 16.9	23 16.0	21 17.4					15 24.1	35 10.3	20 18.5
31 11.8	32 11.5	31 11.6	Cost of Sales/Payables				24 15.4	41 8.8	24 15.3
45 8.2	42 8.7	50 7.3					56 6.6	56 6.5	39 9.3
4.6	6.9	4.8					3.7	4.8	6.1
8.0	12.3	8.9	Sales/Working Capital				8.0	10.2	11.0
13.4	30.2	18.1					14.1	17.9	51.8
9.8	8.9	9.4					9.4	8.0	22.3
(54) 2.5	(49) 3.7	(54) 4.9	EBIT/Interest				6.6	(17) 5.2	6.5
.5	.9	1.0					2.7	.0	1.0
13.6	9.1	10.1	Net Profit + Depr., Dep.,						
(20) 3.8	(19) 3.4	(18) 4.0	Amort./Cur. Mat. L/T/D						
.5	1.7	1.1							
.2	.3	.3					.3	.1	.5
.4	.6	.5	Fixed/Worth				.7	.4	.9
1.4	2.5	1.1					1.4	.6	2.0
.4	.7	.8					.5	.8	1.0
1.1	1.8	1.8	Debt/Worth				1.0	1.6	2.8
3.4	8.2	6.3					4.3	3.8	10.4
33.7	38.0	38.1	% Profit Before Taxes/Tangible				33.5	35.9	53.5
(55) 13.9	(46) 23.6	(49) 24.7	Net Worth				24.0	(17) 15.8	(16) 29.2
-.2	3.1	6.5					10.0	5.7	3.5
14.6	13.0	15.2	% Profit Before Taxes/Total				18.0	10.0	18.7
5.2	5.3	6.4	Assets				7.1	6.8	7.4
-1.3	-.2	.2					4.1	.4	.1
19.4	23.5	27.7					12.9	44.3	20.8
11.9	10.9	10.8	Sales/Net Fixed Assets				7.7	24.8	7.4
5.9	6.3	5.6					6.1	7.3	4.3
2.4	2.6	2.8					2.8	3.0	2.8
2.0	2.2	2.1	Sales/Total Assets				2.2	2.2	1.8
1.5	1.4	1.4					1.7	1.2	1.4
1.0	1.0	.9					1.0	.8	1.0
(51) 1.7	(47) 1.6	(51) 1.6	% Depr., Dep., Amort./Sales				1.8	1.2	(16) 1.8
3.0	2.6	2.4					3.5	2.4	2.3
3.1	2.8	1.7	% Officers', Directors',						
(15) 5.6	(14) 7.1	(15) 2.8	Owners' Comp/Sales						
11.9	9.8	8.7							
3671619M	3738437M	2506396M	Net Sales ($)	691M	9291M	12141M	72828M	269669M	2141776M
2103864M	2126958M	1412260M	Total Assets ($)	359M	6001M	6202M	37835M	151017M	1210846M

© RMA 2005

M = $ thousand   MM = $ million
See Pages 11 through 21 for Explanation of Ratios and Data

Current Data Sorted By Assets   **Comparative Historical Data**

0-500M	500M-2MM	2-10MM	10-50MM	50-100MM	100-250MM	Type of Statement	4/1/00-3/31/01 ALL	4/1/01-3/31/02 ALL
	2	3	9	1	1	Unqualified	9	10
		11	3			Reviewed	8	9
	4	1				Compiled	5	5
1	1	2				Tax Returns	1	1
1		7	5		1	Other	17	11
	20 (4/1-9/30/04)		33 (10/1/04-3/31/05)				40	36
2	7	24	17	1	2	**NUMBER OF STATEMENTS**	40	36
%	%	%	%	%	%		%	%

ASSETS

0-500M	500M-2MM	2-10MM	10-50MM	50-100MM	100-250MM		ALL 40	ALL 36
		7.5	13.8			Cash & Equivalents	7.2	4.5
		34.9	24.2			Trade Receivables (net)	30.7	26.6
		30.1	27.8			Inventory	25.5	29.2
		2.7	1.6			All Other Current	3.1	1.2
		75.2	67.3			Total Current	66.5	61.4
		17.0	26.5			Fixed Assets (net)	20.7	25.8
		3.1	2.8			Intangibles (net)	7.0	7.6
		4.7	3.4			All Other Non-Current	5.8	5.2
		100.0	100.0			Total	100.0	100.0

LIABILITIES

0-500M	500M-2MM	2-10MM	10-50MM	50-100MM	100-250MM		ALL 40	ALL 36
		13.9	7.3			Notes Payable-Short Term	11.3	11.1
		2.0	3.3			Cur. Mat.-L/T/D	4.9	6.6
		12.9	11.0			Trade Payables	16.6	12.6
		.1	.2			Income Taxes Payable	.4	.4
		9.4	15.0			All Other Current	8.6	9.7
		38.4	36.8			Total Current	41.8	40.3
		10.6	17.3			Long-Term Debt	17.3	19.9
		.2	1.0			Deferred Taxes	.6	.4
		2.9	5.7			All Other Non-Current	4.6	3.9
		48.0	39.2			Net Worth	35.8	35.4
		100.0	100.0			Total Liabilities & Net Worth	100.0	100.0

INCOME DATA

0-500M	500M-2MM	2-10MM	10-50MM	50-100MM	100-250MM		ALL 40	ALL 36
		100.0	100.0			Net Sales	100.0	100.0
		30.6	24.6			Gross Profit	29.1	29.1
		27.1	17.1			Operating Expenses	22.8	26.0
		3.5	7.4			Operating Profit	6.4	3.1
		.7	1.1			All Other Expenses (net)	1.9	2.5
		2.8	6.4			Profit Before Taxes	4.5	.6

RATIOS

0-500M	500M-2MM	2-10MM	10-50MM	50-100MM	100-250MM		ALL 40	ALL 36
		3.0	3.9			Current	2.5	2.3
		2.0	1.9				1.6	1.8
		1.4	1.4				1.1	1.2
		1.7	2.2			Quick	1.3	1.4
		1.0	1.0				.9	.7
		.7	.7				.6	.5
	44	8.3	45 8.1			Sales/Receivables	43 8.6	40 9.1
	56	6.5	48 7.6				51 7.1	48 7.6
	69	5.3	57 6.4				72 5.1	59 6.2
	42	8.6	63 5.8			Cost of Sales/Inventory	36 10.2	41 8.8
	84	4.4	77 4.7				58 6.3	82 4.4
	143	2.6	115 3.2				101 3.6	134 2.7
	20	17.9	22 16.8			Cost of Sales/Payables	21 17.2	23 15.8
	30	12.3	27 13.3				36 10.1	29 12.4
	40	9.1	40 9.1				58 6.3	47 7.7
		3.1	2.5			Sales/Working Capital	4.8	4.6
		6.2	5.1				9.1	8.1
		12.1	11.6				26.4	33.8
		9.4	16.3			EBIT/Interest	6.0	4.7
	(22)	3.8	(14) 3.4				(36) 2.0	2.0
		1.2	1.0				.4	-.8
						Net Profit + Depr., Dep., Amort./Cur. Mat. L /T/D	7.1	5.8
							(10) 3.7	(13) 1.6
							.6	1.1
		.1	.3			Fixed/Worth	.3	.3
		.3	.6				.8	.6
		.8	2.4				1.7	1.8
		.6	.6			Debt/Worth	1.0	1.0
		1.0	1.2				2.2	1.8
		2.4	7.0				5.8	4.5
		33.7	32.0			% Profit Before Taxes/Tangible Net Worth	68.8	24.4
	(23)	11.4	(15) 13.9				(35) 31.3	(31) 5.9
		1.1	6.2				-1.0	-2.8
		15.5	14.4			% Profit Before Taxes/Total Assets	14.6	7.6
		6.3	6.5				5.1	2.7
		.5	.8				-2.5	-2.6
		56.6	15.3			Sales/Net Fixed Assets	28.2	19.3
		16.6	6.4				13.8	8.5
		5.7	3.6				5.1	3.6
		2.9	2.2			Sales/Total Assets	2.6	2.4
		1.9	1.7				1.8	1.8
		1.4	1.2				1.4	1.4
		.9	1.7			% Depr., Dep., Amort./Sales	.7	.9
	(23)	1.8	(16) 2.7				(33) 2.1	(35) 2.6
		3.7	4.3				4.5	3.9
						% Officers', Directors', Owners' Comp/Sales	1.6	1.3
							(11) 4.0	(10) 4.8
							5.2	5.8
2261M	15184M	243034M	552054M	90389M	451134M	Net Sales ($)	1745025M	1045029M
609M	6691M	116363M	319852M	73840M	283087M	Total Assets ($)	1248659M	682594M

M = $ thousand   MM = $ million
See Pages 11 through 21 for Explanation of Ratios and Data

Comparative Historical Data | | | | **Current Data Sorted By Sales** | | | | | |

			Type of Statement						
12	14	16	Unqualified	1	1	1	1	4	8
10	8	14	Reviewed		3		2	8	1
5	4	5	Compiled			3	1	1	
2	3	4	Tax Returns		2	1	1		
18	13	14	Other	1		2	3	3	5
4/1/02-3/31/03 ALL	4/1/03-3/31/04 ALL	4/1/04-3/31/05 ALL		0-1MM	1-3MM	3-5MM	5-10MM	10-25MM	25MM & OVER
				20 (4/1-9/30/04)			33 (10/1/04-3/31/05)		
47	42	53	**NUMBER OF STATEMENTS**	2	6	8	7	16	14
%	%	%	**ASSETS**	%	%	%	%	%	%
8.2	8.7	9.1	Cash & Equivalents					10.0	6.0
26.6	31.9	31.8	Trade Receivables (net)					34.4	28.9
27.0	24.5	27.9	Inventory					23.8	30.8
3.9	2.6	1.9	All Other Current					3.1	2.3
65.7	67.7	70.7	Total Current					71.3	68.0
21.7	24.2	22.5	Fixed Assets (net)					21.4	27.7
7.0	3.3	3.2	Intangibles (net)					2.4	2.2
5.6	4.7	3.6	All Other Non-Current					4.9	2.1
100.0	100.0	100.0	Total					100.0	100.0
			LIABILITIES						
9.6	12.2	11.0	Notes Payable-Short Term					10.7	9.2
4.2	4.4	2.3	Cur. Mat.-L/T/D					2.0	3.3
12.8	13.4	13.0	Trade Payables					13.3	13.8
.4	.0	.2	Income Taxes Payable					.2	.5
7.0	10.1	11.6	All Other Current					16.8	12.5
34.0	40.2	38.0	Total Current					43.0	39.3
14.7	19.0	14.6	Long-Term Debt					10.9	17.5
.6	.4	.4	Deferred Taxes					.5	.7
5.7	7.3	5.9	All Other Non-Current					3.3	6.9
45.1	33.2	41.0	Net Worth					42.2	35.6
100.0	100.0	100.0	Total Liabilities & Net Worth					100.0	100.0
			INCOME DATA						
100.0	100.0	100.0	Net Sales					100.0	100.0
28.0	27.1	28.9	Gross Profit					26.4	23.9
24.9	24.3	23.7	Operating Expenses					20.3	18.0
3.1	2.8	5.2	Operating Profit					6.1	5.9
1.9	1.9	.7	All Other Expenses (net)					.9	1.4
1.1	.9	4.5	Profit Before Taxes					5.3	4.5
			RATIOS						
3.5	2.7	3.1						2.6	2.6
2.0	1.7	2.0	Current					1.8	1.6
1.4	1.3	1.4						1.3	1.2
1.8	1.3	1.7						1.9	1.2
.9	1.0	1.0	Quick					1.0	.8
.6	.6	.7						.7	.6
40 9.0	44 8.4	43 8.6						44 8.3	46 7.9
52 7.1	52 7.0	51 7.2	Sales/Receivables					56 6.6	51 7.1
62 5.9	68 5.4	65 5.6						64 5.7	60 6.1
38 9.5	39 9.3	43 8.6						34 10.6	59 6.2
79 4.6	67 5.5	75 4.9	Cost of Sales/Inventory					64 5.7	69 5.3
124 2.9	99 3.7	119 3.1						94 3.9	108 3.4
21 17.2	16 23.3	21 17.3						22 16.4	23 15.8
30 12.2	26 14.2	30 12.2	Cost of Sales/Payables					30 12.0	33 10.9
42 8.6	49 7.4	42 8.7						40 9.2	44 8.3
3.2	4.0	3.9						3.3	4.5
6.2	7.5	6.1	Sales/Working Capital					8.0	8.8
12.4	14.1	12.4						12.5	15.3
7.6	8.0	8.6						31.7	16.3
(44) 3.5	(41) 2.0	(47) 3.6	EBIT/Interest					(14) 8.2	(13) 4.7
.6	-.5	1.2						2.2	.2
2.0		13.3	Net Profit + Depr., Dep.,						
(15) 1.2		(11) 2.8	Amort./Cur. Mat. L/T/D						
.9		1.7							
.3	.3	.2						.1	.4
.6	.6	.6	Fixed/Worth					.6	.6
1.4	3.3	1.2						.9	2.3
.6	.6	.6						.8	.6
1.3	1.9	1.2	Debt/Worth					1.2	1.3
5.7	9.0	3.4						3.1	5.3
23.4	23.6	34.3	% Profit Before Taxes/Tangible					36.7	49.5
(42) 5.3	(35) 7.4	(47) 12.6	Net Worth					(15) 23.5	(12) 14.5
-2.8	-3.7	2.0						9.0	.1
8.1	10.1	16.0	% Profit Before Taxes/Total					16.4	22.1
3.3	1.6	6.5	Assets					10.6	6.4
-1.6	-3.3	.8						2.6	-2.0
18.2	31.1	22.7						53.7	13.8
9.5	9.0	10.5	Sales/Net Fixed Assets					13.6	7.9
4.2	3.8	5.0						4.4	4.4
2.5	2.4	2.5						2.6	2.5
1.7	1.9	1.8	Sales/Total Assets					2.0	1.8
1.2	1.3	1.3						1.3	1.5
1.6	.8	1.2						.9	1.6
(43) 2.6	(37) 1.9	(50) 2.3	% Depr., Dep., Amort./Sales					(15) 1.6	2.4
4.2	3.9	3.8						2.7	4.3
2.2	3.9	3.3	% Officers', Directors',						
(14) 5.3	(11) 5.6	(16) 5.8	Owners' Comp/Sales						
6.9	7.4	8.4							
1006134M	756217M	1354056M	Net Sales ($)	1818M	12195M	32030M	51825M	253059M	1003129M
732385M	521832M	800442M	Total Assets ($)	1311M	4926M	34065M	29906M	139409M	590825M

M = $ thousand   MM = $ million
See Pages 11 through 21 for Explanation of Ratios and Data

Current Data Sorted By Assets   **Comparative Historical Data**

0-500M	500M-2MM	2-10MM	10-50MM	50-100MM	100-250MM	Type of Statement	4/1/00-3/31/01 ALL	4/1/01-3/31/02 ALL
	1	5	4	2	3	Unqualified	9	13
	4	8				Reviewed	25	13
	1	4				Compiled	10	7
	2	1				Tax Returns	2	1
	3	9	1	1	2	Other	13	17
	11 (4/1-9/30/04)	40 (10/1/04-3/31/05)						
	11	**27**	**5**	**3**	**5**	**NUMBER OF STATEMENTS**	**59**	**51**
%	%	%	%	%	%	**ASSETS**	%	%
	7.0	7.7				Cash & Equivalents	6.9	5.4
	46.0	32.2				Trade Receivables (net)	38.0	37.0
	24.9	29.9				Inventory	22.3	23.4
	.7	1.7				All Other Current	5.0	5.5
	78.6	71.5				Total Current	72.3	71.3
	16.7	20.4				Fixed Assets (net)	18.7	18.6
	1.3	2.9				Intangibles (net)	3.6	3.4
	3.5	5.2				All Other Non-Current	5.4	6.1
	100.0	100.0				Total	100.0	100.0
						LIABILITIES		
	10.0	19.7				Notes Payable-Short Term	16.6	14.7
	3.5	2.4				Cur. Mat.-L/T/D	2.3	3.6
	20.0	13.7				Trade Payables	19.6	19.7
	.4	.6				Income Taxes Payable	.2	.3
	15.3	9.0				All Other Current	11.3	11.3
	49.2	45.4				Total Current	50.0	49.6
	8.3	10.7				Long-Term Debt	11.3	10.1
	.4	.4				Deferred Taxes	.5	.2
	20.0	5.3				All Other Non-Current	3.9	3.9
	22.2	38.2				Net Worth	34.3	35.7
	100.0	100.0				Total Liabilities & Net Worth	100.0	100.0
						INCOME DATA		
	100.0	100.0				Net Sales	100.0	100.0
	29.3	28.0				Gross Profit	28.0	29.7
	25.4	22.7				Operating Expenses	22.9	24.3
	4.0	5.3				Operating Profit	5.0	5.5
	−1.1	1.4				All Other Expenses (net)	1.3	1.4
	5.0	3.9				Profit Before Taxes	3.8	4.1
						RATIOS		
	3.1	2.2					2.4	2.4
	1.5	1.4				Current	1.4	1.5
	1.0	1.2					1.0	1.1
	1.5	1.1					1.3	1.5
	1.2	.8				Quick	.8	.8
	.9	.6					.6	.6
	(37) 9.9	(40) 9.0					(44) 8.4	(39) 9.5
	(49) 7.5	(49) 7.4				Sales/Receivables	(53) 6.9	(50) 7.3
	(74) 4.9	(63) 5.8					(75) 4.9	(66) 5.5
	(13) 27.8	(53) 6.9					(29) 12.6	(27) 13.6
	(34) 10.7	(61) 5.9				Cost of Sales/Inventory	(55) 6.6	(54) 6.7
	(90) 4.1	(91) 4.0					(79) 4.6	(71) 5.1
	(14) 26.2	(20) 18.6					(20) 18.6	(20) 18.0
	(24) 15.5	(29) 12.7				Cost of Sales/Payables	(34) 10.6	(33) 11.2
	(55) 6.6	(40) 9.0					(47) 7.7	(52) 7.0
	5.0	4.4					5.5	6.5
	8.1	11.5				Sales/Working Capital	12.5	9.3
	187.0	24.8					−200.8	82.8
		15.2					6.3	9.6
		(25) 5.5				EBIT/Interest	(56) 2.7	(49) 3.3
		1.4					1.2	1.0
						Net Profit + Depr., Dep.,	3.9	5.9
						Amort./Cur. Mat. L /T/D	(12) 2.1	(19) 3.1
							.0	.7
	.1	.2					.2	.3
	.2	.5				Fixed/Worth	.6	.5
	3.5	1.4					2.2	.9
	.5	.6					.8	.8
	1.8	2.2				Debt/Worth	2.6	2.1
	24.9	5.6					11.5	5.1
		50.8				% Profit Before Taxes/Tangible	54.8	58.8
		(25) 24.7				Net Worth	(54) 21.6	(47) 20.8
		4.9					5.1	3.5
	30.6	19.7					12.1	12.5
	7.7	6.1				% Profit Before Taxes/Total	4.8	6.4
	3.2	.9				Assets	1.1	.0
	103.6	24.7					45.1	35.2
	26.8	12.9				Sales/Net Fixed Assets	17.7	13.9
	17.2	7.8					5.7	7.3
	4.2	2.5					3.0	3.4
	3.0	2.3				Sales/Total Assets	2.5	2.3
	2.1	1.6					1.8	1.7
		.5					.8	.7
		(23) 1.8				% Depr., Dep., Amort./Sales	(52) 1.5	(47) 1.6
		3.0					2.8	2.8
		3.0					4.3	.8
		(15) 5.0				% Officers', Directors',	(22) 7.1	(19) 5.1
		8.4				Owners' Comp/Sales	9.4	8.8
	41576M	296427M	230199M	260429M	705236M	Net Sales ($)	1311627M	1322964M
	14385M	133495M	119092M	183562M	844975M	Total Assets ($)	978033M	821729M

(0-500M column: DATA NOT AVAILABLE)

M = $ thousand   MM = $ million
See Pages 11 through 21 for Explanation of Ratios and Data

Comparative Historical Data

Current Data Sorted By Sales

4/1/02-3/31/03 ALL	4/1/03-3/31/04 ALL	4/1/04-3/31/05 ALL		0-1MM	1-3MM	3-5MM	5-10MM	10-25MM	25MM & OVER
			Type of Statement						
12	9	15	Unqualified			1	2	4	8
12	14	12	Reviewed		2	2	5	3	
9	8	5	Compiled			1	1	3	
2	1	3	Tax Returns		2	1			
9	6	16	Other		1	2	4	5	4
					11 (4/1-9/30/04)		40 (10/1/04-3/31/05)		
44	38	51	**NUMBER OF STATEMENTS**		5	7	12	15	12
%	%	%	**ASSETS**	%	%	%	%	%	%
7.4	7.4	8.4	Cash & Equivalents	DATA NOT AVAILABLE			7.2	6.9	11.8
36.2	37.4	33.3	Trade Receivables (net)				36.2	34.7	25.3
21.7	25.0	26.1	Inventory				27.3	32.2	17.0
4.7	3.9	2.6	All Other Current				1.9	1.8	6.1
69.9	73.7	70.3	Total Current				72.6	75.5	60.2
22.7	18.1	19.1	Fixed Assets (net)				19.7	18.1	18.7
2.8	4.0	4.6	Intangibles (net)				4.2	1.1	12.0
4.7	4.2	5.9	All Other Non-Current				3.6	5.3	9.1
100.0	100.0	100.0	Total				100.0	100.0	100.0
			LIABILITIES						
11.2	13.3	13.5	Notes Payable-Short Term				24.3	18.9	3.0
2.8	2.9	2.6	Cur. Mat.-L/T/D				2.9	1.8	2.2
16.0	16.2	14.4	Trade Payables				17.0	13.4	10.5
.3	.2	.5	Income Taxes Payable				.3	.9	.4
10.3	9.1	10.4	All Other Current				8.3	9.5	10.2
40.6	41.7	41.4	Total Current				52.8	44.5	26.3
10.4	8.9	11.1	Long-Term Debt				7.8	12.8	10.1
.1	.3	.4	Deferred Taxes				.5	.5	.7
3.4	4.3	8.4	All Other Non-Current				19.0	8.1	4.4
45.6	44.8	38.6	Net Worth				19.9	34.1	58.5
100.0	100.0	100.0	Total Liabilities & Net Worth				100.0	100.0	100.0
			INCOME DATA						
100.0	100.0	100.0	Net Sales				100.0	100.0	100.0
30.4	27.8	28.1	Gross Profit				29.2	25.8	27.0
26.7	24.4	22.7	Operating Expenses				22.8	18.9	20.0
3.7	3.5	5.4	Operating Profit				6.4	6.9	7.0
.6	.7	.6	All Other Expenses (net)				.8	1.2	.4
3.0	2.8	4.7	Profit Before Taxes				5.6	5.7	6.5
			RATIOS						
3.1	3.3	3.1					1.8	2.5	3.6
1.8	1.9	1.6	Current				1.2	1.7	2.9
1.3	1.3	1.2					1.1	1.3	1.4
1.6	2.0	1.5					1.1	1.1	2.3
1.1	1.1	1.0	Quick				.7	.8	1.5
.7	.8	.7					.6	.6	.8
44 8.4	**44** 8.3	**42** 8.6					**43** 8.6	**40** 9.1	**49** 7.4
54 6.8	**52** 7.0	**50** 7.3	Sales/Receivables				**50** 7.3	**47** 7.7	**60** 6.1
71 5.2	**73** 5.0	**63** 5.8					**62** 5.9	**63** 5.8	**65** 5.6
22 16.5	**28** 13.1	**39** 9.3					**41** 9.0	**51** 7.2	**37** 9.8
47 7.7	**46** 7.9	**61** 5.9	Cost of Sales/Inventory				**58** 6.3	**65** 5.6	**66** 5.5
76 4.8	**77** 4.7	**90** 4.1					**83** 4.4	**92** 4.0	**84** 4.4
21 17.1	**16** 23.2	**21** 17.6					**22** 16.8	**19** 19.1	**26** 14.1
30 12.1	**29** 12.5	**30** 12.4	Cost of Sales/Payables				**33** 11.2	**28** 12.9	**32** 11.5
41 9.0	**48** 7.7	**45** 8.2					**44** 8.4	**40** 9.2	**61** 6.0
4.2	4.6	4.4					7.9	3.8	2.3
7.3	6.4	7.0	Sales/Working Capital				17.1	7.0	4.8
20.0	16.1	19.8					147.5	24.8	8.1
17.5	25.1	16.3					34.6	15.2	40.5
(38) 4.5	(36) 5.8	(47) 6.2	EBIT/Interest				4.5	(13) 8.2	6.8
1.1	1.4	2.0					1.9	2.9	4.8
5.7	3.0	13.1							
(17) 2.3	(11) .8	(14) 2.8	Net Profit + Depr., Dep., Amort./Cur. Mat. L/T/D						
-.3	.0	.9							
.2	.1	.2					.3	.1	.2
.4	.3	.5	Fixed/Worth				1.0	.5	.4
1.0	1.1	1.3					2.2	1.1	1.0
.6	.5	.5					.9	1.1	.4
1.1	1.6	1.6	Debt/Worth				2.9	2.0	.9
2.9	2.5	3.9					23.5	8.0	1.5
38.1	33.3	54.7					59.7	52.5	48.2
(42) 16.4	(35) 18.7	(46) 21.2	% Profit Before Taxes/Tangible Net Worth				(11) 24.7	(13) 31.3	20.0
3.2	6.1	5.2					7.0	8.6	1.4
14.9	14.5	16.7					29.0	21.2	12.8
8.3	6.1	7.4	% Profit Before Taxes/Total Assets				9.4	9.3	7.5
.3	.6	1.7					1.4	3.3	.9
37.3	52.7	29.9					51.9	29.9	11.2
14.1	17.1	12.3	Sales/Net Fixed Assets				14.8	12.9	8.4
5.4	6.8	6.5					8.5	10.1	4.4
3.0	3.1	2.6					3.3	2.7	1.9
2.3	2.2	2.2	Sales/Total Assets				2.4	2.3	1.3
1.6	1.8	1.5					2.0	1.9	1.1
1.0	.7	.8					.3	.8	1.6
(40) 1.7	(35) 1.5	(43) 1.9	% Depr., Dep., Amort./Sales				(10) 1.4	(14) 1.9	(11) 2.6
3.1	2.5	2.8					2.1	2.4	3.4
1.3	1.1	2.7							
(18) 6.0	(16) 4.6	(20) 4.9	% Officers', Directors', Owners' Comp/Sales						
11.8	8.0	8.2							
1233063M	**974613M**	**1533867M**	Net Sales ($)		**11422M**	**29280M**	**90532M**	**225754M**	**1176879M**
695708M	**609541M**	**1295509M**	Total Assets ($)		**6832M**	**12718M**	**37905M**	**100899M**	**1137155M**

M = $ thousand MM = $ million

See Pages 11 through 21 for Explanation of Ratios and Data

Current Data Sorted By Assets   Comparative Historical Data

0-500M	500M-2MM	2-10MM	10-50MM	50-100MM	100-250MM	Type of Statement	4/1/00-3/31/01 ALL	4/1/01-3/31/02 ALL
		4	6	3	1	Unqualified	14	17
	5	12	3			Reviewed	15	21
2	4	5				Compiled	19	18
1	4	1				Tax Returns	3	1
2	3	21	6		5	Other	23	32
25 (4/1-9/30/04)			63 (10/1/04-3/31/05)					
5	16	43	15	3	6	**NUMBER OF STATEMENTS**	74	89
%	%	%	%	%	%	**ASSETS**	%	%
	16.1	10.0	5.7			Cash & Equivalents	8.3	8.0
	38.9	27.6	29.1			Trade Receivables (net)	32.1	28.2
	25.2	32.2	29.8			Inventory	32.6	30.0
	1.6	2.3	3.2			All Other Current	2.9	3.9
	81.9	72.1	67.9			Total Current	75.9	70.1
	10.2	17.0	19.5			Fixed Assets (net)	16.7	19.4
	2.8	4.7	3.5			Intangibles (net)	2.5	5.3
	5.1	6.2	9.2			All Other Non-Current	4.9	5.2
	100.0	100.0	100.0			Total	100.0	100.0
						LIABILITIES		
	13.2	10.7	16.5			Notes Payable-Short Term	10.2	9.2
	1.8	4.0	1.7			Cur. Mat.-L/T/D	2.9	3.8
	12.3	16.3	9.7			Trade Payables	13.8	11.5
	.0	.3	.1			Income Taxes Payable	.8	.2
	8.2	11.6	12.6			All Other Current	11.1	10.3
	35.5	42.8	40.5			Total Current	38.8	35.0
	4.7	12.4	6.5			Long-Term Debt	10.0	14.8
	.0	.3	.4			Deferred Taxes	.4	.4
	2.9	5.0	6.5			All Other Non-Current	5.0	4.4
	56.9	39.5	46.1			Net Worth	45.8	45.4
	100.0	100.0	100.0			Total Liabilities & Net Worth	100.0	100.0
						INCOME DATA		
	100.0	100.0	100.0			Net Sales	100.0	100.0
	41.0	38.3	28.5			Gross Profit	36.2	35.3
	35.9	31.6	22.4			Operating Expenses	29.5	30.7
	5.1	6.7	6.1			Operating Profit	6.6	4.6
	.8	.6	1.0			All Other Expenses (net)	.8	1.5
	4.4	6.1	5.1			Profit Before Taxes	5.8	3.1
						RATIOS		
	5.3	2.2	2.8				3.1	3.6
	3.5	1.5	1.4			Current	2.1	2.1
	1.3	1.3	1.2				1.5	1.4
	2.7	1.3	1.5				1.8	1.9
	2.2	.8	.7			Quick	1.2	1.1
	.9	.6	.6				.7	.7
39 9.4	38 9.6	56 6.5					44 8.2	40 9.1
46 8.0	47 7.8	65 5.6				Sales/Receivables	54 6.8	49 7.4
66 5.6	60 6.1	74 4.9					64 5.7	58 6.3
31 11.7	55 6.7	60 6.1					51 7.2	58 6.3
66 5.5	91 4.0	83 4.4				Cost of Sales/Inventory	95 3.9	87 4.2
147 2.5	155 2.3	140 2.6					132 2.8	137 2.7
12 31.2	21 17.7	15 25.0					19 19.3	17 21.1
31 11.8	39 9.4	25 14.8				Cost of Sales/Payables	32 11.5	29 12.5
43 8.5	62 5.9	56 6.5					50 7.2	42 8.7
	3.6	5.1	4.5				3.8	3.4
	5.2	7.6	7.7			Sales/Working Capital	5.7	6.2
	13.7	11.5	12.0				9.3	9.7
	6.1	15.9	10.3				13.4	7.2
	(12) 2.5	(38) 6.8	(13) 3.6			EBIT/Interest	(64) 4.9	(79) 2.0
	1.2	1.6	1.8				1.9	.8
		3.1				Net Profit + Depr., Dep.,	9.5	4.6
		(10) 1.7				Amort./Cur. Mat. L /T/D	(22) 3.4	(26) 1.8
		.8					1.0	.7
	.1	.2	.2				.2	.2
	.2	.4	.5			Fixed/Worth	.3	.4
	.4	1.0	.9				.7	1.1
	.2	.8	.5				.5	.5
	.8	1.8	1.4			Debt/Worth	1.2	1.4
	1.8	3.8	3.2				2.5	3.8
	42.0	64.7	30.6				39.7	36.1
	8.0	(39) 19.3	18.3			% Profit Before Taxes/Tangible Net Worth	(71) 16.4	(84) 12.2
	.7	6.5	5.2				8.6	-.6
	21.2	20.3	9.8				17.1	12.9
	2.8	8.1	5.6			% Profit Before Taxes/Total Assets	7.8	3.0
	.3	.8	3.4				3.0	-.7
	79.3	32.9	14.9				25.8	21.8
	31.8	16.9	11.5			Sales/Net Fixed Assets	15.4	13.0
	14.7	7.6	4.6				9.0	7.3
	3.2	2.6	2.1				2.5	2.7
	2.7	2.0	1.5			Sales/Total Assets	2.1	2.0
	1.9	1.5	1.2				1.8	1.4
	.4	1.0	1.3				1.0	1.0
	(11) 1.2	(34) 1.8	(13) 2.1			% Depr., Dep., Amort./Sales	(63) 1.9	(79) 2.1
	1.9	2.5	2.8				3.0	3.7
		3.8				% Officers', Directors',	3.1	2.6
		(13) 7.4				Owners' Comp/Sales	(30) 4.7	(29) 4.2
		11.4					8.2	6.9
4474M	46132M	412377M	484889M	450396M	1375871M	Net Sales ($)	1359444M	2160234M
1325M	18116M	205973M	299798M	241991M	954109M	Total Assets ($)	797774M	1597313M

© RMA 2005

M = $ thousand   MM = $ million

See Pages 11 through 21 for Explanation of Ratios and Data

Comparative Historical Data | **Current Data Sorted By Sales**

Current period groupings: 25 (4/1-9/30/04) covers 0-1MM and 1-3MM; 63 (10/1/04-3/31/05) covers 3-5MM through 25MM & Over.

4/1/02-3/31/03 ALL	4/1/03-3/31/04 ALL	4/1/04-3/31/05 ALL	Type of Statement	0-1MM	1-3MM	3-5MM	5-10MM	10-25MM	25MM & OVER
19	17	14	Unqualified			1	1	3	9
16	23	20	Reviewed		3	4	5	5	3
15	14	11	Compiled	2		6	2	1	
4	7	6	Tax Returns		5	1			
26	23	37	Other	1	3	1	14	10	8
80	84	88	**NUMBER OF STATEMENTS**	3	11	13	22	19	20
%	%	%	**ASSETS**	%	%	%	%	%	%
8.6	8.6	10.7	Cash & Equivalents		9.4	18.1	8.0	12.5	8.0
27.1	31.1	30.6	Trade Receivables (net)		38.9	36.7	24.4	31.4	28.4
31.1	28.1	28.7	Inventory		27.0	23.1	34.2	33.3	22.1
2.3	3.4	2.5	All Other Current		2.4	1.5	1.2	4.1	3.3
69.2	71.2	72.5	Total Current		77.8	79.4	67.8	81.2	61.8
18.5	17.1	16.3	Fixed Assets (net)		12.6	9.7	20.1	13.5	22.4
6.7	5.0	4.3	Intangibles (net)		4.0	7.8	3.1	2.2	6.0
5.6	6.7	6.8	All Other Non-Current		5.6	3.1	9.0	3.0	9.8
100.0	100.0	100.0	Total		100.0	100.0	100.0	100.0	100.0
			LIABILITIES						
11.3	10.4	10.8	Notes Payable-Short Term		4.0	15.3	13.0	11.3	8.7
2.6	3.3	2.8	Cur. Mat.-L/T/D		1.5	3.4	2.5	4.9	1.5
13.0	13.9	14.4	Trade Payables		13.0	15.7	16.6	13.8	11.7
.3	.1	.2	Income Taxes Payable		.0	.3	.4	.0	.4
11.3	14.6	11.3	All Other Current		7.9	10.9	11.4	12.9	12.1
38.5	42.3	39.4	Total Current		26.3	45.6	43.8	42.8	34.3
11.4	10.7	9.8	Long-Term Debt		7.7	6.5	13.9	8.2	7.6
.3	.4	.2	Deferred Taxes		.0	.0	.5	.1	.4
8.9	7.6	5.4	All Other Non-Current		9.4	3.5	7.4	2.0	6.4
41.0	38.9	45.1	Net Worth		56.6	44.3	34.4	46.9	51.3
100.0	100.0	100.0	Total Liabilities & Net Worth		100.0	100.0	100.0	100.0	100.0
			INCOME DATA						
100.0	100.0	100.0	Net Sales		100.0	100.0	100.0	100.0	100.0
32.3	35.5	36.1	Gross Profit		39.2	44.9	37.3	34.5	28.5
28.4	32.0	30.6	Operating Expenses		33.6	40.0	31.7	26.1	24.2
3.9	3.5	5.5	Operating Profit		5.6	4.9	5.6	8.4	4.2
1.3	.6	.7	All Other Expenses (net)		.7	.6	.7	.5	.6
2.6	2.9	4.8	Profit Before Taxes		4.9	4.4	4.9	7.9	3.6
			RATIOS						
3.1	2.8	3.3			7.0	3.8	1.9	5.0	2.8
1.8	1.7	1.7	Current		3.8	1.9	1.5	1.5	1.7
1.3	1.1	1.3			1.7	1.2	1.3	1.3	1.2
1.6	1.6	1.9			2.7	2.5	1.0	3.2	1.9
.9	.8	1.0	Quick		2.1	1.1	.6	1.1	.9
.6	.6	.6			1.3	.8	.5	.6	.7
40 9.1	40 9.0	40 9.1			39 9.4	38 9.7	30 12.3	40 9.2	56 6.5
51 7.2	50 7.3	51 7.2	Sales/Receivables		48 7.6	47 7.7	42 8.7	49 7.5	62 5.9
63 5.8	63 5.8	66 5.5			62 5.8	72 5.1	56 6.5	67 5.4	72 5.1
44 8.2	45 8.0	50 7.4			29 12.4	40 9.2	63 5.8	55 6.7	47 7.8
93 3.9	87 4.2	83 4.4	Cost of Sales/Inventory		53 6.9	80 4.6	97 3.8	86 4.2	73 5.0
133 2.7	118 3.1	130 2.8			164 2.2	114 3.2	172 2.1	140 2.6	114 3.2
17 21.4	18 20.2	19 19.1			11 33.9	19 19.0	21 17.6	15 25.0	25 14.7
32 11.6	26 13.8	33 11.0	Cost of Sales/Payables		21 17.7	41 8.8	41 8.8	24 15.5	34 10.8
50 7.2	44 8.3	54 6.8			33 11.1	75 4.8	68 5.3	50 7.3	53 6.9
3.9	4.5	4.3			3.1	4.7	6.1	3.5	4.3
7.1	7.9	7.2	Sales/Working Capital		5.7	7.6	8.0	6.7	7.4
13.9	23.7	11.8			7.3	20.5	12.8	11.5	13.5
7.1	9.3	14.5				13.0		13.4	28.3	16.5
(72) 3.0	(74) 3.7	(73) 5.3	EBIT/Interest		(12) 2.7		(20) 5.2	(15) 14.0	(17) 5.3
-.1	1.0	1.5			1.2		1.2	2.4	1.4
5.3	5.9	7.0							28.4
(24) 1.7	(26) 2.5	(23) 2.6	Net Profit + Depr., Dep., Amort./Cur. Mat. L/T/D						(11) 5.8
.5	1.2	.9							1.7
.2	.2	.2			.0	.1	.3	.1	.2
.5	.5	.3	Fixed/Worth		.2	.2	.6	.3	.5
1.0	1.4	.9			.5	1.3	1.1	.7	.9
.6	.5	.5			.2	.5	1.0	.4	.4
1.7	1.8	1.2	Debt/Worth		.6	1.9	2.0	1.2	.9
3.3	5.3	3.1			1.5	8.7	7.0	2.6	2.9
32.7	33.0	43.2			45.1	40.7	38.2	68.4	29.0
(72) 13.1	(76) 9.7	(81) 18.3	% Profit Before Taxes/Tangible Net Worth	(10) 11.6	(12) 13.0	(20) 18.5	(18) 19.4	(19) 16.1	
-7.2	.7	2.9			.3	.8	3.3	11.3	1.1
12.6	12.7	16.6			31.4	13.1	16.3	32.8	11.5
4.9	4.4	5.6	% Profit Before Taxes/Total Assets		16.8	4.0	5.1	10.3	5.7
-2.2	-.8	.8			.5	.5	.7	3.4	.7
24.2	27.0	32.4			85.1	123.6	27.8	25.4	14.7
13.3	14.5	14.5	Sales/Net Fixed Assets		23.7	46.2	10.9	18.5	10.9
5.7	7.1	7.7			9.2	15.3	5.8	9.8	4.3
2.4	2.8	2.7			3.6	3.0	2.6	2.9	2.4
1.9	2.1	2.0	Sales/Total Assets		2.0	2.7	2.1	1.9	1.5
1.3	1.5	1.4			1.4	1.8	1.5	1.3	1.2
1.2	1.0	1.0			.2		.9	1.1	1.3
(72) 2.3	(74) 1.8	(67) 1.8	% Depr., Dep., Amort./Sales		(10) 1.2		(16) 2.1	(15) 1.4	(17) 2.4
3.6	3.0	2.8			2.4		2.7	2.2	3.8
2.6	1.2	2.4							
(26) 4.0	(33) 3.9	(24) 6.7	% Officers', Directors', Owners' Comp/Sales						
8.3	8.6	10.1							
2134011M	2087681M	2774139M	Net Sales ($)	1205M	21252M	50879M	171568M	288526M	2240709M
1715695M	1247591M	1721312M	Total Assets ($)	738M	10565M	22465M	93791M	156169M	1437584M

M = $ thousand   MM = $ million
See Pages 11 through 21 for Explanation of Ratios and Data

Current Data Sorted By Assets

Comparative Historical Data

						Type of Statement		
	1	5	11	2	2	Unqualified	9	9
	2	9	2			Reviewed	14	16
	6	3				Compiled	8	12
1	2	1	1			Tax Returns	3	4
2	3	9	7		2	Other	15	21
	11 (4/1-9/30/04)		60 (10/1/04-3/31/05)				4/1/00-3/31/01	4/1/01-3/31/02
0-500M	500M-2MM	2-10MM	10-50MM	50-100MM	100-250MM		ALL	ALL
3	14	27	21	2	4	NUMBER OF STATEMENTS	49	62
%	%	%	%	%	%	ASSETS	%	%
	2.9	6.7	3.4			Cash & Equivalents	6.1	8.2
	35.0	23.8	32.2			Trade Receivables (net)	31.0	27.3
	34.2	31.5	28.0			Inventory	28.0	28.3
	1.1	1.6	2.2			All Other Current	1.2	1.9
	73.2	63.6	65.9			Total Current	66.3	65.7
	17.3	20.5	22.7			Fixed Assets (net)	24.3	24.7
	2.8	4.9	3.2			Intangibles (net)	3.9	4.8
	6.6	11.0	8.3			All Other Non-Current	5.5	4.8
	100.0	100.0	100.0			Total	100.0	100.0
						LIABILITIES		
	11.4	13.1	14.8			Notes Payable-Short Term	9.6	14.6
	2.6	3.1	1.7			Cur. Mat.-L/T/D	4.8	3.2
	24.0	15.5	17.3			Trade Payables	16.9	11.9
	.1	.5	.4			Income Taxes Payable	.1	.7
	10.5	10.7	9.4			All Other Current	7.9	7.6
	48.7	42.8	43.6			Total Current	39.2	38.1
	11.1	12.5	11.8			Long-Term Debt	13.1	9.2
	.0	1.0	.3			Deferred Taxes	.3	.3
	12.8	5.7	5.8			All Other Non-Current	4.5	6.2
	27.4	38.0	38.5			Net Worth	42.9	46.1
	100.0	100.0	100.0			Total Liabilities & Net Worth	100.0	100.0
						INCOME DATA		
	100.0	100.0	100.0			Net Sales	100.0	100.0
	30.4	30.4	21.4			Gross Profit	31.2	30.8
	27.3	25.6	16.7			Operating Expenses	23.4	27.0
	3.1	4.8	4.7			Operating Profit	7.8	3.8
	-.3	.9	1.0			All Other Expenses (net)	.9	1.4
	3.4	3.9	3.7			Profit Before Taxes	6.9	2.4
						RATIOS		
	2.2	2.2	2.0				2.7	2.8
	1.6	1.5	1.7			Current	1.8	1.9
	1.2	1.0	1.3				1.2	1.1
	1.2	1.2	1.1				1.5	1.7
	.8	.7	.9			Quick	1.0	.9
	.6	.4	.7				.6	.6
32 11.3	40 9.2	45 8.0					38 9.5	35 10.4
45 8.1	43 8.4	55 6.6				Sales/Receivables	47 7.7	42 8.6
54 6.8	48 7.6	69 5.3					61 6.0	54 6.8
35 10.4	58 6.2	43 8.6					32 11.3	42 8.6
56 6.5	98 3.7	61 6.0				Cost of Sales/Inventory	55 6.7	66 5.5
88 4.1	114 3.2	81 4.5					99 3.7	90 4.1
25 14.6	23 16.0	22 16.5					22 16.4	16 22.4
37 9.9	29 12.5	35 10.4				Cost of Sales/Payables	33 11.2	25 14.6
49 7.5	51 7.1	60 6.1					50 7.3	40 9.0
	7.0	5.1	5.3				5.1	4.5
	11.7	12.7	8.2			Sales/Working Capital	9.0	6.9
	24.2	-145.4	18.2				23.6	43.0
	9.6	8.3	14.5				14.5	6.1
(13)	4.7	(23) 3.5	(20) 5.2			EBIT/Interest	(43) 2.8	(55) 2.7
	2.2	1.6	4.6				1.6	.2
			12.4			Net Profit + Depr., Dep.,		
		(11) 3.6				Amort./Cur. Mat. L./T/D		
			-.1					
	.3	.1	.4				.3	.2
	.6	.4	.5			Fixed/Worth	.6	.5
	NM	2.1	2.9				1.6	1.4
	1.0	.8	.7				.6	.5
	2.3	1.7	1.9			Debt/Worth	1.2	1.1
	NM	4.1	12.1				4.5	3.4
	52.9	38.9	43.8			% Profit Before Taxes/Tangible	59.0	27.8
(11)	30.7	(23) 27.2	(18) 27.9			Net Worth	(45) 32.1	(56) 13.9
	9.5	4.5	10.9				5.8	3.0
	15.8	15.0	18.8			% Profit Before Taxes/Total	26.3	11.4
	11.2	5.1	9.2			Assets	7.8	5.2
	2.9	2.2	4.1				1.8	-.2
	114.9	32.0	13.4				27.8	24.4
	22.1	8.7	10.1			Sales/Net Fixed Assets	9.8	10.6
	8.3	6.5	6.8				6.3	5.3
	3.5	2.7	2.7				3.2	3.0
	3.1	2.2	2.2			Sales/Total Assets	2.4	2.1
	2.3	1.5	1.6				1.7	1.6
	.5	1.2	1.0				.9	1.1
(13)	1.3	(22) 2.0	(18) 1.5			% Depr., Dep., Amort./Sales	(40) 1.9	(55) 2.1
	2.4	2.7	4.3				3.2	4.0
	1.9					% Officers', Directors',	1.9	2.5
(10)	2.6					Owners' Comp/Sales	(18) 3.4	(24) 4.5
	4.2						7.6	9.6
3106M	56207M	284914M	876624M	226383M	1222461M	Net Sales ($)	1139771M	1576117M
879M	18803M	147019M	405397M	162413M	810233M	Total Assets ($)	711333M	986444M

M = $ thousand   MM = $ million
See Pages 11 through 21 for Explanation of Ratios and Data

Comparative Historical Data | Current Data Sorted By Sales

					Type of Statement						
	12		12		21	Unqualified		1	1	1	7	11
	19		14		13	Reviewed		2	2	3	4	2
	8		10		9	Compiled		2	4	2	1	
	3		5		5	Tax Returns	1	2		1	1	
	19		28		23	Other	2	1		5	9	6
	4/1/02-3/31/03 ALL		4/1/03-3/31/04 ALL		4/1/04-3/31/05 ALL			11 (4/1-9/30/04)			60 (10/1/04-3/31/05)	
							0-1MM	1-3MM	3-5MM	5-10MM	10-25MM	25MM & OVER
	61		69		71	NUMBER OF STATEMENTS	3	8	7	12	22	19
	%		%		%	ASSETS	%	%	%	%	%	%
	7.3		5.5		4.8	Cash & Equivalents				4.6	5.6	3.3
	25.9		30.4		29.0	Trade Receivables (net)				31.6	25.9	32.1
	28.7		28.9		30.4	Inventory				32.1	32.4	27.2
	2.0		1.8		1.7	All Other Current				1.6	1.9	2.5
	63.9		66.7		65.9	Total Current				69.9	65.9	65.1
	25.7		22.3		20.6	Fixed Assets (net)				13.9	21.5	23.6
	5.2		3.8		4.3	Intangibles (net)				2.5	2.9	4.3
	5.2		7.3		9.2	All Other Non-Current				13.7	9.7	7.0
	100.0		100.0		100.0	Total				100.0	100.0	100.0
						LIABILITIES						
	12.8		12.4		12.2	Notes Payable-Short Term				16.7	13.2	12.2
	4.3		3.6		2.7	Cur. Mat.-L/T/D				.9	1.8	1.6
	13.3		16.7		17.0	Trade Payables				22.2	15.4	14.8
	.3		.2		.3	Income Taxes Payable				.6	.2	.4
	8.4		8.5		10.0	All Other Current				9.2	9.1	11.0
	39.0		41.5		42.2	Total Current				49.7	39.8	40.0
	15.9		15.6		13.0	Long-Term Debt				3.7	12.7	13.7
	.4		.2		.5	Deferred Taxes				.3	.9	.4
	6.8		6.5		7.3	All Other Non-Current				14.2	5.2	8.1
	37.9		36.2		36.9	Net Worth				32.1	41.4	37.7
	100.0		100.0		100.0	Total Liabilities & Net Worth				100.0	100.0	100.0
						INCOME DATA						
	100.0		100.0		100.0	Net Sales				100.0	100.0	100.0
	27.0		28.0		28.7	Gross Profit				33.7	27.6	23.2
	25.8		24.2		23.5	Operating Expenses				29.8	21.5	16.9
	1.2		3.8		5.2	Operating Profit				3.9	6.1	6.4
	1.0		1.2		.7	All Other Expenses (net)				.5	.5	1.5
	.2		2.6		4.4	Profit Before Taxes				3.4	5.5	4.9
						RATIOS						
	2.6		2.4		2.4					1.8	2.5	2.8
	1.6		1.6		1.6	Current				1.5	1.7	1.8
	1.1		1.2		1.2					1.0	1.3	1.1
	1.4		1.3		1.2					1.2	1.2	1.6
	.7		.9		.8	Quick				.6	.9	1.0
	.5		.6		.6					.4	.5	.7
38	9.7	40	9.1	42	8.7				33	11.0	42 8.8	46 8.0
45	8.1	48	7.6	47	7.7	Sales/Receivables			47	7.8	46 7.9	50 7.2
52	7.0	60	6.1	56	6.5				62	5.8	58 6.3	59 6.2
46	7.9	51	7.2	42	8.8				41	8.8	59 6.2	41 8.8
66	5.5	69	5.3	70	5.2	Cost of Sales/Inventory			75	4.8	77 4.8	53 6.9
98	3.7	97	3.7	106	3.4				136	2.7	107 3.4	81 4.5
21	17.8	25	14.9	23	16.0				28	12.9	21 17.7	21 17.8
28	13.1	34	10.9	32	11.5	Cost of Sales/Payables			38	9.6	29 12.5	32 11.5
40	9.1	43	8.5	45	8.1				56	6.5	59 6.1	37 9.9
	4.7		5.3		5.2					6.4	4.2	4.5
	8.8		9.5		8.5	Sales/Working Capital				12.3	7.5	8.2
	34.6		25.0		26.4					NM	19.2	25.7
	7.3		10.2		13.9						16.1	25.2
(55)	1.6	(65)	3.9	(65)	5.3	EBIT/Interest				(21) 5.8	(18) 6.2
	-.7		.7		2.3						2.5	3.9
	4.5		4.6		12.5	Net Profit + Depr., Dep.,					12.4	
(22)	1.7	(16)	2.5	(23)	4.2	Amort./Cur. Mat. L/T/D				(10) 2.9	
	.6		.9		2.1						1.7	
	.2		.2		.2					.1	.2	.3
	.9		.6		.5	Fixed/Worth				.2	.5	.8
	2.5		2.7		2.0					.8	1.6	2.0
	.8		.8		.8					.9	.5	.7
	2.0		2.0		1.9	Debt/Worth				1.8	1.5	1.9
	5.9		6.7		7.5					6.3	3.8	7.2
	24.1		46.5		52.4	% Profit Before Taxes/Tangible				42.4	65.5	52.4
(54)	5.6	(60)	18.6	(60)	30.1	Net Worth				28.7	(20) 33.2	(16) 29.0
	-12.5		3.8		11.6					(10) 4.4	11.6	24.8
	11.0		14.7		17.3	% Profit Before Taxes/Total				14.7	16.5	19.7
	1.8		5.6		10.7	Assets				7.6	10.9	14.3
	-4.7		-.7		3.2					2.4	4.3	4.9
	21.2		28.6		30.3					48.5	19.1	13.5
	9.5		10.4		10.1	Sales/Net Fixed Assets				21.4	9.5	10.1
	5.1		5.7		7.1					8.4	6.3	7.1
	2.8		2.8		2.8					3.4	2.6	2.7
	1.9		2.1		2.3	Sales/Total Assets				2.5	2.1	2.3
	1.3		1.6		1.5					1.6	1.6	1.5
	1.4		.9		.8					.5	1.3	1.0
(57)	2.5	(64)	1.7	(61)	1.7	% Depr., Dep., Amort./Sales				(10) 1.3	(20) 2.0	(15) 1.3
	4.3		3.2		2.7					2.7	2.5	3.4
	3.0		2.4		2.0	% Officers', Directors',						
(19)	6.8	(20)	4.6	(22)	3.4	Owners' Comp/Sales						
	8.9		7.2		7.5							
	1462498M		1619881M		2669695M	Net Sales ($)	2449M	18960M	29116M	84805M	371600M	2162765M
	940265M		1017852M		1544744M	Total Assets ($)	1644M	14062M	17302M	45485M	204327M	1261924M

M = $ thousand   MM = $ million
See Pages 11 through 21 for Explanation of Ratios and Data

Current Data Sorted By Assets   **Comparative Historical Data**

0-500M	500M-2MM	2-10MM	10-50MM	50-100MM	100-250MM	Type of Statement	4/1/00-3/31/01 ALL	4/1/01-3/31/02 ALL
	2	16	14	2	8	Unqualified	38	33
	14	25	2		1	Reviewed	30	25
3	15	9				Compiled	25	26
9	13	4				Tax Returns	14	12
2	13	25	19	2	2	Other	39	52
	36 (4/1-9/30/04)		164 (10/1/04-3/31/05)					
14	57	79	35	4	11	**NUMBER OF STATEMENTS**	146	148
%	%	%	%	%	%	**ASSETS**	%	%
8.0	10.2	8.5	9.5		21.1	Cash & Equivalents	8.5	7.2
45.3	33.0	32.1	24.2		24.2	Trade Receivables (net)	30.9	28.8
18.0	32.6	33.1	24.8		18.1	Inventory	29.3	29.1
4.7	1.0	3.3	2.6		3.7	All Other Current	3.1	2.6
76.0	76.7	76.9	61.1		67.2	Total Current	71.7	67.7
19.0	13.0	15.3	22.9		13.9	Fixed Assets (net)	17.7	20.5
2.7	6.0	3.1	8.1		12.2	Intangibles (net)	5.2	5.8
2.3	4.2	4.7	7.9		6.7	All Other Non-Current	5.5	6.0
100.0	100.0	100.0	100.0		100.0	Total	100.0	100.0
						LIABILITIES		
52.8	14.9	12.3	10.4		1.2	Notes Payable-Short Term	19.1	12.3
7.2	2.6	2.7	3.5		7.4	Cur. Mat.-L/T/D	3.9	3.6
33.4	19.5	15.0	11.0		12.2	Trade Payables	15.6	15.5
.0	.2	.5	.4		1.1	Income Taxes Payable	.4	.3
14.4	10.0	11.0	14.5		10.5	All Other Current	10.5	11.8
107.9	47.2	41.5	39.7		32.3	Total Current	49.4	43.5
26.2	12.6	10.2	8.1		5.2	Long-Term Debt	11.5	12.5
.1	.1	.3	.6		.8	Deferred Taxes	.7	.3
4.5	6.8	5.2	4.8		3.8	All Other Non-Current	4.9	4.8
-38.7	33.3	42.8	46.9		57.9	Net Worth	33.5	38.8
100.0	100.0	100.0	100.0		100.0	Total Liabilities & Net Worth	100.0	100.0
						INCOME DATA		
100.0	100.0	100.0	100.0		100.0	Net Sales	100.0	100.0
45.3	38.7	31.3	33.2		36.5	Gross Profit	33.9	34.4
43.3	34.1	24.7	27.0		26.9	Operating Expenses	27.3	30.5
2.1	4.6	6.5	6.2		9.7	Operating Profit	6.6	3.9
1.5	.8	.9	1.8		.0	All Other Expenses (net)	1.2	1.7
.6	3.7	5.6	4.4		9.7	Profit Before Taxes	5.4	2.2
						RATIOS		
1.9	3.4	3.4	2.9		3.6		3.2	2.4
.9	1.8	1.9	1.7		2.3	Current	1.7	1.6
.6	1.2	1.3	1.0		1.4		1.3	1.2
1.2	1.9	1.5	1.6		2.2		1.5	1.4
.6	1.0	1.0	.8		1.4	Quick	.9	.8
.3	.6	.6	.5		1.1		.6	.5
23 15.9	31 11.8	42 8.8	43 8.6		45 8.0		38 9.7	34 10.6
37 9.9	43 8.4	47 7.8	52 7.0		57 6.4	Sales/Receivables	49 7.5	46 7.9
59 6.1	57 6.4	67 5.4	72 5.1		79 4.6		68 5.4	63 5.8
0 UND	29 12.8	55 6.6	46 7.9		42 8.6		41 8.8	37 9.9
17 21.9	78 4.7	78 4.7	94 3.9		65 5.6	Cost of Sales/Inventory	70 5.2	70 5.2
58 6.3	127 2.9	124 2.9	125 2.9		97 3.8		114 3.2	124 2.9
10 37.0	20 17.9	17 21.2	24 15.2		19 18.7		22 16.7	17 21.1
34 10.7	44 8.3	31 11.6	33 11.1		39 9.3	Cost of Sales/Payables	35 10.3	31 11.9
82 4.4	59 6.2	54 6.8	45 8.2		49 7.5		51 7.1	51 7.1
9.0	4.9	4.0	4.2		2.1		4.3	4.6
-89.4	8.3	6.3	7.3		4.0	Sales/Working Capital	7.3	8.8
-5.8	24.9	11.8	-67.5		9.9		18.8	22.6
4.6	19.4	22.6	19.2		242.4		14.4	7.5
(12) 2.1	(50) 3.9	(70) 4.0	(31) 3.1		(10) 48.4	EBIT/Interest	(130) 3.9	(127) 2.6
-3.3	1.0	1.7	1.5		4.5		1.8	.5
		7.1	6.3				6.3	4.8
	(20) 2.0	(14) 1.9				Net Profit + Depr., Dep., Amort./Cur. Mat. L/T/D	(40) 2.5	(42) 1.5
		.5	.3				1.0	.9
.1	.1	.1	.3		.2		.2	.2
1.2	.3	.3	.4		.3	Fixed/Worth	.4	.5
NM	1.3	.6	1.1		.9		1.0	1.2
.8	.8	.6	.4		.3		.7	.7
8.7	2.2	1.5	1.0		.6	Debt/Worth	1.7	1.8
-2.2	9.5	3.1	5.6		3.5		3.7	4.3
151.4	59.9	49.9	26.3		39.3		48.2	32.1
(10) 6.0	(46) 25.5	(73) 21.5	(29) 15.9		(10) 21.5	% Profit Before Taxes/Tangible Net Worth	(135) 19.6	(131) 13.7
-9.8	9.3	2.4	3.7		12.3		5.4	1.1
17.9	17.9	21.9	13.4		17.6		19.1	12.6
2.1	6.0	6.9	5.4		13.6	% Profit Before Taxes/Total Assets	7.9	3.7
-17.4	.6	1.2	.5		4.8		2.1	.1
190.2	91.0	40.5	12.8		20.3		36.3	29.4
22.9	32.0	17.9	6.5		9.1	Sales/Net Fixed Assets	15.7	12.6
15.0	21.4	9.0	4.8		7.7		8.1	6.3
5.2	3.4	2.6	1.9		1.9		2.8	3.0
3.6	2.8	2.2	1.5		1.4	Sales/Total Assets	2.1	2.1
3.1	1.9	1.6	1.1		.9		1.6	1.5
	.4	.9	1.6				.7	1.0
	(42) 1.0	(69) 1.4	(30) 2.1			% Depr., Dep., Amort./Sales	(125) 1.5	(120) 1.9
	2.0	2.5	4.2				2.7	3.3
4.4	2.7	2.1					3.1	1.9
(11) 10.7	(30) 4.7	(35) 2.8				% Officers', Directors', Owners' Comp/Sales	(50) 6.0	(52) 5.0
15.8	9.0	5.4					7.9	7.8
14463M	194085M	831141M	1340029M	344699M	2438536M	Net Sales ($)	4657993M	3816132M
3715M	69367M	373378M	865850M	308895M	1663671M	Total Assets ($)	2953162M	2380296M

© RMA 2005   M = $ thousand   MM = $ million
See Pages 11 through 21 for Explanation of Ratios and Data

Comparative Historical Data — **Current Data Sorted By Sales**

	4/1/02-3/31/03 ALL	4/1/03-3/31/04 ALL	4/1/04-3/31/05 ALL	Type of Statement	0-1MM (36, 4/1-9/30/04)	1-3MM (36)	3-5MM (164, 10/1/04-3/31/05)	5-10MM	10-25MM	25MM & OVER
	38	49	42	Unqualified		1	1	5	12	23
	38	45	42	Reviewed		5	5	16	14	2
	19	40	27	Compiled	2	8	6	10	1	
	15	17	26	Tax Returns	7	10	5	4		
	56	61	63	Other	2	9	7	12	15	18
	166	212	200	NUMBER OF STATEMENTS	11	33	24	47	42	43
	%	%	%	**ASSETS**	%	%	%	%	%	%
	9.4	10.7	9.7	Cash & Equivalents	10.7	7.4	10.9	10.9	7.3	11.7
	29.7	29.2	31.1	Trade Receivables (net)	23.2	32.7	31.8	36.0	32.5	24.7
	27.3	26.9	29.4	Inventory	26.6	31.7	35.0	31.5	30.4	21.7
	3.4	3.7	2.6	All Other Current	5.2	.7	2.2	1.8	4.3	2.9
	69.7	70.4	72.8	Total Current	65.7	72.5	80.0	80.2	74.4	61.0
	19.3	18.4	16.2	Fixed Assets (net)	26.6	16.2	10.2	13.0	18.0	18.6
	5.4	5.4	6.0	Intangibles (net)	4.3	6.1	6.9	2.2	3.3	12.6
	5.6	5.8	5.1	All Other Non-Current	3.4	5.3	2.8	4.6	4.3	7.8
	100.0	100.0	100.0	Total	100.0	100.0	100.0	100.0	100.0	100.0
				LIABILITIES						
	9.7	14.0	14.7	Notes Payable-Short Term	49.8	18.6	16.8	11.7	13.1	6.2
	4.2	3.2	3.4	Cur. Mat.-L/T/D	4.2	4.5	3.4	2.1	2.9	4.2
	15.2	15.2	16.6	Trade Payables	15.5	19.3	19.2	18.9	16.4	10.9
	.4	.4	.4	Income Taxes Payable	.1	.1	.2	.3	.3	.8
	11.4	11.6	11.5	All Other Current	5.3	15.0	10.5	10.3	12.4	11.3
	40.8	44.4	46.5	Total Current	74.8	57.6	50.1	43.3	45.2	33.5
	13.5	11.7	11.5	Long-Term Debt	31.0	17.3	11.2	8.0	9.8	7.8
	.2	.3	.3	Deferred Taxes	.0	.1	.1	.2	.6	.6
	4.9	6.9	5.6	All Other Non-Current	16.3	4.7	9.1	3.5	4.3	5.0
	40.6	36.8	36.1	Net Worth	-22.2	20.4	29.5	44.9	40.2	53.2
	100.0	100.0	100.0	Total Liabilities & Net Worth	100.0	100.0	100.0	100.0	100.0	100.0
				INCOME DATA						
	100.0	100.0	100.0	Net Sales	100.0	100.0	100.0	100.0	100.0	100.0
	35.8	33.0	35.1	Gross Profit	44.5	45.5	35.0	32.8	27.9	34.4
	31.2	30.4	29.3	Operating Expenses	42.0	41.4	32.5	25.5	22.8	25.3
	4.7	2.6	5.9	Operating Profit	2.5	4.0	2.5	7.3	5.1	9.2
	1.3	1.2	1.1	All Other Expenses (net)	1.6	1.5	.5	.6	1.2	1.4
	3.4	1.5	4.8	Profit Before Taxes	1.0	2.6	2.0	6.7	3.9	7.8
				RATIOS						
	2.9	2.8	3.0	Current	4.5	2.9	3.4	3.4	2.8	2.9
	1.8	1.7	1.8		1.7	1.5	1.8	1.9	1.7	1.8
	1.3	1.3	1.2		.7	.9	1.3	1.2	1.2	1.4
	1.6	1.5	1.6	Quick	2.1	1.5	1.9	1.8	1.5	1.7
	1.0	.9	1.0		.8	.8	.8	1.1	.9	1.1
	.7	.6	.6		.2	.5	.6	.7	.6	.6
	36 10.2	39 9.4	38 9.7	Sales/Receivables	27 13.4	30 12.0	34 10.6	42 8.8	40 9.0	42 8.6
	49 7.5	49 7.5	47 7.8		33 11.1	47 7.7	46 8.0	46 7.9	52 7.1	48 7.6
	64 5.7	63 5.8	66 5.5		58 6.3	69 5.3	65 5.6	62 5.9	76 4.8	66 5.5
	41 8.8	42 8.8	45 8.1	Cost of Sales/Inventory	0 UND	23 15.5	57 6.4	45 8.1	46 7.9	42 8.6
	81 4.5	68 5.4	78 4.7		94 3.9	99 3.7	85 4.3	67 5.4	64 5.7	86 4.2
	136 2.7	113 3.2	121 3.0		127 2.9	168 2.2	128 2.9	117 3.1	114 3.2	109 3.4
	19 19.6	19 19.6	20 18.0	Cost of Sales/Payables	14 27.0	19 19.3	8 45.4	15 24.5	20 18.1	23 15.8
	33 11.0	36 10.3	34 10.6		45 8.1	45 8.1	37 10.0	32 11.4	35 10.3	31 11.7
	52 7.1	57 6.4	57 6.4		64 5.7	75 4.9	64 5.7	54 6.8	55 6.7	45 8.2
	4.1	4.0	4.3	Sales/Working Capital	2.3	4.5	5.5	4.2	4.3	3.8
	6.4	6.5	7.4		9.6	7.5	8.3	7.0	8.4	7.0
	14.6	17.2	19.6		-8.9	-83.6	14.4	19.6	17.7	10.7
	11.3	8.5	19.1	EBIT/Interest	5.1	6.7	15.7	52.1	20.6	38.3
	(151) 3.5	(190) 2.7	(177) 3.9		(10) 1.4	(29) 2.3	(22) 3.8	(40) 5.3	(37) 3.1	(39) 8.1
	1.1	.2	1.5		-4.5	.7	-.3	1.9	1.0	2.7
	6.5	3.7	7.3	Net Profit + Depr., Dep., Amort./Cur. Mat. L/T/D				4.5	7.1	18.8
	(48) 2.2	(56) 1.6	(53) 2.7				(11) 1.8	(12) 2.4	(20) 5.5	
	1.2	.6	.6					.5	.0	.7
	.2	.2	.2	Fixed/Worth	.4	.1	.1	.1	.2	.2
	.4	.4	.3		1.5	.4	.3	.2	.4	.3
	1.3	1.4	1.2		-.2	8.5	.9	.5	1.2	.9
	.7	.6	.5	Debt/Worth	1.3	.8	.9	.5	.6	.4
	1.6	1.6	1.6		2.6	2.9	2.7	1.6	1.4	.7
	4.1	5.0	5.6		-3.6	NM	9.8	2.4	5.5	3.9
	45.1	26.2	46.9	% Profit Before Taxes/Tangible Net Worth		62.1	59.3	61.2	34.4	35.8
	(146) 17.2	(182) 8.2	(170) 20.1			(25) 18.8	(20) 23.2	(44) 31.7	(38) 18.6	(35) 19.2
	2.9	-.6	3.9			.1	2.4	6.0	.0	10.6
	15.7	9.9	17.7	% Profit Before Taxes/Total Assets	5.8	15.2	17.5	32.6	17.3	16.9
	5.6	2.6	6.1		2.2	4.5	5.2	8.3	6.0	10.3
	.4	-1.3	1.4		-16.9	.0	-1.3	2.5	.0	3.6
	27.1	34.1	41.5	Sales/Net Fixed Assets	23.2	48.3	85.1	59.1	28.9	15.2
	12.9	14.0	17.3		12.7	25.1	31.3	26.1	13.5	9.6
	6.2	6.3	7.5		2.0	11.0	19.3	11.0	6.2	6.5
	2.9	2.7	3.0	Sales/Total Assets	3.2	3.1	3.3	3.2	2.6	2.0
	1.9	2.0	2.2		1.9	2.3	2.6	2.4	2.2	1.6
	1.4	1.4	1.5		1.3	1.2	1.9	1.9	1.6	1.2
	1.3	1.0	.8	% Depr., Dep., Amort./Sales		.5	.4	.6	.9	1.6
	(141) 2.1	(180) 1.9	(161) 1.5			(23) 1.5	(17) 1.0	(43) 1.1	(35) 1.6	(34) 2.1
	3.6	3.3	2.8			3.3	2.2	1.9	2.9	2.9
	2.3	2.7	2.4	% Officers', Directors', Owners' Comp/Sales		3.4	2.9	2.2	2.1	
	(56) 4.8	(57) 4.8	(78) 3.7			(20) 8.8	(15) 4.7	(24) 3.3	(10) 2.6	
	9.6	10.0	8.3			12.4	9.7	5.7	2.9	
	5163052M	5077280M	5162953M	Net Sales ($)	7705M	61313M	92352M	316334M	620763M	4064486M
	3039831M	3455707M	3284876M	Total Assets ($)	7744M	33054M	39689M	153046M	317068M	2734275M

© RMA 2005

M = $ thousand   MM = $ million
See Pages 11 through 21 for Explanation of Ratios and Data

Current Data Sorted By Assets   Comparative Historical Data

						Type of Statement		
			4	3	2	3	Unqualified	8	10
			3	3			Reviewed	6	6
		1	3	2			Compiled	9	7
		1					Tax Returns	1	1
1	2	7	5	1		Other	10	18

0-500M	500M-2MM	2-10MM	10-50MM	50-100MM	100-250MM		4/1/00-3/31/01 ALL	4/1/01-3/31/02 ALL
	6 (4/1-9/30/04)		35 (10/1/04-3/31/05)					
1	4	17	13	3	3	**NUMBER OF STATEMENTS**	34	42
%	%	%	%	%	%	**ASSETS**	%	%
		7.3	9.1			Cash & Equivalents	7.5	9.7
		16.2	17.1			Trade Receivables (net)	18.7	22.7
		48.9	33.5			Inventory	32.2	40.5
		1.1	2.4			All Other Current	7.5	3.8
		73.5	62.1			Total Current	66.0	76.7
		16.3	27.9			Fixed Assets (net)	23.4	18.1
		4.0	4.5			Intangibles (net)	3.7	1.8
		6.2	5.4			All Other Non-Current	6.9	3.4
		100.0	100.0			Total	100.0	100.0
						LIABILITIES		
		22.8	10.0			Notes Payable-Short Term	12.9	16.2
		3.1	3.0			Cur. Mat.-L/T/D	6.2	4.9
		10.8	18.2			Trade Payables	14.5	18.4
		.6	.1			Income Taxes Payable	.0	.1
		15.3	10.2			All Other Current	10.8	12.1
		52.6	41.5			Total Current	44.5	51.7
		6.5	26.1			Long-Term Debt	11.4	10.6
		1.4	.6			Deferred Taxes	.3	.5
		6.6	6.9			All Other Non-Current	3.9	8.0
		32.9	25.0			Net Worth	39.9	29.1
		100.0	100.0			Total Liabilities & Net Worth	100.0	100.0
						INCOME DATA		
		100.0	100.0			Net Sales	100.0	100.0
		22.8	21.5			Gross Profit	22.7	19.3
		18.1	19.0			Operating Expenses	19.7	16.5
		4.7	2.5			Operating Profit	3.0	2.8
		1.1	3.6			All Other Expenses (net)	-.6	1.2
		3.6	-1.1			Profit Before Taxes	3.6	1.6
						RATIOS		
		2.2	2.2				2.0	2.2
		1.2	1.3			Current	1.3	1.5
		1.0	1.1				1.1	1.1
		.7	1.5				.8	1.0
		.4	.7			Quick	.5	.6
		.2	.2				.3	.3
		7 51.5	10 37.7				13 28.7	15 25.0
		13 28.7	40 9.0			Sales/Receivables	28 13.0	32 11.5
		45 8.2	58 6.3				49 7.4	44 8.3
		42 8.8	32 11.4				24 15.4	31 11.9
		76 4.8	74 4.9			Cost of Sales/Inventory	63 5.8	69 5.3
		166 2.2	128 2.9				95 3.9	120 3.1
		8 47.0	15 24.8				11 31.9	15 25.2
		15 24.8	48 7.5			Cost of Sales/Payables	23 15.9	24 14.9
		34 10.6	63 5.8				40 9.0	45 8.1
		6.0	6.4				5.1	6.0
		15.8	14.4			Sales/Working Capital	19.8	13.9
		-167.1	36.6				82.7	38.5
		4.9					13.9	6.8
		(12) 2.1				EBIT/Interest	(29) 3.4	(41) 2.7
		-1.5					1.5	.6
							3.6	
						Net Profit + Depr., Dep., Amort./Cur. Mat. L /T/D	(13) 2.0	
							.5	
		.3	.3				.3	.2
		.8	.7			Fixed/Worth	.6	.5
		-21.2	NM				1.2	7.9
		1.1	.6				.7	.9
		2.0	3.3			Debt/Worth	1.5	2.6
		-112.9	NM				4.3	72.0
		55.4	32.3				40.2	45.0
		(12) 21.2	(10) 13.8			% Profit Before Taxes/Tangible Net Worth	(30) 19.5	(33) 14.6
		6.5	3.0				7.1	1.1
		13.8	7.5				15.3	16.8
		6.1	3.4			% Profit Before Taxes/Total Assets	5.2	4.7
		-1.1	-7.6				2.0	-.7
		40.5	24.4				33.1	27.6
		22.0	11.9			Sales/Net Fixed Assets	10.7	18.3
		12.0	3.3				4.2	8.9
		3.9	2.4				3.6	3.3
		2.7	1.8			Sales/Total Assets	2.5	2.7
		1.7	1.6				1.5	1.8
		.6	.7				.9	.7
		.9	(11) 2.5			% Depr., Dep., Amort./Sales	(29) 1.9	(34) 1.1
		1.5	6.0				3.7	1.7
							1.9	1.4
						% Officers', Directors', Owners' Comp/Sales	(14) 3.6	(12) 3.2
							7.6	4.9
245M	20370M	253254M	504165M	324084M	1004085M	Net Sales ($)	1263475M	3770399M
102M	4380M	91284M	259988M	198373M	486785M	Total Assets ($)	567760M	1054083M

M = $ thousand   MM = $ million
See Pages 11 through 21 for Explanation of Ratios and Data

Comparative Historical Data | Current Data Sorted By Sales

			Type of Statement						
14	13	12	Unqualified				3	2	7
9	9	6	Reviewed				1	2	3
5	8	6	Compiled			1	2	2	1
1	2	1	Tax Returns						
15	11	16	Other	1	1	1	4	4	6
4/1/02-3/31/03	4/1/03-3/31/04	4/1/04-3/31/05		6 (4/1-9/30/04)			35 (10/1/04-3/31/05)		
ALL	ALL	ALL		0-1MM	1-3MM	3-5MM	5-10MM	10-25MM	25MM & OVER
44	43	41	NUMBER OF STATEMENTS	1	1	2	10	10	17
%	%	%	ASSETS	%	%	%	%	%	%
9.7	6.6	8.1	Cash & Equivalents				7.6	8.0	7.9
17.5	18.9	18.5	Trade Receivables (net)				17.2	16.2	16.5
36.4	35.0	38.0	Inventory				50.6	38.8	34.1
3.7	2.6	1.7	All Other Current				1.3	2.4	1.8
67.4	63.1	66.3	Total Current				76.7	65.5	60.4
21.9	23.5	20.5	Fixed Assets (net)				16.5	24.8	18.1
4.0	5.3	7.9	Intangibles (net)				.0	6.8	14.9
6.8	8.1	5.4	All Other Non-Current				6.9	2.9	6.6
100.0	100.0	100.0	Total				100.0	100.0	100.0
			LIABILITIES						
13.1	15.1	14.3	Notes Payable-Short Term				15.8	7.1	18.1
4.9	3.5	2.5	Cur. Mat.-L/T/D				2.1	3.8	2.5
14.7	16.3	16.4	Trade Payables				13.5	15.8	18.5
.6	.5	.3	Income Taxes Payable				.2	.7	.1
16.8	14.3	13.9	All Other Current				22.9	15.3	9.5
50.1	49.6	47.4	Total Current				54.5	42.7	48.8
36.1	15.5	14.6	Long-Term Debt				4.2	8.3	20.9
.5	.7	.9	Deferred Taxes				.5	2.3	.6
11.2	9.9	7.3	All Other Non-Current				10.9	5.6	6.3
2.1	24.3	29.8	Net Worth				30.0	41.1	23.5
100.0	100.0	100.0	Total Liabilities & Net Worth				100.0	100.0	100.0
			INCOME DATA						
100.0	100.0	100.0	Net Sales				100.0	100.0	100.0
21.9	24.2	21.4	Gross Profit				29.5	20.5	15.3
18.9	21.9	18.0	Operating Expenses				25.5	14.9	11.7
3.0	2.3	3.4	Operating Profit				4.0	5.6	3.6
.9	1.0	2.0	All Other Expenses (net)				-.2	1.9	3.7
2.1	1.3	1.4	Profit Before Taxes				4.2	3.7	-.1
			RATIOS						
2.0	1.7	1.7					3.5	2.0	1.5
1.3	1.2	1.3	Current				1.2	1.4	1.3
1.0	1.0	1.1					1.0	1.0	1.0
.9	.8	1.0					1.1	1.2	.8
.5	.5	.5	Quick				.4	.5	.5
.3	.3	.2					.2	.2	.2
8 45.5	9 40.9	9 42.2					10 36.5	6 58.6	10 37.7
28 12.8	31 11.8	28 13.0	Sales/Receivables				27 13.5	14 26.2	28 13.0
56 6.6	54 6.7	53 6.9					63 5.8	44 8.3	53 6.9
40 9.1	31 11.6	34 10.8					57 6.4	30 12.2	34 10.8
59 6.2	68 5.4	62 5.9	Cost of Sales/Inventory				120 3.0	50 7.2	55 6.6
105 3.5	107 3.4	119 3.1					201 1.8	84 4.3	87 4.2
10 35.8	11 32.2	11 33.4					12 30.2	10 37.6	13 27.1
26 14.1	29 12.6	32 11.5	Cost of Sales/Payables				29 12.7	18 20.3	44 8.3
54 6.8	48 7.7	54 6.8					35 10.3	50 7.3	63 5.8
7.0	8.5	8.1					3.0	8.6	10.9
17.3	16.5	13.5	Sales/Working Capital				15.7	13.8	14.4
-84.1	-194.0	116.3					NM	NM	-137.4
11.4	6.2	5.8							11.9
(37) 2.9	(35) 2.6	(29) 1.9	EBIT/Interest					(12) 2.5	2.5
.9	.4	-1.5							-.1
8.2	3.4	5.2	Net Profit + Depr., Dep.,						
(14) 2.3	(13) 1.3	(12) 1.2	Amort./Cur. Mat. L/T/D						
1.3	1.0	-2.0							
.3	.4	.3					.2	.3	.4
1.2	1.2	1.0	Fixed/Worth				.9	.5	1.6
-3.1	4.9	-6.3					-30.5	4.2	-.6
1.8	1.2	.9					.5	.7	1.0
4.7	3.8	2.6	Debt/Worth				3.5	1.7	7.4
-14.8	45.6	-34.0					-143.0	7.7	-3.9
39.3	40.8	43.4	% Profit Before Taxes/Tangible						43.2
(31) 23.7	(34) 11.4	(29) 14.7	Net Worth					(10) 14.7	14.7
10.5	-3.9	4.3							11.8
10.6	12.8	9.0	% Profit Before Taxes/Total				10.3	16.4	7.5
4.9	3.7	4.8	Assets				3.5	12.3	4.8
-.4	-.8	-3.4					-4.7	-5.3	-1.3
34.5	39.1	27.3					44.9	21.6	35.3
11.6	10.5	17.0	Sales/Net Fixed Assets				23.9	13.8	17.0
5.8	4.3	6.6					10.9	9.3	6.3
3.2	3.0	3.4					3.8	3.9	3.0
2.3	2.1	2.3	Sales/Total Assets				2.0	2.6	2.3
1.5	1.3	1.6					1.4	1.9	1.6
.7	.6	.6					.8	.6	.6
(38) 1.6	(38) 2.2	(38) 1.1	% Depr., Dep., Amort./Sales				1.3	.8	(15) 1.6
2.5	4.1	3.0					2.6	1.6	3.4
.8	.4		% Officers', Directors',						
(10) 1.4	(12) 2.5		Owners' Comp/Sales						
2.9	4.2								
2437935M	1977885M	2106203M	Net Sales ($)	245M	2281M	7434M	76538M	171236M	1848469M
1205527M	1209060M	1040912M	Total Assets ($)	102M	1241M	16151M	43524M	71536M	908358M

M = $ thousand   MM = $ million
See Pages 11 through 21 for Explanation of Ratios and Data

Current Data Sorted By Assets   Comparative Historical Data

Type of Statement counts (current data columns: 26 (4/1-9/30/04); 153 (10/1/04-3/31/05)):

Type of Statement	0-500M	500M-2MM	2-10MM	10-50MM	50-100MM	100-250MM	4/1/00-3/31/01 ALL	4/1/01-3/31/02 ALL
Unqualified		1	7	19	11	9	13	13
Reviewed		6	24	7			12	17
Compiled	2	9	7	1			15	12
Tax Returns	2	7	3				4	3
Other	4	13	18	17	9	3	23	20
NUMBER OF STATEMENTS	8	36	59	44	20	12	67	65

	0-500M %	500M-2MM %	2-10MM %	10-50MM %	50-100MM %	100-250MM %	4/1/00 %	4/1/02 %
ASSETS								
Cash & Equivalents		7.2	4.7	1.9	6.6	6.0	3.3	5.7
Trade Receivables (net)		24.3	22.8	23.4	21.4	22.4	19.9	21.9
Inventory		37.2	37.7	32.2	20.3	23.0	41.2	34.3
All Other Current		2.5	1.7	3.6	1.1	2.0	2.4	3.8
Total Current		71.2	66.9	61.1	49.4	53.4	66.8	65.7
Fixed Assets (net)		20.1	24.8	26.7	34.0	28.8	22.0	23.4
Intangibles (net)		3.0	2.5	4.4	8.8	13.9	5.7	5.5
All Other Non-Current		5.8	5.9	7.9	7.8	3.9	5.5	5.4
Total		100.0	100.0	100.0	100.0	100.0	100.0	100.0
LIABILITIES								
Notes Payable-Short Term		13.8	16.0	13.3	10.8	1.5	19.2	20.7
Cur. Mat.-L/T/D		4.6	4.1	4.0	3.6	3.9	2.7	2.7
Trade Payables		26.8	16.3	15.5	15.9	15.9	18.9	14.5
Income Taxes Payable		.1	.1	.9	.2	.4	.1	.4
All Other Current		10.5	12.2	10.7	9.5	9.1	9.4	9.6
Total Current		55.8	48.7	44.4	39.9	30.8	50.3	47.9
Long-Term Debt		15.8	13.7	15.4	12.5	33.8	15.9	16.3
Deferred Taxes		.0	.2	.7	2.5	1.2	.6	.6
All Other Non-Current		2.9	5.5	5.4	13.5	1.4	4.4	2.2
Net Worth		25.4	32.0	34.1	31.5	32.8	28.9	33.0
Total Liabilities & Net Worth		100.0	100.0	100.0	100.0	100.0	100.0	100.0
INCOME DATA								
Net Sales		100.0	100.0	100.0	100.0	100.0	100.0	100.0
Gross Profit		27.8	24.3	20.6	17.1	15.8	21.6	23.9
Operating Expenses		25.1	21.0	15.4	11.9	11.1	17.7	21.2
Operating Profit		2.6	3.3	5.2	5.1	4.8	3.9	2.7
All Other Expenses (net)		.9	.5	.5	3.3	1.7	1.6	1.5
Profit Before Taxes		1.7	2.8	4.7	1.8	3.1	2.3	1.2
RATIOS								
Current		2.1	2.7	2.4	2.8	2.6	2.1	2.2
		1.3	1.5	1.5	1.3	1.7	1.5	1.5
		.9	1.1	1.0	.7	1.3	1.1	1.1
Quick		1.0	1.3	1.0	1.6	1.4	.9	1.3
		.7	.6	.6	.7	.9	.6	.6
		.3	.4	.3	.5	.7	.3	.4
Sales/Receivables		16 22.5	28 13.1	28 13.0	34 10.6	34 10.8	24 15.3	22 16.5
		32 11.3	39 9.5	36 10.1	50 7.2	46 7.9	35 10.4	36 10.3
		40 9.2	51 7.2	53 6.9	60 6.1	64 5.7	47 7.7	51 7.2
Cost of Sales/Inventory		32 11.6	45 8.1	34 10.8	25 14.5	34 10.6	53 6.9	41 9.0
		61 6.0	71 5.2	66 5.5	45 8.1	42 8.6	73 5.0	65 5.6
		98 3.7	119 3.1	100 3.6	81 4.5	76 4.8	113 3.2	114 3.2
Cost of Sales/Payables		16 22.5	15 23.7	16 23.1	16 22.7	24 15.0	17 20.9	15 25.0
		32 11.4	28 13.2	33 11.1	26 14.2	36 10.1	34 10.6	25 14.7
		70 5.2	51 7.1	41 8.9	54 6.8	49 7.4	53 6.9	43 8.5
Sales/Working Capital		9.2	5.8	5.6	5.1	4.5	6.8	5.2
		18.0	10.3	13.8	20.9	8.4	10.2	12.3
		-147.5	48.1	NM	-9.3	27.7	33.8	29.5
EBIT/Interest		5.3	7.2	22.0	17.9	7.0	7.5	4.9
		(35) 2.2	(55) 3.4	6.2	3.7	(11) 2.9	(66) 1.9	(60) 2.0
		-.2	1.4	2.4	.9	1.9	.5	.4
Net Profit + Depr., Dep., Amort./Cur. Mat. L/T/D			4.4	11.7	8.0		9.3	6.6
			(15) 3.7	(16) 3.7	(11) 2.0		(23) 4.5	(19) 1.7
			1.2	1.5	.7		1.2	.5
Fixed/Worth		.3	.4	.3	.7	.7	.3	.3
		.8	.8	.7	1.5	1.4	.8	.7
		-10.7	1.7	2.1	26.8	NM	8.8	1.3
Debt/Worth		1.3	.8	.8	.8	.9	1.1	.8
		2.1	2.0	1.8	3.8	3.8	2.8	2.1
		-41.9	5.8	4.3	92.7	NM	72.5	4.4
% Profit Before Taxes/Tangible Net Worth		51.6	43.4	42.6	32.9		33.1	27.8
		(26) 20.2	(52) 22.3	(40) 24.6	(16) 14.6		(51) 15.8	(56) 10.1
		-.8	6.6	12.0	2.7		2.4	.1
% Profit Before Taxes/Total Assets		11.5	13.2	15.5	9.1	6.4	10.7	9.1
		4.0	5.2	7.4	5.0	4.3	3.3	3.9
		-3.4	1.3	2.6	-1.3	1.3	-2.2	-2.1
Sales/Net Fixed Assets		44.0	27.9	26.1	6.7	13.1	20.3	19.8
		22.7	9.6	9.7	5.1	9.6	11.9	11.1
		8.3	5.6	6.0	3.7	5.8	5.8	5.3
Sales/Total Assets		4.3	2.9	2.6	1.9	2.4	3.0	2.8
		3.0	2.2	2.1	1.7	1.9	2.2	2.0
		2.0	1.7	1.5	1.2	1.5	1.6	1.7
% Depr., Dep., Amort./Sales		.7	.8	.7	2.0		.5	1.0
		(27) 1.2	(47) 1.5	(38) 1.7	(19) 3.1		(62) 1.2	(56) 1.6
		2.8	2.8	3.1	5.5		2.3	3.4
% Officers', Directors', Owners' Comp/Sales		1.8	1.1	1.1			1.2	1.7
		(21) 3.0	(21) 2.7	(14) 1.8			(21) 2.3	(21) 2.4
		6.4	4.1	2.6			4.3	6.9
Net Sales ($)	10140M	125462M	648780M	1868849M	2372983M	3705035M	2750223M	2534872M
Total Assets ($)	2293M	40140M	266702M	870140M	1460978M	1972167M	1551030M	1338318M

M = $ thousand   MM = $ million
See Pages 11 through 21 for Explanation of Ratios and Data

Comparative Historical Data | Current Data Sorted By Sales

4/1/02-3/31/03 ALL	4/1/03-3/31/04 ALL	4/1/04-3/31/05 ALL	Type of Statement	0-1MM	1-3MM	3-5MM	5-10MM	10-25MM	25MM & OVER
44	49	47	Unqualified		1		3	4	39
31	40	37	Reviewed		1	5	9	13	9
15	24	19	Compiled	1	4	5	9		
9	7	12	Tax Returns		8	4			
41	60	64	Other	4	10	5	8	13	24
				26 (4/1-9/30/04)			153 (10/1/04-3/31/05)		
140	180	179	NUMBER OF STATEMENTS	5	24	19	29	30	72
%	%	%	ASSETS	%	%	%	%	%	%
5.1	6.1	5.1	Cash & Equivalents		6.4	5.0	6.5	3.6	4.3
24.4	23.8	23.3	Trade Receivables (net)		16.6	26.1	26.4	20.3	24.0
27.3	28.4	32.6	Inventory		38.2	31.7	32.8	38.9	28.8
3.3	2.8	2.2	All Other Current		2.4	2.6	1.2	2.3	2.7
60.1	61.1	63.2	Total Current		63.5	65.4	66.9	65.1	59.9
28.3	25.7	25.5	Fixed Assets (net)		25.2	27.8	23.3	26.0	26.4
5.0	6.2	4.9	Intangibles (net)		3.7	2.0	2.8	2.4	7.3
6.6	7.0	6.4	All Other Non-Current		7.7	4.8	7.0	6.5	6.5
100.0	100.0	100.0	Total		100.0	100.0	100.0	100.0	100.0
			LIABILITIES						
16.5	11.8	13.5	Notes Payable-Short Term		13.5	17.2	14.1	16.2	11.2
5.5	4.5	4.0	Cur. Mat.-L/T/D		4.4	3.5	3.3	6.5	3.6
16.2	16.6	18.0	Trade Payables		23.1	15.3	18.9	15.8	17.1
.2	.3	.3	Income Taxes Payable		.1	.1	.1	.4	.5
11.7	10.2	11.4	All Other Current		13.4	6.2	13.0	8.0	11.4
50.0	43.3	47.3	Total Current		54.5	42.2	49.4	46.9	43.8
15.1	15.5	16.0	Long-Term Debt		24.8	13.2	12.8	14.1	15.9
.7	.9	.6	Deferred Taxes		.0	.0	.0	.8	1.1
6.3	6.7	5.7	All Other Non-Current		4.6	3.0	5.3	5.1	7.2
27.9	33.6	30.4	Net Worth		16.1	41.5	32.5	33.1	31.9
100.0	100.0	100.0	Total Liabilities & Net Worth		100.0	100.0	100.0	100.0	100.0
			INCOME DATA						
100.0	100.0	100.0	Net Sales		100.0	100.0	100.0	100.0	100.0
24.7	24.0	22.9	Gross Profit		29.7	31.0	24.7	22.4	17.9
22.0	20.4	19.0	Operating Expenses		27.2	28.5	20.7	18.0	13.4
2.8	3.6	3.9	Operating Profit		2.5	2.5	4.0	4.5	4.5
1.3	.9	.9	All Other Expenses (net)		1.0	.3	.6	.4	1.4
1.4	2.7	3.0	Profit Before Taxes		1.6	2.2	3.4	4.1	3.1
			RATIOS						
2.2	2.6	2.4	Current		1.7	2.8	3.0	2.6	2.4
1.3	1.5	1.5			1.2	2.0	1.5	1.6	1.4
.9	1.0	1.0			.8	1.1	.9	1.1	1.0
1.1	1.3	1.2	Quick		.9	1.9	1.5	1.1	1.1
.7	.7	.7			.4	.6	.7	.6	.7
.4	.4	.4			.1	.5	.4	.3	.5
27 13.3	27 13.5	28 13.1	Sales/Receivables	6 58.4	29 12.6	32 11.6	22 16.9		29 12.8
38 9.5	39 9.4	37 10.0		28 12.8	40 9.2	42 8.7	32 11.6		40 9.1
54 6.8	53 7.0	52 7.0		41 9.0	55 6.6	51 7.2	47 7.8		55 6.6
30 12.1	29 12.4	35 10.6	Cost of Sales/Inventory	44 8.4	46 7.9	31 11.9	45 8.1		32 11.4
54 6.7	52 7.0	60 6.1		66 5.6	61 5.9	60 6.1	76 4.8		51 7.2
88 4.2	86 4.3	96 3.8		132 2.8	115 3.2	108 3.4	132 2.8		87 4.2
19 19.1	17 21.5	16 23.1	Cost of Sales/Payables	15 23.7	18 20.0	20 18.3	12 30.4		16 22.2
32 11.6	30 12.1	31 12.0		42 8.6	23 16.2	34 10.8	27 13.8		32 11.4
44 8.3	46 7.9	46 7.9		86 4.2	45 8.1	58 6.3	41 8.9		45 8.2
6.3	5.9	6.3	Sales/Working Capital	10.8	5.7	5.8	6.9		6.0
16.2	12.7	12.9		25.7	7.5	9.5	10.3		14.6
-34.3	-337.7	-999.8		-24.6	101.2	-45.2	NM		111.8
6.9	8.3	9.2	EBIT/Interest	3.0	4.2	17.3	7.3		19.6
(131) 3.0	(174) 3.4	(172) 3.6		(23) 1.5	(18) 2.9	(28) 4.6	(28) 2.9		(71) 5.3
.5	1.1	1.4		-.7	1.0	1.7	1.6		1.9
5.8	8.3	7.3	Net Profit + Depr., Dep., Amort./Cur. Mat. L/T/D					8.4	7.8
(50) 2.6	(63) 3.2	(50) 3.7						(15) 3.2	(28) 4.0
.8	.9	1.5						1.2	1.5
.5	.4	.4	Fixed/Worth		.7	.2	.3	.3	.4
.9	.8	.9			1.7	.6	.5	.8	.9
3.7	3.1	2.6			-4.8	1.9	10.4	1.8	2.2
1.0	1.0	.9	Debt/Worth		1.6	.7	.4	1.0	.9
2.3	2.4	2.4			9.5	1.4	2.0	2.1	3.1
16.0	12.5	8.6			-27.9	3.7	194.3	5.2	6.4
45.9	44.1	43.3	% Profit Before Taxes/Tangible Net Worth	54.2	30.1	46.7	36.7		41.7
(114) 15.0	(151) 15.9	(148) 21.8		(17) 30.0	(17) 11.0	(23) 40.5	(28) 19.5		(61) 18.6
1.2	3.4	6.6		-6.6	.4	13.1	7.2		6.1
12.2	12.6	12.3	% Profit Before Taxes/Total Assets	10.6	7.8	19.6	11.0		11.4
4.3	4.1	5.5		1.3	5.5	10.0	5.7		5.5
-1.4	.0	.9		-5.7	.6	2.5	1.6		1.3
18.6	22.7	27.6	Sales/Net Fixed Assets	29.4	36.9	40.1	24.2		16.8
8.4	9.3	9.6		13.1	7.8	11.3	11.3		8.9
4.4	5.0	5.6		6.5	4.9	6.5	5.5		5.4
2.9	3.0	3.0	Sales/Total Assets	3.8	3.5	2.9	3.2		2.6
2.0	2.1	2.2		2.3	2.3	2.4	2.1		2.0
1.5	1.5	1.6		1.4	1.6	1.8	1.5		1.7
.9	1.1	.8	% Depr., Dep., Amort./Sales		.9	.8	.9	.6	.7
(122) 2.4	(149) 2.2	(144) 1.8			(17) 2.1	(14) 1.7	(22) 1.9	(26) 1.5	(62) 2.0
4.4	3.8	3.1			3.0	3.7	4.4	2.9	3.2
1.6	1.4	1.5	% Officers', Directors', Owners' Comp/Sales		1.8		1.3		.8
(39) 3.5	(51) 3.1	(58) 2.6			(15) 3.2		(11) 3.1		(15) 1.8
5.2	4.9	4.2			5.9		4.0		2.6
6781114M	8332021M	8731249M	Net Sales ($)	3449M	49838M	71580M	209020M	452774M	7944588M
3949744M	4708671M	4612420M	Total Assets ($)	1360M	27998M	34325M	98488M	238062M	4212187M

© RMA 2005

M = $ thousand   MM = $ million
See Pages 11 through 21 for Explanation of Ratios and Data

Current Data Sorted By Assets   Comparative Historical Data

0-500M	500M-2MM	2-10MM	10-50MM	50-100MM	100-250MM	Type of Statement	9 / 13 / 17 / 1 / 21 4/1/00-3/31/01	8 / 10 / 20 / 4 / 21 4/1/01-3/31/02
	1	5	12		3	Unqualified	9	8
	9	5	2			Reviewed	13	10
2	3	6	1	1		Compiled	17	20
	4	1			1	Tax Returns	1	4
		9	10	1		Other	21	21
	17 (4/1-9/30/04)		58 (10/1/04-3/31/05)				ALL	ALL
2	17	26	25	2	3	NUMBER OF STATEMENTS	61	63
%	%	%	%	%	%	**ASSETS**	%	%
	10.7	6.6	4.4			Cash & Equivalents	7.1	8.5
	22.4	16.2	22.3			Trade Receivables (net)	18.3	17.0
	42.1	43.9	38.0			Inventory	38.6	36.1
	2.0	2.2	1.7			All Other Current	4.3	3.6
	77.1	68.9	66.4			Total Current	68.3	65.2
	16.6	23.9	23.4			Fixed Assets (net)	22.4	25.3
	2.8	3.7	6.2			Intangibles (net)	5.3	5.0
	3.4	3.5	4.1			All Other Non-Current	3.9	4.5
	100.0	100.0	100.0			Total	100.0	100.0
						LIABILITIES		
	32.5	11.4	16.7			Notes Payable-Short Term	15.4	16.8
	1.4	4.5	2.4			Cur. Mat.-L/T/D	2.6	6.6
	13.7	20.3	16.6			Trade Payables	14.3	11.1
	.0	.2	.1			Income Taxes Payable	.3	.0
	14.6	11.5	7.3			All Other Current	7.5	7.1
	62.2	48.0	43.1			Total Current	40.1	41.7
	7.9	12.5	18.0			Long-Term Debt	13.6	15.1
	.0	.3	.6			Deferred Taxes	.2	.4
	10.5	10.5	4.6			All Other Non-Current	1.8	4.8
	19.4	28.6	33.8			Net Worth	44.2	37.9
	100.0	100.0	100.0			Total Liabilities & Net Worth	100.0	100.0
						INCOME DATA		
	100.0	100.0	100.0			Net Sales	100.0	100.0
	29.3	19.0	16.3			Gross Profit	20.1	19.3
	27.4	17.4	11.0			Operating Expenses	15.4	19.4
	1.9	1.6	5.3			Operating Profit	4.6	.0
	.5	.7	.5			All Other Expenses (net)	1.0	1.5
	1.3	.9	4.8			Profit Before Taxes	3.7	−1.5
						RATIOS		
	2.3	2.2	2.4				3.0	3.1
	1.4	1.5	1.5			Current	1.8	1.7
	1.0	1.1	1.1				1.2	1.0
	.9	.7	1.0				1.0	1.4
	.4	.5	.5			Quick	.6	.5
	.3	.3	.4				.3	.3
	11 34.1	8 46.4	23 15.5				13 28.1	14 26.1
	28 13.1	16 22.4	26 14.0			Sales/Receivables	25 14.5	25 14.6
	37 9.9	36 10.0	46 8.0				34 10.8	38 9.5
	43 8.5	42 8.6	60 6.1				39 9.5	40 9.1
	66 5.5	80 4.6	71 5.2			Cost of Sales/Inventory	64 5.7	63 5.8
	95 3.8	112 3.3	81 4.5				78 4.7	96 3.8
	13 28.9	14 26.5	14 27.0				10 38.0	7 50.5
	22 17.0	28 12.9	22 16.8			Cost of Sales/Payables	19 19.5	18 19.8
	42 8.7	45 8.1	36 10.1				27 13.3	32 11.3
	8.7	6.2	6.4				5.5	5.0
	21.7	15.5	10.1			Sales/Working Capital	11.3	10.3
	NM	40.9	33.7				34.5	−236.0
	29.2	7.3	8.9				17.1	3.8
	(14) 4.5	(25) 4.2	(24) 4.3			EBIT/Interest	(56) 3.9	(58) 1.5
	1.7	.7	2.7				1.8	−1.1
						Net Profit + Depr., Dep.,	5.8	3.7
						Amort./Cur. Mat. L /T/D	(16) 2.0	(16) 1.2
							1.3	−.5
	.2	.4	.3				.2	.3
	.6	.8	.7			Fixed/Worth	.5	.8
	NM	1.5	1.9				1.7	1.7
	.9	1.1	.9				.6	.7
	9.8	2.4	2.3			Debt/Worth	1.3	1.9
	−10.3	4.8	18.5				3.7	4.4
	62.1	32.1	74.3			% Profit Before Taxes/Tangible	44.1	23.5
	(12) 35.8	(23) 15.3	(22) 25.0			Net Worth	(54) 20.6	(55) 8.0
	2.8	3.5	15.1				11.0	−8.5
	19.3	9.9	16.6			% Profit Before Taxes/Total	16.5	8.0
	3.6	5.8	8.4			Assets	7.7	1.7
	−1.0	−2.6	4.3				2.9	−6.2
	99.4	48.4	35.3				32.6	37.1
	32.2	15.4	9.0			Sales/Net Fixed Assets	14.0	13.3
	10.7	5.9	6.0				7.6	5.2
	4.5	3.9	3.2				3.7	3.7
	3.1	2.8	2.5			Sales/Total Assets	2.8	2.2
	2.1	1.7	1.9				2.0	1.5
	.7	.5	.8				.7	.6
	(12) 1.2	(24) .9	(22) 1.3			% Depr., Dep., Amort./Sales	(51) 1.2	(54) 1.6
	1.7	2.8	1.8				2.0	3.4
							1.2	1.7
						% Officers', Directors',	(16) 2.2	(22) 4.3
						Owners' Comp/Sales	3.0	9.1
1253M	78524M	411390M	1443611M	222935M	1257743M	Net Sales ($)	2994514M	1468186M
133M	21148M	128197M	612116M	116230M	482145M	Total Assets ($)	1226578M	786603M

M = $ thousand   MM = $ million
See Pages 11 through 21 for Explanation of Ratios and Data

Comparative Historical Data | Current Data Sorted By Sales

Type of Statement

4/1/02-3/31/03	4/1/03-3/31/04	4/1/04-3/31/05	Type of Statement	0-1MM	1-3MM	3-5MM	5-10MM	10-25MM	25MM & OVER
19	16	20	Unqualified				2	1	17
11	14	8	Reviewed			1	1	4	2
15	19	17	Compiled	1	3	2	6	4	1
3	10	6	Tax Returns	2	2	1		1	
25	26	24	Other		3		4	6	11
ALL	ALL	ALL		17 (4/1-9/30/04)			58 (10/1/04-3/31/05)		

Main Data

Period/size columns: Historical ALL (4/1/02-3/31/03 | 4/1/03-3/31/04 | 4/1/04-3/31/05); Current sorted by sales (0-1MM | 1-3MM | 3-5MM | 5-10MM | 10-25MM | 25MM & OVER).

Hist 1	Hist 2	Hist 3	Item	0-1MM	1-3MM	3-5MM	5-10MM	10-25MM	25MM & OVER
73	85	75	NUMBER OF STATEMENTS	3	8	4	13	16	31
%	%	%	ASSETS	%	%	%	%	%	%
7.6	6.6	6.3	Cash & Equivalents				5.7	8.7	3.9
17.4	16.5	19.7	Trade Receivables (net)				17.7	15.5	21.8
37.6	38.3	40.6	Inventory				46.4	44.1	37.1
3.7	3.6	1.9	All Other Current				1.2	2.8	1.7
66.4	65.0	68.6	Total Current				71.0	71.1	64.5
27.0	28.6	23.2	Fixed Assets (net)				23.4	21.9	24.2
2.7	2.4	4.7	Intangibles (net)				3.2	3.4	6.6
3.9	4.0	3.6	All Other Non-Current				2.5	3.6	4.6
100.0	100.0	100.0	Total				100.0	100.0	100.0
			LIABILITIES						
14.0	15.3	17.3	Notes Payable-Short Term				14.8	9.7	15.5
4.4	4.4	3.0	Cur. Mat.-L/T/D				2.3	5.5	2.7
14.3	17.9	17.1	Trade Payables				17.0	18.9	16.1
.1	.1	.1	Income Taxes Payable				.0	.4	.1
9.0	7.9	10.5	All Other Current				13.1	10.1	8.8
41.8	45.7	48.1	Total Current				47.2	44.6	43.1
19.5	18.6	19.3	Long-Term Debt				10.7	11.2	18.7
.5	.5	.3	Deferred Taxes				.2	.3	.5
6.6	5.7	7.9	All Other Non-Current				7.5	11.3	4.2
31.6	29.5	24.4	Net Worth				34.5	32.6	33.4
100.0	100.0	100.0	Total Liabilities & Net Worth				100.0	100.0	100.0
			INCOME DATA						
100.0	100.0	100.0	Net Sales				100.0	100.0	100.0
22.4	21.8	21.0	Gross Profit				20.6	20.9	17.0
19.1	19.9	17.6	Operating Expenses				18.5	17.4	11.9
3.2	1.9	3.3	Operating Profit				2.1	3.5	5.1
1.5	.9	.6	All Other Expenses (net)				.4	.7	.5
1.8	1.0	2.7	Profit Before Taxes				1.7	2.8	4.6
			RATIOS						
2.5	2.4	2.2	Current				2.1	2.6	2.1
1.6	1.4	1.5					1.4	1.9	1.5
1.1	1.0	1.1					1.2	1.2	1.2
1.1	.9	.9	Quick				.8	1.2	1.0
.6	(84) .5	.5					.5	.4	.6
.4	.3	.3					.3	.3	.4
14 26.2	10 36.0	11 33.4	Sales/Receivables				8 47.9	8 43.7	22 16.5
23 15.6	22 16.9	25 14.6					15 25.0	14 26.6	26 14.0
39 9.3	36 10.1	38 9.6					36 10.2	25 14.7	45 8.1
43 8.5	38 9.6	44 8.4	Cost of Sales/Inventory				49 7.4	40 9.1	41 8.9
65 5.6	63 5.8	69 5.3					70 5.2	66 5.5	67 5.4
94 3.9	111 3.3	95 3.8					118 3.1	94 3.9	80 4.6
12 29.9	14 26.9	13 27.3	Cost of Sales/Payables				14 25.7	9 42.3	13 27.3
26 13.8	26 14.2	22 16.8					23 16.1	24 15.3	20 18.1
42 8.6	46 7.9	40 9.2					40 9.1	41 8.9	35 10.3
5.4	7.0	6.6	Sales/Working Capital				8.1	6.0	6.6
12.1	16.5	14.7					16.7	10.2	13.9
30.5	−89.6	42.1					34.5	47.0	33.8
5.5	6.2	11.3	EBIT/Interest				18.6	24.4	12.1
(67) 2.3	(76) 2.1	(70) 4.3					3.7	(15) 4.8	(30) 4.4
−.1	.9	2.2					1.5	1.8	2.9
13.2	6.7	6.4	Net Profit + Depr., Dep., Amort./Cur. Mat. L/T/D						10.3
(20) 3.1	(19) 1.6	(15) 2.8							(11) 4.6
1.3	.5	1.5							2.8
.3	.3	.3	Fixed/Worth				.3	.1	.3
.8	.8	.8					.8	.7	.7
1.8	3.8	3.9					1.6	1.0	2.3
.7	1.1	1.1	Debt/Worth				.9	.8	1.1
2.3	2.2	2.9					2.9	1.4	2.3
7.4	14.3	18.0					5.2	3.6	18.0
37.4	35.9	55.7	% Profit Before Taxes/Tangible Net Worth				49.3	37.7	56.9
(62) 7.9	(73) 10.2	(62) 23.2					(12) 12.6	(14) 16.9	(27) 24.5
−1.0	.4	12.0					2.8	14.3	15.4
8.1	8.4	15.4	% Profit Before Taxes/Total Assets				12.9	18.6	15.7
2.6	2.8	6.9					2.4	7.8	8.7
−2.4	−1.2	1.6					1.0	−.9	4.6
36.3	48.6	54.6	Sales/Net Fixed Assets				45.6	65.8	37.8
10.6	8.9	13.1					13.1	21.6	9.2
5.3	5.0	6.6					6.7	6.6	6.0
3.5	3.4	3.6	Sales/Total Assets				4.5	4.5	3.5
2.5	2.3	2.6					2.9	3.1	2.5
1.6	1.7	1.8					1.7	1.9	2.0
.9	.8	.7	% Depr., Dep., Amort./Sales				.6	.6	.7
(69) 1.6	(75) 1.7	(63) 1.3					(11) 1.2	(14) 1.1	(27) 1.4
2.8	3.0	2.2					2.6	3.0	2.0
.9	2.2	.7	% Officers', Directors', Owners' Comp/Sales						
(17) 1.9	(23) 3.0	(16) 2.6							
3.9	5.6	5.4							
2274558M	1987891M	3415456M	Net Sales ($)	2250M	16728M	16485M	93563M	256821M	3029609M
1054498M	815219M	1359969M	Total Assets ($)	768M	9170M	6567M	35972M	92592M	1214900M

M = $ thousand   MM = $ million
See Pages 11 through 21 for Explanation of Ratios and Data

Current Data Sorted By Assets   **Comparative Historical Data**

Type of Statement

Type of Statement	0-500M	500M-2MM	2-10MM	10-50MM	50-100MM	100-250MM		4/1/00-3/31/01 ALL	4/1/01-3/31/02 ALL
Unqualified		1	1	9		4		12	10
Reviewed		4	4	3				5	4
Compiled	2	5	3	1				14	19
Tax Returns								1	
Other	1	5	2	3				14	10

Date ranges: 6 (4/1-9/30/04) — 45 (10/1/04-3/31/05)

	0-500M	500M-2MM	2-10MM	10-50MM	50-100MM	100-250MM		4/1/00-3/31/01 ALL	4/1/01-3/31/02 ALL
NUMBER OF STATEMENTS	3	17	11	16		4		46	43
	%	%	%	%	%	%		%	%
ASSETS									
Cash & Equivalents		14.9	9.5	4.3				9.8	8.6
Trade Receivables (net)		15.2	23.5	24.9				20.8	17.1
Inventory		42.1	47.7	47.1				41.0	41.6
All Other Current		1.4	.8	2.5				.5	2.2
Total Current		73.7	81.4	78.8				72.0	69.4
Fixed Assets (net)		18.2	11.4	13.6				16.5	18.0
Intangibles (net)		1.6	4.3	3.1				7.9	8.9
All Other Non-Current		6.5	2.8	4.5				3.6	3.7
Total		100.0	100.0	100.0				100.0	100.0
LIABILITIES									
Notes Payable-Short Term		13.4	23.1	17.5				12.3	10.6
Cur. Mat.-L/T/D		1.4	1.0	3.8				4.2	2.6
Trade Payables		18.3	14.0	23.8				14.5	20.8
Income Taxes Payable		.0	.0	.4				.0	.3
All Other Current		5.4	16.9	14.9				19.4	19.6
Total Current		38.6	55.0	60.4				50.4	53.9
Long-Term Debt		11.6	2.2	4.8				8.6	8.7
Deferred Taxes		.2	.0	.1				.1	.0
All Other Non-Current		11.7	18.7	5.7				5.1	1.0
Net Worth		37.8	24.1	29.0				35.8	36.4
Total Liabilities & Net Worth		100.0	100.0	100.0				100.0	100.0
INCOME DATA									
Net Sales		100.0	100.0	100.0				100.0	100.0
Gross Profit		24.0	15.5	13.9				19.7	19.4
Operating Expenses		19.2	12.9	12.0				17.2	17.8
Operating Profit		4.8	2.6	2.0				2.5	1.6
All Other Expenses (net)		1.4	.8	.5				−1.9	.9
Profit Before Taxes		3.4	1.8	1.5				4.4	.6
RATIOS									
Current		3.6	2.2	2.0				2.0	2.2
		1.9	1.3	1.3				1.5	1.3
		1.5	1.0	1.1				1.1	1.0
Quick		2.1	1.3	1.1				1.2	1.1
		.7	.6	.5				.5	.5
		.4	.2	.3				.3	.2
Sales/Receivables		5 71.3	5 69.5	14 26.7				10 35.7	5 69.1
		11 34.2	17 22.1	19 19.5				17 21.5	15 24.4
		24 15.3	28 13.0	29 12.8				28 13.0	30 12.3
Cost of Sales/Inventory		27 13.4	33 10.9	35 10.3				29 12.6	34 10.8
		43 8.4	47 7.7	40 9.1				50 7.2	58 6.3
		93 3.9	89 4.1	60 6.1				64 5.7	99 3.7
Cost of Sales/Payables		8 47.1	3 125.9	12 31.1				9 40.5	11 33.3
		16 23.1	8 48.0	21 17.8				14 26.0	21 17.7
		31 11.9	23 15.7	30 12.0				26 14.0	48 7.6
Sales/Working Capital		6.4	9.7	8.8				10.0	6.6
		10.7	25.2	26.6				15.6	18.9
		19.0	693.2	110.5				56.1	−324.2
EBIT/Interest		26.7		13.5				11.6	4.4
		6.9	(15)	5.0				(38) 5.0	(42) 1.2
		1.2		2.5				1.3	−1.1
Net Profit + Depr., Dep., Amort./Cur. Mat. L /T/D									
Fixed/Worth		.2	.2	.2				.2	.2
		.3	.6	.6				.5	.5
		4.2	4.3	1.7				1.4	1.2
Debt/Worth		.6	1.5	.8				.9	.7
		1.2	3.2	4.0				1.7	1.5
		9.7	25.7	10.9				4.8	6.5
% Profit Before Taxes/Tangible Net Worth		71.5		132.2				53.0	36.4
	(14)	28.3	(14)	17.5				(38) 20.5	(37) 4.5
		12.4		11.5				8.4	−7.0
% Profit Before Taxes/Total Assets		31.1	27.6	11.8				21.8	14.9
		11.3	2.6	5.1				8.4	1.3
		.1	−1.0	2.0				2.1	−5.6
Sales/Net Fixed Assets		42.0	65.3	78.3				62.3	59.1
		30.2	50.9	37.6				30.1	22.3
		11.7	17.6	19.6				11.4	11.8
Sales/Total Assets		5.2	4.9	5.7				5.3	4.0
		3.9	4.4	4.7				4.2	2.9
		2.5	3.6	3.3				2.9	2.2
% Depr., Dep., Amort./Sales		.5	.2	.2				.3	.4
	(16)	1.0	.5	(15) .5				(38) .7	(39) .8
		1.5	1.5	.5				1.1	1.8
% Officers', Directors', Owners' Comp/Sales		1.8						.4	.9
	(10)	2.6						(12) 1.1	(10) 1.7
		4.5						3.0	4.3
Net Sales ($)	4709M	86044M	202548M	1687351M		2584135M		1916332M	1957345M
Total Assets ($)	1099M	22300M	50798M	366497M		611139M		568225M	616750M

(Columns 50-100MM and 100-250MM marked **DATA NOT AVAILABLE** for the body data.)

© RMA 2005

M = $ thousand   MM = $ million
See Pages 11 through 21 for Explanation of Ratios and Data

Comparative Historical Data   **Current Data Sorted By Sales**

H1	H2	H3		C1	C2	C3	C4	C5	C6
			Type of Statement						
12	7	15	Unqualified				1		14
8	11	11	Reviewed		1	2	1	3	4
6	8	9	Compiled		2	1	3	1	2
2	2	5	Tax Returns	2			1	1	1
18	15	11	Other		2	2	4	1	2
4/1/02- 3/31/03 ALL	4/1/03- 3/31/04 ALL	4/1/04- 3/31/05 ALL		0-1MM	1-3MM	3-5MM	5-10MM	10-25MM	25MM & OVER
					6 (4/1-9/30/04)		45 (10/1/04-3/31/05)		
46	43	51	**NUMBER OF STATEMENTS**	2	5	5	10	6	23
%	%	%	**ASSETS**	%	%	%	%	%	%
9.9	9.7	9.3	Cash & Equivalents				16.2		6.6
14.3	17.7	22.5	Trade Receivables (net)				20.3		24.9
42.5	43.5	44.8	Inventory				42.0		44.1
1.8	1.9	1.8	All Other Current				2.2		2.7
68.5	72.8	78.4	Total Current				80.7		78.3
21.1	19.7	14.5	Fixed Assets (net)				15.0		14.8
3.5	3.6	2.6	Intangibles (net)				.5		2.3
6.9	3.9	4.5	All Other Non-Current				3.8		4.5
100.0	100.0	100.0	Total				100.0		100.0
			LIABILITIES						
14.3	29.7	17.0	Notes Payable-Short Term				6.6		15.0
3.0	2.6	2.0	Cur. Mat.-L/T/D				.8		3.1
17.5	15.8	20.5	Trade Payables				20.4		21.5
.1	.3	.1	Income Taxes Payable				.0		.3
14.0	11.8	12.6	All Other Current				13.3		16.6
49.0	60.2	52.2	Total Current				41.1		56.7
9.1	7.6	6.2	Long-Term Debt				3.6		4.1
.2	.2	.1	Deferred Taxes				.0		.1
4.5	5.5	10.3	All Other Non-Current				4.3		5.9
37.1	26.5	31.2	Net Worth				50.9		33.3
100.0	100.0	100.0	Total Liabilities & Net Worth				100.0		100.0
			INCOME DATA						
100.0	100.0	100.0	Net Sales				100.0		100.0
21.3	20.0	18.5	Gross Profit				21.6		15.2
17.9	17.4	15.2	Operating Expenses				16.9		12.8
3.4	2.6	3.4	Operating Profit				4.7		2.4
.6	.3	.9	All Other Expenses (net)				.3		.6
2.8	2.3	2.5	Profit Before Taxes				4.4		1.8
			RATIOS						
2.0	2.0	2.2					4.9		2.1
1.4	1.4	1.5	Current				2.0		1.5
1.1	1.1	1.1					1.4		1.1
1.0	1.2	1.1					3.7		1.0
.4	.6	.6	Quick				.8		.5
.2	.2	.3					.6		.3
7 52.7	7 49.2	8 46.0					7 49.8		14 25.4
15 24.8	16 23.4	17 22.0	Sales/Receivables				12 31.7		20 18.7
22 16.6	23 16.1	28 13.2					19 19.4		28 13.0
33 11.0	33 11.2	33 10.9					26 14.2		33 10.9
53 6.9	42 8.7	41 9.0	Cost of Sales/Inventory				31 11.9		36 10.0
114 3.2	99 3.7	69 5.3					50 7.2		56 6.5
8 46.3	7 53.5	8 47.0					8 48.4		11 31.8
17 20.9	13 28.3	18 20.1	Cost of Sales/Payables				14 25.7		19 18.7
36 10.2	28 13.1	30 12.0					21 17.7		30 12.0
7.2	9.0	8.0					7.4		9.7
14.3	20.0	17.0	Sales/Working Capital				16.8		22.3
99.0	36.6	73.4					28.9		89.3
9.7	20.0	14.5					205.9		15.4
(43) 4.8	(40) 5.7	(48) 5.8	EBIT/Interest				11.2	(21)	6.9
1.0	1.6	1.1					1.0		2.3
2.9			Net Profit + Depr., Dep.,						
(10) 1.8			Amort./Cur. Mat. L/T/D						
.5									
.1	.2	.2					.1		.2
.4	.5	.5	Fixed/Worth				.3		.5
1.5	1.1	2.7					.6		1.3
.8	.8	.8					.4		.9
1.7	1.9	2.2	Debt/Worth				.9		1.8
4.9	6.8	10.4					2.8		7.3
51.5	69.1	76.2	% Profit Before Taxes/Tangible				71.5		93.0
(41) 20.4	(36) 32.1	(44) 22.9	Net Worth				44.0	(21)	16.6
4.6	10.3	13.1					4.3		10.3
16.9	20.7	18.0	% Profit Before Taxes/Total				44.4		16.9
8.0	9.9	6.9	Assets				25.2		6.5
.8	3.0	1.3					1.0		1.9
82.7	62.0	65.3					52.3		84.3
22.5	21.7	35.9	Sales/Net Fixed Assets				33.7		35.9
9.0	11.1	16.7					20.0		16.7
4.4	5.1	5.2					7.2		5.5
2.8	3.6	4.0	Sales/Total Assets				4.7		4.6
1.9	2.6	2.7					3.9		3.5
.3	.4	.2					.2		.2
(40) 1.1	(37) .6	(47) .5	% Depr., Dep., Amort./Sales				.5	(21)	.5
2.2	1.3	1.1					.8		.9
1.0	.4	.5	% Officers', Directors',						
(15) 1.8	(12) 1.0	(16) 2.0	Owners' Comp/Sales						
7.0	1.7	4.1							
2977942M	3695188M	4564787M	Net Sales ($)	1134M	9670M	21228M	77659M	90886M	4364210M
1123845M	1107221M	1051833M	Total Assets ($)	613M	4704M	6923M	19103M	26334M	994156M

© RMA 2005   M = $ thousand   MM = $ million
See Pages 11 through 21 for Explanation of Ratios and Data

Current Data Sorted By Assets   Comparative Historical Data

Type of Statement	0-500M	500M-2MM	2-10MM	10-50MM	50-100MM	100-250MM		4/1/00-3/31/01 ALL	4/1/01-3/31/02 ALL
Unqualified		1	5	7	3			14	9
Reviewed	3	3	8	2				10	12
Compiled	1	2	1					10	9
Tax Returns								2	1
Other	1	6	6	5	2	1		7	17
		6 (4/1-9/30/04)		51 (10/1/04-3/31/05)					
NUMBER OF STATEMENTS	5	12	20	14	5	1		43	48

Item	0-500M	500M-2MM	2-10MM	10-50MM	50-100MM	100-250MM	4/1/00-3/31/01 ALL	4/1/01-3/31/02 ALL
	%	%	%	%	%	%	%	%
ASSETS								
Cash & Equivalents		4.7	9.2	4.0			6.7	4.7
Trade Receivables (net)		30.6	32.5	28.2			33.8	31.0
Inventory		24.1	26.8	31.0			24.6	26.0
All Other Current		5.1	1.9	1.3			1.2	.9
Total Current		64.4	70.5	64.5			66.4	62.6
Fixed Assets (net)		28.0	20.0	24.3			25.3	26.8
Intangibles (net)		2.3	3.1	5.8			4.1	3.7
All Other Non-Current		5.2	6.4	5.3			4.3	6.8
Total		100.0	100.0	100.0			100.0	100.0
LIABILITIES								
Notes Payable-Short Term		10.5	13.0	13.9			14.7	20.7
Cur. Mat.-L/T/D		.8	2.9	2.6			3.8	5.8
Trade Payables		16.8	16.8	18.5			20.7	19.1
Income Taxes Payable		.1	2.3	.1			.1	.8
All Other Current		10.9	9.2	10.8			10.9	9.7
Total Current		39.2	44.2	46.0			50.3	56.1
Long-Term Debt		16.9	8.6	8.5			14.2	16.8
Deferred Taxes		.0	.0	.5			.1	.2
All Other Non-Current		1.2	4.1	3.3			2.7	5.0
Net Worth		42.8	43.2	41.7			32.7	21.9
Total Liabilities & Net Worth		100.0	100.0	100.0			100.0	100.0
INCOME DATA								
Net Sales		100.0	100.0	100.0			100.0	100.0
Gross Profit		33.7	31.8	24.9			28.0	30.9
Operating Expenses		29.4	25.7	21.7			26.4	30.9
Operating Profit		4.3	6.1	3.2			1.6	.0
All Other Expenses (net)		-.1	1.0	2.6			1.1	1.5
Profit Before Taxes		4.4	5.1	.6			.5	-1.5
RATIOS								
Current		4.0	3.0	3.4			2.3	1.6
		1.7	1.7	1.2			1.4	1.2
		.9	1.1	1.0			1.0	.8
Quick		1.7	1.8	1.8			1.3	1.0
		1.2	.9	.8			.8	.7
		.4	.5	.4			.6	.5
Sales/Receivables	24 / 15.1	33 / 11.2	37 / 9.9				31 / 11.9	35 / 10.5
	38 / 9.7	48 / 7.6	45 / 8.0				47 / 7.8	46 / 8.0
	52 / 7.0	59 / 6.2	63 / 5.8				60 / 6.1	57 / 6.4
Cost of Sales/Inventory	11 / 32.7	20 / 18.1	48 / 7.6				20 / 18.7	26 / 13.9
	34 / 10.6	58 / 6.3	71 / 5.1				47 / 7.7	59 / 6.1
	85 / 4.3	80 / 4.6	121 / 3.0				72 / 5.1	109 / 3.4
Cost of Sales/Payables	19 / 19.3	18 / 20.7	27 / 13.7				21 / 17.8	23 / 16.1
	25 / 14.6	34 / 10.7	38 / 9.6				36 / 10.2	35 / 10.3
	35 / 10.4	46 / 8.0	59 / 6.2				49 / 7.4	53 / 6.8
Sales/Working Capital		4.3	5.2	4.4			6.7	10.1
		11.5	8.3	15.5			12.7	22.6
		-31.6	60.8	NM			189.6	-26.0
EBIT/Interest		38.9	83.8	26.9			5.5	3.6
		(10) 10.5	(17) 7.0	2.5			(42) 2.0	(46) 1.7
		2.1	-.3	-.2			.9	-.6
Net Profit + Depr., Dep., Amort./Cur. Mat. L/T/D							2.8	3.1
							(12) 1.5	(13) 1.4
							1.0	.2
Fixed/Worth		.2	.2	.4			.4	.4
		.5	.4	* .8			.9	1.3
		4.9	.9	1.6			1.8	8.0
Debt/Worth		.4	.5	.6			1.0	1.3
		1.7	1.3	3.2			1.8	2.6
		5.3	3.0	4.4			6.0	28.2
% Profit Before Taxes/Tangible Net Worth		96.6	61.7	25.9			33.9	35.9
		(10) 32.1	(18) 32.5	10.9			(36) 16.8	(39) 10.2
		3.8	3.6	-7.2			1.4	-9.9
% Profit Before Taxes/Total Assets		28.1	28.6	11.8			12.0	6.7
		11.9	10.8	4.5			2.6	1.7
		2.7	-2.1	-2.0			-1.6	-7.8
Sales/Net Fixed Assets		32.2	35.2	13.6			32.3	35.8
		16.4	18.1	10.6			11.9	11.8
		6.5	6.8	5.6			4.9	4.8
Sales/Total Assets		3.4	3.3	2.5			3.7	3.2
		3.2	2.7	2.2			2.2	2.2
		2.1	1.8	1.7			1.7	1.6
% Depr., Dep., Amort./Sales		.6	.6	1.6			1.0	.9
		(10) 1.0	(19) 1.7	(13) 2.6			(38) 2.2	(43) 2.2
		1.8	2.3	3.2			4.1	3.8
% Officers', Directors', Owners' Comp/Sales							2.9	3.3
							(13) 4.7	(14) 6.4
							7.1	11.3
Net Sales ($)	5110M	33069M	262319M	727146M	863902M	218322M	1681638M	1181055M
Total Assets ($)	1437M	11846M	106771M	319890M	436083M	100502M	693692M	556228M

© RMA 2005   M = $ thousand   MM = $ million
See Pages 11 through 21 for Explanation of Ratios and Data

Comparative Historical Data | **Current Data Sorted By Sales**

Comp. Hist. 1	Comp. Hist. 2	Comp. Hist. 3	Type of Statement	0-1MM	1-3MM	3-5MM	5-10MM	10-25MM	25MM & OVER
23	21	15	Unqualified			1	1	2	11
11	11	11	Reviewed		1		3	5	2
14	10	7	Compiled	1	4	1	1		
2	4	3	Tax Returns		2	1			
12	15	21	Other	1	4	1	4	4	7
4/1/02-3/31/03 ALL	4/1/03-3/31/04 ALL	4/1/04-3/31/05 ALL			6 (4/1-9/30/04)		51 (10/1/04-3/31/05)		
62	61	57	**NUMBER OF STATEMENTS**	2	11	4	9	11	20
%	%	%	**ASSETS**	%	%	%	%	%	%
7.0	6.9	6.6	Cash & Equivalents		5.8			9.9	4.1
29.9	28.5	30.9	Trade Receivables (net)		28.8			31.8	31.3
27.2	26.5	27.4	Inventory		23.0			26.3	27.5
2.4	3.2	2.5	All Other Current		5.4			2.4	1.7
66.5	65.2	67.4	Total Current		63.0			70.3	64.6
25.5	24.3	22.6	Fixed Assets (net)		29.0			20.6	23.8
3.3	3.5	3.8	Intangibles (net)		.6			3.4	5.4
4.7	7.0	6.2	All Other Non-Current		7.4			5.7	6.2
100.0	100.0	100.0	Total		100.0			100.0	100.0
			LIABILITIES						
14.7	13.4	12.2	Notes Payable-Short Term		7.6			5.0	14.1
4.8	3.0	2.0	Cur. Mat.-L/T/D		.4			3.5	2.0
17.9	21.3	17.5	Trade Payables		11.6			17.1	21.4
.5	.5	.9	Income Taxes Payable		.0			1.8	.2
10.2	10.7	10.8	All Other Current		12.5			7.7	11.0
48.0	48.9	43.3	Total Current		32.1			35.0	48.7
16.5	13.6	10.1	Long-Term Debt		21.5			9.2	6.6
.2	.2	.1	Deferred Taxes		.0			.2	.2
4.6	6.0	3.3	All Other Non-Current		1.3			6.8	3.3
30.8	31.3	43.2	Net Worth		45.0			48.8	41.1
100.0	100.0	100.0	Total Liabilities & Net Worth		100.0			100.0	100.0
			INCOME DATA						
100.0	100.0	100.0	Net Sales		100.0			100.0	100.0
28.6	30.7	30.2	Gross Profit		38.5			30.7	19.8
26.2	26.6	25.3	Operating Expenses		34.1			22.7	16.5
2.4	4.1	4.8	Operating Profit		4.5			8.0	3.3
.5	.7	1.2	All Other Expenses (net)		−.2			.4	1.9
1.9	3.4	3.7	Profit Before Taxes		4.6			7.6	1.4
			RATIOS						
2.4	2.5	3.2	Current		4.5			3.2	2.0
1.3	1.5	1.7	Current		2.3			2.3	1.2
1.0	.9	1.1	Current		.9			1.2	1.1
1.3	1.4	1.7	Quick		1.8			2.0	1.3
.9	.8	1.0	Quick		1.3			1.0	.9
.4	.5	.5	Quick		.4			.8	.4
28 13.0	28 13.3	33 11.1	Sales/Receivables		11 34.0			43 8.6	38 9.6
38 9.5	37 9.9	46 8.0	Sales/Receivables		29 12.7			56 6.6	47 7.8
59 6.2	50 7.3	57 6.4	Sales/Receivables		50 7.3			64 5.7	61 6.0
20 18.3	25 14.3	20 18.2	Cost of Sales/Inventory		10 36.0			22 16.4	20 18.4
57 6.4	52 7.0	54 6.8	Cost of Sales/Inventory		30 12.0			63 5.8	56 6.6
102 3.6	92 4.0	105 3.5	Cost of Sales/Inventory		54 6.8			80 4.6	115 3.2
18 20.6	18 20.0	20 18.7	Cost of Sales/Payables		6 56.2			22 16.5	28 13.3
35 10.5	32 11.3	31 11.8	Cost of Sales/Payables		20 18.5			40 9.1	38 9.6
51 7.2	55 6.6	45 8.2	Cost of Sales/Payables		37 10.0			65 5.6	57 6.4
6.3	7.3	4.9	Sales/Working Capital		4.7			4.1	7.4
19.8	11.6	10.3	Sales/Working Capital		10.4			5.7	17.2
215.1	−51.2	45.5	Sales/Working Capital		−37.1			24.6	67.5
10.3	20.5	27.1	EBIT/Interest		38.9				15.8
(58) 2.7	(58) 6.2	(51) 6.5	EBIT/Interest		(10) 11.7				(19) 1.9
1.0	1.1	−.3	EBIT/Interest		−3.8				−2.0
7.4		11.6	Net Profit + Depr., Dep., Amort./Cur. Mat. L/T/D						
(18) 1.7		(13) 2.6	Net Profit + Depr., Dep., Amort./Cur. Mat. L/T/D						
.6		.8	Net Profit + Depr., Dep., Amort./Cur. Mat. L/T/D						
.4	.4	.2	Fixed/Worth		.2			.1	.4
.9	.8	.5	Fixed/Worth		.3			.4	.8
3.4	3.5	1.2	Fixed/Worth		1.3			1.0	1.6
.9	.9	.6	Debt/Worth		.4			.4	.8
1.7	1.7	1.2	Debt/Worth		.9			.9	2.1
21.1	15.4	4.1	Debt/Worth		2.4			3.0	4.6
38.7	70.6	54.3	% Profit Before Taxes/Tangible Net Worth		77.0			74.1	29.0
(50) 15.0	(51) 26.3	(52) 17.6	% Profit Before Taxes/Tangible Net Worth		(10) 31.4			(10) 39.9	11.7
3.1	5.5	3.6	% Profit Before Taxes/Tangible Net Worth		−7.0			4.9	−9.0
12.5	19.3	16.8	% Profit Before Taxes/Total Assets		32.4			32.1	13.8
3.3	10.2	8.5	% Profit Before Taxes/Total Assets		14.0			11.4	4.5
.4	1.1	−.2	% Profit Before Taxes/Total Assets		−9.8			5.7	−2.6
32.4	28.8	29.0	Sales/Net Fixed Assets		35.7			28.3	15.6
14.1	13.4	13.8	Sales/Net Fixed Assets		18.4			14.9	11.3
6.7	6.3	6.0	Sales/Net Fixed Assets		5.6			6.4	5.2
3.1	3.2	3.3	Sales/Total Assets		3.9			2.9	2.8
2.2	2.2	2.4	Sales/Total Assets		3.1			2.3	2.2
1.8	1.9	1.9	Sales/Total Assets		2.1			1.8	1.7
1.0	1.0	.9	% Depr., Dep., Amort./Sales		.5			1.4	1.2
(55) 2.0	(54) 1.7	(49) 1.7	% Depr., Dep., Amort./Sales		(10) 1.0			1.8	(17) 1.9
3.0	2.8	2.4	% Depr., Dep., Amort./Sales		1.8			2.9	3.0
2.7	3.1	3.2	% Officers', Directors', Owners' Comp/Sales						
(25) 4.0	(21) 5.4	(20) 4.5	% Officers', Directors', Owners' Comp/Sales						
8.2	10.0	6.7	% Officers', Directors', Owners' Comp/Sales						
2279129M	2597199M	2109868M	Net Sales ($)	1346M	19630M	16086M	72154M	170486M	1830166M
1006021M	1201629M	976529M	Total Assets ($)	551M	7215M	11954M	29834M	76843M	850132M

© RMA 2005

M = $ thousand   MM = $ million

See Pages 11 through 21 for Explanation of Ratios and Data

Current Data Sorted By Assets   Comparative Historical Data

	0-500M	500M-2MM	2-10MM	10-50MM	50-100MM	100-250MM	Type of Statement	4/1/00-3/31/01 ALL	4/1/01-3/31/02 ALL
		26 (4/1-9/30/04)		105 (10/1/04-3/31/05)			Unqualified	27	24
	1	3	6	8	9	5	Reviewed	54	29
	1	6	16	15			Compiled	18	23
			12	2			Tax Returns	5	2
			1				Other	39	56
	2	3	16	15	8	2			
NUMBER OF STATEMENTS	4	12	51	40	17	7	**NUMBER OF STATEMENTS**	143	134
	%	%	%	%	%	%	**ASSETS**	%	%
		5.1	3.9	8.0	3.1		Cash & Equivalents	5.5	6.7
		33.2	31.6	31.0	24.8		Trade Receivables (net)	28.0	26.1
		17.4	23.3	17.4	11.6		Inventory	19.2	15.7
		3.0	1.3	1.6	7.0		All Other Current	1.3	2.1
		58.8	60.1	58.0	46.5		Total Current	54.1	50.5
		26.4	32.6	36.6	44.0		Fixed Assets (net)	37.4	38.0
		10.3	1.8	1.2	6.6		Intangibles (net)	2.9	3.5
		4.5	5.5	4.2	2.9		All Other Non-Current	5.6	8.0
		100.0	100.0	100.0	100.0		Total	100.0	100.0
							LIABILITIES		
		10.7	13.6	13.3	8.2		Notes Payable-Short Term	12.8	11.0
		6.1	5.3	2.6	6.9		Cur. Mat.-L/T/D	5.4	5.8
		16.7	18.1	19.8	13.9		Trade Payables	16.4	15.6
		.9	.1	.2	.0		Income Taxes Payable	.1	.2
		15.0	8.5	8.0	10.7		All Other Current	9.1	8.5
		49.4	45.6	44.0	39.8		Total Current	43.7	41.1
		17.7	17.0	14.7	19.6		Long-Term Debt	16.6	18.4
		.0	.7	1.1	2.1		Deferred Taxes	.7	.6
		13.9	4.4	4.8	5.7		All Other Non-Current	4.4	3.4
		19.0	32.3	35.4	32.8		Net Worth	34.7	36.5
		100.0	100.0	100.0	100.0		Total Liabilities & Net Worth	100.0	100.0
							INCOME DATA		
		100.0	100.0	100.0	100.0		Net Sales	100.0	100.0
		29.4	19.6	16.7	17.0		Gross Profit	21.6	22.9
		26.8	16.2	12.7	11.3		Operating Expenses	17.9	20.4
		2.7	3.4	3.9	5.7		Operating Profit	3.8	2.5
		.4	.2	.3	1.7		All Other Expenses (net)	2.0	1.7
		2.3	3.1	3.7	4.0		Profit Before Taxes	1.8	.8
							RATIOS		
		3.3	2.2	2.0	1.6			2.0	2.1
		1.3	1.3	1.3	1.2		Current	1.3	1.3
		.5	.9	.9	1.0			.9	.8
		1.8	1.2	1.3	1.0			1.2	1.4
		1.0	.7	.9	.7		Quick	.8	.7
		.3	.5	.6	.6			.5	.5
	29 12.7	39 9.3	50 7.3	47 7.8				37 9.9	36 10.2
	46 7.9	55 6.7	60 6.1	56 6.5		Sales/Receivables	49 7.4	51 7.2
	58 6.3	76 4.8	70 5.2	65 5.6			59 6.3	63 5.8
	19 18.8	31 11.6	21 17.7	16 22.9			22 16.8	22 16.6
	27 13.7	48 7.5	34 10.7	27 13.5		Cost of Sales/Inventory	36 10.1	35 10.5
	70 5.2	71 5.1	53 6.9	43 8.5			56 6.5	54 6.7
	18 20.7	21 17.3	25 14.5	26 14.2			18 20.1	18 20.3
	33 11.0	33 11.2	41 8.9	33 11.2		Cost of Sales/Payables	30 12.2	31 11.9
	53 6.9	52 7.1	59 6.2	51 7.1			46 7.9	56 6.5
	6.5	5.5	6.1	9.7			7.5	7.8
	116.1	14.7	15.3	24.1		Sales/Working Capital	23.2	18.0
	-7.1	-29.5	NM	-536.9			-39.2	-21.7
	5.5	6.6	15.1	6.3			5.7	3.5
	(10) 3.4	(47) 3.2	(36) 2.5	(16) 3.1		EBIT/Interest	(133) 2.0	(123) 2.0
	1.8	1.1	-1.0	1.9			.7	-.2
		6.9	7.8					5.7	3.3
		(10) 1.9	(17) 2.1			Net Profit + Depr., Dep.,	(44) 2.2	(37) 1.9
		.9	1.2			Amort./Cur. Mat. L /T/D	1.1	.8
	.2	.5	.6	1.3			.6	.6
	2.6	1.1	1.1	1.7		Fixed/Worth	1.4	1.5
	-.4	2.9	2.7	4.0			3.1	3.4
	.3	.8	.8	1.6			1.0	.7
	4.1	2.2	2.6	2.4		Debt/Worth	2.1	2.3
	-2.3	7.8	4.9	6.2			7.5	6.6
		39.6	39.1	21.2			31.5	28.4
		(45) 15.5	(39) 12.2	(14) 11.4		% Profit Before Taxes/Tangible	(128) 10.7	(122) 10.0
		2.9	-3.7	3.2		Net Worth	-.9	-4.3
	15.0	12.3	11.4	9.6			10.4	8.9
	7.4	3.3	3.8	4.6		% Profit Before Taxes/Total	2.9	2.7
	.9	.2	-3.2	1.8		Assets	-1.0	-3.3
	27.5	16.7	9.2	6.8			9.4	8.9
	12.7	6.3	5.3	3.5		Sales/Net Fixed Assets	5.1	4.9
	5.6	3.6	3.7	2.2			3.4	3.3
	3.3	2.6	2.3	2.2			2.6	2.3
	2.5	1.8	1.9	1.6		Sales/Total Assets	2.0	1.7
	2.1	1.5	1.4	1.1			1.6	1.4
	1.3	1.7	2.2	3.3			1.9	2.9
	(10) 2.8	(48) 2.7	(36) 3.3	(16) 4.9		% Depr., Dep., Amort./Sales	(132) 3.4	(122) 4.2
	4.9	3.9	5.0	6.2			4.9	6.2
		1.5	.6					1.7	2.0
		(22) 2.9	(11) 2.1			% Officers', Directors',	(48) 5.1	(43) 4.2
		4.2	3.9			Owners' Comp/Sales	9.7	8.7
	7050M	36867M	527757M	1623587M	1988576M	1788486M	Net Sales ($)	4586216M	4247742M
	1469M	14305M	251072M	940195M	1180826M	1056118M	Total Assets ($)	2699165M	2532193M

© RMA 2005

M = $ thousand   MM = $ million
See Pages 11 through 21 for Explanation of Ratios and Data

Comparative Historical Data   Current Data Sorted By Sales

			Type of Statement			26 (4/1-9/30/04)		105 (10/1/04-3/31/05)	
25	31	28	Unqualified			1	2	3	22
43	34	35	Reviewed		2	6	7	10	10
19	22	21	Compiled		3	4	8	5	1
3	3	3	Tax Returns	1	1	1			
49	63	44	Other		2	4	3	12	23
4/1/02-3/31/03 ALL	4/1/03-3/31/04 ALL	4/1/04-3/31/05 ALL		0-1MM	1-3MM	3-5MM	5-10MM	10-25MM	25MM & OVER
139	153	131	**NUMBER OF STATEMENTS**	1	8	16	20	30	56
%	%	%	**ASSETS**	%	%	%	%	%	%
6.5	6.3	5.5	Cash & Equivalents			6.6	4.1	7.6	4.2
26.9	28.2	29.7	Trade Receivables (net)			30.8	29.9	32.6	29.8
15.2	15.3	18.2	Inventory			17.9	27.3	19.3	15.8
2.7	2.8	2.6	All Other Current			2.6	1.9	1.0	3.5
51.4	52.6	56.1	Total Current			57.9	63.2	60.6	53.2
40.2	38.6	35.8	Fixed Assets (net)			36.0	30.9	32.4	39.0
1.9	3.0	3.6	Intangibles (net)			.5	3.5	.9	3.9
6.5	5.9	4.5	All Other Non-Current			5.6	2.4	6.1	3.9
100.0	100.0	100.0	Total			100.0	100.0	100.0	100.0
			LIABILITIES						
12.6	12.9	12.3	Notes Payable-Short Term			4.2	13.9	15.5	10.8
5.5	5.3	4.8	Cur. Mat.-L/T/D			3.8	4.9	5.5	4.1
14.2	16.4	17.8	Trade Payables			12.9	17.0	19.7	19.3
.1	.2	.2	Income Taxes Payable			.9	.1	.1	.1
9.2	8.8	9.2	All Other Current			7.4	13.3	4.6	9.8
41.7	43.6	44.1	Total Current			29.2	49.2	45.4	44.1
23.8	20.7	16.3	Long-Term Debt			15.3	14.1	16.1	15.8
.7	.9	1.1	Deferred Taxes			.6	.4	.9	1.7
5.6	7.1	7.7	All Other Non-Current			24.3	2.5	4.9	5.2
28.2	27.6	30.8	Net Worth			30.6	33.8	32.7	33.2
100.0	100.0	100.0	Total Liabilities & Net Worth			100.0	100.0	100.0	100.0
			INCOME DATA						
100.0	100.0	100.0	Net Sales			100.0	100.0	100.0	100.0
22.8	22.8	19.5	Gross Profit			29.4	17.4	18.0	15.7
19.7	19.6	15.6	Operating Expenses			24.3	13.8	12.9	11.8
3.2	3.1	3.9	Operating Profit			5.1	3.7	5.1	3.9
1.9	1.7	.5	All Other Expenses (net)			.3	.4	.6	.8
1.3	1.4	3.4	Profit Before Taxes			4.8	3.2	4.5	3.1
			RATIOS						
1.9	2.1	2.1	Current			2.9	1.8	2.3	1.8
1.3	1.3	1.3				2.4	1.2	1.3	1.2
.8	.9	.9				1.7	.9	.8	.9
1.1	1.4	1.3	Quick			2.1	.9	1.6	1.1
.8	.8	.8				1.3	.6	.9	.7
.5	.5	.5				1.0	.5	.5	.6
38 9.6	41 9.0	42 8.6	Sales/Receivables			37 9.9	41 9.0	42 8.7	48 7.6
51 7.2	56 6.5	56 6.6				49 7.5	53 6.9	50 7.3	60 6.1
62 5.8	68 5.4	67 5.5				73 5.0	60 6.1	77 4.7	68 5.3
23 16.2	23 16.1	21 17.6	Cost of Sales/Inventory			20 18.4	29 12.8	30 12.2	19 18.9
36 10.0	36 10.2	37 9.9				63 5.8	52 7.1	43 8.5	32 11.5
52 7.0	57 6.4	60 6.0				75 4.8	86 4.2	54 6.8	47 7.8
19 19.5	22 16.8	24 15.1	Cost of Sales/Payables			16 23.4	22 16.8	23 15.9	29 12.7
32 11.3	34 10.8	34 10.6				29 12.6	29 12.7	33 11.2	42 8.8
47 7.8	51 7.1	53 6.9				41 8.8	50 7.3	51 7.1	57 6.4
7.5	6.2	6.3	Sales/Working Capital			4.5	6.4	5.5	8.0
16.4	16.1	16.6				6.4	17.1	18.6	22.1
-15.7	-23.2	-29.5				10.6	-30.2	-20.9	-42.1
4.6	5.9	7.6	EBIT/Interest			6.8	6.6	9.3	9.7
(127) 2.0	(138) 2.1	(120) 3.2				(12) 3.7	(19) 2.1	(28) 4.2	(52) 2.8
.6	.0	1.1				1.4	1.1	.7	.3
3.9	4.6	4.5	Net Profit + Depr., Dep., Amort./Cur. Mat. L/T/D						3.8
(38) 1.6	(55) 2.5	(36) 1.9							(22) 1.8
1.0	1.2	1.1							1.3
.7	.6	.6	Fixed/Worth			.4	.6	.4	.7
1.5	1.5	1.3				.8	1.1	1.1	1.5
3.5	4.8	3.3				2.6	2.2	16.3	2.8
1.2	1.0	1.0	Debt/Worth			.3	1.7	.7	1.2
2.7	2.6	2.3				1.4	2.1	1.8	2.6
6.4	7.4	7.8				3.4	5.8	32.9	4.9
32.9	33.8	38.0	% Profit Before Taxes/Tangible Net Worth			36.3	35.3	50.8	32.9
(117) 10.8	(125) 10.3	(113) 14.1				(13) 3.1	(19) 9.8	(26) 18.5	(52) 12.0
1.1	-3.2	1.7				1.1	.7	8.9	-1.0
8.7	10.4	11.5	% Profit Before Taxes/Total Assets			22.2	11.7	10.8	10.8
2.7	3.2	4.6				6.9	3.0	5.9	4.5
-1.4	-2.5	.4				1.0	.1	.3	-.1
8.1	8.3	10.4	Sales/Net Fixed Assets			14.6	17.5	15.5	8.4
4.5	5.0	6.0				4.3	7.3	6.5	4.5
2.9	3.1	3.1				2.9	3.7	3.9	2.7
2.2	2.2	2.4	Sales/Total Assets			3.2	3.0	2.5	2.3
1.8	1.7	1.9				1.6	1.8	2.0	1.9
1.4	1.3	1.5				1.4	1.5	1.5	1.3
2.7	2.4	2.1	% Depr., Dep., Amort./Sales			1.4	1.6	1.6	2.3
(130) 3.9	(139) 3.8	(115) 3.0				(15) 2.6	(19) 2.8	(27) 2.7	(47) 3.9
5.5	5.2	5.0				4.5	4.6	3.6	5.3
1.8	1.7	1.5	% Officers', Directors', Owners' Comp/Sales				1.4	1.2	
(45) 5.9	(48) 4.3	(42) 3.0					(12) 1.9	(10) 2.1	
8.7	7.2	4.5					3.3	3.4	
4277342M	6162709M	5972323M	Net Sales ($)	899M	14276M	66147M	146775M	484630M	5259596M
2717181M	3762789M	3443985M	Total Assets ($)	359M	7952M	35947M	76266M	283918M	3039543M

M = $ thousand   MM = $ million
See Pages 11 through 21 for Explanation of Ratios and Data

Current Data Sorted By Assets   Comparative Historical Data

	0-500M	500M-2MM	2-10MM	10-50MM	50-100MM	100-250MM	Type of Statement	80	81
	2	1	24	43	21	24	Unqualified	80	81
	5	9	50	28	2		Reviewed	56	52
	11	32	27	5		1	Compiled	40	55
	10	7	8				Tax Returns	11	7
	3	20	53	51	14	15	Other	135	120
		101 (4/1-9/30/04)		365 (10/1/04-3/31/05)				4/1/00-3/31/01	4/1/01-3/31/02
	0-500M	500M-2MM	2-10MM	10-50MM	50-100MM	100-250MM		ALL	ALL
	31	69	162	127	37	40	**NUMBER OF STATEMENTS**	322	315
	%	%	%	%	%	%	**ASSETS**	%	%
	12.3	6.4	5.6	5.7	3.1	5.3	Cash & Equivalents	5.0	5.1
	29.3	28.0	27.2	24.2	26.1	24.7	Trade Receivables (net)	24.5	23.9
	17.6	31.2	31.9	24.9	15.8	18.6	Inventory	25.9	26.9
	1.1	1.3	1.9	2.2	3.6	3.9	All Other Current	2.0	2.2
	60.2	66.8	66.7	57.1	48.6	52.5	Total Current	57.4	58.2
	27.4	25.1	24.1	32.9	38.0	33.4	Fixed Assets (net)	31.2	30.5
	2.5	2.1	3.1	3.7	7.9	8.1	Intangibles (net)	6.3	5.9
	9.8	6.0	6.2	6.3	5.5	5.9	All Other Non-Current	5.1	5.4
	100.0	100.0	100.0	100.0	100.0	100.0	Total	100.0	100.0
							LIABILITIES		
	20.5	14.6	10.3	14.2	11.3	7.2	Notes Payable-Short Term	12.0	12.4
	6.9	3.5	4.0	3.5	4.6	5.3	Cur. Mat.-L/T/D	4.0	4.3
	21.1	16.5	18.3	15.7	20.2	20.1	Trade Payables	16.8	18.1
	.0	.2	.3	.2	.3	.6	Income Taxes Payable	.2	.2
	10.4	9.3	10.2	8.9	8.6	11.0	All Other Current	9.1	8.2
	58.9	44.0	43.0	42.5	45.0	44.1	Total Current	42.1	43.2
	16.4	18.4	13.7	15.3	18.2	12.9	Long-Term Debt	19.1	18.2
	.1	.7	.7	.6	1.7	1.9	Deferred Taxes	.7	.6
	11.5	10.2	4.9	6.2	7.3	5.5	All Other Non-Current	5.5	9.6
	13.2	26.8	37.7	35.4	27.8	35.7	Net Worth	32.6	28.4
	100.0	100.0	100.0	100.0	100.0	100.0	Total Liabilities & Net Worth	100.0	100.0
							INCOME DATA		
	100.0	100.0	100.0	100.0	100.0	100.0	Net Sales	100.0	100.0
	39.9	34.9	27.4	22.9	14.8	17.7	Gross Profit	25.3	24.2
	36.3	31.8	23.0	17.9	11.6	13.6	Operating Expenses	21.8	20.4
	3.6	3.1	4.4	5.0	3.1	4.1	Operating Profit	3.4	3.7
	.8	1.1	1.1	1.0	1.9	1.5	All Other Expenses (net)	-.1	1.9
	2.7	2.0	3.4	4.0	1.2	2.7	Profit Before Taxes	3.6	1.9
							RATIOS		
	2.2	3.2	2.6	1.9	1.6	1.8	Current	2.2	2.3
	1.1	1.4	1.6	1.3	1.1	1.3		1.4	1.5
	.7	1.0	1.1	1.0	.8	1.0		1.0	1.0
	1.3	1.4	1.1	1.1	.9	1.0	Quick	1.1	1.2
	.8	(68) .9	.8	.7	.6	.8		.7	.7
	.4	.6	.5	.5	.5	.4		.4	.4
(10)	35.7	(27) 13.6	(32) 11.4	(37) 10.0	(43) 8.6	(37) 10.0	Sales/Receivables	(32) 11.5	(29) 12.7
(34)	10.8	(43) 8.5	(49) 7.5	(50) 7.3	(55) 6.7	(51) 7.2		(43) 8.5	(41) 9.0
(53)	6.8	(59) 6.1	(60) 6.1	(62) 5.9	(62) 5.9	(59) 6.2		(56) 6.6	(53) 6.9
(2)	226.8	(28) 12.9	(40) 9.2	(29) 12.6	(20) 17.8	(23) 15.6	Cost of Sales/Inventory	(29) 12.7	(27) 13.5
(17)	21.6	(61) 6.0	(72) 5.1	(51) 7.2	(37) 9.8	(43) 8.5		(53) 6.9	(50) 7.3
(43)	8.5	(110) 3.3	(116) 3.1	(102) 3.6	(57) 6.4	(76) 4.8		(94) 3.9	(97) 3.8
(13)	28.2	(15) 24.5	(21) 17.6	(24) 15.1	(30) 12.3	(31) 11.9	Cost of Sales/Payables	(20) 18.2	(21) 17.4
(24)	15.0	(35) 10.5	(36) 10.1	(38) 9.7	(44) 8.3	(40) 9.1		(35) 10.6	(33) 11.0
(41)	8.9	(50) 7.3	(55) 6.6	(58) 6.3	(58) 6.3	(56) 6.5		(51) 7.2	(51) 7.1
	12.9	5.1	5.1	5.8	9.0	7.4	Sales/Working Capital	6.5	5.8
	35.6	12.7	8.9	10.3	70.3	16.5		15.3	12.1
	-19.8	-261.9	36.5	323.1	-20.3	356.4		-142.1	-94.3
	3.8	8.9	15.1	13.4	7.4	10.0	EBIT/Interest	6.1	6.7
(25)	1.7	(62) 3.2	(141) 3.8	(114) 3.6	3.5	(36) 4.7		(298) 2.4	(291) 2.4
	1.0	.7	1.0	1.4	.1	1.9		.7	.5
		6.4	4.6	3.2	5.5	5.1	Net Profit + Depr., Dep., Amort./Cur. Mat. L./T/D	5.3	7.1
		(16) 1.7	(45) 1.6	(35) 2.2	(20) 2.0	(15) 2.5		(93) 2.3	(92) 2.4
		1.2	.6	1.4	.9	1.2		1.3	.8
	.5	.2	.2	.5	1.1	.7	Fixed/Worth	.5	.5
	1.7	1.0	.6	1.0	2.1	1.1		1.3	1.2
	-9.1	5.0	1.6	2.8	-37.5	2.4		3.8	3.6
	1.3	.8	.7	1.1	1.6	1.1	Debt/Worth	1.0	1.0
	7.8	2.8	1.8	2.2	4.3	2.3		2.2	2.5
	-19.0	18.5	5.4	5.6	-81.6	8.7		10.0	12.0
(20)	82.7	(57) 47.3	(146) 39.3	(115) 45.7	(27) 33.2	(35) 35.8	% Profit Before Taxes/Tangible Net Worth	(260) 37.0	(259) 40.9
	8.1	19.3	18.4	19.6	21.5	14.9		17.0	18.0
	.0	1.4	3.1	3.2	7.0	7.9		3.3	1.9
	11.8	11.2	15.7	13.9	12.1	9.4	% Profit Before Taxes/Total Assets	12.7	12.5
	3.5	4.3	5.7	6.5	5.9	5.0		5.2	4.9
	.0	.0	.4	.8	-3.2	2.6		-.6	-1.0
	23.3	39.7	29.3	12.4	7.6	11.3	Sales/Net Fixed Assets	14.5	16.0
	14.4	15.8	11.4	6.3	5.1	5.7		7.1	7.4
	6.7	5.7	4.5	3.4	3.0	3.1		4.1	3.7
	4.6	3.5	2.5	2.2	2.2	2.2	Sales/Total Assets	2.6	2.7
	3.4	2.4	2.0	1.8	1.7	1.7		2.0	2.0
	1.8	1.7	1.5	1.2	1.2	1.3		1.4	1.4
	1.1	1.1	1.2	1.8	2.3	1.7	% Depr., Dep., Amort./Sales	1.4	1.2
(26)	3.6	(59) 2.1	(144) 2.1	(115) 3.0	(33) 3.5	(21) 2.4		(274) 2.5	(259) 2.6
	5.5	4.5	4.0	4.9	5.1	3.6		4.2	4.7
	6.6	2.4	1.4	1.3			% Officers', Directors', Owners' Comp/Sales	2.1	2.3
(16)	10.5	(37) 4.4	(58) 3.0	(18) 2.1				(83) 4.0	(69) 3.7
	15.1	6.5	5.1	3.2				7.9	5.9
	27656M	199391M	1801514M	5070210M	4775194M	11553249M	Net Sales ($)	19451627M	18269126M
	8350M	80889M	855938M	2863901M	2628728M	6133678M	Total Assets ($)	11170889M	9938422M

M = $ thousand   MM = $ million
See Pages 11 through 21 for Explanation of Ratios and Data

Comparative Historical Data | Current Data Sorted By Sales

94	105	115	Type of Statement — Unqualified	2	1	2	10	22	78
78	88	94	Reviewed	3	7	7	19	34	24
75	82	76	Compiled	11	21	12	19	9	4
18	23	25	Tax Returns	7	9	3	4	2	
142	152	156	Other	2	15	9	24	40	66
4/1/02-3/31/03 ALL	4/1/03-3/31/04 ALL	4/1/04-3/31/05 ALL		101 (4/1-9/30/04)			365 (10/1/04-3/31/05)		
				0-1MM	1-3MM	3-5MM	5-10MM	10-25MM	25MM & OVER
407	450	466	**NUMBER OF STATEMENTS**	25	53	33	76	107	172
%	%	%	**ASSETS**	%	%	%	%	%	%
7.3	6.6	6.0	Cash & Equivalents	9.9	7.2	7.1	5.1	5.6	5.5
24.4	25.9	26.3	Trade Receivables (net)	24.9	25.8	28.5	27.5	26.2	25.8
24.5	23.7	26.5	Inventory	21.4	28.0	33.5	30.0	28.2	22.9
2.3	2.8	2.2	All Other Current	1.4	.5	2.8	1.8	1.7	3.1
58.6	58.9	61.0	Total Current	57.5	61.5	71.8	64.5	61.7	57.2
31.7	32.6	28.8	Fixed Assets (net)	30.6	28.1	19.2	24.7	29.0	32.2
4.4	2.9	3.9	Intangibles (net)	2.8	3.4	.9	3.7	3.1	5.3
5.4	5.5	6.4	All Other Non-Current	9.1	7.0	8.1	7.2	6.2	5.2
100.0	100.0	100.0	Total	100.0	100.0	100.0	100.0	100.0	100.0
			LIABILITIES						
12.8	12.1	12.5	Notes Payable-Short Term	23.3	13.0	15.8	10.8	11.0	11.8
4.7	4.9	4.1	Cur. Mat.-L/T/D	8.6	3.8	3.9	3.9	3.7	4.0
15.6	15.7	17.8	Trade Payables	19.2	12.5	19.1	16.6	19.2	18.6
.2	.2	.3	Income Taxes Payable	.0	.2	.1	.5	.1	.4
8.8	9.8	9.7	All Other Current	9.4	8.8	11.9	8.5	10.5	9.5
42.1	42.7	44.3	Total Current	60.5	38.3	50.7	40.3	44.5	44.2
17.0	15.4	15.3	Long-Term Debt	18.8	20.4	11.6	15.9	15.8	13.4
.6	.6	.8	Deferred Taxes	.1	.6	.6	.9	.5	1.1
6.0	7.7	6.7	All Other Non-Current	14.5	12.1	5.4	6.0	4.8	5.6
34.3	33.6	32.9	Net Worth	6.2	28.6	31.7	36.8	34.4	35.6
100.0	100.0	100.0	Total Liabilities & Net Worth	100.0	100.0	100.0	100.0	100.0	100.0
			INCOME DATA						
100.0	100.0	100.0	Net Sales	100.0	100.0	100.0	100.0	100.0	100.0
27.8	27.6	26.3	Gross Profit	40.6	36.0	35.3	29.3	24.9	19.1
23.6	24.3	22.1	Operating Expenses	38.5	33.7	31.7	24.4	20.4	14.3
4.1	3.3	4.2	Operating Profit	2.1	2.4	3.6	4.9	4.5	4.7
1.5	1.4	1.1	All Other Expenses (net)	1.1	1.7	.8	.6	1.2	1.2
2.6	1.9	3.1	Profit Before Taxes	1.1	.7	2.7	4.3	3.3	3.5
			RATIOS						
2.3	2.2	2.2	Current	1.5	3.7	2.9	2.7	2.3	1.8
1.4	1.4	1.4		1.0	1.7	1.3	1.6	1.4	1.3
1.0	1.0	1.0		.6	1.0	1.0	1.2	1.0	1.0
1.3	1.2	1.1	Quick	1.2	1.7	1.1	1.1	1.1	1.0
.7	.8	(465) .8		.7	(52) .9	.8	.8	.7	.7
.5	.5	.5		.3	.5	.5	.5	.5	.5
30 12.2	33 10.9	33 11.1	Sales/Receivables	13 28.0	29 12.6	26 14.2	35 10.3	33 11.0	36 10.1
43 8.6	47 7.8	49 7.5		37 9.9	45 8.0	45 8.2	52 7.1	50 7.3	49 7.4
57 6.4	60 6.1	61 6.0		61 6.0	61 6.0	59 6.2	64 5.7	61 6.0	60 6.1
26 14.3	25 14.5	27 13.5	Cost of Sales/Inventory	6 59.4	11 33.9	35 10.4	40 9.1	33 10.9	26 13.9
48 7.6	50 7.3	52 7.1		36 10.2	59 6.2	66 5.6	81 4.5	53 6.9	43 8.6
97 3.8	90 4.1	102 3.6		107 3.4	129 2.8	183 2.0	116 3.1	104 3.5	78 4.7
19 18.8	21 17.7	22 16.4	Cost of Sales/Payables	14 25.9	13 28.6	20 18.1	26 14.0	24 15.4	25 14.6
32 11.5	32 11.3	37 9.8		29 12.5	28 13.0	38 9.6	36 10.2	39 9.4	39 9.5
50 7.3	49 7.5	56 6.6		49 7.4	47 7.7	55 6.6	55 6.6	62 5.9	56 6.6
5.5	5.8	5.8	Sales/Working Capital	13.9	3.9	4.5	4.8	5.4	7.4
11.9	12.8	12.4		UND	12.5	12.1	7.5	10.2	15.3
-838.7	-254.0	-999.8		-13.3	-113.3	79.4	28.7	131.9	NM
7.4	9.9	10.9	EBIT/Interest	3.8	4.4	10.7	12.2	16.4	13.9
(368) 3.2	(415) 3.3	(415) 3.5		(19) 1.5	(45) 2.2	(31) 3.1	(67) 4.4	(97) 3.2	(156) 4.6
1.1	.6	1.1		1.0	-.9	.2	1.6	1.2	1.5
4.7	3.0	4.4	Net Profit + Depr., Dep., Amort./Cur. Mat. L/T/D		20.0		5.2	3.1	4.6
(126) 2.1	(123) 1.8	(137) 2.0			(12) 2.1		(20) 1.9	(33) 1.8	(60) 2.6
.8	1.0	1.1			1.6		.5	.6	1.3
.4	.4	.4	Fixed/Worth	.7	.2	.2	.2	.3	.6
1.0	1.0	.9		3.1	1.2	.7	.7	.8	1.1
2.7	2.7	2.8		-3.2	11.3	1.8	1.6	3.1	2.4
.7	.8	.9	Debt/Worth	2.0	.8	.9	.7	.8	1.1
2.1	2.0	2.5		13.0	2.4	2.9	2.1	2.3	2.3
6.8	5.7	7.6		-7.3	56.8	7.7	4.6	6.6	6.1
38.1	36.5	41.3	% Profit Before Taxes/Tangible Net Worth	60.9	29.5	47.1	40.0	37.7	43.6
(355) 17.3	(399) 14.3	(400) 18.4		(15) 9.9	(42) 8.0	(30) 20.5	(67) 23.0	(95) 20.4	(151) 18.8
2.6	.1	3.1		.0	-1.6	.3	3.9	3.1	6.4
12.0	12.3	12.9	% Profit Before Taxes/Total Assets	10.5	7.4	11.2	15.5	14.4	13.0
5.4	4.8	5.4		3.5	2.9	5.6	5.9	4.8	6.6
.3	-1.4	.4		.0	-2.5	-.5	1.8	.4	1.2
16.3	15.3	20.1	Sales/Net Fixed Assets	29.1	40.2	27.8	29.8	19.4	12.3
7.2	7.0	8.3		10.3	13.2	15.9	9.2	8.5	6.3
3.8	3.6	4.0		3.3	4.1	6.4	4.4	3.8	3.9
2.7	2.7	2.5	Sales/Total Assets	4.6	3.3	3.3	2.5	2.5	2.4
1.9	1.9	1.9		2.2	2.1	2.0	1.9	2.0	1.9
1.4	1.4	1.4		1.3	1.4	1.6	1.5	1.3	1.5
1.7	1.6	1.4	% Depr., Dep., Amort./Sales	2.7	1.1	1.1	1.2	1.2	1.8
(353) 2.9	(379) 3.2	(398) 2.7		(20) 4.7	(46) 2.5	(28) 2.0	(68) 2.1	(96) 2.6	(140) 2.9
5.1	5.6	4.6		7.9	6.9	3.8	3.6	4.2	4.6
2.7	2.7	1.8	% Officers', Directors', Owners' Comp/Sales	6.5	2.9	2.3	1.3	1.6	1.0
(125) 5.0	(142) 4.3	(129) 3.4		(11) 10.5	(28) 5.8	(18) 4.7	(32) 2.1	(30) 3.0	(10) 1.5
9.6	8.4	6.5		14.7	7.5	6.3	5.1	4.1	2.3
20980771M	20574839M	23427214M	Net Sales ($)	13640M	101439M	124281M	562748M	1713688M	20911418M
10373785M	11328667M	12571484M	Total Assets ($)	6772M	64757M	63337M	325971M	1052204M	11058443M

© RMA 2005

M = $ thousand   MM = $ million

See Pages 11 through 21 for Explanation of Ratios and Data

Current Data Sorted By Assets   —   Comparative Historical Data

0-500M	500M-2MM	2-10MM		10-50MM		50-100MM	100-250MM	Type of Statement	4/1/00-3/31/01 ALL	4/1/01-3/31/02 ALL
		7		12		3	2	Unqualified	16	13
1		14		1				Reviewed	16	10
2		3		2				Compiled	5	8
1	1							Tax Returns	2	2
1	3	14		11		2	6	Other	16	27
		18 (4/1-9/30/04)		68 (10/1/04-3/31/05)						
2	7	38		26		5	8	**NUMBER OF STATEMENTS**	55	60
%	%	%		%		%	%	**ASSETS**	%	%
		8.6		5.7				Cash & Equivalents	7.6	7.6
		23.3		15.6				Trade Receivables (net)	19.9	23.3
		41.3		35.3				Inventory	28.0	32.5
		1.5		2.2				All Other Current	3.2	2.3
		74.7		58.8				Total Current	58.6	65.7
		18.5		31.9				Fixed Assets (net)	32.6	24.4
		3.5		1.6				Intangibles (net)	6.2	5.6
		3.3		7.7				All Other Non-Current	2.6	4.2
		100.0		100.0				Total	100.0	100.0
								LIABILITIES		
		14.1		10.4				Notes Payable-Short Term	10.1	12.4
		3.1		5.0				Cur. Mat.-L/T/D	6.5	5.3
		16.9		11.9				Trade Payables	10.8	15.2
		.1		.1				Income Taxes Payable	.4	.5
		8.9		8.0				All Other Current	7.8	8.8
		43.1		35.5				Total Current	35.6	42.2
		10.6		13.2				Long-Term Debt	25.2	19.6
		.4		.5				Deferred Taxes	.7	.4
		3.9		3.9				All Other Non-Current	4.6	4.8
		42.0		47.0				Net Worth	34.0	33.1
		100.0		100.0				Total Liabilities & Net Worth	100.0	100.0
								INCOME DATA		
		100.0		100.0				Net Sales	100.0	100.0
		26.7		27.4				Gross Profit	28.6	31.4
		21.2		20.1				Operating Expenses	23.5	24.5
		5.5		7.3				Operating Profit	5.1	6.9
		.6		.6				All Other Expenses (net)	2.0	2.9
		4.8		6.8				Profit Before Taxes	3.1	4.1
								RATIOS		
		3.0		2.9				Current	2.5	2.3
		1.7		1.7					1.5	1.6
		1.2		1.2					1.1	1.1
		1.5		1.0				Quick	1.1	1.0
		.6		.5					.7	.6
		.4		.3					.5	.4
		30	12.2	26	14.0			Sales/Receivables	29 12.7	32 11.5
		52	7.0	37	10.0				44 8.3	47 7.7
		64	5.7	66	5.6				59 6.2	60 6.1
		71	5.1	95	3.8			Cost of Sales/Inventory	65 5.6	75 4.9
		105	3.5	125	2.9				90 4.0	106 3.4
		160	2.3	196	1.9				133 2.7	144 2.5
		30	12.3	23	15.8			Cost of Sales/Payables	18 20.3	21 17.6
		44	8.3	42	8.6				31 11.9	41 8.9
		64	5.7	64	5.7				53 6.9	55 6.6
		3.3		3.2				Sales/Working Capital	4.2	4.4
		5.2		5.3					8.3	6.7
		15.9		15.0					33.2	31.7
			11.6		17.6			EBIT/Interest	4.6	7.1
		(34)	3.9	(23)	4.6				(53) 2.4	(57) 2.8
			.7		1.5				.9	1.2
			10.4		2.6			Net Profit + Depr., Dep., Amort./Cur. Mat. L /T/D	6.2	9.4
		(12)	2.9	(11)	2.1				(17) 1.9	(23) 3.1
			1.2		.7				.8	1.3
		.1		.4				Fixed/Worth	.4	.3
		.4		.6					1.1	.9
		.8		1.1					2.3	2.8
		.6		.5				Debt/Worth	.8	1.0
		1.7		1.4					2.1	2.4
		3.4		4.7					5.2	10.0
			51.8		36.0			% Profit Before Taxes/Tangible Net Worth	40.4	39.6
		(35)	13.3	(24)	10.3				(47) 16.7	(50) 19.5
			-.3		5.1				-.3	3.1
		17.0		11.0				% Profit Before Taxes/Total Assets	12.0	11.5
		5.7		4.3					6.4	5.4
		-.6		1.6					-.2	.6
		22.7		6.3				Sales/Net Fixed Assets	10.3	17.1
		12.7		4.2					5.8	8.2
		5.0		2.8					3.8	4.4
		2.1		1.6				Sales/Total Assets	2.2	2.3
		1.8		1.3					1.6	1.6
		1.3		1.0					1.2	1.2
			1.1		2.8			% Depr., Dep., Amort./Sales	2.3	1.9
		(33)	2.2	(24)	3.4				(53) 3.4	(54) 3.2
			4.1		6.1				5.8	4.5
			1.5					% Officers', Directors', Owners' Comp/Sales	1.5	1.0
		(11)	4.4						(12) 4.9	(18) 2.9
			5.1						9.6	9.8
1395M	17680M	404914M		640492M		646438M	1252180M	Net Sales ($)	1538713M	1922837M
503M	7351M	227709M		491310M		337737M	1321578M	Total Assets ($)	1226424M	1351872M

© RMA 2005

M = $ thousand   MM = $ million
See Pages 11 through 21 for Explanation of Ratios and Data

Comparative Historical Data						Current Data Sorted By Sales					
15	17	24	Type of Statement					1	11	12	
			Unqualified								
9	21	16	Reviewed				6	7			
8	8	7	Compiled		2	3	1	1	2	1	
	1	2	Tax Returns	1	1	1					
28	26	37	Other	2	3	2	5	14	11		
4/1/02-	4/1/03-	4/1/04-			18 (4/1-9/30/04)		68 (10/1/04-3/31/05)				
3/31/03	3/31/04	3/31/05									
ALL	ALL	ALL		0-1MM	1-3MM	3-5MM	5-10MM	10-25MM	25MM & OVER		
60	73	86	NUMBER OF STATEMENTS	3	6	6	13	34	24		
%	%	%	ASSETS	%	%	%	%	%	%		
7.5	7.8	7.5	Cash & Equivalents				10.8	8.4	5.5		
18.0	21.1	20.5	Trade Receivables (net)				18.0	22.4	18.2		
35.2	33.0	36.5	Inventory				44.8	37.0	34.2		
1.7	4.1	1.9	All Other Current				1.2	2.3	2.0		
62.3	65.9	66.4	Total Current				74.9	70.1	59.9		
27.8	25.8	24.0	Fixed Assets (net)				18.6	23.3	28.5		
6.5	3.9	3.8	Intangibles (net)				2.6	1.3	3.6		
3.4	4.5	5.8	All Other Non-Current				3.9	5.2	8.0		
100.0	100.0	100.0	Total				100.0	100.0	100.0		
			LIABILITIES								
13.2	15.7	13.2	Notes Payable-Short Term				16.0	11.5	11.1		
6.3	4.0	3.8	Cur. Mat.-L/T/D				2.5	5.2	2.2		
13.5	12.3	13.9	Trade Payables				12.8	15.8	11.9		
.2	.9	.5	Income Taxes Payable				.2	.1	1.5		
7.4	8.2	9.3	All Other Current				5.1	9.3	9.3		
40.6	41.0	40.6	Total Current				36.6	41.8	36.0		
19.7	13.6	12.8	Long-Term Debt				9.7	12.1	15.7		
.5	.4	.3	Deferred Taxes				.9	.3	.3		
4.5	6.1	5.2	All Other Non-Current				.9	4.3	5.6		
34.8	38.8	41.1	Net Worth				51.8	41.5	42.4		
100.0	100.0	100.0	Total Liabilities & Net Worth				100.0	100.0	100.0		
			INCOME DATA								
100.0	100.0	100.0	Net Sales				100.0	100.0	100.0		
28.4	29.6	27.6	Gross Profit				24.5	28.8	24.1		
23.1	23.6	21.3	Operating Expenses				20.9	21.7	15.0		
5.3	6.0	6.3	Operating Profit				3.5	7.1	9.0		
1.7	.9	.8	All Other Expenses (net)				.4	.7	.7		
3.6	5.1	5.5	Profit Before Taxes				3.1	6.4	8.4		
			RATIOS								
2.5	2.4	2.8					6.3	3.0	2.6		
1.5	1.6	1.7	Current				2.4	1.7	1.7		
1.1	1.1	1.2					1.3	1.2	1.3		
.9	1.1	1.3					3.3	1.6	1.0		
.6	.7	.6	Quick				.6	.6	.7		
.4	.4	.4					.4	.4	.4		
25	14.8	34	10.6	27	13.6	Sales/Receivables	25	14.7	26	14.0	36	10.2
43	8.5	47	7.8	47	7.7		56	6.5	46	8.0	48	7.6
57	6.4	63	5.8	66	5.6		62	5.9	65	5.6	67	5.4
79	4.6	70	5.2	71	5.1	Cost of Sales/Inventory	84	4.3	69	5.3	87	4.2
110	3.3	99	3.7	115	3.2		145	2.5	107	3.4	139	2.6
151	2.4	151	2.4	172	2.1		256	1.4	130	2.8	189	1.9
22	16.6	20	18.3	26	13.8	Cost of Sales/Payables	15	24.2	30	12.3	24	15.5
40	9.2	33	10.9	41	8.8		45	8.0	43	8.5	33	11.1
51	7.2	56	6.6	57	6.4		64	5.7	58	6.3	48	7.7
3.8		3.4		3.4		Sales/Working Capital	1.8		3.7		3.2	
8.4		6.7		5.3			2.7		5.2		5.7	
25.0		25.0		19.5			13.0		17.5		11.8	
	7.3		9.0		12.2	EBIT/Interest		19.6		16.1		15.4
(57)	2.7	(65)	2.2	(73)	4.2		(11)	3.1	(30)	4.5	(20)	5.0
	.9		.3		1.2			.1		1.3		3.8
	6.2		5.7		6.3	Net Profit + Depr., Dep., Amort./Cur. Mat. L/T/D				4.7		
(25)	1.7	(23)	2.4	(27)	2.2				(11)	2.1		
	.8		.7		1.1					.7		
.4		.3		.2		Fixed/Worth	.1		.2		.2	
.9		.6		.6			.3		.5		.8	
3.0		1.5		1.1			.5		.8		1.3	
1.0		.8		.6		Debt/Worth	.3		.5		.6	
2.2		1.6		1.6			1.1		1.5		1.4	
10.3		4.5		4.7			2.2		4.4		4.0	
	32.2		41.0		39.3	% Profit Before Taxes/Tangible Net Worth		24.1		51.8		39.4
(50)	14.3	(66)	16.7	(74)	12.9			10.8	(31)	14.5	(21)	17.0
	−5.9		−.3		5.1			−7.4		5.0		8.5
12.1		13.4		12.8		% Profit Before Taxes/Total Assets	9.2		19.2		11.6	
5.7		5.3		4.5			4.1		5.3		5.1	
−.7		−1.2		.7			−2.1		1.4		2.6	
13.3		11.4		16.8		Sales/Net Fixed Assets	16.5		16.0		10.9	
7.6		6.9		7.3			9.2		9.3		6.1	
3.6		3.5		3.8			4.7		4.2		3.0	
2.0		2.1		2.0		Sales/Total Assets	1.7		2.2		1.6	
1.4		1.5		1.5			1.3		1.8		1.3	
1.1		1.1		1.0			1.0		1.3		1.0	
	2.1		1.9		1.5	% Depr., Dep., Amort./Sales		1.1		1.8		1.6
(54)	3.4	(60)	3.3	(74)	2.8		(11)	2.7	(29)	3.3	(22)	2.7
	5.3		5.6		4.3			6.6		4.6		4.3
	.9		1.1		1.4	% Officers', Directors', Owners' Comp/Sales				.5		
(18)	2.2	(16)	2.7	(18)	3.4				(10)	1.7		
	5.7		6.7		5.6					4.6		
1626394M	1919575M	2963099M	Net Sales ($)	2053M	12202M	25129M	96561M	532682M	2294472M		
1249752M	1515183M	2386188M	Total Assets ($)	6496M	7495M	15496M	80522M	329698M	1946481M		

© RMA 2005   M = $ thousand   MM = $ million
See Pages 11 through 21 for Explanation of Ratios and Data

Current Data Sorted By Assets **Comparative Historical Data**

						Type of Statement		
1	2	6	17	3	5	Unqualified	37	27
	4	30	10			Reviewed	32	35
3	3	12	1			Compiled	31	35
5	7	3				Tax Returns	9	6
3	11	13	16	1	4	Other	45	55
	38 (4/1-9/30/04)		122 (10/1/04-3/31/05)				4/1/00-3/31/01	4/1/01-3/31/02
0-500M	500M-2MM	2-10MM	10-50MM	50-100MM	100-250MM		ALL	ALL
12	27	64	44	4	9	NUMBER OF STATEMENTS	154	158
%	%	%	%	%	%	ASSETS	%	%
12.8	11.6	7.3	6.5			Cash & Equivalents	6.7	7.4
17.1	27.4	20.5	18.7			Trade Receivables (net)	22.2	20.4
29.6	29.3	36.0	33.7			Inventory	31.9	33.4
7.0	3.8	2.8	2.7			All Other Current	2.2	2.6
66.5	72.1	66.6	61.7			Total Current	63.0	63.8
12.5	19.5	26.4	26.7			Fixed Assets (net)	26.9	25.6
7.3	2.4	2.4	5.5			Intangibles (net)	5.0	6.2
13.7	6.0	4.6	6.2			All Other Non-Current	5.1	4.4
100.0	100.0	100.0	100.0			Total	100.0	100.0
						LIABILITIES		
11.3	13.3	11.9	10.3			Notes Payable-Short Term	11.7	12.2
8.0	2.3	5.5	3.6			Cur. Mat.-L/T/D	5.0	4.4
13.4	12.0	11.0	10.4			Trade Payables	13.3	11.4
.0	.2	.2	.3			Income Taxes Payable	.4	.2
9.1	9.8	7.6	7.9			All Other Current	8.3	7.3
41.7	37.6	36.2	32.6			Total Current	38.6	35.7
15.2	17.7	15.5	19.6			Long-Term Debt	17.8	17.4
.0	.1	.9	1.0			Deferred Taxes	.5	.6
21.3	12.5	5.5	2.9			All Other Non-Current	6.0	5.4
21.4	32.1	41.9	43.9			Net Worth	37.0	40.9
100.0	100.0	100.0	100.0			Total Liabilities & Net Worth	100.0	100.0
						INCOME DATA		
100.0	100.0	100.0	100.0			Net Sales	100.0	100.0
45.2	41.0	32.2	25.5			Gross Profit	31.8	31.1
41.7	36.0	25.3	18.3			Operating Expenses	23.8	24.2
3.5	5.0	6.9	7.2			Operating Profit	8.0	6.9
1.6	1.3	1.1	1.2			All Other Expenses (net)	2.1	2.3
1.9	3.7	5.8	6.0			Profit Before Taxes	5.9	4.6
						RATIOS		
3.9	5.1	2.8	2.6			Current	3.2	3.4
2.3	2.6	2.0	1.9				1.7	1.9
.9	1.3	1.4	1.3				1.1	1.3
1.2	2.7	1.4	1.3			Quick	1.4	1.5
.7	1.5	.7	.7				.7	.8
.3	.6	.5	.4				.5	.4
(4) 95.3	(21) 17.0	(30) 12.2	(35) 10.3			Sales/Receivables	(30) 12.0	(31) 11.6
(19) 18.9	(46) 8.0	(45) 8.1	(47) 7.7				(46) 7.9	(47) 7.8
(35) 10.4	(65) 5.6	(54) 6.8	(62) 5.9				(62) 5.9	(61) 6.0
(3) 110.9	(38) 9.7	(62) 5.9	(73) 5.0			Cost of Sales/Inventory	(57) 6.3	(64) 5.7
(47) 7.8	(91) 4.0	(111) 3.3	(135) 2.7				(97) 3.7	(108) 3.4
(171) 2.1	(140) 2.6	(165) 2.2	(172) 2.1				(154) 2.4	(158) 2.3
(5) 79.2	(6) 66.0	(15) 24.0	(20) 18.3			Cost of Sales/Payables	(20) 18.2	(16) 22.4
(18) 19.8	(27) 13.5	(30) 12.1	(32) 11.5				(35) 10.4	(30) 12.1
(48) 7.5	(52) 7.0	(45) 8.2	(49) 7.5				(54) 6.8	(53) 6.9
4.1	3.5	3.3	3.0			Sales/Working Capital	3.6	3.4
7.7	6.0	5.6	5.2				6.8	5.7
NM	17.1	11.4	9.8				24.0	12.5
	25.1	12.5	7.7			EBIT/Interest	7.3	6.8
	(23) 5.5	(61) 4.0	(41) 4.5				(141) 3.0	(148) 3.2
	2.5	1.4	1.7				1.4	1.5
		3.3	3.6			Net Profit + Depr., Dep.,	4.5	5.6
		(14) 1.7	(20) 1.7			Amort./Cur. Mat. L /T/D	(51) 1.8	(45) 2.2
		.9	1.0				.9	1.1
.1	.1	.3	.3			Fixed/Worth	.3	.3
.2	.3	.6	.7				.7	.6
-1.1	1.8	1.5	1.2				1.9	1.7
.4	.4	.7	.8			Debt/Worth	.8	.7
2.0	2.0	1.3	1.5				1.7	1.7
-3.5	8.3	3.3	2.7				4.4	4.2
	67.8	37.4	41.7			% Profit Before Taxes/Tangible	43.8	41.9
	(24) 31.0	(62) 17.3	(43) 13.4			Net Worth	(133) 20.3	(136) 18.2
	7.2	3.6	5.7				7.3	5.2
27.0	20.1	16.2	10.6			% Profit Before Taxes/Total	17.5	12.4
10.9	8.9	6.8	5.7			Assets	7.4	6.0
-2.5	2.3	.8	2.2				2.5	1.5
56.4	90.4	21.6	11.9			Sales/Net Fixed Assets	18.4	17.9
31.0	17.8	6.7	6.4				7.2	6.8
20.2	8.3	3.5	3.1				3.3	3.6
5.9	3.2	2.1	1.8			Sales/Total Assets	2.2	2.2
3.1	2.2	1.5	1.2				1.6	1.5
1.3	1.5	1.2	1.0				1.1	1.1
	.9	1.2	1.5			% Depr., Dep., Amort./Sales	1.2	1.2
	(15) 2.3	(60) 3.3	(42) 2.4				(135) 2.7	(133) 2.9
	5.5	5.8	4.8				4.8	4.6
	4.0	2.2	1.6			% Officers', Directors',	2.2	2.3
	(15) 5.1	(24) 3.9	(11) 2.4			Owners' Comp/Sales	(56) 3.9	(51) 4.5
	8.8	5.1	3.1				6.1	7.7
11255M	80240M	514190M	1326246M	323699M	2248766M	Net Sales ($)	3097232M	3594038M
3281M	30330M	314032M	950625M	227212M	1615676M	Total Assets ($)	2646328M	3251509M

M = $ thousand   MM = $ million
See Pages 11 through 21 for Explanation of Ratios and Data

Comparative Historical Data   **Current Data Sorted By Sales**

			Type of Statement						
23	33	34	Unqualified	2	1		3	12	16
34	29	44	Reviewed		7	4	14	14	5
22	28	19	Compiled	2	4	2	8	3	
14	12	15	Tax Returns	4	5	3	3		
48	38	48	Other	2	8	8	7	11	12
4/1/02-3/31/03 ALL	4/1/03-3/31/04 ALL	4/1/04-3/31/05 ALL		38 (4/1-9/30/04)			122 (10/1/04-3/31/05)		
				0-1MM	1-3MM	3-5MM	5-10MM	10-25MM	25MM & OVER
141	140	160	NUMBER OF STATEMENTS	10	25	17	35	40	33
%	%	%	ASSETS	%	%	%	%	%	%
8.1	8.1	8.3	Cash & Equivalents	6.4	13.7	11.8	5.8	7.3	6.6
20.3	21.1	20.9	Trade Receivables (net)	14.0	19.1	23.5	22.5	20.6	21.7
33.6	32.8	33.4	Inventory	34.8	26.2	33.5	34.8	35.9	33.8
3.9	3.6	3.4	All Other Current	9.6	3.5	3.6	2.6	1.9	4.1
65.9	65.5	66.0	Total Current	64.9	62.5	72.4	65.8	65.7	66.1
24.6	23.2	23.8	Fixed Assets (net)	13.6	24.9	19.6	29.0	24.8	21.7
4.4	6.3	4.4	Intangibles (net)	8.6	3.0	4.1	2.0	3.8	7.6
5.1	4.9	5.8	All Other Non-Current	12.9	9.6	3.9	3.3	5.8	4.6
100.0	100.0	100.0	Total	100.0	100.0	100.0	100.0	100.0	100.0
			LIABILITIES						
11.3	8.9	11.5	Notes Payable-Short Term	.1	14.0	17.9	9.5	12.5	10.6
4.3	4.0	4.3	Cur. Mat.-L/T/D	7.8	6.7	2.4	5.1	3.9	2.3
12.0	12.7	11.3	Trade Payables	7.2	9.2	14.7	10.5	12.5	11.8
.2	.4	.2	Income Taxes Payable	.0	.3	.0	.1	.2	.6
8.1	8.4	8.4	All Other Current	11.9	6.4	6.2	8.9	8.0	9.9
35.9	34.3	35.8	Total Current	27.0	36.6	41.1	34.1	37.2	35.2
17.3	19.1	17.2	Long-Term Debt	14.1	23.7	15.3	17.7	14.9	16.3
.5	.5	.7	Deferred Taxes	.3	.4	.7	.8	1.3	.4
5.2	8.1	8.3	All Other Non-Current	10.2	14.6	8.1	6.2	4.7	9.8
41.2	38.0	38.0	Net Worth	48.0	24.8	34.8	41.2	41.9	38.3
100.0	100.0	100.0	Total Liabilities & Net Worth	100.0	100.0	100.0	100.0	100.0	100.0
			INCOME DATA						
100.0	100.0	100.0	Net Sales	100.0	100.0	100.0	100.0	100.0	100.0
31.5	31.8	32.5	Gross Profit	45.5	43.3	37.2	31.3	27.9	24.6
26.7	25.8	26.0	Operating Expenses	39.5	39.2	27.8	25.4	21.2	17.5
4.8	6.0	6.4	Operating Profit	6.0	4.0	9.4	5.9	6.8	7.1
1.7	1.7	1.3	All Other Expenses (net)	1.5	2.1	.9	.9	1.2	1.3
3.1	4.4	5.2	Profit Before Taxes	4.5	1.9	8.5	5.0	5.6	5.8
			RATIOS						
3.4	3.1	3.3	Current	5.4	4.7	5.5	2.5	2.8	3.0
1.9	1.9	2.0		3.0	1.9	2.1	2.1	1.6	2.0
1.4	1.4	1.4		1.9	1.2	1.1	1.7	1.3	1.4
1.6	1.4	1.6	Quick	1.8	2.6	2.0	1.2	1.3	1.5
.7	.8	.8		1.0	.7	1.3	1.0	.7	.7
.5	.5	.5		.5	.4	.6	.5	.4	.5
30 12.2	32 11.6	29 12.7	Sales/Receivables	17 21.1	18 20.5	21 17.7	33 10.9	30 12.2	43 8.6
42 8.7	44 8.3	45 8.0		42 8.6	35 10.3	47 7.8	43 8.4	45 8.1	56 6.5
59 6.2	58 6.3	58 6.3		91 4.0	47 7.8	61 6.0	52 7.0	56 6.5	64 5.7
43 8.5	56 6.5	61 6.0	Cost of Sales/Inventory	40 9.2	6 58.6	63 5.8	60 6.1	67 5.4	65 5.6
102 3.6	100 3.7	110 3.3		187 2.0	83 4.4	104 3.5	109 3.3	125 2.9	102 3.6
168 2.2	155 2.4	166 2.2		407 .9	150 2.4	151 2.4	183 2.0	156 2.3	175 2.1
16 22.7	18 19.8	17 21.8	Cost of Sales/Payables	0 UND	6 57.4	7 55.6	17 21.8	24 15.0	26 14.2
32 11.3	30 12.3	31 11.6		33 10.9	16 22.5	27 13.5	33 11.2	32 11.4	43 8.5
50 7.3	45 8.1	47 7.8		79 4.6	33 11.0	49 7.4	45 8.0	48 7.5	49 7.5
3.5	3.6	3.3	Sales/Working Capital	1.1	4.1	2.3	3.8	3.4	3.2
5.6	5.2	5.3		2.9	6.0	5.8	5.0	7.0	5.0
10.2	10.8	11.0		7.9	65.1	23.8	7.3	14.7	7.2
7.8	8.4	9.3	EBIT/Interest		16.3	30.0	10.3	8.5	9.3
(131) 3.5	(127) 4.4	(143) 4.5			(21) 5.6	3.5	(34) 3.6	(35) 4.8	(31) 4.8
1.3	1.5	1.7			1.3	1.9	1.2	2.5	2.0
6.2	5.4	4.5	Net Profit + Depr., Dep., Amort./Cur. Mat. L/T/D					3.6	11.1
(48) 2.2	(49) 1.9	(44) 1.9						(16) 1.9	(17) 2.6
1.1	.7	1.0						1.4	.8
.3	.3	.2	Fixed/Worth	.0	.1	.2	.3	.2	.3
.7	.6	.5		.2	.5	.3	.6	.5	.6
1.5	1.8	1.5		NM	5.0	2.0	1.5	1.3	.8
.7	.8	.7	Debt/Worth	.3	.4	1.0	.7	.8	.9
1.4	1.6	1.7		1.0	2.0	1.9	1.4	1.3	1.7
4.2	5.5	3.3		NM	25.4	8.3	3.3	3.2	2.6
32.5	38.5	41.7	% Profit Before Taxes/Tangible Net Worth		52.0	81.6	38.4	37.1	41.7
(131) 13.3	(121) 17.3	(148) 17.3			(20) 22.7	(16) 11.8	(34) 15.4	(39) 24.0	(31) 16.2
3.4	5.8	5.9			8.0	6.0	4.5	7.5	7.7
12.2	12.8	16.3	% Profit Before Taxes/Total Assets	10.8	20.4	23.1	16.4	14.0	13.8
5.8	6.0	6.5		2.2	9.5	5.4	5.2	8.2	6.1
.7	1.6	2.0		−3.0	1.0	1.8	1.2	3.1	2.7
21.5	20.8	22.7	Sales/Net Fixed Assets	26.0	53.2	93.5	14.4	18.5	12.7
8.5	8.3	8.1		17.8	19.0	8.3	5.6	7.6	7.0
3.5	4.1	3.8		5.2	3.0	3.4		3.7	4.5
2.4	2.4	2.2	Sales/Total Assets	2.0	3.3	2.3	2.4	2.1	1.9
1.5	1.6	1.5		1.0	2.1	1.5	1.5	1.6	1.4
1.1	1.1	1.1		.6	1.2	1.1	1.2	1.1	1.1
1.3	1.6	1.2	% Depr., Dep., Amort./Sales		.6	2.4	1.4	1.1	1.4
(126) 2.9	(122) 2.7	(136) 2.8			(19) 1.8	(12) 4.4	(34) 3.9	(39) 2.2	(30) 2.1
5.1	4.6	4.8			5.9	8.0	6.4	4.8	3.5
2.4	1.9	2.2	% Officers', Directors', Owners' Comp/Sales		2.7		1.9	2.2	
(45) 4.0	(47) 3.9	(59) 4.0			(13) 5.4		(15) 3.6	(10) 3.9	
6.9	7.4	6.6			9.4		5.0	6.6	
3239654M	3458681M	4504396M	Net Sales ($)	4772M	48951M	67378M	258605M	644360M	3480330M
2388627M	2662666M	3141156M	Total Assets ($)	5949M	30354M	45960M	176530M	473691M	2408672M

© RMA 2005   M = $ thousand   MM = $ million
See Pages 11 through 21 for Explanation of Ratios and Data

Current Data Sorted By Assets   **Comparative Historical Data**

0-500M	500M-2MM	2-10MM	10-50MM	50-100MM	100-250MM	Type of Statement	4/1/00-3/31/01 ALL	4/1/01-3/31/02 ALL
			6	1	2	Unqualified	11	11
			1			Reviewed	6	10
	1	2				Compiled	3	8
		1				Tax Returns	1	
1		3	3	2	1	Other	7	11
	5 (4/1-9/30/04)		19 (10/1/04-3/31/05)					
1	1	6	10	3	3	**NUMBER OF STATEMENTS**	28	40
%	%	%	%	%	%	**ASSETS**	%	%
			2.6			Cash & Equivalents	6.9	8.4
			24.1			Trade Receivables (net)	26.4	23.3
			41.0			Inventory	25.0	23.6
			1.4			All Other Current	1.0	3.8
			69.2			Total Current	59.4	59.1
			20.1			Fixed Assets (net)	23.4	26.9
			6.2			Intangibles (net)	9.7	7.6
			4.5			All Other Non-Current	7.4	6.4
			100.0			Total	100.0	100.0
						LIABILITIES		
			29.7			Notes Payable-Short Term	13.5	11.7
			1.6			Cur. Mat.-L/T/D	4.3	4.9
			23.3			Trade Payables	14.2	13.7
			.2			Income Taxes Payable	.6	.3
			12.0			All Other Current	13.3	11.6
			66.8			Total Current	46.0	42.2
			18.0			Long-Term Debt	10.4	16.9
			.1			Deferred Taxes	.7	.4
			3.7			All Other Non-Current	3.1	2.0
			11.5			Net Worth	39.7	38.6
			100.0			Total Liabilities & Net Worth	100.0	100.0
						INCOME DATA		
			100.0			Net Sales	100.0	100.0
			18.2			Gross Profit	23.5	32.3
			18.1			Operating Expenses	19.8	25.7
			.1			Operating Profit	3.7	6.6
			2.2			All Other Expenses (net)	.7	2.3
			-2.1			Profit Before Taxes	3.0	4.3
						RATIOS		
			2.3			Current	2.2	2.2
			1.1				1.3	1.3
			.7				1.0	1.1
			.8			Quick	1.4	1.3
			.6				.7	.7
			.3				.5	.5
			36 10.1			Sales/Receivables	31 11.8	31 11.6
			48 7.6				46 7.9	48 7.6
			56 6.5				57 6.4	57 6.4
			53 6.9			Cost of Sales/Inventory	41 8.9	36 10.0
			86 4.2				61 5.9	68 5.4
			124 2.9				95 3.8	107 3.4
			27 13.7			Cost of Sales/Payables	24 15.1	19 18.9
			40 9.1				34 10.7	36 10.2
			47 7.8				48 7.6	47 7.8
			4.3			Sales/Working Capital	6.5	5.9
			29.4				22.0	15.8
			-9.1				-309.2	57.2
						EBIT/Interest	8.5	11.0
							(26) 2.0	(37) 3.1
							.3	.6
						Net Profit + Depr., Dep.,		4.8
						Amort./Cur. Mat. L /T/D		(12) 2.1
								.0
			.4			Fixed/Worth	.3	.4
			1.3				.9	.8
			-1.6				NM	1.5
			1.5			Debt/Worth	.8	.8
			3.6				1.8	2.0
			-6.2				NM	4.3
						% Profit Before Taxes/Tangible	32.5	61.5
						Net Worth	(21) 12.7	(34) 18.4
							-3.7	2.4
			9.8			% Profit Before Taxes/Total	15.9	17.7
			1.1			Assets	5.0	5.5
			-21.2				-1.7	-1.5
			20.2			Sales/Net Fixed Assets	22.3	17.8
			9.7				7.7	8.7
			6.5				5.0	4.1
			3.1			Sales/Total Assets	3.1	2.9
			2.0				1.9	1.8
			1.3				1.4	1.4
						% Depr., Dep., Amort./Sales	.9	1.1
							(25) 2.0	(38) 2.4
							3.1	4.1
						% Officers', Directors',		1.7
						Owners' Comp/Sales	(10)	3.1
								4.4
64M	4426M	59767M	529500M	217639M	1099297M	Net Sales ($)	1400853M	1420812M
36M	1836M	23598M	254218M	200118M	525451M	Total Assets ($)	876343M	930812M

M = $ thousand   MM = $ million
See Pages 11 through 21 for Explanation of Ratios and Data

Comparative Historical Data					Current Data Sorted By Sales					

				Type of Statement						
20	16	9	Unqualified						1	8
10	11	2	Reviewed		1					1
6	7	3	Compiled			1	2			
1			Tax Returns							
15	18	10	Other	1				1	3	5

4/1/02-3/31/03 ALL	4/1/03-3/31/04 ALL	4/1/04-3/31/05 ALL			5 (4/1-9/30/04)			19 (10/1/04-3/31/05)		
				0-1MM	1-3MM	3-5MM	5-10MM	10-25MM	25MM & OVER	
52	52	24	NUMBER OF STATEMENTS	1	1	1	3	4	14	

%	%	%	ASSETS	%	%	%	%	%	%
8.3	10.0	7.6	Cash & Equivalents						1.7
22.2	23.4	22.9	Trade Receivables (net)						21.8
25.2	23.2	31.1	Inventory						36.1
4.2	7.2	3.9	All Other Current						5.0
59.9	63.8	65.4	Total Current						64.6
26.6	25.9	22.7	Fixed Assets (net)						21.1
6.3	3.8	6.9	Intangibles (net)						7.8
7.2	6.4	5.0	All Other Non-Current						6.5
100.0	100.0	100.0	Total						100.0

			LIABILITIES						
9.9	10.8	17.0	Notes Payable-Short Term						18.8
4.4	3.2	2.6	Cur. Mat.-L/T/D						3.0
12.8	15.1	18.6	Trade Payables						19.9
.4	.3	.5	Income Taxes Payable						.5
7.5	10.6	14.6	All Other Current						9.4
35.0	40.0	53.3	Total Current						51.8
17.1	14.5	16.7	Long-Term Debt						14.6
.6	.8	.8	Deferred Taxes						1.3
4.9	6.2	6.3	All Other Non-Current						7.6
42.4	38.6	22.8	Net Worth						24.7
100.0	100.0	100.0	Total Liabilities & Net Worth						100.0

			INCOME DATA						
100.0	100.0	100.0	Net Sales						100.0
31.8	31.4	23.5	Gross Profit						17.3
25.8	24.4	20.6	Operating Expenses						14.7
6.0	6.9	2.9	Operating Profit						2.6
2.8	2.0	1.7	All Other Expenses (net)						1.4
3.2	4.9	1.2	Profit Before Taxes						1.2

			RATIOS						
2.7	2.7	2.1	Current						1.9
1.7	1.8	1.4							1.2
1.2	1.1	1.0							.9
1.5	1.5	1.0	Quick						.7
.8	1.0	.6							.5
.5	.5	.3							.3
28 12.9	31 11.8	31 11.7	Sales/Receivables						34 10.6
41 8.8	44 8.3	46 8.0							43 8.4
58 6.3	57 6.4	57 6.4							50 7.3
36 10.2	24 15.2	47 7.7	Cost of Sales/Inventory						54 6.7
59 6.2	58 6.3	64 5.7							69 5.3
99 3.7	106 3.5	119 3.1							122 3.0
17 22.1	18 20.8	28 13.2	Cost of Sales/Payables						27 13.5
37 9.8	36 10.2	41 8.9							42 8.7
50 7.3	50 7.3	50 7.3							52 7.1
4.7	4.5	5.1	Sales/Working Capital						5.2
7.7	6.1	8.1							16.9
25.4	27.9	NM							-142.0
7.5	14.9	15.4	EBIT/Interest						7.7
2.6	(47) 3.6	(22) 2.4						(13)	1.7
.3	.8	-1.2							-.5
4.0	3.9		Net Profit + Depr., Dep., Amort./Cur. Mat. L/T/D						
(24) 2.6	(15) 2.4								
1.3	.9								
.4	.3	.4	Fixed/Worth						.5
.7	.6	.8							.9
1.6	1.5	-2.2							-2.8
.7	.7	1.1	Debt/Worth						1.5
1.5	1.4	2.1							2.9
3.5	3.9	-6.9							-9.9
25.7	35.1	50.2	% Profit Before Taxes/Tangible Net Worth						27.1
(47) 9.1	(45) 19.2	(16) 20.6						(10)	14.6
-4.1	1.6	8.0							3.8
8.3	13.7	16.7	% Profit Before Taxes/Total Assets						8.4
4.1	6.8	7.3							2.2
-1.9	-.4	-11.4							-5.5
16.3	17.7	19.9	Sales/Net Fixed Assets						20.2
6.9	7.8	8.9							9.5
4.5	3.9	5.3							6.5
2.2	2.5	2.8	Sales/Total Assets						2.8
1.8	1.9	2.0							2.0
1.3	1.3	1.3							1.4
1.5	1.5	1.6	% Depr., Dep., Amort./Sales						1.7
(48) 2.7	(46) 2.5	(21) 2.0						(12)	2.1
4.0	4.6	2.9							2.9
1.8			% Officers', Directors', Owners' Comp/Sales						
(10) 3.6									
6.2									
2880013M	2780317M	1910693M	Net Sales ($)	64M	2194M	4426M	22066M	66264M	1815679M
1560121M	1579372M	1005257M	Total Assets ($)	36M	2199M	1836M	9164M	57491M	934531M

M = $ thousand   MM = $ million
See Pages 11 through 21 for Explanation of Ratios and Data

Current Data Sorted By Assets   Comparative Historical Data

0-500M	500M-2MM	2-10MM	10-50MM	50-100MM	100-250MM	Type of Statement	4/1/00-3/31/01 ALL	4/1/01-3/31/02 ALL
		11	16	1	3	Unqualified	22	17
	1	6	8	1		Reviewed	10	11
	1	5	4			Compiled	5	10
1	1	1				Tax Returns		2
	4	5	5	1	1	Other	20	27
	17 (4/1-9/30/04)			59 (10/1/04-3/31/05)				
1	7	28	33	3	4	NUMBER OF STATEMENTS	57	67
%	%	%	%	%	%	**ASSETS**	%	%
		10.6	11.1			Cash & Equivalents	9.7	9.3
		14.8	17.6			Trade Receivables (net)	21.2	21.1
		16.2	12.7			Inventory	8.7	13.2
		9.5	12.6			All Other Current	13.0	12.4
		51.1	54.0			Total Current	52.6	56.0
		39.0	37.4			Fixed Assets (net)	36.2	31.4
		1.0	2.7			Intangibles (net)	3.1	4.2
		8.9	5.9			All Other Non-Current	8.2	8.3
		100.0	100.0			Total	100.0	100.0
						LIABILITIES		
		11.2	10.4			Notes Payable-Short Term	6.4	9.1
		1.8	2.1			Cur. Mat.-L/T/D	5.3	4.0
		10.3	11.1			Trade Payables	12.0	12.5
		.8	.4			Income Taxes Payable	.4	.7
		11.1	14.3			All Other Current	15.4	15.3
		35.2	38.3			Total Current	39.5	41.5
		18.9	22.0			Long-Term Debt	18.2	18.9
		.7	.9			Deferred Taxes	1.2	.9
		3.9	3.0			All Other Non-Current	4.5	3.4
		41.3	35.7			Net Worth	36.5	35.3
		100.0	100.0			Total Liabilities & Net Worth	100.0	100.0
						INCOME DATA		
		100.0	100.0			Net Sales	100.0	100.0
		24.5	23.6			Gross Profit	23.8	24.2
		22.2	17.9			Operating Expenses	20.7	19.8
		2.4	5.7			Operating Profit	3.1	4.4
		1.0	1.1			All Other Expenses (net)	.7	1.5
		1.3	4.6			Profit Before Taxes	2.4	3.0
						RATIOS		
		2.4	2.2				1.9	2.2
		1.2	1.4			Current	1.3	1.4
		1.0	1.1				1.0	1.0
		1.4	1.4				1.4	1.4
		.6	.9			Quick	.8	.8
		.3	.4				.3	.5
		11 34.4	15 24.9				18 19.8	20 18.2
		21 17.4	37 10.0			Sales/Receivables	34 10.6	34 10.7
		45 8.0	59 6.2				55 6.6	57 6.5
		1 280.2	1 414.4				0 UND	1 345.1
		19 18.9	10 37.7			Cost of Sales/Inventory	6 58.7	15 23.7
		73 5.0	55 6.6				31 11.9	45 8.1
		11 31.8	15 24.8				15 23.6	13 29.1
		17 20.9	30 12.3			Cost of Sales/Payables	26 14.2	24 15.4
		28 13.2	49 7.5				39 9.5	42 8.6
		5.0	6.3				6.6	6.6
		24.3	8.6			Sales/Working Capital	20.7	13.1
		NM	41.3				267.5	151.4
		7.5	10.1				9.2	4.8
		(25) 2.7	(28) 5.1			EBIT/Interest	(50) 2.6	(57) 3.1
		-.8	1.4				1.1	1.2
			5.7			Net Profit + Depr., Dep.,	5.3	3.8
		(17)	4.4			Amort./Cur. Mat. L /T/D	(22) 1.8	(23) 2.2
			1.5				.8	1.1
		.4	.7				.4	.5
		.9	1.5			Fixed/Worth	1.0	1.1
		2.0	2.1				1.9	2.1
		.5	1.2				.7	.9
		1.8	2.2			Debt/Worth	1.4	1.8
		3.9	6.0				3.9	5.0
		37.5	39.6			% Profit Before Taxes/Tangible	29.4	34.4
		(27) 7.8	(32) 24.5			Net Worth	(50) 17.1	(57) 18.8
		-10.0	10.0				2.8	3.2
		12.9	11.7			% Profit Before Taxes/Total	12.5	12.5
		2.4	6.7			Assets	6.2	5.7
		-4.1	1.3				.7	.6
		12.9	10.0				13.7	18.1
		5.2	3.6			Sales/Net Fixed Assets	7.1	7.9
		2.8	2.4				3.0	3.8
		2.5	2.0				2.7	2.8
		1.6	1.6			Sales/Total Assets	1.9	2.0
		1.1	1.0				1.3	1.4
		1.6	1.1				.9	.8
		(25) 1.9	(32) 1.8			% Depr., Dep., Amort./Sales	(47) 2.0	(58) 1.6
		4.6	3.1				4.0	4.1
		1.3				% Officers', Directors',	3.4	1.4
		(11) 2.5				Owners' Comp/Sales	(10) 4.1	(18) 2.5
		4.7					8.1	4.5
565M	15597M	251021M	1115004M	305475M	759068M	Net Sales ($)	2774460M	3095069M
334M	6439M	146364M	748101M	198495M	683620M	Total Assets ($)	2024303M	1737249M

M = $ thousand   MM = $ million
See Pages 11 through 21 for Explanation of Ratios and Data

Comparative Historical Data | **Current Data Sorted By Sales**

Type of Statement	4/1/02-3/31/03 ALL	4/1/03-3/31/04 ALL	4/1/04-3/31/05 ALL	0-1MM	1-3MM	3-5MM	5-10MM	10-25MM	25MM & OVER
Unqualified	17	20	31		2	1	5	13	13
Reviewed	16	16	16				2	7	4
Compiled	8	11	10		1	1	6	1	1
Tax Returns	1	2	3	1	1		1		
Other	18	18	16		4	1	4	2	5
					17 (4/1-9/30/04)		59 (10/1/04-3/31/05)		
NUMBER OF STATEMENTS	60	67	76	1	8	3	18	23	23
ASSETS	%	%	%	%	%	%	%	%	%
Cash & Equivalents	11.5	11.3	10.0				7.7	12.8	9.9
Trade Receivables (net)	17.8	21.4	16.2				12.9	18.4	18.8
Inventory	11.7	8.9	14.4				19.5	7.8	12.5
All Other Current	12.4	9.4	10.4				14.4	10.9	11.1
Total Current	53.4	50.9	51.1				54.6	50.0	52.2
Fixed Assets (net)	36.9	34.6	37.9				34.6	41.9	37.5
Intangibles (net)	2.6	4.7	2.6				.5	1.3	4.1
All Other Non-Current	7.2	9.7	8.4				10.4	6.8	6.2
Total	100.0	100.0	100.0				100.0	100.0	100.0
LIABILITIES									
Notes Payable-Short Term	7.5	6.7	9.8				18.8	6.3	5.0
Cur. Mat.-L/T/D	3.6	3.0	2.2				1.5	2.6	2.1
Trade Payables	12.8	12.6	10.4				8.0	11.5	11.5
Income Taxes Payable	1.0	.5	.6				.3	.8	.5
All Other Current	13.2	13.2	12.7				7.6	14.6	16.2
Total Current	38.2	36.0	35.8				36.2	35.9	35.4
Long-Term Debt	17.6	18.1	20.9				16.2	22.5	22.3
Deferred Taxes	1.5	1.2	.8				.9	.8	1.2
All Other Non-Current	3.7	4.8	3.7				1.1	4.7	2.2
Net Worth	39.0	39.8	38.8				45.6	36.2	38.9
Total Liabilities & Net Worth	100.0	100.0	100.0				100.0	100.0	100.0
INCOME DATA									
Net Sales	100.0	100.0	100.0				100.0	100.0	100.0
Gross Profit	25.6	23.6	25.4				22.9	28.0	19.0
Operating Expenses	21.1	19.8	21.1				19.2	21.6	14.4
Operating Profit	4.5	3.9	4.2				3.7	6.4	4.6
All Other Expenses (net)	.7	1.1	.9				1.3	.7	1.0
Profit Before Taxes	3.8	2.8	3.3				2.4	5.7	3.5
RATIOS									
Current	1.9	2.3	2.3				2.9	1.9	2.2
	1.4	1.4	1.4				1.3	1.4	1.6
	1.0	1.1	1.1				1.0	1.1	1.1
Quick	1.3	1.7	1.4				1.5	1.5	1.3
	.8	.9	.8				.5	.9	.9
	.4	.5	.4				.2	.4	.5
Sales/Receivables	10 37.6	23 16.0	13 27.6				8 43.9	16 23.3	18 20.1
	30 12.2	42 8.6	31 11.9				19 19.5	40 9.2	37 9.7
	48 7.7	61 6.0	48 7.7				44 8.2	65 5.6	43 8.4
Cost of Sales/Inventory	0 UND	0 UND	1 339.9				5 73.6	0 UND	1 346.2
	8 46.0	6 59.3	12 31.1				31 11.9	3 116.9	10 37.7
	30 12.4	37 9.8	55 6.6				118 3.1	34 10.7	53 6.9
Cost of Sales/Payables	14 26.9	14 26.0	14 26.2				11 34.7	16 22.8	14 25.9
	21 17.1	22 16.6	25 14.9				17 21.4	34 10.6	27 13.4
	40 9.1	44 8.2	38 9.6				24 15.3	49 7.5	33 10.9
Sales/Working Capital	8.0	6.8	5.7				4.9	5.1	6.6
	17.8	13.1	13.1				12.9	13.1	8.8
	NM	74.3	54.6				NM	49.7	48.6
EBIT/Interest	7.7	8.4	9.5				7.3	10.4	7.8
	(52) 3.5	(54) 3.6	(67) 3.6				(17) 3.5	(20) 6.7	(19) 3.6
	1.2	.7	1.0				.4	1.7	2.0
Net Profit + Depr., Dep., Amort./Cur. Mat. L/T/D	4.2	4.9	9.3					4.8	10.4
	(21) 1.9	(27) 1.7	(32) 4.0				(12) 3.1	(13) 4.5	
	.9	.6	1.6				1.6	1.3	
Fixed/Worth	.5	.5	.5				.4	.8	.8
	1.0	1.0	1.0				.6	1.1	1.0
	1.9	1.7	2.0				1.6	1.9	1.9
Debt/Worth	.7	.7	.7				.5	1.2	.8
	1.9	1.6	1.9				1.3	2.2	2.0
	3.2	3.3	4.5				2.7	4.0	4.6
% Profit Before Taxes/Tangible Net Worth	35.5	35.7	37.3				30.9	46.9	34.6
	(53) 11.4	(60) 17.7	(73) 17.5				8.0	24.7	17.5
	3.5	3.2	1.6				-6.9	3.2	5.2
% Profit Before Taxes/Total Assets	13.0	12.9	11.9				12.5	13.1	8.9
	4.1	5.2	4.9				2.2	11.0	5.0
	.3	-.9	.0				-2.5	1.1	1.5
Sales/Net Fixed Assets	19.5	18.5	11.0				8.4	10.1	10.0
	6.0	6.5	4.4				4.6	3.1	5.1
	2.5	2.6	2.6				3.2	2.0	2.6
Sales/Total Assets	3.1	2.8	2.5				2.3	2.4	2.6
	2.2	1.8	1.6				1.4	1.6	1.7
	1.4	1.1	1.1				1.0	1.1	1.2
% Depr., Dep., Amort./Sales	1.4	.9	1.4				1.6	1.6	.9
	(50) 2.2	(59) 2.1	(70) 1.9				(16) 3.3	(21) 1.9	(21) 1.5
	3.4	4.3	4.3				5.3	3.7	2.7
% Officers', Directors', Owners' Comp/Sales	1.2	1.3	1.3						
	(18) 2.0	(13) 2.3	(19) 2.8						
	5.0	5.7	5.5						
Net Sales ($)	2177901M	2692442M	2446730M	565M	17200M	12037M	132306M	421353M	1863269M
Total Assets ($)	1481224M	1850360M	1783353M	334M	9841M	17054M	101120M	357476M	1297528M

M = $ thousand   MM = $ million
See Pages 11 through 21 for Explanation of Ratios and Data

Current Data Sorted By Assets   Comparative Historical Data

Type of Statement

	0-500M	500M-2MM	2-10MM	10-50MM	50-100MM	100-250MM	Type of Statement	ALL 4/1/00-3/31/01	ALL 4/1/01-3/31/02
Unqualified			4	13	3	1		15	8
Reviewed		4	3	8				12	13
Compiled		1	7					18	19
Tax Returns	4	5	5			1		4	8
Other	1	7	11	4	4	2		32	20
	0-500M	22 (4/1-9/30/04) 500M-2MM	2-10MM	66 (10/1/04-3/31/05) 10-50MM	50-100MM	100-250MM		4/1/00-3/31/01 ALL	4/1/01-3/31/02 ALL
NUMBER OF STATEMENTS	5	17	30	25	7	4		81	68

ASSETS

0-500M	500M-2MM	2-10MM	10-50MM	50-100MM	100-250MM		ALL '00-01	ALL '01-02
%	%	%	%	%	%	ASSETS	%	%
	9.8	11.7	14.7			Cash & Equivalents	11.9	15.0
	7.5	13.9	13.4			Trade Receivables (net)	13.4	11.9
	44.9	38.1	31.5			Inventory	32.5	31.8
	2.1	3.9	4.2			All Other Current	3.0	3.7
	64.3	67.5	63.8			Total Current	60.8	62.4
	27.9	25.6	27.6			Fixed Assets (net)	30.5	28.0
	.2	2.4	3.7			Intangibles (net)	2.8	5.2
	7.6	4.5	4.9			All Other Non-Current	5.8	4.4
	100.0	100.0	100.0			Total	100.0	100.0

LIABILITIES

0-500M	500M-2MM	2-10MM	10-50MM	50-100MM	100-250MM		ALL '00-01	ALL '01-02
	20.1	15.8	8.3			Notes Payable-Short Term	8.2	14.2
	1.4	1.0	2.4			Cur. Mat.-L/T/D	4.4	4.2
	15.6	18.5	13.9			Trade Payables	16.6	12.4
	.0	.4	.4			Income Taxes Payable	.1	.1
	21.4	10.5	14.6			All Other Current	17.4	15.1
	58.6	46.2	39.6			Total Current	46.6	46.0
	15.5	12.1	13.5			Long-Term Debt	16.1	15.7
	.0	.0	1.0			Deferred Taxes	.3	.3
	6.4	4.3	2.2			All Other Non-Current	4.9	4.3
	19.5	37.4	43.6			Net Worth	32.1	33.7
	100.0	100.0	100.0			Total Liabilities & Net Worth	100.0	100.0

INCOME DATA

0-500M	500M-2MM	2-10MM	10-50MM	50-100MM	100-250MM		ALL '00-01	ALL '01-02
	100.0	100.0	100.0			Net Sales	100.0	100.0
	33.7	21.7	22.9			Gross Profit	25.6	26.4
	31.5	16.7	15.9			Operating Expenses	20.3	21.3
	2.2	5.0	7.0			Operating Profit	5.3	5.1
	1.2	.9	.8			All Other Expenses (net)	.9	.8
	.9	4.1	6.2			Profit Before Taxes	4.4	4.4

RATIOS

0-500M	500M-2MM	2-10MM	10-50MM	50-100MM	100-250MM		ALL '00-01	ALL '01-02
	3.1	2.0	2.2			Current	2.1	2.5
	1.1	1.4	1.8				1.5	1.5
	.8	1.1	1.1				1.0	1.0
	1.0	1.2	1.4			Quick	1.2	1.2
	.2	.5	.6				.5	.7
	.1	.2	.2				.3	.3
	0 UND	4 100.6	9 42.7			Sales/Receivables	6 59.7	5 79.0
	6 59.2	15 24.5	22 16.7				15 23.9	15 24.5
	24 15.1	26 14.3	28 12.9				26 14.3	26 14.0
	29 12.7	30 12.3	31 11.7			Cost of Sales/Inventory	27 13.7	24 15.2
	76 4.8	46 8.0	64 5.7				49 7.5	57 6.4
	207 1.8	84 4.3	86 4.2				72 5.1	85 4.3
	17 21.8	11 32.1	15 23.7			Cost of Sales/Payables	13 27.7	8 45.0
	22 16.7	22 16.5	23 16.0				24 15.0	18 20.5
	43 8.5	36 10.2	48 7.6				36 10.1	35 10.3
	6.2	10.4	5.2			Sales/Working Capital	9.4	6.2
	40.7	14.5	9.5				17.0	12.5
	−19.4	51.0	39.6				−129.7	938.4
	17.3	12.3	44.9			EBIT/Interest	14.0	18.7
	(15) 1.2	6.6	(20) 8.8				(71) 3.4	(62) 2.3
	.4	2.3	2.1				1.8	.9
						Net Profit + Depr., Dep., Amort./Cur. Mat. L/T/D	9.8	13.5
							(18) 4.4	(18) 3.0
							.6	1.0
	.4	.3	.3			Fixed/Worth	.5	.3
	1.3	.5	.7				1.0	.8
	−2.6	1.6	2.1				2.5	4.0
	.9	.8	.6			Debt/Worth	.9	.8
	2.4	2.1	1.0				2.0	1.9
	−10.8	4.5	4.0				5.3	64.7
	75.4	65.6	46.5			% Profit Before Taxes/Tangible Net Worth	61.9	58.2
	(12) 20.9	(29) 24.7	(24) 38.3				(69) 29.9	(54) 18.5
	3.8	5.4	14.4				13.2	−.1
	12.2	19.0	27.1			% Profit Before Taxes/Total Assets	19.4	20.5
	3.1	5.6	14.5				10.0	5.9
	−1.8	2.5	3.8				3.3	−.3
	34.2	29.9	21.9			Sales/Net Fixed Assets	17.3	21.9
	11.9	15.3	12.2				11.5	10.7
	6.0	8.2	3.8				6.8	6.6
	3.8	4.2	3.0			Sales/Total Assets	3.9	3.1
	2.6	2.7	2.2				3.0	2.4
	1.2	2.1	1.7				2.1	1.7
	.9	.5	.8			% Depr., Dep., Amort./Sales	.5	.7
	(12) 1.2	(28) .9	(20) 1.5				(72) 1.4	(61) 1.7
	2.0	2.2	3.6				2.6	3.1
		1.3				% Officers', Directors', Owners' Comp/Sales	1.0	1.5
		(13) 1.9					(32) 2.4	(24) 5.3
		2.6					4.6	8.6
4925M	50358M	461224M	1460541M	937004M	866868M	Net Sales ($)	2416601M	1686349M
1391M	17795M	143535M	593706M	532064M	626670M	Total Assets ($)	916809M	741357M

M = $ thousand   MM = $ million
See Pages 11 through 21 for Explanation of Ratios and Data

Comparative Historical Data   Current Data Sorted By Sales

				Type of Statement	0-1MM	1-3MM	3-5MM	5-10MM	10-25MM	25MM & OVER
	15	16	21	Unqualified					6	15
	13	13	15	Reviewed		1	2	2	5	5
	16	17	8	Compiled		1	1		5	1
	9	6	15	Tax Returns	3	4	1	3	3	1
	26	30	29	Other	4	3	2	4	6	10
	4/1/02-3/31/03 ALL	4/1/03-3/31/04 ALL	4/1/04-3/31/05 ALL		22 (4/1-9/30/04)			66 (10/1/04-3/31/05)		
	79	82	88	**NUMBER OF STATEMENTS**	7	9	6	9	25	32
	%	%	%	**ASSETS**	%	%	%	%	%	%
	11.3	9.6	12.4	Cash & Equivalents					5.3	16.8
	12.3	13.5	11.9	Trade Receivables (net)					14.5	12.9
	32.9	33.7	35.4	Inventory					38.3	30.9
	4.8	3.7	3.1	All Other Current					5.4	3.0
	61.3	60.7	62.8	Total Current					63.5	63.6
	30.8	29.7	27.8	Fixed Assets (net)					27.6	25.3
	3.4	3.8	4.3	Intangibles (net)					4.1	6.7
	4.6	5.8	5.1	All Other Non-Current					4.7	4.3
	100.0	100.0	100.0	Total					100.0	100.0
				LIABILITIES						
	9.7	13.7	11.7	Notes Payable-Short Term					14.3	5.9
	2.6	1.8	1.6	Cur. Mat.-L/T/D					1.7	1.8
	16.6	13.2	14.5	Trade Payables					21.5	11.5
	.6	.2	.3	Income Taxes Payable					.4	.5
	14.9	13.1	15.1	All Other Current					9.9	15.5
	44.4	42.0	43.2	Total Current					47.8	35.2
	15.2	12.8	14.0	Long-Term Debt					14.6	10.4
	.3	.3	.4	Deferred Taxes					.7	.4
	3.4	5.0	4.9	All Other Non-Current					1.9	2.6
	36.7	39.9	37.6	Net Worth					35.0	51.4
	100.0	100.0	100.0	Total Liabilities & Net Worth					100.0	100.0
				INCOME DATA						
	100.0	100.0	100.0	Net Sales					100.0	100.0
	25.0	25.3	26.3	Gross Profit					21.9	23.1
	20.0	19.9	21.6	Operating Expenses					18.1	15.6
	5.0	5.4	4.7	Operating Profit					3.8	7.5
	.7	.6	.8	All Other Expenses (net)					1.3	.2
	4.3	4.8	3.9	Profit Before Taxes					2.5	7.3
				RATIOS						
	2.3	2.2	2.2	Current					1.9	3.1
	1.6	1.4	1.5						1.2	1.9
	1.1	1.1	1.1						.9	1.3
	1.2	1.1	1.2	Quick					.7	1.7
	.4	.5	.6						.3	.9
	.2	.3	.2							.3
	5 74.6	7 49.1	3 134.0	Sales/Receivables					9 42.6	5 75.0
	12 31.3	19 19.6	15 24.5						19 19.3	16 22.8
	22 16.3	30 12.2	27 13.5						28 13.2	28 13.1
	31 11.7	25 14.8	29 12.4	Cost of Sales/Inventory					37 9.8	30 12.2
	57 6.5	58 6.3	61 6.0						66 5.6	55 6.6
	83 4.4	110 3.3	111 3.3						101 3.6	79 4.6
	12 30.1	11 33.6	12 31.2	Cost of Sales/Payables					22 16.9	11 33.7
	24 14.9	19 19.3	22 16.6						33 11.1	17 21.2
	40 9.0	39 9.4	36 10.2						47 7.7	29 12.6
	6.1	6.9	5.7	Sales/Working Capital					10.5	4.9
	16.4	13.5	13.6						16.3	9.5
	85.1	54.7	72.0						-92.9	29.9
	17.0	11.5	16.5	EBIT/Interest					9.5	54.1
	(70) 4.1	(73) 3.7	(77) 5.5						6.6	(24) 21.6
	1.6	2.1	1.6						1.4	2.9
	9.1	7.5	9.3	Net Profit + Depr., Dep.,						
	(23) 4.2	(25) 2.9	(12) 2.5	Amort./Cur. Mat. L/T/D						
	1.0	1.7	1.7							
	.4	.4	.3	Fixed/Worth					.4	.3
	.8	.8	.7						.9	.6
	2.5	1.7	2.3						2.1	1.1
	.7	.7	.7	Debt/Worth					.8	.5
	1.9	1.7	1.7						2.0	.9
	6.8	5.0	7.1						4.7	3.2
	47.5	47.8	45.2	% Profit Before Taxes/Tangible					43.2	46.1
	(71) 23.5	(77) 31.5	(77) 25.0	Net Worth					(24) 16.7	(29) 39.0
	6.6	9.7	7.2						3.8	18.6
	19.9	15.9	19.5	% Profit Before Taxes/Total					14.3	27.6
	7.6	7.7	8.0	Assets					6.5	17.4
	1.9	3.1	2.0						.1	4.2
	19.2	23.5	27.0	Sales/Net Fixed Assets					28.0	25.0
	10.0	9.2	12.4						13.1	12.4
	6.2	5.3	5.5						6.5	5.7
	3.5	3.2	3.6	Sales/Total Assets					4.1	3.0
	2.7	2.4	2.3						2.8	2.2
	1.8	1.7	1.7						2.0	1.7
	.8	.8	.8	% Depr., Dep., Amort./Sales					.7	.8
	(75) 1.5	(75) 1.5	(72) 1.5						(23) 1.5	(24) 1.5
	2.3	3.1	2.4						2.4	2.6
	.9	1.1	1.5	% Officers', Directors',						
	(25) 3.0	(30) 2.8	(34) 2.5	Owners' Comp/Sales						
	7.0	6.1	4.3							
	2401837M	3209516M	3780920M	Net Sales ($)	4584M	17447M	24719M	69957M	394457M	3269756M
	1078403M	1611811M	1915161M	Total Assets ($)	3376M	12372M	7411M	34306M	173630M	1684066M

M = $ thousand   MM = $ million
See Pages 11 through 21 for Explanation of Ratios and Data

Current Data Sorted By Assets   **Comparative Historical Data**

0-500M	500M-2MM	2-10MM	10-50MM	50-100MM	100-250MM	Type of Statement	4/1/00-3/31/01 ALL	4/1/01-3/31/02 ALL
		2	2		1	Unqualified	1	3
		2	1			Reviewed	3	4
	1	1				Compiled	4	10
	3	3	3			Tax Returns	1	4
2	2	3		2	2	Other	12	8
	5 (4/1-9/30/04)		22 (10/1/04-3/31/05)					
2	6	11	5		3	NUMBER OF STATEMENTS	21	29
%	%	%	%	%	%	**ASSETS**	%	%
		1.6				Cash & Equivalents	12.4	12.2
		12.2				Trade Receivables (net)	19.9	14.7
		59.0	D	A	T	Inventory	36.0	50.4
		.9				All Other Current	2.6	2.8
		73.7				Total Current	70.9	80.1
		21.2	N	O	T	Fixed Assets (net)	16.5	14.6
		.8				Intangibles (net)	4.9	.9
		4.2				All Other Non-Current	7.7	4.3
		100.0	A	V	A	Total	100.0	100.0
						LIABILITIES		
		35.8	I	L	A	Notes Payable-Short Term	10.9	24.7
		3.1				Cur. Mat.-L/T/D	2.9	4.1
		12.4	B	L	E	Trade Payables	15.5	15.9
		.2				Income Taxes Payable	.7	.1
		6.4				All Other Current	8.3	10.8
		57.9				Total Current	38.3	55.6
		16.9				Long-Term Debt	10.8	8.1
		.0				Deferred Taxes	.1	.1
		1.8				All Other Non-Current	10.9	5.8
		23.3				Net Worth	39.8	30.4
		100.0				Total Liabilities & Net Worth	100.0	100.0
						INCOME DATA		
		100.0				Net Sales	100.0	100.0
		32.7				Gross Profit	33.6	30.9
		27.5				Operating Expenses	27.0	27.4
		5.1				Operating Profit	6.6	3.5
		.5				All Other Expenses (net)	1.4	.3
		4.6				Profit Before Taxes	5.2	3.2
						RATIOS		
		1.6				Current	2.8	2.2
		1.4					1.7	1.5
		1.1					1.4	1.0
		.5				Quick	1.2	.8
		.2					.9	.5
		.1					.6	.1
	3	117.2				Sales/Receivables	9 40.7	1 583.1
	11	32.0					30 12.3	20 18.1
	50	7.3					48 7.7	42 8.6
	93	3.9				Cost of Sales/Inventory	49 7.4	65 5.6
	120	3.1					89 4.1	100 3.6
	224	1.6					119 3.1	155 2.4
	8	47.6				Cost of Sales/Payables	7 50.2	10 37.3
	12	30.8					30 12.1	28 13.1
	57	6.4					54 6.7	48 7.6
		4.9				Sales/Working Capital	4.0	4.6
		17.9					7.5	12.2
		60.1					15.8	97.6
		7.8				EBIT/Interest	11.6	9.4
		3.7					(17) 4.6	(24) 3.2
		2.3					1.9	1.2
						Net Profit + Depr., Dep., Amort./Cur. Mat. L /T/D		
		.2				Fixed/Worth	.2	.3
		.4					.5	.6
		6.4					1.1	.9
		1.5				Debt/Worth	.8	1.2
		1.9					2.0	2.3
		9.4					4.9	7.9
						% Profit Before Taxes/Tangible Net Worth	60.5	63.9
							(19) 38.0	(26) 27.2
							14.6	10.0
		16.8				% Profit Before Taxes/Total Assets	19.2	14.0
		10.9					9.1	6.1
		4.4					4.1	.4
		52.7				Sales/Net Fixed Assets	28.3	64.0
		25.5					18.3	22.7
		5.7					11.6	10.5
		3.5				Sales/Total Assets	3.2	3.1
		1.8					2.6	2.5
		1.7					1.9	2.0
		.9				% Depr., Dep., Amort./Sales	.8	.4
	(10)	1.2					(17) 1.7	(24) 1.3
		2.6					3.6	3.8
						% Officers', Directors', Owners' Comp/Sales		1.6
								(10) 6.9
								13.5
887M	22383M	120751M	164010M		1114864M	Net Sales ($)	2303296M	2003573M
653M	6759M	53507M	119767M		580053M	Total Assets ($)	1036301M	814073M

Comparative Historical Data — Current Data Sorted By Sales

				Type of Statement	0-1MM	1-3MM	3-5MM	5-10MM	10-25MM	25MM & OVER
	3	7	5	Unqualified				1	1	3
	4	3	3	Reviewed		1		1	1	
	4	9	2	Compiled	1				1	
	3	2	6	Tax Returns	1		3	1	1	
	13	12	11	Other	2			1	1	3
	4/1/02-3/31/03 ALL	4/1/03-3/31/04 ALL	4/1/04-3/31/05 ALL			5 (4/1-9/30/04)		22 (10/1/04-3/31/05)		
	27	33	27	**NUMBER OF STATEMENTS**	2	2	4	5	8	6
	%	%	%	**ASSETS**	%	%	%	%	%	%
	7.7	7.7	3.2	Cash & Equivalents						
	19.7	16.9	17.5	Trade Receivables (net)						
	43.4	50.4	52.9	Inventory						
	1.8	3.8	1.1	All Other Current						
	72.4	78.8	74.8	Total Current						
	18.5	13.5	16.7	Fixed Assets (net)						
	3.9	5.4	4.8	Intangibles (net)						
	5.2	2.2	3.7	All Other Non-Current						
	100.0	100.0	100.0	Total						
				LIABILITIES						
	21.2	21.8	28.4	Notes Payable-Short Term						
	3.0	2.3	2.4	Cur. Mat.-L/T/D						
	16.0	18.1	19.1	Trade Payables						
	.3	.2	.3	Income Taxes Payable						
	15.7	15.6	6.5	All Other Current						
	56.2	58.0	56.6	Total Current						
	17.3	11.6	15.6	Long-Term Debt						
	.1	.0	.1	Deferred Taxes						
	5.4	3.0	3.2	All Other Non-Current						
	21.1	27.4	24.5	Net Worth						
	100.0	100.0	100.0	Total Liabilities & Net Worth						
				INCOME DATA						
	100.0	100.0	100.0	Net Sales						
	33.2	28.6	33.7	Gross Profit						
	29.7	29.1	30.3	Operating Expenses						
	3.4	-.5	3.4	Operating Profit						
	.4	.8	1.4	All Other Expenses (net)						
	3.0	-1.2	2.0	Profit Before Taxes						
				RATIOS						
	1.8	1.7	2.1	Current						
	1.4	1.4	1.4							
	1.1	1.0	1.1							
	.9	.7	.6	Quick						
	.6	.5	.4							
	.3	.1	.1							
7	50.5	3 108.1	9 41.6	Sales/Receivables						
31	11.8	25 14.7	31 11.8							
42	8.8	44 8.2	50 7.3							
57	6.4	66 5.5	81 4.5	Cost of Sales/Inventory						
104	3.5	101 3.6	118 3.1							
145	2.5	142 2.6	192 1.9							
13	28.9	11 33.1	12 30.8	Cost of Sales/Payables						
26	13.8	20 18.3	26 14.2							
61	6.0	64 5.7	72 5.1							
	7.1	5.8	5.4	Sales/Working Capital						
	13.5	17.4	9.1							
	28.9	73.2	86.4							
	15.2	8.6	7.8	EBIT/Interest						
(25)	8.1	(29) 5.2	(26) 3.3							
	1.7	-.3	1.1							
				Net Profit + Depr., Dep., Amort./Cur. Mat. L/T/D						
	.2	.1	.1	Fixed/Worth						
	.7	.4	.4							
	3.0	-12.3	6.4							
	1.4	1.3	1.5	Debt/Worth						
	3.0	3.5	2.2							
	11.2	-43.4	12.8							
	62.7	50.4	44.3	% Profit Before Taxes/Tangible Net Worth						
(21)	39.8	(24) 12.6	(21) 30.1							
	23.0	-10.2	5.2							
	17.9	15.9	15.8	% Profit Before Taxes/Total Assets						
	10.9	2.3	5.9							
	2.8	-7.5	2.0							
	71.7	68.2	52.7	Sales/Net Fixed Assets						
	16.4	27.3	26.4							
	7.8	12.6	7.7							
	3.4	3.8	3.2	Sales/Total Assets						
	2.4	2.4	2.0							
	1.7	1.6	1.7							
	.5	.6	.6	% Depr., Dep., Amort./Sales						
(24)	1.0	(26) 1.4	(22) 1.2							
	3.3	2.2	2.6							
		2.3		% Officers', Directors', Owners' Comp/Sales						
		(15) 4.0								
		6.3								
	1921387M	1356278M	1422895M	Net Sales ($)	887M	3518M	17317M	32841M	133829M	1234503M
	846433M	684804M	760739M	Total Assets ($)	653M	2512M	7172M	17036M	93523M	639843M

M = $ thousand   MM = $ million
See Pages 11 through 21 for Explanation of Ratios and Data

Current Data Sorted By Assets | **Comparative Historical Data**

0-500M	500M-2MM	2-10MM	10-50MM	50-100MM	100-250MM	Type of Statement	4/1/00-3/31/01 ALL	4/1/01-3/31/02 ALL
			2			Unqualified	13	11
		4				Reviewed	7	7
1	2	8	1			Compiled	10	11
4	5	4				Tax Returns	2	2
	8	11	8		2	Other	17	21
	13 (4/1-9/30/04)		47 (10/1/04-3/31/05)					
5	15	27	11		2	NUMBER OF STATEMENTS	49	52
%	%	%	%	%	%	**ASSETS**	%	%
	9.2	8.7	7.5	DATA NOT AVAILABLE		Cash & Equivalents	8.3	5.5
	26.9	27.5	23.3			Trade Receivables (net)	20.7	21.8
	32.9	35.6	25.7			Inventory	35.6	36.2
	1.5	3.1	6.3			All Other Current	4.6	4.1
	70.5	74.9	62.8			Total Current	69.2	67.6
	27.3	18.1	20.6			Fixed Assets (net)	18.4	20.1
	1.2	4.1	10.8			Intangibles (net)	5.3	5.4
	1.1	2.9	5.8			All Other Non-Current	7.1	7.0
	100.0	100.0	100.0			Total	100.0	100.0
						LIABILITIES		
	11.0	15.2	15.4			Notes Payable-Short Term	14.9	18.7
	1.5	4.1	3.5			Cur. Mat.-L/T/D	3.6	4.5
	14.2	18.3	14.3			Trade Payables	16.4	15.5
	.0	.6	.7			Income Taxes Payable	.3	.5
	3.3	12.2	11.6			All Other Current	9.6	11.7
	30.1	50.4	45.5			Total Current	44.8	51.0
	16.7	8.8	19.3			Long-Term Debt	17.4	18.0
	.0	.4	.6			Deferred Taxes	.4	.3
	5.8	6.1	8.8			All Other Non-Current	4.4	13.6
	47.5	34.3	25.8			Net Worth	33.1	17.2
	100.0	100.0	100.0			Total Liabilities & Net Worth	100.0	100.0
						INCOME DATA		
	100.0	100.0	100.0			Net Sales	100.0	100.0
	33.6	29.2	26.4			Gross Profit	24.1	24.6
	28.2	25.7	15.7			Operating Expenses	19.9	20.1
	5.4	3.5	10.6			Operating Profit	4.2	4.6
	1.8	.8	4.4			All Other Expenses (net)	.8	2.3
	3.6	2.7	6.2			Profit Before Taxes	3.4	2.3
						RATIOS		
	5.5	1.8	2.3				2.4	2.6
	2.3	1.4	1.2			Current	1.5	1.5
	1.3	1.1	1.0				1.2	1.1
	3.1	1.1	1.6				1.0	1.1
	(14) 1.1	.7	.7			Quick	.6	.6
	.4	.4	.4				.3	.4
	18 20.6	**19** 18.8	**29** 12.5				**10** 35.8	**16** 22.9
	23 15.6	**35** 10.3	**48** 7.7			Sales/Receivables	**31** 11.6	**31** 11.9
	44 8.2	**50** 7.3	**61** 6.0				**54** 6.7	**47** 7.7
	17 21.9	**42** 8.7	**33** 11.1				**31** 11.7	**35** 10.5
	53 6.9	**79** 4.6	**60** 6.1			Cost of Sales/Inventory	**72** 5.1	**60** 6.1
	110 3.3	**113** 3.2	**161** 2.3				**138** 2.6	**122** 3.0
	9 41.1	**20** 18.4	**22** 16.7				**13** 27.3	**14** 26.4
	16 22.6	**34** 10.8	**44** 8.2			Cost of Sales/Payables	**26** 14.1	**24** 15.4
	40 9.1	**44** 8.3	**50** 7.4				**43** 8.5	**36** 10.1
	5.5	5.3	3.3				4.2	6.0
	7.6	15.8	10.2			Sales/Working Capital	9.5	11.9
	18.7	38.9	−110.7				21.5	58.6
	44.6	8.1					5.3	6.3
	(13) 9.8	(25) 3.8				EBIT/Interest	(48) 1.8	(45) 2.3
	.6	2.0					.9	.8
							13.3	13.3
						Net Profit + Depr., Dep., Amort./Cur. Mat. L /T/D	(15) 5.3	(10) 3.6
							1.4	.7
	.1	.1	.2				.3	.3
	.4	.5	1.6			Fixed/Worth	.6	.6
	1.5	2.6	−.4				1.6	8.2
	.4	1.0	.6				.9	1.0
	.8	2.1	3.8			Debt/Worth	2.6	2.7
	3.9	13.4	−4.9				5.9	31.9
	46.4	64.2					41.6	76.9
	(13) 22.9	(24) 28.1				% Profit Before Taxes/Tangible Net Worth	(44) 16.2	(43) 16.7
	10.6	17.6					1.6	3.0
	26.5	15.9	31.6				11.6	12.5
	14.3	6.7	6.1			% Profit Before Taxes/Total Assets	4.2	4.5
	1.2	4.2	−2.0				−.1	.5
	50.0	43.8	20.6				38.0	38.7
	19.2	19.4	11.2			Sales/Net Fixed Assets	12.3	12.3
	5.8	8.1	5.1				7.6	8.1
	4.1	3.5	2.3				3.1	3.3
	3.5	2.5	1.6			Sales/Total Assets	2.1	2.3
	2.3	1.8	1.0				1.3	1.6
	.3	.6	1.2				.7	1.1
	(12) .5	(25) 1.0	(10) 1.8			% Depr., Dep., Amort./Sales	(37) 1.9	(43) 1.7
	2.1	2.4	3.9				3.1	3.6
							2.3	1.1
						% Officers', Directors', Owners' Comp/Sales	(13) 3.5	(17) 2.1
							4.6	4.3
13636M	60144M	291888M	501719M		438841M	Net Sales ($)	1865605M	1862053M
1351M	17691M	109129M	282584M		293316M	Total Assets ($)	1104755M	910409M

M = $ thousand MM = $ million

See Pages 11 through 21 for Explanation of Ratios and Data

Comparative Historical Data | Current Data Sorted By Sales

Type of Statement	4/1/02-3/31/03 ALL	4/1/03-3/31/04 ALL	4/1/04-3/31/05 ALL	13 (4/1-9/30/04) 0-1MM	1-3MM	3-5MM	47 (10/1/04-3/31/05) 5-10MM	10-25MM	25MM & OVER
Unqualified	12	8	2						2
Reviewed	7	12	4				2	2	2
Compiled	8	12	12		1	2	5	4	
Tax Returns	5	9	13		7	1	3	2	
Other	17	24	29	1	1	8	4	7	8
NUMBER OF STATEMENTS	49	65	60	1	9	11	14	15	10
ASSETS	%	%	%	%	%	%	%	%	%
Cash & Equivalents	9.1	9.4	10.4			4.9	21.1	7.5	11.9
Trade Receivables (net)	22.8	24.2	26.2			21.2	23.2	33.0	24.8
Inventory	34.5	29.0	32.4			40.9	35.6	27.4	21.9
All Other Current	3.3	2.6	3.1			.1	3.7	2.0	7.8
Total Current	69.7	65.2	72.0			67.1	83.7	70.0	66.4
Fixed Assets (net)	19.3	24.8	20.4			26.3	14.7	18.0	21.2
Intangibles (net)	4.4	3.9	4.7			2.0	.7	10.4	5.5
All Other Non-Current	6.6	6.1	2.9			4.5	.9	1.7	6.9
Total	100.0	100.0	100.0			100.0	100.0	100.0	100.0
LIABILITIES									
Notes Payable-Short Term	15.3	16.2	16.5			22.3	28.8	7.7	8.2
Cur. Mat.-L/T/D	4.9	4.8	3.3			4.2	2.2	4.3	3.8
Trade Payables	15.1	17.8	17.3			9.8	16.4	19.5	16.5
Income Taxes Payable	.3	.2	.4			.0	.2	.8	.7
All Other Current	11.4	9.1	11.1			14.5	10.0	9.5	13.8
Total Current	46.9	48.1	48.6			50.8	57.7	42.0	43.0
Long-Term Debt	17.8	21.8	14.0			21.4	7.0	4.9	23.0
Deferred Taxes	.2	.2	.3			.5	.3	.1	.8
All Other Non-Current	5.7	9.9	10.8			26.8	2.0	8.2	6.2
Net Worth	29.4	19.9	26.3			.5	33.1	44.9	26.9
Total Liabilities & Net Worth	100.0	100.0	100.0			100.0	100.0	100.0	100.0
INCOME DATA									
Net Sales	100.0	100.0	100.0			100.0	100.0	100.0	100.0
Gross Profit	28.0	27.3	29.0			36.4	24.3	29.7	20.2
Operating Expenses	22.3	25.5	24.1			31.2	21.3	22.4	12.3
Operating Profit	5.6	1.8	4.9			5.2	3.0	7.2	7.8
All Other Expenses (net)	2.4	1.4	1.7			3.4	.3	.8	1.5
Profit Before Taxes	3.3	.4	3.1			1.7	2.7	6.4	6.4
RATIOS									
Current	2.9 / 1.6 / 1.0	2.1 / 1.4 / 1.0	2.3 / 1.5 / 1.1			7.7 / 1.3 / .7	2.9 / 1.6 / 1.3	2.7 / 1.6 / 1.2	2.8 / 1.5 / 1.1
Quick	1.0 / .7 / .4	1.1 / .7 / .4	1.3 / (59) .7 / .4			1.8 / (10) .6 / .2	1.9 / .8 / .4	1.5 / .9 / .5	2.0 / 1.0 / .4
Sales/Receivables	15 24.8 / 31 11.8 / 52 7.0	13 27.2 / 30 12.4 / 46 8.0	18 19.8 / 35 10.5 / 49 7.4		20 18.3 / 35 10.5 / 44 8.2	9 42.1 / 29 12.7 / 52 7.9	22 16.6 / 37 9.9 / 46 7.9	24 15.2 / 50 7.3 / 59 6.2	
Cost of Sales/Inventory	31 11.9 / 70 5.2 / 123 3.0	20 18.1 / 50 7.3 / 100 3.6	24 15.1 / 60 6.1 / 113 3.2		53 6.9 / 90 4.1 / 144 2.5	0 UND / 83 4.4 / 119 3.1	29 12.5 / 53 6.9 / 83 4.4	32 11.6 / 42 8.7 / 63 5.8	
Cost of Sales/Payables	17 21.8 / 25 14.5 / 40 9.1	17 21.3 / 30 12.1 / 42 8.8	15 24.0 / 32 11.5 / 44 8.2		9 39.8 / 25 14.8 / 45 8.0	13 28.9 / 24 15.4 / 45 8.2	16 23.2 / 31 11.6 / 38 9.6	21 17.4 / 39 9.4 / 48 7.6	
Sales/Working Capital	5.5 / 14.3 / 529.2	7.2 / 20.7 / -134.0	5.4 / 11.7 / 39.9			6.3 / 18.7 / -14.5	5.4 / 10.7 / 20.9	5.3 / 15.8 / 38.9	3.2 / 9.0 / NM
EBIT/Interest	10.2 / (46) 2.2 / 1.0	5.5 / (58) 2.0 / .8	21.1 / (50) 3.8 / 1.3				(12) 8.2 / 3.8 / 1.8	(13) 34.0 / 5.3 / 2.4	
Net Profit + Depr., Dep., Amort./Cur. Mat. L/T/D	8.2 / (11) 4.1 / .5	8.1 / (18) .9 / .0	16.4 / (13) 3.0 / .6						
Fixed/Worth	.2 / .7 / 2.6	.5 / 1.0 / -2.6	.2 / .5 / 2.4			.3 / 1.6 / -10.9	.1 / .2 / .9	.2 / .5 / 21.3	.3 / .7 / -.6
Debt/Worth	1.0 / 2.6 / 10.0	1.2 / 4.3 / -9.6	.6 / 2.1 / 19.6			.5 / 3.9 / -36.8	.4 / 1.8 / 5.6	.7 / 1.3 / 87.6	.6 / 2.3 / -5.0
% Profit Before Taxes/Tangible Net Worth	71.9 / (40) 30.9 / 3.9	46.3 / (44) 18.4 / 5.8	52.6 / (48) 27.7 / 13.6				37.8 / (13) 20.1 / 12.5	78.9 / (13) 45.0 / 27.4	
% Profit Before Taxes/Total Assets	19.5 / 6.8 / .5	11.8 / 4.2 / -1.4	16.9 / 6.5 / 2.4			26.5 / 8.2 / .8	14.6 / 5.7 / 2.8	16.9 / 15.7 / 6.1	24.7 / 7.6 / -.6
Sales/Net Fixed Assets	42.5 / 16.3 / 9.9	30.2 / 15.2 / 6.5	43.4 / 17.5 / 7.2			60.4 / 7.2 / 4.3	108.3 / 34.7 / 9.5	36.3 / 19.4 / 11.2	24.5 / 9.6 / 5.0
Sales/Total Assets	3.5 / 2.6 / 1.8	4.2 / 2.6 / 2.1	3.7 / 2.5 / 1.8			3.7 / 2.3 / 1.5	4.2 / 2.7 / 2.1	4.4 / 3.3 / 2.0	2.5 / 1.8 / 1.2
% Depr., Dep., Amort./Sales	.6 / (43) 1.2 / 3.0	.7 / (56) 1.5 / 3.3	.5 / (50) 1.2 / 2.4				.3 / (11) .5 / 1.0	.8 / (14) 1.1 / 2.1	
% Officers', Directors', Owners' Comp/Sales	1.6 / (15) 3.7 / 4.9	2.2 / (29) 5.6 / 8.7	2.7 / (21) 5.2 / 7.6						
Net Sales ($)	1195012M	1516226M	1306228M	783M	16830M	40644M	111893M	241453M	894625M
Total Assets ($)	571390M	747176M	704071M	500M	8905M	32329M	39662M	106334M	516341M

© RMA 2005

M = $ thousand   MM = $ million
See Pages 11 through 21 for Explanation of Ratios and Data

Current Data Sorted By Assets   **Comparative Historical Data**

0-500M	500M-2MM	2-10MM	10-50MM	50-100MM	100-250MM	Type of Statement	4/1/00-3/31/01 ALL	4/1/01-3/31/02 ALL
	1	8	7	4	1	Unqualified	9	12
3	14	21	6			Reviewed	22	17
14	30	20	1	1		Compiled	46	35
28	18	6				Tax Returns	22	26
9	20	26			1	Other	41	37
54 (51 — 4/1-9/30/04) ←			→ 23 (197 — 10/1/04-3/31/05)	5	2	NUMBER OF STATEMENTS	140	127
54	83	81	23	5	2		140	127

%	%	%	%	%	%	**ASSETS**	%	%
7.1	7.6	9.6	9.7			Cash & Equivalents	7.6	7.4
30.2	31.1	28.2	24.7			Trade Receivables (net)	29.1	27.7
16.6	24.4	20.9	21.0			Inventory	22.8	20.8
1.9	1.9	2.4	3.8			All Other Current	1.0	1.8
55.8	65.0	61.2	59.1			Total Current	60.5	57.7
36.0	26.7	29.6	35.9			Fixed Assets (net)	31.6	33.1
1.4	3.8	2.5	.2			Intangibles (net)	3.0	3.8
6.8	4.5	6.8	4.7			All Other Non-Current	4.9	5.4
100.0	100.0	100.0	100.0			Total	100.0	100.0

						LIABILITIES		
10.1	12.4	9.3	8.3			Notes Payable-Short Term	11.0	13.8
7.1	4.9	4.3	2.6			Cur. Mat.-L/T/D	5.9	5.8
15.7	15.3	14.2	14.0			Trade Payables	15.5	14.8
.1	.6	.4	.0			Income Taxes Payable	.6	.3
19.1	14.8	11.5	11.5			All Other Current	12.7	12.3
52.1	48.0	39.7	36.4			Total Current	45.7	46.9
33.1	18.5	15.5	12.9			Long-Term Debt	19.8	21.1
.0	.2	.5	.6			Deferred Taxes	.3	.3
5.9	9.9	8.3	1.7			All Other Non-Current	3.7	5.7
8.9	23.5	36.0	48.3			Net Worth	30.5	26.0
100.0	100.0	100.0	100.0			Total Liabilities & Net Worth	100.0	100.0

						INCOME DATA		
100.0	100.0	100.0	100.0			Net Sales	100.0	100.0
42.4	33.9	32.2	32.8			Gross Profit	32.6	34.6
39.2	30.2	28.2	26.8			Operating Expenses	28.0	30.9
3.2	3.7	4.0	5.9			Operating Profit	4.7	3.8
.7	1.0	.7	.2			All Other Expenses (net)	1.3	1.2
2.5	2.7	3.2	5.7			Profit Before Taxes	3.4	2.6

						RATIOS		
2.4	2.1	2.8	2.7			Current	2.3	1.9
1.3	1.4	1.5	1.6				1.6	1.4
.7	.9	1.1	1.2				1.0	.9
1.4	1.4	1.6	1.5			Quick	1.6	1.2
(53) .8	1.0	.9	.8				.9	.8
.5	.4	.5	.6				.5	.5
0 UND	16 23.3	20 18.3	26 14.0			Sales/Receivables	21 17.3	20 18.3
28 13.0	38 9.6	31 11.7	37 9.7				33 10.9	32 11.4
42 8.7	56 6.5	53 6.8	48 7.6				49 7.5	44 8.3
0 UND	12 29.9	16 23.5	20 18.0			Cost of Sales/Inventory	14 25.5	16 22.6
14 26.8	32 11.3	38 9.6	30 12.2				34 10.7	29 12.4
36 10.0	69 5.3	67 5.5	84 4.4				61 6.0	54 6.8
0 UND	10 36.8	13 27.8	11 31.9			Cost of Sales/Payables	12 30.7	11 33.4
16 22.5	25 14.5	25 14.6	21 17.6				20 18.3	18 19.8
33 11.2	42 8.8	42 8.6	49 7.4				33 11.0	35 10.4
12.4	9.1	6.7	6.9			Sales/Working Capital	8.2	9.7
43.2	16.4	13.1	14.4				13.5	21.2
-55.3	-94.8	60.2	22.6				UND	-60.7
21.5	8.0	12.3	28.3			EBIT/Interest	10.1	7.2
(43) 4.0	(71) 2.1	(71) 3.8	(18) 12.9				(134) 4.0	(117) 3.4
1.0	.4	1.2	3.8				1.4	1.6
	3.3	5.3				Net Profit + Depr., Dep., Amort./Cur. Mat. L/T/D	7.9	4.2
	(12) 2.0	(21) 2.3					(23) 2.1	(23) 1.8
	.2	1.0					1.2	1.1
.5	.4	.3	.4			Fixed/Worth	.4	.5
2.5	1.2	.9	.9				.8	1.2
-2.4	-7.5	2.4	1.4				2.3	UND
1.4	1.0	.7	.4			Debt/Worth	.8	.9
7.2	3.0	2.3	1.1				1.6	2.9
-5.7	-18.3	6.5	2.5				9.4	-56.4
116.5	59.4	56.5	48.1			% Profit Before Taxes/Tangible Net Worth	62.2	58.9
(34) 67.4	(61) 14.5	(72) 22.1	28.9				(117) 31.6	(94) 29.3
18.0	3.2	4.8	10.7				10.3	10.7
26.7	13.5	18.4	22.1			% Profit Before Taxes/Total Assets	20.7	17.4
11.1	4.5	5.2	11.1				8.0	9.4
-.9	-.9	.2	4.5				2.2	1.6
44.4	27.1	21.4	12.3			Sales/Net Fixed Assets	22.6	23.3
16.0	14.6	9.7	5.5				10.5	11.3
8.7	6.9	6.1	4.8				6.1	5.5
6.5	3.9	3.4	2.9			Sales/Total Assets	4.1	4.0
4.2	2.9	2.7	2.5				3.0	3.2
3.0	2.4	2.1	2.0				2.3	2.3
.9	1.0	1.3	1.4			% Depr., Dep., Amort./Sales	1.0	1.1
(42) 1.7	(71) 1.9	(74) 1.7	(19) 1.5				(123) 1.7	(114) 1.9
3.8	2.7	2.6	2.2				2.9	3.1
4.2	2.4	1.2				% Officers', Directors', Owners' Comp/Sales	2.5	2.4
(36) 6.3	(44) 4.1	(44) 1.8					(73) 4.7	(67) 4.2
13.1	5.7	3.1					8.3	7.0
60153M	307518M	977163M	1163003M	1032043M	781442M	Net Sales ($)	2970085M	3060532M
12835M	100018M	357854M	421701M	377172M	343495M	Total Assets ($)	1147010M	1342413M

Comparative Historical Data | | | | **Current Data Sorted By Sales** | | | | | |

			Type of Statement						
20	16	21	Unqualified				4	5	12
29	39	44	Reviewed	1	6	7	10	17	3
49	60	66	Compiled	5	23	14	14	6	4
38	46	52	Tax Returns	16	21	10	4	1	
46	59	65	Other	2	15	9	14	14	11
4/1/02-3/31/03 ALL	4/1/03-3/31/04 ALL	4/1/04-3/31/05 ALL		51 (4/1-9/30/04)			197 (10/1/04-3/31/05)		
				0-1MM	1-3MM	3-5MM	5-10MM	10-25MM	25MM & OVER
182	220	248	NUMBER OF STATEMENTS	24	65	40	46	43	30
%	%	%	**ASSETS**	%	%	%	%	%	%
9.3	8.9	8.3	Cash & Equivalents	7.2	8.5	9.2	7.9	7.0	9.7
24.4	28.7	28.9	Trade Receivables (net)	25.8	28.2	32.0	28.8	33.5	22.8
23.5	20.0	21.4	Inventory	15.3	20.1	21.6	26.0	20.5	23.0
2.2	2.8	2.3	All Other Current	1.1	1.9	1.6	2.1	3.2	4.0
59.5	60.4	60.9	Total Current	49.4	58.7	64.5	64.8	64.2	59.5
33.1	31.6	30.7	Fixed Assets (net)	42.3	29.4	28.6	28.8	28.2	33.3
2.0	2.2	2.7	Intangibles (net)	.2	5.7	.8	1.3	3.0	2.2
5.5	5.8	5.7	All Other Non-Current	8.2	6.2	6.0	5.2	4.6	5.0
100.0	100.0	100.0	Total	100.0	100.0	100.0	100.0	100.0	100.0
			LIABILITIES						
11.7	11.1	10.2	Notes Payable-Short Term	14.1	9.6	10.8	9.6	11.9	6.4
4.9	4.8	4.9	Cur. Mat.-L/T/D	8.5	5.4	3.7	5.1	4.7	2.7
15.1	14.9	14.9	Trade Payables	9.0	16.4	14.7	16.9	14.9	13.3
.3	.3	.4	Income Taxes Payable	.0	.3	.9	.4	.3	.3
12.4	12.7	14.3	All Other Current	13.2	17.7	13.7	15.5	10.0	12.7
44.4	43.8	44.7	Total Current	44.8	49.4	43.9	47.6	41.7	35.3
19.1	21.0	20.0	Long-Term Debt	41.1	24.0	18.3	16.1	12.7	13.5
.2	.5	.3	Deferred Taxes	.0	.1	.4	.2	.5	1.0
4.3	7.4	7.6	All Other Non-Current	7.8	6.6	10.8	12.6	4.0	3.3
31.9	27.3	27.3	Net Worth	6.4	20.0	26.7	23.5	41.1	46.9
100.0	100.0	100.0	Total Liabilities & Net Worth	100.0	100.0	100.0	100.0	100.0	100.0
			INCOME DATA						
100.0	100.0	100.0	Net Sales	100.0	100.0	100.0	100.0	100.0	100.0
35.1	35.2	34.8	Gross Profit	47.9	37.9	33.2	32.7	29.5	31.0
30.6	31.4	30.9	Operating Expenses	45.1	32.9	30.2	30.4	25.0	25.5
4.5	3.7	3.9	Operating Profit	2.8	4.9	3.0	2.3	4.5	5.4
.9	.9	.8	All Other Expenses (net)	1.0	.9	.9	1.0	.5	.3
3.6	2.8	3.1	Profit Before Taxes	1.8	4.0	2.1	1.3	3.9	5.1
			RATIOS						
2.3	2.3	2.4		2.3	2.2	2.3	2.7	2.5	2.1
1.5	1.4	1.5	Current	1.2	1.3	1.5	1.4	1.4	1.6
1.0	1.0	1.0		.7	.9	.9	.9	1.1	1.2
1.6	1.3	1.5		1.6	1.3	1.6	1.6	1.5	1.4
.8	.9 (247)	.9	Quick	.7	(64) .9	1.0	.8	.9	.8
.4	.5	.5		.5	.4	.4	.4	.6	.6
12 29.4	18 19.9	16 23.1		0 UND	7 56.0	13 29.0	22 16.9	27 13.7	22 16.5
28 13.1	33 10.9	32 11.5	Sales/Receivables	27 13.7	28 13.0	38 9.6	34 10.9	33 11.0	30 12.1
44 8.2	47 7.7	49 7.4		46 8.0	44 8.4	53 6.9	53 6.9	63 5.8	45 8.1
17 20.9	15 24.7	12 30.1		0 UND	4 85.1	9 41.9	28 12.9	15 23.6	23 16.2
30 12.0	31 11.7	32 11.6	Cost of Sales/Inventory	9 39.5	23 15.8	26 14.1	40 9.1	32 11.4	31 11.8
61 6.0	50 7.3	58 6.3		44 8.3	53 6.9	69 5.3	73 5.0	57 6.4	49 7.5
11 34.1	13 27.7	10 35.5		0 UND	7 54.1	11 34.7	15 24.3	10 35.8	12 30.6
23 15.9	24 15.4	23 15.6	Cost of Sales/Payables	10 35.1	19 18.7	23 15.6	29 12.4	23 15.6	21 17.7
38 9.7	40 9.1	41 8.9		32 11.6	44 8.2	38 9.7	45 8.1	35 10.4	34 10.8
8.1	8.9	9.0		9.8	11.0	8.1	6.8	8.3	9.3
16.4	18.9	16.4	Sales/Working Capital	192.8	27.1	15.6	15.3	16.5	11.6
−554.4	189.2	−135.2		−47.4	−79.2	−135.3	−42.2	28.9	23.1
12.2	10.6	12.4		21.5	9.3	12.1	7.7	17.3	35.5
(164) 3.9	(197) 3.5	(210) 3.6	EBIT/Interest	(19) 5.4	(52) 2.0	(35) 2.1	(41) 1.6	(39) 5.4	(24) 14.3
1.5	.9	1.0		1.0	.7	.8	−.6	1.9	4.3
5.6	7.3	4.7					3.3	8.9	14.4
(37) 2.5	(47) 3.6	(44) 3.1	Net Profit + Depr., Dep., Amort./Cur. Mat. L/T/D			(10) 1.0	(15) 4.0	(10) 4.5	
1.2	1.4	1.1					.2	1.4	3.1
.3	.4	.4		.4	.5	.3	.4	.3	.4
1.0	1.2	1.0	Fixed/Worth	4.7	1.1	1.0	1.5	.8	.9
3.2	4.9	5.2		−4.1	−1.7	5.1	5.2	1.8	1.4
.7	.9	.9		2.2	.8	.7	1.0	.7	.6
2.2	2.3	2.5	Debt/Worth	7.2	4.5	2.6	3.4	2.0	1.1
7.6	13.5	14.6		−10.1	−5.4	8.2	18.7	4.9	2.5
51.1	53.0	64.7		120.2	95.4	45.3	50.5	56.8	52.4
(157) 24.1	(177) 20.9	(196) 27.5	% Profit Before Taxes/Tangible Net Worth	(17) 86.7	(42) 37.7	(32) 12.9	(37) 14.6	(39) 20.0	(29) 32.9
7.7	3.7	5.2		14.8	2.8	.8	−2.3	10.1	12.1
20.8	15.7	18.6		19.7	25.1	10.6	12.2	18.5	22.7
7.1	6.3	6.7	% Profit Before Taxes/Total Assets	11.1	6.3	4.4	3.2	10.1	14.6
1.7	−.3	.0		−2.7	−.4	−.1	−3.9	3.1	2.4
26.1	23.9	24.4		43.4	32.8	25.6	20.7	24.0	16.7
11.0	11.7	12.3	Sales/Net Fixed Assets	11.3	14.1	14.3	13.0	11.1	8.2
5.5	5.9	6.4		4.5	7.5	6.9	6.6	6.8	5.1
4.0	4.1	4.0		5.0	4.5	4.0	3.5	3.6	3.3
3.0	3.0	3.0	Sales/Total Assets	3.5	3.2	2.8	2.8	2.9	2.8
2.2	2.2	2.3		2.2	2.3	2.2	2.1	2.4	2.4
1.0	1.3	1.1		.8	1.1	1.0	1.1	.8	1.3
(161) 1.8	(186) 2.3	(211) 1.7	% Depr., Dep., Amort./Sales	(20) 2.2	(51) 2.0	(36) 1.9	(40) 1.7	(41) 1.6	(23) 1.5
3.5	3.3	2.8		4.6	2.8	3.1	2.9	2.1	2.4
2.6	1.9	1.8		5.4	3.0	1.7	1.1	1.4	
(92) 5.1	(118) 4.1	(128) 3.8	% Officers', Directors', Owners' Comp/Sales	(18) 11.0	(34) 5.4	(23) 2.9	(25) 1.9	(24) 2.0	
8.4	7.1	6.3		17.0	8.8	5.4	4.4	2.8	
5548249M	5475480M	4321322M	Net Sales ($)	13539M	119998M	159143M	324116M	680279M	3024247M
1677675M	1927569M	1613075M	Total Assets ($)	4013M	42593M	61721M	127851M	245092M	1131805M

M = $ thousand   MM = $ million
See Pages 11 through 21 for Explanation of Ratios and Data

Current Data Sorted By Assets   **Comparative Historical Data**

						Type of Statement		
	1	7	10	4	7	Unqualified	15	8
	2	13	4			Reviewed	13	9
1	5	3	1			Compiled	16	16
1	4	1				Tax Returns	3	1
1	3	9	5			Other	18	16
	19 (4/1-9/30/04)		63 (10/1/04-3/31/05)				4/1/00-3/31/01 ALL	4/1/01-3/31/02 ALL
0-500M	500M-2MM	2-10MM	10-50MM	50-100MM	100-250MM			
3	15	33	20	4	7	NUMBER OF STATEMENTS	65	50
%	%	%	%	%	%	ASSETS	%	%
	3.7	5.5	2.4			Cash & Equivalents	5.7	6.6
	24.0	27.4	20.4			Trade Receivables (net)	26.4	20.1
	39.2	39.7	35.2			Inventory	33.8	35.4
	1.3	2.0	3.8			All Other Current	2.0	4.0
	68.1	74.5	61.8			Total Current	68.0	66.1
	17.1	18.6	28.6			Fixed Assets (net)	21.9	23.2
	2.7	.8	2.0			Intangibles (net)	4.5	5.7
	12.0	6.1	7.6			All Other Non-Current	5.7	5.0
	100.0	100.0	100.0			Total	100.0	100.0
						LIABILITIES		
	12.5	13.9	13.9			Notes Payable-Short Term	10.4	10.9
	1.6	2.0	2.0			Cur. Mat.-L/T/D	2.5	2.9
	25.3	21.5	13.2			Trade Payables	18.1	14.9
	.2	.2	.3			Income Taxes Payable	.6	.3
	7.0	12.2	10.1			All Other Current	14.5	11.4
	46.6	49.8	39.5			Total Current	46.1	40.4
	13.4	11.4	16.2			Long-Term Debt	12.2	14.7
	.0	.5	.1			Deferred Taxes	.3	.1
	3.2	2.6	2.8			All Other Non-Current	4.0	2.3
	36.7	35.7	41.3			Net Worth	37.4	42.5
	100.0	100.0	100.0			Total Liabilities & Net Worth	100.0	100.0
						INCOME DATA		
	100.0	100.0	100.0			Net Sales	100.0	100.0
	24.6	24.8	20.7			Gross Profit	25.3	27.6
	26.7	22.6	18.4			Operating Expenses	20.2	23.1
	-2.1	2.2	2.4			Operating Profit	5.1	4.5
	.2	.5	.3			All Other Expenses (net)	.9	.9
	-2.4	1.7	2.1			Profit Before Taxes	4.3	3.6
						RATIOS		
	2.4	2.6	2.6			Current	2.5	2.7
	1.4	1.5	1.8				1.6	1.8
	1.2	1.1	1.1				1.3	1.3
	1.8	1.3	.9			Quick	1.3	1.4
	.6	.7	.7				(64) .9	.7
	.2	.4	.4				.4	.3
	10 38.3	11 32.8	9 38.6			Sales/Receivables	21 17.7	10 36.5
	21 17.0	35 10.4	27 13.7				36 10.0	30 12.1
	36 10.2	46 8.0	46 8.0				47 7.7	43 8.5
	33 11.0	32 11.4	37 9.7			Cost of Sales/Inventory	35 10.4	36 10.1
	50 7.4	49 7.4	48 7.7				53 6.9	51 7.2
	85 4.3	96 3.8	84 4.4				77 4.8	109 3.3
	9 38.5	15 23.7	8 48.0			Cost of Sales/Payables	14 25.4	8 43.1
	25 14.3	24 15.1	16 23.0				25 14.4	21 17.2
	39 9.4	39 9.3	35 10.3				41 8.8	36 10.1
	6.4	6.1	8.7			Sales/Working Capital	5.5	6.2
	25.5	15.8	13.5				11.4	11.2
	59.4	51.1	37.4				24.6	33.6
	7.6	6.4	11.4			EBIT/Interest	15.2	22.3
	(14) 2.0	(27) 1.5	2.9				(58) 4.6	(45) 4.4
	.3	.1	1.4				1.6	1.2
		6.2	5.0			Net Profit + Depr., Dep., Amort./Cur. Mat. L /T/D	13.5	7.4
		(10) 2.8	(11) 1.9				(18) 3.9	(17) 3.1
		.2	1.6				1.7	.5
	.2	.2	.5			Fixed/Worth	.3	.3
	.8	.5	.6				.5	.7
	1.8	1.8	1.5				1.2	1.7
	.4	.7	.7			Debt/Worth	.6	.6
	2.8	1.8	1.7				1.8	1.6
	14.2	9.3	4.1				4.5	4.4
	16.9	34.0	28.5			% Profit Before Taxes/Tangible Net Worth	49.7	42.4
	(13) 2.8	(30) 8.6	(19) 15.9				(59) 24.8	(43) 23.1
	-89.0	-2.4	2.0				12.1	8.6
	13.1	16.0	10.5			% Profit Before Taxes/Total Assets	18.0	20.3
	1.5	1.2	4.0				10.7	6.7
	-1.0	-4.3	1.2				2.7	.3
	43.2	41.3	16.0			Sales/Net Fixed Assets	38.2	37.6
	29.7	20.6	11.7				17.8	14.3
	17.5	11.6	7.4				9.0	7.9
	6.4	4.2	3.7			Sales/Total Assets	3.8	3.6
	3.4	3.2	3.3				2.6	2.6
	2.4	2.4	2.1				2.1	1.9
	.3	.4	.7			% Depr., Dep., Amort./Sales	.5	.3
	(12) .7	(31) .7	(18) 1.2				(58) .9	(45) .9
	1.2	1.1	1.5				1.6	1.6
		1.8				% Officers', Directors', Owners' Comp/Sales	1.3	1.8
		(14) 2.1					(18) 1.9	(15) 2.2
		4.6					7.3	4.0
4613M	69060M	573529M	1408503M	575502M	2453021M	Net Sales ($)	3515279M	2989636M
1169M	16747M	178242M	462013M	323800M	1092047M	Total Assets ($)	1510296M	1216159M

M = $ thousand   MM = $ million
See Pages 11 through 21 for Explanation of Ratios and Data

Comparative Historical Data | Current Data Sorted By Sales

			Type of Statement	0-1MM	1-3MM	3-5MM	5-10MM	10-25MM	25MM & OVER
23	24	29	Unqualified			1	2	5	21
14	21	19	Reviewed			1	4	7	7
13	21	10	Compiled		2	2	3	1	2
1	7	6	Tax Returns	1	2	1	2		
17	19	18	Other		1	1	2	7	7
4/1/02- 3/31/03 ALL	4/1/03- 3/31/04 ALL	4/1/04- 3/31/05 ALL		|—19 (4/1-9/30/04)—|			|—63 (10/1/04-3/31/05)—|		
68	92	82	**NUMBER OF STATEMENTS**	1	5	6	13	20	37
%	%	%	**ASSETS**	%	%	%	%	%	%
6.2	7.4	4.7	Cash & Equivalents				.8	8.1	3.5
25.9	25.3	23.9	Trade Receivables (net)				29.3	21.7	23.5
32.2	33.4	36.5	Inventory				39.3	39.2	34.5
3.8	2.3	2.6	All Other Current				1.2	2.8	2.7
68.0	68.4	67.7	Total Current				70.6	71.8	64.2
22.5	20.2	20.5	Fixed Assets (net)				21.8	19.7	22.8
2.1	3.2	3.2	Intangibles (net)				1.1	.6	5.2
7.3	8.1	8.6	All Other Non-Current				6.6	7.9	7.7
100.0	100.0	100.0	Total				100.0	100.0	100.0
			LIABILITIES						
8.1	11.5	12.3	Notes Payable-Short Term				19.7	11.6	10.8
2.4	1.8	2.1	Cur. Mat.-L/T/D				2.6	1.8	1.8
15.1	16.4	18.8	Trade Payables				24.1	21.1	15.2
.1	.3	.2	Income Taxes Payable				.1	.3	.2
13.9	12.4	10.6	All Other Current				8.7	14.1	10.4
39.5	42.4	44.0	Total Current				55.2	48.9	38.4
14.6	13.8	13.7	Long-Term Debt				17.8	9.8	16.1
.2	.4	.3	Deferred Taxes				.5	.4	.4
2.7	5.2	3.1	All Other Non-Current				2.9	1.7	3.1
43.0	38.2	38.8	Net Worth				23.6	39.2	42.1
100.0	100.0	100.0	Total Liabilities & Net Worth				100.0	100.0	100.0
			INCOME DATA						
100.0	100.0	100.0	Net Sales				100.0	100.0	100.0
24.3	26.4	25.6	Gross Profit				22.4	28.4	23.1
19.9	24.2	23.8	Operating Expenses				20.4	26.7	19.5
4.3	2.1	1.8	Operating Profit				2.0	1.6	3.7
.4	.6	.5	All Other Expenses (net)				.9	.1	.8
3.9	1.5	1.3	Profit Before Taxes				1.1	1.6	2.9
			RATIOS						
3.3	2.8	2.6	Current				2.5	2.5	2.8
1.7	1.6	1.5					1.3	1.8	1.6
1.2	1.2	1.2					1.1	1.0	1.2
1.5	1.4	1.1	Quick				1.3	1.1	1.1
.8	.7	.7					.6	.7	.8
.5	.5	.4					.2	.3	.5
15 24.0	21 17.8	13 28.0	Sales/Receivables				13 28.6	7 50.6	17 21.8
36 10.3	35 10.3	31 11.9					24 15.3	37 9.8	30 12.3
47 7.7	46 7.9	44 8.3					35 10.6	43 8.5	46 7.9
33 11.2	36 10.1	33 10.9	Cost of Sales/Inventory				32 11.4	31 11.6	37 9.8
46 7.9	52 7.0	49 7.4					39 9.3	62 5.8	47 7.7
74 4.9	88 4.1	87 4.2					83 4.4	137 2.7	75 4.8
11 32.9	14 26.8	13 28.1	Cost of Sales/Payables				12 30.1	14 26.7	12 31.7
19 19.4	21 17.1	25 14.5					25 14.3	29 12.8	23 15.8
28 13.0	37 10.0	38 9.7					36 10.0	49 7.4	35 10.3
5.2	5.8	6.6	Sales/Working Capital				12.3	4.6	7.3
14.2	12.1	15.3					25.5	10.4	13.7
31.3	29.6	41.3					61.4	NM	22.4
20.4	15.3	9.2	EBIT/Interest				4.0	6.5	15.5
(62) 6.9	(83) 3.2	(75) 2.0					1.5	(17) 1.9	(34) 3.6
2.6	.1	.6					.7	-.8	1.4
11.0	7.6	6.1	Net Profit + Depr., Dep.,						6.2
(14) 3.5	(31) 2.9	(27) 2.5	Amort./Cur. Mat. L/T/D					(15) 1.9	
1.1	.5	1.6							1.6
.2	.2	.3	Fixed/Worth				.7	.3	.3
.6	.5	.6					1.0	.5	.6
1.1	1.6	1.6					3.4	1.0	1.6
.4	.6	.7	Debt/Worth				1.4	.6	.7
1.4	1.8	1.9					4.3	1.3	1.9
4.0	5.5	6.8					26.8	8.4	6.0
50.9	34.5	30.9	% Profit Before Taxes/Tangible Net Worth				60.3	31.3	33.5
(62) 23.1	(80) 12.8	(73) 9.3				(11)	2.8	(18) 8.6	(33) 18.5
10.1	-1.0	-1.3					-4.7	-1.9	3.6
18.8	13.4	13.8	% Profit Before Taxes/Total Assets				14.6	14.6	16.6
8.9	4.1	3.2					.6	3.1	4.8
3.1	-1.8	-.9					-.6	-4.8	1.1
32.1	32.1	32.5	Sales/Net Fixed Assets				42.3	23.7	20.8
14.2	15.7	18.1					32.3	16.9	13.6
8.4	9.6	9.6					11.2	10.6	8.1
4.0	3.6	4.2	Sales/Total Assets				5.9	4.2	3.7
3.0	2.9	3.2					3.9	2.7	3.1
2.1	1.9	2.1					2.6	2.0	2.0
.5	.5	.5	% Depr., Dep., Amort./Sales				.4	.4	.5
(57) .9	(79) .9	(70) .9				(12)	.6	(19) .7	(31) 1.2
1.3	1.6	1.4					1.3	1.1	1.5
1.6	1.7	1.7	% Officers', Directors', Owners' Comp/Sales					1.8	
(13) 2.5	(38) 3.0	(27) 2.1						(10) 2.1	
4.5	7.0	4.8						5.3	
5688298M	5091836M	5084228M	Net Sales ($)	927M	9277M	22639M	93289M	323846M	4634250M
2041544M	2110743M	2074018M	Total Assets ($)	279M	3215M	7307M	24859M	125539M	1912819M

M = $ thousand   MM = $ million
See Pages 11 through 21 for Explanation of Ratios and Data

Current Data Sorted By Assets   Comparative Historical Data

0-500M	500M-2MM	2-10MM	10-50MM	50-100MM	100-250MM	Type of Statement	4/1/00-3/31/01 ALL	4/1/01-3/31/02 ALL
		9	5	2	6	Unqualified	22	20
1	6	17	3			Reviewed	20	25
8	14	9	1			Compiled	23	26
9	9	2				Tax Returns	8	15
3	10	18	8	1	2	Other	34	40
	36 (4/1-9/30/04)		107 (10/1/04-3/31/05)					
21	39	55	17	3	8	NUMBER OF STATEMENTS	107	126
%	%	%	%	%	%	ASSETS	%	%
14.5	7.1	7.0	3.1			Cash & Equivalents	4.4	5.7
11.4	18.2	17.8	20.0			Trade Receivables (net)	23.5	21.8
40.1	39.8	43.2	37.2			Inventory	35.2	33.3
3.4	4.9	2.8	2.0			All Other Current	2.6	2.4
69.3	70.0	70.7	62.4			Total Current	65.8	63.3
24.1	22.5	20.6	30.8			Fixed Assets (net)	26.6	27.5
3.7	1.5	2.0	1.7			Intangibles (net)	2.3	2.7
2.8	5.9	6.6	5.2			All Other Non-Current	5.3	6.5
100.0	100.0	100.0	100.0			Total	100.0	100.0
						LIABILITIES		
15.6	9.5	17.3	12.1			Notes Payable-Short Term	14.1	12.6
5.0	4.6	4.7	3.2			Cur. Mat.-L/T/D	4.4	2.7
14.5	14.3	13.1	12.1			Trade Payables	16.6	15.4
.1	.0	.4	.1			Income Taxes Payable	.3	1.5
16.1	14.7	14.7	13.9			All Other Current	12.3	12.7
51.3	43.1	50.3	41.4			Total Current	47.6	44.9
18.5	21.0	12.6	11.2			Long-Term Debt	20.9	21.5
.0	.1	.2	.5			Deferred Taxes	.3	.5
21.2	6.4	7.3	2.7			All Other Non-Current	5.8	6.2
9.0	29.5	29.7	44.2			Net Worth	25.4	26.9
100.0	100.0	100.0	100.0			Total Liabilities & Net Worth	100.0	100.0
						INCOME DATA		
100.0	100.0	100.0	100.0			Net Sales	100.0	100.0
42.5	38.4	28.3	25.6			Gross Profit	27.2	30.9
40.8	36.9	26.5	25.9			Operating Expenses	22.5	27.9
1.7	1.5	1.8	-.4			Operating Profit	4.7	3.0
.5	1.4	.6	.4			All Other Expenses (net)	1.4	1.6
1.2	.1	1.2	-.8			Profit Before Taxes	3.3	1.4
						RATIOS		
3.2	3.0	2.1	2.8				2.6	3.0
1.3	1.7	1.4	1.7			Current	1.5	1.6
.8	1.1	1.0	1.0				1.1	1.1
1.2	1.2	.8	1.3				1.2	1.3
(20) .3	(38) .6	.5	.6			Quick	.7	.7
.1	.3	.2	.3				.4	.4
0 UND	8 48.2	12 29.9	18 20.0				24 15.4	17 21.9
4 86.8	22 16.5	28 13.0	44 8.3			Sales/Receivables	39 9.5	35 10.3
15 24.4	44 8.4	40 9.2	55 6.7				50 7.4	46 7.9
0 UND	27 13.6	47 7.7	69 5.3				41 9.0	39 9.5
64 5.7	101 3.6	107 3.4	80 4.5			Cost of Sales/Inventory	64 5.7	68 5.4
116 3.1	154 2.4	147 2.5	109 3.3				112 3.3	106 3.4
0 UND	13 28.8	11 31.8	12 30.9				15 23.6	13 28.5
18 20.6	29 12.5	23 15.8	25 14.6			Cost of Sales/Payables	25 14.5	22 16.6
35 10.5	42 8.6	39 9.2	41 8.9				38 9.6	41 9.0
6.8	5.1	5.9	4.3				5.4	4.9
15.8	9.9	11.6	9.2			Sales/Working Capital	10.1	11.4
-97.0	72.3	143.6	NM				32.9	96.3
7.4	5.7	8.4	10.5				6.5	5.6
(14) 2.0	(38) 2.1	(53) 2.0	1.4			EBIT/Interest	(101) 2.6	(115) 2.3
.2	.2	.1	-2.9				1.2	.6
		11.1				Net Profit + Depr., Dep.,	6.2	4.6
	(12) 1.3					Amort./Cur. Mat. L /T/D	(37) 2.7	(41) 2.4
	.3						.8	.8
.2	.2	.2	.5				.4	.4
.7	.6	.5	.6			Fixed/Worth	.9	.8
-1.0	2.3	2.4	2.1				2.4	2.6
1.5	.9	1.1	.6				1.3	1.0
5.5	2.1	2.5	.9			Debt/Worth	2.5	2.1
-4.1	5.0	7.7	8.2				5.2	7.3
60.0	29.4	36.1	20.7			% Profit Before Taxes/Tangible	33.3	30.8
(14) 15.2	(32) 11.0	(48) 12.2	1.5			Net Worth	(88) 22.4	(104) 14.2
3.0	.2	-1.4	-23.2				7.3	1.1
29.8	9.8	11.2	10.7			% Profit Before Taxes/Total	14.1	11.0
3.0	3.3	2.3	.9			Assets	7.1	5.2
-.8	-7.4	-1.5	-5.0				1.4	-1.3
67.8	29.0	32.6	11.6				23.4	24.2
22.7	17.2	12.4	6.3			Sales/Net Fixed Assets	10.8	10.5
15.0	8.8	4.9	5.1				5.8	5.4
6.5	3.7	2.7	2.5				3.1	3.7
3.9	2.6	2.2	2.0			Sales/Total Assets	2.4	2.3
3.0	1.9	1.7	1.5				1.7	1.7
.7	.7	.7	1.2				.8	.8
(17) 1.3	(36) 1.8	(46) 1.1	(16) 1.8			% Depr., Dep., Amort./Sales	(94) 1.6	(107) 1.7
2.7	3.8	2.2	3.4				2.9	2.8
2.7	2.8	1.7				% Officers', Directors',	1.1	1.8
(15) 4.0	(27) 3.7	(24) 2.3				Owners' Comp/Sales	(32) 2.4	(44) 3.9
7.8	7.5	3.7					4.8	7.5
21482M	112931M	674403M	694031M	507995M	2013353M	Net Sales ($)	3657140M	4312938M
5168M	40569M	272889M	349502M	193430M	1121887M	Total Assets ($)	2129487M	2256741M

M = $ thousand   MM = $ million
See Pages 11 through 21 for Explanation of Ratios and Data

Comparative Historical Data | **Current Data Sorted By Sales**

4/1/02-3/31/03 ALL	4/1/03-3/31/04 ALL	4/1/04-3/31/05 ALL	Type of Statement	0-1MM	1-3MM	3-5MM	5-10MM	10-25MM	25MM & OVER
					36 (4/1-9/30/04)			107 (10/1/04-3/31/05)	
30	38	22	Unqualified	1	4	3	3	6	13
31	33	27	Reviewed				8	7	4
33	40	32	Compiled	7	8	5	7	4	1
15	19	20	Tax Returns	6	8	4	2		
50	42	42	Other	3	5	6	5	14	9
159	172	143	**NUMBER OF STATEMENTS**	17	25	18	25	31	27
%	%	%	**ASSETS**	%	%	%	%	%	%
7.0	6.5	7.4	Cash & Equivalents	17.2	6.0	6.9	7.4	5.7	4.6
17.4	17.2	17.3	Trade Receivables (net)	14.9	13.5	19.5	15.8	18.3	20.9
39.6	38.9	40.3	Inventory	38.5	43.5	37.1	44.2	40.1	37.2
2.3	2.5	3.3	All Other Current	.3	7.9	3.2	2.4	3.2	2.0
66.2	65.0	68.2	Total Current	70.8	70.9	66.7	69.9	67.3	64.7
26.4	26.4	23.7	Fixed Assets (net)	22.2	24.5	23.6	23.3	21.7	26.8
2.4	2.1	2.3	Intangibles (net)	3.4	1.4	2.7	1.2	2.5	2.8
5.0	6.6	5.7	All Other Non-Current	3.5	3.2	7.0	5.6	8.5	5.7
100.0	100.0	100.0	Total	100.0	100.0	100.0	100.0	100.0	100.0
			LIABILITIES						
12.0	12.0	13.5	Notes Payable-Short Term	16.4	11.2	11.3	11.9	18.8	10.5
3.3	4.4	4.4	Cur. Mat.-L/T/D	7.1	4.3	2.8	5.3	4.9	2.3
13.4	13.7	13.1	Trade Payables	9.8	16.0	12.2	14.3	14.6	10.1
.2	.2	.2	Income Taxes Payable	.0	.1	.0	.4	.4	.1
11.9	13.9	14.7	All Other Current	19.1	13.6	11.8	14.1	15.4	14.4
40.8	44.1	45.7	Total Current	52.4	45.1	38.1	45.9	54.1	37.4
17.2	16.8	16.3	Long-Term Debt	24.7	16.2	17.5	18.7	11.3	13.9
.3	.3	.3	Deferred Taxes	.0	.2	.0	.2	.2	.9
4.9	5.8	8.4	All Other Non-Current	22.3	8.0	6.4	5.6	9.4	3.0
36.8	33.1	29.2	Net Worth	.6	30.5	38.0	29.6	25.0	44.7
100.0	100.0	100.0	Total Liabilities & Net Worth	100.0	100.0	100.0	100.0	100.0	100.0
			INCOME DATA						
100.0	100.0	100.0	Net Sales	100.0	100.0	100.0	100.0	100.0	100.0
33.8	32.1	32.5	Gross Profit	43.5	41.8	34.1	30.0	27.7	23.5
30.8	30.2	30.7	Operating Expenses	43.6	39.4	30.5	26.3	29.8	19.8
3.0	1.9	1.7	Operating Profit	-.1	2.4	3.6	3.7	-2.1	3.7
1.0	.8	.9	All Other Expenses (net)	1.2	1.1	.7	1.2	.3	1.0
2.0	1.1	.8	Profit Before Taxes	-1.2	1.2	2.9	2.5	-2.4	2.7
			RATIOS						
2.7	2.8	2.7		3.1	2.7	3.6	2.5	1.9	3.9
1.7	1.5	1.5	Current	1.4	2.0	1.8	1.5	1.3	2.0
1.2	1.0	1.1		1.0	1.2	1.1	1.1	.9	1.2
1.1	1.0	1.1		1.2	1.1	2.0	.9	.7	1.3
.6 (171)	.5 (141)	.5	Quick	.5 (24)	.3 (17)	.7	.4	.5	.8
.3	.3	.2		.1	.2	.5	.2	.2	.4
6 64.6	6 57.9	8 47.8		2 214.9	0 UND	3 143.4	6 56.7	13 28.2	19 18.7
30 12.1	26 14.1	26 14.2	Sales/Receivables	13 27.4	15 23.6	28 12.8	24 15.0	29 12.7	38 9.5
45 8.2	40 9.1	43 8.6		43 8.4	34 10.8	51 7.2	31 11.7	41 8.9	47 7.8
42 8.6	44 8.2	43 8.6		6 63.3	13 27.3	35 10.4	43 8.5	61 6.0	53 6.9
85 4.3	81 4.5	98 3.7	Cost of Sales/Inventory	115 3.2	92 4.0	56 6.5	112 3.3	104 3.5	79 4.6
135 2.7	124 2.9	139 2.6		218 1.7	183 2.0	139 2.6	158 2.3	124 3.0	104 3.5
15 24.3	12 29.4	11 31.8		0 UND	15 23.8	6 65.3	12 29.4	15 24.6	10 36.2
24 14.9	23 15.6	23 15.8	Cost of Sales/Payables	27 13.6	28 13.3	14 26.6	25 14.3	28 13.2	16 22.6
42 8.7	45 8.1	39 9.3		41 8.9	43 8.4	29 12.6	38 9.7	68 5.4	28 13.1
4.9	5.0	5.3		6.0	5.0	4.8	5.3	6.9	4.3
9.3	11.2	10.0	Sales/Working Capital	9.9	9.5	9.0	9.9	12.8	7.5
25.6	184.0	72.3		-256.5	29.3	169.4	28.5	-22.6	21.2
7.8	8.1	8.2		4.7	6.6	35.5	6.1	3.9	18.0
2.7 (144)	2.2 (156)	2.2 (132)	EBIT/Interest	1.6 (10)	2.7 (24)	2.9	1.6 (24)	.8 (30)	7.7 (26)
1.0	.0	.2		-2.9	.6	1.1	.9	-3.3	1.1
3.6	3.5	8.5	Net Profit + Depr., Dep.,					3.3	8.2
2.5 (50)	1.9 (49)	2.7 (36)	Amort./Cur. Mat. L/T/D					1.1 (12)	3.4 (10)
.9	.2	.9						-1.6	2.4
.3	.3	.3		.2	.2	.3	.3	.2	.3
.6	.7	.6	Fixed/Worth	1.0	.7	.5	.5	.6	.5
1.8	3.0	2.6		-.4	1.7	2.0	5.2	2.6	1.8
.8	.7	.8		.8	1.2	.5	.9	1.1	.4
1.7	1.9	2.3	Debt/Worth	6.1	2.5	1.8	2.4	2.9	1.3
5.2	7.0	7.7		-2.3	5.8	4.5	11.6	7.7	3.3
29.5	31.0	32.5	% Profit Before Taxes/Tangible		47.3	30.6	32.9	32.2	47.3
12.5 (139)	9.0 (146)	12.2 (121)	Net Worth		17.1 (22)	11.8 (15)	11.7 (23)	1.7 (26)	18.1 (26)
.8	-1.9	-1.4			1.0	.7	1.2	-8.5	1.9
11.1	12.7	11.2	% Profit Before Taxes/Total	17.9	17.6	19.2	10.5	6.1	13.0
4.3	3.0	3.0	Assets	2.2	4.4	3.6	3.4	-.5	9.9
.0	-1.4	-2.4		-9.9	-.4	.0	-.7	-5.3	.9
27.9	25.6	29.8		51.6	34.0	28.4	25.2	35.0	18.6
11.1	12.0	13.2	Sales/Net Fixed Assets	17.2	17.7	14.0	11.6	11.7	8.3
5.5	5.8	6.3		6.4	9.1	7.3	6.2	4.9	5.3
3.4	3.3	3.5		5.1	4.2	4.1	2.8	2.7	3.0
2.3	2.3	2.4	Sales/Total Assets	3.0	3.0	2.7	2.3	2.0	2.1
1.7	1.8	1.7		1.4	2.3	2.1	1.9	1.6	1.7
.8	.8	.7		1.1	.7	.7	.6	.7	1.1
1.6 (137)	1.7 (150)	1.5 (124)	% Depr., Dep., Amort./Sales	1.8 (13)	1.8 (23)	1.7 (16)	1.3 (21)	1.2 (28)	1.5 (23)
2.8	2.6	2.8		3.8	3.8	4.0	2.6	2.4	2.8
1.9	1.5	2.3	% Officers', Directors',	3.1	2.7	2.7	1.7	1.4	
3.5 (71)	2.8 (71)	3.0 (71)	Owners' Comp/Sales	6.9 (10)	3.7 (19)	3.0 (13)	2.7 (13)	2.2 (11)	
6.4	5.5	5.8		11.5	6.6	6.1	4.5	3.8	
4800123M	6598606M	4024195M	Net Sales ($)	11998M	45446M	68223M	171796M	478141M	3248591M
2468152M	2915642M	1983445M	Total Assets ($)	5684M	16963M	28636M	75036M	234582M	1622544M

Current Data Sorted By Assets   Comparative Historical Data

			4			Type of Statement	7	4
						Unqualified	7	4
						Reviewed	3	3
1	2	4				Compiled	2	4
3	2	2				Tax Returns	1	2
	2	1	6			Other	9	6
	8 (4/1-9/30/04)		19 (10/1/04-3/31/05)				4/1/00- 3/31/01	4/1/01- 3/31/02
0-500M	500M-2MM	2-10MM	10-50MM	50-100MM	100-250MM		ALL	ALL
4	6	7	10			NUMBER OF STATEMENTS	22	19
%	%	%	%	%	%	ASSETS	%	%
			1.5	D	D	Cash & Equivalents	7.1	9.7
			31.2	A	A	Trade Receivables (net)	24.6	21.9
			28.6	T	T	Inventory	32.1	33.2
			2.0	A	A	All Other Current	1.4	.4
			63.2			Total Current	65.3	65.1
			28.7	N	N	Fixed Assets (net)	20.7	26.4
			3.2	O	O	Intangibles (net)	8.5	4.6
			4.9	T	T	All Other Non-Current	5.5	3.8
			100.0			Total	100.0	100.0
				A	A	LIABILITIES		
			31.3	V	V	Notes Payable-Short Term	15.5	15.9
			2.5	A	A	Cur. Mat.-L/T/D	1.0	7.7
			14.3	I	I	Trade Payables	14.0	16.9
			.0	L	L	Income Taxes Payable	.0	.1
			8.9	A	A	All Other Current	13.7	12.5
			57.1	B	B	Total Current	44.3	53.2
			14.7	L	L	Long-Term Debt	14.0	17.6
			.0	E	E	Deferred Taxes	.3	.0
			1.0			All Other Non-Current	5.7	4.6
			27.2			Net Worth	35.7	24.6
			100.0			Total Liabilities & Net Worth	100.0	100.0
						INCOME DATA		
			100.0			Net Sales	100.0	100.0
			17.4			Gross Profit	30.9	29.9
			14.7			Operating Expenses	26.4	25.3
			2.7			Operating Profit	4.5	4.6
			1.0			All Other Expenses (net)	2.6	2.1
			1.7			Profit Before Taxes	1.9	2.5
						RATIOS		
			1.3				3.3	2.6
			1.2			Current	1.5	1.5
			1.1				1.0	1.0
			.8				2.1	1.4
			.6			Quick	.8	.9
			.4				.4	.2
		35	10.5				34	10.6	7	54.6
		42	8.6			Sales/Receivables	46	7.9	27	13.5
		51	7.2				53	6.8	50	7.2
		27	13.6				57	6.4	33	11.1
		39	9.4			Cost of Sales/Inventory	77	4.7	54	6.8
		70	5.2				105	3.5	85	4.3
		12	30.0				19	19.4	11	32.9
		21	17.7			Cost of Sales/Payables	34	10.6	15	24.7
		30	12.4				55	6.6	33	10.9
			18.9				4.1	7.6
			31.4			Sales/Working Capital	9.2	12.0
			48.7				NM	85.4
			12.7				8.4	16.7
			3.6			EBIT/Interest	(20) 1.4	(17) 5.5
			1.8				-1.2	.4
						Net Profit + Depr., Dep., Amort./Cur. Mat. L /T/D		
			.5				.2	.2
			1.0			Fixed/Worth	.9	.7
			2.5				-5.0	-65.6
			1.9				.8	.6
			3.4			Debt/Worth	2.3	2.5
			5.4				-30.5	-149.5
			68.9			% Profit Before Taxes/Tangible	39.3	77.7
			45.4			Net Worth	(15) -.2	(14) 27.0
			8.5				-35.6	13.6
			15.8			% Profit Before Taxes/Total	14.9	27.7
			5.9			Assets	2.6	17.0
			2.0				-3.8	.7
			20.2				31.2	42.3
			12.1			Sales/Net Fixed Assets	16.2	23.6
			5.3				5.4	5.5
			3.5				3.0	4.5
			2.8			Sales/Total Assets	1.8	2.9
			2.0				1.4	2.1
							.6	.8
						% Depr., Dep., Amort./Sales	(17) 1.9	(16) 1.3
							3.2	2.4
						% Officers', Directors', Owners' Comp/Sales		
6123M	14765M	77668M	622383M			Net Sales ($)	653377M	1533151M
1209M	5153M	33213M	215525M			Total Assets ($)	368097M	386655M

© RMA 2005   M = $ thousand   MM = $ million
See Pages 11 through 21 for Explanation of Ratios and Data

Comparative Historical Data / Current Data Sorted By Sales

	4/1/02-3/31/03 ALL	4/1/03-3/31/04 ALL	4/1/04-3/31/05 ALL	Type of Statement	0-1MM	1-3MM	3-5MM	5-10MM	10-25MM	25MM & OVER
	8	5	4	Unqualified						4
	6	3		Reviewed						
	3	5	7	Compiled		3	1	1	2	
	1	4	7	Tax Returns	2	3			2	
	8	10	9	Other		1	1		1	6
					8 (4/1-9/30/04)			19 (10/1-3/31/05)		
	26	**27**	**27**	**NUMBER OF STATEMENTS**	**2**	**7**	**2**	**1**	**5**	**10**

ASSETS (%)

	4/1/02-3/31/03 ALL	4/1/03-3/31/04 ALL	4/1/04-3/31/05 ALL		25MM & OVER
	%	%	%	ASSETS	%
	12.3	7.6	7.4	Cash & Equivalents	1.5
	22.9	23.0	30.8	Trade Receivables (net)	31.2
	30.5	37.4	30.1	Inventory	28.6
	3.1	3.0	1.9	All Other Current	2.0
	68.7	71.0	70.1	Total Current	63.2
	18.6	20.5	24.4	Fixed Assets (net)	28.7
	5.0	5.2	1.6	Intangibles (net)	3.2
	7.7	3.4	3.8	All Other Non-Current	4.9
	100.0	100.0	100.0	Total	100.0

LIABILITIES

	4/1/02-3/31/03 ALL	4/1/03-3/31/04 ALL	4/1/04-3/31/05 ALL		25MM & OVER
	7.1	21.6	22.6	Notes Payable-Short Term	31.3
	3.1	4.3	5.3	Cur. Mat.-L/T/D	2.5
	14.4	16.3	14.0	Trade Payables	14.3
	.0	.2	.0	Income Taxes Payable	.0
	17.0	9.7	14.2	All Other Current	8.9
	41.7	52.2	56.1	Total Current	57.1
	7.0	12.7	19.9	Long-Term Debt	14.7
	.1	.2	.0	Deferred Taxes	.0
	6.1	14.3	5.4	All Other Non-Current	1.0
	45.1	20.6	18.6	Net Worth	27.2
	100.0	100.0	100.0	Total Liabilities & Net Worth	100.0

INCOME DATA

	4/1/02-3/31/03 ALL	4/1/03-3/31/04 ALL	4/1/04-3/31/05 ALL		25MM & OVER
	100.0	100.0	100.0	Net Sales	100.0
	34.0	34.8	28.6	Gross Profit	17.4
	29.2	30.9	25.0	Operating Expenses	14.7
	4.8	3.9	3.6	Operating Profit	2.7
	.7	1.4	.6	All Other Expenses (net)	1.0
	4.1	2.5	3.0	Profit Before Taxes	1.7

RATIOS

4/1/02-3/31/03 ALL	4/1/03-3/31/04 ALL	4/1/04-3/31/05 ALL		25MM & OVER
4.4	2.1	1.7	Current	1.3
1.5	1.3	1.2		1.2
1.0	1.1	1.0		1.1
2.4	1.2	.9	Quick	.8
1.0	.7	.6		.6
.3	.2	.3		.4
9 41.4	21 17.7	15 24.3	Sales/Receivables	35 10.5
38 9.7	36 10.1	40 9.1		42 8.6
43 8.4	54 6.8	55 6.6		51 7.2
42 8.7	42 8.7	20 18.5	Cost of Sales/Inventory	27 13.6
65 5.6	89 4.1	46 8.0		39 9.4
108 3.4	159 2.3	92 4.0		70 5.2
15 24.6	20 18.0	8 46.6	Cost of Sales/Payables	12 30.0
20 18.0	31 11.9	20 17.9		21 17.7
47 7.7	61 6.0	35 10.5		30 12.4
3.5	6.6	10.4	Sales/Working Capital	18.9
10.4	10.2	19.6		31.4
−778.5	44.9	−147.1		48.7
19.4	10.6	13.9	EBIT/Interest	12.7
(20) 8.1	(25) 3.4	(25) 4.4		3.6
1.3	1.0	1.8		1.8
			Net Profit + Depr., Dep., Amort./Cur. Mat. L/T/D	
.2	.3	.4	Fixed/Worth	.5
.5	.6	1.0		1.0
1.2	6.6	5.4		2.5
.4	1.3	1.7	Debt/Worth	1.9
1.7	3.6	3.5		3.4
5.0	28.2	12.6		5.4
55.0	54.6	87.6	% Profit Before Taxes/Tangible Net Worth	68.9
(24) 11.2	(21) 16.9	(23) 47.7		45.4
1.8	2.2	26.8		8.5
18.3	12.7	19.3	% Profit Before Taxes/Total Assets	15.8
7.5	2.9	9.6		5.9
.7	.5	2.4		2.0
45.4	49.4	84.8	Sales/Net Fixed Assets	20.2
20.1	17.2	16.7		12.1
6.9	5.7	4.5		5.3
3.9	3.2	3.7	Sales/Total Assets	3.5
2.6	2.4	2.8		2.8
1.7	1.6	2.0		2.0
.9	.5	.7	% Depr., Dep., Amort./Sales	
(22) 1.5	(23) 1.3	(23) 1.1		
2.4	1.7	2.8		
	.7		% Officers', Directors', Owners' Comp/Sales	
	(10) 3.0			
	6.2			

Net Sales ($) / Total Assets ($)

	4/1/02-3/31/03 ALL	4/1/03-3/31/04 ALL	4/1/04-3/31/05 ALL		0-1MM	1-3MM	3-5MM	5-10MM	10-25MM	25MM & OVER
Net Sales ($)	1201170M	861292M	720939M		1421M	15899M	8240M	7007M	65989M	622383M
Total Assets ($)	617935M	576796M	255100M		499M	5056M	2873M	4011M	27136M	215525M

© RMA 2005   M = $ thousand   MM = $ million
See Pages 11 through 21 for Explanation of Ratios and Data

Current Data Sorted By Assets   Comparative Historical Data

						Type of Statement	4/1/00-3/31/01	4/1/01-3/31/02
	1	10	20	4	3	Unqualified	19	20
	16	23	5			Reviewed	19	24
3	6	7				Compiled	18	11
5	7	2				Tax Returns	5	12
6	14	23	7	2		Other	31	24
	32 (4/1-9/30/04)		132 (10/1/04-3/31/05)				ALL	ALL
0-500M	500M-2MM	2-10MM	10-50MM	50-100MM	100-250MM			
14	44	65	32	6	3	NUMBER OF STATEMENTS	92	91
%	%	%	%	%	%	**ASSETS**	%	%
3.8	7.3	6.3	8.5			Cash & Equivalents	8.1	7.2
32.0	33.7	24.5	29.0			Trade Receivables (net)	28.9	29.9
23.9	29.0	29.0	23.3			Inventory	23.1	24.8
1.8	2.1	2.3	3.5			All Other Current	2.4	1.7
61.4	72.1	62.1	64.3			Total Current	62.6	63.7
25.5	18.2	27.0	26.1			Fixed Assets (net)	26.3	25.4
1.5	2.5	4.8	4.1			Intangibles (net)	5.4	5.2
12.1	7.2	6.1	5.5			All Other Non-Current	5.7	5.8
100.0	100.0	100.0	100.0			Total	100.0	100.0
						LIABILITIES		
20.6	16.0	15.1	14.1			Notes Payable-Short Term	8.4	16.3
7.9	4.3	3.6	3.3			Cur. Mat.-L/T/D	4.4	4.3
17.3	16.4	13.5	12.6			Trade Payables	14.7	11.3
.0	.1	.3	.2			Income Taxes Payable	.4	.1
4.9	13.2	11.6	13.1			All Other Current	10.0	8.9
50.7	50.0	44.1	43.3			Total Current	37.8	41.0
27.3	12.9	18.1	22.7			Long-Term Debt	15.4	15.3
.0	.4	.5	.3			Deferred Taxes	.7	.2
11.1	7.8	7.6	8.6			All Other Non-Current	5.4	6.3
10.5	29.0	29.7	25.1			Net Worth	40.8	37.3
100.0	100.0	100.0	100.0			Total Liabilities & Net Worth	100.0	100.0
						INCOME DATA		
100.0	100.0	100.0	100.0			Net Sales	100.0	100.0
39.1	32.0	30.0	24.1			Gross Profit	29.2	29.6
33.2	28.7	26.6	20.4			Operating Expenses	23.4	25.5
5.8	3.3	3.4	3.6			Operating Profit	5.7	4.1
3.7	1.1	1.1	1.9			All Other Expenses (net)	.8	1.1
2.1	2.2	2.2	1.7			Profit Before Taxes	5.0	3.0
						RATIOS		
2.6	2.2	1.9	2.2			Current	3.4	3.0
1.3	1.4	1.3	1.6				1.6	1.6
.7	1.0	1.1	1.1				1.2	1.2
2.5	1.3	1.0	1.6			Quick	1.8	1.8
.7	.9	.6	.9				1.1	.9
.3	.6	.4	.5				.7	.6
28 13.1	29 12.4	26 13.9	25 14.6			Sales/Receivables	33 11.1	31 11.9
36 10.0	43 8.5	39 9.2	43 8.4				43 8.4	37 9.8
60 6.1	59 6.2	54 6.8	61 6.0				52 7.0	59 6.2
0 UND	21 17.1	41 8.8	25 14.3			Cost of Sales/Inventory	25 14.5	28 12.9
37 9.8	53 6.9	56 6.5	36 10.0				44 8.2	44 8.3
74 4.9	86 4.3	93 3.9	72 5.1				70 5.2	70 5.2
12 31.5	13 28.8	13 28.2	12 29.5			Cost of Sales/Payables	13 28.3	9 41.3
28 12.9	22 16.4	31 11.9	24 15.3				25 14.6	20 18.5
87 4.2	53 6.9	47 7.7	40 9.2				40 9.1	34 10.8
8.0	6.0	7.6	7.0			Sales/Working Capital	5.8	4.9
34.2	17.2	16.4	12.3				11.1	11.1
-8.3	616.4	64.4	52.4				24.1	29.8
(11) 7.8	(37) 6.2	(60) 9.7	(30) 14.9			EBIT/Interest	(81) 9.8	(85) 7.3
2.1	2.9	3.2	4.6				3.8	3.0
-1.2	1.0	.9	1.6				1.6	1.3
		3.6				Net Profit + Depr., Dep., Amort./Cur. Mat. L /T/D	7.0	4.4
		(15) 2.3					(24) 2.5	(21) 1.7
		.6					1.2	.6
.0	.3	.4	.2			Fixed/Worth	.2	.2
.5	.6	.9	.8				.7	.6
3.0	2.1	2.6	2.1				1.8	1.4
1.7	1.2	1.3	.9			Debt/Worth	.7	.6
5.0	2.4	2.5	2.0				2.0	1.9
-14.7	9.1	8.0	6.2				4.2	3.7
82.8	64.5	41.4	49.8			% Profit Before Taxes/Tangible Net Worth	45.4	39.3
(10) 31.2	(39) 31.7	(56) 14.9	(28) 16.5				(82) 26.3	(81) 18.3
-5.0	3.3	1.5	8.5				9.0	6.8
20.3	12.0	9.6	21.3			% Profit Before Taxes/Total Assets	15.1	13.3
5.9	4.7	4.7	6.1				7.8	6.0
-5.7	-.1	-.4	1.4				2.4	1.4
UND	53.0	24.8	51.6			Sales/Net Fixed Assets	25.8	28.0
32.9	20.2	10.5	11.8				13.6	12.2
7.3	9.8	3.6	4.7				5.4	6.1
3.8	3.6	3.1	3.1			Sales/Total Assets	3.3	3.2
2.9	2.6	2.2	2.3				2.5	2.2
1.1	2.1	1.3	1.9				1.7	1.9
	.6	.8	.6			% Depr., Dep., Amort./Sales	.8	.9
	(40) 1.2	(60) 2.0	(27) 1.4				(83) 1.7	(82) 1.6
	2.6	3.0	3.3				3.1	3.0
	4.0	1.4				% Officers', Directors', Owners' Comp/Sales	1.8	2.2
	(26) 4.8	(23) 3.2					(27) 5.0	(31) 3.0
	7.4	6.9					8.6	6.5
12688M	165951M	699629M	2155011M	667418M	863270M	Net Sales ($)	2057334M	2322959M
3945M	56765M	311214M	638072M	399377M	503563M	Total Assets ($)	1144227M	915293M

M = $ thousand   MM = $ million
See Pages 11 through 21 for Explanation of Ratios and Data

Comparative Historical Data / Current Data Sorted By Sales

			Type of Statement						
30	38	38	Unqualified		1		3	7	27
36	39	44	Reviewed		5	11	14	10	4
25	40	16	Compiled	3	3	3	5	1	1
12	18	14	Tax Returns	2	5	4		3	
43	58	52	Other	4	8	11	12	10	7
4/1/02-3/31/03	4/1/03-3/31/04	4/1/04-3/31/05		0-1MM	32 (4/1-9/30/04) 1-3MM	3-5MM	132 (10/1/04-3/31/05) 5-10MM	10-25MM	25MM & OVER
ALL	ALL	ALL							
146	193	164	**NUMBER OF STATEMENTS**	9	22	29	34	31	39
%	%	%	**ASSETS**	%	%	%	%	%	%
7.1	7.9	6.8	Cash & Equivalents		5.1	5.6	6.9	8.1	8.1
29.2	28.7	28.5	Trade Receivables (net)		31.2	28.6	31.8	24.9	28.0
24.2	25.2	27.1	Inventory		29.5	26.5	25.0	28.2	25.8
1.8	2.7	2.4	All Other Current		.6	3.9	2.7	1.6	2.7
62.3	64.5	64.8	Total Current		66.5	64.5	66.4	62.8	64.7
26.6	24.3	24.5	Fixed Assets (net)		18.4	25.0	25.5	25.8	24.9
4.7	4.2	3.9	Intangibles (net)		6.3	2.8	3.5	3.9	3.9
6.3	7.1	6.9	All Other Non-Current		8.8	7.7	4.5	7.5	6.5
100.0	100.0	100.0	Total		100.0	100.0	100.0	100.0	100.0
			LIABILITIES						
10.7	12.6	14.9	Notes Payable-Short Term		14.2	14.3	14.3	13.0	12.7
3.8	3.4	4.3	Cur. Mat.-L/T/D		9.2	4.7	3.7	3.2	3.5
13.8	14.7	14.6	Trade Payables		13.3	15.3	15.8	14.9	13.0
.3	.2	.2	Income Taxes Payable		.0	.2	.2	.4	.2
9.9	10.9	11.9	All Other Current		6.9	14.2	13.9	10.9	14.1
38.6	41.8	45.9	Total Current		43.6	48.7	48.0	42.4	43.5
18.5	14.4	18.7	Long-Term Debt		23.1	18.0	11.6	16.1	22.1
.4	.4	.4	Deferred Taxes		.2	.3	.7	.3	.4
4.7	10.3	8.1	All Other Non-Current		10.9	3.5	14.1	8.4	4.8
37.8	33.1	26.9	Net Worth		22.2	29.5	25.5	32.8	29.2
100.0	100.0	100.0	Total Liabilities & Net Worth		100.0	100.0	100.0	100.0	100.0
			INCOME DATA						
100.0	100.0	100.0	Net Sales		100.0	100.0	100.0	100.0	100.0
31.1	31.7	29.3	Gross Profit		40.2	31.7	28.2	26.8	22.7
26.6	28.1	26.0	Operating Expenses		36.9	28.3	25.0	23.7	19.9
4.4	3.6	3.3	Operating Profit		3.2	3.4	3.2	3.0	2.9
1.2	1.3	1.5	All Other Expenses (net)		1.2	1.0	1.4	1.3	1.4
3.3	2.3	1.8	Profit Before Taxes		2.0	2.4	1.8	1.7	1.5
			RATIOS						
2.5	2.8	2.2			3.1	1.7	2.1	2.1	2.3
1.6	1.5	1.4	Current		1.5	1.2	1.3	1.4	1.7
1.2	1.1	1.0			1.0	1.0	1.1	1.1	1.1
1.5	1.6	1.3			1.5	1.0	1.1	1.3	1.5
.9	.8	.8	Quick		.9	.6	.8	.7	.9
.6	.5	.5			.4	.4	.5	.5	.5
27 13.4	28 12.9	28 13.0	Sales/Receivables	29 12.4	21 17.4	31 11.9	23 16.0	24 15.2	
39 9.3	39 9.4	41 8.8		44 8.2	45 8.1	41 9.2	39 9.2	41 8.9	
52 7.0	56 6.5	58 6.2		58 6.3	75 4.9	57 6.4	49 7.4	61 6.0	
27 13.4	26 14.1	30 12.3	Cost of Sales/Inventory	44 8.3	21 17.5	28 12.9	32 11.3	27 13.5	
50 7.3	50 7.3	53 6.9		69 5.3	63 5.8	53 6.9	52 7.0	38 9.5	
76 4.8	86 4.2	85 4.3		165 2.2	96 3.8	82 4.5	78 4.7	74 5.0	
16 23.2	14 25.2	13 28.1	Cost of Sales/Payables	18 20.8	12 29.4	13 28.3	12 29.5	14 25.9	
25 14.8	25 14.7	25 14.3		29 12.4	26 13.8	26 14.3	32 11.3	23 15.6	
38 9.6	44 8.4	48 7.7		62 5.9	53 7.0	55 6.7	44 8.2	36 10.1	
6.3	5.4	6.9	Sales/Working Capital		4.1	6.9	9.5	9.3	5.7
11.2	11.0	16.0			12.8	17.4	17.2	15.9	11.6
29.0	109.5	135.3			−625.2	732.3	38.0	89.3	56.3
10.1	9.3	7.9	EBIT/Interest		6.3	5.7	4.5	13.5	14.4
(132) 3.3	(170) 3.0	(147) 3.1		(19) 2.2	(27) 2.6	(28) 2.1	(29) 5.1	(37) 3.9	
.8	.6	.9			.2	1.0	.4	2.2	1.1
3.8	9.3	2.9	Net Profit + Depr., Dep., Amort./Cur. Mat. L/T/D						
(30) 2.2	(42) 2.8	(32) 1.7							
1.1	.7	.4							
.3	.3	.3	Fixed/Worth		.1	.4	.4	.4	.2
.8	.7	.8			.5	.9	.9	.7	.9
1.8	2.2	2.2			NM	4.0	2.6	1.6	2.1
.8	.9	1.3	Debt/Worth		1.4	1.3	1.2	1.2	.7
1.9	1.9	2.6			2.8	3.0	2.6	2.1	1.9
4.1	7.3	8.9			NM	9.2	5.8	6.2	7.5
48.9	41.6	47.6	% Profit Before Taxes/Tangible Net Worth		68.3	64.5	41.4	27.7	41.1
(130) 18.4	(162) 16.9	(141) 16.7		(17) 41.9	(27) 31.7	(28) 11.3	(27) 19.5	(36) 11.8	
2.8	−.1	3.2			1.3	3.2	−7.3	12.6	1.6
15.5	15.4	11.4	% Profit Before Taxes/Total Assets		15.1	9.7	9.3	13.6	12.4
6.5	5.6	4.6			4.8	4.4	3.4	6.6	4.5
.7	−1.0	−.3			−2.5	.2	−1.8	1.9	.3
31.5	31.0	35.1	Sales/Net Fixed Assets		68.3	28.8	29.0	33.6	35.3
10.9	11.2	13.0			21.9	11.8	13.0	11.7	10.6
5.6	5.6	5.4			6.5	4.8	6.3	5.5	5.0
3.2	3.1	3.3	Sales/Total Assets		3.0	3.1	3.6	4.2	3.2
2.4	2.4	2.4			2.3	2.2	2.7	2.4	2.3
1.8	1.7	1.7			1.8	1.3	1.7	1.5	1.9
1.1	.9	.7	% Depr., Dep., Amort./Sales		.7	.7	.7	.8	.6
(120) 1.9	(165) 2.0	(141) 1.8		(19) 1.9	(27) 1.6	(30) 2.0	(29) 1.8	(31) 2.0	
3.5	3.3	3.0			4.0	2.9	2.8	2.3	3.3
1.8	2.7	2.0	% Officers', Directors', Owners' Comp/Sales		3.8	4.6	2.4	1.2	
(56) 4.3	(68) 5.5	(61) 4.4		(15) 4.7	(13) 6.9	(13) 3.2	(13) 1.8		
9.8	9.0	6.9			7.5	10.2	4.4	7.7	
3294535M	4172679M	4563967M	Net Sales ($)	4298M	41966M	112005M	228784M	484281M	3692633M
1622264M	2433545M	1912936M	Total Assets ($)	3278M	22192M	63996M	109697M	228405M	1485368M

© RMA 2005

M = $ thousand   MM = $ million
See Pages 11 through 21 for Explanation of Ratios and Data

Current Data Sorted By Assets   Comparative Historical Data

						Type of Statement	7	6
		3	7			Unqualified	7	6
	3	10	1			Reviewed	13	14
	5	3				Compiled	8	4
1	1	1				Tax Returns	1	4
3	2	10	1	1		Other	16	16
	13 (4/1-9/30/04)		39 (10/1/04-3/31/05)				4/1/00-3/31/01	4/1/01-3/31/02
0-500M	500M-2MM	2-10MM	10-50MM	50-100MM	100-250MM	NUMBER OF STATEMENTS	ALL	ALL
4	11	27	9	1			45	44
%	%	%	%	%	%		%	%
						ASSETS		
	7.9	2.9				Cash & Equivalents	4.8	4.8
	33.3	37.8				Trade Receivables (net)	29.2	31.5
	23.8	29.5				Inventory	24.4	21.5
	7.8	5.3				All Other Current	3.7	2.7
	72.9	75.5				Total Current	62.2	60.5
	20.2	17.0				Fixed Assets (net)	28.8	29.0
	3.7	1.8				Intangibles (net)	4.6	4.7
	3.3	5.8				All Other Non-Current	4.4	5.8
	100.0	100.0				Total	100.0	100.0
						LIABILITIES		
	10.9	18.2				Notes Payable-Short Term	12.6	12.3
	5.0	5.2				Cur. Mat.-L/T/D	5.9	8.6
	21.4	17.3				Trade Payables	15.4	14.2
	.9	.1				Income Taxes Payable	.3	.1
	11.3	15.5				All Other Current	10.0	9.0
	49.6	56.4				Total Current	44.2	44.3
	24.0	11.5				Long-Term Debt	15.5	18.9
	.9	.7				Deferred Taxes	.6	.6
	10.6	7.8				All Other Non-Current	4.3	4.2
	15.0	23.7				Net Worth	35.4	31.9
	100.0	100.0				Total Liabilities & Net Worth	100.0	100.0
						INCOME DATA		
	100.0	100.0				Net Sales	100.0	100.0
	30.3	25.3				Gross Profit	30.6	26.8
	34.3	23.8				Operating Expenses	26.7	24.3
	-4.0	1.5				Operating Profit	3.9	2.5
	.8	1.6				All Other Expenses (net)	1.6	1.4
	-4.8	-.1				Profit Before Taxes	2.3	1.1
						RATIOS		
	2.0	2.1					2.0	2.2
	1.5	1.4				Current	1.5	1.4
	1.2	1.1					1.1	1.1
	1.4	1.1					1.2	1.2
	.9	.7				Quick	.8	.8
	.3	.5					.5	.5
	12 31.7	36 10.3					31 11.7	30 12.1
	42 8.8	50 7.3				Sales/Receivables	44 8.4	42 8.7
	66 5.6	61 6.0					51 7.1	58 6.3
	13 28.5	22 16.5					30 12.3	24 15.4
	33 11.0	50 7.3				Cost of Sales/Inventory	54 6.7	47 7.8
	126 2.9	92 3.9					83 4.4	62 5.9
	14 26.6	21 17.3					18 20.5	15 24.4
	51 7.1	27 13.5				Cost of Sales/Payables	27 13.5	21 17.7
	68 5.4	41 9.0					35 10.4	34 10.6
	9.3	6.5					8.1	8.2
	16.4	15.5				Sales/Working Capital	12.7	13.3
	28.6	40.0					62.0	44.3
	9.2	9.1					5.6	4.5
	1.7	2.0				EBIT/Interest	(43) 2.1	(42) 1.9
	-6.5	.0					1.1	-.1
		2.7				Net Profit + Depr., Dep.,	4.6	4.4
		(10) 1.2				Amort./Cur. Mat. L/T/D	(18) 2.2	(14) 2.2
		.3					1.2	1.0
	.4	.2					.5	.5
	1.1	.6				Fixed/Worth	.9	.8
	-2.4	1.6					2.2	5.5
	2.1	1.1					.9	1.2
	3.8	2.5				Debt/Worth	2.4	1.8
	-8.7	15.3					5.3	11.2
		42.2				% Profit Before Taxes/Tangible	40.6	37.4
		(22) 10.1				Net Worth	(38) 14.4	(36) 13.2
		.5					1.4	-4.0
	16.0	5.4				% Profit Before Taxes/Total	13.5	8.0
	2.1	2.6				Assets	4.4	3.7
	-9.1	-5.7					-.4	-3.2
	47.6	49.4					16.3	18.4
	19.9	19.0				Sales/Net Fixed Assets	10.0	10.6
	8.3	10.4					5.2	5.4
	4.5	3.6					3.6	3.2
	3.0	2.7				Sales/Total Assets	2.7	2.6
	1.9	2.2					1.7	1.9
	.9	.6					1.2	1.3
	(10) 1.5	(24) 1.7				% Depr., Dep., Amort./Sales	(41) 2.3	(42) 2.7
	3.3	2.9					3.1	4.0
		1.7				% Officers', Directors',	2.3	2.0
		(14) 2.5				Owners' Comp/Sales	(19) 4.6	(20) 4.9
		5.8					6.8	6.8
2894M	36851M	327599M	346274M	138985M		Net Sales ($)	738514M	726472M
878M	11544M	113252M	158782M	68445M		Total Assets ($)	418557M	524694M

M = $ thousand   MM = $ million
See Pages 11 through 21 for Explanation of Ratios and Data

Comparative Historical Data | Current Data Sorted By Sales

			Type of Statement	0-1MM	1-3MM	3-5MM	5-10MM	10-25MM	25MM & OVER
12	10	10	Unqualified				2	4	4
10	19	14	Reviewed		1	1	5	6	1
9	14	8	Compiled		3	2	1	2	
4	7	3	Tax Returns	2			1		
16	15	17	Other	4	2	1	3	4	3
4/1/02-3/31/03 ALL	4/1/03-3/31/04 ALL	4/1/04-3/31/05 ALL		13 (4/1-9/30/04)			39 (10/1/04-3/31/05)		
51	65	52	NUMBER OF STATEMENTS	6	6	4	12	16	8
%	%	%	**ASSETS**	%	%	%	%	%	%
5.4	7.4	4.8	Cash & Equivalents				5.7	3.9	
31.4	31.5	35.0	Trade Receivables (net)				35.8	38.7	
26.9	25.0	29.2	Inventory				29.9	30.0	
3.0	3.1	4.8	All Other Current				8.8	2.7	
66.7	66.9	73.7	Total Current				80.1	75.3	
25.3	24.9	18.6	Fixed Assets (net)				14.0	19.1	
2.2	2.0	2.0	Intangibles (net)				1.0	1.0	
5.8	6.2	5.6	All Other Non-Current				4.9	4.6	
100.0	100.0	100.0	Total				100.0	100.0	
			LIABILITIES						
12.2	13.4	19.1	Notes Payable-Short Term				15.3	16.2	
5.0	3.2	4.8	Cur. Mat.-L/T/D				2.7	3.6	
17.7	16.4	17.9	Trade Payables				17.8	18.6	
.1	.3	.3	Income Taxes Payable				.9	.1	
14.3	10.7	13.4	All Other Current				16.7	13.8	
49.4	44.0	55.5	Total Current				53.3	52.4	
18.0	15.3	15.3	Long-Term Debt				15.1	6.5	
1.0	.7	.9	Deferred Taxes				1.3	1.1	
2.2	5.9	11.3	All Other Non-Current				10.3	5.5	
29.5	34.1	17.0	Net Worth				20.0	34.6	
100.0	100.0	100.0	Total Liabilities & Net Worth				100.0	100.0	
			INCOME DATA						
100.0	100.0	100.0	Net Sales				100.0	100.0	
28.1	29.9	27.4	Gross Profit				29.1	25.1	
27.3	27.8	27.0	Operating Expenses				28.2	23.0	
.8	2.1	.4	Operating Profit				.8	2.1	
.7	.6	1.1	All Other Expenses (net)				.9	.7	
.0	1.5	-.7	Profit Before Taxes				-.1	1.4	
			RATIOS						
2.0	2.2	2.2	Current				2.2	1.9	
1.5	1.4	1.5					1.7	1.4	
1.0	1.2	1.1					1.1	1.1	
1.2	1.5	1.3	Quick				1.2	1.2	
.7	.8	.8					.9	.7	
.5	.5	.5					.4	.5	
35 10.5	31 12.0	34 10.6	Sales/Receivables				23 16.1	35 10.3	
45 8.1	41 9.0	48 7.6					43 8.6	49 7.4	
57 6.4	53 6.9	61 6.0					63 5.8	59 6.2	
26 14.0	20 18.1	24 15.5	Cost of Sales/Inventory				16 22.2	22 16.3	
58 6.3	47 7.7	49 7.4					64 5.7	49 7.4	
80 4.5	78 4.7	93 3.9					95 3.8	91 4.0	
18 20.6	13 28.0	20 17.9	Cost of Sales/Payables				21 17.6	22 16.9	
26 14.3	26 13.8	28 12.9					27 13.3	27 13.7	
43 8.6	41 8.8	44 8.3					47 7.7	38 9.5	
7.0	7.1	6.4	Sales/Working Capital				6.4	8.3	
14.7	13.5	14.4					16.0	16.7	
218.0	38.3	32.1					38.2	24.7	
6.9	7.8	9.2	EBIT/Interest				9.8	11.2	
(48) 1.7	(62) 2.3	2.0					2.0	4.8	
-2.9	-.1	-.1					-1.2	1.0	
8.5	4.0	4.2	Net Profit + Depr., Dep.,						
(15) 1.1	(17) 1.4	(20) 1.7	Amort./Cur. Mat. L/T/D						
-1.1	.0	1.0							
.4	.3	.3	Fixed/Worth				.2	.4	
.6	.6	.7					.3	.6	
2.0	1.8	2.8					4.0	1.1	
1.0	1.0	1.3	Debt/Worth				.9	.8	
1.7	1.8	2.6					2.6	2.3	
5.0	4.5	14.7					12.5	4.8	
34.5	42.1	35.4	% Profit Before Taxes/Tangible				53.5	44.2	
(42) 10.5	(58) 13.0	(42) 12.4	Net Worth			(10) 10.7	(15) 17.9	
-13.1	-10.6	1.5					-9.1	5.8	
10.3	12.0	8.8	% Profit Before Taxes/Total				11.7	9.4	
2.4	3.3	2.8	Assets				2.9	4.6	
-8.3	-3.7	-3.8					-5.7	-.2	
24.5	26.2	41.6	Sales/Net Fixed Assets				48.2	60.1	
11.6	13.3	18.5					25.5	14.4	
6.0	7.3	9.2					16.0	9.3	
3.1	3.3	3.6	Sales/Total Assets				3.6	4.3	
2.6	2.6	2.7					2.8	2.9	
2.0	1.9	2.0					2.4	1.9	
1.2	1.0	.8	% Depr., Dep., Amort./Sales				.8	.5	
(47) 2.3	(58) 2.1	(46) 1.6				(10) 1.4	1.7	
3.5	3.0	2.7					2.3	3.1	
1.9	2.7	2.3	% Officers', Directors',						
(22) 4.8	(32) 5.3	(23) 4.2	Owners' Comp/Sales						
7.8	9.4	6.9							
988929M	746383M	852603M	Net Sales ($)	4004M	13235M	14909M	92422M	264572M	463461M
506743M	343192M	352901M	Total Assets ($)	3376M	9906M	6219M	30965M	103462M	198973M

M = $ thousand   MM = $ million
See Pages 11 through 21 for Explanation of Ratios and Data

Current Data Sorted By Assets   Comparative Historical Data

Type of Statement	0-500M	500M-2MM	2-10MM	10-50MM	50-100MM	100-250MM	4/1/00-3/31/01 ALL	4/1/01-3/31/02 ALL
Unqualified	1		4	7	1	1	6	9
Reviewed		4	4	2			17	9
Compiled		1	4				12	8
Tax Returns	1	2	1				2	3
Other	1	6	8	4	1	1	12	19
		10 (4/1-9/30/04)		43 (10/1/04-3/31/05)				
NUMBER OF STATEMENTS	2	13	21	13	2	2	49	48
	%	%	%	%	%	%	%	%
ASSETS								
Cash & Equivalents		2.5	1.9	2.6			9.1	6.7
Trade Receivables (net)		42.5	34.1	33.4			33.1	28.4
Inventory		34.4	22.7	16.7			23.9	24.9
All Other Current		2.4	3.2	1.8			2.4	3.3
Total Current		81.8	62.0	54.4			68.5	63.2
Fixed Assets (net)		14.6	24.2	28.1			24.1	27.9
Intangibles (net)		.0	8.6	10.6			1.9	3.6
All Other Non-Current		3.5	5.1	6.8			5.5	5.4
Total		100.0	100.0	100.0			100.0	100.0
LIABILITIES								
Notes Payable-Short Term		22.9	15.5	13.6			11.3	16.8
Cur. Mat.-L/T/D		.8	2.6	4.4			3.3	4.7
Trade Payables		26.9	14.5	15.6			15.9	16.6
Income Taxes Payable		.3	.4	.2			.1	.2
All Other Current		14.4	12.8	14.0			15.4	10.4
Total Current		65.3	45.8	47.8			46.0	48.8
Long-Term Debt		7.7	17.3	22.3			13.1	13.9
Deferred Taxes		.1	.5	1.0			.1	.3
All Other Non-Current		6.4	3.5	21.4			3.5	7.9
Net Worth		20.6	32.8	7.4			37.2	29.1
Total Liabilities & Net Worth		100.0	100.0	100.0			100.0	100.0
INCOME DATA								
Net Sales		100.0	100.0	100.0			100.0	100.0
Gross Profit		31.9	29.5	23.4			30.5	31.9
Operating Expenses		30.6	24.3	22.7			25.2	27.3
Operating Profit		1.3	5.3	.8			5.2	4.5
All Other Expenses (net)		.5	1.3	3.4			.4	1.5
Profit Before Taxes		.8	3.9	-2.6			4.9	3.0
RATIOS								
Current		1.5	1.6	1.4			2.4	2.5
		1.1	1.4	1.2			1.5	1.3
		1.0	1.1	1.0			1.0	1.0
Quick		1.1	1.3	1.0			1.5	1.3
		.6	.8	.7			1.0	.7
		.4	.5	.6			.6	.5
Sales/Receivables		27 13.4	34 10.9	47 7.7			29 12.6	24 15.3
		44 8.4	46 8.0	68 5.4			39 9.4	39 9.4
		59 6.2	62 5.9	73 5.0			56 6.5	58 6.2
Cost of Sales/Inventory		11 31.8	26 14.0	30 12.3			21 17.4	26 13.8
		41 9.0	42 8.6	46 7.9			39 9.3	50 7.3
		95 3.8	62 5.9	55 6.6			62 5.9	88 4.2
Cost of Sales/Payables		25 14.7	18 20.0	20 18.6			14 25.8	17 20.9
		36 10.1	38 9.6	39 9.2			21 17.3	34 10.7
		66 5.5	42 8.6	50 7.3			32 11.4	49 7.4
Sales/Working Capital		11.9	8.0	11.6			5.9	6.0
		52.1	22.9	20.3			16.8	16.6
		NM	82.2	NM			99.9	-247.5
EBIT/Interest		8.0	8.2	5.3			18.5	8.6
		1.1	(20) 3.9	2.1			(44) 5.3	(44) 2.8
		-2.7	2.0	-.9			2.1	1.1
Net Profit + Depr., Dep., Amort./Cur. Mat. L/T/D							16.1	14.5
							(12) 5.4	(18) 2.3
							2.4	.7
Fixed/Worth		.2	.4	1.2			.3	.4
		.7	1.1	-3.8			.6	1.1
		-8.0	2.4	-1.2			1.4	3.6
Debt/Worth		2.1	1.4	1.7			.6	.8
		2.9	3.1	-14.8			1.9	2.6
		-25.5	7.0	-7.4			4.4	9.7
% Profit Before Taxes/Tangible Net Worth			71.4				64.8	45.4
			(18) 52.7				(46) 33.8	(41) 20.5
			13.0				12.4	7.3
% Profit Before Taxes/Total Assets		14.4	19.5	6.4			21.9	14.9
		.2	12.5	2.3			11.8	6.0
		-5.5	3.2	-15.1			4.1	1.1
Sales/Net Fixed Assets		126.2	32.2	12.2			26.4	21.0
		31.5	11.9	5.8			14.8	11.0
		14.5	4.9	4.6			10.2	6.4
Sales/Total Assets		5.5	3.8	2.2			4.1	3.3
		3.2	2.3	1.8			3.0	2.5
		2.5	1.6	1.6			2.3	1.9
% Depr., Dep., Amort./Sales		.6	.7	1.3			.6	1.0
		(11) 1.2	2.0	(12) 2.6			(45) 1.2	(42) 1.8
		1.6	3.0	3.6			2.8	3.2
% Officers', Directors', Owners' Comp/Sales							2.8	2.2
							(18) 6.9	(16) 4.2
							9.8	9.0
Net Sales ($)	3256M	63153M	256617M	549112M	204527M	264720M	775605M	959993M
Total Assets ($)	752M	16397M	104850M	277229M	121958M	292585M	334625M	459072M

M = $ thousand   MM = $ million

See Pages 11 through 21 for Explanation of Ratios and Data

Comparative Historical Data			Type of Statement	Current Data Sorted By Sales					
13	11	13	Unqualified				1	3	9
17	9	11	Reviewed	1	1		4	4	1
6	5	5	Compiled			1	1	3	
1	1	4	Tax Returns		1	2	1		
17	17	20	Other		3	3	4	5	5
4/1/02-3/31/03 ALL	4/1/03-3/31/04 ALL	4/1/04-3/31/05 ALL		10 (4/1-9/30/04)			43 (10/1/04-3/31/05)		
				0-1MM	1-3MM	3-5MM	5-10MM	10-25MM	25MM & OVER
54	43	53	NUMBER OF STATEMENTS	1	5	6	11	15	15
%	%	%	ASSETS	%	%	%	%	%	%
6.8	7.3	2.8	Cash & Equivalents				.7	3.0	2.7
30.0	35.3	35.4	Trade Receivables (net)				43.6	34.2	31.4
27.0	25.8	22.9	Inventory				26.7	20.1	15.9
3.6	2.7	2.5	All Other Current				1.2	4.0	2.1
67.4	71.1	63.5	Total Current				72.2	61.3	52.1
22.6	17.9	23.0	Fixed Assets (net)				18.0	22.4	28.8
5.0	5.1	7.8	Intangibles (net)				5.4	11.1	12.2
5.1	5.9	5.7	All Other Non-Current				4.4	5.2	6.9
100.0	100.0	100.0	Total				100.0	100.0	100.0
			LIABILITIES						
13.3	16.5	16.0	Notes Payable-Short Term				17.2	16.9	13.4
3.3	3.1	2.6	Cur. Mat.-L/T/D				2.0	3.3	4.1
13.8	19.8	19.0	Trade Payables				23.2	15.1	12.8
.1	.2	.3	Income Taxes Payable				.2	.4	.2
14.2	13.8	13.3	All Other Current				12.9	13.2	12.1
44.7	53.4	51.2	Total Current				55.5	48.9	42.6
8.6	9.9	15.2	Long-Term Debt				13.5	12.4	20.4
.5	.4	.8	Deferred Taxes				.4	.4	2.1
7.1	21.8	9.4	All Other Non-Current				4.1	5.8	19.9
39.1	14.5	23.4	Net Worth				26.5	32.5	15.1
100.0	100.0	100.0	Total Liabilities & Net Worth				100.0	100.0	100.0
			INCOME DATA						
100.0	100.0	100.0	Net Sales				100.0	100.0	100.0
29.7	29.4	28.7	Gross Profit				28.9	25.2	24.5
27.7	28.2	26.0	Operating Expenses				26.3	20.6	21.4
2.0	1.3	2.7	Operating Profit				2.6	4.6	3.1
.5	1.2	1.5	All Other Expenses (net)				.8	1.0	3.5
1.5	.0	1.2	Profit Before Taxes				1.8	3.6	-.4
			RATIOS						
2.3	2.3	1.5					1.5	1.6	1.6
1.7	1.5	1.2	Current				1.3	1.4	1.2
1.2	1.1	1.0					1.1	1.0	1.0
1.4	1.4	1.1					1.1	1.2	1.1
.9	.9	.7	Quick				.7	.8	.7
.5	.6	.5					.5	.5	.6
31 11.9	36 10.1	35 10.4					34 10.9	33 11.2	47 7.7
40 9.2	46 7.9	48 7.7	Sales/Receivables				44 8.3	47 7.8	54 6.8
48 7.6	57 6.4	68 5.4					55 6.6	68 5.3	71 5.2
24 15.2	25 14.6	25 14.4					20 18.2	23 15.9	26 14.2
45 8.2	47 7.7	42 8.6	Cost of Sales/Inventory				50 7.3	36 10.1	38 9.5
74 5.0	68 5.4	60 6.1					78 4.7	52 7.0	58 6.3
15 24.2	23 16.2	20 18.0					32 11.4	14 26.6	20 17.9
22 16.8	40 9.1	38 9.6	Cost of Sales/Payables				39 9.3	26 14.2	36 10.1
36 10.2	60 6.0	46 8.0					46 7.9	41 8.8	44 8.4
7.1	7.5	10.1					10.9	8.0	10.3
11.8	12.4	27.5	Sales/Working Capital				28.0	29.9	20.3
49.8	42.4	106.0					104.0	-271.5	65.0
9.5	6.3	7.6					7.2	10.8	8.2
(51) 3.3	(40) 2.8	(49) 2.9	EBIT/Interest				2.7	(14) 5.9	(14) 2.3
1.1	-1.5	.2					1.1	2.8	-.2
7.7	4.5	8.0	Net Profit + Depr., Dep.,						
(22) 3.1	(15) 2.9	(16) 2.1	Amort./Cur. Mat. L/T/D						
1.7	1.3	1.3							
.3	.3	.5					.3	.5	.7
.5	.8	1.3	Fixed/Worth				.6	1.2	-3.8
1.2	3.4	-3.5					2.5	2.3	-1.8
.7	1.0	1.4					1.6	1.3	.9
1.4	2.6	3.3	Debt/Worth				3.8	2.4	-14.8
3.5	14.6	-17.0					5.2	11.9	-6.3
32.4	38.8	53.5	% Profit Before Taxes/Tangible				59.3	74.6	
(49) 10.1	(34) 10.1	(36) 22.0	Net Worth			(10) 23.9	(12) 52.7	
2.4	-3.5	4.5					.1	21.0	
9.1	10.5	13.2	% Profit Before Taxes/Total				13.1	22.1	7.7
4.5	3.3	4.1	Assets				4.4	15.3	2.6
.7	-3.0	-4.1					.2	4.3	-6.0
35.7	58.7	32.2					110.5	31.7	12.0
13.1	14.5	11.9	Sales/Net Fixed Assets				11.9	20.4	5.3
5.8	8.5	4.7					9.1	4.5	4.3
3.8	3.6	3.6					5.2	4.6	2.0
2.6	2.5	2.3	Sales/Total Assets				2.7	2.3	1.8
1.8	1.7	1.6					2.0	1.6	1.5
1.1	.8	.9					.7	.4	1.9
(49) 2.4	(36) 1.8	(49) 1.9	% Depr., Dep., Amort./Sales			(10) 1.9	1.7	(13) 2.6
3.5	3.0	3.0					2.6	2.8	3.8
1.5	1.9	2.3	% Officers', Directors',						
(25) 3.4	(14) 4.5	(16) 4.6	Owners' Comp/Sales						
7.3	8.2	8.0							
1087681M	1158249M	1341385M	Net Sales ($)	200M	11014M	22758M	84794M	238582M	984037M
589378M	608883M	813771M	Total Assets ($)	260M	6329M	7020M	31218M	100892M	668052M

© RMA 2005   M = $ thousand   MM = $ million
See Pages 11 through 21 for Explanation of Ratios and Data

Current Data Sorted By Assets   Comparative Historical Data

						Type of Statement		
	1	9	13	2	1	Unqualified	17	12
2	14	27	7			Reviewed	46	38
5	18	10	1			Compiled	33	33
9	10	3				Tax Returns	13	5
1	12	22	11	3		Other	28	42
	23 (4/1-9/30/04)		158 (10/1/04-3/31/05)				4/1/00-3/31/01	4/1/01-3/31/02
0-500M	500M-2MM	2-10MM	10-50MM	50-100MM	100-250MM		ALL	ALL
17	55	71	32	5	1	NUMBER OF STATEMENTS	137	130
%	%	%	%	%	%	ASSETS	%	%
9.4	10.8	4.3	4.8			Cash & Equivalents	7.4	8.4
23.2	35.7	32.5	23.6			Trade Receivables (net)	34.4	33.6
23.2	24.6	26.3	22.9			Inventory	23.1	23.1
1.1	1.4	2.1	1.4			All Other Current	2.5	2.7
56.8	72.5	65.3	52.7			Total Current	67.4	67.8
37.6	21.2	27.8	27.9			Fixed Assets (net)	25.2	23.8
1.1	2.5	2.8	14.5			Intangibles (net)	2.3	3.3
4.5	3.8	4.1	4.9			All Other Non-Current	5.1	5.1
100.0	100.0	100.0	100.0			Total	100.0	100.0
						LIABILITIES		
11.7	14.3	16.5	9.1			Notes Payable-Short Term	12.8	13.5
4.3	4.1	3.8	3.9			Cur. Mat.-L/T/D	3.5	4.2
11.3	19.0	17.0	14.3			Trade Payables	16.2	16.0
.0	.2	.1	.2			Income Taxes Payable	.1	.3
9.8	11.7	11.0	11.1			All Other Current	13.5	11.7
37.0	49.4	48.4	38.7			Total Current	46.2	45.8
46.6	18.9	12.3	21.8			Long-Term Debt	14.3	13.7
.3	.1	.7	.2			Deferred Taxes	.2	.2
12.1	5.6	8.6	8.1			All Other Non-Current	4.7	5.2
3.9	26.0	30.1	31.2			Net Worth	34.7	35.0
100.0	100.0	100.0	100.0			Total Liabilities & Net Worth	100.0	100.0
						INCOME DATA		
100.0	100.0	100.0	100.0			Net Sales	100.0	100.0
43.9	31.4	25.8	23.0			Gross Profit	29.3	28.0
38.3	28.4	23.7	16.7			Operating Expenses	25.2	25.9
5.6	3.0	2.1	6.3			Operating Profit	4.1	2.1
1.5	.8	.9	2.1			All Other Expenses (net)	.9	1.0
4.1	2.2	1.2	4.2			Profit Before Taxes	3.2	1.1
						RATIOS		
3.3	2.1	1.9	2.0				2.1	2.4
1.3	1.5	1.5	1.6			Current	1.5	1.6
.8	1.1	1.1	1.1				1.1	1.2
2.1	1.5	1.1	1.3				1.4	1.4
.9	.9	.7	.7			Quick	.9	.9
.2	.6	.5	.5				.6	.7

5	77.5	28	13.0	35	10.6	36	10.1			Sales/Receivables	28	13.2	30	12.4
20	18.3	44	8.3	47	7.7	44	8.2				43	8.5	46	7.9
33	11.0	66	5.5	70	5.2	59	6.2				59	6.2	63	5.8
18	19.8	16	22.6	27	13.5	30	12.3			Cost of Sales/Inventory	22	16.3	23	15.5
31	11.9	38	9.5	46	7.9	48	7.6				40	9.0	40	9.1
52	7.1	78	4.7	76	4.8	85	4.3				61	6.0	58	5.8
7	52.0	17	22.0	18	20.7	22	17.0			Cost of Sales/Payables	13	28.0	15	24.8
18	20.7	25	14.8	30	12.3	28	13.1				27	13.5	26	14.1
32	11.4	50	7.3	44	8.3	37	9.7				41	8.9	38	9.5

	10.8		6.7		6.6		5.6			Sales/Working Capital		7.1		5.9
	38.3		16.9		11.7		12.0					14.2		13.4
	-59.5		52.1		90.0		42.2					65.5		36.5
	8.2		11.4		6.3		8.6			EBIT/Interest		10.4		7.2
(16)	2.9	(52)	2.9	(67)	2.0	(31)	4.8				(129)	3.2	(118)	2.1
	-1.9		.8		.3		1.5					1.3		.3
					6.3		5.8			Net Profit + Depr., Dep., Amort./Cur. Mat. L/T/D		5.1		3.0
		(22)	1.3	(11)	1.3						(39)	2.1	(33)	1.7
			.4		.8							1.3		.2
	.6		.3		.4		.5			Fixed/Worth		.3		.2
	3.4		.7		.9		1.1					.6		.6
	-2.0		13.9		2.3		5.0					1.5		1.9
	1.3		.9		1.2		.9			Debt/Worth		.9		.8
	9.5		2.3		2.1		1.8					2.0		2.0
	-5.4		94.7		8.7		8.9					5.0		5.4
	146.1		58.2		31.9		37.9			% Profit Before Taxes/Tangible Net Worth		49.2		35.8
(12)	50.4	(43)	23.7	(60)	7.5	(26)	18.1				(124)	19.1	(110)	10.8
	-40.1		1.1		-3.4		6.8					3.2		1.8
	38.8		19.9		9.4		12.2			% Profit Before Taxes/Total Assets		15.7		11.5
	12.9		3.7		2.0		6.4					5.9		3.6
	-5.5		-.9		-2.5		1.5					.8		-1.4
	33.7		41.4		22.4		14.8			Sales/Net Fixed Assets		28.7		30.6
	14.7		18.9		10.5		8.5					13.2		12.9
	5.4		8.8		5.3		4.8					8.0		6.8
	6.5		4.1		3.0		2.5			Sales/Total Assets		3.8		3.5
	3.4		3.0		2.3		1.8					2.8		2.5
	3.0		2.1		1.8		1.4					2.2		1.8
	.6		.8		.9		1.4			% Depr., Dep., Amort./Sales		.7		.8
(10)	2.3	(50)	1.7	(69)	1.7	(31)	2.2				(124)	1.4	(114)	1.6
	4.8		3.4		2.8		3.0					2.6		2.6
			3.3		1.6					% Officers', Directors', Owners' Comp/Sales		2.5		2.0
		(31)	4.6	(28)	3.2						(62)	4.4	(49)	4.7
			5.8		6.1							6.9		7.1

17395M	195534M	864002M	1417679M	620753M	148404M	Net Sales ($)	2590621M	2486505M
4311M	64143M	352231M	769673M	349565M	119700M	Total Assets ($)	993511M	1239161M

M = $ thousand   MM = $ million
See Pages 11 through 21 for Explanation of Ratios and Data

Comparative Historical Data / Current Data Sorted By Sales

	4/1/02-3/31/03 ALL	4/1/03-3/31/04 ALL	4/1/04-3/31/05 ALL	Type of Statement	0-1MM	1-3MM	3-5MM	5-10MM	10-25MM	25MM & OVER
	24	18	26	Unqualified	1	1	1	3	5	15
	44	52	50	Reviewed		7	9	11	17	6
	37	38	34	Compiled	3	10	8	7	5	1
	11	23	22	Tax Returns	7	7	4	4		
	56	64	49	Other	1	6	7	11	12	12
						23 (4/1-9/30/04)			158 (10/1/04-3/31/05)	
	172	195	181	**NUMBER OF STATEMENTS**	12	31	29	36	39	34
	%	%	%	**ASSETS**	%	%	%	%	%	%
	7.9	7.7	6.9	Cash & Equivalents	9.1	10.4	10.4	5.0	3.9	5.6
	30.6	30.0	30.7	Trade Receivables (net)	19.3	32.2	29.8	34.6	33.6	26.8
	22.2	22.3	24.8	Inventory	20.3	22.3	24.9	27.0	26.8	23.7
	2.2	2.2	1.7	All Other Current	.8	1.3	1.4	1.6	2.4	2.0
	62.8	62.2	64.1	Total Current	49.4	66.2	66.6	68.3	66.5	58.1
	26.4	27.6	26.9	Fixed Assets (net)	42.9	25.7	27.7	25.7	22.5	28.2
	5.1	4.6	4.7	Intangibles (net)	1.5	4.8	1.6	1.9	6.4	9.2
	5.8	5.5	4.3	All Other Non-Current	6.2	3.3	4.0	4.1	4.5	4.5
	100.0	100.0	100.0	Total	100.0	100.0	100.0	100.0	100.0	100.0
				LIABILITIES						
	11.3	12.3	13.7	Notes Payable-Short Term	9.1	12.8	16.8	17.4	16.0	6.9
	3.4	4.2	3.9	Cur. Mat.-L/T/D	4.8	4.9	3.9	2.4	4.6	3.9
	15.9	13.5	16.3	Trade Payables	7.3	15.2	15.1	19.8	19.6	14.3
	.3	.3	.2	Income Taxes Payable	.0	.1	.0	.2	.1	.3
	12.1	13.1	11.3	All Other Current	9.7	12.7	9.3	11.2	10.8	13.1
	43.1	43.4	45.4	Total Current	30.9	45.7	45.0	51.0	51.2	37.9
	16.2	14.6	19.4	Long-Term Debt	55.8	24.4	19.6	12.5	8.6	21.4
	.4	.4	.5	Deferred Taxes	.5	.0	.6	.9	.1	.9
	7.0	9.0	7.7	All Other Non-Current	3.0	9.8	5.4	5.4	11.8	6.8
	33.3	32.5	27.1	Net Worth	9.8	20.1	29.3	30.1	28.3	32.9
	100.0	100.0	100.0	Total Liabilities & Net Worth	100.0	100.0	100.0	100.0	100.0	100.0
				INCOME DATA						
	100.0	100.0	100.0	Net Sales	100.0	100.0	100.0	100.0	100.0	100.0
	29.7	28.8	28.6	Gross Profit	46.2	36.9	28.2	29.4	22.2	21.5
	26.8	25.7	25.0	Operating Expenses	36.9	32.7	24.7	27.7	20.2	16.8
	2.9	3.1	3.6	Operating Profit	9.4	4.1	3.5	1.6	2.1	4.7
	1.0	.9	1.1	All Other Expenses (net)	3.6	1.2	.7	1.3	.5	1.1
	1.9	2.2	2.4	Profit Before Taxes	5.7	3.0	2.8	.4	1.5	3.6
				RATIOS						
	2.5	2.5	2.0	Current	2.6	2.6	2.0	1.9	1.9	2.1
	1.5	1.6	1.5		1.7	1.5	1.5	1.4	1.3	1.7
	1.0	1.0	1.1		.8	1.1	1.2	1.1	1.0	1.3
	1.6	1.6	1.3	Quick	2.0	1.8	1.3	1.1	1.0	1.4
	.9	.9	.8		1.0	.9	.8	.8	.7	.9
	.5	.6	.5		.4	.5	.6	.6	.5	.5
	31 11.7	31 11.8	28 12.8	Sales/Receivables	4 93.2	25 14.6	24 15.5	28 13.2	36 10.2	35 10.3
	45 8.2	44 8.4	45 8.2		20 18.3	40 9.1	46 7.9	46 8.0	51 7.2	41 8.8
	60 6.1	59 6.2	61 6.0		47 7.8	73 5.0	59 6.2	67 5.5	72 5.1	54 6.8
	26 14.0	25 14.8	24 15.2	Cost of Sales/Inventory	11 33.2	12 31.2	20 17.9	20 18.7	38 9.6	28 13.2
	43 8.5	42 8.7	44 8.3		27 13.6	48 7.6	38 9.5	43 8.6	49 7.5	44 8.3
	72 5.0	67 5.5	77 4.7		39 9.3	80 4.5	83 4.4	71 5.1	82 4.5	75 4.9
	16 22.5	14 25.8	17 21.5	Cost of Sales/Payables	4 83.6	16 22.6	11 32.5	18 20.8	20 17.9	21 17.2
	29 12.5	24 15.1	26 13.8		13 28.5	28 13.0	21 17.0	30 12.3	31 11.7	25 14.4
	48 7.6	38 9.7	43 8.4		24 15.1	48 7.6	49 7.5	45 8.1	57 6.4	35 10.3
	6.4	5.7	6.6	Sales/Working Capital	6.7	5.0	6.5	6.7	7.4	6.4
	12.9	12.0	14.4		15.6	15.4	10.2	17.2	16.1	10.4
	-553.9	284.7	57.4		-48.8	64.2	31.8	60.0	-75.7	22.5
	7.7	8.0	8.4	EBIT/Interest	8.5	5.9	13.2	6.0	5.9	13.4
	(155) 2.6	(176) 3.0	(172) 3.4		(11) 4.6	(29) 2.3	(28) 3.8	(31) 1.9	3.3	5.9
	.2	.7	.9		-2.5	.7	.9	-.9	.5	1.8
	2.4	3.7	6.4	Net Profit + Depr., Dep., Amort./Cur. Mat. L/T/D					6.5	9.1
	(37) 1.1	(52) 2.1	(41) 1.9						(14) 1.3	(13) 1.9
	-.5	.7	.7						.2	.9
	.3	.4	.4	Fixed/Worth	.5	.5	.4	.3	.4	.4
	.9	.9	.9		1.8	1.9	.7	.9	.7	1.0
	2.6	3.6	4.1		9.1	-.7	2.8	1.8	3.9	1.7
	.8	.7	1.1	Debt/Worth	.9	1.5	.9	1.3	1.3	.9
	1.9	1.7	2.2		5.0	5.6	2.1	2.3	2.1	1.8
	7.5	16.2	12.2		31.0	-7.2	3.6	11.6	16.8	5.3
	39.6	38.2	42.2	% Profit Before Taxes/Tangible Net Worth	260.5	57.8	60.8	30.7	34.8	37.9
	(141) 12.5	(157) 12.7	(147) 14.6		(10) 25.9	(21) 25.4	(24) 11.7	(30) 6.2	(32) 12.0	(30) 20.1
	1.2	1.8	.4		-36.4	-.2	-2.4	-3.6	-.5	12.7
	12.9	12.4	12.3	% Profit Before Taxes/Total Assets	38.9	12.9	29.3	9.4	9.8	12.7
	4.3	4.1	4.2		15.3	5.2	4.4	1.6	3.5	7.9
	-2.0	-.7	-.5		-9.5	-1.2	-.1	-6.1	-1.1	2.8
	23.1	22.3	24.8	Sales/Net Fixed Assets	67.7	28.9	29.3	35.4	24.6	19.7
	11.4	10.0	11.3		12.2	14.6	10.1	13.4	13.0	8.5
	6.0	5.5	5.5		3.3	5.5	5.5	5.4	7.9	5.1
	3.1	3.2	3.3	Sales/Total Assets	6.3	3.3	3.9	3.8	3.0	3.0
	2.4	2.3	2.5		3.2	2.6	2.6	2.5	2.3	2.1
	1.8	1.8	1.8		1.8	1.8	1.7	1.9	1.8	1.6
	1.0	1.1	1.0	% Depr., Dep., Amort./Sales		1.5	1.0	.6	.9	1.2
	(151) 1.9	(168) 1.8	(164) 1.8			(26) 2.1	(27) 1.6	(33) 1.8	1.5	(31) 1.5
	2.9	3.3	3.0			3.8	4.1	2.8	2.5	2.6
	2.7	2.1	2.0	% Officers', Directors', Owners' Comp/Sales		3.3	1.8	2.6	1.6	
	(65) 6.1	(71) 3.8	(70) 4.5			(14) 4.8	(17) 4.4	(13) 4.3	(15) 2.9	
	9.7	7.5	6.3			6.9	5.6	6.1	5.2	
	5059905M	3865887M	3263767M	Net Sales ($)	7188M	62581M	110439M	267467M	608014M	2208078M
	1978167M	2109915M	1659623M	Total Assets ($)	13570M	27807M	48147M	113139M	294195M	1162765M

M = $ thousand   MM = $ million
See Pages 11 through 21 for Explanation of Ratios and Data

Current Data Sorted By Assets   Comparative Historical Data

							Type of Statement			
		3	3	1			Unqualified		14	10
	2	3					Reviewed		10	8
3	6	7					Compiled		12	17
2	2	2					Tax Returns		3	5
	3	3	2		2		Other		11	12
	6 (4/1-9/30/04)			38 (10/1/04-3/31/05)					4/1/00-3/31/01	4/1/01-3/31/02
0-500M	500M-2MM	2-10MM	10-50MM	50-100MM	100-250MM				ALL	ALL
5	13	18	5	1	2		NUMBER OF STATEMENTS		50	52
%	%	%	%	%	%		ASSETS		%	%
	11.9	10.3					Cash & Equivalents		6.7	9.4
	24.4	34.8					Trade Receivables (net)		27.2	28.2
	28.2	21.2					Inventory		26.0	23.5
	.7	6.1					All Other Current		2.5	2.4
	65.3	72.4					Total Current		62.4	63.5
	21.6	20.1					Fixed Assets (net)		28.3	28.7
	4.2	1.0					Intangibles (net)		5.3	3.2
	9.0	6.5					All Other Non-Current		4.0	4.6
	100.0	100.0					Total		100.0	100.0
							LIABILITIES			
	4.4	9.8					Notes Payable-Short Term		9.3	7.9
	6.0	2.3					Cur. Mat.-L/T/D		2.6	3.5
	19.9	25.5					Trade Payables		18.6	19.8
	.3	.2					Income Taxes Payable		.1	.1
	8.0	9.3					All Other Current		9.2	8.8
	38.6	47.0					Total Current		39.9	40.2
	13.4	6.9					Long-Term Debt		16.9	15.8
	.2	1.5					Deferred Taxes		.4	.3
	10.1	2.9					All Other Non-Current		5.6	4.1
	37.8	41.6					Net Worth		37.2	39.6
	100.0	100.0					Total Liabilities & Net Worth		100.0	100.0
							INCOME DATA			
	100.0	100.0					Net Sales		100.0	100.0
	37.4	31.2					Gross Profit		31.5	31.3
	33.6	28.2					Operating Expenses		27.8	27.3
	3.8	3.0					Operating Profit		3.7	3.9
	.2	.2					All Other Expenses (net)		.6	.7
	3.7	2.8					Profit Before Taxes		3.1	3.2
							RATIOS			
	3.6	2.9							2.0	2.4
	1.7	1.5					Current		1.5	1.6
	1.2	1.1							1.2	1.1
	2.2	1.7							1.6	1.4
	.8	.8					Quick		.8	.8
	.6	.6							.5	.7
	6 59.0	24 15.1						26 13.9	24 14.9
	34 10.7	37 9.8					Sales/Receivables	35 10.5	33 10.9
	49 7.5	49 7.4						43 8.4	45 8.1
	28 12.9	21 17.6						27 13.6	25 14.7
	48 7.7	27 13.4					Cost of Sales/Inventory	36 10.0	33 11.1
	75 4.9	46 7.9						62 5.9	50 7.4
	14 27.0	20 18.5						18 20.6	18 20.5
	29 12.7	31 11.6					Cost of Sales/Payables	30 12.2	29 12.5
	55 6.6	43 8.5						47 7.7	45 8.1
	7.6	7.1							8.5	7.2
	10.6	13.9					Sales/Working Capital		18.7	16.0
	NM	112.5							36.7	69.0
	36.4	16.3							10.5	9.3
	(12) 5.8	(15) 6.5					EBIT/Interest	(43) 3.4	(46) 3.4
	1.4	1.3							.9	1.1
							Net Profit + Depr., Dep.,		7.4	2.3
							Amort./Cur. Mat. L /T/D	(15) 3.9	(10) 1.0
									1.3	.3
	.3	.2							.5	.4
	.5	.5					Fixed/Worth		.9	.9
	1.7	1.9							2.6	1.5
	.8	.5							.9	.8
	1.3	1.8					Debt/Worth		1.7	1.8
	6.0	4.7							6.0	3.6
	63.0	45.4					% Profit Before Taxes/Tangible		40.3	39.7
	(11) 34.2	(17) 22.2					Net Worth	(45) 18.3	(47) 10.9
	1.5	8.3							2.0	4.2
	31.5	20.4					% Profit Before Taxes/Total		17.7	16.9
	10.0	12.5					Assets		7.1	5.1
	.2	1.8							−.3	.6
	34.1	52.8							19.3	26.6
	19.9	22.3					Sales/Net Fixed Assets		11.4	12.5
	9.7	11.2							7.0	5.6
	4.9	4.2							4.1	4.4
	3.4	3.7					Sales/Total Assets		2.9	3.4
	2.4	2.6							2.1	2.2
	.8	.6							.8	.4
	(12) 1.1	1.2					% Depr., Dep., Amort./Sales	(47) 1.3	(43) 1.1
	1.5	1.5							2.0	2.1
	1.5								1.6	1.4
	(11) 2.3						% Officers', Directors',	(15) 3.1	(21) 2.9
	5.7						Owners' Comp/Sales		5.6	7.2
7091M	52483M	291938M	213088M	167650M	726639M		Net Sales ($)		1281973M	1936706M
1537M	15484M	83489M	78506M	57747M	329985M		Total Assets ($)		603311M	967923M

M = $ thousand   MM = $ million
See Pages 11 through 21 for Explanation of Ratios and Data

Comparative Historical Data | Current Data Sorted By Sales

		Type of Statement			6 (4/1-9/30/04)			38 (10/1/04-3/31/05)	
9	12	7	Unqualified					3	4
9	8	5	Reviewed				1	4	
6	16	16	Compiled	1	5	3	2	4	1
5	5	6	Tax Returns	1	2	1		2	
11	10	10	Other		2	1	1	3	3
4/1/02-3/31/03 ALL	4/1/03-3/31/04 ALL	4/1/04-3/31/05 ALL		0-1MM	1-3MM	3-5MM	5-10MM	10-25MM	25MM & OVER
40	51	44	**NUMBER OF STATEMENTS**	2	9	5	4	16	8
%	%	%	**ASSETS**	%	%	%	%	%	%
7.2	10.1	12.9	Cash & Equivalents					10.6	
29.9	28.1	27.5	Trade Receivables (net)					32.6	
26.7	24.4	23.7	Inventory					20.7	
2.8	3.6	3.1	All Other Current					5.8	
66.6	66.3	67.3	Total Current					69.6	
24.6	22.6	20.2	Fixed Assets (net)					20.0	
3.7	5.0	4.2	Intangibles (net)					1.1	
5.1	6.1	8.3	All Other Non-Current					9.3	
100.0	100.0	100.0	Total					100.0	
			LIABILITIES						
7.6	8.8	6.6	Notes Payable-Short Term					7.9	
3.5	3.2	3.2	Cur. Mat.-L/T/D					2.2	
20.6	20.7	19.3	Trade Payables					25.9	
.3	.1	.2	Income Taxes Payable					.3	
10.6	11.5	12.6	All Other Current					9.3	
42.6	44.4	42.0	Total Current					45.6	
11.5	14.8	9.5	Long-Term Debt					7.0	
1.0	1.0	.7	Deferred Taxes					1.1	
6.9	5.5	6.0	All Other Non-Current					1.9	
38.0	34.3	41.8	Net Worth					44.4	
100.0	100.0	100.0	Total Liabilities & Net Worth					100.0	
			INCOME DATA						
100.0	100.0	100.0	Net Sales					100.0	
32.9	30.6	34.8	Gross Profit					31.1	
30.6	28.0	30.4	Operating Expenses					28.1	
2.3	2.6	4.4	Operating Profit					3.0	
.1	.4	.1	All Other Expenses (net)					.1	
2.3	2.1	4.3	Profit Before Taxes					2.9	
			RATIOS						
2.4	2.5	3.2						2.9	
1.6	1.5	1.6	Current					1.5	
1.3	1.1	1.1						1.1	
1.2	1.4	1.8						1.7	
.9	.9	.8	Quick					.8	
.5	.5	.7						.6	
26 14.3	24 14.9	11 34.4						19 19.6	
33 11.0	33 10.9	32 11.4	Sales/Receivables					34 10.8	
40 9.1	43 8.5	47 7.8						47 7.8	
25 14.7	24 15.1	25 14.5						18 20.5	
35 10.5	33 10.9	34 10.9	Cost of Sales/Inventory					29 12.5	
65 5.6	51 7.1	54 6.8						39 9.4	
21 17.5	17 22.1	16 22.6						21 17.7	
32 11.3	28 13.1	28 13.0	Cost of Sales/Payables					29 12.4	
40 9.2	44 8.3	41 9.0						40 9.1	
9.1	8.3	7.7						7.7	
14.1	16.0	13.9	Sales/Working Capital					18.0	
28.0	37.6	52.0						93.1	
12.5	10.2	21.0						30.6	
(35) 2.9	(47) 3.0	(34) 7.9	EBIT/Interest					(14) 10.3	
.4	1.0	3.2						2.7	
5.6	7.9	15.7	Net Profit + Depr., Dep.,						
(14) 2.5	(21) 2.8	(10) 3.9	Amort./Cur. Mat. L/T/D						
.8	1.1	1.3							
.4	.3	.2						.2	
.6	.7	.5	Fixed/Worth					.5	
1.5	1.6	1.7						1.6	
.8	.9	.7						.5	
1.7	2.1	1.3	Debt/Worth					1.4	
3.5	3.6	5.1						4.5	
39.0	36.3	47.2	% Profit Before Taxes/Tangible					27.3	
(36) 19.0	(45) 18.6	(38) 27.4	Net Worth					(15) 21.7	
−1.3	9.0	13.4						13.2	
18.3	10.4	23.9	% Profit Before Taxes/Total					18.8	
4.0	6.0	12.4	Assets					11.9	
−1.3	.3	2.9						2.0	
24.5	28.4	39.6						49.9	
17.2	15.5	19.3	Sales/Net Fixed Assets					22.5	
8.8	9.1	10.6						12.0	
4.2	4.5	4.3						4.2	
3.2	3.2	3.5	Sales/Total Assets					3.8	
2.4	2.1	2.5						2.6	
.9	.8	.5						.8	
(31) 1.3	(49) 1.3	(41) 1.1	% Depr., Dep., Amort./Sales					1.1	
2.2	2.4	1.5						1.6	
.8	2.1	1.6	% Officers', Directors',						
(19) 5.2	(21) 3.7	(19) 2.9	Owners' Comp/Sales						
9.8	8.9	5.7							
2348527M	1498861M	1458889M	Net Sales ($)	1429M	20647M	19706M	25326M	274690M	1117091M
621198M	643153M	566748M	Total Assets ($)	374M	5863M	7494M	7681M	83973M	461363M

M = $ thousand   MM = $ million
See Pages 11 through 21 for Explanation of Ratios and Data

Current Data Sorted By Assets   Comparative Historical Data

							Type of Statement		
				3			Unqualified	3	6
	2		4	2			Reviewed	6	4
	2		2				Compiled	7	4
2		1					Tax Returns	3	2
1	1		1	5			Other	9	7
	5 (4/1-9/30/04)			20 (10/1/04-3/31/05)				4/1/00- 3/31/01	4/1/01- 3/31/02
0-500M	500M-2MM	2-10MM	10-50MM	50-100MM	100-250MM			ALL	ALL
3	5	7	10				NUMBER OF STATEMENTS	28	23
%	%	%	%	%	%		ASSETS	%	%
			6.9				Cash & Equivalents	9.6	9.4
			28.1	D	D		Trade Receivables (net)	34.0	26.8
			29.8	A	A		Inventory	31.7	32.9
			2.9	T	T		All Other Current	3.7	4.5
			67.7	A	A		Total Current	79.0	73.6
			25.5				Fixed Assets (net)	16.0	19.5
			3.1	N	N		Intangibles (net)	1.7	4.1
			3.7	O	O		All Other Non-Current	3.3	2.8
			100.0	T	T		Total	100.0	100.0
							LIABILITIES		
			10.0	A	A		Notes Payable-Short Term	12.9	15.3
			2.2	V	V		Cur. Mat.-L/T/D	2.0	3.2
			15.1	A	A		Trade Payables	22.3	14.9
			.1	I	I		Income Taxes Payable	.7	.2
			11.2	L	L		All Other Current	10.5	11.2
			38.6	A	A		Total Current	48.4	44.7
			13.1	B	B		Long-Term Debt	6.0	11.7
			1.0	L	L		Deferred Taxes	.1	.1
			1.1	E	E		All Other Non-Current	5.1	2.7
			46.2				Net Worth	40.4	40.7
			100.0				Total Liabilities & Net Worth	100.0	100.0
							INCOME DATA		
			100.0				Net Sales	100.0	100.0
			34.9				Gross Profit	30.2	33.2
			29.5				Operating Expenses	25.8	28.6
			5.5				Operating Profit	4.4	4.6
			.9				All Other Expenses (net)	.1	.4
			4.6				Profit Before Taxes	4.3	4.2
							RATIOS		
			3.0					3.2	2.5
			2.2				Current	1.7	1.5
			1.2					1.3	1.2
			1.8					1.6	1.4
			.8				Quick	.9	.7
			.6					.6	.4
		31	11.9					29 12.4	12 30.1
		35	10.3				Sales/Receivables	41 9.0	33 11.2
		71	5.1					54 6.7	49 7.5
		48	7.6					29 12.5	31 11.9
		74	4.9				Cost of Sales/Inventory	54 6.8	53 6.9
		107	3.4					86 4.3	96 3.8
		19	19.7					16 22.9	10 36.0
		26	14.3				Cost of Sales/Payables	35 10.5	26 14.0
		53	6.9					46 7.9	43 8.4
			3.6					5.2	5.9
			6.8				Sales/Working Capital	9.2	13.3
			18.3					28.0	26.1
								18.9	8.3
							EBIT/Interest	(27) 5.9	(20) 3.4
								3.0	1.5
							Net Profit + Depr., Dep., Amort./Cur. Mat. L./T/D		
			.4					.2	.2
			.6				Fixed/Worth	.4	.3
			1.3					.9	1.3
			.6					.5	.5
			1.1				Debt/Worth	1.2	1.9
			5.4					4.1	4.9
								47.6	52.1
							% Profit Before Taxes/Tangible Net Worth	(25) 30.0	(21) 20.5
								3.9	3.1
			12.0					23.0	19.6
			6.5				% Profit Before Taxes/Total Assets	11.5	9.8
			4.1					2.0	.9
			16.1					76.4	77.1
			9.4				Sales/Net Fixed Assets	29.2	22.9
			6.3					7.9	8.6
			2.8					5.0	4.2
			2.1				Sales/Total Assets	2.7	2.5
			1.6					2.0	1.9
								.5	.7
							% Depr., Dep., Amort./Sales	(24) 1.1	(19) 1.3
								1.7	2.0
								1.7	1.3
							% Officers', Directors', Owners' Comp/Sales	(13) 4.3	(11) 2.5
								7.3	5.2
7187M	28973M	121125M	427145M				Net Sales ($)	616957M	615910M
945M	6866M	37659M	195689M				Total Assets ($)	270706M	263273M

M = $ thousand   MM = $ million
See Pages 11 through 21 for Explanation of Ratios and Data

	Comparative Historical Data				Current Data Sorted By Sales					
				Type of Statement					1	2
	5	5	3	Unqualified				4	3	1
	9	7	8	Reviewed				1	2	
	6	11	4	Compiled		1				
	1	6	2	Tax Returns	1		1			
	10	9	8	Other		2			1	5
	4/1/02-	4/1/03-	4/1/04-			5 (4/1-9/30/04)			20 (10/1/04-3/31/05)	
	3/31/03	3/31/04	3/31/05		0-1MM	1-3MM	3-5MM	5-10MM	10-25MM	25MM & OVER
	ALL	ALL	ALL							
	31	38	25	**NUMBER OF STATEMENTS**	1	3	1	5	7	8
	%	%	%	**ASSETS**	%	%	%	%	%	%
	6.4	10.7	6.9	Cash & Equivalents						
	31.5	28.7	33.1	Trade Receivables (net)						
	32.9	33.4	32.2	Inventory						
	2.0	2.4	2.1	All Other Current						
	72.8	75.2	74.4	Total Current						
	19.1	16.1	18.1	Fixed Assets (net)						
	3.0	4.3	3.3	Intangibles (net)						
	5.1	4.4	4.2	All Other Non-Current						
	100.0	100.0	100.0	Total						
				LIABILITIES						
	14.4	15.5	14.2	Notes Payable-Short Term						
	3.5	4.0	2.9	Cur. Mat.-L/T/D						
	21.2	24.3	23.9	Trade Payables						
	.1	.1	.0	Income Taxes Payable						
	11.9	10.2	15.5	All Other Current						
	51.0	54.1	56.5	Total Current						
	12.1	14.1	16.0	Long-Term Debt						
	.3	.2	.4	Deferred Taxes						
	6.3	10.6	4.2	All Other Non-Current						
	30.3	21.1	22.8	Net Worth						
	100.0	100.0	100.0	Total Liabilities & Net Worth						
				INCOME DATA						
	100.0	100.0	100.0	Net Sales						
	33.8	32.6	30.2	Gross Profit						
	29.9	28.9	27.1	Operating Expenses						
	3.9	3.7	3.1	Operating Profit						
	.8	.7	.7	All Other Expenses (net)						
	3.1	3.0	2.4	Profit Before Taxes						
				RATIOS						
	1.9	2.2	2.2							
	1.3	1.5	1.4	Current						
	1.1	1.1	1.1							
	1.1	1.1	1.0							
	.8	.6	.7	Quick						
	.5	.4	.5							
23	15.8	20	18.6	28	13.2	Sales/Receivables				
36	10.2	30	12.2	33	11.1					
47	7.8	42	8.7	42	8.7					

35	10.3	35	10.4	42	8.7	Cost of Sales/Inventory
52	7.0	54	6.7	62	5.9	
84	4.4	87	4.2	88	4.1	
26	14.1	20	18.3	18	20.8	Cost of Sales/Payables
36	10.2	33	10.9	26	14.3	
52	7.1	62	5.8	49	7.4	
	7.6		7.3		8.8	Sales/Working Capital
	20.9		17.3		16.9	
	56.7		110.4		50.8	
	12.8		11.0		12.1	EBIT/Interest
(28)	4.0	(32)	2.6	(24)	3.0	
	1.7		.3		.8	
	2.6					Net Profit + Depr., Dep., Amort./Cur. Mat. L/T/D
(12)	1.7					
	.4					
	.3		.3		.2	Fixed/Worth
	.6		.9		.7	
	1.6		−2.3		−3.5	
	1.4		1.3		1.0	Debt/Worth
	2.9		2.5		2.6	
	9.7		−11.6		−22.1	
	75.6		54.3		30.8	% Profit Before Taxes/Tangible Net Worth
(28)	26.5	(25)	21.8	(17)	13.8	
	6.1		3.9		5.3	
	16.8		14.2		10.8	% Profit Before Taxes/Total Assets
	9.6		4.7		4.1	
	1.1		−1.9		−.7	
	48.7		52.8		43.5	Sales/Net Fixed Assets
	28.1		30.4		23.5	
	8.5		10.2		9.4	
	4.3		4.7		4.5	Sales/Total Assets
	3.2		3.3		2.8	
	2.4		2.1		2.2	
	.7		.9		.8	% Depr., Dep., Amort./Sales
(27)	1.2	(33)	1.3	(22)	1.1	
	3.2		2.9		2.5	
	2.8		2.2		2.1	% Officers', Directors', Owners' Comp/Sales
(18)	4.9	(19)	4.7	(13)	3.2	
	7.8		6.2		6.7	

Net Sales ($) / Total Assets ($)								
705594M	640636M	584430M	Net Sales ($)	712M	7979M	3732M	40730M	130200M	401077M
270216M	276014M	241159M	Total Assets ($)	121M	2287M	425M	18530M	53556M	166240M

M = $ thousand   MM = $ million
See Pages 11 through 21 for Explanation of Ratios and Data

Current Data Sorted By Assets   Comparative Historical Data

0-500M	500M-2MM	2-10MM	10-50MM	50-100MM	100-250MM	Type of Statement	4/1/00-3/31/01 ALL	4/1/01-3/31/02 ALL
	2	1	3	1		Unqualified	5	4
		4	2			Reviewed	6	4
1	1	1				Compiled	5	3
	1	1				Tax Returns		1
	4	6	2		1	Other	3	3
	6 (4/1-9/30/04)		25 (10/1/04-3/31/05)					
1	8	13	7	1	1	NUMBER OF STATEMENTS	19	15
%	%	%	%	%	%	**ASSETS**	%	%
		5.8				Cash & Equivalents	9.8	10.5
		32.4				Trade Receivables (net)	26.9	28.7
		17.5				Inventory	28.5	27.0
		2.2				All Other Current	1.5	5.5
		57.9				Total Current	66.6	71.7
		27.1				Fixed Assets (net)	22.2	16.9
		11.7				Intangibles (net)	5.0	8.1
		3.2				All Other Non-Current	6.2	3.2
		100.0				Total	100.0	100.0
						LIABILITIES		
		7.7				Notes Payable-Short Term	12.7	11.9
		3.3				Cur. Mat.-L/T/D	2.2	1.5
		12.6				Trade Payables	11.0	11.9
		.2				Income Taxes Payable	.0	.0
		6.0				All Other Current	10.3	10.5
		29.9				Total Current	36.2	35.7
		25.0				Long-Term Debt	13.0	10.7
		.3				Deferred Taxes	.9	.8
		10.0				All Other Non-Current	3.2	19.3
		34.9				Net Worth	46.7	33.5
		100.0				Total Liabilities & Net Worth	100.0	100.0
						INCOME DATA		
		100.0				Net Sales	100.0	100.0
		40.5				Gross Profit	37.9	36.5
		34.8				Operating Expenses	32.0	31.9
		5.7				Operating Profit	5.9	4.6
		1.7				All Other Expenses (net)	1.2	2.1
		3.9				Profit Before Taxes	4.7	2.5
						RATIOS		
		4.1					3.4	7.1
		2.2				Current	1.5	2.1
		1.2					1.3	1.3
		3.5					2.7	2.9
		1.0				Quick	.8	1.1
		.7					.6	.6
		47 7.8					42 8.7	42 8.8
		56 6.6				Sales/Receivables	58 6.3	56 6.6
		93 3.9					73 5.0	79 4.6
		44 8.2					65 5.6	55 6.7
		65 5.6				Cost of Sales/Inventory	92 4.0	99 3.7
		80 4.5					156 2.3	142 2.6
		27 13.6					19 19.5	19 19.0
		39 9.3				Cost of Sales/Payables	34 10.7	24 15.0
		52 7.0					53 6.9	43 8.6
		3.2					4.2	2.7
		6.3				Sales/Working Capital	6.4	4.4
		12.4					12.9	12.6
		11.6					11.0	12.7
		5.6				EBIT/Interest	(16) 3.8	2.2
		2.6					1.2	1.2
						Net Profit + Depr., Dep., Amort./Cur. Mat. L./T/D		
		.2					.2	.2
		.9				Fixed/Worth	.5	.4
		18.6					1.9	21.3
		1.5					.8	.9
		3.2				Debt/Worth	1.4	2.8
		36.5					2.7	234.4
		80.5				% Profit Before Taxes/Tangible	38.7	67.6
	(11)	46.8				Net Worth	(18) 20.4	(12) 23.3
		20.0					.2	-12.0
		18.9				% Profit Before Taxes/Total	19.6	17.4
		10.2				Assets	6.6	3.0
		3.5					-1.8	.3
		29.1					17.5	27.7
		5.9				Sales/Net Fixed Assets	9.7	15.0
		1.8					6.4	11.6
		2.0					2.1	2.0
		1.5				Sales/Total Assets	1.9	1.7
		.7					1.3	1.1
		.9					.6	.7
	(10)	3.1				% Depr., Dep., Amort./Sales	(16) 1.6	(10) 1.5
		5.1					4.0	3.2
						% Officers', Directors', Owners' Comp/Sales		
1336M	22278M	108520M	241290M	94700M	59462M	Net Sales ($)	536103M	279878M
143M	10588M	74597M	142086M	50461M	125667M	Total Assets ($)	381331M	187493M

© RMA 2005

M = $ thousand   MM = $ million
See Pages 11 through 21 for Explanation of Ratios and Data

Comparative Historical Data / Current Data Sorted By Sales

			Type of Statement	0-1MM	1-3MM	3-5MM	5-10MM	10-25MM	25MM & OVER
7	5	7	Unqualified		1		2		4
7	8	6	Reviewed			1	2	3	
6	3	3	Compiled		2		1		
3	1	2	Tax Returns		1		1		
6	9	13	Other		4	3	1	3	2
4/1/02-3/31/03 ALL	4/1/03-3/31/04 ALL	4/1/04-3/31/05 ALL		0-1MM	6 (4/1-9/30/04)		25 (10/1/04-3/31/05)		
29	26	31	**NUMBER OF STATEMENTS**		8	4	7	6	6
%	%	%	**ASSETS**	%	%	%	%	%	%
12.0	13.2	10.5	Cash & Equivalents						
24.1	28.7	29.2	Trade Receivables (net)	D					
28.7	26.7	24.8	Inventory	A					
2.0	3.0	3.0	All Other Current	T					
66.9	71.5	67.6	Total Current	A					
21.8	20.1	19.6	Fixed Assets (net)						
4.9	3.2	9.1	Intangibles (net)	N					
6.4	5.3	3.8	All Other Non-Current	O					
100.0	100.0	100.0	Total	T					
			LIABILITIES	A					
9.8	7.2	6.5	Notes Payable-Short Term	V					
3.6	3.0	2.6	Cur. Mat.-L/T/D	A					
10.9	9.9	12.7	Trade Payables	I					
.0	.0	.1	Income Taxes Payable	L					
12.8	13.3	13.1	All Other Current	A					
37.1	33.4	35.1	Total Current	B					
11.7	11.8	15.3	Long-Term Debt	L					
.2	.3	.6	Deferred Taxes	E					
14.5	20.6	15.2	All Other Non-Current						
36.4	33.9	33.9	Net Worth						
100.0	100.0	100.0	Total Liabilities & Net Worth						
			INCOME DATA						
100.0	100.0	100.0	Net Sales						
39.4	41.1	43.7	Gross Profit						
34.2	34.6	37.4	Operating Expenses						
5.2	6.4	6.2	Operating Profit						
2.0	1.3	1.6	All Other Expenses (net)						
3.2	5.1	4.6	Profit Before Taxes						
			RATIOS						
3.3	3.9	3.7							
1.7	2.6	2.2	Current						
1.2	1.7	1.3							
2.5	2.7	3.2							
.9	1.5	1.1	Quick						
.5	.7	.5							
(33) 11.1	(40) 9.2	(39) 9.3							
(48) 7.7	(54) 6.8	(56) 6.6	Sales/Receivables						
(61) 6.0	(75) 4.9	(76) 4.8							
(48) 7.7	(49) 7.4	(56) 6.5							
(84) 4.3	(73) 5.0	(72) 5.1	Cost of Sales/Inventory						
(120) 3.0	(134) 2.7	(121) 3.0							
(15) 24.5	(21) 17.5	(28) 13.3							
(26) 14.2	(32) 11.3	(48) 7.5	Cost of Sales/Payables						
(66) 5.5	(51) 7.2	(63) 5.8							
3.1	3.1	3.1							
6.9	4.3	6.0	Sales/Working Capital						
27.7	10.4	14.1							
9.1	25.2	31.8							
(26) 1.8	(20) 6.7	(26) 6.1	EBIT/Interest						
.7	1.0	1.2							
			Net Profit + Depr., Dep., Amort./Cur. Mat. L/T/D						
.2	.2	.2							
.4	.3	.7	Fixed/Worth						
6.2	.8	4.2							
.7	.3	.4							
1.7	.7	1.6	Debt/Worth						
11.2	2.3	21.0							
39.6	40.4	51.6							
(25) 5.9	(23) 21.6	(25) 23.5	% Profit Before Taxes/Tangible Net Worth						
−12.1	.8	3.0							
12.8	21.3	15.7							
1.6	6.5	8.3	% Profit Before Taxes/Total Assets						
−1.1	−1.1	.4							
19.6	29.0	37.8							
12.9	11.9	12.6	Sales/Net Fixed Assets						
8.3	6.7	5.5							
2.5	2.4	1.9							
1.9	2.1	1.7	Sales/Total Assets						
1.5	1.2	1.2							
.9	.9	1.0							
(24) 1.5	(23) 1.9	(25) 2.0	% Depr., Dep., Amort./Sales						
2.9	2.6	3.3							
			% Officers', Directors', Owners' Comp/Sales						
450081M	481210M	527586M	Net Sales ($)		15564M	16518M	51202M	105081M	339221M
468453M	653902M	403542M	Total Assets ($)		11876M	19103M	30070M	66363M	276130M

M = $ thousand   MM = $ million
See Pages 11 through 21 for Explanation of Ratios and Data

Current Data Sorted By Assets   **Comparative Historical Data**

	0-500M	500M-2MM	2-10MM	10-50MM	50-100MM	100-250MM	Type of Statement	4/1/00-3/31/01 ALL	4/1/01-3/31/02 ALL
	1	1	10	21	5	10	Unqualified	38	31
	1	2	17	3			Reviewed	25	16
		3	4	1			Compiled	18	18
	6	2	2				Tax Returns	3	1
	4	5	19	21	6	4	Other	26	36
		34 (4/1-9/30/04)			114 (10/1/04-3/31/05)				
	12	13	52	46	11	14	NUMBER OF STATEMENTS	110	102
	%	%	%	%	%	%	ASSETS	%	%
	15.6	9.0	10.3	10.8	24.7	13.9	Cash & Equivalents	11.5	9.0
	33.2	27.2	26.5	23.3	15.0	18.9	Trade Receivables (net)	25.6	25.3
	18.7	28.4	29.9	20.6	12.3	17.4	Inventory	26.4	23.8
	1.9	4.3	1.9	2.6	1.2	1.7	All Other Current	4.2	3.4
	69.4	69.0	68.6	57.3	53.2	52.0	Total Current	67.7	61.5
	21.8	16.5	21.3	22.6	20.1	17.8	Fixed Assets (net)	18.5	21.8
	3.2	6.9	5.9	14.9	24.1	24.2	Intangibles (net)	7.3	10.0
	5.5	7.6	4.2	5.1	2.6	6.0	All Other Non-Current	6.4	6.8
	100.0	100.0	100.0	100.0	100.0	100.0	Total	100.0	100.0
							LIABILITIES		
	11.7	9.3	9.3	5.9	2.2	4.4	Notes Payable-Short Term	8.1	8.9
	.9	1.6	5.4	2.8	2.6	1.9	Cur. Mat.-L/T/D	3.0	3.7
	14.3	16.3	12.1	9.0	7.4	9.0	Trade Payables	11.9	14.6
	.0	.5	.5	.6	.7	.4	Income Taxes Payable	.8	.4
	16.2	8.3	11.5	12.9	9.9	7.0	All Other Current	8.5	9.9
	43.2	36.0	38.8	31.3	22.8	22.6	Total Current	32.3	37.3
	34.1	20.2	12.5	15.1	9.9	15.2	Long-Term Debt	12.5	14.1
	.0	.0	.4	.8	1.2	1.2	Deferred Taxes	.5	.7
	9.0	26.8	6.8	5.6	3.6	6.4	All Other Non-Current	3.8	5.5
	13.0	17.0	41.5	47.3	62.6	54.5	Net Worth	50.9	42.4
	100.0	100.0	100.0	100.0	100.0	100.0	Total Liabilities & Net Worth	100.0	100.0
							INCOME DATA		
	100.0	100.0	100.0	100.0	100.0	100.0	Net Sales	100.0	100.0
	53.6	52.5	40.8	43.1	52.8	43.2	Gross Profit	42.9	43.1
	44.3	44.8	32.6	31.0	40.7	29.8	Operating Expenses	37.8	36.7
	9.3	7.7	8.2	12.1	12.1	13.4	Operating Profit	5.2	6.4
	.1	1.7	.7	1.5	2.6	.9	All Other Expenses (net)	.5	2.5
	9.3	5.9	7.5	10.7	9.4	12.5	Profit Before Taxes	4.7	3.9
							RATIOS		
	4.6	3.3	3.5	3.8	6.8	3.8	Current	3.0	3.3
	1.6	2.6	1.7	1.7	2.0	2.4		2.4	1.7
	.9	1.5	1.3	1.2	1.2	1.5		1.5	1.1
	3.0	1.9	2.1	1.9	6.4	2.1	Quick	1.7	1.7
	.9	1.2	.9	1.0	1.2	1.4		1.1	1.0
	.7	.8	.6	.6	.7	.8		.7	.6
Sales/Receivables	32 11.3	38 9.5	37 10.0	43 8.6	40 9.1	49 7.5	Sales/Receivables	42 8.8	40 9.0
	44 8.3	47 7.8	44 8.4	55 6.7	43 8.6	54 6.7		53 6.8	55 6.7
	50 7.3	61 6.0	56 6.5	67 5.4	74 4.9	66 5.5		63 5.7	68 5.4
	6 66.0	53 6.9	65 5.6	64 5.7	58 6.3	74 4.9	Cost of Sales/Inventory	58 6.3	52 7.0
	41 9.0	95 3.9	78 4.7	88 4.1	75 4.9	87 4.2		108 3.4	99 3.7
	74 5.0	165 2.2	112 3.3	115 3.2	111 3.3	140 2.6		152 2.4	147 2.5
	6 58.1	18 20.6	18 20.0	24 15.3	15 24.3	29 12.5	Cost of Sales/Payables	23 15.8	25 14.4
	40 9.2	41 8.9	31 11.9	34 10.8	42 8.7	38 9.6		35 10.3	40 9.0
	57 6.4	93 3.9	45 8.1	49 7.5	94 3.9	48 7.5		58 6.3	60 6.1
	4.8	4.0	4.1	3.3	1.5	2.6	Sales/Working Capital	3.0	3.7
	12.9	4.3	7.3	8.6	5.4	4.8		5.1	6.3
	-42.9	14.1	16.5	19.7	34.9	9.4		8.3	79.7
		7.7	24.7	26.1		210.2	EBIT/Interest	11.2	9.1
	(11) 4.5	(45) 4.6	(39) 6.6		(12) 9.2			(94) 2.9	(95) 2.5
	2.0	2.4	2.3		1.9			1.3	.6
			7.8	18.0			Net Profit + Depr., Dep., Amort./Cur. Mat. L /T/D	12.9	8.7
		(14) 5.3	(15) 6.0					(36) 4.1	(38) 2.0
		1.3	2.0					1.7	1.2
	.1	.1	.2	.4	.2	.2	Fixed/Worth	.2	.2
	-14.1	.5	.5	.7	.8	.6		.3	.6
	-1.3	-2.0	1.6	2.3	2.9	-2.0		.9	2.0
	.6	.6	.5	.6	.2	.3	Debt/Worth	.5	.5
	-46.6	1.1	1.6	1.7	1.4	1.0		1.0	1.3
	-8.1	-5.5	4.3	4.8	5.1	-11.6		2.5	4.9
			64.7	61.7		31.0	% Profit Before Taxes/Tangible Net Worth	36.1	31.0
		(44) 28.3	(38) 33.9		(10) 20.7			(103) 15.8	(84) 15.6
		7.4	9.9		10.9			2.8	-.6
	71.2	22.2	21.2	22.5	19.0	16.9	% Profit Before Taxes/Total Assets	13.9	14.8
	20.7	13.0	9.9	10.5	10.5	10.7		5.8	4.6
	.7	1.5	2.9	3.6	3.3	4.7		1.1	-.1
	61.6	60.3	38.5	13.5	13.9	8.7	Sales/Net Fixed Assets	31.7	18.6
	13.1	15.6	10.6	6.6	7.6	5.2		9.9	8.0
	7.9	8.6	5.4	4.0	4.4	3.6		4.9	4.0
	4.2	2.7	2.7	1.9	1.3	1.6	Sales/Total Assets	2.2	2.2
	2.8	1.9	2.0	1.4	1.0	1.1		1.7	1.6
	2.5	1.6	1.7	1.0	.7	.6		1.1	1.0
		.5	.9	1.9		2.2	% Depr., Dep., Amort./Sales	.8	1.4
	(12)	1.0	(47) 1.9	(41) 3.0		(10) 3.7		(86) 2.3	(87) 3.6
		4.0	3.1	5.1		5.6		4.1	5.1
			3.0				% Officers', Directors', Owners' Comp/Sales	3.2	3.0
		(17)	5.3					(30) 4.9	(22) 5.1
			6.8					6.6	9.7
	14217M	32584M	496642M	1567034M	849613M	2871537M	Net Sales ($)	3980666M	2976576M
	4303M	15463M	234846M	1077402M	831297M	2203898M	Total Assets ($)	3214797M	2687381M

M = $ thousand   MM = $ million
See Pages 11 through 21 for Explanation of Ratios and Data

Comparative Historical Data			Type of Statement	Current Data Sorted By Sales					
			Unqualified		1	1	7	9	30
51	51	48	Reviewed	1	1	3	9	8	1
27	20	23	Compiled	1	2	1	3	1	
20	17	8	Tax Returns	1	5	2	2		
3	8	10	Other	1	9	4	6	15	25
49	37	59			34 (4/1-9/30/04)		114 (10/1/04-3/31/05)		
4/1/02-3/31/03 ALL	4/1/03-3/31/04 ALL	4/1/04-3/31/05 ALL		0-1MM	1-3MM	3-5MM	5-10MM	10-25MM	25MM & OVER
150	133	148	NUMBER OF STATEMENTS	3	18	11	27	33	56
%	%	%	ASSETS	%	%	%	%	%	%
12.2	11.9	12.2	Cash & Equivalents		13.3	17.0	10.6	10.6	13.0
23.6	24.5	24.6	Trade Receivables (net)		29.7	20.9	25.7	27.1	21.3
21.3	23.8	23.5	Inventory		19.4	32.0	28.1	27.0	18.6
4.0	3.1	2.2	All Other Current		3.3	1.9	2.4	1.4	2.5
61.2	63.3	62.5	Total Current		65.6	71.9	66.9	66.1	55.5
23.4	20.3	20.9	Fixed Assets (net)		20.1	18.5	22.6	20.2	21.6
8.4	9.2	11.7	Intangibles (net)		9.5	4.7	5.6	7.8	19.0
6.9	7.2	5.0	All Other Non-Current		4.7	5.0	4.9	5.9	3.9
100.0	100.0	100.0	Total		100.0	100.0	100.0	100.0	100.0
			LIABILITIES						
6.9	7.3	7.4	Notes Payable-Short Term		9.7	9.5	5.3	11.5	5.0
4.1	4.9	3.4	Cur. Mat.-L/T/D		3.6	3.1	5.5	3.2	2.5
11.6	11.9	11.0	Trade Payables		12.7	14.5	13.0	9.7	9.6
.8	.7	.5	Income Taxes Payable		.2	.4	1.0	.3	.6
12.3	10.8	11.5	All Other Current		13.0	17.2	11.3	6.8	12.1
35.7	35.6	33.9	Total Current		39.2	44.7	36.2	31.5	29.8
12.7	11.8	15.8	Long-Term Debt		30.0	15.6	16.0	12.1	13.8
.6	.7	.6	Deferred Taxes		.0	.0	.4	.7	1.0
5.1	7.1	8.1	All Other Non-Current		11.7	21.5	9.7	4.9	5.6
45.9	44.6	41.6	Net Worth		19.1	18.2	37.8	50.8	49.8
100.0	100.0	100.0	Total Liabilities & Net Worth		100.0	100.0	100.0	100.0	100.0
			INCOME DATA						
100.0	100.0	100.0	Net Sales		100.0	100.0	100.0	100.0	100.0
44.2	46.4	44.7	Gross Profit		52.5	53.6	37.5	43.4	44.3
35.3	37.6	34.5	Operating Expenses		41.8	47.0	28.9	32.1	33.0
8.9	8.9	10.3	Operating Profit		10.7	6.5	8.6	11.3	11.3
1.7	1.5	1.1	All Other Expenses (net)		1.0	.9	.6	1.4	1.4
7.2	7.4	9.1	Profit Before Taxes		9.7	5.7	8.0	9.9	9.9
			RATIOS						
3.5	3.6	3.7			4.5	3.2	3.4	5.5	3.6
2.0	2.1	1.8	Current		2.6	1.7	1.7	2.1	1.7
1.2	1.3	1.3			.9	.9	1.4	1.3	1.2
2.1	2.0	2.0			2.6	1.2	2.0	3.6	1.8
1.1	1.1	1.0	Quick		1.3	.8	1.0	.9	1.0
.6	.6	.7			.7	.6	.6	.7	.7
37 9.8	38 9.6	40 9.2		29 12.5	26 13.9	41 9.0	40 9.1	43 8.6	
48 7.6	47 7.7	48 7.7	Sales/Receivables	44 8.2	37 9.9	49 7.5	45 8.0	53 6.9	
62 5.9	59 6.2	60 6.1		53 6.8	46 8.0	62 5.9	61 6.0	67 5.5	
48 7.7	61 6.0	59 6.2		12 30.6	48 7.6	58 6.3	69 5.3	61 5.9	
80 4.6	92 4.0	80 4.5	Cost of Sales/Inventory	43 8.5	114 3.2	79 4.6	79 4.6	85 4.3	
122 3.0	134 2.7	114 3.2		100 3.6	206 1.8	113 3.2	113 3.2	111 3.3	
22 16.9	23 16.0	20 17.8		13 28.3	17 21.5	18 20.6	22 16.9	23 16.1	
31 11.6	34 10.7	35 10.5	Cost of Sales/Payables	38 9.6	37 9.9	31 11.8	32 11.4	35 10.3	
57 6.4	62 5.9	51 7.1		63 5.8	101 3.6	56 6.5	47 7.8	53 6.9	
3.4	3.3	4.0			4.1	3.7	4.2	3.4	3.5
6.1	6.1	6.7	Sales/Working Capital		5.1	5.2	7.4	7.2	6.8
16.9	17.9	18.5			−78.4	−68.8	12.0	14.0	22.1
19.4	21.4	18.4			19.6		28.2	21.3	31.9
(130) 5.3	(119) 5.4	(123) 5.0	EBIT/Interest		(13) 4.5		(26) 5.5	(26) 5.2	(47) 6.8
1.8	1.8	2.3			1.5		1.8	2.4	1.6
15.3	16.4	7.8	Net Profit + Depr., Dep.,				8.7		19.1
(56) 2.8	(49) 4.8	(43) 3.9	Amort./Cur. Mat. L/T/D				(12) 5.3		(19) 3.9
1.2	2.0	1.6					.7		1.8
.2	.2	.2			.1	.1	.3	.2	.4
.5	.5	.6	Fixed/Worth		1.2	.4	.7	.4	.7
1.4	1.2	2.9			−3.8	3.4	2.1	1.9	2.9
.4	.5	.5			.5	.7	.7	.3	.6
1.3	1.5	1.6	Debt/Worth		NM	1.3	1.8	1.4	1.6
3.1	4.1	7.2			−6.9	11.2	6.1	3.9	6.6
44.5	47.4	61.2	% Profit Before Taxes/Tangible				66.1	59.1	62.7
(135) 22.7	(119) 24.6	(115) 27.6	Net Worth			(22) 28.2	(29) 32.9	(44) 26.0	
7.3	10.0	8.2					6.7	8.5	11.1
17.1	17.6	21.5	% Profit Before Taxes/Total		26.6	18.5	20.4	22.4	20.2
9.1	9.8	10.7	Assets		19.1	7.5	13.0	7.8	10.9
2.0	3.1	3.4			3.5	2.4	2.8	3.6	4.0
18.3	21.2	24.0			68.7	41.4	19.2	34.0	11.9
7.4	8.7	8.5	Sales/Net Fixed Assets		21.5	15.6	7.2	8.1	7.0
4.3	4.7	4.6			7.7	6.7	5.7	4.1	4.4
2.2	2.4	2.4			4.0	2.6	2.5	2.7	1.9
1.6	1.7	1.7	Sales/Total Assets		2.6	2.0	1.9	1.9	1.3
1.2	1.3	1.2			1.7	1.6	1.5	1.0	.9
1.6	1.5	1.1			.5	.6	1.6	.7	1.9
(124) 2.7	(115) 2.7	(125) 2.5	% Depr., Dep., Amort./Sales		(12) 1.7	(10) 1.0	(26) 2.5	(29) 2.4	(47) 3.1
5.0	4.5	4.5			4.2	2.1	3.5	4.6	5.1
2.6	3.0	2.0	% Officers', Directors',						
(41) 4.9	(38) 5.5	(32) 4.5	Owners' Comp/Sales						
10.5	8.8	7.2							
5087628M	4767366M	5831627M	Net Sales ($)	1818M	29128M	43555M	187871M	526424M	5042831M
4240409M	3752560M	4367209M	Total Assets ($)	847M	14817M	21330M	110825M	369208M	3850182M

M = $ thousand   MM = $ million
See Pages 11 through 21 for Explanation of Ratios and Data

Current Data Sorted By Assets   Comparative Historical Data

0-500M	500M-2MM	2-10MM	10-50MM	50-100MM	100-250MM	Type of Statement	4/1/00-3/31/01 ALL	4/1/01-3/31/02 ALL
1	3	8	11	5	3	Unqualified	19	23
	11	18	2			Reviewed	9	8
2	10	6	2			Compiled	16	16
2	5					Tax Returns	8	7
3	9	16	11	1	7	Other	35	31
	27 (4/1-9/30/04)			109 (10/1/04-3/31/05)				
8	38	48	26	6	10	NUMBER OF STATEMENTS	87	85
%	%	%	%	%	%	**ASSETS**	%	%
	8.1	8.4	10.4		9.4	Cash & Equivalents	9.4	8.2
	30.9	28.1	24.0		17.8	Trade Receivables (net)	30.6	27.1
	23.6	27.6	24.9		19.7	Inventory	23.4	23.9
	1.6	1.9	1.8		3.3	All Other Current	1.7	3.2
	64.3	66.0	61.2		50.2	Total Current	65.0	62.3
	20.1	24.6	24.2		14.2	Fixed Assets (net)	19.6	23.2
	8.5	3.1	9.5		29.0	Intangibles (net)	8.2	8.9
	7.1	6.3	5.0		6.6	All Other Non-Current	7.2	5.6
	100.0	100.0	100.0		100.0	Total	100.0	100.0
						LIABILITIES		
	12.3	9.5	7.7		1.7	Notes Payable-Short Term	10.5	9.6
	4.6	3.4	4.4		2.8	Cur. Mat.-L/T/D	2.7	3.1
	16.9	13.6	13.2		8.8	Trade Payables	13.9	13.9
	.0	.6	.0		.3	Income Taxes Payable	.5	.2
	13.3	9.4	11.9		4.8	All Other Current	21.5	10.3
	47.1	36.4	37.2		18.4	Total Current	49.1	37.2
	15.6	14.6	11.6		20.2	Long-Term Debt	13.0	13.7
	.2	.5	.5		.6	Deferred Taxes	.5	.8
	11.7	2.1	7.9		5.3	All Other Non-Current	4.2	12.1
	25.4	46.3	42.8		55.5	Net Worth	33.5	36.2
	100.0	100.0	100.0		100.0	Total Liabilities & Net Worth	100.0	100.0
						INCOME DATA		
	100.0	100.0	100.0		100.0	Net Sales	100.0	100.0
	49.0	44.2	37.5		42.4	Gross Profit	45.1	42.7
	44.4	35.7	30.3		29.3	Operating Expenses	38.0	37.1
	4.6	8.4	7.2		13.1	Operating Profit	7.1	5.6
	.4	.1	1.6		2.2	All Other Expenses (net)	1.0	1.7
	4.2	8.4	5.6		10.8	Profit Before Taxes	6.2	3.9
						RATIOS		
	2.1	3.2	2.6		3.9	Current	3.6	3.6
	1.4	2.2	2.0		2.5		1.8	2.0
	1.0	1.2	1.1		1.5		1.1	1.2
	1.5	2.1	1.5		2.2	Quick	2.2	2.2
	.8	1.0	.9		1.0		1.0	.9
	.5	.6	.6		.7		.6	.6
20 18.0	32 11.5	41 8.8		48 7.7		Sales/Receivables	41 8.8	38 9.7
41 8.8	42 8.8	50 7.3		51 7.2			51 7.2	50 7.3
58 6.3	59 6.1	58 6.3		60 6.0			66 5.5	64 5.7
21 17.8	41 8.9	49 7.4		76 4.8		Cost of Sales/Inventory	40 9.0	34 10.8
65 5.6	70 5.2	83 4.4		84 4.3			75 4.9	75 4.9
92 4.0	114 3.2	131 2.8		127 2.9			112 3.3	111 3.3
13 27.7	13 27.3	21 17.6		32 11.5		Cost of Sales/Payables	17 20.9	18 19.9
40 9.1	26 14.0	42 8.7		38 9.7			33 11.0	31 11.8
68 5.3	54 6.7	52 7.1		44 8.4			55 6.6	50 7.3
	6.9	4.6	4.5		3.2	Sales/Working Capital	4.3	4.3
	19.6	7.9	6.7		5.7		8.0	7.1
	NM	23.0	38.6		10.8		95.4	18.8
	32.9	30.2	14.1			EBIT/Interest	14.6	14.1
	(33) 3.0	(42) 8.9	(22) 4.7				(78) 4.0	(75) 3.7
	.7	3.5	1.2				1.2	1.5
		5.2	11.0			Net Profit + Depr., Dep., Amort./Cur. Mat. L /T/D	13.1	14.8
		(16) 2.9	(13) 2.6				(25) 3.5	(26) 2.4
		1.3	1.2				1.7	1.0
	.3	.2	.3		.2	Fixed/Worth	.2	.2
	.9	.5	.8		.5		.6	.6
	-3.1	1.0	2.0		-2.4		1.7	1.6
	1.2	.5	.7		.7	Debt/Worth	.4	.5
	2.5	1.5	1.6		1.4		1.5	1.6
	-37.3	2.6	5.7		-6.8		4.2	6.1
	75.3	68.6	61.4			% Profit Before Taxes/Tangible Net Worth	47.3	37.0
	(27) 31.0	(47) 28.2	(23) 22.5				(70) 24.8	(70) 18.4
	4.2	11.0	10.9				6.6	5.7
	18.7	24.1	18.3		18.2	% Profit Before Taxes/Total Assets	19.5	15.6
	3.7	10.2	6.0		6.1		9.9	7.1
	-.4	4.6	.6		.6		1.5	1.8
	28.1	25.6	10.7		23.1	Sales/Net Fixed Assets	28.8	28.1
	18.0	9.9	7.7		7.7		13.5	11.4
	9.9	6.0	4.7		4.3		6.5	4.6
	3.6	2.8	2.0		1.6	Sales/Total Assets	2.8	2.9
	2.6	2.3	1.8		.9		2.1	1.8
	1.9	1.7	1.2		.7		1.4	1.3
	1.2	1.1	1.7			% Depr., Dep., Amort./Sales	1.1	1.0
	(29) 2.2	(44) 1.7	(22) 2.7				(71) 1.8	(68) 2.2
	3.9	3.1	5.0				3.1	3.9
	2.9	2.0				% Officers', Directors', Owners' Comp/Sales	2.7	3.3
	(17) 5.3	(13) 5.1					(30) 8.2	(25) 7.4
	11.9						13.2	12.5
11216M	119211M	525733M	1093981M	560123M	1661513M	Net Sales ($)	2713630M	2653408M
2200M	43490M	232020M	645689M	406563M	1420469M	Total Assets ($)	1960648M	2028680M

M = $ thousand   MM = $ million
See Pages 11 through 21 for Explanation of Ratios and Data

Comparative Historical Data / Current Data Sorted By Sales

Current data period groupings: **27 (4/1-9/30/04)** covers 0-1MM and 1-3MM; **109 (10/1/04-3/31/05)** covers 3-5MM through 25MM & OVER.

	4/1/02-3/31/03 ALL	4/1/03-3/31/04 ALL	4/1/04-3/31/05 ALL	0-1MM	1-3MM	3-5MM	5-10MM	10-25MM	25MM & OVER
Type of Statement									
Unqualified	41	32	31			4	2	7	18
Reviewed	18	25	31		5	7	7	9	3
Compiled	14	21	20		8	2	6	2	2
Tax Returns	4	14	7	3	3	1			
Other	37	43	47	3	5	3	9	12	15
NUMBER OF STATEMENTS	114	135	136	6	21	17	24	30	38
ASSETS	%	%	%	%	%	%	%	%	%
Cash & Equivalents	6.5	7.8	8.8		6.8	7.1	8.9	8.9	8.7
Trade Receivables (net)	28.5	25.6	26.5		26.7	25.3	29.7	28.5	23.8
Inventory	23.0	26.8	26.5		26.5	27.8	28.1	25.1	25.0
All Other Current	3.1	2.7	2.0		2.2	1.0	2.5	2.5	1.8
Total Current	61.1	62.9	63.7		62.2	61.2	69.3	64.9	59.3
Fixed Assets (net)	24.3	22.3	22.1		16.8	26.4	21.7	24.0	22.5
Intangibles (net)	8.4	7.9	7.9		11.4	4.0	5.1	5.0	13.2
All Other Non-Current	6.2	6.9	6.2		9.6	8.4	3.9	6.1	5.1
Total	100.0	100.0	100.0		100.0	100.0	100.0	100.0	100.0
LIABILITIES									
Notes Payable-Short Term	9.3	10.8	10.0		10.1	20.2	11.1	7.4	7.9
Cur. Mat.-L/T/D	3.7	3.8	3.8		3.0	5.5	2.8	3.5	3.4
Trade Payables	13.0	15.0	14.0		13.9	17.9	12.0	13.8	13.3
Income Taxes Payable	.6	.7	.3		.0	.0	.5	.6	.1
All Other Current	10.5	13.9	11.5		11.3	16.3	8.5	10.6	12.3
Total Current	37.2	44.2	39.6		38.3	59.9	34.9	35.8	37.0
Long-Term Debt	13.8	16.5	14.2		20.5	16.1	11.2	11.8	14.0
Deferred Taxes	.5	.4	.4		.1	.1	.4	.6	.7
All Other Non-Current	5.5	7.0	6.2		14.2	1.3	7.6	3.2	5.8
Net Worth	42.9	31.9	39.5		26.9	22.6	46.0	48.6	42.5
Total Liabilities & Net Worth	100.0	100.0	100.0		100.0	100.0	100.0	100.0	100.0
INCOME DATA									
Net Sales	100.0	100.0	100.0		100.0	100.0	100.0	100.0	100.0
Gross Profit	43.9	43.9	44.6		49.7	45.3	45.6	43.1	39.4
Operating Expenses	37.9	38.2	37.2		42.9	42.8	38.3	34.4	30.5
Operating Profit	6.0	5.8	7.4		6.8	2.5	7.3	8.8	8.9
All Other Expenses (net)	1.0	1.1	.7		.0	.7	-.2	.6	1.8
Profit Before Taxes	5.0	4.6	6.7		6.8	1.8	7.5	8.2	7.2
RATIOS									
Current	3.3	2.7	3.1		3.7	2.1	3.7	3.1	2.7
	1.9	1.6	1.8		1.7	1.2	2.0	2.2	1.7
	1.2	1.1	1.1		1.0	.9	1.2	1.2	1.2
Quick	1.9	1.5	1.6		1.5	1.1	2.8	1.8	1.5
	1.0	.8	(135) .9		(20) 1.2	.6	1.2	1.0	.9
	.6	.5	.5		.4	.4	.5	.7	.6
Sales/Receivables	38 9.6	33 11.2	32 11.3		4 85.6	18 20.5	33 11.2	31 11.6	42 8.6
	47 7.7	45 8.0	47 7.8		44 8.2	29 12.4	49 7.5	39 9.3	52 7.1
	59 6.2	60 6.1	59 6.2		67 5.4	48 7.7	69 5.3	54 6.8	60 6.0
Cost of Sales/Inventory	37 10.0	39 9.4	41 8.9		11 33.3	32 11.6	37 9.8	39 9.3	68 5.4
	67 5.5	73 5.0	77 4.7		78 4.7	71 5.2	85 4.3	60 6.1	86 4.2
	108 3.4	116 3.2	118 3.1		139 2.6	86 4.2	124 3.0	95 3.8	123 3.0
Cost of Sales/Payables	20 18.2	19 18.9	17 21.3		6 63.6	9 40.9	17 22.1	13 28.4	24 15.0
	33 11.1	33 11.0	35 10.5		46 7.9	48 7.6	27 13.8	26 14.0	42 8.7
	52 7.0	67 5.4	57 6.4		93 3.9	69 5.3	50 7.3	51 7.1	55 6.7
Sales/Working Capital	4.4	4.9	4.8		5.4	7.6	3.9	5.7	4.0
	9.0	10.2	9.3		10.7	37.0	7.6	8.9	9.0
	22.9	44.1	36.6		NM	-60.5	20.3	36.5	21.4
EBIT/Interest	17.7	19.2	26.6		49.1	7.0	22.2	56.3	22.5
	(100) 3.8	(119) 4.2	(120) 5.1		(18) 5.3	(15) 1.2	(21) 9.4	(26) 8.9	(34) 4.7
	1.7	1.4	1.8		2.1	-4.0	3.2	3.3	2.0
Net Profit + Depr., Dep., Amort./Cur. Mat. L/T/D	8.0	11.8	6.2						12.0
	(42) 2.7	(42) 2.4	(42) 2.6						(20) 2.6
	1.5	1.3	1.2						1.2
Fixed/Worth	.3	.3	.3		.1	.2	.2	.3	.3
	.7	.7	.7		1.2	1.0	.5	.6	.8
	1.5	2.1	1.9		-2.1	-2.7	1.1	.9	3.6
Debt/Worth	.6	.9	.7		.9	.9	.6	.6	.8
	1.5	1.9	1.7		3.0	1.8	1.6	1.4	1.8
	4.7	6.5	5.2		-6.4	-14.1	3.3	2.6	8.9
% Profit Before Taxes/Tangible Net Worth	48.2	58.5	62.9		503.4	43.9	65.6	73.5	59.5
	(99) 19.9	(111) 21.2	(114) 25.0		(15) 40.2	(11) 6.0	(23) 26.3	(29) 26.1	(31) 21.3
	4.7	9.2	8.6		17.3	-41.7	12.1	9.2	7.7
% Profit Before Taxes/Total Assets	20.1	16.0	19.0		20.5	16.0	20.1	29.2	13.7
	6.9	6.6	7.7		7.8	.9	10.8	8.8	7.2
	1.8	1.2	1.1		1.7	-9.2	5.6	3.7	1.1
Sales/Net Fixed Assets	20.7	25.0	24.0		56.8	31.0	26.1	23.7	11.7
	10.4	13.2	10.4		23.2	17.6	11.2	11.1	7.3
	4.9	6.2	6.0		11.2	8.1	6.8	6.2	4.4
Sales/Total Assets	2.8	2.9	2.8		2.7	3.6	3.2	3.1	2.1
	2.1	2.2	2.1		2.2	2.8	2.2	2.5	1.5
	1.4	1.6	1.5		1.5	2.2	1.6	1.9	1.0
% Depr., Dep., Amort./Sales	1.5	1.3	1.2		1.2	.9	1.2	1.0	1.6
	(95) 2.3	(110) 2.1	(111) 2.2		(14) 2.1	(15) 2.2	(20) 1.6	(27) 2.1	(32) 2.7
	3.6	3.6	3.8		3.8	3.2	3.4	4.5	4.5
% Officers', Directors', Owners' Comp/Sales	4.2	3.8	2.4		3.8				
	(28) 5.6	(46) 5.5	(35) 5.1		(10) 6.2				
	11.8	11.4	7.3		18.5				
Net Sales ($)	3874420M	3888843M	3971777M	4462M	39030M	66507M	171958M	438489M	3251331M
Total Assets ($)	2543257M	2369452M	2750431M	2133M	22032M	28890M	85824M	217448M	2394104M

M = $ thousand   MM = $ million

See Pages 11 through 21 for Explanation of Ratios and Data

Current Data Sorted By Assets   Comparative Historical Data

						Type of Statement		
		2	5	3	2	Unqualified	8	9
	2	2	2			Reviewed	7	3
	1	1	1			Compiled	7	9
2		1				Tax Returns	4	
	3	5	6		1	Other	9	10
0-500M	500M-2MM	2-10MM	10-50MM	50-100MM	100-250MM		4/1/00-3/31/01 ALL	4/1/01-3/31/02 ALL
		5 (4/1-9/30/04)	33 (10/1/04-3/31/05)					
2	6	10	14	4	2	NUMBER OF STATEMENTS	35	31
%	%	%	%	%	%	**ASSETS**	%	%
		11.1	9.7			Cash & Equivalents	8.2	9.8
		25.0	27.5			Trade Receivables (net)	32.3	23.6
		27.9	21.4			Inventory	26.2	24.9
		3.2	2.8			All Other Current	1.7	2.9
		67.1	61.4			Total Current	68.3	61.3
		27.5	22.5			Fixed Assets (net)	17.3	25.6
		.8	8.6			Intangibles (net)	6.5	6.5
		4.6	7.5			All Other Non-Current	7.9	6.6
		100.0	100.0			Total	100.0	100.0
						LIABILITIES		
		10.1	3.4			Notes Payable-Short Term	9.8	10.0
		1.6	3.2			Cur. Mat.-L/T/D	4.3	2.5
		9.6	10.1			Trade Payables	12.7	8.5
		.2	.1			Income Taxes Payable	.6	.8
		8.1	9.5			All Other Current	9.2	13.2
		29.6	26.3			Total Current	36.6	35.0
		12.5	12.6			Long-Term Debt	14.2	11.7
		.1	.8			Deferred Taxes	.4	.7
		1.5	14.6			All Other Non-Current	6.2	2.2
		56.3	45.7			Net Worth	42.7	50.4
		100.0	100.0			Total Liabilities & Net Worth	100.0	100.0
						INCOME DATA		
		100.0	100.0			Net Sales	100.0	100.0
		48.2	43.4			Gross Profit	45.9	45.9
		36.3	36.4			Operating Expenses	40.9	38.8
		11.9	7.0			Operating Profit	5.0	7.1
		−.3	.6			All Other Expenses (net)	.8	.3
		12.1	6.4			Profit Before Taxes	4.2	6.7
						RATIOS		
		4.7	3.8				3.1	3.0
		2.5	2.8			Current	2.1	1.7
		1.7	1.7				1.3	1.5
		2.1	2.5				1.5	1.5
		1.3	1.6			Quick	1.1	1.0
		.6	1.0				.8	.7
		29 12.7	40 9.2				39 9.2	42 8.8
		38 9.7	49 7.5			Sales/Receivables	49 7.5	46 8.0
		47 7.8	51 7.1				60 6.1	58 6.3
		34 10.7	39 9.5				27 13.4	63 5.8
		97 3.8	63 5.8			Cost of Sales/Inventory	93 3.9	91 4.0
		186 2.0	95 3.8				165 2.2	166 2.2
		14 26.1	20 18.7				19 19.1	16 22.4
		29 12.6	25 14.6			Cost of Sales/Payables	31 11.6	26 14.1
		36 10.0	38 9.6				54 6.8	47 7.8
		3.4	4.3				3.3	3.4
		5.8	6.4			Sales/Working Capital	5.8	5.2
		12.6	9.3				17.6	16.2
			16.9				10.2	9.9
		(13)	12.1			EBIT/Interest	(31) 3.5	(25) 6.4
			3.8				2.3	1.7
						Net Profit + Depr., Dep.,	4.5	
						Amort./Cur. Mat. L /T/D	(15) 1.8	
							.8	
		.2	.3				.2	.2
		.4	.7			Fixed/Worth	.5	.5
		.9	7.9				.9	1.1
		.2	.4				.7	.6
		.8	1.3			Debt/Worth	1.4	1.2
		1.5	25.1				2.5	2.2
		57.4	56.1				48.5	48.7
		31.3	(12) 27.1			% Profit Before Taxes/Tangible Net Worth	(32) 22.4	(29) 22.9
		15.6	16.5				11.6	11.8
		21.7	25.3				15.9	20.3
		10.8	12.5			% Profit Before Taxes/Total Assets	7.6	11.3
		6.5	5.6				3.9	3.9
		16.3	19.1				25.4	16.5
		9.8	10.6			Sales/Net Fixed Assets	15.6	8.5
		3.8	6.1				6.1	5.0
		2.8	2.7				2.8	2.5
		2.5	1.9			Sales/Total Assets	2.0	1.9
		1.1	1.7				1.2	1.3
		.9	1.4				.9	.6
		1.8	(13) 1.9			% Depr., Dep., Amort./Sales	(31) 1.6	(28) 2.1
		2.8	3.6				2.6	4.2
						% Officers', Directors',	3.3	
						Owners' Comp/Sales	(12) 7.4	
							16.2	
1510M	20400M	120854M	593279M	611511M	180605M	Net Sales ($)	824534M	1082709M
636M	7078M	54082M	260153M	298625M	270488M	Total Assets ($)	426351M	679408M

© RMA 2005

M = $ thousand   MM = $ million
See Pages 11 through 21 for Explanation of Ratios and Data

Comparative Historical Data | Current Data Sorted By Sales

			Type of Statement	0-1MM	1-3MM	3-5MM	5-10MM	10-25MM	25MM & OVER
9	11	12	Unqualified				1	2	9
6	6	4	Reviewed		1	1			2
3	4	4	Compiled			1	1	1	2
5	3	3	Tax Returns	2					
16	13	15	Other		1	2	3	4	5
4/1/02-3/31/03 ALL	4/1/03-3/31/04 ALL	4/1/04-3/31/05 ALL			5 (4/1-9/30/04)			33 (10/1/04-3/31/05)	
39	37	38	NUMBER OF STATEMENTS	2	2	4	6	8	16
%	%	%	ASSETS	%	%	%	%	%	%
9.8	11.2	9.1	Cash & Equivalents						8.5
24.2	20.5	25.8	Trade Receivables (net)						25.7
24.9	22.0	24.4	Inventory						22.0
2.0	4.7	2.6	All Other Current						3.7
60.9	58.5	61.9	Total Current						59.9
25.5	26.3	24.2	Fixed Assets (net)						23.0
8.6	10.9	7.6	Intangibles (net)						13.2
5.0	4.4	6.3	All Other Non-Current						4.0
100.0	100.0	100.0	Total						100.0
			LIABILITIES						
7.1	5.6	13.2	Notes Payable-Short Term						7.5
2.9	4.5	2.0	Cur. Mat.-L/T/D						2.7
11.7	8.9	13.3	Trade Payables						8.7
.3	.3	.1	Income Taxes Payable						.1
11.6	11.4	9.2	All Other Current						10.9
33.6	30.6	37.8	Total Current						29.9
13.1	19.1	14.1	Long-Term Debt						11.7
.5	.9	.9	Deferred Taxes						2.0
6.2	6.8	9.5	All Other Non-Current						10.6
46.5	42.5	37.7	Net Worth						45.8
100.0	100.0	100.0	Total Liabilities & Net Worth						100.0
			INCOME DATA						
100.0	100.0	100.0	Net Sales						100.0
49.3	50.1	44.5	Gross Profit						42.8
41.3	42.7	36.6	Operating Expenses						33.8
8.0	7.4	7.9	Operating Profit						8.9
.8	.8	.5	All Other Expenses (net)						.2
7.1	6.5	7.3	Profit Before Taxes						8.7
			RATIOS						
3.0	3.0	3.4	Current						3.3
1.7	2.1	2.2							1.9
1.3	1.4	1.4							1.5
1.7	1.5	1.8	Quick						1.7
1.1	1.0	1.3							1.0
.7	.8	.7							.7
32 11.5	34 10.8	34 10.8	Sales/Receivables						38 9.7
44 8.3	45 8.0	43 8.5							49 7.5
52 7.1	53 6.9	50 7.3							50 7.2
44 8.2	53 6.9	49 7.5	Cost of Sales/Inventory						58 6.3
83 4.4	90 4.1	74 5.0							67 5.5
132 2.8	169 2.2	111 3.3							106 3.4
18 19.8	22 16.3	19 19.2	Cost of Sales/Payables						20 18.1
29 12.8	34 10.8	29 12.6							25 14.6
53 6.8	43 8.5	44 8.2							45 8.1
4.3	3.6	4.4	Sales/Working Capital						4.8
8.6	6.1	8.0							8.4
23.4	15.9	13.2							11.3
16.6	13.6	17.1	EBIT/Interest						17.4
(34) 6.0	(35) 5.3	(35) 8.3							11.3
1.7	2.8	3.4							6.0
10.9	5.5	19.6	Net Profit + Depr., Dep., Amort./Cur. Mat. L/T/D						
(12) 1.9	(15) 2.5	(13) 2.9							
.9	1.0	2.0							
.3	.5	.2	Fixed/Worth						.3
.6	.7	.6							.8
1.3	1.6	1.2							1.4
.7	.5	.5	Debt/Worth						.5
1.6	1.3	1.2							1.5
3.2	2.9	3.4							3.4
61.9	33.5	66.1	% Profit Before Taxes/Tangible Net Worth						67.9
(37) 22.8	(31) 22.0	(34) 36.9						(15)	48.0
4.9	10.1	18.1							19.9
21.6	18.9	21.7	% Profit Before Taxes/Total Assets						23.9
10.2	9.9	10.8							14.2
1.6	3.1	5.7							9.6
16.8	11.3	24.7	Sales/Net Fixed Assets						11.6
8.9	5.9	8.7							6.7
4.9	3.8	4.5							4.6
3.0	2.5	2.9	Sales/Total Assets						2.8
2.1	1.6	2.3							2.0
1.3	1.1	1.5							1.5
1.3	1.6	1.0	% Depr., Dep., Amort./Sales						1.7
(32) 2.1	(35) 2.3	(35) 2.0						(15)	2.3
3.5	3.8	4.0							4.0
2.0	3.9	2.9	% Officers', Directors', Owners' Comp/Sales						
(13) 4.2	(10) 5.6	(11) 4.2							
11.1	29.7	6.6							
1192985M	1391907M	1528159M	Net Sales ($)	1510M	3464M	16936M	46018M	157490M	1302741M
703756M	1001476M	891062M	Total Assets ($)	636M	1662M	5416M	31452M	70265M	781631M

© RMA 2005

M = $ thousand   MM = $ million
See Pages 11 through 21 for Explanation of Ratios and Data

Current Data Sorted By Assets   Comparative Historical Data

0-500M	500M-2MM	2-10MM	10-50MM	50-100MM	100-250MM	Type of Statement	4/1/00-3/31/01 ALL	4/1/01-3/31/02 ALL
	1	1				Unqualified	6	7
	2	4	1			Reviewed	7	5
3	5	4	1			Compiled	6	6
2	1			1	2	Tax Returns	2	2
1	1	6	3	3	1	Other	9	4
	6 (4/1-9/30/04)		37 (10/1/04-3/31/05)					
6	10	15	5	4	3	**NUMBER OF STATEMENTS**	30	24
%	%	%	%	%	%	**ASSETS**	%	%
	7.5	8.1				Cash & Equivalents	10.9	10.0
	32.2	29.0				Trade Receivables (net)	26.0	29.3
	25.5	29.0				Inventory	22.3	26.6
	.3	3.2				All Other Current	2.2	2.5
	65.5	69.2				Total Current	61.5	68.3
	26.5	20.6				Fixed Assets (net)	27.8	20.7
	.8	3.2				Intangibles (net)	7.6	6.9
	7.2	6.9				All Other Non-Current	3.2	4.0
	100.0	100.0				Total	100.0	100.0
						LIABILITIES		
	16.7	7.7				Notes Payable-Short Term	9.9	9.7
	1.7	4.3				Cur. Mat.-L/T/D	4.5	7.6
	23.0	19.3				Trade Payables	13.3	15.3
	1.1	.2				Income Taxes Payable	.0	.3
	7.7	16.1				All Other Current	12.0	15.1
	50.1	47.6				Total Current	39.8	48.0
	13.6	11.4				Long-Term Debt	15.7	16.1
	.0	.2				Deferred Taxes	.6	.4
	3.0	6.4				All Other Non-Current	4.4	5.7
	33.3	34.4				Net Worth	39.5	29.9
	100.0	100.0				Total Liabilities & Net Worth	100.0	100.0
						INCOME DATA		
	100.0	100.0				Net Sales	100.0	100.0
	38.6	46.8				Gross Profit	38.9	39.9
	36.6	39.8				Operating Expenses	34.9	35.9
	2.0	7.0				Operating Profit	4.0	4.0
	-.2	2.2				All Other Expenses (net)	1.3	1.6
	2.2	4.9				Profit Before Taxes	2.7	2.4
						RATIOS		
	1.9	2.1					2.2	2.4
	1.5	1.5				Current	1.5	1.7
	1.0	1.0					1.1	1.2
	1.2	1.1					1.9	1.6
	.7	.7				Quick	.8	.9
	.4	.4					.5	.6
	28 12.9	28 13.0					33 11.0	40 9.1
	38 9.7	37 9.8				Sales/Receivables	40 9.1	45 8.1
	47 7.8	57 6.4					49 7.5	65 5.6
	25 14.6	36 10.2					25 14.7	31 11.7
	48 7.6	78 4.7				Cost of Sales/Inventory	45 8.1	84 4.3
	84 4.4	164 2.2					122 3.0	137 2.7
	24 15.1	20 18.3					18 20.4	24 15.3
	39 9.4	41 8.9				Cost of Sales/Payables	25 14.7	34 10.7
	54 6.7	72 5.1					43 8.5	67 5.4
	10.9	5.9					6.9	4.1
	16.2	18.0				Sales/Working Capital	12.0	9.1
	-249.8	210.2					67.3	17.1
		15.4					4.8	7.0
		(13) 2.8				EBIT/Interest	(27) 2.6	(22) 4.5
		-1.6					1.1	.5
						Net Profit + Depr., Dep., Amort./Cur. Mat. L./T/D		
	.1	.3					.5	.4
	.8	.6				Fixed/Worth	.8	.6
	3.3	1.8					2.2	1.4
	.9	.8					.9	.7
	2.1	2.5				Debt/Worth	1.9	1.3
	4.8	8.0					5.7	13.9
		67.7					42.0	41.9
		(14) 22.9				% Profit Before Taxes/Tangible Net Worth	(27) 17.0	(19) 17.2
		-23.7					2.5	8.3
	16.5	17.7					12.4	15.9
	5.9	7.6				% Profit Before Taxes/Total Assets	6.5	5.5
	-1.7	-5.3					-.1	-2.6
	116.7	24.9					18.1	23.6
	16.8	18.3				Sales/Net Fixed Assets	13.0	11.7
	7.1	10.0					5.6	6.8
	3.9	3.1					3.2	3.0
	3.4	2.6				Sales/Total Assets	2.2	2.2
	1.9	2.2					1.4	1.4
		1.7					1.5	.7
		(14) 2.1				% Depr., Dep., Amort./Sales	(26) 2.7	(22) 1.8
		2.9					3.7	2.9
							.6	
						% Officers', Directors', Owners' Comp/Sales	(11) 3.5	
							12.6	
4028M	38211M	160445M	140230M	362890M	440799M	Net Sales ($)	617718M	600720M
1293M	12716M	67960M	115925M	269456M	465260M	Total Assets ($)	414992M	365308M

M = $ thousand   MM = $ million
See Pages 11 through 21 for Explanation of Ratios and Data

Comparative Historical Data   Current Data Sorted By Sales

			Type of Statement	0-1MM	1-3MM	3-5MM	5-10MM	10-25MM	25MM & OVER
7	4	6	Unqualified				2	1	3
9	7	7	Reviewed		1	1	4		1
5	12	12	Compiled	2	2	4	3	1	
3	3	3	Tax Returns	2		1			
11	10	15	Other	1	2			7	5
4/1/02-3/31/03 ALL	4/1/03-3/31/04 ALL	4/1/04-3/31/05 ALL			6 (4/1-9/30/04)		37 (10/1/04-3/31/05)		
35	36	43	**NUMBER OF STATEMENTS**	5	5	6	9	9	9
%	%	%	**ASSETS**	%	%	%	%	%	%
9.3	5.9	10.0	Cash & Equivalents						
26.9	28.6	22.6	Trade Receivables (net)						
27.1	26.4	23.2	Inventory						
2.6	2.1	3.6	All Other Current						
65.9	63.0	59.4	Total Current						
20.2	29.0	22.0	Fixed Assets (net)						
9.1	3.0	13.0	Intangibles (net)						
4.7	5.0	5.5	All Other Non-Current						
100.0	100.0	100.0	Total						
			LIABILITIES						
9.0	8.5	7.1	Notes Payable-Short Term						
4.8	5.8	3.5	Cur. Mat.-L/T/D						
14.2	25.3	14.9	Trade Payables						
.4	.4	.4	Income Taxes Payable						
10.4	7.2	11.3	All Other Current						
38.8	47.1	37.2	Total Current						
19.1	16.6	16.8	Long-Term Debt						
.4	.4	.6	Deferred Taxes						
6.7	10.4	4.0	All Other Non-Current						
35.0	25.4	41.3	Net Worth						
100.0	100.0	100.0	Total Liabilities & Net Worth						
			INCOME DATA						
100.0	100.0	100.0	Net Sales						
47.1	41.7	50.7	Gross Profit						
40.8	37.5	44.1	Operating Expenses						
6.2	4.2	6.6	Operating Profit						
1.3	.9	1.6	All Other Expenses (net)						
4.9	3.3	5.0	Profit Before Taxes						
			RATIOS						
2.5	2.1	2.8	Current						
1.8	1.5	1.7							
1.2	1.2	1.0							
1.6	1.2	1.5	Quick						
1.0	.9	.8							
.5	.5	.5							
23 16.1	26 14.3	23 15.9	Sales/Receivables						
38 9.7	38 9.7	37 9.8							
47 7.8	50 7.3	51 7.1							
32 11.5	28 13.2	31 11.9	Cost of Sales/Inventory						
89 4.1	81 4.5	76 4.8							
132 2.8	129 2.8	141 2.6							
22 16.7	24 15.5	23 16.0	Cost of Sales/Payables						
31 11.8	39 9.4	38 9.6							
51 7.2	105 3.5	72 5.1							
7.5	6.7	5.7	Sales/Working Capital						
9.3	14.0	11.5							
19.4	43.4	210.2							
13.9	10.0	17.3	EBIT/Interest						
(32) 6.0	(33) 3.7	(38) 7.9							
2.3	1.3	1.2							
6.9	7.1	6.8	Net Profit + Depr., Dep.,						
(13) 3.2	(12) 4.7	(15) 4.5	Amort./Cur. Mat. L/T/D						
1.2	1.2	1.4							
.4	.5	.3	Fixed/Worth						
.6	.9	.6							
1.9	3.1	1.8							
1.0	1.1	.7	Debt/Worth						
2.3	2.7	1.4							
13.1	8.4	7.2							
63.8	54.4	64.2	% Profit Before Taxes/Tangible						
(29) 34.2	(31) 23.6	(38) 29.7	Net Worth						
16.6	5.2	3.9							
23.2	16.1	17.7	% Profit Before Taxes/Total						
8.5	5.3	8.6	Assets						
4.2	1.1	.8							
24.3	22.5	22.5	Sales/Net Fixed Assets						
14.0	10.9	11.9							
10.1	5.2	8.1							
3.5	4.2	3.4	Sales/Total Assets						
2.4	2.4	2.4							
1.8	1.6	1.4							
1.6	1.6	1.3	% Depr., Dep., Amort./Sales						
(27) 2.0	(35) 2.3	(38) 2.1							
3.1	3.4	3.2							
3.9	3.9	3.3	% Officers', Directors',						
(19) 8.4	(13) 6.3	(13) 6.6	Owners' Comp/Sales						
16.5	10.0	15.6							
959250M	1168847M	1146603M	Net Sales ($)	2910M	11441M	22306M	64434M	131045M	914467M
544800M	726982M	932610M	Total Assets ($)	796M	13994M	7527M	24610M	124417M	761266M

M = $ thousand   MM = $ million
See Pages 11 through 21 for Explanation of Ratios and Data

Current Data Sorted By Assets   Comparative Historical Data

0-500M	500M-2MM	2-10MM	10-50MM	50-100MM	100-250MM	Type of Statement	4/1/00-3/31/01 ALL	4/1/01-3/31/02 ALL
1		2	1			Unqualified	2	6
7	5					Reviewed	3	3
10	1					Compiled	12	14
4	4	1				Tax Returns	5	1
						Other	6	5
		13 (4/1-9/30/04)		23 (10/1/04-3/31/05)				
22	10	3	1			**NUMBER OF STATEMENTS**	28	29
%	%	%	%	%	%	**ASSETS**	%	%
16.4	14.4					Cash & Equivalents	13.6	13.2
27.7	41.7					Trade Receivables (net)	32.2	31.3
4.7	5.3					Inventory	8.6	7.5
2.5	2.9					All Other Current	1.5	.5
51.4	64.2					Total Current	55.9	52.5
37.6	19.5					Fixed Assets (net)	27.7	32.5
6.1	1.2					Intangibles (net)	6.9	8.1
4.9	15.1					All Other Non-Current	9.6	6.9
100.0	100.0					Total	100.0	100.0
						LIABILITIES		
6.8	7.4					Notes Payable-Short Term	14.4	9.6
6.8	2.1					Cur. Mat.-L/T/D	9.4	5.1
6.1	8.4					Trade Payables	16.8	10.1
.1	.2					Income Taxes Payable	.3	.3
9.9	9.5					All Other Current	8.8	12.1
29.8	27.5					Total Current	49.7	37.1
23.6	27.6					Long-Term Debt	26.9	20.5
.0	1.7					Deferred Taxes	1.0	.5
8.2	2.4					All Other Non-Current	2.5	8.4
38.3	40.7					Net Worth	19.9	33.5
100.0	100.0					Total Liabilities & Net Worth	100.0	100.0
						INCOME DATA		
100.0	100.0					Net Sales	100.0	100.0
						Gross Profit		
93.4	98.1					Operating Expenses	93.5	94.8
6.6	1.9					Operating Profit	6.5	5.2
-.2	-.3					All Other Expenses (net)	1.3	.8
6.8	2.2					Profit Before Taxes	5.2	4.4
						RATIOS		
3.9	3.4						2.3	2.4
1.4	2.5					Current	1.5	1.4
1.2	2.0						.9	1.0
2.9	2.9						2.1	2.1
1.4	2.5					Quick	1.0	1.2
1.0	1.5						.7	.8
0 UND	38 9.7						16 23.1	33 11.1
34 10.9	41 8.8					Sales/Receivables	38 9.5	39 9.4
36 10.0	48 7.6						46 8.0	43 8.5
						Cost of Sales/Inventory		
						Cost of Sales/Payables		
10.4	6.7						9.4	8.9
27.3	9.9					Sales/Working Capital	19.5	23.0
UND	56.4						-241.6	403.3
22.2							6.8	9.0
(12) 8.4						EBIT/Interest	(25) 2.0	(25) 3.3
2.7							.9	1.7
						Net Profit + Depr., Dep., Amort./Cur. Mat. L /T/D		
.2	.1						.5	.4
1.0	.4					Fixed/Worth	1.4	1.3
-18.2	.8						-3.2	6.7
.4	.5						1.0	.6
2.8	.8					Debt/Worth	2.6	1.9
-24.7	1.8						-6.5	11.7
109.1						% Profit Before Taxes/Tangible Net Worth	62.9	41.6
(16) 66.9							(19) 17.8	(23) 19.3
1.1							.0	11.5
57.8	15.6					% Profit Before Taxes/Total Assets	28.3	16.9
17.9	8.1						8.3	10.8
-.5	1.9						.4	2.5
65.8	34.7						35.6	21.1
14.7	24.0					Sales/Net Fixed Assets	19.1	12.6
8.3	11.9						8.5	7.4
7.0	5.2						6.0	4.3
4.6	3.4					Sales/Total Assets	3.4	3.4
3.7	3.2						2.3	2.3
1.2							1.8	1.3
(16) 2.0						% Depr., Dep., Amort./Sales	(21) 1.9	(23) 2.1
5.5							3.0	2.7
8.2						% Officers', Directors', Owners' Comp/Sales	3.9	5.5
(13) 19.4							(16) 8.4	(14) 8.3
27.0							21.2	20.2
26376M	39599M	27346M	59343M			Net Sales ($)	167618M	266698M
5628M	9823M	9322M	18707M			Total Assets ($)	51104M	134024M

Note: Columns 2-10MM (partially), 10-50MM, 50-100MM, and 100-250MM marked "DATA NOT AVAILABLE."

M = $ thousand   MM = $ million
See Pages 11 through 21 for Explanation of Ratios and Data

Comparative Historical Data / Current Data Sorted By Sales

			Type of Statement						
5	4	1	Unqualified						1
4	5	3	Reviewed		1		1	1	
12	10	12	Compiled	3	5	3	1		
7	20	11	Tax Returns	7	3		1		
7	8	9	Other	1	5	3			
4/1/02-3/31/03 ALL	4/1/03-3/31/04 ALL	4/1/04-3/31/05 ALL		13 (4/1-9/30/04) 0-1MM	1-3MM	3-5MM	23 (10/1/04-3/31/05) 5-10MM	10-25MM	25MM & OVER
35	47	36	**NUMBER OF STATEMENTS**	11	14	6	3	1	1
%	%	%	**ASSETS**	%	%	%	%	%	%
13.4	18.8	14.9	Cash & Equivalents	18.9	17.2				
25.1	23.4	32.3	Trade Receivables (net)	16.4	35.6				
5.4	5.0	5.5	Inventory	6.0	4.4				
1.7	4.4	2.6	All Other Current	.0	4.1				
45.6	51.6	55.3	Total Current	41.3	61.3				
34.6	35.7	31.1	Fixed Assets (net)	46.3	26.7				
8.4	5.0	4.2	Intangibles (net)	5.8	5.1				
11.4	7.7	9.3	All Other Non-Current	6.6	6.9				
100.0	100.0	100.0	Total	100.0	100.0				
			LIABILITIES						
12.2	12.7	6.8	Notes Payable-Short Term	3.9	8.6				
9.9	5.4	5.2	Cur. Mat.-L/T/D	10.1	3.6				
8.8	8.9	7.1	Trade Payables	5.7	7.2				
.2	.6	.1	Income Taxes Payable	.0	.2				
12.3	12.8	10.4	All Other Current	8.9	10.2				
43.4	40.4	29.6	Total Current	28.6	29.8				
23.6	36.3	24.0	Long-Term Debt	23.8	20.9				
.2	.4	.6	Deferred Taxes	.0	.1				
12.0	9.1	7.0	All Other Non-Current	11.3	4.1				
20.8	13.6	38.9	Net Worth	36.3	45.1				
100.0	100.0	100.0	Total Liabilities & Net Worth	100.0	100.0				
			INCOME DATA						
100.0	100.0	100.0	Net Sales	100.0	100.0				
			Gross Profit						
90.4	93.8	95.1	Operating Expenses	92.0	95.6				
9.6	6.2	4.9	Operating Profit	8.0	4.4				
1.1	.5	-.2	All Other Expenses (net)	-.3	-.1				
8.5	5.7	5.1	Profit Before Taxes	8.3	4.5				
			RATIOS						
2.9	3.0	3.1		3.7	4.4				
1.4	1.4	1.8	Current	1.4	1.8				
.7	.8	1.3		1.0	1.3				
2.4	2.6	2.6		2.7	3.5				
1.1	1.1	1.6	Quick	1.4	1.5				
.6	.6	1.0		.8	1.1				
0 UND	0 UND	5 78.3		0 UND	36 10.2				
31 11.9	35 10.4	36 10.1	Sales/Receivables	4 85.0	37 10.0				
39 9.5	40 9.2	42 8.7		35 10.4	43 8.5				
			Cost of Sales/Inventory						
			Cost of Sales/Payables						
9.1	9.7	9.2		12.7	8.2				
29.2	22.9	17.7	Sales/Working Capital	85.0	13.1				
-26.2	-48.9	79.0		UND	32.2				
14.2	14.8	15.1			15.1				
(29) 4.7	(36) 3.6	(22) 7.3	EBIT/Interest		(10) 5.4				
.1	.1	2.5			-.1				
8.8			Net Profit + Depr., Dep.,						
(11) 1.1			Amort./Cur. Mat. L/T/D						
.5									
.3	.3	.2		.3	.2				
1.0	1.0	.6	Fixed/Worth	2.3	.4				
-6.0	-10.2	2.4		-3.5	1.3				
.6	.7	.5		.2	.4				
2.5	2.0	1.2	Debt/Worth	2.9	1.2				
-17.1	-16.8	3.9		-4.7	3.7				
69.5	74.5	85.2	% Profit Before Taxes/Tangible		85.2				
(26) 20.9	(33) 8.9	(28) 20.7	Net Worth		(12) 20.7				
-2.4	-1.6	3.2			-2.1				
32.7	37.7	24.6	% Profit Before Taxes/Total	113.3	28.1				
14.5	4.1	11.3	Assets	15.5	13.8				
-2.7	-1.4	2.0		-3.0	1.5				
19.6	29.3	32.9		30.5	45.3				
12.3	14.2	16.1	Sales/Net Fixed Assets	15.7	14.9				
7.8	8.5	10.0		6.6	9.5				
5.3	7.0	5.2		7.9	4.7				
3.9	3.9	4.1	Sales/Total Assets	5.1	3.8				
2.5	2.3	3.2		3.5	3.2				
1.5	1.5	1.3		1.0					
(33) 2.0	(38) 2.3	(27) 2.1	% Depr., Dep., Amort./Sales	(10) 1.8					
3.6	3.6	3.5		7.2					
3.3	7.3	8.0							
(20) 7.6	(27) 12.6	(18) 11.8	% Officers', Directors',						
13.0	27.5	25.7	Owners' Comp/Sales						
249153M	708512M	152664M	Net Sales ($)	6151M	25740M	24825M	21293M	15312M	59343M
120317M	195688M	43480M	Total Assets ($)	1499M	6681M	6848M	5842M	3903M	18707M

M = $ thousand   MM = $ million
See Pages 11 through 21 for Explanation of Ratios and Data

Current Data Sorted By Assets

Comparative Historical Data

	0-500M	500M-2MM	2-10MM	10-50MM	50-100MM	100-250MM	Type of Statement	4/1/00-3/31/01 ALL	4/1/01-3/31/02 ALL
			10	23	4	4	Unqualified	27	30
		5	38	17	1	2	Reviewed	44	34
	1	12	7	3			Compiled	17	11
	4	6	1				Tax Returns	9	11
	2	7	22	16	2	7	Other	19	23
		48 (4/1-9/30/04)		146 (10/1/04-3/31/05)					
NUMBER OF STATEMENTS	7	30	78	59	7	13		116	109
	%	%	%	%	%	%	**ASSETS**	%	%
		7.3	4.5	3.1		2.5	Cash & Equivalents	5.7	6.0
		26.1	31.9	30.5		27.4	Trade Receivables (net)	30.6	27.5
		39.9	46.2	53.2		55.0	Inventory	45.6	48.4
		1.6	.8	1.6		1.7	All Other Current	.4	.9
		74.9	83.3	88.4		86.5	Total Current	82.3	82.7
		17.3	9.9	5.5		5.2	Fixed Assets (net)	12.3	11.0
		1.4	1.6	1.2		5.6	Intangibles (net)	1.5	1.9
		6.4	5.2	4.9		2.7	All Other Non-Current	3.9	4.4
		100.0	100.0	100.0		100.0	Total	100.0	100.0
							LIABILITIES		
		26.4	27.0	31.4		36.2	Notes Payable-Short Term	23.7	20.8
		2.4	2.7	1.3		1.1	Cur. Mat.-L/T/D	1.7	2.8
		16.8	20.6	14.7		15.4	Trade Payables	18.5	18.1
		.2	.3	.3		.1	Income Taxes Payable	.4	.2
		5.6	5.6	7.1		4.1	All Other Current	7.8	8.2
		51.4	56.2	54.8		56.9	Total Current	52.2	50.1
		12.7	5.7	5.2		1.7	Long-Term Debt	6.5	5.0
		.0	1.1	.7		1.7	Deferred Taxes	.1	.1
		6.2	3.8	4.7		10.8	All Other Non-Current	4.7	5.1
		29.7	33.2	34.5		28.9	Net Worth	36.5	39.8
		100.0	100.0	100.0		100.0	Total Liabilities & Net Worth	100.0	100.0
							INCOME DATA		
		100.0	100.0	100.0		100.0	Net Sales	100.0	100.0
		37.1	26.3	22.3		24.7	Gross Profit	29.9	28.2
		34.3	24.5	18.0		18.1	Operating Expenses	26.4	24.6
		2.8	1.9	4.3		6.6	Operating Profit	3.5	3.6
		2.2	1.3	1.5		1.7	All Other Expenses (net)	1.1	1.9
		.7	.5	2.9		4.9	Profit Before Taxes	2.4	1.7
							RATIOS		
		2.4	1.9	2.1		1.9		2.1	2.4
		1.7	1.4	1.5		1.5	Current	1.5	1.7
		1.2	1.2	1.3		1.3		1.2	1.3
		1.0	.9	.9		.8		1.0	1.0
		.6	.6	.6		.5	Quick	.6	.7
		.4	.4	.4		.4		.4	.4
	20 18.4	32 11.4	57 6.4		56 6.5			29 12.8	28 13.1
	44 8.4	56 6.5	78 4.7		80 4.5		Sales/Receivables	51 7.2	50 7.4
	72 5.1	79 4.6	102 3.6		116 3.1			90 4.1	82 4.5
	56 6.5	65 5.6	111 3.3		141 2.6			56 6.5	70 5.2
	116 3.1	106 3.4	187 1.9		193 1.9		Cost of Sales/Inventory	124 2.9	123 3.0
	199 1.8	218 1.7	279 1.3		310 1.2			228 1.6	228 1.6
	9 41.9	18 20.0	25 14.7		22 16.5			16 22.7	18 20.1
	37 9.7	45 8.1	34 10.9		67 5.5		Cost of Sales/Payables	40 9.0	37 9.9
	113 3.2	78 4.7	79 4.6		88 4.2			74 4.9	74 4.9
		3.2	5.1	2.4		3.6		3.8	3.3
		6.4	8.0	4.8		5.0	Sales/Working Capital	6.9	5.9
		14.1	14.5	8.3		6.2		13.1	14.3
		5.6	5.4	5.6		9.4		5.5	5.7
	(28) 2.3	(75) 2.2	(56) 2.7		(12) 2.3		EBIT/Interest	(112) 2.2	(102) 2.1
		.9	1.0	1.5		1.3		1.2	1.1
			4.4	9.7			Net Profit + Depr., Dep., Amort./Cur. Mat. L/T/D	10.4	7.1
		(14) 2.7	(19) 3.3					(30) 4.0	(21) 3.3
			1.0	.9				1.8	1.6
		.0	.1	.0		.1		.1	.1
		.2	.3	.1		.1	Fixed/Worth	.2	.2
		1.5	.5	.4		.3		.6	.5
		.9	1.3	1.4		1.7		1.0	.8
		2.4	2.5	2.3		2.5	Debt/Worth	2.1	1.6
		7.3	4.0	3.6		7.8		4.2	3.7
		46.3	25.3	23.7		77.6	% Profit Before Taxes/Tangible Net Worth	29.9	28.8
		(27) 10.5	(76) 9.6	(56) 9.6		(12) 13.3		(108) 13.0	(106) 8.5
		.0	-.1	3.8		2.0		3.2	.9
		9.3	7.4	5.9		14.5	% Profit Before Taxes/Total Assets	8.2	8.5
		2.3	2.8	3.4		3.8		4.5	2.8
		-.5	.0	1.0		.4		.8	.5
		99.6	70.3	143.2		81.8		101.4	78.0
		33.8	29.4	47.5		56.0	Sales/Net Fixed Assets	26.0	29.0
		10.5	15.5	16.3		14.6		12.7	12.6
		2.6	2.7	1.8		1.5		2.7	2.6
		1.8	1.9	1.3		1.3	Sales/Total Assets	1.9	1.8
		1.5	1.4	1.0		1.0		1.3	1.2
		.3	.4	.3		.4		.4	.3
	(25) .9	(71) .9	(54) .6		(10) .8		% Depr., Dep., Amort./Sales	(98) .9	(94) .8
		1.7	1.6	1.0		1.5		1.7	1.4
		2.8	1.4	1.1				1.4	1.5
	(22) 7.2	(47) 3.0	(26) 2.3				% Officers', Directors', Owners' Comp/Sales	(64) 2.5	(67) 2.6
		10.3	4.0	3.4				4.4	6.7
	9258M	74452M	932003M	4438197M	672094M	2506941M	Net Sales ($)	2886243M	3218461M
	1633M	35050M	384350M	1276789M	510800M	2011080M	Total Assets ($)	1701624M	1760996M

M = $ thousand   MM = $ million
See Pages 11 through 21 for Explanation of Ratios and Data

Comparative Historical Data | Current Data Sorted By Sales

Hist 1	Hist 2	Hist 3	Type of Statement	0-1MM	1-3MM	3-5MM	5-10MM	10-25MM	25MM & OVER
15	28	41	Unqualified			2	5	16	18
53	54	63	Reviewed		4	6	19	21	13
13	19	23	Compiled	3	10	2	3	4	1
6	7	11	Tax Returns	3	7		1		
19	34	56	Other	2	6	5	8	17	18
4/1/02-3/31/03	4/1/03-3/31/04	4/1/04-3/31/05		48 (4/1-9/30/04)			146 (10/1/04-3/31/05)		
ALL	ALL	ALL							
106	142	194	NUMBER OF STATEMENTS	8	27	15	36	58	50

ASSETS

Hist 1 %	Hist 2 %	Hist 3 %		0-1MM %	1-3MM %	3-5MM %	5-10MM %	10-25MM %	25MM & OVER %
7.7	6.1	5.0	Cash & Equivalents		9.0	3.6	6.9	3.8	2.0
30.7	30.0	30.2	Trade Receivables (net)		27.3	28.6	30.2	31.6	31.3
44.6	46.1	47.5	Inventory		39.4	47.6	44.2	50.3	52.3
1.0	1.6	1.2	All Other Current		1.4	1.3	.8	.9	1.7
84.0	83.7	83.9	Total Current		77.1	81.0	82.1	86.6	87.2
10.3	9.4	9.3	Fixed Assets (net)		15.4	9.6	9.4	8.9	4.9
1.8	1.8	1.8	Intangibles (net)		2.4	3.0	1.9	.9	2.3
3.9	5.1	5.0	All Other Non-Current		5.1	6.4	6.5	3.6	5.6
100.0	100.0	100.0	Total		100.0	100.0	100.0	100.0	100.0

LIABILITIES

Hist 1	Hist 2	Hist 3		0-1MM	1-3MM	3-5MM	5-10MM	10-25MM	25MM & OVER
18.2	22.4	28.9	Notes Payable-Short Term		27.1	27.8	26.2	30.9	31.9
1.6	1.3	2.2	Cur. Mat.-L/T/D		3.6	3.9	1.4	2.4	1.4
18.6	17.4	18.0	Trade Payables		17.1	13.5	20.2	18.1	18.3
.2	.4	.4	Income Taxes Payable		.1	.2	.5	.3	.6
9.4	9.8	6.8	All Other Current		6.9	6.5	5.3	5.3	6.5
48.0	51.3	56.2	Total Current		54.8	51.9	53.5	57.0	58.7
5.5	5.5	6.4	Long-Term Debt		18.5	9.2	5.1	4.3	2.3
.0	.1	.8	Deferred Taxes		.0	.4	.3	1.6	.8
2.3	4.4	4.9	All Other Non-Current		3.2	1.9	5.5	4.0	5.2
44.2	38.7	31.8	Net Worth		23.4	36.5	35.5	33.1	33.0
100.0	100.0	100.0	Total Liabilities & Net Worth		100.0	100.0	100.0	100.0	100.0

INCOME DATA

Hist 1	Hist 2	Hist 3		0-1MM	1-3MM	3-5MM	5-10MM	10-25MM	25MM & OVER
100.0	100.0	100.0	Net Sales		100.0	100.0	100.0	100.0	100.0
32.3	28.7	26.6	Gross Profit		37.3	32.9	27.8	25.0	18.7
28.5	25.0	23.6	Operating Expenses		35.5	27.9	24.7	21.9	14.6
3.8	3.7	3.0	Operating Profit		1.8	5.0	3.0	3.1	4.0
.9	1.2	1.5	All Other Expenses (net)		2.2	2.2	1.2	1.5	1.0
2.9	2.6	1.5	Profit Before Taxes		-.5	2.9	1.9	1.6	3.0

RATIOS

Hist 1	Hist 2	Hist 3		0-1MM	1-3MM	3-5MM	5-10MM	10-25MM	25MM & OVER
2.7	2.3	2.0	Current		2.4	2.0	2.2	1.9	1.7
1.7	1.6	1.5			1.6	1.4	1.5	1.5	1.4
1.3	1.3	1.2			1.1	1.4	1.3	1.2	1.2
1.1	1.1	.9	Quick		1.0	1.0	1.2	.8	.7
.8	.7	.6			.7	.6	.6	.6	.5
.5	.5	.4			.5	.4	.4	.4	.4
35 10.5	41 8.8	39 9.5	Sales/Receivables	13 27.5	42 8.7	31 11.9	43 8.4	51 7.2	
59 6.2	68 5.3	62 5.9		41 9.0	64 5.7	59 6.2	64 5.7	69 5.3	
89 4.1	91 4.0	87 4.2		79 4.6	100 3.7	91 4.0	89 4.1	96 3.8	
69 5.3	75 4.9	79 4.6	Cost of Sales/Inventory	48 7.6	95 3.8	70 5.2	83 4.4	102 3.6	
122 3.0	129 2.8	143 2.6		127 2.9	216 1.7	115 3.2	138 2.6	159 2.3	
215 1.7	225 1.6	220 1.7		208 1.8	310 1.2	217 1.7	247 1.5	209 1.7	
18 19.8	19 19.4	16 22.2	Cost of Sales/Payables	9 42.4	6 61.9	28 13.1	20 18.4	19 19.4	
47 7.8	44 8.4	38 9.5		35 10.5	25 14.4	59 6.1	39 9.3	32 11.3	
83 4.4	82 4.5	84 4.4		77 4.8	92 4.1	88 4.1	75 4.9	84 4.4	
3.6	3.4	3.6	Sales/Working Capital		3.6	3.0	4.8	3.0	3.9
6.1	6.0	6.4			7.2	5.5	6.2	7.1	5.9
9.9	10.4	12.2			25.1	8.6	12.9	12.4	9.2
6.3	5.6	6.1	EBIT/Interest		6.5	5.4	6.4	5.6	8.0
(99) 2.0	(128) 2.6	(184) 2.3		(26) 2.1	2.4	(33) 1.4	(55) 2.6	(48) 2.6	
1.1	1.3	1.2			-.6	1.0	.9	1.3	1.6
6.9	8.5	8.3	Net Profit + Depr., Dep.,					8.5	24.0
(24) 2.1	(22) 2.0	(41) 3.2	Amort./Cur. Mat. L/T/D					(18) 3.2	(14) 4.3
1.3	.7	1.1						.9	1.7
.1	.0	.0	Fixed/Worth		.0	.1	.1	.0	.0
.2	.2	.2			.5	.2	.2	.3	.1
.4	.4	.5			3.1	.5	.4	.5	.2
.7	.8	1.4	Debt/Worth		1.2	.6	1.2	1.5	1.4
1.6	1.9	2.5			2.6	2.7	2.4	2.4	2.5
3.2	3.6	4.3			17.0	3.6	4.2	3.8	4.4
20.2	27.4	27.9	% Profit Before Taxes/Tangible		61.6	19.8	29.0	26.4	25.7
(104) 8.7	(138) 9.8	(183) 10.6	Net Worth		(24) 14.6	(14) 8.7	(34) 5.4	11.3	(47) 12.8
1.3	1.8	1.5			-.3	-.3	-.4	4.3	3.5
7.8	8.1	7.2	% Profit Before Taxes/Total		11.2	5.0	6.7	6.1	7.5
2.5	2.3	3.1	Assets		2.2	3.3	1.0	3.8	3.7
.3	.5	.3			-4.3	.1	-.5	1.4	.9
83.8	147.0	108.0	Sales/Net Fixed Assets		96.9	51.8	60.9	105.1	185.9
29.9	39.3	36.5			29.0	17.0	33.5	31.7	63.4
13.0	15.1	15.9			10.5	7.4	15.7	14.2	26.0
2.5	2.3	2.4	Sales/Total Assets		3.0	1.9	2.7	2.4	2.1
1.9	1.7	1.7			1.8	1.4	2.0	1.7	1.4
1.2	1.2	1.2			1.4	.9	1.2	1.2	1.1
.3	.3	.3	% Depr., Dep., Amort./Sales		.3	.3	.5	.4	.3
(90) .8	(120) .7	(170) .7		(22) 1.1	(14) .7	(31) 1.1	(54) .7	(43) .5	
1.4	1.5	1.4			2.4	1.8	1.9	1.3	1.0
1.9	2.0	1.4	% Officers', Directors',		3.5	2.1	1.5	1.0	.5
(59) 3.7	(77) 4.3	(106) 3.0	Owners' Comp/Sales	(21) 5.2	(12) 3.4	(21) 3.5	(30) 2.0	(17) 1.1	
7.6	7.9	5.2			9.3	4.0	5.6	3.4	2.3
3428601M	4471002M	8632945M	Net Sales ($)	5135M	54457M	60255M	257547M	985383M	7270168M
1944476M	3082481M	4219702M	Total Assets ($)	4771M	31199M	79950M	168072M	643975M	3291735M

M = $ thousand   MM = $ million
See Pages 11 through 21 for Explanation of Ratios and Data

	Current Data Sorted By Assets							Comparative Historical Data	
			3 8	3 1			Type of Statement		
1 2	7 5 1		5	2			Unqualified Reviewed Compiled Tax Returns Other		
	6 (4/1-9/30/04)			32 (10/1/04-3/31/05)				4/1/00- 3/31/01	4/1/01- 3/31/02
0-500M	500M-2MM	2-10MM	10-50MM	50-100MM	100-250MM			ALL	ALL
3	13	16	6			NUMBER OF STATEMENTS			
%	%	%	%	%	%	ASSETS		%	%
	8.0	10.6		D	D	Cash & Equivalents		D	D
	36.6	35.8		A	A	Trade Receivables (net)		A	A
	24.0	28.2		T	T	Inventory		T	T
	.1	.5		A	A	All Other Current		A	A
	68.6	75.1				Total Current			
	24.1	16.5		N	N	Fixed Assets (net)		N	N
	3.9	2.0		O	O	Intangibles (net)		O	O
	3.4	6.4		T	T	All Other Non-Current		T	T
	100.0	100.0				Total			
				A	A	LIABILITIES		A	A
	13.2	17.6		V	V	Notes Payable-Short Term		V	V
	4.4	1.7		A	A	Cur. Mat.-L/T/D		A	A
	14.6	20.2		I	I	Trade Payables		I	I
	.1	.4		L	L	Income Taxes Payable		L	L
	6.0	10.8		A	A	All Other Current		A	A
	38.3	50.8		B	B	Total Current		B	B
	10.7	6.1		L	L	Long-Term Debt		L	L
	.0	1.2		E	E	Deferred Taxes		E	E
	2.0	4.3				All Other Non-Current			
	48.9	37.7				Net Worth			
	100.0	100.0				Total Liabilities & Net Worth			
	100.0	100.0				INCOME DATA Net Sales			
	40.6	30.5				Gross Profit			
	35.4	25.6				Operating Expenses			
	5.2	4.9				Operating Profit			
	1.0	.6				All Other Expenses (net)			
	4.2	4.3				Profit Before Taxes			
	5.4	2.8				RATIOS			
	2.1	1.6				Current			
	1.1	1.0							
	2.8	1.2							
	1.2	.9				Quick			
	.8	.7							
33	11.1　39	9.3							
44	8.3　48	7.7				Sales/Receivables			
67	5.4　53	6.9							
14	25.6　17	21.1							
61	5.9　57	6.4				Cost of Sales/Inventory			
87	4.2　105	3.5							
10	36.5　19	19.7							
26	14.2　24	15.3				Cost of Sales/Payables			
51	7.1　58	6.3							
	5.1	4.8							
	7.9	11.4				Sales/Working Capital			
	323.4	748.1							
	12.9	48.0							
	(10)　4.0　(15)	8.6				EBIT/Interest			
	1.3	2.2							
						Net Profit + Depr., Dep., Amort./Cur. Mat. L /T/D			
	.1	.2							
	.4	.3				Fixed/Worth			
	1.2	1.0							
	.8	.6							
	1.6	1.7				Debt/Worth			
	2.5	3.9							
	40.9	80.4				% Profit Before Taxes/Tangible			
	16.5　(14)	29.2				Net Worth			
	4.7	5.9							
	25.5	21.7				% Profit Before Taxes/Total			
	7.7	11.6				Assets			
	1.9	.6							
	84.2	69.9							
	19.4	18.5				Sales/Net Fixed Assets			
	7.7	15.8							
	3.4	3.4							
	2.7	2.7				Sales/Total Assets			
	2.3	2.2							
	.6	.7							
	(11)　2.4	1.1				% Depr., Dep., Amort./Sales			
	3.0	2.5							
	4.6					% Officers', Directors',			
	(10)　8.7					Owners' Comp/Sales			
	10.5								
3221M	40642M	209375M	232222M			Net Sales ($)			
791M	15671M	80260M	147604M			Total Assets ($)			

M = $ thousand　　MM = $ million
See Pages 11 through 21 for Explanation of Ratios and Data

Comparative Historical Data / Current Data Sorted By Sales

4/1/02-3/31/03 ALL	4/1/03-3/31/04 ALL	4/1/04-3/31/05 ALL	Type of Statement	0-1MM	1-3MM	3-5MM	5-10MM	10-25MM	25MM & OVER
5	2	6	Unqualified					4	2
18	17	17	Reviewed	1	3	4	3	5	1
8	11	7	Compiled	1	3	3		3	
2	2	1	Tax Returns			1			
9	4	7	Other				3	3	1
				6 (4/1-9/30/04)			32 (10/1/04-3/31/05)		
42	36	38	**NUMBER OF STATEMENTS**	2	6	8	6	12	4
%	%	%	**ASSETS**	%	%	%	%	%	%
8.2	8.0	8.7	Cash & Equivalents					10.7	
36.8	36.1	33.5	Trade Receivables (net)					29.8	
21.7	21.1	25.0	Inventory					27.4	
.7	1.4	.4	All Other Current					.5	
67.4	66.6	67.6	Total Current					68.4	
23.3	25.8	21.8	Fixed Assets (net)					22.2	
2.9	2.8	3.6	Intangibles (net)					4.8	
6.4	4.8	7.0	All Other Non-Current					4.6	
100.0	100.0	100.0	Total					100.0	
			LIABILITIES						
16.6	16.3	16.7	Notes Payable-Short Term					10.0	
3.3	4.3	4.0	Cur. Mat.-L/T/D					3.4	
15.6	16.7	16.1	Trade Payables					18.1	
.2	.2	.2	Income Taxes Payable					.5	
10.3	13.2	7.8	All Other Current					8.6	
46.0	50.5	44.8	Total Current					40.5	
14.9	12.9	11.3	Long-Term Debt					9.8	
.5	.3	.5	Deferred Taxes					.1	
13.5	7.8	9.0	All Other Non-Current					4.7	
24.8	28.5	34.4	Net Worth					44.8	
100.0	100.0	100.0	Total Liabilities & Net Worth					100.0	
			INCOME DATA						
100.0	100.0	100.0	Net Sales					100.0	
35.4	35.0	33.9	Gross Profit					33.7	
30.6	31.2	28.9	Operating Expenses					24.7	
4.9	3.9	5.0	Operating Profit					8.9	
2.5	.8	1.1	All Other Expenses (net)					1.1	
2.4	3.0	4.0	Profit Before Taxes					7.8	
			RATIOS						
2.5	2.5	2.7	Current					2.8	
1.4	1.2	1.5						1.6	
1.0	.9	.9						1.0	
1.4	1.4	1.4	Quick					1.2	
1.0	1.0	1.0						1.0	
.6	.5	.7						.7	
38 9.7	36 10.3	35 10.3	Sales/Receivables					39 9.3	
49 7.5	43 8.4	47 7.8						48 7.7	
62 5.9	54 6.7	55 6.6						60 6.1	
10 35.0	12 31.2	18 20.0	Cost of Sales/Inventory					22 16.3	
43 8.5	31 11.6	57 6.4						70 5.2	
69 5.3	87 4.2	96 3.8						105 3.5	
17 21.6	20 18.2	14 25.9	Cost of Sales/Payables					23 16.2	
29 12.5	31 11.9	25 14.8						32 11.5	
41 9.0	48 7.7	53 6.9						63 5.8	
7.6	7.8	6.0	Sales/Working Capital					4.8	
10.8	22.2	11.7						11.4	
NM	−69.8	−51.9						NM	
9.0	15.7	18.3	EBIT/Interest					57.5	
(39) 3.1	(34) 3.9	(33) 4.7						10.3	
1.2	.5	1.3						3.4	
4.9	9.4	10.3	Net Profit + Depr., Dep., Amort./Cur. Mat. L/T/D						
(11) 2.5	(11) 7.1	(14) 2.4							
.8	1.7	.5							
.3	.2	.2	Fixed/Worth					.2	
.8	.7	.4						.4	
2.2	3.8	1.9						1.3	
1.2	1.0	.9	Debt/Worth					.6	
2.3	2.6	1.9						1.7	
6.7	12.5	4.2						2.0	
51.1	45.2	62.7	% Profit Before Taxes/Tangible Net Worth					76.1	
(35) 17.7	(31) 26.6	(33) 23.4						(11) 30.0	
2.6	4.1	4.6						6.2	
22.8	16.1	21.4	% Profit Before Taxes/Total Assets					24.0	
5.7	5.2	6.7						15.4	
.6	−2.0	.3						3.9	
37.7	41.9	36.4	Sales/Net Fixed Assets					32.4	
14.6	16.9	17.7						18.0	
7.5	6.2	11.2						9.2	
3.3	3.4	3.5	Sales/Total Assets					3.2	
2.8	2.6	2.7						2.5	
2.2	2.0	2.1						1.8	
.7	.6	.8	% Depr., Dep., Amort./Sales					.9	
(40) 1.5	(35) 1.8	(36) 1.5						1.5	
3.5	3.6	2.9						3.3	
3.5	2.8	2.5	% Officers', Directors', Owners' Comp/Sales						
(24) 6.2	(24) 5.8	(20) 5.9							
9.6	9.8	9.0							
379084M	229232M	485460M	Net Sales ($)	1255M	12755M	29853M	43955M	196698M	200944M
155099M	90881M	244326M	Total Assets ($)	353M	6399M	9710M	15768M	117589M	94507M

M = $ thousand   MM = $ million
See Pages 11 through 21 for Explanation of Ratios and Data

Current Data Sorted By Assets   **Comparative Historical Data**

Type of Statement	0-500M	500M-2MM	2-10MM	10-50MM	50-100MM	100-250MM		4/1/00-3/31/01 ALL	4/1/01-3/31/02 ALL
Unqualified	.1		18	20	2	7		40	31
Reviewed		5	20	5				27	18
Compiled	3	5	11					25	27
Tax Returns	6	9	3	1				8	8
Other	3	21	17	20	3	1		38	56
		40 (4/1-9/30/04)		141 (10/1/04-3/31/05)					
NUMBER OF STATEMENTS	13	40	69	46	5	8		138	140
ASSETS	%	%	%	%	%	%		%	%
Cash & Equivalents	7.2	6.7	4.4	7.5				5.8	6.4
Trade Receivables (net)	24.4	25.6	25.3	26.1				26.2	24.6
Inventory	40.7	34.5	38.1	36.0				36.2	36.5
All Other Current	8.1	1.4	2.7	3.4				2.2	2.0
Total Current	80.6	68.2	70.5	73.0				70.4	69.5
Fixed Assets (net)	10.6	18.1	18.8	14.4				18.3	17.9
Intangibles (net)	6.5	4.0	3.4	8.5				6.4	6.3
All Other Non-Current	2.3	9.7	7.3	4.2				4.9	6.3
Total	100.0	100.0	100.0	100.0				100.0	100.0
LIABILITIES									
Notes Payable-Short Term	11.9	24.7	17.1	12.0				15.5	17.8
Cur. Mat.-L/T/D	9.4	1.6	2.1	2.7				3.2	3.5
Trade Payables	26.2	16.9	13.6	11.1				14.6	14.8
Income Taxes Payable	.0	.0	.3	.1				.3	.2
All Other Current	18.8	6.7	8.0	10.8				8.8	8.5
Total Current	66.3	49.9	41.1	36.8				42.4	44.8
Long-Term Debt	21.5	14.8	13.8	11.8				12.0	11.9
Deferred Taxes	.0	.0	.3	.5				.4	.3
All Other Non-Current	7.3	5.2	6.2	6.7				7.5	5.9
Net Worth	4.9	30.1	38.7	44.2				37.7	37.1
Total Liabilities & Net Worth	100.0	100.0	100.0	100.0				100.0	100.0
INCOME DATA									
Net Sales	100.0	100.0	100.0	100.0				100.0	100.0
Gross Profit	42.4	41.4	34.5	35.1				36.1	36.5
Operating Expenses	38.1	38.1	29.7	28.4				30.2	31.1
Operating Profit	4.3	3.3	4.8	6.7				5.8	5.4
All Other Expenses (net)	1.1	1.2	1.1	1.0				1.8	1.6
Profit Before Taxes	3.3	2.1	3.7	5.6				4.0	3.8
RATIOS									
Current	2.4 / 2.0 / .9	2.2 / 1.5 / 1.1	3.0 / 1.8 / 1.2	3.2 / 2.1 / 1.5				2.6 / 1.7 / 1.3	2.8 / 1.7 / 1.2
Quick	1.0 / .4 / .1	1.1 / .6 / .4	1.2 / .8 / .4	1.5 / 1.0 / .6				1.3 / .8 / .5	1.4 / .7 / .5
Sales/Receivables	0 UND / 29 12.8 / 47 7.7	17 21.8 / 35 10.4 / 53 6.8	30 12.3 / 44 8.4 / 65 5.6	39 9.3 / 51 7.2 / 70 5.2				29 12.8 / 46 7.9 / 70 5.2	23 15.8 / 43 8.5 / 70 5.2
Cost of Sales/Inventory	29 12.6 / 79 4.6 / 156 2.3	25 14.5 / 102 3.6 / 164 2.2	66 5.5 / 100 3.7 / 163 2.2	81 4.5 / 107 3.4 / 147 2.5				61 6.0 / 103 3.5 / 143 2.5	61 5.9 / 102 3.6 / 157 2.3
Cost of Sales/Payables	6 58.6 / 22 16.3 / 66 5.5	17 21.3 / 36 10.0 / 74 4.9	16 23.0 / 29 12.8 / 50 7.3	17 21.4 / 32 11.4 / 49 7.4				17 20.9 / 31 11.9 / 46 7.9	17 21.4 / 26 13.9 / 46 7.9
Sales/Working Capital	7.5 / 12.7 / -27.6	5.1 / 9.7 / 60.8	4.9 / 7.3 / 15.4	3.4 / 5.3 / 8.8				4.6 / 7.3 / 18.7	4.1 / 7.3 / 26.3
EBIT/Interest	(11) 5.0 / 2.9 / -.7	(36) 9.4 / 3.8 / .7	(65) 10.5 / 3.9 / 1.4	(43) 12.7 / 4.8 / 1.3				(128) 6.8 / 3.0 / 1.3	(135) 6.9 / 2.9 / 1.1
Net Profit + Depr., Dep., Amort./Cur. Mat. L /T/D		(18) 10.1 / 4.0 / 1.2		(17) 8.5 / 3.8 / 1.4				(47) 12.2 / 3.4 / 1.6	(40) 6.0 / 2.4 / .9
Fixed/Worth	.0 / 8.0 / -2.9	.1 / .8 / NM	.1 / .3 / 1.2	.2 / .4 / .7				.2 / .4 / 1.1	.2 / .5 / 1.1
Debt/Worth	3.7 / 187.0 / -6.9	1.0 / 2.1 / NM	.8 / 2.1 / 4.2	.6 / 1.2 / 3.9				.8 / 1.7 / 3.7	.7 / 1.7 / 4.7
% Profit Before Taxes/Tangible Net Worth		(30) 41.1 / 17.3 / -1.0	(64) 36.2 / 11.1 / 4.5	(41) 29.5 / 17.6 / 4.2				(118) 39.5 / 19.3 / 5.3	(122) 46.7 / 18.5 / 3.3
% Profit Before Taxes/Total Assets	20.6 / 2.2 / -15.4	14.0 / 6.0 / -1.8	12.2 / 4.6 / .7	13.4 / 6.5 / 1.6				13.6 / 7.0 / 1.9	13.8 / 5.1 / .6
Sales/Net Fixed Assets	UND / 57.5 / 9.3	57.7 / 29.0 / 9.4	39.7 / 16.8 / 7.2	36.1 / 19.3 / 7.1				33.5 / 13.6 / 6.4	41.6 / 16.3 / 7.4
Sales/Total Assets	5.7 / 3.5 / 1.6	3.0 / 2.1 / 1.5	2.5 / 2.1 / 1.4	2.5 / 1.7 / 1.1				2.8 / 2.0 / 1.3	2.8 / 2.0 / 1.3
% Depr., Dep., Amort./Sales		(30) .6 / 1.0 / 2.3	(61) .8 / 1.3 / 2.3	(42) .7 / 1.9 / 2.7				(123) .9 / 1.7 / 3.0	(118) .8 / 1.5 / 2.8
% Officers', Directors', Owners' Comp/Sales		(21) 2.8 / 4.8 / 7.9	(21) 2.1 / 3.4 / 6.5					(44) 2.4 / 3.5 / 6.0	(57) 2.2 / 3.3 / 5.6
Net Sales ($)	9876M	114174M	710470M	1760999M	462653M	1882759M		4012056M	3668534M
Total Assets ($)	2660M	46111M	344934M	1030787M	332320M	1103677M		2534972M	2366382M

© RMA 2005

M = $ thousand   MM = $ million
See Pages 11 through 21 for Explanation of Ratios and Data

Comparative Historical Data			Type of Statement	Current Data Sorted By Sales					
41	45	48	Unqualified	1		4	7	11	29
31	38	30	Reviewed		5	4	7	11	3
24	31	19	Compiled	2	4	5	4	4	
8	16	19	Tax Returns	4	7	2	3	2	1
57	49	65	Other	4	17	7	5	13	19
4/1/02-3/31/03 ALL	4/1/03-3/31/04 ALL	4/1/04-3/31/05 ALL		40 (4/1-9/30/04)			141 (10/1/04-3/31/05)		
				0-1MM	1-3MM	3-5MM	5-10MM	10-25MM	25MM & OVER
161	179	181	**NUMBER OF STATEMENTS**	11	33	18	26	41	52
%	%	%	**ASSETS**	%	%	%	%	%	%
6.5	6.5	5.8	Cash & Equivalents	3.9	6.6	5.7	6.0	4.0	7.0
23.9	25.8	25.8	Trade Receivables (net)	27.3	21.9	22.2	23.6	28.3	28.2
37.9	38.8	36.7	Inventory	31.3	34.1	43.5	33.1	39.9	36.4
3.0	2.7	3.0	All Other Current	10.4	1.0	.7	2.6	3.4	3.4
71.3	73.8	71.2	Total Current	72.9	63.6	72.1	65.2	75.6	75.0
18.2	15.5	16.7	Fixed Assets (net)	10.3	21.3	18.4	24.3	12.1	14.4
5.8	5.1	5.6	Intangibles (net)	7.2	5.4	1.3	3.2	7.2	6.9
4.6	5.7	6.4	All Other Non-Current	9.6	9.7	8.2	7.3	5.0	3.8
100.0	100.0	100.0	Total	100.0	100.0	100.0	100.0	100.0	100.0
			LIABILITIES						
15.3	16.1	17.1	Notes Payable-Short Term	16.2	21.2	19.8	17.9	16.3	14.2
3.6	3.2	2.6	Cur. Mat.-L/T/D	9.9	2.1	1.5	3.6	1.5	2.2
12.9	14.9	14.5	Trade Payables	22.9	13.8	13.1	15.3	15.6	12.2
.5	.2	.2	Income Taxes Payable	.0	.0	.3	.2	.4	.2
9.5	10.9	9.3	All Other Current	21.6	4.8	7.8	8.0	8.9	11.1
41.8	45.3	43.7	Total Current	70.7	41.9	42.4	44.9	42.7	39.9
13.3	12.7	13.6	Long-Term Debt	29.8	19.9	7.9	17.9	7.8	10.5
.2	.3	.3	Deferred Taxes	.0	.0	.3	.1	.5	.3
7.2	5.3	6.1	All Other Non-Current	9.2	4.4	7.7	4.5	5.9	6.9
37.4	36.4	36.3	Net Worth	-9.7	33.8	41.6	32.6	43.1	42.4
100.0	100.0	100.0	Total Liabilities & Net Worth	100.0	100.0	100.0	100.0	100.0	100.0
			INCOME DATA						
100.0	100.0	100.0	Net Sales	100.0	100.0	100.0	100.0	100.0	100.0
35.8	35.1	36.7	Gross Profit	47.5	42.5	39.4	35.0	32.5	34.0
31.2	30.1	31.6	Operating Expenses	42.4	39.8	35.7	29.2	27.2	27.2
4.6	5.0	5.1	Operating Profit	5.1	2.7	3.6	5.9	5.3	6.8
1.4	1.1	1.1	All Other Expenses (net)	1.8	.8	1.7	1.3	1.3	.6
3.2	3.9	4.1	Profit Before Taxes	3.4	1.9	1.9	4.6	4.0	6.2
			RATIOS						
3.1	2.5	2.8		2.7	2.9	2.8	2.3	2.8	3.0
1.9	1.7	1.8	Current	1.0	1.8	1.7	1.5	1.8	2.0
1.4	1.3	1.2		.6	1.1	1.3	1.1	1.3	1.3
1.4	1.2	1.3		1.0	1.2	.9	1.2	1.2	1.5
.8	.7	.8	Quick	.4	.6	.6	.9	.7	1.0
.5	.4	.4		.1	.3	.4	.4	.5	.5
26 14.0	26 14.3	30 12.2		0 UND	17 20.9	19 19.5	26 13.8	37 9.9	38 9.5
42 8.6	43 8.5	45 8.2	Sales/Receivables	45 8.1	40 9.2	34 10.7	39 9.5	48 7.6	58 6.3
63 5.8	65 5.6	66 5.5		113 3.2	60 6.1	61 6.0	47 7.7	65 5.6	73 5.0
68 5.3	66 5.5	66 5.5		0 UND	44 8.3	53 6.9	35 10.3	72 5.1	78 4.7
103 3.5	97 3.8	101 3.6	Cost of Sales/Inventory	123 3.0	117 3.1	112 3.3	93 3.9	97 3.8	96 3.8
147 2.5	148 2.5	160 2.3		160 2.3	211 1.7	160 2.3	158 2.3	149 2.5	145 2.5
18 20.8	15 24.5	17 21.2		4 87.0	16 23.0	18 20.8	11 34.1	17 21.5	19 19.3
28 13.0	27 13.4	32 11.3	Cost of Sales/Payables	35 10.3	38 9.6	26 14.2	28 13.2	31 11.6	33 11.0
42 8.8	50 7.3	52 7.1		86 4.3	74 4.9	43 8.4	53 6.8	44 8.2	52 7.1
3.9	4.8	4.1		2.7	3.7	4.9	6.2	4.9	3.6
6.5	7.7	7.4	Sales/Working Capital	91.7	9.0	8.8	10.8	6.3	6.1
13.4	17.0	15.6		-22.3	47.3	15.6	27.0	9.6	10.0
12.0	9.9	10.4		5.6	5.5	8.1	24.1	9.0	16.1
(155) 4.2	(168) 3.4	(167) 4.1	EBIT/Interest	(10) 2.3	(27) 2.9	4.2	(25) 2.0	(39) 4.1	(48) 7.2
1.3	1.5	1.3		.5	.0	2.1	.8	1.7	2.4
13.5	8.5	9.5	Net Profit + Depr., Dep.,					12.6	11.3
(52) 3.6	(41) 2.0	(43) 3.8	Amort./Cur. Mat. L/T/D				(16)	4.5	(14) 4.6
1.4	.9	1.3						1.4	2.0
.2	.2	.1		.2	.1	.1	.2	.1	.2
.4	.4	.4	Fixed/Worth	-3.9	1.0	.3	.9	.3	.4
1.5	1.0	1.2		-.1	13.8	1.5	2.3	.5	.7
.7	.8	.8		6.2	.8	.5	.9	.8	.6
1.7	1.7	2.1	Debt/Worth	-11.4	2.4	1.6	2.9	1.8	1.4
6.8	5.0	5.4		-3.8	125.3	4.3	5.0	2.6	4.0
45.3	43.0	40.7	% Profit Before Taxes/Tangible		43.5	32.5	44.4	29.0	43.9
(138) 21.1	(155) 18.8	(154) 16.8	Net Worth	(26) 21.9	(17) 13.3	(23) 11.3	(38) 11.4	(47) 20.5	
8.8	4.9	3.8			-4.8	7.2	-5.3	3.6	10.0
13.8	14.6	13.1	% Profit Before Taxes/Total	13.0	14.4	8.3	18.0	12.1	15.5
7.2	5.9	6.0	Assets	1.8	6.5	5.6	6.0	4.6	9.1
1.7	1.3	.6		-12.1	-6.4	2.9	-1.9	1.0	2.6
34.2	44.9	46.5		431.0	52.6	54.2	24.7	58.7	32.4
14.6	20.2	18.4	Sales/Net Fixed Assets	13.3	23.3	19.8	10.8	30.7	15.7
6.4	8.9	7.8		9.2	5.8	9.5	4.0	10.3	7.8
2.7	2.8	2.7		3.5	2.8	3.4	2.6	2.9	2.5
1.9	2.2	1.9	Sales/Total Assets	1.6	1.8	2.2	2.0	2.2	1.7
1.4	1.5	1.4		.9	1.2	1.8	1.4	1.4	1.4
.9	.8	.8			.7	.8	.9	.6	.8
(140) 1.7	(153) 1.4	(150) 1.5	% Depr., Dep., Amort./Sales	(25)	1.9 (14)	1.2 (25)	1.8 (35)	1.1 (45)	2.0
2.8	2.5	2.5			3.2	2.0	3.2	1.7	2.6
2.4	2.8	2.3	% Officers', Directors',		3.6	2.9	2.2		
(50) 3.8	(53) 5.2	(56) 4.5	Owners' Comp/Sales	(17) 6.0	(10) 3.9	(10) 4.0			
6.4	7.6	7.0			8.7	5.5	5.8		
4644019M	3741566M	4940931M	Net Sales ($)	5386M	62856M	71282M	178898M	605381M	4017128M
3046700M	2069605M	2860489M	Total Assets ($)	3202M	41659M	32860M	107014M	322124M	2353630M

© RMA 2005

M = $ thousand   MM = $ million
See Pages 11 through 21 for Explanation of Ratios and Data

Current Data Sorted By Assets   Comparative Historical Data

0-500M	500M-2MM	2-10MM	10-50MM	50-100MM	100-250MM	Type of Statement	4/1/00-3/31/01 ALL	4/1/01-3/31/02 ALL
		4	7	2	1	Unqualified	9	15
	2	6				Reviewed	5	9
1	2	3	1			Compiled	11	4
2	1					Tax Returns	3	1
1	6	5	7	3	3	Other	23	16
	6 (4/1-9/30/04)		52 (10/1/04-3/31/05)					
4	11	18	15	5	5	**NUMBER OF STATEMENTS**	51	45
%	%	%	%	%	%	**ASSETS**	%	%
	7.6	5.5	2.4			Cash & Equivalents	11.4	10.6
	16.8	36.8	31.6			Trade Receivables (net)	27.2	27.1
	46.8	32.2	24.2			Inventory	31.0	35.1
	3.2	.1	4.6			All Other Current	.9	1.2
	74.3	74.7	62.9			Total Current	70.5	73.9
	14.7	14.0	12.7			Fixed Assets (net)	17.0	16.6
	5.5	2.8	14.0			Intangibles (net)	7.2	5.1
	5.5	8.5	10.5			All Other Non-Current	5.3	4.4
	100.0	100.0	100.0			Total	100.0	100.0
						LIABILITIES		
	48.9	19.3	15.2			Notes Payable-Short Term	15.2	12.6
	2.3	1.8	1.1			Cur. Mat.-L/T/D	4.0	3.0
	15.7	17.5	13.5			Trade Payables	11.6	10.9
	.7	.2	.9			Income Taxes Payable	.4	.2
	7.9	8.7	9.8			All Other Current	9.7	12.2
	75.4	47.5	40.5			Total Current	41.0	38.9
	13.3	7.7	11.1			Long-Term Debt	32.6	13.3
	.0	.0	.3			Deferred Taxes	.6	.6
	6.6	3.6	1.3			All Other Non-Current	5.2	4.3
	4.7	41.2	46.7			Net Worth	20.8	42.9
	100.0	100.0	100.0			Total Liabilities & Net Worth	100.0	100.0
						INCOME DATA		
	100.0	100.0	100.0			Net Sales	100.0	100.0
	45.3	37.9	34.8			Gross Profit	36.0	35.9
	44.7	33.1	26.4			Operating Expenses	31.2	31.0
	.6	4.8	8.4			Operating Profit	4.9	4.9
	1.4	1.3	1.8			All Other Expenses (net)	.7	1.0
	−.8	3.5	6.6			Profit Before Taxes	4.2	3.9
						RATIOS		
	2.8	2.6	2.1				2.6	3.9
	1.8	1.7	1.6			Current	1.8	1.9
	1.0	1.2	1.1				1.2	1.3
	.8	1.6	1.3				1.7	1.8
	.4	.9	.7			Quick	1.0	1.1
	.2	.4	.5				.5	.5
	13 27.9	45 8.1	46 7.9				23 16.1	22 16.9
	21 17.2	63 5.8	66 5.5			Sales/Receivables	57 6.4	48 7.6
	91 4.0	102 3.6	85 4.3				78 4.7	67 5.5
104 3.5		65 5.6	43 8.4				51 7.1	50 7.3
170 2.1		112 3.3	88 4.2			Cost of Sales/Inventory	102 3.6	105 3.5
231 1.6		154 2.4	116 3.2				143 2.5	139 2.6
21 17.4		20 18.0	20 18.6				15 24.5	12 29.8
23 15.9		35 10.6	44 8.3			Cost of Sales/Payables	32 11.6	23 15.6
121 3.0		86 4.3	63 5.8				45 8.0	41 8.9
	2.8	3.6	4.3				4.2	3.2
	7.2	5.3	9.3			Sales/Working Capital	7.2	6.9
	−33.5	13.9	44.4				24.1	15.5
	14.5	9.3	58.7				12.4	6.6
	3.4	(16) 3.3	(13) 14.7			EBIT/Interest	(45) 2.9	(38) 3.1
	−1.1	1.1	.9				1.7	.3
						Net Profit + Depr., Dep.,	13.5	
						Amort./Cur. Mat. L /T/D	(10) 4.2	
							2.0	
	.2	.1	.1				.2	.1
	1.3	.3	.5			Fixed/Worth	.4	.4
	−2.3	.5	.9				1.2	1.1
	.8	.7	.8				.6	.4
	9.0	1.3	1.3			Debt/Worth	1.6	1.7
	−24.8	6.0	4.0				5.1	5.8
		38.8	74.9				50.6	31.8
		(17) 5.9	(12) 35.7			% Profit Before Taxes/Tangible Net Worth	(46) 25.4	(39) 19.4
		.9	18.8				9.3	−.7
	22.2	16.1	31.9				15.2	14.2
	3.5	3.2	15.1			% Profit Before Taxes/Total Assets	6.4	8.4
	−16.9	.1	−1.8				2.3	−1.5
	57.9	54.0	34.6				27.6	37.1
	16.3	12.2	26.2			Sales/Net Fixed Assets	14.5	14.9
	7.8	6.9	8.3				7.2	6.3
	2.5	2.0	2.2				2.9	2.8
	1.6	1.7	1.8			Sales/Total Assets	1.9	2.0
	.9	1.3	1.1				1.4	1.4
		.7					.8	.8
		(16) 1.8				% Depr., Dep., Amort./Sales	(41) 1.8	(37) 1.8
		4.6					2.7	3.3
							1.3	1.7
						% Officers', Directors', Owners' Comp/Sales	(15) 4.4	(11) 5.5
							9.4	12.8
5924M	28581M	151795M	658450M	569871M	3290488M	Net Sales ($)	1705639M	1629691M
1104M	11035M	88297M	383267M	342786M	924897M	Total Assets ($)	897073M	1105639M

M = $ thousand   MM = $ million
See Pages 11 through 21 for Explanation of Ratios and Data

Comparative Historical Data				**Current Data Sorted By Sales**					

Hist 1	Hist 2	Hist 3	Type of Statement	0-1MM	1-3MM	3-5MM	5-10MM	10-25MM	25MM & OVER
15	10	14	Unqualified				2	3	9
9	9	8	Reviewed	1	2		1	4	
5	8	7	Compiled	1	1	2	1	2	
2	2	4	Tax Returns	1	1		1		1
21	26	25	Other	2	5	2	2	4	10
4/1/02-3/31/03 ALL	4/1/03-3/31/04 ALL	4/1/04-3/31/05 ALL		6 (4/1-9/30/04)			52 (10/1/04-3/31/05)		
52	55	58	**NUMBER OF STATEMENTS**	5	9	4	7	13	20
%	%	%	**ASSETS**	%	%	%	%	%	%
8.1	6.9	6.7	Cash & Equivalents					4.1	3.6
26.9	28.0	27.3	Trade Receivables (net)					34.2	26.8
29.4	28.6	29.8	Inventory					31.8	21.5
3.3	2.0	4.2	All Other Current					3.0	8.2
67.6	65.4	67.9	Total Current					73.1	60.2
19.2	19.5	14.8	Fixed Assets (net)					13.3	14.1
8.5	8.6	9.2	Intangibles (net)					4.6	19.1
4.7	6.5	8.1	All Other Non-Current					9.1	6.6
100.0	100.0	100.0	Total					100.0	100.0
			LIABILITIES						
20.8	12.8	21.3	Notes Payable-Short Term					17.7	13.1
2.4	1.4	1.5	Cur. Mat.-L/T/D					1.5	1.4
13.6	14.3	14.7	Trade Payables					12.4	13.8
.1	.2	.8	Income Taxes Payable					.3	1.6
11.9	14.3	8.9	All Other Current					11.3	7.4
48.9	43.1	47.1	Total Current					43.2	37.3
12.1	12.6	10.1	Long-Term Debt					4.4	15.0
.5	.2	.4	Deferred Taxes					.0	1.2
4.8	6.6	3.9	All Other Non-Current					3.5	.9
33.8	37.5	38.5	Net Worth					48.9	45.7
100.0	100.0	100.0	Total Liabilities & Net Worth					100.0	100.0
			INCOME DATA						
100.0	100.0	100.0	Net Sales					100.0	100.0
38.6	36.4	39.5	Gross Profit					39.5	34.1
33.3	33.3	33.9	Operating Expenses					32.7	25.0
5.3	3.1	5.6	Operating Profit					6.8	9.0
1.2	1.0	1.4	All Other Expenses (net)					-.1	1.9
4.1	2.2	4.2	Profit Before Taxes					6.9	7.1
			RATIOS						
2.5	2.5	2.6	Current					2.3	2.6
1.6	1.5	1.6						1.6	1.6
1.1	1.2	1.1						1.4	1.1
1.5	1.4	1.6	Quick					1.5	1.5
.7	.8	.8						.9	.7
.5	.5	.4						.4	.6
32 11.6	34 10.9	32 11.5	Sales/Receivables					47 7.8	41 9.0
49 7.5	47 7.7	58 6.3						67 5.4	65 5.6
67 5.4	90 4.1	88 4.2						99 3.7	78 4.7
47 7.8	45 8.0	60 6.1	Cost of Sales/Inventory					64 5.7	43 8.5
97 3.8	86 4.3	98 3.7						108 3.4	85 4.3
136 2.7	132 2.8	143 2.6						195 1.9	110 3.3
20 18.7	15 24.3	21 17.6	Cost of Sales/Payables					16 22.3	25 14.6
37 9.9	31 11.6	37 9.8						35 10.4	45 8.2
55 6.6	59 6.2	70 5.2						58 6.3	62 5.9
5.3	4.5	4.1	Sales/Working Capital					3.9	5.2
8.9	9.6	7.4						5.4	9.3
29.2	29.6	28.8						11.6	23.5
9.1	17.9	26.4	EBIT/Interest					39.3	45.8
(47) 3.5	(49) 2.5	(49) 3.7					(11) 4.4		(16) 10.3
1.2	-.5	.9						1.7	1.1
6.1			Net Profit + Depr., Dep.,						
(13) 1.7			Amort./Cur. Mat. L/T/D						
-1.5									
.2	.2	.1	Fixed/Worth					.1	.1
.5	.5	.4						.2	.5
5.4	6.2	2.2						.4	6.3
.8	.7	.7	Debt/Worth					.7	.8
1.7	1.5	1.5						1.0	2.3
13.7	18.0	12.3						1.5	70.0
49.1	39.1	76.9	% Profit Before Taxes/Tangible					52.3	79.8
(42) 25.5	(42) 10.2	(49) 29.9	Net Worth					20.9	(16) 44.2
3.3	-3.2	3.8						4.2	20.0
16.8	15.4	23.4	% Profit Before Taxes/Total					23.4	30.8
7.4	2.0	9.3	Assets					12.8	11.9
.9	-7.4	.1						1.5	.5
31.1	31.3	54.9	Sales/Net Fixed Assets					55.0	37.4
11.8	13.0	18.5						20.2	24.5
6.4	5.9	7.5						7.0	7.3
2.6	2.6	2.3	Sales/Total Assets					2.2	2.4
1.9	1.8	1.7						1.8	1.8
1.2	1.3	1.1						1.2	1.1
1.3	.5	.9	% Depr., Dep., Amort./Sales					.8	1.1
(41) 1.8	(43) 1.7	(40) 1.8					(10)	1.4	(10) 1.9
3.8	3.5	4.2						2.6	4.5
1.8	.8	1.7	% Officers', Directors',						
(16) 4.3	(18) 2.7	(14) 3.6	Owners' Comp/Sales						
10.6	8.0	7.9							
1643236M	1767138M	4705109M	Net Sales ($)	3292M	16621M	15149M	50043M	218614M	4401390M
1156975M	1131890M	1751386M	Total Assets ($)	3406M	9648M	9212M	24458M	149339M	1555323M

© RMA 2005

M = $ thousand   MM = $ million
See Pages 11 through 21 for Explanation of Ratios and Data

Current Data Sorted By Assets   Comparative Historical Data

Type of Statement	0-500M	500M-2MM	2-10MM	10-50MM	50-100MM	100-250MM		4/1/00-3/31/01 ALL	4/1/01-3/31/02 ALL
Unqualified		1	12	12	3	3		27	30
Reviewed		19	28	4				52	48
Compiled	9	16	9	2				37	48
Tax Returns	12	13	1			1		19	11
Other	11	14	17	14	3	1		49	71
	39 (4/1-9/30/04)			166 (10/1/04-3/31/05)					
NUMBER OF STATEMENTS	32	63	67	32	6	5		184	208

ASSETS	%	%	%	%	%	%		%	%
Cash & Equivalents	8.3	7.0	6.0	4.7				8.1	7.6
Trade Receivables (net)	38.8	40.3	38.4	33.7				36.5	34.5
Inventory	10.1	18.8	21.4	21.9				18.9	19.2
All Other Current	.6	3.5	2.3	6.6				2.2	2.8
Total Current	57.8	69.6	68.1	66.9				65.7	64.2
Fixed Assets (net)	32.8	23.1	23.5	24.7				25.8	24.8
Intangibles (net)	2.9	2.4	3.6	2.4				3.3	4.4
All Other Non-Current	6.5	4.9	4.8	6.0				5.1	6.6
Total	100.0	100.0	100.0	100.0				100.0	100.0

LIABILITIES									
Notes Payable-Short Term	31.7	12.1	13.4	9.9				13.5	14.3
Cur. Mat.-L/T/D	10.1	5.0	3.7	4.1				3.5	4.6
Trade Payables	16.1	18.7	18.2	15.6				15.8	14.2
Income Taxes Payable	.0	.5	.3	.2				.5	.3
All Other Current	17.4	16.7	12.8	14.0				13.4	13.3
Total Current	75.3	52.9	48.3	43.8				46.7	46.7
Long-Term Debt	32.0	16.0	15.3	14.0				18.5	15.3
Deferred Taxes	.0	.3	.4	.5				.3	.3
All Other Non-Current	6.5	6.5	3.5	4.2				2.8	4.4
Net Worth	-13.8	24.3	32.4	37.5				31.6	33.4
Total Liabilities & Net Worth	100.0	100.0	100.0	100.0				100.0	100.0

INCOME DATA									
Net Sales	100.0	100.0	100.0	100.0				100.0	100.0
Gross Profit	52.3	39.3	29.9	28.5				35.9	37.4
Operating Expenses	47.9	36.2	26.3	24.3				31.9	34.5
Operating Profit	4.4	3.1	3.5	4.2				4.0	2.9
All Other Expenses (net)	2.0	.8	.9	.1				1.3	1.2
Profit Before Taxes	2.4	2.3	2.6	4.2				2.7	1.8

RATIOS	0-500M	500M-2MM	2-10MM	10-50MM	50-100MM	100-250MM		ALL	ALL
Current	1.9	2.0	2.0	2.4				2.0	2.2
	1.2	1.3	1.4	1.6				1.4	1.3
	.7	1.0	1.1	1.1				1.1	1.0
Quick	1.7	1.2	1.4	1.4				1.3	1.3
	.9	1.0	1.0	.8				1.0	.9
	.5	.7	.6	.6				.7	.6
Sales/Receivables	22 16.7	38 9.5	44 8.2	44 8.3				39 9.4	36 10.2
	39 9.4	49 7.5	57 6.4	56 6.5				55 6.6	47 7.7
	51 7.2	63 5.8	75 4.9	73 5.0				67 5.4	66 5.5
Cost of Sales/Inventory	2 155.6	11 32.1	18 20.5	25 14.8				21 17.8	18 20.1
	15 23.9	31 11.7	44 8.3	54 6.7				41 8.8	42 8.7
	32 11.4	74 4.9	63 5.8	94 3.9				63 5.8	68 5.4
Cost of Sales/Payables	9 41.8	21 17.8	19 19.0	23 15.7				21 17.4	19 19.6
	32 11.5	32 11.4	33 11.0	30 12.2				34 10.6	31 11.9
	60 6.1	54 6.7	49 7.5	55 6.7				48 7.6	47 7.8
Sales/Working Capital	14.7	8.9	6.4	5.0				7.0	7.2
	50.5	16.3	12.4	9.1				14.4	14.6
	-10.0	150.3	49.2	40.4				62.6	141.6
EBIT/Interest	6.7	11.0	8.8	11.6				6.9	6.0
	(26) 2.0	(58) 3.7	(61) 3.0	(29) 5.9				(166) 2.3	(189) 2.0
	-.5	1.4	1.6	2.1				1.1	.6
Net Profit + Depr., Dep., Amort./Cur. Mat. L/T/D			2.3	4.7				10.0	3.3
			(19) 1.0	(11) 3.0				(54) 2.6	(58) 1.3
			.4	1.4				1.0	.3
Fixed/Worth	1.0	.3	.3	.3				.3	.3
	4.9	1.0	.9	.7				.8	.9
	-2.9	3.1	1.6	2.4				2.5	2.6
Debt/Worth	2.1	1.1	1.3	.9				1.1	.9
	17.8	2.5	2.8	1.9				2.5	2.7
	-7.9	7.3	6.3	3.8				5.1	7.9
% Profit Before Taxes/Tangible Net Worth	311.1	82.1	45.8	32.1				38.2	38.4
	(20) 38.1	(55) 30.9	(61) 18.1	(29) 19.6				(161) 17.3	(176) 13.2
	5.7	7.5	4.0	9.2				2.3	-1.9
% Profit Before Taxes/Total Assets	14.2	16.4	14.0	11.6				14.3	12.4
	4.3	8.7	5.7	7.6				4.8	4.2
	-4.3	1.0	1.4	2.1				.7	-1.4
Sales/Net Fixed Assets	19.4	29.0	21.2	20.8				21.8	23.3
	12.9	14.9	12.6	10.3				12.0	11.2
	8.9	8.3	6.7	4.2				6.2	6.2
Sales/Total Assets	4.7	3.7	3.1	2.0				3.1	3.3
	3.5	2.8	2.4	2.0				2.5	2.5
	2.5	2.3	1.8	1.6				1.9	1.8
% Depr., Dep., Amort./Sales	2.1	1.1	1.0	1.0				1.1	1.2
	(25) 2.7	(51) 1.7	(62) 1.5	(28) 2.0				(172) 2.0	(184) 2.2
	5.5	3.6	2.7	3.0				3.5	3.3
% Officers', Directors', Owners' Comp/Sales	4.5	3.0	2.0					3.3	3.3
	(23) 5.9	(34) 5.6	(24) 2.9					(79) 6.6	(83) 6.2
	11.7	8.9	7.1					10.5	9.0
Net Sales ($)	33469M	221101M	788281M	1437653M	699586M	1383437M		2838591M	2908360M
Total Assets ($)	8298M	74375M	317127M	707577M	454729M	756553M		1504345M	1677484M

M = $ thousand   MM = $ million
See Pages 11 through 21 for Explanation of Ratios and Data

Comparative Historical Data / Current Data Sorted By Sales

				Type of Statement						
33	27	31		Unqualified			1	5	9	16
74	62	51		Reviewed		7	9	15	16	4
36	42	36		Compiled	4	13	9	5	4	1
30	37	27		Tax Returns	8	12	4	1	1	1
58	64	60		Other	7	11	5	11	7	19
4/1/02-3/31/03 ALL	4/1/03-3/31/04 ALL	4/1/04-3/31/05 ALL			39 (4/1-9/30/04)			166 (10/1/04-3/31/05)		
					0-1MM	1-3MM	3-5MM	5-10MM	10-25MM	25MM & OVER
231	232	205		NUMBER OF STATEMENTS	19	43	28	37	37	41
%	%	%		ASSETS	%	%	%	%	%	%
6.6	8.8	6.5		Cash & Equivalents	6.5	8.2	7.0	6.7	5.2	5.2
35.3	35.6	37.4		Trade Receivables (net)	37.9	35.6	40.0	39.9	41.1	31.8
18.5	17.6	18.6		Inventory	6.9	17.5	20.9	17.8	22.1	21.3
3.0	3.2	3.2		All Other Current	.6	3.0	1.7	3.0	2.5	6.2
63.4	65.2	65.7		Total Current	51.9	64.3	69.6	67.4	71.0	64.5
26.4	24.3	25.4		Fixed Assets (net)	37.4	27.1	24.6	21.9	22.1	24.9
4.3	5.0	3.4		Intangibles (net)	2.8	3.3	1.2	6.2	1.2	4.7
6.0	5.5	5.5		All Other Non-Current	7.8	5.3	4.7	4.5	5.7	6.0
100.0	100.0	100.0		Total	100.0	100.0	100.0	100.0	100.0	100.0
				LIABILITIES						
13.8	14.3	14.8		Notes Payable-Short Term	38.0	14.5	12.4	12.8	13.9	8.5
4.0	4.8	5.1		Cur. Mat.-L/T/D	11.9	6.2	4.3	4.6	3.0	3.4
16.9	16.4	17.2		Trade Payables	17.7	14.3	15.4	19.5	21.5	15.3
.2	.5	.3		Income Taxes Payable	.0	.1	.3	.7	.4	.3
12.0	13.3	14.9		All Other Current	23.7	12.0	12.7	16.8	14.0	14.4
46.8	49.2	52.2		Total Current	91.3	47.0	45.0	54.3	52.8	41.9
17.4	18.1	18.7		Long-Term Debt	31.6	23.7	15.3	15.0	12.9	18.6
.4	.3	.4		Deferred Taxes	.0	.3	.2	.5	.4	.9
4.7	5.7	5.2		All Other Non-Current	5.3	8.2	5.5	4.4	1.7	5.5
30.7	26.8	23.5		Net Worth	−28.2	20.9	34.0	25.8	32.2	33.1
100.0	100.0	100.0		Total Liabilities & Net Worth	100.0	100.0	100.0	100.0	100.0	100.0
				INCOME DATA						
100.0	100.0	100.0		Net Sales	100.0	100.0	100.0	100.0	100.0	100.0
37.1	36.8	36.3		Gross Profit	52.3	44.5	38.6	30.7	29.8	29.9
34.8	34.4	32.5		Operating Expenses	50.0	41.8	33.8	26.8	25.6	25.2
2.3	2.4	3.8		Operating Profit	2.3	2.6	4.8	3.9	4.2	4.7
.9	1.1	.9		All Other Expenses (net)	1.0	2.2	1.0	.2	.5	.6
1.4	1.3	2.9		Profit Before Taxes	1.3	.4	3.8	3.7	3.8	4.0
				RATIOS						
2.0	1.9	2.1		Current	1.3	2.0	2.2	1.9	2.0	2.4
1.3	1.3	1.3			1.0	1.4	1.4	1.4	1.3	1.7
1.0	1.0	1.0			.6	1.1	1.1	1.0	1.1	1.1
1.4	1.4	1.4		Quick	1.2	1.6	1.6	1.3	1.3	1.4
(230) .9	.9	1.0			.9	1.0	1.0	1.0	1.0	.9
.6	.6	.6			.4	.5	.7	.6	.6	.6
36 10.0	36 10.2	38 9.5		Sales/Receivables	22 16.6	33 11.1	40 9.1	35 10.6	45 8.1	43 8.5
52 7.1	50 7.2	50 7.3			47 7.8	48 7.6	51 7.2	46 7.9	53 6.9	53 6.9
65 5.6	65 5.6	70 5.2			62 5.8	62 5.9	62 5.9	75 4.9	75 4.4	71 5.1
18 20.4	15 24.3	13 27.6		Cost of Sales/Inventory	0 UND	9 38.8	20 18.5	10 36.3	16 23.4	25 14.6
42 8.7	35 10.5	37 10.0			14 26.8	31 11.6	33 10.9	32 11.4	46 7.9	55 6.7
68 5.4	65 5.6	68 5.4			25 14.3	74 4.9	99 3.7	55 6.6	64 5.7	85 4.3
19 18.9	18 20.7	20 18.6		Cost of Sales/Payables	16 22.9	16 22.1	20 18.1	15 24.7	25 14.8	22 16.5
35 10.5	34 10.8	33 11.1			34 10.8	32 11.5	32 11.5	33 11.0	33 11.0	33 11.1
54 6.8	55 6.6	54 6.7			74 5.0	60 6.1	38 9.6	54 6.8	52 7.0	53 6.8
7.0	7.2	6.8		Sales/Working Capital	23.8	9.1	5.4	7.5	6.7	5.0
16.6	17.2	15.7			−274.3	16.2	11.1	14.8	17.4	8.9
289.1	−131.4	119.9			−8.6	76.5	115.7	213.5	67.7	27.9
6.7	7.9	8.9		EBIT/Interest	5.5	7.0	10.2	11.0	10.1	12.3
(214) 2.3	(214) 2.2	(185) 3.3			(15) 1.5	(37) 2.3	(25) 3.4	(36) 3.4	(34) 4.8	(38) 4.3
−.3	−.5	1.5			−.5	.9	2.5	1.4	2.3	1.9
6.4	3.3	4.0		Net Profit + Depr., Dep., Amort./Cur. Mat. L/T/D						5.3
(74) 2.9	(54) 2.0	(46) 1.5								(14) 2.5
1.0	.8	1.0								1.4
.4	.3	.4		Fixed/Worth	1.3	.5	.3	.3	.3	.4
1.0	1.0	1.0			5.8	1.3	.8	1.0	.8	.8
4.0	4.4	3.3			−4.2	10.8	1.6	3.7	1.3	3.0
1.0	1.3	1.2		Debt/Worth	2.3	1.4	1.1	1.0	1.3	.9
3.0	3.0	2.7			29.4	2.5	2.4	3.3	2.2	2.6
10.4	19.5	10.6			−8.3	40.3	4.5	50.7	5.4	10.3
36.9	42.0	56.4		% Profit Before Taxes/Tangible Net Worth	273.8	85.3	39.4	72.9	46.9	39.0
(192) 10.9	(185) 13.1	(172) 22.0			(12) 43.9	(33) 26.9	23.3	(29) 16.7	(35) 21.5	(35) 21.7
−2.1	−5.1	5.6			3.8	1.5	3.4	3.7	10.3	10.3
10.5	11.4	14.0		% Profit Before Taxes/Total Assets	15.9	12.3	14.9	14.2	18.2	13.7
3.2	2.8	6.3			2.3	4.8	7.1	5.7	6.5	6.6
−2.9	−3.8	1.2			−7.3	−.9	1.3	.9	3.0	2.3
23.4	26.3	21.6		Sales/Net Fixed Assets	13.3	21.8	22.3	28.7	30.6	19.3
12.0	13.0	12.7			9.1	12.8	13.9	14.9	12.6	9.7
6.1	7.2	6.9			5.4	7.0	6.7	9.3	7.3	5.7
3.3	3.3	3.4		Sales/Total Assets	3.9	4.0	3.1	4.2	3.2	2.5
2.4	2.5	2.5			2.5	2.9	2.6	2.8	2.6	2.0
1.7	1.9	1.9			2.2	2.0	1.9	1.9	2.0	1.6
1.3	1.0	1.1		% Depr., Dep., Amort./Sales	2.5	1.5	.6	1.0	.9	1.0
(210) 2.2	(190) 1.9	(172) 1.9			(16) 4.7	(33) 2.9	(25) 1.5	(31) 1.8	(35) 1.3	(32) 1.9
3.5	3.8	3.4			5.6	4.7	3.6	2.7	1.9	3.2
2.8	3.1	2.4		% Officers', Directors', Owners' Comp/Sales	5.9	3.2	1.5	3.0	1.9	
(106) 5.4	(103) 5.1	(84) 5.2			(12) 8.9	(28) 5.2	(17) 4.9	(15) 4.3	(11) 2.1	
8.4	8.8	9.4			13.2	7.9	8.8	5.1		
3857546M	3314701M	4563527M		Net Sales ($)	10451M	83352M	109263M	253255M	600210M	3506996M
1723297M	1589472M	2318659M		Total Assets ($)	4092M	36772M	47393M	113950M	257556M	1858896M

M = $ thousand   MM = $ million
See Pages 11 through 21 for Explanation of Ratios and Data

Current Data Sorted By Assets   Comparative Historical Data

0-500M	500M-2MM	2-10MM	10-50MM	50-100MM	100-250MM		4/1/00-3/31/01 ALL	4/1/01-3/31/02 ALL
						Type of Statement		
		4	7	3		Unqualified	7	13
1	5	14	2	2		Reviewed	20	14
1	9	5	2			Compiled	19	15
2	3	1				Tax Returns	4	3
1	4	14	4			Other	24	27
	27 (4/1-9/30/04)		57 (10/1/04-3/31/05)					
5	21	38	15	5		**NUMBER OF STATEMENTS**	74	72
%	%	%	%	%	%	**ASSETS**	%	%
	7.1	6.5	6.8			Cash & Equivalents	6.4	5.8
	38.4	31.0	24.6			Trade Receivables (net)	30.9	27.9
	33.8	28.2	19.4			Inventory	26.0	26.2
	.8	1.2	3.3			All Other Current	1.3	1.0
	80.1	66.9	54.1			Total Current	64.6	60.9
	12.9	27.7	33.6			Fixed Assets (net)	26.8	27.1
	.9	1.1	5.2			Intangibles (net)	1.8	6.2
	6.1	4.3	7.2			All Other Non-Current	6.8	5.8
	100.0	100.0	100.0			Total	100.0	100.0
						LIABILITIES		
	10.0	10.2	12.7			Notes Payable-Short Term	14.1	10.6
	2.4	6.3	3.5			Cur. Mat.-L/T/D	4.1	4.1
	23.6	19.1	7.6			Trade Payables	17.3	15.5
	.3	.2	.1			Income Taxes Payable	.3	.3
	6.6	7.0	8.4			All Other Current	8.2	8.1
	42.9	42.7	32.4			Total Current	44.1	38.6
	7.7	12.8	14.4			Long-Term Debt	13.2	17.6
	6.0	.6	.9			Deferred Taxes	.4	.3
	.9	2.1	8.6			All Other Non-Current	5.3	3.5
	42.4	41.7	43.7			Net Worth	37.0	40.0
	100.0	100.0	100.0			Total Liabilities & Net Worth	100.0	100.0
						INCOME DATA		
	100.0	100.0	100.0			Net Sales	100.0	100.0
	35.7	26.1	29.1			Gross Profit	31.4	32.4
	30.8	22.8	21.4			Operating Expenses	26.6	29.1
	4.8	3.4	7.7			Operating Profit	4.8	3.3
	.2	.5	2.0			All Other Expenses (net)	1.3	1.6
	4.7	2.8	5.8			Profit Before Taxes	3.5	1.7
						RATIOS		
	2.8	2.7	3.7				2.5	2.4
	2.2	1.7	2.5			Current	1.4	1.6
	1.5	1.2	1.1				1.0	1.1
	1.6	1.7	2.9				1.5	1.4
	1.2	1.0	1.6			Quick	.7	.9
	.7	.5	.5				.5	.6
	35 10.3	40 9.0	41 8.9				34 10.6	33 11.2
	46 7.9	48 7.5	49 7.4			Sales/Receivables	46 7.9	45 8.1
	56 6.5	58 6.3	56 6.6				59 6.2	53 6.9
	34 10.7	36 10.1	34 10.7				29 12.5	29 12.6
	77 4.7	51 7.1	55 6.6			Cost of Sales/Inventory	51 7.2	56 6.5
	117 3.1	91 4.0	66 5.5				86 4.2	97 3.8
	23 15.7	22 16.9	10 36.2				21 17.4	17 21.9
	43 8.6	34 10.8	23 16.1			Cost of Sales/Payables	33 11.1	30 12.1
	60 6.1	46 8.0	34 10.8				46 8.0	44 8.2
	5.1	5.3	4.3				6.4	6.4
	8.2	10.1	6.3			Sales/Working Capital	13.1	10.1
	13.5	21.1	45.5				606.7	38.9
	25.1	11.3	65.4				5.9	6.1
	(18) 8.1	(35) 4.7	10.8			EBIT/Interest	(67) 2.1	(68) 2.1
	6.2	2.2	1.9				.9	-.1
		15.5				Net Profit + Depr., Dep.,	5.3	3.6
		(10) 2.1				Amort./Cur. Mat. L /T/D	(26) 1.9	(24) 1.4
		1.4					.3	.3
	.1	.3	.3				.3	.3
	.2	.7	.6			Fixed/Worth	.9	.7
	.5	1.5	2.6				1.6	1.6
	.6	.7	.4				.8	.7
	1.1	1.3	1.0			Debt/Worth	1.9	1.7
	3.6	4.1	3.7				5.6	4.5
	51.6	34.4	45.1			% Profit Before Taxes/Tangible	39.7	40.7
	(19) 19.5	(36) 17.9	(13) 35.4			Net Worth	(68) 16.4	(63) 7.7
	2.6	5.5	15.4				2.3	-8.4
	19.3	12.1	29.2			% Profit Before Taxes/Total	13.2	9.5
	8.8	6.5	10.6			Assets	4.9	3.5
	1.6	2.0	3.9				.3	-3.1
	68.5	29.6	10.6				23.1	20.3
	23.6	9.0	6.1			Sales/Net Fixed Assets	10.5	9.4
	11.5	4.6	3.2				5.6	5.1
	3.7	3.1	2.2				3.1	3.3
	2.6	2.1	1.7			Sales/Total Assets	2.5	2.2
	2.0	1.6	1.5				1.9	1.6
	.3	1.2	1.3				.9	1.1
	(15) 1.1	(36) 2.2	(13) 2.8			% Depr., Dep., Amort./Sales	(68) 2.0	(69) 2.1
	1.9	3.7	6.8				3.6	4.4
		1.9				% Officers', Directors',	3.2	3.1
		(12) 5.1				Owners' Comp/Sales	(23) 5.5	(23) 6.0
		5.9					6.6	8.0
4358M	74751M	358253M	483600M	575174M		Net Sales ($)	1018133M	1309405M
1338M	24138M	153901M	275247M	315172M		Total Assets ($)	534598M	833285M

(Column 100-250MM: DATA NOT AVAILABLE)

© RMA 2005

M = $ thousand   MM = $ million
See Pages 11 through 21 for Explanation of Ratios and Data

Comparative Historical Data | Current Data Sorted By Sales

			Type of Statement						
18	9	14	Unqualified		2	2		10	
24	22	22	Reviewed	3	3	9	6	1	
13	17	17	Compiled	2	2	3	5	4	1
3	5	6	Tax Returns	2	3	3	1		1
21	22	25	Other	1	4	3	9	3	5
4/1/02-3/31/03	4/1/03-3/31/04	4/1/04-3/31/05			27 (4/1-9/30/04)			57 (10/1/04-3/31/05)	
ALL	ALL	ALL		0-1MM	1-3MM	3-5MM	5-10MM	10-25MM	25MM & OVER
79	75	84	NUMBER OF STATEMENTS	5	12	11	26	13	17
%	%	%	**ASSETS**	%	%	%	%	%	%
8.4	6.9	7.6	Cash & Equivalents		10.9	8.0	4.8	5.8	8.8
28.0	27.9	30.8	Trade Receivables (net)		26.9	33.6	33.4	31.2	27.4
24.5	26.0	26.7	Inventory		24.8	40.1	29.9	17.7	21.2
1.5	1.4	1.4	All Other Current		.7	.6	2.1	1.0	1.7
62.4	62.2	66.4	Total Current		63.3	82.3	70.2	55.7	59.1
25.4	26.8	25.6	Fixed Assets (net)		25.3	14.8	24.3	36.6	28.6
5.5	5.1	2.6	Intangibles (net)		1.4	.0	1.2	.6	7.9
6.7	6.0	5.4	All Other Non-Current		10.0	2.8	4.3	7.0	4.4
100.0	100.0	100.0	Total		100.0	100.0	100.0	100.0	100.0
			LIABILITIES						
10.6	10.9	13.1	Notes Payable-Short Term		31.6	9.1	15.9	5.9	5.8
3.6	3.0	4.3	Cur. Mat.-L/T/D		2.5	2.9	7.1	3.1	4.4
13.4	13.4	16.7	Trade Payables		23.1	21.3	19.7	11.2	9.8
.5	.4	.2	Income Taxes Payable		.0	1.1	.0	.0	.1
8.4	8.2	8.1	All Other Current		5.6	7.0	8.4	6.9	10.5
36.5	35.9	42.4	Total Current		62.8	41.4	51.1	27.3	30.6
14.9	15.5	11.4	Long-Term Debt		11.9	8.3	9.3	16.6	13.4
.6	.7	2.0	Deferred Taxes		.4	.0	.5	.9	1.0
5.0	5.2	3.2	All Other Non-Current		1.9	.5	2.7	.3	9.8
43.0	42.6	41.1	Net Worth		23.0	49.9	36.4	54.9	45.3
100.0	100.0	100.0	Total Liabilities & Net Worth		100.0	100.0	100.0	100.0	100.0
			INCOME DATA						
100.0	100.0	100.0	Net Sales		100.0	100.0	100.0	100.0	100.0
29.4	31.4	31.0	Gross Profit		37.1	31.2	24.6	31.0	31.3
26.5	29.1	26.0	Operating Expenses		34.0	28.0	22.6	22.8	21.9
2.9	2.3	5.0	Operating Profit		3.1	3.2	2.0	8.1	9.4
1.4	1.0	.7	All Other Expenses (net)		.4	.3	.8	.5	1.4
1.5	1.2	4.3	Profit Before Taxes		2.7	2.9	1.2	7.6	8.0
			RATIOS						
3.1	3.0	2.9			2.8	4.8	2.3	4.0	3.2
1.8	1.8	1.8	Current		2.4	2.5	1.5	2.1	1.8
1.1	1.2	1.3			.9	1.4	1.2	1.5	1.3
1.9	2.0	1.8			1.6	2.1	1.2	2.8	2.3
1.0	.8	1.1	Quick		1.3	1.5	.8	1.8	1.4
.7	.6	.6			.6	.7	.5	1.0	.6
38 9.5	33 10.9	39 9.3		34 10.6	39 9.4	42 8.8	41 9.0	37 9.9	
47 7.8	42 8.7	48 7.6	Sales/Receivables	45 8.1	50 7.3	48 7.5	48 7.6	47 7.7	
56 6.5	52 7.0	56 6.5		61 6.0	56 6.5	55 6.6	58 6.3	57 6.4	
32 11.4	31 11.9	35 10.4		22 16.8	47 7.8	34 10.8	32 11.4	31 11.7	
57 6.4	59 6.2	56 6.5	Cost of Sales/Inventory	72 5.1	87 4.2	51 7.1	46 8.0	57 6.4	
91 4.0	82 4.5	90 4.1		110 3.3	139 2.6	86 4.3	57 6.4	71 5.2	
17 22.0	15 24.9	20 18.6		22 16.3	24 15.5	23 15.9	11 34.2	14 25.2	
26 14.2	27 13.7	33 11.2	Cost of Sales/Payables	40 9.1	45 8.2	33 11.2	18 20.4	28 13.1	
46 8.0	41 8.9	47 7.8		71 5.1	51 7.2	50 7.3	34 10.8	38 9.5	
5.1	5.2	5.2			5.6	3.0	7.3	4.8	4.3
8.3	8.5	8.4	Sales/Working Capital		7.2	6.2	12.0	9.0	6.8
33.0	34.4	18.0			-28.7	13.0	26.0	14.5	24.8
9.7	9.2	19.4			15.0	19.9	10.6	64.1	37.8
(71) 2.4	(66) 2.9	(75) 6.8	EBIT/Interest	(10) 6.7	6.5	(23) 3.9	(12) 12.9	(16) 10.3	
1.3	1.2	2.4			.3	2.9	2.2	2.3	4.8
3.9	3.3	15.3	Net Profit + Depr., Dep.,						
(31) 1.9	(22) 2.1	(26) 2.9	Amort./Cur. Mat. L/T/D						
1.0	1.4	1.3							
.3	.3	.2			.2	.1	.2	.4	.3
.5	.6	.5	Fixed/Worth		.5	.2	.5	.7	.6
1.3	1.6	1.5			NM	.5	1.9	1.1	2.3
.5	.5	.6			.6	.3	.8	.4	.6
1.4	1.6	1.1	Debt/Worth		1.0	.9	1.6	1.0	1.5
4.2	3.0	3.7			NM	5.0	4.5	1.8	3.6
36.2	28.2	45.3	% Profit Before Taxes/Tangible		53.3	34.3	45.1	69.3	
(71) 10.2	(69) 9.9	(76) 22.0	Net Worth		16.8	(24) 16.8	20.1	(16) 35.2	
3.0	3.5	6.9			5.4	4.0	5.9	20.1	
10.4	10.3	20.3	% Profit Before Taxes/Total		28.5	11.4	10.4	30.2	26.0
4.0	3.7	8.2	Assets		5.2	8.8	5.3	8.6	16.3
.9	.7	2.6			1.1	3.2	1.8	2.5	6.0
18.4	23.8	29.6			33.8	83.5	37.5	11.2	12.7
9.5	11.1	9.8	Sales/Net Fixed Assets		12.5	23.6	11.6	6.3	8.7
4.7	4.3	5.9			7.5	7.7	6.4	2.8	3.7
3.0	3.1	3.1			2.6	3.6	3.3	3.4	2.4
2.1	2.3	2.1	Sales/Total Assets		2.2	2.1	2.3	2.2	2.0
1.6	1.5	1.7			1.9	2.0	1.9	1.4	1.6
1.5	1.1	1.1					1.2	1.2	1.3
(71) 2.4	(69) 2.2	(71) 2.1	% Depr., Dep., Amort./Sales			(23) 1.9	2.7	(14) 2.5	
4.3	4.2	3.5					2.9	4.7	3.6
2.6	3.4	2.5	% Officers', Directors',						
(26) 6.6	(22) 5.4	(24) 5.6	Owners' Comp/Sales						
10.4	9.0	8.1							
1564329M 983407M	807149M 462118M	1496136M 769796M	Net Sales ($) Total Assets ($)	3622M - 2249M	24430M 11839M	45080M 20015M	184697M 93432M	206962M 100981M	1031345M 541280M

M = $ thousand   MM = $ million
See Pages 11 through 21 for Explanation of Ratios and Data

Current Data Sorted By Assets							Comparative Historical Data	

						Type of Statement		
		1	1	1		Unqualified	8	6
1		3	2			Reviewed	7	4
	1	2	2			Compiled	2	6
2	1					Tax Returns		2
1	2	3	5	1	4	Other	8	11
	8 (4/1-9/30/04)		26 (10/1/04-3/31/05)				4/1/00-3/31/01 ALL	4/1/01-3/31/02 ALL
0-500M	500M-2MM	2-10MM	10-50MM	50-100MM	100-250MM	NUMBER OF STATEMENTS	25	29
4	5	9	10	2	4			
%	%	%	%	%	%	**ASSETS**	%	%
			8.7			Cash & Equivalents	6.2	6.0
			23.5			Trade Receivables (net)	23.0	20.3
			41.5			Inventory	42.3	42.1
			2.3			All Other Current	1.4	1.7
			76.0			Total Current	72.9	70.1
			14.3			Fixed Assets (net)	16.1	24.0
			5.2			Intangibles (net)	6.4	3.0
			4.5			All Other Non-Current	4.6	2.9
			100.0			Total	100.0	100.0
						LIABILITIES		
			12.1			Notes Payable-Short Term	13.3	10.5
			1.2			Cur. Mat.-L/T/D	2.8	2.9
			12.5			Trade Payables	14.8	20.3
			.1			Income Taxes Payable	.3	.1
			6.7			All Other Current	8.3	13.6
			32.5			Total Current	39.5	47.5
			11.9			Long-Term Debt	10.1	20.1
			.3			Deferred Taxes	.8	.2
			3.6			All Other Non-Current	5.3	10.7
			51.8			Net Worth	44.4	21.5
			100.0			Total Liabilities & Net Worth	100.0	100.0
						INCOME DATA		
			100.0			Net Sales	100.0	100.0
			30.3			Gross Profit	32.8	37.4
			24.2			Operating Expenses	26.7	30.0
			6.1			Operating Profit	6.1	7.4
			1.4			All Other Expenses (net)	2.5	1.5
			4.6			Profit Before Taxes	3.7	5.9
						RATIOS		
			4.0				3.0	3.0
			3.6			Current	1.9	2.2
			1.4				1.5	1.4
			1.5				1.1	1.3
			1.3			Quick	.7	.8
			.6				.5	.4
		34	10.7				29 12.7	24 15.0
		59	6.2			Sales/Receivables	47 7.8	41 9.0
		82	4.5				55 6.6	49 7.5
		102	3.6				88 4.2	84 4.4
		168	2.2			Cost of Sales/Inventory	130 2.8	122 3.0
		181	2.0				167 2.2	189 1.9
		26	13.9				13 27.6	18 20.0
		32	11.6			Cost of Sales/Payables	31 11.6	27 13.4
		133	2.7				60 6.1	54 6.8
			2.3				3.5	3.5
			3.0			Sales/Working Capital	5.2	5.1
			5.7				9.5	8.8
							6.4	9.1
						EBIT/Interest	(23) 3.3	(25) 2.9
							2.0	2.0
						Net Profit + Depr., Dep., Amort./Cur. Mat. L/T/D		
			.1				.3	.3
			.3			Fixed/Worth	.4	.7
			1.8				.7	1.4
			.3				.8	.9
			.8			Debt/Worth	1.2	1.4
			6.9				3.2	4.4
							37.9	41.6
						% Profit Before Taxes/Tangible Net Worth	(23) 23.4	(26) 28.8
							12.7	10.0
			24.3				12.5	18.4
			8.4			% Profit Before Taxes/Total Assets	8.7	9.8
			1.7				2.5	3.8
			27.0				30.1	21.0
			16.8			Sales/Net Fixed Assets	11.9	10.5
			4.5				6.9	4.1
			2.0				2.3	2.4
			1.4			Sales/Total Assets	1.9	1.8
			1.1				1.4	1.4
							.6	1.1
						% Depr., Dep., Amort./Sales	(22) 1.4	(25) 1.4
							2.3	3.5
						% Officers', Directors', Owners' Comp/Sales		
6224M	10621M	77714M	242938M	170708M	903244M	Net Sales ($)	1285774M	1795553M
1308M	5474M	45567M	199356M	126566M	690199M	Total Assets ($)	852921M	858513M

M = $ thousand   MM = $ million
See Pages 11 through 21 for Explanation of Ratios and Data

Comparative Historical Data   Current Data Sorted By Sales

			Type of Statement						
11	4	3	Unqualified					1	2
5	8	7	Reviewed	1		2	1	2	1
3	9	5	Compiled			2	1	1	1
3	2	3	Tax Returns	1	2				
6	8	16	Other	1	2	1	3	3	6
4/1/02-3/31/03 ALL	4/1/03-3/31/04 ALL	4/1/04-3/31/05 ALL		0-1MM	1-3MM	3-5MM	5-10MM	10-25MM	25MM & OVER
					8 (4/1-9/30/04)		26 (10/1/04-3/31/05)		
28	31	34	**NUMBER OF STATEMENTS**	3	4	5	5	7	10
%	%	%	**ASSETS**	%	%	%	%	%	%
7.4	8.8	9.9	Cash & Equivalents						7.4
22.9	22.9	17.4	Trade Receivables (net)						19.5
36.4	36.9	37.0	Inventory						32.8
2.4	4.2	3.1	All Other Current						2.9
69.0	72.8	67.3	Total Current						62.6
18.8	16.3	19.1	Fixed Assets (net)						18.2
1.9	5.2	4.6	Intangibles (net)						5.6
10.3	5.7	9.0	All Other Non-Current						13.6
100.0	100.0	100.0	Total						100.0
			LIABILITIES						
9.3	10.9	11.8	Notes Payable-Short Term						11.0
1.7	3.2	1.9	Cur. Mat.-L/T/D						2.2
12.4	8.9	11.6	Trade Payables						11.9
.2	.4	.1	Income Taxes Payable						.2
16.1	10.3	12.0	All Other Current						6.5
39.8	33.7	37.5	Total Current						31.7
12.3	13.6	16.7	Long-Term Debt						11.3
.6	.3	.4	Deferred Taxes						.2
7.3	9.0	7.5	All Other Non-Current						8.6
39.9	43.4	38.0	Net Worth						48.1
100.0	100.0	100.0	Total Liabilities & Net Worth						100.0
			INCOME DATA						
100.0	100.0	100.0	Net Sales						100.0
35.5	36.9	36.9	Gross Profit						36.4
28.8	30.9	30.9	Operating Expenses						25.8
6.7	6.0	5.9	Operating Profit						10.5
1.1	1.3	1.2	All Other Expenses (net)						1.4
5.6	4.7	4.7	Profit Before Taxes						9.2
			RATIOS						
3.6	4.5	3.8	Current						3.7
2.6	2.5	2.3							2.4
1.2	1.6	1.1							1.2
1.8	2.3	1.5	Quick						1.4
.9	1.1	.8							1.0
.5	.5	.4							.4
27 13.4	31 11.8	17 21.6	Sales/Receivables						37 9.9
40 9.2	39 9.2	39 9.2							43 8.5
54 6.7	60 6.1	50 7.3							56 6.6
89 4.1	79 4.6	89 4.1	Cost of Sales/Inventory						95 3.8
130 2.8	142 2.6	148 2.5							111 3.3
156 2.3	200 1.8	172 2.1							153 2.4
16 22.1	13 28.4	19 19.6	Cost of Sales/Payables						29 12.7
24 15.0	19 19.2	30 12.0							48 7.6
44 8.2	40 9.1	59 6.2							59 6.2
3.1	2.8	3.4	Sales/Working Capital						3.4
4.6	4.4	5.3							4.2
15.8	6.3	35.8							56.0
12.4	10.9	11.5	EBIT/Interest						
(21) 4.6	(26) 3.7	(30) 3.9							
1.6	1.4	.6							
	10.8	8.0	Net Profit + Depr., Dep., Amort./Cur. Mat. L/T/D						
	(14) 4.7	(13) 4.2							
	1.5	2.3							
.2	.1	.2	Fixed/Worth						.2
.3	.4	.4							.4
1.6	.9	4.4							1.0
.4	.5	.4	Debt/Worth						.4
1.0	1.5	1.4							1.3
5.5	4.1	10.2							4.1
33.7	47.4	42.3	% Profit Before Taxes/Tangible Net Worth						44.5
(26) 16.5	(26) 21.8	(28) 24.5							35.4
4.8	2.4	6.6							19.6
16.8	15.9	16.8	% Profit Before Taxes/Total Assets						19.2
10.5	9.7	8.9							13.0
2.6	1.5	1.7							9.1
23.9	52.4	26.4	Sales/Net Fixed Assets						16.2
10.7	15.0	11.9							6.7
5.4	6.3	5.7							5.9
2.2	2.2	2.3	Sales/Total Assets						1.8
1.7	1.7	1.5							1.5
1.5	1.2	1.3							1.2
1.1	.9	1.0	% Depr., Dep., Amort./Sales						1.3
(25) 2.0	(28) 1.7	(30) 1.6							1.7
4.2	3.9	3.0							2.8
			% Officers', Directors', Owners' Comp/Sales						
1044715M	931567M	1411449M	Net Sales ($)	2035M	7298M	17317M	36012M	117246M	1231541M
708892M	602255M	1068470M	Total Assets ($)	1826M	42737M	10015M	24759M	83110M	906023M

© RMA 2005

M = $ thousand   MM = $ million
See Pages 11 through 21 for Explanation of Ratios and Data

Current Data Sorted By Assets   Comparative Historical Data

0-500M	500M-2MM	2-10MM	10-50MM	50-100MM	100-250MM	Type of Statement		
	1 2 1	4 5 2 1	1			Unqualified Reviewed Compiled Tax Returns Other	5 4 5 13	7 5 5 17
		4 (4/1-9/30/04)		23 (10/1/04-3/31/05)			4/1/00- 3/31/01 ALL	4/1/01- 3/31/02 ALL
	4	15	7		1	NUMBER OF STATEMENTS	27	34
%	%	%	%	%	%	ASSETS	%	%
		4.0				Cash & Equivalents	9.3	8.6
		24.1				Trade Receivables (net)	24.2	24.3
		43.3				Inventory	30.4	29.7
		.4				All Other Current	1.3	.7
		71.8				Total Current	65.3	63.4
		23.9				Fixed Assets (net)	22.7	23.4
		.4				Intangibles (net)	5.4	7.8
		3.9				All Other Non-Current	6.6	5.4
		100.0				Total	100.0	100.0
						LIABILITIES		
		6.4				Notes Payable-Short Term	8.0	9.0
		3.0				Cur. Mat.-L/T/D	6.0	3.9
		13.7				Trade Payables	9.3	8.9
		.2				Income Taxes Payable	.4	.4
		7.7				All Other Current	7.1	7.9
		31.0				Total Current	30.8	30.1
		16.8				Long-Term Debt	17.0	18.9
		1.2				Deferred Taxes	.9	.5
		4.7				All Other Non-Current	7.4	6.6
		46.3				Net Worth	43.9	43.9
		100.0				Total Liabilities & Net Worth	100.0	100.0
						INCOME DATA		
		100.0				Net Sales	100.0	100.0
		26.3				Gross Profit	35.8	35.9
		23.4				Operating Expenses	27.0	26.8
		2.9				Operating Profit	8.8	9.1
		.7				All Other Expenses (net)	1.8	2.0
		2.1				Profit Before Taxes	7.0	7.2
						RATIOS		
		3.2					5.0	4.1
		2.0				Current	2.8	2.8
		1.7					1.3	1.7
		1.5					2.7	2.1
		.9				Quick	1.3	1.3
		.5					.6	.6
	32	11.3					36 10.1	34 10.9
	36	10.0				Sales/Receivables	42 8.6	37 9.9
	47	7.8					56 6.5	48 7.7
	62	5.9					68 5.4	56 6.5
	88	4.2				Cost of Sales/Inventory	92 4.0	73 5.0
	126	2.9					112 3.3	112 3.3
	12	31.4					11 33.0	12 29.9
	25	14.7				Cost of Sales/Payables	28 13.3	20 18.0
	44	8.3					44 8.4	29 12.7
		4.6					3.5	4.1
		5.8				Sales/Working Capital	6.3	5.7
		8.8					16.4	8.1
		5.2					7.1	6.5
	(14)	2.5				EBIT/Interest	(22) 2.7	(29) 3.6
		1.5					1.2	2.0
						Net Profit + Depr., Dep., Amort./Cur. Mat. L /T/D		
		.2					.3	.3
		.5				Fixed/Worth	.9	.6
		.7					1.5	1.1
		.5					.4	.5
		1.3				Debt/Worth	1.7	1.4
		2.1					5.9	3.2
		19.9					39.0	76.1
		9.0				% Profit Before Taxes/Tangible Net Worth	(24) 17.8	(31) 17.9
		2.6					2.9	8.1
		5.9					20.2	21.1
		3.0				% Profit Before Taxes/Total Assets	10.9	9.1
		1.6					1.9	3.5
		21.9					17.5	19.7
		11.8				Sales/Net Fixed Assets	8.1	12.7
		4.7					5.4	5.0
		2.8					2.5	2.7
		2.2				Sales/Total Assets	1.8	2.0
		2.0					1.4	1.5
		.9					.7	.6
	(14)	1.7				% Depr., Dep., Amort./Sales	(17) 2.4	(21) 3.1
		2.0					3.5	3.8
						% Officers', Directors', Owners' Comp/Sales		2.9
							(10) 4.7	
								8.0
	14717M	133894M	336553M		256397M	Net Sales ($)	706405M	1098407M
	5317M	58307M	149885M		231662M	Total Assets ($)	504017M	666614M

D A T A   N O T   A V A I L A B L E   (columns 0-500M and 50-100MM)

M = $ thousand   MM = $ million
See Pages 11 through 21 for Explanation of Ratios and Data

Comparative Historical Data				Current Data Sorted By Sales					

				Type of Statement						
12	9	5	Unqualified		1	2	1	1	
6	8	6	Reviewed	1		2	3		
1	7	4	Compiled	1	1	2			
1		1	Tax Returns			1			
10	11	11	Other		1		3	7	
4/1/02- 3/31/03 ALL	4/1/03- 3/31/04 ALL	4/1/04- 3/31/05 ALL		4 (4/1-9/30/04)			23 (10/1/04-3/31/05)		
				0-1MM	1-3MM	3-5MM	5-10MM	10-25MM	25MM & OVER
30	35	27	**NUMBER OF STATEMENTS**	2	3	7	7	8
%	%	%	**ASSETS**	%	%	%	%	%	%
7.1	7.0	6.9	Cash & Equivalents						
22.9	24.0	24.7	Trade Receivables (net)						
37.2	32.5	36.4	Inventory						
1.2	1.5	.9	All Other Current						
68.5	65.0	68.9	Total Current						
22.1	21.2	22.2	Fixed Assets (net)						
3.5	6.4	3.6	Intangibles (net)						
5.9	7.4	5.3	All Other Non-Current						
100.0	100.0	100.0	Total						
			LIABILITIES						
8.1	12.8	6.8	Notes Payable-Short Term						
7.1	3.1	2.9	Cur. Mat.-L/T/D						
9.0	10.9	13.0	Trade Payables						
.5	.1	.1	Income Taxes Payable						
7.6	8.1	7.9	All Other Current						
32.4	35.0	30.9	Total Current						
14.8	11.2	15.4	Long-Term Debt						
.8	.6	.7	Deferred Taxes						
4.6	9.5	4.7	All Other Non-Current						
47.4	43.7	48.4	Net Worth						
100.0	100.0	100.0	Total Liabilities & Net Worth						
			INCOME DATA						
100.0	100.0	100.0	Net Sales						
32.5	29.8	30.8	Gross Profit						
26.9	23.4	25.5	Operating Expenses						
5.6	6.4	5.3	Operating Profit						
1.7	1.5	1.1	All Other Expenses (net)						
3.9	4.9	4.2	Profit Before Taxes						
			RATIOS						
3.7	3.9	4.7							
2.2	1.6	2.0	Current						
1.5	1.3	1.7							
2.0	2.1	1.9							
1.0	.7	1.1	Quick						
.5	.5	.5							
33 11.1	35 10.3	33 11.1							
36 10.1	44 8.3	36 10.0	Sales/Receivables						
44 8.2	49 7.4	48 7.7							
70 5.2	67 5.5	58 6.2							
96 3.8	80 4.6	78 4.7	Cost of Sales/Inventory						
122 3.0	97 3.7	116 3.1							
12 30.1	11 32.0	11 31.8							
21 17.8	24 15.2	30 12.1	Cost of Sales/Payables						
32 11.4	48 7.6	44 8.3							
4.4	4.6	3.7							
5.4	6.5	5.8	Sales/Working Capital						
10.7	17.3	9.7							
5.8	7.3	13.6							
(26) 4.2	(30) 4.2	(25) 2.6	EBIT/Interest						
1.5	1.8	1.5							
3.1	2.9		Net Profit + Depr., Dep.,						
(10) 2.4	(11) 2.0		Amort./Cur. Mat. L/T/D						
1.2	.7								
.2	.3	.2							
.5	.6	.5	Fixed/Worth						
1.0	1.1	.8							
.7	.6	.4							
1.3	1.6	1.3	Debt/Worth						
2.1	2.5	2.3							
28.4	31.4	31.1	% Profit Before Taxes/Tangible						
(29) 16.0	(31) 19.1	(25) 12.4	Net Worth						
7.9	8.5	4.5							
15.7	16.0	12.9	% Profit Before Taxes/Total						
7.1	5.4	4.1	Assets						
1.2	1.8	1.6							
21.8	17.9	20.2							
9.6	9.5	11.8	Sales/Net Fixed Assets						
5.7	6.1	6.8							
2.5	2.4	2.8							
2.1	2.0	2.1	Sales/Total Assets						
1.6	1.6	1.8							
1.4	1.3	1.1							
(23) 2.0	(27) 1.9	(21) 1.8	% Depr., Dep., Amort./Sales						
4.4	3.1	3.2							
		2.2	% Officers', Directors',						
	(10)	5.3	Owners' Comp/Sales						
		8.6							
786875M	682567M	741561M	Net Sales ($)	3673M	13402M	48571M	82965M	592950M
434339M	385610M	445171M	Total Assets ($)	2074M	6879M	23013M	31658M	381547M

M = $ thousand   MM = $ million
See Pages 11 through 21 for Explanation of Ratios and Data

Current Data Sorted By Assets | **Comparative Historical Data**

	0-500M	500M-2MM	2-10MM	10-50MM	50-100MM	100-250MM	Type of Statement	4/1/00-3/31/01 ALL	4/1/01-3/31/02 ALL
		3	33	33	8	13	Unqualified	67	55
	10	27	58	12	1		Reviewed	76	81
	15	32	35	2	2		Compiled	102	76
	10	38	12	2		1	Tax Returns	32	22
	10	35	61	44	7	4	Other	128	113
		100 (4/1-9/30/04)			396 (10/1/04-3/31/05)				
	35	135	199	93	16	18	**NUMBER OF STATEMENTS**	405	347
	%	%	%	%	%	%	**ASSETS**	%	%
	14.1	10.0	6.7	7.1	7.3	6.7	Cash & Equivalents	7.5	7.5
	23.4	28.9	28.1	25.2	22.6	19.9	Trade Receivables (net)	27.5	25.1
	20.8	27.4	27.1	28.3	27.9	22.1	Inventory	26.4	27.5
	5.9	2.8	2.6	4.2	1.1	5.7	All Other Current	2.7	2.3
	64.2	69.1	64.5	64.9	58.8	54.4	Total Current	64.1	62.4
	29.9	20.8	25.5	21.3	25.1	25.4	Fixed Assets (net)	25.9	26.5
	1.0	4.2	3.8	6.8	11.3	13.9	Intangibles (net)	4.1	4.8
	4.9	6.0	6.2	6.9	4.7	6.4	All Other Non-Current	5.9	6.3
	100.0	100.0	100.0	100.0	100.0	100.0	Total	100.0	100.0
							LIABILITIES		
	13.4	12.7	10.6	10.9	8.9	3.1	Notes Payable-Short Term	12.5	12.8
	7.0	3.4	3.7	3.5	2.7	4.0	Cur. Mat.-L/T/D	3.7	4.2
	14.4	16.8	15.4	14.8	11.8	12.1	Trade Payables	16.5	15.3
	1.1	.3	.2	.4	.0	.3	Income Taxes Payable	.4	.4
	21.0	10.1	9.7	10.5	11.9	10.2	All Other Current	11.2	11.8
	57.0	43.1	39.6	40.1	35.3	29.7	Total Current	44.3	44.5
	41.8	18.8	14.0	16.4	21.5	17.0	Long-Term Debt	16.5	18.4
	.0	.2	.6	.6	1.1	2.1	Deferred Taxes	.5	.3
	11.1	7.1	5.6	5.5	3.5	6.9	All Other Non-Current	11.2	5.1
	-9.8	30.8	40.2	37.4	38.7	44.3	Net Worth	27.5	31.7
	100.0	100.0	100.0	100.0	100.0	100.0	Total Liabilities & Net Worth	100.0	100.0
							INCOME DATA		
	100.0	100.0	100.0	100.0	100.0	100.0	Net Sales	100.0	100.0
	48.5	41.1	32.7	28.2	31.1	31.7	Gross Profit	35.7	36.0
	45.7	36.4	28.3	21.9	24.1	24.8	Operating Expenses	30.3	30.9
	2.9	4.7	4.4	6.4	7.1	6.8	Operating Profit	5.4	5.0
	1.1	1.3	.9	1.3	1.1	1.3	All Other Expenses (net)	1.7	1.8
	1.7	3.3	3.5	5.1	6.0	5.6	Profit Before Taxes	3.7	3.2
							RATIOS		
	2.9	2.7	2.7	3.0	2.9	2.7		2.3	2.2
	1.4	1.7	1.6	1.6	1.8	2.0	Current	1.4	1.5
	.8	1.2	1.1	1.2	1.1	1.4		1.1	1.1
	1.9	1.5	1.6	1.4	1.6	1.2		1.3	1.2
	.9	.9	.9	.7	.9	1.0	Quick	.8	.8
	.4	.5	.5	.5	.6	.7		.5	.4
	(1) 255.6	(25) 14.6	(32) 11.5	(35) 10.4	(37) 10.0	(33) 11.2		(31) 11.7	(29) 12.6
	16 22.7	37 9.8	46 7.9	50 7.3	56 6.6	48 7.7	Sales/Receivables	44 8.3	44 8.2
	37 10.0	54 6.8	59 6.1	66 5.5	65 5.6	56 6.5		58 6.3	57 6.4
	0 UND	27 13.7	33 11.0	45 8.1	53 6.9	42 8.7		33 11.0	35 10.4
	26 13.8	56 6.5	64 5.7	72 5.1	81 4.5	80 4.6	Cost of Sales/Inventory	62 5.9	69 5.3
	65 5.6	110 3.3	111 3.3	128 2.9	158 2.3	121 3.0		106 3.4	119 3.1
	1 323.5	16 22.3	19 19.0	21 17.5	22 16.2	21 17.7		18 20.4	18 20.8
	15 24.9	30 12.0	32 11.6	34 10.7	37 10.0	34 10.6	Cost of Sales/Payables	34 10.6	33 11.1
	40 9.0	57 6.4	55 6.6	54 6.8	45 8.2	52 7.1		56 6.5	58 6.3
	11.1	5.5	4.7	3.6	3.8	4.2		6.0	5.3
	24.3	9.8	8.8	8.7	7.0	5.8	Sales/Working Capital	11.5	10.1
	-26.9	29.7	41.1	23.1	25.4	19.2		53.3	47.1
	7.3	8.0	13.6	16.6	12.2	10.0		7.1	5.1
	(28) 2.0	(115) 3.4	(179) 5.0	(86) 4.0	7.5	5.9	EBIT/Interest	(360) 2.7	(312) 2.2
	-1.5	1.2	1.1	1.9	3.6	2.5		1.2	.7
		3.7	4.8	15.5		15.6	Net Profit + Depr., Dep.,	5.0	3.5
		(13) 1.3	(53) 2.3	(31) 3.3		(10) 3.1	Amort./Cur. Mat. L /T/D	(108) 2.3	(83) 2.0
		.8	1.1	1.5		1.8		1.0	1.1
	.4	.2	.3	.2	.5	.4		.3	.3
	3.6	.6	.6	.7	.9	.8	Fixed/Worth	.8	.9
	-1.5	2.5	1.8	1.6	1.9	1.9		2.2	2.5
	1.4	1.0	.7	.7	.8	.9		1.0	.8
	5.6	2.3	1.7	2.3	2.8	2.0	Debt/Worth	2.0	2.2
	-3.4	8.7	4.9	4.9	5.6	3.7		5.9	7.4
	72.8	63.3	43.7	54.0	75.6	44.3	% Profit Before Taxes/Tangible	54.2	40.0
	(22) 18.4	(115) 19.4	(181) 16.6	(81) 27.5	(14) 35.2	(17) 29.2	Net Worth	(343) 21.8	(296) 16.6
	-.8	3.3	2.6	9.3	12.3	6.9		5.9	1.8
	19.0	14.2	14.8	16.7	13.9	10.8	% Profit Before Taxes/Total	16.6	12.6
	4.0	5.3	6.5	7.4	10.2	7.1	Assets	6.4	4.7
	-10.7	.6	.8	2.2	3.1	3.8		.9	-.7
	53.3	50.6	25.8	21.7	12.7	12.8		26.3	21.0
	18.8	17.7	10.6	9.5	5.4	5.8	Sales/Net Fixed Assets	10.7	9.4
	7.7	8.9	4.9	5.1	4.2	3.7		4.9	4.7
	7.0	3.7	2.8	2.2	2.2	1.8		3.1	2.9
	3.4	2.6	2.0	1.7	1.4	1.5	Sales/Total Assets	2.2	2.0
	2.4	1.8	1.4	1.3	1.1	1.2		1.6	1.4
	1.1	.9	1.0	1.0	1.8	1.6		.9	.9
	(21) 2.0	(104) 1.6	(184) 2.2	(86) 1.7	(14) 2.4	(14) 2.6	% Depr., Dep., Amort./Sales	(344) 1.9	(315) 1.9
	3.9	3.4	4.0	3.2	3.0	4.7		3.5	3.7
	4.9	3.2	2.1	1.3				2.3	3.0
	(19) 10.1	(68) 4.7	(59) 3.5	(18) 2.1			% Officers', Directors', Owners' Comp/Sales	(137) 5.3	(124) 5.6
	16.3	7.7	6.0	5.8				9.4	9.5
	47707M	427019M	2086456M	3413069M	1571108M	4081244M	Net Sales ($)	9498145M	7990472M
	10308M	150895M	970667M	1934485M	995071M	2391231M	Total Assets ($)	5274911M	4961708M

M = $ thousand   MM = $ million
See Pages 11 through 21 for Explanation of Ratios and Data

Comparative Historical Data / Current Data Sorted By Sales

Comparative Historical Data			Type of Statement	Current Data Sorted By Sales					
83	85	90	Unqualified	1	1	4	9	27	48
89	92	98	Reviewed	2	12	20	29	22	13
65	121	79	Compiled	5	21	14	23	16	
34	55	68	Tax Returns	12	28	10	11	6	1
142	171	161	Other	10	30	14	32	35	40
4/1/02-3/31/03 ALL	4/1/03-3/31/04 ALL	4/1/04-3/31/05 ALL		100 (4/1-9/30/04)			396 (10/1/04-3/31/05)		
				0-1MM	1-3MM	3-5MM	5-10MM	10-25MM	25MM & OVER
413	524	496	**NUMBER OF STATEMENTS**	30	92	62	104	106	102
%	%	%	**ASSETS**	%	%	%	%	%	%
8.2	7.5	8.2	Cash & Equivalents	9.3	11.5	7.9	8.0	6.3	7.3
24.7	26.4	27.0	Trade Receivables (net)	16.9	24.2	28.8	29.4	28.3	27.3
25.8	26.9	26.8	Inventory	19.0	25.6	27.5	26.0	31.2	26.1
2.9	3.0	3.3	All Other Current	1.3	3.9	3.5	2.6	2.8	4.2
61.6	63.7	65.3	Total Current	46.5	65.2	67.7	66.1	68.7	64.9
26.8	24.8	23.7	Fixed Assets (net)	36.4	26.3	21.0	24.6	19.8	22.4
5.6	5.6	4.9	Intangibles (net)	7.1	2.9	4.3	4.0	4.7	7.5
6.0	5.9	6.1	All Other Non-Current	9.9	5.5	7.0	5.3	6.8	5.2
100.0	100.0	100.0	Total	100.0	100.0	100.0	100.0	100.0	100.0
			LIABILITIES						
11.8	11.8	11.1	Notes Payable-Short Term	10.8	10.2	14.5	9.8	12.0	10.3
4.0	3.4	3.8	Cur. Mat.-L/T/D	7.7	4.0	2.9	4.1	2.9	3.5
14.4	15.2	15.3	Trade Payables	9.8	13.6	16.1	16.2	16.1	16.5
.2	.3	.3	Income Taxes Payable	.0	.1	.8	.4	.1	.4
10.7	11.6	10.8	All Other Current	18.6	9.7	11.0	10.9	8.6	11.7
41.0	42.3	41.4	Total Current	47.0	37.7	45.3	41.4	39.8	42.4
18.5	16.1	18.1	Long-Term Debt	49.0	24.2	16.5	12.7	11.3	16.9
.5	.5	.5	Deferred Taxes	.1	.3	.4	.5	.5	1.0
5.5	6.0	6.4	All Other Non-Current	9.9	6.0	7.9	6.8	5.8	4.8
34.5	35.0	33.7	Net Worth	−6.0	31.8	29.8	38.6	42.7	34.9
100.0	100.0	100.0	Total Liabilities & Net Worth	100.0	100.0	100.0	100.0	100.0	100.0
			INCOME DATA						
100.0	100.0	100.0	Net Sales	100.0	100.0	100.0	100.0	100.0	100.0
35.5	34.5	35.2	Gross Profit	51.8	44.0	37.0	34.5	29.7	27.6
30.5	30.0	30.3	Operating Expenses	43.8	41.1	32.7	30.3	24.6	20.9
5.1	4.5	4.9	Operating Profit	8.0	2.9	4.3	4.1	5.1	6.7
1.4	1.1	1.1	All Other Expenses (net)	3.8	1.0	.8	1.0	.6	1.2
3.6	3.3	3.8	Profit Before Taxes	4.2	2.0	3.5	3.1	4.4	5.5
			RATIOS						
2.4	2.6	2.8		4.6	2.8	2.6	2.8	3.1	2.4
1.5	1.6	1.6	Current	1.7	1.8	1.5	1.7	1.7	1.5
1.1	1.1	1.1		.8	1.2	1.1	1.1	1.2	1.1
1.3	1.4	1.5		1.9	1.4	1.6	1.8	1.7	1.2
.8	.8	.9	Quick	.9	.9	.8	.9	.8	.9
.5	.5	.5		.5	.5	.5	.6	.5	.5

28	13.1	29	12.6	29	12.8	Sales/Receivables	10	37.9	17	21.7	30	12.3	29	12.4	30	12.0	34	10.8
41	8.9	42	8.6	45	8.2		37	10.0	36	10.0	45	8.0	45	8.2	45	8.1	48	7.5
54	6.8	60	6.1	58	6.3		70	5.2	54	6.7	63	5.8	58	6.3	56	6.6	60	6.1
35	10.5	36	10.1	33	11.2	Cost of Sales/Inventory	0	UND	28	13.0	34	10.7	29	12.6	35	10.4	41	8.9
61	6.0	65	5.6	64	5.7		53	6.9	69	5.3	67	5.5	61	6.0	69	5.3	64	5.7
102	3.6	103	3.5	114	3.2		154	2.4	146	2.5	113	3.2	102	3.6	110	3.3	100	3.7
17	21.9	18	20.2	18	20.7	Cost of Sales/Payables	0	UND	8	48.2	14	25.5	20	18.6	18	19.9	22	16.4
32	11.4	32	11.3	32	11.3		30	12.2	30	12.0	36	10.2	29	12.4	32	11.5	34	10.6
49	7.5	53	6.9	54	6.7		76	4.8	63	5.8	58	6.3	53	6.8	45	8.0	51	7.2

5.6	5.1	4.9	Sales/Working Capital	5.1	5.1	4.6	5.2	4.8	4.6
10.8	9.8	9.5		9.8	9.8	12.0	9.0	8.2	9.6
43.7	49.2	34.4		−27.6	24.9	63.1	47.6	25.0	26.2

	8.2		11.0		11.2	EBIT/Interest		4.4		7.4		16.7		9.0		23.7		14.3
(370)	3.2	(470)	3.6	(442)	4.2		(26)	1.6	(75)	3.4	(55)	3.9	(90)	3.7	(98)	7.0	(98)	6.1
	1.2		1.1		1.3			−2.4		.8		1.4		1.3		1.2		2.6
	4.6		7.4		5.3	Net Profit + Depr., Dep., Amort./Cur. Mat. L/T/D						1.5		5.1		5.6		14.3
(101)	2.6	(119)	2.7	(113)	2.6						(12)	1.0	(22)	2.5	(26)	2.7	(43)	3.3
	1.2		1.2		1.2							.4		1.0		1.4		1.7

.3	.3	.2	Fixed/Worth	.5	.3	.2	.2	.2	.3
.8	.7	.7		5.5	.8	.8	.6	.5	.7
2.8	2.3	2.0		−1.4	2.3	2.8	1.8	1.3	1.6
.9	.8	.8	Debt/Worth	1.0	.8	1.1	.7	.6	1.0
2.2	2.0	2.0		8.2	2.3	2.6	1.8	1.4	2.6
6.4	6.1	5.8		−3.3	6.6	22.4	4.8	4.2	4.9

	47.3		46.2		49.5	% Profit Before Taxes/Tangible Net Worth		45.5		66.6		40.4		37.7		44.1		62.6
(351)	20.7	(444)	20.9	(430)	20.6		(19)	11.2	(81)	12.2	(49)	12.1	(96)	17.2	(93)	20.9	(92)	33.6
	4.3		2.4		3.5			−2.1		−1.5		1.7		2.7		3.7		13.1
14.5	15.0	15.6	% Profit Before Taxes/Total Assets	8.0	15.7	11.0	16.6	17.1	16.2
6.1	6.3	6.4		3.0	4.5	5.6	6.2	8.3	9.0
.7	.3	.9		−11.1	−.8	.8	1.3	.6	3.5
24.7	26.1	29.2	Sales/Net Fixed Assets	16.7	33.9	44.9	34.3	29.3	17.9
9.5	11.0	11.7		6.9	12.4	16.0	12.6	14.9	9.1
4.6	4.9	5.2		1.8	4.6	5.9	5.0	6.9	4.9
2.9	3.0	2.9	Sales/Total Assets	2.4	3.4	3.5	3.4	2.9	2.6
2.0	2.2	2.1		1.5	2.4	2.2	2.1	2.3	1.8
1.4	1.5	1.4		.7	1.5	1.5	1.5	1.6	1.4

	1.2		1.0		1.0	% Depr., Dep., Amort./Sales		1.5		1.2		.9		.9		.7		1.0
(365)	2.3	(434)	2.1	(423)	2.0		(21)	3.9	(68)	2.3	(52)	2.0	(93)	2.6	(96)	1.6	(93)	1.8
	4.4		3.6		3.8			6.7		4.4		4.3		4.9		2.5		3.1
	2.7		2.5		2.4	% Officers', Directors', Owners' Comp/Sales		7.3		3.4		3.3		2.4		1.7		.8
(138)	4.4	(168)	4.7	(167)	4.5		(16)	14.1	(41)	4.9	(25)	4.6	(39)	3.8	(30)	3.3	(16)	1.8
	9.7		7.9		7.7			20.5		8.1		6.6		8.0		5.7		5.6

9936618M	11791398M	11626603M	Net Sales ($)	17519M	188433M	234205M	753009M	1733792M	8699645M
6460579M	6922041M	6452657M	Total Assets ($)	15401M	135452M	118751M	417685M	873654M	4891714M

M = $ thousand   MM = $ million
See Pages 11 through 21 for Explanation of Ratios and Data

WHOLESALE TRADE

WHOLESALE—Automobile and Other Motor Vehicle Merchant Wholesalers   NAICS 423110   (SIC 5012)

Current Data Sorted By Assets   **Comparative Historical Data**

Type of Statement	0-500M	500M-2MM	2-10MM	10-50MM	50-100MM	100-250MM		4/1/00-3/31/01 ALL	4/1/01-3/31/02 ALL
Unqualified		2	8	27	6	5		28	27
Reviewed		7	28	23	2			58	55
Compiled	2	26	33	14	7			68	77
Tax Returns	10	21	14	3				24	27
Other	4	17	50	38	5	6		69	72
		52 (4/1-9/30/04)		292 (10/1/04-3/31/05)					
NUMBER OF STATEMENTS	16	73	133	98	13	11		247	258

	0-500M %	500M-2MM %	2-10MM %	10-50MM %	50-100MM %	100-250MM %		ALL %	ALL %
ASSETS									
Cash & Equivalents	13.9	6.6	8.3	5.8	4.6	5.4		8.3	7.6
Trade Receivables (net)	15.1	18.3	19.5	19.3	10.7	23.1		17.0	17.4
Inventory	40.6	49.4	49.5	45.9	39.8	35.5		49.2	47.0
All Other Current	2.1	4.3	2.2	3.5	3.7	1.8		2.4	3.4
Total Current	71.7	78.7	79.5	74.6	58.7	65.9		76.9	75.3
Fixed Assets (net)	23.0	13.8	14.9	17.8	24.3	23.5		16.7	17.2
Intangibles (net)	.2	1.1	1.5	2.5	7.0	2.7		2.1	2.2
All Other Non-Current	5.1	6.4	4.1	5.1	9.9	7.9		4.4	5.3
Total	100.0	100.0	100.0	100.0	100.0	100.0		100.0	100.0
LIABILITIES									
Notes Payable-Short Term	39.1	28.6	32.7	40.2	37.8	21.1		30.9	29.0
Cur. Mat.-L/T/D	8.9	1.8	2.7	2.7	5.3	7.4		3.5	3.9
Trade Payables	6.1	12.3	13.1	9.8	9.8	10.2		12.3	13.0
Income Taxes Payable	.0	.1	.3	.3	.1	.4		.1	.1
All Other Current	2.5	9.7	7.9	8.8	6.7	9.8		9.0	8.8
Total Current	56.7	52.5	56.7	61.8	59.7	48.9		55.9	54.9
Long-Term Debt	19.8	12.3	9.8	9.2	19.9	21.5		10.6	11.6
Deferred Taxes	.0	.0	.2	.6	1.3	1.9		.4	.3
All Other Non-Current	24.9	5.7	4.6	3.2	6.7	3.7		4.3	4.2
Net Worth	-1.4	29.5	28.7	25.3	12.5	23.9		28.8	28.9
Total Liabilities & Net Worth	100.0	100.0	100.0	100.0	100.0	100.0		100.0	100.0
INCOME DATA									
Net Sales	100.0	100.0	100.0	100.0	100.0	100.0		100.0	100.0
Gross Profit	31.6	21.4	22.4	19.2	24.9	31.1		18.9	20.7
Operating Expenses	26.0	20.5	19.6	16.8	22.3	25.5		16.9	18.5
Operating Profit	5.6	.9	2.8	2.3	2.6	5.6		2.0	2.1
All Other Expenses (net)	.7	.1	.5	-.2	.9	3.7		.5	.7
Profit Before Taxes	4.8	.8	2.3	2.5	1.7	2.0		1.5	1.4

RATIOS	0-500M	500M-2MM	2-10MM	10-50MM	50-100MM	100-250MM		ALL	ALL
Current	2.3	2.6	1.9	1.4	1.1	1.6		1.9	2.0
	1.2	1.6	1.3	1.2	1.0	1.1		1.3	1.3
	.7	1.2	1.1	1.0	.9	.9		1.1	1.0
Quick	1.4	.9	.8	.5	.3	1.1		.7	.7
	.5	.5	.5	.4	.3	.3	(246)	.4 (254)	.4
	.0	.2	.2	.2	.2	.2		.2	.2
Sales/Receivables	0 UND	1 563.6	7 55.1	11 34.5	6 57.6	15 24.7		5 71.8	5 71.4
	8 47.0	7 50.2	17 21.1	21 17.4	16 22.4	32 11.4		13 27.7	14 26.6
	30 12.0	37 9.9	40 9.1	34 10.6	23 15.9	61 6.0		25 14.4	30 12.3
Cost of Sales/Inventory	0 UND	22 16.7	33 11.2	45 8.2	44 8.4	34 10.7		28 13.0	27 13.6
	44 8.3	42 8.7	61 5.9	65 5.6	66 5.5	101 3.6		61 5.9	53 6.9
	73 5.0	90 4.1	96 3.8	99 3.7	79 4.6	225 1.6		100 3.7	98 3.7
Cost of Sales/Payables	0 UND	0 848.3	4 86.0	5 73.1	5 71.6	13 28.0		3 119.9	3 119.6
	2 216.6	6 59.3	11 33.8	12 31.6	9 42.4	16 23.2		9 41.0	10 37.6
	17 21.9	21 17.1	34 10.7	22 16.8	24 15.4	56 6.5		25 14.7	28 12.9
Sales/Working Capital	7.7	9.0	9.9	12.7	67.1	6.2		10.7	8.9
	82.6	15.1	17.7	27.2	-397.3	13.7		26.5	24.8
	-50.9	60.6	52.4	118.5	-40.8	-34.3		89.2	227.0
EBIT/Interest	12.5	5.3	7.5	8.8	4.0			3.7	4.0
	(14) 2.1	(62) 2.4	(123) 2.9	(89) 4.1	(11) 2.6		(228)	1.8 (234)	1.8
	-.7	1.1	1.6	2.0	1.1			1.0	1.0
Net Profit + Depr., Dep., Amort./Cur. Mat. L/T/D			7.9	4.6				2.2	2.3
			(20) 2.6	(26) 1.9			(40)	1.4 (44)	1.1
			.9	1.3				.6	.1
Fixed/Worth	.0	.1	.1	.2	.7	.3		.1	.1
	.5	.2	.4	.7	3.2	2.6		.6	.5
	NM	2.1	1.2	1.7	-4.8	3.4		1.6	1.8
Debt/Worth	.9	.9	1.3	2.2	3.5	2.8		1.2	1.4
	3.4	2.2	2.7	3.8	17.3	6.7		3.3	3.2
	-7.4	31.8	8.9	6.6	-19.6	7.9		8.4	8.7
% Profit Before Taxes/Tangible Net Worth	99.4	37.8	34.9	41.3		19.9		38.7	37.7
	(11) 31.1	(61) 14.5	(120) 17.7	(92) 21.1		(10) 12.6	(226)	16.7 (237)	13.4
	-50.0	3.8	5.9	8.7		5.6		3.0	1.5
% Profit Before Taxes/Total Assets	30.6	12.0	9.4	8.5	7.6	4.1		9.2	8.3
	4.4	4.3	3.8	4.2	5.1	1.5		3.5	3.0
	-6.7	.3	1.6	1.5	1.2	.8		.2	.0
Sales/Net Fixed Assets	649.1	260.9	129.3	68.2	34.9	30.3		142.3	129.7
	233.4	57.2	39.0	27.1	15.1	7.5		38.4	35.3
	10.7	20.2	15.9	9.5	6.3	2.1		12.6	10.5
Sales/Total Assets	6.8	8.0	4.4	3.9	3.1	2.5		5.9	5.2
	4.7	4.2	3.3	2.8	3.0	1.7		3.6	3.3
	2.2	2.8	2.3	2.0	2.1	.7		2.4	2.0
% Depr., Dep., Amort./Sales	.1	.2	.3	.3	.5			.2	.2
	(13) .2	(54) .6	(109) .5	(92) .6	(12) 1.6		(192)	.6 (211)	.6
	3.7	2.2	1.4	1.9	4.8			1.5	1.9
% Officers', Directors', Owners' Comp/Sales		.9	.8	.3				.4	.6
		(40) 1.6	(61) 1.7	(32) 1.3			(122)	1.5 (111)	1.5
		2.4	3.5	1.3				3.4	3.9
Net Sales ($)	29307M	520411M	2297807M	6093637M	2525166M	2733889M		12100085M	8221409M
Total Assets ($)	5176M	81601M	626207M	2075289M	935751M	1639776M		3188924M	2512613M

M = $ thousand   MM = $ million
See Pages 11 through 21 for Explanation of Ratios and Data

Comparative Historical Data / Current Data Sorted By Sales

4/1/02-3/31/03 ALL	4/1/03-3/31/04 ALL	4/1/04-3/31/05 ALL	Type of Statement	0-1MM	1-3MM	3-5MM	5-10MM	10-25MM	25MM & OVER
30	40	48	Unqualified			2	2	3	41
74	55	60	Reviewed	1	3	3	10	18	25
69	82	68	Compiled	2	11	10	12	19	14
29	50	48	Tax Returns	3	12	2	13	12	6
95	127	120	Other	2	15	6	17	29	51
					52 (4/1-9/30/04)		292 (10/1/04-3/31/05)		
297	354	344	**NUMBER OF STATEMENTS**	8	41	23	54	81	137
%	%	%	**ASSETS**	%	%	%	%	%	%
8.2	8.5	7.3	Cash & Equivalents		5.6	10.0	6.4	9.7	5.7
16.4	16.4	18.8	Trade Receivables (net)		16.9	17.0	22.1	18.3	18.5
48.1	47.1	47.2	Inventory		47.7	49.2	49.6	46.3	48.0
4.9	3.4	3.1	All Other Current		2.0	2.5	2.1	4.3	3.1
77.7	75.4	76.4	Total Current		72.2	78.7	80.1	78.6	75.3
14.7	16.8	16.5	Fixed Assets (net)		21.1	15.8	12.8	14.7	16.8
1.9	2.3	1.9	Intangibles (net)		.1	2.8	3.0	1.1	2.4
5.8	5.4	5.2	All Other Non-Current		6.6	2.7	4.1	5.6	5.5
100.0	100.0	100.0	Total		100.0	100.0	100.0	100.0	100.0
			LIABILITIES						
34.1	34.2	34.1	Notes Payable-Short Term		32.6	24.6	29.9	30.4	40.0
3.8	3.1	3.0	Cur. Mat.-L/T/D		3.3	2.2	1.8	2.3	3.4
11.2	11.7	11.4	Trade Payables		8.7	10.7	15.0	12.9	10.4
.1	.1	.2	Income Taxes Payable		.0	.0	.2	.4	.3
11.4	10.4	8.3	All Other Current		4.4	6.9	9.0	10.1	8.7
60.6	59.5	57.1	Total Current		49.1	44.5	55.8	56.1	62.7
10.4	11.2	11.4	Long-Term Debt		18.6	7.7	12.3	8.6	9.8
.5	.4	.4	Deferred Taxes		.1	.2	.1	.2	.7
2.6	4.4	5.5	All Other Non-Current		14.4	3.2	4.4	4.1	4.7
26.0	24.5	25.7	Net Worth		17.8	44.5	27.3	31.1	22.1
100.0	100.0	100.0	Total Liabilities & Net Worth		100.0	100.0	100.0	100.0	100.0
			INCOME DATA						
100.0	100.0	100.0	Net Sales		100.0	100.0	100.0	100.0	100.0
19.1	21.5	22.1	Gross Profit		34.3	24.9	22.9	20.9	17.1
17.5	19.5	19.6	Operating Expenses		32.2	20.5	20.6	17.8	15.3
1.7	2.0	2.5	Operating Profit		2.1	4.4	2.3	3.2	1.8
.2	.2	.4	All Other Expenses (net)		1.4	.7	.2	.1	.2
1.5	1.8	2.1	Profit Before Taxes		.7	3.7	2.1	3.1	1.6

RATIOS

4/1/02-3/31/03 ALL	4/1/03-3/31/04 ALL	4/1/04-3/31/05 ALL	Ratio	0-1MM	1-3MM	3-5MM	5-10MM	10-25MM	25MM & OVER
1.7	1.7	1.8	Current		2.3	3.4	2.0	1.9	1.3
1.2	1.2	1.3			1.6	2.0	1.4	1.4	1.1
1.1	1.0	1.0			.9	1.2	1.1	1.1	1.0
.6	.7	.7	Quick		.9	1.2	.9	.8	.5
(294) .3	(353) .4	.4			.4	.7	.5	.4	.4
.2	.2	.2			.2	.2	.2	.2	.2
4 94.1	5 77.7	6 61.1	Sales/Receivables		7 52.5	0 UND	5 71.6	3 118.9	7 48.9
12 29.4	14 26.9	17 21.6			20 18.1	11 33.4	20 18.2	15 23.9	17 22.0
27 13.5	30 12.1	36 10.1			52 7.0	45 8.1	47 7.8	33 11.1	29 12.7
28 13.1	30 12.2	34 10.8	Cost of Sales/Inventory		39 9.2	33 11.1	36 10.1	23 16.1	39 9.5
54 6.8	59 6.2	60 6.1			82 4.4	78 4.7	61 5.9	44 8.2	60 6.1
96 3.8	96 3.8	93 3.9			130 2.8	156 2.3	111 3.3	87 4.2	86 4.3
3 122.3	3 116.9	3 119.0	Cost of Sales/Payables		0 UND	0 UND	4 99.6	3 135.1	4 85.7
8 44.9	9 39.5	10 36.6			10 37.9	11 32.0	12 29.9	10 38.3	10 37.5
20 18.1	24 15.4	26 14.0			37 9.9	34 10.8	39 9.3	34 10.7	18 20.8
11.1	10.6	10.4	Sales/Working Capital		4.7	3.2	9.3	10.3	17.4
26.1	23.9	21.1			13.1	9.1	13.6	18.7	34.3
112.8	158.2	109.2			−104.6	32.9	31.8	48.4	337.0
5.5	7.4	6.8	EBIT/Interest		3.8	12.1	6.0	9.4	7.1
(261) 2.2	(311) 2.6	(308) 3.0			(38) 1.7	(18) 4.6	(47) 2.5	(73) 3.8	(125) 3.3
1.2	1.3	1.5			−.5	1.1	1.5	1.8	1.9
4.7	4.9	5.1	Net Profit + Depr., Dep., Amort./Cur. Mat. L/T/D				2.6		6.4
(49) 1.8	(64) 1.3	(58) 2.5					(10) 1.5		(37) 2.6
.9	.7	1.0					.9		1.1
.1	.2	.2	Fixed/Worth		.2	.1	.1	.1	.2
.4	.5	.5			.8	.2	.3	.3	.8
1.5	1.7	1.7			6.8	.4	1.7	.9	2.0
1.6	1.7	1.5	Debt/Worth		1.3	.4	1.2	1.1	2.5
3.7	3.7	3.2			3.3	1.1	2.8	2.2	4.4
8.8	9.5	9.2			52.3	2.8	13.7	7.4	8.4
33.6	41.2	38.1	% Profit Before Taxes/Tangible Net Worth		37.6	35.3	31.2	34.8	41.9
(265) 15.6	(319) 18.0	(302) 17.9			(34) 11.1	(21) 17.1	(46) 10.2	(73) 19.8	(123) 22.3
4.1	4.5	6.2			−1.2	5.4	5.5	8.8	9.4
8.3	10.4	9.1	% Profit Before Taxes/Total Assets		6.0	19.4	7.8	11.1	8.1
3.7	3.6	4.1			2.0	7.8	3.2	6.0	3.9
.5	.9	1.3			−5.7	1.3	1.4	2.3	1.5
146.1	115.2	107.5	Sales/Net Fixed Assets		53.0	90.8	217.6	207.9	84.5
46.9	38.3	33.8			20.5	48.8	37.3	48.5	35.1
15.9	11.8	12.0			5.9	17.2	18.6	15.9	11.6
5.7	4.9	4.6	Sales/Total Assets		3.6	4.2	4.6	5.6	4.6
3.5	3.1	3.1			2.2	3.0	3.1	3.6	3.3
2.3	2.1	2.2			1.3	1.5	2.3	2.4	2.4
.2	.3	.3	% Depr., Dep., Amort./Sales		.4	.3	.3	.2	.3
(243) .5	(287) .6	(285) .6			(33) 1.8	(17) .9	(46) .6	(59) .5	(123) .5
1.6	1.9	1.8			3.4	1.8	1.6	1.8	1.1
.5	.7	.6	% Officers', Directors', Owners' Comp/Sales		2.1	1.5	1.1	.5	.3
(137) 1.1	(144) 1.6	(143) 1.3			(20) 3.6	(10) 2.8	(29) 2.2	(42) 1.0	(40) .7
2.7	3.0	3.2			8.2	8.3	3.1	2.4	1.1
9467805M	13877628M	14200217M	Net Sales ($)	4172M	82331M	86137M	402364M	1388118M	12237095M
3122431M	4503498M	5363800M	Total Assets ($)	2698M	61403M	38217M	161996M	535173M	4564313M

Current Data Sorted By Assets   Comparative Historical Data

						Type of Statement		
1	3	20	29	12	6	Unqualified	69	58
4	16	74	25	1		Reviewed	162	117
14	49	52	4			Compiled	162	154
19	29	19			1	Tax Returns	45	36
7	26	51	35	7	1	Other	159	177
	117 (4/1-9/30/04)			388 (10/1/04-3/31/05)			4/1/00-3/31/01	4/1/01-3/31/02
0-500M	500M-2MM	2-10MM	10-50MM	50-100MM	100-250MM		ALL	ALL
45	123	216	93	20	8	NUMBER OF STATEMENTS	597	542
%	%	%	%	%	%	**ASSETS**	%	%
7.4	8.1	5.7	3.7	1.3		Cash & Equivalents	5.3	5.2
23.2	25.4	24.6	23.2	22.9		Trade Receivables (net)	24.5	24.1
44.1	45.0	49.6	47.7	50.3		Inventory	48.4	48.0
1.5	1.5	1.2	2.5	1.4		All Other Current	1.7	1.7
76.2	80.1	81.1	77.0	75.8		Total Current	79.9	79.0
16.0	11.7	10.5	14.4	11.3		Fixed Assets (net)	12.2	12.5
1.9	2.8	2.7	3.1	8.5		Intangibles (net)	2.6	3.3
5.9	5.5	5.7	5.4	4.4		All Other Non-Current	5.2	5.1
100.0	100.0	100.0	100.0	100.0		Total	100.0	100.0
						LIABILITIES		
13.1	13.6	17.3	20.5	14.3		Notes Payable-Short Term	16.1	16.8
3.2	3.1	1.9	2.1	2.1		Cur. Mat.-L/T/D	3.2	3.0
22.8	22.9	23.0	20.8	17.6		Trade Payables	22.8	22.1
.2	.1	.2	.1	.4		Income Taxes Payable	.2	.1
17.2	9.4	6.5	7.7	8.1		All Other Current	7.7	8.5
56.4	49.1	49.0	51.2	42.5		Total Current	50.1	50.6
19.5	13.0	7.8	7.9	16.9		Long-Term Debt	11.5	13.1
.0	.1	.2	.2	.2		Deferred Taxes	.2	.1
8.8	3.4	5.9	6.0	4.7		All Other Non-Current	4.1	4.0
15.3	34.4	37.2	34.8	35.6		Net Worth	34.2	32.2
100.0	100.0	100.0	100.0	100.0		Total Liabilities & Net Worth	100.0	100.0
						INCOME DATA		
100.0	100.0	100.0	100.0	100.0		Net Sales	100.0	100.0
39.8	32.3	30.2	28.3	33.9		Gross Profit	31.4	31.6
38.6	28.2	26.6	24.7	29.1		Operating Expenses	28.6	28.8
1.2	4.1	3.6	3.6	4.8		Operating Profit	2.8	2.8
1.3	.9	.4	.6	.9		All Other Expenses (net)	1.0	.9
-.1	3.3	3.2	2.9	4.0		Profit Before Taxes	1.8	1.9
						RATIOS		
2.7	2.7	2.4	2.1	2.3			2.6	2.4
1.4	1.7	1.6	1.4	1.8		Current	1.6	1.6
.9	1.2	1.3	1.1	1.4			1.2	1.2
.9	1.1	.9	.7	.8			1.0	.9
(44) .5	.7	.6	.5	.6		Quick	.6	.6
.3	.4	.4	.4	.3			.4	.3
6 58.1	18 20.9	24 15.5	28 13.1	31 11.7			25 14.9	24 15.1
17 22.0	31 11.8	34 10.9	34 10.6	36 10.2		Sales/Receivables	33 10.9	33 11.1
31 11.7	41 8.9	46 7.9	48 7.6	55 6.6			45 8.0	44 8.3
39 9.3	47 7.8	67 5.4	73 5.0	102 3.6			68 5.4	68 5.4
71 5.2	87 4.2	105 3.5	107 3.4	120 3.0		Cost of Sales/Inventory	110 3.3	105 3.5
118 3.1	130 2.8	156 2.3	161 2.3	164 2.2			160 2.3	149 2.5
12 30.4	24 14.9	24 15.3	28 13.2	31 11.9			27 13.3	24 15.1
37 9.8	39 9.3	41 9.0	44 8.3	43 8.5		Cost of Sales/Payables	44 8.4	41 8.8
67 5.4	55 6.6	63 5.8	67 5.4	58 6.3			64 5.7	64 5.7
6.2	5.1	4.7	5.4	4.9			4.6	5.1
20.5	8.4	8.2	9.5	7.6		Sales/Working Capital	8.5	9.1
-56.6	34.5	16.2	29.9	11.4			18.3	18.6
3.9	13.3	13.2	7.3	10.4			5.1	5.8
(38) 1.6	(107) 3.4	(200) 4.2	(81) 3.7	5.5		EBIT/Interest	(546) 2.2	(498) 2.4
-2.8	1.4	1.7	1.7	2.8			1.1	1.1
	6.8	6.8	9.1	7.0			4.0	4.1
	(18) 2.3	(63) 2.9	(33) 3.5	(12) 3.7		Net Profit + Depr., Dep., Amort./Cur. Mat. L /T/D	(142) 1.9	(138) 1.8
	1.1	1.0	1.6	2.0			.6	.9
.2	.1	.1	.1	.2			.1	.1
1.0	.2	.2	.3	.3		Fixed/Worth	.3	.3
-.4	.8	.7	1.1	.6			.8	.9
1.2	.9	.9	1.2	1.8			.9	1.0
3.5	2.1	1.8	2.1	2.2		Debt/Worth	2.2	2.3
-6.2	6.5	4.9	4.3	3.2			4.6	5.6
47.4	47.6	39.0	28.4	37.3			28.3	30.2
(31) 20.3	(109) 14.0	(197) 17.2	(84) 14.7	(18) 28.2		% Profit Before Taxes/Tangible Net Worth	(533) 10.6	(485) 14.2
-2.7	3.3	5.9	6.9	11.6			2.5	3.2
11.4	14.6	12.4	11.0	15.7			10.1	9.6
2.7	4.3	5.5	5.4	8.2		% Profit Before Taxes/Total Assets	3.4	3.6
-9.4	.4	1.5	1.9	3.9			.5	.4
132.8	114.9	93.0	64.4	56.7			54.3	58.6
36.8	42.9	41.8	34.9	20.8		Sales/Net Fixed Assets	29.1	29.8
15.8	19.6	20.5	13.4	13.7			15.2	15.7
5.4	3.7	3.2	2.8	3.0			3.1	3.2
3.6	2.8	2.4	2.3	1.9		Sales/Total Assets	2.4	2.5
2.8	2.1	1.8	1.7	1.7			1.9	1.9
.5	.3	.4	.5	.6			.6	.5
(37) 1.1	(89) .8	(182) .9	(83) .8	(19) 1.0		% Depr., Dep., Amort./Sales	(503) 1.0	(463) .9
1.9	1.3	1.5	1.7	1.5			1.5	1.5
4.7	2.4	1.0					1.8	1.6
(26) 8.0	(73) 4.2	(86) 2.6	(18) 1.9			% Officers', Directors', Owners' Comp/Sales	(265) 3.1	(238) 3.4
12.2	6.5	5.8	3.2				5.7	5.8
57748M	437938M	2663709M	4193535M	3210699M	2371519M	Net Sales ($)	12480272M	13619002M
13516M	149863M	1028778M	1810761M	1439233M	1447184M	Total Assets ($)	6324437M	5987632M

M = $ thousand   MM = $ million
See Pages 11 through 21 for Explanation of Ratios and Data

Comparative Historical Data | | | | **Current Data Sorted By Sales**

			Type of Statement	0-1MM	1-3MM	3-5MM	5-10MM	10-25MM	25MM & OVER
59	57	71	Unqualified	2	2	2	5	13	47
125	112	120	Reviewed	2	4	15	31	41	27
129	134	119	Compiled	9	26	33	25	24	2
68	54	68	Tax Returns	8	23	8	21	7	1
136	129	127	Other	5	20	12	20	38	32
4/1/02- 3/31/03 ALL	4/1/03- 3/31/04 ALL	4/1/04- 3/31/05 ALL		117 (4/1-9/30/04)		388 (10/1/04-3/31/05)			
517	486	505	**NUMBER OF STATEMENTS**	26	75	70	102	123	109
%	%	%	**ASSETS**	%	%	%	%	%	%
5.6	6.6	5.8	Cash & Equivalents	5.7	6.9	6.5	7.0	6.4	3.2
23.4	23.7	24.3	Trade Receivables (net)	14.9	23.9	24.5	25.6	24.8	24.8
49.1	48.3	47.5	Inventory	42.1	45.7	49.6	47.4	47.5	48.7
2.0	1.6	1.6	All Other Current	1.6	1.5	1.5	.8	1.7	2.2
80.1	80.2	79.2	Total Current	64.3	78.0	82.0	80.7	80.3	78.9
12.1	11.9	12.2	Fixed Assets (net)	26.2	12.8	10.0	11.1	10.5	12.6
3.1	2.8	3.1	Intangibles (net)	2.8	2.6	3.5	3.3	2.2	3.9
4.7	5.1	5.6	All Other Non-Current	6.6	6.6	4.4	4.9	7.0	4.6
100.0	100.0	100.0	Total	100.0	100.0	100.0	100.0	100.0	100.0
			LIABILITIES						
16.3	15.3	16.4	Notes Payable-Short Term	16.1	13.2	19.5	16.0	14.5	19.1
2.7	3.0	2.3	Cur. Mat.-L/T/D	3.7	2.2	3.7	2.4	1.7	1.9
22.2	22.0	22.3	Trade Payables	18.6	19.8	22.6	23.0	23.8	22.4
.2	.2	.2	Income Taxes Payable	.2	.1	.2	.2	.3	.2
9.3	10.0	8.4	All Other Current	17.7	13.7	6.4	5.5	7.4	7.8
50.7	50.4	49.6	Total Current	56.2	48.9	52.4	47.0	47.6	51.5
12.5	11.3	10.5	Long-Term Debt	27.0	14.8	9.5	9.7	7.1	8.9
.1	.2	.1	Deferred Taxes	.0	.0	.1	.1	.2	.3
4.9	5.2	5.5	All Other Non-Current	8.6	4.9	5.4	4.9	7.3	3.7
31.8	32.8	34.2	Net Worth	8.2	31.5	32.6	38.2	37.7	35.7
100.0	100.0	100.0	Total Liabilities & Net Worth	100.0	100.0	100.0	100.0	100.0	100.0
			INCOME DATA						
100.0	100.0	100.0	Net Sales	100.0	100.0	100.0	100.0	100.0	100.0
32.5	31.5	31.3	Gross Profit	46.4	34.8	32.3	30.6	28.2	29.0
29.8	28.6	27.8	Operating Expenses	40.0	32.0	29.2	27.6	24.2	25.1
2.7	2.9	3.6	Operating Profit	6.5	2.8	3.1	2.9	4.0	3.9
.6	.7	.7	All Other Expenses (net)	2.3	.9	.9	.2	.6	.4
2.1	2.2	2.9	Profit Before Taxes	4.2	1.9	2.3	2.7	3.3	3.4
			RATIOS						
2.5	2.5	2.5		2.7	2.6	2.4	2.8	2.3	2.0
1.7	1.7	1.6	Current	1.4	1.7	1.7	1.6	1.6	1.5
1.3	1.3	1.2		.8	1.0	1.2	1.3	1.3	1.2
.9	1.0	.9		.8	1.0	1.0	1.1	1.0	.8
.6 (485)	.6 (504)	.6	Quick	(25) .4	.6	.5	.7	.6	.5
.4	.4	.4		.1	.4	.4	.4	.4	.4
23 15.9	23 16.2	23 16.0		0 UND	15 24.9	25 14.5	23 16.0	27 13.6	27 13.4
33 11.1	32 11.3	33 11.1	Sales/Receivables	13 28.3	29 12.6	35 10.6	32 11.4	36 10.2	33 10.9
42 8.6	44 8.4	44 8.3		30 12.0	39 9.3	52 7.1	44 8.4	46 7.9	47 7.8
65 5.6	64 5.7	60 6.1		49 7.5	45 8.2	61 5.9	60 6.1	60 6.0	73 5.0
106 3.4	103 3.6	101 3.6	Cost of Sales/Inventory	114 3.2	86 4.2	101 3.6	93 3.9	103 3.5	103 3.5
165 2.2	161 2.3	150 2.4		259 1.4	152 2.4	189 1.9	147 2.5	151 2.4	142 2.6
24 15.2	24 15.0	25 14.8		22 16.8	18 20.2	30 12.1	22 16.7	25 14.4	29 12.8
38 9.6	38 9.7	41 8.9	Cost of Sales/Payables	60 6.1	35 10.4	42 8.7	37 9.9	42 8.6	42 8.7
65 5.6	63 5.8	62 5.9		79 4.6	55 6.7	62 5.9	59 6.2	66 5.5	60 6.1
4.7	4.5	5.2		4.5	5.2	5.0	5.0	5.3	6.4
8.2	8.5	8.7	Sales/Working Capital	17.3	8.2	7.0	8.7	8.1	10.3
16.2	18.5	21.4		-44.5	96.1	18.7	16.4	16.3	19.2
6.7	8.6	11.2		5.3	6.4	8.2	14.9	12.4	10.8
2.8 (478)	3.1 (449)	3.8 (454)	EBIT/Interest	2.1 (22)	2.6 (62)	2.6 (65)	4.4 (96)	4.3 (109)	4.7 (100)
1.2	1.3	1.5		-2.1	.6	1.1	2.3	1.8	2.5
4.6	5.6	7.5				5.7	6.4	8.7	8.9
2.0 (146)	2.6 (128)	3.0 (136)	Net Profit + Depr., Dep., Amort./Cur. Mat. L/T/D		(15) 2.3	(25) 3.3	(36) 2.6	(48) 4.3
1.0	1.2	1.3				.9	1.2	1.4	2.0
.1	.1	.1		.2	.1	.1	.1	.1	.1
.3	.3	.3	Fixed/Worth	1.3	.4	.3	.2	.2	.3
.7	.8	1.1		NM	3.1	1.6	1.0	.5	.8
.9	.9	1.0		1.7	.9	.8	.7	.9	1.3
2.0	2.1	2.1	Debt/Worth	4.9	2.1	2.2	1.9	1.8	2.1
4.9	5.0	5.2		NM	8.2	11.1	5.8	3.9	4.0
29.9	35.6	37.2		62.2	39.4	31.7	42.1	28.7	37.3
13.2 (457)	16.1 (441)	16.3 (446)	% Profit Before Taxes/Tangible Net Worth	19.6 (20)	11.4 (59)	14.1 (58)	19.7 (92)	15.1 (115)	23.4 (102)
2.8	3.4	5.1		-22.9	.0	3.2	7.3	5.1	8.9
9.6	11.1	11.8		11.5	10.1	9.5	13.4	11.8	11.9
3.9	4.3	5.2	% Profit Before Taxes/Total Assets	3.0	2.4	3.2	5.9	5.2	7.0
.5	.8	1.2		-10.6	-1.7	.3	2.0	2.0	2.6
64.7	78.4	84.6		152.8	65.2	117.5	112.0	82.5	71.5
34.2	36.2	39.2	Sales/Net Fixed Assets	16.8	34.8	51.7	45.0	48.8	34.4
17.0	16.4	17.5		3.6	15.4	18.5	21.1	23.7	15.3
3.2	3.2	3.2		3.2	3.8	3.1	3.4	3.2	3.0
2.4	2.5	2.5	Sales/Total Assets	1.9	2.9	2.3	2.6	2.5	2.5
1.9	1.9	1.9		1.0	2.0	1.8	1.9	1.8	2.0
.5	.5	.4		.5	.6	.3	.4	.4	.5
1.0 (454)	.9 (409)	.9 (416)	% Depr., Dep., Amort./Sales	1.8 (20)	1.1 (60)	.8 (56)	.9 (76)	.7 (108)	.8 (96)
1.5	1.5	1.6		4.1	1.7	1.6	1.5	1.3	1.4
2.0	1.6	2.0		7.2	3.2	2.0	2.2	1.4	.8
3.4 (217)	3.0 (204)	3.4 (204)	% Officers', Directors', Owners' Comp/Sales	9.3 (13)	4.7 (40)	3.2 (48)	3.0 (44)	2.4 (38)	2.0 (21)
6.1	5.5	6.8		13.0	8.0	6.4	5.8	4.1	4.1
12106376M	11589002M	12935148M	Net Sales ($)	15947M	142342M	279697M	737450M	1987030M	9772682M
5971613M	5069221M	5889335M	Total Assets ($)	11929M	59303M	144444M	328199M	886916M	4458544M

M = $ thousand   MM = $ million
See Pages 11 through 21 for Explanation of Ratios and Data

Current Data Sorted By Assets　　　　　　Comparative Historical Data

0-500M	500M-2MM	2-10MM	10-50MM	50-100MM	100-250MM	Type of Statement	4/1/00-3/31/01 ALL	4/1/01-3/31/02 ALL
		2	10	4	3	Unqualified	16	19
1	10	22	13	2		Reviewed	44	33
5	11	18	3	1		Compiled	61	62
7	7	7	3		1	Tax Returns	15	20
10	11	10	9	1	1	Other	46	38
	30 (4/1-9/30/04)		142 (10/1/04-3/31/05)					
23	39	59	38	8	5	**NUMBER OF STATEMENTS**	182	172
%	%	%	%	%	%	**ASSETS**	%	%
16.6	9.3	5.0	2.3			Cash & Equivalents	6.1	5.9
24.4	24.8	31.2	27.3			Trade Receivables (net)	28.3	26.2
32.2	35.2	40.6	40.3			Inventory	38.9	40.5
1.7	2.1	1.6	3.9			All Other Current	1.8	2.0
74.8	71.5	78.3	73.9			Total Current	75.1	74.6
17.5	19.4	15.4	19.3			Fixed Assets (net)	18.1	18.5
.8	5.9	2.1	2.3			Intangibles (net)	2.0	1.7
6.9	3.2	4.2	4.5			All Other Non-Current	4.8	5.2
100.0	100.0	100.0	100.0			Total	100.0	100.0
						LIABILITIES		
14.7	15.0	12.6	11.1			Notes Payable-Short Term	10.9	11.5
2.6	2.4	1.8	1.9			Cur. Mat.-L/T/D	3.1	3.4
44.3	28.6	37.2	35.9			Trade Payables	33.7	34.4
.1	.2	.2	.1			Income Taxes Payable	.2	.2
7.0	8.7	6.5	5.7			All Other Current	7.6	8.7
68.7	55.0	58.4	54.7			Total Current	55.5	58.1
9.9	10.2	8.5	8.2			Long-Term Debt	11.3	11.8
.0	.0	.4	.6			Deferred Taxes	.2	.2
10.6	2.7	3.4	1.9			All Other Non-Current	2.8	4.5
10.8	32.0	29.4	34.6			Net Worth	30.1	25.4
100.0	100.0	100.0	100.0			Total Liabilities & Net Worth	100.0	100.0
						INCOME DATA		
100.0	100.0	100.0	100.0			Net Sales	100.0	100.0
43.8	34.3	24.2	25.7			Gross Profit	28.1	27.5
43.8	31.8	22.4	23.8			Operating Expenses	26.7	26.2
-.1	2.5	1.7	1.9			Operating Profit	1.4	1.3
.0	.7	-.2	-.1			All Other Expenses (net)	-.6	.1
-.1	1.8	1.9	2.0			Profit Before Taxes	2.0	1.2
						RATIOS		
2.0	1.8	1.6	1.6				1.8	1.8
1.4	1.2	1.3	1.3			Current	1.4	1.4
.8	1.0	1.1	1.1				1.1	1.1
1.5	.9	.8	.7				.9	.8
.6	(38) .6	.6	.5			Quick	.6	.5
.3	.4	.4	.4				.4	.4
8　48.6	15　25.0	25　14.6	28　13.0				23　16.0	19　18.9
16　22.2	28　12.9	39　9.5	36　10.1			Sales/Receivables	34　10.8	30　12.2
28　13.2	38　9.5	47　7.8	49　7.4				47　7.8	42　8.8
34　10.7	26　14.1	50　7.3	61　6.0				46　8.0	49　7.4
47　7.7	57　6.4	66　5.6	77　4.7			Cost of Sales/Inventory	70　5.2	67　5.4
69　5.3	77　4.8	80　4.6	105　3.5				91　4.0	87　4.2
24　15.0	23　15.9	43　8.5	49　7.5				31　11.9	31　11.9
47　7.8	43　8.5	60　6.1	67　5.4			Cost of Sales/Payables	55　6.6	55　6.7
81　4.5	68　5.4	76　4.8	88　4.1				84　4.3	76　4.8
12.8	10.8	10.5	7.9				8.5	8.3
25.4	20.0	16.1	14.5			Sales/Working Capital	14.9	15.6
-21.3	110.2	31.3	38.5				86.8	78.2
7.3	7.6	11.8	13.4				7.1	6.7
(13) 2.8	(32) 3.7	(56) 3.4	(37) 4.5			EBIT/Interest	(171) 2.7	(161) 2.6
-2.8	1.6	2.0	3.2				1.3	1.1
		7.8	6.5			Net Profit + Depr., Dep.,	4.8	3.1
	(25) 2.5	(17) 3.3				Amort./Cur. Mat. L /T/D	(60) 2.4	(53) 2.0
	1.9	2.2					1.0	1.2
.3	.2	.2	.3				.3	.3
.7	.5	.4	.5			Fixed/Worth	.6	.6
-1.0	1.5	.9	.9				1.4	1.6
1.0	1.2	1.6	1.1				1.3	1.1
4.4	2.4	2.7	2.0			Debt/Worth	2.2	2.6
-8.7	7.0	4.8	4.3				6.2	6.3
41.9	41.2	33.0	26.6			% Profit Before Taxes/Tangible	26.3	25.0
(15) 9.9	(33) 21.8	(56) 15.5	14.0			Net Worth	(166) 13.2	(155) 14.0
-14.1	4.1	7.6	10.1				5.5	4.8
9.7	10.3	12.0	7.7			% Profit Before Taxes/Total	8.8	7.9
.8	4.3	4.2	4.5			Assets	3.8	3.7
-9.3	1.5	1.6	2.7				1.0	.5
84.8	46.3	52.5	30.4				41.4	46.0
32.8	29.6	30.6	14.7			Sales/Net Fixed Assets	22.1	20.5
15.9	11.9	12.1	8.7				12.1	11.1
5.6	4.1	3.8	3.1				3.7	3.9
4.5	3.3	2.9	2.6			Sales/Total Assets	3.0	3.1
2.8	2.5	2.5	2.1				2.4	2.4
.6	.8	.4	.7				.6	.6
(14) 1.1	(32) 1.5	(51) .9	(35) 1.2			% Depr., Dep., Amort./Sales	(170) 1.1	(151) 1.2
2.1	2.0	1.5	1.7				1.9	2.0
	2.5	1.1	.6			% Officers', Directors',	1.1	1.2
	(22) 3.3	(27) 1.8	(15) 1.0			Owners' Comp/Sales	(79) 2.1	(76) 2.5
	5.3	2.4	2.1				5.4	5.0
23047M	165578M	867953M	2223674M	1365352M	1744925M	Net Sales ($)	4965611M	4923476M
5806M	46581M	284149M	865931M	587055M	757505M	Total Assets ($)	1852848M	1882247M

© RMA 2005　　　　　　　M = $ thousand　　MM = $ million
See Pages 11 through 21 for Explanation of Ratios and Data

Comparative Historical Data				Current Data Sorted By Sales					
			Type of Statement					2	17
20	16	19	Unqualified					13	18
34	43	48	Reviewed	1	5	3	8	11	4
43	68	38	Compiled	2	5	5	11	4	4
22	13	25	Tax Returns	3	8	1	6	10	11
38	45	42	Other	6	11	1	3		
4/1/02-3/31/03	4/1/03-3/31/04	4/1/04-3/31/05		30 (4/1-9/30/04)			142 (10/1/04-3/31/05)		
ALL	ALL	ALL		0-1MM	1-3MM	3-5MM	5-10MM	10-25MM	25MM & OVER
157	185	172	**NUMBER OF STATEMENTS**	12	29	10	27	40	54
%	%	%	**ASSETS**	%	%	%	%	%	%
7.1	6.0	6.8	Cash & Equivalents	15.6	13.2	11.3	6.6	4.1	2.6
27.1	27.9	27.8	Trade Receivables (net)	23.6	21.6	22.6	28.8	31.9	29.7
39.0	38.9	38.2	Inventory	28.7	32.7	33.2	38.4	42.4	41.1
2.4	2.5	2.3	All Other Current	3.8	1.0	1.0	1.6	3.4	2.3
75.7	75.3	75.1	Total Current	71.7	68.5	68.0	75.3	81.8	75.6
18.6	17.4	17.5	Fixed Assets (net)	19.8	21.5	19.3	17.5	13.5	17.6
1.8	2.0	3.1	Intangibles (net)	1.5	5.6	7.0	3.1	.6	3.1
3.9	5.3	4.3	All Other Non-Current	7.0	4.4	5.7	4.1	4.1	3.7
100.0	100.0	100.0	Total	100.0	100.0	100.0	100.0	100.0	100.0
			LIABILITIES						
10.9	12.5	13.8	Notes Payable-Short Term	19.0	12.3	15.9	10.3	15.5	13.6
3.3	2.9	2.1	Cur. Mat.-L/T/D	3.5	1.3	5.2	2.7	1.4	1.7
31.0	33.0	35.0	Trade Payables	51.0	28.8	34.5	31.1	39.1	33.8
.2	.1	.2	Income Taxes Payable	.2	.2	.0	.1	.2	.2
7.8	9.0	7.2	All Other Current	8.7	10.0	5.0	9.4	3.8	7.3
53.1	57.5	58.3	Total Current	82.5	52.5	60.6	53.5	60.0	56.6
10.8	12.5	9.0	Long-Term Debt	8.3	12.5	12.8	9.7	6.5	8.1
.2	.2	.3	Deferred Taxes	.0	.0	.0	.5	.2	.5
3.3	4.8	4.3	All Other Non-Current	15.1	5.4	.9	4.4	1.8	3.7
32.6	25.0	28.1	Net Worth	−5.9	29.5	25.6	31.9	31.5	31.1
100.0	100.0	100.0	Total Liabilities & Net Worth	100.0	100.0	100.0	100.0	100.0	100.0
			INCOME DATA						
100.0	100.0	100.0	Net Sales	100.0	100.0	100.0	100.0	100.0	100.0
28.1	28.5	29.3	Gross Profit	49.5	38.4	31.9	26.1	23.9	25.0
26.0	26.7	27.5	Operating Expenses	47.6	36.8	31.2	24.3	21.9	23.2
2.1	1.8	1.8	Operating Profit	1.9	1.5	.7	1.8	2.0	1.9
.1	.1	.1	All Other Expenses (net)	2.5	−.2	.7	−.7	.1	.1
1.9	1.7	1.6	Profit Before Taxes	−.6	1.7	.0	2.5	1.8	1.8
			RATIOS						
2.1	1.8	1.7		1.7	2.0	1.4	2.0	1.5	1.6
1.4	1.3	1.3	Current	1.1	1.3	1.1	1.4	1.2	1.3
1.1	1.1	1.1		.7	1.1	.6	1.2	1.2	1.1
1.1	.8	.8		.8	1.2	.7	.8	.8	.7
.6	.5 (171)	.6	Quick	.6	(28) .7	.5	.6	.5	.5
.4	.4	.4		.3	.4	.4	.5	.4	.4
20 18.1	20 18.3	22 16.7		4 84.6	15 24.9	13 28.2	21 17.2	26 13.9	28 13.0
33 11.1	33 11.0	33 11.0	Sales/Receivables	15 24.7	25 14.7	30 12.4	32 11.5	39 9.4	40 9.2
44 8.3	46 7.9	45 8.1		33 11.2	33 11.2	41 9.0	45 8.0	48 7.6	52 7.0
46 7.9	48 7.7	47 7.7		24 15.2	36 10.1	32 11.3	40 9.0	48 7.6	63 5.8
67 5.4	68 5.4	66 5.5	Cost of Sales/Inventory	53 6.9	58 6.3	49 7.5	62 5.9	66 5.5	75 4.9
89 4.1	93 3.9	84 4.4		80 4.6	75 4.9	95 3.8	79 4.6	84 4.4	100 3.7
27 13.5	32 11.3	35 10.5		23 15.8	22 16.9	38 9.6	29 12.4	47 7.8	40 9.2
52 7.0	55 6.7	57 6.4	Cost of Sales/Payables	51 7.2	47 7.7	60 6.0	46 8.0	61 6.0	62 5.9
76 4.8	81 4.5	79 4.6		101 3.6	71 5.2	84 4.4	70 5.2	81 4.5	84 4.4
7.5	8.1	9.3		13.0	10.5	11.9	9.3	10.6	8.1
14.3	16.5	16.7	Sales/Working Capital	122.0	14.8	64.4	15.8	14.9	14.0
49.6	76.1	49.8		−17.7	77.0	−12.7	31.3	28.8	42.4
10.0	10.9	10.7			6.4		12.3	7.9	13.7
(144) 3.8	(170) 4.4	(151) 4.0	EBIT/Interest		(21) 3.0		(25) 3.9	(37) 5.5	(53) 4.5
1.7	1.7	1.9			1.7		1.8	2.4	2.6
5.4	8.4	6.6	Net Profit + Depr., Dep.,				9.1	6.9	11.7
(46) 2.2	(56) 2.8	(61) 2.5	Amort./Cur. Mat. L/T/D				(10) 2.4	(16) 2.6	(24) 3.4
1.0	1.4	1.9					1.7	2.3	2.2
.2	.2	.2		.5	.3	.1	.2	.2	.2
.6	.5	.5	Fixed/Worth	NM	.5	.7	.5	.3	.5
1.2	1.3	1.4		−.3	70.7	NM	1.4	.8	1.1
1.0	1.3	1.4		1.1	1.0	1.7	1.3	1.7	1.4
2.3	2.5	2.6	Debt/Worth	NM	2.6	2.7	2.5	2.5	2.2
5.3	5.7	6.0		−5.4	142.5	NM	5.2	4.1	5.5
28.7	36.2	32.4	% Profit Before Taxes/Tangible		41.7		44.2	33.0	29.2
(142) 16.8	(167) 16.3	(152) 15.7	Net Worth		(23) 19.0		(25) 16.3	20.2	(50) 14.8
6.2	6.3	7.9			−1.7		8.9	7.6	9.8
9.2	9.4	8.8	% Profit Before Taxes/Total	6.2	9.6	6.8	17.4	12.8	7.7
4.5	4.0	4.2	Assets	−2.3	6.2	3.0	4.2	4.3	4.5
1.3	1.2	1.4		−21.5	1.5	−1.3	1.4	2.1	1.9
44.2	47.2	50.5		88.6	55.2	46.7	47.3	75.6	38.8
23.2	25.6	25.5	Sales/Net Fixed Assets	23.0	29.1	27.8	29.8	34.1	19.2
11.3	12.4	11.1		15.5	10.2	9.8	11.6	15.4	8.9
3.7	3.6	3.8		5.7	3.8	3.9	4.2	3.8	3.1
3.1	3.0	2.8	Sales/Total Assets	4.6	3.0	3.0	3.0	3.0	2.7
2.4	2.3	2.3		2.8	2.4	2.4	2.3	2.6	2.1
.6	.7	.6			.8		.7	.4	.5
(140) 1.1	(164) 1.1	(144) 1.1	% Depr., Dep., Amort./Sales		(24) 1.8		(25) 1.3	(34) .8	(49) 1.1
1.7	1.9	1.7			2.4		1.6	1.5	1.5
1.2	1.2	1.2			2.7		1.6	1.1	.6
(63) 2.9	(75) 2.4	(75) 2.3	% Officers', Directors', Owners' Comp/Sales		(14) 2.9		(13) 3.4	(19) 1.4	(17) 1.0
5.4	4.6	5.1			4.3		6.8	2.1	2.2
5131183M	5543145M	6390529M	Net Sales ($)	7553M	53490M	40644M	195573M	654738M	5438531M
1977439M	2207185M	2547027M	Total Assets ($)	2462M	19893M	14127M	65702M	238035M	2206808M

© RMA 2005

M = $ thousand   MM = $ million

See Pages 11 through 21 for Explanation of Ratios and Data

Current Data Sorted By Assets   Comparative Historical Data

0-500M	500M-2MM	2-10MM	10-50MM	50-100MM	100-250MM	Type of Statement	4/1/00-3/31/01 ALL	4/1/01-3/31/02 ALL
1			1			Unqualified	3	1
	2	4	2			Reviewed	8	6
4	3	7				Compiled	21	21
3	8	2				Tax Returns	9	9
	5	6				Other	10	11
	10 (4/1-9/30/04)		38 (10/1/04-3/31/05)					
8	18	19	3			**NUMBER OF STATEMENTS**	51	48
%	%	%	%	%	%	**ASSETS**	%	%
	2.6	7.9		DATA	DATA	Cash & Equivalents	7.5	5.9
	18.8	19.7		NOT	NOT	Trade Receivables (net)	18.8	19.7
	47.5	39.0		AVAILABLE	AVAILABLE	Inventory	40.8	46.4
	.1	3.8				All Other Current	2.1	.6
	69.0	70.5				Total Current	69.1	72.6
	25.1	19.7				Fixed Assets (net)	24.2	20.0
	.2	3.2				Intangibles (net)	2.6	1.1
	5.6	6.6				All Other Non-Current	5.1	7.3
	100.0	100.0				Total	100.0	100.0
						LIABILITIES		
	12.2	12.6				Notes Payable-Short Term	16.1	24.4
	2.9	2.5				Cur. Mat.-L/T/D	7.6	3.4
	12.0	9.5				Trade Payables	12.1	14.3
	.1	.0				Income Taxes Payable	.4	.1
	6.5	10.5				All Other Current	6.9	6.3
	33.7	35.1				Total Current	43.3	48.5
	23.1	23.0				Long-Term Debt	19.3	15.2
	.0	.0				Deferred Taxes	.2	.1
	7.1	4.6				All Other Non-Current	5.3	6.6
	36.0	37.4				Net Worth	32.0	29.7
	100.0	100.0				Total Liabilities & Net Worth	100.0	100.0
						INCOME DATA		
	100.0	100.0				Net Sales	100.0	100.0
	43.7	30.7				Gross Profit	38.9	41.5
	37.7	27.9				Operating Expenses	34.8	39.9
	6.0	2.8				Operating Profit	4.2	1.6
	.6	1.4				All Other Expenses (net)	.7	1.6
	5.4	1.4				Profit Before Taxes	3.5	.0
						RATIOS		
	5.0	4.1					3.6	2.6
	1.9	2.1				Current	1.9	1.6
	1.4	1.3					1.3	1.2
	1.0	1.8					1.0	.9
	.5	.5				Quick	.7	.5
	.3	.3					.3	.2
	9 42.2	10 36.3					9 39.2	10 36.1
	24 15.1	22 16.9				Sales/Receivables	21 17.7	24 15.4
	37 9.9	57 6.4					39 9.5	40 9.2
	50 7.3	56 6.6					49 7.5	64 5.7
	123 3.0	84 4.4				Cost of Sales/Inventory	90 4.0	99 3.7
	271 1.3	135 2.7					143 2.5	197 1.9
	10 36.2	6 64.0					6 66.1	5 67.1
	21 17.3	16 22.2				Cost of Sales/Payables	15 23.9	18 20.3
	42 8.7	33 11.1					44 8.3	54 6.8
	5.2	4.3					4.8	5.2
	9.3	5.4				Sales/Working Capital	8.5	10.3
	11.7	16.0					22.1	35.0
	9.9	10.4					4.4	4.0
	5.3	(17) 4.3				EBIT/Interest	(44) 2.5	(45) 2.0
	1.8	.2					.7	1.2
						Net Profit + Depr., Dep.,	2.1	4.4
						Amort./Cur. Mat. L/T/D	(13) 1.4	(10) 1.6
							.4	.9
	.2	.1					.2	.3
	.4	.3				Fixed/Worth	.5	.6
	1.1	8.9					1.3	2.8
	1.1	.5					.7	1.0
	2.0	1.8				Debt/Worth	1.5	1.9
	3.7	16.2					6.1	12.5
	79.2	33.7				% Profit Before Taxes/Tangible	23.9	40.4
	18.1	(16) 8.4				Net Worth	(43) 10.3	(39) 16.0
	3.8	3.1					.6	3.1
	21.3	17.2				% Profit Before Taxes/Total	13.9	8.1
	7.8	2.8				Assets	4.5	4.3
	1.2	.2					-.1	.7
	40.1	111.4					27.5	41.7
	12.7	22.3				Sales/Net Fixed Assets	11.9	13.3
	7.9	7.6					6.4	9.7
	3.9	3.0					3.6	3.2
	2.6	2.3				Sales/Total Assets	2.3	2.4
	1.6	1.3					1.9	1.8
	.6	.4					.6	.8
	1.6	(14) 1.6				% Depr., Dep., Amort./Sales	(48) 1.6	(41) 1.3
	2.9	4.5					2.4	2.3
							2.5	2.8
						% Officers', Directors',	(29) 4.7	(28) 6.0
						Owners' Comp/Sales	7.7	10.7
7363M	62651M	164036M	204105M			Net Sales ($)	504683M	225853M
2314M	20636M	73916M	63557M			Total Assets ($)	359838M	95152M

M = $ thousand   MM = $ million
See Pages 11 through 21 for Explanation of Ratios and Data

Comparative Historical Data				Current Data Sorted By Sales					
			Type of Statement						
1	5	2	Unqualified		1				1
16	12	8	Reviewed		1	1	2	4	
11	10	14	Compiled	2	4	3	3	2	
18	12	13	Tax Returns	4	2	3	3	1	
16	13	11	Other	2	5		1	3	
4/1/02-3/31/03 ALL	4/1/03-3/31/04 ALL	4/1/04-3/31/05 ALL		10 (4/1-9/30/04)			38 (10/1/04-3/31/05)		
				0-1MM	1-3MM	3-5MM	5-10MM	10-25MM	25MM & OVER
62	52	48	**NUMBER OF STATEMENTS**	8	13	7	9	10	1
%	%	%	**ASSETS**	%	%	%	%	%	%
4.9	7.2	5.9	Cash & Equivalents		3.4			9.8	
17.1	16.6	18.2	Trade Receivables (net)		8.3			30.0	
41.4	46.5	44.5	Inventory		42.3			36.5	
1.7	2.0	1.9	All Other Current		3.8			3.9	
65.0	72.3	70.6	Total Current		57.8			80.1	
24.9	21.3	21.0	Fixed Assets (net)		29.5			14.7	
4.1	2.5	3.4	Intangibles (net)		3.1			.2	
6.0	3.9	5.0	All Other Non-Current		9.6			5.1	
100.0	100.0	100.0	Total		100.0			100.0	
			LIABILITIES						
17.4	16.3	14.1	Notes Payable-Short Term		9.1			13.1	
4.9	6.9	2.7	Cur. Mat.-L/T/D		4.7			1.4	
10.4	10.6	12.5	Trade Payables		7.2			17.9	
.1	.0	.0	Income Taxes Payable		.0			.0	
12.4	14.0	8.4	All Other Current		7.4			16.2	
45.1	47.8	37.9	Total Current		28.4			48.6	
14.6	18.4	23.7	Long-Term Debt		39.9			9.7	
.2	.0	.0	Deferred Taxes		.0			.2	
4.7	3.1	5.1	All Other Non-Current		13.2			2.7	
35.4	30.7	33.3	Net Worth		18.5			38.8	
100.0	100.0	100.0	Total Liabilities & Net Worth		100.0			100.0	
			INCOME DATA						
100.0	100.0	100.0	Net Sales		100.0			100.0	
42.1	41.6	38.3	Gross Profit		45.3			28.0	
40.8	38.1	33.1	Operating Expenses		41.1			26.6	
1.3	3.5	5.2	Operating Profit		4.1			1.4	
.8	.4	1.1	All Other Expenses (net)		3.0			.1	
.5	3.0	4.1	Profit Before Taxes		1.2			1.3	
			RATIOS						
2.6	2.9	3.0			6.0			6.1	
1.5	1.6	1.8	Current		1.6			1.6	
1.0	1.2	1.3			1.3			1.1	
1.0	.9	1.0			.9			3.8	
(61) .5	(51) .6	(47) .5	Quick		(12) .4			.8	
.2	.2	.3			.3			.4	
7 53.5	3 113.1	7 50.2			7 53.8			14 25.3	
25 14.8	21 17.4	21 17.0	Sales/Receivables		21 17.2			30 12.3	
34 10.8	34 10.7	40 9.2			29 12.7			65 5.6	
51 7.2	60 6.1	60 6.0			89 4.1			36 10.2	
108 3.4	103 3.5	97 3.8	Cost of Sales/Inventory		158 2.3			71 5.2	
148 2.5	197 1.9	178 2.1			215 1.7			83 4.4	
6 59.9	4 93.9	7 51.1			0 UND			7 50.5	
20 18.5	17 21.2	20 18.4	Cost of Sales/Payables		26 14.0			16 22.6	
33 11.2	49 7.4	39 9.4			72 5.1			34 10.7	
5.7	5.3	4.4			4.0			5.2	
12.7	8.2	7.4	Sales/Working Capital		8.5			11.8	
-618.5	22.2	15.0			17.9			60.2	
6.3	7.3	8.4			5.8				
(58) 3.4	(50) 4.3	(45) 4.8	EBIT/Interest		1.5				
1.0	1.3	1.3			-2.1				
3.0			Net Profit + Depr., Dep.,						
(13) 1.7			Amort./Cur. Mat. L/T/D						
.9									
.2	.2	.2			.7			.1	
.6	.4	.4	Fixed/Worth		1.3			.3	
1.9	1.2	3.6			35.2			2.9	
.8	1.0	1.1			2.4			.4	
1.6	1.9	2.1	Debt/Worth		5.8			2.2	
7.3	4.2	6.3			40.5			9.4	
25.3	48.2	57.3	% Profit Before Taxes/Tangible		167.7				
(52) 12.2	(45) 17.0	(41) 22.5	Net Worth		(11) 11.4				
1.1	3.6	4.0			-21.8				
9.8	13.0	16.9	% Profit Before Taxes/Total		17.7			20.6	
3.7	5.2	3.9	Assets		1.3			7.6	
-1.3	1.0	.5			-7.0			1.2	
36.0	46.8	66.8			23.6			195.6	
14.8	18.5	20.0	Sales/Net Fixed Assets		8.8			30.9	
5.8	9.1	8.5			5.5			18.9	
3.5	3.9	3.6			3.1			3.5	
2.5	2.5	2.5	Sales/Total Assets		2.0			3.1	
1.7	1.7	1.7			.9			2.3	
.8	.9	.6			1.9				
(56) 1.5	(42) 1.8	(39) 1.6	% Depr., Dep., Amort./Sales		(11) 2.4				
3.2	3.5	4.1			7.1				
2.8	4.3	3.5	% Officers', Directors',						
(30) 5.7	(23) 7.1	(20) 5.8	Owners' Comp/Sales						
10.2	10.2	10.0							
1313761M	1108505M	438155M	Net Sales ($)	4590M	25032M	28917M	65486M	142595M	171535M
660255M	491545M	160423M	Total Assets ($)	3786M	15858M	16060M	30251M	51959M	42509M

M = $ thousand   MM = $ million
See Pages 11 through 21 for Explanation of Ratios and Data

Current Data Sorted By Assets   Comparative Historical Data

						Type of Statement		
		20	22	3	1	Unqualified	27	25
	18	45	15	1		Reviewed	101	66
4	17	14	1			Compiled	69	66
6	17	6			1	Tax Returns	22	25
7	21	31	27		1	Other	75	96
	47 (4/1-9/30/04)		231 (10/1/04-3/31/05)				4/1/00-3/31/01	4/1/01-3/31/02
0-500M	500M-2MM	2-10MM	10-50MM	50-100MM	100-250MM		ALL	ALL
17	73	116	65	4	3	**NUMBER OF STATEMENTS**	294	278
%	%	%	%	%	%	**ASSETS**	%	%
5.3	9.1	6.7	7.8			Cash & Equivalents	9.3	8.7
17.3	34.1	44.0	36.0			Trade Receivables (net)	41.5	37.3
39.3	36.3	27.7	31.7			Inventory	27.0	29.3
3.3	2.4	2.7	4.3			All Other Current	2.8	2.9
65.2	82.0	81.1	79.8			Total Current	80.7	78.1
16.2	11.7	10.1	11.2			Fixed Assets (net)	12.4	13.2
.0	.6	2.3	2.4			Intangibles (net)	2.2	2.1
18.5	5.8	6.4	6.6			All Other Non-Current	4.7	6.5
100.0	100.0	100.0	100.0			Total	100.0	100.0
						LIABILITIES		
12.8	15.5	16.6	20.1			Notes Payable-Short Term	15.4	15.4
1.3	2.8	1.8	1.3			Cur. Mat.-L/T/D	2.1	3.0
23.9	22.7	19.9	18.7			Trade Payables	23.4	21.5
.1	.6	.2	.2			Income Taxes Payable	.3	.2
29.0	17.4	16.6	15.2			All Other Current	16.9	15.7
67.1	59.0	55.1	55.5			Total Current	58.1	55.8
31.1	11.2	5.6	4.6			Long-Term Debt	7.3	8.5
.0	.1	.2	.9			Deferred Taxes	.1	.2
7.6	5.3	4.7	5.4			All Other Non-Current	3.8	5.3
-5.9	24.5	34.4	33.6			Net Worth	30.6	30.2
100.0	100.0	100.0	100.0			Total Liabilities & Net Worth	100.0	100.0
						INCOME DATA		
100.0	100.0	100.0	100.0			Net Sales	100.0	100.0
35.5	31.0	28.5	27.9			Gross Profit	28.9	29.0
35.7	28.5	26.0	24.7			Operating Expenses	25.9	27.3
-.2	2.5	2.5	3.2			Operating Profit	3.0	1.6
.0	.7	.3	.2			All Other Expenses (net)	.3	.5
-.2	1.8	2.2	3.0			Profit Before Taxes	2.7	1.1
						RATIOS		
2.7	2.2	2.4	2.0				1.9	2.0
.9	1.5	1.4	1.4			Current	1.3	1.4
.6	1.1	1.1	1.2				1.1	1.1
.8	1.2	1.3	1.2				1.2	1.2
(16) .4	.9	1.0	.8			Quick	(277) .9	.8
.1	.4	.4	.6				.6	.5
0 UND	9 42.0	33 11.0	28 13.0				25 14.6	19 19.4
7 49.5	30 12.3	44 8.2	42 8.7			Sales/Receivables	41 8.9	35 10.4
30 12.1	50 7.3	62 5.9	54 6.8				61 6.0	53 6.9
2 152.0	16 22.4	11 31.8	17 21.2				12 31.3	11 32.3
44 8.2	36 10.1	35 10.4	46 7.9			Cost of Sales/Inventory	30 12.2	32 11.6
71 5.2	140 2.6	86 4.2	91 4.0				75 4.9	85 4.3
13 28.8	14 26.9	16 22.6	15 24.3				16 23.3	13 27.5
20 18.2	28 12.9	27 13.6	26 14.1			Cost of Sales/Payables	29 12.6	26 14.1
38 9.7	45 8.0	39 9.2	43 8.5				46 7.9	43 8.4
7.4	6.7	7.2	7.9				8.6	9.2
-107.4	14.5	15.2	12.0			Sales/Working Capital	18.0	18.6
-12.1	174.0	31.1	29.9				59.0	67.1
28.3	10.8	11.5	11.1				8.2	6.3
(13) 5.7	(68) 4.0	(104) 3.1	(54) 4.1			EBIT/Interest	(269) 3.0	(253) 2.5
-2.2	.9	1.3	1.4				1.5	.6
		10.5	13.6			Net Profit + Depr., Dep.,	9.6	4.4
	(20) 2.7	(19) 4.9				Amort./Cur. Mat. L/T/D	(83) 3.2	(63) 1.9
	.6	2.7					1.2	.6
.2	.1	.1	.1				.2	.1
1.4	.3	.3	.3			Fixed/Worth	.4	.4
-.4	1.5	.7	1.1				1.0	1.1
1.1	1.1	.8	1.2				1.3	1.2
15.7	2.1	2.1	2.3			Debt/Worth	2.8	2.6
-4.0	15.0	5.3	4.6				6.6	7.0
95.4	51.3	36.6	42.7			% Profit Before Taxes/Tangible	52.5	41.4
(11) 21.4	(60) 20.2	(106) 16.3	(60) 22.5			Net Worth	(268) 21.8	(246) 14.9
-6.2	1.7	3.3	5.7				8.3	1.3
28.6	13.6	11.6	15.2			% Profit Before Taxes/Total	14.7	11.5
5.4	6.3	4.2	4.6			Assets	5.7	4.0
-4.5	.2	.9	.9				2.2	-.8
133.3	86.6	124.0	65.4				84.0	85.8
27.7	42.0	45.2	41.1			Sales/Net Fixed Assets	43.4	45.0
15.3	22.2	20.6	24.4				20.0	22.1
5.7	5.0	4.1	3.8				4.6	5.0
4.0	3.3	3.3	3.1			Sales/Total Assets	3.5	3.8
3.2	2.3	2.5	2.6				2.5	2.6
	.4	.3	.4				.4	.4
	(57) .6	(92) .6	(59) .7			% Depr., Dep., Amort./Sales	(248) .6	(235) .6
	.9	1.0	1.0				1.1	1.0
3.8	2.3	1.3	1.0				1.7	1.7
(10) 5.6	(42) 3.4	(46) 2.8	(10) 1.4			% Officers', Directors', Owners' Comp/Sales	(126) 3.9	(135) 2.7
10.9	6.2	4.7	4.5				6.2	5.5
22163M	347067M	1743505M	4203705M	957343M	1333234M	Net Sales ($)	7568717M	6617749M
4677M	88604M	512299M	1307444M	327365M	528143M	Total Assets ($)	2630439M	1949524M

M = $ thousand   MM = $ million
See Pages 11 through 21 for Explanation of Ratios and Data

Comparative Historical Data / Current Data Sorted By Sales

				Type of Statement	0-1MM	1-3MM	3-5MM	5-10MM	10-25MM	25MM & OVER
	35	45	46	Unqualified			1	4	11	30
	71	75	79	Reviewed		3	8	19	32	17
	52	62	36	Compiled	3	11	6	9	5	2
	18	31	30	Tax Returns	3	12	7	4	1	3
	61	62	87	Other	3	10	9	16	18	31
	4/1/02-3/31/03 ALL	4/1/03-3/31/04 ALL	4/1/04-3/31/05 ALL		47 (4/1-9/30/04)	231 (10/1/04-3/31/05)				
	237	275	278	NUMBER OF STATEMENTS	9	36	31	52	67	83
	%	%	%	ASSETS	%	%	%	%	%	%
	9.7	8.2	7.4	Cash & Equivalents		7.5	7.5	7.1	8.1	6.8
	38.2	36.9	37.6	Trade Receivables (net)		25.0	28.7	38.9	47.4	39.5
	29.9	30.2	31.7	Inventory		43.1	39.0	29.8	23.3	31.1
	3.1	3.1	3.3	All Other Current		.5	4.5	1.3	4.4	4.3
	80.9	78.5	80.0	Total Current		76.1	79.7	77.1	83.2	81.8
	11.8	13.1	11.3	Fixed Assets (net)		14.5	10.0	11.8	10.6	10.3
	1.4	1.8	1.7	Intangibles (net)		.6	2.0	1.5	2.2	2.0
	6.0	6.6	7.0	All Other Non-Current		8.8	8.3	9.6	4.1	5.9
	100.0	100.0	100.0	Total		100.0	100.0	100.0	100.0	100.0
				LIABILITIES						
	16.2	16.3	17.0	Notes Payable-Short Term		12.4	22.2	15.3	15.9	19.3
	2.3	2.1	1.9	Cur. Mat.-L/T/D		3.0	1.7	2.7	1.2	1.5
	20.6	21.2	20.7	Trade Payables		23.7	14.2	21.9	19.4	22.0
	.2	.3	.3	Income Taxes Payable		.5	.8	.1	.2	.2
	15.4	17.0	17.2	All Other Current		20.1	18.3	14.4	18.3	16.1
	54.7	56.9	57.1	Total Current		59.7	57.3	54.4	54.9	59.2
	7.4	8.0	8.5	Long-Term Debt		12.8	16.6	4.8	5.1	5.2
	.1	.1	.3	Deferred Taxes		.0	.1	.4	.1	.7
	5.0	4.5	5.1	All Other Non-Current		6.1	11.9	2.7	2.8	5.1
	32.8	30.5	29.0	Net Worth		21.4	14.1	37.6	37.1	29.9
	100.0	100.0	100.0	Total Liabilities & Net Worth		100.0	100.0	100.0	100.0	100.0
				INCOME DATA						
	100.0	100.0	100.0	Net Sales		100.0	100.0	100.0	100.0	100.0
	28.9	28.9	29.4	Gross Profit		35.3	29.7	30.5	28.8	26.2
	27.6	27.0	26.8	Operating Expenses		32.3	28.6	28.0	25.4	23.2
	1.3	1.9	2.6	Operating Profit		3.0	1.1	2.4	3.4	3.0
	.3	.3	.4	All Other Expenses (net)		.4	.7	.3	.3	.3
	1.0	1.6	2.2	Profit Before Taxes		2.6	.5	2.1	3.1	2.7
				RATIOS						
	2.0	2.1	2.2	Current		2.3	3.1	2.1	2.4	1.8
	1.5	1.3	1.4			1.4	1.7	1.5	1.3	1.3
	1.1	1.1	1.1			.9	1.0	1.1	1.2	1.1
	1.3	1.2	1.2	Quick		1.1	1.5	1.3	1.5	1.1
	.9	.9	(277) .9		(35) .5	.5	.8	1.0	1.0	.8
	.6	.5	.5			.3	.3	.5	.7	.5
23	15.6	22 16.6	24 15.3	Sales/Receivables	0 822.8	23 16.0	25 14.8	31 11.8	30 12.2	
38	9.7	37 9.8	39 9.3		25 14.5	33 11.1	40 9.1	43 8.5	43 8.5	
56	6.5	51 7.1	56 6.5		54 6.8	58 6.3	62 5.9	60 6.1	54 6.8	
11	31.9	12 31.1	15 23.8	Cost of Sales/Inventory	26 14.2	23 15.7	16 22.4	8 43.0	17 21.7	
36	10.1	38 9.7	39 9.3		87 4.2	65 5.6	37 9.9	25 14.5	40 9.2	
86	4.2	88 4.1	94 3.9		146 2.5	143 2.6	95 3.8	52 7.0	86 4.2	
13	27.9	16 23.1	15 24.3	Cost of Sales/Payables	12 30.7	11 32.5	18 20.3	14 25.2	15 24.0	
25	14.7	25 14.6	26 13.8		38 9.7	21 17.5	31 12.0	23 15.9	27 13.6	
43	8.5	44 8.3	42 8.7		56 6.5	33 11.1	46 7.9	35 10.4	45 8.0	
	7.3	9.0	7.4	Sales/Working Capital		6.0	5.4	7.0	8.2	8.8
	15.0	17.9	14.9			14.0	12.8	13.0	16.9	15.0
	42.3	92.0	47.9			-49.5	UND	64.9	37.3	30.5
	8.0	11.1	12.7	EBIT/Interest		23.1	5.6	10.7	14.5	11.9
(207)	2.3	(248) 3.1	(246) 4.0		(32) 3.5	(30) 2.9	(45) 4.2	(58) 3.9	(75) 4.5	
	.4	.6	1.3			.7	-1.1	1.5	1.4	1.6
	9.8	8.6	12.6	Net Profit + Depr., Dep., Amort./Cur. Mat. L/T/D				13.2	20.4	
(62)	2.8	(53) 2.5	(54) 4.4				(12) 3.9	(25) 5.6		
	.9	.1	1.5					.7	3.1	
	.1	.1	.1	Fixed/Worth		.1	.1	.1	.1	.1
	.3	.3	.3			.6	.4	.2	.3	.3
	1.2	1.0	1.0			3.7	-1.0	.7	.6	.8
	1.0	1.1	.9	Debt/Worth		1.5	.5	.8	.7	1.3
	2.0	2.6	2.2			2.3	2.2	1.6	2.3	3.0
	5.7	6.4	6.4			25.7	-6.1	3.1	3.8	5.4
	32.0	37.8	46.6	% Profit Before Taxes/Tangible Net Worth		65.8	33.3	39.6	51.9	48.6
(210)	12.8	(248) 15.8	(244) 20.3		(29) 22.6	(22) 12.9	(48) 14.9	(62) 21.5	(76) 28.7	
	.8	2.2	4.3			7.2	-4.4	4.3	3.4	7.7
	10.7	11.4	13.6	% Profit Before Taxes/Total Assets		18.8	8.1	12.3	16.8	12.9
	3.2	3.9	5.5			4.7	2.4	6.5	5.6	6.0
	-1.3	-.6	.7			.1	-4.7	.9	1.2	.9
	106.8	91.7	86.2	Sales/Net Fixed Assets		90.9	93.7	85.0	149.2	83.8
	45.6	41.9	41.7			33.2	37.2	46.7	46.2	47.8
	23.9	20.4	20.7			13.7	23.8	18.0	23.7	25.7
	4.5	4.6	4.2	Sales/Total Assets		4.0	4.3	4.4	4.5	4.1
	3.4	3.5	3.3			2.8	2.8	3.0	3.7	3.5
	2.6	2.6	2.5			2.1	2.0	2.5	3.0	2.7
	.3	.4	.4	% Depr., Dep., Amort./Sales		.4	.3	.4	.3	.4
(209)	.7	(223) .7	(224) .7		(25) .7	(25) .8	(39) .6	(53) .6	(77) .7	
	1.1	1.1	1.0			1.2	1.0	.8	1.0	.7
	1.8	1.8	1.9	% Officers', Directors', Owners' Comp/Sales		2.8	2.6	1.7	1.0	.8
(110)	2.9	(107) 3.4	(108) 3.3		(26) 4.5	(16) 3.3	(29) 3.6	(21) 2.3	(13) 1.3	
	5.6	5.6	5.6			8.0	5.4	5.4	4.9	3.0
	6014937M	6550326M	8607017M	Net Sales ($)	5613M	76638M	123802M	378523M	1151210M	6871231M
	1775488M	1960598M	2768532M	Total Assets ($)	3548M	29288M	50906M	132875M	338367M	2213548M

M = $ thousand   MM = $ million
See Pages 11 through 21 for Explanation of Ratios and Data

Current Data Sorted By Assets / Comparative Historical Data

Type of Statement	0-500M	500M-2MM	2-10MM	10-50MM	50-100MM	100-250MM		4/1/00-3/31/01 ALL	4/1/01-3/31/02 ALL
Unqualified		5	15	27	3	3		38	34
Reviewed	1	12	44	16	1			75	60
Compiled	1	21	16	1				56	69
Tax Returns	8	16	8					12	18
Other	6	17	30	22	2	1		66	69
	16	41 (4/1-9/30/04)		235 (10/1/04-3/31/05)					
NUMBER OF STATEMENTS	16	71	113	66	6	4		247	250

ASSETS (%)

	0-500M	500M-2MM	2-10MM	10-50MM	50-100MM	100-250MM		ALL	ALL
Cash & Equivalents	15.0	8.9	6.5	5.4				7.0	8.0
Trade Receivables (net)	22.7	30.9	33.9	32.3				31.8	31.3
Inventory	32.5	38.4	42.0	39.1				38.7	39.6
All Other Current	6.1	2.8	1.8	2.8				2.4	2.3
Total Current	76.2	81.0	84.2	79.6				80.0	81.1
Fixed Assets (net)	20.1	12.0	10.0	9.8				11.8	12.0
Intangibles (net)	1.4	1.2	1.0	4.1				2.0	1.9
All Other Non-Current	2.4	5.8	4.8	6.5				6.3	5.0
Total	100.0	100.0	100.0	100.0				100.0	100.0

LIABILITIES

	0-500M	500M-2MM	2-10MM	10-50MM				ALL	ALL
Notes Payable-Short Term	33.6	13.4	19.8	18.3				16.5	19.2
Cur. Mat.-L/T/D	15.2	2.5	1.7	2.1				2.9	2.1
Trade Payables	11.1	23.7	23.2	21.9				21.1	20.0
Income Taxes Payable	.0	.3	.2	.1				.3	.3
All Other Current	7.1	13.7	9.3	7.9				10.3	9.5
Total Current	67.1	53.5	54.1	50.4				51.1	51.0
Long-Term Debt	34.8	9.4	5.7	6.6				8.4	7.7
Deferred Taxes	.0	.2	.1	.2				.2	.3
All Other Non-Current	18.2	5.7	5.5	3.9				5.4	5.1
Net Worth	-20.0	31.2	34.7	38.9				35.0	35.9
Total Liabilities & Net Worth	100.0	100.0	100.0	100.0				100.0	100.0

INCOME DATA

	0-500M	500M-2MM	2-10MM	10-50MM				ALL	ALL
Net Sales	100.0	100.0	100.0	100.0				100.0	100.0
Gross Profit	47.3	32.5	29.0	30.2				30.6	32.5
Operating Expenses	40.4	30.7	26.6	25.3				27.3	29.8
Operating Profit	6.9	1.8	2.4	4.9				3.3	2.7
All Other Expenses (net)	1.9	.4	.3	.1				.1	.8
Profit Before Taxes	5.0	1.4	2.1	4.8				3.2	1.9

RATIOS

	0-500M	500M-2MM	2-10MM	10-50MM				ALL	ALL
Current	2.5 / 2.0 / 1.4	2.8 / 1.6 / 1.1	2.2 / 1.5 / 1.2	2.5 / 1.5 / 1.2				2.3 / 1.6 / 1.2	2.3 / 1.6 / 1.2
Quick	1.6 / 1.2 / .1	1.3 / (70) .8 / .5	1.0 / .8 / .5	1.1 / .7 / .5				1.2 / .7 / .5	1.3 / .7 / .5
Sales/Receivables	0 UND / 13 27.5 / 33 11.1	17 22.0 / 36 10.2 / 53 6.8	32 11.5 / 43 8.5 / 61 6.0	30 12.0 / 39 9.5 / 52 7.0				23 15.5 / 35 10.3 / 48 7.6	24 15.0 / 37 9.8 / 51 7.2
Cost of Sales/Inventory	3 108.6 / 79 4.6 / 140 2.6	22 16.3 / 72 5.1 / 142 2.6	43 8.5 / 71 5.1 / 122 3.0	48 7.6 / 67 5.5 / 127 2.9				35 10.3 / 71 5.2 / 115 3.2	34 10.6 / 66 5.5 / 131 2.8
Cost of Sales/Payables	5 70.7 / 17 21.5 / 36 10.0	17 20.9 / 38 9.6 / 57 6.4	18 20.5 / 33 11.2 / 62 5.9	20 18.1 / 32 11.5 / 58 6.3				17 21.6 / 30 12.2 / 51 7.2	14 25.4 / 28 13.1 / 47 7.8
Sales/Working Capital	7.5 / 12.1 / 28.9	4.6 / 9.4 / 48.2	5.7 / 10.2 / 21.7	6.2 / 10.6 / 19.2				6.1 / 10.4 / 23.6	5.7 / 10.8 / 24.7
EBIT/Interest	12.0 / (15) 6.8 / 1.3	9.2 / (60) 3.1 / .5	10.3 / (104) 4.3 / 2.0	27.1 / (60) 6.5 / 3.4				10.3 / (227) 2.9 / 1.5	6.3 / (225) 2.6 / 1.2
Net Profit + Depr., Dep., Amort./Cur. Mat. L/T/D		9.1 / (10) 2.7 / 1.0	36.3 / (30) 7.7 / 1.7	22.7 / (28) 4.1 / 2.0				8.4 / (54) 3.1 / 1.2	14.4 / (57) 3.9 / 1.0
Fixed/Worth	.1 / .5 / -3.4	.1 / .2 / .8	.1 / .2 / .6	.1 / .2 / .6				.1 / .2 / .6	.1 / .2 / .6
Debt/Worth	1.2 / 2.5 / -5.0	.8 / 2.0 / 10.4	.9 / 2.0 / 4.6	.9 / 2.3 / 4.2				.9 / 2.0 / 4.2	.8 / 1.9 / 3.8
% Profit Before Taxes/Tangible Net Worth	74.4 / (10) 18.2 / .3	51.4 / (64) 17.6 / 1.1	40.7 / (109) 19.3 / 5.3	49.0 / (62) 27.8 / 14.6				49.7 / (232) 20.7 / 6.3	38.8 / (230) 13.2 / 3.2
% Profit Before Taxes/Total Assets	65.1 / 16.6 / .3	14.5 / 4.5 / -.4	11.0 / 5.0 / 1.5	17.7 / 9.0 / 3.1				15.1 / 5.7 / 1.3	11.9 / 4.0 / .7
Sales/Net Fixed Assets	829.0 / 40.3 / 10.5	117.6 / 45.2 / 15.8	106.8 / 44.0 / 23.2	92.5 / 48.7 / 18.6				89.1 / 43.4 / 20.5	86.2 / 43.9 / 21.9
Sales/Total Assets	8.3 / 3.9 / 2.4	3.7 / 3.0 / 2.1	3.8 / 2.8 / 2.0	3.8 / 2.9 / 2.1				4.0 / 3.0 / 2.2	4.0 / 3.0 / 2.2
% Depr., Dep., Amort./Sales	.2 / (10) 1.0 / 7.3	.4 / (58) .7 / 1.7	.3 / (100) .5 / .9	.3 / (61) .6 / .9				.3 / (210) .6 / .9	.3 / (218) .6 / .9
% Officers', Directors', Owners' Comp/Sales	4.5 / (10) 6.1 / 9.4	2.7 / (43) 4.7 / 6.8	1.3 / (50) 3.0 / 4.9	.8 / (18) 2.1 / 4.8				1.9 / (118) 3.3 / 6.3	2.0 / (119) 3.5 / 6.5
Net Sales ($)	22598M	264107M	1545569M	3922384M	970451M	1081963M		5319108M	5771850M
Total Assets ($)	4967M	87015M	528345M	1364171M	369953M	555962M		1835590M	2151623M

M = $ thousand   MM = $ million
See Pages 11 through 21 for Explanation of Ratios and Data

Comparative Historical Data | Current Data Sorted By Sales

			Type of Statement						
41	52	53	Unqualified	1	1		7	12	32
67	73	74	Reviewed		4	9	14	25	22
45	65	39	Compiled	1	9	12	10	6	1
24	34	32	Tax Returns	4	12	5	8	2	1
77	74	78	Other	4	6	13	14	16	25
4/1/02-3/31/03 ALL	4/1/03-3/31/04 ALL	4/1/04-3/31/05 ALL		0-1MM	41 (4/1-9/30/04) 1-3MM	3-5MM	235 (10/1/04-3/31/05) 5-10MM	10-25MM	25MM & OVER
254	298	276	NUMBER OF STATEMENTS	10	32	39	53	61	81

%	%	%	**ASSETS**	%	%	%	%	%	%
6.4	7.3	7.2	Cash & Equivalents	18.6	8.7	10.5	4.7	7.7	4.8
32.8	31.9	32.1	Trade Receivables (net)	19.5	22.1	28.7	34.8	34.5	35.7
39.8	39.0	39.7	Inventory	32.6	47.2	34.3	41.1	41.1	38.1
2.6	2.9	2.5	All Other Current	2.6	3.3	3.4	2.5	2.0	2.2
81.5	81.2	81.5	Total Current	73.3	81.3	77.0	83.0	85.4	80.9
11.5	11.6	11.1	Fixed Assets (net)	15.9	16.3	12.7	10.7	9.5	9.0
2.5	2.5	2.2	Intangibles (net)	2.4	.3	2.8	.8	.2	4.9
4.5	4.7	5.3	All Other Non-Current	8.5	2.1	7.4	5.5	4.8	5.2
100.0	100.0	100.0	Total	100.0	100.0	100.0	100.0	100.0	100.0

			LIABILITIES						
16.0	15.4	18.5	Notes Payable-Short Term	4.6	28.1	16.6	18.5	16.1	19.2
3.6	2.2	2.9	Cur. Mat.-L/T/D	22.9	1.6	2.4	2.0	1.8	2.6
21.8	21.9	22.1	Trade Payables	14.9	16.9	24.6	22.7	24.3	21.8
.3	.2	.2	Income Taxes Payable	.0	.2	.2	.3	.1	.2
10.4	12.8	9.9	All Other Current	6.2	12.6	8.4	11.4	10.9	8.4
52.0	52.6	53.7	Total Current	48.6	59.4	52.2	54.9	53.3	52.2
9.1	8.3	8.9	Long-Term Debt	10.1	12.1	15.3	9.7	5.0	7.0
.1	.1	.2	Deferred Taxes	.0	.3	.1	.1	.1	.3
4.6	6.7	6.0	All Other Non-Current	2.5	14.2	5.8	6.7	3.5	4.8
34.2	32.2	31.2	Net Worth	38.8	14.1	26.6	28.6	38.1	35.8
100.0	100.0	100.0	Total Liabilities & Net Worth	100.0	100.0	100.0	100.0	100.0	100.0

			INCOME DATA						
100.0	100.0	100.0	Net Sales	100.0	100.0	100.0	100.0	100.0	100.0
31.4	32.6	31.3	Gross Profit	51.9	37.2	31.9	30.5	28.5	28.9
28.3	29.1	28.0	Operating Expenses	48.7	34.8	29.2	28.9	25.3	23.8
3.0	3.5	3.3	Operating Profit	3.2	2.4	2.7	1.6	3.2	5.2
.5	.7	.5	All Other Expenses (net)	.4	1.3	.8	.2	-.2	.7
2.5	2.8	2.8	Profit Before Taxes	2.8	1.1	1.9	1.4	3.4	4.5

			RATIOS						
2.4	2.3	2.4		5.3	3.6	2.5	2.3	2.3	2.3
1.6	1.6	1.5	Current	1.7	1.9	1.6	1.5	1.5	1.4
1.3	1.2	1.2		1.4	1.1	1.1	1.1	1.2	1.2
1.3	1.2	1.2		1.8	1.3	1.2	1.2	1.1	1.1
.7	.7 (275)	.7	Quick	1.0 (31)	.6	.9	.8	.7	.7
.5	.5	.5		.2	.3	.5	.4	.6	.6
29 12.5	28 12.9	28 13.1		0 UND	6 57.2	19 19.1	32 11.5	30 12.1	31 11.8
38 9.6	40 9.2	41 9.0	Sales/Receivables	25 14.4	31 11.8	39 9.3	48 7.5	41 9.0	41 8.9
55 6.7	58 6.3	56 6.6		42 8.7	60 6.1	56 6.5	62 5.9	52 7.1	55 6.7
38 9.6	43 8.5	43 8.5		36 10.1	27 13.7	15 24.5	52 7.0	39 9.4	46 7.9
72 5.1	73 5.0	72 5.1	Cost of Sales/Inventory	135 2.7	122 3.0	69 5.3	76 4.8	60 6.1	63 5.8
123 3.0	126 2.9	127 2.9		438 .8	178 2.1	135 2.7	136 2.7	116 3.2	91 4.0
18 20.5	20 18.6	18 20.6		10 35.5	9 42.8	19 19.2	18 20.4	18 20.7	20 18.1
32 11.3	35 10.5	32 11.5	Cost of Sales/Payables	45 8.1	29 12.6	40 9.0	33 11.1	31 11.7	30 12.0
55 6.7	59 6.2	58 6.3		123 3.0	72 5.1	58 6.3	57 6.4	57 6.4	51 7.2
5.2	5.4	5.5		2.2	4.0	5.8	4.8	6.2	7.0
10.0	9.9	10.6	Sales/Working Capital	6.5	7.1	13.6	8.6	13.3	11.5
23.9	23.8	23.9		12.5	43.9	36.3	27.9	21.2	20.7
11.9	10.7	13.0			7.3	13.4	5.7	14.7	25.2
(230) 3.6	(269) 3.7	(249) 4.7	EBIT/Interest	(30) 1.8	(33) 4.8	(50) 3.7	(51) 5.0	(78) 6.5
1.5	1.4	1.6			.5	1.3	1.3	2.7	3.4
12.0	9.0	21.1					8.0	90.2	28.9
(58) 4.5	(62) 3.6	(72) 5.0	Net Profit + Depr., Dep., Amort./Cur. Mat. L/T/D			(15) 2.1	(16) 16.6	(34) 6.5
1.3	1.2	1.7					1.0	1.6	2.8
.1	.1	.1		.0	.1	.1	.1	.1	.1
.2	.2	.2	Fixed/Worth	.2	.4	.3	.2	.2	.2
.7	.8	.7		.9	2.5	1.3	.9	.5	.6
.9	1.2	.9		.4	1.0	.7	.9	.9	.9
2.1	2.3	2.1	Debt/Worth	.8	1.8	1.7	2.5	1.9	2.4
4.0	4.9	4.9		NM	116.7	8.4	6.1	4.3	4.5
41.6	43.7	43.2			26.5	57.1	40.7	41.0	49.2
(233) 19.2	(268) 19.2	(254) 21.5	% Profit Before Taxes/Tangible Net Worth	(26) 10.0	(33) 11.8	(51) 14.9	(60) 19.4	(76) 29.5
5.3	5.3	5.3			-.6	1.9	3.1	6.1	18.2
12.8	13.5	16.3		20.1	13.4	16.8	10.0	15.4	19.4
5.4	4.7	6.2	% Profit Before Taxes/Total Assets	13.1	.9	6.4	3.3	5.7	8.6
1.4	.7	1.3		-10.0	-.9	.6	.9	2.5	4.4
94.4	90.2	107.1		UND	82.1	90.8	151.2	97.3	84.5
48.0	43.2	44.2	Sales/Net Fixed Assets	8.5	41.2	30.5	51.7	41.1	48.7
20.0	19.0	20.3		5.3	12.8	13.8	22.2	24.2	26.0
3.9	3.7	3.8		2.5	3.5	3.8	3.4	4.2	3.8
3.0	2.9	2.9	Sales/Total Assets	1.4	2.6	2.9	2.7	3.1	3.1
2.1	2.0	2.1		1.0	1.4	2.0	2.0	2.5	2.2
.4	.4	.3			.3	.4	.3	.3	.3
(210) .7	(246) .7	(237) .6	% Depr., Dep., Amort./Sales	(23) .9	(33) .8	(48) .5	(52) .4	(73) .5
1.1	1.1	1.1			2.1	1.6	1.1	.8	1.0
1.5	2.0	1.6			3.8	2.9	1.7	1.2	.5
(117) 3.3	(143) 3.6	(123) 3.9	% Officers', Directors', Owners' Comp/Sales	(20) 6.3	(25) 5.0	(25) 3.3	(20) 2.3	(28) 1.7
7.5	6.2	5.7			9.9	6.5	5.0	4.6	4.6
7510151M	8648537M	7807072M	Net Sales ($)	7252M	61974M	152098M	380913M	1026862M	6177973M
2980970M	3625644M	2910413M	Total Assets ($)	4903M	32242M	62176M	155303M	375695M	2280094M

© RMA 2005

M = $ thousand   MM = $ million
See Pages 11 through 21 for Explanation of Ratios and Data

Current Data Sorted By Assets / Comparative Historical Data

						Type of Statement		
1	5	46	93	30	12	Unqualified	138	137
3	41	140	66	1		Reviewed	230	175
10	81	57	13			Compiled	194	179
10	41	26	3			Tax Returns	39	52
9	48	84	55	6	6	Other	194	218
171 (4/1-9/30/04)			716 (10/1/04-3/31/05)				4/1/00-3/31/01	4/1/01-3/31/02
0-500M	**500M-2MM**	**2-10MM**	**10-50MM**	**50-100MM**	**100-250MM**		**ALL**	**ALL**
33	216	353	230	37	18	**NUMBER OF STATEMENTS**	795	761
%	%	%	%	%	%	**ASSETS**	%	%
9.6	7.1	4.4	4.1	2.0	2.6	Cash & Equivalents	5.2	5.4
31.8	38.1	34.7	33.2	33.8	33.5	Trade Receivables (net)	35.3	35.0
25.5	31.7	37.1	36.9	33.7	26.9	Inventory	34.7	34.0
7.2	2.6	1.9	2.6	3.3	4.8	All Other Current	2.3	2.4
74.1	79.6	78.2	76.8	72.9	67.9	Total Current	77.5	76.8
16.3	13.0	15.2	15.7	21.2	17.8	Fixed Assets (net)	15.6	15.7
5.4	1.0	1.6	1.1	1.3	6.3	Intangibles (net)	1.3	1.5
4.2	6.5	5.0	6.3	4.6	8.1	All Other Non-Current	5.6	6.0
100.0	100.0	100.0	100.0	100.0	100.0	Total	100.0	100.0
						LIABILITIES		
22.2	18.6	21.8	23.1	19.0	16.2	Notes Payable-Short Term	20.9	21.5
3.0	2.8	2.6	2.0	3.7	2.6	Cur. Mat.-L/T/D	2.9	3.0
19.9	19.2	14.8	13.4	12.2	13.1	Trade Payables	14.8	14.8
.2	.2	.3	.1	.1	.9	Income Taxes Payable	.3	.2
14.6	9.2	8.4	7.9	8.4	8.6	All Other Current	7.8	7.8
59.8	50.0	47.9	46.4	43.4	41.4	Total Current	46.7	47.2
19.7	9.5	8.9	9.0	16.8	18.2	Long-Term Debt	9.4	9.9
.0	.1	.3	.3	.7	.5	Deferred Taxes	.3	.2
10.4	5.3	3.8	2.3	2.5	3.3	All Other Non-Current	3.4	3.4
10.2	35.1	39.1	42.0	36.6	36.6	Net Worth	40.3	39.2
100.0	100.0	100.0	100.0	100.0	100.0	Total Liabilities & Net Worth	100.0	100.0
						INCOME DATA		
100.0	100.0	100.0	100.0	100.0	100.0	Net Sales	100.0	100.0
23.4	21.9	19.5	18.6	20.0	19.5	Gross Profit	19.3	20.2
21.1	20.0	16.4	15.1	16.4	14.3	Operating Expenses	16.5	17.7
2.4	1.9	3.0	3.5	3.7	5.2	Operating Profit	2.8	2.6
1.2	.2	.4	.3	.0	.5	All Other Expenses (net)	.4	.5
1.2	1.7	2.7	3.2	3.7	4.6	Profit Before Taxes	2.3	2.0
						RATIOS		
3.5	2.5	2.3	2.5	2.9	2.9		2.5	2.7
1.3	1.6	1.6	1.6	1.5	1.6	Current	1.6	1.6
.7	1.2	1.3	1.2	1.3	1.1		1.3	1.2
2.0	1.4	1.3	1.3	1.5	1.6		1.4	1.4
.9	.9	.8	.8	.8	.8	Quick	(793) .8	(760) .8
.3	.5	.5	.5	.6	.6		.5	.5
2 149.3	**20** 18.4	**23** 15.9	**25** 14.4	**27** 13.3	**26** 14.3		**23** 15.8	**23** 15.6
21 17.7	**33** 11.2	**34** 10.9	**35** 10.4	**37** 10.0	**33** 11.0	Sales/Receivables	**32** 11.4	**33** 11.0
43 8.4	**47** 7.8	**45** 8.1	**45** 8.1	**51** 7.2	**52** 7.1		**43** 8.5	**45** 8.2
0 UND	**14** 25.5	**29** 12.4	**35** 10.4	**43** 8.4	**26** 14.0		**24** 15.1	**27** 13.7
14 25.4	**41** 8.9	**46** 7.9	**47** 7.7	**51** 7.2	**33** 11.0	Cost of Sales/Inventory	**45** 8.2	**44** 8.3
45 8.1	**70** 5.2	**73** 5.0	**66** 5.5	**66** 5.6	**52** 7.0		**65** 5.6	**70** 5.2
3 124.0	**9** 41.8	**9** 42.2	**11** 34.7	**11** 33.8	**12** 30.6		**8** 46.5	**8** 44.7
14 26.6	**19** 19.5	**16** 22.7	**15** 24.5	**16** 23.3	**15** 24.3	Cost of Sales/Payables	**14** 25.3	**15** 24.1
38 9.5	**36** 10.2	**25** 14.7	**23** 16.1	**23** 15.7	**22** 16.9		**25** 14.8	**25** 14.5
10.3	6.9	7.2	6.7	6.8	6.4		7.3	6.9
22.9	13.7	12.9	12.1	12.2	14.2	Sales/Working Capital	13.0	12.7
-21.3	41.1	26.0	22.0	20.0	49.1		30.4	27.2
10.8	8.0	13.0	15.5	10.1	10.2		6.3	6.6
(27) 4.1	(197) 3.2	(336) 4.3	(220) 6.6	6.8	(17) 6.9	EBIT/Interest	(746) 2.5	(717) 2.7
-1.0	1.5	2.2	3.3	4.1	3.1		1.4	1.4
	5.6	7.2	10.8	11.7	5.0		5.5	7.8
	(42) 3.6	(101) 3.1	(84) 5.6	(21) 3.1	(11) 2.8	Net Profit + Depr., Dep., Amort./Cur. Mat. L /T/D	(231) 2.2	(193) 2.6
	1.4	1.5	2.4	1.8	1.2		1.1	1.1
.0	.1	.1	.1	.3	.5		.1	.1
.2	.3	.3	.3	.5	.7	Fixed/Worth	.3	.3
UND	.8	.8	.7	.8	.8		.7	.7
1.1	.9	.8	.7	1.3	1.2		.7	.8
3.4	1.9	1.7	1.6	2.0	2.2	Debt/Worth	1.7	1.7
-4.5	4.4	3.5	3.1	2.5	5.2		3.4	3.5
112.0	40.9	40.0	38.2	43.9	49.3		33.0	30.5
(23) 37.7	(198) 15.9	(336) 20.5	(227) 22.7	28.0	37.3	% Profit Before Taxes/Tangible Net Worth	(757) 16.6	(722) 14.6
8.6	2.5	9.4	11.7	16.1	22.2		5.3	4.3
20.9	13.0	15.3	13.9	12.1	16.2		12.6	12.0
9.5	4.8	6.5	8.6	9.7	10.7	% Profit Before Taxes/Total Assets	5.8	5.4
-3.3	.9	2.4	4.0	5.3	6.2		1.6	1.2
UND	182.2	88.6	70.9	47.3	61.3		75.2	74.1
154.6	49.1	29.3	26.3	15.8	21.0	Sales/Net Fixed Assets	31.5	29.1
16.7	20.1	13.3	11.9	8.3	10.8		14.6	13.4
8.0	5.2	4.5	4.3	3.7	4.8		4.9	4.5
4.9	3.7	3.3	3.2	3.0	3.1	Sales/Total Assets	3.6	3.4
2.1	2.6	2.5	2.4	2.4	2.3		2.6	2.5
.1	.2	.4	.3	.5	.3		.3	.3
(16) .8	(173) .6	(303) .8	(211) .7	(35) .9	(16) .8	% Depr., Dep., Amort./Sales	(727) .7	(670) .7
1.6	1.2	1.4	1.2	1.5	1.3		1.2	1.3
1.8	1.5	1.0	.6				1.4	1.4
(14) 3.3	(136) 3.0	(132) 1.7	(53) 1.6			% Officers', Directors', Owners' Comp/Sales	(343) 2.3	(300) 2.2
7.3	4.8	2.9	3.0				4.6	3.9
78929M	1213242M	6477631M	16618198M	8222538M	11730330M	Net Sales ($)	32327033M	30549731M
9647M	265773M	1744474M	4688569M	2505100M	3095096M	Total Assets ($)	8731406M	8448941M

M = $ thousand MM = $ million

See Pages 11 through 21 for Explanation of Ratios and Data

Comparative Historical Data | | | **Current Data Sorted By Sales**

Hist 1	Hist 2	Hist 3	Type of Statement	0-1MM	1-3MM	3-5MM	5-10MM	10-25MM	25MM & OVER
173	176	187	Unqualified	1		4	3	31	148
250	285	251	Reviewed	3	8	14	50	79	97
150	232	161	Compiled	7	26	26	43	33	26
49	65	80	Tax Returns	5	14	12	25	18	6
212	201	208	Other	7	19	16	36	55	75
4/1/02-3/31/03 ALL	4/1/03-3/31/04 ALL	4/1/04-3/31/05 ALL		171 (4/1-9/30/04)			716 (10/1/04-3/31/05)		
834	959	887	NUMBER OF STATEMENTS	23	67	72	157	216	352
%	%	%	ASSETS	%	%	%	%	%	%
5.6	5.2	5.1	Cash & Equivalents	14.2	6.9	7.2	4.6	5.4	3.6
34.3	36.4	35.0	Trade Receivables (net)	16.9	31.5	37.1	34.4	33.9	37.4
34.7	33.8	35.0	Inventory	15.7	37.3	30.2	36.7	36.0	35.4
2.4	2.8	2.6	All Other Current	9.3	3.6	3.0	2.2	1.9	2.4
77.1	78.2	77.6	Total Current	56.1	79.2	77.4	78.0	77.2	78.8
15.8	15.0	15.1	Fixed Assets (net)	25.7	11.9	16.1	15.2	15.8	14.4
1.4	1.6	1.6	Intangibles (net)	7.7	.7	.9	1.9	1.7	1.2
5.7	5.2	5.7	All Other Non-Current	10.5	8.2	5.6	4.9	5.3	5.6
100.0	100.0	100.0	Total	100.0	100.0	100.0	100.0	100.0	100.0
			LIABILITIES						
21.3	21.5	21.1	Notes Payable-Short Term	17.7	19.3	19.6	18.8	21.1	23.1
2.8	2.6	2.5	Cur. Mat.-L/T/D	3.8	4.1	2.2	2.8	2.8	2.0
14.3	15.2	15.5	Trade Payables	10.2	17.8	18.5	16.7	15.6	14.3
.2	.2	.2	Income Taxes Payable	.3	.1	.3	.3	.2	.2
8.3	8.5	8.7	All Other Current	18.7	7.9	9.1	7.8	8.7	8.6
46.9	48.0	48.1	Total Current	50.7	49.3	49.7	46.3	48.3	48.2
9.7	9.6	10.0	Long-Term Debt	31.3	10.6	11.4	10.7	8.0	9.1
.2	.2	.3	Deferred Taxes	.0	.1	.1	.4	.3	.3
3.6	4.6	3.9	All Other Non-Current	12.5	9.2	4.7	3.3	4.1	2.4
39.6	37.6	37.7	Net Worth	5.4	30.9	34.1	39.2	39.3	40.1
100.0	100.0	100.0	Total Liabilities & Net Worth	100.0	100.0	100.0	100.0	100.0	100.0
			INCOME DATA						
100.0	100.0	100.0	Net Sales	100.0	100.0	100.0	100.0	100.0	100.0
21.0	20.2	20.0	Gross Profit	29.8	25.2	23.3	21.9	19.3	17.4
18.7	18.2	17.1	Operating Expenses	28.2	23.6	20.8	19.3	16.2	13.9
2.4	2.1	2.9	Operating Profit	1.5	1.6	2.5	2.5	3.0	3.5
.5	.3	.3	All Other Expenses (net)	1.6	.4	.1	.4	.4	.2
1.9	1.7	2.6	Profit Before Taxes	−.1	1.2	2.4	2.2	2.6	3.3
			RATIOS						
2.6	2.5	2.4	Current	4.7	3.2	2.2	2.6	2.3	2.4
1.6	1.6	1.6		1.2	1.6	1.5	1.7	1.6	1.6
1.3	1.2	1.2		.5	1.0	1.2	1.3	1.2	1.2
1.4	1.4	1.3	Quick	2.4	1.4	1.4	1.4	1.3	1.3
.8	.8	.8		.6	.8	.9	.8	.7	.8
.5	.6	.5		.2	.5	.6	.5	.5	.6
23 16.1	25 14.8	23 15.8	Sales/Receivables	2 191.7	20 18.0	30 12.3	23 15.6	22 16.8	24 14.9
33 11.2	35 10.3	34 10.8		31 11.9	38 9.6	40 9.2	33 11.2	33 11.1	33 10.9
43 8.4	47 7.8	45 8.0		64 5.7	51 7.1	55 6.6	44 8.2	43 8.6	45 8.1
27 13.5	27 13.6	27 13.4	Cost of Sales/Inventory	0 UND	26 14.1	18 19.8	27 13.7	27 13.4	30 12.3
46 7.9	45 8.2	45 8.0		1 257.3	66 5.5	49 7.4	47 7.8	48 7.6	42 8.7
71 5.2	68 5.4	68 5.3		126 2.9	116 3.1	78 4.7	77 4.7	73 5.0	58 6.3
8 44.8	9 41.6	9 40.2	Cost of Sales/Payables	3 112.5	8 47.0	12 31.0	11 33.4	9 40.2	9 42.1
14 25.9	16 22.8	16 22.9		26 13.8	24 15.2	23 16.0	19 19.4	16 22.6	14 26.1
25 14.4	26 14.3	26 13.8		60 6.1	56 6.6	40 9.2	29 12.5	24 14.9	21 17.7
6.7	6.8	7.1	Sales/Working Capital	4.0	4.6	6.3	7.1	7.3	7.7
12.6	12.2	13.1		38.3	9.1	12.8	11.6	13.6	14.0
28.1	27.9	27.3		−6.8	79.3	33.9	21.0	29.0	25.0
8.3	8.7	12.2	EBIT/Interest	3.5	8.5	7.9	8.4	12.3	16.9
(783) 3.1	(906) 3.4	(834) 4.9		(17) .3	(61) 2.4	(69) 3.7	(145) 3.4	(201) 3.9	(341) 7.1
1.4	1.5	2.2		−5.8	.5	1.5	1.8	2.3	3.5
8.2	6.5	7.9	Net Profit + Depr., Dep., Amort./Cur. Mat. L/T/D			5.3	8.1	6.7	10.5
(231) 2.7	(267) 2.7	(260) 3.6			(16) 3.8	(42) 2.6	(60) 2.7	(132) 5.0	
1.3	1.4	1.7				1.6	1.4	1.4	2.3
.1	.1	.1	Fixed/Worth	.1	.1	.2	.1	.1	.1
.3	.3	.3		1.3	.2	.4	.3	.3	.3
.7	.7	.8		−1.1	1.2	1.2	.9	.8	.7
.7	.8	.8	Debt/Worth	1.4	.7	1.1	.9	.8	.8
1.7	1.8	1.8		5.3	2.2	2.1	1.5	1.8	1.7
3.3	4.0	3.7		−2.7	9.4	4.5	3.4	3.6	3.1
30.4	30.1	40.6	% Profit Before Taxes/Tangible Net Worth	40.0	52.4	38.5	36.2	38.2	45.5
(783) 14.0	(904) 14.1	(839) 21.4		(16) 13.8	(58) 8.7	(66) 22.0	(146) 13.4	(207) 18.1	(346) 27.8
3.8	3.7	8.6		−29.5	−1.5	2.0	3.7	9.5	14.8
11.5	10.6	14.7	% Profit Before Taxes/Total Assets	9.5	10.0	13.0	10.9	14.9	16.2
4.9	4.5	7.0		3.4	3.0	6.3	4.8	6.4	9.7
1.0	1.0	2.6		−10.4	−1.7	1.2	1.4	2.7	4.8
71.8	90.4	94.6	Sales/Net Fixed Assets	47.0	116.5	128.9	95.9	94.2	93.2
28.8	29.9	31.6		17.1	50.9	25.7	30.5	31.7	33.4
13.3	13.2	13.5		3.7	16.2	12.9	13.5	12.2	14.9
4.7	4.5	4.6	Sales/Total Assets	2.0	3.7	4.2	4.8	4.7	4.8
3.4	3.3	3.4		1.5	2.6	3.2	3.3	3.5	3.6
2.4	2.4	2.4		1.1	2.0	2.2	2.3	2.5	2.8
.4	.4	.3	% Depr., Dep., Amort./Sales	1.0	.2	.3	.4	.4	.2
(748) .8	(841) .7	(754) .7		(16) 1.9	(48) .7	(57) 1.0	(136) .7	(184) .8	(313) .6
1.5	1.4	1.3		3.8	1.0	1.8	1.4	1.4	1.1
1.3	1.2	1.1	% Officers', Directors', Owners' Comp/Sales	2.6	2.1	1.7	1.3	1.0	.6
(321) 2.3	(377) 2.3	(337) 2.0		(11) 4.8	(40) 3.8	(40) 3.8	(81) 2.1	(91) 1.5	(74) 1.5
4.1	4.1	3.8		13.8	5.9	5.0	3.6	2.7	2.8
33518828M	37478425M	44340868M	Net Sales ($)	13743M	137943M	287880M	1128268M	3566356M	39206678M
9925911M	10990805M	12308659M	Total Assets ($)	9634M	59602M	104627M	390380M	1196364M	10548052M

Current Data Sorted By Assets   **Comparative Historical Data**

						Type of Statement		
	3	11	19	5	4	Unqualified	41	28
1	14	58	20			Reviewed	99	76
6	20	46	3			Compiled	84	84
1	14	13	1			Tax Returns	19	20
4	26	40	17	3	2	Other	75	81
	44 (4/1-9/30/04)		287 (10/1/04-3/31/05)				4/1/00-3/31/01	4/1/01-3/31/02
0-500M	500M-2MM	2-10MM	10-50MM	50-100MM	100-250MM		ALL	ALL
12	77	168	60	8	6	NUMBER OF STATEMENTS	318	289
%	%	%	%	%	%	ASSETS	%	%
15.6	8.7	6.9	4.7			Cash & Equivalents	6.4	7.3
26.5	33.8	30.1	27.8			Trade Receivables (net)	32.0	31.7
12.8	29.4	33.1	32.3			Inventory	28.5	27.7
2.0	1.6	1.5	3.5			All Other Current	2.1	2.3
56.9	73.5	71.6	68.3			Total Current	68.9	69.1
29.4	20.9	21.3	22.4			Fixed Assets (net)	22.5	22.2
9.9	1.8	1.6	1.8			Intangibles (net)	2.0	2.4
3.8	3.8	5.5	7.5			All Other Non-Current	6.6	6.4
100.0	100.0	100.0	100.0			Total	100.0	100.0
						LIABILITIES		
22.1	11.3	13.4	13.9			Notes Payable-Short Term	13.5	13.2
6.1	2.6	3.0	2.6			Cur. Mat.-L/T/D	3.7	3.8
13.9	25.2	20.6	17.3			Trade Payables	18.6	19.9
.0	.1	.3	.5			Income Taxes Payable	.2	.2
13.6	12.6	7.4	8.3			All Other Current	7.4	9.5
55.7	51.7	44.6	42.7			Total Current	43.3	46.7
17.9	15.5	10.8	13.3			Long-Term Debt	12.6	14.2
.0	.4	.3	.4			Deferred Taxes	.3	.3
2.5	6.8	3.8	4.7			All Other Non-Current	4.7	3.6
23.9	25.7	40.4	38.9			Net Worth	39.0	35.3
100.0	100.0	100.0	100.0			Total Liabilities & Net Worth	100.0	100.0
						INCOME DATA		
100.0	100.0	100.0	100.0			Net Sales	100.0	100.0
38.1	32.3	29.1	29.8			Gross Profit	28.6	29.1
37.6	28.8	24.3	24.0			Operating Expenses	24.9	25.4
.5	3.5	4.8	5.8			Operating Profit	3.7	3.7
.2	.3	.1	.6			All Other Expenses (net)	.5	.8
.3	3.3	4.7	5.2			Profit Before Taxes	3.1	2.9
						RATIOS		
2.0	2.2	2.3	2.2			Current	2.5	2.5
1.1	1.5	1.6	1.6				1.6	1.6
.6	1.2	1.2	1.3				1.2	1.1
1.8	1.3	1.3	1.1			Quick	1.4	1.5
.8	.8	.8	.8				.9	.9
.3	.6	.5	.5				.6	.6
11 32.2	28 13.0	31 11.7	36 10.1			Sales/Receivables	31 12.0	30 12.3
22 16.6	37 9.8	40 9.0	48 7.5				39 9.4	39 9.4
50 7.3	57 6.5	51 7.2	61 6.0				50 7.2	54 6.7
0 UND	11 32.5	33 11.0	35 10.4			Cost of Sales/Inventory	24 15.3	26 14.2
6 57.9	49 7.5	59 6.2	72 5.1				48 7.6	50 7.4
38 9.6	89 4.1	91 4.0	140 2.6				79 4.6	84 4.3
0 UND	21 17.1	19 19.6	25 14.7			Cost of Sales/Payables	17 21.7	18 20.3
13 27.9	41 9.0	35 10.5	38 9.6				30 12.1	34 10.8
32 11.4	69 5.3	62 5.9	64 5.7				45 8.0	53 6.8
8.2	6.5	5.6	4.8			Sales/Working Capital	6.2	6.2
NM	12.6	9.9	8.6				10.8	10.7
−11.2	34.5	20.5	16.2				29.7	32.9
	9.4	19.0	12.5			EBIT/Interest	9.0	9.6
	(67) 3.7	(154) 6.6	(55) 4.8				(298) 3.2	(270) 3.4
	.9	2.3	2.3				1.3	1.3
	3.9	6.2	9.3			Net Profit + Depr., Dep.,	5.5	4.8
	(12) 2.2	(53) 2.5	(25) 3.9			Amort./Cur. Mat. L./T/D	(81) 2.6	(86) 2.0
	1.2	1.4	1.9				1.3	1.3
.3	.1	.2	.2			Fixed/Worth	.2	.2
1.5	.4	.5	.5				.5	.5
5.6	2.9	1.1	1.2				1.2	1.4
.9	1.2	.8	.8			Debt/Worth	.7	.7
4.4	2.3	1.7	1.7				1.7	1.8
NM	6.3	3.2	3.8				3.9	5.4
	47.4	43.8	35.0			% Profit Before Taxes/Tangible	40.3	32.5
	(63) 26.5	(160) 26.1	(56) 20.0			Net Worth	(295) 14.9	(250) 15.4
	3.2	8.6	8.8				3.7	4.9
21.0	17.0	16.7	14.6			% Profit Before Taxes/Total	14.6	13.6
1.3	5.9	8.8	5.5			Assets	5.1	6.6
−15.2	−.2	2.8	3.2				1.2	1.2
51.9	88.1	41.8	27.9			Sales/Net Fixed Assets	43.9	48.6
12.1	25.9	16.0	13.8				18.5	17.0
4.3	8.7	7.6	5.8				7.7	7.1
3.9	3.9	3.3	2.4			Sales/Total Assets	3.6	3.6
2.8	3.0	2.6	2.1				2.9	2.7
2.4	1.9	1.8	1.4				2.0	1.9
	.5	.8	.8			% Depr., Dep., Amort./Sales	.6	.6
	(61) 1.6	(144) 1.3	(55) 1.5				(288) 1.3	(259) 1.4
	3.7	2.9	2.6				2.6	2.6
	1.8	1.3	.7			% Officers', Directors',	1.8	1.8
	(38) 3.9	(68) 3.0	(14) 1.9			Owners' Comp/Sales	(146) 3.0	(137) 3.0
	6.3	5.5	4.0				5.7	5.6
10965M	275335M	1839340M	2275984M	982810M	2401980M	Net Sales ($)	4953773M	4301438M
3460M	94021M	734506M	1138736M	528090M	948551M	Total Assets ($)	2134382M	2150228M

M = $ thousand   MM = $ million
See Pages 11 through 21 for Explanation of Ratios and Data

Comparative Historical Data				Current Data Sorted By Sales					

Type of Statement

39	37	42	Unqualified		1	2	4	6	29
73	73	93	Reviewed	1	6	10	25	36	15
59	70	75	Compiled	1	13	18	22	17	4
25	35	29	Tax Returns	2	5	8	6	6	2
65	71	92	Other	5	14	11	24	20	18

4/1/02-3/31/03 ALL	4/1/03-3/31/04 ALL	4/1/04-3/31/05 ALL		44 (4/1-9/30/04)		287 (10/1/04-3/31/05)			
				0-1MM	1-3MM	3-5MM	5-10MM	10-25MM	25MM & OVER
261	286	331	**NUMBER OF STATEMENTS**	9	39	49	81	85	68
%	%	%	**ASSETS**	%	%	%	%	%	%
6.9	7.6	7.1	Cash & Equivalents		10.1	6.7	6.1	8.3	4.3
29.4	30.1	30.1	Trade Receivables (net)		28.7	25.7	32.0	34.5	27.5
27.2	28.5	30.9	Inventory		26.0	30.8	35.1	28.6	33.7
2.6	3.5	1.9	All Other Current		1.9	1.6	1.3	1.6	3.2
66.1	69.7	70.0	Total Current		66.7	64.9	74.5	73.0	68.7
25.7	24.0	22.4	Fixed Assets (net)		23.6	28.2	18.4	20.1	23.0
2.2	1.8	2.2	Intangibles (net)		5.0	1.9	1.6	1.1	2.6
6.1	4.6	5.4	All Other Non-Current		4.7	5.1	5.6	5.8	5.8
100.0	100.0	100.0	Total		100.0	100.0	100.0	100.0	100.0
			LIABILITIES						
13.9	11.6	13.2	Notes Payable-Short Term		14.2	12.5	11.7	11.6	15.4
4.4	3.6	2.9	Cur. Mat.-L/T/D		3.9	3.4	3.0	2.9	2.2
17.9	20.5	20.5	Trade Payables		20.7	21.2	24.6	20.4	17.3
.3	.3	.2	Income Taxes Payable		.0	.1	.1	.5	.3
8.8	8.7	9.1	All Other Current		10.0	9.8	6.7	7.8	9.6
45.3	44.6	45.9	Total Current		48.7	47.0	46.3	43.2	44.9
13.4	12.4	12.9	Long-Term Debt		18.6	19.2	9.6	10.6	11.1
.6	.4	.4	Deferred Taxes		.1	.3	.3	.6	.6
4.2	5.4	4.7	All Other Non-Current		6.5	4.4	6.0	3.3	4.5
36.5	37.2	36.0	Net Worth		26.1	29.0	37.8	42.3	38.9
100.0	100.0	100.0	Total Liabilities & Net Worth		100.0	100.0	100.0	100.0	100.0
			INCOME DATA						
100.0	100.0	100.0	Net Sales		100.0	100.0	100.0	100.0	100.0
30.0	31.2	30.2	Gross Profit		39.2	30.2	28.0	27.4	28.3
26.3	27.5	25.6	Operating Expenses		35.1	25.2	24.3	22.2	23.3
3.8	3.7	4.6	Operating Profit		4.2	5.0	3.7	5.1	5.0
.5	.5	.3	All Other Expenses (net)		.6	.4	.0	.1	.3
3.2	3.2	4.3	Profit Before Taxes		3.6	4.6	3.6	5.0	4.7
			RATIOS						
2.6	2.5	2.2	Current		2.0	2.3	2.2	2.4	2.0
1.6	1.6	1.6			1.3	1.4	1.6	1.7	1.5
1.1	1.2	1.2			1.0	1.0	1.3	1.3	1.2
1.4	1.4	1.3	Quick		1.5	1.2	1.3	1.5	.9
.8	.8	.8			.7	.7	.8	.9	.7
.5	.6	.5			.3	.5	.5	.7	.5
28 12.9	27 13.3	31 11.7	Sales/Receivables		20 18.4	26 13.9	32 11.4	33 11.1	33 11.1
38 9.6	42 8.7	40 9.1			44 8.4	34 10.7	40 9.2	43 8.4	40 9.2
51 7.2	55 6.7	54 6.7			65 5.6	47 7.8	52 7.0	53 6.8	56 6.5
21 17.4	23 15.6	25 14.6	Cost of Sales/Inventory		13 28.9	8 46.6	35 10.3	25 14.6	40 9.0
47 7.8	52 7.0	57 6.4			40 9.1	52 7.0	60 6.1	46 8.0	63 5.8
76 4.8	87 4.2	94 3.9			92 4.0	114 3.2	91 4.0	77 4.7	110 3.3
17 21.7	20 18.1	20	Cost of Sales/Payables		25 14.9	16 23.2	24 15.2	19 18.9	21 17.7
28 12.9	34 10.8	35 10.3			53 6.9	38 9.5	41 8.8	30 12.2	35 10.3
49 7.4	60 6.1	62 5.9			87 4.2	59 6.2	63 5.8	59 6.2	58 6.3
6.1	5.8	5.9	Sales/Working Capital		6.0	5.8	5.6	6.2	5.9
11.1	10.3	10.1			13.7	13.1	9.9	9.6	11.1
32.6	27.2	23.7			703.0	NM	17.6	18.7	23.2
11.2	11.2	13.7	EBIT/Interest		9.1	10.9	13.4	24.9	23.0
(242) 4.4	(263) 4.0	(297) 5.4			(34) 2.7	(44) 3.5	(74) 5.2	(77) 8.2	(63) 5.6
1.6	1.6	1.9			.8	1.6	1.8	3.3	2.4
5.5	5.5	6.5	Net Profit + Depr., Dep., Amort./Cur. Mat. L/T/D			5.7	3.0	6.5	9.7
(76) 2.9	(86) 2.0	(100) 2.7				(14) 2.2	(22) 2.0	(31) 3.1	(27) 4.4
1.2	1.0	1.5				1.7	1.4	1.4	2.4
.2	.2	.2	Fixed/Worth		.1	.2	.2	.2	.3
.5	.6	.5			.5	.8	.5	.5	.6
1.4	1.5	1.3			10.0	3.6	1.0	.9	1.2
.7	.8	.9	Debt/Worth		1.2	1.3	.9	.8	.8
1.8	2.1	1.9			3.6	2.0	1.8	1.3	2.1
5.2	4.7	3.9			112.0	9.3	3.4	3.0	3.9
36.7	34.8	45.6	% Profit Before Taxes/Tangible Net Worth		53.7	53.8	43.7	42.5	41.1
(243) 16.8	(268) 17.4	(301) 24.3			(31) 26.5	(39) 27.6	(77) 22.7	(81) 26.1	(65) 20.1
5.2	5.1	8.1			.0	5.3	4.6	12.0	12.9
12.4	13.6	16.2	% Profit Before Taxes/Total Assets		17.5	16.5	14.6	19.7	15.5
6.3	5.5	7.0			4.7	5.7	6.4	10.0	7.3
1.0	1.1	2.2			-.5	1.0	1.5	3.9	3.3
36.2	40.5	44.1	Sales/Net Fixed Assets		60.9	46.2	45.2	43.0	30.3
15.2	14.9	16.0			20.9	13.7	17.7	16.3	15.8
5.4	5.9	6.7			4.6	4.2	9.5	8.0	6.2
3.5	3.5	3.3	Sales/Total Assets		3.3	3.6	3.4	3.3	2.8
2.6	2.5	2.5			2.3	2.2	2.7	2.6	2.2
1.8	1.8	1.7			1.3	1.5	1.9	2.0	1.7
.9	.9	.8	% Depr., Dep., Amort./Sales		.5	.8	.7	.8	.8
(237) 1.6	(241) 1.7	(279) 1.5			(31) 2.4	(42) 2.7	(66) 1.2	(75) 1.2	(59) 1.3
3.1	3.2	3.2			4.8	6.1	2.6	2.4	2.5
1.8	1.7	1.4	% Officers', Directors', Owners' Comp/Sales		3.2	1.7	2.1	1.1	.5
(101) 3.3	(119) 3.0	(128) 3.1			(19) 4.3	(23) 2.8	(32) 3.4	(37) 1.6	(13) 1.2
5.6	5.5	5.8			9.5	5.4	5.6	4.0	3.5
4514090M	6530346M	7786414M	Net Sales ($)	4236M	77174M	192232M	598147M	1268259M	5646366M
2246143M	3016236M	3447364M	Total Assets ($)	4247M	40825M	112669M	253590M	553026M	2483007M

M = $ thousand   MM = $ million
See Pages 11 through 21 for Explanation of Ratios and Data

WHOLESALE—Roofing, Siding, and Insulation Material Merchant Wholesalers NAICS 423330 (SIC 5033)

Current Data Sorted By Assets							Comparative Historical Data	
						Type of Statement		
		9	6	3	4	Unqualified	13	15
	3	19	14			Reviewed	30	36
3	13	12	5			Compiled	30	27
3	9	1				Tax Returns	7	18
2	7	31	12	2		Other	47	48
	20 (4/1-9/30/04)		138 (10/1/04-3/31/05)				4/1/00-3/31/01	4/1/01-3/31/02
0-500M	500M-2MM	2-10MM	10-50MM	50-100MM	100-250MM		ALL	ALL
8	32	72	37	5	4	**NUMBER OF STATEMENTS**	127	144
%	%	%	%	%	%	**ASSETS**	%	%
	5.4	4.4	4.9			Cash & Equivalents	5.6	6.5
	38.0	43.4	37.8			Trade Receivables (net)	37.1	38.1
	34.2	34.5	33.4			Inventory	30.1	28.1
	3.0	2.0	3.9			All Other Current	3.0	3.1
	80.6	84.2	80.1			Total Current	75.8	75.7
	12.6	11.2	12.8			Fixed Assets (net)	16.0	16.2
	1.1	1.1	3.2			Intangibles (net)	2.3	2.3
	5.7	3.4	3.9			All Other Non-Current	5.9	5.8
	100.0	100.0	100.0			Total	100.0	100.0
						LIABILITIES		
	16.1	17.0	18.4			Notes Payable-Short Term	16.0	13.9
	3.3	2.5	1.9			Cur. Mat.-L/T/D	3.1	2.7
	35.7	32.9	24.1			Trade Payables	23.5	26.3
	.4	.2	.4			Income Taxes Payable	.3	.3
	7.5	6.6	7.3			All Other Current	7.1	7.6
	63.1	59.1	52.1			Total Current	49.9	50.7
	10.4	8.2	7.8			Long-Term Debt	11.7	9.1
	.0	.2	.2			Deferred Taxes	.1	.6
	.9	3.7	4.2			All Other Non-Current	3.2	2.2
	25.6	28.8	35.7			Net Worth	35.1	37.4
	100.0	100.0	100.0			Total Liabilities & Net Worth	100.0	100.0
						INCOME DATA		
	100.0	100.0	100.0			Net Sales	100.0	100.0
	26.1	22.5	25.8			Gross Profit	24.1	23.8
	26.0	19.0	21.4			Operating Expenses	21.1	21.4
	.1	3.5	4.4			Operating Profit	3.0	2.5
	.1	.4	.3			All Other Expenses (net)	.7	.6
	.0	3.0	4.1			Profit Before Taxes	2.3	1.9
						RATIOS		
	2.0	1.7	2.7			Current	2.2	2.2
	1.4	1.4	1.4				1.5	1.5
	1.1	1.2	1.1				1.2	1.1
	1.0	1.0	1.5			Quick	1.1	1.3
	.8	.7	.8				.8	.8
	.5	.6	.5				.6	.6
	29 12.4	40 9.2	35 10.4			Sales/Receivables	28 13.1	33 11.1
	41 8.9	51 7.2	44 8.2				43 8.5	43 8.5
	56 6.5	66 5.6	59 6.2				57 6.4	54 6.7
	36 10.2	34 10.7	40 9.2			Cost of Sales/Inventory	29 12.7	25 14.5
	54 6.7	50 7.3	55 6.7				47 7.8	43 8.6
	79 4.6	71 5.2	79 4.6				65 5.6	64 5.7
	27 13.4	29 12.6	25 14.3			Cost of Sales/Payables	19 19.0	24 15.2
	49 7.4	44 8.3	34 10.6				32 11.4	33 11.0
	65 5.6	69 5.3	59 6.2				48 7.6	52 7.1
	8.2	8.8	6.7			Sales/Working Capital	7.4	7.7
	14.2	13.6	11.9				14.6	12.9
	60.6	27.2	64.4				28.6	34.4
	11.5	16.3	23.2			EBIT/Interest	5.7	6.6
	(29) 4.1	7.3	(34) 6.4				(116) 2.8	(132) 3.2
	1.5	2.0	3.3				1.4	1.4
		8.9				Net Profit + Depr., Dep.,	6.2	6.9
		(15) 4.1				Amort./Cur. Mat. L /T/D	(39) 2.0	(32) 3.4
		1.1					1.1	1.5
	.1	.2	.2			Fixed/Worth	.2	.2
	.3	.3	.4				.4	.4
	1.4	.7	.9				1.0	.9
	1.0	1.6	1.2			Debt/Worth	1.2	.8
	3.0	2.5	2.3				2.0	1.8
	8.3	5.4	4.8				4.2	4.0
	60.4	68.7	57.0			% Profit Before Taxes/Tangible	39.0	33.6
	(26) 14.2	(70) 26.0	(36) 31.9			Net Worth	(121) 18.1	(135) 17.6
	3.3	6.4	16.2				4.2	5.0
	10.0	15.2	14.9			% Profit Before Taxes/Total	10.2	10.9
	5.5	6.8	9.3			Assets	5.6	6.0
	.2	1.5	4.8				1.4	1.4
	100.9	66.4	48.5			Sales/Net Fixed Assets	51.9	49.4
	45.7	34.3	32.7				28.1	27.0
	17.3	21.6	15.2				16.2	14.8
	3.9	3.6	3.7			Sales/Total Assets	3.7	3.9
	3.2	3.1	2.8				3.2	3.3
	2.4	2.7	2.2				2.6	2.6
	.5	.5	.6			% Depr., Dep., Amort./Sales	.6	.7
	(25) .7	(67) .7	(33) .9				(114) 1.0	(126) 1.0
	1.4	1.3	1.4				1.5	1.6
	2.5	1.4	1.3			% Officers', Directors',	1.7	1.3
	(19) 3.9	(22) 2.6	(10) 2.4			Owners' Comp/Sales	(49) 3.1	(58) 2.9
	5.7	4.1	11.4				5.4	5.3
6543M	127051M	1151662M	2096178M	931275M	1510749M	Net Sales ($)	3643300M	4047037M
1799M	38380M	377746M	716593M	333738M	707494M	Total Assets ($)	1248705M	1406217M

M = $ thousand   MM = $ million
See Pages 11 through 21 for Explanation of Ratios and Data

Comparative Historical Data | Current Data Sorted By Sales

Type of Statement									
20	24	22	Unqualified				1	5	16
25	38	36	Reviewed		2		6	12	16
32	38	33	Compiled	3	6	4	7	7	6
9	12	13	Tax Returns	1	4	3	5		
35	55	54	Other	2	3	2	8	21	18
4/1/02-3/31/03	4/1/03-3/31/04	4/1/04-3/31/05			20 (4/1-9/30/04)		138 (10/1/04-3/31/05)		
ALL	ALL	ALL		0-1MM	1-3MM	3-5MM	5-10MM	10-25MM	25MM & OVER
121	167	158	**NUMBER OF STATEMENTS**	6	15	9	27	45	56
%	%	%	**ASSETS**	%	%	%	%	%	%
6.6	5.9	5.5	Cash & Equivalents		8.3		4.4	4.8	3.8
36.8	41.1	39.9	Trade Receivables (net)		30.1		41.0	44.8	40.5
29.6	28.9	33.3	Inventory		34.1		33.4	34.1	32.8
3.3	2.5	2.6	All Other Current		5.2		2.4	1.6	3.2
76.3	78.4	81.3	Total Current		77.6		81.3	85.3	80.2
15.6	13.5	12.2	Fixed Assets (net)		10.0		13.4	10.7	11.9
3.1	2.9	2.3	Intangibles (net)		3.0		1.5	1.4	3.8
5.0	5.2	4.2	All Other Non-Current		9.3		3.9	2.5	4.0
100.0	100.0	100.0	Total		100.0		100.0	100.0	100.0
			LIABILITIES						
15.4	16.1	16.1	Notes Payable-Short Term		12.9		14.3	15.3	18.7
3.4	2.7	2.6	Cur. Mat.-L/T/D		2.9		2.9	2.7	2.2
25.4	29.1	30.8	Trade Payables		37.4		31.7	33.1	27.7
.2	.3	.3	Income Taxes Payable		.1		.5	.2	.4
7.1	7.2	6.9	All Other Current		5.6		7.1	6.6	7.2
51.6	55.4	56.7	Total Current		58.9		56.5	58.0	56.2
8.7	8.5	9.4	Long-Term Debt		13.6		9.3	9.5	7.3
.2	.4	.2	Deferred Taxes		.0		.4	.1	.4
2.3	4.2	3.8	All Other Non-Current		6.2		3.1	3.1	4.1
37.2	31.5	29.9	Net Worth		21.3		30.7	29.3	32.0
100.0	100.0	100.0	Total Liabilities & Net Worth		100.0		100.0	100.0	100.0
			INCOME DATA						
100.0	100.0	100.0	Net Sales		100.0		100.0	100.0	100.0
25.1	23.9	24.1	Gross Profit		24.2		23.6	23.5	23.9
21.9	21.4	21.0	Operating Expenses		25.7		21.0	19.7	19.6
3.2	2.6	3.0	Operating Profit		-1.5		2.6	3.8	4.3
.7	.2	.3	All Other Expenses (net)		.2		.4	.5	.3
2.5	2.4	2.7	Profit Before Taxes		-1.7		2.2	3.3	4.0
			RATIOS						
2.2	2.0	2.0			2.3		2.0	1.9	1.8
1.4	1.4	1.4	Current		1.4		1.4	1.4	1.4
1.1	1.1	1.1			1.0		1.1	1.2	1.1
1.2	1.2	1.1			1.0		1.3	1.2	1.0
.8	.8	.7	Quick		.6		.7	.7	.7
.6	.6	.6			.4		.6	.6	.6
33 11.2	32 11.3	33 11.1		21 17.1		30 12.3	41 8.9	39 9.4	
45 8.0	44 8.3	47 7.8	Sales/Receivables	40 9.1		41 8.9	51 7.1	52 7.0	
57 6.4	56 6.5	62 5.9		57 6.5		60 6.1	69 5.3	61 6.0	
28 13.0	27 13.4	36 10.1		37 9.8		21 17.8	38 9.6	36 10.0	
46 7.9	43 8.5	50 7.3	Cost of Sales/Inventory	56 6.5		43 8.5	52 7.0	49 7.4	
70 5.2	63 5.8	74 5.0		171 2.1		71 5.1	73 5.0	71 5.1	
25 14.8	25 14.4	26 13.9		20 18.4		16 22.2	30 12.0	26 14.0	
36 10.2	40 9.2	43 8.5	Cost of Sales/Payables	48 7.6		41 8.9	44 8.3	37 9.8	
53 6.8	56 6.5	66 5.6		76 4.8		63 5.8	71 5.2	62 5.8	
7.8	8.4	8.2			6.0		8.5	8.2	8.7
13.1	14.2	13.4	Sales/Working Capital		13.4		18.4	13.4	13.0
35.9	49.6	32.6			-140.6		47.6	26.3	66.7
11.4	12.0	13.8			8.2		12.0	19.8	16.2
(112) 4.7	(158) 4.6	(148) 6.4	EBIT/Interest	(12) 2.9		5.6	(44) 7.5	(54) 7.6	
2.0	1.9	2.4			-1.8		1.5	2.2	3.9
11.2	12.1	9.6						11.7	12.5
(39) 4.2	(40) 4.4	(31) 4.5	Net Profit + Depr., Dep., Amort./Cur. Mat. L/T/D				(10) 6.4	(12) 8.6	
2.1	1.8	2.6						3.2	4.2
.2	.2	.2			.0		.2	.2	.2
.4	.4	.4	Fixed/Worth		.2		.3	.3	.4
1.2	1.2	.9			1.8		1.2	.7	.8
.7	1.1	1.3			.9		1.3	1.5	1.3
2.0	2.5	2.6	Debt/Worth		3.0		3.1	2.6	2.4
5.0	7.4	6.4			99.4		6.6	5.0	6.0
40.1	48.3	62.2			44.5		69.3	51.5	72.6
(110) 19.8	(146) 19.9	(146) 26.7	% Profit Before Taxes/Tangible Net Worth	(12) 13.0	(25) 29.3	(43) 21.8	(54) 38.9	
7.0	7.2	8.7			-16.1		1.5	7.8	24.5
12.1	11.7	14.5			10.0		13.3	14.5	16.6
6.7	6.1	7.5	% Profit Before Taxes/Total Assets		4.6		8.4	6.9	10.3
2.3	1.3	2.5			-5.4		1.1	3.0	5.3
54.0	76.3	67.4			393.0		90.8	66.9	52.1
24.7	33.6	37.9	Sales/Net Fixed Assets		59.6		40.7	32.8	38.8
13.0	16.5	19.0			11.2		18.3	24.0	19.0
3.8	3.8	3.7			3.7		3.9	3.5	3.7
2.9	3.2	3.1	Sales/Total Assets		3.1		3.3	3.1	3.0
2.4	2.6	2.5			2.2		2.8	2.5	2.4
.6	.5	.5			.4		.5	.5	.5
(110) .9	(149) .8	(137) .7	% Depr., Dep., Amort./Sales	(10) .7	(23) 1.0	(41) .7	(51) .8	
1.6	1.5	1.3			1.7		1.4	1.2	1.3
1.5	1.6	2.0					1.5	2.3	1.2
(51) 3.3	(63) 3.1	(54) 2.9	% Officers', Directors', Owners' Comp/Sales			(14) 2.7	(13) 2.8	(14) 2.4	
5.2	4.4	4.9					4.6	5.0	5.5
3588154M	5180301M	5823458M	Net Sales ($)	2677M	26642M	36312M	194801M	722118M	4840908M
1327075M	1925093M	2175750M	Total Assets ($)	2547M	14246M	11791M	63771M	255587M	1827808M

M = $ thousand   MM = $ million
See Pages 11 through 21 for Explanation of Ratios and Data

Current Data Sorted By Assets   **Comparative Historical Data**

	0-500M	500M-2MM	2-10MM	10-50MM	50-100MM	100-250MM	Type of Statement	4/1/00-3/31/01 ALL	4/1/01-3/31/02 ALL
	1	1	13	19	3	1	Unqualified	22	24
	1	14	61	20			Reviewed	46	42
	3	21	25				Compiled	72	68
	10	16	13	2		1	Tax Returns	18	16
	4	18	29	7	1	2	Other	63	64
		55 (4/1-9/30/04)		231 (10/1/04-3/31/05)					
NUMBER OF STATEMENTS	19	70	141	48	4	4		221	214
	%	%	%	%	%	%	**ASSETS**	%	%
	7.5	10.4	5.3	5.3			Cash & Equivalents	7.4	7.3
	35.5	38.0	39.7	34.9			Trade Receivables (net)	38.4	37.1
	22.4	29.2	31.4	28.5			Inventory	30.5	29.8
	2.0	2.2	2.8	2.0			All Other Current	1.8	2.9
	67.4	79.8	79.2	70.6			Total Current	78.0	77.2
	22.2	13.6	13.9	20.6			Fixed Assets (net)	16.3	16.9
	.9	1.6	2.4	3.0			Intangibles (net)	2.0	1.4
	9.0	5.0	4.6	5.7			All Other Non-Current	3.7	4.6
	100.0	100.0	100.0	100.0			Total	100.0	100.0
							LIABILITIES		
	37.7	19.2	18.0	13.7			Notes Payable-Short Term	16.1	14.2
	4.3	3.4	2.3	3.9			Cur. Mat.-L/T/D	3.1	3.8
	14.4	24.1	19.7	16.5			Trade Payables	20.8	20.2
	.0	.6	.3	.2			Income Taxes Payable	.2	.3
	6.7	9.8	9.6	9.5			All Other Current	9.1	9.9
	63.2	57.2	50.1	43.7			Total Current	49.2	48.4
	25.2	12.3	7.4	9.5			Long-Term Debt	9.8	10.1
	.0	.1	.3	.5			Deferred Taxes	.1	.2
	16.9	4.8	3.2	1.7			All Other Non-Current	4.3	3.7
	-5.2	25.7	39.1	44.7			Net Worth	36.6	37.6
	100.0	100.0	100.0	100.0			Total Liabilities & Net Worth	100.0	100.0
							INCOME DATA		
	100.0	100.0	100.0	100.0			Net Sales	100.0	100.0
	34.8	27.2	25.8	24.2			Gross Profit	26.3	26.8
	29.2	23.1	22.2	18.4			Operating Expenses	22.7	23.2
	5.6	4.1	3.6	5.8			Operating Profit	3.6	3.6
	.5	.6	.1	.3			All Other Expenses (net)	.1	.6
	5.1	3.5	3.5	5.5			Profit Before Taxes	3.5	2.9
							RATIOS		
	3.4	2.0	2.4	2.4				2.5	2.5
	1.4	1.5	1.5	1.7			Current	1.6	1.6
	.8	1.1	1.2	1.2				1.2	1.2
	2.1	1.4	1.3	1.6				1.4	1.5
	.8	.9	.9	.9			Quick	.9	.9
	.5	.6	.6	.6				.6	.6
	23 15.8	29 12.7	34 10.7	31 11.9				33 11.1	32 11.5
	34 10.7	41 8.9	43 8.4	45 8.2			Sales/Receivables	41 8.8	40 9.2
	57 6.4	58 6.3	59 6.1	60 6.0				58 6.3	55 6.6
	0 UND	20 18.3	28 12.9	30 12.1				26 14.1	27 13.4
	33 11.0	43 8.6	47 7.8	47 7.7			Cost of Sales/Inventory	45 8.0	44 8.4
	59 6.2	81 4.5	69 5.3	63 5.8				69 5.3	65 5.6
	0 UND	15 23.9	17 22.0	12 30.0				15 23.8	16 23.3
	22 16.3	30 12.0	26 14.1	19 18.8			Cost of Sales/Payables	28 13.2	28 13.1
	33 11.1	52 7.1	42 8.7	38 9.5				46 7.9	42 8.6
	8.5	6.8	7.2	5.7				6.9	6.8
	17.1	12.8	11.0	10.2			Sales/Working Capital	11.6	11.0
	-50.0	43.1	25.7	18.9				26.6	27.6
	6.7	11.6	13.7	22.7				10.6	9.4
	(14) 3.8	(65) 3.9	(134) 5.6	(44) 9.6			EBIT/Interest	(201) 4.1	(196) 3.4
	.1	1.3	2.6	4.2				1.8	1.4
		4.2	11.1	13.2			Net Profit + Depr., Dep.,	5.9	5.8
		(10) 1.4	(32) 4.6	(17) 2.5			Amort./Cur. Mat. L/T/D	(50) 3.0	(49) 2.4
		.8	2.1	1.9				1.8	1.2
	.1	.1	.2	.2				.2	.2
	1.4	.4	.3	.3			Fixed/Worth	.4	.4
	-3.4	1.8	.6	1.2				.8	.9
	2.6	1.5	.8	.7				.9	.8
	4.8	2.7	1.8	1.5			Debt/Worth	2.0	1.9
	-10.7	11.1	4.2	2.7				3.9	3.8
	139.3	68.4	48.6	41.1			% Profit Before Taxes/Tangible	47.7	40.6
	(14) 95.6	(60) 32.1	(136) 22.8	(46) 26.9			Net Worth	(209) 23.6	(199) 17.0
	31.0	9.2	10.1	18.5				8.2	5.6
	32.3	17.2	14.4	17.4			% Profit Before Taxes/Total	16.9	15.1
	16.5	7.9	7.6	11.0			Assets	7.1	6.0
	4.8	.9	3.1	7.0				2.5	1.7
	255.3	81.4	61.4	35.5				56.6	51.2
	27.0	32.9	31.8	21.8			Sales/Net Fixed Assets	28.8	27.5
	10.1	15.8	15.4	7.4				14.3	13.0
	5.1	3.9	3.7	3.4				4.1	3.8
	3.8	3.0	3.1	2.9			Sales/Total Assets	3.2	3.2
	2.8	2.4	2.4	1.8				2.5	2.6
	.3	.5	.5	.6				.4	.4
	(10) 1.5	(56) .9	(119) .8	(45) 1.2			% Depr., Dep., Amort./Sales	(194) .9	(187) .9
	4.9	1.9	1.3	1.7				1.5	1.5
		2.4	1.7				% Officers', Directors',	1.3	1.5
		(40) 3.5	(50) 2.5				Owners' Comp/Sales	(100) 2.7	(77) 3.3
		7.1	4.4					6.4	6.6
	19564M	247657M	1998124M	3022217M	907783M	2394213M	Net Sales ($)	5536528M	6138628M
	5033M	75895M	639477M	1058807M	306874M	572258M	Total Assets ($)	1952682M	2096909M

M = $ thousand   MM = $ million
See Pages 11 through 21 for Explanation of Ratios and Data

Comparative Historical Data | Current Data Sorted By Sales

Type of Statement	4/1/02-3/31/03	4/1/03-3/31/04	4/1/04-3/31/05	0-1MM	1-3MM	3-5MM	5-10MM	10-25MM	25MM & OVER
Unqualified	36	33	38	1	1		1	14	21
Reviewed	83	94	96		6	7	21	38	24
Compiled	44	81	49	3	12	6	19	5	4
Tax Returns	20	30	42	6	10	8	8	6	4
Other	58	70	61	2	12	8	11	17	11
	ALL	ALL	ALL	**55 (4/1-9/30/04)**			**231 (10/1/04-3/31/05)**		
NUMBER OF STATEMENTS	241	308	286	12	41	29	60	80	64
ASSETS	%	%	%	%	%	%	%	%	%
Cash & Equivalents	6.7	7.0	6.9	13.5	7.8	9.8	6.7	5.5	5.6
Trade Receivables (net)	36.7	36.9	37.8	26.2	35.8	39.0	39.7	39.1	37.6
Inventory	30.3	30.5	29.6	20.2	30.3	22.6	31.8	31.3	30.0
All Other Current	2.1	2.9	2.5	.4	3.3	1.5	2.6	3.1	1.9
Total Current	75.8	77.3	76.8	60.3	77.2	72.8	80.7	79.0	75.1
Fixed Assets (net)	17.2	15.3	15.8	24.9	15.9	18.4	12.8	13.3	19.0
Intangibles (net)	1.8	2.3	2.2	1.5	1.1	2.1	2.8	2.8	2.1
All Other Non-Current	5.2	5.1	5.1	12.5	5.9	6.7	3.7	4.9	3.9
Total	100.0	100.0	100.0	100.0	100.0	100.0	100.0	100.0	100.0
LIABILITIES									
Notes Payable-Short Term	14.3	15.9	18.8	57.9	18.8	19.0	16.7	17.9	14.4
Cur. Mat.-L/T/D	2.6	2.5	3.0	3.2	4.0	3.7	3.0	2.1	3.0
Trade Payables	19.0	20.5	19.8	5.5	23.2	20.2	23.5	17.9	18.8
Income Taxes Payable	.3	.3	.3	.3	.7	.2	.4	.3	.2
All Other Current	9.8	9.1	9.4	4.9	10.5	11.8	7.0	9.1	10.8
Total Current	46.0	48.2	51.2	71.7	57.1	54.8	50.6	47.4	47.2
Long-Term Debt	9.4	8.7	10.2	26.8	16.7	13.6	6.8	6.8	8.7
Deferred Taxes	.3	.3	.3	.0	.0	.2	.1	.4	.5
All Other Non-Current	2.4	4.7	4.2	18.7	7.4	2.9	4.0	3.2	1.5
Net Worth	41.8	38.2	34.1	-17.3	18.7	28.5	38.4	42.2	42.1
Total Liabilities & Net Worth	100.0	100.0	100.0	100.0	100.0	100.0	100.0	100.0	100.0
INCOME DATA									
Net Sales	100.0	100.0	100.0	100.0	100.0	100.0	100.0	100.0	100.0
Gross Profit	26.5	27.0	26.6	39.3	29.2	26.9	26.5	25.7	23.7
Operating Expenses	23.1	24.2	22.3	30.5	25.2	22.6	23.6	21.3	19.0
Operating Profit	3.3	2.9	4.3	8.8	4.0	4.3	2.9	4.4	4.8
All Other Expenses (net)	.5	.2	.3	.7	.7	.5	.1	.2	.2
Profit Before Taxes	2.9	2.7	4.0	8.1	3.3	3.8	2.8	4.2	4.6
RATIOS									
Current	2.7	2.4	2.3	4.2	2.1	1.7	2.4	2.5	2.4
	1.7	1.6	1.5	1.2	1.4	1.3	1.5	1.6	1.7
	1.2	1.2	1.2	.7	1.0	1.1	1.3	1.2	1.2
Quick	1.5	1.4	1.4	3.3	1.5	1.5	1.2	1.5	1.5
	.9	.9	.9	.8	.8	.8	.9	.9	.9
	.6	.6	.6	.4	.4	.6	.7	.7	.6
Sales/Receivables	29 12.5	31 11.8	31 11.8	0 UND	29 12.6	29 12.4	31 11.8	34 10.7	31 11.9
	41 8.9	42 8.8	43 8.4	43 8.5	46 8.0	40 9.1	43 8.5	42 8.6	44 8.3
	56 6.6	57 6.4	59 6.2	68 5.4	62 5.9	62 5.9	61 6.0	60 6.0	53 6.8
Cost of Sales/Inventory	25 14.9	27 13.4	27 13.7	0 UND	11 33.3	0 UND	29 12.6	29 12.4	27 13.6
	47 7.8	51 7.2	46 8.0	31 11.9	46 7.9	34 10.7	47 7.7	47 7.8	46 7.9
	76 4.8	74 5.0	72 5.1	100 3.6	91 4.0	77 4.7	71 5.1	79 4.6	59 6.2
Cost of Sales/Payables	16 22.8	15 23.6	14 26.0	0 UND	17 21.2	9 40.2	21 17.1	12 29.3	13 28.4
	26 13.8	28 12.9	26 14.1	0 UND	33 11.1	23 16.1	30 12.2	21 17.7	24 15.4
	40 9.1	47 7.8	43 8.5	42 8.7	62 5.9	50 7.3	41 8.9	40 9.2	44 8.2
Sales/Working Capital	6.7	7.0	6.9	5.1	6.7	9.0	6.8	6.7	8.5
	10.2	10.3	11.3	9.4	11.6	16.4	11.3	10.1	11.2
	24.6	28.2	31.2	-11.3	-133.8	67.0	21.5	22.6	20.5
EBIT/Interest	10.7	11.5	13.7		9.0	11.9	13.0	14.5	20.4
	(225) 4.2	(273) 4.2	(264) 5.7		(40) 4.4	(28) 3.2	(55) 4.7	(74) 5.7	(60) 9.2
	1.9	2.0	2.4		1.0	1.1	2.2	2.9	4.6
Net Profit + Depr., Dep., Amort./Cur. Mat. L/T/D	9.3	10.0	9.5				10.4	13.5	9.6
	(68) 4.1	(67) 2.7	(64) 3.4			(12) 2.8	(20) 5.6	(23) 2.9	
	2.0	1.4	1.4				1.3	2.6	1.9
Fixed/Worth	.1	.1	.2	.0	.1	.2	.2	.2	.1
	.3	.3	.3	1.1	.8	.7	.2	.3	.4
	.8	1.0	.9	-2.4	2.2	2.5	.5	.6	1.0
Debt/Worth	.6	.7	.9	1.0	1.7	1.4	1.1	.6	.8
	1.3	1.9	2.0	3.9	3.5	2.9	1.9	1.6	1.6
	3.0	4.3	4.7	-6.2	18.6	13.8	3.9	4.2	2.9
% Profit Before Taxes/Tangible Net Worth	34.7	38.0	55.3		88.1	85.4	33.6	41.2	54.3
	(223) 19.3	(276) 17.9	(264) 26.9		(34) 53.6	(25) 29.6	(58) 15.5	(77) 24.2	(62) 30.4
	5.1	5.9	12.0		14.5	2.1	6.1	11.0	20.5
% Profit Before Taxes/Total Assets	14.0	13.1	16.8	38.0	19.4	14.1	13.5	14.4	17.5
	6.5	6.3	9.4	17.1	7.8	7.3	5.8	8.5	11.4
	1.6	1.9	3.5	8.0	-.1	.2	2.0	4.1	7.0
Sales/Net Fixed Assets	51.3	61.9	60.4	UND	88.0	41.5	72.7	61.4	46.1
	27.3	29.2	28.5	23.7	25.3	19.6	35.5	31.4	24.8
	12.4	13.8	13.8	9.0	14.6	11.6	14.1	20.7	11.1
Sales/Total Assets	3.9	3.9	3.7	5.0	3.4	3.9	3.7	3.7	3.9
	3.0	3.1	3.0	2.6	2.7	3.0	3.1	3.0	3.1
	2.4	2.3	2.4	1.3	2.2	2.4	2.4	2.5	2.5
% Depr., Dep., Amort./Sales	.5	.5	.5		.4	.6	.6	.5	.5
	(215) .9	(267) .9	(235) .9	(30) .9	(22) 1.0	(48) .8	(73) .8	(55) .9	
	1.8	1.7	1.6		1.9	2.3	1.6	1.3	1.4
% Officers', Directors', Owners' Comp/Sales	1.5	1.7	1.9		2.4	2.9	1.7	1.7	
	(91) 3.6	(129) 3.0	(106) 3.1	(21) 4.4	(17) 3.9	(28) 2.4	(28) 2.8		
	6.1	7.1	5.8		9.3	5.2	3.5	5.8	
Net Sales ($)	6640747M	7411626M	8589558M	6256M	83414M	113349M	454509M	1287329M	6644701M
Total Assets ($)	2477175M	2488647M	2658344M	3678M	34674M	40023M	156608M	484395M	1938966M

M = $ thousand   MM = $ million
See Pages 11 through 21 for Explanation of Ratios and Data

Current Data Sorted By Assets   Comparative Historical Data

0-500M	500M-2MM	2-10MM	10-50MM	50-100MM	100-250MM	Type of Statement	4/1/00-3/31/01 ALL	4/1/01-3/31/02 ALL
		2	1		1	Unqualified	6	4
	1	10	3			Reviewed	13	16
	1	2				Compiled	19	14
	2				1	Tax Returns	4	2
1	2	6	1	1		Other	13	11
	7 (4/1-9/30/04)			28 (10/1/04-3/31/05)				
1	6	20	5	1	2	**NUMBER OF STATEMENTS**	55	47
%	%	%	%	%	%	**ASSETS**	%	%
		17.8				Cash & Equivalents	6.6	7.9
		30.9				Trade Receivables (net)	33.4	29.2
		31.1				Inventory	36.7	40.5
		2.5				All Other Current	.8	2.1
		82.3				Total Current	77.5	79.8
		8.2				Fixed Assets (net)	12.5	12.0
		2.9				Intangibles (net)	4.2	2.2
		6.5				All Other Non-Current	5.8	6.0
		100.0				Total	100.0	100.0
						LIABILITIES		
		14.9				Notes Payable-Short Term	15.1	14.0
		1.5				Cur. Mat.-L/T/D	4.6	6.1
		22.8				Trade Payables	23.7	20.2
		.1				Income Taxes Payable	.1	.1
		8.6				All Other Current	6.9	7.7
		48.0				Total Current	50.4	48.0
		2.2				Long-Term Debt	11.1	8.4
		.0				Deferred Taxes	.2	.2
		18.8				All Other Non-Current	2.6	11.6
		31.0				Net Worth	35.7	31.8
		100.0				Total Liabilities & Net Worth	100.0	100.0
						INCOME DATA		
		100.0				Net Sales	100.0	100.0
		28.4				Gross Profit	29.3	28.6
		25.6				Operating Expenses	25.8	27.0
		2.8				Operating Profit	3.5	1.6
		.5				All Other Expenses (net)	.8	.5
		2.3				Profit Before Taxes	2.7	1.1
						RATIOS		
		3.0				Current	2.1	2.9
		1.7					1.6	1.8
		1.2					1.2	1.3
		1.8				Quick	1.3	1.3
		.9					.8	.8
		.6					.5	.5
		15 23.8				Sales/Receivables	28 13.0	25 14.7
		35 10.5					39 9.3	35 10.4
		48 7.6					54 6.8	49 7.5
		27 13.3				Cost of Sales/Inventory	38 9.7	39 9.3
		53 6.8					53 6.9	73 5.0
		79 4.6					104 3.5	100 3.6
		19 19.0				Cost of Sales/Payables	22 16.8	15 24.4
		37 9.8					36 10.1	30 12.0
		46 8.0					56 6.5	49 7.4
		5.9				Sales/Working Capital	5.6	6.0
		12.0					12.4	9.1
		25.4					30.1	17.8
		22.7				EBIT/Interest	4.5	4.4
		(16) 1.9					(50) 2.5	(40) 2.2
		.3					1.1	.8
						Net Profit + Depr., Dep., Amort./Cur. Mat. L /T/D	5.4	2.9
							(17) 1.4	(10) .5
							.4	−2.4
		.0				Fixed/Worth	.1	.0
		.2					.3	.2
		.5					.7	.7
		.5				Debt/Worth	.9	.7
		1.4					2.4	1.7
		4.6					4.9	4.3
		17.1				% Profit Before Taxes/Tangible Net Worth	24.9	22.8
		(18) 8.4					(51) 13.4	(45) 9.6
		−3.5					3.8	.8
		10.6				% Profit Before Taxes/Total Assets	9.8	9.6
		3.2					4.7	4.2
		−1.6					.4	.1
		123.2				Sales/Net Fixed Assets	102.3	130.4
		77.5					53.3	49.3
		28.2					11.9	22.2
		3.8				Sales/Total Assets	3.7	3.6
		3.1					2.9	2.9
		2.5					2.0	2.0
		.1				% Depr., Dep., Amort./Sales	.4	.3
		(16) .5					(45) .8	(39) .8
		2.4					1.9	1.3
						% Officers', Directors', Owners' Comp/Sales	1.4	1.8
							(29) 3.7	(21) 2.8
							5.5	5.2
1002M	28168M	383639M	310433M	168677M	772696M	Net Sales ($)	1636524M	745579M
404M	7621M	111698M	107943M	52931M	248869M	Total Assets ($)	617435M	278045M

M = $ thousand   MM = $ million
See Pages 11 through 21 for Explanation of Ratios and Data

Comparative Historical Data / Current Data Sorted By Sales

	4/1/02-3/31/03 ALL	4/1/03-3/31/04 ALL	4/1/04-3/31/05 ALL	Type of Statement	0-1MM	1-3MM	3-5MM	5-10MM	10-25MM	25MM & OVER
	8	7	4	Unqualified					2	2
	21	18	14	Reviewed				4	4	6
	7	10	3	Compiled				2	1	
	1		3	Tax Returns		1	1			1
	6	10	11	Other		2	1	1	4	3
					0-1MM	7 (4/1-9/30/04) 1-3MM	3-5MM	28 (10/1/04-3/31/05) 5-10MM	10-25MM	25MM & OVER
	43	45	35	NUMBER OF STATEMENTS		3	2	7	11	12
	%	%	%	**ASSETS**	%	%	%	%	%	%
	7.5	9.6	14.0	Cash & Equivalents	DATA NOT AVAILABLE				5.4	20.5
	32.9	28.3	30.0	Trade Receivables (net)					38.5	29.8
	39.4	36.0	34.2	Inventory					33.6	29.2
	1.7	1.9	3.0	All Other Current					4.5	4.5
	81.6	75.9	81.1	Total Current					82.0	84.0
	10.9	14.8	9.7	Fixed Assets (net)					6.1	7.3
	1.2	4.6	1.9	Intangibles (net)					3.5	.7
	6.4	4.8	7.3	All Other Non-Current					8.4	8.0
	100.0	100.0	100.0	Total					100.0	100.0
				LIABILITIES						
	18.9	14.7	16.4	Notes Payable-Short Term					22.2	11.8
	1.4	3.0	1.3	Cur. Mat.-L/T/D					1.4	.5
	21.4	19.8	24.3	Trade Payables					27.2	25.9
	.8	.1	.3	Income Taxes Payable					.2	.4
	10.8	13.5	9.0	All Other Current					8.1	12.6
	53.3	51.0	51.2	Total Current					59.1	51.3
	6.7	11.1	5.1	Long-Term Debt					1.4	3.6
	.1	.1	.0	Deferred Taxes					.0	.0
	6.0	5.6	11.2	All Other Non-Current					33.7	1.2
	33.8	32.2	32.6	Net Worth					5.8	43.9
	100.0	100.0	100.0	Total Liabilities & Net Worth					100.0	100.0
				INCOME DATA						
	100.0	100.0	100.0	Net Sales					100.0	100.0
	30.2	31.1	31.4	Gross Profit					28.4	30.2
	28.2	29.8	27.1	Operating Expenses					25.7	24.4
	2.0	1.2	4.3	Operating Profit					2.6	5.8
	.4	.6	.5	All Other Expenses (net)					1.5	.1
	1.7	.6	3.8	Profit Before Taxes					1.2	5.7
				RATIOS						
	2.0	2.1	2.6	Current					1.9	2.7
	1.5	1.5	1.6						1.3	2.0
	1.2	1.2	1.2						1.2	1.4
	1.1	1.0	1.4	Quick					.9	1.5
	.6	.7	.7						.6	1.1
	.5	.5	.5						.4	.7
	27 13.4	23 16.1	16 23.1	Sales/Receivables					32 11.4	15 23.8
	36 10.1	37 9.7	34 10.8						36 10.2	26 13.8
	63 5.8	54 6.7	54 6.7						48 7.6	55 6.6
	39 9.2	35 10.4	38 9.5	Cost of Sales/Inventory					15 24.0	36 10.2
	69 5.3	65 5.6	54 6.8						53 6.9	46 7.9
	104 3.5	108 3.4	80 4.6						77 4.7	61 6.0
	15 25.0	14 25.9	18 20.0	Cost of Sales/Payables					23 15.9	7 51.5
	37 9.9	31 11.7	37 9.9						42 8.7	27 13.3
	52 7.0	55 6.7	53 6.9						48 7.6	47 7.7
	5.1	5.2	5.6	Sales/Working Capital					10.4	5.9
	9.8	9.7	11.8						16.2	7.4
	29.3	27.8	27.5						27.5	24.4
	5.8	7.6	21.4	EBIT/Interest					4.8	
(39)	1.9	(38) 2.2	(28) 3.8						(10) 1.7	
	.3	-.7	.9						.0	
				Net Profit + Depr., Dep., Amort./Cur. Mat. L/T/D						
	.1	.1	.1	Fixed/Worth					.1	.0
	.2	.5	.2						.2	.1
	.8	1.3	.5						1.0	.4
	.9	1.3	.8	Debt/Worth					1.1	.5
	2.2	3.2	1.5						4.5	1.0
	4.7	6.3	4.0						6.5	2.5
	32.7	32.4	33.1	% Profit Before Taxes/Tangible Net Worth						58.0
(38)	10.9	(37) 5.8	(31) 12.6							(11) 24.6
	.4	-4.8	3.6							5.9
	8.3	6.4	13.4	% Profit Before Taxes/Total Assets					5.2	33.5
	2.5	2.4	5.2						3.0	10.8
	-1.5	-3.4	1.5						-3.5	3.1
	162.6	112.7	125.3	Sales/Net Fixed Assets					116.9	234.6
	42.7	34.9	44.5						77.7	108.6
	18.2	11.3	20.1						38.4	21.4
	3.4	3.3	4.1	Sales/Total Assets					4.6	4.2
	2.8	2.8	3.1						3.3	3.1
	2.1	1.9	2.5						2.6	2.6
	.5	.6	.3	% Depr., Dep., Amort./Sales						.2
(31)	.9	(39) .8	(30) .5						(10)	.5
	2.1	2.1	1.9							2.0
	1.4	2.2	1.0	% Officers', Directors', Owners' Comp/Sales						
(18)	4.1	(20) 3.1	(12) 2.6							
	7.5	8.0	7.2							
	909694M	846712M	1664615M	Net Sales ($)		4043M	8333M	51636M	190881M	1409722M
	332852M	302451M	529466M	Total Assets ($)		2052M	2382M	26757M	57818M	440457M

M = $ thousand   MM = $ million
See Pages 11 through 21 for Explanation of Ratios and Data

Current Data Sorted By Assets   Comparative Historical Data

0-500M	500M-2MM	2-10MM	10-50MM	50-100MM	100-250MM	Type of Statement	4/1/00-3/31/01 ALL	4/1/01-3/31/02 ALL
	2	8	11	1	1	Unqualified	24	14
4	13	34	2			Reviewed	40	39
8	24	13	2			Compiled	50	51
3	6	2				Tax Returns	11	18
	14	18	5			Other	49	46
	50 (4/1-9/30/04)			121 (10/1/04-3/31/05)				
15	59	75	20	1	1	NUMBER OF STATEMENTS	174	168
%	%	%	%	%	%	**ASSETS**	%	%
20.4	8.9	8.0	9.0			Cash & Equivalents	9.1	8.0
21.6	33.2	35.1	24.1			Trade Receivables (net)	33.4	32.3
31.2	33.7	28.5	22.4			Inventory	31.3	33.7
1.2	1.8	3.6	5.4			All Other Current	1.9	2.5
74.4	77.6	75.2	60.8			Total Current	75.8	76.6
17.7	15.4	12.0	21.1			Fixed Assets (net)	14.7	13.4
3.7	2.2	4.7	5.2			Intangibles (net)	3.1	3.3
4.1	4.8	8.1	12.9			All Other Non-Current	6.4	6.8
100.0	100.0	100.0	100.0			Total	100.0	100.0
						LIABILITIES		
14.8	13.4	14.1	11.8			Notes Payable-Short Term	12.7	14.1
8.9	3.9	3.7	4.3			Cur. Mat.-L/T/D	3.7	3.8
20.0	20.7	18.5	10.6			Trade Payables	19.0	19.4
.1	.2	.7	.3			Income Taxes Payable	.3	.3
9.9	13.2	14.8	15.1			All Other Current	16.8	14.3
53.7	51.3	51.8	42.1			Total Current	52.5	51.9
27.7	12.4	8.1	11.5			Long-Term Debt	10.5	11.5
.0	.1	.4	.9			Deferred Taxes	.1	.1
25.3	10.0	5.3	6.4			All Other Non-Current	6.7	5.4
-6.7	26.1	34.5	39.2			Net Worth	30.2	31.2
100.0	100.0	100.0	100.0			Total Liabilities & Net Worth	100.0	100.0
						INCOME DATA		
100.0	100.0	100.0	100.0			Net Sales	100.0	100.0
46.8	38.0	37.4	38.5			Gross Profit	37.6	37.2
43.9	36.0	35.0	34.1			Operating Expenses	35.2	35.4
2.8	2.1	2.5	4.4			Operating Profit	2.4	1.8
1.5	-.3	-.2	.5			All Other Expenses (net)	.2	.7
1.4	2.4	2.6	3.9			Profit Before Taxes	2.2	1.1
						RATIOS		
3.3	2.2	2.0	2.0			Current	2.2	2.2
1.4	1.6	1.5	1.3				1.5	1.5
.9	1.1	1.2	1.1				1.1	1.1
2.3	1.2	1.2	1.0			Quick	1.3	1.2
.6	.8	.8	.8				.8	(167) .7
.3	.6	.6	.5				.5	.5
0 UND	25 14.4	30 12.3	38 9.7			Sales/Receivables	28 12.9	26 13.8
18 20.1	31 11.6	42 8.8	44 8.4				37 9.9	35 10.5
33 11.2	38 9.7	52 7.1	58 6.3				52 7.1	48 7.6
13 28.9	31 11.6	36 10.3	49 7.5			Cost of Sales/Inventory	29 12.5	28 13.2
35 10.5	60 6.1	62 5.9	55 6.6				62 5.9	71 5.2
132 2.8	100 3.6	90 4.1	99 3.7				98 3.7	111 3.3
9 40.8	15 23.8	19 19.1	19 19.2			Cost of Sales/Payables	19 19.4	16 22.5
20 18.1	33 11.0	33 11.2	24 15.0				32 11.5	31 12.0
51 7.2	47 7.7	49 7.5	41 8.9				48 7.5	49 7.4
8.3	6.9	7.4	6.5			Sales/Working Capital	7.3	6.5
15.9	11.4	12.7	13.0				12.5	11.2
-57.0	45.9	26.0	33.2				37.9	37.8
8.5	9.0	11.9	11.6			EBIT/Interest	6.7	5.0
(12) 5.3	(51) 4.7	(65) 4.2	(18) 5.7				(158) 2.8	(157) 2.3
-5.1	1.1	1.6	1.7				1.3	.9
	4.9	5.1				Net Profit + Depr., Dep., Amort./Cur. Mat. L./T/D	8.5	6.5
	(17) 2.3	(19) 1.0					(47) 2.3	(39) 2.2
	.2	.4					1.0	.8
.0	.2	.1	.2			Fixed/Worth	.1	.2
.4	.5	.3	.6				.4	.3
-.5	.9	1.4	1.4				1.2	1.3
.7	1.0	1.0	1.3			Debt/Worth	1.1	.9
-21.3	2.1	2.3	1.6				2.5	2.3
-3.9	6.4	6.3	5.0				5.8	7.6
	45.5	46.3	28.2			% Profit Before Taxes/Tangible Net Worth	39.5	32.8
	(52) 18.6	(62) 13.1	(19) 13.6				(151) 15.3	(142) 11.8
	3.4	3.2	2.7				4.8	1.1
20.1	12.7	15.5	10.0			% Profit Before Taxes/Total Assets	11.3	8.9
3.5	6.7	5.9	4.3				4.6	3.3
-7.6	.7	1.1	1.2				1.0	-.5
598.0	63.5	66.4	39.4			Sales/Net Fixed Assets	71.5	66.6
66.4	30.3	33.7	13.5				33.9	34.2
18.6	15.2	18.9	4.6				14.3	15.3
5.8	5.2	3.6	2.3			Sales/Total Assets	4.0	4.1
4.2	3.6	2.9	2.0				3.1	2.9
2.7	2.4	2.1	1.5				2.1	2.2
	.8	.6	.6			% Depr., Dep., Amort./Sales	.5	.6
	(48) 1.1	(67) 1.1	(14) 2.3				(143) 1.2	(131) 1.2
	2.2	2.1	8.9				2.1	2.3
5.9	2.5	1.7				% Officers', Directors', Owners' Comp/Sales	2.0	2.7
(10) 9.6	(33) 3.6	(22) 3.1					(77) 4.4	(76) 4.1
18.8	5.4	5.0					7.3	7.0
16661M	258810M	958342M	810393M	139097M	684036M	Net Sales ($)	4751168M	2382591M
3858M	74611M	331069M	456544M	51536M	136197M	Total Assets ($)	1698219M	1160945M

© RMA 2005

M = $ thousand   MM = $ million
See Pages 11 through 21 for Explanation of Ratios and Data

Comparative Historical Data — Current Data Sorted By Sales

4/1/02-3/31/03 ALL	4/1/03-3/31/04 ALL	4/1/04-3/31/05 ALL	Type of Statement	0-1MM	1-3MM	3-5MM	5-10MM	10-25MM	25MM & OVER
22	13	23	Unqualified		4	6	4	6	13
55	43	49	Reviewed		7		19	18	2
39	54	43	Compiled	4	7	2	22	7	1
18	12	16	Tax Returns	5	4	6	16	7	1
43	37	40	Other	1		5			6
				50 (4/1-9/30/04)			121 (10/1/04-3/31/05)		
177	**159**	**171**	NUMBER OF STATEMENTS	10	22	19	61	36	23

ASSETS

%	%	%		%	%	%	%	%	%
8.4	9.1	9.4	Cash & Equivalents	20.1	11.8	9.1	9.0	6.3	8.8
31.8	33.3	32.0	Trade Receivables (net)	13.8	27.6	27.4	35.7	35.9	32.2
30.9	30.4	29.9	Inventory	36.3	33.4	36.2	30.2	25.7	24.3
2.8	3.3	3.0	All Other Current	1.2	.8	3.1	2.8	3.9	4.7
74.0	76.1	74.3	Total Current	71.3	73.6	75.9	77.8	71.7	70.1
16.4	14.5	14.6	Fixed Assets (net)	13.6	18.5	18.3	12.1	14.3	15.6
2.9	3.4	3.9	Intangibles (net)	5.1	4.2	1.5	2.5	6.0	5.5
6.7	6.1	7.1	All Other Non-Current	9.9	3.7	4.2	7.6	8.1	8.8
100.0	100.0	100.0	Total	100.0	100.0	100.0	100.0	100.0	100.0

LIABILITIES

14.7	13.1	13.7	Notes Payable-Short Term	14.7	14.0	10.2	15.0	11.9	15.3
4.2	3.9	4.2	Cur. Mat.-L/T/D	12.0	4.6	3.5	3.8	3.5	3.4
19.1	19.5	18.6	Trade Payables	14.4	17.7	20.5	21.0	18.0	14.4
.3	.5	.5	Income Taxes Payable	.0	.3	.1	.9	.2	.3
13.1	16.3	13.8	All Other Current	13.9	9.5	13.2	13.4	15.7	16.2
51.3	53.3	50.8	Total Current	54.9	46.1	47.5	54.2	49.4	49.6
11.8	9.0	11.8	Long-Term Debt	26.7	16.3	12.1	9.9	8.9	10.6
.2	.2	.3	Deferred Taxes	.0	.1	.2	.4	.2	.6
5.1	7.9	8.7	All Other Non-Current	43.9	9.5	4.6	6.7	6.3	5.3
31.6	29.7	28.3	Net Worth	-25.6	28.1	35.7	28.7	35.2	33.9
100.0	100.0	100.0	Total Liabilities & Net Worth	100.0	100.0	100.0	100.0	100.0	100.0

INCOME DATA

100.0	100.0	100.0	Net Sales	100.0	100.0	100.0	100.0	100.0	100.0
39.9	38.1	38.3	Gross Profit	46.2	45.2	41.6	35.2	39.8	31.3
37.2	35.5	35.7	Operating Expenses	40.8	44.5	38.2	32.9	37.3	28.2
2.7	2.7	2.6	Operating Profit	5.4	.7	3.4	2.3	2.6	3.1
.6	.2	.0	All Other Expenses (net)	2.0	.1	-.6	-.4	.3	.3
2.2	2.5	2.5	Profit Before Taxes	3.4	.6	4.0	2.7	2.3	2.7

RATIOS

2.2	2.1	2.0	Current	3.4	2.8	2.2	2.2	1.9	1.9
1.5	1.4	1.5		1.4	1.6	1.5	1.4	1.5	1.3
1.1	1.1	1.1		1.2	1.0	1.1	1.1	1.2	1.1
1.3	1.1	1.2	Quick	1.7	1.2	1.5	1.2	1.3	1.1
.8	.8	.8		.5	.8	.7	.8	.9	.9
.5	.5	.6		.2	.5	.5	.6	.6	.6
25 14.4	29 12.5	27 13.4	Sales/Receivables	0 UND	24 15.4	22 16.3	28 13.1	32 11.4	37 9.8
33 11.0	37 9.9	36 10.2		17 21.1	30 12.3	29 12.7	34 10.7	42 8.8	46 7.9
46 7.9	49 7.5	47 7.8		35 10.4	41 8.8	36 10.2	47 7.8	50 7.4	59 6.2
25 14.6	34 10.8	35 10.5	Cost of Sales/Inventory	16 22.1	33 11.1	54 6.8	27 13.3	28 13.1	40 9.0
64 5.7	67 5.4	60 6.1		106 3.5	67 5.5	68 5.4	62 5.9	57 6.4	50 7.2
101 3.6	104 3.5	95 3.8		190 1.9	112 3.3	121 3.0	82 4.4	84 4.3	83 4.4
19 19.4	14 25.4	15 23.8	Cost of Sales/Payables	0 UND	13 28.2	22 16.9	16 23.2	15 25.1	20 18.5
30 12.1	29 12.6	32 11.5		14 25.2	38 9.5	38 9.7	31 11.8	33 11.2	28 13.3
50 7.3	55 6.7	46 7.9		30 12.1	56 6.6	51 7.1	45 8.1	45 8.2	41 8.8
7.2	7.7	7.4	Sales/Working Capital	6.5	6.5	6.2	7.2	7.8	8.6
14.7	13.6	12.7		16.7	9.1	8.7	13.2	16.5	12.2
65.7	33.8	40.7		NM	NM	42.8	57.2	25.7	35.4
9.6	9.7	10.8	EBIT/Interest		6.8	21.8	9.3	17.0	7.9
(156) 3.2	(143) 3.3	(148) 4.5		(20) 2.2	(14) 5.9	(54) 4.8	(32) 4.9	(21) 4.1
1.1	1.4	1.3			-4.9	-.7	1.6	1.0	1.4
4.9	3.3	4.9	Net Profit + Depr., Dep.,				3.7	5.4	
(47) 1.6	(37) 1.7	(43) 1.6	Amort./Cur. Mat. L/T/D			(15) 1.1	(10) 1.1	
1.0	1.0	.4					.2	.4	
.1	.2	.1	Fixed/Worth	.0	.1	.2	.1	.2	.1
.3	.4	.4		.7	.5	.5	.3	.4	.5
1.5	1.3	1.3		-.4	NM	1.2	.9	1.6	1.5
.9	.9	1.0	Debt/Worth	1.1	1.0	1.0	1.0	1.2	1.3
2.0	2.3	2.1		-13.9	1.9	1.8	2.3	2.3	1.7
6.4	5.9	8.8		-2.2	NM	6.3	5.2	11.3	8.3
37.4	38.4	43.9	% Profit Before Taxes/Tangible		49.5	54.9	39.1	46.3	35.3
(151) 16.8	(138) 15.1	(141) 15.6	Net Worth	(17) 15.6	(18) 21.8	(53) 15.7	(30) 14.4	(19) 13.6
4.0	3.7	3.2			2.7	.6	3.8	.4	2.7
12.7	10.3	14.2	% Profit Before Taxes/Total	30.9	10.5	22.5	13.3	19.3	9.0
5.5	4.5	5.4	Assets	7.6	3.5	7.3	6.7	5.4	3.6
.7	.7	.7		-1.3	-5.0	2.4	1.4	-.3	.4
71.3	69.3	66.7	Sales/Net Fixed Assets	UND	73.4	58.7	64.0	68.9	102.3
30.6	29.1	30.9		25.5	35.3	22.8	35.8	28.2	35.5
13.5	12.7	14.5		12.5	11.3	10.4	19.3	16.4	9.3
4.3	4.0	4.3	Sales/Total Assets	7.4	4.6	5.2	4.3	4.3	3.1
3.1	3.0	3.0		2.7	3.2	3.1	3.4	2.9	2.3
2.2	2.1	2.1		1.5	1.4	1.9	2.3	2.1	2.0
.6	.5	.6	% Depr., Dep., Amort./Sales		.7	1.0	.6	.6	.5
(147) 1.1	(138) 1.0	(140) 1.1		(15) 1.5	(16) 1.4	(53) 1.0	(34) 1.0	(17) .7
2.3	2.3	2.4			3.7	2.9	2.1	2.1	2.3
2.3	2.4	2.4	% Officers', Directors',		4.7	1.9	2.4		
(74) 3.7	(60) 4.1	(65) 3.7	Owners' Comp/Sales	(14) 5.6	(13) 3.6	(22) 3.1		
5.9	6.5	5.8			6.7	4.1	4.7		
4393130M	4532127M	2867339M	Net Sales ($)	5670M	48604M	69233M	445160M	580316M	1718356M
1340931M	1116344M	1053815M	Total Assets ($)	3390M	19293M	24168M	156477M	235861M	614626M

Current Data Sorted By Assets   Comparative Historical Data

Type of Statement	0-500M	500M-2MM	2-10MM	10-50MM	50-100MM	100-250MM	4/1/00-3/31/01 ALL	4/1/01-3/31/02 ALL
Unqualified		1	20	14	3	5	45	46
Reviewed		13	22	7	1		51	39
Compiled	5	11	14	3			67	52
Tax Returns	9	14	7				24	16
Other	6	24	29	16	7	4	95	117
		43 (4/1-9/30/04)		192 (10/1/04-3/31/05)				
NUMBER OF STATEMENTS	20	63	92	40	11	9	282	270
ASSETS	%	%	%	%	%	%	%	%
Cash & Equivalents	16.9	11.1	11.3	13.1	8.5		9.6	11.8
Trade Receivables (net)	37.6	43.2	44.2	44.1	29.7		48.0	44.3
Inventory	18.0	20.5	24.6	21.3	23.8		22.3	19.6
All Other Current	4.5	1.6	1.9	5.2	2.2		2.5	3.2
Total Current	77.0	76.4	82.0	83.7	64.2		82.5	78.9
Fixed Assets (net)	16.6	13.1	7.2	8.4	6.7		10.5	11.0
Intangibles (net)	3.4	4.8	3.8	2.4	17.9		2.9	4.8
All Other Non-Current	3.0	5.7	7.0	5.4	11.2		4.2	5.2
Total	100.0	100.0	100.0	100.0	100.0		100.0	100.0
LIABILITIES								
Notes Payable-Short Term	44.0	16.6	16.2	15.8	6.6		17.4	16.5
Cur. Mat.-L/T/D	1.5	2.4	2.3	.7	1.2		2.5	2.6
Trade Payables	17.9	25.1	26.3	27.5	12.4		29.6	26.8
Income Taxes Payable	.0	.3	.4	1.0	.5		.3	.4
All Other Current	14.1	10.0	9.1	18.4	28.0		12.5	11.9
Total Current	77.6	54.3	54.3	63.4	48.7		62.3	58.1
Long-Term Debt	12.3	7.8	5.2	6.5	6.6		6.8	5.8
Deferred Taxes	.0	.2	.2	.3	.5		.2	.2
All Other Non-Current	10.0	10.2	7.1	7.3	.4		3.8	5.9
Net Worth	.1	27.6	33.2	22.5	43.7		26.9	30.0
Total Liabilities & Net Worth	100.0	100.0	100.0	100.0	100.0		100.0	100.0
INCOME DATA								
Net Sales	100.0	100.0	100.0	100.0	100.0		100.0	100.0
Gross Profit	43.2	35.4	29.7	28.6	25.8		29.2	31.3
Operating Expenses	38.4	32.6	25.3	25.3	21.4		27.2	28.9
Operating Profit	4.8	2.8	4.4	3.2	4.4		2.0	2.4
All Other Expenses (net)	.6	-.1	.3	.1	.7		.7	.6
Profit Before Taxes	4.2	2.9	4.1	3.1	3.8		1.3	1.8
RATIOS								
Current	3.3 / 1.4 / .7	2.5 / 1.5 / 1.0	2.1 / 1.5 / 1.2	1.8 / 1.3 / 1.1	1.9 / 1.4 / .9		1.9 / 1.3 / 1.1	2.2 / 1.4 / 1.0
Quick	2.9 / 1.3 / .3	1.7 / 1.0 / .6	1.5 / 1.1 / .8	1.2 / 1.0 / .7	1.2 / .8 / .5		1.3 / .9 / .7	1.5 / 1.0 / .7
Sales/Receivables	10 35.7 / 31 11.6 / 49 7.4	22 16.6 / 38 9.7 / 53 6.9	29 12.4 / 42 8.6 / 57 6.4	27 13.6 / 45 8.1 / 75 4.9	48 7.6 / 54 6.7 / 87 4.2		30 12.2 / 42 8.8 / 60 6.1	27 13.5 / 40 9.2 / 58 6.3
Cost of Sales/Inventory	0 UND / 13 28.2 / 62 5.9	7 51.9 / 20 18.1 / 41 8.9	6 66.0 / 29 12.8 / 62 5.9	6 66.0 / 19 19.4 / 47 7.8	22 16.7 / 45 8.0 / 63 5.8		8 46.7 / 24 15.0 / 44 8.3	6 58.2 / 20 17.9 / 42 8.7
Cost of Sales/Payables	9 42.0 / 28 13.0 / 51 7.1	19 19.2 / 28 12.9 / 54 6.8	15 23.9 / 32 11.3 / 48 7.6	25 14.7 / 35 10.3 / 59 6.2	5 79.9 / 27 13.3 / 41 8.9		18 20.1 / 35 10.5 / 59 6.2	16 23.1 / 33 11.2 / 51 7.1
Sales/Working Capital	7.9 / 82.2 / -15.1	8.1 / 16.1 / 999.8	9.0 / 16.5 / 34.4	9.0 / 15.6 / 38.6	5.9 / 11.2 / -19.7		10.6 / 22.4 / 119.5	9.4 / 20.5 / 142.8
EBIT/Interest	(15) 11.0 / 4.0 / .8	(52) 9.6 / 2.9 / .8	(83) 33.2 / 7.4 / 1.7	(35) 36.3 / 5.4 / 2.8			(242) 9.7 / 2.3 / .9	(232) 10.7 / 2.5 / .1
Net Profit + Depr., Dep., Amort./Cur. Mat. L /T/D			(13) 27.0 / 11.3 / 5.2				(53) 10.5 / 2.6 / .2	(40) 11.5 / 3.1 / .8
Fixed/Worth	.1 / 1.1 / -.5	.1 / .4 / 3.2	.1 / .2 / .4	.1 / .2 / 1.2	.1 / .2 / 1.3		.1 / .3 / 1.2	.1 / .4 / 1.4
Debt/Worth	.9 / 19.3 / -3.5	1.2 / 3.3 / 13.8	.9 / 2.7 / 9.5	1.4 / 3.4 / 8.5	.8 / 2.4 / 6.2		1.2 / 3.0 / 8.6	1.0 / 2.8 / 12.0
% Profit Before Taxes/Tangible Net Worth	(11) 166.7 / 25.3 / .6	(50) 58.2 / 33.6 / 8.2	(82) 63.9 / 29.3 / 6.7	(34) 53.0 / 27.6 / 11.2	(10) 47.4 / 23.4 / 5.6		(246) 61.1 / 20.2 / 2.6	(219) 66.0 / 24.5 / 2.4
% Profit Before Taxes/Total Assets	41.3 / 7.4 / -6.3	19.3 / 5.3 / .4	19.3 / 7.2 / 1.8	10.3 / 6.8 / 1.4	9.4 / 5.6 / 1.3		15.7 / 4.6 / -.1	16.9 / 4.8 / -1.3
Sales/Net Fixed Assets	314.1 / 62.5 / 21.4	255.1 / 77.3 / 25.6	232.6 / 83.9 / 36.2	200.8 / 45.5 / 20.9	293.9 / 26.3 / 7.1		181.1 / 61.9 / 25.5	151.5 / 61.3 / 25.5
Sales/Total Assets	7.2 / 4.7 / 2.5	5.8 / 3.9 / 2.5	4.7 / 3.8 / 2.8	4.8 / 3.4 / 1.8	3.1 / 2.2 / .6		5.8 / 4.0 / 2.9	5.6 / 4.1 / 2.6
% Depr., Dep., Amort./Sales	(14) .4 / .8 / 1.4	(41) .3 / .7 / 1.4	(70) .2 / .4 / 1.0	(33) .1 / .4 / 1.1			(212) .2 / .5 / 1.2	(213) .2 / .5 / 1.3
% Officers', Directors', Owners' Comp/Sales	(13) 2.1 / 6.4 / 12.5	(31) 2.2 / 5.1 / 8.2	(39) .9 / 2.6 / 5.7				(107) 1.2 / 3.2 / 6.2	(84) 1.6 / 2.9 / 6.4
Net Sales ($)	28697M	324680M	1868293M	2529574M	1637284M	5333841M	12454389M	13556740M
Total Assets ($)	4778M	79075M	409255M	754654M	855748M	1555720M	3332339M	3877026M

M = $ thousand   MM = $ million

See Pages 11 through 21 for Explanation of Ratios and Data

Comparative Historical Data | Current Data Sorted By Sales

Type of Statement	4/1/02-3/31/03 ALL	4/1/03-3/31/04 ALL	4/1/04-3/31/05 ALL	0-1MM	1-3MM	3-5MM	5-10MM	10-25MM	25MM & OVER
Unqualified	58	53	43			1	4	10	28
Reviewed	53	52	43	1	1	15	14		12
Compiled	42	54	33	3	7	1	8	9	5
Tax Returns	29	20	30	5	9	4	8	2	2
Other	100	99	86	4	10	12	16	16	28
				43 (4/1-9/30/04)			192 (10/1/04-3/31/05)		
NUMBER OF STATEMENTS	282	278	235	13	26	19	51	51	75

ASSETS	%	%	%	%	%	%	%	%	%
Cash & Equivalents	13.7	13.8	12.0	10.1	13.9	15.2	12.5	9.5	12.3
Trade Receivables (net)	41.7	43.3	42.5	26.0	37.4	39.1	44.2	46.7	43.8
Inventory	19.1	19.4	22.3	19.0	17.7	15.7	25.0	23.7	23.4
All Other Current	2.7	2.7	2.6	3.3	4.0	1.9	1.2	1.9	3.7
Total Current	77.2	79.2	79.5	58.4	72.9	71.9	82.9	81.9	83.2
Fixed Assets (net)	12.0	10.2	9.7	24.7	17.3	7.5	9.2	7.6	6.7
Intangibles (net)	4.8	5.1	4.8	1.9	6.5	10.8	3.9	3.1	4.9
All Other Non-Current	6.0	5.6	6.1	15.1	3.2	9.8	4.0	7.4	5.2
Total	100.0	100.0	100.0	100.0	100.0	100.0	100.0	100.0	100.0

LIABILITIES									
Notes Payable-Short Term	15.3	14.2	17.6	51.6	19.7	14.9	17.4	13.1	14.9
Cur. Mat.-L/T/D	2.7	2.0	1.9	1.0	3.7	1.9	1.8	1.6	1.8
Trade Payables	24.8	25.8	25.3	16.4	16.4	20.6	26.4	28.5	28.1
Income Taxes Payable	.3	.3	.4	.0	.0	.0	.6	.7	.5
All Other Current	13.7	16.7	12.3	15.7	8.9	7.0	8.9	16.1	13.9
Total Current	56.8	59.1	57.6	84.7	48.7	44.5	55.2	59.9	59.3
Long-Term Debt	6.2	3.8	6.8	20.9	10.2	11.3	6.1	2.4	5.5
Deferred Taxes	.2	.2	.2	.0	.4	.0	.2	.3	.2
All Other Non-Current	5.9	7.3	7.9	11.4	10.7	14.1	7.8	7.6	4.9
Net Worth	30.9	29.7	27.6	-17.0	30.0	30.2	30.6	29.8	30.2
Total Liabilities & Net Worth	100.0	100.0	100.0	100.0	100.0	100.0	100.0	100.0	100.0

INCOME DATA									
Net Sales	100.0	100.0	100.0	100.0	100.0	100.0	100.0	100.0	100.0
Gross Profit	33.4	32.4	31.6	57.6	44.9	34.1	32.0	30.4	22.6
Operating Expenses	30.9	29.5	27.9	46.6	42.5	30.2	28.5	26.4	19.7
Operating Profit	2.5	2.9	3.7	11.1	2.4	4.0	3.5	4.0	2.9
All Other Expenses (net)	.3	.2	.2	1.6	-.4	.0	.3	.2	.2
Profit Before Taxes	2.2	2.7	3.5	9.5	2.8	4.0	3.2	3.8	2.6

RATIOS									
Current	2.1	1.9	2.1	2.0	2.9	2.5	2.2	2.0	1.9
	1.4	1.3	1.4	.7	1.9	1.6	1.4	1.4	1.4
	1.1	1.1	1.1	.4	1.1	1.0	1.2	1.1	1.1
Quick	1.5	1.4	1.5	1.7	2.2	2.3	1.7	1.5	1.2
	1.0	1.0	1.0	.3	1.6	1.2	1.0	1.1	1.0
	.7	.7	.7	.2	.4	.7	.7	.8	.7
Sales/Receivables	27 13.7	28 13.0	27 13.4	11 33.5	29 12.7	22 16.5	28 13.2	29 12.5	26 13.8
	39 9.4	44 8.3	41 9.0	38 9.7	38 9.7	38 9.6	39 9.3	42 8.8	46 7.9
	60 6.1	61 6.0	60 6.1	74 4.9	54 6.8	63 5.8	57 6.4	57 6.4	65 5.6
Cost of Sales/Inventory	5 74.9	6 64.3	5 67.0	0 UND	0 UND	1 326.6	14 26.9	6 62.8	5 69.6
	21 17.7	20 18.6	25 14.7	42 8.8	21 17.4	14 25.7	28 12.9	23 15.5	22 16.7
	43 8.5	43 8.5	58 6.3	115 3.2	60 6.1	63 5.8	53 6.9	58 6.3	54 6.8
Cost of Sales/Payables	18 20.1	19 19.1	20 18.3	26 14.2	15 24.8	14 25.3	18 19.8	20 17.9	20 18.4
	31 11.7	33 11.2	31 11.7	84 4.4	35 10.3	28 12.9	27 13.4	35 10.4	31 11.7
	53 6.9	52 7.0	53 6.8	178 2.1	50 7.3	41 8.9	54 6.8	49 7.5	48 7.5
Sales/Working Capital	8.1	9.4	8.9	65.9	4.9	6.3	8.2	9.8	9.4
	19.5	21.3	16.1	-5.5	12.0	22.4	14.7	15.7	19.0
	118.0	102.4	66.7	-2.2	NM	-134.1	64.6	31.5	39.5
EBIT/Interest	13.6	16.1	17.7	11.9	5.4	10.8	15.9	38.3	27.0
	(235) 3.5	(230) 3.8	(200) 5.4	(11) 4.1	(19) 1.7	(14) 2.4	(44) 3.4	(45) 10.6	(67) 7.1
	1.0	1.1	1.7	.8	.3	.9	1.3	3.2	2.0
Net Profit + Depr., Dep., Amort./Cur. Mat. L/T/D	10.4	9.9	22.5						25.7
	(54) 3.9	(44) 2.9	(32) 8.1						(15) 10.1
	1.0	.7	2.4						1.1
Fixed/Worth	.1	.1	.1	.1	.0	.0	.1	.1	.1
	.3	.3	.2	15.9	.5	.1	.3	.2	.2
	1.3	.9	1.2	-.4	NM	-1.7	1.2	.4	.4
Debt/Worth	.9	1.1	1.1	1.6	.7	.7	1.3	.9	1.3
	2.4	2.3	2.9	-243.0	3.2	5.0	2.5	2.4	3.0
	8.4	11.2	11.3	-2.6	NM	-8.5	9.6	11.4	6.6
% Profit Before Taxes/Tangible Net Worth	59.8	54.3	60.1		47.2	105.3	72.9	68.2	52.3
	(244) 21.0	(233) 20.9	(195) 28.3		(20) 17.9	(13) 41.3	(45) 27.2	(43) 36.6	(68) 27.2
	1.5	2.4	6.8		1.2	9.3	7.0	8.2	6.1
% Profit Before Taxes/Total Assets	14.8	14.9	16.2	21.9	20.4	14.7	19.7	22.4	10.3
	5.6	4.5	6.6	5.9	3.0	6.6	6.7	9.2	6.2
	-.2	.3	.8	-4.6	-1.2	.8	.5	2.5	1.2
Sales/Net Fixed Assets	150.2	170.3	233.5	330.6	413.0	457.0	208.5	178.1	271.0
	51.7	51.8	77.3	16.2	45.3	81.4	67.8	90.5	86.5
	20.4	26.5	26.4	3.1	17.7	18.7	30.4	46.9	23.1
Sales/Total Assets	5.3	5.2	5.0	3.5	5.2	4.5	4.9	5.3	5.0
	3.8	3.6	3.6	2.2	2.5	3.2	3.8	4.0	3.7
	2.4	2.5	2.5	.9	1.9	1.6	3.2	2.8	2.5
% Depr., Dep., Amort./Sales	.3	.3	.2		.7	.4	.2	.2	.1
	(209) .7	(203) .6	(172) .5		(16) 1.1	(11) .6	(35) .7	(41) .4	(61) .4
	1.6	1.4	1.1		1.7	1.2	.9		1.0
% Officers', Directors', Owners' Comp/Sales	2.0	1.7	1.2		2.7		2.0	1.1	.5
	(92) 4.0	(92) 3.5	(87) 3.5		(13) 5.9		(28) 3.8	(19) 2.7	(13) .7
	7.4	7.0	6.9		10.8		5.7	5.8	1.4
Net Sales ($)	11349666M	10856361M	11722369M	8006M	53944M	73820M	380234M	812026M	10394339M
Total Assets ($)	3768482M	4016309M	3659230M	8478M	22534M	34510M	111923M	244536M	3237249M

M = $ thousand   MM = $ million
See Pages 11 through 21 for Explanation of Ratios and Data

Current Data Sorted By Assets

Comparative Historical Data

Type of Statement								
		6	11	2	4	Unqualified	8	14
2	18	30	5			Reviewed	58	49
5	22	10	2	1		Compiled	53	46
7	18	3		1		Tax Returns	16	13
6	27	27	9	1	1	Other	36	53
	46 (4/1-9/30/04)		171 (10/1/04-3/31/05)				4/1/00-3/31/01	4/1/01-3/31/02
0-500M	500M-2MM	2-10MM	10-50MM	50-100MM	100-250MM		ALL	ALL
20	85	76	27	4	5	**NUMBER OF STATEMENTS**	171	175
%	%	%	%	%	%	**ASSETS**	%	%
17.3	9.0	5.1	10.6			Cash & Equivalents	6.8	6.1
21.9	35.2	33.5	34.3			Trade Receivables (net)	35.9	34.8
37.6	32.8	32.7	29.4			Inventory	33.9	36.5
3.0	2.1	4.0	4.4			All Other Current	2.0	2.0
79.9	79.1	75.3	78.7			Total Current	78.5	79.4
11.4	12.4	13.8	11.0			Fixed Assets (net)	12.7	12.7
1.5	1.9	3.7	4.0			Intangibles (net)	2.8	2.9
7.2	6.6	7.2	6.3			All Other Non-Current	6.0	5.0
100.0	100.0	100.0	100.0			Total	100.0	100.0
						LIABILITIES		
37.5	14.4	21.2	9.3			Notes Payable-Short Term	13.9	15.9
3.6	2.5	2.0	1.4			Cur. Mat.-L/T/D	3.5	3.6
19.1	24.3	20.5	22.3			Trade Payables	21.5	21.6
.0	.2	.2	.3			Income Taxes Payable	.2	.2
31.9	9.5	16.4	16.0			All Other Current	11.1	9.6
92.2	50.9	60.2	49.2			Total Current	50.2	50.9
24.8	12.1	8.2	7.0			Long-Term Debt	8.4	9.8
.0	.0	.1	.3			Deferred Taxes	.2	.2
24.5	3.5	3.3	6.0			All Other Non-Current	4.1	4.2
-41.5	33.4	28.2	37.5			Net Worth	37.1	35.0
100.0	100.0	100.0	100.0			Total Liabilities & Net Worth	100.0	100.0
						INCOME DATA		
100.0	100.0	100.0	100.0			Net Sales	100.0	100.0
31.8	31.6	28.5	27.9			Gross Profit	29.6	30.1
30.4	28.5	27.2	21.6			Operating Expenses	27.2	27.6
1.3	3.1	1.3	6.3			Operating Profit	2.3	2.5
.7	.1	.4	.6			All Other Expenses (net)	.2	.4
.6	3.0	.9	5.7			Profit Before Taxes	2.1	2.2
						RATIOS		
2.4	2.7	2.0	2.2				2.3	2.2
1.2	1.4	1.5	1.5			Current	1.6	1.6
.7	1.1	1.1	1.1				1.2	1.2
.9	1.3	1.1	1.7				1.3	1.2
.5	.9	.8	.8			Quick	.8	.8
.3	.5	.4	.6				.6	.6
0 UND	22 16.9	27 13.7	41 9.0				28 13.2	28 13.0
22 16.2	35 10.5	46 7.9	48 7.7			Sales/Receivables	43 8.5	40 9.0
31 11.8	51 7.2	62 5.9	75 4.9				59 6.1	56 6.5
10 35.7	24 14.9	34 10.8	26 14.1				29 12.8	35 10.3
37 10.0	49 7.4	62 5.9	55 6.6			Cost of Sales/Inventory	54 6.8	61 6.0
97 3.8	76 4.8	103 3.6	168 2.2				98 3.7	97 3.8
0 UND	19 19.0	17 21.4	20 18.0				17 21.9	18 20.3
15 25.0	30 12.2	31 11.7	33 11.1			Cost of Sales/Payables	29 12.4	29 12.5
41 8.8	55 6.6	56 6.5	81 4.5				49 7.5	53 6.9
9.8	6.8	6.7	4.5				6.0	6.3
44.0	15.1	10.5	8.5			Sales/Working Capital	11.2	11.6
-41.3	40.2	26.5	24.3				27.7	27.5
12.8	19.5	8.0	25.2				8.1	7.8
(16) 1.4	(80) 6.1	(73) 3.0	(24) 8.7			EBIT/Interest	(157) 3.4	(163) 2.9
-2.7	1.7	1.3	5.4				1.3	1.3
	3.0	8.6				Net Profit + Depr., Dep.,	7.1	4.1
	(15) 1.3	(21) 2.4				Amort./Cur. Mat. L./T/D	(49) 3.5	(48) 2.5
	.2	.8					1.2	1.1
.0	.1	.1	.1				.1	.1
1.8	.2	.3	.3			Fixed/Worth	.3	.3
-.1	.8	.9	.6				.8	.9
3.3	.9	1.0	.8				.9	1.0
19.5	2.7	2.3	2.6			Debt/Worth	1.8	1.9
-2.3	5.7	4.4	4.9				5.1	5.0
250.0	52.6	35.3	53.6			% Profit Before Taxes/Tangible	36.0	33.1
(11) 26.2	(76) 26.9	(70) 12.4	30.8			Net Worth	(156) 14.0	(158) 15.0
.0	8.1	3.9	20.3				1.1	3.0
18.3	16.4	7.5	15.2			% Profit Before Taxes/Total	10.8	12.2
1.3	6.8	3.1	8.0			Assets	5.0	4.1
-10.0	1.8	1.0	5.8				.2	.8
898.0	98.7	128.8	55.5				97.0	81.8
97.9	43.5	34.9	35.4			Sales/Net Fixed Assets	37.3	43.6
18.7	22.0	15.8	12.2				17.1	15.4
6.8	4.3	3.5	3.4				3.8	3.9
4.5	3.4	2.5	2.0			Sales/Total Assets	3.0	3.0
3.0	2.6	1.8	1.2				2.2	2.2
	.4	.3	.4				.3	.3
(61)	.8	(60) .7	(23) .8			% Depr., Dep., Amort./Sales	(149) .8	(147) .7
	1.3	1.4	1.8				1.3	1.5
3.5	1.7	1.3				% Officers', Directors',	2.5	2.2
(11) 6.2	(45) 3.7	(23) 2.9				Owners' Comp/Sales	(99) 4.5	(86) 3.5
12.6	7.4	4.1					7.0	6.4
20163M	356837M	934302M	1268101M	591528M	1710487M	Net Sales ($)	2585062M	3186365M
4638M	98471M	348785M	533201M	286179M	712324M	Total Assets ($)	1002487M	1222633M

M = $ thousand　　MM = $ million
See Pages 11 through 21 for Explanation of Ratios and Data

Comparative Historical Data | Current Data Sorted By Sales

			Type of Statement						
26	20	23	Unqualified				2	6	15
63	58	55	Reviewed	2	7	6	17	17	6
43	66	40	Compiled	4	11	5	14	3	3
17	24	28	Tax Returns	4	12	5	6	1	
58	57	71	Other	2	13	12	19	18	7
4/1/02-3/31/03	4/1/03-3/31/04	4/1/04-3/31/05			46 (4/1-9/30/04)			171 (10/1/04-3/31/05)	
ALL	ALL	ALL		0-1MM	1-3MM	3-5MM	5-10MM	10-25MM	25MM & OVER
207	225	217	**NUMBER OF STATEMENTS**	12	43	28	58	45	31
%	%	%	**ASSETS**	%	%	%	%	%	%
7.1	8.7	8.4	Cash & Equivalents	18.8	10.2	6.9	7.7	6.9	6.5
33.4	33.6	33.0	Trade Receivables (net)	21.1	27.8	33.9	34.0	38.2	34.7
35.7	34.1	32.8	Inventory	35.9	34.0	31.6	33.5	29.6	34.5
2.7	2.8	3.1	All Other Current	3.2	3.2	1.2	4.0	3.0	3.0
78.9	79.2	77.3	Total Current	78.9	75.1	73.7	79.3	77.6	78.8
11.8	12.0	12.9	Fixed Assets (net)	10.5	13.1	14.1	15.2	9.7	12.7
3.4	3.5	3.0	Intangibles (net)	.1	4.5	4.8	.9	3.3	4.1
5.9	5.3	6.8	All Other Non-Current	10.5	7.3	7.4	4.5	9.3	4.5
100.0	100.0	100.0	Total	100.0	100.0	100.0	100.0	100.0	100.0
			LIABILITIES						
14.8	14.0	18.3	Notes Payable-Short Term	33.9	20.8	16.6	14.8	21.1	12.7
2.9	2.8	2.3	Cur. Mat.-L/T/D	5.2	2.1	3.8	1.6	2.2	1.3
22.0	19.9	22.0	Trade Payables	16.3	22.2	22.9	22.9	22.9	19.9
.1	.2	.2	Income Taxes Payable	.0	.1	.3	.1	.3	.3
11.3	12.0	14.7	All Other Current	10.8	17.5	11.7	11.0	21.7	12.2
51.2	48.8	57.4	Total Current	66.2	62.6	55.3	50.4	68.2	46.4
8.7	10.7	11.4	Long-Term Debt	26.7	13.8	11.2	13.1	4.3	9.3
.1	.2	.1	Deferred Taxes	.0	.0	.1	.0	.3	.4
3.8	4.8	5.6	All Other Non-Current	36.1	5.3	2.7	3.3	2.9	5.2
36.3	35.5	25.4	Net Worth	−29.0	18.2	30.7	33.2	24.4	38.7
100.0	100.0	100.0	Total Liabilities & Net Worth	100.0	100.0	100.0	100.0	100.0	100.0
			INCOME DATA						
100.0	100.0	100.0	Net Sales	100.0	100.0	100.0	100.0	100.0	100.0
29.9	33.1	29.8	Gross Profit	35.2	34.7	31.6	27.7	29.3	24.1
27.3	29.7	26.9	Operating Expenses	34.5	32.1	29.3	25.5	25.9	18.7
2.5	3.4	2.9	Operating Profit	.7	2.6	2.2	2.2	3.4	5.4
.5	.4	.4	All Other Expenses (net)	1.4	.7	.1	−.2	.7	.2
2.1	3.0	2.6	Profit Before Taxes	−.7	2.0	2.1	2.4	2.7	5.1
			RATIOS						
2.3	2.7	2.3		2.0	3.0	1.9	2.2	2.0	2.7
1.5	1.7	1.4	Current	1.4	1.4	1.3	1.5	1.4	1.7
1.2	1.2	1.1		.7	.9	1.1	1.2	1.1	1.3
1.2	1.4	1.2		.9	1.1	1.0	1.3	1.3	1.6
.8	(224) .9	.8	Quick	.5	.7	.9	.8	.8	.8
.5	.6	.5		.2	.4	.5	.5	.5	.6
28 13.0	24 15.3	23 15.7		0 UND	21 17.0	18 20.0	25 14.5	32 11.3	37 9.9
41 8.9	40 9.1	40 9.1	Sales/Receivables	23 15.9	31 11.9	39 9.3	39 9.5	47 7.7	45 8.1
54 6.7	56 6.5	57 6.4		32 11.3	47 7.8	63 5.8	58 6.3	73 5.0	55 6.6
32 11.6	26 13.8	27 13.5		10 34.8	36 10.1	29 12.6	19 19.7	23 15.9	33 11.1
63 5.8	64 5.7	55 6.6	Cost of Sales/Inventory	36 10.3	69 5.3	50 7.2	52 7.0	56 6.5	55 6.6
106 3.5	101 3.6	96 3.8		102 3.6	127 2.9	80 4.6	89 4.1	81 4.5	87 4.2
18 20.8	15 24.2	17 21.3		0 UND	18 19.7	21 17.2	16 23.0	17 21.3	20 18.0
32 11.5	27 13.4	31 11.9	Cost of Sales/Payables	1 322.0	31 11.9	34 10.7	30 12.2	32 11.5	30 12.1
54 6.8	51 7.1	55 6.7		62 5.9	70 5.2	47 7.8	57 6.4	63 5.8	39 9.3
5.8	5.2	6.2		10.8	4.0	8.3	6.1	7.6	5.1
10.9	9.6	12.6	Sales/Working Capital	28.3	12.0	16.5	11.2	12.7	10.9
42.1	35.3	38.9		−34.9	−69.6	157.2	28.9	34.5	22.0
9.5	14.5	15.9		13.8	10.4	14.0	15.4	18.0	25.2
(192) 3.4	(207) 5.3	(201) 4.4	EBIT/Interest	(10) 2.5	(38) 2.9	(27) 3.2	(55) 3.3	(43) 6.1	(28) 7.4
1.0	1.9	1.5		−.2	−.6	.6	1.3	2.7	3.9
7.0	10.0	5.9	Net Profit + Depr., Dep.,				2.4	17.0	9.4
(59) 1.9	(48) 2.9	(49) 2.8	Amort./Cur. Mat. L/T/D				(11) 1.2	(13) 4.3	(12) 4.5
.4	1.2	1.1					.7	1.3	2.8
.1	.1	.1		.0	.1	.1	.1	.1	.1
.3	.3	.3	Fixed/Worth	1.0	.5	* .3	.3	.2	.3
.9	1.0	.9		−.5	2.1	1.4	1.0	.5	.5
.9	.7	1.1		2.6	.9	1.6	1.2	.7	1.1
2.0	2.1	2.7	Debt/Worth	12.0	3.3	2.6	2.5	2.3	2.3
6.4	6.0	6.6		−2.9	24.4	4.8	5.7	4.5	4.4
39.2	38.4	49.0	% Profit Before Taxes/Tangible		43.0	46.3	49.9	50.6	49.0
(188) 13.9	(197) 18.1	(193) 20.0	Net Worth		(35) 19.2	(24) 12.9	(53) 14.6	(43) 17.8	27.6
1.9	5.8	7.1			6.8	−.4	3.2	9.3	17.5
11.8	13.1	12.9	% Profit Before Taxes/Total	18.3	13.0	8.9	13.8	9.8	15.5
3.7	5.2	5.3	Assets	2.4	4.9	5.3	4.1	5.5	8.3
.3	1.7	1.5		−8.6	−3.9	−.3	.9	2.7	5.3
95.3	95.4	110.1		UND	76.6	90.5	108.5	135.6	92.2
40.5	39.7	41.5	Sales/Net Fixed Assets	193.0	34.1	38.9	41.8	38.9	44.0
19.9	18.2	16.6		18.7	13.8	18.4	14.8	18.8	12.3
3.7	4.0	4.1		7.0	3.3	4.4	4.3	4.2	3.6
2.9	3.0	3.0	Sales/Total Assets	4.6	2.8	3.3	3.1	2.6	2.9
2.2	2.1	2.1		3.0	2.0	2.3	2.2	1.7	2.0
.5	.4	.4			.7	.3	.3	.3	.3
(177) .8	(178) .8	(158) .8	% Depr., Dep., Amort./Sales		(29) 1.0	(22) .8	(41) .7	(33) .8	(29) .6
1.5	1.4	1.3			2.2	1.3	1.5	1.4	1.2
2.0	2.0	1.7	% Officers', Directors',		2.8	1.2	1.8	1.2	
(84) 3.3	(91) 4.3	(84) 3.3	Owners' Comp/Sales		(22) 4.9	(14) 2.1	(21) 3.3	(14) 1.9	
5.3	7.8	7.0			4.8		5.3	3.7	
4072011M	4326397M	4881418M	Net Sales ($)	7553M	88948M	116337M	397575M	697849M	3573156M
1719271M	1835567M	1983598M	Total Assets ($)	1870M	42248M	40288M	158146M	309879M	1431167M

M = $ thousand   MM = $ million
See Pages 11 through 21 for Explanation of Ratios and Data

Current Data Sorted By Assets | Comparative Historical Data

						Type of Statement		
	5	21	23	6	6	Unqualified	46	43
	20	34	8	3		Reviewed	46	39
8	26	24	3			Compiled	68	59
14	32	9				Tax Returns	22	25
10	41	41	20	7	2	Other	72	69
	72 (4/1-9/30/04)			288 (10/1/04-3/31/05)			4/1/00-3/31/01	4/1/01-3/31/02
0-500M	500M-2MM	2-10MM	10-50MM	50-100MM	100-250MM		ALL	ALL
32	124	129	54	13	8	NUMBER OF STATEMENTS	254	235
%	%	%	%	%	%	**ASSETS**	%	%
13.5	8.7	8.7	7.9	2.3		Cash & Equivalents	8.4	8.8
32.9	37.2	35.7	31.2	27.2		Trade Receivables (net)	38.4	36.1
28.1	27.1	27.5	25.9	26.2		Inventory	27.9	29.4
3.9	2.3	2.0	2.4	2.8		All Other Current	1.8	2.5
78.5	75.3	74.0	67.5	58.5		Total Current	76.4	76.8
12.1	13.9	14.8	19.7	13.8		Fixed Assets (net)	13.3	13.6
3.1	3.7	6.2	6.4	23.6		Intangibles (net)	4.8	4.8
6.3	7.0	5.0	6.4	4.1		All Other Non-Current	5.5	4.8
100.0	100.0	100.0	100.0	100.0		Total	100.0	100.0
						LIABILITIES		
28.3	14.6	11.5	15.4	9.1		Notes Payable-Short Term	14.7	13.8
3.9	2.8	3.4	2.3	3.2		Cur. Mat.-L/T/D	2.7	3.5
26.0	24.2	21.7	14.2	18.8		Trade Payables	25.8	22.6
.0	.4	.1	.4	.5		Income Taxes Payable	.4	.4
15.2	11.1	9.8	11.0	7.8		All Other Current	9.1	9.7
73.3	53.1	46.5	43.3	39.4		Total Current	52.7	49.9
20.9	12.2	10.9	14.4	25.7		Long-Term Debt	11.1	12.8
.0	.2	.3	.3	.8		Deferred Taxes	.2	.3
3.8	5.8	4.7	3.1	4.8		All Other Non-Current	4.8	4.0
1.9	28.7	37.5	38.6	29.2		Net Worth	31.2	33.0
100.0	100.0	100.0	100.0	100.0		Total Liabilities & Net Worth	100.0	100.0
						INCOME DATA		
100.0	100.0	100.0	100.0	100.0		Net Sales	100.0	100.0
47.7	40.5	38.6	43.3	36.5		Gross Profit	38.2	36.1
42.3	36.8	33.2	35.7	26.9		Operating Expenses	33.5	32.3
5.5	3.7	5.4	7.6	9.6		Operating Profit	4.7	3.9
1.6	.5	.6	1.4	.8		All Other Expenses (net)	.5	.7
3.9	3.2	4.9	6.2	8.8		Profit Before Taxes	4.2	3.2
						RATIOS		
2.5	2.0	2.3	2.5	2.3		Current	2.4	2.4
1.4	1.4	1.6	1.7	1.5			1.5	1.5
.7	1.1	1.2	1.1	1.1			1.1	1.2
1.8	1.4	1.6	1.4	1.2		Quick	1.5	1.4
.6	(123) .9	.9	1.0	.8			.9	.8
.3	.6	.6	.6	.5			.6	.6
9 42.8	30 12.2	33 11.0	44 8.4	35 10.4		Sales/Receivables	36 10.1	33 11.1
22 16.6	43 8.5	46 8.0	50 7.3	57 6.4			48 7.6	44 8.2
47 7.7	60 6.1	63 5.8	72 5.1	72 5.1			62 5.9	62 5.9
19 19.6	20 18.0	33 11.1	38 9.7	35 10.3		Cost of Sales/Inventory	31 11.6	32 11.3
35 10.3	46 7.9	53 6.9	66 5.5	57 6.4			57 6.4	58 6.3
129 2.8	91 4.0	95 3.9	103 3.5	133 2.8			88 4.2	86 4.3
6 64.3	21 17.1	24 15.1	22 16.4	28 13.1		Cost of Sales/Payables	26 13.9	23 15.9
33 11.2	36 10.1	44 8.3	32 11.3	38 9.6			48 7.6	40 9.0
78 4.7	67 5.5	71 5.1	48 7.5	64 5.7			76 4.8	64 5.7
9.8	6.9	6.5	3.8	4.4		Sales/Working Capital	5.7	6.4
19.4	14.4	11.7	9.2	20.3			10.5	12.0
-12.1	66.4	28.3	38.9	34.3			36.9	35.5
10.3	13.9	14.0	16.8	34.1		EBIT/Interest	10.5	9.0
(25) 2.1	(107) 4.8	(111) 5.8	(49) 5.1	4.5			(222) 3.3	(207) 2.7
-4.2	1.6	1.8	2.0	3.7			1.4	1.4
	2.4	5.6	14.3			Net Profit + Depr., Dep.,	4.4	5.1
(11) 1.3	(29) 1.9	(18) 4.5				Amort./Cur. Mat. L /T/D	(53) 2.3	(60) 2.5
.7	1.1	2.2					1.4	1.2
.0	.1	.1	.2	.3		Fixed/Worth	.1	.1
.7	.4	.4	.4	7.2			.3	.3
-.3	1.8	1.3	1.6	-5.4			.9	1.2
.8	1.1	.9	.9	4.3		Debt/Worth	1.0	1.0
6.5	2.6	2.2	2.1	21.0			2.4	2.5
-3.5	13.6	6.4	6.5	-25.8			6.1	7.0
171.3	54.3	52.0	55.3			% Profit Before Taxes/Tangible	50.8	49.2
(21) 58.2	(105) 22.6	(117) 25.9	(48) 24.6			Net Worth	(226) 23.0	(207) 19.7
9.6	6.8	9.7	13.9				7.3	6.5
30.4	16.6	16.7	16.3	18.8		% Profit Before Taxes/Total	18.1	14.5
7.1	5.7	7.7	7.9	7.6		Assets	5.8	5.4
-20.5	1.6	1.8	2.2	5.5			1.7	.7
356.6	147.0	83.4	58.1	46.9		Sales/Net Fixed Assets	94.7	97.5
43.4	43.9	32.4	16.2	21.8			36.9	33.1
19.8	17.8	10.3	5.7	6.1			15.0	13.9
6.6	4.1	3.6	3.4	4.0		Sales/Total Assets	3.7	3.9
4.2	2.9	2.5	2.0	1.7			2.9	3.1
2.4	1.9	1.8	1.0	.9			2.0	2.0
.3	.3	.4	.4	.6		% Depr., Dep., Amort./Sales	.4	.4
(20) .6	(91) .8	(111) .9	(52) 1.5	2.0			(204) .8	(197) .9
1.6	1.5	2.4	4.3	4.9			1.8	2.0
3.6	2.6	1.7				% Officers', Directors',	3.0	2.3
(16) 6.7	(60) 5.6	(44) 3.3				Owners' Comp/Sales	(96) 4.9	(107) 4.3
11.6	9.5	5.6					7.6	7.9
46103M	518054M	1670761M	2759918M	2118003M	1856979M	Net Sales ($)	5790492M	6149914M
9326M	148360M	613788M	1252004M	882948M	1291350M	Total Assets ($)	2460510M	2942797M

© RMA 2005

M = $ thousand   MM = $ million
See Pages 11 through 21 for Explanation of Ratios and Data

Comparative Historical Data | Current Data Sorted By Sales

			Type of Statement						
61	49	61	Unqualified		3	2	6	19	31
46	61	62	Reviewed	1	4	10	20	16	11
51	79	61	Compiled	4	16	9	17	7	8
37	48	55	Tax Returns	12	15	11	12	5	8
87	102	121	Other	9	25	9	18	35	25
4/1/02-3/31/03 ALL	4/1/03-3/31/04 ALL	4/1/04-3/31/05 ALL		72 (4/1-9/30/04) 0-1MM	1-3MM	3-5MM	288 (10/1/04-3/31/05) 5-10MM	10-25MM	25MM & OVER
282	339	360	**NUMBER OF STATEMENTS**	26	63	41	73	82	75
%	%	%	**ASSETS**	%	%	%	%	%	%
8.9	9.4	8.7	Cash & Equivalents	12.5	9.4	6.5	9.9	9.7	5.9
35.5	35.8	34.7	Trade Receivables (net)	19.5	36.8	38.0	35.5	35.4	34.6
27.7	27.7	26.9	Inventory	22.8	27.6	29.9	25.2	26.0	28.9
2.5	2.7	2.4	All Other Current	5.8	2.8	1.4	1.1	2.6	2.5
74.6	75.6	72.7	Total Current	60.5	76.6	75.8	71.7	73.7	72.0
15.2	14.1	14.9	Fixed Assets (net)	17.8	14.7	16.0	16.8	15.0	11.7
4.5	4.7	6.4	Intangibles (net)	6.1	3.8	3.1	6.8	5.2	11.5
5.7	5.5	5.9	All Other Non-Current	15.6	4.9	5.1	4.7	6.1	4.8
100.0	100.0	100.0	Total	100.0	100.0	100.0	100.0	100.0	100.0
			LIABILITIES						
14.3	15.0	14.5	Notes Payable-Short Term	23.9	13.5	19.9	14.0	9.6	14.7
4.0	2.7	3.0	Cur. Mat.-L/T/D	5.1	2.7	4.9	3.8	1.9	2.1
23.0	21.9	21.5	Trade Payables	18.0	24.0	21.2	22.0	22.0	19.7
.4	.4	.3	Income Taxes Payable	.6	.4	.1	.1	.1	.4
10.6	12.4	10.8	All Other Current	15.4	10.2	12.2	8.3	11.7	10.5
52.3	52.3	50.0	Total Current	63.1	50.8	58.4	48.2	45.2	47.5
10.8	11.2	13.8	Long-Term Debt	25.7	17.9	8.4	11.4	9.6	15.9
.1	.3	.3	Deferred Taxes	.0	.3	.0	.4	.4	.5
5.4	5.3	4.8	All Other Non-Current	1.2	7.5	5.2	4.3	5.7	3.2
31.3	30.9	31.0	Net Worth	10.0	23.4	28.1	35.7	39.1	32.9
100.0	100.0	100.0	Total Liabilities & Net Worth	100.0	100.0	100.0	100.0	100.0	100.0
			INCOME DATA						
100.0	100.0	100.0	Net Sales	100.0	100.0	100.0	100.0	100.0	100.0
38.2	39.3	40.7	Gross Profit	55.3	44.8	40.8	39.7	41.2	32.3
33.4	34.7	35.2	Operating Expenses	51.4	40.3	36.4	34.6	34.6	26.0
4.8	4.7	5.4	Operating Profit	3.9	4.5	4.4	5.1	6.6	6.3
.6	.7	.8	All Other Expenses (net)	2.0	.5	.9	.9	.4	1.1
4.2	4.0	4.6	Profit Before Taxes	1.9	4.0	3.6	4.2	6.2	5.2
			RATIOS						
2.4	2.3	2.3	Current	2.4	2.2	1.8	2.7	2.3	2.3
1.5	1.5	1.5		.9	1.5	1.3	1.6	1.7	1.5
1.1	1.1	1.1		.6	1.2	1.1	1.2	1.2	1.1
1.5	1.5	1.5	Quick	1.3	1.5	1.0	1.6	1.7	1.3
.9 (338)	.9 (359)	.9		(25) .5	1.0	.8	.9	1.0	1.0
.5	.6	.6		.2	.5	.6	.6	.7	.6
33 11.1	32 11.4	31 11.8	Sales/Receivables	0 UND	34 10.8	29 12.6	30 12.3	32 11.6	37 9.8
43 8.6	43 8.4	45 8.1		19 19.5	53 6.9	47 7.8	41 8.8	44 8.2	48 7.7
59 6.2	60 6.1	62 5.9		61 6.0	75 4.8	57 6.4	58 6.3	63 5.8	61 6.0
26 14.2	30 12.1	31 11.9	Cost of Sales/Inventory	22 16.3	28 13.2	33 11.1	29 12.8	31 11.7	31 11.7
55 6.6	52 7.0	53 6.9		52 7.1	66 5.5	60 6.1	52 7.0	50 7.3	53 7.0
85 4.3	93 3.9	95 3.8		161 2.3	121 3.0	80 4.6	99 3.7	87 4.2	88 4.1
22 16.6	21 17.2	23 16.1	Cost of Sales/Payables	6 61.1	23 16.1	19 19.2	21 17.0	24 15.5	25 14.8
38 9.5	37 9.7	36 10.1		62 5.9	46 7.9	36 10.1	34 10.8	41 9.0	32 11.3
65 5.6	65 5.6	67 5.4		99 3.7	87 4.2	58 6.3	71 5.1	69 5.3	46 7.9
6.2	6.6	6.4	Sales/Working Capital	5.3	5.2	10.7	7.4	5.9	5.9
12.8	11.8	12.5		NM	10.2	18.9	12.1	10.7	13.0
53.0	43.7	39.2		-7.2	50.5	60.3	41.8	26.2	37.4
13.4	17.5	13.4	EBIT/Interest	8.0	12.3	9.4	13.6	24.6	13.5
(249) 4.0	(304) 4.9	(313) 4.9		(21) 2.1	(53) 2.9	(36) 4.2	(65) 5.0	(68) 8.0	(70) 5.2
1.5	1.7	1.6		-5.2	1.4	1.9	1.4	1.8	2.5
6.2	6.2	6.2	Net Profit + Depr., Dep., Amort./Cur. Mat. L/T/D				4.6	11.0	8.5
(70) 2.7	(61) 2.2	(70) 2.2				(18) 1.8	(15) 4.0	(28) 3.5	
1.0	1.3	1.3					1.2	1.2	1.9
.1	.1	.1	Fixed/Worth	.3	.0	.2	.1	.1	.1
.4	.5	.4		2.5	.5	.5	.4	.3	.4
1.2	1.4	1.9		-.9	6.3	1.4	1.4	1.2	4.8
1.0	1.0	1.0	Debt/Worth	1.3	.9	1.2	.9	.7	1.2
2.4	2.8	2.6		6.9	2.7	2.5	2.2	2.0	4.1
7.1	9.1	10.0		-9.1	67.3	4.4	6.0	6.2	16.6
53.4	64.6	56.8	% Profit Before Taxes/Tangible Net Worth	46.9	74.5	47.5	56.8	54.0	60.0
(247) 28.3	(292) 27.9	(302) 25.5		(17) 22.3	(48) 22.8	(37) 24.7	(65) 20.8	(75) 25.9	(60) 32.9
7.8	8.7	9.8		-59.2	4.2	9.1	9.2	13.7	13.2
20.0	16.4	17.1	% Profit Before Taxes/Total Assets	17.2	18.2	13.2	17.6	19.4	15.9
6.8	7.6	7.2		3.7	4.6	7.7	8.1	9.1	7.6
1.4	1.9	1.7		-16.2	.9	2.6	.8	2.1	2.9
94.6	109.0	102.5	Sales/Net Fixed Assets	140.3	166.6	59.1	85.2	96.8	119.6
33.4	34.4	36.4		18.2	35.4	37.1	29.2	43.0	38.7
11.0	11.6	10.2		8.4	16.2	17.7	7.4	10.4	9.8
3.9	4.1	3.9	Sales/Total Assets	3.3	3.8	4.0	4.0	4.0	3.9
3.0	2.9	2.7		2.1	2.1	2.9	2.8	2.8	2.9
2.0	2.0	1.7		.9	1.6	2.4	1.8	1.8	1.6
.4	.4	.4	% Depr., Dep., Amort./Sales	1.1	.3	.5	.3	.4	.3
(229) 1.1	(274) .9	(291) .9		(15) 1.6	(45) .9	(31) 1.0	(64) 1.0	(70) .9	(66) .8
2.2	2.1	2.3		4.1	1.6	1.5	3.1	2.4	2.5
2.4	2.3	2.4	% Officers', Directors', Owners' Comp/Sales	4.3	3.3	2.1	2.9	1.7	1.5
(113) 4.4	(126) 4.8	(128) 4.5		(11) 9.0	(26) 6.3	(25) 3.7	(35) 4.8	(20) 3.2	(11) 1.7
6.9	9.3	8.9		19.7	9.4	8.8	9.6	10.5	3.3
7298734M	8207933M	8969818M	Net Sales ($)	16888M	127087M	162030M	497015M	1196096M	6970702M
3289113M	3520025M	4197776M	Total Assets ($)	12335M	60110M	57623M	238679M	585698M	3243331M

M = $ thousand   MM = $ million
See Pages 11 through 21 for Explanation of Ratios and Data

Current Data Sorted By Assets   Comparative Historical Data

0-500M	500M-2MM	2-10MM	10-50MM	50-100MM	100-250MM	Type of Statement	4/1/00-3/31/01 ALL	4/1/01-3/31/02 ALL
		3	2			Unqualified	3	3
	2	2	1			Reviewed	9	7
	3	1				Compiled	8	6
	4					Tax Returns	1	1
2	2		2			Other	11	10
	7 (4/1-9/30/04)		17 (10/1/04-3/31/05)					
2	11	6	5			NUMBER OF STATEMENTS	32	27
%	%	%	%	%	%	**ASSETS**	%	%
	3.0			D	D	Cash & Equivalents	5.7	4.2
	28.9			A	A	Trade Receivables (net)	31.4	30.7
	46.1			T	T	Inventory	38.6	40.2
	2.5			A	A	All Other Current	2.6	3.1
	80.6					Total Current	78.3	78.3
	11.8			N	N	Fixed Assets (net)	10.5	9.9
	1.0			O	O	Intangibles (net)	4.4	4.6
	6.6			T	T	All Other Non-Current	6.8	6.9
	100.0					Total	100.0	100.0
				A	A	**LIABILITIES**		
	12.8			V	V	Notes Payable-Short Term	15.5	19.1
	25.7			A	A	Cur. Mat.-L/T/D	2.6	2.6
	34.5			I	I	Trade Payables	24.4	22.3
	.0			L	L	Income Taxes Payable	.3	.3
	11.9			A	A	All Other Current	8.2	8.9
	84.9			B	B	Total Current	51.0	53.1
	15.9			L	L	Long-Term Debt	11.9	5.9
	.1			E	E	Deferred Taxes	.2	.5
	4.7					All Other Non-Current	3.1	2.5
	-5.6					Net Worth	33.8	38.0
	100.0					Total Liabilities & Net Worth	100.0	100.0
						INCOME DATA		
	100.0					Net Sales	100.0	100.0
	45.1					Gross Profit	36.2	41.2
	47.1					Operating Expenses	32.0	33.6
	-2.0					Operating Profit	4.2	7.6
	1.9					All Other Expenses (net)	1.3	1.3
	-3.9					Profit Before Taxes	2.9	6.2
						RATIOS		
	2.3						1.9	2.0
	1.1					Current	1.7	1.6
	1.0						1.2	1.1
	.7						1.1	1.1
	.5					Quick	.9	.6
	.2						.5	.5
30	12.1						33 11.2	36 10.3
44	8.4					Sales/Receivables	44 8.3	44 8.2
56	6.5						64 5.7	61 6.0
72	5.1						40 9.2	40 9.2
144	2.5					Cost of Sales/Inventory	95 3.8	121 3.0
192	1.9						198 1.8	184 2.0
27	13.6						21 17.7	19 18.9
116	3.1					Cost of Sales/Payables	43 8.5	38 9.7
173	2.1						75 4.8	109 3.4
	6.6						4.9	4.8
	43.3					Sales/Working Capital	8.4	10.6
	-132.9						25.6	46.2
	9.1						7.1	9.4
	(10) 2.8					EBIT/Interest	(28) 2.5	(23) 3.8
	-1.2						1.5	2.0
						Net Profit + Depr., Dep., Amort./Cur. Mat. L/T/D		
	.1						.1	.1
	10.0					Fixed/Worth	.3	.3
	-.1						.9	.7
	2.0						1.1	.9
	484.5					Debt/Worth	1.8	1.4
	-7.1						4.5	5.4
						% Profit Before Taxes/Tangible Net Worth	40.6 / (29) 20.4 / 10.4	55.5 / (26) 29.9 / 13.1
	8.5						11.7	17.3
	3.9					% Profit Before Taxes/Total Assets	5.4	7.6
	-9.3						2.0	3.0
	126.3						99.5	92.7
	94.1					Sales/Net Fixed Assets	23.8	23.6
	13.7						15.1	15.9
	3.6						3.6	3.3
	2.3					Sales/Total Assets	2.6	2.1
	1.7						1.6	1.7
						% Depr., Dep., Amort./Sales	.3 / (22) .8 / 1.9	.3 / (19) .8 / 1.7
						% Officers', Directors', Owners' Comp/Sales	1.7 / (15) 4.0 / 7.2	2.2 / (11) 3.8 / 5.9
2428M	28729M	97139M	155088M			Net Sales ($)	1126344M	829448M
646M	11365M	36208M	76092M			Total Assets ($)	685586M	467092M

M = $ thousand   MM = $ million
See Pages 11 through 21 for Explanation of Ratios and Data

Comparative Historical Data / Current Data Sorted By Sales

			Type of Statement						
4	6	5	Unqualified			2	1	2	
6	11	5	Reviewed		2		1	2	
5	3	4	Compiled	2	1		1		
2	6	4	Tax Returns	3	1				
11	11	6	Other	1	3			2	
4/1/02- 3/31/03	4/1/03- 3/31/04	4/1/04- 3/31/05			7 (4/1-9/30/04)			17 (10/1/04-3/31/05)	
ALL	ALL	ALL		0-1MM	1-3MM	3-5MM	5-10MM	10-25MM	25MM & OVER
28	37	24	**NUMBER OF STATEMENTS**	1	8	4	2	5	4
%	%	%	**ASSETS**	%	%	%	%	%	%
5.6	6.1	4.8	Cash & Equivalents						
30.0	28.4	27.5	Trade Receivables (net)						
37.7	36.4	39.0	Inventory						
2.9	4.8	2.5	All Other Current						
76.2	75.7	73.8	Total Current						
13.8	12.7	15.7	Fixed Assets (net)						
7.4	4.9	3.9	Intangibles (net)						
2.6	6.7	6.6	All Other Non-Current						
100.0	100.0	100.0	Total						
			LIABILITIES						
17.1	20.3	12.2	Notes Payable-Short Term						
3.9	3.6	13.9	Cur. Mat.-L/T/D						
30.0	23.3	24.0	Trade Payables						
.2	.0	.0	Income Taxes Payable						
9.5	9.1	10.8	All Other Current						
60.7	56.4	60.9	Total Current						
17.2	14.4	12.4	Long-Term Debt						
.1	.1	.1	Deferred Taxes						
4.0	9.9	7.8	All Other Non-Current						
18.1	19.3	18.8	Net Worth						
100.0	100.0	100.0	Total Liabilities & Net Worth						
			INCOME DATA						
100.0	100.0	100.0	Net Sales						
42.5	42.7	40.3	Gross Profit						
39.3	40.1	40.0	Operating Expenses						
3.2	2.5	.3	Operating Profit						
1.5	.6	1.6	All Other Expenses (net)						
1.7	1.9	-1.3	Profit Before Taxes						
			RATIOS						
2.3	2.2	2.3							
1.6	1.6	1.4	Current						
1.1	1.3	1.0							
1.2	1.3	1.3							
.8	.7	.6	Quick						
.5	.4	.3							
26 13.9	30 12.1	31 11.8							
38 9.6	39 9.3	40 9.1	Sales/Receivables						
49 7.5	51 7.1	50 7.3							
37 10.0	39 9.4	58 6.3							
103 3.5	110 3.3	93 3.9	Cost of Sales/Inventory						
193 1.9	182 2.0	184 2.0							
27 13.3	28 13.1	16 22.8							
54 6.8	51 7.2	56 6.5	Cost of Sales/Payables						
97 3.8	89 4.1	116 3.1							
5.5	5.3	6.4							
13.1	9.9	12.9	Sales/Working Capital						
35.9	18.2	159.3							
10.6	8.5	10.8							
(26) 3.2	(33) 3.1	(23) 2.0	EBIT/Interest						
1.6	.3	-1.0							
3.7	2.8		Net Profit + Depr., Dep.,						
(10) 1.5	(12) 1.7		Amort./Cur. Mat. L/T/D						
.5	.4								
.2	.2	.2							
.5	.4	.8	Fixed/Worth						
-.5	1.8	NM							
.9	.9	1.0							
2.8	2.1	2.1	Debt/Worth						
-6.2	14.3	NM							
54.4	46.8	26.4							
(20) 24.1	(30) 12.6	(18) 13.3	% Profit Before Taxes/Tangible Net Worth						
3.8	-10.8	-5.0							
17.7	14.4	12.3							
4.2	6.0	2.7	% Profit Before Taxes/Total Assets						
1.2	-2.3	-6.1							
89.1	52.2	93.1							
27.3	24.3	29.9	Sales/Net Fixed Assets						
10.7	12.0	9.3							
3.9	3.4	3.5							
3.1	2.3	2.2	Sales/Total Assets						
1.8	1.6	1.7							
.4	.5	.6							
(24) .9	(31) 1.1	(20) 1.0	% Depr., Dep., Amort./Sales						
2.3	2.1	2.9							
1.8	2.1	2.9							
(13) 4.1	(15) 4.1	(10) 5.5	% Officers', Directors', Owners' Comp/Sales						
6.9	4.7	15.5							
942463M	1431629M	283384M	Net Sales ($)	380M	15383M	15394M	17393M	92411M	142423M
644790M	781412M	124311M	Total Assets ($)	224M	6180M	5607M	10027M	46870M	55403M

M = $ thousand   MM = $ million
See Pages 11 through 21 for Explanation of Ratios and Data

Current Data Sorted By Assets   Comparative Historical Data

						Type of Statement		
		2	3	2	2	Unqualified	11	10
	6	15	4			Reviewed	13	23
1	6	5	1			Compiled	11	23
5	6					Tax Returns	4	11
1	6	10	2	1		Other	20	17
	16 (4/1-9/30/04)		62 (10/1/04-3/31/05)				4/1/00-3/31/01	4/1/01-3/31/02
0-500M	500M-2MM	2-10MM	10-50MM	50-100MM	100-250MM		ALL	ALL
7	24	32	10	3	2	NUMBER OF STATEMENTS	59	84
%	%	%	%	%	%	ASSETS	%	%
	11.3	4.3	4.0			Cash & Equivalents	6.6	8.6
	41.5	37.7	35.2			Trade Receivables (net)	32.7	38.1
	28.6	31.3	29.9			Inventory	34.4	30.5
	1.9	3.9	4.3			All Other Current	2.2	2.8
	83.3	77.2	73.4			Total Current	75.9	79.9
	9.6	14.4	10.8			Fixed Assets (net)	12.8	13.3
	.7	5.4	10.0			Intangibles (net)	4.9	2.5
	6.4	3.1	5.9			All Other Non-Current	6.4	4.3
	100.0	100.0	100.0			Total	100.0	100.0
						LIABILITIES		
	12.1	17.4	19.1			Notes Payable-Short Term	13.3	17.0
	3.7	2.9	1.8			Cur. Mat.-L/T/D	6.4	3.1
	26.7	28.7	20.7			Trade Payables	24.1	22.1
	.7	.1	.1			Income Taxes Payable	.4	.3
	15.2	6.0	7.2			All Other Current	11.7	11.2
	58.3	55.2	48.9			Total Current	55.9	53.6
	4.1	6.0	12.9			Long-Term Debt	9.4	10.5
	.0	.0	.3			Deferred Taxes	.2	.1
	5.3	1.5	4.1			All Other Non-Current	2.4	3.0
	32.2	37.3	33.9			Net Worth	32.2	32.7
	100.0	100.0	100.0			Total Liabilities & Net Worth	100.0	100.0
						INCOME DATA		
	100.0	100.0	100.0			Net Sales	100.0	100.0
	33.3	31.0	38.2			Gross Profit	33.7	32.4
	31.8	28.3	33.6			Operating Expenses	30.3	28.9
	1.5	2.8	4.6			Operating Profit	3.4	3.5
	1.0	1.1	.7			All Other Expenses (net)	.2	.6
	.6	1.6	3.9			Profit Before Taxes	3.3	2.9
						RATIOS		
	2.2	2.3	3.3				2.3	2.2
	1.5	1.2	1.4			Current	1.4	1.5
	1.0	1.1	1.0				1.1	1.1
	1.8	1.0	1.4				1.1	1.3
	.8	.7	.9			Quick	.7	.8
	.6	.6	.5				.5	.6

		28	12.9	40	9.2	43	8.6				Sales/Receivables	32	11.5	32	11.4

Note: The following ratio blocks use turn-day counts.

							Ratio	Hist 01		Hist 02	
	28	12.9	40	9.2	43	8.6	Sales/Receivables	32	11.5	32	11.4
	42	8.7	46	7.9	46	7.9		43	8.5	45	8.1
	52	7.0	54	6.7	54	6.8		63	5.8	63	5.8
	26	14.3	38	9.6	34	10.7	Cost of Sales/Inventory	43	8.5	27	13.4
	49	7.5	63	5.7	78	4.7		75	4.9	57	6.4
	64	5.7	106	3.4	122	3.0		125	2.9	102	3.6
	16	23.5	27	13.7	26	13.8	Cost of Sales/Payables	26	14.3	20	18.6
	44	8.4	48	7.6	40	9.1		42	8.6	35	10.4
	62	5.9	77	4.7	58	6.3		64	5.7	54	6.8
		8.2		6.3		4.9	Sales/Working Capital		6.1		6.4
		13.8		18.0		16.0			12.1		13.6
		185.4		81.3		NM			67.0		37.0
		15.4		10.5		13.7	EBIT/Interest		11.6		8.8
	(21)	3.7	(29)	4.1		4.8		(57)	4.2	(78)	3.4
		.3		1.9		2.5			1.1		1.4
							Net Profit + Depr., Dep., Amort./Cur. Mat. L/T/D		9.6		7.6
								(12)	4.2	(22)	3.5
									.7		1.1
		.1		.2		.2	Fixed/Worth		.1		.1
		.2		.4		.6			.4		.3
		4.8		4.3		NM			.7		1.0
		.9		.7		1.3	Debt/Worth		.7		.9
		1.8		2.5		2.5			2.1		2.5
		10.3		23.9		NM			7.5		5.3
		63.0		28.2			% Profit Before Taxes/Tangible Net Worth		45.1		42.8
	(20)	14.6	(27)	12.9				(48)	22.2	(73)	19.6
		.4		8.2					6.8		8.8
		13.2		8.6		14.4	% Profit Before Taxes/Total Assets		14.1		13.3
		3.3		6.0		7.6			5.4		6.1
		-3.7		2.5		2.9			1.3		1.8
		161.5		70.9		111.9	Sales/Net Fixed Assets		65.1		84.2
		59.4		28.8		44.6			30.7		32.6
		22.1		9.9		12.1			13.5		14.0
		4.5		3.3		3.0	Sales/Total Assets		3.5		3.6
		3.6		2.6		2.5			2.6		2.8
		2.5		1.9		2.0			2.1		2.2
		.3		.7			% Depr., Dep., Amort./Sales		.5		.3
	(17)	.9	(31)	1.0				(48)	1.0	(69)	1.0
		1.8		2.7					1.8		2.0
		2.1		.9			% Officers', Directors', Owners' Comp/Sales		2.9		2.2
	(16)	3.9	(14)	2.7				(29)	4.1	(43)	4.1
		8.5		3.4					6.5		7.7
11122M	105813M	404716M	634737M	237714M	299975M	Net Sales ($)	1043551M	1377547M
2215M	29140M	152658M	235776M	199849M	325457M	Total Assets ($)	496450M	717330M

M = $ thousand   MM = $ million
See Pages 11 through 21 for Explanation of Ratios and Data

Comparative Historical Data | | | **Current Data Sorted By Sales**

	4/1/02-3/31/03 ALL	4/1/03-3/31/04 ALL	4/1/04-3/31/05 ALL	Type of Statement	0-1MM	1-3MM	3-5MM	5-10MM	10-25MM	25MM & OVER
	15	14	9	Unqualified				1	1	7
	36	28	25	Reviewed	1		2	8	10	4
	14	21	13	Compiled	1	1	1	8	1	1
	13	12	11	Tax Returns	2	5	4			
	23	24	20	Other		5	1	5	5	4
						16 (4/1-9/30/04)			62 (10/1/04-3/31/05)	
NUMBER OF STATEMENTS	101	99	78		4	11	8	22	17	16
ASSETS	%	%	%		%	%	%	%	%	%
Cash & Equivalents	8.4	7.8	6.9			14.1		5.7	3.1	6.3
Trade Receivables (net)	34.6	34.4	38.6			40.9		43.6	40.1	29.6
Inventory	31.0	33.2	29.5			23.9		30.8	34.9	26.0
All Other Current	3.0	2.6	3.0			1.9		4.2	2.2	4.1
Total Current	76.9	78.1	77.9			80.8		84.3	80.3	66.0
Fixed Assets (net)	11.5	12.6	12.4			12.1		10.9	12.1	14.7
Intangibles (net)	5.7	4.7	5.4			6.3		2.3	4.2	14.2
All Other Non-Current	5.8	4.7	4.3			.8		2.5	3.4	5.1
Total	100.0	100.0	100.0			100.0		100.0	100.0	100.0
LIABILITIES										
Notes Payable-Short Term	14.0	13.0	16.1			12.5		14.8	22.5	15.0
Cur. Mat.-L/T/D	3.7	2.7	3.0			2.7		3.7	3.3	2.8
Trade Payables	22.5	22.5	24.6			15.0		31.0	32.5	15.5
Income Taxes Payable	.2	.2	.3			.0		.4	.0	.1
All Other Current	10.7	11.2	10.5			27.8		8.6	4.6	10.1
Total Current	51.1	49.5	54.5			58.0		58.5	62.9	43.5
Long-Term Debt	8.2	7.5	8.0			7.8		3.9	5.1	15.5
Deferred Taxes	.3	.2	.1			.0		.0	.1	.6
All Other Non-Current	4.0	7.2	3.6			16.0		.5	1.5	3.3
Net Worth	36.5	35.5	33.7			18.2		37.2	30.4	37.2
Total Liabilities & Net Worth	100.0	100.0	100.0			100.0		100.0	100.0	100.0
INCOME DATA										
Net Sales	100.0	100.0	100.0			100.0		100.0	100.0	100.0
Gross Profit	35.4	32.1	33.7			41.8		31.4	27.7	38.5
Operating Expenses	31.6	28.8	30.9			39.4		29.9	24.5	33.1
Operating Profit	3.7	3.4	2.9			2.4		1.5	3.2	5.3
All Other Expenses (net)	.3	.9	.9			.0		1.0	.9	1.0
Profit Before Taxes	3.4	2.5	1.9			2.4		.5	2.3	4.4
RATIOS										
Current	2.5	2.3	2.3			2.9		2.4	1.9	2.9
	1.6	1.5	1.3			1.5		1.4	1.2	1.4
	1.1	1.2	1.0			1.0		1.1	1.0	1.0
Quick	1.4	1.2	1.3			2.5		1.4	.8	1.3
	.8	.8	.8			.9		.8	.6	.8
	.6	.6	.6			.6		.5	.5	.6
Sales/Receivables	31 11.9	31 11.8	34 10.6			27 13.6		38 9.5	40 9.1	36 10.1
	42 8.8	41 8.9	45 8.0			43 8.4		45 8.2	46 7.9	46 7.9
	54 6.7	53 6.9	55 6.7			55 6.7		57 6.4	58 6.3	55 6.7
Cost of Sales/Inventory	28 13.0	30 12.0	31 11.9			15 25.1		22 17.0	42 8.6	28 13.0
	60 6.1	64 5.7	57 6.4			34 10.8		60 6.1	57 6.4	91 4.0
	101 3.6	113 3.2	103 3.6			76 4.8		94 3.9	110 3.3	139 2.6
Cost of Sales/Payables	19 19.1	23 15.6	22 16.4			9 39.3		24 15.4	34 10.6	22 16.6
	36 10.0	42 8.6	43 8.5			19 19.6		48 7.6	55 6.7	36 10.0
	65 5.7	61 6.0	62 5.8			45 8.0		67 5.4	76 4.8	55 6.7
Sales/Working Capital	6.1	5.6	6.4			8.2		5.2	8.3	4.8
	11.9	11.2	15.0			39.6		11.7	20.5	8.8
	36.2	23.9	142.2			−225.1		139.5	84.0	152.4
EBIT/Interest	16.8	11.4	12.0			13.6		10.4	11.5	11.9
	(87) 5.0	(88) 4.8	(70) 4.0			(10) 3.9		(18) 3.9	5.2	(15) 3.7
	1.4	1.9	1.9			.5		−2.5	2.1	2.1
Net Profit + Depr., Dep., Amort./Cur. Mat. L/T/D	7.6	6.0	5.1							
	(18) 3.4	(19) 3.1	(15) 1.9							
	1.3	1.7	1.2							
Fixed/Worth	.1	.1	.2			.4		.1	.2	.2
	.3	.3	.4			12.2		.4	.3	.6
	.8	1.0	5.6			−.8		3.7	3.4	NM
Debt/Worth	.8	.9	.8			1.4		.6	1.1	.9
	1.9	2.2	2.5			107.4		1.9	3.2	2.5
	6.6	5.2	26.3			−5.5		25.8	22.7	NM
% Profit Before Taxes/Tangible Net Worth	48.5	40.7	54.2					45.9	44.7	48.0
	(84) 22.4	(86) 17.8	(62) 14.8					(18) 14.5	(15) 12.5	(12) 17.1
	5.4	4.5	3.3					1.1	8.2	4.3
% Profit Before Taxes/Total Assets	15.8	11.2	10.5			22.8		9.3	8.7	9.4
	7.1	6.5	5.5			6.6		4.9	5.5	6.8
	1.2	1.5	1.4			−.8		−1.8	2.0	3.1
Sales/Net Fixed Assets	119.2	77.0	91.5			108.0		112.2	88.2	53.0
	35.9	32.8	34.2			57.9		57.8	32.3	13.7
	15.6	13.1	12.3			13.4		13.1	15.3	7.1
Sales/Total Assets	3.6	3.8	3.7			5.2		3.8	3.7	2.9
	2.8	2.7	2.8			3.4		2.6	3.2	2.2
	2.2	2.1	2.1			2.4		2.1	2.4	1.2
% Depr., Dep., Amort./Sales	.5	.5	.5					.6	.3	.5
	(80) 1.0	(81) 1.1	(65) .9					(17) 1.0	.8	(13) 1.0
	2.2	2.3	2.5					1.7	2.9	3.0
% Officers', Directors', Owners' Comp/Sales	1.8	2.2	1.9			2.1				
	(44) 4.5	(48) 4.2	(38) 3.1			(11) 3.2				
	7.5	7.4	7.3			5.0				
Net Sales ($)	1761758M	1402368M	1694077M		2478M	25382M	35357M	154909M	269374M	1206577M
Total Assets ($)	665712M	620267M	945095M		1669M	8507M	9977M	61332M	93301M	770309M

M = $ thousand   MM = $ million
See Pages 11 through 21 for Explanation of Ratios and Data

Current Data Sorted By Assets   **Comparative Historical Data**

Type of Statement

0-500M	500M-2MM	2-10MM	10-50MM	50-100MM	100-250MM	Type of Statement	4/1/00-3/31/01 ALL	4/1/01-3/31/02 ALL
	3	20	51	19	18	Unqualified	104	104
1	22	94	57	5	2	Reviewed	148	134
7	40	49	11			Compiled	113	116
8	17	11				Tax Returns	22	20
9	30	47	41	9	7	Other	147	168
116 (4/1-9/30/04)			462 (10/1/04-3/31/05)					
0-500M	500M-2MM	2-10MM	10-50MM	50-100MM	100-250MM			
25	112	221	160	33	27	**NUMBER OF STATEMENTS**	534	542

ASSETS

0-500M	500M-2MM	2-10MM	10-50MM	50-100MM	100-250MM		ALL	ALL
%	%	%	%	%	%	**ASSETS**	%	%
11.5	9.3	5.8	4.5	3.1	3.6	Cash & Equivalents	4.5	4.4
37.1	39.8	37.1	33.7	29.0	28.9	Trade Receivables (net)	34.4	31.6
16.6	33.8	38.9	44.3	44.7	45.0	Inventory	40.5	39.4
.2	2.8	1.7	2.0	1.3	2.2	All Other Current	1.2	1.4
65.5	85.6	83.5	84.5	78.0	79.8	Total Current	80.6	76.9
18.8	10.3	11.2	11.3	14.6	14.8	Fixed Assets (net)	14.3	16.3
1.8	1.0	.8	.9	2.8	1.5	Intangibles (net)	1.9	1.5
13.9	3.1	4.4	3.3	4.5	3.9	All Other Non-Current	3.2	5.3
100.0	100.0	100.0	100.0	100.0	100.0	Total	100.0	100.0

LIABILITIES

0-500M	500M-2MM	2-10MM	10-50MM	50-100MM	100-250MM	**LIABILITIES**	ALL	ALL
24.8	13.6	20.2	23.7	18.5	16.0	Notes Payable-Short Term	22.6	22.0
5.6	2.7	1.6	1.3	2.3	1.5	Cur. Mat.-L/T/D	2.2	2.7
20.2	29.9	24.7	23.2	16.3	18.8	Trade Payables	22.8	20.7
.0	.1	.4	.2	.3	.6	Income Taxes Payable	.2	.2
8.4	6.6	7.1	6.8	11.9	9.5	All Other Current	6.9	7.5
59.1	53.0	54.0	55.2	49.2	46.4	Total Current	54.7	53.1
20.8	10.6	6.6	6.3	8.0	7.3	Long-Term Debt	8.5	9.5
.1	.1	.1	.2	.4	.8	Deferred Taxes	.2	.2
4.0	7.3	5.1	3.7	3.6	4.6	All Other Non-Current	3.4	4.3
15.9	29.1	34.2	34.6	38.7	40.8	Net Worth	33.2	32.8
100.0	100.0	100.0	100.0	100.0	100.0	Total Liabilities & Net Worth	100.0	100.0

INCOME DATA

0-500M	500M-2MM	2-10MM	10-50MM	50-100MM	100-250MM	**INCOME DATA**	ALL	ALL
100.0	100.0	100.0	100.0	100.0	100.0	Net Sales	100.0	100.0
29.4	25.7	22.3	19.2	22.5	17.3	Gross Profit	21.8	22.2
25.3	21.4	17.5	13.1	11.2	9.0	Operating Expenses	18.1	19.5
4.2	4.3	4.9	6.1	11.3	8.3	Operating Profit	3.6	2.6
.9	.6	.4	.3	1.5	.6	All Other Expenses (net)	1.2	1.2
3.3	3.7	4.5	5.8	9.8	7.7	Profit Before Taxes	2.4	1.4

RATIOS

0-500M	500M-2MM	2-10MM	10-50MM	50-100MM	100-250MM	**RATIOS**	ALL	ALL
3.6	2.4	2.2	2.2	2.4	2.3	Current	2.2	2.4
1.5	1.6	1.5	1.4	1.5	1.8		1.4	1.4
.9	1.2	1.2	1.2	1.2	1.3		1.1	1.1
2.6	1.4	1.3	1.0	1.1	.9	Quick	1.0	1.1
1.2	1.0	.7	.7	.7	.7	(533)	.6	.7
.5	.6	.5	.5	.4	.6		.5	.4
15 24.3	28 13.2	33 11.0	35 10.4	36 10.0	32 11.3	Sales/Receivables	34 10.7	32 11.3
29 12.8	41 9.0	44 8.3	45 8.2	46 8.0	47 7.8		45 8.2	41 8.9
58 6.3	54 6.8	55 6.7	54 6.8	51 7.1	60 6.1		53 6.9	52 7.0
0 UND	20 18.6	37 10.0	51 7.1	64 5.7	71 5.1	Cost of Sales/Inventory	43 8.4	43 8.5
18 20.1	50 7.3	65 5.6	77 4.8	95 3.8	89 4.1		73 5.0	74 4.9
59 6.2	84 4.3	99 3.7	111 3.3	119 3.1	114 3.2		109 3.3	112 3.3
2 165.6	20 18.2	20 18.6	21 17.4	13 27.6	23 15.8	Cost of Sales/Payables	21 17.7	21 17.3
17 21.3	34 10.7	35 10.6	36 10.2	30 12.4	33 11.1		35 10.4	32 11.4
37 10.0	56 6.5	57 6.4	53 6.9	46 7.9	51 7.2		52 7.0	49 7.5
8.7	7.1	5.8	5.4	5.0	5.4	Sales/Working Capital	6.1	6.0
12.1	11.5	11.6	9.9	9.7	6.1		13.0	11.4
−38.9	21.5	25.2	20.9	23.8	14.8		36.5	34.8
9.0	19.7	18.3	21.6	46.0	50.1	EBIT/Interest	5.3	4.5
(16) 6.3	(102) 6.2	(205) 7.8	(153) 10.0	(30) 10.8	14.0		(492) 2.4	(511) 1.9
1.1	2.1	2.8	4.6	5.3	4.7		1.2	.7
	7.5	18.1	27.1	373.4		Net Profit + Depr., Dep., Amort./Cur. Mat. L /T/D	7.6	3.8
	(15) 3.1	(44) 6.6	(40) 6.9	(10) 30.5			(119) 2.6	(113) 1.8
	2.3	1.7	3.9	3.1			1.0	.4
.1	.1	.1	.1	.2	.1	Fixed/Worth	.1	.1
.6	.2	.2	.2	.3	.3		.4	.4
−11.8	.7	.7	.6	.7	.7		1.0	1.1
1.3	1.0	1.0	1.0	.9	.8	Debt/Worth	1.0	1.0
2.5	2.5	2.4	2.2	2.1	1.7		2.7	2.3
−36.5	7.6	5.1	4.4	3.3	3.9		6.2	5.5
189.3	75.9	73.6	72.6	72.0	79.7	% Profit Before Taxes/Tangible Net Worth	36.3	28.1
(18) 39.2	(97) 31.1	(214) 39.1	(153) 41.4	(32) 53.3	43.3		(499) 17.8	(505) 9.9
7.8	10.2	15.8	24.4	27.7	21.1		4.2	−.9
29.2	20.5	22.0	20.1	33.4	28.2	% Profit Before Taxes/Total Assets	11.6	7.7
13.4	8.3	8.6	11.9	17.3	15.1		4.4	3.0
.4	2.2	3.1	6.3	7.9	6.3		.8	−.9
403.2	196.8	206.7	144.0	54.1	34.2	Sales/Net Fixed Assets	90.9	67.0
29.9	60.4	47.5	30.9	15.2	15.8		27.8	23.3
11.3	24.5	16.3	17.1	8.8	10.2		12.4	10.6
7.3	4.6	3.8	3.3	3.0	3.0	Sales/Total Assets	3.5	3.3
3.4	3.3	2.9	2.6	2.3	2.3		2.6	2.5
2.3	2.6	2.1	2.0	2.0	1.9		2.0	1.9
.4	.3	.2	.2	.4	.4	% Depr., Dep., Amort./Sales	.4	.4
(15) .8	(81) .7	(188) .6	(141) .6	(31) 1.1	(26) 1.0		(459) .8	(464) 1.0
4.1	1.4	1.4	1.2	1.6	1.3		1.5	1.9
2.0	1.6	1.3	.7			% Officers', Directors', Owners' Comp/Sales	1.6	1.5
(11) 3.6	(70) 3.2	(102) 2.3	(38) 1.5				(228) 2.7	(226) 2.8
7.6	5.2	4.8	3.7				4.7	5.2
35229M	541028M	3467935M	9299110M	5727860M	10589487M	Net Sales ($)	17540303M	18199922M
7137M	135424M	1073175M	3377361M	2322149M	4223099M	Total Assets ($)	7562167M	8315400M

M = $ thousand   MM = $ million
See Pages 11 through 21 for Explanation of Ratios and Data

Comparative Historical Data   Current Data Sorted By Sales

Hist 1	Hist 2	Hist 3	Type of Statement	0-1MM	1-3MM	3-5MM	5-10MM	10-25MM	25MM & OVER
119	96	111	Unqualified			1	9	11	90
165	169	181	Reviewed		8	12	28	56	77
88	127	107	Compiled	5	18	20	26	24	14
25	30	36	Tax Returns	3	7	7	15	2	2
161	150	143	Other	4	13	21	26	15	64
4/1/02-3/31/03 ALL	4/1/03-3/31/04 ALL	4/1/04-3/31/05 ALL		116 (4/1-9/30/04)			462 (10/1/04-3/31/05)		
558	572	578	NUMBER OF STATEMENTS	12	46	61	104	108	247
%	%	%	**ASSETS**	%	%	%	%	%	%
5.5	5.2	6.1	Cash & Equivalents	14.5	7.9	9.2	7.8	6.1	3.9
31.7	33.9	35.8	Trade Receivables (net)	36.9	34.2	34.0	37.0	37.5	35.4
40.6	37.5	39.1	Inventory	17.8	30.0	33.0	38.4	38.6	43.8
1.7	2.0	1.9	All Other Current	.2	1.7	2.6	2.7	1.1	1.8
79.5	78.6	82.9	Total Current	69.4	73.8	78.7	86.0	83.3	84.9
15.2	15.0	11.8	Fixed Assets (net)	20.6	16.6	15.5	9.1	11.7	10.7
1.7	1.6	1.1	Intangibles (net)	.0	1.8	1.0	1.1	.8	1.1
3.6	4.8	4.2	All Other Non-Current	10.0	7.8	4.8	3.8	4.2	3.3
100.0	100.0	100.0	Total	100.0	100.0	100.0	100.0	100.0	100.0
			LIABILITIES						
21.3	21.3	19.8	Notes Payable-Short Term	6.1	18.2	14.4	17.0	21.8	22.4
2.9	2.2	1.9	Cur. Mat.-L/T/D	.1	6.4	2.7	2.1	1.1	1.3
21.0	23.3	24.4	Trade Payables	13.3	26.6	22.3	27.4	25.1	23.4
.2	.1	.3	Income Taxes Payable	.0	.0	.2	.3	.3	.3
6.3	7.0	7.3	All Other Current	10.5	7.4	4.1	7.3	7.0	8.2
51.6	53.9	53.7	Total Current	30.0	58.7	43.7	54.1	55.3	55.6
9.1	8.9	8.0	Long-Term Debt	30.8	10.3	16.8	6.9	5.6	5.9
.3	.2	.2	Deferred Taxes	.1	.1	.1	.2	.1	.3
4.0	5.9	5.0	All Other Non-Current	5.2	12.8	5.3	4.4	5.2	3.6
35.0	31.0	33.1	Net Worth	33.8	18.2	34.1	34.4	33.8	34.7
100.0	100.0	100.0	Total Liabilities & Net Worth	100.0	100.0	100.0	100.0	100.0	100.0
			INCOME DATA						
100.0	100.0	100.0	Net Sales	100.0	100.0	100.0	100.0	100.0	100.0
22.2	20.8	22.2	Gross Profit	35.6	30.6	28.7	23.8	20.7	18.4
19.5	18.6	16.6	Operating Expenses	29.9	28.5	24.1	18.8	15.4	11.5
2.7	2.2	5.6	Operating Profit	5.7	2.1	4.6	4.9	5.4	6.9
.9	.7	.5	All Other Expenses (net)	1.7	.5	.7	.5	.3	.5
1.9	1.5	5.1	Profit Before Taxes	4.0	1.6	3.9	4.4	5.1	6.4
			RATIOS						
2.4	2.1	2.3	Current	6.1	2.4	2.8	2.2	2.3	2.1
1.5	1.4	1.5		3.6	1.3	2.0	1.6	1.4	1.4
1.1	1.1	1.2		1.3	.9	1.2	1.3	1.2	1.2
1.1	1.1	1.2	Quick	3.7	1.5	1.9	1.3	1.3	1.0
.7	.7	.8		2.2	.7	1.1	.9	.7	.7
.4	.5	.5		1.2	.4	.5	.6	.5	.5
33 11.1	37 10.0	32 11.3	Sales/Receivables	26 14.0	32 11.5	33 11.1	30 12.1	34 10.8	33 11.1
43 8.5	44 8.2	44 8.4		33 11.2	46 8.0	44 8.2	44 8.3	45 8.1	42 8.6
53 6.9	55 6.6	54 6.7		80 4.6	63 5.8	59 6.1	53 6.8	58 6.3	51 7.1
45 8.2	39 9.3	36 10.1	Cost of Sales/Inventory	0 UND	15 24.8	30 12.3	29 12.7	36 10.0	45 8.2
76 4.8	69 5.3	67 5.4		43 8.5	75 4.9	66 5.6	63 5.8	62 5.9	73 5.0
115 3.2	103 3.5	101 3.6		64 5.7	118 3.1	107 3.4	105 3.5	89 4.1	107 3.4
19 19.0	21 17.0	19 18.9	Cost of Sales/Payables	6 64.7	21 17.4	18 20.6	20 18.0	19 19.2	19 18.9
32 11.3	37 9.9	34 10.8		20 18.6	49 7.5	41 9.0	34 10.7	34 10.6	32 11.5
51 7.2	54 6.8	53 6.8		34 10.6	103 3.5	60 6.0	58 6.3	54 6.8	48 7.6
5.3	5.9	5.9	Sales/Working Capital	6.0	6.8	4.3	5.8	6.5	6.0
10.4	12.7	10.8		10.7	11.0	7.6	10.5	15.1	10.4
29.2	35.5	23.1		12.1	-69.7	15.4	20.1	26.7	24.6
6.4	6.5	21.3	EBIT/Interest		10.6	19.4	20.5	17.1	28.6
(527) 2.5	(525) 2.5	(533) 8.6			(40) 3.0	(54) 6.4	(97) 6.0	(98) 8.6	(239) 11.2
1.1	1.0	2.9			1.0	2.0	2.4	3.3	4.9
6.0	4.8	20.5	Net Profit + Depr., Dep., Amort./Cur. Mat. L/T/D				6.5	23.7	36.1
(134) 2.2	(113) 2.2	(119) 6.7				(23) 2.9	(24) 12.5	(59) 9.4	
.9	.8	2.7					1.9	3.0	3.8
.1	.1	.1	Fixed/Worth	.1	.1	.1	.1	.1	.1
.3	.4	.2		.5	.5	.2	.2	.3	.2
1.1	1.0	.7		.9	NM	.9	.6	.7	.6
1.0	1.2	1.0	Debt/Worth	.5	1.3	.8	.9	1.2	1.0
2.2	2.6	2.4		2.3	3.0	1.7	2.4	2.4	2.3
5.5	5.8	4.9		7.7	-117.5	5.4	6.3	5.2	4.2
27.4	31.8	72.6	% Profit Before Taxes/Tangible Net Worth	130.9	46.9	60.9	60.8	78.8	81.2
(515) 12.3	(523) 12.0	(541) 39.2		(11) 34.9	(34) 21.5	(52) 20.4	(99) 27.3	(107) 40.3	(238) 46.1
2.0	1.9	16.9		3.7	7.8	2.7	13.5	18.0	25.7
8.7	8.1	22.3	% Profit Before Taxes/Total Assets	28.8	17.0	26.2	19.2	22.5	24.2
3.4	3.1	10.6		9.2	4.7	6.7	7.9	10.6	13.3
.2	.1	3.9		-1.9	.0	.9	3.2	4.2	7.1
85.6	88.1	155.9	Sales/Net Fixed Assets	51.7	96.3	126.2	153.6	210.8	203.8
23.7	24.5	37.8		27.9	30.0	37.5	58.8	42.9	32.6
10.2	11.0	15.5		8.0	10.3	10.7	20.4	16.7	15.4
3.4	3.3	3.7	Sales/Total Assets	4.4	3.3	4.1	4.0	3.8	3.6
2.4	2.6	2.8		2.5	2.3	2.7	3.0	2.9	2.8
1.8	1.9	2.1		1.6	1.7	1.6	2.3	2.3	2.1
.4	.4	.3	% Depr., Dep., Amort./Sales		.6	.6	.3	.2	.2
(490) .9	(489) 1.0	(482) .7			(42) 1.2	(42) 1.3	(80) .9	(93) .5	(220) .6
1.8	1.8	1.3			2.8	2.6	1.4	1.2	1.1
1.6	1.3	1.2	% Officers', Directors', Owners' Comp/Sales		2.4	1.8	1.7	1.1	.5
(233) 3.0	(246) 2.6	(229) 2.5			(24) 4.5	(32) 3.2	(57) 3.2	(45) 1.7	(66) 1.3
5.8	4.4	4.9			6.5	6.6	7.1	3.6	3.7
19160328M	19353011M	29660649M	Net Sales ($)	8155M	90132M	236338M	745677M	1783252M	26797095M
8476257M	8142997M	11138345M	Total Assets ($)	3096M	44463M	126943M	267525M	673818M	10022500M

M = $ thousand   MM = $ million
See Pages 11 through 21 for Explanation of Ratios and Data

Current Data Sorted By Assets   **Comparative Historical Data**

0-500M	500M-2MM	2-10MM	10-50MM	50-100MM	100-250MM	Type of Statement	4/1/00-3/31/01 ALL	4/1/01-3/31/02 ALL
		4	1	1		Unqualified	8	3
	1	4	1			Reviewed	7	4
1	3	5	1			Compiled	7	8
						Tax Returns	3	2
3	5	5	31			Other	14	13
	5 (4/1-9/30/04)		31 (10/1/04-3/31/05)					
1	7	14	11	2	1	NUMBER OF STATEMENTS	39	30
%	%	%	%	%	%	**ASSETS**	%	%
		9.3	10.7			Cash & Equivalents	12.5	12.0
		25.5	33.4			Trade Receivables (net)	36.2	44.6
		20.0	15.9			Inventory	17.7	13.8
		3.3	1.3			All Other Current	3.9	3.3
		58.1	61.2			Total Current	70.3	73.7
		23.7	16.6			Fixed Assets (net)	16.6	16.1
		2.2	5.3			Intangibles (net)	3.0	2.4
		16.0	16.9			All Other Non-Current	10.2	7.8
		100.0	100.0			Total	100.0	100.0
						LIABILITIES		
		15.6	11.9			Notes Payable-Short Term	12.7	14.3
		9.6	3.2			Cur. Mat.-L/T/D	4.6	2.8
		20.1	26.5			Trade Payables	25.6	29.5
		.1	.0			Income Taxes Payable	.2	.4
		7.0	10.1			All Other Current	5.0	7.7
		52.5	51.7			Total Current	48.1	54.7
		10.3	10.8			Long-Term Debt	7.5	5.4
		.1	.2			Deferred Taxes	2.4	.1
		1.4	8.7			All Other Non-Current	6.0	6.3
		35.7	28.5			Net Worth	36.1	33.5
		100.0	100.0			Total Liabilities & Net Worth	100.0	100.0
						INCOME DATA		
		100.0	100.0			Net Sales	100.0	100.0
		25.5	11.9			Gross Profit	11.3	13.2
		17.1	7.7			Operating Expenses	12.6	11.4
		8.5	4.2			Operating Profit	-1.2	1.8
		-1.4	-.8			All Other Expenses (net)	-1.4	.1
		9.9	5.0			Profit Before Taxes	.2	1.6
						RATIOS		
		1.5	2.0				2.2	2.1
		1.1	1.2			Current	1.5	1.4
		.8	.7				1.1	1.0
		.9	1.4				1.8	1.5
		.6	.7			Quick	1.0	1.0
		.4	.5				.7	.7
		11 34.2	18 19.9				28 12.9	29 12.6
		19 19.0	33 11.1			Sales/Receivables	41 9.0	41 8.9
		31 11.6	38 9.7				52 7.0	48 7.7
		0 UND	2 150.3				1 414.3	0 UND
		0 UND	10 37.0			Cost of Sales/Inventory	25 14.7	7 55.9
		36 10.1	49 7.5				74 4.9	46 7.9
		8 44.8	16 23.4				18 20.6	17 21.3
		25 14.6	26 13.9			Cost of Sales/Payables	32 11.5	27 13.8
		36 10.1	34 10.9				49 7.5	41 8.9
		14.7	11.3				5.6	7.0
		541.1	27.7			Sales/Working Capital	13.6	15.0
		-30.5	-18.2				43.9	NM
		13.7	17.5				5.5	12.5
		(13) 4.0	6.5			EBIT/Interest	(37) 1.8	(29) 4.0
		3.0	1.0				.7	.9
						Net Profit + Depr., Dep.,	5.0	
						Amort./Cur. Mat. L /T/D	(11) 2.3	
							1.4	
		.0	.1				.0	.1
		.8	.4			Fixed/Worth	.5	.5
		1.5	.8				.8	1.2
		1.3	2.1				.7	.6
		2.7	3.2			Debt/Worth	2.2	2.7
		3.3	31.0				5.7	11.8
		42.7	102.3			% Profit Before Taxes/Tangible	22.2	34.9
		24.6	50.4			Net Worth	(35) 9.8	(26) 11.0
		15.9	13.1				-.1	1.4
		17.9	23.1			% Profit Before Taxes/Total	5.7	9.7
		7.0	6.2			Assets	1.9	3.6
		3.8	.2				-.9	.0
		860.5	420.0			Sales/Net Fixed Assets	395.1	585.0
		41.1	55.6				35.3	57.9
		5.9	8.0				6.6	8.9
		7.1	5.7			Sales/Total Assets	4.6	6.6
		3.7	3.9				2.7	3.6
		1.6	1.3				1.4	2.0
		.1				% Depr., Dep., Amort./Sales	.2	.0
		(12) .8					(30) 1.1	(22) .8
		3.0					3.8	2.3
						% Officers', Directors',	1.1	.6
						Owners' Comp/Sales	(17) 1.7	(12) 1.4
							4.2	2.8
390M	46256M	377815M	979072M	311959M	172692M	Net Sales ($)	1895273M	1310440M
233M	8903M	83874M	300913M	139964M	203487M	Total Assets ($)	686262M	314316M

© RMA 2005   M = $ thousand   MM = $ million
See Pages 11 through 21 for Explanation of Ratios and Data

Comparative Historical Data | **Current Data Sorted By Sales**

			Type of Statement	0-1MM	1-3MM	3-5MM	5-10MM	10-25MM	25MM & OVER
7	5	6	Unqualified						6
5	6	6	Reviewed			2			4
5	8	10	Compiled	1		1	1	4	3
5	4		Tax Returns						
11	16	14	Other	1			3	2	8
4/1/02-3/31/03	4/1/03-3/31/04	4/1/04-3/31/05			5 (4/1-9/30/04)		31 (10/1/04-3/31/05)		
ALL	ALL	ALL							
33	39	36	**NUMBER OF STATEMENTS**	1	3	1	4	6	21
%	%	%	**ASSETS**	%	%	%	%	%	%
15.2	8.0	10.9	Cash & Equivalents						8.3
40.0	36.6	32.4	Trade Receivables (net)						34.2
16.8	20.0	17.5	Inventory						20.6
3.0	7.7	1.9	All Other Current						1.3
75.0	72.3	62.6	Total Current						64.4
16.3	16.2	20.0	Fixed Assets (net)						18.8
1.8	.9	2.5	Intangibles (net)						4.0
6.9	10.6	14.8	All Other Non-Current						12.9
100.0	100.0	100.0	Total						100.0
			LIABILITIES						
15.6	13.5	16.0	Notes Payable-Short Term						12.3
2.4	1.7	5.2	Cur. Mat.-L/T/D						5.4
30.5	25.2	23.4	Trade Payables						23.0
.4	.1	.2	Income Taxes Payable						.2
4.3	11.0	7.7	All Other Current						10.4
53.2	51.5	52.5	Total Current						51.3
9.9	12.6	11.2	Long-Term Debt						9.2
.3	.8	.2	Deferred Taxes						.3
4.6	4.6	4.9	All Other Non-Current						5.1
32.1	30.5	31.3	Net Worth						34.1
100.0	100.0	100.0	Total Liabilities & Net Worth						100.0
			INCOME DATA						
100.0	100.0	100.0	Net Sales						100.0
12.0	19.1	19.3	Gross Profit						12.3
10.2	15.5	13.9	Operating Expenses						8.5
1.8	3.7	5.4	Operating Profit						3.8
.1	.5	-1.0	All Other Expenses (net)						-.6
1.7	3.2	6.4	Profit Before Taxes						4.4
			RATIOS						
2.2	2.2	1.6	Current						1.7
1.5	1.4	1.2							1.2
1.0	1.0	.9							1.1
1.7	1.2	1.1	Quick						1.2
1.0	.8	.7							.7
.8	.6	.5							.5
28 13.0	24 15.3	18 20.2	Sales/Receivables						18 20.2
42 8.6	34 10.7	27 13.5							33 11.1
48 7.5	45 8.0	41 8.9							40 9.1
0 UND	0 UND	0 UND	Cost of Sales/Inventory						4 101.2
23 15.9	19 19.4	9 39.5							19 18.9
45 8.1	67 5.5	50 7.3							53 6.9
16 22.4	14 25.4	11 32.3	Cost of Sales/Payables						12 31.1
26 14.0	28 12.9	25 14.4							25 14.7
54 6.7	51 7.2	35 10.4							29 12.7
6.2	7.0	13.0	Sales/Working Capital						13.0
16.6	23.2	40.9							27.7
121.5	-999.8	-54.9							541.1
12.7	8.6	13.7	EBIT/Interest						16.7
(31) 4.4	(32) 3.6	(33) 6.3							(20) 7.4
2.0	1.8	2.1							4.2
			Net Profit + Depr., Dep., Amort./Cur. Mat. L/T/D						
.0	.0	.0	Fixed/Worth						.1
.4	.4	.4							.4
1.2	1.7	1.1							.9
.9	1.3	1.4	Debt/Worth						1.4
1.9	3.3	2.9							2.7
16.3	8.6	8.3							5.1
34.7	47.2	91.2	% Profit Before Taxes/Tangible Net Worth						93.4
(28) 14.9	(36) 17.9	(35) 25.3							30.0
5.4	7.7	9.8							9.5
9.6	9.3	21.4	% Profit Before Taxes/Total Assets						22.4
3.5	4.1	6.4							6.7
1.6	1.2	2.5							3.0
726.5	547.3	475.1	Sales/Net Fixed Assets						667.3
60.1	38.0	47.9							63.6
13.1	6.7	6.8							8.8
4.6	5.7	5.6	Sales/Total Assets						7.2
3.1	2.3	3.7							3.9
2.0	1.3	1.6							1.8
.1	.0	.2	% Depr., Dep., Amort./Sales						.0
(26) .6	(28) .6	(27) .6							(18) .4
3.0	1.6	2.7							1.2
1.5	.5		% Officers', Directors', Owners' Comp/Sales						
(12) 2.1	(14) 1.2								
3.8	2.8								
1028991M	2095719M	1888184M	Net Sales ($)	390M	5244M	3538M	26856M	81727M	1770429M
377306M	743046M	737374M	Total Assets ($)	233M	9971M	2331M	7483M	29880M	687476M

M = $ thousand   MM = $ million
See Pages 11 through 21 for Explanation of Ratios and Data

Current Data Sorted By Assets — Comparative Historical Data

						Type of Statement		
3	4	23	46	6	6	Unqualified	75	64
1	25	95	33	3		Reviewed	144	121
8	39	39	5			Compiled	156	129
11	25	10				Tax Returns	28	13
4	28	48	20	6	1	Other	113	123
	98 (4/1-9/30/04)			391 (10/1/04-3/31/05)			4/1/00-3/31/01	4/1/01-3/31/02
0-500M	500M-2MM	2-10MM	10-50MM	50-100MM	100-250MM		ALL	ALL
27	121	215	104	15	7	NUMBER OF STATEMENTS	516	450
%	%	%	%	%	%	ASSETS	%	%
11.3	8.0	5.4	5.6	3.1		Cash & Equivalents	5.9	5.7
39.7	37.5	39.7	41.6	37.7		Trade Receivables (net)	39.1	37.7
30.5	34.8	34.2	32.2	35.1		Inventory	34.5	36.0
.8	2.1	2.1	3.3	3.2		All Other Current	2.2	2.4
82.3	82.5	81.3	82.8	79.0		Total Current	81.7	81.7
10.8	10.4	10.7	10.3	10.3		Fixed Assets (net)	11.4	11.1
4.2	1.9	2.6	2.1	7.6		Intangibles (net)	2.3	2.2
2.7	5.3	5.4	4.9	3.1		All Other Non-Current	4.5	5.0
100.0	100.0	100.0	100.0	100.0		Total	100.0	100.0
						LIABILITIES		
21.5	13.6	15.8	16.1	7.0		Notes Payable-Short Term	16.3	18.1
4.2	3.0	2.2	1.2	2.0		Cur. Mat.-L/T/D	2.6	2.8
27.9	25.7	23.8	24.4	21.2		Trade Payables	25.1	22.6
.2	.2	.2	.2	.1		Income Taxes Payable	.3	.2
16.9	10.4	8.3	9.5	7.3		All Other Current	9.1	7.9
70.8	53.0	50.4	51.3	37.7		Total Current	53.5	51.6
7.1	11.3	8.9	7.4	16.3		Long-Term Debt	7.9	8.6
.0	.1	.1	.2	.3		Deferred Taxes	.2	.2
2.1	3.2	6.3	3.1	3.5		All Other Non-Current	3.5	3.2
20.0	32.4	34.3	37.9	42.3		Net Worth	34.9	36.4
100.0	100.0	100.0	100.0	100.0		Total Liabilities & Net Worth	100.0	100.0
						INCOME DATA		
100.0	100.0	100.0	100.0	100.0		Net Sales	100.0	100.0
40.9	31.6	26.3	23.3	25.5		Gross Profit	27.9	27.5
37.4	29.1	23.2	20.0	20.7		Operating Expenses	24.9	24.9
3.5	2.5	3.1	3.3	4.7		Operating Profit	2.9	2.6
.5	.3	.6	.0	.7		All Other Expenses (net)	.5	.6
3.0	2.3	2.5	3.3	4.0		Profit Before Taxes	2.4	2.0
						RATIOS		
1.8	2.3	2.1	2.2	3.3			2.2	2.4
1.3	1.6	1.6	1.6	2.3	Current	1.5	1.6
.9	1.2	1.2	1.2	1.4		1.2	1.2
1.1	1.4	1.2	1.5	1.7		1.3	1.3
.8	.9	.9	.9	1.3	Quick	(515) .9	.8
.5	.6	.7	.6	.8		.6	.6
25 14.9	32 11.5	40 9.0	42 8.6	42 8.7		38 9.7	38 9.6
31 11.6	43 8.6	49 7.4	50 7.3	50 7.3	Sales/Receivables	47 7.7	47 7.8
49 7.4	55 6.7	60 6.1	62 5.9	56 6.5		58 6.3	58 6.3
8 45.3	31 11.7	36 10.2	38 9.7	45 8.1		38 9.5	38 9.5
51 7.2	58 6.3	59 6.2	49 7.4	61 6.0	Cost of Sales/Inventory	56 6.6	60 6.1
70 5.2	101 3.6	89 4.1	69 5.3	83 4.4		86 4.2	96 3.8
11 32.3	26 14.0	28 13.2	28 12.9	29 12.5		25 14.3	25 14.9
31 11.9	37 10.0	40 9.2	36 10.2	34 10.8	Cost of Sales/Payables	38 9.6	35 10.4
74 4.9	60 6.1	52 7.0	50 7.3	45 8.2		55 6.6	49 7.4
9.4	5.8	6.1	6.7	3.9		6.4	6.1
21.7	10.7	9.2	10.4	6.1	Sales/Working Capital	10.9	9.9
−50.9	21.3	18.3	20.8	12.9		22.1	19.3
27.6	9.3	10.6	19.3	14.1		7.5	6.1
(22) 2.2	(108) 3.6	(196) 4.3	(97) 8.2	(14) 7.5	EBIT/Interest	(473) 3.0	(412) 2.3
.4	1.5	2.0	3.4	3.8		1.4	1.1
	7.3	6.9	21.8			7.3	5.5
	(22) 2.4	(60) 2.7	(35) 5.8		Net Profit + Depr., Dep., Amort./Cur. Mat. L /T/D	(148) 3.2	(125) 1.9
	1.4	1.2	2.5			1.1	.4
.1	.1	.1	.1	.1		.1	.1
.4	.2	.2	.2	.2	Fixed/Worth	.3	.3
−.7	.8	.5	.5	.5		.6	.6
1.2	1.0	1.0	1.0	1.0		1.0	.9
3.6	2.0	1.8	1.9	1.8	Debt/Worth	2.0	1.9
−12.7	5.3	4.1	3.1	2.9		4.2	4.0
93.4	26.2	32.4	34.9	41.5	% Profit Before Taxes/Tangible Net Worth	34.4	28.1
(18) 50.3	(105) 11.3	(204) 15.7	(98) 20.3	(14) 21.6		(469) 17.0	(419) 11.4
9.0	3.3	5.5	10.6	11.9		5.1	1.5
26.1	10.0	10.5	12.4	12.5		11.1	9.7
5.5	3.8	4.6	7.5	9.3	% Profit Before Taxes/Total Assets	4.9	3.1
−1.1	.8	1.7	3.7	6.8		1.3	.3
193.0	112.5	82.7	85.7	85.9		86.6	72.2
89.1	46.0	41.6	44.6	27.9	Sales/Net Fixed Assets	41.9	38.7
21.2	22.1	22.3	17.5	14.0		20.6	19.0
5.2	3.8	3.4	3.5	3.5		3.6	3.6
3.9	3.1	2.9	3.0	2.8	Sales/Total Assets	3.0	2.8
3.2	2.3	2.3	2.2	2.0		2.4	2.3
.4	.4	.3	.3	.4		.3	.4
(16) .6	(101) .8	(183) .6	(95) .5	(14) .6	% Depr., Dep., Amort./Sales	(433) .6	(388) .7
1.7	1.5	1.1	.8	.8		1.0	1.2
5.9	2.5	1.4	.7			1.7	1.4
(13) 8.2	(68) 4.9	(94) 2.5	(22) 1.3		% Officers', Directors', Owners' Comp/Sales	(207) 3.5	(183) 2.9
12.6	8.6	4.5	3.3			7.0	5.2
32672M	478287M	2979032M	6899378M	3024095M	2536877M	Net Sales ($)	15243008M	14324383M
7940M	149710M	1054278M	2320426M	1091921M	1049909M	Total Assets ($)	5383763M	5209199M

© RMA 2005

M = $ thousand MM = $ million

See Pages 11 through 21 for Explanation of Ratios and Data

Comparative Historical Data				Current Data Sorted By Sales					
Type of Statement									
77	82	88	Unqualified	2	2	2	6	17	59
155	142	157	Reviewed	2	8	10	36	66	37
99	137	91	Compiled	5	17	16	29	19	5
38	27	46	Tax Returns	5	24	5	6	6	
113	130	107	Other	2	15	10	20	31	29
4/1/02-3/31/03 ALL	4/1/03-3/31/04 ALL	4/1/04-3/31/05 ALL		98 (4/1-9/30/04)			391 (10/1/04-3/31/05)		
				0-1MM	1-3MM	3-5MM	5-10MM	10-25MM	25MM & OVER
482	518	489	**NUMBER OF STATEMENTS**	14	66	43	97	139	130
%	%	%	**ASSETS**	%	%	%	%	%	%
6.5	5.4	6.4	Cash & Equivalents	7.1	9.1	8.4	6.0	6.3	4.6
38.2	38.3	39.6	Trade Receivables (net)	39.0	33.0	38.3	36.9	41.1	43.9
34.4	35.2	33.5	Inventory	38.1	35.6	31.7	34.7	32.5	32.9
2.4	2.5	2.3	All Other Current	2.5	1.6	1.7	1.9	2.2	3.3
81.4	81.3	81.8	Total Current	86.8	79.3	80.2	79.5	82.1	84.6
11.6	10.9	10.6	Fixed Assets (net)	6.8	11.9	12.5	12.7	10.0	8.8
1.9	2.2	2.6	Intangibles (net)	4.2	2.8	2.9	2.5	2.1	2.7
5.1	5.5	5.0	All Other Non-Current	2.2	6.0	4.4	5.4	5.9	3.8
100.0	100.0	100.0	Total	100.0	100.0	100.0	100.0	100.0	100.0
			LIABILITIES						
16.9	16.5	15.5	Notes Payable-Short Term	21.9	15.9	13.2	15.0	15.8	15.4
2.5	2.1	2.3	Cur. Mat.-L/T/D	2.4	3.1	4.3	2.6	2.1	1.1
24.1	23.8	24.6	Trade Payables	22.2	23.2	26.5	24.3	23.8	25.8
.2	.2	.2	Income Taxes Payable	.2	.1	.2	.2	.2	.3
8.5	9.4	9.5	All Other Current	18.9	13.3	5.4	8.0	9.1	9.6
52.1	52.0	52.0	Total Current	65.6	55.6	49.6	50.1	51.0	52.1
7.9	8.2	9.2	Long-Term Debt	2.4	14.2	18.9	9.3	6.1	7.5
.2	.3	.2	Deferred Taxes	.0	.0	.2	.2	.2	.1
4.2	4.6	4.5	All Other Non-Current	4.0	1.8	10.5	5.5	4.5	3.0
35.6	34.9	34.1	Net Worth	28.0	28.4	20.8	34.9	38.1	37.2
100.0	100.0	100.0	Total Liabilities & Net Worth	100.0	100.0	100.0	100.0	100.0	100.0
			INCOME DATA						
100.0	100.0	100.0	Net Sales	100.0	100.0	100.0	100.0	100.0	100.0
28.6	28.1	27.7	Gross Profit	37.5	34.8	32.2	29.9	25.7	22.0
26.8	25.9	24.6	Operating Expenses	35.2	31.5	29.7	26.9	22.5	18.8
1.8	2.1	3.1	Operating Profit	2.2	3.3	2.6	2.9	3.1	3.2
.4	.4	.4	All Other Expenses (net)	.7	.4	.6	.5	.3	.3
1.5	1.8	2.7	Profit Before Taxes	1.5	2.8	1.9	2.5	2.8	3.0
			RATIOS						
2.4	2.2	2.2	Current	2.4	2.2	2.3	2.2	2.2	2.2
1.6	1.6	1.6		1.5	1.6	1.5	1.7	1.6	1.6
1.2	1.2	1.2		.9	1.1	1.2	1.3	1.2	1.3
1.3	1.2	1.3	Quick	1.2	1.3	1.5	1.2	1.3	1.4
.9	(517) .9	.9		.8	.7	1.0	.9	.9	.9
.6	.6	.6		.3	.4	.6	.6	.7	.7
38 9.5	38 9.6	38 9.5	Sales/Receivables	26 13.9	29 12.5	33 11.1	36 10.1	42 8.7	42 8.7
47 7.8	47 7.7	48 7.6		41 8.9	39 9.3	45 8.1	45 8.1	49 7.4	51 7.2
58 6.3	60 6.1	60 6.1		61 6.0	51 7.1	58 6.2	57 6.5	61 6.0	61 5.9
38 9.7	39 9.3	35 10.5	Cost of Sales/Inventory	21 17.7	32 11.3	28 13.1	34 10.8	35 10.5	36 10.2
57 6.4	58 6.3	55 6.7		77 4.7	65 5.7	52 7.0	66 5.6	55 6.6	47 7.7
87 4.2	96 3.8	83 4.4		126 2.9	120 3.1	104 3.5	90 4.0	78 4.7	67 5.4
24 15.0	26 14.0	27 13.4	Cost of Sales/Payables	14 26.4	25 14.7	23 15.7	26 14.2	27 13.3	31 11.6
36 10.2	39 9.4	38 9.7		30 12.4	35 10.4	44 8.4	40 9.1	38 9.6	37 10.0
52 7.0	53 6.9	52 7.0		116 3.1	66 5.5	61 6.0	55 6.0	50 7.4	49 7.5
5.8	5.8	6.1	Sales/Working Capital	4.5	4.8	5.9	6.7	5.7	6.9
9.8	9.8	10.2		9.5	11.1	11.0	9.6	9.3	10.5
20.3	19.2	20.9		−113.4	31.0	21.7	18.0	21.3	20.0
8.4	8.3	12.8	EBIT/Interest	16.8	12.9	5.5	8.5	11.8	18.9
(436) 2.9	(473) 3.0	(443) 4.8		(11) 1.3	(58) 4.5	(36) 2.8	(90) 3.7	(127) 4.9	(121) 8.2
1.1	1.4	2.0		−.8	1.0	1.3	1.5	2.2	3.5
6.6	6.0	11.3	Net Profit + Depr., Dep., Amort./Cur. Mat. L/T/D			3.3	6.1	12.0	18.6
(126) 2.5	(131) 2.0	(126) 3.5			(10) 1.3	(28) 2.6	(36) 2.7	(43) 10.2
.9	.8	1.6				1.0	1.0	1.5	2.5
.1	.1	.1	Fixed/Worth	.0	.1	.1	.1	.1	.1
.2	.3	.2		.3	.3	.2	.3	.2	.2
.6	.6	.6		NM	3.2	.8	.6	.5	.5
.9	1.0	1.0	Debt/Worth	.9	1.0	1.0	1.0	1.0	1.0
1.7	1.9	2.0		3.6	2.4	2.2	1.8	1.7	1.9
3.9	4.2	4.3		−33.2	58.4	3.9	4.7	4.0	3.2
27.0	24.6	33.4	% Profit Before Taxes/Tangible Net Worth	55.2	38.2	19.7	32.1	31.8	36.8
(437) 11.0	(470) 10.9	(446) 16.1		(10) 17.9	(51) 12.2	(37) 8.8	(92) 13.5	(133) 16.2	(123) 20.0
2.1	2.1	5.6		−6.1	3.7	3.8	2.4	6.6	11.0
10.0	8.2	10.9	% Profit Before Taxes/Total Assets	13.6	11.9	6.5	9.5	10.9	12.2
3.4	3.1	5.1		2.2	4.1	2.8	4.7	4.7	7.4
.3	.5	1.6		−8.8	.0	.5	.9	2.1	3.8
77.7	77.9	92.7	Sales/Net Fixed Assets	715.5	89.8	144.9	62.7	95.1	103.0
41.0	40.9	42.0		101.9	44.0	40.8	35.6	44.4	51.8
17.8	19.7	20.7		18.4	20.1	18.0	19.0	22.3	21.6
3.6	3.5	3.5	Sales/Total Assets	3.8	3.6	3.6	3.4	3.4	3.7
2.9	2.8	3.0		3.2	2.7	2.9	2.9	3.0	3.0
2.2	2.2	2.3		2.1	1.9	2.1	2.2	2.3	2.7
.4	.4	.3	% Depr., Dep., Amort./Sales		.5	.3	.4	.3	.3
(433) .7	(439) .7	(416) .6			(50) 1.1	(38) .6	(87) .8	(118) .6	(115) .5
1.1	1.3	1.1			1.7	1.6	1.3	1.1	.7
1.6	1.6	1.7	% Officers', Directors', Owners' Comp/Sales		3.8	2.5	1.8	1.1	1.0
(200) 3.5	(210) 3.3	(198) 3.3			(34) 6.2	(24) 4.3	(52) 3.4	(59) 2.3	(24) 1.2
6.5	6.0	6.3			9.2	7.3	7.5	4.2	2.1
13318029M	15885782M	15950341M	Net Sales ($)	10362M	132257M	167963M	696970M	2250294M	12692495M
4906663M	5952139M	5674184M	Total Assets ($)	4268M	53266M	63283M	265421M	866046M	4421900M

M = $ thousand   MM = $ million
See Pages 11 through 21 for Explanation of Ratios and Data

Current Data Sorted By Assets   **Comparative Historical Data**

						Type of Statement		
	1	8	14	7	2	Unqualified	23	27
	4	13	10			Reviewed	24	21
1	10	12	2			Compiled	28	27
5	4	3				Tax Returns	8	3
3	12	16	9		2	Other	43	34
	29 (4/1-9/30/04)			109 (10/1/04-3/31/05)			4/1/00-3/31/01 ALL	4/1/01-3/31/02 ALL
0-500M	500M-2MM	2-10MM	10-50MM	50-100MM	100-250MM			
9	31	52	35	7	4	NUMBER OF STATEMENTS	126	112
%	%	%	%	%	%	**ASSETS**	%	%
	7.8	10.9	7.7			Cash & Equivalents	6.7	7.5
	30.7	32.5	30.7			Trade Receivables (net)	33.2	34.5
	41.4	39.9	39.6			Inventory	40.7	39.2
	4.2	.6	3.6			All Other Current	1.4	.9
	84.2	83.9	81.6			Total Current	82.1	82.2
	8.6	10.4	11.6			Fixed Assets (net)	9.0	9.2
	.5	.6	1.5			Intangibles (net)	2.8	3.1
	6.7	5.1	5.3			All Other Non-Current	6.2	5.5
	100.0	100.0	100.0			Total	100.0	100.0
						LIABILITIES		
	13.8	17.7	20.2			Notes Payable-Short Term	17.3	19.8
	1.3	1.5	1.2			Cur. Mat.-L/T/D	1.8	1.9
	21.9	21.8	23.2			Trade Payables	24.8	23.2
	.3	.1	.1			Income Taxes Payable	.2	.1
	14.5	9.0	10.0			All Other Current	7.7	8.1
	51.7	50.1	54.7			Total Current	51.8	53.1
	8.7	6.9	4.2			Long-Term Debt	6.4	6.1
	.2	.0	.1			Deferred Taxes	.1	.0
	4.9	2.8	6.5			All Other Non-Current	5.6	9.0
	34.6	40.2	34.5			Net Worth	36.1	31.8
	100.0	100.0	100.0			Total Liabilities & Net Worth	100.0	100.0
						INCOME DATA		
	100.0	100.0	100.0			Net Sales	100.0	100.0
	32.0	24.8	21.6			Gross Profit	23.2	24.5
	29.8	19.7	17.5			Operating Expenses	21.2	21.8
	2.2	5.1	4.1			Operating Profit	2.0	2.8
	.5	.4	.2			All Other Expenses (net)	−.5	.4
	1.7	4.7	3.9			Profit Before Taxes	2.5	2.4
						RATIOS		
	2.6	2.9	2.1				2.4	2.6
	1.6	1.5	1.4			Current	1.6	1.5
	1.2	1.3	1.2				1.2	1.1
	1.2	1.3	1.1				1.2	1.2
	.7	.8	.7			Quick	.8	.7
	.4	.6	.4				.5	.5
	21 17.7	24 15.0	20 18.6				28 13.1	28 13.0
	30 12.1	32 11.3	33 10.9			Sales/Receivables	38 9.5	36 10.2
	45 8.1	49 7.4	51 7.2				53 6.9	51 7.1
	35 10.5	34 10.8	45 8.1				40 9.1	34 10.8
	91 4.0	61 6.0	65 5.6			Cost of Sales/Inventory	59 6.1	58 6.3
	124 2.9	84 4.4	88 4.1				87 4.2	82 4.4
	16 23.5	13 27.6	22 16.6				22 16.8	17 21.9
	36 10.1	27 13.4	26 13.8			Cost of Sales/Payables	37 9.9	32 11.6
	58 6.3	43 8.4	44 8.3				54 6.8	50 7.3
	6.5	5.8	6.9				6.2	6.1
	8.7	9.8	12.7			Sales/Working Capital	10.8	11.0
	17.5	18.8	27.3				22.6	32.6
	6.3	21.5	21.3				10.8	8.0
	(25) 2.2	(42) 5.1	(34) 5.3			EBIT/Interest	(113) 3.5	(101) 2.7
	1.2	2.0	1.9				1.4	1.1
						Net Profit + Depr., Dep.,	9.2	7.0
						Amort./Cur. Mat. L./T/D	(22) 2.8	(15) 2.3
							1.7	1.1
	.1	.1	.1				.1	.1
	.2	.2	.3			Fixed/Worth	.2	.2
	.9	.6	.6				.5	.5
	.7	.5	1.1				.9	.7
	2.0	1.8	2.3			Debt/Worth	2.1	1.7
	6.7	4.1	5.1				5.6	6.5
	39.8	61.6	55.3				41.7	34.0
	(29) 8.0	(50) 20.5	34.1			% Profit Before Taxes/Tangible Net Worth	(117) 16.6	(102) 13.6
	2.4	7.5	3.7				5.1	1.4
	10.9	21.3	18.4				14.3	16.3
	3.3	6.5	9.3			% Profit Before Taxes/Total Assets	5.3	4.9
	.2	2.4	.9				1.4	.5
	159.7	134.3	87.0				159.9	123.0
	48.5	45.1	34.9			Sales/Net Fixed Assets	49.5	52.6
	21.2	29.6	18.5				22.9	25.3
	4.0	4.2	3.6				3.8	4.1
	3.2	3.3	3.0			Sales/Total Assets	3.1	3.3
	2.1	2.4	2.4				2.3	2.6
	.3	.1	.3				.3	.2
	(23) .7	(47) .4	(31) .5			% Depr., Dep., Amort./Sales	(103) .5	(96) .4
	.9	.7	.7				1.0	.9
	2.2	.9	.9				1.2	1.3
	(18) 3.7	(25) 1.6	(10) 1.4			% Officers', Directors', Owners' Comp/Sales	(46) 2.2	(36) 2.4
	4.7	3.7	3.4				4.0	5.9
15390M	134018M	835259M	2226154M	1485059M	3371545M	Net Sales ($)	3829733M	3644936M
2891M	40588M	251099M	748603M	441947M	702792M	Total Assets ($)	1408712M	1321958M

© RMA 2005

M = $ thousand   MM = $ million
See Pages 11 through 21 for Explanation of Ratios and Data

Comparative Historical Data   Current Data Sorted By Sales

		Comparative Historical Data			Current Data Sorted By Sales					
Type of Statement										
Unqualified	33	37	32				3	4	25	
Reviewed	30	37	27			2	8	7	10	
Compiled	25	29	25		1	7	6	6	5	
Tax Returns	8	9	12	2	6		1	3	.5	
Other	41	31	42	2	8	3	9	6	14	
	4/1/02-3/31/03 ALL	4/1/03-3/31/04 ALL	4/1/04-3/31/05 ALL	29 (4/1-9/30/04)			109 (10/1/04-3/31/05)			
				0-1MM	1-3MM	3-5MM	5-10MM	10-25MM	25MM & OVER	
NUMBER OF STATEMENTS	137	143	138	4	15	12	27	26	54	
ASSETS	%	%	%	%	%	%	%	%	%	
Cash & Equivalents	8.6	9.0	9.4		9.7	9.1	8.5	10.0	8.5	
Trade Receivables (net)	32.4	30.3	30.3		24.8	18.9	34.2	33.5	32.8	
Inventory	40.5	39.5	40.3		37.0	51.2	39.5	40.9	40.3	
All Other Current	1.8	2.1	2.4		2.1	.8	2.1	.5	2.9	
Total Current	83.3	81.0	82.5		73.5	79.9	84.3	85.0	84.6	
Fixed Assets (net)	10.2	11.1	10.5		14.8	13.9	8.5	9.9	9.2	
Intangibles (net)	2.6	1.6	1.1		2.2	.0	.3	1.1	1.6	
All Other Non-Current	3.9	6.4	5.9		9.5	6.1	6.9	4.0	4.6	
Total	100.0	100.0	100.0		100.0	100.0	100.0	100.0	100.0	
LIABILITIES										
Notes Payable-Short Term	18.4	17.6	16.7		9.5	19.8	15.1	19.8	18.4	
Cur. Mat.-L/T/D	2.9	1.7	1.5		.1	5.4	2.4	.9	.9	
Trade Payables	22.9	21.9	23.4		28.7	20.3	18.2	24.6	24.9	
Income Taxes Payable	.1	.2	.1		.0	.5	.2	.2	.1	
All Other Current	11.6	10.7	10.2		11.5	16.8	7.1	6.7	11.1	
Total Current	55.8	52.1	52.1		49.8	62.7	43.0	52.1	55.5	
Long-Term Debt	4.0	7.1	7.0		18.7	7.7	8.4	4.4	3.7	
Deferred Taxes	.0	.1	.1		.1	.1	.2	.0	.1	
All Other Non-Current	6.1	4.7	4.5		5.6	1.9	6.4	2.3	5.3	
Net Worth	34.0	36.1	36.3		25.8	27.6	42.0	41.2	35.4	
Total Liabilities & Net Worth	100.0	100.0	100.0		100.0	100.0	100.0	100.0	100.0	
INCOME DATA										
Net Sales	100.0	100.0	100.0		100.0	100.0	100.0	100.0	100.0	
Gross Profit	24.4	25.8	25.9		39.6	34.3	27.4	21.7	19.4	
Operating Expenses	21.0	21.9	21.9		36.1	31.6	23.8	18.1	15.7	
Operating Profit	3.4	3.8	3.9		3.5	2.7	3.6	3.7	3.7	
All Other Expenses (net)	.4	.0	.3		.5	.7	.4	−.1	.0	
Profit Before Taxes	3.0	3.8	3.6		3.0	2.0	3.3	3.7	3.6	
RATIOS										
Current	2.4	2.3	2.3		2.6	1.7	3.8	2.3	2.1	
	1.6	1.5	1.5		1.5	1.5	2.0	1.5	1.4	
	1.2	1.2	1.2		1.1	1.0	1.5	1.2	1.2	
Quick	1.2	1.1	1.2		1.2	.7	2.1	1.2	1.1	
	.8	.8	.7		.7	.4	1.0	.9	.7	
	.5	.5	.5		.5	.2	.6	.6	.5	
Sales/Receivables	23 15.8	22 16.5	22 17.0	19 19.1	9 39.8	25 14.8	23 16.2	23 15.8		
	36 10.2	34 10.7	31 11.7	30 12.1	22 16.5	38 9.6	30 12.1	31 11.6		
	50 7.3	56 6.6	47 7.8	48 7.5	38 9.6	50 7.3	42 8.7	47 7.7		
Cost of Sales/Inventory	36 10.3	38 9.5	40 9.0	53 6.8	46 7.9	30 12.4	36 10.1	42 8.7		
	62 5.9	64 5.7	64 5.7	82 4.5	101 3.6	67 5.5	60 6.1	58 6.3		
	93 3.9	94 3.9	90 4.1	154 2.4	135 2.7	106 3.4	76 4.8	76 4.8		
Cost of Sales/Payables	15 24.8	19 19.0	18 20.6	37 10.0	19 18.8	11 33.1	11 32.7	20 17.9		
	28 13.0	33 11.1	30 12.3	50 7.4	41 8.9	21 17.5	27 13.4	28 13.0		
	47 7.8	50 7.3	47 7.7	78 4.7	61 6.0	42 8.7	41 8.9	44 8.4		
Sales/Working Capital	5.9	5.9	6.5		5.6	6.8	5.5	5.9	7.3	
	10.8	11.5	11.1		12.2	12.7	7.7	11.0	13.1	
	25.2	24.5	24.9		44.5	NM	11.3	39.1	25.1	
EBIT/Interest	13.3	14.5	17.9		22.0	4.3	5.8	24.4	21.1	
	(119) 4.3	(129) 4.6	(119) 4.9	(12) 3.1	(11) 1.9	(22) 2.7	(24) 11.0	(48) 6.5		
	2.1	2.0	1.9		2.0	1.2	1.5	2.6	2.1	
Net Profit + Depr., Dep., Amort./Cur. Mat. L/T/D	7.9	14.9	38.2						54.8	
	(20) 5.3	(30) 6.0	(29) 5.0					(15) 10.0		
	1.5	2.0	1.8						4.5	
Fixed/Worth	.1	.1	.1		.2	.1	.1	.1	.1	
	.2	.2	.2		.7	.3	.1	.2	.2	
	.4	.5	.6		1.9	1.0	.6	.5	.6	
Debt/Worth	.6	.9	.9		2.0	1.7	.5	.7	1.1	
	1.5	2.0	2.0		3.2	2.9	1.2	1.8	2.3	
	4.4	4.2	5.0		8.3	7.1	3.2	4.6	5.0	
% Profit Before Taxes/Tangible Net Worth	46.9	46.8	57.8		141.4	38.0	76.6	58.8	53.0	
	(128) 21.9	(131) 19.3	(132) 20.6	(13) 39.4	(11) 11.2	(25) 11.4	22.9	(53) 27.3		
	6.2	5.9	6.4		9.3	.7	3.1	10.1	6.6	
% Profit Before Taxes/Total Assets	16.6	15.4	17.2		12.8	10.3	13.4	21.8	17.5	
	6.6	6.3	5.9		4.7	3.0	2.7	8.4	8.4	
	1.7	1.8	1.5		2.3	.5	.9	3.7	1.6	
Sales/Net Fixed Assets	204.5	162.5	133.5		100.5	261.5	96.5	232.8	112.0	
	71.0	46.2	44.5		18.9	41.4	41.8	85.3	45.9	
	24.1	18.9	24.0		10.0	30.1	28.8	33.4	23.7	
Sales/Total Assets	4.5	4.0	4.1		4.0	4.2	3.9	4.8	4.0	
	3.3	3.1	3.3		2.8	2.9	3.4	3.3	3.4	
	2.4	2.2	2.5		1.8	2.2	2.1	2.7	2.7	
% Depr., Dep., Amort./Sales	.2	.2	.2		.9		.3	.1	.2	
	(114) .4	(121) .5	(116) .5	(11) 1.6		(23) .5	(24) .3	(47) .4		
	1.0	1.0	.9		2.0		.9	.5	.6	
% Officers', Directors', Owners' Comp/Sales	1.0	1.5	1.2				1.5	.8	.9	
	(62) 1.9	(57) 2.5	(58) 2.4				(13) 2.9	(16) 1.5	(14) 1.5	
	3.4	4.2	4.1				4.8	2.6	3.4	
Net Sales ($)	5568675M	4973883M	8067425M	2402M	29612M	48255M	198173M	423389M	7365594M	
Total Assets ($)	1808552M	1668329M	2187920M	3118M	12732M	16595M	69090M	137050M	1949335M	

© RMA 2005

M = $ thousand   MM = $ million

See Pages 11 through 21 for Explanation of Ratios and Data

Current Data Sorted By Assets   Comparative Historical Data

						Type of Statement	53	55
	4	20	29	8	9	Unqualified	53	55
2	18	66	11			Reviewed	90	84
3	21	25	3		1	Compiled	103	91
6	15	8		1		Tax Returns	20	18
8	25	44		6	6	Other	98	109
	81 (4/1-9/30/04)			266 (10/1/04-3/31/05)			4/1/00-3/31/01	4/1/01-3/31/02
0-500M	500M-2MM	2-10MM	10-50MM	50-100MM	100-250MM		ALL	ALL
19	83	163	51	15	16	NUMBER OF STATEMENTS	364	357
%	%	%	%	%	%	ASSETS	%	%
17.2	7.9	7.7	9.1	19.6	8.2	Cash & Equivalents	7.8	8.5
36.1	36.0	37.6	35.2	28.6	36.1	Trade Receivables (net)	38.5	33.1
24.5	34.4	35.4	34.8	25.6	28.5	Inventory	33.1	36.8
1.4	1.9	2.5	3.9	2.7	3.2	All Other Current	2.4	2.9
79.2	80.2	83.2	82.9	76.5	76.0	Total Current	81.8	81.4
8.1	11.5	8.0	10.2	7.7	9.6	Fixed Assets (net)	10.8	10.3
5.2	2.7	2.8	1.7	8.7	7.3	Intangibles (net)	2.2	2.6
7.5	5.6	6.0	5.2	7.1	7.2	All Other Non-Current	5.2	5.7
100.0	100.0	100.0	100.0	100.0	100.0	Total	100.0	100.0
						LIABILITIES		
17.7	16.0	16.3	16.1	13.4	4.7	Notes Payable-Short Term	17.4	17.0
1.3	2.5	1.4	2.9	1.0	3.4	Cur. Mat.-L/T/D	2.2	2.6
28.1	21.3	25.7	24.3	17.0	16.8	Trade Payables	24.6	20.8
.0	.3	.4	.3	.7	.2	Income Taxes Payable	.4	.2
29.0	10.6	8.7	8.2	18.8	11.6	All Other Current	8.7	9.7
76.1	50.7	52.5	51.8	50.9	36.6	Total Current	53.3	50.3
12.3	9.5	6.5	5.6	5.8	16.8	Long-Term Debt	8.9	9.0
.0	.1	.2	.3	.4	.1	Deferred Taxes	.2	.2
2.9	3.6	3.3	4.1	7.3	.9	All Other Non-Current	3.6	3.2
8.7	36.1	37.6	38.2	35.6	45.7	Net Worth	34.0	37.4
100.0	100.0	100.0	100.0	100.0	100.0	Total Liabilities & Net Worth	100.0	100.0
						INCOME DATA		
100.0	100.0	100.0	100.0	100.0	100.0	Net Sales	100.0	100.0
45.9	34.1	29.1	26.4	25.5	22.8	Gross Profit	29.9	30.5
39.5	33.4	25.7	21.2	22.9	16.8	Operating Expenses	26.1	28.4
6.4	.7	3.4	5.3	2.7	6.0	Operating Profit	3.8	2.1
.5	.2	.4	.2	.6	.6	All Other Expenses (net)	.5	.6
5.9	.5	3.0	5.0	2.1	5.4	Profit Before Taxes	3.3	1.5
						RATIOS		
2.8	2.4	2.3	2.2	2.2	2.9	Current	2.1	2.6
1.3	1.6	1.7	1.6	1.6	2.3		1.5	1.7
.9	1.1	1.2	1.2	1.0	1.5		1.2	1.2
1.8	1.4	1.2	1.1	1.7	1.8	Quick	1.2	1.3
.9	.8	.9	.8	.9	1.1		.8	.8
.3	.6	.6	.6	.5	.9		.6	.6
20 18.2	27 13.4	35 10.6	36 10.2	43 8.5	46 7.9	Sales/Receivables	35 10.5	29 12.5
24 15.0	38 9.7	45 8.2	47 7.7	48 7.6	59 6.2		47 7.8	41 8.9
40 9.2	52 7.0	56 6.5	61 6.0	59 6.2	71 5.1		57 6.4	53 6.8
14 25.8	29 12.6	34 10.8	49 7.4	51 7.1	28 13.0	Cost of Sales/Inventory	32 11.4	35 10.3
40 9.2	56 6.5	61 6.0	63 5.8	75 4.9	65 5.7		57 6.4	64 5.7
59 6.2	90 4.1	98 3.7	96 3.8	77 4.7	79 4.6		84 4.3	103 3.6
20 18.1	14 25.6	23 16.1	32 11.4	8 43.1	24 15.5	Cost of Sales/Payables	21 17.6	17 21.7
46 7.9	29 12.8	39 9.4	41 8.8	44 8.3	34 10.8		35 10.6	31 11.7
78 4.7	48 7.6	61 6.0	53 6.9	64 5.7	54 6.8		60 6.1	51 7.2
9.2	6.4	5.2	6.0	3.6	4.2	Sales/Working Capital	6.9	5.1
16.5	12.7	10.0	9.0	6.1	5.5		11.7	9.4
-49.2	43.6	22.9	23.4	88.2	8.1		26.3	26.0
27.3	12.2	11.8	14.7	50.2	34.3	EBIT/Interest	8.9	7.7
(13) 7.5	(72) 3.2	(143) 4.9	(43) 4.6	(12) 5.5	(15) 8.1		(326) 3.4	(312) 2.3
3.2	.2	1.8	2.3	1.6	3.9		1.6	-.3
	4.3	8.8	29.4			Net Profit + Depr., Dep.,	11.5	10.8
	(11) 2.9	(28) 4.2	(17) 6.0			Amort./Cur. Mat. L./T/D	(77) 3.3	(74) 1.5
	.2	1.7	1.9				1.4	-.1
.0	.1	.1	.1	.1	.0	Fixed/Worth	.1	.1
.2	.2	.2	.2	.2	.1		.2	.2
UND	.7	.5	.6	.6	.3		.6	.7
1.0	.6	.9	1.0	1.0	.6	Debt/Worth	1.1	.7
2.7	2.1	1.9	1.9	2.0	1.5		2.3	1.8
-28.8	5.4	4.4	4.5	8.3	3.5		5.4	4.6
143.6	32.6	41.3	49.3	36.9	36.0	% Profit Before Taxes/Tangible	63.5	36.5
(14) 22.8	(75) 12.9	(154) 17.9	(49) 23.7	(13) 16.2	25.8	Net Worth	(333) 23.2	(325) 12.2
16.0	.3	5.2	6.9	4.7	16.1		5.9	-4.7
65.9	12.8	12.6	14.1	7.5	15.6	% Profit Before Taxes/Total	16.5	11.7
16.4	3.2	5.0	6.3	4.7	10.2	Assets	6.6	3.9
.9	-3.5	1.5	2.4	1.1	4.1		1.6	-3.2
684.5	156.8	125.6	83.1	60.6	143.0	Sales/Net Fixed Assets	127.3	109.9
102.0	52.5	54.4	45.2	21.6	85.7		50.3	45.4
44.2	20.6	24.8	18.1	13.4	19.1		21.9	19.8
5.6	4.3	3.7	3.3	2.8	2.6	Sales/Total Assets	4.0	3.9
4.9	3.2	2.9	2.9	1.7	2.3		3.0	2.9
3.1	2.6	2.2	2.1	1.2	2.1		2.4	2.1
	.5	.4	.4	.5	.2	% Depr., Dep., Amort./Sales	.3	.3
	(59) .9	(139) .6	(47) .8	(11) 1.1	(10) .5		(304) .6	(286) .7
	1.7	1.2	1.3	2.7	1.0		1.2	1.2
6.7		1.7	.6			% Officers', Directors',	1.7	2.1
(10) 12.2	(38) 5.3	(56) 3.0	(16) 1.1			Owners' Comp/Sales	(165) 4.0	(151) 3.8
14.7		7.8	5.5	5.0			7.9	7.3
27159M	333964M	2317970M	2830444M	2105269M	5279967M	Net Sales ($)	10906307M	10238234M
5868M	95262M	791157M	1110724M	1039529M	2383750M	Total Assets ($)	3822813M	4019967M

M = $ thousand   MM = $ million

See Pages 11 through 21 for Explanation of Ratios and Data

Comparative Historical Data / Current Data Sorted By Sales

				Type of Statement						
73		67		70	Unqualified		1	3	2	17	47
103		99		97	Reviewed	1	9	11	24	39	13
79		72		53	Compiled	1	5	14	11	20	2
20		44		30	Tax Returns	3	11	6	4	4	2
114		123		97	Other	7	13	12	19	22	24

						81 (4/1-9/30/04)		266 (10/1/04-3/31/05)		

4/1/02-3/31/03 ALL		4/1/03-3/31/04 ALL		4/1/04-3/31/05 ALL		0-1MM	1-3MM	3-5MM	5-10MM	10-25MM	25MM & OVER
389		405		347	**NUMBER OF STATEMENTS**	12	39	46	60	102	88
%		%		%	**ASSETS**	%	%	%	%	%	%
8.9		9.6		9.0	Cash & Equivalents	12.3	10.2	9.3	9.0	7.7	9.4
36.2		36.2		36.3	Trade Receivables (net)	27.7	36.5	34.8	34.3	38.4	37.3
33.9		32.8		33.7	Inventory	30.5	31.1	33.5	35.1	35.8	32.1
2.6		2.3		2.5	All Other Current	2.8	1.3	1.9	3.8	2.0	3.1
81.6		80.9		81.6	Total Current	73.2	79.0	79.5	82.2	83.9	81.9
10.0		10.9		9.2	Fixed Assets (net)	15.0	9.9	10.8	9.1	8.3	8.6
3.1		2.5		3.2	Intangibles (net)	6.5	4.2	2.6	2.3	2.5	3.9
5.3		5.7		6.0	All Other Non-Current	5.3	6.9	7.1	6.4	5.3	5.6
100.0		100.0		100.0	Total	100.0	100.0	100.0	100.0	100.0	100.0
					LIABILITIES						
15.2		16.0		15.6	Notes Payable-Short Term	16.5	16.5	15.3	15.5	16.7	14.1
2.5		2.3		2.0	Cur. Mat.-L/T/D	2.2	2.5	2.1	2.1	1.3	2.3
23.1		23.6		23.8	Trade Payables	26.1	19.9	20.4	24.8	26.3	23.2
.3		.4		.4	Income Taxes Payable	.4	.1	.3	.8	.2	.3
10.2		10.6		10.8	All Other Current	43.1	12.2	8.8	8.7	8.4	10.9
51.3		52.9		52.4	Total Current	88.3	51.1	46.9	52.0	52.9	50.8
7.0		7.5		7.8	Long-Term Debt	8.7	10.4	13.7	6.9	4.0	8.5
.1		.2		.2	Deferred Taxes	.0	.0	.2	.3	.2	.2
5.4		5.4		3.5	All Other Non-Current	3.6	5.3	2.6	3.2	2.4	4.8
36.1		34.0		36.0	Net Worth	-.6	33.1	36.6	37.6	40.4	35.8
100.0		100.0		100.0	Total Liabilities & Net Worth	100.0	100.0	100.0	100.0	100.0	100.0
					INCOME DATA						
100.0		100.0		100.0	Net Sales	100.0	100.0	100.0	100.0	100.0	100.0
29.5		31.3		30.4	Gross Profit	41.9	43.4	33.4	31.5	27.8	23.8
27.5		29.0		27.1	Operating Expenses	37.8	41.1	32.2	28.2	24.1	19.5
2.0		2.3		3.3	Operating Profit	4.1	2.3	1.3	3.3	3.7	4.3
.4		.6		.4	All Other Expenses (net)	1.3	.5	.3	.3	.1	.5
1.6		1.7		2.9	Profit Before Taxes	2.8	1.7	1.0	3.0	3.6	3.7
					RATIOS						
2.5		2.5		2.4		2.2	2.9	2.4	2.9	2.2	2.3
1.7		1.6		1.6	Current	1.2	1.6	1.8	1.6	1.7	1.6
1.2		1.2		1.2		.8	1.0	1.2	1.2	1.2	1.2
1.3		1.4		1.4		1.1	1.5	1.6	1.6	1.3	1.3
.9		.9		.9	Quick	.7	.9	.8	.8	.9	.9
.6		.6		.6		.3	.6	.6	.6	.6	.6

32	11.4	33	11.0	33	11.0		21	17.5	24	15.0	30	12.1	33	11.0	34	10.6	37	9.8
42	8.6	44	8.2	45	8.2	Sales/Receivables	30	12.0	33	11.2	39	9.3	43	8.5	45	8.1	48	7.6
56	6.5	57	6.5	56	6.6		72	5.0	51	7.1	58	6.3	51	7.2	56	6.5	60	6.1
31	11.7	30	12.0	34	10.7		31	11.8	31	11.8	33	11.0	34	10.6	31	11.6	43	8.5
58	6.2	58	6.3	61	6.0	Cost of Sales/Inventory	87	4.2	49	7.4	64	5.7	62	5.9	60	6.1	61	5.9
95	3.8	102	3.6	91	4.0		210	1.7	119	3.1	89	4.1	95	3.8	103	3.5	77	4.7
22	16.6	20	18.0	22	17.0		22	16.4	15	24.3	14	25.9	20	18.2	23	15.9	28	13.1
36	10.2	37	9.7	38	9.6	Cost of Sales/Payables	76	4.8	36	10.1	29	12.6	41	8.9	39	9.5	38	9.5
50	7.3	58	6.3	56	6.5		118	3.1	57	6.4	47	7.8	62	5.9	56	6.5	52	7.0
	5.4		5.6		5.4			5.4		5.8		5.4		5.1		5.7		5.7
	9.4		10.6		10.2	Sales/Working Capital		23.3		14.5		9.5		10.8		10.6		8.6
	25.7		31.6		24.2			-11.1		110.1		23.1		23.1		20.3		23.4
	8.0		10.7		13.4					20.6		8.8		20.7		13.8		15.0
(344)	2.5	(355)	2.8	(298)	4.9	EBIT/Interest			(33)	5.6	(41)	2.3	(51)	4.6	(88)	6.1	(77)	5.1
	.4		.9		1.6					1.5		-1.2		1.6		2.7		2.0
	8.2		8.5		11.0	Net Profit + Depr., Dep.,										8.8		32.2
(88)	2.6	(67)	2.4	(64)	4.2	Amort./Cur. Mat. L/T/D									(20)	3.4	(24)	5.9
	.7		.7		1.1												1.3		1.4
	.1		.1		.1			.1		.0		.1		.0		.1		.1
	.2		.2		.2	Fixed/Worth		.7		.2		.3		.2		.2		.2
	.6		.8		.6			UND		.8		.7		.6		.4		.6
	.8		.8		.9			1.9		.6		1.0		.5		.9		1.2
	1.8		1.9		1.9	Debt/Worth		15.4		1.7		2.0		1.9		1.7		2.1
	4.9		6.2		4.6			UND		38.7		3.6		5.8		3.4		4.6
	33.2		31.1		40.8	% Profit Before Taxes/Tangible		29.3		123.1		26.8		31.8		46.2		47.5
(357)	10.0	(358)	9.3	(321)	17.9	Net Worth	(10)	4.9	(31)	22.4	(42)	8.7	(55)	15.7	(100)	22.5	(83)	23.7
	-1.7		.1		4.3			-14.3		4.9		-4.2		4.1		6.3		6.9
	10.1		10.8		13.5	% Profit Before Taxes/Total		18.1		27.2		12.3		12.5		13.4		14.8
	3.0		3.0		5.2	Assets		.2		6.1		3.1		4.4		6.7		6.7
	-1.2		-.7		1.0			.7				-3.8		1.0		2.1		2.0
	118.9		125.1		125.2			343.5		240.9		103.0		146.7		111.4		116.9
	52.2		49.4		52.5	Sales/Net Fixed Assets		54.9		52.6		43.0		53.5		52.5		53.6
	22.0		19.8		21.8			6.7		17.7		14.1		24.5		27.8		21.6
	3.9		3.9		3.7			3.5		5.0		3.6		3.8		3.8		3.6
	3.0		2.9		2.9	Sales/Total Assets		1.6		3.3		2.9		2.9		2.9		2.9
	2.1		2.1		2.2			1.3		2.3		2.2		2.0		2.3		2.2
	.4		.4		.4			.5		.4		.4		.4		.4		.3
(317)	.7	(318)	.9	(272)	.7	% Depr., Dep., Amort./Sales			(23)	1.0	(34)	.9	(50)	.5	(88)	.7	(71)	.6
	1.3		1.5		1.3					2.8		1.5		1.1		1.2		1.2
	2.3		2.0		2.1	% Officers', Directors',				4.8		3.0		2.0		1.4		.6
(159)	3.7	(155)	4.0	(122)	4.1	Owners' Comp/Sales			(21)	7.6	(23)	4.1	(21)	5.4	(34)	2.6	(19)	1.1
	6.7		6.9		7.1					11.7		6.1		6.7		5.1		4.2

11788056M		11739736M		12894773M	Net Sales ($)	7502M	84507M	184928M	454672M	1604480M	10558684M
4517429M		4526974M		5426290M	Total Assets ($)	4794M	31698M	73347M	180998M	614853M	4520600M

© RMA 2005

M = $ thousand   MM = $ million

See Pages 11 through 21 for Explanation of Ratios and Data

Current Data Sorted By Assets   Comparative Historical Data

						Type of Statement		
	2	7	19	3	5	Unqualified	35	31
2	14	38	14	2		Reviewed	71	65
5	10	26	2			Compiled	91	92
10	10	4				Tax Returns	19	24
3	11	25	14	2	1	Other	76	72
	42 (4/1-9/30/04)		185 (10/1/04-3/31/05)				4/1/00-3/31/01	4/1/01-3/31/02
0-500M	500M-2MM	2-10MM	10-50MM	50-100MM	100-250MM		ALL	ALL
20	47	100	49	5	6	**NUMBER OF STATEMENTS**	292	284
%	%	%	%	%	%	**ASSETS**	%	%
8.6	6.0	5.5	4.9			Cash & Equivalents	5.2	6.1
24.2	33.9	32.6	28.8			Trade Receivables (net)	29.1	28.5
39.4	43.7	42.8	44.0			Inventory	44.4	44.6
.3	1.4	.9	1.3			All Other Current	1.8	1.5
72.5	85.0	81.9	79.0			Total Current	80.5	80.6
17.6	10.5	10.2	13.5			Fixed Assets (net)	11.5	12.6
3.3	.6	2.9	1.4			Intangibles (net)	2.2	1.7
6.6	3.9	5.1	6.1			All Other Non-Current	5.8	5.0
100.0	100.0	100.0	100.0			Total	100.0	100.0
						LIABILITIES		
22.2	16.4	17.9	19.8			Notes Payable-Short Term	17.8	15.5
5.5	2.4	2.1	2.8			Cur. Mat.-L/T/D	2.7	2.8
17.8	23.8	18.6	18.2			Trade Payables	19.4	18.4
.5	.0	.2	.5			Income Taxes Payable	.3	.2
24.0	5.9	6.1	7.5			All Other Current	7.8	8.2
69.9	48.5	44.9	48.9			Total Current	47.9	45.1
37.0	9.2	7.9	8.2			Long-Term Debt	9.4	11.2
.0	.1	.1	.4			Deferred Taxes	.1	.1
18.5	8.8	3.4	4.1			All Other Non-Current	3.3	3.6
-25.5	33.4	43.8	38.4			Net Worth	39.3	39.9
100.0	100.0	100.0	100.0			Total Liabilities & Net Worth	100.0	100.0
						INCOME DATA		
100.0	100.0	100.0	100.0			Net Sales	100.0	100.0
40.1	31.1	31.9	28.5			Gross Profit	32.3	32.0
42.1	27.6	28.8	24.1			Operating Expenses	28.9	28.8
-2.1	3.5	3.2	4.4			Operating Profit	3.4	3.2
1.9	.5	.2	.3			All Other Expenses (net)	.9	.8
-4.0	3.0	3.0	4.1			Profit Before Taxes	2.5	2.4
						RATIOS		
2.5	2.8	2.5	2.7			Current	2.6	2.6
1.3	1.9	1.8	1.5				1.7	1.9
.6	1.3	1.4	1.2				1.3	1.4
.9	1.5	1.3	1.3			Quick	1.2	1.2
.5	.9	.8	.7		(291)		.7	.7
.2	.5	.6	.4				.5	.5
5 75.4	28 13.3	33 11.0	33 11.0			Sales/Receivables	28 12.9	27 13.6
26 13.8	42 8.6	43 8.6	43 8.5				40 9.1	37 10.0
46 7.9	51 7.2	52 7.0	53 6.9				51 7.1	48 7.6
0 UND	43 8.6	58 6.3	64 5.7			Cost of Sales/Inventory	57 6.4	55 6.7
77 4.7	93 3.9	85 4.3	93 3.9				91 4.0	94 3.9
129 2.8	130 2.8	134 2.7	158 2.3				148 2.5	147 2.5
11 34.4	16 22.8	21 17.1	20 17.9			Cost of Sales/Payables	20 18.0	20 18.7
29 12.5	36 10.1	34 10.8	36 10.1				34 10.7	30 12.0
59 6.2	53 6.9	49 7.4	47 7.7				51 7.1	48 7.6
7.0	4.5	5.2	5.0			Sales/Working Capital	5.2	5.0
18.5	6.8	7.7	7.5				8.2	7.3
-17.8	16.9	12.3	19.7				14.1	13.3
2.4	17.3	10.8	11.7			EBIT/Interest	6.7	5.8
(16) .8	(41) 3.5	(92) 4.6	(44) 6.7				(268) 2.8	(262) 2.4
-5.4	1.2	2.1	2.3				1.1	1.2
		9.4	19.6			Net Profit + Depr., Dep.,	7.3	8.4
	(20) 3.1	(20) 3.1				Amort./Cur. Mat. L./T/D	(84) 3.1	(75) 1.9
		1.3	1.3				.8	.7
.1	.1	.1	.1			Fixed/Worth	.1	.1
UND	.2	.2	.2				.2	.3
-.3	.9	.4	.9				.6	.6
2.4	.7	.8	.7			Debt/Worth	.7	.7
UND	1.5	1.3	2.2				1.6	1.6
-2.7	6.1	2.4	4.2				3.6	3.4
31.8	43.6	31.1	41.0			% Profit Before Taxes/Tangible	27.7	28.4
(10) 1.7	(40) 11.7	(96) 13.6	(46) 23.5			Net Worth	(272) 13.3	(269) 10.9
-18.8	.7	4.2	9.7				2.0	2.4
5.9	11.9	10.3	13.8			% Profit Before Taxes/Total	11.8	9.8
-.3	4.7	5.3	7.0			Assets	4.2	4.1
-18.7	.2	4.2	4.1				.5	.7
207.8	163.6	80.2	59.3			Sales/Net Fixed Assets	64.9	62.5
37.6	36.9	37.7	28.5				30.1	30.5
14.8	20.2	17.4	13.6				17.0	14.9
5.3	3.9	3.3	2.7			Sales/Total Assets	3.2	3.3
3.9	2.7	2.7	2.3				2.6	2.6
2.2	2.4	2.0	1.7				2.0	2.0
.9	.5	.4	.5			% Depr., Dep., Amort./Sales	.4	.5
(16) 2.0	(34) 1.0	(87) .7	(47) .8				(261) .8	(242) .8
2.8	1.4	1.4	1.1				1.4	1.5
7.1	2.2	2.2				% Officers', Directors',	2.5	2.4
(13) 9.2	(23) 3.3	(52) 3.9				Owners' Comp/Sales	(129) 4.5	(135) 4.0
13.1	7.2	7.5					8.9	7.0
17929M	191198M	1158147M	2008968M	796966M	2578872M	Net Sales ($)	6071706M	6055185M
4725M	60162M	427939M	857175M	394704M	940656M	Total Assets ($)	2509039M	2506478M

© RMA 2005

M = $ thousand   MM = $ million
See Pages 11 through 21 for Explanation of Ratios and Data

Comparative Historical Data | Current Data Sorted By Sales

			Type of Statement						
45	39	36	Unqualified			1	4	5	26
74	69	68	Reviewed	2	5	10	9	28	14
45	63	43	Compiled	4	5	9	13	11	1
22	27	24	Tax Returns	5	8	5	1	1	
59	58	56	Other	2	11	2	15	11	15
4/1/02-3/31/03 ALL	4/1/03-3/31/04 ALL	4/1/04-3/31/05 ALL		42 (4/1-9/30/04)			185 (10/1/04-3/31/05)		
				0-1MM	1-3MM	3-5MM	5-10MM	10-25MM	25MM & OVER
245	256	227	NUMBER OF STATEMENTS	13	29	27	46	56	56
%	%	%	ASSETS	%	%	%	%	%	%
6.1	5.1	5.6	Cash & Equivalents	6.1	7.9	6.4	5.7	4.3	5.1
29.0	31.3	30.8	Trade Receivables (net)	18.8	26.3	29.4	34.8	33.6	30.3
43.2	42.6	43.5	Inventory	47.2	39.1	41.9	43.3	45.8	43.5
2.4	2.3	1.2	All Other Current	.4	1.6	.8	.8	.8	1.9
80.7	81.2	81.0	Total Current	72.6	75.0	78.5	84.6	84.6	80.8
12.4	11.7	11.7	Fixed Assets (net)	14.7	15.6	13.1	10.9	9.2	11.5
2.3	2.0	2.2	Intangibles (net)	3.4	6.9	.7	1.5	1.0	2.1
4.6	5.1	5.1	All Other Non-Current	9.2	2.6	7.7	3.1	5.2	5.6
100.0	100.0	100.0	Total	100.0	100.0	100.0	100.0	100.0	100.0
			LIABILITIES						
16.2	17.6	18.1	Notes Payable-Short Term	24.0	15.4	17.9	16.3	20.6	17.2
3.2	2.1	2.8	Cur. Mat.-L/T/D	7.3	2.3	1.6	2.6	2.4	3.0
17.3	18.4	19.5	Trade Payables	18.7	17.3	19.6	20.8	18.8	20.5
.2	.2	.3	Income Taxes Payable	.1	.3	.0	.1	.3	.5
6.6	6.9	8.2	All Other Current	8.1	15.9	4.5	5.0	8.3	8.5
43.4	45.1	48.8	Total Current	58.2	51.1	43.7	44.9	50.4	49.7
10.3	10.4	11.2	Long-Term Debt	48.6	15.6	8.4	9.1	5.0	9.6
.2	.1	.2	Deferred Taxes	.0	.0	.1	.0	.2	.4
4.4	6.0	6.3	All Other Non-Current	12.7	12.4	12.9	2.0	2.9	5.4
41.6	38.3	33.5	Net Worth	-19.5	20.8	35.0	44.0	41.5	35.0
100.0	100.0	100.0	Total Liabilities & Net Worth	100.0	100.0	100.0	100.0	100.0	100.0
			INCOME DATA						
100.0	100.0	100.0	Net Sales	100.0	100.0	100.0	100.0	100.0	100.0
32.9	32.2	31.6	Gross Profit	41.4	36.9	34.2	31.4	29.8	27.3
29.6	29.2	28.4	Operating Expenses	45.0	35.3	30.8	27.2	26.5	22.5
3.3	3.0	3.2	Operating Profit	-3.5	1.5	3.4	4.1	3.3	4.8
.6	.5	.5	All Other Expenses (net)	1.9	.9	.5	.1	.3	.3
2.7	2.5	2.8	Profit Before Taxes	-5.4	.6	2.9	4.1	2.9	4.4
			RATIOS						
3.0	2.8	2.5		2.4	2.9	3.3	2.9	2.1	2.3
1.9	1.8	1.7	Current	1.3	2.2	1.8	2.0	1.6	1.6
1.4	1.4	1.3		.7	1.1	1.3	1.4	1.4	1.2
1.4	1.2	1.2		.8	1.4	1.3	1.4	1.0	1.2
.8	.8	.8	Quick	.6	.8	.9	1.0	.7	.7
.5	.5	.5		.1	.4	.5	.6	.5	.4
31 11.7	32 11.6	31 11.8		4 98.3	25 14.4	34 10.6	32 11.4	31 11.6	34 10.8
40 9.1	43 8.4	43 8.6	Sales/Receivables	22 16.8	42 8.6	46 8.0	43 8.5	42 8.8	43 8.4
50 7.4	54 6.7	51 7.1		46 8.0	51 7.1	55 6.6	48 7.5	50 7.3	53 6.9
58 6.3	55 6.6	55 6.7		72 5.1	40 9.1	64 5.7	53 6.9	51 7.2	62 5.9
93 3.9	92 3.9	90 4.1	Cost of Sales/Inventory	94 3.9	109 3.3	101 3.6	80 4.6	87 4.2	90 4.1
142 2.6	138 2.7	136 2.7		211 1.7	167 2.2	155 2.4	117 3.1	134 2.7	134 2.7
17 20.9	18 20.2	20 18.2		5 72.8	22 16.8	14 26.2	19 19.0	19 19.2	23 15.9
30 12.0	32 11.5	35 10.5	Cost of Sales/Payables	36 10.0	35 10.5	38 9.6	35 10.5	32 11.6	40 9.1
46 7.9	52 7.0	51 7.2		77 4.7	50 7.3	57 6.4	52 7.0	43 8.4	50 7.3
4.4	4.8	5.0		5.8	3.8	4.3	4.5	5.4	5.3
7.1	7.3	7.8	Sales/Working Capital	15.5	6.8	5.9	7.6	8.6	8.3
12.0	12.5	15.5		-20.4	73.9	11.4	13.1	13.5	18.6
	8.0		8.7		11.5		2.6	4.9	15.0	18.7	10.3	12.6
(225) 3.3	(230) 2.7	(204) 4.1	EBIT/Interest	(10) -.3	(23) 3.0	(25) 3.5	(42) 4.4	(53) 5.4	(51) 7.3
1.5	1.2	1.9		-6.9	.8	1.1	2.1	2.0	2.7
4.7	5.7	11.3						6.6	14.3
(80) 1.3	(73) 2.3	(56) 3.4	Net Profit + Depr., Dep., Amort./Cur. Mat. L/T/D				(16) 2.3	(27) 4.2
.6	.9	1.3						.9	2.0
.1	.1	.1		.2	.1	.0	.1	.1	.1
.2	.3	.2	Fixed/Worth	-1.3	.7	.1	.3	.2	.2
.6	.6	.6		-.4	NM	.6	.4	.4	1.0
.7	.7	.8		2.2	.9	.7	.7	.9	.9
1.4	1.8	1.7	Debt/Worth	-15.0	2.3	1.4	1.4	1.4	2.3
3.2	4.0	3.8		-3.4	NM	3.5	2.4	2.8	4.2
25.7	30.9	36.4	% Profit Before Taxes/Tangible Net Worth	33.2	25.8	30.5	29.9	52.9
(227) 10.6	(238) 11.2	(200) 17.4		(22) 5.1	(24) 8.5	(44) 11.1	(54) 18.7	(50) 28.8
3.6	1.8	5.2		-4.3	1.4	2.8	6.2	12.5
10.2	9.2	11.5	% Profit Before Taxes/Total Assets	7.8	7.8	9.5	10.9	12.0	16.1
4.5	3.9	6.0		-.3	2.0	3.0	4.7	6.8	8.8
1.0	.8	1.7		-21.7	-1.1	.2	1.7	2.3	4.4
69.2	67.9	72.5		142.4	48.7	136.1	76.0	90.5	57.3
30.6	32.8	34.0	Sales/Net Fixed Assets	31.9	21.8	26.3	34.0	47.0	28.7
16.0	15.8	17.2		12.9	11.7	14.2	17.3	28.8	17.0
3.2	3.2	3.4		5.0	3.9	2.8	3.6	3.5	3.0
2.6	2.5	2.6	Sales/Total Assets	2.3	2.6	2.4	2.9	2.7	2.5
1.9	1.8	2.0		2.1	1.6	1.8	2.1	2.1	1.9
.5	.4	.5		1.6	.7	.4	.4	.4	.4
(216) .9	(221) .8	(194) .8	% Depr., Dep., Amort./Sales	(10) 2.2	(24) 1.2	(18) 1.1	(41) .8	(48) .7	(53) .7
1.5	1.4	1.5		2.9	2.1	2.2	1.4	1.3	1.0
1.7	2.0	2.2			3.3	2.5	2.0	2.2	1.1
(102) 3.9	(111) 3.8	(96) 4.4	% Officers', Directors', Owners' Comp/Sales	(15) 7.7	(14) 4.9	(24) 3.9	(24) 2.7	(10) 4.6
8.1	7.2	8.6			10.2	7.3	5.9	5.6	8.3
5149064M	5259142M	6752080M	Net Sales ($)	5890M	58021M	109973M	337402M	873730M	5367064M
2242163M	2278013M	2685361M	Total Assets ($)	2438M	31073M	50331M	137550M	337534M	2126435M

© RMA 2005

M = $ thousand   MM = $ million
See Pages 11 through 21 for Explanation of Ratios and Data

Current Data Sorted By Assets   **Comparative Historical Data**

						Type of Statement		
	7	18	24	3	2	Unqualified	53	54
2	17	81	32	2		Reviewed	110	85
7	27	30	5			Compiled	110	95
10	12	13	1			Tax Returns	17	14
8	15	38	14	4	2	Other	78	93
	61 (4/1-9/30/04)			313 (10/1/04-3/31/05)			4/1/00-3/31/01	4/1/01-3/31/02
0-500M	.500M-2MM	2-10MM	10-50MM	50-100MM	100-250MM		ALL	ALL
27	78	180	76	9	4	**NUMBER OF STATEMENTS**	368	341
%	%	%	%	%	%	**ASSETS**	%	%
14.8	9.9	5.0	3.3			Cash & Equivalents	5.5	6.3
25.8	36.4	35.4	34.8			Trade Receivables (net)	35.2	33.9
31.5	36.2	40.6	40.8			Inventory	38.9	38.3
.8	2.0	2.1	4.0			All Other Current	1.5	1.8
72.9	84.6	83.2	82.8			Total Current	81.1	80.2
12.2	9.8	9.9	9.7			Fixed Assets (net)	11.9	12.9
3.2	.8	1.5	3.0			Intangibles (net)	2.0	2.1
11.7	4.9	5.5	4.4			All Other Non-Current	4.9	4.8
100.0	100.0	100.0	100.0			Total	100.0	100.0
						LIABILITIES		
12.0	12.4	14.7	20.9			Notes Payable-Short Term	15.9	16.2
2.2	3.3	1.9	1.2			Cur. Mat.-L/T/D	3.0	2.6
16.4	26.0	21.1	20.4			Trade Payables	23.6	21.3
.0	.5	.6	.6			Income Taxes Payable	.4	.5
9.1	8.0	10.5	9.2			All Other Current	8.3	9.1
39.7	50.2	48.7	52.2			Total Current	51.2	49.7
18.9	8.2	6.2	7.4			Long-Term Debt	8.3	8.2
.0	.1	.2	.1			Deferred Taxes	.3	.3
6.6	2.5	4.6	2.9			All Other Non-Current	3.9	3.6
34.8	39.0	40.3	37.4			Net Worth	36.3	38.2
100.0	100.0	100.0	100.0			Total Liabilities & Net Worth	100.0	100.0
						INCOME DATA		
100.0	100.0	100.0	100.0			Net Sales	100.0	100.0
41.9	27.9	28.4	25.5			Gross Profit	27.3	28.1
38.1	25.7	25.4	21.9			Operating Expenses	25.0	25.7
3.9	2.1	3.0	3.7			Operating Profit	2.2	2.4
.6	.0	.1	.1			All Other Expenses (net)	.5	.3
3.3	2.1	2.8	3.6			Profit Before Taxes	1.7	2.1
						RATIOS		
7.7	2.3	2.4	2.0			Current	2.2	2.4
1.9	1.7	1.7	1.5				1.6	1.6
1.2	1.3	1.3	1.2				1.3	1.2
3.5	1.2	1.1	1.0			Quick	1.1	1.2
1.1	.9	.8	.7				.8	.8
.6	.7	.6	.5				.6	.5
9 41.0	32 11.3	37 9.9	40 9.2			Sales/Receivables	35 10.5	33 10.9
31 11.8	41 9.0	44 8.4	44 8.2				42 8.6	42 8.7
44 8.2	51 7.2	52 7.0	53 6.9				54 6.8	52 7.0
29 12.5	38 9.5	51 7.2	51 7.1			Cost of Sales/Inventory	44 8.3	41 8.9
61 5.9	62 5.9	77 4.7	76 4.8				72 5.1	73 5.0
92 4.0	91 4.0	109 3.4	97 3.8				100 3.7	106 3.4
5 69.0	22 16.3	25 14.6	29 12.8			Cost of Sales/Payables	25 14.7	24 15.1
18 20.3	38 9.5	36 10.0	37 9.8				38 9.7	35 10.4
66 5.6	57 6.5	51 7.2	45 8.1				50 7.3	49 7.4
5.9	5.2	5.3	6.1			Sales/Working Capital	5.7	5.7
11.8	9.4	8.8	10.1				10.2	9.5
26.1	17.5	15.1	16.9				19.8	18.7
8.6	10.8	14.5	13.7			EBIT/Interest	5.6	6.3
(23) 4.5	(68) 4.0	(160) 4.9	(72) 8.6				(339) 2.3	(309) 2.6
.4	1.7	2.2	3.8				1.3	1.3
	16.9	12.8	16.2			Net Profit + Depr., Dep., Amort./Cur. Mat. L /T/D	5.9	8.8
	(22) 3.5	(62) 3.1	(40) 4.7				(109) 2.1	(98) 2.5
	1.0	1.3	2.5				1.2	1.1
.1	.1	.1	.1			Fixed/Worth	.1	.1
.3	.2	.2	.2				.3	.3
4.2	.5	.4	.5				.6	.6
.5	.8	.8	.9			Debt/Worth	.8	.7
1.7	1.7	1.5	2.0				1.9	1.7
19.4	3.0	3.1	3.8				4.0	4.2
60.1	32.0	29.4	44.0			% Profit Before Taxes/Tangible Net Worth	30.3	25.9
(21) 17.6	(73) 12.3	(170) 13.8	(74) 26.5				(340) 12.6	(314) 13.0
.6	2.8	6.3	16.7				3.3	3.7
23.0	12.7	11.3	12.3			% Profit Before Taxes/Total Assets	9.5	10.1
6.2	4.9	5.1	9.2				4.1	4.8
-1.0	1.1	2.5	5.0				.7	.8
141.6	122.3	68.7	59.1			Sales/Net Fixed Assets	63.8	68.4
49.0	51.4	37.0	33.0				33.0	30.5
22.6	20.9	22.3	21.3				17.2	16.3
4.7	3.8	3.3	3.0			Sales/Total Assets	3.5	3.4
3.7	3.1	2.8	2.8				2.9	2.8
2.7	2.4	2.2	2.4				2.3	2.3
.5	.4	.4	.4			% Depr., Dep., Amort./Sales	.4	.5
(17) 1.3	(59) .9	(157) .6	(74) .6				(313) .7	(281) .8
2.2	1.7	1.0	.9				1.3	1.3
4.1	2.7	1.7	.9			% Officers', Directors', Owners' Comp/Sales	1.6	1.6
(13) 8.8	(34) 4.1	(76) 3.0	(21) 1.8				(170) 3.2	(154) 3.2
15.1	6.3	5.4	3.8				5.8	6.3
31839M	300385M	2237778M	4431210M	1556443M	1425448M	Net Sales ($)	7623907M	8816414M
8950M	96691M	816948M	1617207M	584702M	711165M	Total Assets ($)	3141044M	3166708M

© RMA 2005

M = $ thousand   MM = $ million
See Pages 11 through 21 for Explanation of Ratios and Data

Comparative Historical Data / Current Data Sorted By Sales

			Type of Statement						
62	57	54	Unqualified		3	5	9	11	26
137	126	134	Reviewed	2	4	7	32	56	33
60	92	69	Compiled	4	13	16	19	13	4
22	37	36	Tax Returns	7	11	5	8	4	1
66	70	81	Other	3	11	6	18	19	24
4/1/02-3/31/03	4/1/03-3/31/04	4/1/04-3/31/05		61 (4/1-9/30/04)			313 (10/1/04-3/31/05)		
ALL	ALL	ALL		0-1MM	1-3MM	3-5MM	5-10MM	10-25MM	25MM & OVER
347	382	374	**NUMBER OF STATEMENTS**	16	42	39	86	103	88
%	%	%	**ASSETS**	%	%	%	%	%	%
6.0	6.4	6.3	Cash & Equivalents	8.7	14.2	9.3	7.2	4.0	2.5
32.9	33.8	34.6	Trade Receivables (net)	24.7	26.7	34.4	35.4	38.4	34.9
40.1	39.3	39.0	Inventory	36.5	31.9	40.2	39.7	38.8	41.8
2.9	3.1	2.4	All Other Current	.4	2.1	1.4	1.6	2.9	3.5
81.9	82.5	82.2	Total Current	70.3	74.9	85.2	83.9	84.1	82.7
11.8	11.2	10.3	Fixed Assets (net)	11.1	13.6	8.8	10.0	9.4	10.7
1.5	1.6	1.8	Intangibles (net)	.2	3.0	1.7	1.2	1.6	2.2
4.8	4.7	5.7	All Other Non-Current	18.4	8.5	4.2	4.9	4.9	4.4
100.0	100.0	100.0	Total	100.0	100.0	100.0	100.0	100.0	100.0
			LIABILITIES						
17.2	17.1	15.4	Notes Payable-Short Term	14.6	9.3	11.8	11.5	18.0	20.6
2.9	1.9	2.0	Cur. Mat.-L/T/D	2.9	2.6	2.8	2.8	1.5	1.2
20.6	21.2	21.5	Trade Payables	18.7	19.8	24.0	20.7	22.5	21.3
.3	.4	.5	Income Taxes Payable	.0	.5	.4	.9	.3	.5
11.1	9.9	9.6	All Other Current	8.4	7.1	9.0	11.0	10.1	9.3
52.2	50.6	49.0	Total Current	44.6	39.3	48.0	47.0	52.5	52.9
7.8	6.7	8.0	Long-Term Debt	22.6	10.9	9.7	7.0	5.3	7.4
.2	.2	.1	Deferred Taxes	.0	.1	.1	.3	.1	.1
2.9	5.1	3.9	All Other Non-Current	11.0	1.1	3.7	6.1	2.8	3.1
36.9	37.4	38.9	Net Worth	21.8	48.6	38.5	39.6	39.2	36.5
100.0	100.0	100.0	Total Liabilities & Net Worth	100.0	100.0	100.0	100.0	100.0	100.0
			INCOME DATA						
100.0	100.0	100.0	Net Sales	100.0	100.0	100.0	100.0	100.0	100.0
28.5	28.6	28.7	Gross Profit	40.1	33.8	29.0	29.3	26.6	25.8
26.5	26.5	25.6	Operating Expenses	35.2	32.1	26.9	26.1	23.5	22.3
1.9	2.1	3.0	Operating Profit	4.9	1.7	2.1	3.1	3.1	3.5
.1	.2	.1	All Other Expenses (net)	1.0	-.2	.3	.0	.2	.1
1.9	1.9	2.9	Profit Before Taxes	3.9	1.9	1.8	3.1	2.9	3.4
			RATIOS						
2.2	2.4	2.3		6.9	3.3	2.4	2.6	2.2	2.0
1.5	1.6	1.7	Current	1.7	1.9	1.7	1.8	1.6	1.5
1.2	1.2	1.3		.9	1.4	1.3	1.3	1.3	1.2
1.1	1.2	1.2		2.1	1.5	1.2	1.4	1.1	.9
.7	.8	.8	Quick	.7	1.0	.9	.9	.8	.7
.5	.5	.5		.5	.7	.7	.6	.5	.5
34	10.8	34	10.8	36	10.1		23	15.6	22	16.9	34	10.9	35	10.5	38	9.6	39	9.4

						Sales/Receivables						
34	10.8	34	10.8	36	10.1		23	15.6	22	16.9	34	10.9	35	10.5	38	9.6	39	9.4
41	8.8	43	8.5	43	8.5	Sales/Receivables	37	9.8	37	9.9	42	8.7	43	8.4	44	8.4	44	8.2
51	7.2	54	6.7	52	7.1		49	7.4	50	7.4	57	6.5	52	7.0	52	7.0	52	7.0
48	7.7	45	8.1	47	7.8		39	9.4	38	9.5	47	7.7	41	9.0	45	8.1	54	6.7
73	5.0	76	4.8	73	5.0	Cost of Sales/Inventory	74	4.9	62	5.9	85	4.3	73	5.0	69	5.3	73	5.0
108	3.4	108	3.4	98	3.7		131	2.8	98	3.7	115	3.2	110	3.3	91	4.0	93	3.9
24	15.5	24	15.4	25	14.7		13	28.9	16	22.6	30	12.0	20	17.8	26	14.3	28	12.9
33	11.1	37	9.8	37	10.0	Cost of Sales/Payables	28	13.1	36	10.3	38	9.5	36	10.1	36	10.2	37	9.9
48	7.6	50	7.3	50	7.3		76	4.8	58	6.3	58	6.3	50	7.3	45	7.2	45	8.2

	6.0		5.5		5.6			3.0		4.8		4.6		4.9		6.2		6.3
	10.0		9.7		9.5	Sales/Working Capital		12.2		8.8		8.6		8.9		9.5		10.4
	19.6		18.7		16.1			NM		14.0		13.4		14.5		15.6		18.0
	9.3		9.8		12.6			8.6		10.7		5.8		14.8		13.5		13.3
(321)	3.3	(346)	3.8	(336)	5.3	EBIT/Interest	(15)	2.5	(31)	6.1	(36)	3.7	(76)	5.8	(93)	4.3	(85)	8.1
	1.5		1.5		2.4			.4		1.2		1.6		2.2		2.0		3.8
	8.6		8.1		13.6	Net Profit + Depr., Dep.,								19.1		13.8		15.6
(125)	3.0	(121)	3.6	(134)	4.0	Amort./Cur. Mat. L/T/D					(32)	3.3	(37)	4.2	(47)	5.0
	1.1		1.6		1.6									1.6		1.2		2.6
	.1		.1		.1			.0		.1		.1		.1		.1		.1
	.3		.2		.2	Fixed/Worth		.3		.2		.2		.2		.2		.2
	.6		.5		.5			NM		.6		.5		.4		.4		.6
	.9		.8		.8			.9		.5		.8		.8		.8		1.1
	1.9		1.8		1.7	Debt/Worth		2.2		1.2		1.7		1.6		1.8		1.9
	3.8		3.7		3.2			NM		2.3		9.3		3.1		3.1		3.8
	26.1		27.4		34.0	% Profit Before Taxes/Tangible		47.6		32.1		26.7		35.7		28.7		42.5
(321)	11.6	(353)	13.9	(351)	17.8	Net Worth	(12)	23.5	(39)	6.7	(35)	5.6	(81)	18.4	(98)	13.0	(86)	27.5
	4.1		3.5		6.3			-.9		.2		1.2		6.9		7.8		16.8
	9.5		9.7		12.3	% Profit Before Taxes/Total		19.7		13.2		8.9		13.8		10.8		12.3
	4.1		4.6		6.0	Assets		1.7		5.5		3.3		6.3		4.7		9.1
	1.0		1.0		2.3			-4.3		.0		.8		2.6		2.4		5.2
	67.5		65.0		75.2			295.1		84.7		103.6		91.1		64.9		62.5
	33.9		34.1		37.5	Sales/Net Fixed Assets		35.6		44.2		44.7		37.5		39.8		33.0
	18.3		19.4		20.9			16.0		13.5		19.4		22.2		23.7		20.6
	3.4		3.3		3.4			3.8		3.7		3.3		3.4		3.4		3.2
	2.8		2.8		2.9	Sales/Total Assets		2.4		2.8		2.8		2.8		3.0		2.8
	2.2		2.3		2.2			1.8		1.9		2.1		2.2		2.3		2.5
	.4		.5		.4			1.0		.5		.5		.4		.5		.3
(305)	.7	(333)	.7	(320)	.7	% Depr., Dep., Amort./Sales	(11)	1.9	(30)	.8	(30)	.8	(70)	.8	(94)	.6	(85)	.6
	1.2		1.1		1.1			3.1		2.1		1.5		1.1		1.0		.9
	1.7		1.6		1.7	% Officers', Directors',		3.5		3.6		1.8		1.7		.9
(158)	3.3	(156)	2.8	(146)	3.3	Owners' Comp/Sales	(25)	5.0	(17)	5.4	(41)	3.1	(34)	2.5	(24)	1.7
	6.5		5.3		5.9			11.6		7.6		4.8		3.7		5.1
8244861M	8629070M	9983103M	Net Sales ($)	11270M	88728M	151944M	616152M	1638376M	7476633M
3147672M	3384389M	3835663M	Total Assets ($)	5173M	47917M	61705M	235595M	618509M	2866764M

© RMA 2005

M = $ thousand   MM = $ million
See Pages 11 through 21 for Explanation of Ratios and Data

Current Data Sorted By Assets   Comparative Historical Data

						Type of Statement		
1	6	9	26	3	1	Unqualified	41	41
1	16	42	19		1	Reviewed	60	49
5	24	21	2			Compiled	67	61
8	8	6				Tax Returns	8	12
3	7	35	10		1	Other	59	74
	45 (4/1-9/30/04)		210 (10/1/04-3/31/05)				4/1/00-3/31/01 ALL	4/1/01-3/31/02 ALL
0-500M	500M-2MM	2-10MM	10-50MM	50-100MM	100-250MM			
18	61	113	57	5	1	NUMBER OF STATEMENTS	235	237
%	%	%	%	%	%	**ASSETS**	%	%
14.7	7.7	4.4	4.3			Cash & Equivalents	4.7	5.5
27.1	40.5	42.2	35.8			Trade Receivables (net)	40.4	39.5
15.3	33.3	35.9	41.0			Inventory	35.4	35.4
.5	1.9	2.6	1.6			All Other Current	2.2	2.5
57.6	83.4	85.2	82.7			Total Current	82.8	82.9
27.3	10.0	9.0	11.9			Fixed Assets (net)	10.6	10.4
11.0	1.1	.8	1.4			Intangibles (net)	1.7	2.1
4.1	5.4	5.0	3.9			All Other Non-Current	4.8	4.6
100.0	100.0	100.0	100.0			Total	100.0	100.0
						LIABILITIES		
11.4	14.3	19.3	21.7			Notes Payable-Short Term	18.2	18.4
4.5	1.9	1.5	1.2			Cur. Mat.-L/T/D	2.6	2.7
17.2	25.0	24.3	16.2			Trade Payables	23.7	23.1
.0	.1	.3	.1			Income Taxes Payable	.3	.2
8.0	9.6	10.9	9.0			All Other Current	9.9	9.1
41.0	50.8	56.3	48.1			Total Current	54.7	53.6
30.8	9.6	8.3	7.8			Long-Term Debt	6.9	8.8
.0	.4	.3	.3			Deferred Taxes	.3	.2
15.0	2.5	4.6	3.9			All Other Non-Current	3.8	2.4
13.3	36.6	30.4	39.9			Net Worth	34.4	35.0
100.0	100.0	100.0	100.0			Total Liabilities & Net Worth	100.0	100.0
						INCOME DATA		
100.0	100.0	100.0	100.0			Net Sales	100.0	100.0
42.7	30.5	26.9	24.3			Gross Profit	26.9	27.6
38.9	27.4	24.1	21.3			Operating Expenses	23.6	24.8
3.8	3.1	2.7	2.9			Operating Profit	3.3	2.8
1.7	.5	.1	.0			All Other Expenses (net)	.5	.4
2.0	2.6	2.6	2.9			Profit Before Taxes	2.8	2.4
						RATIOS		
3.5	2.5	2.1	2.4				2.0	2.2
1.4	1.6	1.5	1.8			Current	1.5	1.5
.9	1.2	1.2	1.3				1.2	1.2
2.1	1.6	1.1	1.3				1.2	1.2
1.2	.9	.8	.9			Quick	.8	.9
.6	.7	.6	.6				.6	.5
0 UND	33 11.2	37 9.8	40 9.2				36 10.0	36 10.2
33 11.0	40 9.1	47 7.8	47 7.8			Sales/Receivables	45 8.1	44 8.3
44 8.3	55 6.7	61 6.0	58 6.3				60 6.1	57 6.4
0 UND	19 18.9	25 14.7	51 7.1				30 12.1	27 13.6
1 336.9	44 8.3	60 6.1	81 4.5			Cost of Sales/Inventory	58 6.3	62 5.9
41 8.8	78 4.7	99 3.7	100 3.7				94 3.9	95 3.9
0 UND	21 17.2	24 15.3	19 19.2				23 15.9	21 17.5
24 15.2	34 10.9	39 9.5	30 12.3			Cost of Sales/Payables	34 10.6	35 10.4
38 9.7	53 6.9	52 7.0	39 9.4				51 7.1	54 6.7
6.1	6.6	6.1	4.9				6.5	6.0
55.1	11.2	10.8	7.5			Sales/Working Capital	10.3	10.4
-76.6	24.0	20.2	12.4				18.2	18.8
6.7	16.8	12.4	11.0				8.4	10.1
(15) 1.3	(55) 7.3	(105) 4.2	(55) 5.4			EBIT/Interest	(219) 2.9	(216) 3.0
-2.3	1.7	2.0	3.0				1.4	1.4
	12.5	8.0	8.7			Net Profit + Depr., Dep.,	11.1	10.0
	(13) 2.0	(35) 2.7	(17) 3.7			Amort./Cur. Mat. L /T/D	(82) 2.9	(66) 2.7
	.8	1.7	1.8				1.1	1.2
.0	.0	.1	.1				.1	.1
2.2	.1	.2	.3			Fixed/Worth	.2	.2
-2.7	.8	.6	.5				.6	.5
1.8	.7	1.0	.9				1.1	1.0
18.3	1.6	2.2	1.8			Debt/Worth	2.2	1.9
-6.7	5.7	4.1	3.1				4.0	4.0
77.8	45.4	29.4	31.8			% Profit Before Taxes/Tangible	38.8	33.3
(11) 43.0	(55) 24.0	(103) 14.2	(56) 15.8			Net Worth	(224) 17.0	(220) 14.3
-6.6	4.4	4.4	10.5				4.7	5.2
37.9	19.3	10.9	10.6			% Profit Before Taxes/Total	14.0	12.9
2.4	10.1	5.1	6.3			Assets	5.3	4.9
-9.0	1.3	1.8	4.3				1.4	1.3
UND	174.0	92.7	95.6				103.9	93.9
29.5	55.2	47.0	36.0			Sales/Net Fixed Assets	41.2	41.2
11.8	23.6	24.7	12.5				21.8	21.6
6.3	4.4	3.6	3.0				3.6	3.7
4.1	3.5	2.9	2.6			Sales/Total Assets	3.0	2.9
2.6	2.7	2.4	2.2				2.4	2.3
1.0	.3	.4	.4				.3	.3
(10) 2.3	(47) .5	(94) .7	(55) .5			% Depr., Dep., Amort./Sales	(205) .6	(200) .6
3.2	1.3	1.1	.9				1.1	1.0
	2.6	1.7				% Officers', Directors',	2.5	2.1
	(31) 4.4	(49) 3.2				Owners' Comp/Sales	(92) 4.2	(89) 4.2
	5.9	5.1					7.7	7.9
22704M	260722M	1529565M	3268315M	953925M	416661M	Net Sales ($)	6244865M	5180293M
4753M	73546M	511851M	1231215M	350018M	154662M	Total Assets ($)	1897579M	1906642M

© RMA 2005

M = $ thousand   MM = $ million
See Pages 11 through 21 for Explanation of Ratios and Data

Comparative Historical Data   **Current Data Sorted By Sales**

				Type of Statement	1	2	2	5	6	30
51		50	46	Unqualified	1	2	2	5	6	30
68		80	79	Reviewed		5	4	21	28	21
40		63	52	Compiled	2	10	12	14	9	5
21		19	22	Tax Returns	6	5	6	2	2	1
54		65	56	Other	1	4	6	13	20	12
4/1/02-3/31/03		4/1/03-3/31/04	4/1/04-3/31/05		45 (4/1-9/30/04)			210 (10/1/04-3/31/05)		
ALL		ALL	ALL		0-1MM	1-3MM	3-5MM	5-10MM	10-25MM	25MM & OVER
234		277	255	NUMBER OF STATEMENTS	10	26	30	55	65	69
%		%	%	ASSETS	%	%	%	%	%	%
6.1		5.9	5.9	Cash & Equivalents	14.9	10.1	8.2	4.7	5.0	3.8
40.0		40.1	39.2	Trade Receivables (net)	20.9	27.4	41.3	43.7	43.7	37.4
33.7		33.7	35.2	Inventory	22.6	37.4	27.8	34.6	34.7	40.4
2.9		2.8	2.1	All Other Current	1.1	.8	2.7	2.5	2.1	2.0
82.6		82.4	82.3	Total Current	59.5	75.6	80.1	85.6	85.4	83.7
10.8		10.6	11.2	Fixed Assets (net)	27.4	12.8	13.6	8.7	9.4	10.8
1.7		1.1	1.7	Intangibles (net)	9.8	5.4	.8	.3	1.3	1.2
4.8		5.8	4.7	All Other Non-Current	3.2	6.2	5.6	5.4	3.9	4.3
100.0		100.0	100.0	Total	100.0	100.0	100.0	100.0	100.0	100.0
				LIABILITIES						
18.6		18.0	18.4	Notes Payable-Short Term	8.7	17.0	9.7	18.7	20.2	22.2
2.7		1.8	1.7	Cur. Mat.-L/T/D	2.4	3.2	1.6	1.6	1.2	1.5
22.2		23.7	22.0	Trade Payables	10.4	19.8	28.2	23.1	25.3	17.8
.2		.2	.2	Income Taxes Payable	.0	.0	.1	.3	.3	.2
10.5		12.7	9.9	All Other Current	1.9	9.6	6.1	12.3	11.6	9.4
54.2		56.4	52.2	Total Current	23.4	49.6	45.7	56.1	58.6	51.1
9.3		7.4	10.0	Long-Term Debt	46.9	10.3	9.6	6.9	10.4	6.7
.3		.2	.3	Deferred Taxes	.0	.0	.8	.4	.2	.3
4.2		5.2	4.6	All Other Non-Current	10.4	8.2	4.7	2.0	5.1	4.0
32.1		30.8	32.9	Net Worth	19.3	31.9	39.1	34.6	25.7	38.0
100.0		100.0	100.0	Total Liabilities & Net Worth	100.0	100.0	100.0	100.0	100.0	100.0
				INCOME DATA						
100.0		100.0	100.0	Net Sales	100.0	100.0	100.0	100.0	100.0	100.0
27.2		27.3	28.2	Gross Profit	37.4	38.5	31.8	28.0	26.9	22.8
24.8		24.9	25.2	Operating Expenses	32.3	35.0	27.7	25.5	24.2	20.1
2.3		2.4	3.0	Operating Profit	5.1	3.4	4.1	2.5	2.7	2.7
.3		.2	.3	All Other Expenses (net)	1.9	1.8	.2	-.1	.2	.0
2.0		2.2	2.7	Profit Before Taxes	3.2	1.6	3.8	2.6	2.5	2.8
				RATIOS						
2.1		2.1	2.3		6.3	2.6	2.5	2.0	2.2	2.2
1.5		1.5	1.6	Current	2.3	1.8	1.8	1.5	1.5	1.6
1.2		1.2	1.2		1.3	1.1	1.4	1.2	1.2	1.3
1.2		1.2	1.3		3.8	1.6	1.7	1.2	1.1	1.1
.8		.8	.9	Quick	1.5	.8	1.0	.9	.9	.8
.6		.6	.6		.9	.4	.7	.6	.7	.6

35	10.3	36	10.1	36	10.1		0	UND	16	22.4	33	11.2	35	10.4	37	9.7	39	9.3
44	8.2	46	8.0	44	8.2	Sales/Receivables	35	10.5	36	10.2	45	8.0	44	8.2	47	7.7	46	8.0
59	6.2	57	6.5	57	6.4		50	7.3	49	7.4	61	5.9	59	6.2	59	6.2	56	6.5
28	13.2	23	15.9	25	14.5		0	UND	5	73.7	11	32.4	27	13.7	23	15.7	49	7.4
60	6.1	60	6.1	65	5.6	Cost of Sales/Inventory	27	13.7	65	5.6	40	9.1	54	6.8	55	6.6	75	4.9
88	4.2	90	4.1	94	3.9		147	2.5	135	2.7	77	4.7	89	4.1	96	3.8	95	3.8
19	18.8	22	16.9	21	17.0		0	UND	13	27.3	27	13.8	24	15.0	24	15.5	19	19.2
34	10.8	34	10.6	34	10.8	Cost of Sales/Payables	13	28.9	36	10.2	43	8.5	38	9.6	36	10.1	28	13.2
51	7.2	52	7.0	48	7.6		39	9.4	71	5.2	55	6.6	52	7.0	49	7.5	38	9.5

	6.7		6.3		6.1		3.6	5.4	6.2	6.5	7.3	6.0
	10.7		10.2		10.3	Sales/Working Capital	8.7	9.4	9.4	12.2	11.0	9.1
	21.7		23.8		20.5		171.3	58.3	13.8	20.5	21.8	17.2

	7.7		10.2		12.4				12.8		15.7		11.7		12.8		12.3
(221)	3.1	(251)	3.9	(236)	4.9	EBIT/Interest		(23)	2.0	(26)	7.4	(53)	5.2	(59)	4.9	(67)	5.2
	1.3		1.5		2.1				-1.3		2.0		2.1		2.5		3.1
	8.9		11.5		8.0	Net Profit + Depr., Dep.,							8.0		9.6		7.9
(72)	2.2	(76)	3.8	(67)	2.7	Amort./Cur. Mat. L/T/D					(20)	2.6	(19)	2.9	(19)	3.7
	.7		1.6		1.5								1.2		1.4		1.7

	.1		.1		.1		.0	.0	.1	.1	.1	.1
	.3		.3		.2	Fixed/Worth	1.8	.1	.2	.2	.3	.3
	.6		.6		.7		-2.7	7.3	1.1	.5	.8	.4
	1.0		.9		.9		1.8	.7	.7	1.0	.9	1.0
	2.0		2.2		2.0	Debt/Worth	8.3	1.8	1.5	2.0	2.6	1.9
	5.5		4.7		4.4		-4.2	20.2	3.8	3.2	6.5	3.3

	30.3		32.4		35.0				34.9		45.7		34.7		31.2		38.4
(213)	11.7	(250)	17.3	(231)	16.7	% Profit Before Taxes/Tangible Net Worth		(21)	17.5	(29)	22.0	(51)	10.4	(56)	18.6	(68)	17.4
	2.8		4.8		5.7				-5.8		7.1		4.4		10.0		10.3

	9.8		11.7		13.1		38.8	13.9	16.7	16.4	12.9	11.2
	3.7		5.4		6.3	% Profit Before Taxes/Total Assets	5.7	2.1	10.0	3.6	7.6	6.3
	.6		1.2		1.8		-1.3	-4.1	3.7	1.9	1.7	4.1
	99.6		89.7		103.4		UND	286.4	73.3	144.3	99.0	88.8
	41.0		41.8		45.8	Sales/Net Fixed Assets	27.0	58.4	31.5	47.5	52.3	38.9
	20.5		20.1		22.1		4.3	23.1	18.7	25.0	24.7	16.9
	3.6		3.7		3.8		4.1	4.2	4.2	3.9	3.8	3.3
	3.0		3.0		2.9	Sales/Total Assets	3.1	3.0	3.2	2.9	3.1	2.8
	2.5		2.4		2.4		2.1	2.4	2.2	2.5	2.4	2.4

	.4		.4		.4				.3		.3		.4		.4		.4
(205)	.7	(239)	.7	(212)	.6	% Depr., Dep., Amort./Sales		(18)	.6	(25)	.7	(43)	.6	(54)	.7	(67)	.5
	1.1		1.1		1.1				2.3		1.3		1.0		1.1		
	2.0		1.6		2.0				2.2		2.7		2.3		2.2		.5
(95)	4.1	(103)	4.2	(96)	3.7	% Officers', Directors', Owners' Comp/Sales		(13)	4.2	(14)	3.8	(25)	4.3	(26)	3.7	(14)	1.3
	7.4		7.2						6.8		6.0		5.6		6.7		3.6

7508305M		8306197M	6451892M	Net Sales ($)	6596M	52213M	124330M	404702M	1019991M	4844060M
2562428M		2847397M	2326045M	Total Assets ($)	2800M	21373M	42650M	138830M	352956M	1767436M

© RMA 2005   M = $ thousand   MM = $ million

See Pages 11 through 21 for Explanation of Ratios and Data

Current Data Sorted By Assets   Comparative Historical Data

0-500M	500M-2MM	2-10MM	10-50MM	50-100MM	100-250MM	Type of Statement	4/1/00-3/31/01 ALL	4/1/01-3/31/02 ALL
	1	3	3	1		Unqualified	12	9
	7	9	3	1		Reviewed	9	9
1	4	6	4			Compiled	13	12
1	2	3				Tax Returns	3	4
1	5	7	1			Other	19	18
	7 (4/1-9/30/04)		56 (10/1/04-3/31/05)					
0-500M	500M-2MM	2-10MM	10-50MM	50-100MM	100-250MM	**NUMBER OF STATEMENTS**		
3	19	28	11	2			56	52
%	%	%	%	%	%	**ASSETS**	%	%
	6.4	5.7	3.3			Cash & Equivalents	4.8	8.7
	34.1	28.4	27.8			Trade Receivables (net)	35.4	34.3
	43.9	39.9	51.6			Inventory	37.4	36.8
	.4	3.5	1.2			All Other Current	3.4	1.3
	84.8	77.5	83.9			Total Current	81.0	81.1
	7.1	13.9	8.8			Fixed Assets (net)	12.3	11.7
	1.3	2.0	4.2			Intangibles (net)	1.6	1.4
	6.8	6.7	3.1			All Other Non-Current	5.1	5.9
	100.0	100.0	100.0			Total	100.0	100.0
						LIABILITIES		
	15.8	20.3	15.9			Notes Payable-Short Term	19.9	17.6
	1.7	2.6	1.1			Cur. Mat.-L/T/D	2.7	2.8
	24.2	20.6	21.0			Trade Payables	21.6	22.4
	.1	.3	.1			Income Taxes Payable	.4	.2
	5.6	7.8	3.9			All Other Current	8.8	9.3
	47.4	51.5	42.1			Total Current	53.4	52.3
	7.1	8.9	8.8			Long-Term Debt	9.2	7.8
	.0	.1	.4			Deferred Taxes	.1	.1
	4.9	3.8	3.4			All Other Non-Current	4.6	4.1
	40.6	35.7	45.2			Net Worth	32.7	35.7
	100.0	100.0	100.0			Total Liabilities & Net Worth	100.0	100.0
						INCOME DATA		
	100.0	100.0	100.0			Net Sales	100.0	100.0
	26.6	24.3	25.5			Gross Profit	27.1	27.7
	24.9	22.1	21.8			Operating Expenses	25.0	25.8
	1.7	2.2	3.7			Operating Profit	2.1	2.0
	.2	.4	.8			All Other Expenses (net)	.0	.3
	1.5	1.8	3.0			Profit Before Taxes	2.1	1.7
						RATIOS		
	2.7	2.1	3.3				2.2	2.2
	1.7	1.4	2.4			Current	1.5	1.6
	1.4	1.1	1.4				1.2	1.2
	1.5	.9	1.2				1.2	1.3
	.9	.6	.8			Quick	.7	.8
	.6	.5	.5				.6	.5
	28 13.2	33 11.0	34 10.9				31 11.8	32 11.4
	36 10.1	40 9.2	40 9.1			Sales/Receivables	40 9.2	41 8.9
	52 7.0	51 7.2	50 7.4				51 7.2	56 6.5
	48 7.7	55 6.7	86 4.2				29 12.5	35 10.5
	56 6.5	69 5.3	114 3.2			Cost of Sales/Inventory	73 5.0	75 4.8
	133 2.7	125 2.9	162 2.3				112 3.2	111 3.3
	28 12.9	21 17.6	31 11.6				19 19.3	24 15.3
	42 8.7	32 11.4	45 8.2			Cost of Sales/Payables	32 11.5	32 11.5
	50 7.3	62 5.9	51 7.1				48 7.7	55 6.7
	5.4	4.5	4.1				5.6	5.6
	8.4	11.6	4.8			Sales/Working Capital	11.3	11.0
	18.1	29.2	11.3				27.2	20.7
	6.7	7.5	8.2				4.4	5.5
	(17) 3.9	(25) 3.5	6.0			EBIT/Interest	(49) 2.5	(47) 3.4
	1.5	1.6	2.7				1.3	1.3
						Net Profit + Depr., Dep.,	5.6	5.8
						Amort./Cur. Mat. L/T/D	(19) 3.2	(17) 2.5
							2.0	1.1
	.1	.1	.1				.1	.1
	.1	.3	.2			Fixed/Worth	.3	.2
	.2	.6	.4				.7	.5
	.6	1.5	.6				.8	.8
	1.3	2.6	1.5			Debt/Worth	2.0	1.8
	3.9	4.1	3.4				3.8	4.1
	30.3	47.9	24.3			% Profit Before Taxes/Tangible	28.9	22.3
	(18) 7.8	20.8	(10) 14.0			Net Worth	(51) 13.4	(49) 9.9
	1.8	2.6	9.7				2.7	2.8
	8.4	10.7	9.1			% Profit Before Taxes/Total	10.2	7.5
	4.3	4.6	7.9			Assets	4.9	3.7
	.8	.5	2.3				1.0	.8
	127.0	84.2	133.6				79.9	97.5
	74.9	46.5	33.4			Sales/Net Fixed Assets	44.5	36.2
	19.8	14.9	16.3				19.2	15.3
	4.0	3.1	2.7				3.6	3.7
	2.8	2.6	2.2			Sales/Total Assets	2.9	2.7
	2.3	1.8	1.9				2.4	2.1
	.2	.4	.5				.4	.3
	(13) .5	(23) .7	(10) 1.0			% Depr., Dep., Amort./Sales	(48) 1.0	(47) .8
	1.2	1.5	1.4				1.4	1.3
		2.3				% Officers', Directors',	2.0	1.6
		(12) 4.5				Owners' Comp/Sales	(27) 4.5	(23) 3.8
		5.1					7.8	5.7
4436M	76099M	344602M	530711M	237311M		Net Sales ($)	1345271M	866947M
1066M	24439M	143417M	233480M	115301M		Total Assets ($)	543656M	325725M

Note: Columns 50-100MM and 100-250MM are marked "DATA NOT AVAILABLE" for the Assets, Liabilities, Income Data, and Ratios sections.

© RMA 2005

M = $ thousand   MM = $ million
See Pages 11 through 21 for Explanation of Ratios and Data

Comparative Historical Data | Current Data Sorted By Sales

11	9	8	Type of Statement		3	1	1		6
11	17	20	Unqualified				1	1		6
15	24	15	Reviewed		3	2	4	9	2
6	1	6	Compiled		1	2	5	3	4
14	17	14	Tax Returns	1		2	1	2	
			Other	1	4		6	2	1

4/1/02-3/31/03 ALL	4/1/03-3/31/04 ALL	4/1/04-3/31/05 ALL		0-1MM	1-3MM	3-5MM	5-10MM	10-25MM	25MM & OVER
					7 (4/1-9/30/04)		56 (10/1/04-3/31/05)		
57	68	63	**NUMBER OF STATEMENTS**	2	8	7	17	16	13
%	%	%		%	%	%	%	%	%
			ASSETS						
9.1	4.9	5.7	Cash & Equivalents				4.3	7.1	4.5
28.7	27.9	30.2	Trade Receivables (net)				25.3	32.0	29.3
37.1	41.4	42.9	Inventory				40.3	45.6	46.6
1.5	2.2	2.0	All Other Current				5.5	.4	1.4
76.5	76.5	80.8	Total Current				75.4	85.1	81.8
13.7	15.4	11.5	Fixed Assets (net)				14.6	8.4	12.2
3.2	3.4	2.0	Intangibles (net)				1.3	2.2	3.5
6.7	4.7	5.6	All Other Non-Current				8.6	4.3	2.5
100.0	100.0	100.0	Total				100.0	100.0	100.0
			LIABILITIES						
14.4	20.3	17.0	Notes Payable-Short Term				18.4	23.7	12.0
2.0	1.7	2.0	Cur. Mat.-L/T/D				2.1	.5	3.7
20.0	19.1	21.2	Trade Payables				23.3	18.3	24.4
.3	.3	.2	Income Taxes Payable				.2	.2	.2
8.0	5.7	6.2	All Other Current				6.5	5.4	7.0
44.8	47.0	46.7	Total Current				50.5	48.2	47.3
10.0	7.7	8.8	Long-Term Debt				11.3	5.7	5.7
.2	.3	.2	Deferred Taxes				.1	.1	.4
5.9	6.2	4.4	All Other Non-Current				2.4	5.3	2.8
39.2	38.9	39.9	Net Worth				35.7	40.7	43.7
100.0	100.0	100.0	Total Liabilities & Net Worth				100.0	100.0	100.0
			INCOME DATA						
100.0	100.0	100.0	Net Sales				100.0	100.0	100.0
28.6	27.2	26.6	Gross Profit				25.7	22.9	24.2
26.2	24.9	23.9	Operating Expenses				22.6	21.6	20.1
2.4	2.3	2.7	Operating Profit				3.1	1.3	4.1
.1	.1	.4	All Other Expenses (net)				.5	.3	.5
2.2	2.2	2.3	Profit Before Taxes				2.6	1.0	3.6
			RATIOS						
2.4	2.5	2.7					1.9	3.6	3.2
1.7	1.5	1.6	Current				1.4	1.8	1.4
1.3	1.2	1.3					1.2	1.2	1.2
1.4	1.0	1.2					.9	1.4	.9
(56) .7	(67) .7	.7	Quick				.6	.7	.7
.6	.4	.5					.4	.6	.5
27 13.7	30 12.3	32 11.6					29 12.7	32 11.4	33 11.1
34 10.8	38 9.7	37 10.0	Sales/Receivables				34 10.7	42 8.7	36 10.1
46 7.9	48 7.5	50 7.2					41 8.9	51 7.1	46 7.9
28 13.3	52 7.0	53 6.9					53 6.9	57 6.4	64 5.7
66 5.5	75 4.9	83 4.4	Cost of Sales/Inventory				61 6.0	107 3.4	100 3.7
104 3.5	116 3.1	125 2.9					118 3.1	128 2.9	119 3.1
18 20.0	21 17.7	25 14.8					23 16.1	20 18.1	28 13.1
29 12.6	33 11.2	38 9.6	Cost of Sales/Payables				40 9.2	28 13.0	48 7.6
44 8.2	53 6.9	51 7.1					68 5.3	35 10.5	53 6.9
6.1	5.4	4.6					6.1	3.6	4.4
9.2	10.8	8.4	Sales/Working Capital				15.1	6.3	7.6
29.5	26.4	18.8					35.9	21.0	22.7
6.1	8.5	9.4					6.3	13.0	18.6
(49) 2.9	(63) 3.6	(58) 4.4	EBIT/Interest				(16) 4.5	(14) 3.0	7.1
1.9	1.9	2.4					1.6	1.7	3.6
6.2	8.2	7.7	Net Profit + Depr., Dep.,						
(13) 2.8	(18) 3.3	(17) 2.7	Amort./Cur. Mat. L/T/D						
.6	1.8	1.5							
.1	.1	.1					.0	.1	.2
.3	.3	.2	Fixed/Worth				.2	.2	.3
.9	.8	.5					.9	.4	.8
.6	.8	.8					1.2	.8	.5
1.5	2.3	2.0	Debt/Worth				2.3	2.1	1.6
4.3	3.9	3.9					3.4	4.5	4.0
33.8	28.1	45.3	% Profit Before Taxes/Tangible				60.3	30.7	44.2
(53) 12.7	(65) 14.7	(61) 17.0	Net Worth				19.5	16.4	(12) 18.6
4.9	7.5	4.0					1.1	3.8	11.8
11.0	9.1	11.6	% Profit Before Taxes/Total				11.6	8.2	11.9
4.3	4.5	5.2	Assets				5.2	4.2	8.1
2.1	2.3	1.2					.4	.6	4.3
92.1	80.4	89.7					217.1	90.2	90.0
32.7	25.4	42.1	Sales/Net Fixed Assets				60.7	71.1	16.4
14.7	9.8	16.1					11.0	23.6	12.0
3.6	3.2	3.2					3.3	3.1	3.2
2.8	2.5	2.6	Sales/Total Assets				2.6	2.5	2.3
2.2	2.0	2.0					1.9	1.8	1.9
.3	.5	.4					.3	.3	.6
(53) 1.0	(61) .9	(51) .7	% Depr., Dep., Amort./Sales				(13) .6	(13) .7	(12) .9
2.0	1.6	1.4					1.2	1.3	1.8
1.7	1.6	2.3	% Officers', Directors',						
(25) 3.5	(28) 4.0	(27) 4.3	Owners' Comp/Sales						
5.9	4.7	5.1							
1026409M	1292654M	1193159M	Net Sales ($)	1221M	16064M	27468M	123439M	235514M	789453M
394096M	583901M	517703M	Total Assets ($)	733M	6817M	9950M	57157M	100222M	342824M

© RMA 2005

M = $ thousand   MM = $ million

See Pages 11 through 21 for Explanation of Ratios and Data

Current Data Sorted By Assets | Comparative Historical Data

0-500M	500M-2MM	2-10MM	10-50MM	50-100MM	100-250MM	Type of Statement	4/1/00-3/31/01 ALL	4/1/01-3/31/02 ALL
2	13	22	51	21	17	Unqualified	78	91
3	27	53	20	2		Reviewed	54	68
8	9	21	11	1		Compiled	63	73
8	9	7	1			Tax Returns	20	17
5	13	35	24	7	9	Other	93	98
	54 (4/1-9/30/04)			327 (10/1/04-3/31/05)				
18	62	138	107	30	26	**NUMBER OF STATEMENTS**	308	347
%	%	%	%	%	%	**ASSETS**	%	%
15.5	7.2	6.2	3.6	2.6	3.0	Cash & Equivalents	5.0	5.1
24.6	20.4	25.5	17.3	20.3	20.3	Trade Receivables (net)	19.2	18.6
40.2	53.6	40.3	51.1	47.2	51.4	Inventory	49.7	49.9
.5	1.2	2.2	2.8	2.9	1.2	All Other Current	1.7	2.0
80.8	82.5	74.1	74.9	73.0	75.9	Total Current	75.6	75.7
12.5	13.0	19.6	20.7	22.5	20.4	Fixed Assets (net)	18.4	17.8
.0	.7	.7	1.3	.4	1.1	Intangibles (net)	1.5	2.0
6.7	3.9	5.5	3.2	4.2	2.6	All Other Non-Current	4.5	4.5
100.0	100.0	100.0	100.0	100.0	100.0	Total	100.0	100.0
						LIABILITIES		
12.2	28.3	24.6	30.1	31.1	24.9	Notes Payable-Short Term	28.3	29.0
7.4	2.5	3.9	6.3	2.7	1.3	Cur. Mat.-L/T/D	4.6	4.6
22.3	15.7	17.6	11.1	12.6	18.9	Trade Payables	14.2	12.3
.0	.1	.4	.4	1.5	.3	Income Taxes Payable	.3	.2
11.7	5.6	8.3	7.8	7.4	12.1	All Other Current	10.4	7.1
53.6	52.1	54.8	55.7	55.3	57.5	Total Current	57.8	53.3
23.4	12.5	9.6	13.2	18.0	7.3	Long-Term Debt	11.8	12.4
.0	.1	.8	1.1	.6	.6	Deferred Taxes	.6	.6
17.9	2.9	4.0	3.1	1.1	2.1	All Other Non-Current	2.2	2.3
5.0	32.4	30.8	26.8	25.0	32.4	Net Worth	27.5	31.4
100.0	100.0	100.0	100.0	100.0	100.0	Total Liabilities & Net Worth	100.0	100.0
						INCOME DATA		
100.0	100.0	100.0	100.0	100.0	100.0	Net Sales	100.0	100.0
29.1	26.6	26.5	22.6	19.4	22.5	Gross Profit	25.3	25.0
28.5	23.7	22.7	18.8	14.3	17.2	Operating Expenses	21.4	22.0
.6	2.8	3.8	3.8	5.0	5.3	Operating Profit	3.8	3.0
.0	.9	.5	.9	1.1	.7	All Other Expenses (net)	1.2	1.5
.6	2.0	3.3	2.9	4.0	4.6	Profit Before Taxes	2.6	1.5
						RATIOS		
2.3	2.4	1.8	1.7	1.6	1.5		1.8	1.9
1.6	1.5	1.4	1.3	1.3	1.3	Current	1.4	1.4
1.0	1.2	1.1	1.1	1.1	1.2		1.1	1.2
1.3	.9	1.0	.5	.7	.6		.7	.8
.8	(61) .5	.6	.4	.4	.4	Quick	.4	.4
.3	.2	.3	.2	.3	.3		.2	.2
6 64.9	11 33.2	26 14.0	23 16.0	33 11.0	37 9.8		21 17.4	20 18.2
27 13.6	30 12.2	39 9.4	35 10.6	42 8.7	47 7.8	Sales/Receivables	34 10.9	35 10.3
39 9.3	48 7.6	55 6.6	47 7.8	51 7.1	53 6.9		48 7.6	50 7.3
11 31.9	60 6.1	38 9.7	83 4.4	57 6.4	109 3.4		63 5.8	65 5.6
77 4.7	95 3.9	85 4.3	139 2.6	115 3.2	154 2.4	Cost of Sales/Inventory	132 2.8	139 2.6
142 2.6	146 2.5	166 2.2	214 1.7	185 2.0	204 1.8		202 1.8	211 1.7
6 62.6	3 111.6	12 31.5	10 36.3	15 24.7	23 15.6		11 34.4	10 37.3
39 9.5	30 12.2	28 13.0	19 19.0	25 14.4	66 5.5	Cost of Sales/Payables	22 16.4	22 16.9
65 5.6	53 6.9	60 6.1	37 9.9	35 10.3	85 4.3		50 7.3	46 8.0
5.8	4.2	6.3	5.9	6.1	5.5		5.4	4.7
9.8	9.3	11.0	9.6	11.7	7.3	Sales/Working Capital	9.6	9.4
UND	22.7	36.1	20.1	25.5	16.8		23.6	20.9
15.0	5.0	7.8	5.1	8.3	12.5		4.1	2.7
(11) 1.5	(57) 2.1	(130) 3.4	(104) 2.9	4.2	(25) 6.0	EBIT/Interest	(294) 1.9	(327) 1.6
−1.0	1.0	1.8	1.8	2.4	5.1		1.2	1.1
		5.5	9.4			Net Profit + Depr., Dep.,	6.0	6.8
	(44) 2.9	(44) 2.4				Amort./Cur. Mat. L./T/D	(86) 1.7	(96) 2.2
		1.4	1.3				.9	1.0
.0	.1	.1	.2	.1	.3		.2	.2
.2	.3	.3	.5	.4	.5	Fixed/Worth	.4	.3
NM	1.6	1.2	1.3	1.4	1.0		1.2	1.1
1.6	1.1	1.4	1.9	2.5	1.7		1.4	1.4
3.8	2.2	2.6	3.3	2.9	2.2	Debt/Worth	2.7	2.5
−17.7	8.5	4.5	5.2	4.1	3.3		5.2	4.8
56.8	49.2	29.1	27.8	47.8	28.8	% Profit Before Taxes/Tangible	24.6	19.4
(13) 22.0	(55) 13.5	(134) 15.6	(104) 15.7	24.2	22.4	Net Worth	(290) 13.6	(324) 9.9
1.3	.2	7.6	9.5	19.7	19.6		5.2	1.6
14.6	8.9	9.4	6.8	8.8	7.9	% Profit Before Taxes/Total	7.4	5.6
4.9	2.7	4.2	4.1	6.2	7.3	Assets	3.5	2.4
−.9	.0	1.7	1.9	3.5	6.2		1.0	.4
UND	110.2	57.4	39.4	53.5	16.9		45.8	48.5
57.7	34.8	26.3	18.4	20.6	13.1	Sales/Net Fixed Assets	19.7	20.2
15.9	10.8	6.2	5.8	4.6	4.6		7.0	6.9
4.9	3.4	2.8	2.0	2.0	1.8		2.5	2.4
2.8	2.2	2.0	1.6	1.7	1.6	Sales/Total Assets	2.2	1.7
1.8	1.6	1.5	1.3	1.4	1.4		1.3	1.3
	.6	.6	.6	.4	.7		.6	.5
	(46) 1.3	(121) 1.2	(89) 1.1	(16) 1.0	(15) 1.2	% Depr., Dep., Amort./Sales	(250) 1.1	(275) 1.1
	3.4	4.3	4.9	4.1	3.0		2.4	2.7
	1.4	1.6	.6			% Officers', Directors',	1.3	1.2
	(32) 3.4	(48) 3.0	(25) 1.2			Owners' Comp/Sales	(116) 2.7	(116) 2.3
	6.7	5.0	2.2				5.2	4.8
17620M	193420M	1465165M	4420635M	3975884M	7061198M	Net Sales ($)	11979638M	15253088M
4427M	76233M	673010M	2625350M	2296767M	4379647M	Total Assets ($)	8238796M	10382354M

© RMA 2005

M = $ thousand   MM = $ million
See Pages 11 through 21 for Explanation of Ratios and Data

Comparative Historical Data | Current Data Sorted By Sales

Type of Statement	4/1/02-3/31/03 ALL	4/1/03-3/31/04 ALL	4/1/04-3/31/05 ALL	0-1MM	1-3MM	3-5MM	5-10MM	10-25MM	25MM & OVER
Unqualified	94	90	111		3	4	23	81	
Reviewed	66	81	90	5	6	9	26	27	17
Compiled	55	74	62	5	15	14	11	11	6
Tax Returns	21	31	25	7	5	4	5	3	1
Other	66	89	93	4	8	12	13	23	33
				54 (4/1-9/30/04)			327 (10/1/04-3/31/05)		
NUMBER OF STATEMENTS	302	365	381	21	34	42	59	87	138
ASSETS	%	%	%	%	%	%	%	%	%
Cash & Equivalents	5.3	6.5	5.6	10.8	8.4	10.2	5.4	4.7	3.3
Trade Receivables (net)	18.4	18.9	21.5	12.2	23.3	20.0	28.4	20.9	20.4
Inventory	48.7	46.3	46.8	56.0	41.3	49.1	36.6	46.4	50.7
All Other Current	1.7	2.3	2.1	.3	2.2	1.2	2.1	2.7	2.2
Total Current	74.1	73.9	76.0	79.2	75.3	80.5	72.5	74.8	76.7
Fixed Assets (net)	20.0	20.2	18.8	14.5	19.1	15.9	21.9	18.6	19.0
Intangibles (net)	1.0	1.0	.8	.6	.7	.1	.6	1.0	1.1
All Other Non-Current	4.8	4.9	4.4	5.7	5.0	3.4	4.9	5.7	3.2
Total	100.0	100.0	100.0	100.0	100.0	100.0	100.0	100.0	100.0
LIABILITIES									
Notes Payable-Short Term	29.7	27.4	26.7	23.6	20.2	29.1	23.5	24.3	31.0
Cur. Mat.-L/T/D	4.9	4.6	4.2	5.9	4.3	3.4	3.8	5.5	3.5
Trade Payables	12.6	14.2	15.4	12.1	19.2	13.9	18.2	15.0	14.4
Income Taxes Payable	.3	.3	.4	.0	.1	.1	.2	.6	.7
All Other Current	6.4	7.5	8.1	8.6	7.6	5.2	7.3	10.1	8.0
Total Current	53.8	53.9	54.8	50.3	51.2	51.8	53.0	55.5	57.6
Long-Term Debt	11.3	12.2	12.2	21.1	18.2	10.4	10.0	11.0	11.8
Deferred Taxes	.7	.7	.7	.0	.1	.5	1.0	1.1	.6
All Other Non-Current	2.9	3.6	3.9	10.1	5.6	5.0	3.6	3.4	2.6
Net Worth	31.2	29.6	28.4	18.5	24.9	32.3	32.5	29.0	27.4
Total Liabilities & Net Worth	100.0	100.0	100.0	100.0	100.0	100.0	100.0	100.0	100.0
INCOME DATA									
Net Sales	100.0	100.0	100.0	100.0	100.0	100.0	100.0	100.0	100.0
Gross Profit	25.7	26.7	24.7	32.1	32.9	26.1	26.7	23.7	20.9
Operating Expenses	23.1	23.3	21.0	28.9	30.5	22.5	22.1	20.8	16.6
Operating Profit	2.6	3.3	3.7	3.2	2.4	3.6	4.6	2.9	4.2
All Other Expenses (net)	1.0	.8	.7	.9	.9	1.0	.6	.4	.7
Profit Before Taxes	1.6	2.5	3.0	2.3	1.5	2.6	4.0	2.5	3.5

RATIOS

Ratio	Hist 02/03	Hist 03/04	Hist 04/05	0-1MM	1-3MM	3-5MM	5-10MM	10-25MM	25MM & OVER
Current	1.9	1.9	1.8	3.3	2.1	2.2	1.8	1.8	1.6
	1.4	1.4	1.4	1.6	1.4	1.5	1.4	1.3	1.3
	1.1	1.1	1.1	1.1	1.1	1.2	1.1	1.1	1.1
Quick	.7	.8	.8	1.2	1.0	1.3	1.0	.8	.6
	.4	(364) .4	(380) .5	.6	(33) .5	.5	.6	.5	.4
	.2	.3	.3	.2	.3	.2	.3	.2	.3
Sales/Receivables	25 14.7	22 16.4	23 15.8	0 UND	21 17.1	19 18.9	30 12.1	23 16.0	27 13.7
	35 10.6	36 10.0	37 9.8	25 14.7	36 10.1	36 10.0	42 8.6	35 10.4	39 9.5
	47 7.7	51 7.2	51 7.2	40 9.1	55 6.6	50 7.3	60 6.1	52 7.0	50 7.4
Cost of Sales/Inventory	66 5.5	63 5.8	59 6.2	77 4.7	37 9.8	69 5.3	34 10.9	54 6.7	82 4.5
	131 2.8	116 3.1	109 3.3	160 2.3	98 3.7	99 3.7	73 5.0	96 3.8	127 2.9
	218 1.7	192 1.9	179 2.0	392 .9	197 1.9	181 2.0	119 3.1	191 1.9	183 2.0
Cost of Sales/Payables	11 32.3	10 37.9	11 32.3	1 638.5	17 21.2	3 126.3	15 24.4	10 35.1	12 30.2
	24 15.5	26 13.9	25 14.6	24 15.1	41 8.9	25 14.6	31 11.8	19 19.0	24 15.2
	45 8.1	54 6.8	52 7.0	63 5.8	74 4.9	45 8.1	54 6.8	44 8.3	47 7.7
Sales/Working Capital	4.7	4.9	5.6	2.3	4.3	4.3	7.1	6.3	6.1
	8.9	8.7	10.0	3.8	11.7	8.5	12.1	10.5	9.9
	22.4	29.1	25.3	175.8	29.8	27.4	45.9	28.4	21.5
EBIT/Interest	4.0	4.8	6.6	6.8	4.1	5.5	8.5	6.5	7.1
	(293) 1.9	(342) 2.1	(357) 3.3	(15) 1.2	(30) 2.1	(37) 2.4	(56) 3.3	(85) 2.7	(134) 4.5
	1.0	1.2	1.7	-1.0	.9	1.5	1.8	1.5	2.4
Net Profit + Depr., Dep., Amort./Cur. Mat. L/T/D	4.7	5.1	9.4				6.8	5.5	15.9
	(91) 1.9	(99) 2.1	(108) 3.3				(18) 2.9	(37) 2.3	(42) 4.7
	.7	.7	1.4				1.6	1.2	2.2
Fixed/Worth	.2	.2	.1	.0	.1	.1	.1	.1	.2
	.4	.4	.4	.2	.6	.2	.4	.3	.5
	1.2	1.3	1.2	2.2	2.4	1.7	1.2	1.1	1.1
Debt/Worth	1.4	1.4	1.6	1.0	1.5	1.2	1.4	1.5	1.9
	2.5	2.7	2.8	3.5	2.3	3.0	2.3	2.8	3.0
	4.9	5.1	5.1	NM	14.5	7.0	5.2	4.5	4.8
% Profit Before Taxes/Tangible Net Worth	20.5	22.4	30.6	37.5	32.9	50.4	49.2	22.2	31.6
	(289) 8.9	(341) 10.3	(362) 18.0	(16) 11.6	(29) 13.9	(39) 11.7	(83) 17.5	(136) 12.5	22.4
	1.3	2.6	7.8	.1	-.1	3.5	7.8	6.4	14.0
% Profit Before Taxes/Total Assets	5.9	6.4	8.4	8.0	8.9	9.5	12.4	8.2	7.8
	2.3	2.8	4.5	.7	2.6	3.5	4.9	3.3	6.0
	.1	.6	1.7	-.3	-.3	1.0	2.0	.9	3.5
Sales/Net Fixed Assets	44.2	40.0	53.3	UND	88.9	77.9	53.1	51.6	41.3
	16.5	18.3	22.4	26.8	21.3	34.8	22.0	26.5	16.9
	5.8	5.8	6.4	5.0	7.8	10.7	6.3	7.6	6.0
Sales/Total Assets	2.3	2.4	2.6	2.5	2.9	3.2	2.9	2.6	2.2
	1.6	1.7	1.8	1.7	1.9	2.0	2.3	1.9	1.7
	1.3	1.3	1.4	.8	1.4	1.4	1.6	1.4	1.5
% Depr., Dep., Amort./Sales	.7	.6	.6	2.3	.8	.7	.8	.6	.5
	(233) 1.4	(294) 1.3	(295) 1.2	(12) 3.8	(26) 2.1	(30) .9	(50) 1.6	(77) 1.0	(100) 1.0
	3.8	3.8	3.8	4.6	4.4	3.1	5.2	4.4	3.3
% Officers', Directors', Owners' Comp/Sales	1.2	1.7	1.1		2.5	1.7	1.0	.9	.4
	(108) 2.4	(120) 3.3	(116) 2.7		(16) 5.7	(23) 3.0	(28) 2.5	(25) 2.2	(18) 1.0
	5.1	5.8	5.6		12.1	6.3	4.2	4.3	2.0
Net Sales ($)	12809676M	13540286M	17133922M	10873M	72340M	169299M	446766M	1349620M	15085024M
Total Assets ($)	8543757M	9136908M	10055434M	10470M	41700M	98493M	236555M	834837M	8833379M

M = $ thousand   MM = $ million
See Pages 11 through 21 for Explanation of Ratios and Data

Current Data Sorted By Assets   **Comparative Historical Data**

0-500M	500M-2MM	2-10MM	10-50MM	50-100MM	100-250MM	Type of Statement	4/1/00-3/31/01 ALL	4/1/01-3/31/02 ALL
		10	8	9		Unqualified	36	47
1	7	42	17	1		Reviewed	76	87
5	35	52	5			Compiled	114	124
4	16	21	6			Tax Returns	35	38
2	16	42	18	1	1	Other	102	117
	50 (4/1-9/30/04)		269 (10/1/04-3/31/05)					
12	74	167	54	11	1	**NUMBER OF STATEMENTS**	363	413
%	%	%	%	%	%	**ASSETS**	%	%
16.9	7.0	5.1	4.2	1.8		Cash & Equivalents	4.3	5.5
16.8	14.0	13.7	12.9	21.6		Trade Receivables (net)	15.1	14.6
39.5	59.2	65.7	64.8	57.1		Inventory	60.8	60.8
1.4	1.7	1.8	2.3	1.8		All Other Current	2.2	1.7
74.6	81.8	86.4	84.2	82.3		Total Current	82.4	82.5
18.5	12.7	9.4	9.2	9.7		Fixed Assets (net)	11.7	11.5
.2	.7	.4	1.5	2.0		Intangibles (net)	.9	1.0
6.6	4.8	3.9	5.1	6.0		All Other Non-Current	5.0	5.1
100.0	100.0	100.0	100.0	100.0		Total	100.0	100.0
						LIABILITIES		
11.1	21.5	26.4	27.6	25.9		Notes Payable-Short Term	25.7	25.5
5.7	2.5	1.5	1.8	1.2		Cur. Mat.-L/T/D	3.0	2.0
9.3	20.2	19.2	22.4	20.6		Trade Payables	20.6	20.6
.0	.1	.2	.4	.3		Income Taxes Payable	.2	.3
3.1	9.0	10.1	11.4	17.0		All Other Current	7.5	10.6
29.1	53.3	57.4	63.6	65.1		Total Current	57.0	59.0
17.5	13.2	5.6	8.5	8.2		Long-Term Debt	9.5	8.3
.0	.0	.4	.3	.2		Deferred Taxes	.2	.2
8.4	4.8	3.4	1.3	.4		All Other Non-Current	3.4	3.1
44.9	28.6	33.3	26.4	26.2		Net Worth	30.0	29.4
100.0	100.0	100.0	100.0	100.0		Total Liabilities & Net Worth	100.0	100.0
						INCOME DATA		
100.0	100.0	100.0	100.0	100.0		Net Sales	100.0	100.0
30.6	24.3	20.2	19.1	19.4		Gross Profit	22.1	21.8
25.9	22.0	17.9	17.0	16.1		Operating Expenses	20.0	19.8
4.7	2.3	2.3	2.1	3.3		Operating Profit	2.1	2.0
.1	.5	-.1	-.6	.1		All Other Expenses (net)	.6	.6
4.6	1.8	2.3	2.7	3.3		Profit Before Taxes	1.5	1.4
						RATIOS		
8.4	2.2	1.9	1.6	1.7			1.9	1.8
4.7	1.5	1.4	1.3	1.2	Current	1.4	1.4
1.2	1.2	1.2	1.1	1.1		1.2	1.2
5.2	.7	.6	.5	.7			.6	.6
1.0	.3	.2	.2	.3	Quick	(362) .3	.3
.4	.1	.1	.1	.1		.1	.1
0 UND	5 70.5	6 58.4	5 80.2	7 53.4			8 47.3	7 55.8
8 47.2	11 32.8	14 26.6	11 33.9	39 9.3		Sales/Receivables	17 21.0	15 24.5
45 8.1	30 12.0	31 11.9	41 9.0	54 6.8		36 10.1	36 10.1
11 33.7	66 5.5	90 4.0	100 3.6	90 4.1			86 4.2	84 4.4
65 5.6	111 3.3	125 2.9	129 2.8	116 3.2		Cost of Sales/Inventory	135 2.7	124 3.0
164 2.2	168 2.2	172 2.1	187 2.0	157 2.3		185 2.0	177 2.1
0 UND	5 68.5	7 48.7	10 35.9	22 16.4			9 39.9	9 39.7
0 UND	26 14.2	23 16.0	31 11.8	32 11.5		Cost of Sales/Payables	30 12.3	28 13.2
18 20.4	63 5.8	53 6.8	76 4.8	60 6.1		74 4.9	64 5.7
2.4	5.5	5.7	6.1	8.9			5.6	6.2
5.4	9.0	9.0	11.3	18.2		Sales/Working Capital	9.8	10.3
51.1	22.1	14.9	25.8	20.8		21.1	20.6
	5.8	8.6	10.1	13.4			4.0	4.8
	(71) 2.2	(164) 3.8	(53) 4.6	6.0		EBIT/Interest	(345) 1.9	(400) 2.2
	.8	1.9	2.2	5.7		1.1	1.2
	4.3	4.8	9.0			Net Profit + Depr., Dep.,	4.3	4.6
	(11) 1.7	(61) 2.4	(14) 2.8			Amort./Cur. Mat. L/T/D	(106) 2.0	(110) 2.1
	-.3	1.2	1.7			.8	1.0
.1	.1	.1	.2	.2			.1	.1
.3	.3	.2	.3	.4		Fixed/Worth	.3	.3
1.7	.9	.4	.7	.6		.8	.7
.2	1.1	1.3	1.8	2.4			1.4	1.3
1.4	2.6	2.3	3.5	3.5		Debt/Worth	2.6	2.7
15.0	7.2	4.2	7.0	6.0		6.3	5.4
125.8	43.8	25.4	31.3	46.0		% Profit Before Taxes/Tangible	22.1	22.7
19.1	(63) 10.2	(163) 13.2	(52) 22.8	(10) 27.7		Net Worth	(340) 9.8	(391) 11.0
2.3	1.3	6.0	11.1	20.0		2.4	2.8
28.2	6.4	6.6	8.1	11.5		% Profit Before Taxes/Total	6.3	6.8
4.4	2.3	3.8	4.7	6.6		Assets	2.5	3.2
.9	-.6	1.7	1.8	3.9		.4	.6
132.4	83.4	70.4	69.5	46.4			61.5	61.8
68.1	40.0	36.9	28.9	29.6		Sales/Net Fixed Assets	33.7	33.2
12.6	15.0	18.8	15.5	17.5		14.5	14.9
5.4	3.4	3.0	2.8	2.8			2.9	3.0
3.2	2.6	2.3	2.3	2.2		Sales/Total Assets	2.2	2.3
1.5	1.9	1.8	1.8	1.9		1.7	1.8
	.4	.5	.4	.4			.5	.5
	(65) .9	(148) .7	(45) .6	(10) .4		% Depr., Dep., Amort./Sales	(333) .8	(381) .7
	1.7	1.2	1.0	.6		1.3	1.2
	1.3	.8	.7			% Officers', Directors',	1.1	1.0
	(44) 2.3	(92) 1.6	(15) 1.1			Owners' Comp/Sales	(176) 2.1	(198) 1.9
	4.6	3.6	2.6			3.9	3.4
13030M	263049M	1992861M	2466077M	1673860M	337315M	Net Sales ($)	5450021M	7273178M
3771M	91659M	806373M	1139044M	701656M	195242M	Total Assets ($)	2580664M	3302610M

M = $ thousand   MM = $ million
See Pages 11 through 21 for Explanation of Ratios and Data

Comparative Historical Data | Current Data Sorted By Sales

Type of Statement

4/1/02-3/31/03	4/1/03-3/31/04	4/1/04-3/31/05	Type of Statement	0-1MM	1-3MM	3-5MM	5-10MM	10-25MM	25MM & OVER
40	28	27	Unqualified			1	3	4	19
75	68	68	Reviewed		3	6	16	24	19
95	103	97	Compiled	7	17	19	27	18	9
36	50	47	Tax Returns	2	12	5	10	12	6
106	84	80	Other	2	8	9	18	25	18
4/1/02-3/31/03 ALL	4/1/03-3/31/04 ALL	4/1/04-3/31/05 ALL		50 (4/1-9/30/04)		269 (10/1/04-3/31/05)			
352	333	319	**NUMBER OF STATEMENTS**	11	40	40	74	83	71

4/1/02-3/31/03	4/1/03-3/31/04	4/1/04-3/31/05		0-1MM	1-3MM	3-5MM	5-10MM	10-25MM	25MM & OVER
%	%	%	**ASSETS**	%	%	%	%	%	%
5.8	6.4	5.7	Cash & Equivalents	7.8	6.2	10.2	4.8	5.6	3.6
14.3	14.7	14.0	Trade Receivables (net)	13.3	15.1	12.9	13.2	14.5	14.5
61.7	60.4	62.7	Inventory	45.2	55.4	57.8	68.3	63.0	66.3
1.9	2.5	1.9	All Other Current	.5	.8	2.9	1.8	1.8	2.2
83.8	84.0	84.3	Total Current	66.9	77.5	83.9	88.0	84.9	86.6
10.7	10.5	10.5	Fixed Assets (net)	32.3	14.6	11.1	8.1	9.1	8.6
1.0	1.0	.7	Intangibles (net)	.0	.9	.5	.5	.9	.7
4.6	4.4	4.5	All Other Non-Current	.8	7.0	4.5	3.3	5.2	4.0
100.0	100.0	100.0	Total	100.0	100.0	100.0	100.0	100.0	100.0
			LIABILITIES						
26.7	24.8	24.9	Notes Payable-Short Term	15.6	25.0	17.7	31.7	22.6	26.0
2.3	2.3	1.9	Cur. Mat.-L/T/D	7.5	2.3	2.6	1.7	1.4	1.5
20.1	19.7	19.6	Trade Payables	4.7	18.2	19.1	14.7	23.5	23.4
.3	.2	.2	Income Taxes Payable	.1	.0	.0	.3	.2	.5
9.1	8.7	10.0	All Other Current	2.1	5.1	13.9	8.9	9.7	13.4
58.4	55.8	56.7	Total Current	30.0	50.7	53.2	57.3	57.3	64.8
8.4	8.3	8.4	Long-Term Debt	15.8	15.6	11.2	5.8	6.4	6.6
.2	.2	.3	Deferred Taxes	.0	.4	.0	.3	.3	.3
3.3	3.7	3.4	All Other Non-Current	9.5	3.8	6.2	2.9	3.1	1.8
29.6	32.0	31.2	Net Worth	44.7	29.5	29.4	33.8	33.0	26.5
100.0	100.0	100.0	Total Liabilities & Net Worth	100.0	100.0	100.0	100.0	100.0	100.0
			INCOME DATA						
100.0	100.0	100.0	Net Sales	100.0	100.0	100.0	100.0	100.0	100.0
22.1	22.5	21.3	Gross Profit	37.1	27.5	21.8	21.9	18.4	18.0
20.2	20.9	18.9	Operating Expenses	32.8	25.4	19.2	19.2	16.5	15.6
1.9	1.7	2.4	Operating Profit	4.3	2.1	2.6	2.7	1.8	2.4
.3	.0	.0	All Other Expenses (net)	.9	.9	-.1	.1	-.5	-.1
1.6	1.7	2.4	Profit Before Taxes	3.3	1.2	2.7	2.6	2.4	2.6
			RATIOS						
1.8	2.0	2.0		8.7	2.2	2.4	1.9	1.8	1.6
1.4	1.4	1.4	Current	2.0	1.5	1.6	1.5	1.4	1.3
1.2	1.2	1.2		1.1	1.1	1.2	1.3	1.2	1.1
.6	.7	.6		1.1	.7	.8	.5	.6	.5
(351) .3	.3	.3	Quick	.7	.3	.3	.3	.3	.2
.1	.1	.1		.2	.1	.2	.1	.1	.1
7 49.7	6 60.8	6 65.0		0 UND	8 48.4	9 38.7	5 66.8	5 73.1	5 66.6
15 24.2	16 23.2	13 28.9	Sales/Receivables	6 59.2	20 18.2	20 18.6	12 31.0	11 31.8	12 31.7
33 10.9	35 10.3	32 11.3		45 8.1	44 8.4	23 15.8	31 11.9	31 11.8	38 9.6
91 4.0	85 4.3	90 4.1		44 8.3	80 4.6	81 4.5	101 3.6	81 4.5	90 4.1
130 2.8	127 2.9	124 2.9	Cost of Sales/Inventory	146 2.5	166 2.2	119 3.1	139 2.6	109 3.4	111 3.3
184 2.0	176 2.1	172 2.1		326 1.1	224 1.6	189 1.9	173 2.1	158 2.3	153 2.4
9 40.9	8 43.1	7 49.8		0 UND	4 83.5	8 45.7	6 61.8	8 43.5	10 35.8
24 15.0	26 14.0	24 15.3	Cost of Sales/Payables	0 UND	36 10.3	21 17.3	20 18.3	28 12.8	32 11.5
63 5.8	65 5.6	57 6.4		7 52.3	68 5.3	57 6.5	47 7.8	57 6.5	65 5.6
5.7	5.4	5.7		2.1	4.5	4.5	5.7	6.1	7.7
9.6	9.3	9.3	Sales/Working Capital	3.7	7.6	6.5	8.4	10.7	13.4
19.2	17.1	18.5		62.3	23.4	14.3	11.6	19.9	23.4
5.7	6.0	9.2			5.7	6.5	8.4	9.7	11.0
(335) 2.2	(318) 2.8	(308) 3.8	EBIT/Interest		(39) 1.7	(39) 2.6	(73) 3.5	(81) 4.0	(69) 5.4
1.1	1.3	1.7			.1	1.8	1.5	2.0	2.6
4.6	4.7	5.3	Net Profit + Depr., Dep.,			6.6	3.7	4.9	9.3
(105) 2.1	(86) 2.2	(92) 2.6	Amort./Cur. Mat. L/T/D			(12) 3.0	(25) 1.7	(26) 2.6	(23) 3.3
1.3	1.1	1.2				.6	1.1	1.3	1.8
.1	.1	.1		.1	.1	.1	.1	.1	.2
.3	.3	.3	Fixed/Worth	1.4	.3	.3	.2	.3	.3
.7	.6	.5		1.8	1.2	.8	.4	.4	.6
1.3	1.3	1.3		.2	1.3	1.0	1.2	1.4	2.0
2.6	2.6	2.6	Debt/Worth	1.3	2.0	3.1	2.1	2.6	3.5
5.4	4.8	5.0		18.8	17.8	6.6	4.3	4.2	6.0
27.2	27.6	31.1	% Profit Before Taxes/Tangible	88.9	26.3	48.2	21.5	26.3	36.1
(334) 11.0	(316) 11.3	(301) 14.5	Net Worth	(10) 2.8	(34) 8.1	(35) 12.5	(72) 11.7	(81) 13.6	(69) 23.9
2.6	2.8	5.8		1.4	-1.6	4.6	4.9	-6.1	15.4
6.6	7.4	7.2	% Profit Before Taxes/Total	3.2	6.1	7.2	6.6	6.4	10.0
2.7	3.2	3.8	Assets	.9	1.3	3.5	3.7	4.1	6.1
.3	.6	1.3		.0	-2.4	1.3	1.0	1.7	2.7
66.2	69.7	70.7		78.0	67.1	65.2	87.2	71.7	70.7
32.6	35.3	35.5	Sales/Net Fixed Assets	8.2	22.8	40.2	39.3	38.2	36.1
15.7	15.8	16.9		1.9	12.2	12.8	18.6	21.4	20.4
2.9	3.0	3.0		2.3	2.6	2.9	3.0	3.4	3.1
2.2	2.3	2.4	Sales/Total Assets	1.4	2.0	2.2	2.3	2.8	2.5
1.7	1.7	1.8		1.0	1.5	1.5	1.9	2.1	2.0
.5	.5	.4			.6	.4	.4	.5	.4
(309) .8	(296) .8	(274) .7	% Depr., Dep., Amort./Sales		(35) .9	(38) .7	(63) .7	(73) .8	(59) .6
1.3	1.3	1.2			3.2	1.3	1.2	1.2	.8
.9	1.0	.9			1.5	1.2	1.1	.7	.7
(172) 1.7	(167) 2.2	(160) 1.8	% Officers', Directors', Owners' Comp/Sales		(21) 3.0	(23) 1.9	(47) 2.2	(41) 1.5	(21) 1.0
3.6	3.9	3.8			5.1	2.9	4.4	2.8	2.3
6345308M	6326221M	6746192M	Net Sales ($)	6060M	79686M	157277M	524047M	1253187M	4725935M
2872954M	2858546M	2937745M	Total Assets ($)	5301M	48167M	87483M	234459M	540463M	2021872M

M = $ thousand   MM = $ million
See Pages 11 through 21 for Explanation of Ratios and Data

Current Data Sorted By Assets   **Comparative Historical Data**

Type of Statement	0-500M	500M-2MM	2-10MM	10-50MM	50-100MM	100-250MM		
Unqualified		13	55	105	22	6	160	163
Reviewed	5	83	201	49			308	255
Compiled	15	126	111	11			356	328
Tax Returns	25	50	20	3	1		62	58
Other	21	88	125	46	8	7	283	334
	273 (4/1-9/30/04)			923 (10/1/04-3/31/05)			4/1/00-3/31/01	4/1/01-3/31/02
	0-500M	500M-2MM	2-10MM	10-50MM	50-100MM	100-250MM	ALL	ALL
NUMBER OF STATEMENTS	66	360	512	214	31	13	1169	1138
	%	%	%	%	%	%	%	%
ASSETS								
Cash & Equivalents	12.7	8.3	6.7	4.6	2.6	3.5	6.2	6.1
Trade Receivables (net)	35.4	36.6	34.8	30.2	26.1	26.5	34.8	31.9
Inventory	24.0	36.2	35.5	34.9	40.7	45.3	34.8	36.3
All Other Current	1.5	1.3	2.3	2.6	3.9	1.8	2.5	2.3
Total Current	73.6	82.4	79.3	72.3	73.4	77.1	78.3	76.5
Fixed Assets (net)	17.5	11.4	13.3	19.6	18.2	11.1	14.6	15.9
Intangibles (net)	1.3	1.3	1.8	2.7	3.0	4.2	1.7	2.1
All Other Non-Current	7.6	-4.9	5.6	5.3	5.4	7.6	5.5	5.4
Total	100.0	100.0	100.0	100.0	100.0	100.0	100.0	100.0
LIABILITIES								
Notes Payable-Short Term	21.3	15.7	17.1	17.1	17.7	17.8	17.0	17.5
Cur. Mat.-L/T/D	4.3	3.2	3.1	3.3	4.4	1.2	3.5	3.6
Trade Payables	27.0	23.8	21.6	16.6	17.7	17.8	21.9	20.2
Income Taxes Payable	.1	.2	.3	.3	.7	.3	.2	.2
All Other Current	11.5	8.5	10.3	11.0	13.8	11.5	9.9	9.6
Total Current	64.1	51.3	52.4	48.2	54.3	48.6	52.6	51.2
Long-Term Debt	21.4	9.7	8.3	11.4	12.6	11.2	9.3	10.0
Deferred Taxes	.0	.2	.4	.8	.5	.1	.3	.3
All Other Non-Current	6.2	5.8	2.9	4.3	2.5	4.2	2.9	3.5
Net Worth	8.3	33.0	36.1	35.3	30.1	36.0	35.0	34.9
Total Liabilities & Net Worth	100.0	100.0	100.0	100.0	100.0	100.0	100.0	100.0
INCOME DATA								
Net Sales	100.0	100.0	100.0	100.0	100.0	100.0	100.0	100.0
Gross Profit	38.8	32.3	28.7	27.5	25.0	23.8	29.1	30.2
Operating Expenses	34.0	30.0	25.9	23.8	20.9	19.0	26.4	28.2
Operating Profit	4.7	2.3	2.8	3.7	4.0	4.8	2.7	2.1
All Other Expenses (net)	.8	.3	.3	.4	.3	.2	.5	.8
Profit Before Taxes	3.9	2.0	2.5	3.3	3.7	4.6	2.2	1.3
RATIOS								
Current	1.7	2.6	2.2	2.0	1.6	2.2	2.0	2.2
	1.1	1.7	1.5	1.4	1.4	1.9	1.4	1.5
	.8	1.2	1.2	1.1	1.2	1.2	1.2	1.2
Quick	1.3	1.4	1.1	1.0	.7	1.3	1.1	1.1
	(65) .8	.9	.8	.7	.6	.5	(1168) .8	.7
	.5	.6	.5	.5	.4	.3	.5	.5
Sales/Receivables	19 19.0	31 11.6	36 10.1	37 9.8	38 9.6	43 8.4	34 10.7	31 11.7
	34 10.6	42 8.6	45 8.1	46 7.9	47 7.8	45 8.1	44 8.3	42 8.8
	53 6.9	57 6.4	56 6.5	57 6.4	60 6.1	66 5.6	57 6.5	54 6.7
Cost of Sales/Inventory	4 83.6	30 12.1	36 10.0	50 7.3	54 6.8	63 5.8	33 11.1	39 9.3
	26 14.2	58 6.2	61 6.0	70 5.2	87 4.2	122 3.0	61 6.0	65 5.6
	66 5.5	111 3.3	102 3.6	115 3.2	168 2.2	198 1.8	105 3.5	113 3.2
Cost of Sales/Payables	14 26.8	20 18.2	21 17.2	18 19.9	19 18.9	29 12.5	20 17.9	19 18.9
	35 10.6	34 10.8	35 10.5	28 13.0	38 9.7	42 8.6	34 10.7	33 11.0
	60 6.1	57 6.4	56 6.5	48 7.6	57 6.4	77 4.7	56 6.5	55 6.6
Sales/Working Capital	12.0	5.5	6.1	6.0	7.2	4.0	6.5	5.8
	44.0	9.7	10.7	11.3	9.3	7.0	11.6	10.8
	-35.0	20.9	24.6	33.5	24.2	11.3	27.8	26.8
EBIT/Interest	27.5	9.2	10.4	13.2	8.0	11.1	5.6	4.7
	(55) 4.6	(321) 3.1	(468) 3.8	(200) 4.9	4.1	6.2	(1069) 2.4	(1040) 1.8
	1.3	1.1	1.7	2.4	3.0	4.1	1.2	.6
Net Profit + Depr., Dep., Amort./Cur. Mat. L /T/D		2.8	3.9	11.0	6.9		4.6	4.0
		(73) 1.7	(146) 1.8	(76) 3.8	(14) 3.0		(333) 1.6	(327) 1.6
		.9	.9	1.6	1.3		.7	.5
Fixed/Worth	.0	.1	.1	.2	.2	.1	.1	.1
	.5	.3	.3	.6	.8	.3	.3	.3
	4.2	.9	.8	1.4	1.4	1.0	.9	.9
Debt/Worth	1.1	1.0	1.0	1.2	1.9	1.0	1.0	1.0
	6.7	2.0	2.0	2.3	2.9	2.0	2.1	2.1
	-11.1	5.6	4.2	4.9	4.3	5.6	4.5	4.6
% Profit Before Taxes/Tangible Net Worth	117.8	37.5	34.0	36.7	46.6	30.8	30.7	26.3
	(48) 41.2	(323) 12.5	(475) 14.1	(204) 20.1	(12) 22.8	23.3	(1103) 13.2	(1055) 9.0
	2.6	1.3	4.5	9.9	11.5	14.5	3.2	-1.2
% Profit Before Taxes/Total Assets	25.3	11.8	10.4	10.8	11.9	7.9	9.3	7.9
	7.1	4.1	4.2	6.3	4.9	6.6	3.8	2.5
	.4	.1	1.4	2.9	2.7	5.0	.7	-1.2
Sales/Net Fixed Assets	999.8	105.6	73.4	48.5	43.0	61.5	65.3	62.9
	40.8	41.7	31.9	16.7	17.0	15.4	29.1	27.9
	12.8	19.2	14.5	7.5	8.2	7.6	12.2	10.8
Sales/Total Assets	5.6	3.9	3.5	2.9	2.4	2.3	3.6	3.5
	3.9	3.0	2.6	2.3	2.1	1.6	2.7	2.6
	2.9	2.2	2.0	1.7	1.5	1.2	1.9	1.9
% Depr., Dep., Amort./Sales	.7	.4	.4	.5	.5	.8	.4	.5
	(37) 1.6	(270) .9	(447) .9	(192) 1.0	(25) 1.1	(11) 1.4	(1016) .9	(982) .9
	3.1	1.7	1.6	3.2	1.9	3.0	1.7	2.0
% Officers', Directors', Owners' Comp/Sales	4.3	2.8	1.7	1.0			2.2	2.1
	(37) 6.7	(179) 4.8	(205) 3.0	(36) 2.0			(488) 3.9	(425) 3.7
	9.5	8.6	6.1	3.3			6.4	6.4
Net Sales ($)	85867M	1366611M	6361428M	10384664M	4238777M	3927933M	22384003M	22282756M
Total Assets ($)	17978M	439730M	2354168M	4503896M	2147824M	2211876M	10677430M	11082306M

© RMA 2005

M = $ thousand   MM = $ million
See Pages 11 through 21 for Explanation of Ratios and Data

Comparative Historical Data / Current Data Sorted By Sales

		Comparative Historical Data		Type of Statement	273 (4/1-9/30/04)			923 (10/1/04-3/31/05)		
					0-1MM	1-3MM	3-5MM	5-10MM	10-25MM	25MM & OVER
	214	201	201	Unqualified	2	4	6	18	53	120
	378	341	338	Reviewed		29	45	99	109	54
	294	353	263	Compiled	11	61	64	73	44	10
	81	109	99	Tax Returns	15	37	18	17	10	2
	307	310	295	Other	13	54	35	62	68	63
	4/1/02-3/31/03 ALL	4/1/03-3/31/04 ALL	4/1/04-3/31/05 ALL							
NUMBER OF STATEMENTS	1274	1314	1196		41	185	168	269	284	249
ASSETS	%	%	%		%	%	%	%	%	%
Cash & Equivalents	6.7	6.9	7.0		12.5	10.6	8.3	6.0	6.3	4.3
Trade Receivables (net)	33.0	32.9	34.2		26.7	31.2	35.0	35.8	36.6	32.9
Inventory	36.0	35.7	35.2		28.4	35.9	35.2	36.2	35.0	35.1
All Other Current	2.3	2.9	2.0		.9	1.5	1.8	1.9	1.9	3.1
Total Current	77.9	78.5	78.5		68.5	79.1	80.2	80.0	79.9	75.4
Fixed Assets (net)	14.9	14.2	14.2		18.7	13.9	12.8	12.6	13.8	16.9
Intangibles (net)	1.9	1.8	1.8		2.1	1.3	1.9	1.3	1.7	2.8
All Other Non-Current	5.3	5.5	5.5		10.6	5.7	5.1	6.1	4.7	4.8
Total	100.0	100.0	100.0		100.0	100.0	100.0	100.0	100.0	100.0
LIABILITIES										
Notes Payable-Short Term	17.9	17.8	16.9		25.0	17.3	14.6	14.8	18.3	17.6
Cur. Mat.-L/T/D	3.6	3.4	3.2		3.2	3.8	3.2	3.4	3.1	2.9
Trade Payables	20.9	20.8	21.5		19.7	22.8	21.6	23.6	21.7	18.3
Income Taxes Payable	.2	.2	.3		.0	.2	.3	.2	.3	.3
All Other Current	10.2	10.4	10.0		11.1	9.2	8.1	9.6	10.4	11.8
Total Current	52.8	52.5	52.0		59.1	53.3	47.8	51.6	53.9	50.9
Long-Term Debt	9.4	9.2	10.2		28.1	11.9	10.0	7.6	8.3	10.8
Deferred Taxes	.2	.3	.4		.0	.2	.4	.3	.5	.4
All Other Non-Current	3.6	4.0	4.2		6.8	4.2	5.5	4.5	3.5	3.3
Net Worth	34.0	33.9	33.3		6.0	30.3	36.4	36.0	33.8	34.5
Total Liabilities & Net Worth	100.0	100.0	100.0		100.0	100.0	100.0	100.0	100.0	100.0
INCOME DATA										
Net Sales	100.0	100.0	100.0		100.0	100.0	100.0	100.0	100.0	100.0
Gross Profit	30.4	30.8	30.0		41.7	37.6	30.8	29.4	27.1	25.6
Operating Expenses	28.6	28.6	27.0		36.0	35.0	28.3	26.9	24.1	22.0
Operating Profit	1.8	2.1	3.0		5.7	2.6	2.5	2.5	3.0	3.6
All Other Expenses (net)	.7	.5	.4		1.6	.4	.3	.3	.3	.3
Profit Before Taxes	1.1	1.6	2.6		4.1	2.2	2.2	2.2	2.7	3.3
RATIOS										
Current	2.1	2.2	2.2		2.0	2.8	2.5	2.1	2.2	1.9
	1.5	1.5	1.5		1.1	1.6	1.7	1.6	1.4	1.4
	1.2	1.2	1.2		.7	1.2	1.2	1.2	1.1	1.2
Quick	1.2	1.2	1.2		1.1	1.4	1.4	1.1	1.1	1.1
	.7	.8	(1195) .8		.5	(184) .8	.9	.8	.8	.7
	.5	.5	.5		.3	.5	.6	.6	.5	.5
Sales/Receivables	33 11.0	34 10.7	34 10.6		30 12.0	27 13.5	33 11.0	34 10.7	37 9.9	37 10.0
	44 8.3	44 8.3	44 8.3		41 9.0	41 8.8	44 8.2	44 8.3	45 8.0	45 8.2
	55 6.7	56 6.6	56 6.5		77 4.7	57 6.4	59 6.2	56 6.5	56 6.5	55 6.6
Cost of Sales/Inventory	36 10.1	37 9.9	36 10.1		3 123.7	29 12.8	35 10.4	33 11.0	36 10.0	43 8.5
	67 5.4	66 5.6	61 5.9		61 6.0	77 4.7	58 6.3	62 5.9	59 6.2	65 5.6
	110 3.3	112 3.3	107 3.4		156 2.3	171 2.1	109 3.4	102 3.6	88 4.2	99 3.7
Cost of Sales/Payables	21 17.7	20 18.3	20 18.1		16 23.1	17 21.0	21 17.3	23 16.1	19 18.8	19 18.9
	34 10.8	34 10.8	33 11.0		45 8.2	38 9.7	35 10.4	35 10.3	32 11.4	28 12.8
	54 6.8	55 6.6	55 6.7		103 3.5	74 5.0	57 6.4	55 6.6	51 7.1	46 8.0
Sales/Working Capital	5.7	5.6	6.1		2.7	4.3	5.4	6.3	6.5	6.9
	10.6	10.6	10.8		36.7	9.3	8.4	10.7	12.2	11.3
	28.4	26.4	27.2		-13.8	28.0	20.0	20.2	30.1	28.7
EBIT/Interest	5.6	6.5	10.2		6.5	8.8	7.4	10.2	11.5	12.9
	(1163) 2.2	(1200) 2.6	(1088) 3.8		(34) 2.0	(160) 2.9	(148) 2.9	(245) 3.6	(263) 3.8	(238) 5.6
	.7	1.0	1.7		.7	1.0	.8	1.6	1.8	2.7
Net Profit + Depr., Dep., Amort./Cur. Mat. L/T/D	4.5	3.8	5.8			4.5	2.7	2.6	6.3	11.6
	(386) 1.7	(322) 1.5	(316) 2.1			(32) 2.0	(41) 1.2	(64) 1.3	(92) 2.3	(86) 4.6
	.6	.6	1.0			1.0	.5	.7	1.2	1.6
Fixed/Worth	.1	.1	.1		.0	.1	.1	.1	.1	.2
	.4	.3	.3		.4	.3	.3	.3	.3	.5
	1.0	1.0	1.0		3.8	1.4	.9	.7	1.0	1.2
Debt/Worth	.9	.9	1.0		2.1	.9	.8	1.0	1.0	1.3
	2.0	2.1	2.2		6.6	2.1	1.8	1.8	2.2	2.3
	4.7	5.2	5.1		-7.5	8.5	4.8	4.4	4.6	4.3
% Profit Before Taxes/Tangible Net Worth	23.6	29.3	37.3		88.9	39.0	35.0	32.3	36.0	46.4
	(1166) 8.4	(1201) 9.6	(1093) 15.4		(29) 4.8	(157) 12.2	(153) 8.3	(252) 13.9	(264) 15.2	(238) 23.0
	.0	1.0	4.5		-.8	1.5	.6	3.9	6.1	12.4
% Profit Before Taxes/Total Assets	7.3	8.5	11.1		18.4	12.6	9.1	10.9	10.6	12.0
	2.6	3.0	4.6		2.9	4.0	3.4	4.1	4.8	7.1
	-.6	.1	1.4		-.4	-.1	-.3	1.3	1.7	3.5
Sales/Net Fixed Assets	64.9	67.0	76.0		UND	104.6	83.5	81.1	85.4	57.9
	29.3	28.5	30.9		19.9	30.9	37.1	33.9	36.3	20.3
	11.7	12.5	12.9		7.0	12.7	16.6	16.9	14.1	8.7
Sales/Total Assets	3.5	3.4	3.6		3.5	3.8	3.7	3.7	3.6	3.3
	2.6	2.6	2.7		1.9	2.6	2.6	2.8	2.5	2.5
	1.8	1.8	1.9		.9	1.6	2.0	2.0	2.1	1.9
% Depr., Dep., Amort./Sales	.6	.5	.5		.9	.7	.4	.5	.4	.5
	(1126) 1.0	(1124) 1.0	(982) .9		(21) 2.3	(135) 1.1	(134) .9	(218) .9	(255) .8	(219) .9
	1.9	1.8	1.9		5.3	2.4	1.8	1.6	1.6	2.5
% Officers', Directors', Owners' Comp/Sales	2.2	2.1	2.0		6.2	4.0	2.5	2.0	1.2	.8
	(522) 4.0	(520) 4.2	(457) 4.0		(15) 8.3	(103) 6.6	(82) 5.1	(130) 3.6	(93) 2.3	(34) 1.9
	6.4	7.1	7.2		15.5	10.1	9.0	5.3	4.1	2.9
Net Sales ($)	23734568M	25007693M	26365280M		23501M	369544M	679303M	1925273M	4609458M	18758201M
Total Assets ($)	11655315M	12303643M	11675472M		18893M	174763M	294643M	798561M	1879422M	8509190M

M = $ thousand   MM = $ million
See Pages 11 through 21 for Explanation of Ratios and Data

Current Data Sorted By Assets | | | | | | | | **Comparative Historical Data**

0-500M	500M-2MM	2-10MM	10-50MM	50-100MM	100-250MM	Type of Statement	ALL 676	ALL 623
1	7	30	36	4	1	Unqualified	88	85
2	43	104	22			Reviewed	164	136
6	58	60	3			Compiled	191	198
5	21	15	1			Tax Returns	42	33
8	38	67	27	4	4	Other	191	171
	138 (4/1-9/30/04)		429 (10/1/04-3/31/05)				4/1/00-3/31/01	4/1/01-3/31/02
22	167	276	89	8	5	NUMBER OF STATEMENTS	676	623
%	%	%	%	%	%	**ASSETS**	%	%
13.7	6.4	5.9	3.8			Cash & Equivalents	5.1	6.0
36.2	36.1	34.2	33.1			Trade Receivables (net)	35.5	32.7
28.3	36.0	37.7	36.8			Inventory	36.8	37.6
2.5	2.3	1.4	3.1			All Other Current	1.9	2.1
80.7	80.8	79.2	76.8			Total Current	79.4	78.3
14.0	12.1	12.9	13.0			Fixed Assets (net)	12.3	13.2
.4	2.7	1.9	3.5			Intangibles (net)	3.2	3.1
4.7	4.4	5.9	6.7			All Other Non-Current	5.2	5.3
100.0	100.0	100.0	100.0			Total	100.0	100.0
						LIABILITIES		
14.9	14.9	16.7	16.1			Notes Payable-Short Term	17.0	17.4
1.4	3.0	2.3	2.5			Cur. Mat.-L/T/D	2.5	2.8
26.3	22.7	21.6	22.5			Trade Payables	21.7	19.7
.0	.1	.4	.2			Income Taxes Payable	.3	.3
12.2	6.6	7.1	7.1			All Other Current	7.3	7.8
55.0	47.5	48.1	48.4			Total Current	48.8	48.0
7.3	10.8	8.7	11.7			Long-Term Debt	9.7	9.0
.1	.3	.3	.6			Deferred Taxes	.1	.2
3.1	5.1	4.5	1.3			All Other Non-Current	4.0	3.3
34.5	36.3	38.3	38.0			Net Worth	37.2	39.4
100.0	100.0	100.0	100.0			Total Liabilities & Net Worth	100.0	100.0
						INCOME DATA		
100.0	100.0	100.0	100.0			Net Sales	100.0	100.0
34.9	31.6	29.0	27.1			Gross Profit	29.5	29.5
31.8	27.8	25.9	22.5			Operating Expenses	26.2	26.7
3.1	3.8	3.1	4.6			Operating Profit	3.3	2.8
–.4	.6	.3	.3			All Other Expenses (net)	.7	.8
3.6	3.2	2.8	4.4			Profit Before Taxes	2.6	2.0
						RATIOS		
3.0	2.6	2.4	2.2				2.6	2.8
1.7	1.7	1.7	1.6			Current	1.6	1.7
1.2	1.3	1.2	1.3				1.2	1.2
1.5	1.5	1.2	1.1				1.3	1.3
1.1	.9	.8	.8			Quick	.8	.8
.6	.6	.6	.6				.6	.5
28 13.1	33 11.0	37 9.8	37 9.9				36 10.3	33 11.1
46 8.0	42 8.8	44 8.3	44 8.3			Sales/Receivables	44 8.3	41 8.9
57 6.4	50 7.3	52 7.0	55 6.6				53 6.8	50 7.3
18 19.8	33 11.0	42 8.7	42 8.7				41 8.8	42 8.7
56 6.6	58 6.3	62 5.5	66 5.9			Cost of Sales/Inventory	62 5.9	67 5.5
100 3.6	96 3.8	106 3.4	102 3.6				99 3.7	106 3.5
20 18.4	22 16.6	23 16.0	24 15.2				22 16.4	18 19.8
43 8.4	35 10.6	35 10.4	39 9.4			Cost of Sales/Payables	34 10.8	30 12.2
71 5.1	52 7.0	50 7.3	55 6.6				50 7.3	49 7.4
4.6	5.8	5.4	5.4				5.7	5.2
9.5	9.0	9.2	8.6			Sales/Working Capital	9.6	9.4
NM	21.3	21.9	18.3				22.9	24.2
9.7	10.9	11.7	11.5				7.4	6.6
(15) 4.0	(147) 4.2	(256) 4.5	(85) 5.9			EBIT/Interest	(599) 2.7	(560) 2.2
1.0	1.8	1.6	2.7				1.3	.9
	5.8	9.1	6.9				6.6	4.7
	(35) 2.3	(91) 2.8	(34) 3.2			Net Profit + Depr., Dep., Amort./Cur. Mat. L /T/D	(215) 3.0	(166) 1.9
	.7	1.3	1.9				1.3	.7
.1	.1	.1	.1				.1	.1
.3	.3	.2	.3			Fixed/Worth	.3	.3
1.0	.9	.7	.6				.8	.7
.6	.7	.8	.9				.8	.7
1.5	1.6	1.6	1.9			Debt/Worth	1.9	1.6
6.0	5.2	4.2	4.0				4.5	4.0
34.2	42.7	36.7	44.2				34.9	30.5
(19) 16.2	(141) 15.8	(258) 14.6	(84) 23.2			% Profit Before Taxes/Tangible Net Worth	(624) 15.1	(572) 11.4
2.5	3.4	4.2	9.2				3.7	.7
12.8	12.8	12.6	14.2				12.1	10.9
6.0	6.6	4.7	7.4			% Profit Before Taxes/Total Assets	4.9	4.1
–.3	1.4	1.4	2.5				.8	–.1
141.6	120.6	77.6	79.1				70.0	71.1
36.9	42.6	38.9	30.6			Sales/Net Fixed Assets	35.0	34.0
13.5	19.4	14.2	12.9				16.7	16.2
3.7	3.9	3.5	3.4				3.7	3.6
3.1	3.0	2.7	2.6			Sales/Total Assets	2.9	2.8
2.5	2.2	2.1	1.9				2.1	2.0
.5	.4	.5	.4				.4	.4
(13) .8	(131) .8	(248) .8	(84) .7			% Depr., Dep., Amort./Sales	(579) .8	(542) .8
2.0	1.4	1.3	1.4				1.4	1.4
5.2	3.1	2.1	.5				2.2	2.1
(11) 7.9	(81) 4.9	(112) 3.5	(19) 1.7			% Officers', Directors', Owners' Comp/Sales	(301) 3.8	(284) 3.9
17.5	7.4	6.0	3.8				6.6	6.1
25305M	636546M	3429700M	4830321M	661505M	1650285M	Net Sales ($)	12758597M	10931687M
6915M	201270M	1245400M	1812018M	508402M	652443M	Total Assets ($)	5395088M	4580510M

Comparative Historical Data — Current Data Sorted By Sales

			Type of Statement						
85	92	79	Unqualified	1	3	5	7	22	41
182	177	171	Reviewed	2	12	25	46	61	25
130	157	127	Compiled	5	26	31	38	21	6
42	56	42	Tax Returns	2	14	9	10	5	2
167	165	148	Other	4	19	18	36	38	33
4/1/02-3/31/03 ALL	4/1/03-3/31/04 ALL	4/1/04-3/31/05 ALL		138 (4/1-9/30/04)			429 (10/1/04-3/31/05)		
				0-1MM	1-3MM	3-5MM	5-10MM	10-25MM	25MM & OVER
606	647	567	NUMBER OF STATEMENTS	14	74	88	137	147	107
%	%	%	**ASSETS**	%	%	%	%	%	%
7.0	6.0	6.0	Cash & Equivalents	14.2	8.4	5.1	5.8	6.5	3.8
31.9	33.4	34.5	Trade Receivables (net)	26.1	31.3	32.7	36.6	34.7	36.1
36.8	37.6	36.5	Inventory	36.8	34.6	37.6	36.9	36.1	37.2
2.0	2.0	2.0	All Other Current	1.8	3.5	2.1	1.1	1.7	2.2
77.6	79.0	79.0	Total Current	78.8	77.8	77.6	80.4	79.0	79.3
13.5	12.3	12.6	Fixed Assets (net)	14.4	13.6	15.3	11.8	12.9	10.1
4.2	3.5	2.8	Intangibles (net)	.3	4.6	1.6	1.2	2.9	4.7
4.7	5.1	5.6	All Other Non-Current	6.0	4.0	5.5	6.7	5.2	5.9
100.0	100.0	100.0	Total	100.0	100.0	100.0	100.0	100.0	100.0
			LIABILITIES						
16.8	16.4	16.1	Notes Payable-Short Term	23.9	15.8	12.8	16.6	15.2	18.5
3.6	2.6	2.5	Cur. Mat.-L/T/D	5.2	3.1	2.7	2.0	2.4	2.3
19.6	21.8	22.1	Trade Payables	17.9	19.4	22.4	22.1	21.7	24.7
.2	.2	.3	Income Taxes Payable	.0	.2	.1	.2	.4	.5
8.0	8.6	7.1	All Other Current	7.1	9.5	6.7	6.3	7.5	6.4
48.2	49.7	48.1	Total Current	54.1	48.1	44.8	47.2	47.2	52.4
10.5	9.4	9.8	Long-Term Debt	4.6	13.3	11.9	7.7	9.5	9.4
.2	.2	.3	Deferred Taxes	.2	.4	.2	.4	.3	.3
4.0	4.5	4.2	All Other Non-Current	6.2	6.5	5.1	4.1	3.8	2.0
37.1	36.2	37.6	Net Worth	34.9	31.6	37.9	40.7	39.1	36.0
100.0	100.0	100.0	Total Liabilities & Net Worth	100.0	100.0	100.0	100.0	100.0	100.0
			INCOME DATA						
100.0	100.0	100.0	Net Sales	100.0	100.0	100.0	100.0	100.0	100.0
30.5	30.3	29.9	Gross Profit	48.2	32.5	30.8	29.9	29.6	25.5
28.3	27.5	26.1	Operating Expenses	37.3	29.3	27.9	27.2	25.4	20.8
2.2	2.8	3.8	Operating Profit	10.9	3.2	2.9	2.7	4.3	4.6
.6	.6	.4	All Other Expenses (net)	.9	.7	.3	.2	.2	.6
1.7	2.2	3.4	Profit Before Taxes	10.0	2.5	2.6	2.5	4.0	4.0
			RATIOS						
2.7	2.5	2.4	Current	3.1	2.8	2.5	2.5	2.5	2.1
1.7	1.7	1.7		1.9	1.7	1.8	1.7	1.7	1.6
1.2	1.2	1.3		.9	1.3	1.3	1.3	1.2	1.2
1.3	1.3	1.3	Quick	1.5	1.5	1.3	1.3	1.4	1.0
.8	.8	.8		.9	.9	.8	.9	.9	.8
.5	.6	.6		.3	.5	.6	.6	.6	.6
33 11.0	34 10.7	35 10.3	Sales/Receivables	41 8.9	32 11.4	34 10.9	38 9.6	35 10.3	37 10.0
41 9.0	43 8.6	43 8.4		47 7.7	41 8.8	42 8.8	44 8.2	43 8.6	44 8.3
51 7.2	54 6.8	53 6.9		60 6.1	56 6.5	54 6.8	52 7.0	51 7.1	54 6.8
42 8.7	44 8.4	41 8.9	Cost of Sales/Inventory	52 7.0	20 18.1	42 8.7	40 9.1	42 8.6	38 9.5
69 5.3	71 5.2	62 5.9		133 2.8	66 5.5	65 5.6	61 5.9	62 5.9	57 6.4
110 3.3	114 3.2	104 3.5		375 1.0	120 3.0	111 3.3	104 3.5	90 4.0	98 3.7
20 18.2	23 16.0	23 16.1	Cost of Sales/Payables	30 12.1	16 22.4	23 15.7	24 15.1	22 16.5	24 15.3
33 11.2	34 10.6	35 10.4		56 6.5	33 10.9	38 9.6	35 10.3	33 11.1	39 9.3
48 7.6	52 7.1	51 7.1		141 2.6	51 7.1	55 6.6	50 7.2	48 7.6	52 6.8
5.2	5.4	5.5	Sales/Working Capital	3.0	4.4	5.4	5.7	5.6	6.3
9.2	8.4	9.1		5.1	7.7	8.9	8.9	8.9	11.9
24.7	21.0	20.9		-9.5	16.3	18.8	21.1	22.1	20.5
6.7	8.0	11.0	EBIT/Interest	12.9	8.5	8.3	11.6	14.9	11.9
(550) 2.6	(592) 3.0	(515) 4.6		(10) 4.6	(64) 3.1	(77) 3.3	(127) 5.0	(133) 5.4	(104) 6.1
1.0	1.3	1.7		1.8	.8	1.6	1.6	2.0	2.5
5.0	4.5	8.0	Net Profit + Depr., Dep., Amort./Cur. Mat. L/T/D			5.3	8.9	6.8	10.5
(181) 1.7	(169) 1.8	(167) 2.8			(24) 1.8	(44) 2.7	(44) 3.4	(46) 4.1	
.6	.9	1.4				.5	1.3	1.5	1.9
.1	.1	.1	Fixed/Worth	.0	.1	.1	.1	.1	.1
.3	.3	.3		.1	.3	.4	.2	.2	.3
1.0	.8	.8		2.0	1.5	1.1	.6	.6	.7
.8	.8	.8	Debt/Worth	.6	.8	.7	.7	.7	1.2
1.7	1.8	1.7		1.8	1.9	1.6	1.4	1.6	2.1
5.1	5.0	4.6		NM	13.6	4.8	4.1	4.2	5.5
25.3	30.4	41.3	% Profit Before Taxes/Tangible Net Worth	52.4	41.4	36.0	28.9	47.0	44.3
(534) 10.4	(575) 11.9	(511) 16.4		(11) 16.7	(59) 15.4	(78) 10.2	(126) 11.1	(138) 20.0	(99) 23.4
1.9	2.6	4.7		11.2	.0	2.3	3.4	7.2	9.2
9.6	9.5	13.0	% Profit Before Taxes/Total Assets	16.1	14.1	9.9	11.9	13.8	14.2
3.5	3.9	5.8		7.7	4.5	3.6	4.9	7.4	7.1
.1	.6	1.6		3.6	-.6	.8	1.3	2.0	2.4
71.0	79.4	89.1	Sales/Net Fixed Assets	UND	85.9	88.5	93.1	74.6	87.9
31.7	34.8	38.5		44.3	34.8	26.2	42.1	41.0	38.8
14.4	16.2	15.1		9.6	13.4	11.7	14.9	15.9	18.5
3.5	3.4	3.6	Sales/Total Assets	2.1	3.2	3.5	3.7	3.7	3.7
2.8	2.7	2.8		1.3	2.6	2.7	2.8	2.9	2.9
2.0	2.0	2.1		.9	2.0	2.1	2.1	2.2	2.3
.5	.5	.4	% Depr., Dep., Amort./Sales		.6	.6	.4	.5	.3
(535) .9	(541) .9	(485) .8			(52) 1.0	(75) 1.0	(124) .8	(131) .8	(97) .6
1.6	1.5	1.3			1.8	1.8	1.3	1.2	1.1
2.3	2.3	2.2	% Officers', Directors', Owners' Comp/Sales		2.9	3.2	2.5	2.0	.7
(250) 3.8	(246) 4.0	(225) 4.0			(43) 5.6	(39) 4.6	(62) 4.4	(50) 3.3	(27) 2.0
6.4	6.4	6.5			9.2	7.0	6.5	5.2	3.8
12091072M	12143638M	11233662M	Net Sales ($)	7511M	150537M	353764M	1003133M	2265995M	7452722M
5488228M	5110697M	4426448M	Total Assets ($)	5843M	65762M	146023M	393094M	934096M	2881630M

© RMA 2005

M = $ thousand   MM = $ million

See Pages 11 through 21 for Explanation of Ratios and Data

Current Data Sorted By Assets | Comparative Historical Data

0-500M	500M-2MM	2-10MM	10-50MM	50-100MM	100-250MM	Type of Statement	4/1/00-3/31/01 ALL	4/1/01-3/31/02 ALL
	1	4	3		1	Unqualified	14	13
2	7	25	4			Reviewed	42	37
4	11	11	1			Compiled	41	38
6	10	2				Tax Returns	12	12
5	15	18	4		1	Other	46	48
	36 (4/1-9/30/04)			99 (10/1/04-3/31/05)			4/1/00-3/31/01	4/1/01-3/31/02
17	44	60	12		2	NUMBER OF STATEMENTS	155	148
%	%	%	%	%	%	**ASSETS**	%	%
5.8	5.9	6.8	8.5			Cash & Equivalents	6.2	7.6
29.6	38.4	33.8	22.9			Trade Receivables (net)	33.4	29.1
36.6	35.0	31.4	34.9			Inventory	32.9	34.8
1.6	1.5	2.8	2.5			All Other Current	2.0	3.2
73.6	80.9	74.8	68.8			Total Current	74.4	74.6
18.0	10.3	14.4	18.0			Fixed Assets (net)	16.0	16.4
5.2	3.8	4.6	3.8			Intangibles (net)	3.6	3.6
3.3	5.0	6.2	9.5			All Other Non-Current	6.0	5.3
100.0	100.0	100.0	100.0			Total	100.0	100.0
						LIABILITIES		
9.9	15.5	15.1	20.4			Notes Payable-Short Term	17.4	14.9
3.5	2.0	2.6	1.9			Cur. Mat.-L/T/D	3.4	3.1
25.6	27.9	19.6	13.4			Trade Payables	20.5	20.3
.1	.1	.4	.1			Income Taxes Payable	.2	.1
7.4	10.1	9.0	8.4			All Other Current	10.4	8.6
46.5	55.6	46.9	44.2			Total Current	51.9	47.0
21.1	8.4	9.9	9.7			Long-Term Debt	11.8	12.8
.0	.1	.4	.0			Deferred Taxes	.1	.1
3.6	6.2	4.9	26.4			All Other Non-Current	4.3	5.0
28.7	29.7	37.9	19.6			Net Worth	31.9	35.0
100.0	100.0	100.0	100.0			Total Liabilities & Net Worth	100.0	100.0
						INCOME DATA		
100.0	100.0	100.0	100.0			Net Sales	100.0	100.0
35.6	29.7	28.4	35.6			Gross Profit	33.1	35.4
31.4	27.8	24.5	29.6			Operating Expenses	30.9	32.6
4.2	1.9	3.9	6.1			Operating Profit	2.3	2.8
.2	.4	.2	2.8			All Other Expenses (net)	.5	.8
4.0	1.5	3.7	3.3			Profit Before Taxes	1.8	2.1
						RATIOS		
2.3	2.0	2.3	2.3			Current	2.4	2.4
1.7	1.6	1.4	1.4				1.5	1.5
1.1	1.2	1.1	1.2				1.1	1.2
1.3	1.2	1.2	.7			Quick	1.2	1.2
.8	.8	.8	.6				.8	.8
.5	.6	.6	.4				.5	.5
15 23.7	25 14.5	31 11.6	17 21.1			Sales/Receivables	28 13.2	20 18.4
28 13.1	40 9.0	40 9.0	24 15.1				38 9.7	34 10.8
40 9.1	48 7.7	51 7.2	43 8.5				51 7.1	45 8.1
10 38.0	32 11.6	34 10.6	41 8.9			Cost of Sales/Inventory	37 10.0	38 9.7
47 7.7	53 6.9	47 7.8	82 4.4				55 6.6	57 6.4
71 5.1	80 4.5	70 5.2	92 3.9				87 4.2	93 3.9
21 17.6	21 17.2	18 20.3	18 20.1			Cost of Sales/Payables	17 21.0	17 21.8
44 8.4	33 11.1	30 12.1	25 14.4				31 11.9	31 11.8
48 7.6	49 7.4	40 9.2	36 10.1				51 7.2	55 6.7
9.9	8.0	7.4	9.4			Sales/Working Capital	7.0	6.4
15.2	12.2	13.6	21.3				12.9	11.2
38.1	25.2	53.1	28.7				32.5	25.9
9.2	5.5	19.3	13.8			EBIT/Interest	6.4	5.5
(14) 4.6	(37) 1.9	(56) 4.2	(10) 4.2				(145) 2.7	(133) 2.1
2.7	.5	1.6	2.2				1.4	1.0
		16.0				Net Profit + Depr., Dep., Amort./Cur. Mat. L /T/D	5.0	4.1
	(22) 2.8						(42) 1.9	(35) 1.6
		1.4					.9	.7
.3	.2	.1	.3			Fixed/Worth	.2	.2
.6	.3	.4	1.1				.4	.4
NM	NM	.9	4.1				.9	1.1
.9	.9	.9	1.7			Debt/Worth	.9	.9
4.3	2.3	2.2	3.4				2.1	2.5
NM	NM	6.8	21.1				4.4	5.1
76.0	27.0	44.1	55.2			% Profit Before Taxes/Tangible Net Worth	33.4	32.9
(13) 28.8	(33) 8.7	(56) 16.1	(10) 22.1				(137) 16.5	(130) 11.0
.9	.8	5.9	6.8				4.6	.4
23.6	7.6	14.4	11.7			% Profit Before Taxes/Total Assets	11.4	10.7
10.8	1.8	6.6	9.4				5.9	3.2
2.8	.1	1.8	.5				1.1	-.3
107.0	81.2	69.1	22.5			Sales/Net Fixed Assets	55.9	56.5
39.7	38.7	35.2	16.6				30.3	26.0
15.3	24.8	16.0	8.1				15.3	12.3
5.6	4.4	3.8	4.4			Sales/Total Assets	4.1	3.9
4.0	3.5	2.8	3.0				3.1	3.1
2.5	2.8	2.2	1.3				2.2	2.3
.4	.5	.5	.8			% Depr., Dep., Amort./Sales	.5	.5
(14) .8	(36) .9	(50) .8	1.3				(134) 1.0	(127) .8
1.5	1.4	1.4	1.9				1.6	1.8
3.3	2.0	2.0				% Officers', Directors', Owners' Comp/Sales	2.6	2.5
(12) 5.3	(25) 3.1	(26) 2.7					(75) 4.9	(71) 3.9
7.0	5.2	4.8					7.9	7.0
18079M	187496M	845156M	683638M		586642M	Net Sales ($)	2310040M	1840596M
4819M	51846M	277313M	230255M		319377M	Total Assets ($)	910571M	707049M

(Middle columns 50-100MM and 100-250MM: DATA NOT AVAILABLE)

M = $ thousand   MM = $ million
See Pages 11 through 21 for Explanation of Ratios and Data

Comparative Historical Data				Type of Statement	Current Data Sorted By Sales					
15	13	9		Unqualified		1			4	4
57	57	38		Reviewed	1	3	6	9	10	9
34	42	27		Compiled	1	5	5	9	7	
17	20	18		Tax Returns	2	6	5	4	1	
38	36	43		Other	3	9	6	11	8	6
4/1/02-3/31/03 ALL	4/1/03-3/31/04 ALL	4/1/04-3/31/05 ALL			0-1MM	36 (4/1-9/30/04) 1-3MM	3-5MM	99 (10/1/04-3/31/05) 5-10MM	10-25MM	25MM & OVER
161	168	135		**NUMBER OF STATEMENTS**	7	23	23	33	30	19
%	%	%		**ASSETS**	%	%	%	%	%	%
5.7	5.4	6.5		Cash & Equivalents	6.8	6.1	7.3	5.9	6.1	
31.5	32.0	33.5		Trade Receivables (net)	36.5	33.4	33.9	37.6	27.4	
35.8	34.8	33.5		Inventory	36.4	32.7	31.3	31.5	38.8	
3.3	2.4	2.2		All Other Current	2.8	2.3	1.7	1.9	3.0	
76.4	74.6	75.7		Total Current	82.5	74.6	74.2	76.9	75.2	
13.8	14.8	13.7		Fixed Assets (net)	11.5	16.4	11.6	12.3	13.2	
4.8	4.2	5.0		Intangibles (net)	2.1	3.3	6.5	4.4	7.8	
5.0	6.4	5.6		All Other Non-Current	3.9	5.7	7.6	6.4	3.8	
100.0	100.0	100.0		Total	100.0	100.0	100.0	100.0	100.0	
				LIABILITIES						
15.9	15.3	14.9		Notes Payable-Short Term	10.4	17.0	12.9	16.4	19.8	
4.4	3.3	2.5		Cur. Mat.-L/T/D	2.4	1.5	3.2	2.3	2.4	
23.4	21.2	22.4		Trade Payables	27.5	19.3	24.8	20.9	20.0	
.1	.1	.2		Income Taxes Payable	.1	.3	.2	.4	.2	
9.5	10.6	9.1		All Other Current	10.3	11.4	8.8	9.4	6.5	
53.2	50.6	49.1		Total Current	50.7	49.5	49.9	49.4	48.9	
12.7	11.2	11.3		Long-Term Debt	12.8	8.5	11.1	9.0	11.4	
.2	.2	.2		Deferred Taxes	.0	.3	.3	.4	.0	
4.6	5.1	7.0		All Other Non-Current	2.9	12.1	5.3	8.6	7.9	
29.3	32.9	32.3		Net Worth	33.5	29.7	33.3	32.6	31.7	
100.0	100.0	100.0		Total Liabilities & Net Worth	100.0	100.0	100.0	100.0	100.0	
				INCOME DATA						
100.0	100.0	100.0		Net Sales	100.0	100.0	100.0	100.0	100.0	
32.4	31.6	30.5		Gross Profit	32.2	30.3	27.3	30.5	29.7	
30.1	28.9	26.9		Operating Expenses	29.0	28.3	23.4	26.2	26.2	
2.3	2.7	3.6		Operating Profit	3.2	1.9	3.9	4.3	3.5	
.6	.7	.5		All Other Expenses (net)	-.3	.1	.4	1.3	.7	
1.7	2.0	3.1		Profit Before Taxes	3.4	1.8	3.5	3.0	2.8	
				RATIOS						
2.0	2.1	2.2			2.2	2.5	2.4	2.1	2.0	
1.4	1.4	1.6		Current	1.7	1.4	1.6	1.5	1.4	
1.1	1.1	1.2			1.3	1.1	1.1	1.1	1.2	
1.0	1.0	1.2			1.2	1.3	1.5	1.2	.7	
.7	.7	.7		Quick	.8	.7	.8	.8	.6	
.5	.5	.6			.7	.5	.6	.7	.5	
26 14.1	23 16.2	25 14.8		Sales/Receivables	23 16.1	25 14.4	24 15.0	33 10.9	18 20.5	
35 10.4	37 9.8	38 9.7			38 9.7	40 9.1	40 9.1	41 8.9	24 14.9	
47 7.8	49 7.5	48 7.6			53 6.9	51 7.2	51 7.1	51 7.2	41 9.0	
37 9.8	35 10.4	34 10.8		Cost of Sales/Inventory	36 10.2	29 12.4	29 12.4	37 9.9	36 10.1	
58 6.3	55 6.6	51 7.2			67 5.4	54 6.8	43 8.5	56 6.6	46 7.9	
86 4.2	83 4.4	77 4.7			85 4.3	76 4.8	69 5.3	77 4.7	92 4.0	
21 17.3	19 19.3	20 18.4		Cost of Sales/Payables	22 16.3	15 24.6	17 21.8	20 18.3	24 15.1	
34 10.8	32 11.6	31 11.6			44 8.4	31 12.0	27 13.4	34 10.8	32 11.5	
54 6.7	49 7.5	45 8.1			49 7.4	43 8.5	42 8.8	45 8.1	38 9.6	
7.8	7.5	7.9		Sales/Working Capital	6.5	7.9	8.8	7.3	9.3	
13.9	15.3	12.8			8.9	14.8	15.6	11.6	18.7	
40.5	62.4	29.4			28.3	32.7	67.8	43.2	24.7	
8.0	9.6	9.2		EBIT/Interest	8.6	9.1	17.7	19.1	9.8	
(150) 3.0	(161) 3.8	(119) 3.4			(17) 3.1	(22) 2.3	(29) 2.8	(27) 4.3	(18) 4.5	
1.0	1.5	1.4			1.3	-.9	1.2	2.0	2.9	
4.5	5.3	5.4		Net Profit + Depr., Dep., Amort./Cur. Mat. L/T/D			17.7	2.9		
(52) 1.7	(50) 2.6	(36) 2.4					(10) 3.8	(10) 1.8		
.6	1.2	1.1					.7	1.3		
.2	.1	.2		Fixed/Worth	.2	.2	.2	.2	.2	
.5	.4	.4			.4	.3	.5	.4	.6	
1.4	1.3	1.9			1.0	1.9	NM	1.0	1.1	
1.1	1.0	1.0		Debt/Worth	.7	1.0	.8	1.0	1.6	
2.7	2.5	2.3			1.9	2.5	2.0	2.8	3.2	
7.9	5.9	7.9			6.1	7.9	NM	7.7	5.3	
48.5	40.0	44.0		% Profit Before Taxes/Tangible Net Worth	43.8	37.2	40.0	42.8	54.2	
(140) 17.9	(143) 18.4	(113) 14.8			(19) 16.5	(19) 8.7	(25) 16.5	(28) 18.3	(17) 22.4	
1.6	4.7	3.3			3.4	-9.6	2.4	7.9	9.9	
13.3	12.8	14.0		% Profit Before Taxes/Total Assets	20.5	7.7	16.2	13.1	11.8	
4.5	5.3	4.8			4.7	1.2	4.6	6.3	7.9	
.3	1.2	1.0			1.6	-4.3	.5	2.0	3.3	
69.6	73.3	71.9		Sales/Net Fixed Assets	82.9	61.7	80.5	61.2	71.9	
30.4	31.0	33.3			32.2	37.9	33.1	37.3	33.2	
16.0	14.9	18.5			18.4	18.6	21.4	15.8	16.1	
4.0	4.2	4.3		Sales/Total Assets	5.1	3.8	4.4	4.1	4.4	
3.1	3.2	3.4			3.4	3.2	3.1	3.4	3.8	
2.4	2.4	2.4			2.5	2.1	2.3	2.4	2.8	
.6	.5	.5		% Depr., Dep., Amort./Sales	.6	.6	.5	.5	.5	
(146) 1.0	(148) .9	(113) .9			(19) 1.1	(21) 1.0	(25) .8	(26) .8	(17) .7	
1.6	1.6	1.6			1.5	1.5	1.6	1.1	1.4	
1.8	1.9	2.1		% Officers', Directors', Owners' Comp/Sales	2.9	2.2	2.1	1.7		
(77) 3.0	(84) 3.0	(65) 3.1			(15) 4.4	(14) 3.0	(16) 2.8	(12) 2.7		
5.6	5.5	6.1			7.0	5.0	8.5	4.0		
2602970M 1003723M	2781291M 1005096M	2321011M 883610M		Net Sales ($) Total Assets ($)	3776M 1671M	42851M 14317M	93953M 32278M	247190M 89234M	448658M 178975M	1484583M 567135M

Current Data Sorted By Assets   **Comparative Historical Data**

0-500M	500M-2MM	2-10MM	10-50MM	50-100MM	100-250MM	Type of Statement	ALL 4/1/00-3/31/01	ALL 4/1/01-3/31/02
	2	12	8	1		Unqualified	18	22
5	13	28	12			Reviewed	30	28
6	14	16	1			Compiled	38	42
2	12	13				Tax Returns	22	13
2	10	18	8	3	1	Other	42	48
	35 (4/1-9/30/04)		150 (10/1/04-3/31/05)					
13	51	87	29	4	1	**NUMBER OF STATEMENTS**	150	153
%	%	%	%	%	%	**ASSETS**	%	%
16.3	8.7	6.8	6.0			Cash & Equivalents	6.5	6.1
22.6	25.4	26.1	20.7			Trade Receivables (net)	27.0	25.0
33.4	44.5	38.0	41.0			Inventory	42.2	43.6
3.9	1.3	3.0	2.8			All Other Current	2.2	2.4
76.2	80.0	74.0	70.5			Total Current	77.9	77.1
11.0	12.6	17.9	17.7			Fixed Assets (net)	14.9	14.9
4.4	1.5	2.1	4.2			Intangibles (net)	1.5	2.3
8.0	5.9	6.0	7.6			All Other Non-Current	5.8	5.7
100.0	100.0	100.0	100.0			Total	100.0	100.0
						LIABILITIES		
28.2	11.8	21.1	22.9			Notes Payable-Short Term	17.5	21.1
2.2	3.3	3.4	4.2			Cur. Mat.-L/T/D	3.9	3.3
17.7	20.8	19.2	11.1			Trade Payables	19.5	16.9
.0	.1	.3	.1			Income Taxes Payable	.2	.3
10.8	12.1	11.6	6.3			All Other Current	9.5	6.9
58.9	48.1	55.5	44.7			Total Current	50.5	48.6
10.4	10.9	10.6	12.3			Long-Term Debt	11.6	11.2
.0	.3	.5	.6			Deferred Taxes	.4	.5
4.6	6.7	4.0	2.5			All Other Non-Current	3.7	3.7
25.6	34.0	29.4	39.9			Net Worth	33.8	36.0
100.0	100.0	100.0	100.0			Total Liabilities & Net Worth	100.0	100.0
						INCOME DATA		
100.0	100.0	100.0	100.0			Net Sales	100.0	100.0
30.3	32.6	26.1	26.8			Gross Profit	25.9	29.9
29.8	30.6	22.6	21.5			Operating Expenses	22.5	26.2
.4	2.1	3.5	5.3			Operating Profit	3.5	3.7
.9	.3	.3	.3			All Other Expenses (net)	1.0	1.3
-.5	1.8	3.2	5.0			Profit Before Taxes	2.5	2.4
						RATIOS		
1.7	2.3	1.9	2.2				2.5	2.4
1.3	1.7	1.4	1.4			Current	1.6	1.5
1.1	1.2	1.0	1.2				1.2	1.2
1.3	1.1	.9	.9				1.1	1.0
.7	.7	.6	.5			Quick	.6	.6
.3	.3	.4	.4				.4	.4
0 UND	18 20.1	18 20.2	20 18.1				24 15.5	21 17.2
11 34.5	31 11.9	38 9.5	44 8.2			Sales/Receivables	42 8.7	36 10.2
28 13.1	53 7.0	60 6.1	67 5.4				55 6.6	55 6.7
9 39.1	49 7.4	30 12.1	50 7.3				51 7.2	48 7.5
39 9.3	99 3.7	60 6.1	67 5.5			Cost of Sales/Inventory	84 4.3	88 4.1
94 3.9	174 2.1	119 3.1	144 2.5				141 2.6	175 2.1
0 UND	18 20.4	16 22.3	16 23.5				19 19.5	18 20.0
4 88.8	32 11.4	32 11.5	30 12.2			Cost of Sales/Payables	35 10.3	33 11.2
36 10.2	62 5.9	68 5.4	47 7.8				60 6.1	54 6.8
9.0	4.8	6.8	5.0				4.3	4.6
21.3	8.6	14.6	11.4			Sales/Working Capital	8.4	9.2
205.8	30.6	999.8	20.6				23.2	19.3
12.8	8.2	9.1	11.7				4.9	6.4
(10) 2.6	(45) 2.4	(79) 3.0	5.3			EBIT/Interest	(137) 2.2	(143) 2.4
-1.0	1.1	1.6	3.1				1.1	1.0
	5.6	9.5					4.7	4.3
	(12) 1.6	(20) 3.2				Net Profit + Depr., Dep., Amort./Cur. Mat. L/T/D	(34) 1.9	(38) 2.0
	-.1	1.3					.4	.5
.0	.0	.1	.1				.1	.1
.2	.3	.3	.3			Fixed/Worth	.3	.3
-8.9	.8	2.3	.9				.8	.8
1.2	.8	.8					1.0	.9
14.2	1.7	2.7	2.2			Debt/Worth	2.1	1.9
-114.2	6.7	6.9	3.4				4.6	3.9
	39.2	38.7	36.0				34.4	32.0
	(47) 9.8	(75) 19.5	20.9			% Profit Before Taxes/Tangible Net Worth	(138) 12.8	(141) 11.7
	1.1	6.0	9.6				3.1	1.5
14.9	13.3	11.7	11.1				9.4	9.0
.0	3.3	4.2	5.7			% Profit Before Taxes/Total Assets	3.8	4.4
-4.9	.2	1.6	4.6				.4	.2
UND	116.5	106.0	66.4				91.5	59.9
95.0	39.8	32.9	25.7			Sales/Net Fixed Assets	34.7	28.4
35.8	15.7	11.9	8.4				11.7	10.6
7.2	3.2	3.5	2.5				3.2	3.2
6.2	2.6	2.5	1.8			Sales/Total Assets	2.2	2.2
1.9	2.0	1.5	1.2				1.5	1.4
	.5	.3	.4				.4	.4
	(40) 1.0	(70) .7	(24) 1.1			% Depr., Dep., Amort./Sales	(123) .7	(131) .9
	2.0	2.3	2.3				1.9	1.9
	2.5	1.7					2.3	2.5
	(27) 4.9	(35) 2.6				% Officers', Directors', Owners' Comp/Sales	(68) 3.2	(61) 4.0
	9.0	5.9					5.5	8.8
20864M	187919M	1190870M	1056859M	741374M	297866M	Net Sales ($)	3167475M	3578296M
3222M	66245M	435220M	581082M	303939M	134095M	Total Assets ($)	1926911M	1817840M

M = $ thousand   MM = $ million
See Pages 11 through 21 for Explanation of Ratios and Data

Comparative Historical Data

Current Data Sorted By Sales

4/1/02-3/31/03 ALL	4/1/03-3/31/04 ALL	4/1/04-3/31/05 ALL	Type of Statement	0-1MM	1-3MM	3-5MM	5-10MM	10-25MM	25MM & OVER
					35 (4/1-9/30/04)		150 (10/1/04-3/31/05)		
22	20	23	Unqualified			1	2	5	15
52	63	53	Reviewed	1	3	10	14	16	9
37	46	36	Compiled	2	10	7	7	9	1
15	18	31	Tax Returns	2	14	5	6	4	
47	44	42	Other	2	6	6	9	10	9
173	191	185	**NUMBER OF STATEMENTS**	7	33	29	38	44	34
%	**%**	**%**	**ASSETS**	**%**	**%**	**%**	**%**	**%**	**%**
8.0	8.4	7.7	Cash & Equivalents		7.6	11.7	9.6	6.8	4.6
26.1	25.8	24.6	Trade Receivables (net)		18.5	23.2	26.4	29.2	22.7
43.8	42.4	40.0	Inventory		44.5	42.8	32.3	37.2	44.3
2.6	2.0	2.6	All Other Current		1.8	1.4	1.7	4.3	2.0
80.5	78.5	74.9	Total Current		72.4	79.1	70.0	77.4	73.6
12.2	13.4	16.0	Fixed Assets (net)		19.2	14.9	20.4	13.3	14.9
1.9	1.8	2.6	Intangibles (net)		1.6	.9	2.5	3.2	3.8
5.5	6.3	6.4	All Other Non-Current		6.8	5.2	7.0	6.0	7.7
100.0	100.0	100.0	Total		100.0	100.0	100.0	100.0	100.0
			LIABILITIES						
19.4	18.5	19.2	Notes Payable-Short Term		16.0	17.2	17.0	17.4	25.6
2.9	3.1	3.4	Cur. Mat.-L/T/D		3.6	2.5	3.7	4.4	2.2
21.2	19.4	18.0	Trade Payables		16.8	18.8	20.7	18.6	14.6
.1	.2	.2	Income Taxes Payable		.0	.1	.4	.2	.3
9.1	10.3	10.8	All Other Current		10.2	10.1	9.2	15.3	9.1
52.7	51.6	51.7	Total Current		46.7	48.7	51.0	55.9	51.7
8.4	8.5	11.3	Long-Term Debt		15.8	11.3	14.2	5.8	11.5
.5	.7	.4	Deferred Taxes		.7	.1	.3	.3	.8
4.1	4.6	4.5	All Other Non-Current		5.3	7.3	6.1	2.7	1.7
34.3	34.7	32.0	Net Worth		31.5	32.6	28.3	35.4	34.2
100.0	100.0	100.0	Total Liabilities & Net Worth		100.0	100.0	100.0	100.0	100.0
			INCOME DATA						
100.0	100.0	100.0	Net Sales		100.0	100.0	100.0	100.0	100.0
28.8	29.6	28.1	Gross Profit		37.3	34.3	28.8	22.6	19.4
26.1	26.6	24.8	Operating Expenses		35.6	31.0	25.0	19.5	15.0
2.7	2.9	3.2	Operating Profit		1.8	3.3	3.9	3.2	4.4
.4	.6	.4	All Other Expenses (net)		.9	.4	-.2	-.1	1.0
2.3	2.3	2.8	Profit Before Taxes		.9	3.0	4.1	3.3	3.4
			RATIOS						
2.3	2.2	2.1	Current		2.2	2.7	2.0	2.0	1.9
1.5	1.5	1.4			1.7	1.6	1.4	1.4	1.4
1.2	1.2	1.1			1.1	1.2	.9	1.0	1.2
1.0	1.2	1.0	Quick		.9	1.1	1.1	1.0	.9
.6	.6	.6			.5	.8	.7	.6	.5
.4	.4	.4			.4	.4	.4	.4	.3
21 17.5	21 17.1	17 22.0	Sales/Receivables		13 27.8	17 21.9	27 13.3	17 22.0	13 28.5
37 9.9	37 9.8	35 10.4			31 11.7	33 11.0	47 7.7	32 11.4	32 11.3
49 7.5	56 6.5	58 6.3			61 6.0	49 7.4	58 6.3	56 6.5	51 7.2
49 7.5	42 8.7	36 10.1	Cost of Sales/Inventory		42 8.6	51 7.2	27 13.6	29 12.6	42 8.7
78 4.7	82 4.4	67 5.4			100 3.7	129 2.8	58 6.2	59 6.2	59 6.2
136 2.7	146 2.5	137 2.7			210 1.7	198 1.8	93 3.9	100 3.7	118 3.1
19 19.3	17 21.4	16 23.5	Cost of Sales/Payables		4 90.6	20 18.2	19 18.9	16 22.6	10 36.6
37 9.8	36 10.2	30 12.2			30 12.2	40 9.1	42 8.7	24 15.2	24 15.4
56 6.5	61 5.9	60 6.1			67 5.4	76 4.8	68 7.8	47 7.8	41 8.8
5.5	5.0	5.2	Sales/Working Capital		4.4	4.3	8.1	7.3	5.5
9.9	10.0	11.7			9.3	5.8	12.5	14.6	16.5
21.6	30.3	63.3			63.9	38.9	-99.8	281.2	34.2
10.3	6.6	9.0	EBIT/Interest		3.7	6.2	8.1	12.7	8.8
(159) 2.4	(176) 2.9	(168) 3.4			(30) 1.5	(27) 3.2	(33) 3.6	(39) 3.5	4.3
.9	1.1	1.5			-.5	1.1	1.6	1.8	2.6
5.8	8.1	7.0	Net Profit + Depr., Dep., Amort./Cur. Mat. L/T/D					8.0	11.9
(52) 1.9	(52) 2.5	(41) 2.5						(10) 3.6	(13) 2.5
.6	1.0	1.3						2.5	1.3
.1	.1	.1	Fixed/Worth		.1	.1	.1	.1	.2
.2	.2	.3			.4	.3	.7	.3	.3
.9	.8	1.3			2.4	1.4	4.5	.9	1.0
.9	1.0	1.1	Debt/Worth		1.0	.8	1.1	1.0	1.1
2.1	2.2	2.4			1.9	2.5	2.9	2.2	2.4
5.1	4.3	6.8			16.5	6.1	17.5	5.7	4.1
31.1	31.9	38.7	% Profit Before Taxes/Tangible Net Worth		27.0	36.3	40.4	45.0	39.6
(158) 9.6	(180) 12.5	(164) 15.8			(29) 5.9	(27) 11.9	(30) 22.5	(41) 15.2	(32) 26.2
1.4	2.4	4.7			-4.6	5.1	9.7	6.0	11.6
9.0	8.7	11.7	% Profit Before Taxes/Total Assets		5.5	11.3	15.0	12.6	10.6
3.7	3.7	4.6			1.4	3.2	5.5	5.0	5.8
-.1	.3	1.1			-3.6	.3	1.8	1.8	3.6
82.6	100.5	105.5	Sales/Net Fixed Assets		100.0	103.8	119.6	144.8	68.1
38.0	37.8	33.5			32.2	33.1	28.9	51.6	31.2
18.5	15.4	11.8			7.6	9.1	5.4	17.2	11.3
3.5	3.5	3.3	Sales/Total Assets		3.0	2.7	3.2	3.9	3.9
2.4	2.2	2.5			2.0	2.4	2.4	2.8	2.7
1.7	1.5	1.6			1.3	1.7	1.4	2.0	1.9
.4	.4	.4	% Depr., Dep., Amort./Sales		.5	.5	.3	.3	.4
(152) .8	(149) .9	(143) .9			(26) 1.2	(23) 1.2	(29) 1.0	(35) .5	(29) .9
1.4	1.9	2.0			2.5	1.7	3.5	1.6	1.2
2.2	2.1	2.0	% Officers', Directors', Owners' Comp/Sales		3.7	2.5	2.4	1.3	
(81) 3.6	(85) 3.5	(74) 3.5			(22) 5.1	(16) 6.0	(12) 2.8	(15) 2.5	
6.5	7.4	6.4			7.5	11.4	3.5	4.4	
3290884M	3128529M	3495752M	Net Sales ($)	2973M	68577M	110857M	286748M	676767M	2349830M
1621311M	1520257M	1523803M	Total Assets ($)	1749M	44243M	61991M	181081M	290657M	944082M

© RMA 2005

M = $ thousand   MM = $ million
See Pages 11 through 21 for Explanation of Ratios and Data

Current Data Sorted By Assets   **Comparative Historical Data**

Type of Statement	0-500M	500M-2MM	2-10MM	10-50MM	50-100MM	100-250MM	4/1/00-3/31/01 ALL	4/1/01-3/31/02 ALL
Unqualified		2	8	25	5	5	21	18
Reviewed	3	10	45	6			59	45
Compiled	5	24	24		1		67	47
Tax Returns	12	21	8				18	20
Other	6	15	31	13	3	3	63	61
		45 (4/1-9/30/04)		230 (10/1/04-3/31/05)				
NUMBER OF STATEMENTS	26	72	116	44	9	8	228	191
ASSETS	%	%	%	%	%	%	%	%
Cash & Equivalents	8.6	7.5	5.7	4.7			5.7	5.5
Trade Receivables (net)	24.3	25.4	26.2	32.7			26.3	29.6
Inventory	43.7	44.2	48.4	38.5			48.7	46.1
All Other Current	4.8	3.3	2.4	4.3			2.1	2.7
Total Current	81.5	80.4	82.6	80.2			82.8	84.0
Fixed Assets (net)	12.7	10.5	10.3	11.9			9.6	9.2
Intangibles (net)	3.0	3.3	2.0	3.8			3.0	2.6
All Other Non-Current	2.8	5.9	5.1	4.1			4.6	4.3
Total	100.0	100.0	100.0	100.0			100.0	100.0
LIABILITIES								
Notes Payable-Short Term	17.7	22.4	19.5	20.5			21.6	18.8
Cur. Mat.-L/T/D	7.6	1.7	1.3	1.8			2.4	3.6
Trade Payables	21.8	18.5	19.3	18.2			20.2	22.3
Income Taxes Payable	.0	.2	.2	.2			.2	.3
All Other Current	19.8	9.4	7.5	11.6			8.5	8.4
Total Current	67.0	52.3	47.9	52.4			52.9	53.5
Long-Term Debt	12.7	14.1	6.2	6.1			7.7	7.3
Deferred Taxes	.0	.2	.1	.1			.1	.1
All Other Non-Current	26.2	7.2	4.9	4.6			6.1	8.0
Net Worth	-5.7	26.2	41.0	36.8			33.2	31.1
Total Liabilities & Net Worth	100.0	100.0	100.0	100.0			100.0	100.0
INCOME DATA								
Net Sales	100.0	100.0	100.0	100.0			100.0	100.0
Gross Profit	31.1	34.5	30.1	30.2			29.6	29.9
Operating Expenses	33.5	31.7	26.6	26.1			26.1	26.3
Operating Profit	-2.4	2.8	3.4	4.1			3.5	3.6
All Other Expenses (net)	.7	1.1	.4	.1			1.2	1.4
Profit Before Taxes	-3.1	1.7	3.0	4.0			2.3	2.2
RATIOS								
Current	2.4	2.7	2.5	1.8			2.2	2.2
	1.7	1.6	1.7	1.4			1.5	1.6
	.8	1.1	1.3	1.2			1.2	1.2
Quick	1.2	1.0	1.2	1.2			1.0	1.0
	.5	.5	.6	.6			.6	.6
	.2	.3	.4	.4			.3	.4
Sales/Receivables	0 UND	12 30.3	20 18.6	29 12.7			15 24.3	20 18.0
	21 17.4	23 16.1	37 10.0	55 6.6			36 10.1	37 10.0
	34 10.6	51 7.2	50 7.3	79 4.6			59 6.2	64 5.7
Cost of Sales/Inventory	32 11.5	32 11.5	60 6.1	71 5.1			64 5.7	59 6.1
	78 4.7	100 3.6	105 3.5	109 3.4			103 3.5	92 3.9
	204 1.8	154 2.4	171 2.1	140 2.6			146 2.5	142 2.6
Cost of Sales/Payables	5 68.4	14 27.0	15 24.8	14 26.3			16 23.1	17 21.0
	16 23.1	26 13.8	30 12.2	30 12.3			33 11.0	37 9.9
	58 6.3	53 6.9	57 6.4	55 6.7			57 6.4	55 6.6
Sales/Working Capital	4.6	5.0	4.7	4.8			5.3	5.2
	9.6	8.3	7.7	9.6			9.7	9.6
	-21.9	77.8	12.7	14.2			21.9	20.3
EBIT/Interest	8.8	8.1	10.4	20.6			5.9	7.5
	(22) 3.1	(65) 2.2	(105) 4.7	(41) 5.2			(211) 2.5	(179) 2.6
	-1.3	.2	1.6	2.3			1.2	1.2
Net Profit + Depr., Dep., Amort./Cur. Mat. L/T/D			7.9	17.5			4.6	6.6
		(26) 4.5		(19) 5.0			(40) 1.8	(36) 2.1
		.8		1.7			.9	.7
Fixed/Worth	.0	.1	.1	.1			.1	.1
	.7	.4	.2	.4			.2	.2
	-.5	3.7	.5	.5			.7	.8
Debt/Worth	.9	1.0	.7	1.2			1.1	1.0
	4.1	2.5	1.8	2.5			2.3	2.2
	-3.4	66.5	3.5	3.8			6.0	7.4
% Profit Before Taxes/Tangible Net Worth	52.6	61.6	36.5	39.2			35.7	35.0
	(15) 14.0	(56) 27.7	(110) 16.4	(42) 24.9			(203) 19.0	(171) 17.7
	1.6	-3.2	4.0	5.8			5.4	2.4
% Profit Before Taxes/Total Assets	13.7	14.3	12.2	12.7			11.4	12.4
	1.1	3.1	5.5	5.6			5.1	4.8
	-11.8	-2.6	.9	1.8			.9	.6
Sales/Net Fixed Assets	226.6	156.6	120.3	51.1			108.3	137.2
	49.2	53.6	45.4	30.2			47.2	46.7
	17.8	14.6	19.7	13.7			20.9	20.8
Sales/Total Assets	4.4	4.2	3.1	2.7			3.5	3.5
	2.8	2.8	2.3	2.3			2.6	2.6
	1.8	1.9	1.8	1.6			1.8	1.8
% Depr., Dep., Amort./Sales	.2	.3	.3	.4			.3	.2
	(16) .9	(54) .8	(97) .6	(42) .7			(188) .6	(155) .6
	1.7	1.8	1.1	1.6			1.2	1.2
% Officers', Directors', Owners' Comp/Sales	2.3	2.1	1.6				1.9	2.1
	(12) 6.2	(50) 4.0	(60) 2.5				(109) 3.5	(82) 3.5
	11.8	6.5	5.1				5.8	5.8
Net Sales ($)	41136M	270861M	1351266M	2429169M	1556610M	2300873M	4261310M	4683020M
Total Assets ($)	7507M	85754M	512003M	996424M	653456M	1347450M	1910389M	2237151M

M = $ thousand   MM = $ million
See Pages 11 through 21 for Explanation of Ratios and Data

Comparative Historical Data | **Current Data Sorted By Sales**

			Type of Statement						
49	39	45	Unqualified		3	1	4	9	28
59	64	64	Reviewed	1	4	9	18	25	7
45	52	54	Compiled	6	12	12	12	10	2
29	39	41	Tax Returns	8	13	9	6	4	1
57	83	71	Other	8	6	6	18	14	19
4/1/02-3/31/03 ALL	4/1/03-3/31/04 ALL	4/1/04-3/31/05 ALL		45 (4/1-9/30/04) 0-1MM	1-3MM	3-5MM	230 (10/1/04-3/31/05) 5-10MM	10-25MM	25MM & OVER
239	277	275	**NUMBER OF STATEMENTS**	23	38	37	58	62	57
%	%	%	**ASSETS**	%	%	%	%	%	%
6.2	7.4	6.2	Cash & Equivalents	9.2	4.7	7.4	8.8	4.6	4.1
29.2	27.2	26.9	Trade Receivables (net)	14.2	24.7	28.9	24.2	31.1	30.5
44.1	44.4	45.4	Inventory	51.3	44.8	44.7	42.9	47.8	43.6
2.5	3.7	3.2	All Other Current	9.8	1.5	.8	2.5	3.3	3.8
82.0	82.6	81.6	Total Current	84.5	75.6	81.7	78.3	86.7	82.0
10.2	10.5	10.8	Fixed Assets (net)	10.7	13.3	10.8	12.0	7.8	11.2
3.1	1.7	2.8	Intangibles (net)	3.6	6.2	1.9	2.5	1.3	2.7
4.7	5.2	4.8	All Other Non-Current	1.1	4.9	5.6	7.2	4.2	4.0
100.0	100.0	100.0	Total	100.0	100.0	100.0	100.0	100.0	100.0
			LIABILITIES						
19.3	19.5	19.8	Notes Payable-Short Term	19.9	18.7	22.1	17.8	21.6	19.2
3.3	1.9	2.1	Cur. Mat.-L/T/D	6.9	3.5	2.2	.8	1.0	1.6
21.2	22.5	19.5	Trade Payables	13.3	19.3	18.9	16.1	21.8	23.7
.2	.3	.2	Income Taxes Payable	.0	.0	.3	.3	.2	.3
8.2	8.4	9.8	All Other Current	12.8	10.4	7.7	8.9	12.5	7.5
52.2	52.6	51.5	Total Current	52.9	52.0	51.2	43.9	57.2	52.3
8.7	8.9	9.2	Long-Term Debt	19.8	15.5	12.1	7.2	3.1	7.6
.0	.1	.1	Deferred Taxes	.0	.2	.1	.1	.1	.1
5.5	5.3	7.4	All Other Non-Current	9.4	13.6	7.6	7.2	6.8	3.3
33.5	33.1	31.8	Net Worth	18.2	18.7	28.9	41.6	32.9	36.7
100.0	100.0	100.0	Total Liabilities & Net Worth	100.0	100.0	100.0	100.0	100.0	100.0
			INCOME DATA						
100.0	100.0	100.0	Net Sales	100.0	100.0	100.0	100.0	100.0	100.0
30.7	32.1	30.9	Gross Profit	32.2	38.5	34.4	32.1	26.9	26.0
26.9	28.4	28.0	Operating Expenses	35.0	35.7	31.2	27.8	24.5	22.0
3.8	3.7	2.9	Operating Profit	-2.8	2.8	3.3	4.3	2.4	4.0
.7	.3	.5	All Other Expenses (net)	1.6	1.4	.6	.0	.2	.4
3.1	3.3	2.3	Profit Before Taxes	-4.4	1.4	2.6	4.3	2.2	3.6
			RATIOS						
2.6	2.7	2.5	Current	9.0	2.6	2.7	3.3	1.9	2.2
1.6	1.6	1.6		2.0	1.7	1.6	1.9	1.5	1.4
1.2	1.2	1.2		1.4	1.1	1.1	1.3	1.2	1.2
1.2	1.1	1.1	Quick	2.7	.8	1.1	1.4	1.0	1.0
.7	.6	.6		.3	.5	.6	.7	.6	.6
.4	.4	.4		.1	.3	.4	.5	.4	.4
20 18.7	18 20.5	19 19.3	Sales/Receivables	0 UND	14 25.2	15 24.0	18 20.7	19 18.9	28 13.0
35 10.5	34 10.8	35 10.5		19 19.1	27 13.6	37 9.9	30 12.0	39 9.5	40 9.1
58 6.3	55 6.6	55 6.6		40 9.2	53 6.8	58 6.3	45 8.0	65 5.6	59 6.2
49 7.4	52 7.1	55 6.6	Cost of Sales/Inventory	101 3.6	52 7.0	55 6.6	45 8.2	53 6.9	65 5.7
83 4.4	96 3.8	105 3.5		198 1.8	147 2.5	114 3.2	92 4.0	87 4.2	103 3.6
142 2.6	150 2.4	153 2.4		348 1.0	199 1.8	161 2.3	147 2.5	144 2.5	119 3.1
12 29.6	14 26.5	14 26.1	Cost of Sales/Payables	0 UND	14 25.2	17 22.0	11 32.6	13 27.0	18 20.5
29 12.5	36 10.1	29 12.5		20 18.5	30 12.3	31 11.8	27 13.6	29 12.7	37 9.8
55 6.7	63 5.8	57 6.4		57 6.4	52 7.0	62 5.9	47 7.7	56 6.5	59 6.2
4.6	4.6	4.7	Sales/Working Capital	1.7	4.6	4.7	4.6	5.4	4.7
9.8	8.4	8.0		4.3	7.1	7.6	7.0	8.7	9.8
25.2	19.6	18.1		10.4	84.9	41.0	15.0	15.5	18.0
9.3	10.4	10.2	EBIT/Interest	8.7	7.6	5.8	11.7	10.4	17.4
(220) 3.4	(245) 4.3	(249) 4.1		(19) 1.0	(33) 2.0	(35) 3.1	(50) 5.2	(59) 4.8	(53) 5.2
1.5	1.6	1.2		-4.3	-.8	1.0	1.8	1.2	2.3
11.7	6.7	12.4	Net Profit + Depr., Dep., Amort./Cur. Mat. L/T/D				8.0	16.3	22.3
(48) 2.7	(56) 3.4	(60) 4.7					(12) 3.7	(17) 5.8	(22) 6.9
1.0	1.2	1.3					-3.8	1.0	4.3
.1	.1	.1	Fixed/Worth	.0	.1	.1	.0	.1	.1
.3	.2	.2		.2	.4	.4	.2	.2	.3
.7	.7	.8		-.6	-1.4	.8	.7	.5	.5
.9	.8	.9	Debt/Worth	.9	.7	1.0	.7	1.2	1.2
2.2	2.2	2.2		2.8	3.4	2.3	1.1	2.4	2.2
6.0	5.4	5.1		-5.5	-6.8	13.5	3.2	3.9	4.1
46.5	44.6	40.9	% Profit Before Taxes/Tangible Net Worth	47.8	41.6	49.0	42.1	37.4	46.0
(213) 18.2	(244) 18.8	(240) 19.8		(16) 5.8	(25) 24.7	(32) 13.9	(55) 17.6	(56) 18.8	(56) 28.5
5.0	4.2	3.8		-21.0	4.3	.4	5.2	4.0	7.9
14.8	14.4	12.7	% Profit Before Taxes/Total Assets	12.4	12.6	9.8	18.7	11.2	12.7
6.1	6.7	4.9		-5.8	2.5	3.9	6.9	4.8	8.0
1.3	1.1	.3		-13.9	-6.1	.0	1.1	1.2	1.9
101.6	108.9	109.0	Sales/Net Fixed Assets	247.5	100.8	240.2	136.0	100.1	82.2
41.9	44.7	42.9		33.0	29.2	43.8	33.6	58.8	34.1
20.2	22.0	17.6		9.8	11.8	18.8	16.3	29.7	18.3
3.7	3.5	3.2	Sales/Total Assets	2.3	3.1	3.8	3.2	4.1	3.0
2.7	2.5	2.4		1.4	2.4	2.3	2.7	2.7	2.5
1.8	1.9	1.8		.9	1.4	1.8	1.9	1.9	1.9
.4	.4	.3	% Depr., Dep., Amort./Sales	.4	.7	.3	.3	.3	.4
(204) .7	(223) .7	(224) .6		(12) 1.3	(29) 1.3	(27) .5	(47) .6	(56) .5	(53) .6
1.2	1.2	1.3		3.4	3.2	1.1	1.6	.7	1.1
2.2	1.9	1.8	% Officers', Directors', Owners' Comp/Sales		2.3	2.3	2.1	1.2	.5
(105) 3.4	(131) 3.8	(131) 3.4			(25) 4.6	(26) 4.0	(29) 3.4	(34) 1.9	(10) 1.3
6.4	6.6	6.1			8.5	5.5	7.3	4.6	2.7
6009307M	7230294M	7949915M	Net Sales ($)	11853M	76750M	141637M	430391M	969675M	6319609M
2664158M	3231689M	3602594M	Total Assets ($)	9362M	40882M	62440M	184976M	413336M	2891598M

Current Data Sorted By Assets **Comparative Historical Data**

Type of Statement	0-500M	500M-2MM	2-10MM	10-50MM	50-100MM	100-250MM		4/1/00-3/31/01 ALL	4/1/01-3/31/02 ALL
Unqualified		2	7	12	2	1		20	13
Reviewed			12	4				26	22
Compiled	3	10	6					32	36
Tax Returns	6	8	7					10	6
Other	3	8	10		5	1		24	41
		23 (4/1-9/30/04)			90 (10/1/04-3/31/05)				
NUMBER OF STATEMENTS	12	28	42	22	7	2		112	118
ASSETS	%	%	%	%	%	%		%	%
Cash & Equivalents	17.9	11.8	7.6	6.3				6.5	7.9
Trade Receivables (net)	19.2	23.7	29.4	28.7				26.7	25.9
Inventory	40.3	35.8	41.1	40.7				44.0	39.8
All Other Current	2.2	3.2	2.7	6.0				3.2	3.1
Total Current	79.7	74.5	80.7	81.7				80.4	76.8
Fixed Assets (net)	12.1	12.5	13.0	6.1				10.7	13.9
Intangibles (net)	.9	4.5	1.6	7.5				3.0	3.9
All Other Non-Current	7.3	8.5	4.7	4.7				5.9	5.3
Total	100.0	100.0	100.0	100.0				100.0	100.0
LIABILITIES									
Notes Payable-Short Term	32.9	16.4	18.1	19.2				20.1	18.1
Cur. Mat.-L/T/D	1.9	1.3	2.5	3.3				2.6	2.8
Trade Payables	28.9	17.0	22.3	17.7				15.3	15.7
Income Taxes Payable	.1	.1	.0	.0				.4	.1
All Other Current	6.0	6.9	9.5	12.0				9.8	10.1
Total Current	69.7	41.8	52.5	52.3				48.2	46.8
Long-Term Debt	12.3	14.6	5.7	2.9				5.2	7.2
Deferred Taxes	.3	.0	.2	.0				.1	.2
All Other Non-Current	4.8	7.1	5.4	6.9				5.3	5.9
Net Worth	12.8	36.6	36.3	37.9				41.2	39.9
Total Liabilities & Net Worth	100.0	100.0	100.0	100.0				100.0	100.0
INCOME DATA									
Net Sales	100.0	100.0	100.0	100.0				100.0	100.0
Gross Profit	39.5	44.7	35.2	34.4				36.2	37.9
Operating Expenses	39.2	41.4	33.4	30.2				33.0	33.2
Operating Profit	.2	3.3	1.7	4.2				3.2	4.6
All Other Expenses (net)	.6	1.7	.6	1.2				.8	1.1
Profit Before Taxes	-.4	1.5	1.2	3.0				2.4	3.5
RATIOS									
Current	2.5	2.9	2.1	2.8				2.6	2.6
	1.2	1.6	1.4	1.6				1.6	1.6
	.8	1.3	1.2	1.2				1.2	1.2
Quick	1.0	1.7	1.0	1.1				1.1	1.3
	.5	.8	.6	.7				.7 (117)	.7
	.3	.3	.4	.4				.4	.4
Sales/Receivables	7 52.7	13 28.0	27 13.6	26 14.1				26 13.8	24 15.2
	19 19.6	23 15.8	42 8.7	39 9.3				37 9.9	40 9.1
	31 11.9	58 6.3	68 5.4	66 5.5				60 6.1	56 6.5
Cost of Sales/Inventory	33 10.9	50 7.4	52 7.0	63 5.8				64 5.7	58 6.3
	95 3.8	113 3.2	97 3.8	90 4.1				113 3.2	101 3.6
	133 2.7	158 2.3	160 2.3	196 1.9				211 1.7	225 1.6
Cost of Sales/Payables	0 UND	12 31.1	29 12.6	16 23.1				16 23.4	15 24.1
	32 11.5	35 10.4	46 7.9	36 10.1				32 11.5	31 11.9
	84 4.3	52 7.0	73 5.0	62 5.9				54 6.8	55 6.7
Sales/Working Capital	5.9	4.6	4.6	4.7				4.0	4.0
	510.9	9.4	10.1	7.7				8.8	8.8
	-14.6	16.6	18.6	19.6				20.5	19.0
EBIT/Interest		14.6	3.9	12.8				6.1	7.0
		(25) 2.4	(37) 1.8	(20) 5.6				(105) 2.1	(106) 2.8
		-2.1	.0	1.3				1.0	1.2
Net Profit + Depr., Dep., Amort./Cur. Mat. L /T/D			7.9					5.0	5.4
		(10)	2.8					(26) 2.9	(19) 2.2
			-1.2					.6	1.0
Fixed/Worth	.0	.1	.1	.1				.1	.1
	.4	.3	.3	.1				.2	.3
	-4.0	1.0	1.1	.2				.6	.7
Debt/Worth	1.2	.6	1.1	.8				.7	.8
	139.5	1.6	1.5	1.7				1.9	1.5
	-5.3	4.4	8.6	4.0				3.5	3.1
% Profit Before Taxes/Tangible Net Worth		48.3	21.8	49.6				35.9	45.2
	(23)	15.2	(38) 4.8	(18) 20.7				(107) 16.8	(107) 14.6
		-10.8	-3.8	2.9				.7	1.8
% Profit Before Taxes/Total Assets	16.9	18.2	7.3	12.0				14.1	17.0
	-.2	3.8	1.4	8.9				3.8	6.5
	-3.8	-7.1	-1.8	.4				.0	.5
Sales/Net Fixed Assets	126.4	98.0	61.4	89.2				77.7	70.4
	45.6	30.3	30.8	42.6				33.8	31.0
	18.2	9.5	11.3	20.9				17.1	8.7
Sales/Total Assets	5.4	3.3	3.0	2.9				3.0	3.1
	3.3	2.8	2.2	2.4				2.2	2.2
	2.0	1.6	1.7	1.5				1.5	1.4
% Depr., Dep., Amort./Sales		.7	.5	.2				.4	.4
	(20)	1.1	(35) .9	(19) .4				(92) .6	(97) .8
		2.1	1.7	1.4				1.6	2.0
% Officers', Directors', Owners' Comp/Sales		2.3	2.3					2.3	2.0
	(14)	5.2	(20) 4.7					(57) 3.7	(57) 3.4
		9.5	8.2					6.3	5.8
Net Sales ($)	15193M	82815M	437985M	1122076M	1073569M	566501M		2555777M	2799544M
Total Assets ($)	3056M	29850M	180494M	518063M	509643M	291051M		1279213M	1484520M

M = $ thousand   MM = $ million
See Pages 11 through 21 for Explanation of Ratios and Data

Comparative Historical Data | Current Data Sorted By Sales

4/1/02-3/31/03 ALL	4/1/03-3/31/04 ALL	4/1/04-3/31/05 ALL	Type of Statement	0-1MM	1-3MM	3-5MM	5-10MM	10-25MM	25MM & OVER
28	21	24	Unqualified		1	1	4	5	13
31	21	16	Reviewed		1	2	3	7	3
25	34	19	Compiled	2	5	7	3	2	
17	27	21	Tax Returns	3	11	2	4	1	
37	30	33	Other	6	2	3	4	5	13
				23 (4/1-9/30/04)			90 (10/1/04-3/31/05)		
138	133	113	**NUMBER OF STATEMENTS**	11	20	15	18	20	29
%	%	%	**ASSETS**	%	%	%	%	%	%
10.2	10.3	9.0	Cash & Equivalents	9.8	11.0	4.4	23.6	4.8	3.7
26.7	25.8	25.9	Trade Receivables (net)	12.7	27.8	22.5	19.7	40.2	25.3
39.5	38.6	39.7	Inventory	42.3	39.0	48.9	26.8	39.6	42.6
2.9	3.9	3.5	All Other Current	2.9	1.1	3.7	4.4	2.1	5.7
79.4	78.6	78.2	Total Current	67.6	78.9	79.4	74.5	86.7	77.3
12.0	10.9	12.1	Fixed Assets (net)	17.2	9.9	13.7	17.5	7.3	10.8
3.4	4.2	3.8	Intangibles (net)	7.7	1.5	1.0	2.8	1.8	7.3
5.3	6.4	6.0	All Other Non-Current	7.5	9.7	5.8	5.1	4.2	4.6
100.0	100.0	100.0	Total	100.0	100.0	100.0	100.0	100.0	100.0
			LIABILITIES						
14.8	15.0	20.0	Notes Payable-Short Term	24.6	17.2	24.5	15.5	19.9	20.5
2.7	1.8	2.3	Cur. Mat.-L/T/D	1.8	1.3	1.8	3.1	1.7	3.4
18.8	19.0	19.9	Trade Payables	10.5	25.4	17.7	18.3	26.4	17.2
.2	.1	.1	Income Taxes Payable	.0	.1	.3	.0	.0	.0
10.5	9.8	8.9	All Other Current	4.4	9.4	6.6	9.4	5.7	13.4
47.1	45.7	51.1	Total Current	41.3	53.4	50.9	46.4	53.8	54.5
7.0	8.3	9.0	Long-Term Debt	18.4	15.2	7.6	5.0	4.1	7.7
.1	.1	.1	Deferred Taxes	.0	.2	.3	.0	.1	.0
5.1	5.4	6.1	All Other Non-Current	7.2	8.5	4.0	4.8	7.3	5.0
40.8	40.5	33.7	Net Worth	33.1	22.7	37.2	43.9	34.7	32.8
100.0	100.0	100.0	Total Liabilities & Net Worth	100.0	100.0	100.0	100.0	100.0	100.0
			INCOME DATA						
100.0	100.0	100.0	Net Sales	100.0	100.0	100.0	100.0	100.0	100.0
36.4	37.5	38.4	Gross Profit	46.4	43.8	41.0	40.6	28.3	35.9
31.3	32.4	35.6	Operating Expenses	48.6	39.8	39.5	39.0	25.5	30.6
5.0	5.1	2.8	Operating Profit	-2.2	4.0	1.5	1.7	2.8	5.3
.6	.7	.8	All Other Expenses (net)	2.7	1.1	1.2	.2	.6	.3
4.4	4.4	2.0	Profit Before Taxes	-5.0	3.0	.3	1.5	2.2	5.0
			RATIOS						
3.1	3.3	2.3	Current	7.2	2.8	2.3	4.3	2.3	2.1
1.7	1.8	1.5		1.6	1.6	1.5	1.4	1.7	1.4
1.2	1.1	1.2		.8	1.0	1.2	1.0	1.2	1.0
1.6	1.5	1.1	Quick	2.7	1.3	.9	3.0	1.5	1.0
.8	(132) .8	.6		.4	.7	.4	.8	.7	.5
.5	.5	.3		.3	.5	.2	.4	.6	.2
23 15.9	20 18.6	19 19.3	Sales/Receivables	11 32.8	11 34.5	18 19.8	8 44.2	30 12.3	19 19.6
39 9.2	37 9.8	32 11.2		25 14.8	33 11.0	27 13.4	24 15.5	50 7.3	32 11.2
56 6.5	51 7.1	60 6.1		50 7.3	94 3.9	75 4.9	41 8.9	79 4.6	58 6.3
53 6.9	46 8.0	61 5.9	Cost of Sales/Inventory	103 3.6	55 6.6	91 4.0	23 15.7	34 10.7	65 5.6
95 3.8	92 4.0	100 3.6		146 2.5	113 3.2	124 2.9	83 4.4	83 4.4	99 3.7
145 2.5	154 2.4	155 2.4		231 1.6	174 2.1	364 1.0	135 2.7	108 3.4	130 2.8
13 28.0	16 23.2	18 20.7	Cost of Sales/Payables	7 51.7	10 34.8	27 13.5	32 11.4	23 15.7	16 22.4
30 12.0	34 10.6	37 9.9		30 12.3	46 8.0	34 10.7	41 8.8	35 10.5	35 10.4
60 6.1	55 6.7	66 5.5		84 4.3	84 4.4	93 3.9	59 6.2	66 5.5	59 6.3
4.0	4.3	4.7	Sales/Working Capital	2.8	3.2	4.4	4.4	5.9	5.2
7.3	9.6	9.6		5.4	8.8	8.4	13.4	11.1	9.7
20.5	30.8	23.6		-33.5	NM	13.3	NM	16.8	NM
17.1	23.5	8.7	EBIT/Interest		12.5	3.8	7.4	10.6	10.9
(126) 6.6	(122) 5.4	(97) 2.4			(17) 2.4	1.6	(13) 2.1	(17) 3.3	(26) 7.3
1.5	1.6	.3			-.9	-2.3	.6	.3	1.5
11.6	15.8	13.4	Net Profit + Depr., Dep., Amort./Cur. Mat. L/T/D						
(30) 4.1	(21) 3.5	(21) 4.4							
2.6	2.7	.0							
.1	.1	.1	Fixed/Worth	.0	.1	.1	.1	.1	.1
.2	.2	.3		.4	.3	.2	.5	.3	.2
.6	.6	1.0		-15.7	NM	1.3	1.0	.7	.8
.6	.7	1.0	Debt/Worth	1.1	1.0	1.0	.9	.6	1.0
1.5	1.4	1.6		2.5	1.7	1.4	1.5	2.9	1.9
4.2	3.6	7.0		-53.7	-5.8	5.3	3.8	19.5	5.3
56.0	64.6	42.4	% Profit Before Taxes/Tangible Net Worth		28.9	26.7	22.2	49.9	53.1
(126) 25.1	(121) 28.3	(94) 13.3			(14) 8.4	(13) 4.5	3.3	(18) 18.9	(23) 31.5
3.4	5.9	-1.9			-7.6	-14.1	-4.9	6.6	16.6
18.2	21.9	12.9	% Profit Before Taxes/Total Assets	.8	19.3	10.4	7.4	10.8	21.1
7.4	8.8	3.9		-1.8	6.4	.9	1.4	4.6	10.7
.7	1.3	-1.8		-22.7	-3.6	-7.5	-1.5	-.3	3.3
132.4	119.0	77.6	Sales/Net Fixed Assets	56.2	110.2	101.5	44.7	83.3	83.1
45.3	38.0	31.4		22.9	36.7	24.9	25.4	49.1	40.5
11.9	17.7	14.4		7.8	15.4	8.6	7.4	22.5	17.2
3.2	3.8	3.2	Sales/Total Assets	3.0	3.3	3.2	3.1	4.5	2.8
2.4	2.5	2.4		1.6	2.6	1.6	2.4	2.5	2.5
1.7	1.6	1.6		1.0	1.4	1.2	1.8	1.8	1.8
.4	.3	.5	% Depr., Dep., Amort./Sales		.7	.9	.8	.4	.2
(116) .8	(97) .8	(86) .9			(14) .8	(12) 1.2	(13) 1.0	(19) .6	(22) .6
1.8	1.7	1.7			2.1	2.8	3.2	1.3	1.4
2.2	1.8	2.3	% Officers', Directors', Owners' Comp/Sales		1.8				
(64) 4.7	(57) 3.8	(45) 5.0			(10) 5.9				
9.6	9.6	9.6			8.6				
3583895M	4031151M	3298139M	Net Sales ($)	7198M	40097M	58097M	127844M	318351M	2746552M
1683325M	1598133M	1532157M	Total Assets ($)	5136M	20202M	33717M	73740M	126460M	1272902M

© RMA 2005

M = $ thousand   MM = $ million

See Pages 11 through 21 for Explanation of Ratios and Data

WHOLESALE—Recyclable Material Merchant Wholesalers NAICS 423930 (SIC 5093)

Current Data Sorted By Assets   **Comparative Historical Data**

	0-500M	500M-2MM	2-10MM	10-50MM	50-100MM	100-250MM	Type of Statement	4/1/00-3/31/01 ALL	4/1/01-3/31/02 ALL
		1	9	11	11	5	Unqualified	33	20
	2	14	52	25	1		Reviewed	71	74
	4	21	34	2			Compiled	91	72
	12	14	11	1			Tax Returns	24	14
	6	12	35	17	4	2	Other	60	70
	70 (4/1-9/30/04)			236 (10/1/04-3/31/05)					
NUMBER OF STATEMENTS	24	62	141	56	16	7	**NUMBER OF STATEMENTS**	279	250
	%	%	%	%	%	%	**ASSETS**	%	%
	23.4	12.3	9.8	8.5	7.0		Cash & Equivalents	7.4	6.5
	19.9	26.0	31.1	34.8	35.6		Trade Receivables (net)	28.2	26.5
	15.3	20.0	20.8	22.4	22.6		Inventory	20.8	21.9
	.9	1.3	2.7	2.7	1.5		All Other Current	3.3	3.2
	59.5	59.5	64.4	68.4	66.6		Total Current	59.6	58.1
	31.9	28.7	26.8	24.1	26.3		Fixed Assets (net)	31.4	32.9
	1.0	4.4	1.0	1.7	3.1		Intangibles (net)	2.5	2.6
	7.7	7.4	7.8	5.7	3.9		All Other Non-Current	6.4	6.3
	100.0	100.0	100.0	100.0	100.0		Total	100.0	100.0
							LIABILITIES		
	11.3	9.3	11.8	9.9	11.0		Notes Payable-Short Term	14.9	15.7
	2.3	4.0	3.8	2.7	3.0		Cur. Mat.-L/T/D	4.0	4.4
	13.2	18.6	19.8	23.2	22.1		Trade Payables	15.6	15.6
	.0	.2	.4	.4	.6		Income Taxes Payable	.3	.1
	13.4	6.8	7.6	8.8	8.8		All Other Current	7.4	8.2
	40.1	39.0	43.3	44.8	45.5		Total Current	42.2	44.0
	21.4	15.1	14.5	9.1	15.7		Long-Term Debt	14.0	16.0
	1.3	.0	.6	.4	1.2		Deferred Taxes	.3	.6
	6.6	7.8	4.9	4.0	3.0		All Other Non-Current	4.1	5.2
	30.6	38.0	36.6	41.6	34.6		Net Worth	39.4	34.3
	100.0	100.0	100.0	100.0	100.0		Total Liabilities & Net Worth	100.0	100.0
							INCOME DATA		
	100.0	100.0	100.0	100.0	100.0		Net Sales	100.0	100.0
	33.5	33.2	26.7	20.3	17.7		Gross Profit	25.3	25.4
	28.3	27.9	20.2	11.9	10.9		Operating Expenses	22.2	24.1
	5.2	5.3	6.5	8.4	6.8		Operating Profit	3.1	1.3
	.3	.6	.3	.2	.9		All Other Expenses (net)	.8	1.0
	4.9	4.7	6.2	8.1	5.9		Profit Before Taxes	2.3	.3
							RATIOS		
	3.7	2.7	2.5	2.6	2.0		Current	2.5	2.0
	1.6	1.5	1.5	1.5	1.4			1.5	1.4
	.7	1.0	1.1	1.1	1.1			1.0	1.0
	2.6	1.7	1.8	1.9	1.2		Quick	1.4	1.2
	1.0	.9	.9	.9	1.0			.9	.8
	.4	.5	.6	.6	.8			.5	.4
	0 UND	11 34.4	19 18.8	30 12.3	35 10.4		Sales/Receivables	18 20.4	20 17.9
	7 49.2	24 15.4	34 10.7	37 9.9	44 8.2			30 12.3	32 11.5
	18 20.2	38 9.6	46 8.0	50 7.4	57 6.4			40 9.1	44 8.3
	1 361.6	8 48.5	8 46.0	16 22.9	10 36.0		Cost of Sales/Inventory	10 35.4	12 31.5
	7 50.9	17 22.0	21 17.8	26 13.9	22 16.6			26 14.3	28 13.2
	22 16.6	55 6.6	39 9.3	43 8.6	57 6.4			54 6.8	57 6.5
	2 175.4	9 39.0	13 29.1	11 31.8	22 16.5		Cost of Sales/Payables	7 53.8	10 35.3
	7 53.0	22 16.2	25 14.3	29 12.6	28 13.0			18 20.1	22 16.5
	20 17.9	38 9.5	42 8.7	45 8.2	46 8.0			32 11.3	38 9.6
	15.3	9.1	8.0	7.0	9.3		Sales/Working Capital	7.9	8.5
	39.7	19.8	15.8	15.0	17.6			19.0	18.3
	-97.8	-999.8	63.9	55.6	103.0			252.5	-839.8
	12.0	15.6	30.2	52.2	49.7		EBIT/Interest	5.2	3.4
	(15) 4.7	(57) 5.8	(134) 9.7	(51) 10.7	16.1			(255) 2.3	(228) 1.2
	1.7	2.5	4.8	6.0	4.1			1.1	-.2
			10.8	18.1			Net Profit + Depr., Dep., Amort./Cur. Mat. L./T/D	6.8	3.7
			(43) 4.4	(18) 3.3				(67) 2.2	(56) 1.7
			2.3	2.3				1.2	.7
	.2	.3	.3	.3	.6		Fixed/Worth	.3	.4
	1.3	.7	.7	.7	.9			.7	.8
	-2.0	2.0	1.4	1.2	1.6			1.8	2.6
	.5	.9	.7	.8	.9		Debt/Worth	.7	.8
	2.0	1.8	2.1	1.6	2.7			1.7	2.2
	-11.0	4.4	4.8	3.4	6.0			4.8	5.9
	95.4	60.2	72.1	88.3	85.9		% Profit Before Taxes/Tangible Net Worth	31.4	20.0
	(17) 55.6	(56) 36.0	(130) 50.9	(55) 56.3	(15) 53.1			(255) 11.7	(216) 2.7
	24.3	15.3	20.3	28.8	31.2			1.8	-8.8
	45.7	27.8	28.4	39.5	29.5		% Profit Before Taxes/Total Assets	11.3	6.8
	26.4	9.6	13.5	21.4	16.8			4.0	.6
	4.2	3.9	5.8	8.9	7.3			.3	-4.1
	63.9	49.9	33.2	26.2	22.7		Sales/Net Fixed Assets	28.7	20.8
	24.5	17.3	14.5	14.9	9.7			10.4	9.2
	11.6	9.6	7.1	9.0	8.5			5.7	4.5
	10.0	6.0	4.6	4.5	3.7		Sales/Total Assets	4.5	4.0
	5.2	4.0	3.6	3.2	3.2			3.1	2.7
	3.7	2.8	2.2	2.6	2.1			2.1	1.9
	.8	.6	.8	.4	.9		% Depr., Dep., Amort./Sales	.7	.7
	(19) 1.8	(49) 1.6	(126) 1.5	(53) 1.1	(15) 1.6			(247) 1.9	(230) 2.2
	3.0	3.8	3.5	1.8	1.9			3.6	4.2
	3.3	2.0	1.0	.3			% Officers', Directors', Owners' Comp/Sales	1.3	1.6
	(14) 5.6	(42) 4.4	(67) 2.6	(20) .9				(136) 2.8	(118) 2.9
	9.8	7.1	4.1	1.8				5.1	5.9
	47279M	472102M	2674464M	3855872M	3246601M	3365752M	Net Sales ($)	7738759M	6627604M
	6863M	77045M	723657M	1078199M	1053910M	1168105M	Total Assets ($)	3121685M	2739115M

M = $ thousand   MM = $ million
See Pages 11 through 21 for Explanation of Ratios and Data

Comparative Historical Data   **Current Data Sorted By Sales**

Type of Statement	4/1/02-3/31/03 ALL	4/1/03-3/31/04 ALL	4/1/04-3/31/05 ALL	0-1MM	1-3MM	3-5MM	5-10MM	10-25MM	25MM & OVER
Unqualified	26	37	37		1	2	2	5	27
Reviewed	79	84	94	1	4	8	12	25	44
Compiled	71	86	61	3	7	7	16	20	8
Tax Returns	15	28	38	4	8	5	12	7	2
Other	70	72	76	4	6	4	14	15	33
				70 (4/1-9/30/04)			*236 (10/1/04-3/31/05)*		
NUMBER OF STATEMENTS	261	307	306	12	26	26	56	72	114
ASSETS	%	%	%	%	%	%	%	%	%
Cash & Equivalents	8.0	8.7	10.9	31.6	14.2	9.3	11.2	11.6	7.7
Trade Receivables (net)	25.5	28.4	30.0	16.5	20.1	21.1	25.8	31.4	37.0
Inventory	20.4	19.9	21.2	15.5	16.4	16.7	22.2	19.8	24.2
All Other Current	2.8	3.1	2.2	.1	1.6	1.4	1.5	2.9	2.6
Total Current	56.6	60.0	64.3	63.8	52.3	48.5	60.8	65.6	71.5
Fixed Assets (net)	33.6	30.4	26.8	30.6	32.9	32.3	30.9	26.9	21.7
Intangibles (net)	2.7	2.4	1.9	.8	4.4	4.6	.8	2.3	1.2
All Other Non-Current	7.1	7.2	7.0	4.8	10.4	14.6	7.5	5.2	5.6
Total	100.0	100.0	100.0	100.0	100.0	100.0	100.0	100.0	100.0
LIABILITIES									
Notes Payable-Short Term	13.9	13.5	10.8	9.5	9.5	13.2	12.1	8.2	11.7
Cur. Mat.-L/T/D	5.0	4.6	3.4	1.5	4.5	2.9	3.9	4.8	2.4
Trade Payables	15.2	17.9	19.8	8.9	15.6	12.3	18.9	19.6	24.2
Income Taxes Payable	.2	.2	.3	.0	.0	.0	.3	.7	.3
All Other Current	8.0	8.1	8.4	10.0	11.5	7.3	6.0	6.7	10.0
Total Current	42.2	44.3	42.7	29.8	41.0	35.8	41.1	40.0	48.6
Long-Term Debt	16.0	14.8	14.3	18.3	28.6	19.8	16.6	11.2	10.2
Deferred Taxes	.4	.4	.6	.0	1.2	.1	.7	.4	.6
All Other Non-Current	7.9	7.5	5.3	5.6	9.6	7.1	4.4	5.1	4.5
Net Worth	33.5	33.1	37.1	46.3	19.7	37.3	37.2	43.4	36.1
Total Liabilities & Net Worth	100.0	100.0	100.0	100.0	100.0	100.0	100.0	100.0	100.0
INCOME DATA									
Net Sales	100.0	100.0	100.0	100.0	100.0	100.0	100.0	100.0	100.0
Gross Profit	26.9	26.8	26.7	40.2	41.6	38.4	31.6	25.7	17.4
Operating Expenses	23.3	22.7	20.2	32.2	36.2	31.0	26.8	18.1	10.8
Operating Profit	3.6	4.1	6.5	8.0	5.5	7.5	4.9	7.7	6.6
All Other Expenses (net)	.8	.4	.4	1.6	1.0	.4	.0	.3	.3
Profit Before Taxes	2.9	3.7	6.2	6.4	4.5	7.1	4.9	7.3	6.3
RATIOS									
Current	2.1	2.1	2.6	10.3	2.8	2.9	2.2	2.6	2.1
	1.4	1.4	1.5	2.3	1.3	1.3	1.5	1.7	1.4
	1.0	1.0	1.1	.9	.8	.8	1.1	1.2	1.1
Quick	1.4	1.3	1.8	9.9	1.7	1.8	1.3	2.0	1.5
	.8	.8	.9	2.2	.9	.8	.9	1.1	.9
	.5	.5	.6	.3	.5	.4	.5	.6	.7
Sales/Receivables	19 19.4	17 21.3	17 21.9	0 UND	9 38.8	11 33.4	8 43.1	21 17.5	28 13.0
	32 11.5	36 10.2	33 11.2	15 24.7	17 21.8	31 11.9	28 13.0	32 11.5	36 10.0
	43 8.5	50 7.3	45 8.1	32 11.5	45 8.1	41 8.9	47 7.8	43 8.4	47 7.7
Cost of Sales/Inventory	10 34.9	10 36.0	9 41.3	5 80.8	5 73.4	0 UND	8 47.5	9 38.5	11 34.6
	24 15.0	25 14.4	21 17.5	25 14.8	12 31.4	18 19.9	23 16.1	17 21.3	24 15.5
	59 6.2	53 6.9	43 8.5	102 3.6	71 5.1	67 5.4	63 5.8	37 10.0	39 9.3
Cost of Sales/Payables	9 41.6	11 32.9	12 31.6	4 87.5	5 79.8	15 25.1	10 36.0	11 32.1	12 30.0
	22 16.5	26 14.0	25 14.9	16 22.9	22 16.4	28 12.8	28 13.1	25 14.7	25 14.8
	35 10.3	44 8.3	41 9.0	23 15.7	57 6.4	42 8.6	51 7.2	39 9.4	38 9.7
Sales/Working Capital	8.7	8.6	8.0	3.9	7.8	7.2	7.7	8.2	9.2
	19.5	22.2	16.9	15.7	26.8	36.6	16.6	14.2	18.7
	-514.0	577.6	101.7	NM	-52.7	-65.9	107.9	53.9	69.3
EBIT/Interest	6.5	11.3	31.2		12.2	14.2	25.2	60.2	41.2
	(239) 2.9	(284) 4.6	(280) 9.5	(22) 2.8	(24) 9.2	(53) 7.8	(68) 12.0	(108) 10.3	
	1.3	1.7	4.0		1.8	2.3	2.7	6.0	4.8
Net Profit + Depr., Dep., Amort./Cur. Mat. L/T/D	3.9	4.7	11.3				7.3	12.0	12.4
	(55) 2.3	(67) 2.5	(82) 4.0			(13) 2.8	(25) 4.5	(38) 4.1	
	1.3	1.8	2.2				1.2	3.1	2.3
Fixed/Worth	.4	.4	.3	.1	.7	.4	.3	.3	.3
	.9	.9	.7	.5	1.3	.7	.7	.6	.7
	2.9	2.2	1.6	2.6	-2.1	2.6	1.7	1.5	1.2
Debt/Worth	.8	.9	.8	.2	1.8	.7	.9	.6	.9
	1.9	2.1	1.9	1.1	3.1	1.8	1.6	1.3	2.2
	7.2	5.4	4.7	2.1	-12.5	5.7	3.1	3.5	4.9
% Profit Before Taxes/Tangible Net Worth	42.1	48.6	74.1	58.1	86.0	60.6	55.4	80.2	87.1
	(224) 14.6	(280) 21.7	(280) 49.0	(10) 42.9	(19) 34.9	(22) 40.2	(53) 26.5	(67) 60.5	(109) 56.3
	4.2	8.5	21.2	26.6	5.5	21.2	10.5	37.6	28.3
% Profit Before Taxes/Total Assets	12.1	15.4	31.7	46.3	40.0	26.8	20.0	41.0	32.3
	4.5	7.1	14.3	15.9	6.5	14.0	10.3	20.7	16.3
	1.0	2.0	5.5	-5.8	2.6	3.7	3.6	11.3	5.7
Sales/Net Fixed Assets	21.2	24.5	34.4	55.5	44.4	19.0	28.4	31.6	51.7
	9.5	10.6	15.2	20.8	8.7	10.0	12.1	18.0	19.6
	4.9	5.6	8.3	5.8	4.6	5.3	6.0	8.8	9.9
Sales/Total Assets	4.1	4.3	4.9	4.7	5.3	3.7	4.7	4.7	5.2
	2.8	2.9	3.6	2.6	3.0	2.8	3.2	3.8	3.7
	2.0	2.0	2.5	1.4	1.9	1.7	1.8	2.8	3.0
% Depr., Dep., Amort./Sales	1.1	1.0	.6	1.9	.8	.7	.8	.9	.4
	(236) 2.5	(275) 2.3	(268) 1.4	(10) 3.4	(20) 2.4	(21) 2.1	(50) 2.0	(64) 1.6	(103) .9
	4.3	4.0	2.0	4.5	4.3	5.0	4.9	3.0	1.6
% Officers', Directors', Owners' Comp/Sales	1.6	1.2	1.2		3.0	3.6	1.8	1.0	.5
	(116) 3.3	(146) 2.8	(147) 2.7	(12) 4.3	(18) 7.0	(33) 3.5	(35) 2.2	(41) 1.1	
	5.6	5.8	5.1		6.3	10.8	5.3	3.9	2.3
Net Sales ($)	8714155M	10470261M	13662070M	7761M	50914M	103451M	405751M	1194553M	11899640M
Total Assets ($)	3566350M	3946381M	4107779M	5516M	24326M	46457M	159954M	353569M	3517957M

M = $ thousand   MM = $ million
See Pages 11 through 21 for Explanation of Ratios and Data

Current Data Sorted By Assets   **Comparative Historical Data**

0-500M	500M-2MM	2-10MM	10-50MM	50-100MM	100-250MM	Type of Statement	4/1/00-3/31/01 ALL	4/1/01-3/31/02 ALL
		6	12	3	1	Unqualified	26	32
	9	29	24	2	3	Reviewed	49	44
7	11	19	1			Compiled	45	35
6	14	6				Tax Returns	14	9
1	7	11	14	6	6	Other	25	26
	52 (4/1-9/30/04)		146 (10/1/04-3/31/05)					
14	41	71	51	11	10	**NUMBER OF STATEMENTS**	159	146
%	%	%	%	%	%	**ASSETS**	%	%
19.1	13.6	5.8	3.5	3.3	1.9	Cash & Equivalents	5.6	6.3
18.5	24.9	34.4	33.3	31.1	28.9	Trade Receivables (net)	30.6	30.5
51.0	52.1	49.1	55.1	46.2	55.9	Inventory	50.4	49.5
2.5	1.0	2.3	.9	.9	1.3	All Other Current	1.1	1.5
91.0	91.6	91.7	92.8	81.5	88.0	Total Current	87.7	87.8
4.5	4.3	3.9	3.1	4.8	3.5	Fixed Assets (net)	5.5	5.5
.9	.0	1.2	.5	2.3	3.9	Intangibles (net)	2.2	2.1
3.6	4.1	3.2	-3.6	11.4	4.6	All Other Non-Current	4.6	4.6
100.0	100.0	100.0	100.0	100.0	100.0	Total	100.0	100.0
						LIABILITIES		
10.4	15.7	19.6	31.1	22.6	20.3	Notes Payable-Short Term	21.5	21.4
1.6	1.4	1.1	1.2	.6	.4	Cur. Mat.-L/T/D	1.0	1.4
18.0	23.2	28.3	24.8	21.9	20.6	Trade Payables	21.3	20.6
.2	.1	.1	.2	.0	.0	Income Taxes Payable	.4	.2
8.8	8.2	5.5	8.4	12.7	8.5	All Other Current	8.9	7.1
38.9	48.6	54.5	65.7	57.9	49.8	Total Current	53.1	50.7
24.8	4.3	2.6	1.9	10.0	11.6	Long-Term Debt	4.1	4.9
.0	.0	.0	.0	.8	.0	Deferred Taxes	.1	.1
5.7	4.0	4.0	3.3	1.9	5.8	All Other Non-Current	7.0	5.4
30.5	43.1	38.7	29.2	29.4	32.7	Net Worth	35.7	38.9
100.0	100.0	100.0	100.0	100.0	100.0	Total Liabilities & Net Worth	100.0	100.0
						INCOME DATA		
100.0	100.0	100.0	100.0	100.0	100.0	Net Sales	100.0	100.0
37.4	32.5	27.5	19.1	25.2	23.7	Gross Profit	27.0	30.3
33.2	27.8	23.7	15.9	20.7	20.1	Operating Expenses	22.9	26.4
4.2	4.7	3.9	3.3	4.5	3.6	Operating Profit	4.2	3.9
.5	-.1	1.4	.5	1.4	2.5	All Other Expenses (net)	.9	1.5
3.7	4.8	2.5	2.8	3.1	1.1	Profit Before Taxes	3.3	2.4
						RATIOS		
6.3	3.5	2.3	1.6	1.8	3.1		2.6	2.8
3.4	2.2	1.6	1.3	1.4	1.7	Current	1.6	1.7
1.6	1.4	1.3	1.2	1.2	1.2		1.3	1.3
2.9	1.4	1.1	.8	.8	1.0		1.0	1.1
.9	.9	.7	.6	.5	.5	Quick	.6	.7
.4	.5	.4	.3	.3	.3		.4	.4
0 UND	2 152.8	36 10.2	53 6.9	52 7.0	64 5.7		24 15.2	30 12.0
14 25.3	22 16.5	65 5.7	72 5.1	82 4.4	82 4.5	Sales/Receivables	52 7.1	60 6.1
71 5.2	77 4.7	112 3.2	99 3.7	112 3.3	103 3.5		78 4.7	85 4.3
59 6.1	67 5.5	76 4.8	77 4.7	75 4.9	130 2.8		64 5.7	73 5.0
115 3.2	106 3.5	156 2.3	148 2.5	134 2.7	176 2.1	Cost of Sales/Inventory	125 2.9	144 2.5
217 1.7	264 1.4	248 1.5	223 1.6	259 1.4	434 .8		183 2.0	208 1.8
8 46.4	14 25.8	28 13.0	29 12.5	37 9.8	30 12.1		20 18.0	24 15.4
15 24.1	49 7.5	69 5.3	64 5.7	49 7.4	64 5.7	Cost of Sales/Payables	44 8.3	50 7.2
36 10.1	88 4.1	127 2.9	104 3.5	101 3.6	142 2.6		77 4.7	84 4.4
2.4	2.8	3.0	4.5	4.2	2.2		3.8	3.6
4.9	6.3	5.0	7.3	5.3	3.1	Sales/Working Capital	6.3	5.7
9.0	14.5	8.8	15.0	14.6	8.3		13.9	11.5
10.2	25.4	7.9	7.5	7.9	7.4		6.3	5.1
(11) 3.6	(34) 6.2	(65) 2.9	(48) 2.8	2.0	1.4	EBIT/Interest	(150) 2.3	(138) 1.6
.4	2.2	1.3	1.7	1.7	.1		1.4	1.0
			15.6			Net Profit + Depr., Dep.,		18.7	9.8
			(10) 5.6			Amort./Cur. Mat. L/T/D	(25) 2.8	(20) 4.4
			1.5				1.3	.0
.0	.0	.0	.0	.0	.0		.0	.0
.1	.0	.1	.1	.1	.1	Fixed/Worth	.1	.1
.5	.2	.2	.2	.2	.4		.3	.3
.8	.4	1.0	1.6	1.6	1.6		.8	.7
2.1	1.4	2.1	3.0	2.2	2.4	Debt/Worth	2.3	1.9
UND	4.8	3.6	5.1	7.6	9.6		6.2	5.3
161.7	44.1	27.4	35.3	17.2	13.1	% Profit Before Taxes/Tangible	31.7	24.3
(11) 17.0	(39) 22.0	(69) 9.1	15.3	(10) 10.3	3.5	Net Worth	(148) 14.6	(139) 7.8
2.7	4.6	1.4	4.9	5.2	-12.4		4.7	.5
14.7	19.9	7.7	7.5	9.9	5.5	% Profit Before Taxes/Total	9.7	8.4
7.8	7.0	2.7	3.1	3.0	.5	Assets	3.7	2.3
-.4	1.7	.4	1.0	1.0	-1.9		1.3	.1
UND	999.8	422.6	532.2	222.3	130.2		340.6	221.6
123.5	169.3	82.5	129.7	56.9	33.0	Sales/Net Fixed Assets	107.1	81.5
28.5	43.3	33.8	45.2	34.4	16.4		37.5	28.1
3.5	3.3	2.4	2.4	2.0	1.6		3.0	2.7
2.5	2.2	1.7	1.6	1.6	1.3	Sales/Total Assets	2.0	1.9
1.9	1.4	1.2	1.4	1.0	.8		1.5	1.4
	.2	.1	.1	.2	.3		.1	.1
	(25) .6	(58) .4	(44) .2	(10) .6	.7	% Depr., Dep., Amort./Sales	(120) .2	(124) .4
	1.0	.7	.6	1.1	1.5		.7	.9
5.0	2.8	2.0	.4				1.3	1.6
(11) 9.7	(28) 5.4	(47) 3.0	(26) 1.0			% Officers', Directors',	(98) 2.9	(90) 3.9
10.8	8.7	6.2	2.8			Owners' Comp/Sales	5.8	6.2
11200M	141838M	702723M	5300307M	1150975M	1723969M	Net Sales ($)	3690061M	5830063M
3850M	51380M	347653M	1112806M	753816M	1407242M	Total Assets ($)	2045063M	2244197M

M = $ thousand   MM = $ million
See Pages 11 through 21 for Explanation of Ratios and Data

Comparative Historical Data / Current Data Sorted By Sales

	4/1/02-3/31/03	4/1/03-3/31/04	4/1/04-3/31/05		0-1MM	1-3MM	3-5MM	5-10MM	10-25MM	25MM & OVER
				Type of Statement		52 (4/1-9/30/04)		146 (10/1/04-3/31/05)		
	17	21	22	Unqualified			2	3	2	15
	60	73	67	Reviewed	1	6	6	13	21	20
	29	41	38	Compiled	8	5	8	12	4	1
	20	26	26	Tax Returns	6	8	7	4	1	
	30	31	45	Other	1	5	3	7	6	23
	ALL 156	ALL 192	ALL 198	**NUMBER OF STATEMENTS**	16	24	26	39	34	59
	%	%	%	**ASSETS**	%	%	%	%	%	%
	8.1	8.0	7.4	Cash & Equivalents	18.2	7.2	8.3	8.1	8.1	3.4
	32.0	29.4	30.6	Trade Receivables (net)	18.4	19.8	32.3	30.0	37.9	33.6
	48.0	50.5	51.6	Inventory	51.5	62.7	50.1	51.5	46.6	50.7
	2.2	2.4	1.6	All Other Current	2.0	1.0	4.3	1.5	.4	1.2
	90.3	90.4	91.2	Total Current	90.1	90.7	95.1	91.0	93.1	88.9
	3.8	4.8	3.8	Fixed Assets (net)	6.6	3.3	3.1	4.8	2.3	3.9
	.8	1.1	.9	Intangibles (net)	.1	.6	.1	1.3	1.2	1.3
	5.1	3.7	4.1	All Other Non-Current	3.3	5.3	1.7	2.9	3.5	5.9
	100.0	100.0	100.0	Total	100.0	100.0	100.0	100.0	100.0	100.0
				LIABILITIES						
	13.7	14.6	21.3	Notes Payable-Short Term	10.4	23.0	16.0	16.8	24.9	26.8
	1.2	.8	1.2	Cur. Mat.-L/T/D	.5	.9	4.0	.6	.7	.8
	28.5	24.8	24.9	Trade Payables	18.9	19.5	31.0	28.1	24.1	24.2
	.3	.2	.1	Income Taxes Payable	.3	.0	.2	.0	.0	.2
	10.4	14.0	7.6	All Other Current	7.4	6.9	4.9	8.8	7.0	8.6
	54.1	54.4	55.0	Total Current	37.5	50.4	56.1	54.4	56.8	60.6
	4.6	4.6	5.2	Long-Term Debt	13.6	7.7	5.3	4.2	.2	5.5
	.1	.0	.1	Deferred Taxes	.0	.0	.1	.1	.0	.2
	5.1	4.6	3.9	All Other Non-Current	7.6	6.5	3.5	4.1	2.0	3.1
	36.2	36.4	35.8	Net Worth	41.2	35.5	35.1	37.2	41.0	30.7
	100.0	100.0	100.0	Total Liabilities & Net Worth	100.0	100.0	100.0	100.0	100.0	100.0
				INCOME DATA						
	100.0	100.0	100.0	Net Sales	100.0	100.0	100.0	100.0	100.0	100.0
	27.1	27.0	26.8	Gross Profit	38.5	35.6	27.4	29.3	19.5	22.2
	24.0	24.2	22.8	Operating Expenses	35.6	32.5	23.7	25.4	15.4	17.7
	3.1	2.8	3.9	Operating Profit	2.9	3.1	3.7	3.9	4.1	4.5
	.9	.7	.8	All Other Expenses (net)	.5	.6	.4	1.2	.6	1.1
	2.3	2.1	3.1	Profit Before Taxes	2.4	2.6	3.3	2.7	3.5	3.4
				RATIOS						
	2.4	2.6	2.5	Current	5.9	3.2	2.6	2.3	2.3	1.9
	1.7	1.7	1.5		3.1	2.2	1.5	1.6	1.4	1.4
	1.3	1.3	1.3		1.7	1.2	1.3	1.3	1.3	1.2
	1.1	1.0	1.0	Quick	2.6	.9	1.3	1.1	1.2	.8
	.8	.6	.7		.9	.6	.8	.7	.7	.6
	.4	.4	.4		.4	.3	.4	.4	.4	.3
28	13.3	21 · 17.1	25 · 14.4	Sales/Receivables	0 · UND	2 · 214.2	13 · 27.8	21 · 17.5	36 · 10.1	52 · 7.0
60	6.1	57 · 6.4	64 · 5.7		20 · 18.7	53 · 6.9	72 · 5.1	60 · 6.1	71 · 5.1	66 · 5.5
91	4.0	89 · 4.1	90 · 4.1		78 · 4.7	84 · 4.3	84 · 4.3	88 · 4.2	109 · 3.4	94 · 3.9
66	5.5	67 · 5.5	74 · 4.9	Cost of Sales/Inventory	68 · 5.3	111 · 3.3	74 · 4.9	71 · 5.2	56 · 6.5	63 · 5.8
121	3.0	135 · 2.7	141 · 2.6		189 · 1.9	253 · 1.4	114 · 3.2	158 · 2.3	111 · 3.3	137 · 2.7
193	1.9	240 · 1.5	249 · 1.5		370 · 1.0	390 · .9	234 · 1.6	213 · 1.7	178 · 2.1	191 · 1.9
35	10.4	27 · 13.4	23 · 15.8	Cost of Sales/Payables	13 · 27.6	23 · 16.2	24 · 15.5	23 · 15.7	25 · 14.6	30 · 12.3
62	5.9	57 · 6.4	58 · 6.2		21 · 17.1	51 · 7.2	77 · 4.7	71 · 5.1	60 · 6.0	57 · 6.4
104	3.5	104 · 3.5	103 · 3.5		104 · 3.5	143 · 2.6	106 · 3.4	131 · 2.8	88 · 4.2	101 · 3.6
	3.5	3.0	3.3	Sales/Working Capital	1.5	2.2	3.7	3.0	3.7	4.2
	5.9	6.2	5.5		2.9	4.1	5.2	5.1	6.0	7.3
	10.1	10.6	10.0		7.6	12.7	8.2	9.4	8.9	15.3
	7.6	7.7	10.2	EBIT/Interest	14.5	5.7	25.5	9.0	7.1	13.7
(143)	2.6	(173) 2.5	(179) 3.3		(11) 3.6	(21) 2.9	(25) 5.5	(35) 3.3	(30) 2.6	(57) 3.4
	1.2	1.2	1.5		.3	1.0	1.6	1.1	1.8	1.6
	11.6	31.0	11.4	Net Profit + Depr., Dep., Amort./Cur. Mat. L/T/D						14.1
(17)	3.0	(16) 2.4	(25) 3.1						(12)	5.8
	.3	.5	.4							1.9
	.0	.0	.0	Fixed/Worth	.0	.0	.0	.0	.0	.0
	.0	.1	.1		.1	.0	.0	.1	.0	.1
	.1	.1	.2		.3	.3	.2	.1	.1	.2
	.8	.9	.9	Debt/Worth	.6	.8	.8	1.0	.8	1.5
	2.0	2.1	2.2		1.1	1.9	2.2	2.7	2.2	2.5
	3.9	4.0	4.6		4.1	7.0	4.8	4.6	3.5	5.1
	28.2	28.8	32.8	% Profit Before Taxes/Tangible Net Worth	43.0	28.0	36.0	25.0	26.3	37.6
(148)	9.5	(185) 7.8	(190) 11.7		(14) 13.1	(23) 4.5	(23) 24.2	(38) 6.3	9.9	(58) 15.4
	1.7	1.0	3.3		-1.5	-.2	8.9	.8	5.2	4.9
	8.2	8.1	9.3	% Profit Before Taxes/Total Assets	14.2	10.1	9.0	8.1	5.8	9.5
	2.6	2.6	3.4		7.0	1.9	6.2	3.0	2.6	4.0
	.3	.3	.9		-1.1	-.1	1.5	.1	1.2	1.0
	384.4	342.9	486.1	Sales/Net Fixed Assets	UND	195.0	999.8	314.7	504.4	532.2
	147.0	84.7	99.8		123.5	74.6	179.6	82.5	144.0	80.3
	43.4	39.5	35.0		17.5	35.0	36.1	35.1	52.0	34.1
	2.8	2.8	2.5	Sales/Total Assets	3.3	2.0	2.5	2.8	2.6	2.4
	1.9	1.7	1.8		2.0	1.4	2.1	1.9	1.8	1.7
	1.4	1.3	1.3		1.1	1.2	1.2	1.2	1.4	1.3
	.1	.1	.1	% Depr., Dep., Amort./Sales		.4	.2	.1	.1	.1
(121)	.3	(146) .4	(153) .4			(19) .8	(17) .4	(30) .4	(29) .2	(52) .2
	.8	.7	.9			1.1	.5	.8	.7	.9
	1.5	1.7	1.2	% Officers', Directors', Owners' Comp/Sales	6.7	4.5	2.7	2.2	.8	.4
(98)	3.4	(117) 3.3	(124) 3.0		(10) 9.8	(19) 7.3	(19) 4.3	(24) 2.9	(22) 1.3	(30) .8
	6.1	6.5	6.7		11.2	10.5	6.8	4.3	3.1	2.4
	2335235M	8943155M	9031012M	Net Sales ($)	10434M	46442M	101127M	275446M	578700M	8018863M
	1285957M	2724792M	3676747M	Total Assets ($)	7511M	34323M	59205M	160093M	370916M	3044699M

M = $ thousand   MM = $ million
See Pages 11 through 21 for Explanation of Ratios and Data

Current Data Sorted By Assets   **Comparative Historical Data**

						Type of Statement		
1	3	14	13	5	1	Unqualified	42	38
1	30	62	7	2		Reviewed	67	56
10	47	43	7	2	2	Compiled	101	84
34	48	21	2			Tax Returns	46	31
17	47	47	19	5	2	Other	82	98
	89 (4/1-9/30/04)		401 (10/1/04-3/31/05)				4/1/00-3/31/01	4/1/01-3/31/02
0-500M	500M-2MM	2-10MM	10-50MM	50-100MM	100-250MM		ALL	ALL
63	175	187	48	12	5	**NUMBER OF STATEMENTS**	338	307
%	%	%	%	%	%	**ASSETS**	%	%
19.2	7.4	6.5	6.4	9.9		Cash & Equivalents	9.3	9.1
27.1	34.6	34.6	29.2	23.2		Trade Receivables (net)	33.6	33.4
28.3	35.1	37.8	38.2	24.8		Inventory	34.2	34.0
1.2	2.4	1.9	2.5	4.4		All Other Current	2.6	2.8
75.8	79.5	80.8	76.3	62.3		Total Current	79.6	79.3
15.3	11.8	10.3	13.9	12.2		Fixed Assets (net)	12.5	13.0
2.5	1.7	3.1	5.9	19.1		Intangibles (net)	2.9	3.4
6.4	7.0	5.8	3.9	6.3		All Other Non-Current	5.0	4.2
100.0	100.0	100.0	100.0	100.0		Total	100.0	100.0
						LIABILITIES		
16.7	15.9	15.8	19.4	12.9		Notes Payable-Short Term	16.8	17.2
5.4	2.6	2.6	2.1	1.7		Cur. Mat.-L/T/D	2.2	2.8
20.5	24.3	23.8	19.9	13.2		Trade Payables	22.5	22.9
.1	.1	.2	.4	.3		Income Taxes Payable	.3	.2
17.3	7.8	9.5	8.6	10.8		All Other Current	9.1	9.8
60.1	50.8	51.8	50.4	38.8		Total Current	51.0	52.7
26.1	11.1	7.5	11.4	11.2		Long-Term Debt	10.8	9.4
.0	.1	.2	.4	.6		Deferred Taxes	.1	.1
5.4	4.7	5.5	5.1	5.3		All Other Non-Current	4.0	3.9
8.5	33.3	35.0	32.7	44.1		Net Worth	34.2	33.9
100.0	100.0	100.0	100.0	100.0		Total Liabilities & Net Worth	100.0	100.0
						INCOME DATA		
100.0	100.0	100.0	100.0	100.0		Net Sales	100.0	100.0
36.5	30.8	28.3	27.8	39.6		Gross Profit	30.7	30.2
34.3	28.2	24.9	23.1	26.2		Operating Expenses	25.7	27.2
2.2	2.6	3.4	4.7	13.4		Operating Profit	5.0	3.0
.6	.3	.5	.8	7.0		All Other Expenses (net)	.9	.7
1.6	2.3	3.0	4.0	6.4		Profit Before Taxes	4.1	2.3
						RATIOS		
4.3	2.5	2.3	2.2	2.8		Current	2.5	2.3
1.7	1.5	1.6	1.6	1.7			1.6	1.5
1.1	1.2	1.2	1.1	1.3			1.2	1.1
1.8	1.3	1.2	.9	1.4		Quick	1.4	1.3
(62) 1.2	.8	.7	.7	.9			.9	.8
.6	.6	.5	.5	.6			.5	.5
0 UND	27 13.5	30 12.0	30 12.2	35 10.3		Sales/Receivables	28 13.2	29 12.6
23 16.2	39 9.3	43 8.4	43 8.5	42 8.7			41 9.0	40 9.0
33 11.1	51 7.2	56 6.5	64 5.7	64 5.7			56 6.6	56 6.5
2 148.6	27 13.6	35 10.4	48 7.6	73 5.0		Cost of Sales/Inventory	28 13.3	31 11.6
33 11.0	55 6.7	62 5.9	86 4.2	99 3.7			61 6.0	64 5.7
79 4.6	94 3.9	113 3.2	134 2.7	147 2.5			108 3.4	108 3.4
3 127.8	16 22.1	21 17.0	16 22.7	23 16.1		Cost of Sales/Payables	15 23.9	14 25.7
16 22.5	35 10.4	36 10.2	32 11.4	37 9.9			32 11.5	31 11.7
42 8.8	59 6.2	53 6.9	65 5.6	86 4.2			58 6.3	53 6.9
9.2	6.2	5.5	5.1	2.9		Sales/Working Capital	5.6	5.5
15.5	12.1	9.9	7.5	5.0			10.0	10.9
66.4	38.3	22.6	20.8	16.1			26.2	36.9
13.8	12.8	14.1	8.2	14.1		EBIT/Interest	8.8	6.6
(49) 2.7	(157) 3.8	(173) 4.7	(44) 4.1	7.1			(298) 2.9	(260) 2.5
.0	1.4	1.8	1.9	3.6			1.4	1.0
	3.8	5.6	46.7			Net Profit + Depr., Dep.,	19.6	6.9
	(24) 1.5	(31) 2.1	(12) 2.6			Amort./Cur. Mat. L /T/D	(56) 2.5	(53) 2.5
	.2	.5	1.3				1.0	1.4
.0	.1	.1	.1	.2		Fixed/Worth	.1	.1
.3	.2	.2	.3	.9			.2	.3
6.5	.8	.7	1.8	NM			.8	1.0
.7	.8	1.1	1.1	.7		Debt/Worth	.8	.8
2.9	2.2	2.3	2.8	2.9			1.9	2.3
−79.5	6.5	5.7	6.2	NM			4.5	5.9
108.8	53.9	50.7	60.0			% Profit Before Taxes/Tangible	47.7	40.9
(47) 31.6	(154) 17.7	(174) 19.5	(42) 27.9			Net Worth	(307) 21.3	(272) 14.7
2.2	2.1	6.4	7.2				5.5	3.3
28.2	15.5	13.4	14.8	11.6		% Profit Before Taxes/Total	16.7	11.1
8.2	5.4	5.6	6.3	6.9		Assets	6.3	4.3
−5.9	.6	1.5	1.8	3.8			1.7	.1
688.0	155.8	129.1	120.4	44.7		Sales/Net Fixed Assets	125.7	94.2
51.2	51.6	52.0	44.4	34.5			40.4	36.1
24.8	21.8	23.5	11.6	7.5			17.8	16.5
6.9	4.4	3.6	2.5	2.6		Sales/Total Assets	4.0	3.6
4.3	3.1	2.8	2.2	1.3			2.9	2.8
3.1	2.2	2.1	1.6	.9			2.1	2.1
.3	.3	.3	.2	.5		% Depr., Dep., Amort./Sales	.3	.4
(36) 1.0	(129) .8	(155) .6	(43) .5	(10) 2.2			(265) .7	(242) .8
1.6	1.5	1.3	1.3	2.7			1.6	1.5
3.5	2.1	1.5				% Officers', Directors',	2.4	2.1
(34) 8.3	(99) 3.6	(86) 3.4				Owners' Comp/Sales	(165) 4.4	(134) 3.8
11.9	6.8	5.9					8.0	7.8
103936M	717545M	2553724M	2653241M	1823813M	2957847M	Net Sales ($)	7684634M	5995687M
18139M	205903M	860921M	995302M	995740M	952686M	Total Assets ($)	3315155M	2617032M

M = $ thousand   MM = $ million
See Pages 11 through 21 for Explanation of Ratios and Data

Comparative Historical Data | Current Data Sorted By Sales

			Type of Statement						
59	55	37	Unqualified		2	1	5	7	22
90	104	102	Reviewed	1	10	17	24	42	8
93	139	109	Compiled	4	27	13	25	31	9
42	92	105	Tax Returns	13	35	17	24	14	2
92	110	137	Other	10	30	23	19	26	29
4/1/02-3/31/03 ALL	4/1/03-3/31/04 ALL	4/1/04-3/31/05 ALL		89 (4/1-9/30/04)			401 (10/1/04-3/31/05)		
				0-1MM	1-3MM	3-5MM	5-10MM	10-25MM	25MM & OVER
376	500	490	**NUMBER OF STATEMENTS**	28	104	71	97	120	70
%	%	%	**ASSETS**	%	%	%	%	%	%
9.3	9.3	8.6	Cash & Equivalents	12.6	11.2	10.8	6.9	5.9	8.3
32.5	30.7	32.8	Trade Receivables (net)	19.5	29.5	33.2	36.5	35.7	32.7
34.9	34.8	35.0	Inventory	34.3	33.9	32.4	37.2	38.1	31.6
2.4	2.5	2.1	All Other Current	3.1	2.4	2.3	1.0	2.0	2.9
79.2	77.4	78.6	Total Current	69.4	77.1	78.7	81.6	81.6	75.5
13.0	13.1	11.8	Fixed Assets (net)	18.2	13.8	10.8	10.9	9.9	12.3
3.2	3.1	3.4	Intangibles (net)	8.8	2.3	1.5	1.5	3.2	7.9
4.6	6.4	6.1	All Other Non-Current	3.6	6.9	9.1	6.1	5.3	4.3
100.0	100.0	100.0	Total	100.0	100.0	100.0	100.0	100.0	100.0
			LIABILITIES						
18.1	15.6	16.3	Notes Payable-Short Term	19.0	16.4	14.5	13.8	16.8	19.7
2.7	3.5	2.9	Cur. Mat.-L/T/D	3.3	4.0	2.4	2.6	2.8	2.1
22.6	22.3	22.8	Trade Payables	14.6	21.4	22.1	27.2	23.0	22.2
.3	.3	.2	Income Taxes Payable	.0	.2	.1	.3	.2	.3
10.1	9.2	9.8	All Other Current	13.5	14.0	8.8	8.9	7.5	8.1
53.7	50.9	51.9	Total Current	50.5	56.0	47.9	52.7	50.2	52.4
7.8	10.2	11.7	Long-Term Debt	25.5	19.7	8.9	9.1	6.5	9.8
.1	.1	.2	Deferred Taxes	.0	.0	.2	.1	.2	.3
4.8	5.4	5.2	All Other Non-Current	4.3	6.8	3.7	4.7	6.7	2.7
33.6	33.4	31.0	Net Worth	19.7	17.5	39.2	33.4	36.3	34.8
100.0	100.0	100.0	Total Liabilities & Net Worth	100.0	100.0	100.0	100.0	100.0	100.0
			INCOME DATA						
100.0	100.0	100.0	Net Sales	100.0	100.0	100.0	100.0	100.0	100.0
31.2	30.5	30.5	Gross Profit	42.6	36.5	29.5	26.5	28.6	26.7
28.0	27.6	27.2	Operating Expenses	44.1	33.4	26.2	23.9	24.9	20.5
3.2	2.9	3.4	Operating Profit	-1.6	3.2	3.3	2.6	3.7	6.2
.7	.3	.6	All Other Expenses (net)	1.4	.7	.4	.1	.2	1.9
2.5	2.5	2.7	Profit Before Taxes	-3.0	2.4	2.8	2.5	3.5	4.4
			RATIOS						
2.3	2.5	2.5		3.9	2.8	2.9	2.4	2.4	2.1
1.5	1.5	1.6	Current	1.6	1.7	1.5	1.6	1.6	1.6
1.1	1.2	1.2		1.0	1.2	1.2	1.2	1.2	1.1
1.3	1.4	1.3		1.7	1.5	1.5	1.2	1.2	1.1
.8	.8	.8	Quick	.8	.8	.8	.8	.8	.7
.5	.5	.5		.3	.5	.6	.6	.6	.5

27	13.4	23	15.6	26	14.1	Sales/Receivables	11	33.3	20	17.8	19	19.0	28	13.1	30	12.2	29	12.6
41	8.9	39	9.4	40	9.2		24	15.0	37	9.7	39	9.2	40	9.2	40	9.0	41	8.9
56	6.5	52	7.0	54	6.8		58	6.3	53	6.9	53	6.9	51	7.1	56	6.5	55	6.7
34	10.9	29	12.5	27	13.4	Cost of Sales/Inventory	48	7.6	25	14.6	19	19.2	26	13.9	31	11.7	27	13.4
67	5.4	60	6.1	58	6.3		75	4.9	64	5.7	54	6.7	51	7.1	57	6.4	71	5.1
109	3.4	104	3.5	110	3.3		278	1.3	144	2.5	88	4.1	84	4.3	108	3.4	113	3.2
18	20.8	16	23.3	17	21.5	Cost of Sales/Payables	10	36.8	9	42.1	12	29.5	20	18.1	22	16.7	17	21.7
33	10.9	31	11.9	33	11.0		39	9.5	36	10.2	36	12.4	35	10.3	36	10.2	30	12.0
57	6.4	53	6.8	55	6.7		73	5.0	65	5.6	58	6.3	53	6.9	50	7.3	47	7.8

5.7		5.4		5.7	Sales/Working Capital	5.2	4.9	5.8	7.4	6.1	5.2
11.7		11.6		10.9		11.3	10.9	13.8	10.1	10.3	9.0
41.9		32.3		31.3		UND	31.7	38.8	23.8	19.3	80.9

	8.9		12.6		12.9	EBIT/Interest		2.8		8.1		15.7		9.7		16.0		13.1
(336)	3.0	(436)	3.7	(440)	4.0		(23)	.7	(85)	2.3	(65)	4.2	(88)	3.9	(113)	5.2	(66)	5.1
	1.2		1.5		1.6			-5.2		.7		1.7		1.7		2.3		2.5
	10.9		7.0		5.8	Net Profit + Depr., Dep., Amort./Cur. Mat. L/T/D								2.1		9.2		26.6
(80)	2.4	(81)	2.1	(76)	2.1								(18)	.8	(25)	3.2	(17)	7.6
	.8		.9		.6									.2		1.6		1.9
	.1		.1		.1	Fixed/Worth		.1		.0		.1		.1		.1		.1
	.3		.3		.3			.5		.3		.2		.2		.2		.4
	1.0		1.0		.9			-3.8		1.8		.5		.6		.6		1.5
	.9		.8		.9	Debt/Worth		.9		.8		.6		1.0		1.1		1.2
	2.3		2.1		2.3			5.0		2.8		1.6		2.5		2.0		2.9
	5.7		5.5		6.5			-12.3		14.5		5.1		4.9		5.0		8.3
	43.0		48.8		55.1	% Profit Before Taxes/Tangible Net Worth		98.0		54.9		63.8		39.2		64.4		64.5
(335)	14.0	(441)	20.2	(430)	21.6		(19)	12.7	(83)	21.8	(65)	17.8	(89)	17.1	(112)	26.4	(62)	31.0
	3.4		4.3		5.2			-44.4		2.9		2.1		4.2		8.2		9.3
	12.4		13.6		15.0	% Profit Before Taxes/Total Assets		13.1		14.6		16.6		14.8		15.3		15.6
	3.9		5.4		6.0			-.6		5.2		6.1		4.9		6.7		6.6
	.7		1.1		1.1			-12.2		.2		.6		1.5		2.3		2.2
	100.8		103.6		140.8	Sales/Net Fixed Assets		255.9		160.1		146.7		106.8		143.7		118.7
	36.7		43.8		49.7			38.4		37.7		62.0		47.4		55.9		53.8
	15.4		17.5		21.6			6.6		18.1		26.3		26.3		30.0		14.9
	3.8		3.9		4.2	Sales/Total Assets		3.8		4.2		4.4		4.5		4.0		4.5
	2.7		2.9		3.0			2.0		2.8		3.1		3.3		3.1		2.5
	2.1		2.0		2.0			1.2		1.9		2.1		2.3		2.2		1.8
	.3		.4		.3	% Depr., Dep., Amort./Sales		.8		.4		.3		.4		.3		.2
(320)	.8	(398)	.8	(376)	.7		(12)	2.6	(72)	1.0	(53)	.8	(77)	.7	(101)	.5	(61)	.6
	1.6		1.6		1.4			9.2		2.3		1.3		1.4		1.1		1.4
	2.1		1.8		1.9	% Officers', Directors', Owners' Comp/Sales		6.6		3.0		2.0		1.8		1.1		1.6
(191)	3.8	(235)	3.6	(229)	3.8		(11)	11.5	(53)	5.0	(39)	3.5	(57)	3.6	(59)	2.9	(10)	3.7
	6.9		6.8		7.3			8.6		8.8		8.6		6.0		5.1		7.9

8031202M	8572306M	10810106M	Net Sales ($)	16429M	199710M	276129M	690312M	1855065M	7772461M
3333586M	3850170M	4028691M	Total Assets ($)	15341M	83977M	98488M	237500M	694164M	2899221M

M = $ thousand   MM = $ million
See Pages 11 through 21 for Explanation of Ratios and Data

Current Data Sorted By Assets   Comparative Historical Data

0-500M	500M-2MM	2-10MM	10-50MM	50-100MM	100-250MM	Type of Statement	4/1/00-3/31/01 ALL	4/1/01-3/31/02 ALL
		5	13	3	2	Unqualified	20	18
	1	21	4			Reviewed	18	20
2	6	12	1			Compiled	23	22
2	5	1				Tax Returns	3	7
5	7	15	10	4	2	Other	34	27
	22 (4/1-9/30/04)		99 (10/1/04-3/31/05)					
9	19	54	28	7	4	**NUMBER OF STATEMENTS**	98	94
%	%	%	%	%	%	**ASSETS**	%	%
	5.4	5.6	2.1			Cash & Equivalents	3.2	7.5
	44.4	42.5	42.5			Trade Receivables (net)	52.2	49.6
	28.0	21.9	29.5			Inventory	23.6	21.9
	1.3	3.2	2.0			All Other Current	1.3	2.0
	79.0	73.3	76.1			Total Current	80.3	81.1
	8.6	19.1	9.2			Fixed Assets (net)	13.3	12.7
	3.7	3.1	6.0			Intangibles (net)	2.1	2.6
	8.7	4.5	8.6			All Other Non-Current	4.2	3.6
	100.0	100.0	100.0			Total	100.0	100.0
						LIABILITIES		
	17.7	17.0	21.4			Notes Payable-Short Term	22.5	21.3
	3.5	3.2	1.6			Cur. Mat.-L/T/D	2.0	3.3
	25.9	20.8	22.3			Trade Payables	27.7	29.7
	.1	.2	.0			Income Taxes Payable	.0	.1
	10.3	11.3	9.3			All Other Current	7.9	6.3
	57.4	52.4	54.8			Total Current	60.1	60.7
	12.9	11.2	13.3			Long-Term Debt	9.0	25.4
	.0	.2	.2			Deferred Taxes	.2	.1
	5.8	1.1	6.1			All Other Non-Current	4.3	3.5
	23.9	35.0	25.7			Net Worth	26.3	10.2
	100.0	100.0	100.0			Total Liabilities & Net Worth	100.0	100.0
						INCOME DATA		
	100.0	100.0	100.0			Net Sales	100.0	100.0
	31.3	24.3	18.3			Gross Profit	20.8	21.9
	28.5	20.7	15.4			Operating Expenses	18.3	19.4
	2.9	3.6	2.9			Operating Profit	2.5	2.5
	.3	.4	1.2			All Other Expenses (net)	.7	1.2
	2.5	3.2	1.7			Profit Before Taxes	1.8	1.3
						RATIOS		
	2.3	2.2	1.9			Current	1.9	1.9
	1.6	1.4	1.5				1.4	1.4
	.8	1.1	1.2				1.1	1.1
	1.3	1.3	1.1			Quick	1.3	1.4
	.9	.9	.8				1.0	1.0
	.4	.6	.6				.7	.7
	35 10.5	33 11.1	32 11.4			Sales/Receivables	37 9.9	34 10.8
	42 8.6	44 8.3	42 8.7				43 8.4	42 8.6
	51 7.2	55 6.6	48 7.6				54 6.8	52 7.0
	14 26.0	10 37.6	20 18.3			Cost of Sales/Inventory	11 32.6	6 56.5
	39 9.3	23 16.2	38 9.6				27 13.5	23 15.5
	62 5.9	46 7.9	62 5.9				49 7.4	47 7.7
	22 16.3	15 23.8	18 19.8			Cost of Sales/Payables	18 20.1	16 22.9
	37 9.8	25 14.5	25 14.5				27 13.4	25 14.4
	49 7.4	38 9.7	36 10.0				45 8.1	43 8.5
	10.2	7.7	9.5			Sales/Working Capital	10.3	9.6
	22.3	20.1	14.1				21.2	17.3
	-20.0	72.8	41.4				67.7	62.5
	5.3	9.0	5.1			EBIT/Interest	5.3	5.5
	(15) 2.8	(48) 3.3	(26) 3.1				(95) 1.9	(88) 1.6
	1.7	1.4	1.3				1.1	.8
		4.7				Net Profit + Depr., Dep.,		18.2	6.7
		(10) 2.3				Amort./Cur. Mat. L./T/D	(11) 3.5	(19) 3.4
		.6					.9	1.0
	.1	.1	.1			Fixed/Worth	.1	.1
	.2	.4	.2				.3	.3
	-3.6	1.1	.8				1.1	1.4
	1.5	1.0	1.9			Debt/Worth	1.5	1.6
	3.8	2.0	3.5				3.4	3.5
	-21.8	6.1	8.3				8.3	8.2
	70.9	38.6	31.6			% Profit Before Taxes/Tangible	52.1	30.5
	(14) 13.5	(49) 11.0	(25) 12.7			Net Worth	(87) 17.4	(82) 10.4
	4.0	3.0	3.5				4.0	.0
	9.7	11.8	6.9			% Profit Before Taxes/Total	11.6	7.4
	4.5	3.4	3.0			Assets	3.1	2.5
	1.4	.6	.6				.2	-.8
	295.4	309.3	407.4			Sales/Net Fixed Assets	297.9	288.3
	56.9	48.6	77.4				59.5	71.1
	18.3	6.0	28.8				15.7	21.2
	5.4	4.9	4.2			Sales/Total Assets	5.0	5.4
	4.0	3.2	3.5				4.1	4.2
	2.6	1.8	3.0				3.0	2.8
	.2	.2	.1			% Depr., Dep., Amort./Sales	.1	.1
	(14) .8	(42) .7	(23) .2				(78) .4	(73) .3
	1.5	2.9	.6				1.0	.8
	2.6	1.4				% Officers', Directors',	1.3	1.1
	(11) 3.8	(18) 2.6				Owners' Comp/Sales	(38) 2.7	(46) 2.2
	7.5	4.5					7.4	4.6
9510M	101124M	870073M	2684202M	2343091M	1895024M	Net Sales ($)	7002943M	5800813M
1798M	22471M	236751M	662011M	546768M	835668M	Total Assets ($)	1740162M	1339112M

M = $ thousand   MM = $ million
See Pages 11 through 21 for Explanation of Ratios and Data

Comparative Historical Data | Current Data Sorted By Sales

Type of Statement	4/1/02-3/31/03 ALL	4/1/03-3/31/04 ALL	4/1/04-3/31/05 ALL	0-1MM	1-3MM	3-5MM	5-10MM	10-25MM	25MM & OVER
Unqualified	22	27	23				2	3	18
Reviewed	20	35	26		1	3	3	7	12
Compiled	16	23	21	1	3	3	7	4	3
Tax Returns	7	16	8	3	2	1	2		
Other	29	32	43	2	8	2	5	9	17

Periods: 22 (4/1-9/30/04) · 99 (10/1/04-3/31/05)

	4/1/02-3/31/03 ALL	4/1/03-3/31/04 ALL	4/1/04-3/31/05 ALL	0-1MM	1-3MM	3-5MM	5-10MM	10-25MM	25MM & OVER
NUMBER OF STATEMENTS	94	133	121	6	14	9	19	23	50

ASSETS (%)

Metric	02-03	03-04	04-05	0-1MM	1-3MM	3-5MM	5-10MM	10-25MM	25MM
Cash & Equivalents	7.4	7.6	5.1		8.1		5.3	5.8	2.4
Trade Receivables (net)	43.1	39.8	42.3		29.8		40.1	46.2	47.9
Inventory	25.1	24.3	25.2		23.4		22.8	27.8	27.8
All Other Current	3.1	3.5	2.5		2.5		3.5	1.9	2.4
Total Current	78.7	75.2	75.1		63.8		71.6	81.7	80.6
Fixed Assets (net)	13.0	16.1	13.8		15.2		18.3	11.6	8.4
Intangibles (net)	4.2	3.2	4.2		8.0		5.7	1.3	3.9
All Other Non-Current	4.1	5.4	6.9		13.0		4.3	5.4	7.1
Total	100.0	100.0	100.0		100.0		100.0	100.0	100.0

LIABILITIES

Metric	02-03	03-04	04-05	0-1MM	1-3MM	3-5MM	5-10MM	10-25MM	25MM
Notes Payable-Short Term	18.9	17.2	18.0		13.6		10.4	19.4	22.0
Cur. Mat.-L/T/D	3.9	3.4	2.4		3.1		2.7	2.8	1.2
Trade Payables	25.2	22.9	23.3		25.6		17.9	24.5	25.3
Income Taxes Payable	.1	.3	.2		.2		.1	.2	.1
All Other Current	6.6	7.6	11.6		22.7		13.3	13.0	8.5
Total Current	54.7	51.3	55.6		65.3		44.4	60.0	57.2
Long-Term Debt	12.3	11.4	12.0		15.8		14.2	7.7	10.2
Deferred Taxes	.1	.1	.1		.0		.4	.0	.2
All Other Non-Current	8.6	6.6	4.1		4.2		6.0	.3	3.4
Net Worth	24.3	30.5	28.2		14.7		35.1	32.1	29.1
Total Liabilities & Net Worth	100.0	100.0	100.0		100.0		100.0	100.0	100.0

INCOME DATA

Metric	02-03	03-04	04-05	0-1MM	1-3MM	3-5MM	5-10MM	10-25MM	25MM
Net Sales	100.0	100.0	100.0		100.0		100.0	100.0	100.0
Gross Profit	24.5	25.3	23.7		37.3		28.8	19.4	16.0
Operating Expenses	21.7	23.0	20.3		29.9		22.8	16.9	13.9
Operating Profit	2.8	2.3	3.3		7.4		5.9	2.4	2.1
All Other Expenses (net)	.7	.7	.6		.8		1.4	.3	.4
Profit Before Taxes	2.1	1.6	2.8		6.5		4.6	2.1	1.7

RATIOS

Metric	02-03	03-04	04-05	0-1MM	1-3MM	3-5MM	5-10MM	10-25MM	25MM
	2.0	2.1	2.1		2.9		2.5	2.1	1.7
Current	1.4	1.4	1.5		1.4		1.8	1.3	1.5
	1.1	1.2	1.1		.7		1.4	1.1	1.2
	1.4	1.3	1.3		2.0		1.6	1.3	1.2
Quick	.9	(132) .9	.9		.5		1.0	.9	.9
	.6	.6	.6		.4		.7	.6	.6
	34 10.8	32 11.5	32 11.6		18 20.3		43 8.5	30 12.1	31 11.7
Sales/Receivables	42 8.7	41 8.9	42 8.6		32 11.4		49 7.4	37 9.9	41 8.9
	53 6.9	50 7.4	51 7.1		45 8.2		53 6.9	60 6.1	49 7.5
	9 39.6	10 36.7	12 30.5		0 UND		13 27.4	3 115.3	17 21.9
Cost of Sales/Inventory	29 12.7	32 11.4	28 12.9		48 7.6		32 11.3	26 14.2	30 12.3
	58 6.3	60 6.1	56 6.5		86 4.2		74 5.0	48 7.6	47 7.7
	20 18.6	17 21.4	18 20.2		23 15.9		16 22.8	12 29.6	18 20.5
Cost of Sales/Payables	32 11.6	27 13.5	27 13.7		41 8.8		25 14.4	26 14.1	24 15.3
	44 8.2	44 8.2	39 9.4		62 5.9		37 9.9	37 9.8	36 10.1
	8.2	8.6	8.9		5.8		7.0	10.5	10.1
Sales/Working Capital	18.0	15.7	17.7		24.5		9.5	19.5	18.6
	63.8	41.9	76.7		-14.9		17.4	42.4	48.8
	5.0	7.2	8.1		46.1		9.3	13.7	6.4
EBIT/Interest	(85) 2.4	(117) 2.4	(105) 3.3		(10) 5.9		(16) 4.8	(21) 2.2	(46) 3.4
	1.4	1.0	1.4		.6		1.7	1.3	1.9
	6.0	7.0	5.2						8.6
Net Profit + Depr., Dep., Amort./Cur. Mat. L/T/D	(27) 1.8	(27) 1.8	(23) 2.3						(11) 2.3
	.5	.4	.6						.6
	.1	.1	.1		.2		.1	.0	.1
Fixed/Worth	.4	.4	.3		.7		.4	.1	.2
	1.6	1.2	1.0		-.8		1.3	.5	.5
	1.4	1.0	1.2		.8		.8	1.0	1.8
Debt/Worth	3.6	2.6	2.6		NM		2.2	1.9	3.2
	16.9	10.0	8.3		-3.5		4.6	6.9	7.3
	60.7	38.1	42.6				55.0	32.7	35.0
% Profit Before Taxes/Tangible Net Worth	(80) 12.7	(117) 10.4	(105) 13.0				(17) 21.2	(21) 8.4	(47) 13.0
	2.9	.7	4.3				6.5	-.3	4.9
	11.5	9.7	10.4		37.6		12.7	11.6	7.4
% Profit Before Taxes/Total Assets	3.0	2.8	3.6		10.5		4.5	1.8	3.7
	.7	.1	.7		-1.2		1.7	-.4	1.3
	208.4	219.1	254.0		141.0		470.8	510.7	397.2
Sales/Net Fixed Assets	48.9	40.7	57.4		27.4		22.9	105.8	85.6
	16.9	11.3	16.7		9.1		6.1	21.1	36.3
	4.9	4.9	4.8		4.6		4.0	5.5	5.5
Sales/Total Assets	3.7	3.5	3.7		2.9		2.4	4.0	4.1
	2.3	2.4	2.5		1.0		1.8	3.1	3.2
	.2	.2	.1				.4	.1	.1
% Depr., Dep., Amort./Sales	(79) .5	(100) .6	(93) .5				(14) 1.7	(16) .4	(43) .2
	1.1	1.6	1.5				3.4	1.0	.5
	1.2	1.8	1.3						.6
% Officers', Directors', Owners' Comp/Sales	(33) 2.9	(54) 2.8	(40) 2.5						(11) .7
	4.3	5.3	4.3						1.6
Net Sales ($)	5845889M	7168953M	7903024M	3751M	30133M	37623M	137663M	373348M	7320506M
Total Assets ($)	1733911M	1758740M	2305467M	2884M	15597M	21529M	62088M	107897M	2095472M

Current Data Sorted By Assets   Comparative Historical Data

0-500M	500M-2MM	2-10MM	10-50MM	50-100MM	100-250MM	Type of Statement	4/1/00-3/31/01 ALL	4/1/01-3/31/02 ALL
	3	6	5	1	3	Unqualified	9	13
1	9	20	4			Reviewed	29	29
1	11	12				Compiled	44	44
1	4	2				Tax Returns	10	13
5	12	11	4	3	1	Other	40	45
	28 (4/1-9/30/04)		91 (10/1/04-3/31/05)					
8	39	51	13	4	4	NUMBER OF STATEMENTS	132	144
%	%	%	%	%	%	**ASSETS**	%	%
	6.3	7.1	4.7			Cash & Equivalents	6.4	8.0
	42.7	37.3	36.3			Trade Receivables (net)	41.9	39.9
	26.9	29.3	25.5			Inventory	24.8	24.7
	1.5	3.9	3.6			All Other Current	2.9	2.8
	77.4	77.6	70.1			Total Current	76.0	75.3
	11.8	13.4	14.4			Fixed Assets (net)	13.8	14.8
	3.5	2.5	12.2			Intangibles (net)	5.7	4.5
	7.4	6.5	3.3			All Other Non-Current	4.5	5.4
	100.0	100.0	100.0			Total	100.0	100.0
						LIABILITIES		
	13.1	15.7	4.6			Notes Payable-Short Term	14.4	15.7
	2.3	2.3	2.2			Cur. Mat.-L/T/D	2.9	4.4
	22.9	21.8	16.6			Trade Payables	24.5	22.7
	.2	.1	.2			Income Taxes Payable	.1	.2
	14.7	10.1	12.2			All Other Current	9.9	10.7
	53.3	50.0	35.8			Total Current	51.9	53.7
	13.2	10.3	24.7			Long-Term Debt	11.9	9.2
	.2	.2	.3			Deferred Taxes	.2	.3
	4.4	4.4	10.8			All Other Non-Current	5.7	4.3
	28.9	35.1	28.4			Net Worth	30.4	32.4
	100.0	100.0	100.0			Total Liabilities & Net Worth	100.0	100.0
						INCOME DATA		
	100.0	100.0	100.0			Net Sales	100.0	100.0
	34.4	34.7	35.2			Gross Profit	32.0	32.4
	33.3	30.9	29.3			Operating Expenses	30.4	31.1
	1.0	3.8	6.0			Operating Profit	1.7	1.3
	.5	.4	1.8			All Other Expenses (net)	.7	.9
	.6	3.4	4.2			Profit Before Taxes	.9	.4
						RATIOS		
	2.1 1.5 1.1	2.2 1.6 1.2	2.7 2.0 1.5			Current	2.1 1.4 1.1	2.3 1.5 1.1
	1.4 .9 .7	1.4 .9 .6	1.8 1.1 .9			Quick	1.4 .9 .7	1.5 .9 .6
	32 11.5 38 9.7 50 7.4	32 11.2 41 8.9 49 7.4	36 10.0 47 7.8 56 6.5			Sales/Receivables	33 11.0 42 8.6 54 6.8	29 12.5 36 10.0 47 7.8
	11 33.6 29 12.5 67 5.5	23 16.2 39 9.3 107 3.4	20 18.5 39 9.3 111 3.3			Cost of Sales/Inventory	15 23.6 31 11.8 65 5.6	14 25.8 28 12.8 68 5.4
	18 20.8 24 15.2 46 8.0	21 17.2 32 11.4 43 8.5	24 15.0 36 10.2 43 8.6			Cost of Sales/Payables	20 17.9 36 10.1 54 6.7	16 22.8 28 12.9 44 8.2
	8.2 13.7 74.1	6.6 10.7 29.3	4.5 8.2 14.0			Sales/Working Capital	8.3 14.8 44.0	8.5 16.2 68.1
	6.7 (36) 3.3 .7	9.7 (45) 3.8 1.8	11.9 (12) 4.1 1.7			EBIT/Interest	5.5 (118) 2.0 1.0	5.2 (128) 1.7 .5
		5.1 (15) 3.5 1.0				Net Profit + Depr., Dep., Amort./Cur. Mat. L /T/D	4.5 (25) 1.8 .8	4.1 (27) 2.0 .3
	.1 .2 1.0	.1 .3 .8	.2 .6 NM			Fixed/Worth	.2 .4 2.2	.1 .4 1.1
	1.1 2.4 7.8	1.0 1.9 4.5	1.0 1.9 NM			Debt/Worth	1.1 3.0 10.3	1.0 2.0 7.2
	42.5 (34) 13.1 1.7	46.8 (46) 17.7 5.9	33.9 (10) 20.5 12.4			% Profit Before Taxes/Tangible Net Worth	32.4 (117) 9.4 1.2	33.3 (127) 7.5 -3.2
	8.0 2.9 -1.5	14.9 4.4 1.6	10.4 7.7 1.9			% Profit Before Taxes/Total Assets	9.6 2.4 .0	10.7 2.1 -1.6
	156.8 44.8 22.2	80.0 42.0 16.3	43.8 16.0 12.2			Sales/Net Fixed Assets	76.4 29.7 16.8	90.4 35.7 15.9
	4.9 4.2 3.1	4.6 3.1 2.2	4.0 2.6 1.8			Sales/Total Assets	4.6 3.6 2.3	5.1 3.7 2.6
	.3 (31) .8 1.4	.4 (47) .7 1.5	.7 (11) 1.3 1.9			% Depr., Dep., Amort./Sales	.5 (109) .9 1.5	.3 (119) .7 1.1
	2.5 (25) 4.0 6.7	1.4 (28) 2.7 5.2				% Officers', Directors', Owners' Comp/Sales	3.4 (68) 5.2 8.7	2.3 (78) 4.3 7.1
7077M	190112M	772391M	953933M	1078985M	1032842M	Net Sales ($)	3025040M	2744718M
1557M	47955M	230200M	322325M	287380M	605844M	Total Assets ($)	1426719M	1107299M

M = $ thousand   MM = $ million
See Pages 11 through 21 for Explanation of Ratios and Data

Comparative Historical Data   Current Data Sorted By Sales

'02-03	'03-04	'04-05	Type of Statement	0-1MM	1-3MM	3-5MM	5-10MM	10-25MM	25MM & OVER
15	19	18	Unqualified		1	1	2	3	11
46	36	34	Reviewed		4	3	9	13	5
26	34	24	Compiled	1	2	8	5	7	1
16	19	7	Tax Returns	1	2		3	1	
36	29	36	Other	4	7	4	4	8	9
4/1/02-3/31/03 ALL	4/1/03-3/31/04 ALL	4/1/04-3/31/05 ALL			28 (4/1-9/30/04)			91 (10/1/04-3/31/05)	
139	137	119	**NUMBER OF STATEMENTS**	6	16	16	23	32	26
%	%	%	**ASSETS**	%	%	%	%	%	%
7.6	7.3	6.3	Cash & Equivalents		7.9	6.5	4.2	7.0	6.1
40.5	39.7	39.7	Trade Receivables (net)		38.8	36.7	40.9	43.0	40.4
27.8	26.3	28.0	Inventory		29.9	21.6	30.5	30.3	23.5
1.7	2.1	2.8	All Other Current		1.2	2.9	5.6	2.2	2.5
77.6	75.4	76.7	Total Current		77.7	67.7	81.2	82.5	72.5
14.4	14.3	13.0	Fixed Assets (net)		11.0	23.2	10.5	10.4	14.8
2.9	3.8	4.0	Intangibles (net)		.9	1.5	2.9	1.6	7.4
5.1	6.6	6.2	All Other Non-Current		10.3	7.6	5.4	5.6	5.3
100.0	100.0	100.0	Total		100.0	100.0	100.0	100.0	100.0
			LIABILITIES						
14.5	18.2	13.7	Notes Payable-Short Term		12.8	10.6	15.4	17.7	11.7
3.1	3.2	3.0	Cur. Mat.-L/T/D		5.7	1.9	2.4	1.6	3.4
25.6	23.6	21.8	Trade Payables		26.2	19.7	19.5	25.0	21.3
.4	.1	.2	Income Taxes Payable		.2	.2	.1	.1	.4
10.3	11.4	13.0	All Other Current		10.4	8.2	10.9	8.7	16.0
53.8	56.6	51.6	Total Current		55.4	40.5	48.3	53.0	52.8
10.4	9.4	13.0	Long-Term Debt		13.6	16.5	12.9	7.7	17.3
.1	.2	.2	Deferred Taxes		.0	.2	.4	.1	.4
6.3	5.6	5.2	All Other Non-Current		6.1	2.7	3.3	4.0	8.5
29.4	28.3	29.9	Net Worth		24.9	40.1	35.1	35.1	21.0
100.0	100.0	100.0	Total Liabilities & Net Worth		100.0	100.0	100.0	100.0	100.0
			INCOME DATA						
100.0	100.0	100.0	Net Sales		100.0	100.0	100.0	100.0	100.0
31.0	33.0	34.1	Gross Profit		42.6	39.9	33.2	29.6	31.4
28.7	30.9	31.9	Operating Expenses		39.2	37.1	31.0	26.7	26.3
2.2	2.1	2.2	Operating Profit		3.4	2.7	2.2	2.9	5.1
.4	.6	.6	All Other Expenses (net)		.6	.3	.7	.2	1.3
1.8	1.5	1.7	Profit Before Taxes		2.8	2.5	1.5	2.7	3.8
			RATIOS						
2.1	2.1	2.2	Current		1.9	2.9	2.3	2.0	2.2
1.6	1.4	1.6			1.6	1.6	2.0	1.5	1.5
1.1	1.1	1.1			1.0	1.1	1.3	1.2	1.0
1.3	1.3	1.4	Quick		1.3	1.6	1.1	1.4	1.3
.9	.9	.9			.7	1.1	.9	.9	.9
.6	.6	.7			.5	.7	.8	.7	.7
30 12.0	30 12.1	32 11.4	Sales/Receivables		30 12.0	29 12.6	32 11.4	31 11.7	39 9.3
39 9.3	39 9.4	41 8.9			42 8.6	39 9.3	43 8.4	38 9.6	47 7.8
50 7.3	48 7.6	50 7.3			49 7.5	54 6.8	50 7.3	45 8.1	63 5.8
17 22.0	14 26.7	16 23.5	Cost of Sales/Inventory		12 30.0	4 100.3	18 19.9	21 17.1	19 19.3
35 10.4	36 10.0	38 9.6			65 5.7	16 22.3	40 9.1	37 9.8	37 10.0
75 4.9	89 4.1	90 4.1			176 2.1	77 4.7	73 5.0	79 4.6	83 4.4
20 18.0	19 19.4	20 17.9	Cost of Sales/Payables		22 16.4	13 27.5	20 17.9	20 18.0	27 13.7
32 11.5	31 11.7	31 11.9			33 10.9	38 9.6	28 13.0	28 13.0	36 10.2
48 7.6	46 7.9	42 8.7			99 3.7	60 6.1	42 8.7	39 9.3	41 8.9
7.4	7.3	7.1	Sales/Working Capital		5.7	6.2	6.9	8.9	6.4
13.4	16.5	12.8			10.7	15.4	10.6	13.7	14.0
65.0	47.2	38.1			NM	64.3	22.8	35.6	NM
8.1	8.0	7.7	EBIT/Interest		6.1	5.0	7.2	10.8	14.3
(126) 2.6	(130) 2.7	(106) 3.7			(13) 1.7	(13) 1.8	5.0	(31) 3.9	(22) 4.1
1.1	.9	1.5			-1.7	-.2	2.0	2.1	1.6
4.5	5.6	5.1	Net Profit + Depr., Dep., Amort./Cur. Mat. L/T/D						
(29) 1.9	(29) 2.2	(27) 1.6							
1.0	.7	.8							
.1	.2	.1	Fixed/Worth		.1	.2	.1	.1	.3
.4	.3	.3			.2	.5	.2	.2	.7
1.8	1.5	1.5			NM	1.1	.8	.5	NM
1.0	.8	1.1	Debt/Worth		1.0	.8	.9	1.0	1.5
2.4	2.0	2.1			6.7	2.0	2.0	1.7	3.5
10.9	9.3	7.3			-39.6	5.9	3.5	4.3	NM
41.0	35.1	42.4	% Profit Before Taxes/Tangible Net Worth		81.1	46.2	39.3	46.8	32.1
(117) 13.9	(111) 13.1	(102) 16.6			(11) 11.7	14.6	(22) 14.3	(30) 17.7	(20) 22.9
1.1	.0	4.2			-11.5	-2.6	5.2	5.9	10.6
11.4	11.3	11.2	% Profit Before Taxes/Total Assets		12.0	11.1	8.7	15.5	13.4
3.6	3.4	4.0			2.4	2.8	4.4	4.2	8.2
.2	-.9	1.1			-5.3	-1.3	2.4	1.6	2.0
95.8	98.4	85.3	Sales/Net Fixed Assets		77.6	45.8	156.8	84.8	60.4
40.9	40.4	40.3			29.1	20.9	62.3	57.9	26.2
14.0	17.5	16.3			18.0	8.4	11.8	26.5	12.4
4.7	5.1	4.7	Sales/Total Assets		4.8	5.0	4.6	5.2	4.2
3.6	3.8	3.5			3.2	3.5	3.4	3.6	3.0
2.5	2.2	2.3			1.7	1.9	2.4	3.0	2.0
.4	.4	.4	% Depr., Dep., Amort./Sales		.3	.6	.3	.4	.4
(119) .7	(111) .9	(99) .8			(11) 1.2	(14) 1.3	(21) .5	(28) .6	(22) .9
1.5	1.7	1.4			1.9	1.6	1.4	1.3	1.6
1.7	1.7	1.7	% Officers', Directors', Owners' Comp/Sales		4.0		2.1	.8	
(57) 2.7	(66) 3.9	(58) 4.0			(11) 5.6		(16) 3.9	(16) 1.8	
4.7	7.9	6.6			10.3		7.9	3.9	
2738593M	3510132M	4035340M	Net Sales ($)	3164M	35100M	67117M	173732M	502316M	3253911M
980509M	1274490M	1495261M	Total Assets ($)	1926M	15005M	24948M	56118M	136595M	1260669M

M = $ thousand   MM = $ million
See Pages 11 through 21 for Explanation of Ratios and Data

Current Data Sorted By Assets   Comparative Historical Data

	0-500M	500M-2MM	2-10MM	10-50MM	50-100MM	100-250MM	Type of Statement	4/1/00-3/31/01 ALL	4/1/01-3/31/02 ALL
			7	13	2	1	Unqualified	26	28
		12	40	17	3		Reviewed	65	56
	2	12	15	3			Compiled	56	62
	6	9	5				Tax Returns	12	10
	3	17	18	12	2	1	Other	51	62
		47 (4/1-9/30/04)			151 (10/1/04-3/31/05)				
NUMBER OF STATEMENTS	11	50	85	45	5	2		210	218

ASSETS
	0-500M %	500M-2MM %	2-10MM %	10-50MM %	50-100MM %	100-250MM %		%	%
Cash & Equivalents	9.1	5.9	4.3	4.6				5.4	5.3
Trade Receivables (net)	34.7	46.2	41.5	40.1				41.9	41.6
Inventory	35.7	28.8	30.7	30.8				27.9	26.8
All Other Current	3.6	1.7	1.9	2.4				3.0	2.1
Total Current	83.1	82.6	78.5	77.9				78.3	75.9
Fixed Assets (net)	8.4	10.6	13.7	14.7				13.5	14.9
Intangibles (net)	4.0	.8	1.9	2.0				2.8	3.2
All Other Non-Current	4.5	6.0	5.9	5.4				5.4	6.1
Total	100.0	100.0	100.0	100.0				100.0	100.0

LIABILITIES
	0-500M	500M-2MM	2-10MM	10-50MM					
Notes Payable-Short Term	11.8	15.9	16.4	24.0				16.4	16.3
Cur. Mat.-L/T/D	4.4	4.7	2.7	2.4				2.5	2.6
Trade Payables	21.0	33.8	28.7	23.5				27.7	23.9
Income Taxes Payable	.0	.1	.1	.4				.3	.3
All Other Current	12.1	6.6	6.5	6.9				7.2	7.4
Total Current	49.3	61.1	54.4	57.2				54.1	50.4
Long-Term Debt	14.6	8.5	11.1	9.5				10.3	13.1
Deferred Taxes	.0	.1	.1	.5				.2	.1
All Other Non-Current	11.1	2.0	4.5	3.8				2.7	3.0
Net Worth	25.0	28.3	29.8	29.0				32.7	33.5
Total Liabilities & Net Worth	100.0	100.0	100.0	100.0				100.0	100.0

INCOME DATA
	0-500M	500M-2MM	2-10MM	10-50MM					
Net Sales	100.0	100.0	100.0	100.0				100.0	100.0
Gross Profit	35.5	25.2	22.7	19.4				25.2	24.7
Operating Expenses	30.1	23.1	21.5	16.8				22.8	22.0
Operating Profit	5.4	2.1	1.2	2.6				2.5	2.6
All Other Expenses (net)	.8	.0	.1	.4				.6	.7
Profit Before Taxes	4.6	2.1	1.2	2.1				1.9	2.0

RATIOS
	0-500M	500M-2MM	2-10MM	10-50MM				Hist 4/1/00-3/31/01	Hist 4/1/01-3/31/02
	2.9	2.3	2.1	1.7				2.1	2.2
Current	1.5	1.4	1.5	1.3				1.4	1.4
	1.2	1.0	1.2	1.1				1.1	1.1
	1.2	1.3	1.2	1.0				1.2	1.4
Quick	.8	.9	.8	.8				.8	.9
	.7	.6	.6	.6				.6	.6
	17 21.4	32 11.4	32 11.5	33 11.1				31 11.6	31 11.9
Sales/Receivables	29 12.6	39 9.3	39 9.4	42 8.6				38 9.5	37 9.8
	39 9.3	46 7.9	51 7.2	54 6.8				47 7.7	46 7.9
	22 16.2	19 18.8	30 12.2	29 12.5				24 15.5	22 16.5
Cost of Sales/Inventory	69 5.3	33 11.0	41 8.9	42 8.6				36 10.0	35 10.4
	104 3.5	53 6.8	53 6.8	58 6.2				53 6.9	50 7.4
	4 98.2	19 18.9	20 18.1	21 17.1				20 18.6	17 21.4
Cost of Sales/Payables	42 8.7	32 11.5	32 11.3	28 12.9				30 12.0	25 14.3
	49 7.5	49 7.5	53 6.9	43 8.5				45 8.1	41 8.9
	6.9	7.5	8.9	9.7				9.5	8.9
Sales/Working Capital	11.3	19.3	13.8	20.1				17.5	15.9
	38.9	356.6	28.6	51.5				50.8	46.0
	36.0	14.0	12.2	12.5				6.6	6.0
EBIT/Interest	(10) 7.6	(46) 3.9	(81) 4.0	(43) 4.9				(196) 2.5	(201) 2.5
	1.3	.8	1.4	1.9				1.2	1.2
			4.0	6.6				4.4	12.5
Net Profit + Depr., Dep., Amort./Cur. Mat. L /T/D			(27) 2.0	(19) 3.8				(53) 2.8	(49) 3.5
			1.1	1.8				1.5	1.1
	.0	.1	.1	.2				.1	.1
Fixed/Worth	.3	.2	.3	.6				.3	.3
	-2.2	1.7	.8	1.2				.9	.9
	1.3	.9	1.1	1.2				1.0	1.1
Debt/Worth	3.2	2.5	2.4	3.0				2.4	2.4
	-16.0	26.4	5.1	5.6				6.7	6.0
		50.3	32.5	42.6				44.1	37.8
% Profit Before Taxes/Tangible Net Worth		(41) 11.0	(77) 12.0	(41) 20.6				(194) 16.0	(200) 16.0
		-.2	3.6	13.1				4.0	3.1
	29.3	12.8	10.9	10.4				11.0	10.8
% Profit Before Taxes/Total Assets	16.7	3.9	3.4	6.1				4.4	3.9
	.0	-.4	.5	2.1				1.1	.4
	999.8	187.5	139.1	66.9				107.1	106.9
Sales/Net Fixed Assets	41.6	80.0	49.4	35.2				41.3	44.9
	31.8	27.5	16.5	11.7				16.9	16.4
	5.8	5.2	4.2	4.0				4.8	4.8
Sales/Total Assets	4.6	4.3	3.7	3.2				3.9	3.9
	2.0	3.2	3.0	2.3				2.9	2.9
		.2	.2	.4				.3	.3
% Depr., Dep., Amort./Sales		(38) .6	(74) .5	(41) .6				(175) .7	(185) .6
		1.1	1.1	1.2				1.1	1.2
		2.2	1.5	.6				1.6	1.7
% Officers', Directors', Owners' Comp/Sales		(29) 3.9	(40) 2.4	(12) .8				(101) 2.8	(94) 3.1
		5.1	4.0	3.0				5.4	5.6
Net Sales ($)	14202M	304802M	1507201M	3090084M	958461M	988334M		7452738M	7009773M
Total Assets ($)	3362M	67256M	387525M	947969M	311954M	252405M		2294125M	2172496M

M = $ thousand   MM = $ million
See Pages 11 through 21 for Explanation of Ratios and Data

Comparative Historical Data | **Current Data Sorted By Sales**

4/1/02-3/31/03 ALL	4/1/03-3/31/04 ALL	4/1/04-3/31/05 ALL	Type of Statement	0-1MM	1-3MM	3-5MM	5-10MM	10-25MM	25MM & OVER
18	26	23	Unqualified				1	4	18
80	78	70	Reviewed		1	1	13	30	25
54	59	32	Compiled	1	2	7	10	9	3
17	15	20	Tax Returns	2	5	6	4	3	
50	49	53	Other	2	6	4	13	10	18
					47 (4/1-9/30/04)		151 (10/1/04-3/31/05)		
219	227	198	**NUMBER OF STATEMENTS**	5	14	18	41	56	64
%	%	%	**ASSETS**	%	%	%	%	%	%
6.2	5.6	5.0	Cash & Equivalents		4.1	7.7	3.9	5.3	3.9
40.8	39.3	42.1	Trade Receivables (net)		40.6	41.7	41.5	44.2	42.7
29.0	29.4	30.4	Inventory		28.4	29.7	33.5	29.8	29.7
2.7	2.4	2.1	All Other Current		2.5	1.3	1.1	1.7	2.8
78.6	76.6	79.6	Total Current		75.7	80.3	80.0	81.0	79.1
13.8	15.3	12.7	Fixed Assets (net)		13.7	15.8	12.9	12.2	12.1
2.6	2.0	1.8	Intangibles (net)		.2	1.2	2.0	1.8	1.5
5.0	6.1	5.9	All Other Non-Current		10.4	2.7	5.1	5.0	7.3
100.0	100.0	100.0	Total		100.0	100.0	100.0	100.0	100.0
			LIABILITIES						
14.1	16.7	17.5	Notes Payable-Short Term		11.6	18.9	13.9	17.4	21.2
2.9	2.7	3.2	Cur. Mat.-L/T/D		4.5	4.8	3.4	3.4	2.1
27.0	25.7	28.3	Trade Payables		29.2	32.2	26.6	30.8	27.2
.2	.2	.2	Income Taxes Payable		.0	.0	.1	.2	.3
6.9	8.4	6.9	All Other Current		5.6	5.3	7.1	6.6	7.1
51.0	53.7	56.1	Total Current		50.9	61.3	51.1	58.3	57.9
11.3	12.3	10.7	Long-Term Debt		7.6	10.9	14.2	8.9	10.0
.2	.2	.2	Deferred Taxes		.0	.0	.1	.2	.4
2.9	3.9	4.0	All Other Non-Current		1.4	2.4	6.0	3.2	3.0
34.6	29.9	29.1	Net Worth		40.1	25.5	28.6	29.5	28.7
100.0	100.0	100.0	Total Liabilities & Net Worth		100.0	100.0	100.0	100.0	100.0
			INCOME DATA						
100.0	100.0	100.0	Net Sales		100.0	100.0	100.0	100.0	100.0
23.3	24.9	23.2	Gross Profit		29.7	25.4	24.3	22.3	19.5
21.7	22.8	21.2	Operating Expenses		25.0	24.2	23.0	20.8	17.4
1.6	2.1	2.0	Operating Profit		4.7	1.2	1.3	1.5	2.2
.3	.6	.2	All Other Expenses (net)		−.3	.0	.4	.1	.2
1.3	1.5	1.9	Profit Before Taxes		5.0	1.2	1.0	1.4	2.0
			RATIOS						
2.3	2.2	2.1	Current		2.7	2.2	2.4	2.1	1.9
1.6	1.5	1.5			1.5	1.2	1.6	1.5	1.3
1.1	1.1	1.1			1.2	1.0	1.2	1.2	1.1
1.4	1.2	1.2	Quick		1.0	1.1	1.5	1.2	1.1
.9	.8	.8			.8	.8	.9	.8	.8
.6	.6	.6			.6	.6	.6	.7	.6
30 12.3	29 12.5	31 11.6	Sales/Receivables	29 12.4	33 11.2	30 12.0	33 11.1	31 11.6	
36 10.1	38 9.7	39 9.3		42 8.8	39 9.3	40 9.1	40 9.2	40 9.0	
45 8.1	46 8.0	51 7.2		90 4.0	55 6.6	48 7.7	50 7.3	52 7.1	
22 16.4	24 15.2	27 13.7	Cost of Sales/Inventory	17 22.0	23 15.8	30 12.0	27 13.6	24 15.5	
34 10.7	37 9.9	39 9.3		48 7.6	32 11.6	39 9.3	41 8.9	38 9.5	
52 7.0	56 6.6	57 6.4		86 4.2	76 4.8	61 6.0	53 6.8	47 7.8	
19 19.0	20 18.3	20 18.1	Cost of Sales/Payables	22 16.6	18 19.8	19 19.3	20 18.2	21 17.3	
27 13.4	27 13.4	32 11.5		42 8.6	37 9.8	32 11.5	33 11.0	29 12.4	
42 8.7	43 8.6	49 7.4		90 4.1	51 7.2	55 6.7	48 7.6	40 9.2	
8.5	9.1	8.1	Sales/Working Capital		6.2	6.3	7.8	8.4	10.6
14.1	15.5	16.2			11.9	24.4	12.4	15.5	20.9
36.3	57.6	45.2			37.9	NM	27.8	26.8	82.2
10.4	8.6	12.6	EBIT/Interest		22.0	7.5	11.0	13.2	12.7
(198) 3.0	(209) 3.2	(187) 4.3			(11) 8.1	(17) 3.1	(40) 3.3	(53) 3.8	(61) 5.5
1.4	1.3	1.4			1.0	−1.6	.9	1.5	2.2
6.8	3.6	5.5	Net Profit + Depr., Dep., Amort./Cur. Mat. L/T/D					2.9	11.9
(54) 2.2	(61) 1.7	(55) 2.2						(19) 1.8	(24) 3.4
1.0	.6	1.0						1.1	1.8
.1	.1	.1	Fixed/Worth		.0	.1	.1	.1	.1
.3	.3	.3			.2	.9	.3	.3	.3
1.1	1.0	1.1			.8	NM	.7	1.2	.9
.9	1.0	1.1	Debt/Worth		.6	1.0	.9	1.5	1.2
2.2	2.3	2.6			1.2	3.0	2.1	2.4	3.0
6.1	6.1	6.8			5.3	NM	6.4	6.6	5.6
32.2	36.5	43.8	% Profit Before Taxes/Tangible Net Worth		52.8	52.9	45.2	31.2	45.5
(198) 11.3	(204) 14.6	(173) 17.2			(13) 13.6	(14) 27.5	(36) 8.9	(49) 11.9	(59) 22.4
2.2	3.1	4.3			−.6	1.7	2.4	4.4	10.7
8.3	9.3	11.3	% Profit Before Taxes/Total Assets		21.0	12.2	10.5	10.3	11.4
3.5	4.3	4.8			4.9	5.7	2.9	3.5	6.4
.6	.7	.6			−.2	−2.8	−.1	.3	1.8
140.4	117.5	141.4	Sales/Net Fixed Assets		370.1	104.6	150.0	147.6	147.2
54.6	48.4	50.0			39.4	56.6	53.9	48.8	50.7
17.9	14.2	17.0			20.6	9.2	17.4	17.4	23.8
4.9	4.9	4.6	Sales/Total Assets		4.7	4.9	4.5	4.9	4.6
3.9	3.8	3.7			2.6	3.7	3.8	3.7	3.6
3.0	3.0	2.8			1.5	2.6	2.9	3.3	2.8
.3	.4	.3	% Depr., Dep., Amort./Sales		.4	.2	.2	.3	
(180) .7	(198) .7	(164) .5			(15) .7	(32) .8	(49) .4	(57) .5	
1.3	1.3	1.1			1.9	1.2	1.1	.5	
1.3	1.4	1.6	% Officers', Directors', Owners' Comp/Sales		2.5	1.9	.9	.7	
(100) 2.3	(103) 2.8	(86) 2.8			(12) 3.9	(19) 4.0	(30) 2.4	(17) 1.6	
5.2	5.2	4.3			5.4	3.9	3.9	2.9	
6844926M	6172435M	6863084M	Net Sales ($)	3133M	24675M	70926M	305557M	907777M	5551016M
1786517M	1754045M	1970471M	Total Assets ($)	1273M	11185M	22508M	86791M	269618M	1579096M

© RMA 2005

M = $ thousand   MM = $ million
See Pages 11 through 21 for Explanation of Ratios and Data

Current Data Sorted By Assets   Comparative Historical Data

Type of Statement	0-500M	500M-2MM	2-10MM	10-50MM	50-100MM	100-250MM	4/1/00-3/31/01 ALL	4/1/01-3/31/02 ALL
Unqualified	1	1	18	17	8	9	42	36
Reviewed		3	22	9	1		35	31
Compiled	6	11	11	3	1		36	36
Tax Returns	8	8	4	1			8	8
Other	5	10	21	21	4	7	43	61
	43 (4/1-9/30/04)			167 (10/1/04-3/31/05)				
	0-500M	500M-2MM	2-10MM	10-50MM	50-100MM	100-250MM		
NUMBER OF STATEMENTS	20	33	76	51	14	16	164	172
ASSETS	%	%	%	%	%	%	%	%
Cash & Equivalents	11.8	13.7	8.7	11.3	7.0	9.9	8.6	7.6
Trade Receivables (net)	25.7	32.0	36.6	28.1	28.2	28.8	34.1	35.2
Inventory	36.3	37.4	34.3	33.8	29.5	27.9	32.6	35.0
All Other Current	3.1	1.6	2.0	1.9	1.0	2.9	3.6	2.4
Total Current	76.9	84.7	81.7	75.0	65.8	69.5	78.9	80.2
Fixed Assets (net)	6.4	7.9	11.9	14.2	13.9	9.0	9.5	9.3
Intangibles (net)	6.9	4.0	1.4	6.0	12.7	14.7	6.2	5.3
All Other Non-Current	9.8	3.4	4.9	4.8	7.6	6.7	5.4	5.3
Total	100.0	100.0	100.0	100.0	100.0	100.0	100.0	100.0
LIABILITIES								
Notes Payable-Short Term	8.2	12.8	17.4	14.7	7.9	4.9	15.5	17.3
Cur. Mat.-L/T/D	3.6	2.5	2.7	3.3	1.8	1.0	2.7	2.1
Trade Payables	22.8	24.8	25.4	27.4	25.9	27.6	28.0	27.6
Income Taxes Payable	.0	.2	.5	.4	.5	.2	.3	.3
All Other Current	21.5	23.4	8.5	12.3	9.3	7.2	8.3	10.2
Total Current	56.2	63.7	54.4	58.2	45.3	40.9	54.8	57.5
Long-Term Debt	7.0	16.4	7.3	11.9	18.4	17.4	9.5	9.0
Deferred Taxes	.0	.0	.6	.3	.2	.7	.3	.2
All Other Non-Current	3.2	10.5	3.3	5.8	2.0	9.0	3.2	4.4
Net Worth	33.6	9.5	34.4	23.8	34.1	31.9	32.1	28.9
Total Liabilities & Net Worth	100.0	100.0	100.0	100.0	100.0	100.0	100.0	100.0
INCOME DATA								
Net Sales	100.0	100.0	100.0	100.0	100.0	100.0	100.0	100.0
Gross Profit	38.8	30.1	30.7	32.3	25.0	26.7	29.3	25.2
Operating Expenses	33.2	27.9	26.0	27.0	17.4	18.6	25.3	21.5
Operating Profit	5.6	2.2	4.7	5.2	7.6	8.0	3.9	3.8
All Other Expenses (net)	.5	.5	.1	.5	.9	2.7	.7	.6
Profit Before Taxes	5.0	1.7	4.6	4.7	6.7	5.3	3.3	3.1
RATIOS								
Current	2.4	3.4	2.0	1.6	2.2	2.5	2.0	1.9
	1.5	1.7	1.5	1.3	1.6	1.7	1.5	1.4
	1.0	1.2	1.2	1.1	1.1	1.2	1.1	1.1
Quick	1.1	1.9	1.2	1.1	1.2	1.6	1.1	1.0
	.6	(32) .9	.8	.6	.9	.9	.8	.7
	.4	.5	.5	.5	.6	.6	.5	.5
Sales/Receivables	0 UND	10 34.9	27 13.4	14 25.8	25 14.3	21 17.6	26 13.8	23 15.5
	12 30.2	27 13.5	38 9.7	36 10.2	34 10.6	39 9.4	38 9.5	36 10.1
	31 11.7	42 8.7	49 7.4	56 6.5	50 7.3	50 7.3	53 6.9	48 7.5
Cost of Sales/Inventory	6 62.4	27 13.7	25 14.4	33 11.0	24 15.1	22 16.3	28 13.0	26 14.1
	32 11.4	39 9.4	56 6.6	68 5.3	53 6.9	36 10.2	57 6.4	45 8.2
	70 5.2	67 5.4	85 4.3	115 3.2	87 4.2	65 5.6	96 3.8	91 4.0
Cost of Sales/Payables	0 UND	13 28.3	17 21.9	26 14.1	28 13.0	28 12.8	25 14.6	19 19.1
	20 18.3	20 18.5	37 9.9	39 9.3	36 10.0	32 11.4	39 9.3	33 11.1
	44 8.2	40 9.1	57 6.4	63 5.8	45 8.1	49 7.5	60 6.1	52 7.1
Sales/Working Capital	10.6	7.2	6.8	8.9	5.7	4.8	6.7	8.3
	21.1	14.5	13.5	18.0	14.1	14.3	15.2	17.3
	UND	68.3	38.2	36.1	NM	41.2	33.0	66.5
EBIT/Interest	13.8	26.6	15.3	24.3	17.7	6.5	8.9	9.4
	(11) 2.8	(30) 8.3	(64) 5.4	(48) 9.7	(12) 4.2	(13) 3.4	(142) 2.6	(149) 2.9
	1.0	1.3	2.5	3.1	-1.1	2.1	1.2	1.3
Net Profit + Depr., Dep., Amort./Cur. Mat. L./T/D			5.9	14.6			12.8	9.9
		(18) 2.4	(16) 2.6				(30) 2.9	(43) 2.9
			.9	1.8			.8	1.4
Fixed/Worth	.0	.0	.1	.2	.1	.1	.1	.1
	.1	.2	.2	.4	.9	.6	.3	.4
	UND	.6	.6	1.8	NM	1.7	1.0	1.3
Debt/Worth	.9	.8	1.0	2.1	1.6	1.3	1.2	1.3
	1.3	2.3	2.0	3.6	3.7	9.4	2.9	3.1
	UND	392.9	6.2	8.8	NM	NM	12.0	15.0
% Profit Before Taxes/Tangible Net Worth	151.0	131.9	81.1	66.0	121.9	35.6	60.8	59.7
	(17) 49.5	(26) 37.8	(71) 37.3	(43) 30.8	(11) 24.4	(12) 21.9	(143) 21.4	(150) 24.9
	7.7	14.7	15.4	21.6	-1.2	7.8	6.2	8.2
% Profit Before Taxes/Total Assets	30.1	21.7	24.2	17.5	29.1	9.6	15.0	13.8
	13.3	10.6	8.2	8.8	7.6	7.0	5.4	5.3
	.9	1.1	3.8	3.7	-1.3	2.0	.8	1.0
Sales/Net Fixed Assets	UND	391.3	177.1	128.2	80.1	163.3	169.2	186.2
	439.2	105.9	50.4	55.5	41.7	77.0	63.4	69.5
	83.5	56.4	25.7	12.3	12.0	36.8	24.9	28.3
Sales/Total Assets	8.2	6.9	4.3	3.9	4.8	6.3	4.6	5.4
	4.9	4.7	3.6	2.8	2.9	2.9	3.0	3.5
	3.9	3.0	2.5	2.0	1.5	.9	2.0	2.4
% Depr., Dep., Amort./Sales		.2	.2	.2	.1	.1	.1	.2
		(22) .6	(63) .5	(45) .7	(12) .5	(11) .1	(125) .4	(135) .4
		.7	.9	1.7	1.8	1.4	1.1	1.0
% Officers', Directors', Owners' Comp/Sales		1.6	1.7				1.6	.9
		(17) 2.2	(31) 2.6				(61) 3.7	(63) 2.5
		7.9	5.5				6.8	5.9
Net Sales ($)	37929M	224460M	1441329M	3429434M	3399647M	9987631M	13489394M	13926323M
Total Assets ($)	5504M	38063M	381389M	1089602M	985347M	2749003M	3674212M	3705696M

M = $ thousand   MM = $ million
See Pages 11 through 21 for Explanation of Ratios and Data

Comparative Historical Data			Type of Statement	Current Data Sorted By Sales					
60	55	54	Unqualified	1		1	4	14	34
52	42	35	Reviewed			2	4	13	16
37	51	32	Compiled	3	5	4	4	12	4
18	28	21	Tax Returns	4	5	1	5	5	1
66	67	68	Other	1	7	2	12	11	35
4/1/02-3/31/03 ALL	4/1/03-3/31/04 ALL	4/1/04-3/31/05 ALL		43 (4/1-9/30/04)			167 (10/1/04-3/31/05)		
				0-1MM	1-3MM	3-5MM	5-10MM	10-25MM	25MM & OVER
233	243	210	**NUMBER OF STATEMENTS**	9	17	10	29	55	90
%	%	%	**ASSETS**	%	%	%	%	%	%
9.4	9.1	10.4	Cash & Equivalents		10.8	11.7	16.1	10.1	8.3
34.2	33.2	31.6	Trade Receivables (net)		30.1	46.4	28.2	35.4	30.7
31.4	32.5	34.1	Inventory		34.3	28.5	34.6	34.7	33.3
3.9	4.1	2.0	All Other Current		4.0	.0	1.0	2.8	1.9
78.9	78.8	78.1	Total Current		79.3	86.6	79.9	83.0	74.2
10.3	10.6	11.2	Fixed Assets (net)		7.3	11.0	14.9	9.1	12.4
4.9	4.8	5.2	Intangibles (net)		5.9	1.2	2.7	2.8	7.1
5.9	5.8	5.4	All Other Non-Current		7.6	1.3	2.5	5.0	6.3
100.0	100.0	100.0	Total		100.0	100.0	100.0	100.0	100.0
			LIABILITIES						
13.9	14.3	13.5	Notes Payable-Short Term		12.6	15.3	8.5	17.2	13.9
1.6	1.7	2.7	Cur. Mat.-L/T/D		2.5	1.5	3.1	2.7	2.4
27.3	26.5	25.7	Trade Payables		30.4	20.9	23.1	27.0	27.1
.2	.5	.4	Income Taxes Payable		.0	.0	.3	.3	.6
12.5	12.2	13.0	All Other Current		7.6	65.5	9.2	7.4	10.9
55.6	55.2	55.3	Total Current		53.1	103.2	44.2	54.7	54.8
9.3	9.4	11.4	Long-Term Debt		20.5	8.8	13.8	6.3	12.4
.4	.3	.3	Deferred Taxes		.0	.0	.0	.7	.4
3.2	5.6	5.4	All Other Non-Current		2.4	2.6	13.5	3.9	4.7
31.5	29.5	27.6	Net Worth		23.9	-14.6	28.5	34.4	27.7
100.0	100.0	100.0	Total Liabilities & Net Worth		100.0	100.0	100.0	100.0	100.0
			INCOME DATA						
100.0	100.0	100.0	Net Sales		100.0	100.0	100.0	100.0	100.0
29.0	29.4	31.1	Gross Profit		33.9	30.5	33.7	34.6	26.4
24.4	25.6	26.1	Operating Expenses		31.3	30.9	29.2	29.0	20.9
4.6	3.8	5.0	Operating Profit		2.6	-.4	4.5	5.5	5.5
.6	.7	.6	All Other Expenses (net)		.6	-.6	.6	.1	.9
4.0	3.1	4.4	Profit Before Taxes		2.0	.2	3.9	5.5	4.6
			RATIOS						
2.0	2.1	2.0	Current		3.1	2.7	2.8	2.0	1.8
1.4	1.5	1.5			1.5	1.5	1.7	1.5	1.4
1.1	1.2	1.2			1.1	.9	1.4	1.2	1.1
1.2	1.3	1.2	Quick		2.0	1.6	1.7	1.3	1.1
.8 (242)	.8 (209)	.8			.6	1.0 (28)	1.0	.8	.7
.5	.5	.5			.3	.7	.6	.6	.5
23 16.2	22 16.9	19 19.0	Sales/Receivables	19 19.0	26 14.3	13 27.8	25 14.5	19 18.8
34 10.7	35 10.5	35 10.5		30 12.1	38 9.6	33 11.2	38 9.7	33 11.0
47 7.8	50 7.2	47 7.7		41 8.9	56 6.5	50 7.3	51 7.2	46 8.0
22 16.6	22 16.8	26 14.3	Cost of Sales/Inventory	27 13.4	26 14.3	25 14.4	26 14.0	25 14.5
44 8.3	46 7.9	48 7.5		49 7.5	33 11.0	47 7.8	63 5.8	43 8.5
80 4.6	91 4.0	89 4.1		73 5.0	51 7.1	85 4.3	107 3.4	89 4.1
21 17.5	18 19.8	19 19.5	Cost of Sales/Payables	22 16.7	11 34.6	15 24.9	19 19.6	22 16.7
34 10.7	35 10.4	33 11.0		33 11.0	19 18.8	23 16.1	41 9.0	34 10.7
54 6.8	57 6.4	55 6.6		58 6.3	46 7.9	73 5.0	62 5.8	49 7.5
8.3	8.0	7.3	Sales/Working Capital		8.6	6.4	6.0	6.8	9.6
16.8	13.7	15.2			14.8	12.9	9.4	13.7	20.8
58.8	39.3	41.4			NM	-627.4	31.1	37.5	50.8
17.5	16.4	19.4	EBIT/Interest		3.2		29.7	18.9	22.3
(207) 5.9	(208) 4.7	(178) 5.7			(12) 2.1		(24) 7.3	(47) 6.3	(81) 6.2
2.0	2.0	2.2			-3.4		1.9	2.5	3.1
10.9	9.7	10.0	Net Profit + Depr., Dep., Amort./Cur. Mat. L/T/D					3.5	14.6
(51) 3.7	(53) 3.4	(45) 2.5						(11) 2.3	(28) 5.3
1.6	1.3	1.1						.8	1.6
.1	.1	.1	Fixed/Worth		.0	.0	.1	.1	.1
.2	.3	.3			.0	.3	.3	.2	.4
.9	1.0	1.0			.5	UND	.8	.6	1.6
1.2	1.2	1.1	Debt/Worth		1.0	.7	1.0	1.0	1.6
2.7	2.7	2.6			2.3	3.2	2.0	2.5	3.6
8.0	9.8	10.3			393.3	-118.8	7.4	5.1	13.0
83.3	67.5	79.1	% Profit Before Taxes/Tangible Net Worth		85.1		94.9	83.0	65.2
(202) 33.4	(211) 27.0	(180) 32.1			(14) 24.4		(26) 34.9	(50) 35.6	(76) 32.7
11.7	10.0	15.2			7.0		8.6	18.1	17.5
21.6	18.7	21.1	% Profit Before Taxes/Total Assets		21.7	15.2	28.0	27.5	17.0
7.3	6.6	8.8			5.9	7.1	11.0	13.3	8.7
2.2	2.0	3.2			-4.0	-8.1	1.6	4.3	3.4
239.2	201.6	215.5	Sales/Net Fixed Assets		UND	UND	224.2	218.8	134.8
71.7	74.2	68.7			416.8	126.4	72.3	63.1	58.9
28.4	24.9	21.6			41.0	13.5	12.9	25.8	19.1
5.2	5.1	5.0	Sales/Total Assets		5.6	5.0	5.9	4.9	5.0
3.7	3.3	3.5			3.9	3.7	3.2	3.5	3.5
2.3	2.2	2.4			2.7	3.0	2.4	2.4	2.3
.2	.2	.2	% Depr., Dep., Amort./Sales		.2		.2	.2	.1
(189) .5	(191) .5	(159) .5			(10) .6		(22) .6	(45) .5	(74) .5
1.1	1.2	1.0			1.0		1.8	1.0	1.3
1.4	1.0	1.6	% Officers', Directors', Owners' Comp/Sales		3.2		1.9	1.5	.5
(88) 3.1	(89) 3.1	(69) 2.6			(10) 8.0		(16) 2.7	(20) 2.5	(19) 1.7
6.8	6.0	7.2			10.5		6.5	3.1	5.2
16011067M	19945843M	18520430M	Net Sales ($)	3947M	33873M	39988M	227093M	893056M	17322473M
4402941M	5595421M	5248908M	Total Assets ($)	1606M	10291M	10895M	83399M	297531M	4845186M

M = $ thousand   MM = $ million
See Pages 11 through 21 for Explanation of Ratios and Data

Current Data Sorted By Assets   Comparative Historical Data

	0-500M	500M-2MM	2-10MM	10-50MM	50-100MM	100-250MM	Type of Statement	4/1/00-3/31/01 ALL	4/1/01-3/31/02 ALL
		2	17	11		1	Unqualified	25	18
	1	8	33	7			Reviewed	57	36
	8	14	10	1			Compiled	36	35
	3	10	3				Tax Returns	5	12
	4	13	18	6		3	Other	33	26
		45 (4/1-9/30/04)			128 (10/1/04-3/31/05)				
NUMBER OF STATEMENTS	16	47	81	25		4		156	127

0-500M	500M-2MM	2-10MM	10-50MM	50-100MM	100-250MM		4/1/00-3/31/01 ALL	4/1/01-3/31/02 ALL
%	%	%	%	%	%	**ASSETS**	%	%
9.5	14.9	5.3	5.7			Cash & Equivalents	7.8	8.2
32.1	28.6	29.8	25.5			Trade Receivables (net)	36.2	32.9
38.6	35.6	43.3	46.3			Inventory	41.2	40.2
.0	2.2	2.1	4.3			All Other Current	2.2	2.0
80.2	81.3	80.6	81.8			Total Current	87.4	83.2
13.6	11.5	8.7	9.6			Fixed Assets (net)	6.2	8.6
3.1	1.3	3.9	2.8			Intangibles (net)	1.7	2.8
3.2	5.9	6.8	5.8			All Other Non-Current	4.7	5.3
100.0	100.0	100.0	100.0			Total	100.0	100.0
						LIABILITIES		
12.1	14.1	15.5	22.7			Notes Payable-Short Term	21.8	19.9
4.4	1.6	2.3	1.1			Cur. Mat.-L/T/D	1.5	1.5
11.4	25.0	22.2	16.1			Trade Payables	22.7	22.3
.0	.2	.2	.2			Income Taxes Payable	.2	.1
11.6	6.1	8.2	15.2			All Other Current	8.5	8.6
39.5	46.9	48.3	55.4			Total Current	54.7	52.4
13.1	10.1	6.2	4.1			Long-Term Debt	6.0	7.3
.0	.2	.1	.0			Deferred Taxes	.1	.0
6.1	2.3	5.6	5.4			All Other Non-Current	5.0	4.2
41.3	40.4	39.8	35.0			Net Worth	34.3	35.9
100.0	100.0	100.0	100.0			Total Liabilities & Net Worth	100.0	100.0
						INCOME DATA		
100.0	100.0	100.0	100.0			Net Sales	100.0	100.0
36.8	35.0	32.5	27.9			Gross Profit	27.4	28.6
33.7	31.4	29.4	25.1			Operating Expenses	23.9	25.9
3.1	3.6	3.1	2.8			Operating Profit	3.5	2.8
.9	.6	.4	.5			All Other Expenses (net)	1.3	.9
2.2	3.0	2.7	2.3			Profit Before Taxes	2.2	1.9
						RATIOS		
3.2	2.7	2.6	1.8				2.0	2.3
2.1	1.8	1.6	1.5			Current	1.6	1.6
1.5	1.3	1.3	1.2				1.3	1.3
1.6	1.6	1.1	.6				1.1	1.1
.8	1.0	.7	.5			Quick	.8	.7
.6	.5	.5	.4				.5	.5
23 15.7	17 21.6	29 12.4	24 15.0				33 11.0	29 12.7
38 9.5	32 11.4	40 9.1	44 8.3			Sales/Receivables	49 7.4	42 8.7
75 4.8	50 7.3	59 6.2	57 6.4				64 5.7	60 6.0
22 16.3	23 15.9	58 6.3	58 6.3				45 8.1	43 8.5
84 4.4	62 5.9	88 4.1	110 3.3			Cost of Sales/Inventory	76 4.8	76 4.8
235 1.6	134 2.7	136 2.7	146 2.5				123 3.0	122 3.0
4 88.1	19 19.2	21 17.4	10 35.4				22 16.5	19 19.0
26 14.1	33 11.1	39 9.5	31 11.6			Cost of Sales/Payables	35 10.3	37 9.9
37 9.9	62 5.9	58 6.3	53 6.9				55 6.7	53 6.9
3.6	4.7	4.5	5.8				5.4	5.2
4.0	9.4	8.0	7.6			Sales/Working Capital	9.3	9.1
18.6	23.7	17.5	19.7				15.0	16.7
	13.9	9.3	9.2				4.5	5.3
	(38) 3.5	(71) 4.4	(22) 2.2			EBIT/Interest	(145) 1.8	(117) 1.9
	.9	1.7	1.0				1.2	.7
		29.8				Net Profit + Depr., Dep.,	15.9	7.8
	(14) 6.1					Amort./Cur. Mat. L /T/D	(33) 3.9	(21) 2.3
	1.8						1.1	.1
.0	.0	.0	.1				.0	.1
.3	.2	.2	.2			Fixed/Worth	.1	.1
.9	.7	.4	.6				.3	.5
.8	.5	.8	1.4				1.1	1.0
1.7	1.0	1.5	2.4			Debt/Worth	2.2	2.0
4.2	3.2	3.2	4.3				4.4	3.2
34.4	45.0	30.7	33.1			% Profit Before Taxes/Tangible	31.2	30.8
(14) 11.0	(41) 12.1	(75) 14.9	14.4			Net Worth	(145) 14.1	(117) 12.0
-2.2	.5	4.8	.9				3.9	.2
10.8	14.2	11.2	10.4			% Profit Before Taxes/Total	10.8	10.0
2.6	3.1	4.8	3.4			Assets	3.9	3.6
-.3	-.5	2.1	.4				.8	-.5
UND	194.8	166.8	123.7				221.5	128.3
56.7	54.7	58.6	39.7			Sales/Net Fixed Assets	87.7	56.8
16.0	15.4	19.5	17.9				33.7	23.8
5.0	4.5	3.2	2.7				3.4	3.6
2.2	3.2	2.4	2.4			Sales/Total Assets	2.5	2.6
1.6	1.8	1.9	1.8				2.0	2.0
	.3	.3	.1				.2	.2
	(30) .8	(57) .5	(22) .5			% Depr., Dep., Amort./Sales	(118) .4	(102) .4
	1.8	1.1	1.2				.8	.9
	2.8	1.8	.9				1.7	1.8
	(31) 5.3	(43) 3.5	(12) 3.5			% Officers', Directors', Owners' Comp/Sales	(88) 3.6	(63) 4.1
	8.5	7.4	9.7				6.5	6.6
16011M	202177M	979198M	1001200M		1062509M	Net Sales ($)	2531112M	2603218M
5277M	55357M	365754M	442324M		544143M	Total Assets ($)	985999M	994942M

© RMA 2005

M = $ thousand   MM = $ million
See Pages 11 through 21 for Explanation of Ratios and Data

Comparative Historical Data — **Current Data Sorted By Sales**

4/1/02-3/31/03 ALL	4/1/03-3/31/04 ALL	4/1/04-3/31/05 ALL	Type of Statement	0-1MM	1-3MM	3-5MM	5-10MM	10-25MM	25MM & OVER
20	23	31	Unqualified		1	1	7	6	17
62	50	49	Reviewed	1	3	7	15	17	6
20	46	33	Compiled	7	8	4	6	7	1
8	12	16	Tax Returns	2	8	4	1	1	1
32	31	44	Other	1	8	8	10	11	6
				45 (4/1-9/30/04)			128 (10/1/04-3/31/05)		
142	162	173	**NUMBER OF STATEMENTS**	11	27	24	39	42	30
%	%	%	**ASSETS**	%	%	%	%	%	%
9.6	8.6	8.3	Cash & Equivalents	13.2	7.4	11.9	8.7	5.8	7.2
31.9	33.2	28.9	Trade Receivables (net)	24.2	28.2	27.9	29.9	31.1	27.6
37.8	36.8	41.3	Inventory	45.2	39.7	38.2	37.3	43.9	45.3
2.3	3.8	2.3	All Other Current	.0	2.1	1.8	2.1	3.7	1.8
81.7	82.3	80.7	Total Current	82.6	77.4	79.8	77.9	84.5	82.0
8.3	9.2	10.2	Fixed Assets (net)	7.2	11.9	9.1	14.1	7.5	9.6
3.7	3.1	2.9	Intangibles (net)	3.5	5.3	.4	2.9	2.5	3.1
6.2	5.4	6.2	All Other Non-Current	6.7	5.4	10.7	5.0	5.6	5.3
100.0	100.0	100.0	Total	100.0	100.0	100.0	100.0	100.0	100.0
			LIABILITIES						
13.0	15.9	15.5	Notes Payable-Short Term	15.7	15.3	14.4	14.1	15.9	17.6
1.8	1.5	2.3	Cur. Mat.-L/T/D	2.1	4.3	1.3	2.3	1.8	2.1
22.5	23.2	21.0	Trade Payables	5.9	20.3	23.3	20.2	24.1	22.2
.3	.2	.2	Income Taxes Payable	.0	.1	.3	.1	.2	.1
11.4	12.6	8.9	All Other Current	5.3	7.5	3.6	10.7	8.2	14.5
49.1	53.4	47.9	Total Current	29.1	47.5	42.9	47.4	50.3	56.4
6.5	8.0	8.0	Long-Term Debt	15.5	14.4	6.9	6.9	5.0	5.8
.0	.0	.1	Deferred Taxes	.0	.0	.3	.3	.0	.0
5.0	4.0	4.8	All Other Non-Current	1.4	6.6	3.7	4.4	4.9	5.5
39.4	34.6	39.3	Net Worth	54.0	31.5	46.3	41.0	39.8	32.3
100.0	100.0	100.0	Total Liabilities & Net Worth	100.0	100.0	100.0	100.0	100.0	100.0
			INCOME DATA						
100.0	100.0	100.0	Net Sales	100.0	100.0	100.0	100.0	100.0	100.0
29.4	32.0	33.0	Gross Profit	42.1	36.4	31.2	35.9	29.7	28.8
26.6	29.1	29.8	Operating Expenses	36.5	34.4	27.0	32.7	26.1	26.7
2.9	3.0	3.2	Operating Profit	5.6	2.0	4.3	3.2	3.6	2.1
1.1	.8	.5	All Other Expenses (net)	1.5	.9	.5	.4	.2	.5
1.8	2.2	2.7	Profit Before Taxes	4.1	1.2	3.8	2.7	3.3	1.6
			RATIOS						
2.3	2.3	2.6	Current	4.9	2.3	3.1	2.2	2.7	1.8
1.7	1.6	1.6		2.6	1.6	1.7	1.6	1.7	1.4
1.3	1.3	1.3		2.1	1.2	1.3	1.3	1.3	1.2
1.4	1.2	1.2	Quick	2.6	1.3	1.8	1.2	1.2	.8
.8	.8	.7		.8	.8	.8	.8	.7	.5
.5	.5	.4		.6	.4	.5	.5	.5	.4
29 12.6	27 13.8	25 14.8	Sales/Receivables	24 15.0	23 15.9	22 16.4	25 14.8	28 13.1	26 14.2
44 8.2	45 8.1	37 9.9		45 8.1	34 10.6	37 10.0	37 9.8	39 9.4	34 10.8
59 6.1	64 5.7	57 6.4		75 4.9	67 5.5	53 6.9	59 6.2	57 6.4	51 7.1
39 9.4	41 8.9	49 7.4	Cost of Sales/Inventory	119 3.1	43 8.5	31 11.7	48 7.6	49 7.4	50 7.2
79 4.6	74 4.9	86 4.2		210 1.7	89 4.1	68 5.4	89 4.1	78 4.7	94 3.9
120 3.0	113 3.2	143 2.5		304 1.2	191 1.9	161 2.3	133 2.7	128 2.9	127 2.9
22 16.6	23 16.1	19 19.0	Cost of Sales/Payables	3 107.2	12 30.9	16 22.5	21 17.2	13 28.4	18 20.6
43 8.6	35 10.4	35 10.3		29 12.4	37 9.7	33 11.0	32 11.3	39 9.3	40 9.1
60 6.1	56 6.6	58 6.3		36 10.3	63 5.8	62 5.9	51 7.1	60 6.0	52 7.1
4.7	4.5	4.2	Sales/Working Capital	2.7	3.6	3.7	5.9	4.6	7.0
8.5	8.5	8.1		3.5	8.1	8.2	8.3	8.5	10.6
14.8	17.4	18.0		3.9	32.6	16.1	13.1	17.4	21.1
11.1	12.5	8.0	EBIT/Interest		2.2	11.2	13.7	11.5	8.2
(121) 3.0	(139) 3.5	(143) 3.5		(16) 1.4	(22) 3.0	(36) 5.4	(35) 4.8	(26) 2.4	
1.3	1.5	1.4			.8	-.4	2.0	1.8	1.2
13.0	7.0	18.1	Net Profit + Depr., Dep., Amort./Cur. Mat. L/T/D						
(24) 3.3	(33) 3.6	(27) 3.4							
1.9	1.1	1.5							
.0	.0	.0	Fixed/Worth	.0	.0	.0	.0	.1	.1
.1	.1	.2		.1	.2	.1	.2	.2	.2
.4	.6	.6		.8	1.2	.6	.7	.4	.8
.8	.9	.8	Debt/Worth	.5	.8	.5	.8	.9	1.4
1.6	1.9	1.6		.9	2.4	.9	1.3	1.6	2.5
3.2	3.9	3.7		2.0	80.1	2.6	3.2	3.2	4.2
34.6	31.9	34.2	% Profit Before Taxes/Tangible Net Worth	22.9	50.8	44.8	37.7	33.2	33.1
(130) 13.1	(148) 16.1	(159) 14.4		(10) 7.2	(21) 3.3	(21) 13.6	(38) 11.6	(40) 20.4	(29) 14.4
2.4	4.2	2.3		-1.5	-1.5	-.1	3.4	6.3	2.9
12.2	10.7	11.3	% Profit Before Taxes/Total Assets	9.3	5.0	22.2	12.0	15.0	9.0
4.9	4.4	3.8		3.9	2.0	5.4	4.2	6.7	3.1
.7	1.3	.7		.0	-.5	-3.1	1.8	1.6	.5
192.9	177.4	178.3	Sales/Net Fixed Assets	UND	124.4	494.2	118.6	192.0	157.9
63.4	71.5	52.1		72.8	50.1	57.3	42.5	57.7	43.0
25.5	22.6	17.5		11.8	17.4	14.9	13.5	33.0	15.1
3.4	3.4	3.4	Sales/Total Assets	1.8	3.9	4.2	3.2	3.4	3.1
2.5	2.7	2.6		1.6	2.1	2.2	2.5	2.9	2.6
1.9	2.1	1.8		1.3	1.5	1.7	2.1	2.3	2.1
.2	.3	.3	% Depr., Dep., Amort./Sales		.5	.3	.3	.2	.2
(108) .5	(130) .6	(120) .7		(18) .9	(15) .7	(27) .8	(29) .5	(24) .5	
.9	1.0	1.3			1.6	1.2	1.9	1.1	1.1
2.1	2.3	2.1	% Officers', Directors', Owners' Comp/Sales		3.0	1.4	2.1	1.8	1.8
(70) 3.9	(80) 3.7	(95) 4.0		(20) 5.9	(13) 4.0	(20) 3.7	(26) 3.4	(11) 3.6	
8.3	8.3	7.9			9.0	5.6	5.4	10.1	10.1
4975807M	3096674M	3261095M	Net Sales ($)	6354M	52281M	96134M	279394M	687932M	2139000M
1803017M	1227163M	1412855M	Total Assets ($)	3958M	27401M	44604M	114928M	273925M	948039M

M = $ thousand   MM = $ million
See Pages 11 through 21 for Explanation of Ratios and Data

Current Data Sorted By Assets   Comparative Historical Data

Type of Statement

0-500M	500M-2MM	2-10MM	10-50MM	50-100MM	100-250MM	Type of Statement	4/1/00-3/31/01 ALL	4/1/01-3/31/02 ALL
		5	14		3	Unqualified	34	22
	4	26	9			Reviewed	32	31
2	7	7				Compiled	30	29
3	6					Tax Returns	9	4
1	9	6	8	2	3	Other	32	34
	22 (4/1-9/30/04)		93 (10/1/04-3/31/05)					
6	26	44	31	2	6	NUMBER OF STATEMENTS	137	120

Assets, Liabilities, Income Data (%)

0-500M	500M-2MM	2-10MM	10-50MM	50-100MM	100-250MM		4/1/00-3/31/01 ALL	4/1/01-3/31/02 ALL
%	%	%	%	%	%	**ASSETS**	%	%
	12.3	13.4	6.7			Cash & Equivalents	8.3	10.6
	35.4	26.7	35.2			Trade Receivables (net)	31.8	29.7
	39.3	41.4	41.3			Inventory	41.0	41.1
	.7	2.0	1.8			All Other Current	2.5	2.2
	87.7	83.4	85.0			Total Current	83.6	83.6
	6.7	9.9	5.9			Fixed Assets (net)	8.7	7.7
	.7	2.0	4.1			Intangibles (net)	2.6	2.1
	5.0	4.7	5.0			All Other Non-Current	5.1	6.6
	100.0	100.0	100.0			Total	100.0	100.0
						LIABILITIES		
	11.6	17.7	24.6			Notes Payable-Short Term	26.5	21.3
	2.6	2.1	1.2			Cur. Mat.-L/T/D	1.6	1.9
	24.6	22.5	13.1			Trade Payables	16.3	18.6
	.2	.2	.2			Income Taxes Payable	.2	.3
	6.8	7.2	6.3			All Other Current	6.9	7.5
	45.8	49.7	45.4			Total Current	51.5	49.7
	11.3	5.2	6.4			Long-Term Debt	4.8	4.8
	.1	.1	.1			Deferred Taxes	.1	.2
	4.2	8.5	4.0			All Other Non-Current	4.3	5.0
	38.5	36.5	44.0			Net Worth	39.2	40.4
	100.0	100.0	100.0			Total Liabilities & Net Worth	100.0	100.0
						INCOME DATA		
	100.0	100.0	100.0			Net Sales	100.0	100.0
	32.9	30.9	26.5			Gross Profit	29.1	29.1
	27.7	27.5	21.7			Operating Expenses	25.9	25.7
	5.3	3.4	4.8			Operating Profit	3.3	3.4
	1.1	.6	.7			All Other Expenses (net)	1.0	1.2
	4.1	2.8	4.0			Profit Before Taxes	2.2	2.2

Ratios

0-500M	500M-2MM	2-10MM	10-50MM	50-100MM	100-250MM		4/1/00-3/31/01 ALL	4/1/01-3/31/02 ALL
						RATIOS		
	4.3	3.8	2.9				2.7	2.6
	1.9	1.7	1.8			Current	1.7	1.7
	1.4	1.4	1.3				1.2	1.3
	2.0	2.0	1.6				1.2	1.5
	1.1	.9	.9			Quick	.8	.8
	.6	.4	.5				.4	.5
25	14.8	27 13.6	45 8.1				27 13.3	25 14.7
44	8.3	42 8.6	61 6.0			Sales/Receivables	38 9.5	41 9.0
77	4.7	57 6.4	89 4.1				63 5.8	59 6.2
48	7.7	52 7.1	61 6.0				42 8.7	42 8.6
63	5.8	107 3.4	116 3.2			Cost of Sales/Inventory	87 4.2	90 4.1
141	2.6	165 2.2	153 2.4				143 2.6	142 2.6
17	21.1	20 18.2	11 33.2				14 26.2	19 18.9
42	8.7	35 10.4	26 14.1			Cost of Sales/Payables	28 13.1	31 11.9
69	5.3	70 5.2	51 7.1				55 6.7	55 6.7
	3.8	3.8	3.0				5.1	4.8
	6.0	6.0	5.6			Sales/Working Capital	8.5	7.5
	34.1	12.5	11.2				20.7	16.0
	30.5	13.3	10.2				5.4	5.5
	(25) 8.8	(38) 3.7	(30) 3.9			EBIT/Interest	(126) 2.6	(104) 2.5
	3.1	1.7	1.7				1.1	1.3
		9.1				Net Profit + Depr., Dep.,	10.1	5.4
		(11) 4.4				Amort./Cur. Mat. L /T/D	(32) 2.5	(16) 1.8
		1.3					1.1	.4
	.0	.0	.0				.0	.0
	.1	.1	.1			Fixed/Worth	.1	.1
	.2	.5	.3				.5	.4
	.6	.5	.6				.8	.6
	1.9	1.5	1.2			Debt/Worth	1.7	1.9
	4.4	5.5	3.2				4.1	4.9
	80.7	31.6	31.6			% Profit Before Taxes/Tangible	32.8	38.2
	(24) 31.9	(41) 18.2	(29) 16.3			Net Worth	(125) 15.3	(112) 18.3
	11.6	4.9	4.7				2.7	3.1
	24.5	12.0	17.0			% Profit Before Taxes/Total	12.7	13.5
	9.8	5.9	6.1			Assets	4.5	5.3
	3.4	1.1	2.0				.5	1.1
	979.0	199.2	181.5				214.3	218.7
	152.6	66.1	83.4			Sales/Net Fixed Assets	58.6	61.7
	42.4	23.3	26.1				18.8	24.9
	3.8	2.7	2.3				3.4	3.4
	3.1	2.1	2.0			Sales/Total Assets	2.5	2.6
	1.7	1.8	1.6				1.8	1.8
	.3	.2	.2				.2	.2
	(12) .6	(37) .5	(29) .5			% Depr., Dep., Amort./Sales	(108) .5	(92) .5
	.9	1.0	.9				1.3	1.3
	2.9	1.4	1.4				1.7	1.7
	(12) 4.2	(23) 3.8	(12) 2.5			% Officers', Directors', Owners' Comp/Sales	(64) 3.2	(62) 3.0
	6.4	6.3	10.2				7.3	5.5
5095M	120618M	496586M	1349617M	395371M	1472963M	Net Sales ($)	4316287M	3579198M
1713M	32328M	211003M	670922M	134211M	861050M	Total Assets ($)	1882129M	1611309M

M = $ thousand   MM = $ million
See Pages 11 through 21 for Explanation of Ratios and Data

Comparative Historical Data | | | | | **Current Data Sorted By Sales**

					Type of Statement						
46		43		22		Unqualified				8	14
60		46		39		Reviewed		5	16	10	8
24		24		16		Compiled	2	3	4	3	3	1
10		19		9		Tax Returns	4	3		1	1	1
27		31		29		Other		5	4	3	3	13
4/1/02-		4/1/03-		4/1/04-				22 (4/1-9/30/04)		93 (10/1/04-3/31/05)	
3/31/03		3/31/04		3/31/05							
ALL		ALL		ALL			0-1MM	1-3MM	3-5MM	5-10MM	10-25MM	25MM & OVER
167		163		115		**NUMBER OF STATEMENTS**	6	11	13	23	25	37
%		%		%		**ASSETS**	%	%	%	%	%	%
8.9		10.7		11.5		Cash & Equivalents		13.3	12.3	14.7	11.2	7.4
33.3		31.5		30.7		Trade Receivables (net)		26.0	35.0	28.0	28.0	36.3
40.9		40.9		40.6		Inventory		39.1	43.1	38.9	42.0	38.3
1.9		1.6		1.6		All Other Current		.3	.4	1.6	2.4	1.6
85.0		84.7		84.5		Total Current		78.8	90.9	83.3	83.6	83.5
8.2		9.4		8.0		Fixed Assets (net)		12.8	2.4	10.2	11.6	5.4
1.8		1.7		2.9		Intangibles (net)		1.3	.0	3.8	.4	6.1
4.9		4.3		4.6		All Other Non-Current		7.0	6.7	2.8	4.4	5.0
100.0		100.0		100.0		Total		100.0	100.0	100.0	100.0	100.0
						LIABILITIES						
18.2		15.6		17.9		Notes Payable-Short Term		12.0	15.2	10.8	24.0	20.5
3.0		3.5		1.8		Cur. Mat.-L/T/D		4.1	.6	3.5	1.0	1.2
19.6		18.2		19.9		Trade Payables		20.1	18.4	23.0	25.0	14.3
.3		.3		.2		Income Taxes Payable		.0	.3	.3	.2	.1
10.6		11.9		7.2		All Other Current		10.4	3.9	6.1	6.8	7.4
51.6		49.5		47.0		Total Current		46.7	38.4	43.8	56.9	43.6
7.7		9.0		7.2		Long-Term Debt		16.9	4.6	6.2	6.0	6.6
.1		.1		.1		Deferred Taxes		.0	.2	.3	.0	.1
3.6		4.5		6.1		All Other Non-Current		5.3	5.1	9.7	6.6	4.0
37.0		36.9		39.6		Net Worth		31.1	51.8	40.1	30.3	45.7
100.0		100.0		100.0		Total Liabilities & Net Worth		100.0	100.0	100.0	100.0	100.0
						INCOME DATA						
100.0		100.0		100.0		Net Sales		100.0	100.0	100.0	100.0	100.0
28.6		30.3		30.2		Gross Profit		31.3	33.6	32.1	29.0	29.2
24.3		27.1		25.7		Operating Expenses		27.4	28.9	28.8	25.2	23.3
4.3		3.2		4.5		Operating Profit		3.9	4.8	3.3	3.8	5.9
1.0		.9		.8		All Other Expenses (net)		1.5	.3	.7	.8	.7
3.2		2.3		3.7		Profit Before Taxes		2.4	4.5	2.6	3.1	5.1
						RATIOS						
2.9		3.0		3.3				5.3	5.2	3.5	3.6	2.9
1.6		1.7		1.8		Current		1.5	2.2	1.8	1.6	1.8
1.3		1.3		1.4				1.0	1.6	1.3	1.3	1.5
1.3		1.6		1.9				3.1	4.1	2.0	1.8	1.8
.8	(162)	.9		1.0		Quick		.7	1.0	1.2	.9	1.0
.5		.5		.5				.4	.7	.4	.7	.6
25	14.4	26	13.9	31	11.7		13	28.6	35	10.4	26	14.2	28	13.2	38	9.7
42	8.6	43	8.5	46	7.9	Sales/Receivables	39	9.3	54	6.7	43	8.5	43	8.5	54	6.8
73	5.0	58	6.3	69	5.3		83	4.4	82	4.5	50	7.4	63	5.8	71	5.1
40	9.1	42	8.6	53	6.9		47	7.8	61	6.0	50	7.3	49	7.5	45	8.1
80	4.6	93	3.9	99	3.7	Cost of Sales/Inventory	55	6.6	104	3.5	82	4.5	114	3.2	109	3.3
133	2.8	140	2.6	153	2.4		175	2.1	175	2.1	156	2.3	154	2.4	146	2.5
17	21.5	14	26.8	17	21.0		27	13.5	10	37.8	22	16.5	24	15.1	14	26.2
30	12.1	33	11.0	34	10.8	Cost of Sales/Payables	57	6.4	50	7.2	38	9.7	34	10.8	26	14.1
51	7.2	51	7.2	64	5.7		68	5.3	72	5.0	53	6.9	90	4.1	40	9.2
	5.1		4.1		3.7			4.4		3.7		3.3		3.8		3.6
	7.4		7.2		5.8	Sales/Working Capital		6.5		3.9		6.5		8.3		5.8
	16.2		15.3		12.5			−149.1		5.5		18.4		12.2		11.9
	8.0		12.6		13.2					59.1		15.7		10.2		11.4
(149)	4.4	(140)	4.3	(104)	4.6	EBIT/Interest		(12)	6.0	(22)	4.1	(22)	3.4	(35)	5.7
	1.9		2.2		1.8					4.1		1.8		1.6		3.0
	17.3		18.5		9.9	Net Profit + Depr., Dep.,									19.0
(36)	4.8	(38)	4.4	(25)	4.2	Amort./Cur. Mat. L/T/D								(13)	4.1
	1.3		1.8		2.2										2.2
	.0		.0		.0				.0	.0	.0	.1	.0
	.1		.1		.1	Fixed/Worth		.3	.0	.1	.1	.1
	.4		.4		.3			3.3	.1	.7	.5	.2
	.8		.6		.5			.3	.2	.4	.6	.6
	1.9		1.6		1.5	Debt/Worth		3.0	.8	1.9	1.5	1.3
	4.0		3.0		4.3			51.7	3.6	5.6	4.0	3.1
	39.7		36.8		40.6	% Profit Before Taxes/Tangible			50.9	38.8	32.5	51.0
(153)	25.4	(152)	16.8	(105)	18.5	Net Worth			19.2	(21)	18.2	(24)	13.9	(34)	23.3
	6.3		5.7		6.8				2.6	7.4	3.5	9.6
	13.9		12.2		16.0	% Profit Before Taxes/Total		19.5	21.2	12.5	13.6	19.9
	7.7		6.4		7.8	Assets		8.1	9.6	6.9	5.0	9.5
	2.4		1.6		2.0			−3.9	2.8	1.1	4.3
	225.2		153.2		247.5			564.3	462.3	201.8	140.8	212.2
	61.8		63.0		70.2	Sales/Net Fixed Assets		47.3	183.7	53.9	50.0	94.6
	24.6		23.5		23.7			19.2	57.9	23.5	14.1	24.6
	3.3		3.7		3.2			4.0	3.2	3.6	2.6	2.7
	2.6		2.5		2.1	Sales/Total Assets		2.2	2.3	2.0	2.2	2.1
	1.9		1.8		1.7			1.2	1.6	1.7	1.8	1.7
	.2		.3		.2					.3	.4	.2
(133)	.5	(130)	.6	(89)	.6	% Depr., Dep., Amort./Sales		(17)	.6	(22)	.7	(34)	.5
	1.1		1.2		1.0				1.0	1.1	1.1
	1.4		1.8		1.8	% Officers', Directors',			2.6	1.2	1.4
(83)	2.8	(75)	3.3	(52)	4.1	Owners' Comp/Sales		(13)	6.3	(12)	1.8	(11)	2.7
	5.2		5.0		8.1			10.0	5.1	8.6
6396311M		5946811M		3840250M		Net Sales ($)	4566M	20658M	49303M	162333M	383890M	3219500M
2806483M		2883669M		1911227M		Total Assets ($)	3080M	10022M	25748M	82188M	176325M	1613864M

© RMA 2005

M = $ thousand   MM = $ million
See Pages 11 through 21 for Explanation of Ratios and Data

Current Data Sorted By Assets   **Comparative Historical Data**

	0-500M	500M-2MM	2-10MM	10-50MM	50-100MM	100-250MM	4/1/00-3/31/01 ALL	4/1/01-3/31/02 ALL
Type of Statement								
Unqualified		2	3	13	5	2	22	18
Reviewed	2	8	18	8	1	1	29	28
Compiled	5	10	5	1			16	16
Tax Returns	2	3	3			1	8	4
Other		7	11	13	6	3	27	21
	29 (4/1-9/30/04)			104 (10/1/04-3/31/05)				
NUMBER OF STATEMENTS	9	30	40	35	12	7	102	87
	%	%	%	%	%	%	%	%
ASSETS								
Cash & Equivalents		13.8	12.9	8.5	6.9		9.6	8.9
Trade Receivables (net)		25.8	27.1	33.3	39.2		32.0	29.7
Inventory		45.3	40.2	34.6	36.3		39.9	45.9
All Other Current		1.3	2.3	2.9	3.0		3.8	3.4
Total Current		86.2	82.4	79.3	85.3		85.3	87.9
Fixed Assets (net)		5.3	5.2	10.3	3.7		8.0	5.7
Intangibles (net)		.6	2.6	.5	4.1		1.4	.9
All Other Non-Current		8.0	9.7	10.0	6.8		5.3	5.5
Total		100.0	100.0	100.0	100.0		100.0	100.0
LIABILITIES								
Notes Payable-Short Term		13.5	19.6	17.9	29.3		21.4	21.6
Cur. Mat.-L/T/D		1.6	.2	.6	1.8		2.3	3.0
Trade Payables		18.6	18.1	16.7	15.9		19.5	14.7
Income Taxes Payable		.2	.1	.2	1.6		.4	.3
All Other Current		9.5	7.7	10.3	1.6		7.1	7.9
Total Current		43.4	45.7	45.5	50.2		50.7	47.5
Long-Term Debt		6.1	2.3	2.7	13.7		5.2	3.6
Deferred Taxes		.0	.1	.1	.7		.1	.2
All Other Non-Current		8.1	3.3	3.6	3.6		7.4	6.4
Net Worth		42.4	48.6	48.0	31.8		36.6	42.4
Total Liabilities & Net Worth		100.0	100.0	100.0	100.0		100.0	100.0
INCOME DATA								
Net Sales		100.0	100.0	100.0	100.0		100.0	100.0
Gross Profit		37.4	35.1	32.7	29.6		33.1	32.5
Operating Expenses		33.2	31.1	27.1	16.7		27.7	27.4
Operating Profit		4.2	4.0	5.7	12.9		5.4	5.1
All Other Expenses (net)		.7	−.4	.2	2.3		1.3	1.4
Profit Before Taxes		3.5	4.4	5.5	10.6		4.1	3.7
RATIOS								
Current		4.5	3.3	2.7	2.3		2.5	2.8
		2.0	1.7	1.7	1.9		1.7	1.8
		1.3	1.3	1.3	1.4		1.2	1.4
Quick		2.6	1.8	1.4	1.6		1.3	1.6
		.9	.9	1.0	1.1		.8 (86)	.7
		.5	.5	.5	.6		.4	.4
Sales/Receivables	15 24.0	15 24.1	25 14.4	37 9.8			26 14.1	24 15.3
	34 10.8	36 10.1	56 6.5	60 6.1			41 8.9	39 9.5
	46 7.9	54 6.8	72 5.0	82 4.4			60 6.1	54 6.8
Cost of Sales/Inventory	41 8.8	40 9.2	53 6.9	46 7.9			41 9.0	55 6.6
	103 3.5	83 4.4	67 5.4	65 5.6			76 4.8	83 4.4
	199 1.8	143 2.6	127 2.9	111 3.3			124 2.9	130 2.8
Cost of Sales/Payables	6 58.7	9 40.8	18 20.1	22 16.9			11 33.9	11 32.7
	20 18.4	25 14.5	33 11.1	31 11.7			28 13.0	20 18.3
	47 7.8	51 7.1	45 8.1	38 9.5			47 7.8	40 9.0
Sales/Working Capital		3.4	3.9	3.6	4.6		5.3	4.6
		6.7	7.7	7.5	6.7		7.8	8.0
		22.2	17.2	16.1	9.5		17.7	13.5
EBIT/Interest		12.3	21.3	18.8	34.1		7.2	6.7
		(25) 4.4	(33) 5.5	(32) 6.9	(10) 8.5		(95) 2.4	(82) 2.4
		1.7	1.8	2.4	2.5		1.5	1.3
Net Profit + Depr., Dep., Amort./Cur. Mat. L./T/D							44.9	15.8
							(15) 9.1	(12) 7.3
							1.2	.9
Fixed/Worth		.0	.0	.1	.0		.0	.0
		.1	.1	.1	.1		.1	.1
		.2	.2	.4	.2		.3	.2
Debt/Worth		.5	.4	.5	.8		.8	.6
		1.0	1.2	1.1	1.2		1.8	1.4
		2.7	2.7	2.1	2.6		3.5	2.9
% Profit Before Taxes/Tangible Net Worth		30.7	47.2	59.1	72.9		56.0	57.2
		(28) 17.6	(39) 14.7	26.5	(11) 48.4		(95) 20.9	(83) 15.9
		6.6	4.6	12.4	13.1		4.3	3.5
% Profit Before Taxes/Total Assets		14.2	20.8	24.4	40.6		20.9	16.1
		6.6	7.3	10.1	20.8		7.3	6.2
		3.1	2.6	4.7	9.2		2.1	1.2
Sales/Net Fixed Assets		475.8	304.0	112.1	550.9		248.3	145.2
		131.3	132.0	52.2	141.9		83.5	61.6
		26.1	32.3	21.1	28.8		24.8	33.9
Sales/Total Assets		3.6	3.7	3.1	3.1		3.5	3.7
		2.4	2.4	2.6	2.8		2.8	2.7
		1.8	1.9	1.7	1.7		2.1	2.2
% Depr., Dep., Amort./Sales		.1	.1	.3			.2	.2
		(19) .3	(28) .4	(29) .6			(76) .4	(74) .4
		1.1	.6	1.2			.8	.7
% Officers', Directors', Owners' Comp/Sales		1.0	1.5	1.8			1.6	1.5
		(14) 2.5	(25) 2.8	(15) 3.0			(56) 3.4	(53) 2.8
		4.6	4.9	8.0			7.5	7.2
Net Sales ($)	15890M	122360M	559713M	2294272M	2092141M	5188411M	2494434M	2642957M
Total Assets ($)	3293M	36471M	191613M	845844M	867770M	1015856M	1060506M	1003499M

M = $ thousand   MM = $ million
See Pages 11 through 21 for Explanation of Ratios and Data

Comparative Historical Data / Current Data Sorted By Sales

Current Data period coverage: **29 (4/1-9/30/04)** and **104 (10/1/04-3/31/05)**

4/1/02-3/31/03 ALL	4/1/03-3/31/04 ALL	4/1/04-3/31/05 ALL	Type of Statement	0-1MM	1-3MM	3-5MM	5-10MM	10-25MM	25MM & OVER
43	40	25	Unqualified		1		1	5	18
47	61	38	Reviewed	2	4	4	5	13	10
13	25	21	Compiled	3	9	3	3	2	
10	14	9	Tax Returns		3	1	2	2	1
27	28	40	Other	1	2	5	6	2	24
140	168	133	**NUMBER OF STATEMENTS**	6	19	13	17	25	53
%	%	%	**ASSETS**	%	%	%	%	%	%
10.9	10.1	10.6	Cash & Equivalents		10.8	13.8	8.9	13.8	8.4
31.7	30.2	30.3	Trade Receivables (net)		27.2	24.5	31.5	25.0	35.6
38.2	39.1	38.7	Inventory		45.1	44.3	40.6	39.5	34.5
3.0	3.2	3.1	All Other Current		1.1	1.4	.6	4.1	2.6
83.7	82.5	82.7	Total Current		84.1	84.0	81.6	82.4	81.1
6.8	7.9	6.7	Fixed Assets (net)		6.5	9.4	3.0	6.4	7.9
1.7	1.6	1.7	Intangibles (net)		.7	.9	3.5	1.9	1.9
7.8	7.9	8.9	All Other Non-Current		8.7	5.7	11.9	9.3	9.0
100.0	100.0	100.0	Total		100.0	100.0	100.0	100.0	100.0
			LIABILITIES						
16.6	14.4	18.5	Notes Payable-Short Term		18.7	13.4	22.0	15.0	20.0
2.9	1.0	1.0	Cur. Mat.-L/T/D		2.7	.0	.5	.2	1.0
19.1	19.2	17.6	Trade Payables		11.7	13.6	28.8	19.8	17.6
.1	.3	.3	Income Taxes Payable		.2	.1	.1	.1	.5
10.9	11.7	9.0	All Other Current		6.8	10.2	7.0	8.0	10.4
49.6	46.5	46.3	Total Current		40.1	37.3	58.5	43.1	49.5
4.7	3.8	6.1	Long-Term Debt		9.1	4.7	1.6	3.1	8.2
.1	.1	.1	Deferred Taxes		.0	.0	.0	.3	.1
5.5	4.6	4.7	All Other Non-Current		10.4	8.7	.0	1.7	3.5
40.1	45.0	42.8	Net Worth		40.4	49.2	39.9	51.8	38.7
100.0	100.0	100.0	Total Liabilities & Net Worth		100.0	100.0	100.0	100.0	100.0
			INCOME DATA						
100.0	100.0	100.0	Net Sales		100.0	100.0	100.0	100.0	100.0
30.6	32.7	34.0	Gross Profit		40.2	37.4	32.7	32.0	32.2
27.1	28.6	28.7	Operating Expenses		36.8	31.9	30.0	27.9	24.8
3.5	4.1	5.2	Operating Profit		3.3	5.5	2.8	4.0	7.4
.6	.6	.3	All Other Expenses (net)		.8	.1	-.4	-.1	.6
2.9	3.4	5.0	Profit Before Taxes		2.5	5.4	3.2	4.2	6.8
			RATIOS						
2.7	2.9	3.0			4.4	3.7	1.7	3.2	2.5
1.7	1.8	1.8	Current		2.0	2.5	1.4	2.1	1.7
1.3	1.3	1.3			1.3	1.6	1.2	1.4	1.3
1.4	1.7	1.6			2.7	3.1	.9	1.8	1.5
.8	.9	.9	Quick		1.2	1.0	.6	.9	1.0
.5	.5	.5			.3	.5	.4	.5	.6
20 18.4	21 17.2	19 19.4			29 12.6	19 19.7	17 21.0	8 43.2	25 14.5
40 9.0	41 8.9	40 9.2	Sales/Receivables		38 9.6	32 11.4	41 9.0	24 14.9	52 7.0
62 5.9	59 6.1	63 5.8			48 7.6	40 9.1	58 6.3	53 6.9	74 4.9
42 8.6	44 8.4	45 8.1			96 3.8	32 11.3	46 7.9	27 13.3	46 7.9
75 4.9	73 5.0	79 4.6	Cost of Sales/Inventory		114 3.2	135 2.7	79 4.6	74 4.9	61 6.0
125 2.9	125 2.9	132 2.8			201 1.8	213 1.7	127 2.9	132 2.8	90 4.1
12 29.8	14 26.3	13 28.3			1 248.3	2 158.4	12 29.3	15 24.7	18 20.0
29 12.8	28 13.0	28 13.3	Cost of Sales/Payables		25 14.5	17 21.5	37 9.8	26 14.1	29 12.5
54 6.8	45 8.2	46 7.9			47 7.8	44 8.2	55 6.7	52 7.0	37 9.9
4.7	4.4	3.8			3.3	2.9	6.1	3.6	5.0
8.4	7.3	7.5	Sales/Working Capital		5.3	4.3	13.6	7.7	8.0
16.8	15.3	17.4			14.5	12.8	29.3	23.7	16.1
10.8	12.1	20.2			9.0		12.0	18.3	29.5
(127) 3.4	(149) 4.0	(112) 6.3	EBIT/Interest		(16) 3.0	(15)	3.6	(22) 5.6	(48) 8.7
1.5	1.3	2.0			1.2		1.4	1.7	2.8
26.0	15.9	14.4	Net Profit + Depr., Dep.,						15.3
(21) 2.4	(17) 4.3	(17) 3.1	Amort./Cur. Mat. L/T/D					(11)	7.2
.2	1.5	1.4							2.0
.0	.0	.0			.0	.0	.0	.0	.0
.1	.1	.1	Fixed/Worth		.1	.2	.1	.1	.1
.3	.3	.3			.3	.2	.1	.1	.3
.5	.6	.6			.4	.5	.9	.4	.7
1.4	1.2	1.2	Debt/Worth		.9	1.2	1.8	.9	1.3
3.7	3.2	2.8			2.1	2.8	4.3	2.3	3.0
45.9	44.2	53.4			27.3	44.8	51.0	64.0	81.5
(127) 17.7	(161) 15.1	(126) 22.7	% Profit Before Taxes/Tangible Net Worth	(17)	6.1	25.4	(16) 15.4	(24) 12.6	(51) 37.5
3.4	3.4	7.8			-.9	10.1	3.0	4.7	17.3
16.4	17.6	21.7			8.8	18.7	11.3	24.0	28.9
6.8	6.0	8.7	% Profit Before Taxes/Total Assets		3.1	9.0	4.4	6.8	15.5
1.2	1.0	3.2			-.2	5.1	1.3	3.1	7.0
237.0	208.6	262.3			282.6	UND	886.3	273.0	152.0
81.9	77.8	90.1	Sales/Net Fixed Assets		55.0	31.9	219.7	93.2	82.6
33.1	31.6	30.7			18.1	13.1	30.0	39.0	29.8
3.5	3.6	3.5			3.4	3.2	3.8	4.7	3.4
2.8	2.6	2.6	Sales/Total Assets		2.3	2.1	2.4	2.6	2.8
1.9	1.9	1.8			1.5	1.8	1.8	2.0	2.3
.2	.2	.2			.3		.1	.1	.2
(113) .4	(131) .4	(96) .4	% Depr., Dep., Amort./Sales		(12) .7	(12)	.3	(19) .4	(43) .5
.8	.8	.8			1.1		.6	.7	.9
1.8	1.8	1.5					1.3	1.2	1.2
(67) 2.7	(87) 3.6	(69) 2.8	% Officers', Directors', Owners' Comp/Sales				(12) 2.6	(17) 2.4	(23) 2.8
5.7	5.4	5.3					4.3	4.5	6.4
4643589M	6778016M	10272787M	Net Sales ($)	4148M	37719M	48239M	128473M	432973M	9621235M
1751217M	2668216M	2960847M	Total Assets ($)	2456M	20320M	21216M	57841M	175101M	2683913M

M = $ thousand   MM = $ million
See Pages 11 through 21 for Explanation of Ratios and Data

Current Data Sorted By Assets   Comparative Historical Data

		2	2	3	2	Type of Statement	12	7
	5	17	8			Unqualified	21	14
1	2	4				Reviewed	8	15
3	5	3				Compiled	2	4
	2	6	4	4	1	Tax Returns	22	27
						Other		
	12 (4/1-9/30/04)		62 (10/1/04-3/31/05)				4/1/00-3/31/01 ALL	4/1/01-3/31/02 ALL
0-500M	500M-2MM	2-10MM	10-50MM	50-100MM	100-250MM			
4	14	32	14	7	3	**NUMBER OF STATEMENTS**	65	67
%	%	%	%	%	%	**ASSETS**	%	%
	15.0	8.5	5.4			Cash & Equivalents	9.5	8.4
	29.1	32.2	35.8			Trade Receivables (net)	35.5	31.8
	42.5	43.0	32.0			Inventory	39.7	41.3
	1.1	1.5	4.8			All Other Current	2.5	3.9
	87.7	85.2	78.0			Total Current	87.2	85.3
	6.5	7.6	7.4			Fixed Assets (net)	5.4	6.9
	1.1	1.0	4.8			Intangibles (net)	2.3	3.0
	4.7	6.2	9.8			All Other Non-Current	5.2	4.8
	100.0	100.0	100.0			Total	100.0	100.0
						LIABILITIES		
	12.2	18.6	22.4			Notes Payable-Short Term	24.4	19.9
	1.6	.5	.2			Cur. Mat.-L/T/D	.8	3.7
	28.2	21.3	22.0			Trade Payables	16.4	16.8
	.0	.1	.1			Income Taxes Payable	.2	.1
	5.7	5.3	5.6			All Other Current	7.3	10.9
	47.8	45.8	50.3			Total Current	49.0	51.3
	10.8	3.3	1.8			Long-Term Debt	22.6	5.8
	.0	.0	.9			Deferred Taxes	.3	.3
	4.0	3.8	.1			All Other Non-Current	7.9	6.2
	37.5	47.1	46.8			Net Worth	20.1	36.4
	100.0	100.0	100.0			Total Liabilities & Net Worth	100.0	100.0
						INCOME DATA		
	100.0	100.0	100.0			Net Sales	100.0	100.0
	39.1	31.9	35.0			Gross Profit	31.7	33.2
	33.3	28.6	29.5			Operating Expenses	27.9	29.4
	5.9	3.4	5.5			Operating Profit	3.8	3.8
	1.2	.6	.2			All Other Expenses (net)	1.2	2.1
	4.7	2.8	5.3			Profit Before Taxes	2.7	1.7
						RATIOS		
	4.9	2.7	3.0			Current	3.0	3.0
	1.6	1.6	1.5				1.8	1.7
	1.3	1.3	1.2				1.5	1.4
	2.6	1.8	2.1			Quick	1.3	1.3
	.8	.8	(13) .9				(65) .9	.8
	.4	.5	.7				.6	.5
6	61.8	29 12.5	37 9.9			Sales/Receivables	39 9.4	39 9.3
39	9.4	49 7.4	53 6.9				52 7.0	52 7.0
120	3.0	75 4.9	74 4.9				67 5.4	75 4.9
21	17.3	59 6.2	33 11.2			Cost of Sales/Inventory	58 6.3	64 5.7
127	2.9	103 3.5	63 5.8				92 4.0	107 3.4
279	1.3	157 2.3	112 3.3				139 2.6	146 2.5
14	25.4	23 16.2	24 15.4			Cost of Sales/Payables	13 27.4	18 20.5
62	5.9	41 8.9	35 10.3				27 13.4	35 10.3
99	3.7	77 4.7	52 7.0				53 6.9	61 6.0
	4.4	4.0	4.5			Sales/Working Capital	3.9	3.9
	7.1	6.9	10.8				6.6	5.6
	17.2	11.2	16.3				10.3	12.6
	6.6	8.1	17.5			EBIT/Interest	5.5	6.3
	(11) 2.7	(30) 3.4	(12) 4.2				(60) 3.1	(62) 2.1
	1.2	1.3	3.3				1.7	.7
						Net Profit + Depr., Dep., Amort./Cur. Mat. L /T/D	45.2	4.9
							(11) 9.0	(12) 1.3
							1.3	.1
	.0	.0	.1			Fixed/Worth	.1	.1
	.2	.1	.1				.1	.1
	.3	.3	.2				.3	.4
	1.0	.5	.6			Debt/Worth	.7	.8
	2.2	1.3	2.1				1.8	1.5
	3.7	2.7	2.8				3.3	4.0
	56.8	24.4	82.4			% Profit Before Taxes/Tangible Net Worth	30.7	41.8
	(13) 23.1	(31) 6.5	43.8				(59) 17.8	(59) 16.4
	3.1	.3	10.7				5.7	1.8
	19.5	12.7	21.4			% Profit Before Taxes/Total Assets	13.8	11.7
	7.3	3.3	10.5				6.4	3.1
	1.1	.2	4.2				2.4	-.8
	375.5	565.1	121.1			Sales/Net Fixed Assets	124.5	118.1
	35.5	102.7	67.7				57.5	54.7
	17.0	32.0	43.6				32.9	27.0
	4.1	2.7	3.5			Sales/Total Assets	3.0	2.6
	1.8	2.2	2.8				2.2	2.2
	1.3	1.7	2.2				1.6	1.6
	.1	.1	.2			% Depr., Dep., Amort./Sales	.3	.4
	(11) .9	(24) .5	(12) .3				(54) .6	(48) .6
	1.2	1.6	.9				.9	1.1
	4.1	1.8				% Officers', Directors', Owners' Comp/Sales	1.6	3.4
	(12) 5.0	(16) 4.0					(26) 3.7	(29) 5.9
	6.6	11.8					8.7	9.2
2947M	52778M	327329M	761490M	846937M	651478M	Net Sales ($)	2458430M	2223563M
1093M	16445M	134708M	271555M	499979M	399454M	Total Assets ($)	1358014M	1313875M

© RMA 2005

M = $ thousand   MM = $ million
See Pages 11 through 21 for Explanation of Ratios and Data

Comparative Historical Data | **Current Data Sorted By Sales**

Type of Statement

	4/1/02-3/31/03	4/1/03-3/31/04	4/1/04-3/31/05	Type of Statement	0-1MM	1-3MM	3-5MM	5-10MM	10-25MM	25MM & OVER
	21	16	9	Unqualified		5	3	8	2	7
	26	30	30	Reviewed		2	1		6	8
	8	14	7	Compiled		2	1	1	4	
	5	6	11	Tax Returns	4			1	1	1
	26	19	17	Other		1	2	4	1	9
	ALL	ALL	ALL		12 (4/1-9/30/04)		62 (10/1/04-3/31/05)			
	86	85	74	**NUMBER OF STATEMENTS**	4	10	7	14	14	25

Assets / Liabilities / Income Data

4/1/02-3/31/03 %	4/1/03-3/31/04 %	4/1/04-3/31/05 %		0-1MM %	1-3MM %	3-5MM %	5-10MM %	10-25MM %	25MM & OVER %
			ASSETS						
9.4	11.3	10.5	Cash & Equivalents		8.1		8.9	9.2	12.1
35.8	31.3	31.8	Trade Receivables (net)		33.3		37.5	27.8	30.2
37.8	38.5	37.9	Inventory		42.9		37.1	50.0	29.3
2.6	2.8	2.1	All Other Current		1.3		1.0	2.3	3.6
85.6	83.8	82.2	Total Current		85.6		84.5	89.3	75.2
7.2	6.0	7.4	Fixed Assets (net)		6.4		7.4	7.2	7.8
2.2	4.1	3.5	Intangibles (net)		2.9		.0	.5	8.5
5.0	6.1	6.8	All Other Non-Current		5.1		8.0	3.0	8.5
100.0	100.0	100.0	Total		100.0		100.0	100.0	100.0
			LIABILITIES						
18.2	17.5	15.4	Notes Payable-Short Term		16.5		19.0	17.4	13.9
1.4	.8	.8	Cur. Mat.-L/T/D		2.8		.5	.5	.3
18.8	18.7	23.2	Trade Payables		28.1		23.1	20.9	17.4
.2	.1	.1	Income Taxes Payable		.0		.1	.0	.2
8.6	9.6	6.0	All Other Current		7.9		8.1	4.7	6.5
47.1	46.8	45.5	Total Current		55.4		50.7	43.7	38.3
8.2	3.5	4.7	Long-Term Debt		9.1		4.3	2.6	3.0
.2	.1	.3	Deferred Taxes		.1		.0	.0	.8
5.0	3.9	3.5	All Other Non-Current		6.5		2.9	2.3	1.6
39.5	45.8	45.9	Net Worth		28.9		42.1	51.5	56.3
100.0	100.0	100.0	Total Liabilities & Net Worth		100.0		100.0	100.0	100.0
			INCOME DATA						
100.0	100.0	100.0	Net Sales		100.0		100.0	100.0	100.0
32.6	34.4	35.2	Gross Profit		37.1		27.5	33.6	37.1
27.9	30.1	30.1	Operating Expenses		32.1		25.1	30.2	29.0
4.7	4.4	5.1	Operating Profit		5.0		2.3	3.4	8.1
1.3	.5	.6	All Other Expenses (net)		1.0		.5	.6	.4
3.4	3.8	4.5	Profit Before Taxes		3.9		1.8	2.8	7.7

Ratios

4/1/02-3/31/03	4/1/03-3/31/04	4/1/04-3/31/05		0-1MM	1-3MM	3-5MM	5-10MM	10-25MM	25MM & OVER
2.7	3.3	3.2			3.6		2.5	3.4	4.4
2.0	1.8	1.6	Current		1.4		1.4	2.0	1.9
1.4	1.3	1.3			1.1		1.3	1.5	1.4
1.8	1.6	2.0			1.7		1.8	1.8	2.8
1.0	(73) .9	.8	Quick		.7		.9	(24) .7	1.0
.7	.5	.6			.4		.5	.4	.8
41 8.9	34 10.7	29 12.8		0 UND			29 12.4	24 15.0	36 10.1
56 6.5	48 7.6	49 7.4	Sales/Receivables	82 4.5			57 6.4	35 10.5	51 7.2
70 5.2	69 5.3	76 4.8		124 2.9			76 4.8	51 7.1	71 5.1
47 7.7	49 7.5	52 7.1			82 4.4		38 9.6	50 7.3	51 7.1
84 4.4	87 4.2	95 3.8	Cost of Sales/Inventory		138 2.7		96 3.8	107 3.4	74 4.9
138 2.6	147 2.5	145 2.5			204 1.8		136 2.7	149 2.5	103 3.6
18 20.3	14 26.8	23 16.1			44 8.3		30 12.3	6 56.6	21 17.5
29 12.5	38 9.7	39 9.2	Cost of Sales/Payables		68 5.4		36 10.1	30 12.1	36 10.0
56 6.5	61 6.0	77 4.8			119 3.1		58 6.3	76 4.8	52 7.0
3.8	3.7	3.8			2.5		4.9	4.0	3.5
5.1	5.7	6.9	Sales/Working Capital		5.9		7.9	5.8	6.2
11.2	13.0	11.9			107.2		15.1	12.0	11.8
9.2	12.7	12.0					4.5	11.3	102.4
(77) 3.5	(77) 3.5	(63) 4.0	EBIT/Interest		(13) 2.6		(11) 4.0	(21) 7.9	...
1.5	1.1	1.7			-.5		1.4	3.3	
15.8									
(12) 4.4			Net Profit + Depr., Dep., Amort./Cur. Mat. L/T/D						
.3									
.0	.0	.0			.0		.0	.0	.1
.1	.1	.1	Fixed/Worth		.1		.1	.0	.1
.3	.2	.3			1.4		.2	.3	.3
.6	.5	.5			1.7		.6	.5	.3
1.5	1.2	1.5	Debt/Worth		4.1		1.5	1.0	1.5
2.9	2.9	3.2			36.9		3.4	1.9	2.7
38.1	35.1	52.2					21.5	32.6	77.5
(80) 14.8	(80) 12.9	(71) 19.3	% Profit Before Taxes/Tangible Net Worth				12.8	(24) 11.9	26.4
5.4	3.0	2.4					-1.9	.3	13.2
13.2	15.5	17.0			11.1		9.8	18.3	21.8
5.2	4.7	6.6	% Profit Before Taxes/Total Assets		2.6		3.9	4.2	13.4
1.3	.7	.8			-.2		-.8	.2	6.4
175.9	236.7	277.3			UND		499.6	685.8	95.8
62.5	68.4	72.9	Sales/Net Fixed Assets		57.4		90.2	169.2	56.4
23.9	22.0	18.0			14.5		50.6	23.0	17.4
2.9	2.8	2.9			2.4		2.8	3.7	3.3
2.3	2.2	2.2	Sales/Total Assets		1.4		2.3	2.5	2.2
1.6	1.7	1.7			1.3		1.9	2.2	1.7
.2	.2	.2					.1	.1	.3
(67) .5	(57) .7	(56) .7	% Depr., Dep., Amort./Sales				(10) .4	(11) .3	(21) .7
1.1	1.0	1.2					.9	1.6	1.1
2.5	1.8	2.3							
(34) 3.6	(38) 3.1	(36) 4.2	% Officers', Directors', Owners' Comp/Sales						
6.2	5.1	6.3							
3251254M	3078885M	2642959M	Net Sales ($)	2200M	18365M	27863M	105048M	198582M	2290901M
1737943M	1720042M	1323234M	Total Assets ($)	1671M	12523M	13330M	43784M	72900M	1179026M

Current Data Sorted By Assets   **Comparative Historical Data**

	0-500M	500M-2MM	2-10MM	10-50MM	50-100MM	100-250MM	Type of Statement	ALL 4/1/00-3/31/01	ALL 4/1/01-3/31/02
	2	1	12	32	12	15	Unqualified	73	62
	1	10	55	25	1		Reviewed	79	72
	6	32	34	11	1		Compiled	69	77
	15	13	16	3			Tax Returns	31	21
	7	26	31	33	7	7	Other	79	97
	\u200b	114 (4/1-9/30/04)			294 (10/1/04-3/31/05)				
	31	82	148	104	21	22	NUMBER OF STATEMENTS	331	329
	%	%	%	%	%	%	ASSETS	%	%
	15.6	8.4	7.4	5.1	5.0	5.2	Cash & Equivalents	6.5	6.9
	15.4	25.6	34.0	31.3	22.9	16.5	Trade Receivables (net)	34.4	32.5
	31.0	29.3	32.1	29.1	25.6	25.9	Inventory	29.7	30.4
	6.0	3.5	2.5	2.7	6.2	3.6	All Other Current	1.7	1.9
	68.0	66.9	76.0	68.2	59.7	51.3	Total Current	72.2	71.8
	18.9	25.7	17.1	23.8	21.2	33.7	Fixed Assets (net)	18.3	19.5
	3.3	2.5	1.4	2.2	12.6	7.3	Intangibles (net)	2.3	2.8
	9.8	4.9	5.6	5.8	6.5	7.7	All Other Non-Current	7.2	6.0
	100.0	100.0	100.0	100.0	100.0	100.0	Total	100.0	100.0
							LIABILITIES		
	22.4	14.0	16.1	14.7	9.2	6.2	Notes Payable-Short Term	16.3	18.1
	3.5	3.2	2.4	2.2	3.1	3.9	Cur. Mat.-L/T/D	2.1	2.7
	17.9	24.3	24.2	21.8	18.1	12.4	Trade Payables	23.9	23.2
	.1	.1	.2	.3	.2	.4	Income Taxes Payable	.2	.2
	9.7	7.5	7.2	9.1	12.7	20.8	All Other Current	8.5	8.3
	53.6	49.1	50.0	48.1	43.2	43.7	Total Current	51.0	52.5
	23.1	19.2	9.7	13.7	18.3	22.5	Long-Term Debt	12.2	12.6
	.1	.2	.1	.7	1.1	.4	Deferred Taxes	.3	.3
	7.4	10.7	4.6	4.0	5.8	9.9	All Other Non-Current	3.2	3.7
	15.8	20.7	35.6	33.4	31.6	23.5	Net Worth	33.2	30.9
	100.0	100.0	100.0	100.0	100.0	100.0	Total Liabilities & Net Worth	100.0	100.0
							INCOME DATA		
	100.0	100.0	100.0	100.0	100.0	100.0	Net Sales	100.0	100.0
	26.3	21.4	17.0	17.9	15.5	20.2	Gross Profit	18.0	18.6
	21.1	20.4	15.4	14.9	12.5	18.4	Operating Expenses	16.0	16.6
	5.2	1.0	1.5	3.0	3.0	1.8	Operating Profit	2.0	2.0
	.3	.1	-.2	.7	1.1	1.4	All Other Expenses (net)	.4	.3
	4.9	.9	1.7	2.3	2.0	.4	Profit Before Taxes	1.6	1.7
							RATIOS		
	3.5	2.1	2.3	1.8	1.8	2.3	Current	2.1	2.1
	1.6	1.4	1.5	1.4	1.4	1.3		1.4	1.4
	.8	.9	1.1	1.2	1.1	1.0		1.1	1.1
	1.6	1.2	1.3	1.1	.8	.8	Quick	1.1	1.1
	.6	.7	.8	.7	.6	.5		.8 (328)	1.1
	.3	.3	.5	.5	.4	.4		.6	.5
	0 UND	1 303.6	18 20.7	13 29.1	8 47.0	7 55.1	Sales/Receivables	16 23.1	12 29.3
	5 70.1	16 23.5	26 14.1	21 17.4	15 23.7	13 27.2		26 14.3	24 15.3
	14 26.2	28 13.1	41 8.9	31 11.6	20 17.9	29 12.6		36 10.2	35 10.5
	11 34.6	14 25.6	18 20.5	15 23.8	16 22.3	17 21.4	Cost of Sales/Inventory	16 23.0	17 21.4
	14 25.9	24 15.4	28 12.8	25 14.4	26 13.8	31 12.0		25 14.4	26 13.9
	27 13.6	36 10.1	42 8.7	34 10.7	36 10.2	41 9.0		42 8.8	41 8.8
	4 87.2	8 45.4	10 36.3	10 38.0	11 33.3	7 54.4	Cost of Sales/Payables	11 32.8	10 36.2
	8 44.3	17 21.2	19 19.4	16 22.2	16 22.1	14 25.5		18 20.6	19 19.7
	18 19.8	34 10.6	32 11.3	25 14.6	21 17.2	25 14.7		31 11.6	30 12.2
	12.5	12.3	9.8	16.9	17.5	12.0	Sales/Working Capital	12.6	13.8
	57.7	30.2	18.9	26.9	30.6	41.5		25.6	26.3
	-55.2	-181.7	62.7	73.0	198.4	NM		121.8	71.0
	10.9	8.1	11.0	11.3	5.0	5.1	EBIT/Interest	5.5	7.0
	(20) 3.0	(72) 2.3	(135) 2.9	(97) 4.3	(19) 3.1	(21) 1.7		(302) 2.8	(301) 2.7
	1.6	.2	1.4	2.1	2.1	1.4		1.6	1.5
			4.2	12.4			Net Profit + Depr., Dep., Amort./Cur. Mat. L./T/D	6.6	5.9
			(35) 2.9	(41) 4.5				(107) 2.8	(89) 2.1
			1.0	2.2				1.7	1.1
	.1	.3	.1	.3	.4	.6	Fixed/Worth	.2	.2
	1.0	1.0	.5	.6	1.1	1.5		.5	.5
	-1.5	10.4	1.0	1.2	NM	11.2		1.1	1.1
	.8	1.4	.9	1.2	1.9	2.2	Debt/Worth	1.0	.9
	3.9	4.7	2.2	2.5	3.1	3.8		2.5	2.3
	-13.4	49.8	4.8	4.5	NM	83.8		5.2	5.3
	134.8	48.5	33.2	33.0	26.1	21.0	% Profit Before Taxes/Tangible Net Worth	35.9	34.0
	(21) 38.4	(64) 19.7	(138) 15.5	(100) 18.8	(16) 11.4	(19) 15.9		(313) 16.0	(293) 16.1
	7.4	4.4	2.9	9.9	2.2	7.0		6.1	6.4
	22.1	14.3	10.9	10.7	7.8	3.6	% Profit Before Taxes/Total Assets	10.0	10.5
	9.5	4.8	4.1	5.5	4.7	2.3		4.9	4.5
	2.6	-.5	1.0	3.0	1.9	.9		1.5	1.1
	338.8	91.8	89.3	78.3	136.9	27.8	Sales/Net Fixed Assets	106.9	86.1
	118.3	29.6	40.5	27.4	22.1	10.8		38.6	37.4
	23.3	13.0	17.6	11.6	10.6	6.8		15.2	17.5
	12.1	7.5	6.1	7.0	7.2	5.4	Sales/Total Assets	6.8	6.9
	8.0	5.9	4.6	4.8	4.0	3.8		5.0	5.0
	4.8	3.8	3.2	3.4	2.9	2.3		3.4	3.5
	.3	.3	.3	.3	.3	.7	% Depr., Dep., Amort./Sales	.3	.3
	(16) .8	(66) 1.0	(129) .6	(95) .6	(18) .8	(15) 1.2		(285) .6	(279) .6
	1.4	1.6	1.0	1.0	1.2	2.0		1.0	1.1
	2.2	1.3	.9	.4			% Officers', Directors', Owners' Comp/Sales	.9	.8
	(12) 5.4	(43) 2.2	(66) 1.9	(26) 1.0				(128) 1.7	(120) 1.8
	8.4	3.8	2.7	2.3				2.9	2.8
	64088M	535896M	3665363M	12246956M	7557172M	13572329M	Net Sales ($)	36848127M	38266351M
	7310M	91894M	729951M	2216955M	1488978M	3487892M	Total Assets ($)	6785522M	7102157M

© RMA 2005

M = $ thousand   MM = $ million
See Pages 11 through 21 for Explanation of Ratios and Data

Comparative Historical Data | Current Data Sorted By Sales

91	75	74	Type of Statement						
91	75	74	Unqualified	1	2	1		3	67
82	82	92	Reviewed	1		1	9	33	48
60	88	84	Compiled	3	6	11	19	24	21
28	43	47	Tax Returns	7	7	6	10	13	4
115	100	111	Other	3	7	9	19	20	53
4/1/02-3/31/03 ALL	4/1/03-3/31/04 ALL	4/1/04-3/31/05 ALL		114 (4/1-9/30/04)			294 (10/1/04-3/31/05)		
				0-1MM	1-3MM	3-5MM	5-10MM	10-25MM	25MM & OVER
376	388	408	NUMBER OF STATEMENTS	15	22	28	57	93	193
%	%	%	**ASSETS**	%	%	%	%	%	%
7.6	7.0	7.4	Cash & Equivalents	21.7	9.3	9.4	7.1	8.8	5.2
32.3	30.6	28.7	Trade Receivables (net)	19.4	23.2	17.0	26.0	32.4	30.7
30.5	30.6	30.0	Inventory	26.3	24.4	30.5	33.1	29.4	30.3
2.5	2.7	3.3	All Other Current	7.4	6.6	5.0	2.7	2.3	3.0
72.8	71.0	69.4	Total Current	74.8	63.5	61.9	68.9	73.0	69.1
18.2	19.9	21.8	Fixed Assets (net)	17.1	25.6	26.5	23.4	17.6	22.6
2.3	3.1	2.9	Intangibles (net)	2.9	1.8	2.2	2.0	3.3	3.1
6.7	6.0	6.0	All Other Non-Current	5.2	9.1	9.4	5.7	6.1	5.2
100.0	100.0	100.0	Total	100.0	100.0	100.0	100.0	100.0	100.0
			LIABILITIES						
15.5	14.9	14.9	Notes Payable-Short Term	41.3	8.9	10.1	15.9	13.5	14.6
3.0	2.9	2.7	Cur. Mat.-L/T/D	.9	2.0	4.9	4.8	2.2	2.2
24.3	24.8	22.2	Trade Payables	7.0	22.9	23.6	23.0	25.0	21.4
.2	.3	.2	Income Taxes Payable	.2	.1	.1	.0	.3	.2
9.4	9.0	9.0	All Other Current	6.5	8.0	12.8	8.9	6.4	10.0
52.4	51.8	48.9	Total Current	56.0	41.9	51.6	52.7	47.3	48.5
11.1	11.5	14.8	Long-Term Debt	26.4	16.2	27.5	14.6	11.3	13.7
.3	.3	.4	Deferred Taxes	.0	.6	.2	.1	.2	.6
4.4	5.5	6.2	All Other Non-Current	6.3	11.1	15.2	5.8	6.1	4.5
31.7	30.9	29.7	Net Worth	11.3	30.2	5.7	26.8	35.1	32.8
100.0	100.0	100.0	Total Liabilities & Net Worth	100.0	100.0	100.0	100.0	100.0	100.0
			INCOME DATA						
100.0	100.0	100.0	Net Sales	100.0	100.0	100.0	100.0	100.0	100.0
18.5	19.2	18.9	Gross Profit	31.7	31.4	23.6	20.0	18.3	15.8
16.4	17.5	16.7	Operating Expenses	22.5	26.4	19.3	18.4	16.3	14.6
2.1	1.8	2.2	Operating Profit	9.2	4.9	4.3	1.6	2.0	1.2
.1	.3	.3	All Other Expenses (net)	.1	.4	3.1	.1	.1	.1
2.0	1.5	1.9	Profit Before Taxes	9.1	4.5	1.2	1.5	1.9	1.2
			RATIOS						
2.0	2.0	2.1		4.7	3.6	1.8	2.2	2.2	1.9
1.4	1.4	1.4	Current	2.3	1.8	1.3	1.3	1.5	1.4
1.1	1.1	1.1		1.3	.9	.8	.9	1.2	1.1
1.2	1.1	1.2		2.3	2.1	.8	1.1	1.4	1.1
(375) .8	.7	.7	Quick	1.1	.7	.4	.7	.8	.7
.5	.5	.5		.4	.4	.2	.3	.5	.5
13 27.7	13 28.5	8 46.1		0 UND	2 149.9	0 999.8	2 231.4	16 22.8	12 30.6
24 15.3	23 15.7	21 17.4	Sales/Receivables	9 41.1	15 24.8	3 122.6	24 15.2	25 14.7	20 18.1
32 11.4	34 10.9	32 11.3		31 11.7	37 9.8	23 15.7	36 10.0	39 9.3	30 12.3
16 22.3	18 20.5	16 23.5		1 399.0	4 103.0	13 28.5	18 20.7	16 23.4	16 22.2
25 14.6	28 13.1	26 14.0	Cost of Sales/Inventory	27 13.7	25 14.8	20 18.5	27 13.5	29 12.7	25 14.7
39 9.3	42 8.8	38 9.6		73 5.0	66 5.6	38 9.6	48 7.6	42 8.7	35 10.5
11 34.1	12 31.3	9 40.8		0 UND	7 52.1	6 62.8	8 48.5	11 32.5	10 36.1
19 19.1	19 19.5	16 22.2	Cost of Sales/Payables	7 49.2	26 14.2	18 20.2	15 24.2	20 18.2	16 22.7
31 11.8	33 11.1	28 13.2		22 16.5	64 5.7	35 10.5	33 11.1	37 9.8	23 15.5
13.6	12.9	12.4		7.4	3.8	17.4	11.7	9.9	16.6
25.5	24.2	25.6	Sales/Working Capital	12.6	13.3	59.4	45.8	16.8	26.5
89.3	119.9	122.2		57.7	-121.8	-50.8	-101.3	51.7	80.4
11.0	9.1	9.7			10.3	4.3	10.6	10.7	9.9
(345) 3.5	(346) 3.2	(364) 3.1	EBIT/Interest		(16) 2.4	(23) 1.8	(55) 2.6	(84) 2.6	(180) 3.7
1.7	1.6	1.5			-3.2	-1.9	1.5	1.2	1.9
7.6	5.4	7.7						3.6	10.5
(123) 2.8	(115) 2.5	(106) 2.7	Net Profit + Depr., Dep., Amort./Cur. Mat. L/T/D				(17) 2.9	(74) 3.1	
1.1	1.3	1.4						1.7	1.4
.2	.2	.2		.0	.2	.4	.3	.2	.3
.5	.6	.6	Fixed/Worth	.4	.8	2.6	.6	.5	.7
1.2	1.5	2.0		-.4	2.1	NM	8.6	1.3	1.5
1.0	1.1	1.1		.3	1.0	1.0	1.0	1.0	1.2
2.5	2.5	2.6	Debt/Worth	3.8	2.2	8.5	3.7	2.0	2.7
5.3	5.7	7.3		-13.4	11.0	-58.6	24.5	5.1	5.1
42.6	36.8	36.0		134.5	49.6	66.7	43.8	34.6	32.2
(346) 16.9	(350) 15.7	(358) 17.5	% Profit Before Taxes/Tangible Net Worth	(10) 29.3	(19) 16.7	(20) 22.9	(47) 19.3	(82) 11.9	(180) 18.8
6.6	5.9	5.5		-.4	.0	3.9	6.9	2.3	9.3
11.0	9.9	11.0		42.9	11.0	12.4	12.8	11.4	10.2
4.9	4.6	4.5	% Profit Before Taxes/Total Assets	9.6	3.2	4.7	4.7	3.8	4.7
1.7	1.6	1.4		.0	-4.3	-3.1	1.6	.6	2.3
109.5	109.3	90.1		UND	157.7	129.5	94.4	90.9	77.4
38.6	36.5	32.3	Sales/Net Fixed Assets	165.0	20.3	21.1	32.5	36.8	29.2
17.1	13.5	14.0		14.7	6.3	14.8	14.4	17.8	12.9
7.0	6.7	6.9		7.3	5.5	8.0	7.5	6.2	7.2
5.0	4.8	4.9	Sales/Total Assets	2.8	2.7	5.7	5.4	4.6	5.0
3.6	3.4	3.4		2.1	1.7	3.7	3.5	3.2	3.8
.3	.3	.3			.7	.2	.4	.3	.3
(334) .6	(332) .6	(339) .6	% Depr., Dep., Amort./Sales		(14) 1.2	(20) 1.0	(49) .9	(80) .6	(172) .6
1.0	1.1	1.2			1.7	1.6	1.7	1.2	1.0
.8	.9	.9			2.5	1.3	1.2	1.1	.5
(147) 1.6	(150) 1.9	(149) 1.9	% Officers', Directors', Owners' Comp/Sales		(10) 4.4	(11) 3.8	(25) 2.1	(48) 1.8	(50) 1.1
3.5	3.5	3.6			6.0	7.8	2.6	2.9	2.5
46405571M	37065431M	37641804M	Net Sales ($)	7488M	44165M	114396M	391316M	1518205M	35566234M
8110994M	7774508M	8022980M	Total Assets ($)	3177M	35389M	40971M	91671M	431966M	7419806M

M = $ thousand   MM = $ million
See Pages 11 through 21 for Explanation of Ratios and Data

Current Data Sorted By Assets   Comparative Historical Data

Type of Statement

Type	0-500M	500M-2MM	2-10MM	10-50MM	50-100MM	100-250MM		4/1/00-3/31/01 ALL	4/1/01-3/31/02 ALL
Unqualified		1	8	16	4	3		25	21
Reviewed	2	8	15	6				24	20
Compiled	3	7	7	1				29	26
Tax Returns	1							3	1
Other			13	9	2	1		21	27
		32 (4/1-9/30/04)		75 (10/1/04-3/31/05)			NUMBER OF STATEMENTS	102	95
	6	16	43	32	6	4			

Main Data

0-500M	500M-2MM	2-10MM	10-50MM	50-100MM	100-250MM		4/1/00-3/31/01 ALL	4/1/01-3/31/02 ALL
%	%	%	%	%	%	**ASSETS**	%	%
	6.9	7.0	4.4			Cash & Equivalents	5.5	6.2
	27.9	36.9	30.7			Trade Receivables (net)	33.8	30.0
	18.9	33.6	34.2			Inventory	26.2	29.3
	3.8	3.5	2.8			All Other Current	3.2	1.8
	57.5	81.0	72.1			Total Current	68.8	67.3
	30.9	11.3	16.9			Fixed Assets (net)	22.5	22.5
	2.2	2.9	3.2			Intangibles (net)	1.4	2.5
	9.3	4.8	7.8			All Other Non-Current	7.3	7.7
	100.0	100.0	100.0			Total	100.0	100.0
						LIABILITIES		
	13.8	19.5	20.8			Notes Payable-Short Term	18.8	17.4
	3.5	2.0	1.3			Cur. Mat.-L/T/D	2.6	2.3
	30.1	25.6	21.0			Trade Payables	20.0	22.4
	.4	.2	.1			Income Taxes Payable	.1	.1
	11.1	5.5	7.1			All Other Current	9.6	6.9
	59.0	52.9	50.4			Total Current	51.1	49.1
	41.1	7.7	9.5			Long-Term Debt	14.3	13.1
	.0	.2	.7			Deferred Taxes	.5	.4
	2.4	3.7	4.6			All Other Non-Current	8.2	6.0
	-2.6	35.5	34.8			Net Worth	25.8	31.4
	100.0	100.0	100.0			Total Liabilities & Net Worth	100.0	100.0
						INCOME DATA		
	100.0	100.0	100.0			Net Sales	100.0	100.0
	24.1	18.7	16.3			Gross Profit	20.8	19.1
	25.5	16.6	14.2			Operating Expenses	18.4	17.5
	-1.3	2.1	2.1			Operating Profit	2.4	1.6
	1.6	.0	.1			All Other Expenses (net)	.8	.6
	-3.0	2.1	2.0			Profit Before Taxes	1.6	1.0
						RATIOS		
	1.8	2.4	2.1			Current	1.8	2.0
	1.3	1.5	1.4				1.4	1.4
	1.0	1.1	1.2				1.1	1.1
	1.1	1.1	1.3			Quick	1.2	1.2
	.8	.8	.7				.8	.7
	.4	.6	.4				.6	.5
	(9) 39.0	(22) 16.9	(22) 16.8			Sales/Receivables	(16) 23.0	(15) 24.0
	(15) 24.6	(26) 14.0	(26) 14.1				(26) 13.9	(23) 16.0
	(34) 10.9	(33) 11.0	(35) 10.4				(35) 10.4	(31) 11.9
	(8) 44.4	(25) 14.6	(19) 19.5			Cost of Sales/Inventory	(13) 28.4	(15) 23.6
	(25) 14.6	(35) 10.5	(29) 12.7				(23) 15.8	(26) 14.0
	(38) 9.6	(45) 8.2	(50) 7.2				(39) 9.4	(44) 8.3
	(12) 29.9	(15) 24.1	(14) 25.6			Cost of Sales/Payables	(12) 30.7	(13) 28.6
	(16) 22.3	(22) 16.7	(18) 19.9				(19) 19.3	(20) 18.4
	(44) 8.3	(31) 11.8	(27) 13.3				(27) 13.7	(29) 12.8
	29.8	9.9	13.1			Sales/Working Capital	12.9	11.5
	52.0	19.5	22.5				32.5	27.8
	-219.4	49.3	51.3				107.3	75.4
	3.8	12.0	14.6			EBIT/Interest	4.4	6.0
	(14) 2.0	(36) 4.7	(30) 4.7				(95) 2.3	(89) 2.1
	-.8	1.9	2.5				1.3	.9
		4.6	32.9			Net Profit + Depr., Dep.,	6.0	4.9
		(10) 1.5	(14) 6.8			Amort./Cur. Mat. L/T/D	(32) 3.4	(30) 2.2
		.7	3.1				1.3	1.2
	.3	.1	.2			Fixed/Worth	.2	.2
	1.0	.2	.5				.6	.7
	-2.4	.6	.9				1.6	1.4
	1.2	.9	.9			Debt/Worth	1.2	1.1
	3.0	3.0	2.2				2.6	2.2
	-8.2	6.4	6.2				6.4	4.5
	30.4	47.6	28.3			% Profit Before Taxes/Tangible	31.8	28.1
	(11) 13.4	(39) 26.7	(29) 17.1			Net Worth	(91) 13.6	(86) 12.2
	1.1	10.7	11.6				4.9	4.5
	9.6	13.4	9.5			% Profit Before Taxes/Total	9.6	7.4
	4.0	6.2	5.0			Assets	4.7	3.6
	-14.7	2.1	3.4				1.3	.0
	54.4	380.1	67.1			Sales/Net Fixed Assets	124.1	140.6
	22.0	74.1	39.0				32.7	29.5
	4.6	26.2	14.6				11.8	11.5
	7.6	5.8	6.2			Sales/Total Assets	6.4	6.2
	4.3	4.0	4.3				4.8	4.7
	2.6	3.2	2.6				3.1	3.3
	.6	.1	.3			% Depr., Dep., Amort./Sales	.2	.3
	(13) 1.8	(37) .3	(29) .6				(79) .6	(76) .8
	4.2	.8	.9				1.5	1.4
		.6				% Officers', Directors',	.7	.6
		(12) 1.3				Owners' Comp/Sales	(38) 1.5	(31) 1.0
		4.6					3.5	3.3
8956M	110405M	1105173M	3139223M	1603890M	2794647M	Net Sales ($)	6186473M	7289274M
1398M	20231M	233909M	683043M	383375M	669595M	Total Assets ($)	1301164M	1872773M

M = $ thousand   MM = $ million

See Pages 11 through 21 for Explanation of Ratios and Data

Comparative Historical Data / Current Data Sorted By Sales

Comparative Historical Data			Type of Statement						
27	21	32	Unqualified				1	4	27
24	33	21	Reviewed				2	8	11
17	22	18	Compiled	1	2	2	4	8	8
6	9	3	Tax Returns	1	1	1			
38	35	33	Other	1	3		5	9	15
4/1/02-3/31/03	4/1/03-3/31/04	4/1/04-3/31/05		32 (4/1-9/30/04)			75 (10/1/04-3/31/05)		
ALL	ALL	ALL		0-1MM	1-3MM	3-5MM	5-10MM	10-25MM	25MM & OVER
112	120	107	**NUMBER OF STATEMENTS**	3	6	3	12	29	54
%	%	%	**ASSETS**	%	%	%	%	%	%
7.0	4.8	6.8	Cash & Equivalents				11.0	8.5	4.0
28.2	32.1	31.8	Trade Receivables (net)				27.3	37.2	33.0
31.1	29.9	31.9	Inventory				28.8	30.0	35.9
4.0	3.6	3.1	All Other Current				3.6	2.3	3.7
70.3	70.4	73.5	Total Current				70.6	78.0	76.7
20.1	20.4	17.3	Fixed Assets (net)				23.6	12.1	14.6
1.5	3.5	2.7	Intangibles (net)				1.6	4.7	2.1
8.2	5.6	6.5	All Other Non-Current				4.2	5.2	6.6
100.0	100.0	100.0	Total				100.0	100.0	100.0
			LIABILITIES						
17.2	18.4	19.4	Notes Payable-Short Term				16.1	17.7	23.2
2.7	3.0	2.0	Cur. Mat.-L/T/D				2.5	2.5	1.3
23.4	23.7	24.4	Trade Payables				22.7	25.4	24.1
.2	.2	.2	Income Taxes Payable				.2	.3	.2
8.5	7.2	7.8	All Other Current				5.4	5.9	6.7
52.0	52.5	53.9	Total Current				46.9	51.8	55.4
11.8	17.2	17.2	Long-Term Debt				12.7	8.3	8.1
.3	.2	.3	Deferred Taxes				.0	.2	.5
4.1	6.2	5.1	All Other Non-Current				9.9	2.6	3.3
31.8	23.8	23.4	Net Worth				30.5	37.1	32.6
100.0	100.0	100.0	Total Liabilities & Net Worth				100.0	100.0	100.0
			INCOME DATA						
100.0	100.0	100.0	Net Sales				100.0	100.0	100.0
19.4	20.1	18.5	Gross Profit				23.7	18.9	15.0
16.4	18.0	16.9	Operating Expenses				22.0	16.6	13.2
3.0	2.1	1.6	Operating Profit				1.7	2.3	1.8
.2	.6	.3	All Other Expenses (net)				.6	.2	-.1
2.8	1.5	1.2	Profit Before Taxes				1.1	2.2	1.9
			RATIOS						
2.0	1.9	2.1	Current				3.2	2.2	1.9
1.4	1.3	1.3					1.7	1.4	1.3
1.1	1.0	1.1					1.0	1.2	1.1
1.1	1.0	1.1	Quick				1.3	1.1	1.0
.7	(119) .7	.7					.9	.8	.7
.5	.5	.4					.5	.7	.4
15 23.6	17 21.3	18 20.7	Sales/Receivables				14 26.2	22 16.9	18 20.0
23 15.7	26 14.0	25 14.4					21 17.3	26 14.0	25 14.3
34 10.6	34 10.8	36 10.0					32 11.4	49 7.4	33 11.0
18 20.0	19 18.9	19 18.7	Cost of Sales/Inventory				17 21.9	27 13.7	18 19.9
28 13.1	29 12.5	31 11.7					30 12.2	35 10.5	29 12.7
55 6.7	48 7.6	48 7.6					42 8.7	44 8.2	52 7.1
14 26.0	15 24.5	14 25.4	Cost of Sales/Payables				13 28.4	17 22.1	15 24.7
20 18.1	21 17.6	21 17.0					26 14.0	21 17.3	21 17.4
31 11.9	32 11.4	31 11.8					75 4.9	31 11.7	28 13.1
11.4	12.2	11.9	Sales/Working Capital				6.6	9.2	13.2
25.8	26.8	24.5					22.3	20.1	25.0
60.7	134.5	59.5					NM	41.6	57.1
8.3	6.8	11.6	EBIT/Interest				5.1	12.9	13.1
(95) 3.4	(108) 3.2	(93) 4.2				(11) 3.1	(23) 4.0	(50) 4.9	
1.5	1.4	1.8					1.2	2.0	2.5
7.6	5.0	16.3	Net Profit + Depr., Dep.,						22.6
(24) 2.0	(27) 2.3	(33) 4.3	Amort./Cur. Mat. L/T/D					(20)	4.8
1.2	1.6	1.3							2.0
.1	.2	.1	Fixed/Worth				.0	.1	.1
.5	.6	.5					.9	.2	.5
1.2	2.4	1.2					2.9	.8	.8
.9	1.2	1.1	Debt/Worth				.7	.9	1.0
2.4	3.2	3.1					5.6	2.9	3.2
5.7	10.3	9.2					12.2	5.5	5.4
48.9	35.9	35.3	% Profit Before Taxes/Tangible				36.4	42.4	34.6
(104) 16.1	(105) 20.3	(92) 21.3	Net Worth			(10) 15.7	(26) 21.4	(50) 21.3	
6.8	6.5	11.4					6.3	13.3	11.3
10.5	10.5	11.0	% Profit Before Taxes/Total				9.5	12.9	10.1
5.2	4.0	5.4	Assets				6.1	7.1	5.6
1.8	.9	2.6					.8	2.7	3.0
160.6	115.3	162.3	Sales/Net Fixed Assets				358.9	237.6	160.2
31.5	40.1	47.2					21.6	74.1	48.4
13.4	12.3	14.2					8.0	28.6	15.3
6.1	6.2	6.1	Sales/Total Assets				5.2	5.6	6.3
4.4	4.2	4.2					3.8	4.0	4.7
2.7	2.6	2.7					2.5	2.6	3.4
.3	.3	.2	% Depr., Dep., Amort./Sales					.1	.2
(93) .6	(101) .7	(91) .5					(25)	.5	(47) .4
1.4	1.4	1.1						.9	.8
.7	.8	.7	% Officers', Directors',					.5	.7
(35) 1.1	(50) 1.1	(31) 1.7	Owners' Comp/Sales					(10) .7	(11) 1.3
1.6	3.4	4.0						2.8	2.1
7518107M	7619135M	8762294M	Net Sales ($)	1664M	10525M	10785M	88709M	502205M	8148406M
2098292M	1736706M	1991551M	Total Assets ($)	1402M	3482M	3108M	37772M	141619M	1804168M

M = $ thousand   MM = $ million
See Pages 11 through 21 for Explanation of Ratios and Data

Current Data Sorted By Assets   Comparative Historical Data

0-500M	500M-2MM	2-10MM	10-50MM	50-100MM	100-250MM	Type of Statement	4/1/00-3/31/01 ALL	4/1/01-3/31/02 ALL
		4	6	2	2	Unqualified	19	14
	2	7	11			Reviewed	16	12
	4	5	1			Compiled	18	18
3	1	6				Tax Returns	4	3
1	5	5	9			Other	18	19
	19 (4/1-9/30/04)		55 (10/1/04-3/31/05)					
4	12	27	27	2	2	**NUMBER OF STATEMENTS**	75	66
%	%	%	%	%	%	**ASSETS**	%	%
	13.6	9.0	11.5			Cash & Equivalents	6.9	8.9
	37.4	44.6	37.1			Trade Receivables (net)	41.7	42.0
	21.0	20.3	21.3			Inventory	22.8	20.1
	2.0	1.2	2.5			All Other Current	2.1	1.5
	73.9	75.0	72.5			Total Current	73.5	72.4
	20.7	15.8	17.2			Fixed Assets (net)	18.7	20.7
	1.9	1.7	1.3			Intangibles (net)	2.3	2.0
	3.5	7.5	9.0			All Other Non-Current	5.4	4.9
	100.0	100.0	100.0			Total	100.0	100.0
						LIABILITIES		
	5.4	7.3	12.6			Notes Payable-Short Term	16.1	8.8
	3.8	1.7	1.2			Cur. Mat.-L/T/D	2.5	2.6
	31.7	40.2	29.1			Trade Payables	34.4	31.3
	.0	.4	.5			Income Taxes Payable	.2	.1
	3.1	8.2	9.3			All Other Current	8.7	11.1
	44.0	57.7	52.6			Total Current	61.9	53.9
	17.3	8.1	7.0			Long-Term Debt	10.4	10.6
	.0	.0	.1			Deferred Taxes	.3	.2
	16.0	1.9	.5			All Other Non-Current	1.9	1.4
	22.7	32.2	39.7			Net Worth	25.4	33.9
	100.0	100.0	100.0			Total Liabilities & Net Worth	100.0	100.0
						INCOME DATA		
	100.0	100.0	100.0			Net Sales	100.0	100.0
	19.0	15.0	17.2			Gross Profit	17.6	17.2
	16.8	14.0	12.8			Operating Expenses	16.4	15.5
	2.2	1.0	4.4			Operating Profit	1.2	1.7
	-.3	-.3	.2			All Other Expenses (net)	.5	-.1
	2.5	1.3	4.2			Profit Before Taxes	.7	1.8
						RATIOS		
	2.5	1.8	1.8			Current	1.7	1.6
	1.4	1.4	1.3				1.3	1.4
	1.1	.9	1.1				1.0	1.1
	1.8	1.4	1.3			Quick	1.1	1.3
	1.3	1.0	.9				.9	.9
	.5	.6	.7				.6	.6
	14 25.8	18 20.5	20 18.3			Sales/Receivables	23 16.2	20 18.4
	26 14.2	23 16.0	26 14.2				29 12.7	24 15.0
	39 9.5	35 10.4	36 10.3				39 9.5	35 10.4
	1 319.0	7 55.0	8 43.0			Cost of Sales/Inventory	9 41.7	6 58.4
	25 14.8	14 26.7	17 21.8				15 23.7	13 27.9
	49 7.5	23 15.7	33 11.2				32 11.4	25 14.5
	24 15.2	18 20.6	18 20.7			Cost of Sales/Payables	20 18.6	15 23.9
	29 12.5	20 18.1	28 13.0				30 12.2	25 14.7
	43 8.5	37 9.9	40 9.2				41 8.9	31 11.7
	8.7	14.4	14.6			Sales/Working Capital	16.9	17.6
	23.3	29.3	27.1				34.1	32.3
	112.7	-196.2	61.2				-999.8	95.1
	8.7	18.4	49.7			EBIT/Interest	9.8	12.4
	(10) 3.9	(24) 8.3	(25) 7.9				(65) 3.0	(54) 3.7
	1.3	2.0	3.5				1.5	1.8
						Net Profit + Depr., Dep.,	9.4	12.0
						Amort./Cur. Mat. L /T/D	(16) 3.1	(14) 5.8
							1.1	1.8
	.0	.0	.2			Fixed/Worth	.1	.1
	1.0	.4	.4				.6	.4
	NM	1.0	.8				1.5	1.1
	2.2	1.3	.6			Debt/Worth	1.4	1.4
	3.4	2.1	2.2				2.9	2.2
	-15.8	6.3	3.6				6.5	5.0
		34.0	55.1			% Profit Before Taxes/Tangible	41.5	38.4
		(26) 16.9	(26) 24.0			Net Worth	(68) 18.3	(62) 19.6
		6.8	12.8				9.6	10.9
	15.0	11.5	19.6			% Profit Before Taxes/Total	10.0	13.0
	7.8	4.7	8.4			Assets	5.2	6.2
	4.6	2.2	3.2				1.0	2.1
	UND	567.8	220.4			Sales/Net Fixed Assets	288.6	310.1
	57.6	62.0	36.9				32.6	32.5
	8.6	16.1	15.3				15.7	13.9
	6.6	6.2	6.4			Sales/Total Assets	6.4	7.9
	3.9	5.4	4.6				5.2	5.9
	3.0	4.7	3.0				3.3	3.3
		.1	.2			% Depr., Dep., Amort./Sales	.2	.1
		(24) .6	(22) .7				(61) .6	(56) .7
		1.7	.9				1.3	1.2
		1.2	.5			% Officers', Directors',	.8	.9
		(14) 2.1	(11) .8			Owners' Comp/Sales	(31) 1.8	(33) 1.7
		3.1	2.3				3.3	3.4
6040M	77174M	979897M	2644976M	792498M	1648836M	Net Sales ($)	4999538M	4944394M
940M	15828M	148290M	534441M	140033M	280680M	Total Assets ($)	1145947M	980688M

© RMA 2005

M = $ thousand   MM = $ million
See Pages 11 through 21 for Explanation of Ratios and Data

Comparative Historical Data | **Current Data Sorted By Sales**

Type of Statement				0-1MM	1-3MM	3-5MM	5-10MM	10-25MM	25MM & OVER
19	12	14	Unqualified					1	13
19	19	20	Reviewed				2	3	15
13	21	10	Compiled			1	1	5	3
10	9	10	Tax Returns	1				5	1
21	11	20	Other	1	3		2	4	10
4/1/02-3/31/03 ALL	4/1/03-3/31/04 ALL	4/1/04-3/31/05 ALL		19 (4/1-9/30/04)			55 (10/1/04-3/31/05)		
82	72	74	**NUMBER OF STATEMENTS**	2	6	1	5	18	42
%	%	%	**ASSETS**	%	%	%	%	%	%
8.0	7.1	11.2	Cash & Equivalents					7.5	11.1
39.3	36.8	38.9	Trade Receivables (net)					47.6	39.7
21.8	25.0	21.6	Inventory					19.3	19.6
1.2	2.2	2.1	All Other Current					.8	2.6
70.3	71.2	73.8	Total Current					75.2	72.9
21.3	20.4	17.4	Fixed Assets (net)					16.8	16.6
2.2	2.3	1.5	Intangibles (net)					3.0	1.1
6.2	6.1	7.2	All Other Non-Current					4.9	9.4
100.0	100.0	100.0	Total					100.0	100.0
			LIABILITIES						
6.7	8.3	9.5	Notes Payable-Short Term					10.1	9.5
4.4	2.7	1.9	Cur. Mat.-L/T/D					2.2	1.4
31.9	33.3	33.0	Trade Payables					39.9	33.7
.2	.2	.3	Income Taxes Payable					.3	.4
13.3	11.0	9.9	All Other Current					5.9	8.9
56.4	55.4	54.7	Total Current					58.4	54.1
13.2	15.4	12.1	Long-Term Debt					9.8	7.2
.1	.2	.1	Deferred Taxes					.0	.1
4.1	3.1	3.7	All Other Non-Current					1.5	1.2
26.2	25.8	29.5	Net Worth					30.3	37.5
100.0	100.0	100.0	Total Liabilities & Net Worth					100.0	100.0
			INCOME DATA						
100.0	100.0	100.0	Net Sales					100.0	100.0
18.6	19.3	16.7	Gross Profit					17.9	13.9
17.2	17.3	14.2	Operating Expenses					15.9	11.0
1.5	2.0	2.5	Operating Profit					2.0	2.9
.0	.1	-.2	All Other Expenses (net)					.3	.0
1.4	1.9	2.7	Profit Before Taxes					1.7	2.9
			RATIOS						
1.6	1.9	1.9	Current					1.7	1.7
1.2	1.3	1.4						1.4	1.3
1.0	1.0	1.1						.9	1.1
1.3	1.2	1.4	Quick					1.4	1.2
.8	.7	.9						1.0	.9
.5	.5	.6						.6	.7
16 22.6	20 18.0	18 20.5	Sales/Receivables					18 19.8	18 19.9
22 16.3	25 14.3	23 15.7						29 12.6	23 15.9
34 10.7	33 11.1	35 10.3						41 8.8	35 10.6
6 59.1	10 37.3	8 45.2	Cost of Sales/Inventory					6 61.7	6 57.3
17 21.5	20 18.0	17 21.2						14 26.7	17 21.9
35 10.3	35 10.4	31 11.9						23 15.7	28 13.2
14 25.9	22 16.7	18 20.6	Cost of Sales/Payables					19 19.0	18 20.9
24 15.3	30 12.3	25 14.4						27 13.3	23 15.7
39 9.5	40 9.1	34 10.6						45 8.0	32 11.3
17.4	12.4	14.3	Sales/Working Capital					15.5	17.9
42.9	29.5	26.6						28.8	29.3
-877.5	430.7	91.2						-51.2	67.9
12.2	26.7	18.3	EBIT/Interest					18.0	29.9
(67) 4.1	(63) 4.9	(66) 6.7					(15)	4.8	(39) 8.5
1.7	1.7	2.2						1.0	4.2
14.4	4.0	46.0	Net Profit + Depr., Dep., Amort./Cur. Mat. L/T/D						48.3
(11) 1.8	(16) 2.0	(12) 9.2							(10) 9.2
1.3	.5	4.1							4.4
.1	.1	.1	Fixed/Worth					.0	.2
.7	.6	.5						.4	.4
1.5	2.0	1.2						2.1	.8
1.3	1.2	1.2	Debt/Worth					1.3	1.2
2.9	2.8	2.2						3.4	1.9
6.1	6.1	5.5						10.7	3.4
39.8	50.4	45.6	% Profit Before Taxes/Tangible Net Worth					32.1	51.4
(74) 21.0	(62) 17.2	(66) 23.7					(17)	15.0	(41) 24.2
7.5	6.8	12.3						1.5	12.5
12.3	12.7	12.9	% Profit Before Taxes/Total Assets					8.7	13.7
4.9	4.5	6.5						3.4	6.8
1.0	1.3	2.7						.0	3.9
327.9	279.5	286.4	Sales/Net Fixed Assets					675.8	257.7
32.3	31.5	45.6						63.1	36.8
12.9	10.2	15.0						24.1	15.0
8.2	6.2	6.5	Sales/Total Assets					6.5	7.5
5.2	4.7	5.1						5.5	5.0
3.2	2.9	3.5						4.5	3.7
.2	.2	.2	% Depr., Dep., Amort./Sales					.1	.2
(68) .9	(60) .9	(62) .7					(15)	1.0	(35) .4
2.0	1.8	1.4						2.2	1.0
.6	.7	.7	% Officers', Directors', Owners' Comp/Sales					1.1	.5
(35) 1.9	(34) 1.7	(28) 1.6					(10)	1.9	(16) 1.1
4.4	3.7	3.3						2.9	3.6
7227127M	3861329M	6149421M	Net Sales ($)	956M	12989M	4818M	36119M	298634M	5795905M
1273075M	917385M	1120212M	Total Assets ($)	236M	4094M	1569M	9649M	82699M	1021965M

© RMA 2005   M = $ thousand   MM = $ million
See Pages 11 through 21 for Explanation of Ratios and Data

Current Data Sorted By Assets   Comparative Historical Data

	0-500M	500M-2MM	2-10MM	10-50MM	50-100MM	100-250MM		4/1/00-3/31/01 ALL	4/1/01-3/31/02 ALL
Type of Statement									
Unqualified			2	9	4	3		8	6
Reviewed			6	1				19	17
Compiled	1	5	2	1				10	22
Tax Returns	1	1	5	1				1	2
Other	1	4	3	1		1		16	12
		17 (4/1-9/30/04)		34 (10/1/04-3/31/05)					
NUMBER OF STATEMENTS	3	10	18	12	5	3		54	59
	%	%	%	%	%	%		%	%
ASSETS									
Cash & Equivalents		5.6	10.0	5.5				3.1	6.2
Trade Receivables (net)		57.1	33.5	41.4				39.1	37.3
Inventory		17.7	17.6	25.3				17.7	15.7
All Other Current		5.0	-6.5	.2				1.9	3.5
Total Current		85.4	67.7	72.4				61.8	62.8
Fixed Assets (net)		12.5	23.9	21.7				27.3	27.1
Intangibles (net)		.0	2.6	.9				3.1	2.0
All Other Non-Current		2.1	5.7	5.0				7.7	8.1
Total		100.0	100.0	100.0				100.0	100.0
LIABILITIES									
Notes Payable-Short Term		23.0	11.9	17.6				18.0	14.2
Cur. Mat.-L/T/D		1.2	2.6	6.9				2.9	3.3
Trade Payables		37.5	24.9	19.1				25.1	24.2
Income Taxes Payable		.0	.4	.0				.3	.3
All Other Current		10.4	7.5	8.0				6.6	8.4
Total Current		72.0	47.3	51.6				52.9	50.3
Long-Term Debt		4.3	12.5	7.9				14.1	11.5
Deferred Taxes		.0	.1	.0				.8	1.1
All Other Non-Current		9.1	8.0	2.7				4.1	3.9
Net Worth		14.5	32.0	37.8				28.1	33.2
Total Liabilities & Net Worth		100.0	100.0	100.0				100.0	100.0
INCOME DATA									
Net Sales		100.0	100.0	100.0				100.0	100.0
Gross Profit		10.6	14.6	11.0				11.5	15.0
Operating Expenses		10.3	12.3	8.8				10.5	13.4
Operating Profit		.2	2.3	2.2				1.0	1.6
All Other Expenses (net)		-.5	-.4	.1				1.1	.7
Profit Before Taxes		.7	2.8	2.1				-.1	1.0
RATIOS									
Current		2.0	2.3	1.8				1.8	1.6
		1.2	1.4	1.6				1.2	1.2
		.9	1.0	1.1				1.0	1.0
Quick		1.4	1.5	1.2				1.3	1.2
		1.0	.9	1.0				.8	.8
		.6	.7	.6				.5	.6
Sales/Receivables		16 23.2	12 29.3	18 20.3				18 20.3	16 23.3
		21 17.5	18 20.4	22 16.3				22 16.7	22 16.6
		26 14.2	21 17.8	32 11.4				30 12.2	28 12.9
Cost of Sales/Inventory		2 205.8	7 53.6	8 43.1				6 63.4	4 97.0
		6 65.5	11 32.3	12 29.4				10 35.4	8 44.0
		18 20.6	14 25.3	24 15.4				23 16.2	24 15.0
Cost of Sales/Payables		6 56.8	8 47.3	9 41.8				10 35.5	11 34.7
		18 20.5	14 26.7	11 31.8				17 21.0	16 23.0
		29 12.5	20 18.2	18 20.7				23 15.8	22 16.4
Sales/Working Capital		25.3	12.5	12.8				19.6	20.9
		117.2	40.8	30.3				50.1	50.1
		-531.3	NM	NM				-498.6	-335.0
EBIT/Interest			6.6	12.6				7.3	6.8
			(16) 2.6	(11) 3.5				(49) 2.2	(54) 2.6
			.8	1.6				1.0	1.4
Net Profit + Depr., Dep., Amort./Cur. Mat. L/T/D								6.6	5.2
								(13) 2.3	(15) 1.9
								1.2	.5
Fixed/Worth		.1	.3	.1				.2	.3
		.4	.8	.5				1.0	.8
		NM	1.6	1.1				2.1	1.6
Debt/Worth		1.8	1.0	1.0				1.1	.9
		4.0	2.2	1.6				2.6	2.2
		NM	5.7	2.9				7.0	5.8
% Profit Before Taxes/Tangible Net Worth			65.0	28.1				35.9	30.8
			(16) 16.1	(11) 13.4				(49) 11.6	(54) 12.2
			1.0	5.6				1.6	3.9
% Profit Before Taxes/Total Assets		18.9	19.0	13.3				9.5	7.8
		6.4	3.1	5.9				3.5	3.8
		-3.0	.1	2.0				.0	.7
Sales/Net Fixed Assets		UND	100.8	773.4				138.4	81.0
		202.8	36.8	23.7				31.1	29.5
		51.0	21.9	14.5				7.1	7.7
Sales/Total Assets		14.3	9.8	9.0				7.6	9.0
		10.1	7.5	7.2				5.6	5.8
		7.1	5.2	3.8				2.9	2.9
% Depr., Dep., Amort./Sales			.2					.3	.2
			(15) .4					(45) .6	(51) .6
			1.7					1.8	1.7
% Officers', Directors', Owners' Comp/Sales			.4					.5	.4
			(12) .7					(23) 1.2	(19) 1.6
			3.2					2.3	1.8
Net Sales ($)	6056M	132790M	587070M	1583208M	1126903M	596438M		3567733M	3082997M
Total Assets ($)	858M	10500M	84993M	245781M	325099M	527889M		1174366M	843677M

M = $ thousand   MM = $ million
See Pages 11 through 21 for Explanation of Ratios and Data

Comparative Historical Data | **Current Data Sorted By Sales**

4/1/02-3/31/03 ALL	4/1/03-3/31/04 ALL	4/1/04-3/31/05 ALL		0-1MM	1-3MM	3-5MM	5-10MM	10-25MM	25MM & OVER
			Type of Statement			17 (4/1-9/30/04)		34 (10/1/04-3/31/05)	
9	15	18	Unqualified					1	17
17	16	8	Reviewed			1		2	5
14	14	9	Compiled	1		2	1	2	3
	4	7	Tax Returns		1		1	4	1
11	14	9	Other		1	1		2	5
51	63	51	**NUMBER OF STATEMENTS**	1	2	4	2	11	31
%	%	%	**ASSETS**	%	%	%	%	%	%
5.4	4.4	7.9	Cash & Equivalents					14.0	5.6
43.8	41.8	38.1	Trade Receivables (net)					39.5	37.9
19.0	17.6	19.2	Inventory					13.4	22.3
1.4	2.1	3.6	All Other Current					2.2	2.9
69.5	66.0	68.8	Total Current					69.1	68.7
21.6	24.1	24.6	Fixed Assets (net)					22.1	25.4
1.6	1.8	1.5	Intangibles (net)					3.8	1.2
7.3	8.1	5.1	All Other Non-Current					5.1	4.7
100.0	100.0	100.0	Total					100.0	100.0
			LIABILITIES						
14.8	15.8	14.2	Notes Payable-Short Term					12.8	14.8
4.1	2.3	3.4	Cur. Mat.-L/T/D					2.9	4.1
30.0	27.1	23.0	Trade Payables					18.4	21.9
.1	.3	.2	Income Taxes Payable					.7	.0
8.6	12.9	7.6	All Other Current					11.2	7.8
57.6	58.4	48.3	Total Current					46.0	48.6
11.5	10.8	13.6	Long-Term Debt					11.5	12.1
.5	.2	.0	Deferred Taxes					.2	.0
4.7	4.8	6.6	All Other Non-Current					5.5	5.2
25.6	25.8	31.4	Net Worth					36.8	34.1
100.0	100.0	100.0	Total Liabilities & Net Worth					100.0	100.0
			INCOME DATA						
100.0	100.0	100.0	Net Sales					100.0	100.0
11.8	16.8	14.7	Gross Profit					16.1	13.9
11.0	14.7	12.1	Operating Expenses					11.5	11.1
.8	2.1	2.6	Operating Profit					4.6	2.8
.4	.1	-.1	All Other Expenses (net)					.0	.2
.4	2.0	2.7	Profit Before Taxes					4.6	2.6
			RATIOS						
1.7	1.5	2.2						2.5	2.0
1.3	1.2	1.5	Current					1.6	1.4
1.0	.9	1.1						1.0	1.2
1.2	1.0	1.5						1.7	1.2
.8	.7	1.0	Quick					1.1	.9
.6	.6	.6						.8	.6
16 22.6	19 19.7	16 22.4						13 28.0	17 22.0
20 18.5	23 15.9	20 17.9	Sales/Receivables					20 18.3	21 17.7
25 14.8	29 12.6	26 14.3						24 15.5	35 10.4
4 82.9	4 96.6	6 60.8						4 83.8	8 48.5
9 42.8	10 37.7	12 29.9	Cost of Sales/Inventory					8 45.6	13 27.3
20 17.9	21 17.8	23 15.7						14 25.5	33 11.2
9 38.5	10 34.8	8 47.5						3 137.7	9 42.1
18 20.2	18 20.5	14 26.5	Cost of Sales/Payables					10 37.7	14 25.8
23 16.1	23 16.2	22 16.6						17 21.5	19 18.8
23.4	19.3	12.8						11.8	12.1
45.2	60.4	32.8	Sales/Working Capital					33.0	31.5
-304.0	-121.4	160.9						177.4	62.8
9.0	11.2	11.7							12.4
(46) 3.0	(56) 3.6	(45) 3.7	EBIT/Interest					(29)	3.7
1.2	2.2	1.7							2.0
6.3	7.0	7.3	Net Profit + Depr., Dep.,						
(10) 1.5	(14) 2.2	(12) 4.4	Amort./Cur. Mat. L/T/D						
-1.0	1.4	2.0							
.1	.2	.2						.1	.3
.6	.8	.6	Fixed/Worth					.4	.6
2.2	1.8	1.8						1.8	1.6
1.6	1.4	1.0						.8	1.2
2.8	3.0	1.9	Debt/Worth					1.3	1.9
7.4	6.9	7.3						3.9	5.4
52.6	52.4	53.8	% Profit Before Taxes/Tangible						28.3
(48) 20.5	(55) 27.9	(45) 20.8	Net Worth					(29)	18.3
2.1	5.3	4.9							5.9
9.2	12.0	12.9	% Profit Before Taxes/Total					45.4	10.9
4.3	5.9	6.6	Assets					14.0	5.5
.4	1.7	1.1						.6	2.1
351.3	189.1	159.6						293.8	111.9
48.7	40.9	36.3	Sales/Net Fixed Assets					55.2	25.5
19.2	9.6	12.7						13.6	12.7
11.1	9.2	9.3						8.5	10.9
8.1	6.6	6.9	Sales/Total Assets					7.1	6.9
5.4	3.1	3.2						3.1	3.2
.1	.3	.2							.3
(42) .4	(47) .5	(39) .5	% Depr., Dep., Amort./Sales					(23)	.4
.7	1.6	1.7							.8
.3	.4	.4	% Officers', Directors',						.2
(15) 1.5	(25) 1.2	(19) 1.4	Owners' Comp/Sales					(10)	.7
2.1	4.4	3.5							3.3
4229564M	5564678M	4032465M	Net Sales ($)	912M	3582M	17045M	14740M	185861M	3810325M
1108107M	1685077M	1195120M	Total Assets ($)	484M	695M	2131M	4089M	36100M	1151621M

Current Data Sorted By Assets   **Comparative Historical Data**

0-500M	500M-2MM	2-10MM	10-50MM	50-100MM	100-250MM	Type of Statement	4/1/00-3/31/01 ALL	4/1/01-3/31/02 ALL
		6	8	3	1	Unqualified	12	15
	4	14	3	1		Reviewed	23	22
2	7	13				Compiled	26	19
3	3	3				Tax Returns	6	10
3	1	1	6	1	1	Other	15	24
	29 (4/1-9/30/04)		55 (10/1/04-3/31/05)					
8	15	37	17	5	2	**NUMBER OF STATEMENTS**	82	90
%	%	%	%	%	%	**ASSETS**	%	%
	7.3	6.7	4.7			Cash & Equivalents	7.6	7.9
	30.9	27.4	27.3			Trade Receivables (net)	27.7	26.6
	36.7	37.9	36.3			Inventory	35.8	33.9
	2.0	1.5	4.3			All Other Current	2.8	1.8
	77.0	73.5	72.7			Total Current	73.8	70.3
	14.3	17.7	19.1			Fixed Assets (net)	18.5	20.4
	6.2	3.7	.2			Intangibles (net)	3.0	2.6
	2.6	5.2	8.0			All Other Non-Current	4.6	6.6
	100.0	100.0	100.0			Total	100.0	100.0
						LIABILITIES		
	15.8	17.1	23.5			Notes Payable-Short Term	26.4	21.3
	5.1	2.1	1.9			Cur. Mat.-L/T/D	2.3	3.1
	20.9	18.0	16.1			Trade Payables	18.3	21.1
	.2	.4	.0			Income Taxes Payable	.3	.2
	6.7	6.5	8.3			All Other Current	6.6	8.1
	48.7	44.0	49.9			Total Current	53.8	53.8
	8.7	14.3	6.0			Long-Term Debt	13.2	13.1
	.5	.4	.1			Deferred Taxes	.3	.2
	1.4	5.0	5.0			All Other Non-Current	2.7	5.6
	40.7	36.3	39.0			Net Worth	30.0	27.2
	100.0	100.0	100.0			Total Liabilities & Net Worth	100.0	100.0
						INCOME DATA		
	100.0	100.0	100.0			Net Sales	100.0	100.0
	24.8	22.6	20.9			Gross Profit	24.2	25.3
	22.1	20.4	19.5			Operating Expenses	20.3	23.1
	2.7	2.2	1.3			Operating Profit	3.9	2.2
	.4	.5	.6			All Other Expenses (net)	.8	.8
	2.2	1.6	.8			Profit Before Taxes	3.1	1.3
						RATIOS		
	1.8	2.9	2.3			Current	2.2	2.1
	1.7	1.6	1.4				1.4	1.4
	1.4	1.1	1.2				1.1	1.0
	1.3	1.3	1.2			Quick	1.0	1.0
	1.0	.7	.5				.7	.7
	.5	.5	.4				.5	.4
	13 28.7	23 15.7	24 14.9			Sales/Receivables	16 22.6	14 25.4
	25 14.9	28 13.0	35 10.6				27 13.7	25 14.8
	34 10.7	42 8.8	36 10.1				39 9.4	37 9.7
	21 17.1	31 11.9	32 11.3			Cost of Sales/Inventory	22 16.6	21 17.7
	29 12.7	41 9.0	58 6.3				43 8.4	42 8.7
	70 5.2	69 5.3	101 3.6				74 4.9	83 4.4
	5 72.8	8 44.4	12 30.0			Cost of Sales/Payables	9 42.9	10 36.4
	21 17.5	19 19.6	26 14.0				20 18.1	21 17.4
	36 10.1	37 9.9	38 9.6				42 8.7	38 9.6
	11.5	7.4	5.8			Sales/Working Capital	9.8	9.4
	16.5	12.2	14.0				16.1	23.2
	23.6	39.4	34.5				49.1	NM
	8.3	7.2	6.5			EBIT/Interest	7.4	4.3
	(13) 3.4	2.7	4.9				(72) 2.5	(80) 2.0
	1.6	1.5	1.3				1.5	1.1
		14.9				Net Profit + Depr., Dep.,	6.8	9.0
		(11) 2.2				Amort./Cur. Mat. L /T/D	(17) 3.0	(28) 3.1
		1.4					1.5	1.3
	.1	.2	.1			Fixed/Worth	.2	.2
	.3	.5	.4				.4	.6
	.6	1.5	.9				1.0	1.4
	1.2	.9	.7			Debt/Worth	1.0	1.0
	1.7	2.0	2.3				2.4	3.0
	3.2	5.7	5.0				5.2	9.7
	66.2	24.7	38.3			% Profit Before Taxes/Tangible	36.3	34.3
	14.4	(34) 13.6	16.3			Net Worth	(75) 20.7	(77) 12.9
	4.9	5.5	2.9				9.9	3.1
	20.3	7.5	8.8			% Profit Before Taxes/Total	12.6	10.6
	4.8	3.4	7.0			Assets	5.8	4.0
	2.4	1.3	.7				1.5	.4
	215.2	58.1	79.3			Sales/Net Fixed Assets	76.4	92.2
	87.9	31.5	25.6				26.0	23.4
	22.6	10.0	10.5				11.7	8.7
	7.9	5.1	4.5			Sales/Total Assets	5.2	5.8
	4.0	3.5	2.7				3.6	3.6
	2.9	2.1	1.4				2.8	2.3
	.3	.4	.3			% Depr., Dep., Amort./Sales	.4	.3
	(12) .4	(33) .9	(14) .9				(68) .7	(80) .9
	1.7	1.9	2.9				1.5	1.9
		.9				% Officers', Directors',	.9	1.1
		(16) 1.4				Owners' Comp/Sales	(39) 1.8	(39) 2.2
		3.6					3.1	3.6
13448M	96024M	659789M	980324M	967132M	699740M	Net Sales ($)	2350082M	6495206M
2158M	16967M	177558M	356226M	362621M	348261M	Total Assets ($)	917634M	950996M

M = $ thousand   MM = $ million
See Pages 11 through 21 for Explanation of Ratios and Data

Comparative Historical Data / Current Data Sorted By Sales

	4/1/02-3/31/03 ALL	4/1/03-3/31/04 ALL	4/1/04-3/31/05 ALL	Type of Statement	0-1MM	1-3MM	3-5MM	5-10MM	10-25MM	25MM & OVER
	15	17	18	Unqualified				1	6	11
	21	25	22	Reviewed		1		4	8	9
	21	26	22	Compiled		6	2	5	9	
	5	13	9	Tax Returns	1	2	4		2	
	21	17	13	Other	1	2		2		8
						29 (4/1-9/30/04)			55 (10/1/04-3/31/05)	
	ALL	ALL	ALL		0-1MM	1-3MM	3-5MM	5-10MM	10-25MM	25MM & OVER
NUMBER OF STATEMENTS	83	98	84		2	10	7	12	25	28
ASSETS	%	%	%		%	%	%	%	%	%
Cash & Equivalents	6.9	7.1	6.2			4.7		5.3	6.6	5.3
Trade Receivables (net)	24.3	25.1	27.0			24.4		24.2	28.4	28.7
Inventory	33.9	34.2	36.0			27.1		38.2	35.9	42.3
All Other Current	3.4	2.0	2.0			1.8		1.4	1.8	3.1
Total Current	68.5	68.4	71.2			58.0		69.1	72.7	79.5
Fixed Assets (net)	21.8	21.6	19.2			30.9		22.5	19.9	12.9
Intangibles (net)	2.7	3.1	3.0			3.8		3.6	3.1	1.0
All Other Non-Current	7.1	7.0	6.7			7.3		4.8	4.3	6.7
Total	100.0	100.0	100.0			100.0		100.0	100.0	100.0
LIABILITIES										
Notes Payable-Short Term	19.4	17.3	17.4			19.0		8.5	16.9	22.4
Cur. Mat.-L/T/D	2.6	4.2	2.7			2.7		2.5	4.3	1.3
Trade Payables	15.6	17.5	18.0			16.3		24.5	17.3	17.9
Income Taxes Payable	.2	.2	.2			.0		.6	.1	.3
All Other Current	5.2	7.2	10.1			6.7		6.6	5.8	10.6
Total Current	43.1	46.4	48.5			44.8		42.8	44.4	52.5
Long-Term Debt	15.1	13.0	11.1			16.8		16.1	9.8	5.7
Deferred Taxes	.4	.3	.3			.6		.6	.4	.1
All Other Non-Current	3.6	4.2	3.6			.2		8.6	5.8	.9
Net Worth	37.9	36.2	36.6			37.6		32.0	39.7	40.7
Total Liabilities & Net Worth	100.0	100.0	100.0			100.0		100.0	100.0	100.0
INCOME DATA										
Net Sales	100.0	100.0	100.0			100.0		100.0	100.0	100.0
Gross Profit	26.1	25.1	24.5			39.4		28.1	19.2	19.5
Operating Expenses	23.5	23.3	22.3			36.3		26.3	17.1	17.1
Operating Profit	2.6	1.8	2.2			3.1		1.9	2.1	2.4
All Other Expenses (net)	.4	.4	.5			.8		.5	.5	.2
Profit Before Taxes	2.2	1.3	1.7			2.3		1.3	1.6	2.2
RATIOS										
Current	2.6	2.4	2.5			2.4		2.2	2.7	3.0
	1.5	1.5	1.5			1.3		1.7	1.7	1.5
	1.1	1.1	1.1			1.0		1.3	1.1	1.2
Quick	1.3	1.1	1.2			1.8		.9	1.0	1.3
	.7	.7	.7			.6		.7	.7	.6
	.4	.4	.3			.6		.6	.5	.5
Sales/Receivables	18 20.7	15 24.4	21 17.4			4 97.9		16 22.5	22 16.4	24 15.1
	25 14.4	25 14.9	28 12.9			19 19.2		22 16.5	26 13.9	33 11.0
	35 10.4	34 10.8	36 10.1			31 11.9		32 11.6	37 10.0	36 10.1
Cost of Sales/Inventory	27 13.6	25 14.7	29 12.7			11 32.7		24 15.4	29 12.6	34 10.7
	45 8.1	44 8.4	41 8.8			26 13.8		48 7.6	33 11.2	58 6.3
	82 4.4	76 4.8	80 4.5			79 4.6		84 4.3	59 6.1	99 3.7
Cost of Sales/Payables	10 37.4	11 34.5	8 45.0			0 UND		13 28.3	5 69.5	13 28.4
	19 19.6	19 19.1	23 16.1			11 34.2		27 13.3	17 21.0	25 14.8
	34 10.7	34 10.8	38 9.7			38 9.6		53 7.0	37 9.9	37 10.0
Sales/Working Capital	8.1	9.3	7.7			9.5		7.3	9.2	7.9
	15.8	15.9	15.4			14.9		12.8	16.0	13.9
	59.0	50.2	70.0			−402.1		36.8	32.0	39.1
EBIT/Interest	6.8	7.6	7.8					8.7	4.9	13.1
	(78) 3.0	(91) 2.9	(80) 3.2					3.1	(24) 2.4	5.7
	1.6	1.4	1.3					1.4	1.3	1.9
Net Profit + Depr., Dep., Amort./Cur. Mat. L/T/D	8.2	6.2	11.7						3.9	
	(31) 3.2	(23) 2.6	(26) 2.1						(11) 1.6	
	1.9	.7	1.3						.4	
Fixed/Worth	.2	.2	.2			.3		.3	.1	.1
	.6	.4	.4			.9		.4	.6	.3
	1.2	1.0	1.2			2.2		1.6	1.1	.7
Debt/Worth	.8	.7	.9			.9		1.7	.8	.5
	2.1	1.8	2.1			2.1		2.1	1.9	2.2
	5.2	5.4	4.6			4.2		3.2	5.7	4.4
% Profit Before Taxes/Tangible Net Worth	39.3	29.3	32.0			75.1		32.3	27.9	38.6
	(78) 20.3	(89) 14.1	(80) 13.5			2.4		20.4	(27) 12.7	21.6
	5.2	4.3	4.3			−31.0		9.2	4.7	5.7
% Profit Before Taxes/Total Assets	11.3	9.3	9.4			17.8		7.2	10.9	10.5
	5.2	4.1	4.4			1.5		4.8	2.8	7.4
	2.6	.7	.6			−4.1		1.5	.7	2.0
Sales/Net Fixed Assets	60.7	93.6	87.5			68.5		57.7	94.1	87.8
	25.8	28.1	28.4			23.7		27.4	35.7	26.7
	6.3	8.4	9.7			4.6		6.5	9.2	21.3
Sales/Total Assets	4.9	5.4	5.3			6.9		4.8	6.7	5.0
	3.3	3.6	3.5			4.2		3.5	3.5	3.4
	2.0	2.2	2.1			2.3		2.1	2.0	2.1
% Depr., Dep., Amort./Sales	.4	.4	.3						.3	.3
	(73) 1.2	(80) .9	(69) 1.0						.8	(21) .7
	2.4	2.3	1.7						2.2	1.0
% Officers', Directors', Owners' Comp/Sales	.7	1.0	1.0						.9	.6
	(34) 2.0	(44) 2.2	(37) 1.9						(10) 1.2	(10) 1.0
	3.1	4.5	3.9						1.9	3.0
Net Sales ($)	2835489M	3815719M	3416457M		856M	17842M	30031M	90116M	403529M	2874083M
Total Assets ($)	1069297M	1220582M	1263791M		612M	5149M	15593M	29726M	152884M	1059827M

M = $ thousand   MM = $ million
See Pages 11 through 21 for Explanation of Ratios and Data

Current Data Sorted By Assets   Comparative Historical Data

						Type of Statement		
	1	18	19	4	3	Unqualified	33	34
	7	44	9		2	Reviewed	54	54
5	19	17	3			Compiled	60	42
9	15	8	1		1	Tax Returns	22	18
2	11	18	8	2	1	Other	52	63
	54 (4/1-9/30/04)		173 (10/1/04-3/31/05)				4/1/00-3/31/01	4/1/01-3/31/02
0-500M	500M-2MM	2-10MM	10-50MM	50-100MM	100-250MM		ALL	ALL
16	53	105	40	6	7	NUMBER OF STATEMENTS	221	211
%	%	%	%	%	%	ASSETS	%	%
20.9	12.5	5.8	3.0			Cash & Equivalents	9.1	8.5
27.7	39.2	39.5	32.7			Trade Receivables (net)	39.8	36.7
16.8	23.6	30.3	40.2			Inventory	27.5	30.0
2.7	3.0	2.8	2.1			All Other Current	1.9	2.6
68.1	78.3	78.4	78.0			Total Current	78.3	77.7
20.5	14.5	15.4	14.1			Fixed Assets (net)	14.6	14.7
10.0	2.0	1.5	1.8			Intangibles (net)	1.6	2.1
1.5	5.1	4.8	6.1			All Other Non-Current	5.5	5.5
100.0	100.0	100.0	100.0			Total	100.0	100.0
						LIABILITIES		
16.1	17.9	25.1	29.6			Notes Payable-Short Term	20.8	21.1
4.6	2.0	2.0	1.2			Cur. Mat.-L/T/D	2.3	2.2
17.1	27.5	28.9	16.2			Trade Payables	25.4	24.5
.1	.0	.1	.0			Income Taxes Payable	.2	.3
15.8	5.5	6.3	6.5			All Other Current	8.8	6.6
53.8	52.9	62.4	53.4			Total Current	57.5	54.7
12.7	6.7	7.9	11.2			Long-Term Debt	8.2	8.4
.0	.4	.4	.0			Deferred Taxes	.2	.2
1.8	8.7	4.1	3.7			All Other Non-Current	3.9	4.7
31.7	31.4	25.2	31.7			Net Worth	30.3	31.9
100.0	100.0	100.0	100.0			Total Liabilities & Net Worth	100.0	100.0
						INCOME DATA		
100.0	100.0	100.0	100.0			Net Sales	100.0	100.0
23.4	14.5	13.4	12.2			Gross Profit	15.2	14.4
23.2	13.0	11.8	9.4			Operating Expenses	13.2	12.3
.2	1.5	1.6	2.8			Operating Profit	2.0	2.1
−.3	.3	.4	.3			All Other Expenses (net)	−.1	.6
.5	1.2	1.3	2.5			Profit Before Taxes	2.1	1.5
						RATIOS		
6.1	2.2	1.6	2.1				1.9	2.0
1.2	1.4	1.2	1.4			Current	1.3	1.4
.8	1.1	1.0	1.1				1.1	1.1
2.0	1.5	1.0	1.0				1.2	1.3
.9	1.0	.7	.7			Quick	.8	.8
.6	.7	.5	.5				.6	.5
0 UND	16 22.6	23 16.0	27 13.7				21 17.2	19 19.1
9 41.0	23 15.5	31 11.7	37 9.8			Sales/Receivables	29 12.5	28 13.2
23 15.5	36 10.0	38 9.6	44 8.4				39 9.3	39 9.5
0 UND	3 106.3	12 31.7	27 13.7				8 47.0	10 37.8
0 UND	13 28.3	25 14.9	44 8.3			Cost of Sales/Inventory	24 15.3	26 14.0
11 33.5	36 10.1	47 7.8	73 5.0				47 7.8	50 7.4
0 UND	3 117.0	11 32.6	7 53.3				8 45.6	8 43.7
1 381.7	17 21.7	24 15.0	19 19.6			Cost of Sales/Payables	21 17.7	20 18.2
12 29.7	35 10.5	36 10.2	29 12.7				33 11.1	33 11.2
8.8	9.8	13.8	6.7				11.3	11.6
NM	28.8	33.8	18.9			Sales/Working Capital	26.3	22.1
−75.1	97.9	193.9	45.7				96.6	73.1
6.8	9.0	6.5	6.1				5.5	5.5
(11) 1.7	(49) 2.9	(99) 2.5	(39) 3.4			EBIT/Interest	(197) 2.4	(194) 2.3
−8.5	1.0	1.4	1.7				1.3	1.3
		9.8	15.9			Net Profit + Depr., Dep.,	9.0	8.4
	(29) 4.0	(12) 3.4				Amort./Cur. Mat. L/T/D	(50) 2.8	(42) 4.3
		2.0	.2				1.4	1.7
.1	.1	.1	.0				.1	.1
9.1	.4	.3	.3			Fixed/Worth	.4	.4
−1.2	1.2	1.3	.7				.9	.9
.3	1.1	1.7	1.4				1.1	1.1
15.9	3.3	3.9	2.9			Debt/Worth	2.8	2.8
−8.2	7.4	8.0	5.8				6.7	6.1
	52.8	35.5	32.6			% Profit Before Taxes/Tangible	36.7	40.2
	(49) 19.2	(97) 20.4	(39) 16.0			Net Worth	(202) 18.0	(198) 15.3
	1.4	3.8	7.3				7.3	5.1
10.8	10.8	7.7	10.3			% Profit Before Taxes/Total	10.5	9.3
5.2	3.3	3.3	4.1			Assets	4.7	4.7
−11.2	.2	1.2	1.5				1.3	1.2
349.0	269.6	309.3	538.7				203.8	213.5
65.9	70.7	69.3	63.4			Sales/Net Fixed Assets	56.9	69.7
21.3	27.6	19.7	14.1				24.3	22.4
11.6	7.7	6.1	4.5				7.3	6.3
7.0	5.9	4.5	3.2			Sales/Total Assets	4.9	4.5
3.6	3.5	3.1	2.5				3.2	3.1
.3	.3	.1	.1				.2	.2
(13) .5	(42) .6	(84) .5	(36) .2			% Depr., Dep., Amort./Sales	(181) .5	(171) .4
1.8	1.1	1.0	.8				1.0	1.0
2.4	1.0	.8	.8				1.1	.8
(11) 5.3	(33) 2.2	(46) 1.3	(14) 1.1			% Officers', Directors',	(102) 1.9	(101) 1.6
5.9	4.1	1.7	2.5			Owners' Comp/Sales	3.4	2.9
37221M	364328M	2282042M	3090883M	1950076M	4455663M	Net Sales ($)	8525579M	7580109M
4579M	61503M	488988M	940276M	476663M	1193361M	Total Assets ($)	2312729M	2353453M

M = $ thousand   MM = $ million
See Pages 11 through 21 for Explanation of Ratios and Data

Comparative Historical Data | **Current Data Sorted By Sales**

4/1/02-3/31/03 ALL	4/1/03-3/31/04 ALL	4/1/04-3/31/05 ALL	Type of Statement	0-1MM	1-3MM	3-5MM	5-10MM	10-25MM	25MM & OVER
						54 (4/1-9/30/04)		173 (10/1/04-3/31/05)	
42	46	45	Unqualified			3	4	8	30
64	73	62	Reviewed		1	2	4	28	27
46	54	44	Compiled	1	3	10	8	14	8
16	26	34	Tax Returns	2	8	3	14	3	4
61	56	42	Other	1	3	3	6	13	16
229	255	227	**NUMBER OF STATEMENTS**	4	15	21	36	66	85
%	%	%	**ASSETS**	%	%	%	%	%	%
9.3	8.0	8.0	Cash & Equivalents		18.4	10.3	12.5	5.8	4.9
36.1	36.0	36.4	Trade Receivables (net)		19.9	35.0	35.0	41.8	36.1
30.0	30.6	30.1	Inventory		25.2	17.5	31.1	27.6	37.0
2.5	3.0	3.0	All Other Current		2.3	1.2	3.2	2.3	4.2
77.9	77.6	77.6	Total Current		65.8	63.9	81.8	77.5	82.3
15.4	16.1	15.3	Fixed Assets (net)		21.9	23.4	12.6	16.6	12.0
1.9	2.2	2.3	Intangibles (net)		6.1	4.9	.3	1.7	1.3
4.8	4.1	4.9	All Other Non-Current		6.2	7.9	5.2	4.2	4.4
100.0	100.0	100.0	Total		100.0	100.0	100.0	100.0	100.0
			LIABILITIES						
21.3	22.0	23.9	Notes Payable-Short Term		18.4	19.4	18.8	24.8	26.8
2.3	2.9	2.1	Cur. Mat.-L/T/D		1.0	4.9	1.6	2.3	1.8
25.1	25.0	24.6	Trade Payables		17.8	18.9	27.5	30.8	22.2
.4	.1	.1	Income Taxes Payable		.0	.0	.2	.1	.1
6.7	7.5	7.0	All Other Current		8.4	10.6	6.5	6.3	6.7
55.7	57.4	57.7	Total Current		45.7	53.9	54.6	64.3	57.7
8.7	8.7	8.7	Long-Term Debt		8.6	8.2	7.8	9.1	8.3
.2	.3	.3	Deferred Taxes		.0	.4	.3	.4	.3
5.3	5.3	5.3	All Other Non-Current		2.8	6.8	8.1	5.1	4.6
30.1	28.3	28.0	Net Worth		42.9	30.8	29.2	21.1	29.2
100.0	100.0	100.0	Total Liabilities & Net Worth		100.0	100.0	100.0	100.0	100.0
			INCOME DATA						
100.0	100.0	100.0	Net Sales		100.0	100.0	100.0	100.0	100.0
14.8	15.5	14.2	Gross Profit		20.6	23.6	12.1	13.2	11.7
12.6	13.8	12.5	Operating Expenses		19.0	21.0	10.3	11.8	9.6
2.2	1.7	1.8	Operating Profit		1.6	2.6	1.8	1.4	2.1
.4	.4	.3	All Other Expenses (net)		−.4	.0	.5	.4	.4
1.7	1.2	1.5	Profit Before Taxes		2.1	2.6	1.3	1.0	1.7
			RATIOS						
2.0	1.9	1.9	Current		5.7	1.8	2.1	1.7	1.9
1.4	1.3	1.3			1.7	1.3	1.5	1.2	1.4
1.1	1.1	1.1			.9	1.0	1.1	1.0	1.1
1.3	1.1	1.1	Quick		2.1	1.3	1.3	1.0	1.0
.8	.7	.7			1.1	.9	.8	.8	.7
.5	.5	.5			.4	.4	.4	.5	.5
21 17.3	21 17.3	20 18.5	Sales/Receivables		2 184.7	18 19.9	17 21.3	22 16.4	22 16.2
28 13.0	29 12.7	30 12.2			15 24.1	32 11.4	24 15.0	31 11.6	32 11.5
39 9.4	37 9.9	39 9.4			24 15.1	47 7.8	37 10.0	41 8.9	39 9.4
7 52.8	10 36.1	8 47.3	Cost of Sales/Inventory		0 UND	2 147.6	4 91.1	10 37.3	17 21.5
27 13.6	27 13.4	26 14.2			13 27.2	13 27.2	22 16.6	23 15.8	37 9.9
54 6.8	56 6.5	49 7.5			60 6.1	50 7.4	46 7.9	38 9.6	65 5.7
10 37.9	11 34.3	7 53.4	Cost of Sales/Payables		1 561.0	4 94.5	3 120.9	12 31.7	7 50.3
21 17.4	23 16.0	20 18.1			4 100.0	17 21.7	16 23.2	24 15.4	20 18.1
33 11.1	36 10.1	33 11.1			43 8.5	33 11.2	34 10.8	38 9.7	30 12.2
11.5	11.0	10.9	Sales/Working Capital		6.1	9.1	7.9	15.1	11.0
25.4	25.1	28.9			15.2	19.6	32.4	40.1	22.0
73.9	95.1	126.0			−135.6	NM	181.2	−930.2	63.0
8.0	7.0	6.9	EBIT/Interest		11.2	5.5	5.8	5.6	10.0
(205) 2.9	(232) 2.9	(211) 2.6			(12) 1.9	(20) 2.2	(32) 3.0	(62) 2.3	(83) 3.5
1.3	1.2	1.4			−5.5	−.1	1.7	1.1	1.7
5.9	6.0	9.2	Net Profit + Depr., Dep., Amort./Cur. Mat. L/T/D					4.8	16.1
(57) 2.1	(68) 2.2	(55) 4.0						(19) 3.7	(27) 4.5
1.2	.5	1.3						1.0	.7
.1	.1	.1	Fixed/Worth		.0	.2	.0	.1	.1
.3	.4	.4			.6	.8	.3	.5	.3
1.2	1.3	1.1			−11.9	1.9	1.6	2.9	.6
1.2	1.4	1.4	Debt/Worth		.2	1.3	1.1	1.7	1.5
2.8	3.4	3.4			1.5	2.8	3.7	4.5	3.1
6.9	7.3	8.0			−65.5	4.6	13.1	8.2	6.2
37.4	33.8	40.1	% Profit Before Taxes/Tangible Net Worth		24.0	47.5	48.6	34.7	41.3
(205) 17.3	(228) 15.1	(206) 19.4			(11) 12.9	(19) 3.0	(33) 27.1	(58) 20.4	(83) 21.8
5.1	4.3	4.5			−1.6	−3.0	3.5	3.7	7.6
10.2	8.2	9.4	% Profit Before Taxes/Total Assets		9.3	11.3	9.6	7.0	10.0
4.1	3.6	3.7			4.0	1.4	3.4	3.2	4.2
.9	.4	.8			−1.2	−2.1	.3	.5	1.5
198.2	237.2	306.5	Sales/Net Fixed Assets		233.5	55.3	870.5	297.1	534.7
68.9	63.1	64.5			34.0	25.8	80.8	87.0	70.8
20.3	17.4	20.2			8.3	14.4	28.9	17.1	27.4
6.5	6.4	6.4	Sales/Total Assets		7.2	6.0	8.4	6.4	5.6
4.5	4.3	4.4			3.1	4.0	5.9	4.5	4.4
3.1	2.8	2.9			1.9	2.1	2.8	3.5	2.9
.2	.1	.2	% Depr., Dep., Amort./Sales		.3	.7	.2	.1	.1
(202) .4	(216) .4	(184) .5			(11) .8	(19) 1.4	(27) .6	(52) .5	(72) .4
1.0	1.0	1.0			1.2	1.8	1.0	1.0	.7
.8	.1	.9	% Officers', Directors', Owners' Comp/Sales		2.6		1.2	.8	.7
(102) 1.7	(116) 1.8	(107) 1.6			(15) 4.0		(22) 1.6	(25) 1.2	(34) 1.1
3.3	3.3	3.8			5.1		3.2	1.9	2.7
6922029M	9754170M	12180213M	Net Sales ($)	1514M	27939M	81064M	265546M	1034770M	10769380M
1934479M	2682957M	3165370M	Total Assets ($)	633M	11118M	36358M	64224M	253075M	2799962M

© RMA 2005   M = $ thousand   MM = $ million
See Pages 11 through 21 for Explanation of Ratios and Data

Current Data Sorted By Assets   Comparative Historical Data

Type of Statement	0-500M	500M-2MM	2-10MM	10-50MM	50-100MM	100-250MM	4/1/00-3/31/01 ALL	4/1/01-3/31/02 ALL
Unqualified		1	15	13	6	1	29	21
Reviewed		9	34	5			49	35
Compiled	1	13	21	3			49	44
Tax Returns	4	11	5				10	7
Other	4	10	14	14	3	1	43	52
	35 (4/1-9/30/04)			153 (10/1/04-3/31/05)				
NUMBER OF STATEMENTS	9	44	89	35	9	2	180	159
ASSETS	%	%	%	%	%	%	%	%
Cash & Equivalents		6.7	6.3	3.6			7.3	6.1
Trade Receivables (net)		42.3	44.3	38.5			39.2	39.3
Inventory		22.6	25.1	26.9			24.3	25.4
All Other Current		1.2	2.5	1.3			1.5	1.9
Total Current		72.7	78.2	70.3			72.3	72.8
Fixed Assets (net)		19.0	15.1	20.4			19.0	19.9
Intangibles (net)		1.2	2.3	5.0			2.5	2.0
All Other Non-Current		7.0	4.4	4.3			6.3	5.4
Total		100.0	100.0	100.0			100.0	100.0
LIABILITIES								
Notes Payable-Short Term		16.5	20.0	21.1			16.2	14.2
Cur. Mat.-L/T/D		4.8	1.7	1.9			2.8	2.9
Trade Payables		21.9	21.9	21.2			23.3	22.3
Income Taxes Payable		.1	.0	.1			.1	.3
All Other Current		7.2	6.3	7.7			7.1	7.7
Total Current		50.4	49.9	51.9			49.4	47.4
Long-Term Debt		12.9	8.3	11.6			10.1	10.2
Deferred Taxes		.1	.1	.0			.1	.1
All Other Non-Current		7.8	4.9	4.7			2.7	3.5
Net Worth		28.8	36.8	31.7			37.6	38.8
Total Liabilities & Net Worth		100.0	100.0	100.0			100.0	100.0
INCOME DATA								
Net Sales		100.0	100.0	100.0			100.0	100.0
Gross Profit		17.6	14.2	11.2			14.7	14.8
Operating Expenses		17.3	12.5	8.9			13.1	13.1
Operating Profit		.3	1.7	2.4			1.6	1.7
All Other Expenses (net)		.4	.1	.5			.0	.3
Profit Before Taxes		–.1	1.6	1.8			1.6	1.3
RATIOS								
Current		2.3	2.3	1.9			2.0	2.4
		1.8	1.4	1.3			1.4	1.5
		1.1	1.2	1.1			1.1	1.1
Quick		1.5	1.6	1.3			1.3	1.4
		1.0	.9	.8			.9	1.0
		.7	.7	.5			.6	.6
Sales/Receivables		16 22.8	17 20.9	18 20.6			15 23.6	14 25.4
		22 16.7	22 16.2	24 15.4			20 17.9	20 18.3
		26 13.9	29 12.5	29 12.7			28 12.9	29 12.7
Cost of Sales/Inventory		7 52.1	8 46.2	10 35.1			9 41.3	9 42.3
		15 24.9	16 22.8	20 18.7			16 23.5	16 23.4
		25 14.8	23 16.0	33 11.0			25 14.6	25 14.7
Cost of Sales/Payables		8 43.3	8 43.6	9 39.4			8 43.8	7 49.3
		15 24.1	12 30.2	14 26.4			14 25.9	12 29.4
		20 18.5	20 18.4	17 21.0			20 18.3	17 21.1
Sales/Working Capital		12.2	14.8	19.1			17.4	15.7
		29.7	31.8	30.4			35.6	28.6
		158.9	65.0	83.2			75.0	76.6
EBIT/Interest		6.6	10.9	13.8			6.0	7.7
		(42) 2.7	(82) 4.2	5.9			(163) 2.8	(142) 3.5
		1.5	2.0	2.4			1.3	1.4
Net Profit + Depr., Dep., Amort./Cur. Mat. L./T/D			14.6				8.3	7.1
			(20) 2.0				(40) 2.3	(27) 2.5
			1.3				1.2	1.3
Fixed/Worth		.2	.1	.2			.1	.2
		.5	.3	.6			.4	.4
		1.7	1.0	2.0			1.0	1.1
Debt/Worth		.9	1.0	1.4			.9	.7
		2.2	2.4	3.1			2.1	1.9
		9.5	5.2	5.8			3.8	3.8
% Profit Before Taxes/Tangible Net Worth		29.7	41.0	64.3			37.2	39.2
		(39) 15.5	(86) 17.1	(33) 25.4			(173) 13.9	(153) 16.0
		1.3	6.8	13.8			4.0	3.6
% Profit Before Taxes/Total Assets		11.0	10.4	13.0			12.4	12.7
		3.9	5.4	7.8			4.7	5.5
		.3	2.0	3.0			.9	.6
Sales/Net Fixed Assets		130.4	368.8	158.2			144.6	170.0
		58.9	91.2	37.0			54.0	45.6
		14.9	18.2	9.6			19.3	18.1
Sales/Total Assets		8.7	9.3	7.9			9.1	9.3
		6.4	6.5	5.6			6.4	6.6
		4.0	4.6	3.5			4.6	4.7
% Depr., Dep., Amort./Sales		.2	.1	.2			.2	.1
		(39) .5	(82) .4	(33) .4			(159) .5	(137) .5
		1.2	.9	1.0			1.1	1.1
% Officers', Directors', Owners' Comp/Sales		1.3	.7				.7	.9
		(30) 2.2	(51) 1.1				(94) 1.3	(76) 1.6
		3.4	2.0				3.2	2.8
Net Sales ($)	19631M	376883M	3014968M	4187409M	4020768M	685933M	9145826M	9204596M
Total Assets ($)	2833M	53520M	423353M	736492M	697810M	233638M	1598945M	1455704M

M = $ thousand   MM = $ million
See Pages 11 through 21 for Explanation of Ratios and Data

Comparative Historical Data | Current Data Sorted By Sales

4/1/02-3/31/03 ALL	4/1/03-3/31/04 ALL	4/1/04-3/31/05 ALL	Type of Statement	0-1MM	1-3MM	3-5MM	5-10MM	10-25MM	25MM & OVER
					35 (4/1-9/30/04)		153 (10/1/04-3/31/05)		
33	33	36	Unqualified		1		1	1	33
56	51	48	Reviewed		1		4	19	24
45	60	38	Compiled		2	5	6	12	13
17	22	20	Tax Returns		4	4	4	8	
45	43	46	Other	3	2	3	4	12	22
196	209	188	NUMBER OF STATEMENTS	3	10	12	19	52	92
%	%	%	ASSETS	%	%	%	%	%	%
7.3	8.0	6.4	Cash & Equivalents		19.2	5.5	3.5	9.1	4.0
39.3	39.5	41.1	Trade Receivables (net)		29.2	19.6	48.4	42.6	43.0
25.6	23.8	24.4	Inventory		9.6	35.1	15.3	24.8	26.3
1.9	1.9	1.9	All Other Current		1.5	1.4	3.0	2.6	1.4
74.2	73.2	73.8	Total Current		59.5	61.6	70.2	79.1	74.7
17.6	18.8	18.3	Fixed Assets (net)		20.5	30.1	25.1	13.6	17.5
2.3	2.5	3.1	Intangibles (net)		8.1	3.3	.1	2.3	3.6
5.9	5.5	4.8	All Other Non-Current		11.9	4.9	4.6	5.0	4.1
100.0	100.0	100.0	Total		100.0	100.0	100.0	100.0	100.0
			LIABILITIES						
15.2	16.7	19.4	Notes Payable-Short Term		22.3	23.4	21.7	15.5	20.3
3.6	2.4	2.5	Cur. Mat.-L/T/D		2.6	3.3	6.9	2.0	1.8
24.4	22.5	21.6	Trade Payables		13.2	12.5	19.8	23.0	22.9
.4	.1	.1	Income Taxes Payable		.3	.0	.1	.0	.1
10.8	9.5	6.8	All Other Current		8.3	4.2	4.9	7.3	7.3
54.4	51.2	50.4	Total Current		46.8	43.5	53.4	47.9	52.3
9.4	10.9	11.8	Long-Term Debt		21.0	24.2	18.0	8.1	10.0
.1	.1	.1	Deferred Taxes		.0	.0	.3	.1	.1
4.5	4.2	5.5	All Other Non-Current		6.0	7.3	7.0	4.8	5.4
31.6	33.6	32.2	Net Worth		26.3	25.1	21.2	39.1	32.2
100.0	100.0	100.0	Total Liabilities & Net Worth		100.0	100.0	100.0	100.0	100.0
			INCOME DATA						
100.0	100.0	100.0	Net Sales		100.0	100.0	100.0	100.0	100.0
15.9	14.7	15.3	Gross Profit		25.0	20.2	21.7	15.2	11.2
14.5	13.6	13.7	Operating Expenses		26.7	20.4	19.5	13.5	9.4
1.4	1.1	1.6	Operating Profit		-1.7	-.2	2.2	1.7	1.8
.2	.3	.3	All Other Expenses (net)		.6	.5	.4	.1	.3
1.2	.8	1.3	Profit Before Taxes		-2.3	-.7	1.8	1.6	1.5
			RATIOS						
1.9	2.1	2.1	Current		2.6	2.6	2.5	2.6	1.8
1.4	1.4	1.4			1.9	1.9	1.4	1.7	1.3
1.1	1.1	1.1			.8	.8	1.1	1.2	1.1
1.3	1.4	1.5	Quick		2.1	1.0	1.6	1.7	1.3
.9	.9	.9			1.4	.8	1.0	1.1	.8
.6	.7	.6			.7	.4	.8	.7	.6
15 23.8	15 23.6	16 22.5	Sales/Receivables		13 27.3	15 18.4	20 18.4	17 21.3	16 23.4
20 18.7	21 17.6	22 16.5			20 18.4	21 17.3	25 14.8	22 16.3	21 17.3
27 13.6	29 12.8	28 13.0			34 10.7	26 14.3	52 7.0	27 13.6	28 13.1
9 40.5	8 44.9	8 45.4	Cost of Sales/Inventory		1 292.8	22 16.8	4 91.4	8 46.2	9 41.5
16 23.1	14 25.4	16 23.3			5 67.5	34 10.6	13 27.9	15 24.0	16 23.3
28 13.1	25 14.8	25 14.4			31 11.8	72 5.1	22 16.2	22 16.9	25 14.4
9 41.1	7 50.1	9 41.1	Cost of Sales/Payables		1 338.0	7 55.0	11 34.0	9 39.7	9 41.1
15 25.0	13 28.9	13 27.2			14 25.5	16 22.8	15 24.2	13 28.1	13 28.5
21 17.5	19 18.8	20 18.6			28 13.2	23 15.9	20 18.4	20 18.6	18 20.5
18.0	17.5	14.7	Sales/Working Capital		7.9	8.6	13.4	12.4	20.4
30.2	30.8	31.4			24.7	12.4	46.2	26.1	36.5
88.5	106.1	75.5			-15.7	NM	175.3	66.1	76.5
11.5	9.6	10.4	EBIT/Interest			4.6	7.8	13.8	10.4
(174) 4.2	(190) 4.4	(176) 4.2				1.9	(18) 4.0	(49) 4.6	(88) 4.9
1.7	1.8	1.8				-.7	2.1	1.9	2.1
10.3	8.1	7.4	Net Profit + Depr., Dep., Amort./Cur. Mat. L/T/D					5.3	8.9
(41) 4.4	(40) 2.3	(35) 2.0						(10) 1.3	(18) 2.8
2.2	1.2	.8						.4	1.3
.1	.1	.1	Fixed/Worth		.3	.5	.2	.1	.1
.4	.4	.5			.8	1.4	.7	.3	.6
1.3	1.4	1.2			NM	7.7	2.4	.8	1.3
1.0	1.0	1.1	Debt/Worth		.6	2.0	.7	.6	1.4
2.3	2.5	2.5			3.6	3.0	2.5	1.6	2.8
5.8	5.4	5.9			-4.2	19.7	11.6	5.5	5.6
41.8	41.1	43.3	% Profit Before Taxes/Tangible Net Worth			56.5	28.5	33.2	47.5
(174) 17.6	(192) 19.2	(173) 21.1			(10) 10.3		(16) 20.7	(49) 17.3	(88) 24.6
6.8	5.1	7.0			-14.0		5.3	5.0	11.9
12.6	10.9	11.4	% Profit Before Taxes/Total Assets		17.0	8.8	14.6	11.9	11.1
5.5	5.6	5.6			-1.0	3.1	5.7	4.7	6.7
1.6	1.7	1.7			-30.8	-4.2	2.5	1.7	2.8
194.4	240.6	198.4	Sales/Net Fixed Assets		113.2	26.9	85.5	185.6	319.6
59.9	62.3	51.1			18.8	16.8	28.1	79.2	76.0
19.6	17.5	14.2			12.8	10.6	14.5	29.2	13.8
9.4	8.8	8.6	Sales/Total Assets		6.3	6.2	7.8	9.4	9.4
6.2	6.5	6.2			3.8	4.1	5.3	6.7	6.7
4.3	4.3	4.2			2.3	2.5	4.0	4.7	4.7
.2	.1	.2	% Depr., Dep., Amort./Sales			.4	.3	.2	.1
(166) .6	(186) .4	(170) .4				1.3	(18) .6	(47) .4	(84) .3
1.1	1.0	1.0				2.8	1.1	.7	1.0
.9	.6	.6	% Officers', Directors', Owners' Comp/Sales				1.1		.5
(98) 1.5	(102) 1.3	(95) 1.6					(12) 2.3	(37) 1.6	(32) .8
3.0	3.1	2.8					5.7	2.3	1.9
13207090M	15440484M	12305592M	Net Sales ($)	1850M	18634M	49280M	149639M	871153M	11215036M
2138740M	2404669M	2147646M	Total Assets ($)	1455M	5958M	13398M	36348M	152599M	1937888M

M = $ thousand   MM = $ million
See Pages 11 through 21 for Explanation of Ratios and Data

WHOLESALE—Fresh Fruit and Vegetable Merchant Wholesalers NAICS 424480 (SIC 5148)

Current Data Sorted By Assets

Comparative Historical Data

Type of Statement	0-500M	500M-2MM	2-10MM	10-50MM	50-100MM	100-250MM		4/1/00-3/31/01 ALL	4/1/01-3/31/02 ALL
Unqualified	1	3	11	20	6	3		31	41
Reviewed	3	9	30	19	1	1		49	38
Compiled	3	19	33	7				87	91
Tax Returns	5	15	8					16	19
Other	3	12	24	19	2	1		68	71
		86 (4/1-9/30/04)		172 (10/1/04-3/31/05)					
NUMBER OF STATEMENTS	15	58	106	65	9	5		251	260
ASSETS	%	%	%	%	%	%		%	%
Cash & Equivalents	7.5	13.7	9.4	8.1				8.3	9.8
Trade Receivables (net)	39.4	40.1	44.0	38.0				40.8	40.2
Inventory	10.6	11.6	9.5	9.9				10.4	10.3
All Other Current	1.7	1.7	3.9	7.1				5.6	5.7
Total Current	59.2	67.1	66.8	63.1				65.1	66.0
Fixed Assets (net)	28.7	23.2	22.4	23.9				23.5	23.6
Intangibles (net)	.7	1.2	3.7	5.0				3.5	2.9
All Other Non-Current	11.3	8.4	7.2	8.0				7.9	7.5
Total	100.0	100.0	100.0	100.0				100.0	100.0
LIABILITIES									
Notes Payable-Short Term	9.3	11.0	9.9	10.5				9.8	10.2
Cur. Mat.-L/T/D	4.2	3.0	2.4	2.6				2.7	2.2
Trade Payables	48.0	32.8	33.6	28.7				31.7	29.4
Income Taxes Payable	.0	.1	.1	.1				.4	.2
All Other Current	16.0	9.5	9.0	8.9				8.9	10.1
Total Current	77.5	56.4	55.0	50.9				53.5	52.1
Long-Term Debt	8.6	8.6	9.2	11.6				12.7	12.0
Deferred Taxes	.2	.2	.4	.4				.6	.5
All Other Non-Current	5.4	7.8	4.9	3.6				2.5	3.0
Net Worth	8.3	27.0	30.5	33.5				30.7	32.4
Total Liabilities & Net Worth	100.0	100.0	100.0	100.0				100.0	100.0
INCOME DATA									
Net Sales	100.0	100.0	100.0	100.0				100.0	100.0
Gross Profit	29.5	20.6	18.7	21.0				19.5	20.7
Operating Expenses	27.6	19.9	17.0	17.5				17.8	18.3
Operating Profit	1.9	.7	1.7	3.5				1.6	2.5
All Other Expenses (net)	.6	.2	.3	1.5				.3	.6
Profit Before Taxes	1.4	.5	1.4	2.0				1.3	1.9
RATIOS									
Current	1.4	2.1	1.6	1.6				1.8	1.8
	1.0	1.2	1.2	1.2				1.3	1.3
	.6	.9	1.0	1.0				1.0	1.0
Quick	1.1	1.8	1.2	1.3				1.5	1.3
	.7	.9	1.0	.9				1.0	1.0
	.4	.5	.7	.6				.7	.7
Sales/Receivables	13 27.5	13 28.2	22 16.9	26 14.2				22 16.7	21 17.0
	20 18.1	24 15.0	29 12.7	30 12.1				30 12.2	29 12.7
	33 10.9	31 11.7	39 9.2	39 9.3				39 9.4	40 9.1
Cost of Sales/Inventory	0 999.8	1 515.0	2 160.4	4 93.1				2 179.3	2 162.1
	6 66.3	5 69.8	6 65.2	8 46.9				5 69.6	6 59.4
	10 38.2	13 28.0	12 30.7	25 14.7				13 27.6	17 21.7
Cost of Sales/Payables	14 26.8	12 30.0	17 21.9	19 19.2				13 28.7	15 23.9
	30 12.3	25 14.5	26 14.3	26 14.1				23 15.6	25 14.5
	47 7.8	45 8.2	36 10.1	47 7.8				37 9.9	39 9.3
Sales/Working Capital	48.0	21.2	18.8	15.6				16.8	15.9
	-523.0	63.1	71.6	31.7				36.8	36.2
	-24.9	-71.0	-215.9	NM				-999.8	316.9
EBIT/Interest	17.4	8.2	16.2	20.6				7.8	11.1
	(11) 11.8	(46) 2.4	(96) 5.5	(57) 6.3				(226) 3.1	(231) 3.2
	2.4	-.8	1.3	1.6				1.1	1.5
Net Profit + Depr., Dep., Amort./Cur. Mat. L./T/D			10.0	8.5				6.6	9.5
		(35) 4.8	(23) 4.1					(70) 2.9	(69) 3.2
			1.9	1.4				1.5	1.5
Fixed/Worth	.2	.2	.3	.2				.2	.2
	2.1	.8	.7	.8				.6	.6
	4.5	3.2	1.8	1.7				1.7	1.6
Debt/Worth	1.7	1.0	1.3	1.2				1.1	1.1
	4.5	3.3	3.0	2.3				2.1	2.4
	105.0	10.6	5.1	5.5				6.9	5.9
% Profit Before Taxes/Tangible Net Worth	218.1	50.2	45.9	44.2				43.1	44.1
	(12) 25.6	(48) 9.4	(97) 21.0	(59) 25.4				(228) 15.9	(235) 18.8
	-.5	-17.9	3.8	4.3				3.9	5.6
% Profit Before Taxes/Total Assets	28.3	10.7	12.7	12.2				12.9	13.3
	11.2	2.5	4.7	4.9				4.6	4.8
	-.5	-3.8	.6	1.5				.5	1.2
Sales/Net Fixed Assets	176.0	199.0	108.8	112.4				101.3	145.5
	49.0	36.1	38.2	26.0				32.2	31.3
	11.0	10.7	14.8	7.3				13.2	9.9
Sales/Total Assets	9.6	8.8	7.3	6.4				7.1	7.5
	8.0	6.1	5.5	4.8				5.4	5.2
	3.2	3.7	3.4	1.7				2.9	2.5
% Depr., Dep., Amort./Sales	.2	.2	.4	.3				.3	.2
	(11) .5	(43) .7	(92) .8	(52) .7				(216) .7	(220) .6
	2.3	1.7	1.6	2.1				1.4	1.6
% Officers', Directors', Owners' Comp/Sales	1.5	1.3	.8	.6				.9	1.1
	(11) 2.2	(32) 1.6	(54) 1.6	(16) 1.3				(112) 1.9	(97) 2.1
	2.8	4.2	2.5	2.1				3.9	3.5
Net Sales ($)	51023M	508700M	2674272M	5917986M	1658770M	2029273M		8111533M	8760071M
Total Assets ($)	4645M	74342M	491141M	1468781M	607934M	750703M		2406271M	2460326M

© RMA 2005

M = $ thousand   MM = $ million
See Pages 11 through 21 for Explanation of Ratios and Data

Comparative Historical Data / Current Data Sorted By Sales

			Type of Statement	0-1MM	1-3MM	3-5MM	5-10MM	10-25MM	25MM & OVER
40	42	44	Unqualified			1	5	9	29
64	60	63	Reviewed	1	2	3	8	18	31
65	84	62	Compiled	2	4	5	7	23	21
28	23	28	Tax Returns		7	4	7	8	2
59	52	61	Other	1	4	4	8	14	30
4/1/02-3/31/03 ALL	4/1/03-3/31/04 ALL	4/1/04-3/31/05 ALL		86 (4/1-9/30/04)			172 (10/1/04-3/31/05)		
256	261	258	**NUMBER OF STATEMENTS**	4	17	17	35	72	113
%	%	%	**ASSETS**	%	%	%	%	%	%
10.2	11.5	9.7	Cash & Equivalents		12.4	8.9	11.1	10.9	8.2
39.9	39.9	40.2	Trade Receivables (net)		25.8	40.6	32.8	40.2	44.8
9.9	10.6	10.2	Inventory		17.1	15.7	9.1	8.0	10.4
5.2	5.6	4.3	All Other Current		3.7	.8	4.7	5.7	4.1
65.3	67.6	64.5	Total Current		59.0	65.9	57.7	64.8	67.5
23.7	21.7	24.3	Fixed Assets (net)		31.3	23.1	33.3	24.2	20.3
2.8	2.0	3.3	Intangibles (net)		.1	1.0	3.0	3.2	4.4
8.2	8.8	7.9	All Other Non-Current		9.6	10.0	6.0	7.8	7.9
100.0	100.0	100.0	Total		100.0	100.0	100.0	100.0	100.0
			LIABILITIES						
8.6	9.6	10.1	Notes Payable-Short Term		13.5	13.1	7.9	12.9	8.0
2.6	2.6	2.7	Cur. Mat.-L/T/D		4.0	1.9	2.9	2.5	2.3
30.1	29.6	32.0	Trade Payables		25.5	33.8	25.7	28.9	34.8
.3	.2	.1	Income Taxes Payable		.1	.1	.1	.1	.1
9.5	10.9	9.6	All Other Current		6.1	6.7	13.7	7.4	9.9
51.1	52.9	54.6	Total Current		49.2	55.6	50.3	51.9	55.2
11.4	10.6	10.2	Long-Term Debt		10.4	12.5	12.9	12.3	7.7
.3	.5	.4	Deferred Taxes		.2	.0	.0	.8	.4
2.7	4.1	5.3	All Other Non-Current		16.9	10.9	8.8	3.3	2.9
34.4	31.9	29.6	Net Worth		23.3	20.9	28.0	31.7	33.8
100.0	100.0	100.0	Total Liabilities & Net Worth		100.0	100.0	100.0	100.0	100.0
			INCOME DATA						
100.0	100.0	100.0	Net Sales		100.0	100.0	100.0	100.0	100.0
20.3	20.1	20.3	Gross Profit		34.8	24.5	25.2	19.6	15.5
17.6	17.7	18.1	Operating Expenses		32.7	22.6	24.4	17.7	12.7
2.7	2.4	2.1	Operating Profit		2.1	1.9	.8	1.9	2.8
.2	.2	.7	All Other Expenses (net)		.4	1.0	.6	.4	.8
2.4	2.2	1.5	Profit Before Taxes		1.7	.9	.2	1.5	2.0
			RATIOS						
1.8	1.9	1.6			2.6	1.7	2.1	1.8	1.6
1.2	1.3	1.2	Current		1.1	1.2	1.2	1.2	1.2
1.0	1.0	1.0			.9	.7	.8	.9	1.0
1.4	1.3	1.3			1.8	1.3	1.8	1.3	1.2
1.0	1.0	.9	Quick		.7	.8	.8	.9	1.0
.7	.7	.6			.4	.5	.5	.8	.7
20 17.8	20 17.9	20 18.1		15 24.0	12 29.8	15 24.3	20 18.1	23 16.0	
27 13.4	26 13.8	28 13.0	Sales/Receivables	23 15.8	35 10.5	27 13.6	28 13.1	28 13.0	
36 10.1	35 10.4	38 9.6		36 10.1	62 5.9	39 9.4	37 9.9	38 9.7	
2 170.2	2 171.0	3 137.2		4 101.5	1 301.5	1 251.8	3 126.4	3 141.3	
6 66.2	6 62.6	6 59.0	Cost of Sales/Inventory	14 26.1	12 29.2	10 35.6	6 65.8	6 63.6	
13 27.1	15 24.5	15 24.7		66 5.5	62 5.8	30 12.3	10 37.8	11 32.4	
13 27.1	14 26.7	16 22.3		13 29.1	21 17.1	14 25.7	12 29.6	17 21.5	
23 15.6	23 16.0	26 14.1	Cost of Sales/Payables	34 10.6	47 7.8	24 15.5	25 14.4	24 15.3	
35 10.3	35 10.5	39 9.4		73 5.0	61 6.0	52 7.0	36 10.2	35 10.4	
18.1	15.5	19.4			5.9	7.8	14.0	14.1	24.0
46.1	40.2	54.2	Sales/Working Capital		58.8	29.8	42.5	51.2	56.7
422.9	540.8	-137.1			-52.1	-32.5	-36.6	-133.3	313.7
14.1	17.7	16.0			12.7	6.8	12.0	14.2	20.8
(233) 4.4	(240) 4.4	(224) 4.9	EBIT/Interest	(14) 1.5	(15) 2.3	(32) 2.0	(61) 3.8	(99) 6.7	
1.5	1.6	1.4			-2.2	.3	-1.1	1.4	2.5
10.7	6.0	8.5						8.9	8.5
(63) 4.4	(71) 2.5	(76) 3.8	Net Profit + Depr., Dep., Amort./Cur. Mat. L/T/D					(24) 5.1	(40) 4.7
1.5	1.4	1.8						1.8	2.2
.2	.2	.3			.5	.2	.4	.2	.3
.6	.6	.8	Fixed/Worth		1.5	1.0	1.2	.8	.7
1.4	1.3	2.1			4.8	2.4	5.4	2.0	1.3
1.0	1.0	1.2			1.3	2.0	.8	1.1	1.3
2.3	2.4	2.9	Debt/Worth		4.3	4.4	2.9	2.4	2.6
4.7	6.3	7.0			20.3	NM	90.7	5.7	4.7
38.9	44.7	46.6			32.8	46.6	38.5	45.9	50.3
(233) 17.2	(241) 18.7	(229) 21.0	% Profit Before Taxes/Tangible Net Worth	(14) -.6	(13) 12.9	(28) 13.1	(65) 17.3	(107) 25.6	
5.6	5.8	3.5			-36.4	-26.8	-27.4	2.8	8.7
12.7	13.8	12.8			7.7	9.7	11.6	14.2	13.2
4.9	5.3	4.9	% Profit Before Taxes/Total Assets		.5	2.6	3.2	3.9	6.8
1.2	1.3	.6			-8.6	-4.0	-9.1	.7	2.0
107.4	113.8	112.6			37.3	84.1	38.7	138.3	126.8
33.7	36.6	28.5	Sales/Net Fixed Assets		7.4	17.5	16.5	40.3	37.9
12.9	12.9	10.3			5.4	9.9	4.0	11.7	15.6
7.6	7.4	7.2			6.7	6.0	7.0	7.5	7.4
5.4	5.6	5.4	Sales/Total Assets		2.4	4.3	4.1	5.5	5.9
3.1	3.0	2.8			1.3	2.2	1.6	3.2	4.2
.3	.2	.3			.6	.5	.3	.3	.2
(220) .7	(228) .7	(212) .8	% Depr., Dep., Amort./Sales	(14) 1.3	(12) 1.4	(29) 1.5	(58) .8	(96) .6	
1.6	1.6	1.7			4.6	2.4	4.0	1.6	1.3
1.2	1.0	.9			1.5		.9	1.3	.6
(112) 1.8	(119) 1.6	(114) 1.6	% Officers', Directors', Owners' Comp/Sales	(11) 2.2		(18) 1.6	(31) 1.7	(45) 1.2	
3.8	2.9	2.5			4.4		4.7	2.4	2.3
16464379M	15963884M	12840024M	Net Sales ($)	2287M	29262M	64856M	258239M	1200499M	11284881M
2426680M	2996720M	3397546M	Total Assets ($)	987M	26550M	21245M	110305M	407683M	2830776M

© RMA 2005   M = $ thousand   MM = $ million
See Pages 11 through 21 for Explanation of Ratios and Data

Current Data Sorted By Assets | Comparative Historical Data

Type of Statement	0-500M	500M-2MM	2-10MM	10-50MM	50-100MM	100-250MM	4/1/00-3/31/01 ALL	4/1/01-3/31/02 ALL
Unqualified		2	16	30	9	2	51	44
Reviewed		9	50	17	1		53	45
Compiled	.6	16	15	5			75	57
Tax Returns	10	17	7	1			29	21
Other	8	16	26	20	3	3	72	85
		67 (4/1-9/30/04)			222 (10/1/04-3/31/05)			
NUMBER OF STATEMENTS	24	60	114	73	13	5	280	252
ASSETS	%	%	%	%	%	%	%	%
Cash & Equivalents	9.9	7.5	6.0	7.7	8.1		7.7	7.1
Trade Receivables (net)	29.1	28.5	30.7	26.3	14.2		30.8	28.7
Inventory	25.7	30.7	28.0	31.5	28.5		28.7	28.3
All Other Current	.5	2.3	3.2	2.6	4.5		1.8	2.0
Total Current	65.2	69.0	67.9	68.1	55.3		69.0	66.2
Fixed Assets (net)	26.1	19.6	20.5	21.7	27.0		22.2	23.3
Intangibles (net)	.5	6.0	3.2	3.1	11.1		3.3	4.7
All Other Non-Current	8.2	5.4	8.4	7.2	6.6		5.6	5.8
Total	100.0	100.0	100.0	100.0	100.0		100.0	100.0
LIABILITIES								
Notes Payable-Short Term	13.2	15.5	14.1	14.5	18.9		17.6	17.7
Cur. Mat.-L/T/D	5.1	4.8	2.7	2.0	2.1		3.0	5.1
Trade Payables	21.5	23.9	25.9	22.3	11.8		22.6	21.3
Income Taxes Payable	.0	.3	.1	.3	.9		.2	.2
All Other Current	12.6	7.6	7.3	7.7	6.8		7.0	7.4
Total Current	52.4	52.2	50.1	46.8	40.5		50.4	51.8
Long-Term Debt	19.2	14.2	12.2	9.8	15.0		13.5	12.9
Deferred Taxes	.2	.1	.3	.6	.8		.2	.3
All Other Non-Current	26.8	4.1	4.7	3.8	7.1		4.0	5.9
Net Worth	1.5	29.4	32.7	39.0	36.7		31.8	29.1
Total Liabilities & Net Worth	100.0	100.0	100.0	100.0	100.0		100.0	100.0
INCOME DATA								
Net Sales	100.0	100.0	100.0	100.0	100.0		100.0	100.0
Gross Profit	35.4	30.7	25.1	22.6	29.9		27.7	29.0
Operating Expenses	31.8	28.1	22.2	19.1	24.9		24.8	25.5
Operating Profit	3.6	2.7	2.9	3.5	5.0		2.9	3.5
All Other Expenses (net)	.8	.4	.2	.0	2.0		.7	1.1
Profit Before Taxes	2.8	2.3	2.6	3.5	3.0		2.2	2.4
RATIOS								
Current	2.5	2.0	1.9	2.0	2.5		1.9	1.9
	1.5	1.4	1.3	1.3	1.7		1.4	1.2
	.9	1.0	1.1	1.1	1.1		1.0	1.0
Quick	1.6	1.1	1.1	1.2	1.4		1.1	1.1
	.7	.7	.8	.6	.6		.8	.6
	.3	.5	.5	.4	.3		.5	.4
Sales/Receivables	2 231.0	18 20.2	22 16.8	20 17.8	14 25.9		21 17.0	20 17.8
	26 13.8	25 14.6	29 12.5	27 13.4	22 16.5		30 12.4	31 11.9
	37 9.8	34 10.7	40 9.0	36 10.1	36 10.2		42 8.8	40 9.0
Cost of Sales/Inventory	7 51.9	20 17.9	17 21.9	22 16.7	41 9.0		17 21.0	20 18.5
	20 18.2	41 8.8	31 11.8	36 10.0	65 5.6		34 10.8	36 10.3
	49 7.5	77 4.7	68 5.4	69 5.3	92 4.0		70 5.2	70 5.2
Cost of Sales/Payables	4 86.0	13 28.2	16 22.9	16 22.9	14 26.4		14 25.7	14 26.7
	19 19.4	27 13.4	27 13.7	27 13.6	26 14.0		27 13.7	29 12.7
	37 9.9	45 8.2	43 8.4	40 9.2	37 9.9		47 7.8	42 8.7
Sales/Working Capital	10.4	11.2	10.8	8.7	9.4		9.5	10.0
	22.3	25.2	22.7	19.8	13.6		23.0	30.8
	-39.0	542.7	117.6	77.2	158.6		145.5	-205.4
EBIT/Interest	8.5	12.4	13.6	19.5	17.2		7.1	6.5
	(19) 2.9	(53) 2.8	(106) 4.0	(66) 5.0	4.8		(263) 2.8	(225) 2.7
	-1.0	.9	1.4	2.1	2.0		1.3	1.1
Net Profit + Depr., Dep., Amort./Cur. Mat. L/T/D			7.2	7.6			8.8	6.8
			(38) 2.1	(29) 4.0			(74) 3.8	(66) 3.0
			1.3	1.4			1.9	1.5
Fixed/Worth	.3	.2	.1	.2	.3		.2	.2
	.8	.5	.4	.5	.8		.6	.7
	NM	NM	1.7	1.4	NM		1.8	3.4
Debt/Worth	.6	.9	.9	.7	1.0		1.0	1.1
	4.4	1.8	2.5	2.2	3.8		2.4	3.1
	-28.8	NM	5.5	5.2	NM		6.6	10.4
% Profit Before Taxes/Tangible Net Worth	48.8	49.0	51.4	38.6	37.4		39.7	52.8
	(17) 18.1	(45) 16.8	(104) 22.4	(69) 21.2	(10) 14.8		(245) 17.5	(213) 18.8
	7.0	3.3	4.7	8.2	9.5		6.3	5.7
% Profit Before Taxes/Total Assets	13.6	14.8	15.1	15.0	11.5		12.3	12.8
	6.1	7.2	5.5	6.3	4.2		5.5	5.0
	.9	.2	1.0	2.3	2.0		1.3	.2
Sales/Net Fixed Assets	51.0	65.5	134.0	54.6	56.2		66.5	92.3
	22.0	22.7	32.5	22.0	6.4		26.3	20.8
	10.8	13.2	10.5	10.3	4.3		8.6	7.0
Sales/Total Assets	5.8	5.6	5.5	4.8	2.5		5.1	4.8
	4.3	3.8	3.4	3.0	2.2		3.5	3.1
	3.3	2.6	2.3	2.1	1.6		2.2	2.1
% Depr., Dep., Amort./Sales	.8	.4	.3	.3	.7		.4	.3
	(19) 1.4	(49) 1.0	(102) .7	(65) .7	(12) 2.4		(242) .9	(204) 1.2
	3.2	2.5	1.8	1.9	3.6		2.6	2.9
% Officers', Directors', Owners' Comp/Sales	1.3	.9	.6	1.0			1.2	1.3
	(13) 2.7	(24) 3.8	(46) 1.5	(17) 1.5			(116) 2.6	(106) 2.8
	7.1	8.2	3.8	3.9			4.8	5.3
Net Sales ($)	33021M	309112M	2299153M	5092186M	1908206M	2176712M	11568284M	9770632M
Total Assets ($)	6770M	72884M	585470M	1488662M	860658M	820546M	3381548M	2947910M

M = $ thousand   MM = $ million
See Pages 11 through 21 for Explanation of Ratios and Data

Comparative Historical Data | Current Data Sorted By Sales

Type of Statement

56	53	59	Unqualified			1	3	13	42
79	67	77	Reviewed		2	8	12	22	33
52	78	42	Compiled	1	9	6	9	11	6
30	35	35	Tax Returns	6	8	7	5	6	3
80	95	76	Other	3	15	6	11	11	30

4/1/02-3/31/03 ALL	4/1/03-3/31/04 ALL	4/1/04-3/31/05 ALL		0-1MM	67 (4/1-9/30/04) 1-3MM	3-5MM	222 (10/1/04-3/31/05) 5-10MM	10-25MM	25MM & OVER
297	328	289	NUMBER OF STATEMENTS	10	34	28	40	63	114

ASSETS

%	%	%		%	%	%	%	%	%
7.8	8.0	7.1	Cash & Equivalents	10.5	8.8	4.2	7.5	8.5	6.1
29.0	27.5	28.1	Trade Receivables (net)	20.8	25.3	28.0	26.4	26.8	31.0
28.4	28.6	29.3	Inventory	24.1	27.9	28.4	27.3	25.8	32.9
2.3	3.3	2.7	All Other Current	.2	.9	2.2	5.6	2.7	2.6
67.5	67.5	67.2	Total Current	55.5	62.9	62.9	66.9	63.8	72.6
21.8	22.0	21.3	Fixed Assets (net)	28.5	22.6	27.4	20.9	22.5	18.3
4.9	3.8	4.2	Intangibles (net)	1.1	7.3	2.9	5.1	4.5	3.3
5.8	6.7	7.3	All Other Non-Current	14.9	7.2	6.8	7.2	9.2	5.8
100.0	100.0	100.0	Total	100.0	100.0	100.0	100.0	100.0	100.0

LIABILITIES

13.5	13.2	14.6	Notes Payable-Short Term	14.3	12.6	18.7	11.6	13.9	15.6
4.9	2.8	3.1	Cur. Mat.-L/T/D	10.8	5.6	2.5	3.2	2.8	1.9
22.8	20.6	23.3	Trade Payables	13.8	19.8	21.7	26.0	22.6	25.1
.2	.2	.2	Income Taxes Payable	.0	.1	.2	.2	.2	.3
10.0	10.2	7.9	All Other Current	5.3	10.4	7.9	6.6	8.6	7.3
51.3	47.0	49.1	Total Current	44.2	48.4	51.1	47.7	48.1	50.2
15.0	12.0	12.9	Long-Term Debt	23.8	18.2	16.6	16.5	10.7	9.4
.2	.3	.3	Deferred Taxes	.0	.1	.2	.5	.3	.4
4.3	6.1	6.5	All Other Non-Current	1.1	21.1	5.2	3.6	7.0	3.7
29.2	34.5	31.2	Net Worth	31.0	12.1	26.8	31.6	33.8	36.3
100.0	100.0	100.0	Total Liabilities & Net Worth	100.0	100.0	100.0	100.0	100.0	100.0

INCOME DATA

100.0	100.0	100.0	Net Sales	100.0	100.0	100.0	100.0	100.0	100.0
28.0	27.3	26.7	Gross Profit	44.3	40.1	32.0	26.5	26.0	20.4
24.4	24.6	23.5	Operating Expenses	41.0	36.0	27.8	24.1	23.7	16.9
3.6	2.7	3.2	Operating Profit	3.3	4.0	4.2	2.5	2.3	3.6
.7	.6	.3	All Other Expenses (net)	2.3	.4	.5	.1	.2	.3
3.0	2.1	2.9	Profit Before Taxes	1.0	3.7	3.7	2.4	2.1	3.3

RATIOS

1.9	2.2	2.0		3.0	1.9	2.1	2.4	1.8	2.0
1.3	1.4	1.4	Current	1.4	1.3	1.3	1.6	1.3	1.3
1.0	1.1	1.1		.6	.9	1.0	1.0	1.0	1.1
1.2	1.2	1.2		1.7	1.2	1.2	1.2	1.0	1.2
.7	.7	.7	Quick	.6	.7	.8	.7	.7	.7
.4	.5	.5		.3	.4	.5	.4	.5	.5

21	17.5	19	19.3	20	18.3	Sales/Receivables	0	UND	20	17.9	21	17.5	21	17.5	19	19.2	20	18.2
30	12.3	28	13.1	27	13.4		21	17.3	30	12.3	33	11.1	30	12.3	27	13.4	26	13.9
40	9.2	39	9.5	38	9.7		42	8.7	42	8.8	58	6.2	37	9.8	36	10.1	36	10.2
21	17.1	18	20.1	19	18.8	Cost of Sales/Inventory	7	55.9	17	21.7	26	13.9	20	18.3	17	21.2	21	17.7
36	10.1	34	10.7	36	10.2		29	12.6	40	9.0	45	8.2	37	9.9	30	12.4	35	10.5
70	5.2	64	5.7	68	5.4		56	6.6	80	4.6	92	4.0	62	5.9	72	5.1	61	6.0
16	23.2	13	28.5	14	25.6	Cost of Sales/Payables	0	UND	11	34.6	22	16.4	17	21.9	14	26.0	14	25.6
25	14.5	23	15.6	26	13.9		15	24.1	28	13.2	34	10.8	28	12.8	25	14.7	26	14.1
48	7.6	43	8.4	43	8.6		35	10.5	52	7.0	64	5.7	47	7.8	43	8.4	37	9.8

10.1	8.8	10.2		9.8	7.3	6.2	8.3	12.0	10.6
24.7	20.4	21.5	Sales/Working Capital	19.3	29.6	18.8	15.9	23.0	21.1
NM	73.5	123.5		-6.5	-39.2	357.5	542.7	-999.8	51.4

	11.1		10.9		12.8	EBIT/Interest				9.8		11.0		14.6		12.7		18.4
(267)	3.8	(294)	3.8	(262)	3.8				(29)	3.5	(26)	2.2	(37)	2.9	(56)	3.4	(106)	5.0
	1.7		1.6		1.5					.1		.5		1.3		.9		2.6
	7.2		7.5		6.7	Net Profit + Depr., Dep., Amort./Cur. Mat. L/T/D								6.0		6.8		9.8
(81)	2.8	(77)	2.5	(81)	2.4								(13)	1.4	(21)	2.0	(42)	3.6
	1.6		1.2		1.0									.4		.7		1.7

.2	.1	.2		.1	.2	.1	.2	.1	.1
.7	.6	.5	Fixed/Worth	.7	.9	.8	.5	.5	.5
2.3	1.4	1.7		-7.6	NM	6.3	3.4	2.7	1.1
1.0	.8	.9		.4	.9	.9	.8	.8	1.1
2.8	2.2	2.3	Debt/Worth	3.1	2.2	2.5	2.2	2.5	2.5
8.5	5.9	6.8		-31.4	-24.8	12.0	5.2	9.4	4.9

	51.8		43.7		46.5	% Profit Before Taxes/Tangible Net Worth				48.8		63.3		40.1		44.4		49.2
(250)	25.2	(299)	17.2	(249)	20.2				(25)	16.4	(24)	22.9	(33)	20.2	(52)	17.3	(109)	22.7
	8.4		6.0		6.1					-2.7		2.1		4.8		5.1		8.4
	13.8		12.1		14.3	% Profit Before Taxes/Total Assets				14.9		13.4		12.2		17.0		13.8		15.2
	5.8		5.0		6.0					2.5		7.1		4.6		5.4		5.5		6.8
	1.6		1.2		1.1					-3.5		-1.2		-.5		.8		.8		2.3

81.5	95.5	71.6		57.6	41.3	42.0	48.0	82.3	114.8
23.8	24.7	25.1	Sales/Net Fixed Assets	14.1	20.3	21.2	19.9	26.8	37.2
8.4	9.5	10.2		6.2	8.8	4.5	11.6	8.0	12.4
4.8	4.9	5.1		4.4	4.5	4.1	5.1	5.2	5.7
3.2	3.2	3.3	Sales/Total Assets	3.8	3.3	2.7	3.3	3.2	3.7
2.1	2.3	2.3		2.0	1.7	1.6	2.4	2.1	2.5

	.4		.3		.3	% Depr., Dep., Amort./Sales				.8		.6		.4		.3		.2
(267)	1.0	(284)	1.1	(251)	.9				(23)	2.6	(25)	1.1	(37)	1.3	(58)	1.0	(100)	.5
	2.2		2.5		2.2					4.3		2.5		2.1		2.3		1.4
	1.3		.9		.9	% Officers', Directors', Owners' Comp/Sales				2.0		1.3		1.3		.5		.5
(121)	2.1	(124)	1.8	(102)	2.0				(17)	4.8	(13)	2.0	(13)	3.8	(26)	1.3	(29)	1.2
	4.9		4.1		5.3					7.9		8.0		6.3		2.9		3.5

11973503M	16128443M	11818390M	Net Sales ($)	6173M	65784M	107095M	297046M	1089748M	10252544M
3314922M	4214197M	3834990M	Total Assets ($)	2143M	31642M	51334M	112410M	429641M	3207820M

© RMA 2005   M = $ thousand   MM = $ million
See Pages 11 through 21 for Explanation of Ratios and Data

Current Data Sorted By Assets							Comparative Historical Data	
						Type of Statement		
1	17	87	68	10	7	Unqualified	72	163
3	17	54	8		1	Reviewed	69	60
	5	11	1			Compiled	22	21
1	7	2	1			Tax Returns	4	3
2	6	18	8	5	2	Other	39	44
	195 (4/1-9/30/04)		147 (10/1/04-3/31/05)				4/1/00-3/31/01 ALL	4/1/01-3/31/02 ALL
0-500M	500M-2MM	2-10MM	10-50MM	50-100MM	100-250MM			
7	52	172	86	15	10	NUMBER OF STATEMENTS	206	291
%	%	%	%	%	%	**ASSETS**	%	%
	13.3	9.9	7.3	5.9	7.0	Cash & Equivalents	9.5	9.2
	18.2	15.2	13.4	21.4	28.0	Trade Receivables (net)	19.8	16.4
	28.1	32.8	35.4	35.4	26.1	Inventory	29.3	30.1
	4.5	7.1	7.6	6.8	9.7	All Other Current	3.1	3.5
	64.0	65.1	63.6	69.5	70.8	Total Current	61.7	59.2
	26.1	27.8	29.0	22.9	19.8	Fixed Assets (net)	28.2	32.0
	.7	.4	.2	.8	.7	Intangibles (net)	2.6	1.3
	9.2	6.7	7.2	6.8	8.7	All Other Non-Current	7.5	7.5
	100.0	100.0	100.0	100.0	100.0	Total	100.0	100.0
						LIABILITIES		
	17.0	14.5	19.6	26.3	15.7	Notes Payable-Short Term	16.1	14.8
	1.4	1.9	2.2	.9	1.6	Cur. Mat.-L/T/D	2.4	2.4
	20.2	18.4	18.7	20.4	20.0	Trade Payables	18.0	15.5
	.6	.3	.3	.1	1.2	Income Taxes Payable	.3	.5
	6.7	11.2	10.1	9.2	16.3	All Other Current	9.8	8.1
	46.0	46.3	50.9	56.9	54.9	Total Current	46.5	41.3
	8.6	7.9	11.7	14.1	10.4	Long-Term Debt	11.0	10.0
	.4	1.4	1.1	.8	.5	Deferred Taxes	.8	1.1
	.4	1.9	1.2	.5	2.0	All Other Non-Current	1.9	1.6
	44.7	42.4	35.2	27.7	32.3	Net Worth	39.9	46.1
	100.0	100.0	100.0	100.0	100.0	Total Liabilities & Net Worth	100.0	100.0
						INCOME DATA		
	100.0	100.0	100.0	100.0	100.0	Net Sales	100.0	100.0
	12.7	11.4	9.4	7.4	8.5	Gross Profit	16.1	14.2
	11.9	9.8	7.8	6.2	6.7	Operating Expenses	14.3	12.3
	.9	1.6	1.7	1.2	1.8	Operating Profit	1.8	1.8
	.0	.4	.2	.2	.1	All Other Expenses (net)	-.2	.3
	.9	1.2	1.5	1.0	1.7	Profit Before Taxes	2.0	1.5
						RATIOS		
	2.4	1.8	1.5	1.4	1.5		1.7	2.0
	1.4	1.4	1.2	1.3	1.3	Current	1.3	1.4
	1.0	1.2	1.1	1.1	1.2		1.1	1.1
	1.1	.9	.7	.9	.8		.9	1.0
	.7	.5	.3	.3	.6	Quick	.5	.5
	.4	.2	.2	.2	.4		.3	.3
	1 283.1	**2** 149.3	**1** 253.2	**10** 36.9	**12** 30.1		**10** 36.9	**6** 57.9
	11 34.4	**11** 33.0	**10** 36.5	**14** 25.8	**20** 18.2	Sales/Receivables	**19** 19.0	**14** 25.4
	31 11.6	**25** 14.7	**25** 14.5	**17** 21.5	**47** 7.8		**36** 10.2	**30** 12.0
	7 52.1	**15** 25.1	**30** 12.2	**13** 28.5	**12** 31.1		**19** 18.7	**18** 19.8
	26 13.9	**43** 8.5	**45** 8.1	**31** 11.8	**24** 15.5	Cost of Sales/Inventory	**43** 8.4	**39** 9.4
	52 7.0	**65** 5.6	**75** 4.9	**59** 6.2	**40** 9.0		**84** 4.4	**72** 5.1
	2 177.5	**7** 53.9	**9** 41.3	**7** 50.7	**7** 49.7		**9** 40.2	**6** 56.5
	11 32.2	**14** 25.8	**20** 18.3	**12** 30.4	**19** 18.7	Cost of Sales/Payables	**21** 17.5	**17** 21.6
	37 9.8	**32** 11.4	**38** 9.7	**28** 12.9	**27** 13.7		**39** 9.4	**30** 12.3
	14.9	10.9	14.6	23.3	18.1		9.7	10.0
	34.8	21.2	29.2	43.2	25.4	Sales/Working Capital	22.1	21.9
	NM	39.2	57.7	123.9	64.1		96.6	48.2
	4.5	5.6	6.3	8.8			3.8	4.5
	(48) 1.9	(166) 3.2	(85) 3.1	(12) 3.2		EBIT/Interest	(192) 2.1	(278) 2.5
	.8	1.5	1.8	2.2			1.1	1.4
	7.3	7.1	6.7				4.8	7.3
	(15) 3.7	(58) 3.2	(35) 4.3			Net Profit + Depr., Dep., Amort./Cur. Mat. L /T/D	(56) 2.5	(110) 4.2
	2.0	1.0	1.7				1.2	2.0
	.3	.4	.6	.4	.1		.4	.5
	.6	.6	.8	.6	.6	Fixed/Worth	.8	.7
	1.2	.9	1.2	1.5	1.0		1.3	1.1
	.5	.7	1.1	1.9	1.4		.8	.6
	1.3	1.5	1.8	2.3	2.9	Debt/Worth	1.8	1.2
	4.0	2.6	3.9	6.1	4.3		3.8	2.7
	15.1	17.7	17.5	24.6	32.1		19.0	16.2
	(49) 3.1	(169) 7.9	(84) 9.9	16.1	20.2	% Profit Before Taxes/Tangible Net Worth	(202) 8.4	(289) 8.4
	-.4	1.7	5.3	8.4	11.8		1.5	3.5
	5.5	6.8	5.9	5.5	6.5		6.5	6.9
	1.7	3.1	3.3	4.9	5.3	% Profit Before Taxes/Total Assets	2.7	3.6
	-.8	.7	1.6	2.3	4.3		.4	1.3
	57.0	24.2	15.8	83.8	819.9		20.4	18.4
	24.9	11.7	9.9	16.1	26.1	Sales/Net Fixed Assets	9.5	9.0
	9.8	7.4	7.1	10.6	6.8		5.6	6.0
	6.9	4.5	3.7	4.3	7.1		3.8	4.3
	4.3	3.2	3.0	4.2	3.5	Sales/Total Assets	2.5	2.9
	2.9	2.2	2.1	3.3	2.1		1.8	2.0
	.4	.7	.7	.1	.1		.8	.9
	(49) .9	(164) 1.2	(83) 1.2	(13) 1.0	.6	% Depr., Dep., Amort./Sales	(198) 1.4	(276) 1.5
	1.2	1.9	1.6	1.1	1.4		2.3	2.2
	.4	.6					.6	.5
	(12) 1.3	(32) 1.3				% Officers', Directors', Owners' Comp/Sales	(65) 1.5	(47) 1.0
	2.0	2.6					2.4	1.9
5897M	**327152M**	**2962072M**	**5616717M**	**6176667M**	**9401687M**	Net Sales ($)	**7795755M**	**13281679M**
1495M	**66323M**	**835483M**	**1777625M**	**1092480M**	**1521591M**	Total Assets ($)	**2675684M**	**3718139M**

M = $thousand MM = $million

See Pages 11 through 21 for Explanation of Ratios and Data

Comparative Historical Data						Type of Statement	Current Data Sorted By Sales					
	175		180		190	Unqualified	1	1	5	32	54	97
	71		71		83	Reviewed	2	5	8	20	32	16
	19		23		17	Compiled		3	1	7	5	1
	8		7		11	Tax Returns	2	3	1	1	2	2
	38		34		41	Other		3	3	6	13	16
	4/1/02-3/31/03		4/1/03-3/31/04		4/1/04-3/31/05		195 (4/1-9/30/04)			147 (10/1/04-3/31/05)		
	ALL		ALL		ALL		0-1MM	1-3MM	3-5MM	5-10MM	10-25MM	25MM & OVER
	311		315		342	NUMBER OF STATEMENTS	5	15	18	66	106	132
	%		%		%	ASSETS	%	%	%	%	%	%
	8.2		9.0		9.6	Cash & Equivalents		14.8	7.2	9.1	10.6	8.8
	18.8		16.4		15.7	Trade Receivables (net)		17.9	19.1	16.4	12.5	17.5
	31.7		30.4		32.7	Inventory		27.7	33.3	34.0	34.1	31.0
	4.1		7.7		6.8	All Other Current		1.2	5.2	6.7	6.7	7.8
	62.8		63.4		64.8	Total Current		61.6	64.8	66.2	63.9	65.2
	29.0		28.1		27.6	Fixed Assets (net)		24.0	26.7	25.8	29.3	27.5
	.5		.6		.5	Intangibles (net)		1.3	.8	.4	.4	.4
	7.7		7.9		7.1	All Other Non-Current		13.1	7.7	7.6	6.4	6.8
	100.0		100.0		100.0	Total		100.0	100.0	100.0	100.0	100.0
						LIABILITIES						
	17.0		17.0		17.2	Notes Payable-Short Term		19.9	23.5	15.7	15.2	17.6
	2.4		2.0		1.8	Cur. Mat.-L/T/D		1.5	1.8	1.4	2.3	1.7
	15.0		17.4		18.7	Trade Payables		15.4	21.3	17.7	16.7	21.2
	.5		.3		.4	Income Taxes Payable		.3	.4	.5	.4	.4
	8.1		9.0		10.4	All Other Current		6.7	7.6	10.0	12.2	9.9
	43.0		45.8		48.5	Total Current		43.7	54.6	45.3	46.8	50.7
	9.6		9.1		9.2	Long-Term Debt		8.7	9.8	6.5	9.4	10.5
	1.0		1.1		1.1	Deferred Taxes		.1	.7	1.2	1.3	1.1
	2.0		2.1		1.9	All Other Non-Current		.5	5.6	1.3	1.0	1.4
	44.4		41.9		39.3	Net Worth		47.1	29.4	45.7	41.4	36.3
	100.0		100.0		100.0	Total Liabilities & Net Worth		100.0	100.0	100.0	100.0	100.0
						INCOME DATA						
	100.0		100.0		100.0	Net Sales		100.0	100.0	100.0	100.0	100.0
	13.7		10.6		11.2	Gross Profit		25.0	18.2	14.0	9.3	7.7
	12.1		9.5		9.7	Operating Expenses		21.3	14.4	12.1	8.2	6.6
	1.6		1.1		1.5	Operating Profit		3.8	3.8	1.9	1.1	1.1
	.1		.1		.2	All Other Expenses (net)		−.2	3.8	.4	−.1	.0
	1.5		1.0		1.3	Profit Before Taxes		3.9	−.1	1.5	1.2	1.2
						RATIOS						
	2.0		1.8		1.7			3.3	2.4	2.0	1.6	1.5
	1.4		1.3		1.3	Current		1.6	1.1	1.5	1.3	1.3
	1.2		1.1		1.1			.8	.9	1.2	1.2	1.1
	1.0		1.0		.9			1.0	.9	.9	.7	.9
	.5		.5		.5	Quick		.6	.7	.5	.4	.4
	.3		.2		.2			.4	.4	.2	.1	.2
7	49.5	2	188.3	2	166.6		3	124.4	4	100.6	4	82.5	1	549.7	2	166.6

Sales/Receivables and following mixed-count columns:

Count	Hist 1		Hist 2		Hist 3	Label	0-1MM		1-3MM		3-5MM		5-10MM		10-25MM		25MM & OVER
7	49.5	2	188.3	2	166.6	Sales/Receivables	3	124.4	4	100.6	4	82.5	1	549.7	2	166.6
15	23.7	12	29.9	12	31.6		14	26.0	22	16.5	17	21.9	8	46.4	11	32.2
33	11.1	28	12.9	25	14.7		52	7.1	40	9.2	37	9.8	20	18.7	22	16.9
21	17.4	13	27.6	14	25.6	Cost of Sales/Inventory	14	26.2	9	38.6	21	17.7	21	17.4	12	29.5
42	8.7	34	10.7	39	9.5		39	9.3	32	11.3	49	7.5	42	8.7	32	11.5
75	4.9	71	5.2	66	5.6		120	3.0	81	4.5	85	4.3	60	6.0	58	6.3
6	64.2	6	65.2	7	54.5	Cost of Sales/Payables	5	68.1	5	71.9	7	52.9	4	95.5	9	41.6
14	25.4	15	25.0	15	24.0		28	12.8	25	14.7	17	21.4	11	32.0	17	21.4
29	12.7	31	11.8	32	11.4		60	6.1	43	8.5	46	8.0	27	13.5	30	12.2

	9.1		11.5		12.4	Sales/Working Capital		4.3	10.1	8.2	15.3	20.2
	18.1		23.1		24.6			17.8	36.9	11.0	22.6	38.6
	41.2		46.5		53.3			−38.2	−101.3	29.7	39.5	67.2

		6.7		6.0		5.9	EBIT/Interest		13.4		6.2		5.3		5.6		7.4
(291)	3.2	(302)	2.7	(326)	3.0		(13)	3.0		2.6	(62)	2.4	(102)	3.3	(127)	3.1
	1.5		1.2		1.5			1.2		−.5		1.2		1.5		1.8

	6.5		5.1		6.7	Net Profit + Depr., Dep., Amort./Cur. Mat. L/T/D					7.2		6.2		8.0
(107)	3.5	(107)	2.7	(116)	3.5					(17)	3.0	(42)	3.8	(48)	3.4
	1.8		1.4		1.6						1.1		1.4		1.7

	.4		.4		.4	Fixed/Worth		.1	.4	.3	.4	.5
	.7		.7		.7			.5	.9	.5	.7	.7
	1.0		1.0		1.1			2.0	1.9	.8	1.0	1.1

	.7		.7		.8	Debt/Worth		.2	.9	.6	.8	1.1
	1.4		1.4		1.6			1.3	2.4	1.2	1.6	1.8
	2.6		3.5		3.2			4.3	8.3	2.1	2.6	4.0

	16.4		15.6		17.6	% Profit Before Taxes/Tangible Net Worth		20.9		15.6		14.3		15.9		23.3
(308)	8.8	(304)	7.2	(332)	8.9		(14)	6.2	(16)	9.0	(64)	5.9	(104)	8.9	(130)	12.0
	3.0		.8		2.5			−.3		−5.7		1.4		1.5		5.1

	7.1		5.7		6.3	% Profit Before Taxes/Total Assets		8.7	7.1	5.2	6.4	6.4
	3.4		2.8		3.2			1.7	2.2	2.8	3.1	3.9
	1.0		.4		.9			.4	−3.5	.5	.7	1.7

	20.5		24.7		27.5	Sales/Net Fixed Assets		40.6	61.1	24.3	23.7	28.4
	10.2		11.3		11.8			13.3	10.2	10.1	11.8	12.9
	6.3		6.9		7.6			7.2	5.7	6.5	7.4	8.8

	4.0		4.6		4.5	Sales/Total Assets		3.8	4.3	3.9	4.7	5.3
	2.9		3.1		3.3			2.2	2.9	2.8	3.3	3.6
	2.0		2.1		2.3			1.8	1.8	1.8	2.2	2.8

	.9		.7		.6	% Depr., Dep., Amort./Sales		.6	.8	.6	.7	.5
(295)	1.5	(304)	1.2	(323)	1.1		(12)	1.2	1.3	(65)	1.4	(100)	1.2	(125)	1.0
	2.0		1.8		1.7			2.3	3.0	2.0	1.7	1.3

	.4		.5		.5	% Officers', Directors', Owners' Comp/Sales				.7	.5	.3
(53)	1.3	(55)	1.2	(51)	1.2				(15)	1.5	(16)	1.1	(11)	.5
	2.3		2.7		2.3					2.9	2.2	1.0

| | 11453395M | | 19166626M | | 24490192M | Net Sales ($) | 1988M | 32138M | 78144M | 479818M | 1706546M | 22191558M |
| | 3716276M | | 4703707M | | 5294997M | Total Assets ($) | 2993M | 15134M | 36565M | 222726M | 578402M | 4439177M |

M = $ thousand   MM = $ million
See Pages 11 through 21 for Explanation of Ratios and Data

Current Data Sorted By Assets

Comparative Historical Data

0-500M	500M-2MM	2-10MM	10-50MM	50-100MM	100-250MM	Type of Statement	4/1/00-3/31/01 ALL	4/1/01-3/31/02 ALL
			1	1	1	Unqualified	1	3
	3	2				Reviewed	4	6
	3	5	1			Compiled	10	11
5	1	2				Tax Returns	5	2
1	3	3			1	Other	6	4
	8 (4/1-9/30/04)		25 (10/1/04-3/31/05)					
6	10	12	2	1	2	NUMBER OF STATEMENTS	26	26
%	%	%	%	%	%	ASSETS	%	%
	16.3	7.2				Cash & Equivalents	12.1	19.7
	24.4	13.8				Trade Receivables (net)	22.6	18.3
	24.4	20.7				Inventory	25.8	17.6
	9.6	15.4				All Other Current	2.1	4.1
	74.7	57.1				Total Current	62.6	59.7
	17.6	24.1				Fixed Assets (net)	29.0	23.0
	.5	9.0				Intangibles (net)	3.3	6.8
	7.1	9.8				All Other Non-Current	5.2	10.4
	100.0	100.0				Total	100.0	100.0
						LIABILITIES		
	19.3	16.3				Notes Payable-Short Term	18.4	15.7
	.3	1.9				Cur. Mat.-L/T/D	1.6	3.7
	6.1	10.8				Trade Payables	11.0	9.5
	.1	.0				Income Taxes Payable	.4	.0
	23.5	19.7				All Other Current	15.7	16.9
	49.3	48.8				Total Current	47.1	45.9
	4.7	15.7				Long-Term Debt	11.2	14.8
	.0	.1				Deferred Taxes	.2	.0
	3.5	18.7				All Other Non-Current	1.7	1.2
	42.5	16.7				Net Worth	39.7	38.1
	100.0	100.0				Total Liabilities & Net Worth	100.0	100.0
						INCOME DATA		
	100.0	100.0				Net Sales	100.0	100.0
	29.8	43.4				Gross Profit	19.7	29.4
	22.3	38.8				Operating Expenses	15.7	22.9
	7.5	4.5				Operating Profit	3.9	6.6
	4.9	2.2				All Other Expenses (net)	−.1	−.1
	2.6	2.4				Profit Before Taxes	4.0	6.7
						RATIOS		
	7.2	1.8					2.6	1.9
	1.7	1.2				Current	1.2	1.2
	.8	.8					1.0	.9
	6.6	1.0					2.1	1.3
	.8	(11) .7				Quick	(25) .9	.8
	.3	.1					.4	.4
	1 365.9	0 827.6					2 240.9	2 154.7
	6 63.7	9 39.6				Sales/Receivables	8 43.1	13 27.6
	27 13.5	22 16.5					23 15.7	37 9.8
	0 UND	4 85.6					1 427.8	1 435.8
	9 40.7	14 26.9				Cost of Sales/Inventory	14 26.0	13 27.4
	37 9.9	141 2.6					30 12.0	39 9.2
	0 UND	0 785.4					1 691.6	1 523.7
	1 655.4	19 18.8				Cost of Sales/Payables	3 123.3	6 62.0
	11 33.5	107 3.4					10 35.2	30 12.3
	28.5	14.3					18.1	7.3
	444.3	87.2				Sales/Working Capital	76.7	86.6
	−21.9	−57.6					UND	−61.2
		30.6					14.5	21.4
		4.4				EBIT/Interest	(22) 3.9	(22) 3.5
		1.8					1.2	1.0
						Net Profit + Depr., Dep., Amort./Cur. Mat. L/T/D		
	.1	.4					.2	.2
	.4	.8				Fixed/Worth	.6	.5
	2.3	NM					1.5	2.0
	.1	.8					.4	.9
	1.8	3.1				Debt/Worth	2.5	2.7
	8.3	NM					4.4	6.2
						% Profit Before Taxes/Tangible Net Worth	34.5	35.3
							(24) 14.3	(23) 12.8
							3.6	6.3
	40.2	6.6					16.0	12.1
	8.3	3.2				% Profit Before Taxes/Total Assets	6.1	6.0
	.2	1.5					1.3	.0
	613.5	35.5					227.3	120.7
	57.7	14.6				Sales/Net Fixed Assets	34.4	39.9
	19.3	4.2					9.4	5.3
	30.6	4.9					11.5	10.2
	6.1	3.0				Sales/Total Assets	7.7	3.2
	2.5	.8					3.2	1.2
		.6					.1	.1
		1.3				% Depr., Dep., Amort./Sales	(24) .3	(24) .5
		6.2					2.4	2.6
						% Officers', Directors', Owners' Comp/Sales	.2	
							(10) 1.1	
							2.1	
50332M	304158M	179436M	158298M	898636M	434042M	Net Sales ($)	532591M	1007041M
1600M	11626M	55554M	37082M	52504M	422769M	Total Assets ($)	244064M	420733M

© RMA 2005

M = $ thousand   MM = $ million
See Pages 11 through 21 for Explanation of Ratios and Data

Comparative Historical Data　　　　　　　　　　Current Data Sorted By Sales

	1	2	3	Type of Statement	0-1MM	1-3MM	3-5MM	5-10MM	10-25MM	25MM & OVER
	1	2	3	Unqualified						
	9	5	5	Reviewed		1			3	1
	9	9	9	Compiled		1		1	4	1
	9	5	8	Tax Returns	1	2	2	2	1	2
	5	7	8	Other	1	2		2	2	1
	4/1/02-3/31/03	4/1/03-3/31/04	4/1/04-3/31/05			8 (4/1-9/30/04)			25 (10/1/04-3/31/05)	
	ALL	ALL	ALL							
	28	28	33	NUMBER OF STATEMENTS	2	6	2	4	10	9
	%	%	%	**ASSETS**	%	%	%	%	%	%
	18.3	6.6	8.9	Cash & Equivalents					10.0	
	22.5	24.9	16.8	Trade Receivables (net)					17.9	
	24.8	26.8	26.1	Inventory					30.9	
	3.2	11.9	8.6	All Other Current					1.4	
	68.8	70.3	60.5	Total Current					60.3	
	20.5	18.9	25.5	Fixed Assets (net)					23.8	
	1.7	2.7	3.9	Intangibles (net)					7.7	
	9.0	8.1	10.1	All Other Non-Current					8.2	
	100.0	100.0	100.0	Total					100.0	
				LIABILITIES						
	29.6	25.8	19.7	Notes Payable-Short Term					20.2	
	3.9	1.6	1.2	Cur. Mat.-L/T/D					1.1	
	8.5	8.0	7.5	Trade Payables					12.6	
	.0	.2	.1	Income Taxes Payable					.0	
	8.1	16.7	14.9	All Other Current					4.0	
	50.0	52.4	43.4	Total Current					37.8	
	12.5	10.2	16.9	Long-Term Debt					7.7	
	.1	.1	.1	Deferred Taxes					.0	
	2.8	1.1	8.4	All Other Non-Current					4.5	
	34.5	36.2	31.2	Net Worth					50.0	
	100.0	100.0	100.0	Total Liabilities & Net Worth					100.0	
				INCOME DATA						
	100.0	100.0	100.0	Net Sales					100.0	
	16.3	26.4	29.2	Gross Profit					21.0	
	13.3	23.7	25.1	Operating Expenses					19.1	
	2.9	2.7	4.1	Operating Profit					1.9	
	.1	.2	2.1	All Other Expenses (net)					-.1	
	2.9	2.5	2.0	Profit Before Taxes					2.0	
				RATIOS						
	2.8	2.5	3.4						2.4	
	1.2	1.2	1.3	Current					1.5	
	.9	1.0	.9						1.0	
	1.8	1.2	1.6							
	.8 (27)	.6 (30)	.8	Quick						
	.4	.1	.4							
	3 132.1	0 884.6	0 782.2						0 UND	
	8 44.2	13 29.1	8 44.2	Sales/Receivables					8 47.8	
	21 17.6	28 13.1	21 17.5						24 15.2	
	1 494.7	3 137.5	2 167.7						2 151.8	
	11 33.4	9 38.6	14 26.2	Cost of Sales/Inventory					8 43.1	
	24 15.3	31 11.7	47 7.8						70 5.2	
	1 590.1	0 UND	0 999.8						0 UND	
	2 154.2	2 149.3	5 80.8	Cost of Sales/Payables					4 82.7	
	12 31.7	29 12.4	24 15.1						73 5.0	
	15.2	11.1	12.5						15.7	
	102.9	77.4	124.2	Sales/Working Capital					27.3	
	-385.6	-206.0	-508.8						NM	
	6.1	4.9	11.6							
	2.1 (22)	1.9 (25)	2.9 (31)	EBIT/Interest						
	.9	.6	1.3							
				Net Profit + Depr., Dep., Amort./Cur. Mat. L/T/D						
	.2	.2	.3						.1	
	.7	.5	.7	Fixed/Worth					.5	
	1.4	1.2	2.5						.9	
	.8	.9	.6						.5	
	2.7	2.6	2.1	Debt/Worth					1.3	
	7.9	5.4	8.5						3.2	
	53.1	35.4	40.9							
	17.0 (25)	6.0 (26)	15.1 (28)	% Profit Before Taxes/Tangible Net Worth						
	2.4	-2.0	2.3							
	12.4	5.1	9.4						11.5	
	5.0	2.7	3.3	% Profit Before Taxes/Total Assets					4.9	
	1.0	.1	.3						.8	
	167.0	92.5	73.8						613.5	
	68.0	38.0	34.4	Sales/Net Fixed Assets					65.9	
	20.5	15.9	8.2						13.0	
	28.5	8.3	14.0						36.3	
	7.7	5.6	5.3	Sales/Total Assets					4.5	
	4.0	2.3	2.3						3.0	
	.2	.4	.3							
	.4 (25)	.7 (25)	.8 (29)	% Depr., Dep., Amort./Sales						
	.8	2.1	2.3							
	.1	.4	.4							
	.9 (11)	1.7 (12)	1.8 (16)	% Officers', Directors', Owners' Comp/Sales						
	2.2	3.8	5.3							
	619901M	525627M	2024902M	Net Sales ($)	1773M	9060M	7429M	31184M	192105M	1783351M
	276406M	284026M	581135M	Total Assets ($)	3292M	13777M	570M	6268M	37309M	519919M

© RMA 2005　　　　M = $ thousand　　MM = $ million
See Pages 11 through 21 for Explanation of Ratios and Data

Current Data Sorted By Assets   **Comparative Historical Data**

	0-500M	500M-2MM	2-10MM	10-50MM	50-100MM	100-250MM	Type of Statement	4/1/00-3/31/01 ALL	4/1/01-3/31/02 ALL
		1	5	17	3	4	Unqualified	26	28
		2	12	8			Reviewed	16	16
	1	6	8	2			Compiled	22	21
	3	5	5	3			Tax Returns	4	7
	1	3	11	7	3		Other	19	20
		46 (4/1-9/30/04)			64 (10/1/04-3/31/05)				
	5	17	41	37	6	4	**NUMBER OF STATEMENTS**	87	92
	%	%	%	%	%	%	**ASSETS**	%	%
		8.5	7.7	9.3			Cash & Equivalents	10.8	9.3
		26.1	32.0	31.5			Trade Receivables (net)	30.7	30.9
		28.2	32.1	33.1			Inventory	31.2	27.4
		4.1	5.1	3.2			All Other Current	3.7	5.7
		66.8	77.0	77.1			Total Current	76.5	73.3
		16.3	14.6	15.2			Fixed Assets (net)	15.5	17.3
		2.3	.7	.3			Intangibles (net)	1.4	2.0
		14.5	7.7	7.4			All Other Non-Current	6.6	7.8
		100.0	100.0	100.0			Total	100.0	100.0
							LIABILITIES		
		26.4	19.2	17.8			Notes Payable-Short Term	24.2	25.4
		1.7	1.1	3.0			Cur. Mat.-L/T/D	1.9	1.5
		21.3	22.6	23.4			Trade Payables	16.5	18.9
		.1	.9	.2			Income Taxes Payable	.4	.3
		9.9	9.8	11.2			All Other Current	10.4	10.2
		59.4	53.6	55.6			Total Current	53.4	56.3
		8.4	8.4	9.5			Long-Term Debt	7.8	7.6
		.3	.2	.6			Deferred Taxes	.2	.2
		1.3	3.5	4.1			All Other Non-Current	2.1	3.7
		30.6	34.3	30.2			Net Worth	36.6	32.1
		100.0	100.0	100.0			Total Liabilities & Net Worth	100.0	100.0
							INCOME DATA		
		100.0	100.0	100.0			Net Sales	100.0	100.0
		25.6	18.9	15.7			Gross Profit	16.4	19.6
		23.4	16.5	11.9			Operating Expenses	13.4	17.3
		2.2	2.4	3.8			Operating Profit	3.0	2.4
		.5	−.3	.6			All Other Expenses (net)	.1	.6
		1.8	2.7	3.3			Profit Before Taxes	3.0	1.7
							RATIOS		
		1.5	2.2	1.6			Current	1.8	1.7
		1.2	1.4	1.3				1.3	1.3
		.9	1.2	1.1				1.1	1.1
		.9	1.0	1.0			Quick	1.1	1.0
		.5	.7	.7				.7	.7
		.3	.5	.5				.4	.4
	4	94.4	24 15.2	23 16.1			Sales/Receivables	21 17.4	17 21.3
	25	14.5	31 11.8	33 11.2				33 11.1	30 12.0
	50	7.2	45 8.1	55 6.6				53 6.8	46 7.9
	0	UND	26 14.2	22 16.8			Cost of Sales/Inventory	12 30.4	12 30.7
	45	8.1	45 8.1	42 8.8				46 7.9	33 11.0
	105	3.5	85 4.3	84 4.3				99 3.7	72 5.1
	5	70.0	12 31.0	15 24.0			Cost of Sales/Payables	5 74.3	5 66.7
	19	19.7	21 17.4	26 14.2				15 24.7	20 18.7
	59	6.2	47 7.8	50 7.3				35 10.3	40 9.1
		13.4	7.4	10.0			Sales/Working Capital	8.1	9.9
		69.0	17.6	18.2				17.8	22.3
		−77.5	25.2	31.9				74.9	90.8
		11.2	9.4	10.0			EBIT/Interest	5.2	5.2
		1.5	(38) 3.8	(36) 4.1				(79) 2.3	(81) 2.6
		1.0	1.7	2.3				1.4	.9
			13.5	4.7			Net Profit + Depr., Dep., Amort./Cur. Mat. L/T/D	16.4	7.0
			(10) 4.2	(12) 2.3				(16) 3.5	(17) 2.8
			3.3	1.6				1.0	1.0
		.0	.2	.1			Fixed/Worth	.1	.1
		.5	.4	.4				.3	.5
		.9	.7	.9				.8	1.0
		1.1	.9	1.8			Debt/Worth	.9	1.2
		3.4	2.0	2.5				1.9	2.3
		22.0	4.9	5.4				4.7	7.0
		40.4	52.5	36.3			% Profit Before Taxes/Tangible Net Worth	41.2	33.8
	(15)	15.0	(40) 22.7	22.9				(83) 20.9	(85) 14.2
		1.2	6.8	11.1				7.0	−.4
		15.1	15.5	11.0			% Profit Before Taxes/Total Assets	11.9	9.8
		1.9	6.0	5.4				5.2	3.8
		.0	1.5	1.6				1.4	.0
		999.8	95.5	208.7			Sales/Net Fixed Assets	105.2	140.3
		30.3	35.1	22.3				30.4	26.8
		10.9	12.0	7.1				10.1	7.7
		4.8	4.7	4.1			Sales/Total Assets	4.3	4.2
		3.1	3.3	2.9				2.9	3.1
		2.1	2.3	1.8				1.8	2.0
		.7	.3	.3			% Depr., Dep., Amort./Sales	.2	.1
	(12)	1.7	(37) .8	(33) .9				(77) .6	(80) .6
		2.7	1.9	2.1				1.4	1.9
			.8				% Officers', Directors', Owners' Comp/Sales	.7	.8
			(17) 1.7					(21) 1.7	(31) 1.6
			3.4					3.4	4.2
	7184M	89118M	788940M	2655853M	1236124M	1841918M	Net Sales ($)	2481803M	3762915M
	1570M	20370M	212918M	879715M	497468M	695926M	Total Assets ($)	984881M	1604253M

© RMA 2005

M = $ thousand   MM = $ million

See Pages 11 through 21 for Explanation of Ratios and Data

Comparative Historical Data   Current Data Sorted By Sales

Type of Statement

	4/1/02-3/31/03 ALL	4/1/03-3/31/04 ALL	4/1/04-3/31/05 ALL		0-1MM	1-3MM	3-5MM	5-10MM	10-25MM	25MM & OVER
Unqualified	33	44	30					5	1	24
Reviewed	22	25	22			1		1	8	12
Compiled	19	36	17		1	2	2	4	7	1
Tax Returns	12	10	16		1	5	1	2	4	3
Other	19	21	25			3	1	5	6	10
						46 (4/1-9/30/04)		**64 (10/1/04-3/31/05)**		
NUMBER OF STATEMENTS	105	136	110		2	11	4	17	26	50

ASSETS (%)

	H1 %	H2 %	H3 %		0-1MM %	1-3MM %	3-5MM %	5-10MM %	10-25MM %	25MM & OVER %
Cash & Equivalents	9.0	9.9	8.9			8.3		5.5	7.5	10.4
Trade Receivables (net)	29.9	28.5	29.6			28.5		27.5	30.5	32.4
Inventory	32.3	30.8	31.5			38.6		28.7	32.9	31.6
All Other Current	4.5	6.5	4.0			1.1		8.6	4.1	3.5
Total Current	75.7	75.7	74.0			76.6		70.3	74.9	77.9
Fixed Assets (net)	15.5	16.7	16.6			15.0		18.9	13.8	14.2
Intangibles (net)	1.5	.9	.8			1.6		2.4	.4	.3
All Other Non-Current	7.4	6.7	8.6			6.8		8.4	10.8	7.6
Total	100.0	100.0	100.0			100.0		100.0	100.0	100.0

LIABILITIES

	H1	H2	H3		0-1MM	1-3MM	3-5MM	5-10MM	10-25MM	25MM & OVER
Notes Payable-Short Term	19.1	19.5	19.5			23.2		31.7	17.6	16.8
Cur. Mat.-L/T/D	1.9	2.2	2.9			1.6		1.7	1.1	2.3
Trade Payables	21.3	20.7	21.4			18.6		22.5	23.9	21.3
Income Taxes Payable	.3	.3	.5			.0		1.5	.3	.4
All Other Current	10.4	10.7	10.6			12.2		5.3	12.0	12.2
Total Current	53.0	53.4	54.9			55.6		62.7	54.8	52.9
Long-Term Debt	8.3	10.0	8.5			10.1		7.4	8.2	8.1
Deferred Taxes	.1	.2	.3			.2		.1	.3	.5
All Other Non-Current	3.4	2.5	5.0			3.9		2.6	2.4	3.7
Net Worth	35.2	33.9	31.3			30.2		27.3	34.3	34.8
Total Liabilities & Net Worth	100.0	100.0	100.0			100.0		100.0	100.0	100.0

INCOME DATA

	H1	H2	H3		0-1MM	1-3MM	3-5MM	5-10MM	10-25MM	25MM & OVER
Net Sales	100.0	100.0	100.0			100.0		100.0	100.0	100.0
Gross Profit	17.5	18.4	19.7			37.4		25.1	15.8	13.0
Operating Expenses	14.6	16.1	16.4			30.9		22.7	12.5	9.9
Operating Profit	2.9	2.4	3.3			6.5		2.4	3.3	3.1
All Other Expenses (net)	.2	.1	.1			.5		.3	-.1	.1
Profit Before Taxes	2.7	2.2	3.2			5.9		2.1	3.4	3.0

RATIOS (values shown as upper / median / lower)

	H1	H2	H3		0-1MM	1-3MM	3-5MM	5-10MM	10-25MM	25MM & OVER
Current	2.0 / 1.4 / 1.1	2.0 / 1.4 / 1.2	1.7 / 1.3 / 1.1			1.8 / 1.3 / 1.1		2.0 / 1.2 / 1.0	2.1 / 1.4 / 1.2	1.7 / 1.4 / 1.2
Quick	1.3 / .7 / .3	1.2 / .7 / .3	1.0 / .7 / .4			.9 / .7 / .4		.8 / .6 / .3	.9 / .7 / .4	1.1 / .7 / .6
Sales/Receivables	19 — 19.5 / 32 — 11.2 / 47 — 7.7	19 — 18.9 / 30 — 12.0 / 46 — 7.9	22 — 16.5 / 31 — 11.8 / 48 — 7.6			13 — 28.0 / 34 — 10.8 / 61 — 6.0		17 — 21.8 / 41 — 8.9 / 65 — 5.6	23 — 15.5 / 29 — 12.5 / 42 — 8.7	22 — 16.6 / 32 — 11.4 / 48 — 7.6
Cost of Sales/Inventory	15 — 23.8 / 43 — 8.5 / 87 — 4.2	11 — 31.9 / 36 — 10.0 / 85 — 4.3	20 — 17.9 / 45 — 8.2 / 88 — 4.2			21 — 17.2 / 102 — 3.6 / 224 — 1.6		1 — 366.2 / 56 — 6.5 / 118 — 3.1	25 — 14.7 / 44 — 8.2 / 71 — 5.1	16 — 22.5 / 37 — 9.8 / 57 — 6.5
Cost of Sales/Payables	8 — 47.5 / 21 — 17.2 / 45 — 8.1	9 — 40.3 / 23 — 15.8 / 52 — 7.0	12 — 30.1 / 22 — 16.2 / 47 — 7.7			14 — 26.0 / 26 — 13.9 / 91 — 4.0		18 — 20.4 / 30 — 12.4 / 58 — 6.3	9 — 39.0 / 23 — 15.9 / 57 — 6.4	14 — 25.6 / 22 — 16.2 / 35 — 10.3
Sales/Working Capital	8.3 / 15.7 / 42.5	7.7 / 16.3 / 34.1	7.6 / 19.0 / 47.9			3.1 / 18.9 / 104.7		6.7 / 21.2 / -274.9	7.5 / 18.6 / 53.5	10.7 / 18.4 / 29.2
EBIT/Interest	9.5 / (92) 3.9 / 1.5	9.7 / (125) 4.2 / 1.4	10.4 / (105) 3.9 / 1.5			67.8 / 1.5 / 1.1		5.9 / (16) 2.5 / .9	10.7 / 4.7 / 1.4	10.4 / (47) 4.3 / 2.5
Net Profit + Depr., Dep., Amort./Cur. Mat. L/T/D	6.1 / (20) 2.6 / 1.0	4.5 / (26) 2.6 / 1.2	8.2 / (29) 3.9 / 2.1							7.6 / (18) 3.4 / 1.8
Fixed/Worth	.1 / .3 / .9	.1 / .3 / .8	.1 / .5 / .9			.4 / .6 / .9		.4 / .7 / 1.0	.1 / .3 / .7	.1 / .4 / .6
Debt/Worth	.9 / 2.3 / 5.8	.9 / 2.3 / 4.3	1.3 / 2.3 / 5.3			1.3 / 4.2 / 9.0		.9 / 2.4 / 25.5	.9 / 2.4 / 5.3	1.5 / 2.2 / 4.2
% Profit Before Taxes/Tangible Net Worth	37.7 / (99) 18.5 / 7.4	39.1 / (130) 15.9 / 2.9	38.7 / (105) 20.5 / 5.9			193.1 / 28.5 / 1.0		87.4 / (14) 14.0 / 3.8	41.1 / 22.8 / 11.9	36.0 / 16.3 / 10.8
% Profit Before Taxes/Total Assets	10.9 / 6.0 / 1.1	10.9 / 4.8 / .5	13.4 / 5.1 / 1.3			36.2 / 1.9 / .0		12.5 / 3.6 / .2	15.5 / 6.7 / 1.2	11.3 / 5.8 / 2.3
Sales/Net Fixed Assets	230.9 / 35.7 / 12.2	153.6 / 28.3 / 8.8	81.7 / 25.9 / 9.7			47.5 / 32.5 / 11.0		64.2 / 15.3 / 6.6	156.9 / 35.4 / 9.1	190.9 / 26.2 / 14.1
Sales/Total Assets	5.2 / 3.0 / 1.8	4.4 / 2.9 / 1.8	4.5 / 3.1 / 2.0			5.4 / 2.3 / 1.6		4.1 / 3.3 / 1.6	4.6 / 3.1 / 2.3	4.9 / 3.3 / 2.4
% Depr., Dep., Amort./Sales	.1 / (92) .6 / 1.4	.2 / (114) .7 / 2.1	.4 / (95) 1.1 / 2.1					.6 / (16) 1.6 / 3.6	.4 / (21) 1.1 / 1.9	.2 / (44) .8 / 1.4
% Officers', Directors', Owners' Comp/Sales	.8 / (35) 1.0 / 2.0	.8 / (40) 1.7 / 4.4	.7 / (35) 1.5 / 3.3							.2 / (10) .6 / 1.4
Net Sales ($)	4717060M	7992666M	6619137M		375M	22952M	15041M	124794M	453281M	6002694M
Total Assets ($)	1918402M	2352861M	2307967M		414M	10303M	7461M	67781M	204028M	2017980M

© RMA 2005   M = $ thousand   MM = $ million

See Pages 11 through 21 for Explanation of Ratios and Data

Current Data Sorted By Assets / Comparative Historical Data

0-500M	500M-2MM	2-10MM	10-50MM	50-100MM	100-250MM	Type of Statement	4/1/00-3/31/01 ALL	4/1/01-3/31/02 ALL
		4	10	2	3	Unqualified	15	15
2	7	16	7			Reviewed	25	22
5	8	6	2			Compiled	39	32
2	8	3				Tax Returns	6	4
1	8	15	8	3	3	Other	39	34
18 (4/1-9/30/04)		105 (10/1/04-3/31/05)						
10	31	44	27	5	6	NUMBER OF STATEMENTS	124	107
%	%	%	%	%	%	**ASSETS**	%	%
19.2	7.1	6.7	2.9			Cash & Equivalents	6.3	6.1
37.5	37.2	40.7	44.7			Trade Receivables (net)	41.4	39.1
14.4	31.5	27.0	32.3			Inventory	27.3	26.7
5.3	.7	1.7	.7			All Other Current	2.7	3.1
76.5	76.5	76.1	80.6			Total Current	77.8	75.0
22.2	16.4	16.3	14.3			Fixed Assets (net)	14.1	17.3
.0	.4	3.0	2.7			Intangibles (net)	3.1	3.5
1.3	6.8	4.6	2.4			All Other Non-Current	5.0	4.2
100.0	100.0	100.0	100.0			Total	100.0	100.0
						LIABILITIES		
7.8	17.1	13.5	21.0			Notes Payable-Short Term	15.5	16.8
.9	2.1	1.2	1.8			Cur. Mat.-L/T/D	2.1	3.5
23.5	31.0	30.7	29.1			Trade Payables	31.3	26.4
.0	.1	.4	.0			Income Taxes Payable	.3	.0
10.3	6.5	7.3	5.6			All Other Current	7.7	7.5
42.5	56.9	53.1	57.6			Total Current	57.0	54.3
2.8	12.2	6.7	11.9			Long-Term Debt	9.3	11.0
.0	.0	.2	.2			Deferred Taxes	.3	.3
3.2	5.9	4.9	3.2			All Other Non-Current	3.3	3.4
51.5	25.0	35.2	27.1			Net Worth	30.2	30.9
100.0	100.0	100.0	100.0			Total Liabilities & Net Worth	100.0	100.0
						INCOME DATA		
100.0	100.0	100.0	100.0			Net Sales	100.0	100.0
32.6	29.0	23.9	18.0			Gross Profit	21.3	23.3
31.3	26.8	19.1	14.5			Operating Expenses	18.4	20.1
1.3	2.2	4.9	3.6			Operating Profit	2.8	3.2
-.5	.1	1.0	.7			All Other Expenses (net)	.9	1.1
1.8	2.1	3.9	2.8			Profit Before Taxes	1.9	2.1
						RATIOS		
4.0	2.2	2.2	2.0				1.8	2.1
1.8	1.4	1.4	1.4			Current	1.4	1.3
1.3	1.0	1.1	1.1				1.1	1.1
2.8	1.4	1.3	1.1				1.2	1.1
1.2	.8	.9	.9			Quick	.8	.8
.9	.4	.7	.6				.6	.6
0 UND	**29** 12.5	**35** 10.3	**42** 8.7				**35** 10.4	**33** 11.2
34 10.8	**41** 8.9	**43** 8.6	**53** 6.9			Sales/Receivables	**46** 8.0	**41** 8.9
41 8.9	**50** 7.3	**59** 6.2	**69** 5.3				**57** 6.4	**55** 6.6
0 UND	**28** 13.2	**21** 17.3	**31** 11.8				**18** 20.4	**24** 15.3
4 90.5	**49** 7.5	**37** 9.8	**49** 7.4			Cost of Sales/Inventory	**38** 9.5	**41** 8.9
60 6.1	**77** 4.7	**65** 5.6	**70** 5.2				**74** 4.9	**59** 6.2
0 UND	**26** 14.2	**26** 13.9	**28** 12.9				**26** 13.8	**24** 15.4
20 18.0	**42** 8.7	**43** 8.5	**36** 10.1			Cost of Sales/Payables	**41** 8.9	**35** 10.5
51 7.2	**64** 5.7	**62** 5.9	**57** 6.3				**59** 6.2	**49** 7.4
9.3	5.5	8.2	7.8				8.0	9.1
12.1	13.3	13.7	15.4			Sales/Working Capital	18.1	15.1
91.0	-388.4	40.5	30.1				55.6	73.3
	9.7	26.7	11.6				6.4	4.7
	(30) 3.8	(41) 5.8	(26) 4.6			EBIT/Interest	(107) 2.9	(94) 2.5
	1.1	3.0	2.3				1.7	1.1
		13.0					4.8	4.1
		(10) 9.8				Net Profit + Depr., Dep., Amort./Cur. Mat. L /T/D	(24) 2.2	(25) 2.3
		2.9					.9	.4
.1	.2	.1	.1				.1	.1
.3	.6	.4	.4			Fixed/Worth	.3	.5
.5	1.5	.9	1.0				1.1	2.1
.2	1.3	1.1	2.1				1.4	1.1
.8	3.6	2.2	3.5			Debt/Worth	2.7	2.9
4.3	10.2	6.0	7.6				6.8	7.7
126.1	33.9	77.4	54.1				56.8	54.7
24.5	(28) 16.5	(42) 28.5	(26) 27.9			% Profit Before Taxes/Tangible Net Worth	(117) 27.2	(95) 22.2
-11.0	5.3	12.1	17.0				10.4	6.0
45.6	8.9	19.3	11.5				12.0	11.8
7.1	3.4	8.4	6.8			% Profit Before Taxes/Total Assets	5.7	5.2
-7.5	.9	2.6	2.4				2.1	.8
209.0	51.0	83.5	195.7				251.1	131.0
29.7	29.0	34.9	44.4			Sales/Net Fixed Assets	48.2	33.8
14.4	9.5	12.2	10.6				14.2	9.8
8.3	4.1	4.0	3.2				4.2	4.2
6.2	3.0	3.2	2.8			Sales/Total Assets	3.1	3.0
3.6	2.1	2.4	2.4				2.4	2.2
	.5	.4	.2				.2	.3
	(27) 1.0	(38) .7	(23) .8			% Depr., Dep., Amort./Sales	(93) .8	(88) .8
	1.7	1.3	1.4				1.6	2.3
	1.6	.9					1.3	1.2
	(19) 4.0	(15) 1.8				% Officers', Directors', Owners' Comp/Sales	(62) 3.2	(45) 2.2
	6.4	3.7					5.7	5.3
14751M	121916M	690097M	1444206M	1144770M	2069868M	Net Sales ($)	3539057M	4350616M
2681M	39415M	215978M	523091M	378081M	796610M	Total Assets ($)	1414313M	1742837M

M = $ thousand MM = $ million

See Pages 11 through 21 for Explanation of Ratios and Data

Comparative Historical Data | Current Data Sorted By Sales

4/1/02-3/31/03 ALL	4/1/03-3/31/04 ALL	4/1/04-3/31/05 ALL	Type of Statement	0-1MM	1-3MM	3-5MM	5-10MM	10-25MM	25MM & OVER
18	16	19	Unqualified				2	2	15
30	28	32	Reviewed		4	1	9	8	10
24	39	21	Compiled	3	7	2	4	3	2
6	11	13	Tax Returns		4	4	2	2	1
42	40	38	Other	2	7	5	3	2	17
					18 (4/1-9/30/04)		105 (10/1/04-3/31/05)		
120	134	123	**NUMBER OF STATEMENTS**	5	18	12	20	23	45
%	%	%	**ASSETS**	%	%	%	%	%	%
5.4	6.2	6.7	Cash & Equivalents		14.5	11.9	5.7	4.9	4.1
40.1	38.6	40.5	Trade Receivables (net)		38.8	30.4	38.6	46.8	44.4
29.9	28.2	28.2	Inventory		25.6	26.8	28.0	29.3	30.0
1.9	3.2	1.6	All Other Current		2.5	.6	2.6	.7	1.1
77.4	76.1	77.0	Total Current		81.4	69.7	74.9	81.7	79.6
17.2	16.1	16.3	Fixed Assets (net)		13.9	25.2	13.2	12.9	14.4
1.7	2.5	2.5	Intangibles (net)		.0	.2	3.9	2.5	3.8
3.8	5.3	4.1	All Other Non-Current		4.7	4.9	8.0	2.9	2.3
100.0	100.0	100.0	Total		100.0	100.0	100.0	100.0	100.0
			LIABILITIES						
14.5	17.0	16.1	Notes Payable-Short Term		14.5	11.6	18.4	14.3	18.8
2.6	2.5	1.5	Cur. Mat.-L/T/D		1.4	2.7	1.9	.7	1.4
27.5	26.5	29.1	Trade Payables		29.2	19.1	31.2	37.1	29.3
.4	.1	.2	Income Taxes Payable		.2	.0	.2	.4	.1
10.9	7.8	7.6	All Other Current		7.6	4.2	7.4	5.9	8.7
55.9	54.0	54.4	Total Current		52.9	37.6	59.2	58.5	58.3
9.8	7.9	9.4	Long-Term Debt		6.3	20.0	6.7	7.0	10.6
.2	.1	.1	Deferred Taxes		.0	.0	.3	.1	.2
3.7	6.7	4.4	All Other Non-Current		6.9	4.6	3.8	4.6	2.6
30.4	31.3	31.6	Net Worth		33.9	37.7	30.1	29.8	28.3
100.0	100.0	100.0	Total Liabilities & Net Worth		100.0	100.0	100.0	100.0	100.0
			INCOME DATA						
100.0	100.0	100.0	Net Sales		100.0	100.0	100.0	100.0	100.0
25.5	23.7	23.7	Gross Profit		28.3	33.7	25.4	21.8	16.4
22.4	21.4	20.1	Operating Expenses		24.5	29.6	20.9	17.9	12.5
3.0	2.2	3.6	Operating Profit		3.8	4.1	4.6	3.9	3.9
.6	.7	.6	All Other Expenses (net)		.0	.4	.8	.9	.6
2.5	1.6	3.1	Profit Before Taxes		3.9	3.7	3.7	3.1	3.3
			RATIOS						
2.0	2.0	2.1	Current		3.1	3.4	1.8	2.3	1.8
1.4	1.4	1.4			1.5	2.1	1.3	1.4	1.3
1.1	1.1	1.1			1.1	1.5	1.0	1.1	1.1
1.1	1.3	1.3	Quick		2.3	2.3	1.2	1.0	1.1
.8	.9	.9			1.1	1.4	.8	.9	.8
.6	.6	.6			.4	.7	.5	.7	.6
34 10.8	36 10.1	35 10.3	Sales/Receivables		26 14.0	27 13.4	31 11.7	36 10.3	38 9.6
43 8.5	46 8.0	44 8.3			41 9.0	29 12.5	41 8.9	45 8.0	49 7.4
59 6.2	60 6.1	59 6.2			54 6.8	45 8.0	66 5.5	59 6.2	69 5.3
28 13.1	22 16.4	25 14.9	Cost of Sales/Inventory		0 UND	29 12.4	21 17.8	9 38.5	26 14.2
46 7.9	50 7.3	44 8.2			39 9.4	40 9.1	49 7.5	37 10.0	48 7.6
75 4.8	73 5.0	67 5.4			83 4.4	74 4.9	73 5.0	59 6.2	64 5.7
25 14.5	23 15.9	26 14.2	Cost of Sales/Payables		15 23.7	17 21.5	23 16.0	34 10.8	28 13.2
39 9.4	38 9.7	39 9.3			34 10.9	28 13.0	46 8.0	47 7.7	38 9.5
58 6.3	56 6.5	57 6.3			51 7.2	42 8.8	62 5.8	72 5.1	56 6.5
7.4	7.7	7.8	Sales/Working Capital		5.5	5.2	7.7	9.0	8.5
15.3	13.3	14.2			13.0	8.9	18.6	11.8	16.4
47.2	39.9	41.7			91.0	12.7	NM	50.4	30.8
9.0	11.5	14.2	EBIT/Interest		49.1	9.5	21.3	12.6	14.8
(105) 4.2	(122) 2.3	(115) 5.3		(17)	6.3	(11) 4.6	(19) 5.3	(22) 4.6	(42) 6.0
1.2	.3	2.0			1.9	.8	2.0	1.7	2.7
7.1	7.1	19.3	Net Profit + Depr., Dep., Amort./Cur. Mat. L/T/D						23.9
(27) 3.2	(23) 1.8	(23) 9.7						(12)	8.1
1.4	.0	3.2							3.6
.1	.1	.1	Fixed/Worth		.2	.2	.2	.1	.1
.4	.4	.4			.4	.5	.4	.6	.4
1.1	1.4	1.0			.6	1.8	1.2	1.5	.9
1.2	1.0	1.1	Debt/Worth		.6	1.1	.9	1.1	1.8
2.3	2.4	2.9			3.7	1.6	3.0	2.9	3.3
5.0	7.4	7.7			10.6	2.4	8.3	10.2	7.5
46.9	40.1	63.7	% Profit Before Taxes/Tangible Net Worth		79.2	31.5	35.0	82.8	68.8
(108) 19.5	(116) 17.0	(115) 24.9		(17)	31.6	13.3	(18) 25.4	(21) 20.6	(42) 31.9
3.6	-1.2	12.4			15.1	.0	8.2	11.8	18.0
12.7	13.1	14.9	% Profit Before Taxes/Total Assets		22.9	18.4	14.9	14.8	15.5
5.0	3.4	6.2			4.7	4.8	5.1	6.1	8.0
.4	-.9	2.1			2.5	.0	1.1	1.9	2.8
130.4	160.3	140.5	Sales/Net Fixed Assets		151.6	44.3	44.4	88.1	370.1
32.4	34.9	33.8			34.3	15.1	30.7	47.9	64.4
9.7	9.4	10.6			16.3	6.0	13.2	13.5	10.7
3.9	3.6	3.9	Sales/Total Assets		6.1	4.0	3.9	4.2	3.4
3.0	2.8	3.0			3.3	2.8	3.0	3.5	2.9
2.3	2.2	2.3			1.9	2.4	1.9	2.6	2.4
.3	.2	.4	% Depr., Dep., Amort./Sales		.4	.6	.3	.4	.1
(101) 1.0	(117) .9	(102) .8		(14)	1.4	(11) 1.7	(19) .9	(19) .7	(36) .7
2.2	2.6	1.6			2.0	2.7	1.3	1.3	1.3
1.6	1.4	1.3	% Officers', Directors', Owners' Comp/Sales		2.1				.9
(59) 3.7	(59) 3.4	(46) 2.3		(10)	5.3			(11)	1.8
5.7	5.5	5.2			12.0				3.7
4533156M	4946476M	5485608M	Net Sales ($)	2254M	36121M	51219M	145908M	349024M	4901082M
1499030M	1567468M	1955856M	Total Assets ($)	6277M	12463M	19174M	58735M	106689M	1752518M

© RMA 2005   M = $ thousand   MM = $ million
See Pages 11 through 21 for Explanation of Ratios and Data

Current Data Sorted By Assets   **Comparative Historical Data**

Type of Statement	0-500M	500M-2MM	2-10MM	10-50MM	50-100MM	100-250MM		4/1/00-3/31/01 ALL	4/1/01-3/31/02 ALL
Unqualified		2	19	40	4	3		47	49
Reviewed		9	54	24		2		72	70
Compiled	5	18	21	2	2			82	62
Tax Returns	10	14	5	1				17	13
Other	4	19	43	11	7	3		73	75
		58 (4/1-9/30/04)			262 (10/1/04-3/31/05)				
NUMBER OF STATEMENTS	19	62	142	78	13	6		291	269
	%	%	%	%	%	%	**ASSETS**	%	%
	17.1	9.9	6.2	5.6	15.6		Cash & Equivalents	7.8	7.3
	44.1	41.1	40.5	38.9	29.3		Trade Receivables (net)	39.1	38.2
	17.2	21.9	28.8	25.2	16.5		Inventory	26.4	26.5
	1.5	3.3	2.7	2.3	2.8		All Other Current	1.8	2.1
	79.8	76.2	78.3	72.1	64.2		Total Current	75.2	74.0
	15.4	14.3	14.7	19.3	25.3		Fixed Assets (net)	16.8	17.7
	2.6	1.7	1.9	3.1	6.2		Intangibles (net)	2.5	2.7
	2.2	7.8	5.1	5.5	4.2		All Other Non-Current	5.5	5.5
	100.0	100.0	100.0	100.0	100.0		Total	100.0	100.0
							LIABILITIES		
	25.0	17.6	16.6	13.0	8.1		Notes Payable-Short Term	15.2	15.8
	5.8	2.4	1.9	2.4	3.1		Cur. Mat.-L/T/D	2.7	2.8
	25.4	27.7	28.8	26.1	15.8		Trade Payables	27.8	28.3
	.0	.2	.2	.2	1.4		Income Taxes Payable	.2	.3
	16.1	9.8	8.0	8.0	6.6		All Other Current	8.7	7.8
	72.3	57.8	55.5	49.7	34.8		Total Current	54.6	55.0
	7.8	7.1	6.6	12.2	14.2		Long-Term Debt	9.0	8.8
	.0	.1	.1	.5	.4		Deferred Taxes	.3	.3
	11.1	1.8	4.4	2.5	13.2		All Other Non-Current	3.4	3.3
	8.7	33.2	33.3	35.0	37.4		Net Worth	32.7	32.7
	100.0	100.0	100.0	100.0	100.0		Total Liabilities & Net Worth	100.0	100.0
							INCOME DATA		
	100.0	100.0	100.0	100.0	100.0		Net Sales	100.0	100.0
	36.4	30.6	24.0	24.3	34.6		Gross Profit	27.7	27.3
	28.9	28.4	20.8	20.6	27.4		Operating Expenses	24.2	23.8
	7.5	2.2	3.1	3.7	7.2		Operating Profit	3.5	3.5
	.6	.5	.4	.1	2.8		All Other Expenses (net)	.5	.6
	6.9	1.7	2.7	3.5	4.4		Profit Before Taxes	3.0	3.0
							RATIOS		
	2.3	1.9	1.8	2.2	2.9			1.9	1.9
	1.4	1.3	1.4	1.4	1.7		Current	1.3	1.3
	.9	1.0	1.2	1.1	1.2			1.1	1.1
	1.5	1.3	1.2	1.4	2.1			1.2	1.2
	1.0	.9	.8	.8	.9		Quick	.8	.8
	.6	.7	.6	.6	.7			.6	.6
	24 15.0	31 11.7	37 9.9	42 8.7	38 9.7			39 9.4	34 10.8
	38 9.7	43 8.5	47 7.7	48 7.7	51 7.2		Sales/Receivables	47 7.7	43 8.5
	59 6.2	61 6.0	54 6.8	61 6.0	65 5.7			57 6.4	52 7.0
	0 831.0	10 35.7	27 13.4	28 13.0	17 21.4			23 15.8	20 18.4
	14 26.0	31 11.9	46 8.0	46 7.9	58 6.3		Cost of Sales/Inventory	46 8.0	44 8.3
	59 6.2	63 5.8	68 5.4	63 5.8	82 4.5			72 5.1	74 5.0
	5 67.3	20 18.4	28 13.2	32 11.5	22 16.8			28 13.0	26 13.8
	26 14.2	44 8.3	43 8.6	45 8.1	50 7.4		Cost of Sales/Payables	44 8.3	39 9.4
	42 8.6	68 5.3	62 5.9	56 6.5	66 5.5			62 5.9	62 5.9
	7.4	9.4	8.0	7.4	3.6			8.0	9.2
	33.6	24.0	14.7	14.2	8.2		Sales/Working Capital	15.5	18.6
	−45.1	−189.4	33.6	39.3	32.6			66.5	68.3
	21.3	16.4	13.0	14.5	13.1			7.8	8.0
	(14) 7.2	(51) 4.8	(128) 5.8	(72) 6.6	(12) 3.2		EBIT/Interest	(268) 3.0	(249) 2.7
	2.6	.3	2.2	3.0	1.0			1.3	1.5
			8.0	11.5			Net Profit + Depr., Dep.,	5.9	9.7
		(33) 4.4	(31) 4.4				Amort./Cur. Mat. L/T/D	(74) 2.6	(69) 2.8
		2.0	1.7					.8	1.6
	.0	.0	.1	.1	.2			.1	.1
	.2	.3	.2	.4	.5		Fixed/Worth	.3	.5
	33.0	1.4	1.0	1.1	1.9			1.3	1.2
	1.3	.7	1.1	1.1	.9			1.1	1.1
	7.4	2.8	2.2	2.1	2.4		Debt/Worth	2.6	2.4
	−13.4	7.9	4.8	5.6	4.1			6.5	6.1
	544.2	47.3	48.6	48.3	40.2		% Profit Before Taxes/Tangible	45.7	43.7
	(14) 122.7	(53) 13.8	(132) 24.9	(75) 22.5	(12) 8.4		Net Worth	(265) 18.5	(243) 19.3
	5.1	2.9	9.9	8.0	1.3			4.5	6.2
	51.8	13.8	14.5	13.0	20.9		% Profit Before Taxes/Total	11.7	13.5
	14.2	5.0	6.6	7.7	2.9		Assets	5.7	5.2
	4.2	.3	2.9	2.8	.0			1.1	1.0
	UND	240.7	174.2	103.8	29.4			133.7	115.2
	71.7	40.9	55.5	24.3	11.3		Sales/Net Fixed Assets	32.5	26.3
	14.6	14.0	15.0	6.4	4.4			8.8	9.7
	5.2	4.4	4.1	3.5	2.7			3.8	4.1
	4.5	3.4	3.0	2.7	2.1		Sales/Total Assets	3.0	3.1
	3.2	2.2	2.4	2.0	.9			1.9	2.0
		.4	.2	.3	.6			.3	.3
	(43) 1.0	(123) .6	(72) 1.1	2.2			% Depr., Dep., Amort./Sales	(248) .9	(224) .9
	1.6	1.7	2.2	2.6				2.1	2.3
		2.6	1.4	.8				2.2	2.1
	(28) 5.6	(62) 2.6	(13) 1.1				% Officers', Directors',	(117) 3.8	(97) 3.6
	8.8	4.8	3.1				Owners' Comp/Sales	6.7	5.7
	25738M	252472M	2254217M	3968613M	2079725M	1841323M	Net Sales ($)	5966497M	7543428M
	5761M	73605M	702708M	1544863M	930188M	848210M	Total Assets ($)	2529317M	3596464M

© RMA 2005   M = $ thousand   MM = $ million
See Pages 11 through 21 for Explanation of Ratios and Data

Comparative Historical Data / Current Data Sorted By Sales

			Type of Statement						
59	65	68	Unqualified	1	1	1	3	13	49
89	78	87	Reviewed		3	7	11	38	28
43	67	48	Compiled	3	9	6	16	10	4
14	28	30	Tax Returns	4	10	5	7	3	1
87	88	87	Other		15	6	18	21	27
4/1/02-	4/1/03-	4/1/04-			58 (4/1-9/30/04)		262 (10/1/04-3/31/05)		
3/31/03	3/31/04	3/31/05		0-1MM	1-3MM	3-5MM	5-10MM	10-25MM	25MM & OVER
ALL	ALL	ALL							
292	326	320	NUMBER OF STATEMENTS	8	38	25	55	85	109
%	%	%	ASSETS	%	%	%	%	%	%
7.0	7.3	7.8	Cash & Equivalents		12.2	10.1	6.6	7.5	6.1
37.3	37.7	39.8	Trade Receivables (net)		41.3	34.6	41.3	39.2	41.5
25.7	24.7	25.3	Inventory		20.4	19.4	26.1	29.5	24.4
2.3	2.7	2.7	All Other Current		2.2	4.4	1.5	4.2	2.0
72.4	72.4	75.5	Total Current		76.1	68.5	75.6	80.4	74.0
19.3	19.0	16.5	Fixed Assets (net)		15.5	19.8	16.5	13.1	17.7
2.6	2.5	2.5	Intangibles (net)		1.4	2.4	2.6	1.9	3.0
5.7	6.1	5.6	All Other Non-Current		7.0	9.3	5.4	4.7	5.3
100.0	100.0	100.0	Total		100.0	100.0	100.0	100.0	100.0
			LIABILITIES						
14.2	15.3	15.8	Notes Payable-Short Term		23.3	16.1	12.6	15.9	14.0
3.4	3.4	2.4	Cur. Mat.-L/T/D		5.2	2.1	2.2	1.4	2.4
26.7	25.8	26.9	Trade Payables		24.2	24.4	27.8	30.7	25.7
.3	.4	.2	Income Taxes Payable		.3	.2	.1	.1	.4
10.1	9.7	9.0	All Other Current		13.4	7.7	8.3	7.7	8.5
54.6	54.6	54.3	Total Current		66.4	50.5	51.0	55.8	50.9
8.8	9.0	8.7	Long-Term Debt		6.3	10.8	5.7	6.8	10.6
.2	.3	.3	Deferred Taxes		.0	.1	.0	.3	.5
3.7	5.4	4.1	All Other Non-Current		2.3	3.0	3.9	3.2	4.6
32.8	30.7	32.6	Net Worth		25.0	35.5	39.3	34.0	33.4
100.0	100.0	100.0	Total Liabilities & Net Worth		100.0	100.0	100.0	100.0	100.0
			INCOME DATA						
100.0	100.0	100.0	Net Sales		100.0	100.0	100.0	100.0	100.0
27.2	26.9	26.4	Gross Profit		33.2	30.1	33.1	22.5	21.5
23.9	23.7	22.9	Operating Expenses		30.1	27.6	30.1	19.0	17.8
3.4	3.2	3.5	Operating Profit		3.1	2.6	3.0	3.5	3.8
.6	.6	.5	All Other Expenses (net)		.1	1.0	.2	.4	.4
2.8	2.6	3.1	Profit Before Taxes		3.1	1.6	2.8	3.2	3.3
			RATIOS						
1.9	1.9	2.0	Current		1.9	2.0	2.2	1.9	2.1
1.3	1.3	1.4			1.2	1.1	1.5	1.4	1.4
1.1	1.1	1.1			.8	1.0	1.1	1.2	1.2
1.2	1.2	1.3	Quick		1.3	1.1	1.3	1.3	1.3
.8	.8	.8			.9	.8	.9	.8	.9
.6	.6	.6			.6	.6	.7	.6	.7

36	10.1	35	10.5	37	9.9	Sales/Receivables	31	12.0	28	13.2	34	10.6	37	10.0	42	8.7
43	8.5	44	8.4	47	7.8		43	8.5	39	9.2	51	7.2	45	8.1	48	7.6
55	6.7	54	6.7	57	6.5		63	5.8	54	6.8	61	6.0	51	7.2	58	6.3
23	15.7	22	16.8	21	17.2	Cost of Sales/Inventory	9	40.9	8	45.0	28	12.9	28	13.0	22	16.9
42	8.8	42	8.7	43	8.6		28	13.1	37	10.0	51	7.1	43	8.5	44	8.3
71	5.2	66	5.5	66	5.6		63	5.8	97	3.8	79	4.6	67	5.4	58	6.3
26	13.9	24	15.1	26	13.9	Cost of Sales/Payables	13	27.2	21	17.1	25	14.6	30	12.4	27	13.8
43	8.5	40	9.0	42	8.6		37	9.9	46	8.0	49	7.5	43	8.5	38	9.6
57	6.4	60	6.1	61	6.0		76	4.8	66	5.5	68	5.4	61	6.0	51	7.2

8.4		8.8		7.7	Sales/Working Capital	11.1	6.5	7.5	7.9	7.9
16.5		18.1		15.9		27.2	31.8	14.0	14.2	14.9
70.5		68.1		51.4		-27.1	UND	38.1	30.1	33.8
10.3		10.4		13.4	EBIT/Interest	20.2	8.0	14.2	13.5	12.9
(252) 3.4		(293) 3.8		(283) 5.8		(31) 4.8	(22) 2.6	(50) 6.0	(74) 5.9	(101) 6.6
1.6		1.5		2.1		-3.9	1.8	2.9	1.8	3.0
6.9		6.3		8.4	Net Profit + Depr., Dep., Amort./Cur. Mat. L/T/D				7.4	8.5
(74) 3.2		(90) 2.9		(80) 3.8					(28) 4.1	(39) 3.9
1.4		1.3		1.5					1.9	1.6
.1		.1		.1	Fixed/Worth	.0	.0	.1	.1	.1
.4		.4		.3		.2	.4	.2	.2	.4
1.2		1.4		1.1		11.4	1.4	1.1	.9	1.1
1.0		1.1		1.0	Debt/Worth	.9	.8	.8	1.0	1.2
2.3		2.7		2.4		2.8	3.4	2.0	2.0	2.3
5.5		7.0		5.7		NM	5.6	3.6	5.3	4.9
34.4		45.6		48.9	% Profit Before Taxes/Tangible Net Worth	140.7	41.4	43.0	51.9	47.1
(267) 16.9		(288) 17.8		(292) 22.4		(29) 13.8	(24) 11.0	(53) 23.0	(77) 17.6	(105) 29.3
5.3		5.5		8.0		-4.0	2.2	10.5	8.4	9.6
11.0		12.3		14.1	% Profit Before Taxes/Total Assets	32.4	7.1	13.9	13.8	14.2
4.7		5.0		6.8		8.3	4.3	7.0	6.7	8.0
1.0		1.2		2.0		-3.7	1.1	2.0	1.9	2.9
121.5		150.3		182.4	Sales/Net Fixed Assets	425.3	UND	105.0	204.1	244.9
22.8		28.4		36.3		45.3	35.7	32.4	57.8	29.3
8.5		7.6		10.6		14.4	5.5	12.5	18.3	7.8
3.8		4.0		4.0	Sales/Total Assets	4.6	4.3	3.9	4.1	3.8
3.0		2.9		3.0		3.2	2.5	2.9	3.0	3.2
2.1		2.0		2.1		2.2	1.7	2.4	2.1	2.2
.4		.3		.3	% Depr., Dep., Amort./Sales	.4	.8	.3	.2	.2
(254) 1.1		(277) 1.0		(264) .9		(26) 1.0	(16) 2.6	(47) .8	(76) .6	(95) 1.1
2.4		2.3		2.0		2.1	4.2	1.7	1.4	2.0
1.6		1.6		1.5	% Officers', Directors', Owners' Comp/Sales	4.0	4.2	1.9	1.2	.6
(108) 3.0		(120) 3.2		(114) 3.1		(16) 5.2	(11) 6.6	(26) 2.8	(40) 2.4	(18) 1.0
5.8		6.4		6.1		8.8	10.0	5.6	4.2	2.8

9030310M	10899313M	10422088M	Net Sales ($)	4252M	74778M	100465M	412644M	1438527M	8391422M
3629266M	3803343M	4105335M	Total Assets ($)	4256M	26227M	46209M	147107M	514595M	3366941M

M = $ thousand   MM = $ million

Current Data Sorted By Assets

Comparative Historical Data

						Type of Statement		
	8	5	23	8	9	Unqualified	51	44
5	26	50	26			Reviewed	92	83
2	6	43	9			Compiled	87	104
	13	10	22	18	2	Tax Returns	17	18
		22		18	2	Other	82	77
	109 (4/1-9/30/04)		179 (10/1/04-3/31/05)				4/1/00-3/31/01	4/1/01-3/31/02
0-500M	500M-2MM	2-10MM	10-50MM	50-100MM	100-250MM		ALL	ALL
7	53	130	76	10	12	**NUMBER OF STATEMENTS**	329	326
%	%	%	%	%	%	**ASSETS**	%	%
	11.6	7.4	6.6	7.7	6.0	Cash & Equivalents	8.5	9.3
	35.7	33.5	28.8	37.4	26.8	Trade Receivables (net)	28.3	24.8
	15.2	13.9	13.0	19.5	16.5	Inventory	12.7	12.3
	1.9	2.4	3.3	1.2	1.0	All Other Current	2.9	4.2
	64.4	57.3	51.7	65.7	50.2	Total Current	52.4	50.6
	27.4	32.5	37.7	23.2	41.1	Fixed Assets (net)	37.5	38.6
	3.0	3.3	4.3	6.3	1.4	Intangibles (net)	3.0	3.1
	5.2	6.9	6.2	4.8	7.3	All Other Non-Current	7.1	7.7
	100.0	100.0	100.0	100.0	100.0	Total	100.0	100.0
						LIABILITIES		
	10.0	8.6	11.4	14.5	9.2	Notes Payable-Short Term	8.8	9.2
	4.1	4.3	2.9	1.9	1.0	Cur. Mat.-L/T/D	4.2	4.5
	28.6	26.6	25.0	24.4	20.1	Trade Payables	22.9	19.4
	.2	.2	.2	1.3	.1	Income Taxes Payable	.2	.2
	8.4	7.2	7.4	8.9	8.3	All Other Current	7.3	8.6
	51.3	46.9	46.8	50.9	38.7	Total Current	43.4	41.9
	21.5	17.8	17.7	14.1	19.1	Long-Term Debt	20.0	22.3
	.2	.7	1.3	2.4	.6	Deferred Taxes	.6	.7
	9.0	3.1	3.8	1.4	3.4	All Other Non-Current	2.5	2.4
	18.0	31.5	30.4	31.2	38.1	Net Worth	33.4	32.7
	100.0	100.0	100.0	100.0	100.0	Total Liabilities & Net Worth	100.0	100.0
						INCOME DATA		
	100.0	100.0	100.0	100.0	100.0	Net Sales	100.0	100.0
	14.9	12.4	9.7	7.2	16.5	Gross Profit	13.6	15.3
	14.5	11.5	9.2	6.2	8.6	Operating Expenses	13.3	14.1
	.4	.8	.5	1.0	7.9	Operating Profit	.4	1.1
	.0	−.2	−.3	.0	.3	All Other Expenses (net)	−.2	.0
	.4	1.0	.8	1.0	7.6	Profit Before Taxes	.6	1.1
						RATIOS		
	1.7	1.6	1.3	2.2	1.6		1.5	1.8
	1.2	1.3	1.1	1.2	1.3	Current	1.2	1.3
	.9	1.0	.9	.9	1.1		.9	1.0
	1.4	1.2	1.0	1.4	1.2		1.1	1.3
	.9	1.0	.7	.9	.9	Quick	.8	.8
	.6	.7	.5	.6	.6		.6	.5

14	26.0	12	30.3	10	35.7	10	35.3	14	25.5	Sales/Receivables	11	33.8	10	35.8
22	16.5	18	20.4	15	23.9	18	20.4	21	17.6		19	18.9	16	23.0
31	11.6	31	11.9	25	14.7	34	10.6	27	13.6		30	12.0	25	14.4
5	75.7	4	97.3	4	90.3	5	70.1	3	144.4	Cost of Sales/Inventory	5	70.3	5	68.1
8	43.8	8	44.1	8	43.5	10	35.9	10	35.8		10	37.9	9	41.3
18	20.8	16	23.3	13	29.2	15	24.5	31	11.6		16	22.3	15	24.3
10	36.3	12	30.4	12	31.2	10	35.8	12	30.3	Cost of Sales/Payables	13	27.1	10	36.5
16	22.4	17	22.1	15	24.4	12	30.9	21	17.3		18	20.7	14	25.5
25	14.9	22	16.3	22	16.3	16	22.2	24	14.9		24	15.5	20	17.8

	23.0	26.9	43.9	12.2	20.9	Sales/Working Capital	25.4	19.1
	58.7	53.9	227.5	83.6	40.9		64.6	48.7
	−91.5	−909.8	−110.3	−314.3	101.1		−175.5	−310.4

	3.9		4.4		7.2	14.9		EBIT/Interest		4.4		5.1
(50)	1.9	(123)	2.5		2.6	4.4			(312)	2.0	(314)	2.0
	.3		1.3		1.6	2.8				1.1		1.0

	2.8		3.1		3.5		Net Profit + Depr., Dep., Amort./Cur. Mat. L/T/D		5.0		3.2
(16)	2.1	(49)	1.9	(29)	2.0			(129)	2.2	(105)	1.8
	.9		1.1		1.4				1.1		.9

	.7	.5	.9	.6	.7	Fixed/Worth	.7	.6
	1.6	1.0	1.6	1.0	1.0		1.3	1.2
	9.8	2.1	2.8	1.6	1.3		2.5	2.8
	1.8	1.3	1.5	1.9	.9	Debt/Worth	1.3	1.0
	4.4	2.5	3.3	4.1	1.8		2.4	2.3
	35.6	5.0	6.1	7.2	7.0		4.6	5.3

	34.9		22.6		22.0		41.6	% Profit Before Taxes/Tangible Net Worth		20.3		21.0
(42)	5.1	(120)	8.9	(72)	13.0		16.9		(304)	9.3	(292)	10.1
	−12.8		2.6		4.0		12.3			1.6		1.8

	5.3	5.1	5.3	7.9	9.2	% Profit Before Taxes/Total Assets	7.1	7.2
	1.5	2.6	2.9	4.8	6.0		2.6	2.8
	−2.3	.8	1.1	2.6	3.7		.1	.1
	63.1	39.7	32.3	118.9	33.9	Sales/Net Fixed Assets	28.3	30.0
	25.1	20.2	15.2	29.5	12.2		12.8	12.6
	11.2	9.4	8.6	16.3	2.8		7.2	7.1
	9.5	8.2	8.3	11.1	5.9	Sales/Total Assets	6.7	7.1
	5.7	5.6	6.2	7.2	3.7		4.7	4.9
	3.2	4.2	4.4	4.2	1.8		3.2	3.4

	.6		.6		.5		.4	% Depr., Dep., Amort./Sales		.7		.7
(43)	1.2	(122)	1.0	(72)	.9	(11)	.5		(312)	1.3	(312)	1.2
	1.8		1.5		1.4		3.0			2.0		1.9

	.6		.3		.1		% Officers', Directors', Owners' Comp/Sales		.4		.5
(26)	1.6	(57)	.6	(15)	.3			(134)	.9	(124)	.8
	2.3		1.8		.9				1.8		1.8

9567M	447203M	4244072M	10116687M	5112509M	8229673M	Net Sales ($)	18895336M	16865574M
1956M	65662M	655740M	1552527M	674844M	1938736M	Total Assets ($)	4097681M	3945537M

M = $ thousand   MM = $ million
See Pages 11 through 21 for Explanation of Ratios and Data

Comparative Historical Data   **Current Data Sorted By Sales**

Current data sub-periods: 109 (4/1–9/30/04) covers 0-1MM, 1-3MM, 3-5MM; 179 (10/1/04–3/31/05) covers 5-10MM, 10-25MM, 25MM & OVER.

4/1/02-3/31/03 ALL	4/1/03-3/31/04 ALL	4/1/04-3/31/05 ALL	Type of Statement	0-1MM	1-3MM	3-5MM	5-10MM	10-25MM	25MM & OVER
41	53	45	Unqualified				1	1	43
94	96	84	Reviewed		2	1	2	22	57
88	103	83	Compiled	4	5	8	12	27	27
13	13	18	Tax Returns		3	1	3	7	4
66	57	58	Other		3		5	10	36
302	322	288	**NUMBER OF STATEMENTS**	4	13	16	21	67	167
%	%	%	**ASSETS**	%	%	%	%	%	%
8.4	8.8	8.0	Cash & Equivalents		9.9	10.1	10.5	6.7	7.8
27.2	26.6	32.3	Trade Receivables (net)		23.3	31.6	30.9	35.9	32.1
12.7	13.6	14.3	Inventory		15.0	14.1	14.9	16.3	13.6
3.9	4.9	2.6	All Other Current		3.2	.9	1.6	2.3	2.7
52.2	53.9	57.2	Total Current		51.4	56.6	57.9	61.3	56.2
37.8	35.6	32.9	Fixed Assets (net)		38.6	21.7	36.0	29.3	34.4
2.4	3.4	3.5	Intangibles (net)		6.2	6.9	1.5	3.1	3.4
7.6	7.1	6.5	All Other Non-Current		3.7	14.7	4.7	6.3	6.0
100.0	100.0	100.0	Total		100.0	100.0	100.0	100.0	100.0
			LIABILITIES						
9.0	7.7	9.9	Notes Payable-Short Term		17.3	4.9	9.8	9.5	10.1
4.5	4.0	3.7	Cur. Mat.-L/T/D		4.0	3.1	4.5	4.5	3.2
22.6	21.9	25.8	Trade Payables		11.8	13.8	25.1	28.3	27.6
.2	.2	.2	Income Taxes Payable		.2	.3	.2	.1	.3
7.3	9.2	8.1	All Other Current		7.2	10.1	9.5	7.9	7.2
43.5	43.1	47.6	Total Current		40.4	32.2	49.3	50.3	48.3
21.2	20.0	18.1	Long-Term Debt		22.1	24.0	24.6	16.3	17.5
.6	.8	.8	Deferred Taxes		.4	.0	.4	.4	1.1
2.5	4.4	4.3	All Other Non-Current		7.7	8.8	4.8	5.0	3.2
32.2	31.6	29.1	Net Worth		29.4	35.0	20.9	27.9	30.0
100.0	100.0	100.0	Total Liabilities & Net Worth		100.0	100.0	100.0	100.0	100.0
			INCOME DATA						
100.0	100.0	100.0	Net Sales		100.0	100.0	100.0	100.0	100.0
13.1	13.4	12.5	Gross Profit		27.5	26.5	16.3	11.2	9.5
12.9	12.7	11.5	Operating Expenses		24.1	21.6	16.6	11.0	8.5
.2	.6	1.0	Operating Profit		3.4	4.8	-.3	.2	1.0
-.2	-.3	-.2	All Other Expenses (net)		.0	-.5	.0	-.5	-.1
.5	.9	1.2	Profit Before Taxes		3.4	5.3	-.3	.7	1.1

RATIOS

4/1/02-3/31/03 ALL	4/1/03-3/31/04 ALL	4/1/04-3/31/05 ALL		0-1MM	1-3MM	3-5MM	5-10MM	10-25MM	25MM & OVER
1.6	1.7	1.6	Current		2.4	4.9	1.8	1.7	1.4
1.2	1.2	1.2			1.1	2.2	1.3	1.3	1.2
1.0	1.0	.9			.9	1.2	1.0	1.0	.9
1.1	1.1	1.2	Quick		1.1	3.6	1.5	1.2	1.1
.8	.8	.8			.8	1.5	.9	.9	.8
.6	.6	.6			.4	.9	.6	.7	.6
12 31.5	10 36.7	12 30.0	Sales/Receivables		16 23.0	24 15.2	13 28.6	14 25.5	11 34.4
18 20.0	17 21.9	18 20.3			26 13.9	32 11.5	21 17.8	23 15.8	15 24.1
27 13.4	28 13.0	29 12.7			50 7.4	55 6.7	29 12.6	35 10.4	23 15.6
6 65.7	5 69.5	4 86.6	Cost of Sales/Inventory		10 37.3	7 53.3	5 74.3	5 70.2	3 110.6
9 38.8	9 40.0	9 42.7			22 16.5	15 24.9	11 33.1	9 42.5	7 50.7
16 23.1	16 22.7	16 23.5			37 10.0	41 9.0	23 15.7	17 21.6	12 30.6
13 28.0	11 31.8	11 32.4	Cost of Sales/Payables		4 83.8	8 43.0	11 32.7	13 27.8	11 32.6
18 20.7	16 22.7	16 22.6			19 19.4	16 22.6	20 18.5	16 22.1	16 23.4
24 15.3	22 16.5	23 16.0			32 11.4	38 9.6	27 13.6	24 15.4	21 17.5
22.5	22.0	25.4	Sales/Working Capital		9.4	6.5	23.4	20.5	36.3
73.3	59.4	68.9			34.4	12.0	47.9	49.4	95.0
-251.1	-296.9	-189.3			-77.6	67.7	-543.8	-136.0	-198.7
4.2	6.0	5.1	EBIT/Interest		19.2	10.5	2.8	4.0	5.1
(285) 1.9	(308) 2.8	(273) 2.5			(12) 1.9	(14) 5.6	.6	(62) 2.4	(161) 2.7
.5	1.4	1.4			1.8	1.9	-1.5	.3	1.7
3.5	4.2	3.4	Net Profit + Depr., Dep., Amort./Cur. Mat. L/T/D					3.2	4.0
(107) 2.1	(116) 2.3	(103) 2.1						(21) 2.3	(67) 2.1
1.0	1.2	1.2						1.2	1.3
.7	.6	.6	Fixed/Worth		.8	.1	.7	.5	.7
1.2	1.3	1.2			1.6	1.2	1.4	.9	1.2
2.4	2.7	2.6			7.1	NM	6.7	2.2	2.4
1.1	1.2	1.5	Debt/Worth		1.3	.8	1.5	1.5	1.5
2.4	2.5	3.0			3.4	1.5	2.8	2.9	3.1
4.5	5.5	6.3			14.5	NM	12.5	5.5	5.9
18.7	23.8	24.7	% Profit Before Taxes/Tangible Net Worth		74.4	36.3	11.8	22.0	24.4
(285) 6.2	(292) 10.6	(261) 11.3			(11) 35.0	(12) 14.8	(19) -1.5	(59) 6.0	(157) 12.0
-2.8	3.5	2.6			1.8	8.8	-14.2	-2.7	5.0
5.3	6.2	6.1	% Profit Before Taxes/Total Assets		14.2	11.4	3.8	5.5	5.6
1.9	3.1	2.9			4.0	6.2	-.6	2.2	3.1
-1.6	.8	.8			.5	1.7	-4.6	-1.0	1.5
29.0	32.0	39.4	Sales/Net Fixed Assets		10.7	59.3	25.7	48.3	40.1
12.8	15.1	19.6			9.0	27.2	12.9	21.2	20.6
7.3	8.1	9.3			6.0	6.3	8.5	12.2	10.5
6.5	7.3	8.4	Sales/Total Assets		3.0	5.7	6.4	8.4	9.4
4.8	4.9	5.7			2.5	2.8	5.1	5.2	6.7
3.5	3.5	4.0			2.0	1.0	4.1	4.1	4.6
.8	.7	.5	% Depr., Dep., Amort./Sales		1.2	.4	.8	.6	.5
(288) 1.3	(302) 1.1	(261) 1.0			(12) 1.9	(10) 1.7	(19) 1.3	(60) .9	(157) .9
1.9	1.8	1.5			4.3	4.2	2.2	1.2	1.3
.4	.4	.3	% Officers', Directors', Owners' Comp/Sales				.6	.4	.2
(114) .7	(109) .8	(101) .7					(13) 1.6	(35) 1.0	(39) .3
1.7	1.3	2.0					2.6	2.0	.8
17000300M	23448757M	28159711M	Net Sales ($)	2571M	23736M	64239M	151246M	1151621M	26766298M
3854471M	4747891M	4889465M	Total Assets ($)	1281M	10804M	34210M	32321M	238287M	4572562M

© RMA 2005

M = $ thousand   MM = $ million

See Pages 11 through 21 for Explanation of Ratios and Data

WHOLESALE—Petroleum and Petroleum Products Merchant Wholesalers (except Bulk Stations and Terminals) NAICS 424720 (SIC 5172)

Current Data Sorted By Assets | **Comparative Historical Data**

Type of Statement

	0-500M	500M-2MM	2-10MM	10-50MM	50-100MM	100-250MM	Type of Statement	ALL 4/1/00-3/31/01	ALL 4/1/01-3/31/02
	1	4	13	53	14	12	Unqualified	81	83
	1	16	101	54	3		Reviewed	137	139
	5	30	63	17	4		Compiled	141	143
	8	9	20				Tax Returns	33	21
	2	23	46	34	7	5	Other	128	103
		189 (4/1-9/30/04)		356 (10/1/04-3/31/05)					
NUMBER OF STATEMENTS	17	82	243	162	24	17		520	489

ASSETS	%	%	%	%	%	%		%	%
Cash & Equivalents	11.3	10.7	9.7	7.6	7.6	8.2		8.2	8.7
Trade Receivables (net)	39.9	39.7	36.3	32.0	30.8	36.3		32.0	28.7
Inventory	19.8	14.6	12.7	11.6	13.5	11.0		13.3	13.1
All Other Current	3.8	3.5	3.4	3.2	6.2	2.5		2.6	3.6
Total Current	74.7	68.5	62.1	54.4	58.1	58.0		56.0	54.1
Fixed Assets (net)	17.5	23.7	27.0	34.7	30.6	29.1		33.1	34.2
Intangibles (net)	4.1	1.7	2.8	3.4	3.7	3.9		3.4	2.6
All Other Non-Current	3.7	6.1	8.1	7.6	7.6	9.1		7.5	9.2
Total	100.0	100.0	100.0	100.0	100.0	100.0		100.0	100.0

LIABILITIES									
Notes Payable-Short Term	9.1	12.5	11.6	10.9	8.0	9.0		10.8	9.4
Cur. Mat.-L/T/D	3.4	4.6	3.6	3.4	3.0	1.8		4.5	4.2
Trade Payables	37.3	27.1	27.9	28.0	25.9	28.8		25.5	22.2
Income Taxes Payable	.1	.2	.2	.3	.0	.4		.3	.3
All Other Current	14.8	8.9	7.0	6.4	11.4	6.1		7.5	8.1
Total Current	64.7	53.2	50.2	49.0	48.4	46.1		48.6	44.2
Long-Term Debt	8.0	15.9	16.6	19.2	20.2	21.5		18.4	20.4
Deferred Taxes	.0	.3	.6	.9	.8	1.1		.6	.7
All Other Non-Current	7.3	7.6	2.8	2.8	1.6	2.5		3.8	4.1
Net Worth	20.1	23.0	29.8	28.2	29.0	28.9		28.5	30.6
Total Liabilities & Net Worth	100.0	100.0	100.0	100.0	100.0	100.0		100.0	100.0

INCOME DATA									
Net Sales	100.0	100.0	100.0	100.0	100.0	100.0		100.0	100.0
Gross Profit	19.4	17.2	12.8	10.7	8.5	8.8		14.0	14.5
Operating Expenses	16.7	16.4	11.9	9.9	7.3	9.7		13.3	13.6
Operating Profit	2.7	.9	.9	.8	1.2	-.9		.7	.9
All Other Expenses (net)	.4	.2	-.1	-.1	-.3	.2		-.2	.1
Profit Before Taxes	2.3	.6	1.1	1.0	1.5	-1.1		.9	.8

RATIOS

Current									
	2.0	1.9	1.5	1.3	1.4	1.3		1.5	1.6
	1.5	1.3	1.3	1.1	1.1	1.2		1.1	1.2
	1.0	1.0	1.0	.9	1.0	1.0		.9	.9

Quick									
	1.4	1.4	1.2	1.0	1.0	1.1		1.1	1.1
	.8	.9	.9	.8	.7	.9		.8	.8
	.5	.6	.7	.5	.5	.5		.6	.5

Sales/Receivables	0-500M	500M-2MM	2-10MM	10-50MM	50-100MM	100-250MM	ALL	ALL
	3 / 109.8	14 / 26.7	12 / 30.5	10 / 38.0	8 / 44.3	16 / 23.2	13 / 27.5	11 / 33.7
	24 / 15.1	22 / 16.3	21 / 17.3	19 / 19.0	13 / 27.2	24 / 15.4	23 / 15.8	19 / 19.7
	47 / 7.8	38 / 9.7	35 / 10.6	30 / 12.2	21 / 17.0	27 / 13.4	36 / 10.1	31 / 11.7

Cost of Sales/Inventory								
	1 / 335.7	1 / 131.0	3 / 126.7	3 / 119.3	3 / 114.3	3 / 125.7	4 / 93.7	4 / 92.4
	6 / 65.3	8 / 44.3	7 / 49.5	7 / 49.2	8 / 48.5	6 / 56.7	9 / 40.8	8 / 43.7
	53 / 6.9	18 / 20.0	15 / 23.9	14 / 26.1	10 / 35.6	12 / 30.6	19 / 19.7	17 / 22.0

Cost of Sales/Payables								
	6 / 59.0	9 / 41.9	11 / 32.6	12 / 30.1	10 / 38.0	9 / 42.6	14 / 26.1	11 / 33.6
	11 / 32.3	15 / 25.0	16 / 22.3	17 / 21.3	12 / 30.1	19 / 19.0	20 / 18.6	16 / 22.6
	60 / 6.0	36 / 10.3	25 / 14.5	26 / 13.9	19 / 19.6	27 / 13.8	28 / 13.1	23 / 15.7

Sales/Working Capital								
	13.5	18.0	21.7	35.9	35.7	29.1	23.0	22.2
	36.1	48.3	54.1	124.7	120.6	60.2	76.3	66.6
	NM	NM	-682.5	-113.1	-411.9	NM	-108.4	-164.9

EBIT/Interest								
		(70) 6.0	(229) 7.6	(157) 8.2	11.3	10.4	(489) 4.3	(467) 4.3
		2.1	3.0	2.9	4.0	2.9	1.9	2.1
		.9	1.5	1.7	2.2	1.8	1.1	1.3

Net Profit + Depr., Dep., Amort./Cur. Mat. L/T/D								
		(19) 3.5	(71) 4.5	(68) 3.9	(13) 67.1		(171) 3.6	(184) 3.6
		1.7	2.1	2.3	3.9		1.9	2.1
		.8	1.2	1.5	1.7		1.1	1.1

Fixed/Worth								
	.1	.3	.4	.7	.4	.5	.5	.6
	.7	.9	.9	1.4	1.1	1.4	1.4	1.2
	6.6	1.9	2.0	2.6	1.9	2.4	3.0	2.5

Debt/Worth								
	1.4	1.2	1.5	2.0	1.7	2.3	1.5	1.3
	4.2	2.5	2.6	3.3	3.2	3.4	3.0	2.5
	21.3	13.0	5.0	5.3	5.6	5.0	6.6	5.4

% Profit Before Taxes/Tangible Net Worth								
	(14) 66.9	(68) 32.5	(223) 31.9	(152) 33.6	(23) 40.3	(15) 29.4	(471) 26.6	(458) 25.6
	22.6	10.6	14.6	15.2	24.5	18.5	11.9	12.4
	-3.8	.7	3.8	6.8	6.7	10.5	3.5	3.6

% Profit Before Taxes/Total Assets								
	15.0	8.2	8.1	7.1	11.1	6.0	6.8	6.6
	4.7	3.3	3.1	3.7	6.2	4.4	2.6	3.2
	-2.8	-.2	1.1	1.5	1.5	2.4	.6	.8

Sales/Net Fixed Assets								
	866.0	86.6	65.6	38.1	96.2	57.1	37.2	34.1
	44.3	30.5	25.2	17.0	18.8	23.5	15.9	15.7
	19.6	13.5	13.0	8.2	9.4	6.7	8.4	8.4

Sales/Total Assets								
	12.8	9.5	8.8	8.0	11.3	8.8	6.7	6.8
	4.7	6.1	5.9	5.5	6.6	5.9	4.4	4.8
	3.6	3.3	3.9	3.7	3.7	3.1	3.2	3.4

% Depr., Dep., Amort./Sales								
	(14) .3	(69) .4	(224) .4	(155) .5	(13) .1	.3	(479) .7	(455) .5
	1.2	.9	.8	.9	.8	.6	1.1	1.0
	2.0	1.8	1.5	1.5	1.6	1.1	1.9	1.7

% Officers', Directors', Owners' Comp/Sales								
		(35) .6	(101) .4	(46) .2			(217) .5	(204) .5
		1.2	.8	.4			1.0	1.0
		2.1	1.5	.9			2.4	2.5

	0-500M	500M-2MM	2-10MM	10-50MM	50-100MM	100-250MM		ALL	ALL
Net Sales ($)	48990M	747521M	8635661M	21029847M	14766104M	16794146M		33720477M	37729184M
Total Assets ($)	5301M	97592M	1258879M	3500286M	1609606M	2568173M		7138620M	6740149M

M = $ thousand   MM = $ million
See Pages 11 through 21 for Explanation of Ratios and Data

Comparative Historical Data | Current Data Sorted By Sales

Type of Statement

	4/1/02-3/31/03	4/1/03-3/31/04	4/1/04-3/31/05	0-1MM	1-3MM	3-5MM	5-10MM	10-25MM	25MM & OVER
Unqualified	91	95	97	1	1	2	1	4	88
Reviewed	168	174	175		4	3	14	43	111
Compiled	128	162	115	1	12	7	15	34	46
Tax Returns	29	45	41	2	6	3	2	9	19
Other	165	117	117	2	6	9	7	26	67

Current periods: 189 (4/1-9/30/04), 356 (10/1/04-3/31/05). Historical columns: ALL.

	4/1/02-3/31/03 ALL	4/1/03-3/31/04 ALL	4/1/04-3/31/05 ALL	0-1MM	1-3MM	3-5MM	5-10MM	10-25MM	25MM & OVER
NUMBER OF STATEMENTS	581	593	545	6	29	24	39	116	331
ASSETS	%	%	%	%	%	%	%	%	%
Cash & Equivalents	9.1	8.9	9.1		11.4	11.5	8.0	9.7	8.7
Trade Receivables (net)	30.6	30.8	35.4		28.1	35.5	32.8	38.2	35.2
Inventory	13.1	12.4	12.9		19.2	13.3	15.8	14.7	11.1
All Other Current	3.4	4.2	3.5		6.5	2.2	1.4	2.3	4.0
Total Current	56.2	56.4	60.8		65.2	62.5	58.0	64.9	58.9
Fixed Assets (net)	32.4	33.0	28.7		27.7	26.9	29.9	25.5	30.1
Intangibles (net)	3.3	2.6	2.9		2.2	5.1	5.7	2.9	2.5
All Other Non-Current	8.1	8.0	7.5		4.9	5.4	6.4	6.7	8.4
Total	100.0	100.0	100.0		100.0	100.0	100.0	100.0	100.0
LIABILITIES									
Notes Payable-Short Term	10.0	9.4	11.2		14.8	9.6	14.7	10.8	10.7
Cur. Mat.-L/T/D	4.0	3.7	3.6		3.9	5.2	5.0	3.8	3.1
Trade Payables	24.3	24.5	28.0		20.8	25.1	19.2	28.4	29.5
Income Taxes Payable	.2	.2	.2		.2	.2	.1	.1	.4
All Other Current	8.2	7.8	7.5		13.6	8.5	5.7	6.9	7.4
Total Current	46.8	45.6	50.6		53.3	48.6	44.7	50.1	51.0
Long-Term Debt	18.6	19.8	17.3		16.5	26.5	20.1	15.3	17.3
Deferred Taxes	.7	.8	.6		.3	.1	.6	.5	.8
All Other Non-Current	3.4	3.7	3.6		9.4	5.4	6.6	4.3	2.4
Net Worth	30.5	30.0	27.9		20.6	19.4	28.0	29.6	28.6
Total Liabilities & Net Worth	100.0	100.0	100.0		100.0	100.0	100.0	100.0	100.0
INCOME DATA									
Net Sales	100.0	100.0	100.0		100.0	100.0	100.0	100.0	100.0
Gross Profit	15.3	14.5	12.7		28.4	24.3	19.3	14.3	9.0
Operating Expenses	14.2	13.3	11.8		26.7	23.0	18.1	13.2	8.4
Operating Profit	1.1	1.2	.9		1.7	1.2	1.2	1.1	.6
All Other Expenses (net)	.1	-.1	-.1		.8	.4	-.2	.0	-.2
Profit Before Taxes	1.0	1.3	1.0		.9	.8	1.5	1.1	.8
RATIOS									
Current	1.6	1.7	1.5		2.4	1.9	1.8	1.8	1.4
	1.2	1.2	1.2		1.4	1.4	1.4	1.3	1.1
	.9	.9	1.0		1.0	1.0	1.0	1.0	.9
Quick	1.1	1.2	1.2		1.5	1.3	1.2	1.3	1.0
	.8	.8	.9		.8	.9	.9	1.0	.8
	.6	.6	.6		.4	.6	.6	.7	.6
Sales/Receivables	12 / 29.8	10 / 36.3	11 / 31.9	19 / 19.0	30 / 12.1	19 / 19.5	13 / 28.5	10 / 37.4	
	22 / 16.5	20 / 18.7	21 / 17.7	35 / 10.5	35 / 10.4	26 / 14.0	27 / 13.7	16 / 22.5	
	35 / 10.4	32 / 11.3	34 / 10.9	50 / 7.3	53 / 6.8	43 / 8.5	38 / 9.5	26 / 13.9	
Cost of Sales/Inventory	4 / 104.1	3 / 125.2	3 / 124.6	8 / 47.8	7 / 51.9	6 / 59.5	4 / 91.1	2 / 156.7	
	9 / 41.5	8 / 47.2	8 / 48.5	21 / 17.4	14 / 26.0	13 / 27.1	8 / 44.4	5 / 68.5	
	19 / 19.5	17 / 22.0	15 / 24.7	54 / 6.7	26 / 13.8	41 / 8.8	18 / 20.5	11 / 33.8	
Cost of Sales/Payables	13 / 27.8	11 / 32.8	11 / 33.0	8 / 44.6	14 / 25.9	8 / 44.8	11 / 32.2	11 / 33.4	
	19 / 18.8	16 / 22.6	16 / 22.5	34 / 10.6	29 / 12.4	21 / 17.7	17 / 21.5	15 / 24.3	
	29 / 12.7	25 / 14.7	26 / 14.3	49 / 7.5	43 / 8.8	42 / 8.8	24 / 15.0	22 / 16.2	
Sales/Working Capital	20.2	19.2	24.9		10.1	10.5	12.6	17.5	36.7
	69.3	58.0	65.8		32.4	25.7	29.5	41.1	100.1
	-114.2	-299.2	-338.2		NM	NM	491.1	451.8	-171.1
EBIT/Interest	4.9	7.5	7.8		6.4	3.9	9.4	5.0	9.6
	(536) 2.1	(556) 3.1	(506) 3.0		(22) 1.7	(20) 1.6	(36) 4.2	(109) 2.6	(315) 3.2
	1.1	1.6	1.5		.2	-.3	1.5	1.4	1.7
Net Profit + Depr., Dep., Amort./Cur. Mat. L/T/D	3.7	4.3	4.1					3.7	4.8
	(197) 1.8	(211) 2.2	(179) 2.3					(36) 2.2	(124) 2.4
	1.0	1.3	1.3					1.3	1.4
Fixed/Worth	.5	.5	.4		.3	.5	.3	.4	.5
	1.2	1.1	1.0		1.0	1.6	1.0	.8	1.2
	2.5	2.2	2.2		NM	-16.9	3.6	1.9	2.2
Debt/Worth	1.3	1.4	1.6		1.1	1.6	1.4	1.3	1.7
	2.7	2.5	2.8		2.8	12.1	2.5	2.2	2.9
	6.3	5.5	5.5		NM	-71.2	17.6	5.1	5.0
% Profit Before Taxes/Tangible Net Worth	25.9	31.0	32.7		31.9	32.5	38.1	35.9	32.2
	(533) 11.6	(551) 15.0	(495) 15.1		(22) 9.8	(17) 11.7	(33) 17.4	(104) 13.3	(313) 15.2
	2.1	4.7	4.3		-2.3	-.2	3.3	2.2	6.5
% Profit Before Taxes/Total Assets	6.3	8.3	7.7		7.2	4.8	9.2	7.9	7.2
	2.9	3.8	3.6		2.7	1.1	4.0	2.8	3.8
	.3	1.3	1.1		-.9	-1.4	.4	.4	1.4
Sales/Net Fixed Assets	39.0	43.7	61.3		33.6	30.3	75.1	68.1	64.4
	15.3	17.6	22.6		13.8	13.7	18.2	26.5	24.6
	8.3	8.6	10.6		6.5	4.2	6.4	12.7	11.7
Sales/Total Assets	6.7	7.3	8.7		4.8	4.4	6.3	7.8	9.9
	4.5	5.0	5.8		3.1	3.1	4.0	5.8	6.6
	3.1	3.4	3.6		2.1	1.9	2.2	3.5	4.5
% Depr., Dep., Amort./Sales	.7	.5	.4		1.1	1.0	.9	.5	.4
	(537) 1.2	(553) 1.1	(499) .9		(26) 2.0	(20) 1.6	(27) 1.5	(110) .9	(312) .7
	1.9	1.8	1.5		3.1	2.1	2.6	1.7	1.3
% Officers', Directors', Owners' Comp/Sales	.4	.5	.3		1.8		1.2	.6	.2
	(215) 1.0	(226) 1.0	(190) .8		(14) 2.6		(17) 2.2	(46) .8	(104) .5
	2.2	2.1	1.4		4.5		3.1	1.4	1.0
Net Sales ($)	38916855M	49397957M	62022269M	3546M	63849M	98525M	282146M	1919993M	59654210M
Total Assets ($)	8502091M	9152452M	9039837M	1975M	26672M	51012M	121661M	407873M	8430644M

© RMA 2005

M = $ thousand   MM = $ million
See Pages 11 through 21 for Explanation of Ratios and Data

WHOLESALE—Beer and Ale Merchant Wholesalers   NAICS 424810 (SIC 5181)

Current Data Sorted By Assets | **Comparative Historical Data**

Type of Statement

0-500M	500M-2MM	2-10MM	10-50MM	50-100MM	100-250MM	Type of Statement	90	91
	2	25	56	17	10	Unqualified	90	91
4	19	71	23			Reviewed	123	82
4	13	40	6		1	Compiled	111	112
1	11	6	2	8	4	Tax Returns	15	16
		40	38			Other	125	124
	53 (4/1-9/30/04)		352 (10/1/04-3/31/05)				4/1/00-3/31/01 ALL	4/1/01-3/31/02 ALL
9	49	182	125	25	15	NUMBER OF STATEMENTS	464	425

0-500M %	500M-2MM %	2-10MM %	10-50MM %	50-100MM %	100-250MM %		464 ALL %	425 ALL %
						ASSETS		
	14.6	13.1	11.3	8.7	8.4	Cash & Equivalents	10.8	12.0
	7.0	10.3	10.4	7.2	12.3	Trade Receivables (net)	10.7	10.9
	31.7	22.0	16.6	15.7	14.9	Inventory	22.7	21.4
	1.6	2.2	2.1	1.9	3.7	All Other Current	2.6	2.6
	54.8	47.6	40.3	33.5	39.4	Total Current	46.9	46.9
	26.0	25.7	21.2	22.0	17.2	Fixed Assets (net)	23.9	23.3
	11.3	16.2	29.3	34.3	31.3	Intangibles (net)	18.0	19.5
	7.8	10.5	9.2	10.1	12.1	All Other Non-Current	11.3	10.3
	100.0	100.0	100.0	100.0	100.0	Total	100.0	100.0
						LIABILITIES		
	10.2	6.7	4.1	1.9	3.0	Notes Payable-Short Term	8.3	8.4
	3.1	3.5	3.3	3.0	2.6	Cur. Mat.-L/T/D	4.8	4.6
	15.1	11.2	9.1	8.9	11.3	Trade Payables	10.9	11.3
	.1	.2	.1	.1	.2	Income Taxes Payable	.2	.2
	5.6	8.4	6.9	6.9	5.4	All Other Current	8.3	7.8
	34.1	29.9	23.5	20.8	22.5	Total Current	32.4	32.2
	16.4	21.3	28.5	38.0	30.6	Long-Term Debt	22.6	23.0
	.2	.5	.3	.3	.9	Deferred Taxes	.3	.3
	3.1	3.6	3.3	7.0	4.4	All Other Non-Current	4.1	3.1
	46.2	44.8	44.5	33.9	41.6	Net Worth	40.5	41.4
	100.0	100.0	100.0	100.0	100.0	Total Liabilities & Net Worth	100.0	100.0
						INCOME DATA		
	100.0	100.0	100.0	100.0	100.0	Net Sales	100.0	100.0
	25.4	26.1	25.3	26.5	26.7	Gross Profit	24.8	25.2
	22.8	22.8	21.1	21.2	18.8	Operating Expenses	21.6	22.0
	2.6	3.3	4.2	5.2	7.9	Operating Profit	3.1	3.1
	.4	.3	.5	.6	-.2	All Other Expenses (net)	.3	.5
	2.2	3.0	3.7	4.6	8.1	Profit Before Taxes	2.8	2.6
						RATIOS		
	2.9	2.6	2.6	2.4	2.5		2.3	2.4
	1.6	1.7	1.7	1.3	1.7	Current	1.4	1.4
	1.1	1.1	1.1	.9	1.2		1.0	1.0
	1.2	1.5	1.6	1.3	1.3		1.1	1.3
	.5	.8	.8	.4	.7	Quick	(461) .6	.6
	.2	.3	.4	.3	.3		.3	.3
0 999.8	1 334.8	2 175.3	2 226.8	3 143.0			2 242.5	1 245.5
2 220.5	4 93.0	7 48.7	3 107.5	5 78.9		Sales/Receivables	4 81.6	5 78.0
6 61.7	19 19.7	22 16.9	14 26.6	36 10.1			19 19.4	19 19.3
17 21.7	16 23.1	16 23.4	17 22.0	16 22.3			16 23.3	14 25.7
25 14.6	21 17.7	23 16.1	23 15.7	29 12.5		Cost of Sales/Inventory	24 15.5	22 16.3
33 11.0	29 12.8	30 12.0	28 13.2	42 8.7			34 10.8	32 11.4
3 135.3	6 62.9	8 45.0	9 38.8	13 27.4			6 57.3	6 59.8
12 29.9	11 33.0	13 27.6	17 20.9	22 16.7		Cost of Sales/Payables	12 31.4	12 31.5
18 20.8	16 22.1	18 20.5	20 18.6	29 12.6			18 20.1	18 20.6
	13.8	13.7	11.0	10.9	10.5		14.4	13.0
	31.2	22.5	24.7	51.9	18.9	Sales/Working Capital	33.3	32.3
	151.7	141.9	144.9	-204.3	43.9		978.1	-491.4
	13.0	19.2	15.8	11.6	19.7		8.1	9.4
(43)	4.0	(157) 6.2	(113) 4.4	(24) 5.9	6.7	EBIT/Interest	(415) 3.0	(385) 3.5
	1.4	3.0	2.8	3.2	4.3		1.4	1.8
		5.3	20.1			Net Profit + Depr., Dep.,	5.1	4.0
	(45)	2.8	(26) 3.2			Amort./Cur. Mat. L /T/D	(107) 2.3	(95) 1.9
		1.3	.9				1.0	1.2
	.3	.3	.4	1.1	.7		.3	.3
	.8	.7	1.9	9.3	-4.2	Fixed/Worth	.9	.9
	3.3	5.2	-1.3	-.3	-.6		-62.8	-5.4
	.4	.6	.8	1.5	1.0		.7	.7
	1.6	1.6	3.3	12.7	-35.6	Debt/Worth	2.1	2.1
	6.0	19.5	-4.0	-1.9	-3.8		-75.8	-12.2
	48.0	50.0	69.0	78.0		% Profit Before Taxes/Tangible	59.4	60.3
(40)	18.9	(144) 30.7	(79) 34.1	(13) 39.9		Net Worth	(344) 28.1	(303) 29.8
	.6	11.9	16.5	21.2			10.0	12.0
	26.3	19.3	18.2	15.8	28.4		17.1	16.5
	6.9	10.6	9.4	10.5	13.9	% Profit Before Taxes/Total Assets	8.0	7.4
	.3	4.2	4.5	8.3	7.3		2.3	3.2
	65.1	39.6	35.8	33.2	95.3		39.2	39.5
	29.9	23.2	17.2	11.1	16.6	Sales/Net Fixed Assets	20.0	21.7
	13.0	11.8	9.2	8.4	9.6		10.5	10.6
	8.5	5.5	4.1	2.8	3.7		5.3	5.3
	5.3	4.3	3.0	2.5	2.6	Sales/Total Assets	4.0	3.9
	4.4	3.2	2.2	2.3	2.3		2.9	2.8
	.8	.9	.7	.9	.5		.7	.7
(36)	1.1	(162) 1.3	(111) 1.2	(23) 1.4	(13) 1.0	% Depr., Dep., Amort./Sales	(418) 1.2	(391) 1.3
	1.7	1.8	1.6	1.7	1.6		1.8	1.9
	1.6	1.2	.6				1.0	1.0
(36)	2.9	(76) 1.9	(22) 1.0			% Officers', Directors', Owners' Comp/Sales	(191) 1.9	(152) 1.9
	5.9	2.7	1.9				3.3	3.3
9411M	408248M	4079006M	7988139M	4986461M	5782398M	Net Sales ($)	17313697M	20861310M
2246M	67789M	926048M	2723656M	1842270M	2009154M	Total Assets ($)	5233445M	6552343M

M = $ thousand   MM = $ million
See Pages 11 through 21 for Explanation of Ratios and Data

Comparative Historical Data				Current Data Sorted By Sales					
			Type of Statement			2	1	17	92
104	96	110	Unqualified				7	46	43
115	106	98	Reviewed			2			
68	98	69	Compiled	2	2	5	11	29	20
19	22	26	Tax Returns	3	3	2	6	8	4
120	87	102	Other	1	1	3	8	33	56
4/1/02-3/31/03	4/1/03-3/31/04	4/1/04-3/31/05		53 (4/1-9/30/04)			352 (10/1/04-3/31/05)		
ALL	ALL	ALL		0-1MM	1-3MM	3-5MM	5-10MM	10-25MM	25MM & OVER
426	409	405	**NUMBER OF STATEMENTS**	6	6	12	33	133	215
%	%	%	**ASSETS**	%	%	%	%	%	%
10.9	12.3	12.4	Cash & Equivalents			9.0	15.0	13.6	11.2
10.1	9.2	9.9	Trade Receivables (net)			10.6	7.5	9.7	10.3
21.6	20.9	21.1	Inventory			31.8	23.8	21.9	19.0
2.7	2.6	2.2	All Other Current			1.3	2.3	2.1	2.2
45.4	45.0	45.5	Total Current			52.6	48.6	47.3	42.7
24.0	23.5	23.5	Fixed Assets (net)			20.5	26.0	25.2	22.3
20.9	21.3	21.3	Intangibles (net)			19.7	15.4	17.2	25.4
9.7	10.1	9.7	All Other Non-Current			7.2	9.9	10.4	9.7
100.0	100.0	100.0	Total			100.0	100.0	100.0	100.0
			LIABILITIES						
7.9	6.4	6.1	Notes Payable-Short Term			11.3	5.8	6.9	4.9
4.5	4.3	3.3	Cur. Mat.-L/T/D			2.3	2.4	3.8	3.2
10.8	10.1	11.3	Trade Payables			11.8	13.9	10.4	10.5
.2	.2	.1	Income Taxes Payable			.1	.0	.2	.1
9.0	7.7	7.6	All Other Current			2.6	6.4	7.2	8.0
32.4	28.8	28.4	Total Current			28.1	28.6	28.6	26.8
25.2	23.3	24.3	Long-Term Debt			28.7	16.9	19.6	27.9
.3	.4	.4	Deferred Taxes			.0	.1	.5	.4
3.6	4.6	4.6	All Other Non-Current			2.7	3.7	3.9	3.6
38.5	42.9	42.3	Net Worth			40.5	50.8	47.3	41.4
100.0	100.0	100.0	Total Liabilities & Net Worth			100.0	100.0	100.0	100.0
			INCOME DATA						
100.0	100.0	100.0	Net Sales			100.0	100.0	100.0	100.0
25.0	25.9	25.8	Gross Profit			25.0	25.3	26.3	25.4
21.3	22.3	22.0	Operating Expenses			23.3	22.0	23.0	21.1
3.7	3.6	3.8	Operating Profit			1.7	3.3	3.3	4.2
.6	.4	.4	All Other Expenses (net)			.7	.1	.2	.4
3.1	3.2	3.4	Profit Before Taxes			1.0	3.1	3.1	3.9
			RATIOS						
2.2	2.6	2.5				3.0	2.9	2.7	2.4
1.4	1.6	1.6	Current			1.9	1.7	1.7	1.6
1.0	1.0	1.1				1.2	1.1	1.1	1.1
1.1	1.5	1.4				1.1	1.4	1.5	1.4
(425) .6	.7	.7	Quick			.6	.7	.8	.7
.3	.3	.3				.1	.3	.3	.3
1 263.5	1 280.5	1 291.0		0 UND	0 999.8	1 353.5	2 210.4		
4 96.1	3 106.9	4 93.8	Sales/Receivables	2 147.4	2 148.8	4 84.1	4 92.8		
18 19.8	17 21.3	19 19.4		22 16.8	18 20.8	19 19.7	19 19.2		
14 25.9	14 26.2	16 23.0		24 15.3	17 21.3	16 22.6	15 23.6		
24 15.5	22 16.3	22 16.4	Cost of Sales/Inventory	38 9.6	26 14.3	21 17.0	22 16.9		
32 11.4	31 11.8	30 12.1		73 5.0	32 11.3	29 12.7	29 12.6		
6 61.7	6 62.2	7 54.7		8 43.2	3 105.8	6 62.7	8 48.5		
11 32.2	12 31.7	13 28.9	Cost of Sales/Payables	14 26.7	11 34.0	11 31.7	13 27.7		
17 21.7	17 21.6	18 19.8		27 13.6	19 19.0	18 20.6	18 19.7		
14.1	12.9	12.3				10.3	12.5	13.4	12.3
33.6	25.7	23.4	Sales/Working Capital			14.8	21.7	22.1	27.0
-288.5	812.4	151.2				22.1	90.9	120.0	253.9
10.9	15.8	15.6				2.9	14.6	20.7	15.5
(382) 4.3	(357) 6.0	(359) 5.5	EBIT/Interest	(10) 1.8	(26) 5.9	(119) 5.5	(196) 5.9		
2.1	2.5	2.8				1.6	1.2	2.9	3.2
5.3	5.8	6.2	Net Profit + Depr., Dep.,					5.1	15.6
(92) 2.4	(90) 2.9	(88) 3.0	Amort./Cur. Mat. L/T/D					(29) 2.8	(49) 3.2
1.3	1.6	1.4						1.3	1.4
.4	.3	.3				.2	.3	.3	.4
1.1	.9	1.0	Fixed/Worth			2.0	.7	.7	1.3
-2.0	-3.3	-3.9				NM	NM	4.4	-1.3
.8	.6	.7				.7	.4	.6	.9
2.7	2.0	2.1	Debt/Worth			4.2	1.2	1.4	2.9
-7.5	-10.2	-9.5				NM	NM	15.6	-5.0
57.7	61.8	55.8	% Profit Before Taxes/Tangible				45.8	50.4	69.6
(286) 30.5	(291) 30.9	(286) 30.4	Net Worth				(25) 16.3	(107) 28.3	(138) 35.9
13.2	13.3	12.4					.8	11.4	18.3
17.7	18.0	18.7	% Profit Before Taxes/Total			6.3	25.6	18.5	18.9
9.3	10.6	10.1	Assets			1.6	11.9	9.4	10.7
3.5	4.2	4.1				1.2	.4	4.0	5.5
37.8	40.2	41.4				54.4	43.7	38.8	40.2
20.5	20.6	22.1	Sales/Net Fixed Assets			17.2	24.4	22.6	20.4
10.3	10.5	10.7				9.2	11.9	11.3	10.0
5.4	5.1	5.1				3.8	5.3	5.7	4.9
3.7	3.9	3.7	Sales/Total Assets			2.7	4.5	4.1	3.5
2.8	2.6	2.6				2.3	2.7	3.1	2.5
.7	.8	.8					1.0	.9	.7
(389) 1.2	(368) 1.2	(349) 1.2	% Depr., Dep., Amort./Sales				(27) 1.4	(115) 1.3	(193) 1.1
1.7	1.8	1.7					2.5	1.9	1.5
.9	1.1	1.2	% Officers', Directors',				1.3	1.3	.8
(147) 1.8	(153) 1.9	(141) 1.9	Owners' Comp/Sales				(22) 2.3	(57) 1.9	(47) 1.4
3.4	3.1	3.4					4.2	2.9	2.7
23254343M	19066643M	23253663M	Net Sales ($)	3901M	10031M	47821M	244386M	2223502M	20724022M
6905645M	5799261M	7571163M	Total Assets ($)	2182M	9139M	18068M	69428M	665641M	6806705M

© RMA 2005

M = $ thousand   MM = $ million

See Pages 11 through 21 for Explanation of Ratios and Data

WHOLESALE—Wine and Distilled Alcoholic Beverage Merchant Wholesalers NAICS 424820 (SIC 5182)

Current Data Sorted By Assets | **Comparative Historical Data**

						Type of Statement		
1	1	7	17	4	10	Unqualified	27	35
3	3	15	6		1	Reviewed	27	26
1	4	16	1		1	Compiled	23	18
2	5	3				Tax Returns	4	8
	3	8	19	5	8	Other	37	26
38 (4/1-9/30/04)			106 (10/1/04-3/31/05)				4/1/00- 3/31/01	4/1/01- 3/31/02
0-500M	500M-2MM	2-10MM	10-50MM	50-100MM	100-250MM		ALL	ALL
7	16	49	43	9	20	**NUMBER OF STATEMENTS**	118	113
%	%	%	%	%	%		%	%
						ASSETS		
	8.0	5.9	3.9		4.4	Cash & Equivalents	6.1	6.8
	15.6	23.6	25.4		22.6	Trade Receivables (net)	24.8	26.6
	52.9	42.9	44.0		36.7	Inventory	39.8	39.3
	.6	5.1	2.3		2.8	All Other Current	4.2	4.1
	77.1	77.5	75.5		66.5	Total Current	75.0	76.8
	9.2	9.7	9.6		10.1	Fixed Assets (net)	12.7	9.8
	4.1	6.8	8.8		14.1	Intangibles (net)	6.1	5.1
	9.6	6.1	6.1		9.3	All Other Non-Current	6.2	8.2
	100.0	100.0	100.0		100.0	Total	100.0	100.0
						LIABILITIES		
	19.7	11.0	15.8		13.0	Notes Payable-Short Term	10.7	11.5
	1.6	1.4	2.1		3.0	Cur. Mat.-L/T/D	2.8	1.4
	23.2	27.1	23.7		19.2	Trade Payables	25.5	24.9
	.2	.2	.2		.7	Income Taxes Payable	.4	.2
	10.2	11.8	14.5		7.5	All Other Current	14.7	10.0
	54.8	51.5	56.2		43.4	Total Current	54.0	48.0
	10.7	8.7	10.1		17.0	Long-Term Debt	12.7	12.1
	.0	.3	.1		1.0	Deferred Taxes	.1	.1
	5.5	3.2	5.6		6.7	All Other Non-Current	2.9	4.5
	29.1	36.3	28.0		31.9	Net Worth	30.3	35.2
	100.0	100.0	100.0		100.0	Total Liabilities & Net Worth	100.0	100.0
						INCOME DATA		
	100.0	100.0	100.0		100.0	Net Sales	100.0	100.0
	26.7	25.7	23.0		24.2	Gross Profit	26.4	27.1
	28.2	23.1	20.5		19.6	Operating Expenses	21.8	22.8
	-1.5	2.6	2.4		4.6	Operating Profit	4.6	4.2
	.6	.2	-.2		.6	All Other Expenses (net)	1.0	.5
	-2.1	2.4	2.6		4.0	Profit Before Taxes	3.6	3.7
						RATIOS		
	3.7	2.2	2.1		1.9		2.0	2.5
	1.6	1.4	1.3		1.5	Current	1.4	1.6
	.9	1.2	1.1		1.2		1.1	1.1
	1.7	1.0	.7		.8		.9	1.2
	.3	.6	.5		.6	Quick	(117) .6	(112) .7
	.1	.3	.3		.4		.3	.4
	0 777.9	11 34.5	10 38.1		22 16.8		9 40.0	14 25.9
	4 84.5	21 17.4	36 10.2		35 10.4	Sales/Receivables	32 11.4	33 11.1
	48 7.6	43 8.4	51 7.2		48 7.6		50 7.3	48 7.6
	24 15.0	32 11.2	52 7.1		47 7.7		38 9.5	36 10.2
	65 5.6	58 6.3	64 5.7		63 5.8	Cost of Sales/Inventory	54 6.8	54 6.7
	121 3.0	89 4.1	83 4.4		90 4.0		95 3.9	79 4.6
	6 63.8	23 16.1	21 17.5		26 13.9		20 18.5	22 16.8
	28 12.8	38 9.7	32 11.4		34 10.7	Cost of Sales/Payables	34 10.6	35 10.5
	78 4.7	53 6.1	60 6.1		49 7.5		54 6.8	51 7.1
	4.7	6.9	9.0		7.2		7.3	6.6
	12.7	15.1	17.2		12.9	Sales/Working Capital	14.3	12.2
	-215.6	36.8	68.5		25.9		51.8	32.9
	7.1	18.7	12.3		15.7		14.2	11.3
	(12) 1.5	(45) 5.7	(42) 4.8		(19) 4.4	EBIT/Interest	(102) 4.4	(100) 4.1
	-1.0	1.4	1.8		3.2		2.0	1.8
		22.9	18.6			Net Profit + Depr., Dep.,		9.6	15.3
		(10) 9.5	(10) 5.4			Amort./Cur. Mat. L/T/D	(23) 1.7	(24) 4.6
		4.4	2.2				.8	2.0
	.0	.1	.1		.2		.1	.1
	.5	.2	.5		.5	Fixed/Worth	.3	.2
	NM	.8	-3.9		NM		2.1	.9
	.9	.9	1.5		1.2		1.2	1.1
	2.6	1.9	3.9		3.4	Debt/Worth	2.6	2.5
	NM	4.7	-30.7		NM		12.3	4.9
	24.1	54.4	38.8		45.3	% Profit Before Taxes/Tangible	62.9	63.0
	(12) 7.6	(43) 17.4	(30) 14.9		(15) 27.6	Net Worth	(95) 26.6	(100) 27.9
	-8.9	4.8	5.8		18.5		11.7	9.6
	14.0	10.4	12.1		9.5	% Profit Before Taxes/Total	16.6	17.1
	2.0	4.4	5.9		6.9	Assets	8.9	7.5
	-4.4	.8	2.4		4.2		3.0	2.1
	85.6	205.8	146.4		119.0		128.9	136.2
	61.2	57.8	51.8		38.7	Sales/Net Fixed Assets	54.4	57.8
	30.8	33.0	25.2		14.5		18.4	25.4
	6.2	5.0	3.5		3.7		4.2	4.3
	3.8	3.7	2.8		2.7	Sales/Total Assets	3.2	3.4
	1.7	2.6	2.4		1.4		2.1	2.4
	.2	.3	.3		.2		.2	.3
	(10) .6	(39) .5	(35) .5		(16) .5	% Depr., Dep., Amort./Sales	(99) .6	(94) .6
	1.0	.9	.9		1.1		1.2	1.2
		2.4				% Officers', Directors',	1.3	1.2
		(20) 3.7				Owners' Comp/Sales	(41) 2.6	(43) 2.3
		8.5					5.4	3.7
6192M	67332M	851535M	3326537M	2204149M	7606744M	Net Sales ($)	6825800M	8735615M
2115M	16729M	250235M	1089883M	628875M	3087457M	Total Assets ($)	2396430M	2994651M

© RMA 2005

M = $ thousand   MM = $ million
See Pages 11 through 21 for Explanation of Ratios and Data

Comparative Historical Data | Current Data Sorted By Sales

			Type of Statement						
47	47	39	Unqualified	1	1	1	1	4	32
30	22	26	Reviewed	1	1		4	9	11
21	41	24	Compiled	1	3		7	10	3
10	13	8	Tax Returns		3	1	2	2	
45	28	47	Other	3	2	3	1	8	30
4/1/02-3/31/03	4/1/03-3/31/04	4/1/04-3/31/05			38 (4/1-9/30/04)			106 (10/1/04-3/31/05)	
ALL	ALL	ALL		0-1MM	1-3MM	3-5MM	5-10MM	10-25MM	25MM & OVER
153	151	144	**NUMBER OF STATEMENTS**	5	10	5	15	33	76
%	%	%	**ASSETS**	%	%	%	%	%	%
7.5	7.6	5.9	Cash & Equivalents		10.2		10.0	4.8	4.3
23.1	25.5	22.2	Trade Receivables (net)		18.8		16.7	23.0	24.9
42.5	42.2	43.6	Inventory		43.3		50.1	42.2	42.3
2.8	4.0	3.3	All Other Current		1.1		2.5	6.2	2.7
75.9	79.3	75.0	Total Current		73.4		79.2	76.2	74.2
10.1	8.8	9.8	Fixed Assets (net)		6.4		9.0	9.5	9.1
6.8	5.7	8.1	Intangibles (net)		3.4		6.4	7.3	10.0
7.2	6.2	7.1	All Other Non-Current		16.8		5.3	7.1	6.7
100.0	100.0	100.0	Total		100.0		100.0	100.0	100.0
			LIABILITIES						
12.2	13.1	14.4	Notes Payable-Short Term		8.5		12.2	10.2	15.1
2.3	1.6	1.8	Cur. Mat.-L/T/D		1.7		.9	1.7	2.1
24.6	27.8	23.9	Trade Payables		16.6		27.1	28.1	22.8
.2	.2	.2	Income Taxes Payable		.4		.1	.2	.3
11.6	11.8	11.8	All Other Current		7.8		10.3	13.0	12.5
50.8	54.6	52.1	Total Current		35.0		50.5	53.3	52.8
10.8	8.6	11.5	Long-Term Debt		15.6		5.3	10.3	12.3
.2	.2	.3	Deferred Taxes		.7		.1	.1	.3
3.9	5.8	5.8	All Other Non-Current		7.1		2.8	4.3	5.4
34.3	30.8	30.3	Net Worth		41.6		41.3	31.9	29.1
100.0	100.0	100.0	Total Liabilities & Net Worth		100.0		100.0	100.0	100.0
			INCOME DATA						
100.0	100.0	100.0	Net Sales		100.0		100.0	100.0	100.0
25.6	24.8	25.0	Gross Profit		28.8		28.4	24.2	22.6
21.8	21.7	22.6	Operating Expenses		25.4		27.5	22.3	19.0
3.8	3.0	2.4	Operating Profit		3.4		.9	1.9	3.6
.2	.1	.2	All Other Expenses (net)		.9		.2	-.2	.2
3.6	2.9	2.2	Profit Before Taxes		2.5		.7	2.2	3.3
			RATIOS						
2.3	2.2	2.4	Current		16.0		2.4	2.0	2.0
1.5	1.5	1.4			3.0		1.4	1.4	1.4
1.1	1.1	1.1			2.1		1.1	1.1	1.1
1.0	.9	.8	Quick		3.8		1.5	.9	.7
.6	.6	.5			1.0		.3	.5	.6
.4	.4	.3			.4		.1	.3	.4
13 27.9	12 30.8	8 44.7	Sales/Receivables		0 UND		3 104.4	8 47.9	15 24.5
31 11.9	32 11.3	28 12.9			22 16.4		7 55.7	21 17.4	33 11.1
48 7.5	50 7.3	46 8.0			55 6.7		48 7.6	42 8.7	45 8.1
41 8.8	44 8.3	46 7.9	Cost of Sales/Inventory		25 14.7		25 14.7	29 12.6	51 7.2
62 5.9	60 6.1	64 5.7			74 5.0		64 5.7	56 6.5	60 6.1
94 3.9	83 4.4	83 4.4			218 1.7		167 2.2	81 4.5	76 4.8
18 19.8	22 16.9	20 17.8	Cost of Sales/Payables		0 UND		7 52.2	17 21.2	22 16.7
37 9.9	39 9.5	34 10.8			39 9.3		41 8.9	36 10.2	31 11.7
55 6.6	59 6.2	52 7.0			87 4.2		72 5.1	52 7.0	48 7.6
6.7	6.5	7.3	Sales/Working Capital		2.9		5.0	7.9	9.1
13.5	13.6	14.9			6.2		9.1	16.7	15.5
53.5	44.7	41.6			32.2		42.3	58.6	36.1
14.4	14.1	13.5	EBIT/Interest				7.8	29.8	14.0
(136) 4.8	(131) 4.7	(131) 5.2					(12) 3.1	(31) 5.7	(74) 5.8
2.2	2.0	1.6					-.7	1.8	3.1
11.1	10.8	17.2	Net Profit + Depr., Dep.,						13.9
(31) 3.2	(33) 3.8	(30) 6.9	Amort./Cur. Mat. L/T/D						(20) 4.8
1.7	1.9	2.8							2.4
.1	.1	.1	Fixed/Worth		.0		.0	.1	.1
.3	.2	.3			.1		.1	.4	.3
.9	.8	2.2			2.4		.7	2.0	2.2
1.0	1.3	1.0	Debt/Worth		.7		.6	1.1	1.5
2.3	2.6	2.4			1.6		1.3	1.8	3.5
8.3	7.8	30.6			15.6		15.3	19.6	39.1
59.1	41.4	42.3	% Profit Before Taxes/Tangible				17.2	54.4	49.5
(129) 28.9	(129) 23.0	(112) 18.6	Net Worth				(12) 9.2	(27) 20.2	(58) 21.3
14.5	8.6	6.5					.5	9.9	14.2
16.6	13.6	12.0	% Profit Before Taxes/Total		15.7		5.9	12.1	13.1
6.7	5.9	5.6	Assets		3.4		3.7	4.4	7.3
2.9	1.8	1.2			-2.8		.0	1.0	2.8
145.1	171.3	127.0	Sales/Net Fixed Assets		999.8		149.9	99.7	129.3
48.2	68.5	55.1			75.4		54.7	52.6	50.9
22.5	27.5	26.3			24.4		27.2	33.0	23.4
4.3	4.4	4.4	Sales/Total Assets		4.2		5.8	5.0	4.0
2.9	3.0	3.1			2.1		3.7	3.7	3.0
2.2	2.3	2.3			1.2		2.2	2.8	2.4
.3	.3	.3	% Depr., Dep., Amort./Sales				.3	.3	.3
(130) .6	(118) .5	(113) .5					(12) .7	(27) .4	(61) .5
1.2	.9	.9					1.2	.8	.9
2.1	1.5	2.0	% Officers', Directors',				2.2	3.0	
(52) 3.1	(43) 3.0	(37) 3.7	Owners' Comp/Sales				(13) 3.7	(12) 4.1	
4.5	4.2	9.2					9.0	10.3	
13860149M	12147541M	14062489M	Net Sales ($)	2844M	16087M	18807M	114486M	565592M	13344673M
5053116M	4547167M	5075294M	Total Assets ($)	1866M	9274M	22842M	43145M	171481M	4826686M

M = $ thousand   MM = $ million
See Pages 11 through 21 for Explanation of Ratios and Data

Current Data Sorted By Assets   Comparative Historical Data

Type of Statement	0-500M	500M-2MM	2-10MM	10-50MM	50-100MM	100-250MM	4/1/00-3/31/01 ALL	4/1/01-3/31/02 ALL
Unqualified	1	47	331	213	28	16	73	672
Reviewed	2	21	55	5			68	79
Compiled	2	26	26	4			79	87
Tax Returns	8	17	5	2			26	27
Other	6	29	47	26	7	1	64	159
		418 (4/1-9/30/04)		507 (10/1/04-3/31/05)			310	1024
NUMBER OF STATEMENTS	19	140	464	250	35	17	310	1024
ASSETS	%	%	%	%	%	%	%	%
Cash & Equivalents	15.2	7.6	5.8	4.7	4.4	4.3	6.5	6.4
Trade Receivables (net)	31.1	20.3	16.3	15.1	13.7	21.3	28.5	20.3
Inventory	29.8	30.4	29.0	27.4	29.9	32.4	28.4	26.0
All Other Current	3.8	5.2	8.0	10.4	12.7	9.0	2.6	3.0
Total Current	79.8	63.6	59.2	57.6	60.7	67.0	66.1	55.7
Fixed Assets (net)	14.7	23.7	25.3	24.5	22.4	19.3	24.7	26.1
Intangibles (net)	.1	.9	.4	.4	1.0	1.8	1.4	.7
All Other Non-Current	5.4	11.9	15.1	17.5	15.9	11.9	7.8	17.6
Total	100.0	100.0	100.0	100.0	100.0	100.0	100.0	100.0
LIABILITIES								
Notes Payable-Short Term	20.5	12.0	14.7	17.6	15.7	11.7	16.6	12.9
Cur. Mat.-L/T/D	.5	1.9	1.8	1.7	1.2	1.2	3.1	2.2
Trade Payables	24.8	15.6	17.5	19.0	21.5	23.1	18.9	17.5
Income Taxes Payable	.0	.3	.3	.5	.4	.2	.3	.4
All Other Current	11.4	8.3	6.0	6.1	10.2	11.8	8.8	5.6
Total Current	57.2	37.9	40.3	44.8	48.9	48.1	47.6	38.5
Long-Term Debt	13.1	10.0	6.6	9.1	11.8	15.7	11.9	8.8
Deferred Taxes	.0	.2	.3	.5	.6	.8	.4	.3
All Other Non-Current	3.6	3.6	1.0	1.0	1.8	3.6	3.5	1.3
Net Worth	26.2	48.2	51.8	44.6	36.9	31.8	36.6	51.1
Total Liabilities & Net Worth	100.0	100.0	100.0	100.0	100.0	100.0	100.0	100.0
INCOME DATA								
Net Sales	100.0	100.0	100.0	100.0	100.0	100.0	100.0	100.0
Gross Profit	28.9	22.2	15.5	13.3	12.0	17.3	23.2	19.5
Operating Expenses	28.7	21.2	14.3	11.9	10.1	13.7	22.0	18.1
Operating Profit	.2	1.0	1.2	1.4	1.9	3.5	1.2	1.4
All Other Expenses (net)	1.5	-.7	-.7	-.5	-.2	.1	-.3	-.3
Profit Before Taxes	-1.3	1.7	1.9	1.9	2.1	3.4	1.5	1.7
RATIOS								
Current	2.9	2.9	1.9	1.4	1.4	1.8	2.0	1.9
	1.9	1.7	1.4	1.3	1.2	1.3	1.4	1.4
	.8	1.2	1.2	1.2	1.1	1.2	1.1	1.2
Quick	1.5	1.4	.8	.6	.5	.7	1.1	1.0
	1.0	.8	.5	.4	.4	.5	(309) .7	(1023) .7
	.2	.4	.3	.3	.2	.3	.5	.4
Sales/Receivables	1 506.5	13 29.1	13 27.7	11 34.5	7 50.6	9 38.9	22 16.8	18 20.5
	20 18.0	23 16.1	22 16.9	19 19.3	13 27.6	36 10.1	33 10.9	28 13.0
	39 9.5	36 10.1	34 10.7	32 11.3	26 13.9	57 6.4	55 6.6	41 8.9
Cost of Sales/Inventory	6 56.6	25 14.4	33 10.9	30 12.3	26 14.2	35 10.6	27 13.4	32 11.3
	29 12.8	52 7.0	53 6.8	45 8.1	43 8.6	67 5.5	50 7.2	50 7.3
	78 4.7	83 4.4	75 4.9	64 5.7	71 5.1	86 4.3	85 4.3	74 4.9
Cost of Sales/Payables	0 UND	9 39.6	16 23.0	19 19.4	17 21.2	26 14.3	13 27.7	18 19.9
	12 29.3	18 19.7	28 13.2	29 12.8	29 12.5	40 9.1	28 13.2	29 12.5
	37 10.0	34 10.7	42 8.7	49 7.4	43 8.4	63 5.8	47 7.8	46 7.8
Sales/Working Capital	7.6	6.3	8.1	14.8	16.5	6.4	7.5	8.6
	13.0	11.7	14.5	19.7	29.3	15.6	19.2	17.1
	-75.3	30.2	28.5	31.9	40.1	25.4	68.3	30.4
EBIT/Interest	5.7	9.5	7.9	6.6	6.8	7.5	4.5	5.2
	(14) 2.1	(122) 3.6	(437) 3.7	(247) 3.7	(32) 4.0	(16) 4.3	(291) 1.9	(954) 2.7
	-.1	1.0	1.7	2.1	2.7	2.8	1.2	1.4
Net Profit + Depr., Dep., Amort./Cur. Mat. L/T/D		6.3	6.1	6.5	9.5		6.0	7.0
		(16) 3.7	(207) 4.1	(171) 4.2	(25) 4.3		(98) 3.0	(558) 3.9
		1.4	2.4	2.7	3.5		1.5	2.4
Fixed/Worth	.0	.2	.3	.4	.5	.4	.3	.3
	.5	.4	.5	.5	.6	.6	.6	.5
	6.5	.9	.7	.7	.7	.9	1.2	.7
Debt/Worth	.8	.3	.5	.8	1.0	1.2	.8	.5
	2.7	.9	.9	1.2	1.5	2.2	1.8	.9
	14.9	2.6	1.5	2.0	2.9	3.9	4.4	1.7
% Profit Before Taxes/Tangible Net Worth	116.2	16.2	13.4	14.6	19.1	28.8	23.1	12.6
	(16) 20.3	(129) 6.9	(457) 7.3	(249) 9.0	(34) 12.6	(16) 17.2	(294) 9.2	(1004) 7.2
	1.9	.8	3.1	5.0	8.7	13.4	2.7	2.6
% Profit Before Taxes/Total Assets	16.6	8.3	6.7	5.9	6.3	9.7	7.3	6.3
	3.8	3.9	3.8	4.1	5.0	5.9	2.9	3.6
	.0	.1	1.2	2.0	3.4	3.6	.6	1.2
Sales/Net Fixed Assets	UND	26.3	14.6	13.7	17.8	13.5	30.2	13.4
	49.8	14.0	9.4	9.9	11.3	11.7	12.1	8.7
	17.6	7.3	6.8	7.3	7.8	7.6	6.0	6.2
Sales/Total Assets	8.2	3.8	2.9	3.0	3.5	2.7	3.4	2.8
	5.3	2.5	2.2	2.3	2.7	2.2	2.5	2.1
	3.1	1.9	1.7	1.9	1.8	1.6	1.9	1.7
% Depr., Dep., Amort./Sales		.8	1.2	1.2	1.0	.9	.8	1.3
		(128) 1.4	(458) 1.7	(246) 1.7	(33) 1.3	(16) 1.2	(293) 1.5	(1003) 1.9
		2.3	2.3	2.1	2.0	2.0	2.7	2.5
% Officers', Directors', Owners' Comp/Sales		1.2	.8	.2			1.0	1.2
		(36) 2.6	(38) 1.3	(10) .5			(117) 2.1	(122) 2.7
		4.3	2.5	2.6			3.9	4.6
Net Sales ($)	29046M	517725M	5756461M	13487351M	6374223M	6921809M	9869077M	26944641M
Total Assets ($)	5366M	177139M	2390411M	5358285M	2176839M	2509327M	4547045M	11979821M

Comparative Historical Data   Current Data Sorted By Sales

			Type of Statement						
609	598	636	Unqualified	2	31	35	124	199	245
93	77	83	Reviewed	2	11	11	26	25	8
62	76	58	Compiled	1	9	11	20	7	10
20	22	32	Tax Returns	2	11	9	6	3	1
131	105	116	Other	3	27	14	24	17	31
4/1/02-3/31/03	4/1/03-3/31/04	4/1/04-3/31/05		418 (4/1-9/30/04)			507 (10/1/04-3/31/05)		
ALL	ALL	ALL		0-1MM	1-3MM	3-5MM	5-10MM	10-25MM	25MM & OVER
915	878	925	NUMBER OF STATEMENTS	10	89	80	200	251	295
%	%	%	ASSETS	%	%	%	%	%	%
5.8	5.8	5.9	Cash & Equivalents	6.5	7.8	7.2	6.8	5.6	4.5
20.8	16.7	16.9	Trade Receivables (net)	30.2	19.1	17.4	16.7	16.8	15.9
28.4	29.2	28.9	Inventory	23.7	30.8	31.7	28.8	28.0	28.6
3.4	7.9	8.3	All Other Current	5.4	3.7	6.7	7.8	8.8	10.2
58.4	59.6	60.0	Total Current	65.8	61.5	63.0	60.1	59.3	59.2
25.5	25.1	24.4	Fixed Assets (net)	24.1	23.4	22.2	25.5	24.9	24.1
.7	.4	.5	Intangibles (net)	.3	1.0	.3	.6	.4	.6
15.5	14.8	15.1	All Other Non-Current	9.9	14.1	14.5	13.8	15.4	16.2
100.0	100.0	100.0	Total	100.0	100.0	100.0	100.0	100.0	100.0
			LIABILITIES						
15.3	15.7	15.2	Notes Payable-Short Term	20.5	14.5	14.4	13.6	15.4	16.3
2.0	2.1	1.7	Cur. Mat.-L/T/D	1.3	1.8	1.6	1.7	1.9	1.7
16.6	17.3	18.0	Trade Payables	11.8	16.0	15.8	16.1	18.0	20.6
.3	.3	.3	Income Taxes Payable	.0	.1	.1	.2	.4	.5
5.9	6.2	6.7	All Other Current	4.3	6.9	6.7	6.9	6.1	7.1
40.0	41.5	42.0	Total Current	37.9	39.3	38.5	38.6	41.9	46.2
8.6	8.9	8.3	Long-Term Debt	27.5	10.1	6.1	6.6	7.3	9.7
.3	.3	.4	Deferred Taxes	.0	.2	.1	.4	.4	.5
1.6	1.5	1.5	All Other Non-Current	4.1	4.2	1.5	1.3	.9	1.3
49.5	47.8	47.9	Net Worth	30.5	46.2	53.9	53.2	49.6	42.3
100.0	100.0	100.0	Total Liabilities & Net Worth	100.0	100.0	100.0	100.0	100.0	100.0
			INCOME DATA						
100.0	100.0	100.0	Net Sales	100.0	100.0	100.0	100.0	100.0	100.0
19.5	16.5	16.1	Gross Profit	45.7	23.8	19.7	17.5	14.3	12.4
18.5	15.3	14.8	Operating Expenses	43.0	23.0	19.1	16.2	13.0	10.9
1.0	1.2	1.3	Operating Profit	2.7	.7	.6	1.4	1.2	1.5
−.7	−.6	−.6	All Other Expenses (net)	4.7	−1.2	−.9	−.7	−.7	−.3
1.7	1.8	1.8	Profit Before Taxes	−2.0	2.0	1.5	2.1	1.9	1.8
			RATIOS						
1.9	1.8	1.8		3.9	2.6	2.5	2.4	1.7	1.4
1.4	1.4	1.4	Current	2.1	1.8	1.6	1.5	1.4	1.3
1.2	1.2	1.2		1.0	1.2	1.2	1.2	1.2	1.2
1.0	.8	.8		1.2	1.3	1.3	.9	.8	.6
.7	(877) .5	.5	Quick	.7	.7	.7	.6	.5	.4
.4	.3	.3		.5	.4	.3	.4	.3	.3
19 18.8	12 30.1	12 30.7		10 37.4	11 32.8	13 28.1	14 25.9	13 27.7	10 37.2
29 12.5	22 16.6	21 17.5	Sales/Receivables	37 10.0	26 14.3	26 14.3	22 16.3	21 17.4	16 22.2
43 8.5	35 10.4	34 10.6		59 6.2	51 7.1	37 9.8	35 10.3	33 11.2	31 11.8
37 9.9	34 10.8	31 11.9		0 UND	35 10.5	40 9.1	34 10.7	32 11.6	27 13.5
56 6.5	54 6.7	51 7.2	Cost of Sales/Inventory	78 4.7	69 5.3	64 5.7	57 6.4	48 7.6	41 8.8
78 4.7	82 4.5	74 4.9		127 2.9	100 3.6	94 3.9	79 4.6	66 5.5	62 5.8
17 21.0	16 22.8	15 24.0		0 UND	11 34.5	12 29.7	14 26.7	16 22.5	18 20.6
28 13.0	27 13.4	27 13.7	Cost of Sales/Payables	12 29.4	26 14.2	23 16.0	26 14.2	28 12.9	28 13.2
44 8.3	48 7.7	43 8.4		74 4.9	51 7.2	44 8.3	42 8.7	41 8.9	45 8.2
8.3	8.5	8.9		4.4	5.1	5.9	6.9	11.0	15.6
14.5	15.3	16.5	Sales/Working Capital	10.3	8.3	9.7	12.4	16.5	23.0
28.0	27.2	30.4		NM	26.0	25.5	22.3	26.8	35.5
7.0	7.5	7.6			8.6	6.8	10.2	8.0	6.1
(848) 3.3	(820) 3.6	(868) 3.7	EBIT/Interest	(78) 3.3	(71) 4.1	(184) 4.6	(240) 3.9	(288) 3.6
1.6	1.7	1.8			.9	1.0	1.8	1.9	2.3
7.1	6.8	6.5			12.6	5.3	6.8	6.7
(441) 3.9	(431) 4.1	(427) 4.1	Net Profit + Depr., Dep., Amort./Cur. Mat. L/T/D	(13) 7.0	(60) 3.9	(143) 4.2	(202) 4.2
2.3	2.4	2.6			1.3	2.2	2.7	2.6
.3	.3	.3		.1	.2	.2	.3	.4	.4
.5	.5	.5	Fixed/Worth	.9	.4	.4	.4	.5	.6
.8	.7	.7		2.8	1.3	.7	.8	.7	.7
.5	.6	.6		.7	.3	.3	.4	.6	.9
1.0	1.1	1.1	Debt/Worth	2.7	.9	.7	.8	1.0	1.3
1.9	2.0	1.9		11.1	2.6	2.1	1.6	1.5	2.3
13.7	14.3	14.7			17.5	10.0	13.3	14.7	15.8
(892) 7.2	(859) 7.8	(901) 8.3	% Profit Before Taxes/Tangible Net Worth	(80) 6.1	(76) 5.3	(195) 7.2	(249) 8.5	(292) 10.1
2.6	2.6	3.5			−.5	1.3	3.1	3.7	5.6
6.5	6.4	6.7		16.5	7.4	5.6	7.3	7.7	6.1
3.5	3.7	3.9	% Profit Before Taxes/Total Assets	3.6	3.4	3.0	3.9	4.0	4.3
1.1	1.2	1.4		.6	−.5	.4	1.1	1.5	2.2
14.1	14.3	15.7		UND	21.9	22.0	14.4	14.9	15.3
8.7	9.2	10.2	Sales/Net Fixed Assets	22.5	11.4	11.1	9.0	10.0	10.7
6.1	6.6	7.2		5.0	4.8	7.2	6.5	7.2	8.0
2.8	2.8	3.1		6.1	2.8	2.8	2.9	3.0	3.4
2.1	2.1	2.3	Sales/Total Assets	2.0	1.9	2.0	2.1	2.4	2.6
1.7	1.7	1.8		1.0	1.4	1.7	1.7	1.8	2.0
1.3	1.3	1.1			1.0	1.1	1.3	1.2	1.1
(895) 1.8	(855) 1.8	(890) 1.7	% Depr., Dep., Amort./Sales	(81) 1.5	(73) 1.6	(193) 1.9	(249) 1.7	(288) 1.5
2.6	2.4	2.2			3.6	2.3	2.4	2.2	2.0
1.0	1.0	.7			2.0	.7	.8	.5	.3
(90) 2.0	(88) 2.0	(95) 1.8	% Officers', Directors', Owners' Comp/Sales	(25) 3.3	(15) 2.1	(20) 1.3	(18) 1.2	(15) 1.5
4.7	4.6	3.5			4.9	2.8	4.3	1.9	3.0
25548291M	25830804M	33086615M	Net Sales ($)	6832M	189950M	311067M	1479601M	4117713M	26981452M
11719920M	11382384M	12617367M	Total Assets ($)	4441M	116495M	157423M	720214M	1800309M	9818485M

Current Data Sorted By Assets · **Comparative Historical Data**

Current data date spans: **18 (4/1-9/30/04)** covers 0-500M, 500M-2MM, 2-10MM · **35 (10/1/04-3/31/05)** covers 10-50MM, 50-100MM, 100-250MM

Historical columns: **4/1/00-3/31/01 ALL** · **4/1/01-3/31/02 ALL**

	0-500M	500M-2MM	2-10MM	10-50MM	50-100MM	100-250MM	4/1/00-3/31/01 ALL	4/1/01-3/31/02 ALL
Type of Statement								
Unqualified			2	4	2	2	11	7
Reviewed		2	7	1			12	12
Compiled	1	2	2				8	10
Tax Returns	5	5	1				1	1
Other	1	4	5	5		2	17	10
NUMBER OF STATEMENTS	7	13	17	10	2	4	49	40
	%	%	%	%	%	%	%	%
ASSETS								
Cash & Equivalents		10.1	2.4	12.6			9.2	5.6
Trade Receivables (net)		21.6	40.5	27.1			33.4	34.0
Inventory		39.9	27.4	34.7			26.4	30.0
All Other Current		.9	4.4	10.5			2.9	5.1
Total Current		72.4	74.8	84.8			71.9	74.6
Fixed Assets (net)		13.6	18.5	8.2			10.7	16.1
Intangibles (net)		4.7	2.3	2.8			10.0	3.0
All Other Non-Current		9.3	4.4	4.1			7.3	6.3
Total		100.0	100.0	100.0			100.0	100.0
LIABILITIES								
Notes Payable-Short Term		5.9	14.8	15.8			10.1	11.3
Cur. Mat.-L/T/D		6.7	2.0	2.4			2.3	1.9
Trade Payables		25.4	30.1	28.6			37.9	31.4
Income Taxes Payable		.1	.0	.2			.1	.3
All Other Current		7.4	7.5	4.7			9.1	12.7
Total Current		45.5	54.4	51.7			59.5	57.6
Long-Term Debt		10.9	13.2	3.9			9.6	10.6
Deferred Taxes		.3	.3	.6			.1	.5
All Other Non-Current		5.1	2.7	.4			3.0	4.1
Net Worth		38.1	29.5	43.3			27.8	27.4
Total Liabilities & Net Worth		100.0	100.0	100.0			100.0	100.0
INCOME DATA								
Net Sales		100.0	100.0	100.0			100.0	100.0
Gross Profit		39.7	31.6	39.9			32.7	37.5
Operating Expenses		40.6	29.0	33.7			28.7	33.7
Operating Profit		–.9	2.6	6.2			3.9	3.8
All Other Expenses (net)		.9	.3	.7			.6	1.3
Profit Before Taxes		–1.8	2.3	5.4			3.3	2.5
RATIOS								
Current		2.5	1.9	3.0			1.7	2.3
		1.5	1.4	1.6			1.3	1.5
		1.2	1.1	1.3			1.0	1.0
Quick		1.2	1.1	1.8			1.0	1.0
		.8	.8	.6			.7	.7
		.4	.4	.5			.5	.5
Sales/Receivables		22 16.5	33 11.1	25 14.5			27 13.3	28 13.1
		27 13.5	49 7.4	47 7.7			42 8.8	40 9.1
		55 6.6	77 4.8	72 5.1			68 5.4	75 4.9
Cost of Sales/Inventory		32 11.6	10 38.2	18 20.6			13 28.1	25 14.8
		104 3.5	56 6.6	104 3.5			55 6.6	71 5.1
		493 .7	124 2.9	224 1.6			116 3.2	164 2.2
Cost of Sales/Payables		32 11.3	24 15.3	25 14.5			45 8.1	29 12.7
		60 6.1	71 5.1	58 6.3			75 4.8	63 5.8
		66 5.5	90 4.1	192 1.9			102 3.6	98 3.7
Sales/Working Capital		4.4	6.0	3.0			6.7	4.6
		7.8	16.1	5.0			19.3	7.8
		130.4	42.6	7.1			NM	–336.6
EBIT/Interest		17.0	13.9				23.1	7.4
		3.2	(16) 3.2				(48) 4.3	(37) 2.3
		1.5	1.5				1.0	.4
Net Profit + Depr., Dep., Amort./Cur. Mat. L /T/D							3.4	4.5
							(14) 1.2	(14) 2.2
							.5	1.1
Fixed/Worth		.0	.2	.1			.2	.1
		.7	.6	.1			.4	.4
		1.0	2.5	.3			–1.1	3.4
Debt/Worth		1.1	1.0	.8			1.8	.8
		2.4	3.5	1.8			3.1	2.3
		3.3	17.2	3.2			–25.1	23.4
% Profit Before Taxes/Tangible Net Worth		55.0	28.6	28.4			72.1	26.6
		13.9	(15) 15.6	17.4			(36) 27.1	(33) 8.4
		.4	1.4	7.5			4.5	–5.9
% Profit Before Taxes/Total Assets		18.2	7.2	13.7			13.5	11.4
		4.7	2.4	6.7			5.5	3.3
		.6	1.0	2.4			.2	–1.6
Sales/Net Fixed Assets		96.6	37.2	50.2			62.3	71.6
		24.1	21.9	34.0			32.1	32.1
		7.9	10.0	17.5			20.2	9.6
Sales/Total Assets		3.9	3.5	2.3			3.2	3.2
		2.0	2.7	1.8			2.3	2.1
		1.1	2.0	1.3			1.6	1.6
% Depr., Dep., Amort./Sales		.5	.6				.5	.5
		(12) 1.3	1.1				(37) .8	(34) 1.0
		3.6	2.0				1.7	1.5
% Officers', Directors', Owners' Comp/Sales							1.9	1.6
							(16) 3.5	(16) 4.2
							5.1	5.2
Net Sales ($)	13203M	34555M	243996M	326808M	240167M	1092245M	2120225M	1372156M
Total Assets ($)	2066M	13235M	91255M	206549M	142051M	748750M	1116616M	650863M

Comparative Historical Data | Current Data Sorted By Sales

			Type of Statement	0-1MM	1-3MM	3-5MM	5-10MM	10-25MM	25MM & OVER
10	14	10	Unqualified					3	7
10	12	10	Reviewed		3			7	
4	13	5	Compiled		2	1	1	1	
5	5	11	Tax Returns	3	4	2	1	1	1
15	17	17	Other	3		1	1	6	6
4/1/02- 3/31/03 ALL	4/1/03- 3/31/04 ALL	4/1/04- 3/31/05 ALL			18 (4/1-9/30/04)		35 (10/1/04-3/31/05)		
44	61	53	**NUMBER OF STATEMENTS**	6	9	4	3	18	13
%	%	%	**ASSETS**	%	%	%	%	%	%
7.2	9.8	8.9	Cash & Equivalents					4.2	12.0
24.8	30.1	29.9	Trade Receivables (net)					39.3	27.3
29.5	31.2	30.0	Inventory					29.8	23.1
5.3	7.4	4.1	All Other Current					4.4	8.6
66.8	78.5	72.9	Total Current					77.7	71.0
14.8	15.8	15.3	Fixed Assets (net)					16.1	11.1
6.2	2.7	5.3	Intangibles (net)					1.8	12.0
12.1	3.0	6.5	All Other Non-Current					4.4	5.9
100.0	100.0	100.0	Total					100.0	100.0
			LIABILITIES						
8.4	8.2	10.4	Notes Payable-Short Term					18.4	8.3
1.5	3.2	3.0	Cur. Mat.-L/T/D					1.3	2.6
31.1	29.6	31.1	Trade Payables					29.9	26.5
.8	.5	.1	Income Taxes Payable					.0	.1
16.5	11.8	8.9	All Other Current					7.1	12.6
58.3	53.3	53.5	Total Current					56.7	50.2
17.2	8.0	10.3	Long-Term Debt					9.9	6.6
.3	.3	.3	Deferred Taxes					.2	.4
6.0	2.4	2.4	All Other Non-Current					2.1	.6
18.1	36.0	33.5	Net Worth					31.0	42.2
100.0	100.0	100.0	Total Liabilities & Net Worth					100.0	100.0
			INCOME DATA						
100.0	100.0	100.0	Net Sales					100.0	100.0
38.0	38.4	36.8	Gross Profit					32.6	35.5
33.8	32.8	34.8	Operating Expenses					29.5	28.8
4.2	5.5	2.0	Operating Profit					3.2	6.8
1.3	.4	.1	All Other Expenses (net)					.1	.4
2.9	5.2	1.9	Profit Before Taxes					3.0	6.4
			RATIOS						
2.3 / 1.2 / .9	2.5 / 1.4 / 1.1	2.0 / 1.4 / 1.0	Current					1.8 / 1.3 / 1.1	2.4 / 1.4 / 1.0
.9 / .6 / .4	1.3 / .8 / .5	1.1 / .7 / .5	Quick					1.1 / .7 / .4	1.4 / .8 / .5
18 20.8 / 40 9.0 / 49 7.4	25 14.8 / 44 8.4 / 58 6.3	23 15.9 / 44 8.3 / 67 5.5	Sales/Receivables					30 12.4 / 51 7.1 / 85 4.3	24 14.9 / 47 7.7 / 64 5.7
22 16.9 / 72 5.1 / 130 2.8	17 20.9 / 58 6.3 / 151 2.4	16 23.3 / 66 5.5 / 126 2.9	Cost of Sales/Inventory					11 33.1 / 56 6.6 / 139 2.6	15 24.2 / 97 3.8 / 108 3.4
28 12.9 / 65 5.6 / 91 4.0	19 19.7 / 55 6.6 / 100 3.6	31 11.6 / 62 5.9 / 91 4.0	Cost of Sales/Payables					21 17.4 / 75 4.9 / 101 3.6	35 10.4 / 62 5.9 / 96 3.8
6.1 / 19.1 / -34.4	4.8 / 11.6 / 37.4	4.7 / 11.0 / 128.9	Sales/Working Capital					5.4 / 12.7 / 40.4	4.5 / 8.9 / NM
6.9 / (42) 2.8 / 1.0	21.3 / (52) 6.3 / 1.7	17.6 / (45) 3.5 / 1.8	EBIT/Interest					17.1 / (17) 3.3 / 1.9	84.7 / (10) 11.9 / 2.1
4.7 / (13) 1.9 / .7	7.3 / (18) 3.2 / 1.9	8.3 / (13) 2.1 / 1.2	Net Profit + Depr., Dep., Amort./Cur. Mat. L/T/D						
.2 / .8 / -9.6	.1 / .3 / 1.1	.1 / .6 / 1.3	Fixed/Worth					.1 / .4 / 1.8	.1 / .6 / 1.1
1.4 / 5.8 / -22.2	.9 / 2.2 / 3.7	1.1 / 2.7 / 7.1	Debt/Worth					1.1 / 3.3 / 8.5	1.1 / 2.7 / 8.7
34.3 / (30) 11.8 / 7.2	82.3 / (55) 25.8 / 6.7	37.5 / (47) 17.1 / 3.6	% Profit Before Taxes/Tangible Net Worth					27.6 / (17) 17.1 / 6.6	61.7 / (11) 24.5 / 8.1
8.8 / 3.9 / .1	21.9 / 7.0 / 1.8	9.6 / 4.4 / .7	% Profit Before Taxes/Total Assets					7.3 / 3.1 / 1.9	15.5 / 8.4 / 3.7
46.3 / 25.2 / 11.2	66.9 / 30.4 / 12.4	48.6 / 27.7 / 10.6	Sales/Net Fixed Assets					42.6 / 31.8 / 13.1	47.0 / 17.8 / 12.1
3.1 / 2.2 / 1.3	4.3 / 2.3 / 1.6	3.4 / 2.3 / 1.5	Sales/Total Assets					3.2 / 2.4 / 1.7	2.3 / 1.8 / 1.5
.6 / (40) 1.1 / 1.9	.7 / (49) 1.2 / 1.8	.6 / (49) 1.2 / 2.4	% Depr., Dep., Amort./Sales					.5 / (17) 1.1 / 1.7	1.2 / (12) 1.3 / 2.5
1.8 / (19) 4.9 / 10.5	3.5 / (15) 4.5 / 9.6	2.6 / (18) 5.7 / 13.5	% Officers', Directors', Owners' Comp/Sales						
2318839M	2431982M	1950974M	Net Sales ($)	3788M	17732M	15723M	21404M	275884M	1616443M
1349296M	1293115M	1203906M	Total Assets ($)	3408M	9350M	4034M	3376M	145805M	1037933M

© RMA 2005

M = $ thousand   MM = $ million

See Pages 11 through 21 for Explanation of Ratios and Data

Current Data Sorted By Assets   Comparative Historical Data

Type of Statement							4/1/00-3/31/01 ALL	4/1/01-3/31/02 ALL
Unqualified							13	18
Reviewed							28	21
Compiled							39	39
Tax Returns							11	13
Other							42	52

Statement type counts (Current Data):

0-500M	500M-2MM	2-10MM	10-50MM	50-100MM	100-250MM	Type
		10	8	1	1	Unqualified
	8	19	3			Reviewed
6	12	13	2			Compiled
6	12	2				Tax Returns
3	11	15	11			Other

50 (4/1-9/30/04) 93 (10/1/04-3/31/05)

0-500M	500M-2MM	2-10MM	10-50MM	50-100MM	100-250MM		4/1/00-3/31/01 ALL	4/1/01-3/31/02 ALL
15	43	59	24	1	1	**NUMBER OF STATEMENTS**	133	143
%	%	%	%	%	%	**ASSETS**	%	%
14.8	10.9	7.4	6.8			Cash & Equivalents	6.8	8.0
24.7	22.9	26.4	32.1			Trade Receivables (net)	26.1	24.4
22.2	27.3	26.0	22.4			Inventory	27.0	27.9
.1	1.5	3.3	3.1			All Other Current	2.8	2.8
61.8	62.7	63.1	64.4			Total Current	62.7	63.1
29.3	25.2	26.4	22.7			Fixed Assets (net)	25.9	27.1
3.2	2.5	3.6	4.3			Intangibles (net)	2.9	3.5
5.7	9.7	6.9	8.7			All Other Non-Current	8.5	6.2
100.0	100.0	100.0	100.0			Total	100.0	100.0
						LIABILITIES		
23.5	17.6	16.1	15.5			Notes Payable-Short Term	11.3	12.1
9.1	3.5	4.4	1.4			Cur. Mat.-L/T/D	4.1	4.1
28.5	16.6	17.5	14.7			Trade Payables	19.2	16.3
.3	.2	.5	.5			Income Taxes Payable	.7	.8
5.5	7.3	8.8	9.6			All Other Current	8.6	11.3
66.9	45.2	47.3	41.7			Total Current	43.9	44.6
27.7	23.6	13.1	6.6			Long-Term Debt	13.8	13.1
.0	.3	.4	.8			Deferred Taxes	.8	.5
7.5	8.8	2.2	2.6			All Other Non-Current	4.9	4.7
-2.1	22.2	36.9	48.3			Net Worth	36.6	37.1
100.0	100.0	100.0	100.0			Total Liabilities & Net Worth	100.0	100.0
						INCOME DATA		
100.0	100.0	100.0	100.0			Net Sales	100.0	100.0
46.1	36.9	35.6	29.8			Gross Profit	36.7	35.1
45.8	37.0	33.0	28.3			Operating Expenses	33.2	30.8
.2	-.1	2.5	1.6			Operating Profit	3.5	4.3
.7	1.1	.2	-.6			All Other Expenses (net)	1.1	1.1
-.5	-1.2	2.3	2.2			Profit Before Taxes	2.4	3.2
						RATIOS		
1.9	2.7	2.0	2.0			Current	2.3	2.5
1.1	1.4	1.3	1.4				1.4	1.4
.4	.8	1.0	1.2				1.0	1.0
1.6	1.7	1.0	1.1			Quick	1.2	1.1
.4	.7	.8	.8				.7 (142)	.7
.2	.4	.4	.6				.4	.4
4 102.7	13 27.5	15 24.1	29 12.7			Sales/Receivables	16 22.3	16 23.3
18 20.0	20 18.1	30 12.3	38 9.5				31 11.9	29 12.4
31 11.7	34 10.8	49 7.5	68 5.4				44 8.3	42 8.6
0 UND	6 65.6	8 46.9	15 23.7			Cost of Sales/Inventory	17 22.1	13 27.3
9 42.6	36 10.3	50 7.2	42 8.6				39 9.3	42 8.6
52 7.0	63 5.8	126 2.9	91 4.0				130 2.8	122 3.0
0 UND	10 38.0	16 23.0	16 22.8			Cost of Sales/Payables	12 31.4	12 31.4
25 14.7	23 16.2	30 12.1	25 14.7				28 13.2	25 14.7
72 5.0	37 9.9	55 6.7	33 11.0				43 8.4	47 7.8
12.8	9.4	6.5	5.4			Sales/Working Capital	6.4	5.9
65.6	19.6	23.3	15.4				17.9	18.1
-11.1	-49.1	-750.3	30.7				492.1	-367.2
10.2	4.1	7.8	16.9			EBIT/Interest	4.9	6.6
(13) 1.1	(40) 1.7	(53) 3.0	(22) 2.8				(127) 2.3	(125) 2.7
-3.2	-.2	1.1	1.3				1.0	1.1
		11.7	10.8			Net Profit + Depr., Dep., Amort./Cur. Mat. L /T/D	5.6	5.8
	(20) 4.4	(11) 4.2					(40) 2.5	(36) 1.8
	1.6	1.4					1.1	.4
.5	.2	.2	.2			Fixed/Worth	.3	.3
2.6	.7	.8	.5				.6	.7
-2.5	6.1	1.4	1.0				2.2	1.7
1.4	.8	.7	.7			Debt/Worth	.8	.8
8.0	3.1	1.7	1.4				1.7	1.6
-13.1	35.6	4.8	3.0				6.3	5.1
	43.1	36.0	15.5			% Profit Before Taxes/Tangible Net Worth	24.8	38.2
	(35) 13.5	(53) 11.5	8.2				(117) 12.5	(126) 15.1
	-.9	3.0	1.5				1.1	1.6
22.4	11.0	12.2	8.6			% Profit Before Taxes/Total Assets	9.7	14.2
.5	2.1	3.5	3.0				4.2	4.9
-15.7	-2.8	.5	.7				-.1	.4
92.6	34.0	40.0	78.2			Sales/Net Fixed Assets	36.5	30.4
20.2	23.3	15.3	15.7				12.7	12.8
15.1	7.6	4.5	6.3				6.3	5.9
5.8	5.0	3.9	3.3			Sales/Total Assets	4.4	4.3
4.7	3.3	2.4	2.6				2.9	2.9
3.3	2.2	1.6	1.4				1.7	1.8
1.1	.7	.9	.5			% Depr., Dep., Amort./Sales	.6	.7
(10) 3.2	(31) 1.3	(51) 1.8	1.2				(120) 1.3	(131) 1.3
3.8	3.1	2.7	2.0				2.9	2.6
	2.3	1.5				% Officers', Directors', Owners' Comp/Sales	2.1	1.9
	(27) 5.2	(26) 2.3					(64) 3.6	(71) 3.4
	7.6	4.8					6.2	5.8
19257M	188434M	696888M	1245379M	65397M	208268M	Net Sales ($)	2433654M	2659100M
3714M	49103M	275748M	489162M	66977M	133278M	Total Assets ($)	1530192M	1577073M

© RMA 2005

M = $ thousand   MM = $ million
See Pages 11 through 21 for Explanation of Ratios and Data

Comparative Historical Data / Current Data Sorted By Sales

	4/1/02-3/31/03 ALL	4/1/03-3/31/04 ALL	4/1/04-3/31/05 ALL		0-1MM	1-3MM	3-5MM	5-10MM	10-25MM	25MM & OVER
						50 (4/1-9/30/04)			93 (10/1/04-3/31/05)	
Type of Statement										
Unqualified	22	20	20					3	8	9
Reviewed	32	34	30		1	3	1	11	13	1
Compiled	33	37	33		4	4	6	11	7	1
Tax Returns	14	22	20		7	5	6	2		
Other	40	39	40		11	4	4	4	10	11
NUMBER OF STATEMENTS	141	152	143		12	23	17	31	38	22
	%	%	%		%	%	%	%	%	%
ASSETS										
Cash & Equivalents	7.9	7.4	9.0		3.3	13.0	10.9	7.7	11.2	4.8
Trade Receivables (net)	25.4	26.1	26.0		22.3	18.0	21.9	25.5	29.2	35.0
Inventory	27.4	24.8	25.4		40.5	27.6	27.1	24.5	22.3	20.4
All Other Current	3.6	3.6	2.4		.0	1.4	2.4	1.4	4.1	3.2
Total Current	64.3	61.8	62.9		66.1	60.0	62.3	59.0	66.7	63.3
Fixed Assets (net)	25.9	27.9	25.6		28.7	26.2	26.4	28.6	23.7	22.0
Intangibles (net)	2.7	2.4	3.6		.5	5.7	1.1	5.6	.9	6.7
All Other Non-Current	7.1	7.9	7.9		4.7	8.0	10.1	6.8	8.7	7.9
Total	100.0	100.0	100.0		100.0	100.0	100.0	100.0	100.0	100.0
LIABILITIES										
Notes Payable-Short Term	11.3	14.3	17.0		35.4	11.2	14.7	20.7	14.2	14.4
Cur. Mat.-L/T/D	4.4	4.0	4.1		2.4	7.0	4.7	7.0	1.8	1.5
Trade Payables	15.5	19.5	18.0		23.9	14.0	20.4	15.2	18.3	20.5
Income Taxes Payable	.8	.7	.5		.0	.2	.0	.6	.6	1.0
All Other Current	9.3	8.0	8.1		7.6	5.5	4.1	7.6	10.9	10.5
Total Current	41.3	46.5	47.7		69.3	38.0	43.8	51.1	45.7	47.8
Long-Term Debt	15.9	15.8	16.9		34.4	21.9	25.3	13.6	12.6	7.4
Deferred Taxes	.4	.3	.4		.0	.1	.1	.5	.6	.9
All Other Non-Current	5.2	5.4	4.8		6.4	6.8	13.3	3.1	2.3	2.2
Net Worth	37.2	32.0	30.2		−10.1	33.2	17.5	31.7	38.9	41.8
Total Liabilities & Net Worth	100.0	100.0	100.0		100.0	100.0	100.0	100.0	100.0	100.0
INCOME DATA										
Net Sales	100.0	100.0	100.0		100.0	100.0	100.0	100.0	100.0	100.0
Gross Profit	35.4	35.0	36.2		50.1	37.5	41.4	33.4	34.2	30.5
Operating Expenses	32.6	33.2	34.7		53.4	37.5	42.5	31.5	30.1	28.2
Operating Profit	2.8	1.8	1.4		−3.3	.0	−1.0	1.9	4.1	2.3
All Other Expenses (net)	1.1	.5	.5		3.0	1.5	−.8	.5	.1	−.4
Profit Before Taxes	1.7	1.3	1.0		−6.4	−1.5	−.2	1.4	4.0	2.7
RATIOS										
Current	2.7 / 1.5 / 1.0	2.4 / 1.5 / .9	2.0 / 1.4 / .9		1.8 / 1.1 / .5	3.0 / 1.7 / .8	4.5 / 1.4 / .8	2.1 / 1.1 / .9	2.5 / 1.5 / 1.0	1.7 / 1.3 / 1.1
Quick	1.5 / .8 / .4	1.3 / .7 / .4	1.1 / .7 / .4		.7 / .4 / .2	1.7 / .5 / .2	2.1 / .9 / .6	1.0 / .6 / .4	1.4 / 1.0 / .5	.9 / .8 / .6
Sales/Receivables	18 19.9 / 30 12.1 / 46 8.0	16 22.8 / 29 12.5 / 43 8.5	15 24.2 / 29 12.5 / 46 8.0		4 87.6 / 25 14.8 / 59 6.2	4 90.0 / 19 18.9 / 42 8.7	17 20.9 / 20 17.8 / 34 10.9	15 24.2 / 29 12.6 / 53 6.9	12 31.3 / 29 12.4 / 39 9.3	31 11.7 / 42 8.7 / 63 5.8
Cost of Sales/Inventory	14 27.0 / 44 8.3 / 119 3.1	10 36.8 / 36 10.2 / 100 3.7	8 46.9 / 38 9.5 / 84 4.3		17 20.9 / 104 3.5 / 360 1.0	0 UND / 28 13.2 / 290 1.3	0 UND / 48 7.6 / 71 5.1	14 26.1 / 38 9.5 / 67 5.4	1 454.0 / 33 10.9 / 86 4.3	15 24.4 / 38 9.7 / 73 5.0
Cost of Sales/Payables	12 31.1 / 24 15.1 / 40 9.2	14 26.2 / 28 13.0 / 51 7.2	13 28.2 / 25 14.7 / 49 7.4		17 21.2 / 62 5.9 / 131 2.8	5 81.0 / 24 15.3 / 58 6.3	12 30.0 / 31 11.7 / 42 8.7	12 30.0 / 20 18.5 / 37 9.9	14 26.2 / 24 14.9 / 50 7.3	17 21.3 / 27 13.3 / 52 7.0
Sales/Working Capital	5.1 / 14.9 / NM	7.4 / 20.4 / −58.4	7.8 / 20.7 / −221.9		4.2 / 43.9 / −8.5	5.6 / 15.0 / −18.8	8.7 / 14.1 / −49.1	9.6 / 49.4 / −49.1	6.5 / 19.6 / 237.7	9.4 / 16.6 / 46.5
EBIT/Interest	(126) 6.6 / 2.6 / 1.1	(144) 6.5 / 2.2 / .2	(130) 6.2 / 2.3 / .7		(11) 2.1 / 1.0 / −3.8	(21) 4.1 / 1.5 / −.3	(15) 2.7 / 1.5 / −1.3	4.7 / 2.6 / 1.1	(33) 20.4 / 4.8 / 1.7	(19) 7.4 / 2.8 / 1.4
Net Profit + Depr., Dep., Amort./Cur. Mat. L/T/D	(46) 5.4 / 2.9 / .8	(33) 11.5 / 1.8 / .5	(38) 9.3 / 4.4 / 1.4					(10) 8.1 / 4.3 / 1.3	(13) 13.0 / 5.8 / 2.6	(11) 8.8 / 2.7 / 1.3
Fixed/Worth	.2 / .6 / 2.2	.3 / .8 / 3.1	.2 / .7 / 2.6		.3 / 4.6 / NM	.1 / .7 / 11.5	.1 / .7 / 3.0	.3 / .9 / 4.7	.2 / .5 / 1.5	.2 / .8 / 1.1
Debt/Worth	.8 / 1.6 / 5.1	1.0 / 1.8 / 7.6	.9 / 2.0 / 5.9		3.6 / 105.7 / −5.3	.4 / 1.7 / 24.2	.9 / 2.2 / 4.8	.9 / 2.2 / 5.4	1.6 / 1.6 / 3.9	1.0 / 1.8 / 3.9
% Profit Before Taxes/Tangible Net Worth	(122) 31.3 / 9.0 / 1.6	(131) 39.1 / 13.2 / .0	(123) 37.2 / 10.9 / 1.8			(18) 62.1 / 2.8 / −1.2	(14) 15.2 / 6.6 / −18.6	(26) 44.3 / 10.9 / .7	(35) 50.1 / 20.1 / 3.9	29.5 / 11.3 / 2.2
% Profit Before Taxes/Total Assets	10.8 / 3.8 / .2	11.0 / 3.8 / −1.3	11.5 / 2.9 / .0		3.5 / −.1 / −36.5	8.6 / 1.5 / −3.5	6.5 / 1.3 / −12.3	13.0 / 4.3 / .5	17.8 / 6.5 / 1.6	10.3 / 3.4 / .8
Sales/Net Fixed Assets	37.7 / 18.0 / 4.9	32.5 / 13.9 / 5.9	40.0 / 18.4 / 5.9		28.8 / 17.3 / 5.0	51.9 / 19.3 / 3.5	56.7 / 16.4 / 5.3	28.6 / 19.3 / 4.8	57.6 / 19.5 / 6.4	58.1 / 18.5 / 6.4
Sales/Total Assets	3.9 / 2.7 / 1.6	4.5 / 2.8 / 2.0	4.4 / 2.9 / 1.8		4.1 / 2.0 / 1.2	4.6 / 3.1 / 1.1	4.5 / 2.9 / 2.1	5.0 / 2.8 / 1.8	4.4 / 3.3 / 1.9	3.9 / 2.9 / 1.9
% Depr., Dep., Amort./Sales	(126) .7 / 1.3 / 3.3	(134) .7 / 1.8 / 3.1	(117) .7 / 1.6 / 3.1			(15) 1.3 / 2.5 / 7.2	(12) .5 / 1.5 / 4.2	(30) .9 / 1.6 / 2.8	(32) .7 / 1.1 / 2.1	(20) .5 / 1.2 / 1.9
% Officers', Directors', Owners' Comp/Sales	(70) 2.0 / 4.4 / 6.8	(70) 2.1 / 4.1 / 7.7	(67) 1.9 / 4.3 / 6.9			(13) 2.6 / 5.1 / 10.1	(12) 2.3 / 5.9 / 7.6	(18) 2.3 / 4.2 / 5.8	(12) .8 / 1.6 / 2.2	
Net Sales ($)	3535376M	3306810M	2423623M		8090M	48922M	64549M	232394M	597419M	1472249M
Total Assets ($)	1981117M	1381783M	1017982M		5100M	32700M	25038M	97583M	227335M	630226M

© RMA 2005

M = $ thousand   MM = $ million

See Pages 11 through 21 for Explanation of Ratios and Data

WHOLESALE—Tobacco and Tobacco Product Merchant Wholesalers NAICS 424940 (SIC 5194)

Current Data Sorted By Assets							Comparative Historical Data	

		7	14	4	1	Type of Statement		
1	4	30	10			Unqualified	13	14
2	3	23	2			Reviewed	26	31
5	4	3				Compiled	31	40
	5	7			3	Tax Returns	4	7
						Other	12	23
	28 (4/1-9/30/04)		105 (10/1/04-3/31/05)				4/1/00-3/31/01	4/1/01-3/31/02
0-500M	500M-2MM	2-10MM	10-50MM	50-100MM	100-250MM		ALL	ALL
8	16	70	31	4	4	NUMBER OF STATEMENTS	86	115
%	%	%	%	%	%	ASSETS	%	%
	9.1	10.1	10.0			Cash & Equivalents	7.0	9.1
	27.8	32.5	34.4			Trade Receivables (net)	35.0	33.7
	34.9	38.0	30.2			Inventory	38.6	37.0
	.4	2.2	1.8			All Other Current	2.2	1.8
	72.2	82.9	76.3			Total Current	82.7	81.6
	11.2	10.7	15.6			Fixed Assets (net)	10.7	10.4
	4.8	1.4	1.4			Intangibles (net)	1.9	2.3
	11.8	5.1	6.7			All Other Non-Current	4.7	5.8
	100.0	100.0	100.0			Total	100.0	100.0
						LIABILITIES		
	21.5	19.8	30.7			Notes Payable-Short Term	21.5	20.8
	.8	1.1	1.8			Cur. Mat.-L/T/D	2.7	2.7
	10.5	17.5	12.8			Trade Payables	16.5	16.1
	.0	.2	.1			Income Taxes Payable	.4	1.0
	2.9	5.7	7.3			All Other Current	6.8	10.6
	35.8	44.4	52.7			Total Current	47.9	51.2
	12.2	6.9	8.3			Long-Term Debt	5.3	6.8
	.0	.2	.2			Deferred Taxes	.1	.1
	.9	5.0	3.1			All Other Non-Current	1.8	3.1
	51.0	43.5	35.6			Net Worth	44.9	38.8
	100.0	100.0	100.0			Total Liabilities & Net Worth	100.0	100.0
						INCOME DATA		
	100.0	100.0	100.0			Net Sales	100.0	100.0
	20.4	8.2	8.2			Gross Profit	11.5	11.2
	13.1	7.2	7.1			Operating Expenses	10.0	9.9
	7.3	1.0	1.1			Operating Profit	1.5	1.2
	–.1	.0	–.2			All Other Expenses (net)	.1	.2
	7.4	1.0	1.4			Profit Before Taxes	1.3	1.0
						RATIOS		
	2.2	3.3	2.3				2.8	2.3
	1.6	1.7	1.3			Current	1.8	1.7
	1.4	1.3	1.2				1.2	1.2
	1.5	1.7	1.4				1.5	1.2
	.8	.9	.7			Quick	.8	.8
	.6	.6	.6				.5	.6

													Sales/Receivables				

	7	54.8	10	35.5	11	33.6					Sales/Receivables	11	33.3	9	38.8
	15	24.0	15	25.0	17	21.3						17	22.1	14	26.3
	28	13.2	20	17.9	21	17.7						22	16.5	21	17.4
	14	26.0	11	33.6	11	34.6					Cost of Sales/Inventory	12	29.6	10	37.7
	23	15.8	15	23.8	13	28.6						18	19.9	16	22.4
	48	7.6	25	14.4	24	15.0						29	12.4	26	14.1
	0	UND	3	105.6	2	152.8					Cost of Sales/Payables	4	99.7	3	108.0
	4	87.8	6	62.0	5	73.3						7	53.1	6	57.8
	19	18.7	12	31.3	10	36.0						15	23.7	11	32.7

		9.8		14.9		12.1			Sales/Working Capital	13.0	15.6
		20.0		25.1		51.4				26.5	30.3
		58.5		47.9		90.9				57.0	61.3
		20.9		12.2		15.1			EBIT/Interest	8.6	8.0
	(13)	3.3	(66)	3.6	(29)	3.5				(75) 2.7	(100) 3.1
		.6		1.6		1.6				1.4	1.8
				15.7					Net Profit + Depr., Dep., Amort./Cur. Mat. L /T/D	9.4	7.0
			(24)	3.7						(26) 2.9	(30) 3.5
				2.7						1.5	1.6
		.0		.1		.2			Fixed/Worth	.1	.1
		.1		.2		.5				.2	.3
		.7		.6		.8				.6	.5
		.4		.5		1.2			Debt/Worth	.6	.8
		1.2		1.4		2.5				1.2	1.9
		2.6		3.7		5.7				2.7	3.7
		49.2		19.6		28.1			% Profit Before Taxes/Tangible Net Worth	25.4	36.8
	(15)	3.0	(65)	12.4		16.1				(79) 14.2	(106) 17.2
		.6		6.1		6.5				6.7	7.8
		14.1		8.2		9.3			% Profit Before Taxes/Total Assets	11.5	11.6
		1.7		4.8		3.6				6.1	5.4
		.5		1.5		1.2				1.7	1.9
		439.5		361.2		155.1			Sales/Net Fixed Assets	167.8	203.7
		117.2		115.0		62.6				83.1	93.2
		29.0		47.3		42.2				53.4	48.6
		9.7		10.4		10.6			Sales/Total Assets	10.5	11.1
		5.1		8.0		8.2				8.0	8.7
		2.6		6.6		5.8				5.8	5.9
		.1		.1		.2			% Depr., Dep., Amort./Sales	.1	.1
	(11)	.4	(67)	.2		.3				(78) .2	(90) .2
		1.0		.4		.4				.5	.5
		1.0		.4		.2			% Officers', Directors', Owners' Comp/Sales	.4	.3
	(10)	2.2	(31)	.7	(10)	.3				(48) 1.0	(53) .8
		3.5		.9		.9				3.2	1.7

21671M	139264M	3180501M	4911808M	1308736M	1882798M	Net Sales ($)	8456705M	10666140M
1649M	22213M	365263M	635945M	288843M	654277M	Total Assets ($)	1089099M	1542566M

© RMA 2005

M = $ thousand   MM = $ million
See Pages 11 through 21 for Explanation of Ratios and Data

Comparative Historical Data | Current Data Sorted By Sales

			Type of Statement	0-1MM	1-3MM	3-5MM	5-10MM	10-25MM	25MM & OVER
20	30	26	Unqualified				1	1	24
37	30	45	Reviewed			2		8	34
35	44	30	Compiled		2	2	1	6	20
5	10	12	Tax Returns	2	3	1	1	3	2
18	20	20	Other		1	2	2	4	11
4/1/02-3/31/03	4/1/03-3/31/04	4/1/04-3/31/05		28 (4/1-9/30/04)			105 (10/1/04-3/31/05)		
ALL	ALL	ALL							
115	134	133	**NUMBER OF STATEMENTS**	2	6	7	5	22	91
%	%	%	**ASSETS**	%	%	%	%	%	%
8.4	9.0	10.1	Cash & Equivalents					12.7	9.2
32.9	30.0	30.6	Trade Receivables (net)					22.3	34.7
35.7	38.2	35.5	Inventory					46.4	33.6
2.1	3.4	2.0	All Other Current					1.3	2.6
79.1	80.7	78.3	Total Current					82.7	80.1
11.8	11.0	12.6	Fixed Assets (net)					12.9	11.2
2.4	1.7	2.4	Intangibles (net)					1.7	1.9
6.7	6.6	6.7	All Other Non-Current					2.7	6.8
100.0	100.0	100.0	Total					100.0	100.0
			LIABILITIES						
23.8	21.2	21.7	Notes Payable-Short Term					20.2	24.6
2.0	2.5	1.5	Cur. Mat.-L/T/D					1.5	1.3
16.2	17.5	15.7	Trade Payables					13.8	16.6
.7	.3	.3	Income Taxes Payable					.1	.4
8.1	10.0	7.1	All Other Current					3.7	6.8
50.9	51.4	46.1	Total Current					39.3	49.6
8.1	6.6	8.9	Long-Term Debt					9.3	6.5
.1	.1	.2	Deferred Taxes					.2	.2
2.6	3.0	4.7	All Other Non-Current					2.7	4.5
38.2	38.8	40.1	Net Worth					48.6	39.1
100.0	100.0	100.0	Total Liabilities & Net Worth					100.0	100.0
			INCOME DATA						
100.0	100.0	100.0	Net Sales					100.0	100.0
10.1	10.3	10.5	Gross Profit					12.1	7.7
8.8	8.5	8.5	Operating Expenses					10.4	6.3
1.3	1.8	2.0	Operating Profit					1.8	1.3
.3	.0	.1	All Other Expenses (net)					.1	.2
1.0	1.8	2.0	Profit Before Taxes					1.7	1.1
			RATIOS						
2.3	2.4	2.7	Current					3.3	2.5
1.5	1.5	1.5						2.0	1.5
1.2	1.2	1.2						1.4	1.2
1.2	1.1	1.4	Quick					1.5	1.4
.7	.8	.8						1.0	.8
.5	.5	.6						.6	.6
10 35.0	8 46.4	10 37.9	Sales/Receivables					7 49.8	11 33.6
16 23.5	14 25.4	15 23.7						13 29.1	16 23.4
22 16.4	21 17.4	21 17.7						20 17.9	21 17.7
10 35.6	11 33.3	11 33.7	Cost of Sales/Inventory					15 24.7	11 34.6
18 19.8	17 21.8	16 23.5						25 14.6	13 27.5
26 14.0	26 14.1	25 14.5						53 6.9	20 17.9
3 114.8	3 124.4	3 120.8	Cost of Sales/Payables					3 124.5	3 114.0
7 55.8	7 56.1	5 70.6						6 64.5	5 73.0
13 28.3	14 25.6	12 30.7						19 18.8	11 33.6
16.9	18.0	14.4	Sales/Working Capital					8.3	16.8
29.4	27.1	29.6						17.9	34.1
89.9	73.4	64.9						25.3	70.5
8.2	9.7	10.0	EBIT/Interest					18.3	11.3
(104) 3.0	(118) 4.4	(119) 3.5						(18) 2.4	(88) 3.7
1.6	2.0	1.6						.9	1.8
4.0	9.2	15.3	Net Profit + Depr., Dep., Amort./Cur. Mat. L/T/D						16.3
(32) 2.1	(36) 3.9	(32) 3.8							(29) 3.9
.9	1.7	2.7							2.9
.1	.1	.1	Fixed/Worth					.1	.1
.3	.2	.3						.1	.3
.8	.6	.7						.6	.7
.8	.7	.7	Debt/Worth					.6	.7
1.9	1.7	1.7						1.2	1.8
4.2	4.0	4.2						1.8	4.3
27.1	30.3	28.3	% Profit Before Taxes/Tangible Net Worth					19.9	24.7
(108) 14.5	(128) 16.9	(122) 14.3						(21) 7.8	(85) 14.5
4.6	8.3	6.2						1.7	6.8
9.6	10.9	9.2	% Profit Before Taxes/Total Assets					9.8	8.1
4.3	6.3	4.4						4.5	4.7
1.6	2.3	1.0						.8	1.5
221.2	231.9	236.8	Sales/Net Fixed Assets					191.7	230.1
91.8	106.1	85.8						115.7	85.7
39.1	44.4	41.6						30.1	44.4
10.5	11.3	10.5	Sales/Total Assets					8.7	10.9
8.1	8.3	7.8						6.7	8.2
5.9	6.1	5.5						4.3	6.8
.2	.1	.1	% Depr., Dep., Amort./Sales					.2	.1
(101) .3	(117) .3	(120) .3						(19) .5	(89) .2
.6	.4	.5						.8	.4
.3	.4	.3	% Officers', Directors', Owners' Comp/Sales						.3
(55) .6	(56) .6	(53) .7							(34) .6
1.5	1.2	1.3							.9
14527330M	15858677M	11444778M	Net Sales ($)	749M	10741M	26929M	33012M	406376M	10966971M
2024399M	2381544M	1968190M	Total Assets ($)	39M	4950M	27818M	11103M	84712M	1839568M

M = $ thousand   MM = $ million

© RMA 2005

See Pages 11 through 21 for Explanation of Ratios and Data

Current Data Sorted By Assets   Comparative Historical Data

0-500M	500M-2MM	2-10MM	10-50MM	50-100MM	100-250MM	Type of Statement	4/1/00-3/31/01 ALL	4/1/01-3/31/02 ALL
		2	4		1	Unqualified	5	5
	1	6	7			Reviewed	7	11
	6	2	2			Compiled	17	16
1	6	1	1			Tax Returns	2	5
	5	7	6	1		Other	17	10
	14 (4/1-9/30/04)		44 (10/1/04-3/31/05)					
1	18	18	19		2	**NUMBER OF STATEMENTS**	48	47
%	%	%	%	%	%	**ASSETS**	%	%
	6.8	7.5	7.5			Cash & Equivalents	5.4	5.7
	24.8	33.7	28.8			Trade Receivables (net)	35.2	31.0
	40.4	32.2	41.5			Inventory	36.4	36.3
	4.2	4.8	4.0			All Other Current	2.3	2.8
	76.2	78.2	81.9			Total Current	79.4	75.8
	15.8	10.4	8.6			Fixed Assets (net)	11.2	14.2
	.5	7.0	2.5			Intangibles (net)	2.9	3.6
	7.6	4.4	7.0			All Other Non-Current	6.5	6.4
	100.0	100.0	100.0			Total	100.0	100.0
						LIABILITIES		
	9.9	15.6	11.9			Notes Payable-Short Term	15.0	16.2
	2.3	1.6	1.5			Cur. Mat.-L/T/D	2.3	4.7
	17.9	20.7	19.0			Trade Payables	28.9	21.7
	.0	.5	.3			Income Taxes Payable	.5	.1
	16.1	9.9	10.1			All Other Current	7.3	9.2
	46.3	48.3	42.8			Total Current	54.0	52.0
	10.7	8.2	9.8			Long-Term Debt	6.0	7.8
	.0	.2	.3			Deferred Taxes	.1	.1
	.7	5.5	3.0			All Other Non-Current	3.6	7.3
	42.3	37.8	44.1			Net Worth	36.3	32.7
	100.0	100.0	100.0			Total Liabilities & Net Worth	100.0	100.0
						INCOME DATA		
	100.0	100.0	100.0			Net Sales	100.0	100.0
	31.8	37.2	32.6			Gross Profit	34.0	35.4
	30.2	36.2	30.8			Operating Expenses	31.7	33.9
	1.6	1.0	1.7			Operating Profit	2.3	1.5
	-.1	.4	.7			All Other Expenses (net)	-.3	.5
	1.8	.6	1.0			Profit Before Taxes	2.7	1.1
						RATIOS		
	2.7	3.1	3.0				2.2	2.3
	1.7	1.4	2.0			Current	1.5	1.4
	1.3	1.1	1.5				1.1	1.1
	1.6	1.5	1.4				1.0	1.0
	.6	.8	.8			Quick	.8	.7
	.4	.5	.6				.5	.5
	26 14.0	27 13.5	34 10.6				33 11.0	30 12.0
	37 9.8	37 9.8	41 8.9			Sales/Receivables	40 9.0	44 8.3
	44 8.4	48 7.7	65 5.6				52 7.0	56 6.5
	52 7.1	33 11.1	54 6.7				48 7.6	41 8.8
	84 4.3	61 6.0	88 4.2			Cost of Sales/Inventory	72 5.0	77 4.8
	132 2.8	136 2.7	135 2.7				107 3.4	124 2.9
	12 30.3	23 15.8	22 17.0				25 14.5	27 13.5
	37 9.9	36 10.0	36 10.0			Cost of Sales/Payables	49 7.5	42 8.7
	67 5.4	51 7.1	62 5.9				62 5.9	65 5.6
	6.1	6.1	3.7				5.4	4.9
	7.1	14.6	7.1			Sales/Working Capital	11.0	12.4
	21.2	40.0	9.6				31.4	41.0
	5.8	16.1	17.6				7.5	7.1
	(14) 3.8	(13) 4.0	(18) 4.6			EBIT/Interest	(43) 3.5	(44) 2.8
	1.4	1.9	.3				1.5	1.1
			8.5			Net Profit + Depr., Dep.,	10.5	4.6
		(13) 1.7				Amort./Cur. Mat. L /T/D	(12) 2.7	(14) 1.0
			-1.1				.8	.0
	.1	.2	.1				.1	.2
	.2	.3	.2			Fixed/Worth	.3	.5
	.9	.9	.4				.8	1.5
	.8	1.0	.4				.7	.8
	1.1	2.6	1.3			Debt/Worth	1.7	2.5
	3.2	7.0	4.4				5.0	10.2
	33.7	48.5	35.0			% Profit Before Taxes/Tangible	37.0	54.3
	(16) 11.2	(16) 17.6	(17) 23.4			Net Worth	(44) 16.5	(41) 14.5
	1.7	2.8	3.2				5.2	1.2
	8.7	14.3	17.0			% Profit Before Taxes/Total	9.8	10.7
	2.9	6.6	4.8			Assets	5.5	4.2
	.5	1.0	-3.7				1.2	.0
	107.8	80.9	103.6				96.5	52.9
	29.4	36.4	37.8			Sales/Net Fixed Assets	27.3	24.2
	9.9	22.1	18.7				16.4	11.7
	3.1	4.4	3.1				3.9	3.4
	2.6	2.8	2.5			Sales/Total Assets	2.8	2.7
	1.5	1.7	1.5				2.1	1.9
	1.1	.4	.5				.5	.6
	(14) 1.3	(15) .6	(17) .8			% Depr., Dep., Amort./Sales	(39) 1.0	(41) 1.2
	2.0	1.2	1.2				1.8	1.9
	2.7						1.8	1.6
	(13) 4.0					% Officers', Directors', Owners' Comp/Sales	(20) 3.2	(17) 3.1
	5.7						5.7	4.5
854M	53789M	244016M	1103734M		650360M	Net Sales ($)	1422184M	728449M
365M	22276M	74342M	470331M		460112M	Total Assets ($)	786782M	313524M

(50-100MM column: DATA NOT AVAILABLE)

M = $ thousand   MM = $ million
See Pages 11 through 21 for Explanation of Ratios and Data

Comparative Historical Data   **Current Data Sorted By Sales**

			Type of Statement	0-1MM	1-3MM	3-5MM	5-10MM	10-25MM	25MM & OVER
10	7	7	Unqualified			1		2	4
20	16	14	Reviewed		1	1	1	4	7
16	20	10	Compiled		2	4	1	1	2
9	14	8	Tax Returns	1	3	3		1	
15	10	19	Other		2	5	1	3	8
4/1/02-3/31/03 ALL	4/1/03-3/31/04 ALL	4/1/04-3/31/05 ALL		14 (4/1-9/30/04)			44 (10/1/04-3/31/05)		
70	67	58	**NUMBER OF STATEMENTS**	1	8	14	3	11	21
%	%	%	**ASSETS**	%	%	%	%	%	%
8.4	9.8	7.3	Cash & Equivalents			7.6		6.5	6.5
30.2	30.3	28.5	Trade Receivables (net)			29.1		43.2	26.7
39.8	35.0	37.9	Inventory			37.9		27.0	41.9
1.5	4.0	4.1	All Other Current			7.4		1.4	4.6
79.9	79.1	77.7	Total Current			81.9		78.1	79.7
11.9	12.4	11.1	Fixed Assets (net)			11.5		10.7	6.5
3.5	3.2	4.2	Intangibles (net)			.4		6.4	5.2
4.7	5.4	7.0	All Other Non-Current			6.2		4.8	8.6
100.0	100.0	100.0	Total			100.0		100.0	100.0
			LIABILITIES						
11.9	11.8	13.0	Notes Payable-Short Term			8.5		23.9	10.6
2.1	4.6	1.8	Cur. Mat.-L/T/D			1.3		1.2	1.4
24.9	24.0	19.0	Trade Payables			19.7		27.8	18.1
.4	.2	.2	Income Taxes Payable			.1		.5	.3
7.7	10.6	11.9	All Other Current			13.2		5.8	10.5
47.0	51.2	46.0	Total Current			42.8		59.2	40.9
9.5	8.4	9.4	Long-Term Debt			8.6		2.4	9.1
.2	.3	.2	Deferred Taxes			.0		.1	.3
6.6	5.7	3.2	All Other Non-Current			1.6		7.5	3.3
36.6	34.5	41.3	Net Worth			47.0		30.9	46.4
100.0	100.0	100.0	Total Liabilities & Net Worth			100.0		100.0	100.0
			INCOME DATA						
100.0	100.0	100.0	Net Sales			100.0		100.0	100.0
33.3	32.8	33.6	Gross Profit			34.7		34.4	31.2
30.0	30.2	32.1	Operating Expenses			31.9		32.6	29.1
3.4	2.6	1.5	Operating Profit			2.7		1.7	2.2
.4	.0	.3	All Other Expenses (net)			.1		.6	.4
2.9	2.5	1.3	Profit Before Taxes			2.6		1.2	1.8
			RATIOS						
3.1	2.3	3.0				3.2		1.6	3.0
1.7	1.6	1.7	Current			1.8		1.3	2.0
1.3	1.2	1.2				1.2		1.1	1.5
1.5	1.3	1.4				1.8		1.5	1.4
.8	.8	.7	Quick			.6		.8	.8
.5	.5	.5				.5		.6	.5
31 11.9	27 13.3	29 12.7				32 11.4		31 11.6	29 12.8
40 9.1	36 10.1	39 9.2	Sales/Receivables			39 9.4		47 7.7	41 8.9
50 7.4	47 7.8	48 7.7				43 8.6		70 5.3	53 6.9
50 7.3	39 9.3	54 6.8				39 9.3		7 54.5	54 6.8
75 4.9	64 5.7	84 4.4	Cost of Sales/Inventory			96 3.8		56 6.6	84 4.3
123 3.0	108 3.4	130 2.8				133 2.7		87 4.2	132 2.8
26 13.9	21 17.1	20 18.4				14 27.0		24 15.4	23 15.6
42 8.7	37 9.9	40 9.1	Cost of Sales/Payables			42 8.8		48 7.7	44 8.3
64 5.7	68 5.4	59 6.2				72 5.0		51 7.2	61 6.0
5.5	6.5	4.4				6.8		7.5	3.7
9.8	11.5	8.1	Sales/Working Capital			7.1		16.5	7.7
15.9	23.8	20.4				14.9		39.1	14.1
11.1	11.0	10.6						5.7	18.2
(61) 3.6	(58) 3.6	(48) 4.2	EBIT/Interest				(10)	3.6	(19) 8.6
1.6	1.6	1.4						.6	2.1
15.2	15.7	8.5	Net Profit + Depr., Dep.,						8.5
(20) 6.2	(19) 5.6	(20) 2.5	Amort./Cur. Mat. L/T/D						(11) 6.8
3.5	1.2	-.2							-1.7
.1	.1	.1				.0		.2	.1
.3	.3	.2	Fixed/Worth			.2		.4	.1
.9	1.0	.8				.4		.8	.4
.6	.8	.6				.7		1.2	.5
1.7	1.8	1.4	Debt/Worth			1.2		4.3	1.2
5.9	6.5	6.7				2.3		6.6	5.1
36.6	26.9	38.0				41.0		27.5	32.3
(61) 18.5	(59) 14.5	(50) 15.5	% Profit Before Taxes/Tangible			8.1	(10)	14.6	(18) 20.3
6.4	3.4	2.2	Net Worth			1.4		-2.1	5.9
13.4	9.9	12.0				12.3		14.2	14.9
5.8	5.3	4.8	% Profit Before Taxes/Total			3.9		2.8	6.7
1.9	1.0	.5	Assets			.8		-.2	.3
67.2	84.9	94.1				191.6		77.6	111.4
32.7	38.4	33.3	Sales/Net Fixed Assets			59.2		37.8	41.9
16.3	13.8	18.4				25.9		23.6	22.7
3.6	3.6	3.2				3.1		4.6	3.6
2.9	2.9	2.6	Sales/Total Assets			2.6		2.9	2.5
2.0	2.3	1.6				2.0		1.7	1.7
.5	.5	.5				.5			.5
(62) .9	(55) .7	(47) .8	% Depr., Dep., Amort./Sales			(10) .7			(18) .7
1.5	1.5	1.3				1.4			1.0
1.5	1.4	2.0				2.4			
(26) 3.6	(29) 3.0	(25) 3.1	% Officers', Directors', Owners' Comp/Sales			(10) 3.3			
5.7	4.8	5.6				5.5			
2530535M	1736261M	2052753M	Net Sales ($)	854M	15045M	51425M	21363M	175389M	1788677M
1341270M	738140M	1027426M	Total Assets ($)	365M	10567M	21191M	8614M	62925M	923764M

M = $ thousand   MM = $ million
See Pages 11 through 21 for Explanation of Ratios and Data

Current Data Sorted By Assets

Comparative Historical Data

Type of Statement	0-500M	500M-2MM	2-10MM	10-50MM	50-100MM	100-250MM		4/1/00-3/31/01 ALL	4/1/01-3/31/02 ALL
Unqualified	1	4	24	26	7	7		65	57
Reviewed	18	17	79	14	1			118	107
Compiled	30	49	29	6				135	140
Tax Returns	15	49	19	1				36	29
Other	15	32	48	32	3	11		119	132
	94 (4/1-9/30/04)			428 (10/1/04-3/31/05)					
NUMBER OF STATEMENTS	64	151	199	79	11	18		473	465
ASSETS	%	%	%	%	%	%		%	%
Cash & Equivalents	17.2	10.0	7.5	6.1	13.7	5.1		8.8	8.8
Trade Receivables (net)	23.2	31.6	32.3	32.9	21.3	23.2		32.2	30.8
Inventory	32.4	34.8	38.0	34.9	30.2	33.0		34.4	35.6
All Other Current	1.1	1.8	3.6	3.2	2.3	3.4		2.2	2.4
Total Current	73.9	78.2	81.3	77.2	67.5	64.7		77.6	77.7
Fixed Assets (net)	14.9	14.4	11.2	14.2	21.9	16.1		13.7	13.2
Intangibles (net)	4.7	1.9	2.2	2.8	8.6	11.1		2.9	3.4
All Other Non-Current	6.5	5.5	5.2	5.9	1.9	8.2		5.7	5.7
Total	100.0	100.0	100.0	100.0	100.0	100.0		100.0	100.0
LIABILITIES									
Notes Payable-Short Term	19.7	16.6	16.9	19.3	16.9	17.5		17.0	18.6
Cur. Mat.-L/T/D	6.2	2.7	2.6	1.5	5.6	4.2		3.0	3.4
Trade Payables	24.2	23.8	21.7	19.5	14.3	9.9		20.5	19.9
Income Taxes Payable	.1	.1	.3	.2	.0	.4		.3	.3
All Other Current	10.9	10.6	7.7	11.8	13.0	11.5		10.6	9.4
Total Current	61.1	53.8	49.1	52.2	49.9	43.4		51.4	51.6
Long-Term Debt	16.7	11.1	6.7	7.2	14.2	12.3		9.0	9.3
Deferred Taxes	.0	.1	.1	.3	.2	1.0		.2	.2
All Other Non-Current	5.6	7.4	4.8	6.6	12.4	3.4		7.5	5.9
Net Worth	16.5	27.7	39.2	33.7	23.3	40.0		32.1	33.1
Total Liabilities & Net Worth	100.0	100.0	100.0	100.0	100.0	100.0		100.0	100.0
INCOME DATA									
Net Sales	100.0	100.0	100.0	100.0	100.0	100.0		100.0	100.0
Gross Profit	39.3	32.8	30.6	29.7	30.8	29.6		34.2	32.9
Operating Expenses	36.2	30.6	27.0	25.4	24.8	21.3		30.6	29.2
Operating Profit	3.1	2.2	3.6	4.3	6.1	8.2		3.5	3.8
All Other Expenses (net)	.3	.5	.2	.5	2.0	2.3		.5	.9
Profit Before Taxes	2.7	1.7	3.4	3.7	4.1	5.9		3.1	2.9
RATIOS									
Current	3.1	2.4	2.6	1.9	1.8	2.2		2.3	2.5
	1.4	1.4	1.6	1.4	1.4	1.7		1.5	1.5
	.8	1.1	1.3	1.2	1.1	1.3		1.1	1.1
Quick	1.4	1.2	1.3	1.0	.9	.9		1.2	1.2
	.8	.8	.8	.7	.7	.6		.8	.8
	.3	.4	.5	.5	.5	.5		.5	.5
Sales/Receivables	4　93.3	22　16.5	26　13.8	31　11.8	12　30.8	26　13.9		26　13.9	23　15.8
	22　16.4	32　11.4	39　9.3	49　7.4	38　9.7	44　8.3		41　8.9	36　10.0
	41　9.0	47　7.8	55　6.6	58　6.3	56　6.5	72　5.0		56　6.5	51　7.1
Cost of Sales/Inventory	11　34.5	18　19.8	40　9.2	37　9.8	34　10.6	51　7.1		29　12.5	32　11.6
	37　9.8	45　8.1	70　5.2	75　4.9	72　5.0	95　3.8		67　5.4	67　5.5
	112　3.3	114　3.2	126　2.9	119　3.1	137　2.7	150　2.4		122　3.0	125　2.9
Cost of Sales/Payables	5　78.7	14　25.4	16　22.6	17　21.6	12　30.6	12　31.5		16　22.2	14　25.5
	35　10.4	31　11.9	32　11.5	27　13.6	29　12.5	33　11.1		32　11.4	30　12.2
	58　6.3	57　6.4	49　7.5	53　6.9	38　9.6	43　8.4		57　6.4	47　7.7
Sales/Working Capital	7.3	5.7	5.1	6.1	5.4	3.4		5.6	5.6
	26.9	13.6	9.6	10.4	13.3	5.9		10.8	11.3
	−48.5	131.9	20.8	29.9	30.6	30.3		39.2	35.7
EBIT/Interest	9.3	7.6	14.6	15.1	10.6	14.7		7.6	7.2
	(51) 3.3	(131) 2.8	(185) 5.3	(74) 3.7	(10) 3.9	3.1		(417) 2.9	(417) 2.6
	.7	.9	1.9	1.6	2.1	1.0		1.4	1.0
Net Profit + Depr., Dep., Amort./Cur. Mat. L/T/D		15.8	9.6	16.0				9.6	6.5
		(13) 1.3	(42) 2.6	(16) 2.9				(108) 2.8	(92) 2.5
		.0	1.2	2.1				1.0	.8
Fixed/Worth	.1	.1	.1	.1	.4	.2		.1	.1
	.5	.2	.2	.3	.7	.4		.3	.3
	20.1	2.2	.6	1.2	1.9	1.2		.9	1.1
Debt/Worth	.6	.9	.8	1.0	1.6	.8		1.0	.9
	4.1	2.6	1.8	2.4	3.3	1.6		2.2	2.3
	−60.1	12.6	3.7	6.2	14.3	4.3		5.4	7.2
% Profit Before Taxes/Tangible Net Worth	146.3	42.1	43.6	59.0	87.3	37.1		53.1	45.3
	(47) 40.0	(123) 15.6	(188) 20.6	(72) 19.7	(10) 34.3	(15) 19.8		(431) 21.0	(409) 16.6
	1.0	.3	6.5	6.7	11.5	2.0		5.9	2.5
% Profit Before Taxes/Total Assets	28.4	13.3	14.9	14.6	13.1	18.0		14.5	13.0
	9.9	3.7	5.9	5.4	4.8	5.8		5.9	5.3
	−.4	−.1	2.0	1.5	3.0	.2		1.7	.2
Sales/Net Fixed Assets	149.0	131.4	115.5	81.1	26.1	38.9		91.1	97.4
	40.5	56.6	46.7	30.2	14.4	11.1		34.7	39.9
	22.3	14.5	19.2	14.2	6.2	5.3		14.4	14.8
Sales/Total Assets	5.7	4.6	3.7	3.2	3.3	2.3		3.9	3.8
	4.2	3.1	2.8	2.4	2.4	1.8		2.7	2.8
	2.1	2.1	2.0	2.0	1.1	1.1		1.9	2.0
% Depr., Dep., Amort./Sales	.7	.3	.3	.4	1.2	.4		.3	.3
	(37) 1.1	(120) .7	(168) .6	(70) .8	(10) 1.8	(13) 2.2		(390) .7	(371) .7
	2.1	2.0	1.2	1.8	3.1	3.1		1.6	1.6
% Officers', Directors', Owners' Comp/Sales	3.3	2.2	1.5	.8				2.2	2.2
	(31) 5.7	(89) 4.5	(98) 2.8	(17) 1.6				(234) 3.9	(207) 4.0
	12.9	8.0	4.3	3.4				6.2	7.0
Net Sales ($)	73993M	629229M	2884091M	5081904M	1772152M	6155967M		11594361M	12510145M
Total Assets ($)	16908M	173406M	932392M	1714419M	779725M	3078916M		5276685M	4922863M

© RMA 2005

M = $ thousand　　MM = $ million

See Pages 11 through 21 for Explanation of Ratios and Data

Comparative Historical Data | Current Data Sorted By Sales

Hist 1	Hist 2	Hist 3	Type of Statement	0-1MM	1-3MM	3-5MM	5-10MM	10-25MM	25MM & OVER
76	74	68	Unqualified		1	2	3	21	41
132	127	112	Reviewed		7	14	22	48	21
94	174	102	Compiled	14	31	15	20	16	6
53	72	99	Tax Returns	15	39	14	17	14	
128	151	141	Other	11	19	11	21	30	49
4/1/02-3/31/03 ALL	4/1/03-3/31/04 ALL	4/1/04-3/31/05 ALL		94 (4/1-9/30/04)			428 (10/1/04-3/31/05)		
483	598	522	NUMBER OF STATEMENTS	40	97	56	83	129	117
%	%	%	**ASSETS**	%	%	%	%	%	%
9.2	8.5	9.3	Cash & Equivalents	14.4	11.7	11.4	8.0	7.9	6.8
31.5	31.8	30.5	Trade Receivables (net)	18.9	25.1	33.7	33.0	34.5	31.3
35.2	34.0	35.6	Inventory	36.7	34.9	37.1	38.1	35.1	33.8
2.5	3.1	2.7	All Other Current	1.1	1.9	1.7	3.3	3.6	2.9
78.4	77.4	78.0	Total Current	71.1	73.6	83.8	82.3	81.2	74.9
12.6	14.3	13.4	Fixed Assets (net)	17.3	17.0	10.6	10.7	11.0	15.0
3.3	2.9	2.9	Intangibles (net)	4.6	3.0	2.4	.9	2.5	4.6
5.8	5.4	5.6	All Other Non-Current	6.9	6.5	3.2	6.1	5.3	5.5
100.0	100.0	100.0	Total	100.0	100.0	100.0	100.0	100.0	100.0
			LIABILITIES						
16.4	16.9	17.6	Notes Payable-Short Term	11.0	21.6	17.3	15.8	17.1	18.4
3.4	2.9	3.0	Cur. Mat.-L/T/D	7.2	3.4	2.4	3.4	2.1	2.5
21.4	20.4	21.7	Trade Payables	21.2	18.5	23.2	23.9	25.0	18.6
.3	.3	.2	Income Taxes Payable	.2	.1	.3	.1	.1	.2
10.1	10.3	9.8	All Other Current	6.6	11.8	9.7	9.6	7.7	11.6
51.6	50.8	52.2	Total Current	46.1	55.4	52.9	52.8	52.0	51.1
9.9	10.8	9.6	Long-Term Debt	19.6	15.9	9.7	5.5	5.9	8.1
.2	.3	.2	Deferred Taxes	.0	.1	.1	.1	.1	.3
5.8	6.7	6.0	All Other Non-Current	7.9	5.2	11.2	3.2	5.6	6.1
32.5	31.5	31.9	Net Worth	26.4	23.4	26.1	38.4	36.4	34.3
100.0	100.0	100.0	Total Liabilities & Net Worth	100.0	100.0	100.0	100.0	100.0	100.0
			INCOME DATA						
100.0	100.0	100.0	Net Sales	100.0	100.0	100.0	100.0	100.0	100.0
33.1	33.7	32.1	Gross Profit	43.9	39.3	29.7	29.6	29.1	28.5
29.2	30.4	28.7	Operating Expenses	38.5	38.0	26.9	25.7	26.2	23.3
3.9	3.3	3.4	Operating Profit	5.4	1.3	2.8	3.9	2.9	5.1
.8	.6	.5	All Other Expenses (net)	.4	.5	.8	.3	.0	.9
3.1	2.7	3.0	Profit Before Taxes	5.0	.8	2.0	3.5	3.0	4.2
			RATIOS						
2.6	2.4	2.4		3.5	3.1	2.1	2.4	2.4	1.9
1.6	1.5	1.5	Current	1.4	1.5	1.5	1.5	1.5	1.4
1.2	1.1	1.2		.9	1.0	1.2	1.2	1.2	1.2
1.3	1.2	1.2		1.3	1.4	1.2	1.1	1.3	1.1
(482) .8	.8	.8	Quick	.8	.8	.9	.8	.8	.7
.5	.5	.5		.3	.4	.4	.5	.5	.5
23 15.7	24 15.2	23 16.0		5 72.0	20 18.7	25 14.4	24 15.4	27 13.4	24 15.0
38 9.6	38 9.6	36 10.1	Sales/Receivables	21 17.6	31 11.7	35 10.4	36 10.2	39 9.3	42 8.6
55 6.7	54 6.7	53 6.9		58 6.3	47 7.8	59 6.2	54 6.7	52 7.1	56 6.5
33 10.9	28 13.0	29 12.5		21 17.3	20 18.6	29 12.7	28 12.9	32 11.4	30 12.0
65 5.6	60 6.1	59 6.2	Cost of Sales/Inventory	93 3.9	65 5.6	54 6.7	54 6.8	57 6.4	61 5.9
118 3.1	113 3.2	119 3.1		320 1.1	154 2.4	118 3.1	111 3.3	97 3.8	112 3.3
18 20.5	14 25.3	16 22.7		17 22.0	10 35.7	14 26.3	18 20.7	18 20.7	16 23.0
34 9.5	30 12.2	31 11.6	Cost of Sales/Payables	38 9.5	28 13.3	31 12.0	35 10.4	31 11.8	26 13.8
54 6.7	53 6.9	50 7.3		84 4.4	53 6.9	50 7.3	61 6.0	49 7.4	41 8.9
5.1	5.6	5.5		2.3	4.4	5.8	5.6	6.1	6.0
10.0	11.0	11.4	Sales/Working Capital	11.7	11.2	10.4	12.0	10.9	12.7
32.6	40.2	34.9		−79.8	NM	35.1	31.9	28.2	33.6
9.1	9.8	11.4		14.1	5.2	4.8	12.5	13.3	19.2
(433) 3.6	(538) 3.6	(469) 3.9	EBIT/Interest	(32) 5.4	(84) 2.1	(47) 2.0	(76) 5.2	(120) 5.1	(110) 5.1
1.5	1.3	1.4		1.1	.6	.9	2.1	1.8	2.1
5.8	7.8	5.6					18.3	4.2	7.1
(105) 2.4	(114) 2.8	(87) 2.4	Net Profit + Depr., Dep., Amort./Cur. Mat. L/T/D			(12) 3.6	(29) 1.7	(31) 2.8	
1.0	1.2	1.0					1.3	.5	1.9
.1	.1	.1		.1	.1	.1	.1	.1	.1
.3	.3	.3	Fixed/Worth	.5	.5	.2	.2	.2	.3
1.0	1.1	1.1		5.8	NM	1.9	.5	.8	1.1
.8	.9	.8		.6	.6	1.0	.6	.8	1.0
2.2	2.3	2.2	Debt/Worth	2.6	2.8	2.9	1.8	2.1	2.2
7.4	6.2	6.2		32.4	−16.3	13.3	3.4	4.5	5.9
46.1	47.6	49.3		135.0	37.5	43.0	42.7	48.9	58.3
(423) 19.7	(522) 18.3	(455) 19.5	% Profit Before Taxes/Tangible Net Worth	(33) 21.2	(70) 6.2	(46) 16.6	(79) 21.5	(120) 19.5	(107) 26.8
4.9	4.7	3.9		5.5	.0	.3	8.6	4.6	11.4
13.3	13.5	15.3		35.2	10.4	12.6	18.1	13.5	16.7
6.1	4.9	5.4	% Profit Before Taxes/Total Assets	10.7	2.5	2.9	6.9	5.3	6.6
.9	.7	1.0		.5	−1.9	.0	2.6	1.3	2.0
116.6	118.1	114.0		137.2	98.8	138.0	163.3	120.9	79.3
44.2	39.0	41.5	Sales/Net Fixed Assets	35.0	35.4	57.5	48.1	53.0	30.2
16.7	13.2	15.3		10.3	11.1	16.6	22.4	19.9	11.4
3.8	4.0	4.1		4.3	3.9	4.4	4.4	4.3	3.6
2.8	2.7	2.8	Sales/Total Assets	2.0	2.6	2.9	3.0	3.2	2.6
2.0	2.0	2.0		1.3	1.7	2.0	2.2	2.2	2.0
.4	.3	.3		.9	.5	.3	.2	.3	.4
(391) .7	(479) .7	(418) .7	% Depr., Dep., Amort./Sales	(21) 1.3	(76) 1.1	(41) .7	(64) .6	(115) .6	(101) .8
1.6	1.7	1.6		4.5	2.5	1.3	1.1	1.2	2.0
2.0	2.1	1.7		3.4	3.1	2.5	1.8	1.4	.9
(229) 3.3	(288) 4.0	(236) 3.4	% Officers', Directors', Owners' Comp/Sales	(15) 10.2	(59) 5.5	(35) 3.8	(44) 3.0	(60) 2.5	(23) 1.5
6.4	7.5	6.4		14.6	8.0	8.1	4.6	4.1	3.9
15430283M	17271926M	16597336M	Net Sales ($)	20890M	186387M	225730M	598213M	2001642M	13564474M
6132325M	6292023M	6695766M	Total Assets ($)	12064M	83391M	87723M	213764M	699217M	5599607M

M = $ thousand   MM = $ million
See Pages 11 through 21 for Explanation of Ratios and Data

Current Data Sorted By Assets   Comparative Historical Data

						Type of Statement		
2	1	1	12	1	2	Unqualified		
1	3	10	7			Reviewed		
2	9	7	2			Compiled		
5	6	2				Tax Returns		
1	3	11	6		2	Other		
	22 (4/1-9/30/04)			72 (10/1/04-3/31/05)			4/1/00-3/31/01 ALL	4/1/01-3/31/02 ALL
0-500M	500M-2MM	2-10MM	10-50MM	50-100MM	100-250MM	NUMBER OF STATEMENTS		
11	22	31	25	1	4			
%	%	%	%	%	%	**ASSETS**	%	%
29.7	7.2	10.8	7.5			Cash & Equivalents	D	D
33.0	49.4	36.3	26.3			Trade Receivables (net)	A	A
21.4	18.4	32.5	34.1			Inventory	T	T
1.8	.9	2.2	1.5			All Other Current	A	A
85.9	75.9	81.8	69.3			Total Current		
5.0	14.6	10.6	14.3			Fixed Assets (net)	N	N
4.7	2.6	2.6	7.9			Intangibles (net)	O	O
4.4	7.0	4.9	8.4			All Other Non-Current	T	T
100.0	100.0	100.0	100.0			Total		
						LIABILITIES	A	A
18.2	21.4	18.0	26.8			Notes Payable-Short Term	V	V
1.3	2.9	2.5	1.9			Cur. Mat.-L/T/D	A	A
20.7	24.7	28.2	16.5			Trade Payables	I	I
.5	.1	.6	.3			Income Taxes Payable	L	L
6.3	7.3	10.9	7.6			All Other Current	A	A
47.0	56.4	60.2	53.0			Total Current	B	B
6.2	12.6	6.2	13.7			Long-Term Debt	L	L
.2	.1	.3	.9			Deferred Taxes	E	E
4.3	10.0	2.4	5.9			All Other Non-Current		
42.3	20.8	30.8	26.4			Net Worth		
100.0	100.0	100.0	100.0			Total Liabilities & Net Worth		
						INCOME DATA		
100.0	100.0	100.0	100.0			Net Sales		
21.0	31.3	25.1	22.4			Gross Profit		
18.7	30.4	20.9	18.9			Operating Expenses		
2.2	.9	4.2	3.5			Operating Profit		
.2	1.2	.3	.2			All Other Expenses (net)		
2.0	−.2	3.8	3.3			Profit Before Taxes		
						RATIOS		
6.5	2.1	1.6	1.8					
2.3	1.3	1.4	1.2			Current		
1.2	1.0	1.1	1.1					
5.7	1.5	1.1	1.1					
1.2	1.0	.7	.5			Quick		
.6	.7	.6	.3					
0 UND	23 15.9	17 21.2	26 13.8					
22 16.8	35 10.3	30 12.2	37 9.8			Sales/Receivables		
52 7.0	56 6.5	47 7.7	49 7.5					
0 UND	3 113.6	5 70.8	21 17.2					
5 74.6	16 22.1	30 12.3	61 6.0			Cost of Sales/Inventory		
48 7.6	50 7.3	73 5.0	102 3.6					
0 UND	5 74.1	13 28.3	17 21.2					
15 24.9	26 14.1	30 12.1	28 13.1			Cost of Sales/Payables		
34 10.7	52 7.0	49 7.4	37 9.8					
7.0	11.3	7.7	8.6					
17.0	26.9	12.8	23.0			Sales/Working Capital		
47.4	−449.7	88.0	62.8					
	6.6	14.3	13.4					
(20) 1.0	(28) 5.9	(23) 3.7				EBIT/Interest		
	−2.6	1.9	2.0					
			11.3					
		(10) 4.3				Net Profit + Depr., Dep., Amort./Cur. Mat. L/T/D		
			2.2					
.0	.2	.1	.3					
.0	.7	.3	.9			Fixed/Worth		
.2	−1.6	.7	3.1					
.2	.8	1.4	2.4					
1.0	8.9	2.6	3.5			Debt/Worth		
12.2	−22.0	5.0	15.8					
	40.7	42.2	76.5					
(15) 11.9	(29) 30.6	(22) 29.4				% Profit Before Taxes/Tangible Net Worth		
	−4.4	3.6	7.2					
21.9	11.6	16.0	14.4					
13.9	1.8	6.5	6.2			% Profit Before Taxes/Total Assets		
−2.2	−10.8	1.2	1.6					
UND	127.2	231.0	49.6					
958.5	42.4	84.9	31.2			Sales/Net Fixed Assets		
130.8	18.5	25.3	8.6					
9.2	7.4	6.1	3.3					
5.7	4.0	3.4	2.3			Sales/Total Assets		
3.3	2.6	2.5	1.9					
	.4	.2	.7					
(16) .7	(24) .6	(21) 1.0				% Depr., Dep., Amort./Sales		
	1.1	1.0	1.9					
	2.1	1.5						
(11) 5.1	(12) 3.1					% Officers', Directors', Owners' Comp/Sales		
	11.8	10.2						
24088M	134898M	664980M	1629808M	196743M	648121M	Net Sales ($)		
3270M	26367M	149510M	617443M	63225M	625616M	Total Assets ($)		

M = $ thousand   MM = $ million
See Pages 11 through 21 for Explanation of Ratios and Data

Comparative Historical Data | Current Data Sorted By Sales

			Type of Statement						
	7	19	Unqualified		2	2		1	14
	9	21	Reviewed	1		1	4	3	12
1	6	18	Compiled	1	1	4	4	5	3
2	2	13	Tax Returns		8	1	3		1
	7	23	Other		1	2	5	4	11
					22 (4/1-9/30/04)		72 (10/1/04-3/31/05)		
4/1/02-3/31/03	4/1/03-3/31/04	4/1/04-3/31/05		0-1MM	1-3MM	3-5MM	5-10MM	10-25MM	25MM & OVER
ALL	ALL	ALL							
3	31	94	NUMBER OF STATEMENTS	2	12	10	16	13	41
%	%	%	ASSETS	%	%	%	%	%	%
	8.2	11.1	Cash & Equivalents		27.5	10.8	19.0	5.8	5.3
	34.6	36.2	Trade Receivables (net)		30.0	43.4	44.7	31.1	33.5
	27.0	28.3	Inventory		28.1	21.1	16.5	37.5	33.1
	2.5	1.6	All Other Current		1.8	1.4	2.5	1.2	1.5
	72.3	77.2	Total Current		87.4	76.7	82.7	75.6	73.5
	17.0	12.0	Fixed Assets (net)		4.2	13.0	12.0	17.0	12.4
	1.5	4.1	Intangibles (net)		.9	3.3	2.3	.5	6.3
	9.2	6.7	All Other Non-Current		7.6	7.0	3.1	6.9	7.8
	100.0	100.0	Total		100.0	100.0	100.0	100.0	100.0
			LIABILITIES						
	19.4	22.4	Notes Payable-Short Term		15.6	19.4	13.2	19.1	28.8
	2.0	2.2	Cur. Mat.-L/T/D		.0	2.1	3.3	1.7	2.5
	24.3	22.3	Trade Payables		22.1	29.3	21.6	23.7	20.6
	.6	.4	Income Taxes Payable		.4	.1	.3	.0	.7
	7.8	8.6	All Other Current		4.7	4.8	19.4	6.7	7.1
	54.1	56.0	Total Current		42.9	55.7	57.7	51.2	59.7
	11.2	9.7	Long-Term Debt		16.2	4.0	5.8	12.1	10.4
	.2	.4	Deferred Taxes		.2	.4	.2	.1	.7
	6.5	5.5	All Other Non-Current		17.8	3.4	1.2	5.0	4.5
	28.0	28.4	Net Worth		23.0	36.6	35.1	31.6	24.7
	100.0	100.0	Total Liabilities & Net Worth		100.0	100.0	100.0	100.0	100.0
			INCOME DATA						
	100.0	100.0	Net Sales		100.0	100.0	100.0	100.0	100.0
	28.6	26.1	Gross Profit		32.2	35.1	33.0	20.9	22.0
	26.7	22.8	Operating Expenses		31.8	32.5	27.0	19.2	17.9
	2.0	3.3	Operating Profit		.4	2.6	6.0	1.7	4.1
	.4	.5	All Other Expenses (net)		1.3	−.8	.4	.5	.6
	1.5	2.8	Profit Before Taxes		−.9	3.4	5.6	1.3	3.5
			RATIOS						
	1.7	1.9			10.3	5.3	2.8	1.9	1.5
	1.4	1.3	Current		2.6	1.2	1.5	1.4	1.2
	1.1	1.1			1.5	1.0	1.1	1.1	1.1
	1.1	1.2			7.2	4.6	2.2	1.0	1.1
	.8	.8	Quick		1.2	.8	1.3	.7	.6
	.4	.5			.7	.6	.8	.5	.4
22 16.9	21 17.7			0 UND	35 10.3	22 16.3	14 25.7	22 16.6	
33 11.2	33 11.2	Sales/Receivables		23 15.7	48 7.6	32 11.2	29 12.5	33 11.1	
46 7.9	50 7.3			46 8.0	84 4.3	56 6.5	40 9.2	49 7.5	
6 58.5	6 64.6			4 99.4	13 27.3	0 UND	13 29.1	17 21.6	
39 9.4	33 10.9	Cost of Sales/Inventory		26 14.0	35 10.5	5 69.7	42 8.6	55 6.6	
89 4.1	83 4.4			74 4.9	60 6.1	65 5.6	80 4.5	98 3.7	
20 18.4	9 38.7			0 UND	30 12.2	0 UND	7 54.7	13 27.1	
31 11.9	29 12.5	Cost of Sales/Payables		21 17.3	42 8.8	11 33.0	44 8.3	28 13.1	
54 6.8	44 8.4			53 6.9	58 6.2	50 7.3	52 7.0	36 10.2	
	8.1	7.3			6.3	3.8	6.4	10.1	10.1
	21.0	20.1	Sales/Working Capital		10.0	14.9	12.3	18.9	26.8
	59.4	102.8			17.1	NM	152.6	52.0	149.3
	5.4	12.7					90.8	13.9	10.6
(28) 2.0	(84) 3.8	EBIT/Interest			(14) 5.8	9.3	(39) 3.9		
	1.5	1.1					−1.6	1.2	1.9
		5.3	Net Profit + Depr., Dep.,						12.8
	(23) 2.6	Amort./Cur. Mat. L/T/D						(12) 4.3	
		1.0							2.1
	.2	.1			.0	.1	.1	.1	.1
	.5	.3	Fixed/Worth		.1	.2	.3	.3	.7
	2.3	1.1			−1.9	NM	1.0	.8	1.2
	1.5	1.4			.3	.7	.6	1.4	2.6
	2.9	3.5	Debt/Worth		5.5	4.0	1.7	2.4	3.8
	7.8	13.6			−11.5	NM	123.9	4.4	14.2
	31.4	53.6					100.4	36.4	56.3
(27) 15.3	(80) 28.6	% Profit Before Taxes/Tangible Net Worth			(14) 24.6	21.8	(37) 30.6		
	6.3	5.9					3.0	2.4	8.1
	9.4	15.4			20.8	7.4	24.0	14.6	13.4
	2.9	5.8	% Profit Before Taxes/Total Assets		12.8	2.8	11.8	4.9	5.8
	1.4	.8			−10.6	−1.8	1.4	.5	1.7
	89.8	182.5			UND	74.9	147.0	164.8	100.7
	28.8	47.4	Sales/Net Fixed Assets		412.8	31.6	94.8	29.0	41.3
	10.7	17.3			39.1	9.7	14.3	21.4	15.9
	4.7	5.7			6.0	3.3	7.1	6.4	5.3
	3.2	3.1	Sales/Total Assets		4.9	2.7	3.5	3.9	2.9
	2.3	2.3			2.7	1.9	2.2	3.0	2.1
	.3	.4					.2	.2	.5
(26) 1.0	(70) .8	% Depr., Dep., Amort./Sales			(13) .4	(11) .4	(32) .9		
	2.6	1.4					1.3	.9	1.3
	2.3	1.4							.8
(13) 2.9	(32) 3.1	% Officers', Directors', Owners' Comp/Sales					(11) 1.6		
	8.8	8.8							2.6
11079M	658740M	3298638M	Net Sales ($)	1665M	21405M	40912M	113454M	174873M	2946329M
4181M	239422M	1485431M	Total Assets ($)	571M	5654M	29617M	36745M	44976M	1367868M

© RMA 2005

M = $ thousand   MM = $ million
See Pages 11 through 21 for Explanation of Ratios and Data

RETAIL TRADE

Current Data Sorted By Assets   Comparative Historical Data

						Type of Statement		
	1	33	92	20	10	Unqualified	147	143
1	8	192	160	8	2	Reviewed	385	366
1	37	69	40	2	1	Compiled	201	247
10	49	167	38	1		Tax Returns	161	182
15	103	1297	845	39	8	Other	1209	1135
	164 (4/1-9/30/04)		3085 (10/1/04-3/31/05)				4/1/00-3/31/01	4/1/01-3/31/02
0-500M	500M-2MM	2-10MM	10-50MM	50-100MM	100-250MM		ALL	ALL
27	198	1758	1175	70	21	NUMBER OF STATEMENTS	2103	2073
%	%	%	%	%	%	ASSETS	%	%
10.2	9.3	9.5	11.7	10.5	8.8	Cash & Equivalents	7.2	9.0
6.7	7.6	5.6	5.6	10.9	8.0	Trade Receivables (net)	8.2	8.7
66.8	66.1	68.5	60.2	50.8	46.8	Inventory	66.7	62.1
3.8	2.1	3.2	3.9	3.3	2.8	All Other Current	2.9	3.1
87.5	85.2	86.8	81.5	75.5	66.5	Total Current	84.9	82.8
9.3	9.5	7.1	9.3	13.9	18.7	Fixed Assets (net)	8.9	10.4
1.9	1.2	2.8	4.3	2.9	5.3	Intangibles (net)	1.4	1.8
.9	4.1	3.3	4.8	7.7	9.5	All Other Non-Current	4.7	5.0
100.0	100.0	100.0	100.0	100.0	100.0	Total	100.0	100.0
						LIABILITIES		
37.1	46.8	57.1	54.4	47.5	33.2	Notes Payable-Short Term	56.2	51.3
8.0	2.2	1.6	1.4	3.1	4.4	Cur. Mat.-L/T/D	2.2	1.8
1.6	6.7	3.9	3.8	4.4	6.8	Trade Payables	4.5	4.8
.0	.1	.1	.2	.1	.2	Income Taxes Payable	.1	.2
35.1	11.7	12.4	12.1	9.7	19.2	All Other Current	9.1	10.3
81.8	67.4	75.2	71.8	64.8	63.8	Total Current	72.2	68.4
6.8	7.8	4.6	6.0	11.6	14.1	Long-Term Debt	7.0	7.7
.0	.2	.0	.1	.4	.1	Deferred Taxes	.1	.1
11.9	7.1	2.9	2.6	1.3	1.5	All Other Non-Current	2.1	2.7
−1.2	17.5	17.3	19.5	21.8	20.4	Net Worth	18.5	21.1
100.0	100.0	100.0	100.0	100.0	100.0	Total Liabilities & Net Worth	100.0	100.0
						INCOME DATA		
100.0	100.0	100.0	100.0	100.0	100.0	Net Sales	100.0	100.0
14.9	16.7	12.5	12.5	12.9	14.4	Gross Profit	12.5	12.9
14.0	17.3	12.5	11.8	11.4	12.5	Operating Expenses	11.5	11.8
.9	−.6	.0	.7	1.5	1.9	Operating Profit	1.0	1.1
.3	−.3	−.6	−.6	−.6	−.1	All Other Expenses (net)	.1	−.1
.7	−.3	.6	1.3	2.1	2.0	Profit Before Taxes	.9	1.2
						RATIOS		
1.7	1.6	1.3	1.2	1.3	1.2		1.3	1.4
1.2	1.2	1.1	1.1	1.1	1.1	Current	1.2	1.2
1.0	1.0	1.0	1.0	1.0	.9		1.0	1.1
.5	.4	.3	.3	.4	.4		.3	.4
.3 (194)	.2 (1755)	.2 (1174)	.2	.3	.3	Quick	.2 (2092)	.2 (2066)
.1	.1	.1	.1	.2	.2		.1	.1
0 UND	1 292.7	1 309.4	1 287.9	3 120.6	8 48.1		3 137.2	3 135.7
0 999.8	3 109.5	4 102.1	4 91.7	9 41.1	10 37.0	Sales/Receivables	5 68.3	5 69.0
10 37.0	8 43.1	7 51.8	8 43.5	21 17.7	15 25.1		9 38.9	10 38.0
38 9.6	52 7.0	58 6.3	55 6.6	56 6.5	62 5.9		52 7.1	43 8.4
71 5.1	76 4.8	78 4.7	71 5.1	69 5.3	71 5.1	Cost of Sales/Inventory	66 5.5	58 6.3
110 3.3	106 3.4	101 3.6	89 4.1	83 4.4	80 4.6		82 4.4	75 4.9
0 UND	1 260.7	1 248.3	2 212.9	3 135.5	4 85.1		2 232.3	2 242.9
0 UND	4 95.0	3 136.1	3 122.1	4 98.2	6 61.1	Cost of Sales/Payables	3 138.9	3 138.5
3 113.4	11 34.1	5 76.8	5 74.1	6 59.1	8 43.7		5 77.2	5 75.6
7.8	11.7	19.4	22.3	19.3	25.0		20.0	18.9
29.4	28.6	35.0	39.8	42.1	57.0	Sales/Working Capital	37.4	33.5
UND	180.6	122.3	128.9	177.8	−78.0		136.3	101.5
15.6	3.9	5.0	7.8	11.3	15.2		3.6	5.2
(15) 4.7	(161) 1.5	(1390) 1.8	(927) 2.9	(58) 4.7	(17) 3.4	EBIT/Interest	(1915) 1.8	(1813) 2.4
.8	−.8	.7	1.4	2.8	1.4		1.0	1.3
		5.3	10.7	22.6		Net Profit + Depr., Dep.,	5.5	5.3
		(63) 1.8	(101) 2.3	(18) 3.6		Amort./Cur. Mat. L /T/D	(207) 2.3	(196) 2.0
		.7	.9	1.7			.9	.9
.0	.1	.1	.2	.2	.4		.2	.2
.3	.4	.4	.5	.7	1.5	Fixed/Worth	.4	.4
UND	7.2	1.1	1.3	1.5	2.9		1.2	1.1
1.8	1.9	3.2	3.3	2.7	3.5		2.9	2.4
6.3	6.0	6.0	6.2	4.6	5.8	Debt/Worth	5.4	4.5
−57.0	81.9	16.0	13.1	8.4	16.3		12.1	10.1
931.8	33.1	36.1	52.2	48.3	46.8	% Profit Before Taxes/Tangible	40.6	48.0
(20) 29.0	(156) 9.8	(1517) 13.3	(1073) 26.3	(66) 26.7	(18) 22.1	Net Worth	(1900) 17.6	(1884) 24.0
.0	−13.7	.1	9.3	14.1	10.6		3.2	8.3
7.1	5.9	5.9	7.8	8.4	5.6	% Profit Before Taxes/Total	6.7	9.4
.0	1.0	1.8	3.7	4.8	2.2	Assets	2.6	4.2
−1.4	−3.9	−.5	.9	2.8	1.1		.2	1.1
UND	258.4	183.3	131.2	79.6	60.4		162.4	150.6
127.9	79.2	84.3	64.1	33.4	19.0	Sales/Net Fixed Assets	77.7	75.6
37.0	35.6	42.1	29.6	12.9	8.3		36.6	34.4
6.3	5.2	4.6	4.3	3.9	3.7		5.1	5.6
4.0	3.8	3.7	3.5	3.1	2.5	Sales/Total Assets	4.2	4.4
2.8	2.7	3.0	2.9	2.4	2.1		3.4	3.5
.2	.1	.1	.1	.2	.3		.1	.1
(11) .8	(138) .3	(1489) .2	(1077) .2	(65) .4	(16) .4	% Depr., Dep., Amort./Sales	(1828) .2	(1849) .2
1.8	.6	.4	.4	.7	.6		.4	.4
	.6	.3	.2	.2		% Officers', Directors',	.3	.3
	(118) 1.2	(1171) .6	(764) .4	(30) .4		Owners' Comp/Sales	(1281) .6	(1267) .6
	2.4	1.0	.8	.6			1.1	1.1
30538M	1058297M	40035309M	82171814M	15951211M	8701113M	Net Sales ($)	82391859M	84318247M
5026M	251015M	10169685M	22774602M	4641131M	3209382M	Total Assets ($)	20994435M	20152169M

© RMA 2005

M = $ thousand   MM = $ million
See Pages 11 through 21 for Explanation of Ratios and Data

Comparative Historical Data   Current Data Sorted By Sales

Hist 1	Hist 2	Hist 3	Type of Statement	0-1MM	1-3MM	3-5MM	5-10MM	10-25MM	25MM & OVER
172	150	156	Unqualified	1	1	1	3	25	126
444	413	371	Reviewed	1	2	4	22	95	247
218	191	150	Compiled	1	14	16	18	36	65
252	251	265	Tax Returns	6	15	20	38	98	88
1340	1646	2307	Other	21	27	41	197	684	1337
4/1/02-3/31/03 ALL	4/1/03-3/31/04 ALL	4/1/04-3/31/05 ALL		164 (4/1-9/30/04)			3085 (10/1/04-3/31/05)		
2426	2651	3249	NUMBER OF STATEMENTS	29	59	82	278	938	1863
%	%	%	ASSETS	%	%	%	%	%	%
9.3	9.4	10.3	Cash & Equivalents	7.7	10.2	8.6	8.8	8.8	11.4
8.1	7.8	5.9	Trade Receivables (net)	6.0	11.1	5.4	6.0	5.2	6.0
63.2	64.1	64.8	Inventory	57.1	55.6	67.8	68.1	69.2	62.4
2.7	2.8	3.4	All Other Current	4.0	2.2	2.6	2.8	3.0	3.8
83.3	84.2	84.4	Total Current	74.8	79.1	84.4	85.6	86.2	83.6
10.2	9.5	8.3	Fixed Assets (net)	17.9	14.4	9.6	8.1	7.2	8.4
1.5	1.6	3.3	Intangibles (net)	3.7	1.7	1.9	2.7	2.9	3.7
5.0	4.8	4.0	All Other Non-Current	3.3	4.8	4.0	3.6	3.7	4.3
100.0	100.0	100.0	Total	100.0	100.0	100.0	100.0	100.0	100.0
			LIABILITIES						
52.3	51.9	54.9	Notes Payable-Short Term	42.6	40.8	43.4	54.1	56.8	55.3
2.3	1.8	1.7	Cur. Mat.-L/T/D	4.2	3.8	3.5	1.4	2.0	1.3
4.4	5.1	4.0	Trade Payables	3.3	4.5	4.8	5.6	3.9	3.8
.1	.2	.1	Income Taxes Payable	.0	.1	.1	.1	.2	.1
10.5	12.2	12.5	All Other Current	23.8	15.4	15.5	10.8	11.8	12.6
69.6	71.1	73.3	Total Current	73.9	64.5	67.3	72.1	74.6	73.3
7.6	6.7	5.5	Long-Term Debt	13.6	7.4	7.8	7.2	5.3	5.1
.2	.1	.1	Deferred Taxes	.9	.0	.1	.1	.1	.1
2.7	3.1	3.1	All Other Non-Current	10.4	8.5	7.2	4.4	3.0	2.5
19.9	19.0	18.0	Net Worth	.6	19.7	17.7	16.2	17.0	19.1
100.0	100.0	100.0	Total Liabilities & Net Worth	100.0	100.0	100.0	100.0	100.0	100.0
			INCOME DATA						
100.0	100.0	100.0	Net Sales	100.0	100.0	100.0	100.0	100.0	100.0
12.9	13.1	12.8	Gross Profit	23.9	23.0	18.7	13.9	12.8	11.8
12.2	12.6	12.5	Operating Expenses	21.2	24.1	18.2	14.7	12.9	11.3
.7	.4	.3	Operating Profit	2.7	-1.1	.4	-.7	-.1	.6
-.5	-.6	-.6	All Other Expenses (net)	.1	.1	-.4	-.5	-.7	-.6
1.2	1.0	.8	Profit Before Taxes	2.6	-1.2	.8	-.3	.5	1.2
			RATIOS						
1.3	1.3	1.3		1.4	1.9	1.5	1.4	1.3	1.3
1.2	1.2	1.1	Current	1.1	1.2	1.2	1.2	1.1	1.1
1.1	1.0	1.0		.9	.9	1.1	1.1	1.0	1.0
.3	.3	.3		.4	.6	.4	.3	.3	.3
(2416) .2	(2649) .2	(3241) .2	Quick	.2	.2	(80) .2	(277) .1	(935) .2	(1861) .2
.1	.1	.1		.1	.1	.1	.1	.1	.1
3 121.4	3 123.7	1 295.5		0 UND	1 544.0	2 202.5	1 302.1	1 251.4	1 309.3
6 64.4	6 63.5	4 97.4	Sales/Receivables	7 51.0	6 64.2	4 86.7	3 115.6	4 91.5	4 100.8
10 36.9	10 35.5	8 46.9		15 24.1	25 14.7	13 28.9	8 47.0	8 48.6	8 47.1
51 7.2	56 6.5	57 6.4		44 8.3	52 7.0	66 5.5	75 4.9	66 5.5	52 7.1
67 5.5	73 5.0	75 4.9	Cost of Sales/Inventory	86 4.3	118 3.1	91 4.0	100 3.7	86 4.3	67 5.5
86 4.3	91 4.0	95 3.8		217 1.7	153 2.4	155 2.4	129 2.8	106 3.4	83 4.4
2 232.9	2 210.8	2 232.8		0 UND	1 264.3	1 286.2	2 212.3	2 229.5	2 233.0
3 128.8	3 122.8	3 127.7	Cost of Sales/Payables	0 UND	5 67.0	5 79.8	3 105.0	3 125.9	3 133.8
5 71.9	5 70.6	5 72.6		9 41.5	19 19.2	11 34.1	7 48.8	5 69.6	4 81.1
18.4	17.4	19.7		4.7	5.0	7.1	11.7	18.1	23.5
32.9	31.2	36.6	Sales/Working Capital	26.9	14.0	20.4	22.8	33.8	41.8
97.6	101.7	128.0		-11.8	-31.5	67.1	89.5	123.0	132.3
8.3	7.8	6.1		7.3	4.7	5.7	3.1	3.7	7.9
(1801) 3.0	(1861) 2.9	(2568) 2.3	EBIT/Interest	(17) 1.5	(48) .7	(66) 1.5	(223) 1.1	(754) 1.6	(1460) 3.0
1.3	1.1	1.0		-2.0	-3.0	.7	-.7	.5	1.4
5.6	5.1	7.2					1.0	4.3	11.4
(267) 2.0	(221) 2.0	(199) 2.3	Net Profit + Depr., Dep., Amort./Cur. Mat. L/T/D				(12) .4	(30) 1.7	(151) 2.6
.8	.8	.9					-1.4	.7	1.0
.2	.2	.2		.2	.0	.1	.2	.2	.2
.4	.4	.4	Fixed/Worth	3.1	.5	.3	.5	.4	.5
1.3	1.2	1.3		-5.5	4.8	3.4	3.1	1.2	1.2
2.6	2.8	3.2		2.6	1.3	1.9	3.1	3.2	3.2
5.0	5.2	5.2	Debt/Worth	17.7	6.0	4.6	6.5	6.7	5.8
11.5	11.0	14.7		-18.6	24.0	30.4	37.0	15.8	12.8
43.7	41.9	43.6		931.8	30.6	28.9	23.6	30.4	51.7
(2213) 22.0	(2405) 19.8	(2850) 19.0	% Profit Before Taxes/Tangible Net Worth	(20) 19.0	(48) 4.5	(67) 9.9	(224) 5.7	(804) 10.3	(1687) 26.2
6.1	4.9	2.7		.0	-31.0	-1.8	-13.5	-2.0	8.8
7.7	6.9	6.7		5.7	5.9	6.2	3.5	4.9	8.2
3.7	3.0	2.7	% Profit Before Taxes/Total Assets	.0	.2	1.4	.5	1.4	3.7
.7	.4	.0		-3.3	-10.2	-1.3	-3.7	-.8	.8
139.2	138.4	160.0		UND	125.7	242.1	163.7	164.6	157.7
69.2	66.3	75.5	Sales/Net Fixed Assets	37.0	65.9	59.3	59.9	74.3	78.3
29.8	31.7	36.1		3.4	11.9	22.8	29.5	40.2	37.4
4.8	4.5	4.5		4.0	3.1	4.5	3.8	4.2	4.7
4.0	3.7	3.6	Sales/Total Assets	2.6	1.9	3.0	2.9	3.4	3.9
3.2	3.0	2.9		.5	1.0	1.9	2.3	2.8	3.2
.1	.1	.1		1.0	.3	.2	.1	.1	.1
(2165) .3	(2313) .3	(2796) .2	% Depr., Dep., Amort./Sales	(12) 3.0	(32) .5	(63) .3	(202) .3	(786) .2	(1701) .2
.4	.4	.4		15.0	2.1	.6	.6	.4	.4
.3	.3	.3			.9	.8	.5	.3	.2
(1447) .6	(1642) .5	(2097) .5	% Officers', Directors', Owners' Comp/Sales		(29) 2.0	(42) 1.4	(166) .8	(631) .6	(1224) .4
1.2	1.1	1.0			4.6	2.3	1.5	1.0	.8
110677099M	120083741M	147948282M	Net Sales ($)	11385M	116980M	322355M	2105173M	16188769M	129203620M
29006137M	33325223M	41050841M	Total Assets ($)	31681M	81068M	152200M	879576M	5308480M	34597836M

M = $ thousand   MM = $ million
See Pages 11 through 21 for Explanation of Ratios and Data

Current Data Sorted By Assets   Comparative Historical Data

	1	3	4	5		2	Type of Statement	9	16
	1	8	16	3			Unqualified	31	32
	42	70	22	1		1	Reviewed	152	129
	102	101	34	1		2	Compiled	109	145
	17	68	54	11		1	Tax Returns	100	115
							Other		

Unqualified: 1 / 3 / 4 / 5 / — / 2 → Historical 9 / 16
Reviewed: 1 / 8 / 16 / 3 / — / — → Historical 31 / 32
Compiled: 42 / 70 / 22 / 1 / — / 1 → Historical 152 / 129
Tax Returns: 102 / 101 / 34 / 1 / — / 2 → Historical 109 / 145
Other: 17 / 68 / 54 / 11 / — / 1 → Historical 100 / 115

	0-500M	500M-2MM	2-10MM	10-50MM	50-100MM	100-250MM		4/1/00-3/31/01 ALL	4/1/01-3/31/02 ALL
		66 (4/1-9/30/04)		504 (10/1/04-3/31/05)			NUMBER OF STATEMENTS		
	163	250	130	21		6		401	437
ASSETS	%	%	%	%	%	%		%	%
Cash & Equivalents	11.7	8.8	7.3	4.5	D			7.4	6.5
Trade Receivables (net)	7.0	10.1	15.2	32.8	A			11.6	12.0
Inventory	65.5	62.7	55.5	36.4	T			61.7	63.3
All Other Current	1.4	2.0	3.7	1.7	A			3.1	2.3
Total Current	85.7	83.7	81.7	75.5				83.8	84.1
Fixed Assets (net)	11.2	9.4	11.2	5.8	N			11.6	10.8
Intangibles (net)	.8	.9	1.0	1.2	O			1.0	.7
All Other Non-Current	2.2	6.0	6.1	17.4	T			3.6	4.4
Total	100.0	100.0	100.0	100.0				100.0	100.0
LIABILITIES					A				
Notes Payable-Short Term	39.1	39.6	43.1	42.5	V			39.7	41.2
Cur. Mat.-L/T/D	2.7	2.9	1.2	2.2	A			3.3	3.8
Trade Payables	3.8	5.4	6.5	3.0	I			6.1	5.8
Income Taxes Payable	.1	.1	.2	.2	L			.1	.2
All Other Current	14.5	10.9	8.9	10.7	A			10.0	9.7
Total Current	60.2	58.9	59.9	58.7	B			59.3	60.6
Long-Term Debt	19.6	7.9	8.6	11.1	L			11.8	11.8
Deferred Taxes	.0	.0	.0	.1	E			.0	.0
All Other Non-Current	10.8	6.2	5.7	3.4				5.7	7.6
Net Worth	9.5	27.0	25.9	26.7				23.1	20.0
Total Liabilities & Net Worth	100.0	100.0	100.0	100.0				100.0	100.0
INCOME DATA									
Net Sales	100.0	100.0	100.0	100.0				100.0	100.0
Gross Profit	20.2	16.8	19.3	25.6				18.7	17.9
Operating Expenses	18.9	15.1	17.6	20.0				16.2	15.5
Operating Profit	1.3	1.8	1.7	5.6				2.5	2.4
All Other Expenses (net)	.5	.3	.1	1.7				.6	.9
Profit Before Taxes	.8	1.5	1.7	3.9				1.9	1.5
RATIOS									
Current	3.3 / 1.5 / 1.0	2.2 / 1.4 / 1.1	1.8 / 1.3 / 1.1	1.8 / 1.3 / 1.2				2.0 / 1.3 / 1.1	2.1 / 1.3 / 1.1
Quick	.9 / .3 / .1 (159)	.6 / .2 / .1 (247)	.7 / .2 / .1 (129)	1.4 / .4 / .2				.6 / .2 / .1 (396)	.6 / .2 / .1 (432)
Sales/Receivables	0 UND / 0 UND / 5 79.5	0 UND / 2 228.5 / 9 40.7	1 521.7 / 4 96.7 / 15 23.7	2 186.1 / 20 18.6 / 214 1.7				0 UND / 2 194.8 / 9 40.1	0 UND / 2 213.5 / 10 37.1
Cost of Sales/Inventory	36 10.1 / 61 5.9 / 91 4.0	40 9.1 / 61 6.0 / 85 4.3	44 8.4 / 60 6.1 / 87 4.2	30 12.3 / 53 6.9 / 66 5.5				36 10.1 / 56 6.5 / 83 4.4	36 10.2 / 56 6.6 / 83 4.4
Cost of Sales/Payables	0 UND / 0 999.8 / 4 86.7	0 UND / 2 195.2 / 6 60.3	1 277.4 / 3 106.5 / 9 40.6	2 202.4 / 6 58.6 / 8 44.3				0 UND / 2 193.7 / 7 50.5	0 UND / 2 163.4 / 7 55.3
Sales/Working Capital	8.7 / 23.4 / 203.2	8.3 / 20.7 / 70.0	8.6 / 18.8 / 47.5	3.8 / 22.7 / 29.6				9.7 / 25.0 / 107.2	10.0 / 24.3 / 115.2
EBIT/Interest	4.9 / 1.6 / -.8 (124)	5.3 / 2.5 / 1.1 (215)	6.2 / 2.4 / 1.0 (114)	9.9 / 2.5 / 1.6 (18)				3.8 / 1.9 / 1.1 (376)	4.0 / 2.1 / 1.2 (412)
Net Profit + Depr., Dep., Amort./Cur. Mat. L /T/D								7.2 / 2.3 / .5 (24)	8.0 / 1.8 / 1.0 (24)
Fixed/Worth	.0 / .3 / -19.0	.0 / .2 / 1.0	.1 / .3 / .9	.0 / .2 / .3				.1 / .3 / 1.2	.0 / .3 / 1.2
Debt/Worth	1.5 / 6.9 / -23.4	1.1 / 3.2 / 8.5	1.6 / 3.4 / 7.5	1.3 / 3.9 / 6.0				1.6 / 3.8 / 12.8	1.6 / 4.3 / 14.7
% Profit Before Taxes/Tangible Net Worth	77.6 / 29.7 / -2.2 (112)	48.7 / 19.7 / 3.9 (218)	38.5 / 15.0 / 3.7 (119)	45.1 / 26.4 / 7.6 (19)				66.3 / 26.9 / 6.9 (345)	64.6 / 27.9 / 7.4 (371)
% Profit Before Taxes/Total Assets	18.4 / 4.0 / -4.4	12.3 / 5.1 / .4	9.6 / 3.1 / .4	11.3 / 4.3 / 2.0				13.2 / 5.5 / .4	12.9 / 5.4 / .9
Sales/Net Fixed Assets	UND / 148.5 / 38.0	745.9 / 118.0 / 39.2	223.2 / 63.5 / 26.6	332.8 / 90.4 / 21.6				479.3 / 99.1 / 30.9	560.7 / 96.8 / 31.9
Sales/Total Assets	7.5 / 5.1 / 2.8	6.3 / 4.5 / 3.1	5.0 / 3.7 / 2.3	4.8 / 1.4 / 1.0				6.9 / 4.6 / 2.9	6.8 / 4.8 / 3.0
% Depr., Dep., Amort./Sales	.2 / .3 / 1.0 (89)	.1 / .2 / .5 (152)	.1 / .3 / .6 (99)	.1 / .4 / .5 (16)				.1 / .2 / .6 (272)	.1 / .3 / .7 (299)
% Officers', Directors', Owners' Comp/Sales	1.3 / 2.4 / 4.1 (93)	.7 / 1.5 / 2.7 (136)	.6 / 1.2 / 2.3 (84)					.9 / 1.9 / 3.8 (222)	1.0 / 1.8 / 3.6 (246)
Net Sales ($)	260121M	1421692M	2007579M	887422M		3028462M		3285217M	3618290M
Total Assets ($)	44352M	273687M	528864M	361217M		944109M		1018780M	1004302M

M = $ thousand   MM = $ million
See Pages 11 through 21 for Explanation of Ratios and Data

Comparative Historical Data

Current Data Sorted By Sales

18	11	15	Type of Statement						
						66 (4/1-9/30/04)		504 (10/1/04-3/31/05)	
18	11	15	Unqualified		2	2	4	3	6
45	27	28	Reviewed		4	2	9	11	2
152	136	136	Compiled	22	42	26	22	17	7
177	200	240	Tax Returns	41	83	41	37	29	9
111	126	151	Other	9	27	20	42	36	17
4/1/02-3/31/03 ALL	4/1/03-3/31/04 ALL	4/1/04-3/31/05 ALL		0-1MM	1-3MM	3-5MM	5-10MM	10-25MM	25MM & OVER
503	500	570	NUMBER OF STATEMENTS	72	158	89	114	96	41
%	%	%	ASSETS	%	%	%	%	%	%
7.7	7.7	9.1	Cash & Equivalents	10.3	9.3	9.9	9.6	8.1	4.9
11.2	10.3	11.3	Trade Receivables (net)	11.1	11.7	8.7	11.0	12.3	14.3
63.2	63.1	60.9	Inventory	56.2	60.4	62.0	61.7	61.6	64.6
2.5	2.3	2.2	All Other Current	2.7	2.1	1.5	1.6	3.4	2.1
84.5	83.4	83.4	Total Current	80.3	83.5	82.0	83.9	85.3	85.9
10.6	10.8	10.2	Fixed Assets (net)	15.0	10.5	10.2	9.7	8.2	6.2
.8	.9	.9	Intangibles (net)	1.3	.6	1.7	.8	.5	.7
4.1	4.8	5.5	All Other Non-Current	3.4	5.4	6.1	5.6	6.0	7.2
100.0	100.0	100.0	Total	100.0	100.0	100.0	100.0	100.0	100.0
			LIABILITIES						
40.7	39.0	40.5	Notes Payable-Short Term	30.8	37.8	41.5	40.4	49.4	44.7
3.2	3.0	2.4	Cur. Mat.-L/T/D	4.5	2.7	2.0	1.9	1.9	1.1
5.1	4.7	5.0	Trade Payables	3.6	3.7	3.6	6.4	6.9	7.7
.1	.1	.1	Income Taxes Payable	.0	.1	.1	.2	.1	.3
9.5	11.0	11.4	All Other Current	12.8	12.5	12.7	10.3	9.8	7.9
58.7	57.8	59.4	Total Current	51.8	56.9	59.9	59.2	68.1	61.6
11.0	11.1	11.8	Long-Term Debt	24.2	15.0	9.6	6.3	6.9	8.6
.0	.0	.0	Deferred Taxes	.0	.0	.0	.0	.0	.1
8.1	7.4	7.5	All Other Non-Current	18.1	6.5	5.7	5.5	5.5	7.3
22.2	23.6	21.3	Net Worth	5.9	21.6	24.8	29.1	19.5	22.4
100.0	100.0	100.0	Total Liabilities & Net Worth	100.0	100.0	100.0	100.0	100.0	100.0
			INCOME DATA						
100.0	100.0	100.0	Net Sales	100.0	100.0	100.0	100.0	100.0	100.0
19.0	17.8	18.8	Gross Profit	26.3	21.3	17.5	16.9	14.2	15.4
16.5	15.9	17.1	Operating Expenses	25.5	19.2	15.3	14.6	13.1	14.2
2.5	1.8	1.8	Operating Profit	.9	2.1	2.2	2.3	1.1	1.2
.8	.5	.3	All Other Expenses (net)	.7	.4	.1	.7	.0	-.3
1.7	1.3	1.4	Profit Before Taxes	.1	1.7	2.1	1.5	1.1	1.5
			RATIOS						
2.3	2.4	2.2		4.9	2.8	2.3	2.2	1.6	1.6
1.3	1.3	1.4	Current	1.6	1.5	1.4	1.4	1.2	1.3
1.1	1.1	1.1		1.0	1.1	1.1	1.1	1.0	1.2
.6	.6	.7		1.5	.8	.6	.7	.4	.4
(494) .2	(492) .2	(562) .2	Quick	(70) .3	(157) .3	(87) .2	(112) .3	(95) .2	.2
.1	.1	.1		.1	.1	.1	.1	.1	.1
0 UND	0 UND	0 UND		0 UND	0 UND	0 UND	0 UND	0 999.8	1 512.0
2 210.0	2 211.3	2 207.7	Sales/Receivables	0 827.0	1 313.4	1 330.1	2 175.4	3 120.5	4 101.5
10 38.3	9 41.9	10 38.4		10 35.3	13 27.9	7 54.1	9 41.7	8 43.6	14 25.4
38 9.7	40 9.1	39 9.3		41 8.8	45 8.1	39 9.3	36 10.1	29 12.6	42 8.6
62 5.9	60 6.1	60 6.1	Cost of Sales/Inventory	81 4.5	71 5.1	54 6.7	56 6.5	49 7.4	58 6.3
91 4.0	89 4.1	87 4.2		160 2.3	95 3.8	76 4.8	76 4.8	69 5.3	64 5.7
0 UND	0 UND	0 UND		0 UND	0 UND	0 UND	1 645.2	1 596.6	2 209.8
2 229.3	2 211.4	2 194.4	Cost of Sales/Payables	1 379.0	1 362.4	1 330.6	3 105.1	2 164.2	4 90.0
6 62.3	6 63.5	7 55.6		6 57.6	6 63.0	4 82.6	7 49.2	7 51.4	8 44.3
8.2	9.4	8.3		4.2	6.5	8.5	9.2	16.3	14.4
22.0	23.3	21.5	Sales/Working Capital	10.6	16.2	22.2	24.3	31.6	25.5
77.8	101.1	72.5		UND	64.9	57.6	68.0	160.2	47.0
4.9	5.4	5.6		4.9	4.2	5.9	11.1	5.7	8.2
(448) 2.0	(425) 2.4	(476) 2.4	EBIT/Interest	(52) 1.1	(135) 2.0	(72) 2.8	(101) 2.3	(83) 2.5	(33) 4.9
1.0	1.1	.9		-1.8	.6	1.3	1.1	1.3	1.3
3.7	6.0	4.4	Net Profit + Depr., Dep.,						
(23) 2.1	(21) 1.9	(21) 1.6	Amort./Cur. Mat. L/T/D						
.3	.5	.3							
.0	.0	.0		.0	.0	.0	.0	.1	.1
.2	.3	.2	Fixed/Worth	.9	.2	.2	.2	.3	.2
1.2	1.9	1.4		-6.4	2.4	.8	.9	1.1	.4
1.4	1.4	1.3		1.2	1.3	1.1	1.1	2.2	1.6
3.9	3.9	3.6	Debt/Worth	6.3	3.5	3.1	3.1	4.3	3.8
15.8	15.4	17.1		-12.7	35.2	31.0	8.0	10.7	6.3
51.1	54.2	55.9	% Profit Before Taxes/Tangible	63.8	49.2	62.8	51.2	50.7	59.3
(421) 19.3	(410) 20.1	(472) 19.7	Net Worth	(50) 14.8	(125) 18.1	(73) 22.3	(102) 17.1	(83) 24.4	(39) 27.4
3.9	5.7	3.8		-6.2	.8	6.8	3.3	7.6	5.8
12.8	12.2	12.6	% Profit Before Taxes/Total	14.0	13.2	13.8	13.1	11.1	11.4
4.0	4.4	4.5	Assets	1.9	4.0	5.3	4.9	4.5	5.8
.1	.0	-.2		-8.6	-1.9	1.6	.6	1.1	.4
664.1	513.7	578.9		729.5	999.8	999.8	299.0	526.8	374.0
109.1	103.2	110.0	Sales/Net Fixed Assets	65.2	119.4	145.5	91.8	106.8	132.0
31.4	29.6	32.4		12.8	24.8	29.3	46.2	44.7	36.4
6.7	6.5	6.1		4.8	5.4	6.8	6.4	7.8	6.5
4.4	4.4	4.4	Sales/Total Assets	2.6	3.8	4.6	4.9	4.7	5.0
2.5	2.6	2.7		1.7	2.4	2.9	3.6	3.5	3.5
.1	.1	.1		.3	.1	.1	.1	.1	.1
(341) .3	(334) .3	(360) .3	% Depr., Dep., Amort./Sales	(40) .7	(92) .4	(54) .3	(76) .2	(64) .2	(34) .2
.7	.6	.6		2.2	.9	.6	.5	.5	.4
.9	.8	.8		2.2	1.2	1.1	.5	.6	.5
(286) 1.8	(271) 1.7	(325) 1.6	% Officers', Directors', Owners' Comp/Sales	(29) 3.4	(98) 2.4	(49) 1.9	(63) 1.3	(61) 1.1	(25) .8
3.7	2.9	2.9		8.8	3.6	3.2	2.1	1.6	1.7
3975706M	5984214M	7605276M	Net Sales ($)	40762M	309674M	362960M	798882M	1492296M	4600702M
1290717M	2047491M	2152229M	Total Assets ($)	18629M	114455M	108267M	238413M	369055M	1303410M

M = $ thousand   MM = $ million
See Pages 11 through 21 for Explanation of Ratios and Data

Current Data Sorted By Assets | Comparative Historical Data

0-500M	500M-2MM	2-10MM	10-50MM	50-100MM	100-250MM	Type of Statement	4/1/00-3/31/01 ALL	4/1/01-3/31/02 ALL
	2	3	1	1		Unqualified	5	4
	9	29	12			Reviewed	37	35
8	50	51	3			Compiled	168	174
7	38	36	1			Tax Returns	63	45
3	31	56	21	3	2	Other	231	95
62 (4/1-9/30/04)			305 (10/1/04-3/31/05)					
18	130	175	38	4	2	NUMBER OF STATEMENTS	504	353

0-500M	500M-2MM	2-10MM	10-50MM	50-100MM	100-250MM		ALL 504	ALL 353
%	%	%	%	%	%	ASSETS	%	%
8.8	8.6	6.1	7.0			Cash & Equivalents	5.6	7.2
2.8	3.1	2.8	3.4			Trade Receivables (net)	2.7	2.8
62.2	73.8	79.1	78.3			Inventory	76.5	75.8
.0	.4	.8	1.0			All Other Current	.5	.8
73.9	85.9	88.7	89.7			Total Current	85.3	86.5
17.7	11.1	8.1	6.8			Fixed Assets (net)	10.8	9.9
5.6	1.9	1.9	2.8			Intangibles (net)	2.8	2.3
2.9	1.1	1.3	.7			All Other Non-Current	1.1	1.3
100.0	100.0	100.0	100.0			Total	100.0	100.0
						LIABILITIES		
30.4	47.7	54.4	63.8			Notes Payable-Short Term	19.8	23.6
2.9	1.7	3.7	2.8			Cur. Mat.-L/T/D	1.9	1.8
7.0	6.7	5.5	7.7			Trade Payables	38.0	33.4
.0	.2	.1	.1			Income Taxes Payable	.1	.1
7.5	6.9	6.9	5.7			All Other Current	11.3	9.2
47.7	63.1	70.7	80.1			Total Current	71.1	68.1
13.9	8.9	5.9	2.7			Long-Term Debt	5.7	5.6
.1	.0	.0	.0			Deferred Taxes	.0	.0
5.0	3.3	3.3	1.8			All Other Non-Current	1.8	2.2
33.3	24.7	20.1	15.4			Net Worth	21.3	24.0
100.0	100.0	100.0	100.0			Total Liabilities & Net Worth	100.0	100.0
						INCOME DATA		
100.0	100.0	100.0	100.0			Net Sales	100.0	100.0
30.7	22.2	18.6	16.8			Gross Profit	19.3	19.3
26.6	20.3	16.3	14.3			Operating Expenses	15.8	16.2
4.1	1.9	2.3	2.5			Operating Profit	3.5	3.0
1.7	.8	.6	.6			All Other Expenses (net)	2.1	1.5
2.4	1.1	1.7	1.9			Profit Before Taxes	1.4	1.5
						RATIOS		
2.7	1.7	1.4	1.2				1.3	1.4
1.5	1.3	1.2	1.1			Current	1.2	1.2
1.2	1.1	1.1	1.1				1.1	1.1
.7	.3	.2	.2				.2	.2
.2	(129) .1	(174) .1	.1			Quick	(501) .1	(352) .1
.1	.0	.0	.1				.0	.0
0 UND	0 UND	0 999.8	1 540.9				0 999.8	0 999.8
0 UND	1 379.4	2 240.4	2 195.8			Sales/Receivables	1 271.0	2 230.6
7 53.9	4 101.4	4 94.8	5 68.7				4 84.3	4 85.7
48 7.6	106 3.5	109 3.3	115 3.2				99 3.7	95 3.9
112 3.3	143 2.6	137 2.7	136 2.7			Cost of Sales/Inventory	130 2.8	123 3.0
163 2.2	220 1.7	182 2.0	163 2.2				165 2.2	162 2.3
0 UND	0 UND	1 449.3	2 236.1				4 90.3	3 131.2
7 53.1	2 146.5	3 119.9	3 129.2			Cost of Sales/Payables	69 5.3	35 10.3
19 19.3	8 47.3	8 45.5	8 46.1				122 3.5	104 3.5
8.2	6.7	10.5	14.4				12.1	10.5
11.0	14.0	19.2	24.6			Sales/Working Capital	24.1	20.8
NM	31.5	32.8	56.2				67.0	40.6
8.9	3.2	4.3	3.5				2.1	2.4
(17) 1.9	(122) 1.8	(164) 1.9	(35) 2.6			EBIT/Interest	(480) 1.3	(342) 1.5
-.5	1.2	1.2	1.2				1.0	1.1
			21.9				5.7	6.8
		(18)	5.0			Net Profit + Depr., Dep., Amort./Cur. Mat. L/T/D	(68) 2.0	(43) 3.8
			2.4				.9	1.5
.1	.1	.1	.2				.1	.1
.5	.3	.3	.4			Fixed/Worth	.4	.3
6.6	1.2	.7	1.0				1.4	1.1
.7	1.9	3.0	4.4				2.5	2.2
2.2	3.4	5.1	6.9			Debt/Worth	5.3	4.5
19.8	14.8	10.6	16.4				13.6	8.9
82.9	33.8	38.3	44.1				38.0	42.3
(15) 19.1	(118) 9.7	(160) 18.6	(35) 29.8			% Profit Before Taxes/Tangible Net Worth	(457) 17.7	(325) 16.6
-21.3	2.2	6.4	9.1				4.2	4.8
28.3	6.1	7.8	6.2				6.2	6.8
7.8	2.2	2.9	4.0			% Profit Before Taxes/Total Assets	2.3	3.0
-6.7	.6	.9	.8				.4	.7
130.3	136.7	125.1	152.0				174.4	167.7
37.1	57.8	53.8	67.3			Sales/Net Fixed Assets	58.1	59.1
9.0	15.0	26.2	27.9				17.9	19.0
4.7	3.2	3.3	2.9				3.3	3.5
3.1	2.4	2.5	2.6			Sales/Total Assets	2.7	2.8
2.1	1.7	2.0	2.1				2.2	2.2
1.3	.3	.2	.1				.2	.2
(10) 2.0	(106) .6	(134) .4	(33) .4			% Depr., Dep., Amort./Sales	(378) .4	(283) .4
2.8	1.1	.8	.5				.7	.8
3.5	1.3	.9	.4				.9	1.0
(10) 6.7	(79) 2.4	(97) 1.4	(25) .6			% Officers', Directors', Owners' Comp/Sales	(283) 1.6	(219) 1.8
9.1	3.5	2.4					2.7	3.1
22747M	469524M	2203671M	1649382M	578190M	1179484M	Net Sales ($)	6264069M	3978578M
5773M	162599M	808763M	657532M	281794M	404170M	Total Assets ($)	2185681M	1426885M

M = $ thousand   MM = $ million
See Pages 11 through 21 for Explanation of Ratios and Data

Comparative Historical Data / Current Data Sorted By Sales

4/1/02-3/31/03 ALL	4/1/03-3/31/04 ALL	4/1/04-3/31/05 ALL	Type of Statement	0-1MM	1-3MM	3-5MM	5-10MM	10-25MM	25MM & OVER
4	10	7	Unqualified		1		1	3	2
38	49	50	Reviewed		5	3	12	18	12
80	127	112	Compiled	5	29	21	29	22	6
43	94	82	Tax Returns	8	25	13	17	16	3
183	117	116	Other	6	13	19	18	36	24
				62 (4/1-9/30/04)			305 (10/1/04-3/31/05)		
348	397	367	**NUMBER OF STATEMENTS**	19	73	56	77	95	47
%	%	%	**ASSETS**	%	%	%	%	%	%
7.3	7.5	7.1	Cash & Equivalents	6.5	8.0	7.3	6.4	6.7	7.9
2.6	2.6	3.0	Trade Receivables (net)	2.7	1.7	1.8	4.3	3.4	4.0
77.4	77.3	76.2	Inventory	57.3	74.1	80.7	76.3	78.7	76.8
.6	.5	.6	All Other Current	.1	.3	.5	.7	.7	-1.1
87.9	87.8	87.0	Total Current	66.6	84.0	90.3	87.7	89.6	89.7
9.2	9.4	9.6	Fixed Assets (net)	23.9	12.9	7.9	9.5	6.4	7.0
1.8	1.7	2.2	Intangibles (net)	6.3	1.8	.9	1.5	2.8	2.3
1.1	1.1	1.2	All Other Non-Current	3.2	1.3	.9	1.3	1.2	.9
100.0	100.0	100.0	Total	100.0	100.0	100.0	100.0	100.0	100.0
			LIABILITIES						
26.7	23.7	51.7	Notes Payable-Short Term	23.9	45.7	57.8	50.6	57.4	55.5
1.8	2.0	3.1	Cur. Mat.-L/T/D	1.8	1.7	3.2	5.9	1.5	4.0
32.4	33.6	6.3	Trade Payables	2.4	9.2	3.2	6.6	4.4	10.5
.1	.1	.1	Income Taxes Payable	.1	.1	.0	.0	.1	.5
8.4	9.1	6.8	All Other Current	6.6	5.3	5.4	6.8	9.3	5.7
69.4	68.5	68.0	Total Current	34.9	62.1	69.6	70.0	72.7	76.1
5.8	6.5	7.0	Long-Term Debt	29.0	11.7	3.6	6.6	3.5	3.0
.0	.0	.0	Deferred Taxes	.0	.1	.1	.0	.0	.1
2.3	2.6	3.2	All Other Non-Current	2.9	3.4	3.5	2.3	3.8	2.3
22.5	22.3	21.7	Net Worth	33.3	22.5	23.3	21.1	20.1	18.5
100.0	100.0	100.0	Total Liabilities & Net Worth	100.0	100.0	100.0	100.0	100.0	100.0
			INCOME DATA						
100.0	100.0	100.0	Net Sales	100.0	100.0	100.0	100.0	100.0	100.0
20.0	19.3	20.4	Gross Profit	38.9	24.0	20.0	18.7	17.2	16.9
17.3	16.5	18.1	Operating Expenses	32.5	23.0	17.9	16.2	15.0	14.3
2.7	2.7	2.3	Operating Profit	6.4	1.0	2.1	2.5	2.2	2.6
.9	.8	.8	All Other Expenses (net)	2.4	.7	.9	1.0	.3	.5
1.7	2.0	1.5	Profit Before Taxes	4.0	.3	1.2	1.6	1.9	2.1
			RATIOS						
1.4	1.4	1.5	Current	4.6	1.6	1.5	1.4	1.3	1.2
1.2	1.2	1.2		1.8	1.3	1.3	1.2	1.2	1.1
1.1	1.1	1.1		1.0	1.1	1.1	1.1	1.1	1.1
.2	.2	.2	Quick	.8	.3	.1	.2	.2	.2
.1	(395) .1	(365) .1		(18) .2	.1	.1	.2	(94) .1	.1
.0	.0	.0		.1	.0	.0	.0	.1	.1
0 999.8	0 999.8	0 999.8	Sales/Receivables	0 UND	0 UND	0 UND	0 999.8	1 396.1	1 548.7
1 247.7	1 257.6	1 259.3		2 226.0	1 534.0	1 440.3	1 245.6	2 191.6	1 259.3
4 85.7	4 98.8	4 85.3		12 29.9	3 114.3	3 131.8	5 71.6	5 77.8	4 87.9
105 3.5	102 3.6	107 3.4	Cost of Sales/Inventory	118 3.1	120 3.0	120 3.0	102 3.6	97 3.8	99 3.7
137 2.7	129 2.8	138 2.6		224 1.6	180 2.0	140 2.6	135 2.7	122 3.0	117 3.1
178 2.0	165 2.2	189 1.9		378 1.0	256 1.4	221 1.7	176 2.1	155 2.4	142 2.6
2 157.3	3 136.2	1 474.3	Cost of Sales/Payables	0 UND	1 567.3	0 821.8	1 511.8	1 372.0	1 313.2
23 15.7	31 11.8	3 126.7		2 206.0	2 99.9	2 139.4	4 103.0	3 126.7	3 125.7
109 3.3	108 3.4	9 42.3		15 23.6	20 18.1	7 55.6	9 40.7	6 62.3	12 29.5
9.7	9.3	9.2	Sales/Working Capital	2.6	6.0	7.7	11.2	11.9	14.4
17.7	18.6	18.1		5.3	12.0	15.9	18.7	21.0	24.6
38.2	35.3	36.4		-397.0	28.3	31.3	29.9	41.7	39.7
3.2	4.2	4.1	EBIT/Interest	8.5	2.5	2.8	4.1	4.8	4.5
(328) 1.9	(381) 2.4	(344) 2.0		(15) 2.2	(70) 1.5	(53) 1.6	(75) 1.8	(87) 2.5	(44) 2.9
1.3	1.4	1.2		-.4	.7	1.2	1.2	1.4	1.7
5.7	15.6	12.4	Net Profit + Depr., Dep., Amort./Cur. Mat. L/T/D						
(30) 3.2	(39) 5.5	(31) 5.2							
1.2	1.7	2.5							
.1	.1	.1	Fixed/Worth	.0	.1	.1	.1	.1	.2
.3	.3	.3		.7	.5	.3	.3	.3	.4
.9	.9	1.0		6.5	1.7	.8	.8	.6	.9
2.4	2.3	2.5	Debt/Worth	.5	1.9	1.9	2.7	3.2	4.3
4.7	4.4	4.6		2.8	3.6	3.7	4.2	5.2	6.2
9.1	8.5	11.7		19.8	17.0	15.8	7.8	10.4	15.9
44.1	51.7	39.4	% Profit Before Taxes/Tangible Net Worth	35.2	20.1	30.4	37.9	45.9	47.7
(326) 21.1	(374) 23.8	(333) 16.6		(15) 2.5	(64) 8.8	(51) 12.9	(72) 13.5	(87) 22.1	(44) 30.4
7.4	8.5	4.5		-36.3	.5	4.2	4.7	9.3	17.0
6.8	8.8	7.1	% Profit Before Taxes/Total Assets	11.8	4.5	5.3	8.6	7.4	10.7
3.6	4.4	2.8		5.1	1.8	2.2	2.5	4.4	5.1
1.0	1.3	.7		-5.6	-1.2	.6	.9	1.1	2.0
168.5	162.1	127.7	Sales/Net Fixed Assets	197.0	86.1	193.9	133.7	170.6	145.1
61.4	63.2	54.2		9.1	27.3	55.6	56.7	83.3	72.4
22.6	21.6	21.8		4.0	11.9	27.4	24.9	31.2	28.1
3.2	3.4	3.2	Sales/Total Assets	2.1	2.6	3.0	3.5	3.5	3.3
2.6	2.7	2.5		1.1	1.9	2.5	2.5	3.0	2.8
2.0	2.2	1.9		.8	1.5	1.9	2.0	2.2	2.4
.2	.2	.2	% Depr., Dep., Amort./Sales	1.5	.3	.2	.2	.2	.1
(261) .4	(297) .5	(287) .4		(11) 2.1	(61) .9	(40) .4	(59) .3	(76) .4	(40) .3
.9	.8	.9		4.0	1.9	.9	.7	.6	.5
.9	.9	.9	% Officers', Directors', Owners' Comp/Sales	1.5	1.3	1.1	.5	.5	
(214) 1.7	(230) 1.8	(212) 1.6		(46) 2.8	(30) 2.4	(48) 1.8	(53) 1.2	(28) .7	
3.1	2.9	2.8		4.1	3.5	2.4	2.1	1.8	
3908107M	8033582M	6102998M	Net Sales ($)	10947M	150299M	227902M	587657M	1551789M	3574404M
1476923M	2726240M	2320631M	Total Assets ($)	11075M	81298M	99747M	237995M	560469M	1330047M

© RMA 2005

M = $ thousand   MM = $ million
See Pages 11 through 21 for Explanation of Ratios and Data

Current Data Sorted By Assets / Comparative Historical Data

Type of Statement	0-500M	500M-2MM	2-10MM	10-50MM	50-100MM	100-250MM		4/1/00-3/31/01 ALL	4/1/01-3/31/02 ALL
Unqualified		1	4	4				1	4
Reviewed	3	3	38	6				25	20
Compiled	4	26	72	6				78	62
Tax Returns	2	16	31	2				16	27
Other		18	61	10	1			47	65
		43 (4/1-9/30/04)		265 (10/1/04-3/31/05)					
NUMBER OF STATEMENTS	9	64	206	28	1			167	178

Data for columns 50-100MM and 100-250MM: **DATA NOT AVAILABLE**

	0-500M	500M-2MM %	2-10MM %	10-50MM %			4/1/00-3/31/01 ALL %	4/1/01-3/31/02 ALL %
ASSETS								
Cash & Equivalents		7.6	8.5	5.9			8.2	9.6
Trade Receivables (net)		2.8	3.4	3.9			4.1	4.7
Inventory		75.0	67.4	49.7			68.1	66.4
All Other Current		.7	1.7	.9			1.5	1.0
Total Current		86.2	81.0	60.3			81.9	81.8
Fixed Assets (net)		9.1	10.5	19.6			11.1	13.5
Intangibles (net)		1.8	5.0	15.2			3.2	2.3
All Other Non-Current		3.0	3.4	4.9			3.8	2.4
Total		100.0	100.0	100.0			100.0	100.0
LIABILITIES								
Notes Payable-Short Term		38.0	32.6	27.9			31.4	32.4
Cur. Mat.-L/T/D		3.3	3.3	3.2			2.4	1.9
Trade Payables		14.8	12.6	8.8			13.1	11.9
Income Taxes Payable		.1	.1	.4			.2	.3
All Other Current		8.1	8.9	10.7			10.1	9.8
Total Current		64.3	57.6	51.0			57.2	56.3
Long-Term Debt		10.6	7.5	10.9			6.9	10.1
Deferred Taxes		.0	.1	.1			.0	.0
All Other Non-Current		7.5	3.0	4.7			3.1	2.5
Net Worth		17.5	31.9	33.3			32.8	31.1
Total Liabilities & Net Worth		100.0	100.0	100.0			100.0	100.0
INCOME DATA								
Net Sales		100.0	100.0	100.0			100.0	100.0
Gross Profit		20.2	22.2	25.4			21.8	21.6
Operating Expenses		18.9	18.8	20.0			18.0	18.0
Operating Profit		1.3	3.3	5.4			3.8	3.7
All Other Expenses (net)		.0	-.1	.4			.0	.3
Profit Before Taxes		1.3	3.4	5.1			3.8	3.3

RATIOS

	0-500M	500M-2MM	2-10MM	10-50MM		4/1/00-3/31/01 ALL	4/1/01-3/31/02 ALL
Current		1.6	1.8	1.7		1.8	1.8
		1.3	1.3	1.1		1.4	1.3
		1.1	1.2	1.0		1.1	1.2
Quick		.3	.3	.3		.4	.4
	(63)	.1	.2	.1	(163) .2	(177) .2
		.1	.1	.1		.1	.1
Sales/Receivables	0 999.8	2 236.7	3 126.4		1 300.2	1 295.5
	1 254.3	4 98.9	4 83.7		4 100.7	3 108.7
	4 81.3	6 59.4	12 31.1		7 53.2	7 51.2
Cost of Sales/Inventory	89 4.1	92 4.0	90 4.0		78 4.7	76 4.8
	118 3.1	116 3.1	111 3.3		99 3.7	102 3.6
	164 2.2	160 2.3	150 2.4		135 2.7	142 2.6
Cost of Sales/Payables	4 101.6	6 64.9	7 54.2		5 67.5	5 80.1
	7 53.2	10 34.9	15 24.1		11 33.0	11 34.1
	22 16.5	21 17.2	29 12.5		24 15.0	22 16.3
Sales/Working Capital		9.7	7.6	9.9		8.3	8.3
		17.7	11.9	19.6		13.8	12.6
		47.7	25.8	NM		27.4	22.8
EBIT/Interest		5.1	10.3	9.2		11.4	7.8
	(62) 1.6	(192) 4.0	6.5		(152) 3.8	(165) 3.3
		.8	1.8	3.1		1.6	1.7
Net Profit + Depr., Dep., Amort./Cur. Mat. L/T/D			17.1			14.8	24.5
		(28)	7.2		(27) 5.1	(21) 12.3
			2.6			2.5	4.6
Fixed/Worth		.1	.1	.4		.1	.1
		.4	.4	1.5		.3	.3
		2.2	.9	NM		.8	1.0
Debt/Worth		1.6	1.4	1.7		1.1	1.3
		4.9	2.9	5.6		2.7	2.8
		40.7	7.4	NM		6.5	5.9
% Profit Before Taxes/Tangible Net Worth		50.5	50.6	85.2		65.0	53.3
	(51) 25.2	(183) 23.5	(21) 35.6		(157) 30.5	(163) 30.0
		2.8	8.4	10.0		12.6	14.7
% Profit Before Taxes/Total Assets		9.7	14.5	14.4		18.8	16.6
		2.5	7.4	8.2		7.9	7.7
		-1.3	2.1	4.6		2.6	2.8
Sales/Net Fixed Assets		137.9	80.4	45.1		93.3	94.4
		69.5	38.8	15.8		40.6	37.4
		27.0	18.8	5.1		22.4	14.8
Sales/Total Assets		3.5	3.3	2.4		3.9	3.7
		3.0	2.5	1.9		3.0	3.0
		2.3	2.0	1.6		2.4	2.2
% Depr., Dep., Amort./Sales		.3	.3	.4		.3	.3
	(47) .5	(170) .6	(26) .8		(140) .5	(145) .6
		.8	1.0	1.0		.8	1.0
% Officers', Directors', Owners' Comp/Sales		1.3	.9	.5		1.4	1.2
	(39) 1.8	(121) 1.6	(13) 1.3		(97) 2.1	(116) 2.4
		3.3	2.9	2.4		3.5	3.7

	0-500M	500M-2MM	2-10MM	10-50MM	50-100MM		4/1/00-3/31/01 ALL	4/1/01-3/31/02 ALL
Net Sales ($)	13965M	259779M	2374552M	933816M	273192M		1383616M	1807216M
Total Assets ($)	2359M	84122M	924824M	454026M	97203M		457584M	619117M

© RMA 2005

M = $ thousand MM = $ million
See Pages 11 through 21 for Explanation of Ratios and Data

Comparative Historical Data | Current Data Sorted By Sales

					Type of Statement						
	5		6		9		Unqualified								
	24		40		47		Reviewed		2	1	11	27	6
	58		92		107		Compiled	3	9	17	35	39	4
	47		58		53		Tax Returns	3	3	10	19	15	3
	78		77		92		Other	1	8	16	24	38	5
	4/1/02-3/31/03		4/1/03-3/31/04		4/1/04-3/31/05				43 (4/1-9/30/04)		265 (10/1/04-3/31/05)		
	ALL		ALL		ALL			0-1MM	1-3MM	3-5MM	5-10MM	10-25MM	25MM & OVER
	212		273		308		**NUMBER OF STATEMENTS**	7	22	44	91	122	22
	%		%		%		**ASSETS**	%	%	%	%	%	%
	8.7		9.3		8.0		Cash & Equivalents	4.6	6.9	9.0	8.4	8.6
	4.3		3.7		3.4		Trade Receivables (net)	2.6	3.3	2.4	4.0	6.0
	66.4		66.6		67.0		Inventory	75.7	73.1	68.2	64.0	58.1
	1.8		1.4		1.6		All Other Current	3.1	1.1	1.7	1.5	1.9
	81.2		81.1		80.1		Total Current	86.0	84.4	81.3	77.8	74.5
	12.6		12.6		11.4		Fixed Assets (net)	9.1	10.4	9.6	11.8	17.2
	2.9		3.6		5.1		Intangibles (net)	2.7	1.5	6.0	6.3	5.8
	3.3		2.7		3.4		All Other Non-Current	2.2	3.7	3.1	4.1	2.5
	100.0		100.0		100.0		Total	100.0	100.0	100.0	100.0	100.0
							LIABILITIES						
	32.9		31.9		33.3		Notes Payable-Short Term	46.3	36.4	28.9	31.4	35.7
	3.6		2.9		3.2		Cur. Mat.-L/T/D	.7	5.7	3.1	2.9	3.5
	12.2		11.5		13.0		Trade Payables	20.5	14.9	11.7	12.6	9.5
	.3		.1		.1		Income Taxes Payable	.0	.1	.1	.2	.3
	9.5		10.2		9.3		All Other Current	6.5	8.6	10.0	9.2	8.9
	58.5		56.5		58.8		Total Current	74.1	65.6	53.8	56.2	57.9
	9.6		8.1		8.9		Long-Term Debt	9.1	11.3	9.0	7.0	7.9
	.0		.1		.1		Deferred Taxes	.0	.0	.0	.1	.0
	3.3		4.3		4.3		All Other Non-Current	8.7	4.5	4.1	2.8	4.3
	28.6		31.0		28.0		Net Worth	8.2	18.5	33.0	33.9	29.9
	100.0		100.0		100.0		Total Liabilities & Net Worth	100.0	100.0	100.0	100.0	100.0
							INCOME DATA						
	100.0		100.0		100.0		Net Sales	100.0	100.0	100.0	100.0	100.0
	22.1		22.2		22.2		Gross Profit	20.8	19.0	21.3	23.0	27.9
	18.7		19.4		19.4		Operating Expenses	20.4	18.2	18.1	19.0	23.3
	3.3		2.8		2.8		Operating Profit	.3	.8	3.2	4.0	4.6
	.0		–.2		.0		All Other Expenses (net)	1.0	–.6	.3	–.2	–.2
	3.4		2.9		2.8		Profit Before Taxes	–.7	1.4	2.9	4.2	4.8
							RATIOS						
	1.8		1.9		1.7			1.4	1.4	1.8	1.9	1.7
	1.3		1.4		1.3		Current	1.1	1.2	1.4	1.3	1.2
	1.1		1.1		1.1			1.0	1.1	1.2	1.1	1.1
	.4		.4		.3			.1	.3	.4	.3	.5
	.2	(272)	.2	(307)	.2		Quick	.1	.1	.2	.2	.1
	.1		.1		.1			.0	.1	.1	.1	.1
1	316.6	1	377.2	1	335.5			0 UND	0 840.9	1 529.7	2 159.0	3 118.6
4	103.9	3	113.1	3	110.6		Sales/Receivables	2 230.0	3 110.4	2 189.1	4 88.5	4 83.5
7	54.3	6	59.7	6	60.3			4 94.8	7 50.5	4 83.7	7 53.3	7 49.8
77	4.7	83	4.4	90	4.0			113 3.2	90 4.0	93 3.9	86 4.2	73 5.0
112	3.3	107	3.4	116	3.1		Cost of Sales/Inventory	175 2.1	136 2.7	122 3.0	107 3.4	105 3.5
156	2.3	149	2.4	158	2.3			221 1.6	191 1.9	157 2.3	135 2.7	122 3.0
5	80.5	5	76.0	4	81.4			4 90.4	3 110.0	4 87.8	7 55.2	5 73.1
11	34.1	10	34.8	10	35.9		Cost of Sales/Payables	8 46.7	9 42.2	10 38.1	12 31.5	12 30.6
23	15.9	23	16.0	22	16.9			78 4.7	16 22.7	21 17.0	22 16.3	19 18.7
	8.4		8.1		8.1			8.7	8.2	7.3	8.5	9.9
	14.3		13.1		13.2		Sales/Working Capital	23.1	16.7	11.2	14.7	16.2
	35.5		28.2		30.3			NM	49.2	17.0	30.1	69.5
	11.4		10.5		9.2			1.8	4.5	9.3	14.1	10.5
(193)	4.3	(244)	4.0	(292)	3.6		EBIT/Interest	1.2 (43)	1.6 (86)	3.5 (112)	6.0	6.4
	1.6		1.7		1.4			–.3	.9	1.4	2.3	2.8
	13.8		10.5		15.7		Net Profit + Depr., Dep.,				16.8	
(25)	5.6	(36)	3.7	(36)	5.1		Amort./Cur. Mat. L/T/D			(19)	5.0	
	2.0		.7		2.6						1.6	
	.1		.1		.1			.1	.1	.1	.2	.3
	.4		.4		.4		Fixed/Worth	.6	.4	.2	.4	.7
	1.2		1.1		1.4			–.8	1.2	.9	1.1	5.5
	1.4		1.2		1.5			3.5	1.8	1.2	1.2	1.2
	3.0		2.9		3.3		Debt/Worth	11.7	4.6	2.9	3.0	3.3
	7.8		7.1		10.5			–10.6	26.1	7.5	8.1	22.7
	49.3		56.4		52.2		% Profit Before Taxes/Tangible	21.9	40.6	42.5	64.7	85.5
(185)	26.9	(240)	31.3	(263)	24.5		Net Worth	2.7 (15)	14.4 (36)	21.7 (82)	27.6 (108)	48.4 (18)
	12.0		11.6		7.6			–12.9	4.0	6.6	13.9	17.4
	18.4		16.8		13.2		% Profit Before Taxes/Total	2.7	6.1	13.1	15.6	19.1
	6.8		6.8		5.8		Assets	.8	2.7	5.5	9.8	11.3
	2.0		2.5		1.6			–4.1	–.3	1.2	3.3	4.3
	75.3		70.7		84.5			137.7	110.6	109.5	74.6	67.1
	37.3		33.3		40.3		Sales/Net Fixed Assets	56.5	64.1	49.0	32.9	19.1
	15.6		16.8		16.8			20.9	16.1	20.4	18.7	10.7
	3.6		3.7		3.3			3.1	3.3	3.1	3.5	3.4
	2.6		2.8		2.6		Sales/Total Assets	2.1	2.3	2.4	2.8	2.7
	2.0		2.0		2.0			1.8	1.8	1.9	2.1	2.0
	.4		.4		.3			.3	.3	.3	.4	.4
(179)	.6	(226)	.7	(250)	.6		% Depr., Dep., Amort./Sales	.6 (15)	.4 (30)	.5 (75)	.6 (104)	.7 (21)
	1.0		1.2		1.0			1.2	.9	.9	1.0	1.1
	1.2		1.1		1.0			1.6	1.1	.9	.9	.5
(128)	2.0	(155)	1.8	(177)	1.6		% Officers', Directors',	2.1 (10)	1.9 (25)	1.6 (53)	1.6 (72)	1.0 (15)
	4.0		3.7		2.9		Owners' Comp/Sales	3.7	3.4	3.6	2.7	2.8
	2632649M		3333995M		3855304M		Net Sales ($)	4582M	48887M	175135M	655581M	1807868M	1163251M
	985582M		1219524M		1562534M		Total Assets ($)	2745M	36386M	75725M	285090M	717291M	445297M

© RMA 2005

M = $ thousand   MM = $ million
See Pages 11 through 21 for Explanation of Ratios and Data

Current Data Sorted By Assets   Comparative Historical Data

						Type of Statement		
	2	3	1	4		Unqualified	2	5
1	5	20	11			Reviewed	33	37
5	30	37	6			Compiled	118	122
11	32	16	2			Tax Returns	43	32
5	24	38	4			Other	109	62
	44 (4/1-9/30/04)		213 (10/1/04-3/31/05)				4/1/00-3/31/01	4/1/01-3/31/02
0-500M	500M-2MM	2-10MM	10-50MM	50-100MM	100-250MM		ALL	ALL
22	93	114	24	4		NUMBER OF STATEMENTS	305	258
%	%	%	%	%	%	ASSETS	%	%
11.3	7.3	6.6	8.1			Cash & Equivalents	7.1	8.3
3.1	4.1	3.9	2.6		D	Trade Receivables (net)	3.6	4.2
53.5	70.4	75.2	68.3		A	Inventory	72.7	69.3
2.3	1.1	.7	1.3		T	All Other Current	.7	1.2
70.1	82.9	86.4	80.3		A	Total Current	84.1	83.0
26.2	13.0	10.6	11.6			Fixed Assets (net)	11.5	13.0
.5	1.0	1.3	3.8		N	Intangibles (net)	2.3	1.8
3.1	3.1	1.7	4.3		O	All Other Non-Current	2.1	2.3
100.0	100.0	100.0	100.0		T	Total	100.0	100.0
					A	LIABILITIES		
33.1	38.0	53.1	54.1		V	Notes Payable-Short Term	30.7	31.6
4.1	4.2	2.0	4.5		A	Cur. Mat.-L/T/D	1.8	3.3
5.8	7.6	8.2	5.2		I	Trade Payables	20.5	16.4
.0	.1	.1	.6		L	Income Taxes Payable	.1	.2
14.2	7.2	6.7	8.4		A	All Other Current	13.8	12.2
57.1	57.1	70.0	72.7		B	Total Current	67.0	63.6
18.2	12.2	8.7	6.8		L	Long-Term Debt	8.0	10.7
1.8	.0	.0	.2		E	Deferred Taxes	.0	.0
12.8	5.9	1.4	3.3			All Other Non-Current	3.5	3.3
10.1	24.8	19.8	16.9			Net Worth	21.5	22.7
100.0	100.0	100.0	100.0			Total Liabilities & Net Worth	100.0	100.0
						INCOME DATA		
100.0	100.0	100.0	100.0			Net Sales	100.0	100.0
35.8	27.7	21.6	20.3			Gross Profit	22.9	23.6
30.5	24.3	19.2	17.9			Operating Expenses	19.4	20.8
5.3	3.5	2.4	2.4			Operating Profit	3.4	2.8
1.2	1.2	.8	.9			All Other Expenses (net)	1.5	1.5
4.1	2.3	1.6	1.6			Profit Before Taxes	1.9	1.4
						RATIOS		
2.0	1.9	1.4	1.2				1.5	1.6
1.3	1.3	1.2	1.1			Current	1.2	1.2
1.1	1.2	1.1	1.0				1.1	1.1
.5	.3	.2	.2				.2	.3
(21) .3	(92) .1	(113) .1	.1			Quick	(304) .1	.1
.0	.1	.1	.1				.0	.1
0 UND	0 999.8	1 458.3	1 279.8				1 517.3	1 649.9
0 789.7	3 122.3	3 105.1	4 95.2			Sales/Receivables	3 124.8	4 84.9
4 96.1	11 33.5	8 44.9	7 54.0				8 48.4	8 43.8
44 8.2	121 3.0	148 2.5	118 3.1				113 3.2	110 3.3
93 3.9	182 2.0	203 1.8	157 2.3			Cost of Sales/Inventory	169 2.2	162 2.3
173 2.1	260 1.4	265 1.4	219 1.7				235 1.6	229 1.6
0 UND	1 713.7	1 249.6	2 181.1				2 198.4	2 222.7
0 UND	4 100.5	5 79.4	3 106.3			Cost of Sales/Payables	10 35.4	8 47.8
10 36.5	10 36.5	13 27.6	7 56.1				66 5.5	33 10.9
8.2	4.7	7.7	12.6				8.6	7.3
12.9	9.5	13.3	31.0			Sales/Working Capital	15.3	13.8
206.3	23.5	36.1	110.2				38.2	33.4
11.7	4.6	4.0	3.3				3.3	2.9
(19) 3.2	(90) 2.1	(109) 2.0	(23) 1.7			EBIT/Interest	(290) 1.7	(243) 1.6
.1	1.0	1.2	1.2				1.2	1.0
	10.4	5.3				Net Profit + Depr., Dep.,	5.6	7.7
	(10) 5.1	(17) 3.5				Amort./Cur. Mat. L/T/D	(42) 2.9	(29) 3.1
	1.6	1.8					1.1	1.4
.2	.1	.2	.2				.1	.2
.8	.4	.4	.5			Fixed/Worth	.4	.5
UND	1.2	1.2	1.4				1.6	2.1
1.3	1.7	2.6	4.6				2.4	2.1
5.0	4.0	5.8	8.9			Debt/Worth	5.7	4.8
UND	10.1	12.8	22.5				17.4	14.5
92.5	44.4	36.6	56.3			% Profit Before Taxes/Tangible	47.1	32.0
(17) 44.7	(83) 15.1	(103) 14.6	(23) 23.3			Net Worth	(264) 23.7	(224) 12.7
11.4	2.5	5.7	7.6				9.0	2.1
24.6	8.9	5.9	4.5			% Profit Before Taxes/Total	8.0	7.2
6.6	3.8	2.8	2.0			Assets	3.2	2.7
-6.3	-.1	.5	.7				.8	.1
UND	106.5	77.1	90.5				102.3	85.4
17.0	32.8	34.2	35.7			Sales/Net Fixed Assets	40.8	33.8
6.0	10.9	18.0	13.7				15.2	12.3
5.5	2.8	2.4	2.4				2.8	2.7
3.0	2.0	1.8	1.8			Sales/Total Assets	2.0	2.1
1.7	1.4	1.4	1.5				1.5	1.6
1.2	.4	.3	.5				.3	.4
(10) 2.0	(71) .7	(95) .6	(22) .7			% Depr., Dep., Amort./Sales	(242) .6	(213) .7
4.7	1.4	1.1	.9				1.1	1.4
1.8	1.6	1.0				% Officers', Directors',	1.3	1.4
(10) 3.2	(50) 2.4	(56) 1.8				Owners' Comp/Sales	(164) 2.1	(134) 2.3
10.5	3.8	3.3					3.5	4.3
24167M	236756M	958375M	810860M	346571M		Net Sales ($)	3386210M	2159781M
5577M	105619M	494471M	413372M	279864M		Total Assets ($)	1795588M	1123775M

© RMA 2005

M = $ thousand   MM = $ million
See Pages 11 through 21 for Explanation of Ratios and Data

Comparative Historical Data | | Current Data Sorted By Sales

			Type of Statement						
5	8	10	Unqualified		2			2	6
27	37	37	Reviewed	5	5	3	9	15	5
85	94	78	Compiled	5	21	19	23	6	4
46	64	61	Tax Returns	13	20	15	6	5	2
80	75	71	Other	7	19	13	15	14	3
4/1/02- 3/31/03	4/1/03- 3/31/04	4/1/04- 3/31/05		44 (4/1-9/30/04)			213 (10/1/04-3/31/05)		
ALL	ALL	ALL		0-1MM	1-3MM	3-5MM	5-10MM	10-25MM	25MM & OVER
243	278	257	**NUMBER OF STATEMENTS**	25	67	50	53	42	20
%	%	%	**ASSETS**	%	%	%	%	%	%
7.5	8.0	7.5	Cash & Equivalents	7.2	7.0	6.3	7.0	9.3	10.3
3.9	3.8	3.8	Trade Receivables (net)	3.2	4.4	2.0	3.3	5.9	3.6
71.4	70.6	70.7	Inventory	52.6	69.0	80.3	76.1	68.4	64.9
1.0	1.2	1.1	All Other Current	2.0	1.2	.7	.9	.5	2.0
83.9	83.6	83.0	Total Current	64.9	81.6	89.2	87.3	84.2	80.9
12.8	12.7	12.9	Fixed Assets (net)	28.8	14.7	8.2	9.6	12.4	8.8
1.4	1.8	1.4	Intangibles (net)	1.2	.6	1.3	1.0	1.9	4.0
1.9	1.9	2.7	All Other Non-Current	5.1	3.0	1.3	2.1	1.4	6.3
100.0	100.0	100.0	Total	100.0	100.0	100.0	100.0	100.0	100.0
			LIABILITIES						
37.6	34.2	46.0	Notes Payable-Short Term	26.4	38.6	56.2	50.1	50.1	49.9
2.2	3.3	3.3	Cur. Mat.-L/T/D	6.1	3.6	4.3	1.6	1.0	5.2
13.4	15.4	7.4	Trade Payables	1.8	8.5	4.5	9.8	9.5	7.5
.1	.1	.1	Income Taxes Payable	.0	.1	.0	.1	.3	.1
11.3	10.4	7.7	All Other Current	13.6	6.0	6.1	7.5	8.4	9.4
64.6	63.5	64.5	Total Current	47.8	56.9	71.2	69.2	69.3	72.1
11.3	11.4	10.7	Long-Term Debt	24.8	13.7	5.9	8.6	7.3	7.3
.0	.0	.2	Deferred Taxes	1.6	.0	.0	.0	.0	.3
5.3	5.9	4.4	All Other Non-Current	12.6	5.9	2.6	2.3	1.5	5.8
18.7	19.2	20.2	Net Worth	13.2	23.6	20.3	19.9	21.8	14.4
100.0	100.0	100.0	Total Liabilities & Net Worth	100.0	100.0	100.0	100.0	100.0	100.0
			INCOME DATA						
100.0	100.0	100.0	Net Sales	100.0	100.0	100.0	100.0	100.0	100.0
23.7	22.9	25.1	Gross Profit	38.9	28.5	23.7	21.3	19.9	20.8
21.3	20.4	22.0	Operating Expenses	32.3	25.3	21.0	19.5	17.2	17.0
2.4	2.4	3.1	Operating Profit	6.6	3.2	2.7	1.8	2.7	3.8
1.0	.8	1.0	All Other Expenses (net)	1.9	1.2	1.2	.3	.4	1.7
1.4	1.6	2.1	Profit Before Taxes	4.7	2.0	1.6	1.5	2.3	2.1
			RATIOS						
1.6	1.6	1.6	Current	2.0	1.9	1.4	1.5	1.3	1.2
1.2	1.2	1.2	Current	1.2	1.4	1.2	1.2	1.1	1.1
1.1	1.1	1.1	Current	1.1	1.1	1.1	1.1	1.1	1.0
.3	.3	.3	Quick	.5	.4	.2	.3	.3	.2
.1	.1	(254) .1	Quick	(24) .3	(66) .1	(49) .1	.1	.1	.1
.1	.1	.1	Quick	.1	.1	.0	.1	.1	.1
0 939.0	1 656.5	0 779.7	Sales/Receivables	0 UND	0 999.8	0 UND	1 566.6	1 293.0	3 112.5
3 121.2	4 103.9	3 113.0	Sales/Receivables	2 209.0	2 146.3	2 222.0	4 103.0	5 77.7	5 78.3
8 44.9	8 46.5	8 43.6	Sales/Receivables	12 29.8	11 32.5	6 58.7	7 49.7	11 32.2	9 39.7
120 3.0	112 3.3	121 3.0	Cost of Sales/Inventory	75 4.8	126 2.9	132 2.8	123 3.0	108 3.4	93 3.9
169 2.2	166 2.2	182 2.0	Cost of Sales/Inventory	213 1.7	198 1.8	218 1.7	178 2.1	162 2.3	143 2.6
230 1.6	219 1.7	255 1.4	Cost of Sales/Inventory	319 1.1	262 1.4	308 1.2	229 1.6	220 1.7	189 1.9
1 285.1	2 222.8	1 416.1	Cost of Sales/Payables	0 UND	0 833.0	1 640.4	2 191.0	3 139.5	2 181.1
6 60.6	6 58.2	4 92.4	Cost of Sales/Payables	0 UND	4 82.6	2 235.0	7 52.7	5 77.3	3 115.7
23 15.9	37 9.8	11 33.0	Cost of Sales/Payables	4 103.6	13 28.9	8 46.5	18 20.5	11 33.8	5 72.2
6.9	7.1	7.1	Sales/Working Capital	3.9	4.0	7.0	7.7	10.6	14.3
13.8	14.1	13.1	Sales/Working Capital	8.5	9.0	13.2	13.6	18.8	31.0
45.3	42.1	35.5	Sales/Working Capital	51.6	20.6	41.2	34.5	42.6	110.0
3.9	4.3	4.5	EBIT/Interest	5.7	4.5	4.5	4.4	7.1	4.6
(231) 1.7	(267) 2.1	(245) 2.0	EBIT/Interest	(23) 2.1	(65) 1.7	(46) 2.0	(51) 2.6	2.1	1.8
1.1	1.1	1.2	EBIT/Interest	.1	.6	1.1	1.2	1.4	1.5
4.4	6.6	7.0	Net Profit + Depr., Dep., Amort./Cur. Mat. L/T/D						
(39) 2.7	(29) 3.5	(34) 3.9	Net Profit + Depr., Dep., Amort./Cur. Mat. L/T/D						
.1	1.2	1.8	Net Profit + Depr., Dep., Amort./Cur. Mat. L/T/D						
.2	.2	.2	Fixed/Worth	.3	.1	.1	.2	.2	.2
.5	.5	.4	Fixed/Worth	.9	.6	.4	.4	.4	.5
1.8	1.8	1.4	Fixed/Worth	UND	2.4	.9	1.5	1.1	1.3
2.3	2.2	2.3	Debt/Worth	2.1	1.3	2.5	2.3	3.1	5.5
4.8	5.3	5.3	Debt/Worth	7.2	3.4	5.6	4.6	6.4	9.0
15.1	18.2	13.9	Debt/Worth	UND	7.4	11.6	25.1	9.5	17.9
41.3	46.3	44.7	% Profit Before Taxes/Tangible Net Worth	49.9	30.2	55.7	28.8	56.7	58.0
(205) 14.9	(238) 19.3	(229) 17.0	% Profit Before Taxes/Tangible Net Worth	(21) 26.9	(55) 9.0	(47) 18.4	(48) 15.5	(40) 18.4	(18) 30.3
4.8	4.9	5.1	% Profit Before Taxes/Tangible Net Worth	-1.0	1.2	2.6	6.2	8.1	12.9
6.1	7.4	7.2	% Profit Before Taxes/Total Assets	9.1	9.2	7.0	5.9	8.4	8.2
2.6	3.2	3.3	% Profit Before Taxes/Total Assets	3.5	3.5	3.8	3.2	2.9	3.2
.4	.4	.5	% Profit Before Taxes/Total Assets	-3.7	-.9	.2	.5	.9	1.5
77.1	97.7	90.5	Sales/Net Fixed Assets	64.5	75.5	136.2	116.0	91.5	90.5
33.9	31.7	33.5	Sales/Net Fixed Assets	9.5	27.9	38.4	39.3	33.9	42.7
13.5	13.0	11.9	Sales/Net Fixed Assets	3.7	9.3	24.7	21.5	9.3	26.6
2.8	2.8	2.7	Sales/Total Assets	2.3	2.7	2.8	2.6	2.6	2.8
2.0	2.0	1.9	Sales/Total Assets	1.4	1.8	1.8	2.0	1.9	2.0
1.6	1.6	1.5	Sales/Total Assets	.9	1.4	1.3	1.6	1.6	1.5
.4	.4	.4	% Depr., Dep., Amort./Sales	.8	.4	.4	.3	.3	.4
(199) .7	(223) .7	(202) .7	% Depr., Dep., Amort./Sales	(14) 1.8	(55) .9	(35) .6	(42) .7	(38) .6	(18) .6
1.4	1.4	1.3	% Depr., Dep., Amort./Sales	4.0	1.5	1.1	1.2	1.0	.8
1.2	1.3	1.3	% Officers', Directors', Owners' Comp/Sales	.8	1.7	1.6	1.2	1.0	
(127) 2.2	(152) 2.2	(126) 2.0	% Officers', Directors', Owners' Comp/Sales	(10) 2.8	(34) 2.6	(30) 2.0	(28) 2.6	(17) 1.0	
4.3	4.2	3.9	% Officers', Directors', Owners' Comp/Sales	14.6	4.2	3.4	4.4	2.0	
2608261M	2635722M	2376729M	Net Sales ($)	15248M	132210M	195694M	362648M	646677M	1024252M
1169738M	1301147M	1298903M	Total Assets ($)	14338M	72945M	116383M	189131M	322943M	583163M

© RMA 2005

M = $ thousand   MM = $ million
See Pages 11 through 21 for Explanation of Ratios and Data

Current Data Sorted By Assets | Comparative Historical Data

0-500M	500M-2MM	2-10MM	10-50MM	50-100MM	100-250MM	Type of Statement	4/1/00-3/31/01 ALL	4/1/01-3/31/02 ALL
1		9	13	5	3	Unqualified	6	13
	2	27	12	2		Reviewed	17	20
7	18	19	6			Compiled	28	29
15	19	18	1			Tax Returns	17	16
5	7	37	18	1		Other	34	28
28	41 (4/1-9/30/04) 46	110	204 (10/1/04-3/31/05) 50	8	3	**NUMBER OF STATEMENTS**	102	106
%	%	%	%	%	%	**ASSETS**	%	%
15.5	8.9	8.4	8.4			Cash & Equivalents	5.8	8.9
17.5	12.4	13.2	14.1			Trade Receivables (net)	13.0	13.6
45.0	52.7	50.4	49.6			Inventory	53.4	49.9
4.8	1.1	3.0	3.3			All Other Current	2.6	2.1
82.7	75.1	75.0	75.4			Total Current	74.8	74.4
11.8	17.2	17.8	18.2			Fixed Assets (net)	20.2	17.4
2.4	2.0	.9	1.2			Intangibles (net)	1.4	3.0
3.0	5.7	6.3	5.2			All Other Non-Current	3.5	5.2
100.0	100.0	100.0	100.0			Total	100.0	100.0
						LIABILITIES		
41.9	30.5	30.5	38.5			Notes Payable-Short Term	29.9	32.0
1.4	2.7	4.3	5.3			Cur. Mat.-L/T/D	6.2	4.9
6.7	12.2	13.6	8.2			Trade Payables	11.6	8.8
.1	.3	.1	.3			Income Taxes Payable	.3	.2
17.6	6.6	10.4	12.2			All Other Current	10.8	11.7
67.8	52.3	58.9	64.5			Total Current	58.8	57.5
8.1	12.9	15.1	10.0			Long-Term Debt	13.8	10.6
.0	.0	.1	.8			Deferred Taxes	.3	.2
2.9	3.1	3.2	2.5			All Other Non-Current	3.2	3.1
21.1	31.6	22.7	22.3			Net Worth	23.9	28.6
100.0	100.0	100.0	100.0			Total Liabilities & Net Worth	100.0	100.0
						INCOME DATA		
100.0	100.0	100.0	100.0			Net Sales	100.0	100.0
28.7	21.7	19.4	16.1			Gross Profit	21.6	22.7
24.8	18.7	17.9	14.1			Operating Expenses	19.8	19.8
3.9	3.0	1.5	2.0			Operating Profit	1.8	2.9
1.2	.3	.3	.5			All Other Expenses (net)	1.7	2.0
2.7	2.7	1.2	1.5			Profit Before Taxes	.1	.9
						RATIOS		
3.1	2.1	1.9	1.5				1.8	1.9
1.1	1.4	1.2	1.1			Current	1.2	1.2
.8	1.1	1.1	1.0				1.0	1.0
1.5	.8	.7	.6				.6	.7
.3	.4	.4	.3			Quick	.2	.4
.0	.2	.1	.2				.1	.2
0 UND	2 202.0	4 98.8	8 45.1				1 289.0	2 189.8
3 121.6	6 57.7	12 31.3	15 24.3			Sales/Receivables	12 30.5	13 27.6
19 19.0	19 18.9	24 15.4	26 14.2				22 16.5	31 11.8
0 UND	40 9.1	41 8.9	48 7.6				48 7.6	40 9.2
40 9.2	53 6.9	75 4.9	74 5.0			Cost of Sales/Inventory	78 4.7	73 5.0
129 2.8	84 4.3	123 3.0	117 3.1				154 2.4	158 2.3
0 UND	1 260.7	4 84.4	4 92.9				1 313.3	3 120.3
0 UND	9 40.5	12 31.3	8 43.1			Cost of Sales/Payables	6 59.1	10 35.5
6 58.3	22 16.6	30 12.2	16 22.8				20 18.1	22 16.7
17.4	9.7	8.7	9.3				9.7	7.8
48.7	15.3	20.2	41.5			Sales/Working Capital	20.8	17.1
−44.7	66.8	82.2	149.0				473.8	163.2
9.5	9.8	4.6	5.7				2.9	2.7
(22) 3.4	(39) 4.7	(99) 1.8	(43) 2.7			EBIT/Interest	(95) 1.4	(88) 1.6
.8	2.2	1.2	1.6				.9	1.1
		6.5	3.2			Net Profit + Depr., Dep.,	3.4	4.7
		(18) 2.9	(14) 2.2			Amort./Cur. Mat. L/T/D	(21) 1.1	(13) 1.7
		1.1	1.3				.8	.7
.0	.1	.2	.2				.2	.1
.3	.3	.4	.6			Fixed/Worth	.6	.5
3.8	1.4	1.9	1.4				1.7	1.6
1.0	1.3	1.8	2.1				1.9	1.6
8.8	2.8	4.6	4.9			Debt/Worth	3.8	3.3
NM	5.5	11.9	9.2				8.4	13.3
135.5	54.3	30.4	44.6			% Profit Before Taxes/Tangible	33.5	29.1
(21) 55.7	(41) 24.2	(97) 13.6	(46) 19.1			Net Worth	(92) 13.3	(96) 14.3
2.6	9.8	5.4	9.0				2.0	2.2
24.8	19.5	5.5	7.9			% Profit Before Taxes/Total	6.7	5.8
5.0	6.6	2.7	3.2			Assets	2.0	2.5
−.5	2.5	.6	1.4				−.7	.1
UND	282.6	108.9	63.2				76.3	126.6
92.4	32.1	35.5	35.1			Sales/Net Fixed Assets	24.4	37.4
35.2	13.9	10.3	10.0				7.5	10.9
10.3	5.3	3.9	3.6				3.9	4.3
5.5	4.0	2.9	2.6			Sales/Total Assets	2.7	2.9
2.9	3.0	2.0	2.0				2.0	1.8
.2	.5	.2	.3				.3	.3
(13) .4	(28) 1.0	(95) .6	(47) .6			% Depr., Dep., Amort./Sales	(87) .9	(81) .8
1.5	2.5	1.5	1.4				1.7	2.3
1.6	1.3	.5	.3			% Officers', Directors',	.9	.7
(16) 3.6	(28) 1.9	(54) 1.1	(17) .9			Owners' Comp/Sales	(45) 1.9	(48) 2.2
6.8	3.2	2.3	1.5				3.0	5.2
46719M	222682M	1736675M	3144080M	1372119M	1060376M	Net Sales ($)	2685646M	1998818M
7131M	53338M	542391M	1104415M	567325M	470225M	Total Assets ($)	1022045M	877604M

© RMA 2005

M = $ thousand   MM = $ million
See Pages 11 through 21 for Explanation of Ratios and Data

Comparative Historical Data				Current Data Sorted By Sales					
			Type of Statement						
17	34	31	Unqualified		1		3	4	23
31	48	43	Reviewed		1	4	9	16	13
39	54	50	Compiled	3	6	9	15	10	7
39	44	53	Tax Returns	7	15	6	17	8	4
74	75	68	Other	3	8	9	5	19	24
4/1/02-3/31/03	4/1/03-3/31/04	4/1/04-3/31/05		41 (4/1-9/30/04)		204 (10/1/04-3/31/05)			
ALL	ALL	ALL		0-1MM	1-3MM	3-5MM	5-10MM	10-25MM	25MM & OVER
200	255	245	**NUMBER OF STATEMENTS**	13	31	28	49	57	67
%	%	%	**ASSETS**	%	%	%	%	%	%
8.2	8.5	9.3	Cash & Equivalents	8.7	13.5	9.0	5.6	9.9	9.8
12.0	11.0	13.5	Trade Receivables (net)	12.0	17.5	10.7	11.7	13.7	14.3
54.4	51.1	49.5	Inventory	62.3	38.8	46.7	52.0	52.6	48.6
2.4	3.2	3.3	All Other Current	.1	3.7	1.5	2.3	3.6	5.0
77.0	73.9	75.6	Total Current	83.1	73.5	68.0	71.6	79.7	77.7
16.4	18.6	17.3	Fixed Assets (net)	11.2	20.0	22.0	22.9	13.6	14.3
1.3	1.6	1.3	Intangibles (net)	5.0	2.2	.4	.5	1.7	.9
5.3	5.9	5.8	All Other Non-Current	.7	4.3	9.6	5.0	4.9	7.1
100.0	100.0	100.0	Total	100.0	100.0	100.0	100.0	100.0	100.0
			LIABILITIES						
35.5	36.9	33.2	Notes Payable-Short Term	53.0	25.7	30.1	32.8	33.7	34.0
3.5	5.0	3.9	Cur. Mat.-L/T/D	3.8	2.0	2.9	4.4	4.5	4.5
10.5	8.8	11.6	Trade Payables	8.3	13.1	9.4	12.0	12.2	11.5
.2	.2	.2	Income Taxes Payable	.0	.2	.0	.3	.0	.2
8.5	8.9	11.0	All Other Current	4.4	15.7	8.3	7.0	10.0	15.2
58.2	59.8	59.9	Total Current	69.6	56.7	50.8	56.5	60.4	65.3
13.4	14.0	12.8	Long-Term Debt	3.2	16.9	22.7	15.4	10.1	9.1
.3	.3	.3	Deferred Taxes	.0	.1	.0	.1	.1	.8
4.2	5.6	3.1	All Other Non-Current	7.0	1.8	2.8	4.5	2.0	2.9
23.9	20.3	23.9	Net Worth	20.2	24.5	23.8	23.4	27.4	21.8
100.0	100.0	100.0	Total Liabilities & Net Worth	100.0	100.0	100.0	100.0	100.0	100.0
			INCOME DATA						
100.0	100.0	100.0	Net Sales	100.0	100.0	100.0	100.0	100.0	100.0
22.2	21.6	20.1	Gross Profit	31.9	29.8	23.4	20.7	16.5	14.4
20.4	20.0	17.8	Operating Expenses	26.0	27.9	20.6	18.7	14.8	12.4
1.8	1.6	2.3	Operating Profit	5.9	2.0	2.9	2.1	1.8	2.1
1.0	.6	.5	All Other Expenses (net)	1.9	.7	.4	.5	.5	.0
.9	1.0	1.8	Profit Before Taxes	3.9	1.2	2.5	1.5	1.3	2.1
			RATIOS						
1.7	1.6	1.8		2.0	2.6	2.7	1.9	1.8	1.5
1.2	1.2	1.2	Current	1.1	1.5	1.4	1.2	1.2	1.1
1.0	1.0	1.0		.9	.9	1.0	1.1	1.0	1.0
.6	.6	.7		.7	1.6	.8	.6	.8	.6
(197) .3	(253) .3	.3	Quick	.2	.6	.4	.3	.4	.3
.1	.1	.1		.1	.1	.1	.1	.1	.2
3 131.2	3 119.1	4 96.7		0 UND	1 320.9	1 397.5	4 93.2	4 103.1	6 59.1
9 42.5	9 40.5	10 34.9	Sales/Receivables	9 42.3	14 25.4	6 58.1	9 39.8	9 38.8	15 24.9
20 18.0	20 18.3	23 15.9		48 7.6	30 12.1	18 20.8	23 16.1	20 18.2	21 17.1
46 7.9	46 8.0	42 8.8		40 9.1	8 44.8	17 22.0	46 7.9	42 8.7	45 8.1
71 5.1	71 5.2	65 5.6	Cost of Sales/Inventory	155 2.4	57 6.5	66 5.6	75 4.9	63 5.8	60 6.1
113 3.2	108 3.4	114 3.2		358 1.0	141 2.6	92 4.0	119 3.1	108 3.4	106 3.4
2 189.5	2 171.6	2 150.3		0 UND	0 UND	2 202.9	2 157.1	4 93.3	4 89.8
8 47.7	8 48.6	9 40.5	Cost of Sales/Payables	0 UND	7 51.9	15 24.2	10 36.5	9 40.5	9 41.1
21 17.2	20 18.7	21 17.3		34 10.7	40 9.0	21 17.3	27 13.7	21 17.3	17 21.3
10.6	11.2	9.4		6.0	6.1	8.9	9.4	9.9	13.2
24.0	31.8	24.4	Sales/Working Capital	46.7	15.9	17.5	20.7	27.0	46.6
181.0	125.2	109.3		NM	−49.5	153.0	54.3	152.7	110.8
4.5	4.8	6.4		9.3	5.9	7.4	4.5	5.9	7.4
(161) 2.0	(211) 2.2	(211) 2.6	EBIT/Interest	(12) 3.8	(25) 1.5	(25) 3.5	(43) 1.8	(52) 2.2	(54) 3.6
1.2	1.2	1.3		2.4	−1.2	1.7	1.1	1.1	1.9
2.6	2.1	6.1	Net Profit + Depr., Dep.,					6.5	3.6
(28) 1.6	(32) 1.1	(36) 2.3	Amort./Cur. Mat. L/T/D					(11) 2.4	(16) 2.2
.9	.6	1.2						1.2	1.2
.1	.2	.2		.0	.0	.3	.2	.1	.2
.5	.6	.5	Fixed/Worth	.2	.5	.5	.5	.3	.5
2.1	2.2	1.9		2.0	25.6	3.0	2.4	1.1	1.5
1.9	2.3	1.8		2.6	1.2	2.0	1.6	1.1	2.3
4.2	5.2	4.4	Debt/Worth	9.9	5.1	3.7	3.9	4.9	4.5
9.2	12.9	10.7		NM	63.0	14.3	12.5	10.6	9.0
39.9	45.5	40.1	% Profit Before Taxes/Tangible	160.9	66.8	47.3	27.2	37.0	40.7
(181) 13.9	(230) 18.1	(214) 19.3	Net Worth	(10) 55.5	(24) 13.7	(25) 25.3	(42) 13.7	(51) 15.3	(62) 20.3
3.2	4.5	7.4		11.8	−3.6	8.7	4.3	3.9	12.3
8.2	7.5	7.9	% Profit Before Taxes/Total	24.3	10.2	17.1	5.9	7.3	7.9
2.3	3.3	3.7	Assets	7.1	2.0	4.5	2.8	2.4	4.1
.3	.5	.9		2.6	−3.8	2.3	.5	.3	1.8
132.7	122.3	111.8		UND	302.9	71.9	100.8	129.0	71.5
40.5	33.0	40.0	Sales/Net Fixed Assets	34.8	36.9	31.9	21.0	58.3	45.1
10.8	9.4	13.3		13.9	15.5	10.3	8.6	17.8	19.2
4.5	4.1	4.4		4.3	6.7	4.7	3.9	4.1	4.4
3.2	2.9	3.1	Sales/Total Assets	2.5	3.2	3.5	2.8	3.1	3.2
2.2	2.0	2.1		1.2	1.8	1.8	2.0	2.3	2.4
.3	.2	.3			.7	.6	.3	.3	.2
(164) .6	(205) .6	(190) .6	% Depr., Dep., Amort./Sales		(18) 1.4	(20) 1.1	(37) 1.2	(49) .6	(59) .4
1.8	1.8	1.5			4.2	3.2	3.1	1.0	.8
.6	.6	.8			1.3	1.1	1.0	.8	.5
(121) 1.4	(126) 1.5	(116) 1.5	% Officers', Directors', Owners' Comp/Sales	(15) 1.7	(14) 1.9	(24) 1.5	(34) 1.1	(21) 1.5	
3.6	4.0	3.0			3.6	3.5	2.7	2.8	2.0
4549794M	10875377M	7582651M	Net Sales ($)	8046M	64279M	106120M	375090M	975050M	6054066M
1776504M	2851376M	2744825M	Total Assets ($)	5318M	34930M	50364M	169814M	353493M	2130906M

© RMA 2005

M = $ thousand   MM = $ million
See Pages 11 through 21 for Explanation of Ratios and Data

Current Data Sorted By Assets | Comparative Historical Data

Type of Statement	0-500M	500M-2MM	2-10MM	10-50MM	50-100MM	100-250MM		4/1/00-3/31/01 ALL	4/1/01-3/31/02 ALL
Unqualified	1	1	6	9	2	4		16	19
Reviewed	2	23	33	6	1			45	32
Compiled	21	37	27	2	1			100	82
Tax Returns	31	22	8					43	40
Other	10	18	24	12		1		67	77
	57 (4/1-9/30/04)			245 (10/1/04-3/31/05)					
NUMBER OF STATEMENTS	65	101	98	29	4	5		271	250
	%	%	%	%	%	%	**ASSETS**	%	%
Cash & Equivalents	10.0	8.5	5.9	6.3				7.3	6.5
Trade Receivables (net)	15.7	19.9	21.0	19.8				18.0	18.5
Inventory	46.5	51.8	49.4	45.4				46.1	45.7
All Other Current	1.7	1.2	1.9	1.4				2.1	1.5
Total Current	73.9	81.4	78.2	72.8				73.4	72.1
Fixed Assets (net)	20.1	12.9	15.6	15.1				18.4	18.9
Intangibles (net)	2.0	1.3	1.1	4.8				2.5	2.9
All Other Non-Current	3.9	4.4	5.2	7.3				5.7	6.1
Total	100.0	100.0	100.0	100.0				100.0	100.0
							LIABILITIES		
Notes Payable-Short Term	12.5	8.7	10.8	12.8				8.7	9.0
Cur. Mat.-L/T/D	7.0	2.8	3.7	2.7				3.7	3.3
Trade Payables	21.2	22.3	23.0	24.6				24.5	22.5
Income Taxes Payable	.7	.2	.3	.3				.2	.2
All Other Current	7.4	6.0	7.0	6.6				7.2	8.1
Total Current	48.8	40.0	44.8	46.9				44.3	43.0
Long-Term Debt	26.8	14.0	13.1	13.8				16.0	17.5
Deferred Taxes	.0	.1	.2	.2				.2	.2
All Other Non-Current	12.8	4.7	4.1	1.2				5.3	5.0
Net Worth	11.7	41.3	37.7	37.8				34.3	34.3
Total Liabilities & Net Worth	100.0	100.0	100.0	100.0				100.0	100.0
							INCOME DATA		
Net Sales	100.0	100.0	100.0	100.0				100.0	100.0
Gross Profit	40.1	35.4	34.5	35.8				36.8	38.0
Operating Expenses	36.9	32.6	32.2	30.6				34.3	35.4
Operating Profit	3.1	2.8	2.4	5.2				2.5	2.6
All Other Expenses (net)	.7	.3	-.1	.7				.2	.2
Profit Before Taxes	2.5	2.6	2.4	4.5				2.3	2.4
							RATIOS		
Current	3.8	3.3	2.5	2.5				2.8	2.8
	1.9	2.0	1.8	1.5				1.7	1.8
	.9	1.5	1.3	1.2				1.2	1.2
Quick	1.2	1.1	.8	.9				.9	1.0
	.6	.6	(97) .6	.6	.4			.6	.6
	.3	.4	.4	.3				.3	.4
Sales/Receivables	6 62.0	14 25.4	18 20.5	21 17.6				11 34.0	13 27.3
	17 21.9	24 15.2	27 13.3	27 13.4				23 15.7	23 15.8
	26 14.0	34 10.6	38 9.6	44 8.4				33 10.9	33 11.1
Cost of Sales/Inventory	35 10.5	67 5.4	70 5.2	59 6.2				55 6.6	62 5.9
	72 5.1	91 4.0	100 3.6	115 3.2				92 4.0	102 3.6
	130 2.8	146 2.5	154 2.4	186 2.0				137 2.7	150 2.4
Cost of Sales/Payables	16 23.3	26 13.8	29 12.4	42 8.6				27 13.7	24 15.1
	38 9.6	38 9.7	46 7.9	67 5.5				44 8.3	44 8.4
	51 7.2	58 6.3	62 5.9	76 4.8				67 5.4	67 5.5
Sales/Working Capital	4.3	4.6	4.5	5.1				4.9	4.9
	14.0	6.8	7.7	10.1				10.0	9.0
	-104.2	14.4	21.1	16.7				27.8	28.9
EBIT/Interest	6.7	10.2	13.0	19.6				5.7	6.5
	(50) 2.0	(92) 3.4	(92) 4.9	(28) 3.8				(239) 2.7	(225) 2.5
	-.7	1.7	2.1	1.9				1.2	1.2
Net Profit + Depr., Dep., Amort./Cur. Mat. L/T/D		3.8	4.0	11.0				3.8	4.2
		(24) 2.2	(33) 2.3	(10) 2.0				(74) 1.7	(50) 2.5
		1.1	1.1	1.0				.9	.7
Fixed/Worth	.1	.1	.2	.1				.2	.2
	.7	.2	.4	.4				.4	.4
	-5.5	.6	.8	1.1				1.3	1.5
Debt/Worth	.9	.8	1.0	.7				.9	.8
	2.2	1.4	1.7	2.5				1.8	1.9
	-10.2	3.6	3.5	6.5				4.8	5.3
% Profit Before Taxes/Tangible Net Worth	55.8	29.0	30.5	31.3				31.5	34.4
	(45) 10.6	(96) 14.3	(94) 12.0	(26) 22.2				(243) 14.8	(224) 14.1
	-1.2	3.8	4.3	13.4				4.0	3.0
% Profit Before Taxes/Total Assets	14.6	10.4	10.7	12.3				10.0	10.7
	4.1	5.4	4.7	5.8				4.4	4.5
	-3.6	1.6	1.9	3.1				1.0	.5
Sales/Net Fixed Assets	83.4	75.2	41.4	42.1				44.7	38.0
	32.6	32.1	22.8	16.9				20.1	19.5
	11.9	15.9	12.4	11.2				12.1	10.9
Sales/Total Assets	5.7	3.6	3.5	3.5				3.8	3.4
	3.0	3.0	2.7	2.1				2.7	2.6
	2.4	2.2	1.9	1.7				2.0	2.0
% Depr., Dep., Amort./Sales	.7	.5	.7	.7				.8	.8
	(48) 1.3	(85) 1.1	(87) 1.2	(27) 1.3				(245) 1.3	(230) 1.4
	2.0	1.6	1.6	2.1				2.0	2.3
% Officers', Directors', Owners' Comp/Sales	3.7	2.4	1.2					1.9	1.9
	(44) 6.1	(66) 4.0	(44) 2.6					(142) 3.6	(135) 3.3
	8.6	7.6	5.0					6.2	6.3
Net Sales ($)	63352M	340753M	1194769M	1316577M	644467M	1400417M		3246513M	2542901M
Total Assets ($)	17491M	112453M	430760M	610581M	300479M	785064M		1261522M	1099956M

© RMA 2005

M = $ thousand   MM = $ million
See Pages 11 through 21 for Explanation of Ratios and Data

Comparative Historical Data / Current Data Sorted By Sales

4/1/02-3/31/03 ALL	4/1/03-3/31/04 ALL	4/1/04-3/31/05 ALL	Type of Statement	0-1MM	1-3MM	3-5MM	5-10MM	10-25MM	25MM & OVER
29	21	23	Unqualified		1	2		6	14
68	79	65	Reviewed	1	9	11	19	17	8
100	105	88	Compiled	14	22	20	12	16	4
51	90	61	Tax Returns	23	23	4	10	1	
86	95	65	Other	7	15	10	9	10	14
				57 (4/1-9/30/04)			245 (10/1/04-3/31/05)		
334	390	302	**NUMBER OF STATEMENTS**	45	70	47	50	50	40
%	%	%	**ASSETS**	%	%	%	%	%	%
6.1	7.2	7.8	Cash & Equivalents	7.9	9.7	8.8	4.9	8.4	6.1
18.9	18.3	19.2	Trade Receivables (net)	12.3	20.1	18.0	24.6	20.2	19.0
45.8	46.0	48.7	Inventory	50.7	48.6	50.5	50.5	47.6	43.8
2.2	1.7	1.5	All Other Current	1.8	.8	1.4	1.2	2.4	2.1
72.9	73.2	77.3	Total Current	72.7	79.1	78.7	81.1	78.6	71.1
18.4	18.0	15.7	Fixed Assets (net)	21.2	13.8	13.8	14.7	15.5	16.5
2.8	2.9	2.2	Intangibles (net)	1.7	1.9	1.8	.7	.6	7.3
5.9	5.8	4.9	All Other Non-Current	4.3	5.2	5.8	3.5	5.2	5.1
100.0	100.0	100.0	Total	100.0	100.0	100.0	100.0	100.0	100.0
			LIABILITIES						
11.1	10.7	10.4	Notes Payable-Short Term	13.7	9.6	7.8	11.3	10.2	10.2
3.4	3.1	3.9	Cur. Mat.-L/T/D	8.2	3.4	2.9	3.3	3.8	2.4
24.3	22.8	22.6	Trade Payables	17.4	21.7	20.5	26.3	24.9	25.0
.2	.2	.3	Income Taxes Payable	.7	.3	.1	.1	.6	.3
7.2	7.4	6.7	All Other Current	7.5	5.4	6.2	6.9	7.6	7.3
46.2	44.1	44.0	Total Current	47.6	40.4	37.5	47.9	47.0	45.3
18.7	17.6	16.4	Long-Term Debt	31.2	19.0	9.5	15.6	8.8	14.1
.1	.2	.1	Deferred Taxes	.0	.0	.1	.2	.3	.4
5.7	5.8	6.0	All Other Non-Current	10.2	9.8	4.9	3.5	3.1	2.5
29.2	32.2	33.5	Net Worth	11.1	30.8	48.0	32.8	40.8	37.8
100.0	100.0	100.0	Total Liabilities & Net Worth	100.0	100.0	100.0	100.0	100.0	100.0
			INCOME DATA						
100.0	100.0	100.0	Net Sales	100.0	100.0	100.0	100.0	100.0	100.0
35.9	35.8	36.2	Gross Profit	39.9	37.3	35.1	34.5	34.5	35.4
33.2	33.0	33.1	Operating Expenses	37.7	33.0	32.9	32.8	31.6	30.6
2.6	2.8	3.1	Operating Profit	2.2	4.4	2.2	1.6	2.8	4.9
.5	.3	.3	All Other Expenses (net)	.9	.4	.0	.0	.0	.6
2.1	2.5	2.8	Profit Before Taxes	1.2	4.0	2.2	1.7	2.8	4.2
			RATIOS						
2.5	2.8	3.1	Current	4.5	3.4	3.2	2.5	2.4	2.4
1.6	1.7	1.9		2.0	2.2	2.2	1.6	1.7	1.5
1.1	1.2	1.2		.9	1.3	1.6	1.3	1.3	1.2
.9	.9	1.0	Quick	1.0	1.3	1.0	.8	.9	.8
.5	(389) .6	(301) .6		.5	.7	.6	.6	(49) .5	.4
.3	.3	.4		.3	.4	.5	.5	.5	.3
12 31.1	12 30.3	12 29.5	Sales/Receivables	5 67.6	13 28.6	13 27.3	21 17.7	12 29.4	8 43.1
25 14.4	25 14.6	24 15.0		17 21.9	24 15.2	20 18.2	31 11.8	26 14.3	28 13.0
35 10.3	35 10.5	34 10.6		27 13.5	32 11.4	33 11.2	40 9.1	36 10.1	38 9.6
55 6.6	55 6.6	56 6.5	Cost of Sales/Inventory	44 8.2	48 7.7	55 6.7	73 5.0	53 6.9	58 6.3
94 3.9	95 3.8	92 4.0		87 4.2	90 4.0	96 3.8	102 3.6	81 4.5	98 3.7
146 2.5	147 2.5	148 2.5		181 2.0	149 2.4	148 2.5	144 2.5	122 3.0	163 2.2
27 13.7	25 14.4	27 13.5	Cost of Sales/Payables	5 76.4	25 14.5	27 13.6	30 12.0	28 13.0	42 8.6
43 8.5	43 8.5	45 8.2		36 10.1	37 9.9	38 9.5	52 7.0	46 7.9	54 6.7
63 5.8	62 5.9	60 6.1		52 7.0	54 6.7	55 6.6	69 5.3	67 5.4	73 5.0
5.4	5.0	4.5	Sales/Working Capital	2.9	4.2	3.9	4.9	5.1	5.7
10.8	9.5	8.2		7.1	6.8	6.1	8.7	8.7	12.4
35.7	34.2	22.2		-104.2	23.2	12.6	16.4	26.8	31.3
6.1	8.0	10.8	EBIT/Interest	4.2	10.0	8.3	8.2	19.6	18.3
(303) 3.2	(359) 3.2	(271) 3.7		(34) 1.0	(59) 3.4	(44) 3.7	(47) 2.8	(48) 6.7	(39) 5.7
1.2	1.3	1.7		-1.0	2.0	1.8	1.2	2.9	2.4
3.9	3.8	4.1	Net Profit + Depr., Dep., Amort./Cur. Mat. L/T/D			3.8	3.9	4.1	22.3
(84) 2.0	(85) 2.1	(80) 2.3				(16) 1.9	(15) 3.1	(21) 2.9	(17) 4.2
.8	1.0	1.1				.7	1.3	1.1	1.5
.2	.2	.1	Fixed/Worth	.1	.1	.1	.2	.1	.2
.5	.4	.3		.7	.3	.2	.4	.3	.6
1.4	1.3	1.1		-1.4	1.2	.5	.9	.7	1.6
1.1	1.0	.8	Debt/Worth	.9	.8	.6	.9	.9	.8
2.1	2.1	1.7		2.8	1.8	1.1	2.1	1.6	2.8
6.0	5.6	4.9		-5.6	6.3	1.8	4.1	2.4	6.5
34.5	34.4	32.1	% Profit Before Taxes/Tangible Net Worth	31.8	54.7	20.0	22.9	30.3	32.5
(289) 14.6	(348) 14.4	(267) 15.2		(29) 8.5	(63) 18.7	(46) 7.9	(48) 10.2	(47) 17.2	(34) 23.0
2.8	4.0	4.3		-1.2	4.9	2.1	3.5	10.6	14.6
10.4	10.2	10.9	% Profit Before Taxes/Total Assets	9.6	14.4	9.2	6.5	13.4	14.5
4.5	4.9	5.3		.5	7.6	4.1	3.5	6.6	6.2
.4	.9	1.3		-4.9	2.3	1.0	.5	2.4	3.0
51.0	60.9	58.7	Sales/Net Fixed Assets	90.3	66.4	61.6	56.3	54.8	41.3
21.3	22.4	26.0		21.7	33.6	27.8	24.4	27.5	16.5
11.5	11.5	13.2		7.7	18.5	13.3	16.5	12.4	10.1
3.7	3.7	3.6	Sales/Total Assets	3.7	4.0	3.6	3.5	4.0	3.6
2.7	2.7	2.8		2.6	2.9	2.8	2.8	3.0	2.5
2.1	2.0	2.1		1.8	2.2	1.9	2.1	2.1	1.8
.7	.7	.7	% Depr., Dep., Amort./Sales	.7	.5	.7	.6	.7	.6
(300) 1.3	(335) 1.1	(255) 1.2		(31) 1.6	(56) 1.1	(42) 1.1	(45) 1.2	(45) 1.0	(36) 1.3
1.9	2.0	1.7		2.4	1.6	1.6	1.7	1.5	2.0
2.0	1.6	2.0	% Officers', Directors', Owners' Comp/Sales	4.1	2.8	2.0	1.4	1.1	
(171) 3.3	(211) 3.2	(163) 3.9		(30) 6.2	(49) 4.5	(29) 3.3	(27) 2.9	(20) 2.4	
6.3	5.7	7.2		8.9	8.4	4.9	7.2	4.0	
5902652M	6003226M	4960335M	Net Sales ($)	30951M	127313M	185995M	362500M	785014M	3468562M
2551923M	2861223M	2256828M	Total Assets ($)	13553M	47247M	74221M	144867M	291495M	1685445M

M = $ thousand   MM = $ million
See Pages 11 through 21 for Explanation of Ratios and Data

						Type of Statement		
Current Data Sorted By Assets							**Comparative Historical Data**	
	3		1	6	1	Unqualified		
1		3	4			Reviewed	D	D
13	18	14	1			Compiled	A	A
16	13	2			1	Tax Returns	T	T
5	5	1	6	1		Other	A	A
	23 (4/1-9/30/04)		92 (10/1/04-3/31/05)				4/1/00-3/31/01 ALL	4/1/01-3/31/02 ALL
0-500M	500M-2MM	2-10MM	10-50MM	50-100MM	100-250MM			
35	39	20	12	7	2	**NUMBER OF STATEMENTS**	N	N
%	%	%	%	%	%	**ASSETS**	%	%
13.4	8.5	6.4	8.5			Cash & Equivalents	O	O
17.1	21.1	21.5	18.9			Trade Receivables (net)	T	T
36.2	31.5	43.5	37.7			Inventory		
1.6	2.6	.2	6.7			All Other Current	A	A
68.3	63.6	71.7	71.9			Total Current	V	V
24.0	24.5	21.4	21.3			Fixed Assets (net)	A	A
2.7	3.7	.4	.4			Intangibles (net)	I	I
5.0	8.2	6.5	6.4			All Other Non-Current	L	L
100.0	100.0	100.0	100.0			Total	A	A
						LIABILITIES	B	B
8.0	10.0	9.6	13.2			Notes Payable-Short Term	L	L
4.8	4.1	2.9	1.6			Cur. Mat.-L/T/D	E	E
38.0	24.7	36.9	31.8			Trade Payables		
.5	.0	.3	.7			Income Taxes Payable		
11.3	5.1	3.2	10.6			All Other Current		
62.7	43.8	52.9	57.9			Total Current		
28.2	18.6	13.7	12.5			Long-Term Debt		
.0	.2	.0	.3			Deferred Taxes		
5.9	1.1	1.4	2.7			All Other Non-Current		
3.2	36.3	31.9	26.7			Net Worth		
100.0	100.0	100.0	100.0			Total Liabilities & Net Worth		
						INCOME DATA		
100.0	100.0	100.0	100.0			Net Sales		
40.4	37.3	32.0	29.6			Gross Profit		
39.3	36.2	30.3	27.7			Operating Expenses		
1.1	1.1	1.7	1.9			Operating Profit		
.3	.0	.1	-1.0			All Other Expenses (net)		
.8	1.1	1.6	2.8			Profit Before Taxes		
						RATIOS		
1.8	2.2	2.0	1.5					
1.2	1.4	1.2	1.2			Current		
.8	1.0	1.0	1.1					
1.0	1.2	.7	.6					
.5	.7	.5	.5			Quick		
.2	.4	.3	.3					

								Sales/Receivables		
5	75.3	10	37.3	18	20.7	16	22.9			
10	35.7	26	14.2	27	13.4	30	12.2	Sales/Receivables		
19	19.6	39	9.4	37	9.8	36	10.2			
28	12.9	36	10.2	54	6.7	64	5.7			
57	6.4	59	6.2	88	4.1	77	4.7	Cost of Sales/Inventory		
80	4.6	90	4.1	113	3.2	95	3.9			
25	14.5	26	14.3	58	6.3	38	9.6			
37	10.0	44	8.2	68	5.4	64	5.7	Cost of Sales/Payables		
83	4.4	72	5.1	90	4.1	90	4.1			

					Sales/Working Capital		
12.3		7.3	7.4	10.1			
38.5		18.9	27.4	21.0	Sales/Working Capital		
-36.9		-285.5	-406.1	101.5			
	9.8		8.2	7.6	14.5	EBIT/Interest	
(25)	2.8	(34)	2.6	3.6	4.2	EBIT/Interest	
	.2		.9	2.0	2.8		
					Net Profit + Depr., Dep., Amort./Cur. Mat. L /T/D		
.3		.2	.2	.3			
2.5		.6	.7	.7	Fixed/Worth		
-.4		1.4	1.5	1.4			
1.0		.7	1.1	1.7			
5.1		1.5	2.7	3.6	Debt/Worth		
-3.2		5.0	5.2	4.6			
	97.2		17.9	33.3	58.7	% Profit Before Taxes/Tangible Net Worth	
(23)	33.9	(34)	8.2	13.8	27.9	% Profit Before Taxes/Tangible Net Worth	
	.0		-.6	8.7	11.0		
21.0		9.5	7.5	12.5	% Profit Before Taxes/Total Assets		
6.6		2.8	3.9	5.0	% Profit Before Taxes/Total Assets		
-1.7		-.2	2.6	2.7			
91.8		33.1	37.4	28.5	Sales/Net Fixed Assets		
26.5		19.9	15.5	13.6	Sales/Net Fixed Assets		
12.5		9.3	8.0	6.8			
6.4		3.9	3.7	3.7	Sales/Total Assets		
4.2		3.2	2.7	2.6	Sales/Total Assets		
3.1		2.4	2.4	2.1			

								% Depr., Dep., Amort./Sales	
	.6		.9		1.0		.7		
(26)	1.0	(32)	2.0	(18)	1.3	(11)	1.0	% Depr., Dep., Amort./Sales	
	2.3		2.6		2.0		1.6		
	1.3		1.1		.9			% Officers', Directors', Owners' Comp/Sales	
(21)	4.0	(24)	3.1	(14)	1.3			% Officers', Directors', Owners' Comp/Sales	
	6.2		6.0		6.7				

44837M	143624M	204824M	620548M	1009028M	1258872M	Net Sales ($)	
10383M	45141M	75409M	228584M	481534M	308689M	Total Assets ($)	

© RMA 2005

M = $ thousand　　MM = $ million
See Pages 11 through 21 for Explanation of Ratios and Data

Comparative Historical Data | Current Data Sorted By Sales

			Type of Statement						
6	7	11	Unqualified		2		1		8
5	11	8	Reviewed		1		1	3	3
26	31	46	Compiled	4	14	4	18	5	1
16	23	32	Tax Returns	8	15	4	3	1	1
15	21	18	Other	2	6		2	1	6
4/1/02-3/31/03 ALL	4/1/03-3/31/04 ALL	4/1/04-3/31/05 ALL		23 (4/1-9/30/04) 0-1MM	1-3MM	3-5MM	92 (10/1/04-3/31/05) 5-10MM	10-25MM	25MM & OVER
68	93	115	**NUMBER OF STATEMENTS**	14	38	8	25	11	19
%	%	%	**ASSETS**	%	%	%	%	%	%
7.9	9.1	9.3	Cash & Equivalents	7.0	14.8		6.6	4.5	7.4
20.8	20.1	19.6	Trade Receivables (net)	13.1	17.5		26.1	22.6	19.0
41.2	38.9	36.4	Inventory	36.0	32.7		40.1	38.5	41.2
1.5	2.0	2.2	All Other Current	.6	2.0		2.1	5.8	1.5
71.5	70.1	67.5	Total Current	56.7	67.0		75.0	71.4	69.2
21.3	21.0	22.9	Fixed Assets (net)	31.0	24.1		18.8	21.2	19.3
1.3	2.3	3.1	Intangibles (net)	5.1	3.2		1.1	.5	5.9
5.9	6.7	6.5	All Other Non-Current	7.2	5.6		5.2	6.9	5.7
100.0	100.0	100.0	Total	100.0	100.0		100.0	100.0	100.0
			LIABILITIES						
10.0	10.0	10.0	Notes Payable-Short Term	9.5	5.7		9.4	15.3	12.1
3.9	4.4	3.6	Cur. Mat.-L/T/D	11.3	2.4		4.1	2.0	1.3
30.6	25.4	32.3	Trade Payables	31.0	31.7		32.6	35.3	32.8
.3	.2	.3	Income Taxes Payable	.3	.3		.2	.1	.6
8.7	7.1	7.3	All Other Current	13.8	7.1		5.2	3.6	8.8
53.4	47.2	53.4	Total Current	66.0	47.2		51.4	56.2	55.5
17.9	20.9	19.0	Long-Term Debt	50.2	22.6		9.9	11.2	10.1
.0	.2	.1	Deferred Taxes	.0	.3		.3	.2	.2
10.5	5.6	3.7	All Other Non-Current	2.1	3.9		.9	2.1	7.8
18.1	26.2	23.8	Net Worth	−18.2	26.3		37.5	30.3	26.4
100.0	100.0	100.0	Total Liabilities & Net Worth	100.0	100.0		100.0	100.0	100.0
			INCOME DATA						
100.0	100.0	100.0	Net Sales	100.0	100.0		100.0	100.0	100.0
36.5	35.8	35.6	Gross Profit	37.6	42.8		32.8	32.7	26.9
35.2	34.1	34.0	Operating Expenses	39.6	40.3		31.4	30.0	24.0
1.3	1.6	1.6	Operating Profit	−2.0	2.6		1.4	2.7	2.9
.3	.2	.1	All Other Expenses (net)	1.6	.2		−.4	.5	−.3
1.0	1.4	1.5	Profit Before Taxes	−3.5	2.4		1.8	2.1	3.1
			RATIOS						
2.6	2.4	1.9	Current	1.8	2.2		2.2	1.9	1.7
1.5	1.6	1.3		.7	1.6		1.4	1.2	1.2
1.1	1.2	1.0		.5	1.1		1.1	1.0	1.0
1.0	1.1	.9	Quick	.5	1.4		.8	.7	.6
.6	.5	.5		.3	.8		.6	.6	.5
.4	.4	.3		.1	.4		.3	.3	.3
9 40.6	11 34.1	9 40.7	Sales/Receivables	0 UND	6 59.0		18 19.9	27 13.6	16 22.8
20 18.1	23 16.2	19 19.1		7 53.5	14 25.9		29 12.6	38 9.6	27 13.7
32 11.3	32 11.3	33 11.2		19 19.7	28 13.0		34 10.9	60 6.1	33 10.9
30 12.0	38 9.5	45 8.1	Cost of Sales/Inventory	44 8.3	30 12.1		46 7.9	53 6.8	63 5.8
65 5.7	67 5.5	64 5.7		66 5.5	54 6.8		62 5.9	85 4.3	76 4.8
110 3.3	100 3.7	92 4.0		96 3.8	88 4.1		93 3.9	104 3.5	92 4.0
23 15.5	23 15.9	29 12.5	Cost of Sales/Payables	0 UND	25 14.8		33 10.9	58 6.3	35 10.3
44 8.4	41 8.9	51 7.2		37 10.0	38 9.6		54 6.8	64 5.7	61 5.9
67 5.5	64 5.7	81 4.5		95 3.8	81 4.5		71 5.2	140 2.6	84 4.3
6.3	7.0	8.4	Sales/Working Capital	11.6	7.3		7.8	7.3	11.0
14.1	13.4	20.8		−20.0	18.7		17.8	14.3	25.8
93.5	48.0	−285.5		−4.1	139.0		234.6	−999.8	−999.8
11.8	6.5	7.8	EBIT/Interest	3.7	12.5		11.7	11.2	15.7
(62) 2.9	(81) 2.5	(99) 3.3		(12) 1.3	(27) 3.3		(24) 3.5	3.5	(18) 4.5
.7	1.4	1.3		−5.6	1.1		2.1	2.1	2.4
7.2	4.6	10.1	Net Profit + Depr., Dep.,						22.2
(17) 2.3	(25) 2.2	(27) 3.5	Amort./Cur. Mat. L/T/D					(10)	5.5
1.7	1.8	1.6							2.1
.2	.2	.3	Fixed/Worth	1.2	.3		.2	.5	.4
.5	.6	.8		−2.2	.7		.4	.7	.8
1.7	1.4	2.8		−.1	9.8		1.2	1.0	1.8
1.0	1.0	1.0	Debt/Worth	3.8	.6		.9	1.3	1.7
2.6	2.3	2.8		−5.1	1.5		1.8	2.7	3.6
6.9	5.1	12.5		−2.2	31.7		3.7	15.3	6.4
26.6	25.5	36.4	% Profit Before Taxes/Tangible		61.1		25.3	41.3	55.4
(58) 11.5	(80) 11.1	(95) 14.5	Net Worth		(31) 4.1		14.6	18.9	(16) 30.6
1.2	3.5	3.2			−6.0		7.6	11.7	15.4
9.1	10.4	9.9	% Profit Before Taxes/Total	8.0	18.9		9.7	8.0	12.8
2.4	3.3	4.4	Assets	2.3	5.0		4.0	3.9	7.0
−1.1	.9	.3		−32.3	−1.2		2.8	2.5	2.3
54.6	38.8	41.9	Sales/Net Fixed Assets	155.4	49.3		30.1	33.4	30.9
25.8	20.2	19.9		18.9	22.3		20.0	9.3	17.8
12.5	11.0	9.3		1.8	9.4		14.9	6.6	9.3
5.2	4.3	4.2	Sales/Total Assets	4.8	5.6		3.9	3.3	3.6
3.4	3.1	3.2		2.9	3.5		3.6	2.7	2.7
2.6	2.2	2.5		1.0	2.6		2.9	1.8	2.1
.7	.8	.8	% Depr., Dep., Amort./Sales	.6	.7		1.0	1.2	.5
(61) 1.3	(84) 1.5	(94) 1.3		(11) 2.6	(28) 1.1		(22) 1.3	1.6	(16) .9
2.2	2.3	2.3		4.0	2.4		2.0	2.5	1.5
1.1	1.3	1.0	% Officers', Directors',		3.2		.9		
(39) 2.7	(63) 3.1	(67) 2.2	Owners' Comp/Sales		(22) 5.2		(17) 1.4		
4.9	6.0	5.7			6.1		4.4		
1344816M	2988548M	3281733M	Net Sales ($)	9849M	67089M	29997M	162241M	168503M	2844054M
498784M	1010949M	1149740M	Total Assets ($)	5108M	20457M	8957M	48953M	89426M	976839M

M = $ thousand   MM = $ million
See Pages 11 through 21 for Explanation of Ratios and Data

Current Data Sorted By Assets   **Comparative Historical Data**

Type of Statement	0-500M	500M-2MM	2-10MM	10-50MM	50-100MM	100-250MM	ALL 4/1/00-3/31/01	ALL 4/1/01-3/31/02
Unqualified		2	10	27	6	6	37	40
Reviewed	3	18	58	20	2	1	104	88
Compiled	24	69	37	2		1	164	160
Tax Returns	44	72	36	1		1	76	63
Other	21	54	53	27	2	5	134	119
	123 (4/1-9/30/04)			479 (10/1/04-3/31/05)			4/1/00-3/31/01	4/1/01-3/31/02
NUMBER OF STATEMENTS	92	215	194	77	10	14	515	470
ASSETS	%	%	%	%	%	%	%	%
Cash & Equivalents	11.2	7.8	7.7	7.6	13.1	4.3	8.3	8.4
Trade Receivables (net)	12.9	10.5	12.4	12.4	10.8	16.1	16.1	13.7
Inventory	51.1	54.8	52.1	42.9	28.8	33.6	48.9	49.8
All Other Current	1.2	1.4	2.3	2.6	2.0	6.7	1.8	1.8
Total Current	76.4	74.5	74.6	65.5	54.7	60.6	75.1	73.7
Fixed Assets (net)	16.6	16.9	18.4	25.3	22.0	29.2	17.5	18.4
Intangibles (net)	2.3	2.1	1.8	3.2	11.8	4.7	2.2	2.6
All Other Non-Current	4.7	6.5	5.3	6.0	11.5	5.6	5.2	5.3
Total	100.0	100.0	100.0	100.0	100.0	100.0	100.0	100.0
LIABILITIES								
Notes Payable-Short Term	15.4	12.2	11.0	9.2	13.8	11.3	11.9	11.7
Cur. Mat.-L/T/D	5.3	2.9	2.5	1.7	1.7	5.2	2.6	2.7
Trade Payables	19.6	18.3	18.8	19.4	11.4	13.0	19.3	17.8
Income Taxes Payable	.0	.1	.3	.3	.1	.0	.1	.3
All Other Current	18.0	19.6	18.8	20.1	13.5	22.7	17.2	21.6
Total Current	58.2	53.1	51.4	50.6	40.5	52.2	51.1	54.2
Long-Term Debt	19.5	16.8	11.8	12.3	8.5	16.7	11.9	11.3
Deferred Taxes	.2	.0	.1	.1	.5	1.3	.1	.1
All Other Non-Current	4.6	4.9	4.7	3.1	4.4	9.4	4.7	13.5
Net Worth	17.4	25.1	31.9	33.9	46.0	20.3	32.2	20.9
Total Liabilities & Net Worth	100.0	100.0	100.0	100.0	100.0	100.0	100.0	100.0
INCOME DATA								
Net Sales	100.0	100.0	100.0	100.0	100.0	100.0	100.0	100.0
Gross Profit	42.4	41.5	40.3	41.9	42.2	41.5	39.9	41.2
Operating Expenses	38.4	39.7	38.2	39.6	39.4	39.9	37.3	38.8
Operating Profit	3.9	1.8	2.0	2.4	2.8	1.6	2.6	2.4
All Other Expenses (net)	1.0	.5	.2	.1	-1.5	-.5	.1	.4
Profit Before Taxes	2.9	1.3	1.8	2.2	4.3	2.1	2.5	1.9
RATIOS								
Current	2.7	2.4	2.3	1.8	2.3	1.6	2.1	2.3
	1.5	1.5	1.5	1.3	1.2	1.3	1.5	1.5
	1.0	1.1	1.1	1.0	1.1	1.0	1.1	1.1
Quick	.9	.7	.7	.9	1.1	.9	.9	.8
	(90) .4	(212) .2	.3	.3	.6	.2	(513) .4	(464) .4
	.1	.1	.1	.1	.3	.1	.1	.1
Sales/Receivables	0 UND	0 UND	1 438.3	1 342.4	2 156.2	4 99.3	1 294.8	1 650.8
	3 145.8	4 90.6	6 66.0	3 119.0	5 74.3	7 53.0	7 51.0	5 69.2
	18 20.2	16 22.5	27 13.4	23 15.5	10 37.7	21 17.2	28 12.9	23 16.2
Cost of Sales/Inventory	32 11.5	75 4.9	77 4.7	63 5.8	91 4.0	69 5.3	66 5.5	71 5.1
	83 4.4	116 3.1	123 3.0	105 3.5	114 3.2	92 4.0	107 3.4	109 3.4
	142 2.6	164 2.2	176 2.1	135 2.7	131 2.8	113 3.2	155 2.4	163 2.4
Cost of Sales/Payables	7 50.9	19 19.4	19 19.0	25 14.8	29 12.7	25 14.5	19 18.8	19 19.5
	25 14.9	32 11.4	33 11.2	37 9.9	36 10.1	35 10.5	34 10.7	31 11.7
	49 7.5	52 7.0	56 6.5	52 7.0	59 6.1	46 8.0	53 6.9	50 7.3
Sales/Working Capital	7.6	6.2	5.5	8.8	6.2	7.4	6.2	5.9
	18.1	13.0	12.6	26.2	13.7	25.2	13.3	12.3
	190.9	91.0	66.0	NM	207.8	158.3	46.3	58.9
EBIT/Interest	14.5	8.6	10.4	17.8		16.3	8.2	7.0
	(71) 3.4	(180) 2.8	(176) 3.7	(67) 3.7		(13) 6.8	(464) 2.8	(403) 2.5
	-.5	.1	1.3	1.5		1.4	1.3	1.0
Net Profit + Depr., Dep., Amort./Cur. Mat. L/T/D		5.3	6.7	9.1			6.1	4.7
		(25) 2.3	(46) 2.0	(19) 3.9			(104) 2.4	(86) 1.6
		.6	.7	2.0			1.0	.8
Fixed/Worth	.1	.1	.2	.3	.4	.6	.2	.2
	.4	.5	.5	.8	.8	1.3	.5	.5
	-3.9	4.8	1.5	2.5	1.4	-1.0	1.4	1.6
Debt/Worth	.9	1.0	.9	1.2	.6	1.4	.9	.9
	3.5	2.5	2.3	2.5	2.3	2.0	2.3	2.1
	-21.5	20.5	5.9	6.6	3.7	-4.0	5.9	6.0
% Profit Before Taxes/Tangible Net Worth	109.7	37.6	37.6	41.6		32.1	39.0	38.8
	(65) 50.6	(170) 13.3	(170) 15.4	(68) 17.9		(10) 25.6	(454) 15.7	(409) 14.2
	.0	1.7	3.2	3.2		11.4	4.8	2.8
% Profit Before Taxes/Total Assets	35.9	11.1	11.0	13.5	8.6	13.6	12.2	12.4
	10.3	3.6	3.1	5.3	6.8	8.7	5.1	4.2
	-3.9	-1.5	.4	.8	4.4	1.9	1.1	.3
Sales/Net Fixed Assets	257.2	60.0	47.4	30.9	10.3	10.8	49.9	53.6
	40.1	27.7	22.3	13.3	7.5	8.2	25.1	26.0
	17.4	13.1	9.9	7.8	5.9	4.2	10.7	10.6
Sales/Total Assets	6.2	4.0	3.6	3.9	2.3	2.9	4.0	4.0
	4.0	3.0	2.7	2.9	1.6	2.3	2.9	2.8
	2.3	2.1	1.8	2.0	1.1	1.0	2.1	1.8
% Depr., Dep., Amort./Sales	.4	.5	.5	.7		1.1	.5	.5
	(55) 1.1	(178) .9	(164) .8	(65) 1.1		(10) 1.4	(452) .8	(405) .9
	1.8	1.4	1.3	1.5		2.1	1.3	1.3
% Officers', Directors', Owners' Comp/Sales	3.2	2.1	1.0	.7			1.8	1.7
	(48) 5.3	(125) 3.9	(85) 2.2	(21) 1.1			(268) 3.4	(257) 3.3
	6.9	5.5	3.9	2.6			6.0	6.5
Net Sales ($)	107900M	780733M	2422469M	4865240M	1234443M	4832494M	13128939M	9613059M
Total Assets ($)	25098M	242808M	848948M	1617429M	743342M	2179527M	5379060M	3975344M

M = $ thousand   MM = $ million
See Pages 11 through 21 for Explanation of Ratios and Data

Comparative Historical Data				Current Data Sorted By Sales					
			Type of Statement						
64	46	51	Unqualified			1	2	10	38
101	109	102	Reviewed	3	11	8	20	36	24
134	198	133	Compiled	17	45	20	31	16	4
88	154	154	Tax Returns	22	64	26	29	10	3
132	142	162	Other	9	40	26	33	15	39
4/1/02-3/31/03 ALL	4/1/03-3/31/04 ALL	4/1/04-3/31/05 ALL		123 (4/1-9/30/04)			479 (10/1/04-3/31/05)		
				0-1MM	1-3MM	3-5MM	5-10MM	10-25MM	25MM & OVER
519	649	602	**NUMBER OF STATEMENTS**	51	160	81	115	87	108
%	%	%	**ASSETS**	%	%	%	%	%	%
9.7	9.0	8.3	Cash & Equivalents	9.6	7.4	9.0	9.0	7.4	8.3
14.1	12.4	11.9	Trade Receivables (net)	16.0	11.5	8.4	9.5	16.1	12.1
48.0	50.4	50.9	Inventory	46.5	53.2	55.5	55.7	49.2	42.6
2.1	2.2	1.9	All Other Current	1.0	2.2	2.5	.8	1.5	3.2
73.9	74.0	73.0	Total Current	73.2	74.3	75.3	75.0	74.2	66.2
18.5	18.4	18.8	Fixed Assets (net)	18.3	17.9	18.0	16.9	18.0	23.5
2.0	1.8	2.4	Intangibles (net)	2.6	1.9	.7	2.2	2.4	4.4
5.6	5.8	5.8	All Other Non-Current	5.9	5.9	6.0	5.9	5.4	5.9
100.0	100.0	100.0	Total	100.0	100.0	100.0	100.0	100.0	100.0
			LIABILITIES						
9.8	10.4	11.9	Notes Payable-Short Term	20.4	12.8	10.3	9.8	12.0	10.0
2.7	2.3	3.0	Cur. Mat.-L/T/D	5.5	4.0	1.7	2.8	2.2	2.2
18.0	19.1	18.6	Trade Payables	15.0	17.2	18.1	19.3	20.8	20.0
.3	.3	.2	Income Taxes Payable	.1	.0	.2	.3	.1	.3
16.8	18.4	19.1	All Other Current	14.9	17.8	19.5	20.3	19.1	21.5
47.6	50.5	52.8	Total Current	56.0	51.9	49.8	52.5	54.2	54.1
13.8	13.6	14.9	Long-Term Debt	22.0	19.8	11.5	16.2	9.3	10.1
.1	.1	.1	Deferred Taxes	.4	.0	.1	.1	.1	.3
5.5	4.8	4.7	All Other Non-Current	3.4	5.2	6.6	4.0	4.7	3.8
33.0	31.0	27.5	Net Worth	18.3	23.2	32.1	27.2	31.8	31.7
100.0	100.0	100.0	Total Liabilities & Net Worth	100.0	100.0	100.0	100.0	100.0	100.0
			INCOME DATA						
100.0	100.0	100.0	Net Sales	100.0	100.0	100.0	100.0	100.0	100.0
41.1	41.0	41.3	Gross Profit	45.4	42.2	42.3	40.3	38.6	40.5
38.3	38.9	39.0	Operating Expenses	41.2	39.8	39.8	39.1	36.9	37.9
2.8	2.1	2.3	Operating Profit	4.3	2.4	2.5	1.2	1.8	2.6
.4	.5	.4	All Other Expenses (net)	1.7	.6	.5	.0	.1	.0
2.4	1.6	1.9	Profit Before Taxes	2.5	1.8	2.0	1.2	1.7	2.6
			RATIOS						
2.5	2.3	2.3		3.6	2.7	2.7	2.2	2.0	1.6
1.6	1.6	1.4	Current	1.9	1.5	1.5	1.5	1.3	1.2
1.1	1.1	1.1		1.0	1.1	1.1	1.1	1.1	1.0
.9	.9	.8		1.1	.7	.8	.6	.8	.7
.4 (643)	.3 (597)	.3	Quick	.6 (157)	.3 (79)	.2	.3	.3	.3
.1	.1	.1		.1	.1	.1	.1	.1	.1
0 / 826.4	0 / 815.5	0 / 999.8		0 / UND	0 / UND	0 / UND	0 / 999.8	1 / 325.1	2 / 216.3
5 / 73.4	5 / 71.0	4 / 83.0	Sales/Receivables	5 / 72.1	5 / 77.1	4 / 88.0	5 / 70.5	5 / 70.2	4 / 100.3
25 / 14.5	22 / 16.9	18 / 20.3		37 / 10.0	17 / 21.4	15 / 23.7	14 / 26.0	29 / 12.4	14 / 26.9
65 / 5.6	67 / 5.4	68 / 5.4		46 / 8.0	74 / 4.9	77 / 4.7	84 / 4.3	63 / 5.7	61 / 5.9
111 / 3.3	110 / 3.3	114 / 3.2	Cost of Sales/Inventory	120 / 3.0	123 / 3.0	118 / 3.1	122 / 3.0	101 / 3.6	95 / 3.9
158 / 2.3	168 / 2.2	161 / 2.3		208 / 1.8	191 / 1.9	182 / 2.0	164 / 2.2	140 / 2.6	122 / 3.0
19 / 18.8	18 / 19.9	19 / 19.7		11 / 32.0	15 / 23.8	21 / 17.0	18 / 20.1	18 / 20.1	25 / 14.9
32 / 11.3	34 / 10.7	32 / 11.4	Cost of Sales/Payables	22 / 16.3	31 / 12.0	34 / 10.8	32 / 11.4	31 / 11.8	37 / 9.9
53 / 6.9	53 / 6.9	53 / 7.0		63 / 5.8	51 / 7.1	51 / 7.2	58 / 6.3	53 / 6.9	51 / 7.1
5.7	6.1	6.4		4.7	5.5	5.9	6.2	9.5	10.4
11.5	12.5	15.4	Sales/Working Capital	11.4	12.3	10.8	12.7	19.9	28.7
40.7	45.9	112.7		275.0	110.5	37.6	54.0	91.0	NM
10.4	9.3	11.0		5.5	10.1	11.0	8.8	14.3	20.0
(454) 3.3	(556) 3.0	(514) 3.4	EBIT/Interest	(37) 1.4	(138) 2.8	(66) 3.8	(99) 2.7	(83) 4.1	(91) 6.1
1.3	.9	1.0		-1.2	.1	.5	.7	2.0	1.7
9.0	7.7	6.6			5.0	7.1	5.8	4.6	9.1
(108) 3.1	(107) 2.4	(101) 2.6	Net Profit + Depr., Dep., Amort./Cur. Mat. L/T/D		(16) 1.3	(12) 3.1	(21) 1.2	(18) 2.6	(28) 4.2
1.1	.8	.9			.6	.9	.4	1.2	2.0
.1	.2	.2		.1	.1	.2	.2	.2	.4
.4	.5	.6	Fixed/Worth	.4	.6	.4	.5	.6	.8
1.5	1.5	2.8		-135.0	NM	1.5	2.1	1.6	2.5
.9	.9	1.0		.9	1.0	.8	.9	1.0	1.2
2.1	2.1	2.8	Debt/Worth	2.9	2.8	2.2	2.3	2.5	2.6
5.4	6.5	11.8		-299.0	NM	5.5	10.4	6.6	7.0
36.9	32.3	42.4		69.9	53.6	39.8	35.0	45.5	42.5
(462) 15.1	(559) 13.1	(492) 17.2	% Profit Before Taxes/Tangible Net Worth	(38) 23.9	(120) 13.0	(68) 13.0	(98) 14.0	(78) 18.3	(90) 22.9
4.5	1.5	3.0		-1.5	1.9	1.4	1.7	4.7	8.1
12.1	11.2	13.1		13.6	13.2	11.1	12.3	12.8	14.3
4.9	3.7	4.5	% Profit Before Taxes/Total Assets	2.3	3.5	3.6	2.7	4.6	7.1
1.0	-.3	.1		-6.9	-2.7	.1	-1.4	.8	2.2
53.7	52.0	53.1		195.7	55.3	56.7	59.7	56.2	32.2
25.3	23.4	24.2	Sales/Net Fixed Assets	25.6	25.0	26.0	27.7	27.6	13.9
9.5	10.5	10.2		8.4	12.9	10.3	13.7	10.8	8.1
3.9	4.1	4.0		4.1	4.1	3.6	3.7	4.4	4.2
2.8	2.8	2.9	Sales/Total Assets	2.1	2.7	3.0	3.1	3.3	3.1
1.9	1.9	2.0		1.5	1.9	2.1	2.2	2.3	2.2
.6	.5	.5		.7	.4	.4	.5	.6	.7
(430) .9	(560) .9	(480) .9	% Depr., Dep., Amort./Sales	(33) 1.3	(123) 1.0	(69) .9	(93) .7	(76) .8	(86) 1.1
1.5	1.5	1.5		2.3	1.5	1.5	1.0	1.2	1.5
1.7	1.8	1.6		3.8	2.9	2.3	1.3	1.0	.5
(267) 3.6	(333) 3.5	(282) 3.3	% Officers', Directors', Owners' Comp/Sales	(21) 6.6	(89) 4.1	(50) 3.9	(57) 2.3	(40) 1.8	(25) .9
6.2	6.0	5.5		8.5	6.5	6.6	4.1	3.6	1.6
13686982M	13964407M	14243279M	Net Sales ($)	30369M	318247M	318898M	823105M	1397034M	11355626M
5623144M	5469454M	5657152M	Total Assets ($)	15460M	143281M	129504M	316849M	530224M	4521834M

M = $ thousand   MM = $ million
See Pages 11 through 21 for Explanation of Ratios and Data

Current Data Sorted By Assets / Comparative Historical Data

0-500M	500M-2MM	2-10MM	10-50MM	50-100MM	100-250MM	Type of Statement		
2	1	7	5	2		Unqualified	6	7
3	13	21	4			Reviewed	42	26
17	39	21	2		1	Compiled	93	70
53	46	12				Tax Returns	42	24
14	25	33	11			Other	50	49
67 (4/1-9/30/04)			265 (10/1/04-3/31/05)				4/1/00-3/31/01	4/1/01-3/31/02
							ALL	ALL
89	124	94	22	2	1	NUMBER OF STATEMENTS	233	176
%	%	%	%	%	%	ASSETS	%	%
10.9	8.5	7.8	5.2			Cash & Equivalents	8.4	8.7
23.5	28.5	28.7	26.7			Trade Receivables (net)	28.5	27.3
37.5	36.9	37.1	35.5			Inventory	35.5	36.3
1.0	2.8	3.2	4.5			All Other Current	2.2	2.9
72.9	76.5	76.7	71.9			Total Current	74.6	75.2
20.6	14.2	14.9	15.7			Fixed Assets (net)	15.9	15.5
3.0	3.0	2.6	5.5			Intangibles (net)	3.1	3.1
3.4	6.3	5.8	6.8			All Other Non-Current	6.5	6.1
100.0	100.0	100.0	100.0			Total	100.0	100.0
						LIABILITIES		
10.4	10.3	13.4	16.8			Notes Payable-Short Term	11.5	11.1
4.6	2.0	2.4	2.1			Cur. Mat.-L/T/D	3.3	2.8
22.4	20.7	20.3	22.4			Trade Payables	21.3	19.2
.2	.3	.2	.5			Income Taxes Payable	.3	.2
12.4	16.6	14.6	14.5			All Other Current	13.4	16.0
49.9	49.9	50.8	56.3			Total Current	49.7	49.3
22.5	10.3	10.0	7.8			Long-Term Debt	13.5	10.4
.0	.1	.2	.0			Deferred Taxes	.2	.0
5.0	4.5	3.0	1.3			All Other Non-Current	3.2	2.8
22.7	35.2	36.0	34.6			Net Worth	33.4	37.3
100.0	100.0	100.0	100.0			Total Liabilities & Net Worth	100.0	100.0
						INCOME DATA		
100.0	100.0	100.0	100.0			Net Sales	100.0	100.0
35.2	34.8	34.6	32.7			Gross Profit	36.0	35.8
32.9	32.6	31.3	28.4			Operating Expenses	32.6	33.5
2.3	2.2	3.3	4.3			Operating Profit	3.3	2.3
.3	.0	.2	.6			All Other Expenses (net)	.5	.1
2.1	2.2	3.1	3.7			Profit Before Taxes	2.9	2.2
						RATIOS		
3.8	2.3	2.4	1.7			Current	2.4	2.3
1.8	1.6	1.5	1.3				1.5	1.6
1.0	1.2	1.2	1.0				1.1	1.2
1.6	1.3	1.5	1.0			Quick	1.4	1.2
(88) .7	.7	.7	.7				(232) .8	.7
.2	.4	.4	.1				.4	.4
0 UND	9 39.6	15 24.7	3 118.2			Sales/Receivables	12 31.5	11 32.1
13 27.8	23 16.1	30 12.0	36 10.0				26 14.2	26 14.1
26 14.3	39 9.4	44 8.4	48 7.7				40 9.1	40 9.1
10 36.4	24 15.5	31 11.7	31 11.8			Cost of Sales/Inventory	24 15.2	31 12.0
39 9.4	47 7.8	61 6.0	60 6.1				48 7.6	50 7.3
80 4.6	85 4.3	105 3.5	131 2.8				82 4.4	87 4.2
6 64.2	15 24.5	17 21.5	20 18.2			Cost of Sales/Payables	14 25.8	14 25.4
21 17.2	25 14.6	27 13.4	32 11.6				25 14.6	25 14.8
40 9.2	42 8.8	41 8.9	52 7.1				39 9.4	36 10.1
8.6	8.0	6.7	8.0			Sales/Working Capital	7.6	7.4
22.2	12.9	13.6	14.6				14.9	14.4
800.9	39.4	30.5	NM				45.6	36.3
22.0	17.4	13.6	15.4			EBIT/Interest	10.2	17.2
(62) 5.6	(109) 5.0	(88) 4.7	(20) 7.5				(197) 3.6	(154) 3.5
.6	1.3	2.5	3.1				1.5	1.1
	3.0	5.6				Net Profit + Depr., Dep., Amort./Cur. Mat. L./T/D	8.2	3.5
	(10) 2.0	(21) 2.9					(47) 3.5	(27) 1.6
	1.4	.7					1.6	.6
.1	.1	.2	.1			Fixed/Worth	.2	.1
.6	.3	.3	.4				.4	.4
−19.6	1.1	.9	1.5				1.1	.9
.5	.7	.9	1.4			Debt/Worth	.9	.7
2.6	1.8	1.8	3.5				1.8	1.7
−128.4	5.2	4.6	7.9				5.7	4.4
84.4	52.1	44.2	46.4			% Profit Before Taxes/Tangible Net Worth	49.6	41.0
(65) 42.2	(109) 20.4	(88) 20.9	(19) 21.5				(211) 20.6	(159) 14.8
3.6	1.5	9.5	9.6				6.7	2.4
29.6	17.5	15.7	12.1			% Profit Before Taxes/Total Assets	15.1	11.8
7.2	6.0	7.9	5.8				7.2	6.3
−3.4	.4	2.4	2.6				1.8	.4
84.5	80.0	63.9	54.7			Sales/Net Fixed Assets	67.6	76.1
41.5	44.9	34.5	43.1				37.5	34.3
18.8	22.6	15.2	13.8				19.8	17.6
7.3	5.1	4.2	3.9			Sales/Total Assets	5.0	5.0
4.9	4.0	3.2	2.9				4.0	3.8
3.2	2.9	2.3	2.0				2.8	2.5
.5	.4	.3	.4			% Depr., Dep., Amort./Sales	.5	.5
(57) .9	(104) .6	(90) .7	(19) .6				(201) .9	(148) .8
1.3	1.3	1.1	.9				1.3	1.3
3.4	2.2	1.6				% Officers', Directors', Owners' Comp/Sales	2.5	2.3
(59) 5.3	(85) 3.3	(56) 2.5					(133) 4.6	(102) 3.7
7.6	6.3	5.2					8.1	6.4
108539M	536352M	1280865M	1096361M	433769M	414305M	Net Sales ($)	2130384M	1434764M
21279M	132040M	395364M	397416M	131796M	103984M	Total Assets ($)	579375M	437711M

M = $ thousand   MM = $ million
See Pages 11 through 21 for Explanation of Ratios and Data

Comparative Historical Data				Current Data Sorted By Sales					
			Type of Statement						
11	15	17	Unqualified	2			3	4	8
46	48	41	Reviewed	1	6	5	11	11	7
83	107	80	Compiled	11	21	18	14	11	5
77	99	111	Tax Returns	25	46	13	20	7	
66	81	83	Other	6	15	10	25	15	12
4/1/02-3/31/03	4/1/03-3/31/04	4/1/04-3/31/05		67 (4/1-9/30/04)			265 (10/1/04-3/31/05)		
ALL	ALL	ALL		0-1MM	1-3MM	3-5MM	5-10MM	10-25MM	25MM & OVER
283	350	332	**NUMBER OF STATEMENTS**	45	88	46	73	48	32
%	%	%	**ASSETS**	%	%	%	%	%	%
9.9	9.4	8.7	Cash & Equivalents	10.2	9.9	8.6	7.6	9.3	4.9
26.2	27.6	26.8	Trade Receivables (net)	16.6	26.5	25.7	30.4	30.4	30.4
34.5	34.7	36.9	Inventory	43.4	35.2	39.0	36.3	35.2	33.1
2.6	2.8	2.5	All Other Current	.6	1.8	3.4	3.5	2.6	3.3
73.1	74.4	74.9	Total Current	70.9	73.5	76.6	77.8	77.6	71.7
16.9	16.7	16.5	Fixed Assets (net)	22.1	17.8	15.0	13.1	15.4	16.1
3.3	2.5	3.1	Intangibles (net)	4.3	3.7	2.9	1.4	2.3	5.7
6.6	6.3	5.5	All Other Non-Current	2.7	5.0	5.5	7.7	4.7	6.6
100.0	100.0	100.0	Total	100.0	100.0	100.0	100.0	100.0	100.0
			LIABILITIES						
11.9	13.1	11.7	Notes Payable-Short Term	14.1	8.2	12.6	10.5	14.8	14.6
3.8	3.7	2.8	Cur. Mat.-L/T/D	3.2	4.3	1.3	2.6	1.7	2.6
21.4	22.4	22.0	Trade Payables	18.9	21.4	21.6	20.0	24.0	29.7
.4	.2	.2	Income Taxes Payable	.2	.1	.5	.3	.2	.4
12.9	16.7	14.7	All Other Current	10.6	15.6	10.7	18.4	13.1	18.0
50.5	56.2	51.4	Total Current	47.0	49.5	46.7	51.9	53.9	65.2
12.8	10.8	13.3	Long-Term Debt	20.8	18.0	10.4	11.6	7.8	5.8
.1	.0	.1	Deferred Taxes	.1	.1	.1	.1	.2	.0
4.8	5.5	4.0	All Other Non-Current	7.0	3.7	6.7	2.6	2.7	1.4
31.9	27.5	31.3	Net Worth	25.1	28.7	36.1	33.8	35.5	27.6
100.0	100.0	100.0	Total Liabilities & Net Worth	100.0	100.0	100.0	100.0	100.0	100.0
			INCOME DATA						
100.0	100.0	100.0	Net Sales	100.0	100.0	100.0	100.0	100.0	100.0
35.5	35.5	34.9	Gross Profit	38.2	36.1	35.1	32.3	34.3	33.5
33.3	33.1	32.2	Operating Expenses	36.8	33.3	31.9	30.1	30.9	29.9
2.1	2.4	2.7	Operating Profit	1.4	2.7	3.2	2.2	3.5	3.7
.3	.2	.2	All Other Expenses (net)	.3	.2	.2	.2	-.2	.4
1.9	2.3	2.5	Profit Before Taxes	1.1	2.5	3.0	2.0	3.7	3.3
			RATIOS						
2.4	2.3	2.5		4.1	2.7	2.4	2.1	1.9	1.7
1.5	1.4	1.5	Current	1.9	1.6	1.7	1.6	1.4	1.3
1.1	1.1	1.1		1.0	1.2	1.2	1.1	1.2	1.0
1.4	1.3	1.3		1.3	1.6	1.3	1.1	1.4	1.1
(282) .8	.7 (331)	.7	Quick	.4 (87)	.7	.7	.7	.7	.7
.4	.3	.3		.4	.4	.4	.4	.4	.2
10 35.5	10 37.4	6 56.3		0 UND	5 68.0	8 45.4	13 28.3	12 30.3	3 114.1
22 16.3	25 14.5	22 16.4	Sales/Receivables	8 45.7	16 22.7	20 18.6	27 13.6	27 13.4	34 10.8
39 9.4	39 9.3	39 9.4		23 15.6	33 11.1	46 7.9	40 9.1	41 9.0	44 8.3
23 16.1	20 18.6	24 15.5		25 14.5	14 25.4	23 15.8	25 14.7	26 13.8	26 14.1
45 8.1	42 8.8	49 7.4	Cost of Sales/Inventory	74 4.9	47 6.7	54 6.7	47 7.7	50 7.4	43 8.4
83 4.4	76 4.8	91 4.0		148 2.5	85 4.3	90 4.1	90 4.1	78 4.7	72 5.0
14 25.9	13 27.4	15 24.8		1 287.0	10 35.3	18 20.3	14 25.9	19 19.5	16 23.1
24 15.2	25 14.8	25 14.7	Cost of Sales/Payables	28 12.8	23 15.6	27 13.6	23 15.7	29 12.5	26 14.1
40 9.1	41 8.9	42 8.7		66 5.5	42 8.8	46 7.9	33 10.9	40 9.1	44 8.2
8.0	8.8	7.8		5.2	8.2	6.2	8.5	8.3	9.2
14.7	18.5	14.7	Sales/Working Capital	12.8	17.7	10.9	14.7	16.9	18.3
66.7	127.1	69.5		UND	80.8	28.7	52.7	51.9	NM
11.1	10.7	17.2		7.5	20.4	25.6	10.4	15.6	15.2
(248) 3.7	(292) 3.4	(282) 5.1	EBIT/Interest	(32) 1.8	(72) 5.2	(38) 5.9	(67) 4.5	(44) 4.9	(29) 7.7
1.4	1.1	1.6		-.9	1.5	1.4	2.1	2.8	3.7
5.9	6.9	5.2	Net Profit + Depr., Dep.,					5.6	
(58) 2.0	(63) 2.3	(41) 2.6	Amort./Cur. Mat. L/T/D				(15) 2.7		
1.1	.7	1.0						.5	
.2	.2	.1		.1	.1	.1	.2	.2	.1
.4	.4	.3	Fixed/Worth	.5	.4	.3	.3	.3	.4
1.5	1.6	1.6		-3.8	3.8	1.4	.9	.7	3.2
.9	.9	.7		.5	.6	.7	.9	.8	1.2
2.2	2.4	1.9	Debt/Worth	1.3	2.4	1.4	1.9	2.3	1.7
6.8	8.5	7.1		-14.9	18.6	5.4	4.2	4.9	31.5
48.0	56.2	56.0	% Profit Before Taxes/Tangible	66.6	70.2	55.9	45.0	46.7	42.1
(244) 18.7	(294) 20.8	(282) 21.2	Net Worth	(32) 9.6	(71) 21.1	(41) 28.8	(67) 20.4	(46) 21.8	(25) 21.5
5.8	2.5	5.9		-1.6	2.0	8.5	6.0	11.8	12.1
16.3	16.7	17.8	% Profit Before Taxes/Total	23.1	22.6	25.0	15.7	15.8	16.3
6.0	5.7	6.9	Assets	1.0	6.3	8.4	7.7	8.2	8.6
1.1	.7	1.0		-7.4	.3	1.3	2.5	2.4	4.3
62.0	66.5	73.5		76.0	86.6	86.6	69.6	80.3	58.0
32.2	35.3	40.5	Sales/Net Fixed Assets	25.0	47.5	34.6	45.7	38.0	43.1
17.0	18.1	18.5		10.4	20.0	18.2	22.8	19.1	18.5
5.1	5.5	5.2		5.5	6.1	4.6	5.2	4.8	4.9
3.8	3.9	3.8	Sales/Total Assets	2.9	4.1	3.6	4.0	3.6	4.0
2.6	2.9	2.7		1.7	3.0	2.7	2.7	2.7	2.6
.5	.4	.4		.5	.5	.5	.4	.3	.4
(246) .8	(293) .8	(273) .7	% Depr., Dep., Amort./Sales	(28) .9	(69) .8	(40) .6	(62) .6	(46) .7	(28) .6
1.4	1.3	1.2		2.6	1.4	1.1	1.1	1.0	.9
2.4	2.2	2.2	% Officers', Directors',	5.3	2.7	2.6	1.7	1.4	1.2
(177) 4.1	(217) 3.9	(207) 3.5	Owners' Comp/Sales	(27) 7.5	(66) 4.7	(28) 3.4	(48) 2.5	(27) 2.7	(11) 1.6
7.1	6.7	6.4		15.0	7.4	4.6	3.9	5.3	2.2
3123689M	4792539M	3870191M	Net Sales ($)	23861M	166963M	185170M	523786M	792011M	2178400M
966821M	1275570M	1181879M	Total Assets ($)	10382M	51122M	57782M	163719M	261167M	637707M

© RMA 2005

M = $ thousand   MM = $ million

See Pages 11 through 21 for Explanation of Ratios and Data

Current Data Sorted By Assets   Comparative Historical Data

0-500M	500M-2MM	2-10MM	10-50MM	50-100MM	100-250MM	Type of Statement	4/1/00-3/31/01 ALL	4/1/01-3/31/02 ALL
	1	1	4	2	1	Unqualified	11	17
	3	11	1			Reviewed	14	12
12	23	11				Compiled	37	38
22	23	8	1			Tax Returns	38	23
8	17	10	6	1	2	Other	39	44
33 (4/1-9/30/04)			135 (10/1/04-3/31/05)				139	134
42	67	41	12	3	3	NUMBER OF STATEMENTS	139	134
%	%	%	%	%	%	**ASSETS**	%	%
13.7	7.4	7.0	4.2			Cash & Equivalents	8.0	9.0
16.8	17.2	19.2	16.4			Trade Receivables (net)	16.3	11.1
39.1	51.2	46.6	32.0			Inventory	48.8	50.7
.5	1.9	2.2	6.9			All Other Current	1.6	2.2
70.1	77.7	75.0	59.6			Total Current	74.8	73.0
21.7	13.3	18.9	26.9			Fixed Assets (net)	17.6	19.8
2.6	2.2	1.8	6.7			Intangibles (net)	2.6	2.9
5.6	6.9	4.3	6.8			All Other Non-Current	5.1	4.3
100.0	100.0	100.0	100.0			Total	100.0	100.0
						LIABILITIES		
13.4	11.4	14.7	11.4			Notes Payable-Short Term	12.0	11.5
4.6	2.3	2.2	1.0			Cur. Mat.-L/T/D	3.1	3.3
18.0	17.3	19.5	17.1			Trade Payables	19.1	21.3
.2	.3	.2	.3			Income Taxes Payable	.3	.2
13.0	16.2	14.4	11.3			All Other Current	12.7	13.6
49.2	47.5	51.0	41.1			Total Current	47.3	50.0
17.1	15.3	9.6	14.7			Long-Term Debt	13.7	13.2
.0	.0	.1	.0			Deferred Taxes	.2	.1
6.2	2.7	5.7	3.8			All Other Non-Current	7.3	5.9
27.5	34.6	33.6	40.3			Net Worth	31.6	30.7
100.0	100.0	100.0	100.0			Total Liabilities & Net Worth	100.0	100.0
						INCOME DATA		
100.0	100.0	100.0	100.0			Net Sales	100.0	100.0
43.9	43.0	44.6	34.9			Gross Profit	40.0	43.9
40.0	40.5	42.2	31.0			Operating Expenses	36.8	40.9
3.9	2.4	2.4	3.9			Operating Profit	3.2	3.0
.1	.7	.6	.9			All Other Expenses (net)	1.0	1.1
3.9	1.7	1.8	3.0			Profit Before Taxes	2.2	1.9
						RATIOS		
2.6	2.4	2.9	1.6			Current	2.5	2.4
1.4	1.8	1.6	1.4				1.6	1.6
1.1	1.2	1.0	1.1				1.2	1.1
1.3	1.0	.9	.9			Quick	.9	.7
.5	.5	.5	.5				(137) .5	(132) .4
.2	.2	.2	.1				.2	.1
0 UND	3 139.8	1 492.2	3 122.5			Sales/Receivables	0 UND	0 UND
14 25.7	19 18.9	25 14.6	15 24.1				15 24.4	5 75.1
27 13.7	32 11.6	40 9.1	50 7.2				32 11.3	19 19.0
24 15.1	57 6.4	89 4.1	53 6.9			Cost of Sales/Inventory	55 6.6	70 5.2
75 4.9	136 2.7	118 3.1	92 4.0				102 3.6	111 3.3
124 2.9	201 1.8	189 1.9	110 3.3				172 2.1	165 2.2
6 57.1	14 25.4	22 16.9	23 15.8			Cost of Sales/Payables	17 21.8	22 16.4
25 14.4	34 10.7	39 9.4	36 10.2				35 10.5	41 8.8
52 7.0	68 5.3	73 5.0	52 7.1				58 6.3	65 5.7
6.9	5.0	3.8	8.3			Sales/Working Capital	5.5	6.6
19.9	8.7	11.3	16.5				9.8	11.9
92.4	24.2	427.7	38.4				35.9	118.6
22.1	14.2	10.6	25.5			EBIT/Interest	8.1	10.1
(34) 2.4	(58) 3.0	(37) 4.0	(11) 3.1				(121) 2.8	(128) 2.7
-.9	.3	1.7	1.9				1.1	1.0
			13.3			Net Profit + Depr., Dep., Amort./Cur. Mat. L /T/D	8.3	6.9
			(12) 4.1				(23) 1.8	(19) 2.4
			2.3				.9	.6
.2	.1	.2	.2			Fixed/Worth	.2	.2
.4	.3	.5	.8				.5	.5
-4.2	.8	1.1	2.6				2.3	1.7
.5	.8	.7	.9			Debt/Worth	.8	1.1
2.9	1.6	2.3	1.6				2.1	2.1
-9.2	4.7	5.0	6.0				10.1	6.5
88.0	44.1	38.3	29.5			% Profit Before Taxes/Tangible Net Worth	35.3	37.0
(30) 23.8	(59) 11.2	(37) 11.5	18.2				(115) 15.8	(116) 17.3
2.9	-4.6	4.1	4.6				2.1	2.2
23.9	11.7	9.1	9.0			% Profit Before Taxes/Total Assets	12.7	13.8
6.5	3.1	5.0	5.3				4.5	4.9
-3.0	-2.6	1.0	.6				.2	-.3
70.8	62.9	47.0	21.1			Sales/Net Fixed Assets	52.4	45.8
27.5	37.4	23.7	9.4				22.4	20.2
10.5	20.3	8.0	4.4				11.0	10.4
5.0	3.7	3.3	2.6			Sales/Total Assets	3.6	3.9
3.6	2.6	2.2	2.1				2.7	3.0
2.2	1.8	1.6	1.4				2.1	2.1
.7	.5	.6	.8			% Depr., Dep., Amort./Sales	.6	.5
(30) 1.5	(51) .9	(39) 1.0	1.3				(112) 1.0	(109) 1.0
2.2	1.2	1.8	2.7				1.7	1.7
4.3	1.8	2.1				% Officers', Directors', Owners' Comp/Sales	3.2	2.5
(24) 5.3	(46) 3.9	(25) 3.3					(74) 4.6	(71) 4.9
7.7	7.3	5.6					8.2	8.0
45609M	208151M	389274M	588034M	788776M	945498M	Net Sales ($)	4367134M	4128381M
12381M	71877M	157878M	280277M	226343M	364038M	Total Assets ($)	1661508M	1700341M

© RMA 2005

M = $ thousand   MM = $ million
See Pages 11 through 21 for Explanation of Ratios and Data

Comparative Historical Data | Current Data Sorted By Sales

			Type of Statement	0-1MM	1-3MM	3-5MM	5-10MM	10-25MM	25MM & OVER
20	15	9	Unqualified		1			2	6
9	19	15	Reviewed		2			9	
34	57	46	Compiled	9	13	13	7	4	
27	51	54	Tax Returns	11	28	9	5	1	
31	34	44	Other	8	13	3	5	1	9
4/1/02-3/31/03 ALL	4/1/03-3/31/04 ALL	4/1/04-3/31/05 ALL		33 (4/1-9/30/04)			135 (10/1/04-3/31/05)		
121	176	168	**NUMBER OF STATEMENTS**	28	57	27	19	22	15
%	%	%	**ASSETS**	%	%	%	%	%	%
10.9	10.5	8.7	Cash & Equivalents	16.5	7.1	7.7	6.8	7.2	7.0
11.1	11.8	17.0	Trade Receivables (net)	14.1	12.9	27.1	22.7	19.4	9.3
51.1	51.1	45.4	Inventory	35.7	55.8	37.2	45.2	48.0	34.8
2.3	2.2	2.2	All Other Current	.7	.6	3.5	2.6	2.0	8.4
75.4	75.5	73.3	Total Current	66.9	76.4	75.5	77.2	76.7	59.4
17.6	16.3	18.1	Fixed Assets (net)	22.0	15.9	20.3	12.5	16.3	25.5
3.2	3.3	2.8	Intangibles (net)	5.0	1.9	.5	.7	2.4	9.8
3.9	4.9	5.7	All Other Non-Current	6.0	5.8	3.7	9.5	4.6	5.2
100.0	100.0	100.0	Total	100.0	100.0	100.0	100.0	100.0	100.0
			LIABILITIES						
10.3	9.8	12.4	Notes Payable-Short Term	13.7	9.9	14.5	11.7	20.9	4.5
3.7	2.4	2.9	Cur. Mat.-L/T/D	3.4	3.7	1.9	1.7	2.1	3.6
20.3	18.7	18.0	Trade Payables	12.7	18.0	21.3	17.9	19.8	19.1
.2	.3	.3	Income Taxes Payable	.4	.3	.0	.5	.0	.3
13.9	16.8	14.6	All Other Current	16.3	14.0	13.7	14.0	16.0	14.0
48.5	48.0	48.2	Total Current	46.4	46.0	51.4	45.7	58.9	41.6
13.4	15.8	14.1	Long-Term Debt	15.2	17.2	15.3	9.8	7.6	13.0
.3	.2	.1	Deferred Taxes	.0	.0	.0	.2	.0	.7
6.7	6.7	4.3	All Other Non-Current	3.0	4.8	3.8	4.1	7.8	1.1
31.1	29.4	33.3	Net Worth	35.3	32.0	29.6	40.3	25.7	43.6
100.0	100.0	100.0	Total Liabilities & Net Worth	100.0	100.0	100.0	100.0	100.0	100.0
			INCOME DATA						
100.0	100.0	100.0	Net Sales	100.0	100.0	100.0	100.0	100.0	100.0
44.5	43.9	43.0	Gross Profit	47.4	43.6	41.1	44.2	39.8	39.7
40.4	40.1	40.1	Operating Expenses	44.0	40.1	39.8	41.2	37.3	35.8
4.1	3.8	2.9	Operating Profit	3.4	3.4	1.3	3.0	2.5	3.9
.9	.7	.5	All Other Expenses (net)	.2	.6	.9	.1	.7	.5
3.3	3.1	2.4	Profit Before Taxes	3.1	2.9	.4	2.9	1.8	3.4
			RATIOS						
2.6	2.6	2.4		3.7	2.5	2.4	2.4	2.1	1.8
1.7	1.8	1.7	Current	1.5	1.8	1.7	1.9	1.1	1.6
1.1	1.1	1.1		1.1	1.2	1.2	1.4	1.0	1.0
.9	.9	1.0		1.6	.7	1.1	1.5	.8	.6
(117) .4	(175) .5	.5	Quick	.5	.4	.5	.5	.5	.4
.2	.1	.2		.2	.2	.4	.2	.1	.1
0 UND	0 UND	1 282.6		0 UND	2 209.6	10 35.9	0 941.9	1 430.1	2 188.3
3 116.9	5 76.3	18 19.8	Sales/Receivables	20 18.5	10 35.3	28 13.1	27 13.5	10 36.6	7 54.6
25 14.9	26 13.8	33 11.0		32 11.3	27 13.7	42 8.7	36 10.0	43 8.5	20 17.8
65 5.6	62 5.8	55 6.7		26 14.1	68 5.4	17 21.4	67 5.4	54 6.7	51 7.2
117 3.1	117 3.1	103 3.6	Cost of Sales/Inventory	91 4.0	145 2.5	87 4.2	107 3.4	98 3.7	79 4.6
169 2.2	173 2.1	179 2.0		189 1.9	221 1.7	166 2.2	156 2.3	173 2.1	91 4.0
16 22.8	15 24.3	15 23.6		0 UND	18 19.8	14 25.5	12 31.2	19 19.5	23 15.9
38 9.7	34 10.7	35 10.5	Cost of Sales/Payables	21 17.2	36 10.2	35 10.5	29 12.7	36 10.2	36 10.3
62 5.8	59 6.2	65 5.6		71 5.2	67 5.5	65 5.6	67 5.4	55 6.6	72 5.1
6.0	5.4	5.3		4.2	4.5	6.0	4.2	9.3	8.8
11.6	10.3	11.1	Sales/Working Capital	19.6	8.7	9.6	11.3	40.6	15.7
33.4	45.8	56.0		140.2	55.1	20.5	24.2	453.4	-233.1
15.9	18.1	15.4		18.6	16.3	4.0	13.7	12.5	33.2
(98) 3.8	(144) 4.5	(145) 3.1	EBIT/Interest	(21) 1.2	(49) 2.6	(23) 2.0	(18) 6.7	(21) 4.0	(13) 22.5
1.3	1.6	.9		-1.0	.6	.1	1.7	2.4	7.3
12.6	9.9	5.5	Net Profit + Depr., Dep.,						
(26) 5.1	(22) 3.7	(27) 3.0	Amort./Cur. Mat. L/T/D						
1.7	2.3	1.5							
.1	.1	.1		.2	.1	.2	.1	.2	.3
.5	.4	.4	Fixed/Worth	.4	.3	.5	.3	.6	.8
1.4	1.8	1.6		6.1	5.3	.8	.8	1.3	3.5
.7	.9	.8		.5	.7	1.0	.6	1.1	.8
1.8	2.0	1.9	Debt/Worth	1.9	1.8	2.4	1.3	2.8	1.1
6.0	7.4	5.9		22.4	16.1	4.4	3.9	9.3	4.5
38.3	44.6	44.3	% Profit Before Taxes/Tangible	60.4	35.9	50.0	67.8	43.5	31.6
(99) 20.9	(144) 20.6	(143) 16.1	Net Worth	(22) 22.0	(45) 13.4	(24) 10.2	(20) 11.0	20.5	(13) 23.5
5.6	5.2	1.5		-3.7	-2.4	-3.4	5.1	14.5	7.4
15.6	15.3	13.1	% Profit Before Taxes/Total	20.8	11.4	6.7	15.2	12.7	15.2
6.7	6.8	4.6	Assets	3.4	3.9	3.5	5.0	5.9	8.4
1.4	.9	-1.0		-5.9	-1.6	-3.2	2.3	2.2	3.3
63.2	71.6	58.5		97.0	63.8	38.3	90.5	59.8	31.0
24.0	27.8	27.8	Sales/Net Fixed Assets	25.9	32.2	28.8	49.8	26.4	18.2
11.0	12.4	9.9		4.6	14.1	8.1	14.2	10.2	6.4
4.2	4.1	3.8		4.1	3.8	3.9	3.8	4.1	3.3
3.0	2.9	2.6	Sales/Total Assets	2.1	2.6	2.6	2.7	2.9	2.7
2.1	2.0	1.8		1.5	1.8	1.6	1.8	2.1	2.1
.5	.5	.6		1.0	.4	.6	.8	.6	.8
(99) .9	(146) .9	(137) 1.0	% Depr., Dep., Amort./Sales	(15) 1.6	(47) .9	(25) 1.0	(15) .9	(21) .9	(14) 1.2
1.5	1.7	1.7		3.3	1.6	2.1	1.4	1.3	2.5
2.3	3.1	2.0	% Officers', Directors',	4.6	3.2	1.5	1.8	1.8	
(64) 4.1	(90) 5.3	(100) 4.3	Owners' Comp/Sales	(16) 5.6	(36) 4.9	(19) 3.8	(12) 3.1	(14) 2.8	
9.1	9.0	7.1		10.8	7.7	7.2	6.2	4.0	
3773673M	3204599M	2965342M	Net Sales ($)	17602M	108003M	107759M	131183M	322768M	2278027M
1754528M	1338139M	1112794M	Total Assets ($)	8867M	47671M	48008M	58140M	123278M	826830M

© RMA 2005

M = $ thousand   MM = $ million

See Pages 11 through 21 for Explanation of Ratios and Data

Current Data Sorted By Assets   Comparative Historical Data

0-500M	500M-2MM	2-10MM	10-50MM	50-100MM	100-250MM	Type of Statement	9	8
		1	2	1	2	Unqualified	9	8
	2	8	2			Reviewed	11	18
15	20	10	1			Compiled	36	25
10	10	8				Tax Returns	18	12
4	13	7	3		1	Other	19	22
31 (4/1-9/30/04)		89 (10/1/04-3/31/05)					4/1/00-3/31/01 ALL	4/1/01-3/31/02 ALL
29	45	34	8	1	3	**NUMBER OF STATEMENTS**	93	85
%	%	%	%	%	%	**ASSETS**	%	%
11.9	7.1	10.6				Cash & Equivalents	9.3	9.6
13.1	16.5	13.8				Trade Receivables (net)	17.5	14.9
51.9	51.0	50.2				Inventory	46.2	47.5
1.7	2.5	2.0				All Other Current	2.5	2.0
78.7	77.0	76.7				Total Current	75.5	74.1
18.2	14.8	17.3				Fixed Assets (net)	17.6	17.2
1.0	4.3	.8				Intangibles (net)	1.9	4.5
2.1	3.9	5.2				All Other Non-Current	5.0	4.2
100.0	100.0	100.0				Total	100.0	100.0
						LIABILITIES		
15.4	18.9	5.7				Notes Payable-Short Term	19.7	13.2
4.6	2.5	2.9				Cur. Mat.-L/T/D	3.1	1.9
27.8	21.5	23.1				Trade Payables	21.3	23.4
.0	.1	.5				Income Taxes Payable	.3	.2
12.9	15.7	20.1				All Other Current	11.2	12.1
60.7	58.7	52.4				Total Current	55.5	50.8
36.9	9.2	9.7				Long-Term Debt	12.7	10.9
.1	.1	.2				Deferred Taxes	.2	.0
3.2	5.1	3.2				All Other Non-Current	6.1	4.9
-1.0	26.9	34.5				Net Worth	25.5	33.4
100.0	100.0	100.0				Total Liabilities & Net Worth	100.0	100.0
						INCOME DATA		
100.0	100.0	100.0				Net Sales	100.0	100.0
40.4	34.0	30.3				Gross Profit	31.8	29.7
37.9	33.1	27.9				Operating Expenses	29.9	26.9
2.5	.9	2.4				Operating Profit	1.9	2.8
.5	.4	.0				All Other Expenses (net)	.0	.5
2.0	.6	2.4				Profit Before Taxes	1.9	2.4
						RATIOS		
2.5	1.8	2.2					1.9	2.3
1.9	1.3	1.4				Current	1.3	1.5
.9	1.1	1.1					1.1	1.1
1.1	.6	.7					.8	.8
.5	.4	.4				Quick	.4	.5
.1	.2	.2					.2	.2
0 UND	5 74.4	5 68.8					6 58.0	4 85.9
9 39.6	15 24.9	14 25.7				Sales/Receivables	13 28.5	11 32.9
21 17.5	24 15.3	31 11.9					27 13.7	21 17.1
43 8.6	53 6.8	69 5.3					50 7.2	45 8.1
83 4.4	90 4.1	96 3.8				Cost of Sales/Inventory	74 4.9	66 5.5
146 2.5	158 2.3	130 2.8					98 3.7	102 3.6
5 71.3	18 20.1	17 21.8					12 29.4	17 21.4
27 13.4	37 9.9	46 8.0				Cost of Sales/Payables	30 12.1	30 12.1
67 5.5	58 6.3	70 5.2					53 6.9	50 7.3
6.7	6.9	6.2					8.0	8.5
15.5	15.7	13.2				Sales/Working Capital	16.6	14.5
-53.2	65.6	39.7					53.8	47.2
3.0	8.4	13.9					5.6	8.3
(25) 1.8	(42) 2.1	(29) 4.6				EBIT/Interest	(83) 2.4	(77) 3.5
.6	-.8	1.6					1.2	1.1
						Net Profit + Depr., Dep.,	12.9	11.3
						Amort./Cur. Mat. L /T/D	(20) 4.6	(20) 4.0
							1.3	1.9
.3	.2	.2					.2	.2
.8	.5	.5				Fixed/Worth	.6	.5
-3.8	2.2	.9					1.5	1.2
1.3	1.3	1.2					1.4	1.0
6.1	3.5	2.2				Debt/Worth	2.9	2.4
-19.0	7.8	5.5					5.1	6.0
69.4	45.2	39.7				% Profit Before Taxes/Tangible	33.7	39.8
(20) 22.4	(37) 11.5	(32) 19.7				Net Worth	(85) 16.9	(77) 22.4
.6	-7.9	3.4					5.2	3.0
13.8	10.6	12.6				% Profit Before Taxes/Total	9.4	13.6
4.0	2.3	4.3				Assets	4.5	5.5
-.7	-2.6	.8					1.2	.6
59.1	70.9	54.0					62.3	59.5
28.1	33.7	22.1				Sales/Net Fixed Assets	32.7	33.9
12.4	13.0	7.7					12.4	15.1
5.0	4.4	3.6					4.4	4.4
3.3	2.8	2.8				Sales/Total Assets	3.4	3.5
2.4	1.9	2.0					2.4	2.6
.9	.6	.5					.5	.6
(24) 1.7	(36) 1.2	(28) .9				% Depr., Dep., Amort./Sales	(81) .8	(72) .8
2.8	1.5	1.1					1.4	1.3
3.6	1.7	.7					2.2	1.8
(16) 6.5	(26) 2.6	(12) 2.2				% Officers', Directors',	(56) 3.4	(49) 3.4
9.7	5.3	5.7				Owners' Comp/Sales	7.5	5.5
30655M	161034M	442169M	349369M	375647M	1972844M	Net Sales ($)	4103666M	2299005M
8558M	48900M	154301M	131142M	79645M	382565M	Total Assets ($)	1224477M	725432M

M = $ thousand   MM = $ million
See Pages 11 through 21 for Explanation of Ratios and Data

Comparative Historical Data | Current Data Sorted By Sales

8	13	6	Type of Statement						
15	10	12	Unqualified					1	5
34	41	46	Reviewed			2	1	6	3
22	21	29	Compiled	8	18	5	9	6	
34	28	27	Tax Returns	9	4	6	6	3	1
			Other	3	10	4	3	4	3

4/1/02-3/31/03 ALL	4/1/03-3/31/04 ALL	4/1/04-3/31/05 ALL		31 (4/1-9/30/04)			89 (10/1/04-3/31/05)		
				0-1MM	1-3MM	3-5MM	5-10MM	10-25MM	25MM & OVER
113	113	120	NUMBER OF STATEMENTS	20	32	17	19	20	12
%	%	%	**ASSETS**	%	%	%	%	%	%
11.0	11.6	9.3	Cash & Equivalents	13.5	4.4	9.8	11.6	9.3	10.7
15.4	14.4	14.8	Trade Receivables (net)	11.0	15.7	15.2	18.9	14.3	12.5
46.5	44.0	50.5	Inventory	50.6	51.9	49.1	49.8	50.0	50.4
2.6	3.0	2.5	All Other Current	1.9	4.0	1.1	2.0	.5	6.1
75.5	73.1	77.1	Total Current	76.9	76.1	75.2	82.3	74.0	79.8
16.4	18.6	16.7	Fixed Assets (net)	19.3	15.2	20.5	10.9	19.6	15.7
2.4	2.5	2.2	Intangibles (net)	1.2	5.7	.9	.4	1.0	1.5
5.7	5.8	3.9	All Other Non-Current	2.6	3.0	3.5	6.4	5.4	3.0
100.0	100.0	100.0	Total	100.0	100.0	100.0	100.0	100.0	100.0
			LIABILITIES						
14.1	13.5	14.7	Notes Payable-Short Term	11.5	20.7	19.1	6.8	7.0	22.6
3.7	2.0	2.9	Cur. Mat.-L/T/D	2.7	3.5	4.2	3.3	2.2	.8
25.6	22.4	23.1	Trade Payables	20.1	21.0	37.5	19.7	21.0	22.0
.5	.2	.2	Income Taxes Payable	.0	.0	.5	.3	.2	.4
12.1	12.9	16.3	All Other Current	15.7	11.5	11.2	22.0	23.1	17.0
55.9	51.1	57.2	Total Current	50.1	56.7	72.5	52.1	53.5	62.8
11.8	12.1	16.3	Long-Term Debt	26.5	16.8	25.7	7.5	10.8	7.4
.1	.1	.1	Deferred Taxes	.1	.1	.1	.3	.0	.0
4.4	4.1	4.2	All Other Non-Current	3.9	5.7	6.8	1.6	1.3	6.3
27.8	32.7	22.2	Net Worth	19.4	20.6	-5.1	38.4	34.4	23.5
100.0	100.0	100.0	Total Liabilities & Net Worth	100.0	100.0	100.0	100.0	100.0	100.0
			INCOME DATA						
100.0	100.0	100.0	Net Sales	100.0	100.0	100.0	100.0	100.0	100.0
33.0	35.7	34.5	Gross Profit	45.4	32.0	37.4	31.1	30.4	31.6
30.6	33.7	32.5	Operating Expenses	42.5	31.3	35.3	29.2	27.5	29.0
2.4	2.0	2.0	Operating Profit	2.9	.7	2.0	1.9	2.9	2.6
.2	.1	.3	All Other Expenses (net)	.7	.5	.1	.0	.2	-.2
2.2	2.0	1.7	Profit Before Taxes	2.2	.2	1.9	2.0	2.8	2.8
			RATIOS						
1.9	2.0	2.1	Current	2.8	2.0	1.6	2.8	1.8	1.7
1.4	1.4	1.4		1.9	1.3	1.3	1.5	1.2	1.2
1.1	1.2	1.1		1.0	1.0	1.0	1.2	1.0	1.0
.8	.9	.7	Quick	1.8	.8	.5	1.4	.6	.9
.4	.5	.4		.6	.4	.4	.5	.3	.4
.2	.3	.2		.1	.1	.1	.3	.2	.2
4 87.0	4 90.5	5 76.4	Sales/Receivables	0 UND	5 71.5	5 70.6	6 60.4	5 74.7	4 83.2
11 33.4	12 31.7	12 29.7		9 39.7	17 21.5	15 23.6	15 23.8	9 39.5	8 45.6
23 16.0	25 14.3	24 15.0		27 13.6	35 10.5	24 15.3	25 14.8	20 18.3	20 18.5
41 8.9	48 7.7	53 6.9	Cost of Sales/Inventory	48 7.7	53 6.9	66 5.5	31 11.8	56 6.5	55 6.7
66 5.5	75 4.9	88 4.1		107 3.4	133 2.8	95 3.8	59 6.2	89 4.1	70 5.2
108 3.4	112 3.3	142 2.6		164 2.2	202 1.8	144 2.5	97 3.7	112 3.3	89 4.1
14 25.6	20 17.9	15 24.2	Cost of Sales/Payables	2 236.2	18 19.8	30 12.1	10 37.3	17 21.9	10 36.0
32 11.5	36 10.1	36 10.1		30 12.0	36 10.3	57 6.4	18 19.8	36 10.0	22 16.8
55 6.6	56 6.5	60 6.1		71 5.1	64 5.7	77 4.7	45 8.1	59 6.2	47 7.7
8.2	7.7	6.9	Sales/Working Capital	6.0	5.7	9.6	6.5	9.4	9.4
20.2	14.6	15.0		8.5	14.3	13.5	14.9	25.3	40.4
61.6	36.5	92.0		NM	-146.3	NM	44.2	NM	117.8
15.0	12.7	8.3	EBIT/Interest	3.7	3.2	12.7	16.1	12.6	23.7
(99) 5.1	(104) 4.3	(106) 2.4		(16) 1.5	(31) 1.2	(16) 5.5	(16) 7.0	(17) 5.3	(10) 3.2
1.8	.7	.6		.5	-.7	-1.9	1.7	3.4	-.6
4.1	5.8	7.3	Net Profit + Depr., Dep., Amort./Cur. Mat. L/T/D						
(24) 2.0	(24) 3.0	(17) 1.8							
1.1	.7	.5							
.2	.2	.2	Fixed/Worth	.5	.2	.2	.2	.2	.3
.5	.4	.6		.8	.6	.6	.2	.6	.5
1.0	1.3	1.8		NM	-3.1	5.5	.5	1.4	1.3
1.3	1.1	1.3	Debt/Worth	1.5	1.3	1.3	.9	1.6	1.6
2.6	2.4	3.3		5.5	4.9	3.2	2.2	2.7	3.2
6.0	5.4	8.6		NM	-19.2	NM	4.3	4.9	5.8
45.8	42.3	42.1	% Profit Before Taxes/Tangible Net Worth	41.2	48.5	47.6	43.2	42.9	39.2
(99) 23.9	(104) 17.7	(100) 18.4		(15) 27.0	(22) 3.0	(13) 14.7	16.5	21.4	(11) 24.5
8.9	2.5	.2		3.6	-12.9	-11.8	4.4	5.2	-4.5
12.0	12.1	12.6	% Profit Before Taxes/Total Assets	14.8	6.8	15.2	13.4	15.8	17.9
5.5	4.7	3.7		3.1	1.0	7.7	3.7	5.6	8.4
2.3	-.3	-.4		-1.5	-1.9	-4.8	1.3	1.5	-.8
66.3	52.9	60.2	Sales/Net Fixed Assets	53.8	45.2	100.1	90.0	51.0	52.6
33.2	33.3	26.9		28.3	15.7	20.7	60.4	27.7	37.2
13.2	12.8	11.3		10.0	10.5	6.9	19.8	11.1	15.7
4.7	4.2	4.1	Sales/Total Assets	4.1	3.7	4.2	5.7	3.9	4.1
3.6	3.3	3.0		2.9	2.2	3.0	4.2	3.3	3.7
2.6	2.2	2.1		2.2	1.7	1.8	2.4	2.2	2.6
.5	.6	.6	% Depr., Dep., Amort./Sales	1.2	1.1	.4	.3	.5	.4
(98) .8	(91) 1.0	(98) 1.1		(16) 2.0	(26) 1.4	(13) 1.2	(16) .7	(17) .8	(10) .7
1.3	1.9	1.5		2.8	1.7	1.4	1.1	1.1	1.1
2.1	2.2	1.8	% Officers', Directors', Owners' Comp/Sales	5.9	1.8	1.5	1.0		
(60) 3.3	(62) 5.1	(55) 3.3		(12) 7.9	(15) 2.6	(10) 3.8	(10) 2.4		
6.0	8.0	6.2		9.8	5.1	7.1	3.7		
3877474M	7706028M	3331718M	Net Sales ($)	14379M	56027M	63186M	141850M	340538M	2715738M
1293632M	1830548M	805111M	Total Assets ($)	5258M	26829M	24492M	40109M	121165M	587258M

© RMA 2005

M = $ thousand   MM = $ million
See Pages 11 through 21 for Explanation of Ratios and Data

Current Data Sorted By Assets   Comparative Historical Data

						Type of Statement		
	2	3	4	1		Unqualified	17	15
	2	14	3			Reviewed	16	15
6	13	3				Compiled	33	13
13	12	2			1	Tax Returns	12	15
3	15	13	2	2	1	Other	30	31
	24 (4/1-9/30/04)		91 (10/1/04-3/31/05)				4/1/00-3/31/01	4/1/01-3/31/02
0-500M	500M-2MM	2-10MM	10-50MM	50-100MM	100-250MM		ALL	ALL
22	44	35	9	3	2	**NUMBER OF STATEMENTS**	108	89
%	%	%	%	%	%	**ASSETS**	%	%
7.7	8.8	16.8				Cash & Equivalents	9.6	9.4
10.6	25.5	22.0				Trade Receivables (net)	19.3	20.8
47.8	35.0	37.7				Inventory	41.6	39.8
7.6	1.8	3.9				All Other Current	2.3	2.9
73.7	71.1	80.4				Total Current	72.8	72.9
13.7	18.1	12.7				Fixed Assets (net)	19.1	17.8
4.3	3.5	1.0				Intangibles (net)	2.5	2.4
8.3	7.3	5.9				All Other Non-Current	5.6	6.9
100.0	100.0	100.0				Total	100.0	100.0
						LIABILITIES		
17.9	11.9	10.8				Notes Payable-Short Term	10.5	15.2
9.0	2.4	2.6				Cur. Mat.-L/T/D	3.4	5.7
25.1	25.3	31.1				Trade Payables	24.6	25.9
.0	.1	.3				Income Taxes Payable	.6	.3
10.1	11.3	14.4				All Other Current	9.1	9.8
62.1	51.0	59.3				Total Current	48.2	56.9
17.5	14.4	4.6				Long-Term Debt	10.6	14.4
.0	.4	.2				Deferred Taxes	.1	.1
11.0	4.0	1.8				All Other Non-Current	4.1	3.1
9.4	30.2	34.1				Net Worth	37.0	25.5
100.0	100.0	100.0				Total Liabilities & Net Worth	100.0	100.0
						INCOME DATA		
100.0	100.0	100.0				Net Sales	100.0	100.0
50.3	34.6	32.6				Gross Profit	35.6	36.3
50.8	31.5	29.7				Operating Expenses	32.8	34.7
-.5	3.0	2.8				Operating Profit	2.8	1.6
.4	.6	.0				All Other Expenses (net)	-.6	.2
-.9	2.4	2.8				Profit Before Taxes	3.4	1.4
						RATIOS		
1.9	2.2	1.9					2.2	2.0
1.2	1.4	1.4				Current	1.5	1.4
.7	1.0	1.1					1.2	1.1
.5	1.3	1.1					1.0	.9
.2	.7	.7				Quick	.6 (88)	.6
.1	.3	.3					.3	.2
0 UND	13 28.6	5 74.4					5 75.6	6 64.3
2 213.4	25 14.6	18 20.0				Sales/Receivables	14 25.3	17 21.6
11 33.0	43 8.5	39 9.3					40 9.1	41 8.9
54 6.8	23 16.1	30 12.2					38 9.6	41 8.9
70 5.2	67 5.5	58 6.3				Cost of Sales/Inventory	72 5.1	69 5.3
133 2.7	110 3.3	100 3.6					102 3.6	103 3.6
24 15.2	26 13.8	23 16.0					21 17.6	20 17.9
32 11.4	43 8.4	40 9.0				Cost of Sales/Payables	32 11.6	38 9.6
70 5.2	68 5.4	79 4.6					57 6.4	61 5.9
14.6	6.2	10.9					7.3	8.7
41.4	16.8	15.7				Sales/Working Capital	13.2	16.9
-38.6	NM	111.6					37.3	59.2
6.3	9.5	42.9					11.4	7.0
(20) 1.3	(39) 2.5	(28) 10.0				EBIT/Interest	(96) 3.3	(80) 1.5
-4.6	.8	1.3					1.5	.5
						Net Profit + Depr., Dep.,	10.9	11.6
						Amort./Cur. Mat. L./T/D	(32) 2.7	(20) 3.1
							.8	1.3
.2	.1	.2					.2	.2
.5	.5	.4				Fixed/Worth	.4	.5
-3.8	2.9	.5					1.1	1.8
1.3	.8	1.2					.8	1.0
3.5	3.9	2.3				Debt/Worth	2.0	2.5
-11.2	11.5	4.6					4.3	10.9
82.8	41.6	45.8				% Profit Before Taxes/Tangible	53.2	31.9
(15) 8.7	(37) 17.1	(33) 21.5				Net Worth	(101) 19.8	(72) 14.0
-13.8	1.4	.3					5.3	.3
17.0	14.5	19.0				% Profit Before Taxes/Total	16.2	13.4
1.6	3.2	7.8				Assets	6.5	2.3
-5.7	-.5	.1					1.5	-1.9
164.3	87.1	83.4					64.4	54.9
40.0	23.9	26.8				Sales/Net Fixed Assets	29.8	23.4
18.4	9.9	18.4					9.9	14.2
6.7	4.1	4.4					4.5	4.5
3.6	3.0	3.3				Sales/Total Assets	3.1	3.2
2.6	2.2	2.4					2.2	2.3
.5	.7	.4					.5	.6
(14) 1.1	(32) 1.4	(33) .9				% Depr., Dep., Amort./Sales	(92) .9	(72) .9
1.9	2.4	1.4					1.7	1.6
3.3	1.3	.7					2.2	2.3
(10) 5.3	(22) 4.3	(12) 2.3				% Officers', Directors',	(43) 6.0	(48) 4.8
8.5	10.1	5.7				Owners' Comp/Sales	9.9	7.9
20121M	161166M	592817M	563535M	699290M	973132M	Net Sales ($)	5914361M	5368160M
5466M	49849M	149516M	183423M	213955M	240978M	Total Assets ($)	2068152M	1514114M

© RMA 2005

M = $ thousand   MM = $ million
See Pages 11 through 21 for Explanation of Ratios and Data

Comparative Historical Data

Current Data Sorted By Sales

			Type of Statement						
12	13	10	Unqualified		1		1	2	6
22	18	19	Reviewed		1	1	3	10	4
28	25	23	Compiled	3	7	5	4	1	3
26	22	27	Tax Returns	8	12	4	4	2	
22	36	36	Other	5	8	5	6	7	5
4/1/02-	4/1/03-	4/1/04-			24 (4/1-9/30/04)			91 (10/1/04-3/31/05)	
3/31/03	3/31/04	3/31/05		0-1MM	1-3MM	3-5MM	5-10MM	10-25MM	25MM & OVER
ALL	ALL	ALL							
110	114	115	**NUMBER OF STATEMENTS**	16	29	15	16	21	18
%	%	%	**ASSETS**	%	%	%	%	%	%
10.1	10.4	11.3	Cash & Equivalents	4.7	11.0	7.7	20.0	8.8	15.6
17.3	17.0	21.5	Trade Receivables (net)	10.7	19.0	25.1	26.8	24.2	24.5
40.2	42.0	39.2	Inventory	44.2	37.6	39.5	35.7	39.8	39.7
2.9	3.1	3.6	All Other Current	9.1	2.8	1.0	1.4	5.7	1.7
70.4	72.4	75.6	Total Current	68.7	70.4	73.3	83.8	78.6	81.5
21.3	18.5	15.2	Fixed Assets (net)	19.2	15.4	15.7	12.7	16.1	12.0
2.8	3.0	2.7	Intangibles (net)	2.8	5.7	2.5	.4	1.8	1.2
5.4	6.2	6.4	All Other Non-Current	9.4	8.5	8.5	3.1	3.5	5.3
100.0	100.0	100.0	Total	100.0	100.0	100.0	100.0	100.0	100.0
			LIABILITIES						
14.1	13.7	13.4	Notes Payable-Short Term	25.5	10.0	10.0	7.7	16.4	12.3
4.7	2.9	3.6	Cur. Mat.-L/T/D	6.4	4.9	2.7	4.6	2.1	.9
21.4	21.0	27.2	Trade Payables	20.0	22.3	31.3	35.1	29.5	28.4
.4	.2	.2	Income Taxes Payable	.0	.0	.5	.3	.2	.0
10.2	11.8	11.8	All Other Current	11.5	10.4	11.0	12.4	13.3	12.9
50.9	49.5	56.2	Total Current	63.4	47.6	55.5	60.2	61.5	54.7
15.2	16.0	10.8	Long-Term Debt	12.0	20.9	10.1	6.4	6.3	3.2
.2	.1	.2	Deferred Taxes	.0	.0	.6	.7	.3	.1
4.0	5.8	5.0	All Other Non-Current	12.2	3.9	1.5	6.4	2.5	4.9
29.8	28.5	27.7	Net Worth	12.5	27.5	32.3	26.2	29.4	37.2
100.0	100.0	100.0	Total Liabilities & Net Worth	100.0	100.0	100.0	100.0	100.0	100.0
			INCOME DATA						
100.0	100.0	100.0	Net Sales	100.0	100.0	100.0	100.0	100.0	100.0
36.2	35.9	36.9	Gross Profit	52.6	38.6	34.2	30.5	32.6	33.4
34.0	33.5	34.5	Operating Expenses	57.9	33.8	30.8	26.8	30.3	29.7
2.2	2.4	2.4	Operating Profit	−5.3	4.8	3.4	3.7	2.2	3.7
.4	.6	.4	All Other Expenses (net)	.6	.5	.3	−.1	.4	.6
1.8	1.7	2.0	Profit Before Taxes	−5.8	4.3	3.1	3.8	1.8	3.2
			RATIOS						
2.1	2.3	2.0		1.7	2.5	1.9	2.5	1.5	2.2
1.4	1.5	1.4	Current	1.1	1.7	1.4	1.3	1.3	1.5
1.1	1.1	1.0		.7	1.0	1.0	1.0	1.1	1.2
1.0	.9	1.1		.3	1.2	.8	1.3	.9	1.2
(109) .5	.5	.6	Quick	.2	.6	.7	.9	.4	.8
.2	.2	.2		.1	.3	.2	.4	.2	.4
4 97.6	3 109.7	6 57.8		0 UND	7 52.5	9 39.4	10 36.9	4 97.7	5 76.3
15 25.0	13 28.1	18 20.1	Sales/Receivables	5 67.9	18 20.6	18 19.9	26 14.2	17 21.7	12 29.8
35 10.4	31 11.7	38 9.7		24 15.2	46 9.2	40 9.2	51 7.2	43 8.4	35 10.3
34 10.6	43 8.4	32 11.3		57 6.5	52 7.1	24 15.0	19 19.4	31 11.8	31 11.8
63 5.8	73 5.0	66 5.5	Cost of Sales/Inventory	104 3.5	76 4.8	51 7.2	63 5.8	58 6.3	46 8.0
113 3.2	125 2.9	110 3.3		195 1.9	114 3.2	91 4.0	110 3.3	111 3.3	77 4.8
17 20.9	13 28.6	24 15.2		22 16.3	32 11.5	35 10.4	16 22.8	24 15.0	16 22.6
32 11.5	33 11.1	43 8.5	Cost of Sales/Payables	36 10.3	43 8.5	51 7.1	67 5.4	35 10.5	24 15.4
50 7.4	52 7.0	71 5.1		93 3.9	69 5.3	65 5.6	82 4.4	66 5.5	80 4.6
9.6	6.5	9.1		12.7	5.3	7.7	6.9	13.3	10.1
17.4	16.3	17.8	Sales/Working Capital	NM	10.7	18.7	18.4	16.0	13.5
113.7	54.2	−999.8		−14.2	NM	−89.0	NM	140.2	29.4
11.7	13.5	14.7		1.8	14.3	7.8	14.1	20.1	236.0
(94) 2.8	(96) 2.4	(100) 3.1	EBIT/Interest	(14) −2.9	(26) 2.6	3.6	(12) 6.4	(18) 3.1	(15) 18.2
.8	1.0	.7		−6.9	.7	1.7	1.1	1.1	3.5
8.4	8.3	6.7	Net Profit + Depr., Dep.,						
(26) 2.9	(21) 1.1	(17) 2.8	Amort./Cur. Mat. L/T/D						
1.2	.2	.7							
.2	.2	.2		.2	.1	.2	.1	.3	.2
.6	.5	.4	Fixed/Worth	.6	.4	.3	.5	.4	.3
2.0	2.2	2.6		NM	12.4	.9	1.8	2.6	.5
1.1	1.0	.9		1.4	.7	1.1	1.1	1.5	.8
2.1	2.8	2.7	Debt/Worth	4.2	2.4	2.3	4.2	2.3	1.5
5.9	9.5	8.8		NM	NM	4.9	14.3	6.9	3.7
51.1	45.7	51.0	% Profit Before Taxes/Tangible	10.1	81.7	53.1	62.6	41.0	57.2
(95) 20.4	(94) 12.1	(97) 20.0	Net Worth	(12) −12.4	(22) 17.7	(13) 21.6	(14) 28.0	(20) 19.7	(16) 26.5
1.0	1.8	−.2		−106.4	−1.8	8.7	−5.2	.6	14.8
15.7	17.2	17.6	% Profit Before Taxes/Total	2.3	21.5	15.5	19.7	14.1	23.0
4.7	3.5	4.3	Assets	−4.3	4.6	3.3	6.0	6.4	9.4
−.7	−.1	−.6		−29.9	−.1	2.6	−1.3	.2	2.0
51.0	52.7	83.4		61.6	130.4	87.6	139.9	46.2	109.8
21.4	21.8	27.9	Sales/Net Fixed Assets	28.5	22.3	34.3	38.4	24.0	32.0
10.4	11.3	13.9		10.2	10.1	11.7	20.6	17.5	20.0
4.8	3.8	4.6		6.2	4.0	4.9	4.5	4.5	5.7
3.3	2.9	3.2	Sales/Total Assets	2.6	2.5	3.4	3.2	3.3	4.3
2.4	2.3	2.4		1.6	1.8	2.7	2.5	2.6	3.2
.6	.5	.6		.4	.9	.5	.8	.5	.3
(92) 1.0	(85) 1.0	(92) 1.0	% Depr., Dep., Amort./Sales	(11) 1.0	(19) 1.7	(13) 1.2	(13) 1.1	(20) .9	(16) .6
2.0	1.7	1.8		2.4	2.7	2.0	2.0	1.3	1.1
2.2	3.1	1.4			1.7	1.5			
(58) 4.4	(46) 5.4	(47) 3.5	% Officers', Directors', Owners' Comp/Sales	(15) 4.3	(10) 2.0				
10.4	13.2	8.4			5.3	9.3			
3303419M	3856514M	3010061M	Net Sales ($)	10176M	58162M	60175M	107240M	345879M	2428429M
915993M	1111974M	843187M	Total Assets ($)	3983M	25347M	18811M	36363M	108730M	649953M

© RMA 2005

M = $ thousand   MM = $ million
See Pages 11 through 21 for Explanation of Ratios and Data

Current Data Sorted By Assets   Comparative Historical Data

						Type of Statement		
2	2	5	4	1		Unqualified	10	7
2	5	14	1			Reviewed	23	19
8	11	5	1			Compiled	37	26
13	10	6				Tax Returns	21	19
7	16	12	6	1	1	Other	43	34
	32 (4/1-9/30/04)			101 (10/1/04-3/31/05)			4/1/00-3/31/01	4/1/01-3/31/02
0-500M	500M-2MM	2-10MM	10-50MM	50-100MM	100-250MM		ALL	ALL
32	44	42	12	2	1	NUMBER OF STATEMENTS	134	105
%	%	%	%	%	%	**ASSETS**	%	%
17.4	11.2	9.5	3.1			Cash & Equivalents	11.3	11.8
33.7	34.7	42.8	34.1			Trade Receivables (net)	44.6	36.2
17.9	22.0	24.3	19.4			Inventory	16.9	22.9
6.7	3.8	1.9	3.9			All Other Current	2.8	2.7
75.7	71.7	78.6	60.5			Total Current	75.6	73.6
12.1	17.7	10.0	17.9			Fixed Assets (net)	13.7	15.5
3.4	4.0	5.2	8.4			Intangibles (net)	4.4	5.2
8.8	6.6	6.3	13.2			All Other Non-Current	6.3	5.7
100.0	100.0	100.0	100.0			Total	100.0	100.0
						LIABILITIES		
11.9	20.7	14.4	15.7			Notes Payable-Short Term	17.3	15.3
19.7	3.2	1.5	1.2			Cur. Mat.-L/T/D	4.5	3.9
31.1	22.6	32.8	21.3			Trade Payables	27.9	23.9
1.2	.4	.2	3.2			Income Taxes Payable	.5	.9
13.9	11.5	10.3	14.2			All Other Current	13.5	13.9
77.7	58.4	59.2	55.5			Total Current	63.7	58.0
22.4	11.3	6.3	9.2			Long-Term Debt	9.2	17.2
.0	.1	.3	.7			Deferred Taxes	.2	.2
7.8	5.4	6.3	2.2			All Other Non-Current	5.9	6.0
-8.0	24.8	28.0	32.5			Net Worth	21.0	18.7
100.0	100.0	100.0	100.0			Total Liabilities & Net Worth	100.0	100.0
						INCOME DATA		
100.0	100.0	100.0	100.0			Net Sales	100.0	100.0
51.9	39.5	29.4	32.9			Gross Profit	36.4	37.8
48.1	33.0	26.9	27.2			Operating Expenses	35.7	36.6
3.8	6.5	2.5	5.8			Operating Profit	.6	1.2
.5	1.8	.5	1.5			All Other Expenses (net)	-.8	.6
3.2	4.7	2.0	4.3			Profit Before Taxes	1.4	.7
						RATIOS		
1.6	2.0	1.6	1.8				2.0	2.0
1.3	1.3	1.3	1.3			Current	1.2	1.3
.9	1.0	1.1	.9				.9	1.0
1.2	1.3	1.2	1.2				1.4	1.5
.8	.8	.9	.8			Quick	.9	.8
.4	.5	.6	.4				.6	.6

17	21.6	24	15.3	27	13.6	31	11.9	Sales/Receivables	24	15.0	20	18.1

17	21.6	24	15.3	27	13.6	31	11.9			Sales/Receivables	24	15.0	20	18.1
23	16.2	32	11.3	48	7.6	47	7.8				43	8.5	32	11.4
39	9.4	45	8.2	66	5.5	78	4.7				59	6.2	51	7.1
1	314.9	12	30.4	12	31.5	10	34.8			Cost of Sales/Inventory	4	97.9	7	55.2
25	14.8	28	13.1	27	13.7	27	13.6				15	23.8	19	19.0
59	6.2	50	7.3	71	5.1	69	5.3				33	11.0	41	8.9
17	20.9	18	19.8	23	15.9	15	25.0			Cost of Sales/Payables	17	20.9	14	25.3
37	9.8	29	12.6	42	8.7	39	9.4				30	12.0	24	15.3
82	4.4	50	7.4	70	5.2	65	5.6				55	6.6	47	7.7

13.2	11.3	9.9	8.9			Sales/Working Capital	10.8	9.8
22.3	23.1	19.0	19.4				24.5	20.2
-37.9	NM	103.3	-111.3				-111.6	-463.5

	9.5		10.2		15.2		6.0				7.9		5.1
(26)	4.0	(34)	2.9	(39)	4.2	(11)	3.7	EBIT/Interest	(125)	2.5	(95)	1.8
	1.2		.3		.7		1.4			.8		-1.3

											4.8		3.5
								Net Profit + Depr., Dep., Amort./Cur. Mat. L /T/D	(23)	1.8	(14)	.2
										-1.4		-2.2

.2	.2	.1	.2			Fixed/Worth	.1	.2
1.2	.5	.3	.8				.5	.6
-.7	2.0	.6	4.5				3.9	UND
2.3	1.2	1.5	1.3			Debt/Worth	1.2	1.0
54.9	2.2	3.3	5.3				4.0	2.5
-7.9	6.9	8.0	43.6				36.8	UND

	131.7		80.8		55.0		82.8			63.5		42.1
(17)	94.9	(35)	19.3	(39)	20.6	(10)	9.5	% Profit Before Taxes/Tangible Net Worth	(106)	16.5	(79)	10.6
	23.5		5.3		-2.5		-2.9			1.5		-3.3

37.9	22.7	10.5	9.8			% Profit Before Taxes/Total Assets	12.0	9.7
11.3	6.3	4.0	2.9				3.5	3.1
1.0	.5	-1.0	.8				-1.0	-2.8
122.8	95.6	193.8	83.8			Sales/Net Fixed Assets	104.0	102.8
48.3	34.3	73.6	24.3				37.4	37.0
22.9	12.2	21.2	6.4				18.4	20.3
6.0	4.9	4.4	4.7			Sales/Total Assets	5.4	5.8
4.7	4.0	3.1	3.3				3.8	3.8
2.8	2.7	2.4	.7				2.6	2.8

	.5		.3		.2					.3		.3
(18)	1.0	(36)	.9	(32)	.6			% Depr., Dep., Amort./Sales	(103)	.9	(77)	.9
	2.1		1.7		1.0					1.6		1.9
	3.6		1.6		1.0					2.1		2.2
(15)	7.4	(19)	3.5	(19)	2.3			% Officers', Directors', Owners' Comp/Sales	(59)	3.7	(47)	4.0
	10.0		5.6		6.1					7.9		7.8

35320M	183949M	623311M	645784M	683034M	501304M	Net Sales ($)	2895438M	1903357M
7713M	45486M	178573M	241820M	159577M	204447M	Total Assets ($)	892218M	553124M

© RMA 2005

M = $ thousand   MM = $ million
See Pages 11 through 21 for Explanation of Ratios and Data

Comparative Historical Data			Type of Statement	Current Data Sorted By Sales					
16	14	14	Unqualified	1	2	1	2	2	6
19	15	22	Reviewed		2		5	10	3
25	33	25	Compiled	4	5	7	6	3	
22	29	29	Tax Returns	9	9	6	1	1	3
31	44	43	Other	7	10	4	8	8	6
				32 (4/1-9/30/04)			101 (10/1/04-3/31/05)		
4/1/02-3/31/03 ALL	4/1/03-3/31/04 ALL	4/1/04-3/31/05 ALL		0-1MM	1-3MM	3-5MM	5-10MM	10-25MM	25MM & OVER
113	135	133	NUMBER OF STATEMENTS	21	28	20	22	24	18
%	%	%	**ASSETS**	%	%	%	%	%	%
13.4	12.7	11.5	Cash & Equivalents	16.3	15.9	7.8	11.2	7.5	8.9
37.8	38.6	36.9	Trade Receivables (net)	25.6	36.7	36.6	41.5	44.9	34.3
20.8	19.9	21.7	Inventory	16.1	19.3	22.6	21.9	19.3	34.1
2.5	3.5	3.8	All Other Current	9.6	2.4	2.9	4.2	2.2	2.1
74.5	74.7	73.9	Total Current	67.6	74.3	69.9	78.7	73.9	79.4
15.5	15.5	13.8	Fixed Assets (net)	15.3	12.4	19.7	13.6	9.6	13.8
3.4	2.5	4.7	Intangibles (net)	4.4	5.7	4.1	1.2	7.9	4.0
6.6	7.3	7.6	All Other Non-Current	12.6	7.6	6.2	6.5	8.6	2.8
100.0	100.0	100.0	Total	100.0	100.0	100.0	100.0	100.0	100.0
			LIABILITIES						
12.9	16.8	16.0	Notes Payable-Short Term	15.1	16.4	22.2	13.1	17.2	11.2
3.5	2.2	6.4	Cur. Mat.-L/T/D	25.2	6.3	2.6	2.0	1.1	1.3
27.2	23.9	27.8	Trade Payables	28.2	22.7	25.7	28.7	28.9	35.3
.1	.4	.8	Income Taxes Payable	1.7	.6	.4	.1	1.3	.5
14.4	14.6	11.7	All Other Current	14.3	9.7	15.7	8.5	14.7	7.4
58.0	57.8	62.7	Total Current	84.5	55.7	66.6	52.4	63.1	55.6
13.4	10.1	12.0	Long-Term Debt	24.0	21.3	9.5	5.3	3.5	5.7
.1	.2	.2	Deferred Taxes	.0	.0	.6	.1	.2	.3
6.5	7.7	6.0	All Other Non-Current	11.5	5.8	5.4	4.0	3.7	6.3
22.0	24.2	19.1	Net Worth	−20.0	17.1	17.9	38.2	29.5	32.1
100.0	100.0	100.0	Total Liabilities & Net Worth	100.0	100.0	100.0	100.0	100.0	100.0
			INCOME DATA						
100.0	100.0	100.0	Net Sales	100.0	100.0	100.0	100.0	100.0	100.0
34.8	38.4	38.1	Gross Profit	62.1	43.9	35.8	31.1	32.0	20.4
34.5	34.9	33.7	Operating Expenses	55.1	39.1	32.4	24.7	28.7	19.1
.3	3.5	4.5	Operating Profit	7.0	4.9	3.4	6.3	3.3	1.3
.3	.8	1.0	All Other Expenses (net)	1.4	.4	.9	2.3	.7	.6
.0	2.7	3.4	Profit Before Taxes	5.6	4.4	2.5	4.1	2.5	.7
			RATIOS						
2.1	2.0	1.8	Current	1.7	2.0	1.4	2.1	1.6	2.0
1.3	1.3	1.3		1.3	1.4	1.1	1.4	1.2	1.4
.9	1.0	1.0		.6	.9	.8	1.2	1.0	1.2
1.5	1.3	1.2	Quick	1.1	1.5	.9	1.6	1.3	1.2
.9	1.0	.8		.4	1.0	.6	.9	.9	.8
.6	.6	.5		.3	.6	.5	.6	.6	.4
17　21.0	23　16.1	21　17.6	Sales/Receivables	17　21.5	23　16.2	25　14.5	18　20.6	29　12.4	16　22.9
30　12.1	36　10.2	34　10.6		26　14.3	36　10.2	34　10.6	34　10.8	49　7.4	32　11.5
46　7.9	55　6.6	54　6.8		45　8.1	46　7.9	49　7.4	64　5.7	76　4.8	47　7.7
5　74.0	5　78.8	9　38.9	Cost of Sales/Inventory	0　UND	5　72.3	12　30.1	6　58.4	10　38.0	12　31.1
17　21.1	21　17.6	27　13.3		31　11.9	28　12.9	25　14.6	28　13.1	20　17.9	28　13.1
43　8.5	52　7.0	55　6.7		88　4.2	50　7.3	48　7.6	40　9.1	50　7.3	54　6.8
16　22.5	17　21.8	20　18.4	Cost of Sales/Payables	18　20.0	19　18.9	20　18.3	18　20.4	21　17.1	21　17.5
28　13.0	30　12.4	37　10.0		59　6.2	35　10.4	38　9.7	33　11.0	41　8.9	34　10.8
47　7.7	59　6.2	62　5.9		141　2.6	55　6.6	58　6.3	59　6.2	72　5.0	47　7.8
10.0	8.5	9.9	Sales/Working Capital	5.9	13.3	13.0	8.8	12.3	9.1
25.5	20.3	21.1		23.4	19.1	68.5	12.4	19.9	21.4
−135.0	184.7	−624.0		−10.0	NM	−22.4	45.9	145.5	56.3
6.6	12.0	10.5	EBIT/Interest	7.6	12.7	6.1	53.1	5.7	14.5
(101)　2.0	(117)　3.1	(112)　3.5		(17)　2.9	(22)　3.5	(15)　2.2	(20)　7.2	(22)　3.3	(16)　6.2
−.5	.5	1.0		1.0	.4	−.3	−.2	1.4	2.8
2.9	7.7	2.9	Net Profit + Depr., Dep., Amort./Cur. Mat. L/T/D						
(16)　.4	(13)　2.0	(20)　1.5							
−.6	.7	.1							
.1	.1	.1	Fixed/Worth	.2	.1	.2	.1	.1	.2
.5	.4	.5		39.0	.4	1.4	.3	.4	.4
8.2	1.5	2.4		−.3	−4.4	NM	.6	.8	1.1
1.1	1.1	1.4	Debt/Worth	2.0	1.4	2.3	1.0	1.4	1.0
2.6	2.6	3.0		100.0	2.5	6.0	1.9	3.9	2.3
48.1	9.6	23.5		−5.9	−10.6	NM	3.9	13.9	8.1
37.7	58.6	80.7	% Profit Before Taxes/Tangible Net Worth	133.0	113.8	104.2	85.4	43.9	59.7
(88)　7.7	(111)　20.3	(104)　24.7		(11)　84.2	(18)　24.7	(15)　19.9	19.3	(21)　29.4	(17)　20.6
−.6	2.1	5.1		7.3	−7.2	4.2	−8.3	3.4	8.2
9.5	17.1	16.4	% Profit Before Taxes/Total Assets	38.6	21.7	14.3	23.6	8.9	10.9
2.4	6.2	5.2		3.7	10.7	4.5	6.8	3.4	4.7
−3.4	2.1	.4		−1.3	3.6	−2.1	−3.2	.8	1.9
85.2	153.4	121.3	Sales/Net Fixed Assets	64.5	331.0	173.3	122.0	130.4	118.8
36.3	35.1	44.1		41.8	52.0	23.7	65.6	56.2	52.2
21.0	15.2	18.3		10.9	19.2	9.9	19.3	29.2	19.7
6.0	5.0	5.0	Sales/Total Assets	4.9	5.6	4.9	5.1	4.7	6.0
4.5	3.8	3.7		2.9	4.2	3.7	3.8	3.1	4.4
2.8	2.5	2.5		1.6	2.7	2.5	2.5	2.4	3.2
.5	.3	.4	% Depr., Dep., Amort./Sales	.6	.5	.4	.3	.2	.4
(94)　1.0	(95)　1.0	(95)　.9		(13)　1.6	(17)　.9	(15)　1.6	(16)　.6	(20)　.5	(14)　.8
1.7	2.1	1.8		3.1	1.9	3.3	1.2	1.2	1.1
2.5	2.8	1.6	% Officers', Directors', Owners' Comp/Sales		2.3				
(50)　4.9	(55)　5.6	(55)　3.9		(17)　4.6					
8.9	9.2	7.6		8.0					
1525249M	1680193M	2672702M	Net Sales ($)	10326M	58273M	76885M	160846M	359016M	2007356M
466649M	612290M	837616M	Total Assets ($)	5553M	19610M	30769M	45723M	180359M	555602M

M = $ thousand　　MM = $ million
See Pages 11 through 21 for Explanation of Ratios and Data

Current Data Sorted By Assets   **Comparative Historical Data**

0-500M	500M-2MM	2-10MM	10-50MM	50-100MM	100-250MM	Type of Statement	4/1/00-3/31/01	4/1/01-3/31/02
1 2	2 1	6 6 2 1 3	2 2			Unqualified / Reviewed / Compiled / Tax Returns / Other	2 / 10 / 12 / 10 / 6	1 / 8 / 19 / 3 / 10
		11 (4/1-9/30/04)		17 (10/1/04-3/31/05)			ALL	ALL
3	6	15	4			NUMBER OF STATEMENTS	40	41
%	%	%	%	%	%		%	%
		16.5		D	D	**ASSETS** Cash & Equivalents	6.0	11.3
		10.5		A	A	Trade Receivables (net)	13.8	11.1
		47.7		T	T	Inventory	47.2	41.7
		2.6		A	A	All Other Current	.6	2.6
		77.3				Total Current	67.5	66.7
		17.6		N	N	Fixed Assets (net)	23.2	26.0
		1.2		O	O	Intangibles (net)	5.5	2.6
		3.8		T	T	All Other Non-Current	3.7	4.8
		100.0				Total	100.0	100.0
				A	A	**LIABILITIES**		
		7.9		V	V	Notes Payable-Short Term	8.7	4.6
		3.6		A	A	Cur. Mat.-L/T/D	4.3	4.7
		25.6		I	I	Trade Payables	24.2	22.8
		.4		L	L	Income Taxes Payable	.4	.2
		6.5		A	A	All Other Current	9.8	8.5
		44.1		B	B	Total Current	47.4	40.8
		6.0		L	L	Long-Term Debt	22.4	21.5
		.1		E	E	Deferred Taxes	.3	.0
		2.2				All Other Non-Current	2.5	3.9
		47.7				Net Worth	27.4	33.8
		100.0				Total Liabilities & Net Worth	100.0	100.0
						INCOME DATA		
		100.0				Net Sales	100.0	100.0
		31.8				Gross Profit	37.4	40.6
		29.6				Operating Expenses	35.2	37.8
		2.2				Operating Profit	2.2	2.8
		.3				All Other Expenses (net)	1.1	.6
		1.8				Profit Before Taxes	1.2	2.2
						RATIOS		
		2.6				Current	2.1	2.8
		1.7					1.6	1.6
		1.4					1.1	1.3
		1.2				Quick	.7	.9
		.7					.4	.6
		.2					.2	.3
		4 103.6				Sales/Receivables	7 52.4	4 92.9
		6 56.9					10 35.9	8 43.8
		17 21.8					25 14.6	25 14.8
		66 5.5				Cost of Sales/Inventory	67 5.5	56 6.6
		75 4.9					103 3.5	90 4.1
		93 3.9					153 2.4	128 2.9
		22 16.8				Cost of Sales/Payables	24 15.0	27 13.3
		36 10.1					48 7.6	48 7.6
		48 7.6					75 4.9	69 5.3
		8.3				Sales/Working Capital	7.3	5.7
		10.9					11.2	10.5
		15.8					112.7	21.2
		37.6				EBIT/Interest	4.6	8.5
		(13) 2.1					(36) 2.0	(36) 2.7
		-1.0					1.1	1.1
						Net Profit + Depr., Dep., Amort./Cur. Mat. L /T/D		
		.1				Fixed/Worth	.3	.2
		.3					.8	.8
		.6					NM	1.6
		.4				Debt/Worth	1.2	.8
		1.1					3.4	2.1
		3.9					-44.9	5.9
		16.8				% Profit Before Taxes/Tangible Net Worth	21.3	47.1
		12.7					(29) 8.8	(35) 8.8
		-12.4					1.6	-1.2
		11.8				% Profit Before Taxes/Total Assets	8.6	15.6
		4.1					3.1	3.2
		-1.5					.6	-.1
		49.5				Sales/Net Fixed Assets	39.0	39.6
		25.8					17.2	14.3
		14.1					6.9	6.7
		4.3				Sales/Total Assets	3.7	3.2
		3.4					2.9	2.7
		2.2					1.7	2.1
		.9				% Depr., Dep., Amort./Sales	.7	1.2
		1.8					(35) 2.0	(36) 2.4
		2.5					4.1	4.9
		1.0				% Officers', Directors', Owners' Comp/Sales	1.6	1.6
		(12) 2.9					(21) 4.9	(23) 4.6
		7.0					8.5	9.1
2416M	25236M	245692M	219724M			Net Sales ($)	812005M	1436310M
1013M	7326M	57287M	76361M			Total Assets ($)	217566M	400728M

© RMA 2005

M = $ thousand   MM = $ million
See Pages 11 through 21 for Explanation of Ratios and Data

Comparative Historical Data | Current Data Sorted By Sales

				Type of Statement $	0-1MM	1-3MM	3-5MM	5-10MM	10-25MM	25MM & OVER
		1		Unqualified				5	1	2
12	12	8		Reviewed	1	2	2	3	1	2
5	6	9		Compiled	1			1	2	2
5	9	5		Tax Returns			1	1	1	
5	10	6		Other						
4/1/02-3/31/03	4/1/03-3/31/04	4/1/04-3/31/05					11 (4/1-9/30/04)		17 (10/1/04-3/31/05)	
ALL	ALL	ALL								
27	38	28		NUMBER OF STATEMENTS	2	2	3	10	5	6
%	%	%		**ASSETS**	%	%	%	%	%	%
11.2	8.4	12.5		Cash & Equivalents				13.9		
17.0	14.6	9.2		Trade Receivables (net)				9.8		
31.6	43.3	45.1		Inventory				44.7		
1.7	1.9	1.9		All Other Current				1.8		
61.4	68.2	68.7		Total Current				70.2		
29.7	24.4	22.3		Fixed Assets (net)				24.3		
2.8	2.3	3.6		Intangibles (net)				1.5		
6.2	5.1	5.4		All Other Non-Current				4.0		
100.0	100.0	100.0		Total				100.0		
				LIABILITIES						
4.2	7.0	11.3		Notes Payable-Short Term				8.9		
4.8	5.8	3.6		Cur. Mat.-L/T/D				4.5		
15.7	22.2	24.2		Trade Payables				26.2		
.4	.1	.8		Income Taxes Payable				1.0		
9.6	7.5	6.2		All Other Current				4.8		
34.8	42.6	46.1		Total Current				45.4		
12.5	17.8	10.8		Long-Term Debt				9.2		
.1	.2	.2		Deferred Taxes				.1		
6.1	3.6	4.1		All Other Non-Current				2.5		
46.6	35.8	38.8		Net Worth				42.8		
100.0	100.0	100.0		Total Liabilities & Net Worth				100.0		
				INCOME DATA						
100.0	100.0	100.0		Net Sales				100.0		
46.0	41.6	37.0		Gross Profit				34.1		
41.2	39.2	34.8		Operating Expenses				33.4		
4.8	2.5	2.1		Operating Profit				.7		
.7	1.2	.5		All Other Expenses (net)				.3		
4.1	1.3	1.7		Profit Before Taxes				.4		
				RATIOS						
3.0	2.6	2.1						2.8		
1.8	1.6	1.5		Current				1.5		
1.2	1.1	1.2						1.4		
1.8	1.1	.8						1.2		
.9	.4	.5 (27)		Quick				.6		
.3	.2	.2						.2		
6 56.2	5 70.3	4 94.8						3 115.6		
15 23.9	11 32.5	6 56.8		Sales/Receivables				6 63.0		
37 9.8	35 10.5	11 33.7						13 28.8		
46 8.0	52 7.1	66 5.5						65 5.6		
85 4.3	95 3.9	77 4.8		Cost of Sales/Inventory				71 5.1		
106 3.5	127 2.9	123 3.0						95 3.8		
13 29.1	29 12.5	21 17.5						22 16.5		
33 11.1	45 8.2	41 8.9		Cost of Sales/Payables				40 9.2		
72 5.1	71 5.1	53 6.9						57 6.4		
6.8	6.9	8.5						7.9		
8.6	12.6	11.6		Sales/Working Capital				11.6		
41.3	48.9	27.3						17.9		
19.3	6.5	17.5								
(21) 5.5	(34) 2.3	(24) 2.2		EBIT/Interest						
1.5	.7	-.7								
				Net Profit + Depr., Dep., Amort./Cur. Mat. L/T/D						
.2	.2	.2						.3		
.6	.7	.6		Fixed/Worth				.6		
1.2	2.0	1.2						.7		
.4	.6	.7						.4		
1.1	1.6	1.4		Debt/Worth				1.4		
3.0	8.5	4.3						4.1		
46.9	45.7	22.4		% Profit Before Taxes/Tangible						
(24) 17.8	(32) 5.9	(25) 8.0		Net Worth						
1.3	.3	-4.1								
21.2	9.7	10.6		% Profit Before Taxes/Total				8.3		
8.5	3.3	2.7		Assets				-.6		
.0	-1.0	-2.7						-7.8		
45.1	58.5	46.2						36.3		
15.3	19.0	19.0		Sales/Net Fixed Assets				19.0		
3.3	4.2	6.9						10.7		
4.3	3.9	4.2						4.7		
2.3	2.5	2.9		Sales/Total Assets				3.0		
1.6	1.9	2.1						2.2		
.7	1.0	.9								
(25) 2.3	(35) 2.3	(27) 1.9		% Depr., Dep., Amort./Sales						
6.3	4.9	3.5								
3.1	1.8	.9								
(17) 4.5	(25) 4.5	(19) 3.6		% Officers', Directors', Owners' Comp/Sales						
9.9	7.7	7.0								
202022M	482466M	493068M		Net Sales ($)	1280M	2626M	9755M	73492M	74300M	331615M
66779M	161700M	141987M		Total Assets ($)	632M	1334M	3985M	24700M	21350M	89986M

© RMA 2005

M = $ thousand   MM = $ million
See Pages 11 through 21 for Explanation of Ratios and Data

Current Data Sorted By Assets   **Comparative Historical Data**

						Type of Statement		
1	6	24	30	6	4	Unqualified	70	78
8	28	112	46	1	1	Reviewed	186	203
15	60	58	7	1		Compiled	206	221
11	38	16	1			Tax Returns	67	59
	34	56	17	3		Other	150	161
	76 (4/1-9/30/04)			507 (10/1/04-3/31/05)			4/1/00- 3/31/01	4/1/01- 3/31/02
0-500M	500M-2MM	2-10MM	10-50MM	50-100MM	100-250MM		ALL	ALL
35	166	266	101	10	5	NUMBER OF STATEMENTS	679	722
%	%	%	%	%	%	ASSETS	%	%
10.4	6.1	5.1	3.9	6.9		Cash & Equivalents	7.2	6.8
30.0	28.2	33.5	30.7	30.1		Trade Receivables (net)	29.0	29.7
32.8	40.0	35.1	31.5	29.4		Inventory	33.5	33.1
6.4	1.6	1.6	2.4	2.7		All Other Current	2.7	2.6
79.6	75.9	75.3	68.5	69.2		Total Current	72.3	72.2
14.1	15.7	17.0	23.1	24.4		Fixed Assets (net)	18.7	19.3
2.3	1.8	1.3	1.6	1.2		Intangibles (net)	1.8	1.6
4.0	6.6	6.4	6.8	5.2		All Other Non-Current	7.1	6.9
100.0	100.0	100.0	100.0	100.0		Total	100.0	100.0
						LIABILITIES		
22.1	13.4	14.7	16.1	16.8		Notes Payable-Short Term	14.5	14.8
4.1	3.3	2.2	2.4	1.1		Cur. Mat.-L/T/D	3.3	3.4
20.8	21.3	16.5	14.0	10.6		Trade Payables	15.4	15.2
.1	.2	.3	.2	.3		Income Taxes Payable	.2	.2
10.5	8.2	8.5	7.7	8.8		All Other Current	8.4	7.8
57.5	46.4	42.1	40.4	37.7		Total Current	41.7	41.4
32.1	15.1	11.6	13.4	17.2		Long-Term Debt	12.0	13.4
.0	.1	.3	.4	.6		Deferred Taxes	.2	.2
14.8	5.1	3.8	3.6	1.6		All Other Non-Current	3.5	3.6
-4.5	33.4	42.2	42.2	42.9		Net Worth	42.6	41.4
100.0	100.0	100.0	100.0	100.0		Total Liabilities & Net Worth	100.0	100.0
						INCOME DATA		
100.0	100.0	100.0	100.0	100.0		Net Sales	100.0	100.0
33.3	28.4	25.4	26.2	30.0		Gross Profit	26.3	26.9
32.7	26.5	22.5	22.1	22.0		Operating Expenses	23.9	24.3
.6	2.0	2.8	4.0	7.9		Operating Profit	2.4	2.6
.2	.1	.0	-.2	.7		All Other Expenses (net)	.2	.5
.4	1.9	2.8	4.2	7.2		Profit Before Taxes	2.2	2.1
						RATIOS		
2.4	2.8	2.6	2.3	3.2			2.7	2.9
1.8	1.8	1.8	1.6	1.7		Current	1.8	1.8
1.1	1.2	1.4	1.3	1.4			1.3	1.3
1.4	1.3	1.3	1.2	1.8			1.4	1.5
(34) .8	(164) .8	.9	.9	.8	.9	Quick	(721) .9	.9
.4	.5	.6	.6	.7			.5	.6
5 71.0	21 17.5	29 12.8	32 11.2	31 11.8			24 15.2	26 14.0
22 16.9	33 11.1	38 9.5	41 8.8	43 8.5		Sales/Receivables	34 10.7	37 10.0
44 8.2	45 8.1	51 7.1	49 7.5	52 7.1			45 8.1	48 7.6
5 67.2	40 9.1	39 9.3	41 8.9	40 9.2			38 9.7	38 9.7
37 9.9	70 5.2	56 6.6	53 6.9	52 7.0		Cost of Sales/Inventory	53 6.9	54 6.7
78 4.7	102 3.6	76 4.8	69 5.3	99 3.7			77 4.7	80 4.6
4 100.5	18 20.5	16 22.3	17 21.7	18 20.4			13 27.4	15 23.8
27 13.4	30 12.0	23 15.7	21 17.0	22 16.7		Cost of Sales/Payables	21 17.5	23 16.0
46 8.0	45 8.1	36 10.1	29 12.6	25 14.8			33 11.2	34 10.8
7.5	6.1	6.2	6.7	5.9			6.0	5.5
13.3	9.7	8.8	11.0	6.8		Sales/Working Capital	9.8	9.9
60.1	23.1	14.2	18.5	15.7			18.9	19.0
10.4	8.1	11.3	13.5	27.5			6.5	5.9
(29) 4.4	(157) 3.1	(251) 4.6	(98) 7.2	8.3		EBIT/Interest	(634) 2.5	(675) 2.5
-.2	1.2	2.1	3.7	6.0			1.3	1.2
	4.0	7.4	6.3			Net Profit + Depr., Dep.,	4.6	5.8
	(35) 1.5	(94) 3.1	(36) 3.6			Amort./Cur. Mat. L /T/D	(190) 1.9	(198) 2.4
	.3	1.8	2.5				.8	.9
.1	.2	.2	.3	.3			.2	.2
1.1	.4	.4	.5	.6		Fixed/Worth	.4	.4
-.9	1.1	.7	.8	.8			.9	.9
1.0	.9	.7	.9	.9			.7	.6
25.1	1.8	1.4	1.6	1.8		Debt/Worth	1.4	1.5
-4.6	6.9	2.9	2.4	2.2			3.0	3.3
140.5	36.2	31.5	38.0	45.6		% Profit Before Taxes/Tangible	30.2	26.1
(22) 57.5	(144) 12.9	(256) 17.1	(100) 23.0	36.9		Net Worth	(639) 12.7	(677) 10.9
2.0	2.5	6.7	14.5	24.8			3.7	2.8
26.3	11.6	12.7	14.9	19.3		% Profit Before Taxes/Total	10.6	9.7
3.6	4.3	6.2	9.0	15.8		Assets	5.2	4.3
-5.0	.6	2.6	5.7	8.5			1.1	.7
256.2	49.7	38.0	25.9	18.5			38.7	38.0
40.1	25.6	22.2	14.2	13.0		Sales/Net Fixed Assets	20.2	18.6
24.2	12.6	11.1	8.9	7.6			10.8	9.7
6.4	4.0	3.7	3.4	2.8			3.8	3.7
4.1	3.0	2.9	2.8	2.6		Sales/Total Assets	3.0	2.8
3.1	2.3	2.2	2.2	1.7			2.3	2.2
.5	.6	.7	.8	1.0			.6	.7
(21) .8	(145) 1.0	(238) .9	(98) 1.1	1.2		% Depr., Dep., Amort./Sales	(620) 1.0	(673) 1.0
1.7	1.9	1.5	1.6	1.8			1.5	1.6
1.3	1.6	1.2	.7			% Officers', Directors',	1.4	1.4
(19) 4.9	(97) 3.2	(132) 2.4	(28) 1.3			Owners' Comp/Sales	(337) 2.5	(372) 2.7
9.0	5.0	3.7	2.6				4.4	4.8
47139M	647845M	3878522M	5923131M	1628797M	1573122M	Net Sales ($)	13104662M	13646997M
10450M	196438M	1292054M	2140484M	713952M	806684M	Total Assets ($)	4920189M	5227226M

© RMA 2005

M = $ thousand   MM = $ million
See Pages 11 through 21 for Explanation of Ratios and Data

Comparative Historical Data | **Current Data Sorted By Sales**

H1	H2	H3	Type of Statement	0-1MM	1-3MM	3-5MM	5-10MM	10-25MM	25MM & OVER
85	82	70	Unqualified		2	1	5	15	47
211	199	189	Reviewed		13	15	32	70	59
183	220	133	Compiled	5	28	24	31	36	9
77	90	70	Tax Returns	7	28	10	18	6	1
159	142	121	Other	3	22	17	25	33	21
4/1/02-3/31/03 ALL	4/1/03-3/31/04 ALL	4/1/04-3/31/05 ALL		76 (4/1-9/30/04)			507 (10/1/04-3/31/05)		
715	733	583	**NUMBER OF STATEMENTS**	15	93	67	111	160	137
%	%	%	**ASSETS**	%	%	%	%	%	%
5.9	6.0	5.5	Cash & Equivalents	10.1	5.6	3.5	7.8	6.5	2.8
30.1	30.4	31.2	Trade Receivables (net)	30.3	24.7	28.7	31.2	34.8	32.8
34.4	33.1	35.5	Inventory	33.7	39.1	41.9	34.3	34.3	32.5
2.2	3.1	2.1	All Other Current	5.1	3.5	1.6	1.1	1.5	2.4
72.5	72.6	74.3	Total Current	79.1	73.0	75.7	74.4	77.2	70.5
19.4	19.6	17.8	Fixed Assets (net)	14.4	16.9	15.5	17.9	16.3	21.5
1.6	1.8	1.6	Intangibles (net)	2.9	2.2	2.9	1.5	.7	1.4
6.4	6.0	6.4	All Other Non-Current	3.6	7.8	5.9	6.3	5.9	6.6
100.0	100.0	100.0	Total	100.0	100.0	100.0	100.0	100.0	100.0
			LIABILITIES						
16.1	16.3	15.0	Notes Payable-Short Term	8.2	17.2	15.5	12.4	15.4	15.8
3.7	3.1	2.6	Cur. Mat.-L/T/D	7.2	3.2	3.2	2.4	2.2	2.1
15.8	16.1	17.5	Trade Payables	21.5	18.9	20.5	17.6	16.8	15.4
.2	.3	.2	Income Taxes Payable	.3	.1	.4	.3	.2	.3
7.9	8.0	8.4	All Other Current	8.8	7.1	9.2	8.2	9.1	8.2
43.8	43.8	43.8	Total Current	46.1	46.4	48.7	40.9	43.7	41.8
12.4	13.4	14.3	Long-Term Debt	34.4	21.4	15.6	12.5	10.5	12.5
.2	.2	.3	Deferred Taxes	.0	.1	.1	.1	.4	.4
3.9	4.5	4.7	All Other Non-Current	11.0	8.9	4.3	3.6	4.1	3.1
39.7	38.1	36.9	Net Worth	8.5	23.2	31.4	42.9	41.2	42.2
100.0	100.0	100.0	Total Liabilities & Net Worth	100.0	100.0	100.0	100.0	100.0	100.0
			INCOME DATA						
100.0	100.0	100.0	Net Sales	100.0	100.0	100.0	100.0	100.0	100.0
26.9	26.7	27.0	Gross Profit	38.1	31.1	26.8	26.8	25.4	25.0
25.0	24.4	24.2	Operating Expenses	37.0	30.0	24.9	23.4	22.7	21.0
1.9	2.2	2.8	Operating Profit	1.0	1.1	2.0	3.4	2.7	4.0
.2	.1	.0	All Other Expenses (net)	.9	-.1	.2	.2	.0	-.1
1.7	2.1	2.7	Profit Before Taxes	.1	1.2	1.7	3.2	2.8	4.1
			RATIOS						
2.8	2.7	2.6	Current	3.6	3.0	2.7	2.8	2.5	2.3
1.7	1.7	1.8		2.0	1.9	1.6	2.1	1.8	1.7
1.3	1.3	1.3		1.3	1.2	1.2	1.4	1.4	1.3
1.4	1.4	1.3	Quick	1.3	1.2	1.2	1.5	1.4	1.2
.8	(728) .8	(580) .9		.7	(92) .7	(65) .8	1.0	.9	.9
.6	.6	.6		.4	.4	.6	.6	.6	.7
25 14.5	27 13.5	27 13.7	Sales/Receivables	13 29.1	19 19.4	27 13.5	25 14.8	29 12.8	32 11.5
35 10.3	38 9.6	37 9.8		27 13.6	29 12.7	35 10.3	36 10.2	38 9.6	40 9.1
46 7.9	49 7.4	49 7.5		61 6.0	46 7.9	48 7.6	49 7.5	52 7.1	49 7.5
37 9.8	38 9.7	38 9.5	Cost of Sales/Inventory	8 47.9	45 8.2	48 7.5	34 10.7	37 9.9	39 9.4
55 6.6	55 6.7	56 6.5		73 5.0	78 4.7	80 4.6	54 6.7	52 7.0	47 7.7
80 4.6	77 4.7	83 4.4		120 3.0	114 3.2	101 3.6	81 4.5	71 5.2	63 5.8
15 24.5	15 23.8	17 22.0	Cost of Sales/Payables	4 89.0	16 22.2	22 16.9	14 25.4	16 22.8	17 21.7
22 16.7	24 15.3	24 15.0		34 10.8	31 11.6	32 11.2	25 14.6	22 16.7	21 17.5
34 10.6	36 10.1	38 9.5		73 5.0	50 7.2	50 7.3	41 9.0	35 10.4	27 13.7
6.1	5.9	6.2	Sales/Working Capital	5.0	5.2	5.5	5.9	6.6	7.1
10.2	9.7	9.5		8.2	8.8	9.2	7.9	9.2	11.2
21.1	20.0	18.1		24.0	26.5	25.1	18.1	15.2	17.9
7.5	8.7	11.2	EBIT/Interest	4.4	7.8	7.1	13.0	9.4	15.5
(671) 3.0	(676) 3.5	(550) 4.8		(12) .5	(87) 2.9	(62) 2.8	(104) 5.3	(151) 4.3	(134) 7.7
1.2	1.5	2.0		-1.7	.8	1.0	2.0	2.3	3.8
6.2	4.5	6.7	Net Profit + Depr., Dep., Amort./Cur. Mat. L/T/D		4.0	2.7	7.4	5.9	9.7
(211) 2.5	(197) 2.0	(173) 3.0			(16) 1.3	(16) 1.5	(29) 4.5	(55) 2.8	(55) 3.9
1.1	.9	1.4			.3	.6	2.0	2.0	2.5
.2	.2	.2	Fixed/Worth	.0	.2	.2	.2	.2	.3
.4	.4	.4		.6	.5	.5	.4	.3	.5
1.0	1.0	.9		126.0	3.8	1.3	.9	.6	.8
.7	.8	.8	Debt/Worth	.6	1.0	.8	.6	.8	.9
1.6	1.7	1.6		2.5	2.0	2.4	1.4	1.4	1.5
3.2	3.5	3.2		-4.7	21.1	10.2	2.8	3.2	2.3
26.2	28.8	36.1	% Profit Before Taxes/Tangible Net Worth	125.1	36.1	32.8	38.4	31.1	38.0
(657) 11.7	(672) 15.1	(537) 18.3		(10) 1.3	(75) 10.9	(56) 13.0	(104) 17.1	(156) 17.2	(136) 24.2
2.9	3.6	7.5		-23.7	1.6	2.2	6.6	6.6	15.7
9.7	11.1	13.1	% Profit Before Taxes/Total Assets	28.2	9.9	11.8	15.8	12.7	16.7
4.2	4.9	6.4		.0	3.6	4.0	5.9	6.1	9.7
.7	.9	2.3		-10.6	-.9	.4	2.7	2.4	5.9
35.7	37.4	40.6	Sales/Net Fixed Assets	UND	45.5	45.5	40.7	50.7	27.9
18.5	18.7	21.4		40.1	22.6	23.1	20.3	26.7	16.7
10.6	10.0	10.8		8.5	9.1	13.6	10.6	14.0	9.8
3.6	3.6	3.7	Sales/Total Assets	5.0	3.9	3.5	3.8	3.8	3.7
2.9	2.8	2.9		3.0	2.5	2.7	3.0	3.1	3.0
2.2	2.2	2.3		2.1	1.9	2.3	2.2	2.4	2.4
.8	.8	.7	% Depr., Dep., Amort./Sales		.8	.7	.7	.6	.8
(649) 1.1	(658) 1.2	(515) 1.0			(80) 1.5	(61) .9	(95) 1.0	(140) .9	(131) 1.0
1.7	1.8	1.6			2.1	1.5	1.9	1.5	1.5
1.4	1.5	1.3	% Officers', Directors', Owners' Comp/Sales		1.4	1.8	1.4	.9	.9
(363) 2.6	(352) 2.5	(277) 2.6			(55) 3.3	(35) 3.0	(63) 2.4	(76) 2.7	(41) 1.7
5.2	4.7	4.2			5.3	4.2	4.5	3.6	2.6
18228380M	16176286M	13698556M	Net Sales ($)	10542M	190275M	263802M	802562M	2492170M	9939205M
6348597M	6394768M	5160062M	Total Assets ($)	3964M	78202M	109858M	311879M	874147M	3782012M

© RMA 2005

M = $ thousand   MM = $ million
See Pages 11 through 21 for Explanation of Ratios and Data

Current Data Sorted By Assets　　　　**Comparative Historical Data**

0-500M	500M-2MM	2-10MM	10-50MM	50-100MM	100-250MM	Type of Statement	4/1/00-3/31/01 ALL	4/1/01-3/31/02 ALL
	3	1				Unqualified	6	4
	9	6				Reviewed	15	15
5	9	4	2		1	Compiled	30	23
10	9	3				Tax Returns	8	11
1	4	1				Other	19	22
	5 (4/1-9/30/04)		54 (10/1/04-3/31/05)					
16	25	15	2		1	**NUMBER OF STATEMENTS**	78	75
%	%	%	%	%	%	**ASSETS**	%	%
8.5	8.4	3.8				Cash & Equivalents	7.4	8.3
27.7	32.4	31.8				Trade Receivables (net)	27.5	27.5
37.6	34.7	35.2				Inventory	32.7	32.3
.3	2.1	3.3				All Other Current	1.8	3.4
74.1	77.6	74.2				Total Current	69.4	71.5
21.0	17.4	14.2				Fixed Assets (net)	21.4	17.6
2.7	.6	4.4				Intangibles (net)	2.1	1.8
2.2	4.5	7.2				All Other Non-Current	7.1	9.1
100.0	100.0	100.0				Total	100.0	100.0
						LIABILITIES		
14.5	13.0	12.9				Notes Payable-Short Term	10.8	9.8
2.3	2.4	2.4				Cur. Mat.-L/T/D	3.1	4.3
26.2	23.1	22.6				Trade Payables	20.2	20.7
.9	1.1	.7				Income Taxes Payable	.3	.2
11.6	6.2	12.0				All Other Current	8.0	8.8
55.5	45.7	50.7				Total Current	42.4	43.9
37.2	12.0	17.0				Long-Term Debt	17.9	14.5
.0	.2	.0				Deferred Taxes	.4	.2
3.5	5.8	3.1				All Other Non-Current	3.4	6.1
3.8	36.3	29.2				Net Worth	36.0	35.3
100.0	100.0	100.0				Total Liabilities & Net Worth	100.0	100.0
						INCOME DATA		
100.0	100.0	100.0				Net Sales	100.0	100.0
35.1	41.3	26.1				Gross Profit	38.0	36.6
33.0	38.8	25.4				Operating Expenses	35.6	34.5
2.1	2.5	.6				Operating Profit	2.5	2.1
.8	.2	-1.1				All Other Expenses (net)	.6	.6
1.3	2.4	1.7				Profit Before Taxes	1.8	1.5
						RATIOS		
2.5	2.8	2.3					2.7	2.5
1.7	1.7	1.3				Current	1.9	1.6
.9	1.2	1.1					1.2	1.2
1.3	1.5	1.1					1.5	1.5
.8	.8	.7				Quick	.8	.7
.3	.5	.4					.4	.5
13 28.4	20 18.0	23 16.1					19 18.7	21 17.3
22 16.5	30 12.3	40 9.2				Sales/Receivables	31 11.8	33 11.1
37 9.8	43 8.6	49 7.5					50 7.2	49 7.5
20 18.0	28 13.1	26 14.0					34 10.6	28 12.9
51 7.2	54 6.8	47 7.7				Cost of Sales/Inventory	74 4.9	69 5.3
105 3.5	85 4.3	129 2.8					107 3.4	111 3.3
24 15.3	19 19.5	20 18.7					22 16.7	24 15.0
33 11.1	32 11.4	45 8.1				Cost of Sales/Payables	38 9.6	37 9.8
41 9.0	59 6.2	61 6.0					62 5.9	57 6.4
8.0	6.9	6.1					5.7	6.4
12.7	10.7	18.0				Sales/Working Capital	8.8	9.2
-110.2	18.7	29.2					31.8	33.3
13.6	13.0	4.4					8.6	2.7
(14) 4.4	(23) 6.1	2.1				EBIT/Interest	(69) 2.9	(61) 1.5
.9	2.0	1.3					1.0	.4
							9.7	2.2
						Net Profit + Depr., Dep., Amort./Cur. Mat. L /T/D	(22) 3.7	(20) 1.3
							2.0	.2
.2	.3	.2					.2	.2
2.0	.4	.4				Fixed/Worth	.4	.3
40.4	.9	1.6					1.2	1.3
1.4	.6	1.9					.8	.7
4.7	1.6	3.4				Debt/Worth	1.5	1.9
127.0	2.9	8.3					4.2	4.7
107.4	38.0	37.4					37.5	19.5
(13) 56.9	(23) 11.9	16.3				% Profit Before Taxes/Tangible Net Worth	(69) 13.6	(66) 8.0
2.8	3.9	3.8					1.3	-1.2
31.8	11.2	5.3					10.6	7.6
5.5	6.4	2.3				% Profit Before Taxes/Total Assets	4.7	2.1
.0	2.0	1.0					.1	-.6
176.4	50.7	57.6					37.6	51.0
26.3	23.9	30.5				Sales/Net Fixed Assets	19.6	28.0
11.4	14.0	13.4					9.1	12.3
6.7	4.6	4.0					3.5	3.9
3.9	3.6	2.7				Sales/Total Assets	2.7	2.6
2.3	2.8	1.9					1.9	1.8
.3	.6	.8					.8	.4
(10) 1.3	(22) 1.1	(13) 1.0				% Depr., Dep., Amort./Sales	(71) 1.5	(67) .9
3.9	1.6	2.1					2.0	1.7
.8	1.8						2.9	3.2
(10) 3.4	(15) 3.4					% Officers', Directors', Owners' Comp/Sales	(33) 5.5	(41) 5.6
7.7	7.0						7.7	10.6
29598M	99885M	170933M	144712M		275534M	Net Sales ($)	611988M	442215M
4678M	28050M	61221M	60110M		218483M	Total Assets ($)	269624M	185875M

(Center columns 10-50MM, 50-100MM, 100-250MM: DATA NOT AVAILABLE)

© RMA 2005

M = $ thousand   MM = $ million
See Pages 11 through 21 for Explanation of Ratios and Data

Comparative Historical Data | Current Data Sorted By Sales

			Type of Statement						
2	5	4	Unqualified				2	1	3
21	25	9	Reviewed			2	4	3	
27	24	18	Compiled	5	1	6	4	1	1
11	26	22	Tax Returns	3	8	7	2	2	
19	17	6	Other		4				
4/1/02-3/31/03	4/1/03-3/31/04	4/1/04-3/31/05		5 (4/1-9/30/04)		54 (10/1/04-3/31/05)			
ALL	ALL	ALL		0-1MM	1-3MM	3-5MM	5-10MM	10-25MM	25MM & OVER
80	97	59	NUMBER OF STATEMENTS	8	13	15	12	7	4

%	%	%	ASSETS	%	%	%	%	%	%
9.6	10.9	7.1	Cash & Equivalents		7.3	8.6	5.5		
22.0	21.7	30.1	Trade Receivables (net)		35.7	33.0	29.2		
38.0	37.2	34.6	Inventory		33.7	28.5	44.2		
2.2	2.5	2.6	All Other Current		1.1	1.8	2.9		
71.8	72.3	74.4	Total Current		77.7	71.8	81.8		
12.5	12.4	17.4	Fixed Assets (net)		17.2	18.6	12.9		
1.8	1.3	3.3	Intangibles (net)		1.1	2.1	2.0		
13.9	14.0	4.9	All Other Non-Current		4.0	7.5	3.4		
100.0	100.0	100.0	Total		100.0	100.0	100.0		

			LIABILITIES						
9.7	9.8	13.4	Notes Payable-Short Term		10.1	11.0	11.1		
2.5	2.4	2.5	Cur. Mat.-L/T/D		1.2	2.2	3.3		
24.0	23.6	23.1	Trade Payables		30.9	17.1	28.0		
.6	.4	.9	Income Taxes Payable		.0	1.4	1.3		
8.9	6.3	9.3	All Other Current		9.4	4.8	10.0		
45.7	42.6	49.2	Total Current		51.7	36.5	53.8		
7.8	12.1	20.0	Long-Term Debt		14.1	20.0	11.0		
.0	.1	.1	Deferred Taxes		.0	.2	.1		
15.8	16.6	4.5	All Other Non-Current		.0	5.0	6.5		
30.6	28.6	26.2	Net Worth		34.2	38.4	28.6		
100.0	100.0	100.0	Total Liabilities & Net Worth		100.0	100.0	100.0		

			INCOME DATA						
100.0	100.0	100.0	Net Sales		100.0	100.0	100.0		
34.8	34.3	35.3	Gross Profit		35.6	38.0	35.8		
33.7	33.7	33.6	Operating Expenses		31.1	36.0	34.7		
1.1	.6	1.7	Operating Profit		4.4	2.0	1.0		
.2	.2	.0	All Other Expenses (net)		.2	-.7	-.6		
.9	.4	1.7	Profit Before Taxes		4.3	2.7	1.6		

			RATIOS						
2.7	3.1	2.5	Current		2.5	3.0	2.3		
1.6	1.8	1.6			1.5	1.9	1.8		
1.2	1.2	1.2			1.0	1.5	1.1		
1.2	1.7	1.3	Quick		1.6	2.7	1.1		
.6	.6	.8			.9	1.1	.6		
.3	.3	.5			.5	.7	.4		
16 23.1	15 25.2	19 18.9	Sales/Receivables		22 16.5	22 16.6	16 22.4		
25 14.4	24 14.9	30 12.3			31 11.9	32 11.3	24 14.9		
40 9.1	39 9.4	43 8.4			43 8.6	57 6.4	38 9.6		
49 7.4	45 8.1	26 14.0	Cost of Sales/Inventory		20 18.5	18 20.7	32 11.5		
81 4.5	78 4.7	48 7.6			48 7.7	47 7.7	70 5.2		
134 2.7	129 2.8	96 3.8			85 4.3	81 4.5	141 2.6		
19 19.7	19 19.1	20 18.5	Cost of Sales/Payables		28 13.2	20 18.0	21 17.2		
43 8.5	42 8.8	33 11.0			37 9.8	30 12.3	44 8.2		
83 4.4	79 4.6	50 7.3			67 5.5	39 9.3	60 6.0		
5.8	5.3	7.0	Sales/Working Capital		8.2	7.2	6.0		
8.4	8.3	13.1			12.3	8.2	11.9		
26.5	21.1	28.4			NM	17.1	72.2		
7.2	10.3	8.7	EBIT/Interest		48.0	9.8	7.7		
(68) 2.6	(77) 1.8	(55) 3.5		(12)	9.8	(13) 4.6	(11) 3.4		
-1.7	-1.4	1.2			3.6	2.2	1.2		
2.6	4.3	5.7	Net Profit + Depr., Dep., Amort./Cur. Mat. L/T/D						
(26) .9	(29) .4	(10) 3.3							
-2.1	-4.6	2.3							
.1	.1	.2	Fixed/Worth		.2	.2	.1		
.3	.3	.4			.4	.3	.4		
.9	1.3	2.0			1.6	1.5	1.2		
.7	.8	1.4	Debt/Worth		1.0	.6	.8		
2.3	3.0	2.5			2.5	1.8	2.3		
11.8	9.8	8.2			6.1	3.0	5.3		
29.9	33.4	56.7	% Profit Before Taxes/Tangible Net Worth		123.1	35.1	38.0		
(68) 8.3	(82) 5.9	(53) 16.3			56.9	(14) 13.5	(11) 16.5		
-9.7	-4.9	3.9			11.4	3.9	3.9		
9.2	9.5	10.6	% Profit Before Taxes/Total Assets		35.1	10.5	10.6		
3.0	1.9	3.7			11.1	6.4	4.0		
-4.2	-4.1	.3			3.5	2.6	.5		
88.4	61.9	53.4	Sales/Net Fixed Assets		143.9	51.0	49.6		
31.4	32.8	26.4			30.2	22.0	28.1		
14.7	14.6	12.5			11.8	11.5	21.6		
3.6	3.8	4.5	Sales/Total Assets		4.8	5.0	4.6		
2.7	3.0	3.4			3.5	3.1	3.6		
1.7	1.8	2.1			3.3	1.9	2.4		
.6	.6	.6	% Depr., Dep., Amort./Sales			.6	.3		
(64) 1.0	(84) 1.0	(47) 1.1				1.1	(11) .9		
1.6	1.6	1.8				1.6	1.3		
4.1	2.7	1.9	% Officers', Directors', Owners' Comp/Sales						
(44) 5.4	(61) 5.2	(31) 3.4							
7.2	8.8	7.0							
531518M	774643M	720662M	Net Sales ($)	5315M	24796M	57905M	83212M	103903M	445531M
328263M	450890M	372542M	Total Assets ($)	2223M	6816M	23096M	29022M	29028M	282357M

M = $ thousand   MM = $ million
See Pages 11 through 21 for Explanation of Ratios and Data

Current Data Sorted By Assets   Comparative Historical Data

	0-500M	500M-2MM	2-10MM	10-50MM	50-100MM	100-250MM	Type of Statement	4/1/00-3/31/01 ALL	4/1/01-3/31/02 ALL
	1	1	7	9	1	2	Unqualified	9	11
	1	19	27	4			Reviewed	38	42
	16	54	20	4			Compiled	88	85
	18	28	10	3		1	Tax Returns	44	34
	9	38	26	5		3	Other	67	57
	__50 (4/1-9/30/04)__			__257 (10/1/04-3/31/05)__					
NUMBER OF STATEMENTS	45	140	90	25	1	6		246	229
	%	%	%	%	%	%	**ASSETS**	%	%
	6.2	7.0	5.3	2.8			Cash & Equivalents	5.9	6.1
	15.0	13.2	15.7	20.5			Trade Receivables (net)	12.2	13.3
	54.7	51.0	47.8	43.6			Inventory	52.0	48.9
	1.3	1.5	1.3	1.4			All Other Current	1.3	1.3
	77.2	72.8	70.1	68.3			Total Current	71.4	69.6
	10.0	16.1	17.9	25.0			Fixed Assets (net)	17.3	17.8
	4.0	2.0	2.5	.3			Intangibles (net)	1.9	3.1
	8.8	9.1	9.5	6.5			All Other Non-Current	9.4	9.5
	100.0	100.0	100.0	100.0			Total	100.0	100.0
							LIABILITIES		
	11.5	9.8	10.2	13.8			Notes Payable-Short Term	8.7	8.0
	3.7	3.8	3.5	2.0			Cur. Mat.-L/T/D	3.7	3.8
	11.8	15.4	15.4	14.9			Trade Payables	15.7	15.6
	.1	.2	.3	.3			Income Taxes Payable	.2	.2
	9.7	5.8	6.8	6.9			All Other Current	7.1	8.1
	36.7	35.0	36.2	37.9			Total Current	35.3	35.6
	24.9	22.9	17.2	14.6			Long-Term Debt	19.2	20.6
	.0	.1	.3	.8			Deferred Taxes	.1	.1
	5.1	5.5	4.0	3.3			All Other Non-Current	4.8	6.3
	33.3	36.5	42.3	43.4			Net Worth	40.6	37.4
	100.0	100.0	100.0	100.0			Total Liabilities & Net Worth	100.0	100.0
							INCOME DATA		
	100.0	100.0	100.0	100.0			Net Sales	100.0	100.0
	37.0	37.4	33.3	30.4			Gross Profit	35.0	35.3
	35.0	34.0	31.1	26.6			Operating Expenses	33.1	33.1
	2.0	3.4	2.1	3.8			Operating Profit	1.9	2.2
	.3	.6	-.4	.2			All Other Expenses (net)	.1	.4
	1.6	2.9	2.5	3.7			Profit Before Taxes	1.8	1.8
							RATIOS		
	6.0	3.4	3.1	2.7			Current	3.8	3.7
	2.8	2.3	2.2	1.8				2.1	2.2
	1.5	1.5	1.5	1.4				1.5	1.4
	1.3	1.1	1.1	1.1			Quick	1.0	1.0
	.7	.6	.5	.7				.5	.5
	.4	.3	.3	.3				.3	.2
	6 57.5	7 53.9	6 63.5	6 56.2			Sales/Receivables	8 43.2	7 49.8
	14 26.0	14 25.7	20 18.2	34 10.8				14 26.7	15 24.5
	29 12.6	25 14.7	35 10.4	51 7.2				25 14.6	27 13.4
	79 4.6	81 4.5	74 4.9	54 6.7			Cost of Sales/Inventory	88 4.2	81 4.5
	130 2.8	117 3.1	113 3.2	84 4.3				120 3.0	121 3.0
	219 1.7	159 2.3	156 2.3	137 2.7				178 2.0	163 2.2
	8 45.5	19 19.6	21 17.5	18 20.6			Cost of Sales/Payables	17 21.3	18 20.0
	19 18.8	27 13.4	30 12.2	29 12.5				29 12.8	29 12.7
	38 9.5	44 8.2	41 8.9	38 9.5				48 7.7	46 7.9
	3.5	4.4	4.6	5.1			Sales/Working Capital	4.2	4.4
	5.8	6.8	7.0	9.4				6.4	6.7
	14.9	10.4	11.7	16.7				11.8	12.9
	5.2	9.9	8.7	14.7			EBIT/Interest	5.0	4.8
	(38) 2.4	(131) 3.1	(85) 4.5	(24) 6.5				(225) 2.1	(213) 2.1
	.7	1.2	1.4	2.9				.7	1.1
		2.5	4.0				Net Profit + Depr., Dep., Amort./Cur. Mat. L /T/D	3.8	4.5
		(19) 1.0	(27) 1.2					(58) 1.7	(53) 2.0
		.4	.7					.7	1.1
	.1	.1	.2	.2			Fixed/Worth	.1	.2
	.3	.4	.4	.5				.4	.4
	2.1	1.1	1.1	1.4				1.1	1.1
	.6	.6	.7	.6			Debt/Worth	.7	.6
	2.1	1.8	1.5	1.6				1.6	1.7
	46.7	6.7	3.4	2.7				3.8	4.8
	36.4	30.5	26.9	32.5			% Profit Before Taxes/Tangible Net Worth	27.7	27.6
	(35) 7.3	(123) 13.8	(87) 11.7	(24) 19.4				(224) 9.9	(203) 10.4
	-1.2	5.9	4.0	9.5				.1	1.6
	10.4	13.4	9.9	10.7			% Profit Before Taxes/Total Assets	9.4	9.1
	4.7	4.7	4.5	8.5				3.6	3.2
	-.2	.8	1.0	4.4				-1.2	.2
	86.3	51.5	38.8	33.9			Sales/Net Fixed Assets	49.2	40.5
	40.4	24.2	16.8	13.0				21.0	20.4
	14.0	10.5	9.0	6.6				9.4	8.7
	3.5	3.3	2.8	3.2			Sales/Total Assets	3.1	3.0
	2.4	2.6	2.5	2.5				2.3	2.4
	1.9	1.9	2.0	1.9				1.8	1.8
	.6	.6	.7	.7			% Depr., Dep., Amort./Sales	.7	.7
	(29) 1.0	(112) 1.2	(81) 1.2	(22) 1.1				(222) 1.1	(200) 1.2
	1.9	2.2	1.8	1.7				2.0	2.2
	2.8	2.1	1.4				% Officers', Directors', Owners' Comp/Sales	2.9	2.0
	(28) 4.4	(87) 3.9	(42) 2.2					(132) 4.6	(136) 4.0
	7.9	7.3	3.6					7.0	6.1
	39148M	386636M	981920M	1263409M	96447M	2578604M	Net Sales ($)	2771100M	2517327M
	14825M	145681M	391770M	497744M	85059M	880739M	Total Assets ($)	990644M	1153657M

© RMA 2005

M = $ thousand   MM = $ million
See Pages 11 through 21 for Explanation of Ratios and Data

Comparative Historical Data | **Current Data Sorted By Sales**

			Type of Statement						
17	17	21	Unqualified	1	1		1	6	12
54	52	51	Reviewed	1	11	9	14	13	3
110	109	94	Compiled	12	38	24	8	6	6
52	78	60	Tax Returns	16	21	8	8	3	4
76	89	81	Other	11	21	17	15	9	8
4/1/02-3/31/03 ALL	4/1/03-3/31/04 ALL	4/1/04-3/31/05 ALL		| 50 (4/1-9/30/04) |			| 257 (10/1/04-3/31/05) |		
				0-1MM	1-3MM	3-5MM	5-10MM	10-25MM	25MM & OVER
309	345	307	**NUMBER OF STATEMENTS**	41	92	58	46	37	33
%	%	%	**ASSETS**	%	%	%	%	%	%
6.0	6.4	6.1	Cash & Equivalents	5.1	6.8	8.4	5.6	3.9	4.2
13.8	13.6	14.6	Trade Receivables (net)	10.3	12.1	15.8	15.6	20.6	17.1
50.5	50.1	50.0	Inventory	57.7	50.7	49.8	46.7	46.2	48.3
1.8	1.9	1.4	All Other Current	.6	2.0	1.6	.9	1.2	1.6
72.2	71.9	72.2	Total Current	73.6	71.5	75.6	68.8	71.8	71.2
17.0	16.7	16.6	Fixed Assets (net)	14.1	17.6	11.5	19.6	17.9	20.3
1.7	1.5	2.3	Intangibles (net)	3.9	2.7	2.1	2.9	.7	.8
9.2	9.8	8.9	All Other Non-Current	8.4	8.2	10.8	8.6	9.6	7.7
100.0	100.0	100.0	Total	100.0	100.0	100.0	100.0	100.0	100.0
			LIABILITIES						
11.3	9.4	10.4	Notes Payable-Short Term	16.3	8.7	8.2	11.0	9.9	11.9
3.5	2.9	3.5	Cur. Mat.-L/T/D	4.0	3.1	4.2	3.1	4.5	2.5
15.5	15.3	14.7	Trade Payables	8.5	13.9	17.2	17.2	16.0	15.1
.2	.2	.2	Income Taxes Payable	.1	.2	.3	.1	.3	.3
7.0	7.3	6.9	All Other Current	9.3	6.2	5.9	6.7	6.5	8.1
37.4	34.9	35.7	Total Current	38.2	32.0	35.9	38.2	37.2	37.8
19.0	20.6	21.3	Long-Term Debt	23.4	27.0	18.5	19.2	13.9	19.0
.1	.1	.2	Deferred Taxes	.0	.1	.2	.1	.5	.7
5.0	5.1	4.9	All Other Non-Current	7.4	5.3	5.0	4.6	1.9	4.0
38.5	39.2	37.9	Net Worth	31.1	35.6	40.5	37.9	46.5	38.5
100.0	100.0	100.0	Total Liabilities & Net Worth	100.0	100.0	100.0	100.0	100.0	100.0
			INCOME DATA						
100.0	100.0	100.0	Net Sales	100.0	100.0	100.0	100.0	100.0	100.0
35.7	36.1	35.6	Gross Profit	39.1	37.2	35.7	34.6	31.3	32.7
33.1	33.9	32.6	Operating Expenses	35.9	34.1	32.8	32.0	29.1	28.9
2.5	2.3	3.0	Operating Profit	3.2	3.1	2.9	2.6	2.2	3.8
.2	-.1	.2	All Other Expenses (net)	2.1	.0	-.1	.0	-.4	.0
2.3	2.3	2.7	Profit Before Taxes	1.1	3.1	3.0	2.6	2.7	3.8
			RATIOS						
3.7	3.7	3.5	Current	6.8	4.3	2.9	3.3	3.0	2.5
2.2	2.4	2.3		2.9	2.5	2.3	2.1	2.0	2.0
1.5	1.5	1.5		1.2	1.6	1.8	1.2	1.5	1.5
1.1	1.1	1.1	Quick	1.2	1.3	1.2	1.1	1.0	1.0
(308) .5	.6	.6		.6	.5	.7	.5	.6	.5
.2	.3	.3		.2	.2	.3	.3	.3	.2
7 49.8	6 56.5	6 58.1	Sales/Receivables	6 60.4	7 55.8	7 52.8	6 60.8	9 39.1	3 110.5
14 26.5	14 26.3	15 24.0		14 26.0	13 28.9	17 21.4	18 19.8	27 13.6	12 31.7
29 12.4	28 13.2	31 11.6		30 12.2	23 16.2	28 13.2	34 10.6	42 8.7	43 8.5
85 4.3	80 4.6	76 4.8	Cost of Sales/Inventory	130 2.8	86 4.2	71 5.2	67 5.4	54 6.8	58 6.3
120 3.0	120 3.0	116 3.1		220 1.7	125 2.9	103 3.5	110 3.3	100 3.6	87 4.2
171 2.1	174 2.1	161 2.3		320 1.1	170 2.1	135 2.7	127 2.9	148 2.5	145 2.5
17 21.3	18 20.6	18 20.7	Cost of Sales/Payables	7 49.3	16 22.8	18 20.1	21 17.3	21 17.8	18 20.6
30 12.3	28 13.2	28 13.0		24 14.9	27 13.6	29 12.8	30 12.0	30 12.2	29 12.5
50 7.4	44 8.3	42 8.8		40 9.1	43 8.4	42 8.6	43 8.5	37 9.8	35 10.5
4.2	4.0	4.4	Sales/Working Capital	2.3	3.8	5.3	5.6	5.5	5.3
7.0	6.2	6.8		4.7	5.9	7.0	8.0	7.5	9.1
12.3	12.1	12.6		12.7	9.2	9.7	27.5	10.8	16.0
8.1	7.8	9.1	EBIT/Interest	4.5	9.0	9.9	7.4	11.1	14.7
(269) 2.8	(314) 3.1	(285) 3.7		(35) 1.7	(85) 3.0	(55) 3.6	(44) 3.6	(34) 5.3	(32) 8.7
1.1	1.2	1.4		.2	1.3	1.8	1.2	3.5	3.5
5.5	5.2	5.1	Net Profit + Depr., Dep., Amort./Cur. Mat. L/T/D		4.3			4.1	22.8
(73) 2.4	(74) 1.9	(63) 2.0			(16) 1.3			(17) 2.3	(12) 7.0
.5	1.1	.7			.7			.9	2.4
.2	.1	.1	Fixed/Worth	.1	.1	.1	.2	.1	.2
.4	.4	.4		.6	.5	.2	.5	.3	.5
1.0	.9	1.1		NM	2.1	.7	1.6	.7	1.0
.7	.6	.7	Debt/Worth	.6	.7	.6	.9	.6	.8
1.5	1.5	1.7		2.8	2.0	1.4	1.8	1.1	1.4
3.7	4.1	4.6		NM	7.8	3.4	7.2	2.1	2.7
29.2	29.6	30.2	% Profit Before Taxes/Tangible Net Worth	35.8	35.1	26.6	41.4	24.6	34.0
(277) 11.9	(315) 12.3	(274) 13.6		(31) 1.5	(79) 11.8	(54) 13.7	(44) 18.1	(36) 13.8	(30) 19.4
2.2	3.0	4.2		-3.8	3.2	6.3	4.0	5.6	8.9
11.5	10.4	11.2	% Profit Before Taxes/Total Assets	10.4	11.5	14.1	11.7	10.0	12.7
4.7	4.5	5.2		1.3	4.7	4.9	4.9	6.3	8.7
.2	.6	1.0		-1.6	.9	2.5	.8	2.7	3.8
41.1	42.9	49.9	Sales/Net Fixed Assets	65.4	45.4	99.3	42.7	47.9	39.9
19.6	21.5	21.1		14.8	21.9	31.5	17.3	17.7	17.1
9.2	10.9	9.8		7.4	9.8	14.3	10.4	8.0	8.1
3.1	3.0	3.2	Sales/Total Assets	2.3	2.9	3.5	3.1	3.0	3.5
2.4	2.4	2.5		1.7	2.4	2.8	2.6	2.5	2.7
1.8	1.8	1.9		1.3	1.9	2.2	2.3	2.2	2.0
.7	.7	.7	% Depr., Dep., Amort./Sales	.8	.7	.5	.8	.7	.6
(266) 1.2	(291) 1.2	(249) 1.2		(27) 1.5	(74) 1.3	(47) 1.0	(38) 1.4	(35) .9	(28) .9
2.0	2.0	2.0		2.8	2.7	1.9	2.3	1.4	1.6
2.3	2.1	1.7	% Officers', Directors', Owners' Comp/Sales	3.3	2.5	1.5	1.3	1.6	
(168) 4.0	(201) 3.4	(164) 3.5		(22) 6.6	(56) 4.4	(41) 3.3	(20) 2.5	(16) 2.0	
7.0	5.7	6.2		8.7	7.5	5.0			
3762671M	4042329M	5346164M	Net Sales ($)	26742M	172253M	218871M	340641M	578201M	4009456M
1607310M	1667038M	2015818M	Total Assets ($)	16144M	81836M	85074M	139454M	237628M	1455682M

M = $ thousand   MM = $ million
See Pages 11 through 21 for Explanation of Ratios and Data

Current Data Sorted By Assets   Comparative Historical Data

						Type of Statement		
	2	8	12	3	3	Unqualified		
1	14	26	16		1	Reviewed		
15	20	20	2			Compiled		
19	22	21	2			Tax Returns		
5	25	36	10	2	2	Other		
	42 (4/1-9/30/04)		245 (10/1/04-3/31/05)				4/1/00-3/31/01 ALL	4/1/01-3/31/02 ALL
0-500M	500M-2MM	2-10MM	10-50MM	50-100MM	100-250MM			
40	83	111	42	6	5	**NUMBER OF STATEMENTS**		
%	%	%	%	%	%	**ASSETS**	%	%
12.6	7.9	6.7	6.1			Cash & Equivalents		
28.9	27.8	37.1	31.6			Trade Receivables (net)	D	D
35.1	38.4	30.0	34.4			Inventory	A	A
2.3	1.9	2.3	3.0			All Other Current	T	T
78.9	75.9	76.1	75.2			Total Current	A	A
15.6	16.1	17.8	15.3			Fixed Assets (net)		
2.0	1.5	1.1	.6			Intangibles (net)	N	N
3.6	6.5	5.0	8.9			All Other Non-Current	O	O
100.0	100.0	100.0	100.0			Total	T	T
						LIABILITIES	A	A
21.3	13.7	12.2	18.0			Notes Payable-Short Term	V	V
6.5	3.5	2.6	2.8			Cur. Mat.-L/T/D	A	A
20.9	20.9	20.3	16.0			Trade Payables	I	I
.8	.2	.4	.4			Income Taxes Payable	L	L
8.7	7.6	8.0	7.3			All Other Current	A	A
58.2	46.0	43.5	44.6			Total Current	B	B
18.6	13.5	10.7	10.6			Long-Term Debt	L	L
.1	.0	.2	.4			Deferred Taxes	E	E
16.0	3.0	4.8	1.1			All Other Non-Current		
7.1	37.5	40.8	43.4			Net Worth		
100.0	100.0	100.0	100.0			Total Liabilities & Net Worth		
						INCOME DATA		
100.0	100.0	100.0	100.0			Net Sales		
34.6	32.5	26.2	26.4			Gross Profit		
32.2	29.4	23.1	22.4			Operating Expenses		
2.4	3.0	3.1	4.0			Operating Profit		
.4	.3	.0	-.1			All Other Expenses (net)		
2.0	2.7	3.1	4.1			Profit Before Taxes		
						RATIOS		
2.1	2.8	2.5	2.8			Current		
1.4	1.7	1.7	1.6					
1.0	1.2	1.3	1.2					
1.6	1.2	1.7	1.3			Quick		
.6	.7	1.0	.9					
.3	.4	.7	.5					
10 35.2	18 20.1	33 11.0	30 12.0			Sales/Receivables		
24 14.9	29 12.7	45 8.1	43 8.6					
35 10.3	43 8.5	64 5.7	50 7.3					
12 29.7	36 10.1	32 11.4	41 8.9			Cost of Sales/Inventory		
39 9.5	66 5.6	51 7.2	53 6.9					
85 4.3	108 3.4	67 5.4	77 4.7					
12 30.7	17 21.6	18 19.9	14 25.9			Cost of Sales/Payables		
26 14.0	28 13.3	27 13.3	24 15.3					
60 6.0	54 6.7	49 7.4	37 9.8					
9.2	5.9	5.5	5.8			Sales/Working Capital		
16.8	11.3	9.1	10.9					
-354.9	28.9	18.6	21.0					
19.5	10.2	11.0	14.3			EBIT/Interest		
(36) 3.1	(70) 3.5	(102) 4.0	(39) 7.0					
-1.3	1.4	2.1	3.4					
		8.7	10.0			Net Profit + Depr., Dep., Amort./Cur. Mat. L /T/D		
		(22) 2.3	(15) 4.8					
		1.3	1.8					
.1	.1	.1	.2			Fixed/Worth		
.8	.4	.3	.3					
-4.6	1.4	1.1	.6					
1.6	.7	.7	.6			Debt/Worth		
5.1	1.8	1.6	1.5					
-8.5	4.8	4.0	3.0					
101.3	41.4	35.4	36.6			% Profit Before Taxes/Tangible Net Worth		
(26) 34.2	(72) 17.7	(108) 18.2	22.1					
13.2	6.3	6.2	14.7					
22.3	17.1	13.2	15.1			% Profit Before Taxes/Total Assets		
8.4	5.5	5.3	8.2					
-3.4	.7	2.4	4.1					
251.6	64.3	49.8	56.7			Sales/Net Fixed Assets		
28.0	30.6	25.5	21.2					
13.3	12.0	10.1	11.4					
6.1	3.9	3.5	3.3			Sales/Total Assets		
3.9	3.1	2.8	2.8					
2.8	2.3	2.1	2.2					
.3	.7	.5	.5			% Depr., Dep., Amort./Sales		
(27) 1.6	(62) 1.3	(104) .9	(39) 1.0					
3.2	2.3	1.6	1.5					
3.4	1.6	1.5	1.0			% Officers', Directors', Owners' Comp/Sales		
(19) 6.5	(43) 3.1	(56) 2.7	(13) 2.0					
7.8	5.5	5.3	3.6					
48320M	299213M	1397467M	2477879M	1045610M	2366626M	Net Sales ($)		
11215M	95353M	481005M	914777M	501941M	784342M	Total Assets ($)		

© RMA 2005

M = $ thousand   MM = $ million

See Pages 11 through 21 for Explanation of Ratios and Data

Comparative Historical Data | Current Data Sorted By Sales

4/1/02-3/31/03 ALL	4/1/03-3/31/04 ALL	4/1/04-3/31/05 ALL	Type of Statement	0-1MM	1-3MM	3-5MM	5-10MM	10-25MM	25MM & OVER
29	27	28	Unqualified			2	2	6	18
76	74	58	Reviewed	1	4	10	9	19	15
61	78	57	Compiled	7	16	11	13	7	3
26	59	64	Tax Returns	9	20	11	14	7	3
37	67	80	Other	4	13	14	20	14	15
				42 (4/1-9/30/04)			245 (10/1/04-3/31/05)		
229	305	287	**NUMBER OF STATEMENTS**	21	53	48	58	53	54
%	%	%	**ASSETS**	%	%	%	%	%	%
6.7	6.8	7.8	Cash & Equivalents	14.4	8.5	7.7	8.1	6.5	5.7
32.1	32.9	32.0	Trade Receivables (net)	24.5	23.3	31.0	34.2	41.1	33.3
31.8	32.1	33.5	Inventory	33.2	38.3	36.0	33.6	27.9	32.3
3.1	1.9	2.5	All Other Current	2.6	2.3	1.9	2.4	2.3	3.2
73.6	73.6	75.8	Total Current	74.8	72.3	76.6	78.3	77.8	74.5
17.3	18.4	16.9	Fixed Assets (net)	20.1	18.1	16.7	16.7	13.6	17.9
1.7	2.0	1.4	Intangibles (net)	2.5	2.2	.7	.4	2.0	1.5
7.3	6.0	5.9	All Other Non-Current	2.6	7.4	5.9	4.6	6.7	6.1
100.0	100.0	100.0	Total	100.0	100.0	100.0	100.0	100.0	100.0
			LIABILITIES						
16.7	15.9	14.8	Notes Payable-Short Term	20.0	18.7	11.8	11.6	13.2	16.5
3.7	3.6	3.4	Cur. Mat.-L/T/D	9.1	4.1	2.7	3.2	2.3	2.5
19.7	19.9	19.6	Trade Payables	22.1	16.2	22.9	20.6	22.0	15.4
.2	.2	.4	Income Taxes Payable	.1	.8	.0	.6	.2	.5
7.5	7.3	7.9	All Other Current	9.1	7.4	7.8	6.4	8.4	9.1
47.7	46.9	46.1	Total Current	60.3	47.2	45.3	42.4	46.0	44.0
13.4	12.5	13.0	Long-Term Debt	21.1	17.7	10.5	13.7	7.2	12.1
.3	.3	.2	Deferred Taxes	.1	.0	.1	.2	.2	.5
5.8	4.1	5.2	All Other Non-Current	20.1	6.7	4.3	3.9	3.8	1.3
32.8	36.3	35.6	Net Worth	-1.6	28.4	39.8	39.7	42.8	42.1
100.0	100.0	100.0	Total Liabilities & Net Worth	100.0	100.0	100.0	100.0	100.0	100.0
			INCOME DATA						
100.0	100.0	100.0	Net Sales	100.0	100.0	100.0	100.0	100.0	100.0
29.3	29.5	29.2	Gross Profit	38.3	33.9	33.1	25.1	24.8	26.5
27.5	27.9	26.0	Operating Expenses	37.4	30.9	29.7	22.5	20.9	21.9
1.8	1.7	3.3	Operating Profit	.9	2.9	3.4	2.6	3.9	4.6
.4	.2	.1	All Other Expenses (net)	1.2	.0	.3	.0	-.1	.1
1.4	1.5	3.2	Profit Before Taxes	-.3	2.9	3.2	2.6	4.1	4.5
			RATIOS						
2.3	2.4	2.6		1.8	2.8	2.7	2.9	2.5	2.5
1.6	1.6	1.7	Current	1.4	1.5	1.7	1.8	1.7	1.6
1.2	1.2	1.2		1.0	1.1	1.2	1.4	1.2	1.3
1.3	1.3	1.5		.9	1.1	1.9	1.7	1.7	1.2
(228) .8	.8	.9	Quick	.6	.6	.8	.9	1.1	.9
.5	.6	.5		.2	.4	.6	.7	.7	.7
28 13.1	29 12.8	25 14.5		10 35.5	12 30.7	26 14.2	29 12.6	34 10.6	31 11.6
39 9.3	40 9.2	37 9.9	Sales/Receivables	24 15.5	24 15.3	34 10.7	40 9.1	47 7.8	43 8.6
54 6.8	55 6.7	50 7.3		35 10.4	37 9.8	48 7.6	61 5.9	64 5.7	47 7.8
33 11.2	34 10.8	34 10.6		11 32.8	35 10.5	37 9.9	34 10.7	25 14.7	37 9.9
51 7.1	56 6.5	52 7.0	Cost of Sales/Inventory	56 6.5	69 6.5	57 6.6	55 6.6	45 8.1	47 7.7
88 4.1	83 4.4	82 4.5		178 2.1	124 2.9	105 3.5	69 5.3	61 6.0	71 5.2
19 19.6	18 20.6	15 23.6		24 15.1	12 30.1	18 19.9	18 20.5	15 24.3	14 25.6
33 11.0	30 12.3	26 13.8	Cost of Sales/Payables	35 10.3	26 14.1	34 10.6	27 13.3	27 13.7	24 15.5
46 8.0	49 7.5	47 7.8		84 4.4	53 6.8	54 6.7	48 7.7	50 7.1	31 11.7
6.1	6.1	6.0		7.2	6.8	5.6	5.1	6.4	6.4
11.2	11.3	11.1	Sales/Working Capital	13.8	14.2	11.2	7.8	9.1	12.6
28.5	29.2	25.4		-269.5	91.1	27.7	17.2	17.9	21.0
5.7	7.6	11.6		3.2	10.5	12.5	7.2	23.5	14.9
(212) 2.3	(277) 3.1	(256) 4.2	EBIT/Interest	(20) 1.4	(45) 2.4	(41) 3.7	(52) 3.7	(48) 6.0	(50) 6.9
.9	1.3	1.8		-6.7	.8	2.1	1.9	2.6	3.5
3.5	6.4	7.3	Net Profit + Depr., Dep.,				9.3	8.9	7.2
(65) 1.8	(82) 2.5	(56) 3.9	Amort./Cur. Mat. L/T/D				(13) 4.2	(12) 2.9	(20) 5.0
.6	1.1	1.1					1.6	1.2	2.5
.2	.2	.1		.3	.1	.1	.1	.1	.2
.4	.4	.4	Fixed/Worth	.8	.7	.4	.3	.3	.4
1.0	1.1	1.1		-1.9	2.3	.8	1.3	.9	.8
.9	.8	.8		1.4	1.0	.5	.6	.6	.9
1.9	2.0	1.8	Debt/Worth	6.0	2.3	1.6	1.8	1.3	1.5
4.9	4.8	4.4		-3.4	16.8	4.0	4.8	3.8	2.8
29.5	30.0	39.2	% Profit Before Taxes/Tangible	44.2	72.5	39.2	33.3	47.9	41.7
(207) 11.2	(282) 11.7	(259) 20.4	Net Worth	(13) 13.2	(43) 22.5	(43) 18.4	(55) 14.7	(51) 19.4	27.1
1.5	2.0	7.9		-34.0	2.3	6.1	3.5	11.3	16.3
8.4	8.6	15.4	% Profit Before Taxes/Total	9.1	20.4	17.0	10.2	14.4	18.3
2.8	3.7	6.5	Assets	1.2	5.2	6.9	4.6	7.3	9.8
-.2	.4	2.3		-16.1	-.3	1.7	2.1	3.5	4.8
49.1	55.9	58.6		64.0	97.1	56.8	71.5	49.9	55.1
25.2	22.7	25.5	Sales/Net Fixed Assets	16.0	26.8	30.2	25.4	27.8	22.1
11.1	11.0	11.4		10.0	11.3	12.1	9.6	13.2	11.2
3.8	3.7	3.9		5.3	4.1	3.9	3.6	4.0	4.0
2.8	2.9	3.0	Sales/Total Assets	2.8	3.3	3.1	2.8	3.0	3.0
2.0	2.0	2.2		1.9	1.8	2.2	2.2	2.2	2.5
.6	.6	.6		1.2	.6	.6	.5	.5	.5
(203) 1.1	(267) 1.1	(242) 1.0	% Depr., Dep., Amort./Sales	(17) 2.5	(35) 1.5	(41) 1.2	(51) 1.0	(48) .9	(50) .9
1.9	2.1	1.9		3.8	2.5	2.3	1.8	1.3	1.5
1.8	1.6	1.6	% Officers', Directors',	3.4	2.3	1.6	1.6	1.5	1.0
(122) 3.7	(170) 3.2	(132) 3.0	Owners' Comp/Sales	(12) 6.9	(30) 3.8	(23) 3.1	(29) 2.6	(22) 1.8	(16) 2.1
7.3	5.9	6.4		12.9	7.3	5.6	5.8	3.3	4.1
4412425M	6489973M	7635115M	Net Sales ($)	12779M	106261M	196546M	429168M	861052M	6029309M
1992379M	2450443M	2788633M	Total Assets ($)	5133M	40844M	74388M	168790M	323385M	2176093M

© RMA 2005   M = $ thousand   MM = $ million
See Pages 11 through 21 for Explanation of Ratios and Data

Current Data Sorted By Assets   Comparative Historical Data

0-500M	500M-2MM	2-10MM	10-50MM	50-100MM	100-250MM	Type of Statement	4/1/00-3/31/01 ALL	4/1/01-3/31/02 ALL
			1			Unqualified		
2	1	2	1			Reviewed		
4	8	4	1			Compiled		
5	6	2				Tax Returns		
1	5	5	1			Other		
	8 (4/1-9/30/04)		40 (10/1/04-3/31/05)					
12	20	13	3			NUMBER OF STATEMENTS		
%	%	%	%	%	%	ASSETS	%	%
9.4	8.9	10.3				Cash & Equivalents		
11.0	12.7	11.7				Trade Receivables (net)		
52.2	47.9	51.5				Inventory		
.0	1.0	2.6				All Other Current		
72.6	70.5	76.1				Total Current		
20.1	23.7	17.2				Fixed Assets (net)		
.2	1.7	.1				Intangibles (net)		
7.1	4.1	6.7				All Other Non-Current		
100.0	100.0	100.0				Total		
						LIABILITIES		
38.7	22.5	18.1				Notes Payable-Short Term		
2.4	3.5	1.7				Cur. Mat.-L/T/D		
14.7	12.3	13.9				Trade Payables		
.1	.1	.2				Income Taxes Payable		
4.9	12.9	17.5				All Other Current		
60.9	51.3	51.3				Total Current		
14.0	21.8	13.4				Long-Term Debt		
.0	.3	1.1				Deferred Taxes		
8.7	6.5	1.8				All Other Non-Current		
16.3	20.1	32.4				Net Worth		
100.0	100.0	100.0				Total Liabilities & Net Worth		
						INCOME DATA		
100.0	100.0	100.0				Net Sales		
34.8	27.6	22.7				Gross Profit		
33.4	25.9	21.7				Operating Expenses		
1.4	1.7	1.0				Operating Profit		
1.2	1.1	−.9				All Other Expenses (net)		
.2	.5	1.9				Profit Before Taxes		
						RATIOS		
2.1	2.5	2.5						
1.2	1.4	1.4				Current		
.7	1.2	1.1						
.5	1.3	1.0						
.3	.3	.4				Quick		
.1	.1	.1						
3 115.1	3 135.7	6 61.9						
7 49.2	14 26.9	12 31.1				Sales/Receivables		
16 22.2	22 16.6	24 15.1						
38 9.7	42 8.6	55 6.6						
76 4.8	79 4.6	103 3.5				Cost of Sales/Inventory		
120 3.0	170 2.1	134 2.7						
3 123.7	8 47.3	8 48.0						
16 23.0	17 21.6	21 17.0				Cost of Sales/Payables		
33 11.1	29 12.7	42 8.6						
6.6	8.3	7.0						
48.9	13.2	17.5				Sales/Working Capital		
−21.2	17.7	44.2						
5.4	3.9	13.3						
(10) 2.5	(19) 2.5	3.7				EBIT/Interest		
.0	1.0	1.4						
						Net Profit + Depr., Dep., Amort./Cur. Mat. L /T/D		
.1	.2	.2						
.7	.7	.5				Fixed/Worth		
NM	3.3	1.4						
1.2	1.4	1.1						
2.9	3.5	2.7				Debt/Worth		
NM	10.3	5.4						
	40.9	35.7						
	(17) 13.9	19.4				% Profit Before Taxes/Tangible Net Worth		
	1.5	2.5						
13.3	6.2	6.0						
6.8	2.0	5.0				% Profit Before Taxes/Total Assets		
−4.0	.1	.8						
114.2	85.1	38.1						
19.9	19.0	15.6				Sales/Net Fixed Assets		
15.2	6.2	8.9						
6.9	4.2	3.4						
4.4	2.6	2.6				Sales/Total Assets		
2.3	2.1	2.3						
.7	.8	.5						
(10) 1.5	(16) 1.2	1.0				% Depr., Dep., Amort./Sales		
2.9	3.0	2.3						
	1.3							
	(17) 2.7					% Officers', Directors', Owners' Comp/Sales		
	6.0							
11653M	54357M	167288M	145745M			Net Sales ($)		
2671M	19275M	61352M	49655M			Total Assets ($)		

(Columns 50-100MM, 100-250MM, and both Comparative Historical Data columns 4/1/00-3/31/01 ALL and 4/1/01-3/31/02 ALL are marked: DATA NOT AVAILABLE)

M = $ thousand   MM = $ million
See Pages 11 through 21 for Explanation of Ratios and Data

Comparative Historical Data | Current Data Sorted By Sales

Type of Statement				8 (4/1-9/30/04)		40 (10/1/04-3/31/05)			
Unqualified	1	5	1	1	2			1	2
Reviewed	2	6	6	3	6			1	
Compiled	12	17	16	4	4	2	4	1	1
Tax Returns	8	11	14	4	2	2	2		1
Other	2	6	11	2	2			3	
	4/1/02-3/31/03 ALL	4/1/03-3/31/04 ALL	4/1/04-3/31/05 ALL	0-1MM	1-3MM	3-5MM	5-10MM	10-25MM	25MM & OVER
NUMBER OF STATEMENTS	25	45	48	10	14	8	6	6	4
	%	%	%	%	%	%	%	%	%
ASSETS									
Cash & Equivalents	6.5	7.9	9.6	8.6	9.5				
Trade Receivables (net)	12.8	11.1	12.3	8.3	11.7				
Inventory	50.7	50.6	51.0	51.1	46.0				
All Other Current	.6	1.2	1.2	.1	.2				
Total Current	70.6	70.8	74.1	68.1	67.4				
Fixed Assets (net)	24.9	22.9	19.8	21.4	27.8				
Intangibles (net)	.1	1.3	.8	2.0	.4				
All Other Non-Current	4.3	4.9	5.4	8.4	4.4				
Total	100.0	100.0	100.0	100.0	100.0				
LIABILITIES									
Notes Payable-Short Term	17.2	21.5	25.6	30.7	27.4				
Cur. Mat.-L/T/D	2.7	2.2	2.5	2.9	2.4				
Trade Payables	16.2	15.0	14.3	14.2	10.3				
Income Taxes Payable	.0	.1	.1	.0	.2				
All Other Current	12.3	7.7	12.1	3.8	17.8				
Total Current	48.4	46.5	54.7	51.6	58.2				
Long-Term Debt	22.3	20.0	16.3	27.4	19.1				
Deferred Taxes	.0	.4	.4	.0	.1				
All Other Non-Current	.1	5.6	6.2	7.3	6.9				
Net Worth	29.2	27.5	22.4	13.7	15.7				
Total Liabilities & Net Worth	100.0	100.0	100.0	100.0	100.0				
INCOME DATA									
Net Sales	100.0	100.0	100.0	100.0	100.0				
Gross Profit	33.2	28.9	27.4	34.4	27.5				
Operating Expenses	31.1	26.7	25.9	32.4	26.5				
Operating Profit	2.0	2.2	1.5	1.9	1.1				
All Other Expenses (net)	1.7	.8	.6	1.7	.8				
Profit Before Taxes	.4	1.4	1.0	.2	.2				
RATIOS									
Current	2.9 / 1.6 / 1.1	2.2 / 1.5 / 1.2	2.2 / 1.4 / 1.1	2.9 / 1.4 / .8	2.1 / 1.4 / .7				
Quick	1.1 / .3 / .1	1.1 / (44) .3 / .2	1.0 / .4 / .1	.6 / .3 / .2	1.3 / .3 / .1				
Sales/Receivables	2 227.8 / 13 28.8 / 25 14.8	4 82.3 / 12 31.3 / 25 14.4	4 90.5 / 13 28.2 / 22 16.5	3 130.7 / 7 49.7 / 18 20.8	2 149.1 / 14 26.5 / 18 20.7				
Cost of Sales/Inventory	52 7.0 / 102 3.6 / 177 2.1	67 5.4 / 113 3.2 / 148 2.5	47 7.8 / 81 4.5 / 137 2.7	62 5.8 / 107 3.4 / 151 2.4	33 11.0 / 70 5.2 / 92 4.0				
Cost of Sales/Payables	3 141.7 / 22 16.8 / 63 5.8	9 39.0 / 22 16.9 / 48 7.6	7 49.1 / 20 18.1 / 32 11.3	4 93.6 / 21 17.8 / 33 11.0	7 55.6 / 11 32.0 / 26 14.0				
Sales/Working Capital	6.7 / 12.2 / 54.1	5.5 / 11.0 / 27.9	8.1 / 15.2 / 51.3	4.3 / 20.0 / -32.2	10.9 / 15.8 / -20.0				
EBIT/Interest	3.5 / (24) 1.4 / .5	5.9 / (44) 2.3 / 1.1	5.2 / (45) 3.0 / 1.1		3.4 / (12) 1.5 / -1.9				
Net Profit + Depr., Dep., Amort./Cur. Mat. L/T/D									
Fixed/Worth	.2 / .5 / 2.7	.2 / .5 / 2.7	.1 / .6 / 2.1	.2 / .6 / -1.0	.3 / .9 / 6.7				
Debt/Worth	.9 / 2.4 / 10.2	1.0 / 2.7 / 12.6	1.4 / 3.0 / 10.3	1.3 / 2.9 / -4.6	1.3 / 3.5 / 14.6				
% Profit Before Taxes/Tangible Net Worth	17.7 / (22) 5.6 / -5.3	33.8 / (38) 10.9 / 2.3	40.6 / (42) 15.2 / 2.6		35.0 / (13) 5.2 / -21.8				
% Profit Before Taxes/Total Assets	7.3 / .8 / -1.9	7.1 / 3.2 / .4	7.8 / 4.4 / .4	11.5 / 6.3 / -6.9	6.1 / 1.3 / -3.5				
Sales/Net Fixed Assets	49.4 / 18.6 / 6.3	51.1 / 16.8 / 5.4	84.8 / 21.1 / 10.1	71.9 / 19.9 / 6.2	66.6 / 16.7 / 5.7				
Sales/Total Assets	3.4 / 2.5 / 1.8	2.9 / 2.5 / 1.8	4.2 / 2.9 / 2.3	5.2 / 2.6 / 1.8	4.5 / 4.0 / 2.2				
% Depr., Dep., Amort./Sales	.8 / (21) 1.3 / 2.8	.7 / (36) 1.3 / 2.9	.7 / (41) 1.1 / 2.7		.8 / (13) 1.3 / 5.7				
% Officers', Directors', Owners' Comp/Sales	1.8 / (12) 4.0 / 7.9	1.6 / (23) 3.5 / 6.6	1.1 / (31) 2.4 / 6.0						
Net Sales ($)	109976M	309638M	379043M	6424M	28942M	29539M	44381M	93445M	176312M
Total Assets ($)	44047M	136258M	132953M	2912M	9240M	12091M	20156M	31492M	57062M

M = $ thousand   MM = $ million
See Pages 11 through 21 for Explanation of Ratios and Data

Current Data Sorted By Assets   Comparative Historical Data

Type of Statement								
1	1	3	8		2	Unqualified	5	9
1	15	28	4			Reviewed	45	38
27	35	17				Compiled	81	61
30	17	4			1	Tax Returns	42	31
9	18	11	11			Other	51	59
	44 (4/1-9/30/04)			199 (10/1/04-3/31/05)			4/1/00-3/31/01	4/1/01-3/31/02
0-500M	500M-2MM	2-10MM	10-50MM	50-100MM	100-250MM		ALL	ALL
68	86	63	23		3	**NUMBER OF STATEMENTS**	224	198
%	%	%	%	%	%	**ASSETS**	%	%
8.7	5.9	6.0	4.0			Cash & Equivalents	9.0	8.1
10.5	14.8	14.5	19.6			Trade Receivables (net)	12.3	13.1
35.6	38.8	35.5	41.8			Inventory	38.5	36.2
.6	1.6	2.3	2.1			All Other Current	2.0	2.2
55.5	61.1	58.3	67.5			Total Current	61.7	59.7
36.9	30.2	33.6	25.3			Fixed Assets (net)	29.8	32.6
2.0	2.8	1.0	2.5			Intangibles (net)	2.5	2.1
5.7	5.9	7.0	4.7			All Other Non-Current	6.0	5.6
100.0	100.0	100.0	100.0			Total	100.0	100.0
						LIABILITIES		
23.6	12.8	13.5	8.0			Notes Payable-Short Term	13.0	14.1
8.5	4.4	3.7	3.6			Cur. Mat.-L/T/D	4.2	4.6
13.4	17.1	14.0	15.3			Trade Payables	16.6	13.8
.1	.1	.9	1.7			Income Taxes Payable	.2	.5
10.4	9.4	10.1	14.4			All Other Current	9.5	9.2
56.1	43.7	42.2	43.1			Total Current	43.6	42.2
33.6	20.1	13.6	15.5			Long-Term Debt	20.3	23.0
.0	.3	.7	2.1			Deferred Taxes	.5	.7
9.6	3.9	5.5	1.5			All Other Non-Current	4.6	5.3
.7	32.0	38.0	37.8			Net Worth	31.1	28.7
100.0	100.0	100.0	100.0			Total Liabilities & Net Worth	100.0	100.0
						INCOME DATA		
100.0	100.0	100.0	100.0			Net Sales	100.0	100.0
43.4	33.8	34.6	32.1			Gross Profit	39.1	41.7
41.3	32.2	32.5	27.0			Operating Expenses	35.4	38.0
2.1	1.6	2.1	5.1			Operating Profit	3.7	3.8
1.4	.2	.2	.5			All Other Expenses (net)	.7	1.3
.7	1.4	1.9	4.6			Profit Before Taxes	3.0	2.4
						RATIOS		
2.8	2.5	1.9	1.9				2.3	2.8
1.3	1.5	1.4	1.6			Current	1.6	1.5
.6	1.0	1.0	1.3				1.0	1.0
1.0	1.0	.9	.9				1.0	1.2
(67) .2	.3	.5	.6			Quick	(222) .4 (197) .4	
.1	.2	.1	.3				.2	.2
0 UND	4 93.7	6 62.3	16 22.8				3 131.3	4 102.9
6 61.7	12 31.7	12 29.2	40 9.1			Sales/Receivables	10 35.1	11 34.6
15 24.1	31 11.8	35 10.4	56 6.5				25 14.5	31 11.8
16 22.9	34 10.7	32 11.4	62 5.9				38 9.6	36 10.2
51 7.1	79 4.6	79 4.6	126 2.9			Cost of Sales/Inventory	79 4.6	76 4.8
122 3.0	123 3.0	158 2.3	279 1.3				133 2.8	136 2.7
0 UND	7 50.9	16 22.3	25 14.7				11 32.9	10 36.5
15 25.0	25 14.4	31 11.9	50 7.3			Cost of Sales/Payables	26 14.1	24 15.0
39 9.3	55 6.7	52 7.0	63 5.8				51 7.1	47 7.8
7.6	7.2	6.2	3.8				7.4	6.8
20.7	18.7	11.3	8.3			Sales/Working Capital	14.1	13.8
-22.7	-113.1	173.3	18.9				NM	NM
7.4	5.8	9.2	9.1				6.0	5.8
(63) 1.4	(82) 2.7	(62) 3.7	(22) 4.7			EBIT/Interest	(211) 2.5	(191) 2.1
-1.0	.5	1.2	1.5				1.3	1.1
	2.8	5.4	5.0				4.1	4.6
	(18) 1.7	(20) 2.4	(10) 1.8			Net Profit + Depr., Dep., Amort./Cur. Mat. L /T/D	(51) 2.2	(44) 2.1
	1.0	1.0	1.5				.9	.9
.6	.3	.4	.4				.3	.4
5.8	.9	.7	.7			Fixed/Worth	.8	1.0
-2.1	3.3	1.5	1.3				2.7	3.3
1.4	.8	.8	1.2				.7	.9
10.6	2.0	1.6	1.8			Debt/Worth	2.0	2.1
-5.3	8.0	3.9	3.9				9.7	10.3
82.8	23.6	24.6	42.2				36.6	32.6
(40) 15.3	(71) 12.5	(59) 13.4	20.6			% Profit Before Taxes/Tangible Net Worth	(189) 16.7	(165) 16.9
-2.2	1.8	2.8	3.0				5.1	2.6
16.6	7.9	10.9	11.7				12.8	11.0
1.3	3.5	3.9	7.1			% Profit Before Taxes/Total Assets	5.0	4.2
-11.4	-.4	.1	1.0				1.1	.4
34.3	21.4	17.7	13.1				31.9	22.1
13.5	11.1	8.4	7.3			Sales/Net Fixed Assets	12.0	10.2
5.0	5.4	3.7	4.4				5.7	4.8
4.7	4.0	3.2	2.7				3.8	3.7
3.4	2.6	2.1	1.9			Sales/Total Assets	2.7	2.5
1.9	2.0	1.4	1.1				1.9	1.7
1.1	.9	.9	1.1				.9	1.1
(53) 2.4	(80) 1.9	(60) 1.7	1.6			% Depr., Dep., Amort./Sales	(201) 1.8	(178) 1.9
4.6	3.5	3.2	3.5				3.0	3.5
3.2	1.9	1.9					2.9	2.4
(32) 4.9	(51) 3.1	(25) 3.7				% Officers', Directors', Owners' Comp/Sales	(131) 4.3	(109) 3.9
6.5	4.5	6.9					6.6	6.6
70840M	285350M	640611M	871333M		2678991M	Net Sales ($)	1244198M	3090997M
19446M	100442M	284248M	475969M		343593M	Total Assets ($)	558422M	988547M

(50-100MM column: DATA NOT AVAILABLE)

M = $ thousand   MM = $ million
See Pages 11 through 21 for Explanation of Ratios and Data

Comparative Historical Data			Type of Statement	Current Data Sorted By Sales					
23	20	15	Unqualified	1	1	1	1	4	8
42	51	48	Reviewed	1 / 7	7 / 9	9 / 14	14 / 14	14 / 3	3
86	86	79	Compiled	20	28	11	16	4	
54	54	52	Tax Returns	17	21	8	4	1	1
52	56	49	Other	7	14	8	6	6	8
4/1/02-3/31/03 ALL	4/1/03-3/31/04 ALL	4/1/04-3/31/05 ALL		44 (4/1-9/30/04)			199 (10/1/04-3/31/05)		
				0-1MM	1-3MM	3-5MM	5-10MM	10-25MM	25MM & OVER
257	267	243	NUMBER OF STATEMENTS	45	71	37	41	29	20
%	%	%	**ASSETS**	%	%	%	%	%	%
8.7	8.9	6.6	Cash & Equivalents	8.0	6.7	5.9	6.7	5.3	6.2
13.9	13.5	14.1	Trade Receivables (net)	6.2	13.4	16.9	16.1	16.0	21.8
33.8	37.9	37.1	Inventory	39.1	36.9	33.6	37.4	41.4	32.8
2.8	2.1	1.6	All Other Current	.5	1.6	1.0	1.2	3.3	3.3
59.2	62.4	59.4	Total Current	53.7	58.6	57.5	61.5	66.1	64.0
33.4	30.2	32.5	Fixed Assets (net)	41.1	30.9	33.8	31.0	27.6	26.9
2.1	1.3	2.1	Intangibles (net)	.7	3.4	2.6	.7	1.6	3.1
5.3	6.1	6.0	All Other Non-Current	4.4	7.1	6.1	6.8	4.7	6.0
100.0	100.0	100.0	Total	100.0	100.0	100.0	100.0	100.0	100.0
			LIABILITIES						
14.0	14.2	15.5	Notes Payable-Short Term	23.3	17.1	11.7	12.9	15.1	5.8
5.3	4.9	5.2	Cur. Mat.-L/T/D	3.3	8.6	4.6	4.2	2.9	4.0
14.1	14.9	15.0	Trade Payables	11.0	14.3	15.3	17.6	17.0	17.1
.4	.5	.5	Income Taxes Payable	.2	.0	.2	1.0	1.3	.7
7.2	9.4	10.5	All Other Current	7.4	10.0	11.1	11.5	9.1	17.5
41.0	44.0	46.7	Total Current	45.3	50.1	43.0	47.2	45.5	45.1
21.5	21.6	22.0	Long-Term Debt	38.7	23.5	22.0	9.9	13.3	15.9
.4	.5	.5	Deferred Taxes	.0	.2	1.2	1.0	.6	.6
6.8	3.6	5.7	All Other Non-Current	8.6	6.8	6.9	1.8	4.8	1.7
30.3	30.3	25.2	Net Worth	7.5	19.4	26.9	40.0	35.8	36.8
100.0	100.0	100.0	Total Liabilities & Net Worth	100.0	100.0	100.0	100.0	100.0	100.0
			INCOME DATA						
100.0	100.0	100.0	Net Sales	100.0	100.0	100.0	100.0	100.0	100.0
39.3	37.6	36.5	Gross Profit	43.3	37.2	40.5	30.8	28.7	33.8
36.7	35.1	34.2	Operating Expenses	42.3	34.9	37.0	29.5	27.0	28.7
2.6	2.5	2.2	Operating Profit	1.0	2.3	3.5	1.3	1.7	5.0
.8	.8	.6	All Other Expenses (net)	2.0	.4	.5	.0	-.3	.4
1.9	1.8	1.7	Profit Before Taxes	-1.0	2.0	3.0	1.2	2.0	4.6
			RATIOS						
2.8	2.7	2.1	Current	3.1	2.5	2.4	2.1	1.8	1.7
1.6	1.6	1.4		1.3	1.4	1.4	1.5	1.5	1.5
1.1	1.1	1.0		.6	.9	.9	1.0	1.1	1.3
1.4	1.2	1.0	Quick	.9	1.0	1.1	.8	.7	1.2
(254) .6	.5	(242) .4		(44) .2	.4	.5	.5	.3	.6
.2	.2	.1		.0	.1	.2	.2	.1	.3
3 / 138.8	3 / 130.0	3 / 113.4	Sales/Receivables	0 / UND	4 / 100.1	3 / 112.5	7 / 52.9	4 / 92.5	4 / 89.8
9 / 39.5	12 / 30.8	11 / 34.7		6 / 58.0	10 / 35.0	16 / 23.1	13 / 28.0	10 / 35.2	39 / 9.3
29 / 12.7	26 / 13.8	32 / 11.4		15 / 24.1	23 / 16.0	32 / 11.4	34 / 10.6	34 / 10.9	58 / 6.3
28 / 13.1	36 / 10.3	29 / 12.5	Cost of Sales/Inventory	27 / 13.5	37 / 9.9	28 / 13.1	27 / 13.7	35 / 10.4	36 / 10.1
68 / 5.4	71 / 5.1	78 / 4.7		91 / 4.0	79 / 4.6	67 / 5.5	55 / 6.7	87 / 4.2	80 / 4.6
125 / 2.9	121 / 3.0	140 / 2.6		251 / 1.5	133 / 2.7	108 / 3.4	135 / 2.7	155 / 2.4	122 / 3.0
9 / 40.4	10 / 34.8	7 / 50.2	Cost of Sales/Payables	0 / UND	7 / 54.3	14 / 26.3	10 / 37.1	9 / 40.7	19 / 19.3
23 / 15.9	22 / 16.9	25 / 14.7		17 / 22.0	18 / 19.9	28 / 13.0	23 / 15.8	34 / 10.6	34 / 10.6
42 / 8.6	48 / 7.7	53 / 6.9		72 / 5.1	38 / 9.6	59 / 6.2	48 / 7.6	52 / 7.0	52 / 7.0
7.0	6.4	6.9	Sales/Working Capital	4.8	7.0	7.6		5.3	6.2
13.9	12.7	16.2		13.8	18.0	28.4	17.6	11.3	12.3
96.2	58.9	-121.3		-9.5	-88.7	-68.3	542.2	41.0	117.1
6.7	5.7	7.4	EBIT/Interest	3.3	6.6	6.6	7.3	10.2	13.8
(241) 2.6	(246) 2.3	(232) 2.7		(41) 1.3	(70) 2.2	(33) 2.6	(40) 3.7	4.5	(19) 8.1
.8	.9	.6		-1.2	-.1	.3	1.6	.8	3.5
5.0	4.5	4.5	Net Profit + Depr., Dep., Amort./Cur. Mat. L/T/D		6.0	1.6	4.2		
(54) 2.2	(56) 2.1	(51) 2.0			(11) 2.0	(11) 1.1	(12) 2.4		
1.0	1.0	1.1			.6	.4	1.8		
.4	.3	.4	Fixed/Worth	.4	.4	.4	.2	.4	.4
.9	.8	1.0		4.6	1.2	1.1	.7	.6	.6
4.3	2.3	4.6		-2.1	36.0	7.0	1.2	1.8	.9
.8	.8	1.0	Debt/Worth	1.4	.8	1.7	.7	.9	1.1
1.8	1.9	2.3		8.8	3.0	2.8	1.4	1.8	1.8
8.7	6.8	12.5		-4.7	76.7	NM	2.4	4.0	3.1
35.5	37.3	33.6	% Profit Before Taxes/Tangible Net Worth	38.2	29.2	37.0	17.6	35.5	42.2
(217) 12.6	(230) 14.0	(195) 14.4		(26) 11.8	(55) 10.9	(28) 21.8	(40) 8.9	(27) 13.7	(19) 21.4
2.2	2.7	2.6		-8.4	-2.6	5.2	2.7	4.3	8.6
10.8	11.3	9.8	% Profit Before Taxes/Total Assets	10.5	8.4	14.9	8.0	9.7	17.2
4.3	4.0	3.5		1.3	3.4	4.3	2.8	5.0	8.7
-.7	.0	-.7		-10.5	-2.2	-1.3	1.0	-.8	2.3
22.3	26.0	21.8	Sales/Net Fixed Assets	18.9	23.8	21.3	28.9	15.0	20.8
10.6	12.2	10.9		6.1	11.8	11.1	11.9	11.5	12.3
4.7	5.1	4.6		3.0	5.2	4.7	4.4	6.0	6.4
4.4	3.7	3.8	Sales/Total Assets	3.4	3.9	4.2	4.2	3.7	3.3
2.7	2.6	2.5		1.9	2.6	3.0	2.8	2.6	2.1
1.7	1.9	1.6		1.3	1.6	1.7	1.8	1.6	1.7
1.2	1.0	1.0	% Depr., Dep., Amort./Sales	1.2	1.1	.8	.8	1.0	1.0
(233) 2.0	(238) 1.9	(218) 2.0		(36) 3.6	(62) 2.4	(33) 1.9	(39) 1.7	1.5	(19) 1.2
3.3	3.5	3.5		6.3	4.1	4.0	2.9	2.9	2.1
2.5	1.9	2.0	% Officers', Directors', Owners' Comp/Sales	2.9	3.0	2.0	1.6		
(133) 4.3	(118) 3.9	(116) 3.5		(19) 4.9	(38) 3.9	(23) 2.9	(22) 2.4		
6.4	6.0	5.9		6.8	6.3	5.1	5.9		
5991720M	3424385M	4547125M	Net Sales ($)	25304M	136025M	148292M	284631M	460626M	3492247M
1298190M	1226801M	1223698M	Total Assets ($)	14420M	63636M	80589M	140732M	212090M	712231M

M = $ thousand   MM = $ million
See Pages 11 through 21 for Explanation of Ratios and Data

Current Data Sorted By Assets   —   Comparative Historical Data

Type of Statement	0-500M	500M-2MM	2-10MM	10-50MM	50-100MM	100-250MM	4/1/00-3/31/01	4/1/01-3/31/02
Unqualified	2	3	10	33	13	18	101	91
Reviewed	35	11	43	19	4	1	130	122
Compiled	87	83	75	12	4		256	251
Tax Returns	24	108	37	1	1	1	141	138
Other		62	74	31	7	12	253	274
	160 (4/1-9/30/04)			651 (10/1/04-3/31/05)			ALL	ALL
NUMBER OF STATEMENTS	148	267	239	96	29	32	881	876

	0-500M %	500M-2MM %	2-10MM %	10-50MM %	50-100MM %	100-250MM %	ALL %	ALL %
ASSETS								
Cash & Equivalents	12.6	14.3	14.9	10.8	11.8	8.9	11.9	11.7
Trade Receivables (net)	3.9	4.8	4.8	5.2	4.2	6.4	4.8	4.8
Inventory	42.1	30.4	25.5	21.6	21.1	22.0	26.6	25.5
All Other Current	2.5	2.7	2.4	1.8	2.7	2.7	2.5	2.4
Total Current	61.1	52.2	47.6	39.4	39.7	40.0	45.9	44.3
Fixed Assets (net)	26.5	35.0	37.2	48.8	49.3	45.3	41.1	42.1
Intangibles (net)	6.4	3.9	3.7	4.0	2.4	5.5	4.8	5.1
All Other Non-Current	6.0	8.8	11.4	7.9	8.7	9.3	8.2	8.5
Total	100.0	100.0	100.0	100.0	100.0	100.0	100.0	100.0
LIABILITIES								
Notes Payable-Short Term	5.4	4.7	2.9	4.4	3.9	1.1	5.1	4.1
Cur. Mat.-L/T/D	3.5	3.5	4.5	4.2	4.4	4.0	4.2	4.5
Trade Payables	20.3	17.2	16.4	18.3	17.2	15.9	18.2	17.3
Income Taxes Payable	.3	.1	.1	.2	.2	.3	.2	.1
All Other Current	15.9	13.2	8.3	7.7	10.5	12.9	10.6	9.8
Total Current	45.5	38.7	32.2	34.8	36.3	34.3	38.3	35.8
Long-Term Debt	28.1	28.8	28.4	24.7	29.6	21.5	31.5	32.2
Deferred Taxes	.1	.1	.2	1.2	.6	.9	.3	.3
All Other Non-Current	15.3	5.5	3.1	3.9	3.3	6.3	4.7	6.3
Net Worth	11.1	26.9	36.0	35.5	30.3	36.9	25.1	25.4
Total Liabilities & Net Worth	100.0	100.0	100.0	100.0	100.0	100.0	100.0	100.0
INCOME DATA								
Net Sales	100.0	100.0	100.0	100.0	100.0	100.0	100.0	100.0
Gross Profit	24.3	24.0	24.9	24.8	25.7	23.8	23.4	23.5
Operating Expenses	23.3	23.2	23.7	23.1	23.0	22.0	22.9	22.1
Operating Profit	.9	.8	1.2	1.7	2.7	1.8	.4	1.3
All Other Expenses (net)	-.3	-.6	-.5	.2	.3	.5	-.9	-.1
Profit Before Taxes	1.3	1.4	1.7	1.5	2.4	1.3	1.3	1.4

RATIOS

Ratio	0-500M	500M-2MM	2-10MM	10-50MM	50-100MM	100-250MM	ALL 4/1/00-3/31/01	ALL 4/1/01-3/31/02
Current	5.1	2.6	2.4	1.6	1.4	1.4	2.0	2.0
	1.5	1.5	1.5	1.1	1.0	1.2	1.3	1.3
	1.0	1.0	1.1	.8	.8	1.0	.9	.9
Quick	1.1	1.0	1.0	.7	.6	.5	.9	.9
	(145) .4	(266) .5	.6	.4	.3	.3	(874) .4	(866) .4
	.1	.2	.2	.2	.2	.3	.2	.2
Sales/Receivables	0 UND	0 999.8	0 808.1	1 284.5	1 292.7	2 152.8	0 781.9	0 999.8
	0 999.8	1 413.1	1 254.5	3 145.1	3 108.7	4 81.5	2 211.7	2 205.1
	2 230.7	3 142.9	3 124.4	3 87.0	5 67.1	7 55.7	4 90.2	4 81.6
Cost of Sales/Inventory	14 26.6	15 23.7	18 20.8	15 23.8	14 25.7	19 18.7	14 26.6	13 27.7
	23 15.7	24 15.5	24 15.5	22 16.7	21 17.8	26 13.9	21 17.4	20 18.1
	39 9.4	32 11.3	31 12.0	27 13.6	33 11.2	33 11.1	30 12.4	30 12.5
Cost of Sales/Payables	0 UND	5 72.8	9 39.4	12 29.7	13 28.9	15 24.7	8 45.0	8 47.8
	8 46.8	11 33.9	14 26.2	17 21.1	17 21.3	19 19.0	14 25.4	14 26.0
	16 23.4	19 19.5	20 18.2	25 14.3	29 12.6	23 15.9	21 17.1	21 17.7
Sales/Working Capital	14.4	17.5	16.1	33.3	36.9	41.2	22.0	21.7
	40.1	36.9	35.3	83.7	474.8	80.7	63.6	61.5
	UND	-999.8	196.5	-63.8	-55.6	NM	-103.4	-112.1
EBIT/Interest	7.9	10.8	10.4	10.3	11.2	7.8	5.6	6.0
	(98) 2.2	(212) 2.8	(216) 3.5	(88) 3.4	(28) 4.8	(25) 3.2	(777) 2.3	(788) 2.4
	.0	.9	1.3	1.6	1.5	1.3	.9	1.1
Net Profit + Depr., Dep., Amort./Cur. Mat. L/T/D		4.3	3.8	5.7	6.5		5.2	4.5
		(24) 1.4	(48) 1.7	(44) 2.4	(14) 3.5		(174) 2.4	(164) 2.4
		.4	1.0	1.7	2.2		1.2	1.2
Fixed/Worth	.3	.5	.4	.9	1.0	1.0	.7	.7
	2.2	1.3	1.1	1.5	1.9	1.4	2.0	1.9
	-2.0	48.0	3.8	4.0	6.2	3.3	10.3	16.4
Debt/Worth	.9	1.0	.7	.9	1.1	.9	1.1	1.2
	9.5	3.1	2.1	1.9	3.1	2.1	3.2	3.2
	-4.8	89.4	5.5	5.2	9.2	5.4	20.0	33.3
% Profit Before Taxes/Tangible Net Worth	90.9	63.4	38.4	35.1	35.2	25.5	46.2	46.9
	(94) 22.6	(206) 28.2	(206) 17.1	(87) 18.3	(26) 17.5	(27) 16.5	(702) 20.8	(687) 21.3
	.8	7.4	6.6	6.7	3.6	4.8	4.3	6.4
% Profit Before Taxes/Total Assets	15.6	17.3	13.7	11.3	14.7	9.8	12.3	13.3
	4.6	5.8	5.9	5.7	5.9	4.4	5.0	5.1
	-3.3	-.1	1.0	1.7	1.2	.7	-.2	.7
Sales/Net Fixed Assets	170.3	56.2	32.2	15.4	12.9	11.2	32.2	28.1
	43.5	21.5	16.7	8.9	9.8	8.8	14.2	13.5
	14.2	9.2	7.9	5.2	6.7	6.8	6.7	6.4
Sales/Total Assets	12.7	8.2	6.7	5.4	4.9	4.9	7.3	7.3
	7.2	5.9	4.9	4.4	4.5	4.3	5.1	4.9
	4.2	3.9	3.4	3.2	3.6	3.3	3.5	3.4
% Depr., Dep., Amort./Sales	.4	.6	.8	1.1	1.1	1.3	.7	.7
	(104) 1.0	(229) 1.0	(221) 1.2	(94) 1.4	(26) 1.6	(16) 1.6	(812) 1.2	(811) 1.3
	1.9	1.6	1.9	1.9	1.9	1.9	1.8	2.0
% Officers', Directors', Owners' Comp/Sales	1.3	.8	.5	.3			.8	.7
	(74) 2.5	(130) 1.3	(89) 1.1	(11) .4			(325) 1.5	(332) 1.5
	4.5	2.3	2.0	11.5			2.5	2.9
Net Sales ($)	347210M	1919364M	5734552M	11076969M	8958469M	20007900M	49658617M	53849076M
Total Assets ($)	39682M	298185M	1095337M	2376394M	2032347M	4998032M	12009782M	12261760M

© RMA 2005

M = $ thousand   MM = $ million
See Pages 11 through 21 for Explanation of Ratios and Data

Comparative Historical Data | Current Data Sorted By Sales

			Type of Statement						
103	86	77	Unqualified			2	1	6	68
108	114	80	Reviewed		2	6	9	16	47
182	223	209	Compiled	7	24	23	57	63	35
158	209	235	Tax Returns	31	52	42	66	28	16
207	224	210	Other	8	27	15	36	45	79
4/1/02-3/31/03	4/1/03-3/31/04	4/1/04-3/31/05		160 (4/1-9/30/04)			651 (10/1/04-3/31/05)		
ALL	ALL	ALL		0-1MM	1-3MM	3-5MM	5-10MM	10-25MM	25MM & OVER
758	856	811	**NUMBER OF STATEMENTS**	46	105	88	169	158	245
%	%	%	**ASSETS**	%	%	%	%	%	%
12.4	13.0	13.5	Cash & Equivalents	16.1	11.2	10.4	13.6	18.6	11.6
4.9	4.6	4.7	Trade Receivables (net)	2.0	3.8	4.3	5.5	4.7	5.3
28.6	29.0	29.4	Inventory	27.4	34.2	35.2	30.2	28.4	25.7
3.0	3.0	2.5	All Other Current	2.8	2.6	3.6	1.5	2.6	2.5
48.9	49.6	50.0	Total Current	48.2	51.9	53.5	50.7	54.4	45.1
38.6	37.1	36.7	Fixed Assets (net)	32.2	37.8	34.2	36.0	30.8	42.2
3.8	4.1	4.3	Intangibles (net)	14.8	4.3	2.4	3.8	4.5	3.4
8.6	9.2	9.0	All Other Non-Current	4.7	6.1	9.9	9.5	10.4	9.4
100.0	100.0	100.0	Total	100.0	100.0	100.0	100.0	100.0	100.0
			LIABILITIES						
4.1	4.2	4.1	Notes Payable-Short Term	4.4	5.0	5.8	4.5	2.6	3.7
4.7	4.5	4.0	Cur. Mat.-L/T/D	1.3	4.2	3.5	3.8	4.4	4.3
19.2	17.8	17.6	Trade Payables	5.6	14.8	19.8	18.3	17.8	19.6
.3	.2	.2	Income Taxes Payable	.5	.2	.2	.0	.2	.2
11.3	11.5	11.5	All Other Current	16.5	12.4	13.2	13.0	10.1	9.4
39.6	38.2	37.3	Total Current	28.2	36.5	42.6	39.6	35.1	37.3
29.0	28.3	27.8	Long-Term Debt	35.3	30.8	33.9	27.8	26.1	24.0
.3	.3	.3	Deferred Taxes	.1	.0	.1	.1	.3	.7
6.8	7.5	6.4	All Other Non-Current	13.0	10.0	9.6	7.0	4.1	3.4
24.4	25.7	28.2	Net Worth	23.4	22.6	13.9	25.5	34.4	34.6
100.0	100.0	100.0	Total Liabilities & Net Worth	100.0	100.0	100.0	100.0	100.0	100.0
			INCOME DATA						
100.0	100.0	100.0	Net Sales	100.0	100.0	100.0	100.0	100.0	100.0
24.9	24.0	24.4	Gross Profit	33.3	24.1	22.3	22.9	25.2	24.2
23.6	23.0	23.3	Operating Expenses	29.8	23.5	21.7	22.3	24.1	22.7
1.3	1.0	1.2	Operating Profit	3.5	.5	.6	.6	1.1	1.6
-.1	-.2	-.3	All Other Expenses (net)	.0	.0	-.4	-.8	-.6	.0
1.4	1.3	1.5	Profit Before Taxes	3.5	.6	1.0	1.4	1.7	1.6
			RATIOS						
2.2	2.3	2.4		9.9	5.0	2.8	2.3	2.7	1.6
1.3	1.4	1.4	Current	2.1	1.9	1.5	1.5	1.6	1.2
.9	.9	.9		1.1	1.0	.9	.9	1.1	.9
.8	.9	1.0		2.4	1.4	.9	1.0	1.3	.7
(746) .4	(846) .4	(807) .5	Quick	(45) .8	(103) .4	.4	(168) .5	.7	.4
.2	.2	.2		.3	.1	.1	.2	.3	.2
0 999.8	0 999.8	0 999.8		0 UND	0 UND	0 UND	0 999.8	0 999.8	1 324.1
2 237.9	1 284.9	1 285.2	Sales/Receivables	0 UND	1 651.7	1 362.9	1 341.1	1 284.0	2 152.0
4 90.8	4 102.2	3 112.1		0 UND	2 181.8	3 115.7	3 137.5	3 131.6	4 82.5
16 23.2	15 24.5	15 23.6		20 18.0	16 23.1	13 28.4	14 26.1	16 22.6	16 23.5
23 16.0	23 15.7	23 15.7	Cost of Sales/Inventory	35 10.3	28 13.2	24 15.0	22 16.4	22 16.8	22 16.2
32 11.3	32 11.4	32 11.5		70 5.2	43 8.6	36 10.1	29 12.8	30 12.1	28 13.0
8 45.4	7 52.4	7 52.9		0 UND	1 268.3	5 77.2	5 74.2	8 45.1	12 29.9
14 25.7	14 27.0	13 28.0	Cost of Sales/Payables	3 107.0	8 43.5	11 34.0	11 33.2	13 28.0	16 22.1
21 17.0	21 17.5	20 18.3		15 25.1	18 20.1	18 20.5	19 19.3	19 19.4	23 16.0
19.7	19.7	17.7		7.1	12.8	16.4	21.5	15.7	29.2
55.5	47.6	43.1	Sales/Working Capital	17.6	27.4	37.1	42.4	33.1	72.4
-98.7	-168.2	-469.4		134.1	288.8	-237.3	-226.1	173.4	-135.9
6.6	7.8	9.8		3.6	6.8	6.2	11.3	11.8	11.1
(662) 2.9	(720) 2.9	(667) 3.1	EBIT/Interest	(28) 1.5	(80) 2.2	(68) 1.9	(141) 3.0	(131) 3.6	(219) 4.1
1.2	1.1	1.0		.1	.1	.3	1.0	1.6	1.4
4.6	4.6	4.5					5.4	4.5	5.6
(164) 2.1	(165) 2.1	(139) 2.1	Net Profit + Depr., Dep., Amort./Cur. Mat. L/T/D			(17) 1.3	(35) 1.8	(76) 2.4
1.3	1.0	1.3					.7	1.1	1.7
.6	.5	.5		.3	.4	.5	.5	.3	.7
1.6	1.4	1.3	Fixed/Worth	3.1	1.7	1.5	1.7	1.0	1.3
7.2	9.0	8.3		-1.3	-15.2	-7.0	96.6	3.8	3.2
1.1	1.0	.9		.7	.8	1.0	1.1	.7	.9
2.8	2.7	2.8	Debt/Worth	5.9	5.8	4.0	3.2	2.1	2.1
16.9	23.0	23.8		-2.8	-32.1	-12.0	215.8	11.0	5.2
50.2	50.0	50.4		80.2	63.9	48.4	70.6	64.0	36.0
(606) 21.5	(685) 20.0	(646) 20.1	% Profit Before Taxes/Tangible Net Worth	(31) 24.1	(76) 20.2	(62) 16.2	(130) 21.7	(128) 25.3	(219) 18.3
6.7	5.1	6.6		-.6	6.0	.4	8.0	8.6	5.0
12.9	13.0	14.3		14.4	11.8	13.4	14.0	17.5	13.6
5.7	5.5	5.5	% Profit Before Taxes/Total Assets	6.2	3.1	4.3	5.3	6.7	5.9
.9	.2	.3		-1.7	-5.4	-2.2	.0	2.1	1.1
34.5	40.9	43.0		53.0	83.3	62.4	59.5	55.3	25.5
14.7	16.8	16.9	Sales/Net Fixed Assets	12.9	18.9	22.6	19.4	23.1	12.1
7.6	7.4	8.3		4.2	5.5	9.3	9.8	10.4	7.8
7.3	7.5	7.5		5.0	7.2	9.4	9.1	7.6	6.8
5.2	5.1	5.3	Sales/Total Assets	3.1	4.8	5.7	6.0	5.5	5.1
3.5	3.5	3.6		1.6	2.9	3.7	3.7	4.2	3.9
.8	.7	.7		1.1	.6	.6	.6	.7	.8
(678) 1.2	(753) 1.2	(690) 1.2	% Depr., Dep., Amort./Sales	(32) 2.2	(81) 1.1	(73) 1.1	(149) 1.0	(139) 1.2	(216) 1.2
1.8	1.9	1.9		3.2	2.4	2.0	1.7	1.9	1.7
.6	.6	.8		2.9	1.4	1.0	.7	.6	.4
(283) 1.4	(347) 1.3	(306) 1.4	% Officers', Directors', Owners' Comp/Sales	(23) 4.4	(45) 2.6	(51) 1.5	(80) 1.2	(65) 1.0	(42) 1.2
2.6	2.7	2.7		8.9	3.7	2.5	1.7	2.1	2.5
51828206M	55884406M	48044464M	Net Sales ($)	28543M	199169M	344077M	1218768M	2492600M	43761307M
12471756M	12111223M	10839977M	Total Assets ($)	12898M	58516M	73737M	258139M	510420M	9926267M

M = $ thousand   MM = $ million
See Pages 11 through 21 for Explanation of Ratios and Data

Current Data Sorted By Assets

Comparative Historical Data

0-500M	500M-2MM	2-10MM	10-50MM	50-100MM	100-250MM	Type of Statement	4/1/00-3/31/01 ALL	4/1/01-3/31/02 ALL
1		1	2	2	1	Unqualified		
1	1	5	4			Reviewed		
45	5	2	1			Compiled		
6	18	3				Tax Returns		
	7	6	1	2		Other		
	12 (4/1-9/30/04)		102 (10/1/04-3/31/05)					
53	**31**	**17**	**8**	**4**	**1**	**NUMBER OF STATEMENTS**		
%	%	%	%	%	%	**ASSETS**	%	%
10.0	12.6	8.3				Cash & Equivalents		
2.3	3.5	7.0				Trade Receivables (net)	D	D
37.3	17.9	17.7				Inventory	A	A
1.0	2.9	2.6				All Other Current	T	T
50.5	36.9	35.5				Total Current	A	A
28.0	49.3	55.1				Fixed Assets (net)		
15.5	8.3	1.3				Intangibles (net)	N	N
5.9	5.5	8.1				All Other Non-Current	O	O
100.0	100.0	100.0				Total	T	T
						LIABILITIES	A	A
8.7	4.6	6.3				Notes Payable-Short Term	V	V
4.0	2.6	3.0				Cur. Mat.-L/T/D	A	A
12.0	10.2	16.0				Trade Payables	I	I
.0	.2	.6				Income Taxes Payable	L	L
17.5	8.3	9.2				All Other Current	A	A
42.2	25.8	34.9				Total Current	B	B
27.8	41.0	32.1				Long-Term Debt	L	L
.0	.0	.0				Deferred Taxes	E	E
17.5	5.1	1.6				All Other Non-Current		
12.6	28.1	31.4				Net Worth		
100.0	100.0	100.0				Total Liabilities & Net Worth		
						INCOME DATA		
100.0	100.0	100.0				Net Sales		
21.8	18.9	21.1				Gross Profit		
20.3	16.2	18.4				Operating Expenses		
1.5	2.7	2.7				Operating Profit		
-.2	1.0	2.7				All Other Expenses (net)		
1.7	1.7	.0				Profit Before Taxes		
						RATIOS		
7.6	7.4	1.3						
1.8	1.7	1.0				Current		
.6	.9	.6						
1.1	4.1	.6						
(51) .3	.6	.4				Quick		
.1	.2	.2						
0 UND	0 UND	3 135.5						
0 UND	0 745.9	4 100.7				Sales/Receivables		
1 674.8	2 147.2	8 46.5						
11 31.9	13 28.4	9 41.5						
22 16.9	17 22.1	13 28.8				Cost of Sales/Inventory		
39 9.5	27 13.7	29 12.6						
0 UND	0 UND	6 60.5						
2 230.5	6 60.6	12 30.1				Cost of Sales/Payables		
7 56.0	18 20.7	21 17.2						
16.1	14.4	49.2						
34.7	25.9	-623.9				Sales/Working Capital		
-40.0	-243.2	-37.2						
5.8	5.0	11.3						
(35) 1.4	(25) 1.4	(13) 3.4				EBIT/Interest		
-1.5	.0	.3						
						Net Profit + Depr., Dep., Amort./Cur. Mat. L/T/D		
.3	.6	.8						
2.3	3.3	1.4				Fixed/Worth		
-1.0	-4.6	7.4						
1.2	1.1	1.3						
13.4	4.1	2.7				Debt/Worth		
-2.9	-9.5	7.5						
81.4	32.1	40.5						
(29) 18.1	(21) 8.3	(16) 14.8				% Profit Before Taxes/Tangible Net Worth		
.9	-11.9	-3.4						
22.0	6.9	10.6						
2.6	1.5	3.4				% Profit Before Taxes/Total Assets		
-9.1	-3.1	-1.5						
313.6	22.5	28.8						
33.0	10.4	12.2				Sales/Net Fixed Assets		
11.5	3.0	2.8						
11.0	5.9	9.5						
6.8	3.5	6.4				Sales/Total Assets		
3.8	2.3	2.1						
.6	1.0	.8						
(39) 1.2	(27) 1.5	(16) 1.0				% Depr., Dep., Amort./Sales		
2.3	2.0	2.2						
1.1	.6							
(28) 3.0	(16) 1.2					% Officers', Directors', Owners' Comp/Sales		
4.3	1.9							
83876M	150488M	395162M	823840M	1427884M	829326M	Net Sales ($)		
11503M	32359M	72251M	151593M	309168M	131522M	Total Assets ($)		

© RMA 2005

M = $ thousand   MM = $ million
See Pages 11 through 21 for Explanation of Ratios and Data

Comparative Historical Data | Current Data Sorted By Sales

			Type of Statement	0-1MM	1-3MM	3-5MM	5-10MM	10-25MM	25MM & OVER
2	7	7	Unqualified		1			2	6
3	6	10	Reviewed						8
9	14	9	Compiled	1		2		1	1
16	39	66	Tax Returns	26	26	8	4	2	1
6	10	22	Other	4	6	2	3	5	5
4/1/02-3/31/03	4/1/03-3/31/04	4/1/04-3/31/05		12 (4/1-9/30/04)			102 (10/1/04-3/31/05)		
ALL	ALL	ALL							
36	76	114	NUMBER OF STATEMENTS	31	33	12	7	10	21
%	%	%	ASSETS	%	%	%	%	%	%
13.3	11.8	10.0	Cash & Equivalents	11.8	8.0	12.1		10.7	6.5
4.4	4.8	3.8	Trade Receivables (net)	.6	3.0	7.4		5.5	7.4
24.3	29.2	26.8	Inventory	33.5	28.5	20.0		24.2	19.8
2.5	2.6	2.0	All Other Current	.5	1.2	.6		6.1	3.6
44.6	48.4	42.6	Total Current	46.5	40.7	40.1		46.5	37.3
46.5	38.6	41.4	Fixed Assets (net)	32.9	40.5	44.6		51.0	51.6
3.4	6.9	10.0	Intangibles (net)	18.4	11.2	6.6		.8	2.7
5.5	6.1	5.9	All Other Non-Current	2.2	7.6	8.7		1.8	8.4
100.0	100.0	100.0	Total	100.0	100.0	100.0		100.0	100.0
			LIABILITIES						
10.9	2.8	6.5	Notes Payable-Short Term	5.0	12.2	6.7		1.9	3.5
4.3	2.3	3.4	Cur. Mat.-L/T/D	5.3	2.5	.8		4.8	3.3
10.4	12.8	13.0	Trade Payables	4.4	14.2	11.5		19.0	21.7
.2	.4	.2	Income Taxes Payable	.0	.0	.0		1.4	.2
8.4	9.1	12.5	All Other Current	22.0	6.0	20.0		3.6	10.1
34.2	27.4	35.6	Total Current	36.7	34.9	39.1		30.6	38.8
33.8	35.9	33.4	Long-Term Debt	29.7	45.2	18.3		47.9	27.3
.2	.2	.2	Deferred Taxes	.0	.0	.0		.5	.7
6.0	7.3	10.2	All Other Non-Current	15.7	15.4	1.7		3.7	3.7
25.7	29.1	20.6	Net Worth	17.9	4.5	40.9		17.2	29.4
100.0	100.0	100.0	Total Liabilities & Net Worth	100.0	100.0	100.0		100.0	100.0
			INCOME DATA						
100.0	100.0	100.0	Net Sales	100.0	100.0	100.0		100.0	100.0
23.0	19.8	20.6	Gross Profit	27.9	16.7	17.7		19.5	19.0
21.0	18.8	18.7	Operating Expenses	22.9	16.7	15.1		19.2	18.3
2.0	1.0	2.0	Operating Profit	4.9	.1	2.7		.3	.7
1.0	-.7	.6	All Other Expenses (net)	1.7	.5	.1		.0	-.1
1.0	1.8	1.4	Profit Before Taxes	3.2	-.4	2.5		.3	.9
			RATIOS						
1.8	4.0	4.1		15.8	5.6	9.1		2.3	1.2
1.4	1.7	1.4	Current	2.4	1.7	1.5		1.4	1.0
.8	1.2	.7		.6	.6	.5		.9	.7
1.1	1.2	1.1		4.0	1.3	2.7		1.1	.6
(35) .6	(73) .6	(112) .4	Quick	.3	(31) .4	.6		.4	.4
.2	.3	.1		.0	.1	.1		.1	.2
0 UND	0 UND	0 UND		0 UND	0 UND	0 871.6		0 809.4	2 183.1
1 442.0	2 240.6	0 905.3	Sales/Receivables	0 UND	0 UND	2 170.3		3 118.8	4 100.7
5 66.9	4 81.4	4 99.3		0 UND	2 164.0	2 146.7		7 48.9	5 72.0
11 33.6	12 31.4	11 32.3		22 16.9	12 31.0	5 77.3		9 40.3	11 34.5
16 23.3	20 18.6	17 21.8	Cost of Sales/Inventory	37 9.9	18 20.3	10 36.5		14 26.1	13 27.4
36 10.1	31 11.7	34 10.9		56 6.6	26 13.9	24 15.2		29 12.7	16 22.4
0 UND	1 377.5	0 UND		0 UND	0 UND	1 267.3		5 69.9	8 43.5
8 45.6	10 37.4	5 69.9	Cost of Sales/Payables	1 351.0	3 112.4	5 71.6		14 26.6	13 27.2
16 22.2	15 23.8	16 23.1		5 79.3	15 23.7	12 30.6		18 20.3	21 17.2
20.2	18.4	18.9		8.1	19.0	15.2		23.0	89.5
45.3	32.5	59.7	Sales/Working Capital	24.9	42.2	60.5		41.7	999.8
NM	95.4	-54.8		-21.6	-38.4	-67.7		-476.5	-50.1
4.8	7.0	6.3		5.9	3.9				9.5
(29) 2.5	(63) 2.8	(86) 1.8	EBIT/Interest	(18) 2.1	(29) 1.0				(20) 2.4
.4	1.0	.4		.2	-1.9				1.4
			Net Profit + Depr., Dep., Amort./Cur. Mat. L/T/D						
.7	.7	.7		.2	.8	.6		.8	.8
2.3	1.6	2.6	Fixed/Worth	3.7	9.5	2.1		5.0	1.4
UND	-15.7	-6.2		-.9	-1.6	-2.3		NM	4.3
1.2	.9	1.2		1.4	1.9	.4		2.5	1.1
3.5	2.1	4.3	Debt/Worth	5.1	392.0	1.9		8.0	2.7
UND	-30.1	-9.1		-2.7	-3.5	-15.8		NM	5.3
32.3	39.8	50.6		63.9	62.2				33.1
(28) 8.9	(54) 17.1	(77) 10.1	% Profit Before Taxes/Tangible Net Worth	(17) 17.6	(18) 8.2				(19) 10.1
-2.0	2.3	-.2		1.2	-97.4				.8
9.5	12.6	11.3		21.8	5.9	35.1		7.0	6.2
2.1	6.0	2.4	% Profit Before Taxes/Total Assets	4.9	-.1	10.6		-.4	3.2
-2.1	-.8	-2.3		-.7	-9.1	-.2		-7.4	.3
35.3	59.2	44.7		94.4	129.8	30.7		63.7	27.5
12.2	15.7	13.4	Sales/Net Fixed Assets	12.7	15.3	15.4		12.1	10.6
4.7	5.6	6.4		4.6	4.0	10.2		3.8	6.8
5.8	8.6	9.3		6.8	10.8	10.3		9.8	9.3
4.0	5.1	5.4	Sales/Total Assets	3.7	5.4	6.1		7.4	6.3
2.8	3.2	2.7		1.8	2.5	4.3		2.6	4.4
.7	.7	.8		.8	.6	.6			.9
(35) 1.3	(66) 1.4	(94) 1.3	% Depr., Dep., Amort./Sales	(21) 1.8	(27) 1.3	(10) 1.4			(20) 1.1
2.4	2.6	2.2		3.6	2.5	1.9			1.6
.6	.9	.7		3.0	.6				
(19) 2.0	(40) 2.2	(52) 1.7	% Officers', Directors', Owners' Comp/Sales	(16) 4.2	(14) 2.3				
4.6	4.0	3.7		7.3	3.2				
621739M	823084M	3710576M	Net Sales ($)	19571M	61930M	49818M	50877M	152050M	3376330M
150665M	176185M	708396M	Total Assets ($)	12798M	17602M	8509M	8185M	36109M	625193M

M = $ thousand   MM = $ million
See Pages 11 through 21 for Explanation of Ratios and Data

Current Data Sorted By Assets   Comparative Historical Data

						Type of Statement		
3						Unqualified	2	2
5	7	4	1			Reviewed	4	8
6	4	3	2			Compiled	9	14
2	4	4	1			Tax Returns	11	7
						Other	15	20
10 (4/1-9/30/04)			36 (10/1/04-3/31/05)				4/1/00-3/31/01	4/1/01-3/31/02
0-500M	500M-2MM	2-10MM	10-50MM	50-100MM	100-250MM		ALL	ALL
16	15	11	4			**NUMBER OF STATEMENTS**	41	51
%	%	%	%	%	%	**ASSETS**	%	%
14.0	6.1	5.8				Cash & Equivalents	15.9	19.1
8.7	23.0	31.7				Trade Receivables (net)	13.0	14.5
16.6	17.3	26.4				Inventory	15.4	18.4
1.3	.9	1.5				All Other Current	2.7	5.3
40.6	47.2	65.4				Total Current	47.1	57.3
47.3	34.1	25.9				Fixed Assets (net)	38.3	29.8
4.7	4.4	.0				Intangibles (net)	4.9	4.8
7.2	14.3	8.7				All Other Non-Current	9.7	8.0
100.0	100.0	100.0				Total	100.0	100.0
				DATA	DATA	**LIABILITIES**		
1.7	9.9	13.5		NOT	NOT	Notes Payable-Short Term	9.2	12.9
6.5	3.2	2.0		AVAILABLE	AVAILABLE	Cur. Mat.-L/T/D	3.4	3.3
12.8	26.3	22.4				Trade Payables	16.8	20.4
.0	.0	.0				Income Taxes Payable	.2	.1
11.7	3.7	10.0				All Other Current	8.4	14.5
32.7	43.1	47.9				Total Current	38.0	51.2
36.0	25.1	14.4				Long-Term Debt	26.0	18.6
.3	.0	.0				Deferred Taxes	.3	.1
21.7	10.2	4.8				All Other Non-Current	1.0	3.2
9.2	21.7	32.9				Net Worth	34.7	26.9
100.0	100.0	100.0				Total Liabilities & Net Worth	100.0	100.0
						INCOME DATA		
100.0	100.0	100.0				Net Sales	100.0	100.0
35.4	25.0	21.8				Gross Profit	33.4	35.1
34.0	22.9	22.8				Operating Expenses	31.9	32.9
1.4	2.1	-1.0				Operating Profit	1.6	2.2
.1	.3	.3				All Other Expenses (net)	-.3	.7
1.3	1.8	-1.3				Profit Before Taxes	1.9	1.5
						RATIOS		
2.9	2.0	2.6					2.1	1.7
1.4	1.7	1.2				Current	1.4	1.1
.8	.7	1.1					.8	.8
1.1	1.6	1.5					1.4	1.0
.7	.7	.8				Quick	(40) .7	(50) .6
.5	.1	.3					.5	.3
0 UND	0 UND	6 56.2					0 UND	1 390.5
2 168.2	16 22.6	18 19.8				Sales/Receivables	4 87.5	5 75.5
9 42.0	23 15.7	35 10.6					21 17.5	17 21.8
5 75.1	8 46.3	14 26.0					9 42.1	9 41.1
12 30.1	13 28.5	21 17.5				Cost of Sales/Inventory	19 18.8	21 17.8
20 18.0	26 14.0	70 5.3					33 11.1	38 9.6
0 UND	10 37.0	7 48.8					6 59.2	6 57.4
10 34.9	19 19.5	19 19.4				Cost of Sales/Payables	20 18.7	22 16.6
17 21.9	36 10.2	24 15.4					31 11.6	34 10.6
20.0	12.1	24.0					14.4	17.8
55.2	46.3	33.8				Sales/Working Capital	39.0	145.0
-200.6	-15.7	67.1					-65.6	-44.3
7.4	20.1						6.4	5.6
(12) 3.4	(14) 4.1					EBIT/Interest	(34) 2.4	(42) 2.5
1.3	.9						.9	.9
						Net Profit + Depr., Dep., Amort./Cur. Mat. L /T/D		
.8	.1	.0					.3	.4
5.2	2.2	.3				Fixed/Worth	1.1	1.1
-1.3	-7.2	1.8					NM	3.2
1.3	1.4	1.1					.7	1.1
5.2	6.3	1.9				Debt/Worth	2.3	2.5
-3.9	-28.7	5.3					NM	31.8
50.2	104.3	35.9				% Profit Before Taxes/Tangible Net Worth	44.3	41.8
(10) 6.3	(11) 36.9	8.4					(31) 20.8	(40) 22.6
-22.2	-23.9	1.2					1.2	.1
14.9	23.2	14.4				% Profit Before Taxes/Total Assets	19.9	15.7
4.4	6.9	3.2					5.8	7.9
-1.4	.3	.4					-.1	.0
38.2	107.6	UND					29.1	33.8
13.2	10.8	75.6				Sales/Net Fixed Assets	10.6	17.0
8.2	5.6	6.9					6.3	8.8
8.6	7.2	6.7					6.7	4.8
5.9	3.5	4.4				Sales/Total Assets	3.9	3.7
4.8	1.8	1.9					2.5	3.0
.8	.4						1.0	.5
(12) 1.5	(14) .6					% Depr., Dep., Amort./Sales	(39) 1.5	(43) 1.5
4.0	2.3						3.7	2.7
1.7							1.7	1.8
(10) 3.2						% Officers', Directors', Owners' Comp/Sales	(24) 3.5	(23) 3.4
8.5							4.0	6.1
25437M	66327M	284945M	1246303M			Net Sales ($)	1014155M	1132588M
4322M	13248M	50639M	130076M			Total Assets ($)	358046M	309376M

© RMA 2005

M = $ thousand   MM = $ million
See Pages 11 through 21 for Explanation of Ratios and Data

Comparative Historical Data / Current Data Sorted By Sales

			Type of Statement						
5	3		Unqualified		2	1		2	3
7	10	8	Reviewed	2	7	1	3	1	1
13	20	15	Compiled	3	6	1			2
7	26	12	Tax Returns						
12	10	11	Other	1	2	2	1	4	1
4/1/02-3/31/03	4/1/03-3/31/04	4/1/04-3/31/05		10 (4/1-9/30/04)			36 (10/1/04-3/31/05)		
ALL	ALL	ALL		0-1MM	1-3MM	3-5MM	5-10MM	10-25MM	25MM & OVER
44	69	46	NUMBER OF STATEMENTS	6	17	5	4	7	7
%	%	%	ASSETS	%	%	%	%	%	%
10.8	13.4	8.7	Cash & Equivalents		10.2				
11.7	15.6	20.0	Trade Receivables (net)		8.2				
22.8	21.8	20.4	Inventory		18.6				
3.1	1.6	1.4	All Other Current		.4				
48.4	52.4	50.5	Total Current		37.5				
33.6	34.8	36.4	Fixed Assets (net)		45.5				
4.3	3.4	3.1	Intangibles (net)		3.9				
13.6	9.4	10.0	All Other Non-Current		13.1				
100.0	100.0	100.0	Total		100.0				
			LIABILITIES						
8.7	8.1	8.1	Notes Payable-Short Term		3.8				
6.4	2.0	4.5	Cur. Mat.-L/T/D		4.8				
17.6	19.1	20.0	Trade Payables		13.5				
.5	.2	.0	Income Taxes Payable		.0				
8.9	9.1	9.3	All Other Current		5.4				
42.1	38.4	42.0	Total Current		27.6				
30.3	22.9	25.5	Long-Term Debt		31.9				
.1	.1	.1	Deferred Taxes		.3				
8.4	11.1	13.0	All Other Non-Current		24.7				
19.0	27.5	19.4	Net Worth		15.6				
100.0	100.0	100.0	Total Liabilities & Net Worth		100.0				
			INCOME DATA						
100.0	100.0	100.0	Net Sales		100.0				
32.3	29.7	27.3	Gross Profit		30.7				
31.0	27.4	26.1	Operating Expenses		29.0				
1.2	2.3	1.2	Operating Profit		1.8				
-.1	-.3	.1	All Other Expenses (net)		.1				
1.4	2.7	1.1	Profit Before Taxes		1.7				
			RATIOS						
2.9 1.2 .7	2.4 1.6 .9	2.1 1.3 .8	Current		2.5 1.5 .7				
1.5 (42) .6 .3	1.7 (68) .8 .4	1.2 .7 .3	Quick		1.1 .7 .3				
0 UND 1 253.7 18 20.6	0 UND 3 124.0 19 19.3	1 454.5 8 47.9 23 15.6	Sales/Receivables		0 UND 2 217.0 11 32.7				
10 35.1 22 16.3 39 9.4	7 54.3 13 27.6 39 9.3	8 47.4 16 22.6 35 10.5	Cost of Sales/Inventory		8 44.1 14 25.3 25 14.4				
7 56.1 15 23.6 24 15.4	2 187.0 11 31.8 23 15.6	6 58.6 14 26.5 24 15.1	Cost of Sales/Payables		2 223.3 12 30.6 22 16.2				
18.2 124.9 -34.1	11.0 40.5 -276.7	19.0 47.9 -162.0	Sales/Working Capital		18.8 49.6 -62.3				
14.5 (39) 4.1 1.3	11.7 (50) 3.1 .8	12.0 (39) 3.8 1.6	EBIT/Interest		6.1 (14) 2.8 .8				
			Net Profit + Depr., Dep., Amort./Cur. Mat. L/T/D						
.2 1.6 -10.0	.2 .9 4.7	.2 1.8 280.1	Fixed/Worth		.9 1.9 -19.4				
.7 2.8 -21.0	.7 1.7 8.7	1.3 3.7 NM	Debt/Worth		1.4 4.1 -37.1				
48.1 (32) 24.4 9.4	54.4 (55) 21.2 4.3	38.9 (35) 9.0 .3	% Profit Before Taxes/Tangible Net Worth		65.2 (12) 6.9 -17.4				
13.1 7.4 .8	22.5 7.6 1.4	16.0 4.1 .4	% Profit Before Taxes/Total Assets		14.9 4.1 .8				
43.4 18.1 8.5	43.2 19.6 8.9	85.5 15.2 7.0	Sales/Net Fixed Assets		22.0 10.7 5.9				
6.6 4.4 3.2	8.2 5.3 3.0	7.7 5.4 2.6	Sales/Total Assets		6.1 4.6 2.1				
.7 (36) 1.8 3.5	.6 (58) 1.3 2.6	.4 (35) 1.2 2.2	% Depr., Dep., Amort./Sales		.6 (14) 1.3 2.3				
1.2 (22) 2.8 5.5	1.2 (36) 2.5 4.4	1.1 (23) 1.9 4.5	% Officers', Directors', Owners' Comp/Sales						
668565M	604548M	1623012M	Net Sales ($)	3563M	33356M	21136M	25679M	101615M	1437663M
145917M	118385M	198285M	Total Assets ($)	1116M	9852M	9094M	2798M	32562M	142863M

M = $ thousand   MM = $ million
See Pages 11 through 21 for Explanation of Ratios and Data

RETAIL—Fruit and Vegetable Markets   NAICS 445230 (SIC 5148, 5431)

Current Data Sorted By Assets | **Comparative Historical Data**

Type of Statement		2	2
Unqualified		2	2
Reviewed		4	3
Compiled		12	5
Tax Returns		5	2
Other		5	6

0-500M	500M-2MM	2-10MM	10-50MM	50-100MM	100-250MM		4/1/00-3/31/01 ALL	4/1/01-3/31/02 ALL
							1	1
	5	1					3	1
1	4	3					1	
2	1	1					1	
	7 (4/1-9/30/04)		14 (10/1/04-3/31/05)					
4	10	7				**NUMBER OF STATEMENTS**	28	18
%	%	%	%	%	%	**ASSETS**	%	%
17.1			D	D	D	Cash & Equivalents	18.0	14.9
18.8			A	A	A	Trade Receivables (net)	13.7	8.4
17.5			T	T	T	Inventory	15.4	18.4
.3			A	A	A	All Other Current	1.0	5.6
53.7						Total Current	48.0	47.2
34.4			N	N	N	Fixed Assets (net)	39.3	44.8
8.5			O	O	O	Intangibles (net)	3.3	3.4
3.3			T	T	T	All Other Non-Current	9.3	1.9
100.0						Total	100.0	100.0
						LIABILITIES		
6.2			A	A	A	Notes Payable-Short Term	7.0	11.2
1.6			V	V	V	Cur. Mat.-L/T/D	5.1	4.9
36.9			A	A	A	Trade Payables	23.9	28.2
.1			I	I	I	Income Taxes Payable	.1	.1
11.3			L	L	L	All Other Current	15.6	10.5
56.0			A	A	A	Total Current	51.8	54.9
20.4			B	B	B	Long-Term Debt	15.4	31.1
.0			L	L	L	Deferred Taxes	.3	.6
10.4			E	E	E	All Other Non-Current	2.6	6.0
13.3						Net Worth	29.9	7.4
100.0						Total Liabilities & Net Worth	100.0	100.0
						INCOME DATA		
100.0						Net Sales	100.0	100.0
24.1						Gross Profit	31.6	32.1
25.6						Operating Expenses	27.7	28.2
-1.5						Operating Profit	3.9	3.9
-.3						All Other Expenses (net)	.7	.6
-1.2						Profit Before Taxes	3.2	3.3
						RATIOS		
2.3						Current	1.4	1.2
1.1							1.0	.8
.7							.6	.5
1.0						Quick	1.0	.9
.7							.6	.3
.1							.3	.1
0 UND						Sales/Receivables	0 UND	0 UND
0 966.6							1 401.6	1 482.7
28 13.1							14 25.2	6 63.1
6 64.8						Cost of Sales/Inventory	4 86.6	6 63.2
10 34.8							10 35.3	16 23.5
20 18.1							15 23.8	38 9.6
17 21.2						Cost of Sales/Payables	8 43.3	12 29.3
27 13.6							14 25.7	28 13.0
40 9.0							33 11.2	33 10.9
31.9						Sales/Working Capital	62.0	82.5
536.2							392.3	-58.5
-41.6							-28.6	-20.2
						EBIT/Interest	(22) 7.4	(15) 4.4
							3.0	2.2
							1.1	.3
						Net Profit + Depr., Dep., Amort./Cur. Mat. L /T/D		
1.0						Fixed/Worth	.4	.6
1.8							1.2	5.0
-1.0							7.5	-3.1
1.9						Debt/Worth	.9	2.7
4.7							2.0	6.5
-2.7							13.3	-9.1
						% Profit Before Taxes/Tangible Net Worth	(22) 91.3	(12) 112.1
							29.3	38.8
							2.7	-2.1
10.8						% Profit Before Taxes/Total Assets	21.8	17.6
2.1							7.6	5.7
-11.9							1.1	-1.2
47.8						Sales/Net Fixed Assets	48.2	34.3
25.4							21.7	12.6
10.1							10.8	3.2
8.0						Sales/Total Assets	9.9	8.4
6.5							7.6	4.1
4.7							4.3	2.2
.4						% Depr., Dep., Amort./Sales	.5	.7
.9							(24) 1.0	(17) 1.4
1.3							1.9	2.0
						% Officers', Directors', Owners' Comp/Sales	.8	
							(16) 2.2	
							7.2	
10062M	79430M	183069M				Net Sales ($)	364631M	460484M
911M	12644M	27085M				Total Assets ($)	59929M	117165M

© RMA 2005

M = $ thousand   MM = $ million
See Pages 11 through 21 for Explanation of Ratios and Data

Comparative Historical Data | Current Data Sorted By Sales

4/1/02-3/31/03 ALL	4/1/03-3/31/04 ALL	4/1/04-3/31/05 ALL	Type of Statement	0-1MM	1-3MM	3-5MM	5-10MM	10-25MM	25MM & OVER
6	3	1	Unqualified						1
10	7	2	Reviewed				1		1
8	8	8	Compiled				6	2	
2	6	6	Tax Returns	1		1	1	2	
	2	4	Other	1	1	1	1	1	
					7 (4/1-9/30/04)			14 (10/1/04-3/31/05)	
26	26	21	**NUMBER OF STATEMENTS**	2	1	2	9	5	2
%	%	%	**ASSETS**	%	%	%	%	%	%
17.0	13.5	17.8	Cash & Equivalents						
11.0	12.1	14.7	Trade Receivables (net)						
19.7	24.3	19.5	Inventory						
1.9	5.4	3.9	All Other Current						
49.6	55.2	55.8	Total Current						
41.6	36.7	35.2	Fixed Assets (net)						
3.3	2.6	4.5	Intangibles (net)						
5.6	5.5	4.4	All Other Non-Current						
100.0	100.0	100.0	Total						
			LIABILITIES						
6.4	7.8	4.4	Notes Payable-Short Term						
3.4	5.1	3.3	Cur. Mat.-L/T/D						
21.6	24.3	30.9	Trade Payables						
.1	.2	.2	Income Taxes Payable						
10.8	8.0	14.6	All Other Current						
42.3	45.4	53.4	Total Current						
24.2	16.0	18.6	Long-Term Debt						
.3	.4	.4	Deferred Taxes						
5.8	13.9	16.2	All Other Non-Current						
27.4	24.4	11.4	Net Worth						
100.0	100.0	100.0	Total Liabilities & Net Worth						
			INCOME DATA						
100.0	100.0	100.0	Net Sales						
33.9	31.4	29.2	Gross Profit						
29.6	28.9	28.4	Operating Expenses						
4.3	2.5	.8	Operating Profit						
.5	.7	.4	All Other Expenses (net)						
3.8	1.8	.4	Profit Before Taxes						
			RATIOS						
2.3	2.0	2.3	Current						
1.2	1.6	1.1							
.7	.8	.9							
1.3	1.0	1.5	Quick						
.6	.5	.8							
.2	.1	.1							
0 UND	0 UND	0 UND	Sales/Receivables						
1 546.5	1 540.0	0 933.4							
15 24.8	20 18.2	13 29.0							
3 113.9	9 38.5	5 77.7	Cost of Sales/Inventory						
11 32.1	18 20.7	10 35.1							
21 17.2	45 8.2	21 17.7							
4 93.6	5 66.9	12 30.5	Cost of Sales/Payables						
9 41.1	19 19.6	23 16.0							
27 13.4	40 9.0	32 11.3							
34.3	15.9	32.6	Sales/Working Capital						
126.4	44.1	169.0							
-37.2	-48.5	-89.8							
12.5	11.4	18.4	EBIT/Interest						
(18) 4.1	(21) 5.3	(17) 2.6							
.6	.5	-1.9							
			Net Profit + Depr., Dep., Amort./Cur. Mat. L/T/D						
.5	.5	.8	Fixed/Worth						
1.9	1.1	1.7							
NM	5.4	NM							
.6	.7	1.4	Debt/Worth						
2.7	2.0	5.7							
NM	8.9	NM							
123.5	80.4	342.1	% Profit Before Taxes/Tangible Net Worth						
(20) 34.9	(22) 31.3	(16) 19.8							
5.0	6.1	5.3							
37.2	19.5	25.2	% Profit Before Taxes/Total Assets						
12.6	8.0	4.4							
-.4	-1.5	-7.1							
36.4	51.5	51.0	Sales/Net Fixed Assets						
21.6	18.5	31.6							
10.5	6.4	8.4							
10.9	9.4	10.5	Sales/Total Assets						
7.4	5.5	6.6							
4.2	2.8	4.3							
.8	.7	.4	% Depr., Dep., Amort./Sales						
(22) 1.0	(24) 1.4	(19) .8							
1.6	2.3	1.6							
1.4	1.4		% Officers', Directors', Owners' Comp/Sales						
(16) 3.2	(11) 2.5								
7.8									
496352M	861702M	272561M	Net Sales ($)	1336M	1634M	7473M	62831M	71543M	127744M
68140M	319351M	40640M	Total Assets ($)	879M	50M	791M	14176M	14812M	9932M

M = $ thousand   MM = $ million
See Pages 11 through 21 for Explanation of Ratios and Data

Current Data Sorted By Assets

Comparative Historical Data

						Type of Statement		
		1	2	1		Unqualified	2	2
		1	2			Reviewed	2	2
	1	1				Compiled	7	6
11						Tax Returns	5	7
3	2	2	3			Other	6	3
	11 (4/1-9/30/04)		19 (10/1/04-3/31/05)				4/1/00-3/31/01	4/1/01-3/31/02
0-500M	500M-2MM	2-10MM	10-50MM	50-100MM	100-250MM		ALL	ALL
14	3	5	7	1		**NUMBER OF STATEMENTS**	22	20
%	%	%	%	%	%	**ASSETS**	%	%
12.0						Cash & Equivalents	19.9	26.0
7.1					D	Trade Receivables (net)	9.1	11.7
16.2					A	Inventory	20.3	19.6
1.6					T	All Other Current	1.4	3.9
36.9					A	Total Current	50.6	61.3
44.7						Fixed Assets (net)	37.5	27.6
9.8					N	Intangibles (net)	4.8	1.3
8.7					O	All Other Non-Current	6.8	9.8
100.0					T	Total	100.0	100.0
					A	**LIABILITIES**		
12.5					V	Notes Payable-Short Term	8.2	7.4
5.4					A	Cur. Mat.-L/T/D	2.6	2.3
12.0					I	Trade Payables	14.7	14.1
.1					L	Income Taxes Payable	.3	.1
9.9					A	All Other Current	13.6	15.9
39.9					B	Total Current	39.3	39.7
52.8					L	Long-Term Debt	29.0	12.8
.0					E	Deferred Taxes	.2	.0
9.4						All Other Non-Current	5.5	5.8
−2.1						Net Worth	25.9	41.7
100.0						Total Liabilities & Net Worth	100.0	100.0
						INCOME DATA		
100.0						Net Sales	100.0	100.0
65.2						Gross Profit	50.4	49.1
67.0						Operating Expenses	47.4	44.1
−1.8						Operating Profit	3.1	4.9
1.7						All Other Expenses (net)	2.2	2.4
−3.5						Profit Before Taxes	.8	2.5
						RATIOS		
3.0							2.1	2.7
.9						Current	1.3	1.5
.5							.6	1.0
2.0							1.3	1.6
.7						Quick	.6	.9
.2							.1	.3
0	UND						0	UND	0	UND
0	UND					Sales/Receivables	1	295.4	0	UND
2	175.4						22	16.5	20	17.9
13	28.6						13	28.5	8	45.0
21	17.4					Cost of Sales/Inventory	46	7.9	41	8.9
54	6.8						78	4.7	78	4.7
12	31.4						15	24.2	2	153.3
36	10.1					Cost of Sales/Payables	29	12.5	10	36.6
63	5.8						53	6.9	35	10.5
27.9							6.1	5.9
−105.1						Sales/Working Capital	43.9	26.2
−13.9							−24.7	UND
3.6							4.3	8.5
(13) −.3						EBIT/Interest	(19) 2.0	(15) 3.6
−5.4							.1	2.0
						Net Profit + Depr., Dep., Amort./Cur. Mat. L./T/D		
.7							.3	.2
NM						Fixed/Worth	2.7	.6
−1.1							UND	2.3
1.0							1.0	.7
NM						Debt/Worth	3.0	1.4
−3.3							UND	9.9
						% Profit Before Taxes/Tangible Net Worth	87.3	39.6
							(17) 31.4	(19) 24.4
							−.7	.0
10.0							16.4	17.2
−.5						% Profit Before Taxes/Total Assets	7.4	9.6
−24.2							−3.3	.8
15.5							35.8	88.8
6.2						Sales/Net Fixed Assets	7.9	28.8
5.1							3.3	6.5
4.5							4.1	7.0
3.0						Sales/Total Assets	2.7	3.5
2.1							1.7	2.6
1.4							1.3	.2
(13) 4.0						% Depr., Dep., Amort./Sales	(19) 2.0	(19) .9
6.5							4.6	2.2
						% Officers', Directors', Owners' Comp/Sales		3.4
							(12) 7.1
							15.8
9824M	11652M	71489M	373214M	62863M		Net Sales ($)	181389M	149106M
3030M	3870M	20337M	138670M	71906M		Total Assets ($)	63586M	41218M

M = $ thousand   MM = $ million
See Pages 11 through 21 for Explanation of Ratios and Data

Comparative Historical Data					Current Data Sorted By Sales					

			Type of Statement							
3	4	4	Unqualified					1	1	3
4	3	3	Reviewed					1		2
4	6	2	Compiled			1	1			
16	9	11	Tax Returns	9	2		1		2	3
9	8	10	Other	1	3		1		2	3
4/1/02-3/31/03 ALL	4/1/03-3/31/04 ALL	4/1/04-3/31/05 ALL		11 (4/1-9/30/04)			19 (10/1/04-3/31/05)			
				0-1MM	1-3MM	3-5MM	5-10MM	10-25MM	25MM & OVER	
36	30	30	**NUMBER OF STATEMENTS**	10	5	1	2	4	8	
%	%	%	**ASSETS**	%	%	%	%	%	%	
11.1	12.4	9.6	Cash & Equivalents	14.9						
9.0	9.0	9.7	Trade Receivables (net)	5.8						
26.6	22.9	24.0	Inventory	16.8						
1.5	3.0	3.1	All Other Current	.4						
48.3	47.4	46.5	Total Current	37.9						
34.9	38.6	38.6	Fixed Assets (net)	45.1						
9.3	7.0	5.7	Intangibles (net)	8.5						
7.5	7.1	9.3	All Other Non-Current	8.5						
100.0	100.0	100.0	Total	100.0						
			LIABILITIES							
9.0	8.5	10.5	Notes Payable-Short Term	11.6						
3.8	4.9	4.2	Cur. Mat.-L/T/D	7.6						
13.9	15.2	14.8	Trade Payables	9.5						
.1	.1	.3	Income Taxes Payable	.0						
6.1	9.9	9.6	All Other Current	11.4						
32.8	38.7	39.3	Total Current	40.1						
29.6	22.6	33.8	Long-Term Debt	67.6						
.3	.6	.7	Deferred Taxes	.0						
10.5	6.2	19.1	All Other Non-Current	10.5						
26.9	32.1	7.1	Net Worth	−18.2						
100.0	100.0	100.0	Total Liabilities & Net Worth	100.0						
			INCOME DATA							
100.0	100.0	100.0	Net Sales	100.0						
53.2	47.8	50.6	Gross Profit	64.3						
49.9	45.4	50.4	Operating Expenses	68.5						
3.4	2.4	.2	Operating Profit	−4.1						
1.2	1.0	1.2	All Other Expenses (net)	2.3						
2.2	1.5	−1.0	Profit Before Taxes	−6.4						
			RATIOS							
2.7	2.0	2.4		3.8						
1.6	1.1	1.3	Current	1.0						
.8	.9	.7		.4						
1.2	.9	1.2		2.0						
.5	(29) .7	.5	Quick	.9						
.3	.1	.1		.2						
0 UND	0 UND	0 UND		0 UND						
2 195.2	1 366.0	1 353.5	Sales/Receivables	0 UND						
20 18.6	18 20.7	19 18.9		0 UND						
18 20.3	21 17.3	16 23.2		13 28.6						
43 8.4	50 7.3	54 6.8	Cost of Sales/Inventory	17 21.9						
121 3.0	94 3.9	99 3.7		62 5.9						
11 32.5	9 42.0	9 38.5		0 UND						
23 15.9	17 21.3	22 16.7	Cost of Sales/Payables	29 12.5						
54 6.8	68 5.3	60 6.1		45 8.2						
8.5	15.6	10.6		27.9						
22.4	61.6	37.5	Sales/Working Capital	NM						
−58.7	−45.6	−35.0		−13.9						
10.8	13.5	11.5								
(32) 2.5	(26) 1.4	(28) 2.3	EBIT/Interest							
.6	−.9	−.6								
			Net Profit + Depr., Dep., Amort./Cur. Mat. L/T/D							
.4	.4	.4		.6						
1.3	1.6	1.5	Fixed/Worth	−8.7						
4.0	9.7	−11.6		−.8						
1.0	.8	.9		1.6						
3.6	2.3	2.4	Debt/Worth	−20.8						
UND	26.9	−25.2		−2.0						
40.6	44.4	51.9	% Profit Before Taxes/Tangible Net Worth							
(27) 20.1	(24) 10.0	(22) 19.6								
9.6	.0	5.5								
11.6	18.5	11.4	% Profit Before Taxes/Total Assets	3.9						
2.9	3.0	4.3		−9.5						
−2.3	−4.4	−2.7		−43.2						
32.7	21.0	24.3	Sales/Net Fixed Assets	20.8						
6.8	6.9	6.2		6.5						
4.2	3.7	4.2		4.2						
4.5	5.0	4.0	Sales/Total Assets	4.7						
2.5	2.6	2.8		3.2						
2.0	1.8	1.7		1.7						
.9	.6	.7	% Depr., Dep., Amort./Sales							
(34) 2.4	(29) 1.9	(28) 2.5								
4.4	3.0	4.5								
2.7	5.7		% Officers', Directors', Owners' Comp/Sales							
(14) 3.7	(14) 9.2									
11.0	15.6									
458803M	424666M	529042M	Net Sales ($)	5138M	5835M	3322M	12793M	60843M	441111M	
176495M	126725M	237813M	Total Assets ($)	1498M	2356M	1281M	4317M	26563M	201798M	

M = $ thousand   MM = $ million
See Pages 11 through 21 for Explanation of Ratios and Data

Current Data Sorted By Assets

Comparative Historical Data

0-500M	500M-2MM	2-10MM	10-50MM	50-100MM	100-250MM	Type of Statement	6	7
	1	2	5	2	2	Unqualified	6	7
2	2	4	2			Reviewed	14	13
7	8	3	1		1	Compiled	19	26
43	20	3	3	1		Tax Returns	29	29
8	8	7	5	2	5	Other	31	36
	17 (4/1-9/30/04)			127 (10/1/04-3/31/05)			4/1/00-3/31/01 ALL	4/1/01-3/31/02 ALL
60	39	19	13	5	8	**NUMBER OF STATEMENTS**	99	111
%	%	%	%	%	%	**ASSETS**	%	%
13.2	10.6	9.1	4.3			Cash & Equivalents	10.7	10.9
2.3	11.3	16.7	9.2			Trade Receivables (net)	9.7	8.5
17.2	11.8	18.0	17.9			Inventory	21.9	20.3
2.6	2.8	2.9	3.4			All Other Current	3.0	3.6
35.3	36.5	46.6	34.7			Total Current	45.2	43.3
38.3	44.6	39.9	50.0			Fixed Assets (net)	43.2	39.3
16.3	11.4	4.3	8.2			Intangibles (net)	5.3	7.8
9.8	7.5	9.2	7.1			All Other Non-Current	6.2	9.6
100.0	100.0	100.0	100.0			Total	100.0	100.0
						LIABILITIES		
13.2	5.8	15.8	9.4			Notes Payable-Short Term	5.0	8.8
7.5	4.8	3.1	9.2			Cur. Mat.-LT/D	5.1	3.7
10.8	15.0	13.9	15.7			Trade Payables	17.6	14.3
.2	.0	.0	.2			Income Taxes Payable	.3	.1
12.7	15.2	8.1	10.0			All Other Current	9.1	12.5
44.5	40.9	40.8	44.5			Total Current	37.0	39.4
31.3	39.3	25.8	22.6			Long-Term Debt	27.8	29.9
.0	.0	.0	1.6			Deferred Taxes	.2	.1
22.8	12.6	2.3	5.3			All Other Non-Current	4.6	4.9
1.1	7.3	31.1	25.9			Net Worth	30.7	25.7
100.0	100.0	100.0	100.0			Total Liabilities & Net Worth	100.0	100.0
						INCOME DATA		
100.0	100.0	100.0	100.0			Net Sales	100.0	100.0
56.2	52.8	39.9	42.4			Gross Profit	39.4	41.8
52.4	48.1	36.8	37.5			Operating Expenses	35.6	37.8
3.8	4.7	3.1	4.9			Operating Profit	3.8	4.0
1.5	2.7	.1	.9			All Other Expenses (net)	1.0	.7
2.2	2.0	3.0	4.1			Profit Before Taxes	2.8	3.3
						RATIOS		
1.9	1.6	1.9	1.2			Current	2.9	2.3
.9	1.1	1.1	.9				1.5	1.2
.4	.5	.7	.4				.8	.7
1.1	1.4	1.1	.6			Quick	(97) 1.3	1.0
.3	.8	.7	.4				.5	.5
.0	.2	.3	.1				.2	.2
0 UND	0 UND	1 411.9	2 225.3			Sales/Receivables	0 UND	0 UND
0 UND	5 69.1	5 77.6	7 48.8				2 187.8	2 201.2
0 UND	23 15.7	39 9.3	33 10.9				23 15.7	15 23.7
6 61.2	10 37.8	10 38.2	9 42.4			Cost of Sales/Inventory	12 30.3	10 36.0
13 28.5	15 25.1	14 25.6	29 12.7				24 15.0	20 18.2
31 11.8	50 7.3	34 10.8	64 5.7				61 5.9	56 6.6
0 UND	11 34.0	9 38.7	17 21.5			Cost of Sales/Payables	6 65.4	5 68.7
8 45.5	27 13.5	21 17.1	30 12.0				19 19.3	17 21.2
33 11.0	65 5.6	40 9.1	69 5.3				33 11.1	34 10.9
24.2	16.8	19.1	22.7			Sales/Working Capital	10.7	11.8
UND	74.0	47.3	-55.0				34.0	85.5
-15.0	-17.4	-24.4	-8.9				-55.6	-40.7
(45) 8.7	(37) 5.8	(17) 7.6	8.9			EBIT/Interest	(86) 6.5	7.8
4.1	2.7	4.0	2.8				3.0	2.9
.5	-.7	2.3	2.0				1.1	1.1
						Net Profit + Depr., Dep., Amort./Cur. Mat. L /T/D	(16) 2.6	(13) 2.4
							1.6	1.3
							1.2	.4
.8	.8	.6	1.2			Fixed/Worth	.7	.5
7.3	3.3	1.1	2.7				1.8	1.7
-.7	-4.2	4.8	NM				4.6	5.6
1.0	1.5	1.1	2.1			Debt/Worth	.9	1.0
10.5	4.3	1.9	2.9				2.6	2.8
-2.7	-4.4	6.6	NM				7.8	10.5
(32) 119.4	(26) 65.6	(16) 37.5	(10) 37.1			% Profit Before Taxes/Tangible Net Worth	(78) 48.6	(91) 58.4
62.0	33.8	17.1	18.9				19.6	38.5
23.9	-1.5	4.5	10.6				3.9	6.8
26.8	13.0	16.0	8.7			% Profit Before Taxes/Total Assets	18.4	20.4
10.7	5.3	6.7	6.3				6.8	10.0
-2.5	-4.1	2.2	2.9				1.0	.8
32.6	23.2	22.3	9.1			Sales/Net Fixed Assets	26.1	36.4
14.6	6.2	11.5	6.7				8.8	10.7
5.0	2.9	6.1	3.8				4.4	4.1
7.4	4.4	4.8	3.8			Sales/Total Assets	5.5	6.0
3.5	3.0	3.9	2.6				3.4	3.6
2.2	1.7	2.1	1.5				2.2	2.0
(47) 1.5	(36) 1.0	.8	1.7			% Depr., Dep., Amort./Sales	(90) .8	(85) .7
2.1	2.2	1.7	2.4				1.7	1.8
5.2	6.3	3.8	4.0				3.1	3.5
(28) 1.8	(14) 2.3					% Officers', Directors', Owners' Comp/Sales	(42) 2.1	(46) 2.4
5.0	3.4						3.3	4.9
8.3	8.8						6.9	9.0
63915M	152193M	379674M	901286M	1957433M	6235588M	Net Sales ($)	2835967M	3062246M
13630M	39807M	93041M	262646M	368135M	1277600M	Total Assets ($)	951943M	1085150M

M = $ thousand   MM = $ million
See Pages 11 through 21 for Explanation of Ratios and Data

Comparative Historical Data   Current Data Sorted By Sales

Type of Statement									
Unqualified	11	12	12			2			10
Reviewed	11	15	10	1	1	1	1	4	2
Compiled	14	26	20	4	6	1	5	2	2
Tax Returns	39	55	67	34	25	3	1	2	2
Other	38	41	35	5	8	1	4	4	12
	4/1/02-3/31/03	4/1/03-3/31/04	4/1/04-3/31/05	17 (4/1-9/30/04)			127 (10/1/04-3/31/05)		
	ALL	ALL	ALL	0-1MM	1-3MM	3-5MM	5-10MM	10-25MM	25MM & OVER
NUMBER OF STATEMENTS	113	149	144	44	40	8	12	12	28
ASSETS	%	%	%	%	%	%	%	%	%
Cash & Equivalents	12.0	13.6	11.5	14.3	11.4		11.1	9.7	10.9
Trade Receivables (net)	8.1	8.0	7.4	2.1	4.8		15.7	19.3	10.1
Inventory	21.6	20.4	15.6	13.1	12.9		19.6	14.6	17.0
All Other Current	1.4	2.4	3.0	2.0	3.8		2.5	4.1	3.2
Total Current	43.1	44.5	37.5	31.5	32.9		48.9	47.7	41.2
Fixed Assets (net)	40.4	37.3	41.7	41.9	43.3		33.4	38.2	45.8
Intangibles (net)	9.4	10.6	11.7	17.5	15.3		6.8	1.7	3.8
All Other Non-Current	7.1	7.6	9.1	8.9	8.4		11.0	12.4	9.2
Total	100.0	100.0	100.0	100.0	100.0		100.0	100.0	100.0
LIABILITIES									
Notes Payable-Short Term	4.8	7.6	10.0	8.4	11.4		15.6	7.9	3.6
Cur. Mat.-L/T/D	3.4	5.4	5.8	6.6	7.9		2.7	3.6	5.1
Trade Payables	14.1	12.6	12.4	4.8	13.9		20.6	16.3	15.6
Income Taxes Payable	.1	.3	.2	.2	.1		.1	.0	.3
All Other Current	12.4	13.5	12.0	10.8	16.0		6.1	10.3	13.6
Total Current	34.9	39.4	40.5	30.8	49.3		45.1	38.2	38.2
Long-Term Debt	29.8	29.0	29.5	43.3	30.2		17.0	17.7	17.4
Deferred Taxes	.2	.2	.3	.0	.0		.0	.2	1.5
All Other Non-Current	7.4	7.5	13.8	16.1	18.9		3.9	2.3	14.1
Net Worth	27.7	23.9	15.9	9.6	1.7		34.0	41.6	28.8
Total Liabilities & Net Worth	100.0	100.0	100.0	100.0	100.0		100.0	100.0	100.0
INCOME DATA									
Net Sales	100.0	100.0	100.0	100.0	100.0		100.0	100.0	100.0
Gross Profit	43.7	44.2	51.5	60.7	53.4		50.3	39.9	41.8
Operating Expenses	39.4	40.6	47.1	55.9	49.4		45.2	36.6	37.2
Operating Profit	4.2	3.6	4.4	4.8	4.0		5.1	3.4	4.6
All Other Expenses (net)	1.9	.8	1.5	2.3	2.3		.1	.2	.1
Profit Before Taxes	2.3	2.8	3.0	2.6	1.7		4.9	3.2	4.5
RATIOS									
	2.1	2.3	2.0	2.1	1.6		1.6	1.5	3.1
Current	1.4	1.3	1.1	1.1	.9		1.1	1.1	1.8
	.8	.5	.5	.4	.4		.8	.7	.9
	1.1	1.2	1.2	1.7	1.2		1.1	1.1	1.9
Quick	(112) .6	.5	.6	.6	.4		.7	.6	.8
	.3	.3	.3	.1	.0		.2	.3	.3
	0 UND	0 UND	0 UND	0 UND	0 UND		0 838.7	1 349.6	0 UND
Sales/Receivables	2 166.5	1 514.7	1 413.6	0 UND	0 UND		4 94.5	7 55.5	4 84.4
	13 28.2	9 40.3	8 43.4	0 UND	6 59.2		32 11.3	34 10.6	11 34.0
	10 36.3	9 40.8	8 44.6	8 45.7	4 85.5		12 29.6	9 40.7	10 38.0
Cost of Sales/Inventory	21 17.0	21 17.6	14 25.7	15 24.7	10 35.8		19 19.7	16 22.7	15 24.4
	55 6.7	55 6.7	39 9.3	30 12.3	37 9.8		66 5.6	38 9.7	50 7.4
	7 51.6	5 70.8	4 92.9	0 UND	3 115.6		21 17.3	11 33.4	0 UND
Cost of Sales/Payables	19 18.8	16 22.1	20 18.6	8 43.3	11 32.3		33 11.1	21 17.7	19 18.8
	36 10.3	39 9.3	40 9.2	34 10.6	61 6.0		54 6.7	51 7.1	33 11.1
	12.8	11.5	19.4	15.5	35.1		15.1	17.1	13.7
Sales/Working Capital	43.5	54.1	105.3	UND	NM		NM	64.5	43.7
	-59.3	-18.3	-18.9	-16.5	-12.2		-35.8	-24.1	NM
	7.4	10.0	8.0	7.4	9.0		6.5	15.0	19.4
EBIT/Interest	(87) 1.8	(127) 2.7	(118) 3.4	(32) 3.3	(36) 4.3		(11) 3.1	(10) 3.7	(21) 3.1
	.6	.6	1.2	.7	-.2		.9	2.7	2.0
Net Profit + Depr., Dep.,	36.4	3.7	15.9						
Amort./Cur. Mat. L/T/D	(10) 3.1	(17) 1.6	(15) 2.5						
	1.7	.7	1.1						
	.5	.5	.7	.8	1.0		.3	.3	.4
Fixed/Worth	1.6	1.6	2.0	7.3	12.7		1.1	.7	.8
	11.0	UND	-2.4	-.8	-.7		3.1	1.5	2.5
	1.0	1.1	1.0	1.4	.9		1.5	.8	.2
Debt/Worth	2.4	3.0	3.1	10.2	13.8		3.0	1.7	1.2
	104.3	-104.0	-5.5	-2.7	-2.7		4.6	3.2	3.2
% Profit Before Taxes/Tangible	60.5	58.9	88.5	94.0	174.6		86.5	30.9	72.0
Net Worth	(86) 27.5	(111) 25.6	(97) 31.3	(24) 37.1	(23) 62.8		(11) 19.7	19.3	(24) 18.7
	1.0	8.1	11.4	18.1	26.6		-.3	4.5	11.8
% Profit Before Taxes/Total	19.5	17.5	22.1	23.8	25.1		18.8	14.1	35.5
Assets	5.2	6.6	7.8	9.4	9.9		5.7	6.5	8.4
	-1.1	-1.2	.6	-1.9	-5.3		.9	1.7	2.6
	26.0	26.6	22.2	21.6	26.6		39.1	30.0	19.1
Sales/Net Fixed Assets	8.9	9.8	11.2	6.8	13.0		13.8	12.2	10.8
	4.1	4.6	4.3	3.2	5.9		6.4	3.4	4.4
	5.2	4.9	5.5	3.3	6.9		4.8	4.6	8.0
Sales/Total Assets	2.9	3.0	3.3	2.2	4.0		4.4	3.6	4.4
	1.9	1.9	2.0	1.5	2.7		2.9	2.1	2.3
	1.1	1.1	1.0	2.1	1.1		.9	.6	.8
% Depr., Dep., Amort./Sales	(91) 2.3	(128) 2.1	(122) 2.1	(35) 4.2	(35) 1.8		(10) 1.0	1.6	(22) 1.9
	4.6	5.2	5.0	8.4	5.4		4.3	4.2	3.5
	1.7	1.3	1.5	1.6	2.4				
% Officers', Directors',	(49) 3.2	(58) 3.6	(56) 3.4	(15) 5.0	(21) 5.1				
Owners' Comp/Sales	7.1	6.9	8.6	12.9	8.0				
Net Sales ($)	3984586M	8270538M	9690089M	26611M	75805M	33209M	86141M	212092M	9256231M
Total Assets ($)	1305885M	1823912M	2054859M	12463M	21314M	20966M	24227M	74559M	1901330M

M = $ thousand   MM = $ million
See Pages 11 through 21 for Explanation of Ratios and Data

Current Data Sorted By Assets   Comparative Historical Data

Type of Statement	0-500M	500M-2MM	2-10MM	10-50MM	50-100MM	100-250MM		4/1/00-3/31/01 ALL	4/1/01-3/31/02 ALL
Unqualified	1	1	3	4				8	8
Reviewed	14	8	14	2				18	25
Compiled	64	26	9	1				59	63
Tax Returns	15	57	10					52	39
Other		14	11	3	1	1		29	43
	53 (4/1-9/30/04)			206 (10/1/04-3/31/05)				166	178
NUMBER OF STATEMENTS	94	106	47	10	1	1		166	178
	%	%	%	%	%	%	**ASSETS**	%	%
Cash & Equivalents	11.8	13.3	10.5	2.4				11.6	12.9
Trade Receivables (net)	1.0	1.5	4.5	3.7				1.9	2.3
Inventory	52.2	48.4	42.6	53.4				50.2	45.8
All Other Current	1.4	2.3	1.7	2.0				1.0	1.9
Total Current	66.5	65.4	59.4	61.5				64.8	62.8
Fixed Assets (net)	12.9	17.9	23.9	14.1				19.2	18.2
Intangibles (net)	12.8	8.5	8.5	17.6				8.5	11.3
All Other Non-Current	7.8	8.2	8.2	6.8				7.5	7.7
Total	100.0	100.0	100.0	100.0				100.0	100.0
							LIABILITIES		
Notes Payable-Short Term	7.6	8.0	9.4	13.8				7.5	6.7
Cur. Mat.-L/T/D	3.3	3.0	3.2	2.8				3.8	3.8
Trade Payables	18.8	24.8	19.0	25.8				20.8	21.4
Income Taxes Payable	.1	.1	.2	.3				.4	.3
All Other Current	12.3	11.2	9.2	5.7				12.7	8.7
Total Current	42.1	47.1	40.9	48.4				45.2	40.8
Long-Term Debt	26.8	14.9	19.0	13.9				20.0	19.7
Deferred Taxes	.0	.6	.2	.0				.1	.1
All Other Non-Current	9.8	9.5	4.3	3.3				8.5	8.8
Net Worth	21.3	27.9	35.6	34.3				26.2	30.6
Total Liabilities & Net Worth	100.0	100.0	100.0	100.0				100.0	100.0
							INCOME DATA		
Net Sales	100.0	100.0	100.0	100.0				100.0	100.0
Gross Profit	22.7	22.0	24.0	23.8				22.2	23.3
Operating Expenses	21.5	20.0	21.5	21.0				20.0	21.2
Operating Profit	1.2	2.1	2.4	2.8				2.2	2.0
All Other Expenses (net)	–.6	–.4	–.1	.3				.0	.0
Profit Before Taxes	1.8	2.4	2.5	2.5				2.2	2.0
							RATIOS		
Current	3.6	2.8	2.5	1.7				2.8	3.3
	1.8	1.6	1.4	1.2				1.5	1.7
	1.1	1.0	1.1	1.0				1.0	1.0
Quick	.8	.7	.9					.7	.9
	(90) .3	(103) .3	.3					(163) .3	(177) .4
	.1	.1	.1					.1	.1
Sales/Receivables	0 UND	0 UND	0 999.8	1 267.9				0 UND	0 UND
	0 UND	0 UND	1 382.0	2 153.2				0 UND	0 UND
	0 812.4	1 389.1	5 67.2	7 53.3				1 331.8	2 153.2
Cost of Sales/Inventory	31 11.6	41 8.8	43 8.6	53 6.8				35 10.5	33 11.0
	46 7.9	60 6.1	57 6.4	70 5.2				48 7.6	54 6.8
	70 5.2	85 4.3	86 4.3	86 4.3				66 5.6	73 5.0
Cost of Sales/Payables	1 364.5	9 39.5	10 37.4	20 18.1				3 126.5	2 150.0
	12 30.6	26 14.1	28 13.0	33 11.1				18 20.3	22 16.6
	31 11.6	46 7.9	43 8.5	50 7.2				36 10.1	39 9.4
Sales/Working Capital	9.8	8.2	9.0	11.6				10.2	8.7
	20.0	14.6	17.4	63.6				23.4	18.5
	203.9	–999.8	83.0	–514.9				–269.2	136.8
EBIT/Interest	11.4	15.6	17.7	8.1				7.0	5.8
	(62) 3.1	(89) 3.8	(43) 3.8	3.6				(142) 3.1	(156) 3.0
	–.8	1.6	2.1	3.0				1.7	1.8
Net Profit + Depr., Dep., Amort./Cur. Mat. L/T/D			5.4					5.5	6.3
			(13) 2.5					(21) 2.1	(22) 2.7
			1.4					1.7	1.2
Fixed/Worth	.1	.1	.3	.2				.2	.2
	.5	.5	1.0	.7				.9	.6
	–.6	–6.5	3.7	NM				–3.7	6.7
Debt/Worth	.8	.9	.8	1.7				1.1	1.2
	5.4	2.7	2.2	2.0				3.6	2.9
	–4.5	–20.9	8.9	NM				–9.2	UND
% Profit Before Taxes/Tangible Net Worth	73.0	50.6	38.2					59.4	49.6
	(56) 38.9	(74) 25.2	(40) 21.5					(116) 23.4	(134) 19.5
	13.3	10.2	12.0					8.9	6.0
% Profit Before Taxes/Total Assets	23.4	13.4	12.1	10.6				12.6	13.3
	9.1	6.1	6.6	6.7				6.2	5.2
	.0	1.9	2.5	3.6				1.8	1.8
Sales/Net Fixed Assets	252.7	117.9	56.1	53.4				93.3	96.4
	64.4	37.9	16.9	40.2				35.1	31.7
	26.7	14.6	7.8	22.2				13.1	13.2
Sales/Total Assets	7.5	4.7	4.4	4.0				6.1	5.4
	4.9	3.8	3.6	3.4				4.1	4.1
	3.0	2.8	2.4	2.7				3.0	2.8
% Depr., Dep., Amort./Sales	.5	.3	.5	.7				.3	.4
	(59) .8	(84) .7	(43) 1.0	.8				(132) .7	(151) .8
	1.7	1.4	1.4	1.0				1.4	1.3
% Officers', Directors', Owners' Comp/Sales	2.7	1.6	1.1					1.3	1.7
	(56) 4.0	(59) 2.3	(19) 1.8					(101) 2.6	(98) 2.6
	5.8	3.6	3.1					4.4	4.4
Net Sales ($)	127284M	439975M	713167M	693056M	116003M	1236050M		3887787M	2379452M
Total Assets ($)	24106M	107828M	207940M	201299M	69374M	246952M		922775M	728649M

M = $ thousand   MM = $ million
See Pages 11 through 21 for Explanation of Ratios and Data

Comparative Historical Data | Current Data Sorted By Sales

12	11	8	Type of Statement		1			2	5
12	11	8	Unqualified		1			2	5
23	23	25	Reviewed		1			12	2
67	67	50	Compiled	2	21	6	12	6	3
107	130	131	Tax Returns	38	56	25	9	3	2
49	48	45	Other	9	11	6	5	6	8
4/1/02-3/31/03 ALL	4/1/03-3/31/04 ALL	4/1/04-3/31/05 ALL		53 (4/1-9/30/04)			206 (10/1/04-3/31/05)		
				0-1MM	1-3MM	3-5MM	5-10MM	10-25MM	25MM & OVER
258	279	259	**NUMBER OF STATEMENTS**	49	90	39	34	29	18
%	%	%	**ASSETS**	%	%	%	%	%	%
11.9	10.5	11.7	Cash & Equivalents	7.8	13.9	13.2	12.8	12.0	5.8
2.0	2.0	2.0	Trade Receivables (net)	1.6	.9	2.1	1.5	3.7	6.0
48.5	50.2	48.7	Inventory	49.8	47.1	52.1	54.6	42.2	46.0
1.0	1.1	1.8	All Other Current	1.5	1.4	3.1	.9	3.0	1.9
63.4	63.8	64.3	Total Current	60.7	63.3	70.5	69.9	60.9	59.7
18.2	17.8	17.0	Fixed Assets (net)	19.2	14.8	18.7	13.7	21.6	17.7
12.2	11.1	10.7	Intangibles (net)	13.2	12.8	3.6	7.3	9.8	16.1
6.1	7.3	8.0	All Other Non-Current	6.8	9.1	7.2	9.1	7.7	6.5
100.0	100.0	100.0	Total	100.0	100.0	100.0	100.0	100.0	100.0
			LIABILITIES						
8.1	8.9	8.3	Notes Payable-Short Term	9.2	4.8	11.3	6.4	15.0	9.8
3.5	2.9	3.2	Cur. Mat.-L/T/D	6.6	1.9	2.2	2.3	3.1	4.0
20.6	20.2	21.5	Trade Payables	13.3	23.1	24.9	25.3	20.6	22.9
.2	.5	.1	Income Taxes Payable	.0	.1	.0	.3	.5	.0
10.4	10.8	11.0	All Other Current	11.8	12.2	10.7	8.8	10.8	7.9
42.8	43.3	44.1	Total Current	40.9	42.1	49.1	43.0	50.0	44.5
20.6	23.1	20.0	Long-Term Debt	34.9	18.1	16.4	15.0	15.9	13.3
.0	.0	.3	Deferred Taxes	.0	.7	.0	.1	.2	.1
9.3	8.2	8.4	All Other Non-Current	15.6	9.2	8.9	2.7	2.9	3.3
27.2	25.4	27.1	Net Worth	8.6	29.8	25.7	39.3	30.9	38.7
100.0	100.0	100.0	Total Liabilities & Net Worth	100.0	100.0	100.0	100.0	100.0	100.0
			INCOME DATA						
100.0	100.0	100.0	Net Sales	100.0	100.0	100.0	100.0	100.0	100.0
23.0	23.3	22.7	Gross Profit	25.3	22.1	20.7	21.0	24.4	23.3
20.9	21.7	20.8	Operating Expenses	24.4	20.2	18.8	19.0	21.4	21.6
2.1	1.6	1.9	Operating Profit	1.0	1.9	1.8	2.0	3.0	1.7
.1	-.3	-.3	All Other Expenses (net)	-.5	-.5	-.6	.3	-.1	-.2
2.0	1.9	2.2	Profit Before Taxes	1.4	2.5	2.5	1.7	3.1	2.0
			RATIOS						
3.2	3.0	2.7		3.2	3.1	3.0	2.5	2.4	1.7
1.6	1.6	1.6	Current	1.8	1.8	1.4	1.8	1.3	1.3
1.0	1.0	1.0		.9	1.1	1.0	1.0	.9	1.0
.8	.8	.7		.7	.9	.6	.6	1.0	.4
(254) .3	(275) .3	(251) .3	Quick	(47) .2	(86) .3	(38) .2	.3	.3	(17) .2
.1	.1	.1		.1	.1	.1	.1	.1	.1
0 UND	0 UND	0 UND		0 UND	0 UND	0 UND	0 UND	0 999.8	0 999.8
0 UND	0 UND	0 UND	Sales/Receivables	0 UND	0 UND	0 999.8	0 999.8	1 347.1	2 176.5
1 288.4	2 208.0	1 277.0		1 292.8	1 720.3	1 278.3	2 176.3	3 121.5	7 53.8
38 9.7	37 9.9	38 9.7		39 9.4	38 9.7	34 10.9	40 9.1	23 15.9	42 8.6
53 6.9	55 6.6	55 6.6	Cost of Sales/Inventory	60 6.1	57 6.4	57 6.5	55 6.7	45 8.1	56 6.5
72 5.1	80 4.6	80 4.6		92 3.9	83 4.4	80 4.6	80 4.6	61 6.0	69 5.3
0 852.8	1 495.0	5 68.9		0 UND	7 49.1	8 45.1	3 141.2	8 43.7	15 23.7
19 19.1	19 19.2	23 15.7	Cost of Sales/Payables	9 42.4	25 14.4	27 13.7	29 12.8	25 14.5	27 13.7
37 9.8	39 9.3	40 9.2		31 12.0	45 8.0	34 10.7	47 7.7	32 11.3	36 10.1
9.6	9.0	9.0		8.9	7.8	12.2	8.3	10.5	12.9
17.8	19.3	18.4	Sales/Working Capital	16.5	14.2	26.2	14.6	18.1	27.1
486.0	441.2	320.9		-67.2	85.1	-275.8	NM	-83.5	-527.4
9.0	8.0	14.0		4.2	13.5	13.0	15.4	30.7	11.7
(209) 3.7	(231) 3.1	(206) 3.6	EBIT/Interest	(32) 2.1	(63) 3.3	(35) 3.7	(32) 4.8	(27) 6.9	(17) 3.3
1.3	1.0	1.3		-1.3	1.1	1.6	1.6	2.9	1.9
5.5	4.7	3.9	Net Profit + Depr., Dep., Amort./Cur. Mat. L/T/D						
(31) 3.5	(24) 2.4	(26) 2.0							
1.1	.9	1.1							
.2	.2	.1		.1	.1	.2	.1	.3	.2
.8	.9	.5	Fixed/Worth	8.8	.4	.5	.3	1.0	.7
-3.9	-3.5	-3.1		-.3	-4.1	-3.5	1.4	NM	2.4
1.2	1.2	.9		.9	1.1	1.2	.8	.8	1.7
3.3	3.7	2.8	Debt/Worth	-31.6	3.1	2.8	1.7	1.9	2.0
-15.1	-17.1	-9.4		-3.0	-9.8	-30.5	5.3	NM	9.4
66.0	66.8	50.0	% Profit Before Taxes/Tangible Net Worth	76.6	61.2	55.4	39.1	46.5	35.3
(180) 23.6	(198) 30.8	(179) 29.2		(23) 41.9	(60) 33.8	(29) 24.9	(30) 19.2	(22) 31.4	(15) 23.9
7.4	8.0	12.0		18.6	10.8	13.2	8.5	12.7	11.5
15.6	14.2	15.5	% Profit Before Taxes/Total Assets	18.6	15.5	14.0	11.9	17.5	11.5
6.3	5.7	6.6		4.9	6.2	8.3	6.1	9.6	6.0
.9	.6	1.0		-3.6	.8	2.7	1.9	4.1	1.4
130.6	111.1	119.3	Sales/Net Fixed Assets	255.2	147.3	101.6	119.4	71.7	76.8
37.8	39.3	42.4		38.6	45.2	55.4	60.8	23.7	34.3
14.3	14.7	14.9		10.8	15.6	16.9	23.5	13.8	12.9
5.7	5.4	5.3	Sales/Total Assets	6.0	5.4	6.0	5.3	5.9	4.6
4.0	3.9	3.9		3.2	3.5	4.3	4.4	4.3	3.7
2.7	2.8	2.8		2.1	2.6	3.6	3.7	3.2	3.1
.4	.3	.4	% Depr., Dep., Amort./Sales	.5	.4	.3	.3	.3	.6
(196) .8	(218) .8	(197) .8		(33) 1.8	(61) .9	(32) .6	(27) .7	(27) .8	(17) .9
1.6	1.4	1.4		3.5	1.3	1.2	1.0	1.3	1.3
1.6	1.6	1.6	% Officers', Directors', Owners' Comp/Sales	2.7	2.3	1.8	1.2	1.1	
(141) 2.7	(158) 2.4	(139) 2.8		(29) 4.2	(48) 3.5	(18) 2.3	(21) 2.2	(15) 1.6	
3.9	4.1	4.5		6.1	5.5	2.9	3.4	1.9	
2716956M	2481219M	3325535M	Net Sales ($)	31998M	166080M	153665M	233472M	488888M	2251432M
825839M	699740M	857499M	Total Assets ($)	12141M	58727M	43303M	59265M	129127M	554936M

© RMA 2005   **M = $ thousand   MM = $ million**
See Pages 11 through 21 for Explanation of Ratios and Data

Current Data Sorted By Assets   Comparative Historical Data

						Type of Statement		
1	4	6	1		2	Unqualified	13	14
9	12	2	2			Reviewed	24	19
11	43	17	1			Compiled	73	63
16	51	10				Tax Returns	42	50
16	21	23	9	3	2	Other	51	52

0-500M	500M-2MM	2-10MM	10-50MM	50-100MM	100-250MM		4/1/00-3/31/01 ALL	4/1/01-3/31/02 ALL
	54 (4/1-9/30/04)		206 (10/1/04-3/31/05)					
43	125	66	18	4	4	NUMBER OF STATEMENTS	203	198
%	%	%	%	%	%	ASSETS	%	%
17.0	11.3	11.7	10.2			Cash & Equivalents	9.3	10.8
14.2	24.7	29.3	24.1			Trade Receivables (net)	23.3	22.4
44.0	39.6	29.4	34.4			Inventory	41.0	42.4
4.0	1.3	2.6	5.6			All Other Current	2.4	2.9
79.3	76.9	72.9	74.4			Total Current	76.0	78.5
13.1	11.8	15.7	11.8			Fixed Assets (net)	13.0	12.5
2.4	5.0	3.5	7.8			Intangibles (net)	5.6	4.2
5.2	6.3	7.9	6.1			All Other Non-Current	5.4	4.8
100.0	100.0	100.0	100.0			Total	100.0	100.0
						LIABILITIES		
10.2	6.9	10.5	5.4			Notes Payable-Short Term	7.9	7.3
3.7	3.1	2.8	2.3			Cur. Mat.-L/T/D	3.2	3.3
24.8	21.4	23.3	24.6			Trade Payables	23.4	24.6
.0	.1	.1	.2			Income Taxes Payable	.2	.2
11.2	7.8	5.4	11.1			All Other Current	8.7	7.7
49.8	39.2	42.0	43.6			Total Current	43.4	43.2
14.9	15.1	11.6	12.3			Long-Term Debt	17.6	16.2
.0	.0	.2	.3			Deferred Taxes	.2	.1
17.5	3.0	5.0	1.8			All Other Non-Current	5.3	6.1
17.7	42.6	41.1	41.9			Net Worth	33.5	34.4
100.0	100.0	100.0	100.0			Total Liabilities & Net Worth	100.0	100.0
						INCOME DATA		
100.0	100.0	100.0	100.0			Net Sales	100.0	100.0
30.2	23.9	28.3	19.3			Gross Profit	25.4	26.2
27.0	21.3	24.0	17.4			Operating Expenses	23.0	23.1
3.2	2.6	4.3	1.9			Operating Profit	2.4	3.1
.1	.2	-.2	-.6			All Other Expenses (net)	.1	.4
3.1	2.4	4.5	2.6			Profit Before Taxes	2.3	2.7
						RATIOS		
3.0	3.6	3.0	2.2			Current	2.8	3.1
1.8	2.2	1.8	1.9				1.9	2.0
1.1	1.4	1.3	1.2				1.4	1.4
1.1	1.7	1.7	1.1			Quick	1.3	1.2
.6	1.0	.9	.7			(202)	.8	.8
.3	.5	.6	.5				.5	.5
1 244.8	9 41.2	14 26.1	12 31.7			Sales/Receivables	10 35.8	9 40.7
10 37.8	17 21.6	23 15.9	16 22.3				17 21.7	16 23.3
16 22.8	24 15.1	38 9.7	28 12.9				26 14.2	24 15.1
26 13.8	27 13.7	22 16.3	12 29.3			Cost of Sales/Inventory	28 13.1	28 13.1
36 10.0	33 11.2	34 10.7	37 9.8				41 9.0	38 9.7
60 6.1	44 8.2	43 8.6	67 5.4				55 6.6	56 6.5
10 35.3	9 39.7	15 24.0	14 25.7			Cost of Sales/Payables	15 25.0	13 29.2
18 20.8	16 22.6	24 15.4	29 12.5				20 18.1	21 17.2
36 12.8	28 12.8	42 8.7	37 9.8				31 11.6	36 10.2
8.5	8.9	8.2	9.8			Sales/Working Capital	8.9	8.1
17.0	13.3	14.4	11.3				13.6	12.3
111.1	28.0	29.3	46.0				29.2	25.7
26.1	14.3	26.1	25.1			EBIT/Interest	10.1	11.1
(30) 7.0	(103) 6.1	(61) 9.6	(15) 12.0				(178) 4.5	(171) 4.4
.9	1.9	2.5	3.6				1.5	1.7
	9.2	6.2				Net Profit + Depr., Dep.,		7.4
	(16) 5.7	(13) 2.9				Amort./Cur. Mat. L/T/D	(45) 2.4	(33) 1.8
	1.3	1.2					1.4	1.1
.1	.1	.2	.2			Fixed/Worth	.1	.1
.5	.2	.4	.2				.4	.4
13.8	.6	.8	.8				1.7	1.0
.9	.6	.9	1.0			Debt/Worth	.8	.8
3.2	1.3	1.6	1.9				1.8	1.9
-164.0	5.3	4.1	3.8				20.3	6.5
147.5	49.2	62.0	42.8			% Profit Before Taxes/Tangible	50.0	53.6
(32) 66.2	(110) 21.0	(62) 29.7	(17) 29.6			Net Worth	(161) 23.4	(167) 24.2
24.4	6.5	12.8	8.3				7.8	8.0
36.8	19.2	24.9	16.0			% Profit Before Taxes/Total	17.0	18.3
16.1	8.2	10.6	8.9			Assets	8.4	9.1
-.4	2.1	3.3	2.4				1.8	2.1
123.1	143.9	62.5	89.1			Sales/Net Fixed Assets	125.8	132.5
48.3	75.6	32.4	46.2				52.0	53.6
29.4	36.1	19.7	21.5				25.0	26.7
7.7	6.6	5.1	5.2			Sales/Total Assets	6.1	6.4
5.5	5.4	4.1	4.2				4.8	4.7
3.5	4.2	3.2	3.1				3.6	3.6
.3	.2	.5	.6			% Depr., Dep., Amort./Sales	.3	.3
(32) .5	(93) .4	(57) .7	(14) .8				(165) .5	(164) .5
1.1	1.0	1.1	1.1				.9	.9
.7	1.8	.7				% Officers', Directors',	2.2	1.9
(13) 3.7	(81) 3.5	(32) 1.9				Owners' Comp/Sales	(110) 3.4	(113) 3.2
7.3	6.3	4.0					5.0	5.9
76715M	718703M	1067809M	1599690M	1090133M	2417013M	Net Sales ($)	4140120M	3554242M
13067M	134139M	263527M	350740M	300565M	643857M	Total Assets ($)	1465235M	937743M

M = $ thousand   MM = $ million
See Pages 11 through 21 for Explanation of Ratios and Data

Comparative Historical Data / Current Data Sorted By Sales

Hist 4/1/02-3/31/03 ALL	Hist 4/1/03-3/31/04 ALL	Hist 4/1/04-3/31/05 ALL		0-1MM	1-3MM	3-5MM	5-10MM	10-25MM	25MM & OVER
			Type of Statement						
12	23	14	Unqualified				1	2	11
23	22	23	Reviewed				5	12	4
79	87	72	Compiled	2	16	12	27	12	3
68	79	77	Tax Returns	6	16	23	25	6	1
61	60	74	Other	7	9	9	14	16	19
				54 (4/1-9/30/04)			206 (10/1/04-3/31/05)		
243	271	260	**NUMBER OF STATEMENTS**	15	41	46	72	48	38
%	%	%	**ASSETS**	%	%	%	%	%	%
11.6	10.5	12.1	Cash & Equivalents	12.4	15.4	13.0	10.5	11.7	11.1
23.6	24.9	23.7	Trade Receivables (net)	12.1	17.9	20.1	27.7	29.8	23.4
39.8	37.4	37.7	Inventory	32.3	39.5	41.5	40.0	32.1	36.2
3.0	2.4	2.4	All Other Current	4.2	3.4	1.1	1.7	2.5	3.0
78.0	75.2	75.9	Total Current	60.9	76.2	75.7	80.0	76.0	73.8
12.6	13.8	13.4	Fixed Assets (net)	22.4	13.4	13.0	11.3	12.9	14.7
3.9	4.6	4.3	Intangibles (net)	1.3	5.5	6.3	3.0	3.2	5.6
5.6	6.5	6.4	All Other Non-Current	15.4	4.9	4.9	5.7	7.9	5.9
100.0	100.0	100.0	Total	100.0	100.0	100.0	100.0	100.0	100.0
			LIABILITIES						
8.5	7.4	8.4	Notes Payable-Short Term	13.1	10.1	2.6	8.0	12.3	7.8
2.9	3.8	3.0	Cur. Mat.-L/T/D	4.2	3.6	2.2	2.7	3.9	2.3
24.3	25.3	22.5	Trade Payables	8.8	24.2	20.8	23.0	25.9	23.3
.2	.3	.1	Income Taxes Payable	.1	.0	.3	.0	.2	.1
7.4	9.0	8.0	All Other Current	24.8	5.5	9.3	6.6	5.0	9.1
43.4	45.8	42.1	Total Current	50.9	43.5	35.1	40.2	47.2	42.7
14.1	13.9	14.3	Long-Term Debt	15.9	15.1	15.9	13.7	11.1	15.8
.1	.1	.1	Deferred Taxes	.0	.0	.0	.0	.3	.2
3.7	6.0	5.9	All Other Non-Current	11.5	14.4	4.9	2.7	4.9	3.1
38.8	34.1	37.6	Net Worth	21.7	27.0	44.0	43.4	36.5	38.1
100.0	100.0	100.0	Total Liabilities & Net Worth	100.0	100.0	100.0	100.0	100.0	100.0
			INCOME DATA						
100.0	100.0	100.0	Net Sales	100.0	100.0	100.0	100.0	100.0	100.0
25.4	26.6	25.8	Gross Profit	46.3	25.7	23.9	24.8	26.1	21.9
21.7	23.3	22.8	Operating Expenses	43.9	21.5	20.4	22.6	22.6	19.0
3.8	3.3	3.1	Operating Profit	2.4	4.2	3.5	2.2	3.5	2.9
.1	.2	.0	All Other Expenses (net)	.4	.1	.2	.1	-.2	-.3
3.7	3.1	3.1	Profit Before Taxes	2.0	4.0	3.3	2.1	3.6	3.2
			RATIOS						
3.0 / 1.9 / 1.3	2.7 / 1.8 / 1.2	3.1 / 2.0 / 1.3	Current	3.9 / 1.2 / .8	3.7 / 2.3 / 1.1	4.8 / 2.5 / 1.5	3.0 / 2.1 / 1.4	2.2 / 1.8 / 1.2	2.4 / 1.8 / 1.3
1.5 / .8 / .5	1.4 / .7 / .5	1.6 / .8 / .5	Quick	1.3 / .5 / .2	1.9 / .7 / .4	2.2 / 1.0 / .4	1.6 / 1.0 / .5	1.3 / .8 / .6	1.2 / .8 / .5
8 44.1 / 16 23.1 / 26 14.2	10 36.9 / 18 20.4 / 26 14.1	9 41.2 / 16 22.6 / 26 14.2	Sales/Receivables	0 UND / 14 26.5 / 42 8.7	3 138.1 / 12 30.1 / 24 15.1	6 57.6 / 14 26.8 / 22 16.7	9 40.4 / 19 19.3 / 26 13.8	14 27.0 / 20 18.3 / 30 12.1	11 32.3 / 15 24.4 / 30 12.3
25 14.8 / 35 10.6 / 50 7.2	25 14.6 / 36 10.2 / 49 7.4	26 14.1 / 35 10.4 / 48 7.6	Cost of Sales/Inventory	36 10.1 / 94 3.9 / 181 2.0	28 13.3 / 36 10.1 / 53 6.8	26 13.8 / 36 10.1 / 45 8.2	26 14.1 / 32 11.6 / 42 8.6	22 16.9 / 31 11.9 / 41 8.9	22 16.4 / 38 9.7 / 62 5.9
14 26.1 / 21 17.2 / 31 11.9	16 23.5 / 22 16.2 / 34 10.6	11 32.7 / 19 18.8 / 33 11.1	Cost of Sales/Payables	0 UND / 32 11.2 / 64 5.7	10 37.4 / 16 22.4 / 34 10.8	8 47.3 / 15 24.5 / 27 13.6	12 29.6 / 18 20.6 / 29 12.5	16 23.4 / 23 16.0 / 34	15 23.8 / 23 16.2 / 35 10.5
9.3 / 14.4 / 29.9	9.6 / 14.0 / 42.3	8.8 / 13.6 / 35.5	Sales/Working Capital	6.2 / 17.9 / -8.5	7.6 / 12.3 / 104.1	8.2 / 11.0 / 26.0	9.9 / 13.6 / 26.1	10.6 / 17.0 / 48.5	9.1 / 12.5 / 25.3
21.0 / (201) 6.8 / 3.0	19.3 / (219) 6.0 / 2.5	18.9 / (216) 6.5 / 2.2	EBIT/Interest	37.2 / (12) 1.0 / -1.6	12.5 / (30) 5.4 / 2.1	21.3 / (37) 10.6 / 3.3	12.7 / (59) 5.0 / 1.6	21.3 / (46) 9.5 / 2.9	24.9 / (32) 8.8 / 2.5
10.1 / (43) 1.9 / 1.0	5.9 / (54) 2.1 / 1.5	7.9 / (39) 3.8 / 1.3	Net Profit + Depr., Dep., Amort./Cur. Mat. L/T/D					(13) 7.8 / 2.9 / 1.3	
.1 / .3 / .7	.1 / .4 / 1.2	.1 / .3 / .8	Fixed/Worth	.1 / .5 / -3.0	.1 / .5 / 17.2	.1 / .2 / .8	.1 / .2 / .5	.2 / .4 / .8	.2 / .3 / .8
.7 / 1.7 / 4.9	.8 / 2.0 / 7.3	.7 / 1.7 / 5.5	Debt/Worth	.7 / 12.6 / -14.3	.5 / 2.5 / 84.9	.5 / 1.6 / 8.7	.5 / 1.4 / 3.1	.6 / 1.6 / 4.1	.9 / 2.1 / 4.8
77.9 / (221) 37.0 / 13.8	64.2 / (229) 28.2 / 12.3	58.3 / (227) 26.1 / 9.3	% Profit Before Taxes/Tangible Net Worth		127.1 / (32) 33.0 / 13.1	75.9 / (41) 32.3 / 16.2	39.5 / (66) 15.3 / 4.9	70.1 / (44) 39.6 / 14.2	51.2 / (35) 25.2 / 9.3
25.7 / 13.1 / 5.4	20.0 / 9.8 / 3.5	20.4 / 9.6 / 2.4	% Profit Before Taxes/Total Assets	30.2 / -.3 / -5.7	24.7 / 12.9 / 3.8	25.4 / 13.2 / 4.7	18.9 / 5.8 / 1.8	27.9 / 10.8 / 4.3	17.2 / 8.1 / 3.1
127.2 / 54.5 / 25.7	129.0 / 47.4 / 23.4	109.4 / 50.7 / 24.9	Sales/Net Fixed Assets	40.4 / 12.3 / 9.2	112.7 / 53.7 / 35.7	261.5 / 81.0 / 26.3	123.0 / 62.5 / 35.1	86.9 / 35.2 / 25.2	85.3 / 31.3 / 15.0
6.6 / 5.0 / 3.9	5.9 / 4.8 / 3.8	6.3 / 4.8 / 3.6	Sales/Total Assets	3.3 / 2.3 / 1.4	6.7 / 4.7 / 3.6	6.5 / 5.3 / 4.2	6.8 / 5.5 / 4.1	6.2 / 4.9 / 3.8	5.2 / 4.1 / 3.3
.3 / (202) .6 / .9	.4 / (214) .7 / 1.1	.3 / (204) .6 / 1.1	% Depr., Dep., Amort./Sales	.7 / (10) 1.2 / 3.1	.3 / (31) .4 / 1.0	.2 / (36) .4 / 1.3	.3 / (53) .5 / .8	.5 / (42) .7 / 1.1	.5 / (32) .8 / 1.0
1.7 / (133) 3.2 / 6.1	1.6 / (139) 2.9 / 4.9	1.5 / (129) 2.9 / 5.2	% Officers', Directors', Owners' Comp/Sales		.9 / (18) 2.7 / 6.1	1.4 / (31) 3.1 / 5.1	2.2 / (47) 4.2 / 7.0	.4 / (26) 1.8 / 2.9	
8911436M	7189290M	6970063M	Net Sales ($)	8996M	83335M	179791M	504249M	699700M	5493992M
1658825M	1885664M	1705895M	Total Assets ($)	5500M	22219M	41313M	103293M	152986M	1380584M

© RMA 2005   M = $ thousand   MM = $ million

See Pages 11 through 21 for Explanation of Ratios and Data

RETAIL—Cosmetics, Beauty Supplies, and Perfume Stores NAICS 446120 (SIC 5087, 5122, 5999)

Current Data Sorted By Assets							Comparative Historical Data	
	1	2		1	1	**Type of Statement**		
		1				Unqualified	6	4
2	1	2				Reviewed	6	3
7	1	2		1		Compiled	6	5
1	2	2	3			Tax Returns		1
	5 (4/1-9/30/04)		24 (10/1/04-3/31/05)			Other	5	5
							4/1/00-3/31/01	4/1/01-3/31/02
0-500M	500M-2MM	2-10MM	10-50MM	50-100MM	100-250MM		ALL	ALL
10	5	9	3	1	1	**NUMBER OF STATEMENTS**	23	18
%	%	%	%	%	%		%	%
						ASSETS		
8.2						Cash & Equivalents	3.4	4.5
10.4						Trade Receivables (net)	16.0	20.5
38.0						Inventory	41.6	38.2
6.6						All Other Current	1.8	1.7
63.2						Total Current	62.9	64.9
22.3						Fixed Assets (net)	12.0	14.4
8.9						Intangibles (net)	8.3	12.1
5.7						All Other Non-Current	16.8	8.6
100.0						Total	100.0	100.0
						LIABILITIES		
1.2						Notes Payable-Short Term	13.7	11.8
5.1						Cur. Mat.-L/T/D	5.1	4.2
16.6						Trade Payables	19.7	20.9
.2						Income Taxes Payable	.1	.0
2.5						All Other Current	17.7	7.5
25.7						Total Current	56.3	44.4
28.9						Long-Term Debt	10.7	13.2
.2						Deferred Taxes	.2	.2
3.6						All Other Non-Current	5.4	8.6
41.4						Net Worth	27.5	33.6
100.0						Total Liabilities & Net Worth	100.0	100.0
						INCOME DATA		
100.0						Net Sales	100.0	100.0
43.8						Gross Profit	39.0	39.3
39.5						Operating Expenses	35.2	37.4
4.3						Operating Profit	3.8	1.9
.7						All Other Expenses (net)	1.1	.6
3.6						Profit Before Taxes	2.7	1.3
						RATIOS		
11.1							1.6	2.3
3.4						Current	1.2	1.4
1.3							.8	1.2
2.8							.5	1.0
.6						Quick	.3	.5
.1							.2	.4
0 UND							13 27.6	17 22.0
0 UND						Sales/Receivables	17 21.0	26 14.2
30 12.3							33 10.9	30 12.0
42 8.7							53 6.9	50 7.3
103 3.5						Cost of Sales/Inventory	88 4.2	83 4.4
249 1.5							117 3.1	96 3.8
0 UND							17 21.9	29 12.7
37 9.8						Cost of Sales/Payables	40 9.1	41 9.0
66 5.5							67 5.5	60 6.1
3.6							9.2	10.0
6.3						Sales/Working Capital	22.6	17.3
22.3							−15.4	32.7
							5.4	2.9
						EBIT/Interest	(20) 2.1	(17) 1.5
							.3	.8
						Net Profit + Depr., Dep., Amort./Cur. Mat. L /T/D		
.1							.1	.3
.5						Fixed/Worth	.6	.6
−6.1							2.4	NM
.2							1.5	1.5
1.0						Debt/Worth	3.1	2.9
−15.4							46.2	NM
							35.0	14.8
						% Profit Before Taxes/Tangible Net Worth	(19) 11.6	(14) 7.4
							−11.5	−2.2
13.6							11.0	8.7
8.8						% Profit Before Taxes/Total Assets	4.0	2.4
.0							−2.6	−.4
73.7							73.7	58.1
20.3						Sales/Net Fixed Assets	42.8	28.2
4.2							21.4	15.9
4.1							3.9	3.6
2.0						Sales/Total Assets	2.7	2.8
1.4							1.5	2.3
							.5	.6
						% Depr., Dep., Amort./Sales	(13) .9	(14) 1.1
							2.0	1.7
						% Officers', Directors', Owners' Comp/Sales		
6022M	16875M	116205M	143253M	135918M	221273M	Net Sales ($)	813510M	734070M
1897M	5360M	46055M	60332M	69413M	230192M	Total Assets ($)	411685M	335168M

M = $ thousand   MM = $ million
See Pages 11 through 21 for Explanation of Ratios and Data

Comparative Historical Data

Current Data Sorted By Sales

				Type of Statement						
4	1	4		Unqualified			1		1	3
7	4	2		Reviewed			1		1	
12	10	5		Compiled	2	1	1		1	
7	8	10		Tax Returns	4	3	1	2		2
10	14	8		Other	1	1	1	1	2	2
4/1/02- 3/31/03 ALL	4/1/03- 3/31/04 ALL	4/1/04- 3/31/05 ALL				5 (4/1-9/30/04)			24 (10/1/04-3/31/05)	
					0-1MM	1-3MM	3-5MM	5-10MM	10-25MM	25MM & OVER
40	37	29		NUMBER OF STATEMENTS	7	5	4	3	5	5
%	%	%		ASSETS	%	%	%	%	%	%
13.8	13.5	6.9		Cash & Equivalents						
15.1	13.1	17.5		Trade Receivables (net)						
36.4	41.6	38.6		Inventory						
1.7	3.5	4.5		All Other Current						
67.0	71.6	67.5		Total Current						
23.7	20.4	21.9		Fixed Assets (net)						
5.3	2.6	5.2		Intangibles (net)						
4.0	5.4	5.4		All Other Non-Current						
100.0	100.0	100.0		Total						
				LIABILITIES						
7.8	15.9	11.4		Notes Payable-Short Term						
3.3	3.5	3.0		Cur. Mat.-L/T/D						
18.4	20.8	18.7		Trade Payables						
.1	.1	.1		Income Taxes Payable						
14.1	8.4	6.6		All Other Current						
43.6	48.7	39.8		Total Current						
16.7	17.6	15.9		Long-Term Debt						
.4	.0	.7		Deferred Taxes						
9.3	2.9	4.0		All Other Non-Current						
29.9	30.7	39.5		Net Worth						
100.0	100.0	100.0		Total Liabilities & Net Worth						
				INCOME DATA						
100.0	100.0	100.0		Net Sales						
46.3	45.2	39.2		Gross Profit						
39.4	39.7	34.5		Operating Expenses						
6.9	5.5	4.7		Operating Profit						
1.2	.8	.6		All Other Expenses (net)						
5.7	4.7	4.1		Profit Before Taxes						
				RATIOS						
2.4	2.6	4.5								
1.6	1.5	1.5		Current						
1.1	1.1	1.3								
1.4	1.4	1.2								
.5	.4	.4		Quick						
.2	.2	.2								
0 UND	0 UND	0 UND								
16 22.2	15 24.7	18 20.5		Sales/Receivables						
35 10.5	24 15.1	46 8.0								
53 6.9	52 7.0	45 8.1								
70 5.2	85 4.3	103 3.5		Cost of Sales/Inventory						
126 2.9	166 2.2	167 2.2								
17 21.1	7 53.7	13 28.2								
45 8.0	39 9.2	31 11.7		Cost of Sales/Payables						
58 6.2	66 5.5	56 6.5								
5.1	8.8	4.4								
14.2	14.0	11.8		Sales/Working Capital						
102.7	81.2	31.6								
8.5	8.9	13.9								
(33) 3.4	(32) 2.8	(21) 5.3		EBIT/Interest						
1.2	−1.0	3.0								
6.2	14.9			Net Profit + Depr., Dep.,						
(10) 3.0	(10) 3.9			Amort./Cur. Mat. L/T/D						
1.5	.2									
.2	.2	.1								
.7	.6	.5		Fixed/Worth						
5.4	1.3	1.6								
1.5	.9	.5								
2.4	2.7	1.5		Debt/Worth						
12.8	5.3	6.5								
57.8	54.3	40.9		% Profit Before Taxes/Tangible						
(32) 31.4	(34) 20.6	(25) 24.1		Net Worth						
10.9	−8.8	12.6								
31.0	19.2	13.0		% Profit Before Taxes/Total						
6.2	6.1	9.3		Assets						
.8	−5.1	4.3								
47.8	40.8	76.1								
19.1	21.8	23.7		Sales/Net Fixed Assets						
7.5	7.3	5.1								
3.8	4.0	3.6								
2.7	2.7	2.5		Sales/Total Assets						
1.9	1.8	1.8								
.6	.6	.3								
(37) 1.6	(29) 1.1	(25) .8		% Depr., Dep., Amort./Sales						
2.8	1.9	2.8								
1.9	1.4	1.4								
(22) 2.8	(19) 2.0	(15) 2.0		% Officers', Directors',						
8.5	2.9	8.5		Owners' Comp/Sales						
1222654M	268304M	639546M		Net Sales ($)	1508M	9018M	17123M	24114M	77580M	510203M
574402M	94998M	413249M		Total Assets ($)	888M	2129M	8067M	9310M	34954M	357901M

M = $ thousand   MM = $ million
See Pages 11 through 21 for Explanation of Ratios and Data

RETAIL—Optical Goods Stores NAICS 446130 (SIC 5995)

Current Data Sorted By Assets   **Comparative Historical Data**

	0-500M	500M-2MM	2-10MM	10-50MM	50-100MM	100-250MM	Type of Statement	4/1/00-3/31/01 ALL	4/1/01-3/31/02 ALL
				3		1	Unqualified	3	1
	1	2	2				Reviewed	6	3
	3	3	3				Compiled	21	18
	13	7	3				Tax Returns	15	19
	7	4	6	2		1	Other	23	15
	6 (4/1-9/30/04)			52 (10/1/04-3/31/05)					
NUMBER OF STATEMENTS	24	16	11	5		2		68	56

	0-500M %	500M-2MM %	2-10MM %	10-50MM %	50-100MM %	100-250MM %		4/1/00-3/31/01 ALL %	4/1/01-3/31/02 ALL %
ASSETS									
Cash & Equivalents	10.5	8.7	13.4					8.5	8.2
Trade Receivables (net)	11.2	13.3	12.5					14.8	11.6
Inventory	31.6	33.1	30.0					35.9	38.0
All Other Current	1.7	1.1	1.2					2.6	2.2
Total Current	55.0	56.2	57.1					61.8	60.1
Fixed Assets (net)	23.0	24.9	33.5					24.4	22.2
Intangibles (net)	4.7	9.8	2.7					8.2	9.6
All Other Non-Current	17.3	9.1	6.8					5.6	8.3
Total	100.0	100.0	100.0					100.0	100.0
LIABILITIES									
Notes Payable-Short Term	6.0	9.7	8.9					12.7	9.1
Cur. Mat.-L/T/D	5.4	6.9	2.6					4.5	4.1
Trade Payables	11.0	14.2	15.4					21.5	17.8
Income Taxes Payable	.0	.2	.2					.2	.1
All Other Current	8.9	2.8	18.4					15.8	9.8
Total Current	31.3	33.8	45.5					54.6	40.8
Long-Term Debt	29.6	13.5	16.5					19.5	19.0
Deferred Taxes	.0	.0	.0					.3	.0
All Other Non-Current	6.9	3.1	1.6					5.2	10.9
Net Worth	32.2	49.6	36.5					20.4	29.2
Total Liabilities & Net Worth	100.0	100.0	100.0					100.0	100.0
INCOME DATA									
Net Sales	100.0	100.0	100.0					100.0	100.0
Gross Profit	56.0	51.8	53.8					48.0	53.0
Operating Expenses	50.8	46.5	47.3					45.3	47.1
Operating Profit	5.2	5.3	6.5					2.7	5.9
All Other Expenses (net)	1.1	.0	1.9					1.0	1.3
Profit Before Taxes	4.1	5.3	4.6					1.7	4.6

(columns 10-50MM, 50-100MM, 100-250MM marked "DATA NOT AVAILABLE")

RATIOS

	0-500M	500M-2MM	2-10MM		4/1/00-3/31/01 ALL	4/1/01-3/31/02 ALL
Current	4.2	2.3	1.9		2.1	2.6
	2.2	1.8	1.6		1.3	1.5
	.9	1.4	.9		.8	1.0
Quick	1.4	1.1	1.4		1.0	.8
	.8	(15) .8	.6		.4	.4
	.3	.2	.1		.2	.2
Sales/Receivables	0 UND	5 68.9	5 74.5		1 433.1	1 543.8
	4 89.2	11 33.5	9 40.7		9 41.6	5 75.4
	22 16.7	17 21.7	33 11.0		27 13.6	16 23.5
Cost of Sales/Inventory	51 7.2	28 12.8	45 8.2		37 9.9	53 6.9
	87 4.2	63 5.8	76 4.8		80 4.6	92 4.0
	118 3.1	165 2.2	178 2.0		125 2.9	165 2.2
Cost of Sales/Payables	1 305.5	10 37.6	25 14.6		19 19.7	14 26.7
	17 21.9	29 12.8	33 11.2		39 9.3	38 9.7
	33 11.1	60 6.1	72 5.1		66 5.5	76 4.8
Sales/Working Capital	8.0	8.1	8.5		7.7	7.6
	13.8	13.7	10.4		29.2	16.2
	-72.9	32.1	-54.2		-39.3	NM
EBIT/Interest	4.6	20.3	16.4		9.7	8.4
	(15) 4.0	(14) 2.4	(10) 11.8		(63) 2.0	(47) 2.4
	-.2	-3.7	6.2		-.5	1.0
Net Profit + Depr., Dep., Amort./Cur. Mat. L/T/D					5.9	
					(12) 1.7	
					.6	
Fixed/Worth	.1	.2	.3		.3	.1
	.9	.5	.7		.9	.9
	NM	1.0	4.0		-14.8	-25.8
Debt/Worth	.4	.7	1.1		1.0	.8
	2.8	1.3	1.9		3.0	2.8
	NM	2.1	7.2		-33.6	-115.3
% Profit Before Taxes/Tangible Net Worth	100.0	49.3	79.6		66.5	63.2
	(18) 33.9	(15) 27.4	15.1		(49) 14.7	(41) 28.2
	.7	-6.7	3.1		-1.8	7.0
% Profit Before Taxes/Total Assets	29.2	25.2	18.7		22.9	20.3
	11.2	11.5	7.3		3.7	7.1
	-1.9	-3.3	1.3		-2.8	.6
Sales/Net Fixed Assets	52.8	37.7	22.7		49.8	84.2
	19.0	15.0	10.4		19.2	21.1
	8.6	8.6	3.9		7.3	7.5
Sales/Total Assets	4.4	4.5	3.1		4.6	4.4
	3.5	2.5	2.2		2.9	2.6
	2.3	1.8	1.6		2.1	1.7
% Depr., Dep., Amort./Sales	.6	.8	1.3		.8	.6
	(16) 1.9	(15) 1.5	(10) 1.8		(59) 1.6	(42) 1.1
	4.5	3.3	3.0		3.2	2.6
% Officers', Directors', Owners' Comp/Sales	3.9				2.3	3.3
	(13) 12.4				(36) 4.6	(33) 7.4
	16.3				8.3	13.1

	0-500M	500M-2MM	2-10MM	10-50MM	100-250MM		4/1/00-3/31/01	4/1/01-3/31/02
Net Sales ($)	19091M	48341M	93453M	172203M	440530M		3779428M	3870264M
Total Assets ($)	5284M	14676M	40734M	76036M	244095M		698573M	811087M

M = $ thousand   MM = $ million
See Pages 11 through 21 for Explanation of Ratios and Data

Comparative Historical Data | Current Data Sorted By Sales

			Type of Statement						
4	6	4	Unqualified						4
6	3	5	Reviewed	1	2	1	1		
13	16	6	Compiled	2	3		1		
29	19	23	Tax Returns	12	5	1	4	1	
13	17	20	Other	5	6	1	1	5	2
4/1/02- 3/31/03 ALL	4/1/03- 3/31/04 ALL	4/1/04- 3/31/05 ALL		6 (4/1-9/30/04) 0-1MM	1-3MM	3-5MM	52 (10/1/04-3/31/05) 5-10MM	10-25MM	25MM & OVER
65	61	58	**NUMBER OF STATEMENTS**	20	16	3	7	6	6
%	%	%	**ASSETS**	%	%	%	%	%	%
10.6	12.8	9.9	Cash & Equivalents	11.7	7.2				
11.1	14.0	12.4	Trade Receivables (net)	6.9	17.5				
33.5	29.1	29.6	Inventory	30.8	34.3				
1.9	2.9	1.5	All Other Current	2.2	.1				
57.1	58.8	53.4	Total Current	51.5	59.1				
25.5	22.3	26.0	Fixed Assets (net)	24.1	20.0				
6.8	12.4	8.8	Intangibles (net)	10.1	4.0				
10.6	6.5	11.9	All Other Non-Current	14.2	16.8				
100.0	100.0	100.0	Total	100.0	100.0				
			LIABILITIES						
5.7	4.2	7.6	Notes Payable-Short Term	3.6	12.4				
6.5	5.8	4.8	Cur. Mat.-L/T/D	8.6	3.5				
19.4	15.6	13.5	Trade Payables	10.1	12.9				
.1	.4	.1	Income Taxes Payable	.0	.0				
10.8	11.1	9.0	All Other Current	4.6	10.3				
42.6	37.2	35.0	Total Current	26.8	39.1				
25.4	22.9	20.0	Long-Term Debt	33.0	15.1				
.1	.2	.4	Deferred Taxes	.0	.0				
8.6	4.7	5.6	All Other Non-Current	7.9	1.0				
23.2	35.1	39.0	Net Worth	32.4	44.8				
100.0	100.0	100.0	Total Liabilities & Net Worth	100.0	100.0				
			INCOME DATA						
100.0	100.0	100.0	Net Sales	100.0	100.0				
52.0	54.8	54.1	Gross Profit	58.0	53.8				
45.6	47.4	48.0	Operating Expenses	51.3	49.8				
6.4	7.4	6.1	Operating Profit	6.7	4.0				
1.3	.8	1.2	All Other Expenses (net)	1.6	–.3				
5.1	6.5	4.9	Profit Before Taxes	5.1	4.3				
			RATIOS						
2.5	2.7	2.9	Current	4.6	2.7				
1.5	1.6	1.7		2.7	1.8				
.8	1.1	1.0		1.1	1.1				
.8	1.2	1.4	Quick	1.4	1.0				
.4	.7	(57) .7		1.0	.6				
.2	.3	.3		.2	.3				
0 UND	1 522.5	3 121.7	Sales/Receivables	0 UND	2 162.2				
5 66.7	8 48.3	9 42.8		4 89.2	11 33.5				
16 23.1	34 10.8	20 18.3		12 31.1	23 15.9				
48 7.6	28 13.0	44 8.4	Cost of Sales/Inventory	61 6.0	42 8.7				
85 4.3	77 4.7	77 4.8		94 3.9	64 5.7				
112 3.3	132 2.8	128 2.9		134 2.7	149 2.5				
10 35.6	13 28.4	10 36.2	Cost of Sales/Payables	0 UND	10 38.3				
33 10.9	33 11.1	28 13.2		14 26.2	26 13.9				
61 6.0	57 6.4	60 6.1		33 11.1	58 6.3				
7.9	6.2	8.4	Sales/Working Capital	7.9	7.5				
22.0	15.3	14.0		13.0	14.7				
–63.9	72.5	–107.1		NM	115.0				
8.7	18.9	12.0	EBIT/Interest	4.2	17.2				
(54) 3.8	(49) 5.5	(44) 4.1		(14) 1.2	(11) 4.1				
.4	1.4	.9		–1.6	.6				
			Net Profit + Depr., Dep., Amort./Cur. Mat. L/T/D						
.2	.2	.3	Fixed/Worth	.3	.1				
1.2	.7	.8		1.1	.4				
–3.3	22.4	4.0		–1.5	1.2				
1.1	.5	.6	Debt/Worth	.4	.6				
2.7	1.5	1.9		2.8	1.4				
–8.0	UND	11.5		–5.1	4.2				
45.9	85.5	74.1	% Profit Before Taxes/Tangible Net Worth	77.3	92.1				
(40) 22.5	(47) 33.9	(49) 30.3		(13) 30.3	23.9				
–4.2	6.2	2.3		–3.4	–1.1				
16.3	22.6	23.1	% Profit Before Taxes/Total Assets	29.2	22.0				
7.9	9.1	9.6		13.3	9.1				
–2.5	1.0	.7		–3.8	–.3				
63.1	49.7	34.8	Sales/Net Fixed Assets	34.3	60.3				
17.4	14.9	14.3		9.9	22.2				
6.7	7.2	7.7		7.6	12.6				
4.7	5.3	4.1	Sales/Total Assets	4.1	4.5				
2.9	2.7	2.7		2.6	3.3				
1.9	1.9	1.9		1.8	2.4				
.7	.6	.8	% Depr., Dep., Amort./Sales	1.8	.6				
(53) 1.2	(40) 1.7	(47) 1.8		(13) 2.6	(14) .9				
2.3	3.7	3.2		5.1	1.8				
2.8	2.2	2.5	% Officers', Directors', Owners' Comp/Sales	4.1					
(34) 7.1	(34) 6.2	(29) 4.5		(10) 7.4					
14.3	9.9	13.6		17.7					
1961848M	885572M	773618M	Net Sales ($)	10077M	31644M	11974M	49584M	68187M	602152M
575206M	539594M	380825M	Total Assets ($)	4427M	10521M	6226M	17575M	33959M	308117M

M = $ thousand   MM = $ million
See Pages 11 through 21 for Explanation of Ratios and Data

Current Data Sorted By Assets   **Comparative Historical Data**

	0-500M	500M-2MM	2-10MM	10-50MM	50-100MM	100-250MM	Type of Statement	4/1/00-3/31/01 ALL	4/1/01-3/31/02 ALL
	2	1	14	34	8	8	Unqualified		
		3	24	19	2		Reviewed		
	30	39	33	6		1	Compiled		
	71	68	22	2	1	1	Tax Returns		
	26	36	33	24	5	5	Other		
	86 (4/1-9/30/04)		432 (10/1/04-3/31/05)						
NUMBER OF STATEMENTS	129	147	126	85	16	15			
	%	%	%	%	%	%	**ASSETS**	%	%
	13.2	8.0	7.5	8.0	7.7	5.4	Cash & Equivalents	D	D
	5.1	6.0	8.9	8.7	7.9	6.9	Trade Receivables (net)	A	A
	33.3	15.6	11.2	11.7	14.1	15.3	Inventory	T	T
	1.7	1.7	2.5	3.6	1.7	2.2	All Other Current	A	A
	53.3	31.3	30.1	32.0	31.4	29.7	Total Current		
	28.3	57.2	57.5	58.3	57.5	63.6	Fixed Assets (net)	N	N
	10.8	4.5	3.5	2.5	5.7	2.9	Intangibles (net)	O	O
	7.6	7.1	8.9	7.2	5.4	3.8	All Other Non-Current	T	T
	100.0	100.0	100.0	100.0	100.0	100.0	Total		
							LIABILITIES	A	A
	6.8	4.3	3.7	4.3	.2	1.0	Notes Payable-Short Term	V	V
	2.6	3.6	3.6	4.8	2.7	2.9	Cur. Mat.-L/T/D	A	A
	17.6	13.5	14.9	16.4	13.1	14.9	Trade Payables	I	I
	.1	.0	.1	.3	.1	.1	Income Taxes Payable	L	L
	14.3	7.0	7.1	8.2	8.2	7.7	All Other Current	A	A
	41.4	28.4	29.4	33.9	24.4	26.6	Total Current	B	B
	30.9	49.1	42.2	34.2	39.7	32.6	Long-Term Debt	L	L
	.5	.1	.3	1.0	1.0	.8	Deferred Taxes	E	E
	19.8	8.2	4.7	2.5	6.5	4.8	All Other Non-Current		
	7.4	14.2	23.4	28.3	28.5	35.2	Net Worth		
	100.0	100.0	100.0	100.0	100.0	100.0	Total Liabilities & Net Worth		
							INCOME DATA		
	100.0	100.0	100.0	100.0	100.0	100.0	Net Sales		
	15.4	14.1	14.5	16.1	11.8	14.1	Gross Profit		
	15.1	13.2	13.5	14.6	10.8	12.4	Operating Expenses		
	.2	.8	1.0	1.5	1.0	1.7	Operating Profit		
	-.2	.3	.1	.1	-.2	.4	All Other Expenses (net)		
	.5	.6	.9	1.4	1.1	1.3	Profit Before Taxes		
							RATIOS		
	3.1	2.6	1.6	1.2	1.4	1.6			
	1.5	1.4	1.1	1.0	1.0	1.0	Current		
	.9	.8	.8	.7	.9	.7			
	1.3	1.1	.8	.7	.9	.6			
	(124) .5	.5	(125) .6	.5	.4	.4	Quick		
	.2	.2	.3	.3	.3	.2			
	0 UND	0 UND	1 437.7	2 147.8	2 191.9	2 148.9			
	1 622.3	1 257.3	4 100.7	5 71.3	4 90.3	4 87.8	Sales/Receivables		
	2 167.3	4 84.0	9 41.9	8 43.9	6 64.4	8 45.6			
	7 52.7	7 54.7	7 55.5	7 55.1	8 44.1	7 53.8			
	10 35.8	9 40.2	9 40.0	10 38.3	11 33.5	12 29.2	Cost of Sales/Inventory		
	15 23.9	14 26.0	13 27.6	13 27.5	15 24.7	16 22.9			
	0 UND	2 201.4	5 75.9	10 36.8	8 45.6	8 44.8			
	4 98.7	7 49.8	9 38.8	13 29.1	13 27.6	16 23.1	Cost of Sales/Payables		
	9 38.7	13 28.1	16 22.7	18 19.9	17 21.9	24 15.2			
	34.2	31.4	41.1	82.3	40.6	46.2			
	69.2	96.4	253.8	-302.9	-480.6	-999.8	Sales/Working Capital		
	-673.2	-86.5	-73.9	-43.7	-154.7	-62.1			
	6.1	3.4	3.7	4.0	4.3	8.9			
	(69) 1.9	(132) 1.7	(119) 1.8	(80) 2.3	(14) 2.0	(14) 2.8	EBIT/Interest		
	-.1	.7	.9	1.4	1.3	1.5			
		2.8	4.3	3.4			Net Profit + Depr., Dep.,		
		(13) 1.7	(20) 1.5	(35) 2.0			Amort./Cur. Mat. L/T/D		
		1.5	.8	1.2					
	.2	1.3	1.3	1.5	1.6	1.2			
	1.5	4.7	3.1	2.2	2.4	2.4	Fixed/Worth		
	-1.6	-7.8	26.8	5.8	5.4	3.8			
	.9	2.1	1.9	1.7	1.9	.9			
	4.6	6.3	4.3	2.6	3.3	2.0	Debt/Worth		
	-3.5	-11.7	34.2	7.3	8.1	9.3			
	61.7	47.9	27.2	21.1	24.1	20.8	% Profit Before Taxes/Tangible		
	(81) 23.4	(101) 20.0	(103) 10.0	(79) 10.4	(15) 13.2	(14) 17.0	Net Worth		
	3.8	2.6	-3.0	4.6	6.7	2.2			
	20.9	8.4	5.1	5.4	6.4	7.8	% Profit Before Taxes/Total		
	6.3	3.2	2.9	2.9	3.2	3.1	Assets		
	-3.0	-.9	-.4	1.0	1.0	1.2			
	306.8	24.4	16.3	13.7	9.1	9.8			
	59.3	7.1	7.2	7.0	5.9	5.7	Sales/Net Fixed Assets		
	17.6	3.9	3.9	4.9	4.5	5.2			
	18.0	8.7	6.9	6.5	4.8	5.6			
	10.7	4.3	4.4	4.4	3.9	4.3	Sales/Total Assets		
	7.1	2.8	2.5	3.2	2.8	2.8			
	.3	.9	.9	.9	.9	.9			
	(87) .6	(125) 1.4	(119) 1.4	(82) 1.2	(14) 1.3	(13) 1.3	% Depr., Dep., Amort./Sales		
	1.4	2.3	2.3	1.7	1.7	1.5			
	.7	.6	.4	.3			% Officers', Directors',		
	(75) 1.5	(72) 1.0	(44) .7	(26) .5			Owners' Comp/Sales		
	2.3	1.8	1.4	.7					
	352577M	948314M	3178488M	9408890M	4913980M	10814349M	Net Sales ($)		
	30833M	154019M	595956M	1963713M	1225269M	2231182M	Total Assets ($)		

M = $ thousand MM = $ million
See Pages 11 through 21 for Explanation of Ratios and Data

Comparative Historical Data | Current Data Sorted By Sales

			Type of Statement						
31	49	67	Unqualified		1	6	1	3	56
47	54	48	Reviewed		1			9	38
101	152	109	Compiled	2	23	21	21	20	22
134	221	165	Tax Returns	11	69	38	27	13	7
113	126	129	Other	3	23	22	17	21	43
4/1/02-3/31/03	4/1/03-3/31/04	4/1/04-3/31/05			86 (4/1-9/30/04)		432 (10/1/04-3/31/05)		
ALL	ALL	ALL		0-1MM	1-3MM	3-5MM	5-10MM	10-25MM	25MM & OVER
426	602	518	**NUMBER OF STATEMENTS**	16	117	87	66	66	166
%	%	%	**ASSETS**	%	%	%	%	%	%
9.9	11.4	9.1	Cash & Equivalents	13.6	9.1	10.2	10.6	7.1	8.2
6.8	5.9	7.0	Trade Receivables (net)	6.5	2.5	4.7	6.5	11.1	10.0
19.4	21.0	18.2	Inventory	30.2	22.0	21.1	16.9	15.0	14.7
2.5	1.8	2.2	All Other Current	.0	1.1	2.4	2.1	2.3	3.1
38.7	40.0	36.5	Total Current	50.4	34.7	38.4	36.2	35.5	36.0
47.8	46.6	50.4	Fixed Assets (net)	44.4	48.6	47.4	50.1	50.5	54.0
6.1	6.3	5.5	Intangibles (net)	4.2	7.4	6.0	9.0	4.9	2.8
7.4	7.1	7.6	All Other Non-Current	1.1	9.3	8.2	4.7	9.0	7.2
100.0	100.0	100.0	Total	100.0	100.0	100.0	100.0	100.0	100.0
			LIABILITIES						
3.6	3.6	4.5	Notes Payable-Short Term	6.3	5.1	3.8	7.4	4.3	3.3
3.8	3.5	3.5	Cur. Mat.-L/T/D	.5	3.3	4.2	2.5	3.5	4.0
15.4	15.3	15.3	Trade Payables	12.2	11.0	13.1	15.3	17.6	19.0
.2	.3	.1	Income Taxes Payable	.0	.0	.1	.1	.1	.2
8.1	8.5	9.1	All Other Current	22.0	7.0	12.4	5.7	8.3	9.3
31.1	31.2	32.6	Total Current	41.0	26.4	33.7	30.9	33.9	35.8
37.5	37.2	39.7	Long-Term Debt	33.4	46.2	40.7	49.2	38.4	31.9
.2	.2	.4	Deferred Taxes	.0	.5	.1	.2	.3	.8
10.0	12.1	9.2	All Other Non-Current	9.2	20.5	8.1	8.6	2.8	4.5
21.2	19.2	18.1	Net Worth	16.4	6.5	17.4	11.0	24.7	27.0
100.0	100.0	100.0	Total Liabilities & Net Worth	100.0	100.0	100.0	100.0	100.0	100.0
			INCOME DATA						
100.0	100.0	100.0	Net Sales	100.0	100.0	100.0	100.0	100.0	100.0
17.1	16.2	14.7	Gross Profit	24.1	15.4	15.7	13.5	13.0	14.0
16.1	15.5	13.9	Operating Expenses	27.4	14.5	13.7	12.9	12.5	13.2
1.0	.7	.9	Operating Profit	-3.4	1.0	2.0	.7	.5	.8
-.1	-.2	.1	All Other Expenses (net)	-.6	.3	.6	.1	-.1	-.2
1.2	.9	.8	Profit Before Taxes	-2.7	.7	1.4	.6	.7	1.0
			RATIOS						
2.4	2.4	2.1		3.0	3.5	3.2	2.0	1.5	1.2
1.3	1.3	1.2	Current	1.6	1.5	1.8	1.2	1.1	1.0
.8	.8	.8		.7	.8	.8	.7	.8	.8
1.0	1.0	.9		2.5	1.2	1.7	1.0	.9	.7
(423) .5	(599) .5	(512) .5	Quick	.5	(116) .4	(84) .6	(65) .5	.6	(165) .5
.2	.2	.2		.2	.2	.2	.2	.3	.3
0 UND	0 UND	0 999.8		0 UND	0 UND	0 UND	0 UND	1 679.7	2 158.5
2 176.0	2 241.6	2 169.4	Sales/Receivables	0 UND	0 889.5	2 238.5	1 258.4	3 115.5	5 80.8
5 70.7	4 87.8	6 65.1		6 61.7	2 185.7	3 116.4	4 81.2	8 43.3	8 44.0
8 48.4	7 50.4	7 54.2		16 23.3	8 43.6	6 59.7	6 65.3	5 73.5	7 53.8
12 30.7	10 35.4	9 38.6	Cost of Sales/Inventory	28 12.9	12 29.6	8 43.0	8 46.5	9 41.4	9 39.8
17 21.2	16 22.4	14 26.8		70 5.3	16 22.2	11 32.1	12 31.4	12 31.3	13 27.6
3 126.2	3 134.4	3 132.2		0 UND	0 UND	0 756.3	2 177.6	5 76.6	9 42.5
10 37.1	8 43.9	9 42.4	Cost of Sales/Payables	9 42.9	4 91.8	5 67.8	8 48.5	9 41.9	13 28.6
17 21.7	15 24.6	14 25.9		61 5.9	10 36.2	10 36.1	12 30.6	13 27.1	17 21.7
29.8	28.9	36.8		6.8	29.8	27.2	36.6	52.7	74.6
86.2	86.9	133.8	Sales/Working Capital	22.3	67.4	59.4	123.4	133.1	-480.6
-78.2	-88.3	-90.7		-13.0	-91.4	-101.8	-94.5	-89.3	-77.0
3.8	4.9	4.2		3.2	3.4	4.8	3.7	5.2	4.3
(343) 1.8	(473) 2.0	(428) 1.9	EBIT/Interest	(10) .1	(83) 1.4	(61) 1.7	(61) 1.8	(61) 1.9	(152) 2.4
.6	.9	1.0		-12.9	.2	1.0	.8	1.1	1.3
3.1	3.4	3.2	Net Profit + Depr., Dep.,					3.2	2.9
(70) 1.8	(77) 2.0	(81) 1.8	Amort./Cur. Mat. L/T/D				(11) 1.8	(55) 1.8
.8	1.0	1.2						1.5	1.2
.8	.8	1.0		.3	.9	.4	1.2	1.0	1.2
2.9	2.6	2.7	Fixed/Worth	2.6	8.7	2.4	7.9	2.4	2.2
32.0	-77.1	60.5		29.6	-2.7	116.7	-4.1	16.7	5.6
1.6	1.4	1.6		1.6	1.7	1.0	3.1	1.8	1.7
4.1	3.9	4.2	Debt/Worth	6.7	11.5	3.4	13.9	3.9	2.9
206.4	-49.3	122.9		48.0	-5.1	-76.3	-10.1	19.0	7.9
55.7	48.3	36.5	% Profit Before Taxes/Tangible	51.3	53.9	49.8	51.6	23.0	23.9
(323) 17.8	(436) 18.7	(393) 14.0	Net Worth	(13) 5.2	(66) 22.3	(65) 23.2	(43) 27.2	(54) 11.7	(152) 11.2
3.2	3.3	2.9		-42.8	2.5	3.2	4.3	.7	3.8
10.1	10.7	8.5	% Profit Before Taxes/Total	4.6	11.5	14.2	8.6	6.3	6.4
3.5	3.9	3.2	Assets	1.0	2.5	4.5	4.0	2.5	3.2
-.5	-.3	.0		-17.1	-3.3	-.1	-.4	-.1	.9
46.7	54.5	35.4		48.1	55.1	98.2	47.1	33.0	18.1
9.7	11.7	10.1	Sales/Net Fixed Assets	9.5	9.3	9.3	10.7	14.3	9.4
4.0	4.7	4.9		1.6	4.2	4.2	4.7	4.9	5.7
8.8	10.4	9.4		4.4	10.0	12.5	11.9	9.8	7.7
5.0	5.3	5.4	Sales/Total Assets	2.9	5.5	4.8	6.6	5.6	5.4
2.8	3.1	3.2		1.4	2.7	2.9	3.3	3.3	3.7
.8	.7	.8		1.2	.7	.6	.7	.8	.8
(367) 1.3	(500) 1.3	(440) 1.2	% Depr., Dep., Amort./Sales	(10) 2.0	(94) 1.5	(68) 1.4	(55) 1.3	(57) 1.2	(156) 1.2
2.2	2.2	1.9		8.3	2.5	2.9	2.1	2.1	1.5
.6	.6	.5			.8	.6	.5	.3	.3
(186) 1.2	(296) 1.2	(221) .9	% Officers', Directors', Owners' Comp/Sales	(64) 1.5	(39) 1.1	(34) .9	(26) .6	(49) .5
2.3	2.2	1.8			2.2	1.9	1.5	1.1	1.4
14422843M	21648159M	29616598M	Net Sales ($)	10133M	236517M	327625M	459345M	1065571M	27517407M
3391229M	5099025M	6200972M	Total Assets ($)	6409M	66061M	121389M	93388M	255160M	5658565M

© RMA 2005

M = $ thousand   MM = $ million
See Pages 11 through 21 for Explanation of Ratios and Data

Current Data Sorted By Assets   Comparative Historical Data

						Type of Statement		
	1	10	34	18	7	Unqualified	61	70
4	11	40	37	2	1	Reviewed	83	88
27	41	22	5		1	Compiled	189	175
100	66	23	4	1	1	Tax Returns	196	146
14	34	42	35	4	3	Other	204	210
	100 (4/1-9/30/04)		487 (10/1/04-3/31/05)				4/1/00- 3/31/01	4/1/01- 3/31/02
0-500M	500M-2MM	2-10MM	10-50MM	50-100MM	100-250MM		ALL	ALL
145	153	137	115	25	12	NUMBER OF STATEMENTS	733	689
%	%	%	%	%	%	**ASSETS**	%	%
18.6	8.1	9.5	8.7	10.8	8.7	Cash & Equivalents	10.3	10.7
7.8	7.3	9.5	10.2	6.3	7.1	Trade Receivables (net)	8.6	8.0
31.2	12.8	11.7	11.6	9.8	7.8	Inventory	17.0	15.6
2.1	1.7	2.7	1.9	1.2	1.5	All Other Current	1.9	2.4
59.7	29.9	33.4	32.4	28.0	25.2	Total Current	37.8	36.7
21.2	53.9	55.3	56.9	60.3	53.9	Fixed Assets (net)	50.5	51.6
12.5	11.2	3.8	2.8	2.8	13.5	Intangibles (net)	5.7	4.2
6.6	5.1	7.5	7.9	8.9	7.4	All Other Non-Current	6.0	7.5
100.0	100.0	100.0	100.0	100.0	100.0	Total	100.0	100.0
						LIABILITIES		
6.3	4.3	3.1	3.2	.8	1.6	Notes Payable-Short Term	5.0	4.0
2.0	2.1	4.3	3.8	5.6	3.4	Cur. Mat.-L/T/D	3.6	3.4
15.5	11.3	15.6	18.2	13.1	14.0	Trade Payables	15.0	15.3
.1	.1	.2	.1	.2	.0	Income Taxes Payable	.2	.2
20.0	8.9	8.6	7.4	5.5	8.0	All Other Current	10.0	8.6
43.8	26.7	31.8	32.7	25.2	26.9	Total Current	33.8	31.3
18.0	52.7	37.5	32.5	34.7	33.2	Long-Term Debt	35.4	37.2
.0	.2	.4	.7	1.6	1.0	Deferred Taxes	.5	.4
12.8	7.8	4.0	3.3	2.9	11.6	All Other Non-Current	7.7	7.9
25.4	12.6	26.4	30.8	35.6	27.2	Net Worth	22.7	23.2
100.0	100.0	100.0	100.0	100.0	100.0	Total Liabilities & Net Worth	100.0	100.0
						INCOME DATA		
100.0	100.0	100.0	100.0	100.0	100.0	Net Sales	100.0	100.0
15.4	15.4	13.3	13.3	13.3	14.4	Gross Profit	17.0	17.8
15.0	14.3	12.2	12.3	11.5	13.3	Operating Expenses	16.5	16.5
.4	1.1	1.1	1.0	1.9	1.1	Operating Profit	.4	1.3
–.6	.3	.1	–.5	.3	–.1	All Other Expenses (net)	–.5	.4
1.0	.8	1.1	1.4	1.6	1.1	Profit Before Taxes	1.0	1.0
						RATIOS		
4.2	2.7	1.6	1.2	1.4	1.1		1.9	2.0
1.8	1.5	1.1	.9	1.0	.9	Current	1.2	1.2
.9	.8	.7	.7	.7	.6		.8	.7
1.4	1.2	1.0	.8	.9	.8		1.0	1.1
.7	(152) .6	.5	.5	.6	.6	Quick	(728) .5	(680) .5
.3	.2	.3	.2	.2	.2		.3	.3
0 UND	0 UND	1 368.2	2 179.9	2 172.9	2 194.6		1 590.2	1 544.3
1 549.8	1 266.3	3 134.7	4 89.1	3 104.8	5 71.5	Sales/Receivables	3 120.7	3 119.7
3 139.8	4 84.0	7 49.3	8 43.6	8 45.9	9 42.6		8 46.8	7 52.3
5 71.4	6 66.1	6 65.0	5 69.6	6 58.3	3 112.6		7 53.1	6 59.5
8 46.2	8 46.8	9 41.6	9 39.7	6 40.8	6 59.3	Cost of Sales/Inventory	10 36.4	9 38.6
13 27.3	15 23.8	13 27.1	13 28.2	16 23.3	11 32.3		15 24.0	14 25.9
0 999.8	0 914.5	5 69.5	11 33.9	10 37.3	9 40.7		5 73.5	5 74.4
3 110.0	5 78.7	11 33.0	13 27.7	14 25.9	15 23.8	Cost of Sales/Payables	11 33.5	10 36.0
9 39.3	11 33.0	14 25.4	18 20.8	17 21.1	18 20.8		17 20.9	16 22.5
30.8	31.7	43.9	99.6	46.8	166.0		33.9	31.7
53.9	76.4	248.7	–247.4	999.8	–149.9	Sales/Working Capital	115.7	138.7
–371.0	–105.4	–58.4	–50.6	–72.6	–40.2		–59.2	–66.0
14.3	4.3	5.1	4.9	5.2	3.8		3.9	4.3
(66) 2.6	(141) 1.9	(128) 2.0	(111) 2.7	(24) 2.1	(10) 2.5	EBIT/Interest	(617) 1.7	(593) 1.8
.2	.8	1.1	1.3	1.3	1.4		.8	.9
	6.4	3.9	3.2	4.4		Net Profit + Depr., Dep.,	3.4	3.5
	(12) 2.6	(29) 1.8	(31) 2.3	(11) 2.3		Amort./Cur. Mat. L /T/D	(125) 1.9	(107) 1.8
	1.1	1.3	1.5	1.9			1.0	1.1
.0	1.6	1.2	1.2	1.2	1.7		1.0	.9
.8	11.9	2.5	2.4	2.1	3.4	Fixed/Worth	2.7	2.4
–18.7	–3.3	6.6	4.1	3.5	–15.1		39.9	12.7
.9	2.6	1.6	1.7	1.0	1.6		1.3	1.2
3.7	15.1	3.6	2.9	2.6	3.9	Debt/Worth	3.8	3.2
–11.6	–5.9	8.9	5.6	3.8	–21.9		74.3	21.5
100.0	44.3	33.1	31.8	23.3		% Profit Before Taxes/Tangible	38.5	40.6
(99) 33.7	(86) 23.3	(119) 11.8	(106) 16.2	12.6		Net Worth	(563) 15.6	(552) 16.1
6.2	10.4	2.0	6.3	4.0			2.6	3.1
17.5	8.9	7.2	7.2	7.6	4.9		9.4	9.5
7.2	4.0	3.5	3.1	3.5	4.4	% Profit Before Taxes/Total Assets	3.5	3.8
–2.1	–.7	.2	.9	1.1	3.1		–.5	.0
999.8	25.1	18.6	15.0	11.6	10.0		29.1	29.1
137.9	8.0	8.9	8.2	5.7	7.5	Sales/Net Fixed Assets	9.4	9.3
31.0	3.6	4.5	4.7	4.3	5.2		4.3	4.2
19.7	7.7	7.9	6.6	4.7	5.9		8.4	8.5
12.6	4.4	5.1	4.5	3.5	4.6	Sales/Total Assets	4.5	4.9
7.9	2.7	3.1	3.1	2.7	2.8		2.9	2.9
.2	.8	.7	.9	.9			.7	.7
(84) .4	(129) 1.4	(129) 1.2	(109) 1.3	(24) 1.3		% Depr., Dep., Amort./Sales	(647) 1.4	(610) 1.3
1.1	2.3	1.9	1.8	1.7			2.1	2.0
.6	.6	.3	.3				.6	.5
(73) 1.3	(67) 1.1	(52) .6	(22) .5			% Officers', Directors', Owners' Comp/Sales	(310) 1.3	(287) 1.1
2.5	2.1	1.1	.9				2.5	2.6
446252M	956630M	4137129M	14449214M	7108288M	7771840M	Net Sales ($)	31251754M	31464232M
33139M	163486M	682604M	2664956M	1711130M	1855156M	Total Assets ($)	7149574M	7024439M

© RMA 2005

M = $ thousand   MM = $ million
See Pages 11 through 21 for Explanation of Ratios and Data

Comparative Historical Data — **Current Data Sorted By Sales**

78	91	70	Type of Statement						
92	99	95	Unqualified			1		3	66
156	194	95	Reviewed		2	3		16	64
168	205	195	Compiled	5	24	14	18	22	12
183	152	132	Tax Returns	13	74	47	31	20	10
			Other	3	19	17	17	17	64

4/1/02-3/31/03 ALL	4/1/03-3/31/04 ALL	4/1/04-3/31/05 ALL		100 (4/1-9/30/04)			487 (10/1/04-3/31/05)		
				0-1MM	1-3MM	3-5MM	5-10MM	10-25MM	25MM & OVER
677	741	587	**NUMBER OF STATEMENTS**	21	119	82	71	78	216
%	%	%	**ASSETS**	%	%	%	%	%	%
9.6	12.1	11.3	Cash & Equivalents	18.9	12.7	11.2	11.9	9.0	10.4
7.5	7.9	8.4	Trade Receivables (net)	6.2	5.9	4.8	9.1	10.3	10.6
15.1	16.7	16.6	Inventory	26.2	21.7	17.9	17.8	14.9	12.6
2.4	2.8	2.0	All Other Current	.2	1.2	3.4	2.3	2.2	2.1
34.6	39.4	38.4	Total Current	51.5	41.6	37.3	41.0	36.3	35.7
53.7	47.7	47.0	Fixed Assets (net)	31.4	41.8	42.2	43.4	52.0	52.6
4.4	6.2	7.8	Intangibles (net)	9.2	12.2	13.6	10.0	5.1	3.3
7.2	6.7	6.8	All Other Non-Current	7.9	4.4	6.9	5.6	6.6	8.4
100.0	100.0	100.0	Total	100.0	100.0	100.0	100.0	100.0	100.0
			LIABILITIES						
4.6	4.1	4.1	Notes Payable-Short Term	3.7	4.8	4.7	5.3	4.6	3.0
3.9	3.4	3.1	Cur. Mat.-L/T/D	4.9	1.9	1.7	2.3	4.9	3.8
14.8	15.4	14.8	Trade Payables	11.5	10.3	11.0	13.0	16.9	18.9
.1	.2	.1	Income Taxes Payable	.0	.1	.1	.1	.2	.1
10.1	11.1	11.1	All Other Current	17.0	13.0	10.4	15.5	9.0	9.1
33.6	34.1	33.2	Total Current	37.1	30.0	27.9	36.1	35.6	34.9
38.8	37.6	35.5	Long-Term Debt	27.3	39.5	44.5	36.6	37.4	29.5
.4	.3	.4	Deferred Taxes	.0	.0	.0	.1	.3	.8
6.5	8.2	7.1	All Other Non-Current	11.1	12.0	8.6	8.4	5.6	3.7
20.7	19.9	23.8	Net Worth	24.6	18.5	19.0	18.8	21.0	31.2
100.0	100.0	100.0	Total Liabilities & Net Worth	100.0	100.0	100.0	100.0	100.0	100.0
			INCOME DATA						
100.0	100.0	100.0	Net Sales	100.0	100.0	100.0	100.0	100.0	100.0
17.8	16.0	14.4	Gross Profit	28.2	17.2	13.4	13.1	12.9	12.8
16.9	14.9	13.4	Operating Expenses	25.2	16.3	12.3	12.6	12.5	11.8
.9	1.2	.9	Operating Profit	3.1	.9	1.1	.5	.4	1.0
.2	.1	-.1	All Other Expenses (net)	-.5	-.1	.3	.3	-.5	-.3
.7	1.1	1.1	Profit Before Taxes	3.6	1.0	.8	.2	.9	1.3
			RATIOS						
1.8	2.1	2.1		7.7	3.6	3.8	3.1	1.5	1.3
1.1	1.2	1.1	Current	3.0	1.8	1.7	1.2	1.0	1.0
.7	.8	.8		1.3	.8	.9	.8	.7	.7
.9	1.1	1.0		1.9	1.5	1.3	1.1	.9	.8
(673) .5	(737) .5	(586) .6	Quick	1.1	(118) .7	.7	.6	.5	.5
.2	.3	.3		.4	.2	.3	.3	.3	.3
1 535.9	0 945.0	0 999.8		0 UND	0 UND	0 UND	0 UND	1 392.0	2 175.9
3 126.6	2 149.4	2 169.8	Sales/Receivables	0 UND	0 744.0	0 906.1	2 218.7	2 168.8	4 98.7
7 52.1	6 56.6	6 63.2		3 110.7	3 106.9	2 178.8	4 92.6	8 43.7	8 45.1
7 54.2	6 59.3	5 66.4		12 29.3	7 50.7	5 71.1	5 79.8	5 74.0	5 72.1
10 35.8	9 40.3	8 43.3	Cost of Sales/Inventory	19 18.7	11 31.9	7 56.0	7 51.5	7 51.0	8 43.2
15 24.8	15 25.1	14 26.6		40 9.1	18 20.3	10 38.3	11 34.0	12 31.2	12 29.2
4 84.2	3 110.9	2 157.1		0 UND	0 999.8	0 782.2	1 401.1	3 126.9	10 37.6
11 32.8	10 37.0	9 41.5	Cost of Sales/Payables	4 104.0	3 109.3	3 105.3	5 78.2	10 34.9	13 28.2
17 21.3	15 23.9	14 25.8		16 23.5	11 34.2	8 48.2	11 34.7	15 25.1	17 22.1
36.4	31.7	38.0		9.7	26.5	38.5	43.5	50.5	75.1
281.9	135.4	166.4	Sales/Working Capital	18.2	45.5	61.8	145.3	658.3	-391.1
-47.0	-77.9	-80.4		95.2	-101.0	-713.8	-85.0	-64.9	-56.0
3.6	4.4	5.0			4.1	3.8	4.7	5.3	5.7
(592) 1.7	(620) 2.0	(480) 2.1	EBIT/Interest	(82) 1.8	(56) 1.8	(60) 1.8	(71) 2.2	(202) 2.8	
.4	1.0	1.1		.7	1.0	.5	1.0	1.4	
3.9	4.1	3.9	Net Profit + Depr., Dep.,					5.0	4.0
(100) 1.7	(110) 2.1	(86) 2.2	Amort./Cur. Mat. L/T/D				(13) 1.9	(61) 2.3	
1.1	1.2	1.3						1.3	1.5
1.1	.9	.9		.0	.6	.7	.7	1.2	1.0
2.8	2.5	2.5	Fixed/Worth	1.5	5.6	3.9	2.4	2.5	2.2
57.7	-33.5	51.3		6.9	-2.9	-4.5	-5.6	23.1	3.9
1.6	1.6	1.6		.8	1.8	1.8	1.4	2.2	1.5
4.0	4.0	3.8	Debt/Worth	3.9	8.0	8.0	8.7	3.6	2.9
90.4	-31.6	UND		11.5	-4.9	-7.4	-7.2	49.2	5.7
34.1	44.0	40.7	% Profit Before Taxes/Tangible	85.0	65.8	73.3	39.6	41.2	31.1
(514) 12.8	(537) 18.5	(442) 18.5	Net Worth	(17) 26.2	(72) 23.0	(50) 30.3	(45) 16.3	(61) 18.8	(197) 15.6
-.5	5.7	4.7		-3.9	8.1	8.1	-1.2	3.2	6.1
7.6	9.8	9.7	% Profit Before Taxes/Total	13.4	14.9	12.8	9.0	8.9	7.4
2.4	3.9	4.1	Assets	5.1	4.5	3.9	3.1	4.4	3.9
-2.2	.3	.4		-.9	-.2	-2.7	-1.6	.5	1.1
21.4	37.3	46.0		UND	113.0	205.9	97.7	34.1	18.8
8.0	10.2	11.8	Sales/Net Fixed Assets	45.9	16.5	19.6	15.1	11.7	10.1
4.0	4.5	5.1		5.9	3.6	4.5	5.3	5.6	5.3
7.6	9.3	9.7		8.9	12.4	15.5	15.7	10.1	8.1
4.2	4.8	5.6	Sales/Total Assets	5.9	5.1	6.3	5.7	6.1	5.5
2.6	3.0	3.3		1.2	2.3	3.3	4.0	3.8	3.3
1.0	.7	.6		1.4	.4	.4	.6	.7	.7
(602) 1.6	(640) 1.3	(484) 1.2	% Depr., Dep., Amort./Sales	(11) 2.4	(87) 1.3	(59) 1.3	(53) 1.2	(72) 1.2	(202) 1.2
2.4	2.1	1.8		4.6	2.9	2.1	1.8	1.7	1.6
.5	.5	.5	% Officers', Directors',		1.0	.5	.4	.4	.2
(265) 1.3	(295) 1.2	(219) 1.0	Owners' Comp/Sales		(56) 1.7	(35) .9	(37) .7	(33) .6	(49) .5
2.5	2.3	1.9			2.9	1.9	1.4	1.0	1.1
35663735M	39432358M	34869353M	Net Sales ($)	14567M	242305M	316050M	489509M	1211156M	32595766M
8588246M	8559978M	7110471M	Total Assets ($)	6447M	71919M	67195M	109549M	248153M	6607208M

M = $ thousand   MM = $ million
See Pages 11 through 21 for Explanation of Ratios and Data

Current Data Sorted By Assets   Comparative Historical Data

						Type of Statement		
1	1	3	2	1	3	Unqualified	14	9
1	1	6	1			Reviewed	19	20
13	17	6	1			Compiled	35	31
7	4	1				Tax Returns	12	12
5	9	3	4	2		Other	22	26
		23 (4/1-9/30/04)		68 (10/1/04-3/31/05)			4/1/00-3/31/01	4/1/01-3/31/02
0-500M	500M-2MM	2-10MM	10-50MM	50-100MM	100-250MM		ALL	ALL
26	32	19	8	3	3	**NUMBER OF STATEMENTS**	102	98
%	%	%	%	%	%	**ASSETS**	%	%
9.2	15.9	7.1				Cash & Equivalents	11.0	11.3
3.3	11.0	6.6				Trade Receivables (net)	8.0	8.0
73.1	50.2	48.7				Inventory	53.7	52.1
.8	.3	2.4				All Other Current	1.1	1.6
86.4	77.3	64.8				Total Current	73.8	73.0
10.2	17.9	19.7				Fixed Assets (net)	17.2	19.1
.3	.9	.6				Intangibles (net)	2.2	2.5
3.1	3.9	14.9				All Other Non-Current	6.7	5.4
100.0	100.0	100.0				Total	100.0	100.0
						LIABILITIES		
13.3	14.9	13.6				Notes Payable-Short Term	9.7	13.0
1.5	1.1	4.1				Cur. Mat.-L/T/D	3.1	4.0
20.1	24.1	21.9				Trade Payables	17.7	18.6
2.7	.1	.0				Income Taxes Payable	.5	.1
7.5	14.9	10.7				All Other Current	11.7	10.0
45.1	55.1	50.4				Total Current	42.8	45.8
13.1	8.3	15.1				Long-Term Debt	11.3	13.4
.0	.0	.0				Deferred Taxes	.0	.1
3.4	2.0	1.0				All Other Non-Current	3.9	5.6
38.3	34.5	33.4				Net Worth	42.0	35.1
100.0	100.0	100.0				Total Liabilities & Net Worth	100.0	100.0
						INCOME DATA		
100.0	100.0	100.0				Net Sales	100.0	100.0
45.7	45.3	46.9				Gross Profit	43.6	43.1
41.3	44.6	47.3				Operating Expenses	40.9	41.4
4.4	.7	-.4				Operating Profit	2.7	1.8
.4	.0	-.2				All Other Expenses (net)	.8	1.0
4.0	.7	-.2				Profit Before Taxes	1.9	.8
						RATIOS		
3.1	3.6	2.3					3.4	2.7
2.0	1.8	1.5				Current	1.9	1.7
1.5	1.1	.9					1.2	1.2
.5	1.3	.4					1.0	.9
.2	.5	.3				Quick	(101) .3	.4
.0	.2	.1					.1	.1
0 UND	0 UND	0 999.8					0 999.8	0 UND
0 UND	6 60.8	4 81.5				Sales/Receivables	3 116.7	3 123.9
2 150.9	23 15.9	24 15.4					17 21.6	21 17.6
97 3.8	94 3.9	105 3.5					84 4.4	89 4.1
144 2.5	134 2.7	160 2.3				Cost of Sales/Inventory	125 2.9	143 2.6
238 1.5	219 1.7	231 1.6					187 2.0	210 1.7
21 17.0	32 11.5	31 11.6					15 24.3	20 17.9
35 10.6	50 7.4	65 5.6				Cost of Sales/Payables	31 11.7	40 9.0
53 6.9	71 5.1	88 4.1					67 5.4	68 5.3
4.7	3.5	5.8					4.7	4.9
8.1	9.7	12.9				Sales/Working Capital	6.7	7.3
16.2	72.2	-20.3					25.5	45.9
41.3	8.3	9.4					9.0	3.8
(20) 6.2	(24) 1.1	(17) 1.5				EBIT/Interest	(93) 2.7	(81) 1.6
2.0	-1.6	-.7					.8	-.1
						Net Profit + Depr., Dep.,	4.4	2.9
						Amort./Cur. Mat. L/T/D	(23) 1.8	(18) 1.5
							.7	.4
.0	.1	.2					.1	.2
.2	.4	.4				Fixed/Worth	.3	.4
.6	1.4	2.9					.9	1.2
.6	.4	.8					.5	.7
1.1	1.0	1.2				Debt/Worth	1.4	1.9
4.9	9.8	3.6					3.2	4.6
60.7	32.6	20.3				% Profit Before Taxes/Tangible	26.1	20.8
(22) 18.4	(27) 3.1	(15) 6.4				Net Worth	(94) 9.3	(87) 5.6
3.4	-4.3	-5.1					-1.5	-6.9
31.2	12.0	11.1				% Profit Before Taxes/Total	10.1	7.0
6.4	.3	2.0				Assets	4.4	1.6
2.3	-4.6	-3.9					-.7	-2.4
148.0	26.0	31.4					73.0	60.8
75.2	19.3	14.9				Sales/Net Fixed Assets	23.1	20.0
17.7	13.3	8.5					11.1	7.7
4.4	3.4	2.9					3.3	3.1
3.1	2.6	2.1				Sales/Total Assets	2.7	2.3
2.2	1.6	1.6					2.0	1.7
.3	.6	.7					.4	.5
(14) .5	(25) 1.0	(17) 1.3				% Depr., Dep., Amort./Sales	(85) .8	(78) 1.1
1.0	1.7	2.0					1.7	2.3
5.8	2.3					% Officers', Directors',	3.4	2.1
(14) 9.6	(22) 4.1					Owners' Comp/Sales	(48) 6.2	(51) 4.2
15.3	8.3						11.2	8.6
23173M	110879M	184155M	285046M	508619M	1243554M	Net Sales ($)	2460728M	1355894M
7106M	37565M	79686M	127964M	194553M	494192M	Total Assets ($)	1024157M	689294M

M = $ thousand   MM = $ million
See Pages 11 through 21 for Explanation of Ratios and Data

Comparative Historical Data | Current Data Sorted By Sales

			Type of Statement						
9	14	10	Unqualified		1	1		3	5
19	14	9	Reviewed	1	1	1		5	
23	35	37	Compiled	9	16	6	4	1	1
15	21	12	Tax Returns	7	2	2		1	
20	21	23	Other	3	7	4	1	4	4
4/1/02-3/31/03	4/1/03-3/31/04	4/1/04-3/31/05		23 (4/1-9/30/04)			68 (10/1/04-3/31/05)		
ALL	ALL	ALL		0-1MM	1-3MM	3-5MM	5-10MM	10-25MM	25MM & OVER
86	105	91	**NUMBER OF STATEMENTS**	20	27	14	6	14	10
%	%	%	**ASSETS**	%	%	%	%	%	%
10.9	13.8	10.5	Cash & Equivalents	6.3	16.9	10.7		8.5	6.1
8.6	6.5	6.5	Trade Receivables (net)	2.5	8.7	7.3		10.6	1.5
48.8	51.1	56.8	Inventory	72.4	55.7	52.4		48.4	51.6
1.4	2.2	1.0	All Other Current	.6	1.0	1.1		2.0	.5
69.7	73.6	74.7	Total Current	81.8	82.3	71.5		69.5	59.7
20.7	19.8	18.6	Fixed Assets (net)	14.1	13.8	18.2		21.6	33.4
2.3	.8	.6	Intangibles (net)	.3	.1	2.4		.2	.4
7.4	5.7	6.1	All Other Non-Current	3.8	3.8	8.0		8.8	6.4
100.0	100.0	100.0	Total	100.0	100.0	100.0		100.0	100.0
			LIABILITIES						
7.8	10.2	13.4	Notes Payable-Short Term	13.6	19.6	11.3		12.5	5.0
2.7	2.4	2.3	Cur. Mat.-L/T/D	2.1	.7	3.8		2.9	4.5
16.5	25.8	21.6	Trade Payables	19.3	17.1	26.1		23.0	23.0
.2	.6	.9	Income Taxes Payable	2.2	1.0	.2		.0	.4
10.9	11.8	10.9	All Other Current	7.1	16.3	11.7		8.7	9.5
38.0	50.8	49.1	Total Current	44.2	54.7	53.2		47.2	42.3
17.4	11.6	11.4	Long-Term Debt	18.3	9.0	7.0		17.8	5.3
.1	.2	.1	Deferred Taxes	.0	.0	.2		.0	.4
5.2	4.0	2.7	All Other Non-Current	5.0	1.8	1.5		3.0	3.5
39.3	33.4	36.8	Net Worth	32.5	34.5	38.2		32.0	48.4
100.0	100.0	100.0	Total Liabilities & Net Worth	100.0	100.0	100.0		100.0	100.0
			INCOME DATA						
100.0	100.0	100.0	Net Sales	100.0	100.0	100.0		100.0	100.0
45.8	44.5	44.6	Gross Profit	47.3	47.8	41.1		41.9	38.7
43.9	41.5	42.7	Operating Expenses	43.9	45.9	41.2		40.1	35.6
1.9	2.9	1.9	Operating Profit	3.4	1.9	-.1		1.8	3.1
.6	.6	.2	All Other Expenses (net)	.7	-.6	.7		1.1	.2
1.3	2.3	1.7	Profit Before Taxes	2.7	2.5	-.8		.7	2.9
			RATIOS						
3.3	2.4	2.7	Current	3.2	3.6	3.0		2.6	2.1
2.1	1.6	1.8		1.9	2.3	1.4		1.9	1.4
1.3	1.1	1.2		1.4	1.2	1.0		1.3	1.1
1.1	.8	.7	Quick	.5	1.1	1.1		.6	.3
.4	(104) .3	.2		.2	.6	.2		.4	.1
.2	.1	.1		.0	.1	.1		.1	.1
0 UND	0 UND	0 UND	Sales/Receivables	0 UND	0 UND	0 UND		0 999.8	1 573.2
4 98.9	3 139.5	1 244.2		0 UND	1 244.2	4 96.4		5 76.4	1 257.6
20 18.2	12 31.3	11 34.5		3 109.6	26 14.2	25 14.9		11 32.9	4 87.3
90 4.0	84 4.3	96 3.8	Cost of Sales/Inventory	116 3.1	100 3.7	85 4.3		93 3.9	70 5.3
134 2.7	129 2.8	145 2.5		195 1.9	131 2.8	149 2.4		124 2.9	115 3.2
194 1.9	216 1.7	228 1.6		275 1.3	239 1.5	164 2.2		190 1.9	175 2.1
16 22.8	33 10.9	30 12.1	Cost of Sales/Payables	21 17.8	29 12.4	29 12.4		27 13.6	26 13.9
40 9.2	58 6.3	45 8.2		42 8.7	39 9.3	56 6.5		39 9.3	53 6.9
61 6.0	99 3.7	72 5.1		77 4.7	65 5.6	71 5.2		70 5.2	91 4.0
3.9	4.9	4.8	Sales/Working Capital	3.7	3.6	9.0		5.1	6.4
6.6	9.2	8.7		8.1	6.6	13.0		7.9	23.2
19.7	43.8	30.2		19.1	15.7	-94.4		15.2	NM
6.5	7.8	12.1	EBIT/Interest	9.5	55.3	2.8		12.3	
(75) 1.6	(80) 2.2	(74) 2.2		(17) 2.7	(20) 2.0	(11) -.1		(13) 1.4	
-.8	.6	-.1		1.1	-.2	-14.2		-.1	
4.5	15.1	3.7	Net Profit + Depr., Dep., Amort./Cur. Mat. L/T/D						
(19) .5	(17) 1.2	(13) .4							
-1.1	.6	-.3							
.2	.2	.1	Fixed/Worth	.1	.1	.2		.2	.4
.4	.4	.4		.3	.2	.5		.3	.9
.9	1.4	1.1		.8	1.3	NM		1.4	1.0
.7	.8	.6	Debt/Worth	.8	.5	.7		.8	.6
1.3	1.7	1.1		2.2	1.0	1.1		1.6	1.1
4.3	5.0	4.7		6.0	10.9	NM		4.0	1.6
25.5	28.6	33.5	% Profit Before Taxes/Tangible Net Worth	33.6	47.9	16.1		29.9	36.7
(77) 8.0	(91) 9.4	(78) 9.7		(17) 10.3	(22) 8.8	(11) 3.1		(12) 14.4	11.0
-3.1	2.1	-.1		2.2	-1.5	-5.1		-5.1	7.1
8.7	10.0	13.3	% Profit Before Taxes/Total Assets	14.8	26.3	11.6		12.9	14.1
1.4	3.2	2.6		3.8	2.2	.3		4.2	5.8
-4.6	.0	-1.8		1.3	-1.8	-11.7		-2.5	2.7
48.4	52.3	44.2	Sales/Net Fixed Assets	82.2	88.8	28.8		38.1	12.1
16.3	19.6	18.7		26.5	25.1	18.6		15.4	7.7
7.8	9.3	9.7		11.7	16.7	12.3		8.2	6.2
3.1	3.2	3.5	Sales/Total Assets	4.2	3.5	3.5		3.2	3.3
2.4	2.3	2.6		2.6	2.6	2.7		2.5	2.8
1.8	1.7	1.9		1.9	1.4	1.9		1.6	2.1
.6	.5	.6	% Depr., Dep., Amort./Sales	.4	.4	.8		.5	
(75) 1.4	(84) 1.3	(69) 1.0		(13) .8	(18) .7	(11) 1.1		1.2	
2.3	2.1	1.9		1.4	1.1	2.0		2.0	
3.5	2.9	2.2	% Officers', Directors', Owners' Comp/Sales	5.3	2.9				
(48) 6.0	(61) 5.0	(47) 5.5		(13) 10.6	(16) 5.5				
9.8	8.5	8.7		16.0	8.7				
3169188M	1927539M	2355426M	Net Sales ($)	12770M	50648M	55860M	39945M	226276M	1969927M
1231664M	799246M	941066M	Total Assets ($)	5550M	24538M	22530M	18070M	101654M	768724M

Current Data Sorted By Assets   Comparative Historical Data

0-500M	500M-2MM	2-10MM	10-50MM	50-100MM	100-250MM	Type of Statement	4/1/00-3/31/01 ALL	4/1/01-3/31/02 ALL
1	2	4	6		2	Unqualified	12	16
7	8	12	2	1		Reviewed	15	16
10	7	5	1	1		Compiled	25	30
7	3	5	3		6	Tax Returns	12	11
						Other	29	24
20 (4/1-9/30/04)			73 (10/1/04-3/31/05)					
25	20	26	12	2	8	**NUMBER OF STATEMENTS**	93	97
%	%	%	%	%	%	**ASSETS**	%	%
6.5	12.9	16.8	17.1			Cash & Equivalents	11.6	13.8
2.7	10.3	5.0	11.0			Trade Receivables (net)	5.8	7.0
55.7	45.4	47.2	41.2			Inventory	54.7	47.8
.1	1.7	2.3	3.9			All Other Current	2.3	1.7
65.0	70.4	71.2	73.2			Total Current	74.5	70.4
26.1	16.7	16.8	22.1			Fixed Assets (net)	17.8	22.0
2.0	.2	.8	.6			Intangibles (net)	2.7	3.0
6.9	12.6	11.2	4.1			All Other Non-Current	5.0	4.7
100.0	100.0	100.0	100.0			Total	100.0	100.0
						LIABILITIES		
24.8	8.3	6.7	14.9			Notes Payable-Short Term	11.4	12.2
5.0	2.5	2.2	1.1			Cur. Mat.-L/T/D	2.7	3.2
8.7	17.7	24.7	22.4			Trade Payables	16.8	16.2
.4	.3	.7	.0			Income Taxes Payable	.6	.4
7.4	10.3	14.5	12.5			All Other Current	13.0	10.4
46.4	39.2	48.8	51.1			Total Current	44.5	42.5
17.7	13.9	4.1	5.1			Long-Term Debt	10.0	13.6
.0	.0	.2	.1			Deferred Taxes	.1	.1
6.1	5.1	2.9	3.3			All Other Non-Current	5.4	4.1
29.8	41.9	43.9	40.4			Net Worth	40.1	39.8
100.0	100.0	100.0	100.0			Total Liabilities & Net Worth	100.0	100.0
						INCOME DATA		
100.0	100.0	100.0	100.0			Net Sales	100.0	100.0
43.5	37.5	45.8	45.5			Gross Profit	41.0	42.9
38.9	36.1	43.1	45.1			Operating Expenses	37.7	40.2
4.6	1.3	2.7	.3			Operating Profit	3.3	2.7
1.7	1.4	.0	−.1			All Other Expenses (net)	.9	1.1
2.9	.0	2.7	.5			Profit Before Taxes	2.4	1.5
						RATIOS		
3.5	3.8	2.0	1.8				2.7	2.6
1.7	2.3	1.4	1.7			Current	1.9	1.7
.8	1.1	1.1	1.1				1.3	1.2
.5	1.1	1.0	1.0				.7	1.0
.1	.5	.4	.6			Quick	(92) .4	.4
.0	.1	.1	.2				.1	.2
0 UND	0 UND	0 UND	1 256.8				0 UND	0 UND
0 UND	5 74.6	1 571.0	4 83.8			Sales/Receivables	2 235.8	2 168.0
5 71.7	25 14.4	4 94.4	30 12.1				10 37.3	10 36.5
69 5.3	56 6.6	54 6.8	67 5.5				66 5.5	62 5.9
118 3.1	101 3.6	91 4.0	97 3.7			Cost of Sales/Inventory	114 3.2	92 4.0
175 2.1	200 1.8	156 2.3	116 3.1				167 2.2	150 2.4
0 UND	12 29.6	25 14.9	31 11.8				23 15.9	20 18.0
11 32.6	30 12.3	45 8.1	48 7.6			Cost of Sales/Payables	34 10.7	34 10.7
32 11.4	50 7.4	104 3.5	72 5.1				46 7.9	50 7.3
5.2	4.0	8.2	5.2				4.9	5.8
14.9	6.5	14.7	15.2			Sales/Working Capital	10.1	11.1
NM	754.6	45.8	58.0				19.7	42.1
5.5	13.9	23.0					10.1	9.9
(21) 2.5	(18) 4.6	(22) 6.2				EBIT/Interest	(78) 2.5	(80) 2.3
−.3	.2	2.0					.9	.9
						Net Profit + Depr., Dep.,	9.3	19.7
						Amort./Cur. Mat. L /T/D	(17) 2.5	(13) 2.3
							.7	1.2
.1	.1	.2	.1				.2	.2
.6	.2	.3	.4			Fixed/Worth	.4	.5
1.4	.6	.7	.9				1.0	1.3
.6	.6	.8	1.0				.6	.6
2.1	1.1	1.4	1.7			Debt/Worth	1.3	1.0
9.9	3.1	2.4	1.9				3.0	5.7
104.0	49.3	29.6	25.4				35.8	37.4
(21) 31.8	(19) 12.2	(24) 14.1	(11) 16.3			% Profit Before Taxes/Tangible Net Worth	(83) 13.5	(81) 14.4
4.9	−3.5	6.0	4.9				3.5	.4
19.3	12.6	17.2	15.5				12.3	13.0
8.9	4.9	5.3	7.1			% Profit Before Taxes/Total Assets	4.5	5.2
−.8	−1.2	2.1	1.9				.7	−.3
121.4	75.2	36.9	59.7				54.7	43.2
20.4	31.7	21.7	13.3			Sales/Net Fixed Assets	20.0	19.8
7.8	9.7	16.8	8.0				9.9	9.0
4.2	3.0	4.6	3.9				3.8	3.9
2.9	2.5	3.4	3.1			Sales/Total Assets	2.6	2.8
2.1	2.0	2.3	2.0				2.0	2.1
.7	.4	.7					.6	.5
(14) 1.4	(17) .7	(22) 1.0				% Depr., Dep., Amort./Sales	(75) .9	(80) .9
2.1	1.6	1.8					1.5	1.9
3.9	3.7	1.7					3.1	2.9
(13) 5.9	(10) 5.3	(13) 2.2				% Officers', Directors', Owners' Comp/Sales	(41) 5.7	(47) 5.0
7.5	6.7	3.6					8.7	8.1
19251M	62987M	385730M	625512M	573754M	3213924M	Net Sales ($)	3945383M	5014957M
6070M	22083M	105264M	211193M	186656M	1357950M	Total Assets ($)	1384310M	1984938M

M = $ thousand   MM = $ million
See Pages 11 through 21 for Explanation of Ratios and Data

Comparative Historical Data | Current Data Sorted By Sales

4/1/02-3/31/03 ALL	4/1/03-3/31/04 ALL	4/1/04-3/31/05 ALL	Type of Statement	0-1MM	1-3MM	3-5MM	5-10MM	10-25MM	25MM & OVER
24	20	12	Unqualified			1		2	9
17	24	17	Reviewed		3	2	1	6	5
21	34	21	Compiled	9	4		6	1	1
12	18	17	Tax Returns	8	6	2	1		
29	22	26	Other	6	3		3	5	9
					20 (4/1-9/30/04)		73 (10/1/04-3/31/05)		
103	118	93	NUMBER OF STATEMENTS	23	16	5	11	14	24
%	%	%	ASSETS	%	%	%	%	%	%
12.2	12.7	13.4	Cash & Equivalents	6.0	6.9		8.3	18.7	20.0
6.9	7.7	6.2	Trade Receivables (net)	2.3	8.4		12.7	5.5	7.2
47.1	44.6	46.6	Inventory	61.7	41.4		53.5	43.9	35.2
2.4	1.8	2.0	All Other Current	.0	2.2		1.4	1.8	4.4
68.6	66.7	68.2	Total Current	70.0	59.0		75.9	69.9	66.9
21.1	22.7	21.1	Fixed Assets (net)	24.6	21.1		17.6	15.2	23.5
3.3	3.0	1.8	Intangibles (net)	2.2	.3		.6	.9	4.0
6.9	7.6	8.9	All Other Non-Current	3.2	19.7		5.9	14.1	5.6
100.0	100.0	100.0	Total	100.0	100.0		100.0	100.0	100.0
			LIABILITIES						
10.0	8.4	12.5	Notes Payable-Short Term	27.5	8.8		4.9	8.8	7.4
2.8	4.8	2.8	Cur. Mat.-L/T/D	5.6	2.7		3.2	1.6	1.1
19.1	18.8	17.8	Trade Payables	8.9	9.1		31.9	24.3	22.1
.5	.5	.4	Income Taxes Payable	.3	.3		.0	.5	.4
9.7	11.9	11.5	All Other Current	5.4	11.6		12.8	12.5	14.1
42.0	44.3	45.0	Total Current	47.5	32.5		52.8	47.7	45.2
10.9	14.2	10.9	Long-Term Debt	21.4	12.7		8.3	1.7	8.0
.1	.1	.2	Deferred Taxes	.0	.0		.0	.4	.4
3.9	8.3	4.9	All Other Non-Current	9.1	2.8		4.5	1.8	5.4
43.2	33.0	39.1	Net Worth	22.0	52.0		34.3	48.4	41.0
100.0	100.0	100.0	Total Liabilities & Net Worth	100.0	100.0		100.0	100.0	100.0
			INCOME DATA						
100.0	100.0	100.0	Net Sales	100.0	100.0		100.0	100.0	100.0
42.0	41.2	42.6	Gross Profit	43.0	39.5		42.0	47.9	42.1
38.3	39.2	40.1	Operating Expenses	38.8	38.2		39.6	47.5	38.7
3.7	2.0	2.5	Operating Profit	4.2	1.4		2.4	.4	3.4
.6	.8	.8	All Other Expenses (net)	2.1	1.4		.2	.1	.2
3.1	1.2	1.7	Profit Before Taxes	2.1	.0		2.2	.3	3.2
			RATIOS						
2.6	2.5	3.0		3.8	3.8		2.9	2.0	1.9
1.7	1.7	1.6	Current	1.8	2.5		1.5	1.5	1.6
1.2	1.0	1.1		1.1	1.0		1.0	1.0	1.3
.9	1.0	1.0		.5	1.0		.5	1.1	1.0
.3	.4	.4	Quick	.1	.4		.3	.4	.6
.1	.1	.1		.1	.0		.1	.1	.4
0 UND	0 UND	0 UND		0 UND	0 UND		0 UND	0 UND	1 287.8
3 142.0	2 239.2	1 251.3	Sales/Receivables	0 UND	2 172.9		2 157.0	1 571.0	3 135.8
11 34.4	12 30.2	9 40.7		6 65.5	25 14.6		26 14.2	14 25.7	9 41.2
66 5.5	48 7.6	59 6.1		102 3.6	16 22.2		40 9.0	54 6.8	43 8.5
106 3.5	99 3.7	99 3.7	Cost of Sales/Inventory	153 2.4	92 4.0		92 4.0	92 4.0	80 4.6
151 2.4	148 2.5	151 2.4		246 1.5	139 2.6		201 1.8	130 2.8	100 3.6
24 15.5	16 22.5	13 27.2		5 67.0	0 UND		24 15.4	28 13.1	28 13.2
37 10.0	34 10.6	32 11.3	Cost of Sales/Payables	14 25.3	17 22.0		55 6.6	41 8.9	47 7.8
56 6.5	56 6.5	53 6.9		32 11.3	42 8.7		103 3.6	81 4.5	56 6.5
5.2	5.7	5.3		4.5	5.3		4.8	6.5	8.4
9.9	13.1	12.4	Sales/Working Capital	8.3	8.2		11.5	14.7	15.2
48.5	NM	45.1		43.7	NM		-264.3	NM	28.1
21.7	8.6	13.3		4.2	11.5		29.6	14.5	183.2
(88) 3.8	(104) 2.5	(76) 4.0	EBIT/Interest	(21) 2.3	(14) 3.5		(10) 9.3	(10) 3.0	(18) 13.0
1.1	-.3	1.7		.2	-3.8		3.6	1.9	3.3
16.4	8.1	12.2	Net Profit + Depr., Dep.,						
(21) 2.5	(20) 2.0	(16) 2.1	Amort./Cur. Mat. L/T/D						
-.4	.6	1.1							
.3	.3	.2		.1	.1		.1	.2	.3
.5	.6	.5	Fixed/Worth	.6	.2		.4	.3	.6
1.0	4.5	.9		2.9	.6		1.0	.6	.9
.6	.7	.7		.7	.5		1.1	.4	.9
1.1	1.4	1.5	Debt/Worth	3.1	.8		2.0	1.0	1.6
2.5	24.2	3.3		13.0	2.1		4.1	2.4	2.3
34.4	25.7	46.8	% Profit Before Taxes/Tangible	96.2	45.4		44.6	38.0	39.0
(92) 11.3	(94) 11.4	(84) 18.4	Net Worth	(19) 28.6	11.0		(10) 15.6	(13) 14.1	(22) 21.4
3.3	-1.1	4.8		2.0	-26.0		6.0	4.2	13.2
13.8	10.4	16.7	% Profit Before Taxes/Total	13.3	23.1		16.5	15.4	25.9
5.5	3.3	6.2	Assets	5.8	8.0		4.6	3.5	11.0
.4	-2.2	1.3		-2.5	-8.7		1.7	1.5	3.2
41.1	33.3	43.7		121.4	54.8		37.9	50.7	28.9
16.3	17.8	20.4	Sales/Net Fixed Assets	15.5	34.1		18.6	22.6	12.5
8.4	7.8	8.5		5.8	13.0		11.3	19.8	8.5
3.7	4.1	4.0		3.4	4.0		4.2	5.2	4.4
2.6	2.6	2.7	Sales/Total Assets	2.3	2.7		3.1	3.4	3.1
1.9	1.9	2.1		1.8	2.1		2.4	2.5	2.4
.6	.7	.6		1.0	.3		.5	.9	1.3
(81) 1.1	(93) 1.3	(68) 1.1	% Depr., Dep., Amort./Sales	(12) 1.8	(15) .9		(10) .8	(12) 1.0	(15) 2.3
2.0	2.3	2.1		2.9	1.2		1.8	1.7	2.6
2.3	2.8	2.1	% Officers', Directors',	4.2					
(47) 4.6	(52) 4.8	(37) 4.5	Owners' Comp/Sales	(12) 5.8					
6.8	7.4	6.4		6.8					
5888365M	6287443M	4881158M	Net Sales ($)	13442M	30898M	19878M	77631M	227916M	4511393M
2599071M	2660875M	1889216M	Total Assets ($)	7359M	11870M	9966M	26316M	81712M	1751993M

M = $ thousand   MM = $ million
See Pages 11 through 21 for Explanation of Ratios and Data

RETAIL—Family Clothing Stores NAICS 448140 (SIC 5651)

Current Data Sorted By Assets | Comparative Historical Data

Type of Statement	0-500M	500M-2MM	2-10MM	10-50MM	50-100MM	100-250MM		4/1/00-3/31/01 ALL	4/1/01-3/31/02 ALL
Unqualified			6	6	1	1		15	8
Reviewed		3		3				14	15
Compiled	3	7	1					19	17
Tax Returns	10	5	6	6				18	25
Other	5	5	2		2			34	29
		17 (4/1-9/30/04)		55 (10/1/04-3/31/05)					
NUMBER OF STATEMENTS	18	20	15	15	3	1		100	94

	%	%	%	%	%	%		%	%
ASSETS									
Cash & Equivalents	13.9	10.5	10.6	13.4				11.5	13.8
Trade Receivables (net)	.2	3.9	7.6	5.6				5.6	6.0
Inventory	64.3	56.5	47.7	48.0				48.1	47.0
All Other Current	1.0	.2	2.1	2.4				1.7	2.5
Total Current	79.4	71.2	68.0	69.5				66.8	69.3
Fixed Assets (net)	9.4	17.9	27.1	23.0				23.8	18.6
Intangibles (net)	.8	4.2	1.4	1.8				4.1	4.2
All Other Non-Current	10.3	6.6	3.5	5.8				5.3	7.9
Total	100.0	100.0	100.0	100.0				100.0	100.0
LIABILITIES									
Notes Payable-Short Term	20.5	13.9	7.5	9.1				9.0	8.3
Cur. Mat.-L/T/D	5.1	.9	2.2	2.0				3.0	1.6
Trade Payables	17.1	17.8	16.2	13.3				15.4	17.5
Income Taxes Payable	.3	.1	.1	.1				.2	.1
All Other Current	5.0	3.9	6.6	13.7				9.7	13.4
Total Current	48.0	36.6	32.6	38.2				37.4	40.9
Long-Term Debt	10.6	19.5	15.4	12.5				17.8	11.6
Deferred Taxes	.1	.0	.0	.1				.0	.5
All Other Non-Current	6.0	5.2	1.3	3.2				4.7	4.2
Net Worth	35.4	38.7	50.7	46.0				40.0	42.8
Total Liabilities & Net Worth	100.0	100.0	100.0	100.0				100.0	100.0
INCOME DATA									
Net Sales	100.0	100.0	100.0	100.0				100.0	100.0
Gross Profit	42.8	48.1	40.6	42.6				41.0	41.2
Operating Expenses	37.8	43.6	37.4	39.4				37.3	38.8
Operating Profit	5.0	4.4	3.2	3.2				3.7	2.4
All Other Expenses (net)	.9	.1	-.2	-.2				1.2	.1
Profit Before Taxes	4.1	4.3	3.5	3.4				2.5	2.3
RATIOS									
Current	3.5 / 1.8 / 1.1	2.8 / 1.9 / 1.5	3.4 / 2.0 / 1.4	3.0 / 1.8 / 1.3				3.8 / 2.0 / 1.2	3.7 / 2.0 / 1.3
Quick	.8 / (17) .2 / .1	.4 / .3 / .1	.9 / .5 / .1	.9 / .3 / .1				.9 / (99) .4 / .1	.9 / .4 / .1
Sales/Receivables	0 UND / 0 UND / 0 UND	0 UND / 0 UND / 7 54.0	0 UND / 2 162.5 / 5 80.7	0 UND / 2 149.0 / 11 33.5				0 UND / 2 165.3 / 9 38.7	0 UND / 1 329.7 / 12 31.5
Cost of Sales/Inventory	87 4.2 / 134 2.7 / 215 1.7	129 2.8 / 171 2.1 / 290 1.3	91 4.0 / 125 2.9 / 211 1.7	61 6.0 / 107 3.4 / 121 3.0				64 5.7 / 125 2.9 / 181 2.0	60 6.1 / 107 3.4 / 181 2.0
Cost of Sales/Payables	14 25.2 / 25 14.3 / 62 5.8	21 17.1 / 40 9.1 / 74 4.9	17 22.0 / 36 10.1 / 71 5.2	21 17.6 / 30 12.0 / 43 8.6				13 28.2 / 32 11.6 / 56 6.5	10 34.8 / 33 11.2 / 60 6.1
Sales/Working Capital	3.8 / 10.1 / NM	4.0 / 6.6 / 16.5	5.3 / 8.1 / 12.7	7.5 / 9.6 / 16.2				4.7 / 8.5 / 28.9	4.6 / 8.7 / 24.9
EBIT/Interest	4.9 / (14) 3.0 / 1.0	12.6 / (18) 2.6 / -.9	12.0 / 4.7 / 1.3	18.9 / (14) 3.2 / 2.0				11.1 / (89) 3.8 / 1.2	13.2 / (79) 2.6 / .0
Net Profit + Depr., Dep., Amort./Cur. Mat. L /T/D								5.0 / (19) 2.6 / 1.6	5.5 / (15) 1.4 / .2
Fixed/Worth	.0 / .2 / NM	.2 / .4 / 1.0	.1 / .3 / 1.6	.2 / .4 / .8				.2 / .5 / 1.2	.1 / .4 / .9
Debt/Worth	.4 / 1.3 / NM	.7 / 1.1 / 3.7	.4 / 1.0 / 2.0	.6 / 1.5 / 3.3				.7 / 1.3 / 3.7	.6 / 1.1 / 3.4
% Profit Before Taxes/Tangible Net Worth	61.3 / (14) 15.6 / 2.2	87.1 / (18) 24.2 / -1.0	26.6 / 13.2 / 1.7	45.5 / (14) 9.4 / 3.2				51.6 / (87) 18.7 / 4.7	45.2 / (84) 11.0 / .7
% Profit Before Taxes/Total Assets	26.4 / 6.8 / 1.9	25.4 / 4.0 / -2.3	15.7 / 6.0 / .5	21.1 / 2.7 / 2.1				18.4 / 6.6 / 1.0	20.9 / 5.0 / -2.0
Sales/Net Fixed Assets	UND / 62.2 / 22.9	29.1 / 17.3 / 7.7	40.6 / 16.1 / 3.2	30.2 / 15.1 / 8.7				36.0 / 13.0 / 7.9	58.7 / 20.2 / 8.5
Sales/Total Assets	4.1 / 3.1 / 2.3	3.3 / 2.2 / 1.5	3.6 / 2.4 / 1.5	3.7 / 3.1 / 2.0				3.7 / 2.4 / 1.6	3.7 / 2.6 / 1.7
% Depr., Dep., Amort./Sales		.4 / (16) .9 / 1.6	.6 / (13) 1.0 / 1.3	1.1 / 1.4 / 1.8				.6 / (79) 1.1 / 2.3	.6 / (77) .9 / 1.7
% Officers', Directors', Owners' Comp/Sales	2.6 / (13) 6.7 / 10.3	2.1 / 5.1 / 7.6						2.8 / (40) 4.4 / 8.2	1.3 / (44) 6.0 / 10.0
Net Sales ($)	15858M	49661M	162392M	980375M	721423M	367207M		4621503M	2271378M
Total Assets ($)	5027M	21006M	63090M	321242M	230018M	100399M		1857394M	830749M

© RMA 2005

M = $ thousand   MM = $ million
See Pages 11 through 21 for Explanation of Ratios and Data

Comparative Historical Data   Current Data Sorted By Sales

4/1/02-3/31/03 ALL	4/1/03-3/31/04 ALL	4/1/04-3/31/05 ALL	Type of Statement	17 (4/1-9/30/04) 0-1MM	55 (10/1/04-3/31/05) 1-3MM	3-5MM	5-10MM	10-25MM	25MM & OVER
6	11	8	Unqualified					2	6
14	14	7	Reviewed		3			2	2
19	16	16	Compiled		11	2	1	2	
12	17	17	Tax Returns	10	3	1	3		
23	19	24	Other	4	4	3	1	4	8
74	77	72	**NUMBER OF STATEMENTS**	14	21	6	5	10	16
%	%	%	**ASSETS**	%	%	%	%	%	%
10.0	11.0	12.5	Cash & Equivalents	13.7	11.3			12.0	14.4
5.4	3.0	4.0	Trade Receivables (net)	2.6	.8			15.8	1.9
49.5	52.7	54.5	Inventory	61.2	54.9			50.9	50.4
4.4	2.6	1.5	All Other Current	.5	.8			1.3	3.2
69.4	69.3	72.4	Total Current	77.9	67.8			80.0	69.8
19.2	21.3	19.0	Fixed Assets (net)	10.5	20.5			16.0	23.4
3.1	2.8	2.1	Intangibles (net)	2.1	2.8			1.7	.9
8.4	6.6	6.5	All Other Non-Current	9.6	9.0			2.3	5.9
100.0	100.0	100.0	Total	100.0	100.0			100.0	100.0
			LIABILITIES						
14.2	12.5	12.6	Notes Payable-Short Term	17.6	19.1			13.2	7.5
3.3	3.2	2.5	Cur. Mat.-L/T/D	6.4	1.2			2.1	1.8
18.3	18.6	17.0	Trade Payables	13.0	17.8			16.0	18.1
.2	.2	.2	Income Taxes Payable	.0	.3			.2	.1
10.2	12.7	7.1	All Other Current	2.4	4.3			10.6	13.2
46.2	47.1	39.3	Total Current	39.3	42.8			42.0	40.8
14.4	15.1	14.4	Long-Term Debt	13.6	20.7			8.9	10.3
.1	.0	.1	Deferred Taxes	.0	.1			.1	.3
5.3	8.1	3.9	All Other Non-Current	7.7	5.2			.5	3.1
34.0	29.7	42.3	Net Worth	39.5	31.3			48.5	45.5
100.0	100.0	100.0	Total Liabilities & Net Worth	100.0	100.0			100.0	100.0
			INCOME DATA						
100.0	100.0	100.0	Net Sales	100.0	100.0			100.0	100.0
42.9	43.1	43.3	Gross Profit	42.1	46.7			34.8	42.1
40.4	40.8	39.3	Operating Expenses	38.0	42.4			31.9	38.3
2.5	2.3	4.1	Operating Profit	4.1	4.3			2.9	3.8
−.2	.1	.2	All Other Expenses (net)	.1	.4			−.4	.2
2.7	2.2	3.9	Profit Before Taxes	4.0	3.9			3.2	3.7
			RATIOS						
2.6	2.9	3.1	Current	3.9	2.8			3.4	2.7
1.8	1.7	1.9		2.2	1.8			1.7	1.9
1.1	1.0	1.4		1.5	1.2			1.4	1.3
.6	.7	.7	Quick	.8	.3			1.0	.7
.3	.2	(71) .3		(13) .3	.2			.6	.3
.1	.0	.1		.1	.0			.1	.1
0 UND	0 UND	0 UND	Sales/Receivables	0 UND	0 UND			0 UND	0 UND
2 192.5	1 567.0	0 UND		0 UND	0 UND			5 71.7	1 293.6
8 47.4	3 104.6	4 93.5		0 UND	0 UND			55 6.7	3 130.1
55 6.6	85 4.3	89 4.1	Cost of Sales/Inventory	109 3.3	85 4.3			83 4.4	62 5.9
112 3.2	131 2.8	126 2.9		148 2.5	175 2.1			110 3.3	102 3.6
190 1.9	189 1.9	214 1.7		286 1.3	254 1.4			151 2.4	120 3.0
18 20.0	20 18.0	19 19.5	Cost of Sales/Payables	0 UND	18 20.6			22 16.6	18 20.3
35 10.4	34 10.8	35 10.5		23 15.7	37 10.0			32 11.3	33 11.2
60 6.1	54 6.8	62 5.9		40 9.2	84 4.4			53 6.8	43 8.6
5.7	5.3	4.4	Sales/Working Capital	2.9	4.2			5.8	7.9
11.4	11.6	8.4		6.8	7.9			8.3	11.5
74.8	106.9	18.0		25.3	25.0			11.8	23.2
16.2	10.9	11.4	EBIT/Interest	4.7	8.6				21.7
(65) 4.5	(61) 2.5	(64) 3.5		(11) 3.0	(19) 2.5				(15) 4.7
1.1	−1.2	1.1		.4	−.6				2.0
12.2	4.5	4.4	Net Profit + Depr., Dep., Amort./Cur. Mat. L/T/D						
(18) 2.5	(17) 1.3	(16) 2.5							
.9	.5	1.1							
.1	.1	.1	Fixed/Worth	.0	.2			.1	.3
.5	.4	.3		.1	.8			.2	.4
1.2	1.4	1.0		NM	1.9			.8	.8
.6	.7	.6	Debt/Worth	.5	.6			.4	.6
1.2	1.3	1.1		1.3	1.2			1.3	1.1
3.1	4.5	2.3		NM	5.1			2.1	3.0
39.9	44.4	48.8	% Profit Before Taxes/Tangible Net Worth	78.6	61.7				40.7
(66) 10.4	(63) 17.9	(65) 14.0		(11) 7.2	(18) 18.5				14.8
1.8	−2.4	2.8		−.5	.9				4.8
15.4	16.7	20.8	% Profit Before Taxes/Total Assets	27.6	18.1			16.8	26.5
4.6	6.0	5.2		4.7	6.3			6.3	4.9
.3	−2.9	1.3		.5	−1.9			2.5	2.2
51.4	46.7	47.2	Sales/Net Fixed Assets	UND	45.7			116.5	31.8
16.3	18.0	19.3		34.6	18.2			22.7	15.2
9.6	8.4	9.5		18.8	6.9			7.0	9.9
3.8	3.7	3.6	Sales/Total Assets	3.5	3.3			4.1	3.9
2.6	2.5	2.8		2.9	2.2			2.6	3.5
2.1	2.0	1.9		1.7	1.5			1.9	2.7
.6	.7	.6	% Depr., Dep., Amort./Sales		.4				1.1
(59) 1.4	(67) 1.4	(57) 1.1			(18) 1.0				1.3
2.0	2.2	1.5			2.2				1.7
2.4	2.0	2.2	% Officers', Directors', Owners' Comp/Sales		2.7				
(33) 4.2	(31) 4.8	(33) 5.6			(14) 5.7				
10.4	11.5	7.7			8.0				
4825866M	2444685M	2296916M	Net Sales ($)	8414M	37906M	22149M	35638M	191498M	2001311M
1176618M	775885M	740782M	Total Assets ($)	4461M	22580M	10467M	12287M	93482M	597505M

© RMA 2005

M = $ thousand   MM = $ million

See Pages 11 through 21 for Explanation of Ratios and Data

Current Data Sorted By Assets   **Comparative Historical Data**

Type of Statement	0-500M	500M-2MM	2-10MM	10-50MM	50-100MM	100-250MM	4/1/00-3/31/01 ALL	4/1/01-3/31/02 ALL
Unqualified		1	2				2	1
Reviewed		4	4	1			8	5
Compiled	5	5	3				16	11
Tax Returns	13	7	2				4	3
Other	5	8	6	2	1	1	7	12
	14 (4/1-9/30/04)			57 (10/1/04-3/31/05)				
NUMBER OF STATEMENTS	23	25	17	3	2	1	37	32
ASSETS	%	%	%	%	%	%	%	%
Cash & Equivalents	12.4	9.5	11.9				11.8	12.9
Trade Receivables (net)	6.6	17.7	12.8				17.5	13.1
Inventory	53.1	41.7	51.0				50.5	46.4
All Other Current	.8	1.7	3.4				2.5	4.2
Total Current	72.9	70.7	79.0				82.4	76.6
Fixed Assets (net)	22.1	17.9	12.7				10.8	15.6
Intangibles (net)	1.3	7.0	.1				2.3	1.2
All Other Non-Current	3.7	4.3	8.2				4.6	6.6
Total	100.0	100.0	100.0				100.0	100.0
LIABILITIES								
Notes Payable-Short Term	13.0	13.4	13.5				14.8	10.0
Cur. Mat.-L/T/D	5.6	2.1	2.6				1.3	5.7
Trade Payables	17.7	22.8	21.9				20.2	18.1
Income Taxes Payable	.0	.2	.5				.3	.2
All Other Current	13.0	12.9	9.8				16.7	12.3
Total Current	49.4	51.4	48.3				53.2	46.3
Long-Term Debt	17.1	11.1	5.9				9.8	9.9
Deferred Taxes	.0	.2	.0				.2	.0
All Other Non-Current	8.1	3.1	4.5				4.1	12.1
Net Worth	25.4	34.2	41.3				32.6	31.8
Total Liabilities & Net Worth	100.0	100.0	100.0				100.0	100.0
INCOME DATA								
Net Sales	100.0	100.0	100.0				100.0	100.0
Gross Profit	50.4	48.0	45.4				45.1	48.6
Operating Expenses	47.0	44.1	40.0				42.0	44.8
Operating Profit	3.4	3.9	5.5				3.1	3.8
All Other Expenses (net)	.4	.3	1.4				.7	.6
Profit Before Taxes	3.0	3.6	4.0				2.4	3.2
RATIOS								
Current	3.1	1.6	1.9				3.2	2.4
	2.0	1.5	1.6				1.5	1.6
	1.0	1.0	1.4				1.3	1.2
Quick	1.3	1.2	1.0				1.3	1.0
	.3	.4	.4				.7	.5
	.1	.2	.1				.2	.2
Sales/Receivables	0 UND	0 UND	2 179.1				2 240.3	0 UND
	0 UND	14 26.6	6 60.0				24 15.4	15 24.0
	14 26.6	48 7.6	41 8.8				41 8.9	37 9.8
Cost of Sales/Inventory	79 4.6	56 6.5	89 4.1				95 3.9	99 3.7
	120 3.1	80 4.6	137 2.7				163 2.2	160 2.3
	173 2.1	152 2.4	190 1.9				241 1.5	272 1.3
Cost of Sales/Payables	0 UND	25 14.3	33 11.0				12 29.7	14 25.7
	26 14.1	46 7.9	57 6.5				55 6.6	39 9.3
	61 6.0	72 5.1	68 5.3				94 3.9	86 4.3
Sales/Working Capital	6.8	9.0	5.8				3.8	4.3
	10.8	16.2	9.2				6.0	7.5
	UND	106.6	20.1				15.7	15.8
EBIT/Interest	15.8	13.8	69.8				7.6	5.2
	(17) 4.5	(22) 6.5	5.7				(29) 2.1	(30) 2.1
	-2.6	1.0	1.7				.9	1.2
Net Profit + Depr., Dep., Amort./Cur. Mat. L /T/D								
Fixed/Worth	.3	.1	.1				.1	.1
	.7	.5	.2				.2	.3
	18.7	1.1	.6				.6	.6
Debt/Worth	.5	.9	.9				.8	.8
	6.1	2.1	1.7				2.0	1.6
	42.3	5.5	2.4				5.3	4.6
% Profit Before Taxes/Tangible Net Worth	92.9	92.1	64.5				27.7	28.8
	(19) 39.0	(22) 35.0	25.3				(34) 8.3	(29) 7.6
	10.2	6.7	2.7				1.0	.8
% Profit Before Taxes/Total Assets	25.5	21.3	20.2				8.8	10.4
	8.6	6.6	8.5				3.9	2.9
	-7.3	.7	1.5				-.3	.4
Sales/Net Fixed Assets	52.0	115.3	70.0				124.9	87.3
	20.5	21.5	28.0				28.1	19.2
	8.8	10.9	13.2				12.7	10.0
Sales/Total Assets	4.9	4.1	3.4				3.0	3.0
	3.5	2.9	3.0				2.3	2.0
	2.2	2.2	1.7				1.5	1.3
% Depr., Dep., Amort./Sales	.5	.5	.6				.4	.3
	(14) .9	(20) 1.2	(14) 1.2				(30) .9	(24) .9
	1.8	2.1	2.0				1.4	1.7
% Officers', Directors', Owners' Comp/Sales	2.7	3.0					5.9	4.3
	(13) 5.8	(16) 3.7					(21) 8.1	(14) 7.8
	13.2	5.5					13.6	15.1
Net Sales ($)	16190M	86005M	190951M	158477M	332955M	337028M	247516M	226186M
Total Assets ($)	5190M	25386M	66844M	54880M	137156M	244131M	97396M	95629M

M = $ thousand   MM = $ million

See Pages 11 through 21 for Explanation of Ratios and Data

Comparative Historical Data / **Current Data Sorted By Sales**

	4/1/02-3/31/03 ALL	4/1/03-3/31/04 ALL	4/1/04-3/31/05 ALL	0-1MM	1-3MM	3-5MM	5-10MM	10-25MM	25MM & OVER
Type of Statement									
Unqualified	2	2	5			2	1		2
Reviewed	6	9	9	1	2	1	2	2	1
Compiled	10	12	13	3	4	3	3		
Tax Returns	8	10	22	14	2	1	3	2	
Other	9	5	22	4	7	2	3	2	4
				14 (4/1-9/30/04)			57 (10/1/04-3/31/05)		
NUMBER OF STATEMENTS	35	38	71	22	15	9	12	6	7
ASSETS	%	%	%	%	%	%	%	%	%
Cash & Equivalents	15.6	12.1	10.5	11.6	7.9		14.0		
Trade Receivables (net)	15.0	13.4	12.8	6.6	13.9		20.5		
Inventory	49.7	46.1	48.1	52.9	42.8		42.0		
All Other Current	3.1	1.4	1.7	.9	.8		4.9		
Total Current	83.3	73.0	73.1	72.0	65.3		81.4		
Fixed Assets (net)	11.8	18.0	17.8	20.5	22.7		13.6		
Intangibles (net)	.8	2.1	3.7	3.8	2.9		.3		
All Other Non-Current	4.0	7.0	5.4	3.8	9.1		4.7		
Total	100.0	100.0	100.0	100.0	100.0		100.0		
LIABILITIES									
Notes Payable-Short Term	10.7	12.0	13.0	12.7	14.0		8.2		
Cur. Mat.-L/T/D	2.3	4.1	3.3	6.1	1.3		2.4		
Trade Payables	23.5	20.3	20.5	17.9	19.2		24.4		
Income Taxes Payable	.1	.2	.2	.0	.6		.4		
All Other Current	11.0	9.5	12.1	14.5	14.2		9.7		
Total Current	47.6	46.1	49.1	51.2	49.3		45.1		
Long-Term Debt	13.2	13.2	12.9	18.3	14.6		6.8		
Deferred Taxes	.1	.1	.1	.0	.2		.2		
All Other Non-Current	4.6	7.5	5.9	8.1	1.8		3.1		
Net Worth	34.5	33.1	31.9	22.3	34.1		44.8		
Total Liabilities & Net Worth	100.0	100.0	100.0	100.0	100.0		100.0		
INCOME DATA									
Net Sales	100.0	100.0	100.0	100.0	100.0		100.0		
Gross Profit	46.6	48.4	47.4	49.9	50.1		45.5		
Operating Expenses	43.7	43.6	43.5	46.5	46.6		42.8		
Operating Profit	3.0	4.8	4.0	3.5	3.6		2.7		
All Other Expenses (net)	.4	.8	.7	.6	.4		-.1		
Profit Before Taxes	2.5	4.0	3.3	2.9	3.2		2.8		
RATIOS									
Current	3.7	2.3	2.3	3.3	2.0		2.0		
	1.7	1.7	1.6	1.4	1.5		1.6		
	1.2	1.2	1.1	.9	1.0		1.5		
Quick	1.1	1.0	1.1	1.3	.8		1.4		
	.6	.4	.4	.3	.3		.5		
	.3	.2	.1	.1	.1		.2		
Sales/Receivables	0 999.8	0 UND	0 UND	0 UND	0 UND		2 195.0		
	14 26.7	7 49.7	4 92.2	0 UND	4 92.2		14 26.9		
	45 8.1	34 10.6	37 9.8	24 15.0	50 7.4		43 8.4		
Cost of Sales/Inventory	70 5.2	58 6.3	63 5.8	72 5.0	67 5.5		63 5.8		
	163 2.2	118 3.1	106 3.4	145 2.5	89 4.1		103 3.5		
	245 1.5	218 1.7	173 2.1	194 1.9	127 2.9		185 2.0		
Cost of Sales/Payables	22 16.5	23 16.2	19 19.0	0 UND	9 38.4		28 12.8		
	53 6.9	58 6.3	45 8.1	28 13.1	46 7.9		55 6.7		
	117 3.1	102 3.6	65 5.6	86 4.2	80 4.6		74 5.0		
Sales/Working Capital	3.9	5.3	6.8	4.4	8.3		4.4		
	7.7	8.6	11.9	15.0	12.8		9.1		
	22.1	47.9	73.5	-20.7	73.5		14.0		
EBIT/Interest	18.9	14.9	13.8	8.7	15.5		123.7		
	(29) 2.8	(34) 5.6	(62) 4.6	(16) 3.2	(14) 4.0		(11) 5.7		
	-.3	1.5	1.3	-2.8	2.2		.8		
Net Profit + Depr., Dep., Amort./Cur. Mat. L/T/D			3.8						
		(11) .9							
			.5						
Fixed/Worth	.1	.1	.2	.3	.2		.0		
	.4	.4	.5	1.4	.6		.2		
	.6	1.4	2.5	UND	.8		.5		
Debt/Worth	.6	.6	.8	.6	.6		.5		
	1.2	1.7	2.1	8.9	1.9		1.7		
	3.0	3.5	8.1	UND	5.2		2.4		
% Profit Before Taxes/Tangible Net Worth	30.7	53.4	74.2	96.4	65.5		32.8		
	(31) 6.7	(32) 14.4	(63) 30.4	(17) 29.6	(14) 28.4		(11) 19.0		
	-3.7	1.8	7.5	4.7	9.8		2.2		
% Profit Before Taxes/Total Assets	15.0	16.6	18.7	24.2	18.3		14.0		
	3.6	8.4	6.6	4.9	8.4		8.3		
	-1.9	.5	1.1	-8.9	5.5		.0		
Sales/Net Fixed Assets	76.8	46.9	62.7	70.1	25.3		195.7		
	25.5	20.0	24.5	21.0	16.1		43.0		
	12.6	10.3	9.6	6.8	9.0		12.0		
Sales/Total Assets	4.2	3.9	3.9	5.0	3.8		4.1		
	2.6	2.7	3.0	2.6	3.3		3.0		
	1.5	1.9	2.1	1.8	2.4		1.8		
% Depr., Dep., Amort./Sales	.3	.6	.5	.4	.9		.4		
	(26) 1.0	(32) 1.3	(53) 1.1	(14) .9	(11) 1.3		(10) 1.1		
	2.2	1.8	1.9	2.0	2.1		2.4		
% Officers', Directors', Owners' Comp/Sales	3.3	2.9	2.7	2.9	3.0				
	(19) 5.9	(20) 4.7	(35) 4.8	(12) 6.9	(10) 3.6				
	9.2	8.1	7.5	13.7	5.6				
Net Sales ($)	228341M	241121M	1121606M	12448M	28992M	35031M	79040M	104400M	861695M
Total Assets ($)	84298M	102693M	533587M	6112M	11682M	14552M	30826M	28746M	441669M

M = $ thousand   MM = $ million
See Pages 11 through 21 for Explanation of Ratios and Data

RETAIL—Other Clothing Stores NAICS 448190 (SIC 5621, 5632, 5699)

Current Data Sorted By Assets							Comparative Historical Data	
1	1	5	4	2	1	Type of Statement		
1	6	15				Unqualified	9	10
4	17	8				Reviewed	13	16
23	20	4			1	Compiled	35	30
10	8	18	7	1		Tax Returns	22	10
						Other	29	30
	35 (4/1-9/30/04)		122 (10/1/04-3/31/05)				4/1/00-3/31/01	4/1/01-3/31/02
0-500M	500M-2MM	2-10MM	10-50MM	50-100MM	100-250MM		ALL	ALL
39	52	50	11	3	2	NUMBER OF STATEMENTS	108	96
%	%	%	%	%	%	ASSETS	%	%
8.5	8.6	7.8	5.7			Cash & Equivalents	9.3	8.9
9.9	8.7	17.5	18.7			Trade Receivables (net)	11.4	13.8
53.0	55.1	44.4	44.0			Inventory	46.6	46.2
.4	1.6	2.1	1.4			All Other Current	1.8	2.3
71.8	74.1	71.7	69.8			Total Current	69.1	71.2
17.5	18.7	20.7	21.6			Fixed Assets (net)	20.5	22.5
6.0	1.4	2.4	2.4			Intangibles (net)	4.1	2.3
4.7	5.9	5.2	6.2			All Other Non-Current	6.3	4.0
100.0	100.0	100.0	100.0			Total	100.0	100.0
						LIABILITIES		
13.4	18.9	9.8	20.5			Notes Payable-Short Term	17.0	10.1
3.3	2.1	2.3	1.5			Cur. Mat.-L/T/D	4.0	4.6
15.1	21.1	24.5	16.9			Trade Payables	24.7	21.9
.1	.3	.4	.0			Income Taxes Payable	.1	.3
10.2	8.6	10.0	9.2			All Other Current	10.8	11.4
42.1	51.1	47.0	48.3			Total Current	56.6	48.3
24.9	11.4	10.7	8.5			Long-Term Debt	14.8	17.6
.1	.0	.0	.0			Deferred Taxes	.1	.2
4.9	4.2	3.8	8.7			All Other Non-Current	6.0	7.8
28.0	33.4	38.6	34.5			Net Worth	22.3	26.1
100.0	100.0	100.0	100.0			Total Liabilities & Net Worth	100.0	100.0
						INCOME DATA		
100.0	100.0	100.0	100.0			Net Sales	100.0	100.0
47.1	44.3	44.1	41.6			Gross Profit	42.2	43.3
41.6	40.8	40.1	35.1			Operating Expenses	39.1	39.6
5.5	3.5	4.0	6.5			Operating Profit	3.1	3.7
.9	.4	.2	.5			All Other Expenses (net)	1.2	1.0
4.5	3.2	3.8	6.0			Profit Before Taxes	2.0	2.8
						RATIOS		
5.2	2.9	2.1	2.1				2.1	2.4
3.3	1.7	1.6	1.3			Current	1.4	1.5
1.1	1.0	1.2	1.2				1.0	1.1
1.3	.7	.8	.9				.7	.9
.6	.3	.5	.3			Quick	(107) .3	.4
.2	.1	.2	.1				.1	.1
0 UND	0 UND	1 728.8	0 UND				0 UND	0 999.8
2 188.0	3 107.4	10 37.6	11 34.0			Sales/Receivables	3 129.0	4 103.9
27 13.4	18 20.6	48 7.6	46 7.9				27 13.6	35 10.5
49 7.4	81 4.5	61 6.0	61 6.0				57 6.4	61 6.0
130 2.8	146 2.5	125 2.9	101 3.6			Cost of Sales/Inventory	102 3.6	120 3.0
189 1.9	274 1.3	192 1.9	144 2.5				158 2.3	192 1.9
9 40.5	12 31.2	32 11.4	13 28.8				23 15.6	20 18.0
28 13.0	41 8.8	49 7.5	40 9.1			Cost of Sales/Payables	49 7.5	47 7.7
47 7.8	78 4.7	87 4.2	55 6.6				70 4.7	78 4.7
4.5	4.3	5.9	10.2				7.8	5.6
7.7	9.7	9.6	14.4			Sales/Working Capital	15.4	10.9
46.0	UND	25.0	34.5				163.1	52.0
10.3	18.7	19.2	252.7				6.0	6.9
(29) 2.8	(45) 4.7	(47) 5.9	10.7			EBIT/Interest	(99) 2.1	(80) 3.2
-.3	1.7	1.9	3.7				.5	1.6
						Net Profit + Depr., Dep., Amort./Cur. Mat. L /T/D	7.2	5.8
							(23) 2.3	(15) 1.6
							.5	.9
.1	.1	.1	.1				.2	.2
.5	.3	.5	.3			Fixed/Worth	.7	.6
-9.4	1.6	1.1	.9				2.7	1.9
.4	.7	.8	.8				1.1	.9
1.8	1.9	1.6	2.4			Debt/Worth	2.8	3.0
-25.2	5.5	4.6	3.2				13.8	5.6
56.7	40.8	51.2	71.5			% Profit Before Taxes/Tangible Net Worth	50.3	71.6
(28) 31.7	(45) 17.2	(44) 18.9	(10) 48.8				(90) 23.0	(86) 29.5
10.2	5.5	6.8	20.8				3.0	7.0
25.1	15.0	21.9	37.8			% Profit Before Taxes/Total Assets	15.9	17.9
12.9	6.0	6.5	15.9				5.2	6.6
-2.3	1.0	1.5	8.1				-.8	1.2
63.4	50.3	64.0	63.9				52.3	40.1
27.3	28.0	14.4	15.4			Sales/Net Fixed Assets	23.8	19.1
9.0	7.9	8.7	11.7				10.6	8.0
3.5	3.3	3.7	3.8				4.2	4.0
2.6	2.4	2.4	2.7			Sales/Total Assets	2.9	2.6
2.2	1.5	1.9	2.3				2.0	1.8
.4	.5	.5					.4	.5
(26) 1.0	(42) .9	(46) 1.2				% Depr., Dep., Amort./Sales	(86) 1.0	(78) 1.2
2.6	1.5	2.0					1.9	2.2
3.1	2.7	1.7					2.2	2.7
(23) 5.9	(29) 3.9	(27) 3.0				% Officers', Directors', Owners' Comp/Sales	(59) 4.2	(46) 4.3
9.7	10.3	7.2					8.0	7.3
32826M	150749M	529109M	848057M	337987M	1400650M	Net Sales ($)	2197795M	1276487M
11317M	56967M	203913M	291889M	205897M	273621M	Total Assets ($)	674623M	552182M

M = $ thousand   MM = $ million
See Pages 11 through 21 for Explanation of Ratios and Data

Comparative Historical Data | | | | **Current Data Sorted By Sales**

			Type of Statement						
14	22	14	Unqualified	1		1	2	3	7
21	19	22	Reviewed		4	3	9	6	
27	47	29	Compiled	4	9	6	8	2	
35	35	48	Tax Returns	21	16	4	4	2	1
43	33	44	Other	10	6	4	5	9	10
4/1/02-3/31/03 ALL	4/1/03-3/31/04 ALL	4/1/04-3/31/05 ALL		35 (4/1-9/30/04)			122 (10/1/04-3/31/05)		
				0-1MM	1-3MM	3-5MM	5-10MM	10-25MM	25MM & OVER
140	156	157	**NUMBER OF STATEMENTS**	36	35	18	28	22	18
%	%	%	**ASSETS**	%	%	%	%	%	%
11.8	10.5	8.3	Cash & Equivalents	7.8	6.5	8.2	9.0	11.2	7.8
10.3	12.9	12.6	Trade Receivables (net)	7.1	7.0	22.8	14.3	17.8	15.5
43.0	45.5	50.0	Inventory	57.5	54.5	40.3	48.1	44.8	45.5
2.5	2.8	1.4	All Other Current	1.5	.4	3.6	1.6	1.2	1.3
67.6	71.7	72.3	Total Current	73.9	68.3	74.9	72.9	75.1	70.1
23.2	19.1	19.2	Fixed Assets (net)	13.6	24.1	19.7	20.1	17.6	20.8
3.5	3.1	3.2	Intangibles (net)	7.2	1.3	.8	1.1	3.7	3.8
5.7	6.1	5.3	All Other Non-Current	5.3	6.3	4.7	5.9	3.6	5.3
100.0	100.0	100.0	Total	100.0	100.0	100.0	100.0	100.0	100.0
			LIABILITIES						
9.1	11.4	14.7	Notes Payable-Short Term	18.1	20.2	11.0	8.3	8.4	18.9
4.8	2.5	2.6	Cur. Mat.-L/T/D	1.8	4.7	1.1	1.4	2.7	3.5
17.5	20.3	20.1	Trade Payables	15.0	19.5	18.1	25.5	27.1	16.2
.5	.3	.3	Income Taxes Payable	.0	.1	.9	.0	.8	.3
10.1	14.0	9.6	All Other Current	9.5	10.7	5.7	8.1	12.0	11.0
42.1	48.5	47.3	Total Current	44.4	55.1	36.7	43.3	51.0	49.7
22.3	14.2	14.4	Long-Term Debt	21.9	18.6	10.2	7.5	11.0	9.9
.0	.2	.1	Deferred Taxes	.0	.1	.0	.1	.0	.2
12.6	8.9	4.6	All Other Non-Current	4.3	6.0	1.5	5.6	1.4	7.8
23.0	28.2	33.7	Net Worth	29.3	20.1	51.7	43.5	36.6	32.3
100.0	100.0	100.0	Total Liabilities & Net Worth	100.0	100.0	100.0	100.0	100.0	100.0
			INCOME DATA						
100.0	100.0	100.0	Net Sales	100.0	100.0	100.0	100.0	100.0	100.0
44.3	43.5	44.5	Gross Profit	46.5	45.2	44.8	43.5	42.7	42.8
39.1	39.3	40.0	Operating Expenses	40.6	43.4	41.3	38.4	37.6	36.6
5.2	4.1	4.5	Operating Profit	5.9	1.8	3.4	5.1	5.0	6.2
1.3	.6	.4	All Other Expenses (net)	1.1	.6	-.9	.5	.1	.3
3.9	3.5	4.1	Profit Before Taxes	4.9	1.1	4.4	4.6	4.9	5.9
			RATIOS						
2.8	2.5	3.0		4.7	3.1	5.0	2.6	2.1	2.0
1.8	1.6	1.7	Current	2.5	1.3	2.0	1.8	1.6	1.3
1.2	1.2	1.1		1.5	.8	1.4	1.2	1.2	1.1
1.0	.9	1.0		1.3	.5	3.4	.8	.9	.8
.4	.4	.4	Quick	.5	.3	.8	.4	.5	.3
.1	.2	.1		.1	.0	.2	.1	.4	.1
0 UND	0 UND	0 UND		0 UND	0 UND	1 265.4	0 897.5	0 999.8	0 UND
2 207.1	4 87.0	5 71.4	Sales/Receivables	0 UND	2 231.9	19 19.3	4 98.2	7 53.3	6 62.1
27 13.3	37 10.0	30 12.2		25 14.5	12 31.1	57 6.4	30 12.0	44 8.2	46 7.9
58 6.3	65 5.6	63 5.8		81 4.5	80 4.6	55 6.6	61 6.0	55 6.6	58 6.3
112 3.3	119 3.1	132 2.8	Cost of Sales/Inventory	179 2.0	139 2.6	116 3.1	125 2.9	87 4.2	107 3.4
184 2.0	191 1.9	200 1.8		268 1.4	254 1.4	198 1.8	183 2.0	167 2.2	150 2.4
14 25.3	16 22.3	20 18.5		6 60.9	14 26.9	17 21.0	35 10.4	28 12.8	14 26.2
37 9.8	37 9.8	40 9.0	Cost of Sales/Payables	29 12.4	32 11.4	41 9.0	49 7.4	47 7.8	34 10.8
59 6.1	69 5.3	70 5.2		89 4.1	67 5.5	53 6.9	98 3.7	67 5.5	57 6.4
5.1	5.1	5.2		3.8	5.3	3.9	5.4	7.3	9.8
9.2	9.2	9.7	Sales/Working Capital	5.8	11.3	8.2	9.3	15.3	15.0
35.0	24.5	45.1		20.8	-33.8	15.7	18.0	28.1	42.1
8.9	9.8	17.4		10.7	10.3	21.0	18.7	31.9	64.5
(129) 3.8	(135) 3.5	(137) 4.7	EBIT/Interest	(27) 4.3	(30) 2.2	(14) 3.3	6.4	(20) 11.5	7.6
1.4	1.2	1.5		1.0	-.6	1.8	2.0	3.1	3.3
3.8	5.5	3.5	Net Profit + Depr., Dep.,						
(23) 2.6	(33) 3.1	(19) 1.5	Amort./Cur. Mat. L/T/D						
.6	.8	.0							
.2	.1	.1		.0	.1	.1	.2	.1	.2
.5	.5	.5	Fixed/Worth	.2	1.0	.2	.4	.5	.8
1.8	1.4	1.6		-2.4	8.8	.6	.7	1.0	2.5
.7	.8	.7		.4	1.1	.3	.5	1.0	1.4
1.8	1.7	1.9	Debt/Worth	1.5	2.7	.9	1.4	1.5	2.6
6.6	5.3	6.7		-8.7	52.3	2.5	3.4	6.9	8.1
51.5	51.8	52.1	% Profit Before Taxes/Tangible	74.5	35.8	23.4	38.2	68.2	68.9
(123) 24.3	(136) 24.5	(131) 22.5	Net Worth	(26) 25.1	(27) 21.4	(17) 9.2	(27) 18.4	(18) 46.9	(16) 48.8
5.7	6.3	8.7		7.8	8.4	3.5	6.1	17.2	11.7
19.1	16.7	20.9	% Profit Before Taxes/Total	24.6	15.1	12.3	19.8	29.0	36.6
8.4	6.9	7.7	Assets	7.1	5.2	3.5	6.5	18.3	13.2
1.4	1.1	1.0		.0	-6.5	1.1	1.5	5.9	4.4
53.3	57.4	61.1		152.5	39.2	43.0	36.5	88.1	47.0
16.6	18.8	20.8	Sales/Net Fixed Assets	40.1	15.4	17.3	22.7	21.3	17.9
7.5	8.1	8.5		8.6	5.9	6.6	10.8	9.5	10.1
3.6	3.5	3.5		3.0	3.2	4.0	3.4	4.2	3.9
2.5	2.5	2.5	Sales/Total Assets	2.2	2.5	2.3	2.6	3.4	2.7
1.6	1.6	1.9		1.3	1.6	1.9	2.2	2.3	2.2
.7	.6	.5		.4	.6	.8	.6	.4	.4
(111) 1.1	(122) 1.2	(128) 1.1	% Depr., Dep., Amort./Sales	(24) 1.0	(28) .9	(14) 1.1	(26) 1.1	(20) 1.1	(16) 1.3
1.8	2.0	2.0		3.9	1.4	1.8	1.5	2.2	2.2
2.9	2.5	2.3	% Officers', Directors',	4.5	3.0	3.1	2.3	.9	
(70) 5.0	(72) 4.6	(80) 4.9	Owners' Comp/Sales	(15) 5.9	(23) 4.0	(11) 7.1	(18) 3.5	(10) 2.0	
9.1	9.2	9.1		11.3	10.2	17.0	8.0	7.2	
3272591M	3527876M	3299378M	Net Sales ($)	25078M	58534M	70748M	194547M	302334M	2648137M
1489348M	1374743M	1043604M	Total Assets ($)	15682M	25885M	33988M	78043M	104055M	785951M

© RMA 2005

M = $ thousand   MM = $ million
See Pages 11 through 21 for Explanation of Ratios and Data

Current Data Sorted By Assets   Comparative Historical Data

0-500M	500M-2MM	2-10MM	10-50MM	50-100MM	100-250MM	Type of Statement	ALL	ALL
		2	5		3	Unqualified	11	5
1	1	7	2			Reviewed	12	13
5	3	7				Compiled	22	28
6	3	1		1		Tax Returns	9	8
5	9	4				Other	16	22
	18 (4/1-9/30/04)		50 (10/1/04-3/31/05)				4/1/00-3/31/01	4/1/01-3/31/02
17	16	21	10	1	3	NUMBER OF STATEMENTS	70	76
%	%	%	%	%	%	ASSETS	%	%
15.1	10.4	13.8	9.1			Cash & Equivalents	11.5	7.4
4.6	2.5	6.5	1.6			Trade Receivables (net)	4.2	6.9
62.6	69.6	56.5	61.1			Inventory	60.6	66.0
1.0	1.4	.5	2.4			All Other Current	1.1	.8
83.3	83.9	77.4	74.3			Total Current	77.4	81.2
12.6	10.6	13.8	19.9			Fixed Assets (net)	14.0	13.2
2.8	2.5	3.6	.0			Intangibles (net)	3.4	1.1
1.3	3.1	5.2	5.8			All Other Non-Current	5.2	3.9
100.0	100.0	100.0	100.0			Total	100.0	100.0
						LIABILITIES		
8.9	15.7	12.7	5.7			Notes Payable-Short Term	10.7	14.2
6.1	1.7	3.6	2.5			Cur. Mat.-L/T/D	4.3	2.8
19.0	25.4	24.0	14.2			Trade Payables	19.8	19.5
.1	.0	.3	.1			Income Taxes Payable	.1	.1
7.6	8.9	4.8	8.1			All Other Current	6.9	6.3
41.7	51.7	45.3	30.6			Total Current	41.9	43.0
15.9	11.3	5.9	16.5			Long-Term Debt	15.1	12.7
.0	.0	.2	.2			Deferred Taxes	.2	.1
2.2	12.3	3.6	3.7			All Other Non-Current	3.8	6.7
40.3	24.7	45.0	49.0			Net Worth	38.3	36.9
100.0	100.0	100.0	100.0			Total Liabilities & Net Worth	100.0	100.0
						INCOME DATA		
100.0	100.0	100.0	100.0			Net Sales	100.0	100.0
43.7	46.9	39.6	39.8			Gross Profit	40.6	41.0
39.6	45.0	36.9	35.9			Operating Expenses	37.2	37.3
4.1	1.9	2.7	3.9			Operating Profit	3.3	3.7
.7	1.3	.2	.4			All Other Expenses (net)	.5	1.5
3.5	.6	2.5	3.6			Profit Before Taxes	2.8	2.2
						RATIOS		
6.2	3.0	2.6	3.3				3.4	3.5
2.8	1.4	1.9	2.3			Current	2.2	2.0
1.2	1.3	1.3	1.9				1.3	1.3
1.0	.8	.8	.6				.9	.5
.5	(15) .1	.2	.4			Quick	.3	.2
.1	.1	.1	.1				.1	.1
0 UND	0 UND	0 UND	0 UND				0 UND	0 UND
0 UND	1 301.8	1 313.1	2 162.2			Sales/Receivables	1 653.0	2 203.4
3 114.9	3 110.5	3 120.9	3 118.0				4 90.4	7 50.5
84 4.3	121 3.0	70 5.2	85 4.3				92 4.0	113 3.2
168 2.2	245 1.5	128 2.8	155 2.4			Cost of Sales/Inventory	138 2.6	170 2.1
248 1.5	273 1.3	203 1.8	241 1.5				211 1.7	267 1.4
25 14.6	43 8.5	30 12.1	28 13.3				21 17.6	23 15.8
36 10.1	73 5.0	47 7.8	33 11.1			Cost of Sales/Payables	36 10.2	42 8.6
59 6.2	104 3.5	70 5.2	41 9.0				69 5.3	78 4.7
2.8	4.4	4.8	4.0				3.8	3.4
5.4	8.5	10.4	5.4			Sales/Working Capital	6.2	5.9
32.7	17.0	22.8	8.8				18.0	17.7
7.7	3.1	9.6	14.9				7.3	9.1
(12) 3.3	(14) 1.4	(18) 3.9	4.4			EBIT/Interest	(57) 2.6	(68) 2.6
1.2	−1.7	2.2	1.5				.9	.4
							3.4	7.0
						Net Profit + Depr., Dep., Amort./Cur. Mat. L /T/D	(14) 1.1	(19) 2.2
							.3	.5
.0	.1	.1	.2				.1	.1
.2	.3	.2	.3			Fixed/Worth	.3	.3
.8	NM	.7	.7				1.1	.7
.3	.7	.6	.8				.6	.8
1.1	2.8	1.6	1.1			Debt/Worth	1.9	1.7
5.5	−8.1	2.5	1.4				7.6	5.1
33.3	49.5	33.6	45.9				54.9	37.8
(15) 11.8	(11) 5.7	(20) 12.5	7.0			% Profit Before Taxes/Tangible Net Worth	(62) 23.0	(69) 14.7
1.5	−13.9	2.1	1.7				2.8	.9
22.7	12.1	12.3	22.4				18.5	13.4
7.7	1.8	5.9	3.4			% Profit Before Taxes/Total Assets	4.0	5.2
1.1	−8.7	1.0	.9				.0	−.1
229.2	94.3	68.8	29.4				66.3	46.5
41.1	26.7	22.7	14.9			Sales/Net Fixed Assets	28.2	24.8
12.5	13.7	14.0	8.3				11.6	13.4
3.3	3.2	3.7	2.8				3.4	3.1
2.4	2.2	2.8	2.5			Sales/Total Assets	2.4	2.4
1.8	1.9	2.1	1.9				1.7	1.8
.2	.3	.7	.8				.4	.5
(10) .8	(11) .7	(15) .9	1.4			% Depr., Dep., Amort./Sales	(55) .7	(62) .9
1.3	1.1	1.9	1.5				1.4	1.3
4.6		2.0					2.7	2.8
(11) 7.0		(12) 3.1				% Officers', Directors', Owners' Comp/Sales	(32) 3.7	(42) 4.7
15.3		8.4					6.0	7.1
13239M	47873M	291537M	619237M	135037M	1281789M	Net Sales ($)	2465173M	1987311M
4892M	17992M	99933M	258267M	85097M	612935M	Total Assets ($)	1220177M	1062293M

M = $ thousand   MM = $ million
See Pages 11 through 21 for Explanation of Ratios and Data

Comparative Historical Data / Current Data Sorted By Sales

4/1/02-3/31/03 ALL	4/1/03-3/31/04 ALL	4/1/04-3/31/05 ALL	Type of Statement	18 (4/1-9/30/04) 0-1MM	1-3MM	3-5MM	50 (10/1/04-3/31/05) 5-10MM	10-25MM	25MM & OVER
7	7	10	Unqualified		1	1	2	2	8
15	11	11	Reviewed					3	4
25	19	15	Compiled	6	2	2	3	1	1
12	25	10	Tax Returns	5	2	1	2		
18	15	22	Other	6	4	4	2	2	4
77	77	68	**NUMBER OF STATEMENTS**	17	9	8	9	8	17
%	%	%	**ASSETS**	%	%	%	%	%	%
7.3	10.7	12.1	Cash & Equivalents	9.3					9.5
4.5	5.5	4.4	Trade Receivables (net)	4.6					2.6
64.8	61.5	61.9	Inventory	65.7					59.0
3.5	1.1	1.2	All Other Current	2.2					1.8
80.1	78.8	79.5	Total Current	81.8					72.9
11.4	13.5	14.0	Fixed Assets (net)	13.1					21.1
1.5	2.5	2.6	Intangibles (net)	4.2					.8
7.0	5.3	3.8	All Other Non-Current	.9					5.2
100.0	100.0	100.0	Total	100.0					100.0
			LIABILITIES						
8.6	12.9	11.1	Notes Payable-Short Term	13.4					6.0
3.6	2.6	3.4	Cur. Mat.-L/T/D	6.3					1.7
21.0	19.2	21.2	Trade Payables	14.8					17.9
.1	.2	.1	Income Taxes Payable	.1					.2
7.7	12.0	7.3	All Other Current	5.7					8.2
41.0	46.8	43.1	Total Current	40.4					34.0
14.0	9.1	11.0	Long-Term Debt	16.5					10.5
.1	.1	.2	Deferred Taxes	.0					.5
7.1	5.0	5.3	All Other Non-Current	6.9					4.4
37.9	39.0	40.3	Net Worth	36.2					50.6
100.0	100.0	100.0	Total Liabilities & Net Worth	100.0					100.0
			INCOME DATA						
100.0	100.0	100.0	Net Sales	100.0					100.0
40.8	43.7	42.0	Gross Profit	44.5					38.6
38.2	40.2	38.9	Operating Expenses	41.6					34.3
2.6	3.5	3.1	Operating Profit	3.0					4.3
.5	.9	.6	All Other Expenses (net)	1.4					.3
2.1	2.7	2.6	Profit Before Taxes	1.6					4.0
			RATIOS						
3.5	3.1	3.1	Current	7.4					3.0
2.1	1.9	2.0		2.8					2.2
1.4	1.2	1.3		1.2					1.7
.6	.8	.8	Quick	1.0					.6
.2	.2	(67) .3		.5					.3
.0	.0	.1		.1					.1
0 UND	0 UND	0 UND	Sales/Receivables	0 UND					0 UND
1 453.6	0 739.4	1 355.2		0 UND					2 162.2
4 89.2	2 167.2	3 110.7		7 53.9					3 114.4
109 3.3	101 3.6	92 4.0	Cost of Sales/Inventory	146 2.5					85 4.3
178 2.1	177 2.1	163 2.2		227 1.6					124 2.9
282 1.3	256 1.4	243 1.5		299 1.2					221 1.6
30 12.2	21 17.0	30 12.3	Cost of Sales/Payables	22 16.7					30 12.2
49 7.5	38 9.6	41 8.8		33 10.9					35 10.5
83 4.4	71 5.2	70 5.2		68 5.3					48 7.7
3.0	3.7	4.2	Sales/Working Capital	2.5					4.2
5.2	6.5	6.4		3.5					6.2
15.8	18.4	15.4		14.7					11.9
8.2	8.4	9.6	EBIT/Interest	4.6					16.1
(60) 2.1	(58) 3.9	(58) 3.0		(14) 2.4				(16)	7.8
.6	.9	1.3		.5					1.4
6.0	3.8	4.7	Net Profit + Depr., Dep., Amort./Cur. Mat. L/T/D						
(19) 1.6	(12) 2.2	(11) 1.5							
.6	1.0	.5							
.1	.1	.1	Fixed/Worth	.1					.2
.3	.2	.3		.2					.4
.6	.8	.8		10.2					.6
.6	.6	.5	Debt/Worth	.2					.7
1.5	1.6	1.4		2.5					1.0
6.0	4.2	3.1		17.3					1.4
40.4	41.0	33.1	% Profit Before Taxes/Tangible Net Worth	34.4					39.5
(69) 8.9	(68) 15.2	(60) 10.2		(14) 6.8					13.6
.2	.4	1.5		-3.5					1.6
13.0	17.2	14.1	% Profit Before Taxes/Total Assets	10.7					21.6
2.9	6.0	4.2		2.2					7.7
-.7	-.7	.6		-2.0					.8
44.0	61.6	70.9	Sales/Net Fixed Assets	138.1					21.9
28.7	23.7	21.2		39.8					14.2
14.4	13.1	11.4		11.4					8.3
3.1	3.1	3.3	Sales/Total Assets	2.5					3.2
2.2	2.3	2.4		1.9					2.5
1.6	1.7	1.9		1.5					1.9
.6	.6	.5	% Depr., Dep., Amort./Sales	.3					.7
(68) 1.0	(58) .9	(48) .9		(10) .8				(15)	1.2
1.4	1.5	1.5		1.3					1.5
2.2	2.1	1.9	% Officers', Directors', Owners' Comp/Sales	4.9					
(40) 3.9	(44) 3.9	(35) 4.0		(12) 6.6					
8.5	8.5	9.6		11.0					
1794793M	1676790M	2388712M	Net Sales ($)	10101M	18626M	30678M	75070M	119739M	2134498M
797386M	886145M	1079116M	Total Assets ($)	5312M	7246M	13694M	25978M	45429M	981457M

© RMA 2005

M = $ thousand   MM = $ million

See Pages 11 through 21 for Explanation of Ratios and Data

Current Data Sorted By Assets   Comparative Historical Data

	1		2	12	4	3	Type of Statement		13	15
		1	25	14			Unqualified			
1	8	33	4				Reviewed		41	24
5	43	18			1		Compiled		98	88
26	29	12	8	1	8		Tax Returns		45	50
4	11						Other		54	53
	85 (4/1-9/30/04)			188 (10/1/04-3/31/05)					4/1/00-3/31/01	4/1/01-3/31/02
0-500M	500M-2MM	2-10MM	10-50MM	50-100MM	100-250MM				ALL	ALL
36	92	90	38	5	12	**NUMBER OF STATEMENTS**		251	230
%	%	%	%	%	%	**ASSETS**		%	%
11.2	6.6	5.3	4.7		8.1	Cash & Equivalents		6.0	7.1
6.2	5.3	7.2	11.8		15.1	Trade Receivables (net)		9.0	9.8
69.5	74.3	68.8	64.5		50.5	Inventory		67.6	66.7
1.5	.4	1.2	.9		1.5	All Other Current		1.2	1.5
88.4	86.6	82.5	81.8		75.2	Total Current		83.8	85.1
7.1	8.4	11.3	12.3		16.8	Fixed Assets (net)		10.3	9.8
.5	1.7	.4	1.5		1.6	Intangibles (net)		1.8	1.3
4.0	3.3	5.8	4.3		6.4	All Other Non-Current		4.1	3.9
100.0	100.0	100.0	100.0		100.0	Total		100.0	100.0
						LIABILITIES			
12.7	11.3	12.4	13.5		19.4	Notes Payable-Short Term		12.4	11.0
1.0	3.0	2.4	1.9		.2	Cur. Mat.-L/T/D		3.3	4.0
22.5	26.3	23.9	21.0		19.7	Trade Payables		21.1	20.3
.0	.2	.3	.1		.3	Income Taxes Payable		.2	.3
9.3	7.0	8.9	9.4		9.3	All Other Current		8.2	8.2
45.5	47.8	47.8	45.8		48.9	Total Current		45.3	43.8
15.9	13.6	8.8	8.7		8.1	Long-Term Debt		12.8	11.5
.0	.0	.2	.1		2.1	Deferred Taxes		.1	.1
5.4	4.9	5.2	1.6		1.9	All Other Non-Current		3.5	4.3
33.2	33.7	38.0	43.8		38.9	Net Worth		38.4	40.3
100.0	100.0	100.0	100.0		100.0	Total Liabilities & Net Worth		100.0	100.0
						INCOME DATA			
100.0	100.0	100.0	100.0		100.0	Net Sales		100.0	100.0
45.7	44.6	41.4	46.0		40.6	Gross Profit		44.0	45.4
40.6	41.3	37.6	41.5		34.5	Operating Expenses		39.0	41.7
5.1	3.3	3.8	4.5		6.2	Operating Profit		5.1	3.7
.9	1.4	1.1	.3		1.3	All Other Expenses (net)		.8	1.2
4.2	2.0	2.7	4.2		4.9	Profit Before Taxes		4.3	2.5
						RATIOS			
4.3	2.7	2.5	2.5		2.7			3.1	3.4
2.5	1.8	1.8	1.8		1.5	Current		2.0	2.0
1.4	1.4	1.3	1.4		1.2			1.4	1.4
1.0	.4	.5	.6		.6			.6	.7
(35) .2	(91) .2	(89) .2	.3		.5	Quick		(229) .3	.3
.1	.1	.1	.1		.1			.1	.1
0 UND	0 988.1	1 361.3	5 76.4		1 478.9			1 447.6	1 340.3
0 UND	3 117.5	7 48.9	18 20.4		32 11.3	Sales/Receivables		10 38.2	11 32.0
16 22.8	14 26.1	22 16.5	33 10.9		100 3.7			25 14.5	27 13.6
130 2.8	201 1.8	209 1.8	257 1.4		136 2.7			189 1.9	210 1.7
241 1.5	317 1.2	297 1.2	279 1.3		220 1.7	Cost of Sales/Inventory		271 1.3	280 1.3
329 1.1	416 .9	382 1.0	327 1.1		366 1.0			363 1.0	381 1.0
10 36.8	55 6.6	45 8.2	45 8.1		51 7.1			34 10.8	33 11.2
57 6.4	99 3.7	81 4.5	75 4.9		84 4.3	Cost of Sales/Payables		70 5.2	76 4.8
109 3.4	142 2.6	143 2.6	142 2.6		118 3.1			118 3.1	129 2.8
2.5	2.6	2.8	2.8		2.4			2.6	2.4
6.2	4.5	4.7	5.0		6.4	Sales/Working Capital		4.1	4.0
8.6	7.4	10.1	8.4		11.2			8.1	7.7
9.7	6.5	10.3	9.9		11.0			7.4	5.8
(27) 3.6	(86) 2.4	(86) 3.5	(36) 4.6		(11) 6.0	EBIT/Interest		(236) 3.1	(218) 2.7
1.0	1.1	1.6	2.3		1.2			1.7	1.1
	3.5	4.7	5.3			Net Profit + Depr., Dep.,		3.3	2.6
	(13) 1.0	(23) 1.6	(15) 2.8			Amort./Cur. Mat. L/T/D		(61) 1.7	(47) 1.4
	.4	.7	1.3					.7	.5
.0	.1	.1	.1		.1			.1	.1
.2	.2	.3	.3		.4	Fixed/Worth		.2	.2
.5	.6	.6	.5		.8			.5	.5
.5	1.1	.9	.8		.9			.8	.7
1.6	2.1	1.7	1.2		2.4	Debt/Worth		1.8	1.7
7.0	4.5	3.4	2.3		2.7			3.3	3.6
63.2	22.9	23.8	25.5		37.3	% Profit Before Taxes/Tangible		31.4	23.7
(29) 27.0	(79) 10.3	(87) 10.2	16.2		19.2	Net Worth		(235) 14.7	(215) 11.3
-1.8	1.6	4.6	7.4		5.3			5.7	3.0
24.7	7.8	8.2	11.1		13.5	% Profit Before Taxes/Total		10.4	9.3
10.2	3.1	3.3	5.5		6.4	Assets		5.5	4.1
-.7	.3	1.3	2.4		1.5			2.1	1.5
345.8	74.0	52.7	28.3		36.2			57.0	68.5
50.3	29.9	19.6	14.5		10.8	Sales/Net Fixed Assets		26.0	23.8
21.7	13.8	10.4	9.9		7.6			13.2	10.7
3.3	2.1	2.0	1.9		2.1			2.2	2.1
2.2	1.6	1.5	1.5		1.4	Sales/Total Assets		1.7	1.6
1.5	1.2	1.2	1.3		1.0			1.3	1.2
.3	.4	.4	.5		1.1			.3	.3
(17) 1.1	(69) .9	(74) .8	(37) 1.2		(10) 1.5	% Depr., Dep., Amort./Sales		(212) .7	(190) .7
2.0	1.5	1.5	1.9		2.1			1.5	1.4
4.3	4.5	2.1	1.0			% Officers', Directors',		3.7	3.4
(24) 8.4	(68) 5.8	(46) 5.1	(11) 2.2			Owners' Comp/Sales		(143) 6.4	(122) 5.7
15.1	9.1	8.4	4.5					9.7	8.9
26107M	202461M	626423M	1243912M	610132M	2638615M	Net Sales ($)		2957681M	2436196M
10801M	112838M	392786M	750772M	344638M	1647403M	Total Assets ($)		1709668M	1570333M

M = $ thousand   MM = $ million
See Pages 11 through 21 for Explanation of Ratios and Data

Comparative Historical Data | Current Data Sorted By Sales

4/1/02-3/31/03 ALL	4/1/03-3/31/04 ALL	4/1/04-3/31/05 ALL	Type of Statement	0-1MM	1-3MM	3-5MM	5-10MM	10-25MM	25MM & OVER
					85 (4/1-9/30/04)		188 (10/1/04-3/31/05)		
20	22	22	Unqualified		1	1		3	17
47	41	48	Reviewed		10	2	12	17	7
81	98	85	Compiled	12	35	20	9	8	1
72	78	74	Tax Returns	25	25	14	8	1	1
48	73	44	Other	6	6	5	8	7	12
268	312	273	**NUMBER OF STATEMENTS**	43	77	42	37	36	38
%	%	%	**ASSETS**	%	%	%	%	%	%
7.7	7.8	6.5	Cash & Equivalents	8.3	6.7	7.0	6.0	5.3	5.1
8.7	7.9	7.7	Trade Receivables (net)	5.6	5.6	5.5	7.7	10.6	13.8
65.9	67.8	69.1	Inventory	72.1	73.7	68.6	71.2	64.7	58.7
2.0	1.8	.9	All Other Current	1.4	.4	1.0	1.1	.8	1.2
84.3	85.2	84.2	Total Current	87.4	86.5	82.1	86.0	81.4	78.8
10.3	10.0	10.2	Fixed Assets (net)	7.9	7.7	9.4	10.8	13.7	14.7
1.1	1.0	1.1	Intangibles (net)	.4	1.4	1.6	.1	1.4	1.8
4.2	3.7	4.5	All Other Non-Current	4.3	4.4	6.9	3.1	3.5	4.7
100.0	100.0	100.0	Total	100.0	100.0	100.0	100.0	100.0	100.0
			LIABILITIES						
11.1	12.0	12.5	Notes Payable-Short Term	14.2	12.4	8.3	12.0	14.1	14.6
2.8	2.8	2.3	Cur. Mat.-L/T/D	1.3	2.9	2.9	2.0	2.2	2.3
19.0	21.8	23.9	Trade Payables	23.2	25.0	26.8	24.4	21.5	21.0
.1	.2	.2	Income Taxes Payable	.0	.1	.2	.3	.3	.2
9.3	9.3	8.5	All Other Current	7.7	8.3	7.5	6.8	9.5	11.4
42.4	46.1	47.4	Total Current	46.4	48.8	45.7	45.5	47.6	49.4
12.2	9.1	11.2	Long-Term Debt	17.5	13.3	10.3	8.9	7.4	6.5
.1	.1	.2	Deferred Taxes	.0	.0	.1	.1	.3	.8
4.5	6.0	4.5	All Other Non-Current	5.2	5.0	5.0	5.2	2.8	3.3
40.8	38.7	36.7	Net Worth	30.8	32.9	38.8	40.3	41.9	40.1
100.0	100.0	100.0	Total Liabilities & Net Worth	100.0	100.0	100.0	100.0	100.0	100.0
			INCOME DATA						
100.0	100.0	100.0	Net Sales	100.0	100.0	100.0	100.0	100.0	100.0
44.8	44.5	43.7	Gross Profit	46.9	43.5	41.7	40.7	44.7	44.8
40.2	40.3	39.7	Operating Expenses	42.7	39.8	37.9	36.5	41.2	39.8
4.5	4.2	4.0	Operating Profit	4.2	3.8	3.8	4.1	3.5	5.1
1.1	1.0	1.1	All Other Expenses (net)	1.4	1.5	.8	.8	.3	1.4
3.4	3.2	2.9	Profit Before Taxes	2.8	2.3	2.9	3.3	3.2	3.6
			RATIOS						
3.3	2.9	2.7		4.1	2.7	2.5	2.9	3.0	2.3
2.0	2.0	1.8	Current	2.3	1.7	1.9	1.9	1.7	1.7
1.5	1.4	1.4		1.4	1.3	1.5	1.4	1.2	1.3
.7	.6	.5		.6	.5	.5	.5	.6	.5
(267) .3	(309) .3	(270) .2	Quick	(42) .2	(76) .2	(41) .3	.2	.3	.2
.1	.1	.1		.1	.1	.1	.1	.1	.1
2 202.6	0 741.2	1 657.0		0 UND	0 878.8	1 491.4	1 276.0	4 97.7	2 154.5
9 41.3	6 65.2	5 69.2	Sales/Receivables	1 454.0	5 79.8	4 101.1	6 64.3	12 30.1	18 19.8
27 13.6	23 15.7	21 17.2		14 25.6	21 17.6	15 24.2	20 17.9	31 11.8	38 9.5
190 1.9	193 1.9	198 1.8		218 1.7	211 1.7	191 1.9	164 2.2	232 1.6	168 2.2
296 1.2	293 1.2	290 1.3	Cost of Sales/Inventory	335 1.1	330 1.1	252 1.5	295 1.2	276 1.3	260 1.4
401 .9	397 .9	386 .9		522 .7	420 .9	345 1.1	332 1.1	306 1.2	319 1.1
36 10.2	43 8.5	45 8.1		38 9.6	52 7.1	32 11.4	53 7.0	33 11.1	42 8.7
71 5.1	82 4.5	83 4.4	Cost of Sales/Payables	78 4.7	96 3.8	92 4.0	76 4.8	66 5.5	83 4.4
120 3.1	137 2.7	137 2.7		146 2.5	143 2.6	141 2.6	98 3.7	141 2.6	110 3.3
2.3	2.8	2.7		2.1	2.6	3.2	2.9	2.6	4.2
3.7	4.3	4.8	Sales/Working Capital	3.4	4.5	4.8	4.7	5.7	6.0
6.8	6.9	8.2		8.2	8.0	7.2	7.9	12.0	8.5
6.8	9.5	8.1		7.3	5.2	11.6	11.3	11.3	11.3
(245) 2.7	(287) 3.7	(251) 3.0	EBIT/Interest	(36) 1.8	(71) 2.3	(39) 4.1	(34) 3.8	(35) 3.2	(36) 5.0
1.2	1.2	1.3		.5	1.2	1.6	1.8	1.8	2.1
3.4	5.9	5.4			6.2	2.6		4.5	12.1
(63) 1.4	(59) 2.3	(57) 1.8	Net Profit + Depr., Dep., Amort./Cur. Mat. L/T/D		(10) 1.4	(10) 1.3		(12) 1.5	(16) 5.0
.4	.9	1.0			.3	.9		.6	3.0
.1	.1	.1		.0	.1	.1	.1	.2	.1
.2	.2	.3	Fixed/Worth	.2	.2	.3	.2	.4	.3
.5	.5	.5		1.0	.5	.5	.6	.6	.6
.7	.7	.9		.4	1.1	.8	.9	.8	.8
1.4	1.6	1.8	Debt/Worth	1.9	2.4	1.7	1.5	1.5	1.8
3.2	3.6	3.7		-28.9	5.1	3.6	3.0	3.5	2.6
22.8	27.2	26.7		44.6	33.1	22.9	25.5	26.3	26.7
(248) 10.2	(291) 11.2	(249) 13.3	% Profit Before Taxes/Tangible Net Worth	(32) 10.9	(70) 10.0	(39) 7.9	(36) 12.8	(35) 16.2	(37) 18.4
1.4	2.3	4.1		-1.9	3.8	3.3	6.0	6.5	9.5
9.7	10.0	10.4		12.9	8.1	8.1	10.7	10.9	12.6
3.7	4.2	4.1	% Profit Before Taxes/Total Assets	2.2	3.0	3.5	4.3	4.4	6.3
.7	.6	.7		-1.6	.6	1.4	2.1	1.7	1.8
68.0	59.1	60.4		285.0	96.1	77.2	61.1	22.1	28.5
25.1	21.0	22.9	Sales/Net Fixed Assets	32.8	29.6	30.4	27.0	12.5	14.6
9.9	10.9	11.4		11.5	14.6	13.3	11.6	9.7	10.0
2.0	2.1	2.1		2.4	2.1	2.1	2.5	2.1	2.2
1.5	1.6	1.6	Sales/Total Assets	1.4	1.4	1.8	1.7	1.5	1.7
1.2	1.2	1.2		1.1	1.1	1.4	1.4	1.4	1.4
.5	.5	.5		.6	.4	.3	.5	.5	1.0
(230) .9	(255) .9	(212) 1.0	% Depr., Dep., Amort./Sales	(22) 1.2	(57) .9	(35) .5	(28) .8	(35) 1.1	(35) 1.3
1.5	1.6	1.7		3.1	1.5	1.2	1.6	1.6	2.2
3.2	3.3	2.9		5.8	4.3	3.3	.9	1.2	
(165) 5.7	(176) 5.7	(152) 5.4	% Officers', Directors', Owners' Comp/Sales	(29) 8.1	(53) 5.4	(27) 7.7	(21) 4.9	(14) 2.3	
9.3	9.9	9.2		9.5	9.5	9.5	7.0	4.0	
2669230M	3684724M	5347650M	Net Sales ($)	25896M	148987M	157566M	263135M	566450M	4185616M
1688615M	2398164M	3259238M	Total Assets ($)	18493M	119471M	96451M	161993M	386000M	2476830M

Current Data Sorted By Assets   Comparative Historical Data

						Type of Statement		
3	2	5	6	3	4	Unqualified	13	16
22	13	27	4			Reviewed	36	35
44	40	29	1		1	Compiled	107	92
14	29	5	1	1		Tax Returns	41	52
	26	18	4		1	Other	70	58
	56 (4/1-9/30/04)			245 (10/1/04-3/31/05)			4/1/00-3/31/01	4/1/01-3/31/02
0-500M	500M-2MM	2-10MM	10-50MM	50-100MM	100-250MM		ALL	ALL
83	110	84	15	4	5	NUMBER OF STATEMENTS	267	253
%	%	%	%	%	%	ASSETS	%	%
10.2	8.3	7.5	4.0			Cash & Equivalents	6.3	8.3
3.5	10.8	9.2	7.7			Trade Receivables (net)	7.5	6.3
62.7	58.7	58.9	56.7			Inventory	60.3	60.5
.3	1.6	1.4	1.0			All Other Current	1.7	1.8
76.9	79.3	77.0	69.3			Total Current	75.9	76.9
17.2	13.6	16.1	21.8			Fixed Assets (net)	16.8	15.4
1.8	2.8	1.7	3.8			Intangibles (net)	3.2	3.2
4.1	4.3	5.2	5.1			All Other Non-Current	4.1	4.5
100.0	100.0	100.0	100.0			Total	100.0	100.0
						LIABILITIES		
21.5	15.3	15.1	15.0			Notes Payable-Short Term	13.1	13.1
3.7	1.8	2.8	.8			Cur. Mat.-L/T/D	3.5	3.0
23.0	22.3	23.8	26.1			Trade Payables	24.2	23.1
.2	.1	.2	.1			Income Taxes Payable	.3	.3
10.2	7.1	7.9	8.4			All Other Current	8.9	8.9
58.6	46.5	49.8	50.3			Total Current	50.0	48.4
25.7	13.8	12.2	14.6			Long-Term Debt	15.7	12.1
.0	.1	.1	.0			Deferred Taxes	.1	.1
8.8	8.7	5.4	4.3			All Other Non-Current	5.2	5.2
6.9	30.9	32.5	30.7			Net Worth	28.9	34.3
100.0	100.0	100.0	100.0			Total Liabilities & Net Worth	100.0	100.0
						INCOME DATA		
100.0	100.0	100.0	100.0			Net Sales	100.0	100.0
38.9	36.8	37.3	38.3			Gross Profit	36.1	37.7
36.3	34.3	35.7	34.8			Operating Expenses	33.9	34.8
2.5	2.5	1.6	3.5			Operating Profit	2.2	2.9
.9	.5	.7	.9			All Other Expenses (net)	1.2	.9
1.6	2.0	.9	2.6			Profit Before Taxes	1.0	1.9
						RATIOS		
3.0	3.4	2.1	1.7			Current	2.3	2.7
1.7	1.8	1.5	1.4				1.6	1.7
1.0	1.2	1.2	1.1				1.1	1.2
.7	.8	.6	.3			Quick	.5	.5
(81) .3	(109) .3	(83) .2	.2				(265) .2	(251) .2
.1	.1	.1	.1				.0	.1
0 UND	0 999.8	0 999.8	2 200.3			Sales/Receivables	0 951.0	0 UND
0 UND	4 102.6	2 184.6	4 90.7				3 111.8	2 196.0
5 80.2	24 15.1	16 22.4	7 51.9				15 25.1	10 36.0
94 3.9	74 4.9	101 3.6	109 3.4			Cost of Sales/Inventory	96 3.8	92 4.0
136 2.7	141 2.6	145 2.5	142 2.6				138 2.6	135 2.7
189 1.9	230 1.6	198 1.8	185 2.0				192 1.9	183 2.0
12 31.3	20 18.6	30 12.2	45 8.1			Cost of Sales/Payables	27 13.3	25 14.7
36 10.1	33 11.1	53 6.8	56 6.5				45 8.1	46 7.9
73 5.0	69 5.3	83 4.4	77 4.7				77 4.8	69 5.3
4.8	3.8	6.9	6.7			Sales/Working Capital	5.1	5.2
9.5	6.6	10.4	10.3				9.5	8.8
-121.0	31.6	20.0	52.0				29.4	23.4
4.9	10.9	8.1	9.8			EBIT/Interest	3.9	6.9
(70) 1.3	(98) 3.0	(79) 3.3	5.0				(250) 1.9	(227) 2.3
-.5	1.1	1.2	2.2				.8	1.0
	3.6	5.2				Net Profit + Depr., Dep.,	8.7	7.4
	(15) 1.6	(19) 2.7				Amort./Cur. Mat. L./T/D	(49) 2.0	(42) 2.4
	-.3	1.2					1.0	1.2
.2	.1	.1	.3			Fixed/Worth	.2	.1
.8	.3	.4	.4				.5	.4
-1.4	2.4	1.1	2.8				1.9	1.2
1.2	.7	1.0	1.3			Debt/Worth	1.0	.8
6.1	2.1	2.0	3.7				2.3	2.0
-12.1	11.6	3.9	5.3				9.6	6.3
65.4	36.9	31.9	47.2			% Profit Before Taxes/Tangible	26.1	35.5
(53) 16.7	(90) 13.6	(76) 14.8	(14) 30.7			Net Worth	(224) 10.3	(220) 14.2
-3.4	2.4	4.0	7.1				1.6	1.3
11.8	12.4	9.8	7.7			% Profit Before Taxes/Total	8.3	10.7
2.0	3.7	3.6	6.2			Assets	2.9	4.2
-4.2	.2	.3	1.7				-.7	.0
56.3	103.9	74.9	22.6			Sales/Net Fixed Assets	62.0	63.0
26.2	32.1	27.0	15.2				23.9	24.8
12.6	12.4	11.6	6.4				9.9	11.8
3.6	3.5	3.3	2.6			Sales/Total Assets	3.2	3.4
2.8	2.5	2.5	2.2				2.5	2.5
2.2	1.7	1.7	1.5				1.9	1.9
.6	.4	.5	.9			% Depr., Dep., Amort./Sales	.5	.5
(57) 1.2	(83) .8	(77) .8	1.6				(235) 1.0	(214) 1.0
2.2	1.5	1.4	2.3				2.1	1.8
4.0	2.4	1.8				% Officers', Directors',	2.1	2.3
(58) 5.3	(74) 4.6	(36) 3.0				Owners' Comp/Sales	(147) 3.8	(141) 4.3
7.7	6.1						6.3	7.0
62383M	357247M	953140M	665666M	640625M	1586401M	Net Sales ($)	3994007M	3380517M
22203M	123651M	365010M	306939M	342317M	932684M	Total Assets ($)	1704586M	1413097M

M = $ thousand   MM = $ million
See Pages 11 through 21 for Explanation of Ratios and Data

Comparative Historical Data | Current Data Sorted By Sales

			Type of Statement						
26	19	20	Unqualified		1	1	1	3	14
45	47	47	Reviewed	4	7	9	10	13	4
84	103	91	Compiled	19	29	11	19	13	
56	102	80	Tax Returns	30	30	8	7	3	2
74	71	63	Other	16	15	13	6	6	7
4/1/02-3/31/03 ALL	4/1/03-3/31/04 ALL	4/1/04-3/31/05 ALL		0-1MM	1-3MM	3-5MM	5-10MM	10-25MM	25MM & OVER
				56 (4/1-9/30/04)			245 (10/1/04-3/31/05)		
285	342	301	**NUMBER OF STATEMENTS**	69	82	42	43	38	27
%	%	%	**ASSETS**	%	%	%	%	%	%
7.1	8.4	8.4	Cash & Equivalents	9.9	8.7	7.8	7.6	8.2	6.0
8.8	6.9	8.1	Trade Receivables (net)	2.7	7.2	14.7	8.7	11.0	9.7
60.1	60.0	59.4	Inventory	58.8	62.0	58.3	59.1	63.2	50.1
1.1	1.8	1.2	All Other Current	.5	1.4	.9	2.2	1.0	1.1
77.0	77.1	77.1	Total Current	71.9	79.4	81.8	77.5	83.4	66.9
15.1	15.8	16.0	Fixed Assets (net)	20.5	14.6	13.1	15.2	11.7	20.0
3.5	3.4	2.3	Intangibles (net)	2.3	3.2	1.3	1.3	1.6	4.2
4.4	3.7	4.6	All Other Non-Current	5.3	2.9	3.8	5.9	3.3	8.9
100.0	100.0	100.0	Total	100.0	100.0	100.0	100.0	100.0	100.0
			LIABILITIES						
13.0	14.2	16.8	Notes Payable-Short Term	23.2	15.4	16.0	12.7	16.5	13.1
3.4	2.7	2.5	Cur. Mat.-L/T/D	3.9	2.5	1.4	1.6	3.6	1.0
24.8	23.6	22.9	Trade Payables	19.9	20.9	24.2	23.6	31.2	22.0
.2	.2	.2	Income Taxes Payable	.2	.2	.2	.1	.2	.2
9.2	9.2	8.3	All Other Current	12.2	4.7	6.2	10.5	8.2	9.2
50.7	49.9	50.7	Total Current	59.3	43.6	48.0	48.5	59.6	45.4
12.9	13.7	16.8	Long-Term Debt	34.1	15.0	11.3	7.7	6.1	16.3
.1	.1	.1	Deferred Taxes	.0	.0	.0	.2	.1	.2
6.4	7.8	7.3	All Other Non-Current	11.5	8.1	7.2	4.6	2.2	6.2
29.9	28.5	25.0	Net Worth	-4.9	33.2	33.4	39.0	32.0	31.9
100.0	100.0	100.0	Total Liabilities & Net Worth	100.0	100.0	100.0	100.0	100.0	100.0
			INCOME DATA						
100.0	100.0	100.0	Net Sales	100.0	100.0	100.0	100.0	100.0	100.0
36.2	37.5	37.6	Gross Profit	39.0	37.5	36.7	37.8	36.7	36.2
34.2	35.3	35.2	Operating Expenses	37.1	35.3	35.1	34.9	34.0	31.9
2.0	2.1	2.4	Operating Profit	1.9	2.3	1.6	2.9	2.7	4.3
.9	.6	.7	All Other Expenses (net)	1.6	.6	.5	.2	.1	.9
1.1	1.5	1.7	Profit Before Taxes	.3	1.7	1.1	2.7	2.6	3.4
			RATIOS						
2.5	2.5	2.5	Current	3.0	3.4	3.9	2.2	1.7	1.9
1.6	1.6	1.6		1.5	1.8	1.9	1.6	1.4	1.6
1.1	1.2	1.2		.8	1.2	1.2	1.2	1.2	1.0
.7	.6	.7	Quick	.7	.7	1.1	.7	.6	.3
(283) .2	(336) .2	(297) .2		.2	(79) .3	(41) .3	.3	.2	.2
.1	.1	.1		.1	.1	.1	.1	.1	.1
0 999.8	0 UND	0 UND	Sales/Receivables	0 UND	0 UND	1 692.5	0 999.8	0 777.5	1 327.2
3 115.8	2 168.4	2 173.2		0 UND	2 213.7	5 75.5	2 198.8	5 75.3	3 105.8
14 25.8	11 33.8	13 27.6		7 53.8	16 22.1	30 12.2	16 22.7	15 24.6	12 30.3
88 4.2	91 4.0	94 3.9	Cost of Sales/Inventory	97 3.8	106 3.4	70 5.2	83 4.4	97 3.8	109 3.4
133 2.7	138 2.6	141 2.6		159 2.3	154 2.4	131 2.8	123 3.0	121 3.0	140 2.6
189 1.9	211 1.7	206 1.8		238 1.5	221 1.7	231 1.6	189 1.9	154 2.4	169 2.2
27 13.7	21 17.0	21 17.5	Cost of Sales/Payables	16 23.3	16 23.5	20 18.6	27 13.7	37 10.0	39 9.4
49 7.4	47 7.8	42 8.8		38 9.7	34 10.7	39 9.4	39 9.5	57 6.4	52 7.0
81 4.5	78 4.7	77 4.7		69 5.3	83 4.4	81 4.5	72 5.0	87 4.2	72 5.1
5.5	5.3	4.8	Sales/Working Capital	4.3	3.6	4.7	6.9	8.6	6.0
10.3	9.5	9.1		8.2	6.5	6.6	9.5	12.2	10.3
34.1	28.4	30.9		-35.2	26.8	26.4	21.9	27.8	433.6
6.6	7.8	7.9	EBIT/Interest	4.2	7.1	16.6	8.7	13.3	10.2
(259) 2.1	(305) 2.3	(270) 2.9		(55) 1.1	(73) 1.9	(39) 3.1	(40) 3.9	5.6	(25) 5.2
.9	.7	1.1		-1.0	.4	1.1	1.5	2.2	2.2
10.6	6.8	5.2	Net Profit + Depr., Dep., Amort./Cur. Mat. L/T/D		2.1		7.8	18.3	
(48) 2.1	(57) 2.3	(50) 2.1			(14) .7		(10) 2.8	(12) 3.7	
.9	.8	.7			-.4		1.0	2.7	
.1	.1	.1	Fixed/Worth	.3	.1	.1	.1	.2	.2
.4	.4	.4		2.3	.4	.3	.3	.4	.4
1.3	2.3	2.8		-.5	2.8	1.5	.8	.8	2.8
1.0	.9	1.0	Debt/Worth	1.5	.7	.7	.9	1.2	1.2
2.3	2.3	2.5		220.5	2.5	1.6	1.5	2.9	1.6
8.0	10.0	17.1		-5.0	16.1	6.2	3.5	4.7	5.4
29.6	30.1	41.1	% Profit Before Taxes/Tangible Net Worth	78.4	30.2	30.9	39.9	36.2	54.2
(242) 11.9	(289) 12.9	(241) 16.3		(36) 16.5	(66) 12.1	(37) 12.9	(37) 12.7	(24) 21.0	(24) 36.3
.9	-.2	3.4		-8.5	.5	2.0	3.6	8.4	9.9
8.8	10.0	10.4	% Profit Before Taxes/Total Assets	11.1	8.6	10.1	14.1	13.6	10.9
3.2	2.8	3.7		.4	3.0	3.1	4.1	7.5	7.2
-.2	-1.2	-.1		-8.0	-1.5	.1	.9	1.8	2.5
60.9	72.5	76.0	Sales/Net Fixed Assets	48.0	105.5	104.4	66.8	72.3	68.9
27.3	26.6	26.3		19.9	26.6	36.5	31.8	32.7	18.1
12.9	10.7	11.8		8.7	12.0	12.0	14.0	16.3	6.2
3.4	3.4	3.4	Sales/Total Assets	3.0	3.3	3.4	3.8	3.7	3.0
2.5	2.5	2.5		2.3	2.5	2.6	2.9	3.1	2.2
1.9	1.8	1.8		1.5	1.6	2.0	2.0	2.3	1.6
.5	.5	.5	% Depr., Dep., Amort./Sales	.7	.5	.4	.4	.5	.7
(246) .9	(295) 1.0	(239) 1.0		(46) 1.3	(63) 1.0	(32) .8	(40) .7	(34) .7	(24) 1.5
1.8	1.8	1.8		2.2	2.0	1.4	1.3	1.3	2.4
2.2	2.2	2.4	% Officers', Directors', Owners' Comp/Sales	3.3	3.4	2.2	2.2	1.1	
(147) 4.3	(206) 4.1	(173) 4.6		(43) 5.3	(57) 4.9	(28) 4.9	(23) 3.3	(15) 1.7	
7.6	6.8	6.5		6.4	6.4	6.8	5.0	5.6	
4865446M	5641272M	4265462M	Net Sales ($)	36139M	147025M	167607M	307889M	593865M	3012937M
2131079M	2572444M	2092804M	Total Assets ($)	22715M	72497M	72701M	121142M	212385M	1591364M

M = $ thousand   MM = $ million
See Pages 11 through 21 for Explanation of Ratios and Data

Current Data Sorted By Assets | | | | | | **Comparative Historical Data**

Type of Statement

0-500M	500M-2MM	2-10MM	10-50MM	50-100MM	100-250MM	Type of Statement	4/1/00-3/31/01 ALL	4/1/01-3/31/02 ALL
	1	1	2		2	Unqualified	5	7
		2				Reviewed	6	8
4	4	3	1			Compiled	20	15
11	9	1		1		Tax Returns	4	6
5	1	1	2			Other	17	22

7 (4/1-9/30/04) [0-500M, 500M-2MM]   44 (10/1/04-3/31/05) [2-10MM … 100-250MM]

0-500M	500M-2MM	2-10MM	10-50MM	50-100MM	100-250MM		4/1/00-3/31/01 ALL	4/1/01-3/31/02 ALL
20	15	8	5	1	2	**NUMBER OF STATEMENTS**	52	58
%	%	%	%	%	%	**ASSETS**	%	%
11.0	13.1					Cash & Equivalents	9.2	11.5
2.4	1.1					Trade Receivables (net)	9.6	9.5
62.9	68.0					Inventory	56.9	52.8
1.0	.9					All Other Current	3.3	2.8
77.3	83.1					Total Current	79.0	76.5
12.5	9.0					Fixed Assets (net)	13.7	16.1
3.2	.8					Intangibles (net)	2.6	2.3
7.1	7.0					All Other Non-Current	4.6	5.0
100.0	100.0					Total	100.0	100.0
						LIABILITIES		
13.0	11.9					Notes Payable-Short Term	10.0	12.1
2.6	4.7					Cur. Mat.-L/T/D	2.8	4.6
6.2	19.9					Trade Payables	21.5	16.7
.0	.0					Income Taxes Payable	.3	.4
6.3	5.7					All Other Current	12.1	9.7
28.0	42.2					Total Current	46.6	43.6
23.8	18.1					Long-Term Debt	17.5	21.2
.0	.0					Deferred Taxes	.1	.2
11.5	3.2					All Other Non-Current	5.9	9.0
36.7	36.4					Net Worth	29.9	26.1
100.0	100.0					Total Liabilities & Net Worth	100.0	100.0
						INCOME DATA		
100.0	100.0					Net Sales	100.0	100.0
42.0	36.5					Gross Profit	39.0	41.8
37.3	35.6					Operating Expenses	38.1	37.6
4.7	.9					Operating Profit	.9	4.1
.9	.5					All Other Expenses (net)	.0	1.4
3.9	.4					Profit Before Taxes	.8	2.7
						RATIOS		
16.9	4.1						3.0	3.5
4.7	2.4					Current	1.9	2.0
1.5	1.3						1.2	1.2
2.5	.5						.7	1.0
.8	.3					Quick	(51) .4	.4
.1	.2						.1	.1
0 UND	0 UND						0 UND	0 UND
0 UND	0 UND					Sales/Receivables	2 214.3	3 129.4
1 467.5	0 999.8						14 25.2	14 26.1
64 5.7	62 5.9						83 4.4	89 4.1
113 3.2	123 3.0					Cost of Sales/Inventory	129 2.8	122 3.0
194 1.9	173 2.1						183 2.0	170 2.1
0 UND	11 34.1						21 17.0	14 26.6
1 297.3	22 16.7					Cost of Sales/Payables	38 9.5	28 13.0
18 20.7	34 10.6						54 6.8	49 7.5
3.2	5.1						5.1	4.3
9.2	7.3					Sales/Working Capital	9.3	9.1
48.7	15.1						25.7	33.7
19.0	17.5						6.3	11.5
(15) 3.2	(14) 6.6					EBIT/Interest	(47) 1.6	(55) 2.4
.5	3.1						−.3	.9
						Net Profit + Depr., Dep.,	8.4	
						Amort./Cur. Mat. L /T/D	(12) 1.8	
							.9	
.1	.0						.1	.1
.1	.1					Fixed/Worth	.4	.4
NM	3.8						.9	2.2
.3	.4						.8	.9
1.7	1.0					Debt/Worth	1.9	2.6
NM	50.5						4.7	6.7
130.5	82.3					% Profit Before Taxes/Tangible	32.4	52.9
(15) 50.9	(12) 27.1					Net Worth	(44) 11.2	(49) 21.0
5.0	10.3						−15.3	3.3
48.3	18.9					% Profit Before Taxes/Total	14.5	16.0
11.8	9.9					Assets	1.9	4.9
−.4	5.3						−5.0	−.2
282.2	163.9						84.3	67.0
32.3	50.7					Sales/Net Fixed Assets	38.1	29.5
11.6	18.1						14.6	11.4
5.2	4.4						4.2	3.8
3.5	3.0					Sales/Total Assets	3.0	2.9
2.4	2.2						2.1	1.8
.5	.5						.3	.6
(12) 1.3	(11) .7					% Depr., Dep., Amort./Sales	(38) .8	(42) .8
2.8	1.5						1.8	1.7
	1.4					% Officers', Directors',	2.4	2.2
	(10) 3.5					Owners' Comp/Sales	(19) 4.4	(29) 4.0
	5.1						7.1	5.3
23305M	44939M	68860M	267541M	106402M	832630M	Net Sales ($)	1782188M	2127473M
4771M	12989M	31111M	106809M	62032M	412797M	Total Assets ($)	913638M	871882M

M = $ thousand   MM = $ million
See Pages 11 through 21 for Explanation of Ratios and Data

Comparative Historical Data   Current Data Sorted By Sales

			Type of Statement	0-1MM	1-3MM	3-5MM	5-10MM	10-25MM	25MM & OVER
2	4	6	Unqualified				1	1	4
6	4	2	Reviewed			1		1	1
11	13	12	Compiled	1	6	2	1	1	1
14	19	21	Tax Returns	7	10	1	2	1	
18	13	10	Other	4	2		1		3
4/1/02-3/31/03	4/1/03-3/31/04	4/1/04-3/31/05		7 (4/1-9/30/04)			44 (10/1/04-3/31/05)		
ALL	ALL	ALL							
51	53	51	**NUMBER OF STATEMENTS**	12	18	5	4	4	8
%	%	%	**ASSETS**	%	%	%	%	%	%
11.5	10.6	10.5	Cash & Equivalents	9.1	12.2				
5.8	6.4	4.5	Trade Receivables (net)	3.5	1.2				
58.9	56.3	62.0	Inventory	64.8	64.4				
2.8	2.8	1.3	All Other Current	.3	.9				
79.0	76.2	78.3	Total Current	77.7	78.7				
11.3	14.8	12.4	Fixed Assets (net)	13.2	12.1				
4.3	1.9	2.9	Intangibles (net)	4.1	1.5				
5.4	7.1	6.4	All Other Non-Current	5.1	7.7				
100.0	100.0	100.0	Total	100.0	100.0				
			LIABILITIES						
12.7	9.6	15.1	Notes Payable-Short Term	11.3	14.3				
3.8	2.6	4.2	Cur. Mat.-L/T/D	2.0	5.2				
19.7	15.5	12.1	Trade Payables	7.4	13.0				
.2	.3	.0	Income Taxes Payable	.0	.0				
21.1	16.2	7.2	All Other Current	7.4	5.6				
57.5	44.3	38.7	Total Current	28.1	38.1				
16.5	24.7	21.7	Long-Term Debt	28.0	18.0				
.1	.1	.1	Deferred Taxes	.0	.0				
5.0	8.9	6.3	All Other Non-Current	18.0	3.5				
20.9	22.1	33.3	Net Worth	26.0	40.4				
100.0	100.0	100.0	Total Liabilities & Net Worth	100.0	100.0				
			INCOME DATA						
100.0	100.0	100.0	Net Sales	100.0	100.0				
43.1	40.7	40.2	Gross Profit	46.2	40.6				
40.6	37.8	36.5	Operating Expenses	41.4	38.7				
2.6	2.9	3.7	Operating Profit	4.8	1.9				
1.2	.9	.9	All Other Expenses (net)	1.2	.7				
1.4	2.0	2.8	Profit Before Taxes	3.6	1.2				
			RATIOS						
2.8	3.5	4.6		11.9	4.4				
1.5	2.1	2.4	Current	3.6	2.8				
1.1	1.3	1.2		1.5	1.2				
.6	.8	1.1		1.6	.7				
.3	(52) .4	.4	Quick	.8	.4				
.0	.1	.1		.1	.2				
0 UND	0 UND	0 UND		0 UND	0 UND				
1 420.0	0 999.8	0 999.8	Sales/Receivables	0 UND	0 UND				
7 54.8	5 74.7	5 73.5		4 92.2	0 781.8				
87 4.2	90 4.1	81 4.5		106 3.5	75 4.9				
129 2.8	125 2.9	122 3.0	Cost of Sales/Inventory	180 2.0	126 2.9				
216 1.7	175 2.1	197 1.9		208 1.8	179 2.0				
13 27.1	8 48.3	2 219.9		0 UND	2 239.5				
30 12.2	26 13.8	16 22.3	Cost of Sales/Payables	0 UND	16 22.8				
53 6.9	45 8.1	38 9.6		30 12.2	34 10.9				
5.3	5.3	5.0		2.6	4.9				
13.6	8.0	8.6	Sales/Working Capital	4.2	8.8				
57.1	15.8	30.1		34.2	NM				
6.3	7.6	15.3			7.3				
(46) 2.5	(45) 3.4	(45) 4.1	EBIT/Interest	(16)	4.6				
.7	1.4	1.4			1.8				
			Net Profit + Depr., Dep., Amort./Cur. Mat. L/T/D						
.1	.1	.1		.1	.1				
.5	.3	.2	Fixed/Worth	.3	.1				
7.8	1.4	3.8		−1.1	NM				
1.4	.8	.6		.4	.3				
3.6	2.9	2.1	Debt/Worth	2.5	.9				
−28.3	21.9	39.3		−6.3	NM				
51.3	38.0	69.3	% Profit Before Taxes/Tangible		74.4				
(38) 18.3	(42) 15.8	(41) 30.5	Net Worth	(14)	15.5				
1.1	3.4	7.1			6.7				
12.2	11.8	20.6	% Profit Before Taxes/Total	35.9	14.2				
5.9	7.0	9.4	Assets	9.8	8.8				
−1.8	.1	1.8		−6.7	4.0				
59.0	60.0	82.2		64.1	83.6				
32.8	31.8	31.3	Sales/Net Fixed Assets	21.9	37.3				
15.7	15.7	14.0		10.3	16.8				
3.7	3.6	4.2		4.0	4.6				
2.7	2.9	3.1	Sales/Total Assets	2.9	2.9				
1.9	2.2	1.9		1.7	2.1				
.7	.5	.7			.4				
(35) 1.1	(42) 1.0	(37) 1.1	% Depr., Dep., Amort./Sales	(14)	.7				
1.8	1.6	1.5			1.7				
1.8	1.9	1.5	% Officers', Directors',		2.5				
(27) 3.5	(26) 3.5	(27) 4.3	Owners' Comp/Sales	(13)	5.0				
5.1	5.2	5.5			8.6				
1061765M	1353803M	1343677M	Net Sales ($)	6845M	32905M	20928M	29508M	46918M	1206573M
500519M	598381M	630509M	Total Assets ($)	2790M	13068M	4357M	5968M	22688M	581638M

M = $ thousand   MM = $ million
See Pages 11 through 21 for Explanation of Ratios and Data

Current Data Sorted By Assets   Comparative Historical Data

0-500M	500M-2MM	2-10MM	10-50MM	50-100MM	100-250MM	Type of Statement	4/1/00-3/31/01 ALL	4/1/01-3/31/02 ALL
	8	3	2		4	Unqualified	5	3
4	7	16				Reviewed	20	14
6	11	12				Compiled	33	25
1	5	5				Tax Returns	10	15
		7	4	1	1	Other	26	17
	40 (4/1-9/30/04)			57 (10/1/04-3/31/05)				
11	31	43	6	1	5	NUMBER OF STATEMENTS	94	74
%	%	%	%	%	%	**ASSETS**	%	%
21.4	7.9	4.2				Cash & Equivalents	5.7	7.4
8.1	11.5	14.6				Trade Receivables (net)	13.5	9.4
50.2	61.4	56.9				Inventory	54.6	55.6
.0	1.5	3.3				All Other Current	2.9	2.9
79.7	82.3	79.0				Total Current	76.7	75.3
15.6	11.3	15.6				Fixed Assets (net)	17.8	16.9
.8	1.6	.5				Intangibles (net)	1.2	2.4
3.8	4.8	4.9				All Other Non-Current	4.3	5.5
100.0	100.0	100.0				Total	100.0	100.0
						LIABILITIES		
19.7	11.8	18.3				Notes Payable-Short Term	13.9	22.1
2.1	2.5	4.6				Cur. Mat.-L/T/D	3.6	3.8
7.8	20.1	14.1				Trade Payables	20.6	15.8
.0	.2	.5				Income Taxes Payable	.3	.1
24.9	9.4	9.8				All Other Current	10.2	7.3
54.5	44.0	47.3				Total Current	48.5	49.1
12.5	12.6	11.8				Long-Term Debt	17.7	12.8
.0	.0	.7				Deferred Taxes	.4	.2
5.6	3.0	5.4				All Other Non-Current	3.9	4.1
27.3	40.4	34.9				Net Worth	29.5	33.8
100.0	100.0	100.0				Total Liabilities & Net Worth	100.0	100.0
						INCOME DATA		
100.0	100.0	100.0				Net Sales	100.0	100.0
44.0	42.0	41.1				Gross Profit	42.9	45.2
40.1	40.6	39.4				Operating Expenses	39.6	42.4
4.0	1.4	1.7				Operating Profit	3.3	2.8
2.1	.5	.5				All Other Expenses (net)	.5	1.0
1.8	1.0	1.2				Profit Before Taxes	2.8	1.8
						RATIOS		
2.3	2.9	2.0					2.2	2.3
1.6	2.0	1.7				Current	1.6	1.6
1.0	1.4	1.3					1.1	1.3
1.0	.8	.6					.7	.7
.3	.4	.2				Quick	.3	.3
.1	.2	.1					.1	.1
0 UND	4 98.1	7 51.1					5 79.1	3 139.3
7 54.7	13 28.4	18 20.4				Sales/Receivables	16 22.8	11 33.1
34 10.9	30 12.4	42 8.6					33 11.1	22 16.3
27 13.7	146 2.5	155 2.4					119 3.1	134 2.7
91 4.0	206 1.8	218 1.7				Cost of Sales/Inventory	181 2.0	185 2.0
342 1.1	324 1.1	265 1.4					236 1.5	270 1.4
0 UND	13 27.3	17 22.0					24 15.1	15 24.5
11 32.9	37 9.7	52 7.1				Cost of Sales/Payables	54 6.7	39 9.3
26 14.1	134 2.7	90 4.1					94 3.9	70 5.2
4.0	3.2	3.7					4.4	4.4
9.7	5.5	5.8				Sales/Working Capital	8.1	6.5
−166.0	9.0	12.3					20.1	14.9
	4.9	3.9					5.0	4.6
	(27) 1.7	(42) 1.6				EBIT/Interest	(86) 2.3	(72) 2.1
	.6	.9					1.2	1.2
		3.7				Net Profit + Depr., Dep.,	10.9	3.7
	(20) 1.1					Amort./Cur. Mat. L /T/D	(28) 4.3	(27) 1.0
		.1					1.4	.6
.0	.1	.1					.1	.1
.3	.2	.3				Fixed/Worth	.3	.3
UND	.6	.7					1.5	.9
.6	.9	1.2					1.1	1.1
2.0	1.5	2.1				Debt/Worth	2.1	1.9
UND	4.5	3.3					5.1	4.0
	27.0	12.8				% Profit Before Taxes/Tangible	33.4	26.2
	(28) 11.8	6.0				Net Worth	(87) 14.9	(69) 9.6
	−1.0	−.4					3.9	2.8
32.5	8.0	5.5				% Profit Before Taxes/Total	9.0	8.4
.6	3.9	1.8				Assets	4.7	2.7
−15.4	−.9	−.2					.8	.6
UND	103.2	36.6					41.6	43.8
53.1	21.4	16.4				Sales/Net Fixed Assets	22.9	21.3
14.8	11.9	7.7					8.4	8.5
4.0	2.5	2.0					2.6	2.9
1.6	1.9	1.6				Sales/Total Assets	1.9	1.9
1.3	1.6	1.2					1.5	1.5
	.7	.7					.6	.6
	(20) 1.3	(36) 1.3				% Depr., Dep., Amort./Sales	(84) .9	(63) .9
	4.1	2.0					2.5	1.8
	2.5	1.9				% Officers', Directors',	2.7	2.9
	(24) 4.5	(24) 4.5				Owners' Comp/Sales	(39) 5.0	(38) 5.5
	5.8	7.2					8.0	8.5
6588M	74348M	280146M	439811M	89902M	992562M	Net Sales ($)	1193524M	537954M
3160M	36531M	161196M	197480M	52226M	565362M	Total Assets ($)	618313M	259317M

M = $ thousand   MM = $ million
See Pages 11 through 21 for Explanation of Ratios and Data

Comparative Historical Data				Current Data Sorted By Sales					
9	8	9	**Type of Statement** Unqualified			1	2		6
21	19	24	Reviewed		5	7	10	2	
33	34	23	Compiled	4	7	5	5	2	
7	19	22	Tax Returns	6	10	4	1	1	
24	23	19	Other	2	5	2	4		3
4/1/02-3/31/03 ALL	4/1/03-3/31/04 ALL	4/1/04-3/31/05 ALL		40 (4/1-9/30/04)			57 (10/1/04-3/31/05)		
				0-1MM	1-3MM	3-5MM	5-10MM	10-25MM	25MM & OVER
94	103	97	**NUMBER OF STATEMENTS**	12	27	19	21	9	9
%	%	%	**ASSETS**	%	%	%	%	%	%
7.5	6.5	7.0	Cash & Equivalents	20.2	7.6	5.9	2.7		
13.5	14.8	14.1	Trade Receivables (net)	11.5	10.5	15.4	12.6		
58.4	55.9	55.9	Inventory	46.5	59.6	58.1	58.9		
2.6	3.1	2.1	All Other Current	.1	4.4	.7	2.5		
82.0	80.3	79.1	Total Current	78.4	82.1	80.0	76.7		
12.2	14.9	14.9	Fixed Assets (net)	15.9	10.9	14.6	18.3		
1.0	1.0	1.1	Intangibles (net)	.7	1.9	.2	.4		
4.8	3.8	4.9	All Other Non-Current	5.0	5.1	5.2	4.6		
100.0	100.0	100.0	Total	100.0	100.0	100.0	100.0		
			LIABILITIES						
16.3	20.1	17.2	Notes Payable-Short Term	17.3	11.1	16.0	22.6		
3.5	3.5	3.8	Cur. Mat.-L/T/D	1.4	2.9	3.7	6.1		
20.3	14.8	15.5	Trade Payables	7.4	19.0	21.1	10.8		
.4	.3	.4	Income Taxes Payable	.0	.1	.7	.5		
11.3	8.9	11.2	All Other Current	24.1	9.8	5.7	10.5		
51.7	47.6	48.1	Total Current	50.2	43.0	47.3	50.4		
8.7	13.8	12.3	Long-Term Debt	10.9	15.8	9.3	13.0		
.2	.3	.3	Deferred Taxes	.0	.2	.0	1.0		
2.9	5.2	4.1	All Other Non-Current	5.8	6.2	3.4	3.1		
36.5	33.0	35.1	Net Worth	33.0	34.8	40.1	32.5		
100.0	100.0	100.0	Total Liabilities & Net Worth	100.0	100.0	100.0	100.0		
			INCOME DATA						
100.0	100.0	100.0	Net Sales	100.0	100.0	100.0	100.0		
42.6	44.2	41.6	Gross Profit	44.4	42.7	41.0	42.8		
39.6	42.7	39.4	Operating Expenses	43.6	40.2	39.7	40.9		
3.0	1.6	2.2	Operating Profit	.8	2.6	1.3	1.9		
.6	.8	.7	All Other Expenses (net)	1.8	.9	-.7	.9		
2.4	.8	1.5	Profit Before Taxes	-1.1	1.7	2.0	1.0		
			RATIOS						
2.5	2.6	2.3		4.2	3.4	2.3	1.8		
1.7	1.8	1.7	Current	1.7	2.2	1.9	1.7		
1.4	1.3	1.2		1.0	1.3	1.3	1.2		
.8	.9	.8		2.4	.6	.8	.5		
.3	.3	.3	Quick	.5	.4	.3	.2		
.2	.1	.1		.2	.2	.1	.1		
4 83.0	5 80.6	6 61.0		0 UND	3 112.0	7 53.4	7 55.8		
12 29.8	13 28.5	16 23.2	Sales/Receivables	12 29.5	13 28.4	17 21.2	17 21.0		
30 12.2	37 9.8	36 10.3		82 4.4	24 15.1	39 9.5	23 15.5		
112 3.2	132 2.8	131 2.8		33 10.9	155 2.3	144 2.5	157 2.3		
197 1.9	210 1.7	195 1.9	Cost of Sales/Inventory	292 1.3	199 1.8	209 1.8	231 1.6		
248 1.5	262 1.4	273 1.3		376 1.0	316 1.2	239 1.5	278 1.3		
21 17.4	16 22.9	14 25.2		0 UND	14 26.4	17 22.0	14 25.4		
45 8.1	43 8.5	39 9.4	Cost of Sales/Payables	15 24.8	39 9.4	80 4.6	34 10.6		
72 5.1	67 5.5	81 4.5		25 14.4	147 2.5	105 3.5	58 6.3		
4.3	3.9	3.9		1.9	3.0	3.5	4.5		
6.4	5.5	6.3	Sales/Working Capital	6.3	4.8	6.7	7.0		
11.4	14.2	18.3		UND	12.3	10.7	19.9		
7.7	5.6	5.1		19.0	4.6	8.6	3.2		
(84) 3.1	(97) 2.1	(90) 1.7	EBIT/Interest	(10) .8	(25) 1.7	(18) 2.2	(19) 1.5		
1.5	1.0	.8		-3.8	.9	1.0	.1		
5.0	2.9	4.5	Net Profit + Depr., Dep.,				1.9		
(30) 2.6	(33) 1.4	(29) 1.2	Amort./Cur. Mat. L/T/D				(10) 1.0		
.9	.4	.3					-.1		
.1	.1	.1		.0	.1	.1	.3		
.3	.3	.3	Fixed/Worth	.2	.2	.2	.4		
.5	.9	.7		UND	.7	.6	1.0		
.8	1.0	1.0		.4	1.2	.9	1.2		
1.7	2.1	2.0	Debt/Worth	1.8	2.1	1.5	2.1		
2.7	4.4	4.0		UND	7.8	3.0	4.6		
23.1	24.1	24.4	% Profit Before Taxes/Tangible	139.9	27.0	8.5	16.5		
(88) 10.2	(93) 8.6	(92) 7.4	Net Worth	(10) 2.0	(24) 11.8	6.1	7.8		
3.9	.5	.5		-5.7	.4	1.3	-8.1		
8.0	7.2	6.6	% Profit Before Taxes/Total	16.9	8.0	6.5	6.1		
3.9	2.5	1.9	Assets	-.5	2.0	2.4	1.9		
1.2	.0	-.4		-15.2	.1	.5	-1.9		
62.7	55.8	50.9		140.0	103.2	52.5	21.2		
25.5	21.8	16.9	Sales/Net Fixed Assets	16.0	28.2	20.9	14.8		
13.6	9.3	8.4		6.4	11.4	7.7	7.5		
2.6	2.6	2.2		2.8	2.2	2.1	2.2		
2.1	1.8	1.8	Sales/Total Assets	1.5	1.8	1.8	1.9		
1.5	1.3	1.4		1.2	1.4	1.4	1.4		
.5	.7	.7		.3	.4	1.0	.9		
(73) .9	(85) 1.2	(75) 1.3	% Depr., Dep., Amort./Sales	(10) 1.4	(18) 1.1	(12) 1.7	(19) 1.3		
1.8	2.5	2.0		3.2	4.1	2.7	2.2		
3.3	2.3	2.4	% Officers', Directors',		2.5	2.2	1.6		
(44) 5.3	(54) 4.9	(53) 4.8	Owners' Comp/Sales		(23) 4.2	(12) 5.5	(10) 4.2		
8.3	7.9	7.1			5.8	8.8	5.3		
1356408M	1188535M	1883357M	Net Sales ($)	6947M	55291M	70959M	141723M	148940M	1459497M
697829M	715699M	1015955M	Total Assets ($)	5403M	36006M	42978M	82170M	101374M	748024M

M = $ thousand   MM = $ million
See Pages 11 through 21 for Explanation of Ratios and Data

Current Data Sorted By Assets   Comparative Historical Data

							Type of Statement		
	2	5	6		1		Unqualified	10	9
	1	5	2				Reviewed	12	8
3	10	1					Compiled	15	14
8	5	2					Tax Returns	14	7
3	5	9	3	1			Other	22	20
	20 (4/1-9/30/04)		52 (10/1/04-3/31/05)					4/1/00-3/31/01	4/1/01-3/31/02
0-500M	500M-2MM	2-10MM	10-50MM	50-100MM	100-250MM			ALL	ALL
14	23	22	11	1	1	NUMBER OF STATEMENTS		73	58
%	%	%	%	%	%	ASSETS		%	%
7.2	7.4	13.1	10.6			Cash & Equivalents		10.8	13.0
7.6	6.8	6.9	6.6			Trade Receivables (net)		6.0	6.3
50.5	53.7	48.7	45.0			Inventory		54.8	52.0
2.3	3.1	2.1	1.9			All Other Current		2.0	1.2
67.6	71.0	70.8	64.1			Total Current		73.5	72.5
27.0	17.5	23.6	28.3			Fixed Assets (net)		18.7	19.6
1.5	1.3	3.2	.8			Intangibles (net)		2.5	1.6
3.9	10.3	2.4	6.8			All Other Non-Current		5.3	6.3
100.0	100.0	100.0	100.0			Total		100.0	100.0
						LIABILITIES			
12.5	16.0	6.2	9.8			Notes Payable-Short Term		8.0	10.1
3.2	7.6	5.3	.8			Cur. Mat.-L/T/D		2.5	2.8
26.6	21.4	22.2	16.9			Trade Payables		24.6	25.3
.0	.0	.2	.0			Income Taxes Payable		.1	.2
35.3	9.4	7.5	15.0			All Other Current		11.1	10.0
77.6	54.4	41.4	42.6			Total Current		46.3	48.5
13.9	9.7	15.4	10.2			Long-Term Debt		14.0	15.8
.0	.2	.2	.1			Deferred Taxes		.1	.2
23.6	1.6	8.6	2.0			All Other Non-Current		5.4	3.7
-15.1	34.2	34.5	45.1			Net Worth		34.2	31.9
100.0	100.0	100.0	100.0			Total Liabilities & Net Worth		100.0	100.0
						INCOME DATA			
100.0	100.0	100.0	100.0			Net Sales		100.0	100.0
44.9	41.3	42.1	45.7			Gross Profit		40.1	38.7
43.8	41.5	36.8	42.8			Operating Expenses		38.4	36.7
1.1	-.3	5.2	2.9			Operating Profit		1.7	2.0
.8	-.3	.8	1.8			All Other Expenses (net)		-.4	.7
.3	.0	4.5	1.0			Profit Before Taxes		2.2	1.3
						RATIOS			
1.8	2.6	2.9	3.0					2.7	3.0
1.3	1.4	2.2	2.5			Current		1.7	1.5
.6	.8	1.2	1.1					1.1	1.1
.3	.7	1.0	1.5					.8	1.0
.1	.1	.5	.5			Quick		(72) .4	(56) .3
.0	.0	.2	.1					.1	.2

0	UND	0	999.8	0	895.1	2	194.7				Sales/Receivables	1	608.0	0	UND
1	336.4	2	174.2	3	112.8	5	70.9					3	120.8	3	131.2
9	40.0	12	31.0	13	28.1	10	34.8					10	35.7	11	34.5
76	4.8	61	6.0	68	5.3	89	4.1				Cost of Sales/Inventory	86	4.2	80	4.5
101	3.6	120	3.0	109	3.4	118	3.1					123	3.0	104	3.5
132	2.8	221	1.7	185	2.0	231	1.6					187	1.9	145	2.5
0	UND	21	17.1	27	13.4	15	23.8				Cost of Sales/Payables	25	14.6	25	14.8
45	8.1	42	8.7	44	8.3	42	8.7					53	6.9	44	8.4
95	3.8	70	5.2	64	5.7	64	5.7					83	4.4	87	4.2

7.5	5.7	4.9	4.4			Sales/Working Capital		5.0	5.1
20.0	14.2	7.7	5.9					10.6	10.5
-27.3	-21.9	16.1	43.0					31.6	33.7
	8.5	14.5				EBIT/Interest		13.4	8.3
	(21) 2.4	(20) 4.9						(66) 3.7	(51) 2.5
	1.0	1.3						.9	.5
						Net Profit + Depr., Dep., Amort./Cur. Mat. L /T/D		12.3	92.2
								(15) 4.5	(10) 7.1
								1.7	1.6
.4	.3	.2	.3			Fixed/Worth		.2	.2
6.7	.6	.6	.5					.4	.5
-.7	6.0	1.8	1.5					1.5	1.9
1.3	.8	.5	.4			Debt/Worth		.6	.7
24.1	2.0	1.8	1.5					2.4	2.2
-2.5	23.7	3.9	2.5					4.7	5.0
	15.9	88.5	8.7			% Profit Before Taxes/Tangible Net Worth		34.4	39.5
	(19) 10.5	(19) 15.5	(10) 4.3					(64) 17.3	(48) 15.0
	.5	7.8	-4.8					5.2	1.3
15.8	6.8	16.1	4.9			% Profit Before Taxes/Total Assets		11.2	12.1
3.3	3.8	7.9	1.2					5.5	4.4
-14.7	-.4	.6	-3.1					.3	-2.1
56.9	50.0	81.5	20.2			Sales/Net Fixed Assets		51.8	54.9
19.2	18.6	12.8	9.2					19.1	15.1
8.7	8.9	4.6	4.2					8.7	8.6
4.2	4.4	3.0	2.7			Sales/Total Assets		3.5	3.4
3.5	2.4	2.1	1.8					2.6	2.6
2.4	-1.4	1.8	1.7					1.7	1.9
.4	.6	1.0	1.1			% Depr., Dep., Amort./Sales		.6	.7
(11) .9	(18) 1.2	(21) 1.5	(10) 1.4					(63) 1.3	(51) 1.1
1.2	2.1	2.6	1.9					2.1	1.9
	1.8					% Officers', Directors', Owners' Comp/Sales		2.2	2.6
	(12) 3.4							(27) 4.4	(22) 5.6
	7.9							7.7	9.2
13080M	74604M	289026M	471864M	129931M	314315M	Net Sales ($)		923112M	973047M
3763M	25091M	123130M	234837M	57975M	114713M	Total Assets ($)		435597M	425445M

© RMA 2005

M = $ thousand   MM = $ million
See Pages 11 through 21 for Explanation of Ratios and Data

Comparative Historical Data | Current Data Sorted By Sales

	4/1/02-3/31/03 ALL	4/1/03-3/31/04 ALL	4/1/04-3/31/05 ALL	Type of Statement			20 (4/1-9/30/04)			52 (10/1/04-3/31/05)	
					0-1MM	1-3MM	3-5MM	5-10MM	10-25MM	25MM & OVER	
Unqualified	15	13	14			2		2	4	6	
Reviewed	11	8	8			5		5	1	2	
Compiled	14	19	14		3	5	4	1	1	1	
Tax Returns	12	15	15		4	7	1	1	2		
Other	23	26	21		2	4		5	6	4	
NUMBER OF STATEMENTS	75	81	72		9	18	5	14	14	12	

	4/1/02-3/31/03	4/1/03-3/31/04	4/1/04-3/31/05	0-1MM	1-3MM	3-5MM	5-10MM	10-25MM	25MM & OVER
ASSETS (%)									
Cash & Equivalents	12.0	12.1	9.6		6.2		11.1	14.2	8.8
Trade Receivables (net)	7.6	7.0	6.8		5.8		9.7	9.0	4.4
Inventory	46.7	46.9	49.8		51.1		45.9	46.8	49.8
All Other Current	2.7	2.9	2.4		1.6		2.1	2.3	2.0
Total Current	68.9	69.0	68.7		64.7		68.8	72.3	65.0
Fixed Assets (net)	22.3	21.1	23.1		23.8		24.7	22.5	25.7
Intangibles (net)	1.9	2.0	2.2		1.8		2.5	2.6	3.2
All Other Non-Current	7.0	7.9	6.0		9.8		4.0	2.6	6.1
Total	100.0	100.0	100.0		100.0		100.0	100.0	100.0
LIABILITIES									
Notes Payable-Short Term	6.2	5.3	11.0		17.1		6.2	5.5	9.0
Cur. Mat.-L/T/D	2.4	2.4	4.8		8.9		3.4	5.7	.7
Trade Payables	26.5	24.4	22.2		19.4		26.2	19.5	21.3
Income Taxes Payable	.2	.1	.1		.0		.1	.2	.1
All Other Current	11.4	14.7	14.7		27.5		7.3	8.1	14.6
Total Current	46.8	46.9	52.8		72.9		43.2	39.0	45.7
Long-Term Debt	16.1	14.1	12.5		7.6		18.4	8.8	14.1
Deferred Taxes	.2	.1	.1		.0		.0	.3	.0
All Other Non-Current	4.9	6.4	8.1		12.1		.3	4.3	12.9
Net Worth	32.0	32.5	26.4		7.4		38.1	47.6	27.2
Total Liabilities & Net Worth	100.0	100.0	100.0		100.0		100.0	100.0	100.0
INCOME DATA									
Net Sales	100.0	100.0	100.0		100.0		100.0	100.0	100.0
Gross Profit	39.2	40.4	43.3		42.1		45.9	41.4	44.8
Operating Expenses	35.6	38.7	41.0		41.9		41.4	36.1	42.1
Operating Profit	3.6	1.8	2.3		.1		4.4	5.3	2.7
All Other Expenses (net)	.9	1.1	.6		.4		.6	.6	2.1
Profit Before Taxes	2.7	.7	1.7		−.3		3.9	4.7	.6
RATIOS									
Current	2.7	2.7	2.7		2.0		2.9	3.2	2.7
	1.6	1.5	1.5		1.3		1.9	2.3	1.9
	1.0	1.0	.9		.7		1.1	1.2	1.0
Quick	.9	.7	.9		.2		1.2	1.3	.9
	.4	.3	.3		.1		.5	.5	.2
	.1	.2	.1		.0		.1	.4	.1
Sales/Receivables	0 UND	0 999.8	0 964.9		0 UND		0 999.8	0 895.1	2 189.2
	3 128.3	3 120.6	3 143.2		2 178.3		2 198.1	5 74.3	3 128.3
	11 33.1	12 31.5	10 34.9		6 60.0		13 27.2	17 21.9	10 37.9
Cost of Sales/Inventory	65 5.7	68 5.4	76 4.8		76 4.8		53 6.9	77 4.8	89 4.1
	92 4.0	102 3.6	113 3.2		137 2.7		101 3.6	107 3.4	113 3.2
	125 2.9	144 2.5	194 1.9		231 1.6		159 2.3	186 2.0	176 2.1
Cost of Sales/Payables	26 14.2	14 26.8	25 14.9		21 17.5		23 16.0	30 12.2	18 20.5
	44 8.4	42 8.8	44 8.3		47 7.8		43 8.4	41 8.8	43 8.5
	74 4.9	80 4.6	70 5.2		85 4.3		90 4.1	59 6.2	79 4.6
Sales/Working Capital	6.1	6.5	5.8		7.0		6.5	4.1	5.8
	11.2	11.9	11.7		20.8		8.8	6.5	11.2
	112.1	189.6	−85.9		−18.2		NM	16.1	220.0
EBIT/Interest	20.4	11.4	10.7		7.3		11.2	19.2	9.4
	(67) 3.9	(70) 3.2	(59) 2.0		(14) 1.4		(13) 5.8	(12) 10.7	(10) 1.7
	.3	.5	.9		−2.1		1.3	4.3	.1
Net Profit + Depr., Dep., Amort./Cur. Mat. L/T/D	14.4	5.9	12.8						
	(12) 2.9	(14) 1.8	(12) 5.0						
	.5	1.1	1.7						
Fixed/Worth	.3	.2	.3		.4		.4	.1	.4
	.7	.5	.7		.8		.7	.4	1.0
	3.1	66.8	7.1		−1.5		1.5	.8	NM
Debt/Worth	.7	.6	.7		1.3		.7	.4	.6
	2.4	1.8	1.8		1.9		1.9	1.5	1.6
	11.2	165.6	29.2		−14.4		4.2	3.1	NM
% Profit Before Taxes/Tangible Net Worth	67.1	32.5	33.8		14.9		90.3	61.4	
	(64) 16.9	(63) 9.6	(57) 11.7		(12) 4.3		(13) 29.8	(13) 14.3	
	2.9	1.5	1.9		−30.3		7.2	6.9	
% Profit Before Taxes/Total Assets	13.9	8.4	11.1		7.4		15.3	16.1	3.2
	5.5	2.5	3.7		.5		4.3	9.0	.2
	−1.3	−1.3	−.7		−7.8		1.4	5.2	−5.9
Sales/Net Fixed Assets	46.7	66.2	33.1		50.3		23.2	89.9	21.7
	13.4	20.4	15.5		10.9		15.4	13.0	12.2
	6.7	6.6	7.0		7.3		5.2	4.9	5.0
Sales/Total Assets	3.7	4.1	3.5		3.6		4.7	3.1	3.1
	2.8	2.8	2.4		2.3		2.6	2.0	2.4
	2.1	1.8	1.8		1.4		1.9	1.8	1.7
% Depr., Dep., Amort./Sales	.8	.6	.9		.6		1.3	.7	1.1
	(64) 1.4	(67) 1.5	(61) 1.4		(14) 1.4		(12) 1.5	(13) 1.7	(10) 1.4
	2.1	2.5	2.1		2.6		2.1	2.8	
% Officers', Directors', Owners' Comp/Sales	1.6	2.3	1.8		1.6				
	(28) 4.8	(26) 3.4	(23) 3.8		(10) 2.7				
	8.4	9.0			4.7				
Net Sales ($)	2128066M	1311580M	1292820M	5639M	27292M	19183M	105257M	236583M	898866M
Total Assets ($)	1038295M	602563M	559509M	2865M	13093M	5462M	44019M	107646M	386424M

M = $ thousand   MM = $ million
See Pages 11 through 21 for Explanation of Ratios and Data

Current Data Sorted By Assets　　　　　　　　　　　　**Comparative Historical Data**

0-500M	500M-2MM	2-10MM	10-50MM	50-100MM	100-250MM	Type of Statement	4/1/00-3/31/01 ALL	4/1/01-3/31/02 ALL
	1	3	8		1	Unqualified	6	13
		4	2			Reviewed	9	3
	3	3	1			Compiled	6	11
1	2					Tax Returns	6	3
	3	5	2	1	3	Other	15	12
		8 (4/1-9/30/04)	35 (10/1/04-3/31/05)					
1	9	15	13	1	4	**NUMBER OF STATEMENTS**	42	42
%	%	%	%	%	%	**ASSETS**	%	%
		11.2	11.1			Cash & Equivalents	10.6	11.2
		16.1	3.0			Trade Receivables (net)	13.1	10.5
		34.1	39.3			Inventory	43.7	38.0
		1.1	1.5			All Other Current	2.0	6.3
		62.5	54.9			Total Current	69.4	66.0
		17.5	20.6			Fixed Assets (net)	20.9	22.4
		4.4	5.5			Intangibles (net)	2.5	5.5
		15.5	19.0			All Other Non-Current	7.2	6.1
		100.0	100.0			Total	100.0	100.0
						LIABILITIES		
		5.8	4.0			Notes Payable-Short Term	7.8	3.0
		.7	1.5			Cur. Mat.-L/T/D	1.6	2.2
		14.6	19.0			Trade Payables	13.0	12.1
		1.4	.1			Income Taxes Payable	.3	.2
		10.8	6.8			All Other Current	7.1	7.5
		33.3	31.4			Total Current	29.8	25.1
		10.7	10.0			Long-Term Debt	16.4	16.7
		.4	2.4			Deferred Taxes	.2	.7
		3.2	4.1			All Other Non-Current	6.4	2.0
		52.4	52.1			Net Worth	47.2	55.4
		100.0	100.0			Total Liabilities & Net Worth	100.0	100.0
						INCOME DATA		
		100.0	100.0			Net Sales	100.0	100.0
		30.0	38.5			Gross Profit	35.4	33.9
		26.4	36.5			Operating Expenses	35.0	30.4
		3.6	2.0			Operating Profit	.4	3.5
		−.5	−.8			All Other Expenses (net)	−1.2	.7
		4.1	2.8			Profit Before Taxes	1.6	2.8
						RATIOS		
		3.6	5.7				4.5	5.8
		2.8	2.0			Current	2.3	2.6
		1.5	1.1				1.8	1.8
		1.5	2.0				2.2	1.8
		.8	.6			Quick	.8	.8
		.3	.1				.1	.4
		0　999.8	0　UND				1　644.7	1　299.4
		12　30.7	5　67.5			Sales/Receivables	4　91.6	6　57.9
		41　8.8	15　23.8				37　9.8	21　17.0
		4　86.6	65　5.6				59　6.2	50　7.3
		53　6.8	110　3.3			Cost of Sales/Inventory	83　4.4	80　4.6
		89　4.1	196　1.9				146　2.5	113　3.2
		5　68.9	11　34.0				15　23.8	12　30.2
		27　13.4	39　9.4			Cost of Sales/Payables	30　12.1	31　11.9
		42　8.6	84　4.4				51　7.1	48　7.5
		5.9	2.7				4.0	3.9
		9.9	6.9			Sales/Working Capital	6.3	6.3
		22.2	NM				14.1	9.7
		16.4	22.6				6.5	15.4
	(12)	10.0	(11)　5.4			EBIT/Interest	(31)　2.3	(32)　3.4
		3.5	.8				1.0	1.4
						Net Profit + Depr., Dep.,	5.2	
						Amort./Cur. Mat. L /T/D	(13)　1.6	
							.3	
		.1	.2				.1	.2
		.2	.6			Fixed/Worth	.5	.4
		.7	1.3				1.4	1.2
		.5	.2				.5	.2
		.9	1.7			Debt/Worth	1.2	.9
		1.7	8.9				3.0	2.4
		30.3	52.9				27.8	23.6
	(14)	12.4	(12)　9.6			% Profit Before Taxes/Tangible Net Worth	(38)　12.3	(38)　10.7
		.3	−1.4				1.8	1.5
		9.7	13.1				10.9	10.7
		4.1	4.2			% Profit Before Taxes/Total Assets	4.3	4.2
		.9	.8				−1.1	1.0
		95.7	26.6				39.1	48.3
		50.0	16.5			Sales/Net Fixed Assets	12.6	11.2
		12.1	5.2				5.5	6.2
		3.9	3.9				3.6	3.5
		2.7	2.3			Sales/Total Assets	2.3	2.3
		1.4	1.1				1.5	1.3
		.2	.9				.4	.4
	(14)	.4	1.1			% Depr., Dep., Amort./Sales	(32)　1.3	(36)　.9
		1.1	2.4				2.2	2.0
							1.0	1.4
						% Officers', Directors', Owners' Comp/Sales	(13)　3.3	(11)　4.0
							12.0	12.0
1246M	38243M	320938M	983065M	189516M	2057817M	Net Sales ($)	2497356M	3584411M
329M	10953M	75754M	359952M	64703M	607720M	Total Assets ($)	1453887M	1702723M

M = $ thousand　　MM = $ million
See Pages 11 through 21 for Explanation of Ratios and Data

Comparative Historical Data | Current Data Sorted By Sales

4/1/02-3/31/03 ALL	4/1/03-3/31/04 ALL	4/1/04-3/31/05 ALL	Type of Statement	0-1MM	1-3MM	3-5MM	5-10MM	10-25MM	25MM & OVER
17	19	13	Unqualified				3	1	9
11	6	6	Reviewed				3		3
9	9	7	Compiled		4	1	2		2
9	3	3	Tax Returns		1		2		
17	13	14	Other			4	1	2	7
					8 (4/1-9/30/04)		35 (10/1/04-3/31/05)		
63	50	43	NUMBER OF STATEMENTS		5	5	11	3	19
%	%	%	ASSETS	%	%	%	%	%	%
10.0	12.3	11.5	Cash & Equivalents				8.5		7.5
8.4	7.5	14.1	Trade Receivables (net)	D			22.9		8.0
36.4	40.2	36.2	Inventory	A			31.1		44.6
3.0	2.6	1.4	All Other Current	T			2.5		.7
57.8	62.5	63.2	Total Current	A			65.1		60.8
29.3	21.3	20.0	Fixed Assets (net)				17.9		20.8
3.4	3.8	3.3	Intangibles (net)	N			2.4		5.9
9.5	12.4	13.5	All Other Non-Current	O			14.6		12.4
100.0	100.0	100.0	Total	T			100.0		100.0
			LIABILITIES	A					
7.8	6.8	7.2	Notes Payable-Short Term	V			8.8		6.3
1.7	2.7	1.5	Cur. Mat.-L/T/D	A			.5		1.6
14.5	15.3	19.1	Trade Payables	I			23.1		21.3
.2	.5	.8	Income Taxes Payable	L			2.3		.1
10.0	8.2	8.6	All Other Current	A			6.9		9.7
34.2	33.4	37.2	Total Current	B			41.6		38.9
18.1	13.9	9.1	Long-Term Debt	L			5.4		9.5
1.0	.3	1.0	Deferred Taxes	E			.6		1.2
4.2	2.3	4.2	All Other Non-Current				1.1		5.0
42.4	50.1	48.5	Net Worth				51.3		45.4
100.0	100.0	100.0	Total Liabilities & Net Worth				100.0		100.0
			INCOME DATA						
100.0	100.0	100.0	Net Sales				100.0		100.0
36.4	36.0	35.9	Gross Profit				34.1		31.9
32.1	32.2	32.0	Operating Expenses				32.4		28.4
4.3	3.7	3.9	Operating Profit				1.7		3.5
.6	.3	-.5	All Other Expenses (net)				-.7		.5
3.7	3.5	4.4	Profit Before Taxes				2.4		3.0
			RATIOS						
3.5	3.4	3.6					3.3		3.2
1.9	2.1	1.7	Current				1.5		1.5
1.3	1.3	1.3					1.2		.9
1.2	1.1	1.5					1.5		.6
(62) .5	.6	.7	Quick				.8		.4
.2	.2	.3					.3		.1
1 487.8	0 775.3	1 426.2					4 84.8		0 UND
4 82.4	3 130.0	8 45.6	Sales/Receivables				23 16.1		1 361.5
18 20.3	15 23.8	32 11.5					44 8.4		12 30.7
34 10.7	48 7.6	38 9.6					24 15.2		43 8.4
81 4.5	97 3.8	78 4.7	Cost of Sales/Inventory				53 6.8		78 4.7
161 2.3	138 2.6	125 2.9					155 2.4		121 3.0
9 41.3	12 31.2	11 33.3					20 18.2		10 37.1
30 12.3	31 11.9	29 12.4	Cost of Sales/Payables				37 9.9		26 14.0
45 8.1	46 7.9	52 7.0					47 7.8		72 5.1
5.0	3.8	3.8					5.9		6.9
8.6	8.8	10.2	Sales/Working Capital				10.2		17.4
69.8	19.8	26.7					26.7		-98.4
11.9	11.1	21.7							38.6
(53) 4.4	(38) 4.7	(35) 5.4	EBIT/Interest					(16)	19.4
1.5	1.4	2.0							2.3
15.0	7.6	17.5	Net Profit + Depr., Dep.,						
(13) 4.5	(13) 2.2	(11) 4.1	Amort./Cur. Mat. L/T/D						
2.7	.6	2.0							
.2	.1	.2					.1		.2
.6	.4	.4	Fixed/Worth				.3		.6
1.7	.8	.9					.7		1.8
.5	.3	.2					.5		.2
1.3	1.0	1.3	Debt/Worth				1.1		1.7
3.3	3.0	3.7					1.7		10.2
30.8	27.5	41.4	% Profit Before Taxes/Tangible				28.0		118.5
(54) 14.0	(46) 11.6	(41) 14.4	Net Worth				10.0	(18)	19.6
3.1	.4	1.0					1.8		-3.6
12.8	11.8	14.8	% Profit Before Taxes/Total				10.0		19.1
5.2	5.4	4.5	Assets				4.5		5.0
1.5	-1.6	.7					.9		-.5
34.2	49.1	50.0					95.7		36.6
10.0	15.4	16.9	Sales/Net Fixed Assets				15.5		17.7
4.5	8.4	10.7					8.9		10.9
3.8	3.6	3.9					3.9		5.1
2.1	2.4	2.7	Sales/Total Assets				2.7		3.0
1.3	1.6	1.6					1.4		2.3
.6	.5	.5					.3		.5
(53) 1.2	(46) 1.1	(42) 1.0	% Depr., Dep., Amort./Sales				.5	(18)	1.1
2.6	2.2	1.6					1.1		2.1
1.9	2.4	1.5	% Officers', Directors',						
(21) 4.4	(18) 5.3	(15) 4.9	Owners' Comp/Sales						
10.3	11.0	8.8							
4351867M	3779178M	3590825M	Net Sales ($)		9411M	20546M	76205M	53573M	3431090M
2200177M	1427884M	1119411M	Total Assets ($)		12656M	17479M	42579M	28551M	1018146M

Current Data Sorted By Assets   Comparative Historical Data

0-500M	500M-2MM	2-10MM	10-50MM	50-100MM	100-250MM	Type of Statement	4/1/00-3/31/01 ALL	4/1/01-3/31/02 ALL
2		1	7	1		Unqualified	15	21
	1	9	5			Reviewed	22	18
9	19	6				Compiled	65	64
27	17	1			2	Tax Returns	35	44
7	11	13	3	1	4	Other	51	42
26 (4/1-9/30/04)			**121 (10/1/04-3/31/05)**					
45	48	30	16	2	6	NUMBER OF STATEMENTS	188	189
%	%	%	%	%	%	**ASSETS**	%	%
8.4	9.1	9.6	7.7			Cash & Equivalents	9.3	10.5
4.1	6.5	7.1	4.3			Trade Receivables (net)	7.5	7.9
63.1	53.3	47.9	46.9			Inventory	50.9	49.1
2.9	1.3	4.1	1.2			All Other Current	2.6	2.4
78.5	70.2	68.6	60.1			Total Current	70.2	69.9
14.2	21.2	19.8	30.6			Fixed Assets (net)	20.2	21.8
3.1	3.7	4.2	2.5			Intangibles (net)	3.2	2.5
4.2	4.9	7.4	6.8			All Other Non-Current	6.3	5.9
100.0	100.0	100.0	100.0			Total	100.0	100.0
						LIABILITIES		
8.7	13.3	12.2	11.4			Notes Payable-Short Term	11.4	10.4
3.0	2.5	3.7	2.6			Cur. Mat.-L/T/D	2.3	2.8
12.5	13.3	20.0	13.9			Trade Payables	16.3	16.5
.2	.1	.1	.3			Income Taxes Payable	.2	.2
10.7	9.7	10.1	9.2			All Other Current	13.7	10.6
35.1	39.0	46.2	37.4			Total Current	43.9	40.6
22.8	18.2	14.2	20.7			Long-Term Debt	18.2	16.9
.1	.0	.4	.3			Deferred Taxes	.1	.1
20.8	6.3	7.1	2.0			All Other Non-Current	8.8	5.7
21.2	36.5	32.1	39.6			Net Worth	29.1	36.8
100.0	100.0	100.0	100.0			Total Liabilities & Net Worth	100.0	100.0
						INCOME DATA		
100.0	100.0	100.0	100.0			Net Sales	100.0	100.0
39.4	39.1	39.3	38.8			Gross Profit	36.2	37.3
36.7	35.2	37.0	32.5			Operating Expenses	34.1	34.6
2.7	3.9	2.4	6.4			Operating Profit	2.2	2.8
1.1	.8	-.5	1.3			All Other Expenses (net)	.6	.7
1.6	3.0	2.9	5.1			Profit Before Taxes	1.6	2.1
						RATIOS		
5.2	3.6	2.9	3.3			Current	3.1	3.6
2.9	1.9	1.6	1.6				1.9	1.8
1.4	1.2	1.2	1.1				1.1	1.2
.8	.9	1.0	1.1			Quick	.7	.9
(42) .3	.3	.3	.3				(184) .3	(186) .3
.1	.1	.1	.1				.1	.1
0 UND	0 UND	0 UND	1 410.0			Sales/Receivables	0 UND	0 UND
0 UND	2 154.7	2 240.1	2 230.0				1 246.9	1 321.6
2 157.2	15 24.8	12 29.9	3 117.1				13 27.2	10 37.1
59 6.2	70 5.2	52 7.0	64 5.7			Cost of Sales/Inventory	41 8.9	46 8.0
125 2.9	161 2.3	92 4.0	91 4.0				100 3.6	100 3.7
325 1.1	268 1.4	185 2.0	130 2.8				165 2.2	160 2.3
0 UND	4 87.4	11 33.1	4 91.0			Cost of Sales/Payables	9 42.4	9 40.8
23 16.0	27 13.3	28 13.3	28 12.8				23 15.8	25 14.8
46 7.9	50 7.3	40 9.2	47 7.7				44 8.4	45 8.2
3.1	3.4	5.5	5.8			Sales/Working Capital	5.3	4.9
7.8	9.0	13.9	11.8				10.7	9.8
27.5	24.6	38.9	215.2				54.7	37.9
10.9	5.7	10.0	15.7			EBIT/Interest	8.3	7.3
(36) 1.9	(42) 2.9	(27) 3.0	(15) 7.0				(165) 2.9	(167) 2.3
-1.5	.2	.5	2.1				1.0	.6
						Net Profit + Depr., Dep., Amort./Cur. Mat. L /T/D	8.6	5.5
							(31) 3.0	(35) 2.5
							1.5	.5
.1	.1	.2	.2			Fixed/Worth	.2	.2
.4	.3	.5	.6				.6	.4
-2.1	1.7	3.2	3.6				1.8	1.3
1.1	1.0	.8	.5			Debt/Worth	.8	.6
5.3	1.6	1.7	1.9				2.3	1.6
-9.6	4.9	7.1	8.0				9.2	4.7
73.4	25.1	39.6	68.2			% Profit Before Taxes/Tangible Net Worth	38.6	39.1
(31) 25.6	(44) 7.4	(25) 19.5	(14) 34.4				(155) 18.8	(170) 15.1
.0	.5	8.1	8.5				4.7	.3
23.0	7.4	12.9	26.6			% Profit Before Taxes/Total Assets	15.8	12.4
5.4	3.4	4.3	8.2				5.2	4.3
-6.1	.0	.5	3.9				.0	-.2
108.7	67.8	60.0	28.1			Sales/Net Fixed Assets	52.5	55.0
30.1	22.8	28.6	14.7				22.9	22.8
17.6	6.5	8.6	4.9				10.8	10.7
4.7	2.7	5.1	3.7			Sales/Total Assets	4.4	4.3
2.8	2.0	3.1	2.6				2.9	3.1
1.6	1.3	1.6	2.2				2.0	2.3
.5	.7	.5	.6			% Depr., Dep., Amort./Sales	.4	.5
(33) .9	(41) 1.2	(27) 1.1	(15) .9				(162) .7	(163) 1.0
1.8	2.2	1.7	1.5				1.6	1.7
2.5	2.3					% Officers', Directors', Owners' Comp/Sales	1.6	1.9
(26) 4.5	(27) 3.0						(84) 4.3	(93) 4.0
9.4	5.7						7.9	7.5
49562M	115190M	519942M	993725M	387424M	6190817M	Net Sales ($)	5588957M	5638378M
10938M	48846M	143244M	351505M	163086M	871932M	Total Assets ($)	2140993M	2068787M

M = $ thousand   MM = $ million
See Pages 11 through 21 for Explanation of Ratios and Data

Comparative Historical Data | Current Data Sorted By Sales

			Type of Statement						
17	18	11	Unqualified	2				1	8
24	23	15	Reviewed		1		3	4	7
39	54	34	Compiled	5	14	6	4	3	2
39	47	48	Tax Returns	24	14	5	2		3
39	50	39	Other	9	10	1	6	3	10
4/1/02-3/31/03	4/1/03-3/31/04	4/1/04-3/31/05		26 (4/1-9/30/04)			121 (10/1/04-3/31/05)		
ALL	ALL	ALL		0-1MM	1-3MM	3-5MM	5-10MM	10-25MM	25MM & OVER
158	192	147	**NUMBER OF STATEMENTS**	40	39	12	15	11	30
%	%	%	**ASSETS**	%	%	%	%	%	%
10.2	10.2	8.7	Cash & Equivalents	7.9	7.0	12.2	11.3	13.3	7.6
7.8	7.1	5.6	Trade Receivables (net)	3.1	4.6	9.7	13.4	6.2	4.6
48.2	45.0	53.7	Inventory	63.4	53.2	50.3	42.6	49.6	49.7
2.7	3.3	2.4	All Other Current	2.6	1.4	.8	2.1	5.7	3.0
68.9	65.6	70.4	Total Current	77.0	66.3	73.0	69.4	74.8	64.8
22.1	25.1	20.7	Fixed Assets (net)	15.1	24.8	16.8	17.6	22.0	25.6
2.2	2.9	3.3	Intangibles (net)	3.9	3.8	6.3	2.5	.0	2.3
6.8	6.4	5.6	All Other Non-Current	4.0	5.0	4.0	10.5	3.2	7.4
100.0	100.0	100.0	Total	100.0	100.0	100.0	100.0	100.0	100.0
			LIABILITIES						
9.4	10.6	11.0	Notes Payable-Short Term	9.7	11.3	15.9	11.3	6.6	11.8
2.3	2.4	2.9	Cur. Mat.-L/T/D	2.3	2.9	7.1	.9	5.7	1.8
17.0	16.4	14.5	Trade Payables	9.7	11.7	17.4	17.1	14.6	22.0
.3	.3	.2	Income Taxes Payable	.3	.0	.5	.0	.3	.2
8.3	10.8	10.0	All Other Current	13.4	7.9	4.3	8.8	7.2	12.0
37.3	40.4	38.5	Total Current	35.4	33.9	45.1	38.1	34.3	47.9
21.0	18.4	19.3	Long-Term Debt	22.5	25.6	21.1	14.1	5.3	13.6
.1	.2	.1	Deferred Taxes	.1	.0	.0	.0	.5	.4
7.7	10.5	10.8	All Other Non-Current	21.4	9.7	2.8	9.1	.8	5.7
33.8	30.5	31.3	Net Worth	20.6	30.8	31.0	38.7	59.2	32.4
100.0	100.0	100.0	Total Liabilities & Net Worth	100.0	100.0	100.0	100.0	100.0	100.0
			INCOME DATA						
100.0	100.0	100.0	Net Sales	100.0	100.0	100.0	100.0	100.0	100.0
38.2	38.2	39.0	Gross Profit	48.2	34.0	35.1	39.4	39.3	34.2
35.3	35.1	35.6	Operating Expenses	43.6	30.8	34.8	37.0	34.7	31.1
2.9	3.1	3.4	Operating Profit	4.6	3.3	.3	2.4	4.6	3.2
.5	.7	.7	All Other Expenses (net)	1.6	.4	1.1	−.2	.2	.3
2.4	2.5	2.7	Profit Before Taxes	3.0	2.9	−.8	2.6	4.4	2.8
			RATIOS						
3.9	3.2	4.2		5.8	4.0	2.6	3.4	7.0	2.8
2.1	1.8	1.9	Current	2.7	2.4	1.8	1.6	2.1	1.6
1.3	1.1	1.2		1.3	1.2	1.1	1.3	1.2	.9
1.0	.9	.9		.8	.9	1.1	1.2	2.6	.5
.3	.4	(144) .3	Quick	(38) .3	(38) .3	.3	.6	.9	.1
.1	.1	.1		.1	.1	.1	.4	.1	.1
0 UND	0 UND	0 UND		0 UND	0 UND	0 UND	2 210.3	0 UND	0 UND
2 218.6	1 281.8	1 322.0	Sales/Receivables	0 UND	2 189.8	0 UND	7 54.5	2 210.5	1 263.6
8 47.1	8 46.8	5 68.5		2 149.8	10 37.4	14 26.0	22 16.7	6 58.6	3 107.2
41 8.9	34 10.9	58 6.3		117 3.1	53 6.9	31 11.6	51 7.2	49 7.4	48 7.6
104 3.5	87 4.2	121 3.0	Cost of Sales/Inventory	255 1.4	142 2.6	94 3.9	74 4.9	77 4.8	87 4.2
168 2.2	148 2.5	227 1.6		452 .8	215 1.7	226 1.6	162 2.3	169 2.2	132 2.8
10 36.6	10 34.9	5 78.2		0 UND	1 293.0	4 91.9	5 78.2	4 89.6	21 17.6
28 12.9	28 13.1	26 13.8	Cost of Sales/Payables	31 11.8	13 27.1	24 14.9	20 18.1	14 25.8	29 12.6
48 7.6	44 8.3	44 8.2		47 7.8	44 8.2	73 5.0	38 9.7	39 9.5	43 8.5
4.5	5.3	3.9		2.1	3.7	6.2	5.2	5.6	6.9
9.7	12.8	9.7	Sales/Working Capital	5.2	9.2	13.8	10.5	10.9	19.0
29.8	62.2	34.4		12.0	27.1	64.7	45.4	38.4	−202.0
7.1	9.2	8.5		7.4	5.6	5.9	13.5		25.8
(130) 2.9	(160) 3.5	(128) 2.9	EBIT/Interest	(33) 1.9	(34) 2.7	(10) 2.1	(14) 4.0		(29) 5.0
.8	1.4	.2		−1.3	−.2	−2.3	1.6		2.1
10.3	6.8	11.3							17.7
(23) 4.2	(30) 2.4	(21) 2.4	Net Profit + Depr., Dep., Amort./Cur. Mat. L/T/D					(10)	2.6
1.0	1.0	.6							1.8
.2	.2	.1		.1	.1	.1	.1	.1	.2
.5	.6	.5	Fixed/Worth	.5	.7	.3	.2	.4	.7
1.9	2.0	3.7		−1.3	6.1	2.1	1.3	.8	2.0
.7	.8	.9		1.0	1.1	1.0	.6	.2	.9
2.0	1.9	2.2	Debt/Worth	5.8	2.0	1.6	1.4	.5	1.9
6.3	6.1	7.9		−6.5	10.1	6.9	4.2	1.8	5.8
48.8	35.6	38.9		51.8	33.0	24.6	33.9	39.0	67.6
(137) 15.4	(165) 19.9	(122) 18.2	% Profit Before Taxes/Tangible Net Worth	(27) 20.7	(34) 8.3	(10) 6.6	(13) 12.4	24.4	(27) 22.4
2.3	5.6	2.6		.0	−1.8	−2.7	5.8	9.8	5.7
17.3	13.5	12.8		19.5	7.0	11.5	10.6	26.1	19.7
4.8	6.2	4.3	% Profit Before Taxes/Total Assets	3.4	3.2	2.0	3.6	9.9	6.7
−.4	1.3	−1.4		−6.1	−2.3	−4.3	.2	4.8	2.1
57.2	43.0	58.3		57.2	101.8	63.8	45.7	67.4	54.4
21.5	19.4	24.2	Sales/Net Fixed Assets	24.4	21.4	32.0	39.3	24.7	18.2
9.7	7.0	8.3		11.1	3.8	13.7	8.7	8.3	9.7
4.2	4.3	4.1		3.0	3.5	4.6	4.5	6.0	5.1
2.9	2.8	2.6	Sales/Total Assets	1.8	2.0	2.8	2.7	3.2	3.0
2.0	2.0	1.6		.9	1.3	2.2	1.6	2.2	2.5
.7	.6	.6		.7	.5		.7	.5	.5
(131) 1.2	(159) 1.2	(122) 1.1	% Depr., Dep., Amort./Sales	(31) 1.2	(32) 1.3	(12)	1.1	1.3	(27) .9
1.9	2.2	1.8		3.0	2.2		2.1	1.5	1.2
1.6	1.7	2.0		3.7	1.9				
(78) 4.1	(87) 3.5	(64) 3.6	% Officers', Directors', Owners' Comp/Sales	(20) 5.1	(23) 2.6				
7.7	7.0	6.3		10.7	5.6				
5267248M	7597695M	8256660M	Net Sales ($)	19876M	64406M	43916M	110825M	170604M	7847033M
2014509M	2383558M	1589551M	Total Assets ($)	12525M	37384M	15966M	70918M	56184M	1396574M

Current Data Sorted By Assets							Comparative Historical Data	
						Type of Statement		
		1				Unqualified	1	2
	2	4	1			Reviewed	4	4
9	3	2				Compiled	27	24
27	7	2			2	Tax Returns	20	20
5	6	3				Other	17	10
	27 (4/1-9/30/04)		47 (10/1/04-3/31/05)				4/1/00-3/31/01	4/1/01-3/31/02
0-500M	500M-2MM	2-10MM	10-50MM	50-100MM	100-250MM		ALL	ALL
41	18	12	1		2	**NUMBER OF STATEMENTS**	69	60
%	%	%	%	%	%	**ASSETS**	%	%
11.3	12.4	7.9		DATA NOT AVAILABLE		Cash & Equivalents	14.0	10.9
15.3	16.2	10.7				Trade Receivables (net)	17.0	18.8
23.8	18.3	18.6				Inventory	23.4	22.3
1.5	1.6	3.7				All Other Current	2.1	3.1
51.8	48.6	40.8				Total Current	56.5	55.1
32.6	40.1	42.6				Fixed Assets (net)	32.7	33.2
5.9	4.6	9.9				Intangibles (net)	4.6	5.2
9.7	6.8	6.7				All Other Non-Current	6.2	6.4
100.0	100.0	100.0				Total	100.0	100.0
						LIABILITIES		
14.0	3.9	7.0				Notes Payable-Short Term	6.0	8.6
15.1	4.7	2.9				Cur. Mat.-L/T/D	5.2	6.5
26.6	15.3	9.7				Trade Payables	21.2	20.8
.1	.1	.2				Income Taxes Payable	.2	.2
15.3	4.1	7.9				All Other Current	19.5	16.8
71.0	28.1	27.6				Total Current	52.2	52.9
34.7	25.1	18.7				Long-Term Debt	28.9	34.4
.1	.3	.3				Deferred Taxes	.3	.3
17.3	3.2	8.5				All Other Non-Current	6.4	2.9
-23.1	43.3	44.9				Net Worth	12.2	9.5
100.0	100.0	100.0				Total Liabilities & Net Worth	100.0	100.0
						INCOME DATA		
100.0	100.0	100.0				Net Sales	100.0	100.0
57.5	49.9	61.5				Gross Profit	52.8	52.5
55.1	48.5	62.0				Operating Expenses	51.9	50.9
2.3	1.5	-.5				Operating Profit	.8	1.6
.2	-.3	.0				All Other Expenses (net)	.1	.9
2.1	1.8	-.5				Profit Before Taxes	.7	.7
						RATIOS		
1.8	2.6	2.7					2.2	2.5
1.0	1.9	1.9				Current	1.3	1.4
.4	1.1	.9					1.0	.8
1.3	1.5	1.6					1.3	1.5
(40) .4	1.1	.6				Quick	.7	(59) .8
.2	.3	.3					.4	.4
4 97.6	10 36.8	11 33.7					7 54.4	11 33.1
12 30.9	16 23.0	17 21.8				Sales/Receivables	17 21.0	18 20.3
20 17.9	28 12.8	23 15.7					27 13.4	28 13.3
13 28.8	28 13.1	49 7.4					23 15.9	27 13.7
35 10.4	46 8.0	71 5.2				Cost of Sales/Inventory	45 8.1	42 8.7
88 4.1	66 5.5	83 4.4					82 4.5	75 4.9
23 15.9	18 20.2	27 13.6					21 17.7	16 23.3
43 8.4	33 10.9	35 10.3				Cost of Sales/Payables	28 13.0	31 11.7
72 5.1	48 7.6	70 5.2					48 7.6	66 5.6
16.1	8.3	8.9					11.4	8.6
284.0	13.2	11.8				Sales/Working Capital	24.3	34.2
-14.9	NM	NM					-397.8	-66.3
6.9	6.9	15.0					4.0	4.8
(33) 2.1	(15) 1.4	1.4				EBIT/Interest	(60) 1.8	(51) 2.5
.5	-2.8	-4.1					.0	.9
							3.5	3.8
						Net Profit + Depr., Dep., Amort./Cur. Mat. L /T/D	(14) 1.6	(12) 1.9
							.4	1.1
.7	.4	.7					.4	.5
-10.8	.7	1.1				Fixed/Worth	1.3	1.4
-.8	2.6	2.8					-11.4	-2.2
2.5	.5	.5					.9	1.1
-36.4	1.5	1.5				Debt/Worth	2.7	2.3
-3.0	5.5	3.3					-25.7	-6.0
97.9	36.0	26.1					31.7	49.0
(18) 18.1	(16) 12.7	(11) 6.2				% Profit Before Taxes/Tangible Net Worth	(48) 9.8	(40) 10.5
-1.0	-8.1	-28.6					-2.8	-.2
27.2	10.4	11.6					13.4	14.4
6.5	4.1	1.6				% Profit Before Taxes/Total Assets	2.7	2.5
-.7	-4.0	-10.7					-3.2	-1.1
23.5	21.1	7.0					23.5	31.2
13.3	8.4	6.3				Sales/Net Fixed Assets	12.7	13.3
9.2	2.8	4.0					7.4	7.1
6.2	4.8	2.9					4.8	5.3
4.5	2.0	2.3				Sales/Total Assets	3.6	3.5
2.8	1.7	1.7					2.5	2.2
1.2	1.3	1.8					1.1	1.0
(35) 2.0	(17) 2.6	3.9				% Depr., Dep., Amort./Sales	(61) 2.0	(56) 1.7
3.0	3.2	4.4					3.1	2.8
4.4							3.6	3.1
(26) 7.8						% Officers', Directors', Owners' Comp/Sales	(37) 6.7	(38) 5.6
12.6							9.6	7.7
32581M	54210M	122321M	12019M		1590441M	Net Sales ($)	1895855M	467708M
8046M	18467M	52205M	10552M		297530M	Total Assets ($)	500708M	235386M

M = $ thousand MM = $ million

See Pages 11 through 21 for Explanation of Ratios and Data

Comparative Historical Data | Current Data Sorted By Sales

Type of Statement	4/1/02-3/31/03 ALL	4/1/03-3/31/04 ALL	4/1/04-3/31/05 ALL	0-1MM	1-3MM	3-5MM	5-10MM	10-25MM	25MM & OVER
Unqualified	1	3	1					1	
Reviewed	2	5	7		2	2	2	1	
Compiled	26	28	14	7	4	1	1	1	
Tax Returns	34	23	38	20	10	3	2	1	2
Other	12	13	14	4	5	2	2	1	
				27 (4/1-9/30/04)			47 (10/1/04-3/31/05)		
NUMBER OF STATEMENTS	75	72	74	31	21	8	7	5	2
ASSETS	%	%	%	%	%	%	%	%	%
Cash & Equivalents	13.6	7.0	11.4	10.2	10.7				
Trade Receivables (net)	12.9	15.9	14.7	15.5	12.9				
Inventory	22.6	22.7	21.3	25.4	18.4				
All Other Current	2.3	2.0	1.9	1.0	1.9				
Total Current	51.4	47.7	49.3	52.0	43.9				
Fixed Assets (net)	36.7	37.7	36.4	33.0	41.1				
Intangibles (net)	6.7	5.4	6.0	4.7	7.9				
All Other Non-Current	5.2	9.3	8.3	10.3	7.1				
Total	100.0	100.0	100.0	100.0	100.0				
LIABILITIES									
Notes Payable-Short Term	8.7	9.9	9.9	10.8	12.8				
Cur. Mat.-L/T/D	7.1	4.3	10.6	20.2	2.6				
Trade Payables	19.6	20.3	20.9	24.1	21.9				
Income Taxes Payable	.2	.1	.1	.1	.0				
All Other Current	12.8	13.4	11.0	16.1	6.9				
Total Current	48.3	48.0	52.5	71.3	44.2				
Long-Term Debt	37.8	33.6	29.2	34.3	33.7				
Deferred Taxes	.1	.2	.1	.0	.4				
All Other Non-Current	5.8	2.6	11.9	10.0	21.9				
Net Worth	7.9	15.6	6.2	−15.6	−.2				
Total Liabilities & Net Worth	100.0	100.0	100.0	100.0	100.0				
INCOME DATA									
Net Sales	100.0	100.0	100.0	100.0	100.0				
Gross Profit	51.8	51.4	56.3	57.0	53.8				
Operating Expenses	50.9	49.9	54.9	55.5	51.8				
Operating Profit	.9	1.5	1.4	1.5	2.1				
All Other Expenses (net)	.7	.6	.0	.0	−.1				
Profit Before Taxes	.3	1.0	1.4	1.5	2.2				
RATIOS									
Current	2.2	1.8	2.3	1.6	2.3				
	1.2	1.0	1.1	1.0	1.5				
	.7	.6	.6	.4	.6				
Quick	1.2	1.1	1.4	.9	1.6				
	.6	.4	(73) .5	(30) .4	.9				
	.3	.3	.3	.2	.3				
Sales/Receivables	4 102.3	9 39.7	6 62.4	4 96.8	5 67.9				
	14 25.7	15 23.9	14 26.0	15 24.2	12 30.3				
	23 16.2	23 16.0	23 15.9	22 16.8	20 18.2				
Cost of Sales/Inventory	23 15.8	17 20.9	18 20.7	15 25.1	16 22.8				
	44 8.3	40 9.1	47 7.8	46 8.0	40 9.1				
	83 4.4	77 4.7	81 4.5	91 4.0	79 4.6				
Cost of Sales/Payables	19 18.8	22 16.2	24 15.2	23 16.0	17 21.8				
	40 9.1	34 10.8	39 9.2	37 9.8	39 9.4				
	61 6.0	62 5.9	62 5.9	69 5.3	59 6.2				
Sales/Working Capital	10.7	14.4	10.7	18.3	9.5				
	45.4	UND	45.6	284.0	26.8				
	−17.8	−16.5	−21.5	−14.9	−21.9				
EBIT/Interest	5.9	8.2	6.9	6.3	6.9				
	(69) 2.4	(61) 1.7	(63) 1.5	(26) 1.5	(16) 2.4				
	.4	−1.2	−1.4	.5	.4				
Net Profit + Depr., Dep., Amort./Cur. Mat. L/T/D	3.0		1.6						
	(11) 2.3		(11) .7						
	2.0		.2						
Fixed/Worth	.6	.6	.6	.6	.6				
	3.3	1.7	1.7	9.0	1.7				
	−1.4	−2.3	−2.5	−.8	−1.8				
Debt/Worth	1.2	1.2	.7	2.7	.6				
	5.5	5.9	4.0	107.0	5.3				
	−3.4	−5.1	−5.3	−2.8	−3.3				
% Profit Before Taxes/Tangible Net Worth	55.6	57.6	44.7	52.2	34.5				
	(47) 12.9	(47) 12.7	(48) 9.6	(16) 8.1	(12) 16.3				
	1.4	−13.0	−12.4	−6.7	.1				
% Profit Before Taxes/Total Assets	14.2	14.0	16.1	17.8	15.0				
	4.7	3.6	3.7	5.4	5.7				
	−3.1	−6.3	−4.0	−.7	−4.2				
Sales/Net Fixed Assets	30.3	26.6	20.4	25.5	17.2				
	10.5	13.5	12.2	13.3	11.0				
	4.4	4.4	5.6	6.9	4.1				
Sales/Total Assets	4.8	4.9	5.0	5.9	5.2				
	3.1	3.2	3.4	3.8	3.5				
	2.1	2.0	1.9	2.2	1.8				
% Depr., Dep., Amort./Sales	1.2	1.2	1.3	1.1	1.9				
	(62) 2.4	(64) 2.0	(65) 2.5	(28) 1.9	(17) 2.7				
	4.2	3.4	3.9	2.8	3.4				
% Officers', Directors', Owners' Comp/Sales	3.8	4.4	4.1	5.7					
	(47) 5.6	(36) 6.0	(40) 6.8	(21) 10.0					
	9.5	10.0	10.8	13.9					
Net Sales ($)	2627300M	2622449M	1811572M	17467M	33783M	33031M	47787M	89063M	1590441M
Total Assets ($)	648150M	990427M	386800M	5966M	12551M	18655M	14443M	37655M	297530M

M = $ thousand   MM = $ million
See Pages 11 through 21 for Explanation of Ratios and Data

Current Data Sorted By Assets   **Comparative Historical Data**

						Type of Statement		
		2		1		Unqualified		2
	11	13				Reviewed	10	10
13	18	5				Compiled	23	22
12	12	2				Tax Returns	11	7
4	12	4	1	1		Other	15	20
	37 (4/1-9/30/04)			**75 (10/1/04-3/31/05)**			**4/1/00-3/31/01**	**4/1/01-3/31/02**
0-500M	**500M-2MM**	**2-10MM**	**10-50MM**	**50-100MM**	**100-250MM**		**ALL**	**ALL**
29	53	26	2	2		**NUMBER OF STATEMENTS**	59	61
%	%	%	%	%	%	**ASSETS**	%	%
13.5	8.4	5.8				Cash & Equivalents	10.1	9.2
21.1	34.0	34.9				Trade Receivables (net)	28.7	27.3
35.1	36.1	28.8				Inventory	35.3	35.2
3.7	1.6	2.6				All Other Current	1.0	2.8
73.4	80.2	72.2				Total Current	75.0	74.6
18.3	11.4	15.2				Fixed Assets (net)	14.3	14.6
4.4	2.6	4.2				Intangibles (net)	1.9	5.3
4.0	5.8	8.5				All Other Non-Current	8.7	5.6
100.0	100.0	100.0				Total	100.0	100.0
						LIABILITIES		
15.2	12.7	16.8				Notes Payable-Short Term	8.8	9.2
2.4	3.6	3.2				Cur. Mat.-L/T/D	4.6	4.2
36.4	26.6	19.5				Trade Payables	28.4	24.1
.0	.1	.2				Income Taxes Payable	.3	.4
17.1	7.9	10.4				All Other Current	10.2	9.1
71.1	50.8	50.1				Total Current	52.3	47.0
27.1	14.1	9.3				Long-Term Debt	15.8	15.3
.0	.0	.2				Deferred Taxes	.1	.0
9.4	5.1	5.9				All Other Non-Current	4.6	4.7
-7.6	30.0	34.6				Net Worth	27.2	32.9
100.0	100.0	100.0				Total Liabilities & Net Worth	100.0	100.0
						INCOME DATA		
100.0	100.0	100.0				Net Sales	100.0	100.0
40.4	34.0	34.7				Gross Profit	35.2	35.6
39.0	33.0	33.5				Operating Expenses	33.8	34.0
1.4	1.0	1.2				Operating Profit	1.3	1.6
1.1	-.3	.0				All Other Expenses (net)	.3	.4
.3	1.3	1.2				Profit Before Taxes	1.0	1.2
						RATIOS		
1.8	2.3	2.3				Current	2.0	2.2
1.1	1.6	1.6					1.5	1.6
.7	1.2	1.0					1.3	1.3
.6	1.1	1.0				Quick	1.0	1.2
.5	.8	.9					.8	.8
.3	.5	.5					.5	.4
0 UND	23 16.1	27 13.6				Sales/Receivables	12 30.6	6 63.4
18 19.8	32 11.3	39 9.3					28 13.0	27 13.4
28 13.0	39 9.3	48 7.6					38 9.5	35 10.3
13 27.2	23 15.7	28 13.2				Cost of Sales/Inventory	23 16.0	23 15.6
50 7.4	62 5.9	44 8.3					50 7.3	49 7.5
130 2.8	115 3.2	91 4.0					112 3.3	114 3.2
27 13.3	23 16.2	21 17.2				Cost of Sales/Payables	24 15.0	21 17.2
51 7.2	35 10.5	31 11.9					35 10.4	30 12.3
78 4.7	54 6.7	46 7.9					54 6.8	45 8.1
8.7	6.0	6.1				Sales/Working Capital	8.6	7.8
41.6	14.9	14.3					14.9	13.9
-24.7	34.6	273.3					30.2	23.7
7.0	5.7	6.0				EBIT/Interest	4.8	6.0
(27) 1.8	(49) 2.6	(25) 3.6					(56) 2.4	(57) 2.3
-4.0	1.2	1.2					.9	.9
	4.8	5.1				Net Profit + Depr., Dep.,	4.3	1.6
	(10) 2.3	(12) 3.2				Amort./Cur. Mat. L /T/D	(14) .9	(15) .6
	1.0	1.3					-.3	-.9
.3	.1	.2				Fixed/Worth	.2	.2
3.1	.3	.6					.6	.4
-.4	.8	1.3					.9	1.3
2.3	1.3	1.0				Debt/Worth	1.1	1.0
6.2	1.9	2.5					2.5	2.0
-2.4	7.9	10.5					6.5	7.1
29.3	45.2	26.2				% Profit Before Taxes/Tangible	35.7	32.2
(17) 10.2	(48) 11.2	(23) 10.7				Net Worth	(50) 8.6	(55) 11.8
-19.2	.4	4.5					-.1	.9
11.1	7.4	7.8				% Profit Before Taxes/Total	10.0	10.4
3.4	3.6	2.6				Assets	3.9	3.1
-12.7	.2	1.3					-.9	.0
84.4	98.0	63.9				Sales/Net Fixed Assets	59.4	74.6
35.1	41.9	29.8					30.1	34.9
10.0	20.3	12.1					16.6	16.4
5.4	5.0	4.2				Sales/Total Assets	4.9	5.2
3.2	3.8	2.9					3.9	3.5
2.8	2.5	2.1					2.8	2.7
.6	.4	.7				% Depr., Dep., Amort./Sales	.4	.4
(22) 1.1	(45) .9	(23) 1.0					(53) 1.0	(56) .8
1.8	1.7	1.8					1.4	1.2
2.5	1.7	2.0				% Officers', Directors',	1.6	1.5
(12) 5.2	(32) 3.9	(13) 3.2				Owners' Comp/Sales	(30) 3.9	(32) 3.6
9.8	5.6	4.6					6.8	5.9
32542M	242386M	302180M	175179M	238055M		Net Sales ($)	525409M	1167853M
7547M	62790M	99650M	61339M	127475M		Total Assets ($)	132180M	315885M

Columns 10-50MM, 50-100MM, and 100-250MM marked "DATA NOT AVAILABLE" for percentage and ratio sections.

Comparative Historical Data / Current Data Sorted By Sales

			Type of Statement						
4	9	3	Unqualified		3	7	5	2	1
15	23	25	Reviewed					9	1
39	43	36	Compiled	8	9	11	5	3	
31	25	26	Tax Returns	8	8	4	5	1	
27	21	22	Other	2	6	4	5	3	2
4/1/02-3/31/03 ALL	4/1/03-3/31/04 ALL	4/1/04-3/31/05 ALL		37 (4/1-9/30/04) 0-1MM	1-3MM	3-5MM	75 (10/1/04-3/31/05) 5-10MM	10-25MM	25MM & OVER
116	121	112	NUMBER OF STATEMENTS	18	26	26	20	18	4
%	%	%	ASSETS	%	%	%	%	%	%
8.3	9.6	8.9	Cash & Equivalents	18.2	8.2	9.1	5.7	5.5	
28.8	27.4	30.8	Trade Receivables (net)	13.7	22.9	34.9	40.7	42.3	
36.0	33.6	33.6	Inventory	39.9	40.7	27.7	30.6	31.7	
2.0	2.0	2.4	All Other Current	1.1	1.2	5.7	1.7	1.7	
75.0	72.6	75.8	Total Current	73.0	72.9	77.3	78.7	81.1	
14.7	15.3	14.2	Fixed Assets (net)	19.1	15.0	12.4	11.6	13.3	
4.8	4.0	4.0	Intangibles (net)	5.0	4.1	3.9	3.0	.9	
5.4	8.0	6.1	All Other Non-Current	3.0	8.0	6.3	6.6	4.7	
100.0	100.0	100.0	Total	100.0	100.0	100.0	100.0	100.0	
			LIABILITIES						
13.8	12.8	14.2	Notes Payable-Short Term	17.2	12.4	13.8	13.9	15.6	
4.2	6.2	3.1	Cur. Mat.-L/T/D	1.8	5.4	2.6	3.2	2.1	
24.9	23.4	27.2	Trade Payables	36.8	25.5	23.6	28.8	25.1	
.2	.3	.1	Income Taxes Payable	.0	.1	.1	.3	.0	
10.4	10.3	11.2	All Other Current	10.0	12.4	13.0	9.0	9.2	
53.6	53.0	55.8	Total Current	65.8	55.8	53.1	55.2	52.0	
16.3	15.0	16.2	Long-Term Debt	21.4	15.1	22.2	14.3	7.5	
.1	.1	.1	Deferred Taxes	.1	.0	.1	.1	.2	
5.0	5.1	6.6	All Other Non-Current	12.6	8.0	4.1	2.4	5.8	
25.1	26.9	21.3	Net Worth	.1	21.1	20.6	28.1	34.5	
100.0	100.0	100.0	Total Liabilities & Net Worth	100.0	100.0	100.0	100.0	100.0	
			INCOME DATA						
100.0	100.0	100.0	Net Sales	100.0	100.0	100.0	100.0	100.0	
37.7	38.0	35.8	Gross Profit	47.3	34.8	33.9	31.1	34.2	
36.1	35.7	34.7	Operating Expenses	45.2	33.8	32.7	30.6	33.0	
1.6	2.3	1.1	Operating Profit	2.1	1.0	1.1	.5	1.2	
.4	.5	.2	All Other Expenses (net)	1.6	.0	.1	−.8	.3	
1.2	1.8	.9	Profit Before Taxes	.5	1.1	1.1	1.3	.9	
			RATIOS						
1.9	2.0	2.2	Current	1.8	2.4	2.3	1.8	2.1	
1.5	1.5	1.5		1.2	1.4	1.6	1.3	1.6	
1.1	1.1	1.0		.9	.8	1.1	1.1	1.2	
1.1	1.1	1.1	Quick	.7	.8	1.4	1.1	1.2	
.7	.7	.7		.4	.5	.8	1.0	1.0	
.4	.4	.4		.3	.3	.6	.6	.6	
10 36.8	16 22.3	19 19.7	Sales/Receivables	0 UND	5 66.9	25 14.8	27 13.5	28 13.1	
28 13.0	27 13.3	31 11.6		0 UND	22 16.4	35 10.3	33 11.0	39 9.3	
39 9.4	37 9.9	41 9.0		31 11.6	33 11.2	45 8.0	37 9.8	45 8.1	
22 16.8	21 17.6	23 15.8	Cost of Sales/Inventory	32 11.6	48 7.5	22 16.3	19 19.4	12 29.4	
57 6.4	59 6.2	49 7.4		115 3.2	78 4.7	39 9.4	35 10.6	31 11.8	
114 3.2	98 3.7	106 3.4		162 2.2	125 2.9	76 4.8	63 5.8	91 4.0	
20 18.7	19 19.4	23 16.0	Cost of Sales/Payables	45 8.1	18 19.8	17 21.0	24 15.4	21 17.2	
33 11.2	32 11.3	36 10.2		61 6.0	39 9.5	34 10.8	31 11.7	30 12.1	
52 7.0	50 7.2	59 6.2		147 2.5	60 6.1	56 6.5	41 9.0	41 8.9	
9.5	7.2	7.4	Sales/Working Capital	8.2	5.4	5.8	12.5	7.4	
14.8	15.0	17.0		21.2	15.9	13.6	24.8	14.3	
62.6	122.2	640.0		−65.8	−22.4	244.9	59.8	36.9	
6.4	5.6	5.8	EBIT/Interest	4.1	4.8	6.6	5.9	6.0	
(109) 2.5	(113) 2.3	(105) 2.7		1.0	(23) 2.1	(25) 2.7	(17) 3.7	3.2	
−.8	.6	1.0		−4.1	1.0	.9	1.5	1.3	
2.5	2.0	4.6	Net Profit + Depr., Dep., Amort./Cur. Mat. L/T/D						
(22) 1.4	(26) 1.2	(24) 2.6							
.3	.5	1.2							
.2	.2	.2	Fixed/Worth	.1	.2	.2	.2	.1	
.5	.4	.5		1.4	.4	.4	.3	.4	
4.4	2.2	3.1		−.7	−36.3	2.1	.8	1.3	
1.2	1.1	1.4	Debt/Worth	1.8	1.4	1.4	1.2	.8	
3.0	2.4	3.0		5.5	3.5	2.1	3.2	1.8	
33.7	8.7	28.2		−2.4	−60.0	15.7	10.3	5.8	
45.2	38.1	34.4	% Profit Before Taxes/Tangible Net Worth	23.0	51.7	36.3	54.0	24.6	
(92) 19.3	(101) 15.7	(91) 10.7		(13) .0	(19) 9.0	(21) 11.0	(19) 16.2	(16) 10.3	
−1.9	.1	.0		−38.2	.4	1.1	3.2	3.0	
9.9	9.6	7.9	% Profit Before Taxes/Total Assets	7.8	10.3	10.6	8.1	7.2	
4.2	3.4	3.2		.0	2.4	4.6	5.9	2.1	
−3.5	−.7	.0		−12.6	.0	1.0	1.5	.5	
76.8	65.4	74.5	Sales/Net Fixed Assets	82.4	43.2	77.0	110.8	80.1	
37.8	34.1	36.4		31.4	29.2	43.5	53.9	40.1	
18.9	15.8	16.0		9.2	15.4	21.5	22.9	15.5	
5.1	5.0	4.9	Sales/Total Assets	3.3	4.4	4.6	5.9	5.9	
3.6	3.6	3.3		2.9	2.9	3.4	4.9	3.9	
2.6	2.5	2.4		2.1	2.0	2.3	3.4	2.8	
.5	.7	.6	% Depr., Dep., Amort./Sales	.7	.7	.5	.2	.6	
(98) 1.0	(97) 1.0	(93) 1.0		(16) 1.1	(18) 1.4	(23) 1.0	(17) .7	(16) .8	
1.8	2.0	1.8		1.9	1.9	1.9	1.2	1.6	
1.4	2.6	2.0	% Officers', Directors', Owners' Comp/Sales		2.8	1.6	2.1		
(67) 4.1	(66) 4.5	(59) 4.0		(15) 4.5	(16) 3.6	(13) 5.0			
7.2	7.6	7.6		10.4	5.3	6.6			
2400636M	1132458M	990342M	Net Sales ($)	10962M	49685M	108687M	147470M	260304M	413234M
595314M	518896M	358801M	Total Assets ($)	3895M	19167M	35039M	36636M	75250M	188814M

© RMA 2005

M = $ thousand   MM = $ million
See Pages 11 through 21 for Explanation of Ratios and Data

Current Data Sorted By Assets | Comparative Historical Data

0-500M	500M-2MM	2-10MM	10-50MM	50-100MM	100-250MM	Type of Statement	4/1/00-3/31/01 ALL	4/1/01-3/31/02 ALL
	1	4	8	2	1	Unqualified	10	4
	2	14	1	1		Reviewed	17	21
18	21	7	2			Compiled	54	38
39	14	5		1	2	Tax Returns	35	48
8	10	17	2		2	Other	44	53
52 (4/1-9/30/04)			130 (10/1/04-3/31/05)					
65	48	47	13	4	5	**NUMBER OF STATEMENTS**	160	164
%	%	%	%	%	%	**ASSETS**	%	%
11.4	10.4	14.1	9.1			Cash & Equivalents	9.8	10.7
6.6	6.7	7.8	9.8			Trade Receivables (net)	8.9	7.1
55.9	49.6	41.0	45.1			Inventory	50.6	52.1
1.3	2.7	2.3	5.0			All Other Current	2.1	1.0
75.2	69.5	65.2	69.0			Total Current	71.3	70.8
14.1	23.0	23.9	18.6			Fixed Assets (net)	19.1	20.4
4.8	2.9	3.9	5.3			Intangibles (net)	4.7	3.2
6.0	4.7	6.9	7.1			All Other Non-Current	4.9	5.5
100.0	100.0	100.0	100.0			Total	100.0	100.0
						LIABILITIES		
14.2	12.3	9.9	8.4			Notes Payable-Short Term	11.1	13.6
2.7	5.8	2.3	4.2			Cur. Mat.-L/T/D	3.8	2.6
13.8	18.0	20.1	14.5			Trade Payables	14.9	13.9
.6	.7	.1	.1			Income Taxes Payable	.3	.3
13.5	8.1	7.5	7.9			All Other Current	11.3	10.2
44.8	45.0	39.8	35.0			Total Current	41.3	40.6
20.7	13.9	15.2	23.3			Long-Term Debt	22.3	20.5
.0	.0	.2	.2			Deferred Taxes	.1	.1
22.5	9.9	7.5	13.4			All Other Non-Current	7.8	6.8
11.8	31.1	37.3	28.1			Net Worth	28.5	32.1
100.0	100.0	100.0	100.0			Total Liabilities & Net Worth	100.0	100.0
						INCOME DATA		
100.0	100.0	100.0	100.0			Net Sales	100.0	100.0
45.3	51.1	47.1	51.3			Gross Profit	46.2	45.1
44.0	49.8	45.0	48.2			Operating Expenses	42.1	41.8
1.4	1.3	2.1	3.1			Operating Profit	4.1	3.3
1.4	.9	.5	1.8			All Other Expenses (net)	1.7	1.3
.0	.4	1.5	1.3			Profit Before Taxes	2.4	2.0
						RATIOS		
4.9	2.8	3.3	2.9			Current	3.1	3.3
2.4	1.9	1.8	2.0				1.9	1.9
1.2	1.1	1.2	1.4				1.3	1.3
.8	.8	1.3	1.0			Quick	.9	.9
.3	(47) .3	.5	.5				(158) .4	(163) .4
.1	.1	.1	.2				.1	.1
0 UND	0 UND	0 UND	1 317.0			Sales/Receivables	0 UND	0 UND
0 UND	1 626.6	2 214.1	6 61.1				0 752.2	1 472.6
3 116.2	8 44.3	7 51.6	36 10.2				12 29.5	9 40.1
55 6.7	75 4.8	60 6.1	79 4.6			Cost of Sales/Inventory	82 4.5	82 4.5
140 2.6	158 2.3	111 3.3	136 2.7				136 2.7	128 2.8
246 1.5	236 1.5	208 1.8	196 1.9				208 1.8	198 1.8
6 66.3	24 15.3	26 14.1	24 15.4			Cost of Sales/Payables	13 27.8	8 47.2
17 22.0	37 10.0	43 8.5	36 10.2				29 12.6	27 13.7
41 8.9	63 5.8	79 4.6	56 6.5				60 6.1	54 6.7
4.8	5.3	4.6	3.5			Sales/Working Capital	5.1	5.1
8.6	8.4	8.4	10.1				7.5	8.1
46.8	129.8	52.9	18.5				19.0	14.1
7.8	6.6	6.9	7.1			EBIT/Interest	5.8	5.6
(49) 2.4	(44) 1.6	(44) 3.9	3.3				(146) 2.3	(141) 2.3
-.5	-1.5	1.5	-.1				.6	.2
						Net Profit + Depr., Dep., Amort./Cur. Mat. L./T/D	4.1	6.8
							(27) 1.4	(18) 2.9
							.6	1.2
.1	.2	.2	.3			Fixed/Worth	.2	.2
.6	.5	.5	.8				.6	.6
-.8	1.7	1.4	-3.4				3.2	2.5
.5	.8	1.0	1.2			Debt/Worth	.9	.7
7.0	2.1	1.9	3.8				2.2	2.0
-6.1	5.6	3.7	-23.9				11.5	7.1
66.7	29.5	28.9				% Profit Before Taxes/Tangible Net Worth	44.8	45.8
(38) 31.9	(39) 7.1	(43) 16.2					(131) 18.2	(146) 17.0
-9.2	-9.9	4.1					2.3	-1.0
20.8	11.2	9.6	11.1			% Profit Before Taxes/Total Assets	13.7	14.3
5.7	1.6	5.8	5.6				6.1	5.1
-6.7	-6.1	1.2	-5.8				-1.1	-1.6
98.5	43.4	32.8	52.1			Sales/Net Fixed Assets	51.0	44.5
35.9	15.6	16.5	15.8				20.2	17.7
14.1	7.9	5.2	8.1				8.1	7.3
4.5	3.4	3.5	3.2			Sales/Total Assets	3.4	3.6
3.2	2.8	2.2	2.2				2.5	2.5
2.0	1.8	1.4	1.8				1.7	1.7
.4	.6	.9	1.0			% Depr., Dep., Amort./Sales	.6	.6
(52) 1.1	(43) 1.0	(41) 1.8	(11) 2.5				(137) 1.4	(135) 1.3
2.3	2.5	2.5	2.8				2.3	2.2
4.2	2.6	.6				% Officers', Directors', Owners' Comp/Sales	3.2	2.0
(40) 6.3	(31) 5.0	(17) 1.2					(79) 4.8	(80) 4.4
10.0	7.9	4.3					8.1	7.7
57888M	158541M	570193M	684197M	758695M	1624759M	Net Sales ($)	2382520M	3586902M
16720M	55013M	224252M	292684M	295009M	721823M	Total Assets ($)	1324290M	1929581M

© RMA 2005

M = $ thousand   MM = $ million
See Pages 11 through 21 for Explanation of Ratios and Data

Comparative Historical Data | Current Data Sorted By Sales

			Type of Statement						
16	9	16	Unqualified					7	9
20	23	18	Reviewed		1	3	4	7	3
67	63	48	Compiled	12	18	6	7	3	2
45	52	61	Tax Returns	28	22	4	2	2	3
50	44	39	Other	6	9	8	7	2	7
4/1/02-3/31/03	4/1/03-3/31/04	4/1/04-3/31/05		52 (4/1-9/30/04)			130 (10/1/04-3/31/05)		
ALL	ALL	ALL		0-1MM	1-3MM	3-5MM	5-10MM	10-25MM	25MM & OVER
198	191	182	NUMBER OF STATEMENTS	46	50	21	20	21	24
%	%	%	ASSETS	%	%	%	%	%	%
13.5	12.2	11.8	Cash & Equivalents	11.1	11.2	8.5	20.6	10.1	11.2
6.4	9.1	6.9	Trade Receivables (net)	6.2	3.9	10.0	8.4	9.1	8.9
46.8	49.5	49.0	Inventory	55.8	48.0	53.1	37.3	49.8	43.5
1.5	2.0	2.4	All Other Current	1.2	3.0	1.3	1.5	3.4	4.3
68.1	72.7	70.1	Total Current	74.2	66.0	73.0	67.9	72.4	68.0
21.8	19.0	19.8	Fixed Assets (net)	16.9	23.0	16.4	25.3	15.8	20.9
4.2	3.8	4.0	Intangibles (net)	3.6	5.5	5.2	1.4	2.8	3.8
5.8	4.4	6.1	All Other Non-Current	5.3	5.5	5.3	5.4	9.0	7.4
100.0	100.0	100.0	Total	100.0	100.0	100.0	100.0	100.0	100.0
			LIABILITIES						
10.4	13.0	12.0	Notes Payable-Short Term	16.6	10.4	9.8	9.2	12.2	10.4
4.8	4.1	3.5	Cur. Mat.-L/T/D	3.1	4.5	2.1	4.5	2.5	3.8
17.1	17.7	16.7	Trade Payables	10.2	16.6	22.9	17.0	22.4	18.7
.2	.3	.5	Income Taxes Payable	.2	.8	1.5	.2	.0	.1
12.1	10.3	9.9	All Other Current	16.7	7.2	5.4	7.2	9.2	9.4
44.6	45.4	42.6	Total Current	46.7	39.5	41.6	38.1	46.3	42.5
19.8	20.0	17.6	Long-Term Debt	17.5	23.9	14.3	7.9	11.0	21.4
.1	.1	.1	Deferred Taxes	.0	.0	.0	.4	.1	.0
7.4	12.2	14.4	All Other Non-Current	27.5	8.8	3.7	18.3	7.6	12.8
28.1	22.4	25.4	Net Worth	8.2	27.8	40.5	35.3	35.0	23.4
100.0	100.0	100.0	Total Liabilities & Net Worth	100.0	100.0	100.0	100.0	100.0	100.0
			INCOME DATA						
100.0	100.0	100.0	Net Sales	100.0	100.0	100.0	100.0	100.0	100.0
46.7	44.8	47.7	Gross Profit	48.2	45.4	51.5	48.3	47.9	47.7
43.7	42.7	45.9	Operating Expenses	46.8	44.8	49.3	45.3	45.5	44.7
3.0	2.1	1.8	Operating Profit	1.4	.6	2.2	3.0	2.4	3.1
1.0	1.0	1.0	All Other Expenses (net)	1.7	1.0	1.0	.6	.2	.8
2.0	1.1	.8	Profit Before Taxes	−.3	−.3	1.2	2.4	2.2	2.3
			RATIOS						
3.1	3.0	3.4		5.9	3.5	3.7	3.3	2.3	2.6
1.6	1.8	2.0	Current	2.4	2.0	2.3	2.4	1.6	1.6
1.1	1.2	1.2		1.2	1.1	1.4	1.3	1.0	1.3
.9	1.0	.9		.8	.9	1.3	1.9	.6	1.1
(195) .4	(190) .4	(181) .4	Quick	.3	.3	(20) .4	.9	.3	.5
.1	.1	.1		.1	.1	.2	.4	.1	.1
0 UND	0 UND	0 UND		0 UND	0 UND	0 UND	0 UND	0 UND	0 UND
0 UND	0 999.8	1 537.3	Sales/Receivables	0 UND	0 999.8	2 206.7	1 343.1	0 741.9	2 169.7
5 77.5	7 53.2	7 52.2		3 127.7	3 116.9	10 36.4	7 49.4	13 28.5	
75 4.9	69 5.3	66 5.5		100 3.6	51 7.2	87 4.2	48 7.6	60 6.1	64 5.7
128 2.8	130 2.8	129 2.8	Cost of Sales/Inventory	194 1.9	108 3.4	159 2.3	92 4.0	121 3.0	92 4.0
212 1.7	196 1.9	215 1.7		316 1.2	205 1.8	234 1.6	178 2.0	194 1.9	172 2.1
11 31.8	11 32.1	13 28.3		5 69.6	11 33.5	24 14.9	25 14.5	29 12.6	17 21.5
34 10.6	30 12.3	32 11.2	Cost of Sales/Payables	22 16.9	31 11.6	41 8.9	32 11.4	47 7.8	38 9.7
66 5.5	68 5.4	58 6.3		47 7.8	68 5.4	61 6.0	58 6.2	72 5.1	50 7.2
4.6	5.1	4.7		3.5	5.7	5.7	4.3	7.0	4.0
9.6	9.0	8.5	Sales/Working Capital	6.2	10.2	8.4	6.9	12.0	13.1
37.6	38.0	32.7		29.9	124.8	17.1	17.8	−564.3	22.5
7.3	6.4	7.0		7.4	2.9	10.7	6.9	7.0	10.0
(176) 2.3	(174) 2.1	(158) 3.2	EBIT/Interest	(38) 4.1	(40) 1.1	(20) 3.2	(18) 4.9	(19) 3.7	(23) 5.7
.2	−.4	.0		−.9	−.6	−1.0	1.0	1.8	2.4
5.8	7.4	17.0	Net Profit + Depr., Dep.,						
(29) 2.0	(23) 2.0	(22) 3.4	Amort./Cur. Mat. L/T/D						
.2	.6	.4							
.2	.2	.2		.1	.2	.1	.4	.2	.3
.7	.7	.6	Fixed/Worth	1.1	.7	.3	.6	.4	.8
4.0	11.8	8.7		−.8	15.2	1.5	.9	.7	−3.0
.8	.9	.8		1.0	.5	.6	.6	1.3	1.0
2.1	2.7	2.2	Debt/Worth	6.8	2.3	1.6	1.7	1.9	2.3
17.8	−999.8	−48.8		−6.4	NM	7.2	3.8	3.7	−23.1
48.4	40.5	39.9	% Profit Before Taxes/Tangible	66.7	33.9	43.1	25.7	32.9	39.5
(165) 16.1	(143) 11.7	(136) 16.0	Net Worth	(26) 25.8	(38) 6.8	(17) 13.7	(18) 16.2	(20) 18.6	(17) 28.7
−1.5	−2.5	.2		−9.2	−11.2	.2	1.8	9.0	15.7
15.2	14.2	13.4	% Profit Before Taxes/Total	17.9	8.6	19.4	9.0	10.3	13.6
3.8	3.0	4.8	Assets	6.2	.8	4.2	4.6	5.8	9.3
−2.0	−3.5	−4.1		−7.8	−5.5	−6.9	.9	2.8	.8
36.4	62.8	51.5		67.9	68.0	75.3	28.1	56.3	46.3
14.9	25.3	21.8	Sales/Net Fixed Assets	26.1	19.1	32.2	15.4	26.6	15.0
7.6	10.0	8.3		6.2	7.4	11.3	5.7	18.5	8.1
3.1	3.8	3.6		3.3	4.4	3.7	3.4	4.0	3.9
2.4	2.6	2.7	Sales/Total Assets	2.5	3.1	2.8	2.7	2.6	2.8
1.7	1.8	1.8		1.4	1.7	1.7	1.5	2.1	1.9
.8	.7	.6		.6	.5	.4	1.1	.7	1.0
(162) 1.4	(153) 1.2	(153) 1.4	% Depr., Dep., Amort./Sales	(37) 1.4	(43) 1.1	(17) 1.3	(18) 1.8	(19) .9	(19) 1.6
2.4	2.1	2.5		3.4	2.6	2.3	2.0	2.0	2.8
2.5	2.5	2.2	% Officers', Directors',	4.7	3.0		.1		
(90) 4.5	(96) 4.4	(94) 4.7	Owners' Comp/Sales	(27) 7.1	(33) 5.1		(12) 1.2		
7.6	7.4	8.7		17.6	8.6		4.6		
4433152M	3535106M	3854273M	Net Sales ($)	21347M	94825M	81971M	147054M	342303M	3166773M
1910570M	1444149M	1605501M	Total Assets ($)	10973M	50368M	40406M	68832M	124111M	1310811M

M = $ thousand   MM = $ million
See Pages 11 through 21 for Explanation of Ratios and Data

Current Data Sorted By Assets   Comparative Historical Data

			4				Type of Statement		
	1	1					Unqualified	6	7
2	6	4					Reviewed	6	7
20	15	6					Compiled	32	31
13	4	2			1		Tax Returns	16	20
							Other	23	30
	10 (4/1-9/30/04)			69 (10/1/04-3/31/05)				4/1/00-3/31/01	4/1/01-3/31/02
0-500M	500M-2MM	2-10MM	10-50MM	50-100MM	100-250MM			ALL	ALL
35	26	13	4		1	NUMBER OF STATEMENTS		83	95
%	%	%	%	%	%	ASSETS		%	%
24.2	3.6	10.8				Cash & Equivalents		6.9	7.8
4.4	14.1	7.4	D			Trade Receivables (net)		13.9	13.4
32.6	45.8	53.8	A			Inventory		46.5	42.7
3.0	1.2	1.4	T			All Other Current		5.2	5.0
64.2	64.7	73.4	A			Total Current		72.5	68.9
20.6	22.4	22.8				Fixed Assets (net)		17.3	20.7
5.0	1.6	.5	N			Intangibles (net)		3.2	5.2
10.3	11.3	3.2	O			All Other Non-Current		7.0	5.2
100.0	100.0	100.0	T			Total		100.0	100.0
			A			LIABILITIES			
21.9	18.6	6.6	V			Notes Payable-Short Term		20.2	17.7
7.8	1.1	1.6	A			Cur. Mat.-L/T/D		2.5	2.1
6.2	10.4	4.9	I			Trade Payables		8.0	4.5
.1	.0	.1	L			Income Taxes Payable		.1	.1
46.0	9.1	7.4	A			All Other Current		9.4	11.1
82.0	39.2	20.6	B			Total Current		40.3	35.5
13.7	24.6	13.5	L			Long-Term Debt		11.4	16.8
.0	.0	.0	E			Deferred Taxes		.1	.1
31.3	9.3	2.4				All Other Non-Current		5.9	7.9
-26.9	26.9	63.6				Net Worth		42.3	39.7
100.0	100.0	100.0				Total Liabilities & Net Worth		100.0	100.0
						INCOME DATA			
100.0	100.0	100.0				Net Sales		100.0	100.0
52.6	47.4	45.2				Gross Profit		48.7	51.4
48.5	43.0	37.0				Operating Expenses		43.2	43.2
4.1	4.3	8.2				Operating Profit		5.5	8.1
.5	1.1	-.3				All Other Expenses (net)		.0	3.1
3.6	3.2	8.5				Profit Before Taxes		5.5	5.0
						RATIOS			
2.7	5.5	7.7						4.2	5.2
1.2	1.8	3.4				Current		1.9	2.5
.6	1.1	2.9						1.3	1.3
1.2	1.3	1.8						1.4	1.5
(34) .4	.5	.5				Quick		(93) .5	.7
.1	.0	.3						.2	.2
0 UND	0 UND	0 UND						0 UND	0 UND
0 UND	8 47.1	7 54.9				Sales/Receivables		7 53.3	8 46.4
2 183.4	52 7.1	23 16.0						63 5.8	65 5.6
7 50.8	61 6.0	57 6.4						82 4.4	102 3.6
80 4.5	147 2.5	162 2.3				Cost of Sales/Inventory		185 2.0	184 2.0
187 2.0	390 .9	898 .4						371 1.0	299 1.2
0 UND	0 UND	3 106.0						0 UND	0 UND
0 UND	18 20.1	11 34.7				Cost of Sales/Payables		15 23.9	6 56.3
15 23.8	39 9.3	30 12.3						43 8.4	34 10.6
9.4	2.8	1.2						2.5	2.0
59.4	7.6	3.0				Sales/Working Capital		5.3	5.2
-11.9	NM	11.9						23.2	27.0
37.6	7.9	54.9						7.8	6.7
(22) 14.6	3.4	(12) 7.1				EBIT/Interest		(75) 3.5	(85) 2.2
9.7	1.2	2.1						1.5	.9
						Net Profit + Depr., Dep.,			3.3
						Amort./Cur. Mat. L /T/D		(10) 1.1	
									.4
.1	.2	.0						.1	.1
.5	.6	.3				Fixed/Worth		.3	.5
-1.2	13.2	.8						.8	1.2
.5	1.1	.4						.6	.5
4.7	3.2	.5				Debt/Worth		1.5	1.5
-2.8	53.1	1.0						3.5	5.3
136.0	68.2	35.0				% Profit Before Taxes/Tangible		34.3	41.3
(21) 34.2	(21) 23.4	18.2				Net Worth		(78) 17.6	(82) 20.0
19.9	3.0	5.2						4.0	4.3
39.8	19.7	17.1				% Profit Before Taxes/Total		13.4	15.0
19.2	5.3	10.6				Assets		5.8	6.6
-12.3	.7	3.3						1.6	.0
100.5	97.9	56.9						74.8	42.4
23.2	15.2	25.4				Sales/Net Fixed Assets		19.5	14.6
12.1	5.4	3.9						8.6	6.7
8.6	3.3	2.8						2.7	2.4
3.5	2.1	1.6				Sales/Total Assets		1.7	1.5
1.9	1.2	.7						1.0	1.1
.6	1.0	.4						.5	.5
(24) 1.2	(19) 1.4	(12) .6				% Depr., Dep., Amort./Sales		(55) .9	(73) 1.0
2.7	2.8	1.3						1.9	2.2
		2.8						3.7	3.4
	(19) 5.6					% Officers', Directors',		(37) 7.6	(43) 6.0
	10.1					Owners' Comp/Sales		10.6	10.6
32670M	71230M	100329M	99330M		293002M	Net Sales ($)		2215733M	1218085M
8302M	27754M	56380M	78824M		126995M	Total Assets ($)		1149832M	912133M

© RMA 2005

M = $ thousand   MM = $ million

See Pages 11 through 21 for Explanation of Ratios and Data

Comparative Historical Data | Current Data Sorted By Sales

			Type of Statement	0-1MM	1-3MM	3-5MM	5-10MM	10-25MM	25MM & OVER
4	10	4	Unqualified					3	1
5	3	2	Reviewed				2		
23	26	12	Compiled	1	7	2	2		
15	33	41	Tax Returns	19	13	4	4	1	
20	24	20	Other	4	12		1	2	1
4/1/02- 3/31/03 ALL	4/1/03- 3/31/04 ALL	4/1/04- 3/31/05 ALL		10 (4/1-9/30/04)		69 (10/1/04-3/31/05)			
67	96	79	**NUMBER OF STATEMENTS**	24	32	6	9	6	2
%	%	%	**ASSETS**	%	%	%	%	%	%
9.8	7.5	14.1	Cash & Equivalents	22.6	10.6				
14.1	11.9	8.8	Trade Receivables (net)	5.5	6.7				
41.5	44.2	39.3	Inventory	37.2	42.5				
7.2	4.5	2.3	All Other Current	3.3	.5				
72.6	68.0	64.5	Total Current	68.6	60.2				
20.5	21.1	23.5	Fixed Assets (net)	19.3	24.3				
1.9	4.1	3.0	Intangibles (net)	1.2	5.3				
5.0	6.7	9.1	All Other Non-Current	11.0	10.1				
100.0	100.0	100.0	Total	100.0	100.0				
			LIABILITIES						
17.6	11.9	16.9	Notes Payable-Short Term	16.1	17.6				
1.2	2.6	4.3	Cur. Mat.-L/T/D	7.2	3.9				
6.2	8.7	7.5	Trade Payables	5.8	5.2				
.1	.0	.1	Income Taxes Payable	.0	.1				
10.2	7.8	25.0	All Other Current	56.6	12.9				
35.4	31.0	53.8	Total Current	85.7	39.7				
14.4	21.4	18.3	Long-Term Debt	22.9	17.6				
.0	.0	.0	Deferred Taxes	.0	.0				
8.5	9.6	17.5	All Other Non-Current	23.0	22.5				
41.7	38.0	10.5	Net Worth	−31.6	20.2				
100.0	100.0	100.0	Total Liabilities & Net Worth	100.0	100.0				
			INCOME DATA						
100.0	100.0	100.0	Net Sales	100.0	100.0				
55.7	54.2	50.0	Gross Profit	48.1	54.0				
48.0	48.1	45.1	Operating Expenses	47.2	47.2				
7.7	6.1	4.9	Operating Profit	.9	6.8				
2.1	1.1	.6	All Other Expenses (net)	.7	.7				
5.5	4.9	4.3	Profit Before Taxes	.2	6.1				
			RATIOS						
8.3	7.9	4.3		3.5	9.5				
3.8	2.4	2.0	Current	1.9	2.0				
1.4	1.2	1.0		.7	.8				
3.8	2.5	1.6		1.1	1.6				
(63) 1.1	.5	(78) .5	Quick	(23) .3	.4				
.2	.1	.1		.1	.1				
0 UND	0 UND	0 UND		0 UND	0 UND				
11 34.5	8 47.1	2 202.5	Sales/Receivables	0 UND	2 180.8				
59 6.1	49 7.4	20 18.5		2 181.5	10 36.4				
70 5.2	74 5.0	37 9.9		0 UND	64 5.7				
165 2.2	166 2.2	103 3.6	Cost of Sales/Inventory	186 2.0	100 3.6				
332 1.1	349 1.0	241 1.5		533 .7	310 1.2				
0 UND	2 229.9	0 UND		0 UND	0 UND				
11 34.1	15 24.5	9 41.0	Cost of Sales/Payables	2 176.5	6 63.0				
47 7.8	44 8.3	35 10.5		21 17.6	26 14.0				
1.8	2.2	3.0		2.9	3.3				
2.9	4.6	12.0	Sales/Working Capital	14.0	13.5				
10.1	40.9	−311.1		−9.5	−52.5				
10.6	10.5	14.9		10.0	23.2				
(59) 3.8	(86) 3.4	(64) 6.8	EBIT/Interest	(12) 3.9	(31) 10.5				
1.7	1.2	2.1		−1.1	2.7				
			Net Profit + Depr., Dep., Amort./Cur. Mat. L/T/D						
.1	.1	.1		.0	.1				
.2	.4	.5	Fixed/Worth	.3	.6				
1.1	1.7	6.0		−1.5	6.5				
.3	.7	.5		.7	.7				
1.0	1.6	1.8	Debt/Worth	4.1	1.6				
4.2	5.9	53.5		−3.0	18.3				
33.6	45.7	62.8		33.4	131.5				
(59) 16.8	(84) 14.4	(60) 26.5	% Profit Before Taxes/Tangible Net Worth	(13) 17.8	(26) 51.0				
8.5	3.2	5.2		−13.0	6.2				
16.7	15.3	22.1		13.2	37.6				
8.0	7.5	9.9	% Profit Before Taxes/Total Assets	2.7	20.0				
2.2	.7	.5		−21.6	4.0				
51.2	51.2	75.4		UND	37.5				
15.9	16.5	17.8	Sales/Net Fixed Assets	17.0	17.7				
6.9	6.6	6.6		7.3	7.3				
2.2	2.9	4.5		5.6	4.0				
1.5	1.8	2.4	Sales/Total Assets	1.5	2.8				
1.0	1.2	1.2		1.0	1.3				
.4	.6	.6		.9	.7				
(51) 1.2	(74) 1.5	(60) 1.3	% Depr., Dep., Amort./Sales	(14) 2.3	(26) 1.2				
2.5	2.5	2.7		2.9	2.2				
3.3	2.9	2.6			3.1				
(32) 9.1	(45) 6.4	(34) 6.3	% Officers', Directors', Owners' Comp/Sales		(15) 6.1				
11.5	11.5	12.5			14.7				
1064743M	1466037M	596561M	Net Sales ($)	9767M	54759M	23151M	63917M	108638M	336329M
672696M	881940M	298255M	Total Assets ($)	6256M	35181M	13817M	21807M	58673M	162521M

© RMA 2005

M = $ thousand   MM = $ million
See Pages 11 through 21 for Explanation of Ratios and Data

Current Data Sorted By Assets   Comparative Historical Data

Type of Statement	0-500M	500M-2MM	2-10MM	10-50MM	50-100MM	100-250MM		4/1/00-3/31/01 ALL	4/1/01-3/31/02 ALL
Unqualified		7	1	4				7	4
Reviewed	3	35	15	2				30	25
Compiled	7	35	15	2				56	68
Tax Returns	1	13	8	1				17	20
Other			7	2				33	30
		21 (4/1-9/30/04)		137 (10/1/04-3/31/05)					
NUMBER OF STATEMENTS	11	90	46	11				143	147

(Columns 50-100MM and 100-250MM: DATA NOT AVAILABLE)

	0-500M %	500M-2MM %	2-10MM %	10-50MM %	50-100MM %	100-250MM %		4/1/00-3/31/01 %	4/1/01-3/31/02 %
ASSETS									
Cash & Equivalents	12.3	11.8	8.8	2.8				6.1	8.7
Trade Receivables (net)	2.3	8.1	9.4	13.1				6.4	5.7
Inventory	61.1	59.6	58.7	35.8				58.1	57.8
All Other Current	.1	2.5	2.8	3.5				2.5	3.1
Total Current	75.8	82.0	79.6	55.1				73.1	75.3
Fixed Assets (net)	17.8	11.8	14.5	24.1				19.2	15.6
Intangibles (net)	1.3	.5	.1	1.8				2.0	2.1
All Other Non-Current	5.2	5.8	5.8	19.0				5.7	7.1
Total	100.0	100.0	100.0	100.0				100.0	100.0
LIABILITIES									
Notes Payable-Short Term	38.5	45.4	33.4	21.7				37.9	42.0
Cur. Mat.-L/T/D	1.9	.9	3.3	4.1				3.6	3.2
Trade Payables	17.4	5.2	7.0	4.8				6.1	5.4
Income Taxes Payable	.7	.0	.0	.0				.1	.1
All Other Current	12.6	12.5	10.0	5.9				8.1	9.7
Total Current	71.1	64.0	53.7	36.4				55.8	60.5
Long-Term Debt	41.3	5.4	8.7	22.6				9.7	9.4
Deferred Taxes	.0	.0	.0	.2				.1	.1
All Other Non-Current	.7	3.6	7.3	7.5				5.1	6.0
Net Worth	-13.1	27.0	30.2	33.2				29.2	24.1
Total Liabilities & Net Worth	100.0	100.0	100.0	100.0				100.0	100.0
INCOME DATA									
Net Sales	100.0	100.0	100.0	100.0				100.0	100.0
Gross Profit	29.5	23.3	21.7	33.9				24.7	22.0
Operating Expenses	26.0	20.5	20.0	25.6				22.8	20.6
Operating Profit	3.4	2.8	1.7	8.4				1.9	1.4
All Other Expenses (net)	1.4	.3	.5	1.5				.0	.7
Profit Before Taxes	2.0	2.5	1.2	6.8				2.0	.8
RATIOS									
Current	1.8	1.6	2.5	2.6				1.9	1.6
	1.1	1.2	1.3	1.7				1.2	1.2
	.7	1.0	1.1	1.0				1.0	1.0
Quick	.6	.5	.8	.5				.4	.5
	.3	.3	.3	.2			(141) .2	(146) .2
	.1	.1	.2	.0				.1	.1
Sales/Receivables	0 UND	0 UND	5 77.2	0 999.8				1 703.9	0 999.8
	0 UND	3 142.2	10 35.3	28 12.9				3 110.8	4 84.2
	0 733.0	18 20.5	24 15.0	59 6.2				16 23.3	13 27.9
Cost of Sales/Inventory	40 9.0	92 3.9	105 3.5	72 5.1				85 4.3	84 4.4
	97 3.8	130 2.8	141 2.6	163 2.2				131 2.8	120 3.1
	247 1.5	167 2.2	196 1.9	253 1.4				191 1.9	179 2.0
Cost of Sales/Payables	0 UND	0 873.0	2 191.4	12 30.2				1 410.5	0 999.8
	2 152.6	3 131.7	4 82.2	17 21.2				4 95.2	3 127.8
	92 4.0	7 52.4	12 31.3	38 9.5				12 30.7	10 35.5
Sales/Working Capital	13.8	7.5	5.2	2.7				6.6	7.7
	64.5	15.3	11.5	3.9				16.0	22.0
	-7.9	-350.8	56.4	-999.8				131.5	-999.8
EBIT/Interest	7.9	4.0	4.7	31.8				3.4	3.1
	(10) 1.8	(76) 2.1	(40) 1.4	(10) 2.7			(134) 1.6	(137) 1.4
	-1.0	.2	1.0	1.1				.8	.7
Net Profit + Depr., Dep., Amort./Cur. Mat. L /T/D								5.8	7.7
							(19) 1.7	(18) 1.9
								1.0	.4
Fixed/Worth	.3	.1	.2	.3				.2	.2
	-5.4	.4	.4	.5				.6	.6
	-.7	.9	1.0	3.5				1.5	1.7
Debt/Worth	3.4	1.4	.8	1.2				1.3	1.6
	-7.4	3.1	2.7	3.0				3.3	3.8
	-3.6	9.5	11.0	7.1				8.7	16.5
% Profit Before Taxes/Tangible Net Worth		50.0	26.8	25.1				38.7	37.9
	(79)	16.1	(40) 8.3	(10) 15.2			(125) 9.5	(126) 10.2
		2.1	-.5	.8				.5	-5.1
% Profit Before Taxes/Total Assets	23.8	8.1	6.6	10.4				8.0	8.1
	7.5	2.9	1.4	1.6				2.6	1.8
	-10.1	-1.5	-.2	.9				-.8	-1.8
Sales/Net Fixed Assets	104.7	67.5	54.1	16.6				46.0	54.0
	29.9	30.0	19.5	6.6				19.4	20.4
	11.3	12.9	10.1	3.1				7.4	9.5
Sales/Total Assets	5.7	2.9	2.5	2.4				3.0	3.1
	3.0	2.3	1.8	1.2				2.1	2.3
	1.9	1.7	1.5	.5				1.5	1.6
% Depr., Dep., Amort./Sales		.3	.3	1.0				.4	.4
	(76)	.7	(40) .9	(10) 1.7			(130) .8	(134) .7
		1.3	1.4	2.6				2.0	1.6
% Officers', Directors', Owners' Comp/Sales		1.9	1.5					1.4	1.6
	(58)	2.8	(27) 2.2				(57) 2.3	(70) 2.8
		3.8						4.2	4.4
Net Sales ($)	13224M	245453M	305325M	213098M				1045708M	884236M
Total Assets ($)	3947M	105418M	158563M	195966M				651580M	434120M

© RMA 2005

M = $ thousand   MM = $ million
See Pages 11 through 21 for Explanation of Ratios and Data

| Comparative Historical Data | | | | | Current Data Sorted By Sales | | | | | |

				Type of Statement				1	3	1
7		3	5	Unqualified				5	1	1
12		13	16	Reviewed		3	6	5	1	
71		76	55	Compiled	2	24	17	7	5	
18		33	59	Tax Returns	4	30	10	11	3	1
24		22	23	Other	3	9	5	5	1	
4/1/02-		4/1/03-	4/1/04-			21 (4/1-9/30/04)		137 (10/1/04-3/31/05)		
3/31/03		3/31/04	3/31/05							
ALL		ALL	ALL		0-1MM	1-3MM	3-5MM	5-10MM	10-25MM	25MM & OVER
132		147	158	NUMBER OF STATEMENTS	9	66	38	29	13	3
%		%	%	ASSETS	%	%	%	%	%	%
9.1		8.5	10.3	Cash & Equivalents		12.4	11.5	12.3	–2.1	
7.0		8.4	8.4	Trade Receivables (net)		7.4	7.1	8.0	15.6	
54.7		57.7	57.8	Inventory		57.6	56.9	53.8	59.2	
3.5		3.1	2.5	All Other Current		3.2	1.9	2.4	2.7	
74.2		77.7	79.0	Total Current		80.6	77.4	76.5	75.5	
16.9		15.0	13.8	Fixed Assets (net)		13.1	13.4	17.8	14.7	
1.1		.8	.5	Intangibles (net)		.4	.8	.2	1.4	
7.7		6.5	6.7	All Other Non-Current		5.9	8.4	5.5	8.3	
100.0		100.0	100.0	Total		100.0	100.0	100.0	100.0	
				LIABILITIES						
36.0		39.4	39.8	Notes Payable-Short Term		42.1	35.6	46.0	22.5	
2.1		2.8	1.9	Cur. Mat.-L/T/D		1.3	2.0	3.0	2.3	
4.3		9.2	6.5	Trade Payables		6.8	5.9	3.1	11.5	
.1		.1	.1	Income Taxes Payable		.1	.0	.0	.2	
11.5		12.5	11.3	All Other Current		10.3	13.6	11.8	8.3	
54.0		64.0	59.6	Total Current		60.6	57.1	63.9	44.8	
11.0		10.7	10.1	Long-Term Debt		8.0	7.9	5.9	12.5	
.0		.0	.0	Deferred Taxes		.0	.0	.0	.1	
5.9		6.3	4.7	All Other Non-Current		3.3	9.1	3.8	6.0	
29.0		18.9	25.6	Net Worth		28.1	25.9	26.4	36.7	
100.0		100.0	100.0	Total Liabilities & Net Worth		100.0	100.0	100.0	100.0	
				INCOME DATA						
100.0		100.0	100.0	Net Sales		100.0	100.0	100.0	100.0	
24.6		24.7	24.0	Gross Profit		24.3	22.1	23.8	24.4	
22.7		22.5	21.1	Operating Expenses		21.9	19.0	20.9	20.9	
1.9		2.3	2.9	Operating Profit		2.4	3.1	2.9	3.5	
.7		.5	.5	All Other Expenses (net)		.6	.1	.3	1.1	
1.3		1.7	2.4	Profit Before Taxes		1.9	3.0	2.6	2.5	
				RATIOS						
2.1		1.6	1.7			1.6	1.7	1.5	2.7	
1.3		1.2	1.2	Current		1.2	1.3	1.1	1.7	
1.0		1.0	1.0			1.0	1.1	.9	1.2	
.6		.5	.6			.6	.5	.6	.8	
.2	(146)	.2	(156) .3	Quick		.3	.3	(28) .3	(12) .5	
.1		.1	.1			.1	.2	.2	.2	
0 999.8	0	UND	0 999.8		0 UND	1 518.1	0 771.5	5 73.7		
5 68.6	5	80.0	6 64.9	Sales/Receivables	2 181.1	8 48.3	11 34.3	10 37.0		
17 21.1	21	17.2	23 16.2		18 20.8	21 17.0	23 15.6	37 9.8		
84 4.3	82	4.5	92 4.0		100 3.6	92 4.0	61 6.0	105 3.5		
135 2.7	128	2.9	135 2.7	Cost of Sales/Inventory	141 2.6	126 2.9	104 3.5	153 2.4		
179 2.0	178	2.0	188 1.9		196 1.9	188 1.9	139 2.6	244 1.5		
0 UND	1	618.0	1 314.9		0 999.8	1 304.3	1 299.9	6 64.9		
3 104.3	4	93.5	4 89.9	Cost of Sales/Payables	2 155.7	4 83.6	4 84.3	13 27.7		
11 32.3	17	22.1	11 34.1		7 49.4	11 33.3	8 43.3	38 9.7		
5.4		6.2	6.3			6.3	7.5	10.2	3.0	
12.3		19.9	14.0	Sales/Working Capital		13.8	11.9	39.0	5.6	
105.0		UND	544.5			297.8	82.3	–44.5	19.1	
		4.1	4.4 4.9			5.7	3.6	4.9	35.8	
(120) 1.6	(127)	1.8	(136) 1.9	EBIT/Interest	(53) 2.4	(36) 2.0	(26) 1.9	(11) 1.7		
.5		.8	.8			–.2	1.0	1.0	.8	
5.1		2.0	2.4	Net Profit + Depr., Dep.,						
(11) 1.1	(13)	1.6	(11) 1.9	Amort./Cur. Mat. L/T/D						
–.6		.3	.4							
.2		.2	.2			.1	.2	.2	.2	
.4		.5	.4	Fixed/Worth		.4	.3	.6	.4	
1.7		2.1	1.1			.8	1.5	1.1	2.8	
1.1		1.7	1.4			1.3	1.4	1.5	.6	
2.9		4.0	3.4	Debt/Worth		2.9	2.9	3.0	1.8	
7.9		13.9	12.4			8.7	33.1	11.8	10.0	
37.3		52.2	32.4	% Profit Before Taxes/Tangible		51.9	26.4	37.5	13.1	
(115) 9.0	(123)	11.9	(133) 13.8	Net Worth	(57) 13.8	(32) 16.6	(26) 12.9	(11) 8.6		
–1.7		–.5	1.3			2.1	2.2	–1.8	–2.3	
7.5		8.9	8.1	% Profit Before Taxes/Total		8.1	6.9	10.2	8.0	
2.1		2.7	2.3	Assets		2.3	3.9	1.7	1.6	
–1.2		–.9	–.4			–1.4	.0	–.3	–.3	
68.0		54.7	65.2			65.5	62.8	82.9	37.9	
21.6		23.3	25.9	Sales/Net Fixed Assets		25.2	23.4	26.2	16.6	
8.8		11.4	11.5			12.3	11.9	11.1	4.2	
2.8		2.9	2.9			2.8	2.7	3.3	2.6	
2.0		2.1	2.1	Sales/Total Assets		2.0	2.3	2.5	1.6	
1.4		1.4	1.6			1.5	1.6	1.8	1.2	
.4		.4	.3			.3	.4	.2	.5	
(116) .8	(124)	.9	(134) .8	% Depr., Dep., Amort./Sales	(55) .6	(37) .9	(24) .8	(12) 1.1		
1.5		1.5	1.4			1.2	1.5	1.5	1.4	
1.4		1.5	1.7	% Officers', Directors',		2.2	1.6	1.0		
(67) 2.3	(61)	2.7	(91) 2.7	Owners' Comp/Sales	(38) 3.1	(25) 2.3	(20) 1.9			
4.9		4.3	3.8			4.5	3.0	3.4		
617452M		677366M	777100M	Net Sales ($)	5919M	129627M	148008M	205818M	181014M	106714M
512830M		453855M	463894M	Total Assets ($)	4224M	70496M	87156M	109237M	151801M	40980M

© RMA 2005

M = $ thousand   MM = $ million
See Pages 11 through 21 for Explanation of Ratios and Data

Current Data Sorted By Assets / Comparative Historical Data

Type of Statement								
	1	3	12	15	2	3	Unqualified	30	28
	1	15	29	6			Reviewed	43	55
	32	48	39	5			Compiled	125	107
	67	57	14				Tax Returns	109	88
	22	38	32	11	2	4	Other	127	122

	0-500M	500M-2MM	2-10MM	10-50MM	50-100MM	100-250MM		4/1/00-3/31/01 ALL	4/1/01-3/31/02 ALL
	87 (4/1-9/30/04)			371 (10/1/04-3/31/05)					
NUMBER OF STATEMENTS	123	161	126	37	4	7		434	400
	%	%	%	%	%	%	ASSETS	%	%
	14.8	8.7	8.8	8.8			Cash & Equivalents	9.2	9.6
	11.1	17.2	17.9	13.2			Trade Receivables (net)	16.3	15.6
	39.7	42.5	38.2	37.9			Inventory	41.5	41.3
	2.6	1.9	3.4	2.4			All Other Current	1.7	1.7
	68.2	70.4	68.4	62.2			Total Current	68.7	68.2
	20.8	19.6	22.9	27.5			Fixed Assets (net)	21.2	22.5
	6.1	3.2	2.7	3.3			Intangibles (net)	4.1	3.4
	4.9	6.8	6.0	7.0			All Other Non-Current	6.0	5.9
	100.0	100.0	100.0	100.0			Total	100.0	100.0
							LIABILITIES		
	14.3	12.1	12.3	12.9			Notes Payable-Short Term	10.9	11.2
	5.6	3.7	3.0	4.7			Cur. Mat.-L/T/D	3.4	3.6
	17.4	20.0	21.0	18.4			Trade Payables	19.2	18.6
	.1	.1	.2	.2			Income Taxes Payable	.3	.2
	14.7	12.1	11.5	7.9			All Other Current	12.1	10.8
	52.0	48.0	47.9	44.2			Total Current	46.0	44.5
	14.1	17.5	13.4	16.8			Long-Term Debt	17.2	20.0
	.0	.3	.3	.2			Deferred Taxes	.2	.1
	10.5	6.5	3.3	2.1			All Other Non-Current	6.9	7.0
	23.3	27.7	35.0	36.7			Net Worth	29.8	28.4
	100.0	100.0	100.0	100.0			Total Liabilities & Net Worth	100.0	100.0
							INCOME DATA		
	100.0	100.0	100.0	100.0			Net Sales	100.0	100.0
	45.1	38.8	37.9	36.9			Gross Profit	41.1	42.4
	40.8	36.2	34.1	31.4			Operating Expenses	38.1	39.3
	4.3	2.6	3.9	5.5			Operating Profit	3.0	3.2
	.8	.3	.3	.4			All Other Expenses (net)	.4	1.0
	3.5	2.3	3.5	5.0			Profit Before Taxes	2.6	2.2
							RATIOS		
	3.5	2.4	1.9	2.1			Current	2.7	2.7
	1.6	1.5	1.4	1.4				1.6	1.6
	.9	1.1	1.1	1.0				1.1	1.1
	1.5	.9	.9	.9			Quick	1.1	1.1
	(122) .5	.5	(125) .6	.4				(432) .5	(396) .6
	.1	.2	.2	.1				.2	.2
	0 UND	2 180.2	3 120.7	4 104.1			Sales/Receivables	0 777.6	0 999.8
	3 138.3	13 28.8	17 21.4	13 28.4				11 33.5	10 35.6
	16 22.3	33 11.1	39 9.2	32 11.5				35 10.4	35 10.6
	19 18.8	42 8.6	32 11.3	65 5.6			Cost of Sales/Inventory	38 9.6	38 9.5
	58 6.3	87 4.2	72 5.1	116 3.1				84 4.3	80 4.6
	142 2.6	143 2.6	127 2.9	172 2.1				139 2.6	157 2.3
	0 UND	11 32.2	19 19.4	26 14.2			Cost of Sales/Payables	13 29.1	13 28.8
	18 20.8	33 11.0	37 9.7	36 10.1				32 11.4	30 12.0
	41 8.8	60 6.1	65 5.7	64 5.7				64 5.7	64 5.7
	7.2	5.9	6.9	6.2			Sales/Working Capital	6.3	6.1
	19.4	15.0	16.4	13.1				12.5	12.8
	-95.2	58.7	90.2	96.6				75.0	43.7
	9.7	9.8	11.7	18.3			EBIT/Interest	6.8	6.0
	(78) 3.2	(143) 3.4	(116) 5.1	(36) 8.2				(385) 2.8	(345) 2.3
	.2	.9	2.0	2.1				1.1	.7
		3.6	8.4	24.6			Net Profit + Depr., Dep., Amort./Cur. Mat. L/T/D	4.0	4.4
		(16) 1.0	(30) 3.5	(10) 6.3				(56) 1.8	(73) 1.8
		-.1	1.4	2.9				.9	.9
	.2	.2	.2	.3			Fixed/Worth	.2	.2
	.7	.6	.5	.8				.6	.6
	-4.2	4.4	1.5	1.8				2.4	3.5
	.5	1.1	.9	1.0			Debt/Worth	.9	.9
	3.3	2.7	2.3	2.1				2.3	2.5
	-23.0	15.7	5.0	3.8				10.8	13.8
	73.0	53.3	48.6	43.1			% Profit Before Taxes/Tangible Net Worth	50.6	44.1
	(90) 35.3	(130) 18.2	(116) 20.1	(35) 20.3				(357) 17.6	(323) 16.2
	5.2	3.5	6.1	7.1				3.9	1.6
	25.1	13.3	13.9	16.7			% Profit Before Taxes/Total Assets	14.9	12.8
	9.0	5.4	6.7	7.1				5.3	4.6
	-1.6	.0	1.9	2.3				.4	-.9
	80.2	71.7	49.7	19.2			Sales/Net Fixed Assets	53.5	47.8
	26.3	26.1	17.6	9.9				20.5	20.5
	10.8	11.4	8.7	3.7				9.1	8.0
	6.1	4.2	3.9	2.9			Sales/Total Assets	4.1	4.0
	3.9	3.0	2.5	1.9				2.8	2.8
	2.2	1.9	1.9	1.2				1.9	1.8
	.6	.5	.6	.9			% Depr., Dep., Amort./Sales	.6	.6
	(86) 1.3	(128) 1.1	(103) 1.3	(35) 1.4				(350) 1.2	(326) 1.3
	2.5	2.4	2.2	3.2				2.3	2.7
	3.3	1.7	1.9	1.3			% Officers', Directors', Owners' Comp/Sales	2.6	2.3
	(69) 5.3	(85) 3.0	(57) 2.6	(11) 2.3				(223) 4.4	(201) 4.7
	10.4	5.2	5.7	5.5				7.5	7.4
	130183M	557404M	1555753M	1659288M	759002M	2152000M	Net Sales ($)	7133819M	5451211M
	30286M	165886M	525762M	819482M	279155M	1221959M	Total Assets ($)	3315772M	2541233M

M = $ thousand   MM = $ million
See Pages 11 through 21 for Explanation of Ratios and Data

Comparative Historical Data / Current Data Sorted By Sales

Hist 1	Hist 2	Hist 3	Type of Statement	0-1MM	1-3MM	3-5MM	5-10MM	10-25MM	25MM & OVER
36	40	36	Unqualified	1	1	2	3	9	20
53	53	51	Reviewed		10	5	10	21	5
92	137	124	Compiled	25	37	20	22	13	7
102	137	138	Tax Returns	53	47	21	10	7	
102	124	109	Other	14	29	17	15	14	20
4/1/02-3/31/03 ALL	4/1/03-3/31/04 ALL	4/1/04-3/31/05 ALL		87 (4/1-9/30/04)			371 (10/1/04-3/31/05)		
385	491	458	**NUMBER OF STATEMENTS**	93	124	65	60	64	52
%	%	%	**ASSETS**	%	%	%	%	%	%
9.7	10.3	10.4	Cash & Equivalents	13.2	10.1	10.9	7.8	8.4	11.4
15.0	16.0	15.5	Trade Receivables (net)	8.3	13.3	19.1	20.0	22.6	15.1
40.3	41.1	39.9	Inventory	40.9	41.5	40.3	39.0	36.8	38.6
2.4	3.0	2.6	All Other Current	2.1	2.3	2.6	3.5	2.6	3.5
67.3	70.4	68.5	Total Current	64.4	67.2	72.9	70.3	70.3	68.7
23.8	21.3	21.4	Fixed Assets (net)	25.6	21.6	16.3	20.8	21.2	21.0
3.0	3.0	4.1	Intangibles (net)	4.8	4.9	4.4	2.0	1.9	5.5
5.8	5.4	6.1	All Other Non-Current	5.2	6.3	6.4	6.9	6.6	4.7
100.0	100.0	100.0	Total	100.0	100.0	100.0	100.0	100.0	100.0
			LIABILITIES						
12.1	13.9	12.8	Notes Payable-Short Term	13.5	12.4	12.2	15.2	14.5	8.6
3.7	3.3	4.1	Cur. Mat.-L/T/D	4.5	5.0	4.4	2.6	3.0	3.6
19.9	19.0	19.3	Trade Payables	14.5	18.7	20.2	22.3	21.7	21.8
.2	.3	.2	Income Taxes Payable	.1	.1	.2	.1	.2	.7
11.0	11.0	12.3	All Other Current	16.1	11.6	12.3	9.9	11.5	11.1
46.9	47.6	48.7	Total Current	48.7	47.7	49.3	50.2	50.8	45.8
18.7	17.3	15.4	Long-Term Debt	17.4	18.1	17.8	12.4	10.5	11.8
.2	.2	.2	Deferred Taxes	.3	.1	.1	.4	.3	.3
6.8	6.0	6.4	All Other Non-Current	10.9	7.1	5.9	5.1	2.7	3.3
27.5	28.9	29.3	Net Worth	22.7	27.0	26.8	32.0	35.7	38.8
100.0	100.0	100.0	Total Liabilities & Net Worth	100.0	100.0	100.0	100.0	100.0	100.0
			INCOME DATA						
100.0	100.0	100.0	Net Sales	100.0	100.0	100.0	100.0	100.0	100.0
40.6	40.7	40.0	Gross Profit	50.0	39.6	39.2	36.5	36.3	32.5
36.9	36.9	36.2	Operating Expenses	45.9	35.8	36.5	32.9	32.8	27.7
3.6	3.8	3.8	Operating Profit	4.1	3.8	2.7	3.6	3.5	4.8
1.0	.6	.5	All Other Expenses (net)	1.5	.3	.2	.0	.2	.1
2.7	3.2	3.3	Profit Before Taxes	2.6	3.5	2.5	3.5	3.3	4.7
			RATIOS						
2.2	2.6	2.4		4.7	2.4	2.2	1.8	1.9	2.1
1.5	1.5	1.5	Current	1.7	1.4	1.5	1.4	1.3	1.5
1.1	1.1	1.0		.9	1.0	1.1	1.1	1.0	1.3
1.0	1.1	1.0		1.6	.9	1.1	.9	1.0	.9
(383) .5	(490) .5	(456) .5	Quick	.5	(123) .5	.6	.6	.6	(51) .5
.2	.2	.2		.1	.2	.2	.2	.3	.2
0 886.2	1 346.0	1 272.3		0 UND	0 UND	2 176.0	2 229.8	8 45.5	3 136.7
8 45.5	12 31.3	12 31.3	Sales/Receivables	3 109.0	10 36.5	16 22.3	15 24.3	22 16.3	12 30.2
30 12.0	32 11.4	31 11.8		19 18.8	29 12.6	33 11.1	35 10.5	39 9.3	35 10.5
31 11.6	30 12.3	33 11.0		36 10.1	26 14.1	27 13.6	35 10.4	37 9.8	38 9.7
76 4.8	76 4.8	77 4.8	Cost of Sales/Inventory	112 3.3	82 4.5	61 6.0	76 4.8	68 5.4	79 4.6
144 2.5	150 2.4	137 2.7		236 1.5	136 2.7	116 3.1	129 2.8	120 3.1	129 2.8
13 27.9	10 36.9	11 34.0		0 UND	10 37.9	11 34.7	24 15.0	16 22.5	19 18.9
34 10.9	31 12.0	31 11.8	Cost of Sales/Payables	19 19.1	31 11.7	29 12.7	39 9.4	34 10.6	34 10.8
62 5.9	60 6.1	57 6.4		49 7.4	60 6.1	62 5.9	65 5.6	49 7.4	50 7.4
7.0	6.2	6.4		4.4	6.0	7.9	7.5	6.9	6.6
14.5	13.7	15.9	Sales/Working Capital	11.7	17.8	15.0	16.5	20.1	13.8
122.7	72.1	128.2		−77.1	−225.7	37.9	86.8	135.1	39.5
7.7	11.2	11.0		7.1	10.3	9.2	8.8	11.7	25.0
(340) 3.0	(416) 3.4	(383) 4.6	EBIT/Interest	(62) 2.2	(106) 3.8	(54) 3.7	(55) 5.3	(60) 4.8	(46) 10.0
.9	1.1	1.4		−1.5	.8	1.1	2.8	2.0	4.3
7.7	6.8	7.7			2.2		9.1	12.3	19.6
(61) 1.8	(69) 2.7	(67) 2.7	Net Profit + Depr., Dep., Amort./Cur. Mat. L/T/D		(11) 1.3		(13) 3.4	(16) 1.9	(16) 7.1
.8	1.0	1.3			.5		1.1	1.3	3.2
.2	.2	.2		.2	.1	.2	.1	.2	.2
.7	.6	.6	Fixed/Worth	.7	.9	.6	.5	.5	.4
4.1	2.5	2.8		−18.6	UND	1.6	1.3	1.1	1.2
1.0	.8	.9		.6	.9	1.1	.8	1.0	.7
2.4	2.4	2.4	Debt/Worth	3.4	3.1	2.7	2.1	2.2	1.8
13.1	12.9	10.0		−24.1	UND	9.2	7.1	4.4	3.6
45.0	49.0	53.7		64.0	69.1	41.7	53.3	40.0	53.8
(308) 16.3	(400) 20.2	(380) 21.6	% Profit Before Taxes/Tangible Net Worth	(69) 27.0	(94) 23.7	(52) 15.8	(56) 21.8	(62) 16.8	(47) 28.4
1.7	4.3	5.4		−.6	5.2	3.0	10.4	4.5	14.6
13.8	16.5	16.8		24.0	16.8	16.2	15.2	12.3	19.3
5.0	5.6	6.5	% Profit Before Taxes/Total Assets	5.0	6.9	4.9	6.7	5.9	11.1
.0	.3	.8		−5.7	.5	.4	3.9	1.7	3.9
44.9	61.6	64.3		44.6	85.8	73.9	72.5	43.6	71.0
21.9	25.5	22.5	Sales/Net Fixed Assets	16.3	27.7	26.1	20.1	25.0	15.3
8.6	9.5	9.1		5.1	8.7	16.8	10.4	9.1	8.3
4.4	4.4	4.3		4.2	4.1	4.9	4.0	4.3	4.5
2.9	2.8	2.9	Sales/Total Assets	2.4	2.7	3.5	2.8	2.9	2.9
1.9	1.9	1.9		1.4	1.8	2.6	2.1	2.1	1.7
.7	.6	.6		.8	.5	.5	.6	.7	.5
(318) 1.3	(385) 1.3	(361) 1.2	% Depr., Dep., Amort./Sales	(70) 2.0	(92) 1.2	(49) .9	(46) 1.2	(55) 1.1	(49) 1.1
2.7	2.5	2.3		4.1	2.9	1.7	1.8	2.1	1.8
2.3	1.9	2.0		3.4	2.0	2.0	1.7	1.5	1.2
(194) 4.4	(241) 4.0	(222) 3.8	% Officers', Directors', Owners' Comp/Sales	(44) 6.1	(70) 3.8	(35) 4.6	(31) 3.6	(29) 2.3	(13) 2.2
8.0	6.9	7.3		7.3	7.2	7.2	5.7	3.2	6.1
7836384M	7075161M	6813630M	Net Sales ($)	51035M	245773M	252276M	423636M	975138M	4865772M
3363516M	3125457M	3042530M	Total Assets ($)	28672M	110829M	86822M	172884M	396220M	2247103M

© RMA 2005
M = $ thousand   MM = $ million
See Pages 11 through 21 for Explanation of Ratios and Data

Current Data Sorted By Assets   Comparative Historical Data

Type of Statement								4/1/00-3/31/01 ALL	4/1/01-3/31/02 ALL
Unqualified		1	6	17	6	8		25	24
Reviewed		2	16	3	1			18	10
Compiled	1	5	7	1				31	34
Tax Returns	9	3	3					8	12
Other	5	4	11	9	1	4		49	56

	0-500M	500M-2MM	2-10MM	10-50MM	50-100MM	100-250MM			
		32 (4/1-9/30/04)		91 (10/1/04-3/31/05)					
NUMBER OF STATEMENTS	15	15	43	30	8	12		131	136
ASSETS	%	%	%	%	%	%		%	%
Cash & Equivalents	14.2	20.8	10.9	13.5		13.3		9.8	11.5
Trade Receivables (net)	9.4	16.3	17.0	9.4		18.4		16.7	16.0
Inventory	53.2	29.4	45.4	39.4		33.1		40.9	40.0
All Other Current	4.8	7.8	3.9	3.6		3.8		2.9	3.7
Total Current	81.6	74.4	77.3	65.8		68.5		70.3	71.2
Fixed Assets (net)	8.0	13.9	12.4	15.4		18.0		14.6	15.1
Intangibles (net)	2.3	.3	3.9	7.4		5.6		6.3	6.1
All Other Non-Current	8.0	11.4	6.4	11.4		7.8		8.7	8.3
Total	100.0	100.0	100.0	100.0		100.0		100.0	100.0
LIABILITIES									
Notes Payable-Short Term	19.1	16.7	15.1	9.1		2.6		12.0	8.4
Cur. Mat.-L/T/D	.7	3.5	1.1	2.4		1.6		2.4	3.3
Trade Payables	32.8	20.0	31.4	22.2		13.1		24.6	23.2
Income Taxes Payable	.0	.1	.2	.2		.6		.3	.4
All Other Current	19.0	11.1	9.6	13.7		10.3		10.2	9.6
Total Current	71.6	51.4	57.4	47.6		28.2		49.5	44.9
Long-Term Debt	10.9	7.3	5.6	10.5		29.7		9.7	9.9
Deferred Taxes	.0	.2	.0	.3		.4		.1	.2
All Other Non-Current	4.8	1.4	1.5	9.2		2.7		6.4	4.5
Net Worth	12.7	39.7	35.5	32.4		39.0		34.2	40.6
Total Liabilities & Net Worth	100.0	100.0	100.0	100.0		100.0		100.0	100.0
INCOME DATA									
Net Sales	100.0	100.0	100.0	100.0		100.0		100.0	100.0
Gross Profit	31.5	36.8	34.9	46.8		44.7		43.2	45.9
Operating Expenses	31.0	32.7	33.1	43.2		37.5		39.7	41.6
Operating Profit	.4	4.1	1.8	3.6		7.2		3.5	4.3
All Other Expenses (net)	1.1	-.2	.0	-.1		.9		.6	.7
Profit Before Taxes	-.6	4.3	1.9	3.6		6.3		2.9	3.6
RATIOS									
Current	1.7	2.8	2.1	3.1		4.3		2.5	3.2
	1.4	1.5	1.4	1.3		2.8		1.5	1.7
	.9	.9	1.1	1.0		1.6		1.0	1.1
Quick	.9	2.8	.8	1.3		2.1		.9	1.2
	.3	.7	.5	.4		1.2	(130)	.5	.6
	.1	.3	.2	.1		.7		.2	.2
Sales/Receivables	0 UND	4 91.8	1 335.5	3 119.9		7 52.7		3 130.3	3 111.3
	2 160.5	8 43.3	10 34.8	5 79.9		28 13.1		10 38.1	11 33.0
	5 68.8	34 10.8	31 11.9	23 15.6		41 8.9		29 12.4	29 12.7
Cost of Sales/Inventory	11 32.1	16 22.5	31 11.6	68 5.4		51 7.2		49 7.5	48 7.6
	39 9.3	31 11.7	72 5.0	94 3.9		74 4.9		84 4.3	80 4.6
	101 3.6	95 3.8	115 3.2	134 2.7		119 3.1		118 3.1	123 3.0
Cost of Sales/Payables	3 104.8	13 28.7	18 20.1	22 16.4		23 15.8		24 15.0	20 18.0
	25 14.6	27 13.4	33 11.0	44 8.4		27 13.6		37 9.8	35 10.3
	61 6.0	43 8.5	67 5.5	76 4.8		34 10.8		63 5.8	63 5.8
Sales/Working Capital	17.0	6.8	7.6	5.9		4.0		7.7	5.9
	31.0	15.5	17.1	19.8		6.2		14.5	12.5
	-58.0	-55.7	78.5	-279.5		12.8		999.8	108.4
EBIT/Interest		15.7	33.0	85.5		22.4		11.1	14.7
	(14) 4.4	(36) 5.1	(28) 8.3			(10) 11.5		(117) 4.2	(114) 3.9
	1.7	.5	3.3			4.9		1.5	.9
Net Profit + Depr., Dep., Amort./Cur. Mat. L./T/D				16.5				10.0	13.0
			(10) 5.5				(21) 3.7	(22) 4.3
				3.3				.7	1.5
Fixed/Worth	.0	.2	.1	.2		.2		.2	.2
	.3	.5	.3	.5		.5		.4	.4
	-2.1	.8	.9	22.4		.7		1.1	1.2
Debt/Worth	.9	.9	.8	.7		.7		.9	.7
	4.5	1.2	2.1	2.2		1.4		2.0	1.7
	-26.1	6.1	4.8	104.2		2.3		5.2	6.4
% Profit Before Taxes/Tangible Net Worth	102.4	45.6	40.7	58.4		48.3		58.5	56.1
	(11) 13.8	(14) 24.8	(39) 14.4	(24) 23.9		(11) 40.6		(108) 29.5	(116) 28.9
	-62.5	12.7	-3.9	16.2		25.8		8.2	3.2
% Profit Before Taxes/Total Assets	16.2	12.3	16.0	17.7		27.7		17.8	19.1
	2.6	8.2	4.1	8.1		16.4		8.5	7.4
	-6.9	1.6	-1.5	3.8		10.2		.8	.1
Sales/Net Fixed Assets	UND	69.5	114.4	48.8		30.0		54.1	56.1
	118.5	38.2	64.0	30.5		14.2		31.5	30.3
	48.9	12.5	20.7	10.5		9.2		14.5	14.7
Sales/Total Assets	7.5	4.9	5.8	3.9		3.1		4.3	4.9
	5.6	2.7	4.1	2.8		2.4		3.2	3.3
	3.6	2.3	2.6	1.9		2.0		2.2	2.2
% Depr., Dep., Amort./Sales		.4	.4	.6				.5	.6
		(14) .7	(36) .6	(27) 1.2			(105) .8	(104) 1.0
		1.3	1.1	1.5				1.4	1.5
% Officers', Directors', Owners' Comp/Sales		1.2	1.0					1.8	1.8
		(10) 3.9	(19) 1.9				(43) 3.8	(44) 4.0
		8.9	4.3					7.4	8.0
Net Sales ($)	25005M	67888M	953935M	2189253M	1761426M	5417510M		7017402M	7851916M
Total Assets ($)	4049M	16650M	215939M	762349M	630589M	2161218M		2451291M	2784377M

© RMA 2005

M = $ thousand   MM = $ million

See Pages 11 through 21 for Explanation of Ratios and Data

Comparative Historical Data | Current Data Sorted By Sales

Hist 4/1/02-3/31/03 ALL	Hist 4/1/03-3/31/04 ALL	Hist 4/1/04-3/31/05 ALL	Type of Statement	0-1MM	1-3MM	3-5MM	5-10MM	10-25MM	25MM & OVER
44	48	38	Unqualified		1		1	4	32
28	20	22	Reviewed		1	1	1	9	10
24	34	14	Compiled		3	1	3	5	2
9	12	15	Tax Returns	4	6	1	2	2	
51	36	34	Other	1	6	3		7	17
				32 (4/1-9/30/04)			91 (10/1/04-3/31/05)		
156	150	123	**NUMBER OF STATEMENTS**	5	17	6	7	27	61
%	%	%	**ASSETS**	%	%	%	%	%	%
11.9	12.4	12.9	Cash & Equivalents		13.0			14.7	11.2
13.7	12.6	13.8	Trade Receivables (net)		12.0			20.7	11.2
41.2	40.1	42.1	Inventory		49.3			37.6	43.2
4.8	6.0	4.6	All Other Current		5.7			2.3	4.0
71.6	71.1	73.4	Total Current		80.1			75.3	69.6
14.3	15.8	13.9	Fixed Assets (net)		11.0			14.9	14.9
5.5	5.5	4.3	Intangibles (net)		.3			2.1	7.0
8.6	7.6	8.4	All Other Non-Current		8.6			7.7	8.6
100.0	100.0	100.0	Total		100.0			100.0	100.0
			LIABILITIES						
9.0	12.0	12.4	Notes Payable-Short Term		12.5			13.7	8.3
5.6	3.7	1.8	Cur. Mat.-L/T/D		1.6			1.6	1.8
23.5	23.1	26.2	Trade Payables		25.5			28.3	26.4
.3	.3	.2	Income Taxes Payable		.0			.3	.3
12.7	12.6	12.0	All Other Current		24.1			6.9	13.0
51.1	51.7	52.7	Total Current		63.8			50.8	49.8
9.8	9.0	10.4	Long-Term Debt		7.2			6.5	12.2
.2	.2	.2	Deferred Taxes		.1			.2	.2
4.0	4.0	3.8	All Other Non-Current		3.8			.8	5.4
34.9	35.1	32.9	Net Worth		25.1			41.6	32.4
100.0	100.0	100.0	Total Liabilities & Net Worth		100.0			100.0	100.0
			INCOME DATA						
100.0	100.0	100.0	Net Sales		100.0			100.0	100.0
44.2	44.3	38.8	Gross Profit		36.4			35.5	42.0
40.3	41.6	35.7	Operating Expenses		32.4			32.5	38.5
4.0	2.7	3.1	Operating Profit		4.0			3.1	3.5
.6	.5	.2	All Other Expenses (net)		.5			-.1	.2
3.4	2.2	2.8	Profit Before Taxes		3.5			3.1	3.3
			RATIOS						
2.6	2.4	2.8			1.7			2.8	3.1
1.6	1.5	1.4	Current		1.3			1.4	1.4
1.1	1.1	1.1			1.0			1.1	1.1
1.2	1.1	1.1			.8			1.2	1.2
.4	(149) .5	.5	Quick		.3			.6	.4
.1	.1	.1			.1			.3	.1
3 120.2	2 154.3	2 240.3		0 UND				2 184.3	1 273.7
10 36.3	8 47.5	6 58.6	Sales/Receivables	5 68.8				16 23.1	5 66.8
25 14.6	22 16.9	30 12.2		22 16.2				34 10.9	26 14.0
50 7.4	48 7.5	31 11.6		26 14.2				27 13.8	50 7.4
88 4.2	80 4.5	76 4.8	Cost of Sales/Inventory	55 6.6				72 5.1	92 4.0
126 2.9	124 2.9	124 2.9		112 3.2				85 4.3	128 2.8
26 14.3	23 15.8	22 16.5		11 32.0				18 20.1	24 15.5
39 9.4	42 8.6	34 10.7	Cost of Sales/Payables	25 14.5				35 10.3	36 10.1
62 5.9	66 5.6	61 6.0		47 7.8				67 5.5	68 5.4
7.4	6.6	6.8			13.1			7.4	6.4
13.2	14.2	15.5	Sales/Working Capital		31.0			14.8	14.1
57.3	66.8	70.2			NM			60.3	78.1
19.6	17.0	22.4			4.7			34.7	27.1
(135) 6.3	(137) 4.3	(103) 6.2	EBIT/Interest	(14) 2.5			(23) 7.7		(52) 9.1
1.9	.8	2.0			1.6			2.1	4.0
8.2	9.7	7.9	Net Profit + Depr., Dep.,						14.0
(27) 3.2	(38) 3.2	(26) 5.2	Amort./Cur. Mat. L/T/D					(16)	5.7
1.2	.7	2.8							3.8
.1	.2	.1			.1			.1	.2
.4	.4	.3	Fixed/Worth		.5			.3	.4
1.2	1.1	1.0			NM			.4	1.9
.8	.8	.9			1.2			.6	1.0
2.1	2.0	2.0	Debt/Worth		2.8			2.1	2.0
5.7	4.7	5.6			NM			4.2	6.4
67.9	42.1	48.3	% Profit Before Taxes/Tangible		88.0			41.1	57.4
(133) 31.5	(131) 22.3	(107) 23.9	Net Worth	(13) 18.9			(26)	22.1	(51) 24.8
11.9	1.6	4.9			6.4			7.0	12.8
20.0	15.9	18.0	% Profit Before Taxes/Total		13.3			18.9	21.3
9.0	7.2	7.4	Assets		5.7			5.7	9.5
2.0	-.6	1.8			1.4			2.0	3.4
67.1	64.0	88.4			134.2			87.9	71.2
30.6	30.0	38.9	Sales/Net Fixed Assets		48.9			38.2	30.6
15.1	11.2	12.3			23.5			18.4	11.2
4.4	4.5	5.1			6.5			5.1	5.1
3.0	3.0	3.3	Sales/Total Assets		4.0			3.4	3.2
2.2	2.2	2.2			2.4			2.3	2.1
.5	.5	.4			.2			.4	.5
(121) .9	(125) 1.0	(100) .8	% Depr., Dep., Amort./Sales	(12) .6			(26)	.6	(49) 1.1
1.7	1.6	1.4			1.1			1.2	1.5
1.6	1.5	1.1						1.0	
(41) 3.5	(53) 3.7	(40) 2.4	% Officers', Directors', Owners' Comp/Sales				(13)	1.9	
6.9	7.4	5.5						4.9	
12560259M	11705218M	10415017M	Net Sales ($)	2715M	31526M	27291M	47676M	427103M	9878706M
4694180M	4365339M	3790794M	Total Assets ($)	1084M	9048M	12116M	14494M	134707M	3619345M

M = $ thousand   MM = $ million
See Pages 11 through 21 for Explanation of Ratios and Data

Current Data Sorted By Assets   Comparative Historical Data

	0-500M	500M-2MM	2-10MM	10-50MM	50-100MM	100-250MM	Type of Statement	4/1/00-3/31/01 ALL	4/1/01-3/31/02 ALL
			4	4		1	Unqualified	5	8
		4	15	2			Reviewed	18	13
	9	10	8				Compiled	38	29
	4	6	2				Tax Returns	20	10
	4	9	7	4	1		Other	27	27
	31 (4/1-9/30/04)			63 (10/1/04-3/31/05)					
	17	29	36	10	1	1	**NUMBER OF STATEMENTS**	108	87
	%	%	%	%	%	%	**ASSETS**	%	%
	10.3	9.4	8.7	7.6			Cash & Equivalents	8.7	9.8
	4.5	6.4	8.6	10.7			Trade Receivables (net)	8.1	7.8
	18.8	16.1	16.7	14.8			Inventory	16.9	16.8
	.9	1.2	2.5	2.4			All Other Current	1.7	1.9
	34.6	33.1	36.6	35.4			Total Current	35.5	36.3
	50.6	57.6	52.0	54.3			Fixed Assets (net)	52.2	50.7
	2.9	4.2	5.3	4.9			Intangibles (net)	5.0	4.7
	11.8	5.2	6.2	5.4			All Other Non-Current	7.3	8.3
	100.0	100.0	100.0	100.0			Total	100.0	100.0
							LIABILITIES		
	35.6	10.4	5.9	4.1			Notes Payable-Short Term	7.8	8.7
	10.6	8.4	9.0	5.7			Cur. Mat.-L/T/D	8.1	9.1
	10.5	16.5	15.1	21.7			Trade Payables	13.0	12.8
	.4	.2	.1	.1			Income Taxes Payable	.2	.2
	20.1	9.7	6.7	10.1			All Other Current	8.9	9.3
	77.0	45.2	36.8	41.7			Total Current	38.0	40.2
	31.5	27.9	27.9	29.6			Long-Term Debt	31.6	28.6
	.0	.3	.5	2.0			Deferred Taxes	.5	.5
	2.4	7.7	2.8	21.4			All Other Non-Current	7.0	6.9
	-11.0	18.9	31.9	5.3			Net Worth	22.9	23.8
	100.0	100.0	100.0	100.0			Total Liabilities & Net Worth	100.0	100.0
							INCOME DATA		
	100.0	100.0	100.0	100.0			Net Sales	100.0	100.0
	48.0	47.8	51.0	43.0			Gross Profit	46.5	44.4
	44.0	48.3	49.1	43.1			Operating Expenses	44.7	42.8
	4.0	-.5	1.9	-.1			Operating Profit	1.8	1.6
	.1	.1	-.1	1.5			All Other Expenses (net)	.6	.9
	3.9	-.6	2.0	-1.5			Profit Before Taxes	1.2	.7
							RATIOS		
	1.5	1.1	1.3	1.0			Current	1.5	1.5
	.5	.7	.9	.9				1.0	1.0
	.2	.4	.7	.6				.6	.5
	.6	.6	.6	.6			Quick	.8	.9
	(16) .1	.3	.4	.4				.4 (86) .4	
	.0	.1	.2	.3				.2	.2
	0 UND	1 306.4	3 142.3	3 133.2			Sales/Receivables	2 180.0	2 189.2
	0 UND	3 129.4	7 50.3	8 43.1				6 61.1	4 81.7
	6 65.6	8 46.2	17 21.7	20 18.6				13 31.7	12 31.7
	14 25.2	22 17.0	22 16.8	23 15.8			Cost of Sales/Inventory	23 15.8	23 15.6
	24 15.0	32 11.5	37 9.9	28 13.2				36 10.2	34 10.8
	49 7.5	46 8.0	51 7.2	35 10.4				50 7.3	49 7.4
	0 UND	17 21.6	18 20.3	35 10.5			Cost of Sales/Payables	17 21.2	16 22.3
	20 18.5	33 11.2	33 11.2	44 8.3				28 13.0	25 14.4
	31 11.7	43 8.4	49 7.5	67 5.4				50 7.4	41 8.8
	18.1	119.2	21.8	292.8			Sales/Working Capital	21.4	16.6
	-13.2	-44.4	-97.3	-60.7				-761.7	-415.0
	-5.3	-11.3	-22.9	-15.3				-17.2	-15.2
	2.1	3.1	6.8	1.7			EBIT/Interest	3.5	2.9
	(15) 1.2	(28) 1.5	2.6	1.2				(103) 1.6	(82) 1.4
	-.8	-4.6	1.0	-.5				.8	-.7
			2.4				Net Profit + Depr., Dep., Amort./Cur. Mat. L/T/D	6.4	2.6
		(13) 2.2						(20) 2.2	(20) 1.5
			1.5					1.0	.9
	.6	1.0	1.0	2.3			Fixed/Worth	1.1	1.1
	3.5	1.8	1.9	9.0				2.6	2.1
	-1.6	-5.2	3.6	NM				16.0	9.7
	.9	.9	1.2	2.2			Debt/Worth	1.3	1.3
	7.5	1.6	2.3	16.1				3.6	2.6
	-3.2	-7.3	5.2	NM				31.2	21.1
		25.7	39.3				% Profit Before Taxes/Tangible Net Worth	29.9	26.3
		(20) 3.0	(32) 15.0					(85) 15.3	(69) 10.5
		-6.5	.5					3.6	-2.3
	7.8	5.6	8.7	2.0			% Profit Before Taxes/Total Assets	7.5	8.3
	1.2	1.0	4.2	.5				2.5	1.9
	-2.2	-7.1	.0	-8.0				-1.2	-7.2
	13.4	10.4	8.1	8.0			Sales/Net Fixed Assets	8.4	10.4
	5.3	7.0	6.2	5.0				5.4	5.7
	3.4	5.4	3.6	4.0				3.5	3.5
	5.3	4.7	3.9	4.0			Sales/Total Assets	3.6	4.3
	2.7	3.6	3.1	3.6				2.8	2.7
	2.0	2.3	2.2	2.0				2.0	1.9
	1.8	3.5	3.2	1.7			% Depr., Dep., Amort./Sales	4.1	3.5
	(15) 5.2	(28) 4.1	4.8	3.2				(102) 5.9	(81) 5.2
	9.5	6.6	6.4	6.3				8.2	7.3
		2.6	1.0				% Officers', Directors', Owners' Comp/Sales	1.7	1.4
		(15) 3.9	(15) 2.4					(53) 3.6	(37) 4.1
		7.3	4.1					5.1	8.1
	21332M	104901M	412893M	526565M	182782M	72172M	Net Sales ($)	1161028M	2126596M
	5703M	28380M	140459M	182297M	68618M	186407M	Total Assets ($)	566898M	1022916M

M = $ thousand   MM = $ million
See Pages 11 through 21 for Explanation of Ratios and Data

Comparative Historical Data | **Current Data Sorted By Sales**

Current Data date ranges: 31 (4/1-9/30/04); 63 (10/1/04-3/31/05)

4/1/02-3/31/03 ALL	4/1/03-3/31/04 ALL	4/1/04-3/31/05 ALL	Type of Statement	0-1MM	1-3MM	3-5MM	5-10MM	10-25MM	25MM & OVER
10	12	9	Unqualified		1	2	5	2	6
23	23	21	Reviewed				1	11	2
29	44	27	Compiled	3	12	4	6	2	
15	22	12	Tax Returns	4	6	1	1		
33	32	25	Other	2	7	3	5	3	5
110	133	94	NUMBER OF STATEMENTS	9	26	10	18	18	13
%	%	%	**ASSETS**	%	%	%	%	%	%
8.1	9.1	9.0	Cash & Equivalents		8.3	12.4	12.7	5.7	7.8
7.2	6.6	7.3	Trade Receivables (net)		5.0	7.4	5.8	11.2	10.1
15.4	16.5	16.5	Inventory		17.8	14.2	16.6	21.6	13.2
3.1	1.7	1.8	All Other Current		1.6	3.0	2.1	1.6	2.4
33.8	34.0	34.6	Total Current		32.6	37.0	37.1	40.1	33.5
52.4	53.7	53.2	Fixed Assets (net)		58.9	51.3	51.4	48.5	50.9
6.6	4.9	5.4	Intangibles (net)		3.5	3.0	6.0	5.7	11.5
7.2	7.4	6.7	All Other Non-Current		5.1	8.7	5.5	5.6	4.1
100.0	100.0	100.0	Total		100.0	100.0	100.0	100.0	100.0
			LIABILITIES						
7.0	10.8	12.8	Notes Payable-Short Term		24.3	12.6	9.1	3.0	7.9
8.2	10.2	8.6	Cur. Mat.-L/T/D		9.6	6.7	8.6	8.8	5.4
12.6	13.2	15.2	Trade Payables		12.0	14.9	16.2	20.5	22.0
.3	.2	.2	Income Taxes Payable		.2	.6	.1	.1	.1
9.7	8.2	10.5	All Other Current		10.4	15.9	9.0	7.3	11.6
37.8	42.7	47.3	Total Current		56.4	50.6	43.0	39.7	47.0
31.7	29.4	28.5	Long-Term Debt		29.0	16.6	25.7	34.3	25.0
.8	.5	.5	Deferred Taxes		.0	.8	1.0	.1	1.6
9.3	10.0	7.0	All Other Non-Current		5.8	1.0	1.0	8.0	22.1
20.4	17.4	16.7	Net Worth		8.8	31.5	29.3	18.0	4.2
100.0	100.0	100.0	Total Liabilities & Net Worth		100.0	100.0	100.0	100.0	100.0
			INCOME DATA						
100.0	100.0	100.0	Net Sales		100.0	100.0	100.0	100.0	100.0
46.7	47.1	48.7	Gross Profit		48.8	54.4	49.4	45.6	46.7
44.8	46.0	47.4	Operating Expenses		49.5	53.1	47.1	45.1	46.5
1.9	1.1	1.3	Operating Profit		-.7	1.3	2.4	.5	.2
.5	.5	.3	All Other Expenses (net)		-.1	.0	-.1	-.2	2.6
1.3	.6	.9	Profit Before Taxes		-.6	1.3	2.4	.7	-2.4
			RATIOS						
1.5	1.4	1.1			1.4	1.3	1.2	1.5	.9
.9	.9	.8	Current		.6	1.0	.9	1.0	.7
.6	.5	.5			.3	.7	.5	.7	.6
.7	.7	.6			.5	.8	.7	.6	.5
(109) .4	(131) .3	(93) .3	Quick		.5	.5	.3	.4	.4
.2	.1	.1			.1	.3	.1	.2	.2
1 342.1	0 991.3	1 275.9			0 UND	3 135.4	1 293.0	3 108.7	3 126.2
4 94.0	3 128.6	5 69.1	Sales/Receivables		2 150.5	6 61.5	3 139.3	9 41.6	9 40.3
12 29.4	10 35.1	14 26.5			11 33.3	10 38.2	15 24.4	14 25.2	19 19.3
24 15.2	21 17.4	21 17.1			19 19.7	21 17.2	23 16.1	23 16.2	23 15.9
35 10.6	33 11.1	32 11.5	Cost of Sales/Inventory		40 9.0	32 11.5	34 10.8	38 9.7	29 12.7
47 7.7	51 7.1	48 7.7			51 7.1	35 10.3	50 7.4	67 5.5	32 11.3
12 30.0	13 28.7	17 21.0			7 49.4	1 254.7	22 16.9	17 21.1	33 11.1
27 13.6	27 13.3	32 11.4	Cost of Sales/Payables		23 15.7	30 12.1	34 10.7	36 10.1	38 9.6
46 8.0	47 7.7	47 7.8			39 9.4	40 9.1	47 7.7	65 5.6	60 6.1
29.8	34.9	92.3			24.0	46.6	57.1	19.8	-119.4
-93.3	-43.6	-52.9	Sales/Working Capital		-22.0	-240.2	NM	NM	-36.7
-17.7	-12.2	-12.3			-8.9	-19.9	-11.0	-37.9	-15.2
3.6	3.8	4.7			2.5	7.1	6.2	8.3	1.5
(106) 1.6	(128) 1.3	(91) 1.5	EBIT/Interest	(25)	1.1	2.4	(17) 1.7	2.4	1.0
.2	-.4	-.1			-3.7	-1.2	.9	-.2	-.3
3.3	2.8	3.1	Net Profit + Depr., Dep.,						
(24) 1.8	(24) 1.4	(23) 1.9	Amort./Cur. Mat. L/T/D						
1.2	.9	1.3							
1.2	1.2	1.1			1.1	.8	.9	1.2	3.0
2.7	3.0	2.2	Fixed/Worth		2.3	1.2	1.7	1.9	10.2
-16.7	-8.8	-23.8			-1.3	1.9	93.6	4.5	-2.5
1.4	1.3	1.3			.8	.6	1.3	1.5	4.4
4.4	3.7	2.8	Debt/Worth		3.2	1.1	1.9	2.5	17.5
-27.6	-18.0	-47.2			-3.3	2.0	121.4	6.2	-5.5
26.2	35.7	24.8	% Profit Before Taxes/Tangible		20.6		28.5	44.6	
(77) 7.6	(95) 6.7	(69) 6.5	Net Worth	(17)	-1.5	(15) 16.9	(15) 15.6		
-4.7	-8.1	-4.1			-9.3		-1.0	4.1	
8.2	7.6	7.2	% Profit Before Taxes/Total		5.6	8.0	12.8	7.7	2.0
2.0	1.2	2.0	Assets		.6	2.2	2.7	4.2	.0
-2.9	-4.0	-4.0			-3.1	-5.7	-.1	-4.3	-10.0
9.5	9.0	9.3			10.4	9.2	11.6	13.4	8.1
5.0	5.2	6.3	Sales/Net Fixed Assets		6.4	6.7	5.8	7.1	7.6
3.5	3.4	3.7			2.4	4.8	3.7	5.9	4.4
4.2	4.0	4.2			4.5	5.0	4.4	4.4	4.1
2.9	2.9	3.3	Sales/Total Assets		3.2	3.6	3.1	3.4	3.7
1.9	1.9	2.2			1.8	2.2	2.4	3.0	2.3
3.6	3.8	3.1			4.0	2.9	3.6	2.9	1.8
(104) 5.4	(121) 5.4	(90) 4.6	% Depr., Dep., Amort./Sales		5.8	4.0	4.1	4.3	(12) 3.2
7.6	8.3	6.8			10.4	7.0	5.7	5.3	4.8
1.5	1.8	2.1	% Officers', Directors',		2.9				
(50) 4.0	(56) 4.0	(41) 3.8	Owners' Comp/Sales	(12)	4.9				
5.4	7.3	13.1			13.1				
1466779M	2092648M	1320645M	Net Sales ($)	4615M	51348M	36766M	130948M	281722M	815246M
792182M	1185522M	611864M	Total Assets ($)	2695M	25558M	13330M	49244M	86038M	434999M

M = $ thousand   MM = $ million
See Pages 11 through 21 for Explanation of Ratios and Data

Current Data Sorted By Assets

Comparative Historical Data

							Type of Statement		
	4	9	16	3	4		Unqualified	33	20
3	31	53	10	1			Reviewed	90	70
10	37	22					Compiled	77	61
18	11	2					Tax Returns	21	26
4	11	17	13	1	3		Other	36	37
	151 (4/1-9/30/04)		132 (10/1/04-3/31/05)					4/1/00-3/31/01	4/1/01-3/31/02
0-500M	500M-2MM	2-10MM	10-50MM	50-100MM	100-250MM			ALL	ALL
35	94	103	39	5	7		NUMBER OF STATEMENTS	257	214
%	%	%	%	%	%		ASSETS	%	%
17.7	15.9	11.5	5.9				Cash & Equivalents	11.2	16.5
24.5	28.9	28.7	29.3				Trade Receivables (net)	29.0	23.2
14.9	11.6	10.7	8.7				Inventory	10.6	10.9
1.5	1.8	1.8	3.4				All Other Current	2.9	2.5
58.6	58.2	52.6	47.4				Total Current	53.7	53.1
25.1	28.0	29.9	36.0				Fixed Assets (net)	30.8	30.2
5.5	7.4	7.5	8.2				Intangibles (net)	6.9	7.7
10.7	6.4	10.0	8.5				All Other Non-Current	8.6	9.1
100.0	100.0	100.0	100.0				Total	100.0	100.0
							LIABILITIES		
14.6	7.8	10.0	6.9				Notes Payable-Short Term	9.1	6.1
8.2	5.6	3.7	3.6				Cur. Mat.-L/T/D	4.5	4.7
18.0	15.1	17.3	20.5				Trade Payables	18.9	14.6
.0	.1	.1	.4				Income Taxes Payable	.3	.4
20.6	17.5	18.2	15.1				All Other Current	14.3	19.8
61.5	46.1	49.3	46.4				Total Current	47.2	45.6
24.4	18.9	13.3	22.6				Long-Term Debt	20.2	19.8
.1	.5	.5	1.1				Deferred Taxes	.5	.5
4.8	6.7	5.0	4.1				All Other Non-Current	6.6	7.6
9.2	27.8	31.9	25.8				Net Worth	25.5	26.5
100.0	100.0	100.0	100.0				Total Liabilities & Net Worth	100.0	100.0
							INCOME DATA		
100.0	100.0	100.0	100.0				Net Sales	100.0	100.0
22.0	21.7	20.5	16.7				Gross Profit	20.8	22.2
21.8	21.3	19.4	16.3				Operating Expenses	19.3	20.5
.2	.5	1.1	.5				Operating Profit	1.4	1.7
−.1	.0	−.2	.0				All Other Expenses (net)	.3	.1
.3	.5	1.3	.5				Profit Before Taxes	1.2	1.5
							RATIOS		
2.1	1.9	1.4	1.3					1.7	1.7
1.2	1.2	1.1	1.0				Current	1.1	1.1
.8	.9	.8	.8					.8	.8
1.3	1.5	1.1	1.0					1.3	1.3
.8	.8	.8	.8				Quick	.9	.9
.4	.6	.5	.6					.6	.6
0 UND	12 29.4	15 24.8	16 23.0					13 27.7	12 31.6
14 26.0	22 16.9	25 14.8	21 17.5				Sales/Receivables	25 14.4	19 19.4
30 12.2	34 10.9	34 10.9	34 10.8					35 10.5	27 13.7
1 710.4	4 85.7	4 86.1	5 78.4					5 72.5	4 82.0
6 60.4	9 39.3	11 33.9	9 40.0				Cost of Sales/Inventory	10 37.4	9 38.5
11 33.3	15 24.1	19 19.2	14 25.8					16 22.9	16 22.6
0 UND	7 55.6	10 37.3	11 33.1					12 30.8	8 47.5
8 43.6	12 30.2	16 23.5	17 20.9				Cost of Sales/Payables	17 20.9	13 27.9
22 16.9	24 15.3	24 15.0	30 12.2					27 13.7	19 18.7
15.0	19.8	25.8	34.1					17.4	19.5
134.0	49.3	91.8	999.8				Sales/Working Capital	71.8	87.8
−47.3	−80.1	−33.9	−45.7					−51.5	−50.3
4.1	5.5	9.5	5.3					5.7	6.0
(30) 1.7	(85) 2.5	(92) 3.0	(37) 2.8				EBIT/Interest	(237) 2.3	(198) 2.6
−1.4	.3	1.5	1.7					1.0	1.3
	3.7	3.1	3.2				Net Profit + Depr., Dep.,	4.4	3.9
(28)	1.6	(37) 1.9	(17) 1.6				Amort./Cur. Mat. L /T/D	(91) 2.1	(72) 2.1
	.5	1.3	1.1					1.0	1.6
.3	.5	.5	1.0					.6	.5
.7	1.3	1.4	1.9				Fixed/Worth	1.6	1.5
−6.4	13.5	3.5	8.4					134.2	12.5
1.3	1.4	1.4	2.3					1.2	1.4
2.6	3.2	2.8	4.7				Debt/Worth	3.1	3.2
−26.2	41.5	14.4	19.0					447.1	29.3
40.1	27.0	46.6	31.8				% Profit Before Taxes/Tangible	36.0	42.2
(25) .0	(72) 7.5	(90) 13.9	(32) 16.9				Net Worth	(196) 15.7	(167) 19.3
−11.2	−2.9	4.3	3.8					3.1	5.2
8.3	8.8	8.5	6.8				% Profit Before Taxes/Total	9.2	11.3
1.1	3.3	4.0	3.5				Assets	3.9	4.6
−6.5	−.8	1.0	1.0					.1	1.1
104.8	34.0	35.3	22.5					28.4	27.4
38.0	21.1	17.0	13.7				Sales/Net Fixed Assets	15.3	16.6
20.1	10.2	8.0	6.8					8.8	9.3
11.4	6.4	5.4	5.9					5.6	6.1
6.7	4.4	3.7	4.0				Sales/Total Assets	4.0	4.2
4.6	3.1	2.8	2.8					3.0	3.1
.8	.9	1.0	.7					.8	1.0
(28) 1.2	(81) 1.6	(92) 1.5	(38) 1.2				% Depr., Dep., Amort./Sales	(243) 1.5	(201) 1.6
2.4	2.4	2.1	2.3					2.3	2.5
1.5	1.4	.7	.2				% Officers', Directors',	1.5	1.2
(26) 5.0	(68) 2.6	(59) 1.5	(10) .6				Owners' Comp/Sales	(127) 2.6	(127) 2.6
7.9	4.9	2.9	1.4					5.1	5.3
73248M	518703M	2143815M	3262928M	1584359M	1966391M		Net Sales ($)	10346540M	7796994M
9162M	110634M	476268M	758422M	341538M	1081276M		Total Assets ($)	2315204M	2003462M

© RMA 2005

M = $ thousand   MM = $ million
See Pages 11 through 21 for Explanation of Ratios and Data

Comparative Historical Data | Current Data Sorted By Sales

			Type of Statement	0-1MM	1-3MM	3-5MM	5-10MM	10-25MM	25MM & OVER
44	33	36	Unqualified		2		2	5	27
99	96	98	Reviewed	3	3	11	26	35	20
65	90	69	Compiled	3	12	14	21	14	5
34	30	31	Tax Returns	3	10	13	3	1	1
32	33	49	Other	2	5	7	6	5	24
4/1/02-3/31/03 ALL	4/1/03-3/31/04 ALL	4/1/04-3/31/05 ALL		151 (4/1-9/30/04)			132 (10/1/04-3/31/05)		
274	282	283	**NUMBER OF STATEMENTS**	11	32	45	58	60	77
%	%	%	**ASSETS**	%	%	%	%	%	%
12.7	14.7	12.7	Cash & Equivalents	20.2	15.4	14.3	18.2	10.5	7.0
25.0	26.4	28.0	Trade Receivables (net)	14.4	22.9	27.0	27.9	30.7	30.6
10.5	9.4	11.2	Inventory	18.9	12.4	12.5	12.1	11.1	8.3
3.1	2.9	2.1	All Other Current	.0	1.0	2.0	2.3	1.6	3.1
51.3	53.4	53.9	Total Current	53.6	51.7	55.8	60.4	53.8	49.1
32.0	29.5	29.7	Fixed Assets (net)	32.1	31.0	27.1	23.8	31.7	33.3
7.3	8.0	7.9	Intangibles (net)	4.4	8.3	8.0	7.4	7.0	9.3
9.5	9.1	8.5	All Other Non-Current	9.9	9.1	9.2	8.4	7.4	8.4
100.0	100.0	100.0	Total	100.0	100.0	100.0	100.0	100.0	100.0
			LIABILITIES						
8.6	7.9	9.3	Notes Payable-Short Term	15.6	5.4	14.0	7.8	10.9	7.1
5.1	4.1	4.8	Cur. Mat.-L/T/D	16.4	6.0	6.3	3.8	4.0	3.3
16.1	15.4	16.8	Trade Payables	10.9	12.8	17.4	14.3	17.5	20.5
.1	.2	.1	Income Taxes Payable	.0	.1	.1	.0	.2	.3
18.6	18.1	17.7	All Other Current	25.8	12.8	19.8	23.8	14.7	15.0
48.6	45.6	48.8	Total Current	68.7	37.0	57.7	49.7	47.3	46.0
18.9	18.0	18.1	Long-Term Debt	25.5	27.7	20.7	11.9	16.2	17.6
.6	.5	.6	Deferred Taxes	.2	.5	.4	.5	.6	1.0
4.3	5.4	5.6	All Other Non-Current	.5	8.6	8.2	5.8	3.8	4.9
27.6	30.6	26.9	Net Worth	5.2	26.2	13.1	32.2	32.1	30.4
100.0	100.0	100.0	Total Liabilities & Net Worth	100.0	100.0	100.0	100.0	100.0	100.0
			INCOME DATA						
100.0	100.0	100.0	Net Sales	100.0	100.0	100.0	100.0	100.0	100.0
23.1	21.7	20.6	Gross Profit	24.4	27.0	21.8	22.0	20.3	15.7
22.2	20.0	19.8	Operating Expenses	30.3	26.5	21.3	20.3	19.5	14.5
.8	1.8	.8	Operating Profit	-5.9	.5	.6	1.7	.8	1.2
.1	.0	-.1	All Other Expenses (net)	.3	-.2	.3	-.5	.2	-.1
.7	1.7	.8	Profit Before Taxes	-6.2	.7	.3	2.2	.6	1.3
			RATIOS						
1.5	1.8	1.6		1.9	2.8	1.8	1.7	1.5	1.4
1.1	1.1	1.1	Current	1.1	1.3	1.1	1.1	1.1	1.1
.8	.9	.8		.6	.8	.8	.8	.9	.8
1.1	1.4	1.2		1.1	1.9	1.2	1.4	1.3	1.1
.8	.8	.8	Quick	.7	.8	.8	.9	.8	.8
.5	.6	.6		.1	.5	.5	.6	.6	.5
12 30.3	13 28.7	13 29.0		0 UND	10 36.3	6 59.3	15 24.2	16 22.2	13 29.1
22 16.8	21 17.0	23 16.2	Sales/Receivables	9 41.5	19 18.7	21 17.2	25 14.5	24 15.0	22 16.6
33 10.9	33 11.0	34 10.9		34 10.7	31 11.8	39 9.3	33 10.9	33 11.0	33 11.1
5 76.9	4 93.7	4 86.7		2 205.7	3 135.3	4 95.0	5 77.1	5 69.3	3 121.2
11 34.2	9 42.5	10 37.9	Cost of Sales/Inventory	11 33.3	13 28.2	9 40.4	10 36.3	11 34.5	8 44.6
20 18.6	15 23.8	17 21.9		182 2.0	25 14.4	16 23.1	16 22.6	19 19.6	13 27.2
11 34.8	9 42.6	8 43.7		1 308.5	4 99.2	4 90.1	8 44.4	10 35.2	11 34.4
17 21.5	14 25.4	15 25.1	Cost of Sales/Payables	26 13.9	10 38.3	13 27.6	11 31.8	16 22.8	16 23.3
26 14.2	22 16.5	24 15.1		40 9.0	23 15.8	28 12.9	22 16.9	24 15.0	24 15.3
18.9	16.5	22.4		15.0	10.8	22.2	14.5	27.9	31.0
137.2	90.1	104.8	Sales/Working Capital	440.0	95.7	90.3	79.6	67.5	152.4
-29.9	-58.4	-47.3		-7.8	-45.2	-31.1	-37.1	-67.6	-50.5
4.5	7.9	5.9			7.6	3.4	11.0	4.2	8.3
(253) 1.7	(262) 3.2	(256) 2.8	EBIT/Interest		(31) 3.5	(41) 1.1	(52) 4.2	(56) 1.9	(71) 3.3
.1	1.5	1.2			-.1	-.5	1.8	1.2	1.9
2.8	4.9	3.5				2.8	5.3	3.1	3.2
(93) 1.9	(94) 2.3	(92) 1.7	Net Profit + Depr., Dep., Amort./Cur. Mat. L/T/D			(13) .6	(16) 2.2	(28) 2.2	(27) 1.8
.8	1.4	1.0				-.1	1.3	1.1	1.2
.5	.5	.5		.5	.4	.7	.4	.6	.8
1.4	1.3	1.5	Fixed/Worth	.8	1.5	2.1	1.1	1.4	1.6
9.2	6.1	6.5		-.8	NM	-.9	7.7	3.4	3.9
1.3	1.1	1.4		.8	1.3	1.7	1.2	1.3	2.0
3.1	2.9	3.3	Debt/Worth	2.0	3.4	5.2	2.5	2.7	3.3
29.6	15.9	23.5		-2.7	NM	-7.1	17.6	12.7	9.0
22.3	42.0	34.0			43.7	18.6	53.5	27.0	41.3
(216) 8.6	(225) 17.0	(228) 11.6	% Profit Before Taxes/Tangible Net Worth	(24) 10.8	(30) 3.2	(48) 15.7	(52) 8.8	(67) 19.7	
-1.9	5.1	1.0		-18.8	-13.9	4.6	2.8	5.1	
5.8	10.2	7.9		.0	12.6	5.7	12.4	6.4	7.7
1.9	4.4	3.6	% Profit Before Taxes/Total Assets	-2.1	4.6	.7	4.8	2.0	4.4
-2.5	1.3	.2		-19.2	-3.5	-2.7	1.3	.6	1.5
25.1	30.4	35.2		56.8	37.6	35.9	36.8	28.5	35.0
14.0	16.9	18.9	Sales/Net Fixed Assets	13.2	15.4	24.3	21.0	15.5	16.3
7.4	8.7	9.3		7.8	9.7	12.3	9.8	9.0	7.9
5.1	5.6	6.2		11.0	4.9	8.5	5.2	5.9	6.6
3.6	3.9	4.2	Sales/Total Assets	4.8	4.4	4.5	3.8	4.0	4.6
2.7	3.0	3.1		1.1	3.0	3.1	2.9	3.2	3.1
1.1	1.0	.9			1.1	.9	.9	1.1	.4
(260) 1.8	(261) 1.5	(249) 1.4	% Depr., Dep., Amort./Sales		(29) 1.9	(40) 1.5	(50) 1.5	(55) 1.4	(69) 1.1
2.8	2.5	2.3			2.7	2.4	2.4	2.2	1.9
1.3	1.0	.9			4.0	1.2	1.5	.8	.3
(144) 2.7	(139) 2.3	(164) 2.0	% Officers', Directors', Owners' Comp/Sales		(18) 5.8	(37) 2.2	(42) 2.6	(36) 1.6	(23) .6
4.8	4.5	4.7			7.2	4.8	4.1	2.9	.8
9141961M	10788597M	9549444M	Net Sales ($)	5547M	63958M	175873M	426055M	921367M	7956644M
2676901M	3070118M	2777300M	Total Assets ($)	4480M	19971M	42214M	116208M	241731M	2352696M

M = $ thousand MM = $ million
See Pages 11 through 21 for Explanation of Ratios and Data

Current Data Sorted By Assets   **Comparative Historical Data**

Type of Statement	0-500M	500M-2MM	2-10MM	10-50MM	50-100MM	100-250MM		ALL 4/1/00-3/31/01	ALL 4/1/01-3/31/02
Unqualified		1	3	10	1	2		5	11
Reviewed	1	2	13	5				16	9
Compiled		14	9					26	26
Tax Returns	5	5	4					2	5
Other	2	4	10	1				13	14
		36 (4/1-9/30/04)			56 (10/1/04-3/31/05)			4/1/00-3/31/01	4/1/01-3/31/02
NUMBER OF STATEMENTS	8	26	39	16	1	2		62	65

	0-500M	500M-2MM	2-10MM	10-50MM	50-100MM	100-250MM		ALL 01	ALL 02
	%	%	%	%	%	%	**ASSETS**	%	%
		7.3	10.2	6.0			Cash & Equivalents	6.7	9.3
		24.4	20.4	18.9			Trade Receivables (net)	20.1	18.8
		12.9	10.8	8.3			Inventory	11.6	13.0
		3.6	2.4	2.7			All Other Current	2.3	3.4
		48.2	43.8	35.9			Total Current	40.6	44.5
		36.5	40.9	54.0			Fixed Assets (net)	45.2	42.5
		6.6	4.9	5.2			Intangibles (net)	5.1	3.7
		8.7	10.4	4.8			All Other Non-Current	9.0	9.3
		100.0	100.0	100.0			Total	100.0	100.0
							LIABILITIES		
		7.1	7.7	5.1			Notes Payable-Short Term	6.6	5.4
		5.3	3.4	6.8			Cur. Mat.-L/T/D	5.2	3.9
		19.6	14.8	9.6			Trade Payables	15.2	15.0
		.2	.1	.3			Income Taxes Payable	.2	.1
		9.1	11.5	9.6			All Other Current	9.8	12.1
		41.3	37.4	31.4			Total Current	37.1	36.5
		23.4	18.7	23.4			Long-Term Debt	25.5	26.8
		.4	.4	4.0			Deferred Taxes	1.3	.9
		11.4	6.4	2.4			All Other Non-Current	4.0	4.5
		23.6	37.1	38.8			Net Worth	32.2	31.3
		100.0	100.0	100.0			Total Liabilities & Net Worth	100.0	100.0
							INCOME DATA		
		100.0	100.0	100.0			Net Sales	100.0	100.0
		34.3	34.3	37.1			Gross Profit	35.6	33.7
		31.8	31.8	33.9			Operating Expenses	33.1	30.2
		2.5	2.5	3.2			Operating Profit	2.5	3.6
		.5	.3	.3			All Other Expenses (net)	−.2	1.1
		2.0	2.2	2.9			Profit Before Taxes	2.7	2.5
							RATIOS		
		1.8	2.4	1.5				1.5	2.1
		1.1	1.4	1.2			Current	1.1	1.4
		.8	.7	1.0				.7	.8
		1.1	1.5	1.1				1.0	1.5
		.8	.9	.8			Quick	.7	.8
		.5	.5	.5				.5	.4
		14 25.7	14 25.6	21 17.5				13 27.9	12 30.3
		30 12.1	27 13.4	28 13.0			Sales/Receivables	25 14.6	19 19.0
		56 6.5	46 7.9	39 9.5				49 7.5	32 11.6
		8 47.2	9 41.1	13 28.5				12 31.1	8 43.2
		21 17.1	17 21.0	21 17.8			Cost of Sales/Inventory	22 16.6	20 18.4
		43 8.5	30 12.0	41 8.9				40 9.2	38 9.6
		19 19.0	13 28.6	17 20.9				14 26.0	8 43.4
		29 12.5	20 17.9	26 13.9			Cost of Sales/Payables	33 11.1	17 21.4
		55 6.7	45 8.1	39 9.0				51 7.1	30 12.2
		10.9	12.7	17.0				14.7	11.3
		77.4	41.9	50.6			Sales/Working Capital	99.2	27.0
		−36.0	−15.6	NM				−46.1	−32.6
		4.9	15.7	6.7				4.8	6.9
		(25) 2.7	(37) 4.0	(15) 3.0			EBIT/Interest	(58) 2.0	(61) 2.4
		.9	1.1	2.3				.8	1.1
							Net Profit + Depr., Dep.,	4.6	4.2
							Amort./Cur. Mat. L/T/D	(17) 2.3 (20) 2.5	
								1.3	1.9
		.5	.5	1.2				.8	.6
		2.0	1.6	2.0			Fixed/Worth	1.9	1.7
		−3.8	5.5	3.1				6.5	6.0
		.7	.8	1.0				1.3	.8
		4.9	2.0	2.6			Debt/Worth	2.7	2.1
		−9.3	18.7	4.3				9.6	12.9
		38.1	24.5	33.5			% Profit Before Taxes/Tangible	42.0	43.8
		(17) 12.3	(32) 11.1	19.9			Net Worth	(54) 12.0	(55) 21.2
		1.6	.6	11.0				−4.4	4.8
		9.2	12.2	7.7			% Profit Before Taxes/Total	10.0	14.9
		3.4	4.1	4.8			Assets	3.7	6.6
		−.2	.1	2.9				−.6	.5
		15.2	10.3	6.3				12.3	12.8
		7.5	6.2	3.5			Sales/Net Fixed Assets	6.4	7.2
		3.9	3.8	2.6				2.6	3.6
		3.8	3.2	2.7				3.6	4.2
		2.4	2.4	2.1			Sales/Total Assets	2.5	2.6
		1.6	1.6	1.4				1.7	1.9
		2.0	2.2	2.6				1.5	1.0
		(23) 3.3	4.4	3.7			% Depr., Dep., Amort./Sales	(58) 3.8	(54) 2.9
		7.5	5.8	5.2				6.4	4.6
		2.9	.9				% Officers', Directors',	1.3	1.3
		(11) 4.5	(17) 3.3				Owners' Comp/Sales	(27) 3.6	(21) 4.6
		6.3	5.9					11.4	6.8
	8285M	83431M	527694M	869337M	104910M	448600M	Net Sales ($)	870475M	1243826M
	2706M	29137M	165763M	351486M	74573M	345667M	Total Assets ($)	383589M	495602M

M = $ thousand   MM = $ million
See Pages 11 through 21 for Explanation of Ratios and Data

Comparative Historical Data / Current Data Sorted By Sales

Type of Statement									
Unqualified	9	16	17		1	1	2	1	12
Reviewed	21	25	21	1	1	3	3	6	7
Compiled	17	27	23		7	6	7	1	2
Tax Returns	6	18	14	3	7	2	1	1	
Other	16	17	17	2	3	3	5	3	1
	4/1/02-3/31/03 ALL	4/1/03-3/31/04 ALL	4/1/04-3/31/05 ALL	0-1MM	36 (4/1-9/30/04) 1-3MM	3-5MM	56 (10/1/04-3/31/05) 5-10MM	10-25MM	25MM & OVER
NUMBER OF STATEMENTS	69	103	92	6	19	15	18	12	22
ASSETS	%	%	%	%	%	%	%	%	%
Cash & Equivalents	8.3	9.3	8.6		9.5	10.6	10.2	8.0	6.7
Trade Receivables (net)	19.0	21.1	20.6		21.4	15.8	22.2	16.0	24.8
Inventory	9.8	10.8	12.1		18.4	10.9	9.7	16.4	8.2
All Other Current	2.4	2.1	2.6		3.4	2.8	2.0	2.1	3.2
Total Current	39.5	43.3	44.0		52.7	40.1	44.1	42.6	42.8
Fixed Assets (net)	46.5	42.1	42.2		35.0	37.9	38.7	48.2	46.9
Intangibles (net)	7.4	6.9	5.8		5.0	9.2	5.8	3.3	4.7
All Other Non-Current	6.6	7.7	8.0		7.3	12.8	11.5	5.9	5.5
Total	100.0	100.0	100.0		100.0	100.0	100.0	100.0	100.0
LIABILITIES									
Notes Payable-Short Term	5.9	7.4	6.5		6.9	4.6	8.8	8.6	5.6
Cur. Mat.-L/T/D	5.0	6.1	4.3		3.8	6.2	3.9	3.6	4.5
Trade Payables	13.9	14.7	15.1		16.1	13.3	14.5	16.1	15.1
Income Taxes Payable	.1	.3	.1		.2	.1	.0	.1	.2
All Other Current	8.3	10.2	10.4		8.1	9.1	10.5	15.1	8.7
Total Current	33.2	38.8	36.5		35.0	33.4	37.7	43.6	34.2
Long-Term Debt	21.3	22.7	23.0		21.3	17.6	26.4	16.0	19.2
Deferred Taxes	1.4	1.1	1.3		.0	.4	.8	.0	4.3
All Other Non-Current	5.0	7.4	8.4		16.1	9.1	2.8	7.0	2.9
Net Worth	39.1	30.0	30.9		27.6	39.5	32.3	33.4	39.3
Total Liabilities & Net Worth	100.0	100.0	100.0		100.0	100.0	100.0	100.0	100.0
INCOME DATA									
Net Sales	100.0	100.0	100.0		100.0	100.0	100.0	100.0	100.0
Gross Profit	39.9	36.3	35.2		38.4	37.0	36.3	35.0	29.2
Operating Expenses	36.6	33.2	32.4		36.8	34.0	33.6	30.8	27.2
Operating Profit	3.2	3.0	2.8		1.6	3.0	2.7	4.2	2.0
All Other Expenses (net)	.2	.4	.5		.4	.5	.1	.9	-.1
Profit Before Taxes	3.0	2.6	2.3		1.2	2.5	2.6	3.3	2.2
RATIOS									
Current	2.1	1.9	2.0		3.5	2.9	2.6	1.4	1.6
	1.4	1.2	1.3		1.5	1.1	1.5	1.0	1.4
	.8	.8	.9		1.0	.7	.6	.7	1.0
Quick	1.5	1.3	1.3		1.5	1.5	2.0	.7	1.2
	.8	.8	.8		.9	.9	1.1	.5	.9
	.4	.5	.5		.5	.5	.5	.5	.6
Sales/Receivables	15 24.3	16 22.9	16 22.3		13 28.5	19 19.3	21 17.7	12 29.9	18 20.1
	27 13.5	27 13.7	28 13.1		30 12.0	27 13.4	34 10.7	26 13.9	25 14.7
	43 8.5	42 8.7	41 8.9		55 6.7	33 11.0	51 7.2	39 9.3	38 9.7
Cost of Sales/Inventory	15 24.8	8 44.6	10 37.6		13 27.4	9 41.1	9 39.9	18 20.7	6 59.4
	24 15.3	21 17.1	20 18.3		21 17.8	23 15.6	14 26.5	25 14.5	16 23.4
	43 8.4	43 8.5	36 10.0		54 6.8	34 10.7	45 8.1	53 6.9	35 10.3
Cost of Sales/Payables	15 23.9	13 27.7	15 24.1		9 39.8	22 16.4	11 31.9	13 29.1	14 26.3
	27 13.3	30 12.2	27 13.7		26 14.3	26 14.0	30 12.2	22 16.3	23 16.0
	47 7.8	48 7.6	47 7.8		57 6.4	40 9.1	46 8.0	73 5.0	36 10.0
Sales/Working Capital	9.1	12.3	12.8		7.3	13.3	7.6	18.6	17.2
	26.2	47.7	37.2		17.4	125.2	13.3	NM	44.2
	-37.8	-30.7	-45.7		137.5	-11.4	-30.5	-11.0	247.5
EBIT/Interest	7.4	9.6	6.4		5.6	14.7	7.2	18.6	7.0
	(60) 2.8	(90) 3.1	(87) 3.2		(17) 2.7	1.9	(17) 2.7	(10) 4.1	3.8
	.8	1.3	1.2		.2	.6	.4	3.0	2.5
Net Profit + Depr., Dep., Amort./Cur. Mat. L/T/D	3.3	4.4	5.8						4.8
	(27) 2.4	(28) 2.5	(30) 2.1					(13)	2.2
	1.6	1.6	1.3						1.1
Fixed/Worth	.7	.6	.6		.3	.5	.6	.9	.7
	1.5	1.8	1.7		1.5	1.6	2.0	2.1	1.6
	3.1	5.2	8.4		-6.8	-8.9	-7.1	4.3	2.3
Debt/Worth	.8	1.1	.7		.3	.5	.8	1.3	1.0
	1.9	2.6	2.5		3.1	1.2	2.3	2.0	2.3
	5.1	13.0	20.2		-11.8	-19.6	-38.8	10.7	3.5
% Profit Before Taxes/Tangible Net Worth	38.1	41.8	27.7		41.4	21.5	26.1	28.9	36.2
	(62) 15.0	(84) 19.3	(72) 13.4		(14) 11.9	(11) 4.9	(13) 12.3	(11) 15.7	15.8
	5.4	8.3	2.1		1.1	-1.8	-8.4	6.7	10.6
% Profit Before Taxes/Total Assets	10.2	11.1	9.8		9.7	10.9	11.4	11.7	8.9
	4.6	5.7	4.0		1.9	4.1	3.1	5.3	4.2
	-.3	1.1	.5		.0	-1.2	-1.0	2.8	2.7
Sales/Net Fixed Assets	7.8	11.2	10.1		16.8	10.3	9.3	10.6	11.0
	4.7	5.4	6.0		6.4	7.9	6.2	5.9	4.3
	2.6	2.6	2.9		3.6	3.9	4.7	2.7	2.7
Sales/Total Assets	3.0	3.2	3.2		2.6	3.7	3.2	4.0	4.2
	2.1	2.1	2.3		2.3	2.0	2.5	2.5	2.6
	1.6	1.5	1.6		1.6	1.7	1.4	1.6	1.6
% Depr., Dep., Amort./Sales	3.3	2.4	2.3		2.1	2.8	2.8	2.1	1.3
	(63) 5.1	(94) 4.4	(86) 4.1		(15) 6.4	(14) 4.6	4.3	4.2	2.9
	6.5	6.3	6.0		8.6	5.8	6.0	6.0	4.8
% Officers', Directors', Owners' Comp/Sales	1.7	.9	1.6		2.9				
	(29) 3.5	(39) 3.0	(36) 3.3		(11) 3.4				
	5.9	6.0	6.1		4.5				
Net Sales ($)	1187733M	2594680M	2042257M	4589M	37080M	62816M	121285M	198398M	1618089M
Total Assets ($)	712847M	1163755M	969332M	2583M	19182M	32002M	57239M	95218M	763108M

© RMA 2005

M = $ thousand   MM = $ million

See Pages 11 through 21 for Explanation of Ratios and Data

Current Data Sorted By Assets   Comparative Historical Data

Type of Statement								Comp. Hist.	
	1	3	4		3	Unqualified		4	7
	4	5	2			Reviewed		5	2
8	9	7				Compiled		10	17
21	14	5				Tax Returns		2	5
6	11	7	6	1	1	Other		6	9
	16 (4/1-9/30/04)		102 (10/1/04-3/31/05)					4/1/00-3/31/01	4/1/01-3/31/02
0-500M	500M-2MM	2-10MM	10-50MM	50-100MM	100-250MM			ALL	ALL
35	39	27	12	1	4	**NUMBER OF STATEMENTS**		27	40
%	%	%	%	%	%	**ASSETS**		%	%
16.2	11.8	13.7	14.2			Cash & Equivalents		11.3	15.9
19.3	28.3	23.6	12.8			Trade Receivables (net)		21.4	17.8
29.1	25.0	24.6	23.5			Inventory		21.2	20.9
1.8	2.8	.9	3.8			All Other Current		9.8	4.8
66.3	67.9	62.8	54.3			Total Current		63.7	59.4
19.8	17.2	25.4	28.2			Fixed Assets (net)		23.6	26.6
7.0	7.3	5.3	9.2			Intangibles (net)		4.6	4.4
6.9	7.6	6.5	8.3			All Other Non-Current		8.0	9.7
100.0	100.0	100.0	100.0			Total		100.0	100.0
						LIABILITIES			
29.4	8.7	7.1	12.4			Notes Payable-Short Term		12.8	10.8
2.3	4.4	3.0	1.7			Cur. Mat.-L/T/D		4.9	7.0
33.7	22.3	21.9	7.3			Trade Payables		21.1	19.8
.2	.2	.1	.3			Income Taxes Payable		.9	.5
9.7	12.8	10.5	7.2			All Other Current		14.9	13.0
75.3	48.3	42.7	28.8			Total Current		54.6	51.0
28.2	16.7	18.2	8.6			Long-Term Debt		14.9	17.5
.0	.0	.0	.5			Deferred Taxes		.0	.2
10.3	5.6	5.7	2.2			All Other Non-Current		4.9	3.5
−13.8	29.4	33.4	59.9			Net Worth		25.6	27.9
100.0	100.0	100.0	100.0			Total Liabilities & Net Worth		100.0	100.0
						INCOME DATA			
100.0	100.0	100.0	100.0			Net Sales		100.0	100.0
51.3	38.0	32.6	50.7			Gross Profit		50.1	47.1
49.1	35.2	26.3	40.9			Operating Expenses		45.6	43.6
2.2	2.9	6.3	9.8			Operating Profit		4.5	3.5
1.4	.4	1.2	.5			All Other Expenses (net)		1.5	.8
.8	2.5	5.1	9.2			Profit Before Taxes		3.0	2.6
						RATIOS			
3.4	2.6	2.6	3.2					1.9	3.1
1.6	1.5	1.4	1.9			Current		1.1	1.4
.8	.9	.9	1.3					.7	.7
1.8	2.2	1.6	1.8					1.2	2.0
(34) .6	.8	.8	1.3			Quick		.6	.7
.2	.3	.5	.3					.3	.2
0 UND	1 326.7	6 60.6	2 153.5					3 111.1	1 251.3
11 34.7	26 14.0	25 14.3	14 25.9			Sales/Receivables		18 19.8	13 29.0
38 9.5	45 8.1	53 6.9	38 9.5					39 9.4	38 9.5
18 20.4	11 33.0	14 27.0	45 8.1					9 40.5	7 54.3
49 7.4	26 14.1	31 11.7	61 5.9			Cost of Sales/Inventory		34 10.8	32 11.4
104 3.5	57 6.4	77 4.7	122 3.0					104 3.5	63 5.8
0 UND	19 19.6	26 13.9	17 20.9					18 20.3	11 31.9
25 14.6	31 11.7	33 10.9	27 13.4			Cost of Sales/Payables		46 8.0	29 12.5
58 6.3	50 7.3	50 7.3	46 7.9					74 4.9	53 6.9
9.0	7.4	4.9	4.7					12.0	7.3
28.5	17.0	24.1	8.7			Sales/Working Capital		120.1	18.3
−20.3	−106.2	−42.5	31.3					−22.0	−49.4
11.4	9.8	34.8	54.6					9.3	4.8
(28) 2.3	(34) 2.7	(24) 5.7	(11) 31.1			EBIT/Interest		(22) 2.6	(32) 3.5
−1.5	.9	1.5	2.5					−.5	.8
						Net Profit + Depr., Dep., Amort./Cur. Mat. L /T/D			
.2	.1	.2	.1					.2	.2
1.8	.5	1.8	.5			Fixed/Worth		.5	1.0
−.3	−4.4	26.9	.9					5.2	16.3
1.4	.9	1.1	.3					.9	1.0
6.4	3.3	2.3	.8			Debt/Worth		4.6	2.0
−2.6	−9.6	41.4	1.9					26.2	217.2
208.1	46.1	51.9	33.5					91.4	76.9
(20) 66.7	(27) 26.8	(21) 36.9	23.4			% Profit Before Taxes/Tangible Net Worth		(23) 23.7	(31) 24.6
5.3	.6	2.9	5.6					5.9	6.0
23.7	15.0	24.0	25.0					30.6	18.8
3.1	3.1	4.8	11.9			% Profit Before Taxes/Total Assets		4.2	6.9
−12.5	−.6	1.2	1.4					−10.6	.4
238.0	146.3	48.0	28.9					72.3	40.8
25.7	42.9	17.7	19.1			Sales/Net Fixed Assets		16.5	18.7
12.1	14.1	4.8	2.5					5.9	6.3
7.0	4.8	4.7	2.3					5.2	4.1
4.4	3.7	2.3	1.8			Sales/Total Assets		3.1	2.9
2.6	2.5	1.6	1.0					2.0	2.4
.8	.4	.5	.1					.7	.4
(20) 1.6	(30) 1.1	(25) 1.3				% Depr., Dep., Amort./Sales		(20) 2.3	(34) 1.5
3.9	1.9	2.6						5.1	4.9
4.3	1.9	1.0						1.5	2.1
(18) 9.1	(21) 3.2	(14) 2.9				% Officers', Directors', Owners' Comp/Sales		(11) 8.4	(16) 5.0
14.1	5.5	7.3						9.5	10.9
28200M	207717M	364138M	538673M	272824M	1528122M	Net Sales ($)		1344809M	2104725M
7450M	48775M	110383M	278515M	71664M	642137M	Total Assets ($)		469241M	737075M

M = $ thousand   MM = $ million
See Pages 11 through 21 for Explanation of Ratios and Data

Comparative Historical Data | Current Data Sorted By Sales

	4/1/02-3/31/03 ALL	4/1/03-3/31/04 ALL	4/1/04-3/31/05 ALL	Type of Statement	0-1MM	1-3MM	3-5MM	5-10MM	10-25MM	25MM & OVER
	7	12	11	Unqualified		1	1	2	3	5
	8	8	11	Reviewed		1		2	4	3
	8	23	24	Compiled	4	4	5	4	1	
	17	29	40	Tax Returns	7	7	5	7	2	1
	18	25	32	Other	14	11	5	4	7	8
					16 (4/1-9/30/04)			102 (10/1/04-3/31/05)		
	58	97	118	**NUMBER OF STATEMENTS**	25	24	16	19	17	17
	%	%	%	**ASSETS**	%	%	%	%	%	%
	10.9	13.1	14.0	Cash & Equivalents	16.7	11.3	13.2	12.0	18.2	13.1
	19.4	27.3	22.3	Trade Receivables (net)	16.4	25.8	31.7	27.1	16.4	17.9
	21.5	22.8	26.1	Inventory	27.9	25.6	23.5	20.8	29.7	28.9
	5.2	5.2	2.2	All Other Current	1.6	1.2	1.2	4.0	2.1	3.7
	57.1	68.4	64.7	Total Current	62.6	63.9	69.6	63.8	66.4	63.6
	22.6	19.4	21.2	Fixed Assets (net)	22.9	22.5	16.1	22.0	19.8	22.3
	10.9	5.3	6.8	Intangibles (net)	8.5	7.3	7.7	5.4	1.5	9.5
	9.3	6.8	7.3	All Other Non-Current	6.0	6.3	6.6	8.8	12.3	4.6
	100.0	100.0	100.0	Total	100.0	100.0	100.0	100.0	100.0	100.0
				LIABILITIES						
	14.8	15.0	14.5	Notes Payable-Short Term	22.4	23.2	10.6	6.3	8.7	9.5
	7.2	2.4	3.2	Cur. Mat.-L/T/D	1.1	3.2	3.6	7.1	1.7	2.8
	20.2	23.7	23.7	Trade Payables	38.3	19.3	16.2	26.9	21.3	14.1
	.2	.5	.2	Income Taxes Payable	.2	.0	.4	.2	.1	.4
	14.4	14.2	10.8	All Other Current	8.2	8.7	6.7	10.1	20.7	12.5
	56.8	55.8	52.4	Total Current	70.1	54.4	37.5	50.6	52.4	39.3
	14.4	12.2	19.6	Long-Term Debt	29.1	33.1	15.5	13.9	5.5	10.8
	.4	.3	.1	Deferred Taxes	.0	.0	.0	.0	.1	.4
	9.2	8.5	6.4	All Other Non-Current	5.8	16.7	2.8	3.8	3.4	2.3
	19.2	23.2	21.5	Net Worth	-5.0	-4.2	44.2	31.7	38.6	47.2
	100.0	100.0	100.0	Total Liabilities & Net Worth	100.0	100.0	100.0	100.0	100.0	100.0
				INCOME DATA						
	100.0	100.0	100.0	Net Sales	100.0	100.0	100.0	100.0	100.0	100.0
	45.3	41.0	42.5	Gross Profit	53.3	42.4	36.0	37.2	43.4	38.1
	42.1	36.0	37.9	Operating Expenses	49.3	42.3	30.4	31.0	35.9	31.8
	3.2	5.0	4.6	Operating Profit	4.0	.0	5.6	6.2	7.5	6.3
	.8	.9	.9	All Other Expenses (net)	2.7	.1	.1	1.1	.5	.1
	2.4	4.1	3.7	Profit Before Taxes	1.3	.0	5.5	5.0	7.0	6.3
				RATIOS						
	2.3	2.5	2.8	Current	2.4	3.5	3.6	2.0	2.5	2.9
	1.0	1.4	1.7		1.5	1.7	2.1	1.5	1.7	1.5
	.6	.9	.9		.7	.9	1.0	.8	.9	1.0
	.9	1.5	1.8	Quick	1.7	2.4	2.3	1.6	1.5	1.5
	.6	.8	(117) .8		.5	(23) .8	1.4	.9	.7	.7
	.3	.4	.3		.1	.4	.7	.3	.4	.4
	4 86.2	8 47.8	2 216.0	Sales/Receivables	0 UND	0 UND	20 18.0	1 348.5	3 119.5	2 189.7
	23 16.1	23 16.1	21 17.1		13 28.3	28 12.8	39 9.3	26 14.0	6 56.5	14 26.8
	36 10.2	51 7.1	44 8.3		34 10.9	51 7.1	52 6.9	53 6.9	28 12.9	43 8.4
	14 26.1	9 39.6	17 21.8	Cost of Sales/Inventory	13 27.3	17 20.9	12 30.8	14 27.0	12 29.6	29 12.6
	43 8.4	33 10.9	41 8.9		66 5.5	40 9.2	34 10.8	25 14.6	64 5.7	47 7.8
	86 4.2	83 4.4	92 4.0		126 2.9	73 5.0	90 4.1	54 6.8	99 3.7	108 3.4
	17 22.9	16 22.9	17 22.0	Cost of Sales/Payables	0 UND	21 17.2	20 18.1	20 18.2	17 21.8	15 23.8
	36 10.1	36 10.1	31 12.0		25 14.6	36 10.1	31 11.7	37 9.9	28 12.9	28 13.1
	58 6.3	74 4.9	52 7.0		119 3.1	65 5.6	43 8.5	59 6.2	47 7.7	46 8.0
	11.0	6.8	6.4	Sales/Working Capital	3.8	5.9	4.4	7.7	6.8	7.9
	NM	20.0	18.1		41.8	19.4	8.7	19.2	18.0	24.1
	-15.3	-83.4	-53.7		-16.4	-132.0	NM	-33.5	-170.5	-92.4
	13.9	23.8	21.5	EBIT/Interest	9.0	9.2	36.9	34.9	43.3	54.8
	(44) 6.4	(81) 5.0	(100) 3.4		(19) 1.5	(21) 1.5	(15) 2.4	(17) 3.6	(14) 16.2	(14) 16.1
	1.2	1.7	1.1		-2.4	1.0	1.0	1.4	2.7	1.7
		15.2	6.7	Net Profit + Depr., Dep., Amort./Cur. Mat. L/T/D						
		(18) 5.7	(18) 2.6							
		1.7	.9							
	.5	.1	.2	Fixed/Worth	.1	.6	.1	.2	.1	.2
	2.1	.8	.7		1.4	2.6	.5	.5	.4	.4
	-2.3	76.5	-5.1		-.7	-.2	2.1	-31.5	1.9	2.1
	1.1	.9	.8	Debt/Worth	1.3	1.8	.4	1.1	.4	.5
	9.7	3.4	2.8		8.9	5.0	1.5	2.4	1.4	1.5
	-10.1	640.9	-14.1		-2.8	-2.7	8.7	-98.5	5.3	3.1
	145.7	84.3	71.8	% Profit Before Taxes/Tangible Net Worth	148.3	84.9	61.1	58.3	77.9	49.9
	(40) 40.9	(74) 37.4	(84) 30.2		(14) 36.4	(13) 26.8	(13) 11.1	(14) 30.6	(15) 34.3	(15) 31.0
	9.5	14.7	2.6		-22.7	.4	-1.2	6.6	5.7	5.8
	21.8	21.6	23.7	% Profit Before Taxes/Total Assets	22.5	14.1	29.0	24.6	29.1	36.0
	8.3	8.8	5.0		2.0	.5	3.3	5.6	14.8	13.4
	.5	1.9	.1		-9.6	-1.3	-1.0	.7	2.2	1.3
	60.5	106.5	95.2	Sales/Net Fixed Assets	313.0	44.5	192.7	64.4	162.3	39.4
	25.6	33.2	25.6		25.4	27.4	28.1	29.7	48.0	22.4
	8.9	11.0	10.4		6.0	13.6	12.0	10.3	13.3	10.5
	4.9	4.6	4.9	Sales/Total Assets	5.3	5.0	4.3	4.9	6.5	4.1
	3.1	3.1	3.5		2.6	3.7	2.5	4.3	4.2	3.5
	2.2	2.0	1.9		.7	2.5	1.9	2.4	1.8	2.1
	.8	.4	.5	% Depr., Dep., Amort./Sales	.6	1.0	.5	.3	.3	.4
	(43) 1.3	(70) 1.2	(89) 1.3		(15) 1.9	(16) 1.3	(13) 1.5	(17) .8	(15) 1.3	(13) 1.0
	3.1	2.9	2.6		5.3	3.6	2.3	2.2	4.1	2.9
	2.3	1.5	1.9	% Officers', Directors', Owners' Comp/Sales	4.5	4.7		1.0		
	(21) 3.5	(49) 4.0	(54) 4.5		(11) 9.4	(13) 7.9		(12) 2.7		
	12.2	7.7	8.7		15.2	13.3		5.4		
	2169160M	2566658M	2939674M	Net Sales ($)	12088M	39355M	65879M	132087M	283164M	2407101M
	981605M	927219M	1158924M	Total Assets ($)	13971M	15247M	30305M	40239M	121854M	937308M

© RMA 2005

M = $ thousand   MM = $ million
See Pages 11 through 21 for Explanation of Ratios and Data

TRANSPORTATION
AND WAREHOUSING

Current Data Sorted By Assets   Comparative Historical Data

0-500M	500M-2MM	2-10MM	10-50MM	50-100MM	100-250MM	Type of Statement	4/1/00-3/31/01 ALL	4/1/01-3/31/02 ALL
1	1	1	6	2	5	Unqualified	5	1
		5	2			Reviewed	9	2
1			1			Compiled	8	10
2		2				Tax Returns	4	1
2	4	9	7		2	Other	21	20
	12 (4/1-9/30/04)		41 (10/1/04-3/31/05)					
6	5	17	16	2	7	NUMBER OF STATEMENTS	47	34
%	%	%	%	%	%	**ASSETS**	%	%
		10.6	12.7			Cash & Equivalents	9.3	12.6
		12.9	16.2			Trade Receivables (net)	16.4	19.7
		2.9	6.5			Inventory	7.9	8.1
		5.7	3.7			All Other Current	4.0	3.0
		32.1	39.1			Total Current	37.6	43.4
		47.9	51.4			Fixed Assets (net)	51.1	44.0
		2.3	2.7			Intangibles (net)	3.0	5.1
		17.6	6.8			All Other Non-Current	8.3	7.5
		100.0	100.0			Total	100.0	100.0
						LIABILITIES		
		2.7	2.8			Notes Payable-Short Term	9.9	7.4
		6.7	4.6			Cur. Mat.-L/T/D	5.4	5.4
		7.9	19.8			Trade Payables	13.9	15.5
		.0	.1			Income Taxes Payable	.3	.4
		9.1	15.2			All Other Current	14.7	10.2
		26.3	42.5			Total Current	44.1	38.9
		33.6	24.0			Long-Term Debt	29.6	35.3
		.0	.5			Deferred Taxes	1.0	1.1
		9.3	7.8			All Other Non-Current	4.3	6.6
		30.8	25.1			Net Worth	21.0	18.1
		100.0	100.0			Total Liabilities & Net Worth	100.0	100.0
						INCOME DATA		
		100.0	100.0			Net Sales	100.0	100.0
						Gross Profit		
		86.3	93.3			Operating Expenses	93.0	99.4
		13.7	6.7			Operating Profit	7.0	.6
		2.4	3.0			All Other Expenses (net)	2.6	1.9
		11.4	3.7			Profit Before Taxes	4.4	-1.3
						RATIOS		
		3.2	1.3				1.4	1.6
		1.4	.8			Current	.9	1.0
		.6	.6				.4	.8
		2.5	1.0				1.0	1.2
		1.0	.6			Quick	.5	.8
		.4	.4				.3	.4
	5	73.2	11 34.3				10 35.0	16 23.0
	24	15.3	18 20.1			Sales/Receivables	30 12.2	29 12.7
	40	9.1	45 8.0				46 8.0	36 10.0
						Cost of Sales/Inventory		
						Cost of Sales/Payables		
		6.1	42.6				18.2	11.8
		11.0	-57.2			Sales/Working Capital	-113.6	-98.3
		-6.7	-9.6				-7.8	-22.1
		24.4	9.9				4.2	4.2
		4.4	(14) 3.0			EBIT/Interest	(37) 1.7	(30) 1.2
		-2.0	1.6				-.5	-1.0
						Net Profit + Depr., Dep., Amort./Cur. Mat. L/T/D		
		.9	1.0				1.0	.7
		2.0	1.8			Fixed/Worth	2.0	4.6
		NM	164.7				9.9	-6.5
		.7	1.0				1.7	1.7
		2.9	3.3			Debt/Worth	5.3	7.9
		NM	242.1				29.0	-12.7
		103.2	72.2			% Profit Before Taxes/Tangible	86.1	61.7
		(13) 26.1	(13) 34.8			Net Worth	(38) 23.6	(24) 11.9
		4.5	8.7				-7.0	-60.0
		20.7	16.3			% Profit Before Taxes/Total	16.2	11.5
		11.0	6.2			Assets	3.9	1.6
		-6.2	-3.6				-4.1	-8.3
		7.3	9.6				16.6	14.9
		2.1	1.9			Sales/Net Fixed Assets	2.8	5.0
		.8	1.6				1.3	1.9
		3.0	2.6				3.8	4.3
		1.0	1.3			Sales/Total Assets	1.7	1.9
		.5	.8				.8	1.1
		2.7	1.6				1.5	.6
	(14)	5.6	(14) 4.4			% Depr., Dep., Amort./Sales	(40) 4.1	(24) 2.8
		16.1	6.9				12.9	15.1
						% Officers', Directors', Owners' Comp/Sales	1.2	
							(13) 2.1	
							2.9	
8416M	13709M	163710M	655048M	189208M	1737231M	Net Sales ($)	1537747M	3052315M
2042M	6836M	88488M	332266M	163132M	1050605M	Total Assets ($)	723702M	1620630M

Comparative Historical Data | | | | | **Current Data Sorted By Sales**

			Type of Statement	1	2			3	10
12	7	16	Unqualified	1	2			3	10
3	4	7	Reviewed		1	2		2	2
8	8	2	Compiled		1			1	
5	4	4	Tax Returns	2	1	1			
18	12	24	Other	3	6	3	3	2	7
4/1/02-3/31/03 ALL	4/1/03-3/31/04 ALL	4/1/04-3/31/05 ALL		12 (4/1-9/30/04)			41 (10/1/04-3/31/05)		
				0-1MM	1-3MM	3-5MM	5-10MM	10-25MM	25MM & OVER
46	35	53	**NUMBER OF STATEMENTS**	6	11	6	3	8	19
%	%	%	**ASSETS**	%	%	%	%	%	%
13.7	9.4	11.8	Cash & Equivalents		8.6				14.9
12.4	12.9	12.4	Trade Receivables (net)		6.2				17.6
6.7	10.0	4.1	Inventory		2.4				2.8
2.2	5.0	4.3	All Other Current		7.7				5.0
35.0	37.3	32.6	Total Current		24.9				40.2
51.9	50.4	54.0	Fixed Assets (net)		61.6				49.6
2.6	2.0	1.9	Intangibles (net)		2.4				2.1
10.5	10.2	11.5	All Other Non-Current		11.1				8.1
100.0	100.0	100.0	Total		100.0				100.0
			LIABILITIES						
4.4	3.6	5.3	Notes Payable-Short Term		2.3				6.9
6.1	7.1	4.9	Cur. Mat.-L/T/D		4.2				4.1
8.8	8.9	12.9	Trade Payables		11.5				22.6
.8	.2	.0	Income Taxes Payable		.0				.0
13.2	11.9	11.9	All Other Current		9.2				12.4
33.3	31.7	35.1	Total Current		27.2				46.0
25.2	34.1	48.0	Long-Term Debt		77.1				23.3
1.3	2.2	.6	Deferred Taxes		.0				1.1
12.4	7.9	8.5	All Other Non-Current		13.8				6.0
27.9	24.2	7.8	Net Worth		-18.1				23.6
100.0	100.0	100.0	Total Liabilities & Net Worth		100.0				100.0
			INCOME DATA						
100.0	100.0	100.0	Net Sales		100.0				100.0
			Gross Profit						
100.7	96.8	91.5	Operating Expenses		88.2				93.6
-.7	3.2	8.5	Operating Profit		11.8				6.4
1.8	2.4	3.0	All Other Expenses (net)		5.3				.7
-2.5	.8	5.5	Profit Before Taxes		6.5				5.8
			RATIOS						
1.7	2.1	1.7			1.4				1.5
1.0	1.2	1.0	Current		1.2				1.0
.6	.6	.6			.7				.7
1.2	1.2	1.4			1.0				1.3
.7	.6	.8	Quick		.9				.8
.3	.2	.4			.2				.6
9 40.1	9 39.0	7 52.2			1 285.2				10 36.0
25 14.8	25 14.8	15 24.8	Sales/Receivables		15 24.8				14 26.2
38 9.6	45 8.1	37 10.0			32 11.4				45 8.2
			Cost of Sales/Inventory						
			Cost of Sales/Payables						
13.4	5.1	11.9			11.0				16.8
NM	51.9	113.8	Sales/Working Capital		56.5				113.8
-8.0	-8.7	-8.7			-9.3				-14.0
3.0	7.6	12.8							15.4
(42) 1.1	(31) 2.5	(49) 2.9	EBIT/Interest					(18)	4.6
-3.4	.5	.6							2.4
2.4			Net Profit + Depr., Dep.,						
(16) 1.3			Amort./Cur. Mat. L/T/D						
.3									
.8	.7	1.1			1.1				1.0
1.2	1.4	2.3	Fixed/Worth		48.5				1.9
21.4	-10.9	-7.1			-3.0				68.7
.8	.9	1.1			1.4				1.4
1.6	1.8	3.6	Debt/Worth		72.3				2.9
27.4	-12.6	-16.0			-4.1				133.6
34.6	29.5	97.9	% Profit Before Taxes/Tangible						73.7
(36) 5.5	(26) 13.1	(38) 30.0	Net Worth					(15)	53.6
-14.7	5.2	6.9							11.5
8.6	10.9	16.4	% Profit Before Taxes/Total		14.4				22.9
.8	4.2	6.3	Assets		9.9				9.2
-7.6	-1.5	-4.0			-5.4				2.8
6.8	9.2	7.3			6.1				16.4
2.5	3.1	2.1	Sales/Net Fixed Assets		1.6				4.4
1.3	1.3	1.4			.7				1.7
2.9	2.8	2.6			1.9				4.1
1.5	1.4	1.3	Sales/Total Assets		1.2				1.7
.8	.8	.7			.5				1.3
2.3	1.3	1.9	% Depr., Dep., Amort./Sales						.7
(42) 5.5	(27) 6.8	(41) 4.6						(15)	1.8
11.8	12.3	13.2							5.1
1.3		1.2	% Officers', Directors',						
(13) 4.7		(10) 4.8	Owners' Comp/Sales						
18.3		12.3							
3130512M	2641536M	2767322M	Net Sales ($)	3509M	21788M	21783M	25208M	148045M	2546989M
1889746M	1375708M	1643369M	Total Assets ($)	9647M	37040M	24147M	41584M	223932M	1307019M

M = $ thousand   MM = $ million
See Pages 11 through 21 for Explanation of Ratios and Data

	Current Data Sorted By Assets							Comparative Historical Data	
	1	1	7	12	1	1	Type of Statement		
	2	2	7	3			Unqualified	11	16
1	1	1	8	2			Reviewed	8	14
1	5	5	8	1		1	Compiled	17	20
1	10	10	14	11		8	Tax Returns	15	8
		16 (4/1-9/30/04)		90 (10/1/04-3/31/05)			Other	25	33
								4/1/00-	4/1/01-
								3/31/01	3/31/02
0-500M	500M-2MM		2-10MM	10-50MM	50-100MM	100-250MM		ALL	ALL
3	19		44	29	1	10	NUMBER OF STATEMENTS	76	91
%	%		%	%	%	%	ASSETS	%	%
	13.0		8.4	10.7		4.1	Cash & Equivalents	8.6	7.2
	19.5		14.5	12.9		9.5	Trade Receivables (net)	16.2	16.1
	4.6		11.5	10.5		20.3	Inventory	8.2	10.1
	6.0		2.8	7.1		2.4	All Other Current	5.6	3.6
	43.0		37.1	41.2		36.3	Total Current	38.6	37.1
	48.9		50.6	49.7		51.5	Fixed Assets (net)	52.4	50.5
	.9		5.0	.9		9.5	Intangibles (net)	3.0	2.6
	7.2		7.4	8.2		2.7	All Other Non-Current	6.0	9.9
	100.0		100.0	100.0		100.0	Total	100.0	100.0
							LIABILITIES		
	4.4		8.5	6.0		.7	Notes Payable-Short Term	8.9	11.6
	4.7		5.7	6.4		3.1	Cur. Mat.-L/T/D	5.5	5.6
	9.3		10.3	8.6		2.9	Trade Payables	10.4	7.9
	.1		.2	.2		3.0	Income Taxes Payable	.7	.4
	16.3		9.3	12.6		8.1	All Other Current	16.1	9.7
	34.9		34.0	33.7		17.7	Total Current	41.6	35.3
	45.1		44.3	37.0		29.5	Long-Term Debt	37.1	44.8
	.1		1.1	2.7		2.3	Deferred Taxes	.8	1.1
	15.9		4.3	2.4		2.4	All Other Non-Current	14.6	2.9
	4.0		16.3	24.2		48.0	Net Worth	5.9	15.9
	100.0		100.0	100.0		100.0	Total Liabilities & Net Worth	100.0	100.0
							INCOME DATA		
	100.0		100.0	100.0		100.0	Net Sales	100.0	100.0
							Gross Profit		
	89.3		96.6	94.1		89.8	Operating Expenses	97.0	93.9
	10.7		3.4	5.9		10.2	Operating Profit	3.0	6.1
	4.2		3.2	1.2		2.0	All Other Expenses (net)	−.2	3.5
	6.4		.2	4.7		8.2	Profit Before Taxes	3.2	2.6
							RATIOS		
	1.7		1.9	1.6		2.6		2.0	2.0
	1.0		1.1	1.2		2.4	Current	1.2	1.2
	.7		.6	.8		1.3		.6	.7
	1.4		1.1	1.1		1.2		1.3	1.2
	.8		.7	.7		.4	Quick	.6	.7
	.7		.4	.4		.3		.2	.4
	0 UND		16 23.4	13 27.1		20 17.8		1 380.3	13 28.4
	25 14.8		27 13.4	25 14.7		27 13.7	Sales/Receivables	23 15.8	29 12.8
	47 7.8		40 9.1	43 8.4		64 5.7		46 7.9	51 7.2
							Cost of Sales/Inventory		
							Cost of Sales/Payables		
	11.8		6.1	8.5		2.6		8.5	8.1
	UND		50.4	24.2		4.1	Sales/Working Capital	43.2	33.0
	−24.2		−14.6	−31.4		13.3		−15.5	−17.8
	5.2		8.6	7.4		8.3		4.4	3.2
(12)	2.4	(40)	1.4	2.8		2.2	EBIT/Interest	(65) 1.8	(77) 1.7
	.8		−.2	1.5		1.1		.4	.6
			3.4	4.0					3.6
		(11)	2.0	(13) 1.4			Net Profit + Depr., Dep., Amort./Cur. Mat. L /T/D		(22) 2.1
			1.3	.7					.7
	1.9		.9	.8		.8		.9	.9
	9.9		2.5	1.7		.9	Fixed/Worth	2.3	2.2
	−4.4		−5.4	3.4		NM		−34.1	22.5
	2.5		1.9	1.5		.6		1.2	1.7
	10.3		5.0	2.7		1.0	Debt/Worth	3.7	3.8
	−13.2		−9.9	4.9		NM		−36.2	59.1
	195.8		33.1	27.8				54.5	51.2
(13)	75.0	(29)	11.9	(26) 19.9			% Profit Before Taxes/Tangible Net Worth	(54) 21.2	(72) 14.1
	15.0		−7.6	7.4				4.5	−3.8
	15.3		7.1	8.4		7.5		14.4	8.0
	4.8		1.5	4.7		2.8	% Profit Before Taxes/Total Assets	3.6	2.5
	−2.5		−5.6	1.8		−.4		−3.9	−2.7
	135.7		8.2	10.0		2.4		8.6	8.1
	3.8		3.1	2.0		1.6	Sales/Net Fixed Assets	2.9	2.8
	1.2		1.4	1.2		1.4		1.5	1.5
	4.2		2.4	2.1		1.4		2.8	2.6
	2.0		1.4	1.2		.7	Sales/Total Assets	1.6	1.6
	.9		.9	.7		.7		.8	.9
	.2		3.0	2.4				1.6	2.0
(15)	6.8	(40)	7.0	(24) 5.2			% Depr., Dep., Amort./Sales	(63) 6.2	(78) 5.1
	18.8		12.5	11.7				14.6	10.2
			1.3					2.7	2.1
		(12)	2.1				% Officers', Directors', Owners' Comp/Sales	(27) 6.4	(28) 3.8
			4.1					11.7	6.3
5207M	64556M		465364M	1131106M	46195M	1704439M	Net Sales ($)	1083773M	1847007M
1093M	24419M		216141M	654231M	51195M	1632666M	Total Assets ($)	834097M	1475534M

M = $ thousand   MM = $ million
See Pages 11 through 21 for Explanation of Ratios and Data

Comparative Historical Data   Current Data Sorted By Sales

16	19	22	Type of Statement						
13	13	13	Unqualified		1	2	4	6	9
16	25	11	Reviewed	2	2	1	2	5	1
13	7	16	Compiled		4	2	2	2	1
36	47	44	Tax Returns	2	2	5	5	1	1
4/1/02-3/31/03	4/1/03-3/31/04	4/1/04-3/31/05	Other	4	5	4	5	12	14
ALL	ALL	ALL			16 (4/1-9/30/04)			90 (10/1/04-3/31/05)	
				0-1MM	1-3MM	3-5MM	5-10MM	10-25MM	25MM & OVER
94	111	106	NUMBER OF STATEMENTS	8	14	14	18	26	26
%	%	%	ASSETS	%	%	%	%	%	%
7.4	10.2	9.6	Cash & Equivalents		14.2	4.8	13.7	6.9	10.8
17.5	17.6	15.0	Trade Receivables (net)		11.6	14.0	15.4	16.0	19.5
8.1	7.0	10.5	Inventory		1.6	9.2	8.4	12.5	14.6
4.0	6.0	4.4	All Other Current		8.4	6.5	1.0	3.6	5.7
37.1	40.7	39.5	Total Current		35.8	34.4	38.5	39.1	50.7
51.4	50.6	50.2	Fixed Assets (net)		46.9	53.4	54.1	49.7	40.2
1.4	2.2	3.4	Intangibles (net)		4.2	5.3	1.6	2.5	4.8
10.0	6.5	6.9	All Other Non-Current		13.2	6.9	5.7	8.7	4.4
100.0	100.0	100.0	Total		100.0	100.0	100.0	100.0	100.0
			LIABILITIES						
9.2	10.5	6.1	Notes Payable-Short Term		4.1	15.0	2.1	10.5	2.7
6.3	7.5	5.4	Cur. Mat.-L/T/D		5.7	7.0	4.7	6.8	3.5
9.8	9.7	8.8	Trade Payables		5.2	8.8	6.6	10.6	13.1
.5	.6	.4	Income Taxes Payable		.2	.3	.2	.1	1.3
8.1	10.6	11.3	All Other Current		7.2	8.3	12.8	9.4	18.9
33.8	38.8	32.2	Total Current		22.5	39.4	26.5	37.4	39.5
40.9	40.8	40.9	Long-Term Debt		39.6	47.6	47.3	32.0	30.4
1.1	1.1	1.5	Deferred Taxes		1.1	1.3	1.3	1.5	2.4
3.0	8.8	6.2	All Other Non-Current		4.4	23.9	4.4	2.3	2.5
21.2	10.4	19.2	Net Worth		32.5	-12.1	20.6	26.9	25.2
100.0	100.0	100.0	Total Liabilities & Net Worth		100.0	100.0	100.0	100.0	100.0
			INCOME DATA						
100.0	100.0	100.0	Net Sales		100.0	100.0	100.0	100.0	100.0
			Gross Profit						
94.1	94.2	94.0	Operating Expenses		90.2	96.8	101.6	96.1	92.3
5.9	5.8	6.0	Operating Profit		9.8	3.2	-1.6	3.9	7.7
2.1	3.6	2.5	All Other Expenses (net)		3.5	5.3	.6	-.2	1.3
3.7	2.1	3.5	Profit Before Taxes		6.3	-2.2	-2.2	4.2	6.4
			RATIOS						
1.9	2.1	1.9			3.0	2.1	3.0	1.3	2.4
1.1	1.3	1.2	Current		1.3	1.3	1.3	1.0	1.5
.8	.8	.7			.7	.6	.6	.8	1.0
1.3	1.4	1.2			1.5	1.2	1.8	.9	1.3
(93) .7	.7	.7	Quick		.9	.5	.8	.7	.8
.4	.3	.4			.7	.2	.6	.5	.3
17 21.9	15 24.3	15 24.6		16 23.1	0 UND	14 26.1	18 20.5	16 22.5	
27 13.3	28 13.0	26 14.0	Sales/Receivables	31 11.8	25 14.5	27 13.4	26 13.9	27 13.7	
37 9.8	44 8.2	42 8.8		52 7.0	37 9.9	54 6.7	42 8.8	47 7.7	
			Cost of Sales/Inventory						
			Cost of Sales/Payables						
10.1	6.4	6.4			4.0	13.9	3.8	16.3	5.1
40.3	25.4	26.9	Sales/Working Capital		13.6	45.0	37.9	104.8	11.0
-23.2	-19.0	-24.8			-23.5	-11.0	-15.7	-23.3	269.9
5.3	5.9	7.3			5.4	2.0	2.6	9.4	10.8
(85) 2.2	(91) 2.0	(95) 2.0	EBIT/Interest	(11) 1.6	.8	(14) 1.1	(25) 3.1	5.8	
.9	.0	.7			.6	-1.0	-1.2	1.6	1.6
4.1	5.0	3.6	Net Profit + Depr., Dep.,					21.0	4.6
(23) 2.7	(26) 1.7	(33) 2.0	Amort./Cur. Mat. L/T/D				(10) 1.3	(12) 2.6	
1.1	1.2	1.3						.6	2.0
1.0	1.1	.9			.4	1.4	.9	1.2	.8
2.9	2.9	2.1	Fixed/Worth		2.5	NM	1.9	2.0	1.8
NM	-5.8	NM			6.1	-1.1	-4.9	3.8	-11.8
1.3	1.7	1.4			.8	2.0	.5	1.4	1.2
4.2	4.4	4.2	Debt/Worth		4.9	NM	8.9	2.7	2.2
NM	-13.2	-150.4			10.9	-2.6	-10.0	4.9	-13.8
(71) 50.3	(74) 33.9	(79) 53.9	% Profit Before Taxes/Tangible		110.6		32.7	32.3	65.9
25.8	13.1	18.3	Net Worth		(13) 22.4	(11) 7.3	(23) 21.2	(19) 16.4	
5.3	4.9	3.4			2.9		-24.0	10.7	5.5
11.9	8.1	8.8	% Profit Before Taxes/Total		15.4	4.9	6.9	9.9	19.7
5.2	3.2	3.3	Assets		3.9	-1.5	1.2	5.8	5.4
-.2	-3.1	-1.8			-.3	-6.5	-12.1	2.3	1.3
8.4	8.5	8.7			37.2	11.0	11.8	8.3	17.4
2.7	2.6	2.9	Sales/Net Fixed Assets		3.1	3.5	1.9	3.2	3.5
1.2	1.4	1.4			1.2	1.5	1.1	1.4	1.5
2.7	2.7	2.5			2.2	2.6	1.8	2.7	3.5
1.5	1.6	1.4	Sales/Total Assets		1.2	1.5	1.0	1.4	1.8
.9	1.0	.8			.7	.9	.8	.9	.8
(82) 2.2	(94) 2.9	(90) 2.5	% Depr., Dep., Amort./Sales		3.4	2.2	2.6	2.3	1.9
5.0	6.1	6.7		(10) 8.2	5.5	(17) 7.0	(22) 5.3	(20) 3.8	
9.6	13.2	10.4			18.2	8.3	19.4	9.1	7.4
1.9	2.9	1.7	% Officers', Directors',						
(32) 3.4	(24) 4.7	(24) 3.3	Owners' Comp/Sales						
8.3	7.1	7.0							
1569853M	3378255M	3416867M	Net Sales ($)	3881M	27724M	53811M	121012M	416645M	2793794M
1197104M	2140098M	2579745M	Total Assets ($)	10248M	30930M	47099M	111790M	348759M	2030919M

M = $ thousand   MM = $ million
See Pages 11 through 21 for Explanation of Ratios and Data

Current Data Sorted By Assets   **Comparative Historical Data**

0-500M	500M-2MM	2-10MM	10-50MM	50-100MM	100-250MM	Type of Statement	4/1/00-3/31/01 ALL	4/1/01-3/31/02 ALL
		7				Unqualified		
	1	4				Reviewed		
	3	1	1			Compiled		
1	1	3				Tax Returns		
7	4	8			2	Other		
	10 (4/1-9/30/04)		33 (10/1/04-3/31/05)					
8	9	23	1		2	**NUMBER OF STATEMENTS**		
%	%	%	%	%	%	**ASSETS**	%	%
		8.7		D		Cash & Equivalents		D
		9.9		A		Trade Receivables (net)	D	A
		1.3		T		Inventory	A	T
		1.6		A		All Other Current	T	A
		21.5				Total Current	A	
		73.7		N		Fixed Assets (net)		N
		1.4		O		Intangibles (net)	N	O
		3.5		T		All Other Non-Current	O	T
		100.0				Total	T	
				A		**LIABILITIES**		A
		2.7		V		Notes Payable-Short Term	A	V
		2.1		A		Cur. Mat.-L/T/D	V	A
		9.4		I		Trade Payables	A	I
		.1		L		Income Taxes Payable	I	L
		3.4		A		All Other Current	L	A
		17.6		B		Total Current	A	B
		37.8		L		Long-Term Debt	B	L
		.4		E		Deferred Taxes	L	E
		4.4				All Other Non-Current	E	
		39.8				Net Worth		
		100.0				Total Liabilities & Net Worth		
						INCOME DATA		
		100.0				Net Sales		
						Gross Profit		
		89.6				Operating Expenses		
		10.4				Operating Profit		
		7.2				All Other Expenses (net)		
		3.2				Profit Before Taxes		
						RATIOS		
		2.2						
		1.0				Current		
		.5						
		1.8						
		.9				Quick		
		.3						
	5	78.7						
	22	16.3				Sales/Receivables		
	39	9.3						
						Cost of Sales/Inventory		
						Cost of Sales/Payables		
		10.4						
		142.3				Sales/Working Capital		
		−7.0						
		7.9						
	(20)	1.5				EBIT/Interest		
		.3						
						Net Profit + Depr., Dep., Amort./Cur. Mat. L./T/D		
		1.1						
		2.5				Fixed/Worth		
		4.1						
		.5						
		2.3				Debt/Worth		
		4.6						
		17.4						
	(21)	1.9				% Profit Before Taxes/Tangible Net Worth		
		−8.8						
		3.9						
		1.1				% Profit Before Taxes/Total Assets		
		−3.2						
		1.4						
		.7				Sales/Net Fixed Assets		
		.5						
		.8						
		.6				Sales/Total Assets		
		.5						
		6.7						
	(21)	9.1				% Depr., Dep., Amort./Sales		
		12.5						
						% Officers', Directors', Owners' Comp/Sales		
7355M	18069M	114444M	4014M		448053M	Net Sales ($)		
1694M	9765M	122264M	11176M		342193M	Total Assets ($)		

M = $ thousand   MM = $ million
See Pages 11 through 21 for Explanation of Ratios and Data

Comparative Historical Data				Current Data Sorted By Sales					
	4	7	**Type of Statement**		1	4	1	1	
	8	5	Unqualified		2	3			
1	4	6	Reviewed	2	1	3			
	5	11	Compiled	6	4	1			
	8	14	Tax Returns	2	5	2		3	2
4/1/02- 3/31/03 ALL	4/1/03- 3/31/04 ALL	4/1/04- 3/31/05 ALL	Other		**10 (4/1-9/30/04)**			**33 (10/1/04-3/31/05)**	
1	29	43	**NUMBER OF STATEMENTS**	0-1MM	1-3MM	3-5MM	5-10MM	10-25MM	25MM & OVER
				10	13	13	1	4	2
%	%	%	**ASSETS**	%	%	%	%	%	%
	6.1	8.2	Cash & Equivalents	8.0	6.6	5.8			
	8.1	9.9	Trade Receivables (net)	4.1	7.0	5.5			
	5.9	3.3	Inventory	.4	4.0	6.1			
	1.8	3.2	All Other Current	.4	5.9	2.9			
	22.0	24.7	Total Current	12.9	23.5	20.4			
	63.7	70.2	Fixed Assets (net)	81.9	74.4	73.4			
	.5	1.3	Intangibles (net)	.8	.0	1.0			
	13.9	3.9	All Other Non-Current	4.3	2.0	5.2			
	100.0	100.0	Total	100.0	100.0	100.0			
			LIABILITIES						
	7.8	4.5	Notes Payable-Short Term	6.3	7.2	2.6			
	3.1	3.7	Cur. Mat.-L/T/D	3.1	5.8	3.2			
	7.3	7.9	Trade Payables	.9	5.8	4.6			
	.9	.1	Income Taxes Payable	.0	.0	.2			
	10.9	4.7	All Other Current	6.5	3.7	4.2			
	30.0	21.0	Total Current	16.7	22.7	14.7			
	37.9	36.0	Long-Term Debt	42.9	32.0	45.2			
	.5	.4	Deferred Taxes	.0	.4	.3			
	5.7	11.4	All Other Non-Current	16.6	8.0	11.2			
	25.9	31.2	Net Worth	23.8	37.0	28.6			
	100.0	100.0	Total Liabilities & Net Worth	100.0	100.0	100.0			
			INCOME DATA						
	100.0	100.0	Net Sales	100.0	100.0	100.0			
			Gross Profit						
	100.5	93.6	Operating Expenses	82.8	100.5	94.5			
	-.5	6.4	Operating Profit	17.2	-.5	5.5			
	2.2	4.9	All Other Expenses (net)	14.7	.9	1.3			
	-2.7	1.5	Profit Before Taxes	2.5	-1.4	4.3			
			RATIOS						
	1.3	2.2	Current	2.8	2.4	2.5			
	.7	1.0		.7	1.5	1.0			
	.3	.5		.1	.5	.5			
	1.0	1.7	Quick	2.6	1.7	1.4			
	.6	.8		.6	.5	.6			
	.1	.3		.0	.2	.4			
	2 165.3	3 117.6	Sales/Receivables	0 UND	4 102.4	5 71.3			
	10 36.7	16 23.5		0 UND	9 42.7	22 16.3			
	41 8.9	37 9.8		13 27.8	30 12.2	35 10.5			
			Cost of Sales/Inventory						
			Cost of Sales/Payables						
	17.8	10.4	Sales/Working Capital	11.9	15.5	5.2			
	-27.5	117.8		-94.9	24.8	142.3			
	-6.7	-10.4		-3.4	-9.3	-12.3			
	5.9	4.9	EBIT/Interest		2.0	4.9			
(24)	.8	(38) 1.5			.6	(11) 1.2			
	-1.1	-.8			-2.9	.2			
			Net Profit + Depr., Dep., Amort./Cur. Mat. L/T/D						
	1.0	1.2	Fixed/Worth	1.2	1.2	.9			
	1.7	2.1		2.1	1.9	3.2			
	3.9	12.3		-74.8	3.5	NM			
	.9	.6	Debt/Worth	.5	.8	.5			
	1.5	2.0		1.4	2.0	2.5			
	3.8	11.8		-76.0	3.5	NM			
	24.0	15.4	% Profit Before Taxes/Tangible Net Worth		7.5	16.4			
(24)	1.8	(35) 1.9		(12)	-3.2	(10) -1.0			
	-10.2	-8.7			-15.4	-5.9			
	7.6	4.1	% Profit Before Taxes/Total Assets	10.5	2.4	6.8			
	-.6	.4		.9	-1.9	-2.4			
	-6.1	-3.5		-1.7	-5.9	-3.2			
	5.3	5.5	Sales/Net Fixed Assets	4.4	8.3	3.3			
	1.3	1.2		.7	1.2	.9			
	.6	.6		.3	.5	.5			
	2.1	3.7	Sales/Total Assets	2.5	4.7	1.4			
	.7	.8		.6	1.0	.7			
	.5	.5		.3	.5	.5			
	3.3	5.4	% Depr., Dep., Amort./Sales		5.4	7.4			
(27)	7.1	(35) 7.7		(11)	7.6	8.6			
	9.0	11.3			12.2	12.0			
		3.0	% Officers', Directors', Owners' Comp/Sales						
		(17) 11.3							
		27.2							
506M	93319M	591935M	Net Sales ($)	4530M	25864M	50522M	5823M	57143M	448053M
996M	105106M	487092M	Total Assets ($)	15917M	32920M	73727M	8044M	14291M	342193M

Current Data Sorted By Assets   Comparative Historical Data

0-500M	500M-2MM	2-10MM	10-50MM	50-100MM	100-250MM	Type of Statement	4/1/00-3/31/01 ALL	4/1/01-3/31/02 ALL
		5	7	3	4	Unqualified	16	17
	1	5	1			Reviewed	4	3
1	2	2	2	1		Compiled	6	9
2	1					Tax Returns		1
	6	11	5		3	Other	23	17
	11 (4/1-9/30/04)		56 (10/1/04-3/31/05)					
3	10	23	15	9	7	NUMBER OF STATEMENTS	49	47
%	%	%	%	%	%	**ASSETS**	%	%
	8.8	7.6	14.2			Cash & Equivalents	5.2	5.5
	20.9	16.7	10.6			Trade Receivables (net)	12.6	10.4
	1.4	5.2	1.8			Inventory	4.0	2.8
	1.8	2.0	3.6			All Other Current	1.6	3.5
	32.9	31.5	30.3			Total Current	23.4	22.3
	47.3	54.8	64.8			Fixed Assets (net)	69.3	67.0
	.0	1.0	1.4			Intangibles (net)	3.0	5.6
	19.8	12.7	3.5			All Other Non-Current	4.3	5.1
	100.0	100.0	100.0			Total	100.0	100.0
						LIABILITIES		
	4.3	4.2	1.6			Notes Payable-Short Term	3.1	2.0
	3.6	2.7	3.1			Cur. Mat.-L/T/D	3.8	4.0
	11.9	13.8	5.3			Trade Payables	10.7	6.3
	2.4	.9	.4			Income Taxes Payable	.2	.5
	9.9	6.4	13.3			All Other Current	7.3	9.3
	32.1	28.1	23.7			Total Current	25.2	22.2
	25.1	22.5	27.4			Long-Term Debt	27.8	24.2
	.4	3.7	1.7			Deferred Taxes	5.7	4.8
	9.3	3.7	7.7			All Other Non-Current	6.0	5.5
	33.0	42.1	39.5			Net Worth	35.3	43.5
	100.0	100.0	100.0			Total Liabilities & Net Worth	100.0	100.0
						INCOME DATA		
	100.0	100.0	100.0			Net Sales	100.0	100.0
						Gross Profit		
	83.4	85.8	82.9			Operating Expenses	85.0	84.8
	16.6	14.2	17.1			Operating Profit	15.0	15.2
	2.7	1.3	1.8			All Other Expenses (net)	4.7	3.2
	14.0	12.8	15.4			Profit Before Taxes	10.3	11.9
						RATIOS		
	1.2	2.6	2.4			Current	1.3	1.9
	.9	1.0	1.1				.8	.7
	.6	.8	.8				.5	.5
	1.2	1.9	2.1			Quick	1.0	.9
	.9	.9	.9				.6	.6
	.6	.6	.6				.3	.3
	18 20.2	23 15.9	29 12.8			Sales/Receivables	32 11.5	20 18.5
	37 9.9	39 9.3	51 7.1				52 7.0	44 8.3
	47 7.7	73 5.0	59 6.2				68 5.4	62 5.9
						Cost of Sales/Inventory		
						Cost of Sales/Payables		
	20.7	5.7	4.1			Sales/Working Capital	12.7	8.9
	−67.0	999.8	22.0				−24.7	−13.8
	−9.2	−22.9	−16.9				−5.9	−6.3
		17.9	49.6			EBIT/Interest	4.8	5.7
		(20) 7.8	(14) 13.9				(45) 2.9	(44) 2.6
		2.3	2.9				1.6	1.3
						Net Profit + Depr., Dep., Amort./Cur. Mat. L /T/D	5.5	2.8
							(19) 1.7	(19) 1.6
							.6	1.2
	.5	.8	1.1			Fixed/Worth	1.1	1.1
	1.0	1.4	1.9				2.4	1.8
	2.8	2.7	3.8				4.6	3.7
	1.0	.6	.9			Debt/Worth	.9	.7
	2.5	1.8	1.8				2.0	1.6
	5.6	4.2	4.2				4.5	3.5
	72.1	64.9	35.0			% Profit Before Taxes/Tangible Net Worth	40.2	28.8
	31.3	15.5	25.6				(44) 15.1	(42) 13.8
	9.8	4.8	16.7				3.3	3.9
	19.6	17.3	18.1			% Profit Before Taxes/Total Assets	11.2	10.7
	12.9	6.0	8.6				4.9	4.5
	4.0	2.2	4.4				1.7	1.3
	15.6	4.7	1.8			Sales/Net Fixed Assets	1.4	2.1
	3.2	1.7	1.0				.7	.8
	1.6	.5	.8				.5	.5
	3.0	1.4	1.1			Sales/Total Assets	1.0	1.1
	1.3	.7	.7				.6	.7
	.9	.4	.6				.4	.4
	1.1	2.4	3.1			% Depr., Dep., Amort./Sales	5.6	4.6
	4.8	(18) 7.6	(13) 10.5				(45) 9.0	(44) 8.4
	7.6	16.4	12.0				11.5	11.9
						% Officers', Directors', Owners' Comp/Sales		
913M	29619M	122135M	440934M	362171M	896167M	Net Sales ($)	784972M	1035489M
921M	15716M	110968M	318434M	727996M	960321M	Total Assets ($)	1403382M	1754544M

© RMA 2005

M = $ thousand   MM = $ million
See Pages 11 through 21 for Explanation of Ratios and Data

Comparative Historical Data | Current Data Sorted By Sales

					11 (4/1-9/30/04)			56 (10/1/04-3/31/05)	
Type of Statement	4/1/02-3/31/03 ALL	4/1/03-3/31/04 ALL	4/1/04-3/31/05 ALL	0-1MM	1-3MM	3-5MM	5-10MM	10-25MM	25MM & OVER
Unqualified	17	20	19	2	1		2	7	7
Reviewed	6	2	7		2		4		
Compiled	3	8	8		2	1	2	1	1
Tax Returns	2	1	3		1	1			
Other	17	21	30	3	6	2	7	3	9
NUMBER OF STATEMENTS	45	52	67	8	12	4	15	11	17
ASSETS	%	%	%	%	%	%	%	%	%
Cash & Equivalents	7.0	7.6	9.2		8.3		7.2	12.4	9.8
Trade Receivables (net)	8.7	10.1	14.2		15.1		23.2	10.7	12.3
Inventory	2.5	3.4	3.2		1.3		5.1	6.1	2.8
All Other Current	3.1	3.9	2.0		.6		4.2	2.4	.8
Total Current	21.4	25.0	28.7		25.4		39.7	31.5	25.7
Fixed Assets (net)	66.0	64.3	57.9		64.2		43.6	55.6	61.7
Intangibles (net)	4.1	3.3	1.6		.0		1.7	1.9	3.6
All Other Non-Current	8.6	7.4	11.8		10.4		15.0	11.0	9.0
Total	100.0	100.0	100.0		100.0		100.0	100.0	100.0
LIABILITIES									
Notes Payable-Short Term	5.4	5.6	3.1		1.6		4.8	1.3	2.6
Cur. Mat.-L/T/D	5.1	3.0	3.1		2.3		4.3	2.4	3.3
Trade Payables	7.6	7.1	9.9		6.8		18.4	8.4	6.0
Income Taxes Payable	.5	.2	1.0		2.4		1.2	1.6	.1
All Other Current	8.8	6.2	9.3		5.1		12.7	6.0	13.4
Total Current	27.4	22.1	26.4		18.2		41.4	19.8	25.3
Long-Term Debt	32.8	28.0	24.9		25.6		22.8	21.4	22.4
Deferred Taxes	6.1	5.1	2.7		1.5		2.7	2.5	3.4
All Other Non-Current	10.4	10.6	8.7		6.0		7.4	6.9	15.7
Net Worth	23.3	34.1	37.3		48.7		25.8	49.4	33.2
Total Liabilities & Net Worth	100.0	100.0	100.0		100.0		100.0	100.0	100.0
INCOME DATA									
Net Sales	100.0	100.0	100.0		100.0		100.0	100.0	100.0
Gross Profit									
Operating Expenses	84.5	85.8	86.7		84.8		94.5	88.4	89.4
Operating Profit	15.5	14.2	13.3		15.2		5.5	11.6	10.6
All Other Expenses (net)	4.0	2.1	2.1		2.7		-1.0	4.6	.9
Profit Before Taxes	11.6	12.1	11.2		12.5		6.6	7.1	9.6
RATIOS									
Current	1.7	2.0	2.1		2.5		1.1	2.9	1.5
	.8	1.0	1.0		1.2		1.0	2.4	.9
	.5	.6	.7		.6		.8	1.0	.7
Quick	1.1	1.4	1.6		1.9		.9	2.4	1.0
	.6	.7	.8		1.2		.8	1.8	.7
	.3	.4	.6		.6		.5	.6	.6
Sales/Receivables	18 20.3	18 20.6	29 12.8		17 21.9		35 10.5	23 15.9	48 7.6
	39 9.5	38 9.7	46 7.9		35 10.3		43 8.5	46 8.0	54 6.7
	60 6.1	55 6.7	60 6.1		67 5.4		57 6.4	59 6.2	65 5.7
Cost of Sales/Inventory									
Cost of Sales/Payables									
Sales/Working Capital	8.6	6.2	7.9		3.6		22.0	3.6	15.0
	-19.3	138.4	232.3		50.7		-137.0	5.9	-49.3
	-6.1	-9.1	-16.9		-13.2		-17.5	24.7	-9.8
EBIT/Interest	8.8	9.2	16.4		32.9		10.0		31.4
	(44) 3.9	(50) 3.7	(58) 6.5		(10) 9.8		(13) 4.0		10.0
	1.4	2.3	2.8		2.9		1.6		3.6
Net Profit + Depr., Dep., Amort./Cur. Mat. L/T/D	3.0	13.2	5.4						
	(17) 2.1	(19) 4.5	(20) 2.5						
	1.3	2.2	1.3						
Fixed/Worth	1.4	1.2	.9		.6		1.1	.6	1.4
	2.8	1.9	1.7		1.0		1.6	1.1	2.0
	9.7	5.2	3.1		3.1		3.0	2.7	3.3
Debt/Worth	1.4	1.0	.9		.5		1.8	.2	1.4
	3.2	2.0	2.2		1.4		2.8	1.6	2.2
	10.7	5.8	4.4		2.7		8.0	3.2	7.0
% Profit Before Taxes/Tangible Net Worth	46.1	38.7	62.5		34.0		64.9	45.3	73.1
	(39) 25.7	(46) 20.9	(66) 22.7		19.8		23.0	(10) 18.5	29.4
	9.6	13.2	8.5		4.7		8.7	6.5	12.2
% Profit Before Taxes/Total Assets	13.4	11.8	15.2		17.2		13.4	27.0	12.8
	5.4	6.1	8.1		6.3		5.3	8.6	8.2
	.7	3.5	2.9		3.7		1.6	1.3	3.4
Sales/Net Fixed Assets	2.5	2.1	4.1		3.5		13.7	2.4	2.5
	.9	1.1	1.3		1.5		4.5	1.7	1.1
	.5	.5	.7		.5		1.2	.8	.7
Sales/Total Assets	1.2	1.1	1.3		1.1		3.0	1.2	1.2
	.7	.7	.8		.8		1.4	.7	.8
	.4	.3	.5		.5		.7	.3	.5
% Depr., Dep., Amort./Sales	4.8	4.2	3.1		3.3		2.1		3.6
	(43) 7.1	(48) 7.1	(57) 6.7		(11) 7.0		(13) 3.1	(14) 6.1	
	11.5	12.0	11.5		17.0		9.2		9.7
% Officers', Directors', Owners' Comp/Sales									
Net Sales ($)	1303836M	1592257M	1851939M	3938M	23471M	15264M	111722M	171404M	1526140M
Total Assets ($)	1687835M	1874041M	2134356M	18459M	44149M	18779M	97720M	366182M	1589067M

Current Data Sorted By Assets							Comparative Historical Data	
						Type of Statement		
		4	12	3	13	Unqualified	12	14
	1	3	2			Reviewed	5	4
	5	4	2			Compiled	14	12
2	3					Tax Returns	3	4
2	2	9	5	1	2	Other	10	20
	11 (4/1-9/30/04)		64 (10/1/04-3/31/05)				4/1/00-3/31/01	4/1/01-3/31/02
0-500M	500M-2MM	2-10MM	10-50MM	50-100MM	100-250MM		ALL	ALL
4	11	20	21	4	15	**NUMBER OF STATEMENTS**	44	54
%	%	%	%	%	%	**ASSETS**	%	%
	7.8	9.7	7.7		3.9	Cash & Equivalents	11.1	10.6
	23.1	17.3	14.6		8.7	Trade Receivables (net)	15.5	18.7
	.3	.1	1.7		2.2	Inventory	1.7	2.3
	7.8	2.7	3.5		1.7	All Other Current	3.8	2.0
	39.0	29.9	27.5		16.5	Total Current	32.1	33.5
	53.5	56.7	60.4		70.9	Fixed Assets (net)	61.1	57.3
	6.5	.0	2.8		5.3	Intangibles (net)	1.5	2.4
	1.0	13.5	9.4		7.3	All Other Non-Current	5.3	6.7
	100.0	100.0	100.0		100.0	Total	100.0	100.0
						LIABILITIES		
	4.7	3.6	3.3		1.3	Notes Payable-Short Term	3.8	4.4
	5.1	5.4	5.8		6.1	Cur. Mat.-L/T/D	5.1	4.5
	11.9	4.2	5.7		4.2	Trade Payables	9.5	9.0
	.0	.1	.3		.0	Income Taxes Payable	.2	.5
	1.5	8.9	7.9		3.2	All Other Current	7.8	5.5
	23.2	22.2	22.9		14.8	Total Current	26.4	24.0
	45.1	22.3	35.4		28.4	Long-Term Debt	34.6	34.4
	.0	3.1	2.6		5.4	Deferred Taxes	1.4	2.1
	7.5	6.7	2.6		4.4	All Other Non-Current	2.6	4.4
	24.3	45.7	36.5		47.0	Net Worth	34.9	35.1
	100.0	100.0	100.0		100.0	Total Liabilities & Net Worth	100.0	100.0
						INCOME DATA		
	100.0	100.0	100.0		100.0	Net Sales	100.0	100.0
						Gross Profit		
	83.0	88.3	91.9		87.4	Operating Expenses	91.0	86.8
	17.0	11.7	8.1		12.6	Operating Profit	9.0	13.2
	1.8	1.3	1.8		2.5	All Other Expenses (net)	3.3	4.1
	15.1	10.4	6.2		10.1	Profit Before Taxes	5.7	9.1
						RATIOS		
	2.0	2.4	2.1		1.9		1.6	2.0
	1.3	1.4	1.3		1.2	Current	1.1	1.2
	.8	.6	.6		.8		.6	.8
	1.8	1.9	1.6		1.4		1.3	1.8
	1.3	1.3	1.1		.9	Quick	1.0	1.0
	.6	.6	.6		.6		.5	.6
	10 35.4	23 15.6	14 25.2		35 10.4		21 17.4	24 15.0
	61 6.0	49 7.5	38 9.5		45 8.1	Sales/Receivables	39 9.2	43 8.4
	79 4.6	86 4.2	47 7.8		57 6.4		67 5.4	60 6.1
						Cost of Sales/Inventory		
						Cost of Sales/Payables		
	8.8	3.7	7.2		8.1		9.4	6.0
	17.6	20.4	34.5		31.9	Sales/Working Capital	49.5	23.7
	-39.4	-5.8	-17.2		-24.3		-12.2	-23.1
		11.1	3.5		5.5		(40) 4.1	(46) 6.2
		(17) 5.1	(20) 2.2		(14) 3.7	EBIT/Interest	2.0	2.6
		2.4	.7		2.3		.1	1.7
							(12) 3.9	(13) 3.3
						Net Profit + Depr., Dep., Amort./Cur. Mat. L /T/D	1.2	2.0
							.5	1.4
	1.0	.5	1.1		1.1		1.0	.9
	3.3	1.2	1.9		1.8	Fixed/Worth	1.8	2.0
	-19.4	2.3	4.1		4.5		6.7	4.9
	.9	.4	.9		.6		1.0	.9
	3.9	1.0	1.5		1.6	Debt/Worth	2.3	2.2
	-36.6	2.4	6.1		4.5		7.5	6.7
		31.1	19.0		26.3		(40) 35.6	(50) 58.7
		(18) 14.8	(18) 6.3		17.0	% Profit Before Taxes/Tangible Net Worth	15.3	23.2
		7.2	.4		9.4		-4.4	12.9
	30.9	11.5	7.9		7.0		12.2	13.3
	12.4	6.9	3.2		6.5	% Profit Before Taxes/Total Assets	4.6	7.7
	2.8	4.0	-.1		4.2		-2.3	2.6
	6.1	3.2	4.1		1.1		4.7	5.9
	3.1	1.8	1.7		.8	Sales/Net Fixed Assets	1.4	1.3
	1.2	.7	.8		.6		.8	.7
	1.9	1.6	2.0		.7		2.0	2.5
	1.7	.8	1.1		.6	Sales/Total Assets	.9	.8
	.8	.5	.5		.5		.5	.5
	4.2	3.7	3.0				2.9	3.2
	(10) 5.5	(17) 5.9	(20) 7.7			% Depr., Dep., Amort./Sales	(42) 8.3	(45) 7.1
	8.8	16.7	11.5				10.6	11.1
							.8	
						% Officers', Directors', Owners' Comp/Sales	(10) 5.1	
							7.2	
4730M	38122M	114994M	652141M	285178M	1604647M	Net Sales ($)	1199363M	1952884M
1342M	14347M	110406M	503400M	251983M	2384513M	Total Assets ($)	1331803M	1892663M

M = $ thousand   MM = $ million
See Pages 11 through 21 for Explanation of Ratios and Data

Comparative Historical Data | Current Data Sorted By Sales

Comp. Hist. 1	Comp. Hist. 2	Comp. Hist. 3	Type of Statement	0-1MM	1-3MM	3-5MM	5-10MM	10-25MM	25MM & OVER
29	27	32	Unqualified		1		3	5	23
2	4	6	Reviewed			1		2	2
17	18	11	Compiled	3	2	3	2	2	
4	2	5	Tax Returns	2	3		1	1	
22	21	21	Other		7	4	3	3	4
4/1/02-3/31/03 ALL	4/1/03-3/31/04 ALL	4/1/04-3/31/05 ALL			11 (4/1-9/30/04)		64 (10/1/04-3/31/05)		
74	**72**	**75**	**NUMBER OF STATEMENTS**	5	13	8	11	11	27
%	%	%	**ASSETS**	%	%	%	%	%	%
7.8	7.4	7.7	Cash & Equivalents		5.0		13.2	12.7	5.7
15.8	16.1	16.3	Trade Receivables (net)		24.4		14.7	18.5	14.7
2.2	1.7	1.8	Inventory		3.9		.1	1.5	2.2
1.9	4.3	3.4	All Other Current		5.7		1.8	3.9	2.1
27.6	29.5	29.1	Total Current		38.9		29.8	36.6	24.7
59.4	62.6	59.8	Fixed Assets (net)		46.0		58.4	51.2	62.3
2.2	2.5	2.8	Intangibles (net)		5.5		.0	.8	4.8
10.8	5.4	8.4	All Other Non-Current		9.5		11.8	11.4	8.2
100.0	100.0	100.0	Total		100.0		100.0	100.0	100.0
			LIABILITIES						
3.5	2.3	3.1	Notes Payable-Short Term		2.8		3.4	1.2	1.4
6.6	6.4	5.7	Cur. Mat.-L/T/D		4.5		7.5	3.2	6.1
10.1	7.0	5.8	Trade Payables		6.5		3.8	9.2	6.1
.6	.2	.1	Income Taxes Payable		.0		.2	.2	.1
6.6	6.9	7.0	All Other Current		9.4		8.8	8.2	7.1
27.5	22.9	21.7	Total Current		23.3		23.8	22.1	20.9
43.6	35.1	31.5	Long-Term Debt		30.3		31.2	28.0	29.7
2.8	2.6	3.0	Deferred Taxes		1.8		2.2	3.0	4.7
3.6	5.5	5.4	All Other Non-Current		.0		1.8	8.8	5.6
22.6	33.9	38.4	Net Worth		44.5		41.1	38.1	39.1
100.0	100.0	100.0	Total Liabilities & Net Worth		100.0		100.0	100.0	100.0
			INCOME DATA						
100.0	100.0	100.0	Net Sales		100.0		100.0	100.0	100.0
			Gross Profit						
90.7	90.5	87.8	Operating Expenses		90.9		88.6	90.4	90.3
9.3	9.5	12.2	Operating Profit		9.1		11.4	9.6	9.7
3.9	3.1	1.6	All Other Expenses (net)		-.1		3.3	.0	1.5
5.5	6.3	10.5	Profit Before Taxes		9.2		8.1	9.6	8.2
			RATIOS						
1.8	2.0	2.0	Current		3.2		2.3	2.6	1.9
1.0	1.2	1.3			2.0		1.5	1.4	1.2
.5	.6	.6			.8		.6	1.2	.8
1.8	1.6	1.8	Quick		2.0		2.2	2.5	1.4
.8	1.0	1.1			1.6		1.3	1.3	1.0
.4	.4	.6			.7		.6	.9	.6
14 25.8	19 18.9	25 14.6	Sales/Receivables	0 UND		34 10.8	12 31.6	35 10.4	
38 9.5	39 9.3	41 8.9		64 5.7		41 8.9	41 8.9	42 8.8	
57 6.4	61 6.0	63 5.8		89 4.1		68 5.4	52 7.0	54 6.8	
			Cost of Sales/Inventory						
			Cost of Sales/Payables						
9.8	7.6	7.4	Sales/Working Capital		3.4		3.7	8.0	8.1
-123.6	28.4	25.7			8.4		10.0	17.7	32.6
-8.8	-12.1	-25.8			NM		-6.5	37.8	-25.8
(71) 5.3	(63) 6.4	(66) 5.9	EBIT/Interest		(10) 6.5		(10) 20.9		(26) 5.4
2.2	2.4	3.2			4.2		4.3		2.9
1.1	1.4	1.7			1.0		1.8		1.8
(21) 2.1	(17) 2.0	(19) 3.6	Net Profit + Depr., Dep., Amort./Cur. Mat. L/T/D						(10) 1.9
1.5	1.3	1.9							1.4
1.0	.9	1.4							.6
1.1	1.2	.9	Fixed/Worth		.3		.5	.5	1.2
2.4	2.0	1.8			1.2		1.2	1.3	2.1
4.2	4.9	4.0			NM		4.0	2.4	4.5
1.2	1.0	.8	Debt/Worth		.5		.3	.7	.8
2.9	2.2	1.5			.9		1.2	1.5	1.6
9.0	6.2	4.7			NM		3.9	5.3	4.7
(65) 32.6	(66) 32.7	(66) 53.2	% Profit Before Taxes/Tangible Net Worth		(10) 67.8		(10) 33.7	(10) 76.1	(25) 42.0
17.1	14.9	16.9			12.5		19.3	12.0	16.8
2.6	6.4	6.1			4.3		13.9	-.6	5.3
9.0	8.0	11.2	% Profit Before Taxes/Total Assets		24.8		18.9	9.4	9.8
4.4	3.8	6.5			5.8		8.1	3.4	6.1
.0	1.9	2.8			2.0		5.2	.0	2.6
5.0	4.1	3.2	Sales/Net Fixed Assets		8.4		3.2	5.7	2.4
1.5	1.4	1.3			4.9		2.2	2.7	1.1
.7	.7	.8			.8		.8	.8	.8
1.9	1.8	1.7	Sales/Total Assets		2.8		1.5	2.2	1.4
.9	1.0	.9			1.3		.9	1.5	.7
.5	.5	.5			.5		.7	.5	.6
(69) 3.1	(62) 3.0	(62) 4.1	% Depr., Dep., Amort./Sales		(11) 4.9			(10) 3.3	(20) 2.9
7.2	7.5	7.2			6.6			6.7	8.9
11.0	11.6	11.2			15.0			8.1	9.8
(14) 3.3	(12) 2.3	(15) 2.0	% Officers', Directors', Owners' Comp/Sales						
6.3	6.3	4.8							
9.3	11.5	9.4							
2228680M	2796605M	2699812M	Net Sales ($)	2246M	25448M	29724M	83184M	196517M	2362693M
2818566M	3472287M	3265991M	Total Assets ($)	4807M	34757M	41137M	118856M	194859M	2871575M

M = $ thousand   MM = $ million
See Pages 11 through 21 for Explanation of Ratios and Data

Current Data Sorted By Assets   Comparative Historical Data

Type of Statement	0-500M	500M-2MM	2-10MM	10-50MM	50-100MM	100-250MM		4/1/00-3/31/01 ALL	4/1/01-3/31/02 ALL
Unqualified	1	6	22	29	10	8		53	52
Reviewed	12	51	132	36		1		193	184
Compiled	57	112	84	9	1			297	270
Tax Returns	118	87	26	4		1		144	132
Other	45	121	99	39	5	5		244	257
	172 (4/1-9/30/04)			949 (10/1/04-3/31/05)					
NUMBER OF STATEMENTS	233	377	363	117	16	15		931	895
ASSETS	%	%	%	%	%	%		%	%
Cash & Equivalents	17.9	10.1	7.5	7.1	3.7	5.1		9.2	9.2
Trade Receivables (net)	22.3	30.9	28.9	24.6	23.0	17.9		27.1	26.1
Inventory	1.6	2.2	1.4	1.6	.5	2.1		1.6	1.7
All Other Current	4.3	3.8	4.0	4.2	5.1	4.4		3.9	4.0
Total Current	46.1	47.0	41.8	37.5	32.3	29.5		41.8	41.0
Fixed Assets (net)	41.2	40.5	45.0	51.5	57.8	53.7		46.9	46.5
Intangibles (net)	2.1	2.6	2.6	2.5	3.9	8.8		2.8	3.0
All Other Non-Current	10.6	9.9	10.6	8.5	6.0	8.1		8.5	9.5
Total	100.0	100.0	100.0	100.0	100.0	100.0		100.0	100.0
LIABILITIES									
Notes Payable-Short Term	17.2	8.1	7.5	7.4	2.5	3.3		8.8	9.2
Cur. Mat.-L/T/D	8.8	9.0	8.6	9.1	13.0	8.9		9.0	9.3
Trade Payables	13.2	11.9	10.3	9.3	7.5	8.1		10.0	10.3
Income Taxes Payable	.1	.3	.3	.3	.3	.1		.2	.4
All Other Current	14.7	9.6	9.9	9.1	10.0	9.7		9.1	9.9
Total Current	54.1	38.9	36.7	35.2	33.2	30.1		37.3	39.1
Long-Term Debt	42.0	29.3	25.5	28.4	26.7	25.5		28.0	29.8
Deferred Taxes	.1	.4	1.4	2.4	2.1	6.1		1.0	.9
All Other Non-Current	9.0	5.4	3.5	2.0	3.0	1.8		3.7	4.7
Net Worth	-5.2	26.0	32.9	32.0	35.0	36.5		30.2	25.6
Total Liabilities & Net Worth	100.0	100.0	100.0	100.0	100.0	100.0		100.0	100.0
INCOME DATA									
Net Sales	100.0	100.0	100.0	100.0	100.0	100.0		100.0	100.0
Gross Profit									
Operating Expenses	96.3	96.1	95.5	94.2	92.8	91.3		95.8	96.0
Operating Profit	3.7	3.9	4.5	5.8	7.2	8.7		4.2	4.0
All Other Expenses (net)	1.3	1.0	.8	1.3	-.8	1.4		1.0	1.6
Profit Before Taxes	2.4	2.9	3.7	4.6	8.0	7.4		3.2	2.4

RATIOS

Ratio	0-500M	500M-2MM	2-10MM	10-50MM	50-100MM	100-250MM	4/1/00-3/31/01 ALL	4/1/01-3/31/02 ALL
Current	2.7	2.4	1.8	1.6	1.4	1.5	1.9	1.9
	1.0	1.2	1.1	1.0	1.0	.9	1.1	1.1
	.5	.7	.7	.7	.8	.7	.7	.6
Quick	2.3	2.1	1.6	1.4	1.1	1.0	1.7	1.7
	.8	1.1	1.0	.9	.9	.8	(929) 1.0	1.0
	.3	.6	.6	.6	.7	.4	.6	.5
Sales/Receivables	0 UND	16 22.3	26 13.8	30 12.2	37 9.8	27 13.5	18 20.8	17 21.2
	8 44.8	31 11.8	38 9.7	40 9.1	46 7.9	35 10.5	34 10.6	31 11.6
	31 11.9	46 8.0	48 7.6	49 7.4	54 6.8	45 8.0	49 7.4	46 8.0
Cost of Sales/Inventory								
Cost of Sales/Payables								
Sales/Working Capital	17.4	12.0	12.3	15.5	29.9	13.5	13.2	13.6
	385.5	50.0	60.3	229.0	NM	-71.9	63.2	74.7
	-13.2	-23.6	-24.6	-14.5	-27.3	-18.5	-19.5	-18.6
EBIT/Interest	6.2	8.3	7.5	5.9	8.4	14.7	4.8	4.5
	(188) 2.2	(330) 2.7	(346) 3.3	(111) 3.2	4.5	5.7	(841) 2.2	(809) 1.8
	-.5	.7	1.5	1.8	2.8	2.4	1.0	.5
Net Profit + Depr., Dep., Amort./Cur. Mat. L/T/D	3.0	3.4	2.7	3.2			2.9	2.6
	(12) 1.9	(50) 1.9	(129) 1.5	(58) 1.4			(234) 1.5	(204) 1.3
	-.7	1.3	1.0	1.0			.9	.8
Fixed/Worth	.5	.5	.6	1.0	1.4	.8	.6	.7
	4.6	1.5	1.5	1.8	2.1	3.0	1.6	1.7
	-1.7	11.9	3.4	2.9	3.4	5.2	4.8	6.2
Debt/Worth	1.3	.9	1.0	1.2	1.3	.8	.9	1.0
	11.4	2.9	2.1	2.2	2.0	3.1	2.4	2.6
	-4.1	24.8	5.9	3.7	4.6	7.0	8.5	12.2
% Profit Before Taxes/Tangible Net Worth	98.0	62.7	39.1	35.5	36.9	58.3	40.9	36.3
	(138) 32.3	(299) 25.7	(323) 18.1	(109) 20.1	(15) 28.2	(13) 25.6	(784) 16.0	(729) 12.8
	.6	4.1	4.9	8.1	18.8	16.4	2.3	.4
% Profit Before Taxes/Total Assets	22.8	14.2	12.4	10.2	12.1	12.4	11.8	10.6
	6.6	5.4	5.2	6.1	8.6	10.2	4.7	3.4
	-6.5	-.9	1.3	2.4	4.8	4.4	.2	-2.2
Sales/Net Fixed Assets	53.0	23.5	13.7	7.8	6.0	7.6	14.3	16.2
	12.7	8.1	5.2	4.1	3.0	3.4	6.2	6.4
	4.6	4.2	3.0	2.1	1.9	2.2	2.8	3.0
Sales/Total Assets	7.9	4.6	3.5	2.8	2.2	2.6	4.1	4.1
	4.4	3.2	2.5	2.0	1.6	1.6	2.6	2.7
	2.5	2.1	1.7	1.3	1.3	1.4	1.7	1.7
% Depr., Dep., Amort./Sales	2.2	2.1	1.9	2.6	2.9		2.2	2.2
	(148) 4.4	(311) 4.4	(338) 4.5	(114) 5.2	(14) 4.0		(833) 4.7	(780) 5.3
	10.6	9.1	7.2	8.6	7.0		8.7	9.4
% Officers', Directors', Owners' Comp/Sales	2.6	2.2	1.1	1.0			2.3	2.1
	(114) 5.1	(179) 3.6	(145) 2.2	(27) 1.7			(393) 4.0	(392) 4.0
	9.1	6.4	4.0	4.3			7.5	7.2
Net Sales ($)	299382M	1529917M	4438496M	6394795M	2097688M	4902449M	9682450M	10987562M
Total Assets ($)	58445M	426950M	1651160M	2353354M	1133424M	2265144M	4889124M	4906013M

M = $ thousand   MM = $ million
See Pages 11 through 21 for Explanation of Ratios and Data

Comparative Historical Data | **Current Data Sorted By Sales**

62	63	76	Type of Statement					
			Unqualified	1	2	1	10	18	44
211	214	232	Reviewed	8	27	26	61	70	40
243	301	263	Compiled	32	73	52	59	35	12
163	194	236	Tax Returns	73	81	38	28	10	6
237	253	314	Other	38	68	53	56	51	48
4/1/02-3/31/03	4/1/03-3/31/04	4/1/04-3/31/05		172 (4/1-9/30/04)			949 (10/1/04-3/31/05)		
ALL	ALL	ALL		0-1MM	1-3MM	3-5MM	5-10MM	10-25MM	25MM & OVER
916	1025	1121	**NUMBER OF STATEMENTS**	152	251	170	214	184	150
%	%	%	**ASSETS**	%	%	%	%	%	%
10.2	10.7	10.4	Cash & Equivalents	16.0	11.7	9.8	9.9	8.0	6.8
28.1	28.5	27.5	Trade Receivables (net)	12.2	24.1	31.7	32.5	32.4	31.0
1.9	1.5	1.7	Inventory	1.0	2.6	2.0	1.2	1.5	1.5
4.8	4.6	4.1	All Other Current	4.2	3.2	3.7	4.5	4.8	4.3
45.1	45.3	43.7	Total Current	33.3	41.6	47.2	48.2	46.7	43.7
43.2	42.4	43.7	Fixed Assets (net)	52.7	45.0	39.5	40.0	41.5	45.0
2.7	2.9	2.6	Intangibles (net)	2.5	3.0	1.6	2.8	2.1	3.5
9.0	9.3	10.1	All Other Non-Current	11.5	10.5	11.7	9.0	9.7	7.9
100.0	100.0	100.0	Total	100.0	100.0	100.0	100.0	100.0	100.0
			LIABILITIES						
9.5	8.9	9.6	Notes Payable-Short Term	17.8	9.4	7.5	9.0	6.8	8.0
8.8	10.0	8.9	Cur. Mat.-L/T/D	9.0	9.1	8.7	9.2	8.2	9.2
10.9	11.2	11.3	Trade Payables	6.8	11.9	12.1	11.6	12.3	12.2
.3	.2	.3	Income Taxes Payable	.1	.2	.2	.4	.6	.2
9.7	11.3	10.7	All Other Current	13.8	9.9	9.8	9.6	11.0	11.1
39.3	41.7	40.7	Total Current	47.5	40.5	38.4	39.8	38.9	40.6
25.8	26.3	30.6	Long-Term Debt	48.4	35.9	29.1	24.9	22.0	23.9
.9	.8	1.0	Deferred Taxes	.2	.3	.5	1.1	1.7	2.4
3.7	5.4	5.1	All Other Non-Current	10.4	7.0	3.9	3.7	2.9	2.4
30.4	25.7	22.6	Net Worth	-6.4	16.3	28.1	30.5	34.5	30.8
100.0	100.0	100.0	Total Liabilities & Net Worth	100.0	100.0	100.0	100.0	100.0	100.0
			INCOME DATA						
100.0	100.0	100.0	Net Sales	100.0	100.0	100.0	100.0	100.0	100.0
			Gross Profit						
96.2	95.9	95.6	Operating Expenses	89.3	97.0	96.0	97.1	96.9	95.9
3.8	4.1	4.4	Operating Profit	10.7	3.0	4.0	2.9	3.1	4.1
1.3	.9	1.0	All Other Expenses (net)	4.6	.6	.8	.1	.3	.5
2.5	3.2	3.4	Profit Before Taxes	6.1	2.4	3.3	2.8	2.8	3.6
			RATIOS						
2.0	2.0	2.0	Current	2.6	2.6	2.0	2.0	1.9	1.7
1.2	1.2	1.1		.8	1.1	1.2	1.1	1.2	1.1
.7	.7	.7		.2	.6	.7	.7	.8	.8
1.7	1.7	1.7	Quick	1.9	2.3	1.9	1.8	1.7	1.5
1.0	1.0	1.0		.6	.9	1.0	1.0	1.1	1.0
.6	.6	.6		.2	.4	.6	.6	.7	.6
18 20.5	18 20.1	14 26.8	Sales/Receivables	0 UND	5 72.1	21 17.3	26 13.9	27 13.5	31 11.6
34 10.8	33 11.0	34 10.9		0 UND	25 14.5	33 11.0	37 9.8	36 10.1	39 9.4
46 7.9	46 8.0	45 8.0		31 11.9	42 8.6	48 7.6	50 7.2	48 7.7	46 7.9
			Cost of Sales/Inventory						
			Cost of Sales/Payables						
12.2	12.1	13.5	Sales/Working Capital	13.1	14.1	10.9	12.7	13.7	18.3
53.4	61.9	84.5		-32.8	121.0	56.7	64.4	49.0	65.3
-26.5	-23.1	-19.8		-4.7	-15.0	-39.6	-31.7	-31.0	-27.4
5.5	6.4	7.4	EBIT/Interest	6.3	6.3		8.4	7.6	9.6
(822) 2.1	(917) 2.5	(1006) 3.0		(111) 2.3	(228) 2.2	(151) 3.1	(199) 3.3	(173) 3.2	(144) 4.1
.6	1.0	1.1		-.5	.2	1.1	1.2	1.6	2.4
3.1	2.8	3.0	Net Profit + Depr., Dep., Amort./Cur. Mat. L/T/D		3.5	2.2	2.8	3.1	3.2
(245) 1.5	(234) 1.5	(260) 1.6			(33) 2.0	(29) 1.7	(52) 1.5	(77) 1.6	(63) 1.6
1.0	1.0	1.0			1.2	1.1	1.0	1.0	1.0
.6	.5	.6	Fixed/Worth	1.1	.6	.5	.5	.5	.8
1.4	1.5	1.7		8.4	2.4	1.5	1.5	1.2	1.6
4.0	5.5	8.2		-2.7	-11.9	6.2	3.7	2.8	3.0
.9	.9	1.1	Debt/Worth	1.6	.9	.9	1.0	1.0	1.3
2.2	2.5	2.6		21.9	3.9	2.9	2.1	2.0	2.5
7.7	13.8	17.2		-4.7	-14.4	12.0	6.6	4.3	4.8
38.5	41.6	52.0	% Profit Before Taxes/Tangible Net Worth	100.0	61.5	53.2	44.8	37.4	45.4
(778) 13.5	(825) 14.8	(897) 21.2		(88) 38.2	(180) 23.4	(147) 17.6	(177) 20.2	(168) 17.3	(137) 24.9
-.8	1.8	5.6		6.3	2.7	3.8	4.0	3.8	13.7
11.6	12.8	13.5	% Profit Before Taxes/Total Assets	19.6	13.7	13.3	13.5	12.8	12.4
3.9	4.6	5.8		5.8	4.1	5.7	5.6	6.0	7.8
-1.2	.0	.2		-7.4	-2.7	.8	1.0	1.0	3.2
18.9	20.0	18.3	Sales/Net Fixed Assets	14.7	17.2	24.6	19.2	23.8	16.1
7.3	7.5	6.8		4.3	7.8	7.5	8.7	7.3	6.0
3.3	3.6	3.4		1.6	3.5	4.3	3.9	3.7	3.1
4.3	4.6	4.5	Sales/Total Assets	4.1	4.7	4.7	4.5	4.4	4.1
2.8	2.9	2.8		1.9	3.0	2.9	2.9	2.9	2.6
1.8	1.9	1.8		.8	1.9	2.2	1.9	2.0	1.7
2.2	2.3	2.1	% Depr., Dep., Amort./Sales	4.4	2.5	2.1	1.7	1.7	1.6
(805) 4.5	(864) 4.8	(930) 4.5		(111) 12.0	(197) 5.7	(135) 4.6	(186) 3.3	(173) 3.8	(128) 3.3
8.6	8.2	8.3		19.1	10.7	7.7	6.0	6.1	6.0
2.0	1.8	1.7	% Officers', Directors', Owners' Comp/Sales	3.9	2.7	1.7	1.8	1.1	.5
(379) 3.5	(433) 3.6	(469) 3.2		(53) 7.4	(128) 4.2	(87) 2.8	(96) 2.9	(69) 2.0	(36) 1.3
6.8	6.7	6.6		16.1	7.1	5.2	4.9	3.6	3.2
17213891M	16526700M	19662727M	Net Sales ($)	75936M	478267M	671249M	1544746M	2832101M	14060428M
5894201M	5744381M	7888477M	Total Assets ($)	80684M	252556M	300623M	646253M	1118605M	5489756M

M = $ thousand   MM = $ million
See Pages 11 through 21 for Explanation of Ratios and Data

Current Data Sorted By Assets | | | | | | **Comparative Historical Data**

Type of Statement	0-500M	500M-2MM	2-10MM	10-50MM	50-100MM	100-250MM		4/1/00-3/31/01 ALL	4/1/01-3/31/02 ALL
Unqualified	1	1	31	107	45	32		137	145
Reviewed	5	31	145	70	3	2		205	219
Compiled	31	114	121	20		2		268	309
Tax Returns	63	53	25	2	1	2		74	79
Other	37	77	125	73	11	14		279	368
	170 (4/1-9/30/04)		1072 (10/1/04-3/31/05)						
NUMBER OF STATEMENTS	137	276	447	272	60	50		963	1120
ASSETS	%	%	%	%	%	%		%	%
Cash & Equivalents	16.8	10.0	6.7	6.7	4.0	6.0		6.8	7.4
Trade Receivables (net)	25.9	33.2	33.3	27.4	23.0	25.7		28.0	27.7
Inventory	1.6	2.1	1.4	1.5	1.6	1.2		1.4	1.5
All Other Current	4.6	2.7	3.8	3.2	5.4	4.3		3.1	3.8
Total Current	48.9	48.1	45.2	38.7	34.0	37.3		39.3	40.4
Fixed Assets (net)	39.1	41.9	44.3	50.3	53.4	47.7		49.5	48.1
Intangibles (net)	.7	1.3	1.0	2.2	4.1	9.9		2.9	2.8
All Other Non-Current	11.2	8.7	9.5	8.7	8.5	5.2		8.3	8.7
Total	100.0	100.0	100.0	100.0	100.0	100.0		100.0	100.0
LIABILITIES									
Notes Payable-Short Term	11.4	9.7	9.8	6.7	3.6	3.8		8.2	8.7
Cur. Mat.-L/T/D	13.6	9.0	10.9	10.4	9.4	10.0		10.1	10.8
Trade Payables	12.2	12.6	10.3	10.3	10.1	13.4		9.8	10.7
Income Taxes Payable	.2	.1	.3	.3	.4	.2		.2	.3
All Other Current	19.1	8.9	8.7	8.7	11.4	12.2		10.1	10.3
Total Current	56.5	40.3	39.9	36.3	34.9	39.4		38.4	40.8
Long-Term Debt	36.5	28.3	25.7	25.2	27.6	27.2		27.1	26.2
Deferred Taxes	.3	.4	1.5	2.7	4.2	4.3		1.8	1.8
All Other Non-Current	11.9	5.2	3.6	1.9	3.5	3.5		3.3	3.3
Net Worth	-5.1	25.8	29.2	33.9	29.8	25.5		29.4	27.9
Total Liabilities & Net Worth	100.0	100.0	100.0	100.0	100.0	100.0		100.0	100.0
INCOME DATA									
Net Sales	100.0	100.0	100.0	100.0	100.0	100.0		100.0	100.0
Gross Profit									
Operating Expenses	94.0	94.7	96.6	95.7	94.6	94.3		96.2	96.5
Operating Profit	6.0	5.3	3.4	4.3	5.4	5.7		3.8	3.5
All Other Expenses (net)	1.4	1.2	.6	.6	1.5	1.3		1.1	1.4
Profit Before Taxes	4.6	4.0	2.8	3.7	3.8	4.3		2.7	2.1
RATIOS									
Current	2.4	2.2	1.6	1.6	1.2	1.6		1.6	1.6
	1.0	1.2	1.1	1.0	1.0	1.0		1.0	1.0
	.5	.7	.8	.7	.8	.7		.7	.6
Quick	2.3	2.0	1.5	1.4	1.0	1.3		1.4	1.4
	(135) .8	1.1	1.0	.9	.8	.8		(961) .9	(1118) .9
	.5	.7	.7	.6	.6	.6		.6	.5
Sales/Receivables	0 UND	19 18.9	28 13.0	31 11.6	31 11.7	37 9.7		25 14.6	23 15.6
	10 35.6	31 11.9	37 10.0	39 9.3	39 9.4	42 8.7		35 10.3	33 11.0
	32 11.4	41 8.9	45 8.0	47 7.8	45 8.2	49 7.5		45 8.1	43 8.6
Cost of Sales/Inventory									
Cost of Sales/Payables									
Sales/Working Capital	17.8	15.4	16.8	17.0	59.2	16.7		17.5	18.0
	-740.5	63.3	70.1	438.8	909.1	NM		999.8	793.2
	-13.4	-30.9	-25.4	-21.8	-34.6	-19.8		-18.4	-17.6
EBIT/Interest	9.5	8.1	7.2	8.2	9.2	8.3		4.6	4.0
	(101) 3.4	(246) 3.2	(427) 2.9	(269) 3.8	(57) 3.9	(49) 3.5		(886) 2.1	(1038) 1.7
	-.2	1.2	1.4	1.9	2.7	1.6		.8	.6
Net Profit + Depr., Dep., Amort./Cur. Mat. L /T/D	1.7	3.7	2.4	2.3		3.1		2.1	2.0
	(10) .9	(46) 1.4	(151) 1.4	(131) 1.4	(16) 1.9	1.9		(285) 1.3	(331) 1.2
	.4	1.0	1.0	1.0	1.0	1.0		.9	.8
Fixed/Worth	.3	.6	.7	1.1	1.3	.9		.9	.8
	2.3	1.5	1.5	1.6	2.1	3.1		1.9	1.9
	-2.1	5.6	3.8	3.2	4.4	63.9		4.7	4.7
Debt/Worth	1.0	1.1	1.2	1.1	1.4	1.2		1.1	1.1
	11.8	2.8	2.4	2.4	2.8	3.3		2.6	2.7
	-4.1	12.5	5.7	4.4	5.2	111.5		7.1	7.7
% Profit Before Taxes/Tangible Net Worth	100.0	74.0	45.4	35.0	33.8	36.1		35.9	30.7
	(83) 34.3	(237) 29.4	(408) 21.5	(256) 21.1	(56) 23.7	(39) 24.2		(829) 15.2	(971) 11.3
	.0	6.4	6.0	8.1	15.1	12.2		1.1	-.9
% Profit Before Taxes/Total Assets	23.7	15.0	12.0	10.5	9.6	11.9		10.1	10.0
	7.3	6.3	6.0	6.1	6.0	6.8		4.0	3.2
	-.5	.7	1.2	2.6	3.4	2.0		-.8	-1.6
Sales/Net Fixed Assets	177.2	22.7	14.2	8.4	5.5	6.9		11.7	13.4
	15.3	9.4	6.3	4.1	3.3	3.7		4.9	5.7
	5.5	4.9	3.5	2.5	2.3	2.4		2.6	2.9
Sales/Total Assets	9.2	5.4	4.2	3.1	2.5	2.6		3.9	4.1
	4.7	3.6	2.9	2.2	2.0	1.9		2.5	2.7
	2.3	2.6	2.0	1.7	1.5	1.5		1.6	1.7
% Depr., Dep., Amort./Sales	1.9	1.6	1.8	2.4	3.5	.8		2.0	2.1
	(77) 4.4	(220) 4.3	(412) 4.2	(261) 4.9	(38) 4.5	(13) 2.0		(850) 4.9	(970) 4.9
	10.3	7.8	7.4	8.2	6.9	4.3		8.9	9.0
% Officers', Directors', Owners' Comp/Sales	2.1	1.9	1.0	.9				1.4	1.3
	(54) 4.5	(127) 3.3	(184) 1.7	(65) 1.3				(374) 2.8	(391) 2.7
	6.8	6.7	3.6	5.6				5.8	5.1
Net Sales ($)	205336M	1273928M	6906846M	15420800M	9724220M	16265492M		28189156M	35053547M
Total Assets ($)	32723M	317967M	2227349M	6290279M	4312610M	7232957M		14058029M	16321409M

M = $ thousand   MM = $ million

See Pages 11 through 21 for Explanation of Ratios and Data

Comparative Historical Data | | | **Current Data Sorted By Sales**

			Type of Statement						
189	194	217	Unqualified	1	13	21	5	34	177
229	260	256	Reviewed	4			42	102	74
263	362	286	Compiled	23	47	39	82	70	25
89	131	146	Tax Returns	36	44	21	25	15	5
295	339	337	Other	24	41	34	48	79	111
4/1/02-3/31/03 ALL	4/1/03-3/31/04 ALL	4/1/04-3/31/05 ALL		170 (4/1-9/30/04)			1072 (10/1/04-3/31/05)		
				0-1MM	1-3MM	3-5MM	5-10MM	10-25MM	25MM & OVER
1065	1286	1242	**NUMBER OF STATEMENTS**	88	145	115	202	300	392
%	%	%	**ASSETS**	%	%	%	%	%	%
7.3	7.8	8.4	Cash & Equivalents	14.1	12.1	10.3	8.2	7.7	5.8
28.3	28.4	30.4	Trade Receivables (net)	17.9	24.2	32.9	31.9	32.2	32.6
1.7	1.5	1.6	Inventory	.3	2.8	1.3	1.7	1.5	1.6
4.3	4.2	3.6	All Other Current	5.0	2.9	3.0	3.3	3.3	4.1
41.6	41.9	44.0	Total Current	37.3	41.9	47.5	45.1	44.6	44.1
47.6	46.9	45.1	Fixed Assets (net)	53.4	47.1	41.6	43.6	45.1	44.3
2.3	2.2	1.8	Intangibles (net)	.5	1.0	1.0	1.5	1.1	3.3
8.5	9.0	9.1	All Other Non-Current	8.8	10.0	9.9	9.8	9.2	8.2
100.0	100.0	100.0	Total	100.0	100.0	100.0	100.0	100.0	100.0
			LIABILITIES						
8.7	9.3	8.7	Notes Payable-Short Term	5.7	12.2	8.0	9.3	9.0	7.8
11.0	10.6	10.5	Cur. Mat.-L/T/D	7.7	15.0	10.9	9.8	11.4	9.2
10.6	10.6	11.1	Trade Payables	7.9	10.6	11.8	11.1	10.2	12.5
.2	.3	.2	Income Taxes Payable	.1	.2	.2	.3	.3	.3
10.9	11.5	10.2	All Other Current	10.9	13.6	9.0	9.0	8.7	10.8
41.4	42.2	40.8	Total Current	32.4	51.6	39.9	39.3	39.6	40.6
26.7	26.9	27.5	Long-Term Debt	40.7	34.7	30.8	26.9	25.8	22.6
1.9	1.7	1.6	Deferred Taxes	.4	.3	.7	1.2	1.5	2.8
3.7	4.5	4.5	All Other Non-Current	9.9	7.8	4.7	3.8	3.5	3.1
26.3	24.6	25.6	Net Worth	16.5	5.6	23.8	28.7	29.5	30.8
100.0	100.0	100.0	Total Liabilities & Net Worth	100.0	100.0	100.0	100.0	100.0	100.0
			INCOME DATA						
100.0	100.0	100.0	Net Sales	100.0	100.0	100.0	100.0	100.0	100.0
			Gross Profit						
96.5	96.4	95.5	Operating Expenses	83.1	95.1	95.7	97.3	97.2	96.2
3.5	3.6	4.5	Operating Profit	16.9	4.9	4.3	2.7	2.8	3.8
1.5	1.1	.9	All Other Expenses (net)	6.4	.8	.5	.1	.3	.7
2.0	2.5	3.6	Profit Before Taxes	10.4	4.1	3.8	2.6	2.5	3.1
			RATIOS						
1.5	1.6	1.7	Current	2.7	1.8	2.2	1.8	1.7	1.5
1.0	1.0	1.1		1.0	.9	1.2	1.1	1.1	1.0
.7	.6	.7		.3	.5	.8	.8	.8	.8
1.3	1.4	1.5	Quick	2.6	1.6	1.8	1.5	1.6	1.3
(1063) .8	(1285) .9	(1240) .9		.7	(143) .8	1.1	1.0	1.0	.9
.5	.5	.6		.3	.4	.8	.7	.7	.7
24 15.0	23 15.8	24 15.3	Sales/Receivables	0 UND	1 704.6	20 18.4	26 14.2	27 13.4	32 11.4
35 10.6	34 10.8	35 10.3		7 52.3	27 13.3	31 11.9	35 10.4	36 10.2	39 9.3
43 8.4	43 8.5	45 8.2		37 9.9	41 9.0	42 8.7	44 8.3	44 8.3	47 7.8
			Cost of Sales/Inventory						
			Cost of Sales/Payables						
20.3	17.7	17.3	Sales/Working Capital	8.6	18.0	12.9	16.6	17.7	19.6
UND	352.1	116.3		UND	-112.3	44.5	70.7	81.6	137.3
-18.6	-18.2	-24.4		-6.2	-12.7	-46.8	-31.0	-25.7	-26.2
4.5	5.5	8.1	EBIT/Interest	9.4	6.5	7.0	7.0	7.6	9.2
(996) 2.0	(1185) 2.5	(1149) 3.3		(61) 4.0	(125) 2.1	(106) 3.3	(185) 3.0	(292) 3.1	(380) 3.9
.7	1.0	1.5		1.1	.4	1.2	1.5	1.4	2.0
2.1	2.4	2.4	Net Profit + Depr., Dep., Amort./Cur. Mat. L/T/D	2.0	2.4	1.9	2.4	2.4	2.8
(330) 1.3	(355) 1.4	(363) 1.4		(10) 1.0	(15) 1.3	(17) 1.4	(61) 1.4	(104) 1.3	(156) 1.5
.8	.9	1.0		.4	.9	1.1	.9	1.0	1.1
.8	.8	.8	Fixed/Worth	.5	.9	.7	.8	.7	.8
1.9	1.9	1.6		1.6	2.7	1.6	1.5	1.6	1.6
5.2	5.1	4.5		31.9	-7.6	5.0	4.4	3.9	3.4
1.2	1.2	1.2	Debt/Worth	.9	1.2	1.1	1.1	1.2	1.2
2.7	2.6	2.6		3.6	4.6	2.3	2.6	2.4	2.7
9.0	9.0	8.2		-37.0	-12.5	13.5	8.0	5.7	5.1
33.6	38.3	47.7	% Profit Before Taxes/Tangible Net Worth	86.4	59.5	74.6	50.0	40.7	37.7
(912) 12.7	(1088) 15.9	(1079) 22.6		(65) 27.3	(99) 21.7	(98) 29.3	(183) 25.3	(272) 19.3	(362) 23.0
.4	3.1	7.3		3.0	2.7	7.7	7.6	5.5	11.3
8.6	10.6	12.4	% Profit Before Taxes/Total Assets	16.8	16.0	13.4	12.2	11.9	11.1
3.4	4.1	6.2		6.5	5.3	6.5	7.0	5.4	6.3
-.9	-.1	1.4		.0	-1.7	.0	1.3	1.1	3.0
14.2	15.3	16.3	Sales/Net Fixed Assets	17.5	17.7	22.8	14.4	14.1	15.4
5.6	6.1	6.1		3.4	6.9	9.0	6.9	6.7	5.2
2.9	3.1	3.2		1.4	4.1	4.8	3.7	3.3	2.9
4.2	4.2	4.3	Sales/Total Assets	3.0	5.4	4.7	4.5	4.5	3.8
2.6	2.7	2.8		1.6	3.1	3.6	2.9	3.0	2.5
1.8	1.8	1.9		.6	2.0	2.7	2.0	2.0	1.8
2.3	2.0	2.0	% Depr., Dep., Amort./Sales	4.9	3.0	2.2	1.9	1.9	1.7
(928) 5.3	(1082) 5.0	(1021) 4.4		(57) 14.0	(106) 6.4	(87) 4.8	(185) 4.4	(273) 4.2	(313) 3.5
9.0	8.6	7.8		30.2	10.8	9.2	7.1	7.4	6.3
1.4	1.3	1.2	% Officers', Directors', Owners' Comp/Sales	4.5	2.2	1.7	1.3	.9	.8
(382) 2.5	(422) 2.4	(443) 2.5		(27) 7.4	(58) 3.8	(59) 3.0	(101) 2.2	(120) 1.6	(78) 1.4
5.6	5.0	5.5		12.1	6.7	4.8	4.0	4.7	5.0
43081407M	46794198M	49796622M	Net Sales ($)	36274M	284109M	451897M	1489257M	4999541M	42535544M
18285617M	20034250M	20413885M	Total Assets ($)	40199M	137400M	207374M	605874M	1996384M	17426654M

Current Data Sorted By Assets   **Comparative Historical Data**

0-500M	500M-2MM	2-10MM	10-50MM	50-100MM	100-250MM	Type of Statement	4/1/00-3/31/01 ALL	4/1/01-3/31/02 ALL
						Unqualified		
	3	2	8	1	7	Reviewed		
		8	4			Compiled		
3	6	10	3			Tax Returns		
3	3	1				Other		
	5	7	10	5	3			
	11 (4/1-9/30/04)		81 (10/1/04-3/31/05)					
6	17	28	25	6	10	NUMBER OF STATEMENTS		
%	%	%	%	%	%		%	%
						ASSETS		
	9.7	8.7	6.9		5.8	Cash & Equivalents	D	D
	40.0	37.0	21.3		20.1	Trade Receivables (net)	A	A
	.6	2.9	.6		2.5	Inventory	T	T
	7.1	4.8	6.9		3.9	All Other Current	A	A
	57.4	53.3	35.6		32.2	Total Current		
	32.7	40.8	58.0		64.1	Fixed Assets (net)	N	N
	1.0	1.0	2.2		.3	Intangibles (net)	O	O
	8.9	4.8	4.2		3.4	All Other Non-Current	T	T
	100.0	100.0	100.0		100.0	Total		
						LIABILITIES	A	A
	12.3	6.6	3.4		3.5	Notes Payable-Short Term	V	V
	4.6	10.1	10.2		9.8	Cur. Mat.-L/T/D	A	A
	7.3	10.5	7.8		6.2	Trade Payables	I	I
	.3	.3	.2		.0	Income Taxes Payable	L	L
	5.9	8.7	6.6		10.1	All Other Current	A	A
	30.4	36.3	28.3		29.6	Total Current	B	B
	22.4	22.6	28.7		28.3	Long-Term Debt	L	L
	.0	1.6	5.0		1.0	Deferred Taxes	E	E
	4.8	2.5	.2		2.9	All Other Non-Current		
	42.4	37.0	37.9		38.2	Net Worth		
	100.0	100.0	100.0		100.0	Total Liabilities & Net Worth		
						INCOME DATA		
	100.0	100.0	100.0		100.0	Net Sales		
						Gross Profit		
	100.0	97.4	92.8		95.7	Operating Expenses		
	.0	2.6	7.2		4.3	Operating Profit		
	−.8	.5	.7		1.0	All Other Expenses (net)		
	.8	2.2	6.6		3.2	Profit Before Taxes		
						RATIOS		
	3.3	1.9	1.8		1.8			
	1.8	1.4	1.2		1.1	Current		
	1.3	1.0	.8		.7			
	2.8	1.5	1.4		1.3			
	1.5	1.2	.9		1.0	Quick		
	1.2	.8	.7		.5			
	22 17.0	33 11.2	27 13.3		35 10.5			
	28 13.1	41 9.0	40 9.0		41 9.0	Sales/Receivables		
	37 10.0	45 8.1	43 8.5		44 8.2			
						Cost of Sales/Inventory		
						Cost of Sales/Payables		
	12.7	11.0	13.6		11.8			
	20.9	31.1	47.8		NM	Sales/Working Capital		
	53.3	NM	−38.3		−15.5			
	10.1	7.3	9.4		9.8			
	(13) 2.4	(25) 2.5	3.5		5.3	EBIT/Interest		
	2.0	1.1	2.4		1.7			
		1.3	3.7			Net Profit + Depr., Dep.,		
		(12) 1.2	(14) 1.4			Amort./Cur. Mat. L /T/D		
		1.0	1.3					
	.3	.6	1.1		1.1			
	.7	1.6	1.5		1.5	Fixed/Worth		
	1.6	3.7	3.2		4.2			
	1.0	.8	.8		.8			
	1.4	2.0	2.0		1.5	Debt/Worth		
	2.8	6.9	4.6		4.7			
	29.9	33.4	42.2		24.5	% Profit Before Taxes/Tangible		
	(16) 14.0	17.5	22.1		17.9	Net Worth		
	4.0	3.4	8.2		15.8			
	10.0	13.0	10.6		10.9	% Profit Before Taxes/Total		
	4.6	4.4	5.8		9.4	Assets		
	2.0	1.3	3.9		2.2			
	83.5	16.2	5.2		4.0			
	17.6	7.3	4.0		2.8	Sales/Net Fixed Assets		
	5.5	5.0	2.3		2.0			
	6.6	4.8	2.8		2.2			
	4.4	3.1	1.9		1.8	Sales/Total Assets		
	2.8	2.7	1.6		1.4			
	.5	1.3	4.1			% Depr., Dep., Amort./Sales		
	(13) 3.0	(25) 2.8	6.2					
	7.8	4.0	8.8					
	1.9	.6				% Officers', Directors',		
	(10) 4.4	(13) 1.7				Owners' Comp/Sales		
	9.0	3.6						
13189M	109582M	541847M	1379353M	887803M	2783826M	Net Sales ($)		
1595M	20608M	155530M	675156M	446538M	1496512M	Total Assets ($)		

© RMA 2005

M = $ thousand   MM = $ million
See Pages 11 through 21 for Explanation of Ratios and Data

Comparative Historical Data | **Current Data Sorted By Sales**

	4/1/02-3/31/03 ALL	4/1/03-3/31/04 ALL	4/1/04-3/31/05 ALL	Type of Statement	0-1MM	1-3MM	3-5MM	5-10MM	10-25MM	25MM & OVER
	10	13	18	Unqualified			1	2	3	15
	6	13	15	Reviewed	2	3	1	4	7	5
	8	8	22	Compiled	2	3	1	2	4	8
	2	4	7	Tax Returns	1	2	1	1	1	
	24	15	30	Other	1	2	2		7	18
					11 (4/1-9/30/04)			81 (10/1/04-3/31/05)		
	50	53	92	**NUMBER OF STATEMENTS**	3	7	6	8	22	46
	%	%	%	**ASSETS**	%	%	%	%	%	%
	5.8	8.3	7.4	Cash & Equivalents					8.7	7.1
	29.2	29.7	30.0	Trade Receivables (net)					39.2	25.7
	.7	1.4	1.5	Inventory					.2	1.4
	4.5	4.7	5.3	All Other Current					5.8	4.9
	40.2	44.1	44.2	Total Current					53.9	39.1
	51.3	46.6	48.4	Fixed Assets (net)					40.8	55.8
	.9	1.0	1.4	Intangibles (net)					.7	1.6
	7.6	8.3	5.9	All Other Non-Current					4.6	3.6
	100.0	100.0	100.0	Total					100.0	100.0
				LIABILITIES						
	7.5	13.3	6.7	Notes Payable-Short Term					5.6	3.6
	10.1	7.1	8.9	Cur. Mat.-L/T/D					9.4	10.2
	9.8	9.8	8.0	Trade Payables					10.9	8.4
	.1	.1	.2	Income Taxes Payable					.5	.2
	10.3	8.5	7.6	All Other Current					7.5	9.6
	37.8	38.8	31.4	Total Current					34.0	32.0
	22.4	29.1	29.4	Long-Term Debt					23.3	27.0
	2.6	1.5	2.0	Deferred Taxes					2.2	2.9
	1.9	4.9	2.3	All Other Non-Current					3.1	1.3
	35.3	25.7	35.0	Net Worth					37.4	36.8
	100.0	100.0	100.0	Total Liabilities & Net Worth					100.0	100.0
				INCOME DATA						
	100.0	100.0	100.0	Net Sales					100.0	100.0
				Gross Profit						
	95.2	95.8	96.1	Operating Expenses					96.3	96.0
	4.8	4.2	3.9	Operating Profit					3.7	4.0
	1.2	.6	.2	All Other Expenses (net)					.7	.7
	3.6	3.6	3.6	Profit Before Taxes					3.0	3.3
				RATIOS						
	1.7	1.9	2.0	Current					2.2	1.6
	1.1	1.2	1.3						1.4	1.2
	.7	.7	.9						1.1	.9
	1.5	1.5	1.5	Quick					1.9	1.3
	1.0	1.0	1.1						1.3	1.0
	.6	.6	.8						.9	.8
	31 11.8	31 11.9	28 13.0	Sales/Receivables					32 11.3	30 12.0
	37 10.0	37 9.9	38 9.7						40 9.2	40 9.0
	45 8.1	47 7.8	43 8.5						44 8.3	44 8.3
				Cost of Sales/Inventory						
				Cost of Sales/Payables						
	19.2	14.0	12.7	Sales/Working Capital					11.4	14.4
	86.3	58.6	34.0						23.0	47.8
	-20.4	-23.2	-61.9						166.9	-53.2
	5.8	5.4	9.6	EBIT/Interest					10.0	9.5
(47) 2.9	(50) 2.8	(83) 3.7						(20) 4.6	(44) 3.7
	1.0	1.6	1.9						1.7	2.1
	2.3	2.3	2.2	Net Profit + Depr., Dep.,					2.1	3.2
(12) 1.2	(17) 1.5	(29) 1.4	Amort./Cur. Mat. L/T/D					(10) 1.2	(15) 1.4
	.9	1.1	1.1						1.0	1.1
	.8	.8	.7	Fixed/Worth					.6	1.0
	1.7	1.5	1.4						1.2	1.6
	3.4	2.8	3.2						3.3	3.7
	1.1	1.0	.9	Debt/Worth					1.0	.9
	1.7	1.8	1.7						1.5	1.9
	4.4	5.7	4.6						6.8	4.6
	24.6	32.9	35.5	% Profit Before Taxes/Tangible					37.1	37.2
(49) 14.6	(49) 14.2	(88) 19.1	Net Worth					19.7	19.0
	.2	5.3	7.6						8.8	8.2
	7.6	8.1	11.6	% Profit Before Taxes/Total					16.1	10.3
	4.1	4.1	6.4	Assets					8.7	6.0
	.0	1.8	2.4						2.4	3.5
	11.8	13.7	11.0	Sales/Net Fixed Assets					19.6	5.6
	4.4	5.8	5.3						6.9	3.8
	2.5	3.4	3.2						4.6	2.5
	3.5	4.3	4.1	Sales/Total Assets					5.4	2.9
	2.1	2.7	2.7						3.1	2.1
	1.6	1.7	1.9						2.3	1.7
	2.1	1.7	2.5	% Depr., Dep., Amort./Sales					1.3	3.7
(36) 5.2	(42) 4.8	(72) 4.1						(21) 3.0	(35) 5.3
	9.0	7.9	7.2						4.1	7.8
	.5	.5	1.2	% Officers', Directors',						.8
(12) 1.3	(18) 3.1	(33) 2.8	Owners' Comp/Sales					(10)	2.0
	4.8	5.4	5.8							8.1
	4629554M	3593112M	5715600M	Net Sales ($)	1685M	14517M	24251M	58698M	369559M	5246890M
	2555358M	1683743M	2795939M	Total Assets ($)	665M	27188M	5481M	15823M	124338M	2622444M

M = $ thousand   MM = $ million
See Pages 11 through 21 for Explanation of Ratios and Data

						Type of Statement		
	1	2	3		3	Unqualified		
2	8	15	5			Reviewed		
5	6	6	1			Compiled		
4	5	2				Tax Returns		
1	6	7				Other	4/1/00-3/31/01	4/1/01-3/31/02
	5 (4/1-9/30/04)		77 (10/1/04-3/31/05)				ALL	ALL
0-500M	500M-2MM	2-10MM	10-50MM	50-100MM	100-250MM			
12	26	32	9		3	NUMBER OF STATEMENTS		
%	%	%	%	%	%	ASSETS	%	%
18.7	9.8	7.3		D		Cash & Equivalents	D	D
53.7	21.7	30.5		A		Trade Receivables (net)	A	A
.0	1.4	.2		T		Inventory	T	T
1.3	5.8	2.7		A		All Other Current	A	A
73.7	38.6	40.7				Total Current		
18.2	48.0	34.9		N		Fixed Assets (net)	N	N
1.0	1.2	1.4		O		Intangibles (net)	O	O
7.1	12.1	23.0		T		All Other Non-Current	T	T
100.0	100.0	100.0				Total		
				A		LIABILITIES	A	A
5.4	7.5	6.7		V		Notes Payable-Short Term	V	V
3.4	4.2	4.8		A		Cur. Mat.-L/T/D	A	A
27.0	9.6	8.9		I		Trade Payables	I	I
.0	.1	.6		L		Income Taxes Payable	L	L
4.8	10.2	13.6		A		All Other Current	A	A
40.6	31.7	34.4		B		Total Current	B	B
7.7	28.7	20.7		L		Long-Term Debt	L	L
.0	.6	1.5		E		Deferred Taxes	E	E
4.6	4.5	1.0				All Other Non-Current		
47.0	34.5	42.4				Net Worth		
100.0	100.0	100.0				Total Liabilities & Net Worth		
						INCOME DATA		
100.0	100.0	100.0				Net Sales		
						Gross Profit		
95.9	89.7	93.1				Operating Expenses		
4.1	10.3	6.9				Operating Profit		
1.8	5.9	2.4				All Other Expenses (net)		
2.3	4.4	4.5				Profit Before Taxes		
						RATIOS		
7.4	2.3	1.5						
2.8	1.1	1.1				Current		
1.0	.6	.7						
7.3	1.5	1.4						
2.8	1.0	1.0				Quick		
1.0	.5	.7						
0 UND	0 UND	30 12.2						
29 12.4	21 17.0	41 9.0				Sales/Receivables		
61 6.0	42 8.6	58 6.3						
						Cost of Sales/Inventory		
						Cost of Sales/Payables		
8.0	9.4	13.4						
23.4	69.7	71.0				Sales/Working Capital		
UND	−28.7	−13.9						
	3.3	12.1						
(21)	2.0	(27) 4.0				EBIT/Interest		
	−.3	1.6						
		5.3				Net Profit + Depr., Dep.,		
	(12)	2.6				Amort./Cur. Mat. L /T/D		
		1.4						
.0	.3	.3						
.1	1.3	.9				Fixed/Worth		
.7	4.8	1.8						
.3	1.2	.7						
.8	1.8	1.6				Debt/Worth		
8.7	5.2	2.3						
88.7	28.7	23.5				% Profit Before Taxes/Tangible		
(10) 8.9	(23) 5.2	(30) 14.3				Net Worth		
4.2	−3.3	3.3						
28.1	5.7	11.5				% Profit Before Taxes/Total		
5.3	2.5	4.0				Assets		
.4	−1.6	1.4						
UND	21.4	25.0						
220.0	4.8	10.8				Sales/Net Fixed Assets		
13.5	2.6	4.2						
9.2	4.1	3.8						
5.6	2.5	2.3				Sales/Total Assets		
3.9	1.2	1.7						
	2.1	1.3						
	(23) 3.7	(29) 2.9				% Depr., Dep., Amort./Sales		
	6.6	6.1						
	2.1					% Officers', Directors',		
	(10) 5.0					Owners' Comp/Sales		
	7.2							
23155M	73416M	360241M	545901M		1381931M	Net Sales ($)		
3708M	30180M	147583M	175113M		550219M	Total Assets ($)		

M = $ thousand   MM = $ million
See Pages 11 through 21 for Explanation of Ratios and Data

Comparative Historical Data   **Current Data Sorted By Sales**

			Type of Statement						
1	4	9	Unqualified			1		1	7
11	18	30	Reviewed		7	5	4	11	3
8	10	18	Compiled	3	4	6	1	3	1
2	5	11	Tax Returns	4	5	1	1	1	
7	11	14	Other	2	4		4	4	
4/1/02-	4/1/03-	4/1/04-							
3/31/03	3/31/04	3/31/05			5 (4/1-9/30/04)		77 (10/1/04-3/31/05)		
ALL	ALL	ALL		0-1MM	1-3MM	3-5MM	5-10MM	10-25MM	25MM & OVER
29	48	82	**NUMBER OF STATEMENTS**	9	20	13	10	19	11
%	%	%	**ASSETS**	%	%	%	%	%	%
8.1	12.1	9.5	Cash & Equivalents		7.9	8.6	11.7	8.9	5.6
30.8	30.3	32.0	Trade Receivables (net)		30.1	38.2	27.6	36.7	41.5
1.4	1.7	.5	Inventory		.5	1.9	.3	.1	.3
6.4	5.8	4.3	All Other Current		1.3	3.5	10.2	2.6	9.5
46.7	49.9	46.3	Total Current		39.8	52.3	49.7	48.3	56.8
36.2	34.8	36.2	Fixed Assets (net)		40.1	34.7	33.3	27.0	24.6
1.6	.7	1.9	Intangibles (net)		.6	3.6	.6	1.2	5.6
15.5	14.6	15.6	All Other Non-Current		19.4	9.4	16.5	23.5	13.0
100.0	100.0	100.0	Total		100.0	100.0	100.0	100.0	100.0
			LIABILITIES						
6.4	7.5	6.9	Notes Payable-Short Term		4.0	13.0	1.3	8.3	8.1
5.7	5.5	4.5	Cur. Mat.-L/T/D		5.5	4.3	4.5	4.4	4.5
8.9	9.0	12.2	Trade Payables		12.9	16.2	8.6	10.4	14.8
.1	.2	.3	Income Taxes Payable		.0	1.0	.1	.4	.1
7.6	12.6	11.1	All Other Current		6.8	9.8	11.4	18.6	15.4
28.7	34.8	34.9	Total Current		29.2	44.3	25.9	42.0	42.8
29.1	25.0	20.8	Long-Term Debt		22.9	12.0	26.8	11.2	15.6
.5	.4	1.1	Deferred Taxes		1.3	2.3	1.8	.7	.4
5.9	8.5	3.2	All Other Non-Current		4.3	6.4	.2	1.5	5.4
35.8	31.3	40.0	Net Worth		42.4	34.9	45.4	44.6	35.7
100.0	100.0	100.0	Total Liabilities & Net Worth		100.0	100.0	100.0	100.0	100.0
			INCOME DATA						
100.0	100.0	100.0	Net Sales		100.0	100.0	100.0	100.0	100.0
			Gross Profit						
97.3	92.0	92.9	Operating Expenses		97.0	95.4	95.9	97.7	97.5
2.7	8.0	7.1	Operating Profit		3.0	4.6	4.1	2.3	2.5
2.2	3.6	3.0	All Other Expenses (net)		1.2	2.1	.9	-.7	.0
.5	4.4	4.0	Profit Before Taxes		1.8	2.5	3.2	3.0	2.5
			RATIOS						
2.6	2.9	2.1			3.2	1.9	4.4	1.8	1.4
1.7	1.6	1.2	Current		1.0	1.1	1.6	1.1	1.3
1.0	.8	.8			.4	.8	1.3	.9	1.1
2.4	2.5	1.7			3.1	1.5	4.3	1.6	1.2
1.4	1.2	1.1	Quick		1.0	.8	1.4	1.1	1.1
.8	.7	.7			.3	.7	1.1	.9	.9
25 14.4	19 19.3	21 17.8		14 25.7	20 18.1	28 12.8	33 11.2	42 8.8	
38 9.7	35 10.4	39 9.4	Sales/Receivables	30 12.1	32 11.3	35 10.3	45 8.1	48 7.6	
53 6.8	48 7.6	53 6.9		52 7.1	46 7.9	50 7.3	66 5.5	54 6.8	
			Cost of Sales/Inventory						
			Cost of Sales/Payables						
7.5	7.2	9.8			8.2	12.9	8.2	9.3	18.8
14.3	21.4	46.4	Sales/Working Capital		NM	52.5	15.1	73.6	25.8
NM	-37.2	-61.4			-13.8	-25.9	27.6	-79.4	63.5
9.2	7.6	8.3			4.5	6.4		22.1	8.3
(25) 1.9	(42) 2.9	(66) 3.2	EBIT/Interest	(17) 2.2	(12) 2.6	(17) 5.4	(10) 5.7		
-.1	.9	1.2			-2.6	1.2		1.7	2.1
	7.1	4.2	Net Profit + Depr., Dep.,				6.5		
	(10) 3.9	(27) 2.0	Amort./Cur. Mat. L/T/D				(10) 2.8		
	1.3	1.5					1.5		
.4	.4	.2			.1	.0	.2	.2	.5
.7	.6	.8	Fixed/Worth		.6	1.3	.7	.6	.6
4.4	3.5	2.0			3.2	1.5	2.0	1.2	1.1
.7	.7	.7			.4	1.1	.5	.6	1.5
1.6	1.4	1.7	Debt/Worth		1.9	1.7	1.4	1.6	2.0
11.3	5.6	3.7			4.9	7.7	2.7	2.0	3.1
40.7	34.9	29.7			22.3	28.7	29.7	31.6	42.7
(24) 11.0	(43) 11.2	(74) 11.1	% Profit Before Taxes/Tangible	(18) 5.2	(11) 7.4	16.8	(18) 18.5	(10) 20.5	
.8	-.3	2.9	Net Worth		-.2	2.1	4.3	2.5	1.2
9.0	9.9	10.2			6.3	7.4	13.9	17.3	10.6
1.8	4.7	4.1	% Profit Before Taxes/Total		1.8	2.6	8.1	6.1	7.0
-2.8	-.1	.9	Assets		-2.0	.4	2.3	2.2	1.4
22.8	27.0	28.7			109.8	999.8	33.0	31.3	25.9
9.5	10.8	10.5	Sales/Net Fixed Assets		10.2	6.3	9.0	11.9	16.5
4.3	6.4	4.2			4.2	4.2	4.1	8.4	10.2
4.4	3.8	4.2			4.1	6.7	4.0	4.2	3.9
2.8	3.0	3.0	Sales/Total Assets		3.0	4.0	2.7	2.7	3.2
1.8	2.4	1.8			1.8	1.9	2.0	1.9	2.6
1.5	1.7	1.3			1.8			.9	1.1
(24) 2.6	(44) 3.7	(69) 2.9	% Depr., Dep., Amort./Sales	(16) 3.1		(17) 1.8	(10) 1.5		
4.2	5.5	5.2			4.4			3.0	3.1
	3.3	2.3	% Officers', Directors',						
	(15) 5.1	(21) 2.8	Owners' Comp/Sales						
	12.3	5.0							
272993M	365286M	2384644M	Net Sales ($)	2926M	37938M	53523M	71208M	276961M	1942088M
129279M	141118M	906803M	Total Assets ($)	13578M	23253M	27522M	29420M	103349M	709681M

M = $ thousand   MM = $ million
See Pages 11 through 21 for Explanation of Ratios and Data

Current Data Sorted By Assets   **Comparative Historical Data**

0-500M	500M-2MM	2-10MM	10-50MM	50-100MM	100-250MM	Type of Statement	4/1/00-3/31/01 ALL	4/1/01-3/31/02 ALL
		2			1	Unqualified		
3	8	7	4			Reviewed		
7	9	11	2			Compiled		
18	7	2		2		Tax Returns		
2	13	8		1		Other		
	16 (4/1-9/30/04)		91 (10/1/04-3/31/05)					
30	37	30	8	1	1	**NUMBER OF STATEMENTS**		
%	%	%	%	%	%	**ASSETS**	%	%
22.3	8.7	10.2				Cash & Equivalents	D	D
9.1	25.0	23.1				Trade Receivables (net)	A	A
.1	1.2	.8				Inventory	T	T
2.0	7.5	4.9				All Other Current	A	A
33.5	42.5	38.9				Total Current		
53.8	49.5	46.8				Fixed Assets (net)	N	N
4.3	1.8	2.4				Intangibles (net)	O	O
8.4	6.2	11.8				All Other Non-Current	T	T
100.0	100.0	100.0				Total		
						LIABILITIES	A	A
14.3	7.4	4.3				Notes Payable-Short Term	V	V
12.5	7.3	9.4				Cur. Mat.-L/T/D	A	A
12.5	10.5	8.4				Trade Payables	I	I
.1	.3	.8				Income Taxes Payable	L	L
5.5	8.0	6.9				All Other Current	A	A
44.8	33.5	30.0				Total Current	B	B
75.8	31.5	27.4				Long-Term Debt	L	L
.0	.4	1.6				Deferred Taxes	E	E
4.6	9.0	2.0				All Other Non-Current		
−25.3	25.7	39.0				Net Worth		
100.0	100.0	100.0				Total Liabilities & Net Worth		
						INCOME DATA		
100.0	100.0	100.0				Net Sales		
						Gross Profit		
96.2	94.8	94.3				Operating Expenses		
3.8	5.2	5.7				Operating Profit		
1.0	1.2	.5				All Other Expenses (net)		
2.8	4.0	5.2				Profit Before Taxes		
						RATIOS		
3.1	3.6	1.8				Current		
.9	1.6	1.4						
.3	.7	.6						
3.0	3.6	1.7				Quick		
.8	1.3	1.0						
.2	.5	.5						
0 UND	8 44.8	18 20.1				Sales/Receivables		
0 UND	27 13.6	30 12.0						
19 19.0	36 10.2	55 6.7						
						Cost of Sales/Inventory		
						Cost of Sales/Payables		
23.0	10.4	10.7				Sales/Working Capital		
−314.5	23.1	24.7						
−19.1	−32.3	−13.9						
4.1	9.1	7.5				EBIT/Interest		
(24) 1.0	(34) 4.7	(28) 4.6						
−2.4	1.4	1.8						
						Net Profit + Depr., Dep., Amort./Cur. Mat. L /T/D		
1.1	.8	.5				Fixed/Worth		
NM	2.0	1.2						
−1.2	8.3	3.2						
1.7	1.1	.9				Debt/Worth		
NM	2.3	1.7						
−2.6	11.4	6.3						
136.4	93.1	53.0				% Profit Before Taxes/Tangible Net Worth		
(15) 78.9	(32) 21.2	(29) 21.4						
11.8	3.8	6.2						
27.3	19.0	13.1				% Profit Before Taxes/Total Assets		
5.5	7.4	6.9						
−19.1	1.1	1.9						
25.7	11.5	9.1				Sales/Net Fixed Assets		
11.3	5.9	3.5						
4.4	3.5	2.8						
8.8	4.9	3.0				Sales/Total Assets		
4.7	3.1	2.0						
2.9	2.4	1.4						
3.1	3.4	2.4				% Depr., Dep., Amort./Sales		
(20) 6.1	(32) 7.1	(28) 6.6						
13.0	11.8	11.5						
1.4	2.0	1.4				% Officers', Directors', Owners' Comp/Sales		
(13) 3.7	(14) 3.7	(13) 2.6						
4.7	5.6	5.0						
33718M	138784M	277344M	183012M	57591M	176136M	Net Sales ($)		
6789M	38968M	121169M	127185M	53005M	131819M	Total Assets ($)		

M = $ thousand   MM = $ million

See Pages 11 through 21 for Explanation of Ratios and Data

Comparative Historical Data / Current Data Sorted By Sales

Type of Statement

4/1/02-3/31/03	4/1/03-3/31/04	4/1/04-3/31/05	Type of Statement	0-1MM	1-3MM	3-5MM	5-10MM	10-25MM	25MM & OVER
3	1	3	Unqualified			1		1	1
6	20	22	Reviewed	3	5	1	5	7	1
8	17	29	Compiled	3	8	6	7	4	1
5	20	27	Tax Returns	16	9	1	1		1
10	13	26	Other	2	4	4	13	2	
ALL 32	ALL 71	ALL 107	NUMBER OF STATEMENTS	24	26	13	26	14	4

Current data groupings: 16 (4/1-9/30/04) covers 0-1MM / 1-3MM / 3-5MM; 91 (10/1/04-3/31/05) covers 5-10MM / 10-25MM / 25MM & OVER.

Main Data

4/1/02-3/31/03 ALL	4/1/03-3/31/04 ALL	4/1/04-3/31/05 ALL		0-1MM	1-3MM	3-5MM	5-10MM	10-25MM	25MM & OVER
%	%	%	**ASSETS**	%	%	%	%	%	%
8.4	13.6	13.4	Cash & Equivalents	21.7	11.9	6.4	10.5	12.9	
21.9	19.8	19.4	Trade Receivables (net)	9.5	13.8	26.2	27.7	24.9	
1.8	.7	.8	Inventory	.1	.5	1.2	1.7	.6	
5.4	4.0	4.9	All Other Current	2.8	5.3	1.7	8.4	4.8	
37.4	38.1	38.5	Total Current	34.1	31.4	35.6	48.3	43.2	
54.1	53.3	49.9	Fixed Assets (net)	55.1	56.1	49.4	41.9	49.5	
1.4	1.0	2.6	Intangibles (net)	3.2	3.2	1.3	2.8	1.6	
7.1	7.7	9.0	All Other Non-Current	7.5	9.3	13.7	7.0	5.7	
100.0	100.0	100.0	Total	100.0	100.0	100.0	100.0	100.0	
			LIABILITIES						
18.1	8.1	8.1	Notes Payable-Short Term	7.4	13.1	1.0	10.5	3.3	
6.1	11.8	9.3	Cur. Mat.-L/T/D	9.3	11.9	14.5	4.2	9.9	
11.8	10.1	10.3	Trade Payables	12.8	8.0	13.3	10.3	8.0	
.3	1.0	.4	Income Taxes Payable	.0	.3	.2	1.0	.1	
4.9	7.3	6.9	All Other Current	2.9	6.7	7.1	8.4	8.7	
41.2	38.3	34.9	Total Current	32.4	40.1	36.1	34.5	30.0	
26.2	33.4	41.3	Long-Term Debt	70.2	51.0	29.0	28.9	17.4	
1.1	.9	.7	Deferred Taxes	.2	.8	1.8	.6	.6	
4.7	3.7	5.3	All Other Non-Current	5.4	5.3	4.9	7.7	1.7	
26.8	23.8	17.8	Net Worth	-8.3	2.8	28.3	28.4	50.5	
100.0	100.0	100.0	Total Liabilities & Net Worth	100.0	100.0	100.0	100.0	100.0	
			INCOME DATA						
100.0	100.0	100.0	Net Sales	100.0	100.0	100.0	100.0	100.0	
			Gross Profit						
97.9	96.8	94.6	Operating Expenses	88.5	97.8	97.2	96.5	95.8	
2.1	3.2	5.4	Operating Profit	11.5	2.2	2.8	3.5	4.2	
1.2	.7	.7	All Other Expenses (net)	3.7	.8	-.6	-.8	.5	
.9	2.5	4.6	Profit Before Taxes	7.7	1.4	3.4	4.2	3.7	
			RATIOS						
1.9	1.6	2.7	Current	3.4	2.6	2.7	2.6	2.2	
1.2	1.1	1.4		1.6	.8	1.5	1.5	1.4	
.6	.6	.7		.6	.3	.6	.7	1.0	
1.6	1.4	2.2	Quick	3.1	2.4	2.7	2.2	1.8	
1.0	(70) .9	1.1		1.2	.6	1.2	1.3	1.2	
.3	.5	.5		.4	.2	.6	.6	.7	
10 37.3	2 167.8	3 108.6	Sales/Receivables	0 UND	0 UND	5 72.0	11 34.6	23 15.9	
30 12.3	22 16.8	24 15.2		0 UND	16 22.2	29 12.5	27 13.8	36 10.1	
46 7.9	37 9.8	40 9.2		29 12.8	32 11.5	52 7.0	48 7.5	45 8.0	
			Cost of Sales/Inventory						
			Cost of Sales/Payables						
12.1	24.9	10.6	Sales/Working Capital	9.9	12.2	11.9	8.7	6.8	
36.6	104.2	32.5		69.9	-144.1	61.1	17.6	24.7	
-16.3	-19.8	-24.5		-28.1	-8.7	-24.2	-35.3	NM	
7.0	9.2	8.5	EBIT/Interest	8.7	6.5	7.5	7.6	18.4	
(30) 1.7	(66) 2.9	(95) 3.6		(17) 3.6	(24) 1.2	2.4	(24) 4.7	6.9	
.2	1.0	.8		.7	-2.4	1.4	1.9	2.6	
	3.5	2.7	Net Profit + Depr., Dep.,						
	(13) 1.3	(18) 1.3	Amort./Cur. Mat. L/T/D						
	1.1	.8							
.8	.8	.8	Fixed/Worth	.5	1.0	.6	.8	.5	
1.7	2.3	1.8		5.5	2.5	2.0	1.3	.9	
17.3	10.1	15.0		-2.6	-3.0	6.1	6.2	2.9	
.6	1.1	1.0	Debt/Worth	1.3	1.1	1.0	1.1	.5	
2.1	2.5	2.2		6.0	3.0	1.3	2.2	.8	
20.1	24.8	20.3		-3.9	-5.8	7.5	11.8	2.7	
42.4	63.6	73.2	% Profit Before Taxes/Tangible	97.2	93.0	72.9	101.3	24.7	
(25) 9.1	(59) 22.6	(86) 23.4	Net Worth	(16) 32.4	(17) 11.8	(12) 25.0	(23) 30.7	13.0	
.1	2.6	4.7		7.8	-7.4	3.9	9.7	5.4	
9.8	13.6	18.1	% Profit Before Taxes/Total	32.7	11.6	17.0	18.4	11.1	
2.4	5.7	7.4	Assets	9.9	-.1	10.6	11.6	7.7	
-2.8	.5	.6		-.7	-16.9	1.8	3.5	1.7	
15.9	13.8	12.3	Sales/Net Fixed Assets	23.2	12.0	26.7	17.4	11.0	
3.6	6.0	5.5		4.7	5.4	5.9	8.5	4.7	
2.1	3.2	3.0		2.7	3.4	4.4	3.2	2.3	
3.7	5.0	4.8	Sales/Total Assets	5.1	4.9	5.7	5.4	3.7	
2.2	3.1	2.9		3.1	3.0	3.0	3.1	2.0	
1.1	2.0	1.7		1.2	1.7	1.9	1.9	1.5	
2.3	2.9	3.5	% Depr., Dep., Amort./Sales	7.8	4.1	2.7	1.8	3.4	
(30) 6.9	(65) 6.2	(89) 7.0		(17) 11.3	(22) 6.5	(11) 6.9	(22) 4.8	7.1	
14.7	10.6	11.2		15.9	11.5	12.2	8.3	9.3	
2.2	1.6	1.5	% Officers', Directors',		1.5		1.3		
(11) 5.1	(31) 3.1	(43) 3.3	Owners' Comp/Sales		(12) 3.9		(11) 2.2		
6.4	6.1	4.8			5.5		5.6		
273315M	513206M	866585M	Net Sales ($)	12627M	51242M	51588M	184161M	261192M	305775M
126832M	174196M	478935M	Total Assets ($)	10817M	20029M	19648M	76386M	132025M	220030M

Current Data Sorted By Assets   **Comparative Historical Data**

	0-500M	500M-2MM	2-10MM	10-50MM	50-100MM	100-250MM	Type of Statement	4/1/00-3/31/01 ALL	4/1/01-3/31/02 ALL
			9	11	5	4	Unqualified		
		2	4	6			Reviewed		
	2	10	2	2			Compiled		
	3	3					Tax Returns		
	4	5	6	6	2	2	Other		
		6 (4/1-9/30/04)		82 (10/1/04-3/31/05)					
NUMBER OF STATEMENTS	9	20	21	25	7	6		%	%
	%	%	%	%	%	%	**ASSETS**		
		13.2	8.8	3.4			Cash & Equivalents	D	D
		24.9	31.0	21.5			Trade Receivables (net)	A	A
		1.8	1.5	1.0			Inventory	T	T
		4.8	3.5	6.2			All Other Current	A	A
		44.7	44.9	32.1			Total Current		
		46.2	45.1	57.9			Fixed Assets (net)	N	N
		1.1	2.9	1.5			Intangibles (net)	O	O
		8.0	7.1	8.6			All Other Non-Current	T	T
		100.0	100.0	100.0			Total		
							LIABILITIES	A	A
		11.0	17.3	5.2			Notes Payable-Short Term	V	V
		9.5	6.7	12.6			Cur. Mat.-L/T/D	A	A
		6.5	6.4	7.0			Trade Payables	I	I
		.0	.2	.2			Income Taxes Payable	L	L
		7.7	14.5	10.7			All Other Current	A	A
		34.9	45.1	35.6			Total Current	B	B
		23.3	21.5	28.8			Long-Term Debt	L	L
		1.4	1.6	4.9			Deferred Taxes	E	E
		12.2	3.6	.7			All Other Non-Current		
		28.3	28.2	30.0			Net Worth		
		100.0	100.0	100.0			Total Liabilities & Net Worth		
							INCOME DATA		
		100.0	100.0	100.0			Net Sales		
							Gross Profit		
		99.5	97.4	96.0			Operating Expenses		
		.5	2.6	4.0			Operating Profit		
		.6	.2	.6			All Other Expenses (net)		
		.0	2.4	3.4			Profit Before Taxes		
							RATIOS		
		2.1	1.8	1.3			Current		
		1.5	1.0	1.0					
		.8	.6	.7					
		1.6	1.6	1.1			Quick		
		1.1	.9	.8					
		.7	.6	.5					
		(13) 28.5	(27) 13.7	(31) 11.9			Sales/Receivables		
		(28) 13.0	(33) 11.0	(36) 10.3					
		(43) 8.4	(44) 8.3	(41) 8.8					
							Cost of Sales/Inventory		
							Cost of Sales/Payables		
		12.0	11.6	25.0			Sales/Working Capital		
		36.8	315.5	-999.8					
		-56.1	-15.5	-17.6					
		4.6	11.1	6.7			EBIT/Interest		
		(17) 1.6	(20) 3.3	3.5					
		-.9	-.1	2.0					
				1.2			Net Profit + Depr., Dep.,		
			(14)	1.1			Amort./Cur. Mat. L /T/D		
				.7					
		.7	.9	1.4			Fixed/Worth		
		1.8	1.8	1.9					
		92.9	8.1	3.7					
		.8	1.5	1.6			Debt/Worth		
		1.9	3.4	3.0					
		112.4	11.2	5.4					
		20.3	54.3	43.1			% Profit Before Taxes/Tangible Net Worth		
		(17) .8	(17) 34.3	21.7					
		-11.1	8.0	9.3					
		9.6	14.0	12.0			% Profit Before Taxes/Total Assets		
		.3	5.2	6.3					
		-3.4	.0	2.3					
		14.4	10.9	7.1			Sales/Net Fixed Assets		
		5.6	5.4	3.1					
		3.7	3.7	2.2					
		4.2	3.8	3.0			Sales/Total Assets		
		3.0	2.6	1.9					
		1.8	2.2	1.4					
		2.7	1.9	2.6			% Depr., Dep., Amort./Sales		
		(15) 3.7	3.2	(24) 3.8					
		13.5	6.2	9.1					
		1.2					% Officers', Directors', Owners' Comp/Sales		
		(11) 2.4							
		4.6							
Net Sales ($)	15791M	74298M	312063M	1186684M	1087581M	1924297M			
Total Assets ($)	2416M	25144M	90310M	562382M	589206M	875016M			

M = $ thousand   MM = $ million

See Pages 11 through 21 for Explanation of Ratios and Data

Comparative Historical Data				Current Data Sorted By Sales					
6	11	20	**Type of Statement**					2	18
5	10	17	Unqualified	1	1	1	8	6	
8	12	18	Reviewed	1	2	3	7	3	2
2	6	8	Compiled	2	3		3	3	
11	21	25	Tax Returns	2	5	1	4	4	9
			Other						
4/1/02-	4/1/03-	4/1/04-			6 (4/1-9/30/04)		82 (10/1/04-3/31/05)		
3/31/03	3/31/04	3/31/05		0-1MM	1-3MM	3-5MM	5-10MM	10-25MM	25MM & OVER
ALL	ALL	ALL							
32	60	88	**NUMBER OF STATEMENTS**	5	11	5	15	17	35
%	%	%	**ASSETS**	%	%	%	%	%	%
4.2	7.3	7.2	Cash & Equivalents		5.6		17.6	7.7	3.1
36.4	24.4	25.1	Trade Receivables (net)		23.3		28.0	25.5	24.3
2.0	2.1	1.2	Inventory		.4		.2	1.3	1.3
5.4	4.3	4.3	All Other Current		3.2		6.1	3.5	5.1
47.9	38.1	37.9	Total Current		32.5		52.0	38.0	33.7
42.9	51.6	51.9	Fixed Assets (net)		59.0		41.6	53.1	54.1
2.1	2.8	3.0	Intangibles (net)		1.8		4.1	.2	5.1
7.0	7.5	7.2	All Other Non-Current		6.8		2.4	8.7	7.0
100.0	100.0	100.0	Total		100.0		100.0	100.0	100.0
			LIABILITIES						
4.3	5.4	8.6	Notes Payable-Short Term		2.6		9.0	11.4	6.0
8.3	8.7	9.7	Cur. Mat.-L/T/D		6.7		9.1	8.9	11.5
16.5	10.0	7.4	Trade Payables		11.6		7.4	8.7	6.0
.6	.1	.1	Income Taxes Payable		.0		.3	.0	.1
16.4	10.6	10.3	All Other Current		5.1		9.6	9.9	14.6
46.2	34.8	36.0	Total Current		26.0		35.3	38.8	38.2
18.3	33.4	29.7	Long-Term Debt		57.3		23.0	25.2	27.4
2.1	1.8	3.3	Deferred Taxes		.0		2.1	3.9	5.6
8.8	6.3	5.1	All Other Non-Current		8.2		12.7	1.3	1.8
24.7	23.6	25.8	Net Worth		8.5		26.8	30.7	27.0
100.0	100.0	100.0	Total Liabilities & Net Worth		100.0		100.0	100.0	100.0
			INCOME DATA						
100.0	100.0	100.0	Net Sales		100.0		100.0	100.0	100.0
			Gross Profit						
96.9	97.1	97.6	Operating Expenses		100.1		96.7	97.6	96.7
3.1	2.9	2.4	Operating Profit		-.1		3.3	2.4	3.3
.3	.9	.4	All Other Expenses (net)		.4		.0	-.2	.7
2.8	2.0	2.0	Profit Before Taxes		-.5		3.3	2.7	2.7
			RATIOS						
1.6	1.6	1.6			2.2		2.2	1.6	1.2
1.2	1.1	1.0	Current		1.2		1.6	1.0	.9
.7	.7	.7			.8		1.1	.6	.7
1.2	1.3	1.3			1.9		2.0	1.4	.9
1.0	.9	.8	Quick		.9		1.3	.8	.7
.6	.5	.6			.7		1.0	.5	.5
22 16.3	18 20.2	24 15.4		0 UND		20 18.0	25 14.6	28 13.0	
34 10.8	32 11.4	34 10.8	Sales/Receivables	15 24.1		31 11.9	37 9.9	35 10.4	
56 6.5	40 9.0	41 8.9		37 9.8		43 8.4	46 8.0	40 9.2	
			Cost of Sales/Inventory						
			Cost of Sales/Payables						
16.9	20.8	21.9			23.7		11.8	12.0	59.7
74.1	63.4	661.6	Sales/Working Capital		159.5		16.9	315.5	-64.5
-40.9	-21.6	-25.2			-73.7		112.9	-14.3	-23.9
5.9	4.3	5.8			2.7		9.3	4.6	6.5
(30) 2.8	(57) 2.4	(83) 3.2	EBIT/Interest	(10) 1.3		(12) 5.0	3.4	3.5	
.4	1.3	1.3			.3		1.9	1.6	1.9
	2.6	1.3	Net Profit + Depr., Dep.,						1.2
(14) 1.6	(28) 1.1		Amort./Cur. Mat. L/T/D					(14) 1.1	
	1.2	.8							.7
.7	1.0	1.4			1.9		.6	1.1	1.6
2.0	2.6	2.5	Fixed/Worth		11.8		1.8	1.7	3.0
4.6	6.6	6.5			-1.4		178.7	3.8	4.8
1.1	1.3	1.6			1.8		.7	1.6	1.9
3.0	3.5	3.2	Debt/Worth		11.1		3.2	2.5	3.6
20.3	10.9	10.1			-6.7		444.0	4.6	6.8
67.7	40.2	42.9	% Profit Before Taxes/Tangible		51.1		49.8	37.6	
(27) 17.8	(52) 17.8	(75) 20.7	Net Worth		(12) 31.4	(16) 16.3	(31) 23.4		
6.0	5.1	2.9			-.8		3.5	13.3	
12.5	10.3	11.3	% Profit Before Taxes/Total		21.8		20.2	11.5	10.1
4.7	4.0	5.2	Assets		2.5		6.5	5.2	5.4
-1.3	.4	.4			-4.6		.4	.9	1.3
25.8	9.9	10.4			30.2		19.3	8.7	8.4
6.4	4.7	4.6	Sales/Net Fixed Assets		4.4		8.0	4.0	3.8
3.2	2.7	2.6			4.0		4.6	2.3	2.5
4.8	3.9	3.7			8.2		4.4	3.5	3.0
3.1	2.6	2.5	Sales/Total Assets		3.5		3.2	2.3	2.3
2.0	1.7	1.7			2.7		2.5	1.5	1.6
1.7	2.9	2.2					2.0	2.7	2.0
(25) 4.6	(49) 6.4	(68) 3.8	% Depr., Dep., Amort./Sales		(11) 2.9		5.7	(24) 3.5	
11.6	11.4	8.4					7.4	8.6	6.7
	1.3	1.3	% Officers', Directors',						
(22) 2.9	(28) 2.5		Owners' Comp/Sales						
	9.3	6.5							
1524924M	1981982M	4600714M	Net Sales ($)	2967M	22366M	17871M	94446M	281472M	4181592M
537376M	814504M	2144474M	Total Assets ($)	3274M	7215M	5786M	33265M	144056M	1950878M

© RMA 2005

M = $ thousand   MM = $ million

See Pages 11 through 21 for Explanation of Ratios and Data

Current Data Sorted By Assets   Comparative Historical Data

0-500M	500M-2MM	2-10MM	10-50MM	50-100MM	100-250MM	Type of Statement	4/1/00-3/31/01 ALL	4/1/01-3/31/02 ALL
1		2	1		1	Unqualified	1	1
	2	3	2			Reviewed		3
	5	2		1		Compiled	5	4
10	3	1			1	Tax Returns	3	5
2		2				Other	11	7
	6 (4/1-9/30/04)		33 (10/1/04-3/31/05)					
13	10	10	3	1	2	NUMBER OF STATEMENTS	20	20
%	%	%	%	%	%	**ASSETS**	%	%
13.3	6.8	19.7				Cash & Equivalents	8.3	8.8
8.0	23.5	17.6				Trade Receivables (net)	15.4	10.7
.6	4.0	.0				Inventory	1.3	.4
16.2	3.3	2.2				All Other Current	9.7	2.2
38.2	37.6	39.5				Total Current	34.7	22.2
45.0	51.6	24.4				Fixed Assets (net)	36.1	41.8
7.3	2.9	9.5				Intangibles (net)	14.3	22.2
9.5	7.9	26.5				All Other Non-Current	14.9	13.9
100.0	100.0	100.0				Total	100.0	100.0
						LIABILITIES		
2.0	9.2	2.1				Notes Payable-Short Term	4.1	6.5
2.0	8.9	7.5				Cur. Mat.-L/T/D	9.4	11.1
10.7	7.8	6.4				Trade Payables	5.7	8.0
.0	.0	.7				Income Taxes Payable	.2	.8
28.0	6.9	24.2				All Other Current	10.1	26.1
42.6	32.9	40.7				Total Current	29.4	52.4
29.5	27.7	21.8				Long-Term Debt	21.3	23.1
.0	.0	.0				Deferred Taxes	.4	.3
1.7	17.7	6.7				All Other Non-Current	3.5	6.6
26.2	21.7	30.8				Net Worth	45.4	17.6
100.0	100.0	100.0				Total Liabilities & Net Worth	100.0	100.0
						INCOME DATA		
100.0	100.0	100.0				Net Sales	100.0	100.0
						Gross Profit		
95.7	98.4	90.7				Operating Expenses	88.4	91.6
4.3	1.6	9.3				Operating Profit	11.6	8.4
1.4	−.2	1.0				All Other Expenses (net)	.9	1.2
3.0	1.8	8.4				Profit Before Taxes	10.7	7.2
						RATIOS		
3.9	2.3	1.9				Current	2.3	1.0
.7	1.1	.7					1.0	.7
.3	.7	.4					.3	.3
.9	1.3	1.6				Quick	1.3	.9
.3	.9	.7					.7	.6
.0	.6	.4					.2	.2
0 UND	19 19.2	1 297.2				Sales/Receivables	1 265.3	2 158.4
0 UND	26 14.1	14 26.7					19 19.4	8 43.9
14 25.9	57 6.4	27 13.4					45 8.2	25 14.6
						Cost of Sales/Inventory		
						Cost of Sales/Payables		
30.2	15.7	7.8				Sales/Working Capital	11.1	−206.3
−44.7	110.0	−33.9					NM	−35.9
−5.0	−21.1	−11.1					−10.1	−10.1
		23.9				EBIT/Interest	8.1	8.9
		18.9					(16) 1.8	(19) 5.9
		3.0					1.2	1.5
						Net Profit + Depr., Dep., Amort./Cur. Mat. L /T/D		
.4	1.0	.3				Fixed/Worth	.4	.9
1.4	3.0	1.1					1.0	1.8
NM	−5.5	NM					11.0	−1.0
1.4	1.2	1.7				Debt/Worth	.5	1.2
2.2	4.1	3.4					1.7	3.4
−5.9	−12.8	NM					16.6	−2.9
						% Profit Before Taxes/Tangible Net Worth	28.0	94.6
							(16) 14.1	(12) 27.8
							.8	7.0
29.6	9.9	22.4				% Profit Before Taxes/Total Assets	18.4	19.5
3.5	2.9	17.4					4.8	12.3
−21.0	−5.5	7.2					.9	2.6
25.1	9.9	193.8				Sales/Net Fixed Assets	15.5	7.2
14.4	4.5	7.2					6.7	4.9
4.1	3.2	4.0					3.9	3.1
8.3	3.4	3.8				Sales/Total Assets	3.1	4.0
3.4	2.3	2.2					2.1	2.6
1.1	1.5	1.2					1.3	1.1
						% Depr., Dep., Amort./Sales	2.1	3.6
							(17) 5.3	(18) 6.4
							9.2	11.3
						% Officers', Directors', Owners' Comp/Sales		
12244M	28316M	153860M	86386M	15787M	723093M	Net Sales ($)	361800M	402812M
3027M	12359M	51790M	47561M	61397M	310786M	Total Assets ($)	230618M	269923M

© RMA 2005

M = $ thousand   MM = $ million

See Pages 11 through 21 for Explanation of Ratios and Data

Comparative Historical Data | Current Data Sorted By Sales

	4/1/02-3/31/03 ALL	4/1/03-3/31/04 ALL	4/1/04-3/31/05 ALL	Type of Statement	0-1MM	1-3MM	3-5MM	5-10MM	10-25MM	25MM & OVER
	3	3	4	Unqualified		1			2	1
	2	5	9	Reviewed	1	1	3		2	2
	10	8	7	Compiled		3	3	1	1	
	9	9	12	Tax Returns	5	4	1		1	1
	9	8	7	Other	1	3			2	
					6 (4/1-9/30/04)			33 (10/1/04-3/31/05)		
NUMBER OF STATEMENTS	33	33	39		7	12	7	1	8	4
	%	%	%	ASSETS	%	%	%	%	%	%
	14.3	9.2	13.1	Cash & Equivalents		9.9				
	19.7	26.5	15.7	Trade Receivables (net)		19.1				
	1.0	2.1	1.4	Inventory		.9				
	6.0	8.4	7.1	All Other Current		2.0				
	41.0	46.2	37.2	Total Current		31.9				
	35.0	29.3	40.0	Fixed Assets (net)		42.6				
	13.6	10.1	7.0	Intangibles (net)		10.9				
	10.4	14.4	15.8	All Other Non-Current		14.6				
	100.0	100.0	100.0	Total		100.0				
				LIABILITIES						
	10.0	6.7	4.7	Notes Payable-Short Term		6.0				
	4.7	9.4	5.2	Cur. Mat.-L/T/D		6.7				
	9.1	10.7	7.5	Trade Payables		12.4				
	2.2	1.2	.2	Income Taxes Payable		.0				
	11.7	11.4	18.4	All Other Current		16.4				
	37.6	39.5	36.1	Total Current		41.5				
	21.8	25.9	29.8	Long-Term Debt		34.4				
	.2	1.1	.0	Deferred Taxes		.0				
	5.8	10.5	7.7	All Other Non-Current		9.1				
	34.5	23.1	26.4	Net Worth		15.0				
	100.0	100.0	100.0	Total Liabilities & Net Worth		100.0				
				INCOME DATA						
	100.0	100.0	100.0	Net Sales		100.0				
				Gross Profit						
	88.8	88.4	92.0	Operating Expenses		88.5				
	11.2	11.6	8.0	Operating Profit		11.5				
	2.7	4.4	2.9	All Other Expenses (net)		7.1				
	8.5	7.2	5.1	Profit Before Taxes		4.4				
				RATIOS						
	2.0	2.6	2.1	Current		3.8				
	1.0	1.5	.8			.8				
	.7	.6	.4			.3				
	1.7	1.9	1.2	Quick		3.7				
	1.0	1.1	.7			.7				
	.4	.3	.3			.3				
	3 105.9	8 48.4	0 UND	Sales/Receivables		0 UND				
	18 20.0	36 10.1	16 22.7			20 18.5				
	44 8.3	63 5.8	31 11.9			34 10.7				
				Cost of Sales/Inventory						
				Cost of Sales/Payables						
	8.8	8.0	14.7	Sales/Working Capital		36.9				
	235.5	16.2	-199.0			-39.4				
	-16.6	-13.9	-12.7			-6.4				
	21.8	12.4	19.2	EBIT/Interest						
	(29) 7.5	(25) 4.2	(28) 3.6							
	2.3	1.2	-.2							
			5.8	Net Profit + Depr., Dep., Amort./Cur. Mat. L/T/D						
		(12) 2.1	2.1							
			1.5							
	.5	.4	.4	Fixed/Worth		.2				
	1.7	1.9	1.4			NM				
	NM	-7.2	-41.2			-2.7				
	1.8	1.5	1.3	Debt/Worth		1.4				
	3.1	3.6	2.9			-34.0				
	NM	-13.1	-53.7			-4.6				
	116.4	78.8	99.3	% Profit Before Taxes/Tangible Net Worth						
	(25) 40.4	(22) 46.8	(28) 42.3							
	23.4	18.4	5.2							
	27.6	21.7	20.6	% Profit Before Taxes/Total Assets		19.4				
	11.2	9.5	9.4			3.4				
	3.9	1.7	-2.6			-14.2				
	17.6	32.6	21.5	Sales/Net Fixed Assets		155.5				
	8.5	8.7	6.5			11.0				
	4.4	4.2	4.0			4.0				
	3.9	3.8	3.9	Sales/Total Assets		6.5				
	2.2	2.2	2.4			3.1				
	1.3	1.3	1.2			1.1				
	1.9	2.0	3.4	% Depr., Dep., Amort./Sales						
	(28) 4.7	(27) 4.6	(25) 5.2							
	12.9	9.3	12.9							
	3.1	5.5	2.0	% Officers', Directors', Owners' Comp/Sales						
	(19) 4.7	(17) 8.7	(18) 5.3							
	12.1	10.4	17.0							
	344949M	201552M	1019686M	Net Sales ($)	2756M	20097M	25563M	5237M	127129M	838904M
	233419M	162483M	486920M	Total Assets ($)	1612M	25139M	14069M	1593M	105226M	339281M

M = $ thousand   MM = $ million
See Pages 11 through 21 for Explanation of Ratios and Data

Current Data Sorted By Assets							Comparative Historical Data	

	2	3	1			Type of Statement		
		4				Unqualified		
		1				Reviewed		
1	4	1				Compiled		
6	3		1			Tax Returns		
4			1			Other	4/1/00- 3/31/01 ALL	4/1/01- 3/31/02 ALL
	9 (4/1-9/30/04)			22 (10/1/04-3/31/05)				
0-500M	500M-2MM	2-10MM	10-50MM	50-100MM	100-250MM			
11	9	9	2			NUMBER OF STATEMENTS		
%	%	%	%	%	%	ASSETS	%	%
19.1				D	D	Cash & Equivalents	D	D
2.0				A	A	Trade Receivables (net)	A	A
.1				T	T	Inventory	T	T
2.4				A	A	All Other Current	A	A
23.7						Total Current		
70.0				N	N	Fixed Assets (net)	N	N
2.1				O	O	Intangibles (net)	O	O
4.2				T	T	All Other Non-Current	T	T
100.0						Total		
				A	A	LIABILITIES	A	A
7.4				V	V	Notes Payable-Short Term	V	V
10.0				A	A	Cur. Mat.-L/T/D	A	A
2.0				I	I	Trade Payables	I	I
.0				L	L	Income Taxes Payable	L	L
12.8				A	A	All Other Current	A	A
32.3				B	B	Total Current	B	B
105.6				L	L	Long-Term Debt	L	L
.0				E	E	Deferred Taxes	E	E
20.7						All Other Non-Current		
-58.6						Net Worth		
100.0						Total Liabilities & Net Worth		
						INCOME DATA		
100.0						Net Sales		
						Gross Profit		
86.9						Operating Expenses		
13.1						Operating Profit		
5.8						All Other Expenses (net)		
7.4						Profit Before Taxes		
						RATIOS		
4.0								
.6						Current		
.2								
4.0								
.4						Quick		
.2								
0 UND								
0 UND						Sales/Receivables		
4 83.6								
						Cost of Sales/Inventory		
						Cost of Sales/Payables		
25.1								
-70.5						Sales/Working Capital		
-4.4								
						EBIT/Interest		
						Net Profit + Depr., Dep., Amort./Cur. Mat. L /T/D		
4.0								
-2.6						Fixed/Worth		
-1.2								
6.3								
-4.2						Debt/Worth		
-2.6								
						% Profit Before Taxes/Tangible Net Worth		
42.5								
1.0						% Profit Before Taxes/Total Assets		
-14.8								
8.7								
6.1						Sales/Net Fixed Assets		
1.3								
6.3								
1.7						Sales/Total Assets		
1.0								
						% Depr., Dep., Amort./Sales		
						% Officers', Directors', Owners' Comp/Sales		
6353M	22066M	109497M	111856M			Net Sales ($)		
2163M	10274M	40730M	56182M			Total Assets ($)		

© RMA 2005

M = $ thousand   MM = $ million
See Pages 11 through 21 for Explanation of Ratios and Data

Comparative Historical Data				Current Data Sorted By Sales					
			Type of Statement						
3		6	Unqualified		1	1	2	1	1
1		4	Reviewed				3		1
3	1	6	Compiled	2	2	1	1		
6	7	9	Tax Returns	7	2				
1	4	6	Other	2	2		1		1
4/1/02- 3/31/03 ALL	4/1/03- 3/31/04 ALL	4/1/04- 3/31/05 ALL		0-1MM	9 (4/1-9/30/04) 1-3MM	3-5MM	5-10MM	22 (10/1/04-3/31/05) 10-25MM	25MM & OVER
14	12	31	**NUMBER OF STATEMENTS**	11	7	2	7	1	3
%	%	%	**ASSETS**	%	%	%	%	%	%
8.4	11.7	17.6	Cash & Equivalents	18.1					
7.0	6.9	12.5	Trade Receivables (net)	3.8					
.0	.0	2.5	Inventory	.2					
.3	1.8	3.0	All Other Current	2.4					
15.6	20.4	35.7	Total Current	24.6					
75.8	72.6	54.5	Fixed Assets (net)	66.2					
1.4	.1	4.4	Intangibles (net)	7.3					
7.2	6.9	5.4	All Other Non-Current	1.8					
100.0	100.0	100.0	Total	100.0					
			LIABILITIES						
9.9	10.8	8.1	Notes Payable-Short Term	1.2					
17.2	15.4	9.2	Cur. Mat.-L/T/D	10.0					
4.5	3.8	3.7	Trade Payables	2.1					
.0	.0	.0	Income Taxes Payable	.0					
5.3	18.7	10.8	All Other Current	13.1					
37.0	48.7	31.8	Total Current	26.5					
43.5	41.9	54.1	Long-Term Debt	98.2					
.3	.4	.0	Deferred Taxes	.0					
9.6	5.1	11.5	All Other Non-Current	20.0					
9.7	3.9	2.5	Net Worth	-44.7					
100.0	100.0	100.0	Total Liabilities & Net Worth	100.0					
			INCOME DATA						
100.0	100.0	100.0	Net Sales	100.0					
			Gross Profit						
95.9	98.5	94.1	Operating Expenses	89.5					
4.1	1.5	5.9	Operating Profit	10.5					
3.6	1.1	3.0	All Other Expenses (net)	5.9					
.5	.4	2.9	Profit Before Taxes	4.5					
			RATIOS						
1.5	1.2	2.5		4.0					
.3	.4	1.0	Current	.7					
.1	.1	.4		.3					
1.5	1.2	2.4		4.0					
.3	.3	.8	Quick	.6					
.0	.1	.3		.2					
0 UND	0 UND	0 UND		0 UND					
0 UND	7 50.8	11 32.3	Sales/Receivables	0 UND					
16 23.3	14 26.3	33 11.0		11 32.3					
			Cost of Sales/Inventory						
			Cost of Sales/Payables						
21.9	NM	9.1		4.7					
-10.2	-11.0	215.3	Sales/Working Capital	-155.0					
-3.4	-7.6	-7.3		-4.4					
5.5	4.8	8.4		3.3					
1.8 (11)	.8 (29)	2.3	EBIT/Interest	1.0 (10)					
1.4	-3.1	-1.1		-1.9					
			Net Profit + Depr., Dep., Amort./Cur. Mat. L/T/D						
1.3	2.8	.7		1.2					
3.9	4.9	4.5	Fixed/Worth	-2.6					
-3.1	-5.6	-2.6		-1.2					
.6	2.0	.6		.5					
5.8	5.1	8.5	Debt/Worth	-4.2					
-4.2	-8.9	-4.2		-2.6					
		107.8	% Profit Before Taxes/Tangible Net Worth						
	(21)	9.3							
		1.6							
19.3	22.1	10.9	% Profit Before Taxes/Total Assets	23.7					
4.2	-1.2	2.4		.0					
1.7	-12.9	-2.5		-14.8					
4.1	7.3	11.0		7.0					
2.0	5.7	4.3	Sales/Net Fixed Assets	2.1					
1.2	1.9	1.6		1.2					
2.5	5.2	4.0		3.8					
1.7	3.8	1.7	Sales/Total Assets	1.1					
1.0	1.7	1.0		.8					
9.2		3.4	% Depr., Dep., Amort./Sales						
12.5 (12)	(25)	7.4							
23.2		16.1							
	3.1	2.3	% Officers', Directors', Owners' Comp/Sales						
	4.8 (10)	3.7 (13)							
	11.0	6.7							
44570M	20171M	249772M	Net Sales ($)	4613M	12166M	8143M	47038M	14482M	163330M
25650M	6250M	109349M	Total Assets ($)	3561M	6481M	4181M	26848M	3587M	64691M

M = $ thousand   MM = $ million
See Pages 11 through 21 for Explanation of Ratios and Data

Current Data Sorted By Assets   Comparative Historical Data

0-500M	500M-2MM	2-10MM	10-50MM	50-100MM	100-250MM	Type of Statement	4/1/00-3/31/01 ALL	4/1/01-3/31/02 ALL
1		2	8	2		Unqualified	16	10
	12	33	5			Reviewed	26	24
4	10	16	1			Compiled	30	27
7	2	2				Tax Returns	11	12
1	3	5	2	1		Other	12	14
	46 (4/1-9/30/04)			71 (10/1/04-3/31/05)				
13	27	58	16	3		**NUMBER OF STATEMENTS**	95	87
%	%	%	%	%	%	**ASSETS**	%	%
13.5	10.1	9.2	9.3			Cash & Equivalents	12.6	9.2
10.8	10.9	9.7	12.8			Trade Receivables (net)	10.8	10.1
.5	1.0	1.8	2.7			Inventory	3.3	2.6
1.1	3.3	2.6	2.8			All Other Current	2.6	2.1
26.0	25.3	23.4	27.5			Total Current	29.2	23.9
62.1	62.2	64.6	63.8	DATA	NOT	Fixed Assets (net)	60.5	66.0
3.3	3.1	2.3	1.3	AVAILABLE		Intangibles (net)	3.0	2.1
8.6	9.4	9.7	7.4			All Other Non-Current	7.3	7.9
100.0	100.0	100.0	100.0			Total	100.0	100.0
						LIABILITIES		
12.8	6.0	3.5	3.0			Notes Payable-Short Term	6.1	8.7
15.4	13.8	13.5	13.3			Cur. Mat.-L/T/D	11.1	11.9
2.1	5.4	3.9	3.7			Trade Payables	3.8	3.4
.0	.1	.5	.1			Income Taxes Payable	.3	.1
7.1	8.1	5.4	3.8			All Other Current	6.8	6.9
37.3	33.3	26.7	23.9			Total Current	28.2	31.1
26.6	33.7	32.6	29.0			Long-Term Debt	31.5	37.9
.0	1.1	1.6	3.9			Deferred Taxes	1.7	2.4
10.6	1.3	3.2	2.2			All Other Non-Current	2.6	2.9
25.5	30.6	35.9	41.1			Net Worth	35.9	25.8
100.0	100.0	100.0	100.0			Total Liabilities & Net Worth	100.0	100.0
						INCOME DATA		
100.0	100.0	100.0	100.0			Net Sales	100.0	100.0
						Gross Profit		
96.4	94.7	93.6	93.7			Operating Expenses	94.3	94.1
3.6	5.3	6.4	6.3			Operating Profit	5.7	5.9
1.7	2.8	2.1	1.1			All Other Expenses (net)	2.0	3.1
1.9	2.5	4.3	5.2			Profit Before Taxes	3.7	2.9
						RATIOS		
1.2	1.4	1.3	1.5				1.9	1.2
.8	.9	.8	1.2			Current	1.0	.8
.4	.2	.5	.7				.5	.4
1.1	1.3	1.1	1.3				1.7	1.0
(12) .8	.8	.6	.9			Quick	.8	.7
.5	.2	.3	.5				.4	.3
0 UND	0 UND	5 69.8	21 17.6				3 108.5	4 95.1
0 UND	16 22.6	16 23.3	34 10.7			Sales/Receivables	20 18.5	18 20.5
26 13.9	28 13.2	29 12.6	47 7.7				37 9.8	31 11.8
						Cost of Sales/Inventory		
						Cost of Sales/Payables		
69.2	27.6	28.4	14.2				13.1	29.1
-60.0	-27.2	-23.8	43.3			Sales/Working Capital	194.3	-37.2
-7.1	-10.0	-9.5	-15.4				-11.4	-7.7
3.1	7.6	4.8	4.2				3.4	2.5
(11) 1.0	(24) 3.3	(55) 2.4	3.2			EBIT/Interest	(87) 2.1	(80) 1.4
.1	1.4	1.2	2.0				1.0	.7
	1.9	1.5				Net Profit + Depr., Dep.,	2.2	2.1
	(11) 1.3	(24) 1.1				Amort./Cur. Mat. L/T/D	(42) 1.3	(27) 1.2
	1.0	.9					.9	.9
1.3	1.0	1.4	1.3				1.1	1.3
2.9	1.9	2.2	1.7			Fixed/Worth	2.0	3.1
5.8	8.0	4.1	2.9				5.0	12.7
1.4	.9	1.1	1.0				.9	1.2
3.1	1.8	1.9	1.7			Debt/Worth	2.4	3.2
6.7	12.6	4.7	3.1				5.6	16.2
53.1	48.1	34.4	20.9			% Profit Before Taxes/Tangible	28.2	35.4
(12) 7.2	(21) 17.3	(55) 13.1	14.9			Net Worth	(87) 13.6	(73) 8.7
-37.2	5.1	2.2	12.2				2.1	2.3
12.2	10.9	9.8	8.1			% Profit Before Taxes/Total	8.0	8.4
.0	3.9	4.6	5.9			Assets	4.0	2.1
-14.5	.9	.8	2.9				.0	-.4
7.4	5.4	3.1	3.3				4.2	3.8
3.5	3.6	1.9	1.6			Sales/Net Fixed Assets	2.3	2.1
1.5	1.6	1.3	1.5				1.5	1.4
3.0	2.6	1.8	1.6				2.3	2.0
2.2	2.1	1.3	1.3			Sales/Total Assets	1.4	1.5
1.1	.9	1.0	1.1				1.0	1.0
7.0	5.3	8.3	8.1				5.6	6.8
11.1	(26) 11.0	(56) 11.0	11.2			% Depr., Dep., Amort./Sales	(91) 10.6	(82) 12.1
24.2	14.8	14.9	14.8				15.4	16.2
	3.3	2.3				% Officers', Directors',	2.8	2.9
	(16) 6.2	(31) 4.1				Owners' Comp/Sales	(61) 5.1	(51) 5.3
	8.9	7.7					10.3	10.8
8670M	66347M	410800M	505609M	154342M		Net Sales ($)	2771183M	648580M
3916M	31928M	263123M	344134M	223639M		Total Assets ($)	987457M	452459M

M = $ thousand   MM = $ million
See Pages 11 through 21 for Explanation of Ratios and Data

Comparative Historical Data

Current Data Sorted By Sales

			Type of Statement						
10	11	13	Unqualified	1	1			4	7
43	45	50	Reviewed	1	8	13	17	10	1
32	45	31	Compiled	6	8	10	4	1	2
13	14	11	Tax Returns	7	3			1	
16	13	12	Other	1	5	1	1	3	1
4/1/02- 3/31/03 ALL	4/1/03- 3/31/04 ALL	4/1/04- 3/31/05 ALL		0-1MM	46 (4/1-9/30/04) 1-3MM	3-5MM	5-10MM	71 (10/1/04-3/31/05) 10-25MM	25MM & OVER
114	128	117	**NUMBER OF STATEMENTS**	16	25	24	22	19	11
%	%	%	**ASSETS**	%	%	%	%	%	%
10.9	10.2	9.9	Cash & Equivalents	10.9	10.1	9.5	9.9	8.0	12.1
9.1	11.1	10.4	Trade Receivables (net)	5.3	9.5	8.8	8.0	18.4	14.6
2.5	1.6	1.6	Inventory	.1	.5	1.4	.9	1.7	8.1
1.9	3.4	2.7	All Other Current	1.7	1.7	4.1	3.6	1.3	3.8
24.3	26.3	24.6	Total Current	18.0	21.8	23.7	22.4	29.4	38.7
64.2	62.3	63.3	Fixed Assets (net)	65.3	68.3	64.2	66.0	59.8	48.4
2.3	2.4	2.4	Intangibles (net)	2.7	3.0	1.9	3.1	2.4	.3
9.2	9.0	9.7	All Other Non-Current	14.0	6.9	10.3	8.5	8.4	12.6
100.0	100.0	100.0	Total	100.0	100.0	100.0	100.0	100.0	100.0
			LIABILITIES						
5.6	5.7	5.0	Notes Payable-Short Term	7.9	6.9	3.5	4.0	4.0	3.5
12.7	12.7	13.6	Cur. Mat.-L/T/D	18.3	13.0	13.8	13.5	13.9	7.4
3.5	3.9	4.0	Trade Payables	1.6	3.8	4.9	4.0	3.2	7.4
.3	.2	.3	Income Taxes Payable	.0	.1	.2	.3	.9	.1
11.4	8.9	6.4	All Other Current	5.3	9.4	4.8	4.7	4.9	10.5
33.5	31.4	29.3	Total Current	33.1	33.2	27.2	26.4	27.0	28.9
31.7	31.1	31.7	Long-Term Debt	35.8	33.2	32.0	31.2	31.4	23.7
1.7	2.2	1.6	Deferred Taxes	.0	1.1	1.5	2.0	4.0	.0
2.4	3.8	3.4	All Other Non-Current	11.6	1.2	2.7	2.2	2.1	2.3
30.6	31.4	34.0	Net Worth	19.4	31.3	36.7	38.1	35.6	45.1
100.0	100.0	100.0	Total Liabilities & Net Worth	100.0	100.0	100.0	100.0	100.0	100.0
			INCOME DATA						
100.0	100.0	100.0	Net Sales	100.0	100.0	100.0	100.0	100.0	100.0
			Gross Profit						
93.3	93.2	94.2	Operating Expenses	93.8	93.3	95.4	94.3	93.6	94.6
6.7	6.8	5.8	Operating Profit	6.2	6.7	4.6	5.7	6.4	5.4
2.6	2.3	2.1	All Other Expenses (net)	5.0	2.4	1.0	2.0	1.5	1.2
4.2	4.5	3.7	Profit Before Taxes	1.3	4.4	3.6	3.6	4.9	4.2
			RATIOS						
1.2	1.5	1.4		1.1	1.3	1.4	1.3	1.4	2.6
.7	.8	.8	Current	.5	.9	.8	.8	.9	1.4
.4	.4	.4		.2	.2	.6	.5	.7	.7
1.0	1.2	1.2		1.1	1.3	1.4	1.1	1.3	1.2
.6	.6	(116) .7	Quick	(15) .5	.8	.6	.6	.8	.8
.3	.3	.4		.1	.2	.3	.4	.4	.4
5 77.5	5 80.6	4 92.3		0 UND	1 476.9	4 90.8	7 51.9	19 18.8	19 19.2
13 27.4	20 18.7	17 20.9	Sales/Receivables	0 UND	10 35.6	13 27.5	18 20.9	34 10.8	31 11.7
27 13.5	32 11.4	33 11.2		0 UND	37 10.0	26 13.8	25 14.6	50 7.3	35 10.4
			Cost of Sales/Inventory						
			Cost of Sales/Payables						
39.1	25.0	18.6		NM	32.4	21.7	20.0	14.6	7.4
−26.3	−41.7	−50.5	Sales/Working Capital	−10.2	−22.8	−23.5	−41.7	−53.1	17.7
−7.8	−8.1	−9.3		−2.1	−4.1	−9.1	−11.8	−19.6	−13.9
4.3	5.3	4.5		3.6	4.4	6.1	4.9	4.0	13.1
(106) 2.5	(118) 2.4	(109) 2.6	EBIT/Interest	(13) 2.4	(22) 2.7	2.1	(21) 2.3	(18) 3.2	4.0
1.2	1.4	1.3		.3	1.2	1.0	1.1	2.0	2.0
2.8	2.4	1.6	Net Profit + Depr., Dep.,			1.6	1.3	1.6	
(37) 1.3	(42) 1.5	(46) 1.2	Amort./Cur. Mat. L/T/D		(11) 1.2	(10) 1.0	(11) 1.3		
1.0	1.1	1.0				.7	.8	1.0	
1.2	1.1	1.3		1.8	1.0	1.0	1.4	1.5	.7
2.3	2.2	2.1	Fixed/Worth	4.0	2.2	2.0	2.1	2.0	1.3
6.5	7.1	4.4		NM	6.9	3.6	4.1	4.4	2.2
1.2	1.0	1.1		1.4	1.1	.9	.9	1.5	.6
2.3	2.2	1.9	Debt/Worth	3.4	1.8	1.9	2.0	1.8	1.4
7.6	9.4	4.7		NM	7.1	4.4	4.4	5.5	3.0
41.4	36.7	29.0	% Profit Before Taxes/Tangible	42.4	43.4	19.4	36.2	49.2	21.3
(99) 17.4	(108) 17.9	(107) 14.1	Net Worth	(12) 7.2	(22) 14.7	(23) 9.0	(21) 11.0	(18) 15.5	18.0
6.7	7.7	3.2		−37.2	4.6	−.3	−.1	13.3	8.6
10.6	10.8	9.7	% Profit Before Taxes/Total	7.0	8.3	9.8	11.0	10.9	8.5
5.4	5.5	4.9	Assets	.5	4.7	2.8	2.9	6.2	6.7
1.0	1.9	.8		−11.0	.9	.0	.9	3.8	2.3
3.7	4.5	4.0		4.2	3.6	3.9	4.0	5.0	4.6
2.2	2.5	2.1	Sales/Net Fixed Assets	2.3	1.7	2.3	2.2	2.0	3.2
1.6	1.6	1.4		1.0	1.1	1.8	1.4	1.5	1.6
2.2	2.3	2.2		2.8	2.0	2.3	1.9	2.8	2.0
1.5	1.6	1.4	Sales/Total Assets	1.4	1.1	1.5	1.4	1.4	1.6
1.1	1.1	1.0		.4	.8	1.2	1.1	1.1	.9
7.9	7.9	7.6		8.7	8.3	7.5	8.0	6.8	4.9
(111) 11.9	(120) 11.3	(114) 10.8	% Depr., Dep., Amort./Sales	14.6	12.4	10.2	(19) 10.3	10.9	7.6
15.0	15.9	15.0		37.4	15.9	15.0	13.0	15.0	10.5
2.8	2.1	2.3	% Officers', Directors',		2.8	3.2	.5		
(74) 5.1	(70) 4.4	(62) 4.4	Owners' Comp/Sales	(18) 5.8	(12) 6.3	(11) 2.9			
9.2	9.2	8.9		9.3	8.2	6.2			
997760M	1091983M	1145768M	Net Sales ($)	8735M	43779M	95693M	160865M	312620M	524076M
711077M	768595M	866740M	Total Assets ($)	8678M	39932M	71048M	114265M	211753M	421064M

© RMA 2005

M = $ thousand   MM = $ million

See Pages 11 through 21 for Explanation of Ratios and Data

Current Data Sorted By Assets   Comparative Historical Data

0-500M	500M-2MM	2-10MM	10-50MM	50-100MM	100-250MM	Type of Statement	7 ALL	8 ALL
	1	2	4			Unqualified	7	8
1	6	10	2			Reviewed	4	12
1	5	7	1			Compiled	20	29
6	6	5	1			Tax Returns	1	7
2	5	10	1	1		Other	10	31
0-500M	500M-2MM 18 (4/1-9/30/04)	2-10MM	10-50MM 61 (10/1/04-3/31/05)	50-100MM	100-250MM		ALL 4/1/00-3/31/01	ALL 4/1/01-3/31/02
9	23	34	12	1		NUMBER OF STATEMENTS	42	87
%	%	%	%	%	%	**ASSETS**	%	%
	7.2	6.5	7.3			Cash & Equivalents	7.9	8.3
	9.3	6.6	12.5			Trade Receivables (net)	6.9	8.2
	.7	2.7	1.2			Inventory	1.5	1.9
	5.1	1.5	4.7			All Other Current	2.8	3.6
	22.3	17.3	25.6			Total Current	19.0	22.1
	61.5	72.4	67.4			Fixed Assets (net)	72.7	63.0
	2.7	2.0	.4			Intangibles (net)	1.8	3.4
	13.5	8.2	6.6			All Other Non-Current	6.5	11.4
	100.0	100.0	100.0			Total	100.0	100.0
						LIABILITIES		
	9.5	3.6	2.9			Notes Payable-Short Term	4.1	3.3
	9.4	15.5	9.1			Cur. Mat.-L/T/D	11.2	14.7
	8.1	4.5	3.0			Trade Payables	3.8	6.1
	.5	.2	.8			Income Taxes Payable	.2	.1
	10.9	7.8	7.6			All Other Current	9.7	10.6
	38.4	31.6	23.3			Total Current	29.0	34.7
	50.9	46.3	30.8			Long-Term Debt	46.0	42.2
	1.0	1.7	3.7			Deferred Taxes	.8	1.5
	6.1	6.9	2.5			All Other Non-Current	2.4	6.9
	3.6	13.6	39.8			Net Worth	21.7	14.8
	100.0	100.0	100.0			Total Liabilities & Net Worth	100.0	100.0
						INCOME DATA		
	100.0	100.0	100.0			Net Sales	100.0	100.0
						Gross Profit		
	101.6	96.4	89.6			Operating Expenses	93.4	95.7
	-1.6	3.6	10.4			Operating Profit	6.6	4.3
	.3	3.3	2.2			All Other Expenses (net)	2.7	2.9
	-1.9	.3	8.2			Profit Before Taxes	3.9	1.4
						RATIOS		
	2.3	.9	1.6			Current	1.3	1.2
	.5	.6	1.1				.7	.7
	.2	.2	.6				.2	.3
	1.9	.7	1.5			Quick	1.1	.9
	.4	.3	.7				.5	.5
	.1	.2	.3				.2	.2
0	UND	7 53.0	15 24.0			Sales/Receivables	2 152.2	1 374.0
9	40.0	11 32.2	22 16.6				13 28.8	13 29.0
26	13.8	33 11.0	47 7.8				24 15.4	25 14.8
						Cost of Sales/Inventory		
						Cost of Sales/Payables		
	25.0	-34.8	14.4			Sales/Working Capital	36.9	32.4
	-23.4	-12.1	92.9				-25.8	-16.9
	-5.7	-4.6	-12.1				-6.8	-6.1
	3.1	2.9	7.4			EBIT/Interest	3.6	2.4
(21)	.1	1.5	2.7				1.7	(79) 1.2
	-5.4	.2	1.3				.9	.1
		1.8				Net Profit + Depr., Dep.,	1.8	1.8
	(15)	1.2				Amort./Cur. Mat. L /T/D	(14) 1.1	(20) 1.0
		.6					.7	.7
	1.2	2.2	1.0			Fixed/Worth	1.4	1.4
	-7.5	5.9	1.8				3.4	4.6
	-1.8	32.4	2.9				-26.5	-5.3
	.6	1.9	1.1			Debt/Worth	1.0	1.4
	-9.2	6.9	1.6				3.4	7.0
	-3.9	37.5	2.4				-31.5	-8.1
		18.0	40.9			% Profit Before Taxes/Tangible	27.6	23.5
	(28)	4.2	15.5			Net Worth	(31) 10.2	(58) 6.9
		-27.0	2.9				2.7	-8.7
	5.4	5.8	15.6			% Profit Before Taxes/Total	7.9	7.4
	-2.2	1.3	5.1			Assets	3.2	1.2
	-14.2	-2.8	.8				-.5	-4.1
	7.8	2.3	2.9			Sales/Net Fixed Assets	2.8	4.3
	3.6	1.4	1.5				1.9	2.5
	2.5	1.0	1.4				1.5	1.5
	3.9	1.6	1.3			Sales/Total Assets	2.1	2.7
	2.2	1.1	1.1				1.4	1.6
	1.6	.8	1.0				1.1	1.0
	2.5	7.1	5.3			% Depr., Dep., Amort./Sales	2.5	3.4
(20)	5.6	10.6	8.1				7.6	(80) 8.2
	12.4	16.8	10.6				13.2	14.1
	1.8	.3				% Officers', Directors',	1.4	1.4
(12)	4.4	(10) 1.8				Owners' Comp/Sales	(20) 3.0	(36) 3.1
	8.2	3.6					8.1	7.3
13780M	75486M	217741M	304343M	102795M		Net Sales ($)	303361M	707783M
2855M	28410M	169207M	234314M	74305M		Total Assets ($)	239163M	499154M

(Columns 50-100MM and 100-250MM: DATA NOT AVAILABLE)

Comparative Historical Data			Type of Statement	Current Data Sorted By Sales					
5	7	7	Unqualified		1	1	1	2	2
17	25	18	Reviewed		5	4	5	3	1
27	26	14	Compiled		7	1	3	3	
12	12	18	Tax Returns	3	9		6		
24	19	22	Other	2	6	4	3	5	2
4/1/02-3/31/03	4/1/03-3/31/04	4/1/04-3/31/05		18 (4/1-9/30/04)			61 (10/1/04-3/31/05)		
ALL	ALL	ALL		0-1MM	1-3MM	3-5MM	5-10MM	10-25MM	25MM & OVER
85	89	79	NUMBER OF STATEMENTS	5	28	10	18	13	5
%	%	%	ASSETS	%	%	%	%	%	%
8.1	8.0	8.1	Cash & Equivalents		7.7	7.1	7.6	5.0	
8.4	9.0	8.7	Trade Receivables (net)		8.8	9.0	6.5	12.3	
1.3	2.0	1.9	Inventory		.9	1.0	4.1	1.9	
3.5	5.1	3.0	All Other Current		2.4	4.2	2.9	1.8	
21.2	24.1	21.7	Total Current		19.8	21.3	21.2	21.1	
69.5	64.6	67.2	Fixed Assets (net)		68.6	69.0	67.4	66.0	
1.8	3.4	1.9	Intangibles (net)		3.8	1.3	.3	.5	
7.5	7.9	9.1	All Other Non-Current		7.8	8.3	11.1	12.4	
100.0	100.0	100.0	Total		100.0	100.0	100.0	100.0	
			LIABILITIES						
4.4	6.3	8.4	Notes Payable-Short Term		11.9	2.0	2.2	8.1	
14.0	10.6	11.9	Cur. Mat.-L/T/D		13.5	10.5	12.0	12.9	
5.9	6.2	5.3	Trade Payables		6.2	3.8	5.0	5.8	
.3	.4	.4	Income Taxes Payable		.0	1.6	.1	.1	
8.4	8.3	8.7	All Other Current		9.0	12.2	7.4	5.9	
33.0	31.9	34.7	Total Current		40.7	30.2	26.7	32.8	
52.9	44.9	46.6	Long-Term Debt		50.1	46.8	46.3	38.8	
1.3	1.5	1.6	Deferred Taxes		.9	2.0	1.9	2.5	
8.6	6.6	6.1	All Other Non-Current		10.0	10.3	1.0	3.1	
4.3	15.2	11.1	Net Worth		−1.6	10.7	24.2	22.9	
100.0	100.0	100.0	Total Liabilities & Net Worth		100.0	100.0	100.0	100.0	
			INCOME DATA						
100.0	100.0	100.0	Net Sales		100.0	100.0	100.0	100.0	
			Gross Profit						
94.7	97.0	97.0	Operating Expenses		97.8	97.2	98.2	92.8	
5.3	3.0	3.0	Operating Profit		2.2	2.8	1.8	7.2	
3.3	2.3	2.1	All Other Expenses (net)		3.0	2.5	1.7	1.1	
2.0	.7	.9	Profit Before Taxes		−.8	.4	.0	6.1	
			RATIOS						
1.3	1.3	1.0			1.0	4.7	1.1	1.3	
.7	.8	.6	Current		.4	.5	.7	.7	
.3	.4	.3			.2	.3	.4	.3	
1.0	1.0	1.0			1.0	4.7	.7	.9	
.4	(88) .5	.4	Quick		.4	.3	.4	.6	
.2	.3	.2			.1	.1	.2	.2	
3 126.2	6 65.9	6 62.4		2 170.2	0 UND	0 UND	6 59.2		
12 30.2	15 25.0	11 32.9	Sales/Receivables	16 23.0	9 40.0	10 37.6	23 16.1		
24 15.3	25 14.5	33 11.0		34 10.7	49 7.5	16 22.9	48 7.6		
			Cost of Sales/Inventory						
			Cost of Sales/Payables						
61.0	29.2	110.8			UND	20.1	154.5	92.9	
−19.7	−25.9	−15.2	Sales/Working Capital		−11.7	−11.7	−27.6	−15.2	
−6.8	−7.9	−6.6			−4.0	−4.5	−9.8	−8.3	
2.8	3.6	3.2			2.5	3.5	3.2	3.4	
(82) 1.4	(87) 1.3	(76) 1.7	EBIT/Interest	(27) .9	1.2	(16) 1.8	2.6		
−.1	−.5	−.2			−.5	−.4	−1.2	.9	
1.9	1.8	1.7	Net Profit + Depr., Dep.,						
(30) 1.3	(27) 1.3	(25) 1.2	Amort./Cur. Mat. L/T/D						
1.0	.9	.6							
2.0	1.6	1.6			3.0	4.8	1.3	1.7	
3.5	4.3	4.3	Fixed/Worth		20.1	47.5	2.3	2.9	
−6.7	−25.8	−7.6			−1.8	−6.9	10.5	5.1	
1.8	1.7	1.6			2.7	5.2	1.3	1.4	
3.7	5.5	4.2	Debt/Worth		23.2	84.1	1.9	2.4	
−11.9	−62.9	−9.4			−3.9	−9.4	15.1	11.2	
38.0	34.4	29.5	% Profit Before Taxes/Tangible	33.7		16.5	34.7		
(58) 13.6	(65) 6.1	(55) 6.9	Net Worth	(16) 2.1		(15) 5.3	(11) 14.6		
.9	−6.2	−8.4		−39.5		−9.4	.4		
8.2	6.3	6.7	% Profit Before Taxes/Total		6.1	6.5	6.6	9.7	
2.0	1.7	2.0	Assets		.1	1.0	3.2	3.9	
−3.1	−3.8	−3.4			−6.4	−7.9	−3.8	−.5	
3.9	5.7	4.3			4.1	3.7	7.6	6.5	
2.2	2.4	2.4	Sales/Net Fixed Assets		1.8	2.8	2.2	1.6	
1.3	1.4	1.3			1.0	1.5	1.2	1.4	
2.4	2.7	2.3			2.3	2.3	4.8	2.2	
1.5	1.6	1.5	Sales/Total Assets		1.3	1.7	1.6	1.2	
1.0	1.1	1.1			.8	1.1	1.1	1.1	
5.9	5.2	4.9			4.1	5.7	4.0	5.4	
(80) 9.8	(82) 8.6	(75) 8.6	% Depr., Dep., Amort./Sales	(26) 8.9		8.7	(17) 10.5	7.8	
14.2	12.9	14.4			15.1	21.5	15.6	10.5	
1.5	2.1	1.1	% Officers', Directors',						
(29) 2.8	(35) 3.1	(29) 3.4	Owners' Comp/Sales						
8.6	7.5	6.0							
602158M	723307M	714145M	Net Sales ($)	2859M	58439M	40070M	122169M	214092M	276516M
438034M	471795M	509091M	Total Assets ($)	1528M	59548M	30691M	78811M	163029M	175484M

M = $ thousand   MM = $ million
See Pages 11 through 21 for Explanation of Ratios and Data

Current Data Sorted By Assets | Comparative Historical Data

0-500M	500M-2MM	2-10MM	10-50MM	50-100MM	100-250MM	Type of Statement	4/1/00-3/31/01 ALL	4/1/01-3/31/02 ALL
	5	11	5	3		Unqualified	15	16
2	5	5	2			Reviewed	14	11
5	14	4				Compiled	28	29
6	10	3			1	Tax Returns	17	15
2	7	10	4	1		Other	22	27
	25 (4/1-9/30/04)		80 (10/1/04-3/31/05)					
15	41	33	11	4	1	**NUMBER OF STATEMENTS**	96	98
%	%	%	%	%	%	**ASSETS**	%	%
11.8	9.8	10.6	15.6			Cash & Equivalents	10.2	11.5
22.8	24.1	25.7	31.1			Trade Receivables (net)	21.2	24.9
.0	.2	1.0	.6			Inventory	.7	1.2
1.8	4.9	4.3	6.3			All Other Current	2.3	4.1
36.4	38.9	41.7	53.6			Total Current	34.3	41.7
43.6	44.1	42.8	31.7			Fixed Assets (net)	54.3	47.1
1.0	7.7	2.7	3.1			Intangibles (net)	3.8	4.0
19.0	9.2	12.8	11.6			All Other Non-Current	7.6	7.2
100.0	100.0	100.0	100.0			Total	100.0	100.0
						LIABILITIES		
18.0	11.1	4.4	6.3			Notes Payable-Short Term	15.2	9.2
14.9	13.4	9.3	11.2			Cur. Mat.-L/T/D	9.5	8.1
13.8	10.0	7.9	12.5			Trade Payables	5.4	6.5
.9	.2	.5	.4			Income Taxes Payable	.2	.9
17.7	6.6	12.1	7.3			All Other Current	7.2	8.8
65.4	41.3	34.2	37.8			Total Current	37.6	33.5
45.2	26.5	18.5	13.6			Long-Term Debt	27.0	25.7
1.0	.2	.7	.5			Deferred Taxes	1.0	.7
12.7	8.1	4.2	1.3			All Other Non-Current	4.8	9.0
-24.2	23.9	42.3	46.8			Net Worth	29.7	31.2
100.0	100.0	100.0	100.0			Total Liabilities & Net Worth	100.0	100.0
						INCOME DATA		
100.0	100.0	100.0	100.0			Net Sales	100.0	100.0
						Gross Profit		
98.7	95.3	96.2	97.3			Operating Expenses	92.5	94.9
1.3	4.7	3.8	2.7			Operating Profit	7.5	5.1
2.4	.7	1.8	.1			All Other Expenses (net)	2.2	1.5
-1.2	3.9	2.0	2.6			Profit Before Taxes	5.3	3.5
						RATIOS		
1.1	1.9	3.5	2.7				2.5	2.7
.5	1.2	1.6	1.3			Current	1.1	1.4
.1	.6	.8	.9				.6	.8
1.1	1.9	3.4	2.7				2.3	2.4
.5	1.0	1.1	1.3			Quick	1.0	1.1
.1	.5	.6	.8				.4	.6
0 UND	0 UND	21 17.4	48 7.6				0 738.5	7 54.4
6 56.3	30 12.1	38 9.6	57 6.4			Sales/Receivables	30 12.3	33 11.0
35 10.3	54 6.7	58 6.3	76 4.8				68 5.4	72 5.0
						Cost of Sales/Inventory		
						Cost of Sales/Payables		
119.7	11.1	7.4	5.2				7.8	5.9
-22.3	76.0	17.1	22.4			Sales/Working Capital	95.6	23.2
-7.8	-14.2	-23.3	-61.2				-11.1	-29.0
6.7	5.8	4.4	7.9				7.0	6.9
(13) .3	(37) 1.9	(32) 2.5	(10) 6.2			EBIT/Interest	(85) 3.0	(90) 2.4
-2.7	-1.0	.1	1.1				1.1	.8
						Net Profit + Depr., Dep.,		3.4	4.1
						Amort./Cur. Mat. L/T/D	(26) 1.3	(30) 1.5
							.7	1.0
.7	1.0	.7	.4				.8	.6
-6.0	2.1	1.2	.8			Fixed/Worth	1.6	1.3
-1.1	-33.4	2.3	1.2				6.4	4.1
4.4	1.1	.5	.5				.6	.6
-7.3	3.1	1.1	1.5			Debt/Worth	1.8	2.2
-2.8	-81.8	5.4	2.4				7.9	8.8
	64.8	31.4	26.7			% Profit Before Taxes/Tangible	59.5	40.8
	(30) 8.7	(30) 11.2	6.0			Net Worth	(80) 16.8	(84) 14.7
	-17.4	1.1	4.8				3.8	.4
28.1	10.7	10.0	8.6			% Profit Before Taxes/Total	19.5	14.3
.6	2.8	3.6	3.6			Assets	5.6	5.3
-19.0	-4.5	-1.7	1.0				.8	-.4
46.0	12.1	10.7	13.5				7.9	10.3
13.3	8.1	5.4	5.4			Sales/Net Fixed Assets	3.7	5.1
4.8	4.5	2.7	3.0				1.9	2.4
8.8	4.4	3.2	2.6				2.8	3.5
6.1	2.5	2.3	2.0			Sales/Total Assets	1.9	2.0
2.8	1.8	1.3	1.3				1.3	1.4
	2.9	4.3	2.3				3.5	3.4
	(30) 5.7	(31) 5.3	(10) 3.8			% Depr., Dep., Amort./Sales	(90) 6.0	(90) 6.4
	8.8	8.2	8.0				10.2	9.6
	2.5	1.9					2.5	2.9
	(18) 5.1	(11) 3.5				% Officers', Directors',	(44) 5.5	(41) 5.8
	12.0	5.8				Owners' Comp/Sales	8.6	9.2
28163M	129863M	340821M	355260M	293064M	1786239M	Net Sales ($)	872376M	1147253M
4195M	45757M	152408M	177515M	272968M	176693M	Total Assets ($)	418295M	589032M

M = $ thousand   MM = $ million
See Pages 11 through 21 for Explanation of Ratios and Data

Comparative Historical Data				Current Data Sorted By Sales					

			Type of Statement						
27	24	24	Unqualified	1	4	2	6	4	7
11	15	14	Reviewed	1	2	2	3	5	1
18	25	23	Compiled	2	4	9	6	2	
15	21	20	Tax Returns	6	9	3	1		1
23	30	24	Other	2	6	2	4	7	3
4/1/02-3/31/03 ALL	4/1/03-3/31/04 ALL	4/1/04-3/31/05 ALL		25 (4/1-9/30/04)			80 (10/1/04-3/31/05)		
				0-1MM	1-3MM	3-5MM	5-10MM	10-25MM	25MM & OVER
94	115	105	NUMBER OF STATEMENTS	12	25	18	20	18	12
%	%	%	ASSETS	%	%	%	%	%	%
14.5	12.3	10.8	Cash & Equivalents	11.5	8.7	8.0	13.9	11.8	12.1
24.2	23.3	25.0	Trade Receivables (net)	13.0	25.5	18.2	27.9	32.8	30.0
.6	1.9	1.3	Inventory	.0	.3	.2	.4	1.4	7.1
3.4	4.6	4.3	All Other Current	11.8	5.1	1.2	.9	4.7	4.6
42.7	42.1	41.4	Total Current	36.3	39.6	27.6	43.1	50.7	53.8
42.6	44.6	42.1	Fixed Assets (net)	50.9	43.2	43.1	46.6	36.0	31.4
6.6	5.2	4.7	Intangibles (net)	.1	5.8	8.7	2.5	4.3	5.4
8.1	8.1	11.8	All Other Non-Current	12.7	11.3	20.6	7.8	9.0	9.5
100.0	100.0	100.0	Total	100.0	100.0	100.0	100.0	100.0	100.0
			LIABILITIES						
8.5	11.9	9.8	Notes Payable-Short Term	14.7	11.8	8.5	9.0	5.5	10.6
8.1	8.5	12.1	Cur. Mat.-L/T/D	19.3	15.0	9.6	9.5	8.0	13.3
5.7	6.8	9.9	Trade Payables	3.4	17.8	5.2	5.2	12.4	10.9
1.0	.7	.5	Income Taxes Payable	.3	.5	.1	.7	.7	.4
12.6	15.4	10.2	All Other Current	11.1	16.2	6.3	4.4	12.1	8.9
36.0	43.5	42.4	Total Current	48.8	61.3	29.7	28.9	38.7	44.1
25.6	27.5	26.8	Long-Term Debt	58.5	22.9	28.7	21.1	14.3	28.6
.4	.8	.5	Deferred Taxes	.6	.4	.1	.9	.8	.4
5.0	6.5	6.6	All Other Non-Current	1.1	13.0	9.0	6.4	2.1	2.4
33.1	21.7	23.6	Net Worth	−9.1	2.4	32.5	42.8	44.1	24.5
100.0	100.0	100.0	Total Liabilities & Net Worth	100.0	100.0	100.0	100.0	100.0	100.0
			INCOME DATA						
100.0	100.0	100.0	Net Sales	100.0	100.0	100.0	100.0	100.0	100.0
			Gross Profit						
94.5	94.7	96.1	Operating Expenses	89.8	99.2	96.3	96.4	95.7	95.6
5.5	5.3	3.9	Operating Profit	10.2	.8	3.7	3.6	4.3	4.4
2.3	2.8	1.4	All Other Expenses (net)	5.1	.0	.8	2.0	1.3	1.1
3.2	2.5	2.5	Profit Before Taxes	5.1	.8	3.0	1.6	3.0	3.3
			RATIOS						
2.5	2.6	2.4		1.9	1.8	1.9	3.2	2.7	2.1
1.4	1.1	1.1	Current	1.0	.8	.8	1.5	1.2	1.2
.8	.5	.7		.2	.3	.6	1.1	.8	.9
2.5	2.2	2.3		1.9	1.6	1.6	3.2	2.6	2.1
1.2	.9	1.0	Quick	.6	.5	.8	1.5	1.0	1.0
.7	.3	.5		.1	.2	.6	1.0	.6	.6
11 32.1	2 207.7	7 51.5		0 UND	0 UND	0 UND	12 31.6	25 14.7	38 9.5
39 9.3	25 14.3	34 10.6	Sales/Receivables	3 123.5	29 12.7	30 12.3	39 9.5	37 9.8	58 6.3
64 5.7	57 6.4	56 6.5		53 6.9	50 7.4	49 7.5	55 6.7	66 5.5	76 4.8
			Cost of Sales/Inventory						
			Cost of Sales/Payables						
7.5	8.5	10.1		6.0	13.9	14.4	6.5	7.5	7.9
26.6	73.2	66.1	Sales/Working Capital	95.6	−16.8	−537.1	18.4	48.2	23.3
−27.1	−14.3	−16.0		−3.4	−8.3	−15.0	159.0	−24.6	NM
8.6	6.0	5.9		9.0	5.7	5.6	3.7	9.0	7.6
(85) 2.9	(101) 1.8	(97) 2.1	EBIT/Interest	(10) 1.1	(23) 1.2	(16) 2.7	2.0	(17) 2.7	(11) 2.9
.9	.3	−.3		−1.1	−3.8	1.3	−.8	−.6	1.3
5.5	2.9	2.1	Net Profit + Depr., Dep.,						
(24) 1.6	(24) 1.1	(25) .5	Amort./Cur. Mat. L/T/D						
.9	.6	.2							
.5	.5	.8		1.3	.8	1.0	.7	.6	.3
1.0	1.6	1.5	Fixed/Worth	1.9	11.9	1.7	1.2	1.1	.9
3.5	86.6	104.5		−.8	−1.5	−47.2	2.2	2.4	5.7
.7	.7	.9		1.1	1.0	1.0	.5	.5	.8
1.6	2.8	2.4	Debt/Worth	29.1	107.3	2.8	1.3	1.4	2.4
7.3	133.3	645.0		−4.2	−3.7	−119.1	5.6	4.6	20.3
44.4	40.0	50.6			64.4	55.5	26.9	63.0	32.8
(80) 12.8	(87) 9.6	(80) 10.3	% Profit Before Taxes/Tangible Net Worth	(15) 7.7	(13) 20.1	(18) 3.0	(17) 24.4	(10) 9.7	
1.6	−5.5	−1.1			−37.8	6.0	−6.7	−7.1	4.8
15.0	15.3	11.3		19.6	11.5	13.6	10.1	16.5	8.3
5.1	3.4	3.3	% Profit Before Taxes/Total Assets	2.9	1.0	5.3	.9	3.9	3.2
−.1	−2.8	−3.2		−4.5	−13.7	1.9	−3.5	−4.2	1.8
10.7	12.3	12.8		12.2	16.0	13.0	12.0	12.4	47.3
5.7	6.8	7.6	Sales/Net Fixed Assets	3.4	7.2	8.5	8.4	7.6	8.1
2.7	3.2	3.3		1.0	3.9	3.5	3.5	3.7	3.5
3.1	3.9	4.1		2.8	4.8	4.7	4.9	4.1	2.6
2.1	2.4	2.4	Sales/Total Assets	1.1	2.4	2.4	2.8	2.5	2.1
1.5	1.6	1.5		.5	1.8	1.7	2.0	1.6	1.0
3.2	3.7	3.0			2.8	4.9	3.0	2.9	
(85) 6.5	(97) 5.8	(82) 5.6	% Depr., Dep., Amort./Sales	(16) 6.4	(14) 6.1	(18) 5.1	(17) 5.8		
10.9	8.9	8.2		13.5	12.0	6.4	8.0		
3.0	2.5	2.3					3.2		
(40) 5.5	(38) 4.7	(37) 4.8	% Officers', Directors', Owners' Comp/Sales			(10) 4.7			
10.5	10.5	10.6					6.7		
1518633M	1350314M	2933410M	Net Sales ($)	6633M	50609M	75028M	129577M	311519M	2360044M
727442M	637383M	829536M	Total Assets ($)	7285M	27938M	30686M	55634M	130548M	577445M

M = $ thousand   MM = $ million
See Pages 11 through 21 for Explanation of Ratios and Data

Current Data Sorted By Assets　　　　　　　　　　　　　　Comparative Historical Data

						Type of Statement	4/1/00-3/31/01 ALL	4/1/01-3/31/02 ALL
1		1	2	1	1	Unqualified		
1	1	2				Reviewed		
4		2				Compiled		
4	1	1				Tax Returns		
3	1	3		1		Other		
10 (4/1-9/30/04)			20 (10/1/04-3/31/05)					
0-500M	500M-2MM	2-10MM	10-50MM	50-100MM	100-250MM			
13	3	9	2	2	1	NUMBER OF STATEMENTS		
%	%	%	%	%	%	ASSETS	%	%
17.0						Cash & Equivalents		
8.3						Trade Receivables (net)	D	D
3.7						Inventory	A	A
2.0						All Other Current	T	T
31.0						Total Current	A	A
49.9						Fixed Assets (net)		
5.3						Intangibles (net)	N	N
13.7						All Other Non-Current	O	O
100.0						Total	T	T
						LIABILITIES	A	A
14.5						Notes Payable-Short Term	V	V
8.4						Cur. Mat.-L/T/D	A	A
9.3						Trade Payables	I	I
.0						Income Taxes Payable	L	L
8.2						All Other Current	A	A
40.4						Total Current	B	B
35.3						Long-Term Debt	L	L
.0						Deferred Taxes	E	E
18.1						All Other Non-Current		
6.2						Net Worth		
100.0						Total Liabilities & Net Worth		
						INCOME DATA		
100.0						Net Sales		
						Gross Profit		
88.3						Operating Expenses		
11.7						Operating Profit		
4.6						All Other Expenses (net)		
7.1						Profit Before Taxes		
						RATIOS		
1.4								
.6						Current		
.3								
1.0								
.6						Quick		
.2								
0 UND								
0 UND						Sales/Receivables		
12 29.5								
						Cost of Sales/Inventory		
						Cost of Sales/Payables		
NM								
-21.7						Sales/Working Capital		
-5.0								
						EBIT/Interest		
						Net Profit + Depr., Dep., Amort./Cur. Mat. L./T/D		
1.1								
-6.0						Fixed/Worth		
-2.1								
.9								
-42.7						Debt/Worth		
-4.7								
						% Profit Before Taxes/Tangible Net Worth		
24.5								
1.6						% Profit Before Taxes/Total Assets		
-8.3								
57.0								
6.5						Sales/Net Fixed Assets		
1.0								
5.9								
3.5						Sales/Total Assets		
.8								
						% Depr., Dep., Amort./Sales		
						% Officers', Directors', Owners' Comp/Sales		
9528M	4792M	51453M	30942M	177882M	101043M	Net Sales ($)		
3257M	2822M	43366M	40817M	146693M	103281M	Total Assets ($)		

M = $ thousand　　MM = $ million
See Pages 11 through 21 for Explanation of Ratios and Data

Comparative Historical Data | Current Data Sorted By Sales

Type of Statement

				0-1MM	1-3MM	3-5MM	5-10MM	10-25MM	25MM & OVER
2	2	6	Unqualified	1			1	2	2
1	3	4	Reviewed	1	1	1	1		
2	3	6	Compiled	2	3	1			
6	2	6	Tax Returns	3	3				
2	5	8	Other	2	4				2

4/1/02-3/31/03 ALL	4/1/03-3/31/04 ALL	4/1/04-3/31/05 ALL		0-1MM	10 (4/1-9/30/04) 1-3MM	3-5MM	20 (10/1/04-3/31/05) 5-10MM	10-25MM	25MM & OVER
13	15	30	**NUMBER OF STATEMENTS**	9	11	2	2	2	4
%	%	%	**ASSETS**	%	%	%	%	%	%
6.3	12.0	10.7	Cash & Equivalents		6.8				
2.4	10.3	5.1	Trade Receivables (net)		7.6				
6.0	3.2	3.2	Inventory		1.3				
2.6	.6	2.0	All Other Current		.9				
17.2	26.2	21.0	Total Current		16.5				
69.2	44.6	58.8	Fixed Assets (net)		58.5				
1.0	7.9	3.8	Intangibles (net)		4.1				
12.5	21.3	16.3	All Other Non-Current		20.8				
100.0	100.0	100.0	Total		100.0				
			LIABILITIES						
3.4	7.9	8.1	Notes Payable-Short Term		17.2				
11.8	11.9	5.4	Cur. Mat.-L/T/D		5.8				
4.0	9.9	6.8	Trade Payables		2.6				
.2	.1	.0	Income Taxes Payable		.0				
5.8	11.9	9.9	All Other Current		9.5				
25.3	41.7	30.3	Total Current		35.1				
41.9	34.0	40.3	Long-Term Debt		46.1				
.5	.8	.5	Deferred Taxes		.0				
2.4	6.8	11.6	All Other Non-Current		12.6				
29.9	16.8	17.4	Net Worth		6.3				
100.0	100.0	100.0	Total Liabilities & Net Worth		100.0				
			INCOME DATA						
100.0	100.0	100.0	Net Sales		100.0				
			Gross Profit						
85.1	96.8	88.1	Operating Expenses		86.3				
14.9	3.2	11.9	Operating Profit		13.7				
5.6	2.8	4.6	All Other Expenses (net)		7.1				
9.3	.5	7.3	Profit Before Taxes		6.6				
			RATIOS						
1.3	1.4	1.7			3.2				
.6	.6	.6	Current		.4				
.1	.3	.2			.3				
.6	1.4	1.1			3.2				
.2	.3	.3	Quick		.3				
.1	.1	.1			.1				
0 UND	0 UND	0 UND		0 UND					
3 135.9	12 30.4	1 366.2	Sales/Receivables	0 UND					
6 56.6	37 9.8	10 34.8		30 12.1					
			Cost of Sales/Inventory						
			Cost of Sales/Payables						
57.0	30.7	24.4			37.7				
-17.4	-6.8	-16.4	Sales/Working Capital		-11.2				
-7.9	-2.8	-5.1			-5.4				
5.7	2.7	4.0							
(12) 1.9	(12) 1.2	(22) 2.0	EBIT/Interest						
1.2	.0	.0							
			Net Profit + Depr., Dep., Amort./Cur. Mat. L/T/D						
1.1	1.4	1.3			1.1				
2.3	3.1	3.5	Fixed/Worth		3.5				
4.6	-2.9	-2.5			-2.0				
1.0	3.7	1.1			1.1				
2.0	12.0	3.0	Debt/Worth		4.8				
5.1	-10.0	-6.9			-3.8				
40.5		29.0	% Profit Before Taxes/Tangible Net Worth						
(11) 7.5		(20) 15.3							
2.1		.2							
19.3	8.6	12.0	% Profit Before Taxes/Total Assets		5.3				
2.2	1.5	4.0			3.5				
.6	-4.7	-.2			-16.6				
5.9	9.3	9.0			22.6				
2.2	5.2	2.5	Sales/Net Fixed Assets		5.4				
.6	1.3	.9			.5				
3.3	2.3	3.6			4.3				
1.7	1.5	1.5	Sales/Total Assets		1.7				
.5	.7	.6			.4				
2.8	3.1	3.6							
(11) 12.3	(12) 5.8	(24) 5.8	% Depr., Dep., Amort./Sales						
18.1	9.1	11.2							
		2.5	% Officers', Directors', Owners' Comp/Sales						
	(10)	5.5							
		11.2							
354841M	129082M	375640M	Net Sales ($)	3433M	17161M	8052M	11471M	30942M	304581M
151310M	118849M	340236M	Total Assets ($)	2155M	24035M	7954M	10626M	40817M	254649M

© RMA 2005

M = $ thousand   MM = $ million
See Pages 11 through 21 for Explanation of Ratios and Data

Current Data Sorted By Assets | Comparative Historical Data

						Type of Statement		
						Unqualified	8	4
	2	2	2		1	Reviewed	5	2
1	4	4				Compiled	2	4
2	1	1	2			Tax Returns	4	3
3	2	7	2			Other	17	22
	4 (4/1-9/30/04)		27 (10/1/04-3/31/05)				4/1/00-3/31/01	4/1/01-3/31/02
0-500M	500M-2MM	2-10MM	10-50MM	50-100MM	100-250MM		ALL	ALL
6	9	11	4		1	NUMBER OF STATEMENTS	36	35
%	%	%	%	%	%	**ASSETS**	%	%
		14.1				Cash & Equivalents	12.6	13.4
		3.9				Trade Receivables (net)	8.3	3.5
		1.8		D		Inventory	2.6	4.6
		.3		A		All Other Current	1.4	1.5
		20.1		T		Total Current	25.0	23.0
		57.8		A		Fixed Assets (net)	57.0	63.6
		3.5				Intangibles (net)	1.5	1.8
		18.6		N		All Other Non-Current	16.5	11.7
		100.0		O		Total	100.0	100.0
				T		**LIABILITIES**		
		4.1				Notes Payable-Short Term	8.1	18.0
		4.7		A		Cur. Mat.-L/T/D	7.5	4.6
		3.8		V		Trade Payables	4.6	3.9
		.0		A		Income Taxes Payable	.0	.0
		11.2		I		All Other Current	10.2	14.8
		23.8		L		Total Current	30.4	41.3
		34.1		A		Long-Term Debt	40.6	45.4
		.0		B		Deferred Taxes	.4	.2
		9.3		L		All Other Non-Current	19.3	3.1
		32.8		E		Net Worth	9.3	10.0
		100.0				Total Liabilities & Net Worth	100.0	100.0
						INCOME DATA		
		100.0				Net Sales	100.0	100.0
						Gross Profit		
		86.5				Operating Expenses	85.8	87.1
		13.5				Operating Profit	14.2	12.9
		5.6				All Other Expenses (net)	11.3	7.7
		7.9				Profit Before Taxes	2.8	5.2
						RATIOS		
		2.6					1.4	2.0
		1.2				Current	1.0	.8
		.2					.2	.2
		2.0					1.2	1.3
		.6				Quick	.6	.5
		.1					.2	.1
	0 UND						2 229.3	0 UND
	0 771.9					Sales/Receivables	6 58.3	1 264.9
	4 103.9						25 14.6	8 47.3
						Cost of Sales/Inventory		
						Cost of Sales/Payables		
		6.4					8.2	12.4
		27.4				Sales/Working Capital	NM	-41.5
		-5.7					-6.0	-5.2
							4.8	3.4
						EBIT/Interest	(28) 1.7	(27) 1.8
							.8	.1
						Net Profit + Depr., Dep., Amort./Cur. Mat. L /T/D		
		.7					1.5	1.6
		1.4				Fixed/Worth	2.2	3.6
		27.8					13.7	-30.8
		.4					1.8	1.3
		3.3				Debt/Worth	4.1	4.7
		30.0					15.4	-34.5
						% Profit Before Taxes/Tangible Net Worth	56.7	68.9
							(28) 22.1	(25) 10.3
							.8	-4.9
		18.5					11.1	12.8
		4.2				% Profit Before Taxes/Total Assets	2.4	5.7
		1.0					-1.1	-1.9
		4.4					4.1	5.0
		3.1				Sales/Net Fixed Assets	1.9	2.1
		.4					.9	.9
		1.6					1.6	2.2
		1.2				Sales/Total Assets	1.2	1.6
		.3					.6	.7
							2.9	2.3
						% Depr., Dep., Amort./Sales	(35) 6.1	(33) 6.2
							11.6	10.3
						% Officers', Directors', Owners' Comp/Sales		
6509M	26446M	64419M	124070M		72799M	Net Sales ($)	609221M	367464M
1323M	9577M	58820M	79777M		245762M	Total Assets ($)	753365M	342815M

DATA NOT AVAILABLE (50-100MM column)

Comparative Historical Data | **Current Data Sorted By Sales**

Type of Statement	4/1/02-3/31/03 ALL	4/1/03-3/31/04 ALL	4/1/04-3/31/05 ALL		0-1MM	1-3MM	3-5MM	5-10MM	10-25MM	25MM & OVER
Unqualified	5	6	5					1	1	3
Reviewed	5	8	4			1	1		1	1
Compiled	9	8	7		1	5	1			
Tax Returns	6	4	3		2			1		
Other	11	15	12		4	3	2	3		
					4 (4/1-9/30/04)			27 (10/1/04-3/31/05)		
NUMBER OF STATEMENTS	36	41	31		7	9	4	5	2	4
ASSETS	%	%	%		%	%	%	%	%	%
Cash & Equivalents	15.6	12.0	15.2							
Trade Receivables (net)	4.1	3.7	5.7							
Inventory	3.1	2.6	4.7							
All Other Current	2.9	1.4	1.8							
Total Current	25.7	19.7	27.5							
Fixed Assets (net)	57.9	69.8	58.9							
Intangibles (net)	3.8	3.5	2.6							
All Other Non-Current	12.6	7.1	11.0							
Total	100.0	100.0	100.0							
LIABILITIES										
Notes Payable-Short Term	4.6	11.9	7.5							
Cur. Mat.-L/T/D	6.6	6.4	6.5							
Trade Payables	8.6	6.6	8.9							
Income Taxes Payable	.1	.0	.0							
All Other Current	17.6	13.2	21.6							
Total Current	37.5	38.2	44.5							
Long-Term Debt	47.4	42.1	51.3							
Deferred Taxes	.7	.7	.2							
All Other Non-Current	5.3	9.1	10.1							
Net Worth	9.3	9.9	-6.1							
Total Liabilities & Net Worth	100.0	100.0	100.0							
INCOME DATA										
Net Sales	100.0	100.0	100.0							
Gross Profit										
Operating Expenses	90.3	87.2	88.9							
Operating Profit	9.7	12.8	11.1							
All Other Expenses (net)	5.2	6.4	5.0							
Profit Before Taxes	4.5	6.4	6.1							
RATIOS										
Current	1.5	1.3	2.9							
	.8	.9	1.1							
	.2	.3	.2							
Quick	1.3	1.2	2.3							
	.6	.6	.7							
	.2	.1	.1							
Sales/Receivables	0 UND	0 UND	0 UND							
	2 230.6	1 280.5	0 745.5							
	9 38.7	6 59.0	7 51.7							
Cost of Sales/Inventory										
Cost of Sales/Payables										
Sales/Working Capital	27.1	28.8	10.1							
	-24.6	-64.9	112.3							
	-8.1	-5.8	-6.7							
EBIT/Interest	4.8	6.9	6.5							
	(29) 2.1	(34) 2.1	(28) 2.5							
	.5	.9	.8							
Net Profit + Depr., Dep., Amort./Cur. Mat. L/T/D										
Fixed/Worth	1.2	1.6	1.2							
	2.9	3.8	3.2							
	-7.5	NM	-2.4							
Debt/Worth	1.2	1.5	1.8							
	4.0	3.6	5.9							
	-7.5	-98.3	-4.1							
% Profit Before Taxes/Tangible Net Worth	47.5	49.6	60.6							
	(24) 20.7	(30) 24.7	(19) 20.8							
	-.2	-1.7	7.6							
% Profit Before Taxes/Total Assets	14.8	23.4	18.5							
	5.8	4.5	5.4							
	-2.9	-.8	-1.2							
Sales/Net Fixed Assets	4.7	3.7	6.0							
	2.9	2.0	2.8							
	1.6	.9	1.1							
Sales/Total Assets	2.5	2.5	2.6							
	1.7	1.2	1.5							
	1.1	.7	.9							
% Depr., Dep., Amort./Sales	4.3	4.6	4.1							
	(32) 6.7	(38) 6.6	(26) 5.7							
	10.7	12.8	8.4							
% Officers', Directors', Owners' Comp/Sales	3.8	2.2								
	(15) 7.2	(10) 3.7								
	15.0	11.4								
Net Sales ($)	1380784M	448712M	294243M		3372M	15807M	16520M	37745M	36092M	184707M
Total Assets ($)	624693M	638027M	395259M		9506M	25980M	3451M	21550M	21675M	313097M

M = $ thousand   MM = $ million
See Pages 11 through 21 for Explanation of Ratios and Data

Current Data Sorted By Assets   **Comparative Historical Data**

0-500M	500M-2MM	2-10MM	10-50MM	50-100MM	100-250MM	Type of Statement	4/1/00-3/31/01 ALL	4/1/01-3/31/02 ALL
	2	7	9	3	1	Unqualified	23	17
	2	5	4			Reviewed	19	18
1	18	9	1			Compiled	24	31
3	2	1		1		Tax Returns	9	9
3	6	14	11	3	3	Other	44	43
	15 (4/1-9/30/04)		94 (10/1/04-3/31/05)					
7	30	36	25	7	4	**NUMBER OF STATEMENTS**	119	118
%	%	%	%	%	%	**ASSETS**	%	%
	7.5	7.4	14.3			Cash & Equivalents	6.6	8.8
	24.3	21.6	11.5			Trade Receivables (net)	20.7	22.8
	16.0	12.2	5.3			Inventory	11.9	14.1
	3.3	2.1	9.4			All Other Current	3.1	3.1
	51.1	43.3	40.6			Total Current	42.3	48.8
	37.9	41.1	49.5			Fixed Assets (net)	46.5	39.5
	2.0	7.3	4.5			Intangibles (net)	4.3	2.7
	9.0	8.3	5.4			All Other Non-Current	7.0	9.0
	100.0	100.0	100.0			Total	100.0	100.0
						LIABILITIES		
	10.3	5.1	2.4			Notes Payable-Short Term	7.6	11.4
	7.9	7.5	4.8			Cur. Mat.-L/T/D	4.4	5.5
	11.7	13.0	5.7			Trade Payables	11.2	16.7
	.6	.7	.0			Income Taxes Payable	.4	1.2
	7.3	13.7	9.9			All Other Current	9.3	16.6
	37.8	40.0	22.9			Total Current	32.7	51.4
	22.1	22.1	38.4			Long-Term Debt	29.5	26.5
	1.4	.6	.8			Deferred Taxes	.7	.3
	11.3	4.2	7.8			All Other Non-Current	3.2	24.9
	27.4	33.1	30.2			Net Worth	33.8	-3.1
	100.0	100.0	100.0			Total Liabilities & Net Worth	100.0	100.0
						INCOME DATA		
	100.0	100.0	100.0			Net Sales	100.0	100.0
						Gross Profit		
	92.1	90.6	95.2			Operating Expenses	95.1	95.0
	7.9	9.4	4.8			Operating Profit	4.9	5.0
	3.1	2.9	2.7			All Other Expenses (net)	2.4	3.2
	4.8	6.5	2.1			Profit Before Taxes	2.5	1.9
						RATIOS		
	2.4	1.8	3.0				2.1	2.1
	1.5	1.4	1.5			Current	1.3	1.3
	.9	.9	1.2				.8	.9
	1.8	1.5	2.4				1.4	1.6
	.9	1.0	1.1			Quick	.9	.8
	.3	.5	.4				.4	.4
	(8) 48.3	(15) 23.7	(16) 22.2				(18) 20.8	(16) 22.8
	(25) 14.8	(38) 9.7	(23) 16.1			Sales/Receivables	(29) 12.6	(29) 12.6
	(44) 8.2	(51) 7.1	(38) 9.5				(43) 8.5	(46) 8.0
						Cost of Sales/Inventory		
						Cost of Sales/Payables		
	7.6	10.2	3.4				7.9	8.3
	23.1	20.6	7.4			Sales/Working Capital	23.3	21.8
	-70.9	-67.9	19.6				-28.5	-37.2
	13.8	15.3	4.1				6.4	5.1
	(29) 4.6	(30) 6.9	(21) 2.4			EBIT/Interest	(110) 2.3	(102) 2.2
	1.5	2.0	1.3				.4	1.0
							6.7	2.7
						Net Profit + Depr., Dep., Amort./Cur. Mat. L/T/D	(13) 1.8	(20) 1.7
							1.0	.6
	.5	.6	1.0				.5	.5
	1.3	1.2	3.2			Fixed/Worth	1.4	1.1
	NM	2.6	-5.6				6.3	4.9
	.7	1.1	.9				.7	.8
	1.9	1.7	4.5			Debt/Worth	1.8	2.4
	NM	6.6	-18.7				9.2	6.9
	59.0	74.9	43.8				40.6	39.2
	(23) 37.7	(32) 32.8	(17) 23.3			% Profit Before Taxes/Tangible Net Worth	(99) 17.0	(103) 17.5
	5.4	10.9	1.8				.3	.9
	21.7	19.0	11.7				12.4	12.7
	7.8	10.6	4.3			% Profit Before Taxes/Total Assets	5.2	4.3
	.6	2.3	1.2				-1.6	-1.1
	23.5	25.6	6.1				21.3	22.8
	12.7	5.4	1.8			Sales/Net Fixed Assets	3.9	6.1
	4.2	2.3	1.1				1.3	2.5
	4.2	2.8	1.7				3.1	3.5
	2.9	2.0	.9			Sales/Total Assets	1.8	2.0
	2.0	1.2	.4				.8	1.2
	.9	1.8	2.2				1.1	1.2
	(27) 1.7	(32) 3.4	(21) 5.3			% Depr., Dep., Amort./Sales	(108) 3.4	(110) 2.1
	3.0	7.0	10.1				8.9	4.4
	2.2	1.8					1.6	1.5
	(11) 5.2	(13) 2.6				% Officers', Directors', Owners' Comp/Sales	(34) 2.9	(42) 3.7
	11.9	5.6						7.0
7507M	98364M	370165M	554866M	700278M	514761M	Net Sales ($)	3668045M	2695594M
2159M	32773M	160102M	478116M	521366M	614815M	Total Assets ($)	3253882M	1633782M

M = $ thousand   MM = $ million
See Pages 11 through 21 for Explanation of Ratios and Data

Comparative Historical Data			Type of Statement	Current Data Sorted By Sales					
19	18	22	Unqualified	1	3	1	4	6	7
11	13	11	Reviewed			4	5	2	
22	23	29	Compiled	4	10	7	7		1
13	13	7	Tax Returns	4	1	1	1		1
49	44	40	Other	1	6	4	6	14	9
4/1/02-3/31/03 ALL	4/1/03-3/31/04 ALL	4/1/04-3/31/05 ALL		15 (4/1-9/30/04)			94 (10/1/04-3/31/05)		
				0-1MM	1-3MM	3-5MM	5-10MM	10-25MM	25MM & OVER
114	111	109	NUMBER OF STATEMENTS	10	20	16	23	22	18
%	%	%	**ASSETS**	%	%	%	%	%	%
6.7	7.1	9.9	Cash & Equivalents	3.5	13.3	10.7	4.4	16.6	8.1
17.1	20.3	19.1	Trade Receivables (net)	1.7	20.6	15.8	24.9	13.3	29.5
12.7	14.3	10.2	Inventory	11.1	10.9	18.9	8.7	6.3	8.0
3.4	3.9	4.3	All Other Current	1.6	1.6	8.1	2.8	7.2	3.7
39.8	45.5	43.5	Total Current	17.9	46.3	53.6	40.8	43.4	49.2
44.0	44.4	42.8	Fixed Assets (net)	73.5	46.4	40.3	41.3	38.7	30.9
7.4	5.3	5.2	Intangibles (net)	.1	.7	.1	8.9	8.9	8.3
8.9	4.8	8.5	All Other Non-Current	8.5	6.6	6.0	9.0	9.0	11.5
100.0	100.0	100.0	Total	100.0	100.0	100.0	100.0	100.0	100.0
			LIABILITIES						
10.5	12.6	6.5	Notes Payable-Short Term	5.1	11.6	11.6	3.6	3.5	4.4
5.1	6.3	6.7	Cur. Mat.-L/T/D	18.5	3.6	8.8	5.7	4.3	5.9
10.2	11.0	10.6	Trade Payables	4.3	8.1	10.5	11.7	11.7	14.2
.3	.1	.7	Income Taxes Payable	.0	.4	.5	1.0	.1	1.8
10.4	14.7	10.1	All Other Current	7.3	6.3	19.9	7.5	8.3	13.0
36.4	44.7	34.6	Total Current	35.2	30.0	51.3	29.5	27.9	39.4
31.8	28.2	30.5	Long-Term Debt	54.3	17.7	28.3	27.9	30.7	36.8
.5	.7	.9	Deferred Taxes	.4	.8	.6	1.3	.6	1.1
6.9	7.2	7.0	All Other Non-Current	6.2	2.9	16.0	5.3	8.4	4.8
24.4	19.2	26.9	Net Worth	3.9	48.6	3.8	36.0	32.5	17.9
100.0	100.0	100.0	Total Liabilities & Net Worth	100.0	100.0	100.0	100.0	100.0	100.0
			INCOME DATA						
100.0	100.0	100.0	Net Sales	100.0	100.0	100.0	100.0	100.0	100.0
			Gross Profit						
92.1	97.6	91.0	Operating Expenses	66.0	98.1	94.2	94.0	92.9	88.2
7.9	2.4	9.0	Operating Profit	34.0	1.9	5.8	6.0	7.1	11.8
4.0	2.2	4.0	All Other Expenses (net)	24.6	1.2	2.0	1.7	1.9	3.2
3.9	.1	4.9	Profit Before Taxes	9.4	.7	3.9	4.3	5.2	8.6
			RATIOS						
1.9	1.9	2.2	Current	2.3	3.4	2.0	2.4	2.6	1.7
1.2	1.2	1.4		.3	1.4	1.2	1.7	1.8	1.3
.5	.8	.9		.0	1.0	.9	1.1	1.1	1.0
1.4	1.2	1.6	Quick	.4	2.3	1.0	1.8	2.0	1.3
.6	(110) .7	.9		.1	1.3	.6	1.2	1.3	.8
.2	.3	.5		.0	.7	.3	.6	.5	.7
12　30.5	18　19.9	15　23.9	Sales/Receivables	0　UND	21　17.7	7　51.7	31　11.9	13　28.4	23　15.9
26　13.8	31　11.8	29　12.7		0　UND	28　13.0	16　22.6	42　8.8	17　21.9	38　9.6
42　8.7	46　7.9	45　8.1		18　20.0	42　8.7	40　9.1	61　6.0	34　10.8	56　6.5
			Cost of Sales/Inventory						
			Cost of Sales/Payables						
10.6	9.0	6.8	Sales/Working Capital	NM	5.5	5.3	7.6	4.0	8.5
38.4	27.8	17.9		-3.7	7.8	19.5	13.7	14.1	27.9
-10.0	-30.5	-88.2		-.5	NM	-99.7	45.3	216.6	NM
6.5	5.9	9.7	EBIT/Interest		15.1	6.0	19.9	7.7	6.8
(101) 2.2	(101) 2.3	(95) 3.9			(19) 3.9	(15) 3.0	(22) 7.8	(19) 4.1	(15) 3.7
.9	-.2	1.6			-.2	-.3	1.5	2.3	1.9
4.0	5.6	6.9	Net Profit + Depr., Dep., Amort./Cur. Mat. L/T/D						
(17) 2.3	(18) 2.1	(24) 2.8							
1.3	.8	1.1							
.6	.7	.7	Fixed/Worth	3.9	.3	.9	.5	.8	.5
2.1	1.9	1.5		41.0	1.0	2.0	1.1	1.5	1.4
-42.9	29.9	NM		-2.2	1.7	-1.4	3.1	NM	-2.6
1.0	1.3	1.0	Debt/Worth	5.2	.3	.9	1.1	1.2	1.3
3.7	3.3	2.8		45.1	.7	3.8	1.6	4.5	3.5
-19.8	55.7	NM		-37.6	5.2	-6.8	6.5	NM	-5.5
52.7	34.1	57.4	% Profit Before Taxes/Tangible Net Worth		33.0	59.1	59.7	113.6	43.6
(84) 21.9	(84) 11.6	(82) 29.1		(17) 5.4	(10) 35.0	(20) 29.5	(17) 47.6	(12) 25.1	
3.8	-3.5	9.2			-1.8	17.5	10.9	24.3	12.3
13.1	8.8	17.8	% Profit Before Taxes/Total Assets	4.9	13.7	17.6	21.7	17.4	18.6
4.1	2.3	6.3		1.8	3.1	5.4	12.6	10.6	8.1
-.9	-4.4	1.9		-3.2	-1.6	-3.6	.5	3.7	2.8
16.3	17.0	17.3	Sales/Net Fixed Assets	4.2	16.0	12.0	18.7	17.1	29.4
4.1	4.4	5.2		.3	5.0	6.0	5.9	6.1	5.6
1.5	1.8	1.7		.2	2.0	1.8	2.3	1.8	3.1
2.8	3.1	3.2	Sales/Total Assets	.9	3.1	3.8	3.4	2.8	4.3
1.4	1.7	1.9		.3	2.3	1.9	2.0	2.0	1.7
.8	1.0	.8		.2	1.3	1.2	1.2	1.0	.8
1.5	1.6	1.4	% Depr., Dep., Amort./Sales	10.4	1.3	1.4	1.8	1.1	.7
(102) 3.5	(100) 3.3	(91) 3.1		17.1	(15) 2.2	(15) 1.8	(20) 3.4	(19) 3.1	(12) 2.0
6.7	7.2	7.3		23.4	8.9	7.3	7.5	5.3	5.6
1.4	2.4	2.0	% Officers', Directors', Owners' Comp/Sales				1.8		
(38) 3.0	(31) 4.4	(32) 4.6					(13) 2.2		
7.7	10.1	9.9					5.4		
2105563M	2843563M	2245941M	Net Sales ($)	4207M	38040M	67104M	166590M	355793M	1614207M
2089035M	2128222M	1809331M	Total Assets ($)	12691M	111296M	60169M	120373M	392649M	1112153M

M = $ thousand　　MM = $ million
See Pages 11 through 21 for Explanation of Ratios and Data

Current Data Sorted By Assets | **Comparative Historical Data**

Type of Statement	0-500M	500M-2MM	2-10MM	10-50MM	50-100MM	100-250MM
Unqualified			2			
Reviewed			2			
Compiled	1	1	1	1		
Tax Returns	4	3	2			1
Other	2	2	4		3	

	0-500M	500M-2MM	2-10MM	10-50MM	50-100MM	100-250MM		4/1/00-3/31/01 ALL	4/1/01-3/31/02 ALL
	4 (4/1-9/30/04)			26 (10/1/04-3/31/05)					
NUMBER OF STATEMENTS	7	7	11	4		1			
	%	%	%	%	%	%		%	%
ASSETS									
Cash & Equivalents			9.0						
Trade Receivables (net)			20.9		D			D	D
Inventory			11.1		A			A	A
All Other Current			3.2		T			T	T
Total Current			44.2		A			A	A
Fixed Assets (net)			34.4						
Intangibles (net)			2.8		N			N	N
All Other Non-Current			18.5		O			O	O
Total			100.0		T			T	T
LIABILITIES					A			A	A
Notes Payable-Short Term			6.6		V			V	V
Cur. Mat.-L/T/D			6.1		A			A	A
Trade Payables			15.5		I			I	I
Income Taxes Payable			.1		L			L	L
All Other Current			7.7		A			A	A
Total Current			36.0		B			B	B
Long-Term Debt			26.7		L			L	L
Deferred Taxes			.0		E			E	E
All Other Non-Current			5.9						
Net Worth			31.3						
Total Liabilities & Net Worth			100.0						
INCOME DATA									
Net Sales			100.0						
Gross Profit									
Operating Expenses			95.2						
Operating Profit			4.8						
All Other Expenses (net)			1.9						
Profit Before Taxes			2.9						
RATIOS									
Current			1.5						
			1.2						
			1.0						
Quick			1.2						
			.9						
			.5						
Sales/Receivables			12 29.9						
			31 11.9						
			53 6.9						
Cost of Sales/Inventory									
Cost of Sales/Payables									
Sales/Working Capital			12.2						
			27.7						
			-414.3						
EBIT/Interest			9.8						
			(10) 4.0						
			.3						
Net Profit + Depr., Dep., Amort./Cur. Mat. L /T/D									
Fixed/Worth			.2						
			.9						
			2.0						
Debt/Worth			1.5						
			1.9						
			4.1						
% Profit Before Taxes/Tangible Net Worth			42.9						
			(10) 13.7						
			-.4						
% Profit Before Taxes/Total Assets			9.2						
			5.8						
			-.7						
Sales/Net Fixed Assets			70.8						
			4.0						
			1.3						
Sales/Total Assets			5.6						
			1.8						
			.3						
% Depr., Dep., Amort./Sales									
% Officers', Directors', Owners' Comp/Sales									
Net Sales ($)	11783M	35757M	135214M	176834M		201165M			
Total Assets ($)	1728M	8825M	54633M	87023M		119914M			

© RMA 2005

M = $ thousand   MM = $ million

See Pages 11 through 21 for Explanation of Ratios and Data

Comparative Historical Data				Current Data Sorted By Sales					
1	8	4	Type of Statement						
1	8	4	Unqualified	1			1	1	1
1	5	3	Reviewed		1		1	1	
3	4	3	Compiled	1	1				1
1	2	9	Tax Returns	1	4	2	1	1	
4	6	11	Other	3	1	1		3	3
4/1/02- 3/31/03 ALL	4/1/03- 3/31/04 ALL	4/1/04- 3/31/05 ALL		0-1MM	4 (4/1-9/30/04) 1-3MM	3-5MM	26 (10/1/04-3/31/05) 5-10MM	10-25MM	25MM & OVER
10	25	30	**NUMBER OF STATEMENTS**	6	7	3	3	6	5
%	%	%	**ASSETS**	%	%	%	%	%	%
7.7	7.5	18.2	Cash & Equivalents						
13.1	17.4	15.7	Trade Receivables (net)						
15.9	22.2	15.1	Inventory						
5.0	6.3	3.2	All Other Current						
41.7	53.3	52.1	Total Current						
50.9	39.7	34.5	Fixed Assets (net)						
1.0	2.1	1.7	Intangibles (net)						
6.3	4.8	11.8	All Other Non-Current						
100.0	100.0	100.0	Total						
			LIABILITIES						
4.4	14.4	12.1	Notes Payable-Short Term						
6.3	4.3	5.8	Cur. Mat.-L/T/D						
8.1	9.6	10.5	Trade Payables						
.0	.0	.2	Income Taxes Payable						
6.7	10.7	9.5	All Other Current						
25.5	39.0	38.0	Total Current						
29.8	26.8	29.4	Long-Term Debt						
.2	.6	.0	Deferred Taxes						
13.6	6.2	4.0	All Other Non-Current						
30.9	27.4	28.5	Net Worth						
100.0	100.0	100.0	Total Liabilities & Net Worth						
			INCOME DATA						
100.0	100.0	100.0	Net Sales						
			Gross Profit						
93.6	95.9	92.8	Operating Expenses						
6.4	4.1	7.2	Operating Profit						
3.7	2.4	.9	All Other Expenses (net)						
2.7	1.8	6.3	Profit Before Taxes						
			RATIOS						
2.2	2.2	3.3							
1.6	1.5	1.3	Current						
1.3	1.1	1.0							
1.1	1.3	2.3							
.9	.6	.9	Quick						
.6	.4	.4							
4 84.9	15 24.1	2 242.2							
22 16.3	36 10.3	23 16.2	Sales/Receivables						
38 9.6	57 6.5	37 10.0							
			Cost of Sales/Inventory						
			Cost of Sales/Payables						
11.2	4.8	7.7							
14.7	13.5	24.4	Sales/Working Capital						
34.0	46.2	−144.3							
7.8	5.5	14.8							
1.0	(21) 2.9	(24) 4.2	EBIT/Interest						
−.6	−.4	.4							
			Net Profit + Depr., Dep., Amort./Cur. Mat. L/T/D						
.5	.2	.2							
1.6	1.7	1.0	Fixed/Worth						
5.4	10.8	3.3							
.8	1.0	1.0							
2.6	3.7	2.1	Debt/Worth						
5.1	16.6	5.7							
	41.1	51.9	% Profit Before Taxes/Tangible Net Worth						
(22) 11.8	(25) 25.7								
	−14.3	4.5							
13.2	10.2	16.4	% Profit Before Taxes/Total Assets						
.0	3.6	8.0							
−3.5	−2.9	−.2							
37.9	19.9	41.4							
2.2	6.5	11.2	Sales/Net Fixed Assets						
1.3	1.4	2.4							
2.9	2.6	5.2							
1.4	1.5	2.1	Sales/Total Assets						
1.0	.8	1.1							
1.2	1.0	1.1							
3.3	3.0	(23) 2.8	% Depr., Dep., Amort./Sales						
5.4	6.0	4.8							
		2.0	% Officers', Directors', Owners' Comp/Sales						
	(13) 4.1								
		7.0							
130443M	595538M	560753M	Net Sales ($)	3919M	11801M	10901M	22369M	103248M	408515M
42624M	423689M	272123M	Total Assets ($)	7560M	15130M	2463M	14105M	37009M	195856M

M = $ thousand   MM = $ million
See Pages 11 through 21 for Explanation of Ratios and Data

Current Data Sorted By Assets   **Comparative Historical Data**

						Type of Statement		
						Unqualified	26	19
	1	6	7		7	Reviewed	5	3
	2	4	2	5		Compiled	14	15
	2	2	1		1	Tax Returns	1	3
1	1					Other	22	23
	1	6	6	3	4		4/1/00-3/31/01	4/1/01-3/31/02
0-500M	500M-2MM	2-10MM	10-50MM	50-100MM	100-250MM		ALL	ALL
1	7	18	16	8	12	NUMBER OF STATEMENTS	68	63
%	%	%	%	%	%	ASSETS	%	%
		14.5	12.2		11.1	Cash & Equivalents	9.6	9.2
		19.1	24.8		16.5	Trade Receivables (net)	23.8	22.2
		.7	.6		1.1	Inventory	2.7	3.6
		5.4	6.8		3.8	All Other Current	5.3	3.4
		39.8	44.5		32.4	Total Current	41.3	38.5
		46.7	46.9		46.9	Fixed Assets (net)	46.3	46.5
		1.4	2.1		6.1	Intangibles (net)	2.8	2.5
		12.2	6.6		14.5	All Other Non-Current	9.5	12.5
		100.0	100.0		100.0	Total	100.0	100.0
						LIABILITIES		
		3.9	4.1		.1	Notes Payable-Short Term	7.0	4.9
		5.6	6.1		4.4	Cur. Mat.-L/T/D	5.1	4.4
		18.4	10.7		7.1	Trade Payables	9.0	7.6
		.1	.2		.0	Income Taxes Payable	.2	.2
		10.9	9.6		12.6	All Other Current	10.7	11.5
		38.9	30.6		24.2	Total Current	32.0	28.7
		28.6	23.5		18.5	Long-Term Debt	19.6	20.2
		.0	.4		3.9	Deferred Taxes	.8	.5
		5.2	7.3		11.0	All Other Non-Current	5.8	8.2
		27.2	38.3		42.4	Net Worth	41.7	42.5
		100.0	100.0		100.0	Total Liabilities & Net Worth	100.0	100.0
						INCOME DATA		
		100.0	100.0		100.0	Net Sales	100.0	100.0
						Gross Profit		
		77.6	89.1		91.7	Operating Expenses	92.1	91.1
		22.4	10.9		8.3	Operating Profit	7.9	8.9
		5.2	.4		.7	All Other Expenses (net)	.6	5.0
		17.2	10.6		7.6	Profit Before Taxes	7.3	3.9
						RATIOS		
		1.4	2.5		1.8		1.9	2.2
		1.0	1.8		1.5	Current	1.5	1.4
		.6	.9		1.3		.8	1.0
		1.1	2.0		1.5		1.6	1.8
		.9	1.4		1.3	Quick	1.2	1.2
		.4	.6		1.0		.6	.8
		0 UND	40 9.0		39 9.4		26 13.8	26 14.0
		31 11.9	55 6.6		45 8.1	Sales/Receivables	46 7.9	50 7.4
		55 6.7	69 5.3		53 6.9		65 5.6	62 5.9
						Cost of Sales/Inventory		
						Cost of Sales/Payables		
		12.9	6.1		7.0		7.3	5.9
		NM	8.8		14.6	Sales/Working Capital	16.1	15.2
		−7.9	NM		20.0		−28.9	−129.8
		13.3	8.8		7.4		8.7	5.5
		(13) 3.8	(15) 6.8		(11) 4.4	EBIT/Interest	(60) 2.9	(52) 2.8
		.9	2.6		3.0		1.3	1.4
						Net Profit + Depr., Dep.,	5.5	1.6
						Amort./Cur. Mat. L /T/D	(18) 2.1	(15) 1.2
							1.0	.8
		.6	.5		.6		.7	.7
		1.3	1.6		1.3	Fixed/Worth	1.1	1.0
		5.7	2.2		3.6		2.5	2.2
		1.4	.9		1.0		.6	.7
		2.7	1.9		2.1	Debt/Worth	1.6	1.4
		6.4	2.7		4.1		3.4	3.3
		63.6	46.4		51.5	% Profit Before Taxes/Tangible	47.0	24.6
		(15) 34.4	23.7		27.0	Net Worth	(60) 17.5	(58) 11.5
		5.1	13.2		14.8		3.4	.0
		17.1	17.5		12.1	% Profit Before Taxes/Total	15.2	8.9
		9.8	9.6		6.5	Assets	5.8	4.1
		.9	4.2		4.2		.4	.0
		19.0	14.3		6.3		9.8	8.2
		3.5	3.9		3.1	Sales/Net Fixed Assets	4.6	3.4
		.8	.8		1.0		1.3	1.2
		2.9	2.7		1.6		3.1	2.5
		.9	1.7		.8	Sales/Total Assets	1.5	1.3
		.5	.6		.6		.9	.8
		2.4	2.2				2.1	2.0
		(16) 4.7	3.2			% Depr., Dep., Amort./Sales	(57) 4.5	(54) 3.9
		19.5	6.8				8.5	9.2
						% Officers', Directors',		.1
						Owners' Comp/Sales	(13) 1.9	
								5.6
10944M	25305M	161469M	558076M	848994M	2543331M	Net Sales ($)	3474138M	3780617M
368M	9889M	98690M	312561M	582315M	2140480M	Total Assets ($)	2259898M	2802968M

9 (4/1-9/30/04) 53 (10/1/04-3/31/05)

M = $ thousand   MM = $ million
See Pages 11 through 21 for Explanation of Ratios and Data

Comparative Historical Data | Current Data Sorted By Sales

16	31	26	Type of Statement		5		3	5	13
16	31	26	Unqualified		5		3	5	13
9	10	8	Reviewed	1		2	2	1	2
8	9	6	Compiled	1	1	2	1		1
3	3	2	Tax Returns						
16	22	20	Other		1	1	4	2	12
4/1/02-3/31/03 ALL	4/1/03-3/31/04 ALL	4/1/04-3/31/05 ALL		0-1MM	9 (4/1-9/30/04) 1-3MM	3-5MM	53 (10/1/04-3/31/05) 5-10MM	10-25MM	25MM & OVER
52	75	62	**NUMBER OF STATEMENTS**	2	7	5	11	9	28
%	%	%	**ASSETS**	%	%	%	%	%	%
9.3	10.6	12.7	Cash & Equivalents				22.7		10.7
24.0	21.0	20.1	Trade Receivables (net)				23.9		23.3
3.8	1.8	1.1	Inventory				1.1		1.0
3.9	5.4	6.1	All Other Current				5.5		9.4
40.9	38.8	40.1	Total Current				53.2		44.4
47.3	48.2	46.4	Fixed Assets (net)				33.3		38.7
2.0	2.3	2.9	Intangibles (net)				.0		5.6
9.7	10.6	10.5	All Other Non-Current				13.4		11.4
100.0	100.0	100.0	Total				100.0		100.0
			LIABILITIES						
4.8	4.6	2.7	Notes Payable-Short Term				1.6		.7
4.5	6.1	5.1	Cur. Mat.-L/T/D				3.5		4.9
10.2	8.8	12.0	Trade Payables				23.7		12.0
.3	.1	.1	Income Taxes Payable				.0		.3
10.8	9.7	13.0	All Other Current				7.3		18.5
30.6	29.4	32.9	Total Current				36.1		36.4
21.5	24.1	25.8	Long-Term Debt				22.8		19.0
1.5	1.3	1.1	Deferred Taxes				.0		2.4
7.2	7.2	6.1	All Other Non-Current				4.5		8.7
39.2	38.0	34.0	Net Worth				36.7		33.6
100.0	100.0	100.0	Total Liabilities & Net Worth				100.0		100.0
			INCOME DATA						
100.0	100.0	100.0	Net Sales				100.0		100.0
			Gross Profit						
90.2	88.4	87.2	Operating Expenses				85.5		93.0
9.8	11.6	12.8	Operating Profit				14.5		7.0
3.1	3.1	2.8	All Other Expenses (net)				1.4		1.5
6.7	8.5	9.9	Profit Before Taxes				13.1		5.5
			RATIOS						
2.3	2.6	2.1					2.7		2.0
1.3	1.4	1.3	Current				2.0		1.4
.9	.9	.8					1.0		.9
2.0	1.9	1.7					2.7		1.6
1.2	1.2	1.0	Quick				1.3		1.0
.6	.6	.6					1.0		.6
28 13.1	24 15.5	24 15.3					24 15.4		35 10.4
48 7.6	43 8.6	41 8.8	Sales/Receivables				43 8.5		43 8.5
63 5.8	60 6.1	58 6.3					57 6.4		55 6.6
			Cost of Sales/Inventory						
			Cost of Sales/Payables						
5.9	7.1	7.3					3.2		7.5
17.2	16.3	22.4	Sales/Working Capital				12.4		15.8
-27.8	-51.0	-25.6					-173.8		-38.3
11.5	9.9	8.6							9.0
(45) 3.4	(63) 3.8	(49) 4.4	EBIT/Interest						(25) 4.4
1.1	1.6	2.3							2.4
7.0	3.4	3.5							3.9
(14) 1.5	(25) 2.4	(14) 2.6	Net Profit + Depr., Dep., Amort./Cur. Mat. L/T/D						(12) 2.4
.4	1.0	1.9							1.5
.5	.5	.6					.1		.5
1.4	1.1	1.4	Fixed/Worth				.6		1.3
2.6	3.1	3.9					1.6		4.9
.9	.8	.9					.9		1.0
2.1	1.7	2.3	Debt/Worth				2.3		2.7
4.8	4.7	4.7					3.2		5.2
30.7	47.5	48.2					63.6		50.4
(49) 18.2	(69) 18.8	(55) 24.4	% Profit Before Taxes/Tangible Net Worth				44.7		(25) 28.3
1.7	4.1	12.8					8.5		15.3
11.3	11.4	15.6					19.2		12.1
4.1	5.8	8.0	% Profit Before Taxes/Total Assets				16.8		6.5
.4	1.3	3.2					2.9		3.4
9.9	12.1	13.2					107.0		14.0
3.2	4.1	3.3	Sales/Net Fixed Assets				12.6		5.6
1.2	.9	.9					.8		1.6
2.7	2.5	2.8					3.3		3.2
1.3	1.5	1.3	Sales/Total Assets				2.4		1.7
.8	.6	.6					.6		.8
2.7	2.4	2.3					.5		2.2
(45) 4.4	(65) 4.9	(54) 4.7	% Depr., Dep., Amort./Sales				4.5		(22) 3.4
9.7	8.6	10.1					6.5		5.9
		1.1							
	(12) 2.6	2.6	% Officers', Directors', Owners' Comp/Sales						
		6.1							
2214874M	3894837M	4148119M	Net Sales ($)	1138M	12978M	19463M	81258M	146472M	3886810M
1832275M	3042784M	3144303M	Total Assets ($)	5248M	28195M	23042M	75991M	421642M	2590185M

M = $ thousand   MM = $ million
See Pages 11 through 21 for Explanation of Ratios and Data

Current Data Sorted By Assets   Comparative Historical Data

Type of Statement	0-500M	500M-2MM	2-10MM	10-50MM	50-100MM	100-250MM		4/1/00-3/31/01 ALL	4/1/01-3/31/02 ALL
Unqualified			6	7	3	5		11	15
Reviewed			8	4				14	10
Compiled	1	3	10	3				20	24
Tax Returns		1	3					3	7
Other	1	3	7	2	5	1		22	20
			17 (4/1-9/30/04)	56 (10/1/04-3/31/05)					
NUMBER OF STATEMENTS	2	7	34	16	8	6		70	76
	%	%	%	%	%	%		%	%
ASSETS									
Cash & Equivalents			12.2	6.5				6.9	9.6
Trade Receivables (net)			17.6	11.3				17.5	17.5
Inventory			.4	.8				.9	1.6
All Other Current			3.0	2.1				2.3	2.4
Total Current			33.2	20.6				27.6	31.0
Fixed Assets (net)			56.3	69.3				62.2	58.8
Intangibles (net)			.6	1.8				.8	.4
All Other Non-Current			9.9	8.3				9.3	9.7
Total			100.0	100.0				100.0	100.0
LIABILITIES									
Notes Payable-Short Term			3.7	3.8				4.9	2.8
Cur. Mat.-L/T/D			8.9	6.2				5.6	6.8
Trade Payables			7.1	6.5				8.5	7.6
Income Taxes Payable			.4	.1				.3	.3
All Other Current			9.5	5.2				8.8	7.8
Total Current			29.6	21.8				28.2	25.3
Long-Term Debt			37.1	42.8				36.4	38.5
Deferred Taxes			.8	1.8				1.8	1.5
All Other Non-Current			5.2	7.8				4.3	7.0
Net Worth			27.3	25.9				29.3	27.6
Total Liabilities & Net Worth			100.0	100.0				100.0	100.0
INCOME DATA									
Net Sales			100.0	100.0				100.0	100.0
Gross Profit									
Operating Expenses			85.2	91.0				90.7	88.0
Operating Profit			14.8	9.0				9.3	12.0
All Other Expenses (net)			3.9	5.2				3.9	4.1
Profit Before Taxes			10.9	3.8				5.4	7.9

RATIOS

Ratio	2-10MM	10-50MM	4/1/00-3/31/01 ALL	4/1/01-3/31/02 ALL
Current	1.8	1.8	2.0	2.1
	1.1	.9	1.0	1.2
	.7	.6	.6	.8
Quick	1.7	1.4	2.0	2.0
	.9	.8	.9	1.1
	.5	.5	.5	.6
Sales/Receivables	1 321.6	27 13.5	27 13.6	28 13.2
	37 10.0	44 8.2	45 8.2	46 7.9
	68 5.4	60 6.1	63 5.8	63 5.8
Cost of Sales/Inventory				
Cost of Sales/Payables				
Sales/Working Capital	8.5	10.1	9.3	6.7
	119.1	-106.9	-549.1	20.2
	-10.4	-8.3	-8.4	-32.1
EBIT/Interest	5.6	5.6	6.6	6.0
	(29) 3.4	(14) 2.4	(64) 2.8	(74) 3.0
	.9	.9	.9	1.2
Net Profit + Depr., Dep., Amort./Cur. Mat. L /T/D			2.3	5.1
			(18) 1.6	(21) 2.3
			1.4	1.6
Fixed/Worth	.9	1.1	.9	1.2
	2.2	2.2	1.9	1.7
	4.8	-14.6	6.4	5.9
Debt/Worth	1.5	.9	.8	1.2
	2.8	1.8	1.9	2.0
	6.8	-22.6	5.8	6.5
% Profit Before Taxes/Tangible Net Worth	45.8	38.9	28.5	37.9
	(29) 25.9	(11) 14.3	(61) 13.8	(64) 20.6
	7.7	7.2	5.3	7.5
% Profit Before Taxes/Total Assets	11.9	12.5	11.7	12.2
	4.9	3.4	5.4	5.1
	.3	-2.4	-.2	.6
Sales/Net Fixed Assets	4.8	2.9	3.7	3.9
	1.5	1.4	1.8	1.8
	.5	.7	.8	1.0
Sales/Total Assets	2.4	1.5	2.0	1.8
	1.0	.7	1.0	1.0
	.4	.6	.6	.7
% Depr., Dep., Amort./Sales	2.8	3.0	3.4	4.3
	(31) 6.8	(15) 8.3	(63) 8.6	(73) 6.8
	17.3	13.5	12.3	11.5
% Officers', Directors', Owners' Comp/Sales			2.3	2.3
			(18) 4.7	(19) 5.1
			11.8	8.6

	0-500M	500M-2MM	2-10MM	10-50MM	50-100MM	100-250MM		4/1/00-3/31/01 ALL	4/1/01-3/31/02 ALL
Net Sales ($)	5631M	12112M	246517M	341647M	417955M	476613M		1107754M	1448519M
Total Assets ($)	773M	6950M	187630M	299873M	511213M	793668M		1258486M	1646472M

M = $ thousand   MM = $ million
See Pages 11 through 21 for Explanation of Ratios and Data

Comparative Historical Data			Type of Statement	Current Data Sorted By Sales					
					4	2	1	5	9
16	14	21	Unqualified		1		7	2	2
6	16	12	Reviewed	4	1	3	5	4	
25	21	17	Compiled		2	1		1	
9	12	4	Tax Returns	3	3	2	2	2	7
29	22	19	Other						
4/1/02-3/31/03 ALL	4/1/03-3/31/04 ALL	4/1/04-3/31/05 ALL		17 (4/1-9/30/04)			56 (10/1/04-3/31/05)		
				0-1MM	1-3MM	3-5MM	5-10MM	10-25MM	25MM & OVER
85	85	73	**NUMBER OF STATEMENTS**	7	11	8	15	14	18
%	%	%	**ASSETS**	%	%	%	%	%	%
7.9	8.4	10.1	Cash & Equivalents		4.2		11.2	10.5	5.4
16.1	16.3	14.5	Trade Receivables (net)		8.6		16.3	23.9	12.3
.5	.5	.4	Inventory		.0		.0	1.8	.3
3.5	3.7	3.0	All Other Current		4.8		.8	1.1	5.1
28.1	28.9	28.1	Total Current		17.6		28.3	37.3	23.0
63.3	62.1	62.0	Fixed Assets (net)		75.7		57.2	54.3	70.0
.6	.3	.9	Intangibles (net)		.0		.1	.4	1.8
8.1	8.8	9.0	All Other Non-Current		6.6		14.4	8.1	5.2
100.0	100.0	100.0	Total		100.0		100.0	100.0	100.0
			LIABILITIES						
4.1	3.5	3.9	Notes Payable-Short Term		4.4		5.5	1.4	4.5
9.1	6.4	9.0	Cur. Mat.-L/T/D		18.1		5.7	7.2	6.2
7.4	5.6	5.9	Trade Payables		4.7		4.6	11.5	6.7
.1	.1	.2	Income Taxes Payable		.2		.5	.4	.1
5.9	7.4	6.9	All Other Current		8.7		6.0	9.4	5.9
26.6	23.0	25.9	Total Current		36.1		22.2	29.8	23.4
42.8	38.4	41.3	Long-Term Debt		32.8		42.2	30.2	36.5
1.6	1.5	1.3	Deferred Taxes		.8		.4	1.3	2.9
5.6	3.9	5.9	All Other Non-Current		8.4		9.1	3.7	2.9
23.3	33.1	25.6	Net Worth		21.9		26.1	35.0	34.2
100.0	100.0	100.0	Total Liabilities & Net Worth		100.0		100.0	100.0	100.0
			INCOME DATA						
100.0	100.0	100.0	Net Sales		100.0		100.0	100.0	100.0
			Gross Profit						
91.1	90.1	86.6	Operating Expenses		74.7		90.7	95.0	89.3
8.9	9.9	13.4	Operating Profit		25.3		9.3	5.0	10.7
3.9	4.3	3.8	All Other Expenses (net)		8.4		2.1	1.5	2.6
5.0	5.6	9.6	Profit Before Taxes		16.9		7.2	3.5	8.1
			RATIOS						
1.8	2.9	2.0	Current		1.9		2.0	1.9	1.6
1.0	1.3	1.2			.5		.9	1.2	1.1
.5	.6	.6			.0		.7	.8	.4
1.5	2.3	1.7	Quick		.8		1.8	1.5	1.2
.9	1.0	.9			.1		.9	1.1	.8
.4	.5	.5			.0		.7	.8	.4
16 23.0	17 22.0	26 14.1	Sales/Receivables	0 UND			32 11.3	35 10.3	32 11.5
41 9.0	45 8.2	44 8.2		0 UND			53 6.9	46 8.0	39 9.4
68 5.4	72 5.0	65 5.6		68 5.3			69 5.3	62 5.9	58 6.3
			Cost of Sales/Inventory						
			Cost of Sales/Payables						
8.1	5.7	7.4	Sales/Working Capital		13.6		5.9	11.9	11.4
157.7	26.5	33.4			-5.5		-92.0	23.2	34.7
-11.0	-9.8	-9.4			-1.5		-13.9	-34.2	-6.0
3.7	4.9	6.0	EBIT/Interest		12.7		10.8	6.1	4.5
(81) 2.0	(76) 2.9	(66) 3.4		(10) 5.3		(13) 3.4	(13) 2.9		2.9
1.0	1.2	1.7			-.1		2.0	1.7	1.7
3.5	4.2	3.4	Net Profit + Depr., Dep., Amort./Cur. Mat. L/T/D						
(25) 1.4	(23) 2.0	(19) 1.8							
.8	1.1	1.3							
1.4	1.1	1.0	Fixed/Worth		1.8		1.0	.9	1.5
2.4	2.1	2.0			4.6		2.2	1.5	2.3
11.2	3.8	4.9			-10.1		5.0	2.0	4.1
1.3	1.3	1.3	Debt/Worth		1.4		1.4	.8	1.3
2.7	1.9	1.9			4.3		2.9	1.8	1.7
19.4	5.4	6.8			-13.6		11.1	3.9	3.9
31.2	34.4	40.1	% Profit Before Taxes/Tangible Net Worth				44.1	32.2	34.3
(69) 14.4	(76) 15.5	(61) 17.6			(12) 22.4		(13) 10.6	(17) 12.3	
3.1	4.7	7.6					15.1	6.4	3.0
8.2	11.6	12.3	% Profit Before Taxes/Total Assets		21.0		9.6	10.2	8.1
3.6	4.6	5.1			15.5		6.1	4.5	4.8
.2	1.0	1.3			-3.6		3.3	2.0	1.1
3.5	4.1	3.2	Sales/Net Fixed Assets		2.8		5.4	8.4	1.9
1.9	1.5	1.4			.5		1.4	3.0	1.3
.8	.7	.7			.4		.8	1.5	.7
2.1	1.8	1.6	Sales/Total Assets		1.6		1.6	2.5	1.4
1.0	1.1	.9			.5		.9	1.9	.9
.5	.5	.5			.3		.6	1.0	.6
4.0	3.7	3.2	% Depr., Dep., Amort./Sales		8.2		1.7	2.5	7.5
(81) 8.5	(82) 7.7	(63) 8.9		(10) 15.4		(13) 4.6	3.4	(13) 9.1	
12.3	16.5	13.6			28.6		13.1	8.0	10.6
2.8	1.7	1.9	% Officers', Directors', Owners' Comp/Sales						
(21) 6.1	(19) 4.8	(17) 2.9							
10.4	10.4	10.6							
1422254M	1349410M	1500475M	Net Sales ($)	4720M	21645M	29117M	109723M	228886M	1106384M
1718827M	1604422M	1800107M	Total Assets ($)	21131M	45282M	37272M	167327M	181821M	1347274M

© RMA 2005

M = $ thousand   MM = $ million
See Pages 11 through 21 for Explanation of Ratios and Data

Current Data Sorted By Assets   Comparative Historical Data

Type of Statement	0-500M	500M-2MM	2-10MM	10-50MM	50-100MM	100-250MM		4/1/00-3/31/01 ALL	4/1/01-3/31/02 ALL
Unqualified		1	2	6	2			8	8
Reviewed		1	4	2				4	2
Compiled		5	7	3				10	15
Tax Returns	1	1	1	1				5	2
Other	2	1	13	6	3			11	9
	12 (4/1-9/30/04)			50 (10/1/04-3/31/05)					
NUMBER OF STATEMENTS	3	9	27	18	5			38	36

Columns for current data: 0-500M, 500M-2MM, 2-10MM, 10-50MM, 50-100MM, 100-250MM. The 0-500M, 500M-2MM, 50-100MM and 100-250MM columns show only "%" with data in the 100-250MM column noted as "DATA NOT AVAILABLE".

	2-10MM %	10-50MM %		Item	4/1/00-3/31/01 ALL %	4/1/01-3/31/02 ALL %
				ASSETS		
	12.8	10.0		Cash & Equivalents	10.3	10.8
	21.1	18.4		Trade Receivables (net)	11.1	19.2
	1.3	1.6		Inventory	1.4	2.8
	6.0	2.0		All Other Current	5.8	4.0
	41.1	32.0		Total Current	28.6	36.9
	49.6	57.3		Fixed Assets (net)	58.9	54.7
	4.4	3.1		Intangibles (net)	1.2	2.3
	4.9	7.6		All Other Non-Current	11.4	6.2
	100.0	100.0		Total	100.0	100.0
				LIABILITIES		
	4.6	4.2		Notes Payable-Short Term	7.7	5.1
	5.3	9.5		Cur. Mat.-L/T/D	7.3	6.5
	7.6	5.2		Trade Payables	4.6	12.4
	1.1	.1		Income Taxes Payable	.2	.4
	7.0	10.0		All Other Current	5.5	5.7
	25.6	29.0		Total Current	25.3	30.1
	37.3	27.2		Long-Term Debt	31.2	32.5
	.3	2.4		Deferred Taxes	.8	1.6
	1.9	3.1		All Other Non-Current	7.8	3.8
	34.9	38.2		Net Worth	34.8	32.1
	100.0	100.0		Total Liabilities & Net Worth	100.0	100.0
				INCOME DATA		
	100.0	100.0		Net Sales	100.0	100.0
				Gross Profit		
	80.9	85.7		Operating Expenses	79.7	83.0
	19.1	14.3		Operating Profit	20.3	17.0
	2.5	3.4		All Other Expenses (net)	5.7	4.7
	16.6	10.9		Profit Before Taxes	14.6	12.3
				RATIOS		
	3.4	1.6			1.5	2.1
	1.9	1.1		Current	1.1	1.3
	.8	.6			.6	.7
	2.5	1.4			1.4	1.9
	1.2	1.0		Quick	.8	1.0
	.7	.5			.4	.4
	12 30.2	26 13.8			0 UND	23 15.6
	46 7.9	50 7.3		Sales/Receivables	36 10.1	43 8.4
	71 5.1	102 3.6			62 5.9	67 5.5
				Cost of Sales/Inventory		
				Cost of Sales/Payables		
	3.1	9.3			10.8	7.3
	11.0	40.0		Sales/Working Capital	68.7	16.0
	-19.2	-4.1			-7.5	-12.0
	23.0	13.2			5.2	15.4
	(25) 5.7	(15) 3.1		EBIT/Interest	(32) 2.5	(29) 4.5
	2.4	2.3			.4	1.5
				Net Profit + Depr., Dep.,		5.5
				Amort./Cur. Mat. L./T/D	(10) 1.5	1.5
						.3
	.7	.8			1.0	.7
	1.5	1.3		Fixed/Worth	2.0	1.9
	5.9	3.0			3.8	3.8
	.7	.7			1.1	.7
	2.9	1.4		Debt/Worth	2.0	2.3
	12.8	4.0			4.1	6.6
	61.9	38.5			44.8	45.5
	(22) 38.8	(16) 25.1		% Profit Before Taxes/Tangible Net Worth	(32) 26.9	(31) 18.3
	8.9	10.7			6.2	4.0
	21.3	10.7			19.0	16.6
	9.3	5.6		% Profit Before Taxes/Total Assets	6.3	4.6
	3.4	3.3			-.5	1.2
	17.4	5.7			8.8	6.5
	2.4	1.1		Sales/Net Fixed Assets	1.5	1.6
	1.2	.6			.4	.9
	2.5	2.2			2.4	1.8
	1.3	.8		Sales/Total Assets	.8	1.2
	.4	.4			.4	.5
	2.5	4.1			5.0	2.0
	(25) 7.6	(16) 9.5		% Depr., Dep., Amort./Sales	(31) 12.0	(29) 8.4
	15.1	12.9			17.8	14.5
					2.3	1.7
				% Officers', Directors', Owners' Comp/Sales	(13) 4.6	(10) 3.0
					9.6	7.4

0-500M	500M-2MM	2-10MM	10-50MM	50-100MM				
960M	24438M	247301M	668882M	101920M	Net Sales ($)		390675M	908241M
773M	9460M	147344M	388821M	323097M	Total Assets ($)		725018M	916445M

M = $ thousand   MM = $ million
See Pages 11 through 21 for Explanation of Ratios and Data

Comparative Historical Data / Current Data Sorted By Sales

Type of Statement

4/1/02-3/31/03	4/1/03-3/31/04	4/1/04-3/31/05	Type of Statement	0-1MM	1-3MM	3-5MM	5-10MM	10-25MM	25MM & OVER
16	19	11	Unqualified				3	4	4
10	9	7	Reviewed	1	1		3	2	
11	15	15	Compiled	1	5	6	1	2	
2	8	4	Tax Returns	1		1	2		
24	17	25	Other	3	3	5	1	10	3
ALL	ALL	ALL				12 (4/1-9/30/04)		50 (10/1/04-3/31/05)	
63	68	62	NUMBER OF STATEMENTS	6	9	12	10	18	7

Assets / Liabilities / Income Data (%)

4/1/02-3/31/03	4/1/03-3/31/04	4/1/04-3/31/05		0-1MM	1-3MM	3-5MM	5-10MM	10-25MM	25MM & OVER
%	%	%	**ASSETS**	%	%	%	%	%	%
9.2	15.2	9.7	Cash & Equivalents			8.1	7.6	14.1	
19.7	13.9	18.2	Trade Receivables (net)			14.3	11.5	26.1	
3.2	2.8	2.4	Inventory			3.7	2.0	.6	
5.2	5.0	4.9	All Other Current			3.4	11.8	3.3	
37.4	36.8	35.3	Total Current			29.6	32.8	44.1	
50.6	52.5	54.4	Fixed Assets (net)			62.2	63.3	46.0	
3.6	3.3	2.9	Intangibles (net)			5.5	.4	3.2	
8.3	7.4	7.5	All Other Non-Current			2.7	3.5	6.8	
100.0	100.0	100.0	Total			100.0	100.0	100.0	
			LIABILITIES						
6.1	4.5	4.3	Notes Payable-Short Term			3.3	5.8	3.9	
7.1	6.8	7.2	Cur. Mat.-L/T/D			8.8	6.7	7.7	
7.4	5.9	5.6	Trade Payables			2.6	3.8	11.7	
.2	.2	.5	Income Taxes Payable			.0	.0	1.7	
7.2	7.0	9.8	All Other Current			4.0	4.4	16.2	
27.9	24.3	27.5	Total Current			18.7	20.7	41.1	
24.6	31.5	32.6	Long-Term Debt			45.2	43.2	18.3	
1.1	.7	1.0	Deferred Taxes			.0	1.5	1.2	
4.7	8.1	3.3	All Other Non-Current			4.6	1.0	2.1	
41.6	35.4	35.6	Net Worth			31.6	33.6	37.3	
100.0	100.0	100.0	Total Liabilities & Net Worth			100.0	100.0	100.0	
			INCOME DATA						
100.0	100.0	100.0	Net Sales			100.0	100.0	100.0	
			Gross Profit						
86.3	85.9	83.6	Operating Expenses			85.2	88.6	82.9	
13.7	14.1	16.4	Operating Profit			14.8	11.4	17.1	
3.8	2.6	3.0	All Other Expenses (net)			3.0	3.4	2.4	
10.0	11.6	13.4	Profit Before Taxes			11.7	8.0	14.8	

Ratios

4/1/02-3/31/03	4/1/03-3/31/04	4/1/04-3/31/05	**RATIOS**	0-1MM	1-3MM	3-5MM	5-10MM	10-25MM	25MM & OVER
2.2	3.1	2.5	Current			3.2	2.2	2.0	
1.3	1.4	1.4				1.7	1.6	1.1	
.6	.8	.7				.7	.9	.7	
1.7	2.3	1.9	Quick			2.3	1.4	1.9	
1.0	1.0	1.1				1.0	1.1	1.0	
.5	.5	.5				.6	.3	.5	
18 20.8	16 22.9	13 28.7	Sales/Receivables			12 31.5	2 216.4	18 19.9	
50 7.2	44 8.3	44 8.4				72 5.1	49 7.4	37 9.9	
72 5.1	68 5.3	80 4.5				108 3.4	102 3.6	73 5.0	
			Cost of Sales/Inventory						
			Cost of Sales/Payables						
5.0	5.1	7.0	Sales/Working Capital			4.3	6.4	11.5	
15.7	15.3	20.2				16.4	7.2	120.0	
-16.9	-20.5	-14.7				-16.3	-19.0	-6.9	
7.2	6.3	12.6	EBIT/Interest			10.1	14.5	16.6	
(53) 3.7	(56) 3.5	(56) 4.0				3.9	3.5	(15) 4.0	
1.3	1.0	2.1				2.2	1.9	2.3	
3.5			Net Profit + Depr., Dep.,						
(13) 2.2			Amort./Cur. Mat. L/T/D						
1.1									
.8	.7	.7	Fixed/Worth			1.1	.8	.4	
1.3	1.7	1.4				2.6	1.3	1.4	
2.8	4.5	4.8				NM	NM	4.1	
.6	.7	.7	Debt/Worth			.9	.6	.5	
1.5	1.7	1.8				2.4	1.2	2.9	
4.5	5.1	5.8				NM	NM	4.3	
35.7	33.3	41.7	% Profit Before Taxes/Tangible					59.1	
(57) 14.3	(60) 12.1	(52) 23.8	Net Worth					(17) 25.8	
4.6	4.3	8.5						12.9	
11.5	11.0	13.8	% Profit Before Taxes/Total			10.7	15.3	17.2	
6.7	4.2	6.8	Assets			7.6	6.1	7.4	
.2	.0	3.1				3.0	-.3	4.7	
8.6	9.6	6.1	Sales/Net Fixed Assets			2.5	3.4	29.3	
2.6	1.7	2.1				1.5	1.1	2.9	
1.0	.7	.7				.5	.8	.8	
2.6	1.7	2.1	Sales/Total Assets			1.5	1.3	3.5	
1.2	.9	1.2				.9	.8	1.5	
.5	.5	.4				.4	.6	.4	
2.5	2.6	2.6	% Depr., Dep., Amort./Sales			6.4	3.6	.9	
(52) 6.7	(56) 6.1	(57) 8.6				11.7	10.2	(14) 7.4	
11.8	12.1	14.4				15.4	22.9	9.7	
2.3	2.9	2.9	% Officers', Directors',						
(14) 3.9	(15) 4.7	(16) 4.0	Owners' Comp/Sales						
5.8	9.3	7.3							
2284734M	2054811M	1043501M	Net Sales ($)	2397M	15048M	46374M	73460M	309513M	596709M
1619047M	2075418M	869495M	Total Assets ($)	4995M	38005M	70991M	115203M	407296M	233005M

M = $ thousand   MM = $ million
See Pages 11 through 21 for Explanation of Ratios and Data

TRANSPORTATION—Motor Vehicle Towing NAICS 488410 (SIC 7549)

Current Data Sorted By Assets **Comparative Historical Data**

Type of Statement	0-500M	500M-2MM	2-10MM	10-50MM	50-100MM	100-250MM		4/1/00-3/31/01 ALL	4/1/01-3/31/02 ALL
Unqualified	1	5	2	5		4		6	12
Reviewed	8	13	4	2		2		8	12
Compiled	38	21	4	1				59	50
Tax Returns	8	12	5	7				44	32
Other				1				32	50
		22 (4/1-9/30/04)		121 (10/1/04-3/31/05)					
NUMBER OF STATEMENTS	55	51	22	9		6		149	156
ASSETS	%	%	%	%	%	%		%	%
Cash & Equivalents	11.2	10.9	5.5					10.4	10.9
Trade Receivables (net)	11.1	13.4	13.8					14.9	13.2
Inventory	14.6	11.2	21.1					16.3	15.5
All Other Current	2.5	1.9	2.9					2.3	2.2
Total Current	39.4	37.4	43.3	D				43.8	41.9
Fixed Assets (net)	47.7	51.3	46.4	A				43.8	42.9
Intangibles (net)	6.1	3.0	5.9	T				5.9	8.3
All Other Non-Current	6.8	8.4	4.4	A				6.4	6.9
Total	100.0	100.0	100.0					100.0	100.0
LIABILITIES				N					
Notes Payable-Short Term	5.1	10.4	13.7	O				8.1	12.9
Cur. Mat.-L/T/D	12.2	3.3	7.8	T				6.6	4.8
Trade Payables	9.9	10.9	10.0					13.0	14.3
Income Taxes Payable	.1	.1	.7	A				.2	.2
All Other Current	10.0	9.6	8.5	V				13.3	23.4
Total Current	37.3	34.3	40.7	A				41.3	55.5
Long-Term Debt	49.6	27.0	34.5	I				32.3	32.6
Deferred Taxes	.0	.1	.4	L				.1	.3
All Other Non-Current	29.2	5.7	4.9	A				4.5	5.8
Net Worth	-16.2	32.9	19.5	B				21.8	5.8
Total Liabilities & Net Worth	100.0	100.0	100.0	L				100.0	100.0
INCOME DATA				E					
Net Sales	100.0	100.0	100.0					100.0	100.0
Gross Profit									
Operating Expenses	92.5	94.5	90.1					93.3	96.1
Operating Profit	7.5	5.5	9.9					6.7	3.9
All Other Expenses (net)	1.5	2.9	7.4					3.5	2.8
Profit Before Taxes	6.0	2.6	2.5					3.3	1.0
RATIOS									
Current	3.2	2.2	1.4					2.3	1.9
	1.3	1.2	1.0					1.1	1.1
	.5	.5	.5					.6	.5
Quick	2.0	1.6	.7					1.4	1.3
	(53) .5	.7	.5					.6	.5
	.1	.3	.2					.3	.2
Sales/Receivables	0 UND	3 140.1	1 250.3					1 304.9	2 187.4
	1 363.4	15 24.0	12 30.7					13 27.6	8 47.7
	17 21.9	33 11.0	36 10.1					30 12.1	28 13.0
Cost of Sales/Inventory									
Cost of Sales/Payables									
Sales/Working Capital	11.7	14.5	13.1					12.0	12.5
	57.1	42.0	NM					90.5	83.6
	-19.1	-8.8	-14.2					-20.2	-11.1
EBIT/Interest	8.9	9.2	8.5					5.6	3.4
	(47) 2.4	(44) 3.2	(18) 3.5					(125) 1.8	(132) 1.2
	.0	.5	.0					.8	-.3
Net Profit + Depr., Dep., Amort./Cur. Mat. L /T/D								2.9	1.8
								(12) 1.7	(18) 1.1
								.7	.2
Fixed/Worth	.7	.4	1.0					.6	.7
	6.5	1.4	2.2					2.5	2.7
	-1.3	11.0	NM					UND	-4.1
Debt/Worth	1.5	.7	1.9					1.2	1.4
	20.1	2.0	4.9					3.8	5.5
	-4.0	15.7	NM					UND	-7.9
% Profit Before Taxes/Tangible Net Worth	368.4	60.5	52.5					72.3	73.0
	(30) 72.8	(42) 19.2	(17) 33.0					(113) 23.7	(105) 15.5
	4.1	1.5	10.2					3.8	-1.0
% Profit Before Taxes/Total Assets	33.1	14.2	12.5					17.8	10.7
	4.0	4.8	2.8					4.3	1.6
	-4.8	-.9	-.5					-1.0	-5.4
Sales/Net Fixed Assets	18.4	15.7	33.5					23.2	27.7
	9.7	4.5	5.6					7.7	7.8
	4.8	1.7	1.6					2.7	2.6
Sales/Total Assets	6.0	3.2	3.1					4.9	4.2
	4.3	2.4	2.2					2.6	2.4
	2.0	1.4	1.0					1.5	1.2
% Depr., Dep., Amort./Sales	2.3	1.8	1.1					1.2	1.3
	(38) 5.7	(40) 6.3	(20) 2.7					(133) 3.4	(129) 2.9
	11.5	10.5	7.7					7.2	6.4
% Officers', Directors', Owners' Comp/Sales	2.7	1.8	3.1					2.6	2.9
	(35) 4.6	(27) 3.1	(11) 3.7					(77) 5.5	(73) 5.5
	9.8	5.1	6.5					9.1	9.6
Net Sales ($)	52094M	143777M	301489M	550483M		3002457M		1410357M	1256007M
Total Assets ($)	12338M	52784M	111655M	207192M		1190512M		644535M	841481M

M = $ thousand   MM = $ million
See Pages 11 through 21 for Explanation of Ratios and Data

Comparative Historical Data / Current Data Sorted By Sales

Current Data groupings: **22 (4/1-9/30/04)** covers 0-1MM, 1-3MM, 3-5MM; **121 (10/1/04-3/31/05)** covers 5-10MM, 10-25MM, 25MM & OVER.

Hist 4/1/02-3/31/03 ALL	Hist 4/1/03-3/31/04 ALL	Hist 4/1/04-3/31/05 ALL	Type of Statement	0-1MM	1-3MM	3-5MM	5-10MM	10-25MM	25MM & OVER
8	5	11	Unqualified				1	3	7
15	8	12	Reviewed	1	4	1	3	2	1
37	40	28	Compiled	5	11	4	4		4
38	48	64	Tax Returns	31	21	5	5	2	
38	43	28	Other	9	9	2	3	3	2
136	144	143	**NUMBER OF STATEMENTS**	46	45	12	16	10	14
%	%	%	**ASSETS**	%	%	%	%	%	%
10.7	12.2	10.0	Cash & Equivalents	9.1	11.3	9.0	12.8	6.2	8.9
12.9	12.6	12.8	Trade Receivables (net)	10.2	9.9	11.3	22.3	21.2	14.8
13.6	16.0	14.9	Inventory	7.0	16.5	20.3	11.5	26.6	26.4
3.3	3.5	2.6	All Other Current	1.2	2.6	.2	5.3	3.2	5.9
40.5	44.3	40.3	Total Current	27.5	40.4	40.8	52.0	57.3	56.0
45.5	40.3	47.2	Fixed Assets (net)	63.4	43.3	51.4	35.0	35.6	25.3
6.2	7.8	5.4	Intangibles (net)	4.2	6.5	.8	6.4	2.3	11.2
7.8	7.6	7.1	All Other Non-Current	4.9	9.9	7.0	6.7	4.8	7.6
100.0	100.0	100.0	Total	100.0	100.0	100.0	100.0	100.0	100.0
			LIABILITIES						
7.8	12.7	9.2	Notes Payable-Short Term	5.1	10.9	4.7	7.2	10.9	22.6
6.6	6.2	7.7	Cur. Mat.-L/T/D	13.1	3.8	11.1	5.5	2.6	6.2
11.3	11.7	10.1	Trade Payables	7.3	10.0	13.4	13.7	16.1	7.9
.2	.3	.2	Income Taxes Payable	.1	.1	.1	.1	1.2	.3
19.0	12.3	9.4	All Other Current	8.8	10.3	6.2	9.0	13.8	8.4
44.8	43.2	36.6	Total Current	34.4	35.1	35.5	35.5	44.6	45.4
36.6	29.6	36.8	Long-Term Debt	58.7	31.3	19.1	27.2	19.8	20.5
.2	.1	.2	Deferred Taxes	.0	.0	.3	.6	.1	.4
6.8	21.4	14.7	All Other Non-Current	32.6	7.0	4.9	4.0	9.8	4.5
11.6	5.8	11.8	Net Worth	-25.7	26.5	40.2	32.7	25.7	29.2
100.0	100.0	100.0	Total Liabilities & Net Worth	100.0	100.0	100.0	100.0	100.0	100.0
			INCOME DATA						
100.0	100.0	100.0	Net Sales	100.0	100.0	100.0	100.0	100.0	100.0
			Gross Profit						
95.4	94.5	93.2	Operating Expenses	87.4	95.8	96.3	95.3	99.5	95.0
4.6	5.5	6.8	Operating Profit	12.6	4.2	3.7	4.7	.5	5.0
2.5	2.2	2.8	All Other Expenses (net)	6.7	.9	-.3	2.9	1.0	.1
2.1	3.3	4.0	Profit Before Taxes	5.9	3.4	4.1	1.8	-.5	4.8
			RATIOS						
2.6	2.1	2.2		3.1	2.6	2.1	2.4	1.8	1.6
1.2	1.1	1.2	Current	.7	1.4	1.2	1.4	1.4	1.2
.5	.6	.5		.1	.5	.9	.9	.9	.9
1.5	1.3	1.5		2.0	1.6	1.4	1.4	1.0	.7
.6	.6 (140)	.6	Quick	(45) .5	(44) .5	.6	.8	.6	(13) .4
.2	.3	.2		.1	.2	.7	.5	.3	
1 374.7	0 UND	0 UND		0 UND	0 UND	0 800.2	10 35.4	6 62.2	0 UND
8 44.2	7 49.3	9 41.8	Sales/Receivables	0 UND	7 50.8	5 67.2	28 13.1	22 16.3	15 25.2
26 14.2	30 12.3	31 11.8		34 10.9	24 14.9	21 17.3	45 8.2	70 5.2	26 14.2
			Cost of Sales/Inventory						
			Cost of Sales/Payables						
10.9	13.0	12.4		9.9	12.7	24.0	11.4	6.9	15.0
69.9	95.4	46.1	Sales/Working Capital	-59.7	39.9	43.0	25.8	17.5	51.4
-17.4	-19.2	-18.7		-2.6	-25.8	-109.7	-114.5	-297.6	NM
7.8	6.6	8.9		7.0	8.0	25.0	10.1	9.4	9.3
(116) 2.2	(119) 2.6	(123) 3.0	EBIT/Interest	(35) 2.4	(39) 1.8	9.1	(15) 4.7	2.2	(12) 3.7
.6	.7	.3		.3	-.9	6.3	.0	-5.3	2.9
3.1	2.7	29.3	Net Profit + Depr., Dep.,						
(14) 1.9	(14) 1.7	(16) 3.0	Amort./Cur. Mat. L/T/D						
.9	1.1	2.1							
.7	.6	.6		1.6	.5	1.0	.2	.2	.5
2.3	2.4	2.4	Fixed/Worth	15.4	2.0	1.4	1.1	1.8	1.0
-4.5	-3.5	-9.4		-2.8	-7.5	2.0	4.8	6.5	3.0
1.2	1.3	1.2		2.0	.7	.8	.9	1.6	2.3
4.3	7.0	4.6	Debt/Worth	18.9	7.7	1.3	1.7	2.9	4.8
-10.5	-8.1	-11.8		-5.4	-7.5	3.3	10.1	16.4	23.9
63.2	64.4	91.3	% Profit Before Taxes/Tangible	258.4	189.3	82.1	44.9		132.8
(94) 19.8	(92) 21.2	(102) 29.4	Net Worth	(26) 28.4	(31) 22.7	(11) 40.5	(13) 18.0		(12) 44.7
4.3	2.2	4.5		2.3	1.5	12.3	-.8		11.8
16.8	12.8	17.7	% Profit Before Taxes/Total	18.2	26.3	23.8	14.1	14.1	18.8
4.2	4.2	4.2	Assets	2.2	3.2	15.0	8.5	2.6	12.9
-1.2	-.8	-1.6		-2.9	-10.3	6.6	-2.9	-11.4	2.2
21.2	31.4	18.4		7.4	18.3	16.5	41.1	55.0	27.2
9.1	9.4	6.8	Sales/Net Fixed Assets	2.9	9.7	7.3	12.8	14.9	18.0
2.4	2.6	2.5		.4	3.9	4.1	4.4	3.7	5.8
4.8	4.7	4.4		3.6	5.6	4.0	5.6	5.0	4.2
2.8	2.5	2.6	Sales/Total Assets	1.5	2.7	3.1	3.1	2.5	2.8
1.4	1.3	1.4		.4	2.0	2.7	1.6	1.6	1.5
1.4	1.1	1.7		6.5	1.5		1.5	.5	
(121) 2.7	(113) 3.4	(107) 4.5	% Depr., Dep., Amort./Sales	(36) 12.2	(32) 3.4		(13) 2.8	1.6	
6.9	8.3	9.7		15.9	7.4		6.1	4.0	
2.6	2.5	2.4	% Officers', Directors',	4.0	2.7	1.3			
(65) 4.4	(69) 4.5	(76) 4.2	Owners' Comp/Sales	(22) 7.4	(26) 4.3	(10) 2.3			
9.2	7.1	7.8		12.7	8.1	4.8			
1030257M	1035562M	4050300M	Net Sales ($)	19674M	77561M	46735M	114399M	164422M	3627509M
531101M	578889M	1574481M	Total Assets ($)	25503M	29933M	15815M	55022M	72213M	1375995M

M = $ thousand   MM = $ million
See Pages 11 through 21 for Explanation of Ratios and Data

Current Data Sorted By Assets   Comparative Historical Data

Type of Statement	0-500M	500M-2MM	2-10MM	10-50MM	50-100MM	100-250MM		4/1/00-3/31/01 ALL	4/1/01-3/31/02 ALL
Unqualified	2		2					2	
Reviewed	1	1	4	3				1	1
Compiled	1	1	1					2	1
Tax Returns	5	4	1		1				2
Other	3		7	1		1		3	
		6 (4/1-9/30/04)		32 (10/1/04-3/31/05)					
NUMBER OF STATEMENTS	12	7	14	4	1			8	4

	0-500M %	500M-2MM %	2-10MM %	10-50MM %	50-100MM %	100-250MM %		ALL %	ALL %
ASSETS									
Cash & Equivalents	12.9		9.6						
Trade Receivables (net)	32.8		31.4						
Inventory	2.7		4.8			D			
All Other Current	4.0		1.5			A			
Total Current	52.4		47.2			T			
Fixed Assets (net)	32.6		44.4			A			
Intangibles (net)	6.2		1.0						
All Other Non-Current	8.8		7.5			N			
Total	100.0		100.0			O			
						T			
LIABILITIES									
Notes Payable-Short Term	15.3		6.0			A			
Cur. Mat.-L/T/D	2.4		3.8			V			
Trade Payables	16.9		12.9			A			
Income Taxes Payable	.0		.5			I			
All Other Current	7.0		11.3			L			
Total Current	41.6		34.5			A			
Long-Term Debt	22.5		29.6			B			
Deferred Taxes	.0		1.0			L			
All Other Non-Current	3.9		2.3			E			
Net Worth	32.0		32.6						
Total Liabilities & Net Worth	100.0		100.0						
INCOME DATA									
Net Sales	100.0		100.0						
Gross Profit									
Operating Expenses	99.3		81.9						
Operating Profit	.7		18.1						
All Other Expenses (net)	.1		7.8						
Profit Before Taxes	.6		10.3						

RATIOS	0-500M	500M-2MM	2-10MM	10-50MM	50-100MM	100-250MM		ALL	ALL
Current	2.2		1.7						
	.9		1.1						
	.7		.8						
Quick	2.2		1.4						
	.9		1.0						
	.5		.7						
Sales/Receivables	2 239.9		0 UND						
	23 16.0		45 8.0						
	37 9.9		55 6.7						
Cost of Sales/Inventory									
Cost of Sales/Payables									
Sales/Working Capital	18.7		10.4						
	−558.1		86.0						
	−42.7		−25.3						
EBIT/Interest	9.4								
	(10) 3.1								
	−.8								
Net Profit + Depr., Dep., Amort./Cur. Mat. L./T/D									
Fixed/Worth	.3		.3						
	.8		1.9						
	NM		2.7						
Debt/Worth	.2		1.3						
	3.3		2.6						
	NM		5.1						
% Profit Before Taxes/Tangible Net Worth			44.8						
			30.8						
			14.4						
% Profit Before Taxes/Total Assets	17.2		10.2						
	6.9		6.0						
	−6.0		3.6						
Sales/Net Fixed Assets	75.1		51.3						
	40.0		4.9						
	7.1		1.0						
Sales/Total Assets	7.2		3.5						
	5.0		2.0						
	3.1		.8						
% Depr., Dep., Amort./Sales			.4						
		(12)	2.8						
			11.6						
% Officers', Directors', Owners' Comp/Sales									
Net Sales ($)	16288M	13028M	147768M	260805M	201247M			209601M	63993M
Total Assets ($)	3169M	6941M	68180M	89440M	68636M			119638M	41262M

© RMA 2005

M = $ thousand   MM = $ million
See Pages 11 through 21 for Explanation of Ratios and Data

Comparative Historical Data   Current Data Sorted By Sales

1	5	4	Type of Statement			6 (4/1-9/30/04)		32 (10/1/04-3/31/05)		
				0-1MM	1-3MM	3-5MM	5-10MM	10-25MM	25MM & OVER	
1	5	4	Unqualified	1	1			2		
12	16	9	Reviewed	1	1		1	3	3	
3	12	3	Compiled		2				1	
8	8	9	Tax Returns	3	4	2	3		2	
12	21	13	Other	3	5					
4/1/02-3/31/03 ALL	4/1/03-3/31/04 ALL	4/1/04-3/31/05 ALL								
36	62	38	NUMBER OF STATEMENTS	8	13	2	4	5	6	
%	%	%		%	%	%	%	%	%	

ASSETS

1	5	4		1-3MM
9.1	10.7	11.0	Cash & Equivalents	13.8
28.4	18.2	28.6	Trade Receivables (net)	25.6
5.7	7.6	5.8	Inventory	1.0
.9	5.3	4.2	All Other Current	2.1
44.1	41.9	49.6	Total Current	42.4
36.4	42.9	38.9	Fixed Assets (net)	38.9
3.3	3.8	4.4	Intangibles (net)	8.4
16.1	11.4	7.1	All Other Non-Current	10.3
100.0	100.0	100.0	Total	100.0

LIABILITIES

1	5	4		1-3MM
13.0	8.8	9.1	Notes Payable-Short Term	5.7
4.9	5.9	4.3	Cur. Mat.-L/T/D	3.1
14.3	7.2	12.6	Trade Payables	15.2
.0	.2	.2	Income Taxes Payable	.0
23.8	9.1	13.0	All Other Current	6.5
56.1	31.1	39.2	Total Current	30.5
39.4	27.1	28.8	Long-Term Debt	29.1
.6	1.1	.5	Deferred Taxes	.3
6.5	8.6	4.9	All Other Non-Current	.4
-2.6	32.1	26.7	Net Worth	39.8
100.0	100.0	100.0	Total Liabilities & Net Worth	100.0

INCOME DATA

1	5	4		1-3MM
100.0	100.0	100.0	Net Sales	100.0
			Gross Profit	
88.4	88.9	90.3	Operating Expenses	93.8
11.6	11.1	9.7	Operating Profit	6.2
7.2	5.1	3.5	All Other Expenses (net)	1.8
4.4	5.9	6.3	Profit Before Taxes	4.4

RATIOS

1	5	4		1-3MM
2.0	3.0	2.1	Current	2.2
1.0	1.2	1.2		1.0
.5	.8	.8		.8
2.0	1.8	1.6	Quick	1.8
.8	.9	1.0		1.0
.4	.5	.7		.8
0 UND	3 114.6	9 40.7	Sales/Receivables	0 UND
33 11.0	27 13.4	33 11.2		25 14.4
46 8.0	41 8.9	45 8.1		35 10.4
			Cost of Sales/Inventory	
			Cost of Sales/Payables	
9.0	8.8	13.0	Sales/Working Capital	17.8
151.2	32.4	36.8		-999.8
-14.7	-31.8	-47.3		-76.2
8.1	9.7	6.6	EBIT/Interest	6.1
(22) 3.2	(47) 2.5	(29) 3.9		(11) 4.4
1.7	1.3	1.8		1.9
	2.3		Net Profit + Depr., Dep., Amort./Cur. Mat. L/T/D	
	(16) 1.2			
	.4			
.2	.4	.3	Fixed/Worth	.4
1.2	1.4	1.4		1.2
28.6	5.2	9.5		NM
1.0	.7	1.1	Debt/Worth	.7
4.0	2.7	2.6		1.4
-20.2	8.4	29.3		NM
69.2	23.6	43.2	% Profit Before Taxes/Tangible Net Worth	37.6
(26) 16.9	(51) 12.5	(30) 26.7		(10) 17.9
6.3	2.6	12.0		-4.6
13.8	8.2	11.1	% Profit Before Taxes/Total Assets	17.5
5.6	3.5	7.1		8.3
1.1	.9	3.6		1.3
139.2	32.6	45.9	Sales/Net Fixed Assets	50.7
11.3	5.1	8.9		17.6
2.7	1.5	2.1		2.5
4.3	3.4	4.9	Sales/Total Assets	6.8
2.7	1.9	2.9		4.7
1.4	1.0	1.3		1.4
.6	1.4	.8	% Depr., Dep., Amort./Sales	
(28) 3.1	(50) 3.8	(28) 2.5		
13.1	10.7	7.1		
1.4	1.0	2.8	% Officers', Directors', Owners' Comp/Sales	
(10) 8.0	(15) 2.8	(13) 5.3		
23.2	7.6	8.9		

1	5	4		0-1MM	1-3MM	3-5MM	5-10MM	10-25MM	25MM & OVER
534847M	2020796M	639136M	Net Sales ($)	4183M	24023M	7956M	25954M	78629M	498391M
227142M	728661M	236366M	Total Assets ($)	13140M	17253M	1762M	16210M	34051M	153950M

M = $ thousand   MM = $ million
See Pages 11 through 21 for Explanation of Ratios and Data

Current Data Sorted By Assets   Comparative Historical Data

Statement type counts (top):

	2	6	24	10	8
3	8	52	9	10	1
10	22	18	8	1	
18	19	3	39		
11	25		19		

Type of Statement	36	32
Unqualified	36	32
Reviewed	44	50
Compiled	77	58
Tax Returns	21	27
Other	64	98

0-500M	500M-2MM	2-10MM	10-50MM	50-100MM	100-250MM		4/1/00-3/31/01 ALL	4/1/01-3/31/02 ALL
	55 (4/1-9/30/04)		261 (10/1/04-3/31/05)					
42	76	118	60	11	9	NUMBER OF STATEMENTS	242	265
%	%	%	%	%	%	**ASSETS**	%	%
20.8	10.5	7.6	8.8	11.8		Cash & Equivalents	9.6	9.0
38.9	47.1	57.3	49.0	18.9		Trade Receivables (net)	50.1	47.5
3.0	.9	.6	2.1	5.9		Inventory	.9	1.6
10.7	5.9	5.8	5.8	.6		All Other Current	3.5	4.6
73.6	64.3	71.3	65.6	37.2		Total Current	64.1	62.6
16.2	23.2	18.8	22.8	48.7		Fixed Assets (net)	23.3	25.8
1.4	4.5	3.6	3.0	8.6		Intangibles (net)	4.2	3.3
8.7	8.0	6.3	8.5	5.5		All Other Non-Current	8.4	8.3
100.0	100.0	100.0	100.0	100.0		Total	100.0	100.0
						LIABILITIES		
19.1	11.3	13.0	8.1	7.7		Notes Payable-Short Term	10.2	12.8
9.2	2.7	3.4	3.6	7.1		Cur. Mat.-L/T/D	4.4	5.2
22.2	26.2	29.0	28.8	8.6		Trade Payables	26.4	24.4
.1	.2	.3	.3	.3		Income Taxes Payable	.3	.2
24.7	13.2	11.2	12.2	12.8		All Other Current	12.9	11.5
75.3	53.5	57.0	52.9	36.5		Total Current	54.3	54.1
12.2	15.8	11.4	11.3	28.6		Long-Term Debt	12.5	15.0
.1	.3	.3	.5	4.4		Deferred Taxes	.5	.7
18.3	7.8	5.0	1.2	2.0		All Other Non-Current	4.5	4.4
-5.9	22.6	26.3	34.1	28.4		Net Worth	28.2	25.8
100.0	100.0	100.0	100.0	100.0		Total Liabilities & Net Worth	100.0	100.0
						INCOME DATA		
100.0	100.0	100.0	100.0	100.0		Net Sales	100.0	100.0
						Gross Profit		
97.4	95.4	95.7	95.5	90.6		Operating Expenses	95.6	95.9
2.6	4.6	4.3	4.5	9.4		Operating Profit	4.4	4.1
.4	1.0	.6	.3	3.0		All Other Expenses (net)	.1	1.3
2.2	3.7	3.8	4.1	6.4		Profit Before Taxes	4.3	2.9
						RATIOS		
2.6	2.1	1.7	1.6	1.2			1.8	1.6
1.2	1.2	1.3	1.3	1.0		Current	1.2	1.1
.6	.8	1.0	1.0	.8			.9	.9
2.2	1.9	1.6	1.4	1.1			1.6	1.5
.8	1.1	1.2	1.2	.8		Quick	1.1	1.0
.3	.7	.9	.8	.6			.8	.8
0 UND	22 16.5	35 10.5	36 10.3	24 15.1			26 13.9	27 13.5
21 17.7	40 9.2	46 7.9	45 8.1	40 9.2		Sales/Receivables	41 9.0	38 9.6
38 9.7	57 6.4	61 5.9	55 6.6	51 7.2			62 5.9	56 6.5
						Cost of Sales/Inventory		
						Cost of Sales/Payables		
11.8	12.2	13.9	13.2	24.4			13.0	16.3
88.7	42.7	32.2	33.1	55.2		Sales/Working Capital	44.5	70.3
-17.7	-60.4	218.4	-744.6	-34.5			-79.7	-44.3
15.0	8.8	22.2	31.8	7.9			15.1	10.1
(25) 3.8	(62) 5.0	(107) 5.6	(52) 8.6	3.9		EBIT/Interest	(209) 4.2	(232) 2.7
-1.6	2.6	2.9	4.1	2.8			1.4	1.0
		17.4	23.7				10.3	5.9
	(28) 2.8	(23) 3.5				Net Profit + Depr., Dep., Amort./Cur. Mat. L./T/D	(48) 2.7	(59) 1.8
	1.7	1.7					1.4	.9
.0	.2	.1	.2	.7			.2	.2
.3	.5	.5	.5	2.1		Fixed/Worth	.5	.8
-1.5	4.3	2.2	2.0	6.3			2.2	2.9
.8	1.3	1.5	1.3	1.9			1.2	1.5
8.9	3.3	3.0	2.4	3.7		Debt/Worth	3.0	3.2
-3.5	19.1	10.2	4.0	12.7			8.3	8.0
131.9	84.6	66.7	49.3	35.8			57.9	52.5
(24) 31.6	(60) 33.3	(99) 30.4	(56) 32.2	(10) 28.6		% Profit Before Taxes/Tangible Net Worth	(208) 29.5	(226) 20.1
.9	6.0	12.8	16.7	22.0			9.9	2.9
26.7	18.7	15.9	14.3	10.5			17.8	12.1
6.4	8.0	7.1	8.7	8.0		% Profit Before Taxes/Total Assets	6.8	4.5
-.3	2.4	3.0	3.2	3.0			1.7	.0
UND	128.1	197.9	105.3	4.9			148.1	113.5
229.2	41.8	58.9	28.2	2.7		Sales/Net Fixed Assets	28.9	28.9
33.5	10.1	11.1	8.3	2.1			9.0	6.9
11.3	6.5	5.9	5.7	2.1			6.5	6.2
7.1	4.3	4.3	3.7	1.5		Sales/Total Assets	4.0	3.9
3.3	2.1	2.7	1.9	.4			2.1	2.1
.2	.2	.2	.4	1.5			.3	.3
(19) .6	(62) .5	(98) .5	(53) .8	(10) 6.1		% Depr., Dep., Amort./Sales	(204) 1.0	(210) 1.1
1.8	4.5	1.9	2.5	7.0			3.0	3.4
1.8	1.7	1.1	.3				2.0	1.4
(17) 3.9	(38) 2.6	(46) 2.6	(14) 1.2			% Officers', Directors', Owners' Comp/Sales	(81) 3.8	(92) 3.1
9.9	5.4	4.4	4.0				8.6	9.3
78132M	464582M	2463578M	4672224M	1277945M	2368485M	Net Sales ($)	10580716M	8154428M
9812M	94018M	560544M	1250362M	827152M	1559185M	Total Assets ($)	2591831M	3191010M

© RMA 2005

M = $ thousand   MM = $ million
See Pages 11 through 21 for Explanation of Ratios and Data

Comparative Historical Data | **Current Data Sorted By Sales**

Hist 1	Hist 2	Hist 3	Type of Statement	0-1MM	1-3MM	3-5MM	5-10MM	10-25MM	25MM & OVER
35	44	50	Unqualified				3	7	40
59	65	73	Reviewed	3	6	4	9	23	28
56	74	59	Compiled	3	13	2	13	14	14
31	35	40	Tax Returns	9	14	4	10	3	14
79	84	94	Other	5	17	8	18	18	28
4/1/02-3/31/03 ALL	4/1/03-3/31/04 ALL	4/1/04-3/31/05 ALL		55 (4/1-9/30/04)			261 (10/1/04-3/31/05)		
260	302	316	**NUMBER OF STATEMENTS**	20	50	18	53	65	110
%	%	%	**ASSETS**	%	%	%	%	%	%
8.3	9.2	10.5	Cash & Equivalents	17.4	15.2	9.4	11.3	8.1	8.4
48.5	49.0	48.7	Trade Receivables (net)	30.1	33.3	52.3	45.2	58.1	54.7
1.6	1.1	1.5	Inventory	4.3	.9	.1	1.3	1.0	1.8
5.3	5.7	6.2	All Other Current	11.7	8.5	4.0	3.9	8.2	4.3
63.7	65.0	66.9	Total Current	63.4	58.0	65.7	61.7	75.3	69.3
23.8	24.0	22.0	Fixed Assets (net)	29.6	28.6	21.0	27.3	13.2	20.5
3.5	3.4	3.7	Intangibles (net)	1.2	3.9	6.1	3.1	4.0	3.7
9.0	7.6	7.4	All Other Non-Current	5.7	9.5	7.2	7.9	7.6	6.5
100.0	100.0	100.0	Total	100.0	100.0	100.0	100.0	100.0	100.0
			LIABILITIES						
10.9	11.3	12.0	Notes Payable-Short Term	14.6	13.6	18.4	11.1	11.9	10.3
6.5	5.3	4.2	Cur. Mat.-L/T/D	13.4	6.6	.9	3.8	2.5	3.2
24.2	26.9	26.3	Trade Payables	6.0	19.8	29.2	21.8	33.7	30.2
.3	.3	.2	Income Taxes Payable	.0	.2	.0	.4	.3	.2
13.6	16.1	13.8	All Other Current	26.9	19.6	13.4	8.8	12.4	12.0
55.5	59.9	56.5	Total Current	60.9	59.8	61.9	45.9	60.7	56.0
14.0	12.5	13.5	Long-Term Debt	20.4	19.0	13.6	19.5	7.3	10.5
.7	.7	.5	Deferred Taxes	.0	.0	.1	.4	.3	1.0
4.5	4.2	6.8	All Other Non-Current	2.2	17.2	17.7	3.1	4.0	4.6
25.2	22.7	22.7	Net Worth	16.5	3.9	6.7	31.2	27.7	28.0
100.0	100.0	100.0	Total Liabilities & Net Worth	100.0	100.0	100.0	100.0	100.0	100.0
			INCOME DATA						
100.0	100.0	100.0	Net Sales	100.0	100.0	100.0	100.0	100.0	100.0
			Gross Profit						
96.6	96.2	95.5	Operating Expenses	90.2	94.6	94.2	95.4	97.1	96.2
3.4	3.8	4.5	Operating Profit	9.8	5.4	5.8	4.6	2.9	3.8
.7	.7	.7	All Other Expenses (net)	5.1	.5	.0	.5	.4	.5
2.7	3.1	3.8	Profit Before Taxes	4.8	4.9	5.9	4.1	2.5	3.3
			RATIOS						
1.6	1.5	1.7	Current	4.9	1.8	2.3	2.2	1.7	1.5
1.2	1.1	1.2		1.5	1.0	1.4	1.4	1.3	1.2
.9	.9	.9		.5	.7	.8	.9	1.0	1.0
1.5	1.4	1.6	Quick	4.9	1.6	2.2	2.0	1.6	1.4
1.1	1.0	1.1		.6	.8	1.4	1.3	1.1	1.1
.7	.7	.7		.2	.4	.7	.9	.9	.9
26 13.8	27 13.5	27 13.6	Sales/Receivables	0 UND	5 71.2	28 13.1	23 15.6	35 10.5	33 11.0
38 9.6	41 9.0	43 8.6		12 31.7	36 10.2	39 9.3	43 8.6	47 7.8	43 8.5
55 6.6	53 6.9	56 6.6		96 3.8	58 6.3	68 5.4	60 6.1	60 6.0	52 7.0
			Cost of Sales/Inventory						
			Cost of Sales/Payables						
17.0	17.2	13.4	Sales/Working Capital	3.0	14.1	8.9	11.5	14.1	19.1
52.6	51.8	36.5		48.7	81.3	91.6	27.7	27.0	40.7
-71.7	-54.0	-81.5		-6.4	-17.6	-28.3	-123.5	207.6	-475.6
13.6	15.8	17.2	EBIT/Interest		10.6	33.3	9.6	15.4	34.1
(226) 3.4	(265) 4.7	(266) 5.8		(39) 4.5	8.2	(45) 4.3	(56) 6.1	(100) 7.7	
1.2	1.3	2.7		1.4	3.7	1.8		3.1	
4.9	9.5	15.2	Net Profit + Depr., Dep., Amort./Cur. Mat. L/T/D					12.5	22.2
(63) 1.7	(67) 2.3	(71) 3.0					(21) 4.9	(36) 3.2	
.8	1.3	1.7						1.8	1.7
.2	.2	.2	Fixed/Worth	.0	.1	.2	.2	.1	.2
.6	.7	.5		.3	1.2	.7	.7	.4	.6
2.7	3.9	3.0		26.5	UND	-3.3	3.2	1.3	2.1
1.4	1.6	1.4	Debt/Worth	.3	1.5	1.3	1.0	1.6	1.4
2.9	3.4	2.9		2.7	5.0	3.4	2.9	2.9	2.8
7.3	10.4	12.9		-4.2	-5.8	-16.2	16.5	9.0	5.8
52.9	52.6	65.5	% Profit Before Taxes/Tangible Net Worth	43.6	77.1	76.5	82.2	81.3	51.0
(218) 18.5	(249) 26.3	(256) 31.5		(13) 7.7	(34) 26.5	(12) 43.7	(44) 29.7	(58) 29.4	(95) 33.3
4.9	6.0	10.7		1.5	5.0	20.6	7.7	12.8	17.9
13.1	14.6	15.9	% Profit Before Taxes/Total Assets	15.5	18.9	24.4	15.5	15.9	15.6
5.0	5.5	7.7		1.5	6.9	10.9	6.5	7.8	8.1
.6	.8	2.4		.1	1.6	6.6	1.0	3.2	2.9
110.9	112.8	163.1	Sales/Net Fixed Assets	UND	238.1	93.7	84.3	191.6	151.2
32.4	35.3	45.8		15.0	31.8	36.9	28.6	89.9	48.4
8.2	7.5	9.7		2.6	4.3	10.5	5.4	16.5	11.8
6.0	6.5	6.2	Sales/Total Assets	4.4	7.1	6.2	6.4	6.0	6.4
4.1	4.4	4.2		2.4	2.4	4.0	4.2	4.4	4.5
2.3	2.2	2.0		.7	1.1	1.5	2.7	3.2	2.3
.3	.3	.3	% Depr., Dep., Amort./Sales	1.9	.4	.2	.2	.2	.3
(223) .8	(245) .9	(247) .7		(10) 4.6	(33) 1.8	(14) .8	(45) .9	(54) .4	(91) .6
3.3	3.1	2.8		16.1	5.8	3.3	3.7	1.5	1.9
1.2	1.4	1.1	% Officers', Directors', Owners' Comp/Sales		2.5	1.9	1.0	1.6	.6
(85) 3.2	(90) 3.0	(116) 2.5			(26) 6.7	(10) 3.8	(22) 2.0	(23) 2.2	(31) 1.2
5.7	5.8	5.5			8.4	10.6	2.9	3.9	3.0
6450077M	8711936M	11324946M	Net Sales ($)	8686M	98266M	70228M	379214M	1040995M	9727557M
2086731M	3272862M	4301073M	Total Assets ($)	9112M	66024M	34014M	247262M	354937M	3589724M

Current Data Sorted By Assets   Comparative Historical Data

0-500M	500M-2MM	2-10MM	10-50MM	50-100MM	100-250MM	Type of Statement	4/1/00-3/31/01 ALL	4/1/01-3/31/02 ALL
3	2 2 4	2 8 3	3 2			Unqualified / Reviewed / Compiled / Tax Returns / Other	4 / 9 / 8 / 1 / 12	4 / 12 / 5 / 3 / 16
6 1	3 7	9	3	1				
6 (4/1-9/30/04)			53 (10/1/04-3/31/05)					
10	18	22	8	1		**NUMBER OF STATEMENTS**	34	40
%	%	%	%	%	%	**ASSETS**	%	%
25.9	8.8	9.4				Cash & Equivalents	6.0	8.7
20.8	33.7	30.7				Trade Receivables (net)	35.5	31.9
1.3	9.7	15.5				Inventory	16.0	14.4
.7	6.6	3.3				All Other Current	2.4	4.6
48.6	58.7	58.9				Total Current	59.9	59.6
42.3	32.0	31.9				Fixed Assets (net)	28.6	30.9
1.9	1.3	2.8				Intangibles (net)	2.0	4.5
7.2	8.0	6.5				All Other Non-Current	9.5	5.0
100.0	100.0	100.0				Total	100.0	100.0
						LIABILITIES		
19.6	6.0	14.1				Notes Payable-Short Term	11.1	11.4
6.2	4.3	2.3				Cur. Mat.-L/T/D	6.3	6.8
17.5	17.1	18.4				Trade Payables	14.4	13.8
.0	.0	.2				Income Taxes Payable	.3	.1
8.4	16.8	7.4				All Other Current	7.3	12.9
51.6	44.3	42.5				Total Current	39.5	45.1
20.3	22.5	15.4				Long-Term Debt	11.8	17.9
.1	.0	.0				Deferred Taxes	.2	.2
1.4	35.1	10.5				All Other Non-Current	10.1	8.9
26.5	-1.8	31.6				Net Worth	38.4	27.9
100.0	100.0	100.0				Total Liabilities & Net Worth	100.0	100.0
						INCOME DATA		
100.0	100.0	100.0				Net Sales	100.0	100.0
						Gross Profit		
95.2	94.3	95.9				Operating Expenses	94.7	94.4
4.8	5.7	4.1				Operating Profit	5.3	5.6
.5	1.1	1.9				All Other Expenses (net)	1.1	2.3
4.3	4.5	2.3				Profit Before Taxes	4.2	3.3
						RATIOS		
3.3 / .8 / .3	2.6 / 1.3 / .9	2.7 / 1.3 / 1.0				Current	2.6 / 1.5 / 1.0	2.1 / 1.3 / .9
3.1 / .8 / .3	2.2 / 1.0 / .5	1.9 / .8 / .6				Quick	1.7 / 1.0 / .7	1.3 / .9 / .6
0 UND / 3 133.8 / 41 8.8	30 12.1 / 45 8.2 / 53 6.9	28 12.9 / 43 8.5 / 56 6.5				Sales/Receivables	33 10.9 / 53 6.9 / 71 5.1	29 12.5 / 43 8.4 / 57 6.5
						Cost of Sales/Inventory		
						Cost of Sales/Payables		
12.7 / -55.9 / -15.4	8.5 / 14.5 / NM	5.8 / 25.5 / -68.2				Sales/Working Capital	5.8 / 16.9 / -282.1	7.5 / 20.1 / -55.6
	(14) 8.0 / 3.8 / 2.4	(21) 12.0 / 2.8 / -1.3				EBIT/Interest	(25) 14.1 / 3.9 / .9	(35) 9.5 / 3.2 / 1.1
						Net Profit + Depr., Dep., Amort./Cur. Mat. L./T/D		
.2 / 2.4 / -15.3	.3 / 1.3 / NM	.4 / 1.1 / 5.9				Fixed/Worth	.3 / .6 / 1.3	.4 / 1.2 / NM
1.3 / 3.5 / -19.0	1.2 / 4.0 / NM	.9 / 2.0 / 12.2				Debt/Worth	.9 / 1.6 / 3.2	1.1 / 2.2 / NM
	(14) 71.6 / 33.6 / 4.7	(19) 57.2 / 14.8 / -5.8				% Profit Before Taxes/Tangible Net Worth	(30) 40.3 / 17.8 / 7.1	(30) 40.5 / 24.1 / 9.4
70.8 / 17.4 / -7.8	17.9 / 6.1 / .1	13.4 / 2.1 / -4.2				% Profit Before Taxes/Total Assets	14.8 / 7.1 / .1	14.2 / 7.3 / 1.6
154.8 / 21.2 / 7.8	27.2 / 10.2 / 5.7	21.7 / 10.2 / 4.9				Sales/Net Fixed Assets	23.6 / 15.7 / 5.2	27.2 / 12.4 / 4.1
12.0 / 4.3 / 3.1	3.5 / 2.9 / 1.8	3.5 / 2.2 / 1.7				Sales/Total Assets	3.4 / 2.7 / 1.8	3.6 / 2.8 / 1.3
	(15) 1.3 / 1.9 / 3.9	(21) 1.4 / 3.7 / 5.9				% Depr., Dep., Amort./Sales	(33) .9 / 1.8 / 2.7	(36) 1.2 / 2.3 / 4.1
		(10) 1.6 / 2.6 / 5.3				% Officers', Directors', Owners' Comp/Sales	(16) 3.8 / 5.0 / 11.0	(19) 1.5 / 3.4 / 5.2
13593M	58193M	298610M	547178M	55664M		Net Sales ($)	374749M	554153M
2283M	22241M	111078M	214264M	70098M		Total Assets ($)	140862M	225038M

Note: Columns 10-50MM, 50-100MM, and 100-250MM are marked "DATA NOT AVAILABLE."

M = $ thousand   MM = $ million
See Pages 11 through 21 for Explanation of Ratios and Data

Comparative Historical Data | Current Data Sorted By Sales

			Type of Statement	0-1MM	1-3MM	3-5MM	5-10MM	10-25MM	25MM & OVER
5	5	7	Unqualified			2	1	1	3
11	15	12	Reviewed		4	3	4	1	
7	8	10	Compiled	2	3	2	1	2	
7	10	9	Tax Returns	4	1	3			
21	18	21	Other	1	4	3	4	6	5
4/1/02-3/31/03 ALL	4/1/03-3/31/04 ALL	4/1/04-3/31/05 ALL			6 (4/1-9/30/04)		53 (10/1/04-3/31/05)		
51	56	59	NUMBER OF STATEMENTS	7	9	14	7	13	9
%	%	%	ASSETS	%	%	%	%	%	%
10.4	9.7	11.5	Cash & Equivalents			19.8		8.7	
31.3	31.7	30.4	Trade Receivables (net)			33.4		31.9	
13.0	14.2	11.3	Inventory			8.9		15.0	
1.9	2.7	4.4	All Other Current			5.2		4.0	
56.7	58.3	57.5	Total Current			67.4		59.5	
33.6	31.9	32.9	Fixed Assets (net)			24.7		31.1	
4.8	5.0	3.1	Intangibles (net)			1.6		3.1	
4.9	4.8	6.5	All Other Non-Current			6.4		6.3	
100.0	100.0	100.0	Total			100.0		100.0	
			LIABILITIES						
9.3	7.2	11.4	Notes Payable-Short Term			6.1		17.5	
6.2	5.1	3.8	Cur. Mat.-L/T/D			1.5		2.8	
18.8	17.4	18.4	Trade Payables			17.2		19.7	
.3	.2	.1	Income Taxes Payable			.0		.4	
9.0	10.1	10.9	All Other Current			10.3		7.9	
43.7	40.0	44.7	Total Current			35.0		48.2	
20.4	20.3	18.7	Long-Term Debt			23.7		12.9	
.0	.0	.1	Deferred Taxes			.0		.0	
3.2	7.6	15.1	All Other Non-Current			31.0		7.8	
32.7	32.2	21.5	Net Worth			10.2		31.1	
100.0	100.0	100.0	Total Liabilities & Net Worth			100.0		100.0	
			INCOME DATA						
100.0	100.0	100.0	Net Sales			100.0		100.0	
			Gross Profit						
94.7	94.7	95.1	Operating Expenses			93.2		96.4	
5.3	5.3	4.9	Operating Profit			6.8		3.6	
1.2	1.5	1.4	All Other Expenses (net)			.6		2.2	
4.1	3.8	3.5	Profit Before Taxes			6.2		1.4	
			RATIOS						
2.0	2.4	2.6				3.5		2.3	
1.4	1.4	1.3	Current			2.6		1.1	
.9	1.0	.9				1.5		.9	
1.3	2.0	1.8				3.0		1.5	
.9	.9	.9	Quick			2.2		.6	
.6	.6	.6				1.0		.5	
20 18.5	26 14.0	28 12.9				33 11.1		28 12.9	
39 9.4	45 8.2	41 8.9	Sales/Receivables			43 8.4		38 9.7	
56 6.5	70 5.2	56 6.5				52 7.1		57 6.4	
			Cost of Sales/Inventory						
			Cost of Sales/Payables						
11.6	7.8	6.5				3.7		10.2	
22.7	18.2	29.4	Sales/Working Capital			9.9		39.2	
-55.4	NM	-76.1				52.7		-48.4	
11.1	10.5	9.8				49.0		16.2	
(43) 3.7	(46) 4.7	(51) 3.4	EBIT/Interest		(10)	6.1		1.2	
1.8	1.7	.4				2.1		-2.9	
21.6	17.6	15.1							
(11) 3.2	(11) 5.3	(14) 2.5	Net Profit + Depr., Dep., Amort./Cur. Mat. L/T/D						
1.3	1.4	-.1							
.3	.2	.3				.2		.5	
1.2	1.2	1.1	Fixed/Worth			.5		1.2	
3.3	2.9	4.5				2.9		9.3	
.7	.9	1.1				.6		1.0	
2.3	2.6	2.8	Debt/Worth			2.2		2.2	
6.3	10.4	11.6				6.8		26.9	
48.6	54.9	65.4				76.2		57.2	
(44) 30.7	(49) 28.6	(48) 29.8	% Profit Before Taxes/Tangible Net Worth		(12)	48.7	(11)	14.6	
7.2	9.6	1.4				4.8		-75.6	
19.8	18.1	18.6				26.3		26.3	
8.3	8.0	5.3	% Profit Before Taxes/Total Assets			14.1		.3	
-2.1	1.3	-2.1				2.1		-13.1	
35.8	30.5	27.0				37.9		23.1	
10.0	11.7	11.1	Sales/Net Fixed Assets			17.9		11.8	
4.2	5.2	5.8				7.0		5.6	
4.0	3.6	3.7				3.5		3.6	
2.9	2.9	2.9	Sales/Total Assets			3.2		3.2	
2.1	1.5	1.8				1.9		1.8	
.9	.9	1.2				1.3		1.4	
(43) 1.8	(42) 1.6	(50) 2.6	% Depr., Dep., Amort./Sales		(11)	3.2	(12)	3.7	
4.3	4.7	5.2				4.5		6.1	
1.9	2.9	1.4							
(24) 4.7	(24) 4.8	(25) 3.3	% Officers', Directors', Owners' Comp/Sales						
7.7	8.0	6.2							
766659M	748312M	973238M	Net Sales ($)	4217M	17684M	55308M	47401M	211386M	637242M
289558M	395474M	419964M	Total Assets ($)	2159M	7585M	22553M	26660M	85798M	275209M

M = $ thousand   MM = $ million
See Pages 11 through 21 for Explanation of Ratios and Data

Current Data Sorted By Assets   **Comparative Historical Data**

0-500M	500M-2MM	2-10MM	10-50MM	50-100MM	100-250MM	Type of Statement	4/1/00-3/31/01 ALL	4/1/01-3/31/02 ALL
1	5	4	7	5	3	Unqualified	11	10
3	4	15	3	1		Reviewed	17	17
5	13	5	1	1		Compiled	27	26
9	7	7	1			Tax Returns	11	16
7	18	10	8	2	3	Other	25	25
	23 (4/1-9/30/04)		118 (10/1/04-3/31/05)					
25	47	35	19	9	6	NUMBER OF STATEMENTS	91	94
%	%	%	%	%	%	**ASSETS**	%	%
21.1	9.3	9.8	10.0			Cash & Equivalents	7.4	7.2
30.0	36.6	37.0	17.2			Trade Receivables (net)	30.5	27.9
2.7	4.5	3.0	10.0			Inventory	6.3	4.9
7.3	3.5	2.3	8.8			All Other Current	4.7	6.6
61.2	54.0	52.1	46.0			Total Current	48.9	46.6
20.7	36.7	37.3	43.3			Fixed Assets (net)	39.9	39.8
8.0	2.3	2.3	2.5			Intangibles (net)	3.3	4.8
10.0	7.0	8.2	8.1			All Other Non-Current	7.8	8.9
100.0	100.0	100.0	100.0			Total	100.0	100.0
						LIABILITIES		
2.3	12.3	8.4	11.2			Notes Payable-Short Term	14.0	9.5
7.2	6.8	6.1	7.1			Cur. Mat.-L/T/D	8.6	7.9
19.0	17.5	8.7	6.6			Trade Payables	15.8	12.2
.0	.3	.4	.0			Income Taxes Payable	.2	.2
29.1	15.9	16.7	13.5			All Other Current	11.0	12.6
57.6	52.8	40.2	38.4			Total Current	49.6	42.4
21.9	17.7	17.8	21.3			Long-Term Debt	24.5	25.5
.3	.1	1.2	2.8			Deferred Taxes	.5	1.0
15.9	3.8	3.8	5.5			All Other Non-Current	3.7	3.7
4.3	25.7	37.0	32.1			Net Worth	21.6	27.4
100.0	100.0	100.0	100.0			Total Liabilities & Net Worth	100.0	100.0
						INCOME DATA		
100.0	100.0	100.0	100.0			Net Sales	100.0	100.0
						Gross Profit		
96.1	95.2	94.1	91.0			Operating Expenses	93.2	91.8
3.9	4.8	5.9	9.0			Operating Profit	6.8	8.2
1.1	1.9	.4	2.3			All Other Expenses (net)	1.6	2.7
2.8	2.9	5.5	6.6			Profit Before Taxes	5.2	5.4
						RATIOS		
3.8	2.1	1.9	1.1				1.4	1.7
1.3	1.0	1.2	1.0			Current	1.0	1.1
.8	.7	.9	.7				.5	.7
3.2	2.1	1.5	.9				1.2	1.4
1.1	.9	1.1	.6			Quick	.7 (93)	.9
.6	.4	.8	.3				.3	.3
0 UND	19 19.3	33 11.1	16 22.7				22 16.4	4 92.6
20 18.4	42 8.8	42 8.6	32 11.3			Sales/Receivables	38 9.5	30 12.2
49 7.4	60 6.0	58 6.3	45 8.1				51 7.2	55 6.6
						Cost of Sales/Inventory		
						Cost of Sales/Payables		
11.6	12.6	12.1	17.2				14.7	19.0
43.1	77.5	49.1	-420.2			Sales/Working Capital	-162.8	78.7
-47.7	-13.9	-61.6	-10.9				-8.8	-19.5
8.9	16.0	14.8	7.0				4.5	5.6
(16) 2.7	(40) 6.4	(32) 5.0	(16) 2.7			EBIT/Interest	(77) 1.8	(77) 2.2
.6	.6	1.8	1.3				.7	1.1
		9.0					2.8	3.7
		(11) 1.3				Net Profit + Depr., Dep., Amort./Cur. Mat. L/T/D	(18) 1.2	(23) 2.2
		.9					.4	1.0
.0	.3	.5	.4				.6	.5
.6	1.1	.9	1.3			Fixed/Worth	2.4	1.4
-1.3	-14.5	2.3	2.4				9.2	5.3
.7	.9	1.3	1.4				1.9	.9
5.9	2.2	2.2	2.7			Debt/Worth	4.4	3.0
-4.3	-45.8	3.0	5.7				18.8	25.7
93.2	55.4	59.9	38.3				57.7	49.2
(14) 16.7	(33) 19.7	(34) 26.3	20.3			% Profit Before Taxes/Tangible Net Worth	(74) 22.9	(76) 16.8
-4.0	7.3	4.2	9.4				3.6	4.9
16.3	17.5	15.4	9.3				14.9	16.4
3.4	8.4	7.8	3.7			% Profit Before Taxes/Total Assets	4.1	5.5
-3.1	-.8	1.6	2.1				-1.1	.6
999.8	63.6	36.0	28.0				26.5	31.0
34.4	11.1	7.5	5.1			Sales/Net Fixed Assets	6.9	10.1
11.5	4.7	4.1	1.7				2.7	2.9
8.1	4.3	3.8	2.8				3.7	4.7
4.1	3.2	3.0	1.6			Sales/Total Assets	2.3	2.6
1.8	1.8	1.5	.9				1.3	1.5
.6	.7	1.3	1.2				1.1	1.0
(11) 2.3	(39) 2.6	(33) 4.5	(17) 5.5			% Depr., Dep., Amort./Sales	(79) 4.3	(81) 3.1
7.6	9.6	6.5	16.9				8.8	8.3
4.6	2.3	1.7					2.5	1.7
(11) 5.9	(16) 3.6	(11) 2.2				% Officers', Directors', Owners' Comp/Sales	(35) 4.8	(34) 3.7
10.5	5.8	2.7					6.2	5.4
35467M	217466M	540461M	833543M	984648M	1767749M	Net Sales ($)	1922871M	1222934M
5634M	56208M	183059M	417354M	696261M	1101733M	Total Assets ($)	1221369M	744731M

M = $ thousand   MM = $ million
See Pages 11 through 21 for Explanation of Ratios and Data

Comparative Historical Data   **Current Data Sorted By Sales**

			Type of Statement						
20	20	25	Unqualified	2		5	3	3	12
22	23	26	Reviewed	4	1	5	1	8	7
25	40	25	Compiled	3	5	5	5	5	2
18	32	17	Tax Returns	8	4	2	2	2	1
34	45	48	Other	4	12	6	8	7	11
4/1/02-3/31/03 ALL	4/1/03-3/31/04 ALL	4/1/04-3/31/05 ALL		23 (4/1-9/30/04)		118 (10/1/04-3/31/05)			
				0-1MM	1-3MM	3-5MM	5-10MM	10-25MM	25MM & OVER
119	160	141	**NUMBER OF STATEMENTS**	21	22	23	19	23	33
%	%	%	**ASSETS**	%	%	%	%	%	%
9.5	9.1	11.4	Cash & Equivalents	9.6	18.7	9.4	12.4	11.3	8.5
29.5	29.9	31.4	Trade Receivables (net)	25.9	27.9	33.7	39.5	36.1	27.6
6.1	4.5	4.6	Inventory	3.2	5.6	4.2	.7	4.6	7.2
4.7	4.8	4.6	All Other Current	5.5	2.2	4.7	5.9	4.0	5.1
49.8	48.3	51.9	Total Current	44.2	54.4	52.0	58.6	55.9	48.3
38.6	39.5	36.1	Fixed Assets (net)	39.5	36.0	36.5	28.7	36.9	37.3
3.3	4.8	4.4	Intangibles (net)	8.3	2.3	2.6	3.7	1.9	6.8
8.3	7.3	7.6	All Other Non-Current	8.0	7.3	8.9	9.0	5.3	7.6
100.0	100.0	100.0	Total	100.0	100.0	100.0	100.0	100.0	100.0
			LIABILITIES						
12.3	9.9	8.3	Notes Payable-Short Term	7.6	7.3	7.2	11.8	8.5	7.9
8.4	8.1	6.7	Cur. Mat.-L/T/D	10.5	2.4	7.0	5.7	8.0	6.6
15.9	13.0	13.1	Trade Payables	11.1	18.5	16.0	15.2	11.8	8.3
.3	.3	.3	Income Taxes Payable	.0	.1	.4	.5	.2	.3
12.7	12.0	17.5	All Other Current	39.9	15.7	13.0	11.0	15.1	12.9
49.6	43.3	45.8	Total Current	69.2	43.9	43.7	44.2	43.7	36.0
27.3	25.0	20.4	Long-Term Debt	25.6	23.3	18.5	15.9	17.6	20.7
.6	.5	1.1	Deferred Taxes	.0	1.2	.2	.7	1.0	2.8
5.6	8.4	6.2	All Other Non-Current	10.8	7.1	9.2	2.4	1.0	6.5
16.8	22.8	26.5	Net Worth	-5.5	24.5	28.4	36.7	36.7	33.9
100.0	100.0	100.0	Total Liabilities & Net Worth	100.0	100.0	100.0	100.0	100.0	100.0
			INCOME DATA						
100.0	100.0	100.0	Net Sales	100.0	100.0	100.0	100.0	100.0	100.0
			Gross Profit						
92.4	95.7	94.1	Operating Expenses	96.3	89.8	95.5	95.0	94.2	93.9
7.6	4.3	5.9	Operating Profit	3.7	10.2	4.5	5.0	5.8	6.1
2.6	1.3	1.5	All Other Expenses (net)	4.0	1.1	1.4	1.1	.7	1.1
5.1	3.0	4.4	Profit Before Taxes	-.3	9.2	3.1	3.9	5.1	5.0
			RATIOS						
1.7	1.7	1.9		1.4	3.1	2.4	3.0	1.8	1.7
1.2	1.1	1.1	Current	.9	1.1	1.3	1.2	1.1	1.1
.6	.7	.8		.5	.8	.9	.8	.8	1.0
1.4	1.5	1.6		1.3	2.9	2.4	2.3	1.6	1.5
.9	.9	.9	Quick	.6	1.0	1.1	1.0	.9	.8
.4	.5	.6		.3	.4	.8	.8	.7	.6
9 42.6	18 20.8	21 17.7		9 38.7	0 UND	14 25.2	30 12.2	25 14.7	25 14.7
31 11.8	33 11.2	39 9.5	Sales/Receivables	38 9.7	38 9.6	39 9.4	50 7.3	37 9.9	35 10.5
52 7.0	52 7.0	57 6.4		119 3.1	59 6.2	55 6.7	80 4.6	54 6.8	46 7.9
			Cost of Sales/Inventory						
			Cost of Sales/Payables						
10.9	12.3	11.9		14.8	11.3	11.2	9.2	9.7	14.2
48.0	56.0	66.4	Sales/Working Capital	-50.0	95.8	18.0	43.1	90.3	49.1
-16.6	-19.2	-38.5		-3.5	-35.6	-80.9	-25.6	-29.1	-154.8
8.8	12.2	12.3		4.3	9.4	18.1	22.9	12.9	10.3
(98) 2.7	(144) 2.7	(119) 4.4	EBIT/Interest	(13) 1.3	(17) 5.5	(22) 4.7	(17) 7.1	(21) 5.3	(29) 4.0
1.0	1.0	1.3		-.2	-.8	1.3	1.3	1.3	2.1
3.8	5.7	5.2							4.4
(19) 1.5	(34) 2.5	(31) 2.4	Net Profit + Depr., Dep., Amort./Cur. Mat. L/T/D						(12) 2.4
.6	1.3	1.1							1.2
.6	.6	.4		.1	.4	.3	.4	.2	.5
1.3	1.5	1.1	Fixed/Worth	3.9	1.6	1.1	1.0	1.1	1.3
21.3	14.6	3.9		-1.3	-3.6	6.4	2.1	2.5	3.1
1.2	1.5	1.2		1.9	.9	.4	1.1	1.0	1.8
3.0	3.3	2.7	Debt/Worth	-97.0	3.1	2.4	1.9	2.2	2.7
166.3	59.8	7.0		-2.9	-31.6	16.1	6.8	3.0	4.7
56.2	53.9	57.7		79.8	90.0	48.0	47.8	74.1	45.0
(91) 20.7	(125) 23.4	(114) 20.9	% Profit Before Taxes/Tangible Net Worth	(10) 16.7	(15) 29.8	(18) 11.0	(17) 34.6	(22) 29.5	(32) 20.1
5.4	4.3	8.5		-11.5	5.2	3.3	11.7	7.4	10.8
13.8	17.6	14.7		13.5	19.1	16.1	16.5	16.4	10.7
5.3	3.9	6.9	% Profit Before Taxes/Total Assets	1.8	9.1	6.4	7.8	8.9	5.6
.4	-.1	1.2		-3.4	-1.1	.5	1.6	1.4	2.4
39.8	32.9	46.7		UND	50.8	63.6	92.5	59.4	29.3
8.6	8.1	10.4	Sales/Net Fixed Assets	15.7	10.1	9.4	11.4	7.5	6.4
2.5	3.2	3.3		.9	3.4	4.1	5.9	5.0	2.2
4.9	4.3	4.2		3.5	4.3	4.0	5.6	4.4	3.9
2.5	2.9	2.8	Sales/Total Assets	1.6	2.8	3.1	3.4	3.1	2.0
1.3	1.6	1.4		.5	1.4	1.7	1.7	1.8	1.2
1.1	1.4	1.1		5.8	1.2	.6	.8	.4	1.1
(94) 3.4	(127) 4.0	(109) 3.6	% Depr., Dep., Amort./Sales	(11) 10.9	(14) 4.0	(22) 3.9	(16) 2.7	(20) 4.6	(26) 2.2
9.6	9.8	8.1		24.8	13.9	7.6	5.3	5.5	7.0
1.6	1.8	1.7				2.3			
(35) 3.3	(55) 3.1	(42) 3.0	% Officers', Directors', Owners' Comp/Sales		(11) 3.2				
5.6	5.8	5.9			5.5				
2811780M	3099768M	4379334M	Net Sales ($)	8649M	43483M	89474M	141398M	385440M	3710890M
1581152M	1428162M	2460249M	Total Assets ($)	9193M	31296M	58554M	61907M	170159M	2129140M

© RMA 2005   M = $ thousand   MM = $ million
See Pages 11 through 21 for Explanation of Ratios and Data

Current Data Sorted By Assets | **Comparative Historical Data**

Type of Statement	0-500M	500M-2MM	2-10MM	10-50MM	50-100MM	100-250MM	4/1/00-3/31/01	4/1/01-3/31/02
Unqualified		2	4	5	2	1	10	7
Reviewed	2	3	8				14	15
Compiled	3	4	7	2			17	17
Tax Returns	9	5	1				8	7
Other	6	11	12	7	1		27	33
	11 (4/1-9/30/04)			84 (10/1/04-3/31/05)			ALL	ALL

	0-500M	500M-2MM	2-10MM	10-50MM	50-100MM	100-250MM		ALL	ALL
NUMBER OF STATEMENTS	20	25	32	14	3	1		76	79
	%	%	%	%	%	%	**ASSETS**	%	%
	9.1	11.9	5.6	6.3			Cash & Equivalents	8.2	7.8
	41.6	38.7	42.0	29.2			Trade Receivables (net)	37.3	35.0
	.8	.1	1.1	1.7			Inventory	4.0	2.4
	7.3	6.1	6.2	5.3			All Other Current	2.5	4.0
	58.8	56.8	54.9	42.5			Total Current	52.1	49.1
	30.4	22.5	29.1	37.4			Fixed Assets (net)	32.3	33.6
	3.4	10.3	5.4	12.4			Intangibles (net)	8.3	7.6
	7.4	10.5	10.6	7.8			All Other Non-Current	7.4	9.8
	100.0	100.0	100.0	100.0			Total	100.0	100.0
							LIABILITIES		
	18.2	10.9	17.1	6.8			Notes Payable-Short Term	9.3	9.9
	11.1	5.8	5.2	6.6			Cur. Mat.-L/T/D	7.1	6.8
	12.2	7.4	15.3	11.4			Trade Payables	12.7	13.2
	.0	.3	.2	.1			Income Taxes Payable	.3	.2
	9.3	13.1	15.2	13.0			All Other Current	10.9	9.4
	50.7	37.4	53.0	37.9			Total Current	40.4	39.4
	27.2	16.6	13.5	20.5			Long-Term Debt	24.2	22.2
	.0	.0	.3	1.7			Deferred Taxes	.5	.5
	30.7	9.0	4.5	4.4			All Other Non-Current	4.8	5.6
	-8.7	37.0	28.6	35.6			Net Worth	30.0	32.3
	100.0	100.0	100.0	100.0			Total Liabilities & Net Worth	100.0	100.0
							INCOME DATA		
	100.0	100.0	100.0	100.0			Net Sales	100.0	100.0
							Gross Profit		
	98.7	95.9	96.1	95.0			Operating Expenses	95.3	97.8
	1.3	4.1	3.9	5.0			Operating Profit	4.7	2.2
	.5	.7	.9	1.3			All Other Expenses (net)	1.1	1.3
	.8	3.4	3.0	3.7			Profit Before Taxes	3.7	.9
							RATIOS		
	3.1	2.6	1.3	1.5				2.0	2.0
	1.1	1.5	1.0	1.0			Current	1.3	1.2
	.6	1.1	.7	.9				1.0	.9
	3.0	2.4	1.3	1.2				1.9	1.7
	1.1	1.4	.8	.9			Quick	1.1	1.0
	.4	1.0	.6	.7				.8	.7
	15 24.6	25 14.3	27 13.5	31 11.7				25 14.6	23 16.1
	25 14.6	34 10.8	36 10.0	41 8.9			Sales/Receivables	37 10.0	34 10.7
	31 11.8	40 9.1	47 7.7	50 7.4				45 8.1	43 8.5
							Cost of Sales/Inventory		
							Cost of Sales/Payables		
	28.8	11.8	26.4	17.9				13.1	14.8
	293.4	26.8	217.3	540.5			Sales/Working Capital	41.3	47.1
	-25.7	283.6	-36.7	-58.7				-130.3	-45.5
	7.1	8.9	11.3	10.0				6.4	6.5
	(15) 3.0	(22) 3.9	(30) 2.3	(13) 4.8			EBIT/Interest	(71) 1.6	(72) 1.8
	-.1	1.0	.8	2.2				.0	.1
							Net Profit + Depr., Dep.,	2.1	4.2
							Amort./Cur. Mat. L /T/D	(18) 1.6	(16) 2.3
								.9	1.1
	.8	.2	.4	.8				.7	.5
	-5.5	.6	1.7	2.1			Fixed/Worth	1.4	1.3
	-.5	1.8	7.1	3.2				11.9	10.5
	2.2	.8	1.4	1.9				1.2	.9
	-19.9	2.6	3.1	3.1			Debt/Worth	3.2	2.0
	-3.1	22.0	20.2	7.3				76.0	26.0
		57.6	70.1	73.2			% Profit Before Taxes/Tangible	60.8	43.5
	(20) 31.1	(27) 37.1	(12) 30.5				Net Worth	(58) 18.3	(64) 11.9
		12.4	3.3	10.3				-9.9	-3.7
	38.8	22.5	21.5	10.5			% Profit Before Taxes/Total	16.2	14.5
	6.1	9.4	5.1	6.9			Assets	2.9	3.7
	-8.9	.9	-.1	1.7				-5.1	-2.5
	75.4	66.2	80.3	33.4				51.0	46.0
	30.3	24.5	27.6	5.5			Sales/Net Fixed Assets	14.0	16.5
	11.1	13.4	8.0	2.7				5.8	6.5
	10.4	5.8	6.8	4.6				5.7	5.5
	7.2	4.4	4.8	2.1			Sales/Total Assets	3.9	3.7
	4.9	3.6	2.8	1.2				2.0	2.1
	.3	.5	.6	1.1				1.2	.6
	(19) 1.8	(16) 1.5	(26) 1.8	(13) 4.9			% Depr., Dep., Amort./Sales	(61) 3.0	(65) 2.2
	2.6	3.5	4.0	9.1				4.8	5.0
	3.0		3.2					3.1	2.7
	(14) 5.4		(14) 3.8				% Officers', Directors', Owners' Comp/Sales	(36) 4.5	(33) 5.3
	12.7		9.4					7.0	9.4
	37858M	132178M	636097M	863923M	503237M	208615M	Net Sales ($)	2265852M	1971786M
	5475M	27047M	137862M	298185M	250901M	104664M	Total Assets ($)	1172695M	881604M

M = $ thousand   MM = $ million
See Pages 11 through 21 for Explanation of Ratios and Data

Comparative Historical Data				Current Data Sorted By Sales					
			Type of Statement						
8	15	14	Unqualified		1	1	1	5	7
13	14	13	Reviewed	1	2	1	2	3	4
10	12	16	Compiled		2	3	3	7	1
15	15	15	Tax Returns	4	5	5		1	
19	20	37	Other		8	4	6	10	9
4/1/02- 3/31/03 ALL	4/1/03- 3/31/04 ALL	4/1/04- 3/31/05 ALL			11 (4/1-9/30/04)		84 (10/1/04-3/31/05)		
				0-1MM	1-3MM	3-5MM	5-10MM	10-25MM	25MM & OVER
65	76	95	**NUMBER OF STATEMENTS**	5	18	13	12	26	21
%	%	%	**ASSETS**	%	%	%	%	%	%
6.6	9.8	8.1	Cash & Equivalents		7.5	9.2	13.2	5.1	5.4
37.3	34.9	38.2	Trade Receivables (net)		28.8	48.9	38.4	38.7	39.4
1.9	1.9	.9	Inventory		.0	.2	.9	1.7	.4
5.0	5.2	6.1	All Other Current		8.3	4.4	2.6	6.3	6.5
50.8	51.8	53.3	Total Current		44.8	62.8	55.1	51.8	51.6
31.4	32.0	29.6	Fixed Assets (net)		33.9	29.4	24.0	31.5	28.5
6.7	7.9	7.6	Intangibles (net)		10.1	3.5	7.6	6.1	11.5
11.1	8.3	9.5	All Other Non-Current		11.2	4.2	13.3	10.5	8.4
100.0	100.0	100.0	Total		100.0	100.0	100.0	100.0	100.0
			LIABILITIES						
13.2	11.0	13.5	Notes Payable-Short Term		18.1	12.9	8.3	15.9	13.0
6.3	9.6	7.4	Cur. Mat.-L/T/D		12.4	9.0	4.3	6.6	6.2
15.4	11.7	11.7	Trade Payables		6.6	14.4	6.2	12.5	17.4
1.0	.3	.2	Income Taxes Payable		.0	.0	.9	.0	.1
11.5	15.3	12.8	All Other Current		10.1	12.1	10.8	16.1	13.2
47.3	48.0	45.6	Total Current		47.2	48.5	30.4	51.1	49.9
20.8	20.5	18.5	Long-Term Debt		20.4	25.2	12.4	15.2	12.5
.8	.7	.7	Deferred Taxes		.0	.0	.2	.7	2.4
6.1	6.2	11.1	All Other Non-Current		3.6	27.2	8.8	4.4	5.4
24.9	24.6	24.0	Net Worth		28.9	-.8	48.2	28.6	29.7
100.0	100.0	100.0	Total Liabilities & Net Worth		100.0	100.0	100.0	100.0	100.0
			INCOME DATA						
100.0	100.0	100.0	Net Sales		100.0	100.0	100.0	100.0	100.0
			Gross Profit						
96.2	95.7	96.6	Operating Expenses		95.6	98.6	93.8	95.7	97.9
3.8	4.3	3.4	Operating Profit		4.4	1.4	6.2	4.3	2.1
1.4	1.5	.8	All Other Expenses (net)		.8	.6	.9	.7	1.1
2.5	2.8	2.6	Profit Before Taxes		3.6	.7	5.3	3.6	1.0
			RATIOS						
1.6	1.8	1.9			1.9	2.1	4.3	1.4	1.4
1.2	1.1	1.2	Current		1.1	1.3	1.4	1.0	1.2
.7	.7	.8			.6	.8	.9	.8	.7
1.5	1.5	1.6			1.6	2.0	4.3	1.1	1.2
1.0	.9	1.0	Quick		1.1	1.2	1.4	.8	1.1
.6	.6	.7			.3	.7	.8	.7	.6
25 14.5	20 18.6	23 16.1		1 268.9	23 15.6	28 13.1	28 13.2	30 12.3	
34 10.6	33 11.2	34 10.8	Sales/Receivables	25 14.5	31 11.7	33 11.0	36 10.2	37 9.9	
45 8.1	42 8.6	41 8.9		32 11.4	38 9.7	41 8.8	46 8.0	47 7.8	
			Cost of Sales/Inventory						
			Cost of Sales/Payables						
17.5	18.1	18.1			16.3	18.6	8.2	27.4	23.0
62.3	98.0	70.3	Sales/Working Capital		293.4	52.1	28.4	NM	70.3
-21.6	-32.3	-38.5			-20.9	-74.0	NM	-42.5	-18.8
9.4	10.7	9.1			14.0	8.0		8.4	11.8
(60) 2.6	(68) 4.0	(84) 3.1	EBIT/Interest		(15) 3.8	(12) 2.0		2.7	(19) 3.1
.6	1.1	.9			1.1	-1.4		1.4	1.2
4.4	13.7	4.2	Net Profit + Depr., Dep.,						
(15) 2.5	(18) 5.2	(13) 2.7	Amort./Cur. Mat. L/T/D						
.5	1.4	.7							
.6	.5	.4			.4	.5	.1	.5	.6
1.5	1.4	1.7	Fixed/Worth		1.5	1.8	.5	1.8	2.7
-10.8	-12.6	33.1			-2.8	NM	6.4	3.2	NM
1.0	1.1	1.3			.5	2.0	.2	1.7	2.4
3.8	3.9	3.5	Debt/Worth		3.0	4.7	1.0	2.7	3.9
-13.6	-90.1	-45.4			-4.2	-6.0	7.9	10.8	NM
69.9	82.7	74.4	% Profit Before Taxes/Tangible		97.8			67.9	74.8
(46) 21.0	(55) 32.2	(71) 34.8	Net Worth		(11) 37.3	(10) 31.6		(23) 24.5	(16) 37.1
-1.4	6.1	10.7			27.2	2.8		7.0	13.8
17.3	17.9	19.6	% Profit Before Taxes/Total		24.4	22.4	34.8	14.2	11.5
6.0	8.3	6.9	Assets		13.7	.0	12.5	6.9	6.5
-1.1	.8	-.2			-.3	-16.1	-4.9	1.4	.6
55.1	49.1	60.4			31.5	174.7	59.8	70.0	72.6
14.6	18.6	24.5	Sales/Net Fixed Assets		17.7	19.4	36.4	21.3	25.3
8.0	5.8	7.4			9.6	14.7	10.4	3.0	5.5
5.5	6.0	6.9			7.9	8.7	4.9	6.7	6.1
4.1	4.6	4.6	Sales/Total Assets		4.6	6.6	4.0	4.5	4.6
2.6	2.7	2.8			3.4	4.0	2.8	1.9	2.2
1.0	.7	.7			1.5	.3		.5	.6
(57) 2.0	(63) 1.5	(76) 1.9	% Depr., Dep., Amort./Sales		(15) 2.4	(10) 1.1		(23) 2.3	(16) 1.6
4.9	4.8	4.1			3.5	3.6		5.5	4.8
2.9	1.6	3.0	% Officers', Directors',			2.6			
(36) 4.5	(36) 3.6	(39) 4.0	Owners' Comp/Sales			(10) 4.7			
6.7	6.0	6.9				5.7			
1736132M	2130664M	2381908M	Net Sales ($)	3504M	36872M	48921M	86381M	443437M	1762793M
886343M	959984M	824134M	Total Assets ($)	814M	8632M	10440M	25662M	157869M	620717M

© RMA 2005   M = $ thousand   MM = $ million
See Pages 11 through 21 for Explanation of Ratios and Data

Current Data Sorted By Assets | | | | | | | **Comparative Historical Data**

						Type of Statement		
1	3	9	15	10	4	Unqualified	28	27
4	8	23	7	1	1	Reviewed	44	44
13	17	22	4			Compiled	89	93
27	48	20	2			Tax Returns	36	42
12	38	38	15	4	1	Other	86	127
	46 (4/1-9/30/04)		301 (10/1/04-3/31/05)				4/1/00-3/31/01	4/1/01-3/31/02
0-500M	500M-2MM	2-10MM	10-50MM	50-100MM	100-250MM		ALL	ALL
57	114	112	43	15	6	**NUMBER OF STATEMENTS**	283	333
%	%	%	%	%	%	**ASSETS**	%	%
12.3	7.2	7.6	12.0	6.8		Cash & Equivalents	8.2	9.0
17.6	18.6	17.6	18.6	14.5		Trade Receivables (net)	18.3	17.5
4.6	1.6	1.7	.9	4.3		Inventory	1.6	2.3
3.3	2.3	3.0	3.2	1.4		All Other Current	2.9	4.1
37.8	29.7	29.9	34.7	27.0		Total Current	31.0	33.0
42.8	61.0	56.5	51.1	65.5		Fixed Assets (net)	56.9	54.8
3.3	1.5	3.6	4.3	.5		Intangibles (net)	3.2	3.1
16.0	7.8	10.0	9.9	7.0		All Other Non-Current	8.8	9.2
100.0	100.0	100.0	100.0	100.0		Total	100.0	100.0
						LIABILITIES		
7.5	7.8	6.1	2.6	9.7		Notes Payable-Short Term	5.9	7.3
6.3	4.4	4.4	5.1	4.1		Cur. Mat.-L/T/D	5.9	4.1
16.6	6.5	7.3	6.7	5.8		Trade Payables	6.4	7.5
.0	.2	.2	.6	.1		Income Taxes Payable	.2	.2
30.3	8.6	7.4	7.3	5.1		All Other Current	12.1	11.0
60.7	27.5	25.4	22.4	24.8		Total Current	30.6	30.1
41.5	46.6	39.5	37.7	41.7		Long-Term Debt	39.9	45.1
.0	.0	.6	.9	2.0		Deferred Taxes	.4	.2
4.7	2.9	4.9	3.7	2.0		All Other Non-Current	5.4	5.4
-7.0	23.0	29.6	35.3	29.4		Net Worth	23.8	19.2
100.0	100.0	100.0	100.0	100.0		Total Liabilities & Net Worth	100.0	100.0
						INCOME DATA		
100.0	100.0	100.0	100.0	100.0		Net Sales	100.0	100.0
						Gross Profit		
91.3	74.4	81.9	88.4	88.7		Operating Expenses	83.0	82.6
8.7	25.6	18.1	11.6	11.3		Operating Profit	17.0	17.4
5.2	10.9	9.9	5.5	3.6		All Other Expenses (net)	8.8	9.8
3.5	14.7	8.2	6.1	7.7		Profit Before Taxes	8.2	7.6
						RATIOS		
1.9	2.1	2.2	2.3	1.5		Current	2.0	2.0
.8	1.0	1.2	1.3	1.1			1.1	1.1
.4	.3	.4	.8	.9			.6	.6
1.3	1.6	1.7	2.2	1.2		Quick	1.8	1.7
.7	.9	.8	1.1	.9			(282) 1.0	(332) .8
.3	.2	.4	.7	.7			.4	.4
0 UND	0 UND	1 250.0	32 11.4	35 10.5		Sales/Receivables	5 75.4	0 UND
9 42.6	7 55.8	31 11.8	44 8.4	40 9.2			32 11.6	27 13.5
33 11.1	42 8.8	48 7.6	58 6.3	66 5.5			47 7.7	46 7.9
						Cost of Sales/Inventory		
						Cost of Sales/Payables		
24.9	10.9	9.1	5.0	10.8		Sales/Working Capital	11.8	10.3
-74.2	237.7	38.5	23.4	75.5			103.7	89.5
-7.4	-5.1	-7.6	-24.3	-47.8			-10.9	-11.2
9.1	8.8	9.1	8.3	4.7		EBIT/Interest	7.0	5.3
(37) 1.7	(72) 3.8	(86) 3.6	(37) 3.5	(14) 2.5			(192) 2.9	(228) 2.5
-1.8	2.1	1.4	1.5	2.3			1.4	1.2
		7.0	4.0			Net Profit + Depr., Dep., Amort./Cur. Mat. L/T/D	3.5	5.5
	(21) 2.4	(17) 1.4					(57) 1.8	(46) 1.9
		1.1	.8				1.1	1.0
.4	.7	.7	.6	1.4		Fixed/Worth	.7	.8
3.8	2.9	2.4	1.9	2.8			2.5	2.4
-2.6	20.2	15.1	5.4	3.0			11.9	11.5
1.4	1.3	.8	.8	1.5		Debt/Worth	1.0	1.3
7.1	3.9	3.4	3.1	2.9			2.9	3.4
-3.7	31.5	21.1	7.1	3.7			17.9	20.9
97.0	61.5	45.3	35.6	31.3		% Profit Before Taxes/Tangible Net Worth	49.2	54.2
(35) 36.1	(91) 26.8	(93) 18.2	(37) 20.5	23.3			(227) 20.7	(265) 20.9
6.6	9.2	4.0	7.6	16.9			7.3	4.3
19.2	16.0	10.7	9.6	7.6		% Profit Before Taxes/Total Assets	12.0	12.4
4.6	6.9	4.5	5.2	6.6			5.2	4.3
-6.0	1.9	.6	.6	4.9			1.0	.3
46.7	12.1	11.0	6.4	1.9		Sales/Net Fixed Assets	9.9	12.7
12.5	.7	1.6	2.6	1.2			2.3	2.5
3.6	.2	.3	.6	.7			.4	.4
5.7	2.9	2.4	1.7	1.5		Sales/Total Assets	2.7	2.8
2.9	.5	1.0	1.0	.8			1.2	1.2
1.3	.2	.3	.4	.5			.4	.3
1.3	2.2	2.4	2.8	3.2		% Depr., Dep., Amort./Sales	2.0	1.9
(42) 3.6	(105) 7.8	(101) 7.0	(41) 4.7	(13) 6.0			(261) 5.4	(299) 5.0
9.1	15.0	12.9	9.1	10.8			11.6	11.6
6.2	3.0	1.9				% Officers', Directors', Owners' Comp/Sales	3.0	2.8
(23) 8.5	(29) 5.3	(29) 4.3					(85) 6.0	(96) 7.2
16.9	10.6	9.5					10.1	13.3
56396M	221302M	762263M	1082766M	2401682M	733305M	Net Sales ($)	3933204M	4127997M
16762M	129932M	524504M	868493M	1010091M	795541M	Total Assets ($)	2662078M	3123130M

M = $ thousand   MM = $ million
See Pages 11 through 21 for Explanation of Ratios and Data

Comparative Historical Data | | Current Data Sorted By Sales

			Type of Statement						
26	30	42	Unqualified	3	2	1	5	9	22
61	54	44	Reviewed	3	10	7	10	10	4
68	108	56	Compiled	18	16	6	9	7	
60	66	97	Tax Returns	73	14	7	3		
118	126	108	Other	32	24	8	13	22	9
4/1/02-3/31/03	4/1/03-3/31/04	4/1/04-3/31/05		46 (4/1-9/30/04)			301 (10/1/04-3/31/05)		
ALL	ALL	ALL		0-1MM	1-3MM	3-5MM	5-10MM	10-25MM	25MM & OVER
333	384	347	**NUMBER OF STATEMENTS**	129	66	29	40	48	35
%	%	%	**ASSETS**	%	%	%	%	%	%
8.4	9.6	8.7	Cash & Equivalents	6.3	10.6	10.3	11.3	11.1	6.6
16.3	17.9	17.9	Trade Receivables (net)	3.9	20.1	30.6	28.5	29.2	27.2
2.0	2.3	2.2	Inventory	1.3	2.6	3.6	.9	3.2	3.5
2.3	4.3	2.7	All Other Current	.7	5.3	2.7	2.7	4.8	2.6
29.0	34.0	31.5	Total Current	12.2	38.6	47.1	43.5	48.2	39.8
60.5	54.7	55.5	Fixed Assets (net)	76.7	46.2	39.1	43.4	37.9	46.5
2.5	3.0	2.8	Intangibles (net)	2.4	2.2	2.1	4.2	3.3	4.1
8.0	8.4	10.1	All Other Non-Current	8.7	13.0	11.7	8.9	10.5	9.6
100.0	100.0	100.0	Total	100.0	100.0	100.0	100.0	100.0	100.0
			LIABILITIES						
5.0	5.8	6.6	Notes Payable-Short Term	6.5	6.7	4.6	5.5	7.5	8.7
5.0	4.7	4.7	Cur. Mat.-L/T/D	5.6	4.3	3.9	4.3	4.0	4.4
6.6	7.3	8.4	Trade Payables	5.0	8.0	12.2	8.1	14.4	10.3
.2	.1	.2	Income Taxes Payable	.0	.2	.2	.6	.0	.8
9.9	10.7	11.4	All Other Current	11.8	10.7	15.0	7.2	14.3	9.4
26.6	28.7	31.4	Total Current	29.0	29.9	35.8	25.7	40.2	33.6
42.5	37.6	42.1	Long-Term Debt	63.4	36.9	26.2	27.5	23.1	28.8
.3	.3	.4	Deferred Taxes	.0	.0	1.2	.9	.7	1.1
5.2	7.0	3.9	All Other Non-Current	3.0	3.1	2.5	2.5	8.0	2.8
25.3	26.4	22.3	Net Worth	4.6	30.1	34.3	40.8	28.0	33.6
100.0	100.0	100.0	Total Liabilities & Net Worth	100.0	100.0	100.0	100.0	100.0	100.0
			INCOME DATA						
100.0	100.0	100.0	Net Sales	100.0	100.0	100.0	100.0	100.0	100.0
			Gross Profit						
81.2	84.1	82.2	Operating Expenses	67.7	85.3	91.9	91.5	94.8	93.9
18.8	15.9	17.8	Operating Profit	32.3	14.7	8.1	8.5	5.2	6.1
10.0	8.0	8.6	All Other Expenses (net)	18.0	6.5	1.0	2.6	1.2	1.0
8.8	7.9	9.2	Profit Before Taxes	14.3	8.2	7.1	5.9	3.9	5.1
			RATIOS						
2.4	2.4	2.1		1.4	2.3	3.4	2.3	2.2	1.6
1.1	1.2	1.1	Current	.5	1.3	1.4	1.5	1.2	1.1
.5	.6	.5		.1	.7	.9	1.0	.8	.9
1.8	1.8	1.6		1.2	2.0	2.4	2.3	1.6	1.3
1.0	.9	.9	Quick	.4	1.1	1.2	1.3	.9	1.0
.3	.4	.4		.1	.5	.7	.8	.6	.8
0 UND	2 201.5	0 UND		0 UND	6 56.7	22 16.4	30 12.1	34 10.8	36 10.0
26 14.0	26 13.8	29 12.7	Sales/Receivables	0 UND	32 11.5	39 9.4	42 8.7	41 8.8	44 8.3
43 8.4	44 8.2	46 7.9		6 56.3	46 7.9	48 7.6	65 5.7	51 7.2	62 5.9
			Cost of Sales/Inventory						
			Cost of Sales/Payables						
9.1	9.1	10.2		38.9	7.1	10.3	8.0	9.2	7.6
48.3	42.5	75.5	Sales/Working Capital	-8.2	24.0	26.6	17.8	29.8	75.5
-9.3	-11.3	-8.4		-2.7	-23.7	-108.5	767.1	-21.4	-66.4
6.2	7.8	8.8		4.3	11.8	10.7	12.2	40.3	9.5
(223) 3.1	(273) 2.9	(250) 3.5	EBIT/Interest	(65) 2.9	(47) 2.9	(26) 4.1	(36) 3.6	(43) 3.8	(33) 4.1
1.2	1.1	1.5		1.6	1.4	1.6	1.4	1.3	2.3
5.4	6.5	4.8						5.6	14.4
(59) 2.4	(54) 2.2	(54) 2.0	Net Profit + Depr., Dep., Amort./Cur. Mat. L/T/D				(10) 1.4	(18) 3.7
1.3	1.1	1.0						.8	1.4
.8	.7	.7		2.8	.4	.6	.3	.6	1.0
2.3	2.4	2.6	Fixed/Worth	9.8	1.7	1.2	.9	1.4	1.9
11.8	16.5	19.2		-10.3	9.0	3.8	3.3	4.6	3.0
1.1	1.0	1.0		2.4	.6	.7	.6	1.0	1.4
2.6	3.1	3.6	Debt/Worth	10.5	1.8	1.7	2.0	3.1	3.6
28.8	30.2	30.5		-11.1	30.6	6.6	3.4	9.5	5.6
45.8	52.2	48.6		49.3	67.8	67.9	53.3	34.0	44.4
(267) 19.1	(303) 21.5	(277) 23.5	% Profit Before Taxes/Tangible Net Worth	(85) 24.0	(55) 19.1	(26) 33.9	(36) 18.9	(41) 20.5	(34) 25.7
3.1	3.3	8.1		8.3	6.1	7.6	4.6	3.3	16.5
12.5	12.1	12.3		11.0	13.7	18.1	12.4	11.6	10.9
5.0	4.4	5.5	% Profit Before Taxes/Total Assets	3.7	6.8	12.3	5.9	4.5	7.1
.3	.1	1.3		.5	1.7	1.9	1.2	.5	4.1
9.8	14.1	12.5		.9	25.6	27.3	13.2	14.8	14.8
1.7	2.6	2.4	Sales/Net Fixed Assets	.3	6.5	7.3	5.4	8.8	4.1
.3	.4	.4		.2	.7	2.3	1.3	2.2	1.5
2.9	3.0	2.9		.7	3.9	4.2	2.9	4.2	3.3
1.0	1.2	1.1	Sales/Total Assets	.3	2.1	2.8	1.9	2.2	1.7
.3	.3	.3		.2	.4	1.1	.8	1.1	.9
2.8	2.2	2.2		8.3	1.8	1.4	2.2	1.6	1.9
(294) 5.4	(329) 5.4	(308) 6.0	% Depr., Dep., Amort./Sales	(113) 13.6	(60) 3.9	(27) 1.9	(36) 4.9	(40) 3.5	(32) 3.0
13.5	12.9	13.3		21.2	10.4	4.8	9.1	5.8	4.2
2.5	2.0	2.6		8.4	3.9	2.5	2.2	1.2	
(98) 6.1	(99) 5.2	(92) 6.3	% Officers', Directors', Owners' Comp/Sales	(24) 11.7	(23) 7.6	(14) 4.3	(12) 3.4	(10) 2.1	
11.9		10.0	11.3	14.7	14.8	10.9	8.5	14.4	
4510483M	5285461M	5257714M	Net Sales ($)	53814M	126794M	110012M	293981M	760859M	3912254M
3180936M	4040969M	3345323M	Total Assets ($)	188746M	194409M	79896M	337679M	791992M	1752601M

© RMA 2005   M = $ thousand   MM = $ million
See Pages 11 through 21 for Explanation of Ratios and Data

Current Data Sorted By Assets | **Comparative Historical Data**

Type of Statement

	0-500M	500M-2MM	2-10MM	10-50MM	50-100MM	100-250MM		4/1/00-3/31/01 ALL	4/1/01-3/31/02 ALL
Unqualified		1	6	9		4		19	14
Reviewed		1	11	6	4			12	16
Compiled	2	5	10	2		1		18	22
Tax Returns		3						3	3
Other	1	4	10	3		4		24	24
	12 (4/1-9/30/04)			75 (10/1/04-3/31/05)					
NUMBER OF STATEMENTS	3	14	37	20	4	9		76	79

Data columns below are %, with values present for 500M-2MM, 2-10MM, and 10-50MM.

0-500M	500M-2MM	2-10MM	10-50MM	50-100MM	100-250MM	ITEM	4/1/00-3/31/01 ALL	4/1/01-3/31/02 ALL
%	%	%	%	%	%	**ASSETS**	%	%
	10.5	9.3	8.0			Cash & Equivalents	8.3	7.0
	12.2	19.5	7.0			Trade Receivables (net)	12.4	13.3
	.7	3.5	.5			Inventory	2.1	1.7
	2.9	2.3	5.8			All Other Current	2.0	2.8
	26.4	34.6	21.2			Total Current	24.7	25.0
	63.2	59.8	68.6			Fixed Assets (net)	64.2	64.7
	.8	1.8	.3			Intangibles (net)	3.2	2.0
	9.6	3.9	10.0			All Other Non-Current	7.9	8.3
	100.0	100.0	100.0			Total	100.0	100.0
						LIABILITIES		
	5.2	5.6	8.9			Notes Payable-Short Term	3.7	4.6
	13.9	6.4	3.6			Cur. Mat.-L/T/D	5.3	5.8
	7.5	8.8	2.9			Trade Payables	6.2	5.3
	.2	.0	.8			Income Taxes Payable	.3	.1
	5.0	8.0	2.9			All Other Current	5.8	6.6
	31.8	29.0	19.2			Total Current	21.3	22.4
	29.7	39.8	44.5			Long-Term Debt	41.9	39.6
	.2	.3	.5			Deferred Taxes	.6	.9
	6.8	2.2	4.9			All Other Non-Current	4.8	2.2
	31.5	28.8	30.9			Net Worth	31.5	34.9
	100.0	100.0	100.0			Total Liabilities & Net Worth	100.0	100.0
						INCOME DATA		
	100.0	100.0	100.0			Net Sales	100.0	100.0
						Gross Profit		
	84.3	87.7	83.5			Operating Expenses	85.2	86.0
	15.7	12.3	16.5			Operating Profit	14.8	14.0
	3.4	5.0	7.3			All Other Expenses (net)	6.0	6.7
	12.3	7.3	9.2			Profit Before Taxes	8.7	7.3
						RATIOS		
	2.2	2.8	2.1			Current	2.0	1.9
	.9	1.2	1.3				1.1	1.3
	.1	.8	.6				.6	.7
	1.9	2.3	1.6			Quick	1.7	1.6
	.6	1.1	1.0				1.0	.9
	.1	.5	.4				.5	.5
	0 UND	20 18.1	26 13.8			Sales/Receivables	22 16.4	23 15.5
	18 20.4	30 12.1	37 9.9				36 10.2	37 9.8
	38 9.7	46 8.0	47 7.7				48 7.6	48 7.6
						Cost of Sales/Inventory		
						Cost of Sales/Payables		
	3.9	8.1	5.6			Sales/Working Capital	8.6	9.1
	NM	29.0	18.9				44.3	34.0
	-7.8	-23.8	-11.1				-12.1	-15.5
	8.9	9.7	3.2			EBIT/Interest	3.5	3.9
	(10) 2.1	(35) 2.9	(17) 2.6				(61) 2.4	(65) 1.9
	-.5	1.4	1.7				1.3	1.0
						Net Profit + Depr., Dep., Amort./Cur. Mat. L /T/D	4.7	2.8
							(17) 2.2	(23) 1.7
							1.1	.9
	.7	.8	1.5			Fixed/Worth	1.2	.9
	2.0	1.9	2.1				2.4	2.4
	18.2	8.8	3.7				8.0	4.4
	.9	1.2	1.6			Debt/Worth	1.2	.9
	1.8	2.6	2.3				2.5	2.2
	21.9	10.1	3.7				7.6	4.9
	34.4	46.2	23.3			% Profit Before Taxes/Tangible Net Worth	39.2	28.3
	(12) 8.3	(32) 18.5	(19) 10.9				(65) 22.3	(72) 11.8
	-10.0	5.2	4.9				4.6	1.4
	8.1	13.3	6.0			% Profit Before Taxes/Total Assets	10.9	8.8
	4.0	5.5	2.8				5.1	3.9
	-1.9	1.1	1.6				1.2	.0
	4.7	8.3	1.0			Sales/Net Fixed Assets	2.7	3.9
	2.6	1.3	.7				1.1	1.1
	.2	.9	.4				.5	.5
	3.5	3.1	.8			Sales/Total Assets	1.5	1.6
	1.1	1.0	.5				.7	.7
	.2	.6	.3				.4	.4
	2.5	3.4	7.2			% Depr., Dep., Amort./Sales	2.6	3.5
	12.6	(33) 8.1	(19) 11.1				(67) 6.6	(75) 7.2
	23.1	13.8	13.3				11.2	14.1
		1.3				% Officers', Directors', Owners' Comp/Sales	2.7	2.0
		(11) 5.0					(18) 5.7	(20) 6.3
		7.0					9.6	18.9
4519M	37196M	338985M	272260M	105884M	1958489M	Net Sales ($)	2356701M	988570M
815M	20532M	183073M	459491M	277794M	1363167M	Total Assets ($)	1307986M	1108549M

M = $ thousand   MM = $ million
See Pages 11 through 21 for Explanation of Ratios and Data

	Comparative Historical Data			Type of Statement	**Current Data Sorted By Sales**					
	18	25	24	Unqualified			4	8	5	7
	24	20	18	Reviewed		3	2	4	7	2
	24	34	20	Compiled	3	6	1	5	2	3
	6	8	3	Tax Returns	1			1	1	
	27	39	22	Other	4	7	2	2	2	5
	4/1/02-3/31/03	4/1/03-3/31/04	4/1/04-3/31/05		12 (4/1-9/30/04)			75 (10/1/04-3/31/05)		
	ALL	ALL	ALL		0-1MM	1-3MM	3-5MM	5-10MM	10-25MM	25MM & OVER
NUMBER OF STATEMENTS	99	126	87		8	16	9	20	17	17
ASSETS	%	%	%		%	%	%	%	%	%
Cash & Equivalents	7.1	6.8	8.6			13.2		5.8	13.9	7.0
Trade Receivables (net)	14.9	13.8	15.6			16.0		14.6	20.7	22.6
Inventory	2.6	2.4	2.5			.0		2.4	1.7	7.4
All Other Current	3.4	5.1	3.6			2.0		4.0	3.1	6.9
Total Current	28.0	28.1	30.3			31.2		26.9	39.4	43.9
Fixed Assets (net)	61.3	63.9	62.2			63.9		66.4	54.1	47.1
Intangibles (net)	3.4	2.9	1.2			1.1		1.8	.8	1.8
All Other Non-Current	7.3	5.0	6.3			3.8		4.9	5.7	7.2
Total	100.0	100.0	100.0			100.0		100.0	100.0	100.0
LIABILITIES										
Notes Payable-Short Term	5.1	4.1	7.5			10.3		9.7	5.1	10.3
Cur. Mat.-L/T/D	5.4	4.6	6.2			5.7		10.2	3.3	1.5
Trade Payables	6.9	5.3	6.8			3.0		5.4	10.7	12.7
Income Taxes Payable	.1	.2	.3			.2		.0	.1	1.1
All Other Current	9.6	7.7	6.0			6.3		4.0	8.0	6.9
Total Current	27.2	21.8	26.8			25.6		29.3	27.2	32.4
Long-Term Debt	38.5	39.1	39.0			55.0		33.9	33.3	29.6
Deferred Taxes	.7	.5	.5			.2		.7	.5	1.2
All Other Non-Current	3.9	5.4	3.5			2.4		3.0	3.8	3.1
Net Worth	29.7	33.2	30.0			16.8		33.0	35.2	33.7
Total Liabilities & Net Worth	100.0	100.0	100.0			100.0		100.0	100.0	100.0
INCOME DATA										
Net Sales	100.0	100.0	100.0			100.0		100.0	100.0	100.0
Gross Profit										
Operating Expenses	84.4	89.8	85.6			83.4		86.0	93.7	86.9
Operating Profit	15.6	10.2	14.4			16.6		14.0	6.3	13.1
All Other Expenses (net)	7.9	5.9	5.7			6.0		4.8	2.4	5.8
Profit Before Taxes	7.7	4.2	8.7			10.6		9.1	4.0	7.3
RATIOS										
Current	2.5	2.3	2.2			2.9		3.0	2.2	1.9
	1.2	1.3	1.3			2.0		1.1	1.4	1.3
	.7	.7	.6			.7		.1	1.0	1.1
Quick	1.8	1.8	1.8			2.6		1.7	2.0	1.4
	.9	.9	1.0			1.7		.6	1.3	.9
	.6	.5	.4			.6		.1	.8	.4
Sales/Receivables	21 17.1	26 14.1	19 18.8			23 16.2	7 55.2	30 12.2		20 18.1
	35 10.3	36 10.2	33 11.1			30 12.2	35 10.4	36 10.2		44 8.2
	48 7.7	51 7.1	48 7.6			48 7.5	47 7.7	49 7.5		51 7.2
Cost of Sales/Inventory										
Cost of Sales/Payables										
Sales/Working Capital	9.5	7.6	6.2			3.2		6.6	9.3	7.7
	45.9	32.3	22.4			14.5		NM	15.3	21.1
	-13.6	-20.1	-12.9			-16.0		-6.2	NM	98.5
EBIT/Interest	5.9	5.1	5.1			3.0		13.0	3.8	16.9
	(81) 2.3	(105) 2.5	(76) 2.7			2.1	(17)	3.7	2.4	(15) 3.5
	1.1	1.3	1.6			.8		1.6	1.5	2.2
Net Profit + Depr., Dep., Amort./Cur. Mat. L/T/D	3.2	3.3	4.0							
	(25) 2.5	(28) 2.3	(19) 3.2							
	1.7	1.7	2.1							
Fixed/Worth	1.1	1.1	.9			1.0		.8	.7	.5
	2.6	2.3	2.0			5.6		2.1	1.7	1.9
	6.5	6.7	4.7			NM		8.1	2.9	3.1
Debt/Worth	.9	1.1	1.3			1.7		1.0	1.3	2.0
	2.7	2.2	2.5			10.9		2.3	2.1	2.8
	7.3	9.5	6.5			-27.9		10.7	4.4	3.9
% Profit Before Taxes/Tangible Net Worth	29.4	31.0	26.4			48.4		41.7	20.5	30.6
	(83) 17.4	(107) 12.1	(78) 15.6			(11) 8.1	(18)	16.7	8.6	20.5
	4.3	3.5	4.7			-10.8		3.6	4.8	15.0
% Profit Before Taxes/Total Assets	11.5	7.7	7.5			10.4		11.8	6.6	11.7
	4.7	3.7	3.6			1.6		5.3	2.9	5.6
	.2	.4	1.0			-1.4		1.3	1.7	2.9
Sales/Net Fixed Assets	4.3	4.6	5.3			2.7		3.5	17.0	51.6
	1.3	1.2	1.0			1.0		1.4	1.0	5.2
	.6	.5	.5			.5		.9	.6	.7
Sales/Total Assets	2.2	2.0	2.3			1.4		2.1	3.6	3.2
	.8	.8	.8			.6		1.1	.8	2.1
	.4	.4	.4			.4		.7	.5	.5
% Depr., Dep., Amort./Sales	4.1	4.3	2.9			10.2		4.8	2.2	.9
	(94) 8.1	(116) 8.9	(80) 10.6			(14) 14.0	(18)	8.8	(15) 7.0	(16) 2.5
	13.4	13.4	15.1			22.0		12.8	11.1	10.3
% Officers', Directors', Owners' Comp/Sales	3.1	3.1	3.2							
	(26) 4.1	(40) 4.7	(21) 4.3							
	10.5	9.2	6.5							
Net Sales ($)	2088507M	2401727M	2717333M		2423M	29252M	36122M	135054M	268042M	2246440M
Total Assets ($)	1932700M	2504425M	2304872M		12350M	59368M	86191M	216865M	337046M	1593052M

M = $ thousand   MM = $ million
See Pages 11 through 21 for Explanation of Ratios and Data

Current Data Sorted By Assets   Comparative Historical Data

0-500M	500M-2MM	2-10MM	10-50MM	50-100MM	100-250MM	Type of Statement	4/1/00-3/31/01 ALL	4/1/01-3/31/02 ALL
	7	7	11	1	3	Unqualified	19	19
1	8	11	1			Reviewed	17	13
	3	3	2			Compiled	13	9
4	3					Tax Returns	2	1
		4	4			Other	12	11
	43 (4/1-9/30/04)		30 (10/1/04-3/31/05)					
5	21	25	18	1	3	**NUMBER OF STATEMENTS**	63	53
%	%	%	%	%	%	**ASSETS**	%	%
	15.1	11.6	9.8			Cash & Equivalents	8.7	8.7
	15.7	11.3	12.3			Trade Receivables (net)	17.1	16.7
	16.0	18.7	26.4			Inventory	18.6	21.4
	6.9	5.6	8.6			All Other Current	4.1	5.9
	53.7	47.2	57.0			Total Current	48.6	52.6
	35.4	48.0	34.3			Fixed Assets (net)	43.1	37.7
	1.8	.2	.1			Intangibles (net)	.9	1.8
	9.1	4.6	8.5			All Other Non-Current	7.5	7.9
	100.0	100.0	100.0			Total	100.0	100.0
						LIABILITIES		
	21.0	10.5	14.7			Notes Payable-Short Term	16.5	15.6
	4.0	2.1	5.3			Cur. Mat.-L/T/D	3.4	2.7
	6.8	9.2	11.1			Trade Payables	11.0	11.7
	.1	.2	.1			Income Taxes Payable	.1	.1
	10.7	13.4	12.8			All Other Current	7.9	9.5
	42.5	35.5	44.0			Total Current	38.9	39.6
	9.8	19.5	15.5			Long-Term Debt	20.6	16.8
	.8	1.5	.8			Deferred Taxes	.5	.7
	1.8	.3	3.1			All Other Non-Current	1.2	2.3
	45.1	43.2	36.5			Net Worth	38.8	40.5
	100.0	100.0	100.0			Total Liabilities & Net Worth	100.0	100.0
						INCOME DATA		
	100.0	100.0	100.0			Net Sales	100.0	100.0
						Gross Profit		
	91.2	91.0	97.5			Operating Expenses	92.1	88.3
	8.8	9.0	2.5			Operating Profit	7.9	11.7
	.3	.7	-.1			All Other Expenses (net)	3.2	2.2
	8.5	8.3	2.6			Profit Before Taxes	4.7	9.5
						RATIOS		
	2.4	2.4	1.6				2.0	2.1
	1.2	1.2	1.2			Current	1.2	1.3
	1.0	1.0	1.1				.9	1.0
	1.8	1.5	1.2				1.3	1.7
	.7	.6	.3			Quick	.6	.5
	.3	.2	.2				.2	.2
	5 76.6	5 72.1	5 70.4				7 54.8	9 42.6
	10 35.0	13 28.5	10 36.0			Sales/Receivables	18 19.8	25 14.8
	27 13.6	33 11.0	34 10.6				46 8.0	48 7.6
						Cost of Sales/Inventory		
						Cost of Sales/Payables		
	8.3	8.6	11.5				11.0	8.9
	27.2	21.9	32.6			Sales/Working Capital	21.5	18.3
	NM	NM	141.6				-52.3	-153.8
	4.0	20.9	6.0				3.7	4.9
	(18) 2.4	4.3	(17) 1.8			EBIT/Interest	(54) 1.6	(49) 2.2
	.8	2.5	.3				.9	1.2
						Net Profit + Depr., Dep.,	6.7	11.6
						Amort./Cur. Mat. L./T/D	(16) 3.0	(17) 5.4
							1.2	2.7
	.4	.7	.6				.4	.5
	.7	1.1	.7			Fixed/Worth	1.2	.8
	1.6	2.1	1.3				2.2	1.7
	.5	.4	1.3				.6	.7
	1.2	1.2	2.0			Debt/Worth	2.0	1.6
	3.2	4.2	3.8				5.0	5.0
	21.0	24.8	18.7			% Profit Before Taxes/Tangible	26.0	22.2
	(20) 8.4	(24) 18.1	(17) 6.1			Net Worth	(60) 16.1	(49) 11.1
	.7	7.3	-.6				.2	1.7
	10.7	12.1	8.6			% Profit Before Taxes/Total	10.5	9.8
	3.2	7.1	1.4			Assets	3.4	4.1
	.0	2.0	-1.6				.0	1.1
	27.0	11.5	18.5				12.7	16.0
	17.5	5.7	10.9			Sales/Net Fixed Assets	5.5	5.7
	5.6	1.3	5.0				1.6	2.0
	5.0	3.4	4.5				3.0	3.3
	3.3	2.4	3.3			Sales/Total Assets	2.0	2.0
	1.8	.7	1.1				.9	.9
	.9	1.0	.9				1.2	1.0
	(20) 1.5	(24) 1.8	(17) 1.2			% Depr., Dep., Amort./Sales	(61) 2.4	(51) 1.9
	2.2	4.5	2.5				6.0	4.0
						% Officers', Directors',	2.1	.6
						Owners' Comp/Sales	(15) 4.1	(14) 2.4
							6.8	6.5
2944M	109439M	279702M	958927M	133489M	1818970M	Net Sales ($)	2289660M	660159M
1126M	25204M	119342M	298701M	61766M	554376M	Total Assets ($)	684424M	447097M

M = $ thousand   MM = $ million
See Pages 11 through 21 for Explanation of Ratios and Data

Comparative Historical Data			Type of Statement	Current Data Sorted By Sales					
29	27	29	Unqualified		4	1	4	5	15
22	26	21	Reviewed	3	3	2	10	2	1
11	14	8	Compiled	1		1	3	2	1
5	9	7	Tax Returns	4	2	1			
18	9	8	Other		1		1	3	3
4/1/02-3/31/03	4/1/03-3/31/04	4/1/04-3/31/05		43 (4/1-9/30/04)			30 (10/1/04-3/31/05)		
ALL	ALL	ALL		0-1MM	1-3MM	3-5MM	5-10MM	10-25MM	25MM & OVER
85	85	73	NUMBER OF STATEMENTS	8	10	5	18	12	20
%	%	%	ASSETS	%	%	%	%	%	%
7.3	8.8	11.9	Cash & Equivalents		6.1		15.4	15.6	8.1
17.3	15.1	13.4	Trade Receivables (net)		12.8		16.0	8.6	15.5
20.0	20.0	21.0	Inventory		17.0		19.1	21.5	35.2
6.5	6.1	7.8	All Other Current		7.2		8.1	5.7	8.0
51.1	49.9	54.1	Total Current		43.2		58.6	51.4	66.8
40.9	43.1	38.6	Fixed Assets (net)		46.3		34.9	41.8	26.0
1.3	1.3	.6	Intangibles (net)		.1		.0	.1	.1
6.7	5.7	6.8	All Other Non-Current		10.4		6.5	6.7	7.0
100.0	100.0	100.0	Total		100.0		100.0	100.0	100.0
			LIABILITIES						
13.9	16.1	16.3	Notes Payable-Short Term		19.5		22.4	7.9	21.4
4.1	5.1	3.8	Cur. Mat.-L/T/D		2.7		3.2	1.3	3.9
10.1	10.1	8.1	Trade Payables		2.9		9.6	10.9	10.8
.2	.2	.1	Income Taxes Payable		.3		.1	.3	.1
9.4	11.4	12.0	All Other Current		8.4		10.0	21.1	14.2
37.7	42.9	40.3	Total Current		33.8		45.2	41.6	50.4
17.4	17.2	14.4	Long-Term Debt		13.0		14.7	16.3	8.0
.8	.8	1.0	Deferred Taxes		1.3		.7	2.3	.6
1.6	2.7	1.4	All Other Non-Current		2.2		3.6	.2	.7
42.4	36.5	42.9	Net Worth		49.6		35.8	39.7	40.2
100.0	100.0	100.0	Total Liabilities & Net Worth		100.0		100.0	100.0	100.0
			INCOME DATA						
100.0	100.0	100.0	Net Sales		100.0		100.0	100.0	100.0
			Gross Profit						
89.3	93.2	91.9	Operating Expenses		82.9		97.5	99.4	95.3
10.7	6.8	8.1	Operating Profit		17.1		2.5	.6	4.7
1.5	1.1	.4	All Other Expenses (net)		1.4		−.7	−.2	.4
9.2	5.7	7.7	Profit Before Taxes		15.7		3.2	.8	4.3
			RATIOS						
2.0	1.7	2.3			2.5		2.3	2.3	1.4
1.2	1.2	1.2	Current		1.2		1.1	1.5	1.2
.9	1.0	1.1			1.0		1.0	.9	1.1
1.4	1.1	1.5			1.5		1.7	1.0	1.0
.6	.5	.6	Quick		.6		.7	.6	.3
.2	.2	.3			.2		.3	.2	.2
8 46.3	5 77.7	5 76.6		7 50.9		7 55.4	4 99.4		4 96.3
19 19.4	13 27.3	11 33.3	Sales/Receivables	20 17.8		19 19.4	8 46.3		9 39.6
40 9.0	38 9.6	33 11.1		41 8.9		43 8.6	21 17.2		15 24.9
			Cost of Sales/Inventory						
			Cost of Sales/Payables						
8.5	13.8	8.6			8.7		6.4	10.9	19.6
31.9	35.2	27.2	Sales/Working Capital		19.3		37.5	25.6	34.5
−102.0	UND	152.8			−184.5		241.2	NM	77.9
7.4	6.0	10.8					3.6	6.4	12.6
(82) 3.1	(84) 2.5	(68) 3.4	EBIT/Interest		2.7		3.3	(19) 3.9
1.7	.7	1.4					1.2	2.2	1.4
7.2	5.6	6.0	Net Profit + Depr., Dep.,						
(28) 1.6	(27) 2.7	(20) 2.8	Amort./Cur. Mat. L/T/D						
.8	.2	.2							
.5	.6	.5			.5		.6	.6	.5
1.0	1.0	.9	Fixed/Worth		1.1		.9	1.0	.6
1.8	1.7	1.5			1.7		1.7	3.3	1.3
.6	.7	.5			.3		.9	.5	1.2
1.5	1.5	1.4	Debt/Worth		1.0		1.8	1.2	1.9
3.0	3.9	3.5			3.7		2.8	12.0	4.4
30.0	23.0	26.3	% Profit Before Taxes/Tangible		45.1		13.9	23.5	29.4
(81) 11.1	(78) 9.1	(70) 13.1	Net Worth		22.1	(17) 7.3	(11) 11.6	11.5
4.9	−.3	3.2			13.1		−.3	6.3	3.6
11.0	9.3	11.0	% Profit Before Taxes/Total		28.0		6.4	6.8	10.6
4.3	2.9	4.5	Assets		10.5		2.7	3.7	5.0
1.8	−1.1	.9			3.1		.3	1.4	.8
15.2	15.4	20.7			21.1		20.1	14.3	33.3
6.0	6.7	9.5	Sales/Net Fixed Assets		6.2		9.6	8.8	16.2
2.0	2.0	1.1			.9		3.7	4.3	10.9
3.7	4.0	4.2			2.5		3.6	4.7	6.1
2.0	2.4	2.9	Sales/Total Assets		1.5		3.1	2.7	3.6
.9	.8	1.1			.7		.8	2.1	3.0
1.1	1.0	.9			.9		1.1	.8	.5
(84) 2.0	(82) 1.6	(69) 1.4	% Depr., Dep., Amort./Sales		1.8	(17) 2.1	1.2	(19) .9
5.0	4.2	2.9			4.9		2.8	2.1	1.2
1.4	1.7	2.2	% Officers', Directors',						
(23) 3.2	(19) 2.5	(10) 3.1	Owners' Comp/Sales						
4.9	5.7	5.3							
3018576M	2753223M	3303471M	Net Sales ($)	3454M	19776M	18586M	128393M	174218M	2959044M
1149262M	1063441M	1060515M	Total Assets ($)	4963M	18900M	17691M	95261M	75323M	848377M

M = $ thousand   MM = $ million
See Pages 11 through 21 for Explanation of Ratios and Data

Current Data Sorted By Assets   Comparative Historical Data

0-500M	500M-2MM	2-10MM	10-50MM	50-100MM	100-250MM	Type of Statement	4/1/00-3/31/01 ALL	4/1/01-3/31/02 ALL
	1					Unqualified	3	4
2	1	10	4	1		Reviewed	11	14
2	6	6	2			Compiled	16	24
6	10	3	1			Tax Returns	8	6
2	6	8	10	1	1	Other	12	22
	12 (4/1-9/30/04)		71 (10/1/04-3/31/05)					
12	24	27	17	2	1	**NUMBER OF STATEMENTS**	50	70

0-500M %	500M-2MM %	2-10MM %	10-50MM %	50-100MM %	100-250MM %		%	%
						ASSETS		
15.8	7.4	11.6	16.9			Cash & Equivalents	9.5	10.3
12.8	7.6	25.3	20.2			Trade Receivables (net)	18.3	21.9
3.6	3.1	6.0	.7			Inventory	4.7	4.1
1.9	1.1	2.7	3.1			All Other Current	4.1	5.2
34.1	19.2	45.5	40.9			Total Current	36.6	41.5
42.6	71.5	42.6	44.8			Fixed Assets (net)	51.2	45.4
15.7	1.3	7.4	5.0			Intangibles (net)	2.7	3.9
7.6	8.0	4.5	9.2			All Other Non-Current	9.6	9.3
100.0	100.0	100.0	100.0			Total	100.0	100.0
						LIABILITIES		
26.7	6.5	8.0	6.8			Notes Payable-Short Term	3.8	5.6
5.9	3.5	6.0	3.1			Cur. Mat.-L/T/D	3.9	6.8
5.6	3.9	11.3	10.4			Trade Payables	10.5	13.1
1.0	.0	.4	.1			Income Taxes Payable	.1	.3
3.9	6.3	9.9	8.1			All Other Current	8.1	10.7
43.2	20.2	35.7	28.5			Total Current	26.3	36.5
30.5	52.7	30.6	34.6			Long-Term Debt	33.5	28.7
.0	.2	.8	.6			Deferred Taxes	.7	.7
10.2	3.1	2.4	3.6			All Other Non-Current	6.3	3.3
16.0	23.7	30.5	32.8			Net Worth	33.2	30.9
100.0	100.0	100.0	100.0			Total Liabilities & Net Worth	100.0	100.0
						INCOME DATA		
100.0	100.0	100.0	100.0			Net Sales	100.0	100.0
						Gross Profit		
96.8	73.5	86.4	82.4			Operating Expenses	85.5	87.5
3.2	26.5	13.6	17.6			Operating Profit	14.5	12.5
1.6	12.1	5.6	7.2			All Other Expenses (net)	4.1	4.4
1.6	14.5	8.0	10.3			Profit Before Taxes	10.4	8.1
						RATIOS		
2.6	1.2	1.8	3.0				2.2	1.9
.9	.7	1.0	1.4			Current	1.5	1.3
.6	.2	.6	1.1				.7	.9
2.5	.9	1.6	2.7				1.8	1.5
.9	.5	.9	1.4			Quick	1.0	1.0
.3	.2	.5	1.0				.5	.5
0 UND	0 UND	16 22.7	25 14.4				10 37.4	15 24.2
0 UND	0 UND	32 11.6	41 9.0			Sales/Receivables	32 11.3	34 10.7
31 11.7	35 10.6	43 8.4	61 6.0				48 7.7	49 7.4
						Cost of Sales/Inventory		
						Cost of Sales/Payables		
11.7	29.8	9.4	6.3				6.7	10.1
NM	−21.9	999.8	15.0			Sales/Working Capital	20.1	23.1
−26.1	−3.5	−7.6	96.5				−31.9	−103.3
10.3	8.7	15.1	8.7				11.7	8.2
(11) 1.8	(17) 3.4	(24) 2.8	(15) 3.6			EBIT/Interest	(38) 3.5	(50) 2.6
−5.3	2.3	.7	2.4				2.0	1.4
						Net Profit + Depr., Dep.,		5.0
						Amort./Cur. Mat. L /T/D		(10) 2.1
								.3
.8	1.3	.3	.7				.7	.5
1.7	3.8	1.4	1.4			Fixed/Worth	1.8	2.0
−1.4	−13.9	9.7	2.3				5.8	4.9
.8	1.4	1.3	.9				.6	.9
1.3	3.7	2.9	2.6			Debt/Worth	2.8	3.1
−3.0	−18.6	13.7	6.9				7.7	7.3
	64.9	74.7	36.5			% Profit Before Taxes/Tangible	60.9	71.1
	(16) 33.7	(25) 19.9	(15) 28.2			Net Worth	(45) 35.7	(62) 34.8
	15.4	.2	12.2				8.8	4.8
23.8	14.9	18.1	16.1			% Profit Before Taxes/Total	21.9	20.3
2.8	5.3	3.6	5.5			Assets	7.5	6.6
−15.1	1.9	−.7	3.0				2.4	1.9
28.0	3.6	20.8	11.3				17.3	30.2
6.4	.8	8.3	3.3			Sales/Net Fixed Assets	2.9	4.4
4.5	.2	.7	2.3				.7	.8
5.0	2.0	3.6	2.1				3.5	3.8
2.6	.6	2.1	1.6			Sales/Total Assets	1.5	2.0
1.8	.2	.6	.8				.5	.6
	4.9	.7	2.3			% Depr., Dep., Amort./Sales	1.0	.7
	(23) 9.7	(25) 2.5	(16) 3.7				(48) 2.6	(59) 3.0
	14.5	8.8	4.8				10.0	9.1
						% Officers', Directors',	3.6	2.1
						Owners' Comp/Sales	(11) 5.6	(20) 6.8
							15.0	12.0
12027M	29304M	289205M	613238M	84526M	379424M	Net Sales ($)	584627M	1508166M
3868M	29572M	121702M	377500M	143405M	150357M	Total Assets ($)	427598M	806522M

Comparative Historical Data				Current Data Sorted By Sales					
			Type of Statement						
10	5	6	Unqualified			1	1	1	3
15	19	15	Reviewed	4			4	6	1
6	31	15	Compiled	5	3		2	3	2
7	14	19	Tax Returns	12	5	2			
12	21	28	Other	5	6	2	3	5	7
4/1/02-3/31/03	4/1/03-3/31/04	4/1/04-3/31/05		12 (4/1-9/30/04)			71 (10/1/04-3/31/05)		
ALL	ALL	ALL		0-1MM	1-3MM	3-5MM	5-10MM	10-25MM	25MM & OVER
50	90	83	**NUMBER OF STATEMENTS**	26	14	5	10	15	13
%	%	%	**ASSETS**	%	%	%	%	%	%
8.5	10.7	12.3	Cash & Equivalents	8.6	12.2		12.0	14.7	15.7
29.0	19.5	16.9	Trade Receivables (net)	3.0	15.8		21.7	29.0	30.4
5.4	2.8	3.5	Inventory	.5	5.2		6.7	5.5	2.0
2.3	4.0	2.1	All Other Current	.6	1.4		1.2	4.3	4.0
45.2	36.9	34.9	Total Current	12.8	34.7		41.6	53.6	52.0
43.3	49.5	52.3	Fixed Assets (net)	75.4	51.4		40.2	33.9	40.2
5.3	4.6	6.1	Intangibles (net)	8.2	5.0		12.4	4.2	1.1
6.2	9.0	6.8	All Other Non-Current	3.6	9.0		5.8	8.3	6.6
100.0	100.0	100.0	Total	100.0	100.0		100.0	100.0	100.0
			LIABILITIES						
12.5	7.6	9.8	Notes Payable-Short Term	13.7	8.5		6.1	9.5	10.5
5.4	3.9	4.5	Cur. Mat.-L/T/D	4.4	3.8		4.9	3.8	3.9
12.3	7.2	7.8	Trade Payables	2.2	6.4		13.3	9.1	16.1
.1	.2	.3	Income Taxes Payable	.5	.0		.1	.7	.1
12.2	10.9	13.3	All Other Current	4.6	10.7		8.7	8.9	46.3
42.5	29.8	35.9	Total Current	25.3	29.4		33.1	32.1	76.9
24.3	29.6	37.5	Long-Term Debt	56.4	37.3		33.7	19.3	18.1
.7	.4	.5	Deferred Taxes	.0	.3		.4	1.2	1.2
3.8	6.0	3.9	All Other Non-Current	6.9	4.1		1.2	1.2	4.4
28.7	34.2	22.2	Net Worth	11.4	28.8		31.5	46.2	-.6
100.0	100.0	100.0	Total Liabilities & Net Worth	100.0	100.0		100.0	100.0	100.0
			INCOME DATA						
100.0	100.0	100.0	Net Sales	100.0	100.0		100.0	100.0	100.0
			Gross Profit						
87.6	85.9	83.1	Operating Expenses	70.9	90.1		85.9	87.6	95.7
12.4	14.1	16.9	Operating Profit	29.1	9.9		14.1	12.4	4.3
6.1	6.5	6.9	All Other Expenses (net)	15.0	3.9		4.9	.6	-.2
6.3	7.6	10.0	Profit Before Taxes	14.1	6.0		9.1	11.8	4.5
			RATIOS						
2.6	2.5	1.9		1.0	2.1		2.8	2.5	2.1
1.3	1.2	1.0	Current	.5	1.0		1.2	1.4	1.2
.6	.7	.5		.2	.4		.8	1.0	.9
1.5	1.9	1.6		1.0	2.0		2.7	2.0	1.7
.9	1.0	.9	Quick	.4	.7		.9	1.2	1.0
.5	.5	.4		.2	.4		.8	.8	.9
25 14.4	5 72.3	0 UND		0 UND	12 30.3		35 10.5	30 12.2	29 12.5
44 8.2	36 10.0	29 12.8	Sales/Receivables	0 UND	35 10.5		45 8.2	39 9.4	37 9.8
50 7.4	56 6.5	42 8.6		2 198.8	43 8.6		52 7.0	49 7.5	47 7.7
			Cost of Sales/Inventory						
			Cost of Sales/Payables						
8.2	6.5	11.0		172.9	9.9		7.3	5.9	11.3
31.1	27.7	127.1	Sales/Working Capital	-9.7	NM		NM	16.2	24.8
-10.8	-12.4	-8.5		-2.0	-4.9		-21.2	-431.4	NM
10.7	12.4	9.8		5.8	17.8			64.2	6.7
(42) 2.3	(65) 3.0	(69) 3.4	EBIT/Interest	(18) 3.1	(12) 2.7		(14) 13.5	(12) 3.7	
.3	1.3	1.4		.4	1.0		1.7	2.7	
2.9	1.6	6.0	Net Profit + Depr., Dep.,						
(11) 2.1	(12) 1.2	(21) 2.2	Amort./Cur. Mat. L/T/D						
.7	1.0	1.3							
.5	.5	.7		2.1	.4		.8	.2	.7
2.4	2.1	1.8	Fixed/Worth	14.5	3.2		1.7	.5	1.2
10.2	10.0	17.2		-7.0	NM		15.2	1.8	1.7
.9	.7	1.1		1.3	.7		1.4	.7	1.5
3.0	2.1	2.6	Debt/Worth	14.4	3.1		3.9	1.2	2.6
24.4	15.0	88.6		-9.5	NM		32.5	2.9	4.3
54.1	56.3	57.5	% Profit Before Taxes/Tangible	67.7	58.6			68.7	33.9
(39) 27.7	(78) 21.3	(65) 29.6	Net Worth	(15) 34.7	(11) 17.4			35.0	(12) 19.3
4.6	6.2	10.0		15.4	7.0			8.9	11.6
16.3	12.4	18.0	% Profit Before Taxes/Total	14.1	23.1		8.5	24.8	12.1
4.4	5.3	5.0	Assets	4.2	3.5		5.2	14.9	4.6
-1.9	.4	1.2		.6	-.8		-2.0	3.5	3.0
36.0	11.1	12.8		4.5	14.2		13.7	24.0	28.9
7.0	2.8	3.6	Sales/Net Fixed Assets	.3	3.5		6.8	10.7	4.0
.7	.7	.5		.2	1.2		1.7	2.9	2.6
3.9	2.7	2.8		1.8	2.6		3.6	3.5	3.3
2.2	1.2	1.7	Sales/Total Assets	.3	1.6		1.4	2.1	2.5
.6	.5	.5		.2	.8		.7	1.3	1.6
1.3	1.8	1.7		4.3	1.8		2.2	.7	1.2
(44) 3.0	(76) 6.5	(75) 4.3	% Depr., Dep., Amort./Sales	(23) 10.2	(13) 6.5		3.3	(13) 2.1	(11) 2.4
10.9	12.3	10.2		20.2	12.1		4.1	3.6	5.0
3.6	2.4	2.1	% Officers', Directors',						
(18) 6.1	(20) 4.2	(23) 6.6	Owners' Comp/Sales						
12.4	11.6	11.6							
1170686M	1025539M	1407724M	Net Sales ($)	12952M	27598M	17822M	71805M	241011M	1036536M
482118M	826930M	826404M	Total Assets ($)	31103M	29537M	31146M	57571M	216932M	460115M

© RMA 2005

M = $ thousand   MM = $ million
See Pages 11 through 21 for Explanation of Ratios and Data

INFORMATION

Current Data Sorted By Assets   Comparative Historical Data

0-500M	500M-2MM 12 (4/1-9/30/04)	2-10MM	10-50MM 71 (10/1/04-3/31/05)	50-100MM	100-250MM	Type of Statement	4/1/00-3/31/01 ALL	4/1/01-3/31/02 ALL
	1	3	13	5	5	Unqualified	22	19
	5	10	3		1	Reviewed	12	11
2	6	1	2			Compiled	14	18
2	6	2				Tax Returns	6	8
2	4	4	6			Other	23	32
6	22	20	24	5	6	**NUMBER OF STATEMENTS**	77	88
%	%	%	%	%	%	**ASSETS**	%	%
	18.7	8.2	8.1			Cash & Equivalents	9.1	10.6
	28.3	24.6	16.4			Trade Receivables (net)	24.4	24.2
	2.3	5.9	6.0			Inventory	4.2	3.1
	3.7	1.2	1.8			All Other Current	1.9	2.9
	53.0	39.8	32.3			Total Current	39.6	40.9
	18.9	25.9	26.9			Fixed Assets (net)	34.6	32.0
	18.6	18.3	30.2			Intangibles (net)	17.0	17.1
	9.6	16.1	10.6			All Other Non-Current	8.8	10.1
	100.0	100.0	100.0			Total	100.0	100.0
						LIABILITIES		
	3.3	6.0	1.9			Notes Payable-Short Term	8.0	3.1
	7.7	3.9	4.7			Cur. Mat.-L/T/D	5.1	5.4
	11.8	11.9	9.3			Trade Payables	10.1	8.6
	.0	.3	.0			Income Taxes Payable	.3	.4
	13.1	10.6	12.0			All Other Current	13.6	10.0
	36.0	32.7	28.0			Total Current	37.1	27.5
	36.9	23.1	37.7			Long-Term Debt	28.4	31.2
	.0	.2	.2			Deferred Taxes	.6	.4
	22.2	9.5	11.8			All Other Non-Current	10.4	14.3
	4.9	34.5	22.4			Net Worth	23.4	26.6
	100.0	100.0	100.0			Total Liabilities & Net Worth	100.0	100.0
						INCOME DATA		
	100.0	100.0	100.0			Net Sales	100.0	100.0
	56.0	41.1	44.4			Gross Profit	49.7	49.0
	50.2	36.4	35.6			Operating Expenses	44.6	44.2
	5.8	4.8	8.9			Operating Profit	5.1	4.8
	1.6	1.3	2.5			All Other Expenses (net)	1.5	2.3
	4.3	3.5	6.3			Profit Before Taxes	3.6	2.5
						RATIOS		
	3.0	1.5	1.5				1.8	2.3
	1.9	1.1	1.1			Current	1.3	1.5
	.9	.8	.9				.9	1.0
	2.7	1.2	1.2				1.4	2.0
	1.3	.9	1.0			Quick	1.1	1.2
	.8	.7	.7				.7	.8
	29 12.6	36 10.1	30 12.1				34 10.7	33 11.2
	37 9.8	43 8.5	36 10.0			Sales/Receivables	42 8.8	40 9.1
	44 8.2	54 6.8	40 9.2				51 7.2	50 7.3
	0 UND	0 UND	8 47.7				2 217.8	0 UND
	0 UND	5 77.2	14 25.3			Cost of Sales/Inventory	11 31.8	8 48.5
	19 19.1	14 26.9	35 10.3				21 17.0	18 20.3
	10 37.5	16 22.4	14 26.1				14 26.7	12 30.6
	24 15.2	33 11.1	27 13.7			Cost of Sales/Payables	26 13.9	23 16.1
	70 5.2	52 7.0	46 7.9				53 6.9	44 8.3
	6.1	17.5	20.0				12.0	8.0
	14.4	44.8	50.2			Sales/Working Capital	23.1	18.1
	-30.5	-35.3	-110.7				-109.0	-123.1
	7.9	9.2	9.8				4.2	6.7
	(20) 3.2	(18) 4.3	(23) 4.0			EBIT/Interest	(70) 2.3	(78) 1.9
	.8	1.8	2.6				1.0	.1
			3.9				3.3	4.7
			(11) 1.4			Net Profit + Depr., Dep., Amort./Cur. Mat. L./T/D	(22) 1.5	(17) 1.6
			.8				.8	.8
	.6	.5	.8				.9	.5
	-1.8	1.4	6.7			Fixed/Worth	1.8	2.2
	-.1	4.0	-.4				-3.0	-1.6
	1.0	1.6	1.3				1.5	.8
	-9.0	2.9	49.5			Debt/Worth	3.2	3.7
	-1.5	6.0	-2.8				-6.3	-4.9
	87.3	41.0	76.7				33.2	44.4
	(10) 49.8	(16) 15.6	(13) 32.1			% Profit Before Taxes/Tangible Net Worth	(53) 17.9	(58) 11.7
	5.2	1.0	15.1				1.8	-.4
	26.5	11.4	11.7				13.6	13.5
	6.2	5.8	7.1			% Profit Before Taxes/Total Assets	5.8	4.4
	-2.2	.3	4.3				.1	-2.7
	47.3	26.4	14.0				9.6	15.5
	17.3	9.6	4.9			Sales/Net Fixed Assets	5.7	5.7
	9.2	4.6	3.7				3.0	3.1
	3.7	2.7	1.9				2.5	2.7
	2.5	1.9	1.5			Sales/Total Assets	1.8	1.9
	1.9	1.2	1.1				1.2	1.1
	1.1	1.4	2.9				1.9	1.7
	(15) 1.8	(17) 3.0	(22) 4.0			% Depr., Dep., Amort./Sales	(61) 3.2	(77) 3.6
	4.7	6.0	5.8				6.0	6.4
	2.5						2.7	2.4
	(14) 5.5					% Officers', Directors', Owners' Comp/Sales	(18) 6.0	(22) 5.0
	8.7						9.6	8.4
6548M	62893M	165233M	895745M	430152M	660135M	Net Sales ($)	2398116M	2790753M
1474M	22764M	87626M	532565M	342529M	850359M	Total Assets ($)	1894535M	1735629M

M = $ thousand   MM = $ million
See Pages 11 through 21 for Explanation of Ratios and Data

Comparative Historical Data | **Current Data Sorted By Sales**

4/1/02-3/31/03 ALL	4/1/03-3/31/04 ALL	4/1/04-3/31/05 ALL	Type of Statement	0-1MM	1-3MM	3-5MM	5-10MM	10-25MM	25MM & OVER
27	27	27	Unqualified		1		2	6	18
13	20	19	Reviewed		4	3	5	5	2
12	16	11	Compiled		5	2	2	1	1
9	8	10	Tax Returns	2	3	4	1		
28	26	16	Other	3	2	3	2	2	4
					12 (4/1-9/30/04)		71 (10/1/04-3/31/05)		
89	97	83	NUMBER OF STATEMENTS	5	15	12	12	14	25
%	%	%	**ASSETS**	%	%	%	%	%	%
14.6	13.3	11.9	Cash & Equivalents		19.2	17.6	9.0	8.4	8.6
20.7	20.7	22.1	Trade Receivables (net)		29.7	28.9	19.3	21.4	15.0
3.3	3.5	4.3	Inventory		1.5	3.0	7.9	2.8	5.7
2.7	3.9	2.1	All Other Current		2.1	2.1	4.7	.7	2.0
41.3	41.5	40.4	Total Current		52.4	51.6	40.9	33.3	31.2
33.6	26.6	24.9	Fixed Assets (net)		13.0	26.3	30.2	15.8	33.6
15.6	17.9	23.3	Intangibles (net)		21.1	11.9	18.0	39.1	23.0
9.5	14.0	11.4	All Other Non-Current		13.5	10.2	10.9	11.8	12.1
100.0	100.0	100.0	Total		100.0	100.0	100.0	100.0	100.0
			LIABILITIES						
3.1	4.4	3.2	Notes Payable-Short Term		1.9	4.4	6.8	2.4	2.6
4.7	5.5	5.2	Cur. Mat.-L/T/D		8.1	3.2	7.1	3.8	4.6
8.1	7.3	10.4	Trade Payables		11.5	14.2	10.4	8.6	9.0
.4	.4	.1	Income Taxes Payable		.1	.0	.1	.3	.2
12.6	12.0	11.2	All Other Current		9.5	15.0	10.2	11.6	10.9
28.9	29.7	30.1	Total Current		31.1	36.9	34.7	26.5	27.2
26.3	30.8	31.7	Long-Term Debt		25.0	41.9	33.1	31.7	34.7
.6	.7	.2	Deferred Taxes		.0	.0	.3	.1	.5
7.8	6.4	12.7	All Other Non-Current		24.2	4.0	8.3	9.0	10.2
36.4	32.4	25.3	Net Worth		19.7	17.2	23.6	32.7	27.3
100.0	100.0	100.0	Total Liabilities & Net Worth		100.0	100.0	100.0	100.0	100.0
			INCOME DATA						
100.0	100.0	100.0	Net Sales		100.0	100.0	100.0	100.0	100.0
52.8	50.3	46.4	Gross Profit		50.8	63.0	37.4	47.4	39.6
46.2	42.8	39.4	Operating Expenses		42.4	61.3	32.0	40.6	29.0
6.6	7.5	7.0	Operating Profit		8.4	1.7	5.3	6.9	10.6
1.8	2.7	1.8	All Other Expenses (net)		1.9	−.1	2.2	1.6	2.3
4.8	4.9	5.1	Profit Before Taxes		6.5	1.8	3.1	5.3	8.3
			RATIOS						
2.7	2.8	2.0	Current		3.6	3.0	1.5	1.8	1.5
1.4	1.5	1.3			2.0	1.5	1.1	1.2	1.1
.9	.9	.9			.7	.8	.7	1.0	.8
2.3	2.1	1.5	Quick		3.6	2.7	1.2	1.6	1.1
1.2	1.1	1.0			1.6	1.3	.8	1.1	1.0
.8	.7	.7			.7	.8	.6	.9	.7
30 12.0	31 11.9	30 12.2	Sales/Receivables		36 10.2	29 12.5	30 12.2	32 11.2	30 12.4
36 10.1	37 9.9	37 9.9			39 9.3	35 10.3	39 9.4	38 9.7	33 10.9
48 7.6	45 8.1	45 8.1			48 7.6	43 8.5	48 7.5	51 7.2	38 9.5
0 UND	0 UND	0 UND	Cost of Sales/Inventory		0 UND	0 UND	0 UND	0 UND	4 96.4
8 44.3	8 43.5	7 53.1			0 UND	5 77.9	5 79.7	9 39.8	11 32.2
20 18.7	19 19.3	21 17.6			18 19.9	38 9.6	10 35.0	15 24.4	28 12.8
14 26.1	13 28.7	14 26.6	Cost of Sales/Payables		15 24.3	16 22.7	11 32.8	14 25.7	12 30.9
22 16.9	22 16.6	26 14.1			26 14.0	33 11.0	17 22.1	32 11.3	26 14.1
51 7.2	42 8.6	46 8.0			41 8.8	70 5.2	40 9.0	47 7.7	44 8.3
6.8	6.6	10.1	Sales/Working Capital		6.0	6.8	14.6	15.9	11.4
23.4	16.3	26.8			16.6	18.5	44.8	35.6	56.6
−51.1	−60.8	−34.7			−19.8	−32.1	−17.2	NM	−27.6
9.6	7.8	9.8	EBIT/Interest		9.5	8.8	5.0	13.1	11.1
(74) 3.7	(84) 3.2	(75) 4.3			(13) 3.9	(10) 4.4	2.9	(13) 6.1	(24) 4.8
1.1	1.5	2.0			.8	.5	1.2	2.4	2.6
8.5	3.3	3.8	Net Profit + Depr., Dep.,						
(20) 2.0	(30) 1.4	(20) 1.8	Amort./Cur. Mat. L/T/D						
1.3	.7	.7							
.6	.5	.6	Fixed/Worth		.2	.8	.8	.5	1.2
2.1	1.1	2.5			.9	1.3	2.1	2.0	3.5
−4.0	NM	−.7			−.1	−1.5	−.6	−.5	−5.0
.5	.8	1.2	Debt/Worth		.4	1.2	2.5	.7	2.6
2.4	2.6	3.8			5.7	2.4	3.8	4.2	8.2
−9.2	NM	−4.4			−1.5	−8.9	−4.1	−2.5	−15.3
43.0	67.9	59.0	% Profit Before Taxes/Tangible						88.2
(61) 15.9	(73) 18.8	(53) 23.8	Net Worth					(16)	32.9
1.3	2.5	6.7							9.5
16.1	17.7	14.9	% Profit Before Taxes/Total		46.1	22.4	10.5	14.1	15.6
7.7	6.3	7.1	Assets		11.6	5.8	4.9	9.6	7.3
.8	1.2	1.8			−2.2	−3.0	.4	3.6	5.4
13.1	20.1	28.5	Sales/Net Fixed Assets		201.7	27.9	16.2	37.4	11.3
5.8	6.0	8.9			28.5	13.4	7.0	10.3	4.4
3.1	3.8	4.4			10.0	5.8	4.5	4.6	2.6
2.4	2.4	2.7	Sales/Total Assets		3.8	3.5	2.7	2.4	1.9
1.7	1.7	1.8			2.7	2.5	1.9	1.5	1.5
1.1	1.0	1.2			1.4	1.8	1.1	1.1	1.0
2.1	1.9	1.4	% Depr., Dep., Amort./Sales					1.6	1.9	2.5
(79) 3.8	(86) 3.9	(65) 3.5						3.3	(12) 4.0	(20) 4.1
6.2	6.2	5.7						6.1	5.2	6.1
3.8	2.1	1.8	% Officers', Directors',						
(22) 7.3	(25) 4.8	(25) 5.1	Owners' Comp/Sales						
16.5	8.2	8.7							
1952200M	2374547M	2220706M	Net Sales ($)	3942M	28917M	47305M	89374M	243820M	1807348M
1645529M	2225799M	1837317M	Total Assets ($)	2213M	14529M	20420M	58353M	253232M	1488570M

© RMA 2005

M = $ thousand   MM = $ million
See Pages 11 through 21 for Explanation of Ratios and Data

Current Data Sorted By Assets   Comparative Historical Data

Type of Statement	0-500M	500M-2MM	2-10MM	10-50MM	50-100MM	100-250MM	4/1/00-3/31/01 ALL	4/1/01-3/31/02 ALL
Unqualified	1	1	10	10	3	4	19	23
Reviewed		6	15	3			21	18
Compiled	3	6	2	1			13	13
Tax Returns	7		2	1			6	4
Other	3	5	9	6	2	1	19	28
	20 (4/1-9/30/04)			81 (10/1/04-3/31/05)				
NUMBER OF STATEMENTS	14	18	38	21	5	5	78	86
ASSETS	%	%	%	%	%	%	%	%
Cash & Equivalents	14.2	12.5	17.3	12.4			12.7	11.1
Trade Receivables (net)	37.7	30.0	26.8	16.2			31.9	27.6
Inventory	1.2	10.5	6.1	8.4			6.1	5.5
All Other Current	3.8	7.3	3.3	2.5			2.6	3.8
Total Current	57.0	60.3	53.5	39.5			53.3	48.0
Fixed Assets (net)	12.6	12.8	15.8	19.7			19.9	20.4
Intangibles (net)	13.3	16.8	21.5	28.9			15.8	19.3
All Other Non-Current	17.2	10.2	9.1	11.9			11.0	12.4
Total	100.0	100.0	100.0	100.0			100.0	100.0
LIABILITIES								
Notes Payable-Short Term	31.2	7.0	8.0	4.1			9.5	12.6
Cur. Mat.-L/T/D	7.6	3.6	3.4	4.2			3.9	5.9
Trade Payables	14.5	11.7	12.4	7.7			15.5	14.0
Income Taxes Payable	.7	.7	.0	.4			.4	.3
All Other Current	17.1	17.2	20.4	8.2			20.8	18.4
Total Current	71.2	40.2	44.1	24.6			50.0	51.3
Long-Term Debt	14.9	11.6	24.6	19.8			18.9	20.7
Deferred Taxes	.0	.3	.2	.9			.7	.5
All Other Non-Current	11.1	8.3	24.0	22.9			14.4	14.9
Net Worth	2.8	39.6	7.0	31.8			15.9	12.6
Total Liabilities & Net Worth	100.0	100.0	100.0	100.0			100.0	100.0
INCOME DATA								
Net Sales	100.0	100.0	100.0	100.0			100.0	100.0
Gross Profit	61.4	48.8	45.8	51.0			49.3	47.5
Operating Expenses	61.5	43.2	39.1	42.6			45.0	44.2
Operating Profit	-.1	5.5	6.7	8.4			4.3	3.4
All Other Expenses (net)	.3	.2	1.1	1.3			1.8	1.4
Profit Before Taxes	-.4	5.4	5.6	7.1			2.5	2.0
RATIOS								
Current	1.5	2.9	2.1	2.6			1.8	1.6
	1.0	1.8	1.2	1.6			1.2	1.1
	.5	.9	.7	1.2			.9	.8
Quick	1.3	2.0	1.9	2.1			1.5	1.3
	.9	1.3	1.1	1.2			1.1	.9
	.4	.7	.6	.8			.7	.6
Sales/Receivables	0 UND	31 11.8	23 15.8	30 12.0			28 12.9	30 12.1
	36 10.1	38 9.5	38 9.6	37 9.8			48 7.7	40 9.1
	47 7.8	50 7.2	55 6.6	45 8.1			65 5.6	56 6.5
Cost of Sales/Inventory	0 UND	0 UND	0 UND	10 36.1			0 UND	0 UND
	0 UND	11 34.4	3 111.9	22 16.5			7 50.0	6 57.1
	3 130.5	60 6.1	21 17.5	57 6.4			26 14.2	19 19.1
Cost of Sales/Payables	0 UND	13 27.3	16 23.1	18 20.5			12 30.0	15 24.9
	22 16.7	26 13.8	30 12.1	22 16.8			30 12.0	35 10.3
	97 3.8	48 7.7	49 7.4	46 7.9			80 4.6	71 5.2
Sales/Working Capital	22.2	7.3	7.0	5.0			11.1	13.3
	UND	10.9	24.9	9.6			32.0	42.5
	-12.6	-34.6	-18.8	47.9			-37.1	-17.6
EBIT/Interest	7.0	41.2	17.4	31.9			8.8	7.2
	(11) 5.0	(15) 6.9	(35) 6.0	(20) 7.8			(67) 3.1	(77) 2.5
	1.0	2.3	1.0	4.4			.7	-.2
Net Profit + Depr., Dep., Amort./Cur. Mat. L/T/D				7.4			11.5	5.7
				(10) 2.0			(17) 2.0	(15) 3.1
				1.6			.9	1.6
Fixed/Worth	.3	.1	.6	.3			.5	.4
	-1.6	.4	5.9	-592.2			2.3	4.9
	-.3	-1.5	-.2	-.1			-.5	-.3
Debt/Worth	1.9	.6	2.3	.9			1.5	1.7
	-9.2	1.5	NM	-999.8			8.0	11.4
	-3.3	-7.5	-2.7	-2.0			-3.5	-2.5
% Profit Before Taxes/Tangible Net Worth		57.0	133.1	56.0			62.0	69.3
	(13) 24.7	(19) 39.9	(10) 29.0				(48) 26.0	(48) 24.7
	7.3	19.1	13.1				-8.3	3.7
% Profit Before Taxes/Total Assets	26.4	23.8	23.3	15.9			14.9	12.5
	6.0	8.9	10.1	8.0			7.1	6.9
	-3.0	4.0	.6	5.3			-1.3	-3.6
Sales/Net Fixed Assets	135.6	84.6	48.3	22.5			40.7	35.0
	37.1	25.3	30.4	11.3			21.6	18.0
	19.1	12.7	14.9	5.8			7.6	6.6
Sales/Total Assets	7.1	3.6	3.2	1.8			3.4	3.1
	4.5	2.6	2.4	1.6			2.4	2.1
	3.3	2.2	1.8	1.3			1.6	1.3
% Depr., Dep., Amort./Sales	.8	.5	1.0	1.1			1.1	1.1
	(10) 2.4	(13) .8	(31) 1.4	(17) 1.9			(57) 2.3	(67) 2.5
	4.0	3.4	2.1	3.3			3.8	4.9
% Officers', Directors', Owners' Comp/Sales	2.9						3.7	3.0
	(10) 5.3						(18) 6.2	(20) 5.9
	8.9						9.4	8.9
Net Sales ($)	16387M	67986M	433010M	775667M	387005M	867735M	1377357M	1834711M
Total Assets ($)	3365M	23681M	173780M	500826M	320807M	856261M	969048M	1400420M

M = $ thousand   MM = $ million
See Pages 11 through 21 for Explanation of Ratios and Data

Comparative Historical Data | Current Data Sorted By Sales

	4/1/02-3/31/03 ALL	4/1/03-3/31/04 ALL	4/1/04-3/31/05 ALL	Type of Statement	0-1MM	1-3MM	3-5MM	5-10MM	10-25MM	25MM & OVER
	23	27	29	Unqualified	1		2	3	10	13
	15	25	24	Reviewed		1	6	1	15	1
	20	27	12	Compiled	1	3	4	2	1	1
	5	11	10	Tax Returns	5	1	1	1	2	
	28	26	26	Other	3	6	1	4	3	9
					20 (4/1-9/30/04)			81 (10/1/04-3/31/05)		
NUMBER OF STATEMENTS	91	116	101		10	11	14	11	31	24
ASSETS	%	%	%		%	%	%	%	%	%
Cash & Equivalents	13.7	12.9	14.8		15.7	10.8	11.8	13.7	16.2	16.8
Trade Receivables (net)	26.6	31.0	25.4		24.7	31.5	32.2	24.9	27.9	15.7
Inventory	6.2	5.3	6.4		1.0	3.7	11.3	9.3	6.3	5.7
All Other Current	6.4	4.3	3.8		5.4	5.8	5.1	1.4	4.3	2.0
Total Current	52.9	53.5	50.3		46.8	51.9	60.4	49.3	54.7	40.1
Fixed Assets (net)	19.5	19.2	15.8		11.9	9.6	20.4	13.7	14.0	20.8
Intangibles (net)	16.5	15.4	21.6		31.9	10.6	12.9	31.3	20.2	24.8
All Other Non-Current	11.2	11.9	12.3		9.5	27.9	6.3	5.8	11.0	14.3
Total	100.0	100.0	100.0		100.0	100.0	100.0	100.0	100.0	100.0
LIABILITIES										
Notes Payable-Short Term	4.5	8.1	9.6		18.0	26.0	10.1	5.7	7.4	2.9
Cur. Mat.-L/T/D	5.7	5.2	4.0		9.9	.9	4.9	3.4	3.6	3.1
Trade Payables	13.9	14.4	11.0		11.4	12.1	12.8	9.2	14.0	6.0
Income Taxes Payable	.5	.4	.3		.9	.1	.7	.2	.3	.2
All Other Current	22.5	17.4	16.7		14.5	18.3	21.1	13.5	18.9	12.7
Total Current	47.2	45.5	41.5		54.8	57.4	49.6	32.1	44.1	24.9
Long-Term Debt	21.6	20.3	20.0		24.7	14.5	17.2	31.1	17.4	20.4
Deferred Taxes	.6	.3	.5		.0	.0	.1	.5	.8	.7
All Other Non-Current	13.1	18.9	19.5		7.4	10.7	9.2	22.1	25.2	25.8
Net Worth	17.5	14.9	18.5		13.1	17.4	23.8	14.2	12.4	28.1
Total Liabilities & Net Worth	100.0	100.0	100.0		100.0	100.0	100.0	100.0	100.0	100.0
INCOME DATA										
Net Sales	100.0	100.0	100.0		100.0	100.0	100.0	100.0	100.0	100.0
Gross Profit	46.9	47.9	49.7		51.1	60.7	45.3	49.2	45.1	52.8
Operating Expenses	41.7	41.7	43.7		48.1	61.9	43.6	39.3	38.8	42.1
Operating Profit	5.2	6.3	6.0		3.1	−1.1	1.7	9.9	6.3	10.7
All Other Expenses (net)	1.8	1.2	1.0		.4	.4	1.1	2.1	.6	1.4
Profit Before Taxes	3.4	5.1	5.0		2.6	−1.6	.6	7.8	5.7	9.3
RATIOS										
Current	1.9	2.2	2.2		1.7	1.9	2.2	2.6	1.9	2.6
	1.2	1.3	1.5		1.5	.9	1.7	1.7	1.3	1.6
	.7	.8	.8		.5	.6	.6	.7	1.0	1.0
Quick	1.3	1.7	1.9		1.6	1.3	2.0	2.1	1.9	2.0
	1.1	1.0	1.1		1.1	.8	1.1	1.4	1.1	1.1
	.6	.6	.7		.4	.5	.5	.7	.6	.8
Sales/Receivables	26 14.2	30 12.2	25 14.7		0 UND	22 16.7	27 13.4	19 19.2	31 11.8	21 17.5
	41 9.0	42 8.7	38 9.6		31 11.8	47 7.8	40 9.1	35 10.3	39 9.4	38 9.7
	55 6.7	61 6.0	51 7.2		48 7.6	59 6.1	52 7.1	43 8.4	55 6.6	50 7.2
Cost of Sales/Inventory	0 UND	0 UND	0 UND		0 UND	0 UND	0 UND	0 UND	0 UND	8 43.4
	6 57.6	6 65.6	9 42.6		0 UND	0 UND	16 23.4	3 110.2	5 71.0	24 15.0
	22 16.5	18 20.2	28 12.8		3 130.5	22 16.5	67 5.5	31 11.7	24 15.1	37 9.9
Cost of Sales/Payables	19 19.5	17 21.0	15 24.4		0 UND	14 27.0	17 21.7	7 54.0	18 19.9	17 21.2
	31 11.9	29 12.6	25 14.4		17 21.5	33 11.0	31 11.8	14 25.9	30 12.3	24 15.1
	66 5.6	67 5.5	49 7.5		72 5.1	61 6.0	48 7.6	48 7.7	60 6.1	45 8.2
Sales/Working Capital	7.8	7.4	7.0		15.4	14.2	6.3	5.2	7.5	5.3
	27.2	24.6	21.0		61.1	−38.6	10.9	12.1	22.2	12.5
	−18.0	−17.6	−23.7		−13.2	−5.9	−11.6	−31.4	−228.9	NM
EBIT/Interest	15.1	16.6	15.7				8.1	41.2	29.8	28.8
	(75) 3.5	(96) 4.3	(89) 6.0			(13) 1.7	9.4	(29) 6.0	(20) 8.0	
	.2	1.1	1.5			.2	1.4	1.7	4.0	
Net Profit + Depr., Dep., Amort./Cur. Mat. L/T/D	4.3	5.5	9.1							
	(15) 1.6	(24) 3.0	(21) 2.5							
	.3	1.3	1.7							
Fixed/Worth	.3	.3	.3		.2	.0	.3	.4	.4	.4
	1.2	1.3	2.2		−.9	.7	4.0	−.6	2.2	1.3
	−.3	−.5	−.3		−.2	−.3	−1.5	−.2	−.1	−.7
Debt/Worth	1.4	1.2	1.3		1.1	1.3	.9	.8	1.6	1.2
	4.5	5.4	13.9		−5.7	−10.5	12.3	−3.5	13.0	8.9
	−4.3	−5.7	−2.7		−2.0	−4.2	−6.1	−2.2	−2.4	−3.9
% Profit Before Taxes/Tangible Net Worth	82.5	79.2	70.8						114.7	102.2
	(58) 23.1	(75) 27.4	(54) 32.9					(18) 44.2	(13) 57.8	
	.9	6.5	11.7					19.5	10.6	
% Profit Before Taxes/Total Assets	18.2	20.8	22.0		28.8	7.5	11.7	33.1	20.8	21.4
	7.4	7.9	9.6		24.1	2.4	3.6	14.8	11.6	10.3
	−2.0	.7	1.8		−2.3	.9	−3.9	.8	5.1	5.6
Sales/Net Fixed Assets	47.6	50.7	48.2		91.3	113.0	94.4	47.0	46.1	16.3
	18.6	21.7	22.0		28.7	41.5	22.5	28.0	25.2	8.7
	8.8	6.7	10.3		16.3	22.4	8.7	12.8	15.8	4.3
Sales/Total Assets	3.3	3.7	3.2		5.5	4.2	3.3	3.3	3.2	1.8
	2.2	2.1	2.2		3.5	3.6	2.6	2.2	2.4	1.6
	1.4	1.4	1.5		1.5	1.0	1.7	1.8	1.6	.9
% Depr., Dep., Amort./Sales	1.2	.8	1.0				.5		.9	1.4
	(72) 1.8	(85) 1.5	(77) 1.6			(12) 1.6		(24) 1.3	(19) 2.5	
	3.4	3.5	3.3			6.2		1.8	4.2	
% Officers', Directors', Owners' Comp/Sales	3.5	3.2	3.2							
	(25) 5.5	(39) 5.7	(33) 4.3							
	7.1	8.8	8.3							
Net Sales ($)	2023688M	2220669M	2547790M		5323M	21703M	58088M	72254M	460833M	1929589M
Total Assets ($)	1594281M	1429058M	1878720M		2198M	11599M	24630M	37308M	233702M	1569283M

M = $ thousand   MM = $ million
See Pages 11 through 21 for Explanation of Ratios and Data

Current Data Sorted By Assets   Comparative Historical Data

Type of Statement	0-500M	500M-2MM	2-10MM	10-50MM	50-100MM	100-250MM		4/1/00-3/31/01 ALL	4/1/01-3/31/02 ALL
Unqualified			6	16	7	4		32	33
Reviewed		3	18	5	1			26	22
Compiled	1	3	3					13	15
Tax Returns	3	2	3					10	5
Other	3	3	10	9	4	3		24	38
		28 (4/1-9/30/04)		79 (10/1/04-3/31/05)					
NUMBER OF STATEMENTS	7	11	40	30	12	7		105	113

	500M-2MM %	2-10MM %	10-50MM %	50-100MM %		4/1/00-3/31/01 ALL %	4/1/01-3/31/02 ALL %
ASSETS							
Cash & Equivalents	17.1	8.9	11.8	8.4		8.8	9.1
Trade Receivables (net)	28.2	28.5	22.6	30.8		29.4	28.4
Inventory	20.3	35.3	21.7	18.5		28.3	28.8
All Other Current	3.1	2.8	3.6	3.6		3.0	3.3
Total Current	68.7	75.5	59.7	61.2		69.6	69.5
Fixed Assets (net)	22.5	11.0	18.0	10.7		14.3	13.8
Intangibles (net)	5.0	4.7	10.6	18.5		6.6	7.1
All Other Non-Current	3.8	8.8	11.7	9.6		9.5	9.5
Total	100.0	100.0	100.0	100.0		100.0	100.0
LIABILITIES							
Notes Payable-Short Term	7.8	12.1	5.9	3.5		10.8	20.3
Cur. Mat.-L/T/D	3.0	2.4	2.3	5.2		2.2	2.6
Trade Payables	11.3	16.1	13.2	15.4		17.3	12.9
Income Taxes Payable	.0	.6	1.4	.6		.3	.3
All Other Current	16.4	11.4	12.5	18.0		14.3	17.2
Total Current	38.6	42.5	35.4	42.6		44.9	53.3
Long-Term Debt	13.8	7.6	13.1	21.3		13.2	12.3
Deferred Taxes	.0	.2	.2	1.7		.3	.2
All Other Non-Current	6.1	7.4	7.1	60.1		6.8	7.0
Net Worth	41.5	42.3	44.2	−25.7		34.8	27.3
Total Liabilities & Net Worth	100.0	100.0	100.0	100.0		100.0	100.0
INCOME DATA							
Net Sales	100.0	100.0	100.0	100.0		100.0	100.0
Gross Profit	48.8	48.7	52.2	46.7		51.3	54.2
Operating Expenses	42.7	42.5	45.4	42.4		44.6	48.8
Operating Profit	6.1	6.2	6.8	4.3		6.7	5.3
All Other Expenses (net)	−.1	1.2	.7	2.5		1.0	1.4
Profit Before Taxes	6.2	5.0	6.1	1.8		5.7	4.0
RATIOS							
Current	2.3	2.9	2.7	2.2		2.4	2.5
	1.7	2.0	1.6	1.6		1.6	1.8
	1.0	1.3	1.2	.9		1.3	1.2
Quick	1.7	1.3	1.5	1.4		1.5	1.5
	1.3	1.0	.8	.8		.9	.8
	.5	.7	.7	.6		.5	.5
Sales/Receivables	23 15.6	43 8.5	30 12.0	62 5.9		36 10.1	37 9.7
	49 7.4	54 6.7	48 7.6	81 4.5		62 5.9	60 6.0
	103 3.5	83 4.4	77 4.8	115 3.2		97 3.8	99 3.7
Cost of Sales/Inventory	0 UND	94 3.9	40 9.1	84 4.4		50 7.2	78 4.6
	48 7.6	156 2.3	150 2.4	101 3.6		132 2.8	155 2.4
	143 2.6	277 1.3	216 1.7	144 2.5		248 1.5	285 1.3
Cost of Sales/Payables	2 147.0	37 10.0	28 13.0	26 14.2		32 11.4	23 15.7
	46 7.9	49 7.5	61 6.0	72 5.1		60 6.1	50 7.3
	87 4.2	95 3.8	95 3.8	168 2.2		113 3.2	89 4.1
Sales/Working Capital	2.3	2.9	2.8	2.8		3.4	3.1
	9.7	4.4	4.9	7.2		6.3	5.3
	999.8	19.5	15.1	−39.1		17.8	20.1
EBIT/Interest	14.8	11.0	12.0	9.7		11.3	6.0
	(10) 4.4	(39) 4.6	(27) 6.8	(10) 2.6		(89) 3.3	(97) 2.4
	1.8	2.7	3.2	−.5		.7	.8
Net Profit + Depr., Dep., Amort./Cur. Mat. L/T/D		14.1	5.8			5.1	4.2
		(12) 2.6	(11) 1.6			(23) 1.8	(26) 1.9
		1.4	1.0			1.3	1.0
Fixed/Worth	.0	.1	.2	.1		.1	.1
	.2	.1	.4	1.2		.3	.3
	3.1	.6	1.4	−.2		2.4	1.7
Debt/Worth	.8	.6	.8	.9		.8	.8
	1.2	1.3	1.9	NM		2.0	1.6
	6.6	5.7	3.9	−2.4		25.5	7.4
% Profit Before Taxes/Tangible Net Worth		64.1	43.6			38.7	34.7
		(36) 9.1	(27) 22.6			(84) 22.6	(95) 14.5
		1.4	9.1			3.0	1.6
% Profit Before Taxes/Total Assets	11.3	18.5	13.7	9.6		17.2	10.7
	8.5	4.3	10.0	7.1		6.9	4.2
	4.6	1.0	3.2	−7.7		.2	−.7
Sales/Net Fixed Assets	269.5	94.7	41.9	51.3		55.6	55.1
	23.6	46.7	12.6	19.3		24.0	21.6
	4.8	18.3	4.7	7.3		8.1	8.3
Sales/Total Assets	2.7	2.1	2.1	1.7		2.0	1.9
	1.7	1.7	1.4	1.2		1.6	1.5
	1.2	1.3	1.1	.9		1.2	1.2
% Depr., Dep., Amort./Sales		.4	1.0			.7	.6
		(35) .6	(25) 1.9			(77) 1.3	(87) 1.4
		1.4	3.7			3.0	2.6
% Officers', Directors', Owners' Comp/Sales		4.1				1.5	3.8
		(16) 5.7				(38) 6.3	(30) 6.5
		11.1				10.3	14.6

	0-500M	500M-2MM	2-10MM	10-50MM	50-100MM	100-250MM			
Net Sales ($)	6720M	27432M	389938M	895609M	1058447M	984655M		2479414M	2636435M
Total Assets ($)	1521M	14933M	215352M	603258M	872397M	990925M		1842226M	1975888M

M = $ thousand   MM = $ million
See Pages 11 through 21 for Explanation of Ratios and Data

Comparative Historical Data | | | | **Current Data Sorted By Sales** | | | | |

			Type of Statement		28 (4/1-9/30/04)		79 (10/1/04-3/31/05)		
39	32	33	Unqualified		1	1	4	8	19
21	24	27	Reviewed		1	3	10	7	6
12	12	7	Compiled		4	2	1		
8	8	8	Tax Returns	2	4		2		
29	26	32	Other	3	4		6	9	11
4/1/02-3/31/03	4/1/03-3/31/04	4/1/04-3/31/05		0-1MM	1-3MM	3-5MM	5-10MM	10-25MM	25MM & OVER
ALL	ALL	ALL							
109	102	107	**NUMBER OF STATEMENTS**	5	13	6	22	25	36
%	%	%	**ASSETS**	%	%	%	%	%	%
9.0	10.2	11.4	Cash & Equivalents		14.4		7.8	12.8	11.3
27.8	30.0	26.8	Trade Receivables (net)		25.7		27.6	26.0	26.2
24.5	27.9	26.2	Inventory		23.4		38.3	25.5	19.2
4.0	3.5	3.1	All Other Current		2.7		3.4	2.6	3.9
65.4	71.6	67.6	Total Current		66.2		77.2	66.9	60.5
14.9	14.0	13.6	Fixed Assets (net)		17.1		9.4	15.7	14.1
9.8	6.2	8.3	Intangibles (net)		4.2		4.1	11.3	11.5
9.9	8.3	10.5	All Other Non-Current		12.5		9.2	6.1	13.8
100.0	100.0	100.0	Total		100.0		100.0	100.0	100.0
			LIABILITIES						
14.6	11.5	10.0	Notes Payable-Short Term		15.3		14.5	9.8	3.2
3.8	2.2	2.5	Cur. Mat.-L/T/D		2.8		2.1	2.7	2.8
16.7	17.4	15.4	Trade Payables		6.5		15.2	15.6	13.6
.4	.8	.8	Income Taxes Payable		.0		.2	2.1	.7
13.7	14.0	14.9	All Other Current		30.2		12.4	10.0	15.4
49.2	45.9	43.6	Total Current		54.8		44.3	40.2	35.8
15.7	8.7	10.8	Long-Term Debt		13.7		8.2	12.0	12.7
.3	.1	.6	Deferred Taxes		.0		.4	.0	1.4
10.0	8.6	15.0	All Other Non-Current		6.5		7.0	10.6	22.0
24.9	36.7	30.0	Net Worth		24.9		40.1	37.2	28.2
100.0	100.0	100.0	Total Liabilities & Net Worth		100.0		100.0	100.0	100.0
			INCOME DATA						
100.0	100.0	100.0	Net Sales		100.0		100.0	100.0	100.0
51.3	47.3	49.8	Gross Profit		50.8		50.4	48.4	49.9
46.6	41.5	44.0	Operating Expenses		48.1		45.5	39.8	44.2
4.7	5.7	5.9	Operating Profit		2.8		5.0	8.7	5.7
1.5	1.1	1.0	All Other Expenses (net)		.0		.9	1.2	1.0
3.2	4.6	4.9	Profit Before Taxes		2.8		4.1	7.5	4.7
			RATIOS						
2.3	2.5	2.6			2.7		3.2	3.0	2.6
1.5	1.6	1.8	Current		1.7		2.0	1.5	1.7
1.1	1.1	1.2			.8		1.4	1.2	1.1
1.5	1.5	1.5			1.6		1.8	1.6	1.5
.9	1.0	1.0	Quick		1.2		.9	1.0	.8
.5	.6	.6			.3		.4	.4	.7
39 9.4	45 8.2	37 9.9		14 26.2		45 8.0	36 10.1	39 9.3
56 6.5	66 5.5	56 6.5	Sales/Receivables	48 7.6		59 6.2	56 6.5	58 6.3
84 4.3	109 3.3	84 4.3		97 3.7		90 4.1	78 4.6	94 3.9
28 13.2	57 6.4	46 8.0		0 UND		131 2.8	42 8.7	66 5.5
117 3.1	142 2.6	133 2.7	Cost of Sales/Inventory	89 4.1		194 1.9	123 3.0	108 3.4
182 2.0	202 1.8	215 1.7		233 1.6		328 1.1	185 2.0	156 2.3
22 16.3	30 12.0	26 13.9		0 UND		38 9.6	39 9.3	26 14.1
55 6.6	63 5.8	52 7.0	Cost of Sales/Payables	39 9.4		72 5.1	48 7.6	55 6.7
96 3.8	119 3.1	97 3.8		85 4.3		109 3.4	94 3.9	121 3.0
3.6	3.0	2.8			2.1		2.8	2.9	2.8
7.1	6.4	4.9	Sales/Working Capital		4.8		4.2	7.5	5.5
52.5	37.2	23.0			NM		10.0	26.8	28.8
8.5	9.8	11.1			12.5		8.8	14.0	26.6
(94) 3.4	(90) 4.6	(96) 5.0	EBIT/Interest	(12) 2.9		(21) 4.6	(23) 4.7	(31) 6.8
.7	1.9	2.0			-9.2		1.1	3.9	1.8
4.1	17.4	12.4	Net Profit + Depr., Dep.,						
(25) 2.0	(26) 3.5	(28) 2.5	Amort./Cur. Mat. L/T/D						
.6	1.6	1.3							
.1	.1	.1			.0		.1	.1	.1
.5	.3	.2	Fixed/Worth		.2		.1	.4	.4
2.5	1.0	1.1			5.3		.7	3.2	1.2
.8	.8	.7			.8		.7	.9	.6
1.8	1.7	1.5	Debt/Worth		1.5		1.4	2.8	1.1
26.2	4.9	8.2			25.2		5.5	10.4	9.7
38.2	43.8	46.3	% Profit Before Taxes/Tangible		79.9		46.9	74.6	32.6
(85) 13.4	(89) 21.6	(89) 19.0	Net Worth	(11) 20.6		(20) 14.1	(21) 41.0	(29) 19.0
.1	4.0	3.7			.1		-1.5	6.8	7.9
12.6	13.0	16.0	% Profit Before Taxes/Total		17.9		13.6	17.4	15.6
5.3	5.4	7.4	Assets		6.2		3.8	8.5	8.7
-.1	1.1	1.4			-1.3		-.1	2.0	2.3
37.2	53.8	67.0			261.6		97.1	62.8	48.2
18.3	27.0	28.1	Sales/Net Fixed Assets		23.6		50.5	33.3	19.1
7.8	8.7	6.7			7.3		19.6	4.9	5.7
2.2	2.0	2.1			3.7		2.0	2.0	2.0
1.6	1.4	1.6	Sales/Total Assets		1.3		1.5	1.6	1.2
1.2	1.1	1.1			1.0		1.3	1.4	1.0
.9	.6	.5			.8		.4	.5	.8
(85) 1.8	(81) 1.3	(83) 1.1	% Depr., Dep., Amort./Sales	(10) 1.2		(18) .6	(21) 1.0	(26) 1.7
3.0	3.1	2.1			1.8		1.5	2.1	3.8
3.7	1.6	2.7	% Officers', Directors',				4.1		
(27) 6.5	(28) 5.4	(30) 5.8	Owners' Comp/Sales				(12) 5.6		
11.9	11.2	11.4					11.1		
3564503M	3406644M	3362801M	Net Sales ($)	1626M	29536M	25743M	169584M	405951M	2730361M
2702952M	2675873M	2698386M	Total Assets ($)	630M	32076M	15378M	112737M	276368M	2261197M

© RMA 2005   M = $ thousand   MM = $ million
See Pages 11 through 21 for Explanation of Ratios and Data

Current Data Sorted By Assets							Comparative Historical Data	
		3	1			Type of Statement		
		2				Unqualified		
	3	1				Reviewed		
						Compiled		
	1	7			2	Tax Returns		
	2 (4/1-9/30/04)		18 (10/1/04-3/31/05)			Other	4/1/00-3/31/01	4/1/01-3/31/02
0-500M	500M-2MM	2-10MM	10-50MM	50-100MM	100-250MM		ALL	ALL
	4	13		1	2	NUMBER OF STATEMENTS		
%	%	%	%	%	%	ASSETS	%	%
D		13.8	D			Cash & Equivalents	D	D
A		40.0	A			Trade Receivables (net)	A	A
T		2.9	T			Inventory	T	T
A		.5	A			All Other Current	A	A
		57.2				Total Current		
N		26.8	N			Fixed Assets (net)	N	N
O		2.0	O			Intangibles (net)	O	O
T		14.0	T			All Other Non-Current	T	T
		100.0				Total		
A			A			LIABILITIES	A	A
V		10.0	V			Notes Payable-Short Term	V	V
A		3.1	A			Cur. Mat.-L/T/D	A	A
I		21.9	I			Trade Payables	I	I
L		.4	L			Income Taxes Payable	L	L
A		18.1	A			All Other Current	A	A
B		53.5	B			Total Current	B	B
L		25.2	L			Long-Term Debt	L	L
E		.0	E			Deferred Taxes	E	E
		9.6				All Other Non-Current		
		11.6				Net Worth		
		100.0				Total Liabilities & Net Worth		
						INCOME DATA		
		100.0				Net Sales		
						Gross Profit		
		96.9				Operating Expenses		
		3.1				Operating Profit		
		1.0				All Other Expenses (net)		
		2.1				Profit Before Taxes		
						RATIOS		
		2.4						
		1.0				Current		
		.7						
		2.4						
		1.0				Quick		
		.5						
		30 12.3						
		52 7.0				Sales/Receivables		
		88 4.2						
						Cost of Sales/Inventory		
						Cost of Sales/Payables		
		8.6						
		UND				Sales/Working Capital		
		−14.8						
		18.4						
		(11) 7.6				EBIT/Interest		
		2.7						
						Net Profit + Depr., Dep., Amort./Cur. Mat. L /T/D		
		.3						
		1.4				Fixed/Worth		
		−3.9						
		1.3						
		3.3				Debt/Worth		
		−12.9						
						% Profit Before Taxes/Tangible Net Worth		
		17.1						
		8.6				% Profit Before Taxes/Total Assets		
		−1.4						
		22.7						
		14.1				Sales/Net Fixed Assets		
		4.7						
		3.0						
		2.3				Sales/Total Assets		
		1.4						
		1.2						
		3.6				% Depr., Dep., Amort./Sales		
		5.8						
						% Officers', Directors', Owners' Comp/Sales		
	11195M	153061M		63513M	193399M	Net Sales ($)		
	4412M	59863M		83625M	237575M	Total Assets ($)		

M = $ thousand   MM = $ million
See Pages 11 through 21 for Explanation of Ratios and Data

Comparative Historical Data				Current Data Sorted By Sales					
			Type of Statement						
7	5	4	Unqualified			2	1	1	
6	6	5	Reviewed	1	2	1		1	
10	7	1	Compiled			1			
5	2		Tax Returns						
9	11	10	Other	1	1	1	4	1	2
4/1/02-3/31/03 ALL	4/1/03-3/31/04 ALL	4/1/04-3/31/05 ALL		0-1MM	2 (4/1-9/30/04) 1-3MM	3-5MM	18 (10/1/04-3/31/05) 5-10MM	10-25MM	25MM & OVER
37	31	20	**NUMBER OF STATEMENTS**	1	2	3	8	2	4
%	%	%	**ASSETS**	%	%	%	%	%	%
13.0	12.6	12.8	Cash & Equivalents						
31.3	28.8	37.8	Trade Receivables (net)						
5.9	6.0	3.0	Inventory						
1.6	2.6	.9	All Other Current						
51.8	50.1	54.4	Total Current						
33.2	35.2	24.2	Fixed Assets (net)						
6.5	7.9	9.0	Intangibles (net)						
8.5	6.8	12.3	All Other Non-Current						
100.0	100.0	100.0	Total						
			LIABILITIES						
10.1	9.7	8.7	Notes Payable-Short Term						
4.8	6.7	3.2	Cur. Mat.-L/T/D						
11.5	12.3	17.8	Trade Payables						
.1	.4	.2	Income Taxes Payable						
17.0	24.3	20.8	All Other Current						
43.4	53.4	50.8	Total Current						
18.7	20.4	23.7	Long-Term Debt						
.2	.4	.1	Deferred Taxes						
10.9	10.7	8.3	All Other Non-Current						
26.8	15.2	17.1	Net Worth						
100.0	100.0	100.0	Total Liabilities & Net Worth						
			INCOME DATA						
100.0	100.0	100.0	Net Sales						
			Gross Profit						
94.4	94.9	93.9	Operating Expenses						
5.6	5.1	6.1	Operating Profit						
2.7	2.4	1.1	All Other Expenses (net)						
2.9	2.7	5.0	Profit Before Taxes						
			RATIOS						
2.5	1.4	1.9							
1.5	1.0	1.0	Current						
.9	.5	.6							
2.0	1.2	1.9							
1.3	.8	.9	Quick						
.6	.5	.5							
32 11.5	24 15.3	43 8.5							
43 8.5	52 7.1	54 6.7	Sales/Receivables						
56 6.5	70 5.2	95 3.8							
			Cost of Sales/Inventory						
			Cost of Sales/Payables						
6.6	12.7	11.1							
14.9	−307.4	UND	Sales/Working Capital						
−82.0	−13.0	−13.7							
12.3	6.9	16.5							
(33) 2.5	(25) 2.3	(17) 7.6	EBIT/Interest						
.0	.5	2.7							
	5.6		Net Profit + Depr., Dep.,						
(11) 1.9			Amort./Cur. Mat. L/T/D						
.9									
.4	.9	.4							
1.4	2.1	1.8	Fixed/Worth						
6.9	6.2	−2.5							
1.0	1.9	1.4							
2.6	4.6	3.9	Debt/Worth						
25.4	15.6	−11.6							
51.8	68.3	67.9	% Profit Before Taxes/Tangible						
(31) 31.8	(26) 38.1	(14) 44.2	Net Worth						
−1.6	7.5	17.7							
21.2	14.2	20.9	% Profit Before Taxes/Total						
6.9	4.9	10.0	Assets						
−1.3	−3.1	1.0							
23.3	21.7	19.5							
7.9	7.7	14.2	Sales/Net Fixed Assets						
4.4	3.9	6.3							
3.8	3.4	2.9							
2.3	2.1	2.1	Sales/Total Assets						
1.7	1.3	1.0							
1.3	3.1	1.3							
(29) 3.1	(21) 4.8	(18) 3.6	% Depr., Dep., Amort./Sales						
5.7	8.6	4.7							
3.9	4.6								
(19) 5.8	(11) 7.3		% Officers', Directors', Owners' Comp/Sales						
11.3	10.0								
369160M	642771M	421168M	Net Sales ($)	609M	4395M	11602M	62134M	42573M	299855M
243606M	417495M	385475M	Total Assets ($)	799M	5580M	5259M	32511M	13278M	328048M

M = $ thousand   MM = $ million
See Pages 11 through 21 for Explanation of Ratios and Data

Current Data Sorted By Assets   Comparative Historical Data

						Type of Statement		
		4	13	3	3	Unqualified	22	21
	1	14	6		1	Reviewed	15	11
	4	2				Compiled	13	12
7	3		1			Tax Returns	5	11
3	4	7	9	2	1	Other	38	38
	15 (4/1-9/30/04)		73 (10/1/04-3/31/05)				4/1/00- 3/31/01	4/1/01- 3/31/02
0-500M	500M-2MM	2-10MM	10-50MM	50-100MM	100-250MM		ALL	ALL
10	12	27	29	6	4	NUMBER OF STATEMENTS	93	93
%	%	%	%	%	%	**ASSETS**	%	%
25.4	11.3	5.9	11.3			Cash & Equivalents	8.3	10.4
25.7	33.2	33.6	23.4			Trade Receivables (net)	30.6	26.7
17.5	13.5	13.0	12.1			Inventory	12.8	14.3
2.6	4.0	6.9	3.6			All Other Current	3.5	4.7
71.2	62.0	59.4	50.4			Total Current	55.2	56.1
22.3	26.7	26.8	24.8			Fixed Assets (net)	26.1	26.1
1.4	.3	8.3	15.8			Intangibles (net)	10.1	9.4
5.1	11.1	5.5	9.1			All Other Non-Current	8.6	8.4
100.0	100.0	100.0	100.0			Total	100.0	100.0
						LIABILITIES		
14.0	12.0	10.0	4.0			Notes Payable-Short Term	8.3	15.8
.3	.4	6.6	4.1			Cur. Mat.-L/T/D	5.8	5.2
25.5	24.7	14.0	12.2			Trade Payables	12.0	12.8
.0	.0	.9	.5			Income Taxes Payable	.6	.1
13.4	9.3	12.4	20.6			All Other Current	15.2	15.8
53.2	46.5	43.9	41.3			Total Current	41.9	49.7
15.3	20.2	13.3	16.8			Long-Term Debt	21.9	19.0
.0	.0	.9	.4			Deferred Taxes	.4	.3
36.1	16.7	5.1	8.0			All Other Non-Current	11.9	7.6
-4.5	16.7	36.8	33.4			Net Worth	23.9	23.4
100.0	100.0	100.0	100.0			Total Liabilities & Net Worth	100.0	100.0
						INCOME DATA		
100.0	100.0	100.0	100.0			Net Sales	100.0	100.0
56.3	50.0	36.5	41.9			Gross Profit	47.6	47.5
46.7	43.1	32.5	34.9			Operating Expenses	42.1	43.4
9.6	6.9	4.0	7.0			Operating Profit	5.4	4.1
4.8	4.3	1.0	1.6			All Other Expenses (net)	1.9	1.4
4.8	2.6	2.9	5.4			Profit Before Taxes	3.5	2.7
						RATIOS		
3.9	3.1	1.7	2.3				2.2	2.2
1.7	1.9	1.3	1.4			Current	1.4	1.4
.7	.8	1.1	.8				1.0	.9
3.6	2.3	1.3	1.5				1.8	1.5
1.1	1.6	.9	1.0			Quick	1.0	.8
.4	.6	.6	.6				.6	.5
0 UND	36 10.2	37 9.7	34 10.6				36 10.3	29 12.6
3 104.5	54 6.8	48 7.6	54 6.8			Sales/Receivables	49 7.5	46 7.9
62 5.9	93 3.9	72 5.1	64 5.7				72 5.1	63 5.8
0 UND	0 UND	8 47.9	10 37.4				2 196.8	1 313.9
0 UND	13 27.3	21 17.6	24 15.1			Cost of Sales/Inventory	33 10.9	24 15.1
41 9.0	57 6.4	66 5.6	79 4.6				98 3.7	114 3.2
0 UND	33 11.0	17 21.2	21 17.4				18 20.2	17 21.5
19 19.4	63 5.8	31 11.9	32 11.3			Cost of Sales/Payables	33 10.9	32 11.5
42 8.8	178 2.0	53 6.9	63 5.8				59 6.2	67 5.5
11.0	5.9	8.2	4.8				6.5	6.4
28.8	7.2	22.0	18.5			Sales/Working Capital	13.9	12.8
-751.0	NM	80.5	-13.0				-336.3	-44.9
	11.6	10.6	8.8				9.2	9.5
	(11) 5.8	(26) 2.8	(26) 3.4			EBIT/Interest	(86) 3.3	(81) 2.3
	1.0	.0	.6				.8	.1
			11.4			Net Profit + Depr., Dep.,	4.6	2.8
			(13) 1.5			Amort./Cur. Mat. L /T/D	(26) 2.1	(19) .9
			.9				.8	.5
.0	.1	.6	.4				.4	.3
.5	.7	1.0	.9			Fixed/Worth	1.1	.9
-.5	NM	2.0	-.8				5.5	8.6
.3	1.0	1.5	.8				.8	.7
1.3	5.8	2.3	1.6			Debt/Worth	2.8	2.3
-2.2	-6.5	4.0	-4.6				9.7	UND
		58.1	41.2			% Profit Before Taxes/Tangible	55.7	43.7
	(25)	17.8	(20) 16.4			Net Worth	(72) 24.1	(70) 15.2
		.2	3.9				2.1	-4.4
84.9	11.0	9.5	14.4			% Profit Before Taxes/Total	21.1	18.3
3.8	5.8	3.7	6.5			Assets	6.4	5.0
-41.5	-1.3	-2.5	-.8				-1.0	-2.1
UND	68.5	25.8	21.6				19.4	28.7
134.3	28.7	8.8	9.5			Sales/Net Fixed Assets	12.5	11.8
30.1	2.7	5.7	4.1				5.2	4.8
9.2	3.1	2.6	2.2				2.6	2.7
4.0	2.3	2.3	1.6			Sales/Total Assets	2.0	1.9
3.2	1.1	1.7	1.2				1.4	1.3
		1.7	1.8				.9	.8
	(25)	3.0	(27) 3.3			% Depr., Dep., Amort./Sales	(80) 2.4	(74) 2.3
		4.7	6.5				4.8	5.3
							3.2	3.5
						% Officers', Directors', Owners' Comp/Sales	(32) 4.8	(33) 7.3
							9.7	13.1
16568M	29649M	277669M	1097686M	611643M	552042M	Net Sales ($)	2743577M	1813885M
1948M	15348M	133559M	657619M	416579M	564250M	Total Assets ($)	1650871M	973410M

M = $ thousand   MM = $ million
See Pages 11 through 21 for Explanation of Ratios and Data

Comparative Historical Data | Current Data Sorted By Sales

H: 4/1/02-3/31/03	H: 4/1/03-3/31/04	H: 4/1/04-3/31/05	Type of Statement	0-1MM	1-3MM	3-5MM	5-10MM	10-25MM	25MM & OVER
16	23	23	Unqualified				3	6	14
14	21	22	Reviewed		1		8	10	3
6	17	6	Compiled	1	4		1		
4	9	11	Tax Returns	3	5	1	1	1	
30	23	26	Other	3	4	1	4	2	12
ALL 70	ALL 93	ALL 88		15 (4/1-9/30/04)			73 (10/1/04-3/31/05)		
70	93	88	**NUMBER OF STATEMENTS**	6	10	7	17	19	29
%	%	%	**ASSETS**	%	%	%	%	%	%
11.6	11.4	11.1	Cash & Equivalents		13.5		5.3	9.1	10.6
29.4	27.4	28.2	Trade Receivables (net)		34.2		31.6	25.8	25.9
15.0	15.0	13.1	Inventory		6.7		14.2	14.4	9.3
4.9	6.3	4.6	All Other Current		.8		4.1	3.3	4.7
60.9	60.1	57.0	Total Current		55.1		55.1	52.6	50.5
22.8	20.8	23.9	Fixed Assets (net)		34.1		25.7	30.7	21.1
9.6	9.1	11.2	Intangibles (net)		.3		14.6	9.6	18.3
6.7	10.1	7.9	All Other Non-Current		10.5		4.7	7.1	10.1
100.0	100.0	100.0	Total		100.0		100.0	100.0	100.0
			LIABILITIES						
9.6	10.0	8.0	Notes Payable-Short Term		9.4		9.6	6.8	4.5
5.7	3.3	3.8	Cur. Mat.-L/T/D		.7		6.9	4.7	4.1
18.0	15.5	16.1	Trade Payables		17.9		15.6	9.7	13.7
.3	.4	.5	Income Taxes Payable		.0		.1	.3	.6
23.4	18.5	15.5	All Other Current		13.0		9.9	10.6	23.4
57.1	47.7	43.9	Total Current		40.9		42.1	32.2	46.2
12.6	18.2	16.1	Long-Term Debt		35.0		13.0	15.7	17.4
.4	.4	.5	Deferred Taxes		.0		.3	1.4	.3
18.9	14.8	11.5	All Other Non-Current		34.5		6.1	4.9	8.8
11.1	18.9	28.0	Net Worth		-10.4		38.5	45.8	27.4
100.0	100.0	100.0	Total Liabilities & Net Worth		100.0		100.0	100.0	100.0
			INCOME DATA						
100.0	100.0	100.0	Net Sales		100.0		100.0	100.0	100.0
47.4	47.3	44.1	Gross Profit		47.6		43.2	37.4	43.6
42.4	41.5	37.5	Operating Expenses		43.0		37.3	32.6	36.7
5.0	5.8	6.6	Operating Profit		4.6		5.9	4.8	6.9
.7	.7	2.1	All Other Expenses (net)		1.2		1.8	1.0	1.3
4.3	5.1	4.5	Profit Before Taxes		3.4		4.1	3.9	5.6
			RATIOS						
2.0	2.4	2.2	Current		3.3		1.7	2.4	2.0
1.2	1.3	1.4			1.5		1.3	1.4	1.3
.9	.9	1.0			.9		1.0	1.1	.8
1.5	1.4	1.6	Quick		2.4		1.2	1.4	1.3
.8	.9	.9			1.4		.8	1.0	.8
.5	.5	.6			.4		.4	.7	.6
24 15.1	27 13.7	32 11.4	Sales/Receivables		25 14.6		27 13.3	34 10.7	36 10.1
46 8.0	45 8.0	50 7.3			45 8.1		48 7.6	44 8.3	57 6.4
63 5.8	68 5.4	70 5.2			77 4.8		93 3.9	65 5.6	67 5.5
0 UND	1 381.6	2 203.8	Cost of Sales/Inventory		0 UND		0 UND	12 30.1	5 68.4
20 18.3	19 19.0	20 18.1			13 27.8		30 12.3	23 15.7	20 18.7
106 3.4	90 4.1	74 4.9			20 18.0		79 4.6	123 3.0	71 5.2
19 19.3	19 19.3	19 18.9	Cost of Sales/Payables		24 15.0		27 13.4	12 31.1	26 14.0
38 9.6	40 9.1	34 10.7			43 8.5		47 7.8	20 18.2	35 10.4
88 4.2	77 4.8	66 5.5			88 4.2		76 4.8	39 9.4	70 5.2
6.7	5.6	6.8	Sales/Working Capital		7.0		7.9	4.2	8.1
21.5	16.7	18.8			22.5		16.2	22.0	19.6
-49.2	-24.7	-529.4			NM		NM	37.5	-18.3
13.7	16.8	10.4	EBIT/Interest				8.3	10.5	9.3
(59) 3.9	(85) 4.4	(80) 3.3					(16) 2.4	(18) 3.7	(27) 3.5
1.0	1.3	.6					.0	-1.5	.8
3.3	3.1	10.6	Net Profit + Depr., Dep., Amort./Cur. Mat. L/T/D						11.1
(20) 2.0	(21) 1.4	(26) 2.0							(11) 3.1
.9	.7	.9							1.0
.2	.3	.4	Fixed/Worth		.4		.4	.4	.5
.9	1.3	.9			5.0		.8	1.0	1.7
NM	-2.4	NM			-.5		2.0	2.0	-.6
1.0	1.1	.9	Debt/Worth		1.2		1.4	.6	.9
3.1	4.3	2.3			5.8		2.2	1.6	3.0
NM	-9.0	-8.6			-4.4		6.1	3.6	-3.7
80.9	55.3	52.6	% Profit Before Taxes/Tangible Net Worth				53.7	32.9	47.7
(53) 33.5	(65) 21.3	(64) 17.3					(15) 17.8	(17) 13.7	(17) 16.8
10.0	2.7	3.8					-2.0	-4.8	4.8
26.2	19.1	11.8	% Profit Before Taxes/Total Assets		27.4		10.4	10.8	17.6
8.2	5.3	5.2			3.6		4.1	6.7	6.5
1.5	.9	-1.2			-3.8		-2.0	-3.7	-.8
31.2	34.6	39.7	Sales/Net Fixed Assets		148.8		46.7	11.4	21.6
14.2	13.8	10.3			11.3		20.0	7.9	9.7
6.8	6.6	5.2			2.3		6.4	3.6	5.2
2.8	2.8	2.8	Sales/Total Assets		4.4		2.6	2.5	2.2
2.0	1.9	1.8			2.9		2.0	1.6	1.8
1.4	1.5	1.3			1.4		1.5	1.2	1.2
1.1	.9	1.6	% Depr., Dep., Amort./Sales				1.5	1.8	1.8
(57) 2.4	(80) 2.3	(68) 3.0					(14) 2.3	4.3	(24) 3.1
5.3	4.0	5.0					4.1	5.6	6.3
2.2	3.0	2.1	% Officers', Directors', Owners' Comp/Sales						
(15) 6.1	(31) 6.6	(20) 4.6							
8.5	9.6	8.6							
1983914M	2283126M	2585257M	Net Sales ($)	2374M	18357M	26643M	134058M	302981M	2100844M
1196940M	1405203M	1789303M	Total Assets ($)	3097M	9035M	10243M	78318M	195559M	1493051M

© RMA 2005

M = $ thousand   MM = $ million

See Pages 11 through 21 for Explanation of Ratios and Data

Current Data Sorted By Assets   Comparative Historical Data

0-500M	500M-2MM	2-10MM	10-50MM	50-100MM	100-250MM	Type of Statement	4/1/00-3/31/01 ALL	4/1/01-3/31/02 ALL
	1	9	11	6	13	Unqualified	40	36
1						Reviewed	18	14
1	5	4				Compiled	27	28
3	3	1				Tax Returns	11	9
6	12	12	11	1	5	Other	65	59
	24 (4/1-9/30/04)			92 (10/1/04-3/31/05)				
11	21	35	24	7	18	NUMBER OF STATEMENTS	161	146
%	%	%	%	%	%	ASSETS	%	%
23.5	15.5	25.7	30.3		37.7	Cash & Equivalents	21.0	21.2
36.5	41.9	32.8	30.9		22.3	Trade Receivables (net)	37.4	34.7
4.5	1.3	3.8	3.7		.8	Inventory	3.4	3.2
7.8	2.8	5.3	4.4		3.4	All Other Current	3.5	4.1
72.4	61.5	67.6	69.4		64.2	Total Current	65.4	63.3
9.7	18.1	13.1	11.0		5.2	Fixed Assets (net)	15.5	16.8
8.3	7.4	12.5	12.7		25.0	Intangibles (net)	8.4	10.9
9.6	13.0	6.8	6.9		5.6	All Other Non-Current	10.7	9.0
100.0	100.0	100.0	100.0		100.0	Total	100.0	100.0
						LIABILITIES		
24.8	15.8	4.3	4.2		.4	Notes Payable-Short Term	9.4	10.7
8.8	1.2	.9	1.7		1.5	Cur. Mat.-L/T/D	2.2	2.4
11.5	9.4	7.5	6.4		6.2	Trade Payables	12.7	10.1
2.7	.3	.8	.6		1.9	Income Taxes Payable	.7	1.7
26.7	49.9	24.0	31.1		19.6	All Other Current	20.4	24.0
74.5	76.6	37.5	44.0		29.5	Total Current	45.4	48.9
27.3	12.6	4.8	4.8		6.9	Long-Term Debt	8.7	11.3
20.3	.1	.5	.1		.0	Deferred Taxes	.4	.7
31.7	13.2	11.1	31.1		6.8	All Other Non-Current	8.2	19.6
-53.9	-2.4	46.1	20.0		56.7	Net Worth	37.3	19.6
100.0	100.0	100.0	100.0		100.0	Total Liabilities & Net Worth	100.0	100.0
						INCOME DATA		
100.0	100.0	100.0	100.0		100.0	Net Sales	100.0	100.0
						Gross Profit		
97.8	93.9	92.9	93.8		87.9	Operating Expenses	97.0	95.6
2.2	6.1	7.1	6.2		12.1	Operating Profit	3.0	4.4
.7	1.4	.5	.7		-.1	All Other Expenses (net)	-.7	1.0
1.6	4.8	6.5	5.5		12.2	Profit Before Taxes	3.7	3.4
						RATIOS		
3.6	5.0	2.9	2.6		3.6		3.1	2.5
1.0	1.1	1.9	1.5		2.1	Current	1.7	1.5
.6	.6	1.1	1.1		1.4		1.0	1.0
3.1	4.6	2.8	2.6		3.4		2.7	2.2
1.0	.8	1.5	1.3		2.1	Quick	1.5	1.3
.4	.5	1.1	1.1		1.2		.9	.8
5 71.6	22 16.7	40 9.0	49 7.5		60 6.0		37 9.9	31 11.8
9 38.8	53 6.8	53 6.9	75 4.9		74 5.0	Sales/Receivables	59 6.2	54 6.7
53 6.9	69 5.3	79 4.6	102 3.6		85 4.3		91 4.0	81 4.5
						Cost of Sales/Inventory		
						Cost of Sales/Payables		
7.4	5.5	3.7	3.6		1.2		3.6	5.2
UND	588.8	8.1	6.5		2.9	Sales/Working Capital	11.4	14.2
-29.2	-7.3	28.9	25.9		7.7		-182.0	-414.8
	24.2	66.5	27.4		36.8		27.9	22.6
	(18) 6.7	(22) 9.8	(21) 4.8		(14) 19.6	EBIT/Interest	(119) 3.8	(109) 3.5
	.8	2.8	-1.4		4.0		.2	-1.3
						Net Profit + Depr., Dep.,	14.3	21.9
						Amort./Cur. Mat. L./T/D	(26) 6.7	(19) 3.6
							1.1	-.4
.0	.1	.1	.3		.1		.1	.2
.3	.9	.3	1.1		.1	Fixed/Worth	.3	.5
-.1	-.5	1.6	-.2		.5		1.8	1.9
.6	.4	.6	1.5		.5		.5	.9
-5.1	1.4	1.5	3.5		1.5	Debt/Worth	1.4	1.9
-2.3	-2.9	9.7	-6.0		3.4		16.0	17.0
	103.2	112.7	61.0		31.8	% Profit Before Taxes/Tangible	65.4	81.7
	(14) 28.9	(32) 40.9	(15) 37.5		(15) 16.8	Net Worth	(133) 19.6	(115) 29.8
	-.9	1.9	3.7		6.6		1.8	-8.9
37.8	41.8	21.2	19.2		16.6	% Profit Before Taxes/Total	24.2	24.1
17.6	15.9	11.3	9.7		6.9	Assets	5.7	5.0
-6.1	-.7	.4	-.3		3.5		-1.5	-7.4
UND	76.4	52.4	43.7		39.3		37.2	43.4
63.2	18.6	25.9	26.2		17.7	Sales/Net Fixed Assets	18.9	19.6
33.7	11.8	16.7	9.1		12.4		11.1	9.4
13.9	4.6	3.0	1.9		1.1		3.6	3.8
6.0	3.2	1.7	1.4		.6	Sales/Total Assets	2.1	2.2
4.6	2.3	1.3	1.3		.6		1.2	1.3
	.9	1.3	.9				.9	.6
	(16) 1.7	(21) 2.2	(15) 2.4			% Depr., Dep., Amort./Sales	(116) 1.9	(98) 2.1
	2.2	3.9	3.7				3.6	3.3
						% Officers', Directors',	4.2	4.4
						Owners' Comp/Sales	(43) 6.7	(40) 6.5
							13.3	15.9
27633M	73412M	392006M	785856M	680251M	4221437M	Net Sales ($)	8665951M	5035150M
2608M	21865M	191517M	533126M	563786M	3280150M	Total Assets ($)	5031275M	3608058M

© RMA 2005

M = $ thousand   MM = $ million
See Pages 11 through 21 for Explanation of Ratios and Data

Comparative Historical Data

Current Data Sorted By Sales

			Type of Statement						
50	38	40	Unqualified		1		3	9	27
20	21	12	Reviewed		1	1	5	3	2
17	22	10	Compiled	1	3	2	1	2	1
13	17	7	Tax Returns		1	4	1	1	
60	63	47	Other	4	10	2	9	8	14
4/1/02-3/31/03	4/1/03-3/31/04	4/1/04-3/31/05			24 (4/1-9/30/04)			92 (10/1/04-3/31/05)	
ALL	ALL	ALL		0-1MM	1-3MM	3-5MM	5-10MM	10-25MM	25MM & OVER
160	161	116	**NUMBER OF STATEMENTS**	5	16	9	19	23	44
%	%	%	**ASSETS**	%	%	%	%	%	%
22.6	25.2	26.4	Cash & Equivalents		14.2		27.0	28.4	32.6
33.0	32.9	32.4	Trade Receivables (net)		41.6		28.9	34.1	28.2
3.2	2.7	2.9	Inventory		1.2		1.4	5.6	2.7
5.5	5.0	4.6	All Other Current		5.8		2.7	6.8	4.2
64.3	65.9	66.2	Total Current		62.8		60.1	74.9	67.6
15.0	13.7	11.8	Fixed Assets (net)		15.0		17.1	7.0	9.1
11.7	11.3	14.1	Intangibles (net)		6.8		18.5	11.7	17.7
9.0	9.1	7.8	All Other Non-Current		15.4		4.3	6.4	5.6
100.0	100.0	100.0	Total		100.0		100.0	100.0	100.0
			LIABILITIES						
9.4	14.2	8.4	Notes Payable-Short Term		14.1		8.2	3.6	4.9
3.2	2.9	2.0	Cur. Mat.-L/T/D		1.8		.9	.8	1.6
10.0	9.2	7.9	Trade Payables		10.4		7.9	7.4	7.1
1.5	2.1	1.0	Income Taxes Payable		1.8		.4	.2	1.4
27.7	30.3	31.3	All Other Current		51.2		18.3	37.7	29.0
51.8	58.7	50.5	Total Current		79.3		35.7	49.6	44.0
11.8	9.7	8.9	Long-Term Debt		2.4		5.9	4.8	5.5
.4	.3	2.1	Deferred Taxes		.1		.6	.2	.0
12.1	11.1	16.4	All Other Non-Current		16.4		16.8	22.4	11.7
23.9	20.3	22.1	Net Worth		1.9		41.0	22.9	38.7
100.0	100.0	100.0	Total Liabilities & Net Worth		100.0		100.0	100.0	100.0
			INCOME DATA						
100.0	100.0	100.0	Net Sales		100.0		100.0	100.0	100.0
			Gross Profit						
97.7	94.1	92.9	Operating Expenses		95.1		88.3	94.9	92.0
2.3	5.9	7.1	Operating Profit		4.9		11.7	5.1	8.0
1.2	1.5	.6	All Other Expenses (net)		.9		1.1	.4	.3
1.1	4.3	6.5	Profit Before Taxes		4.0		10.6	4.7	7.7
			RATIOS						
2.2	2.5	3.0			5.2		2.9	2.4	3.0
1.4	1.5	1.6	Current		1.2		2.1	1.5	1.6
1.0	.9	1.1			.4		1.1	1.1	1.2
2.1	2.1	2.8			3.2		2.8	2.4	2.7
1.2	1.3	1.4	Quick		1.0		1.6	1.2	1.4
.8	.7	.9			.4		1.0	1.0	1.1

								Sales/Receivables								
35	10.3	35	10.5	40	9.1		23	16.0			40	9.0	32	11.4	52	7.0
58	6.3	54	6.8	62	5.9		54	6.8			52	7.0	54	6.7	69	5.3
81	4.5	79	4.6	81	4.5		70	5.2			77	4.7	86	4.2	85	4.3

			Cost of Sales/Inventory							
			Cost of Sales/Payables							
4.8	3.9	3.5			6.3		2.8	3.9	2.1	
11.6	13.3	8.3	Sales/Working Capital		NM		8.8	9.6	6.0	
UND	−70.7	451.7			−7.3		38.7	31.2	20.7	

														EBIT/Interest								
	16.1		33.9		32.6			13.3			55.3		93.9		29.6		
(126)	3.8	(122)	6.4	(88)	6.8		(12)	5.6	(16)	7.0	(15)	36.5	(35)	8.4			
	−1.7		.9		1.3			.2			2.5		2.6		.8		

							Net Profit + Depr., Dep., Amort./Cur. Mat. L/T/D								
	7.5		25.0		48.1									9.3	
(26)	3.7	(17)	5.3	(18)	7.6								(11)	4.0	
	1.0		1.9		2.5									1.4	

			Fixed/Worth							
.1	.1	.1			.1		.1	.1	.1	
.6	.4	.4			1.4		.5	.3	.3	
−10.0	5.6	−1.7			−.6		4.8	−.2	NM	

			Debt/Worth							
.8	.7	.6			.4		.5	1.1	.9	
2.5	1.9	2.0			5.0		1.6	3.3	1.7	
−28.5	35.7	−10.6			−6.0		28.7	−4.9	NM	

							% Profit Before Taxes/Tangible Net Worth								
	57.7		62.1		66.3			56.2		151.7		154.9		49.4	
(118)	20.2	(122)	22.4	(83)	26.2		(10)	24.5	(16)	48.0	(16)	22.4	(33)	24.3	
	−4.8		1.4		3.7			−11.0		10.5		−14.8		7.5	

			% Profit Before Taxes/Total Assets							
16.9	20.1	21.0			30.0		37.1	21.8	16.7	
4.6	7.6	10.3			15.1		10.0	9.6	9.0	
−4.8	−2.7	.6			1.6		3.5	−1.0	1.4	

			Sales/Net Fixed Assets							
40.2	46.8	52.5			112.7		52.5	77.5	37.0	
20.0	25.8	24.6			34.8		18.6	40.4	17.9	
9.8	13.2	12.7			11.4		12.9	21.6	10.6	

			Sales/Total Assets							
3.3	3.5	3.3			4.7		2.9	3.3	1.8	
1.8	2.1	1.7			3.3		1.4	1.8	1.3	
1.2	1.3	1.2			2.3		1.2	1.4	.6	

							% Depr., Dep., Amort./Sales								
	1.2		.9		1.2					1.3		.7		1.0	
(96)	2.2	(103)	2.1	(69)	2.2				(13)	2.6	(11)	2.2	(27)	3.2	
	4.6		3.7		4.0					4.5		2.5		4.8	

							% Officers', Directors', Owners' Comp/Sales								
	2.4		4.7		2.1										
(49)	7.2	(36)	6.8	(23)	6.0										
	14.3		15.8		13.0										

5938529M	8110173M	6180595M	Net Sales ($)	3618M	35001M	34557M	133873M	359062M	5614484M	
4998408M	5022127M	4593052M	Total Assets ($)	1316M	11669M	11993M	89953M	196781M	4281340M	

© RMA 2005   **M = $ thousand   MM = $ million**
See Pages 11 through 21 for Explanation of Ratios and Data

INFORMATION—Motion Picture and Video Production   NAICS 512110 (SIC 7812)

Current Data Sorted By Assets   **Comparative Historical Data**

0-500M	500M-2MM	2-10MM	10-50MM	50-100MM	100-250MM	Type of Statement	4/1/00-3/31/01 ALL	4/1/01-3/31/02 ALL
	1	3	1		4	Unqualified	18	13
1	2	15	1			Reviewed	24	17
3	10	3	1			Compiled	24	19
10	8	4	1			Tax Returns	16	14
11	8	11	3	2	1	Other	52	48
	24 (4/1-9/30/04)			80 (10/1/04-3/31/05)				
25	29	36	7	2	5	**NUMBER OF STATEMENTS**	134	111
%	%	%	%	%	%	**ASSETS**	%	%
20.4	14.7	12.8				Cash & Equivalents	11.8	10.4
22.0	23.7	31.4				Trade Receivables (net)	29.2	25.3
3.6	2.6	4.0				Inventory	4.4	6.0
3.6	7.9	2.5				All Other Current	3.4	3.1
49.6	48.9	50.7				Total Current	48.8	44.9
34.2	34.0	36.2				Fixed Assets (net)	34.9	36.2
3.2	3.8	5.5				Intangibles (net)	6.7	7.1
13.1	13.3	7.6				All Other Non-Current	9.5	11.8
100.0	100.0	100.0				Total	100.0	100.0
						LIABILITIES		
42.2	6.8	6.6				Notes Payable-Short Term	12.0	9.3
2.3	7.1	7.4				Cur. Mat.-L/T/D	8.1	5.7
12.6	11.4	13.4				Trade Payables	11.6	10.5
.0	.5	.2				Income Taxes Payable	.4	.4
15.5	14.8	11.3				All Other Current	17.0	17.4
72.6	40.7	38.8				Total Current	49.1	43.3
23.7	17.2	17.8				Long-Term Debt	20.1	21.9
.2	.5	1.0				Deferred Taxes	.7	.4
9.3	10.8	4.3				All Other Non-Current	9.8	7.6
-5.7	30.8	38.1				Net Worth	20.3	26.8
100.0	100.0	100.0				Total Liabilities & Net Worth	100.0	100.0
						INCOME DATA		
100.0	100.0	100.0				Net Sales	100.0	100.0
						Gross Profit		
93.8	92.6	93.2				Operating Expenses	94.2	94.1
6.2	7.4	6.8				Operating Profit	5.8	5.9
.6	1.6	1.9				All Other Expenses (net)	1.5	3.0
5.6	5.8	4.9				Profit Before Taxes	4.2	2.9
						RATIOS		
2.2	2.7	2.2					1.7	2.3
1.1	.9	1.4				Current	1.0	1.0
.4	.5	.9					.6	.7
1.7	1.8	1.9					1.5	1.9
.9	.8	1.3				Quick	.9	.9
.3	.4	.7					.5	.5
2 185.5	16 23.4	22 16.3					19 18.9	12 29.5
19 18.8	49 7.4	40 9.2				Sales/Receivables	43 8.4	43 8.4
42 8.8	69 5.3	61 6.0					65 5.6	73 5.0
						Cost of Sales/Inventory		
						Cost of Sales/Payables		
15.7	7.7	9.0					10.3	7.7
127.0	-138.5	21.9				Sales/Working Capital	234.5	130.3
-9.4	-13.3	-112.3					-16.4	-16.0
10.0	12.8	18.5					8.9	7.3
(19) 3.2	(24) 5.3	(29) 4.6				EBIT/Interest	(119) 2.6	(95) 1.9
-1.5	-1.4	1.1					.7	-.3
						Net Profit + Depr., Dep.,	4.9	5.5
						Amort./Cur. Mat. L /T/D	(33) 2.4	(27) 2.9
							1.4	.6
.3	.2	.5					.3	.3
1.5	.8	.9				Fixed/Worth	1.7	1.2
-6.0	2.5	2.2					36.8	6.7
1.0	.8	1.1					1.2	.8
2.1	1.6	1.9				Debt/Worth	3.6	2.7
-25.0	4.8	7.3					168.8	22.5
175.2	88.5	82.2				% Profit Before Taxes/Tangible	79.6	74.1
(18) 82.7	(26) 14.4	(33) 31.8				Net Worth	(103) 28.9	(91) 21.9
27.1	-11.6	3.1					6.5	2.3
63.0	16.8	25.4				% Profit Before Taxes/Total	18.2	13.9
25.3	6.1	10.2				Assets	6.8	4.2
-1.4	-5.5	.6					.1	-3.5
34.9	22.2	19.4					29.3	28.3
11.3	8.9	7.7				Sales/Net Fixed Assets	9.5	7.5
5.7	4.0	4.3					3.5	3.1
4.1	3.6	4.0					3.2	3.2
3.6	2.1	2.4				Sales/Total Assets	2.2	2.1
3.0	1.3	1.7					1.4	1.4
1.7	1.4	2.2					1.1	1.6
(14) 3.5	(20) 4.2	(32) 4.1				% Depr., Dep., Amort./Sales	(105) 3.7	(85) 4.2
5.5	7.0	7.2					8.8	8.8
6.7	6.9	1.2				% Officers', Directors',	3.1	4.7
(14) 12.6	(11) 13.5	(11) 1.8				Owners' Comp/Sales	(54) 7.6	(41) 9.8
22.5	22.1	9.5					13.9	16.3
27096M	86264M	375324M	342193M	101721M	510324M	Net Sales ($)	2964270M	2170607M
6780M	31578M	137736M	188465M	136356M	692705M	Total Assets ($)	2255285M	2035911M

M = $ thousand   MM = $ million
See Pages 11 through 21 for Explanation of Ratios and Data

Comparative Historical Data   **Current Data Sorted By Sales**

			Type of Statement						
14	16	9	Unqualified	1		1	1	1	5
27	30	19	Reviewed		1	6	9	2	1
25	30	17	Compiled	1	9	1	3	2	1
22	29	23	Tax Returns	10	4	3	4	2	
30	32	36	Other	7	11	1	3	8	6
4/1/02- 3/31/03 ALL	4/1/03- 3/31/04 ALL	4/1/04- 3/31/05 ALL		24 (4/1-9/30/04)			80 (10/1/04-3/31/05)		
				0-1MM	1-3MM	3-5MM	5-10MM	10-25MM	25MM & OVER
118	137	104	NUMBER OF STATEMENTS	19	25	12	20	15	13
%	%	%	**ASSETS**	%	%	%	%	%	%
13.3	14.1	14.1	Cash & Equivalents	27.6	12.2	10.9	14.5	9.1	6.2
25.9	25.5	25.8	Trade Receivables (net)	15.1	23.6	31.9	30.2	31.3	27.2
5.6	4.8	4.2	Inventory	3.6	3.2	1.7	5.9	1.6	9.7
3.7	3.5	4.4	All Other Current	4.6	3.9	3.5	6.4	2.1	5.4
48.5	47.8	48.5	Total Current	50.9	42.9	48.0	57.0	44.1	48.5
31.4	37.0	37.5	Fixed Assets (net)	32.0	42.2	37.1	30.7	40.4	44.0
7.1	5.1	3.9	Intangibles (net)	2.9	2.9	9.0	4.3	4.2	1.2
13.0	10.0	10.1	All Other Non-Current	14.2	11.9	5.9	8.0	11.2	6.3
100.0	100.0	100.0	Total	100.0	100.0	100.0	100.0	100.0	100.0
			LIABILITIES						
16.3	12.2	15.3	Notes Payable-Short Term	32.1	8.4	36.5	7.9	4.7	8.2
8.5	6.0	5.4	Cur. Mat.-L/T/D	1.7	7.8	6.5	8.7	3.8	2.0
15.2	15.8	12.3	Trade Payables	3.2	12.0	22.1	10.2	19.0	12.6
.9	.4	.3	Income Taxes Payable	.1	.5	.2	.4	.0	.4
17.4	19.4	13.6	All Other Current	17.5	10.3	11.4	15.2	9.0	19.6
58.3	53.8	47.0	Total Current	54.6	39.0	76.8	42.4	36.6	42.6
21.9	20.1	21.3	Long-Term Debt	26.5	24.0	14.2	13.2	20.2	29.0
.7	.5	.7	Deferred Taxes	.2	.2	1.6	1.1	.3	1.0
8.9	8.5	12.7	All Other Non-Current	8.4	4.5	22.2	1.5	13.5	41.8
10.1	17.1	18.4	Net Worth	10.2	32.3	−14.8	41.8	29.4	−14.5
100.0	100.0	100.0	Total Liabilities & Net Worth	100.0	100.0	100.0	100.0	100.0	100.0
			INCOME DATA						
100.0	100.0	100.0	Net Sales	100.0	100.0	100.0	100.0	100.0	100.0
			Gross Profit						
95.1	94.6	93.8	Operating Expenses	87.8	92.9	98.2	94.8	94.2	98.3
4.9	5.4	6.2	Operating Profit	12.2	7.1	1.8	5.2	5.8	1.7
2.0	2.2	1.6	All Other Expenses (net)	2.5	1.3	.3	1.7	1.1	2.1
2.8	3.3	4.6	Profit Before Taxes	9.7	5.8	1.5	3.5	4.7	−.4
			RATIOS						
1.7	2.0	2.6		8.9	2.2	2.1	2.7	1.5	4.6
1.0	1.1	1.2	Current	1.1	.9	1.4	1.5	1.2	1.2
.5	.6	.7		.4	.5	.5	1.0	.8	.8
1.4	1.6	1.9		5.7	1.6	1.5	2.5	1.4	4.6
.8	.9	1.1	Quick	1.1	.8	1.3	1.3	1.2	.7
.4	.5	.4		.4	.4	.5	.6	.4	.3
19 19.2	17 20.9	16 22.5		0 UND	5 70.4	25 14.5	23 16.0	17 21.8	13 27.3
43 8.4	37 9.7	39 9.4	Sales/Receivables	24 15.0	31 12.0	48 7.6	40 9.2	39 9.3	46 7.9
62 5.9	59 6.2	59 6.2		63 5.8	48 7.6	64 5.7	67 5.4	45 8.1	108 3.4
			Cost of Sales/Inventory						
			Cost of Sales/Payables						
8.7	9.3	9.0		4.0	11.2	8.3	8.3	21.9	2.8
NM	110.0	39.8	Sales/Working Capital	127.0	−138.5	16.5	12.6	47.0	16.7
−10.6	−12.4	−22.7		−3.5	−10.9	−15.5	−194.1	−32.8	−54.2
5.1	11.0	11.8		13.2	10.3	6.7	24.1	21.1	
(93) 1.7	(119) 3.1	(82) 4.0	EBIT/Interest	(12) 4.2	(22) 5.0	(10) 1.2	(19) 3.9	(11) 4.6	
−.7	−.1	1.0		−6.2	1.1	−2.4	1.0	3.1	
5.1	5.3	7.9	Net Profit + Depr., Dep.,						
(36) 1.9	(26) 2.2	(14) 2.9	Amort./Cur. Mat. L/T/D						
1.0	1.0	.7							
.4	.5	.4		.1	.3	.8	.3	.5	1.7
1.5	1.3	1.5	Fixed/Worth	.4	1.6	1.8	.7	1.4	2.7
15.6	6.5	9.0		9.4	13.5	NM	1.9	7.8	−2.4
1.2	1.0	1.1		.2	.9	1.2	.4	1.3	2.4
3.8	2.8	2.6	Debt/Worth	1.3	2.4	2.6	1.5	3.5	24.8
NM	31.3	22.5		9.0	33.3	NM	5.9	15.7	−12.8
62.8	54.0	96.4	% Profit Before Taxes/Tangible	119.1	147.7		65.2	134.7	
(89) 11.3	(107) 20.3	(86) 33.0	Net Worth	(16) 58.5	(21) 71.4		(19) 24.3	(12) 45.2	
1.3	1.7	2.2		6.9	1.7		−.3	13.2	
13.2	15.9	26.7	% Profit Before Taxes/Total	61.8	38.0	16.7	15.3	27.1	8.0
3.3	5.4	7.4	Assets	7.8	13.2	4.3	10.5	7.5	3.0
−4.6	−4.4	.2		−4.1	−.2	−9.2	.0	3.0	−3.7
31.5	31.6	21.6		22.4	25.8	13.8	19.9	66.0	28.8
10.0	8.1	8.1	Sales/Net Fixed Assets	8.9	9.6	7.5	7.9	9.9	2.8
4.2	3.2	3.9		5.3	3.4	4.3	5.5	5.2	1.0
3.5	3.7	3.9		3.7	3.7	4.2	3.4	5.3	4.2
2.1	2.3	2.6	Sales/Total Assets	2.6	3.2	2.3	2.6	4.0	.8
1.4	1.4	1.4		1.3	1.6	1.7	2.0	1.9	.7
2.0	2.1	1.7		2.2	1.3	1.7	2.0	2.6	
(92) 4.8	(103) 4.5	(71) 4.1	% Depr., Dep., Amort./Sales	(11) 4.0	(17) 4.6	(10) 4.1	(18) 4.0	(10) 4.0	
9.3	10.4	7.1		9.0	6.7	5.5	8.1	7.5	
4.8	4.3	1.8	% Officers', Directors',	10.9	8.2				
(52) 8.5	(63) 8.4	(39) 9.5	Owners' Comp/Sales	(10) 18.7	(12) 11.2				
11.6	15.1	18.1		33.2	17.7				
1579040M	1732238M	1442922M	Net Sales ($)	10003M	43029M	47333M	149425M	226820M	966312M
1312505M	1531232M	1193620M	Total Assets ($)	12950M	19959M	21146M	64849M	122249M	952467M

M = $ thousand   MM = $ million
See Pages 11 through 21 for Explanation of Ratios and Data

Current Data Sorted By Assets | **Comparative Historical Data**

Type of Statement		
Unqualified	15	20
Reviewed	7	6
Compiled	15	15
Tax Returns	10	4
Other	29	31

0-500M	500M-2MM	2-10MM	10-50MM	50-100MM	100-250MM		4/1/00-3/31/01 ALL	4/1/01-3/31/02 ALL
	15 (4/1-9/30/04)		87 (10/1/04-3/31/05)					
11	13	34	26	9	9	NUMBER OF STATEMENTS	76	76
%	%	%	%	%	%	**ASSETS**	%	%
26.4	20.8	9.2	7.6			Cash & Equivalents	9.5	10.9
5.1	.3	1.0	.5			Trade Receivables (net)	1.0	1.3
.7	.9	1.9	.8			Inventory	1.0	1.4
2.8	.3	.9	1.2			All Other Current	3.6	1.5
34.9	22.3	13.0	10.0			Total Current	15.2	15.0
48.4	57.6	77.2	75.7			Fixed Assets (net)	73.8	73.7
1.4	4.8	2.9	3.1			Intangibles (net)	5.0	3.3
15.2	15.3	6.9	11.2			All Other Non-Current	6.0	8.0
100.0	100.0	100.0	100.0			Total	100.0	100.0
						LIABILITIES		
23.1	2.5	5.5	.2			Notes Payable-Short Term	3.4	3.9
3.3	4.7	3.6	2.8			Cur. Mat.-L/T/D	4.8	6.0
16.5	5.2	2.4	3.4			Trade Payables	5.7	7.4
.9	.0	.0	.1			Income Taxes Payable	.1	.0
10.4	5.6	9.9	4.6			All Other Current	12.4	5.8
54.2	18.0	21.6	11.0			Total Current	26.3	23.3
16.7	28.8	44.9	59.7			Long-Term Debt	45.6	40.3
.0	.0	.0	.1			Deferred Taxes	.3	.4
.8	16.9	5.2	4.9			All Other Non-Current	8.4	11.2
28.2	36.2	28.4	24.3			Net Worth	19.3	24.9
100.0	100.0	100.0	100.0			Total Liabilities & Net Worth	100.0	100.0
						INCOME DATA		
100.0	100.0	100.0	100.0			Net Sales	100.0	100.0
						Gross Profit		
88.8	93.4	85.9	90.1			Operating Expenses	90.9	91.2
11.2	6.6	14.1	9.9			Operating Profit	9.1	8.8
2.5	1.0	7.9	3.5			All Other Expenses (net)	4.9	6.3
8.7	5.6	6.2	6.4			Profit Before Taxes	4.2	2.6
						RATIOS		
3.5	4.5	1.4	2.1				1.4	1.5
1.0	1.0	.8	.7			Current	.6	.5
.1	.2	.2	.4				.2	.3
3.5	4.2	1.1	1.6				1.0	.9
1.0	1.0	.5	.6			Quick	.3	.4
.0	.1	.2	.3				.1	.2
0　UND	0　UND	0　UND	0　UND				0　UND	0　UND
0　UND	0　UND	0　UND	2　999.8			Sales/Receivables	0　UND	0　UND
1　335.3	0　UND	1　386.5	2　154.4				2　179.8	3　123.0
						Cost of Sales/Inventory		
						Cost of Sales/Payables		
13.6	6.3	14.2	11.8				38.0	26.0
UND	296.0	-38.3	-28.1			Sales/Working Capital	-16.1	-14.4
-14.9	-8.4	-4.6	-11.0				-6.0	-5.8
	10.4	6.0	4.2				3.9	3.6
	(10) 4.2	(26) 2.7	(24) 1.9			EBIT/Interest	(62) 1.5	(65) 1.7
	1.4	1.2	.9				.7	.5
						Net Profit + Depr., Dep.,		
						Amort./Cur. Mat. L /T/D		
.2	.5	1.5	2.0				2.0	1.4
1.0	2.2	3.4	4.5			Fixed/Worth	4.4	3.9
-3.0	8.8	10.1	61.7				-13.9	20.7
.2	.3	1.3	1.6				1.5	.9
1.0	2.0	3.2	4.0			Debt/Worth	4.4	3.5
-5.6	9.1	10.1	66.2				-15.8	95.9
	31.8	39.6	36.6			% Profit Before Taxes/Tangible	40.2	31.4
	(11) 10.6	(30) 17.0	(21) 17.5			Net Worth	(53) 10.4	(58) 13.6
	2.5	2.6	10.9				3.0	-6.2
95.9	13.3	11.1	9.4			% Profit Before Taxes/Total	11.0	11.3
37.9	8.8	3.6	3.5			Assets	3.7	3.4
21.3	1.9	.2	.0				-2.7	-3.1
28.5	6.2	2.0	1.6				3.1	3.0
10.8	3.2	.9	1.1			Sales/Net Fixed Assets	1.2	1.0
8.0	1.8	.5	.6				.8	.7
7.7	3.3	1.2	1.1				1.8	1.6
5.8	1.7	.7	.7			Sales/Total Assets	1.0	.8
2.5	.9	.5	.5				.6	.6
	2.9	4.6	5.7				4.1	4.6
	(10) 4.2	(30) 7.7	(25) 8.1			% Depr., Dep., Amort./Sales	(67) 6.8	(66) 7.3
	7.5	16.3	10.2				9.6	10.8
							2.9	2.4
						% Officers', Directors',	(22) 5.1	(15) 3.2
						Owners' Comp/Sales	9.4	5.6
17082M	29220M	149823M	494544M	472543M	1240734M	Net Sales ($)	1178865M	2042639M
3079M	15932M	156297M	591558M	622099M	1394914M	Total Assets ($)	1392204M	2252590M

© RMA 2005

M = $ thousand　　MM = $ million
See Pages 11 through 21 for Explanation of Ratios and Data

Comparative Historical Data | **Current Data Sorted By Sales**

			Type of Statement						
27	23	18	Unqualified		1	1	3	4	9
10	14	12	Reviewed	1	2	2	2	4	1
21	15	13	Compiled	2	4	2	4	1	
11	14	11	Tax Returns	3	5	1	1		1
32	34	48	Other	7	11	6	6	4	14
4/1/02- 3/31/03 ALL	4/1/03- 3/31/04 ALL	4/1/04- 3/31/05 ALL		0-1MM	15 (4/1-9/30/04) 1-3MM	3-5MM	5-10MM	87 (10/1/04-3/31/05) 10-25MM	25MM & OVER
101	100	102	**NUMBER OF STATEMENTS**	13	23	12	16	13	25
%	%	%	**ASSETS**	%	%	%	%	%	%
14.0	14.8	12.1	Cash & Equivalents	13.7	18.3	9.2	10.3	9.9	9.1
1.8	1.0	1.2	Trade Receivables (net)	5.2	.4	1.3	.5	.7	.8
1.1	.9	1.1	Inventory	.3	.7	4.1	.6	1.3	.8
1.4	3.2	1.1	All Other Current	.6	.2	2.7	1.3	1.7	1.0
18.3	19.9	15.5	Total Current	19.8	19.6	17.3	12.6	13.6	11.6
71.7	68.5	72.2	Fixed Assets (net)	60.5	68.2	67.4	72.2	76.4	82.0
2.1	3.6	2.8	Intangibles (net)	1.4	4.2	4.3	2.6	1.6	2.2
7.9	8.0	9.5	All Other Non-Current	18.3	8.0	11.0	12.5	8.4	4.2
100.0	100.0	100.0	Total	100.0	100.0	100.0	100.0	100.0	100.0
			LIABILITIES						
3.0	2.6	4.9	Notes Payable-Short Term	21.9	4.5	6.2	.4	.8	.7
5.6	4.7	4.2	Cur. Mat.-L/T/D	3.7	3.4	3.8	2.8	4.7	5.9
6.9	6.6	5.2	Trade Payables	1.8	4.6	13.1	1.8	3.8	6.5
.1	.3	.3	Income Taxes Payable	.0	.4	.2	.1	.1	.7
10.8	10.8	7.2	All Other Current	8.2	5.7	13.3	8.1	5.0	5.5
26.4	24.9	21.7	Total Current	35.7	18.5	36.5	13.3	14.4	19.4
47.2	38.6	44.4	Long-Term Debt	38.3	37.9	27.8	50.9	47.2	56.0
.3	.3	.2	Deferred Taxes	.0	.0	.0	.0	.3	.5
7.3	10.5	6.8	All Other Non-Current	.8	6.4	13.7	6.6	4.4	8.5
18.8	25.7	26.9	Net Worth	25.2	37.1	22.0	29.2	33.7	15.6
100.0	100.0	100.0	Total Liabilities & Net Worth	100.0	100.0	100.0	100.0	100.0	100.0
			INCOME DATA						
100.0	100.0	100.0	Net Sales	100.0	100.0	100.0	100.0	100.0	100.0
			Gross Profit						
86.5	89.4	89.0	Operating Expenses	82.7	89.5	88.5	88.2	90.8	91.5
13.5	10.6	11.0	Operating Profit	17.3	10.5	11.5	11.8	9.2	8.5
5.7	3.7	4.7	All Other Expenses (net)	9.6	6.1	2.6	3.8	1.5	4.3
7.8	7.0	6.3	Profit Before Taxes	7.8	4.5	8.9	8.0	7.7	4.2
			RATIOS						
2.2	1.8	2.0		2.0	4.5	1.1	2.3	1.6	1.1
.7	.9	.7	Current	.3	1.5	.4	.8	.9	.6
.3	.3	.2		.0	.2	.2	.3	.3	.3
1.6	1.6	1.6		1.9	4.3	.9	2.0	1.1	.8
.5	.6	.5	Quick	.3	1.0	.3	.7	.7	.5
.2	.3	.2		.0	.1	.1	.2	.3	.2
0 UND	0 UND	0 UND		0 UND	0 UND	0 UND	0 UND	0 UND	0 UND
0 UND	0 UND	0 UND	Sales/Receivables	0 UND	0 UND	0 UND	2 214.4	0 UND	2 206.5
1 267.3	1 252.7	3 143.6		0 UND	0 UND	3 137.2	5 70.1	1 313.6	4 84.4
			Cost of Sales/Inventory						
			Cost of Sales/Payables						
13.6	12.2	13.6		6.3	7.1	164.9	8.3	21.8	289.3
-24.6	-60.6	-30.9	Sales/Working Capital	-35.1	25.3	-14.9	-117.6	-137.4	-12.0
-7.2	-8.4	-7.7		-1.5	-13.2	-5.3	-7.2	-18.9	-7.6
5.5	6.3	6.3			16.1		4.7	7.3	5.2
(81) 2.5	(89) 2.9	(84) 3.0	EBIT/Interest	(17) 4.3		(12) 2.0	(12) 2.6	2.4	
1.3	1.5	1.4			1.4		.9	1.9	1.0
4.9	3.2	2.8	Net Profit + Depr., Dep.,						
(17) 1.7	(21) 1.8	(13) 1.8	Amort./Cur. Mat. L/T/D						
1.3	1.4	1.3							
1.9	1.7	1.5		.4	.7	1.2	1.3	1.6	2.3
4.2	3.4	3.0	Fixed/Worth	2.5	2.4	2.1	4.5	3.8	3.1
24.2	8.9	10.1		7.4	15.9	9.4	87.5	6.1	17.4
1.5	1.4	1.2		.5	.5	1.1	1.7	1.0	1.8
4.3	3.0	3.1	Debt/Worth	2.0	2.1	1.7	4.1	3.8	3.2
30.5	9.9	11.0		6.6	16.0	10.4	92.3	7.2	18.1
58.8	47.8	41.7	% Profit Before Taxes/Tangible	31.8	91.3	35.7	53.6	68.7	39.8
(80) 32.6	(86) 26.3	(86) 21.9	Net Worth	(11) 10.6	(19) 23.6	(10) 10.6	(13) 13.0	29.8	(20) 26.1
8.4	8.5	7.6		-29.4	2.5	4.9	6.1	15.8	12.7
13.6	14.3	11.9	% Profit Before Taxes/Total	21.4	28.6	16.8	11.5	11.6	9.3
6.0	5.7	5.6	Assets	6.2	5.8	6.7	3.5	7.1	5.1
1.4	2.0	1.2		-2.0	1.3	1.5	.1	3.6	-.7
3.5	4.4	3.1		9.9	8.0	3.3	2.2	2.8	1.6
1.3	1.4	1.2	Sales/Net Fixed Assets	.9	2.4	1.5	.9	1.6	1.2
.8	.9	.7		.3	.6	1.0	.5	.9	.8
1.9	2.1	1.7		2.2	3.7	2.2	1.1	1.9	1.2
1.0	1.0	.9	Sales/Total Assets	.8	.9	1.0	.6	1.1	1.0
.7	.7	.5		.2	.5	.7	.4	.6	.7
3.9	4.8	4.4		2.9	3.6	2.0	5.8	4.5	5.9
(90) 6.5	(91) 6.4	(85) 7.4	% Depr., Dep., Amort./Sales	(10) 8.4	(19) 7.4	(11) 3.9	(15) 7.9	(12) 7.4	(18) 8.4
9.9	9.0	9.9		17.3	16.0	6.9	10.8	9.7	9.1
2.4	2.0	2.4	% Officers', Directors',						
(18) 3.0	(25) 4.0	(18) 4.3	Owners' Comp/Sales						
5.2	7.7	5.8							
2390260M	2758562M	2403946M	Net Sales ($)	7584M	47519M	44997M	116663M	193134M	1994049M
2541116M	2165123M	2783879M	Total Assets ($)	16683M	63474M	48002M	237556M	211207M	2206957M

M = $ thousand   MM = $ million
See Pages 11 through 21 for Explanation of Ratios and Data

Current Data Sorted By Assets   Comparative Historical Data

0-500M	500M-2MM	2-10MM	10-50MM	50-100MM	100-250MM	Type of Statement	4/1/00-3/31/01 ALL	4/1/01-3/31/02 ALL
		2	4	2		Unqualified	6	8
	1	4	1			Reviewed	9	8
2	2	1	1			Compiled	13	10
1	5	1				Tax Returns	3	6
	3	5				Other	14	16
	2 (4/1-9/30/04)		32 (10/1/04-3/31/05)					
3	11	13	5	2		NUMBER OF STATEMENTS	45	48
%	%	%	%	%	%	**ASSETS**	%	%
	8.4	17.6				Cash & Equivalents	9.7	10.6
	41.1	22.5				Trade Receivables (net)	26.2	23.8
	7.0	7.7				Inventory	3.9	3.7
	2.2	4.9				All Other Current	2.3	1.8
	58.7	52.7				Total Current	42.1	39.9
	36.4	40.3				Fixed Assets (net)	45.9	49.7
	.2	3.7				Intangibles (net)	3.5	3.2
	4.7	3.4				All Other Non-Current	8.6	7.2
	100.0	100.0				Total	100.0	100.0
						LIABILITIES		
	9.9	6.6				Notes Payable-Short Term	8.2	10.8
	6.3	5.2				Cur. Mat.-L/T/D	5.9	8.5
	19.0	7.3				Trade Payables	11.9	11.0
	.1	.0				Income Taxes Payable	.8	.1
	11.0	6.1				All Other Current	13.5	11.6
	46.3	25.2				Total Current	40.3	42.0
	13.2	25.2				Long-Term Debt	18.7	18.9
	.1	.1				Deferred Taxes	1.2	.8
	5.8	21.1				All Other Non-Current	3.7	4.3
	34.7	28.3				Net Worth	36.2	33.9
	100.0	100.0				Total Liabilities & Net Worth	100.0	100.0
						INCOME DATA		
	100.0	100.0				Net Sales	100.0	100.0
						Gross Profit		
	94.4	91.8				Operating Expenses	94.7	96.4
	5.6	8.2				Operating Profit	5.3	3.6
	.1	1.6				All Other Expenses (net)	2.0	1.5
	5.6	6.6				Profit Before Taxes	3.2	2.2
						RATIOS		
	3.6	3.8					1.8	1.4
	1.5	2.0				Current	1.1	1.0
	.7	1.2					.7	.5
	3.4	2.7					1.5	1.2
	.8	1.4				Quick	1.0	.8
	.7	1.1					.5	.5
25 14.7	24 14.9						25 14.6	12 29.3
47 7.8	36 10.1					Sales/Receivables	48 7.6	37 9.8
62 5.9	59 6.2						64 5.7	61 6.0
						Cost of Sales/Inventory		
						Cost of Sales/Payables		
	8.7	4.6					10.8	14.5
	17.9	10.5				Sales/Working Capital	92.6	194.5
	−15.3	28.8					−15.5	−11.3
	17.2	49.4					8.1	8.0
	(10) 9.7	5.6				EBIT/Interest	(40) 1.9	(43) 2.8
	2.0	1.6					.8	.7
							4.8	3.7
						Net Profit + Depr., Dep., Amort./Cur. Mat. L /T/D	(12) 2.5	(16) 2.0
							1.4	1.1
	.1	.5					.7	.8
	1.6	1.2				Fixed/Worth	1.3	1.6
	35.3	NM					2.7	3.2
	.5	.7					.8	1.0
	2.2	.9				Debt/Worth	2.0	1.9
	34.9	NM					3.5	5.5
		59.1					43.4	42.7
	(10)	34.9				% Profit Before Taxes/Tangible Net Worth	(40) 18.5	(43) 18.0
		7.6					−.2	−6.6
	24.6	31.7					15.2	14.2
	14.8	13.1				% Profit Before Taxes/Total Assets	5.2	6.2
	1.8	1.2					−1.0	−1.9
	50.4	13.3					9.1	9.4
	10.9	5.7				Sales/Net Fixed Assets	4.3	4.5
	4.5	2.8					2.7	2.7
	4.7	2.9					3.3	3.1
	2.7	2.5				Sales/Total Assets	1.9	2.1
	2.3	1.3					1.4	1.3
							4.0	3.8
						% Depr., Dep., Amort./Sales	(43) 7.7	(46) 7.5
							12.1	13.0
							5.4	2.9
						% Officers', Directors', Owners' Comp/Sales	(24) 9.1	(18) 11.2
							15.4	13.9
3895M	40566M	146856M	201646M	100173M		Net Sales ($)	544950M	2021142M
1232M	11712M	65391M	169275M	138276M		Total Assets ($)	310515M	336113M

(DATA NOT AVAILABLE — 100-250MM column)

© RMA 2005

M = $ thousand   MM = $ million
See Pages 11 through 21 for Explanation of Ratios and Data

Comparative Historical Data / Current Data Sorted By Sales

Type of Statement					0-1MM	1-3MM	3-5MM	5-10MM	10-25MM	25MM & OVER
Unqualified	7	8	8					1	3	4
Reviewed	6	4	6			1		2	2	1
Compiled	10	7	5			3		1	1	1
Tax Returns	4	6	7			4	1	1	1	
Other	17	11	8			2	3	1	1	
	4/1/02-3/31/03 ALL	4/1/03-3/31/04 ALL	4/1/04-3/31/05 ALL			2 (4/1-9/30/04)		32 (10/1/04-3/31/05)		
NUMBER OF STATEMENTS	44	36	34			9	5	6	8	6

Current Data columns (0-1MM … 25MM & OVER) for the items below: **DATA NOT AVAILABLE**

	%	%	%	0-1MM %	1-3MM %	3-5MM %	5-10MM %	10-25MM %	25MM & OVER %
ASSETS									
Cash & Equivalents	11.5	9.6	14.3						
Trade Receivables (net)	22.1	23.4	26.8						
Inventory	7.6	7.3	7.9						
All Other Current	3.0	1.4	3.4						
Total Current	44.2	41.7	52.3						
Fixed Assets (net)	46.2	47.4	41.1						
Intangibles (net)	4.5	1.7	2.7						
All Other Non-Current	5.1	9.2	3.8						
Total	100.0	100.0	100.0						
LIABILITIES									
Notes Payable-Short Term	14.2	13.1	7.4						
Cur. Mat.-L/T/D	7.8	5.1	4.8						
Trade Payables	10.7	8.9	10.7						
Income Taxes Payable	.4	.1	.2						
All Other Current	11.2	10.5	9.5						
Total Current	44.4	37.6	32.7						
Long-Term Debt	16.6	20.8	19.1						
Deferred Taxes	.5	.3	.5						
All Other Non-Current	5.6	12.2	12.4						
Net Worth	32.9	29.1	35.3						
Total Liabilities & Net Worth	100.0	100.0	100.0						
INCOME DATA									
Net Sales	100.0	100.0	100.0						
Gross Profit									
Operating Expenses	96.6	91.4	92.7						
Operating Profit	3.4	8.6	7.3						
All Other Expenses (net)	1.3	3.4	1.1						
Profit Before Taxes	2.0	5.2	6.2						

RATIOS

	4/1/02-3/31/03	4/1/03-3/31/04	4/1/04-3/31/05
Current	1.6 / .9 / .6	1.9 / 1.3 / .8	2.7 / 1.6 / 1.0
Quick	1.3 / .7 / .5	1.5 / 1.0 / .6	1.9 / 1.2 / .8
Sales/Receivables	17 — 21.6 / 40 — 9.2 / 58 — 6.3	28 — 13.0 / 44 — 8.3 / 65 — 5.6	24 — 15.4 / 38 — 9.6 / 61 — 6.0
Cost of Sales/Inventory			
Cost of Sales/Payables			
Sales/Working Capital	10.3 / −46.5 / −10.1	8.0 / 25.1 / −18.0	5.3 / 11.2 / −436.6
EBIT/Interest	7.5 / (40) 2.2 / .4	19.3 / (31) 2.2 / 1.1	36.8 / (33) 5.6 / 1.4
Net Profit + Depr., Dep., Amort./Cur. Mat. L/T/D	3.2 / (14) 1.7 / .8	8.3 / (11) 4.9 / 1.8	7.3 / (12) 3.3 / 2.1
Fixed/Worth	.9 / 1.7 / 9.6	.8 / 2.1 / 6.2	.6 / 1.3 / 3.2
Debt/Worth	.8 / 2.6 / 19.8	.8 / 2.7 / 12.2	.6 / 1.4 / 6.2
% Profit Before Taxes/Tangible Net Worth	46.5 / (36) 13.5 / −7.1	70.0 / (31) 20.9 / 1.0	51.5 / (28) 30.5 / 7.6
% Profit Before Taxes/Total Assets	13.0 / 3.6 / −2.3	22.9 / 6.5 / .3	22.8 / 10.1 / 1.1
Sales/Net Fixed Assets	8.9 / 5.3 / 2.2	9.8 / 5.3 / 1.9	16.1 / 6.4 / 2.8
Sales/Total Assets	3.0 / 1.9 / 1.0	3.0 / 2.0 / 1.0	3.3 / 2.4 / 1.3
% Depr., Dep., Amort./Sales	4.6 / (36) 9.0 / 15.8	5.3 / (26) 8.3 / 12.6	4.0 / (24) 6.7 / 11.3
% Officers', Directors', Owners' Comp/Sales	7.9 / (14) 9.9 / 16.5	6.1 / (13) 9.6 / 14.0	4.2 / (12) 7.5 / 10.1

	02-03	03-04	04-05	0-1MM	1-3MM	3-5MM	5-10MM	10-25MM	25MM & OVER
Net Sales ($)	496261M	1841194M	493136M		15045M	20352M	46583M	119200M	291956M
Total Assets ($)	364354M	753361M	385886M		7778M	8269M	20392M	100386M	249061M

M = $ thousand   MM = $ million
See Pages 11 through 21 for Explanation of Ratios and Data

Current Data Sorted By Assets						Type of Statement	Comparative Historical Data	
1	2	8	10	8	3	Unqualified	28	26
4	3	4	1		1	Reviewed	18	12
2	2	7			1	Compiled	32	23
2	2					Tax Returns	8	6
4	9	18	8	3		Other	47	36
	17 (4/1-9/30/04)		85 (10/1/04-3/31/05)				4/1/00- 3/31/01	4/1/01- 3/31/02
0-500M	500M-2MM	2-10MM	10-50MM	50-100MM	100-250MM		ALL	ALL
13	18	37	19	12	3	NUMBER OF STATEMENTS	133	103
%	%	%	%	%	%	ASSETS	%	%
17.9	16.7	13.7	12.5	8.1		Cash & Equivalents	8.7	8.9
27.5	19.1	16.3	17.8	6.6		Trade Receivables (net)	16.5	15.2
.0	.2	.3	.1	.3		Inventory	.7	.3
1.4	8.7	1.2	3.0	2.0		All Other Current	3.0	2.5
46.8	44.7	31.4	33.5	17.0		Total Current	29.0	26.9
23.9	30.5	28.2	24.2	15.5		Fixed Assets (net)	31.5	29.5
18.8	19.3	26.4	29.8	58.5		Intangibles (net)	27.5	30.5
10.4	5.5	14.0	12.5	9.1		All Other Non-Current	12.0	13.0
100.0	100.0	100.0	100.0	100.0		Total	100.0	100.0
						LIABILITIES		
3.0	1.0	1.4	4.3	.1		Notes Payable-Short Term	1.7	1.8
9.0	5.6	5.7	3.5	2.9		Cur. Mat.-L/T/D	7.7	5.3
2.3	4.4	3.1	7.3	1.1		Trade Payables	4.2	3.9
.0	.1	.1	.0	2.0		Income Taxes Payable	.0	.1
19.8	4.8	5.5	3.4	2.1		All Other Current	9.2	6.1
34.1	15.9	15.8	18.5	8.3		Total Current	23.0	17.3
31.5	44.4	39.7	19.4	50.0		Long-Term Debt	50.0	44.7
.0	.3	.2	.5	1.9		Deferred Taxes	.8	.7
.4	18.3	11.3	6.6	16.6		All Other Non-Current	18.9	18.5
33.8	21.2	33.0	54.9	23.3		Net Worth	7.4	18.8
100.0	100.0	100.0	100.0	100.0		Total Liabilities & Net Worth	100.0	100.0
						INCOME DATA		
100.0	100.0	100.0	100.0	100.0		Net Sales	100.0	100.0
						Gross Profit		
92.6	87.9	85.6	82.9	81.4		Operating Expenses	87.6	91.0
7.4	12.1	14.4	17.1	18.6		Operating Profit	12.4	9.0
2.3	3.3	5.4	4.2	8.1		All Other Expenses (net)	6.5	7.1
5.1	8.7	9.0	12.9	10.5		Profit Before Taxes	5.9	1.9
						RATIOS		
9.0	4.8	3.3	5.1	5.2			3.1	4.1
1.9	2.6	1.8	1.7	2.8		Current	1.7	2.0
1.0	1.6	1.2	1.3	1.3			.9	.9
9.0	3.5	3.1	5.1	4.3			2.9	4.1
1.9	1.8	1.7	1.4	2.4		Quick	1.6	1.8
.9	.9	1.0	1.1	1.1			.7	.8
43　8.4	1　340.3	47　7.8	26　13.9	48　7.6			41　8.9	40　9.1
53　6.9	46　8.0	57　6.4	51　7.2	55　6.7		Sales/Receivables	57　6.4	58　6.3
58　6.3	56　6.5	78　4.7	78　4.7	63　5.8			68　5.4	70　5.2
						Cost of Sales/Inventory		
						Cost of Sales/Payables		
3.9	3.2	3.8	3.6	2.4			5.1	4.9
7.8	8.6	7.2	7.1	4.7		Sales/Working Capital	9.4	9.0
NM	21.6	28.5	23.2	28.4			−81.4	−61.3
	9.7	10.2	7.7	5.1			4.8	4.7
	4.2	(35)　3.9	(12)　5.4	(10)　2.8		EBIT/Interest	(111)　1.7	(90)　1.7
	2.2	1.3	2.6	2.0			.6	.3
						Net Profit + Depr., Dep., Amort./Cur. Mat. L /T/D	5.6	5.6
							(21)　1.8	(15)　1.4
							.6	1.2
.1	.5	.6	.4	NM			.7	.9
.6	NM	4.5	1.1	−.4		Fixed/Worth	−5.2	−3.5
−4.4	−.6	−.8	−22.0	−.1			−.5	−.5
.1	.8	.9	.3	NM			1.5	1.3
1.6	NM	6.4	1.5	−1.8		Debt/Worth	−10.1	−7.6
−5.1	−2.7	−2.4	−66.7	−1.3			−2.0	−2.0
		74.7	80.9			% Profit Before Taxes/Tangible Net Worth	57.4	37.9
	(19)　27.7	(13)　15.5					(58)　24.5	(44)　11.9
	4.6	4.2					3.6	−2.5
28.8	25.6	17.4	14.8	8.2		% Profit Before Taxes/Total Assets	15.4	9.7
3.0	11.6	6.3	7.2	4.0			4.0	2.4
−4.3	5.9	1.4	2.5	2.0			−2.1	−3.5
26.8	11.0	9.0	15.9	7.3		Sales/Net Fixed Assets	6.4	6.9
10.3	4.8	4.3	4.2	3.6			3.2	3.2
5.4	3.5	1.6	2.1	2.4			2.0	1.9
2.6	1.9	1.2	1.0	.6		Sales/Total Assets	1.4	1.4
1.9	1.3	.9	.7	.4			.9	.9
1.3	1.1	.6	.5	.3			.6	.5
1.4	1.0	3.1	3.6	4.7		% Depr., Dep., Amort./Sales	3.7	3.7
(10)　2.0	2.7	(32)　5.2	(15)　5.3	7.6			(123)　7.0	(88)　8.0
4.9	5.1	9.4	7.2	9.7			12.7	12.6
						% Officers', Directors', Owners' Comp/Sales	6.0	4.9
							(21)　11.6	(29)　10.7
							16.3	16.1
7600M	30595M	191736M	323382M	430937M	121877M	Net Sales ($)	1125885M	1170925M
4039M	18151M	188407M	364611M	942561M	374986M	Total Assets ($)	1967011M	1796043M

M = $ thousand　　MM = $ million
See Pages 11 through 21 for Explanation of Ratios and Data

Comparative Historical Data				Type of Statement	Current Data Sorted By Sales					
38	29	32		Unqualified	2	2	4	5	4	15
19	12	12		Reviewed	5	2	2	2	1	
32	20	12		Compiled	3	5	2	1		1
4	11	4		Tax Returns	2	2				
36	35	42		Other	9	10	8	8	5	2
4/1/02-3/31/03	4/1/03-3/31/04	4/1/04-3/31/05			17 (4/1-9/30/04)		85 (10/1/04-3/31/05)			
ALL	ALL	ALL			0-1MM	1-3MM	3-5MM	5-10MM	10-25MM	25MM & OVER
129	107	102		**NUMBER OF STATEMENTS**	21	21	16	16	10	18
%	%	%		**ASSETS**	%	%	%	%	%	%
10.0	10.7	13.6		Cash & Equivalents	16.7	18.9	9.5	13.7	9.2	9.8
15.8	17.0	17.0		Trade Receivables (net)	18.4	18.5	18.6	14.7	18.7	13.5
.2	.3	.2		Inventory	.0	.1	.6	.1	.0	.3
3.2	3.7	3.1		All Other Current	1.0	7.4	2.3	1.0	1.2	4.0
29.2	31.6	33.9		Total Current	36.1	44.9	31.0	29.4	29.1	27.6
27.2	27.6	25.3		Fixed Assets (net)	30.4	24.4	32.3	28.1	18.1	15.8
30.7	28.7	30.0		Intangibles (net)	22.0	20.1	25.9	31.9	37.4	48.7
12.9	12.1	10.8		All Other Non-Current	11.5	10.6	10.8	10.6	15.3	7.9
100.0	100.0	100.0		Total	100.0	100.0	100.0	100.0	100.0	100.0
				LIABILITIES						
2.6	2.9	1.9		Notes Payable-Short Term	2.4	.5	4.7	1.3	3.5	.1
8.2	6.7	5.4		Cur. Mat.-L/T/D	7.5	4.6	5.9	5.9	3.2	4.1
4.5	4.0	3.7		Trade Payables	2.0	3.8	3.4	2.3	4.9	6.5
.2	.0	.3		Income Taxes Payable	.1	.0	.0	.1	2.4	.0
11.8	7.3	6.3		All Other Current	12.9	6.4	5.3	3.3	4.3	3.2
27.3	21.0	17.5		Total Current	24.7	15.2	19.3	12.9	18.2	13.9
43.2	40.6	37.4		Long-Term Debt	46.4	41.0	33.8	28.5	18.1	44.5
.6	.4	.5		Deferred Taxes	.1	.2	.0	.6	.3	1.5
10.5	15.5	10.6		All Other Non-Current	7.3	10.3	13.0	12.3	9.3	11.6
18.4	22.6	34.1		Net Worth	21.5	33.3	34.0	45.6	54.1	28.4
100.0	100.0	100.0		Total Liabilities & Net Worth	100.0	100.0	100.0	100.0	100.0	100.0
				INCOME DATA						
100.0	100.0	100.0		Net Sales	100.0	100.0	100.0	100.0	100.0	100.0
				Gross Profit						
87.7	88.0	85.4		Operating Expenses	92.0	85.4	82.0	87.6	81.5	81.1
12.3	12.0	14.6		Operating Profit	8.0	14.6	18.0	12.4	18.5	18.9
5.6	5.5	4.9		All Other Expenses (net)	4.5	6.5	5.2	1.5	3.3	6.9
6.7	6.5	9.7		Profit Before Taxes	3.4	8.1	12.8	10.9	15.2	12.1
				RATIOS						
3.7	3.9	3.4			3.3	10.2	3.5	3.3	3.7	3.4
1.6	2.0	2.2		Current	1.9	2.9	2.0	2.2	1.9	2.3
.9	1.0	1.2			.9	1.3	1.0	1.3	1.2	1.4
3.4	3.4	3.3			3.3	9.8	3.4	3.3	3.7	3.1
1.5	1.8	1.7		Quick	1.9	1.8	1.6	2.2	1.6	1.5
.8	.9	1.0			.8	.9	.8	1.2	.9	1.1
41 8.8	42 8.7	44 8.2			37 9.8	44 8.2	39 9.3	45 8.1	17 21.6	47 7.7
56 6.5	56 6.5	53 6.9		Sales/Receivables	50 7.2	57 6.4	51 7.1	51 7.2	51 7.1	56 6.5
67 5.4	70 5.2	65 5.6			58 6.3	76 4.8	61 6.0	63 5.8	85 4.3	69 5.3
				Cost of Sales/Inventory						
				Cost of Sales/Payables						
4.5	4.4	3.6			3.9	2.2	4.6	3.9	3.4	3.7
11.1	7.9	7.1		Sales/Working Capital	13.4	6.5	6.7	6.7	8.4	5.1
-52.8	-999.8	29.5			-43.8	21.8	NM	21.4	NM	14.3
7.0	6.9	7.9			4.3	9.8	8.2	10.6		7.0
(113) 2.1	(87) 3.3	(87) 3.9		EBIT/Interest	(16) .3	(20) 3.8	(15) 4.0	(14) 4.4		(14) 4.1
.7	.7	1.6			-1.8	1.2	2.2	2.9		2.0
6.1	3.2	3.6		Net Profit + Depr., Dep.,						3.5
(19) 1.9	(15) 1.7	(19) 1.3		Amort./Cur. Mat. L/T/D					(10) 1.7	
1.2	.6	1.1								1.2
.7	.7	.5			.4	.4	.9	.3	.3	1.3
-4.7	17.3	3.3		Fixed/Worth	7.0	1.3	NM	1.1	.8	-1.0
-.5	-.5	-.7			-1.1	-.8	-.6	-.8	NM	-.2
1.1	1.1	.8			.4	.6	1.2	.4	.7	4.4
-9.1	25.5	7.9		Debt/Worth	-33.8	6.4	NM	3.7	1.8	-2.9
-2.1	-2.0	-2.4			-2.7	-2.6	-2.5	-2.4	NM	-1.4
61.6	75.9	73.4		% Profit Before Taxes/Tangible	31.6	119.5				
(58) 27.8	(55) 31.3	(52) 20.9		Net Worth	(10) 8.0	(12) 30.9				
1.4	6.8	4.6			-5.9	2.1				
15.8	17.0	15.7		% Profit Before Taxes/Total	19.8	20.3	26.1	14.5	26.3	12.3
4.7	6.8	7.2		Assets	3.0	6.3	10.0	7.7	9.5	7.6
-1.0	-1.1	2.1			-6.1	1.0	2.7	5.7	2.2	2.4
9.3	9.0	9.3			16.4	12.5	9.4	7.3	19.4	7.4
3.7	4.1	4.4		Sales/Net Fixed Assets	5.2	5.1	3.6	4.2	5.0	4.2
2.3	2.2	2.4			2.3	1.8	1.8	2.3	2.3	2.7
1.5	1.4	1.4			2.0	1.5	1.3	1.2	1.1	1.1
.9	.9	.9		Sales/Total Assets	1.3	1.0	.8	1.0	.9	.5
.6	.6	.5			.7	.4	.7	.6	.4	.4
3.5	2.4	2.3			1.9	1.4	3.1	2.9		2.8
(117) 5.5	(99) 5.0	(90) 4.8		% Depr., Dep., Amort./Sales	(16) 3.6	(19) 4.6	(14) 4.7	5.3		5.9
9.1	8.5	8.7			7.1	8.7	9.8	8.4		10.2
3.9	4.2	2.6		% Officers', Directors',						
(30) 7.2	(25) 9.1	(22) 5.3		Owners' Comp/Sales						
12.7	11.9	12.9								
1405108M	1106436M	1106127M		Net Sales ($)	13494M	41174M	59769M	113350M	182714M	695626M
2444652M	1714655M	1892755M		Total Assets ($)	20975M	65706M	69334M	139584M	300067M	1297089M

© RMA 2005   M = $ thousand   MM = $ million
See Pages 11 through 21 for Explanation of Ratios and Data

Current Data Sorted By Assets							Comparative Historical Data	

Type of Statement

0-500M	500M-2MM	2-10MM	10-50MM	50-100MM	100-250MM		4/1/00-3/31/01 ALL	4/1/01-3/31/02 ALL
						Type of Statement		
	1	12	22	5	6	Unqualified	37	35
		4				Reviewed	4	8
		3				Compiled	5	9
		1				Tax Returns	3	1
1	2	4	4	1	3	Other	17	19
		30 (4/1-9/30/04)	39 (10/1/04-3/31/05)					
1	3	24	26	6	9	**NUMBER OF STATEMENTS**	66	72
%	%	%	%	%	%	**ASSETS**	%	%
		16.8	12.5			Cash & Equivalents	14.1	9.9
		12.0	10.6			Trade Receivables (net)	13.4	10.9
		.2	1.2			Inventory	1.8	1.1
		4.6	5.1			All Other Current	4.0	7.5
		33.6	29.4			Total Current	33.3	29.4
		52.5	50.0			Fixed Assets (net)	40.1	41.1
		7.0	8.7			Intangibles (net)	12.2	14.0
		7.0	11.9			All Other Non-Current	14.4	15.4
		100.0	100.0			Total	100.0	100.0
						LIABILITIES		
		3.8	2.2			Notes Payable-Short Term	3.7	2.7
		4.2	2.0			Cur. Mat.-L/T/D	5.1	6.3
		5.3	3.9			Trade Payables	5.3	4.7
		.2	.3			Income Taxes Payable	.3	.1
		7.6	6.7			All Other Current	9.8	9.4
		21.1	15.2			Total Current	24.2	23.3
		22.3	21.9			Long-Term Debt	30.6	36.1
		.0	1.0			Deferred Taxes	.4	.3
		10.9	4.9			All Other Non-Current	10.7	10.2
		45.7	56.9			Net Worth	34.1	30.1
		100.0	100.0			Total Liabilities & Net Worth	100.0	100.0
						INCOME DATA		
		100.0	100.0			Net Sales	100.0	100.0
						Gross Profit		
		98.0	93.6			Operating Expenses	90.0	92.6
		2.0	6.4			Operating Profit	10.0	7.4
		2.2	.3			All Other Expenses (net)	.1	5.4
		−.2	6.1			Profit Before Taxes	9.9	2.0
						RATIOS		
		3.1	3.4				3.7	2.5
		1.8	1.8			Current	1.7	1.5
		.6	1.3				.9	.8
		2.4	3.1				3.2	2.1
		1.2	1.6			Quick	1.4	1.1
		.4	.7				.7	.4
		6 56.5	14 25.2				21 17.2	12 31.3
		29 12.4	44 8.2			Sales/Receivables	56 6.6	46 7.9
		56 6.6	65 5.6				67 5.5	71 5.2
						Cost of Sales/Inventory		
						Cost of Sales/Payables		
		5.2	3.0				3.5	4.7
		12.8	7.0			Sales/Working Capital	7.8	10.9
		−9.8	22.5				−69.6	−11.8
		17.3	14.0				10.9	5.2
		(20) 2.2	(21) 3.9			EBIT/Interest	(46) 2.9	(51) 1.2
		−.9	.5				1.0	−.7
						Net Profit + Depr., Dep., Amort./Cur. Mat. L./T/D		
		.7	.6				.5	.6
		1.1	.9			Fixed/Worth	1.1	1.4
		2.1	2.0				NM	−2.3
		.4	.2				.3	.4
		.7	.6			Debt/Worth	1.0	1.5
		6.3	2.1				NM	−7.4
		27.9	10.0				30.9	27.7
		(22) 2.4	(23) 4.1			% Profit Before Taxes/Tangible Net Worth	(50) 13.9	(48) 5.5
		−9.0	−1.0				1.2	−3.9
		13.5	6.8				17.6	10.8
		1.8	2.6			% Profit Before Taxes/Total Assets	5.4	.2
		−4.4	−.3				−.2	−4.9
		4.9	2.7				4.6	4.7
		1.7	1.7			Sales/Net Fixed Assets	2.5	2.2
		1.0	.9				1.5	1.3
		1.4	1.2				1.2	1.3
		.8	.7			Sales/Total Assets	.9	.8
		.6	.5				.6	.5
		5.9	5.6				4.6	4.0
		(22) 8.4	(24) 9.5			% Depr., Dep., Amort./Sales	(56) 6.6	(67) 7.3
		13.7	13.3				10.3	13.2
								2.6
						% Officers', Directors', Owners' Comp/Sales		(13) 4.8
								12.6
571M	6278M	134935M	549154M	491255M	668809M	Net Sales ($)	1553205M	1436797M
153M	4841M	130576M	611511M	444105M	1272513M	Total Assets ($)	2307154M	1906116M

M = $ thousand   MM = $ million
See Pages 11 through 21 for Explanation of Ratios and Data

Comparative Historical Data				Current Data Sorted By Sales					
39	42	46	**Type of Statement** Unqualified	1	4	4	12	9	16
9	9	4	Reviewed	1			1	2	
3	9	3	Compiled		2		1		
4	4	1	Tax Returns			1			
22	19	15	Other	1	2	2	4	1	5
4/1/02-3/31/03 ALL	4/1/03-3/31/04 ALL	4/1/04-3/31/05 ALL		30 (4/1-9/30/04)			39 (10/1/04-3/31/05)		
				0-1MM	1-3MM	3-5MM	5-10MM	10-25MM	25MM & OVER
77	83	69	**NUMBER OF STATEMENTS**	3	8	7	18	12	21
%	%	%	**ASSETS**	%	%	%	%	%	%
9.7	11.3	13.6	Cash & Equivalents				17.0	13.2	9.5
12.9	13.5	12.1	Trade Receivables (net)				8.9	18.1	15.2
1.2	.5	.6	Inventory				.4	.9	.7
5.3	7.2	5.0	All Other Current				5.7	4.0	4.5
29.0	32.4	31.3	Total Current				31.9	36.2	29.9
44.1	41.0	44.9	Fixed Assets (net)				52.9	38.8	32.9
14.6	16.2	10.8	Intangibles (net)				6.3	12.7	18.0
12.3	10.4	13.1	All Other Non-Current				8.8	12.3	19.2
100.0	100.0	100.0	Total				100.0	100.0	100.0
			LIABILITIES						
9.5	4.4	3.3	Notes Payable-Short Term				2.9	.8	1.6
6.0	8.5	3.2	Cur. Mat.-L/T/D				1.5	3.0	3.3
5.4	5.5	4.5	Trade Payables				4.2	2.0	4.7
.0	.1	.3	Income Taxes Payable				.0	.7	.5
8.8	8.9	7.9	All Other Current				5.3	12.1	9.5
29.6	27.4	19.1	Total Current				13.9	18.7	19.6
28.8	28.4	26.0	Long-Term Debt				22.2	14.2	39.4
.4	.2	.5	Deferred Taxes				.4	.0	.3
5.2	8.5	10.3	All Other Non-Current				2.5	16.2	6.8
36.0	35.4	44.1	Net Worth				60.9	50.9	34.0
100.0	100.0	100.0	Total Liabilities & Net Worth				100.0	100.0	100.0
			INCOME DATA						
100.0	100.0	100.0	Net Sales				100.0	100.0	100.0
			Gross Profit						
92.6	92.0	93.5	Operating Expenses				96.7	88.0	89.4
7.4	8.0	6.5	Operating Profit				3.3	12.0	10.6
5.1	5.0	2.1	All Other Expenses (net)				3.4	2.6	2.4
2.4	3.0	4.4	Profit Before Taxes				-.1	9.3	8.3
			RATIOS						
2.8	2.7	3.0					3.7	2.9	1.8
1.3	1.6	1.7	Current				2.2	2.2	1.6
.7	.9	.9					.8	1.3	1.0
1.7	2.1	2.6					3.2	2.9	1.8
1.0	1.2	1.2	Quick				1.5	1.8	1.1
.5	.6	.7					.7	1.1	.8
22 16.7	23 16.1	12 30.4					8 43.6	36 10.0	34 10.6
56 6.5	55 6.6	44 8.3	Sales/Receivables				14 26.1	56 6.5	59 6.2
70 5.2	71 5.1	64 5.7					47 7.8	66 5.5	69 5.3
			Cost of Sales/Inventory						
			Cost of Sales/Payables						
4.6	4.3	3.9					3.1	3.3	5.0
14.1	10.8	8.7	Sales/Working Capital				6.7	6.8	8.7
-15.7	-32.6	-31.2					-30.5	21.8	NM
4.6	7.8	14.3					17.8	18.9	11.4
(60) 2.3	(66) 2.9	(58) 3.1	EBIT/Interest				(14) 1.4	(10) 13.1	(19) 3.7
.3	.3	.7					-1.1	1.9	.9
2.8	2.1		Net Profit + Depr., Dep.,						
(12) 1.5	(10) 1.4		Amort./Cur. Mat. L/T/D						
1.0	.8								
.7	.7	.6					.6	.5	.7
1.4	1.8	1.1	Fixed/Worth				.9	.8	3.3
-3.5	-2.0	5.1					2.1	1.9	-3.6
.4	.3	.4					.3	.2	1.1
2.1	2.0	1.3	Debt/Worth				.5	.4	3.7
-7.0	-3.9	11.2					2.6	5.4	-14.3
21.1	27.5	18.5	% Profit Before Taxes/Tangible				14.4	45.8	10.4
(53) 2.9	(55) 9.1	(57) 3.5	Net Worth				(17) 1.1	(10) 12.2	(14) 3.1
-10.4	-.4	-5.5					-6.7	4.6	-11.7
9.2	9.5	10.2	% Profit Before Taxes/Total				9.2	22.0	9.3
2.3	2.5	2.4	Assets				.4	6.1	4.6
-2.8	-1.9	-1.0					-2.9	3.8	.7
3.7	4.1	3.7					2.9	6.5	4.2
2.1	2.1	1.8	Sales/Net Fixed Assets				1.2	2.4	2.6
1.3	1.3	1.1					.9	1.9	1.6
1.2	1.3	1.2					1.0	1.7	1.3
.9	.8	.8	Sales/Total Assets				.7	1.0	.8
.6	.5	.5					.5	.6	.5
5.2	6.1	5.5					5.1	5.6	3.7
(68) 8.3	(78) 8.1	(61) 8.5	% Depr., Dep., Amort./Sales				(17) 8.3	7.9	(15) 8.6
14.3	13.7	13.2					13.3	12.9	12.8
1.8	1.9		% Officers', Directors',						
(11) 5.6	(15) 5.7		Owners' Comp/Sales						
8.8	27.6								
1486458M	1982516M	1851002M	Net Sales ($)	2235M	18036M	26500M	136060M	197861M	1470310M
2291395M	2475541M	2463699M	Total Assets ($)	5128M	24265M	54008M	277116M	224458M	1878724M

M = $ thousand   MM = $ million
See Pages 11 through 21 for Explanation of Ratios and Data

Current Data Sorted By Assets							**Comparative Historical Data**	
1	3	2	13	7	6	Type of Statement Unqualified	19	27
	2	6	1			Reviewed	12	12
	3					Compiled	10	10
2	3	3				Tax Returns	4	6
1	3	3	7	4	1	Other	26	24
	9 (4/1-9/30/04)		62 (10/1/04-3/31/05)				4/1/00-3/31/01	4/1/01-3/31/02
0-500M	500M-2MM	2-10MM	10-50MM	50-100MM	100-250MM		ALL	ALL
4	14	14	21	11	7	**NUMBER OF STATEMENTS**	71	79
%	%	%	%	%	%	**ASSETS**	%	%
	13.3	12.4	7.9	12.2		Cash & Equivalents	10.4	11.1
	37.6	20.2	13.5	12.4		Trade Receivables (net)	11.8	11.1
	8.6	1.2	4.4	.4		Inventory	1.7	3.0
	5.1	3.4	1.7	3.1		All Other Current	3.6	4.0
	64.5	37.1	27.6	28.0		Total Current	27.4	29.2
	26.3	45.0	45.9	39.3		Fixed Assets (net)	52.3	49.3
	.9	12.7	20.0	27.1		Intangibles (net)	13.7	14.9
	8.3	5.1	6.4	5.6		All Other Non-Current	6.5	6.6
	100.0	100.0	100.0	100.0		Total	100.0	100.0
						LIABILITIES		
	24.9	5.0	7.4	6.8		Notes Payable-Short Term	4.9	4.9
	6.0	5.4	6.4	4.3		Cur. Mat.-L/T/D	4.8	9.7
	9.6	9.5	13.3	3.9		Trade Payables	6.7	7.3
	1.2	.6	.3	.4		Income Taxes Payable	.2	.1
	10.5	10.0	7.7	9.5		All Other Current	8.7	13.1
	52.1	30.5	35.0	24.9		Total Current	25.4	35.0
	8.0	32.0	30.9	38.6		Long-Term Debt	43.8	38.3
	.1	1.4	2.4	3.1		Deferred Taxes	1.0	1.2
	19.9	14.0	9.8	12.6		All Other Non-Current	8.7	10.9
	20.0	22.2	21.9	20.8		Net Worth	21.1	14.6
	100.0	100.0	100.0	100.0		Total Liabilities & Net Worth	100.0	100.0
						INCOME DATA		
	100.0	100.0	100.0	100.0		Net Sales	100.0	100.0
						Gross Profit		
	94.3	84.7	89.3	87.3		Operating Expenses	91.7	94.0
	5.7	15.3	10.7	12.7		Operating Profit	8.3	6.0
	.9	4.1	5.8	5.1		All Other Expenses (net)	7.1	7.5
	4.8	11.2	4.8	7.6		Profit Before Taxes	1.1	-1.5
						RATIOS		
	4.4	1.8	1.1	4.9		Current	1.8	1.3
	1.9	.9	.6	1.0			.9	.8
	1.0	.3	.3	.3			.4	.3
	4.4	1.6	.8	4.3		Quick	1.5	1.0
	1.4	.7	.6	.6			.7	.6
	.6	.2	.1	.3			.3	.2
30	12.3	6 64.7	8 43.8	14 26.2		Sales/Receivables	7 55.1	6 57.5
39	9.3	24 15.2	19 19.1	23 15.9			19 18.9	20 18.2
64	5.7	50 7.3	47 7.7	55 6.6			37 10.0	38 9.7
						Cost of Sales/Inventory		
						Cost of Sales/Payables		
	5.6	12.5	60.8	4.7		Sales/Working Capital	8.5	13.7
	14.1	-216.2	-15.1	-57.8			-123.5	-22.5
	NM	-4.1	-4.7	-11.0			-9.6	-4.6
	40.3	9.8	9.0	47.1		EBIT/Interest	4.8	4.4
	10.3	(11) 6.4	(19) 1.3	1.9			(57) 1.6	(67) 1.3
	2.6	3.1	.2	.8			.4	.1
						Net Profit + Depr., Dep., Amort./Cur. Mat. L./T/D	5.5	12.6
							(15) 2.6	(17) 2.0
							1.2	1.0
	.1	.5	1.0	2.9		Fixed/Worth	1.3	1.2
	.4	1.9	7.7	-6.2			4.7	8.1
	1.4	-4.7	-2.8	-1.3			-3.1	-1.8
	.3	1.8	3.5	5.7		Debt/Worth	1.3	1.8
	1.8	3.9	-15.4	-8.1			5.6	10.8
	8.2	-3.7	-4.4	-3.6			-4.7	-3.7
	91.9		57.4			% Profit Before Taxes/Tangible Net Worth	59.8	45.8
	(12) 29.2		(10) 28.8				(46) 25.3	(46) 13.1
	11.4		9.9				-9.8	-1.0
	27.0	18.3	9.1	9.8		% Profit Before Taxes/Total Assets	14.7	10.4
	14.9	13.2	3.0	1.6			2.7	.9
	2.7	3.7	-1.8	-.7			-5.5	-6.4
	40.7	29.1	17.3	5.9		Sales/Net Fixed Assets	4.7	5.6
	25.3	4.3	1.4	1.6			1.7	1.5
	6.3	.9	.6	.8			1.0	.8
	4.2	3.2	1.9	1.2		Sales/Total Assets	1.8	1.6
	2.9	.8	.7	.5			.9	.7
	2.5	.5	.4	.4			.6	.5
	1.0	1.2	6.9			% Depr., Dep., Amort./Sales	6.0	5.3
	(12) 1.5	(12) 11.9	(17) 17.7				(56) 12.3	(63) 12.9
	6.3	18.1	23.7				22.6	26.0
	3.0					% Officers', Directors', Owners' Comp/Sales	2.6	2.5
	(10) 5.2						(18) 3.4	(22) 5.1
	8.1						7.0	8.5
5327M	46390M	97916M	575382M	729791M	681349M	Net Sales ($)	1305179M	1395217M
1443M	14941M	63315M	522089M	822724M	1115520M	Total Assets ($)	2162517M	2279968M

M = $ thousand   MM = $ million
See Pages 11 through 21 for Explanation of Ratios and Data

Comparative Historical Data			Type of Statement	Current Data Sorted By Sales					
23	21	32	Unqualified	1	2	3	5	8	13
12	10	9	Reviewed		3	2		3	1
6	10	3	Compiled	1	1		1		
15	15	8	Tax Returns		5	1	2		
23	10	19	Other	1	3	2	2	4	7
4/1/02-3/31/03 ALL	4/1/03-3/31/04 ALL	4/1/04-3/31/05 ALL		0-1MM	9 (4/1-9/30/04) 1-3MM	3-5MM	62 (10/1/04-3/31/05) 5-10MM	10-25MM	25MM & OVER
79	66	71	NUMBER OF STATEMENTS	3	14	8	10	15	21
%	%	%	ASSETS	%	%	%	%	%	%
10.1	7.8	10.4	Cash & Equivalents		12.3		1.1	8.2	14.6
15.9	14.4	19.4	Trade Receivables (net)		24.7		21.6	17.6	18.0
3.8	3.5	3.5	Inventory		6.0		1.7	1.0	4.2
3.6	3.9	3.0	All Other Current		4.3		2.1	2.6	3.2
33.4	29.6	36.3	Total Current		47.3		26.5	29.5	40.0
43.7	46.5	40.0	Fixed Assets (net)		36.5		49.8	35.8	34.7
14.6	13.4	17.2	Intangibles (net)		10.8		19.1	22.3	20.0
8.3	10.4	6.5	All Other Non-Current		5.3		4.6	12.4	5.2
100.0	100.0	100.0	Total		100.0		100.0	100.0	100.0
			LIABILITIES						
5.4	8.6	9.1	Notes Payable-Short Term		5.6		3.8	6.5	8.5
7.3	5.8	5.7	Cur. Mat.-L/T/D		7.5		10.6	2.8	4.2
9.9	9.8	9.4	Trade Payables		8.6		5.2	9.6	12.7
.4	.5	.5	Income Taxes Payable		.4		.0	.7	.5
11.9	11.0	9.1	All Other Current		6.7		11.1	9.3	10.1
34.9	35.7	33.8	Total Current		28.8		30.7	28.9	35.9
37.3	30.5	28.1	Long-Term Debt		20.8		26.1	29.9	30.1
.7	1.1	2.1	Deferred Taxes		.1		4.1	5.5	1.2
11.1	14.6	12.7	All Other Non-Current		9.3		7.5	9.6	8.8
16.0	18.1	23.3	Net Worth		41.0		31.5	26.0	24.1
100.0	100.0	100.0	Total Liabilities & Net Worth		100.0		100.0	100.0	100.0
			INCOME DATA						
100.0	100.0	100.0	Net Sales		100.0		100.0	100.0	100.0
			Gross Profit						
94.9	92.8	89.4	Operating Expenses		89.0		92.8	86.9	88.8
5.1	7.2	10.6	Operating Profit		11.0		7.2	13.1	11.2
4.2	2.8	4.2	All Other Expenses (net)		1.6		5.5	4.1	4.5
1.0	4.4	6.4	Profit Before Taxes		9.4		1.7	9.0	6.7
			RATIOS						
1.5	1.4	1.6			5.6		1.6	1.4	1.2
.8	.7	1.0	Current		1.3		.3	.6	1.0
.4	.2	.4			.6		.1	.5	.9
1.3	.9	1.3			5.3		1.3	1.2	.9
.6	.5	.7	Quick		.9		.3	.6	.8
.3	.2	.3			.3		.3	.3	.7
8 44.8	8 43.4	13 27.6		8 45.4		6 62.3	14 26.2		24 15.2
23 15.6	18 19.8	32 11.3	Sales/Receivables	23 15.7		15 24.2	33 11.0		35 10.4
43 8.6	39 9.4	48 7.6		57 6.4		46 7.9	48 7.6		53 6.8
			Cost of Sales/Inventory						
			Cost of Sales/Payables						
14.4	29.0	13.4			5.0		126.4	22.1	33.9
-32.7	-16.2	-406.7	Sales/Working Capital		27.4		-6.8	-18.1	274.3
-6.5	-4.6	-5.9			-24.3		-2.2	-5.8	-38.2
4.9	6.1	14.1			13.7		65.6	17.9	15.0
(66) 1.8	(58) 2.4	(65) 3.8	EBIT/Interest	(12) 6.1		2.6	(13) 2.9		(20) 3.8
.2	.5	.9			3.2		.1	1.1	.7
9.5	2.3	4.6	Net Profit + Depr., Dep.,						
(13) 2.6	(12) 1.5	(14) 3.4	Amort./Cur. Mat. L/T/D						
2.1	1.1	1.6							
.9	.8	.6			.1		.5	1.0	.9
9.2	7.4	2.9	Fixed/Worth		.6		3.7	-8.6	3.3
-1.5	-4.6	-2.8			5.7		-3.7	-.7	-5.7
2.0	2.2	1.8			.4		1.6	2.8	3.9
13.7	13.8	6.8	Debt/Worth		2.7		3.4	-13.0	8.3
-3.9	-5.9	-4.1			NM		-5.0	-2.5	-7.2
48.2	72.5	71.2	% Profit Before Taxes/Tangible		136.6				56.5
(42) 19.7	(37) 34.0	(41) 32.0	Net Worth	(11) 27.6					(11) 46.3
.8	4.6	17.8			-1.6				27.6
14.3	13.7	18.2	% Profit Before Taxes/Total		19.3		16.6	22.0	9.7
1.9	3.6	6.4	Assets		10.1		2.6	13.7	7.2
-3.6	-3.0	-.6			2.6		-3.3	1.1	-1.2
13.9	12.6	23.1			50.1		43.0	16.2	17.3
3.1	3.5	2.1	Sales/Net Fixed Assets		15.1		.9	1.8	2.1
1.0	1.0	.9			1.4		.7	.9	1.5
2.7	3.5	2.9			3.1		2.9	3.1	1.9
1.3	1.3	.9	Sales/Total Assets		2.7		.6	.9	.9
.5	.5	.4			.6		.4	.4	.6
3.0	4.3	1.3			1.2			3.6	.7
(64) 9.9	(54) 11.1	(54) 11.1	% Depr., Dep., Amort./Sales	(12) 5.9			(13) 17.3		(10) 5.2
21.6	20.6	22.7			16.8			22.7	18.9
2.8	2.3	1.7	% Officers', Directors',						
(32) 4.6	(24) 4.1	(21) 4.1	Owners' Comp/Sales						
6.9	5.8	8.5							
2612018M	967640M	2136155M	Net Sales ($)	1895M	26762M	31564M	81180M	262530M	1732224M
2542347M	1261352M	2540032M	Total Assets ($)	6774M	25513M	34533M	144455M	511739M	1817018M

© RMA 2005

M = $ thousand   MM = $ million
See Pages 11 through 21 for Explanation of Ratios and Data

Current Data Sorted By Assets | Comparative Historical Data

0-500M	500M-2MM	2-10MM	10-50MM	50-100MM	100-250MM	Type of Statement	4/1/00-3/31/01 ALL	4/1/01-3/31/02 ALL
2	3	36	73	27	18	Unqualified	42	51
	5	12	1			Reviewed	12	12
2	4	8	1		1	Compiled	23	22
4	4					Tax Returns	14	5
4	5	17	27	6	5	Other	37	52
\<-- 37 (4/1-9/30/04) -->			228 (10/1/04-3/31/05)					
12	21	73	102	33	24	NUMBER OF STATEMENTS	128	142
%	%	%	%	%	%	**ASSETS**	%	%
24.4	10.2	14.4	14.0	10.4	13.8	Cash & Equivalents	12.5	11.0
13.0	33.4	16.4	8.1	8.7	6.3	Trade Receivables (net)	26.0	24.3
4.8	11.2	4.2	3.2	2.5	2.0	Inventory	6.2	5.7
3.8	2.3	5.7	3.3	1.9	2.2	All Other Current	4.0	2.7
45.9	57.1	40.6	28.6	23.5	24.3	Total Current	48.7	43.8
40.1	28.6	39.4	52.4	49.7	53.7	Fixed Assets (net)	34.6	38.0
3.7	10.7	6.9	6.6	16.8	13.3	Intangibles (net)	7.1	7.5
10.2	3.6	13.0	12.4	10.0	8.7	All Other Non-Current	9.6	10.7
100.0	100.0	100.0	100.0	100.0	100.0	Total	100.0	100.0
						LIABILITIES		
2.9	13.1	5.3	2.1	.8	.1	Notes Payable-Short Term	10.6	7.2
6.9	5.1	4.6	3.8	4.5	2.5	Cur. Mat.-L/T/D	3.0	4.7
8.4	21.1	9.7	6.1	7.1	3.3	Trade Payables	15.3	13.8
2.5	.1	.3	.5	.1	.4	Income Taxes Payable	.7	.6
10.9	12.3	10.3	5.4	3.8	3.7	All Other Current	9.9	10.6
31.6	51.8	30.3	17.8	16.4	10.0	Total Current	39.6	36.9
33.6	24.1	20.8	27.6	35.9	31.3	Long-Term Debt	17.9	22.8
.0	.0	.9	1.7	1.0	2.3	Deferred Taxes	2.2	1.9
23.1	4.5	6.7	6.6	4.7	9.6	All Other Non-Current	4.9	8.9
11.6	19.6	41.3	46.3	42.0	46.8	Net Worth	35.6	29.4
100.0	100.0	100.0	100.0	100.0	100.0	Total Liabilities & Net Worth	100.0	100.0
						INCOME DATA		
100.0	100.0	100.0	100.0	100.0	100.0	Net Sales	100.0	100.0
						Gross Profit		
94.5	95.5	86.0	83.9	84.1	83.4	Operating Expenses	89.4	92.1
5.5	4.5	14.0	16.1	15.9	16.6	Operating Profit	10.6	7.9
1.2	3.0	3.6	3.4	5.9	4.8	All Other Expenses (net)	–.6	3.6
4.4	1.6	10.4	12.8	10.0	11.9	Profit Before Taxes	11.2	4.2
						RATIOS		
2.5	1.6	2.2	2.6	2.2	2.9	Current	2.4	2.0
1.0	1.0	1.5	1.7	1.4	2.0		1.3	1.2
.6	.7	.9	1.1	.9	1.3		.9	.8
2.5	1.4	1.9	2.1	1.7	2.5	Quick	1.8	1.6
.9	.9	1.1	1.2	1.1	1.3		1.0	.9
.4	.5	.5	.8	.7	.9		.5	.6
0 UND	21 17.0	18 19.8	13 28.1	21 17.8	19 19.0	Sales/Receivables	33 11.1	28 13.2
7 50.2	39 9.3	34 10.8	30 12.0	37 9.8	36 10.1		49 7.4	49 7.4
33 11.0	51 7.2	46 7.9	41 8.8	53 6.8	47 7.8		70 5.2	69 5.3
						Cost of Sales/Inventory		
						Cost of Sales/Payables		
12.6	12.7	3.6	2.4	4.4	3.0	Sales/Working Capital	4.9	6.7
UND	344.9	12.4	6.5	8.2	5.8		18.4	29.6
–43.3	–16.0	–54.4	44.8	–43.9	19.4		–45.6	–17.2
	9.0	8.6	7.0	6.7	7.5	EBIT/Interest	17.8	7.2
	(18) 3.4	(64) 5.0	(97) 3.9	(32) 3.0	(23) 3.8		(117) 5.4	(127) 2.7
	.5	2.7	2.2	1.5	.6		1.1	.1
		4.6	7.8	5.4		Net Profit + Depr., Dep., Amort./Cur. Mat. L /T/D	12.2	7.2
		(34) 2.8	(62) 3.9	(20) 3.1			(35) 5.2	(45) 2.8
		1.6	2.6	1.9			2.5	.7
.1	.4	.4	.8	1.5	.9	Fixed/Worth	.4	.5
1.0	2.6	1.0	1.2	2.3	1.6		1.0	1.4
5.1	–1.7	2.7	2.4	7.6	3.4		2.6	15.2
.6	1.8	.7	.6	1.2	.7	Debt/Worth	.7	1.0
1.9	12.8	1.5	1.2	2.2	1.3		2.0	2.4
NM	–4.2	3.9	4.2	11.7	3.7		5.4	61.9
	85.0	31.9	21.4	19.6	37.5	% Profit Before Taxes/Tangible Net Worth	60.3	56.0
	(13) 36.6	(63) 14.2	(90) 13.4	(27) 10.3	(23) 16.2		(108) 26.1	(110) 16.8
	11.9	5.9	5.5	3.3	–5.3		7.3	.5
54.5	22.0	11.5	9.5	7.8	10.1	% Profit Before Taxes/Total Assets	21.4	13.9
11.0	8.2	6.1	5.7	5.5	6.6		8.6	4.1
–1.3	.0	2.4	2.6	1.7	–.9		.6	–1.8
141.7	51.4	13.2	1.8	1.8	1.2	Sales/Net Fixed Assets	24.2	18.1
12.1	13.6	1.5	.8	.8	.8		6.6	4.8
4.6	4.3	.8	.5	.6	.6		.9	.7
6.1	4.5	2.2	.8	.8	.6	Sales/Total Assets	3.0	2.9
4.1	3.3	.6	.5	.4	.5		1.7	1.3
2.7	1.6	.4	.3	.3	.4		.5	.5
	.9	5.2	11.9	13.8		% Depr., Dep., Amort./Sales	1.3	1.8
	(18) 2.0	(67) 14.0	(99) 17.4	(27) 22.6			(113) 3.8	(117) 5.4
	8.0	19.7	22.3	25.1			15.0	17.2
						% Officers', Directors', Owners' Comp/Sales	3.7	2.5
							(26) 5.8	(24) 6.2
							8.6	16.6
11181M	78505M	563368M	1801913M	1580263M	3812407M	Net Sales ($)	3140886M	4198759M
2829M	23933M	421472M	2421930M	2480281M	3683192M	Total Assets ($)	3651877M	3852025M

M = $ thousand   MM = $ million
See Pages 11 through 21 for Explanation of Ratios and Data

Comparative Historical Data | Current Data Sorted By Sales

			Type of Statement						
64	60	159	Unqualified	5	20	12	35	39	48
14	14	18	Reviewed		2	6	6	4	
20	31	16	Compiled	3	6	1	3	1	2
6	13	8	Tax Returns	2	4	2			
57	49	64	Other	3	6	7	9	18	21
4/1/02-3/31/03 ALL	4/1/03-3/31/04 ALL	4/1/04-3/31/05 ALL		37 (4/1-9/30/04)		228 (10/1/04-3/31/05)			
				0-1MM	1-3MM	3-5MM	5-10MM	10-25MM	25MM & OVER
161	167	265	**NUMBER OF STATEMENTS**	13	38	28	53	62	71
%	%	%	**ASSETS**	%	%	%	%	%	%
13.1	12.9	13.8	Cash & Equivalents	23.4	11.1	10.9	16.1	13.1	13.5
23.8	23.3	12.5	Trade Receivables (net)	8.6	10.2	10.5	11.3	14.0	14.8
6.4	6.5	4.0	Inventory	2.6	3.9	6.2	2.7	3.7	4.6
4.5	4.8	3.6	All Other Current	1.5	4.7	3.6	5.2	3.0	2.9
47.9	47.5	33.9	Total Current	36.1	29.9	31.2	35.3	33.8	35.8
35.7	35.3	46.1	Fixed Assets (net)	32.8	51.1	44.6	49.7	47.1	43.0
6.7	7.5	8.8	Intangibles (net)	11.5	7.9	7.5	4.1	10.0	11.7
9.7	9.7	11.2	All Other Non-Current	19.5	11.2	16.7	10.9	9.1	9.4
100.0	100.0	100.0	Total	100.0	100.0	100.0	100.0	100.0	100.0
			LIABILITIES						
7.2	6.8	3.5	Notes Payable-Short Term	2.4	3.1	7.6	4.4	3.0	2.2
3.8	4.0	4.2	Cur. Mat.-L/T/D	3.6	5.2	8.3	4.0	3.2	3.2
15.1	13.4	8.3	Trade Payables	6.6	6.0	7.1	5.6	9.1	11.5
.3	.5	.5	Income Taxes Payable	2.3	.3	.3	.6	.2	.3
18.7	15.5	7.2	All Other Current	7.5	5.5	6.2	8.3	6.7	7.9
45.1	40.3	23.7	Total Current	22.4	20.2	29.5	23.0	22.3	25.1
20.9	21.7	27.1	Long-Term Debt	33.1	32.0	24.0	25.9	24.7	27.6
1.4	1.4	1.2	Deferred Taxes	.0	.3	2.6	.9	1.7	1.4
7.2	6.9	7.2	All Other Non-Current	24.3	6.3	3.7	7.3	5.6	7.5
25.4	29.7	40.7	Net Worth	20.2	41.2	40.2	42.9	45.8	38.5
100.0	100.0	100.0	Total Liabilities & Net Worth	100.0	100.0	100.0	100.0	100.0	100.0
			INCOME DATA						
100.0	100.0	100.0	Net Sales	100.0	100.0	100.0	100.0	100.0	100.0
			Gross Profit						
89.7	92.4	85.8	Operating Expenses	90.9	83.0	86.1	82.7	85.4	89.1
10.3	7.6	14.2	Operating Profit	9.1	17.0	13.9	17.3	14.6	10.9
3.4	2.0	3.7	All Other Expenses (net)	4.6	4.6	2.9	3.5	4.1	3.3
6.8	5.7	10.4	Profit Before Taxes	4.4	12.5	11.0	13.8	10.5	7.6
			RATIOS						
2.3	2.3	2.4		2.3	2.6	2.2	3.2	2.5	2.2
1.2	1.3	1.5	Current	1.0	1.7	1.3	2.0	1.3	1.5
.8	.8	1.0		.7	.8	.7	1.1	1.0	1.1
1.8	1.9	1.9		2.3	2.1	1.8	2.8	1.7	1.7
(160) .9	1.0	1.1	Quick	.9	1.1	.8	1.4	1.1	1.1
.6	.5	.6		.7	.4	.4	.7	.7	.7
29 12.8	22 16.7	18 20.8		0 UND	11 32.8	8 44.3	15 25.0	19 18.9	24 15.0
42 8.6	38 9.5	32 11.4	Sales/Receivables	35 10.4	24 15.4	29 12.8	28 12.9	34 10.7	37 9.7
57 6.4	58 6.3	45 8.0		56 6.5	38 9.7	41 9.0	43 8.4	49 7.5	49 7.4
			Cost of Sales/Inventory						
			Cost of Sales/Payables						
5.8	4.8	3.5		11.8	2.6	5.0	2.2	3.8	4.7
23.8	26.7	11.8	Sales/Working Capital	270.0	10.0	23.3	4.4	12.0	13.1
-17.4	-24.9	-351.7		-35.0	-36.3	-10.6	29.9	NM	72.8
7.1	10.5	7.4			7.4	6.3	8.3	11.6	7.4
(140) 3.5	(147) 3.4	(243) 4.0	EBIT/Interest	(35) 3.8	(26) 4.3	(52) 4.6	(56) 3.8	(66) 4.1	
.6	1.0	1.9			2.1	1.4	2.8	1.9	1.3
5.5	6.9	6.1			6.1	3.0	6.6	7.4	9.6
(54) 2.7	(40) 3.3	(123) 3.3	Net Profit + Depr., Dep., Amort./Cur. Mat. L/T/D	(19) 3.1	(16) 2.1	(34) 4.0	(32) 3.7	(21) 4.3	
1.8	1.5	2.2			2.0	1.4	2.6	2.4	1.9
.4	.5	.7		.1	.7	.7	.8	.6	.8
1.3	1.3	1.4	Fixed/Worth	.6	1.4	1.2	1.2	1.3	1.6
5.6	8.1	3.4		-1.7	4.7	2.8	2.2	2.7	6.2
1.0	.7	.7		.7	.6	.8	.7	.6	.8
2.3	2.2	1.5	Debt/Worth	3.1	1.6	1.8	1.3	1.6	2.2
18.9	19.1	4.9		-3.0	4.8	4.9	3.5	3.2	10.1
61.1	54.5	30.0			46.5	36.7	25.5	25.2	36.6
(126) 17.8	(129) 19.6	(225) 13.9	% Profit Before Taxes/Tangible Net Worth	(34) 14.1	(25) 13.4	(45) 14.6	(53) 13.7	(60) 14.2	
4.0	4.3	5.0			3.5	6.0	7.7	5.7	1.1
15.3	13.8	10.9		14.5	14.7	11.3	10.5	10.9	8.7
6.5	6.3	5.8	% Profit Before Taxes/Total Assets	2.6	5.7	4.6	7.0	5.3	6.3
.7	1.1	1.9		-9.6	1.5	1.6	3.8	2.1	.9
24.3	25.1	8.5		38.7	6.3	7.6	3.0	9.0	13.9
6.1	6.9	1.1	Sales/Net Fixed Assets	10.8	1.1	.9	.8	.9	1.5
.9	1.0	.7		1.0	.7	.7	.5	.6	.8
3.6	2.9	1.6		4.7	1.9	1.2	1.2	1.4	1.8
1.6	1.7	.6	Sales/Total Assets	1.6	.5	.5	.5	.6	.7
.5	.5	.4		.3	.3	.3	.3	.4	.4
1.6	1.2	5.5			5.0	12.6	11.5	5.3	2.8
(133) 6.8	(133) 5.3	(226) 16.4	% Depr., Dep., Amort./Sales	(37) 15.9	(26) 17.1	(49) 19.5	(60) 15.4	(46) 12.7	
18.5	16.2	22.2			22.0	21.8	24.2	22.7	20.6
2.6	3.9	3.8	% Officers', Directors', Owners' Comp/Sales						
(23) 4.4	(32) 7.6	(26) 7.4							
11.7	8.9	11.4							
4411090M	4191959M	7847637M	Net Sales ($)	6796M	77116M	107490M	382998M	943775M	6329462M
4385696M	4414003M	9033637M	Total Assets ($)	11459M	153718M	214527M	824807M	1693512M	6135614M

© RMA 2005   M = $ thousand   MM = $ million
See Pages 11 through 21 for Explanation of Ratios and Data

Current Data Sorted By Assets   Comparative Historical Data

0-500M	500M-2MM	2-10MM	10-50MM	50-100MM	100-250MM	Type of Statement	4/1/00-3/31/01 ALL	4/1/01-3/31/02 ALL
		7	22	5	3	Unqualified	20	20
1		6				Reviewed	6	7
4	8					Compiled	12	20
4	3	1				Tax Returns	10	7
	8	12	8	1	1	Other	62	47
17 (4/1-9/30/04)			77 (10/1/04-3/31/05)					
9	19	26	30	6	4	**NUMBER OF STATEMENTS**	110	101
%	%	%	%	%	%	**ASSETS**	%	%
	12.2	11.7	12.3			Cash & Equivalents	12.8	11.8
	24.7	25.8	9.8			Trade Receivables (net)	25.0	22.3
	15.4	12.9	4.9			Inventory	11.6	13.0
	6.6	3.0	3.4			All Other Current	3.1	4.9
	58.9	53.3	30.3			Total Current	52.5	51.9
	24.8	26.9	47.4			Fixed Assets (net)	30.8	30.6
	6.9	5.2	11.3			Intangibles (net)	7.6	8.5
	9.4	14.5	11.0			All Other Non-Current	9.1	9.0
	100.0	100.0	100.0			Total	100.0	100.0
						LIABILITIES		
	8.3	7.0	1.3			Notes Payable-Short Term	3.9	7.0
	9.4	5.8	5.0			Cur. Mat.-L/T/D	4.8	3.8
	22.8	18.4	7.3			Trade Payables	15.9	16.5
	.0	.3	.1			Income Taxes Payable	.7	.4
	15.9	13.6	9.3			All Other Current	10.0	11.7
	56.4	45.2	23.0			Total Current	35.2	39.3
	16.7	22.1	24.2			Long-Term Debt	20.3	18.8
	.0	.1	.7			Deferred Taxes	1.2	1.1
	3.5	8.8	12.0			All Other Non-Current	7.0	10.2
	23.4	23.8	40.1			Net Worth	36.2	30.7
	100.0	100.0	100.0			Total Liabilities & Net Worth	100.0	100.0
						INCOME DATA		
	100.0	100.0	100.0			Net Sales	100.0	100.0
						Gross Profit		
	98.5	92.8	94.4			Operating Expenses	93.5	93.1
	1.5	7.2	5.6			Operating Profit	6.5	6.9
	−.1	1.7	2.3			All Other Expenses (net)	−1.4	2.0
	1.6	5.5	3.3			Profit Before Taxes	7.9	4.9
						RATIOS		
	2.1	1.8	2.3				2.7	2.0
	.9	1.3	1.4			Current	1.6	1.4
	.7	.7	1.0				1.0	.9
	1.4	1.6	1.6				1.8	1.6
	.5	.9	1.0			Quick	1.2	.9
	.2	.4	.5				.7	.6
	8 47.4	22 16.3	21 17.3				29 12.8	25 14.8
	31 12.0	36 10.1	32 11.5			Sales/Receivables	41 9.0	39 9.4
	53 6.9	49 7.5	45 8.2				55 6.7	51 7.2
						Cost of Sales/Inventory		
						Cost of Sales/Payables		
	9.5	7.2	3.8				5.6	8.2
	−121.0	61.5	17.0			Sales/Working Capital	12.8	17.9
	−20.4	−11.4	−641.6				452.9	−49.3
	12.2	35.7	13.9				15.8	8.2
	(15) 1.7	5.4	(29) 1.8			EBIT/Interest	(97) 4.0	(87) 3.3
	−4.3	.9	−2.1				.8	1.1
							21.5	16.4
						Net Profit + Depr., Dep., Amort./Cur. Mat. L/T/D	(24) 7.1	(31) 4.0
							1.8	1.7
	.2	.3	.5				.4	.3
	2.0	1.4	1.5			Fixed/Worth	.9	.8
	−1.8	6.3	NM				NM	3.3
	1.1	.7	.5				.6	.9
	4.0	4.1	1.6			Debt/Worth	1.3	2.2
	−6.0	47.3	NM				NM	18.0
	92.6	58.9	34.7			% Profit Before Taxes/Tangible Net Worth	65.6	51.9
	(14) 34.8	(21) 25.2	(23) 13.3				(83) 25.7	(78) 15.1
	1.6	8.3	−13.5				8.7	3.1
	26.4	19.1	20.1			% Profit Before Taxes/Total Assets	20.1	15.3
	4.9	7.2	4.2				8.4	6.7
	−8.2	−.6	−9.0				.1	.1
	116.8	30.4	7.9			Sales/Net Fixed Assets	27.4	27.3
	26.9	14.7	1.4				9.2	10.0
	4.5	3.7	.8				1.8	2.1
	3.3	3.6	1.3			Sales/Total Assets	3.1	3.5
	2.9	2.5	.8				2.1	2.3
	2.4	1.1	.6				.7	1.1
	.3	.9	7.9			% Depr., Dep., Amort./Sales	1.4	1.6
	(15) 2.3	(23) 1.8	(24) 14.2				(89) 3.5	(83) 2.5
	5.2	8.4	20.1				9.0	7.3
						% Officers', Directors', Owners' Comp/Sales	2.4	2.9
							(29) 7.1	(27) 5.3
							13.0	8.8
11023M	65714M	244782M	734376M	416031M	785099M	Net Sales ($)	4264005M	2664564M
2449M	21446M	112908M	795460M	375634M	541967M	Total Assets ($)	2555831M	2054926M

M = $ thousand   MM = $ million
See Pages 11 through 21 for Explanation of Ratios and Data

Comparative Historical Data | Current Data Sorted By Sales

			Type of Statement						
25	26	37	Unqualified		1	2	9	14	11
10	9	7	Reviewed		2		3	2	
15	24	12	Compiled	2	6	3	1		
5	13	8	Tax Returns	2	4	1		1	
29	30	30	Other		3	4	8	2	6
4/1/02-	4/1/03-	4/1/04-			17 (4/1-9/30/04)		77 (10/1/04-3/31/05)		
3/31/03	3/31/04	3/31/05		0-1MM	1-3MM	3-5MM	5-10MM	10-25MM	25MM & OVER
ALL	ALL	ALL							
84	102	94	**NUMBER OF STATEMENTS**	4	16	10	21	26	17
%	%	%	**ASSETS**	%	%	%	%	%	%
12.6	12.3	14.2	Cash & Equivalents		22.8	16.8	10.2	12.4	13.0
15.4	18.6	18.1	Trade Receivables (net)		19.8	22.6	16.7	18.3	18.1
14.1	13.0	9.5	Inventory		12.9	5.4	13.9	7.3	7.9
3.8	3.1	3.6	All Other Current		2.4	3.1	7.5	2.6	2.6
45.9	47.0	45.4	Total Current		57.9	47.9	48.2	40.5	41.6
35.9	34.3	34.8	Fixed Assets (net)		27.3	29.3	35.1	39.0	35.7
6.5	9.4	8.7	Intangibles (net)		2.3	12.3	5.3	7.9	12.5
11.8	9.3	11.2	All Other Non-Current		12.6	10.5	11.4	12.6	10.2
100.0	100.0	100.0	Total		100.0	100.0	100.0	100.0	100.0
			LIABILITIES						
10.6	9.8	4.2	Notes Payable-Short Term		8.0	3.0	5.4	3.8	1.3
5.3	6.7	6.0	Cur. Mat.-L/T/D		3.7	13.7	6.3	4.9	3.7
17.0	16.3	14.1	Trade Payables		17.5	14.6	20.0	10.4	11.2
.5	.1	.1	Income Taxes Payable		.1	.1	.2	.2	.1
12.9	12.8	12.0	All Other Current		12.9	16.7	11.5	11.3	12.5
46.2	45.8	36.4	Total Current		42.1	48.2	43.4	30.6	28.7
24.8	24.5	23.4	Long-Term Debt		18.1	19.0	26.7	16.5	27.0
1.1	.6	.7	Deferred Taxes		.0	.0	.6	1.2	1.3
4.0	4.8	8.2	All Other Non-Current		10.4	7.1	4.9	13.5	4.6
23.9	24.3	31.3	Net Worth		29.5	25.8	24.4	38.4	38.4
100.0	100.0	100.0	Total Liabilities & Net Worth		100.0	100.0	100.0	100.0	100.0
			INCOME DATA						
100.0	100.0	100.0	Net Sales		100.0	100.0	100.0	100.0	100.0
			Gross Profit						
93.0	90.3	94.1	Operating Expenses		92.6	95.5	96.9	96.2	88.0
7.0	9.7	5.9	Operating Profit		7.4	4.5	3.1	3.8	12.0
1.8	2.9	1.5	All Other Expenses (net)		.8	.5	2.0	1.5	2.4
5.1	6.8	4.4	Profit Before Taxes		6.6	3.9	1.2	2.4	9.5
			RATIOS						
1.8	2.2	2.4			3.1	3.2	2.0	2.1	2.8
1.3	1.2	1.3	Current		1.3	1.1	1.1	1.4	1.4
.7	.6	.8			.8	.5	.6	1.0	1.1
1.3	1.7	1.6			2.3	2.7	1.3	1.6	2.4
.7	.8	.9	Quick		.9	.9	.7	1.0	1.1
.4	.3	.5			.5	.2	.4	.6	.7
18 19.8	17 20.9	17 21.0		8 46.0	11 33.8	18 20.2	22 16.6	25 14.8	
32 11.3	30 12.3	32 11.3	Sales/Receivables	26 13.9	38 9.5	29 12.8	37 9.8	38 9.7	
44 8.3	45 8.2	47 7.7		46 8.0	59 6.2	47 7.7	46 8.0	58 6.3	
			Cost of Sales/Inventory						
			Cost of Sales/Payables						
7.6	7.9	6.8			16.3	4.2	7.3	5.7	5.1
27.3	28.9	24.0	Sales/Working Capital		27.1	NM	35.8	23.5	16.6
−17.0	−12.9	−27.6			−21.9	−10.6	−10.3	−105.9	66.8
6.5	8.8	13.0			7.7		24.3	29.9	11.1
(75) 2.3	(92) 3.0	(85) 2.6	EBIT/Interest	(10) 2.1		5.0	3.4	(16) 5.6	
.4	.5	−.6			−5.0		−1.4	−1.0	1.5
10.5	7.2	11.4	Net Profit + Depr., Dep.,						
(25) 1.6	(19) 2.4	(18) 1.9	Amort./Cur. Mat. L/T/D						
.6	.2	1.1							
.5	.5	.4			.3	.1	.5	.5	.2
1.3	1.7	1.6	Fixed/Worth		1.9	3.8	.8	1.8	1.2
18.5	−87.1	14.7			12.1	−1.4	4.5	NM	2.2
.8	1.3	.7			.7	.5	1.0	.4	.9
2.7	2.6	2.7	Debt/Worth		3.3	5.0	3.4	2.2	1.6
NM	−107.2	52.4			102.9	−5.0	16.7	NM	5.9
51.0	65.1	52.8			218.2		36.0	33.7	57.1
(63) 11.4	(75) 24.3	(73) 24.5	% Profit Before Taxes/Tangible Net Worth	(13) 42.2		(18) 19.2	(20) 8.7	(14) 40.2	
	.9	2.1		16.8		−11.8	2.4	3.0	
14.6	15.6	20.2			45.8	25.0	15.1	12.3	22.6
3.8	4.7	5.8	% Profit Before Taxes/Total Assets		8.5	−.1	4.4	3.1	10.6
−.7	−1.9	−5.7			−5.6	−8.4	−11.4	−8.8	2.2
23.1	28.4	33.7			111.4	21.1	29.0	26.6	36.5
6.2	8.9	6.9	Sales/Net Fixed Assets		27.7	10.1	6.4	2.6	3.6
1.3	1.9	1.3			4.4	3.6	1.1	.9	1.1
3.1	3.2	2.9			5.5	3.1	3.1	2.6	2.0
1.8	1.9	1.8	Sales/Total Assets		2.7	2.8	2.1	.9	1.2
.6	.7	.7			1.8	.9	.7	.6	.7
1.7	1.2	1.5			.6		1.1	1.6	2.1
(68) 3.7	(88) 4.3	(78) 5.0	% Depr., Dep., Amort./Sales	(13) 1.8		(20) 4.2	(21) 10.7	(13) 4.4	
13.8	11.1	15.0			5.0		15.8	18.7	14.6
3.3	3.4	2.1							
(21) 6.5	(33) 7.1	(24) 5.0	% Officers', Directors', Owners' Comp/Sales						
13.8	14.8	8.8							
1681690M	1665469M	2257025M	Net Sales ($)	2054M	31111M	40789M	156350M	444906M	1581815M
1611769M	1455659M	1849864M	Total Assets ($)	1201M	15799M	31121M	151059M	559619M	1091065M

M = $ thousand   MM = $ million
See Pages 11 through 21 for Explanation of Ratios and Data

Current Data Sorted By Assets

Comparative Historical Data

						Type of Statement		
2	3	5	14	3	4	Unqualified	19	12
1	6	11	4			Reviewed	14	13
5	5	3	2			Compiled	23	30
9	7		2			Tax Returns	9	13
4	15	15	12	6	1	Other	58	56
	17 (4/1-9/30/04)		120 (10/1/04-3/31/05)				4/1/00-3/31/01	4/1/01-3/31/02
0-500M	500M-2MM	2-10MM	10-50MM	50-100MM	100-250MM		ALL	ALL
21	36	36	30	9	5	**NUMBER OF STATEMENTS**	123	124
%	%	%	%	%	%	**ASSETS**	%	%
18.3	11.7	11.9	16.5			Cash & Equivalents	10.7	10.4
32.9	38.9	36.9	23.5			Trade Receivables (net)	34.4	30.5
8.2	9.3	6.5	5.9			Inventory	6.9	7.2
3.5	3.8	5.6	4.9			All Other Current	4.5	4.9
62.9	63.6	60.9	50.8			Total Current	56.4	53.0
27.5	20.0	26.4	32.6			Fixed Assets (net)	31.6	30.8
2.0	3.8	4.9	6.6			Intangibles (net)	7.0	8.6
7.6	12.6	7.8	10.1			All Other Non-Current	4.9	7.6
100.0	100.0	100.0	100.0			Total	100.0	100.0
						LIABILITIES		
20.8	14.9	20.6	5.0			Notes Payable-Short Term	10.7	12.5
5.6	4.7	8.9	2.6			Cur. Mat.-L/T/D	6.8	20.3
27.3	17.3	16.4	13.9			Trade Payables	13.3	14.8
.7	.8	.8	.7			Income Taxes Payable	.5	.6
24.7	15.1	11.8	13.8			All Other Current	11.9	11.9
79.0	52.8	58.3	35.9			Total Current	43.3	60.1
16.8	12.1	12.7	18.0			Long-Term Debt	24.2	49.6
.3	.3	.9	.9			Deferred Taxes	.6	.9
11.8	13.2	7.4	5.7			All Other Non-Current	7.2	8.1
−7.9	21.6	20.7	39.5			Net Worth	24.7	−18.7
100.0	100.0	100.0	100.0			Total Liabilities & Net Worth	100.0	100.0
						INCOME DATA		
100.0	100.0	100.0	100.0			Net Sales	100.0	100.0
						Gross Profit		
96.8	95.2	93.1	88.9			Operating Expenses	94.5	96.0
3.2	4.8	6.9	11.1			Operating Profit	5.5	4.0
1.0	.4	1.0	3.2			All Other Expenses (net)	2.1	2.6
2.2	4.4	5.9	7.9			Profit Before Taxes	3.4	1.4
						RATIOS		
1.8	1.9	1.9	2.1				2.2	1.9
1.0	1.4	1.2	1.2			Current	1.5	1.1
.5	.9	.7	1.0				.9	.8
1.6	1.7	1.6	1.7				1.8	1.4
.7	.9	1.0	1.0			Quick	1.1 (123)	.9
.3	.6	.5	.8				.8	.6
0 UND	21 17.3	29 12.7	28 13.1				29 12.7	30 12.0
30 12.1	48 7.6	53 6.9	45 8.1			Sales/Receivables	51 7.2	50 7.2
56 6.5	73 5.0	66 5.6	69 5.3				74 5.0	71 5.1
						Cost of Sales/Inventory		
						Cost of Sales/Payables		
28.9	7.5	9.0	5.1				7.0	8.0
−304.0	26.4	27.3	20.0			Sales/Working Capital	16.7	50.0
−10.5	−126.8	−17.3	NM				−53.3	−21.7
9.1	18.6	11.0	24.2				8.8	6.4
(14) 3.3	(31) 5.3	(33) 4.8	(23) 6.2			EBIT/Interest	(110) 3.0	(106) 2.0
−1.4	−2.1	1.7	2.1				1.0	−1.9
		11.7				Net Profit + Depr., Dep.,	5.3	4.4
	(10)	2.5				Amort./Cur. Mat. L./T/D	(24) 2.0	(19) 1.4
		.9					.5	.7
.2	.2	.2	.3				.4	.4
5.8	.6	.9	.9			Fixed/Worth	1.3	1.6
−.4	2.7	4.1	2.2				7.0	−13.7
1.0	1.3	1.1	.8				.8	1.0
UND	2.4	3.3	2.1			Debt/Worth	2.8	3.9
−2.7	9.8	10.4	4.3				33.5	−39.4
144.4	112.4	76.5	43.4			% Profit Before Taxes/Tangible	72.1	82.8
(11) 62.5	(30) 33.8	(32) 39.8	(28) 25.8			Net Worth	(95) 33.6	(90) 22.5
10.6	7.4	11.7	11.2				2.9	−12.5
54.1	24.7	23.2	14.4			% Profit Before Taxes/Total	24.3	15.9
6.3	9.2	12.1	8.0			Assets	7.3	2.8
−11.6	−2.1	2.5	3.5				−.3	−7.3
127.2	62.3	47.2	31.8				24.9	27.8
34.4	24.4	23.3	7.7			Sales/Net Fixed Assets	10.8	8.9
18.1	10.3	6.0	1.2				3.4	3.4
12.3	3.8	3.5	2.7				3.4	3.4
5.0	3.0	2.7	1.4			Sales/Total Assets	2.5	1.9
2.7	2.3	1.9	.6				1.2	1.0
.3	1.0	.7	1.5				.9	.9
(15) 1.3	(28) 2.1	(32) 1.6	(23) 5.2			% Depr., Dep., Amort./Sales	(103) 2.5	(95) 2.5
4.5	3.7	5.7	13.2				7.0	7.7
1.5	2.5					% Officers', Directors',	2.8	2.5
(11) 11.0	(11) 6.7					Owners' Comp/Sales	(38) 5.5	(37) 6.4
15.4	13.1						9.0	12.7
21823M	210157M	348379M	1069162M	1114583M	1009517M	Net Sales ($)	2601244M	3383617M
4339M	43239M	137199M	687296M	617080M	745350M	Total Assets ($)	2129182M	2991547M

M = $ thousand   MM = $ million
See Pages 11 through 21 for Explanation of Ratios and Data

Comparative Historical Data				Current Data Sorted By Sales					
Type of Statement									
29	29	31	Unqualified	2	1	1	4	9	14
16	18	22	Reviewed		4	5	7	3	3
18	15	13	Compiled	2	3	3	4	1	
11	13	18	Tax Returns	8	4	2	4		
50	52	53	Other	2	10	8	10	9	14
4/1/02-3/31/03 ALL	4/1/03-3/31/04 ALL	4/1/04-3/31/05 ALL		0-1MM	17 (4/1-9/30/04) 1-3MM	3-5MM	120 (10/1/04-3/31/05) 5-10MM	10-25MM	25MM & OVER
124	127	137	**NUMBER OF STATEMENTS**	14	22	19	29	22	31
%	%	%	**ASSETS**	%	%	%	%	%	%
10.9	12.0	14.2	Cash & Equivalents	22.1	10.9	10.5	11.2	16.7	16.3
31.1	31.7	32.2	Trade Receivables (net)	21.0	36.4	35.7	35.5	32.0	29.1
6.0	6.7	7.5	Inventory	6.8	5.8	11.4	7.4	5.8	8.1
3.6	4.8	4.5	All Other Current	3.9	3.9	5.2	3.8	3.8	6.0
51.6	55.2	58.4	Total Current	53.8	57.0	62.8	57.8	58.2	59.5
28.8	28.0	26.9	Fixed Assets (net)	30.6	31.7	17.7	29.3	27.8	24.5
10.6	7.8	4.8	Intangibles (net)	1.2	4.5	6.0	3.7	4.7	7.0
9.0	8.9	9.9	All Other Non-Current	14.3	6.8	13.4	9.2	9.3	9.0
100.0	100.0	100.0	Total	100.0	100.0	100.0	100.0	100.0	100.0
			LIABILITIES						
7.1	12.3	13.8	Notes Payable-Short Term	21.5	18.5	20.9	16.0	6.7	5.5
5.3	4.6	5.6	Cur. Mat.-L/T/D	1.5	11.1	2.5	9.6	3.1	3.5
13.7	18.9	16.9	Trade Payables	14.3	15.9	28.7	16.0	15.8	13.1
.4	.7	.7	Income Taxes Payable	1.0	.1	.4	1.3	.4	.7
15.3	15.9	15.8	All Other Current	31.4	9.5	12.9	12.8	14.1	19.2
41.7	52.5	52.8	Total Current	69.6	55.2	65.5	55.7	40.2	41.9
21.8	18.8	14.6	Long-Term Debt	14.0	21.1	9.4	16.9	11.2	13.8
.6	.6	.6	Deferred Taxes	.4	.4	.2	.7	.7	1.1
4.4	8.2	9.4	All Other Non-Current	20.5	9.7	10.6	7.6	6.6	6.9
31.4	20.0	22.6	Net Worth	-4.5	13.6	14.4	19.1	41.2	36.3
100.0	100.0	100.0	Total Liabilities & Net Worth	100.0	100.0	100.0	100.0	100.0	100.0
			INCOME DATA						
100.0	100.0	100.0	Net Sales	100.0	100.0	100.0	100.0	100.0	100.0
			Gross Profit						
95.1	93.8	93.0	Operating Expenses	95.9	89.6	98.1	97.5	89.9	88.8
4.9	6.2	7.0	Operating Profit	4.1	10.4	1.9	2.5	10.1	11.2
1.8	1.8	1.3	All Other Expenses (net)	.1	1.9	2.1	.7	2.3	.9
3.1	4.4	5.7	Profit Before Taxes	4.1	8.6	-.2	1.7	7.7	10.4
			RATIOS						
2.2	1.7	1.9		1.4	2.2	2.0	1.7	2.7	2.0
1.2	1.2	1.2	Current	.9	1.1	1.4	1.1	1.3	1.4
.8	.8	.9		.5	.7	.8	.7	1.1	1.1
1.7	1.4	1.6		1.3	2.0	1.9	1.6	2.1	1.5
1.0	.9	.9	Quick	.6	.9	.9	.8	1.1	1.0
.6	.5	.6		.2	.5	.5	.6	.8	.8
29 12.7	24 15.5	26 13.8		0 UND	6 63.4	26 14.0	19 18.9	28 12.9	32 11.3
53 6.9	48 7.6	48 7.7	Sales/Receivables	26 13.8	44 8.3	49 7.5	52 7.1	47 7.8	52 7.1
71 5.1	69 5.3	66 5.5		63 5.8	71 5.2	74 4.9	62 5.9	66 5.5	67 5.5
			Cost of Sales/Inventory						
			Cost of Sales/Payables						
7.8	9.0	7.8		131.9	12.3	6.6	11.7	5.1	4.7
18.9	38.8	27.2	Sales/Working Capital	-197.6	76.8	15.6	35.4	20.0	15.7
-23.7	-22.1	-58.0		-6.5	-14.6	-36.4	-12.2	70.7	153.2
8.2	12.6	14.8			16.6	18.1	10.1	25.8	21.0
(109) 2.3	(113) 4.1	(113) 5.4	EBIT/Interest		(19) 5.3	(16) 3.6	(23) 1.7	(19) 6.7	(27) 8.5
-.6	1.0	.5				.7	-1.7	-1.9	4.1	3.2
6.8	5.7	10.5						11.5	
(22) 2.0	(24) 2.8	(30) 3.2	Net Profit + Depr., Dep., Amort./Cur. Mat. L/T/D					(11) 4.0	
.4	1.6	1.8						2.7	
.4	.4	.3		.4	.1	.2	.3	.2	.2
1.0	1.4	.9	Fixed/Worth	UND	1.0	.5	.9	.6	.9
454.5	36.1	4.5		-.4	NM	4.5	20.2	1.7	2.2
.8	1.3	1.1		.9	1.2	1.0	1.2	.9	1.2
3.0	2.9	2.5	Debt/Worth	UND	3.2	2.4	4.0	2.0	1.8
488.7	64.3	14.0		-2.8	NM	10.4	31.4	3.5	4.7
67.5	56.8	80.0			168.6	64.0	104.5	65.9	70.8
(94) 22.6	(96) 22.8	(112) 34.5	% Profit Before Taxes/Tangible Net Worth		(17) 48.8	(15) 31.3	(24) 43.4	31.8	(27) 35.2
-5.5	.9	10.7			16.6	-3.7	-28.1	12.4	17.2
14.5	18.2	23.2		53.4	26.3	18.6	22.2	22.5	22.3
4.8	4.8	8.4	% Profit Before Taxes/Total Assets	2.5	10.3	3.6	8.7	11.3	12.5
-4.0	-.9	-.8		-11.3	1.4	-5.3	-5.9	5.1	4.4
25.5	32.3	51.2		53.6	117.6	51.9	51.8	31.2	38.5
9.9	11.3	18.6	Sales/Net Fixed Assets	26.4	17.0	22.7	25.0	15.1	15.2
4.0	3.8	4.6		6.0	4.3	12.1	3.9	3.8	3.8
3.1	3.7	3.6		19.0	3.6	3.3	4.0	3.6	3.0
2.2	2.2	2.6	Sales/Total Assets	3.0	2.6	2.7	3.1	2.5	2.2
1.2	1.1	1.6		2.4	1.6	1.9	2.2	1.0	1.4
1.6	1.3	.9		.4	.9	.6	.8	1.5	.9
(100) 3.7	(99) 3.4	(108) 2.2	% Depr., Dep., Amort./Sales	(10) 3.1	(16) 2.4	(18) 1.5	(25) 2.5	(17) 2.2	(22) 3.3
6.8	7.0	5.7		10.8	5.0	2.8	6.4	11.3	5.5
2.7	1.8	2.2							
(46) 5.9	(27) 4.9	(34) 6.2	% Officers', Directors', Owners' Comp/Sales						
10.2	7.4	13.3							
4277337M	4144350M	3773621M	Net Sales ($)	6012M	39889M	74010M	205722M	349473M	3098515M
2852199M	3160925M	2234503M	Total Assets ($)	2334M	31264M	90788M	124334M	257088M	1728695M

© RMA 2005
M = $ thousand   MM = $ million
See Pages 11 through 21 for Explanation of Ratios and Data

Current Data Sorted By Assets   Comparative Historical Data

	0-500M	500M-2MM	2-10MM	10-50MM	50-100MM	100-250MM	4/1/00-3/31/01 ALL	4/1/01-3/31/02 ALL
Type of Statement								
Unqualified		3	5	4	4	2	10	13
Reviewed	1	1	4				1	4
Compiled	1	2	2				8	9
Tax Returns	7	3	3				5	3
Other	3	9	6	2		1	20	28
	0-500M	6 (4/1-9/30/04) 500M-2MM	2-10MM	10-50MM	57 (10/1/04-3/31/05) 50-100MM	100-250MM		
NUMBER OF STATEMENTS	12	18	20	6	4	3	44	57
	%	%	%	%	%	%	%	%
ASSETS								
Cash & Equivalents	25.7	11.7	12.9				13.4	15.0
Trade Receivables (net)	20.3	31.3	35.1				38.7	31.8
Inventory	2.1	1.7	2.0				2.6	1.2
All Other Current	1.2	4.5	2.4				2.5	7.3
Total Current	49.4	49.2	52.4				57.2	55.3
Fixed Assets (net)	30.3	27.0	27.6				26.8	28.8
Intangibles (net)	8.2	18.0	3.9				10.4	8.8
All Other Non-Current	12.1	5.9	16.0				5.6	7.1
Total	100.0	100.0	100.0				100.0	100.0
LIABILITIES								
Notes Payable-Short Term	23.2	22.4	5.9				8.7	12.5
Cur. Mat.-L/T/D	13.9	6.7	3.3				5.5	7.7
Trade Payables	6.5	23.6	12.8				14.3	14.5
Income Taxes Payable	.0	.1	.4				.5	.3
All Other Current	15.1	20.7	21.2				20.7	17.6
Total Current	58.7	73.6	43.6				49.7	52.4
Long-Term Debt	18.1	21.1	30.4				14.6	14.6
Deferred Taxes	.0	.8	.3				.6	.5
All Other Non-Current	3.3	26.0	9.3				4.7	5.7
Net Worth	19.8	-21.5	16.4				30.4	26.8
Total Liabilities & Net Worth	100.0	100.0	100.0				100.0	100.0
INCOME DATA								
Net Sales	100.0	100.0	100.0				100.0	100.0
Gross Profit								
Operating Expenses	94.3	93.9	87.0				96.1	95.6
Operating Profit	5.7	6.1	13.0				3.9	4.4
All Other Expenses (net)	.7	2.3	4.5				.8	2.3
Profit Before Taxes	5.0	3.8	8.6				3.1	2.1
RATIOS								
Current	5.9	1.9	2.1				2.7	2.2
	.7	1.0	1.1				1.5	1.0
	.3	.5	.6				.8	.7
Quick	5.4	1.6	2.0				2.5	1.9
	.7	.9	.9				1.3	.9
	.2	.4	.6				.7	.5
Sales/Receivables	0 UND	12 30.0	4 93.9				25 14.4	17 21.2
	0 UND	34 10.9	50 7.3				62 5.9	42 8.8
	43 8.5	60 6.0	73 5.0				85 4.3	68 5.4
Cost of Sales/Inventory								
Cost of Sales/Payables								
Sales/Working Capital	9.9	14.9	5.1				7.1	7.0
	-59.5	NM	43.4				14.2	UND
	-10.5	-6.0	-6.3				-14.2	-10.1
EBIT/Interest		8.6	14.2				13.8	11.1
		(17) 4.1	(15) 3.6				(39) 3.6	(47) 5.1
		.8	1.3				1.6	-.2
Net Profit + Depr., Dep., Amort./Cur. Mat. L/T/D							25.9	13.7
							(13) 1.8	(10) 2.9
							.9	1.4
Fixed/Worth	.3	1.2	.2				.2	.3
	4.6	NM	.9				.7	1.2
	-.2	-.2	-2.5				NM	-30.0
Debt/Worth	.3	2.1	1.7				.9	.9
	6.6	NM	3.3				2.9	2.6
	-2.9	-2.0	-10.3				NM	-53.7
% Profit Before Taxes/Tangible Net Worth			52.5				75.8	51.8
			(13) 24.5				(33) 35.3	(42) 33.1
			10.8				14.0	-3.0
% Profit Before Taxes/Total Assets	59.2	28.9	17.8				22.1	21.7
	.8	10.4	4.1				6.4	12.2
	-2.5	-1.9	1.5				.1	-8.2
Sales/Net Fixed Assets	119.7	25.9	75.3				34.1	34.4
	35.8	13.7	19.7				11.1	12.8
	6.9	5.9	4.9				4.8	4.5
Sales/Total Assets	6.3	3.6	3.0				3.8	3.1
	4.6	3.0	2.5				2.4	2.4
	2.7	1.7	1.1				1.5	1.5
% Depr., Dep., Amort./Sales			1.2				1.7	1.2
			(17) 2.3				(37) 4.3	(46) 3.4
			7.9				7.8	7.0
% Officers', Directors', Owners' Comp/Sales							4.0	2.8
							(14) 10.6	(14) 8.4
							16.1	22.6
Net Sales ($)	11125M	59249M	198629M	266548M	494951M	259628M	1490456M	1316018M
Total Assets ($)	2471M	19209M	89987M	142733M	350458M	420550M	999400M	857076M

© RMA 2005

M = $ thousand   MM = $ million

See Pages 11 through 21 for Explanation of Ratios and Data

Comparative Historical Data   Current Data Sorted By Sales

			Type of Statement						
20	21	18	Unqualified			4	4	1	9
5	11	6	Reviewed	1	1		1	3	
5	12	5	Compiled	1	1	1	2		
7	5	13	Tax Returns	6	4	1	1	1	
28	28	21	Other	3	8	2	2	4	2
4/1/02- 3/31/03	4/1/03- 3/31/04	4/1/04- 3/31/05		6 (4/1-9/30/04)			57 (10/1/04-3/31/05)		
ALL	ALL	ALL		0-1MM	1-3MM	3-5MM	5-10MM	10-25MM	25MM & OVER
65	77	63	NUMBER OF STATEMENTS	11	14	8	10	9	11
%	%	%	ASSETS	%	%	%	%	%	%
17.3	16.3	15.0	Cash & Equivalents	30.7	10.8		5.6		14.8
37.2	30.2	28.4	Trade Receivables (net)	12.7	24.3		36.6		24.1
1.8	3.2	2.0	Inventory	4.2	.7		3.5		2.4
5.1	4.3	2.8	All Other Current	1.9	3.3		1.3		2.3
61.4	53.9	48.1	Total Current	49.5	39.0		47.0		43.6
18.9	25.0	27.1	Fixed Assets (net)	44.0	30.3		15.0		23.6
14.0	13.5	13.4	Intangibles (net)	.8	21.5		17.3		23.8
5.7	7.7	11.4	All Other Non-Current	5.6	9.2		20.6		8.9
100.0	100.0	100.0	Total	100.0	100.0		100.0		100.0
			LIABILITIES						
17.5	13.9	13.0	Notes Payable-Short Term	18.8	10.7		13.9		1.4
6.6	6.7	6.8	Cur. Mat.-L/T/D	5.0	12.4		5.5		6.4
13.8	12.7	13.6	Trade Payables	5.8	8.9		34.9		7.5
.5	.2	.2	Income Taxes Payable	.0	.1		.0		.3
20.9	18.6	17.9	All Other Current	10.4	14.2		13.0		12.2
59.3	52.1	51.5	Total Current	39.9	46.4		67.3		27.7
11.9	16.4	22.8	Long-Term Debt	27.8	21.7		24.2		14.4
.6	.9	.9	Deferred Taxes	.0	1.0		1.9		1.4
7.7	9.7	11.8	All Other Non-Current	1.3	7.9		42.9		3.3
20.4	20.9	13.1	Net Worth	30.9	22.9		-36.2		53.1
100.0	100.0	100.0	Total Liabilities & Net Worth	100.0	100.0		100.0		100.0
			INCOME DATA						
100.0	100.0	100.0	Net Sales	100.0	100.0		100.0		100.0
			Gross Profit						
94.3	93.4	91.6	Operating Expenses	89.3	84.5		95.1		91.9
5.7	6.6	8.4	Operating Profit	10.7	15.5		4.9		8.1
1.0	2.4	2.9	All Other Expenses (net)	4.1	3.8		2.5		3.8
4.7	4.2	5.5	Profit Before Taxes	6.5	11.7		2.4		4.3
			RATIOS						
2.6	2.3	2.2		18.0	1.7		1.6		2.5
1.3	1.2	1.1	Current	3.0	1.0		1.0		2.0
.6	.8	.5		.5	.4		.1		.6
2.3	2.0	2.0		15.1	1.4		1.3		2.0
1.2	1.1	.9	Quick	2.9	.8		.8		1.9
.5	.7	.4		.3	.3		.1		.6
30 12.3	23 16.0	6 62.7		0 UND	0 UND		15 23.9		40 9.2
55 6.6	42 8.6	42 8.8	Sales/Receivables	0 UND	30 12.1		58 6.3		56 6.5
68 5.4	67 5.5	64 5.7		56 6.5	49 7.5		75 4.9		64 5.7
			Cost of Sales/Inventory						
			Cost of Sales/Payables						
5.3	6.6	6.3		4.8	19.6		8.8		3.3
15.3	35.0	57.7	Sales/Working Capital	27.0	NM		NM		9.4
-9.2	-25.7	-7.8		-7.8	-10.8		-3.8		-12.5
40.5	17.6	12.0			15.6				22.6
(49) 4.0	(62) 5.7	(53) 4.1	EBIT/Interest		(11) 7.0				5.0
.0	1.2	.7			3.1				.2
	26.8		Net Profit + Depr., Dep.,						
	(12) 2.5		Amort./Cur. Mat. L/T/D						
	.9								
.1	.2	.2		.2	1.5		.2		.1
.9	1.0	2.9	Fixed/Worth	3.1	NM		-2.4		.5
-.6	-10.7	-.6		6.0	-.1		-.4		3.4
.8	.9	.9		.1	1.7		1.9		.5
3.0	2.2	3.9	Debt/Worth	5.1	NM		-23.6		1.1
-3.6	-13.3	-5.9		13.2	-2.1		-2.3		8.2
109.0	66.2	65.3	% Profit Before Taxes/Tangible						36.8
(42) 31.0	(55) 32.6	(40) 24.9	Net Worth					(10)	25.6
2.1	6.2	1.7							-6.2
24.4	22.0	21.0	% Profit Before Taxes/Total	43.5	53.2		17.5		17.4
6.4	11.3	4.2	Assets	.1	19.2		7.9		4.2
-2.1	1.3	-.7		-3.1	3.1		-11.0		-1.0
50.3	37.5	53.2		15.1	64.9		70.9		29.0
19.7	13.6	15.1	Sales/Net Fixed Assets	6.8	18.8		29.9		8.1
7.9	7.2	4.2		4.0	5.4		9.5		2.9
3.9	3.3	3.6		4.6	5.3		3.8		2.1
2.3	2.3	2.6	Sales/Total Assets	2.6	3.0		3.1		1.0
1.1	1.3	1.6		.8	1.7		.6		.6
.8	1.3	.9							
(48) 2.4	(54) 2.8	(40) 3.2	% Depr., Dep., Amort./Sales						
6.8	5.8	7.6							
3.5	4.6	3.4	% Officers', Directors',						
(11) 10.6	(16) 10.3	(20) 7.2	Owners' Comp/Sales						
17.8	17.9	11.7							
1781868M	2719341M	1290130M	Net Sales ($)	6712M	26790M	32217M	72428M	145721M	1006262M
1744960M	2293677M	1025408M	Total Assets ($)	8243M	19195M	17080M	55374M	43987M	881529M

© RMA 2005   M = $ thousand   MM = $ million
See Pages 11 through 21 for Explanation of Ratios and Data

Current Data Sorted By Assets

Comparative Historical Data

Type of Statement	0-500M	500M-2MM	2-10MM	10-50MM	50-100MM	100-250MM		ALL 117	ALL 123
Unqualified	1	3	15	18	6	5		32	29
		12	10	4					
Reviewed	5	7	6		1			19	18
Compiled	6	6	3					24	28
Tax Returns								10	9
Other	7	22	24	15	8	4		32	39
	40 (4/1-9/30/04)			148 (10/1/04-3/31/05)				4/1/00-3/31/01	4/1/01-3/31/02
NUMBER OF STATEMENTS	19	50	58	37	15	9		117	123
ASSETS	%	%	%	%	%	%		%	%
Cash & Equivalents	25.9	16.5	12.7	23.5	33.8			12.9	13.3
Trade Receivables (net)	33.9	40.3	34.4	23.0	24.8			40.1	35.2
Inventory	8.8	3.5	3.2	1.8	.2			3.7	3.0
All Other Current	2.7	2.3	3.2	5.9	7.4			3.7	4.2
Total Current	71.4	62.5	53.5	54.2	66.2			60.3	55.7
Fixed Assets (net)	12.6	22.0	25.7	21.9	7.4			27.7	28.6
Intangibles (net)	6.0	5.7	7.8	17.5	15.8			5.0	7.7
All Other Non-Current	10.0	9.8	13.0	6.4	10.6			7.0	8.0
Total	100.0	100.0	100.0	100.0	100.0			100.0	100.0
LIABILITIES									
Notes Payable-Short Term	11.1	21.1	13.4	5.0	3.6			10.7	10.9
Cur. Mat.-L/T/D	7.2	4.6	4.6	3.0	7.5			3.8	6.0
Trade Payables	21.1	13.4	14.2	10.7	17.7			11.0	12.3
Income Taxes Payable	.0	.0	.4	.5	.5			1.0	.6
All Other Current	21.7	13.4	14.7	29.3	13.6			17.0	17.0
Total Current	61.0	52.6	47.2	48.5	43.0			43.4	46.8
Long-Term Debt	8.5	22.8	12.3	10.5	4.5			11.2	15.5
Deferred Taxes	.0	.0	1.2	1.0	.0			.7	.6
All Other Non-Current	13.4	4.4	6.8	8.6	9.9			6.7	6.6
Net Worth	17.1	20.1	32.5	31.4	42.6			38.0	30.6
Total Liabilities & Net Worth	100.0	100.0	100.0	100.0	100.0			100.0	100.0
INCOME DATA									
Net Sales	100.0	100.0	100.0	100.0	100.0			100.0	100.0
Gross Profit									
Operating Expenses	97.6	95.3	95.4	95.7	91.1			95.3	95.0
Operating Profit	2.4	4.7	4.6	4.3	8.9			4.7	5.0
All Other Expenses (net)	.3	.8	.7	.8	2.8			.8	2.1
Profit Before Taxes	2.1	3.8	3.9	3.6	6.1			4.0	2.9
RATIOS									
Current	3.8	2.0	1.8	1.6	4.0			2.1	2.2
	1.2	1.4	1.2	1.2	2.0			1.4	1.2
	.7	.9	.8	.8	1.0			1.0	.8
Quick	2.0	1.9	1.7	1.4	3.2			1.9	1.9
	1.0	1.3	1.0	1.0	2.0			1.2	1.0
	.6	.8	.6	.6	.7			.8	.7
Sales/Receivables	0 UND	24 15.4	36 10.0	28 13.3	34 10.7			33 11.0	34 10.9
	22 16.6	43 8.4	51 7.1	47 7.7	65 5.7			53 6.9	49 7.4
	63 5.8	59 6.1	71 5.1	77 4.8	96 3.8			80 4.6	69 5.3
Cost of Sales/Inventory									
Cost of Sales/Payables									
Sales/Working Capital	9.1	11.2	7.0	6.8	1.9			7.9	7.5
	91.2	24.1	20.2	21.9	4.4			22.2	29.2
	-26.2	-61.5	-20.5	-15.5	-999.8			NM	-26.2
EBIT/Interest	2.5	14.0	17.3	70.2	44.1			13.3	7.2
	(11) -1.5	(43) 6.0	(54) 5.7	(29) 5.0	(11) 6.9			(96) 3.8	(101) 2.9
	-15.0	1.9	1.0	2.1	-.3			1.1	1.0
Net Profit + Depr., Dep., Amort./Cur. Mat. L/T/D			7.8	6.4				6.4	4.8
		(21) 3.0	(11) 2.7					(22) 3.3	(37) 2.6
		1.6	1.2					1.7	.9
Fixed/Worth	.0	.2	.3	.3	.1			.3	.3
	.2	.6	.7	1.1	.2			.7	1.0
	UND	22.5	1.2	-6.2	-.7			1.8	4.0
Debt/Worth	.4	.9	.9	1.2	.4			.7	.9
	3.5	2.2	1.8	3.8	1.6			1.9	2.4
	-3.6	64.3	5.4	-21.7	-7.0			5.3	28.1
% Profit Before Taxes/Tangible Net Worth	330.5	69.0	56.0	65.6	48.8			71.8	57.8
	(12) 34.1	(39) 40.2	(50) 24.8	(27) 19.5	(11) 16.3			(102) 27.6	(101) 28.1
	-4.5	3.4	11.5	-1.1	9.4			2.1	2.8
% Profit Before Taxes/Total Assets	19.9	27.2	15.8	13.6	18.6			21.8	18.6
	-4.0	10.4	7.4	5.1	9.0			9.2	5.2
	-10.0	1.6	2.1	-.2	-.7			.3	.0
Sales/Net Fixed Assets	UND	62.8	31.2	35.2	45.6			27.8	30.1
	669.0	27.3	14.8	10.6	21.0			12.2	11.6
	35.5	12.1	4.8	3.9	14.2			5.5	4.3
Sales/Total Assets	6.4	4.6	3.2	2.2	2.3			3.9	3.6
	4.8	3.3	2.0	1.6	1.1			2.6	2.3
	3.0	2.5	1.2	1.0	.7			1.6	1.5
% Depr., Dep., Amort./Sales		.9	1.4	2.0	2.7			1.1	.8
		(31) 2.0	(45) 2.7	(30) 5.3	(10) 3.5			(91) 2.7	(100) 2.8
		4.6	5.9	8.1	5.6			5.0	6.6
% Officers', Directors', Owners' Comp/Sales		4.0	1.3					3.0	3.5
		(20) 6.1	(12) 3.6					(41) 4.7	(32) 5.2
		10.1	8.6					9.2	15.8
Net Sales ($)	22265M	222647M	571447M	1414701M	3102952M	1838816M		4686719M	2648045M
Total Assets ($)	3996M	60207M	263776M	827696M	1054980M	1353729M		1878261M	1426345M

M = $ thousand   MM = $ million
See Pages 11 through 21 for Explanation of Ratios and Data

Comparative Historical Data | Current Data Sorted By Sales

Hist 1	Hist 2	Hist 3	Type of Statement	0-1MM	1-3MM	3-5MM	5-10MM	10-25MM	25MM & OVER
50	45	48	Unqualified	1	1	3	9	11	23
22	27	26	Reviewed	1	1	6	8	6	4
20	41	19	Compiled	1	5	3	6	3	1
21	21	15	Tax Returns	3	5	5	1	1	
60	54	80	Other	4	19	8	11	19	19
4/1/02-3/31/03 ALL	4/1/03-3/31/04 ALL	4/1/04-3/31/05 ALL		40 (4/1-9/30/04)			148 (10/1/04-3/31/05)		
173	188	188	NUMBER OF STATEMENTS	10	31	25	35	40	47
%	%	%	ASSETS	%	%	%	%	%	%
16.5	16.7	18.9	Cash & Equivalents	28.8	13.3	16.6	14.6	19.7	24.4
36.3	33.4	32.5	Trade Receivables (net)	29.4	35.7	27.4	37.9	36.3	26.6
3.6	4.6	3.2	Inventory	3.4	8.9	.7	3.4	2.7	1.0
4.1	4.9	4.0	All Other Current	.3	3.2	3.2	3.3	2.5	7.5
60.5	59.7	58.7	Total Current	61.9	61.1	47.9	59.2	61.2	59.5
19.9	20.4	20.5	Fixed Assets (net)	18.4	22.9	28.9	24.4	17.9	14.3
8.8	9.3	10.7	Intangibles (net)	9.3	2.9	11.6	8.0	9.8	18.4
10.8	10.5	10.1	All Other Non-Current	10.4	13.0	11.7	8.3	11.1	7.8
100.0	100.0	100.0	Total	100.0	100.0	100.0	100.0	100.0	100.0
			LIABILITIES						
11.1	10.1	12.4	Notes Payable-Short Term	12.7	11.9	38.2	8.9	9.5	4.0
4.8	4.3	4.7	Cur. Mat.-L/T/D	1.6	6.1	6.7	5.1	2.4	5.0
14.3	12.1	14.3	Trade Payables	17.4	16.4	9.2	14.6	12.4	16.2
.8	.7	.3	Income Taxes Payable	.0	.0	.4	.2	.4	.3
17.5	18.8	17.9	All Other Current	15.9	16.3	17.0	13.5	18.9	22.2
48.6	46.0	49.5	Total Current	47.6	50.7	71.6	42.4	43.7	47.6
14.2	12.6	13.8	Long-Term Debt	15.2	11.0	22.7	9.8	20.1	8.1
.7	.5	.6	Deferred Taxes	.0	.0	1.1	.3	1.2	.4
7.6	10.0	7.4	All Other Non-Current	3.4	11.6	7.3	7.1	8.1	5.3
29.0	30.9	28.7	Net Worth	33.8	26.8	-2.7	40.4	26.9	38.5
100.0	100.0	100.0	Total Liabilities & Net Worth	100.0	100.0	100.0	100.0	100.0	100.0
			INCOME DATA						
100.0	100.0	100.0	Net Sales	100.0	100.0	100.0	100.0	100.0	100.0
			Gross Profit						
95.5	94.8	95.2	Operating Expenses	91.6	98.7	93.8	97.0	93.8	94.4
4.5	5.2	4.8	Operating Profit	8.4	1.3	6.2	3.0	6.2	5.6
1.0	1.3	.9	All Other Expenses (net)	1.7	1.0	.8	.8	.4	1.2
3.4	3.9	3.9	Profit Before Taxes	6.7	.3	5.4	2.2	5.8	4.4
			RATIOS						
2.0	2.3	2.1	Current	6.5	1.8	1.8	2.1	2.4	2.2
1.4	1.4	1.3		1.1	1.2	1.1	1.4	1.5	1.3
.9	.9	.8		.5	.6	.3	1.0	.9	.9
1.9	2.1	1.8	Quick	6.3	1.7	1.8	2.0	2.2	1.9
1.2	1.1	1.1		1.1	1.0	.9	1.2	1.3	1.2
.7	.7	.7		.5	.5	.3	.9	.8	.7
30 12.1	27 13.4	29 12.8	Sales/Receivables	0 UND	22 16.6	24 15.5	24 15.1	36 10.2	31 11.9
46 7.9	44 8.2	48 7.7		31 11.6	41 8.9	42 8.8	48 7.5	51 7.1	53 6.9
66 5.6	64 5.7	71 5.1		71 5.1	69 5.3	69 5.3	60 6.0	75 4.8	85 4.3
			Cost of Sales/Inventory						
			Cost of Sales/Payables						
7.1	7.7	6.9	Sales/Working Capital	5.0	12.9	9.5	9.2	6.1	3.7
18.8	22.3	21.8		UND	53.9	33.3	18.3	16.6	15.4
-62.6	-76.5	-29.7		-5.8	-13.9	-9.1	-265.7	-62.9	-42.6
12.1	17.1	20.2	EBIT/Interest		7.5	14.4	20.5	44.2	50.0
(147) 4.0	(153) 5.2	(156) 5.0		(23) 1.9	(21) 4.4	(33) 6.8	(37) 10.5	(36) 5.1	
1.0	1.1	.8			-4.3	.7	1.0	2.8	2.1
8.1	10.0	8.8	Net Profit + Depr., Dep., Amort./Cur. Mat. L/T/D					13.8	14.9
(41) 2.8	(47) 4.3	(42) 3.4					(14) 4.3	(12) 7.1	
1.2	1.6	1.6						2.6	1.4
.2	.2	.2	Fixed/Worth	.0	.1	.5	.2	.2	.1
.7	.7	.6		.3	.6	1.2	.6	.5	.7
2.6	4.6	7.2		UND	2.7	-.6	1.2	1.5	-1.0
1.0	.9	.9	Debt/Worth	.4	.9	.9	1.0	.7	1.0
1.9	2.0	2.2		2.3	2.5	3.8	1.8	1.7	3.2
13.9	14.2	168.7		UND	-21.0	-2.8	3.9	5.2	-8.3
63.4	59.2	65.3	% Profit Before Taxes/Tangible Net Worth		80.4	82.8	48.3	62.5	82.5
(142) 22.2	(146) 27.4	(144) 25.7		(22) 19.4	(16) 25.8	(30) 22.3	(34) 33.9	(34) 22.5	
3.3	4.5	5.5			-8.5	1.8	9.7	11.7	.0
18.0	18.5	17.3	% Profit Before Taxes/Total Assets	38.3	15.5	28.6	13.0	22.9	14.0
6.9	7.1	7.5		7.5	2.7	5.6	7.7	10.3	7.2
.3	.3	-.5		-39.5	-9.4	.4	.5	3.0	.0
40.8	52.4	45.7	Sales/Net Fixed Assets	UND	93.3	34.0	49.6	40.5	53.9
16.2	20.2	18.4		UND	28.9	14.2	15.2	17.7	19.1
8.0	9.9	6.6		7.5	5.6	4.2	9.1	8.0	6.8
3.7	4.1	3.7	Sales/Total Assets	5.6	4.2	3.9	4.2	3.5	2.6
2.4	2.5	2.3		3.0	2.8	2.5	3.3	2.0	1.6
1.6	1.4	1.3		1.6	1.9	1.6	1.6	1.6	.9
.9	1.0	1.3	% Depr., Dep., Amort./Sales		.5	1.7	1.8	1.4	.8
(126) 2.1	(135) 2.4	(126) 2.9		(18) 1.4	(17) 3.7	(25) 2.5	(31) 3.0	(33) 3.1	
4.8	5.5	6.6			6.5	8.2	5.0	6.0	7.4
4.4	3.0	2.6	% Officers', Directors', Owners' Comp/Sales				2.4		
(52) 7.2	(53) 6.9	(47) 6.0				(12) 4.8			
14.6	16.1	9.2				8.9			
4280818M	4958372M	7172828M	Net Sales ($)	4732M	64359M	101815M	246227M	610461M	6145234M
2528155M	2868958M	3564384M	Total Assets ($)	2712M	32313M	56558M	131924M	388813M	2952064M

© RMA 2005

M = $ thousand   MM = $ million
See Pages 11 through 21 for Explanation of Ratios and Data

FINANCE
AND INSURANCE

Current Data Sorted By Assets   Comparative Historical Data

						Type of Statement		
	1	3	4		1	Unqualified		
	1	2				Reviewed		
1	1	1				Compiled		
3	1					Tax Returns		
1	3	3		2		Other		
	7 (4/1-9/30/04)			21 (10/1/04-3/31/05)			4/1/00-3/31/01	4/1/01-3/31/02
0-500M	500M-2MM	2-10MM	10-50MM	50-100MM	100-250MM		ALL	ALL
5	7	9	6		1	NUMBER OF STATEMENTS		
%	%	%	%	%	%	ASSETS	%	%
				D		Cash & Equivalents	D	D
				A		Trade Receivables (net)	A	A
				T		Inventory	T	T
				A		All Other Current	A	A
						Total Current		
				N		Fixed Assets (net)	N	N
				O		Intangibles (net)	O	O
				T		All Other Non-Current	T	T
						Total		
				A		LIABILITIES	A	A
				V		Notes Payable-Short Term	V	V
				A		Cur. Mat.-L/T/D	A	A
				I		Trade Payables	I	I
				L		Income Taxes Payable	L	L
				A		All Other Current	A	A
				B		Total Current	B	B
				L		Long-Term Debt	L	L
				E		Deferred Taxes	E	E
						All Other Non-Current		
						Net Worth		
						Total Liabilities & Net Worth		
						INCOME DATA		
						Net Sales		
						Gross Profit		
						Operating Expenses		
						Operating Profit		
						All Other Expenses (net)		
						Profit Before Taxes		
						RATIOS		
						Current		
						Quick		
						Sales/Receivables		
						Cost of Sales/Inventory		
						Cost of Sales/Payables		
						Sales/Working Capital		
						EBIT/Interest		
						Net Profit + Depr., Dep., Amort./Cur. Mat. L /T/D		
						Fixed/Worth		
						Debt/Worth		
						% Profit Before Taxes/Tangible Net Worth		
						% Profit Before Taxes/Total Assets		
						Sales/Net Fixed Assets		
						Sales/Total Assets		
						% Depr., Dep., Amort./Sales		
						% Officers', Directors', Owners' Comp/Sales		
6921M	9433M	13892M	35812M		116039M	Net Sales ($)		
1200M	8971M	31406M	144631M		162104M	Total Assets ($)		

M = $ thousand   MM = $ million
See Pages 11 through 21 for Explanation of Ratios and Data

Comparative Historical Data				Current Data Sorted By Sales					

			Type of Statement						
13	11	9	Unqualified	3	1	2	1	1	1
4	5	3	Reviewed	2	1				
2	5	3	Compiled	2	1				
1	1	4	Tax Returns	3	1				
4	13	9	Other	3	4	1	1		
4/1/02-3/31/03 ALL	4/1/03-3/31/04 ALL	4/1/04-3/31/05 ALL		0-1MM	7 (4/1-9/30/04) 1-3MM	3-5MM	21 (10/1/04-3/31/05) 5-10MM	10-25MM	25MM & OVER
24	35	28	NUMBER OF STATEMENTS	13	7	4	2	1	1
%	%	%	ASSETS	%	%	%	%	%	%
2.7	11.4	9.2	Cash & Equivalents	9.4					
70.2	53.2	44.8	Trade Receivables (net)	53.2					
.0	2.7	6.7	Inventory	7.4					
18.8	15.3	11.7	All Other Current	12.1					
91.7	82.7	72.5	Total Current	82.1					
1.6	5.4	6.0	Fixed Assets (net)	2.4					
.7	2.6	3.7	Intangibles (net)	7.1					
5.9	9.3	17.9	All Other Non-Current	8.4					
100.0	100.0	100.0	Total	100.0					
			LIABILITIES						
30.2	30.3	27.4	Notes Payable-Short Term	25.6					
10.7	4.0	4.5	Cur. Mat.-L/T/D	.9					
.9	5.1	3.9	Trade Payables	2.8					
.0	.0	.3	Income Taxes Payable	.0					
16.0	11.1	9.9	All Other Current	9.3					
57.8	50.5	45.9	Total Current	38.6					
3.9	9.6	13.7	Long-Term Debt	14.0					
.0	.2	.4	Deferred Taxes	.0					
7.3	7.2	9.9	All Other Non-Current	16.3					
30.9	32.6	30.0	Net Worth	31.0					
100.0	100.0	100.0	Total Liabilities & Net Worth	100.0					
			INCOME DATA						
100.0	100.0	100.0	Net Sales	100.0					
			Gross Profit						
75.0	77.1	72.8	Operating Expenses	71.2					
25.0	22.9	27.2	Operating Profit	28.8					
14.1	11.0	9.0	All Other Expenses (net)	6.6					
10.9	11.9	18.2	Profit Before Taxes	22.2					
			RATIOS						
2.4	2.6	2.3		4.0					
1.5	1.7	1.6	Current	1.9					
1.2	1.4	1.1		1.3					
2.3	2.2	1.9		2.5					
1.4	1.5	1.1	Quick	1.4					
1.0	.5	.2		.7					
333 1.1	7 51.9	0 UND		0 UND					
865 .4	480 .8	217 1.7	Sales/Receivables	578 .6					
1578 .2	1155 .3	989 .4		1071 .3					
			Cost of Sales/Inventory						
			Cost of Sales/Payables						
.6	.6	.6		.5					
1.2	1.2	2.1	Sales/Working Capital	.9					
2.4	4.5	15.9		2.8					
3.5	4.6	6.0							
(17) 1.6	(25) 2.8	(20) 3.4	EBIT/Interest						
.9	1.5	2.0							
			Net Profit + Depr., Dep., Amort./Cur. Mat. L/T/D						
.0	.0	.0		.0					
.0	.1	.0	Fixed/Worth	.0					
.1	.3	.1		.1					
1.8	1.1	.9		1.0					
2.8	2.3	2.3	Debt/Worth	1.7					
4.7	9.3	7.3		5.0					
36.0	39.1	45.5		51.3					
(23) 14.6	(33) 16.7	(27) 25.7	% Profit Before Taxes/Tangible Net Worth	(12) 26.9					
−.8	5.2	6.5		3.3					
6.3	6.9	9.4		10.7					
2.2	4.0	5.0	% Profit Before Taxes/Total Assets	4.7					
−.1	2.4	2.3		.5					
196.8	118.3	646.9		UND					
40.6	30.3	74.3	Sales/Net Fixed Assets	85.0					
18.7	15.2	15.1		32.4					
.4	1.3	1.1		.6					
.3	.4	.4	Sales/Total Assets	.4					
.2	.2	.2		.2					
.3	.6	1.0							
(19) .8	(25) 1.6	(16) 1.4	% Depr., Dep., Amort./Sales						
1.2	2.3	2.9							
	3.7	3.0							
	(14) 10.4	(12) 6.7	% Officers', Directors', Owners' Comp/Sales						
	26.8	17.9							
183100M	429621M	182097M	Net Sales ($)	5991M	14006M	15933M	14044M	16084M	116039M
470816M	1046428M	348312M	Total Assets ($)	20314M	54856M	57516M	39584M	13938M	162104M

M = $ thousand   MM = $ million
See Pages 11 through 21 for Explanation of Ratios and Data

Current Data Sorted By Assets   Comparative Historical Data

0-500M	500M-2MM	2-10MM	10-50MM	50-100MM	100-250MM	Type of Statement	4/1/00-3/31/01 ALL	4/1/01-3/31/02 ALL
	1	12	20	5		Unqualified		
	2	15	8			Reviewed		
	3	8	3			Compiled		
2	8	5	2			Tax Returns		
	8	9	7		4	Other		
	13 (4/1-9/30/04)		109 (10/1/04-3/31/05)					
2	22	49	40	5	4	**NUMBER OF STATEMENTS**		
%	%	%	%	%	%	**ASSETS**	%	%
	15.8	6.0	6.0			Cash & Equivalents	D	D
	41.4	52.2	46.7			Trade Receivables (net)	A	A
	5.6	1.3	2.6			Inventory	T	T
	5.7	7.3	11.3			All Other Current	A	A
	68.5	66.9	66.6			Total Current		
	15.1	13.0	8.0			Fixed Assets (net)	N	N
	.3	1.9	.5			Intangibles (net)	O	O
	16.2	18.2	24.9			All Other Non-Current	T	T
	100.0	100.0	100.0			Total		
						LIABILITIES	A	A
	26.6	27.2	40.9			Notes Payable-Short Term	V	V
	4.5	7.9	3.2			Cur. Mat.-L/T/D	A	A
	6.3	2.7	2.0			Trade Payables	I	I
	.0	.2	.1			Income Taxes Payable	L	L
	4.3	5.9	6.1			All Other Current	A	A
	41.7	43.9	52.3			Total Current	B	B
	17.3	18.6	14.9			Long-Term Debt	L	L
	.1	1.2	.4			Deferred Taxes	E	E
	3.7	11.9	7.7			All Other Non-Current		
	37.3	24.5	24.6			Net Worth		
	100.0	100.0	100.0			Total Liabilities & Net Worth		
						INCOME DATA		
	100.0	100.0	100.0			Net Sales		
						Gross Profit		
	75.3	70.8	68.6			Operating Expenses		
	24.7	29.2	31.4			Operating Profit		
	9.4	10.3	13.0			All Other Expenses (net)		
	15.4	18.8	18.5			Profit Before Taxes		
						RATIOS		
	7.2	2.6	1.6					
	1.7	1.4	1.3			Current		
	1.0	.9	1.1					
	7.1	2.4	1.5					
	1.1	1.3	1.3			Quick		
	.6	.4	.4					
0 UND		**27** 13.6		**13** 28.9				
54 6.8		**365** 1.0		**709** .5		Sales/Receivables		
922 .4		**982** .4		**1277** .3				
						Cost of Sales/Inventory		
						Cost of Sales/Payables		
	.5	.8	.8					
	2.3	1.8	1.4			Sales/Working Capital		
	NM	NM	10.1					
	10.1	7.1	4.4					
	(14) 2.4	(31) 2.9	(20) 3.0			EBIT/Interest		
	1.2	1.6	1.7					
						Net Profit + Depr., Dep., Amort./Cur. Mat. L./T/D		
	.0	.0	.0					
	.0	.1	.1			Fixed/Worth		
	1.0	.8	.4					
	.5	1.7	2.1					
	2.6	3.2	4.1			Debt/Worth		
	12.1	7.3	14.8					
	36.8	42.7	42.9					
	16.7	(45) 20.9	(38) 19.0			% Profit Before Taxes/Tangible Net Worth		
	5.2	4.5	8.3					
	11.6	12.9	6.2					
	2.8	4.4	3.1			% Profit Before Taxes/Total Assets		
	1.0	1.1	1.7					
	UND	85.1	155.8					
	63.9	33.2	34.0			Sales/Net Fixed Assets		
	1.8	7.6	8.4					
	.9	.7	.3					
	.4	.4	.2			Sales/Total Assets		
	.2	.2	.2					
		.6	.6					
	(33)	1.1	(25) 1.3			% Depr., Dep., Amort./Sales		
		2.6	4.1					
		5.7						
	(18)	13.9				% Officers', Directors', Owners' Comp/Sales		
		24.0						
523M	32186M	125339M	328114M	378238M	310857M	Net Sales ($)		
861M	24383M	246329M	855430M	372521M	509525M	Total Assets ($)		

M = $ thousand   MM = $ million
See Pages 11 through 21 for Explanation of Ratios and Data

Comparative Historical Data   **Current Data Sorted By Sales**

			Type of Statement						
23	37	38	Unqualified	3	10	4	12	6	3
4	17	25	Reviewed	4	13	2	5		1
3	14	14	Compiled	6	3	3	1	1	
5	8	17	Tax Returns	10	4	1	2		
6	21	28	Other	13	7	3		2	3
4/1/02- 3/31/03 ALL	4/1/03- 3/31/04 ALL	4/1/04- 3/31/05 ALL		13 (4/1-9/30/04) 0-1MM	1-3MM	3-5MM	109 (10/1/04-3/31/05) 5-10MM	10-25MM	25MM & OVER
41	97	122	**NUMBER OF STATEMENTS**	36	37	13	20	9	7
%	%	%	**ASSETS**	%	%	%	%	%	%
8.4	7.6	7.4	Cash & Equivalents	10.5	6.7	3.4	5.8		
37.0	47.4	49.7	Trade Receivables (net)	46.9	47.5	63.0	56.3		
2.4	2.4	2.5	Inventory	.1	2.7	1.5	3.7		
15.2	11.8	7.8	All Other Current	9.1	10.6	6.3	.5		
63.0	69.2	67.4	Total Current	66.6	67.4	74.2	66.3		
7.7	14.4	10.7	Fixed Assets (net)	10.5	13.7	7.4	10.2		
2.3	1.3	1.7	Intangibles (net)	.2	2.6	1.2	.1		
26.9	15.0	20.2	All Other Non-Current	22.6	16.4	17.2	23.5		
100.0	100.0	100.0	Total	100.0	100.0	100.0	100.0		
			LIABILITIES						
31.3	28.4	32.1	Notes Payable-Short Term	28.5	29.8	46.5	36.4		
7.3	6.4	5.2	Cur. Mat.-L/T/D	5.9	5.9	4.7	3.6		
3.9	3.6	3.1	Trade Payables	2.2	2.8	.5	4.8		
.3	.3	.1	Income Taxes Payable	.1	.2	.1	.1		
4.8	7.2	5.9	All Other Current	7.1	5.3	3.7	4.5		
47.6	45.9	46.4	Total Current	43.8	43.9	55.5	49.4		
19.2	20.6	16.7	Long-Term Debt	18.7	18.3	14.8	13.2		
.3	.4	.6	Deferred Taxes	.0	1.1	.1	.0		
11.4	9.4	9.3	All Other Non-Current	8.3	11.4	6.9	8.5		
21.5	23.7	26.9	Net Worth	29.1	25.3	22.7	28.9		
100.0	100.0	100.0	Total Liabilities & Net Worth	100.0	100.0	100.0	100.0		
			INCOME DATA						
100.0	100.0	100.0	Net Sales	100.0	100.0	100.0	100.0		
			Gross Profit						
66.7	70.1	71.9	Operating Expenses	65.4	69.5	72.6	78.6		
33.3	29.9	28.1	Operating Profit	34.6	30.5	27.4	21.4		
19.3	15.3	10.8	All Other Expenses (net)	15.6	10.8	9.0	6.1		
14.0	14.7	17.3	Profit Before Taxes	19.0	19.7	18.4	15.3		
			RATIOS						
2.1 / 1.3 / 1.0	2.4 / 1.4 / 1.0	2.4 / 1.4 / 1.0	Current	4.3 / 1.4 / 1.0	2.5 / 1.6 / .9	1.4 / 1.3 / 1.2	2.9 / 1.3 / 1.1		
1.9 / 1.1 / .1	2.4 / 1.3 / .5	2.2 / 1.3 / .6	Quick	3.7 / 1.3 / .4	2.4 / 1.3 / .3	1.4 / 1.2 / 1.0	2.3 / 1.3 / 1.0		
0 UND / 151 2.4 / 840 .4	15 23.6 / 392 .9 / 1000 .4	17 21.2 / 379 1.0 / 1216 .3	Sales/Receivables	5 73.1 / 490 .7 / 1462 .2	6 57.5 / 394 .9 / 1195 .3	282 1.3 / 973 .4 / 1175 .3	24 15.3 / 276 1.3 / 821 .4		
			Cost of Sales/Inventory						
			Cost of Sales/Payables						
.9 / 1.9 / 48.2	.6 / 1.5 / 35.2	.8 / 1.6 / 22.5	Sales/Working Capital	.5 / 1.5 / 43.4	.6 / 1.0 / NM	1.0 / 1.4 / 3.8	.9 / 3.3 / 11.4		
(22) 5.2 / 2.8 / 1.5	(58) 5.4 / 2.5 / 1.1	(73) 4.9 / 2.7 / 1.3	EBIT/Interest	(19) 3.8 / 1.9 / 1.2	(20) 7.9 / 3.7 / 1.8		(13) 5.8 / 2.7 / 1.0		
			Net Profit + Depr., Dep., Amort./Cur. Mat. L/T/D						
.0 / .1 / .7	.0 / .1 / .5	.0 / .1 / .6	Fixed/Worth	.0 / .0 / 1.0	.0 / .0 / .4	.0 / .1 / .6	.0 / .1 / .4		
2.0 / 5.1 / 19.5	1.6 / 3.4 / 8.4	1.7 / 3.9 / 10.0	Debt/Worth	1.2 / 4.4 / 12.5	1.6 / 2.6 / 13.9	2.1 / 4.1 / 9.0	2.4 / 3.8 / 7.9		
(38) 40.5 / 20.2 / 7.6	(90) 32.8 / 17.0 / 3.0	(114) 39.1 / 19.0 / 6.0	% Profit Before Taxes/Tangible Net Worth	(35) 35.7 / 15.8 / 4.3	(34) 28.5 / 16.3 / 5.0	(11) 36.7 / 25.9 / 3.7	53.0 / 23.9 / 6.6		
6.4 / 1.9 / .7	7.0 / 2.7 / .8	8.4 / 3.3 / 1.1	% Profit Before Taxes/Total Assets	7.1 / 2.4 / .9	9.7 / 4.0 / 1.0	8.3 / 4.4 / 1.9	12.1 / 3.3 / 1.0		
239.4 / 38.9 / 6.6	96.5 / 27.0 / 4.9	170.5 / 37.1 / 7.8	Sales/Net Fixed Assets	UND / 48.5 / 2.8	257.1 / 25.0 / 14.2	47.4 / 33.2 / 7.8	69.4 / 35.9 / 8.8		
.4 / .2 / .1	.5 / .3 / .2	.6 / .3 / .2	Sales/Total Assets	.3 / .2 / .1	.5 / .3 / .2	.5 / .3 / .2	1.0 / .4 / .3		
(29) .6 / 1.4 / 4.6	(66) .7 / 1.7 / 17.9	(72) .7 / 1.3 / 4.1	% Depr., Dep., Amort./Sales	(17) 1.2 / 1.4 / 20.5	(22) .7 / 1.5 / 8.9		(16) .3 / .8 / 3.7		
(11) 8.8 / 15.3 / 33.3	(27) 4.1 / 10.9 / 20.5	(34) 5.5 / 11.9 / 22.0	% Officers', Directors', Owners' Comp/Sales		(14) 4.3 / 11.2 / 15.8				
228813M	591818M	1175257M	Net Sales ($)	16830M	69339M	51812M	133776M	133325M	770175M
1050420M	1512431M	2009049M	Total Assets ($)	98393M	308828M	204352M	401748M	466617M	529111M

M = $ thousand   MM = $ million
See Pages 11 through 21 for Explanation of Ratios and Data

FINANCE—Consumer Lending NAICS 522291 (SIC 6141)

Current Data Sorted By Assets | **Comparative Historical Data**

Type of Statement	0-500M	500M-2MM	2-10MM	10-50MM	50-100MM	100-250MM	4/1/00-3/31/01 ALL	4/1/01-3/31/02 ALL
Unqualified		2	27	33	5	15	40	57
Reviewed	1	4	18	6			16	22
Compiled	5	19	10	1		1	33	45
Tax Returns	6	10	6		1		13	14
Other	2	8	28	16	8	5	72	46
	38 (4/1-9/30/04)			198 (10/1/04-3/31/05)				
NUMBER OF STATEMENTS	14	43	89	56	14	20	174	184

ASSETS	%	%	%	%	%	%	%	%
Cash & Equivalents	25.5	9.8	6.8	7.8	16.0	10.3	6.6	7.1
Trade Receivables (net)	50.7	60.9	61.2	72.4	54.5	57.2	65.4	64.1
Inventory	.0	.4	2.0	.4	.8	1.2	1.8	1.6
All Other Current	2.2	9.9	9.6	3.7	7.6	11.6	8.0	9.7
Total Current	78.4	81.0	79.6	84.3	79.0	80.4	81.8	82.5
Fixed Assets (net)	15.9	6.9	3.7	5.6	8.3	5.4	6.3	5.6
Intangibles (net)	3.4	2.1	.4	2.2	2.6	3.7	1.6	2.5
All Other Non-Current	2.4	10.0	16.2	8.0	10.1	10.5	10.3	9.4
Total	100.0	100.0	100.0	100.0	100.0	100.0	100.0	100.0

LIABILITIES								
Notes Payable-Short Term	38.3	31.9	38.1	35.7	27.8	38.4	36.9	34.3
Cur. Mat.-L/T/D	2.4	1.5	2.8	2.0	5.2	2.4	3.3	3.9
Trade Payables	1.8	1.2	1.3	2.1	1.8	3.3	3.1	1.2
Income Taxes Payable	.0	.1	.1	.1	.0	.1	.1	.1
All Other Current	4.5	11.6	7.4	8.8	18.9	5.2	10.7	11.3
Total Current	47.0	46.2	49.6	48.7	53.7	49.4	54.1	50.9
Long-Term Debt	7.2	8.3	9.5	12.4	14.4	12.8	10.0	12.6
Deferred Taxes	.3	.0	.0	.0	.3	.5	.0	.1
All Other Non-Current	13.6	13.6	10.3	9.6	5.4	7.4	7.8	8.5
Net Worth	32.0	31.8	30.6	29.3	26.2	29.9	28.1	27.9
Total Liabilities & Net Worth	100.0	100.0	100.0	100.0	100.0	100.0	100.0	100.0

INCOME DATA								
Net Sales	100.0	100.0	100.0	100.0	100.0	100.0	100.0	100.0
Gross Profit								
Operating Expenses	80.2	80.7	72.0	68.5	77.1	72.7	74.0	70.8
Operating Profit	19.8	19.3	28.0	31.5	22.9	27.3	26.0	29.2
All Other Expenses (net)	7.7	7.6	12.2	13.6	7.4	6.3	10.9	15.8
Profit Before Taxes	12.1	11.7	15.8	17.8	15.6	21.0	15.1	13.4

RATIOS								
Current	3.7	2.9	2.8	2.5	4.2	2.6	2.5	2.8
	2.0	1.6	1.6	1.5	1.4	1.6	1.4	1.6
	1.2	1.3	1.2	1.2	1.0	1.2	1.2	1.1
Quick	3.7	2.9	2.2	2.5	3.3	1.9	2.3	2.4
	2.0	1.5	1.5	1.5	1.4	1.4	1.3	1.4
	1.2	1.1	1.0	1.1	1.0	1.1	1.0	1.0
Sales/Receivables	0 UND	8 45.7	142 2.6	273 1.3	109 3.3	25 14.8	129 2.8	115 3.2
	188 1.9	632 .6	645 .6	1149 .3	453 .8	220 1.7	746 .5	786 .5
	918 .4	960 .4	1373 .3	1808 .2	1429 .3	1050 .3	1396 .3	1382 .3
Cost of Sales/Inventory								
Cost of Sales/Payables								
Sales/Working Capital	1.2	.8	.6	.4	.8	1.0	.7	.6
	1.8	1.5	1.3	1.0	1.4	2.3	1.3	1.2
	NM	6.7	3.0	2.8	6.1	3.8	7.4	5.8
EBIT/Interest	9.8	4.7	5.4	7.4		20.2	5.6	5.0
	(12) 1.7	(34) 2.0	(59) 2.7	(34) 2.4		(16) 3.4	(88) 2.8	(97) 2.6
	.6	1.3	1.4	1.5		2.1	1.5	1.5
Net Profit + Depr., Dep., Amort./Cur. Mat. L /T/D							8.7	47.1
							(21) .8	(14) 6.8
							.1	.6
Fixed/Worth	.0	.0	.0	.0	.0	.0	.0	.0
	.1	.1	.0	.1	.3	.1	.1	.1
	2.7	.8	.3	.2	.7	.2	.2	.3
Debt/Worth	.8	1.2	1.3	1.9	1.5	1.3	1.4	1.4
	4.7	3.1	3.0	3.8	3.0	4.1	3.8	4.1
	10.7	13.9	6.3	9.8	259.0	8.2	9.5	11.1
% Profit Before Taxes/Tangible Net Worth	70.3	60.2	40.5	42.4	44.4	58.1	43.5	44.6
	(12) 15.5	(39) 15.1	(84) 14.5	(54) 23.8	(12) 15.8	39.7	(168) 18.9	(172) 18.3
	−8.1	4.2	3.3	9.8	7.0	29.6	6.0	4.8
% Profit Before Taxes/Total Assets	16.3	12.6	9.3	7.5	8.4	19.0	9.4	8.8
	2.6	3.1	3.5	3.5	4.5	7.7	4.1	3.6
	−2.2	1.1	1.0	1.7	.8	4.4	1.2	.9
Sales/Net Fixed Assets	UND	305.0	147.7	71.9	50.4	28.8	92.7	186.4
	75.8	36.8	33.6	24.1	12.4	24.6	23.8	26.2
	10.4	12.2	10.6	11.0	3.0	12.2	9.0	10.5
Sales/Total Assets	1.2	1.6	.5	.5	.7	1.2	.6	.6
	.5	.4	.3	.3	.3	.4	.3	.3
	.3	.3	.2	.2	.2	.3	.2	.2
% Depr., Dep., Amort./Sales		.5	.6	.4		.8	.6	.8
	(29)	1.2	(55) 1.8	(43) 1.6		(16) 1.3	(125) 1.3	(113) 1.6
		3.2	2.5	3.3		2.3	2.8	2.7
% Officers', Directors', Owners' Comp/Sales		6.4	4.5	2.4			6.3	4.2
	(18)	15.4	(19) 11.5	(10) 8.0			(39) 13.6	(41) 7.3
		28.7	23.7	23.4			23.2	16.1
Net Sales ($)	4860M	52366M	210539M	699026M	446418M	2162624M	2876359M	2346462M
Total Assets ($)	4893M	45387M	434280M	1231981M	1037870M	2866118M	4511079M	4258053M

M = $ thousand   MM = $ million
See Pages 11 through 21 for Explanation of Ratios and Data

Comparative Historical Data · **Current Data Sorted By Sales**

Hist 1	Hist 2	Hist 3	Type of Statement	0-1MM	1-3MM	3-5MM	5-10MM	10-25MM	25MM & OVER
64	71	82	Unqualified	14	18	12	8	14	16
32	29	29	Reviewed	10	11	4	4		
25	35	35	Compiled	24	4	3	2	1	1
15	15	23	Tax Returns	13	4	4	2		
73	55	67	Other	17	23	3	5	7	12
4/1/02-3/31/03 ALL	4/1/03-3/31/04 ALL	4/1/04-3/31/05 ALL		38 (4/1-9/30/04)			198 (10/1/04-3/31/05)		
209	205	236	**NUMBER OF STATEMENTS**	78	60	26	21	22	29
%	%	%	**ASSETS**	%	%	%	%	%	%
6.3	8.4	9.5	Cash & Equivalents	9.6	4.5	10.4	11.3	10.2	17.2
63.7	63.3	62.4	Trade Receivables (net)	63.7	72.2	61.5	60.2	56.0	46.3
2.8	2.4	1.1	Inventory	.2	.3	2.2	5.2	.9	1.3
11.3	7.3	7.9	All Other Current	12.4	5.0	2.7	6.6	8.6	6.8
84.2	81.4	80.9	Total Current	85.8	82.0	76.8	83.3	75.7	71.5
4.8	6.4	5.9	Fixed Assets (net)	4.3	3.8	8.9	9.0	5.9	9.5
1.7	1.4	1.7	Intangibles (net)	.1	2.1	1.4	.7	3.3	5.3
9.3	10.7	11.5	All Other Non-Current	9.8	12.2	12.9	7.0	15.1	13.7
100.0	100.0	100.0	Total	100.0	100.0	100.0	100.0	100.0	100.0
			LIABILITIES						
35.6	35.2	35.8	Notes Payable-Short Term	39.7	39.0	30.4	35.1	31.3	27.6
3.7	2.5	2.5	Cur. Mat.-L/T/D	2.5	1.0	1.8	4.6	3.9	3.3
2.5	2.6	1.7	Trade Payables	1.0	1.0	1.8	2.6	2.2	3.9
.2	.1	.1	Income Taxes Payable	.0	.1	.1	.0	.0	.1
11.2	8.6	8.8	All Other Current	7.3	11.1	10.4	6.9	11.2	6.5
53.2	49.0	48.9	Total Current	50.5	52.2	44.5	49.2	48.7	41.4
10.4	10.2	10.4	Long-Term Debt	6.0	11.5	16.6	5.2	13.2	15.9
.0	.0	.1	Deferred Taxes	.1	.0	.0	.0	.2	.3
9.5	10.7	10.4	All Other Non-Current	14.9	9.4	6.2	7.5	11.7	5.2
26.9	30.1	30.3	Net Worth	28.5	26.9	32.7	38.1	26.2	37.1
100.0	100.0	100.0	Total Liabilities & Net Worth	100.0	100.0	100.0	100.0	100.0	100.0
			INCOME DATA						
100.0	100.0	100.0	Net Sales	100.0	100.0	100.0	100.0	100.0	100.0
			Gross Profit						
73.9	72.6	73.6	Operating Expenses	74.3	67.2	75.6	75.9	80.4	76.5
26.1	27.4	26.4	Operating Profit	25.7	32.8	24.4	24.1	19.6	23.5
12.0	10.3	10.7	All Other Expenses (net)	13.0	13.3	10.5	7.0	7.4	4.3
14.1	17.1	15.7	Profit Before Taxes	12.7	19.5	13.9	17.1	12.2	19.2
			RATIOS						
2.6	2.8	2.8	Current	3.0	2.0	2.3	2.7	4.4	4.6
1.5	1.5	1.6		1.7	1.5	1.7	1.7	1.4	1.8
1.1	1.2	1.2		1.2	1.2	1.2	1.3	1.1	1.2
2.3	2.4	2.4	Quick	3.0	2.0	2.1	2.1	3.3	3.4
1.3	1.4	1.5		1.6	1.4	1.6	1.5	1.3	1.5
1.0	1.1	1.1		1.1	1.2	1.1	1.1	1.1	1.2
92 4.0 · 95 3.8 · 92 4.0			Sales/Receivables	174 2.1 · 339 1.1	83 4.4 · 14 25.6	29 12.5 · 17 21.8			
633 .6 · 746 .5 · 799 .5				878 .4 · 1005 .4	810 .5 · 649 .6	481 .8 · 97 3.7			
1297 .3 · 1260 .3 · 1280 .3				1301 .3 · 1553 .2	1616 .2 · 1161 .3	1168 .3 · 924 .4			
			Cost of Sales/Inventory						
			Cost of Sales/Payables						
.7	.8	.6	Sales/Working Capital	.4	.6	.7	.8	.7	1.3
1.5	1.5	1.3		1.0	1.0	1.6	2.1	1.4	2.7
5.3	4.0	3.5		2.5	2.7	3.4	11.5	23.8	6.1
6.2	7.1	6.3	EBIT/Interest	4.3	5.3	7.9	12.9	5.5	29.8
(142) 2.6	(144) 3.1	(163) 2.5		(48) 1.9	(41) 2.8	(19) 2.7	(15) 3.3	(16) 2.1	(24) 4.8
1.7	1.8	1.5		1.0	1.5	1.8	1.8	1.5	2.1
19.0	7.9	2.7	Net Profit + Depr., Dep., Amort./Cur. Mat. L/T/D						
(22) 3.6	(17) .6	(17) .9							
.7	.1	.3							
.0	.0	.0	Fixed/Worth	.0	.0	.0	.0	.0	.1
.1	.1	.1		.0	.0	.1	.1	.1	.1
.3	.3	.3		.3	.2	.5	.3	.3	.5
1.5	1.4	1.3	Debt/Worth	1.2	1.9	1.1	1.6	1.6	1.0
4.0	3.3	3.3		3.6	3.6	3.6	2.0	4.0	2.7
10.1	7.7	9.3		9.7	10.9	5.9	4.8	12.3	6.8
48.3	44.6	46.0	% Profit Before Taxes/Tangible Net Worth	31.7	48.2	38.3	58.8	42.0	89.0
(194) 21.1	(196) 23.8	(221) 19.4		(72) 8.1	(55) 20.1	(20) 19.0	(20) 32.8	27.9	(28) 44.7
6.9	9.6	5.6		.9	7.0	7.9	11.0	7.7	29.6
8.7	11.0	10.0	% Profit Before Taxes/Total Assets	5.5	9.1	9.5	14.8	7.5	34.4
3.8	5.1	3.8		2.1	3.3	4.1	6.8	4.3	13.0
1.2	2.2	1.2		.1	1.7	1.6	3.1	1.0	4.9
115.7	103.7	119.2	Sales/Net Fixed Assets	495.0	118.5	67.3	67.8	96.9	28.5
30.1	29.8	27.8		38.8	44.3	17.5	36.8	22.9	16.3
11.7	11.8	10.9		11.7	11.6	6.0	10.0	11.5	10.6
.8	.8	.7	Sales/Total Assets	.4	.5	1.1	1.6	.8	1.6
.3	.3	.3		.3	.3	.4	.5	.4	1.1
.2	.2	.2		.2	.2	.2	.3	.2	.3
.5	.7	.6	% Depr., Dep., Amort./Sales	.6	.6	1.3	.5	1.2	.9
(133) 1.2	(140) 1.3	(159) 1.6		(47) 1.6	(37) 1.1	(21) 2.9	(17) .9	(14) 1.7	(23) 2.1
2.6	2.7	2.8		2.4	2.1	3.7	1.8	4.3	2.5
3.7	2.5	5.5	% Officers', Directors', Owners' Comp/Sales	9.9	7.2	4.8			
(53) 8.8	(37) 8.7	(53) 13.1		(22) 21.2	(14) 10.6	(11) 11.5			
19.4	15.2	26.6		31.4	23.4	21.0			
2669274M	3435391M	3575833M	Net Sales ($)	35648M	119248M	95338M	145034M	358707M	2821858M
4468946M	4823262M	5620529M	Total Assets ($)	173519M	516254M	293172M	319713M	1235543M	3082328M

© RMA 2005

M = $ thousand   MM = $ million

See Pages 11 through 21 for Explanation of Ratios and Data

Current Data Sorted By Assets   Comparative Historical Data

0-500M	500M-2MM	2-10MM	10-50MM	50-100MM	100-250MM	Type of Statement	4/1/00-3/31/01 ALL	4/1/01-3/31/02 ALL
16	27	96	165	44	42	Unqualified	167	131
1	2	5	6			Reviewed	5	4
3	2	7	3		1	Compiled	27	23
20	13	16	4			Tax Returns	13	16
8	14	18	22	4	9	Other	58	60
76 (4/1-9/30/04)			472 (10/1/04-3/31/05)					
NUMBER OF STATEMENTS 48	58	142	200	48	52		270	234
%	%	%	%	%	%	**ASSETS**	%	%
45.8	30.5	16.4	9.5	5.1	10.5	Cash & Equivalents	17.9	15.7
5.3	12.9	30.7	52.3	55.4	52.0	Trade Receivables (net)	22.8	23.2
.2	3.4	5.6	6.4	6.7	4.1	Inventory	9.2	13.5
7.4	16.4	21.0	16.3	12.5	13.8	All Other Current	22.3	19.7
58.6	63.3	73.8	84.5	79.8	80.4	Total Current	72.3	72.0
21.1	18.0	8.5	2.9	3.2	2.6	Fixed Assets (net)	7.7	7.4
.6	.7	3.1	1.6	3.6	1.6	Intangibles (net)	2.9	3.8
19.8	18.0	14.6	11.0	13.5	15.4	All Other Non-Current	17.1	16.7
100.0	100.0	100.0	100.0	100.0	100.0	Total	100.0	100.0
						LIABILITIES		
23.6	23.0	38.6	27.3	28.9	23.2	Notes Payable-Short Term	44.0	47.8
.7	2.4	1.2	1.4	.9	.1	Cur. Mat.-L/T/D	1.2	4.9
6.5	6.8	13.8	38.3	38.4	39.4	Trade Payables	3.7	2.9
.2	.4	.1	.1	.4	.3	Income Taxes Payable	.1	.3
13.1	8.3	6.3	4.8	2.4	11.0	All Other Current	9.1	7.9
44.0	40.9	60.0	71.9	71.1	74.0	Total Current	58.1	63.7
4.4	10.8	6.5	6.9	5.9	4.9	Long-Term Debt	8.3	7.5
.2	.4	.2	.2	.2	.2	Deferred Taxes	.4	.3
2.6	1.7	4.4	1.7	4.5	2.0	All Other Non-Current	2.7	4.0
48.9	46.3	28.8	19.2	18.3	18.9	Net Worth	30.5	24.6
100.0	100.0	100.0	100.0	100.0	100.0	Total Liabilities & Net Worth	100.0	100.0
						INCOME DATA		
100.0	100.0	100.0	100.0	100.0	100.0	Net Sales	100.0	100.0
						Gross Profit		
92.1	83.1	76.8	80.7	69.4	72.2	Operating Expenses	83.6	75.0
7.9	16.9	23.2	19.3	30.6	27.8	Operating Profit	16.4	25.0
1.9	5.4	8.6	8.1	12.2	7.7	All Other Expenses (net)	6.1	10.0
6.0	11.5	14.6	11.3	18.5	20.1	Profit Before Taxes	10.3	15.1
						RATIOS		
4.3	2.8	1.7	1.3	1.3	1.1		1.5	1.5
2.1	1.5	1.3	1.1	1.1	1.1	Current	1.1	1.1
.8	1.1	1.1	1.1	1.0	1.0		1.0	1.0
3.6	2.8	1.3	1.1	1.1	1.1		1.2	1.1
2.0	1.2	1.0	1.1	1.0	1.0	Quick	.7 (233)	.6
.5	.3	.2	.3	.2	.3		.1	.1
0 UND	0 UND	0 UND	15 25.0	30 12.1	22 16.6		0 UND	0 UND
0 UND	0 UND	25 14.5	367 1.0	601 .6	742 .5	Sales/Receivables	16 22.8	15 24.2
3 132.3	14 26.2	378 1.0	787 .5	1456 .3	1193 .3		246 1.5	256 1.4
						Cost of Sales/Inventory		
						Cost of Sales/Payables		
9.7	3.0	1.6	2.4	1.4	2.0		1.7	2.1
41.9	7.9	3.9	4.5	3.2	4.8	Sales/Working Capital	5.0	7.8
-43.8	42.1	18.5	11.3	10.8	22.5		39.4	-53.2
32.8	15.0	6.4	4.2	12.4	8.9		4.0	7.3
(28) 12.6	(46) 2.3	(102) 2.2	(160) 2.1	(33) 2.4	(40) 3.6	EBIT/Interest	(168) 1.5	(147) 2.9
.7	1.2	1.1	1.3	1.0	2.0		.9	1.4
		18.1	27.7			Net Profit + Depr., Dep.,	4.9	7.5
	(16) 8.6	(20) 7.3				Amort./Cur. Mat. L/T/D	(29) 3.4	(23) 3.4
		3.3	.2				.5	.3
.0	.0	.0	.0	.0	.0		.0	.0
.4	.1	.1	.1	.1	.1	Fixed/Worth	.1	.1
1.0	1.2	.4	.2	.2	.2		.4	.4
.2	.4	1.5	3.5	3.9	3.6		1.2	1.7
.6	1.4	2.9	6.5	8.0	8.6	Debt/Worth	3.8	6.3
2.8	3.5	6.0	10.1	14.1	15.8		10.6	16.5
95.2	34.9	38.1	40.9	51.3	80.0	% Profit Before Taxes/Tangible	30.8	66.4
(44) 51.1	(55) 16.8	(134) 15.4	(195) 19.7	(46) 20.6	(51) 34.1	Net Worth	(256) 11.8	(217) 28.5
.0	2.5	3.1	8.1	7.0	14.6		.5	9.3
68.2	14.4	8.9	6.2	5.9	7.8	% Profit Before Taxes/Total	6.0	9.3
29.5	5.0	3.5	2.8	3.2	3.9	Assets	1.9	3.9
.0	.9	.3	.8	.5	1.6		.1	1.3
532.3	86.6	68.5	81.1	59.8	82.3		53.3	85.1
43.3	26.9	28.5	31.3	33.3	35.9	Sales/Net Fixed Assets	22.7	30.6
13.1	8.7	11.9	15.7	18.1	15.6		8.9	12.0
9.9	3.0	.8	.7	.4	.4		.7	.9
5.0	1.1	.5	.4	.3	.3	Sales/Total Assets	.4	.3
2.3	.5	.2	.2	.1	.2		.2	.2
.3	.8	.7	.5	.5	.5		.8	.6
(25) .9	(39) 1.2	(98) 1.2	(147) .9	(39) .9	(28) 1.1	% Depr., Dep., Amort./Sales	(188) 1.7	(151) 1.2
2.3	1.7	2.1	1.5	1.7	1.9		2.8	1.8
7.2	4.6	4.1	2.0	1.3		% Officers', Directors',	5.8	6.3
(22) 13.2	(21) 9.9	(43) 9.3	(67) 4.7	(12) 2.4		Owners' Comp/Sales	(69) 13.0	(48) 8.2
21.4	16.9	24.3	9.7	5.0			21.7	17.0
63342M	159303M	871761M	2710247M	5767960M	2523100M	Net Sales ($)	1980744M	2340148M
10791M	70660M	744151M	4583707M	3510617M	8426002M	Total Assets ($)	6287458M	7426573M

© RMA 2005

M = $ thousand   MM = $ million
See Pages 11 through 21 for Explanation of Ratios and Data

Comparative Historical Data				Current Data Sorted By Sales					
			Type of Statement						
225	427	390	Unqualified	27	67	45	91	96	64
15	12	14	Reviewed	5	8			1	
22	25	16	Compiled	6	7	1		1	1
29	28	53	Tax Returns	30	16	1	5		1
72	75	75	Other	18	17	7	14	7	12
4/1/02-3/31/03 ALL	4/1/03-3/31/04 ALL	4/1/04-3/31/05 ALL		76 (4/1-9/30/04)			472 (10/1/04-3/31/05)		
				0-1MM	1-3MM	3-5MM	5-10MM	10-25MM	25MM & OVER
363	567	548	**NUMBER OF STATEMENTS**	86	115	54	110	105	78
%	%	%	**ASSETS**	%	%	%	%	%	%
16.5	19.7	16.4	Cash & Equivalents	26.0	21.0	15.1	11.6	10.7	14.4
23.9	34.8	38.7	Trade Receivables (net)	16.4	26.2	41.4	46.3	49.4	54.7
10.0	6.3	5.2	Inventory	4.8	4.0	3.8	6.1	7.4	3.8
23.3	18.3	16.2	All Other Current	15.4	18.5	12.2	18.4	19.4	8.8
73.6	79.0	76.4	Total Current	62.5	69.8	72.6	82.4	86.9	81.7
8.6	7.1	7.5	Fixed Assets (net)	14.3	9.2	9.3	5.0	3.7	5.1
3.0	2.2	2.0	Intangibles (net)	.7	1.5	5.0	1.5	1.9	2.9
14.8	11.7	14.1	All Other Non-Current	22.5	19.6	13.2	11.1	7.5	10.4
100.0	100.0	100.0	Total	100.0	100.0	100.0	100.0	100.0	100.0
			LIABILITIES						
43.9	29.3	29.2	Notes Payable-Short Term	33.7	36.7	22.4	30.6	28.7	16.6
3.5	1.6	1.2	Cur. Mat.-L/T/D	2.0	1.7	1.7	.6	1.1	.3
2.8	19.2	25.9	Trade Payables	1.8	9.3	28.2	34.2	36.5	49.8
.5	.4	.2	Income Taxes Payable	.1	.2	.1	.1	.2	.4
10.4	10.5	6.7	All Other Current	7.8	6.5	4.2	6.4	7.5	6.7
61.1	61.0	63.2	Total Current	45.3	54.4	56.6	71.9	74.0	73.8
9.4	6.2	6.7	Long-Term Debt	12.9	11.8	5.5	4.0	2.7	2.6
.2	.3	.2	Deferred Taxes	.2	.3	.2	.3	.2	.1
2.2	2.2	2.8	All Other Non-Current	4.5	3.6	2.0	2.1	2.1	1.9
27.1	30.4	27.1	Net Worth	37.1	29.9	35.7	21.7	21.0	21.5
100.0	100.0	100.0	Total Liabilities & Net Worth	100.0	100.0	100.0	100.0	100.0	100.0
			INCOME DATA						
100.0	100.0	100.0	Net Sales	100.0	100.0	100.0	100.0	100.0	100.0
			Gross Profit						
76.0	77.0	79.1	Operating Expenses	70.0	75.5	86.1	82.9	79.2	84.1
24.0	23.0	20.9	Operating Profit	30.0	24.5	13.9	17.1	20.8	15.9
6.0	5.4	7.7	All Other Expenses (net)	12.9	8.9	7.8	6.2	7.3	2.9
18.0	17.7	13.2	Profit Before Taxes	17.1	15.6	6.2	10.9	13.5	12.9
			RATIOS						
1.8	1.6	1.5		3.7	2.4	1.5	1.3	1.3	1.2
1.1	1.2	1.2	Current	1.3	1.3	1.3	1.1	1.1	1.1
1.0	1.1	1.0		1.0	1.1	1.1	1.0	1.0	1.0
1.4	1.3	1.3		3.6	2.1	1.4	1.2	1.1	1.1
.8	1.1	1.1	Quick	1.0	1.1	1.1	1.1	1.0	1.0
.1	.3	.3		.1	.2	.3	.2	.2	.8
0 UND	0 UND	0 UND		0 UND	0 UND	0 UND	4 86.9	13 28.9	20 18.6
14 27.0	21 17.6	70 5.2	Sales/Receivables	0 UND	13 27.6	70 5.2	321 1.1	367 1.0	285 1.3
203 1.8	446 .8	661 .6		85 4.3	371 1.0	822 .4	632 .6	851 .4	747 .5
			Cost of Sales/Inventory						
			Cost of Sales/Payables						
2.2	2.4	2.2		1.1	1.4	2.5	2.7	2.6	3.8
5.7	5.2	5.3	Sales/Working Capital	6.2	3.6	4.4	4.7	5.4	11.8
48.0	16.8	19.4		−126.7	12.8	14.1	15.5	11.2	47.3
	9.6		8.5		6.6		15.1		8.3		4.0		6.7		4.7		9.2
(234) 3.7	(415) 3.9	(409) 2.3	EBIT/Interest	(43) 2.1	(71) 2.7	(45) 1.8	(91) 2.1	(90) 2.3	(69) 3.1
1.9	2.1	1.2		.6	1.2	.9	1.2	1.3	1.5
24.2	97.2	23.7	Net Profit + Depr., Dep.,				19.7	30.9	94.2
(30) 4.9	(55) 17.3	(52) 7.3	Amort./Cur. Mat. L/T/D			(11) 7.0	(14) 11.7	(12) 13.7
.6	3.5	1.8					−.8	4.8	2.5
.0	.0	.0		.0	.0	.1	.0	.0	.1
.1	.1	.1	Fixed/Worth	.0	.1	.1	.1	.1	.2
.4	.3	.3		.7	.3	.4	.3	.3	.4
1.5	1.4	1.7		.5	.8	1.1	2.8	3.1	2.9
5.5	3.8	4.6	Debt/Worth	2.2	3.1	2.5	5.3	6.7	6.9
12.9	8.2	9.4		6.8	8.3	5.9	9.0	10.8	12.9
64.7	78.4	45.7	% Profit Before Taxes/Tangible	45.6	35.9	34.4	40.3	56.1	80.8
(341) 33.6	(542) 45.2	(525) 19.5	Net Worth	(81) 16.3	(106) 16.1	(51) 13.6	(108) 18.3	(102) 27.9	(77) 34.1
11.6	17.3	5.0		2.8	3.4	−.2	5.0	10.4	16.1
11.9	17.7	9.0	% Profit Before Taxes/Total	10.2	9.3	7.7	6.5	8.7	11.0
4.8	8.2	3.5	Assets	3.3	3.4	2.0	2.7	4.0	5.1
1.7	3.0	.7		.1	.8	−.2	.7	1.5	1.9
80.3	88.2	84.4		UND	123.8	39.8	57.7	53.8	83.1
31.4	34.8	32.0	Sales/Net Fixed Assets	44.2	33.7	23.7	31.1	29.1	37.5
14.2	16.0	14.2		7.5	13.3	13.0	15.8	15.4	24.5
1.1	1.2	.9		1.8	1.1	1.3	.8	.7	1.3
.3	.6	.5	Sales/Total Assets	.3	.5	.6	.5	.4	.5
.2	.3	.2		.1	.2	.3	.3	.3	.3
.6	.4	.5		.3	.7	.6	.5	.3	
(245) 1.1	(424) .8	(376) 1.0	% Depr., Dep., Amort./Sales	(40) 1.6	(71) 1.2	(39) 1.2	(85) 1.0	(86) 1.0	(55) .6
1.9	1.3	1.7		3.3	1.7	1.6	1.5	1.7	1.4
7.3	3.7	2.5		7.3	5.9	6.1	3.2	1.6	.6
(89) 12.4	(183) 9.1	(170) 6.2	% Officers', Directors', Owners' Comp/Sales	(27) 14.4	(33) 13.2	(18) 9.8	(43) 4.3	(31) 3.2	(18) .9
24.0	16.6	14.9		24.8	21.4	14.0	11.4	6.1	2.0
4891252M	17971648M	12095713M	Net Sales ($)	45569M	213306M	206745M	799251M	1645606M	9185236M
10790081M	17170549M	17345928M	Total Assets ($)	260789M	931959M	589963M	2492307M	5043884M	8027026M

© RMA 2005

M = $ thousand   MM = $ million
See Pages 11 through 21 for Explanation of Ratios and Data

Current Data Sorted By Assets — Comparative Historical Data

0-500M	500M-2MM	2-10MM	10-50MM	50-100MM	100-250MM	Type of Statement	4/1/00-3/31/01 ALL	4/1/01-3/31/02 ALL
1			7	1	2	Unqualified	9	14
1						Reviewed	3	2
		1		1		Compiled	2	5
3	1	2				Tax Returns	2	2
	2	1	3	1		Other	4	12
4 (4/1-9/30/04)			**23 (10/1/04-3/31/05)**					
5	3	4	10	3	2	NUMBER OF STATEMENTS	20	35
%	%	%	%	%	%		%	%
						ASSETS		
			24.8			Cash & Equivalents	21.7	17.2
			46.3			Trade Receivables (net)	31.1	11.9
			.0			Inventory	.3	14.7
			9.6			All Other Current	9.5	18.1
			80.7			Total Current	62.6	62.0
			2.4			Fixed Assets (net)	15.5	13.7
			.2			Intangibles (net)	1.7	2.6
			16.7			All Other Non-Current	20.2	21.8
			100.0			Total	100.0	100.0
						LIABILITIES		
			46.9			Notes Payable-Short Term	24.0	39.5
			1.9			Cur. Mat.-L/T/D	4.0	2.6
			.7			Trade Payables	5.9	3.7
			.0			Income Taxes Payable	.0	.3
			2.2			All Other Current	13.2	6.9
			51.7			Total Current	47.0	52.9
			11.2			Long-Term Debt	26.9	15.3
			.0			Deferred Taxes	.0	.1
			2.5			All Other Non-Current	1.7	4.1
			34.6			Net Worth	24.4	27.5
			100.0			Total Liabilities & Net Worth	100.0	100.0
						INCOME DATA		
			100.0			Net Sales	100.0	100.0
						Gross Profit		
			58.0			Operating Expenses	97.9	77.2
			42.0			Operating Profit	2.1	22.8
			20.8			All Other Expenses (net)	−.5	11.2
			21.2			Profit Before Taxes	2.7	11.5
						RATIOS		
			6.2				3.9	1.6
			1.5			Current	1.1	1.2
			1.1				.8	.9
			5.4				3.4	1.2
			1.5			Quick	1.0	.4
			1.1				.7	.1
			6 60.8				0 UND	0 UND
			546 .7			Sales/Receivables	28 13.0	8 44.0
			1504 .2				757 .5	63 5.8
						Cost of Sales/Inventory		
						Cost of Sales/Payables		
			.3				1.6	2.0
			1.0			Sales/Working Capital	21.7	4.1
			3.4				−6.2	−4.4
							7.0	5.3
						EBIT/Interest	(10) 1.7	(23) 2.2
							1.2	1.4
						Net Profit + Depr., Dep., Amort./Cur. Mat. L/T/D		
			.0				.0	.0
			.0			Fixed/Worth	.1	.2
			.2				5.6	.5
			.7				1.5	1.0
			4.3			Debt/Worth	11.2	3.8
			7.8				643.8	16.1
			29.8				95.1	42.4
			13.4			% Profit Before Taxes/Tangible Net Worth	(16) 22.4	(30) 12.4
			9.4				−1.3	3.5
			8.9				6.2	10.0
			4.0			% Profit Before Taxes/Total Assets	2.5	2.9
			1.1				−.8	.3
			UND				UND	61.0
			101.7			Sales/Net Fixed Assets	30.1	18.7
			30.0				10.4	3.7
			.5				1.0	.6
			.2			Sales/Total Assets	.7	.3
			.1				.1	.2
							.7	.6
						% Depr., Dep., Amort./Sales	(12) 2.0	(26) 1.7
							5.9	3.5
						% Officers', Directors', Owners' Comp/Sales		
6034M	449M	3824M	76863M	26512M	37407M	Net Sales ($)	94629M	302628M
1380M	4949M	13893M	277477M	204280M	332343M	Total Assets ($)	405827M	986865M

© RMA 2005

M = $ thousand   MM = $ million
See Pages 11 through 21 for Explanation of Ratios and Data

Comparative Historical Data				Current Data Sorted By Sales					

Type of Statement

13	12	11		1	2	2	3	1	2
	2	1	Unqualified		1				
	2	2	Reviewed						
	3	6	Compiled		2				
1	3	7	Tax Returns	5	1				
3	5		Other	4		1		2	
4/1/02-	4/1/03-	4/1/04-			4 (4/1-9/30/04)			23 (10/1/04-3/31/05)	
3/31/03	3/31/04	3/31/05		0-1MM	1-3MM	3-5MM	5-10MM	10-25MM	25MM & OVER
ALL	ALL	ALL							
17	24	27	NUMBER OF STATEMENTS	10	6	3	3	3	2
%	%	%	ASSETS	%	%	%	%	%	%
20.5	28.5	20.9	Cash & Equivalents	22.2					
16.1	22.0	39.7	Trade Receivables (net)	32.2					
7.4	.3	3.4	Inventory	.3					
14.2	9.0	10.3	All Other Current	7.4					
58.2	59.8	74.3	Total Current	62.1					
17.3	16.0	5.5	Fixed Assets (net)	7.7					
.1	2.2	.5	Intangibles (net)	.3					
24.4	21.9	19.8	All Other Non-Current	29.9					
100.0	100.0	100.0	Total	100.0					
			LIABILITIES						
23.0	14.0	31.0	Notes Payable-Short Term	10.2					
4.0	2.5	1.5	Cur. Mat.-L/T/D	2.1					
6.3	5.0	4.3	Trade Payables	2.2					
.0	.1	.0	Income Taxes Payable	.0					
8.4	11.7	7.5	All Other Current	9.6					
41.6	33.3	44.4	Total Current	24.1					
12.1	11.8	20.3	Long-Term Debt	31.7					
.0	.1	.0	Deferred Taxes	.1					
8.8	6.5	3.0	All Other Non-Current	2.2					
37.5	48.3	32.3	Net Worth	41.9					
100.0	100.0	100.0	Total Liabilities & Net Worth	100.0					
			INCOME DATA						
100.0	100.0	100.0	Net Sales	100.0					
			Gross Profit						
78.5	81.2	67.6	Operating Expenses	60.7					
21.5	18.8	32.4	Operating Profit	39.3					
12.8	4.1	16.7	All Other Expenses (net)	19.5					
8.7	14.7	15.7	Profit Before Taxes	19.8					
			RATIOS						
2.7	4.3	3.8		5.1					
1.3	2.0	1.6	Current	3.5					
1.0	.9	1.1		.3					
1.4	3.2	3.8		5.1					
.8	1.9	1.4	Quick	3.5					
.3	.7	.2		.2					
0 UND	1 337.9	0 UND		0 UND					
13 28.9	19 19.7	246 1.5	Sales/Receivables	101 3.6					
121 3.0	132 2.8	1556 .2		2000 .1					
			Cost of Sales/Inventory						
			Cost of Sales/Payables						
1.3	1.6	.3		.1					
6.3	8.3	1.2	Sales/Working Capital	.8					
−26.3	NM	20.1		−57.0					
11.9	8.1	11.6							
(11) 4.4	(16) 2.7	(15) 2.8	EBIT/Interest						
−2.7	.6	1.5							
			Net Profit + Depr., Dep., Amort./Cur. Mat. L/T/D						
.0	.0	.0		.0					
.1	.0	.1	Fixed/Worth	.0					
.9	1.4	.5		.9					
.5	.5	.9		.8					
2.6	1.2	3.9	Debt/Worth	1.0					
5.2	4.2	12.7		4.7					
43.2	19.9	35.6							
(16) 9.9	(23) 8.4	(23) 11.1	% Profit Before Taxes/Tangible Net Worth						
−5.1	2.7	2.2							
6.9	10.6	8.2		10.1					
3.1	5.4	2.5	% Profit Before Taxes/Total Assets	1.1					
−3.5	−.1	.8		.1					
UND	UND	UND		UND					
35.7	61.5	59.3	Sales/Net Fixed Assets	59.8					
1.5	4.3	18.7		3.2					
1.1	2.5	.7		1.0					
.3	.8	.2	Sales/Total Assets	.1					
.2	.2	.1		.1					
.7	.8	1.1							
(12) 2.2	(12) 1.4	(15) 1.2	% Depr., Dep., Amort./Sales						
5.1	4.1	3.1							
		10.4							
	(10)	15.2	% Officers', Directors', Owners' Comp/Sales						
		28.7							
181237M	514370M	151089M	Net Sales ($)	4083M	14159M	11134M	20194M	39407M	62112M
620572M	282591M	834322M	Total Assets ($)	35877M	85383M	117327M	164265M	179923M	251547M

© RMA 2005   M = $ thousand   MM = $ million
See Pages 11 through 21 for Explanation of Ratios and Data

Current Data Sorted By Assets   Comparative Historical Data

							Type of Statement		96	90
2	5	26	67	22	21		Unqualified		96	90
1	6	20	14				Reviewed		33	33
3	7	12	2				Compiled		32	37
4	12	6	1				Tax Returns		11	14
7	12	28	28	9	9		Other		57	68
	52 (4/1-9/30/04)		272 (10/1/04-3/31/05)						4/1/00-3/31/01	4/1/01-3/31/02
0-500M	500M-2MM	2-10MM	10-50MM	50-100MM	100-250MM				ALL	ALL
17	42	92	112	31	30		NUMBER OF STATEMENTS		229	242
%	%	%	%	%	%		ASSETS		%	%
28.3	18.2	11.2	7.8	5.8	5.8		Cash & Equivalents		8.8	9.3
24.2	34.2	43.8	52.5	58.1	43.5		Trade Receivables (net)		48.9	46.9
8.6	4.4	1.8	2.5	1.8	5.7		Inventory		.6	1.8
7.5	7.9	10.9	9.9	14.6	10.8		All Other Current		13.3	12.7
68.6	64.8	67.6	72.7	80.3	65.7		Total Current		71.5	70.6
23.2	14.5	12.8	10.0	7.3	5.7		Fixed Assets (net)		10.9	11.0
3.1	1.9	1.0	.9	.6	2.0		Intangibles (net)		1.7	1.9
5.0	18.8	18.7	16.3	11.8	26.6		All Other Non-Current		15.9	16.5
100.0	100.0	100.0	100.0	100.0	100.0		Total		100.0	100.0
							LIABILITIES			
21.5	30.1	31.1	29.8	35.7	20.9		Notes Payable-Short Term		41.1	30.9
8.9	1.4	4.7	3.4	4.9	3.5		Cur. Mat.-L/T/D		5.4	5.8
1.2	10.3	3.2	5.1	2.3	3.5		Trade Payables		3.7	4.3
.0	.3	.2	.5	.2	.1		Income Taxes Payable		.1	.1
11.2	12.1	7.1	9.3	1.9	4.0		All Other Current		15.6	9.3
42.9	54.1	46.3	48.2	45.1	32.1		Total Current		66.0	50.5
55.4	12.6	17.4	19.3	23.5	31.9		Long-Term Debt		17.2	18.9
.0	.0	.3	.1	.7	.8		Deferred Taxes		.3	.2
7.7	9.8	5.8	7.7	4.9	8.2		All Other Non-Current		10.6	5.1
−5.8	23.4	30.2	24.6	25.8	26.9		Net Worth		5.9	25.2
100.0	100.0	100.0	100.0	100.0	100.0		Total Liabilities & Net Worth		100.0	100.0
							INCOME DATA			
100.0	100.0	100.0	100.0	100.0	100.0		Net Sales		100.0	100.0
							Gross Profit			
85.0	72.5	70.6	67.1	56.2	63.8		Operating Expenses		68.4	66.1
15.0	27.5	29.4	32.9	43.8	36.2		Operating Profit		31.6	33.9
2.7	11.9	12.8	13.6	18.4	15.0		All Other Expenses (net)		14.1	17.8
12.3	15.6	16.6	19.3	25.5	21.2		Profit Before Taxes		17.5	16.1
							RATIOS			
11.8	3.7	2.4	2.9	3.0	5.6				1.9	2.2
1.3	1.2	1.4	1.4	1.4	2.2		Current		1.3	1.3
.4	.8	.9	1.1	1.2	1.1				1.0	1.1
6.0	3.4	1.9	2.5	2.5	5.2				1.7	1.8
1.1	1.1	1.1	1.3	1.3	1.6		Quick		1.2	1.2
.3	.5	.5	.8	.6	.9				.3	.4

0	UND	0	UND	27	13.7	30	12.0	30	12.3	22	16.7		Sales/Receivables	1	588.6	6	66.1
0	UND	49	7.5	277	1.3	622	.6	1470	.2	189	1.9			406	.9	300	1.2
49	7.4	945	.4	1084	.3	2000	.2	2000	.1	2000	.2			1456	.3	1347	.3

							Cost of Sales/Inventory			
							Cost of Sales/Payables			

2.0	1.1	.6	.5	.2	.4				.6	.6
37.3	5.7	2.2	1.2	.5	1.6		Sales/Working Capital		1.6	2.2
−51.1	−9.7	−33.8	14.3	1.9	5.4				93.9	45.2

	40.0		4.7		5.6		5.1		8.1		12.5				3.8	4.4
(11)	2.0	(22)	2.7	(55)	3.1	(63)	3.1	(12)	4.9	(13)	4.8	EBIT/Interest	(88)	2.4	(107)	2.5
	.2		1.1		1.6		1.9		1.9		2.7				1.4	1.2

				10.4					3.5	3.1
		(10)		2.6		Net Profit + Depr., Dep., Amort./Cur. Mat. L /T/D	(16)	.8	(12)	.2
				.5					.1	.0

.0	.0	.0	.0	.0	.0				.0	.0
.1	.0	.1	.0	.0	.1		Fixed/Worth		.0	.1
−3.1	1.1	.4	.4	.2	.2				.3	.4
1.2	1.4	1.6	1.9	2.1	2.3				1.9	1.8
10.7	5.7	2.6	3.8	3.8	4.0		Debt/Worth		4.4	4.4
−4.5	37.2	6.5	10.8	7.7	6.6				10.6	10.5

	175.3		74.1		39.1		36.3		31.8		28.0				39.4	41.0
(10)	45.7	(36)	23.8	(87)	18.6	(107)	21.2	(30)	19.6	(28)	14.9	% Profit Before Taxes/Tangible Net Worth	(215)	19.2	(230)	17.2
	16.1		2.5		5.5		9.7		10.8		9.8				7.9	4.8

93.8	9.1	8.7	6.8	8.1	7.3				7.3	7.1
13.7	3.7	3.7	3.8	3.2	3.1		% Profit Before Taxes/Total Assets		3.3	3.1
−.5	.5	1.3	1.8	1.0	1.4				.8	.6
UND	UND	225.1	76.1	118.1	89.6				259.5	154.3
82.6	90.1	29.5	29.1	33.1	39.8		Sales/Net Fixed Assets		33.3	38.7
19.5	6.6	5.4	5.0	6.5	8.8				11.7	11.5
9.7	1.1	.7	.4	.2	.9				.4	.6
2.7	.4	.3	.2	.1	.1		Sales/Total Assets		.2	.3
.6	.2	.1	.1	.1	.1				.1	.1

			.6		.6		.8		.4		1.0				.8	.7
		(22)	1.3	(61)	1.9	(79)	1.7	(21)	1.3	(15)	1.4	% Depr., Dep., Amort./Sales	(143)	1.5	(161)	1.3
			2.9		4.6		4.1		4.5		2.2				3.9	4.6

			1.9		3.3					4.4	4.3
		(24)	7.6	(18)	11.4	% Officers', Directors', Owners' Comp/Sales	(51)	7.8	(50)	9.8
			13.0		21.9					18.1	20.2

20541M	69125M	332135M	3487661M	1169592M	2348332M		Net Sales ($)		2070911M	3266833M
3509M	52199M	499252M	2666058M	2223698M	4584528M		Total Assets ($)		6372862M	6101629M

© RMA 2005

M = $ thousand   MM = $ million
See Pages 11 through 21 for Explanation of Ratios and Data

Comparative Historical Data | Current Data Sorted By Sales

			Type of Statement						
116	119	143	Unqualified	18	23	21	29	30	22
40	43	41	Reviewed	11	16	3	8	2	1
29	29	24	Compiled	9	9	1	3	2	
21	32	23	Tax Returns	14	7		1	1	
84	86	93	Other	28	21	7	13	13	11
4/1/02-3/31/03	4/1/03-3/31/04	4/1/04-3/31/05		52 (4/1-9/30/04)		272 (10/1/04-3/31/05)			
ALL	ALL	ALL		0-1MM	1-3MM	3-5MM	5-10MM	10-25MM	25MM & OVER
290	309	324	NUMBER OF STATEMENTS	80	76	32	54	48	34
%	%	%	ASSETS	%	%	%	%	%	%
7.8	10.3	10.8	Cash & Equivalents	13.8	11.1	8.0	10.5	7.7	10.7
45.3	43.0	45.9	Trade Receivables (net)	40.4	47.8	50.6	43.6	53.6	42.8
3.7	3.2	3.1	Inventory	2.2	2.2	.8	2.6	3.8	9.3
12.5	10.5	10.3	All Other Current	9.1	9.6	8.1	16.9	6.4	12.0
69.3	67.0	70.1	Total Current	65.4	70.7	67.4	73.6	71.5	74.8
9.2	11.8	11.4	Fixed Assets (net)	10.3	14.9	5.9	10.0	15.0	8.8
1.8	1.1	1.3	Intangibles (net)	1.3	.9	.3	1.4	1.1	2.7
19.6	20.1	17.2	All Other Non-Current	23.0	13.6	26.3	15.0	12.4	13.8
100.0	100.0	100.0	Total	100.0	100.0	100.0	100.0	100.0	100.0
			LIABILITIES						
30.5	29.9	29.5	Notes Payable-Short Term	34.0	26.2	23.8	36.4	26.7	24.8
4.0	3.6	4.0	Cur. Mat.-L/T/D	2.5	4.6	8.0	5.1	3.3	1.6
2.7	3.0	4.6	Trade Payables	3.4	3.9	2.2	5.2	6.3	8.0
.2	.4	.3	Income Taxes Payable	.1	.3	.3	.9	.0	.2
10.8	9.9	8.0	All Other Current	10.3	8.1	4.4	6.9	5.0	11.5
48.2	46.9	46.4	Total Current	50.2	43.1	38.7	54.5	41.2	46.1
18.1	18.2	21.4	Long-Term Debt	19.2	24.9	35.9	12.9	23.4	15.5
.4	.4	.3	Deferred Taxes	.1	.1	.2	.2	.6	.7
7.1	7.9	7.2	All Other Non-Current	6.9	6.3	6.3	10.0	8.6	4.6
26.2	26.6	24.8	Net Worth	23.6	25.5	18.9	22.4	26.2	33.1
100.0	100.0	100.0	Total Liabilities & Net Worth	100.0	100.0	100.0	100.0	100.0	100.0
			INCOME DATA						
100.0	100.0	100.0	Net Sales	100.0	100.0	100.0	100.0	100.0	100.0
			Gross Profit						
68.0	66.9	68.4	Operating Expenses	65.0	64.7	69.6	69.4	64.5	87.2
32.0	33.1	31.6	Operating Profit	35.0	35.3	30.4	30.6	35.5	12.8
16.1	13.7	13.2	All Other Expenses (net)	16.4	13.8	10.9	14.2	14.2	3.1
15.8	19.4	18.5	Profit Before Taxes	18.6	21.5	19.4	16.4	21.3	9.7
			RATIOS						
2.4	2.6	3.3		3.4	4.0	3.1	1.6	3.8	3.3
1.3	1.3	1.4	Current	1.3	1.5	1.5	1.3	1.5	1.4
1.0	1.0	1.0		1.0	1.0	1.1	1.1	1.1	1.1
1.9	1.9	2.8		3.1	3.1	2.2	1.4	3.7	2.5
1.2	1.2	1.3	Quick	1.2	1.4	1.3	1.1	1.4	1.3
.4	.4	.6		.5	.6	.6	.4	.8	.7
14 26.1	3 136.1	11 34.3		0 UND	0 846.6	29 12.6	8 46.4	27 13.3	19 19.6
302 1.2	245 1.5	287 1.3	Sales/Receivables	722 .5	582 .6	452 .8	253 1.4	310 1.2	93 3.9
1418 .3	1450 .3	1576 .2		1656 .2	1643 .2	2000 .2	1483 .2	1588 .2	184 2.0
			Cost of Sales/Inventory						
			Cost of Sales/Payables						
.6	.5	.5		.4	.4	.3	.7	.4	2.7
1.5	1.9	1.7	Sales/Working Capital	1.7	1.1	.9	1.5	1.8	6.7
34.3	NM	34.0		−68.5	NM	49.9	43.8	11.1	165.1
5.5	7.4	6.1		5.0	5.9	4.9	4.6	8.7	10.5
(149) 2.6	(177) 3.0	(176) 3.2	EBIT/Interest	(29) 1.5	(41) 3.3	(18) 2.8	(30) 2.7	(31) 4.4	(27) 4.8
1.4	1.6	1.6		.7	2.0	1.8	1.3	3.0	2.1
12.2	8.3	4.2							
(18) 3.1	(18) 1.0	(26) 2.2	Net Profit + Depr., Dep., Amort./Cur. Mat. L/T/D						
.6	.2	.4							
.0	.0	.0		.0	.0	.0	.0	.0	.0
.0	.0	.1	Fixed/Worth	.0	.1	.0	.0	.1	.1
.4	.5	.5		.4	.6	.1	.7	1.5	.4
1.5	1.6	1.7		1.7	1.5	1.4	2.1	1.5	1.6
4.2	3.8	3.8	Debt/Worth	5.7	3.3	3.1	5.2	3.8	2.6
9.4	8.8	9.6		25.3	6.7	7.0	10.9	10.5	5.2
40.8	39.8	38.3		47.5	33.9	27.3	38.8	38.3	42.6
(270) 15.0	(286) 18.7	(298) 20.5	% Profit Before Taxes/Tangible Net Worth	(71) 16.5	(70) 18.8	(30) 15.3	(51) 22.6	(42) 25.0	27.9
4.3	7.3	7.4		1.9	8.9	4.1	9.5	12.0	12.3
7.5	8.3	7.7		4.7	8.3	6.2	6.7	10.4	15.0
2.7	3.9	3.6	% Profit Before Taxes/Total Assets	2.0	4.1	3.7	3.5	5.1	6.5
.8	1.3	1.4		.5	1.8	1.1	1.3	2.2	1.7
165.1	227.6	177.7		UND	87.7	81.2	87.8	101.3	113.7
40.1	36.7	32.9	Sales/Net Fixed Assets	122.6	20.6	41.2	30.1	33.4	36.4
8.4	8.4	6.5		6.5	3.2	7.4	8.0	5.0	8.8
.5	.6	.7		.4	.5	.5	.5	1.0	3.0
.2	.2	.2	Sales/Total Assets	.2	.2	.2	.2	.3	1.3
.1	.1	.1		.1	.1	.1	.1	.1	.9
.6	.7	.7		.9	.5	.9	.8	.4	.5
(184) 1.4	(193) 1.7	(206) 1.6	% Depr., Dep., Amort./Sales	(37) 2.2	(50) 1.4	(23) 1.7	(40) 1.6	(31) 1.6	(25) 1.1
3.4	3.5	3.8		4.6	4.9	3.8	4.5	3.8	2.1
4.1	4.0	2.3		8.4	6.7		2.0		
(47) 9.5	(58) 10.5	(57) 9.2	% Officers', Directors', Owners' Comp/Sales	(12) 13.1	(19) 8.6		(15) 10.5		
18.5	26.5	18.6		21.1	13.3		28.8		
3401660M	3195381M	7427386M	Net Sales ($)	36552M	145476M	129725M	377322M	688499M	6049812M
8172679M	8755121M	10029244M	Total Assets ($)	275708M	839833M	910003M	1941794M	2866495M	3195411M

© RMA 2005

M = $ thousand   MM = $ million
See Pages 11 through 21 for Explanation of Ratios and Data

Current Data Sorted By Assets							Comparative Historical Data	
						Type of Statement		
8	16	27	25	8	4	Unqualified	31	36
	2	4	1			Reviewed	3	7
7	3	5	1		1	Compiled	5	9
21		8			2	Tax Returns	5	7
17	10	8	8	1	2	Other	15	19
	24 (4/1-9/30/04)		165 (10/1/04-3/31/05)				4/1/00-3/31/01	4/1/01-3/31/02
0-500M	500M-2MM	2-10MM	10-50MM	50-100MM	100-250MM		ALL	ALL
53	31	52	35	9	9	**NUMBER OF STATEMENTS**	59	78
%	%	%	%	%	%	**ASSETS**	%	%
41.8	28.6	14.1	11.3			Cash & Equivalents	18.0	22.1
9.0	18.3	28.9	20.7			Trade Receivables (net)	22.4	27.2
.0	5.9	7.8	10.9			Inventory	7.1	8.0
8.3	22.3	15.7	34.0			All Other Current	18.6	13.9
59.1	75.1	66.5	77.0			Total Current	66.1	71.2
25.5	14.2	16.7	5.3			Fixed Assets (net)	16.8	13.4
1.2	3.2	1.9	1.3			Intangibles (net)	2.1	1.5
14.2	7.4	14.9	16.4			All Other Non-Current	15.0	13.9
100.0	100.0	100.0	100.0			Total	100.0	100.0
						LIABILITIES		
15.0	22.4	35.6	50.9			Notes Payable-Short Term	41.0	32.5
1.7	2.7	6.8	4.7			Cur. Mat.-L/T/D	3.9	3.3
4.2	3.6	3.5	4.8			Trade Payables	8.8	3.5
.8	.4	.2	.0			Income Taxes Payable	.2	.3
19.2	14.9	13.3	6.0			All Other Current	5.9	8.6
40.9	44.1	59.4	66.4			Total Current	59.8	48.2
8.8	9.7	12.1	9.9			Long-Term Debt	13.8	11.9
.0	.2	.2	.1			Deferred Taxes	.1	.1
1.0	1.4	2.8	1.6			All Other Non-Current	1.2	3.0
49.3	44.5	25.5	22.0			Net Worth	25.1	36.9
100.0	100.0	100.0	100.0			Total Liabilities & Net Worth	100.0	100.0
						INCOME DATA		
100.0	100.0	100.0	100.0			Net Sales	100.0	100.0
						Gross Profit		
90.3	92.4	85.2	81.0			Operating Expenses	74.3	77.6
9.7	7.6	14.8	19.0			Operating Profit	25.7	22.4
.2	3.7	5.1	7.8			All Other Expenses (net)	10.7	7.9
9.5	3.9	9.7	11.2			Profit Before Taxes	15.0	14.5
						RATIOS		
4.7	4.2	1.4	1.4				2.6	3.3
1.9	1.5	1.1	1.2			Current	1.4	1.5
1.0	1.1	.9	1.0				1.1	1.0
4.5	4.0	1.3	1.4				2.5	2.4
1.5	(30) 1.0	.8	.2			Quick	1.0	(76) 1.2
.6	.6	.1	.1				.1	.2
0 UND	0 810.0	1 718.8	0 UND				0 UND	
0 UND	7 53.2	16 22.5	10 36.8			Sales/Receivables	7 55.4	11 33.5
7 55.6	62 5.9	195 1.9	108 3.4				108 3.4	150 2.4
						Cost of Sales/Inventory		
						Cost of Sales/Payables		
9.2	3.2	2.8	1.3				2.8	2.4
34.9	6.5	11.3	4.8			Sales/Working Capital	8.2	7.1
UND	24.8	−25.3	32.0				41.7	42.9
42.0	12.9	14.6	4.0				7.0	20.0
(31) 10.8	(22) 1.2	(44) 3.0	(27) 3.2			EBIT/Interest	(40) 3.5	(55) 5.1
−3.0	−1.5	1.3	1.3				1.9	2.0
						Net Profit + Depr., Dep., Amort./Cur. Mat. L /T/D		
.1	.1	.1	.0				.0	.0
.4	.2	.4	.1			Fixed/Worth	.1	.1
1.0	.5	1.3	.7				.6	.4
.3	.7	1.9	2.7				.9	.5
.7	1.8	4.3	7.3			Debt/Worth	2.4	1.9
3.6	3.3	9.1	12.6				6.0	8.7
183.9	50.0	52.2	60.6			% Profit Before Taxes/Tangible Net Worth	63.2	72.6
(47) 39.3	10.3	(50) 19.8	(34) 26.4				(56) 21.7	(75) 33.5
.0	−5.3	8.0	7.7				6.1	17.2
100.9	19.5	11.6	6.2			% Profit Before Taxes/Total Assets	19.3	27.9
24.9	2.5	4.5	4.0				5.7	7.8
.0	−1.6	.9	1.5				1.4	2.6
250.6	89.5	48.4	89.4			Sales/Net Fixed Assets	60.6	85.6
34.6	26.8	20.8	25.7				26.5	35.0
14.4	13.7	5.4	14.9				12.3	15.6
12.7	4.2	1.3	.8			Sales/Total Assets	2.3	3.3
6.2	1.8	.7	.4				.8	.9
3.2	.7	.4	.2				.3	.3
.5	.5	.5	.5			% Depr., Dep., Amort./Sales	.6	.5
(29) 1.0	(24) 1.0	(45) 1.1	(26) .9				(49) 1.1	(51) .9
2.0	1.6	2.5	1.8				2.3	2.1
7.1		3.3				% Officers', Directors', Owners' Comp/Sales	4.5	7.4
(28) 13.0		(15) 10.0					(10) 8.6	(21) 13.3
18.8		19.9					18.9	31.2
62861M	118882M	452669M	480605M	246200M	3522899M	Net Sales ($)	345572M	479686M
10031M	37813M	269259M	863823M	659151M	1326155M	Total Assets ($)	684055M	1263898M

M = $ thousand   MM = $ million
See Pages 11 through 21 for Explanation of Ratios and Data

Comparative Historical Data | Current Data Sorted By Sales

			Type of Statement						
60	90	88	Unqualified	11	19	7	19	20	12
7	7	7	Reviewed	2	4			1	
6	22	17	Compiled	4	9	1		2	1
11	24	31	Tax Returns	17	9	2	1		2
19	36	46	Other	9	16	9	3	5	4
4/1/02-3/31/03	4/1/03-3/31/04	4/1/04-3/31/05		24 (4/1-9/30/04)			165 (10/1/04-3/31/05)		
ALL	ALL	ALL		0-1MM	1-3MM	3-5MM	5-10MM	10-25MM	25MM & OVER
103	179	189	**NUMBER OF STATEMENTS**	43	57	19	23	28	19
%	%	%	**ASSETS**	%	%	%	%	%	%
20.5	24.2	24.0	Cash & Equivalents	39.6	18.7	26.3	20.8	14.6	20.2
24.2	20.5	19.2	Trade Receivables (net)	9.5	19.8	21.8	27.7	24.6	18.4
5.0	3.0	6.3	Inventory	2.9	3.9	4.0	7.3	7.9	20.1
23.9	18.8	18.3	All Other Current	14.6	18.5	8.7	24.5	29.0	12.2
73.6	66.5	67.8	Total Current	66.6	61.0	60.7	80.3	76.0	70.8
13.0	14.1	16.1	Fixed Assets (net)	15.7	23.4	21.2	5.9	7.4	15.2
1.2	1.1	1.7	Intangibles (net)	2.6	.9	1.3	4.1	.9	1.1
12.2	18.4	14.4	All Other Non-Current	15.1	14.7	16.8	9.7	15.7	13.0
100.0	100.0	100.0	Total	100.0	100.0	100.0	100.0	100.0	100.0
			LIABILITIES						
37.3	31.3	31.2	Notes Payable-Short Term	22.1	26.1	19.4	45.3	46.1	39.3
2.9	3.7	3.7	Cur. Mat.-L/T/D	2.3	5.2	5.2	.9	6.2	.7
4.3	3.6	3.8	Trade Payables	2.0	3.4	3.7	4.6	4.1	8.2
.8	.2	.4	Income Taxes Payable	.9	.0	.3	.5	.2	.2
9.3	11.9	13.3	All Other Current	20.5	10.3	14.7	11.8	9.1	13.1
54.6	50.8	52.4	Total Current	47.9	45.1	43.2	63.1	65.6	61.5
9.6	7.8	10.7	Long-Term Debt	6.9	16.2	13.4	9.3	5.3	9.4
.2	.1	.1	Deferred Taxes	.0	.3	.0	.2	.0	.2
2.4	3.8	1.9	All Other Non-Current	2.1	1.1	1.9	4.4	1.4	1.6
33.2	37.6	34.9	Net Worth	43.1	37.3	41.4	23.1	27.7	27.2
100.0	100.0	100.0	Total Liabilities & Net Worth	100.0	100.0	100.0	100.0	100.0	100.0
			INCOME DATA						
100.0	100.0	100.0	Net Sales	100.0	100.0	100.0	100.0	100.0	100.0
			Gross Profit						
75.7	79.3	86.4	Operating Expenses	86.6	86.2	84.7	82.7	86.2	93.1
24.3	20.7	13.6	Operating Profit	13.4	13.8	15.3	17.3	13.8	6.9
5.2	3.7	4.3	All Other Expenses (net)	3.5	3.8	7.8	6.4	5.1	.8
19.1	16.9	9.3	Profit Before Taxes	9.9	10.0	7.5	10.9	8.7	6.1
			RATIOS						
2.3	2.5	2.5		4.2	3.0	4.3	1.9	1.9	1.2
1.3	1.2	1.2	Current	1.5	1.3	1.5	1.3	1.1	1.0
1.0	1.0	1.0		1.1	1.1	1.0	1.1	1.0	1.0
1.7	2.1	2.0		4.2	2.4	4.0	1.6	1.4	1.1
1.0	1.0 (188)	1.0	Quick	1.1 (56)	1.0	1.4	.9	.6	.9
.1	.3	.2		.4	.3	.3	.1	.1	.1
0 UND	0 UND	0 UND		0 UND	0 UND	0 751.4	2 222.5	1 560.1	0 UND
9 41.5	5 79.0	6 64.3	Sales/Receivables	0 UND	5 69.8	9 39.6	14 25.7	14 25.3	5 78.1
97 3.8	66 5.6	55 6.6		14 26.5	58 6.3	56 6.6	153 2.4	115 3.2	12 31.0
			Cost of Sales/Inventory						
			Cost of Sales/Payables						
1.5	3.0	3.6		4.0	3.6	2.9	2.6	3.7	16.3
7.4	11.7	12.8	Sales/Working Capital	8.5	22.5	12.8	7.9	10.0	70.9
36.7	−310.7	197.5		90.0	117.7	70.1	31.3	308.6	−400.0
9.8	33.2	17.1		23.5	17.9	3.3	10.1	23.9	10.4
(69) 4.7	(111) 5.0	(138) 3.2	EBIT/Interest	(25) 3.0	(44) 3.7	(11) 1.3	(18) 3.6	(23) 2.5	(17) 3.3
2.7	2.2	1.1		.0	1.2	−4.3	1.2	1.3	1.4
18.7	49.0	12.4	Net Profit + Depr., Dep.,						
(12) 5.3	(11) 9.0	(13) .5	Amort./Cur. Mat. L/T/D						
1.9	5.0	.2							
.0	.0	.1		.0	.1	.0	.1	.0	.2
.1	.2	.2	Fixed/Worth	.2	.4	.1	.1	.2	.6
.4	.5	.8		.4	1.1	.8	.9	.7	.8
.9	.5	.7		.3	.7	.5	2.4	1.2	1.0
2.7	2.6	2.7	Debt/Worth	1.1	2.6	2.7	6.8	5.1	4.9
10.2	7.7	8.9		5.3	5.1	8.2	12.1	13.2	18.8
77.7	92.1	63.8	% Profit Before Taxes/Tangible	64.0	56.8	33.1	78.6	71.7	81.4
(99) 32.7	(170) 39.1	(179) 22.2	Net Worth	(38) 8.5	(55) 29.7	(18) 10.6	(22) 19.0	31.7	(18) 45.2
15.5	12.9	1.9		−8.2	6.1	−4.0	7.6	4.2	10.6
17.0	33.3	21.4	% Profit Before Taxes/Total	36.1	28.1	7.8	8.4	6.5	42.9
6.9	9.5	4.7	Assets	3.3	6.0	4.0	4.1	4.9	10.3
2.6	2.5	.4		−1.8	1.6	−.7	.9	.6	.9
107.7	83.6	94.9		113.5	53.2	146.7	95.5	105.9	136.4
30.1	31.1	26.0	Sales/Net Fixed Assets	21.7	21.4	34.1	25.7	31.4	34.5
16.6	16.3	11.8		13.7	7.3	12.1	14.9	15.1	13.8
2.5	3.6	4.5		5.8	6.7	4.5	1.3	1.7	9.9
.6	1.3	1.1	Sales/Total Assets	2.2	1.8	.9	.7	.7	2.6
.2	.4	.4		.4	.5	.3	.4	.3	.7
.5	.5	.4		.7	.7	.3	.3	.4	.2
(70) 1.0	(130) .8	(136) 1.0	% Depr., Dep., Amort./Sales	(25) 1.4	(42) 1.3	(13) .7	(21) .8	(20) .9	(15) .7
1.6	1.5	2.1		2.2	2.4	6.5	1.8	1.7	1.6
5.5	4.8	5.3		5.8					
(25) 14.2	(46) 8.7	(64) 12.4	% Officers', Directors',	(17) 14.5	(25) 11.3				
24.3	17.2	17.4	Owners' Comp/Sales	29.1	16.5				
790544M	3443591M	4884116M	Net Sales ($)	24746M	111857M	72631M	148348M	442538M	4083996M
2085669M	3657573M	3166232M	Total Assets ($)	43014M	159966M	160167M	342682M	1091855M	1368548M

© RMA 2005

M = $ thousand   MM = $ million
See Pages 11 through 21 for Explanation of Ratios and Data

Current Data Sorted By Assets								Comparative Historical Data	
	0-500M	500M-2MM	2-10MM	10-50MM	50-100MM	100-250MM	**Type of Statement**		
		2	8	3	3	3	Unqualified	16	10
		1	2				Reviewed	3	3
	5	6	1	3			Compiled	1	8
	4	3	1				Tax Returns		2
	2	5	9	4	2	3	Other	6	15
		6 (4/1-9/30/04)		64 (10/1/04-3/31/05)				4/1/00-3/31/01 ALL	4/1/01-3/31/02 ALL
	0-500M	500M-2MM	2-10MM	10-50MM	50-100MM	100-250MM	**NUMBER OF STATEMENTS**	ALL	ALL
	11	17	21	10	5	6		26	38
	%	%	%	%	%	%	**ASSETS**	%	%
	50.9	35.1	34.8	27.4			Cash & Equivalents	37.4	36.3
	11.7	24.9	7.5	21.5			Trade Receivables (net)	31.1	22.2
	.4	.1	3.6	4.6			Inventory	1.6	2.0
	15.1	10.2	11.1	3.3			All Other Current	2.8	4.4
	78.2	70.2	57.0	56.8			Total Current	72.9	64.9
	10.8	16.9	11.7	19.1			Fixed Assets (net)	12.6	14.5
	3.1	11.6	4.2	8.3			Intangibles (net)	7.0	4.5
	7.9	1.2	27.1	15.8			All Other Non-Current	7.5	16.1
	100.0	100.0	100.0	100.0			Total	100.0	100.0
							LIABILITIES		
	37.7	27.1	16.9	18.5			Notes Payable-Short Term	29.6	14.5
	1.0	4.0	1.0	1.8			Cur. Mat.-L/T/D	1.8	1.5
	.3	6.0	8.1	16.7			Trade Payables	11.5	17.0
	.2	.0	.1	1.0			Income Taxes Payable	.1	.0
	10.8	22.4	24.4	10.4			All Other Current	14.9	15.0
	50.0	59.5	50.3	48.4			Total Current	58.0	48.0
	26.0	21.1	8.0	25.7			Long-Term Debt	13.7	12.6
	.0	.0	.1	.2			Deferred Taxes	.8	.0
	25.7	.9	8.5	8.3			All Other Non-Current	7.3	13.2
	-1.7	18.4	33.1	17.4			Net Worth	20.2	26.2
	100.0	100.0	100.0	100.0			Total Liabilities & Net Worth	100.0	100.0
							INCOME DATA		
	100.0	100.0	100.0	100.0			Net Sales	100.0	100.0
							Gross Profit		
	86.1	80.9	90.7	80.4			Operating Expenses	82.0	80.1
	13.9	19.1	9.3	19.6			Operating Profit	18.0	19.9
	4.5	11.5	1.9	4.7			All Other Expenses (net)	9.8	7.4
	9.4	7.6	7.4	14.9			Profit Before Taxes	8.2	12.6
							RATIOS		
	2.3	3.0	2.4	1.8				1.5	2.6
	1.5	1.3	1.1	1.4			Current	1.2	1.3
	1.0	.7	.8	1.0				1.0	1.0
	3.3	3.0	1.8	1.6				1.5	2.3
(10)	1.2	1.0	.9	1.4			Quick	1.2	1.2
	.7	.3	.6	.9				1.0	.9
0	UND	0 UND	0 UND	0 UND				0 UND	0 UND
0	UND	9 40.8	1 352.5	49 7.4			Sales/Receivables	24 15.0	9 42.3
25	14.9	181 2.0	105 3.5	133 2.7				2000 .2	114 3.2
							Cost of Sales/Inventory		
							Cost of Sales/Payables		
	3.5	2.6	3.0	2.2				1.0	3.8
	18.8	4.7	29.5	3.7			Sales/Working Capital	4.3	6.4
	UND	-4.1	-14.0	NM				84.2	-190.1
		5.5	34.5	18.9				6.7	6.8
	(11)	3.4	(15) 4.8	5.0			EBIT/Interest	(15) 2.4	(22) 2.8
		2.6	-.1	1.6				.4	.3
							Net Profit + Depr., Dep., Amort./Cur. Mat. L./T/D		
	.0	.1	.1	.2				.1	.1
	.0	1.4	.4	1.2			Fixed/Worth	.5	.4
	-3.3	-1.4	1.8	-3.0				6.3	2.2
	.7	.7	.7	.7				3.1	1.3
	1.8	3.2	7.0	3.4			Debt/Worth	5.8	3.5
	-12.6	-15.3	14.1	-5.4				46.2	13.0
		100.9	57.8				% Profit Before Taxes/Tangible	42.0	63.5
	(12)	33.8	(19) 20.2				Net Worth	(21) 9.4	(33) 23.5
		8.9	-7.4					-1.3	8.8
	76.8	14.3	8.7	21.9			% Profit Before Taxes/Total	7.9	12.4
	27.5	7.6	2.7	5.7			Assets	1.8	5.9
	1.3	1.1	-.5	2.7				-.5	.7
	UND	89.7	78.3	52.0				15.9	36.4
	83.0	16.2	11.5	9.1			Sales/Net Fixed Assets	8.4	12.9
	11.5	3.5	3.8	2.6				5.2	7.7
	3.1	1.9	2.6	1.2				1.2	1.6
	2.6	1.2	.8	1.0			Sales/Total Assets	.7	1.1
	1.4	.8	.1	.5				.1	.3
		1.1	1.3					1.6	.4
	(10)	3.7	(17) 3.6				% Depr., Dep., Amort./Sales	(18) 3.6	(24) 1.8
		8.7	6.6					4.9	4.4
								10.6	3.7
							% Officers', Directors', Owners' Comp/Sales	(10) 26.4	(10) 15.0
								37.7	26.5
	5551M	20901M	260546M	212535M	270469M	283751M	Net Sales ($)	474924M	846763M
	2510M	17090M	112841M	206605M	346564M	956887M	Total Assets ($)	1265405M	1124649M

© RMA 2005

M = $ thousand   MM = $ million

See Pages 11 through 21 for Explanation of Ratios and Data

Comparative Historical Data   **Current Data Sorted By Sales**

			Type of Statement						
14	24	19	Unqualified	2	6	1	1	2	7
5	4	3	Reviewed		1	1	1		
4	15	15	Compiled	7	5			3	
3	5	8	Tax Returns	5	3				
13	18	25	Other	4	6	2	1	7	5
4/1/02-3/31/03 ALL	4/1/03-3/31/04 ALL	4/1/04-3/31/05 ALL		6 (4/1-9/30/04)			64 (10/1/04-3/31/05)		
				0-1MM	1-3MM	3-5MM	5-10MM	10-25MM	25MM & OVER
39	66	70	NUMBER OF STATEMENTS	18	21	4	3	12	12
%	%	%	ASSETS	%	%	%	%	%	%
47.2	33.0	33.2	Cash & Equivalents	42.3	32.9			33.7	23.3
16.2	15.7	17.2	Trade Receivables (net)	17.5	17.4			17.4	20.5
.2	3.0	1.8	Inventory	.3	3.6			.0	3.9
9.4	6.3	10.8	All Other Current	9.3	12.5			6.8	13.1
73.0	58.0	63.1	Total Current	69.4	66.4			57.9	60.8
11.7	12.8	13.3	Fixed Assets (net)	16.6	9.6			9.9	15.8
5.0	7.1	6.5	Intangibles (net)	2.0	9.7			7.3	7.0
10.3	22.1	17.2	All Other Non-Current	12.0	14.3			24.9	16.4
100.0	100.0	100.0	Total	100.0	100.0			100.0	100.0
			LIABILITIES						
18.1	19.3	23.1	Notes Payable-Short Term	29.5	28.2			18.4	16.7
3.4	1.0	2.3	Cur. Mat.-L/T/D	1.5	2.7			1.0	5.2
8.4	8.3	7.3	Trade Payables	5.6	4.6			6.4	15.2
.2	.5	.4	Income Taxes Payable	.1	.0			.0	1.8
9.1	20.3	18.3	All Other Current	14.2	23.3			16.0	11.8
39.2	49.4	51.4	Total Current	51.0	58.9			41.8	50.6
8.7	13.6	17.6	Long-Term Debt	24.5	13.3			20.5	20.8
.0	.3	.2	Deferred Taxes	.0	.0			.0	1.1
10.9	10.1	9.7	All Other Non-Current	20.8	3.0			3.6	3.9
41.2	26.5	21.2	Net Worth	3.8	24.8			34.2	23.5
100.0	100.0	100.0	Total Liabilities & Net Worth	100.0	100.0			100.0	100.0
			INCOME DATA						
100.0	100.0	100.0	Net Sales	100.0	100.0			100.0	100.0
			Gross Profit						
80.9	80.4	84.7	Operating Expenses	87.4	80.0			82.7	91.1
19.1	19.6	15.3	Operating Profit	12.6	20.0			17.3	8.9
5.9	3.8	5.2	All Other Expenses (net)	3.4	10.7			2.6	1.8
13.3	15.8	10.1	Profit Before Taxes	9.2	9.3			14.8	7.1
			RATIOS						
3.6	2.1	2.4	Current	2.4	2.9			2.5	2.3
1.9	1.3	1.3		1.2	1.3			1.5	1.1
1.2	.9	.9		1.0	.7			1.1	.6
3.4	1.5	1.8	Quick	2.3	1.6			2.2	1.6
1.6	1.1	(69) 1.1		(17) 1.1	.9			1.4	.9
1.0	.6	.6		.9	.3			.9	.2
0 UND	0 UND	0 UND	Sales/Receivables	0 UND	0 UND			0 UND	0 UND
1 488.5	2 234.9	7 49.5		0 UND	9 40.8			1 546.6	36 10.2
51 7.2	74 4.9	95 3.8		270 1.4	66 5.5			85 4.3	89 4.1
			Cost of Sales/Inventory						
			Cost of Sales/Payables						
1.9	3.0	2.6	Sales/Working Capital	1.7	2.7			2.8	6.2
3.6	8.7	8.8		11.5	4.7			6.4	25.7
8.8	-13.7	-22.9		UND	-4.1			NM	-7.7
10.3	16.3	18.6	EBIT/Interest	18.6	10.4				37.6
(27) 6.5	(50) 6.8	(52) 4.3		(12) 3.5	(14) 4.2				5.0
2.2	1.3	2.1		.3	2.5				1.3
			Net Profit + Depr., Dep., Amort./Cur. Mat. L/T/D						
.0	.0	.1	Fixed/Worth	.0	.0			.0	.1
.2	.4	.3		.4	.2			.3	.3
.7	3.2	2.9		-3.3	4.8			1.2	2.0
.8	1.3	.8	Debt/Worth	.7	.7			.8	.7
1.9	3.5	5.0		15.7	3.2			4.3	4.0
4.3	12.3	30.2		-11.2	14.1			8.8	17.1
57.3	62.2	57.8	% Profit Before Taxes/Tangible Net Worth	85.8	96.3			46.4	71.8
(38) 30.4	(56) 23.5	(55) 32.5		(12) 13.0	(17) 34.5			(10) 27.2	(10) 37.8
16.2	7.6	7.2		3.5	10.5			5.4	22.8
18.2	14.8	15.5	% Profit Before Taxes/Total Assets	12.8	16.6			22.5	21.2
11.6	6.1	5.6		2.9	7.6			4.9	6.3
2.4	1.1	.9		-.7	2.6			2.0	1.6
92.6	78.1	95.5	Sales/Net Fixed Assets	UND	98.3			307.5	115.9
17.6	12.3	13.9		10.1	23.4			13.9	24.7
7.0	4.4	4.1		2.9	7.2			8.1	4.9
1.6	1.5	2.1	Sales/Total Assets	2.4	2.2			1.8	4.6
1.1	.8	1.0		1.1	1.2			1.0	1.1
.5	.3	.5		.1	.7			.2	.7
.9	1.4	1.2	% Depr., Dep., Amort./Sales	3.3	.8				
(28) 2.4	(43) 3.5	(48) 3.8		(13) 5.8	(14) 1.6				
4.7	5.7	6.7		8.8	6.6				
10.0	7.8	5.8	% Officers', Directors', Owners' Comp/Sales						
(14) 18.7	(20) 17.5	(23) 15.4							
23.3	27.3	18.2							
461249M	1195059M	1053753M	Net Sales ($)	8591M	30110M	13971M	22297M	174565M	804219M
655797M	1646767M	1642497M	Total Assets ($)	36615M	49983M	100228M	141079M	662442M	652150M

© RMA 2005   M = $ thousand   MM = $ million
See Pages 11 through 21 for Explanation of Ratios and Data

Current Data Sorted By Assets   Comparative Historical Data

0-500M	500M-2MM	2-10MM	10-50MM	50-100MM	100-250MM	Type of Statement	4/1/00-3/31/01 ALL	4/1/01-3/31/02 ALL
2	7	19	18	6	3	Unqualified	58	43
	2	4				Reviewed	6	7
2	2	3	1		1	Compiled	10	19
10	4	2				Tax Returns	24	18
3	4	10	8	1	3	Other	33	41
22 (4/1-9/30/04)			93 (10/1/04-3/31/05)					
17	19	38	27	7	7	**NUMBER OF STATEMENTS**	131	128
%	%	%	%	%	%	**ASSETS**	%	%
34.8	36.8	27.7	30.7			Cash & Equivalents	28.3	32.6
14.1	11.1	19.0	19.1			Trade Receivables (net)	19.3	17.4
2.5	5.8	6.3	5.7			Inventory	4.0	3.5
6.7	12.4	8.5	16.2			All Other Current	11.7	11.9
58.0	66.1	61.5	71.7			Total Current	63.3	65.3
22.7	10.7	8.6	8.6			Fixed Assets (net)	19.1	17.6
2.9	1.3	4.2	1.1			Intangibles (net)	4.0	3.9
16.5	21.9	25.7	18.6			All Other Non-Current	13.6	13.2
100.0	100.0	100.0	100.0			Total	100.0	100.0
						LIABILITIES		
7.1	6.2	9.1	10.6			Notes Payable-Short Term	13.3	13.9
7.1	2.1	2.1	.9			Cur. Mat.-L/T/D	2.0	2.2
6.5	11.1	12.4	6.7			Trade Payables	9.5	10.8
.1	.5	.6	.2			Income Taxes Payable	.5	.3
61.0	14.3	16.8	16.1			All Other Current	19.5	25.2
81.9	34.2	41.1	34.6			Total Current	44.6	52.4
30.8	4.5	8.7	13.2			Long-Term Debt	18.0	12.5
.0	.4	.2	1.5			Deferred Taxes	.1	.1
29.2	2.7	2.6	7.6			All Other Non-Current	4.8	7.2
-41.7	58.2	47.4	43.2			Net Worth	32.4	27.7
100.0	100.0	100.0	100.0			Total Liabilities & Net Worth	100.0	100.0
						INCOME DATA		
100.0	100.0	100.0	100.0			Net Sales	100.0	100.0
						Gross Profit		
81.2	82.1	75.5	76.6			Operating Expenses	85.0	83.4
18.8	17.9	24.5	23.4			Operating Profit	15.0	16.6
.5	-.9	6.1	5.1			All Other Expenses (net)	2.5	5.7
18.2	18.9	18.3	18.4			Profit Before Taxes	12.5	10.9
						RATIOS		
3.2	2.7	3.7	3.9				2.9	3.0
1.1	2.1	1.9	1.9			Current	1.3	1.4
.4	1.0	1.0	1.1				.9	.9
2.1	2.2	3.3	3.1				2.4	2.4
.9	1.4	1.6	1.3			Quick	(130) 1.1	(127) 1.2
.3	.4	.4	.4				.5	.4
0 UND	0 UND	3 135.5	0 UND				0 UND	0 UND
0 UND	0 UND	24 15.4	14 26.7			Sales/Receivables	11 33.0	13 27.5
15 24.5	30 12.4	65 5.6	97 3.8				69 5.3	55 6.7
						Cost of Sales/Inventory		
						Cost of Sales/Payables		
10.5	2.4	2.4	1.6				2.7	2.5
65.5	14.7	5.8	4.2			Sales/Working Capital	8.0	7.7
-23.0	-638.6	NM	6.1				-111.7	-178.0
	95.0	39.7	70.2				14.1	18.0
	(10) 21.7	(26) 13.6	(14) 12.8			EBIT/Interest	(83) 3.8	(80) 4.6
	7.6	4.4	1.9				1.3	1.2
							31.4	7.5
						Net Profit + Depr., Dep., Amort./Cur. Mat. L/T/D	(12) 8.4	(15) 4.2
							-.2	.3
.0	.0	.0	.0				.0	.0
.3	.1	.1	.1			Fixed/Worth	.2	.2
3.4	.3	.4	.5				1.2	1.6
.3	.2	.4	.5				.6	.6
4.2	.8	1.0	1.1			Debt/Worth	2.0	1.9
-2.4	2.1	2.7	9.3				9.2	10.2
478.4	171.2	51.9	44.5				70.2	59.2
(12) 64.0	24.6	(34) 19.0	(24) 18.6			% Profit Before Taxes/Tangible Net Worth	(115) 26.3	(109) 27.0
.4	9.0	9.0	4.3				3.9	3.2
280.0	69.9	21.1	17.0				19.4	19.9
60.1	10.9	7.7	4.4			% Profit Before Taxes/Total Assets	6.5	4.8
.2	4.4	5.3	.6				.2	.5
UND	265.3	173.1	82.2				99.7	107.4
93.4	93.4	54.6	25.1			Sales/Net Fixed Assets	34.5	33.3
17.0	51.4	23.0	8.3				10.2	10.4
12.3	6.3	2.7	1.4				3.7	4.0
5.8	3.3	1.2	.8			Sales/Total Assets	1.5	1.6
3.0	1.0	.7	.3				.4	.6
	.4	.6	.7				.6	.6
	(10) .6	(28) 1.0	(17) 1.3			% Depr., Dep., Amort./Sales	(103) 1.3	(83) 1.1
	2.6	1.5	2.6				3.9	2.6
6.5							6.9	6.9
(12) 16.1						% Officers', Directors', Owners' Comp/Sales	(32) 16.7	(37) 11.3
25.0							26.4	22.6
13888M	102791M	313730M	654342M	316547M	411073M	Net Sales ($)	2600797M	3604536M
2126M	24622M	206342M	646630M	435105M	1004899M	Total Assets ($)	3703054M	3685103M

M = $ thousand   MM = $ million
See Pages 11 through 21 for Explanation of Ratios and Data

Comparative Historical Data | | | | Current Data Sorted By Sales | | | | | |

			Type of Statement						
60	50	55	Unqualified	2	7	5	13	13	15
4	2	6	Reviewed	1	1	1	2	1	
19	16	9	Compiled	2	1	1	5		
25	21	16	Tax Returns	9	4	1	1	1	
28	34	29	Other	8	4	1	4	6	6
4/1/02- 3/31/03 ALL	4/1/03- 3/31/04 ALL	4/1/04- 3/31/05 ALL		22 (4/1-9/30/04) 0-1MM	1-3MM	3-5MM	93 (10/1/04-3/31/05) 5-10MM	10-25MM	25MM & OVER
136	123	115	**NUMBER OF STATEMENTS**	22	17	9	25	21	21
%	%	%	**ASSETS**	%	%	%	%	%	%
31.0	32.5	32.3	Cash & Equivalents	23.4	35.6		33.0	31.4	42.8
18.1	15.4	18.4	Trade Receivables (net)	8.0	13.7		20.0	26.2	23.1
4.5	6.1	5.4	Inventory	3.0	5.8		3.4	5.5	4.3
11.9	9.4	11.2	All Other Current	10.9	11.6		10.5	14.6	11.5
65.5	63.4	67.3	Total Current	45.3	66.7		66.8	77.8	81.6
18.0	15.9	10.2	Fixed Assets (net)	18.3	8.9		7.7	6.8	6.9
2.8	2.7	2.5	Intangibles (net)	.7	2.1		5.6	3.1	1.3
13.7	17.9	20.0	All Other Non-Current	35.8	22.3		19.9	12.4	10.2
100.0	100.0	100.0	Total	100.0	100.0		100.0	100.0	100.0
			LIABILITIES						
20.6	15.6	9.0	Notes Payable-Short Term	13.0	15.0		6.9	4.7	8.5
5.0	1.7	2.3	Cur. Mat.-L/T/D	4.9	.1		2.6	1.0	.7
10.9	12.2	11.5	Trade Payables	3.8	8.4		13.1	17.4	15.7
.2	.4	.4	Income Taxes Payable	.1	.1		1.0	.1	.3
22.1	22.0	24.2	All Other Current	24.4	42.0		13.0	24.4	29.0
58.9	52.0	47.4	Total Current	46.2	65.5		36.6	47.6	54.2
13.3	15.3	11.7	Long-Term Debt	18.0	16.5		9.6	7.7	2.3
.1	.1	.5	Deferred Taxes	.0	.0		.3	1.8	.1
6.3	4.7	7.8	All Other Non-Current	5.2	3.2		1.7	3.8	3.1
21.3	27.9	32.6	Net Worth	30.7	14.9		51.8	39.1	40.4
100.0	100.0	100.0	Total Liabilities & Net Worth	100.0	100.0		100.0	100.0	100.0
			INCOME DATA						
100.0	100.0	100.0	Net Sales	100.0	100.0		100.0	100.0	100.0
			Gross Profit						
84.4	81.2	78.6	Operating Expenses	57.2	77.2		82.5	86.9	90.0
15.6	18.8	21.4	Operating Profit	42.8	22.8		17.5	13.1	10.0
1.9	4.0	3.3	All Other Expenses (net)	12.5	6.2		-.5	.1	-.1
13.6	14.8	18.1	Profit Before Taxes	30.4	16.6		18.0	13.0	10.1
			RATIOS						
2.7	3.1	3.1		2.8	8.3		3.0	3.2	2.2
1.3	1.5	1.7	Current	1.2	2.1		2.1	1.5	1.4
.8	.9	1.1		.3	.9		1.1	1.1	1.1
1.9	2.5	2.3		1.4	8.2		2.5	1.9	2.0
(135) 1.1	1.0	1.1	Quick	.6	1.6		1.6	1.1	1.2
.4	.4	.5		.1	.4		.7	.7	.8
0 UND	0 UND	0 UND		0 UND	0 UND		1 258.2	2 181.0	6 58.6
10 38.3	8 43.2	15 24.6	Sales/Receivables	0 UND	3 145.7		22 16.7	36 10.1	27 13.5
65 5.6	50 7.4	75 4.8		20 18.6	54 6.8		42 8.7	165 2.2	160 2.3
			Cost of Sales/Inventory						
			Cost of Sales/Payables						
3.1	2.5	2.4		8.1	2.1		2.9	1.9	3.1
10.7	10.1	5.8	Sales/Working Capital	63.9	4.9		6.3	5.8	4.7
-59.5	-141.5	65.5		-19.7	-263.3		213.5	15.5	10.4
17.4	25.5	38.7			65.8		61.7	101.1	37.9
(95) 3.8	(76) 6.0	(66) 12.1	EBIT/Interest	(10) 24.4		(15) 15.4	(14) 6.5	(12) 15.9
1.5	1.5	2.9			3.3		6.4	-.4	4.3
		3.9	Net Profit + Depr., Dep.,						
	(10) .6		Amort./Cur. Mat. L/T/D						
		-.2							
.0	.0	.0		.0	.0		.0	.0	.1
.2	.1	.1	Fixed/Worth	.1	.0		.1	.1	.1
2.1	1.5	.4		1.2	.2		.2	.7	.4
.7	.4	.4		.4	.2		.4	.5	.7
3.0	2.0	1.3	Debt/Worth	2.1	2.1		.8	1.4	1.5
23.8	11.4	5.2		10.6	5.7		2.2	11.9	8.3
83.9	59.6	62.0		308.1	41.6		95.6	52.5	46.3
(111) 23.6	(102) 22.9	(102) 21.0	% Profit Before Taxes/Tangible Net Worth	(20) 15.4	(15) 11.1	(23) 23.9	(17) 21.1	(19) 28.6
2.9	3.7	6.7		1.9	6.8		4.7	7.8	6.6
26.6	24.2	31.3		191.6	31.0		44.6	26.9	18.1
4.6	6.0	7.6	% Profit Before Taxes/Total Assets	10.0	5.9		10.8	5.5	7.2
.6	.6	1.6		.6	1.5		4.7	.2	1.1
107.8	211.5	178.6		UND	215.3		156.1	144.3	115.1
36.0	47.6	54.2	Sales/Net Fixed Assets	139.7	82.2		61.0	61.7	43.4
15.0	15.1	19.6		10.1	18.5		20.1	28.2	19.4
5.7	4.6	3.0		8.1	3.1		4.0	4.1	2.3
2.0	1.5	1.3	Sales/Total Assets	1.7	1.2		1.6	1.4	1.2
.7	.5	.5		.1	.2		.8	.4	.6
.7	.5	.6			.4		.5	.6	.8
(98) 1.3	(80) 1.0	(69) 1.0	% Depr., Dep., Amort./Sales	(12) .9	(15) 1.2	(13) .9	(14) 1.6
2.5	2.3	1.8			4.3		1.5	1.2	3.1
9.7	8.3	5.1		6.4					
(44) 25.6	(28) 23.3	(32) 13.3	% Officers', Directors', Owners' Comp/Sales	(10) 13.3					
36.2	39.2	27.8		17.0					
8625396M	4213009M	1812371M	Net Sales ($)	11282M	28788M	37878M	183305M	343216M	1207902M
4396194M	2258028M	2319724M	Total Assets ($)	67691M	77570M	81426M	252328M	534508M	1306201M

© RMA 2005

M = $ thousand   MM = $ million
See Pages 11 through 21 for Explanation of Ratios and Data

Current Data Sorted By Assets   Comparative Historical Data

						Type of Statement		
	2	10	20	9	10	Unqualified	31	24
2	3	5	5			Reviewed	16	19
5	3	8	4			Compiled	31	33
10	15	10	2			Tax Returns	19	22
9	19	24	15	3	5	Other	55	47
	16 (4/1-9/30/04)		182 (10/1/04-3/31/05)				4/1/00-3/31/01	4/1/01-3/31/02
0-500M	500M-2MM	2-10MM	10-50MM	50-100MM	100-250MM		ALL	ALL
26	42	57	46	12	15	NUMBER OF STATEMENTS	152	145
%	%	%	%	%	%	ASSETS	%	%
27.9	13.9	11.3	16.1	15.5	13.6	Cash & Equivalents	12.7	11.0
10.1	7.6	16.7	21.1	9.5	2.0	Trade Receivables (net)	14.5	11.7
9.2	3.4	7.7	4.1	2.7	.7	Inventory	5.9	4.8
2.9	1.1	4.7	11.2	12.0	9.7	All Other Current	5.0	7.3
50.1	26.0	40.4	52.4	39.6	26.1	Total Current	38.1	34.8
32.9	38.9	37.9	20.7	16.0	29.2	Fixed Assets (net)	32.2	38.3
.8	2.8	6.1	5.8	5.0	.7	Intangibles (net)	3.9	5.1
16.3	32.3	15.5	21.1	39.5	44.0	All Other Non-Current	25.8	21.9
100.0	100.0	100.0	100.0	100.0	100.0	Total	100.0	100.0
						LIABILITIES		
19.9	12.9	22.1	21.5	11.3	14.1	Notes Payable-Short Term	13.4	36.4
3.2	4.2	3.5	3.0	1.3	2.3	Cur. Mat.-L/T/D	4.4	5.8
28.9	2.6	3.1	4.2	9.3	2.1	Trade Payables	4.2	4.3
.0	.0	.0	.0	.3	.1	Income Taxes Payable	.1	.2
46.4	11.8	3.8	11.1	17.7	8.1	All Other Current	8.9	10.7
98.4	31.5	32.6	39.8	39.9	26.7	Total Current	31.1	57.4
17.2	25.8	26.0	17.7	23.0	15.8	Long-Term Debt	27.7	31.5
.0	.0	.2	.1	.4	.0	Deferred Taxes	.6	.1
12.8	6.5	3.9	4.9	2.2	.3	All Other Non-Current	6.8	4.3
-28.4	36.2	37.3	37.5	34.4	57.2	Net Worth	33.8	6.7
100.0	100.0	100.0	100.0	100.0	100.0	Total Liabilities & Net Worth	100.0	100.0
						INCOME DATA		
100.0	100.0	100.0	100.0	100.0	100.0	Net Sales	100.0	100.0
						Gross Profit		
79.6	64.8	59.8	65.7	74.9	50.2	Operating Expenses	63.3	65.1
20.4	35.2	40.2	34.3	25.1	49.8	Operating Profit	36.7	34.9
3.8	12.5	16.4	10.3	4.0	11.5	All Other Expenses (net)	13.4	14.8
16.5	22.7	23.8	23.9	21.0	38.3	Profit Before Taxes	23.3	20.0
						RATIOS		
4.6	2.1	2.7	2.1	1.7	2.5		2.9	2.2
1.0	.6	1.2	1.2	1.0	.9	Current	1.1	1.0
.4	.1	.2	.7	.5	.2		.5	.3
3.0	2.1	2.3	2.1	1.0	2.5		2.3	1.5
.7	.4	.9	1.0	.5	.3	Quick	.7	.4
.1	.1	.1	.3	.2	.1		.1	.1
0 UND	0 UND	0 UND	2 171.2	0 UND	0 UND		0 UND	0 UND
0 UND	0 UND	0 999.8	62 5.9	14 26.8	0 UND	Sales/Receivables	3 131.0	0 UND
3 113.9	1 249.4	84 4.4	150 2.4	42 8.7	5 70.0		44 8.3	30 12.3
						Cost of Sales/Inventory		
						Cost of Sales/Payables		
9.6	8.1	1.1	1.0	1.5	.8		2.4	2.5
UND	-21.9	38.2	12.1	NM	-21.8	Sales/Working Capital	23.7	254.8
-6.1	-2.7	-2.7	-11.4	-5.7	-1.1		-4.2	-2.8
(15) 21.0	(16) 25.7	(22) 24.8	(28) 15.1	(10) 35.8	(11) 18.9		(81) 6.9	(74) 16.6
6.2	5.5	8.1	3.6	8.2	8.1	EBIT/Interest	2.6	3.7
1.5	-.1	3.7	.5	1.8	3.5		.9	1.1
							6.5	
						Net Profit + Depr., Dep., Amort./Cur. Mat. L/T/D	(14) 1.8	
							.5	
.1	.0	.0	.0	.0	.0		.0	.0
.7	.6	.6	.2	.1	.0	Fixed/Worth	.4	1.1
3.9	4.3	7.6	2.7	.8	1.7		4.5	8.9
1.5	.7	.6	.9		.3		.6	.9
3.7	3.1	2.3	2.3	3.7	1.0	Debt/Worth	2.3	3.2
-6.6	12.4	11.9	16.7	NM	2.5		12.0	394.0
(18) 164.6	(35) 110.1	(49) 45.5	(38) 49.2		21.5		(126) 38.1	(111) 38.8
32.1	21.5	19.6	17.2		8.8	% Profit Before Taxes/Tangible Net Worth	13.4	13.3
5.5	7.0	1.6	4.5		2.4		2.5	2.5
24.3	34.6	15.1	12.4	12.3	11.1		11.5	12.1
13.7	5.9	5.1	4.9	6.7	4.5	% Profit Before Taxes/Total Assets	3.9	4.2
-1.2	.8	.9	.7	2.5	1.2		.7	.7
UND	UND	411.2	101.7	UND	UND		323.2	76.5
33.8	14.7	12.8	12.3	56.1	29.4	Sales/Net Fixed Assets	12.5	7.7
3.7	.3	.2	2.6	4.3	.5		.5	.3
9.1	2.2	1.1	1.0	1.2	.3		1.6	1.1
4.4	.3	.2	.5	.6	.1	Sales/Total Assets	.3	.3
1.1	.1	.1	.1	.1	.1		.1	.1
(17) .8	(28) 1.6	(36) .7	(28) .6				(99) .5	(101) 1.0
1.9	7.4	3.2	2.1			% Depr., Dep., Amort./Sales	2.7	3.9
8.1	23.7	29.2	9.3				11.9	13.5
								2.7	6.2
						% Officers', Directors', Owners' Comp/Sales	(29) 10.6	(21) 14.0
							18.9	30.8
23998M	87921M	282487M	687693M	764375M	650102M	Net Sales ($)	2906187M	2516188M
5831M	51720M	296185M	1062354M	824368M	2454076M	Total Assets ($)	3543389M	2964904M

© RMA 2005

M = $ thousand   MM = $ million
See Pages 11 through 21 for Explanation of Ratios and Data

Comparative Historical Data | Current Data Sorted By Sales

Type of Statement	4/1/02-3/31/03 ALL	4/1/03-3/31/04 ALL	4/1/04-3/31/05 ALL	0-1MM	1-3MM	3-5MM	5-10MM	10-25MM	25MM & OVER
Unqualified	33	28	51	5	9	4	5	13	15
Reviewed	23	28	15	5	4	2	2	1	1
Compiled	24	46	20	10	3	2	1	2	2
Tax Returns	28	40	37	28	8		1		
Other	62	94	75	26	15	4	13	11	6
				16 (4/1-9/30/04)			182 (10/1/04-3/31/05)		
NUMBER OF STATEMENTS	170	236	198	74	39	12	21	28	24
ASSETS	%	%	%	%	%	%	%	%	%
Cash & Equivalents	13.0	10.9	15.6	16.2	11.9	22.8	13.9	20.9	11.0
Trade Receivables (net)	11.0	11.7	13.4	7.3	21.8	9.5	13.4	14.6	18.8
Inventory	6.8	5.1	5.3	6.5	4.3	.2	5.5	4.6	6.6
All Other Current	5.9	7.2	6.0	3.7	5.3	8.8	8.0	8.4	8.5
Total Current	36.6	34.9	40.3	33.7	43.3	41.4	40.8	48.6	44.9
Fixed Assets (net)	38.9	39.5	31.5	44.5	27.2	17.3	22.8	21.2	25.0
Intangibles (net)	4.8	4.6	4.2	1.6	3.6	4.4	9.6	7.5	4.4
All Other Non-Current	19.7	21.0	24.1	20.3	26.0	36.9	26.7	22.8	25.7
Total	100.0	100.0	100.0	100.0	100.0	100.0	100.0	100.0	100.0
LIABILITIES									
Notes Payable-Short Term	15.5	17.7	18.5	17.2	22.8	25.8	18.1	19.0	11.5
Cur. Mat.-L/T/D	3.0	3.2	3.3	4.6	1.8	1.0	3.3	3.1	2.8
Trade Payables	6.5	3.5	7.0	1.4	18.3	.7	3.4	7.3	11.6
Income Taxes Payable	.2	.2	.0	.0	.0	.0	.0	.0	.2
All Other Current	7.3	9.7	13.9	15.5	12.7	10.1	11.2	16.0	13.3
Total Current	32.6	34.3	42.7	38.6	55.6	37.6	36.0	45.4	39.3
Long-Term Debt	36.2	28.7	21.9	31.4	18.9	15.4	14.8	10.0	21.2
Deferred Taxes	.2	.2	.1	.1	.0	.0	.0	.2	.4
All Other Non-Current	5.4	6.3	5.5	4.2	11.2	.7	4.4	6.4	2.2
Net Worth	25.7	30.5	29.8	25.7	14.4	46.3	44.7	38.0	36.8
Total Liabilities & Net Worth	100.0	100.0	100.0	100.0	100.0	100.0	100.0	100.0	100.0
INCOME DATA									
Net Sales	100.0	100.0	100.0	100.0	100.0	100.0	100.0	100.0	100.0
Gross Profit									
Operating Expenses	68.0	62.6	65.0	57.2	63.7	63.5	67.8	74.9	78.3
Operating Profit	32.0	37.4	35.0	42.8	36.3	36.5	32.2	25.1	21.7
All Other Expenses (net)	14.5	13.8	11.4	18.6	12.6	9.1	5.6	2.2	4.0
Profit Before Taxes	17.5	23.6	23.6	24.2	23.8	27.4	26.5	22.9	17.7
RATIOS									
Current	2.3	3.0	2.4	3.0	2.3	10.5	6.7	1.8	1.9
	1.2	1.1	1.1	1.0	1.1	1.2	1.2	1.1	1.2
	.6	.2	.3	.2	.2	.5	.6	.5	.6
Quick	1.8	2.0	2.1	2.8	2.2	10.5	5.3	1.3	1.4
	.8	.6	.7	.3	.7	1.1	.9	.9	.8
	.2	.1	.1	.1	.0	.2	.3	.3	.2
Sales/Receivables	0 UND	0 UND	0 UND	0 UND	0 UND	0 UND	0 UND	0 UND	6 62.0
	1 635.0	1 723.0	0 999.8	0 UND	5 74.8	2 163.5	4 86.9	5 77.9	21 17.4
	31 11.9	32 11.3	47 7.8	0 UND	142 2.6	138 2.6	71 5.2	76 4.8	63 5.8
Cost of Sales/Inventory									
Cost of Sales/Payables									
Sales/Working Capital	2.7	2.7	2.3	2.8	1.0	.7	1.7	4.0	11.9
	22.0	25.9	43.0	UND	63.9	18.3	12.4	33.6	26.1
	-5.5	-3.0	-4.2	-2.2	-2.5	-7.9	-10.5	-9.0	-8.8
EBIT/Interest	10.9	10.8	19.1	11.9	25.9		84.1	30.0	13.7
	(96) 3.6	(132) 4.1	(102) 6.3	(25) 5.6	(16) 7.0		(11) 7.4	(23) 11.7	(22) 4.8
	1.6	1.8	1.5	1.3	1.2		1.8	.9	2.8
Net Profit + Depr., Dep., Amort./Cur. Mat. L/T/D	6.9	8.3	2.7						
	(19) 2.2	(12) 3.9	(14) .9						
	.6	1.4	.3						
Fixed/Worth	.0	.0	.0	.0	.0	.0	.0	.0	.0
	1.0	1.3	.5	1.0	.0	.2	.8	.4	.5
	10.2	4.9	3.3	4.3	2.7	3.9	UND	12.8	1.7
Debt/Worth	1.0	.9	.7	.8	1.0	.1	.2	.3	1.1
	3.9	2.4	2.3	2.6	2.5	1.9	3.5	3.5	1.9
	NM	33.3	12.8	10.2	12.1	13.2	UND	NM	3.7
% Profit Before Taxes/Tangible Net Worth	51.5	50.7	53.4	33.3	60.4	148.6	193.4	72.3	80.7
	(128) 15.7	(191) 18.8	(164) 19.6	(62) 14.4	(33) 19.6	(11) 10.6	(16) 24.4	(21) 21.9	(21) 29.7
	3.7	5.6	3.8	1.5	8.5	-.8	1.0	7.4	6.8
% Profit Before Taxes/Total Assets	11.2	13.4	14.8	9.2	14.8	31.5	45.7	15.9	17.5
	3.7	4.9	5.6	4.9	3.8	6.3	9.7	6.3	10.5
	.4	1.7	1.1	.2	2.2	-.2	1.7	-.4	4.0
Sales/Net Fixed Assets	86.3	76.8	493.1	UND	UND	148.5	UND	451.8	38.6
	5.5	5.2	18.3	.8	50.1	18.7	36.7	27.7	16.7
	.3	.3	.5	.2	1.4	8.2	4.5	4.2	4.3
Sales/Total Assets	1.0	.9	1.6	.4	1.4	2.3	3.1	2.0	2.6
	.3	.3	.3	.2	.2	.4	.9	.7	1.2
	.1	.1	.1	.1	.1	.1	.1	.4	.5
% Depr., Dep., Amort./Sales	1.5	1.2	.9	3.0	1.1		.5	.5	.6
	(124) 5.3	(160) 7.9	(126) 3.0	(47) 15.7	(19) 3.5		(11) 1.7	(20) 1.8	(21) 1.7
	14.5	18.8	16.5	28.0	29.8		13.1	3.8	3.1
% Officers', Directors', Owners' Comp/Sales	1.5	1.5	5.5						
	(31) 8.3	(26) 5.4	(24) 11.5						
	14.0	14.4	21.0						
Net Sales ($)	2562717M	2654025M	2496576M	27107M	68154M	48322M	150410M	460680M	1741903M
Total Assets ($)	3444784M	3810731M	4694534M	196038M	342742M	352482M	802067M	1184194M	1817011M

M = $ thousand   MM = $ million
See Pages 11 through 21 for Explanation of Ratios and Data

Current Data Sorted By Assets   Comparative Historical Data

0-500M	500M-2MM	2-10MM	10-50MM	50-100MM	100-250MM	Type of Statement	4/1/00-3/31/01 ALL	4/1/01-3/31/02 ALL
	2	2	4			Unqualified		
1		1				Reviewed		
1				1	1	Compiled		
2	7	1				Tax Returns		
4	3	8	6	2	2	Other		
	3 (4/1-9/30/04)		45 (10/1/04-3/31/05)					
8	12	12	10	3	3	NUMBER OF STATEMENTS		
%	%	%	%	%	%	**ASSETS**	%	%
	12.8	18.3	13.3			Cash & Equivalents		
	16.3	30.2	14.0			Trade Receivables (net)	D	D
	.0	.4	3.9			Inventory	A	A
	9.0	4.8	11.1			All Other Current	T	T
	38.0	53.7	42.3			Total Current	A	A
	44.0	31.2	26.1			Fixed Assets (net)		
	5.0	2.0	13.4			Intangibles (net)	N	N
	12.9	13.2	18.2			All Other Non-Current	O	O
	100.0	100.0	100.0			Total	T	T
						LIABILITIES	A	A
	6.2	6.1	4.3			Notes Payable-Short Term	V	V
	5.9	1.4	4.2			Cur. Mat.-L/T/D	A	A
	4.5	5.7	2.5			Trade Payables	I	I
	1.0	.0	.0			Income Taxes Payable	L	L
	19.4	25.4	8.3			All Other Current	A	A
	37.0	38.6	19.2			Total Current	B	B
	68.0	23.7	16.1			Long-Term Debt	L	L
	.2	.0	.1			Deferred Taxes	E	E
	2.8	14.7	16.4			All Other Non-Current		
	-8.0	23.0	48.3			Net Worth		
	100.0	100.0	100.0			Total Liabilities & Net Worth		
						INCOME DATA		
	100.0	100.0	100.0			Net Sales		
						Gross Profit		
	76.1	89.6	57.4			Operating Expenses		
	23.9	10.4	42.6			Operating Profit		
	13.0	5.1	13.8			All Other Expenses (net)		
	10.9	5.3	28.9			Profit Before Taxes		
						RATIOS		
	1.9	4.8	8.5			Current		
	.8	1.4	1.8					
	.3	.8	1.3					
	1.2	4.8	5.5			Quick		
	.7	1.4	1.4					
	.3	.4	1.0					
0	UND	0 UND	0 UND			Sales/Receivables		
0	UND	23 15.7	47 7.7					
52	7.0	72 5.1	110 3.3					
						Cost of Sales/Inventory		
						Cost of Sales/Payables		
	8.2	4.1	1.2			Sales/Working Capital		
	-34.4	17.9	7.9					
	-2.3	-35.3	17.2					
						EBIT/Interest		
						Net Profit + Depr., Dep., Amort./Cur. Mat. L/T/D		
	.1	.2	.0			Fixed/Worth		
	72.6	1.3	.3					
	-.9	5.2	2.2					
	1.6	.6	.5			Debt/Worth		
	79.8	4.6	2.0					
	-5.1	14.5	3.7					
		143.9				% Profit Before Taxes/Tangible Net Worth		
	(10)	15.8						
		-3.2						
	28.9	30.0	27.1			% Profit Before Taxes/Total Assets		
	9.2	13.8	6.9					
	-.1	-1.4	.1					
	45.2	43.8	UND			Sales/Net Fixed Assets		
	14.1	24.4	16.0					
	.4	2.8	1.7					
	2.6	3.9	1.2			Sales/Total Assets		
	1.2	2.7	.6					
	.3	.6	.2					
		.9				% Depr., Dep., Amort./Sales		
	(11)	1.6						
		4.9						
						% Officers', Directors', Owners' Comp/Sales		
12063M	17451M	168380M	246025M	23496M	17340M	Net Sales ($)		
1857M	12208M	65016M	203980M	204090M	350067M	Total Assets ($)		

M = $ thousand   MM = $ million
See Pages 11 through 21 for Explanation of Ratios and Data

Comparative Historical Data   Current Data Sorted By Sales

			Type of Statement						
9	15	8	Unqualified	1	1	2	1	2	1
2	1	2	Reviewed		1			1	
6	9	3	Compiled			1	1	1	
2	18	10	Tax Returns	7	3				
13	22	25	Other	4	3	3	4	4	3
4/1/02-3/31/03	4/1/03-3/31/04	4/1/04-3/31/05		3 (4/1-9/30/04)			45 (10/1/04-3/31/05)		
ALL	ALL	ALL		0-1MM	1-3MM	3-5MM	5-10MM	10-25MM	25MM & OVER
32	65	48	**NUMBER OF STATEMENTS**	12	12	6	6	8	4
%	%	%	**ASSETS**	%	%	%	%	%	%
17.3	18.5	15.4	Cash & Equivalents	3.7	10.4				
9.7	10.7	16.0	Trade Receivables (net)	.1	21.9				
1.1	.2	1.3	Inventory	.0	1.8				
5.9	5.3	7.1	All Other Current	1.3	10.1				
34.1	34.8	39.7	Total Current	5.1	44.1				
30.2	34.3	31.8	Fixed Assets (net)	76.8	25.7				
2.5	2.8	5.4	Intangibles (net)	1.2	7.6				
33.2	28.2	23.1	All Other Non-Current	16.8	22.5				
100.0	100.0	100.0	Total	100.0	100.0				
			LIABILITIES						
22.1	18.2	19.5	Notes Payable-Short Term	4.6	49.0				
5.3	3.2	4.7	Cur. Mat.-L/T/D	12.4	2.8				
4.4	4.4	4.0	Trade Payables	.4	7.2				
.1	.3	.5	Income Taxes Payable	.1	1.3				
10.2	23.8	15.6	All Other Current	2.4	20.6				
42.1	49.9	44.5	Total Current	19.9	80.9				
19.8	35.2	42.8	Long-Term Debt	118.2	33.9				
.1	.2	.4	Deferred Taxes	.0	1.2				
6.2	9.3	7.8	All Other Non-Current	7.8	2.7				
31.8	5.5	4.5	Net Worth	−45.9	−18.7				
100.0	100.0	100.0	Total Liabilities & Net Worth	100.0	100.0				
			INCOME DATA						
100.0	100.0	100.0	Net Sales	100.0	100.0				
			Gross Profit						
74.3	76.7	69.7	Operating Expenses	65.7	83.5				
25.7	23.3	30.3	Operating Profit	34.3	16.5				
8.2	9.7	10.9	All Other Expenses (net)	27.5	7.8				
17.5	13.5	19.4	Profit Before Taxes	6.8	8.7				
			RATIOS						
3.0	2.6	3.0		1.3	21.3				
1.3	1.3	1.2	Current	.6	1.8				
.2	.2	.6		.1	.5				
2.5	2.0	1.9		.7	20.5				
.6	.9	1.0	Quick	.5	1.4				
.1	.2	.4		.0	.5				
0 UND	0 UND	0 UND		0 UND	0 UND				
0 UND	1 636.6	1 613.3	Sales/Receivables	0 UND	11 32.6				
21 17.5	29 12.5	52 7.1		0 UND	52 7.0				
			Cost of Sales/Inventory						
			Cost of Sales/Payables						
7.1	6.1	4.8		17.5	6.2				
59.1	46.8	18.1	Sales/Working Capital	−11.1	16.8				
−3.0	−8.3	−19.7		−1.9	−30.1				
21.0	20.0	21.1							
(22) 4.6	(36) 5.6	(27) 4.7	EBIT/Interest						
1.5	2.0	1.6							
			Net Profit + Depr., Dep., Amort./Cur. Mat. L/T/D						
.0	.1	.0		2.5	.1				
.4	.9	.5	Fixed/Worth	5.6	.5				
3.3	6.2	5.9		−38.9	NM				
.4	.8	.5		3.9	.5				
1.5	2.5	2.7	Debt/Worth	79.8	1.4				
8.5	NM	NM		−3.4	−5.1				
72.6	74.7	89.4	% Profit Before Taxes/Tangible						
(27) 10.2	(49) 16.0	(36) 22.8	Net Worth						
2.7	5.4	3.6							
20.2	33.5	21.8	% Profit Before Taxes/Total	8.9	61.1				
4.5	7.2	7.8	Assets	6.8	17.9				
.1	1.0	.9		−2.9	−.8				
310.3	109.7	59.4		.6	46.8				
25.4	15.1	21.2	Sales/Net Fixed Assets	.3	19.5				
.5	.5	2.2		.2	13.3				
2.9	4.1	3.3		.5	8.0				
1.0	2.1	.8	Sales/Total Assets	.2	2.6				
.2	.2	.2		.1	.9				
1.1	1.7	1.0		10.9					
(21) 5.0	(42) 3.2	(32) 2.5	% Depr., Dep., Amort./Sales	(10) 13.5					
13.7	16.6	11.4		21.9					
	10.3		% Officers', Directors',						
	(12) 19.8		Owners' Comp/Sales						
	30.9								
798043M	1268619M	484755M	Net Sales ($)	5281M	24629M	21540M	40182M	150224M	242899M
470421M	600455M	837218M	Total Assets ($)	36311M	88242M	239762M	268071M	106488M	98344M

Current Data Sorted By Assets   Comparative Historical Data

						Type of Statement		
1	6	10	8	1	4	Unqualified	34	36
2	4	1				Reviewed	6	5
3	2	3	2			Compiled	19	26
17	2	2				Tax Returns	8	8
8	8	10	6	2	3	Other	26	31
	14 (4/1-9/30/04)		89 (10/1/04-3/31/05)				4/1/00-3/31/01	4/1/01-3/31/02
0-500M	500M-2MM	2-10MM	10-50MM	50-100MM	100-250MM		ALL	ALL
31	22	26	14	3	7	NUMBER OF STATEMENTS	93	106
%	%	%	%	%	%	**ASSETS**	%	%
37.9	24.7	24.2	29.2			Cash & Equivalents	19.0	23.8
15.0	31.2	30.3	33.1			Trade Receivables (net)	22.5	20.8
.0	1.1	.0	5.6			Inventory	2.1	1.6
1.3	4.6	5.3	2.6			All Other Current	7.3	8.1
54.2	61.6	59.9	70.6			Total Current	51.0	54.3
24.7	16.5	14.8	6.2			Fixed Assets (net)	24.8	23.7
5.5	.0	13.1	14.0			Intangibles (net)	8.3	8.2
15.6	21.9	12.3	9.2			All Other Non-Current	16.0	13.4
100.0	100.0	100.0	100.0			Total	100.0	100.0
						LIABILITIES		
28.1	8.2	5.4	7.4			Notes Payable-Short Term	17.5	10.5
14.5	5.9	3.7	.5			Cur. Mat.-L/T/D	4.6	3.8
5.3	6.5	4.9	3.0			Trade Payables	8.9	6.6
.2	.4	.3	1.1			Income Taxes Payable	.6	1.3
12.9	19.5	14.5	27.5			All Other Current	15.6	21.0
61.0	40.5	28.9	39.5			Total Current	47.2	43.2
17.7	17.0	17.5	4.9			Long-Term Debt	19.3	17.1
.0	.5	.0	.3			Deferred Taxes	.7	.5
15.6	1.7	9.5	5.5			All Other Non-Current	6.3	32.6
5.7	40.3	44.0	49.8			Net Worth	26.5	6.5
100.0	100.0	100.0	100.0			Total Liabilities & Net Worth	100.0	100.0
						INCOME DATA		
100.0	100.0	100.0	100.0			Net Sales	100.0	100.0
						Gross Profit		
87.3	89.0	77.3	84.5			Operating Expenses	84.7	80.4
12.7	11.0	22.7	15.5			Operating Profit	15.3	19.6
2.5	1.2	5.2	.3			All Other Expenses (net)	1.5	6.1
10.2	9.9	17.5	15.2			Profit Before Taxes	13.8	13.5
						RATIOS		
2.5	3.9	4.6	3.6				2.8	3.9
1.1	2.1	2.5	1.7			Current	1.3	1.7
.3	1.2	1.3	1.1				.8	.9
2.4	3.9	4.4	3.5				2.2	3.7
1.1	1.8	2.1	1.6			Quick	1.0	1.4
.3	.9	1.3	1.0				.4	.5
0 UND	4 93.4	0 UND	33 11.1				0 UND	0 UND
0 UND	20 18.4	54 6.7	58 6.2			Sales/Receivables	21 17.1	17 21.1
8 46.6	74 5.0	86 4.3	93 3.9				66 5.5	60 6.1
						Cost of Sales/Inventory		
						Cost of Sales/Payables		
16.4	4.7	2.0	2.8				4.7	4.0
372.0	12.0	6.8	6.8			Sales/Working Capital	17.1	10.8
−17.1	278.0	14.2	32.3				−28.0	−62.9
	31.2	25.7	39.9				19.9	20.8
(20) 4.5	(17) 6.4	(19) 11.4				EBIT/Interest	(59) 5.7	(65) 7.9
1.9	1.1	4.6					1.9	2.1
						Net Profit + Depr., Dep.,	11.4	21.5
						Amort./Cur. Mat. L /T/D	(14) 4.3 (11) .6	
							.5	.2
.0	.1	.1	.0				.1	.1
.8	.2	.2	.1			Fixed/Worth	.8	.4
3.4	2.2	NM	.5				2.3	2.3
.9	.6	.4	.5				.5	.5
2.6	1.6	1.0	1.8			Debt/Worth	1.6	1.8
−6.0	8.1	NM	4.5				8.0	12.9
244.5	84.2	112.9	94.3			% Profit Before Taxes/Tangible	113.2	83.1
(22) 67.5	(20) 20.7	(20) 31.3	(13) 44.0			Net Worth	(75) 25.1	(84) 31.8
10.4	9.0	14.7	7.6				9.3	4.9
59.3	34.3	35.0	30.9			% Profit Before Taxes/Total	33.6	41.5
27.7	12.7	15.0	11.0			Assets	10.1	10.6
3.5	2.6	5.4	2.5				1.7	.8
UND	109.7	83.3	100.3				56.3	67.6
89.1	37.1	28.8	50.4			Sales/Net Fixed Assets	20.3	22.9
18.5	19.0	15.4	21.3				5.7	7.2
13.1	4.6	2.9	2.4				3.2	3.7
7.2	3.1	1.5	1.8			Sales/Total Assets	2.0	1.9
3.1	2.3	1.0	.5				1.0	.7
.6	.4	.7	.7				.7	.7
(14) 1.3	(16) 1.1	(19) 1.3	(10) 1.5			% Depr., Dep., Amort./Sales	(70) 1.6	(77) 1.5
3.6	2.7	3.3	2.2				3.4	3.8
17.0	5.4						6.4	4.8
(19) 25.6	(11) 18.4					% Officers', Directors',	(19) 15.4	(23) 17.1
34.6	34.9					Owners' Comp/Sales	31.9	34.9
51132M	98675M	247791M	666297M	147628M	979022M	Net Sales ($)	2027289M	1937809M
7339M	23166M	133654M	354858M	232211M	1134506M	Total Assets ($)	1164894M	1770290M

© RMA 2005

M = $ thousand   MM = $ million
See Pages 11 through 21 for Explanation of Ratios and Data

Comparative Historical Data | Current Data Sorted By Sales

Type of Statement									
Unqualified	30	27	30	5	3	5	9		8
Reviewed	5	5	7	3	2	2			
Compiled	16	19	8	1	3	1	2	1	
Tax Returns	9	19	21	12	8	1			
Other	35	39	37	3	9	4	5	10	6
	4/1/02-3/31/03 ALL	4/1/03-3/31/04 ALL	4/1/04-3/31/05 ALL	14 (4/1-9/30/04) 0-1MM	89 (10/1/04-3/31/05) 1-3MM	3-5MM	5-10MM	10-25MM	25MM & OVER
NUMBER OF STATEMENTS	95	109	103	16	28	11	14	20	14
ASSETS	%	%	%	%	%	%	%	%	%
Cash & Equivalents	27.8	27.9	29.0	35.2	35.7	17.1	17.7	30.4	26.9
Trade Receivables (net)	22.3	25.2	26.6	14.4	21.7	42.5	32.1	27.3	31.8
Inventory	1.0	2.5	1.0	.0	.0	2.2	.6	.1	4.8
All Other Current	4.2	4.0	3.5	.0	5.1	1.8	6.2	1.9	5.0
Total Current	55.2	59.6	60.1	49.6	62.5	63.6	56.6	59.8	68.5
Fixed Assets (net)	23.7	16.1	16.5	28.9	16.9	11.1	17.0	11.4	12.5
Intangibles (net)	6.8	7.5	6.9	5.1	2.5	17.6	6.7	13.4	.3
All Other Non-Current	14.3	16.9	16.5	16.4	18.1	7.7	19.8	15.4	18.7
Total	100.0	100.0	100.0	100.0	100.0	100.0	100.0	100.0	100.0
LIABILITIES									
Notes Payable-Short Term	17.8	16.6	14.1	35.4	15.8	7.9	9.4	3.6	11.2
Cur. Mat.-L/T/D	3.8	6.3	6.7	2.0	19.9	.8	4.5	1.4	.3
Trade Payables	7.1	5.6	4.8	2.7	5.4	7.2	7.0	3.7	3.8
Income Taxes Payable	1.1	.6	.4	.0	.3	.1	.4	.7	1.1
All Other Current	25.3	24.0	18.6	4.3	12.6	19.9	22.1	23.8	34.6
Total Current	55.1	53.1	44.7	44.4	54.0	35.8	43.5	33.2	51.0
Long-Term Debt	9.1	14.5	15.4	25.8	17.8	16.3	9.6	11.8	9.1
Deferred Taxes	.4	.2	.2	.0	.1	.0	.7	.2	.1
All Other Non-Current	6.6	5.5	8.7	5.2	17.4	1.5	1.4	8.7	8.5
Net Worth	28.9	26.7	31.0	24.5	10.7	46.5	44.9	46.2	31.3
Total Liabilities & Net Worth	100.0	100.0	100.0	100.0	100.0	100.0	100.0	100.0	100.0
INCOME DATA									
Net Sales	100.0	100.0	100.0	100.0	100.0	100.0	100.0	100.0	100.0
Gross Profit									
Operating Expenses	82.0	81.5	82.5	78.4	85.3	91.2	89.6	74.4	79.1
Operating Profit	18.0	18.5	17.5	21.6	14.7	8.8	10.4	25.6	20.9
All Other Expenses (net)	4.2	1.9	3.3	2.2	4.4	.0	.8	5.8	3.6
Profit Before Taxes	13.8	16.6	14.3	19.4	10.3	8.8	9.6	19.8	17.3
RATIOS									
Current	3.0	3.5	3.5	2.5	3.7	3.9	3.4	4.2	2.9
	1.6	1.3	1.8	1.4	2.0	2.4	1.3	2.0	1.3
	.6	.7	1.0	.5	1.0	1.0	.9	1.1	1.1
Quick	2.9	3.0	3.3	2.5	3.6	3.9	2.8	3.9	2.8
	1.3	1.2	1.6	1.4	1.5	2.2	1.1	1.8	1.3
	.6	.5	.8	.5	.9	.8	.2	1.1	.8
Sales/Receivables	0 UND	0 UND	0 UND	0 UND	0 UND	29 12.4	5 73.1	2 174.6	2 240.1
	17 21.0	26 14.2	20 18.1	0 UND	1 350.6	62 5.9	43 8.6	46 8.0	39 9.3
	63 5.7	76 4.8	81 4.5	20 18.0	36 10.1	85 4.3	84 4.3	94 3.9	80 4.5
Cost of Sales/Inventory									
Cost of Sales/Payables									
Sales/Working Capital	4.9	3.5	3.8	7.5	4.0	4.7	3.9	2.8	3.6
	16.8	12.5	13.0	200.6	14.6	10.3	31.4	7.0	8.3
	-22.4	-20.3	-557.6	-11.2	NM	-529.3	-421.8	15.9	48.1
EBIT/Interest	83.8	30.8	32.1		15.4			101.4	
	(65) 14.8	(73) 7.7	(71) 7.6		(21) 4.7			(14) 34.2	
	1.3	2.9	2.5		2.3			14.3	
Net Profit + Depr., Dep., Amort./Cur. Mat. L/T/D	25.3	22.0	16.5						
	(10) 7.9	(14) 3.3	(10) 7.2						
	.2	.8	2.0						
Fixed/Worth	.1	.1	.0	.0	.0	.1	.1	.0	.1
	.5	.2	.2	.7	.2	.2	.3	.1	.2
	4.6	2.1	2.1	NM	2.9	7.5	4.8	.4	.6
Debt/Worth	.5	.6	.6	.6	.6	.6	.3	.4	1.1
	1.5	2.3	1.8	2.4	2.7	.9	2.1	1.1	2.5
	15.6	34.1	9.0	-9.7	20.2	83.0	14.5	5.7	4.8
% Profit Before Taxes/Tangible Net Worth	97.6	94.1	105.5	640.7	95.1		84.2	145.1	116.1
	(72) 55.0	(84) 32.4	(84) 31.3	(11) 25.0	(22) 20.2		(12) 20.5	(17) 83.0	(13) 77.5
	10.6	5.6	10.3	2.4	11.7		5.8	28.1	7.6
% Profit Before Taxes/Total Assets	52.6	50.3	42.2	118.3	42.6	33.2	27.4	61.1	44.7
	18.0	14.5	15.0	19.2	16.0	9.3	13.2	27.9	11.9
	2.0	3.6	3.6	.8	4.6	3.0	5.1	7.1	-.2
Sales/Net Fixed Assets	72.7	79.9	144.3	UND	102.7	132.3	52.0	152.5	117.2
	25.8	30.6	42.5	93.2	49.2	58.8	30.1	62.3	27.1
	8.8	17.6	15.5	4.5	18.8	27.8	15.4	15.4	12.7
Sales/Total Assets	6.2	5.3	5.2	9.5	6.9	7.2	4.8	3.3	2.4
	2.5	2.4	2.4	2.7	3.2	2.7	2.7	1.7	1.9
	1.5	1.0	1.2	.6	1.9	1.5	1.4	.6	1.0
% Depr., Dep., Amort./Sales	.8	.9	.7		.6		1.3	.7	.8
	(71) 1.4	(68) 1.5	(64) 1.3		(17) 1.5		(10) 1.4	(13) 1.0	(10) 1.6
	2.3	2.5	2.6		2.7		2.8	2.1	3.0
% Officers', Directors', Owners' Comp/Sales	6.7	11.9	14.6		16.5				
	(25) 13.6	(36) 20.8	(39) 22.9		(13) 24.6				
	26.3	33.3	33.4		34.9				
Net Sales ($)	2232944M	2033253M	2190545M	7594M	51129M	41671M	118886M	336289M	1634976M
Total Assets ($)	1786634M	1877597M	1885734M	4211M	39685M	17695M	78874M	606088M	1139181M

© RMA 2005

M = $ thousand   MM = $ million
See Pages 11 through 21 for Explanation of Ratios and Data

Current Data Sorted By Assets   Comparative Historical Data

						Type of Statement		
	1	4	2	1	4	Unqualified	17	15
	1	2				Reviewed	4	2
						Compiled	5	9
1	2	1	1			Tax Returns	2	2
1	4	12	4		2	Other	10	14
	8 (4/1-9/30/04)		35 (10/1/04-3/31/05)				4/1/00-3/31/01	4/1/01-3/31/02
0-500M	500M-2MM	2-10MM	10-50MM	50-100MM	100-250MM		ALL	ALL
2	8	19	7	1	6	NUMBER OF STATEMENTS	38	42
%	%	%	%	%	%	ASSETS	%	%
		15.0				Cash & Equivalents	22.9	20.5
		20.6				Trade Receivables (net)	15.3	11.2
		1.6				Inventory	1.3	.9
		3.0				All Other Current	4.8	8.2
		40.2				Total Current	44.3	40.8
		34.8				Fixed Assets (net)	35.1	31.4
		8.2				Intangibles (net)	2.1	3.7
		16.8				All Other Non-Current	18.5	24.1
		100.0				Total	100.0	100.0
						LIABILITIES		
		5.8				Notes Payable-Short Term	7.4	6.6
		4.2				Cur. Mat.-L/T/D	.7	.5
		5.3				Trade Payables	9.0	6.3
		1.3				Income Taxes Payable	.4	.5
		8.8				All Other Current	13.7	23.5
		25.4				Total Current	31.2	37.3
		22.4				Long-Term Debt	28.2	19.5
		1.3				Deferred Taxes	.1	.0
		7.0				All Other Non-Current	2.6	3.7
		43.9				Net Worth	37.9	39.6
		100.0				Total Liabilities & Net Worth	100.0	100.0
						INCOME DATA		
		100.0				Net Sales	100.0	100.0
						Gross Profit		
		76.7				Operating Expenses	69.0	71.6
		23.3				Operating Profit	31.0	28.4
		7.7				All Other Expenses (net)	15.5	12.3
		15.6				Profit Before Taxes	15.5	16.2
						RATIOS		
		5.4					4.4	3.9
		1.4				Current	1.5	1.4
		.4					.8	.4
		3.4					4.1	2.9
		1.4				Quick	1.0	1.0
		.3					.4	.3
	0	UND					0 UND	0 UND
	25	14.8				Sales/Receivables	18 20.0	6 56.6
	121	3.0					62 5.9	37 9.8
						Cost of Sales/Inventory		
						Cost of Sales/Payables		
		2.1					2.4	3.1
		5.2				Sales/Working Capital	17.7	12.8
		-5.6					-78.7	-9.8
		69.3					86.7	27.5
	(10)	4.7				EBIT/Interest	(17) 3.5	(19) 4.7
		1.5					1.8	1.3
						Net Profit + Depr., Dep., Amort./Cur. Mat. L /T/D		
		.1					.0	.0
		.3				Fixed/Worth	.5	.4
		5.6					3.6	2.7
		.2					.6	.3
		1.6				Debt/Worth	2.1	1.2
		10.2					12.2	7.9
		42.1				% Profit Before Taxes/Tangible Net Worth	42.2	24.5
	(16)	21.2					(33) 16.4	(36) 8.1
		9.4					4.1	4.1
		12.7				% Profit Before Taxes/Total Assets	17.0	8.6
		4.8					2.9	3.9
		1.7					.7	.4
		52.8				Sales/Net Fixed Assets	28.6	57.5
		17.1					12.1	14.4
		.4					.3	.3
		1.8				Sales/Total Assets	1.8	1.7
		.6					.6	.6
		.2					.1	.1
		.8				% Depr., Dep., Amort./Sales	.6	.7
	(15)	3.9					(33) 2.1	(29) 3.9
		22.9					13.0	13.0
						% Officers', Directors', Owners' Comp/Sales		
1129M	7780M	81331M	34781M	74541M	247298M	Net Sales ($)	849655M	1004326M
191M	8912M	102340M	249046M	80298M	928637M	Total Assets ($)	1424138M	1581777M

M = $ thousand   MM = $ million
See Pages 11 through 21 for Explanation of Ratios and Data

Comparative Historical Data   **Current Data Sorted By Sales**

Type of Statement	4/1/02-3/31/03 ALL	4/1/03-3/31/04 ALL	4/1/04-3/31/05 ALL	0-1MM	1-3MM	3-5MM	5-10MM	10-25MM	25MM & OVER
Unqualified	16	11	12		2	2	3	2	3
Reviewed	3	2	3		1		1	1	
Compiled	6	10							
Tax Returns	4	1	5	4	1				
Other	15	25	23	8	6	2	6		1
					8 (4/1-9/30/04)		35 (10/1/04-3/31/05)		
NUMBER OF STATEMENTS	44	49	43	12	10	4	10	3	4
	%	%	%	%	%	%	%	%	%
ASSETS									
Cash & Equivalents	21.5	26.0	30.3	32.7	27.8		17.0		
Trade Receivables (net)	12.2	13.7	14.6	9.3	18.0		22.6		
Inventory	.7	2.4	.8	.0	.0		3.0		
All Other Current	5.3	6.8	3.1	4.2	5.0		2.7		
Total Current	39.7	48.9	48.8	46.2	50.8		45.3		
Fixed Assets (net)	34.0	23.5	27.3	39.8	22.8		13.0		
Intangibles (net)	5.6	5.7	5.7	10.5	2.2		1.3		
All Other Non-Current	20.7	21.8	18.2	3.5	24.1		40.5		
Total	100.0	100.0	100.0	100.0	100.0		100.0		
LIABILITIES									
Notes Payable-Short Term	9.8	9.2	5.9	8.4	12.0		.0		
Cur. Mat.-L/T/D	2.0	.9	2.3	1.9	4.4		1.2		
Trade Payables	5.9	5.5	4.8	5.1	.9		8.9		
Income Taxes Payable	.8	.6	.6	.0	.1		2.3		
All Other Current	12.5	16.5	11.5	13.1	5.5		15.2		
Total Current	31.0	32.7	25.2	28.4	22.9		27.6		
Long-Term Debt	14.9	18.4	22.6	34.7	13.0		12.4		
Deferred Taxes	.2	.7	1.0	.0	.4		1.1		
All Other Non-Current	5.4	6.2	5.0	3.4	12.2		2.3		
Net Worth	48.6	42.0	46.3	33.5	51.4		56.6		
Total Liabilities & Net Worth	100.0	100.0	100.0	100.0	100.0		100.0		
INCOME DATA									
Net Sales	100.0	100.0	100.0	100.0	100.0		100.0		
Gross Profit									
Operating Expenses	76.5	78.0	69.0	59.8	63.8		76.1		
Operating Profit	23.5	22.0	31.0	40.2	36.2		23.9		
All Other Expenses (net)	6.7	4.0	9.1	16.8	5.5		6.9		
Profit Before Taxes	16.7	18.0	21.9	23.5	30.7		17.0		
RATIOS									
Current	5.1	7.4	5.8	5.0	5.5		21.3		
	1.4	2.2	2.3	1.6	3.5		3.9		
	.7	1.0	.6	.1	1.1		.8		
Quick	3.1	6.4	5.3	5.0	4.1		21.3		
	1.0	2.0	1.9	1.3	2.2		2.5		
	.3	.4	.6	.1	1.1		.6		
Sales/Receivables	0 UND	0 UND	0 UND	0 UND	0 UND		0 UND		
	15 25.0	25 14.8	9 42.2	0 UND	0 UND		25 14.5		
	39 9.4	43 8.5	64 5.7	61 6.0	68 5.4		98 3.7		
Cost of Sales/Inventory									
Cost of Sales/Payables									
Sales/Working Capital	2.5	1.7	.5	.5	.1		2.4		
	34.6	5.1	3.9	17.3	2.3		5.0		
	-10.4	NM	-11.9	-.6	NM		-142.4		
EBIT/Interest	(23) 30.8	(28) 11.4	(21) 12.7						
	5.4	3.9	4.3						
	2.6	2.0	2.0						
Net Profit + Depr., Dep., Amort./Cur. Mat. L/T/D									
Fixed/Worth	.1	.0	.0	.0	.0		.0		
	.7	.2	.2	.3	.3		.1		
	1.7	2.3	3.1	9.2	8.9		.5		
Debt/Worth	.4	.3	.2	.9	.1		.2		
	.8	1.0	1.3	2.2	1.0		.6		
	5.6	15.0	10.2	19.9	12.0		4.6		
% Profit Before Taxes/Tangible Net Worth	(40) 32.8	(42) 50.2	(38) 40.1	65.1			88.0		
	14.3	16.1	16.8	(10) 26.8			26.2		
	5.2	6.6	4.0	7.3			4.3		
% Profit Before Taxes/Total Assets	11.1	18.2	11.6	12.1	12.6		27.6		
	4.8	6.1	4.6	3.4	7.4		7.9		
	1.3	1.2	1.7	.9	3.4		1.2		
Sales/Net Fixed Assets	31.8	48.2	74.4	UND	26.5		UND		
	12.0	19.7	7.0	1.7	2.1		47.2		
	.3	.6	.7	.2	.6		13.1		
Sales/Total Assets	2.0	1.9	1.3	.3	.9		2.0		
	.6	.6	.3	.2	.3		1.2		
	.2	.2	.1	.1	.1		.2		
% Depr., Dep., Amort./Sales	(35) 1.6	(34) 1.1	(26) 1.1						
	3.1	2.2	3.4						
	16.5	12.3	16.7						
% Officers', Directors', Owners' Comp/Sales									
Net Sales ($)	717600M	725624M	446860M	5083M	20456M	14994M	69122M	59146M	278059M
Total Assets ($)	924996M	1145099M	1369424M	30124M	205062M	64097M	159930M	265381M	644830M

Current Data Sorted By Assets   Comparative Historical Data

						Type of Statement		
1	1	2	4	4	6	Unqualified	8	9
	1					Reviewed		1
3	1					Compiled	1	1
	1	1	2	1	2	Tax Returns	2	2
	1					Other	17	6
	4 (4/1-9/30/04)		26 (10/1/04-3/31/05)				4/1/00- 3/31/01	4/1/01- 3/31/02
0-500M	500M-2MM	2-10MM	10-50MM	50-100MM	100-250MM		ALL	ALL
4	4	3	6	5	8	**NUMBER OF STATEMENTS**	28	19
%	%	%	%	%	%		%	%
						ASSETS		
						Cash & Equivalents	31.9	39.8
						Trade Receivables (net)	4.4	5.6
						Inventory	.1	.0
						All Other Current	4.4	7.0
						Total Current	40.7	52.4
						Fixed Assets (net)	6.6	5.9
						Intangibles (net)	11.2	4.0
						All Other Non-Current	41.5	37.7
						Total	100.0	100.0
						LIABILITIES		
						Notes Payable-Short Term	5.0	11.4
						Cur. Mat.-L/T/D	1.0	.6
						Trade Payables	7.5	5.6
						Income Taxes Payable	.1	.8
						All Other Current	32.9	25.2
						Total Current	46.5	43.6
						Long-Term Debt	7.5	10.7
						Deferred Taxes	.1	.3
						All Other Non-Current	17.9	7.5
						Net Worth	27.9	37.9
						Total Liabilities & Net Worth	100.0	100.0
						INCOME DATA		
						Net Sales	100.0	100.0
						Gross Profit		
						Operating Expenses	109.0	87.8
						Operating Profit	-9.0	12.2
						All Other Expenses (net)	-12.0	2.9
						Profit Before Taxes	3.0	9.4
						RATIOS		
						Current	2.1	5.3
							1.1	2.0
							.3	.5
						Quick	1.7	5.1
							1.0	1.5
							.1	.5
						Sales/Receivables	0 UND	0 UND
							1 531.1	0 UND
							51 7.1	13 28.0
						Cost of Sales/Inventory		
						Cost of Sales/Payables		
						Sales/Working Capital	2.2	.7
							20.7	12.4
							-2.2	-4.5
						EBIT/Interest		
						Net Profit + Depr., Dep., Amort./Cur. Mat. L /T/D		
						Fixed/Worth	.0	.0
							.1	.1
							.7	.3
						Debt/Worth	2.5	.7
							4.6	1.9
							13.6	12.9
						% Profit Before Taxes/Tangible Net Worth	11.9	33.1
							(26) 5.7	(18) 12.3
							1.2	-6.4
						% Profit Before Taxes/Total Assets	1.7	6.6
							.8	2.9
							.0	-.4
						Sales/Net Fixed Assets	441.7	96.3
							20.1	31.9
							4.9	12.5
						Sales/Total Assets	.9	1.8
							.3	.3
							.1	.2
						% Depr., Dep., Amort./Sales	1.1	
							(12) 3.5	
							6.9	
						% Officers', Directors', Owners' Comp/Sales		
5916M	13866M	64920M	136190M	231082M	1073223M	Net Sales ($)	750142M	488174M
599M	4116M	14456M	173450M	328483M	1198204M	Total Assets ($)	1989940M	1122068M

© RMA 2005

M = $ thousand   MM = $ million
See Pages 11 through 21 for Explanation of Ratios and Data

Comparative Historical Data / Current Data Sorted By Sales

				Type of Statement	0-1MM	1-3MM	3-5MM	5-10MM	10-25MM	25MM & OVER
	11	9	18	Unqualified	1	1	2	1	7	6
				Reviewed						
	1	1	1	Compiled	1					
	1	7	4	Tax Returns	2					
	9	3	7	Other		1	1	1		4
	4/1/02-3/31/03	4/1/03-3/31/04	4/1/04-3/31/05			4 (4/1-9/30/04)		26 (10/1/04-3/31/05)		
	ALL	ALL	ALL		0-1MM	1-3MM	3-5MM	5-10MM	10-25MM	25MM & OVER
	21	20	30	NUMBER OF STATEMENTS	4	2	4	3	7	10

	%	%	%	ASSETS	%	%	%	%	%	%
	27.4	38.4	46.8	Cash & Equivalents						47.6
	15.4	14.1	10.6	Trade Receivables (net)						6.1
	4.4	.0	.6	Inventory						1.4
	2.2	7.0	9.5	All Other Current						6.5
	49.3	59.5	67.6	Total Current						61.7
	11.8	13.7	5.7	Fixed Assets (net)						7.8
	4.5	8.1	4.1	Intangibles (net)						.9
	34.3	18.6	22.7	All Other Non-Current						29.6
	100.0	100.0	100.0	Total						100.0
				LIABILITIES						
	1.8	.7	9.1	Notes Payable-Short Term						2.0
	1.7	1.9	.8	Cur. Mat.-L/T/D						.3
	11.0	14.7	11.0	Trade Payables						7.2
	.4	.3	.3	Income Taxes Payable						.5
	34.6	18.2	23.9	All Other Current						22.4
	49.5	35.8	45.1	Total Current						32.4
	6.4	22.3	7.4	Long-Term Debt						5.6
	.2	.7	.6	Deferred Taxes						.5
	10.4	10.5	13.5	All Other Non-Current						18.7
	33.5	30.7	33.4	Net Worth						42.8
	100.0	100.0	100.0	Total Liabilities & Net Worth						100.0
				INCOME DATA						
	100.0	100.0	100.0	Net Sales						100.0
				Gross Profit						
	88.9	86.3	89.0	Operating Expenses						92.8
	11.1	13.7	11.0	Operating Profit						7.2
	5.1	.4	.5	All Other Expenses (net)						−.3
	6.0	13.3	10.5	Profit Before Taxes						7.5

RATIOS

				Ratio						25MM & OVER
	1.8	4.8	2.9	Current						4.6
	1.3	1.9	1.5							2.7
	.8	.9	1.1							1.5
	1.5	4.3	2.6	Quick						3.8
	1.1	1.8	1.2							2.3
	.5	.7	1.0							1.4
0	UND	0 UND	0 UND	Sales/Receivables					0	UND
11	33.8	7 53.1	6 56.8						1	402.6
55	6.6	69 5.3	41 9.0						54	6.7
				Cost of Sales/Inventory						
				Cost of Sales/Payables						
	3.4	1.4	2.0	Sales/Working Capital						2.0
	6.4	6.5	8.1							7.3
	−301.3	NM	42.0							20.9
(13)	41.6	(12) 52.2	(22) 94.4	EBIT/Interest						
	6.4	7.0	9.5							
	1.3	3.4	3.0							
				Net Profit + Depr., Dep., Amort./Cur. Mat. L/T/D						
	.0	.0	.0	Fixed/Worth						.0
	.1	.1	.0							.1
	.6	.5	.2							.2
	.8	.4	.9	Debt/Worth						.8
	1.9	2.1	2.3							1.4
	12.8	13.9	8.2							4.8
(20)	20.7	(16) 42.1	(28) 74.9	% Profit Before Taxes/Tangible Net Worth						77.1
	12.0	15.4	14.9							22.7
	1.1	11.4	8.3							9.6
	8.5	25.3	16.5	% Profit Before Taxes/Total Assets						34.9
	2.8	8.6	5.2							8.2
	.4	2.1	1.2							3.1
	98.4	UND	UND	Sales/Net Fixed Assets						999.8
	26.6	29.3	112.3							90.4
	7.1	14.4	19.3							14.1
	1.2	3.1	3.2	Sales/Total Assets						3.5
	.4	1.2	1.0							1.2
	.2	.2	.2							.4
			.3	% Depr., Dep., Amort./Sales						
		(15)	1.3							
			2.2							
				% Officers', Directors', Owners' Comp/Sales						
	581109M	584720M	1525197M	Net Sales ($)	2614M	4563M	15314M	24192M	106262M	1372252M
	1831986M	997683M	1719308M	Total Assets ($)	1486M	2989M	113391M	171210M	328479M	1101753M

FINANCE—Direct Health and Medical Insurance Carriers   NAICS 524114 (SIC 6321, 6324)

Current Data Sorted By Assets							Comparative Historical Data	

0-500M	500M-2MM	2-10MM	10-50MM	50-100MM	100-250MM	Type of Statement	4/1/00-3/31/01 ALL	4/1/01-3/31/02 ALL
2	2	5	18	6	14	Unqualified	38	36
1	1	2				Reviewed	1	2
1	2				1	Compiled	3	5
2	1	2				Tax Returns	3	
	7	9	10	4	7	Other	19	35
	15 (4/1-9/30/04)			82 (10/1/04-3/31/05)				
6	13	18	28	10	22	**NUMBER OF STATEMENTS**	64	78
%	%	%	%	%	%	**ASSETS**	%	%
	24.1	20.9	49.7	37.9	39.5	Cash & Equivalents	37.9	37.9
	22.5	23.4	11.0	7.6	10.8	Trade Receivables (net)	17.6	16.0
	.0	2.0	.6	.0	.5	Inventory	1.8	1.7
	16.8	5.1	3.3	14.4	2.6	All Other Current	6.2	4.2
	63.4	51.4	64.7	59.9	53.5	Total Current	63.5	59.8
	19.9	25.1	13.3	5.6	9.0	Fixed Assets (net)	14.4	14.0
	8.0	10.7	5.9	14.1	17.1	Intangibles (net)	5.8	5.3
	8.8	12.8	16.1	20.4	20.4	All Other Non-Current	16.3	20.8
	100.0	100.0	100.0	100.0	100.0	Total	100.0	100.0
						LIABILITIES		
	17.9	6.6	1.5	.0	3.6	Notes Payable-Short Term	3.4	3.3
	2.6	4.6	1.4	1.0	1.0	Cur. Mat.-L/T/D	2.3	7.9
	9.8	12.3	10.9	2.5	17.5	Trade Payables	14.7	15.5
	.1	.6	.3	.1	.3	Income Taxes Payable	.3	.4
	25.7	21.2	28.7	34.0	16.1	All Other Current	33.7	29.2
	56.1	45.3	42.8	37.6	38.5	Total Current	54.4	56.2
	6.4	17.0	6.7	8.5	11.6	Long-Term Debt	17.7	30.2
	.0	.8	.1	.4	.8	Deferred Taxes	.1	.3
	5.9	10.3	10.8	10.1	2.6	All Other Non-Current	4.2	6.9
	31.5	26.7	39.6	43.4	46.4	Net Worth	23.7	6.3
	100.0	100.0	100.0	100.0	100.0	Total Liabilities & Net Worth	100.0	100.0
						INCOME DATA		
	100.0	100.0	100.0	100.0	100.0	Net Sales	100.0	100.0
						Gross Profit		
	94.6	91.3	93.1	96.5	92.7	Operating Expenses	97.3	96.1
	5.4	8.7	6.9	3.5	7.3	Operating Profit	2.7	3.9
	.3	1.8	−.3	−.6	−.1	All Other Expenses (net)	−1.2	1.6
	5.1	6.9	7.1	4.2	7.3	Profit Before Taxes	3.9	2.3
						RATIOS		
	5.8	2.9	2.1	3.7	2.5		2.0	1.7
	1.1	1.1	1.6	1.2	1.7	Current	1.3	1.2
	.6	.7	1.1	1.0	.9		.7	.8
	3.8	1.7	2.1	3.7	2.2		1.7	1.5
	.8	1.0	1.4	1.0	1.5	Quick	1.1	1.1
	.6	.7	1.1	.4	.8		.6	.7
	0 UND	**8** 43.6	**5** 77.1	**8** 46.9	**11** 34.6		**6** 65.3	**5** 75.1
	14 26.9	**35** 10.5	**14** 26.1	**18** 20.7	**20** 18.6	Sales/Receivables	**22** 16.5	**15** 24.6
	44 8.3	**55** 6.6	**38** 9.5	**35** 10.4	**42** 8.6		**43** 8.4	**43** 8.6
						Cost of Sales/Inventory		
						Cost of Sales/Payables		
	4.4	7.4	4.2	1.5	4.6		5.9	7.6
	40.8	90.5	10.9	10.8	8.5	Sales/Working Capital	20.7	21.7
	−11.3	−25.8	40.8	NM	−144.1		−14.1	−29.3
		16.8	54.3				36.3	14.4
		(13) 8.7	(10) 26.1			EBIT/Interest	(34) 8.1	(48) 3.9
		2.6	7.0				1.4	.3
							16.4	17.2
						Net Profit + Depr., Dep., Amort./Cur. Mat. L /T/D	(10) 4.9	(14) 1.6
							2.9	.5
	.1	.3	.0	.0	.0		.1	.1
	.6	.7	.1	.1	.1	Fixed/Worth	.3	.4
	−.9	16.5	.8	NM	.9		1.0	1.1
	.5	2.2	.6	.7	.9		1.2	1.4
	9.5	4.0	1.3	1.6	1.3	Debt/Worth	2.1	2.3
	−7.0	36.3	2.5	NM	3.4		4.7	10.9
		73.3	45.2		40.1		62.0	38.9
		(16) 41.8	(24) 18.7		(19) 27.8	% Profit Before Taxes/Tangible Net Worth	(56) 25.2	(66) 15.0
		11.3	8.8		16.7		6.7	1.8
	50.4	11.1	17.6	10.2	17.6		15.1	12.3
	5.8	6.3	8.3	6.5	12.4	% Profit Before Taxes/Total Assets	6.5	4.6
	−4.6	2.1	3.4	.9	6.8		1.1	.0
	112.7	131.8	292.1	536.2	547.1		127.8	141.4
	35.0	16.9	42.4	51.0	82.8	Sales/Net Fixed Assets	34.9	26.0
	14.5	3.3	12.0	19.0	11.1		11.5	9.5
	6.8	3.6	4.0	2.8	3.1		3.8	3.9
	3.9	1.9	2.0	1.0	1.5	Sales/Total Assets	2.4	2.5
	1.0	.5	1.2	.7	1.0		1.5	1.1
	.5	.6	.4		.2		.5	.5
	(10) 1.6	(14) 2.6	(20) .9		(17) .7	% Depr., Dep., Amort./Sales	(41) 1.2	(57) 1.1
	3.4	7.0	2.8		3.1		3.6	3.2
						% Officers', Directors', Owners' Comp/Sales		
15955M	52190M	212174M	2127633M	1422600M	7752452M	Net Sales ($)	9350859M	10723212M
2146M	14383M	88330M	732099M	709999M	3698980M	Total Assets ($)	3623257M	4684062M

M = $ thousand   MM = $ million
See Pages 11 through 21 for Explanation of Ratios and Data

Comparative Historical Data | **Current Data Sorted By Sales**

			Type of Statement	0-1MM	1-3MM	3-5MM	5-10MM	10-25MM	25MM & OVER
49	53	47	Unqualified	1	2	1	1	6	36
3	4	4	Reviewed		1			2	
2	9	4	Compiled			1	2		1
2	2	5	Tax Returns				2		
23	24	37	Other	1	2	1	4	6	17
4/1/02- 3/31/03	4/1/03- 3/31/04	4/1/04- 3/31/05		15 (4/1-9/30/04)			82 (10/1/04-3/31/05)		
ALL	ALL	ALL							
79	92	97	**NUMBER OF STATEMENTS**	6	9	6	7	15	54
%	%	%	**ASSETS**	%	%	%	%	%	%
35.9	41.8	39.9	Cash & Equivalents					21.9	45.7
20.0	17.4	13.8	Trade Receivables (net)					28.0	10.7
1.4	1.5	.7	Inventory					1.1	.4
6.0	5.6	6.2	All Other Current					10.5	4.0
63.3	66.4	60.6	Total Current					61.4	60.9
11.1	12.3	14.1	Fixed Assets (net)					21.3	9.6
6.4	8.3	10.2	Intangibles (net)					2.5	11.8
19.2	13.0	15.1	All Other Non-Current					14.8	17.7
100.0	100.0	100.0	Total					100.0	100.0
			LIABILITIES						
4.0	4.4	5.5	Notes Payable-Short Term					5.9	1.9
1.3	2.0	2.0	Cur. Mat.-L/T/D					5.3	1.3
18.0	16.8	11.8	Trade Payables					11.6	13.3
.5	.4	.3	Income Taxes Payable					.0	.3
25.1	24.7	23.4	All Other Current					26.1	24.7
48.9	48.3	43.0	Total Current					48.9	41.5
9.5	10.2	9.5	Long-Term Debt					14.0	8.1
.4	.3	.4	Deferred Taxes					.1	.5
7.7	7.5	7.7	All Other Non-Current					8.5	6.9
33.4	33.8	39.5	Net Worth					28.4	43.0
100.0	100.0	100.0	Total Liabilities & Net Worth					100.0	100.0
			INCOME DATA						
100.0	100.0	100.0	Net Sales					100.0	100.0
			Gross Profit						
94.2	94.5	91.4	Operating Expenses					90.8	94.6
5.8	5.5	8.6	Operating Profit					9.2	5.4
1.1	–.3	.4	All Other Expenses (net)					.8	–.3
4.7	5.8	8.2	Profit Before Taxes					8.4	5.6
			RATIOS						
1.7	2.1	2.8						2.0	2.2
1.3	1.5	1.4	Current					1.1	1.5
1.0	1.1	1.0						.9	1.0
1.5	1.9	2.5						1.3	2.1
1.2	1.4	1.2	Quick					1.0	1.4
.8	.9	.8						.7	1.0
6 64.9	5 74.2	5 70.2						25 14.8	7 53.3
17 21.5	16 23.4	15 24.3	Sales/Receivables					41 8.8	14 25.2
41 8.9	40 9.2	43 8.6						54 6.7	31 11.8
			Cost of Sales/Inventory						
			Cost of Sales/Payables						
7.5	5.7	4.3						4.1	4.6
16.9	11.1	14.1	Sales/Working Capital					22.5	11.4
–103.7	124.7	–138.2						–57.9	241.6
14.5	34.7	25.8						28.4	38.2
(43) 7.4	(54) 11.0	(42) 9.5	EBIT/Interest				(10)	6.5 (19)	16.4
1.8	2.8	4.6						.8	5.7
7.1	16.6		Net Profit + Depr., Dep.,						
(14) 3.2	(11) 2.6		Amort./Cur. Mat. L/T/D						
1.1	1.5								
.1	.0	.0						.1	.0
.2	.3	.2	Fixed/Worth					.6	.1
.8	1.1	2.3						149.7	.7
1.3	.9	.7						1.5	.7
2.8	2.0	1.7	Debt/Worth					2.4	1.3
9.0	10.8	7.4						405.2	3.1
48.6	54.8	73.3	% Profit Before Taxes/Tangible					64.5	43.5
(72) 16.7	(81) 28.1	(82) 26.9	Net Worth				(12)	19.2 (47)	21.3
3.1	8.7	9.7						6.4	8.7
13.0	18.7	19.8	% Profit Before Taxes/Total					11.6	17.4
5.3	7.6	9.4	Assets					6.0	10.2
.7	1.9	3.0						1.6	4.8
294.7	284.2	275.4						110.2	349.7
44.3	34.5	46.2	Sales/Net Fixed Assets					18.2	65.3
16.3	12.9	12.0						3.8	12.8
4.3	4.3	4.0						3.4	4.0
2.7	2.7	2.0	Sales/Total Assets					2.1	2.3
.9	1.4	.9						.8	1.1
.5	.4	.4						.7	.3
(50) 1.2	(59) 1.3	(67) 1.3	% Depr., Dep., Amort./Sales				(12)	2.0 (37)	.7
3.7	3.4	3.1						5.2	2.3
3.4	2.0	2.2	% Officers', Directors',						
(10) 6.7	(11) 10.4	(15) 4.8	Owners' Comp/Sales						
31.1	33.0	9.9							
12259703M	14514486M	11583004M	Net Sales ($)	2094M	18127M	24647M	50509M	233249M	11254378M
4950434M	5658996M	5245937M	Total Assets ($)	7175M	15215M	17128M	18244M	230509M	4957666M

M = $ thousand   MM = $ million
See Pages 11 through 21 for Explanation of Ratios and Data

Current Data Sorted By Assets   **Comparative Historical Data**

0-500M	500M-2MM	2-10MM	10-50MM	50-100MM	100-250MM	Type of Statement	4/1/00-3/31/01 ALL	4/1/01-3/31/02 ALL
	1	4	14	4	6	Unqualified	14	13
	1	1				Reviewed	3	2
2		2	1			Compiled	8	11
	1					Tax Returns	4	3
2	1	4	7	8	7	Other	31	24
	9 (4/1-9/30/04)		57 (10/1/04-3/31/05)					
4	4	11	22	12	13	**NUMBER OF STATEMENTS**	60	53
%	%	%	%	%	%	**ASSETS**	%	%
		47.3	62.3	50.5	49.8	Cash & Equivalents	41.5	33.1
		17.4	12.2	17.7	6.9	Trade Receivables (net)	25.0	25.5
		.0	.2	.0	.0	Inventory	1.4	.9
		9.4	9.7	8.4	7.3	All Other Current	3.9	5.0
		74.2	84.2	76.7	64.1	Total Current	71.7	64.5
		3.3	3.3	.7	.8	Fixed Assets (net)	6.8	7.8
		6.2	1.1	.5	.3	Intangibles (net)	6.7	5.6
		16.3	11.4	22.1	34.8	All Other Non-Current	14.8	22.1
		100.0	100.0	100.0	100.0	Total	100.0	100.0
						LIABILITIES		
		4.7	4.1	6.0	.6	Notes Payable-Short Term	5.3	19.8
		1.8	.0	.1	.1	Cur. Mat.-L/T/D	2.7	2.6
		30.2	11.4	11.4	12.9	Trade Payables	18.5	20.7
		.0	.3	.7	.3	Income Taxes Payable	.5	.4
		24.5	30.2	36.5	40.2	All Other Current	27.7	23.5
		61.2	45.9	54.7	54.2	Total Current	54.7	67.0
		9.0	1.4	1.1	2.3	Long-Term Debt	6.7	7.3
		.3	.7	.0	.1	Deferred Taxes	.1	.1
		3.3	19.2	20.2	15.5	All Other Non-Current	9.3	13.8
		26.2	32.8	24.0	28.0	Net Worth	29.2	11.7
		100.0	100.0	100.0	100.0	Total Liabilities & Net Worth	100.0	100.0
						INCOME DATA		
		100.0	100.0	100.0	100.0	Net Sales	100.0	100.0
						Gross Profit		
		91.0	90.6	85.1	93.2	Operating Expenses	97.9	88.2
		9.0	9.4	14.9	6.8	Operating Profit	2.1	11.8
		−.3	−4.4	3.8	−2.6	All Other Expenses (net)	−6.3	1.4
		9.3	13.8	11.0	9.3	Profit Before Taxes	8.4	10.5
						RATIOS		
		1.6	3.4	2.2	1.4	Current	1.9	1.7
		1.1	1.7	1.5	1.2		1.5	1.2
		1.0	1.2	.8	.9		1.0	.8
		1.4	2.2	2.2	1.3	Quick	1.7	1.6
		1.1	1.5	1.4	1.2		1.3	1.2
		.9	1.2	.8	.7		.9	.7
		0 UND	12 29.6	1 385.7	0 UND	Sales/Receivables	25 14.6	22 16.6
		15 24.8	51 7.1	34 10.7	55 6.7		55 6.6	66 5.5
		95 3.8	89 4.1	184 2.0	142 2.6		115 3.2	149 2.5
						Cost of Sales/Inventory		
						Cost of Sales/Payables		
		2.0	.7	1.2	1.3	Sales/Working Capital	1.0	1.9
		19.4	2.2	2.0	2.3		2.8	11.8
		−20.9	7.0	−8.4	−13.5		−96.1	−9.4
						EBIT/Interest	9.5	31.7
							(22) 3.8	(25) 9.1
							1.0	3.0
						Net Profit + Depr., Dep., Amort./Cur. Mat. L./T/D		
		.0	.0	.0	.0	Fixed/Worth	.0	.0
		.0	.0	.0	.0		.0	.1
		.2	.2	.1	.0		.6	.4
		2.4	1.1	1.7	2.0	Debt/Worth	1.2	1.8
		3.9	1.6	4.1	2.2		2.2	2.9
		18.7	3.4	NM	7.3		14.7	11.7
		101.5	59.3		17.2	% Profit Before Taxes/Tangible Net Worth	29.9	47.4
	(10) 26.9		(21) 21.9		14.6		(48) 10.9	(44) 22.4
		9.9	7.0		6.0		−1.1	1.4
		7.5	17.2	12.1	4.8	% Profit Before Taxes/Total Assets	12.8	13.9
		3.9	6.9	4.3	3.4		3.7	6.6
		2.5	3.7	−.2	1.3		.1	1.0
		UND	UND	UND	UND	Sales/Net Fixed Assets	UND	264.0
		77.8	127.2	198.4	126.1		98.7	40.9
		16.0	21.3	34.7	32.1		15.6	14.0
		1.2	1.0	.7	.4	Sales/Total Assets	1.3	1.3
		.7	.7	.6	.4		.6	.7
		.3	.5	.4	.2		.4	.5
			.6			% Depr., Dep., Amort./Sales	.9	1.0
		(10)	1.6				(24) 1.8	(23) 1.7
			4.6				3.7	3.6
						% Officers', Directors', Owners' Comp/Sales	9.7	
							(13) 14.2	
							19.1	
3916M	8561M	50453M	399151M	531142M	637335M	Net Sales ($)	1670107M	2164607M
691M	6603M	62725M	583250M	910496M	1961864M	Total Assets ($)	2839553M	2999793M

© RMA 2005

M = $ thousand   MM = $ million
See Pages 11 through 21 for Explanation of Ratios and Data

Comparative Historical Data | Current Data Sorted By Sales

			Type of Statement						
16	13	29	Unqualified		5	1	3	8	12
2	5	2	Reviewed		1	1			
6	11	5	Compiled	1	1	2		1	
	6	1	Tax Returns		1				
26	23	29	Other	1	3	2	2	5	16
4/1/02-	4/1/03-	4/1/04-			9 (4/1-9/30/04)			57 (10/1/04-3/31/05)	
3/31/03	3/31/04	3/31/05							
ALL	ALL	ALL		0-1MM	1-3MM	3-5MM	5-10MM	10-25MM	25MM & OVER
50	58	66	NUMBER OF STATEMENTS	2	11	6	5	14	28
%	%	%	ASSETS	%	%	%	%	%	%
38.5	35.3	51.9	Cash & Equivalents		56.2			54.5	53.9
21.7	21.3	13.2	Trade Receivables (net)		5.5			13.6	12.3
.2	.0	.1	Inventory		.0			.0	.1
8.3	9.9	8.1	All Other Current		9.2			11.8	6.9
68.6	66.6	73.3	Total Current		70.9			79.9	73.2
6.6	6.8	4.9	Fixed Assets (net)		12.9			1.1	2.7
5.8	7.1	2.9	Intangibles (net)		8.4			.0	1.1
19.0	19.5	19.0	All Other Non-Current		7.9			18.9	23.0
100.0	100.0	100.0	Total		100.0			100.0	100.0
			LIABILITIES						
5.8	6.4	4.2	Notes Payable-Short Term		4.2			5.5	3.3
.6	3.5	.7	Cur. Mat.-L/T/D		.0			.0	.1
21.7	15.8	15.0	Trade Payables		13.8			10.2	14.4
.2	.4	.3	Income Taxes Payable		.0			.3	.5
24.5	33.9	30.5	All Other Current		27.1			32.2	34.8
53.0	60.0	50.7	Total Current		45.0			48.3	53.1
6.6	4.7	4.5	Long-Term Debt		8.3			.2	2.0
.0	.0	.3	Deferred Taxes		.0			.1	.5
13.1	11.0	14.1	All Other Non-Current		3.2			12.6	22.9
27.3	24.3	30.4	Net Worth		43.5			38.8	21.6
100.0	100.0	100.0	Total Liabilities & Net Worth		100.0			100.0	100.0
			INCOME DATA						
100.0	100.0	100.0	Net Sales		100.0			100.0	100.0
			Gross Profit						
93.9	93.2	89.5	Operating Expenses		90.1			77.5	91.7
6.1	6.8	10.5	Operating Profit		9.9			22.5	8.3
.1	-1.3	-1.2	All Other Expenses (net)		-1.4			-1.5	-.9
6.0	8.1	11.7	Profit Before Taxes		11.3			24.0	9.2
			RATIOS						
2.2	1.6	1.9			1.9			4.7	1.8
1.3	1.2	1.4	Current		1.5			1.5	1.3
.9	.8	1.1			1.3			1.1	.9
1.6	1.4	1.7			1.7			3.2	1.7
1.2	1.0	1.3	Quick		1.4			1.4	1.2
.7	.6	1.0			1.2			1.1	.9
20 18.1	10 37.0	0 UND		0 UND			0 UND	1 385.7	
58 6.3	48 7.6	32 11.3	Sales/Receivables	15 24.8			25 14.6	39 9.3	
136 2.7	97 3.7	93 3.9		48 7.6			75 4.9	146 2.5	
			Cost of Sales/Inventory						
			Cost of Sales/Payables						
1.6	2.0	1.3			.4			.7	1.5
7.0	17.3	3.2	Sales/Working Capital		3.6			2.2	2.8
-13.7	-15.4	34.9			18.0			9.6	-129.5
20.2	27.1	26.5							55.6
(25) 7.1	(32) 13.9	(25) 15.0	EBIT/Interest					(11) 18.9	
2.1	5.4	4.2							14.4
			Net Profit + Depr., Dep., Amort./Cur. Mat. L/T/D						
.0	.0	.0			.0			.0	.0
.1	.1	.0	Fixed/Worth		.1			.0	.0
.5	.7	.2			.7			.1	.4
1.9	1.7	1.2			.7			1.1	2.0
3.2	2.7	2.2	Debt/Worth		1.5			1.6	2.9
7.3	15.4	5.5			2.6			4.0	7.9
42.7	58.4	56.0			113.3			61.1	47.2
(45) 17.9	(48) 22.1	(60) 18.0	% Profit Before Taxes/Tangible Net Worth	(10) 17.5			31.2	(24) 17.2	
.9	9.9	9.9			6.9			11.6	13.7
9.0	13.6	11.8			40.1			19.5	11.2
3.7	6.0	5.2	% Profit Before Taxes/Total Assets		6.5			7.0	4.8
.5	1.8	2.9			2.8			3.2	2.9
313.3	219.2	UND			UND			UND	700.7
26.9	50.8	100.4	Sales/Net Fixed Assets		77.8			127.2	109.7
11.1	19.5	21.3			8.1			29.7	31.5
.9	1.6	1.0			2.3			.9	.9
.6	.9	.6	Sales/Total Assets		.7			.5	.6
.4	.5	.4			.3			.3	.4
.6	.5	.5							.4
(24) 1.8	(28) 1.2	(26) .9	% Depr., Dep., Amort./Sales					(14) .7	
3.0	3.2	2.7							2.8
		11.2							
	(14) 16.4		% Officers', Directors', Owners' Comp/Sales						
		30.9							
1676326M	1466964M	1630558M	Net Sales ($)	1311M	19208M	24496M	39754M	217509M	1328280M
2734355M	2667977M	3525629M	Total Assets ($)	123M	66436M	31880M	157480M	595371M	2674339M

M = $ thousand   MM = $ million
See Pages 11 through 21 for Explanation of Ratios and Data

FINANCE—Direct Title Insurance Carriers NAICS 524127 (SIC 6361)

Current Data Sorted By Assets   **Comparative Historical Data**

	0-500M	500M-2MM	2-10MM	10-50MM	50-100MM	100-250MM	4/1/00-3/31/01 ALL	4/1/01-3/31/02 ALL
Type of Statement								
Unqualified	1	1	8	10	3	1	8	10
Reviewed			4				4	1
Compiled	1	2	1	1			3	8
Tax Returns	9	3	1				4	9
Other	6	8	3	4	5	6	20	12
		2 (4/1-9/30/04)		75 (10/1/04-3/31/05)				
NUMBER OF STATEMENTS	17	14	17	14	8	7	39	40
ASSETS (%)	%	%	%	%	%	%	%	%
Cash & Equivalents	42.5	33.9	29.1	36.3			33.0	32.4
Trade Receivables (net)	4.0	9.7	10.4	3.9			3.5	6.8
Inventory	.0	.1	.3	.7			1.3	1.5
All Other Current	9.2	8.4	14.9	10.2			6.7	9.9
Total Current	55.6	52.0	54.7	51.0			44.6	50.5
Fixed Assets (net)	25.0	28.8	17.5	14.2			26.5	22.7
Intangibles (net)	.0	3.9	4.6	5.9			10.1	10.0
All Other Non-Current	19.4	15.3	23.2	28.9			18.8	16.8
Total	100.0	100.0	100.0	100.0			100.0	100.0
LIABILITIES								
Notes Payable-Short Term	14.0	9.8	8.8	6.3			4.4	2.8
Cur. Mat.-L/T/D	3.7	1.6	1.9	1.1			4.2	4.1
Trade Payables	3.2	4.9	17.0	11.2			6.5	8.9
Income Taxes Payable	.4	.2	.1	1.7			.2	.3
All Other Current	58.1	17.2	25.5	20.2			19.6	23.4
Total Current	79.4	33.7	53.2	40.5			35.0	39.4
Long-Term Debt	17.9	21.8	14.9	9.1			21.3	21.4
Deferred Taxes	.0	1.0	.5	.9			.2	.4
All Other Non-Current	7.2	4.5	6.0	2.6			9.0	7.5
Net Worth	-4.4	39.0	25.3	47.0			34.5	31.3
Total Liabilities & Net Worth	100.0	100.0	100.0	100.0			100.0	100.0
INCOME DATA								
Net Sales	100.0	100.0	100.0	100.0			100.0	100.0
Gross Profit								
Operating Expenses	87.3	86.2	95.7	89.0			101.3	91.2
Operating Profit	12.7	13.8	4.3	11.0			-1.3	8.8
All Other Expenses (net)	-.2	-.4	.2	.5			-1.3	1.3
Profit Before Taxes	13.0	14.2	4.0	10.4			.0	7.5
RATIOS								
Current	4.4	4.8	1.4	1.9			2.0	1.8
	1.3	1.8	1.1	1.4			1.5	1.4
	.5	1.2	.7	.9			1.1	.9
Quick	3.7	4.8	1.2	1.7			1.9	1.4
	1.2	1.7	1.0	1.3			(38) 1.3	(39) 1.1
	.2	1.0	.4	.5			.7	.7
Sales/Receivables	0 UND	0 UND	2 230.9	3 142.6			0 UND	0 UND
	0 UND	4 92.5	5 72.0	5 72.1			6 64.8	3 136.1
	2 238.9	7 51.2	20 18.5	14 26.8			10 37.4	31 11.9
Cost of Sales/Inventory								
Cost of Sales/Payables								
Sales/Working Capital	8.4	7.9	8.0	6.0			5.6	4.2
	47.3	21.7	48.9	23.1			14.0	29.8
	-102.6	135.1	-35.9	-51.1			85.5	-41.6
EBIT/Interest	127.8		12.7				5.8	19.9
	(10) 53.5		(11) 6.5				(28) 1.0	(30) 4.0
	9.0		-3.0				-.2	.8
Net Profit + Depr., Dep., Amort./Cur. Mat. L /T/D							3.7	
							(11) 1.8	
							-1.5	
Fixed/Worth	.0	.2	.3	.1			.2	.2
	.3	.7	.8	.4			.7	.6
	NM	NM	-2.2	.7			6.9	6.4
Debt/Worth	.4	.3	1.0	.6			.8	1.0
	1.4	.9	3.4	1.2			1.8	1.8
	-4.6	NM	-13.8	4.6			7.4	40.9
% Profit Before Taxes/Tangible Net Worth	704.4	182.3	87.7	72.4			24.6	69.6
	(12) 120.1	(11) 103.7	(11) 37.1	(13) 23.6			(30) 4.2	(31) 16.6
	54.0	3.6	-30.5	7.6			-18.9	.0
% Profit Before Taxes/Total Assets	224.0	116.6	32.8	33.7			10.3	34.6
	66.8	31.1	11.6	14.5			1.9	8.1
	1.6	1.4	-.9	1.9			-5.3	-.4
Sales/Net Fixed Assets	UND	54.2	33.2	35.1			17.2	47.8
	31.9	17.2	21.8	17.4			8.9	15.6
	14.6	8.1	8.9	8.6			3.6	4.6
Sales/Total Assets	10.9	6.2	4.0	3.3			2.1	3.3
	6.2	4.5	2.2	1.5			1.8	1.3
	2.8	2.8	.9	.6			.8	.9
% Depr., Dep., Amort./Sales		.6	1.0				2.0	.8
		(10) 1.3	(14) 1.6				(30) 3.0	(28) 2.3
		2.4	2.2				4.1	4.4
% Officers', Directors', Owners' Comp/Sales								5.2
								(18) 9.9
								34.2
Net Sales ($)	15352M	61837M	242875M	807051M	1218730M	1722421M	867520M	907832M
Total Assets ($)	3128M	13619M	81112M	354319M	539097M	925249M	595951M	844267M

M = $ thousand   MM = $ million

See Pages 11 through 21 for Explanation of Ratios and Data

Comparative Historical Data   Current Data Sorted By Sales

4/1/02-3/31/03 ALL	4/1/03-3/31/04 ALL	4/1/04-3/31/05 ALL	Type of Statement	0-1MM	1-3MM	3-5MM	5-10MM	10-25MM	25MM & OVER
32	18	24	Unqualified	1	2	2	1	5	13
1	1	4	Reviewed				2	2	
6	7	4	Compiled		1	1	2		
10	6	13	Tax Returns	6	6	1			
23	33	32	Other	5	7	1	3	2	14
				2 (4/1-9/30/04)		75 (10/1/04-3/31/05)			
72	65	77	**NUMBER OF STATEMENTS**	12	16	5	8	9	27
%	%	%	**ASSETS**	%	%	%	%	%	%
41.8	37.2	36.6	Cash & Equivalents	31.0	34.4				43.3
6.8	7.0	6.3	Trade Receivables (net)	.9	4.2				4.3
1.4	.5	.2	Inventory	.0	.6				.0
6.0	7.8	10.1	All Other Current	12.7	19.4				5.8
56.0	52.5	53.2	Total Current	44.6	58.6				53.4
22.8	19.2	20.3	Fixed Assets (net)	30.8	16.6				18.2
4.5	5.2	5.6	Intangibles (net)	.0	4.8				10.9
16.7	23.0	20.9	All Other Non-Current	24.7	20.1				17.5
100.0	100.0	100.0	Total	100.0	100.0				100.0
			LIABILITIES						
2.2	8.2	10.0	Notes Payable-Short Term	18.9	7.0				6.3
2.5	3.2	1.9	Cur. Mat.-L/T/D	5.2	.3				1.3
9.4	9.4	8.7	Trade Payables	3.9	1.2				9.3
1.1	1.1	.6	Income Taxes Payable	.5	.2				1.2
21.1	23.3	28.5	All Other Current	70.8	28.2				19.3
36.3	45.3	49.7	Total Current	99.3	36.9				37.5
13.3	7.6	14.3	Long-Term Debt	23.2	9.9				5.4
.5	.6	.5	Deferred Taxes	.0	.1				.4
4.7	6.0	6.7	All Other Non-Current	11.3	.5				9.1
45.2	40.5	28.8	Net Worth	-33.7	52.6				47.6
100.0	100.0	100.0	Total Liabilities & Net Worth	100.0	100.0				100.0
			INCOME DATA						
100.0	100.0	100.0	Net Sales	100.0	100.0				100.0
			Gross Profit						
87.3	83.6	90.1	Operating Expenses	98.5	77.6				91.4
12.7	16.4	9.9	Operating Profit	1.5	22.4				8.6
-.2	1.5	-.1	All Other Expenses (net)	.9	.4				-.6
12.9	15.0	10.0	Profit Before Taxes	.6	22.0				9.2
			RATIOS						
2.9	2.0	2.7		4.0	4.9				2.3
1.6	1.4	1.3	Current	.8	1.8				1.5
1.0	.8	1.0		.2	1.2				1.1
2.5	1.8	2.1		3.0	4.5				2.1
(71) 1.3	1.1	1.3	Quick	.4	1.5				1.4
.7	.6	.6		.0	.5				.9
0 UND	0 UND	0 UND		0 UND	0 UND				1 266.4
5 75.5	4 81.7	4 87.6	Sales/Receivables	0 UND	4 81.6				5 72.0
12 30.2	11 34.3	11 33.0		0 UND	6 58.5				11 32.1
			Cost of Sales/Inventory						
			Cost of Sales/Payables						
5.4	7.6	7.0		10.4	4.6				6.4
12.9	28.3	24.6	Sales/Working Capital	UND	15.3				19.7
250.5	-57.8	-282.5		-6.6	43.5				83.0
48.8	66.6	102.0			62.3				177.8
(41) 15.8	(40) 18.5	(50) 19.4	EBIT/Interest		(11) 60.2			(16)	37.1
2.7	4.5	6.3			5.5				14.3
16.0	22.6	21.0	Net Profit + Depr., Dep.,						
(15) 2.9	(15) 10.3	(13) 6.0	Amort./Cur. Mat. L/T/D						
1.7	3.9	1.6							
.1	.1	.2		.2	.0				.3
.4	.6	.6	Fixed/Worth	1.8	.2				.5
.9	1.3	1.9		-.6	1.0				.8
.5	.6	.6		.6	.3				.7
1.1	1.5	1.5	Debt/Worth	NM	.7				1.5
4.3	4.1	36.1		-2.4	5.4				2.9
117.7	106.6	92.0			211.1				73.4
(64) 59.0	(57) 61.8	(59) 42.7	% Profit Before Taxes/Tangible Net Worth		(15) 87.4			(23)	34.2
21.2	31.6	16.3			4.4				19.6
49.2	50.5	43.8		92.9	157.5				33.2
17.7	26.1	17.8	% Profit Before Taxes/Total Assets	13.9	39.2				18.2
6.0	8.1	2.5		-5.7	4.0				9.8
37.1	42.6	38.7		123.8	204.3				26.7
14.8	19.4	17.4	Sales/Net Fixed Assets	25.3	20.6				16.9
8.0	11.1	9.4		9.7	8.3				9.9
3.9	5.2	5.1		10.1	5.0				3.2
2.5	2.7	2.7	Sales/Total Assets	6.0	2.8				2.3
1.5	1.5	1.3		1.3	.7				1.5
.9	.9	1.1							1.1
(58) 1.5	(45) 1.3	(51) 1.6	% Depr., Dep., Amort./Sales					(18)	1.5
2.1	1.9	2.8							2.4
4.7	3.9	4.8							
(21) 15.1	(12) 9.8	(20) 11.4	% Officers', Directors', Owners' Comp/Sales						
33.1	20.3	23.8							
1648101M	3024670M	4068266M	Net Sales ($)	7563M	25409M	20226M	60627M	132006M	3822435M
964655M	1311922M	1916524M	Total Assets ($)	4625M	42001M	16287M	47893M	47983M	1757735M

M = $ thousand   MM = $ million
See Pages 11 through 21 for Explanation of Ratios and Data

Current Data Sorted By Assets · **Comparative Historical Data**

						Type of Statement		
	1	6	8	4	10	Unqualified	11	11
	1	2				Reviewed	2	
	1	1				Compiled	10	6
	2	1				Tax Returns	3	2
4	2	10	5	5	2	Other	17	15
	5 (4/1-9/30/04)			60 (10/1/04-3/31/05)			4/1/00-3/31/01	4/1/01-3/31/02
0-500M	500M-2MM	2-10MM	10-50MM	50-100MM	100-250MM		ALL	ALL
4	7	20	13	9	12	NUMBER OF STATEMENTS	43	34
%	%	%	%	%	%	**ASSETS**	%	%
		35.3	45.7		38.9	Cash & Equivalents	36.5	35.5
		24.2	10.4		19.8	Trade Receivables (net)	19.8	19.2
		.2	3.4		.1	Inventory	.1	.6
		5.8	3.0		18.5	All Other Current	8.0	9.1
		65.5	62.5		77.2	Total Current	64.4	64.5
		6.1	1.5		5.0	Fixed Assets (net)	9.9	10.1
		4.3	2.3		.5	Intangibles (net)	8.1	5.5
		24.2	33.7		17.4	All Other Non-Current	17.6	19.8
		100.0	100.0		100.0	Total	100.0	100.0
						LIABILITIES		
		5.2	.4		.0	Notes Payable-Short Term	3.0	3.3
		.8	.2		1.1	Cur. Mat.-L/T/D	3.3	1.8
		28.0	7.3		9.7	Trade Payables	22.1	27.8
		.6	.1		.3	Income Taxes Payable	.7	1.1
		28.5	36.6		35.9	All Other Current	22.7	27.9
		63.1	44.6		47.0	Total Current	51.8	61.9
		11.9	5.0		8.8	Long-Term Debt	12.6	13.4
		.0	.1		.6	Deferred Taxes	.2	.4
		17.0	21.0		13.3	All Other Non-Current	12.2	7.5
		8.0	29.4		30.2	Net Worth	23.2	16.9
		100.0	100.0		100.0	Total Liabilities & Net Worth	100.0	100.0
						INCOME DATA		
		100.0	100.0		100.0	Net Sales	100.0	100.0
						Gross Profit		
		89.8	84.6		87.1	Operating Expenses	91.6	90.2
		10.2	15.4		12.9	Operating Profit	8.4	9.8
		.2	.2		1.1	All Other Expenses (net)	-3.7	.1
		9.9	15.2		11.8	Profit Before Taxes	12.1	9.7
						RATIOS		
		5.2	9.6		2.5		2.0	1.7
		1.0	1.6		1.5	Current	1.2	1.1
		.7	1.0		1.2		.9	.7
		5.2	8.8		2.4		1.3	1.3
		1.0	1.6		1.3	Quick	1.0	.8
		.7	.6		.4		.7	.5
		0 UND	1 532.3		0 UND		0 UND	2 181.7
		38 9.6	42 8.7		44 8.4	Sales/Receivables	60 6.1	39 9.4
		117 3.1	94 3.9		78 4.7		131 2.8	81 4.5
						Cost of Sales/Inventory		
						Cost of Sales/Payables		
		2.4	.8		.4		3.9	4.0
		NM	3.3		1.5	Sales/Working Capital	14.0	33.8
		-4.2	-24.1		7.6		-15.1	-8.0
		57.2					7.2	14.0
		(12) 12.7				EBIT/Interest	(19) 2.9	(17) 5.6
		1.1					1.6	2.7
						Net Profit + Depr., Dep., Amort./Cur. Mat. L/T/D		
		.0	.0		.0		.0	.0
		.3	.1		.1	Fixed/Worth	.2	.3
		NM	NM		.2		37.5	2.8
		1.4	1.2		1.3		1.3	1.2
		4.3	2.6		3.4	Debt/Worth	4.7	3.4
		-4.0	NM		9.6		-72.4	-6.3
		108.7	51.2		57.5		78.2	75.1
		(14) 22.6	(10) 27.4		17.8	% Profit Before Taxes/Tangible Net Worth	(32) 40.1	(24) 18.5
		5.1	10.0		3.7		7.1	6.5
		16.7	11.4		9.5		9.5	10.7
		5.1	3.6		2.8	% Profit Before Taxes/Total Assets	5.0	6.4
		.1	1.6		1.2		1.3	2.4
		UND	UND		149.8		308.0	UND
		96.1	75.0		23.6	Sales/Net Fixed Assets	29.1	18.0
		22.6	25.6		12.8		11.4	10.9
		2.0	1.1		1.6		1.5	2.0
		.7	.7		.3	Sales/Total Assets	.6	.6
		.5	.2		.2		.3	.3
							.7	1.5
						% Depr., Dep., Amort./Sales	(26) 1.3	(20) 2.9
							2.9	5.8
						% Officers', Directors', Owners' Comp/Sales		
4267M	9720M	202936M	210763M	437075M	1569031M	Net Sales ($)	836793M	716632M
834M	5597M	111912M	301393M	600039M	2205615M	Total Assets ($)	1392036M	1230033M

M = $ thousand   MM = $ million
See Pages 11 through 21 for Explanation of Ratios and Data

Comparative Historical Data   **Current Data Sorted By Sales**

Type of Statement									
Unqualified	25	25	29	1	4	3	5	6	10
Reviewed		4	3		1	1		1	
Compiled	5	5	2	1		1			
Tax Returns	1	9	3	1	1		1		
Other	25	24	28	5	4	3		4	11
	4/1/02-3/31/03 ALL	4/1/03-3/31/04 ALL	4/1/04-3/31/05 ALL	5 (4/1-9/30/04) 0-1MM	1-3MM	3-5MM	60 (10/1/04-3/31/05) 5-10MM	10-25MM	25MM & OVER
NUMBER OF STATEMENTS	56	67	65	8	10	8	7	11	21
ASSETS	%	%	%	%	%	%	%	%	%
Cash & Equivalents	42.3	40.6	39.1		42.4			40.1	43.0
Trade Receivables (net)	20.4	16.6	16.5		8.3			9.6	21.1
Inventory	.2	.0	.8		.0			.0	.2
All Other Current	8.4	12.2	7.4		9.6			10.2	11.0
Total Current	71.3	69.5	63.7		60.2			60.0	75.3
Fixed Assets (net)	8.8	9.3	8.4		10.8			2.1	6.4
Intangibles (net)	5.2	1.8	3.4		2.9			3.4	2.1
All Other Non-Current	14.7	19.3	24.4		26.0			34.4	16.3
Total	100.0	100.0	100.0		100.0			100.0	100.0
LIABILITIES									
Notes Payable-Short Term	2.6	4.6	3.9		7.1			.5	.0
Cur. Mat.-L/T/D	2.1	2.0	1.0		1.3			.1	1.0
Trade Payables	19.1	20.0	16.3		15.4			4.0	10.8
Income Taxes Payable	.9	1.0	.3		.4			.1	.5
All Other Current	43.4	29.3	30.5		18.1			50.8	35.9
Total Current	68.1	56.8	52.0		42.2			55.4	48.1
Long-Term Debt	8.6	8.6	9.5		8.7			13.0	8.9
Deferred Taxes	.2	.0	.1		.1			.0	.4
All Other Non-Current	6.0	10.2	17.0		24.1			14.7	18.0
Net Worth	17.1	24.4	21.4		24.9			16.9	24.6
Total Liabilities & Net Worth	100.0	100.0	100.0		100.0			100.0	100.0
INCOME DATA									
Net Sales	100.0	100.0	100.0		100.0			100.0	100.0
Gross Profit									
Operating Expenses	86.5	89.0	87.5		81.8			80.2	95.4
Operating Profit	13.5	11.0	12.5		18.2			19.8	4.6
All Other Expenses (net)	1.8	1.2	2.4		.6			11.4	-1.1
Profit Before Taxes	11.7	9.8	10.1		17.6			8.5	5.7
RATIOS									
Current	1.8	2.1	2.6		22.3			5.1	2.6
	1.1	1.3	1.4		7.9			1.5	1.6
	.8	.8	.8		.6			.5	1.1
Quick	1.6	2.0	2.4		21.3			3.9	2.4
	1.0	1.1	1.2		7.6			1.0	1.5
	.5	.5	.7		.6			.4	1.0
Sales/Receivables	0 787.0	2 216.0	0 898.7		0 UND			4 83.5	2 148.7
	40 9.2	22 16.4	23 16.1		0 UND			17 21.0	35 10.3
	127 2.9	100 3.7	81 4.5		13 27.1			49 7.5	71 5.2
Cost of Sales/Inventory									
Cost of Sales/Payables									
Sales/Working Capital	2.1	1.6	1.3		.5			1.3	1.2
	8.7	10.9	8.7		12.8			3.3	4.2
	-8.9	-7.8	-17.7		-21.8			-2.0	53.0
EBIT/Interest	(23) 24.9	(31) 38.6	(36) 39.5						56.7
	3.3	7.2	8.1					(10)	19.4
	1.3	2.2	1.6						2.1
Net Profit + Depr., Dep., Amort./Cur. Mat. L/T/D									
Fixed/Worth	.0	.0	.0		.0			.0	.0
	.2	.1	.1		.4			.1	.1
	2.6	.6	1.5		-6.7			-1.0	.3
Debt/Worth	1.3	1.1	1.2		.9			.2	1.9
	2.9	2.9	3.6		3.7			1.4	4.1
	116.5	13.0	85.1		-14.9			-17.7	23.1
% Profit Before Taxes/Tangible Net Worth	(44) 83.4	(56) 45.4	(51) 51.9						50.9
	22.3	18.6	15.8					(18)	17.8
	4.4	4.4	4.7						5.1
% Profit Before Taxes/Total Assets	15.2	12.3	10.2		9.2			14.6	9.2
	5.6	3.9	2.6		2.8			2.8	2.3
	1.3	.7	.9		1.3			.0	.5
Sales/Net Fixed Assets	899.4	UND	UND		UND			UND	151.9
	28.1	43.5	44.4		91.7			37.0	42.0
	13.6	16.5	16.1		19.1			11.3	16.4
Sales/Total Assets	1.8	2.1	1.6		4.5			1.3	2.0
	.6	.6	.7		.5			.7	.7
	.4	.4	.3		.1			.2	.4
% Depr., Dep., Amort./Sales	(29) .6	(30) 1.0	(31) .9						.4
	1.8	1.8	1.3					(12)	1.0
	2.4	3.5	3.2						2.3
% Officers', Directors', Owners' Comp/Sales		6.9							
		(18) 14.5							
		27.2							
Net Sales ($)	1639878M	2284991M	2433792M	3425M	17768M	33552M	49252M	187503M	2142292M
Total Assets ($)	2254791M	3174501M	3225390M	8996M	52280M	57153M	144796M	612966M	2349199M

© RMA 2005

M = $ thousand   MM = $ million
See Pages 11 through 21 for Explanation of Ratios and Data

Current Data Sorted By Assets | Comparative Historical Data

						Type of Statement		
1	4	42	45	10	14	Unqualified	81	78
13	32	53	17	2		Reviewed	113	93
26	55	47	3			Compiled	148	160
127	75	15	4	1	2	Tax Returns	117	123
45	58	67	41	7	12	Other	170	212
	131 (4/1-9/30/04)		687 (10/1/04-3/31/05)				4/1/00-3/31/01	4/1/01-3/31/02
0-500M	500M-2MM	2-10MM	10-50MM	50-100MM	100-250MM		ALL	ALL
212	224	224	110	20	28	NUMBER OF STATEMENTS	629	666
%	%	%	%	%	%	ASSETS	%	%
31.6	22.9	34.4	29.5	38.8	40.9	Cash & Equivalents	26.0	26.3
11.1	20.1	25.4	25.1	29.8	16.5	Trade Receivables (net)	25.1	23.6
.0	.5	.2	.3	.0	.1	Inventory	.8	.4
5.2	4.3	4.6	7.4	1.8	9.8	All Other Current	4.8	4.6
47.9	47.7	64.7	62.2	70.5	67.2	Total Current	56.6	54.9
21.3	13.8	11.0	7.8	4.6	5.0	Fixed Assets (net)	15.1	14.8
14.8	23.1	10.9	14.3	13.1	15.9	Intangibles (net)	12.5	15.6
16.0	15.4	13.4	15.7	11.8	11.9	All Other Non-Current	15.7	14.6
100.0	100.0	100.0	100.0	100.0	100.0	Total	100.0	100.0
						LIABILITIES		
18.1	8.8	6.3	7.2	1.9	4.7	Notes Payable-Short Term	15.6	11.8
5.8	5.8	2.4	1.8	4.4	2.9	Cur. Mat.-L/T/D	4.4	5.2
16.0	21.2	30.6	25.1	34.5	12.1	Trade Payables	26.1	26.8
.3	.1	.3	.6	1.2	.4	Income Taxes Payable	.4	.3
18.6	13.0	19.8	23.4	21.4	31.8	All Other Current	18.1	18.2
58.7	49.0	59.5	58.1	63.4	51.8	Total Current	64.6	62.3
33.1	27.2	11.7	8.3	8.9	8.1	Long-Term Debt	19.4	21.6
.1	.5	.4	.5	.1	.5	Deferred Taxes	.5	.4
8.3	5.2	5.2	6.1	5.6	20.5	All Other Non-Current	9.5	7.1
-.2	18.2	23.2	27.0	21.9	19.1	Net Worth	5.9	8.5
100.0	100.0	100.0	100.0	100.0	100.0	Total Liabilities & Net Worth	100.0	100.0
						INCOME DATA		
100.0	100.0	100.0	100.0	100.0	100.0	Net Sales	100.0	100.0
						Gross Profit		
89.9	87.3	88.9	87.0	87.2	89.4	Operating Expenses	90.9	89.9
10.1	12.7	11.1	13.0	12.8	10.6	Operating Profit	9.1	10.1
.8	2.1	1.4	-.2	1.0	2.7	All Other Expenses (net)	1.1	1.5
9.3	10.6	9.7	13.2	11.8	7.9	Profit Before Taxes	8.0	8.5
						RATIOS		
2.8	1.6	1.4	1.4	1.4	3.1		1.4	1.4
.9	1.0	1.1	1.1	1.1	1.3	Current	1.0	1.0
.3	.5	.8	.9	.9	.9		.7	.6
2.5	1.4	1.3	1.2	1.4	2.2		1.3	1.2
.8	.9	1.0	1.0	1.1	1.2	Quick	.9	.9
.3	.4	.8	.7	.8	.8		(628) .5	.5

																Sales/Receivables				
0	UND	0	UND	12	31.1	18	20.1	51	7.2	15	23.6		3	112.0	2	185.9
0	UND	18	20.1	47	7.7	62	5.9	107	3.4	55	6.6		40	9.1	33	11.0
13	27.5	59	6.2	108	3.4	140	2.6	173	2.1	117	3.1		113	3.2	105	3.5

| | | | | | | | | | | | | | Cost of Sales/Inventory | | | |

| | | | | | | | | | | | | | Cost of Sales/Payables | | | |

22.5		10.7		6.6		5.0		6.7		1.0		Sales/Working Capital		8.6		10.6
-127.2		-317.2		37.7		22.1		26.8		3.7				-222.0		-213.2
-15.2		-8.0		-17.2		-21.6		-22.4		NM				-9.7		-8.9

												EBIT/Interest		
	20.9		18.4		27.1		57.9		63.5		18.3		11.8	13.6
(148)	6.2	(182)	5.6	(172)	8.8	(73) 19.7	(15) 9.8	(18) 5.7		(482)	4.1	(525)	4.9
	1.0		1.8		3.4		3.6		2.6		2.2		1.6	2.0

												Net Profit + Depr., Dep., Amort./Cur. Mat. L /T/D		
	6.6		4.5		4.9		10.0						5.5	5.0
(10)	2.4	(33)	1.5	(49)	2.5	(24) 5.5				(111)	1.8	(112)	1.7
	.8		.7		1.5		1.5						1.0	.9

												Fixed/Worth		
.2		.1		.2		.1		.1		.0			.2	.2
1.5		1.3		.6		.3		.3		.1			.9	1.2
-.4		-.3		165.3		3.9		NM		-1.1			-1.2	-.5

												Debt/Worth		
.8		1.6		2.4		2.1		2.4		2.6			1.8	1.9
22.0		11.1		7.4		5.2		10.5		5.3			7.5	11.1
-2.6		-2.5		-73.4		88.9		-29.0		-109.1			-8.3	-4.0

												% Profit Before Taxes/Tangible Net Worth		
	212.9		93.9		124.5		90.2		158.5		19.3		80.9	122.4
(113)	67.5	(127)	35.3	(164)	47.1	(86) 35.7	(14) 57.5	(20) 13.0		(418)	29.3	(410)	38.1
	15.5		11.8		15.0		12.2		6.1		7.7		9.4	10.9

												% Profit Before Taxes/Total Assets		
67.3		23.9		16.7		18.2		15.5		7.1			15.9	18.4
16.0		9.1		7.5		7.4		8.5		3.2			5.8	6.6
.0		2.8		2.3		2.1		3.3		.5			1.2	1.7

												Sales/Net Fixed Assets		
195.3		100.2		60.2		67.2		719.3		891.2			45.3	54.0
42.9		33.8		26.0		26.6		18.4		28.8			19.8	21.8
17.0		13.0		11.4		11.4		12.1		11.1			9.1	10.1

												Sales/Total Assets		
10.7		2.9		1.8		1.5		1.0		.8			2.5	2.9
4.7		1.8		1.2		.9		.8		.4			1.3	1.4
2.4		1.0		.7		.5		.6		.3			.8	.8

												% Depr., Dep., Amort./Sales		
	.6		.9		.9		.9		.8		.5		1.1	.9
(116)	1.5	(137)	1.8	(164)	1.8	(76) 1.8	(14) 2.3	(11) 1.5		(456)	2.1	(453)	1.9
	2.9		3.0		2.9		3.0		3.4		3.6		3.5	3.5

												% Officers', Directors', Owners' Comp/Sales		
	10.9		7.0		7.0		5.7						8.2	8.1
(133)	17.6	(135)	14.0	(87)	12.3	(23) 8.5				(292)	15.3	(301)	16.3
	26.2		24.1		22.6		18.6						25.2	27.2

262465M	605444M	1653702M	3015592M	2314280M	3659747M	Net Sales ($)	7968775M	8812942M
48138M	251202M	1069950M	2515517M	1330126M	4556731M	Total Assets ($)	6699025M	7198479M

M = $ thousand   MM = $ million
See Pages 11 through 21 for Explanation of Ratios and Data

Comparative Historical Data | | | Type of Statement | ## Current Data Sorted By Sales

			Type of Statement						
120	110	116	Unqualified	1	10	8	23	32	42
107	116	117	Reviewed	14	34	19	28	12	10
145	159	131	Compiled	21	59	25	14	12	
172	231	224	Tax Returns	109	67	26	8	9	5
206	230	230	Other	40	63	32	34	29	32
4/1/02-3/31/03	4/1/03-3/31/04	4/1/04-3/31/05		131 (4/1-9/30/04)			687 (10/1/04-3/31/05)		
ALL	ALL	ALL		0-1MM	1-3MM	3-5MM	5-10MM	10-25MM	25MM & OVER
750	846	818	**NUMBER OF STATEMENTS**	185	233	110	107	94	89
%	%	%	**ASSETS**	%	%	%	%	%	%
28.7	30.3	30.2	Cash & Equivalents	23.8	28.7	32.8	32.6	34.9	36.4
22.3	21.0	20.0	Trade Receivables (net)	16.7	19.2	20.3	25.9	22.0	19.3
.2	.3	.2	Inventory	.1	.1	.3	.0	.8	.4
4.4	5.1	5.1	All Other Current	4.7	4.4	3.9	6.1	4.9	8.6
55.6	56.6	55.6	Total Current	45.4	52.4	57.3	64.6	62.5	64.7
14.0	13.8	13.7	Fixed Assets (net)	17.9	13.8	16.0	12.3	8.4	15.0
14.3	15.1	15.9	Intangibles (net)	20.0	19.7	10.2	9.2	13.8	8.0
16.1	14.5	14.8	All Other Non-Current	16.7	14.0	16.5	13.9	15.3	11.5
100.0	100.0	100.0	Total	100.0	100.0	100.0	100.0	100.0	100.0
			LIABILITIES						
9.8	10.3	10.0	Notes Payable-Short Term	16.3	12.2	7.9	6.0	5.8	2.7
4.4	3.7	4.2	Cur. Mat.-L/T/D	6.5	4.3	3.4	3.5	2.3	3.1
25.4	25.1	23.0	Trade Payables	13.4	23.3	28.8	30.6	26.5	22.1
.4	.4	.3	Income Taxes Payable	.4	.2	.1	.4	.5	.7
18.9	19.0	18.6	All Other Current	15.2	16.2	14.7	23.2	21.7	27.5
58.8	58.5	56.0	Total Current	51.8	56.1	55.0	63.7	56.9	56.1
19.5	19.3	20.8	Long-Term Debt	36.2	22.5	17.4	15.0	7.9	9.3
.3	.2	.3	Deferred Taxes	.1	.4	.4	.5	.6	.3
6.5	6.7	6.7	All Other Non-Current	10.1	3.7	3.9	8.4	5.2	10.3
14.9	15.2	16.1	Net Worth	1.8	17.4	23.4	12.4	29.5	24.0
100.0	100.0	100.0	Total Liabilities & Net Worth	100.0	100.0	100.0	100.0	100.0	100.0
			INCOME DATA						
100.0	100.0	100.0	Net Sales	100.0	100.0	100.0	100.0	100.0	100.0
			Gross Profit						
89.2	88.4	88.4	Operating Expenses	83.7	88.3	92.1	92.0	89.0	89.4
10.8	11.6	11.6	Operating Profit	16.3	11.7	7.9	8.0	11.0	10.6
1.7	1.3	1.2	All Other Expenses (net)	3.9	1.3	-.4	-.5	.1	.6
9.0	10.3	10.3	Profit Before Taxes	12.4	10.4	8.4	8.5	10.8	10.0
			RATIOS						
1.4	1.4	1.6		2.4	1.6	1.6	1.4	1.5	1.6
1.0	1.0	1.0	Current	1.0	1.0	1.1	1.0	1.1	1.1
.7	.6	.7		.4	.6	.7	.8	.9	.9
1.3	1.3	1.4		2.3	1.4	1.5	1.2	1.3	1.4
(749) 1.0	1.0	1.0	Quick	.9	.9	1.0	.9	1.0	1.0
.5	.5	.5		.3	.5	.6	.7	.8	.6
1 308.0	0 UND	0 UND		0 UND	0 UND	2 172.3	6 59.7	12 30.0	11 34.2
31 11.6	25 14.8	22 16.6	Sales/Receivables	1 525.0	17 21.6	25 14.5	49 7.4	37 9.8	43 8.5
99 3.7	81 4.5	74 4.9		41 8.8	62 5.9	64 5.7	128 2.9	83 4.4	95 3.8
			Cost of Sales/Inventory						
			Cost of Sales/Payables						
8.5	8.7	8.6		7.0	11.9	10.6	8.4	6.5	5.7
179.3	88.9	111.1	Sales/Working Capital	-189.0	-188.7	43.3	345.1	24.5	25.9
-10.2	-14.2	-12.3		-8.5	-9.7	-21.4	-9.5	-24.3	-33.6
15.6	24.4	25.5		10.5	16.3	28.8	46.4	47.3	53.2
(578) 4.8	(635) 6.5	(608) 7.4	EBIT/Interest	(119) 3.4	(188) 5.7	(86) 9.8	(85) 12.5	(69) 15.9	(61) 16.5
1.7	2.3	2.3		.6	2.1	4.1	3.2	3.6	4.1
5.7	6.2	5.9	Net Profit + Depr., Dep.,		4.6	4.6	4.9	7.0	10.0
(139) 2.2	(118) 2.4	(127) 2.5	Amort./Cur. Mat. L/T/D	(32) 1.9	(15) 2.3	(19) 3.1	(25) 2.5	(27) 3.6
.8	1.1	1.3			.9	1.5	1.1	1.4	1.7
.2	.1	.1		.0	.2	.3	.2	.1	.1
.8	.8	.8	Fixed/Worth	1.2	1.3	.6	.7	.3	.6
-1.0	-.7	-.8		-.4	-.3	-6.2	-3.9	4.8	-2.4
1.8	2.2	1.8		1.3	1.8	1.3	2.4	1.7	2.3
9.3	11.4	8.2	Debt/Worth	22.0	20.9	5.2	7.2	5.8	4.8
-5.9	-4.8	-5.8		-2.2	-3.1	-38.4	-29.9	105.3	-106.5
103.0	129.6	120.1	% Profit Before Taxes/Tangible	120.5	90.4	119.6	152.2	160.5	108.0
(486) 35.8	(530) 45.2	(524) 41.7	Net Worth	(100) 45.4	(132) 29.2	(78) 47.6	(74) 58.9	(74) 51.3	(66) 32.7
8.3	13.2	12.9		7.6	9.6	17.6	16.6	18.4	10.1
18.6	23.5	23.6	% Profit Before Taxes/Total	31.3	24.0	26.0	17.4	22.1	18.6
6.9	8.5	8.7	Assets	9.0	9.0	10.6	7.8	8.8	8.3
1.7	2.1	2.3		-.1	1.9	3.7	2.3	3.2	2.8
63.4	85.1	97.1		434.8	91.3	78.3	59.7	80.6	91.6
22.8	28.0	30.9	Sales/Net Fixed Assets	41.4	32.4	28.2	27.0	31.9	25.9
11.0	12.5	12.6		10.3	12.8	12.2	11.9	15.8	12.2
2.7	3.0	3.2		4.4	3.3	4.5	2.2	2.9	2.1
1.4	1.5	1.6	Sales/Total Assets	1.6	1.8	2.1	1.2	1.5	1.1
.8	.9	.9		.7	1.0	1.3	.7	.7	.6
1.0	.9	.8		.8	.8	1.0	.8	.8	.6
(513) 2.0	(541) 1.9	(518) 1.8	% Depr., Dep., Amort./Sales	(96) 2.3	(147) 1.8	(72) 1.9	(78) 1.6	(63) 1.4	(62) 1.5
3.5	3.3	2.9		3.7	3.0	2.9	2.2	2.7	3.0
7.3	7.6	7.8	% Officers', Directors',	11.7	9.4	7.2	6.7	2.2	3.3
(348) 15.4	(409) 14.9	(383) 15.3	Owners' Comp/Sales	(100) 18.4	(135) 15.9	(68) 14.2	(41) 9.4	(27) 5.2	(12) 7.0
25.4	25.0	24.1		27.0	23.5	23.5	22.5	21.8	13.5
13792945M	11758010M	11511230M	Net Sales ($)	95883M	424039M	425174M	773333M	1427358M	8365443M
9239460M	10163077M	9771664M	Total Assets ($)	114990M	376453M	323491M	794563M	1663500M	6498667M

© RMA 2005   **M = $ thousand   MM = $ million**
See Pages 11 through 21 for Explanation of Ratios and Data

Current Data Sorted By Assets   Comparative Historical Data

0-500M	500M-2MM	2-10MM	10-50MM	50-100MM	100-250MM	Type of Statement	4/1/00-3/31/01 ALL	4/1/01-3/31/02 ALL
	2	7	5		2	Unqualified	5	15
	2	3	1			Reviewed		2
2	2	3	1	1		Compiled	6	8
	4	2		1		Tax Returns	4	6
3	10	8	5	4	1	Other	23	21
	2 (4/1-9/30/04)		67 (10/1/04-3/31/05)					
5	20	23	12	6	3	**NUMBER OF STATEMENTS**	38	52
%	%	%	%	%	%	**ASSETS**	%	%
	18.5	19.2	18.1			Cash & Equivalents	19.3	17.5
	12.5	12.8	16.5			Trade Receivables (net)	13.0	15.0
	.0	5.6	.0			Inventory	.1	.7
	13.9	11.4	16.8			All Other Current	4.7	8.5
	44.9	48.9	51.4			Total Current	37.1	41.5
	20.8	23.6	35.7			Fixed Assets (net)	32.2	34.5
	5.2	4.4	.6			Intangibles (net)	5.2	2.4
	29.1	23.0	12.3			All Other Non-Current	25.6	21.5
	100.0	100.0	100.0			Total	100.0	100.0
						LIABILITIES		
	9.4	5.2	8.4			Notes Payable-Short Term	17.1	11.8
	1.7	2.8	2.7			Cur. Mat.-L/T/D	1.5	4.9
	5.9	7.2	3.6			Trade Payables	5.4	2.9
	.2	.1	.0			Income Taxes Payable	.3	.2
	16.2	20.2	7.4			All Other Current	19.5	20.9
	33.3	35.5	22.2			Total Current	43.8	40.6
	15.5	14.1	25.1			Long-Term Debt	22.6	15.2
	.0	.0	.0			Deferred Taxes	1.5	.0
	4.9	5.1	3.9			All Other Non-Current	6.4	11.8
	46.3	45.3	48.9			Net Worth	25.7	32.5
	100.0	100.0	100.0			Total Liabilities & Net Worth	100.0	100.0
						INCOME DATA		
	100.0	100.0	100.0			Net Sales	100.0	100.0
						Gross Profit		
	67.3	74.1	64.5			Operating Expenses	74.1	75.9
	32.7	25.9	35.5			Operating Profit	25.9	24.1
	13.0	3.2	.5			All Other Expenses (net)	-1.9	4.2
	19.7	22.7	35.0			Profit Before Taxes	27.8	19.9
						RATIOS		
	5.5	2.2	8.5				2.8	3.8
	1.5	1.5	1.7			Current	1.2	1.1
	.6	.7	.7				.3	.5
	2.9	2.0	3.2				2.8	2.3
	.8	.8	1.1			Quick	.9	.8
	.3	.3	.4				.1	.1
	0 UND	0 UND	0 UND				0 UND	0 UND
	11 34.7	7 48.9	23 15.9			Sales/Receivables	0 UND	6 57.7
	46 7.9	62 5.9	60 6.0				47 7.7	57 6.4
						Cost of Sales/Inventory		
						Cost of Sales/Payables		
	1.9	3.9	1.4				2.3	2.4
	6.2	13.0	13.2			Sales/Working Capital	82.8	40.0
	-16.5	-27.4	-2.9				-4.3	-6.8
		38.2					59.1	16.5
		(13) 4.4				EBIT/Interest	(25) 7.1	(31) 4.7
		.5					.7	1.4
						Net Profit + Depr., Dep., Amort./Cur. Mat. L /T/D		
	.0	.0	.1				.0	.0
	.0	.2	1.1			Fixed/Worth	.5	.4
	3.6	2.4	3.4				5.0	4.5
	.2	.2	.2				.5	.4
	1.5	1.2	1.0			Debt/Worth	1.8	1.5
	8.4	6.6	2.8				11.7	7.8
	47.4	94.9	26.9				71.4	53.6
	(17) 11.1	(22) 26.2	(10) 14.6			% Profit Before Taxes/Tangible Net Worth	(31) 18.5	(45) 16.6
	2.5	.4	6.1				2.3	5.5
	10.2	24.1	10.6				18.6	15.8
	3.3	11.0	5.9			% Profit Before Taxes/Total Assets	4.9	5.2
	-.5	-.3	1.1				.7	1.5
	982.2	101.8	198.5				70.3	85.6
	62.2	31.0	8.0			Sales/Net Fixed Assets	12.9	16.0
	5.7	4.0	.2				1.6	.5
	2.5	2.6	1.5				2.4	2.6
	1.5	1.0	.3			Sales/Total Assets	.5	.9
	.1	.4	.1				.1	.2
		1.0	.8				1.0	.8
		(15) 2.8	(10) 2.2			% Depr., Dep., Amort./Sales	(22) 2.4	(35) 2.0
		8.5	8.9				8.7	12.4
								5.5
						% Officers', Directors', Owners' Comp/Sales		(10) 17.6
								38.0
6958M	32933M	187353M	265518M	71029M	366737M	Net Sales ($)	781928M	807063M
1055M	21880M	116909M	299804M	393265M	512953M	Total Assets ($)	1066853M	1308947M

M = $ thousand   MM = $ million
See Pages 11 through 21 for Explanation of Ratios and Data

Comparative Historical Data | Current Data Sorted By Sales

			Type of Statement						
16	14	16	Unqualified	3	2	4	3	2	2
2	7	6	Reviewed	1	1		3	1	
6	16	9	Compiled	2	5	1		1	
9	8	7	Tax Returns	4	2			1	
23	18	31	Other	9	5	3	6	2	6
4/1/02- 3/31/03	4/1/03- 3/31/04	4/1/04- 3/31/05			2 (4/1-9/30/04)		67 (10/1/04-3/31/05)		
ALL	ALL	ALL		0-1MM	1-3MM	3-5MM	5-10MM	10-25MM	25MM & OVER
56	63	69	**NUMBER OF STATEMENTS**	19	15	8	12	7	8
%	%	%	**ASSETS**	%	%	%	%	%	%
20.8	19.1	21.4	Cash & Equivalents	30.6	18.1		15.7		
4.9	7.3	12.7	Trade Receivables (net)	2.8	9.9		21.6		
.0	2.2	2.4	Inventory	.0	.0		4.1		
7.1	6.4	12.8	All Other Current	7.1	12.0		32.9		
32.8	35.1	49.3	Total Current	40.6	40.1		74.4		
38.7	29.4	23.8	Fixed Assets (net)	26.2	28.6		19.3		
5.5	6.4	6.0	Intangibles (net)	1.0	4.9		3.6		
23.1	29.2	21.4	All Other Non-Current	32.2	26.4		2.8		
100.0	100.0	100.0	Total	100.0	100.0		100.0		
			LIABILITIES						
11.9	11.6	7.2	Notes Payable-Short Term	7.9	5.8		8.7		
2.0	1.8	2.0	Cur. Mat.-L/T/D	.6	1.5		6.5		
3.9	3.6	6.5	Trade Payables	1.0	5.3		6.6		
.1	.2	.1	Income Taxes Payable	.1	.0		.1		
14.0	16.4	15.2	All Other Current	6.2	17.6		35.6		
31.9	33.5	31.0	Total Current	15.8	30.2		57.6		
35.0	25.2	14.9	Long-Term Debt	18.1	16.2		14.5		
.0	.3	.0	Deferred Taxes	.0	.0		.0		
3.8	5.4	7.8	All Other Non-Current	16.2	4.6		2.1		
29.2	35.6	46.2	Net Worth	49.8	48.9		25.8		
100.0	100.0	100.0	Total Liabilities & Net Worth	100.0	100.0		100.0		
			INCOME DATA						
100.0	100.0	100.0	Net Sales	100.0	100.0		100.0		
			Gross Profit						
65.8	65.5	67.1	Operating Expenses	53.8	66.8		71.9		
34.2	34.5	32.9	Operating Profit	46.2	33.2		28.1		
10.9	10.0	6.4	All Other Expenses (net)	16.8	2.4		5.3		
23.3	24.4	26.4	Profit Before Taxes	29.4	30.8		22.8		
			RATIOS						
2.7	3.8	4.3		20.7	1.7		3.1		
1.1	1.0	1.6	Current	3.1	.8		1.2		
.2	.3	.7		.4	.3		.6		
2.3	2.5	2.8		4.4	1.5		1.9		
.9	.7	.8	Quick	1.4	.7		.6		
.1	.2	.3		.4	.1		.2		
0 UND	0 UND	0 UND		0 UND	0 UND		0 UND		
0 UND	0 UND	6 63.3	Sales/Receivables	0 UND	2 163.8		8 44.2		
15 24.2	20 18.1	47 7.7		8 44.3	50 7.3		66 5.5		
			Cost of Sales/Inventory						
			Cost of Sales/Payables						
3.2	3.4	2.8		.1	6.8		1.2		
55.3	161.9	10.9	Sales/Working Capital	3.1	-66.9		12.0		
-4.5	-3.0	-16.8		-4.2	-13.2		-4.4		
19.1	40.3	48.3			60.9		30.8		
(35) 4.6	(34) 7.9	(40) 7.0	EBIT/Interest	(10) 4.6		(10) 7.1			
1.0	3.8	1.5			2.0		-1.3		
			Net Profit + Depr., Dep., Amort./Cur. Mat. L/T/D						
.0	.0	.0		.0	.0		.0		
1.4	.5	.2	Fixed/Worth	.0	.0		.4		
12.3	5.7	2.0		2.3	2.4		NM		
.6	.4	.2		.0	.7		.7		
1.8	1.7	1.2	Debt/Worth	.4	1.2		6.1		
11.6	7.2	5.0		4.2	3.1		NM		
50.5	42.4	57.7	% Profit Before Taxes/Tangible	16.3	51.5				
(44) 16.5	(52) 19.6	(60) 16.3	Net Worth	(17) 7.5	(14) 26.1				
4.5	3.6	1.5		1.1	2.2				
15.4	20.3	21.8	% Profit Before Taxes/Total	8.5	30.1		11.2		
5.6	5.1	6.3	Assets	2.6	6.1		7.7		
1.3	2.0	.2		.5	1.2		-6.5		
54.4	93.8	680.8		UND	929.3		346.7		
13.1	18.3	42.5	Sales/Net Fixed Assets	82.0	66.0		50.0		
.3	.4	3.9		.2	.4		9.3		
1.9	2.3	2.5		.2	2.7		3.1		
.4	.3	1.0	Sales/Total Assets	.1	1.6		1.0		
.1	.1	.1		.1	.4		.1		
1.7	1.0	1.0							
(36) 4.5	(41) 2.4	(38) 2.4	% Depr., Dep., Amort./Sales						
17.3	13.5	10.9							
5.9	4.5	1.7	% Officers', Directors',						
(10) 17.5	(14) 5.8	(14) 3.6	Owners' Comp/Sales						
27.0	23.0	21.2							
1082698M	762058M	930528M	Net Sales ($)	7532M	29805M	30535M	84461M	122894M	655301M
1360188M	1655011M	1345866M	Total Assets ($)	160686M	72630M	43383M	335421M	319395M	414351M

M = $ thousand   MM = $ million
See Pages 11 through 21 for Explanation of Ratios and Data

FINANCE—Real Estate Investment Trusts NAICS 525930 (SIC 6798)

Current Data Sorted By Assets							Comparative Historical Data	
						Type of Statement		
1	3	8	7		8	Unqualified	15	9
	2	4	1			Reviewed	4	4
1	1	5	2			Compiled	11	13
6	19	9		1		Tax Returns	14	10
1	6	11	13	6	4	Other	12	23
	10 (4/1-9/30/04)		109 (10/1/04-3/31/05)				4/1/00-3/31/01	4/1/01-3/31/02
0-500M	500M-2MM	2-10MM	10-50MM	50-100MM	100-250MM		ALL	ALL
9	31	37	23	7	12	**NUMBER OF STATEMENTS**	56	59
%	%	%	%	%	%	**ASSETS**	%	%
	11.2	4.5	5.5		6.5	Cash & Equivalents	4.2	5.6
	5.1	2.5	6.1		7.5	Trade Receivables (net)	8.0	5.5
	10.5	.4	3.4		7.0	Inventory	3.0	1.4
	2.1	2.1	2.8		.4	All Other Current	2.4	2.5
	28.9	9.4	17.8		21.5	Total Current	17.6	14.9
	62.1	82.3	60.2		63.8	Fixed Assets (net)	59.7	68.1
	.4	1.1	5.8		1.4	Intangibles (net)	3.3	2.7
	8.6	7.2	16.1		13.3	All Other Non-Current	19.3	14.3
	100.0	100.0	100.0		100.0	Total	100.0	100.0
						LIABILITIES		
	10.4	5.8	7.2		25.4	Notes Payable-Short Term	11.9	3.7
	3.0	2.3	2.3		.7	Cur. Mat.-L/T/D	2.2	2.5
	1.1	1.9	.7		1.0	Trade Payables	1.9	1.7
	.0	.0	.2		.0	Income Taxes Payable	.1	.2
	5.9	4.1	4.4		1.9	All Other Current	8.6	4.2
	20.3	14.2	14.7		29.0	Total Current	24.6	12.4
	44.7	45.5	41.1		27.3	Long-Term Debt	49.3	47.8
	.0	.0	.6		.4	Deferred Taxes	.6	.4
	3.5	7.4	5.5		2.9	All Other Non-Current	2.1	4.1
	31.5	33.0	38.1		40.3	Net Worth	23.3	35.4
	100.0	100.0	100.0		100.0	Total Liabilities & Net Worth	100.0	100.0
						INCOME DATA		
	100.0	100.0	100.0		100.0	Net Sales	100.0	100.0
						Gross Profit		
	58.8	58.8	50.0		59.0	Operating Expenses	54.6	57.9
	41.2	41.2	50.0		41.0	Operating Profit	45.4	42.1
	17.1	14.8	15.3		8.0	All Other Expenses (net)	22.4	25.1
	24.1	26.3	34.6		33.0	Profit Before Taxes	23.0	16.9
						RATIOS		
	4.2	1.6	3.3		2.8		2.1	2.8
	1.3	.7	.6		.3	Current	.7	1.2
	.2	.2	.3		.1		.2	.3
	2.1	1.2	3.3		2.8		1.3	2.2
	.3	.5	.4		.2	Quick	.4	1.0
	.1	.1	.2		.1		.1	.3
0 UND	0 UND	0 UND		0 UND			0 UND	0 UND
0 UND	0 UND	9 39.6		4 86.3		Sales/Receivables	0 UND	0 UND
0 UND	28 13.1	46 7.9		14 26.6			28 13.1	16 23.2
						Cost of Sales/Inventory		
						Cost of Sales/Payables		
	1.5	8.7	2.0		2.8		4.1	3.9
	10.1	−4.5	−47.4		−4.6	Sales/Working Capital	−62.1	14.8
	−2.2	−1.6	−1.6		−.6		−2.4	−4.6
	19.8	8.2					8.7	7.4
(15)	4.1	(18) 4.6				EBIT/Interest	(14) 2.8	(15) 2.0
	2.4	2.0					.4	.2
						Net Profit + Depr., Dep., Amort./Cur. Mat. L./T/D		
	.6	1.3	.5		.4		.8	.8
	3.2	3.5	2.8		1.9	Fixed/Worth	2.2	2.7
	7.2	9.9	9.9		2.3		7.7	4.9
	.6	1.0	.7		1.0		1.0	1.0
	3.0	3.1	5.9		1.4	Debt/Worth	2.6	2.2
	11.7	10.4	13.3		3.7		9.1	9.4
	43.3	26.1	26.0		16.4		37.0	22.7
(27)	24.9	(33) 10.4	(19) 13.9		(11) 8.7	% Profit Before Taxes/Tangible Net Worth	(48) 12.8	(51) 8.8
	10.1	−.1	6.6		3.3		5.6	1.6
	10.5	8.8	8.6		6.4		8.1	6.1
	5.7	3.0	6.6		3.2	% Profit Before Taxes/Total Assets	4.0	2.7
	1.1	−.1	1.7		1.8		.8	.2
	4.5	.4	51.5		38.5		6.9	.6
	.3	.2	.2		.2	Sales/Net Fixed Assets	.3	.2
	.1	.1	.1		.1		.2	.1
	.6	.3	.2		.2		.3	.2
	.2	.2	.1		.2	Sales/Total Assets	.2	.2
	.1	.1	.1		.1		.1	.1
	2.8	10.3	7.5				9.0	8.8
(24)	16.4	(33) 15.0	(15) 17.5			% Depr., Dep., Amort./Sales	(45) 16.7	(49) 14.7
	25.3	20.4	21.3				23.5	21.0
						% Officers', Directors', Owners' Comp/Sales		
4559M	35376M	55448M	160055M	637621M	402909M	Net Sales ($)	584982M	502483M
2305M	37163M	170481M	526484M	491263M	2119583M	Total Assets ($)	2405350M	1556252M

© RMA 2005

M = $ thousand   MM = $ million
See Pages 11 through 21 for Explanation of Ratios and Data

Comparative Historical Data | Current Data Sorted By Sales

				Type of Statement						
20		30		27	Unqualified	9	3	4	4	4	3
13		7		7	Reviewed	2	3		1	1	
21		24		9	Compiled	5	4				
30		35		35	Tax Returns	31	1		1	1	1
30		28		41	Other	12	10	7	5	1	5
4/1/02-		4/1/03-		4/1/04-			10 (4/1-9/30/04)		109 (10/1/04-3/31/05)		
3/31/03		3/31/04		3/31/05		0-1MM	1-3MM	3-5MM	5-10MM	10-25MM	25MM & OVER
ALL		ALL		ALL							
114		124		119	NUMBER OF STATEMENTS	59	21	11	11	8	9
%		%		%	ASSETS	%	%	%	%	%	%
10.0		8.6		8.2	Cash & Equivalents	8.8	6.3	11.4	2.5		
6.1		4.1		4.5	Trade Receivables (net)	3.0	1.6	.2	12.6		
2.6		4.1		4.6	Inventory	4.6	1.8	.0	1.5		
1.3		4.9		1.8	All Other Current	1.9	4.0	.7	.5		
19.9		21.6		19.1	Total Current	18.3	13.7	12.3	17.1		
66.3		65.8		66.2	Fixed Assets (net)	74.2	68.6	57.5	52.0		
2.9		1.9		3.0	Intangibles (net)	1.8	1.6	2.4	8.8		
10.9		10.7		11.7	All Other Non-Current	5.8	16.2	27.8	22.0		
100.0		100.0		100.0	Total	100.0	100.0	100.0	100.0		
				LIABILITIES						
6.8		6.0		9.2	Notes Payable-Short Term	8.9	3.9	2.0	6.9		
4.3		4.1		2.1	Cur. Mat.-L/T/D	3.0	1.0	.6	2.9		
1.9		2.3		1.4	Trade Payables	.9	.8	1.1	1.9		
.1		.0		.0	Income Taxes Payable	.0	.2	.0	.0		
4.0		8.4		5.0	All Other Current	5.1	2.7	7.2	4.1		
17.1		20.9		17.7	Total Current	18.1	8.6	11.0	15.9		
52.6		50.9		42.9	Long-Term Debt	56.5	31.5	31.4	32.7		
.1		.4		.2	Deferred Taxes	.0	.6	.0	.0		
4.9		5.1		5.6	All Other Non-Current	3.2	9.0	4.6	13.2		
25.2		22.7		33.6	Net Worth	22.3	50.3	53.0	38.2		
100.0		100.0		100.0	Total Liabilities & Net Worth	100.0	100.0	100.0	100.0		
				INCOME DATA						
100.0		100.0		100.0	Net Sales	100.0	100.0	100.0	100.0		
				Gross Profit						
59.6		56.5		56.7	Operating Expenses	53.5	48.6	70.6	54.9		
40.4		43.5		43.3	Operating Profit	46.5	51.4	29.4	45.1		
24.4		18.8		14.1	All Other Expenses (net)	19.6	11.5	7.3	8.3		
15.9		24.7		29.2	Profit Before Taxes	26.9	39.9	22.0	36.8		
				RATIOS						
3.7		3.8		2.6		2.1	3.7	4.5	1.7		
1.2		1.2		1.0	Current	.9	2.0	1.7	.6		
.3		.4		.3		.2	.4	.2	.3		
2.8		2.3		1.9		1.4	3.3	4.4	1.7		
1.0		.8		.6	Quick	.5	.8	1.2	.6		
.3		.3		.2		.1	.4	.1	.1		
0 UND		0 UND		0 UND		0 UND	0 UND	0 UND	0 UND		
0 UND		0 UND		0 UND	Sales/Receivables	0 UND	0 UND	0 UND	12 30.2		
18 20.1		13 28.4		13 29.2		0 UND	37 9.8	3 116.4	43 8.6		
				Cost of Sales/Inventory						
				Cost of Sales/Payables						
2.4		2.7		4.1		2.9	2.3	1.9	13.1		
26.9		27.1		166.0	Sales/Working Capital	−16.9	18.0	10.1	−774.3		
−4.8		−3.8		−2.0		−1.7	−2.9	−1.5	−2.7		
10.1		7.1		9.0		5.2	8.9				
(40) 3.7	(58)	3.9	(56)	4.4	EBIT/Interest	(22) 4.0	(10) 7.3				
.8		1.9		2.5		2.4	3.0				
				Net Profit + Depr., Dep., Amort./Cur. Mat. L/T/D						
1.1		1.1		.8		1.3	.8	.4	.0		
3.5		2.6		2.3	Fixed/Worth	3.9	1.7	1.0	2.9		
22.8		12.8		7.2		12.2	6.1	5.5	13.0		
1.1		1.1		.8		1.5	.1	.0	.7		
3.6		3.0		2.9	Debt/Worth	3.6	1.2	.4	2.6		
30.6		14.6		11.7		29.1	7.8	14.2	13.3		
30.4		34.5		35.5	% Profit Before Taxes/Tangible Net Worth	39.5	22.0				
(90) 10.2	(100)	13.1	(101)	15.8		(49) 17.5	(19) 10.4				
.3		5.7		4.5		4.9	6.6				
6.7		8.9		9.7	% Profit Before Taxes/Total Assets	6.9	12.2	14.2	17.1		
2.1		4.2		4.4		4.1	6.9	2.9	7.2		
.0		1.4		1.4		.9	2.5	−.6	6.3		
.9		1.6		2.3	Sales/Net Fixed Assets	.4	1.3	4.5	51.5		
.3		.3		.2		.2	.2	.6	.5		
.1		.2		.1		.1	.1	.2	.1		
.3		.4		.4	Sales/Total Assets	.3	.3	.4	.7		
.2		.2		.2		.1	.1	.4	.2		
.1		.1		.1		.1	.1	.2	.1		
8.6		8.7		6.5	% Depr., Dep., Amort./Sales	10.9	8.8				
(93) 14.5	(98)	13.0	(89)	14.6		(51) 15.2	(16) 17.1				
21.8		20.5		21.3		23.1	20.9				
		.9		5.1	% Officers', Directors', Owners' Comp/Sales						
	(11)	6.9	(11)	10.2							
		12.7		23.4							
712817M		1414742M		1295968M	Net Sales ($)	20509M	37077M	41527M	69559M	148064M	979232M
3082546M		3422905M		3347279M	Total Assets ($)	127593M	316861M	288739M	345121M	1119184M	1149781M

M = $ thousand   MM = $ million
See Pages 11 through 21 for Explanation of Ratios and Data

Current Data Sorted By Assets   Comparative Historical Data

						Type of Statement	7	5
1		6	1	3		Unqualified	7	5
		1	1			Reviewed	1	1
1	1					Compiled	10	7
4	2	2	2			Tax Returns	9	8
3	3	3	7	1		Other	11	13
							4/1/00-3/31/01	4/1/01-3/31/02
	5 (4/1-9/30/04)		38 (10/1/04-3/31/05)				ALL	ALL
0-500M	500M-2MM	2-10MM	10-50MM	50-100MM	100-250MM			
9	7	12	11	3	1	NUMBER OF STATEMENTS	38	34
%	%	%	%	%	%	**ASSETS**	%	%
		16.1	38.3			Cash & Equivalents	9.6	13.3
		14.0	2.1			Trade Receivables (net)	13.7	7.7
		1.8	1.6			Inventory	1.4	2.2
		13.4	.3			All Other Current	13.6	11.9
		45.3	42.2			Total Current	38.4	35.2
		18.5	23.9			Fixed Assets (net)	36.4	33.3
		3.3	3.6			Intangibles (net)	3.1	3.6
		32.9	30.2			All Other Non-Current	22.2	28.0
		100.0	100.0			Total	100.0	100.0
						LIABILITIES		
		22.4	19.4			Notes Payable-Short Term	17.7	14.1
		3.7	.4			Cur. Mat.-L/T/D	5.6	6.3
		2.5	2.3			Trade Payables	5.8	6.0
		.0	.1			Income Taxes Payable	.0	.1
		12.2	4.0			All Other Current	4.5	7.0
		40.9	26.1			Total Current	33.6	33.4
		7.7	12.5			Long-Term Debt	30.4	23.6
		.0	.4			Deferred Taxes	.0	.5
		2.5	5.8			All Other Non-Current	6.4	9.2
		48.9	55.2			Net Worth	29.6	33.5
		100.0	100.0			Total Liabilities & Net Worth	100.0	100.0
						INCOME DATA		
		100.0	100.0			Net Sales	100.0	100.0
						Gross Profit		
		68.4	56.6			Operating Expenses	63.2	58.4
		31.6	43.4			Operating Profit	36.8	41.6
		3.5	25.7			All Other Expenses (net)	12.9	12.8
		28.1	17.7			Profit Before Taxes	23.8	28.8
						RATIOS		
		2.4	5.1			Current	3.1	4.5
		1.3	1.4				1.3	1.6
		.4	.9				.4	.4
		1.8	5.1			Quick	2.9	2.6
		.9	1.2				(37) .7	.5
		.1	.9				.1	.1
		0 UND	0 UND			Sales/Receivables	0 UND	0 UND
		23 16.0	2 212.0				0 UND	0 UND
		46 7.9	14 25.3				28 12.8	16 22.4
						Cost of Sales/Inventory		
						Cost of Sales/Payables		
		5.2	.5			Sales/Working Capital	5.0	1.4
		16.4	4.6				52.7	11.6
		−9.5	−15.1				−3.1	−8.1
						EBIT/Interest	10.1	18.1
							(20) 3.9	(17) 4.6
							1.1	1.6
						Net Profit + Depr., Dep., Amort./Cur. Mat. L /T/D		
		.0	.0			Fixed/Worth	.0	.0
		.2	.2				.8	.5
		.6	1.8				20.0	3.3
		.4	.1			Debt/Worth	.4	.4
		.8	.7				3.8	1.6
		3.4	7.6				NM	22.5
		126.4				% Profit Before Taxes/Tangible Net Worth	66.7	44.4
		(11) 28.6					(29) 15.0	(28) 7.7
		5.0					1.4	4.8
		76.2	5.6			% Profit Before Taxes/Total Assets	12.5	11.9
		20.4	1.6				3.8	4.0
		1.0	.8				.9	.8
		147.0	UND			Sales/Net Fixed Assets	69.6	UND
		15.9	9.2				6.1	19.7
		7.1	.2				.3	.3
		3.5	.8			Sales/Total Assets	1.5	1.1
		1.2	.1				.2	.2
		.2	.1				.1	.1
		.5				% Depr., Dep., Amort./Sales	1.1	.7
		(10) 2.6					(28) 4.3	(22) 3.8
		4.8					16.1	16.0
						% Officers', Directors', Owners' Comp/Sales		
10234M	25732M	114952M	84689M	88483M	21925M	Net Sales ($)	425011M	178990M
1899M	8301M	60280M	218302M	173822M	156197M	Total Assets ($)	856874M	932014M

M = $ thousand   MM = $ million

See Pages 11 through 21 for Explanation of Ratios and Data

Comparative Historical Data				Current Data Sorted By Sales					

Type of Statement

			Type of Statement						
8	8	11	Unqualified	2	1	2		2	4
5	5	2	Reviewed				1	1	
4	5	2	Compiled			2			
8	10	10	Tax Returns	6	3			1	
11	17	18	Other	6	4	2	2	3	1
4/1/02-3/31/03	4/1/03-3/31/04	4/1/04-3/31/05			5 (4/1-9/30/04)			38 (10/1/04-3/31/05)	
ALL	ALL	ALL		0-1MM	1-3MM	3-5MM	5-10MM	10-25MM	25MM & OVER
36	45	43	**NUMBER OF STATEMENTS**	14	8	6	3	7	5
%	%	%	**ASSETS**	%	%	%	%	%	%
16.8	18.9	26.3	Cash & Equivalents	43.7					
15.6	12.2	11.8	Trade Receivables (net)	8.1					
1.9	1.7	3.6	Inventory	5.0					
7.4	9.5	9.6	All Other Current	10.6					
41.8	42.3	51.2	Total Current	67.5					
36.5	28.5	20.9	Fixed Assets (net)	11.2					
4.4	4.6	2.7	Intangibles (net)	.8					
17.3	24.6	25.3	All Other Non-Current	20.5					
100.0	100.0	100.0	Total	100.0					
			LIABILITIES						
21.6	12.5	26.9	Notes Payable-Short Term	20.3					
4.9	6.9	2.7	Cur. Mat.-L/T/D	3.5					
5.5	4.7	7.3	Trade Payables	11.0					
.2	.0	.2	Income Taxes Payable	.0					
14.4	10.4	12.4	All Other Current	12.5					
46.5	34.5	49.4	Total Current	47.2					
18.5	18.8	14.2	Long-Term Debt	21.7					
.9	.4	.5	Deferred Taxes	.0					
1.1	2.1	3.5	All Other Non-Current	.1					
33.0	44.2	32.4	Net Worth	31.2					
100.0	100.0	100.0	Total Liabilities & Net Worth	100.0					
			INCOME DATA						
100.0	100.0	100.0	Net Sales	100.0					
			Gross Profit						
68.8	62.0	67.0	Operating Expenses	51.9					
31.2	38.0	33.0	Operating Profit	48.1					
12.9	8.1	10.3	All Other Expenses (net)	15.7					
18.3	29.9	22.7	Profit Before Taxes	32.3					
			RATIOS						
3.1	2.8	2.7		2.7					
1.3	1.0	1.5	Current	1.5					
.4	.5	.5		.9					
2.7	2.4	2.1		2.6					
.9	.7 (42)	1.0	Quick	.9					
.2	.2	.1		.1					
0 UND	0 UND	0 UND		0 UND					
2 238.2	0 UND	2 180.3	Sales/Receivables	0 UND					
44 8.3	50 7.3	30 12.2		36 10.0					
			Cost of Sales/Inventory						
			Cost of Sales/Payables						
2.1	4.8	2.4		1.6					
8.2	221.0	13.5	Sales/Working Capital	8.8					
−6.3	−2.3	−11.6		−55.1					
14.9	24.2	32.0							
5.2 (22)	7.8 (28)	8.7 (26)	EBIT/Interest						
.7	3.2	2.0							
			Net Profit + Depr., Dep., Amort./Cur. Mat. L/T/D						
.1	.0	.0		.0					
1.1	.2	.2	Fixed/Worth	.0					
7.3	1.6	3.0		.2					
.5	.4	.4		.3					
2.0	.8	1.1	Debt/Worth	1.9					
10.6	8.6	10.7		NM					
33.8	83.5	87.0		88.9					
14.8 (32)	38.8 (40)	27.9 (33)	% Profit Before Taxes/Tangible Net Worth	37.4 (11)					
.3	9.1	5.1		5.0					
14.8	29.0	29.4		77.5					
3.5	6.7	7.1	% Profit Before Taxes/Total Assets	16.0					
.0	4.0	.8		1.9					
61.0	127.8	296.7		UND					
12.1	16.1	21.6	Sales/Net Fixed Assets	UND					
.2	.7	6.0		54.9					
2.3	2.3	3.6		3.4					
.4	.6	1.0	Sales/Total Assets	.3					
.1	.1	.1		.1					
1.1	1.2	1.0							
3.6 (22)	3.1 (29)	2.7 (28)	% Depr., Dep., Amort./Sales						
18.7	15.0	6.1							
			% Officers', Directors', Owners' Comp/Sales						
311797M	250539M	346015M	Net Sales ($)	7261M	14205M	22243M	18761M	108959M	174586M
609972M	749735M	618801M	Total Assets ($)	50603M	126633M	61995M	16206M	220930M	142434M

© RMA 2005

M = $ thousand   MM = $ million
See Pages 11 through 21 for Explanation of Ratios and Data

REAL ESTATE
AND RENTAL
AND LEASING

Current Data Sorted By Assets   Comparative Historical Data

						Type of Statement		
6	68	120	30	8	8	Unqualified	110	97
14	20	29	15	1	1	Reviewed	42	43
18	71	58	10	1	1	Compiled	104	123
159	331	190	29	1	3	Tax Returns	249	206
65	106	127	40	2	3	Other	169	243
	128 (4/1-9/30/04)		1407 (10/1/04-3/31/05)				4/1/00-3/31/01	4/1/01-3/31/02
0-500M	500M-2MM	2-10MM	10-50MM	50-100MM	100-250MM		ALL	ALL
262	596	524	124	13	16	NUMBER OF STATEMENTS	674	712
%	%	%	%	%	%	ASSETS	%	%
15.1	5.4	4.9	6.0	13.5	23.2	Cash & Equivalents	7.3	7.8
3.6	2.4	2.0	4.5	3.1	.9	Trade Receivables (net)	3.1	3.0
2.4	2.3	2.7	6.2	3.4	.0	Inventory	2.2	2.2
4.4	1.7	2.2	2.3	9.1	10.6	All Other Current	2.8	3.1
25.5	11.8	11.7	19.0	29.0	34.7	Total Current	15.4	16.1
62.5	79.3	78.5	69.1	36.6	57.4	Fixed Assets (net)	74.0	73.8
2.6	1.3	1.5	1.8	1.1	.8	Intangibles (net)	2.0	1.8
9.5	7.6	8.3	10.2	33.3	7.2	All Other Non-Current	8.6	8.2
100.0	100.0	100.0	100.0	100.0	100.0	Total	100.0	100.0
						LIABILITIES		
11.8	5.6	4.6	6.5	5.6	1.7	Notes Payable-Short Term	6.2	6.8
4.9	3.5	3.7	2.9	2.4	3.9	Cur. Mat.-L/T/D	5.5	4.8
3.5	1.1	1.3	2.7	1.0	1.0	Trade Payables	1.8	3.0
.0	.1	.1	.0	.2	.0	Income Taxes Payable	.1	.1
12.9	5.1	5.3	6.4	4.0	12.2	All Other Current	6.8	7.4
33.0	15.2	15.1	18.6	13.3	18.6	Total Current	20.4	22.2
79.5	73.2	67.1	58.4	40.2	84.2	Long-Term Debt	71.7	75.8
.0	.0	.0	.0	.0	.1	Deferred Taxes	.1	.1
5.0	2.5	2.7	3.2	4.8	8.5	All Other Non-Current	4.4	3.8
-17.5	9.0	15.1	19.8	41.7	-11.4	Net Worth	3.4	-1.9
100.0	100.0	100.0	100.0	100.0	100.0	Total Liabilities & Net Worth	100.0	100.0
						INCOME DATA		
100.0	100.0	100.0	100.0	100.0	100.0	Net Sales	100.0	100.0
						Gross Profit		
72.9	71.9	75.3	75.2	74.2	76.0	Operating Expenses	71.7	71.1
27.1	28.1	24.7	24.8	25.8	24.0	Operating Profit	28.3	28.9
13.8	20.3	21.5	18.4	8.8	18.2	All Other Expenses (net)	19.1	22.3
13.3	7.8	3.3	6.3	16.9	5.7	Profit Before Taxes	9.2	6.6
						RATIOS		
2.6	1.6	1.9	1.9	6.2	3.0		2.0	1.9
.9	.5	.7	.9	1.5	1.3	Current	.7	.7
.2	.2	.2	.3	1.1	.6		.2	.2
2.1	1.2	1.5	1.3	3.7	2.0		1.4	1.4
.6	.4	.4	.4	1.0	1.0	Quick	.5	.4
.2	.1	.1	.1	.5	.5		.1	.1
0 UND	0 UND	0 UND	0 UND	0 UND	0 UND		0 UND	0 UND
0 UND	0 UND	0 UND	2 184.1	6 61.2	2 152.4	Sales/Receivables	0 UND	0 UND
1 551.3	1 254.1	5 79.7	18 20.7	16 22.3	30 12.1		5 71.5	5 77.0
						Cost of Sales/Inventory		
						Cost of Sales/Payables		
9.7	17.0	7.8	4.9	.8	3.9		9.3	7.6
-100.3	-10.3	-18.3	-77.9	6.7	56.8	Sales/Working Capital	-14.8	-18.1
-4.7	-3.1	-3.1	-3.1	14.9	-62.5		-2.9	-3.2
5.2	4.9	5.1	4.7	8.5			5.4	4.7
(140) 3.3	(244) 2.3	(209) 2.0	(48) 2.5	(11) 3.4		EBIT/Interest	(242) 2.7	(251) 2.5
1.6	1.0	.9	1.6	1.7			1.4	1.3
	2.9	4.6				Net Profit + Depr., Dep.,	6.8	4.4
	(10) 1.2	(16) 3.4				Amort./Cur. Mat. L /T/D	(24) 1.2	(19) 1.9
	.2	.5					.6	.5
1.1	2.3	2.0	1.1	.0	1.0		1.8	1.9
6.1	7.9	6.4	4.4	.9	2.8	Fixed/Worth	5.8	7.5
-3.4	-14.5	-30.3	41.0	3.1	-4.8		-13.4	-10.4
1.2	1.9	1.7	1.7	.7	2.5		1.6	1.9
8.2	8.5	6.8	6.4	1.4	4.6	Debt/Worth	6.6	8.8
-5.6	-17.1	-40.0	115.8	4.6	-6.3		-16.6	-11.7
66.5	32.6	28.4	28.2	28.9	124.3	% Profit Before Taxes/Tangible	34.9	34.2
(165) 26.7	(402) 8.2	(372) 5.1	(98) 7.7	9.4	(11) 9.5	Net Worth	(456) 9.8	(462) 8.9
2.1	-4.9	-5.9	-.1	6.5	-6.1		-1.2	-2.7
22.6	6.7	4.7	4.1	6.9	8.0	% Profit Before Taxes/Total	7.5	6.2
6.0	1.9	.7	1.5	3.3	2.2	Assets	1.8	1.4
.0	-1.3	-1.9	-.7	2.0	-2.4		-.9	-1.2
13.9	.6	.5	.8	34.9	41.6		.9	.9
1.0	.3	.2	.2	.9	.3	Sales/Net Fixed Assets	.3	.3
.2	.2	.1	.1	.4	.2		.2	.2
2.0	.4	.3	.3	.4	1.1		.5	.5
.6	.2	.2	.2	.3	.2	Sales/Total Assets	.3	.2
.2	.1	.1	.1	.1	.1		.2	.2
3.1	10.7	11.9	7.1				8.4	8.9
(204) 11.5	(533) 17.8	(472) 19.6	(108) 16.5			% Depr., Dep., Amort./Sales	(600) 15.5	(621) 16.1
19.3	25.5	30.5	28.1				22.9	23.7
4.6	4.1	4.8	1.9			% Officers', Directors',	3.7	3.7
(42) 6.8	(85) 6.6	(67) 7.6	(19) 3.8			Owners' Comp/Sales	(83) 6.3	(86) 6.6
13.8	13.2	14.2	7.9				15.4	12.1
85940M	353187M	873708M	1075443M	399701M	6004000M	Net Sales ($)	2103171M	3874269M
70079M	685363M	2328194M	2599376M	975095M	2632058M	Total Assets ($)	4747680M	5742914M

© RMA 2005   M = $ thousand   MM = $ million
See Pages 11 through 21 for Explanation of Ratios and Data

Comparative Historical Data   **Current Data Sorted By Sales**

Hist 1	Hist 2	Hist 3	Type of Statement	0-1MM	1-3MM	3-5MM	5-10MM	10-25MM	25MM & OVER
154	203	240	Unqualified	138	52	11	14	12	13
55	89	80	Reviewed	33	21	4	12	8	2
118	223	159	Compiled	112	29	13	3	1	1
390	623	713	Tax Returns	597	96	6	5	4	5
234	307	343	Other	216	67	17	24	15	4
4/1/02-3/31/03 ALL	4/1/03-3/31/04 ALL	4/1/04-3/31/05 ALL		128 (4/1-9/30/04)		1407 (10/1/04-3/31/05)			
951	1445	1535	**NUMBER OF STATEMENTS**	1096	265	51	58	40	25
%	%	%	**ASSETS**	%	%	%	%	%	%
7.9	7.6	7.2	Cash & Equivalents	6.0	7.5	12.7	14.2	11.1	21.2
2.8	2.5	2.6	Trade Receivables (net)	1.2	4.0	11.4	5.2	14.4	6.2
1.8	2.8	2.7	Inventory	1.3	4.9	4.6	10.7	11.9	5.8
2.9	3.3	2.5	All Other Current	2.0	2.6	4.8	3.2	8.6	10.8
15.4	16.1	15.1	Total Current	10.5	19.0	33.5	33.3	45.9	44.0
74.5	73.8	74.7	Fixed Assets (net)	81.5	66.1	47.2	53.5	34.7	41.1
1.9	1.4	1.6	Intangibles (net)	1.4	1.9	2.2	1.4	4.1	3.0
8.2	8.7	8.6	All Other Non-Current	6.6	13.1	17.2	11.7	15.3	11.9
100.0	100.0	100.0	Total	100.0	100.0	100.0	100.0	100.0	100.0
			LIABILITIES						
6.4	5.5	6.4	Notes Payable-Short Term	5.9	6.6	12.8	8.2	8.2	5.2
5.0	3.7	3.8	Cur. Mat.-L/T/D	3.6	4.5	2.5	3.5	5.4	1.9
1.8	1.8	1.7	Trade Payables	1.0	2.3	3.7	3.5	8.6	6.1
.1	.1	.1	Income Taxes Payable	.0	.2	.0	.1	.1	.1
6.4	8.4	6.6	All Other Current	5.5	7.4	11.6	9.8	14.8	18.9
19.9	19.5	18.5	Total Current	16.0	20.9	30.7	25.1	37.1	32.1
74.8	69.1	70.8	Long-Term Debt	75.7	66.6	53.1	44.7	33.9	57.5
.1	.1	.0	Deferred Taxes	.0	.1	.1	.1	.2	.0
3.0	5.1	3.2	All Other Non-Current	2.9	3.7	3.3	2.7	4.6	7.2
2.3	6.2	7.5	Net Worth	5.3	8.8	12.9	27.5	24.3	3.2
100.0	100.0	100.0	Total Liabilities & Net Worth	100.0	100.0	100.0	100.0	100.0	100.0
			INCOME DATA						
100.0	100.0	100.0	Net Sales	100.0	100.0	100.0	100.0	100.0	100.0
			Gross Profit						
69.5	72.5	73.6	Operating Expenses	71.1	77.7	78.6	82.0	87.1	83.9
30.5	27.5	26.4	Operating Profit	28.9	22.3	21.4	18.0	12.9	16.1
20.6	19.0	19.3	All Other Expenses (net)	22.3	14.4	11.8	7.2	5.4	7.1
9.8	8.5	7.1	Profit Before Taxes	6.6	7.8	9.6	10.9	7.5	9.0
			RATIOS						
1.9	2.0	1.9	Current	1.7	2.4	2.1	2.9	2.2	1.9
.8	.7	.7		.5	.9	1.1	1.6	1.4	1.3
.2	.2	.2		.2	.2	.5	.7	.6	1.0
1.5	1.3	1.4	Quick	1.2	1.9	1.7	1.9	1.5	1.7
(950) .5	(1442) .4	.4		.4	.4	.6	1.0	.8	1.0
.1	.1	.1		.1	.1	.1	.3	.2	.5
0 UND	0 UND	0 UND	Sales/Receivables	0 UND	0 UND	0 UND	0 UND	0 UND	0 UND
0 UND	0 UND	0 UND		0 UND	0 999.8	3 140.9	3 123.1	11 33.0	3 114.4
3 133.8	3 115.1	3 108.6		1 314.5	6 57.8	32 11.3	17 21.7	30 12.0	22 16.4
			Cost of Sales/Inventory						
			Cost of Sales/Payables						
8.3	8.2	9.5	Sales/Working Capital	13.4	6.7	9.2	4.7	4.1	9.9
-23.8	-17.7	-16.5		-10.5	-58.4	47.5	10.9	21.3	19.1
-3.4	-3.5	-3.3		-2.9	-4.1	-4.4	-11.4	-16.9	111.1
5.6	5.3	5.0	EBIT/Interest	4.2	5.6	24.9	14.9	15.8	48.6
(399) 2.6	(603) 2.4	(656) 2.4		(398) 2.3	(144) 2.3	(32) 3.1	(39) 3.4	(30) 4.5	(13) 6.3
1.3	1.2	1.1		1.0	1.1	1.5	2.0	1.8	1.7
7.7	3.1	3.7	Net Profit + Depr., Dep., Amort./Cur. Mat. L/T/D		2.6		3.6		
(31) 2.7	(38) 1.1	(38) 1.6			(13) .6		(10) 1.9		
1.1	.5	.5			.1		.5		
1.8	1.8	1.9	Fixed/Worth	2.3	1.3	.2	.7	.1	.2
6.0	5.9	6.4		7.9	7.2	2.4	1.8	1.0	2.6
-15.4	-17.4	-20.5		-18.7	-10.5	-21.9	7.2	10.8	277.2
1.6	1.7	1.8	Debt/Worth	1.9	1.5	1.1	.6	1.4	2.4
6.6	6.8	7.4		8.5	9.0	2.8	3.0	4.4	4.8
-18.0	-19.5	-22.6		-20.7	-12.1	-24.3	21.0	23.9	NM
35.7	34.7	35.0	% Profit Before Taxes/Tangible Net Worth	30.5	45.9	53.0	42.6	64.6	141.4
(650) 10.0	(990) 8.8	(1061) 8.9		(744) 6.7	(180) 14.8	(37) 17.4	(49) 12.7	(32) 32.4	(19) 30.6
-.7	-3.4	-4.2		-5.9	-.8	3.4	4.2	10.4	6.5
8.0	7.1	6.8	% Profit Before Taxes/Total Assets	5.9	10.0	10.8	13.5	10.2	20.8
2.3	2.0	1.8		1.3	2.1	4.2	4.2	5.5	6.3
-.6	-1.2	-1.3		-1.6	-.9	.0	1.0	1.9	.9
.9	.9	.8	Sales/Net Fixed Assets	.4	2.1	28.3	11.4	52.6	145.7
.3	.3	.3		.2	.5	2.0	1.0	9.0	6.5
.2	.2	.1		.1	.2	.4	.3	.7	.4
.5	.5	.5	Sales/Total Assets	.3	.8	2.6	1.2	3.0	4.8
.2	.2	.2		.2	.3	.8	.5	1.2	1.4
.2	.1	.1		.1	.2	.2	.2	.3	.3
9.0	9.1	9.3	% Depr., Dep., Amort./Sales	12.9	4.6	.8	1.7	1.0	.4
(827) 16.9	(1251) 16.7	(1335) 17.3		(968) 19.5	(235) 12.3	(40) 3.9	(48) 7.6	(28) 2.7	(16) 1.9
24.1	25.2	26.4		28.5	21.0	14.9	13.0	9.9	11.8
3.7	4.2	4.4	% Officers', Directors', Owners' Comp/Sales	5.0	4.1	2.1	2.2	.7	
(101) 5.7	(194) 6.9	(217) 6.6		(116) 8.3	(60) 6.0	(13) 5.5	(12) 6.7	(12) 2.3	
11.2	13.1	13.3		14.5	8.5	15.6	16.9	17.1	
6268280M	6484580M	8791979M	Net Sales ($)	371430M	446889M	203212M	390245M	608091M	6772112M
6976600M	10533338M	9290165M	Total Assets ($)	2005050M	1640707M	605201M	1124898M	1413750M	2500559M

M = $ thousand   MM = $ million
See Pages 11 through 21 for Explanation of Ratios and Data

Current Data Sorted By Assets | Comparative Historical Data

Type of Statement	0-500M	500M-2MM	2-10MM	10-50MM	50-100MM	100-250MM		4/1/00-3/31/01 ALL	4/1/01-3/31/02 ALL
Unqualified	3	23	73	63	18	21		124	152
Reviewed	11	78	121	46	1	8		183	178
Compiled	84	304	310	71	2	3		507	569
Tax Returns	417	1206	781	77	4	1		785	885
Other	100	361	473	131	29	20		502	587
	234 (4/1-9/30/04)			4606 (10/1/04-3/31/05)					
NUMBER OF STATEMENTS	615	1972	1758	388	54	53		2101	2371
ASSETS	%	%	%	%	%	%		%	%
Cash & Equivalents	10.2	5.2	4.9	5.5	9.9	6.4		5.6	5.2
Trade Receivables (net)	2.9	1.7	1.6	3.3	6.8	4.3		2.3	2.2
Inventory	1.5	.8	1.4	3.2	1.4	7.5		1.7	1.6
All Other Current	2.0	1.4	1.4	2.6	3.4	2.7		2.3	2.6
Total Current	16.6	9.2	9.3	14.5	21.4	20.9		11.9	11.7
Fixed Assets (net)	77.2	84.3	82.3	71.9	58.3	64.9		79.0	80.1
Intangibles (net)	1.9	1.3	1.7	1.8	3.1	2.9		2.5	2.1
All Other Non-Current	4.3	5.1	6.7	11.8	17.2	11.3		6.7	6.1
Total	100.0	100.0	100.0	100.0	100.0	100.0		100.0	100.0
LIABILITIES									
Notes Payable-Short Term	6.5	4.3	4.1	4.4	3.5	2.7		5.2	4.3
Cur. Mat.-L/T/D	6.1	4.8	3.7	3.5	2.4	2.7		5.3	5.7
Trade Payables	2.1	.9	1.0	2.0	4.8	4.8		1.6	1.8
Income Taxes Payable	.0	.0	.1	.0	1.0	.6		.1	.0
All Other Current	8.2	3.7	3.5	4.3	6.1	5.6		6.0	4.8
Total Current	23.0	13.7	12.4	14.2	17.8	16.4		18.2	16.6
Long-Term Debt	65.4	68.6	65.7	55.5	46.3	50.0		67.1	67.1
Deferred Taxes	.1	.1	.0	.3	.6	.8		.1	.1
All Other Non-Current	6.4	2.4	2.8	4.1	5.6	2.0		3.2	2.5
Net Worth	5.2	15.2	19.0	25.9	29.7	30.7		11.4	13.6
Total Liabilities & Net Worth	100.0	100.0	100.0	100.0	100.0	100.0		100.0	100.0
INCOME DATA									
Net Sales	100.0	100.0	100.0	100.0	100.0	100.0		100.0	100.0
Gross Profit									
Operating Expenses	53.0	49.4	52.6	58.0	70.0	69.3		53.0	52.1
Operating Profit	47.0	50.6	47.4	42.0	30.0	30.7		47.0	47.9
All Other Expenses (net)	19.6	24.9	24.8	19.2	12.3	13.8		26.5	28.2
Profit Before Taxes	27.3	25.7	22.6	22.8	17.6	17.0		20.5	19.6
RATIOS									
Current	1.8	1.7	2.0	2.5	2.8	2.1		1.7	1.8
	.6	.5	.6	.9	1.2	1.0		.6	.6
	.2	.1	.2	.2	.4	.4		.1	.1
Quick	1.5	1.4	1.6	1.4	2.4	1.1		1.3	1.3
	(614) .5	(1971) .4	(1755) .4	(387) .5	.9	.7		(2099) .3	(2367) .4
	.1	.1	.1	.1	.3	.2		.1	.1
Sales/Receivables	0 UND	0 UND	0 UND	0 UND	4 94.8	3 124.8		0 UND	0 UND
	0 UND	0 UND	0 UND	2 213.0	13 27.4	8 48.2		0 UND	0 UND
	0 UND	0 UND	2 159.3	20 18.4	50 7.3	36 10.1		5 67.5	3 112.5
Cost of Sales/Inventory									
Cost of Sales/Payables									
Sales/Working Capital	11.5	10.1	6.9	4.1	2.8	5.7		9.8	10.0
	-12.8	-9.3	-12.4	-23.2	22.6	-46.7		-10.2	-11.0
	-2.6	-2.3	-2.5	-2.8	-4.1	-2.7		-2.2	-2.4
EBIT/Interest	8.6	7.7	6.2	6.8	16.8	17.8		6.5	6.2
	(260) 4.5	(727) 4.3	(600) 3.8	(162) 4.1	(32) 4.1	(25) 4.6		(600) 3.5	(667) 3.4
	2.7	2.4	2.1	2.0	1.6	1.7		1.6	1.8
Net Profit + Depr., Dep., Amort./Cur. Mat. L/T/D	2.8	3.9	3.0	4.8		33.7		4.0	3.3
	(13) 1.0	(45) 1.8	(77) 1.5	(43) 1.8		(10) 3.5		(112) 1.8	(123) 1.5
	.0	1.0	.9	.9		1.0		.9	.9
Fixed/Worth	1.6	2.4	2.3	1.5	.7	1.0		2.1	2.2
	4.5	5.4	5.3	3.5	2.9	2.6		5.2	5.6
	-15.0	79.4	43.3	15.7	7.0	6.0		-115.7	254.7
Debt/Worth	1.3	1.9	1.9	1.4	1.0	1.3		1.7	1.9
	4.5	5.3	5.1	4.1	3.3	2.9		5.5	5.6
	-15.6	101.3	50.9	18.7	9.0	6.7		-114.7	617.0
% Profit Before Taxes/Tangible Net Worth	53.8	44.9	40.4	33.7	20.1	24.1		40.9	42.8
	(427) 24.0	(1517) 21.1	(1386) 17.1	(326) 15.4	(47) 13.1	(48) 12.3		(1554) 19.1	(1788) 19.9
	9.5	7.8	6.0	5.8	2.9	4.6		6.2	6.0
% Profit Before Taxes/Total Assets	16.4	9.3	7.1	7.3	6.7	6.8		8.9	8.8
	7.0	4.4	3.6	3.4	3.5	3.4		3.8	3.8
	1.8	1.2	.9	1.2	.3	1.3		.6	.6
Sales/Net Fixed Assets	.9	.3	.3	.4	4.7	1.8		.5	.5
	.3	.2	.2	.2	.3	.3		.2	.2
	.2	.1	.1	.1	.2	.1		.2	.2
Sales/Total Assets	.6	.3	.2	.3	.5	.5		.3	.3
	.3	.2	.2	.2	.2	.2		.2	.2
	.2	.1	.1	.1	.1	.1		.1	.1
% Depr., Dep., Amort./Sales	7.4	11.6	12.4	10.3	3.7	7.9		9.3	9.7
	(543) 13.3	(1835) 16.7	(1633) 18.3	(348) 17.0	(46) 15.5	(43) 15.0		(1976) 14.9	(2225) 15.1
	21.2	23.4	25.8	22.7	24.1	23.7		21.4	21.6
% Officers', Directors', Owners' Comp/Sales	4.2	2.4	2.2	1.8				3.4	3.0
	(58) 7.5	(124) 6.7	(134) 5.1	(52) 4.9				(208) 6.7	(220) 6.3
	13.9	14.1	12.7	10.7				14.0	13.4
Net Sales ($)	132844M	804313M	2921546M	3493718M	2279589M	5668164M		6570280M	8030731M
Total Assets ($)	178875M	2263337M	7676730M	7887209M	3586800M	8001491M		15441100M	18094178M

Comparative Historical Data			Type of Statement	Current Data Sorted By Sales					
183	179	201	Unqualified	59	45	18	20	33	26
217	253	265	Reviewed	138	54	21	28	14	10
559	931	774	Compiled	581	135	27	18	9	4
1645	2273	2486	Tax Returns	2235	196	34	11	7	3
743	1026	1114	Other	741	221	33	56	34	29
				234 (4/1-9/30/04)		4606 (10/1/04-3/31/05)			
4/1/02-3/31/03 ALL	4/1/03-3/31/04 ALL	4/1/04-3/31/05 ALL		0-1MM	1-3MM	3-5MM	5-10MM	10-25MM	25MM & OVER
3347	4662	4840	NUMBER OF STATEMENTS	3754	651	133	133	97	72
%	%	%	ASSETS	%	%	%	%	%	%
5.4	5.6	5.8	Cash & Equivalents	5.3	6.5	8.9	9.5	10.1	10.2
1.9	2.0	2.0	Trade Receivables (net)	.8	3.5	6.1	10.1	10.2	16.7
1.3	1.3	1.4	Inventory	.5	1.8	6.6	5.9	7.7	16.0
1.7	2.7	1.6	All Other Current	1.3	1.8	3.5	4.6	2.3	5.7
10.2	11.6	10.8	Total Current	7.9	13.6	25.0	30.1	30.3	48.6
82.7	80.7	81.2	Fixed Assets (net)	85.5	75.0	61.2	54.0	53.0	37.0
1.5	1.5	1.6	Intangibles (net)	1.4	2.2	3.3	2.2	4.5	2.0
5.6	6.2	6.3	All Other Non-Current	5.2	9.2	10.5	13.7	12.2	12.5
100.0	100.0	100.0	Total	100.0	100.0	100.0	100.0	100.0	100.0
			LIABILITIES						
4.7	5.2	4.5	Notes Payable-Short Term	4.1	5.3	9.8	4.7	4.4	8.6
5.3	4.4	4.4	Cur. Mat.-L/T/D	4.5	4.4	3.9	3.4	2.9	2.3
1.4	1.4	1.3	Trade Payables	.5	1.9	3.5	6.7	7.2	11.6
.0	.0	.1	Income Taxes Payable	.0	.1	.3	.3	.2	.5
5.0	6.1	4.3	All Other Current	3.8	4.7	6.0	8.6	8.0	12.7
16.5	17.1	14.5	Total Current	12.9	16.4	23.6	23.7	22.7	35.7
65.5	61.6	65.6	Long-Term Debt	69.1	61.8	44.9	43.1	44.9	28.6
.1	.1	.1	Deferred Taxes	.0	.1	.0	.6	.8	.3
2.9	5.4	3.3	All Other Non-Current	2.9	4.2	5.1	5.6	3.8	3.1
15.0	15.8	16.5	Net Worth	15.0	17.6	26.3	27.1	27.8	32.3
100.0	100.0	100.0	Total Liabilities & Net Worth	100.0	100.0	100.0	100.0	100.0	100.0
			INCOME DATA						
100.0	100.0	100.0	Net Sales	100.0	100.0	100.0	100.0	100.0	100.0
			Gross Profit						
51.1	52.9	52.2	Operating Expenses	48.2	59.3	69.3	76.1	74.8	89.2
48.9	47.1	47.8	Operating Profit	51.8	40.7	30.7	23.9	25.2	10.8
26.8	24.2	23.5	All Other Expenses (net)	26.2	17.3	12.8	9.3	9.3	3.1
22.1	22.8	24.4	Profit Before Taxes	25.6	23.4	17.9	14.7	15.9	7.8
			RATIOS						
1.7	2.0	1.9	Current	1.8	2.1	2.9	2.7	2.5	2.3
.5	.6	.6		.5	.8	1.0	1.1	1.3	1.3
.1	.1	.2		.1	.2	.3	.5	.6	.8
1.3	1.4	1.5	Quick	1.4	1.5	1.9	1.8	1.8	1.3
(3344) .4	(4658) .4	(4834) .4		(3750) .4	(650) .6	(132) .4	.6	.9	.8
.1	.1	.1		.1	.1	.1	.3	.3	.3
0 UND	0 UND	0 UND	Sales/Receivables	0 UND	0 UND	0 UND	0 UND	4 91.4	3 129.2
0 UND	0 UND	0 UND		0 UND	0 UND	3 145.5	10 34.9	15 23.9	19 19.6
2 209.5	1 247.4	1 447.5		0 UND	11 32.7	19 18.7	30 12.1	44 8.4	48 7.5
			Cost of Sales/Inventory						
			Cost of Sales/Payables						
10.6	7.4	8.0	Sales/Working Capital	8.8	7.7	4.4	7.1	3.5	6.7
-9.3	-10.9	-11.8		-8.3	-30.5	50.9	52.2	15.6	25.4
-2.3	-2.3	-2.4		-2.2	-3.3	-4.4	-6.0	-9.6	-30.5
6.6	6.5	7.2	EBIT/Interest	7.0	6.9	11.2	9.6	9.6	19.1
(1086) 3.8	(1681) 3.7	(1806) 4.1		(1213) 4.3	(320) 3.8	(73) 3.8	(85) 3.7	(61) 3.5	(54) 4.6
2.1	2.0	2.3		2.6	1.6	1.7	1.6	1.5	1.9
3.2	3.4	4.1	Net Profit + Depr., Dep., Amort./Cur. Mat. L/T/D	2.6	3.2	6.9	5.1	8.3	26.4
(181) 1.4	(203) 1.5	(197) 1.8		(94) 1.5	(42) 1.8	(14) 1.9	(18) 2.1	(15) 4.8	(14) 8.3
.7	.9	.9		.9	1.0	.5	1.2	1.3	1.2
2.3	2.1	2.2	Fixed/Worth	2.5	1.7	1.0	.5	.9	.2
5.4	5.1	5.0		5.7	4.3	3.1	2.4	2.6	.8
81.0	57.2	56.8		86.3	69.8	19.9	7.2	7.8	3.5
1.9	1.8	1.7	Debt/Worth	1.9	1.4	1.3	1.5	1.4	1.1
5.2	5.1	4.9		5.4	4.4	3.7	3.5	2.8	2.9
95.0	79.3	71.8		101.8	137.9	38.2	10.7	9.4	7.6
41.8	41.8	42.2	% Profit Before Taxes/Tangible Net Worth	41.4	45.8	50.4	50.3	32.8	34.2
(2574) 19.2	(3610) 18.6	(3751) 19.0		(2887) 19.2	(495) 18.0	(106) 19.2	(117) 20.9	(83) 18.1	(63) 18.0
6.4	6.2	7.0		7.0	6.6	7.2	5.4	6.7	7.4
8.7	8.5	8.7	% Profit Before Taxes/Total Assets	8.4	9.6	11.2	9.4	9.8	12.3
4.0	4.0	4.2		4.0	4.6	4.2	4.7	4.3	6.6
.9	.8	1.2		1.2	1.1	1.1	1.1	1.4	1.8
.4	.4	.4	Sales/Net Fixed Assets	.3	.6	6.9	21.0	10.9	40.8
.2	.2	.2		.2	.3	.4	.6	.7	10.5
.1	.1	.1		.1	.2	.2	.2	.2	1.7
.3	.3	.3	Sales/Total Assets	.2	.4	1.4	2.5	1.4	3.8
.2	.2	.2		.2	.2	.3	.3	.3	1.8
.1	.1	.1		.1	.1	.2	.2	.2	.6
10.9	10.9	11.3	% Depr., Dep., Amort./Sales	12.5	9.2	4.1	1.5	2.7	.4
(3126) 16.3	(4317) 16.4	(4448) 16.8		(3495) 17.6	(582) 15.1	(118) 11.4	(113) 10.5	(84) 9.4	(56) 2.2
22.6	23.4	24.0		24.9	22.1	18.6	17.5	19.9	6.1
3.2	3.3	2.4	% Officers', Directors', Owners' Comp/Sales	2.8	3.5	1.8	1.8	2.2	
(247) 6.5	(386) 6.5	(379) 5.9		(188) 6.8	(96) 7.9	(30) 3.7	(33) 5.4	(23) 2.9	
12.0	13.5	12.8		13.6	14.1	6.3	11.0	7.5	
10075875M	14093877M	15300174M	Net Sales ($)	1203886M	1063889M	522327M	958254M	1503874M	10047944M
22819860M	28533740M	29594442M	Total Assets ($)	7416825M	5207578M	2089717M	3456917M	5507235M	5916170M

© RMA 2005

M = $ thousand   MM = $ million

See Pages 11 through 21 for Explanation of Ratios and Data

| Current Data Sorted By Assets | | | | | | | Comparative Historical Data | |

© RMA 2005

						Type of Statement		
	1	4	1		1	Unqualified		
			2			Reviewed		
2	8	2	1			Compiled		
12	35	15	2			Tax Returns		
4	16	4	1	1		Other		
	6 (4/1-9/30/04)		106 (10/1/04-3/31/05)				4/1/00-3/31/01	4/1/01-3/31/02
0-500M	500M-2MM	2-10MM	10-50MM	50-100MM	100-250MM		ALL	ALL
18	60	25	7	1	1	NUMBER OF STATEMENTS		
%	%	%	%	%	%	ASSETS	%	%
23.7	6.5	4.4				Cash & Equivalents	D	D
.1	1.6	3.4				Trade Receivables (net)	A	A
1.0	.0	2.4				Inventory	T	T
.7	1.1	2.7				All Other Current	A	A
25.5	9.2	13.0				Total Current		
60.0	83.3	80.0				Fixed Assets (net)	N	N
4.9	1.1	.9				Intangibles (net)	O	O
9.5	6.4	6.2				All Other Non-Current	T	T
100.0	100.0	100.0				Total		
						LIABILITIES	A	A
31.4	4.3	3.6				Notes Payable-Short Term	V	V
3.3	8.3	8.2				Cur. Mat.-L/T/D	A	A
2.3	.4	1.9				Trade Payables	I	I
.0	.0	.0				Income Taxes Payable	L	L
8.8	2.8	3.1				All Other Current	A	A
45.9	15.8	16.8				Total Current	B	B
92.9	67.6	63.9				Long-Term Debt	L	L
.0	.0	.2				Deferred Taxes	E	E
1.8	3.0	2.7				All Other Non-Current		
-40.7	13.7	16.3				Net Worth		
100.0	100.0	100.0				Total Liabilities & Net Worth		
						INCOME DATA		
100.0	100.0	100.0				Net Sales		
						Gross Profit		
69.1	64.5	66.3				Operating Expenses		
30.9	35.5	33.7				Operating Profit		
11.8	15.8	22.4				All Other Expenses (net)		
19.2	19.7	11.3				Profit Before Taxes		
						RATIOS		
5.6	1.3	2.7						
.4	.5	.9				Current		
.1	.2	.1						
3.3	1.0	1.4						
.4	.4	.2				Quick		
.1	.1	.1						
0 UND	0 UND	0 UND						
0 UND	0 UND	0 UND				Sales/Receivables		
0 UND	0 UND	3 128.6						
						Cost of Sales/Inventory		
						Cost of Sales/Payables		
11.5	21.5	3.6						
-27.0	-7.6	-69.1				Sales/Working Capital		
-2.9	-2.4	-1.3						
	5.0	6.0						
	(37) 3.2	(11) 3.3				EBIT/Interest		
	2.2	2.1						
						Net Profit + Depr., Dep., Amort./Cur. Mat. L./T/D		
.7	2.3	2.5						
UND	6.7	5.0				Fixed/Worth		
-.5	NM	-12.2						
.7	2.0	2.8						
UND	6.0	5.6				Debt/Worth		
-1.6	NM	-16.4						
228.4	47.3	29.5				% Profit Before Taxes/Tangible Net Worth		
(10) 30.2	(45) 29.7	(18) 15.4						
4.4	2.6	-.3						
27.9	10.1	8.0				% Profit Before Taxes/Total Assets		
11.4	5.6	2.4						
.5	.6	.7						
55.6	.4	.4						
1.3	.3	.2				Sales/Net Fixed Assets		
.3	.2	.1						
3.2	.4	.3						
1.0	.3	.2				Sales/Total Assets		
.3	.2	.1						
5.3	9.6	9.3				% Depr., Dep., Amort./Sales		
(13) 10.7	(57) 14.1	(24) 14.3						
16.4	19.8	22.9						
	4.0					% Officers', Directors', Owners' Comp/Sales		
	(12) 10.8							
	13.0							
5230M	29331M	45385M	54876M	41423M	45599M	Net Sales ($)		
4140M	69286M	78930M	103042M	57641M	146771M	Total Assets ($)		

M = $ thousand　　MM = $ million
See Pages 11 through 21 for Explanation of Ratios and Data

Comparative Historical Data				Current Data Sorted By Sales					

Type of Statement

			Type of Statement						
	4	2	Unqualified					1	
1	1	7	Reviewed	2	2	2		1	
10	13	13	Compiled	11	2	2	2		
29	60	64	Tax Returns	62	2				
10	28	26	Other	18	3	1	2		2
4/1/02-3/31/03 ALL	4/1/03-3/31/04 ALL	4/1/04-3/31/05 ALL		0-1MM	1-3MM	3-5MM	5-10MM	10-25MM	25MM & OVER
					6 (4/1-9/30/04)		106 (10/1/04-3/31/05)		
50	106	112	**NUMBER OF STATEMENTS**	93	9	3	3	1	3

%	%	%	**ASSETS**	%	%	%	%	%	%
4.4	6.2	8.7	Cash & Equivalents	8.5					
.1	2.0	1.9	Trade Receivables (net)	.1					
.0	.2	.7	Inventory	.2					
1.7	1.0	1.4	All Other Current	1.5					
6.2	9.4	12.7	Total Current	10.4					
89.5	82.2	78.0	Fixed Assets (net)	82.6					
1.9	2.1	2.2	Intangibles (net)	1.8					
2.3	6.3	7.1	All Other Non-Current	5.3					
100.0	100.0	100.0	Total	100.0					
			LIABILITIES						
2.4	1.5	8.2	Notes Payable-Short Term	8.9					
5.5	5.5	7.0	Cur. Mat.-L/T/D	7.4					
.3	1.0	1.3	Trade Payables	.6					
.0	.0	.0	Income Taxes Payable	.0					
3.5	3.8	3.8	All Other Current	3.2					
11.7	11.8	20.3	Total Current	20.1					
74.7	74.9	69.9	Long-Term Debt	70.8					
.0	.0	.1	Deferred Taxes	.0					
8.1	9.4	2.6	All Other Non-Current	2.3					
5.5	3.9	7.2	Net Worth	6.8					
100.0	100.0	100.0	Total Liabilities & Net Worth	100.0					
			INCOME DATA						
100.0	100.0	100.0	Net Sales	100.0					
			Gross Profit						
59.2	67.4	65.7	Operating Expenses	62.6					
40.8	32.6	34.3	Operating Profit	37.4					
25.5	19.1	16.5	All Other Expenses (net)	18.4					
15.3	13.5	17.8	Profit Before Taxes	19.0					

			RATIOS						
3.0	3.5	1.7		1.7					
.5	.8	.5	Current	.5					
.2	.2	.2		.1					
1.6	3.1	1.3		1.0					
.3	.7	.4	Quick	.3					
.1	.1	.1		.1					
0 UND	0 UND	0 UND		0 UND					
0 UND	0 UND	0 UND	Sales/Receivables	0 UND					
0 UND	1 432.1	1 390.1		0 UND					
			Cost of Sales/Inventory						
			Cost of Sales/Payables						
8.5	11.1	14.3		15.0					
-9.2	-73.0	-13.2	Sales/Working Capital	-9.7					
-2.9	-3.8	-2.3		-1.8					
6.1	5.2	5.3		5.0					
(16) 3.7	(49) 2.6	(63) 3.3	EBIT/Interest	(49) 3.3					
2.0	1.5	2.1		2.4					
			Net Profit + Depr., Dep., Amort./Cur. Mat. L/T/D						
2.9	2.6	2.1		2.6					
9.9	7.0	5.4	Fixed/Worth	6.7					
-15.3	-13.4	-32.5		-14.1					
2.3	2.6	1.6		2.2					
10.5	7.0	5.6	Debt/Worth	6.3					
-16.3	-15.4	-34.6		-17.6					
51.7	45.4	39.7		39.6					
(33) 16.7	(69) 13.8	(81) 21.5	% Profit Before Taxes/Tangible Net Worth	(66) 24.9					
7.9	3.3	3.9		4.2					
8.9	8.2	10.4		10.6					
3.5	3.3	4.9	% Profit Before Taxes/Total Assets	5.2					
.6	.0	.7		.7					
.4	.6	.7		.5					
.3	.3	.3	Sales/Net Fixed Assets	.3					
.2	.2	.2		.2					
.4	.4	.5		.4					
.3	.2	.3	Sales/Total Assets	.3					
.2	.2	.2		.2					
10.1	10.2	9.0		9.6					
(47) 14.1	(100) 16.2	(102) 13.9	% Depr., Dep., Amort./Sales	(85) 14.1					
18.9	21.4	19.1		19.8					
	4.8	5.1		4.6					
	(17) 9.9	(20) 9.4	% Officers', Directors', Owners' Comp/Sales	(18) 10.4					
	16.8	12.5		12.7					
60200M	145761M	221844M	Net Sales ($)	32319M	16422M	12358M	16829M	20055M	123861M
210527M	426932M	459810M	Total Assets ($)	130963M	62689M	16370M	28383M	3563M	217842M

M = $ thousand   MM = $ million
See Pages 11 through 21 for Explanation of Ratios and Data

REAL ESTATE—Lessors of Other Real Estate Property NAICS 531190 (SIC 6515, 6517, 6519)

Current Data Sorted By Assets — **Comparative Historical Data**

© RMA 2005

M = $ thousand   MM = $ million
See Pages 11 through 21 for Explanation of Ratios and Data

Type of Statement	0-500M	500M-2MM	2-10MM	10-50MM	50-100MM	100-250MM	4/1/00-3/31/01 ALL	4/1/01-3/31/02 ALL
Unqualified	1	14	32	32	8	10	61	52
Reviewed	7	30	55	14	1	3	84	73
Compiled	52	113	120	32	1	1	263	274
Tax Returns	154	429	266	25	1	1	348	306
Other	49	164	198	54	6	5	229	256
	120 (4/1-9/30/04)			1756 (10/1/04-3/31/05)				
NUMBER OF STATEMENTS	263	750	671	157	15	20	985	961
ASSETS	%	%	%	%	%	%	%	%
Cash & Equivalents	13.2	5.0	4.8	6.8	6.6	6.6	5.8	5.8
Trade Receivables (net)	2.6	2.7	2.3	3.8	3.1	2.4	2.6	2.5
Inventory	2.2	2.1	2.6	3.7	4.3	8.9	2.1	2.2
All Other Current	4.4	2.1	2.0	4.0	4.8	1.8	3.8	3.9
Total Current	22.4	11.9	11.7	18.2	18.8	19.8	14.3	14.3
Fixed Assets (net)	68.9	80.2	79.5	70.4	56.0	72.6	76.4	76.6
Intangibles (net)	1.6	1.4	1.7	1.4	1.5	1.0	1.8	1.9
All Other Non-Current	7.1	6.5	7.1	10.0	23.6	6.6	7.6	7.2
Total	100.0	100.0	100.0	100.0	100.0	100.0	100.0	100.0
LIABILITIES								
Notes Payable-Short Term	9.6	5.6	5.6	5.8	7.1	5.0	4.9	6.1
Cur. Mat.-L/T/D	7.5	4.9	4.1	4.1	8.2	3.7	5.0	4.4
Trade Payables	3.1	1.5	1.5	2.1	3.2	2.5	1.6	1.5
Income Taxes Payable	.1	.0	.1	.1	.4	.1	.1	.1
All Other Current	13.5	5.4	4.2	5.1	3.8	3.9	5.9	5.4
Total Current	33.8	17.4	15.5	17.3	22.8	15.2	17.4	17.4
Long-Term Debt	64.0	63.0	58.8	51.8	35.4	50.3	65.5	62.4
Deferred Taxes	.0	.0	.1	.4	1.6	1.1	.1	.2
All Other Non-Current	6.3	3.1	3.6	3.3	3.9	4.4	3.1	3.0
Net Worth	-4.2	16.5	22.0	27.2	36.3	29.0	13.9	16.9
Total Liabilities & Net Worth	100.0	100.0	100.0	100.0	100.0	100.0	100.0	100.0
INCOME DATA								
Net Sales	100.0	100.0	100.0	100.0	100.0	100.0	100.0	100.0
Gross Profit								
Operating Expenses	60.1	53.9	55.5	63.5	77.8	71.3	55.6	53.6
Operating Profit	39.9	46.1	44.5	36.5	22.2	28.7	44.4	46.4
All Other Expenses (net)	15.1	22.4	21.9	16.8	9.7	16.2	23.8	25.6
Profit Before Taxes	24.8	23.7	22.6	19.7	12.5	12.5	20.6	20.8
RATIOS								
Current	2.2	1.7	1.8	2.4	1.4	4.0	2.1	2.1
	.7	.4	.7	1.0	.9	1.6	.7	.7
	.2	.1	.2	.3	.1	.2	.2	.2
Quick	1.6	1.1	1.4	1.4	.9	1.6	1.4	1.2
	.5	(749) .3	(670) .4	.4	.4	.9	(984) .4	(959) .4
	.1	.1	.1	.1	.1	.1	.1	.1
Sales/Receivables	0 UND	0 UND	0 UND	0 UND	0 UND	1 454.8	0 UND	0 UND
	0 UND	0 UND	0 UND	0 999.8	11 31.8	10 38.3	0 UND	0 UND
	0 UND	0 UND	2 170.6	16 23.4	45 8.1	33 11.1	5 78.1	3 138.8
Cost of Sales/Inventory								
Cost of Sales/Payables								
Sales/Working Capital	7.1	13.9	6.9	3.5	6.6	2.1	6.0	5.8
	-22.5	-6.1	-13.0	-86.5	-22.9	15.9	-17.9	-19.8
	-2.2	-2.0	-2.0	-3.6	-.9	-5.7	-2.8	-2.7
EBIT/Interest	9.1	6.8	7.1	5.2	10.8		7.0	5.8
	(130) 5.4	(312) 3.8	(279) 3.6	(76) 2.9	(12) 2.3		(322) 3.5	(310) 3.2
	2.7	1.8	1.9	1.5	.7		1.6	1.7
Net Profit + Depr., Dep., Amort./Cur. Mat. L/T/D		2.3	3.4	3.4			4.3	3.2
		(25) 1.6	(35) 1.4	(22) 1.6			(55) 1.5	(68) 1.3
		.9	.3	.8			.8	.8
Fixed/Worth	1.2	2.1	2.0	1.6	.2	1.5	1.8	1.8
	4.5	4.8	4.4	3.3	2.7	2.8	4.5	4.2
	-8.5	159.0	35.1	10.6	6.4	9.4	701.2	54.8
Debt/Worth	1.0	1.8	1.7	1.4	.6	1.1	1.6	1.6
	7.0	4.6	4.4	3.3	2.9	2.7	4.7	4.3
	-7.0	252.5	41.7	12.0	6.0	9.5	UND	74.8
% Profit Before Taxes/Tangible Net Worth	67.4	44.9	39.0	38.1	47.0	27.5	36.4	37.5
	(177) 27.1	(568) 19.1	(542) 17.6	(137) 13.1	11.5	(18) 11.2	(740) 17.7	(753) 18.1
	7.6	6.6	5.7	2.1	-6.1	-4.5	5.1	5.2
% Profit Before Taxes/Total Assets	26.4	9.5	7.1	7.1	9.2	5.1	9.2	9.3
	8.0	4.5	3.5	3.2	3.2	1.6	3.8	3.8
	1.8	.8	.9	.5	-2.2	-1.3	.8	.6
Sales/Net Fixed Assets	2.7	.4	.3	.6	2.6	.5	.5	.5
	.6	.2	.2	.2	.4	.2	.2	.2
	.2	.1	.1	.1	.3	.2	.2	.2
Sales/Total Assets	1.5	.3	.3	.3	.7	.2	.4	.3
	.4	.2	.2	.2	.2	.2	.2	.2
	.2	.1	.1	.1	.2	.1	.1	.1
% Depr., Dep., Amort./Sales	5.2	10.7	12.0	7.1	5.6	6.5	8.8	8.3
	(215) 12.7	(681) 16.5	(612) 18.6	(144) 15.2	(11) 14.5	(14) 16.7	(915) 15.5	(890) 15.4
	20.5	24.3	27.3	24.1	22.2	23.0	22.9	22.2
% Officers', Directors', Owners' Comp/Sales	4.2	2.7	3.3	2.1			3.2	2.5
	(36) 8.3	(57) 5.5	(59) 6.7	(19) 3.7			(100) 6.3	(102) 6.8
	13.8	11.0	11.3	7.3			17.2	12.9
Net Sales ($)	77010M	403150M	1018452M	1637833M	876762M	1235675M	2663913M	3132616M
Total Assets ($)	71882M	873416M	2931717M	3059711M	1051726M	3202254M	6495661M	6388840M

Comparative Historical Data			Type of Statement	Current Data Sorted By Sales					
95	81	97	Unqualified	28	23	12	8	10	16
110	127	109	Reviewed	57	25	9	6	8	4
293	425	319	Compiled	235	64	9	6	3	2
582	816	875	Tax Returns	759	85	15	10	4	2
387	510	476	Other	321	84	25	18	18	10
4/1/02-3/31/03	4/1/03-3/31/04	4/1/04-3/31/05		120 (4/1-9/30/04)			1756 (10/1/04-3/31/05)		
ALL	ALL	ALL		0-1MM	1-3MM	3-5MM	5-10MM	10-25MM	25MM & OVER
1467	1959	1876	**NUMBER OF STATEMENTS**	1400	281	70	48	43	34
%	%	%	**ASSETS**	%	%	%	%	%	%
5.4	5.9	6.3	Cash & Equivalents	5.4	8.3	11.1	9.9	8.1	9.6
2.3	2.2	2.6	Trade Receivables (net)	1.2	3.3	11.6	12.1	14.3	10.1
1.7	2.5	2.5	Inventory	.9	4.6	8.3	9.9	12.4	16.9
2.7	3.3	2.5	All Other Current	2.1	3.0	4.4	6.7	7.7	2.3
12.1	14.0	14.0	Total Current	9.5	19.3	35.3	38.6	42.5	38.9
79.5	77.5	77.3	Fixed Assets (net)	83.0	68.8	51.4	45.7	45.4	49.0
1.9	1.5	1.5	Intangibles (net)	1.3	1.8	2.0	5.5	.9	1.6
6.5	7.1	7.3	All Other Non-Current	6.2	10.1	11.3	10.2	11.2	10.4
100.0	100.0	100.0	Total	100.0	100.0	100.0	100.0	100.0	100.0
			LIABILITIES						
5.0	5.7	6.2	Notes Payable-Short Term	5.5	8.8	6.7	4.9	8.3	10.9
5.0	4.9	4.9	Cur. Mat.-L/T/D	5.0	4.6	3.9	7.2	4.3	4.4
1.4	1.7	1.8	Trade Payables	.9	2.4	5.7	8.2	8.6	10.1
.0	.1	.1	Income Taxes Payable	.0	.1	.1	.3	.2	.1
6.9	6.7	6.1	All Other Current	5.1	7.8	9.8	11.0	12.3	7.6
18.3	19.1	19.0	Total Current	16.5	23.7	26.2	31.6	33.6	33.0
62.0	58.4	60.4	Long-Term Debt	64.5	57.1	35.1	36.8	37.9	31.8
.1	.1	.1	Deferred Taxes	.0	.1	.5	.3	.8	.8
3.4	5.1	3.8	All Other Non-Current	3.6	3.8	5.3	6.5	2.6	4.6
16.2	17.3	16.7	Net Worth	15.4	15.3	32.8	24.8	25.1	29.7
100.0	100.0	100.0	Total Liabilities & Net Worth	100.0	100.0	100.0	100.0	100.0	100.0
			INCOME DATA						
100.0	100.0	100.0	Net Sales	100.0	100.0	100.0	100.0	100.0	100.0
			Gross Profit						
55.2	55.4	56.6	Operating Expenses	51.7	65.0	69.3	84.9	81.7	88.3
44.8	44.6	43.4	Operating Profit	48.3	35.0	30.7	15.1	18.3	11.7
24.4	21.8	20.6	All Other Expenses (net)	23.7	14.1	10.5	5.0	5.9	6.7
20.4	22.8	22.9	Profit Before Taxes	24.6	21.0	20.2	10.1	12.4	5.0
			RATIOS						
1.9	2.0	1.9		1.7	2.1	3.0	2.0	1.6	1.8
.6	.7	.6	Current	.5	.8	1.3	1.0	1.3	1.2
.2	.2	.1		.1	.2	.6	.6	.7	.7
1.3	1.3	1.3		1.2	1.4	2.7	1.3	1.0	1.3
(1466) .4	(1957) .4	(1874) .4	Quick	(1398) .3	.5	.8	.6	.5	.5
.1	.1	.1		.1	.1	.2	.2	.1	.3
0 UND	0 UND	0 UND		0 UND	0 UND	0 UND	0 999.8	2 150.4	3 113.0
0 UND	0 UND	0 UND	Sales/Receivables	0 UND	0 UND	0 999.8	10 37.6	11 31.8	18 20.7
2 165.0	1 440.5	1 485.1		0 UND	6 57.8	16 23.3	39 9.3	57 6.4	39 9.3
			Cost of Sales/Inventory						
			Cost of Sales/Payables						
9.4	7.7	7.8		9.3	6.9	3.9	6.8	4.8	11.2
-13.2	-14.1	-10.7	Sales/Working Capital	-6.5	-31.7	26.0	NM	17.3	39.3
-2.4	-2.3	-2.1		-1.8	-3.6	-9.0	-12.6	-8.1	-21.5
6.3	7.3	7.2		6.8	8.6	13.6	10.8	11.0	5.9
(515) 3.5	(796) 3.9	(817) 3.8	EBIT/Interest	(514) 4.0	(166) 3.7	(44) 4.0	(35) 3.4	(33) 3.2	(25) 2.8
1.8	1.9	1.8		2.1	1.7	1.8	1.3	1.2	1.1
3.2	3.0	3.0		2.4	2.1				
(92) 1.5	(90) 1.6	(90) 1.5	Net Profit + Depr., Dep., Amort./Cur. Mat. L/T/D	(36) 1.3	(27) 1.4				
.7	.8	.7		.7	.5				
1.9	1.8	1.9		2.2	1.5	.5	.5	.2	.3
4.7	4.5	4.4	Fixed/Worth	4.8	4.1	1.7	3.4	1.7	1.8
65.8	55.1	48.4		59.4	NM	7.2	199.5	10.3	4.9
1.5	1.5	1.6		1.7	1.3	.7	1.3	1.7	1.1
4.6	4.6	4.4	Debt/Worth	4.6	4.6	2.8	4.5	3.2	3.1
85.7	67.1	64.3		74.0	-97.5	11.3	224.9	15.8	7.4
39.0	41.1	41.5	% Profit Before Taxes/Tangible Net Worth	36.5	55.8	67.3	95.2	48.4	56.1
(1121) 17.2	(1520) 18.8	(1457) 18.6		(1082) 17.1	(209) 23.7	(60) 29.2	(37) 45.7	(37) 30.3	(32) 16.4
4.3	5.3	5.7		4.9	8.6	7.1	3.3	11.1	-7.0
9.1	9.6	9.1	% Profit Before Taxes/Total Assets	8.6	11.0	16.6	18.3	10.0	13.0
3.8	4.1	4.3		4.0	5.1	6.2	5.2	5.0	3.4
.6	.8	.8		.8	1.3	.7	.5	1.2	-2.0
.5	.5	.5	Sales/Net Fixed Assets	.3	1.3	16.8	27.2	27.5	35.8
.2	.2	.2		.2	.3	1.4	2.6	1.9	3.6
.1	.1	.1		.1	.2	.4	.4	.3	.5
.4	.3	.3	Sales/Total Assets	.3	.7	2.0	3.3	1.7	3.4
.2	.2	.2		.2	.3	.5	1.2	.6	1.2
.1	.1	.1		.1	.2	.2	.3	.2	.3
10.4	10.0	10.0		12.3	5.3	1.7	1.4	1.1	.4
(1354) 16.5	(1772) 16.7	(1677) 16.9	% Depr., Dep., Amort./Sales	(1264) 18.5	(257) 13.7	(55) 7.6	(41) 6.3	(35) 3.6	(25) 1.8
24.1	24.6	24.8		27.0	21.6	13.6	14.4	15.9	10.1
4.0	3.0	2.8		4.1	3.3	2.5	1.9		
(138) 8.0	(190) 6.0	(176) 6.5	% Officers', Directors', Owners' Comp/Sales	(92) 8.2	(41) 4.9	(18) 5.1	(13) 6.5		
17.5	14.4	12.1		16.7	9.4	8.0	7.7		
4046792M	6817868M	5248882M	Net Sales ($)	461194M	483708M	267289M	343888M	694101M	2998702M
8522017M	11064906M	11190706M	Total Assets ($)	2768464M	1965913M	897637M	738409M	1811221M	3009062M

© RMA 2005

M = $ thousand   MM = $ million

See Pages 11 through 21 for Explanation of Ratios and Data

Current Data Sorted By Assets   **Comparative Historical Data**

Type of Statement	0-500M	500M-2MM	2-10MM	10-50MM	50-100MM	100-250MM		4/1/00-3/31/01 ALL	4/1/01-3/31/02 ALL
Unqualified	3	10	28	31	8	5		76	68
Reviewed	5	17	27	18	3			68	70
Compiled	32	40	40	9				171	212
Tax Returns	207	162	68	6		3		215	250
Other	69	90	88	50	12	7		262	277
	93 (4/1-9/30/04)			945 (10/1/04-3/31/05)					
NUMBER OF STATEMENTS	316	319	251	114	23	15		792	877
ASSETS	%	%	%	%	%	%		%	%
Cash & Equivalents	34.7	15.6	12.0	10.9	17.0	15.9		15.3	15.3
Trade Receivables (net)	6.7	5.2	5.6	8.8	8.2	8.7		7.7	7.0
Inventory	2.6	6.1	10.9	8.8	2.7	6.6		4.6	4.3
All Other Current	4.9	3.7	4.2	7.0	7.4	8.1		6.0	6.2
Total Current	49.0	30.7	32.8	35.4	35.3	39.3		33.5	32.7
Fixed Assets (net)	33.1	52.4	50.6	36.0	30.2	34.9		46.4	49.6
Intangibles (net)	5.9	4.8	4.0	3.4	8.6	1.0		4.1	4.5
All Other Non-Current	12.0	12.2	12.6	25.3	25.9	24.8		15.9	13.2
Total	100.0	100.0	100.0	100.0	100.0	100.0		100.0	100.0
LIABILITIES									
Notes Payable-Short Term	15.6	10.6	10.0	12.6	7.4	.4		9.6	18.5
Cur. Mat.-L/T/D	3.3	3.6	2.8	1.7	2.0	1.8		4.5	7.4
Trade Payables	5.9	3.5	3.1	3.8	8.3	2.2		5.7	4.4
Income Taxes Payable	.1	.2	.1	.3	.1	.1		.1	.1
All Other Current	25.8	12.7	12.4	11.3	11.3	9.0		16.1	15.4
Total Current	50.7	30.6	28.5	29.7	29.1	13.5		36.0	45.9
Long-Term Debt	25.7	41.8	42.7	32.8	26.1	40.5		34.7	38.6
Deferred Taxes	.0	.0	.1	.5	.5	2.3		.3	.3
All Other Non-Current	6.2	5.2	2.8	3.6	3.7	4.4		5.7	6.0
Net Worth	17.3	22.5	25.9	33.4	40.6	39.3		23.4	9.1
Total Liabilities & Net Worth	100.0	100.0	100.0	100.0	100.0	100.0		100.0	100.0
INCOME DATA									
Net Sales	100.0	100.0	100.0	100.0	100.0	100.0		100.0	100.0
Gross Profit									
Operating Expenses	84.3	70.7	72.6	75.4	79.0	77.8		79.0	74.3
Operating Profit	15.7	29.3	27.4	24.6	21.0	22.2		21.0	25.7
All Other Expenses (net)	3.4	12.4	11.1	8.0	7.6	8.0		8.6	13.3
Profit Before Taxes	12.4	16.9	16.2	16.6	13.4	14.1		12.5	12.4
RATIOS									
Current	4.0	2.4	2.2	2.2	1.7	5.1		2.2	2.1
	1.2	.9	1.1	1.3	1.1	1.6		1.0	1.0
	.4	.3	.4	.6	.6	.3		.4	.3
Quick	3.1	1.9	1.4	1.5	1.2	3.7		1.6	1.5
	.9	.7	.6	.7	.6	.5	(791) .6	(876) .6
	.3	.1	.1	.1	.3	.2		.2	.1
Sales/Receivables	0 UND	0 UND	0 UND	0 UND	1 271.8	0 UND		0 UND	0 UND
	0 UND	0 UND	0 999.8	4 96.6	11 31.8	2 178.2		1 706.2	0 UND
	1 359.8	2 148.1	10 36.5	24 15.5	36 10.1	28 13.2		15 24.3	14 26.4
Cost of Sales/Inventory									
Cost of Sales/Payables									
Sales/Working Capital	12.6	8.1	4.7	2.9	6.7	3.7		7.1	8.6
	161.9	-186.1	72.2	21.0	81.6	15.7		275.4	425.8
	-18.0	-4.5	-5.7	-14.1	-7.3	-4.7		-6.5	-6.2
EBIT/Interest	25.7	15.8	14.3	29.0	14.1	10.1		9.8	8.3
	(167) 7.2	(184) 5.1	(156) 5.8	(76) 5.2	(16) 4.2	(11) 5.4	(455) 3.4	(466) 3.3
	2.4	2.3	2.3	1.6	1.6	1.9		1.2	1.1
Net Profit + Depr., Dep., Amort./Cur. Mat. L /T/D		6.4	10.2	3.5				5.7	6.6
		(14) 3.2	(23) 4.4	(20) 1.8			(69) 2.3	(69) 2.3	
		1.0	1.5	.9				1.0	1.1
Fixed/Worth	.0	.5	.3	.1	.3	.1		.4	.5
	.9	3.0	1.9	.7	1.0	.4		1.6	2.3
	20.8	42.3	11.7	3.2	3.3	5.5		11.5	34.1
Debt/Worth	.5	1.5	1.2	1.2	1.0	.7		.9	1.0
	2.9	5.1	4.0	2.8	2.3	1.4		3.1	3.9
	-19.7	128.0	22.4	8.8	6.3	5.7		28.3	563.2
% Profit Before Taxes/Tangible Net Worth	260.9	88.5	81.7	55.2	45.2	27.7		56.6	62.3
	(226) 79.7	(246) 32.1	(210) 31.1	(108) 25.3	(20) 15.0	(13) 17.0	(629) 19.7	(664) 19.1
	18.7	12.1	7.4	7.0	5.2	5.5		4.4	4.6
% Profit Before Taxes/Total Assets	90.2	19.0	15.8	14.2	15.4	9.8		14.2	13.7
	18.8	6.9	6.7	5.7	4.3	8.5		5.1	5.0
	3.9	1.6	1.5	1.1	1.1	1.2		.5	.4
Sales/Net Fixed Assets	347.0	38.7	26.2	32.9	35.5	50.2		30.6	28.4
	47.9	1.6	1.4	6.9	9.1	7.8		5.4	3.5
	6.8	.2	.2	.3	.4	.4		.3	.2
Sales/Total Assets	11.6	2.7	1.7	1.6	2.2	1.5		3.5	3.4
	4.9	.5	.5	.4	.6	.4		.7	.7
	1.7	.2	.2	.2	.2	.2		.2	.2
% Depr., Dep., Amort./Sales	.5	1.3	1.3	1.1	1.4			1.1	1.1
	(177) 1.6	(241) 9.5	(204) 6.5	(88) 2.7	(17) 2.5		(640) 3.8	(706) 4.2	
	4.7	18.6	17.8	14.3	16.8			14.3	15.0
% Officers', Directors', Owners' Comp/Sales	3.0	2.3	2.4	.6				3.6	3.0
	(141) 7.7	(76) 5.6	(46) 4.9	(12) 4.1			(220) 8.2	(209) 7.6	
	18.0	15.1	7.2	8.4				15.7	14.0
Net Sales ($)	417663M	739889M	1524760M	3025150M	2463581M	7140865M		9560377M	13104698M
Total Assets ($)	63895M	350829M	1092455M	2648282M	1651044M	2481408M		7757795M	7612258M

© RMA 2005

M = $ thousand   MM = $ million
See Pages 11 through 21 for Explanation of Ratios and Data

Comparative Historical Data			Type of Statement	Current Data Sorted By Sales					
97	101	85	Unqualified	10	13	6	17	14	25
93	84	70	Reviewed	10	23	8	11	9	9
148	193	121	Compiled	51	41	7	11	10	1
342	469	446	Tax Returns	296	77	27	29	12	5
279	294	316	Other	105	82	30	28	40	31
4/1/02-3/31/03 ALL	4/1/03-3/31/04 ALL	4/1/04-3/31/05 ALL		93 (4/1-9/30/04) 0-1MM	1-3MM	3-5MM	945 (10/1/04-3/31/05) 5-10MM	10-25MM	25MM & OVER
959	1141	1038	**NUMBER OF STATEMENTS**	472	236	78	96	85	71
%	%	%	**ASSETS**	%	%	%	%	%	%
16.5	18.5	20.1	Cash & Equivalents	17.0	23.6	25.2	20.3	19.2	23.9
7.3	6.2	6.3	Trade Receivables (net)	2.5	7.5	8.3	11.3	12.9	10.8
2.9	4.4	6.4	Inventory	3.8	5.9	13.7	11.7	7.5	9.1
5.5	5.6	4.7	All Other Current	3.0	4.8	5.9	9.9	4.0	8.0
32.2	34.8	37.5	Total Current	26.3	41.8	53.0	53.2	43.7	51.6
48.3	45.3	43.6	Fixed Assets (net)	61.0	34.6	25.5	28.3	22.9	22.8
4.8	4.5	4.8	Intangibles (net)	3.4	5.8	6.3	4.5	6.8	7.4
14.8	15.5	14.1	All Other Non-Current	9.3	17.8	15.2	14.0	26.6	18.1
100.0	100.0	100.0	Total	100.0	100.0	100.0	100.0	100.0	100.0
			LIABILITIES						
10.4	9.8	12.0	Notes Payable-Short Term	9.4	15.1	19.6	17.7	7.2	8.3
4.0	4.0	3.1	Cur. Mat.-L/T/D	3.1	3.2	4.2	1.9	3.2	2.2
4.4	4.3	4.3	Trade Payables	2.4	4.2	5.6	5.1	8.8	8.5
.2	.2	.1	Income Taxes Payable	.0	.2	.1	.3	.6	.1
15.5	17.7	16.4	All Other Current	15.8	15.2	19.8	14.6	21.0	16.6
34.5	36.1	35.8	Total Current	30.9	38.0	49.2	39.6	40.8	35.7
35.6	35.3	35.8	Long-Term Debt	49.3	27.8	25.5	21.8	22.0	18.8
.2	.2	.1	Deferred Taxes	.0	.1	.0	.1	.5	.8
6.3	5.6	4.7	All Other Non-Current	3.8	7.1	4.3	3.0	5.7	4.3
23.5	22.8	23.6	Net Worth	16.0	27.1	21.0	35.4	30.9	40.4
100.0	100.0	100.0	Total Liabilities & Net Worth	100.0	100.0	100.0	100.0	100.0	100.0
			INCOME DATA						
100.0	100.0	100.0	Net Sales	100.0	100.0	100.0	100.0	100.0	100.0
			Gross Profit						
76.4	77.4	76.1	Operating Expenses	64.4	83.0	87.7	88.2	87.4	88.3
23.6	22.6	23.9	Operating Profit	35.6	17.0	12.3	11.8	12.6	11.7
10.9	9.5	8.7	All Other Expenses (net)	15.8	4.9	.8	1.7	1.8	.5
12.7	13.1	15.2	Profit Before Taxes	19.7	12.2	11.5	10.0	10.9	11.3
			RATIOS						
2.1	2.5	2.8		3.4	2.8	2.0	2.3	1.9	2.1
1.0	1.0	1.1	Current	.9	1.1	1.1	1.4	1.1	1.3
.3	.3	.4		.2	.4	.7	.8	.6	1.0
1.7	1.8	1.9		2.6	2.0	1.7	1.6	1.6	1.4
(955) .7	(1140) .6	.7	Quick	.6	.7	.8	.8	.8	1.0
.2	.1	.1		.1	.1	.2	.1	.4	.4
0 UND	0 UND	0 UND		0 UND	0 UND	0 UND	0 UND	0 999.8	1 567.8
0 UND	0 UND	0 UND	Sales/Receivables	0 UND	0 UND	1 587.9	2 214.3	4 92.9	4 83.9
10 35.9	7 55.0	6 61.0		0 UND	9 42.5	8 44.1	10 35.9	23 15.7	22 16.3
			Cost of Sales/Inventory						
			Cost of Sales/Payables						
10.5	8.0	7.1		5.0	8.1	9.4	6.7	10.9	10.1
−245.2	536.7	129.7	Sales/Working Capital	−74.6	98.4	108.1	46.7	58.1	35.1
−5.5	−5.5	−9.0		−3.4	−13.2	−32.4	−59.8	−26.9	999.8
14.6	15.0	18.8		10.7	18.8	31.9	30.3	28.2	55.6
(538) 4.4	(657) 4.5	(610) 5.6	EBIT/Interest	(202) 4.3	(159) 6.8	(57) 5.6	(69) 8.2	(65) 9.0	(58) 10.0
1.7	1.7	2.2		2.0	1.9	2.7	2.0	2.2	3.4
8.1	7.7	6.7	Net Profit + Depr., Dep.,	5.0	9.3			8.4	7.3
(76) 2.6	(84) 3.0	(68) 2.7	Amort./Cur. Mat. L/T/D	(12) 2.2	(13) 2.4		(13) 3.9	(20) 3.2
1.0	1.2	1.1		.7	.8			1.4	1.5
.4	.3	.2		.8	.1	.1	.1	.1	.2
1.8	1.7	1.7	Fixed/Worth	3.8	1.1	.7	.6	.5	.5
32.0	20.2	14.0		42.0	10.0	4.0	3.1	3.4	1.7
.9	1.0	1.0		1.2	.7	.8	1.1	.8	.7
3.2	3.2	3.4	Debt/Worth	5.8	2.4	6.7	2.2	3.0	1.7
80.4	51.2	40.8		127.3	38.0	266.6	6.8	11.4	4.7
76.4	83.3	100.0	% Profit Before Taxes/Tangible	86.3	97.4	224.6	137.0	79.5	104.5
(753) 25.2	(892) 28.9	(823) 35.3	Net Worth	(364) 28.6	(183) 35.3	(60) 55.3	(87) 34.5	(69) 40.5	(60) 47.5
7.5	6.6	10.5		7.5	10.9	14.5	9.1	13.7	21.0
18.7	19.8	24.7	% Profit Before Taxes/Total	15.3	35.0	43.8	28.8	31.5	35.8
6.2	6.5	8.1	Assets	5.2	10.5	10.3	10.9	13.4	15.4
.9	.8	1.6		1.2	2.2	4.3	2.0	3.6	8.5
34.4	44.4	72.3		15.3	138.5	270.0	113.6	104.1	51.5
5.3	7.4	9.3	Sales/Net Fixed Assets	.4	19.6	44.8	28.4	25.0	22.8
.3	.3	.3		.2	1.4	10.9	5.0	6.7	9.3
4.0	3.9	4.3		1.8	5.7	8.7	7.0	6.1	6.0
.8	.9	1.1	Sales/Total Assets	.3	2.0	2.6	2.3	2.6	3.3
.2	.2	.2		.1	.5	.9	.6	.7	1.5
1.1	1.1	1.0		4.4	.6	.4	.3	.5	.6
(773) 4.4	(886) 3.9	(736) 3.9	% Depr., Dep., Amort./Sales	(350) 13.3	(152) 2.3	(47) 1.3	(70) 1.1	(63) 1.2	(54) 1.2
15.9	15.7	16.1		20.4	10.7	2.9	2.9	2.1	1.8
2.7	2.8	2.5	% Officers', Directors',	5.2	3.1	1.5	1.0	1.9	.8
(249) 7.2	(312) 7.0	(280) 6.1	Owners' Comp/Sales	(89) 12.4	(88) 6.4	(32) 2.9	(37) 2.4	(22) 3.6	(12) 4.6
16.9	15.1	15.1		21.3	15.6	10.4	6.3	6.6	8.4
10822623M	15572980M	15311908M	Net Sales ($)	173403M	433656M	305526M	663866M	1359397M	12376060M
8423473M	9809390M	8287913M	Total Assets ($)	613207M	837047M	330302M	899466M	1589748M	4018143M

M = $ thousand   MM = $ million
See Pages 11 through 21 for Explanation of Ratios and Data

Current Data Sorted By Assets   Comparative Historical Data

						Type of Statement		
1	5 1	2 1	3 1		1	Unqualified Reviewed		
2 11 8	3 18 6	2 8 9	1 5		1	Compiled Tax Returns Other		
	10 (4/1-9/30/04)			78 (10/1/04-3/31/05)			4/1/00- 3/31/01 ALL	4/1/01- 3/31/02 ALL
0-500M	500M-2MM	2-10MM	10-50MM	50-100MM	100-250MM			
22	33	21	10		2	**NUMBER OF STATEMENTS**		
%	%	%	%	%	%	**ASSETS**	%	%
19.1	10.9	9.2	3.6			Cash & Equivalents		
8.9	5.7	1.6	9.7	D		Trade Receivables (net)	D	D
4.5	4.7	4.6	9.6	A		Inventory	A	A
5.5	5.3	1.5	4.8	T		All Other Current	T	T
38.0	26.6	16.8	27.7	A		Total Current	A	A
40.1	61.4	59.9	47.0			Fixed Assets (net)		
9.0	2.3	1.2	1.2	N		Intangibles (net)	N	N
12.9	9.6	22.1	24.1	O		All Other Non-Current	O	O
100.0	100.0	100.0	100.0	T		Total	T	T
						LIABILITIES		
10.9	6.8	9.1	12.3	A		Notes Payable-Short Term	A	A
4.0	4.5	1.1	4.4	V		Cur. Mat.-L/T/D	V	V
4.8	4.0	1.2	2.0	A		Trade Payables	A	A
.8	.0	.0	.1	I		Income Taxes Payable	I	I
9.8	10.2	4.8	6.7	L		All Other Current	L	L
30.3	25.6	16.2	25.5	A		Total Current	A	A
33.9	62.4	46.2	38.6	B		Long-Term Debt	B	B
.1	.2	.0	.0	L		Deferred Taxes	L	L
5.2	4.0	5.6	.3	E		All Other Non-Current	E	E
30.5	7.7	32.1	35.6			Net Worth		
100.0	100.0	100.0	100.0			Total Liabilities & Net Worth		
						INCOME DATA		
100.0	100.0	100.0	100.0			Net Sales		
						Gross Profit		
79.9	82.4	81.2	64.8			Operating Expenses		
20.1	17.6	18.8	35.2			Operating Profit		
8.0	14.6	8.4	9.0			All Other Expenses (net)		
12.2	3.0	10.4	26.1			Profit Before Taxes		
						RATIOS		
4.4	2.9	1.3	2.1					
1.1	.7	.3	.9			Current		
.5	.4	.2	.3					
2.8	1.9	.8	.8					
.9	.5	.2	.4			Quick		
.4	.1	.0	.1					
0 UND	0 UND	0 UND	0 UND					
0 UND	4 84.4	0 UND	18 20.0			Sales/Receivables		
14 27.0	11 34.4	14 26.7	102 3.6					
						Cost of Sales/Inventory		
						Cost of Sales/Payables		
5.3	12.9	9.7	6.3					
UND	−17.6	−25.0	NM			Sales/Working Capital		
−10.0	−5.0	−5.5	−1.3					
	3.9	19.7						
(18) 1.6	(10) 2.5					EBIT/Interest		
−.3	.9							
						Net Profit + Depr., Dep., Amort./Cur. Mat. L /T/D		
.2	2.0	.5	.2					
1.7	3.4	2.4	1.2			Fixed/Worth		
UND	−7.0	12.2	7.5					
.3	1.7	.7	.7					
2.0	7.2	2.9	3.5			Debt/Worth		
UND	−13.8	36.0	7.9					
119.7	53.5	66.5	52.5			% Profit Before Taxes/Tangible		
(17) 64.3	(22) .1	(18) 28.0	22.1			Net Worth		
10.0	−7.9	.8	11.2					
32.0	8.1	10.9	11.3			% Profit Before Taxes/Total		
14.0	.8	3.9	7.2			Assets		
−.3	−2.3	.9	3.3					
46.3	11.9	9.1	14.0					
15.7	.7	.5	.5			Sales/Net Fixed Assets		
.9	.2	.2	.2					
4.1	1.4	.8	.6					
1.5	.4	.4	.2			Sales/Total Assets		
.6	.2	.2	.1					
1.6	2.9	4.1						
(12) 4.8	(30) 8.8	(14) 15.2				% Depr., Dep., Amort./Sales		
22.4	21.8	22.2						
						% Officers', Directors', Owners' Comp/Sales		
15323M	52152M	48879M	109575M		657330M	Net Sales ($)		
5684M	39910M	90917M	251859M		324006M	Total Assets ($)		

© RMA 2005

M = $ thousand   MM = $ million
See Pages 11 through 21 for Explanation of Ratios and Data

Comparative Historical Data				Current Data Sorted By Sales					
5	8	12	Type of Statement Unqualified	7	1		2		2
3	2	2	Reviewed			1	1		
7	7	7	Compiled	4	3				
16	39	38	Tax Returns	24	10	2	1	1	
10	35	29	Other	11	6	5	4	2	1
4/1/02-3/31/03 ALL	4/1/03-3/31/04 ALL	4/1/04-3/31/05 ALL		10 (4/1-9/30/04) 0-1MM	1-3MM	3-5MM	78 (10/1/04-3/31/05) 5-10MM	10-25MM	25MM & OVER
41	91	88	NUMBER OF STATEMENTS	46	20	8	8	3	3
%	%	%	ASSETS	%	%	%	%	%	%
18.7	14.3	12.6	Cash & Equivalents	11.6	13.9				
6.1	4.6	5.9	Trade Receivables (net)	4.1	6.8				
10.1	5.6	5.1	Inventory	2.0	7.8				
11.2	5.1	4.3	All Other Current	5.1	3.3				
46.1	29.6	27.8	Total Current	22.9	31.8				
43.4	53.5	53.7	Fixed Assets (net)	67.5	42.1				
4.4	4.4	3.6	Intangibles (net)	.5	10.5				
6.1	12.5	14.9	All Other Non-Current	9.1	15.6				
100.0	100.0	100.0	Total	100.0	100.0				
			LIABILITIES						
12.1	17.0	10.3	Notes Payable-Short Term	6.6	11.7				
4.1	3.3	3.5	Cur. Mat.-L/T/D	4.6	1.6				
2.6	4.1	3.3	Trade Payables	2.4	5.1				
.0	.1	.2	Income Taxes Payable	.0	.7				
13.4	10.0	8.4	All Other Current	5.9	14.1				
32.2	34.4	25.6	Total Current	19.4	33.2				
38.5	46.2	48.3	Long-Term Debt	63.5	39.6				
.0	.0	.1	Deferred Taxes	.0	.5				
2.0	2.8	4.2	All Other Non-Current	5.7	1.5				
27.3	16.6	21.8	Net Worth	11.4	25.2				
100.0	100.0	100.0	Total Liabilities & Net Worth	100.0	100.0				
			INCOME DATA						
100.0	100.0	100.0	Net Sales	100.0	100.0				
			Gross Profit						
80.3	74.8	79.7	Operating Expenses	75.4	88.8				
19.7	25.2	20.3	Operating Profit	24.6	11.2				
8.3	14.4	10.8	All Other Expenses (net)	16.6	7.5				
11.5	10.8	9.5	Profit Before Taxes	7.9	3.7				
			RATIOS						
4.2	2.5	1.7		2.9	1.5				
1.8	1.1	.7	Current	.6	1.0				
.7	.3	.4		.3	.3				
2.9	1.6	1.4		2.1	1.3				
.6	.5	(87) .5	Quick	(45) .5	.6				
.1	.1	.2		.1	.1				
0 UND	0 UND	0 UND		0 UND	0 UND				
0 UND	0 UND	1 443.6	Sales/Receivables	0 UND	0 UND				
15 23.7	10 38.2	15 24.2		14 27.0	14 26.8				
			Cost of Sales/Inventory						
			Cost of Sales/Payables						
3.1	7.6	9.1		6.4	22.2				
17.4	65.1	-31.7	Sales/Working Capital	-7.0	UND				
-27.8	-6.0	-5.1		-3.6	-6.8				
22.3	59.1	6.7		2.7	3.2				
(21) 3.7	(46) 3.5	(45) 2.7	EBIT/Interest	(17) 1.6	(10) 1.3				
1.5	1.8	.5		-.4	-2.8				
			Net Profit + Depr., Dep., Amort./Cur. Mat. L/T/D						
.1	.5	.6		1.8	.7				
1.3	3.7	2.5	Fixed/Worth	4.5	5.0				
8.2	-113.8	527.5		-10.7	UND				
.6	1.0	1.2		1.4	1.5				
3.2	6.0	4.2	Debt/Worth	4.7	12.5				
193.9	-127.0	UND		-15.0	UND				
89.5	108.5	65.1	% Profit Before Taxes/Tangible Net Worth	50.9	106.1				
(32) 18.9	(68) 31.7	(68) 22.1		(31) 4.5	(16) 15.1				
4.4	10.1	-4.9		-5.8	-19.7				
46.2	19.4	12.3	% Profit Before Taxes/Total Assets	7.5	9.6				
7.0	4.4	3.7		1.9	2.5				
.0	.3	-.9		-2.1	-5.5				
45.3	22.2	19.6	Sales/Net Fixed Assets	1.2	36.7				
18.3	1.3	.9		.4	11.9				
.2	.2	.2		.2	.3				
4.0	2.7	1.5	Sales/Total Assets	.7	3.9				
.8	.5	.5		.3	2.0				
.2	.2	.2		.1	.3				
1.0	2.5	3.0	% Depr., Dep., Amort./Sales	8.0	2.5				
(29) 4.8	(64) 12.7	(64) 10.1		(36) 16.9	(14) 4.9				
20.4	19.7	21.5		26.5	14.3				
2.9	7.1	3.6	% Officers', Directors', Owners' Comp/Sales						
(12) 9.4	(15) 8.6	(20) 6.5							
14.9	17.8	16.8							
127604M	351077M	883259M	Net Sales ($)	17479M	35495M	29391M	46139M	45035M	709720M
212617M	617598M	712376M	Total Assets ($)	61734M	76476M	63767M	102586M	143924M	263889M

© RMA 2005

M = $ thousand   MM = $ million
See Pages 11 through 21 for Explanation of Ratios and Data

Current Data Sorted By Assets   **Comparative Historical Data**

	0-500M	500M-2MM	2-10MM	10-50MM	50-100MM	100-250MM		4/1/00-3/31/01 ALL	4/1/01-3/31/02 ALL
Type of Statement									
Unqualified			1						
Reviewed			3	1					
Compiled		6	6	2	1	1			
Tax Returns	1	17	6	2					
Other	9	12	11	5	1	1			
	9								
	7 (4/1-9/30/04)			87 (10/1/04-3/31/05)					
NUMBER OF STATEMENTS	19	35	27	10	2	1			
	%	%	%	%	%	%	**ASSETS**	%	%
	21.1	4.9	4.1	6.5			Cash & Equivalents	D	D
	3.1	4.0	2.3	1.0			Trade Receivables (net)	A	A
	4.8	.1	9.5	11.9			Inventory	T	T
	5.7	1.2	3.1	8.6			All Other Current	A	A
	34.8	10.2	19.1	28.0			Total Current		
	48.0	82.4	66.9	66.9			Fixed Assets (net)	N	N
	5.9	2.0	2.1	1.0			Intangibles (net)	O	O
	11.3	5.5	11.9	4.1			All Other Non-Current	T	T
	100.0	100.0	100.0	100.0			Total		
							LIABILITIES	A	A
	21.1	4.2	4.9	4.6			Notes Payable-Short Term	V	V
	4.0	4.6	1.8	3.4			Cur. Mat.-L/T/D	A	A
	19.9	.5	1.0	1.1			Trade Payables	I	I
	.0	.0	.0	.0			Income Taxes Payable	L	L
	16.2	3.6	7.6	8.0			All Other Current	A	A
	61.2	12.9	15.4	17.2			Total Current	B	B
	25.1	78.1	68.7	61.6			Long-Term Debt	L	L
	.0	.0	.0	.0			Deferred Taxes	E	E
	.6	2.7	1.9	4.3			All Other Non-Current		
	13.1	6.3	14.0	17.0			Net Worth		
	100.0	100.0	100.0	100.0			Total Liabilities & Net Worth		
							INCOME DATA		
	100.0	100.0	100.0	100.0			Net Sales		
							Gross Profit		
	84.7	58.6	62.8	69.7			Operating Expenses		
	15.3	41.4	37.2	30.3			Operating Profit		
	10.0	18.8	23.4	19.5			All Other Expenses (net)		
	5.4	22.6	13.8	10.8			Profit Before Taxes		
							RATIOS		
	1.4	2.1	1.9	15.8					
	.6	1.1	.5	1.5			Current		
	.1	.2	.3	.4					
	.9	2.1	.7	4.9					
	.6	.4	.4	.3			Quick		
	.1	.1	.2	.1					
	0 UND	0 UND	0 UND	0 UND					
	0 UND	0 UND	0 UND	0 UND			Sales/Receivables		
	1 283.0	2 174.0	15 24.7	8 48.1					
							Cost of Sales/Inventory		
							Cost of Sales/Payables		
	20.5	11.7	13.6	.5					
	-13.5	185.0	-7.6	11.3			Sales/Working Capital		
	-3.5	-2.7	-2.9	-4.9					
		12.2							
		(15) 2.6					EBIT/Interest		
		2.1							
							Net Profit + Depr., Dep., Amort./Cur. Mat. L /T/D		
	.6	2.4	1.7	2.1					
	3.2	7.5	4.3	4.1			Fixed/Worth		
	-2.8	-18.0	45.9	NM					
	.4	1.9	1.5	2.6					
	5.4	8.3	4.7	8.8			Debt/Worth		
	-4.7	-19.9	75.9	NM					
	42.6	61.1	32.9						
	(12) 30.3	(23) 32.4	(21) 18.8				% Profit Before Taxes/Tangible Net Worth		
	3.8	15.7	6.5						
	14.6	15.2	4.5	7.1					
	1.0	6.9	1.9	1.2			% Profit Before Taxes/Total Assets		
	-22.6	2.8	.7	.2					
	82.7	.6	.5	1.3					
	14.6	.3	.2	.3			Sales/Net Fixed Assets		
	.3	.2	.1	.2					
	5.1	.6	.4	.6					
	.9	.2	.2	.2			Sales/Total Assets		
	.3	.2	.1	.1					
	1.3	5.8	8.5						
	(11) 6.7	(31) 15.0	(25) 20.0				% Depr., Dep., Amort./Sales		
	10.9	21.0	26.0						
							% Officers', Directors', Owners' Comp/Sales		
	16804M	61286M	56904M	89651M	31056M	42430M	Net Sales ($)		
	5096M	40637M	123575M	244591M	147117M	176594M	Total Assets ($)		

© RMA 2005

M = $ thousand   MM = $ million
See Pages 11 through 21 for Explanation of Ratios and Data

Comparative Historical Data   Current Data Sorted By Sales

Type of Statement

	4/1/02-3/31/03 ALL	4/1/03-3/31/04 ALL	4/1/04-3/31/05 ALL	0-1MM	1-3MM	3-5MM	5-10MM	10-25MM	25MM & OVER
Unqualified		4	3				1	1	1
Reviewed	2	1	4	2	1				1
Compiled	5	11	15	9	4		1	1	1
Tax Returns	8	25	34	27	5	1	2	3	
Other	13	18	38	23	9			1	
	4/1/02-3/31/03 ALL	4/1/03-3/31/04 ALL	4/1/04-3/31/05 ALL	7 (4/1-9/30/04) 0-1MM	1-3MM	3-5MM	87 (10/1/04-3/31/05) 5-10MM	10-25MM	25MM & OVER
NUMBER OF STATEMENTS	28	59	94	61	19	1	4	6	3

ASSETS (%)

	4/1/02-3/31/03 ALL	4/1/03-3/31/04 ALL	4/1/04-3/31/05 ALL	0-1MM	1-3MM	3-5MM	5-10MM	10-25MM	25MM & OVER
Cash & Equivalents	12.2	10.0	8.0	8.3	4.5				
Trade Receivables (net)	6.0	1.3	2.9	3.5	.7				
Inventory	.1	2.9	5.0	.6	10.4				
All Other Current	11.0	1.4	3.4	1.4	11.4				
Total Current	29.3	15.7	19.3	13.8	26.9				
Fixed Assets (net)	57.6	67.3	69.7	76.4	58.8				
Intangibles (net)	3.0	4.3	2.7	2.4	3.4				
All Other Non-Current	10.0	12.7	8.3	7.3	10.9				
Total	100.0	100.0	100.0	100.0	100.0				

LIABILITIES

	4/1/02-3/31/03 ALL	4/1/03-3/31/04 ALL	4/1/04-3/31/05 ALL	0-1MM	1-3MM	3-5MM	5-10MM	10-25MM	25MM & OVER
Notes Payable-Short Term	12.6	10.0	7.7	7.7	10.5				
Cur. Mat.-L/T/D	11.8	7.3	3.5	2.9	5.9				
Trade Payables	2.9	.9	4.7	5.4	1.8				
Income Taxes Payable	.0	.0	.0	.0	.0				
All Other Current	15.0	6.3	7.7	4.5	17.2				
Total Current	42.4	24.5	23.7	20.5	35.4				
Long-Term Debt	59.6	49.3	63.5	59.4	84.0				
Deferred Taxes	.0	.0	.0	.0	.0				
All Other Non-Current	21.2	8.9	2.1	2.0	1.4				
Net Worth	-23.2	17.2	10.6	18.1	-20.8				
Total Liabilities & Net Worth	100.0	100.0	100.0	100.0	100.0				

INCOME DATA

	4/1/02-3/31/03 ALL	4/1/03-3/31/04 ALL	4/1/04-3/31/05 ALL	0-1MM	1-3MM	3-5MM	5-10MM	10-25MM	25MM & OVER
Net Sales	100.0	100.0	100.0	100.0	100.0				
Gross Profit									
Operating Expenses	66.9	61.5	66.9	60.6	71.8				
Operating Profit	33.1	38.5	33.1	39.4	28.2				
All Other Expenses (net)	18.2	21.5	19.0	21.0	15.4				
Profit Before Taxes	14.9	17.0	14.1	18.4	12.8				

RATIOS

	4/1/02-3/31/03 ALL	4/1/03-3/31/04 ALL	4/1/04-3/31/05 ALL	0-1MM	1-3MM	3-5MM	5-10MM	10-25MM	25MM & OVER
Current	1.9 / .5 / .2	1.6 / .6 / .1	1.9 / .6 / .2	1.4 / .6 / .2	1.9 / .6 / .1				
Quick	1.2 / (27) .4 / .1	1.3 / .4 / .1	1.3 / .4 / .1	1.2 / .4 / .2	1.1 / .1 / .0				
Sales/Receivables	0 UND / 0 UND / 17 21.4	0 UND / 0 UND / 2 235.2	0 UND / 0 UND / 6 58.4	0 UND / 0 UND / 2 198.0	0 UND / 0 868.5 / 7 53.5				
Cost of Sales/Inventory									
Cost of Sales/Payables									
Sales/Working Capital	6.2 / -15.3 / -2.8	9.1 / -8.1 / -1.5	12.1 / -12.4 / -3.0	14.4 / -9.9 / -2.7	8.7 / -5.3 / -3.4				
EBIT/Interest	(13) 7.2 / 2.5 / -1.4	(25) 6.2 / 4.5 / 1.4	(36) 5.0 / 2.5 / 1.2	(20) 10.5 / 2.4 / -.3					
Net Profit + Depr., Dep., Amort./Cur. Mat. L/T/D									
Fixed/Worth	1.7 / 7.1 / -6.9	1.5 / 3.1 / 14.9	1.8 / 5.5 / -25.6	2.2 / 6.1 / -39.7	1.5 / 3.6 / -3.7				
Debt/Worth	3.1 / 17.0 / -10.6	1.2 / 3.5 / 20.3	1.8 / 6.3 / -27.4	1.6 / 6.7 / -36.4	2.0 / 5.1 / -5.7				
% Profit Before Taxes/Tangible Net Worth	(17) 124.8 / 21.6 / .3	(47) 35.6 / 18.1 / 2.9	(65) 43.9 / 22.2 / 6.9	(42) 43.7 / 23.0 / 5.4	(13) 49.5 / 22.2 / 14.3				
% Profit Before Taxes/Total Assets	18.4 / 5.5 / -.3	8.6 / 3.9 / .7	8.6 / 3.3 / .3	8.3 / 3.4 / -.4	10.2 / 5.7 / 1.2				
Sales/Net Fixed Assets	16.7 / .7 / .2	2.1 / .3 / .1	2.2 / .3 / .2	.5 / .2 / .1	5.9 / .8 / .3				
Sales/Total Assets	2.8 / .4 / .2	.5 / .2 / .1	.7 / .2 / .1	.4 / .2 / .1	2.0 / .5 / .2				
% Depr., Dep., Amort./Sales	(20) 3.2 / 12.8 / 18.6	(53) 7.5 / 16.9 / 23.0	(78) 6.0 / 14.9 / 23.3	(50) 8.7 / 16.6 / 24.5	(15) 3.8 / 10.7 / 20.0				
% Officers', Directors', Owners' Comp/Sales		3.5 / (13) 8.3 / 18.3	2.1 / (16) 8.4 / 19.9						

Net Sales ($) / Total Assets ($)

	4/1/02-3/31/03 ALL	4/1/03-3/31/04 ALL	4/1/04-3/31/05 ALL	0-1MM	1-3MM	3-5MM	5-10MM	10-25MM	25MM & OVER
Net Sales ($)	355842M	275561M	298131M	21256M	34672M	3564M	30566M	92798M	115275M
Total Assets ($)	201341M	532877M	737610M	118959M	107751M	15240M	88011M	214364M	193285M

© RMA 2005

M = $ thousand   MM = $ million
See Pages 11 through 21 for Explanation of Ratios and Data

Current Data Sorted By Assets   **Comparative Historical Data**

						Type of Statement		
2	4	7	5	9		Unqualified		
2	2	6	3	2		Reviewed		
9	14	14	4			Compiled		
62	79	72	14	1		Tax Returns		
20	21	41	20	4	4	Other		
	28 (4/1-9/30/04)		393 (10/1/04-3/31/05)				4/1/00-3/31/01 ALL	4/1/01-3/31/02 ALL
0-500M	500M-2MM	2-10MM	10-50MM	50-100MM	100-250MM			
95	120	140	46	16	4	**NUMBER OF STATEMENTS**		
%	%	%	%	%	%	**ASSETS**	%	%
22.7	12.3	6.3	10.4	6.5		Cash & Equivalents	D	D
5.4	4.5	7.9	3.9	1.7		Trade Receivables (net)	A	A
6.4	12.5	21.1	17.3	16.1		Inventory	T	T
6.8	4.0	4.1	9.2	7.9		All Other Current	A	A
41.3	33.3	39.3	40.9	32.3		Total Current		
41.8	50.9	47.0	36.0	38.9		Fixed Assets (net)		
1.3	2.0	.8	2.8	1.1		Intangibles (net)	N	N
15.6	13.7	12.9	20.4	27.8		All Other Non-Current	O	O
100.0	100.0	100.0	100.0	100.0		Total	T	T
						LIABILITIES	A	A
14.8	13.6	14.6	13.2	12.1		Notes Payable-Short Term	V	V
7.8	3.5	4.4	3.6	6.9		Cur. Mat.-L/T/D	A	A
5.8	3.6	3.4	2.8	22.0		Trade Payables	I	I
.1	.0	.1	.2	.1		Income Taxes Payable	L	L
26.6	7.5	5.7	8.8	8.4		All Other Current	A	A
55.2	28.3	28.2	28.5	49.5		Total Current	B	B
33.0	42.5	39.1	33.3	34.1		Long-Term Debt	L	L
.0	.0	.1	.3	.0		Deferred Taxes	E	E
7.4	4.7	2.4	6.0	7.1		All Other Non-Current		
4.4	24.5	30.2	31.9	9.4		Net Worth		
100.0	100.0	100.0	100.0	100.0		Total Liabilities & Net Worth		
						INCOME DATA		
100.0	100.0	100.0	100.0	100.0		Net Sales		
						Gross Profit		
80.4	67.5	72.5	72.4	71.1		Operating Expenses		
19.6	32.5	27.5	27.6	28.9		Operating Profit		
5.6	13.3	9.9	10.9	4.3		All Other Expenses (net)		
14.0	19.3	17.6	16.7	24.6		Profit Before Taxes		
						RATIOS		
2.4	2.7	3.6	2.7	1.6				
.8	1.1	1.2	1.3	1.1		Current		
.3	.3	.4	.6	.3				
1.2	2.1	1.8	1.4	1.1				
(94) .4	.5	(139) .3	.4	.3		Quick		
.1	.1	.0	.0	.1				
0 UND	0 UND	0 UND	0 UND	0 UND				
0 UND	0 UND	0 UND	0 999.8	2 237.1		Sales/Receivables		
1 392.1	1 578.1	20 18.1	18 20.7	11 32.8				
						Cost of Sales/Inventory		
						Cost of Sales/Payables		
17.2	3.8	2.0	1.3	5.0				
-64.1	45.9	31.7	10.0	NM		Sales/Working Capital		
-5.2	-2.7	-5.9	-11.8	-3.6				
16.1	14.3	22.9	10.0	24.5				
(50) 4.6	(64) 4.3	(85) 7.2	(29) 4.0	(10) 4.9		EBIT/Interest		
.7	2.2	1.8	.9	2.0				
						Net Profit + Depr., Dep., Amort./Cur. Mat. L /T/D		
.0	.2	.2	.0	.1				
1.7	2.0	1.8	.7	1.3		Fixed/Worth		
16.2	9.3	7.0	7.6	6.1				
.7	1.3	1.0	1.2	3.0				
4.7	4.3	3.5	4.1	5.3		Debt/Worth		
-42.3	15.7	10.3	12.5	11.2				
133.3	91.1	53.6	43.6	92.2		% Profit Before Taxes/Tangible Net Worth		
(67) 61.1	(105) 30.9	(118) 20.1	(42) 13.3	(15) 42.2				
7.5	8.0	3.7	3.4	15.4				
51.6	13.2	12.8	9.2	13.6		% Profit Before Taxes/Total Assets		
10.2	5.9	3.5	4.0	6.9				
.3	1.3	.6	.3	1.4				
999.8	43.6	27.0	57.4	175.7		Sales/Net Fixed Assets		
19.6	.8	.9	2.5	9.4				
.9	.2	.2	.2	.2				
5.3	1.0	.9	.8	1.2		Sales/Total Assets		
2.0	.3	.3	.2	.3				
.5	.1	.1	.1	.2				
1.0	2.4	1.1	.4	.2		% Depr., Dep., Amort./Sales		
(55) 5.9	(82) 12.4	(93) 6.6	(32) 4.9	(11) 1.5				
20.5	18.7	18.1	15.1	11.6				
7.8	1.9	1.4				% Officers', Directors', Owners' Comp/Sales		
(27) 13.6	(15) 5.6	(22) 5.2						
23.7	11.9	7.9						
88165M	141480M	487881M	729918M	1159368M	300087M	Net Sales ($)		
24572M	134651M	620283M	1029712M	1092587M	737907M	Total Assets ($)		

© RMA 2005

M = $ thousand   MM = $ million

See Pages 11 through 21 for Explanation of Ratios and Data

	Comparative Historical Data			Type of Statement	Current Data Sorted By Sales					
	7	20	27	Unqualified	4	5	3	4	5	6
	5	14	15	Reviewed	3	5	1	1	1	5
	9	21	41	Compiled	22	9	4	3	2	1
	41	142	228	Tax Returns	152	44	8	14	9	1
	22	74	110	Other	41	34	7	11	5	12
	4/1/02-3/31/03 ALL	4/1/03-3/31/04 ALL	4/1/04-3/31/05 ALL		28 (4/1-9/30/04)		393 (10/1/04-3/31/05)			
					0-1MM	1-3MM	3-5MM	5-10MM	10-25MM	25MM & OVER
NUMBER OF STATEMENTS	84	271	421		222	97	22	33	22	25
	%	%	%	ASSETS	%	%	%	%	%	%
	11.3	13.7	12.5	Cash & Equivalents	9.6	15.0	12.3	17.6	15.5	19.0
	7.8	7.9	5.6	Trade Receivables (net)	4.5	5.5	8.2	8.4	8.6	8.0
	14.6	16.9	14.7	Inventory	8.7	15.3	32.1	19.4	36.7	26.0
	8.7	4.3	5.6	All Other Current	4.6	4.1	3.4	16.4	1.3	11.3
	42.4	42.9	38.4	Total Current	27.3	39.9	56.1	61.8	62.2	64.2
	42.8	41.9	45.0	Fixed Assets (net)	58.7	37.2	27.9	20.6	27.8	16.4
	1.5	1.4	1.5	Intangibles (net)	1.1	.9	1.5	2.8	.6	5.5
	13.4	13.9	15.0	All Other Non-Current	12.8	22.0	14.6	14.8	9.4	13.9
	100.0	100.0	100.0	Total	100.0	100.0	100.0	100.0	100.0	100.0
				LIABILITIES						
	19.9	16.4	14.1	Notes Payable-Short Term	12.2	11.9	19.9	24.4	20.4	16.1
	3.8	5.2	4.9	Cur. Mat.-L/T/D	5.0	5.5	3.3	4.8	2.4	5.0
	3.0	3.1	4.6	Trade Payables	2.1	2.7	7.4	7.4	14.9	18.9
	.1	.1	.1	Income Taxes Payable	.1	.0	.8	.0	.2	.2
	7.5	9.3	11.4	All Other Current	10.8	12.8	9.2	12.3	6.4	16.2
	34.2	34.1	35.1	Total Current	30.1	32.9	40.6	48.9	44.3	56.3
	35.1	34.2	37.7	Long-Term Debt	44.8	38.4	24.2	21.2	24.3	17.0
	.1	.1	.1	Deferred Taxes	.0	.0	.3	.0	.6	.4
	5.3	5.2	4.9	All Other Non-Current	5.7	4.0	.7	3.7	5.7	6.1
	25.3	26.4	22.2	Net Worth	19.3	24.7	34.2	26.2	25.1	20.2
	100.0	100.0	100.0	Total Liabilities & Net Worth	100.0	100.0	100.0	100.0	100.0	100.0
				INCOME DATA						
	100.0	100.0	100.0	Net Sales	100.0	100.0	100.0	100.0	100.0	100.0
				Gross Profit						
	75.1	73.5	72.9	Operating Expenses	65.7	76.2	87.3	80.5	82.0	92.5
	24.9	26.5	27.1	Operating Profit	34.3	23.8	12.7	19.5	18.0	7.5
	11.5	10.3	9.8	All Other Expenses (net)	15.3	5.1	.3	2.2	5.3	1.3
	13.4	16.2	17.4	Profit Before Taxes	19.0	18.8	12.4	17.3	12.7	6.2
				RATIOS						
	3.6	3.2	3.0		2.3	3.7	4.9	3.2	5.0	1.7
	1.3	1.1	1.1	Current	.8	1.4	1.4	1.2	1.3	1.4
	.5	.4	.4		.1	.4	.7	1.0	.8	.6
	1.6	1.5	1.6		1.4	2.9	2.6	1.4	2.3	1.4
	.6	.5	(419) .4	Quick	(221) .3	.4	(21) .6	.5	.4	.4
	.1	.1	.1		.0	.1	.2	.0	.1	.1
	0 UND	0 UND	0 UND		0 UND	0 UND	0 UND	0 UND	0 UND	0 UND
	0 UND	0 UND	0 UND	Sales/Receivables	0 UND	0 UND	2 233.8	1 641.8	1 437.7	4 82.6
	18 20.6	6 58.9	5 67.4		0 UND	11 34.0	23 16.1	15 23.9	10 35.3	20 18.7
				Cost of Sales/Inventory						
				Cost of Sales/Payables						
	2.7	4.0	3.4		3.3	3.0	3.8	3.5	3.1	3.8
	21.0	33.1	58.4	Sales/Working Capital	-37.9	27.7	8.1	13.2	19.6	17.9
	-10.0	-4.1	-4.4		-2.0	-10.2	-49.1	NM	-28.8	-13.3
	15.0	12.4	15.5		11.4	30.8	93.9	44.0	15.7	61.6
	(43) 3.3	(148) 4.9	(239) 4.8	EBIT/Interest	(106) 4.3	(63) 4.9	(15) 19.6	(23) 8.7	(15) 2.3	(17) 4.7
	1.1	1.6	1.6		1.6	1.5	6.5	3.6	1.0	2.1
		6.8	7.0	Net Profit + Depr., Dep.,						
		(10) 2.4	(16) 1.4	Amort./Cur. Mat. L/T/D						
		.2	.4							
	.1	.0	.1		.7	.1	.0	.0	.0	.1
	1.6	1.1	1.6	Fixed/Worth	2.5	.7	.5	.3	.3	.4
	4.7	5.4	8.7		10.2	10.1	1.2	6.2	6.2	1.3
	1.5	1.1	1.1		1.3	.7	.4	.8	.7	1.3
	3.7	3.2	4.2	Debt/Worth	4.6	3.6	2.9	5.2	3.5	2.8
	18.2	16.2	17.5		19.0	40.0	5.6	10.0	15.8	12.1
	72.4	86.9	81.3	% Profit Before Taxes/Tangible	75.0	61.6	94.6	93.3	110.4	77.7
	(71) 17.1	(233) 28.5	(351) 27.1	Net Worth	(183) 18.9	(80) 31.5	(21) 49.8	(28) 40.1	(18) 21.0	(21) 42.2
	1.1	6.8	6.4		1.9	9.8	13.2	3.6	3.6	14.5
	15.3	18.5	15.0	% Profit Before Taxes/Total	10.6	20.4	23.4	36.5	12.5	18.0
	3.4	5.2	5.5	Assets	3.5	8.2	11.6	8.2	3.6	10.3
	.2	.8	.7		.1	1.8	4.4	3.3	.0	3.4
	36.8	246.4	63.9		8.8	77.1	UND	999.8	457.7	239.3
	6.0	6.6	2.4	Sales/Net Fixed Assets	.3	9.1	21.4	19.2	53.5	27.2
	.3	.2	.2		.1	.4	1.8	6.0	.4	11.1
	1.7	2.0	1.6		.7	2.4	2.7	2.8	5.1	3.7
	.5	.5	.4	Sales/Total Assets	.2	.6	1.1	1.1	1.7	1.6
	.2	.2	.2		.1	.2	.7	.3	.2	.9
	1.2	.9	1.2		5.7	1.0	.5	.4	.4	.2
	(57) 4.1	(169) 6.0	(275) 7.2	% Depr., Dep., Amort./Sales	(159) 13.5	(49) 3.2	(11) 1.7	(21) 1.2	(16) 1.8	(19) .6
	13.0	17.8	18.0		23.1	13.0	4.7	4.0	10.7	1.5
	3.7	3.2	2.3	% Officers', Directors',	5.8	4.9				
	(20) 5.7	(50) 5.7	(70) 7.4	Owners' Comp/Sales	(32) 12.1	(16) 8.7				
	19.5	17.9	15.4		22.0	16.7				
	1189726M	3680975M	2906899M	Net Sales ($)	82529M	171062M	86046M	217785M	346117M	2003360M
	907569M	2325955M	3639712M	Total Assets ($)	400459M	516479M	125976M	478508M	789675M	1328615M

M = $ thousand   MM = $ million
See Pages 11 through 21 for Explanation of Ratios and Data

Current Data Sorted By Assets   Comparative Historical Data

0-500M	500M-2MM	2-10MM	10-50MM	50-100MM	100-250MM	Type of Statement	4/1/00-3/31/01 ALL	4/1/01-3/31/02 ALL
		9	10	1	4	Unqualified	16	19
	3	13	6	1		Reviewed	21	27
3	5	13	3		1	Compiled	29	25
9	2	2				Tax Returns	12	10
6	9	13	7	1	3	Other	29	44
20 (4/1-9/30/04)			104 (10/1/04-3/31/05)					
18	19	50	26	3	8	**NUMBER OF STATEMENTS**	107	125
%	%	%	%	%	%	**ASSETS**	%	%
22.1	9.5	11.0	6.0			Cash & Equivalents	6.9	6.7
8.6	7.7	6.9	3.9			Trade Receivables (net)	6.3	4.8
7.6	10.9	17.0	17.5			Inventory	8.0	11.4
3.1	10.0	4.4	10.1			All Other Current	4.2	5.4
41.4	38.0	39.3	37.6			Total Current	25.4	28.4
43.5	55.3	51.1	55.3			Fixed Assets (net)	65.2	64.9
5.9	2.1	1.6	1.1			Intangibles (net)	1.8	1.2
9.2	4.5	8.0	6.1			All Other Non-Current	7.7	5.5
100.0	100.0	100.0	100.0			Total	100.0	100.0
						LIABILITIES		
16.6	28.3	36.3	39.2			Notes Payable-Short Term	31.3	36.4
8.1	8.8	5.4	7.3			Cur. Mat.-L/T/D	10.1	7.8
29.4	3.7	4.6	5.2			Trade Payables	4.6	3.4
.1	.0	.1	.2			Income Taxes Payable	.1	.2
15.4	9.6	6.2	5.4			All Other Current	4.8	5.0
69.6	50.5	52.6	57.3			Total Current	50.8	52.8
32.4	23.3	17.8	23.0			Long-Term Debt	29.3	26.4
.0	.3	.6	1.4			Deferred Taxes	.4	.5
.8	2.0	2.8	1.2			All Other Non-Current	3.7	2.1
-2.7	23.9	26.2	17.1			Net Worth	15.8	18.2
100.0	100.0	100.0	100.0			Total Liabilities & Net Worth	100.0	100.0
						INCOME DATA		
100.0	100.0	100.0	100.0			Net Sales	100.0	100.0
						Gross Profit		
93.1	94.3	94.5	92.9			Operating Expenses	91.7	94.8
6.9	5.7	5.5	7.1			Operating Profit	8.3	5.2
2.3	.2	1.5	4.2			All Other Expenses (net)	3.9	4.9
4.7	5.5	4.0	2.9			Profit Before Taxes	4.4	.3
						RATIOS		
2.8	1.8	1.2	1.2				1.1	1.1
1.0	1.0	.9	1.0			Current	.4	.4
.3	.1	.2	.2				.2	.2
2.5	.9	.7	.3				.9	.5
(17) .4	.3	.3	.2			Quick	.2	.2
.3	.1	.1	.1				.1	.1
0 UND	2 190.0	4 84.3	8 43.8				6 59.3	6 61.7
7 54.8	14 25.3	10 37.8	13 28.4			Sales/Receivables	13 28.2	11 33.4
23 15.6	32 11.4	25 14.5	19 18.9				27 13.5	24 15.5
						Cost of Sales/Inventory		
						Cost of Sales/Payables		
13.6	5.9	10.5	12.7				25.8	25.9
NM	-49.1	-40.0	NM			Sales/Working Capital	-6.0	-6.9
-4.3	-2.5	-2.6	-1.2				-1.6	-1.5
5.9	5.8	4.8	2.6				2.2	1.8
(11) 2.0	(17) 1.3	(44) 1.7	(22) 1.5			EBIT/Interest	(100) 1.3	(120) 1.3
.6	-.7	1.2	1.0				1.0	.7
						Net Profit + Depr., Dep.,	4.3	5.5
						Amort./Cur. Mat. L/T/D	(13) 1.5	(13) 1.5
							1.0	1.1
.0	.2	.3	.8				1.8	1.7
1.4	1.8	2.2	3.6			Fixed/Worth	4.7	4.3
-15.6	-8.2	5.6	9.4				21.2	10.7
.5	1.0	1.8	3.6				3.6	2.7
10.1	2.7	3.9	8.1			Debt/Worth	6.4	4.9
-2.6	-9.4	9.4	14.3				25.6	12.2
102.3	24.8	31.5	30.0			% Profit Before Taxes/Tangible	46.4	25.5
(10) 28.6	(14) 18.9	(46) 13.5	(25) 16.5			Net Worth	(93) 18.3	(105) 9.1
4.2	-6.3	1.8	3.2				3.3	-2.0
28.5	5.3	10.1	3.2			% Profit Before Taxes/Total	6.3	4.6
4.4	1.7	2.0	2.1			Assets	2.0	1.3
-2.8	-4.7	.4	.2				.2	-1.8
UND	8.3	16.6	20.8				4.0	3.6
3.6	3.4	2.3	1.1			Sales/Net Fixed Assets	1.1	1.1
1.0	1.1	.8	.6				.7	.8
7.2	2.2	1.6	.9				1.3	1.2
1.6	1.0	.9	.6			Sales/Total Assets	.8	.8
.8	.6	.5	.5				.6	.6
12.5	3.1	10.0	13.5				15.0	14.2
(11) 25.2	(13) 12.5	(33) 24.7	(17) 28.0			% Depr., Dep., Amort./Sales	(81) 30.2	(104) 28.5
32.9	30.3	40.9	38.5				38.9	39.0
		2.4	1.4				2.1	1.8
	(18) 4.1	(10) 2.5				% Officers', Directors',	(38) 3.9	(46) 4.2
		6.5	7.2			Owners' Comp/Sales	8.6	9.8
10022M	32131M	295905M	414700M	238679M	943896M	Net Sales ($)	1244978M	1095438M
4075M	20681M	235120M	586468M	270125M	1060625M	Total Assets ($)	1473006M	1235842M

M = $ thousand   MM = $ million
See Pages 11 through 21 for Explanation of Ratios and Data

Comparative Historical Data / Current Data Sorted By Sales

		Comparative Historical Data		Type of Statement	20 (4/1-9/30/04)		104 (10/1/04-3/31/05)			
					0-1MM	1-3MM	3-5MM	5-10MM	10-25MM	25MM & OVER
	13	23	24	Unqualified		2	5	2	8	7
	38	30	23	Reviewed	2	2	6	7	5	1
	27	35	25	Compiled	4	8	4	6		3
	16	21	13	Tax Returns	10	2	1			
	46	42	39	Other	9	9	4	5	6	6
	4/1/02-3/31/03 ALL	4/1/03-3/31/04 ALL	4/1/04-3/31/05 ALL							
NUMBER OF STATEMENTS	140	151	124		25	23	20	20	19	17
	%	%	%	**ASSETS**	%	%	%	%	%	%
	8.1	8.4	10.9	Cash & Equivalents	13.7	13.7	9.1	9.8	6.8	11.4
	4.5	6.0	6.5	Trade Receivables (net)	6.5	5.5	5.1	6.7	8.1	7.6
	19.3	8.0	14.2	Inventory	6.0	15.4	19.8	14.8	15.4	16.3
	4.4	11.9	9.5	All Other Current	7.5	3.2	5.7	1.3	13.4	30.4
	36.3	34.3	41.1	Total Current	33.7	37.7	39.7	32.5	43.7	65.6
	56.7	56.6	49.4	Fixed Assets (net)	55.9	54.8	49.1	55.2	48.8	26.8
	3.0	2.8	2.7	Intangibles (net)	2.9	2.8	2.7	1.2	2.0	5.0
	4.0	6.3	6.8	All Other Non-Current	7.6	4.8	8.5	11.1	5.4	2.6
	100.0	100.0	100.0	Total	100.0	100.0	100.0	100.0	100.0	100.0
				LIABILITIES						
	32.0	31.4	33.6	Notes Payable-Short Term	18.5	25.8	40.0	46.4	36.8	40.3
	8.4	7.5	6.3	Cur. Mat.-L/T/D	6.2	12.6	5.5	4.7	6.3	.5
	4.6	5.2	8.2	Trade Payables	11.0	14.5	6.8	3.5	3.0	8.2
	.2	.1	.1	Income Taxes Payable	.0	.1	.0	.2	.1	.3
	6.8	5.3	7.6	All Other Current	14.8	6.8	4.4	7.8	6.6	3.2
	51.9	49.5	55.8	Total Current	50.5	59.8	56.6	62.8	52.8	52.5
	26.8	28.0	22.0	Long-Term Debt	27.6	33.0	12.4	13.9	24.1	17.6
	.5	.6	.7	Deferred Taxes	.0	.8	.5	1.1	1.1	.7
	3.3	4.3	2.2	All Other Non-Current	1.8	.3	4.5	1.7	1.8	3.9
	17.4	17.5	19.3	Net Worth	20.0	6.1	26.0	20.6	20.3	25.3
	100.0	100.0	100.0	Total Liabilities & Net Worth	100.0	100.0	100.0	100.0	100.0	100.0
				INCOME DATA						
	100.0	100.0	100.0	Net Sales	100.0	100.0	100.0	100.0	100.0	100.0
				Gross Profit						
	96.6	94.6	93.4	Operating Expenses	88.4	98.2	95.2	96.4	92.1	89.9
	3.4	5.4	6.6	Operating Profit	11.6	1.8	4.8	3.6	7.9	10.1
	1.5	1.6	1.9	All Other Expenses (net)	3.3	−.3	1.7	2.1	2.9	2.0
	1.8	3.8	4.7	Profit Before Taxes	8.2	2.1	3.1	1.5	5.0	8.1
				RATIOS						
	1.2	1.4	1.4		2.1	1.8	1.2	1.0	1.4	3.8
	.7	.6	1.0	Current	1.0	.5	.9	.3	1.0	1.2
	.2	.2	.2		.2	.1	.2	.2	.4	.9
	.5	.6	.8		1.6	.6	.8	.4	1.4	.8
(138)	.2	(150) .2	(123) .3	Quick	(24) .4	.3	.2	.2	.3	.2
	.1	.1	.1		.4	.1	.1	.1	.1	.1
5	80.5	5 68.8	4 91.2		0 UND	4 93.2	4 93.7	6 61.8	9 38.5	9 39.2
11	32.6	11 33.3	12 30.0	Sales/Receivables	6 59.4	9 38.5	8 46.7	13 27.4	13 27.8	15 24.2
23	15.8	28 12.9	25 14.5		29 12.4	22 16.4	25 14.7	23 15.6	25 14.4	28 13.2
				Cost of Sales/Inventory						
				Cost of Sales/Payables						
	10.5	10.6	9.7		9.7	8.3	17.6	NM	10.9	3.0
	−12.4	−17.2	−55.3	Sales/Working Capital	−49.1	−11.7	−50.5	−2.8	71.9	13.2
	−2.3	−2.5	−2.6		−2.6	−2.5	−3.1	−1.3	−4.3	NM
	3.2	3.3	4.3		9.0	4.3	3.6	4.5	4.2	9.3
(122)	1.6	(133) 1.7	(103) 1.6	EBIT/Interest	(17) 2.0	(22) 1.3	(19) 1.4	(16) 1.5	(15) 2.1	(14) 2.5
	1.0	1.1	1.1		.1	1.0	1.1	.9	1.4	1.5
	11.3	14.8		Net Profit + Depr., Dep.,						
(13)	1.2	(14) 1.7		Amort./Cur. Mat. L/T/D						
	.9	.6								
	.9	.8	.3		.4	.2	.4	.4	.9	.1
	4.2	2.5	2.7	Fixed/Worth	1.7	3.0	2.0	2.7	3.1	.8
	13.5	7.0	8.6		7.3	13.1	5.0	7.2	10.3	8.0
	2.7	1.8	1.8		.7	1.8	1.6	2.0	3.5	2.5
	5.5	4.2	4.5	Debt/Worth	2.6	5.2	3.4	4.1	6.2	6.6
	19.0	11.1	15.6		−14.2	−21.3	123.1	15.8	14.6	11.7
	36.9	26.8	34.1	% Profit Before Taxes/Tangible	42.8	27.8	26.6	27.2	36.2	48.7
(115)	14.7	(133) 14.5	(104) 16.7	Net Worth	(18) 20.4	(17) 9.7	(18) 11.8	(18) 7.3	(18) 19.9	(15) 35.6
	2.2	2.4	3.8		4.2	−1.7	.6	−.3	8.5	12.2
	6.0	7.0	7.0	% Profit Before Taxes/Total	18.4	10.0	6.9	5.5	6.7	9.8
	2.2	2.1	2.3	Assets	4.1	1.7	1.2	1.4	3.0	3.9
	−.8	.3	.4		−1.5	−.6	.0	−.2	1.5	2.1
	11.0	11.3	26.8		21.0	19.9	10.2	32.7	14.1	89.1
	1.6	1.6	2.4	Sales/Net Fixed Assets	1.1	1.4	2.8	2.3	4.0	16.9
	.7	.7	.9		.6	.7	1.0	.7	.6	1.9
	1.4	1.5	1.7		1.6	2.2	1.6	1.7	2.0	1.7
	.8	.7	.9	Sales/Total Assets	.7	.7	.9	1.4	.7	1.1
	.5	.5	.5		.4	.6	.5	.5	.5	.6
	10.6	11.9	8.3		13.6	9.5	12.6	7.0	3.5	
(101)	29.6	(106) 27.8	(76) 24.0	% Depr., Dep., Amort./Sales	(18) 28.1	(16) 28.4	(12) 24.0	(13) 11.3	(12) 17.5	
	42.7	39.1	36.9		56.1	41.2	37.9	39.3	35.5	
	2.2	2.3	2.3	% Officers', Directors',		3.4		1.2		
(47)	3.8	(59) 3.6	(42) 4.1	Owners' Comp/Sales		(10) 4.0		(11) 3.7		
	5.9	7.5	7.3			7.6		6.2		
	1740640M	1420052M	1935333M	Net Sales ($)	10098M	46283M	78677M	139998M	287989M	1372288M
	1788557M	1910056M	2177094M	Total Assets ($)	15343M	56832M	100198M	167200M	370593M	1466928M

M = $ thousand   MM = $ million
See Pages 11 through 21 for Explanation of Ratios and Data

Current Data Sorted By Assets   **Comparative Historical Data**

						Type of Statement		
							22	21
		3	18	3	3	Unqualified	22	21
1	4	10	14		2	Reviewed	13	16
3	5	14	4			Compiled	29	27
6	5	2				Tax Returns	10	9
1	6	11	18	3	1	Other	34	40
	26 (4/1-9/30/04)		111 (10/1/04-3/31/05)				4/1/00-3/31/01	4/1/01-3/31/02
0-500M	500M-2MM	2-10MM	10-50MM	50-100MM	100-250MM		ALL	ALL
11	20	40	54	6	6	**NUMBER OF STATEMENTS**	108	113
%	%	%	%	%	%	**ASSETS**	%	%
14.1	11.3	6.9	4.2			Cash & Equivalents	5.3	4.6
4.2	6.1	8.4	11.0			Trade Receivables (net)	10.1	9.4
.1	12.7	6.3	1.8			Inventory	7.9	10.9
16.4	1.7	8.7	10.6			All Other Current	4.6	6.5
34.8	31.9	30.3	27.7			Total Current	27.8	31.4
62.2	59.4	49.4	43.6			Fixed Assets (net)	57.9	54.4
.0	.0	.2	1.4			Intangibles (net)	.6	.9
3.0	8.7	20.1	27.3			All Other Non-Current	13.7	13.3
100.0	100.0	100.0	100.0			Total	100.0	100.0
						LIABILITIES		
3.3	16.8	20.9	14.2			Notes Payable-Short Term	21.9	24.2
8.8	6.5	8.2	10.4			Cur. Mat.-L/T/D	10.1	11.0
8.5	4.5	4.0	3.3			Trade Payables	3.8	5.3
.0	.0	.1	.3			Income Taxes Payable	.3	.2
13.4	3.6	3.4	2.7			All Other Current	7.0	4.2
34.1	31.4	36.5	30.9			Total Current	43.1	45.0
59.3	42.0	49.2	50.2			Long-Term Debt	35.5	35.3
.0	.0	.6	1.7			Deferred Taxes	1.1	1.5
.7	3.3	3.4	3.4			All Other Non-Current	2.3	1.8
6.0	23.3	10.4	13.8			Net Worth	17.9	16.5
100.0	100.0	100.0	100.0			Total Liabilities & Net Worth	100.0	100.0
						INCOME DATA		
100.0	100.0	100.0	100.0			Net Sales	100.0	100.0
						Gross Profit		
95.8	88.3	87.9	86.3			Operating Expenses	86.7	87.8
4.2	11.7	12.1	13.7			Operating Profit	13.3	12.2
4.4	6.9	6.9	8.2			All Other Expenses (net)	6.6	8.0
-.2	4.8	5.2	5.5			Profit Before Taxes	6.6	4.3
						RATIOS		
2.8	3.2	2.1	2.8			Current	1.2	1.5
1.1	.8	1.2	1.1				.7	.9
.8	.1	.4	.5				.2	.3
1.4	2.5	1.1	1.7			Quick	.7	1.0
.8	.2	.5	.9				.3	.3
.3	.0	.1	.2				.1	.1
0 UND	0 UND	2 221.4	6 59.9			Sales/Receivables	6 59.1	5 67.3
5 66.8	1 300.8	12 29.3	27 13.5				14 26.4	16 22.4
12 30.7	15 24.3	26 14.2	75 4.9				45 8.1	43 8.5
						Cost of Sales/Inventory		
						Cost of Sales/Payables		
8.4	6.5	4.8	4.7			Sales/Working Capital	21.6	8.8
111.7	NM	60.6	12.9				-8.4	-55.4
-14.3	-1.3	-2.7	-2.8				-1.5	-2.1
	3.9	2.3	3.1			EBIT/Interest	2.4	2.0
	(15) 1.3	(34) 1.3	(40) 1.6				(83) 1.5	(90) 1.3
	.2	1.0	1.3				1.1	.9
						Net Profit + Depr., Dep.,	1.6	1.3
						Amort./Cur. Mat. L /T/D	(17) 1.1	(15) .9
							.5	.2
.7	.8	.4	.1			Fixed/Worth	1.3	.8
2.4	3.5	3.9	2.5				3.6	3.2
62.0	133.7	31.5	9.3				14.5	13.1
.9	1.5	4.1	4.2			Debt/Worth	3.0	2.3
2.6	4.7	12.9	9.1				6.0	6.4
-42.8	133.1	51.9	16.5				27.2	21.1
	41.2	56.8	23.0			% Profit Before Taxes/Tangible	40.8	32.0
	(16) 6.0	(35) 20.9	(51) 12.7			Net Worth	(97) 12.0	(101) 11.1
	-10.3	1.5	4.4				4.9	.8
27.0	5.6	3.2	2.2			% Profit Before Taxes/Total	5.1	4.0
-5.4	1.1	1.1	1.2			Assets	2.2	1.5
-15.4	-3.1	.2	.7				.5	-.8
5.9	18.5	38.0	45.5			Sales/Net Fixed Assets	8.7	17.7
1.5	.8	1.5	1.4				1.0	1.2
1.0	.4	.6	.5				.5	.5
1.3	1.1	.8	.5			Sales/Total Assets	1.0	1.0
1.1	.4	.5	.4				.5	.5
.5	.3	.4	.3				.3	.4
	42.9	12.7	9.8			% Depr., Dep., Amort./Sales	6.6	6.9
	(14) 62.4	(30) 31.1	(35) 30.9				(85) 34.9	(87) 32.4
	77.4	64.0	60.8				59.8	64.8
		1.3	1.7			% Officers', Directors',	1.0	1.1
		(14) 4.9	(13) 4.5			Owners' Comp/Sales	(33) 3.8	(38) 3.7
		7.2	7.1				5.0	7.6
4906M	27914M	191375M	475418M	98883M	446754M	Net Sales ($)	1723350M	1565195M
2874M	23293M	206960M	1150177M	448141M	873885M	Total Assets ($)	2390473M	2315637M

M = $ thousand   MM = $ million
See Pages 11 through 21 for Explanation of Ratios and Data

Comparative Historical Data | Current Data Sorted By Sales

			Type of Statement						
16	21	27	Unqualified		2	4	3	14	4
14	33	31	Reviewed	4	8	6	8	4	1
23	43	26	Compiled	7	11	3	4	1	
11	11	13	Tax Returns	9	2			1	1
34	34	40	Other	8	8	8	6	9	1
4/1/02-	4/1/03-	4/1/04-			26 (4/1-9/30/04)		111 (10/1/04-3/31/05)		
3/31/03	3/31/04	3/31/05		0-1MM	1-3MM	3-5MM	5-10MM	10-25MM	25MM & OVER
ALL	ALL	ALL							
98	142	137	NUMBER OF STATEMENTS	28	31	21	21	29	7
%	%	%	ASSETS	%	%	%	%	%	%
5.3	6.3	6.7	Cash & Equivalents	12.1	6.6	5.2	3.5	5.2	
7.6	5.9	8.5	Trade Receivables (net)	3.5	15.8	6.6	2.7	9.6	
8.2	7.4	4.5	Inventory	8.5	5.5	1.8	1.6	4.3	
5.7	8.3	9.7	All Other Current	5.2	12.6	6.6	9.9	10.5	
26.7	27.8	29.4	Total Current	29.4	40.5	20.2	17.8	29.7	
51.6	52.9	49.7	Fixed Assets (net)	62.1	40.6	38.6	66.8	42.3	
.5	.9	.6	Intangibles (net)	.0	.4	2.8	.0	.4	
21.2	18.4	20.3	All Other Non-Current	8.5	18.5	38.4	15.4	27.7	
100.0	100.0	100.0	Total	100.0	100.0	100.0	100.0	100.0	
			LIABILITIES						
17.6	14.8	16.7	Notes Payable-Short Term	13.7	23.4	13.2	13.8	13.0	
9.4	9.8	8.4	Cur. Mat.-L/T/D	7.7	7.6	9.9	12.7	7.1	
4.1	2.5	3.9	Trade Payables	3.5	2.8	1.4	1.3	7.5	
.4	.4	.2	Income Taxes Payable	.0	.1	.1	.6	.0	
6.9	4.9	4.2	All Other Current	6.6	4.1	1.7	1.6	4.3	
38.3	32.4	33.5	Total Current	31.6	38.0	26.4	30.0	32.0	
39.8	46.3	49.0	Long-Term Debt	54.7	43.9	55.3	53.6	48.4	
.7	1.3	.9	Deferred Taxes	.5	.3	1.1	.8	1.9	
5.1	4.0	2.9	All Other Non-Current	2.2	3.8	3.5	1.0	4.2	
16.1	16.0	13.7	Net Worth	11.0	14.0	13.7	14.6	13.6	
100.0	100.0	100.0	Total Liabilities & Net Worth	100.0	100.0	100.0	100.0	100.0	
			INCOME DATA						
100.0	100.0	100.0	Net Sales	100.0	100.0	100.0	100.0	100.0	
			Gross Profit						
88.5	87.8	86.4	Operating Expenses	87.6	83.3	85.3	89.4	89.7	
11.5	12.2	13.6	Operating Profit	12.4	16.7	14.7	10.6	10.3	
6.3	7.7	8.0	All Other Expenses (net)	8.5	11.1	7.3	6.1	6.3	
5.1	4.6	5.6	Profit Before Taxes	3.8	5.6	7.4	4.5	4.0	
			RATIOS						
1.5	2.2	2.5		3.7	1.9	4.4	3.0	2.0	
.9	1.1	1.1	Current	1.0	1.2	1.2	1.1	1.4	
.2	.4	.3		.2	.3	.4	.2	.5	
1.1	1.5	1.5		3.2	1.2	2.5	1.6	1.6	
.3	.5	.6	Quick	.4	.6	.5	.3	1.0	
.1	.1	.1		.1	.1	.2	.1	.2	
6 60.5	3 126.7	3 143.9		0 UND	4 99.6	0 999.8	5 78.2	11 33.7	
16 23.0	14 25.3	14 25.3	Sales/Receivables	1 710.3	13 27.9	18 19.8	14 26.5	24 15.2	
35 10.3	42 8.7	38 9.5		16 22.5	55 6.6	69 5.3	30 12.0	53 6.9	
			Cost of Sales/Inventory						
			Cost of Sales/Payables						
8.8	5.1	4.9		1.6	2.4	4.0	8.3	5.4	
−24.7	29.0	43.8	Sales/Working Capital	NM	40.9	15.3	67.6	20.8	
−1.6	−2.9	−2.6		−1.3	−2.8	−2.1	−1.9	−5.3	
2.8	2.5	3.0		1.9	4.3	2.9	1.9	3.0	
(77) 1.6	(114) 1.5	(106) 1.6	EBIT/Interest	(20) .7	(22) 1.5	(16) 1.3	(17) 1.5	(25) 1.6	
1.1	1.1	1.1		−1.3	1.1	1.0	1.2	1.3	
	4.3	1.3	Net Profit + Depr., Dep.,						
	(17) 1.2	(12) 1.0	Amort./Cur. Mat. L/T/D						
	.3	.2							
.3	.7	.3		1.1	.1	.0	2.2	.1	
2.4	3.2	3.2	Fixed/Worth	4.2	1.6	2.3	3.7	1.5	
8.5	10.3	12.0		145.4	15.9	12.0	9.7	8.8	
2.1	3.3	3.4		1.8	4.1	3.5	3.2	4.3	
5.7	6.9	9.0	Debt/Worth	5.7	12.6	6.7	9.0	9.3	
19.6	22.2	34.8		NM	103.3	24.8	22.1	14.4	
31.5	23.2	35.0		50.3	56.7	33.3	25.3	29.7	
(84) 11.9	(125) 11.6	(122) 12.7	% Profit Before Taxes/Tangible Net Worth	(21) −.4	(27) 20.9	(18) 8.9	(28) 13.8	15.3	
3.7	2.7	2.8		−19.5	.3	3.6	3.8	9.0	
4.0	3.1	3.0		4.5	3.2	2.3	2.1	2.5	
2.0	1.4	1.1	% Profit Before Taxes/Total Assets	−.7	1.1	1.1	1.1	1.7	
.2	.1	.2		−4.9	.1	.5	.4	.9	
23.4	16.3	26.7		1.6	84.2	217.1	2.2	96.9	
1.4	1.0	1.3	Sales/Net Fixed Assets	.8	2.8	1.8	.7	3.1	
.5	.6	.5		.4	.6	.5	.5	.6	
.9	.7	.7		.7	.6	.6	.8	.9	
.5	.5	.4	Sales/Total Assets	.4	.4	.4	.5	.5	
.3	.3	.3		.2	.2	.3	.4	.4	
11.6	12.1	13.6		38.9	27.9	15.5	13.8	4.3	
(69) 36.0	(111) 35.8	(91) 39.6	% Depr., Dep., Amort./Sales	(21) 61.2	(18) 53.5	(13) 34.8	(19) 28.1	(18) 12.3	
59.2	66.0	68.4		77.7	72.3	59.4	54.9	39.0	
1.3	1.4	1.2			2.0				
(30) 3.1	(41) 4.7	(34) 4.1	% Officers', Directors', Owners' Comp/Sales		(12) 5.3				
5.2	7.8	7.1			8.8				
1574265M	1414953M	1245250M	Net Sales ($)	12252M	59512M	78250M	150257M	441496M	503483M
2149498M	2757795M	2705330M	Total Assets ($)	35575M	216015M	277002M	363227M	1007228M	806283M

M = $ thousand   MM = $ million
See Pages 11 through 21 for Explanation of Ratios and Data

Current Data Sorted By Assets   Comparative Historical Data

0-500M	500M-2MM	2-10MM	10-50MM	50-100MM	100-250MM	Type of Statement	4/1/00-3/31/01 ALL	4/1/01-3/31/02 ALL
1		9	27	12	8	Unqualified	28	32
	11	22	17	1		Reviewed	46	41
5	16	20	4			Compiled	50	39
10	9	7				Tax Returns	17	15
12	17	16	20	6	1	Other	41	64
	44 (4/1-9/30/04)			207 (10/1/04-3/31/05)				
28	53	74	68	19	9	**NUMBER OF STATEMENTS**	182	191
%	%	%	%	%	%	**ASSETS**	%	%
12.5	8.6	7.8	6.0	3.7		Cash & Equivalents	6.6	6.8
7.4	11.7	13.2	16.9	6.9		Trade Receivables (net)	9.5	11.6
3.2	5.4	10.0	7.5	7.2		Inventory	8.0	5.6
2.2	2.9	4.0	3.4	3.0		All Other Current	2.6	2.8
25.2	28.5	35.0	33.9	20.8		Total Current	26.7	26.8
66.8	59.1	54.1	56.6	68.7		Fixed Assets (net)	61.5	61.5
.1	1.5	1.7	1.4	.4		Intangibles (net)	1.2	1.6
7.9	10.9	9.3	8.1	10.1		All Other Non-Current	10.6	10.2
100.0	100.0	100.0	100.0	100.0		Total	100.0	100.0
						LIABILITIES		
7.9	17.0	9.4	14.5	5.5		Notes Payable-Short Term	10.5	9.5
14.2	13.6	11.9	10.4	12.1		Cur. Mat.-L/T/D	13.7	12.9
2.3	7.3	6.6	5.3	3.5		Trade Payables	4.8	5.4
.0	.1	.2	.5	.6		Income Taxes Payable	.1	.3
12.7	5.4	5.9	4.8	3.0		All Other Current	5.4	6.3
37.2	43.4	34.1	35.6	24.6		Total Current	34.4	34.4
56.0	35.5	33.9	30.9	48.6		Long-Term Debt	36.1	35.5
.0	.7	1.3	3.0	1.3		Deferred Taxes	1.6	1.8
4.8	2.7	3.3	3.6	2.0		All Other Non-Current	5.2	3.4
1.9	17.7	27.5	26.9	23.5		Net Worth	22.7	24.8
100.0	100.0	100.0	100.0	100.0		Total Liabilities & Net Worth	100.0	100.0
						INCOME DATA		
100.0	100.0	100.0	100.0	100.0		Net Sales	100.0	100.0
						Gross Profit		
92.3	94.3	89.4	90.0	84.6		Operating Expenses	91.5	89.0
7.7	5.7	10.6	10.0	15.4		Operating Profit	8.5	11.0
1.7	3.6	2.7	2.6	6.9		All Other Expenses (net)	4.1	5.7
6.0	2.0	7.9	7.4	8.4		Profit Before Taxes	4.4	5.3
						RATIOS		
2.9	1.2	1.7	1.6	1.3		Current	1.4	1.3
.5	.7	1.0	1.0	.9			.8	.8
.2	.2	.5	.6	.4			.3	.4
2.6	.9	1.3	1.2	.9		Quick	.9	1.1
.4	.4	.5	.6	.5			.4	.5
.2	.1	.2	.3	.3			.2	.2
0 UND	0 UND	4 84.9	22 16.9	10 35.7		Sales/Receivables	0 UND	1 271.0
0 UND	5 71.8	31 11.7	37 9.9	34 10.7			26 13.8	33 11.1
16 22.4	40 9.0	46 8.0	60 6.1	44 8.3			43 8.4	53 6.9
						Cost of Sales/Inventory		
						Cost of Sales/Payables		
10.9	39.8	7.4	8.9	17.7		Sales/Working Capital	17.3	13.8
-9.9	-10.2	97.5	-198.9	-29.6			-16.3	-16.6
-2.4	-1.7	-4.4	-5.4	-5.9			-2.8	-3.7
8.8	3.7	5.1	3.6	2.8		EBIT/Interest	2.4	2.6
(25) 2.6	(48) 1.5	(63) 2.3	(62) 2.3	(18) 2.0			(158) 1.5	(163) 1.5
-1.3	.6	1.3	1.4	1.5			1.0	.9
		2.1	1.6			Net Profit + Depr., Dep.,	2.7	1.8
	(13) 1.2	(27) 1.1				Amort./Cur. Mat. L /T/D	(44) 1.1	(55) 1.2
		1.0	1.0				.6	.6
2.1	1.5	.8	1.4	1.8		Fixed/Worth	1.3	1.1
75.8	3.7	2.1	2.5	2.8			2.4	3.0
-3.6	-589.9	5.4	4.7	5.1			7.8	10.7
1.9	1.9	1.6	1.8	1.9		Debt/Worth	1.5	1.5
138.5	8.0	3.5	3.5	4.0			4.2	3.8
-5.4	-613.6	8.4	7.8	5.5			11.9	13.9
100.0	39.5	33.4	26.4	23.8		% Profit Before Taxes/Tangible	24.9	28.9
(15) 34.2	(39) 12.2	(65) 16.5	(63) 17.1	(18) 13.3		Net Worth	(156) 11.9	(165) 9.7
6.3	-.4	4.0	9.1	6.8			4.0	.0
30.4	7.9	9.0	6.3	4.8		% Profit Before Taxes/Total	6.4	6.4
3.1	2.6	3.1	3.8	2.9		Assets	2.1	1.7
-10.4	-1.3	1.0	1.2	1.6			-.2	-.5
5.0	5.0	6.1	4.8	2.1		Sales/Net Fixed Assets	3.4	3.5
1.6	1.6	1.7	1.4	.8			1.2	1.3
1.0	.7	.5	.7	.5			.6	.6
2.7	2.3	1.9	1.6	1.2		Sales/Total Assets	1.4	1.4
1.1	.8	.8	.8	.7			.7	.7
.6	.5	.3	.4	.5			.5	.5
7.8	7.2	6.4	5.5	7.7		% Depr., Dep., Amort./Sales	6.3	7.6
(15) 26.2	(43) 26.2	(66) 22.0	(62) 13.7	(15) 14.1			(163) 23.0	(168) 23.0
42.1	55.3	40.3	30.2	22.3			52.1	44.4
	2.7	1.1	1.1			% Officers', Directors',	.8	1.4
	(13) 7.2	(13) 3.7	(10) 2.0			Owners' Comp/Sales	(38) 3.0	(46) 2.4
	14.7	9.4	14.7				6.2	5.3
10966M	125320M	438371M	1890516M	1181650M	704776M	Net Sales ($)	2373537M	2663487M
7048M	61457M	362100M	1558538M	1326403M	1438618M	Total Assets ($)	2814550M	3073489M

    M = $ thousand   MM = $ million
See Pages 11 through 21 for Explanation of Ratios and Data

Comparative Historical Data   **Current Data Sorted By Sales**

Hist 1	Hist 2	Hist 3	Type of Statement						
49	56	57	Unqualified	1	7	2	8	10	29
63	50	51	Reviewed	5	13	3	10	12	8
34	49	45	Compiled	14	14	5	8	4	
10	19	26	Tax Returns	18	5	2	1		11
70	76	72	Other	20	15	3	11	12	11
4/1/02-3/31/03	4/1/03-3/31/04	4/1/04-3/31/05		44 (4/1-9/30/04)			207 (10/1/04-3/31/05)		
ALL	ALL	ALL		0-1MM	1-3MM	3-5MM	5-10MM	10-25MM	25MM & OVER
226	250	251	NUMBER OF STATEMENTS	58	54	15	38	38	48
%	%	%	**ASSETS**	%	%	%	%	%	%
6.9	8.7	7.5	Cash & Equivalents	10.3	7.4	9.3	5.4	9.0	4.1
11.7	10.5	12.5	Trade Receivables (net)	5.8	11.8	19.2	15.9	14.0	15.3
8.3	8.7	7.3	Inventory	1.4	3.5	12.4	9.9	11.1	11.8
3.9	4.4	3.7	All Other Current	2.9	4.5	2.8	3.3	4.7	3.7
30.8	32.3	31.0	Total Current	20.5	27.2	43.7	34.5	38.7	34.9
58.3	55.4	58.4	Fixed Assets (net)	65.0	63.3	50.1	52.1	52.0	57.5
.7	1.1	1.2	Intangibles (net)	1.0	1.1	4.6	.3	.9	1.7
10.2	11.2	9.4	All Other Non-Current	13.5	8.3	1.5	13.0	8.4	5.9
100.0	100.0	100.0	Total	100.0	100.0	100.0	100.0	100.0	100.0
			LIABILITIES						
9.2	11.9	12.0	Notes Payable-Short Term	9.9	10.7	19.4	14.7	12.2	11.4
13.0	11.9	12.6	Cur. Mat.-L/T/D	15.6	12.7	11.9	10.1	10.6	12.5
4.1	5.6	5.5	Trade Payables	1.6	3.2	8.4	8.0	8.6	7.7
.3	.4	.3	Income Taxes Payable	.1	.2	.0	.2	.6	.5
7.0	6.0	5.9	All Other Current	7.5	5.5	2.4	6.2	4.7	6.4
33.6	35.8	36.3	Total Current	34.5	32.3	42.2	39.1	36.7	38.5
34.5	31.8	37.0	Long-Term Debt	50.3	41.2	26.2	25.8	29.4	34.5
1.7	2.0	1.7	Deferred Taxes	.2	1.1	2.0	3.3	1.5	3.0
3.4	4.1	3.2	All Other Non-Current	3.9	3.2	.8	7.5	1.0	1.7
26.9	26.4	21.8	Net Worth	11.0	22.3	28.8	24.3	31.5	22.3
100.0	100.0	100.0	Total Liabilities & Net Worth	100.0	100.0	100.0	100.0	100.0	100.0
			INCOME DATA						
100.0	100.0	100.0	Net Sales	100.0	100.0	100.0	100.0	100.0	100.0
			Gross Profit						
87.5	88.0	90.3	Operating Expenses	88.0	90.7	89.1	89.6	89.4	94.0
12.5	12.0	9.7	Operating Profit	12.0	9.3	10.9	10.4	10.6	6.0
5.7	4.1	3.4	All Other Expenses (net)	5.0	2.8	.9	3.5	3.2	2.7
6.8	7.9	6.4	Profit Before Taxes	7.0	6.5	10.0	6.8	7.4	3.3
			RATIOS						
1.5	1.4	1.6	Current	1.9	1.8	1.4	1.6	1.6	1.2
.9	.9	.9		.5	.9	.9	1.0	1.0	1.0
.5	.4	.4		.2	.3	.5	.5	.6	.7
1.0	1.0	1.1	Quick	1.3	1.6	1.1	1.3	1.2	.8
.5	.5	.5		.4	.4	.5	.5	.5	.5
.2	.2	.2		.1	.1	.2	.2	.4	.3
6 · 60.8	1 · 624.3	1 · 311.2	Sales/Receivables	0 · UND	0 · UND	11 · 32.6	15 · 24.0	18 · 19.7	22 · 16.6
29 · 12.5	26 · 14.3	27 · 13.5		0 · UND	16 · 22.2	28 · 12.9	38 · 9.7	34 · 10.8	34 · 10.8
49 · 7.4	45 · 8.2	46 · 8.0		27 · 13.3	52 · 7.0	40 · 9.1	54 · 6.8	47 · 7.8	45 · 8.1
			Cost of Sales/Inventory						
			Cost of Sales/Payables						
10.2	10.2	10.3	Sales/Working Capital	9.6	5.6	7.8	8.4	13.2	24.6
−30.8	−38.2	−56.0		−7.2	−312.3	−97.1	−108.9	NM	−164.3
−5.1	−4.7	−4.0		−1.6	−2.6	−5.5	−4.2	−8.1	−10.2
3.8	4.5	3.7	EBIT/Interest	4.2	3.7	10.8	4.6	3.5	3.1
(191) 1.6	(216) 2.2	(222) 2.0		(52) 1.9	(43) 1.6	(14) 1.9	(36) 2.4	(32) 2.1	(45) 2.1
1.0	1.2	1.2		.5	.7	1.1	1.2	1.5	1.6
1.8	1.9	1.9	Net Profit + Depr., Dep.,				4.2	1.8	3.2
(56) 1.3	(59) 1.3	(53) 1.1	Amort./Cur. Mat. L/T/D			(13) 1.2	(10) 1.3	(18) 1.1
.9	.9	.9					1.0	.9	1.0
.9	1.0	1.3	Fixed/Worth	2.1	1.2	.5	.9	.8	1.6
2.4	2.2	2.7		8.7	3.3	1.5	2.0	1.8	3.2
5.7	5.9	8.2		−7.7	16.0	10.5	4.2	2.7	5.6
1.4	1.3	1.8	Debt/Worth	1.7	1.6	1.0	1.5	1.6	2.5
3.3	3.4	4.1		11.9	4.5	3.4	3.6	2.4	4.3
7.2	9.0	16.2		−11.8	26.0	12.5	13.3	4.4	6.6
28.4	28.3	31.2	% Profit Before Taxes/Tangible	77.7	29.7	34.3	32.4	23.2	29.5
(203) 10.5	(219) 12.8	(209) 16.5	Net Worth	(37) 13.5	(45) 12.6	(13) 21.6	(33) 18.8	(36) 13.5	(45) 20.9
1.4	4.0	6.5		−.1	−1.8	14.2	6.5	8.0	9.9
7.5	8.1	7.8	% Profit Before Taxes/Total	10.7	7.0	9.8	7.9	7.9	5.7
2.4	3.2	3.1	Assets	2.9	2.6	3.1	2.7	3.8	3.9
.1	.8	.8		−4.5	−.2	−.5	.8	1.6	2.3
5.1	6.2	4.5	Sales/Net Fixed Assets	1.8	3.4	11.5	15.9	7.7	5.5
1.3	1.5	1.4		.9	1.2	2.8	1.5	1.7	2.1
.7	.7	.6		.5	.6	.8	.7	.8	1.0
1.7	1.9	1.8	Sales/Total Assets	.9	1.2	2.3	2.0	2.1	2.5
.8	.8	.8		.6	.7	1.4	.7	.9	1.2
.5	.4	.4		.3	.3	.3	.4	.5	.7
7.4	4.7	6.8	% Depr., Dep., Amort./Sales	22.7	11.8	3.4	5.1	5.1	3.7
(194) 24.0	(209) 20.8	(201) 19.2		(43) 38.7	(43) 35.6	(14) 19.6	(33) 17.5	(33) 13.2	(35) 7.7
41.3	44.0	38.8		56.9	58.6	32.0	32.0	26.7	13.2
1.4	1.1	1.3	% Officers', Directors',	4.6	2.2				
(51) 4.0	(54) 2.6	(43) 6.4	Owners' Comp/Sales	(13) 9.8	(12) 6.7				
7.6	6.5	13.4		17.1	14.5				
4354868M	5035189M	4351599M	Net Sales ($)	25967M	100247M	58152M	257176M	597317M	3312740M
4256520M	4880729M	4754164M	Total Assets ($)	66445M	221914M	90704M	471846M	1021948M	2881307M

© RMA 2005

M = $ thousand   MM = $ million
See Pages 11 through 21 for Explanation of Ratios and Data

Current Data Sorted By Assets   **Comparative Historical Data**

						Type of Statement	4/1/00-3/31/01 ALL	4/1/01-3/31/02 ALL
	1	2	5	1	1	Unqualified		
	1	10	3			Reviewed		
7	13	3	2			Compiled		
9	6					Tax Returns		
2	11	8	1	1		Other		
	15 (4/1-9/30/04)		72 (10/1/04-3/31/05)					
0-500M	500M-2MM	2-10MM	10-50MM	50-100MM	100-250MM			
18	32	23	11	2	1	**NUMBER OF STATEMENTS**		
%	%	%	%	%	%	**ASSETS**	%	%
10.0	8.8	7.1	11.2			Cash & Equivalents	D	D
4.3	13.3	12.7	7.7			Trade Receivables (net)	A	A
8.6	17.1	10.0	8.2			Inventory	T	T
.2	4.8	6.3	7.4			All Other Current	A	A
23.1	44.1	36.2	34.4			Total Current		
69.6	44.0	38.8	35.9			Fixed Assets (net)	N	N
.6	3.7	4.1	7.3			Intangibles (net)	O	O
6.6	8.2	20.9	22.4			All Other Non-Current	T	T
100.0	100.0	100.0	100.0			Total		
						LIABILITIES	A	A
9.2	16.2	13.7	3.7			Notes Payable-Short Term	V	V
17.5	8.4	9.0	6.9			Cur. Mat.-L/T/D	A	A
3.0	6.0	5.2	4.7			Trade Payables	I	I
.0	.0	.1	.1			Income Taxes Payable	L	L
4.7	6.4	9.0	10.6			All Other Current	A	A
34.5	37.1	37.0	25.9			Total Current	B	B
44.6	29.9	27.5	34.4			Long-Term Debt	L	L
.2	.5	.5	.6			Deferred Taxes	E	E
15.4	7.3	2.3	1.6			All Other Non-Current		
5.3	25.2	32.7	37.5			Net Worth		
100.0	100.0	100.0	100.0			Total Liabilities & Net Worth		
						INCOME DATA		
100.0	100.0	100.0	100.0			Net Sales		
						Gross Profit		
95.0	88.8	75.2	91.1			Operating Expenses		
5.0	11.2	24.8	8.9			Operating Profit		
.7	4.2	9.3	3.5			All Other Expenses (net)		
4.3	7.0	15.5	5.4			Profit Before Taxes		
						RATIOS		
1.5	2.0	2.2	2.0					
.6	1.4	1.2	1.4			Current		
.4	.4	.4	.8					
.9	1.4	1.0	1.3					
.4	.7	.5	.6			Quick		
.2	.2	.2	.3					
0 UND	0 UND	0 UND	8 46.5					
0 UND	4 97.6	16 23.4	25 14.6			Sales/Receivables		
10 38.2	39 9.4	41 8.9	36 10.2					
						Cost of Sales/Inventory		
						Cost of Sales/Payables		
21.7	5.0	5.5	5.9					
−30.2	19.8	22.7	25.4			Sales/Working Capital		
−11.6	−8.0	−7.6	−43.9					
3.9	4.5	6.7						
(17) .3	(30) 2.3	(17) 3.5				EBIT/Interest		
−2.8	−2.1	1.2						
						Net Profit + Depr., Dep., Amort./Cur. Mat. L /T/D		
2.5	.9	.4	.2					
21.3	1.6	1.3	1.3			Fixed/Worth		
−10.9	8.9	4.6	4.1					
3.6	1.1	1.4	.6					
21.4	3.3	2.2	3.0			Debt/Worth		
−15.7	17.1	7.0	7.5					
302.8	75.7	26.5	40.7			% Profit Before Taxes/Tangible Net Worth		
(12) 32.3	(27) 16.7	(19) 11.4	25.7					
−25.3	−12.2	3.3	7.3					
9.6	12.2	10.2	8.6			% Profit Before Taxes/Total Assets		
−.6	4.1	7.6	4.2					
−14.6	−6.0	1.4	1.9					
5.3	16.4	26.1	19.0			Sales/Net Fixed Assets		
3.8	4.6	4.7	7.1					
1.9	1.7	1.4	2.3					
3.5	2.3	2.1	2.4			Sales/Total Assets		
2.3	1.9	1.0	1.2					
1.3	.8	.2	.5					
5.2	5.4	4.6				% Depr., Dep., Amort./Sales		
(17) 13.3	(19) 15.4	(17) 14.4						
25.3	25.1	30.5						
3.3	8.6					% Officers', Directors', Owners' Comp/Sales		
(10) 10.9	(10) 14.9							
13.3	18.3							
13956M	53226M	166347M	322244M	14495M	78381M	Net Sales ($)		
5344M	30639M	104358M	205144M	114595M	238548M	Total Assets ($)		

© RMA 2005

M = $ thousand   MM = $ million
See Pages 11 through 21 for Explanation of Ratios and Data

Comparative Historical Data				Current Data Sorted By Sales					

			Type of Statement						
7	13	10	Unqualified		2		2	3	3
11	16	14	Reviewed	2	2	4	2	3	1
20	34	25	Compiled	8	14		1	1	1
17	16	15	Tax Returns	9	5	1			
23	26	23	Other	8	8	1	3	2	1
					15 (4/1-9/30/04)		72 (10/1/04-3/31/05)		
4/1/02-3/31/03 ALL	4/1/03-3/31/04 ALL	4/1/04-3/31/05 ALL		0-1MM	1-3MM	3-5MM	5-10MM	10-25MM	25MM & OVER
78	105	87	NUMBER OF STATEMENTS	27	31	6	8	9	6
%	%	%	ASSETS	%	%	%	%	%	%
6.5	6.3	8.8	Cash & Equivalents	6.0	12.4				
10.7	12.6	10.7	Trade Receivables (net)	5.7	8.8				
11.7	10.5	11.8	Inventory	5.5	16.6				
3.6	4.0	4.8	All Other Current	5.5	3.6				
32.5	33.5	36.0	Total Current	22.7	41.4				
54.6	45.8	45.7	Fixed Assets (net)	61.7	41.9				
1.5	4.5	4.3	Intangibles (net)	.3	4.2				
11.5	16.2	14.0	All Other Non-Current	15.3	12.6				
100.0	100.0	100.0	Total	100.0	100.0				
			LIABILITIES						
17.1	13.1	12.0	Notes Payable-Short Term	10.3	18.4				
13.3	9.0	10.1	Cur. Mat.-L/T/D	12.3	11.6				
3.9	8.0	4.9	Trade Payables	1.2	6.0				
.2	.1	.1	Income Taxes Payable	.1	.0				
5.2	6.9	7.2	All Other Current	4.0	5.6				
39.8	37.2	34.1	Total Current	28.0	41.6				
37.4	35.7	33.8	Long-Term Debt	39.8	33.2				
.7	.5	.5	Deferred Taxes	.1	.4				
5.0	11.1	7.2	All Other Non-Current	15.5	3.0				
17.2	15.5	24.4	Net Worth	16.5	21.9				
100.0	100.0	100.0	Total Liabilities & Net Worth	100.0	100.0				
			INCOME DATA						
100.0	100.0	100.0	Net Sales	100.0	100.0				
			Gross Profit						
86.6	84.9	86.1	Operating Expenses	73.0	93.1				
13.4	15.1	13.9	Operating Profit	27.0	6.9				
7.1	7.6	5.2	All Other Expenses (net)	9.7	3.2				
6.3	7.5	8.7	Profit Before Taxes	17.3	3.7				
			RATIOS						
1.5	1.6	2.0		1.7	2.0				
.7	.9	1.1	Current	.6	1.1				
.3	.3	.5		.2	.5				
.8	.9	1.1		.9	1.1				
.3	.5	.5	Quick	.4	.5				
.1	.1	.2		.2	.1				
0 UND	0 UND	0 UND		0 UND	0 UND				
10 38.1	11 33.0	9 40.8	Sales/Receivables	0 UND	3 144.6				
34 10.8	36 10.2	35 10.5		16 22.5	31 11.7				
			Cost of Sales/Inventory						
			Cost of Sales/Payables						
6.9	10.3	5.9		4.6	5.3				
-19.2	-42.8	25.4	Sales/Working Capital	-33.9	92.0				
-3.4	-6.3	-13.0		-4.6	-13.0				
4.4	4.1	4.9		6.5	3.8				
(66) 2.0	(79) 1.7	(73) 2.0	EBIT/Interest	(21) 2.6	(29) 1.9				
.5	.5	-.5		-.4	-2.7				
2.2	3.9	4.7	Net Profit + Depr., Dep.,						
(10) 1.5	(16) 2.0	(12) 1.8	Amort./Cur. Mat. L/T/D						
.2	1.4	.6							
1.0	.6	.6		.8	.9				
2.6	2.5	2.2	Fixed/Worth	3.7	1.6				
59.9	16.1	14.3		UND	50.4				
1.5	1.6	1.5		1.8	1.3				
4.5	4.6	4.3	Debt/Worth	7.1	3.5				
114.1	46.1	18.4		UND	62.3				
42.7	36.5	48.0		148.4	70.9				
(60) 13.8	(81) 14.8	(71) 14.5	% Profit Before Taxes/Tangible Net Worth	(21) 13.7	(24) 14.0				
-1.9	2.1	3.3		4.1	-11.9				
8.6	9.2	10.0		11.1	10.7				
2.2	2.9	3.9	% Profit Before Taxes/Total Assets	2.6	3.9				
-2.1	-.5	-2.9		-2.2	-7.8				
6.2	14.4	14.3		4.1	16.6				
2.5	3.1	4.1	Sales/Net Fixed Assets	2.0	5.2				
.7	1.2	1.6		.6	3.2				
2.1	2.2	2.4		1.6	2.6				
1.1	1.2	1.6	Sales/Total Assets	.7	2.2				
.4	.4	.5		.2	1.2				
8.9	4.7	4.7		13.3	4.1				
(63) 17.5	(75) 14.6	(64) 13.3	% Depr., Dep., Amort./Sales	(21) 24.0	(20) 10.3				
38.8	35.2	24.4		41.8	24.2				
4.4	3.1	3.5			8.5				
(24) 6.2	(42) 6.9	(31) 11.4	% Officers', Directors', Owners' Comp/Sales		(14) 12.4				
12.7	14.8	16.9			17.9				
402941M	593313M	648649M	Net Sales ($)	12167M	57565M	24151M	57228M	142039M	355499M
562564M	637933M	698628M	Total Assets ($)	31290M	67796M	18588M	146054M	111116M	323784M

Current Data Sorted By Assets   **Comparative Historical Data**

Type of Statement									4/1/00-3/31/01 ALL	4/1/01-3/31/02 ALL
Unqualified									4	3
Reviewed									8	5
Compiled									8	9
Tax Returns									7	10
Other									12	13

	0-500M	500M-2MM	2-10MM	10-50MM	50-100MM	100-250MM			4/1/00-3/31/01 ALL	4/1/01-3/31/02 ALL
(Statement type distribution)	1	1	2							
			4	1						
	2	3								
	7	3	2			1				
	3	8	3			1				
		2 (4/1-9/30/04)		40 (10/1/04-3/31/05)						
NUMBER OF STATEMENTS	13	15	11	1		2			39	40
	%	%	%	%	%	%			%	%
ASSETS										
Cash & Equivalents	17.4	9.0	14.6						9.8	14.0
Trade Receivables (net)	.0	2.5	13.1						6.0	3.2
Inventory	12.8	16.9	15.6						18.5	10.8
All Other Current	.8	7.2	1.0						1.1	.5
Total Current	31.0	35.6	44.3						35.5	28.6
Fixed Assets (net)	31.0	36.6	34.5						49.7	53.2
Intangibles (net)	18.4	16.2	7.5						7.2	8.9
All Other Non-Current	19.6	11.6	13.6						7.6	9.4
Total	100.0	100.0	100.0						100.0	100.0
LIABILITIES										
Notes Payable-Short Term	3.3	8.6	12.0						6.5	3.7
Cur. Mat.-L/T/D	4.0	3.9	5.8						8.9	9.3
Trade Payables	13.5	14.5	29.6						17.9	12.4
Income Taxes Payable	.0	.0	.0						.1	.0
All Other Current	13.3	11.9	12.5						12.4	11.1
Total Current	34.2	38.9	59.9						45.9	36.5
Long-Term Debt	21.4	29.0	20.5						27.6	25.9
Deferred Taxes	.8	.0	1.7						.1	.0
All Other Non-Current	4.9	.0	1.7						6.7	10.9
Net Worth	38.8	32.1	16.1						19.6	26.8
Total Liabilities & Net Worth	100.0	100.0	100.0						100.0	100.0
INCOME DATA										
Net Sales	100.0	100.0	100.0						100.0	100.0
Gross Profit										
Operating Expenses	90.9	84.5	92.2						94.2	88.1
Operating Profit	9.1	15.5	7.8						5.8	11.9
All Other Expenses (net)	.9	.8	1.5						2.5	2.5
Profit Before Taxes	8.2	14.7	6.3						3.3	9.4
RATIOS										
Current	2.2	2.5	1.0						1.2	1.7
	.7	1.1	.9						.8	.6
	.3	.6	.5						.4	.3
Quick	1.4	1.4	.8						.7	1.3
	.5	.3	.5						.2	.3
	.2	.2	.2						.1	.1
Sales/Receivables	0 UND	0 UND	5 78.8						0 UND	0 UND
	0 UND	0 UND	11 34.0						4 103.1	0 UND
	0 UND	4 88.0	37 9.8						12 31.5	5 72.5
Cost of Sales/Inventory										
Cost of Sales/Payables										
Sales/Working Capital	8.4	3.7	-352.2						48.6	18.4
	-52.1	57.9	-75.2						-32.5	-18.4
	-10.0	-11.0	-26.2						-8.1	-6.8
EBIT/Interest	34.6	18.9							7.3	7.5
	(10) 20.1	(11) 4.5							(36) 2.1	(34) 4.0
	1.5	.0							1.0	.9
Net Profit + Depr., Dep., Amort./Cur. Mat. L /T/D										
Fixed/Worth	.2	1.0	.6						1.1	1.1
	.8	2.9	1.7						3.0	2.0
	-2.9	-2.8	8.2						-4.1	25.3
Debt/Worth	.5	1.4	1.4						1.6	.9
	1.4	3.4	4.5						3.4	2.7
	-15.3	-12.4	13.1						-16.6	574.7
% Profit Before Taxes/Tangible Net Worth		77.5							60.0	94.9
		(10) 17.7							(27) 33.5	(31) 49.5
		-7.2							10.3	17.0
% Profit Before Taxes/Total Assets	78.3	30.5	28.7						15.1	24.3
	22.6	12.3	16.9						5.2	10.7
	.6	-.8	11.8						-.3	.8
Sales/Net Fixed Assets	35.5	10.9	25.9						12.3	14.7
	21.1	7.8	8.5						5.2	7.1
	5.1	3.2	6.8						1.8	2.2
Sales/Total Assets	4.3	2.4	4.1						3.7	4.0
	2.9	1.7	3.3						1.9	2.4
	1.8	1.0	2.0						1.1	1.2
% Depr., Dep., Amort./Sales									2.2	2.1
									(23) 6.7	(26) 7.0
									24.0	15.6
% Officers', Directors', Owners' Comp/Sales									1.9	2.6
									(11) 4.3	(14) 6.3
									8.9	16.0
Net Sales ($)	9469M	25940M	713380M	18292M		465868M			998401M	443763M
Total Assets ($)	3043M	13537M	50340M	11575M		356591M			750197M	290989M

Columns 10-50MM, 50-100MM, 100-250MM for ratio/percentage data marked: DATA NOT AVAILABLE

M = $ thousand   MM = $ million
See Pages 11 through 21 for Explanation of Ratios and Data

Comparative Historical Data				Current Data Sorted By Sales					
			Type of Statement						
3	10	4	Unqualified	1	1			1	1
2	2	5	Reviewed				1	3	1
9	8	5	Compiled	2	3			1	2
11	7	13	Tax Returns	6	2	2		1	2
14	7	15	Other	7	3	1	2		2
4/1/02- 3/31/03 ALL	4/1/03- 3/31/04 ALL	4/1/04- 3/31/05 ALL		0-1MM	2 (4/1-9/30/04) 1-3MM	3-5MM	40 (10/1/04-3/31/05) 5-10MM	10-25MM	25MM & OVER
39	34	42	**NUMBER OF STATEMENTS**	16	9	3	4	5	5
%	%	%	**ASSETS**	%	%	%	%	%	%
14.5	14.2	12.7	Cash & Equivalents	16.5					
2.5	3.7	4.4	Trade Receivables (net)	.0					
16.7	12.3	14.5	Inventory	15.6					
2.1	.8	3.4	All Other Current	1.7					
35.8	31.1	35.0	Total Current	33.8					
44.3	39.4	37.5	Fixed Assets (net)	30.1					
13.3	19.9	13.7	Intangibles (net)	17.0					
6.6	9.6	13.8	All Other Non-Current	19.1					
100.0	100.0	100.0	Total	100.0					
			LIABILITIES						
5.0	6.4	9.3	Notes Payable-Short Term	2.7					
6.5	4.4	4.5	Cur. Mat.-L/T/D	3.1					
15.6	13.5	17.9	Trade Payables	7.2					
.0	.1	.0	Income Taxes Payable	.0					
10.6	14.2	11.8	All Other Current	13.6					
37.6	38.5	43.6	Total Current	26.6					
31.4	24.3	24.0	Long-Term Debt	33.8					
.0	.3	.7	Deferred Taxes	.6					
8.5	3.3	2.0	All Other Non-Current	.0					
22.6	33.7	29.6	Net Worth	39.0					
100.0	100.0	100.0	Total Liabilities & Net Worth	100.0					
			INCOME DATA						
100.0	100.0	100.0	Net Sales	100.0					
			Gross Profit						
95.1	92.2	88.9	Operating Expenses	82.2					
4.9	7.8	11.1	Operating Profit	17.8					
.4	1.3	1.1	All Other Expenses (net)	1.4					
4.5	6.5	10.0	Profit Before Taxes	16.4					
			RATIOS						
1.9	1.9	1.6		6.3					
1.0	.9	.8	Current	1.6					
.5	.5	.4		.4					
.7	1.1	.9		3.1					
.4	.4	.4	Quick	.9					
.2	.2	.2		.2					
0 UND	0 UND	0 UND		0 UND					
0 UND	1 253.5	0 UND	Sales/Receivables	0 UND					
4 83.6	7 49.7	6 63.6		0 UND					
			Cost of Sales/Inventory						
			Cost of Sales/Payables						
13.1	16.3	9.1		5.4					
−200.4	−67.2	−50.4	Sales/Working Capital	8.9					
−13.1	−12.2	−9.4		−12.9					
14.5	11.1	24.0		25.0					
(26) 5.4	(28) 5.6	(33) 7.7	EBIT/Interest	(11) 18.9					
2.9	−.8	2.3		7.7					
			Net Profit + Depr., Dep., Amort./Cur. Mat. L/T/D						
.5	.9	.7		.3					
1.9	2.0	2.0	Fixed/Worth	.9					
−3.1	−6.0	−11.4		−2.2					
.9	.7	1.3		.7					
3.6	2.8	3.0	Debt/Worth	1.7					
−6.9	−9.0	−26.9		−11.3					
97.4	55.3	110.8		116.7					
(25) 44.8	(23) 40.3	(29) 52.6	% Profit Before Taxes/Tangible Net Worth	(10) 95.1					
20.9	20.7	19.3		51.6					
26.5	22.4	31.4		47.4					
12.5	10.0	16.1	% Profit Before Taxes/Total Assets	26.6					
4.4	.9	4.0		10.3					
14.6	19.0	21.1		25.4					
7.4	6.2	8.0	Sales/Net Fixed Assets	8.0					
3.2	2.4	3.3		3.4					
3.4	4.7	3.4		2.8					
2.5	1.8	2.3	Sales/Total Assets	1.7					
1.2	1.1	1.5		1.0					
1.2	3.4	2.1							
(22) 3.1	(21) 8.5	(20) 6.9	% Depr., Dep., Amort./Sales						
18.8	18.3	13.2							
3.1		3.7							
(16) 6.5		(18) 5.6	% Officers', Directors', Owners' Comp/Sales						
23.3		7.9							
1781445M	756192M	1232949M	Net Sales ($)	8956M	14463M	11990M	25763M	84880M	1086897M
677903M	702539M	435086M	Total Assets ($)	6095M	7106M	3379M	12159M	29856M	376491M

© RMA 2005

M = $ thousand   MM = $ million

See Pages 11 through 21 for Explanation of Ratios and Data

Current Data Sorted By Assets | Comparative Historical Data

0-500M	500M-2MM	2-10MM	10-50MM	50-100MM	100-250MM	Type of Statement	4/1/00-3/31/01 ALL	4/1/01-3/31/02 ALL
		4	5	1	2	Unqualified	9	11
1	5	10	1			Reviewed	21	26
1	5	2	1			Compiled	19	22
1	3	1				Tax Returns	5	12
5	6	7	5			Other	23	43
	13 (4/1-9/30/04)		53 (10/1/04-3/31/05)					
8	19	24	12	1	2	**NUMBER OF STATEMENTS**	77	114
%	%	%	%	%	%	**ASSETS**	%	%
	13.3	10.2	11.5			Cash & Equivalents	6.7	7.9
	12.9	26.5	30.6			Trade Receivables (net)	28.7	24.6
	4.4	7.8	8.6			Inventory	10.1	9.3
	1.3	2.4	2.2			All Other Current	3.2	1.5
	32.0	46.8	52.8			Total Current	48.8	43.3
	56.8	44.6	27.5			Fixed Assets (net)	41.0	46.5
	1.5	.3	11.1			Intangibles (net)	3.9	3.4
	9.7	8.3	8.5			All Other Non-Current	6.3	6.7
	100.0	100.0	100.0			Total	100.0	100.0
						LIABILITIES		
	10.3	8.5	8.8			Notes Payable-Short Term	13.0	10.9
	8.9	9.8	7.9			Cur. Mat.-L/T/D	7.1	10.0
	3.6	9.9	8.1			Trade Payables	11.8	9.3
	1.4	.4	.9			Income Taxes Payable	.5	.8
	3.3	5.2	18.8			All Other Current	7.6	5.7
	27.5	33.9	44.5			Total Current	40.1	36.6
	35.0	24.9	18.4			Long-Term Debt	27.0	27.4
	1.2	1.2	1.0			Deferred Taxes	1.4	.8
	6.3	2.2	5.5			All Other Non-Current	3.5	5.0
	30.0	37.9	30.7			Net Worth	28.1	30.2
	100.0	100.0	100.0			Total Liabilities & Net Worth	100.0	100.0
						INCOME DATA		
	100.0	100.0	100.0			Net Sales	100.0	100.0
						Gross Profit		
	82.9	83.7	93.2			Operating Expenses	88.6	85.0
	17.1	16.3	6.8			Operating Profit	11.4	15.0
	4.3	3.9	4.0			All Other Expenses (net)	5.4	6.1
	12.8	12.4	2.8			Profit Before Taxes	6.0	8.9
						RATIOS		
	3.1	2.1	3.8				2.2	2.1
	1.5	1.4	1.4			Current	1.4	1.3
	.8	.8	.6				.6	.6
	2.6	1.6	3.4				1.7	1.6
	1.4	1.1	1.0			Quick	.9	.9
	.6	.4	.4				.4	.4
0	UND	15 24.3	43 8.5				18 20.5	8 43.8
19	19.7	54 6.7	54 6.8			Sales/Receivables	61 6.0	46 7.9
61	6.0	81 4.5	84 4.3				91 4.0	83 4.4
						Cost of Sales/Inventory		
						Cost of Sales/Payables		
	7.5	5.1	5.2				5.7	6.8
	27.9	12.6	12.7			Sales/Working Capital	14.1	18.1
	-23.9	-16.0	-9.6				-14.9	-9.1
	14.3	10.8					5.4	5.8
(17)	7.0	4.5				EBIT/Interest	(63) 2.5	(95) 2.3
	2.4	1.8					1.0	1.3
		4.2					4.8	3.2
	(10)	2.5				Net Profit + Depr., Dep., Amort./Cur. Mat. L/T/D	(19) 1.8	(21) 1.4
		1.8					1.0	.4
	.7	.5	.3				.6	.6
	2.0	1.0	1.8			Fixed/Worth	1.4	1.6
	6.1	2.2	NM				8.3	4.9
	.8	1.0	.7				1.1	1.2
	1.3	1.5	4.3			Debt/Worth	2.6	2.4
	6.9	3.2	NM				11.8	7.3
	69.7	53.3				% Profit Before Taxes/Tangible	46.2	64.3
(16)	34.2	(23) 31.6				Net Worth	(66) 17.4	(100) 24.2
	6.4	15.3					.4	4.7
	31.0	22.8	15.5			% Profit Before Taxes/Total	14.0	14.9
	12.0	5.8	7.3			Assets	4.8	6.5
	3.3	2.4	-.8				.0	1.2
	6.0	7.5	44.2				11.5	12.5
	2.9	4.6	5.1			Sales/Net Fixed Assets	4.6	4.3
	1.3	1.0	2.4				1.4	1.0
	2.5	2.2	2.2				2.3	2.3
	1.7	1.4	1.8			Sales/Total Assets	1.5	1.4
	.9	.7	.9				.7	.6
	7.7	5.0					1.7	2.6
(15)	10.3	(22) 7.8				% Depr., Dep., Amort./Sales	(70) 5.9	(106) 8.6
	26.6	27.8					12.0	22.4
							1.5	3.9
						% Officers', Directors', Owners' Comp/Sales	(25) 5.1	(29) 6.9
							15.0	15.9
6081M	34099M	173088M	521492M	264936M	771656M	Net Sales ($)	933214M	1774345M
1976M	18901M	119634M	283945M	98824M	218568M	Total Assets ($)	933701M	1401578M

© RMA 2005

M = $ thousand   MM = $ million

See Pages 11 through 21 for Explanation of Ratios and Data

Comparative Historical Data				Current Data Sorted By Sales					
			Type of Statement						
11	10	12	Unqualified			4	1	3	4
15	17	17	Reviewed	2	6		5	2	2
9	17	9	Compiled	3	3	2	1		
14	15	5	Tax Returns	1	3		1		
24	24	23	Other	7	4	2	3	3	4
4/1/02-3/31/03 ALL	4/1/03-3/31/04 ALL	4/1/04-3/31/05 ALL		13 (4/1-9/30/04)			53 (10/1/04-3/31/05)		
				0-1MM	1-3MM	3-5MM	5-10MM	10-25MM	25MM & OVER
73	83	66	**NUMBER OF STATEMENTS**	13	16	8	10	9	10
%	%	%	**ASSETS**	%	%	%	%	%	%
8.1	8.6	11.3	Cash & Equivalents	14.9	11.9		12.6		9.8
30.0	27.9	22.8	Trade Receivables (net)	7.5	16.9		35.1		45.6
11.4	9.1	8.2	Inventory	4.8	7.9		8.2		11.0
2.8	3.5	2.9	All Other Current	2.0	2.4		1.2		2.3
52.4	49.1	45.2	Total Current	29.2	39.1		57.1		68.6
40.4	40.4	43.9	Fixed Assets (net)	59.2	52.2		35.5		16.2
2.2	1.7	3.0	Intangibles (net)	.3	1.7		.5		5.9
5.1	8.8	8.0	All Other Non-Current	11.3	7.0		6.9		9.3
100.0	100.0	100.0	Total	100.0	100.0		100.0		100.0
			LIABILITIES						
10.2	6.9	9.5	Notes Payable-Short Term	12.0	8.9		11.0		11.7
9.2	6.7	8.8	Cur. Mat.-L/T/D	8.6	9.7		7.4		8.1
10.4	12.1	8.2	Trade Payables	1.5	7.8		6.7		14.4
1.2	.7	.7	Income Taxes Payable	.0	1.6		.1		.1
7.7	7.3	7.1	All Other Current	2.2	4.2		4.4		22.5
38.7	33.8	34.3	Total Current	24.4	32.2		29.6		57.0
24.1	29.4	27.9	Long-Term Debt	34.8	40.5		22.9		13.6
.7	1.2	1.0	Deferred Taxes	.0	1.5		1.1		1.2
5.3	7.1	5.0	All Other Non-Current	8.7	6.3		.7		6.4
31.2	28.5	31.9	Net Worth	32.1	19.5		45.7		21.8
100.0	100.0	100.0	Total Liabilities & Net Worth	100.0	100.0		100.0		100.0
			INCOME DATA						
100.0	100.0	100.0	Net Sales	100.0	100.0		100.0		100.0
			Gross Profit						
90.2	89.0	85.1	Operating Expenses	72.6	86.3		89.4		96.7
9.8	11.0	14.9	Operating Profit	27.4	13.7		10.6		3.3
4.2	3.6	4.1	All Other Expenses (net)	7.5	4.4		.5		.5
5.5	7.3	10.7	Profit Before Taxes	19.8	9.3		10.1		2.8
			RATIOS						
2.6	2.5	2.9		7.0	2.7		4.7		2.2
1.5	1.4	1.5	Current	1.5	1.2		2.2		1.4
1.0	.9	.8		.3	.8		1.2		.7
1.8	1.9	2.2		5.3	1.6		4.2		1.7
1.0	1.1	1.2	Quick	1.5	1.0		1.5		1.2
.5	.6	.5		.2	.5		1.0		.6
14 25.5	30 12.1	0 UND		0 UND	0 UND		38 9.6		39 9.3
57 6.4	51 7.1	46 8.0	Sales/Receivables	0 UND	22 17.0		80 4.6		62 5.9
91 4.0	78 4.7	66 5.5		59 6.2	52 7.1		102 3.6		94 3.9
			Cost of Sales/Inventory						
			Cost of Sales/Payables						
5.3	4.2	5.8		4.8	9.4		3.0		7.1
10.1	11.4	16.3	Sales/Working Capital	16.8	34.3		8.6		18.3
NM	−46.8	−16.4		−2.2	−17.3		NM		−11.3
7.4	10.3	11.1		35.8	9.1		21.0		
(61) 2.6	(70) 3.9	(61) 4.6	EBIT/Interest	(12) 5.7	(15) 4.3		4.8		
1.0	1.3	1.7		1.8	.7		1.7		
6.5	9.7	4.5	Net Profit + Depr., Dep.,						
(16) 1.6	(19) 2.3	(17) 2.4	Amort./Cur. Mat. L/T/D						
1.1	1.2	1.3							
.4	.4	.5		.7	.7		.5		.1
1.2	1.1	1.4	Fixed/Worth	1.9	3.5		.8		.9
4.3	5.4	6.0		59.2	−7.3		2.3		NM
1.0	1.0	.9		.9	.8		.5		1.2
2.2	2.3	2.3	Debt/Worth	2.3	4.8		1.2		5.1
7.4	10.7	8.2		59.6	−10.6		3.9		NM
35.0	44.7	69.7	% Profit Before Taxes/Tangible	142.9	41.2		36.7		
(61) 17.8	(69) 24.8	(56) 34.8	Net Worth	(11) 47.6	(11) 28.8		25.1		
1.7	7.1	14.9		7.3	4.6		5.0		
14.0	16.2	23.3	% Profit Before Taxes/Total	25.2	15.9		17.6		21.7
5.0	6.6	9.6	Assets	12.7	7.6		7.3		7.6
−.3	.9	2.0		2.2	.1		.9		1.1
14.2	10.9	9.4		5.9	4.5		9.8		157.2
5.0	4.8	4.0	Sales/Net Fixed Assets	1.3	2.1		6.8		38.9
1.5	1.3	1.4		.3	1.0		3.8		5.9
2.2	2.3	2.4		1.5	2.1		2.3		3.2
1.6	1.6	1.7	Sales/Total Assets	.8	1.6		1.9		2.4
.8	.6	.8		.3	.7		1.2		1.8
3.3	1.8	4.9		8.9	8.8				
(65) 7.6	(74) 7.3	(55) 9.1	% Depr., Dep., Amort./Sales	(10) 19.4	(14) 14.3				
23.1	21.3	19.2		47.0	35.8				
3.5	3.8	2.4	% Officers', Directors',						
(25) 7.5	(26) 6.7	(21) 4.7	Owners' Comp/Sales						
18.1	10.8	14.6							
1214826M	1856903M	1771352M	Net Sales ($)	6273M	29665M	29146M	71217M	157842M	1477209M
903282M	1277565M	741848M	Total Assets ($)	8921M	35093M	22716M	48585M	222980M	403553M

© RMA 2005

M = $ thousand   MM = $ million
See Pages 11 through 21 for Explanation of Ratios and Data

Current Data Sorted By Assets   Comparative Historical Data

Type of Statement

Type of Statement	0-500M	500M-2MM	2-10MM	10-50MM	50-100MM	100-250MM
Unqualified						
Reviewed			3	1	1	
Compiled		1	3			
Tax Returns	3	5	2		1	
Other	7	5	1			
	4	4			1	

Columns (Current Data): 0-500M, 500M-2MM, 2-10MM, 10-50MM, 50-100MM, 100-250MM — dates: 12 (4/1-9/30/04) ... 29 (10/1/04-3/31/05)

Comparative Historical Data columns: 4/1/00-3/31/01 ALL, 4/1/01-3/31/02 ALL

	0-500M	500M-2MM	2-10MM	10-50MM	50-100MM	100-250MM		4/1/00-3/31/01 ALL	4/1/01-3/31/02 ALL
NUMBER OF STATEMENTS	14	15	9	1	2				
	%	%	%	%	%	%		%	%
ASSETS									
Cash & Equivalents	15.1	7.5							
Trade Receivables (net)	5.4	7.6				D		D	D
Inventory	12.1	9.7				A		A	A
All Other Current	1.5	.9				T		T	T
Total Current	34.0	25.7				A		A	A
Fixed Assets (net)	60.0	65.2							
Intangibles (net)	2.6	1.5				N		N	N
All Other Non-Current	3.3	7.6				O		O	O
Total	100.0	100.0				T		T	T
LIABILITIES									
Notes Payable-Short Term	16.5	9.8				A		A	A
Cur. Mat.-L/T/D	10.1	7.2				V		V	V
Trade Payables	6.4	10.2				A		A	A
Income Taxes Payable	.2	.5				I		I	I
All Other Current	15.3	2.2				L		L	L
Total Current	48.5	29.8				A		A	A
Long-Term Debt	53.0	43.4				B		B	B
Deferred Taxes	.0	.2				L		L	L
All Other Non-Current	.7	3.7				E		E	E
Net Worth	-2.4	22.9							
Total Liabilities & Net Worth	100.0	100.0							
INCOME DATA									
Net Sales	100.0	100.0							
Gross Profit									
Operating Expenses	95.7	96.1							
Operating Profit	4.3	3.9							
All Other Expenses (net)	2.4	5.6							
Profit Before Taxes	1.9	-1.7							

RATIOS

Ratio	0-500M	500M-2MM		4/1/00-3/31/01 ALL	4/1/01-3/31/02 ALL
Current	1.8	1.7			
	.8	1.2			
	.2	.5			
Quick	1.0	1.4			
	.5	.6			
	.1	.3			
Sales/Receivables	0 UND	8 48.6			
	3 112.0	25 14.4			
	15 23.6	50 7.3			
Cost of Sales/Inventory					
Cost of Sales/Payables					
Sales/Working Capital	14.5	10.5			
	-56.4	39.4			
	-7.9	-5.2			
EBIT/Interest	5.5	5.7			
	(12) 2.3	(13) 1.4			
	-.2	-1.0			
Net Profit + Depr., Dep., Amort./Cur. Mat. L /T/D					
Fixed/Worth	1.2	1.0			
	4.6	3.1			
	-98.6	-12.8			
Debt/Worth	2.7	.8			
	11.0	2.8			
	-117.4	-18.3			
% Profit Before Taxes/Tangible Net Worth	291.7	25.3			
	(10) 7.3	(11) 16.2			
	-36.4	.6			
% Profit Before Taxes/Total Assets	21.1	9.3			
	6.4	2.7			
	-8.1	-2.8			
Sales/Net Fixed Assets	8.7	3.0			
	4.4	2.3			
	3.3	1.0			
Sales/Total Assets	4.2	1.7			
	3.0	1.2			
	2.3	.9			
% Depr., Dep., Amort./Sales	4.3	9.1			
	(10) 11.1	10.4			
	14.8	18.1			
% Officers', Directors', Owners' Comp/Sales					

	0-500M	500M-2MM	2-10MM	10-50MM	50-100MM
Net Sales ($)	10506M	18647M	44675M	53629M	125438M
Total Assets ($)	3588M	16115M	38616M	17964M	126132M

M = $ thousand   MM = $ million
See Pages 11 through 21 for Explanation of Ratios and Data

Comparative Historical Data / Current Data Sorted By Sales

			Type of Statement						
3	4	4	Unqualified	1	2		1	1	1
3	7	5	Reviewed		1	1	1	1	
4	14	8	Compiled	3	5		1		
6	7	14	Tax Returns	11	2		1		1
		10	Other	4	4				1
4/1/02- 3/31/03 ALL	4/1/03- 3/31/04 ALL	4/1/04- 3/31/05 ALL		0-1MM	1-3MM	3-5MM	5-10MM	10-25MM	25MM & OVER
				12 (4/1-9/30/04)		29 (10/1/04-3/31/05)			
16	32	41	**NUMBER OF STATEMENTS**	19	14	1	3	1	3
%	%	%	**ASSETS**	%	%	%	%	%	%
4.1	4.8	8.5	Cash & Equivalents	8.9	11.8				
10.4	10.0	9.9	Trade Receivables (net)	5.3	12.3				
16.2	10.3	10.5	Inventory	6.4	15.0				
1.0	1.8	1.5	All Other Current	1.1	1.2				
31.7	26.8	30.4	Total Current	21.8	40.3				
57.4	63.7	59.1	Fixed Assets (net)	68.2	47.6				
3.9	4.1	1.7	Intangibles (net)	2.0	1.8				
7.1	5.3	8.8	All Other Non-Current	8.0	10.4				
100.0	100.0	100.0	Total	100.0	100.0				
			LIABILITIES						
22.2	11.7	11.6	Notes Payable-Short Term	11.2	14.4				
15.6	7.1	8.6	Cur. Mat.-L/T/D	8.7	8.4				
4.2	7.0	7.3	Trade Payables	5.4	10.9				
.0	.0	.3	Income Taxes Payable	.2	.5				
3.9	3.9	7.5	All Other Current	11.2	3.2				
45.9	29.7	35.2	Total Current	36.8	37.3				
25.0	46.5	42.2	Long-Term Debt	55.1	37.1				
.1	.3	.2	Deferred Taxes	.0	.2				
13.3	9.9	3.4	All Other Non-Current	1.9	3.9				
15.7	13.6	19.0	Net Worth	6.2	21.4				
100.0	100.0	100.0	Total Liabilities & Net Worth	100.0	100.0				
			INCOME DATA						
100.0	100.0	100.0	Net Sales	100.0	100.0				
			Gross Profit						
93.7	91.8	92.3	Operating Expenses	90.4	95.3				
6.3	8.2	7.7	Operating Profit	9.6	4.7				
4.2	4.5	4.3	All Other Expenses (net)	6.0	4.3				
2.1	3.7	3.4	Profit Before Taxes	3.6	.4				
			RATIOS						
1.6	1.5	1.8		1.7	10.6				
.7	.9	1.0	Current	.5	1.3				
.2	.5	.3		.3	.6				
.6	.8	1.3		.7	7.8				
.2	.5	.6	Quick	.5	.8				
.2	.1	.2		.1	.1				
0 UND	0 UND	0 UND		0 UND	0 UND				
7 50.6	19 19.1	16 22.5	Sales/Receivables	4 88.1	25 14.5				
41 8.9	47 7.8	32 11.3		19 19.0	36 10.1				
			Cost of Sales/Inventory						
			Cost of Sales/Payables						
NM	14.4	12.5		14.5	10.3				
-13.7	-24.5	566.0	Sales/Working Capital	-9.5	19.3				
-4.5	-7.5	-6.3		-3.9	-13.6				
7.7	4.6	6.1		4.3	5.7				
(15) 2.8	(30) 2.1	(37) 1.9	EBIT/Interest	(16) 2.1	(13) 1.3				
-1.2	-1.4	.6		.8	-1.9				
			Net Profit + Depr., Dep., Amort./Cur. Mat. L/T/D						
1.1	1.4	1.0		1.4	.8				
2.8	5.6	2.1	Fixed/Worth	5.2	1.4				
143.7	196.2	19.8		-130.0	NM				
.5	1.0	.9		.8	1.3				
3.4	5.8	3.3	Debt/Worth	8.5	4.2				
345.8	315.9	27.8		-154.0	NM				
37.1	74.5	42.2		75.6	39.0				
(13) 8.3	(25) 25.4	(33) 14.8	% Profit Before Taxes/Tangible Net Worth	(14) 15.4	(11) 17.8				
-49.0	-3.3	-5.6		-13.6	-26.3				
8.7	9.1	10.9		11.5	13.9				
2.6	4.1	4.6	% Profit Before Taxes/Total Assets	4.6	1.5				
-11.6	-10.4	-2.1		-1.5	-11.2				
9.2	3.8	5.9		4.9	10.2				
2.6	2.0	3.0	Sales/Net Fixed Assets	3.4	2.7				
1.4	1.1	1.6		1.0	2.0				
2.5	2.3	2.7		3.2	1.9				
1.4	1.1	1.7	Sales/Total Assets	2.2	1.5				
1.0	.9	.9		.7	.9				
2.2	9.3	8.0		8.2	5.1				
(15) 6.4	15.2	(35) 10.5	% Depr., Dep., Amort./Sales	(16) 12.8	(12) 10.0				
20.7	21.0	18.1		19.4	16.2				
	3.2	3.5		3.5					
	(13) 6.3	(20) 6.0	% Officers', Directors', Owners' Comp/Sales	(11) 6.5					
	8.9	8.7		8.9					
133971M	143433M	252895M	Net Sales ($)	12756M	21805M	4234M	22280M	12753M	179067M
119493M	144675M	202415M	Total Assets ($)	12651M	23557M	4495M	12958M	4658M	144096M

M = $ thousand   MM = $ million
See Pages 11 through 21 for Explanation of Ratios and Data

Current Data Sorted By Assets   Comparative Historical Data

0-500M	500M-2MM	2-10MM	10-50MM	50-100MM	100-250MM	Type of Statement	4/1/00-3/31/01 ALL	4/1/01-3/31/02 ALL
	1	2		2	2	Unqualified		
	3	1	2			Reviewed		
	2	5	2			Compiled		
1		1	1			Tax Returns		
	4	1			1	Other		
	7 (4/1-9/30/04)		25 (10/1/04-3/31/05)					
1	10	10	6	2	3	NUMBER OF STATEMENTS		
%	%	%	%	%	%	ASSETS	%	%
	7.1	21.0				Cash & Equivalents	D	D
	3.3	24.3				Trade Receivables (net)	A	A
	1.7	.0				Inventory	T	T
	1.0	10.0				All Other Current	A	A
	13.0	55.4				Total Current		
	79.6	38.8				Fixed Assets (net)		
	.7	.0				Intangibles (net)	N	N
	6.8	5.8				All Other Non-Current	O	O
	100.0	100.0				Total	T	T
						LIABILITIES	A	A
	.7	.8				Notes Payable-Short Term	V	V
	10.5	3.3				Cur. Mat.-L/T/D	A	A
	3.1	8.2				Trade Payables	I	I
	.0	.0				Income Taxes Payable	L	L
	1.9	10.3				All Other Current	A	A
	16.2	22.6				Total Current	B	B
	68.9	50.0				Long-Term Debt	L	L
	1.4	2.9				Deferred Taxes	E	E
	9.7	10.7				All Other Non-Current		
	3.7	13.7				Net Worth		
	100.0	100.0				Total Liabilities & Net Worth		
						INCOME DATA		
	100.0	100.0				Net Sales		
						Gross Profit		
	82.4	106.0				Operating Expenses		
	17.6	-6.0				Operating Profit		
	10.0	2.9				All Other Expenses (net)		
	7.5	-8.9				Profit Before Taxes		
						RATIOS		
	1.5	5.2						
	.7	2.6				Current		
	.2	1.7						
	1.4	3.5						
	.4	2.2				Quick		
	.2	1.5						
	0 UND	25 14.8						
	0 UND	45 8.1				Sales/Receivables		
	33 10.9	75 4.8						
						Cost of Sales/Inventory		
						Cost of Sales/Payables		
	14.6	2.5						
	NM	4.8				Sales/Working Capital		
	-2.3	9.2						
						EBIT/Interest		
						Net Profit + Depr., Dep., Amort./Cur. Mat. L /T/D		
	1.1	.3						
	4.7	1.1				Fixed/Worth		
	-3.1	-5.7						
	.6	.6						
	4.7	1.4				Debt/Worth		
	-4.8	-9.6						
						% Profit Before Taxes/Tangible Net Worth		
	17.8	9.9						
	4.6	-2.8				% Profit Before Taxes/Total Assets		
	-9.3	-20.2						
	1.8	22.6						
	.7	2.4				Sales/Net Fixed Assets		
	.3	.7						
	1.0	3.2						
	.5	.8				Sales/Total Assets		
	.3	.5						
						% Depr., Dep., Amort./Sales		
						% Officers', Directors', Owners' Comp/Sales		
2760M	7997M	86537M	129823M	33020M	544036M	Net Sales ($)		
145M	12979M	54867M	128944M	116538M	588085M	Total Assets ($)		

© RMA 2005

M = $ thousand   MM = $ million
See Pages 11 through 21 for Explanation of Ratios and Data

Comparative Historical Data | Current Data Sorted By Sales

			Type of Statement	0-1MM	1-3MM	3-5MM	5-10MM	10-25MM	25MM & OVER
2	6	6	Unqualified					4	2
5	5	4	Reviewed	1				3	
8	8	10	Compiled	4	1	1	1	2	1
5	2	5	Tax Returns	2	1	1		1	
4	8	7	Other	1	4	1			1
4/1/02-3/31/03 ALL	4/1/03-3/31/04 ALL	4/1/04-3/31/05 ALL		**7 (4/1-9/30/04)**			**25 (10/1/04-3/31/05)**		
24	29	32	**NUMBER OF STATEMENTS**	8	6	3	1	10	4
%	%	%	**ASSETS**	%	%	%	%	%	%
8.4	13.1	11.6	Cash & Equivalents					10.9	
14.3	11.5	14.8	Trade Receivables (net)					26.4	
1.6	1.2	2.7	Inventory					.1	
3.1	4.3	4.1	All Other Current					5.3	
27.4	30.1	33.2	Total Current					42.7	
69.4	66.4	61.2	Fixed Assets (net)					53.4	
.3	.1	.4	Intangibles (net)					.1	
2.9	3.4	5.2	All Other Non-Current					3.8	
100.0	100.0	100.0	Total					100.0	
			LIABILITIES						
2.9	4.4	5.9	Notes Payable-Short Term					9.4	
11.0	8.2	5.8	Cur. Mat.-L/T/D					4.4	
10.4	9.0	10.2	Trade Payables					4.9	
.4	.4	.0	Income Taxes Payable					.0	
4.1	4.1	5.6	All Other Current					10.8	
28.8	26.1	27.6	Total Current					29.6	
42.7	39.6	47.4	Long-Term Debt					21.9	
1.9	1.9	2.6	Deferred Taxes					6.0	
3.0	3.0	7.0	All Other Non-Current					1.9	
23.6	29.3	15.3	Net Worth					40.6	
100.0	100.0	100.0	Total Liabilities & Net Worth					100.0	
			INCOME DATA						
100.0	100.0	100.0	Net Sales					100.0	
			Gross Profit						
85.4	82.3	90.8	Operating Expenses					92.1	
14.6	17.7	9.2	Operating Profit					7.9	
4.1	4.8	5.2	All Other Expenses (net)					2.3	
10.5	12.9	4.0	Profit Before Taxes					5.6	
			RATIOS						
1.5 / 1.0 / .5	1.6 / 1.0 / .3	2.0 / 1.1 / .3	Current					3.2 / 1.3 / .4	
1.3 / .7 / .3	1.2 / .8 / .2	1.9 / .8 / .3	Quick					2.7 / 1.1 / .4	
18 20.2 / 35 10.3 / 60 6.1	6 65.9 / 29 12.8 / 52 7.1	8 46.6 / 35 10.4 / 69 5.3	Sales/Receivables					25 14.8 / 69 5.3 / 82 4.4	
			Cost of Sales/Inventory						
			Cost of Sales/Payables						
9.3 / NM / -6.2	8.3 / -175.7 / -3.0	7.3 / 108.0 / -3.9	Sales/Working Capital					7.6 / 17.9 / -3.3	
7.8 / (21) 3.5 / .8	7.4 / (22) 3.6 / 1.6	5.2 / (26) 1.8 / .0	EBIT/Interest						
			Net Profit + Depr., Dep., Amort./Cur. Mat. L/T/D						
1.2 / 2.1 / 3.6	.7 / 2.1 / 4.2	.8 / 2.2 / 6.8	Fixed/Worth					.3 / 1.9 / 3.0	
1.0 / 2.3 / 4.3	1.0 / 1.7 / 6.2	.9 / 2.9 / 30.8	Debt/Worth					1.0 / 1.5 / 3.0	
65.2 / (20) 23.4 / 10.3	47.6 / (26) 17.5 / 3.7	40.0 / (26) 14.4 / .9	% Profit Before Taxes/Tangible Net Worth					37.9 / 13.8 / -2.4	
10.9 / 6.9 / -1.6	11.1 / 4.0 / .0	8.6 / 2.6 / -3.6	% Profit Before Taxes/Total Assets					10.0 / 3.6 / -1.2	
2.0 / 1.1 / .5	2.6 / .7 / .4	5.5 / 1.0 / .4	Sales/Net Fixed Assets					22.6 / 1.8 / .5	
1.4 / .8 / .5	1.4 / .5 / .3	1.4 / .7 / .4	Sales/Total Assets					3.2 / 1.2 / .4	
4.8 / (21) 17.2 / 33.5	5.0 / (22) 11.3 / 35.4	4.5 / (27) 19.6 / 36.4	% Depr., Dep., Amort./Sales						
			% Officers', Directors', Owners' Comp/Sales						
395243M	357948M	804173M	Net Sales ($)	4086M	11579M	12590M	5893M	168428M	601597M
467615M	614239M	901558M	Total Assets ($)	12247M	13366M	51025M	6206M	219195M	599519M

M = $ thousand   MM = $ million
See Pages 11 through 21 for Explanation of Ratios and Data

Current Data Sorted By Assets   Comparative Historical Data

Type of Statement	0-500M	500M-2MM	2-10MM	10-50MM	50-100MM	100-250MM	4/1/00-3/31/01 ALL	4/1/01-3/31/02 ALL
Unqualified	2	3	12	24	2	4	26	34
Reviewed	2	11	41	22	2	1	51	46
Compiled	7	15	21	8	1		55	62
Tax Returns	21	10	8	1			21	19
Other	4	9	29	28	8	2	68	72
		51 (4/1-9/30/04)		245 (10/1/04-3/31/05)				
NUMBER OF STATEMENTS	34	48	111	83	13	7	221	233
ASSETS	%	%	%	%	%	%	%	%
Cash & Equivalents	9.7	10.4	6.4	5.3	2.5		7.8	6.7
Trade Receivables (net)	4.2	17.0	20.8	14.6	15.4		15.5	16.4
Inventory	.8	6.0	9.9	13.9	20.1		8.3	9.8
All Other Current	.9	3.0	1.8	2.0	2.0		3.2	2.9
Total Current	15.7	36.4	38.9	35.8	40.1		34.7	35.8
Fixed Assets (net)	70.0	55.9	50.8	58.8	54.2		57.1	56.1
Intangibles (net)	1.4	1.4	1.9	.6	1.0		1.9	1.9
All Other Non-Current	13.0	6.4	8.4	4.9	4.6		6.3	6.2
Total	100.0	100.0	100.0	100.0	100.0		100.0	100.0
LIABILITIES								
Notes Payable-Short Term	19.6	7.4	9.2	8.8	11.6		11.7	11.2
Cur. Mat.-L/T/D	9.5	10.3	9.0	8.3	7.7		9.9	12.0
Trade Payables	2.2	7.2	8.5	6.3	6.2		5.3	6.4
Income Taxes Payable	.0	.2	.4	.3	1.2		.2	.3
All Other Current	3.6	10.2	7.3	3.9	5.9		5.9	6.3
Total Current	34.9	35.3	34.4	27.6	32.6		33.0	36.2
Long-Term Debt	48.0	35.7	29.4	31.3	29.3		30.9	34.0
Deferred Taxes	.0	.4	1.4	1.9	.8		1.2	1.0
All Other Non-Current	2.6	7.7	4.1	3.3	2.5		7.2	3.1
Net Worth	14.5	20.9	30.7	35.9	34.8		27.7	25.7
Total Liabilities & Net Worth	100.0	100.0	100.0	100.0	100.0		100.0	100.0
INCOME DATA								
Net Sales	100.0	100.0	100.0	100.0	100.0		100.0	100.0
Gross Profit								
Operating Expenses	88.2	89.1	89.8	87.4	88.7		89.0	88.4
Operating Profit	11.8	10.9	10.2	12.6	11.3		11.0	11.6
All Other Expenses (net)	3.0	3.0	1.9	3.1	1.9		2.5	5.3
Profit Before Taxes	8.8	7.9	8.3	9.6	9.4		8.4	6.3
RATIOS								
Current	1.4	2.0	1.9	1.8	1.8		2.1	1.7
	.3	1.2	1.2	1.2	1.2		1.1	1.0
	.1	.5	.7	.8	.6		.5	.5
Quick	.9	1.7	1.5	1.3	1.1		1.7	1.4
	.2	.8	.8	.8	.5		.8	.7
	.1	.3	.4	.4	.4		.3	.3
Sales/Receivables	0 UND	0 UND	34 10.7	37 9.8	36 10.1		14 25.8	13 27.9
	0 UND	31 11.7	60 6.1	59 6.2	63 5.8		42 8.7	45 8.1
	0 UND	51 7.2	83 4.4	76 4.8	79 4.6		67 5.4	68 5.4
Cost of Sales/Inventory								
Cost of Sales/Payables								
Sales/Working Capital	26.7	7.0	5.7	5.5	8.0		6.5	8.1
	-14.7	38.1	25.4	23.0	25.0		34.8	UND
	-2.9	-6.7	-9.6	-9.4	-10.7		-7.2	-5.1
EBIT/Interest	8.2	7.7	5.2	6.9	7.6		4.6	4.4
	(25) 1.1	(38) 2.5	(100) 2.6	(75) 2.7	4.0		(193) 2.2	(206) 1.8
	-.6	.7	1.3	1.5	1.8		1.2	1.0
Net Profit + Depr., Dep., Amort./Cur. Mat. L/T/D			2.0	2.6			3.6	2.8
			(36) 1.2	(22) 1.6			(57) 2.0	(60) 1.9
			.8	1.0			1.0	1.1
Fixed/Worth	1.5	.9	.9	.8	.7		.9	1.0
	7.5	3.0	2.1	1.9	1.7		1.9	2.2
	-2.3	NM	4.5	3.9	2.5		5.5	5.5
Debt/Worth	1.0	.7	1.4	1.1	1.3		1.0	1.2
	7.6	3.2	2.3	2.4	2.4		2.2	3.1
	-4.8	NM	6.5	4.2	3.4		6.7	6.8
% Profit Before Taxes/Tangible Net Worth	89.0	50.1	35.6	35.7	27.1		34.7	33.1
	(21) 29.5	(36) 17.9	(101) 16.1	(81) 19.7	15.6		(194) 16.9	(204) 14.3
	-2.1	.4	5.7	5.4	9.4		3.1	2.9
% Profit Before Taxes/Total Assets	21.7	14.2	10.3	9.9	8.4		13.0	11.6
	2.2	4.0	4.3	5.0	5.8		4.1	2.9
	-2.5	-1.9	1.2	1.7	2.0		.2	.3
Sales/Net Fixed Assets	4.4	6.2	5.1	3.8	5.7		4.2	4.4
	1.7	2.6	2.4	1.4	2.2		1.6	1.8
	.7	.8	.9	.7	.7		.8	.8
Sales/Total Assets	2.8	2.1	1.6	1.3	1.5		1.6	1.7
	1.1	1.3	1.2	.9	.9		1.0	1.0
	.5	.6	.7	.5	.6		.6	.6
% Depr., Dep., Amort./Sales	12.6	4.4	5.5	6.2			5.9	4.7
	(25) 36.4	(39) 13.9	(103) 11.2	(74) 13.1			(197) 15.2	(205) 13.8
	67.7	32.4	19.4	22.2			26.3	28.6
% Officers', Directors', Owners' Comp/Sales		3.5	2.1	.5			2.6	2.3
		(14) 4.8	(37) 4.2	(12) 1.1			(59) 4.9	(63) 5.0
		8.8	8.7	2.5			12.6	11.0
Net Sales ($)	16443M	80485M	638423M	1787659M	935559M	1064716M	3309875M	2991172M
Total Assets ($)	8571M	53553M	542378M	1950125M	920817M	1072465M	3487775M	3270932M

© RMA 2005

M = $ thousand   MM = $ million
See Pages 11 through 21 for Explanation of Ratios and Data

Comparative Historical Data | | | **Current Data Sorted By Sales**

4/1/02-3/31/03 ALL	4/1/03-3/31/04 ALL	4/1/04-3/31/05 ALL	Type of Statement	51 (4/1-9/30/04) 0-1MM	1-3MM	3-5MM	245 (10/1/04-3/31/05) 5-10MM	10-25MM	25MM & OVER
37	46	45	Unqualified	1	4	3	6	14	17
54	69	79	Reviewed	6	14	20	14	17	8
54	63	52	Compiled	12	14	5	12	7	2
24	35	40	Tax Returns	27	7	2	4		
69	79	80	Other	8	14	5	19	18	16
238	292	296	**NUMBER OF STATEMENTS**	54	53	35	55	56	43
%	%	%	**ASSETS**	%	%	%	%	%	%
6.5	7.7	6.9	Cash & Equivalents	10.6	5.8	7.6	7.8	5.0	4.5
16.4	15.7	16.2	Trade Receivables (net)	3.8	14.5	20.1	21.4	20.7	18.0
9.1	9.6	10.0	Inventory	3.0	3.9	8.0	12.4	10.2	24.2
2.9	3.3	2.1	All Other Current	2.2	1.4	1.7	2.2	1.6	3.4
35.0	36.3	35.1	Total Current	19.5	25.7	37.3	43.9	37.5	50.1
57.4	55.1	56.1	Fixed Assets (net)	68.2	62.5	51.5	48.6	57.1	44.8
1.9	1.3	1.3	Intangibles (net)	.4	2.7	2.6	1.0	.6	1.0
5.8	7.3	7.5	All Other Non-Current	11.9	9.1	8.6	6.6	4.7	4.1
100.0	100.0	100.0	Total	100.0	100.0	100.0	100.0	100.0	100.0
			LIABILITIES						
10.9	12.1	10.1	Notes Payable-Short Term	13.9	7.9	5.4	11.4	9.2	11.3
11.6	10.9	8.9	Cur. Mat.-L/T/D	8.9	12.6	8.5	6.9	8.8	7.4
5.9	5.7	6.9	Trade Payables	1.9	4.8	9.2	8.5	8.7	9.4
.3	.2	.3	Income Taxes Payable	.0	.3	.8	.4	.1	.6
5.5	7.7	6.4	All Other Current	4.8	7.5	8.0	6.5	6.1	6.0
34.2	36.5	32.6	Total Current	29.4	33.0	31.9	33.7	33.0	34.6
30.6	31.3	33.3	Long-Term Debt	44.3	40.9	26.0	27.6	29.8	27.5
1.2	.9	1.2	Deferred Taxes	.0	.5	1.9	1.7	2.3	.9
3.9	5.0	4.1	All Other Non-Current	4.3	5.4	2.0	7.1	2.8	2.0
30.2	26.2	28.8	Net Worth	21.9	20.2	38.2	29.9	32.0	35.0
100.0	100.0	100.0	Total Liabilities & Net Worth	100.0	100.0	100.0	100.0	100.0	100.0
			INCOME DATA						
100.0	100.0	100.0	Net Sales	100.0	100.0	100.0	100.0	100.0	100.0
			Gross Profit						
89.9	89.7	88.7	Operating Expenses	84.1	84.0	91.0	90.4	92.6	91.4
10.1	10.3	11.3	Operating Profit	15.9	16.0	9.0	9.6	7.4	8.6
4.3	3.3	2.5	All Other Expenses (net)	3.7	4.9	1.4	1.4	1.9	1.4
5.8	7.0	8.7	Profit Before Taxes	12.1	11.1	7.6	8.2	5.5	7.2
			RATIOS						
1.8	1.8	1.8		1.8	1.6	2.0	2.0	1.5	2.0
1.1	1.1	1.1	Current	.5	.8	1.2	1.2	1.2	1.4
.5	.5	.6		.1	.3	.8	.8	.8	1.0
1.3	1.2	1.4		1.5	1.3	2.0	1.7	1.3	1.3
.7	.7	.8	Quick	.4	.7	1.0	.8	.8	.7
.3	.3	.3		.1	.2	.4	.4	.5	.4
25 14.7	12 30.7	20 18.0		0 UND	9 40.3	27 13.6	33 11.0	43 8.5	35 10.5
48 7.6	45 8.1	49 7.4	Sales/Receivables	0 UND	48 7.7	47 7.8	63 5.8	62 5.9	55 6.6
72 5.1	68 5.3	73 5.0		29 12.5	119 3.1	66 5.5	79 4.6	78 4.7	74 4.9
			Cost of Sales/Inventory						
			Cost of Sales/Payables						
6.7	6.6	6.2		6.4	6.9	6.4	5.3	7.6	5.5
51.1	75.9	30.5	Sales/Working Capital	-14.7	-19.0	27.9	27.9	21.0	11.5
-6.6	-4.6	-8.0		-1.9	-2.8	-16.4	-18.2	-18.6	105.8
3.5	5.3	6.4		8.8	5.2	6.1	4.8	6.0	9.1
(216) 2.0	(256) 2.0	(257) 2.7	EBIT/Interest	(38) 2.4	(45) 2.4	(32) 2.3	(48) 2.6	(55) 2.6	(39) 3.7
.6	.6	1.2		-.6	1.0	1.2	1.1	1.4	2.2
2.0	2.3	2.4				1.2	3.1	2.4	25.6
(67) 1.4	(63) 1.5	(69) 1.5	Net Profit + Depr., Dep., Amort./Cur. Mat. L/T/D		(12) .9	(17) 1.6	(20) 1.3	(12) 2.3	
.8	1.1	.9				.7	1.1	.9	1.6
1.0	.9	.9		.9	1.3	.8	.7	1.0	.5
2.0	2.0	2.1	Fixed/Worth	3.7	2.6	1.6	2.0	2.1	1.1
5.5	4.7	5.3		-14.4	10.1	3.9	5.9	4.1	2.0
1.2	1.2	1.3		.6	1.6	.7	1.3	1.4	1.3
2.6	2.4	2.6	Debt/Worth	3.2	2.9	1.9	2.5	2.5	2.4
7.4	6.8	6.5		-17.2	12.3	5.7	8.7	4.1	3.9
32.4	30.4	37.4		53.0	55.0	28.5	43.6	29.4	30.3
(216) 11.8	(252) 14.0	(259) 19.6	% Profit Before Taxes/Tangible Net Worth	(39) 18.8	(43) 19.7	(30) 14.0	(50) 22.0	(54) 18.2	20.3
-1.5	.5	5.5		1.1	2.2	4.3	5.4	5.4	9.4
7.5	9.1	11.6		18.8	12.6	11.9	12.2	8.0	8.3
3.1	3.3	4.5	% Profit Before Taxes/Total Assets	2.9	4.2	5.0	4.4	5.1	5.7
-1.5	-1.1	.8		-2.1	.2	.5	.9	1.5	2.4
4.0	4.7	5.2		2.9	3.6	5.8	5.8	4.7	7.7
1.7	1.8	2.0	Sales/Net Fixed Assets	1.0	1.3	3.0	2.4	1.8	3.4
.8	.8	.8		.4	.6	.9	1.3	1.0	1.1
1.5	1.6	1.6		1.3	1.5	2.2	1.6	1.5	1.8
1.0	1.0	1.0	Sales/Total Assets	.6	.7	1.3	1.2	1.0	1.3
.6	.6	.6		.3	.3	.7	.8	.7	.6
7.2	6.3	5.9		12.5	6.9	6.3	5.5	5.8	2.8
(215) 13.8	(254) 14.1	(254) 12.9	% Depr., Dep., Amort./Sales	(43) 34.5	(49) 19.4	(30) 10.9	(48) 10.6	(53) 11.6	(31) 6.3
28.7	24.2	24.1		71.9	42.9	16.8	18.3	17.7	13.5
2.4	2.3	1.9			4.3	2.2	2.0	.8	
(69) 4.4	(78) 4.6	(74) 3.7	% Officers', Directors', Owners' Comp/Sales		(14) 6.4	(12) 3.6	(22) 3.4	(10) 1.7	
10.1	9.4	8.6			11.6	4.7	8.4	3.4	
3640683M	4330117M	4523285M	Net Sales ($)	20390M	94433M	133781M	385214M	924460M	2965007M
4216745M	4746214M	4547909M	Total Assets ($)	43145M	205114M	125558M	485308M	1008231M	2680553M

M = $ thousand   MM = $ million
See Pages 11 through 21 for Explanation of Ratios and Data

| Current Data Sorted By Assets | | | | | | | Comparative Historical Data | |

	0-500M	500M-2MM	2-10MM	10-50MM	50-100MM	100-250MM	4/1/00-3/31/01 ALL	4/1/01-3/31/02 ALL
Type of Statement								
Unqualified			6	11	4	3	17	11
Reviewed			4	7			9	6
Compiled	2	8	4	1			2	3
Tax Returns	6	8	2				4	2
Other	2	8	8	5			15	10
	12 (4/1-9/30/04)		77 (10/1/04-3/31/05)					
NUMBER OF STATEMENTS	10	24	24	24	4	3	47	32
	%	%	%	%	%	%	%	%
ASSETS								
Cash & Equivalents	9.7	8.1	9.4	5.3			10.2	5.7
Trade Receivables (net)	9.5	15.8	16.3	16.2			16.3	17.3
Inventory	10.1	12.9	5.9	8.9			8.3	4.9
All Other Current	4.0	4.1	5.5	8.9			5.7	9.4
Total Current	33.2	40.9	37.0	39.3			40.5	37.3
Fixed Assets (net)	48.5	53.9	48.9	27.6			39.7	40.7
Intangibles (net)	.0	1.5	1.4	2.3			2.9	.9
All Other Non-Current	18.2	3.8	12.6	30.8			16.9	21.1
Total	100.0	100.0	100.0	100.0			100.0	100.0
LIABILITIES								
Notes Payable-Short Term	31.4	12.5	7.7	11.8			10.4	26.9
Cur. Mat.-L/T/D	13.7	8.4	20.7	12.9			19.4	8.3
Trade Payables	7.7	5.7	8.1	5.5			7.9	7.9
Income Taxes Payable	.2	.1	.0	.1			.6	.1
All Other Current	1.4	6.9	6.6	8.1			6.2	7.0
Total Current	54.3	33.5	43.2	38.5			44.6	50.1
Long-Term Debt	29.8	24.6	33.7	23.6			19.9	26.2
Deferred Taxes	.0	.0	.0	.6			.2	.2
All Other Non-Current	4.3	8.1	7.6	13.6			5.4	13.6
Net Worth	11.7	33.8	15.5	23.7			29.9	9.9
Total Liabilities & Net Worth	100.0	100.0	100.0	100.0			100.0	100.0
INCOME DATA								
Net Sales	100.0	100.0	100.0	100.0			100.0	100.0
Gross Profit								
Operating Expenses	79.6	83.1	92.5	79.8			88.5	89.0
Operating Profit	20.4	16.9	7.5	20.2			11.5	11.0
All Other Expenses (net)	1.8	2.0	3.5	9.3			4.8	8.9
Profit Before Taxes	18.6	14.8	4.1	10.8			6.8	2.1
RATIOS								
Current	1.7	3.1	1.4	1.4			1.8	1.1
	.9	1.2	1.0	1.1			1.0	.7
	.2	.4	.3	.3			.3	.3
Quick	1.2	1.2	1.2	.9			1.4	.9
	.5	.7	.6	.4			.6	.3
	.1	.2	.1	.1			.2	.1
Sales/Receivables	0 UND	0 UND	8 44.2	13 27.7			5 73.6	11 34.4
	13 28.9	20 18.7	38 9.5	35 10.4			34 10.6	32 11.5
	31 11.7	31 11.8	60 6.1	80 4.5			53 6.9	46 7.9
Cost of Sales/Inventory								
Cost of Sales/Payables								
Sales/Working Capital	7.0	6.4	10.2	5.1			9.9	16.2
	NM	52.0	NM	22.8			275.6	-11.8
	-2.3	-4.6	-2.7	-3.1			-2.5	-1.8
EBIT/Interest		13.5	3.6	3.9			4.3	2.0
		(23) 3.0	(20) 1.4	(18) 2.1			(40) 1.8	(25) 1.2
		1.2	.6	1.2			1.4	-1.3
Net Profit + Depr., Dep., Amort./Cur. Mat. L./T/D								
Fixed/Worth	.3	.7	1.3	.0			.2	.3
	2.4	1.8	3.0	.4			1.4	1.8
	NM	3.2	5.8	2.8			3.7	7.1
Debt/Worth	1.0	1.1	2.9	2.4			1.6	2.1
	13.3	2.5	5.1	5.1			3.2	5.8
	NM	5.9	11.4	11.7			7.4	20.5
% Profit Before Taxes/Tangible Net Worth		75.9	44.9	50.5			52.9	30.7
		(23) 26.9	(20) 12.7	(23) 10.2			(42) 18.6	(27) 4.7
		1.6	3.5	4.6			7.3	-12.2
% Profit Before Taxes/Total Assets	34.3	22.5	8.8	5.2			13.3	4.1
	12.0	6.9	1.9	3.2			4.0	.9
	-1.5	.9	-.3	.5			2.1	-6.4
Sales/Net Fixed Assets	15.7	22.8	7.4	96.7			27.3	31.2
	4.8	4.0	2.7	20.7			6.5	4.6
	1.0	.6	1.1	1.2			1.2	1.1
Sales/Total Assets	3.4	3.3	2.1	1.3			2.8	2.6
	1.7	1.9	.9	.4			.9	.8
	.5	.4	.5	.2			.6	.4
% Depr., Dep., Amort./Sales		3.1	1.2	.7			3.0	3.2
		(16) 19.5	(21) 13.9	(19) 5.7			(29) 14.0	(18) 16.5
		44.9	38.2	42.3			27.4	49.0
% Officers', Directors', Owners' Comp/Sales								
Net Sales ($)	7076M	50932M	124156M	358079M	66221M	421968M	1058081M	2171665M
Total Assets ($)	3832M	25554M	93227M	428691M	262429M	467841M	1009956M	896221M

M = $ thousand   MM = $ million
See Pages 11 through 21 for Explanation of Ratios and Data

Comparative Historical Data | **Current Data Sorted By Sales**

			Type of Statement						
12	14	24	Unqualified		1	3	8	7	5
9	9	11	Reviewed	2	3	2	2	1	1
4	15	15	Compiled	4	3	5	3		
5	11	16	Tax Returns	6	7	2	1		
18	20	23	Other	10	6	3	1	1	1
4/1/02-3/31/03 ALL	4/1/03-3/31/04 ALL	4/1/04-3/31/05 ALL		12 (4/1-9/30/04) 0-1MM	1-3MM	3-5MM	77 (10/1/04-3/31/05) 5-10MM	10-25MM	25MM & OVER
48	69	89	**NUMBER OF STATEMENTS**	22	20	15	16	9	7
%	%	%	**ASSETS**	%	%	%	%	%	%
9.4	6.6	7.4	Cash & Equivalents	7.2	12.0	4.4	6.1		
21.8	18.2	16.1	Trade Receivables (net)	3.8	17.0	21.7	16.2		
5.1	5.7	8.7	Inventory	.4	11.1	5.1	15.8		
3.1	8.3	7.1	All Other Current	6.7	8.3	4.8	7.2		
39.4	38.8	39.4	Total Current	18.2	48.4	35.9	45.3		
43.3	43.6	41.4	Fixed Assets (net)	68.5	36.5	29.4	42.6		
1.5	1.9	1.5	Intangibles (net)	1.4	3.2	.2	1.4		
15.8	15.7	17.7	All Other Non-Current	11.8	11.9	34.4	10.7		
100.0	100.0	100.0	Total	100.0	100.0	100.0	100.0		
			LIABILITIES						
13.6	13.4	12.6	Notes Payable-Short Term	19.8	8.7	7.4	15.7		
15.1	13.2	13.9	Cur. Mat.-L/T/D	14.1	14.7	18.2	12.9		
7.9	5.8	6.4	Trade Payables	3.0	4.1	6.9	5.7		
.2	.1	.1	Income Taxes Payable	.1	.2	.1	.0		
6.8	5.7	6.4	All Other Current	1.5	6.4	7.2	6.9		
43.7	38.2	39.5	Total Current	38.5	34.1	39.8	41.2		
27.4	26.1	28.3	Long-Term Debt	34.6	36.9	22.6	24.2		
.4	.3	.3	Deferred Taxes	.0	.0	.0	.4		
7.0	7.7	9.3	All Other Non-Current	3.1	11.9	17.0	6.1		
21.5	27.8	22.7	Net Worth	23.8	17.2	20.7	28.1		
100.0	100.0	100.0	Total Liabilities & Net Worth	100.0	100.0	100.0	100.0		
			INCOME DATA						
100.0	100.0	100.0	Net Sales	100.0	100.0	100.0	100.0		
			Gross Profit						
87.0	82.1	83.9	Operating Expenses	73.6	89.0	78.0	89.5		
13.0	17.9	16.1	Operating Profit	26.4	11.0	22.0	10.5		
10.0	8.8	5.5	All Other Expenses (net)	5.6	4.6	8.1	6.4		
3.1	9.1	10.6	Profit Before Taxes	20.8	6.5	13.9	4.1		
			RATIOS						
1.7	1.6	1.6		1.3	3.1	1.2	2.0		
.7	1.0	1.1	Current	.7	1.4	.9	1.1		
.3	.4	.3		.2	1.1	.1	.3		
1.2	1.1	1.1		.9	3.0	.9	1.2		
.6	.5	.6	Quick	.3	1.0	.6	.5		
.3	.1	.2		.1	.2	.1	.1		
5 74.8	0 UND	1 559.5		0 UND	6 58.9	14 25.2	0 762.5		
29 12.6	22 16.6	27 13.6	Sales/Receivables	0 UND	35 10.3	27 13.6	21 17.6		
67 5.5	56 6.6	50 7.3		26 14.1	58 6.3	135 2.7	49 7.4		
			Cost of Sales/Inventory						
			Cost of Sales/Payables						
6.3	10.3	6.3		6.8	2.1	20.3	5.6		
-15.1	-56.9	70.5	Sales/Working Capital	-4.9	10.3	-4.1	30.7		
-3.1	-3.4	-3.6		-2.2	65.4	-2.1	-6.0		
2.8	4.9	6.6		7.7	5.3	8.0	9.1		
(40) 1.3	(50) 2.3	(72) 2.3	EBIT/Interest	(18) 2.9	(16) 1.5	(11) 3.1	(14) 2.7		
-1.4	1.0	1.1		-1.9	-.7	1.0	1.3		
	3.0	1.9	Net Profit + Depr., Dep.,						
	(10) 1.8	(10) .8	Amort./Cur. Mat. L/T/D						
	.5	.3							
.4	.4	.2		1.9	.1	.1	.4		
1.8	1.4	1.6	Fixed/Worth	2.6	1.1	1.4	1.1		
5.3	3.3	3.4		7.4	19.4	3.0	3.5		
1.9	1.3	1.7		1.3	2.8	2.6	1.0		
3.2	3.8	3.8	Debt/Worth	2.5	8.1	5.6	3.1		
10.9	10.9	11.9		14.3	79.4	10.3	11.0		
39.4	43.6	59.0	% Profit Before Taxes/Tangible	53.8	102.9	77.6	49.4		
(42) 10.3	(62) 14.0	(81) 19.0	Net Worth	(20) 19.9	(16) 20.4	(14) 23.7	(15) 19.0		
-7.2	2.2	4.3		3.5	-2.6	1.7	6.2		
4.4	8.9	9.9	% Profit Before Taxes/Total	18.2	7.3	9.5	11.0		
1.4	2.5	4.2	Assets	5.6	2.4	4.9	4.6		
-6.0	.1	.4		-1.7	-1.8	.5	.8		
15.9	13.0	35.3		2.0	94.2	52.2	21.4		
3.8	3.5	4.4	Sales/Net Fixed Assets	.8	5.7	6.2	4.6		
.8	.9	1.1		.3	1.5	1.6	1.7		
2.2	1.7	2.2		1.0	2.6	1.6	2.7		
.9	.8	.8	Sales/Total Assets	.4	.9	.6	1.4		
.5	.2	.3		.3	.3	.2	.4		
4.3	6.0	1.0		14.1	.5	2.4	.7		
(36) 16.8	(49) 14.8	(64) 11.6	% Depr., Dep., Amort./Sales	(15) 39.3	(15) 11.0	(11) 5.7	(13) 11.7		
60.0	49.7	37.5		66.0	31.4	17.3	50.7		
3.0	2.2	2.2	% Officers', Directors',						
(15) 7.8	(17) 10.2	(24) 5.8	Owners' Comp/Sales						
16.1	23.4	16.2							
832804M	2458878M	1028432M	Net Sales ($)	9802M	38112M	59260M	115169M	148495M	657594M
865207M	1150273M	1281574M	Total Assets ($)	23985M	80837M	183514M	236089M	403728M	353421M

M = $ thousand   MM = $ million
See Pages 11 through 21 for Explanation of Ratios and Data

Current Data Sorted By Assets							Comparative Historical Data	
2	3	18	48	14	10	**Type of Statement**	75	64
5	16	46	24	1	3	Unqualified	100	87
38	69	38	9		1	Reviewed	173	159
39	31	13	1			Compiled	99	91
18	51	44	35	1	2	Tax Returns	185	198
						Other		
109 (4/1-9/30/04)			471 (10/1/04-3/31/05)				4/1/00-3/31/01	4/1/01-3/31/02
0-500M	500M-2MM	2-10MM	10-50MM	50-100MM	100-250MM		ALL	ALL
102	170	159	117	16	16	**NUMBER OF STATEMENTS**	632	599
%	%	%	%	%	%	**ASSETS**	%	%
11.1	7.5	8.5	4.7	2.4	6.0	Cash & Equivalents	7.2	7.7
7.7	13.9	14.7	19.8	11.8	7.3	Trade Receivables (net)	13.8	12.4
5.6	7.2	10.0	6.5	4.4	.9	Inventory	9.4	7.9
5.6	3.8	4.5	8.6	2.9	13.5	All Other Current	3.5	4.4
29.9	32.4	37.6	39.6	21.5	27.7	Total Current	33.9	32.3
60.0	56.9	50.0	40.5	53.7	52.7	Fixed Assets (net)	52.8	53.5
3.3	2.9	2.0	3.0	2.1	2.1	Intangibles (net)	2.8	3.1
6.8	7.7	10.4	16.8	22.8	17.4	All Other Non-Current	10.4	11.1
100.0	100.0	100.0	100.0	100.0	100.0	Total	100.0	100.0
						LIABILITIES		
7.0	13.4	9.6	12.8	9.1	16.4	Notes Payable-Short Term	14.0	12.8
17.9	10.8	9.0	8.6	3.9	13.1	Cur. Mat.-L/T/D	10.5	10.4
3.5	5.7	7.4	5.9	4.9	5.5	Trade Payables	5.9	5.2
.0	.1	.4	.6	.2	.5	Income Taxes Payable	.2	.3
17.5	7.6	7.8	5.5	4.2	3.9	All Other Current	7.6	7.9
46.0	37.8	34.3	33.4	22.3	39.3	Total Current	38.2	36.6
43.7	31.8	27.5	30.3	41.4	33.8	Long-Term Debt	29.3	31.4
.1	.5	.9	2.1	1.5	.9	Deferred Taxes	.5	.5
4.8	4.1	4.3	8.5	6.7	5.5	All Other Non-Current	5.7	5.8
5.3	25.8	32.9	25.8	28.1	20.5	Net Worth	26.3	25.6
100.0	100.0	100.0	100.0	100.0	100.0	Total Liabilities & Net Worth	100.0	100.0
						INCOME DATA		
100.0	100.0	100.0	100.0	100.0	100.0	Net Sales	100.0	100.0
						Gross Profit		
83.7	88.2	84.4	81.3	82.0	73.4	Operating Expenses	83.4	83.3
16.3	11.8	15.6	18.7	18.0	26.6	Operating Profit	16.6	16.7
4.1	3.0	4.5	7.2	10.0	15.1	All Other Expenses (net)	6.6	8.4
12.2	8.9	11.1	11.5	8.0	11.5	Profit Before Taxes	10.1	8.2
						RATIOS		
1.9	1.9	1.8	1.6	2.0	1.4		1.9	1.6
.6	.9	1.1	1.1	1.2	.8	Current	.9	.9
.2	.3	.5	.7	.4	.4		.4	.3
1.4	1.2	1.2	1.1	1.1	1.2		1.3	1.1
(101) .3	.6	.6	(116) .7	.5	.3	Quick	(629) .5	(598) .5
.1	.3	.3	.3	.2	.1		.2	.2
0 UND	0 UND	2 203.3	15 25.0	21 17.2	1 314.2		0 UND	0 UND
0 UND	18 19.9	29 12.4	47 7.8	33 11.0	35 10.5	Sales/Receivables	23 15.8	18 19.8
26 13.9	45 8.0	50 7.2	90 4.1	70 5.2	67 5.5		54 6.8	50 7.4
						Cost of Sales/Inventory		
						Cost of Sales/Payables		
9.8	10.1	6.9	3.6	5.8	5.3		7.1	8.0
−29.4	−38.6	84.8	17.6	65.3	−20.2	Sales/Working Capital	−90.2	−54.0
−3.5	−4.4	−5.8	−9.3	−4.8	−2.8		−4.8	−4.4
6.1	6.5	8.3	5.0	6.5	2.9		5.6	5.4
(74) 2.9	(149) 2.5	(130) 3.1	(98) 3.1	(12) 2.1	(11) 1.7	EBIT/Interest	(499) 2.6	(470) 2.1
.9	.9	1.5	1.6	1.1	1.4		1.1	.9
	5.3	3.2	4.6			Net Profit + Depr., Dep.,	3.6	3.9
(21) 2.5	(36) 1.7	(27) 1.7			Amort./Cur. Mat. L /T/D	(119) 1.8	(93) 1.9
	1.5	1.0	.9				1.1	.9
.9	1.0	.6	.1	.3	.4		.6	.7
2.7	2.7	1.6	1.4	1.6	4.1	Fixed/Worth	1.8	1.9
−4.8	22.6	5.2	4.0	5.2	6.6		7.0	10.2
1.0	.9	1.0	1.0	1.5	4.1		1.0	1.1
3.8	3.2	2.9	3.8	4.4	6.3	Debt/Worth	2.7	3.3
−4.8	28.3	9.3	10.8	6.3	9.0		12.1	18.2
88.8	43.3	37.7	40.3	38.3	41.5	% Profit Before Taxes/Tangible	42.7	41.4
(67) 23.7	(133) 17.6	(137) 20.1	(107) 23.6	13.6	20.1	Net Worth	(544) 20.4	(502) 16.6
.0	4.1	7.8	8.7	5.4	9.8		4.3	1.5
25.3	12.4	11.5	9.1	7.7	8.2	% Profit Before Taxes/Total	14.4	10.3
7.5	4.5	6.2	3.8	2.4	2.8	Assets	5.0	3.6
.0	.2	1.7	1.3	.7	1.2		.6	.0
7.7	6.0	11.6	20.2	5.9	4.0		8.2	7.4
2.5	2.5	2.4	2.4	2.1	1.2	Sales/Net Fixed Assets	2.4	2.3
.9	.9	.6	.8	.4	.5		.9	.8
2.7	2.2	2.0	1.1	1.2	.9		2.0	1.9
1.4	1.2	1.1	.6	.5	.4	Sales/Total Assets	1.1	1.0
.7	.5	.3	.3	.2	.2		.4	.4
6.4	7.9	4.7	1.8	5.2		% Depr., Dep., Amort./Sales	4.3	5.0
(79) 19.8	(142) 14.8	(134) 13.7	(97) 7.9	(10) 17.1			(549) 11.3	(511) 13.0
50.0	35.8	39.5	19.8	42.1			29.7	33.9
8.3	3.5	1.5	2.3			% Officers', Directors',	3.6	3.6
(31) 12.9	(55) 5.9	(38) 3.8	(21) 3.0			Owners' Comp/Sales	(203) 6.5	(170) 6.7
19.7	10.0	6.6	6.3				12.0	12.0
52889M	294642M	896007M	2343780M	877618M	2120188M	Net Sales ($)	6222206M	5228546M
25530M	188078M	703459M	2706653M	1191044M	2785893M	Total Assets ($)	6985457M	6484760M

M = $ thousand   MM = $ million
See Pages 11 through 21 for Explanation of Ratios and Data

Comparative Historical Data | | | | **Current Data Sorted By Sales**

Type of Statement	4/1/02-3/31/03 ALL	4/1/03-3/31/04 ALL	4/1/04-3/31/05 ALL	0-1MM	1-3MM	3-5MM	5-10MM	10-25MM	25MM & OVER
Unqualified	76	74	95	7	11	6	14	29	28
Reviewed	95	104	95	12	26	11	18	19	9
Compiled	121	165	155	63	46	19	18	6	3
Tax Returns	89	85	84	54	20	3	6	1	3
Other	170	176	151	52	32	19	20	19	9
				109 (4/1-9/30/04)			471 (10/1/04-3/31/05)		
NUMBER OF STATEMENTS	551	604	580	188	135	58	76	74	49
ASSETS	%	%	%	%	%	%	%	%	%
Cash & Equivalents	7.8	7.8	7.6	9.4	6.2	7.4	9.6	5.3	5.8
Trade Receivables (net)	13.2	13.4	14.0	7.3	13.6	22.0	17.2	19.3	18.1
Inventory	8.0	8.5	7.3	4.0	6.7	8.9	9.3	13.3	7.5
All Other Current	4.8	5.5	5.5	5.3	4.4	4.6	6.9	6.6	7.0
Total Current	33.8	35.3	34.4	25.9	30.9	42.9	43.0	44.5	38.4
Fixed Assets (net)	54.9	52.4	52.1	63.0	53.4	43.8	43.9	38.5	49.7
Intangibles (net)	2.6	2.7	2.7	3.0	2.4	3.8	1.2	3.1	2.6
All Other Non-Current	8.7	9.6	10.8	8.1	13.3	9.6	11.9	14.0	9.3
Total	100.0	100.0	100.0	100.0	100.0	100.0	100.0	100.0	100.0
LIABILITIES									
Notes Payable-Short Term	12.3	11.1	11.1	10.6	10.0	10.9	12.9	11.6	12.7
Cur. Mat.-L/T/D	10.7	9.2	11.0	14.3	12.1	7.2	8.8	8.0	7.9
Trade Payables	5.3	5.7	5.8	1.9	5.2	7.4	8.6	10.2	9.3
Income Taxes Payable	.4	.3	.3	.0	.3	.5	.4	.3	.9
All Other Current	8.1	7.7	8.8	12.4	5.4	6.4	8.8	8.2	8.1
Total Current	36.8	33.9	37.0	39.3	33.0	32.4	39.5	38.3	38.9
Long-Term Debt	32.8	31.6	32.7	41.1	35.1	24.4	24.6	26.0	26.7
Deferred Taxes	.6	.7	.9	.3	.9	1.1	1.2	1.6	1.2
All Other Non-Current	6.4	7.2	5.3	3.3	6.9	5.2	4.9	8.5	4.2
Net Worth	23.3	26.6	24.1	16.0	24.1	36.9	29.7	25.6	29.0
Total Liabilities & Net Worth	100.0	100.0	100.0	100.0	100.0	100.0	100.0	100.0	100.0
INCOME DATA									
Net Sales	100.0	100.0	100.0	100.0	100.0	100.0	100.0	100.0	100.0
Gross Profit									
Operating Expenses	85.0	85.1	84.4	77.4	86.9	88.5	85.6	89.2	90.3
Operating Profit	15.0	14.9	15.6	22.6	13.1	11.5	14.4	10.8	9.7
All Other Expenses (net)	7.2	5.5	4.9	6.5	4.0	3.8	4.8	4.9	3.2
Profit Before Taxes	7.8	9.3	10.7	16.0	9.1	7.7	9.6	5.9	6.4
RATIOS									
Current	1.7	2.2	1.8	1.7	1.7	2.8	1.7	1.9	1.7
	.9	1.1	1.0	.7	.9	1.3	1.1	1.1	1.1
	.4	.5	.4	.2	.4	.9	.6	.8	.7
Quick	1.1	1.3	1.2	1.2	1.2	1.6	1.1	1.1	1.2
	(550) .5	(603) .6	(578) .5	(187) .4	.5	.9	.6	(73) .6	.7
	.2	.2	.2	.1	.2	.4	.3	.4	.3
Sales/Receivables	0 UND	0 UND	0 UND	0 UND	0 743.5	21 17.7	11 33.6	23 15.8	17 21.8
	21 17.2	23 16.0	26 14.2	0 UND	20 17.9	41 8.8	36 10.3	42 8.6	39 9.3
	51 7.1	51 7.1	52 7.1	33 10.9	48 7.6	57 6.4	64 5.7	61 6.0	63 5.8
Cost of Sales/Inventory									
Cost of Sales/Payables									
Sales/Working Capital	7.6	6.0	7.0	7.6	8.9	3.7	6.0	5.9	10.9
	-124.2	78.8	664.4	-9.1	-47.4	14.9	39.6	37.7	54.0
	-4.2	-5.2	-4.8	-1.9	-7.0	-37.9	-9.2	-17.3	-8.9
EBIT/Interest	5.3	7.0	6.3	6.2	4.7	7.1	9.2	6.2	5.6
	(442) 2.2	(508) 2.6	(474) 2.8	(138) 2.8	(114) 2.4	(48) 2.4	(64) 3.8	(66) 2.4	(44) 3.0
	.9	1.0	1.2	1.0	.9	1.1	2.1	1.4	1.5
Net Profit + Depr., Dep., Amort./Cur. Mat. L/T/D	2.8	4.1	4.1	3.4	6.8	3.0	3.7	16.3	4.6
	(93) 1.9	(101) 1.9	(94) 1.9	(12) 2.0	(19) 1.9	(14) 1.9	(16) 2.1	(18) 1.7	(15) 2.1
	1.2	.9	1.3	1.4	.9	1.4	1.0	.8	1.5
Fixed/Worth	.8	.6	.8	1.1	.8	.3	.3	.5	.7
	2.0	1.7	2.0	3.0	2.2	1.3	1.4	1.7	1.6
	8.2	6.7	8.5	-97.5	17.1	3.2	6.1	4.1	5.9
Debt/Worth	1.2	1.0	1.2	1.2	.9	.8	1.1	2.0	1.5
	3.2	2.8	3.4	3.6	3.4	2.0	2.2	4.2	2.8
	11.9	10.5	15.9	-28.4	32.0	8.9	11.7	7.5	7.3
% Profit Before Taxes/Tangible Net Worth	34.7	42.1	43.2	55.4	41.2	33.8	45.2	41.5	43.5
	(463) 14.7	(502) 15.7	(476) 20.1	(138) 20.9	(107) 15.7	(53) 14.5	(67) 23.9	(66) 21.2	(45) 20.9
	2.1	3.2	6.1	3.8	3.2	2.6	14.8	6.0	8.1
% Profit Before Taxes/Total Assets	10.0	12.8	12.1	16.0	11.5	9.3	13.3	9.9	11.1
	3.6	4.4	5.0	5.7	4.6	3.2	7.4	3.9	5.6
	-.3	.1	.9	.4	.2	.5	2.8	1.1	2.1
Sales/Net Fixed Assets	7.2	7.8	8.2	3.2	9.0	18.9	20.3	22.1	7.4
	2.2	2.3	2.4	.9	2.8	4.3	3.2	4.4	2.4
	.7	.8	.8	.5	1.2	1.6	1.0	2.1	1.3
Sales/Total Assets	1.9	1.9	1.9	1.3	2.1	2.4	2.5	2.2	2.1
	.9	1.0	1.0	.6	1.1	1.5	1.1	1.3	1.3
	.4	.4	.4	.3	.4	.4	.4	.7	.7
% Depr., Dep., Amort./Sales	6.1	5.3	4.7	12.9	6.8	2.6	2.8	2.3	2.6
	(480) 14.6	(515) 14.5	(467) 13.6	(153) 37.4	(111) 14.3	(52) 9.5	(63) 9.1	(59) 7.1	(29) 4.2
	38.9	35.6	37.4	61.7	23.3	18.4	18.7	14.3	10.6
% Officers', Directors', Owners' Comp/Sales	2.6	2.8	3.0	7.3	4.1	2.0	2.3	2.2	
	(154) 6.2	(170) 5.4	(146) 5.8	(35) 11.7	(46) 7.2	(17) 3.2	(22) 4.6	(22) 3.1	
	10.8	9.8	10.5	19.7	16.8	6.2	6.7	5.6	
Net Sales ($)	5763993M	5534936M	6585124M	83739M	245858M	228942M	529872M	1142167M	4354546M
Total Assets ($)	6424267M	6827433M	7600657M	188531M	459027M	435827M	925146M	1843381M	3748745M

M = $ thousand   MM = $ million
See Pages 11 through 21 for Explanation of Ratios and Data

Current Data Sorted By Assets   Comparative Historical Data

	0-500M	500M-2MM	2-10MM	10-50MM	50-100MM	100-250MM	Type of Statement		4/1/00-3/31/01 ALL	4/1/01-3/31/02 ALL
		2	3	8	1	1	Unqualified		10	9
		1	1	1	1		Reviewed		1	1
		1	2				Compiled		1	6
	4	4					Tax Returns			1
	1	3	6	3	1	1	Other		6	29
	\- 6 (4/1-9/30/04) -			\- 38 (10/1/04-3/31/05) -						
	5	11	12	12	2	2	**NUMBER OF STATEMENTS**		18	46
	%	%	%	%	%	%	**ASSETS**		%	%
		6.4	13.9	8.7			Cash & Equivalents		24.6	10.7
		9.6	7.7	24.1			Trade Receivables (net)		17.2	7.0
		1.6	4.9	4.0			Inventory		8.1	4.0
		2.9	8.0	6.9			All Other Current		7.4	6.6
		20.4	34.5	43.7			Total Current		57.3	28.4
		59.9	44.7	26.4			Fixed Assets (net)		19.6	48.9
		9.1	5.0	11.5			Intangibles (net)		10.6	13.3
		10.7	15.9	18.5			All Other Non-Current		12.5	9.4
		100.0	100.0	100.0			Total		100.0	100.0
							LIABILITIES			
		5.2	7.8	3.2			Notes Payable-Short Term		12.1	1.2
		6.3	3.7	3.2			Cur. Mat.-L/T/D		5.2	12.6
		6.2	9.7	12.1			Trade Payables		15.8	10.9
		.0	.1	.6			Income Taxes Payable		.9	.6
		5.1	8.9	11.6			All Other Current		35.8	11.6
		22.7	30.3	30.7			Total Current		69.8	36.9
		60.4	31.9	24.3			Long-Term Debt		15.4	50.2
		.0	.0	3.3			Deferred Taxes		.1	.2
		15.8	3.9	5.1			All Other Non-Current		5.6	8.6
		1.1	33.8	36.6			Net Worth		9.2	4.1
		100.0	100.0	100.0			Total Liabilities & Net Worth		100.0	100.0
							INCOME DATA			
		100.0	100.0	100.0			Net Sales		100.0	100.0
							Gross Profit			
		76.0	76.4	81.9			Operating Expenses		89.3	89.4
		24.0	23.6	18.1			Operating Profit		10.7	10.6
		11.8	2.7	3.4			All Other Expenses (net)		−.3	4.1
		12.3	21.0	14.7			Profit Before Taxes		11.0	6.5
							RATIOS			
		1.2	2.6	1.9					1.9	1.2
		.6	1.1	1.3			Current		1.3	.6
		.2	.4	1.0					.8	.4
		1.0	1.7	1.5					1.6	.6
		.6	.6	1.2			Quick		1.0	.3
		.2	.3	.6					.6	.1
	0 UND	0 908.2	19 19.5						13 28.2	0 UND
	18 20.6	7 52.3	33 11.0				Sales/Receivables		24 15.5	1 280.6
	30 12.2	22 16.6	99 3.7						35 10.4	14 25.9
							Cost of Sales/Inventory			
							Cost of Sales/Payables			
		22.3	16.0	7.5					4.4	36.2
		−23.0	NM	13.9			Sales/Working Capital		12.3	−27.6
		−3.5	−6.7	410.1					−56.8	−14.9
			99.7	21.6					10.4	6.0
		(11)	5.6	6.7			EBIT/Interest	(15)	6.5	(44) 2.3
			4.7	5.2					2.3	1.3
							Net Profit + Depr., Dep., Amort./Cur. Mat. L /T/D			
		1.9	.4	.1					.2	1.4
		4.4	2.4	.7			Fixed/Worth		.5	26.8
		4.8	5.8	2.5					1.2	−3.9
		1.9	.7	1.6					.9	2.5
		3.9	3.1	3.1			Debt/Worth		1.7	39.8
		5.7	16.5	5.0					11.6	−5.7
			145.5	66.4					43.1	172.7
		(10)	66.3	(11) 59.6			% Profit Before Taxes/Tangible Net Worth	(15)	30.4	(27) 29.0
			47.6	32.8					19.1	10.5
		20.3	34.9	20.4					20.0	15.2
		4.4	11.4	14.7			% Profit Before Taxes/Total Assets		7.6	5.7
		−12.2	6.3	7.3					1.0	1.8
		12.7	17.0	72.4					32.2	12.0
		.7	9.3	5.0			Sales/Net Fixed Assets		18.8	6.5
		.2	1.0	2.2					6.1	2.2
		2.0	5.2	1.7					4.6	4.4
		.7	2.3	1.1			Sales/Total Assets		2.2	2.4
		.2	.6	.7					1.0	1.5
			1.8	.7					.5	2.1
			2.4	(10) 5.4			% Depr., Dep., Amort./Sales	(14)	1.3	(39) 3.1
			5.8	7.2					2.4	4.5
							% Officers', Directors', Owners' Comp/Sales			
	2486M	15219M	156957M	402453M	108725M	326691M	Net Sales ($)		500608M	2310662M
	1703M	14960M	57676M	245707M	129570M	355156M	Total Assets ($)		356609M	1242298M

M = $ thousand   MM = $ million

See Pages 11 through 21 for Explanation of Ratios and Data

Comparative Historical Data / Current Data Sorted By Sales

			Type of Statement	0-1MM	1-3MM	3-5MM	5-10MM	10-25MM	25MM & OVER
22	12	15	Unqualified		2	1	1	6	5
1	2	3	Reviewed	2				1	
1	1	3	Compiled	1		1			1
3	7	8	Tax Returns	8					
9	10	15	Other	1	3	3	1	4	3
4/1/02-3/31/03 ALL	4/1/03-3/31/04 ALL	4/1/04-3/31/05 ALL			6 (4/1-9/30/04)			38 (10/1/04-3/31/05)	
36	32	44	NUMBER OF STATEMENTS	12	5	5	2	11	9
%	%	%	**ASSETS**	%	%	%	%	%	%
22.1	14.8	11.3	Cash & Equivalents	6.9				12.7	
13.8	18.3	13.1	Trade Receivables (net)	.8				18.6	
4.9	3.5	2.9	Inventory	.1				5.0	
6.5	7.8	5.1	All Other Current	.5				4.4	
47.2	44.4	32.5	Total Current	8.3				40.7	
28.1	35.3	45.1	Fixed Assets (net)	78.3				40.9	
12.0	6.1	8.4	Intangibles (net)	9.8				1.9	
12.6	14.2	14.0	All Other Non-Current	3.7				16.5	
100.0	100.0	100.0	Total	100.0				100.0	
			LIABILITIES						
4.2	15.4	4.3	Notes Payable-Short Term	.3				6.6	
2.9	4.2	4.1	Cur. Mat.-L/T/D	5.4				2.6	
12.4	10.4	8.2	Trade Payables	1.0				12.2	
2.7	.1	.2	Income Taxes Payable	.0				.1	
11.4	20.3	9.8	All Other Current	2.4				12.0	
33.7	50.3	26.7	Total Current	9.1				33.4	
22.6	20.6	42.2	Long-Term Debt	76.9				23.6	
.8	.9	.9	Deferred Taxes	.0				1.7	
10.1	5.9	10.0	All Other Non-Current	16.8				5.9	
32.9	22.2	20.2	Net Worth	−2.8				35.4	
100.0	100.0	100.0	Total Liabilities & Net Worth	100.0				100.0	
			INCOME DATA						
100.0	100.0	100.0	Net Sales	100.0				100.0	
			Gross Profit						
85.7	73.5	78.9	Operating Expenses	69.7				80.9	
14.3	26.5	21.1	Operating Profit	30.3				19.1	
2.9	5.0	7.8	All Other Expenses (net)	16.8				1.8	
11.4	21.4	13.4	Profit Before Taxes	13.5				17.2	
			RATIOS						
3.0	1.7	1.9	Current	2.6				1.9	
1.6	1.1	1.1		.5				1.4	
.7	.6	.6		.1				.9	
2.7	1.5	1.4	Quick	1.7				1.5	
1.3	.8	.7		.5				1.1	
.5	.3	.3		.1				.5	
6 63.8	0 UND	0 999.8	Sales/Receivables	0 UND				11 32.9	
23 16.0	27 13.5	14 25.5		0 UND				34 10.8	
44 8.4	57 6.4	32 11.3		0 UND				68 5.4	
			Cost of Sales/Inventory						
			Cost of Sales/Payables						
4.1	9.8	11.7	Sales/Working Capital	11.8				11.5	
9.8	54.9	54.8		−17.2				22.2	
−15.2	−4.1	−12.6		−2.3				−26.4	
32.9	62.5	21.4	EBIT/Interest					99.7	
(28) 6.8	(27) 15.7	(36) 6.0						6.3	
2.8	4.9	3.1						5.3	
			Net Profit + Depr., Dep., Amort./Cur. Mat. L/T/D						
.2	.3	.4	Fixed/Worth	4.2				.5	
1.0	1.2	2.5		5.7				1.7	
NM	8.4	8.3		NM				2.5	
.6	.8	1.6	Debt/Worth	3.5				1.1	
2.3	3.0	3.8		6.7				2.2	
NM	13.0	8.7		NM				3.8	
61.7	113.5	80.3	% Profit Before Taxes/Tangible Net Worth					106.2	
(27) 24.6	(25) 47.8	(36) 47.4						68.5	
10.5	20.9	19.6						59.6	
20.6	29.8	19.2	% Profit Before Taxes/Total Assets	7.5				41.2	
6.7	12.7	9.1		4.9				16.1	
3.0	4.9	3.6		−1.9				10.1	
30.9	33.1	17.5	Sales/Net Fixed Assets	.8				13.7	
14.7	7.6	4.2		.2				7.3	
1.6	1.2	.5		.2				1.7	
2.9	2.3	2.8	Sales/Total Assets	.7				5.4	
1.1	1.0	1.1		.2				1.6	
.6	.5	.4		.2				1.0	
1.4	.7	1.2	% Depr., Dep., Amort./Sales	6.0				2.1	
(27) 2.9	(27) 2.4	(39) 5.1		(11) 22.7				5.1	
4.6	6.0	13.1		39.2				6.4	
			% Officers', Directors', Owners' Comp/Sales						
1158123M	484139M	1012531M	Net Sales ($)	4499M	10288M	21080M	13341M	194175M	769148M
771850M	626239M	804772M	Total Assets ($)	13641M	8839M	29516M	86182M	126027M	540567M

© RMA 2005

M = $ thousand   MM = $ million
See Pages 11 through 21 for Explanation of Ratios and Data

PROFESSIONAL, SCIENTIFIC, AND TECHNICAL SERVICES

Current Data Sorted By Assets							Comparative Historical Data	
						Type of Statement		
5	10	22	36	11	18	Unqualified	56	52
10	47	85	41	6	1	Reviewed	155	148
83	84	58	16		1	Compiled	325	305
281	103	41	12	4		Tax Returns	245	283
146	171	167	89	15	10	Other	448	535
	84 (4/1-9/30/04)		1489 (10/1/04-3/31/05)				4/1/00-3/31/01	4/1/01-3/31/02
0-500M	500M-2MM	2-10MM	10-50MM	50-100MM	100-250MM		ALL	ALL
525	415	373	194	36	30	**NUMBER OF STATEMENTS**	1229	1323
%	%	%	%	%	%	**ASSETS**	%	%
33.3	31.3	27.4	34.9	35.8	40.5	Cash & Equivalents	27.2	28.7
7.4	16.3	26.9	20.8	15.6	13.6	Trade Receivables (net)	18.0	17.1
.3	1.1	2.3	1.5	1.5	.0	Inventory	1.4	1.4
13.0	14.5	11.6	12.4	10.0	11.1	All Other Current	11.2	12.7
54.0	63.2	68.1	69.7	62.9	65.3	Total Current	57.7	59.9
27.6	18.3	19.4	20.2	29.1	27.2	Fixed Assets (net)	26.3	25.9
3.4	2.1	1.5	1.3	1.1	1.7	Intangibles (net)	2.8	2.7
15.0	16.4	10.9	8.9	7.0	5.8	All Other Non-Current	13.2	11.5
100.0	100.0	100.0	100.0	100.0	100.0	Total	100.0	100.0
						LIABILITIES		
45.4	24.4	13.4	8.9	4.7	7.6	Notes Payable-Short Term	24.8	30.6
11.3	4.1	2.5	2.6	4.5	2.3	Cur. Mat.-L/T/D	6.0	5.5
2.4	2.8	3.0	3.7	2.5	1.6	Trade Payables	3.0	2.9
.9	.4	.7	.6	.5	.1	Income Taxes Payable	.5	.5
37.1	29.8	26.6	19.0	12.4	15.5	All Other Current	27.0	31.6
97.0	61.4	46.3	34.9	24.6	26.9	Total Current	61.3	71.1
21.5	11.3	10.5	10.1	9.4	12.0	Long-Term Debt	16.2	14.5
.0	.3	1.3	.3	.9	.9	Deferred Taxes	.5	.4
5.6	4.5	4.7	5.5	6.0	2.0	All Other Non-Current	5.6	6.7
-24.1	22.5	37.2	49.3	59.0	58.1	Net Worth	16.6	7.2
100.0	100.0	100.0	100.0	100.0	100.0	Total Liabilities & Net Worth	100.0	100.0
						INCOME DATA		
100.0	100.0	100.0	100.0	100.0	100.0	Net Sales	100.0	100.0
						Gross Profit		
84.8	84.3	79.2	70.4	65.5	66.4	Operating Expenses	81.1	82.2
15.2	15.7	20.8	29.6	34.5	33.6	Operating Profit	18.9	17.8
.7	1.1	1.3	1.0	2.0	1.6	All Other Expenses (net)	.9	1.1
14.5	14.7	19.5	28.6	32.5	32.0	Profit Before Taxes	18.0	16.6
						RATIOS		
1.4	2.3	3.6	5.9	11.7	10.2		3.0	2.9
.7	1.1	1.5	2.6	4.4	5.5	Current	1.2	1.1
.3	.7	1.0	1.2	1.7	2.3		.6	.6
1.1	1.8	3.2	4.9	9.0	9.0		2.4	2.2
(521) .5	(414) .8	1.2	2.0	3.1	5.2	Quick	(1226) 1.0	(1319) .9
.1	.3	.7	.9	1.4	1.6		.3	.3
0 UND	0 UND	0 UND	0 UND	0 UND	0 UND		0 UND	0 UND
0 UND	0 UND	13 29.2	7 49.9	8 47.6	6 65.6	Sales/Receivables	0 UND	0 UND
0 UND	21 17.2	71 5.2	61 6.0	54 6.7	46 8.0		31 11.9	29 12.7
						Cost of Sales/Inventory		
						Cost of Sales/Payables		
65.7	11.5	5.5	4.2	5.3	4.3		8.7	8.9
-63.3	100.9	17.8	8.6	8.9	5.6	Sales/Working Capital	78.4	101.1
-15.2	-19.9	-124.2	45.3	13.9	9.0		-26.9	-27.2
59.0	80.0	170.4	220.8	198.9	83.0		62.7	58.1
(391) 8.7	(343) 11.3	(314) 34.5	(167) 97.3	(28) 100.5	(26) 60.8	EBIT/Interest	(1050) 12.3	(1095) 9.8
1.0	1.2	2.7	16.8	10.2	33.6		1.3	1.3
	8.0	9.4	11.4			Net Profit + Depr., Dep.,	5.7	3.3
	(25) 2.1	(45) 2.0	(23) 3.2			Amort./Cur. Mat. L /T/D	(81) 1.6	(85) 1.3
	.5	1.0	1.3				.5	.4
.3	.1	.1	.2	.3	.2		.2	.2
3.2	.8	.4	.4	.4	.3	Fixed/Worth	.8	.9
-.5	-9.0	2.0	.9	.7	.6		UND	404.0
1.3	.8	.6	.3	.1	.1		.6	.6
UND	3.5	1.6	.7	.6	.4	Debt/Worth	2.3	2.5
-2.7	-41.2	10.8	2.9	1.9	1.8		-48.1	-72.5
905.9	346.9	318.2	297.1	270.0	181.7	% Profit Before Taxes/Tangible	324.8	312.9
(273) 236.1	(301) 79.8	(312) 101.3	(179) 176.8	(35) 203.2	(28) 147.0	Net Worth	(905) 108.3	(979) 111.3
25.5	4.5	14.4	67.7	121.5	104.8		14.6	11.8
243.9	105.5	131.0	167.2	189.5	131.2	% Profit Before Taxes/Total	139.8	129.4
36.0	16.1	27.6	101.2	117.7	94.1	Assets	31.6	28.0
.0	.1	2.5	16.9	76.7	50.8		1.2	.8
241.3	112.7	57.5	30.8	23.6	18.0		59.8	62.3
70.3	45.3	28.4	21.4	14.5	11.9	Sales/Net Fixed Assets	26.7	28.0
28.4	22.6	15.4	13.7	10.2	8.3		14.6	14.7
19.9	8.2	5.4	4.6	5.0	3.8		8.4	9.3
9.6	4.3	3.1	3.1	2.9	2.7	Sales/Total Assets	4.6	4.7
5.3	2.5	2.0	2.0	2.5	1.9		2.6	2.6
.4	.6	.7	1.0	1.4	1.6		.7	.6
(262) .9	(262) .9	(294) 1.3	(172) 1.5	(29) 1.9	(19) 1.9	% Depr., Dep., Amort./Sales	(956) 1.3	(996) 1.1
1.6	1.6	1.8	2.0	2.4	2.3		2.0	1.8
14.8	11.1	8.5	19.5	14.4		% Officers', Directors',	15.4	13.5
(297) 24.8	(217) 23.2	(144) 23.3	(67) 22.5			Owners' Comp/Sales	(553) 28.2	(643) 27.0
35.4	36.7	35.1	33.0				36.5	36.9
1231094M	2611276M	7285496M	17397274M	9508806M	14379759M	Net Sales ($)	32970034M	40990770M
106216M	452762M	1713870M	4307360M	2536481M	4606602M	Total Assets ($)	8933538M	10528285M

© RMA 2005

M = $ thousand   MM = $ million

See Pages 11 through 21 for Explanation of Ratios and Data

Comparative Historical Data | Current Data Sorted By Sales

				Type of Statement						
82		100	102	Unqualified	3	4	2	5	16	72
181		182	190	Reviewed	2	5	16	33	66	68
275		365	242	Compiled	27	61	45	44	43	22
348		459	441	Tax Returns	119	155	59	61	25	22
604		639	598	Other	55	118	79	108	96	142
4/1/02-		4/1/03-	4/1/04-			84 (4/1-9/30/04)		1489 (10/1/04-3/31/05)		
3/31/03		3/31/04	3/31/05							
ALL		ALL	ALL		0-1MM	1-3MM	3-5MM	5-10MM	10-25MM	25MM & OVER
1490		1745	1573	**NUMBER OF STATEMENTS**	206	343	201	251	246	326
%		%	%	**ASSETS**	%	%	%	%	%	%
30.0		31.8	31.7	Cash & Equivalents	32.3	33.7	29.3	28.4	30.3	34.4
17.3		15.8	16.4	Trade Receivables (net)	6.3	12.9	17.9	19.2	23.7	17.7
1.5		1.2	1.2	Inventory	.2	.9	1.6	1.3	2.2	.9
12.4		13.0	12.9	All Other Current	11.1	14.9	14.6	13.4	11.7	11.2
61.2		61.9	62.1	Total Current	49.9	62.4	63.4	62.2	67.9	64.3
24.9		23.6	22.3	Fixed Assets (net)	29.1	18.8	19.4	20.2	21.3	25.9
1.8		2.0	2.2	Intangibles (net)	4.2	2.8	1.3	2.5	1.6	1.3
12.1		12.5	13.3	All Other Non-Current	16.7	15.9	15.9	15.1	9.1	8.5
100.0		100.0	100.0	Total	100.0	100.0	100.0	100.0	100.0	100.0
				LIABILITIES						
24.6		25.4	26.1	Notes Payable-Short Term	33.7	41.0	28.0	29.9	17.3	8.2
5.8		5.2	5.9	Cur. Mat.-L/T/D	11.8	8.4	5.3	3.6	3.6	3.4
2.9		3.1	2.8	Trade Payables	2.2	2.9	2.9	2.7	3.4	2.5
.4		.6	.7	Income Taxes Payable	.0	.5	.7	1.6	.7	.5
30.9		31.4	29.5	All Other Current	32.5	33.5	30.0	31.6	31.5	19.8
64.6		65.7	64.9	Total Current	80.3	86.3	67.0	69.4	56.5	34.4
12.9		12.6	14.3	Long-Term Debt	26.5	16.4	12.7	11.4	10.2	10.9
.4		.4	.5	Deferred Taxes	.0	.2	.7	1.1	.5	.3
6.4		6.2	5.0	All Other Non-Current	7.1	5.7	5.3	3.3	4.1	4.8
15.8		15.1	15.3	Net Worth	−13.9	−8.7	14.3	14.9	28.7	49.7
100.0		100.0	100.0	Total Liabilities & Net Worth	100.0	100.0	100.0	100.0	100.0	100.0
				INCOME DATA						
100.0		100.0	100.0	Net Sales	100.0	100.0	100.0	100.0	100.0	100.0
				Gross Profit						
81.8		82.6	80.8	Operating Expenses	81.2	86.1	85.4	83.7	79.5	70.6
18.2		17.4	19.2	Operating Profit	18.8	13.9	14.6	16.3	20.5	29.4
1.1		1.1	1.0	All Other Expenses (net)	2.5	.5	.4	.7	.7	1.5
17.1		16.3	18.2	Profit Before Taxes	16.3	13.4	14.1	15.6	19.8	27.9
				RATIOS						
2.8		3.0	3.0		1.3	1.8	2.6	2.7	3.6	6.0
1.2		1.2	1.1	Current	.7	.9	1.1	1.2	1.3	2.3
.6		.6	.6		.3	.4	.5	.5	.8	1.1
2.3		2.2	2.3		1.0	1.5	1.8	2.0	3.3	5.2
(1488) .9	(1743)	.9	(1568) .9	Quick	(203) .5	.7	(199) .8	.9	1.0	1.8
.4		.3	.3		.1	.2	.3	.3	.6	.8
0 UND	0	UND	0 UND		0 UND	0 UND	0 UND	0 UND	0 UND	0 UND
0 UND	0	UND	0 UND	Sales/Receivables	0 UND	0 UND	0 UND	0 UND	7 50.6	6 61.5
26 13.8	21	17.6	24 15.4		0 UND	9 40.3	29 12.5	50 7.4	45 8.0	27 13.5
				Cost of Sales/Inventory						
				Cost of Sales/Payables						
8.1		9.0	8.8		40.0	18.3	13.9	8.9	7.7	5.5
63.3		83.3	72.8	Sales/Working Capital	−28.5	−122.9	145.5	−68.5	33.4	12.4
−27.8		−26.8	−25.4		−8.2	−14.1	−24.2	−25.1	−63.4	109.3
92.9		102.4	124.3		31.5	53.7	62.5	129.2	201.7	221.3
(1240) 15.9	(1439)	16.0	(1269) 20.3	EBIT/Interest	(141) 5.5	(264) 7.9	(173) 14.9	(214) 14.2	(199) 43.5	(278) 90.9
1.6		1.4	2.2		.9	1.0	2.0	1.2	2.8	13.2
5.9		7.0	9.5	Net Profit + Depr., Dep.,				4.7	19.1	20.6
(110) 2.1	(118)	2.5	(108) 2.6	Amort./Cur. Mat. L/T/D			(22) 2.0	(31) 2.7	(38) 3.2	
1.1		1.1	1.1					.8	1.1	1.4
.2		.2	.2		.1	.1	.1	.1	.2	.2
.8		.8	.7	Fixed/Worth	2.8	1.5	.8	.6	.6	.4
−29.8		−4.3	−16.7		−1.0	−.5	−1.8	−18.2	99.7	1.1
.6		.6	.6		1.5	1.3	.8	.7	.5	.3
2.5		2.8	2.7	Debt/Worth	69.7	18.5	3.5	2.7	2.1	.8
−28.1		−13.6	−23.3		−3.5	−4.3	−12.9	−41.2	271.3	2.7
319.3		326.7	376.5	% Profit Before Taxes/Tangible	515.6	552.9	454.0	274.2	372.0	334.7
(1082) 100.8	(1228)	113.2	(1128) 133.8	Net Worth	(118) 106.4	(199) 112.8	(137) 141.7	(181) 69.0	(187) 107.6	(306) 186.7
13.5		15.0	17.9		19.0	9.1	13.6	5.9	15.7	83.3
135.6		135.9	152.9	% Profit Before Taxes/Total	132.9	129.5	118.7	108.8	154.7	199.2
29.0		28.6	39.0	Assets	21.7	21.2	35.4	16.2	43.7	114.5
.9		1.0	2.1		.0	.0	.7	.4	3.5	18.4
65.8		85.1	99.6		446.3	191.6	108.1	110.6	73.3	32.3
29.8		35.2	36.0	Sales/Net Fixed Assets	36.1	57.3	59.6	48.6	35.3	20.9
14.9		17.7	18.3		9.4	24.3	27.5	23.9	19.0	13.2
9.0		10.1	9.4		8.9	10.9	12.2	11.2	8.6	6.4
4.6		5.1	4.6	Sales/Total Assets	3.8	5.6	5.5	4.9	4.7	4.2
2.5		2.7	2.5		1.5	2.6	2.8	2.4	2.4	2.6
.8		.7	.7		.9	.3	.6	.6	.7	1.0
(1114) 1.3	(1197)	1.2	(1038) 1.2	% Depr., Dep., Amort./Sales	(97) 1.5	(196) .7	(115) .8	(163) 1.0	(191) 1.3	(276) 1.5
2.0		1.9	1.8		4.3	1.5	1.4	1.6	1.7	2.0
13.5		14.0	12.0	% Officers', Directors',	13.0	11.8	13.1	12.6	11.9	7.2
(702) 24.8	(863)	25.4	(742) 23.6	Owners' Comp/Sales	(106) 22.3	(201) 22.0	(114) 26.0	(123) 23.8	(93) 27.4	(105) 22.5
35.7		36.8	35.4		34.6	34.8	36.0	34.6	37.2	33.4
47477283M		75062906M	52413705M	Net Sales ($)	108330M	648336M	786237M	1825189M	3807034M	45238579M
11504472M		14194758M	13723291M	Total Assets ($)	62530M	238439M	195391M	527759M	1176823M	11522349M

M = $ thousand   MM = $ million
See Pages 11 through 21 for Explanation of Ratios and Data

Current Data Sorted By Assets

Comparative Historical Data

	0-500M	500M-2MM	2-10MM	10-50MM	50-100MM	100-250MM	Type of Statement	4/1/00-3/31/01 ALL	4/1/01-3/31/02 ALL
			9	6			Unqualified	6	3
	2		1				Reviewed	2	4
5	6		4				Compiled	13	13
15	9		4	1			Tax Returns	10	14
11	8		3	2	1	2	Other	3	13
		10 (4/1-9/30/04)		79 (10/1/04-3/31/05)					
31	25	21	9	1	2	**NUMBER OF STATEMENTS**	34	47
%	%	%	%	%	%	**ASSETS**	%	%
42.1	32.9	24.5				Cash & Equivalents	30.8	35.7
1.9	8.0	20.6				Trade Receivables (net)	7.0	13.6
.0	.0	.5				Inventory	.1	.1
5.7	8.5	13.4				All Other Current	5.4	8.1
49.7	49.4	59.0				Total Current	43.3	57.4
25.6	25.3	21.0				Fixed Assets (net)	28.8	21.8
7.9	9.6	6.1				Intangibles (net)	12.3	8.6
16.8	15.6	13.9				All Other Non-Current	15.5	12.2
100.0	100.0	100.0				Total	100.0	100.0
						LIABILITIES		
28.1	4.5	5.6				Notes Payable-Short Term	17.0	10.9
1.6	2.1	1.7				Cur. Mat.-L/T/D	4.9	2.7
7.0	6.1	7.3				Trade Payables	8.3	12.8
.7	.7	.9				Income Taxes Payable	.1	.1
14.4	21.5	24.8				All Other Current	25.3	21.2
51.8	35.0	40.4				Total Current	55.5	47.7
9.8	24.5	16.9				Long-Term Debt	22.5	12.8
.0	.0	.4				Deferred Taxes	.4	.1
9.9	1.9	5.1				All Other Non-Current	10.0	6.5
28.6	38.6	37.2				Net Worth	11.6	32.9
100.0	100.0	100.0				Total Liabilities & Net Worth	100.0	100.0
						INCOME DATA		
100.0	100.0	100.0				Net Sales	100.0	100.0
						Gross Profit		
91.0	82.9	90.1				Operating Expenses	96.3	88.2
9.0	17.1	9.9				Operating Profit	3.7	11.8
−.6	3.2	2.4				All Other Expenses (net)	−2.8	−1.0
9.7	13.9	7.6				Profit Before Taxes	6.5	12.8
						RATIOS		
2.5	3.3	2.8					1.9	3.0
1.0	1.7	1.4				Current	.9	1.1
.6	1.0	1.0					.3	.7
2.5	3.3	2.3					1.6	2.8
1.0	1.2	1.1				Quick	.9	1.0
.2	.9	.6					.3	.6
0 UND	0 UND	1 303.7					0 UND	0 UND
0 UND	1 330.2	7 51.5				Sales/Receivables	0 UND	5 71.6
0 UND	32 11.6	71 5.2					21 17.0	28 13.0
						Cost of Sales/Inventory		
						Cost of Sales/Payables		
9.1	5.8	4.5					9.6	8.3
UND	14.9	14.8				Sales/Working Capital	−44.1	34.3
−23.9	183.5	−26.7					−9.4	−24.1
56.3	54.9	72.3					10.0	35.4
(17) 13.7	(18) 4.0	(17) 7.5				EBIT/Interest	(31) 2.5	(38) 12.3
−5.6	2.0	−2.6					−1.6	3.6
						Net Profit + Depr., Dep., Amort./Cur. Mat. L /T/D		
.0	.3	.2					.4	.3
.6	.8	.5				Fixed/Worth	1.6	.9
−1.5	−23.8	3.3					−1.2	9.4
.3	.8	.6					1.0	.9
1.0	3.0	2.0				Debt/Worth	4.6	4.9
−5.8	−378.3	112.7					−7.2	46.0
258.5	114.3	96.1					93.5	213.2
(23) 93.2	(18) 26.5	(17) 35.7				% Profit Before Taxes/Tangible Net Worth	(23) 16.2	(39) 108.6
29.6	10.9	.8					−5.6	40.6
88.1	37.7	25.3					18.9	42.2
33.8	9.3	7.7				% Profit Before Taxes/Total Assets	3.9	16.3
4.5	4.9	−3.9					−6.4	3.2
UND	83.6	28.2					22.6	34.5
41.6	13.9	16.0				Sales/Net Fixed Assets	12.5	16.5
12.7	5.0	7.6					6.6	8.2
12.7	4.5	2.6					3.8	4.1
5.5	2.3	1.6				Sales/Total Assets	2.4	2.6
3.4	.7	.9					1.4	1.6
.4	1.2	1.0					1.3	.8
(17) 2.2	(17) 2.2	(19) 1.7				% Depr., Dep., Amort./Sales	(31) 2.0	(36) 1.5
3.0	4.9	2.9					4.6	2.6
9.0	2.1						6.8	4.4
(13) 11.5	(13) 6.2					% Officers', Directors', Owners' Comp/Sales	(19) 14.7	(16) 12.8
17.5	8.7						21.8	27.1
40090M	85277M	200963M	255529M	31390M	523065M	Net Sales ($)	272891M	418955M
5951M	28080M	96788M	205679M	57136M	271983M	Total Assets ($)	139338M	190860M

© RMA 2005

M = $ thousand   MM = $ million
See Pages 11 through 21 for Explanation of Ratios and Data

Comparative Historical Data | Current Data Sorted By Sales

4/1/02-3/31/03 ALL	4/1/03-3/31/04 ALL	4/1/04-3/31/05 ALL	Type of Statement	0-1MM	1-3MM	3-5MM	5-10MM	10-25MM	25MM & OVER
6	6	15	Unqualified		2	1	2	7	3
8	5	3	Reviewed		2		1		
12	20	15	Compiled	4	3	4	3	1	
11	25	29	Tax Returns	12	12	3	2		
21	28	27	Other	10	3	3	3	2	6
				10 (4/1-9/30/04)		79 (10/1/04-3/31/05)			
58	84	89	**NUMBER OF STATEMENTS**	26	22	11	11	10	9
%	%	%	**ASSETS**	%	%	%	%	%	%
35.0	33.5	35.2	Cash & Equivalents	43.5	29.6	29.6	38.0	25.8	
11.2	8.5	8.2	Trade Receivables (net)	.9	7.8	18.7	17.8	10.0	
.0	1.4	.1	Inventory	.0	.0	.1	.0	1.0	
9.4	6.6	8.3	All Other Current	8.3	8.3	7.9	8.6	8.3	
55.6	49.9	51.9	Total Current	52.7	45.7	56.3	64.4	45.1	
23.3	26.7	21.9	Fixed Assets (net)	20.6	28.9	19.5	23.3	23.5	
10.1	7.0	8.3	Intangibles (net)	6.6	10.6	10.1	5.4	10.2	
11.0	16.4	18.0	All Other Non-Current	20.1	14.8	14.1	6.9	21.2	
100.0	100.0	100.0	Total	100.0	100.0	100.0	100.0	100.0	
			LIABILITIES						
8.4	10.1	13.3	Notes Payable-Short Term	21.0	17.5	5.2	5.7	11.7	
4.4	1.9	1.6	Cur. Mat.-L/T/D	1.4	1.5	2.9	2.2	1.0	
10.7	6.6	7.2	Trade Payables	5.9	5.7	7.5	4.3	12.4	
.1	.8	.7	Income Taxes Payable	.9	.0	3.0	.1	.6	
30.3	19.1	20.9	All Other Current	21.3	17.7	16.2	30.9	16.3	
53.9	38.6	43.8	Total Current	50.6	42.4	34.7	43.2	42.0	
15.2	15.6	14.7	Long-Term Debt	11.5	32.2	5.1	13.7	6.1	
.0	.2	.2	Deferred Taxes	.0	.0	.0	.0	1.6	
4.2	6.8	7.1	All Other Non-Current	7.5	6.7	8.6	2.1	9.5	
26.6	38.8	34.3	Net Worth	30.4	18.7	51.5	41.0	40.8	
100.0	100.0	100.0	Total Liabilities & Net Worth	100.0	100.0	100.0	100.0	100.0	
			INCOME DATA						
100.0	100.0	100.0	Net Sales	100.0	100.0	100.0	100.0	100.0	
			Gross Profit						
86.7	82.0	88.8	Operating Expenses	82.0	91.5	93.0	86.5	94.0	
13.3	18.0	11.2	Operating Profit	18.0	8.5	7.0	13.5	6.0	
2.3	1.7	1.1	All Other Expenses (net)	2.6	1.2	-.2	1.3	-.1	
11.0	16.3	10.1	Profit Before Taxes	15.4	7.3	7.2	12.2	6.2	
			RATIOS						
2.9	2.2	2.2		3.8	2.1	3.4	2.1	1.5	
1.3	1.4	1.2	Current	1.5	1.2	1.7	1.6	1.1	
.9	.9	.8		.4	.7	1.0	1.1	.8	
2.4	2.1	2.1		3.8	2.1	2.5	1.9	1.4	
1.1	1.1	1.1	Quick	1.1	1.1	1.0	1.2	.9	
.7	.5	.6		.2	.4	.7	.9	.4	
0 UND	0 UND	0 UND		0 UND	0 UND	1 482.8	0 UND	1 451.2	
1 356.1	0 UND	1 482.8	Sales/Receivables	0 UND	0 UND	4 103.3	7 54.0	6 60.3	
23 15.8	13 28.1	15 24.1		0 UND	14 25.7	48 7.6	66 5.5	24 15.2	
			Cost of Sales/Inventory						
			Cost of Sales/Payables						
9.3	8.0	7.7		7.2	6.3	5.9	5.0	14.4	
22.8	29.6	30.0	Sales/Working Capital	43.2	79.8	17.2	36.7	70.3	
-33.3	-57.9	-51.2		-20.8	-29.8	-869.0	193.8	-41.9	
47.3	60.2	61.5		23.0	14.6				
(40) 16.5	(59) 24.0	(60) 12.3	EBIT/Interest	(11) 4.6	(17) 9.1				
2.3	9.1	1.9		-5.9	1.2				
			Net Profit + Depr., Dep., Amort./Cur. Mat. L/T/D						
.3	.2	.1		.0	.4	.1	.3	.4	
.7	.6	.5	Fixed/Worth	.5	2.0	.3	.5	.6	
16.1	3.5	6.1		-31.8	-1.5	1.8	1.2	NM	
.6	.7	.5		.3	.9	.5	.8	.8	
2.4	1.7	1.9	Debt/Worth	1.4	6.0	.6	2.0	1.4	
161.2	9.8	119.5		-560.6	-5.8	3.8	3.0	NM	
208.6	214.0	122.5		258.5	158.7		216.1		
(45) 66.1	(72) 88.2	(68) 37.0	% Profit Before Taxes/Tangible Net Worth	(19) 47.1	(13) 39.6		(10) 50.3		
18.9	37.0	9.2		17.0	4.2		-4.0		
53.3	71.1	36.9		76.3	34.7	76.6	55.5	17.8	
18.8	27.7	10.5	% Profit Before Taxes/Total Assets	15.0	9.0	10.3	25.9	7.4	
4.2	12.6	1.2		4.0	.6	1.0	-7.0	-8.2	
40.0	38.8	99.3		UND	47.0	84.7	51.9	19.0	
17.2	18.0	20.5	Sales/Net Fixed Assets	100.5	18.2	18.3	22.3	14.3	
9.7	7.9	11.7		12.0	5.8	9.5	11.7	12.4	
4.1	4.9	5.2		7.2	4.5	6.5	11.4	4.1	
2.6	2.8	2.5	Sales/Total Assets	3.3	2.3	2.7	3.0	2.5	
1.4	1.4	1.0		.7	1.0	1.1	1.5	1.0	
1.1	1.0	1.0		1.1	.9				
(42) 1.9	(56) 2.0	(59) 1.9	% Depr., Dep., Amort./Sales	(12) 1.8	(17) 2.2				
2.8	3.1	3.1		3.6	4.8				
7.1	6.0	3.6		9.4	4.6				
(28) 13.0	(34) 9.8	(29) 7.4	% Officers', Directors', Owners' Comp/Sales	(10) 16.0	(10) 7.4				
24.0	18.6	15.2		28.3	10.2				
1632585M	551753M	1136314M	Net Sales ($)	14261M	36991M	44202M	76291M	162268M	802301M
532624M	270503M	665617M	Total Assets ($)	11191M	25035M	31919M	29084M	101676M	466712M

M = $ thousand   MM = $ million
See Pages 11 through 21 for Explanation of Ratios and Data

Current Data Sorted By Assets   Comparative Historical Data

0-500M	500M-2MM	2-10MM	10-50MM	50-100MM	100-250MM	Type of Statement	4/1/00-3/31/01 ALL	4/1/01-3/31/02 ALL
2	5	8	3	1	3	Unqualified	16	20
1	4	4	2			Reviewed	14	12
46	39	23	7	2	1	Compiled	101	111
122	29	6	1		2	Tax Returns	74	91
137	153	130	26	4	8	Other	340	352
	198 (4/1-9/30/04)			571 (10/1/04-3/31/05)				
308	230	171	39	7	14	NUMBER OF STATEMENTS	545	586
%	%	%	%	%	%	ASSETS	%	%
22.4	9.6	12.0	12.5		10.9	Cash & Equivalents	12.1	13.0
21.7	40.0	40.2	41.3		30.2	Trade Receivables (net)	39.6	36.8
2.3	5.6	5.5	2.5		2.0	Inventory	3.7	3.9
4.4	6.0	9.1	8.1		13.6	All Other Current	6.8	5.5
50.7	61.2	66.8	64.5		56.7	Total Current	62.2	59.2
22.5	17.1	14.0	14.3		14.1	Fixed Assets (net)	18.8	20.7
12.9	9.2	7.6	5.2		14.3	Intangibles (net)	8.4	8.6
13.8	12.5	11.6	16.0		15.0	All Other Non-Current	10.7	11.5
100.0	100.0	100.0	100.0		100.0	Total	100.0	100.0
						LIABILITIES		
29.4	13.7	9.4	9.9		18.1	Notes Payable-Short Term	18.0	24.9
6.3	3.5	2.6	2.0		3.7	Cur. Mat.-L/T/D	5.0	4.4
2.9	3.1	3.8	5.4		5.1	Trade Payables	3.5	4.1
.8	.8	.8	.7		.3	Income Taxes Payable	.2	.3
23.8	15.4	15.1	15.4		39.1	All Other Current	18.6	20.8
63.1	36.6	31.7	33.4		66.3	Total Current	45.2	54.5
23.5	17.3	12.0	8.3		14.8	Long-Term Debt	16.8	19.1
.1	.1	.7	.0		.7	Deferred Taxes	1.0	.6
10.2	5.8	7.2	8.9		5.8	All Other Non-Current	5.3	6.5
3.2	40.2	48.5	49.3		12.5	Net Worth	31.6	19.3
100.0	100.0	100.0	100.0		100.0	Total Liabilities & Net Worth	100.0	100.0
						INCOME DATA		
100.0	100.0	100.0	100.0		100.0	Net Sales	100.0	100.0
						Gross Profit		
85.2	85.9	85.4	83.3		88.0	Operating Expenses	86.8	86.3
14.8	14.1	14.6	16.7		12.0	Operating Profit	13.2	13.7
.8	2.1	1.5	.8		.7	All Other Expenses (net)	1.7	2.2
14.1	12.1	13.2	15.9		11.3	Profit Before Taxes	11.5	11.5
						RATIOS		
2.3	3.0	4.1	3.3		2.6		3.7	3.4
1.0	1.7	2.2	1.9		1.7	Current	1.8	1.8
.3	1.0	1.5	1.2		.8		1.0	.9
2.2	2.6	3.2	3.0		2.4		2.9	2.8
(307) .8	1.4	1.7	1.5		1.3	Quick	1.5	1.4
.3	.8	1.1	1.1		.2		.3	.8
0 UND	29 12.4	41 9.0	41 8.9		0 UND		28 13.1	8 45.6
0 UND	54 6.8	60 6.1	71 5.1		37 9.9	Sales/Receivables	56 6.5	51 7.1
44 8.3	84 4.4	87 4.2	88 4.2		66 5.5		82 4.4	80 4.6
						Cost of Sales/Inventory		
						Cost of Sales/Payables		
13.8	5.5	4.4	4.9		6.2		5.1	5.5
−487.5	9.8	6.8	7.3		11.0	Sales/Working Capital	9.6	11.8
−14.8	178.0	13.0	15.5		−139.9		172.3	−115.5
28.5	33.6	48.9	99.7		22.5		21.3	21.1
(232) 7.9	(193) 7.5	(144) 12.8	(32) 28.2		(12) 15.8	EBIT/Interest	(476) 5.6	(503) 5.0
1.6	2.7	3.6	3.8		−4.9		1.5	1.5
	3.9	4.3					4.9	2.3
	(11) 1.3	(17) 2.5				Net Profit + Depr., Dep., Amort./Cur. Mat. L /T/D	(32) 1.5	(43) 1.3
	.7	1.4					.8	.5
.2	.1	.1	.1		.2		.2	.1
1.8	.3	.3	.3		.6	Fixed/Worth	.4	.5
−.9	1.8	.8	.4		−.3		2.1	5.0
.9	.6	.6	.6		.7		.5	.6
9.5	1.4	1.2	1.1		2.7	Debt/Worth	1.6	1.6
−2.8	6.5	3.4	3.4		−2.9		9.0	24.1
381.8	116.1	107.8	118.2		132.4	% Profit Before Taxes/Tangible Net Worth	115.3	131.9
(175) 104.0	(193) 39.0	(154) 41.8	(38) 60.2		(10) 109.9		(446) 39.9	(458) 40.5
18.6	8.8	8.9	11.7		84.6		7.5	8.9
103.4	40.0	49.8	55.1		53.3	% Profit Before Taxes/Total Assets	55.5	53.5
32.1	12.8	13.1	19.2		44.6		12.2	13.5
2.8	2.5	3.5	5.1		2.8		1.4	1.8
250.8	71.1	43.8	30.0		52.7		41.3	49.2
39.8	25.4	24.5	16.9		41.0	Sales/Net Fixed Assets	22.2	23.4
15.7	13.7	13.5	11.3		12.9		13.4	12.1
9.8	3.5	3.0	2.9		7.7		4.1	4.7
4.8	2.6	2.4	2.2		2.3	Sales/Total Assets	2.8	2.9
2.9	1.8	1.8	1.7		2.0		2.0	2.1
.7	1.2	1.1	1.2				1.2	1.1
(152) 1.7	(160) 1.7	(128) 1.7	(29) 2.0			% Depr., Dep., Amort./Sales	(396) 1.9	(430) 1.8
2.7	2.7	2.4	2.8				2.7	2.6
14.9	18.3	10.3	12.2				17.1	14.8
(191) 23.6	(117) 24.9	(80) 26.2	(16) 24.3			% Officers', Directors', Owners' Comp/Sales	(285) 25.3	(320) 25.0
33.2	33.1	32.2	31.7				32.9	32.3
359674M	695355M	1716392M	1555545M	1019973M	9020385M	Net Sales ($)	10553101M	6769069M
58128M	257866M	660455M	730528M	471028M	2180533M	Total Assets ($)	2802408M	2956309M

M = $ thousand   MM = $ million
See Pages 11 through 21 for Explanation of Ratios and Data

Comparative Historical Data   **Current Data Sorted By Sales**

				Type of Statement						
22	23	22		Unqualified	2	4	1	5	5	5
11	13	11		Reviewed	1	2	1	4	2	1
112	144	118		Compiled	32	34	16	19	9	8
85	140	160		Tax Returns	84	49	12	11	1	3
382	418	458		Other	106	121	56	93	50	32
4/1/02-3/31/03	4/1/03-3/31/04	4/1/04-3/31/05			198 (4/1-9/30/04)			571 (10/1/04-3/31/05)		
ALL	ALL	ALL			0-1MM	1-3MM	3-5MM	5-10MM	10-25MM	25MM & OVER
612	738	769		NUMBER OF STATEMENTS	225	210	86	132	67	49
%	%	%		**ASSETS**	%	%	%	%	%	%
13.1	14.4	15.5		Cash & Equivalents	18.6	15.4	15.3	11.4	16.7	11.3
36.4	34.7	32.6		Trade Receivables (net)	22.8	29.9	39.4	43.3	38.6	40.0
4.5	4.2	4.0		Inventory	1.9	4.7	5.8	5.2	4.7	3.1
6.7	7.1	6.3		All Other Current	4.5	5.1	7.6	7.6	9.4	10.4
60.7	60.4	58.4		Total Current	47.9	55.0	68.2	67.5	69.4	64.8
19.2	18.2	18.4		Fixed Assets (net)	24.5	18.0	13.7	14.4	14.0	17.7
8.6	10.1	10.1		Intangibles (net)	11.7	13.7	7.8	7.6	5.1	5.7
11.5	11.4	13.0		All Other Non-Current	15.9	13.3	10.3	10.5	11.5	11.8
100.0	100.0	100.0		Total	100.0	100.0	100.0	100.0	100.0	100.0
				LIABILITIES						
18.3	20.0	18.9		Notes Payable-Short Term	23.1	23.8	12.5	16.9	5.6	13.6
5.2	4.8	4.6		Cur. Mat.-L/T/D	6.0	5.5	2.8	2.4	2.4	6.4
3.2	3.5	3.4		Trade Payables	3.2	2.3	2.9	4.5	2.8	7.1
.6	.5	.8		Income Taxes Payable	.8	.7	.5	1.2	.5	.7
19.2	19.0	19.2		All Other Current	19.0	20.3	20.0	16.5	17.3	24.2
46.4	47.8	46.9		Total Current	52.2	52.7	38.6	41.6	28.6	52.1
16.5	19.2	18.0		Long-Term Debt	26.6	17.4	20.3	9.8	10.8	8.4
.4	.2	.2		Deferred Taxes	.1	.1	.2	.5	.6	.2
7.2	7.2	8.0		All Other Non-Current	7.7	11.6	3.1	7.5	6.5	5.3
29.6	25.5	26.9		Net Worth	13.4	18.3	37.8	40.6	53.5	34.1
100.0	100.0	100.0		Total Liabilities & Net Worth	100.0	100.0	100.0	100.0	100.0	100.0
				INCOME DATA						
100.0	100.0	100.0		Net Sales	100.0	100.0	100.0	100.0	100.0	100.0
				Gross Profit						
86.7	85.9	85.4		Operating Expenses	80.8	88.1	87.2	87.9	84.3	85.6
13.3	14.1	14.6		Operating Profit	19.2	11.9	12.8	12.1	15.7	14.4
2.2	2.0	1.3		All Other Expenses (net)	2.4	.7	.6	1.1	1.4	1.0
11.1	12.1	13.3		Profit Before Taxes	16.8	11.1	12.2	11.0	14.3	13.5
				RATIOS						
3.3	3.2	3.0			2.5	2.3	3.4	3.7	5.1	2.6
1.8	1.7	1.6		Current	1.0	1.4	2.2	1.9	2.9	1.7
1.0	.8	.8			.3	.6	1.3	1.3	1.6	1.2
2.8	2.6	2.5			2.2	2.2	2.7	3.3	4.0	2.5
1.4	1.3 (768)	1.3		Quick	.9	1.1	1.6 (131)	1.6	2.0	1.3
.7	.6	.6			.3	.4	.8	1.0	1.1	.8
18 20.1	0 UND	0 UND			0 UND	0 UND	23 16.0	35 10.4	36 10.1	27 13.7
50 7.3	46 7.9	43 8.6		Sales/Receivables	11 34.0	40 9.1	52 7.0	62 5.9	52 7.0	59 6.2
80 4.6	78 4.7	72 5.1			53 6.8	68 5.4	79 4.6	88 4.2	72 5.0	82 4.5
				Cost of Sales/Inventory						
				Cost of Sales/Payables						
5.3	5.7	6.1			8.9	7.3	5.1	4.9	4.0	6.0
10.9	11.9	13.6		Sales/Working Capital	UND	22.6	8.6	8.2	6.8	9.5
-172.1	-72.0	-50.0			-11.4	-32.1	28.9	24.5	13.0	50.4
29.0	36.1	35.6			28.1	29.7	39.7	52.3	61.6	58.8
(507) 7.2	(617) 8.5	(620) 9.1		EBIT/Interest	(157) 8.9	(180) 5.6	(71) 12.2	(116) 9.2	(54) 16.4	(42) 15.8
1.8	2.0	2.4			2.1	1.9	2.4	2.7	5.7	3.5
4.7	3.6	6.0					2.2		11.1	
(42) 1.8	(48) 1.2	(41) 2.2		Net Profit + Depr., Dep., Amort./Cur. Mat. L/T/D		(11) 1.3		(12) 1.9		
.8	.8	1.4				.8		.7		
.1	.1	.1			.1	.1	.1	.1	.1	.2
.4	.4	.4		Fixed/Worth	1.7	.6	.3	.3	.3	.4
4.3	16.9	9.6			-1.4	-1.3	2.2	.8	.7	1.0
.6	.6	.7			1.0	.8	.4	.6	.4	.6
1.7	2.0	1.9		Debt/Worth	7.5	2.5	1.2	1.2	.9	1.3
37.3	-80.8	-212.2			-3.9	-5.4	8.0	5.1	2.2	4.0
121.4	140.4	146.1			260.4	191.7	102.2	116.4	121.5	112.9
(478) 42.9	(548) 53.8	(575) 55.7		% Profit Before Taxes/Tangible Net Worth	(138) 82.8	(144) 56.1	(69) 41.9	(117) 35.8	(64) 51.5	(43) 87.6
6.8	7.8	10.7			24.4	10.4	8.9	3.6	13.6	33.3
49.7	60.3	64.2			82.5	60.1	52.5	49.9	63.8	59.2
13.0	17.2	17.2		% Profit Before Taxes/Total Assets	29.5	14.4	11.7	12.0	22.0	27.4
1.3	1.6	3.1			4.8	2.6	2.4	1.4	5.9	6.4
49.6	64.1	80.3			169.9	94.8	118.9	59.0	45.4	41.0
24.6	27.8	28.4		Sales/Net Fixed Assets	26.2	32.3	32.9	29.2	25.7	18.3
14.1	14.3	14.0			8.7	15.8	16.5	16.7	13.8	12.9
4.2	4.6	4.7			5.5	6.4	4.0	3.6	3.5	3.9
2.8	3.0	3.0		Sales/Total Assets	3.2	3.1	3.0	2.7	2.9	2.7
1.9	2.0	2.0			1.5	2.1	2.2	2.1	2.0	2.1
1.2	1.1	1.1			1.1	.9	1.1	1.1	1.3	.9
(424) 1.9	(494) 1.8	(480) 1.7		% Depr., Dep., Amort./Sales	(115) 2.3	(132) 1.6	(60) 1.6	(92) 1.6	(49) 1.8	(32) 1.9
2.8	2.7	2.6			4.9	2.5	2.2	2.3	2.4	2.5
14.8	13.7	16.0			14.4	16.6	17.4	21.0	10.1	10.9
(322) 24.4	(382) 23.7	(414) 24.5		% Officers', Directors', Owners' Comp/Sales	(126) 20.9	(124) 24.6	(45) 25.1	(69) 29.9	(29) 26.2	(21) 25.5
32.9	31.4	32.8			31.8	32.0	32.0	36.3	31.8	33.2
13192649M	13953421M	14367324M		Net Sales ($)	111537M	379766M	337581M	912518M	1026402M	11599520M
3614046M	4265219M	4358538M		Total Assets ($)	65432M	152598M	135027M	395990M	544055M	3065436M

M = $ thousand   MM = $ million
See Pages 11 through 21 for Explanation of Ratios and Data

Current Data Sorted By Assets   **Comparative Historical Data**

			1				Type of Statement		
							Unqualified		
			1				Reviewed		
			1				Compiled		
2	3						Tax Returns		
10	1						Other		
9	7	4	3		1			4/1/00-3/31/01	4/1/01-3/31/02
		6 (4/1-9/30/04)		37 (10/1/04-3/31/05)				ALL	ALL
0-500M	500M-2MM	2-10MM	10-50MM	50-100MM	100-250MM				
21	11	7	3		1	**NUMBER OF STATEMENTS**			
%	%	%	%	%	%	**ASSETS**		%	%
16.2	21.5			D		Cash & Equivalents		D	D
14.7	33.6			A		Trade Receivables (net)		A	A
.1	.0			T		Inventory		T	T
4.8	8.9			A		All Other Current		A	A
35.7	64.0					Total Current			
23.6	25.5			N		Fixed Assets (net)		N	N
12.6	6.1			O		Intangibles (net)		O	O
28.1	4.5			T		All Other Non-Current		T	T
100.0	100.0					Total			
				A		**LIABILITIES**		A	A
16.7	10.1			V		Notes Payable-Short Term		V	V
4.7	.7			A		Cur. Mat.-L/T/D		A	A
11.7	4.1			I		Trade Payables		I	I
.4	.2			L		Income Taxes Payable		L	L
12.7	10.8			A		All Other Current		A	A
46.1	25.8			B		Total Current		B	B
46.4	13.6			L		Long-Term Debt		L	L
.0	.0			E		Deferred Taxes		E	E
4.0	15.1					All Other Non-Current			
3.4	45.5					Net Worth			
100.0	100.0					Total Liabilities & Net Worth			
						INCOME DATA			
100.0	100.0					Net Sales			
						Gross Profit			
83.2	83.6					Operating Expenses			
16.8	16.4					Operating Profit			
.5	3.6					All Other Expenses (net)			
16.2	12.8					Profit Before Taxes			
						RATIOS			
3.5	18.0								
1.0	2.3					Current			
.2	1.4								
3.5	9.8								
.8	2.2					Quick			
.1	1.3								
0 UND	0 UND								
3 136.5	46 8.0					Sales/Receivables			
17 21.5	88 4.2								
						Cost of Sales/Inventory			
						Cost of Sales/Payables			
22.1	2.9								
-161.8	6.9					Sales/Working Capital			
-17.0	15.3								
9.8									
(15) 7.5						EBIT/Interest			
1.9									
						Net Profit + Depr., Dep., Amort./Cur. Mat. L /T/D			
.3	.1								
-5.0	.5					Fixed/Worth			
-.5	3.6								
1.3	.5								
-19.0	1.9					Debt/Worth			
-3.2	5.2								
						% Profit Before Taxes/Tangible Net Worth			
67.2	50.2								
36.8	29.5					% Profit Before Taxes/Total Assets			
16.4	6.7								
68.1	40.5								
23.7	22.6					Sales/Net Fixed Assets			
11.1	4.9								
6.1	3.8								
3.9	2.8					Sales/Total Assets			
2.3	.7								
						% Depr., Dep., Amort./Sales			
7.4									
(10) 18.0						% Officers', Directors', Owners' Comp/Sales			
29.1									
16801M	29149M	56620M	145124M		338637M	Net Sales ($)			
4123M	11374M	31099M	81064M		152188M	Total Assets ($)			

© RMA 2005

M = $ thousand   MM = $ million
See Pages 11 through 21 for Explanation of Ratios and Data

Comparative Historical Data | Current Data Sorted By Sales

			Type of Statement						
4	1	1	Unqualified					1	
		1	Reviewed	1					
5	5	6	Compiled	1	2	2		1	
2	8	11	Tax Returns	10	1				
5	16	24	Other	8	4	3	4	1	4
4/1/02-3/31/03	4/1/03-3/31/04	4/1/04-3/31/05		6 (4/1-9/30/04)			37 (10/1/04-3/31/05)		
ALL	ALL	ALL		0-1MM	1-3MM	3-5MM	5-10MM	10-25MM	25MM & OVER
16	30	43	**NUMBER OF STATEMENTS**	20	7	5	5	2	4
%	%	%	**ASSETS**	%	%	%	%	%	%
13.6	16.4	15.7	Cash & Equivalents	15.7					
35.2	24.7	27.0	Trade Receivables (net)	15.0					
1.0	1.5	1.1	Inventory	.1					
6.6	7.6	6.6	All Other Current	5.1					
56.4	50.3	50.4	Total Current	35.8					
24.2	19.8	20.8	Fixed Assets (net)	24.9					
7.5	12.7	9.5	Intangibles (net)	12.1					
11.9	17.1	19.3	All Other Non-Current	27.2					
100.0	100.0	100.0	Total	100.0					
			LIABILITIES						
19.3	11.1	14.9	Notes Payable-Short Term	19.5					
8.4	2.1	3.2	Cur. Mat.-L/T/D	4.4					
10.7	5.2	7.5	Trade Payables	11.4					
.0	.2	.3	Income Taxes Payable	.4					
14.9	17.6	11.4	All Other Current	8.6					
53.3	36.2	37.2	Total Current	44.4					
13.4	22.1	29.2	Long-Term Debt	43.7					
.1	.8	.3	Deferred Taxes	.0					
10.9	4.8	7.8	All Other Non-Current	7.3					
22.3	36.1	25.4	Net Worth	4.6					
100.0	100.0	100.0	Total Liabilities & Net Worth	100.0					
			INCOME DATA						
100.0	100.0	100.0	Net Sales	100.0					
			Gross Profit						
90.2	89.9	83.5	Operating Expenses	79.3					
9.8	10.1	16.5	Operating Profit	20.7					
2.5	1.3	2.3	All Other Expenses (net)	2.5					
7.3	8.8	14.2	Profit Before Taxes	18.2					
			RATIOS						
1.9	2.6	4.5	Current	4.7					
1.1	1.6	1.8		1.0					
.7	1.0	.8		.3					
1.3	2.6	4.2	Quick	4.6					
.8	1.2	1.4		.9					
.6	.6	.7		.1					
4 85.7	0 UND	0 UND	Sales/Receivables	0 UND					
52 7.0	37 9.9	18 20.0		3 113.8					
70 5.2	58 6.3	64 5.7		25 14.9					
			Cost of Sales/Inventory						
			Cost of Sales/Payables						
9.8	6.5	4.6	Sales/Working Capital	9.0					
NM	24.2	18.8		NM					
-17.8	UND	-98.5		-17.8					
(12) 15.5	(22) 17.2	(33) 29.4	EBIT/Interest	(13) 8.2					
5.0	4.6	8.2		7.3					
-.5	1.6	2.3		1.5					
			Net Profit + Depr., Dep., Amort./Cur. Mat. L/T/D						
.1	.1	.1	Fixed/Worth	.5					
.8	.7	.6		-7.9					
NM	-2.3	-1.5		-.5					
1.9	.5	.5	Debt/Worth	1.3					
3.9	2.3	2.8		-25.1					
NM	-5.7	-6.8		-3.7					
(12) 265.8	(19) 66.7	(27) 186.4	% Profit Before Taxes/Tangible Net Worth						
28.3	40.3	73.4							
-5.4	1.9	23.2							
25.3	35.8	57.9	% Profit Before Taxes/Total Assets	66.5					
3.8	14.2	25.3		35.6					
-16.8	1.7	7.2		4.8					
148.1	173.1	46.2	Sales/Net Fixed Assets	71.0					
17.1	39.5	23.7		23.4					
6.3	6.1	11.5		7.6					
3.8	3.6	4.6	Sales/Total Assets	5.1					
2.5	2.5	2.8		2.7					
1.7	1.7	1.5		1.3					
(10) 1.9	(15) 1.6	(25) 1.3	% Depr., Dep., Amort./Sales						
2.8	2.4	2.5							
6.0	4.7	3.8							
	(10) 8.3	(14) 5.9	% Officers', Directors', Owners' Comp/Sales						
	22.0	17.6							
	30.9	29.1							
306327M	107761M	586331M	Net Sales ($)	9901M	12755M	17139M	36042M	26733M	483761M
188513M	44878M	279848M	Total Assets ($)	7403M	5671M	4338M	21262M	7922M	233252M

M = $ thousand   MM = $ million
See Pages 11 through 21 for Explanation of Ratios and Data

Current Data Sorted By Assets | Comparative Historical Data

Type of Statement	0-500M	500M-2MM	2-10MM	10-50MM	50-100MM	100-250MM	4/1/00-3/31/01 ALL	4/1/01-3/31/02 ALL
Unqualified	1		8	15	2	3	22	21
Reviewed	5	15	53	13	1		64	59
Compiled	24	36	25				100	79
Tax Returns	44	16	7	1			34	37
Other	29	46	46	16	2		90	97
	52 (4/1-9/30/04)			356 (10/1/04-3/31/05)				
NUMBER OF STATEMENTS	103	113	139	45	5	3	310	293
	%	%	%	%	%	%	%	%
ASSETS								
Cash & Equivalents	23.8	8.5	7.2	8.6			10.1	10.5
Trade Receivables (net)	23.5	55.1	59.2	56.2			50.7	51.0
Inventory	1.1	2.7	1.9	1.9			1.8	2.0
All Other Current	1.4	4.8	6.4	10.1			6.6	6.5
Total Current	49.9	71.1	74.7	76.9			69.2	70.0
Fixed Assets (net)	31.7	18.5	15.1	14.7			19.7	19.3
Intangibles (net)	3.1	2.5	2.4	1.0			1.8	1.7
All Other Non-Current	15.3	7.9	7.9	7.4			9.3	9.1
Total	100.0	100.0	100.0	100.0			100.0	100.0
LIABILITIES								
Notes Payable-Short Term	35.4	14.6	10.1	7.9			15.3	17.3
Cur. Mat.-L/T/D	4.3	3.1	2.5	2.9			4.3	3.8
Trade Payables	10.8	18.4	17.1	16.5			15.4	16.0
Income Taxes Payable	.5	2.8	3.0	2.5			1.4	1.3
All Other Current	29.3	15.3	17.1	23.2			18.0	17.4
Total Current	80.4	54.4	49.6	53.0			54.4	55.8
Long-Term Debt	21.8	10.6	8.5	7.2			10.3	12.2
Deferred Taxes	.1	.5	2.6	1.7			1.9	3.0
All Other Non-Current	3.2	5.5	3.1	2.6			2.9	3.5
Net Worth	-5.4	29.1	36.1	35.5			30.5	25.5
Total Liabilities & Net Worth	100.0	100.0	100.0	100.0			100.0	100.0
INCOME DATA								
Net Sales	100.0	100.0	100.0	100.0			100.0	100.0
Gross Profit								
Operating Expenses	94.8	94.0	94.7	93.1			94.3	94.7
Operating Profit	5.2	6.0	5.3	6.9			5.7	5.3
All Other Expenses (net)	.6	1.5	1.4	.7			1.2	1.3
Profit Before Taxes	4.6	4.5	3.8	6.2			4.6	4.0
RATIOS								
Current	2.3	2.4	2.1	2.0			2.2	2.2
	.7	1.3	1.5	1.4			1.4	1.4
	.2	.9	1.1	1.1			1.0	1.0
Quick	2.2	2.2	1.9	1.8			2.0	1.9
	.7	1.2	1.4	1.3			1.2 (292)	1.3
	.2	.8	1.0	.9			.8	.9
Sales/Receivables	0 UND	47 7.8	71 5.1	65 5.6			39 9.3	46 7.9
	0 UND	71 5.1	94 3.9	92 4.0			75 4.9	70 5.2
	36 10.2	114 3.2	117 3.1	139 2.6			106 3.4	100 3.6
Cost of Sales/Inventory								
Cost of Sales/Payables								
Sales/Working Capital	18.9	6.7	5.7	6.2			6.3	6.9
	-70.0	18.6	9.5	10.8			13.9	16.2
	-14.5	-55.5	37.5	25.0			UND	510.5
EBIT/Interest	22.8	13.6	24.6	66.7			20.2	25.5
	(79) 6.3	(91) 3.7	(121) 7.3	(41) 19.8			(270) 5.6	(257) 6.0
	-2.5	-2.3	2.1	3.9			1.1	1.3
Net Profit + Depr., Dep., Amort./Cur. Mat. L/T/D		5.7	6.4	6.5			9.8	5.1
	(16) 1.7	(45) 2.7	(17) 2.7				(65) 2.7	(65) 2.1
		-.3	.9	1.4			1.0	.6
Fixed/Worth	.2	.1	.2	.2			.2	.2
	3.5	.5	.3	.4			.5	.5
	-1.1	3.8	1.0	.9			1.2	1.3
Debt/Worth	1.0	.8	1.0	.9			.8	1.0
	29.5	2.5	1.9	2.1			2.3	2.2
	-4.5	15.3	5.2	7.0			6.0	7.0
% Profit Before Taxes/Tangible Net Worth	260.0	57.7	49.1	65.1			57.0	61.1
	(59) 100.3	(91) 25.0	(134) 15.3	(43) 29.8			(276) 27.3	(251) 25.6
	20.9	-15.7	2.3	13.3			5.8	3.5
% Profit Before Taxes/Total Assets	51.3	23.6	13.2	23.5			21.9	23.2
	20.0	7.8	5.6	10.8			7.9	7.7
	-7.3	-4.8	.7	3.9			.4	.6
Sales/Net Fixed Assets	107.6	51.2	44.0	43.7			36.5	42.5
	35.7	30.9	25.0	26.9			23.1	22.6
	16.2	17.1	14.5	13.1			13.6	14.0
Sales/Total Assets	14.8	4.0	2.9	2.9			3.9	3.8
	8.0	3.0	2.4	2.3			2.8	2.9
	4.1	2.1	1.9	1.7			2.1	2.1
% Depr., Dep., Amort./Sales	.6	.9	.9	.7			.9	.9
	(65) 1.0	(84) 1.4	(126) 1.5	(37) 1.2			(270) 1.5	(250) 1.5
	1.7	2.1	2.1	2.1			2.2	2.2
% Officers', Directors', Owners' Comp/Sales	9.1	5.9	4.0	4.4			6.4	4.9
	(57) 14.4	(53) 10.2	(40) 6.7	(10) 8.1			(135) 11.2	(118) 10.6
	19.5	17.5	11.7	21.5			17.9	18.3
Net Sales ($)	155698M	439969M	1558160M	3123146M	505377M	1191905M	3751432M	7786079M
Total Assets ($)	20235M	126683M	653757M	881106M	307689M	553713M	1668038M	2153484M

© RMA 2005

M = $ thousand   MM = $ million
See Pages 11 through 21 for Explanation of Ratios and Data

Comparative Historical Data | **Current Data Sorted By Sales**

Type of Statement									
Unqualified	34	36	29		1		3	4	21
Reviewed	74	87	87	2	13	7	21	30	14
Compiled	84	102	85	12	24	21	15	12	1
Tax Returns	51	83	68	22	29	8	6		3
Other	115	122	139	15	36	20	35	21	12
	4/1/02-3/31/03	4/1/03-3/31/04	4/1/04-3/31/05	52 (4/1-9/30/04)			356 (10/1/04-3/31/05)		
	ALL	ALL	ALL	0-1MM	1-3MM	3-5MM	5-10MM	10-25MM	25MM & OVER
NUMBER OF STATEMENTS	358	430	408	51	103	56	80	67	51
ASSETS	%	%	%	%	%	%	%	%	%
Cash & Equivalents	10.3	14.2	11.9	16.3	17.2	10.9	7.2	8.7	9.6
Trade Receivables (net)	49.2	45.0	48.5	24.0	40.5	49.8	61.0	60.4	52.2
Inventory	1.7	1.7	1.9	.2	2.1	4.0	1.5	2.4	.9
All Other Current	6.5	5.7	5.3	2.3	2.1	7.3	5.9	6.2	10.7
Total Current	67.7	66.7	67.6	42.8	61.9	72.0	75.7	77.7	73.3
Fixed Assets (net)	20.1	20.7	20.1	42.4	22.3	16.4	13.8	13.9	15.4
Intangibles (net)	2.2	2.0	2.6	3.3	3.4	1.3	2.4	1.2	3.6
All Other Non-Current	10.0	10.6	9.7	11.5	12.4	10.3	8.1	7.3	7.7
Total	100.0	100.0	100.0	100.0	100.0	100.0	100.0	100.0	100.0
LIABILITIES									
Notes Payable-Short Term	19.0	18.0	17.3	29.6	24.7	19.3	9.5	9.2	10.6
Cur. Mat.-L/T/D	3.9	4.2	3.2	2.4	4.3	3.8	2.7	2.2	2.8
Trade Payables	17.4	15.1	15.7	14.5	11.1	17.7	19.5	16.9	16.4
Income Taxes Payable	1.8	1.8	2.3	.3	2.4	1.7	1.9	3.0	3.3
All Other Current	20.3	19.9	20.6	15.5	24.6	17.4	18.0	20.4	25.5
Total Current	62.4	59.0	59.0	62.3	67.1	59.9	51.6	52.6	58.6
Long-Term Debt	11.8	11.9	12.3	35.5	12.7	9.6	8.1	5.1	7.8
Deferred Taxes	1.8	1.4	1.2	.1	.1	1.6	1.6	2.5	2.0
All Other Non-Current	4.1	5.0	3.7	4.7	1.9	6.8	4.5	2.8	3.0
Net Worth	19.9	22.8	23.7	-2.6	18.2	22.1	34.2	37.1	28.6
Total Liabilities & Net Worth	100.0	100.0	100.0	100.0	100.0	100.0	100.0	100.0	100.0
INCOME DATA									
Net Sales	100.0	100.0	100.0	100.0	100.0	100.0	100.0	100.0	100.0
Gross Profit									
Operating Expenses	97.0	95.2	94.4	88.0	94.6	96.8	96.0	94.5	94.8
Operating Profit	3.0	4.8	5.6	12.0	5.4	3.2	4.0	5.5	5.2
All Other Expenses (net)	1.1	1.0	1.1	3.9	.9	.4	1.0	.7	.5
Profit Before Taxes	2.0	3.8	4.5	8.1	4.5	2.7	3.0	4.8	4.7

RATIOS

	Hist 1	Hist 2	Hist 3	0-1MM	1-3MM	3-5MM	5-10MM	10-25MM	25MM & OVER
Current	2.1	2.2	2.2	2.3	2.7	2.4	2.1	2.1	1.7
	1.4	1.4	1.3	.7	1.3	1.3	1.4	1.4	1.3
	1.0	1.0	.9	.2	.6	.9	1.1	1.1	1.2
Quick	1.8	2.0	1.9	2.2	2.4	2.2	1.7	1.9	1.5
	1.2	(429) 1.2	1.2	.7	1.2	1.2	1.3	1.3	1.2
	.8	.8	.8	.2	.5	.7	1.0	1.0	.9
Sales/Receivables	39 9.2	0 UND	24 14.9	0 UND	0 UND	26 13.9	61 6.0	72 5.1	53 6.9
	72 5.1	65 5.6	73 5.0	0 UND	49 7.4	77 4.7	88 4.2	91 4.0	81 4.5
	103 3.6	97 3.8	108 3.4	53 6.8	104 3.5	109 3.3	112 3.3	115 3.2	110 3.3
Cost of Sales/Inventory									
Cost of Sales/Payables									
Sales/Working Capital	6.6	6.6	6.7	11.8	7.7	6.7	6.5	6.0	8.2
	14.4	18.2	15.9	-40.7	26.8	18.9	12.2	9.7	11.9
	-527.3	-196.0	-119.4	-8.0	-23.1	-44.9	60.2	30.4	23.0
EBIT/Interest	17.3	24.0	25.0	18.4	33.6	14.5	16.8	44.8	41.8
	(291) 4.0	(340) 5.3	(340) 6.9	(36) 6.4	(81) 6.2	(47) 2.5	(71) 4.9	(59) 14.4	(46) 17.0
	-.7	.0	1.1	-1.7	-.9	-2.3	.4	2.8	4.3
Net Profit + Depr., Dep., Amort./Cur. Mat. L/T/D	3.9	4.6	5.9				6.6	6.9	6.5
	(89) 1.8	(90) 1.8	(84) 2.3			(19) 1.9	(25) 2.7	(21) 2.7	
	.2	.4	1.0				.8	1.4	1.2
Fixed/Worth	.2	.2	.2	.6	.1	.1	.2	.2	.2
	.5	.4	.5	3.5	.6	.5	.4	.3	.5
	1.8	1.8	3.1	-1.3	41.5	NM	1.2	.6	1.0
Debt/Worth	1.0	.8	.9	1.7	.6	.9	.9	1.0	1.1
	2.1	2.1	2.5	12.8	2.4	2.5	2.3	2.1	2.8
	9.9	9.1	15.9	-9.3	264.3	-61.2	5.8	5.1	8.7
% Profit Before Taxes/Tangible Net Worth	46.0	60.9	67.1	223.0	112.4	77.3	50.6	55.0	58.3
	(295) 14.9	(360) 18.8	(335) 23.0	(30) 66.9	(79) 35.0	(41) 17.5	(71) 17.0	19.3	(47) 26.8
	-1.4	-.6	3.1	16.9	-1.7	-20.5	2.2	4.6	13.5
% Profit Before Taxes/Total Assets	15.7	27.5	24.1	39.6	33.8	23.6	15.3	15.2	19.9
	3.5	5.3	7.3	19.4	10.4	6.1	6.5	6.1	7.0
	-4.6	-1.2	.0	.3	-3.6	-8.5	-.3	1.6	2.8
Sales/Net Fixed Assets	44.7	54.3	51.1	72.8	59.1	76.7	46.0	43.4	44.3
	25.0	27.9	29.3	14.6	32.4	30.4	31.0	25.5	26.2
	13.7	15.6	15.4	3.6	19.5	17.7	19.7	14.5	15.5
Sales/Total Assets	4.0	4.7	4.4	7.6	10.6	4.2	3.5	3.0	3.3
	2.7	2.9	2.8	3.5	3.6	3.2	2.7	2.4	2.6
	2.1	2.2	2.1	1.0	2.3	2.1	2.2	2.0	1.9
% Depr., Dep., Amort./Sales	1.0	.9	.8	1.1	.7	.8	.8	1.0	.8
	(297) 1.5	(342) 1.4	(319) 1.4	(29) 2.0	(70) 1.0	(48) 1.3	(71) 1.2	(56) 1.6	(45) 1.4
	2.2	2.2	2.0	13.0	2.1	1.9	1.8	2.1	2.0
% Officers', Directors', Owners' Comp/Sales	6.6	6.5	6.1	13.6	7.9	5.9	4.5	2.1	3.6
	(142) 11.1	(183) 11.7	(161) 10.1	(19) 15.0	(59) 12.7	(28) 9.1	(28) 8.5	(16) 5.1	(11) 7.7
	19.7	19.3	19.7	22.1	17.7	22.2	14.7	7.0	21.4
Net Sales ($)	12067603M	9225549M	6974255M	28463M	204085M	213281M	581954M	1091319M	4855153M
Total Assets ($)	3025405M	3051202M	2543183M	20820M	72540M	79425M	225661M	474171M	1670566M

© RMA 2005

M = $ thousand   MM = $ million
See Pages 11 through 21 for Explanation of Ratios and Data

Current Data Sorted By Assets							Comparative Historical Data	

0-500M	500M-2MM	2-10MM	10-50MM	50-100MM	100-250MM	Type of Statement	4/1/00-3/31/01 ALL	4/1/01-3/31/02 ALL
2	1	5	2		4	Unqualified	10	5
3	14	19	2			Reviewed	50	39
9	20	5	1			Compiled	59	50
27	19	1	1			Tax Returns	38	27
14	19	12			3	Other	40	41
	27 (4/1-9/30/04)		158 (10/1/04-3/31/05)					
55	73	42	8		7	NUMBER OF STATEMENTS	197	162
%	%	%	%	%	%	**ASSETS**	%	%
14.0	10.2	8.6				Cash & Equivalents	10.0	9.0
22.3	33.2	43.5				Trade Receivables (net)	28.6	30.1
7.5	10.1	8.6				Inventory	9.8	9.1
2.0	3.3	3.0				All Other Current	4.5	4.0
45.8	56.8	63.7				Total Current	52.9	52.3
39.9	34.8	25.1				Fixed Assets (net)	39.3	39.4
6.0	1.1	2.8				Intangibles (net)	1.9	2.4
8.1	7.3	8.3				All Other Non-Current	5.9	5.9
100.0	100.0	100.0				Total	100.0	100.0
						LIABILITIES		
23.5	10.5	11.8				Notes Payable-Short Term	10.5	14.3
7.6	7.2	4.7				Cur. Mat.-L/T/D	7.5	5.7
8.7	12.8	11.1				Trade Payables	9.8	10.8
.2	.2	1.4				Income Taxes Payable	.5	.5
10.1	9.8	10.1				All Other Current	11.5	12.7
50.1	40.3	39.1				Total Current	39.8	44.0
29.5	21.0	11.9				Long-Term Debt	23.5	24.2
.0	.3	1.3				Deferred Taxes	1.4	1.7
4.8	3.6	3.3				All Other Non-Current	2.7	3.6
15.7	34.7	44.4				Net Worth	32.5	26.5
100.0	100.0	100.0				Total Liabilities & Net Worth	100.0	100.0
						INCOME DATA		
100.0	100.0	100.0				Net Sales	100.0	100.0
						Gross Profit		
93.4	97.0	93.8				Operating Expenses	94.5	94.6
6.6	3.0	6.2				Operating Profit	5.5	5.4
.7	.9	.1				All Other Expenses (net)	.9	1.5
5.9	2.1	6.1				Profit Before Taxes	4.6	3.9
						RATIOS		
1.9	2.5	2.5				Current	2.1	2.3
1.0	1.5	1.6					1.4	1.3
.4	.8	1.2					.9	.9
1.8	1.9	1.9				Quick	1.8	1.7
.7	1.0	1.3					1.0 (161)	.9
.2	.5	.9					.5	.5
0 UND	14 25.2	43 8.5				Sales/Receivables	14 25.5	12 31.4
7 50.3	33 11.0	65 5.6					40 9.2	40 9.2
32 11.2	55 6.6	93 3.9					61 6.0	63 5.8
						Cost of Sales/Inventory		
						Cost of Sales/Payables		
17.6	7.5	6.1				Sales/Working Capital	8.7	8.5
−244.0	17.6	10.5					19.2	20.2
−26.6	−42.8	40.2					−86.0	−58.8
16.0	8.3	21.6				EBIT/Interest	8.1	8.4
(47) 6.3	(69) 2.8	(40) 8.3					(185) 3.8	(149) 3.1
1.4	.2	3.6					1.6	1.2
	6.5	7.3				Net Profit + Depr., Dep., Amort./Cur. Mat. L /T/D	5.2	4.5
	(17) 2.1	(14) 3.6					(54) 2.4	(37) 1.9
	1.2	1.5					1.6	1.2
.4	.4	.2				Fixed/Worth	.5	.6
1.3	.9	.6					1.1	1.1
−1.2	2.9	1.3					2.3	3.3
1.0	.7	.7				Debt/Worth	1.0	1.0
4.0	2.1	1.4					1.9	2.1
−3.2	4.4	2.9					4.4	4.9
136.8	48.2	44.8				% Profit Before Taxes/Tangible Net Worth	63.9	52.1
(37) 45.5	(63) 20.1	(40) 26.8					(179) 25.3	(140) 22.8
10.3	4.3	9.7					7.1	5.1
44.6	16.5	22.5				% Profit Before Taxes/Total Assets	20.3	17.6
20.3	4.8	10.2					8.1	7.4
2.2	−1.7	4.6					2.5	1.0
54.5	19.1	26.2				Sales/Net Fixed Assets	16.0	14.6
14.9	11.1	11.7					7.9	7.9
6.0	6.5	6.3					4.7	4.8
8.9	4.4	2.9				Sales/Total Assets	3.9	3.9
5.6	3.1	2.4					2.8	2.7
2.7	2.2	1.6					1.9	1.8
1.7	2.0	1.3				% Depr., Dep., Amort./Sales	1.9	1.8
(32) 3.4	(62) 3.4	(38) 2.4					(171) 3.8	(146) 3.5
5.4	4.3	3.9					5.4	5.3
3.1	2.9	1.2				% Officers', Directors', Owners' Comp/Sales	3.0	3.0
(38) 7.1	(47) 5.2	(16) 2.3					(115) 5.4	(91) 6.4
13.3	7.5	4.5					8.6	10.2
65086M	256766M	409673M	198446M		4821143M	Net Sales ($)	2018452M	1182525M
11403M	76385M	175404M	142051M		1288869M	Total Assets ($)	814861M	514159M

© RMA 2005

M = $ thousand   MM = $ million
See Pages 11 through 21 for Explanation of Ratios and Data

Comparative Historical Data | **Current Data Sorted By Sales**

4/1/02-3/31/03 ALL	4/1/03-3/31/04 ALL	4/1/04-3/31/05 ALL	Type of Statement	27 (4/1-9/30/04) 0-1MM	1-3MM	3-5MM	158 (10/1/04-3/31/05) 5-10MM	10-25MM	25MM & OVER
8	10	14	Unqualified	2		2	2	2	6
55	41	38	Reviewed	3	8	8	6	10	3
41	48	35	Compiled	5	13	10	6		1
48	50	48	Tax Returns	19	15	9	4	1	
57	58	50	Other	7	15	10	12	2	4
209	207	185	**NUMBER OF STATEMENTS**	36	51	39	30	15	14
%	%	%	**ASSETS**	%	%	%	%	%	%
10.3	8.7	10.5	Cash & Equivalents	15.1	7.9	13.1	8.7	11.4	4.4
31.1	32.7	31.6	Trade Receivables (net)	14.4	31.9	33.4	37.6	55.2	32.4
8.2	8.9	9.0	Inventory	9.0	8.9	9.2	11.9	3.1	8.3
4.6	2.6	3.2	All Other Current	1.3	2.1	5.0	2.0	3.4	9.9
54.1	52.8	54.4	Total Current	39.8	50.7	60.7	60.1	73.2	55.0
38.2	36.3	34.1	Fixed Assets (net)	44.0	39.6	28.5	30.4	17.6	29.3
2.1	2.8	3.7	Intangibles (net)	6.6	2.3	2.8	.6	3.8	10.8
5.6	8.1	7.8	All Other Non-Current	9.3	7.4	7.9	8.9	5.5	4.9
100.0	100.0	100.0	Total	100.0	100.0	100.0	100.0	100.0	100.0
			LIABILITIES						
12.9	15.3	14.5	Notes Payable-Short Term	22.4	14.2	9.3	16.1	13.3	8.0
6.3	7.2	6.5	Cur. Mat.-L/T/D	8.9	7.0	5.3	6.5	3.5	4.4
11.4	11.6	11.4	Trade Payables	6.5	10.1	12.7	11.0	18.9	18.5
1.0	.5	.5	Income Taxes Payable	.4	.1	.2	1.4	1.2	.4
8.5	10.9	10.5	All Other Current	9.2	8.5	10.4	8.8	13.3	21.8
40.1	45.5	43.4	Total Current	47.4	39.8	37.8	43.8	50.2	53.1
22.9	21.2	22.0	Long-Term Debt	29.1	27.1	19.7	18.7	6.0	15.0
1.0	.9	.7	Deferred Taxes	.2	.2	.3	.7	1.7	3.4
4.7	5.9	4.1	All Other Non-Current	2.0	6.9	2.6	2.5	4.5	6.2
31.3	26.6	30.0	Net Worth	21.4	25.9	39.6	34.4	37.7	22.3
100.0	100.0	100.0	Total Liabilities & Net Worth	100.0	100.0	100.0	100.0	100.0	100.0
			INCOME DATA						
100.0	100.0	100.0	Net Sales	100.0	100.0	100.0	100.0	100.0	100.0
			Gross Profit						
95.4	95.2	94.9	Operating Expenses	92.6	96.8	95.3	95.1	93.6	93.8
4.6	4.8	5.1	Operating Profit	7.4	3.2	4.7	4.9	6.4	6.2
1.2	1.0	.9	All Other Expenses (net)	.9	.9	.3	1.6	.2	1.0
3.4	3.8	4.2	Profit Before Taxes	6.5	2.3	4.4	3.2	6.2	5.2
			RATIOS						
2.4	2.4	2.1	Current	2.2	2.2	3.1	1.9	1.8	1.5
1.5	1.3	1.3		.8	1.2	1.8	1.4	1.5	1.1
1.0	.8	.8		.4	.8	1.0	1.0	1.3	.9
2.0	1.7	1.8	Quick	1.7	1.9	2.6	1.5	1.8	1.1
(208) 1.1	1.0	1.0		.6	.9	1.3	1.0	1.3	.8
.6	.5	.5		.2	.4	.6	.7	1.0	.4
10 35.9	14 26.9	11 32.6	Sales/Receivables	0 UND	7 48.7	14 26.6	27 13.5	41 8.9	19 19.1
39 9.3	37 9.9	35 10.4		0 UND	32 11.4	30 12.1	48 7.7	66 5.6	56 6.6
64 5.7	63 5.8	61 6.0		35 10.4	64 5.7	53 6.8	76 4.8	87 4.2	64 5.7
			Cost of Sales/Inventory						
			Cost of Sales/Payables						
7.9	8.6	8.5	Sales/Working Capital	14.0	8.6	5.3	7.5	9.3	10.6
20.4	25.2	24.1		-106.4	29.9	11.6	17.6	11.4	166.5
-472.0	-38.0	-45.2		-11.5	-40.0	663.2	-814.2	24.1	-28.4
9.6	9.0	12.5	EBIT/Interest	16.3	7.2	31.0	9.8	34.6	22.5
(185) 3.2	(184) 3.3	(167) 5.0		(30) 4.6	(48) 3.4	(35) 9.1	(27) 3.8	8.9	(12) 7.6
1.2	1.0	1.5		.7	.4	2.1	-.6	3.6	2.5
3.5	4.0	5.8	Net Profit + Depr., Dep.,						
(46) 2.1	(40) 2.1	(36) 2.2	Amort./Cur. Mat. L/T/D						
1.0	.8	1.4							
.5	.5	.4	Fixed/Worth	.4	.5	.2	.4	.2	1.1
1.0	1.1	1.0		1.6	1.1	.6	.7	.6	1.7
3.1	6.6	4.0		-5.0	27.5	1.9	1.7	.8	NM
.8	.8	.9	Debt/Worth	.7	1.0	.4	.9	1.0	1.8
2.0	1.9	2.3		3.4	2.6	1.7	2.3	1.5	3.7
5.3	24.1	10.1		-4.5	59.2	4.2	4.3	4.9	NM
60.0	55.2	54.4	% Profit Before Taxes/Tangible	84.9	62.9	55.4	32.0	54.5	85.2
(185) 19.9	(166) 24.0	(150) 27.6	Net Worth	(25) 30.6	(41) 21.9	(33) 33.6	(27) 18.6	(13) 44.3	(11) 33.1
2.9	4.5	8.3		3.6	6.3	10.2	-4.3	22.6	21.9
18.8	17.3	21.7	% Profit Before Taxes/Total	36.9	19.3	25.8	16.3	21.3	18.3
6.7	7.1	9.3	Assets	12.4	6.0	11.0	5.6	15.9	9.7
.5	.3	1.8		.1	-.2	4.1	-2.9	6.3	6.1
16.1	19.6	25.4	Sales/Net Fixed Assets	38.9	19.9	31.3	24.0	48.8	21.2
8.5	9.2	12.2		12.1	9.8	15.2	11.1	34.0	14.2
5.4	5.3	6.1		3.5	5.4	10.9	6.3	11.6	4.6
3.9	4.0	5.3	Sales/Total Assets	7.0	5.3	5.9	4.3	4.0	3.7
2.9	2.9	2.9		3.0	3.0	3.4	2.7	2.9	2.5
2.1	2.1	2.0		2.0	1.8	2.4	1.8	2.4	1.7
2.1	1.8	1.6	% Depr., Dep., Amort./Sales	2.1	1.9	1.3	1.6	1.2	
(177) 3.6	(173) 3.2	(141) 3.3		(24) 4.3	(42) 3.6	(27) 2.2	(27) 3.3	(13) 2.1	
5.2	5.2	4.3		9.8	4.7	3.6	4.2	3.4	
2.8	3.2	2.7	% Officers', Directors',	3.2	4.2	2.1	2.0		
(109) 5.5	(112) 5.9	(103) 5.2	Owners' Comp/Sales	(27) 6.9	(33) 5.5	(20) 5.0	(14) 3.5		
11.5	10.2	10.0		14.9	8.2	9.7	8.2		
2790350M	4995040M	5751114M	Net Sales ($)	20174M	96606M	151162M	210874M	218812M	5053486M
1142933M	1816224M	1694112M	Total Assets ($)	10212M	38727M	69863M	116623M	71235M	1387452M

M = $ thousand   MM = $ million
See Pages 11 through 21 for Explanation of Ratios and Data

Current Data Sorted By Assets   Comparative Historical Data

						Type of Statement		
3	25	77	83	17	22	Unqualified	153	180
15	101	186	40			Reviewed	260	232
44	119	59	8			Compiled	277	285
106	74	15	2		2	Tax Returns	103	90
70	125	130	57	14	10	Other	379	360
	180 (4/1-9/30/04)			1224 (10/1/04-3/31/05)			4/1/00-3/31/01	4/1/01-3/31/02
0-500M	500M-2MM	2-10MM	10-50MM	50-100MM	100-250MM		ALL	ALL
238	444	467	190	31	34	NUMBER OF STATEMENTS	1172	1147
%	%	%	%	%	%	ASSETS	%	%
21.9	10.7	9.1	9.4	10.4	7.9	Cash & Equivalents	9.7	10.4
27.8	52.2	53.3	45.8	46.1	34.9	Trade Receivables (net)	51.1	49.6
2.5	3.9	4.6	4.0	1.7	4.4	Inventory	3.6	4.0
4.4	4.5	8.1	12.6	14.6	11.0	All Other Current	6.7	6.5
56.5	71.3	75.2	71.8	72.8	58.3	Total Current	71.0	70.5
29.8	17.0	15.0	15.8	13.5	16.9	Fixed Assets (net)	18.3	18.8
2.2	1.9	2.6	3.6	8.9	14.5	Intangibles (net)	2.5	3.1
11.5	9.7	7.2	8.7	4.8	10.3	All Other Non-Current	8.2	7.6
100.0	100.0	100.0	100.0	100.0	100.0	Total	100.0	100.0
						LIABILITIES		
33.2	13.3	11.3	11.2	8.8	3.0	Notes Payable-Short Term	12.7	14.5
7.2	3.5	3.3	2.4	2.4	5.7	Cur. Mat.-L/T/D	3.9	3.4
8.8	10.9	12.9	12.2	13.2	10.7	Trade Payables	11.5	11.8
.4	.9	2.3	3.8	2.8	1.1	Income Taxes Payable	1.5	1.7
24.7	12.1	15.0	18.8	25.3	18.6	All Other Current	16.6	16.9
74.3	40.7	44.8	48.4	52.4	39.2	Total Current	46.2	48.2
23.7	11.8	8.9	10.3	11.4	14.2	Long-Term Debt	10.0	10.4
.2	1.4	1.5	2.3	.7	1.1	Deferred Taxes	2.8	2.3
10.0	3.6	3.8	5.5	6.7	8.3	All Other Non-Current	4.4	5.2
−8.1	42.5	41.0	33.6	28.7	37.2	Net Worth	36.7	33.9
100.0	100.0	100.0	100.0	100.0	100.0	Total Liabilities & Net Worth	100.0	100.0
						INCOME DATA		
100.0	100.0	100.0	100.0	100.0	100.0	Net Sales	100.0	100.0
						Gross Profit		
94.0	93.6	95.0	94.9	95.1	94.1	Operating Expenses	94.6	95.6
6.0	6.4	5.0	5.1	4.9	5.9	Operating Profit	5.4	4.4
.7	.9	.8	1.8	.7	2.1	All Other Expenses (net)	.9	1.0
5.2	5.5	4.2	3.3	4.3	3.8	Profit Before Taxes	4.5	3.3
						RATIOS		
2.9	3.4	2.6	2.3	2.0	2.2		2.6	2.5
1.0	1.9	1.7	1.6	1.6	1.5	Current	1.6	1.6
.4	1.2	1.3	1.2	1.1	1.3		1.2	1.1
2.8	3.0	2.2	1.7	1.7	1.5		2.2	2.2
(237) .9	1.6	1.4	1.2	1.0	1.1	Quick	1.4 (1146)	1.3
.3	1.0	1.0	1.0	.8	.8		1.0	.9
0 UND	46 8.0	56 6.5	58 6.3	61 6.0	47 7.7		52 7.1	48 7.5
0 UND	71 5.2	78 4.7	76 4.8	74 5.0	69 5.3	Sales/Receivables	76 4.8	71 5.1
57 6.4	100 3.6	110 3.3	102 3.6	97 3.7	94 3.9		103 3.6	97 3.8
						Cost of Sales/Inventory		
						Cost of Sales/Payables		
10.7	4.9	4.8	5.4	4.5	5.2		5.1	5.4
505.8	8.8	8.3	8.5	8.3	10.5	Sales/Working Capital	9.5	10.1
−18.0	26.6	18.8	18.9	42.2	17.2		29.4	39.1
22.0	22.8	24.7	20.1	36.1	31.7		15.6	15.1
(178) 5.3	(377) 6.3	(405) 7.8	(160) 8.0	(26) 10.6	(30) 8.6	EBIT/Interest	(1036) 4.9	(997) 4.3
−.4	1.3	2.2	3.4	4.0	3.3		1.5	1.1
	4.2	7.4	8.1	21.9	22.2	Net Profit + Depr., Dep.,	6.5	6.7
(70)	1.3	(147) 3.0	(90) 3.6	(13) 4.6	(10) 3.7	Amort./Cur. Mat. L /T/D	(334) 2.8	(301) 2.9
	.5	1.2	1.9	2.5	2.0		1.3	1.1
.2	.1	.1	.2	.1	.1		.2	.2
1.1	.3	.3	.4	.3	.3	Fixed/Worth	.4	.4
−1.2	1.0	.7	.8	1.1	2.7		.9	1.0
.7	.5	.7	.9	1.1	1.1		.8	.8
3.1	1.3	1.4	1.8	2.5	2.4	Debt/Worth	1.7	1.7
−4.4	4.1	3.6	3.6	5.5	14.5		3.8	4.0
150.2	54.7	44.1	41.8	52.7	51.3	% Profit Before Taxes/Tangible	52.1	46.7
(153) 60.5	(404) 25.7	(434) 22.3	(174) 21.3	(27) 25.3	(27) 29.4	Net Worth	(1073) 25.6	(1030) 21.6
10.3	4.0	6.8	9.5	17.5	17.2		6.6	4.0
67.9	24.4	17.3	12.7	13.2	11.7	% Profit Before Taxes/Total	18.8	17.5
16.9	9.9	7.6	6.4	8.6	8.3	Assets	8.8	7.1
−2.9	1.1	1.7	2.7	3.4	3.6		1.6	.3
115.5	54.0	50.1	42.9	51.6	46.3		41.5	42.0
34.3	26.2	22.5	19.0	22.9	23.6	Sales/Net Fixed Assets	21.4	20.6
14.1	12.5	12.7	10.6	16.3	11.2		10.9	10.8
12.3	3.6	3.0	2.6	2.8	2.6		3.4	3.5
5.9	2.7	2.4	2.1	2.2	1.8	Sales/Total Assets	2.5	2.6
3.3	2.1	1.8	1.7	1.5	1.2		1.9	2.0
.8	.9	.9	1.0	.9	.7		1.0	.9
(145) 2.1	(338) 1.6	(407) 1.6	(172) 1.7	(25) 1.6	(21) 1.4	% Depr., Dep., Amort./Sales	(994) 1.7	(987) 1.8
3.7	2.6	2.6	2.5	1.9	1.9		2.6	2.8
5.2	4.8	2.3	2.8			% Officers', Directors',	4.9	4.3
(138) 10.2	(190) 7.8	(136) 5.3	(26) 7.5			Owners' Comp/Sales	(395) 8.9	(386) 8.7
17.5	13.5	14.1	17.4				16.1	15.3
399312M	1554882M	5538758M	8335395M	4740024M	14080926M	Net Sales ($)	22650419M	27095055M
56932M	519128M	2118027M	3613349M	2134024M	5648125M	Total Assets ($)	9777165M	11072024M

M = $ thousand   MM = $ million
See Pages 11 through 21 for Explanation of Ratios and Data

Comparative Historical Data				Current Data Sorted By Sales					
226	218	227	**Type of Statement** Unqualified	4	11	12	33	49	118
327	344	342	Reviewed	13	50	46	107	88	38
242	313	230	Compiled	22	79	51	51	22	5
139	169	199	Tax Returns	41	93	32	23	5	5
364	408	406	Other	32	99	64	71	65	75
4/1/02-3/31/03 ALL	4/1/03-3/31/04 ALL	4/1/04-3/31/05 ALL		180 (4/1-9/30/04) 0-1MM	1-3MM	3-5MM	1224 (10/1/04-3/31/05) 5-10MM	10-25MM	25MM & OVER
1298	1452	1404	**NUMBER OF STATEMENTS**	112	332	205	285	229	241
%	%	%	**ASSETS**	%	%	%	%	%	%
11.5	12.0	11.8	Cash & Equivalents	18.9	13.5	12.1	10.6	9.9	9.1
46.6	46.0	47.0	Trade Receivables (net)	28.6	44.5	50.6	50.8	51.4	47.4
3.7	3.7	3.9	Inventory	3.1	3.4	3.7	5.2	3.9	3.5
7.5	8.1	7.2	All Other Current	3.3	4.1	5.8	7.2	9.2	12.4
69.3	69.8	69.9	Total Current	54.0	65.4	72.3	73.8	74.4	72.4
19.7	19.5	18.3	Fixed Assets (net)	34.0	21.3	16.9	15.3	15.4	14.2
2.6	2.6	2.9	Intangibles (net)	1.5	1.9	2.5	2.7	2.9	5.4
8.4	8.1	9.0	All Other Non-Current	10.6	11.4	8.3	8.2	7.3	7.9
100.0	100.0	100.0	Total	100.0	100.0	100.0	100.0	100.0	100.0
			LIABILITIES						
14.2	15.7	15.4	Notes Payable-Short Term	27.4	21.1	14.1	12.7	11.3	10.1
3.5	4.0	3.9	Cur. Mat.-L/T/D	5.2	5.7	3.0	3.1	3.0	3.4
11.0	10.9	11.4	Trade Payables	9.0	10.4	9.5	11.9	13.6	13.1
2.0	1.8	1.7	Income Taxes Payable	.5	.6	.9	2.0	2.9	3.2
17.1	16.6	16.6	All Other Current	17.6	17.8	12.0	15.2	15.9	20.4
47.9	48.9	49.0	Total Current	59.7	55.5	39.5	44.9	46.7	50.2
11.4	11.0	12.7	Long-Term Debt	25.8	17.2	9.8	9.4	9.8	9.5
1.6	1.7	1.3	Deferred Taxes	.0	1.2	1.1	1.6	1.4	1.9
4.9	5.5	5.2	All Other Non-Current	7.6	7.2	4.3	3.2	3.3	6.2
34.2	32.8	31.8	Net Worth	6.9	19.0	45.3	40.8	38.8	32.2
100.0	100.0	100.0	Total Liabilities & Net Worth	100.0	100.0	100.0	100.0	100.0	100.0
			INCOME DATA						
100.0	100.0	100.0	Net Sales	100.0	100.0	100.0	100.0	100.0	100.0
			Gross Profit						
96.1	95.6	94.3	Operating Expenses	88.1	94.9	93.7	95.3	95.1	95.2
3.9	4.4	5.7	Operating Profit	11.9	5.1	6.3	4.7	4.9	4.8
.8	.9	1.0	All Other Expenses (net)	3.8	.7	.8	.6	.9	.8
3.1	3.6	4.7	Profit Before Taxes	8.1	4.5	5.5	4.1	4.0	3.9
			RATIOS						
2.6	2.7	2.7		3.0	3.2	3.9	2.6	2.2	2.2
1.6	1.6	1.6	Current	1.0	1.6	2.2	1.7	1.6	1.5
1.1	1.2	1.1		.4	.9	1.3	1.2	1.2	1.2
2.2	2.2	2.4		2.8	2.9	3.1	2.3	1.8	1.7
1.3	1.3	(1403) 1.3	Quick	.9	1.5	(204) 1.8	1.4	1.3	1.2
.9	.9	.9		.3	.8	1.1	.9	1.0	.9
42 8.7	41 9.0	43 8.4		0 UND	23 16.2	48 7.7	47 7.7	53 6.9	55 6.7
69 5.3	67 5.4	70 5.2	Sales/Receivables	26 14.2	65 5.6	74 5.0	71 5.1	73 5.0	72 5.1
96 3.8	94 3.9	97 3.7		79 4.6	98 3.7	108 3.4	101 3.6	102 3.6	92 4.0
			Cost of Sales/Inventory						
			Cost of Sales/Payables						
5.5	5.4	5.4		6.8	5.7	4.2	5.0	5.7	5.8
10.5	10.1	9.9	Sales/Working Capital	−549.5	12.0	7.5	9.0	9.5	9.5
42.0	41.2	39.0		−8.8	−90.2	20.7	21.6	22.7	24.3
15.8	19.7	22.9		15.7	19.4	46.5	28.7	22.4	23.3
(1127) 4.7	(1221) 5.5	(1176) 7.1	EBIT/Interest	(69) 3.2	(280) 5.4	(169) 9.6	(245) 7.3	(200) 7.3	(213) 8.7
.8	1.2	1.7		−.8	.5	2.2	1.5	2.7	3.9
5.8	6.0	7.5			2.9	7.2	8.6	5.6	9.5
(378) 2.2	(382) 2.4	(338) 2.9	Net Profit + Depr., Dep., Amort./Cur. Mat. L/T/D		(41) 1.1	(36) 1.5	(74) 2.9	(77) 2.4	(110) 4.4
1.0	1.1	1.1			.0	.5	1.1	1.2	2.2
.2	.2	.1		.2	.1	.1	.1	.2	.2
.4	.4	.3	Fixed/Worth	1.5	.4	.2	.3	.3	.3
1.1	1.1	1.1		UND	2.3	.8	.7	.8	.8
.7	.7	.7		.8	.6	.4	.7	.8	1.0
1.6	1.6	1.6	Debt/Worth	2.7	1.6	.9	1.4	1.5	2.1
4.3	4.4	5.0		−15.6	15.1	3.5	4.2	3.6	4.2
45.6	47.7	53.2		100.9	68.8	47.5	45.2	47.9	44.2
(1161) 19.0	(1266) 20.3	(1219) 25.2	% Profit Before Taxes/Tangible Net Worth	(80) 37.6	(265) 25.8	(185) 26.0	(261) 21.9	(210) 26.6	(218) 24.2
2.5	3.1	6.6		6.6	1.6	7.3	6.3	7.9	12.6
17.2	18.7	20.7		31.6	31.4	25.2	18.0	18.4	14.2
6.2	6.8	8.3	% Profit Before Taxes/Total Assets	8.1	8.3	12.8	8.0	7.9	7.2
−.1	.4	1.4		−2.2	−1.2	2.3	1.1	2.1	3.9
43.8	52.8	54.0		54.5	57.5	62.8	52.6	51.3	52.0
20.4	22.8	24.1	Sales/Net Fixed Assets	15.5	23.3	30.3	25.2	21.7	24.4
11.4	11.4	12.4		5.0	11.6	13.7	13.5	12.7	13.6
3.6	3.8	3.6		5.7	4.4	3.7	3.5	3.3	3.1
2.6	2.7	2.6	Sales/Total Assets	2.6	2.8	2.7	2.6	2.5	2.4
2.0	1.9	1.9		1.0	2.1	2.0	2.0	1.9	1.8
1.0	.9	.9		1.2	1.0	.8	.8	.9	.8
(1109) 1.8	(1178) 1.7	(1108) 1.6	% Depr., Dep., Amort./Sales	(74) 2.8	(238) 2.0	(153) 1.5	(239) 1.5	(197) 1.6	(207) 1.4
2.9	2.8	2.6		6.7	3.1	2.5	2.6	2.5	2.2
4.5	4.8	4.1		7.8	5.2	3.3	3.2	1.7	1.3
(480) 8.7	(503) 9.1	(498) 7.8	% Officers', Directors', Owners' Comp/Sales	(50) 14.4	(163) 8.7	(96) 6.9	(99) 6.3	(52) 4.1	(38) 7.5
15.7	15.7	15.0		21.5	14.7	12.5	14.3	13.3	17.4
32002741M	39316018M	34649297M	Net Sales ($)	63431M	648573M	801292M	2013435M	3597452M	27525114M
12962236M	14185757M	14089585M	Total Assets ($)	55231M	258308M	330530M	817859M	1768254M	10859403M

M = $ thousand   MM = $ million
See Pages 11 through 21 for Explanation of Ratios and Data

Current Data Sorted By Assets							Comparative Historical Data	
						Type of Statement		
	1	5	1			Unqualified	5	5
1	6	6				Reviewed	7	6
1	9	4	1			Compiled	11	20
16	5	2				Tax Returns	10	13
4	13	6	3			Other	18	24
	9 (4/1-9/30/04)		75 (10/1/04-3/31/05)				4/1/00-3/31/01	4/1/01-3/31/02
0-500M	500M-2MM	2-10MM	10-50MM	50-100MM	100-250MM		ALL	ALL
22	34	23	5			NUMBER OF STATEMENTS	51	68
%	%	%	%	%	%	**ASSETS**	%	%
24.9	11.6	11.2		DATA NOT AVAILABLE	DATA NOT AVAILABLE	Cash & Equivalents	13.3	10.3
6.6	44.7	38.7				Trade Receivables (net)	34.9	32.7
.0	2.6	3.3				Inventory	3.1	4.9
1.4	3.6	9.2				All Other Current	4.9	5.2
32.9	62.6	62.4				Total Current	56.2	53.1
43.9	23.2	23.6				Fixed Assets (net)	30.3	34.4
6.6	2.0	1.0				Intangibles (net)	3.6	3.5
16.6	12.2	13.0				All Other Non-Current	9.9	9.0
100.0	100.0	100.0				Total	100.0	100.0
						LIABILITIES		
42.7	12.5	11.9				Notes Payable-Short Term	9.1	10.9
8.2	3.4	4.0				Cur. Mat.-L/T/D	7.7	8.6
1.3	5.3	6.2				Trade Payables	8.6	10.9
.1	1.9	3.8				Income Taxes Payable	.9	.7
21.5	8.7	9.5				All Other Current	11.3	12.0
73.8	31.8	35.4				Total Current	37.6	43.0
52.8	19.5	8.2				Long-Term Debt	21.2	29.8
.0	1.0	1.6				Deferred Taxes	1.1	.6
5.1	4.2	3.8				All Other Non-Current	3.8	2.9
-31.5	43.4	51.1				Net Worth	36.3	23.7
100.0	100.0	100.0				Total Liabilities & Net Worth	100.0	100.0
						INCOME DATA		
100.0	100.0	100.0				Net Sales	100.0	100.0
						Gross Profit		
94.0	94.4	91.2				Operating Expenses	92.7	95.2
6.0	5.6	8.8				Operating Profit	7.3	4.8
1.9	.8	.0				All Other Expenses (net)	1.5	2.0
4.1	4.9	8.8				Profit Before Taxes	5.8	2.8
						RATIOS		
3.2	3.6	4.1					3.3	2.9
.6	2.3	1.8				Current	1.9	1.3
.1	1.3	1.1					1.0	.9
2.7	3.4	2.8					2.5	2.1
.6	1.8	1.3				Quick	1.4	1.1
.1	1.2	.9					.9	.7
0 UND	41 9.0	56 6.5					23 15.8	9 40.4
0 UND	66 5.5	73 5.0				Sales/Receivables	68 5.3	57 6.4
0 977.1	82 4.4	103 3.5					94 3.9	86 4.3
						Cost of Sales/Inventory		
						Cost of Sales/Payables		
21.4	5.0	5.0					4.8	6.7
-158.4	8.3	7.4				Sales/Working Capital	11.4	22.6
-18.3	20.8	61.9					-614.2	-140.1
7.8	41.6	62.1					15.1	6.0
(19) 1.5	(32) 6.7	(21) 13.4				EBIT/Interest	(47) 4.7	(64) 2.4
-1.0	1.1	2.1					1.7	.0
							8.0	3.8
						Net Profit + Depr., Dep., Amort./Cur. Mat. L/T/D	(13) 1.6	(12) 1.8
							.6	.2
.7	.1	.2					.4	.4
NM	.7	.5				Fixed/Worth	.8	1.3
-.5	1.5	1.0					2.4	-12.2
.8	.4	.3					.5	.8
NM	1.0	1.1				Debt/Worth	1.6	2.4
-2.0	3.4	2.1					5.3	-52.1
207.8	49.0	56.1					82.1	73.1
(11) 72.1	(29) 26.2	(21) 20.5				% Profit Before Taxes/Tangible Net Worth	(43) 28.9	(50) 15.8
30.3	1.0	5.2					11.6	-2.0
37.9	26.1	36.5					24.6	20.3
8.1	12.0	7.1				% Profit Before Taxes/Total Assets	8.4	4.7
-16.4	1.1	1.2					2.6	-1.8
69.5	49.9	24.7					19.6	17.5
25.9	19.6	13.1				Sales/Net Fixed Assets	10.6	11.3
11.2	5.9	6.7					6.4	5.1
17.3	3.2	2.9					4.1	3.6
7.6	2.4	2.0				Sales/Total Assets	2.1	2.3
3.8	2.1	1.7					1.4	1.8
1.5	1.6	1.6					2.1	1.9
(12) 3.8	(25) 2.6	(19) 2.5				% Depr., Dep., Amort./Sales	(47) 3.3	(54) 3.0
5.8	4.3	3.2					6.7	4.9
8.5	6.5						6.5	5.3
(16) 15.2	(20) 9.3					% Officers', Directors', Owners' Comp/Sales	(27) 11.7	(36) 12.1
21.9	12.7						20.8	14.2
29566M	103913M	260880M	167122M			Net Sales ($)	1197469M	1617520M
3312M	37714M	100800M	104784M			Total Assets ($)	565988M	791060M

M = $thousand MM = $million

See Pages 11 through 21 for Explanation of Ratios and Data

PROFESSIONAL SERVICES—Surveying and Mapping (except Geophysical) Services NAICS 541370 (SIC 7389, 8713)

Comparative Historical Data				Current Data Sorted By Sales					
5	4	7	**Type of Statement** Unqualified		1	2	2	1	1
12	6	13	Reviewed		5	3	2	3	
16	20	15	Compiled	1	4	3	3	2	2
20	17	23	Tax Returns	10	8	2	2		1
25	35	26	Other	2	10	6	2	3	3
4/1/02-3/31/03 ALL	4/1/03-3/31/04 ALL	4/1/04-3/31/05 ALL		9 (4/1-9/30/04) 0-1MM	1-3MM	3-5MM	75 (10/1/04-3/31/05) 5-10MM	10-25MM	25MM & OVER
78	82	84	**NUMBER OF STATEMENTS**	13	28	16	11	9	7
%	%	%	**ASSETS**	%	%	%.	%	%	%
14.3	16.9	14.5	Cash & Equivalents	29.2	11.6	13.1	10.6		
33.2	33.1	32.5	Trade Receivables (net)	6.9	34.9	35.4	46.7		
2.3	2.8	2.0	Inventory	.0	1.7	2.6	2.2		
4.5	5.6	5.1	All Other Current	.8	3.8	2.3	14.2		
54.4	58.5	54.1	Total Current	37.0	52.0	53.5	73.7		
35.5	29.7	29.0	Fixed Assets (net)	43.0	31.0	28.1	14.5		
2.8	3.7	3.8	Intangibles (net)	3.4	4.1	3.5	.3		
7.4	8.2	13.1	All Other Non-Current	16.6	12.9	14.9	11.5		
100.0	100.0	100.0	Total	100.0	100.0	100.0	100.0		
			LIABILITIES						
10.7	17.3	20.0	Notes Payable-Short Term	16.2	31.0	19.9	7.3		
5.5	4.9	4.7	Cur. Mat.-L/T/D	2.8	6.3	5.2	4.5		
5.1	10.2	4.9	Trade Payables	.8	4.9	4.0	8.1		
1.5	1.2	1.8	Income Taxes Payable	.0	2.3	1.5	2.5		
9.9	11.3	12.1	All Other Current	21.8	11.6	10.5	6.0		
32.7	44.9	43.5	Total Current	41.6	56.1	41.1	28.4		
22.8	19.1	25.2	Long-Term Debt	51.2	28.9	23.0	8.1		
.4	.7	.9	Deferred Taxes	.0	.5	.3	2.3		
6.0	4.5	4.5	All Other Non-Current	1.0	8.1	.9	1.6		
38.1	30.8	26.0	Net Worth	6.4	6.3	34.7	59.6		
100.0	100.0	100.0	Total Liabilities & Net Worth	100.0	100.0	100.0	100.0		
			INCOME DATA						
100.0	100.0	100.0	Net Sales	100.0	100.0	100.0	100.0		
			Gross Profit						
93.2	92.0	93.3	Operating Expenses	89.8	97.3	90.3	91.7		
6.8	8.0	6.7	Operating Profit	10.2	2.7	9.7	8.3		
.9	1.3	.9	All Other Expenses (net)	2.5	1.0	.3	.7		
5.9	6.7	5.9	Profit Before Taxes	7.8	1.8	9.3	7.5		
			RATIOS						
4.5	5.3	3.6	Current	3.6	3.2	2.9	7.8		
1.9	2.1	1.8		1.8	1.3	1.4	3.2		
1.0	.9	1.0		.4	.6	1.0	1.4		
4.4	4.0	2.9	Quick	3.4	2.9	2.5	7.8		
1.5	(81) 1.7	1.5		1.8	1.3	1.4	2.3		
.8	.9	.7		.4	.5	.8	1.4		
0 UND	0 UND	0 UND	Sales/Receivables	0 UND	0 753.6	0 UND	58 6.3		
62 5.9	58 6.3	56 6.5		0 UND	52 7.0	72 5.0	65 5.6		
85 4.3	96 3.8	80 4.6		1 461.8	73 5.0	83 4.4	84 4.4		
			Cost of Sales/Inventory						
			Cost of Sales/Payables						
5.4	4.8	5.4	Sales/Working Capital	7.4	5.6	5.2	3.2		
10.6	10.8	12.3		53.5	19.3	11.2	6.8		
-87.9	-570.4	NM		-104.9	-18.2	227.6	16.6		
16.5	25.6	28.2	EBIT/Interest	8.7	14.6	47.9			
(73) 4.4	(71) 5.6	(77) 4.7		(10) 2.3	(27) 2.7	11.8			
.6	.6	1.0		-1.0	.1	1.1			
5.9	10.9	6.3	Net Profit + Depr., Dep., Amort./Cur. Mat. L/T/D						
(19) 2.8	(13) 2.1	(12) 2.0							
1.1	1.4	1.0							
.3	.2	.2	Fixed/Worth	.4	.4	.1	.1		
.9	.6	.7		1.5	1.3	.6	.3		
2.2	1.7	4.2		-1.4	-2.7	1.1	.5		
.6	.5	.4	Debt/Worth	.4	.7	.5	.2		
1.6	1.6	1.5		2.5	2.8	.9	.5		
5.2	4.1	30.8		-2.7	-5.4	1.9	3.5		
77.4	84.8	65.8	% Profit Before Taxes/Tangible Net Worth		45.9	73.3	48.8		
(70) 21.4	(71) 33.7	(65) 26.2			(18) 24.4	(14) 27.4	20.5		
4.7	5.8	6.4			-5.7	8.5	5.0		
33.8	34.7	28.4	% Profit Before Taxes/Total Assets	82.5	18.1	40.6	46.4		
9.7	10.5	10.1		15.4	9.0	14.7	17.1		
-.1	.9	.3		-6.3	-2.1	-.3	1.1		
17.4	26.7	39.5	Sales/Net Fixed Assets	45.5	49.8	46.6	36.2		
10.6	15.9	15.7		16.5	13.6	19.6	16.0		
4.8	7.5	6.8		10.9	5.8	5.5	11.7		
4.0	4.4	4.5	Sales/Total Assets	13.5	4.4	3.7	3.4		
2.5	2.8	2.6		5.0	2.5	2.4	2.6		
1.6	1.9	2.0		3.4	2.1	1.7	1.8		
2.5	2.1	1.6	% Depr., Dep., Amort./Sales	1.4	2.3	1.3			
(68) 3.8	(62) 3.2	(60) 2.6		(10) 2.5	(18) 3.2	(11) 2.1			
6.2	5.7	4.9		5.1	6.4	4.5			
7.7	7.4	6.7	% Officers', Directors', Owners' Comp/Sales		6.6				
(33) 13.1	(38) 11.2	(44) 10.3			(18) 10.2				
16.1	15.0	15.8			11.6				
509371M	1523279M	561481M	Net Sales ($)	7429M	56206M	62539M	74425M	115390M	245492M
248521M	667436M	246610M	Total Assets ($)	1395M	20327M	27776M	30472M	54183M	112457M

M = $ thousand   MM = $ million
See Pages 11 through 21 for Explanation of Ratios and Data

Current Data Sorted By Assets   Comparative Historical Data

0-500M	500M-2MM	2-10MM	10-50MM	50-100MM	100-250MM	Type of Statement	4/1/00-3/31/01 ALL	4/1/01-3/31/02 ALL
	1	11	13	1	4	Unqualified	15	20
1	13	30	5			Reviewed	42	36
5	17	8	3			Compiled	53	54
9	10	3				Tax Returns	15	14
7	18	20	11		1	Other	31	55
42 (4/1-9/30/04)			146 (10/1/04-3/31/05)					
22	59	72	29	1	5	NUMBER OF STATEMENTS	156	179
%	%	%	%	%	%	ASSETS	%	%
7.9	12.3	12.2	12.5			Cash & Equivalents	10.1	7.8
25.2	38.8	36.8	34.5			Trade Receivables (net)	38.5	36.5
6.3	3.9	4.4	2.2			Inventory	2.9	3.9
1.1	4.2	3.0	7.0			All Other Current	3.1	2.8
40.4	59.1	56.3	56.2			Total Current	54.6	51.0
46.1	34.0	32.7	30.3			Fixed Assets (net)	35.7	37.8
5.7	3.0	3.9	6.4			Intangibles (net)	3.9	5.2
7.7	3.9	7.1	7.1			All Other Non-Current	5.9	5.9
100.0	100.0	100.0	100.0			Total	100.0	100.0
						LIABILITIES		
20.0	7.4	7.3	4.4			Notes Payable-Short Term	9.7	10.3
12.4	4.0	4.2	3.8			Cur. Mat.-L/T/D	5.3	6.2
12.1	8.5	7.7	8.3			Trade Payables	9.4	9.4
.3	.3	.2	1.1			Income Taxes Payable	.8	.6
6.5	12.9	12.2	14.9			All Other Current	13.1	11.0
51.3	33.1	31.6	32.6			Total Current	38.2	37.4
35.0	21.4	17.3	14.7			Long-Term Debt	19.5	21.6
.5	1.6	1.0	1.4			Deferred Taxes	1.3	1.2
11.0	8.5	5.0	5.9			All Other Non-Current	4.1	3.8
2.2	35.4	45.2	45.5			Net Worth	36.9	36.0
100.0	100.0	100.0	100.0			Total Liabilities & Net Worth	100.0	100.0
						INCOME DATA		
100.0	100.0	100.0	100.0			Net Sales	100.0	100.0
						Gross Profit		
92.7	91.3	91.0	92.4			Operating Expenses	94.7	93.6
7.3	8.7	9.0	7.6			Operating Profit	5.3	6.4
3.4	3.1	1.5	1.5			All Other Expenses (net)	1.3	1.9
4.0	5.6	7.5	6.1			Profit Before Taxes	4.0	4.4
						RATIOS		
1.8	4.5	3.0	3.3			Current	2.3	2.4
.9	1.8	1.8	1.6				1.5	1.5
.3	1.2	1.3	1.1				1.1	1.0
1.8	3.4	3.0	3.0			Quick	2.1	2.2
(21) 1.0	1.4	1.7	1.3				1.3	1.3
.3	.9	1.2	.7				.9	.8
0 UND	39 9.5	51 7.1	53 6.9			Sales/Receivables	45 8.2	43 8.4
30 12.0	58 6.3	61 6.0	73 5.0				62 5.9	60 6.1
49 7.4	76 4.8	84 4.4	85 4.3				82 4.4	81 4.5
						Cost of Sales/Inventory		
						Cost of Sales/Payables		
11.6	5.4	4.3	4.1			Sales/Working Capital	6.1	6.7
NM	11.8	9.6	8.3				13.3	15.6
-6.3	39.6	20.1	55.5				75.5	-143.9
9.7	19.2	20.5	22.7			EBIT/Interest	8.1	6.2
(18) 2.1	(54) 4.9	(63) 6.5	(28) 8.2				(143) 3.0	(168) 2.9
-2.9	.6	2.5	1.9				.8	1.2
		7.9	6.7			Net Profit + Depr., Dep., Amort./Cur. Mat. L /T/D	4.6	3.6
	(28) 3.6	(16) 3.2					(44) 2.3	(57) 2.2
	1.9	1.7					1.5	1.2
.9	.4	.4	.3			Fixed/Worth	.5	.5
3.3	.8	.6	1.0				.9	1.0
-3.7	2.2	1.4	1.6				2.1	2.7
1.7	.6	.7	.7			Debt/Worth	.8	.9
8.6	1.2	1.4	1.8				1.6	1.8
-9.7	3.8	3.5	2.6				3.7	5.1
121.4	47.2	55.1	39.0			% Profit Before Taxes/Tangible Net Worth	42.7	44.1
(14) 20.1	(52) 22.9	(70) 22.0	(28) 23.7				(137) 19.8	(155) 19.0
-25.2	.4	7.7	14.6				.8	4.6
30.0	21.9	18.6	14.2			% Profit Before Taxes/Total Assets	16.1	15.0
3.8	8.3	8.7	8.9				7.0	6.8
-25.5	-.8	2.9	2.8				-.2	.6
15.4	16.5	13.3	12.5			Sales/Net Fixed Assets	15.3	12.4
6.4	8.3	6.6	6.8				7.1	6.9
3.2	4.6	3.3	3.4				4.3	3.5
4.6	3.1	2.7	2.5			Sales/Total Assets	3.0	2.9
2.7	2.4	1.9	1.6				2.2	2.1
2.0	1.7	1.4	1.0				1.6	1.5
3.1	1.7	2.1	2.4			% Depr., Dep., Amort./Sales	1.7	2.2
(16) 5.1	(52) 3.7	(66) 3.8	(25) 3.5				(143) 4.0	(162) 4.1
9.5	5.3	6.0	6.5				6.3	6.2
3.8	2.5	3.6				% Officers', Directors', Owners' Comp/Sales	4.0	3.2
(12) 7.2	(24) 5.7	(23) 6.2					(63) 7.8	(74) 7.7
16.1	9.9	8.3					12.7	12.6
18111M	166684M	635886M	907193M	69809M	926824M	Net Sales ($)	1993565M	1911441M
5974M	69026M	331295M	533031M	77518M	690394M	Total Assets ($)	1198663M	1356049M

Comparative Historical Data				Current Data Sorted By Sales					
			Type of Statement						
26	23	30	Unqualified		2	1	4	11	12
45	43	49	Reviewed	1	12	6	12	15	3
28	40	30	Compiled	5	7	12	3	3	
16	29	22	Tax Returns	7	8	6	1		
52	51	57	Other	8	10	7	17	7	8
4/1/02-3/31/03	4/1/03-3/31/04	4/1/04-3/31/05		42 (4/1-9/30/04)			146 (10/1/04-3/31/05)		
ALL	ALL	ALL		0-1MM	1-3MM	3-5MM	5-10MM	10-25MM	25MM & OVER
167	186	188	**NUMBER OF STATEMENTS**	21	39	32	37	36	23
%	%	%	**ASSETS**	%	%	%	%	%	%
10.2	11.6	11.9	Cash & Equivalents	6.1	14.9	12.7	12.1	12.4	9.6
36.7	36.3	35.3	Trade Receivables (net)	22.6	32.1	40.7	37.5	38.4	35.9
2.4	3.9	4.1	Inventory	4.0	3.9	3.9	5.9	3.7	2.4
4.1	3.8	3.8	All Other Current	.8	3.8	5.0	2.2	3.6	7.4
53.4	55.5	55.0	Total Current	33.6	54.7	62.4	57.6	58.1	55.3
36.9	33.8	33.8	Fixed Assets (net)	57.2	33.2	32.3	30.5	29.4	27.7
4.2	4.7	5.1	Intangibles (net)	3.1	5.1	1.5	6.8	4.2	10.6
5.5	6.0	6.1	All Other Non-Current	6.0	7.0	3.8	5.1	8.2	6.4
100.0	100.0	100.0	Total	100.0	100.0	100.0	100.0	100.0	100.0
			LIABILITIES						
9.4	8.5	8.2	Notes Payable-Short Term	17.5	7.8	6.8	8.6	6.1	5.5
6.0	4.9	5.0	Cur. Mat.-L/T/D	12.5	4.7	3.7	3.6	4.6	3.1
8.5	8.4	8.5	Trade Payables	9.8	6.5	8.9	8.4	8.9	10.2
.6	.6	.4	Income Taxes Payable	.0	.3	.4	.1	.4	1.2
10.1	11.8	12.3	All Other Current	6.2	13.7	9.9	10.1	15.6	16.8
34.7	34.2	34.4	Total Current	46.1	32.9	29.7	30.8	35.6	36.8
21.3	21.1	20.1	Long-Term Debt	40.2	25.2	14.3	18.3	14.9	11.9
1.1	1.3	1.3	Deferred Taxes	.5	1.5	1.3	1.3	1.0	1.8
4.3	6.7	7.0	All Other Non-Current	7.6	11.8	8.2	5.8	1.9	6.5
38.6	36.8	37.3	Net Worth	5.5	28.5	46.5	43.9	46.5	43.0
100.0	100.0	100.0	Total Liabilities & Net Worth	100.0	100.0	100.0	100.0	100.0	100.0
			INCOME DATA						
100.0	100.0	100.0	Net Sales	100.0	100.0	100.0	100.0	100.0	100.0
			Gross Profit						
92.4	90.9	91.4	Operating Expenses	84.6	89.5	95.1	93.0	92.1	91.7
7.6	9.1	8.6	Operating Profit	15.4	10.5	4.9	7.0	7.9	8.3
1.6	2.3	2.2	All Other Expenses (net)	8.8	2.4	.9	1.3	.7	1.3
5.9	6.8	6.4	Profit Before Taxes	6.6	8.1	4.0	5.7	7.2	7.0
			RATIOS						
2.7	2.9	3.2		2.0	5.1	4.3	3.4	2.3	2.4
1.6	1.6	1.6	Current	.6	1.7	2.3	1.7	1.5	1.3
1.1	1.1	1.1		.2	1.1	1.3	1.3	1.2	1.0
2.3	2.5	2.7		1.9	5.1	3.4	3.4	2.1	1.6
1.4	1.5	(187) 1.4	Quick	(20) .6	1.5	2.0	1.3	1.4	1.2
.9	.9	.9		.2	.9	1.2	.9	1.1	.7
44 8.3	41 9.0	40 9.1		0 UND	34 10.6	40 9.2	52 7.0	50 7.3	51 7.1
68 5.4	60 6.1	60 6.1	Sales/Receivables	31 11.8	57 6.4	63 5.8	60 6.1	60 6.1	73 5.0
87 4.2	78 4.7	79 4.6		62 5.9	76 4.8	78 4.7	84 4.3	85 4.3	82 4.4
			Cost of Sales/Inventory						
			Cost of Sales/Payables						
5.3	5.4	5.3		9.0	3.9	4.5	5.5	5.5	5.2
12.1	11.5	11.3	Sales/Working Capital	-9.7	12.9	7.5	10.1	12.0	17.0
55.6	55.6	48.6		-3.2	112.8	19.2	22.2	20.5	-279.3
11.9	13.8	17.6		4.1	17.3	17.6	19.0	30.2	14.5
(153) 4.0	(161) 3.9	(167) 4.9	EBIT/Interest	(14) 1.4	(34) 4.4	(30) 5.4	(33) 4.3	(35) 10.8	(21) 7.5
1.5	1.4	1.2		-4.2	.6	.2	.9	3.8	1.7
6.2	7.6	7.8						8.9	7.6
(61) 2.5	(56) 2.4	(56) 3.3	Net Profit + Depr., Dep., Amort./Cur. Mat. L/T/D					(21) 3.5	(13) 2.2
1.4	1.6	1.7						1.7	1.5
.4	.4	.4		1.7	.4	.4	.4	.4	.3
1.0	.9	.9	Fixed/Worth	9.7	1.0	.6	.6	.9	1.1
2.0	2.2	1.9		-20.2	2.0	1.3	1.7	1.3	1.7
.7	.7	.7		1.7	.6	.5	.7	.6	1.1
1.6	1.8	1.7	Debt/Worth	11.5	1.6	.8	1.6	1.5	2.4
4.4	4.0	4.1		-28.9	3.8	4.1	3.9	2.4	3.0
51.1	51.3	51.0		39.1	84.8	28.2	47.9	65.4	58.1
(149) 21.4	(167) 25.0	(168) 22.5	% Profit Before Taxes/Tangible Net Worth	(15) 19.0	(33) 20.0	(29) 18.2	(35) 23.5	(35) 25.0	(21) 33.8
5.8	3.9	6.7		-9.8	.7	1.1	11.1	14.9	18.2
19.7	20.7	19.2		11.4	30.0	18.9	19.6	21.7	19.0
7.4	8.4	8.4	% Profit Before Taxes/Total Assets	1.4	9.2	6.5	7.6	11.0	9.1
1.3	1.1	1.1		-9.0	-1.6	-1.1	1.7	6.1	1.4
11.0	14.8	14.7		10.7	15.7	16.9	19.1	13.7	13.6
6.6	7.6	7.2	Sales/Net Fixed Assets	5.0	6.9	8.1	8.4	6.5	7.6
3.4	3.9	3.8		1.4	3.9	3.8	4.6	3.9	3.9
2.8	3.0	2.8		3.7	2.7	3.1	3.1	2.9	2.6
2.0	2.1	2.1	Sales/Total Assets	2.0	2.2	2.5	2.2	1.9	1.7
1.5	1.5	1.4		.9	1.4	1.7	1.3	1.5	1.4
2.4	2.0	2.2		3.3	2.0	1.9	1.3	2.5	2.3
(153) 3.8	(165) 4.0	(165) 3.8	% Depr., Dep., Amort./Sales	(16) 7.3	(34) 4.4	(29) 3.7	(30) 3.7	(34) 3.6	(22) 3.3
7.2	6.6	6.1		16.7	6.2	5.5	5.5	5.8	4.6
3.2	3.5	3.5			3.7	2.4	2.4		
(56) 6.3	(69) 6.6	(63) 6.2	% Officers', Directors', Owners' Comp/Sales		(21) 6.9	(12) 6.2	(13) 6.4		
10.2	14.8	10.1			10.1	9.7	8.3		
2369848M	2266432M	2724507M	Net Sales ($)	11243M	74133M	121392M	249208M	551804M	1716727M
1554297M	1477116M	1707238M	Total Assets ($)	8791M	55054M	61369M	140807M	335579M	1105638M

M = $ thousand   MM = $ million
See Pages 11 through 21 for Explanation of Ratios and Data

Current Data Sorted By Assets   **Comparative Historical Data**

						Type of Statement	4/1/00-3/31/01 ALL	4/1/01-3/31/02 ALL
		1	1			Unqualified		
		2				Reviewed		
		1				Compiled		
3	2	3				Tax Returns		
8	3	3	1			Other		
4	7	1			1			
	6 (4/1-9/30/04)		31 (10/1/04-3/31/05)					
0-500M	500M-2MM	2-10MM	10-50MM	50-100MM	100-250MM			
15	12	8	1		1	**NUMBER OF STATEMENTS**		
%	%	%	%	%	%	**ASSETS**	%	%
15.0	9.8					Cash & Equivalents		
20.6	33.5					Trade Receivables (net)		
20.9	12.0					Inventory		
1.9	5.6					All Other Current		
58.4	61.0					Total Current		
26.7	20.6					Fixed Assets (net)		
.3	9.1					Intangibles (net)		
14.6	9.4					All Other Non-Current		
100.0	100.0					Total		
						LIABILITIES		
42.8	7.2					Notes Payable-Short Term		
.3	2.6					Cur. Mat.-L/T/D		
14.4	13.8					Trade Payables		
.4	.3					Income Taxes Payable		
44.7	19.7					All Other Current		
102.7	43.7					Total Current		
7.3	19.5					Long-Term Debt		
.0	.0					Deferred Taxes		
14.6	4.4					All Other Non-Current		
−24.6	32.4					Net Worth		
100.0	100.0					Total Liabilities & Net Worth		
						INCOME DATA		
100.0	100.0					Net Sales		
						Gross Profit		
97.5	92.0					Operating Expenses		
2.5	8.0					Operating Profit		
.6	3.7					All Other Expenses (net)		
1.9	4.3					Profit Before Taxes		
						RATIOS		
1.0	2.1							
.6	1.4					Current		
.3	.7							
.9	1.9							
.4	.9					Quick		
.1	.4							
0 UND	17 21.1							
12 29.9	34 10.9					Sales/Receivables		
19 19.6	57 6.4							
						Cost of Sales/Inventory		
						Cost of Sales/Payables		
743.0	6.7							
−18.7	13.2					Sales/Working Capital		
−2.8	NM							
11.8								
(11) 1.0						EBIT/Interest		
−1.3								
						Net Profit + Depr., Dep., Amort./Cur. Mat. L /T/D		
.7	.1							
−2.0	.5					Fixed/Worth		
−.3	7.4							
5.3	.8							
−8.5	2.6					Debt/Worth		
−2.2	8.5							
	87.1							
(10)	25.8					% Profit Before Taxes/Tangible Net Worth		
	8.0							
18.5	20.9							
1.6	5.8					% Profit Before Taxes/Total Assets		
−7.0	1.1							
125.1	69.6							
11.2	33.6					Sales/Net Fixed Assets		
7.5	14.9							
6.0	3.4							
3.2	2.6					Sales/Total Assets		
2.1	1.8							
.6								
(10) 1.1						% Depr., Dep., Amort./Sales		
3.0								
4.4								
(10) 6.5						% Officers', Directors', Owners' Comp/Sales		
8.4								
13686M	34230M	68277M	50449M		1224495M	Net Sales ($)		
3455M	14102M	38311M	23962M		105357M	Total Assets ($)		

(Columns 2-10MM, 10-50MM, 50-100MM, 100-250MM show "DATA NOT AVAILABLE" for the ASSETS and LIABILITIES sections; the Comparative Historical Data columns also show "DATA NOT AVAILABLE.")

M = $ thousand   MM = $ million
See Pages 11 through 21 for Explanation of Ratios and Data

Comparative Historical Data   **Current Data Sorted By Sales**

Type of Statement	4/1/02-3/31/03 ALL	4/1/03-3/31/04 ALL	4/1/04-3/31/05 ALL	0-1MM	1-3MM	3-5MM	5-10MM	10-25MM	25MM & OVER
Unqualified		2	2					1	1
Reviewed	1	2	2				1	1	
Compiled	2	6	6		5		1		1
Tax Returns	4	13	15	6	4	2	2		
Other	5	12	12	4	2	6			
				6 (4/1-9/30/04)			31 (10/1/04-3/31/05)		
NUMBER OF STATEMENTS	12	35	37	10	11	8	4	2	2
ASSETS	%	%	%	%	%	%	%	%	%
Cash & Equivalents	32.2	20.1	14.7	9.4	15.0				
Trade Receivables (net)	25.3	20.4	22.4	17.5	26.4				
Inventory	23.0	18.5	22.2	17.0	23.0				
All Other Current	4.4	6.3	3.9	2.8	.0				
Total Current	84.9	65.4	63.2	46.7	64.4				
Fixed Assets (net)	12.0	17.3	21.9	43.4	11.3				
Intangibles (net)	.3	4.8	3.8	.6	9.2				
All Other Non-Current	2.8	12.5	11.2	9.4	15.1				
Total	100.0	100.0	100.0	100.0	100.0				
LIABILITIES									
Notes Payable-Short Term	2.2	11.3	20.7	56.4	12.1				
Cur. Mat.-L/T/D	.8	1.8	1.2	.7	2.7				
Trade Payables	15.8	15.7	15.6	7.2	19.5				
Income Taxes Payable	.0	.1	.3	.7	.2				
All Other Current	41.6	34.1	33.0	29.5	40.6				
Total Current	60.4	63.0	70.8	94.6	75.0				
Long-Term Debt	4.6	13.4	10.5	16.1	6.6				
Deferred Taxes	.0	.7	.2	.0	.0				
All Other Non-Current	.0	5.5	11.2	22.0	4.7				
Net Worth	34.9	17.5	7.3	-32.6	13.6				
Total Liabilities & Net Worth	100.0	100.0	100.0	100.0	100.0				
INCOME DATA									
Net Sales	100.0	100.0	100.0	100.0	100.0				
Gross Profit									
Operating Expenses	94.7	95.1	94.8	92.7	94.2				
Operating Profit	5.3	4.9	5.2	7.3	5.8				
All Other Expenses (net)	.1	.4	1.5	5.7	.2				
Profit Before Taxes	5.3	4.5	3.7	1.6	5.7				
RATIOS									
Current	2.5 / 1.6 / 1.0	1.5 / 1.1 / .8	1.8 / 1.2 / .5	.7 / .6 / .1	1.9 / 1.0 / .3				
Quick	2.3 / 1.0 / .4	1.0 / .6 / .3	1.0 / .6 / .2	.5 / .3 / .1	1.2 / .6 / .3				
Sales/Receivables	12 31.1 / 21 17.3 / 44 8.3	0 UND / 19 19.6 / 57 6.4	2 202.7 / 18 20.1 / 42 8.8	0 UND / 11 32.4 / 22 16.9	8 43.1 / 28 12.9 / 42 8.8				
Cost of Sales/Inventory									
Cost of Sales/Payables									
Sales/Working Capital	7.3 / 11.1 / NM	13.5 / 76.1 / -33.7	7.2 / 58.2 / -8.9	NM / -5.8 / -1.8	8.1 / -411.8 / -8.9				
EBIT/Interest		(28) 21.5 / 2.6 / -1.4	(25) 27.2 / 3.8 / .7						
Net Profit + Depr., Dep., Amort./Cur. Mat. L/T/D									
Fixed/Worth	.1 / .4 / 1.1	.3 / 1.3 / -2.4	.2 / 1.5 / -1.1	7.5 / -1.1 / -.3	.0 / .7 / -4.5				
Debt/Worth	.6 / 1.7 / 7.9	2.0 / 6.9 / -31.3	1.7 / 5.6 / -7.5	7.3 / -6.1 / -2.2	1.7 / 5.6 / -28.8				
% Profit Before Taxes/Tangible Net Worth	(11) 110.0 / 17.0 / -.3	(24) 131.4 / 41.0 / 2.1	(24) 83.7 / 23.2 / 7.3						
% Profit Before Taxes/Total Assets	36.3 / 7.5 / -.8	31.5 / 1.8 / -4.2	20.1 / 4.5 / .7	1.2 / -3.5 / -40.6	44.1 / 15.6 / 3.9				
Sales/Net Fixed Assets	180.0 / 41.4 / 11.0	90.7 / 32.8 / 13.8	53.8 / 24.9 / 9.0	11.1 / 7.9 / 2.6	UND / 32.0 / 28.4				
Sales/Total Assets	5.3 / 2.7 / 2.2	4.9 / 2.7 / 2.1	4.5 / 2.5 / 1.8	3.7 / 2.3 / 1.7	7.1 / 3.4 / 2.9				
% Depr., Dep., Amort./Sales	(11) .3 / 1.0 / 1.5	(24) .5 / 1.1 / 2.2	(26) .6 / 1.0 / 2.4						
% Officers', Directors', Owners' Comp/Sales		(23) 2.7 / 5.0 / 14.4	(23) 2.8 / 5.5 / 7.6						
Net Sales ($)	404830M	174727M	1391137M	5384M	18769M	33001M	27123M	31916M	1274944M
Total Assets ($)	85276M	81486M	185187M	3339M	5807M	15189M	16680M	14853M	129319M

M = $ thousand   MM = $ million
See Pages 11 through 21 for Explanation of Ratios and Data

Current Data Sorted By Assets   **Comparative Historical Data**

Type of Statement

0-500M	500M-2MM	2-10MM	10-50MM	50-100MM	100-250MM		4/1/00-3/31/01 ALL	4/1/01-3/31/02 ALL
	1	6	3		1	Unqualified	9	8
	11	19	1			Reviewed	30	21
8	18	10				Compiled	40	34
22	12	3				Tax Returns	34	23
14	23	20	7		1	Other	37	56
	33 (4/1-9/30/04)		147 (10/1/04-3/31/05)					
44	65	58	11		2	**NUMBER OF STATEMENTS**	150	142

0-500M %	500M-2MM %	2-10MM %	10-50MM %	50-100MM %	100-250MM %		%	%
						ASSETS		
20.5	9.0	12.8	18.3			Cash & Equivalents	9.9	10.0
23.9	37.7	31.7	26.4			Trade Receivables (net)	35.1	35.4
6.8	8.9	9.5	10.7			Inventory	9.9	9.9
.9	2.6	2.9	4.0			All Other Current	3.4	2.6
52.0	58.2	56.9	59.3			Total Current	58.4	57.8
34.3	30.7	33.4	25.7			Fixed Assets (net)	32.4	29.9
7.0	5.5	4.5	7.3			Intangibles (net)	3.0	4.7
6.7	5.6	5.2	7.7			All Other Non-Current	6.2	7.5
100.0	100.0	100.0	100.0			Total	100.0	100.0
						LIABILITIES		
34.7	12.6	8.9	9.4			Notes Payable-Short Term	12.7	13.0
15.0	6.1	5.0	2.5			Cur. Mat.-L/T/D	6.6	5.1
10.3	17.9	14.3	10.0			Trade Payables	16.6	15.3
.3	.9	.2	.2			Income Taxes Payable	.4	.3
20.9	13.6	11.8	17.2			All Other Current	12.8	11.5
81.3	51.0	40.2	39.1			Total Current	49.1	45.3
21.9	24.7	21.5	22.9			Long-Term Debt	20.5	17.7
.0	.3	.4	.3			Deferred Taxes	.6	.7
19.1	3.7	5.5	7.1			All Other Non-Current	4.8	3.5
−22.2	20.3	32.4	30.6			Net Worth	25.0	32.9
100.0	100.0	100.0	100.0			Total Liabilities & Net Worth	100.0	100.0
						INCOME DATA		
100.0	100.0	100.0	100.0			Net Sales	100.0	100.0
						Gross Profit		
94.5	93.9	93.7	93.2			Operating Expenses	94.8	96.8
5.5	6.1	6.3	6.8			Operating Profit	5.2	3.2
1.6	2.5	2.0	2.0			All Other Expenses (net)	1.4	1.4
3.9	3.7	4.3	4.8			Profit Before Taxes	3.8	1.8
						RATIOS		
1.7	1.9	2.2	2.4				2.3	2.5
1.0	1.1	1.4	1.4			Current	1.4	1.5
.3	.7	.9	1.2				1.0	.9
1.5	1.5	1.9	1.8				1.9	2.1
.8	.8	1.0	1.1			Quick	(149) 1.0	(141) 1.1
.3	.5	.7	.7				.7	.7
0 UND	29 12.6	33 11.0	43 8.6				30 12.3	29 12.6
16 22.3	46 7.9	45 8.2	56 6.6			Sales/Receivables	50 7.3	46 7.9
42 8.6	66 5.5	68 5.3	66 5.5				65 5.6	62 5.9
						Cost of Sales/Inventory		
						Cost of Sales/Payables		
12.1	10.6	6.2	7.0				7.9	7.2
UND	50.7	14.6	13.8			Sales/Working Capital	18.3	21.6
−14.4	−15.6	−57.3	27.3				−136.1	−55.4
14.8	13.4	8.5					8.0	11.8
(37) 5.6	(58) 3.2	(50) 3.1				EBIT/Interest	(133) 2.9	(121) 1.7
−1.3	1.2	.5					.7	−1.0
	6.8	4.4				Net Profit + Depr., Dep.,	5.1	5.4
	(10) 3.1	(14) 2.1				Amort./Cur. Mat. L /T/D	(38) 1.8	(31) 2.0
	1.0	1.3					.7	.7
.5	.3	.4	.5				.4	.3
12.5	1.3	1.1	1.2			Fixed/Worth	1.0	.8
−.5	NM	5.6	12.4				5.1	3.7
1.3	.7	.9	.7				.9	.5
12.0	4.8	2.5	2.6			Debt/Worth	2.4	2.4
−2.2	−400.7	9.8	45.3				13.9	13.8
263.8	78.4	42.6	54.5			% Profit Before Taxes/Tangible	62.3	47.4
(26) 53.5	(48) 47.8	(50) 15.0	(10) 35.0			Net Worth	(126) 22.6	(115) 12.9
5.1	11.8	−3.2	15.1				5.0	−14.2
39.7	28.6	11.9	14.3			% Profit Before Taxes/Total	18.4	13.1
9.2	4.5	3.1	7.8			Assets	6.5	2.7
−11.1	.5	−1.5	3.4				.1	−7.8
55.9	42.2	18.2	27.5				25.8	29.0
27.4	13.7	7.9	6.6			Sales/Net Fixed Assets	11.5	11.5
11.3	5.3	3.9	5.0				5.0	5.4
9.0	4.4	3.0	2.9				3.5	3.8
4.6	2.8	2.2	1.8			Sales/Total Assets	2.6	2.8
3.0	1.9	1.5	1.3				1.8	1.9
.8	1.0	1.3					1.2	1.2
(30) 1.6	(50) 2.4	(54) 3.8				% Depr., Dep., Amort./Sales	(131) 2.7	(114) 2.8
4.4	7.4	6.9					5.1	5.3
4.5	3.4	2.4				% Officers', Directors',	3.5	3.9
(24) 9.1	(34) 6.9	(21) 4.1				Owners' Comp/Sales	(79) 6.6	(62) 7.9
16.7	9.9	7.8					13.3	16.9
48559M	221479M	522714M	707368M		352089M	Net Sales ($)	1020759M	1159796M
9344M	72879M	236598M	274121M		375966M	Total Assets ($)	462595M	477362M

M = $ thousand   MM = $ million
See Pages 11 through 21 for Explanation of Ratios and Data

Comparative Historical Data | Current Data Sorted By Sales

	4/1/02-3/31/03 ALL	4/1/03-3/31/04 ALL	4/1/04-3/31/05 ALL	Type of Statement	0-1MM	1-3MM	3-5MM	5-10MM	10-25MM	25MM & OVER
	19	14	11	Unqualified	1			1	5	4
	26	29	31	Reviewed		4	9	10	7	1
	38	41	36	Compiled	5	12	11	6	2	
	16	28	37	Tax Returns	15	12	5	5		
	61	62	65	Other	9	19	10	13	6	8
					33 (4/1-9/30/04)			147 (10/1/04-3/31/05)		
	160	174	180	**NUMBER OF STATEMENTS**	30	47	35	35	20	13
	%	%	%	**ASSETS**	%	%	%	%	%	%
	12.2	13.8	13.6	Cash & Equivalents	16.0	14.4	12.9	8.8	11.6	22.6
	34.9	33.4	31.5	Trade Receivables (net)	15.7	32.4	33.6	41.3	34.4	27.7
	6.8	8.3	8.6	Inventory	7.1	5.8	12.3	8.9	11.1	7.8
	3.2	3.1	2.4	All Other Current	1.1	1.6	3.1	2.6	4.0	3.1
	57.2	58.6	56.0	Total Current	39.9	54.2	62.0	61.6	61.2	61.2
	28.7	29.0	32.1	Fixed Assets (net)	50.5	34.6	24.4	28.3	28.3	17.1
	6.0	4.9	5.8	Intangibles (net)	4.4	5.5	6.3	6.3	2.9	11.8
	8.1	7.4	6.1	All Other Non-Current	5.2	5.7	7.3	3.8	7.6	9.9
	100.0	100.0	100.0	Total	100.0	100.0	100.0	100.0	100.0	100.0
				LIABILITIES						
	14.6	15.4	16.5	Notes Payable-Short Term	19.6	19.5	19.5	14.0	9.8	7.2
	6.1	5.7	7.6	Cur. Mat.-L/T/D	19.6	5.7	3.7	7.4	5.1	2.1
	14.6	13.8	14.2	Trade Payables	9.4	14.4	12.3	19.1	16.7	13.0
	.5	.3	.5	Income Taxes Payable	.1	1.3	.3	.1	.1	.2
	14.4	12.7	15.0	All Other Current	20.0	15.4	15.1	10.7	12.3	17.1
	50.2	47.9	53.8	Total Current	68.8	56.3	50.9	51.4	44.0	39.6
	18.1	17.8	22.7	Long-Term Debt	34.2	29.1	14.7	18.6	17.5	13.9
	.4	.9	.3	Deferred Taxes	.0	.3	.2	.5	.4	.2
	3.7	7.2	8.2	All Other Non-Current	20.3	6.8	2.4	8.1	4.5	7.3
	27.6	26.2	15.0	Net Worth	-23.3	7.6	31.8	21.4	33.5	39.0
	100.0	100.0	100.0	Total Liabilities & Net Worth	100.0	100.0	100.0	100.0	100.0	100.0
				INCOME DATA						
	100.0	100.0	100.0	Net Sales	100.0	100.0	100.0	100.0	100.0	100.0
				Gross Profit						
	95.7	95.1	93.9	Operating Expenses	86.0	95.6	94.7	97.5	95.4	91.7
	4.3	4.9	6.1	Operating Profit	14.0	4.4	5.3	2.5	4.6	8.3
	1.5	.9	2.0	All Other Expenses (net)	7.1	1.6	-.1	1.2	.5	1.7
	2.8	4.0	4.1	Profit Before Taxes	6.8	2.7	5.4	1.3	4.1	6.6
				RATIOS						
	2.3	2.6	2.0		1.4	2.2	2.0	2.0	2.8	2.4
	1.3	1.4	1.2	Current	1.0	1.2	1.4	1.2	1.3	1.5
	.8	1.0	.8		.3	.7	1.0	.7	.9	1.2
	1.9	2.2	1.6		1.3	1.6	1.9	1.8	1.6	2.0
	1.0	1.1	.9	Quick	.5	1.0	1.0	1.0	1.0	1.4
	.6	.7	.6		.2	.5	.7	.6	.7	.9
	30 12.2	28 12.9	20 18.0		0 UND	25 14.6	30 12.2	37 10.0	34 10.7	26 14.0
	46 8.0	46 8.0	41 8.9	Sales/Receivables	0 UND	39 9.5	42 8.6	54 6.8	39 9.4	43 8.4
	68 5.3	64 5.7	61 6.0		36 10.0	63 5.8	67 5.4	73 5.0	59 6.2	75 4.9
				Cost of Sales/Inventory						
				Cost of Sales/Payables						
	7.7	7.4	8.4		18.7	8.7	7.1	8.7	7.0	5.6
	20.2	18.7	31.6	Sales/Working Capital	-484.8	49.8	20.3	38.4	19.1	13.9
	-29.4	UND	-21.8		-8.9	-14.4	-80.5	-23.1	-56.4	34.1
	6.7	14.9	11.5		12.3	11.5	16.4	6.2	18.6	10.3
	(131) 2.3	(150) 2.7	(156) 3.3	EBIT/Interest	(23) 3.5	(41) 3.0	(32) 3.3	(31) 2.2	(19) 7.4	(10) 6.6
	-1.1	.1	.7		-1.8	.9	1.2	-1.1	2.5	2.4
	4.2	3.7	4.2	Net Profit + Depr., Dep.,						
	(30) 1.5	(29) 2.0	(27) 2.2	Amort./Cur. Mat. L/T/D						
	.8	1.2	1.4							
	.3	.3	.4		.9	.5	.2	.4	.4	.3
	.9	.8	1.4	Fixed/Worth	10.4	2.5	.6	1.1	1.3	.6
	4.0	3.8	UND		-1.7	-3.0	2.0	6.7	6.0	1.5
	.8	.8	1.0		1.5	1.1	.7	1.1	.6	.9
	2.1	2.1	4.0	Debt/Worth	10.4	5.3	1.8	4.4	3.6	2.1
	10.9	9.3	UND		-5.0	-12.1	8.6	-25.3	16.2	14.6
	56.2	69.8	65.3	% Profit Before Taxes/Tangible	250.0	71.9	85.9	39.7	47.3	64.6
	(131) 14.5	(146) 21.5	(136) 33.8	Net Worth	(19) 39.9	(31) 47.3	(30) 20.5	(26) 16.3	(18) 27.6	(12) 36.9
	-6.9	-.5	5.0		-9.3	4.9	4.8	-14.5	10.1	17.3
	15.3	21.1	21.5	% Profit Before Taxes/Total	45.3	18.7	28.3	13.6	12.0	19.3
	3.9	3.4	4.6	Assets	4.0	4.5	5.0	2.7	7.2	14.3
	-5.4	-1.3	-1.2		-10.8	-.9	.8	-5.6	2.4	15.2
	27.5	30.8	33.8		35.9	29.5	60.5	58.5	28.2	152.4
	11.3	12.7	12.9	Sales/Net Fixed Assets	11.2	13.5	15.1	13.9	10.9	10.6
	5.5	5.4	5.1		.5	4.9	6.8	5.2	5.3	5.5
	3.9	3.7	4.3		6.2	4.3	4.0	4.6	4.0	4.1
	2.6	2.6	2.8	Sales/Total Assets	3.4	2.7	2.7	3.0	2.7	2.3
	1.7	1.8	1.7		.4	1.8	1.7	2.0	2.0	1.0
	1.1	1.2	1.1		1.2	1.3	.9	.9	1.0	1.3
	(129) 2.8	(145) 2.6	(144) 2.7	% Depr., Dep., Amort./Sales	(20) 4.7	(39) 3.5	(29) 2.3	(27) 2.4	(19) 2.4	(10) 3.3
	5.4	4.9	5.9		11.5	7.5	4.9	6.9	3.8	4.8
	5.0	4.7	3.5		4.0	4.4	2.7	3.4		
	(65) 8.3	(69) 8.4	(82) 6.6	% Officers', Directors', Owners' Comp/Sales	(13) 10.5	(21) 8.3	(21) 5.9	(19) 4.3		
	14.9	18.5	10.6		21.6	11.4	10.2	9.8		
	2099526M	3697087M	1852209M	Net Sales ($)	13773M	87385M	130854M	244154M	293350M	1082693M
	1087583M	1582350M	968908M	Total Assets ($)	15106M	43109M	59201M	99429M	118924M	633139M

M = $ thousand MM = $ million
See Pages 11 through 21 for Explanation of Ratios and Data

Current Data Sorted By Assets   Comparative Historical Data

						Type of Statement		
1	8	33	22	7	8	Unqualified	67	53
1	19	31	3	1		Reviewed	40	45
14	32	13	1		1	Compiled	59	73
24	17	5				Tax Returns	26	29
37	41	43	30	6	6	Other	134	109

54 (4/1-9/30/04)			350 (10/1/04-3/31/05)				4/1/00-3/31/01 ALL	4/1/01-3/31/02 ALL
0-500M	500M-2MM	2-10MM	10-50MM	50-100MM	100-250MM			
77	117	125	56	14	15	**NUMBER OF STATEMENTS**	326	309
%	%	%	%	%	%	**ASSETS**	%	%
23.7	17.9	17.6	21.5	18.8	30.9	Cash & Equivalents	14.8	15.0
33.8	50.6	44.5	42.2	31.5	15.2	Trade Receivables (net)	47.8	44.6
4.3	3.6	3.5	2.0	3.3	1.8	Inventory	3.0	3.6
6.2	3.3	5.4	4.0	2.0	3.2	All Other Current	5.3	4.3
68.0	75.5	71.1	69.7	55.6	51.0	Total Current	71.0	67.5
17.0	11.9	12.5	10.6	7.0	6.9	Fixed Assets (net)	14.1	14.9
5.6	5.7	6.8	11.8	31.8	26.4	Intangibles (net)	8.0	8.0
9.3	7.0	9.6	8.0	5.5	15.7	All Other Non-Current	6.9	9.5
100.0	100.0	100.0	100.0	100.0	100.0	Total	100.0	100.0
						LIABILITIES		
22.8	15.5	8.4	7.5	6.2	.0	Notes Payable-Short Term	19.4	16.8
6.0	3.0	2.2	2.1	1.8	.6	Cur. Mat.-L/T/D	2.9	3.6
14.2	13.5	10.8	11.7	10.9	6.1	Trade Payables	13.7	10.5
1.2	1.0	.6	1.0	.6	.7	Income Taxes Payable	.7	.7
17.7	21.9	23.8	21.6	19.8	14.1	All Other Current	22.3	25.2
61.9	54.9	45.8	43.8	39.4	21.5	Total Current	58.9	56.8
19.0	6.7	6.4	7.3	8.5	6.3	Long-Term Debt	15.0	13.9
.8	.9	.8	.8	2.1	.7	Deferred Taxes	.9	1.1
17.8	9.4	5.4	11.6	15.9	7.8	All Other Non-Current	5.3	13.4
.6	28.1	41.5	36.5	34.1	63.7	Net Worth	19.8	14.8
100.0	100.0	100.0	100.0	100.0	100.0	Total Liabilities & Net Worth	100.0	100.0
						INCOME DATA		
100.0	100.0	100.0	100.0	100.0	100.0	Net Sales	100.0	100.0
						Gross Profit		
94.3	96.2	93.4	94.0	94.1	87.2	Operating Expenses	95.2	95.8
5.7	3.8	6.6	6.0	5.9	12.8	Operating Profit	4.8	4.2
1.1	.6	.6	.8	1.5	.4	All Other Expenses (net)	.8	.9
4.7	3.2	6.1	5.3	4.4	12.4	Profit Before Taxes	4.0	3.3
						RATIOS		
2.7	2.8	2.5	2.6	1.8	3.7		2.4	2.6
1.3	1.4	1.7	1.6	1.3	2.5	Current	1.5	1.5
.8	1.0	1.1	1.1	1.0	2.0		1.0	.9
2.6	2.4	2.3	2.3	1.7	3.6		2.3	2.4
1.1	1.3	1.5	1.4	1.1	2.2	Quick	1.3	1.3
.6	.9	1.0	.7	.7	1.7		.8	.8
0 UND	37 9.7	41 8.8	48 7.6	62 5.9	49 7.4		39 9.2	35 10.4
20 18.5	55 6.7	57 6.4	74 4.9	71 5.1	62 5.9	Sales/Receivables	60 6.1	53 6.9
43 8.5	68 5.4	78 4.7	101 3.6	90 4.1	79 4.6		80 4.6	75 4.9
						Cost of Sales/Inventory		
						Cost of Sales/Payables		
12.8	6.8	5.4	3.0	5.5	1.8		6.4	6.8
34.1	17.2	10.2	7.8	16.5	3.3	Sales/Working Capital	15.0	16.6
-46.2	-999.8	34.4	57.2	NM	5.7		114.0	-103.2
22.9	36.7	59.4	36.8	23.9			18.6	13.2
(53) 3.0	(97) 6.3	(95) 12.0	(40) 4.1	15.3		EBIT/Interest	(258) 5.6	(258) 2.7
-.2	1.4	3.6	1.0	1.5			.8	-2.3
	16.2	16.6	75.8			Net Profit + Depr., Dep.,	17.3	13.2
	(13) 2.6	(19) 6.8	(10) 8.9			Amort./Cur. Mat. L /T/D	(38) 3.7	(45) 6.0
	.0	3.6	1.2				.8	.4
.1	.1	.1	.1	.1	.1		.1	.1
.4	.3	.2	.3	.6	.2	Fixed/Worth	.4	.4
-.6	1.7	.7	1.7	-.1	.5		1.5	2.6
.8	.8	.6	.6	.9	.3		.8	.7
3.8	2.0	1.4	2.8	8.5	.5	Debt/Worth	2.1	2.2
-2.9	15.4	4.4	13.6	-1.8	2.2		12.0	21.6
136.8	76.4	68.9	52.1		43.3	% Profit Before Taxes/Tangible	76.7	77.2
(49) 66.1	(93) 30.2	(110) 39.5	(43) 27.9		(12) 22.6	Net Worth	(263) 40.5	(237) 30.9
24.1	8.8	14.3	14.7		4.3		10.0	-3.1
44.1	31.1	27.4	19.7	8.9	18.9	% Profit Before Taxes/Total	28.6	23.7
19.5	7.9	13.9	7.0	4.8	7.1	Assets	10.6	6.4
1.6	1.4	3.1	-.1	2.4	2.8		.4	-7.2
497.3	103.9	77.5	52.9	48.9	28.9		75.4	66.8
93.6	46.8	33.5	25.5	32.1	21.2	Sales/Net Fixed Assets	30.2	29.6
21.9	18.1	17.1	12.0	14.0	6.1		13.3	13.7
8.7	4.7	3.7	2.6	2.4	1.0		4.3	4.6
6.0	3.4	2.6	1.8	1.3	.8	Sales/Total Assets	3.1	3.2
4.0	2.3	1.7	1.1	.7	.5		1.9	2.0
.5	.4	.4	.8				.5	.6
(28) 1.3	(74) .9	(83) 1.3	(36) 2.0			% Depr., Dep., Amort./Sales	(230) 1.4	(223) 1.5
2.5	2.3	2.7	4.3				2.5	2.8
7.3	4.1	2.4					3.5	2.7
(36) 9.6	(44) 6.4	(24) 3.6				% Officers', Directors',	(98) 5.0	(101) 5.7
21.6	10.4	9.1				Owners' Comp/Sales	9.8	11.6
120858M	497946M	1397874M	1894580M	1677561M	4701715M	Net Sales ($)	9072755M	6299587M
18347M	133685M	540045M	1079860M	1124769M	2518281M	Total Assets ($)	4661605M	2959181M

M = $ thousand   MM = $ million
See Pages 11 through 21 for Explanation of Ratios and Data

Comparative Historical Data						Current Data Sorted By Sales					
				Type of Statement							
64		71		79	Unqualified	1	3	7	10	27	31
66		50		55	Reviewed		11	10	15	12	7
55		71		61	Compiled	5	24	9	17	3	3
35		52		46	Tax Returns	13	16	9	7	1	
113		150		163	Other	14	35	22	32	27	33
4/1/02-		4/1/03-		4/1/04-			54 (4/1-9/30/04)		350 (10/1/04-3/31/05)		
3/31/03		3/31/04		3/31/05		0-1MM	1-3MM	3-5MM	5-10MM	10-25MM	25MM & OVER
ALL		ALL		ALL							
333		394		404	**NUMBER OF STATEMENTS**	33	89	57	81	70	74
%		%		%	**ASSETS**	%	%	%	%	%	%
17.0		20.4		19.9	Cash & Equivalents	24.8	19.7	19.5	16.1	21.9	20.7
42.5		40.3		42.4	Trade Receivables (net)	25.4	40.1	49.2	46.9	45.0	39.9
2.6		3.4		3.4	Inventory	4.4	5.7	1.5	3.9	2.2	2.4
4.7		4.4		4.6	All Other Current	3.7	6.2	3.6	5.1	3.8	3.8
66.8		68.5		70.3	Total Current	58.3	71.7	73.8	72.0	73.0	66.7
15.1		14.2		12.5	Fixed Assets (net)	23.7	12.5	13.6	12.0	10.8	8.9
8.4		7.6		8.5	Intangibles (net)	11.2	5.3	4.3	6.6	8.1	17.1
9.7		9.7		8.7	All Other Non-Current	6.7	10.4	8.4	9.4	8.2	7.3
100.0		100.0		100.0	Total	100.0	100.0	100.0	100.0	100.0	100.0
				LIABILITIES							
14.9		12.2		12.7	Notes Payable-Short Term	23.9	18.8	16.2	10.4	6.1	6.5
5.9		3.5		3.1	Cur. Mat.-L/T/D	9.5	2.8	2.7	2.6	3.1	1.4
13.6		13.3		12.2	Trade Payables	9.6	13.8	12.3	10.8	12.2	12.8
.7		.7		.9	Income Taxes Payable	.4	1.5	1.0	.3	1.1	.7
21.2		23.7		21.3	All Other Current	19.0	16.7	23.0	24.6	24.0	20.3
56.5		53.3		50.1	Total Current	62.4	53.5	55.2	48.6	46.5	41.7
11.7		9.7		9.1	Long-Term Debt	17.7	15.6	5.7	5.5	6.0	7.0
.9		.8		.9	Deferred Taxes	2.1	.2	1.7	.9	.7	.8
7.7		11.2		10.2	All Other Non-Current	20.8	13.6	11.0	4.1	9.4	8.1
23.2		24.9		29.7	Net Worth	−2.9	17.1	26.5	40.9	37.4	42.3
100.0		100.0		100.0	Total Liabilities & Net Worth	100.0	100.0	100.0	100.0	100.0	100.0
				INCOME DATA							
100.0		100.0		100.0	Net Sales	100.0	100.0	100.0	100.0	100.0	100.0
				Gross Profit							
95.8		95.0		94.2	Operating Expenses	93.7	95.0	95.6	94.1	94.6	92.3
4.2		5.0		5.8	Operating Profit	6.3	5.0	4.4	5.9	5.4	7.7
.9		1.2		.7	All Other Expenses (net)	2.3	.9	.5	.2	.6	.7
3.3		3.8		5.0	Profit Before Taxes	4.1	4.2	3.9	5.7	4.7	7.0
				RATIOS							
2.8		2.7		2.7		2.6	2.7	3.1	2.8	2.5	2.5
1.5		1.6		1.6	Current	1.3	1.5	1.4	1.6	1.7	1.6
.9		1.0		1.0		.6	.9	.9	1.1	1.1	1.1
2.6		2.5		2.4		2.4	2.1	2.9	2.2	2.3	2.3
1.3		1.4		1.3	Quick	1.1	1.2	1.2	1.4	1.6	1.4
.8		.8		.9		.5	.8	.9	.9	1.0	1.0

32	11.5	31	11.8	32	11.5	Sales/Receivables	0	UND	10	37.7	42	8.8	36	10.1	43	8.4	48	7.6
51	7.2	52	7.1	54	6.7		12	30.3	46	8.0	55	6.7	53	6.8	57	6.4	67	5.4
73	5.0	71	5.2	74	4.9		54	6.7	68	5.3	70	5.2	78	4.7	77	4.8	82	4.4

Cost of Sales/Inventory

Cost of Sales/Payables

	6.0		5.7		5.9	Sales/Working Capital		9.1		7.2		5.8		5.4		5.5		3.7
	14.7		12.5		14.4			102.8		19.5		14.2		12.0		10.1		11.1
	−63.9		UND		438.1			−15.6		−118.3		−117.7		42.0		42.5		33.9
	21.2		29.8		40.9	EBIT/Interest		6.1		16.1		22.1		48.6		87.7		36.8
(265)	5.2	(305)	5.7	(306)	6.8		(24)	2.3	(66)	5.0	(44)	9.7	(66)	11.2	(54)	13.7	(52)	11.3
	.5		.4		1.7			−7.5		1.4		1.5		3.1		2.5		2.0
	8.2		16.3		16.6	Net Profit + Depr., Dep.,										14.0		91.2
(48)	3.8	(47)	5.7	(47)	6.8	Amort./Cur. Mat. L/T/D									(14)	4.2	(12)	15.0
	.8		1.4		1.9											2.1		3.7
	.1		.1		.1	Fixed/Worth		.0		.1		.1		.1		.1		.1
	.3		.4		.3			1.1		.4		.4		.2		.3		.2
	4.0		1.8		1.9			−.7		UND		1.7		.8		.8		NM
	.6		.8		.6	Debt/Worth		1.1		.8		.8		.6		.6		.6
	2.0		1.8		1.9			38.0		2.3		1.7		1.6		1.6		2.1
	81.9		11.5		15.2			−2.6		−81.2		7.7		4.5		4.7		NM
	67.1		71.9		75.6	% Profit Before Taxes/Tangible		244.4		81.4		73.9		73.7		80.2		54.3
(256)	31.1	(310)	29.9	(315)	36.1	Net Worth	(17)	65.3	(66)	34.6	(46)	41.9	(70)	30.1	(60)	43.2	(56)	27.1
	3.9		3.4		11.9			35.2		8.3		7.4		10.3		17.3		14.9
	25.3		25.4		27.4	% Profit Before Taxes/Total		42.4		30.9		31.0		27.3		30.9		18.9
	8.1		7.8		10.1	Assets		9.1		10.3		10.3		10.8		13.9		7.5
	−3.7		−1.3		1.6			−9.3		1.2		.6		3.2		2.9		2.9
	69.5		72.7		102.7	Sales/Net Fixed Assets		497.3		153.5		93.9		86.1		81.9		80.5
	29.1		29.1		37.7			41.9		47.3		38.5		37.5		28.4		30.8
	14.8		15.0		17.1			10.2		21.8		13.6		17.3		19.5		14.3
	4.4		4.5		4.5	Sales/Total Assets		7.7		5.9		4.5		4.2		4.1		3.2
	3.0		2.8		2.9			4.1		3.8		3.1		2.9		2.6		1.9
	1.9		1.7		1.7			2.5		2.2		2.2		2.0		1.7		1.0
	.7		.8		.5	% Depr., Dep., Amort./Sales		.7		.5		.6		.6		.3		.5
(228)	1.5	(249)	1.7	(234)	1.3		(14)	1.6	(43)	1.0	(32)	1.8	(54)	1.6	(47)	1.0	(44)	1.6
	2.9		3.2		3.0			7.2		2.4		3.5		2.8		2.6		3.6
	3.5		4.1		3.8	% Officers', Directors',		8.5		6.7		5.1		2.9		2.7		
(109)	6.6	(110)	8.2	(112)	7.2	Owners' Comp/Sales	(15)	18.5	(36)	8.4	(15)	8.3	(27)	4.3	(11)	3.7		
	13.4		12.7		12.4			27.0		13.8		17.1		6.7		5.5		
7770564M		8097479M		10290534M	Net Sales ($)	20789M	177895M	221273M	564737M	1072689M	8233151M
3093676M		4566447M		5414987M	Total Assets ($)	11285M	92961M	87581M	265498M	515607M	4442055M

© RMA 2005   **M = $ thousand   MM = $million**
See Pages 11 through 21 for Explanation of Ratios and Data

Current Data Sorted By Assets | Comparative Historical Data

0-500M	500M-2MM	2-10MM	10-50MM	50-100MM	100-250MM	Type of Statement	ALL 4/1/00-3/31/01	ALL 4/1/01-3/31/02
	5	42	33	8	11	Unqualified	83	66
3	21	39	2			Reviewed	57	52
15	25	14			1	Compiled	89	85
15	15	5	1		1	Tax Returns	21	18
19	52	66	27	6	8	Other	115	126
	68 (4/1-9/30/04)		366 (10/1/04-3/31/05)					
52	118	166	63	14	21	NUMBER OF STATEMENTS	365	347
%	%	%	%	%	%	ASSETS	%	%
27.8	12.6	13.5	18.0	14.7	19.5	Cash & Equivalents	15.6	15.5
36.0	50.1	49.7	41.7	40.6	22.7	Trade Receivables (net)	46.8	43.5
5.8	3.0	6.6	4.9	3.1	6.5	Inventory	6.3	6.9
1.5	5.0	6.2	7.4	4.8	4.4	All Other Current	5.9	6.5
71.2	70.8	76.0	72.1	63.1	53.1	Total Current	74.6	72.4
18.7	13.5	11.6	9.6	8.3	13.2	Fixed Assets (net)	14.3	14.3
2.6	7.5	4.5	8.9	23.1	29.7	Intangibles (net)	5.4	6.2
7.6	8.1	7.8	9.4	5.4	4.0	All Other Non-Current	5.7	7.1
100.0	100.0	100.0	100.0	100.0	100.0	Total	100.0	100.0
						LIABILITIES		
39.3	17.6	13.4	8.7	5.7	5.4	Notes Payable-Short Term	12.8	15.5
8.9	2.9	2.0	2.6	6.6	.7	Cur. Mat.-L/T/D	3.1	3.4
17.3	16.5	17.5	18.0	18.6	8.7	Trade Payables	17.5	16.7
.1	.5	1.1	.8	.3	.6	Income Taxes Payable	.6	.7
32.7	18.2	22.5	20.6	18.5	15.7	All Other Current	17.4	19.2
98.3	55.6	56.5	50.8	49.7	31.1	Total Current	51.5	55.5
34.6	10.7	5.9	5.3	4.6	10.7	Long-Term Debt	8.4	7.4
.2	.8	.4	.7	1.4	1.0	Deferred Taxes	.7	.5
10.8	7.1	7.1	3.5	14.5	2.9	All Other Non-Current	5.2	8.9
-43.9	25.7	30.1	39.7	29.8	54.3	Net Worth	34.3	27.8
100.0	100.0	100.0	100.0	100.0	100.0	Total Liabilities & Net Worth	100.0	100.0
						INCOME DATA		
100.0	100.0	100.0	100.0	100.0	100.0	Net Sales	100.0	100.0
						Gross Profit		
97.6	94.3	95.3	94.2	97.4	92.4	Operating Expenses	97.9	96.9
2.4	5.7	4.7	5.8	2.6	7.6	Operating Profit	2.1	3.1
1.0	1.3	.5	.4	.8	.9	All Other Expenses (net)	.0	1.0
1.4	4.4	4.2	5.4	1.8	6.7	Profit Before Taxes	2.1	2.1
						RATIOS		
1.7	2.9	2.0	1.9	2.1	2.7	Current	2.6	2.1
1.1	1.3	1.4	1.4	1.2	1.7		1.4	1.4
.5	1.0	1.0	1.1	1.0	1.0		1.1	1.0
1.5	2.6	1.7	1.7	1.6	2.6	Quick	2.2	1.8
.9	1.2	1.1	1.2	1.0	1.3		1.2	1.1
.4	.8	.8	.9	.8	.7		.9	.7
0 UND	35 10.4	45 8.1	52 7.1	61 6.0	43 8.5	Sales/Receivables	43 8.5	33 11.0
29 12.7	51 7.1	59 6.2	68 5.4	70 5.2	65 5.6		62 5.9	52 7.0
43 8.4	71 5.1	82 4.4	90 4.1	86 4.3	90 4.1		85 4.3	74 4.9
						Cost of Sales/Inventory		
						Cost of Sales/Payables		
17.0	7.2	6.9	4.9	4.7	3.1	Sales/Working Capital	5.4	7.1
583.8	19.3	15.6	10.7	25.9	9.5		12.9	16.8
-14.2	271.5	120.6	26.9	NM	NM		51.1	137.2
23.3	34.3	42.0	26.1	28.5	11.3	EBIT/Interest	16.0	11.7
(44) 3.1	(98) 6.6	(137) 9.0	(50) 10.2	(11) 15.4	(16) 5.8		(293) 3.3	(286) 3.1
-3.3	1.6	2.1	4.5	-1.0	2.1		-.5	.2
		13.9	28.5			Net Profit + Depr., Dep., Amort./Cur. Mat. L /T/D	9.6	15.0
	(31)	3.1	(17) 3.5				(66) 3.5	(63) 3.2
		1.1	1.8				1.5	.9
.0	.1	.1	.1	.2	.2	Fixed/Worth	.1	.2
.8	.4	.3	.3	.4	.7		.3	.4
-.6	2.7	1.8	.6	-1.2	NM		1.2	2.1
1.9	.8	.8	1.1	1.3	.5	Debt/Worth	.8	.8
UND	2.3	2.3	2.5	6.5	1.5		2.3	2.5
-1.9	14.5	8.0	4.8	-4.9	NM		7.3	12.2
150.0	66.1	63.9	60.5	95.3	111.5	% Profit Before Taxes/Tangible Net Worth	67.7	56.8
(27) 74.3	(93) 31.0	(138) 37.0	(59) 32.8	(10) 54.0	(16) 20.7		(321) 25.1	(281) 29.4
37.3	7.7	11.6	10.6	-6.2	7.9		1.0	2.0
39.3	22.6	20.4	16.0	12.8	11.2	% Profit Before Taxes/Total Assets	20.6	19.3
16.8	8.6	10.4	9.2	8.1	7.8		6.3	5.9
-27.0	1.2	3.3	3.2	-4.5	4.2		-1.9	-2.1
515.0	108.5	92.6	78.1	41.1	46.5	Sales/Net Fixed Assets	68.1	71.3
66.0	45.8	47.0	24.2	23.7	21.5		29.4	31.9
17.4	19.4	18.3	14.0	11.1	8.6		12.8	13.8
8.3	4.7	3.7	2.9	2.9	1.5	Sales/Total Assets	3.9	4.6
5.0	3.5	3.0	1.8	1.6	1.3		2.8	3.0
3.8	2.5	2.2	1.3	1.0	.8		1.7	1.9
.6	.6	.4	.8			% Depr., Dep., Amort./Sales	.4	.3
(24) 1.2	(76) 1.1	(125) .9	(43) 1.7				(278) 1.1	(256) .9
4.7	2.3	2.1	5.5				2.5	2.2
9.3	4.6	2.0				% Officers', Directors', Owners' Comp/Sales	2.7	2.5
(25) 12.4	(31) 6.0	(36) 5.4					(87) 6.7	(86) 5.4
25.6	9.1	12.5					11.9	11.9
59034M	492408M	2094696M	3206338M	1685303M	5993271M	Net Sales ($)	9717149M	9228982M
11259M	142381M	739039M	1479008M	927054M	3438875M	Total Assets ($)	5944273M	4871726M

© RMA 2005

M = $ thousand   MM = $ million
See Pages 11 through 21 for Explanation of Ratios and Data

Comparative Historical Data / Current Data Sorted By Sales

					Type of Statement						
	129		103	99	Unqualified		1	1	16	36	45
	70		64	65	Reviewed		9	12	25	15	4
	41		81	55	Compiled	8	16	13	10	6	2
	33		40	37	Tax Returns	11	9	5	8	2	2
	158		144	178	Other	13	26	19	43	40	37
	4/1/02- 3/31/03 ALL		4/1/03- 3/31/04 ALL	4/1/04- 3/31/05 ALL			68 (4/1-9/30/04)			366 (10/1/04-3/31/05)	
	431		432	434	NUMBER OF STATEMENTS	0-1MM 32	1-3MM 61	3-5MM 50	5-10MM 102	10-25MM 99	25MM & OVER 90
	%		%	%	ASSETS	%	%	%	%	%	%
	17.5		16.1	16.0	Cash & Equivalents	28.6	16.9	15.3	14.1	13.7	15.8
	43.8		45.1	45.4	Trade Receivables (net)	22.6	42.7	49.9	50.0	48.9	43.9
	6.4		4.8	5.2	Inventory	5.1	5.6	2.3	5.7	4.9	6.2
	5.2		5.7	5.4	All Other Current	5.3	2.9	3.5	6.1	7.0	5.5
	72.8		71.7	71.9	Total Current	61.5	68.0	71.0	75.9	74.5	71.4
	14.0		13.9	12.6	Fixed Assets (net)	20.3	18.5	11.7	12.2	10.8	9.0
	6.4		7.7	7.6	Intangibles (net)	4.6	6.0	8.8	4.5	6.7	13.4
	6.8		6.7	7.9	All Other Non-Current	13.5	7.5	8.5	7.3	8.0	6.2
	100.0		100.0	100.0	Total	100.0	100.0	100.0	100.0	100.0	100.0
					LIABILITIES						
	15.8		15.7	16.3	Notes Payable-Short Term	59.3	19.1	12.2	15.8	9.7	9.4
	3.1		3.0	3.2	Cur. Mat.-L/T/D	7.0	5.7	2.2	3.0	2.0	2.4
	16.5		18.6	16.9	Trade Payables	14.5	14.6	15.3	16.9	16.5	20.5
	.5		.8	.7	Income Taxes Payable	.0	.3	.6	.5	1.3	.9
	20.5		21.4	21.8	All Other Current	35.8	18.1	24.3	20.1	23.0	18.6
	56.3		59.5	59.0	Total Current	116.6	57.9	54.7	56.5	52.5	51.8
	7.3		12.3	10.7	Long-Term Debt	36.7	22.1	8.0	6.0	6.4	5.5
	.5		.5	.6	Deferred Taxes	.1	.9	1.0	.3	.5	.8
	7.1		8.2	7.1	All Other Non-Current	13.5	8.3	7.0	6.7	6.1	5.5
	28.7		19.6	22.6	Net Worth	−66.8	10.9	29.4	30.6	34.5	36.5
	100.0		100.0	100.0	Total Liabilities & Net Worth	100.0	100.0	100.0	100.0	100.0	100.0
					INCOME DATA						
	100.0		100.0	100.0	Net Sales	100.0	100.0	100.0	100.0	100.0	100.0
					Gross Profit						
	95.7		95.8	95.1	Operating Expenses	90.2	97.4	95.5	96.3	94.0	94.9
	4.3		4.2	4.9	Operating Profit	9.8	2.6	4.5	3.7	6.0	5.1
	.6		.9	.8	All Other Expenses (net)	3.9	1.1	.2	.3	.5	.7
	3.7		3.2	4.1	Profit Before Taxes	5.9	1.4	4.3	3.4	5.6	4.4
					RATIOS						
	2.3		2.2	2.2		2.1	3.0	2.8	2.2	2.0	2.0
	1.4		1.3	1.3	Current	.8	1.4	1.3	1.3	1.5	1.3
	1.0		1.0	1.0		.3	.8	1.0	1.0	1.1	1.1
	2.0		1.8	1.9		1.7	3.0	2.5	1.7	1.7	1.6
	1.2		1.1	1.1	Quick	.6	1.1	1.2	1.1	1.2	1.2
	.7		.8	.8		.2	.7	1.0	.8	.8	.9
36	10.3	35	10.5	38	9.6		0	UND	31	11.9	39	9.3	43	8.4	38	9.6	51	7.2

(Sales/Receivables, EBIT/Interest, etc. — continued below with leading counts)

Hist 1		Hist 2		Hist 3		Item	0-1MM		1-3MM		3-5MM		5-10MM		10-25MM		25MM & OVER
36	10.3	35	10.5	38	9.6	Sales/Receivables	0	UND	31	11.9	39	9.3	43	8.4	38	9.6	51	7.2
57	6.5	56	6.5	55	6.6		18	20.5	46	8.0	57	6.4	58	6.2	57	6.4	67	5.5
78	4.7	76	4.8	77	4.7		33	11.1	67	5.4	80	4.6	80	4.6	77	4.7	84	4.3
						Cost of Sales/Inventory											
						Cost of Sales/Payables											
	6.7		7.1		6.7	Sales/Working Capital		11.7		5.2		7.0		6.6		7.1		5.6
	14.4		17.6		16.9			−95.0		24.5		19.3		16.8		13.5		14.5
	−130.1		−146.6		301.6			−3.4		−23.8		137.1		−227.6		88.7		34.7
	23.5		20.8		31.8	EBIT/Interest		9.8		25.3		40.1		23.4		47.8		46.7
(362)	5.6	(362)	5.6	(356)	7.7		(25)	2.2	(51)	5.0	(42)	5.5	(83)	8.6	(81)	10.1	(74)	10.8
	1.2		1.2		1.7			−4.3		.0		1.3		2.0		3.5		3.1
	29.6		15.3		19.0	Net Profit + Depr., Dep., Amort./Cur. Mat. L/T/D								9.9		22.8		67.6
(64)	6.6	(68)	2.9	(66)	2.9						(11)	2.7	(23)	6.1	(22)	4.4
	1.8		.7		1.2										1.1		1.2		1.6
	.1		.1		.1	Fixed/Worth		.0		.1		.1		.1		.1		.1
	.4		.4		.3			.9		.5		.4		.4		.2		.3
	1.9		3.5		2.1			−.3		−3.6		1.7		4.0		1.1		.8
	.9		.9		.9	Debt/Worth		1.0		.9		.8		.8		.9		1.1
	2.2		3.0		2.5			UND		2.5		2.8		2.4		2.2		2.6
	10.6		74.0		20.3			−1.5		−11.6		7.9		22.1		4.9		6.3
	65.8		65.7		68.6	% Profit Before Taxes/Tangible Net Worth		130.0		68.1		61.1		71.3		63.9		79.0
(349)	33.5	(329)	30.6	(343)	36.6		(16)	37.1	(42)	30.6	(40)	32.5	(80)	30.1	(86)	40.0	(79)	34.2
	4.5		5.3		10.8			−26.5		4.8		7.7		11.6		19.5		11.2
	22.0		17.8		20.3	% Profit Before Taxes/Total Assets		73.3		21.2		26.4		18.6		21.9		13.6
	8.0		8.3		9.8			8.6		8.1		7.2		9.6		12.2		8.3
	.3		.5		1.8			−25.0		−5.2		.6		3.0		4.7		2.4
	75.2		88.5		97.5	Sales/Net Fixed Assets		437.3		85.1		98.7		92.1		95.5		115.7
	32.3		35.4		43.8			66.0		29.2		45.8		44.0		47.3		36.2
	15.9		15.0		16.5			9.2		9.4		22.8		18.3		16.9		17.7
	4.1		4.5		4.2	Sales/Total Assets		8.3		5.0		4.0		4.0		4.1		3.5
	3.0		2.9		3.0			4.0		3.6		3.1		3.1		3.1		2.1
	1.9		1.9		1.9			1.9		1.8		2.5		2.2		1.8		1.3
	.6		.6		.5	% Depr., Dep., Amort./Sales		.6		.9		.6		.5		.4		.4
(318)	1.3	(294)	1.3	(285)	1.1		(14)	2.0	(40)	2.0	(30)	1.2	(76)	1.0	(73)	.8	(52)	1.2
	2.5		2.4		2.6			6.5		4.3		1.9		1.7		2.8		2.0
	3.2		2.6		3.8	% Officers', Directors', Owners' Comp/Sales		12.7		6.6		4.2		3.4		1.7		
(118)	5.9	(101)	6.4	(98)	7.2		(12)	25.6	(18)	9.9	(18)	6.2	(25)	6.5	(18)	3.7		
	13.7		12.9		13.7			30.0		15.1		15.4		11.1		6.8		
11206330M		10013023M		13531050M		Net Sales ($)	17563M		119586M		203466M		727459M		1587311M		10875665M
5921584M		5429026M		6737616M		Total Assets ($)	9597M		54581M		67868M		301133M		706562M		5597875M

Current Data Sorted By Assets   Comparative Historical Data

						Type of Statement		
	2	28	20	6	5	Unqualified	53	45
4	16	37	4			Reviewed	43	29
10	26	12	1		1	Compiled	70	59
36	20	5			1	Tax Returns	36	38
38	47	42	24	5	7	Other	136	135
41 (4/1-9/30/04)			356 (10/1/04-3/31/05)				4/1/00-3/31/01	4/1/01-3/31/02
0-500M	500M-2MM	2-10MM	10-50MM	50-100MM	100-250MM		ALL	ALL
88	111	124	49	11	14	**NUMBER OF STATEMENTS**	338	306
%	%	%	%	%	%	**ASSETS**	%	%
26.9	16.6	12.5	13.4	27.6	16.0	Cash & Equivalents	12.8	12.5
33.2	45.7	49.3	42.9	32.2	22.0	Trade Receivables (net)	50.3	47.5
5.3	4.8	5.5	5.1	.1	1.3	Inventory	3.8	3.4
1.8	2.4	5.2	4.6	4.4	8.8	All Other Current	3.7	4.3
67.2	69.5	72.5	65.9	64.3	48.1	Total Current	70.6	67.7
19.1	17.0	15.2	12.8	14.6	11.7	Fixed Assets (net)	16.8	18.0
5.5	6.2	5.0	13.1	18.9	19.2	Intangibles (net)	6.0	8.0
8.2	7.3	7.3	8.2	2.2	21.0	All Other Non-Current	6.6	6.2
100.0	100.0	100.0	100.0	100.0	100.0	Total	100.0	100.0
						LIABILITIES		
39.0	11.4	13.2	9.6	9.7	3.9	Notes Payable-Short Term	18.2	22.2
3.7	3.3	2.1	3.0	3.3	2.6	Cur. Mat.-L/T/D	4.4	4.2
15.0	13.3	16.4	16.5	8.7	7.8	Trade Payables	14.9	17.7
.1	.8	1.0	.5	19.6	.9	Income Taxes Payable	.6	.5
19.9	21.3	19.3	15.9	20.3	10.3	All Other Current	15.5	18.8
77.6	50.1	52.1	45.5	61.6	25.5	Total Current	53.7	63.4
24.9	12.1	8.7	15.3	7.4	16.7	Long-Term Debt	11.1	9.3
.0	.2	.3	1.2	2.4	.4	Deferred Taxes	1.0	.7
11.9	8.5	6.6	12.5	5.1	5.5	All Other Non-Current	4.7	8.3
-14.4	29.1	32.4	25.5	23.4	51.9	Net Worth	29.5	18.2
100.0	100.0	100.0	100.0	100.0	100.0	Total Liabilities & Net Worth	100.0	100.0
						INCOME DATA		
100.0	100.0	100.0	100.0	100.0	100.0	Net Sales	100.0	100.0
						Gross Profit		
94.5	93.9	92.5	91.9	88.3	95.4	Operating Expenses	96.9	97.2
5.5	6.1	7.5	8.1	11.7	4.6	Operating Profit	3.1	2.8
.7	.8	1.4	1.3	.5	1.4	All Other Expenses (net)	.9	1.6
4.8	5.2	6.1	6.7	11.1	3.3	Profit Before Taxes	2.3	1.2
						RATIOS		
2.2	3.5	1.9	2.3	2.0	4.6		2.4	2.3
1.3	1.7	1.4	1.4	1.3	1.9	Current	1.4	1.3
.6	1.1	1.1	1.1	.8	1.0		1.0	.9
2.0	3.0	1.8	2.1	1.8	4.0		2.2	1.9
1.1	1.5	1.2	1.2	1.3	1.1	Quick	1.2	1.1
.5	.8	.9	.9	.7	.7		.8	.8
0 UND	25 14.6	39 9.4	48 7.6	25 14.5	36 10.0		39 9.3	35 10.4
25 14.6	51 7.1	56 6.5	64 5.7	70 5.2	63 5.8	Sales/Receivables	56 6.5	51 7.1
48 7.6	67 5.4	80 4.5	76 4.8	101 3.6	83 4.4		77 4.7	69 5.3
						Cost of Sales/Inventory		
						Cost of Sales/Payables		
11.5	7.0	7.2	5.9	4.0	2.5		7.3	9.0
101.3	13.2	17.4	11.4	7.0	14.8	Sales/Working Capital	20.5	23.8
-13.5	112.7	64.7	83.2	-17.7	NM		-842.9	-49.6
15.6	28.1	29.9	23.4		9.7		11.6	8.7
(60) 3.5	(88) 8.4	(101) 6.7	(41) 5.6		(11) 4.9	EBIT/Interest	(283) 3.1	(258) 2.3
.6	2.2	2.7	1.7		-1.6		-.3	-1.9
		13.7	7.9			Net Profit + Depr., Dep.,	7.6	8.9
		(27) 5.0	(10) 1.9			Amort./Cur. Mat. L./T/D	(43) 2.7	(46) 2.3
		2.1	.4				.2	.5
.1	.1	.1	.1	.3	.1		.2	.2
1.7	.3	.4	.2	.5	.4	Fixed/Worth	.5	.5
-.3	4.3	1.4	1.5	-.1	2.5		2.7	6.9
1.3	.5	1.0	1.1	1.1	.3		.8	1.0
UND	1.8	2.4	2.8	4.2	2.9	Debt/Worth	2.3	2.8
-2.6	12.3	7.0	9.1	-6.9	15.7		17.2	36.9
118.9	79.2	65.4	55.5		52.2	% Profit Before Taxes/Tangible	75.0	80.1
(45) 60.0	(86) 42.1	(105) 39.6	(40) 32.5		(12) 8.6	Net Worth	(271) 32.9	(237) 24.8
20.0	10.2	15.8	15.2		-6.6		-1.1	.3
51.7	25.8	26.3	20.4	21.3	11.1	% Profit Before Taxes/Total	20.3	20.6
17.6	14.4	10.6	8.1	11.9	4.9	Assets	6.7	4.7
-1.6	2.4	3.6	.9	6.8	-.2		-4.5	-9.2
181.8	94.4	88.1	154.2	54.4	62.3		74.2	74.5
46.8	39.4	36.0	50.8	35.2	16.1	Sales/Net Fixed Assets	29.1	31.4
22.7	17.3	13.1	11.2	9.8	6.2		13.1	13.4
8.7	4.7	4.0	3.4	2.4	1.5		4.8	5.2
4.8	3.7	2.9	2.4	1.8	1.1	Sales/Total Assets	3.3	3.6
3.3	2.4	1.9	1.4	.8	.7		2.3	2.2
.3	.6	.5	.5				.4	.5
(49) .7	(68) 1.1	(99) 1.4	(38) 1.3			% Depr., Dep., Amort./Sales	(244) 1.1	(228) 1.3
2.0	2.3	2.8	3.7				2.3	3.0
6.1	4.0	2.0					3.3	3.5
(44) 9.7	(42) 6.9	(23) 3.6				% Officers', Directors',	(105) 7.2	(89) 6.4
16.6	16.0	7.5				Owners' Comp/Sales	14.9	13.2
107079M	471771M	1530195M	2262449M	1435466M	2986500M	Net Sales ($)	7689152M	6819270M
19597M	132756M	519931M	1054304M	739026M	2445382M	Total Assets ($)	3772035M	3231937M

© RMA 2005

M = $ thousand   MM = $ million

See Pages 11 through 21 for Explanation of Ratios and Data

Comparative Historical Data | **Current Data Sorted By Sales**

4/1/02-3/31/03 ALL	4/1/03-3/31/04 ALL	4/1/04-3/31/05 ALL	Type of Statement	0-1MM	1-3MM	3-5MM	5-10MM	10-25MM	25MM & OVER
65	61	61	Unqualified				12	17	32
42	44	61	Reviewed	2	7	9	25	16	2
47	75	50	Compiled	8	10	10	15	3	4
48	65	62	Tax Returns	23	19	11	7		2
118	126	163	Other	23	30	26	25	26	33
				41 (4/1-9/30/04)			356 (10/1/04-3/31/05)		
320	371	397	**NUMBER OF STATEMENTS**	56	66	56	84	62	73
%	%	%	**ASSETS**	%	%	%	%	%	%
12.9	15.7	17.5	Cash & Equivalents	23.4	20.2	22.0	14.5	13.8	13.6
46.0	43.5	42.5	Trade Receivables (net)	24.1	37.1	40.1	50.7	51.6	46.1
3.6	4.8	4.9	Inventory	5.7	5.5	5.1	4.8	5.5	3.3
3.8	3.8	3.7	All Other Current	2.4	2.1	4.4	4.2	2.6	5.8
66.4	67.8	68.6	Total Current	55.6	64.9	71.6	74.3	73.5	68.8
18.8	16.5	16.1	Fixed Assets (net)	31.3	15.4	13.5	14.1	14.4	11.0
6.8	6.0	7.3	Intangibles (net)	7.3	11.7	2.4	4.5	5.0	12.5
8.1	9.7	7.9	All Other Non-Current	5.8	8.0	12.5	7.1	7.1	7.7
100.0	100.0	100.0	Total	100.0	100.0	100.0	100.0	100.0	100.0
			LIABILITIES						
19.1	16.4	17.6	Notes Payable-Short Term	40.3	19.1	15.2	13.7	13.0	8.8
4.3	3.3	3.0	Cur. Mat.-L/T/D	4.2	3.1	1.4	4.1	2.4	2.2
16.0	14.1	14.7	Trade Payables	12.5	13.1	10.8	17.0	15.4	17.7
.6	.7	1.2	Income Taxes Payable	.1	.1	.5	1.6	.9	3.4
20.6	18.4	19.3	All Other Current	25.2	17.1	17.6	24.0	16.0	15.2
60.7	52.9	55.7	Total Current	82.3	52.4	45.6	60.4	47.8	47.4
11.6	10.6	14.3	Long-Term Debt	31.1	19.1	6.5	11.9	6.5	12.4
.7	.7	.4	Deferred Taxes	.0	.1	.1	.3	.7	.8
8.2	8.9	9.0	All Other Non-Current	11.7	12.1	5.8	8.3	8.6	7.5
18.8	26.9	20.7	Net Worth	−25.1	16.3	42.0	19.0	36.4	31.9
100.0	100.0	100.0	Total Liabilities & Net Worth	100.0	100.0	100.0	100.0	100.0	100.0
			INCOME DATA						
100.0	100.0	100.0	Net Sales	100.0	100.0	100.0	100.0	100.0	100.0
			Gross Profit						
95.5	94.9	93.3	Operating Expenses	88.9	94.2	92.8	94.9	93.5	94.0
4.5	5.1	6.7	Operating Profit	11.1	5.8	7.2	5.1	6.5	6.0
1.3	1.1	1.1	All Other Expenses (net)	3.3	.9	.1	.5	.8	1.1
3.2	4.0	5.7	Profit Before Taxes	7.8	5.0	7.0	4.6	5.7	4.9
			RATIOS						
1.9	2.5	2.4		1.9	2.3	3.9	2.0	2.3	2.5
1.3	1.5	1.4	Current	.9	1.4	1.8	1.4	1.4	1.4
.8	.9	1.0		.2	.9	1.1	1.1	1.1	1.1
1.8	2.2	2.1		1.6	1.9	3.0	1.9	2.3	2.3
1.1	(370) 1.2	1.2	Quick	.7	1.3	1.5	1.2	1.3	1.3
.7	.7	.8		.2	.8	.9	.9	.9	.8
29 12.4	28 13.2	25 14.4		0 UND	21 17.6	22 16.4	36 10.1	41 8.9	46 7.9
48 7.6	50 7.4	51 7.1	Sales/Receivables	21 17.2	45 8.1	50 7.4	56 6.6	59 6.2	64 5.7
66 5.5	73 5.0	72 5.1		44 8.3	63 5.8	69 5.3	74 4.9	75 4.9	79 4.6
			Cost of Sales/Inventory						
			Cost of Sales/Payables						
9.7	7.4	7.1		11.9	8.5	5.8	7.6	6.9	5.8
24.8	15.7	17.8	Sales/Working Capital	−43.0	19.6	13.3	15.2	12.5	16.1
−36.1	−120.3	−468.3		−5.1	−38.4	100.6	72.5	47.3	83.2
15.7	22.2	23.3		11.3	13.2	59.4	25.9	56.3	22.0
(266) 3.6	(294) 4.8	(309) 6.2	EBIT/Interest	(37) 3.2	(48) 3.6	(42) 12.0	(71) 5.8	(51) 7.5	(60) 6.8
.7	1.0	1.9		−3.3	1.4	6.1	1.7	1.7	2.1
9.8	6.7	13.7					16.0	14.7	34.6
(59) 3.0	(44) 2.0	(51) 4.4	Net Profit + Depr., Dep., Amort./Cur. Mat. L/T/D			(15) 5.3	(13) 5.0	(14) 3.8	
1.1	.5	1.2					2.1	1.0	.3
.2	.1	.1		.2	.2	.1	.1	.1	.1
.6	.4	.4	Fixed/Worth	4.6	1.2	.3	.3	.3	.3
13.2	3.0	UND		−.4	−.4	.7	7.5	1.2	1.3
1.1	.7	.9		1.5	.9	.4	1.1	.8	.8
2.8	2.1	2.7	Debt/Worth	UND	3.6	1.4	3.0	2.4	2.3
71.5	17.5	−113.2		−2.2	−3.5	3.7	21.1	6.0	9.3
73.1	74.5	72.4		92.7	87.6	84.4	69.4	67.0	58.0
(244) 28.9	(295) 27.3	(295) 40.7	% Profit Before Taxes/Tangible Net Worth	(28) 44.8	(38) 44.8	(49) 46.6	(66) 43.5	(55) 35.3	(59) 31.5
7.2	3.5	14.4		17.5	18.2	16.5	9.2	9.3	4.5
21.2	24.1	25.9		38.9	27.8	40.5	24.1	27.6	19.0
7.5	8.2	11.3	% Profit Before Taxes/Total Assets	11.5	14.0	19.6	10.1	11.6	8.3
−1.7	.2	2.2		−.8	2.3	5.7	1.8	1.3	1.3
71.3	83.7	101.0		76.7	90.0	92.2	91.0	133.2	141.7
34.8	34.5	39.3	Sales/Net Fixed Assets	38.8	31.1	38.1	40.9	45.4	53.2
13.6	13.0	15.5		8.5	14.5	17.9	18.2	12.9	13.7
4.7	4.7	4.5		6.7	4.8	4.7	4.7	4.4	3.9
3.5	3.2	3.2	Sales/Total Assets	3.6	3.4	3.4	3.7	3.2	2.5
2.4	2.1	2.0		1.3	2.1	2.3	2.4	1.9	1.5
.7	.5	.5		.3	.3	.6	.6	.3	.5
(241) 1.3	(261) 1.2	(266) 1.2	% Depr., Dep., Amort./Sales	(34) 1.5	(36) 1.2	(32) 1.2	(67) .9	(49) 1.3	(48) 1.3
2.9	2.7	2.5		5.9	2.6	1.8	2.3	2.4	3.3
4.0	3.3	4.2		8.1	5.8	2.9	3.6		
(103) 7.3	(109) 6.0	(111) 7.3	% Officers', Directors', Owners' Comp/Sales	(25) 10.0	(32) 8.5	(19) 4.9	(23) 5.3		
11.0	11.4	11.4		23.7	15.5	11.9	9.7		
13319093M	7229200M	8793460M	Net Sales ($)	28917M	122396M	226835M	595911M	999914M	6819487M
3375205M	4250448M	4910996M	Total Assets ($)	23342M	51043M	81448M	225772M	476152M	4053239M

M = $ thousand   MM = $ million
See Pages 11 through 21 for Explanation of Ratios and Data

Current Data Sorted By Assets

Comparative Historical Data

	0-500M	500M-2MM	2-10MM	10-50MM	50-100MM	100-250MM	Type of Statement		4/1/00-3/31/01 ALL	4/1/01-3/31/02 ALL
	2	12	43	36	4	9	Unqualified		85	78
	7	23	39	10	1		Reviewed		68	59
	16	32	13	1			Compiled		80	86
	51	13	6				Tax Returns		40	29
	32	42	49	24	9	4	Other		144	130
	73 (4/1-9/30/04)			404 (10/1/04-3/31/05)						
	108	122	150	71	13	13	NUMBER OF STATEMENTS		417	382
	%	%	%	%	%	%	ASSETS		%	%
	23.7	13.2	15.0	15.6	9.2	18.3	Cash & Equivalents		15.8	16.6
	23.7	42.8	44.2	39.5	23.6	18.7	Trade Receivables (net)		44.2	43.5
	1.7	2.0	4.3	5.0	7.5	4.1	Inventory		1.9	1.6
	3.4	3.8	4.5	6.7	3.3	2.7	All Other Current		5.2	5.5
	52.5	61.9	68.1	66.8	43.7	43.8	Total Current		67.2	67.2
	28.0	16.6	15.1	13.5	9.7	15.7	Fixed Assets (net)		16.8	18.4
	4.5	4.8	5.4	11.7	25.0	30.5	Intangibles (net)		5.3	5.2
	14.9	16.8	11.4	8.1	21.6	10.1	All Other Non-Current		10.7	9.2
	100.0	100.0	100.0	100.0	100.0	100.0	Total		100.0	100.0
							LIABILITIES			
	30.9	15.5	8.7	6.7	5.2	1.2	Notes Payable-Short Term		14.2	14.5
	8.8	4.5	1.9	2.3	4.1	2.9	Cur. Mat.-L/T/D		2.5	3.9
	12.2	11.8	11.7	13.7	4.8	9.0	Trade Payables		12.3	13.0
	.5	.4	.9	.7	1.4	.3	Income Taxes Payable		.8	.9
	22.1	17.7	17.0	25.7	18.3	22.4	All Other Current		19.0	20.3
	74.5	49.9	40.2	49.1	33.8	35.7	Total Current		48.8	52.6
	28.4	10.2	11.5	13.9	13.9	16.1	Long-Term Debt		10.9	11.3
	.1	.7	.6	.8	1.1	1.0	Deferred Taxes		1.3	1.4
	9.6	9.3	8.8	5.7	11.6	6.3	All Other Non-Current		7.1	14.0
	-12.7	29.9	38.9	30.5	39.7	40.9	Net Worth		31.9	20.7
	100.0	100.0	100.0	100.0	100.0	100.0	Total Liabilities & Net Worth		100.0	100.0
							INCOME DATA			
	100.0	100.0	100.0	100.0	100.0	100.0	Net Sales		100.0	100.0
							Gross Profit			
	94.6	93.3	90.4	91.4	92.0	93.3	Operating Expenses		94.4	96.0
	5.4	6.7	9.6	8.6	8.0	6.7	Operating Profit		5.6	4.0
	.6	1.6	2.0	1.3	1.3	.9	All Other Expenses (net)		.4	1.1
	4.9	5.1	7.6	7.3	6.7	5.8	Profit Before Taxes		5.2	2.9
							RATIOS			
	2.4	2.5	3.3	2.0	1.5	2.6	Current		2.7	2.4
	1.1	1.5	1.6	1.3	1.2	1.2			1.5	1.4
	.4	.9	1.1	1.0	1.0	.7			1.0	.9
	2.2	2.2	2.9	1.6	1.2	1.5	Quick		2.4	2.2
	1.1	1.4	1.4	1.0	1.0	1.0			1.4	1.3
	.3	.7	1.0	.8	.7	.5			.9	.8
	0 UND	17 20.9	32 11.3	41 9.0	20 18.6	31 11.6	Sales/Receivables		28 13.3	28 12.8
	0 UND	46 8.0	57 6.4	66 5.5	58 6.3	49 7.4			57 6.5	53 6.9
	31 11.9	71 5.1	85 4.3	87 4.2	67 5.5	62 5.9			82 4.5	77 4.7
							Cost of Sales/Inventory			
							Cost of Sales/Payables			
	24.5	7.5	4.9	5.0	16.9	4.8	Sales/Working Capital		6.6	6.9
	176.3	19.4	9.7	15.2	24.6	13.2			13.0	17.0
	-16.2	-71.8	45.4	637.3	NM	-14.5			399.0	-96.6
	24.7	15.1	46.4	30.2	9.7	34.1	EBIT/Interest		21.7	20.4
	(76) 5.6	(96) 4.2	(120) 10.0	(56) 10.0	(10) 5.4	9.0			(315) 5.2	(310) 3.1
	-.5	-.8	2.1	2.8	1.9	.9			1.4	-1.1
		10.3	24.3	17.1			Net Profit + Depr., Dep., Amort./Cur. Mat. L /T/D		8.2	5.7
		(12) 4.3	(27) 5.0	(20) 4.6					(67) 3.8	(72) 1.9
		.7	1.1	2.4					1.2	.3
	.2	.1	.1	.2	.2	.3	Fixed/Worth		.1	.1
	2.3	.4	.3	.5	.6	3.1			.4	.5
	-.6	3.1	.9	-13.3	-.4	-4.6			1.8	3.6
	.8	.7	.5	1.1	1.5	1.7	Debt/Worth		.7	.8
	6.9	1.9	1.5	3.2	7.4	9.2			2.0	2.4
	-2.7	159.6	4.6	-35.4	-4.2	-18.6			11.0	12.8
	219.4	54.0	73.2	69.3			% Profit Before Taxes/Tangible Net Worth		66.0	64.3
	(63) 73.2	(94) 22.1	(133) 33.8	(51) 28.9					(341) 32.0	(308) 26.8
	6.7	1.1	6.6	13.1					10.6	-.1
	75.7	20.3	28.6	20.7	17.3	12.3	% Profit Before Taxes/Total Assets		25.7	24.6
	20.7	6.9	11.8	9.8	8.0	7.1			9.2	5.1
	-8.5	-1.7	2.1	2.7	3.5	-.6			1.2	-4.3
	150.7	96.7	66.3	57.3	37.9	24.8	Sales/Net Fixed Assets		69.6	71.0
	49.0	39.8	26.4	29.0	22.3	8.6			30.1	26.3
	15.5	16.3	12.3	10.8	16.3	6.8			13.8	12.6
	14.6	4.7	3.4	3.0	2.1	2.2	Sales/Total Assets		4.5	4.6
	6.1	3.2	2.5	2.0	1.5	1.4			3.1	3.1
	3.4	2.2	1.6	1.3	.9	1.1			2.0	2.0
	.4	.6	.7	.8		1.6	% Depr., Dep., Amort./Sales		.7	.6
	(61) .9	(83) 1.0	(119) 1.4	(55) 1.4		(10) 2.6			(303) 1.3	(291) 1.4
	2.1	1.7	2.9	3.2		4.4			2.3	2.6
	5.5	4.3	3.7				% Officers', Directors', Owners' Comp/Sales		5.9	3.8
	(58) 12.3	(39) 7.3	(32) 5.5						(126) 10.9	(102) 8.6
	22.7	14.1	9.7						20.2	18.8
	203374M	443066M	1750048M	3684482M	1574486M	3162938M	Net Sales ($)		13715231M	10003431M
	23750M	128747M	692520M	1485606M	983764M	2078248M	Total Assets ($)		4712385M	3995771M

M = $ thousand   MM = $ million
See Pages 11 through 21 for Explanation of Ratios and Data

Comparative Historical Data | Current Data Sorted By Sales

4/1/02-3/31/03 ALL	4/1/03-3/31/04 ALL	4/1/04-3/31/05 ALL	Type of Statement	0-1MM	1-3MM	3-5MM	5-10MM	10-25MM	25MM & OVER
107	100	106	Unqualified	2	7	9	18	21	49
73	65	79	Reviewed	4	11	13	20	24	7
53	86	62	Compiled	6	28	17	6	4	1
50	65	70	Tax Returns	30	23	6	6	5	
144	150	160	Other	22	31	20	22	34	31
				73 (4/1-9/30/04)			404 (10/1/04-3/31/05)		
427	466	477	**NUMBER OF STATEMENTS**	64	100	65	72	88	88
%	%	%	**ASSETS**	%	%	%	%	%	%
17.6	18.3	16.5	Cash & Equivalents	16.3	15.2	21.7	14.9	17.0	15.2
39.0	35.8	37.3	Trade Receivables (net)	18.7	32.6	35.7	47.3	46.5	39.6
2.3	3.5	3.3	Inventory	.6	4.6	4.0	2.5	3.1	4.4
7.4	6.4	4.3	All Other Current	4.7	5.0	1.3	3.4	4.9	5.8
66.3	63.9	61.5	Total Current	40.4	57.5	62.6	68.0	71.5	65.1
17.2	17.2	18.0	Fixed Assets (net)	34.5	19.2	17.7	12.6	15.4	12.0
5.2	6.2	7.2	Intangibles (net)	6.0	4.0	6.1	6.3	5.3	15.1
11.2	12.7	13.3	All Other Non-Current	18.9	19.4	13.6	13.1	7.9	7.8
100.0	100.0	100.0	Total	100.0	100.0	100.0	100.0	100.0	100.0
			LIABILITIES						
14.7	12.4	14.9	Notes Payable-Short Term	34.9	16.5	15.9	12.6	7.8	6.5
4.0	3.4	4.3	Cur. Mat.-L/T/D	8.5	6.6	3.2	2.8	2.1	2.5
12.9	12.6	11.9	Trade Payables	9.6	12.5	9.8	12.1	12.7	13.6
.8	.7	.7	Income Taxes Payable	.2	.7	.7	.8	.6	.9
20.0	20.4	19.8	All Other Current	22.5	16.1	20.1	15.8	22.0	22.9
52.3	49.5	51.5	Total Current	75.7	52.5	49.6	44.2	45.2	46.4
12.6	13.8	15.6	Long-Term Debt	32.9	14.5	17.4	7.8	13.1	11.6
.8	.7	.5	Deferred Taxes	.0	.6	.3	.5	.7	1.0
8.2	9.0	8.7	All Other Non-Current	5.1	11.2	11.4	10.1	7.3	6.4
26.0	26.9	23.7	Net Worth	−13.8	21.2	21.3	37.3	33.7	34.7
100.0	100.0	100.0	Total Liabilities & Net Worth	100.0	100.0	100.0	100.0	100.0	100.0
			INCOME DATA						
100.0	100.0	100.0	Net Sales	100.0	100.0	100.0	100.0	100.0	100.0
			Gross Profit						
93.3	93.0	92.4	Operating Expenses	90.8	92.0	96.9	92.0	91.1	92.1
6.7	7.0	7.6	Operating Profit	9.2	8.0	3.1	8.0	8.9	7.9
2.7	1.1	1.4	All Other Expenses (net)	2.4	1.8	.7	.6	1.9	1.0
4.0	5.9	6.2	Profit Before Taxes	6.8	6.2	2.4	7.4	7.0	7.0
			RATIOS						
2.6	2.5	2.6	Current	2.3	3.5	2.3	2.9	2.6	2.0
1.5	1.4	1.4		.8	1.5	1.4	1.7	1.5	1.3
.9	.9	.9		.1	1.0	.9	1.1	1.1	1.0
2.2	2.1	2.3	Quick	2.2	3.1	2.1	2.6	2.3	1.6
(426) 1.3	1.2	1.2		.7	1.3	1.3	1.5	1.3	1.1
.8	.7	.7		.1	.6	.8	1.0	1.0	.8
20 18.5	14 26.1	13 28.8	Sales/Receivables	0 UND	0 UND	4 90.4	27 13.4	36 10.1	41 9.0
50 7.3	48 7.6	47 7.7		0 UND	29 12.7	37 9.8	52 7.0	64 5.7	59 6.2
78 4.7	71 5.1	71 5.1		38 9.6	68 5.4	61 6.0	84 4.4	84 4.3	75 4.9
			Cost of Sales/Inventory						
			Cost of Sales/Payables						
5.9	6.8	6.4	Sales/Working Capital	11.6	5.7	7.9	5.8	5.5	7.2
13.5	20.0	21.1		−29.5	32.7	36.0	13.2	12.7	15.9
−169.6	−79.5	−86.2		−6.4	−153.2	−91.5	101.8	47.1	721.2
19.5	24.4	27.8	EBIT/Interest	10.8	15.9	21.2		45.7	30.3
(325) 5.4	(353) 5.3	(371) 6.6		(45) 3.1	(71) 5.4	(52) 4.1	(62) 12.0	(70) 7.7	(71) 9.7
.6	1.4	1.3		−1.0	−1.0	−1.4	3.5	1.3	3.4
6.9	10.0	12.3	Net Profit + Depr., Dep., Amort./Cur. Mat. L/T/D				11.9	15.1	17.1
(82) 2.1	(72) 3.6	(70) 4.2					(12) 5.9	(15) 5.0	(28) 4.0
.9	1.4	1.2					1.7	1.9	1.3
.1	.1	.1	Fixed/Worth	.3	.1	.2	.1	.1	.2
.4	.5	.5		3.6	.4	.5	.4	.3	.5
4.1	3.6	8.8		−.7	UND	−2.3	2.1	1.3	10.5
.7	.8	.7	Debt/Worth	1.4	.5	.8	.5	.7	1.1
2.1	2.3	2.5		16.0	2.0	2.5	1.5	2.0	3.0
32.9	20.7	UND		−1.9	UND	−14.7	12.5	7.2	NM
63.0	79.4	77.9	% Profit Before Taxes/Tangible Net Worth	123.6	110.6	55.0	54.3	76.8	79.8
(331) 27.8	(366) 30.4	(359) 32.1		(38) 21.3	(75) 31.2	(47) 15.6	(58) 27.6	(75) 40.9	(66) 39.2
1.0	5.9	5.3		3.3	3.8	−6.5	8.1	4.6	15.9
22.1	22.1	27.0	% Profit Before Taxes/Total Assets	32.6	31.5	26.3	26.2	31.8	20.8
7.5	9.7	10.5		6.9	10.7	6.4	12.6	15.4	10.4
−1.5	1.2	.5		−8.5	−.7	−4.0	3.3	1.4	3.7
86.8	94.9	76.5	Sales/Net Fixed Assets	59.1	105.6	98.5	78.7	79.5	57.2
32.4	32.1	33.8		13.0	38.8	37.8	36.0	35.1	32.4
13.0	12.6	12.4		3.8	15.8	15.4	18.1	12.9	11.5
4.6	4.3	4.6	Sales/Total Assets	5.1	6.1	5.6	4.6	3.7	3.4
2.8	2.7	2.9		2.6	3.3	3.6	3.1	3.0	2.2
1.7	1.7	1.8		.8	1.9	2.0	2.1	1.9	1.6
.7	.6	.7	% Depr., Dep., Amort./Sales	1.0	.6	.6	.8	.5	.8
(308) 1.6	(334) 1.5	(336) 1.3		(34) 1.7	(69) .9	(49) 1.0	(52) 1.3	(65) 1.3	(67) 1.5
2.8	2.7	2.5		5.6	1.9	2.2	2.5	2.8	2.6
3.4	3.4	4.6	% Officers', Directors', Owners' Comp/Sales	10.4	5.1	4.9	3.7	1.9	
(124) 7.2	(124) 8.3	(140) 7.5		(28) 21.0	(48) 9.0	(17) 5.8	(20) 5.2	(18) 5.9	
17.3	17.9	17.5		36.1	19.5	7.4	9.8	9.5	
14679577M	15248388M	10818394M	Net Sales ($)	32819M	188962M	254229M	515008M	1322827M	8504549M
6044206M	5960291M	5392635M	Total Assets ($)	30076M	119030M	110227M	254140M	581847M	4297315M

© RMA 2005   M = $ thousand   MM = $ million
See Pages 11 through 21 for Explanation of Ratios and Data

Current Data Sorted By Assets   **Comparative Historical Data**

						Type of Statement		
2	3	10	3	1		Unqualified		
	6	5	1			Reviewed		
10	6	3				Compiled		
12	1					Tax Returns		
10	14	15		3		Other		
	18 (4/1-9/30/04)			87 (10/1/04-3/31/05)			4/1/00-3/31/01	4/1/01-3/31/02
0-500M	500M-2MM	2-10MM	10-50MM	50-100MM	100-250MM		ALL	ALL
34	30	33	7	1		NUMBER OF STATEMENTS		
%	%	%	%	%	%	**ASSETS**	%	%
21.6	10.4	11.3				Cash & Equivalents		
39.1	53.2	52.3			D	Trade Receivables (net)	D	D
.1	.1	.0			A	Inventory	A	A
7.6	1.8	7.6			T	All Other Current	T	T
68.3	65.5	71.2			A	Total Current	A	A
18.6	19.2	8.2				Fixed Assets (net)		
6.0	5.8	7.0			N	Intangibles (net)	N	N
7.1	9.5	13.7			O	All Other Non-Current	O	O
100.0	100.0	100.0			T	Total	T	T
						LIABILITIES		
46.1	19.4	18.4			A	Notes Payable-Short Term	A	A
6.4	3.2	.5			V	Cur. Mat.-L/T/D	V	V
9.8	8.0	8.4			A	Trade Payables	A	A
.0	.6	.4			I	Income Taxes Payable	I	I
16.4	17.9	19.3			L	All Other Current	L	L
78.6	49.2	47.1			A	Total Current	A	A
14.4	12.8	6.2			B	Long-Term Debt	B	B
.0	.0	.6			L	Deferred Taxes	L	L
12.3	5.8	5.7			E	All Other Non-Current	E	E
-5.3	32.3	40.5				Net Worth		
100.0	100.0	100.0				Total Liabilities & Net Worth		
						INCOME DATA		
100.0	100.0	100.0				Net Sales		
						Gross Profit		
94.4	91.1	95.3				Operating Expenses		
5.6	8.9	4.7				Operating Profit		
.1	2.2	-.1				All Other Expenses (net)		
5.4	6.8	4.8				Profit Before Taxes		
						RATIOS		
2.0	1.8	2.4						
1.1	1.5	1.4				Current		
.5	1.0	1.0						
1.7	1.7	2.2						
1.1	1.5	1.4				Quick		
.5	.9	.8						
0 UND	9 39.0	31 11.6						
24 15.2	41 9.0	45 8.2				Sales/Receivables		
43 8.5	55 6.6	62 5.9						
						Cost of Sales/Inventory		
						Cost of Sales/Payables		
16.2	13.8	10.7						
185.9	26.8	23.2				Sales/Working Capital		
-14.3	NM	419.3						
17.8	16.2	22.8						
(24) 2.7	(26) 6.6	(27) 10.1				EBIT/Interest		
-2.4	2.7	2.1						
						Net Profit + Depr., Dep., Amort./Cur. Mat. L./T/D		
.1	.1	.1						
NM	.3	.2				Fixed/Worth		
-.4	4.3	.4						
1.5	1.1	.6						
-25.3	1.7	1.7				Debt/Worth		
-3.1	22.1	6.1						
110.1	92.0	59.5				% Profit Before Taxes/Tangible		
(16) 21.3	(25) 37.5	(28) 36.7				Net Worth		
-25.0	20.1	13.2						
40.5	23.3	22.7				% Profit Before Taxes/Total		
11.8	11.1	12.6				Assets		
-9.3	5.6	5.2						
337.1	333.3	180.9						
99.1	75.7	91.8				Sales/Net Fixed Assets		
18.4	20.1	50.1						
12.1	7.4	5.7						
6.8	5.4	4.0				Sales/Total Assets		
3.2	3.4	2.9						
.3	.2	.3						
(25) .6	(21) .6	(25) .5				% Depr., Dep., Amort./Sales		
1.4	1.4	.7						
5.7								
(15) 8.4						% Officers', Directors',		
12.9						Owners' Comp/Sales		
53751M	300581M	719469M	285608M	233572M		Net Sales ($)		
7173M	34918M	152471M	135975M	52136M		Total Assets ($)		

© RMA 2005

M = $ thousand MM = $ million
See Pages 11 through 21 for Explanation of Ratios and Data

Comparative Historical Data / Current Data Sorted By Sales

	4/1/02-3/31/03 ALL	4/1/03-3/31/04 ALL	4/1/04-3/31/05 ALL	0-1MM	1-3MM	3-5MM	5-10MM	10-25MM	25MM & OVER
Type of Statement				18 (4/1-9/30/04)			87 (10/1/04-3/31/05)		
Unqualified	9	13	19	1	2	2	3	4	7
Reviewed	4	5	12		1	1	4	4	2
Compiled	12	13	19	5	5	2	3	3	1
Tax Returns	10	11	13	7	3	2	1		
Other	37	36	42	5	10	4	4	12	7
NUMBER OF STATEMENTS	72	78	105	18	21	11	15	23	17
ASSETS	%	%	%	%	%	%	%	%	%
Cash & Equivalents	13.6	13.4	15.1	10.6	19.1	23.4	6.6	16.6	14.7
Trade Receivables (net)	48.6	47.8	48.2	30.1	41.3	39.6	71.1	53.8	53.5
Inventory	.0	.0	.1	.0	.2	.0	.0	.0	.0
All Other Current	6.4	6.7	5.7	12.2	2.1	.8	1.8	5.6	10.0
Total Current	68.6	68.0	69.0	52.8	62.7	64.0	79.5	76.0	78.3
Fixed Assets (net)	11.1	13.5	14.6	32.9	19.9	7.2	7.2	10.4	5.7
Intangibles (net)	6.3	5.1	6.0	9.0	8.3	1.2	3.8	5.6	5.8
All Other Non-Current	14.0	13.4	10.4	5.3	9.1	27.6	9.6	8.0	10.3
Total	100.0	100.0	100.0	100.0	100.0	100.0	100.0	100.0	100.0
LIABILITIES									
Notes Payable-Short Term	20.5	30.4	27.6	57.0	21.9	24.2	32.5	18.1	14.0
Cur. Mat.-L/T/D	4.7	6.8	3.2	8.1	4.3	1.3	4.5	.6	.2
Trade Payables	7.6	10.6	9.0	10.2	8.0	4.4	8.9	4.5	18.3
Income Taxes Payable	.0	.5	.3	.0	.2	.1	.5	.5	.3
All Other Current	21.3	18.9	18.1	19.1	12.5	11.1	22.1	20.2	22.2
Total Current	54.2	67.1	58.2	94.5	46.9	41.1	68.5	43.9	55.0
Long-Term Debt	6.2	11.0	10.4	25.4	12.9	12.5	3.9	3.6	5.1
Deferred Taxes	.7	.7	.2	.0	.1	.0	.9	.1	.0
All Other Non-Current	11.1	7.5	8.1	16.7	10.1	8.6	2.8	4.9	5.6
Net Worth	27.8	13.7	23.1	-36.6	30.1	37.8	24.0	47.5	34.3
Total Liabilities & Net Worth	100.0	100.0	100.0	100.0	100.0	100.0	100.0	100.0	100.0
INCOME DATA									
Net Sales	100.0	100.0	100.0	100.0	100.0	100.0	100.0	100.0	100.0
Gross Profit									
Operating Expenses	97.5	95.3	93.6	84.8	93.8	97.0	94.6	94.3	98.3
Operating Profit	2.5	4.7	6.4	15.2	6.2	3.0	5.4	5.7	1.7
All Other Expenses (net)	.9	1.0	.7	2.2	.2	.1	1.6	.2	.2
Profit Before Taxes	1.6	3.7	5.7	13.0	5.9	2.9	3.8	5.5	1.5
RATIOS									
Current	2.5	1.9	2.0	1.4	1.9	2.7	1.6	4.2	1.8
	1.5	1.2	1.4	.6	1.2	1.2	1.5	1.6	1.5
	1.0	.8	.9	.3	.8	.8	1.0	1.3	1.1
Quick	2.2	1.9	1.7	1.1	1.8	2.6	1.6	3.6	1.6
	1.3	1.1	1.2	.5	1.2	1.2	1.5	1.6	1.3
	.8	.6	.8	.2	.7	.8	.9	1.2	.9
Sales/Receivables	18 19.8	22 16.6	16 23.5	0 UND	0 UND	0 UND	40 9.1	28 12.8	13 28.8
	46 8.0	36 10.0	39 9.4	14 25.3	36 10.0	29 12.8	54 6.8	41 9.0	43 8.4
	60 6.1	56 6.6	55 6.7	49 7.4	53 6.9	48 7.6	91 4.0	62 5.9	50 7.3
Cost of Sales/Inventory									
Cost of Sales/Payables									
Sales/Working Capital	9.7	11.5	12.6	12.8	14.1	12.3	11.2	6.2	15.7
	20.3	102.2	29.8	-10.6	51.5	105.3	16.6	17.3	30.4
	NM	-34.5	-113.2	-3.9	-74.5	-41.5	241.7	34.3	265.2
EBIT/Interest	19.6	27.0	18.8	29.5	10.4		32.5	64.1	17.6
	(55) 4.0	(63) 4.6	(83) 6.0	(12) 3.5	(17) 1.5		8.5	(17) 10.4	(14) 5.9
	-1.3	1.1	1.6	-3.3	-.8		2.4	5.1	1.9
Net Profit + Depr., Dep., Amort./Cur. Mat. L/T/D									
Fixed/Worth	.1	.1	.1	.8	.2	.0	.0	.1	.1
	.3	.3	.3	-.8	.7	.2	.1	.2	.2
	1.3	4.2	NM	-.2	-9.5	-.6	7.6	.5	.3
Debt/Worth	.8	1.0	1.0	4.4	.9		1.1		1.4
	1.7	3.0	2.4	-3.2	2.4	1.0	1.7	1.6	2.1
	11.4	UND	-30.1	-2.2	-27.2	-11.5	48.3	2.5	8.0
% Profit Before Taxes/Tangible Net Worth	56.1	81.7	84.7		33.3		99.7	80.0	91.8
	(56) 21.2	(59) 30.6	(77) 33.3		(15) .7		(12) 35.3	(20) 46.2	(16) 29.0
	-3.1	3.1	9.7		-10.8		22.8	30.6	7.2
% Profit Before Taxes/Total Assets	18.6	22.0	24.4	27.9	24.0	34.1	20.6	30.3	17.3
	5.9	6.9	11.2	12.0	1.2	13.4	11.0	18.1	7.0
	-5.1	-.2	1.5	-4.5	-4.2	-1.3	3.6	9.9	2.2
Sales/Net Fixed Assets	136.3	201.1	247.3	249.7	180.6	411.3	369.6	102.6	214.2
	54.4	62.4	77.9	17.8	63.7	251.5	205.4	75.2	145.6
	26.2	26.2	21.9	7.1	18.8	20.4	73.4	44.8	70.3
Sales/Total Assets	6.0	6.8	7.7	7.3	10.4	14.8	6.8	6.7	8.9
	4.4	5.0	4.9	3.0	5.2	7.3	5.3	4.8	4.9
	2.5	3.3	3.1	1.3	3.1	2.5	3.1	3.8	3.5
% Depr., Dep., Amort./Sales	.4	.4	.3	.4	.4			.3	.1
	(49) 1.0	(49) .7	(77) .6	(13) 1.1	(16) .7			(19) .5	(14) .4
	1.6	1.2	1.1	6.3	2.4			.7	.7
% Officers', Directors', Owners' Comp/Sales	1.6	1.7	2.3		2.2				
	(28) 4.3	(26) 6.5	(32) 6.1		(11) 6.9				
	11.3	11.4	8.8		10.3				
Net Sales ($)	1966811M	4633613M	1592981M	8810M	42611M	47342M	107732M	335778M	1050708M
Total Assets ($)	698363M	1038069M	382673M	5202M	18508M	12088M	56108M	77232M	213535M

M = $ thousand   MM = $ million
See Pages 11 through 21 for Explanation of Ratios and Data

Current Data Sorted By Assets   Comparative Historical Data

0-500M	500M-2MM	2-10MM	10-50MM	50-100MM	100-250MM	Type of Statement	4/1/00-3/31/01 ALL	4/1/01-3/31/02 ALL
		1	3		4	Unqualified		
		3	2			Reviewed		
	3	3				Compiled		
	2	1				Tax Returns		
4	2	1				Other		
4	4	8	2		1			
8	9	16	7		5	NUMBER OF STATEMENTS		
%	%	%	%	%	%	ASSETS	%	%
		13.4		D		Cash & Equivalents	D	D
		37.9		A		Trade Receivables (net)	A	A
		4.0		T		Inventory	T	T
		2.7		A		All Other Current	A	A
		58.1				Total Current		
		18.0		N		Fixed Assets (net)	N	N
		14.5		O		Intangibles (net)	O	O
		9.3		T		All Other Non-Current	T	T
		100.0				Total		
				A		**LIABILITIES**	A	A
		11.8		V		Notes Payable-Short Term	V	V
		3.7		A		Cur. Mat.-L/T/D	A	A
		10.6		I		Trade Payables	I	I
		.5		L		Income Taxes Payable	L	L
		23.0		A		All Other Current	A	A
		49.7		B		Total Current	B	B
		8.2		L		Long-Term Debt	L	L
		.9		E		Deferred Taxes	E	E
		15.0				All Other Non-Current		
		26.2				Net Worth		
		100.0				Total Liabilities & Net Worth		
						INCOME DATA		
		100.0				Net Sales		
						Gross Profit		
		93.1				Operating Expenses		
		6.9				Operating Profit		
		1.7				All Other Expenses (net)		
		5.2				Profit Before Taxes		
						RATIOS		
		3.0						
		1.1				Current		
		.7						
		2.7						
		1.0				Quick		
		.6						
	33	11.2						
	54	6.8				Sales/Receivables		
	92	4.0						
						Cost of Sales/Inventory		
						Cost of Sales/Payables		
		6.9						
		33.2				Sales/Working Capital		
		-16.3						
		21.6						
	(15)	4.8				EBIT/Interest		
		1.3						
						Net Profit + Depr., Dep., Amort./Cur. Mat. L /T/D		
		.5						
		1.7				Fixed/Worth		
		-2.8						
		3.2						
		8.6				Debt/Worth		
		-13.8						
		111.2				% Profit Before Taxes/Tangible		
	(11)	31.2				Net Worth		
		14.1						
		26.9				% Profit Before Taxes/Total		
		6.4				Assets	•	
		1.0						
		43.3						
		26.8				Sales/Net Fixed Assets		
		9.7						
		3.1						
		2.2				Sales/Total Assets		
		1.4						
		1.1						
	(11)	1.7				% Depr., Dep., Amort./Sales		
		2.8						
						% Officers', Directors', Owners' Comp/Sales		
7423M	31886M	172317M	566796M		1208743M	Net Sales ($)		
1193M	8100M	78284M	151132M		870345M	Total Assets ($)		

M = $ thousand   MM = $ million
See Pages 11 through 21 for Explanation of Ratios and Data

	Comparative Historical Data					Current Data Sorted By Sales					

Type of Statement

					Type of Statement						
	2		6		8	Unqualified				1	7
	3		3		5	Reviewed				1	2
	3		3		6	Compiled		2	2	1	
	3		5		7	Tax Returns		1	2		
	9		18		19	Other	2	3	1		
	4/1/02-3/31/03		4/1/03-3/31/04		4/1/04-3/31/05		2	6	1	2	4	4
	ALL		ALL		ALL			3 (4/1-9/30/04)		42 (10/1/04-3/31/05)	
	20		35		45		0-1MM	1-3MM	3-5MM	5-10MM	10-25MM	25MM & OVER
						NUMBER OF STATEMENTS	4	11	3	7	7	13
	%		%		%	ASSETS	%	%	%	%	%	%
	16.1		15.1		12.9	Cash & Equivalents		10.2				15.2
	38.1		43.3		40.4	Trade Receivables (net)		41.4				34.4
	2.1		3.1		7.2	Inventory		.0				16.4
	7.9		3.5		4.0	All Other Current		2.1				6.4
	64.2		65.0		64.5	Total Current		53.7				72.4
	12.9		15.4		16.0	Fixed Assets (net)		31.5				6.6
	5.7		8.2		9.9	Intangibles (net)		2.7				13.8
	17.1		11.4		9.6	All Other Non-Current		12.0				7.3
	100.0		100.0		100.0	Total		100.0				100.0
						LIABILITIES						
	6.0		11.9		19.1	Notes Payable-Short Term		35.7				9.0
	1.9		3.2		2.5	Cur. Mat.-L/T/D		2.9				1.2
	9.6		13.7		23.0	Trade Payables		31.6				27.2
	.0		.4		.3	Income Taxes Payable		.0				.1
	27.8		12.7		18.5	All Other Current		16.1				20.6
	45.3		41.9		63.3	Total Current		86.3				58.1
	13.6		11.3		10.4	Long-Term Debt		13.5				13.8
	.2		.3		.4	Deferred Taxes		.0				.2
	4.8		9.2		16.2	All Other Non-Current		6.1				17.2
	36.1		37.3		9.8	Net Worth		-5.9				10.8
	100.0		100.0		100.0	Total Liabilities & Net Worth		100.0				100.0
						INCOME DATA						
	100.0		100.0		100.0	Net Sales		100.0				100.0
						Gross Profit						
	88.0		93.7		94.7	Operating Expenses		94.2				93.4
	12.0		6.3		5.3	Operating Profit		5.8				6.6
	.9		1.1		1.8	All Other Expenses (net)		2.5				2.5
	11.1		5.3		3.5	Profit Before Taxes		3.4				4.1
						RATIOS						
	4.7		3.1		1.8			1.2				1.8
	1.7		1.9		1.1	Current		.5				1.3
	.8		1.1		.7			.3				1.1
	3.4		2.6		1.6			1.0				1.4
	1.2		1.4		.9	Quick		.5				1.1
	.6		.8		.5			.3				.6
14	26.8	40	9.2	29	12.5	Sales/Receivables	1	423.3			29	12.6
33	11.0	54	6.8	47	7.8		33	10.9			35	10.3
65	5.6	66	5.5	75	4.9		102	3.6			66	5.5
						Cost of Sales/Inventory						
						Cost of Sales/Payables						
	7.6		5.4		10.3			16.0				8.8
	23.9		13.7		38.4	Sales/Working Capital		-14.3				14.8
	-20.8		51.7		-16.4			-4.1				43.6
	55.7		30.1		22.4							274.2
(13)	28.8	(26)	6.5	(39)	4.8	EBIT/Interest					(11)	6.3
	6.0		.6		-.2							.4
						Net Profit + Depr., Dep., Amort./Cur. Mat. L/T/D						
	.0		.1		.2			.2				.1
	.2		.4		1.3	Fixed/Worth		2.6				.1
	3.0		-3.9		-1.5			-3.3				3.3
	.3		.7		1.8			2.8				1.4
	1.2		1.8		12.3	Debt/Worth		12.3				3.5
	-13.1		-23.9		-7.4			-4.5				65.9
	136.5		125.7		129.1	% Profit Before Taxes/Tangible Net Worth						163.3
(14)	45.5	(25)	32.9	(29)	58.3						(11)	50.9
	22.3		1.0		23.1							23.8
	46.9		28.9		27.5			41.3				24.9
	25.1		12.8		7.9	% Profit Before Taxes/Total Assets		4.3				9.9
	7.4		-2.7		-6.7			-6.0				-2.3
	248.1		80.7		60.2			45.1				618.2
	33.6		45.3		29.0	Sales/Net Fixed Assets		23.9				40.7
	21.8		14.7		18.1			13.3				17.6
	5.5		4.3		4.8			6.2				3.9
	3.9		2.8		3.0	Sales/Total Assets		5.1				3.0
	1.9		2.1		1.6			2.0				1.1
	.4		.5		1.0							.7
(10)	1.7	(20)	1.3	(29)	1.4	% Depr., Dep., Amort./Sales					(10)	1.5
	2.8		2.8		2.0							2.3
			5.4		5.5	% Officers', Directors', Owners' Comp/Sales						
		(13)	13.0	(10)	9.3							
			16.8		14.4							
	343561M		466655M		1987165M	Net Sales ($)	1702M	20776M	11137M	52817M	96324M	1804409M
	211967M		206717M		1109054M	Total Assets ($)	486M	12082M	5897M	22876M	36734M	1030979M

© RMA 2005 M = $ thousand MM = $ million
See Pages 11 through 21 for Explanation of Ratios and Data

Current Data Sorted By Assets

Comparative Historical Data

3 2 5	1 2 8 5	3 4 2 6	4 2 4	1	2	Type of Statement Unqualified Reviewed Compiled Tax Returns Other		
		10 (4/1-9/30/04)		45 (10/1/04-3/31/05)			4/1/00- 3/31/01 ALL	4/1/01- 3/31/02 ALL
0-500M	500M-2MM	2-10MM	10-50MM	50-100MM	100-250MM			
10	16	15	10	2	2	NUMBER OF STATEMENTS		
%	%	%	%	%	%	ASSETS	%	%
24.2	5.0	4.9	6.9			Cash & Equivalents		
32.5	49.3	57.7	52.1			Trade Receivables (net)	D	D
.0	3.7	4.8	.8			Inventory	A	A
9.4	8.5	.9	6.6			All Other Current	T	T
66.2	66.7	68.3	66.3			Total Current	A	A
16.8	18.9	17.9	19.2			Fixed Assets (net)		
.0	.8	5.0	7.7			Intangibles (net)	N	N
17.0	13.6	8.8	6.7			All Other Non-Current	O	O
100.0	100.0	100.0	100.0			Total	T	T
						LIABILITIES	A	A
7.2	10.4	19.4	10.8			Notes Payable-Short Term	V	V
3.7	1.8	3.0	4.0			Cur. Mat.-L/T/D	A	A
11.8	17.1	28.8	36.8			Trade Payables	I	I
.0	.1	.0	.1			Income Taxes Payable	L	L
22.6	15.6	11.4	8.8			All Other Current	A	A
45.3	45.0	62.7	60.5			Total Current	B	B
20.1	9.9	9.7	4.8			Long-Term Debt	L	L
.0	.7	.3	1.4			Deferred Taxes	E	E
4.8	3.2	2.1	2.8			All Other Non-Current		
29.8	41.3	25.2	30.5			Net Worth		
100.0	100.0	100.0	100.0			Total Liabilities & Net Worth		
						INCOME DATA		
100.0	100.0	100.0	100.0			Net Sales		
						Gross Profit		
99.1	96.0	93.9	95.1			Operating Expenses		
.9	4.0	6.1	4.9			Operating Profit		
−.3	.4	1.0	.6			All Other Expenses (net)		
1.2	3.6	5.2	4.2			Profit Before Taxes		
						RATIOS		
8.3	2.1	1.4	1.3					
1.3	1.4	1.1	1.2			Current		
.7	.9	.7	.9					
7.9	1.8	1.3	1.3					
1.0	1.3	1.1	1.0			Quick		
.3	.8	.5	.7					
0 UND	33 10.9	51 7.1	34 10.7					
0 UND	50 7.3	69 5.3	43 8.5			Sales/Receivables		
46 8.0	76 4.8	199 1.8	76 4.8					
						Cost of Sales/Inventory		
						Cost of Sales/Payables		
20.0	8.9	9.9	23.6					
42.8	17.8	35.8	35.2			Sales/Working Capital		
−55.3	−113.5	−11.7	NM					
	23.8	11.7						
	(12) 7.6	(13) 6.6				EBIT/Interest		
	1.1	.7						
						Net Profit + Depr., Dep., Amort./Cur. Mat. L /T/D		
.0	.1	.1	.3					
.0	.3	.3	.6			Fixed/Worth		
1.4	1.0	4.5	1.1					
.9	.9	2.1	1.3					
1.7	1.5	3.7	2.1			Debt/Worth		
19.9	2.5	16.5	6.5					
	39.0	93.4				% Profit Before Taxes/Tangible Net Worth		
	(14) 20.6	(12) 54.8						
	−3.9	4.3						
38.8	15.2	21.9	18.3			% Profit Before Taxes/Total Assets		
10.2	3.8	7.8	6.2					
−.5	−1.7	1.0	2.1					
UND	94.9	100.6	162.9					
UND	48.0	40.5	50.4			Sales/Net Fixed Assets		
41.0	13.2	3.0	10.7					
19.0	5.3	4.3	5.5					
8.8	3.6	1.3	4.1			Sales/Total Assets		
1.9	2.5	1.1	2.4					
	.4	.4						
	(13) .9	(11) 1.8				% Depr., Dep., Amort./Sales		
	2.9	6.7						
						% Officers', Directors', Owners' Comp/Sales		
16892M	80558M	164096M	925501M	126853M	717373M	Net Sales ($)		
2505M	18391M	73881M	235873M	115012M	273820M	Total Assets ($)		

M = $ thousand   MM = $ million
See Pages 11 through 21 for Explanation of Ratios and Data

Comparative Historical Data | | | | **Current Data Sorted By Sales**

	3	9	11	Type of Statement	0-1MM	1-3MM	3-5MM	5-10MM	10-25MM	25MM & OVER
	3	9	11	Unqualified	1		1	2	4	7
	16	8	8	Reviewed	2	4	3	2	3	1
	9	12	13	Compiled					2	
	1	4	2	Tax Returns		2				
	8	18	21	Other	4	3	5	2	2	5
	4/1/02-3/31/03	4/1/03-3/31/04	4/1/04-3/31/05			10 (4/1-9/30/04)			45 (10/1/04-3/31/05)	
	ALL	ALL	ALL							
	37	51	55	**NUMBER OF STATEMENTS**	7	9	9	6	11	13
	%	%	%	**ASSETS**	%	%	%	%	%	%
	8.1	10.7	8.9	Cash & Equivalents					4.3	7.3
	48.5	41.7	47.6	Trade Receivables (net)					65.0	47.1
	.2	.5	2.7	Inventory					.2	1.3
	6.2	5.2	6.0	All Other Current					1.2	6.5
	63.0	58.1	65.2	Total Current					70.7	62.3
	23.3	25.6	19.5	Fixed Assets (net)					9.8	20.5
	3.0	7.1	4.3	Intangibles (net)					7.6	11.4
	10.7	9.2	10.9	All Other Non-Current					11.8	5.9
	100.0	100.0	100.0	Total					100.0	100.0
				LIABILITIES						
	11.8	9.7	12.0	Notes Payable-Short Term					17.4	7.8
	3.3	5.8	3.1	Cur. Mat.-L/T/D					1.6	4.5
	29.3	26.9	22.3	Trade Payables					26.8	30.1
	.3	.2	.1	Income Taxes Payable					.1	.1
	12.6	15.3	13.9	All Other Current					18.2	8.9
	57.3	57.9	51.3	Total Current					64.0	51.3
	9.2	13.3	11.0	Long-Term Debt					3.3	7.7
	.9	1.0	.8	Deferred Taxes					1.4	1.0
	1.9	2.2	2.9	All Other Non-Current					1.1	2.3
	30.6	25.6	33.9	Net Worth					30.2	37.6
	100.0	100.0	100.0	Total Liabilities & Net Worth					100.0	100.0
				INCOME DATA						
	100.0	100.0	100.0	Net Sales					100.0	100.0
				Gross Profit						
	93.9	96.3	95.7	Operating Expenses					93.0	95.5
	6.1	3.7	4.3	Operating Profit					7.0	4.5
	.9	.9	.5	All Other Expenses (net)					.6	.6
	5.2	2.8	3.8	Profit Before Taxes					6.5	3.9
				RATIOS						
	1.3	1.4	1.6						1.6	1.5
	1.1	1.1	1.2	Current					1.2	1.2
	.8	.7	.9						.7	1.1
	1.3	1.2	1.4						1.6	1.5
	1.0	1.0	1.1	Quick					1.1	1.1
	.6	.7	.7						.7	.8
	27 13.3	24 15.1	35 10.4						40 9.2	36 10.1
	35 10.3	39 9.2	51 7.1	Sales/Receivables					54 6.8	42 8.6
	61 6.0	51 7.1	77 4.7						77 4.7	69 5.3
				Cost of Sales/Inventory						
				Cost of Sales/Payables						
	17.2	14.6	11.1						17.9	14.2
	87.3	55.7	33.4	Sales/Working Capital					47.4	32.6
	−61.3	−23.6	−86.4						−11.7	93.3
	36.8	19.1	20.3							77.2
	(32) 8.0	(45) 5.2	(43) 7.3	EBIT/Interest						(12) 8.7
	1.6	1.7	1.8							2.1
	15.2	21.2		Net Profit + Depr., Dep.,						
	(11) 9.8	(11) 3.4		Amort./Cur. Mat. L/T/D						
	2.1	.9								
	.1	.2	.1						.0	.4
	.7	.8	.4	Fixed/Worth					.2	.6
	1.6	6.6	1.4						1.7	.9
	1.4	1.3	1.0						1.3	.8
	3.3	3.2	2.1	Debt/Worth					3.6	2.5
	6.0	10.7	5.8						−15.2	5.1
	76.0	62.7	56.1	% Profit Before Taxes/Tangible						60.1
	(33) 34.9	(42) 22.4	(48) 24.7	Net Worth						(12) 24.7
	13.9	−2.1	4.3							8.2
	25.6	19.4	19.9	% Profit Before Taxes/Total					21.3	19.1
	9.4	6.0	7.0	Assets					7.0	5.5
	2.4	.2	.8						1.6	1.2
	127.2	96.8	181.8						481.9	127.4
	54.6	21.7	43.7	Sales/Net Fixed Assets					100.6	22.4
	7.6	7.6	11.5						40.5	7.2
	5.5	5.6	5.6						6.6	5.0
	4.0	3.4	3.8	Sales/Total Assets					4.3	3.9
	2.4	1.3	1.3						1.2	1.9
	.4	.5	.4							.3
	(31) 1.0	(37) 1.1	(37) .9	% Depr., Dep., Amort./Sales						(10) .9
	2.4	4.5	3.7							2.5
	2.8	1.7	3.6	% Officers', Directors',						
	(13) 4.1	(15) 7.7	(20) 10.1	Owners' Comp/Sales						
	8.9	19.6	16.1							
	998107M	1579899M	2031273M	Net Sales ($)	4652M	20284M	36411M	40569M	180671M	1748686M
	473645M	714540M	719482M	Total Assets ($)	3823M	4517M	22878M	19528M	78009M	590727M

© RMA 2005

M = $ thousand   MM = $ million
See Pages 11 through 21 for Explanation of Ratios and Data

Current Data Sorted By Assets　　　　　　　　　　　　　　　　　　　**Comparative Historical Data**

						Type of Statement		
1	4	14	17	2	4	Unqualified	37	44
2	19	31	4			Reviewed	41	47
13	14	11	1			Compiled	53	60
23	13	4			1	Tax Returns	38	38
13	30	43	15	2	2	Other	81	107
	42 (4/1-9/30/04)		241 (10/1/04-3/31/05)				4/1/00-3/31/01	4/1/01-3/31/02
0-500M	500M-2MM	2-10MM	10-50MM	50-100MM	100-250MM		ALL	ALL
52	80	103	37	4	7	NUMBER OF STATEMENTS	250	296
%	%	%	%	%	%	ASSETS	%	%
34.6	12.1	14.6	13.0			Cash & Equivalents	14.5	14.4
19.7	55.8	53.4	37.1			Trade Receivables (net)	44.1	44.7
.3	2.4	2.1	2.3			Inventory	3.3	3.1
5.7	4.9	4.7	8.6			All Other Current	4.8	5.2
60.2	75.3	74.8	61.0			Total Current	66.6	67.5
19.6	13.6	11.9	15.8			Fixed Assets (net)	20.2	19.4
2.3	2.2	4.0	7.0			Intangibles (net)	3.9	4.1
17.8	8.9	9.3	16.1			All Other Non-Current	9.2	9.0
100.0	100.0	100.0	100.0			Total	100.0	100.0
						LIABILITIES		
34.1	18.8	10.8	5.8			Notes Payable-Short Term	16.0	17.3
4.0	1.5	2.5	2.5			Cur. Mat.-L/T/D	4.6	7.2
13.1	16.6	14.1	15.8			Trade Payables	12.7	12.1
1.9	.7	1.0	1.2			Income Taxes Payable	1.1	.7
21.7	13.7	17.8	22.1			All Other Current	17.0	18.1
74.8	51.3	46.3	47.4			Total Current	51.4	55.4
17.1	6.5	9.3	10.0			Long-Term Debt	12.2	13.3
.0	.8	1.2	1.1			Deferred Taxes	.7	1.0
5.2	5.4	5.5	4.9			All Other Non-Current	15.4	7.9
3.0	35.9	37.7	36.7			Net Worth	20.3	22.4
100.0	100.0	100.0	100.0			Total Liabilities & Net Worth	100.0	100.0
						INCOME DATA		
100.0	100.0	100.0	100.0			Net Sales	100.0	100.0
						Gross Profit		
91.0	95.3	91.1	92.0			Operating Expenses	92.8	94.0
9.0	4.7	8.9	8.0			Operating Profit	7.2	6.0
1.8	1.2	1.9	2.9			All Other Expenses (net)	1.3	2.1
7.2	3.5	7.0	5.1			Profit Before Taxes	5.9	3.9
						RATIOS		
1.9	2.6	2.9	2.3				2.4	2.2
1.1	1.6	1.6	1.4			Current	1.4	1.4
.4	1.1	1.2	1.0				.9	1.0
1.7	2.4	2.6	1.9				2.2	2.0
1.0	1.4	1.5	1.1			Quick	1.2	1.3
.2	1.0	1.1	.6				.8	.8

0	UND	36	10.2	50	7.3	36	10.0	Sales/Receivables	23	15.7	30	12.1
0	UND	63	5.8	72	5.1	62	5.9		62	5.8	58	6.3
38	9.6	88	4.2	100	3.6	98	3.7		91	4.0	88	4.2

						Cost of Sales/Inventory		
						Cost of Sales/Payables		

	20.7		6.6		4.6		4.8	Sales/Working Capital		6.2		7.2
	198.8		14.9		9.5		14.2			17.3		15.9
	-14.8		72.9		21.2		-75.1			-103.0		UND
	23.4		33.3		24.6		26.3			13.8		11.6
(32)	7.5	(67)	5.7	(83)	7.9	(28)	10.5	EBIT/Interest	(200)	4.4	(244)	3.5
	.4		.3		2.3		4.0			1.4		.9
					10.6		4.9	Net Profit + Depr., Dep.,		6.9		8.4
		(19)			5.4	(11)	3.1	Amort./Cur. Mat. L /T/D	(40)	2.1	(50)	3.0
					1.3		1.8			.4		.8
	.1		.1		.1		.1			.2		.2
	.6		.3		.2		.4	Fixed/Worth		.4		.5
	-1.3		.8		.8		.9			2.4		2.3
	.6		.7		.7		1.0			.8		.8
	2.9		1.6		1.7		3.0	Debt/Worth		2.1		2.4
	-4.9		4.0		5.2		4.9			9.7		11.3
	137.7		68.6		74.0		46.1	% Profit Before Taxes/Tangible		75.3		70.3
(34)	69.4	(72)	31.8	(92)	39.9	(33)	24.1	Net Worth	(205)	30.8	(246)	24.1
	7.3		2.5		6.9		6.6			6.5		2.6
	46.5		24.8		33.0		11.1	% Profit Before Taxes/Total		29.3		19.9
	23.3		9.7		9.4		6.3	Assets		10.3		7.0
	-1.6		-2.2		2.1		1.4			.9		-.9
	515.8		106.0		107.6		46.7			56.5		68.4
	99.8		39.5		42.7		23.5	Sales/Net Fixed Assets		26.5		26.5
	29.3		19.5		19.3		8.5			13.0		11.1
	17.4		4.2		3.7		2.5			4.4		4.7
	6.6		3.3		2.5		1.7	Sales/Total Assets		2.8		2.9
	3.6		2.6		1.9		.8			2.0		1.9
	.3		.5		.4		1.0			.7		.5
(28)	.7	(55)	1.1	(76)	1.1	(33)	1.7	% Depr., Dep., Amort./Sales	(196)	1.3	(228)	1.4
	2.1		2.3		2.2		2.5			2.6		2.9
	7.0		5.0		2.2			% Officers', Directors',		5.7		5.1
(27)	11.8	(35)	7.5	(25)	4.3			Owners' Comp/Sales	(95)	9.7	(93)	8.3
	22.0		13.9		8.4					18.6		16.4

105598M	312342M	1450643M	1683010M	651157M	2270422M	Net Sales ($)	7829114M	5708356M
11161M	83650M	463705M	889074M	322471M	1077130M	Total Assets ($)	2100805M	2678111M

M = $ thousand　MM = $ million
See Pages 11 through 21 for Explanation of Ratios and Data

Comparative Historical Data   Current Data Sorted By Sales

			Type of Statement						
58	56	42	Unqualified	1	2	4	3	13	19
40	36	56	Reviewed	3	6	10	14	19	4
38	69	39	Compiled	7	10	7	8	6	1
28	38	41	Tax Returns	12	12	9	6	1	1
102	86	105	Other	8	23	18	19	21	16
4/1/02-3/31/03 ALL	4/1/03-3/31/04 ALL	4/1/04-3/31/05 ALL		42 (4/1-9/30/04) 0-1MM	1-3MM	241 (10/1/04-3/31/05) 3-5MM	5-10MM	10-25MM	25MM & OVER
266	285	283	NUMBER OF STATEMENTS	31	53	48	50	60	41
%	%	%	ASSETS	%	%	%	%	%	%
16.3	14.5	17.6	Cash & Equivalents	33.9	19.1	14.2	13.2	13.4	18.7
43.6	46.0	44.7	Trade Receivables (net)	8.4	46.2	45.7	54.7	57.1	39.1
2.0	2.4	1.8	Inventory	.2	.5	2.1	3.8	1.9	1.9
5.0	5.4	5.6	All Other Current	5.5	3.5	6.0	6.4	3.8	9.5
66.9	68.3	69.7	Total Current	47.9	69.3	68.1	78.0	76.1	69.3
20.1	17.7	14.5	Fixed Assets (net)	24.2	16.9	19.1	8.1	10.6	12.1
5.5	3.7	4.0	Intangibles (net)	4.1	2.0	3.5	3.3	2.0	11.1
7.6	10.3	11.7	All Other Non-Current	23.7	11.8	9.2	10.6	11.3	7.4
100.0	100.0	100.0	Total	100.0	100.0	100.0	100.0	100.0	100.0
			LIABILITIES						
16.1	15.3	16.5	Notes Payable-Short Term	32.9	19.4	18.9	15.5	11.3	6.6
3.8	3.4	2.6	Cur. Mat.-L/T/D	5.5	2.1	1.8	1.8	2.3	3.7
12.3	14.5	14.6	Trade Payables	4.8	18.9	14.4	13.9	16.5	14.8
.7	.8	1.2	Income Taxes Payable	3.3	.2	.9	1.3	.8	1.4
23.4	18.4	17.8	All Other Current	22.4	14.7	15.0	15.9	19.4	21.6
56.3	52.4	52.8	Total Current	68.9	55.3	51.1	48.5	50.3	48.2
11.9	11.4	10.0	Long-Term Debt	18.8	12.5	8.2	9.9	6.4	7.5
.6	.6	.8	Deferred Taxes	.1	.0	1.4	1.6	.6	1.1
6.5	8.1	5.5	All Other Non-Current	1.1	9.8	3.9	5.8	4.0	6.9
24.8	27.5	30.9	Net Worth	11.2	22.5	35.3	34.2	38.7	36.3
100.0	100.0	100.0	Total Liabilities & Net Worth	100.0	100.0	100.0	100.0	100.0	100.0
			INCOME DATA						
100.0	100.0	100.0	Net Sales	100.0	100.0	100.0	100.0	100.0	100.0
			Gross Profit						
94.3	92.4	92.3	Operating Expenses	80.8	94.6	94.7	93.4	93.0	92.9
5.7	7.6	7.7	Operating Profit	19.2	5.4	5.3	6.6	7.0	7.1
1.0	1.3	1.9	All Other Expenses (net)	5.3	1.7	2.2	1.5	.4	2.1
4.7	6.3	5.8	Profit Before Taxes	13.9	3.7	3.1	5.1	6.7	5.1
			RATIOS						
2.5	2.3	2.6	Current	1.9	2.8	2.4	3.0	2.5	2.2
1.4	1.5	1.5		1.1	1.7	1.4	1.7	1.4	1.4
1.0	1.0	1.1		.2	.7	1.1	1.2	1.2	1.2
2.2	2.1	2.4	Quick	1.9	2.7	2.1	2.7	2.0	1.7
1.2	1.3	1.3		1.1	1.6	1.3	1.5	1.4	1.1
.8	.8	.9		.1	.6	.9	1.0	1.0	.9
29 12.8	28 12.8	30 12.2	Sales/Receivables	0 UND	12 30.5	35 10.6	53 7.0	43 8.5	39 9.3
53 6.8	59 6.2	58 6.2		0 UND	56 6.6	50 7.4	76 4.8	65 5.6	59 6.2
86 4.3	92 4.0	88 4.1		33 10.9	86 4.2	85 4.3	92 4.0	92 4.0	91 4.0
			Cost of Sales/Inventory						
			Cost of Sales/Payables						
6.4	6.1	6.0	Sales/Working Capital	14.2	6.3	5.7	5.7	7.0	5.3
14.8	11.7	15.3		82.5	18.6	15.8	9.6	15.1	13.7
-142.2	-170.9	127.5		-4.9	-92.6	72.9	38.6	33.4	55.5
22.0	26.8	26.8	EBIT/Interest	8.0	30.5	20.1	23.7	45.5	28.4
(211) 5.2	(232) 5.9	(220) 7.6		(17) 2.0	(39) 12.0	(41) 5.7	(40) 9.9	(48) 11.2	(35) 8.1
1.6	1.4	1.5		-.2	-.3	.2	2.7	2.5	3.3
9.9	7.0	9.7	Net Profit + Depr., Dep., Amort./Cur. Mat. L/T/D					9.5	3.8
(45) 4.4	(61) 2.5	(44) 3.3						(13) 5.4	(12) 2.4
1.3	1.1	1.4						2.1	1.4
.2	.1	.1	Fixed/Worth	.0	.1	.2	.1	.1	.1
.4	.4	.3		.3	.3	.3	.2	.2	.4
2.2	2.4	1.1		-1.9	3.3	1.0	.8	.8	.9
.8	.7	.7	Debt/Worth	.4	.5	.8	.6	.6	.8
1.9	1.9	1.9		1.9	2.0	1.6	1.8	1.8	3.0
10.2	11.0	6.1		-4.8	21.3	3.6	9.8	5.4	5.1
71.5	74.2	74.0	% Profit Before Taxes/Tangible Net Worth	76.4	94.9	54.9	90.9	74.1	86.4
(216) 29.3	(228) 30.2	(240) 36.5		(21) 21.8	(43) 39.5	(44) 31.6	(43) 27.0	(54) 39.9	(35) 40.8
6.3	7.1	6.5		-2.6	6.2	1.9	7.1	9.3	7.9
21.9	26.7	28.4	% Profit Before Taxes/Total Assets	44.4	35.2	17.8	32.2	31.8	21.4
8.3	9.5	9.6		6.0	15.2	9.0	6.2	11.2	9.2
.8	.8	.5		-2.2	-2.4	-2.4	1.1	2.6	3.2
63.4	91.0	125.2	Sales/Net Fixed Assets	UND	127.6	71.9	156.0	108.5	129.3
27.3	30.3	42.2		63.0	44.9	27.0	60.2	53.9	36.5
12.2	12.3	19.3		7.7	19.4	13.8	24.5	21.6	16.0
4.3	4.3	4.4	Sales/Total Assets	8.8	4.6	4.2	4.2	4.2	3.4
2.8	2.8	3.0		3.2	3.6	3.2	3.0	2.9	2.4
1.9	1.9	1.9		.5	2.5	2.0	2.0	2.0	1.2
.8	.8	.5	% Depr., Dep., Amort./Sales	.6	.5	.9	.5	.3	.9
(197) 1.6	(215) 1.6	(198) 1.2		(11) 1.7	(34) 1.1	(36) 1.8	(40) 1.0	(46) .6	(31) 1.5
3.3	3.0	2.3		3.1	2.4	3.3	1.4	1.8	2.4
3.8	3.9	3.8	% Officers', Directors', Owners' Comp/Sales	10.6	7.0	3.1	1.8	1.2	
(79) 9.4	(82) 9.2	(91) 7.5		(13) 21.3	(23) 11.4	(21) 6.1	(14) 4.7	(16) 3.3	
20.2	17.1	16.5		31.3	17.5	12.9	10.8	4.9	
4831284M	6320753M	6473172M	Net Sales ($)	15969M	101785M	185465M	365424M	951400M	4853129M
2219688M	2648950M	2847191M	Total Assets ($)	21235M	78904M	92124M	151569M	385321M	2118038M

M = $ thousand   MM = $ million
See Pages 11 through 21 for Explanation of Ratios and Data

Current Data Sorted By Assets **Comparative Historical Data**

	0-500M	500M-2MM	2-10MM	10-50MM	50-100MM	100-250MM	Type of Statement	4/1/00-3/31/01 ALL	4/1/01-3/31/02 ALL
	3	2 3	2 7	2 2			Unqualified		
	1	1	1				Reviewed		
	6	3					Compiled		
	2	8	5	2			Tax Returns		
							Other		
	5 (4/1-9/30/04)			45 (10/1/04-3/31/05)					
	12	17	15	6			NUMBER OF STATEMENTS		
	%	%	%	%	%	%	ASSETS	%	%
	23.1	2.2	7.3				Cash & Equivalents		
	35.4	49.1	57.0	D	D		Trade Receivables (net)	D	D
	.2	1.6	.7	A	A		Inventory	A	A
	4.5	2.6	5.3	T	T		All Other Current	T	T
	63.1	55.5	70.3	A	A		Total Current	A	A
	21.7	32.2	20.7				Fixed Assets (net)		
	.0	8.7	1.8	N	N		Intangibles (net)	N	N
	15.1	3.6	7.2	O	O		All Other Non-Current	O	O
	100.0	100.0	100.0	T	T		Total	T	T
							LIABILITIES		
	24.4	13.9	13.2	A	A		Notes Payable-Short Term	A	A
	1.6	3.3	7.6	V	V		Cur. Mat.-L/T/D	V	V
	13.7	17.9	15.2	A	A		Trade Payables	A	A
	.0	1.6	.0	I	I		Income Taxes Payable	I	I
	9.9	10.3	15.6	L	L		All Other Current	L	L
	49.6	47.0	51.8	A	A		Total Current	A	A
	40.0	19.3	8.4	B	B		Long-Term Debt	B	B
	.1	1.3	.7	L	L		Deferred Taxes	L	L
	22.0	3.3	3.0	E	E		All Other Non-Current	E	E
	−11.7	29.1	36.2				Net Worth		
	100.0	100.0	100.0				Total Liabilities & Net Worth		
	100.0	100.0	100.0				INCOME DATA Net Sales		
	96.5	88.7	95.7				Gross Profit		
	3.5	11.3	4.3				Operating Expenses		
	−.2	6.4	1.0				Operating Profit		
	3.6	4.9	3.3				All Other Expenses (net)		
							Profit Before Taxes		
	2.4	1.5	1.9				RATIOS		
	1.5	1.2	1.5				Current		
	1.3	.9	1.1						
	1.8	1.3	1.5						
	1.4	1.2	1.4				Quick		
	.7	.8	1.1						
0 UND	49 7.4	65 5.6							
0 UND	74 4.9	98 3.7				Sales/Receivables		
80 4.6	90 4.1	113 3.2						
							Cost of Sales/Inventory		
							Cost of Sales/Payables		
	11.2	10.9	5.3						
	17.2	26.5	9.4				Sales/Working Capital		
	82.8	−41.0	29.9						
		12.2	11.7						
	(14) 5.0	(14) 3.9				EBIT/Interest		
	1.1	−1.7						
							Net Profit + Depr., Dep., Amort./Cur. Mat. L /T/D		
	.4	.3	.2						
	.7	1.1	.4				Fixed/Worth		
	2.1	UND	1.5						
	.8	1.3	.8						
	2.2	3.4	2.0				Debt/Worth		
	85.3	UND	4.5						
	95.8	111.0	33.6				% Profit Before Taxes/Tangible		
(10) 27.0	(14) 8.4	(14) 24.2				Net Worth		
	−56.8	−2.9	−2.7						
	39.1	23.1	14.6				% Profit Before Taxes/Total		
	19.6	3.2	5.3				Assets		
	−20.5	−.2	−2.5						
	127.3	53.3	37.4						
	26.4	11.9	16.3				Sales/Net Fixed Assets		
	18.7	3.1	4.4						
	9.0	3.5	2.8						
	4.3	2.1	2.1				Sales/Total Assets		
	2.7	1.4	1.8						
		.6	.9						
	(13) 1.3	(14) 2.8				% Depr., Dep., Amort./Sales		
	6.8	3.2						
							% Officers', Directors', Owners' Comp/Sales		
	10650M	49059M	123157M	210972M			Net Sales ($)		
	2302M	19913M	54610M	105140M			Total Assets ($)		

© RMA 2005

M = $ thousand   MM = $ million
See Pages 11 through 21 for Explanation of Ratios and Data

Comparative Historical Data						Type of Statement		Current Data Sorted By Sales					

	1		5		6	Unqualified	1		3			2	
	5		12		15	Reviewed	3	1	1	6	3	1	
	2		8		3	Compiled	1	1		1			
	4		8		9	Tax Returns	4	4	1				
	7		15		17	Other	1	6	4	2	3	1	

	4/1/02- 3/31/03 ALL		4/1/03- 3/31/04 ALL		4/1/04- 3/31/05 ALL		5 (4/1-9/30/04)		45 (10/1/04-3/31/05)				
							0-1MM	1-3MM	3-5MM	5-10MM	10-25MM	25MM & OVER	
	19		48		50	NUMBER OF STATEMENTS	10	12	6	12	6	4	
	%		%		%	ASSETS	%	%	%	%	%	%	
	10.8		13.1		9.6	Cash & Equivalents	7.8	19.2		5.6			
	48.1		50.5		48.1	Trade Receivables (net)	36.8	34.7		59.8			
	1.1		1.0		1.0	Inventory	.2	.0		.8			
	4.8		5.0		5.3	All Other Current	5.4	.6		3.8			
	64.8		69.7		64.0	Total Current	50.3	54.4		70.0			
	27.5		19.8		24.7	Fixed Assets (net)	34.3	27.7		24.1			
	.6		3.4		3.5	Intangibles (net)	.0	12.0		.2			
	7.1		7.1		7.8	All Other Non-Current	15.5	5.8		5.6			
	100.0		100.0		100.0	Total	100.0	100.0		100.0			
						LIABILITIES							
	6.2		14.6		15.0	Notes Payable-Short Term	21.8	14.5		13.3			
	4.2		3.4		4.1	Cur. Mat.-L/T/D	.3	5.0		9.3			
	22.6		18.3		16.1	Trade Payables	14.7	11.8		15.0			
	1.8		.7		.6	Income Taxes Payable	.0	.0		.5			
	10.9		10.4		12.4	All Other Current	10.4	6.3		12.7			
	45.6		47.4		48.1	Total Current	47.3	37.6		50.8			
	13.9		10.2		19.2	Long-Term Debt	58.6	16.5		9.9			
	.2		.2		.9	Deferred Taxes	.2	.0		.1			
	2.0		7.9		7.7	All Other Non-Current	22.7	7.7		1.9			
	38.4		34.2		24.1	Net Worth	-28.7	38.2		37.4			
	100.0		100.0		100.0	Total Liabilities & Net Worth	100.0	100.0		100.0			
						INCOME DATA							
	100.0		100.0		100.0	Net Sales	100.0	100.0		100.0			
						Gross Profit							
	96.2		94.9		93.7	Operating Expenses	88.5	90.7		94.3			
	3.8		5.1		6.3	Operating Profit	11.5	9.3		5.7			
	1.1		.6		2.4	All Other Expenses (net)	10.1	.4		1.1			
	2.7		4.5		3.8	Profit Before Taxes	1.5	8.9		4.7			
						RATIOS							
	2.0		3.2		1.9		1.6	3.1		2.6			
	1.6		1.6		1.4	Current	1.4	1.4		1.5			
	.9		1.0		1.1		.4	1.0		1.1			
	1.9		2.4		1.5		1.4	3.1		2.2			
	1.4		1.4		1.3	Quick	1.2	1.4		1.4			
	.7		.9		1.0		.0	1.0		1.1			
38	9.6	41	8.8	49	7.5		0 UND	0 UND		67 5.5			
65	5.6	81	4.5	76	4.8	Sales/Receivables	0 UND	71 5.2		95 3.9			
93	3.9	99	3.7	101	3.6		86 4.2	85 4.3		111 3.3			
						Cost of Sales/Inventory							
						Cost of Sales/Payables							
	8.5		4.8		7.7		11.0	11.4		5.4			
	13.6		9.5		15.4	Sales/Working Capital	22.5	23.3		12.3			
	-359.8		797.0		63.5		-19.1	NM		39.5			
	17.5		15.2		13.4			16.4		13.7			
(14)	6.0	(37)	5.5	(40)	4.7	EBIT/Interest	(10)	7.4	(11)	5.5			
	-.7		1.3		1.0			1.7		.9			
			18.9			Net Profit + Depr., Dep.,							
		(14)	8.5			Amort./Cur. Mat. L/T/D							
			1.1										
	.2		.2		.3		.5	.3		.3			
	.5		.4		.6	Fixed/Worth	1.1	.7		.5			
	1.6		1.6		2.0		UND	NM		1.9			
	.9		.7		1.0		.6	1.2		.7			
	1.4		1.8		2.0	Debt/Worth	11.0	1.8		2.1			
	4.4		6.2		5.4		UND	NM		4.4			
	80.6		60.9		41.1	% Profit Before Taxes/Tangible				69.6			
(18)	24.2	(44)	27.2	(44)	17.0	Net Worth				25.7			
	5.5		10.7		-3.7					1.6			
	37.7		18.1		19.4	% Profit Before Taxes/Total	25.2	32.4		17.9			
	6.7		11.0		5.7	Assets	3.1	23.1		8.5			
	1.4		2.5		-.9		-24.5	1.2		.8			
	54.1		47.0		51.8		146.6	27.3		30.1			
	15.8		26.7		17.9	Sales/Net Fixed Assets	52.9	21.0		14.1			
	9.3		10.4		5.9		3.4	6.3		4.4			
	5.1		3.6		3.5		5.9	6.2		2.8			
	2.6		2.5		2.6	Sales/Total Assets	3.3	2.6		2.2			
	2.0		2.0		1.8		1.4	1.7		1.6			
	1.0		1.2		.8					1.0			
(14)	2.5	(37)	1.9	(39)	2.2	% Depr., Dep., Amort./Sales				2.8			
	3.5		3.2		3.2					3.2			
	3.6		4.3		1.9	% Officers', Directors',							
(14)	9.3	(17)	6.5	(16)	6.1	Owners' Comp/Sales							
	21.6		19.0		19.3								
	110386M		254586M		393838M	Net Sales ($)	4741M	21531M	20889M	83997M	89741M	172939M	
	46390M		108849M		181965M	Total Assets ($)	3404M	9318M	8295M	37432M	56010M	67506M	

M = $ thousand   MM = $ million
See Pages 11 through 21 for Explanation of Ratios and Data

Current Data Sorted By Assets | **Comparative Historical Data**

0-500M	500M-2MM	2-10MM	10-50MM	50-100MM	100-250MM	Type of Statement	4/1/00-3/31/01 ALL	4/1/01-3/31/02 ALL
	2	1	4	1	1	Unqualified		
1	3	3	1			Reviewed		
3	3	2		1		Compiled		
4	5					Tax Returns		
2	9	7	1	2		Other		
___	___	___	___	___	___			
14 (4/1-9/30/04)			42 (10/1/04-3/31/05)					
10	22	13	6	4	1	**NUMBER OF STATEMENTS**		
%	%	%	%	%	%	**ASSETS**	%	%
12.9	17.0	20.6				Cash & Equivalents	D	D
35.7	45.1	47.8				Trade Receivables (net)	A	A
.2	3.4	3.8				Inventory	T	T
4.6	4.2	6.7				All Other Current	A	A
53.5	69.7	78.9				Total Current		
15.4	17.2	12.6				Fixed Assets (net)		
.1	3.6	1.8				Intangibles (net)	N	N
31.1	9.5	6.7				All Other Non-Current	O	O
100.0	100.0	100.0				Total	T	T
						LIABILITIES	A	A
41.5	7.4	14.2				Notes Payable-Short Term	V	V
.5	1.6	1.9				Cur. Mat.-L/T/D	A	A
6.3	14.4	6.4				Trade Payables	I	I
.0	.2	.9				Income Taxes Payable	L	L
22.6	15.6	21.4				All Other Current	A	A
71.0	39.2	44.8				Total Current	B	B
2.6	9.3	25.0				Long-Term Debt	L	L
.0	.3	3.4				Deferred Taxes	E	E
9.0	5.1	.2				All Other Non-Current		
17.5	46.1	26.7				Net Worth		
100.0	100.0	100.0				Total Liabilities & Net Worth		
						INCOME DATA		
100.0	100.0	100.0				Net Sales		
						Gross Profit		
93.2	93.0	93.3				Operating Expenses		
6.8	7.0	6.7				Operating Profit		
.6	.5	1.6				All Other Expenses (net)		
6.3	6.5	5.0				Profit Before Taxes		
						RATIOS		
2.6	3.1	2.9						
1.0	2.2	2.1				Current		
.1	1.3	1.5						
2.5	2.8	2.7						
1.0	2.0	1.6				Quick		
.1	1.0	1.4						
0 UND	21 17.0	43 8.5						
5 80.4	38 9.6	66 5.5				Sales/Receivables		
60 6.1	67 5.5	99 3.7						
						Cost of Sales/Inventory		
						Cost of Sales/Payables		
13.1	5.1	3.4						
NM	10.8	5.1				Sales/Working Capital		
−9.1	NM	9.4						
	53.9	193.8						
	(15) 7.4	(12) 12.2				EBIT/Interest		
	1.3	7.0						
						Net Profit + Depr., Dep., Amort./Cur. Mat. L /T/D		
.0	.1	.1						
.3	.3	.2				Fixed/Worth		
UND	1.6	.4						
.8	.5	.5						
4.7	1.0	.9				Debt/Worth		
UND	4.9	1.6						
	125.1	46.8						
	(19) 32.2	(12) 20.9				% Profit Before Taxes/Tangible Net Worth		
	2.8	12.5						
58.5	42.5	18.9						
18.4	18.5	10.0				% Profit Before Taxes/Total Assets		
.0	2.2	7.4						
UND	89.0	62.4						
171.4	37.1	38.9				Sales/Net Fixed Assets		
13.4	16.5	10.5						
7.3	5.6	3.1						
5.9	3.8	1.9				Sales/Total Assets		
2.9	2.1	1.4						
	.6	.9						
	(14) 1.3	(10) 2.0				% Depr., Dep., Amort./Sales		
	2.4	3.4						
						% Officers', Directors', Owners' Comp/Sales		
18232M	115698M	190570M	476156M	279834M	47489M	Net Sales ($)		
2487M	24322M	73008M	167809M	268794M	147338M	Total Assets ($)		

M = $ thousand   MM = $ million
See Pages 11 through 21 for Explanation of Ratios and Data

Comparative Historical Data | Current Data Sorted By Sales

			Type of Statement						
1	6	9	Unqualified		1	1	1	1	5
4	9	8	Reviewed	1	1	2	1	2	1
7	9	9	Compiled	2	4	1	1		1
2	7	9	Tax Returns	1	3	3	1		
11	17	21	Other	1	2	3	7	4	4
4/1/02-3/31/03 ALL	4/1/03-3/31/04 ALL	4/1/04-3/31/05 ALL		14 (4/1-9/30/04)			42 (10/1/04-3/31/05)		
				0-1MM	1-3MM	3-5MM	5-10MM	10-25MM	25MM & OVER
25	48	56	**NUMBER OF STATEMENTS**	5	11	10	12	7	11
%	%	%	**ASSETS**	%	%	%	%	%	%
10.9	17.8	15.0	Cash & Equivalents		18.9	14.9	15.2		4.9
36.8	36.2	41.3	Trade Receivables (net)		35.6	40.2	51.6		40.7
7.5	3.9	3.7	Inventory		1.0	4.9	2.0		4.3
3.3	9.0	4.6	All Other Current		4.0	3.6	3.5		3.1
58.6	67.0	64.6	Total Current		59.5	63.6	72.3		53.0
34.1	23.9	16.1	Fixed Assets (net)		17.7	22.8	12.0		12.4
1.5	4.1	6.6	Intangibles (net)		3.5	.3	4.0		23.8
5.9	5.0	12.7	All Other Non-Current		19.4	13.3	11.7		10.8
100.0	100.0	100.0	Total		100.0	100.0	100.0		100.0
			LIABILITIES						
17.4	21.4	13.9	Notes Payable-Short Term		13.0	9.5	27.1		8.4
7.5	5.6	1.6	Cur. Mat.-L/T/D		2.7	1.6	.4		2.5
12.2	14.4	10.3	Trade Payables		7.4	13.3	11.7		12.6
.8	.2	.7	Income Taxes Payable		.1	.3	.0		2.3
17.9	13.9	18.0	All Other Current		21.2	12.9	15.7		19.6
55.9	55.5	44.6	Total Current		44.3	37.7	55.0		45.3
22.3	13.3	13.9	Long-Term Debt		5.7	23.1	3.3		36.9
.5	.5	1.0	Deferred Taxes		.5	3.4	.3		.3
.4	3.6	6.7	All Other Non-Current		.1	4.2	7.0		15.1
20.9	27.2	33.9	Net Worth		49.3	31.6	34.3		2.4
100.0	100.0	100.0	Total Liabilities & Net Worth		100.0	100.0	100.0		100.0
			INCOME DATA						
100.0	100.0	100.0	Net Sales		100.0	100.0	100.0		100.0
			Gross Profit						
95.3	96.9	93.1	Operating Expenses		91.1	90.2	94.3		94.5
4.7	3.1	6.9	Operating Profit		8.9	9.8	5.7		5.5
2.6	.4	1.4	All Other Expenses (net)		.2	4.1	1.1		1.7
2.0	2.6	5.5	Profit Before Taxes		8.6	5.7	4.5		3.7
			RATIOS						
1.7	2.0	2.8			2.8	3.1	2.3		1.7
1.1	1.2	1.8	Current		2.0	2.2	2.0		1.3
.8	.9	.9			.3	.7	1.4		.8
1.6	1.7	2.4			2.8	2.6	2.3		1.6
.9	1.0	1.6	Quick		1.3	1.6	1.7		.9
.6	.6	.8			.2	.7	1.3		.6
33 11.2	31 11.9	24 15.3			2 152.1	0 UND	15 24.7		43 8.5
55 6.6	52 7.1	46 7.9	Sales/Receivables		30 12.2	49 7.4	40 9.0		50 7.4
87 4.2	70 5.2	76 4.8			102 3.6	75 4.8	71 5.2		75 4.9
			Cost of Sales/Inventory						
			Cost of Sales/Payables						
15.0	8.0	5.0			4.2	4.4	5.9		10.9
63.4	25.9	11.5	Sales/Working Capital		14.9	9.3	11.5		18.6
-15.3	-33.9	-96.8			-9.1	-95.2	39.1		-24.8
7.6	9.7	41.5					54.6		
(22) 2.5	(36) 3.9	(42) 15.6	EBIT/Interest				(11) 30.0		
-.3	1.3	5.9					2.7		
		5.4	Net Profit + Depr., Dep.,						
		(12) 2.9	Amort./Cur. Mat. L/T/D						
		1.1							
.3	.2	.1			.0	.2	.1		.2
1.4	.8	.3	Fixed/Worth		.2	.8	.3		.6
NM	2.2	1.7			1.1	NM	1.5		-.1
1.5	.9	.6			.4	.6	.7		1.1
2.8	2.6	1.2	Debt/Worth		.8	3.7	1.0		2.9
-46.4	7.5	6.7			6.0	NM	3.5		-1.9
41.9	75.3	84.5	% Profit Before Taxes/Tangible		156.8		124.4		
(18) 20.7	(41) 20.2	(47) 35.4	Net Worth		35.4	(10) 22.8			
-6.8	.1	11.2			.0		11.1		
10.5	17.0	26.5	% Profit Before Taxes/Total		47.8	25.4	68.6		30.3
4.5	4.5	12.1	Assets		24.7	17.5	14.3		10.5
-6.3	-.1	2.5			.0	5.5	5.5		-6.2
18.1	59.2	80.8			226.8	48.9	442.4		62.1
9.8	13.4	37.7	Sales/Net Fixed Assets		54.7	18.5	54.4		20.2
5.2	7.2	14.3			17.8	9.7	17.5		13.3
3.2	3.5	5.4			6.9	4.4	7.4		3.3
2.3	2.6	3.1	Sales/Total Assets		3.2	3.5	5.4		2.3
1.5	1.7	1.7			1.7	1.2	2.1		.9
1.6	1.8	.7							.8
(19) 2.7	(34) 2.9	(38) 1.5	% Depr., Dep., Amort./Sales						(10) 1.5
5.5	4.6	2.8							4.9
1.6	4.5	3.0	% Officers', Directors',						
(11) 4.9	(18) 7.8	(16) 7.0	Owners' Comp/Sales						
11.3	17.2	12.1							
167223M	372082M	1127979M	Net Sales ($)	2041M	22280M	41017M	85545M	121829M	855267M
80411M	169057M	683758M	Total Assets ($)	928M	8137M	37431M	22437M	48706M	566119M

M = $ thousand   MM = $ million
See Pages 11 through 21 for Explanation of Ratios and Data

Current Data Sorted By Assets   **Comparative Historical Data**

						Type of Statement		
2	3	15	28	4	12	Unqualified	66	44
1	2	15	3			Reviewed	15	13
3	5	8				Compiled	22	30
3	2	2				Tax Returns	5	2
5	15	16	17	6	7	Other	48	40
	55 (4/1-9/30/04)		119 (10/1/04-3/31/05)				4/1/00-3/31/01 ALL	4/1/01-3/31/02 ALL
0-500M	500M-2MM	2-10MM	10-50MM	50-100MM	100-250MM			
14	27	56	48	10	19	NUMBER OF STATEMENTS	156	129
%	%	%	%	%	%	ASSETS	%	%
14.3	25.5	17.5	20.1	17.3	24.8	Cash & Equivalents	17.0	16.1
43.8	39.4	32.3	25.8	22.0	16.8	Trade Receivables (net)	32.4	32.9
10.7	2.8	7.1	1.4	4.8	3.9	Inventory	3.3	3.8
2.3	3.8	7.8	5.3	1.5	10.5	All Other Current	5.7	6.2
71.1	71.4	64.7	52.7	45.6	56.1	Total Current	58.3	59.0
19.6	19.5	24.1	29.8	28.6	16.4	Fixed Assets (net)	26.1	24.1
1.8	1.4	3.1	4.1	15.2	17.5	Intangibles (net)	4.1	5.1
6.8	7.7	8.1	13.5	10.6	10.0	All Other Non-Current	11.4	11.9
100.0	100.0	100.0	100.0	100.0	100.0	Total	100.0	100.0
						LIABILITIES		
38.7	7.4	7.2	2.3	3.5	.9	Notes Payable-Short Term	6.6	8.2
1.8	1.2	2.6	1.6	2.1	1.3	Cur. Mat.-L/T/D	3.3	2.4
12.1	13.0	11.0	8.8	5.6	6.6	Trade Payables	10.0	12.1
.8	.2	.7	.6	2.0	.3	Income Taxes Payable	.7	.8
20.0	17.3	15.6	18.2	11.3	16.3	All Other Current	17.3	15.7
73.5	39.0	37.1	31.6	24.4	25.4	Total Current	37.9	39.2
16.0	12.8	9.7	11.2	11.4	7.3	Long-Term Debt	10.8	11.4
.0	.1	.4	.7	.5	.2	Deferred Taxes	.6	.8
1.0	7.8	6.4	5.8	1.5	13.0	All Other Non-Current	3.7	4.3
8.6	40.3	46.4	50.7	62.1	54.0	Net Worth	47.0	44.4
100.0	100.0	100.0	100.0	100.0	100.0	Total Liabilities & Net Worth	100.0	100.0
						INCOME DATA		
100.0	100.0	100.0	100.0	100.0	100.0	Net Sales	100.0	100.0
						Gross Profit		
99.1	93.7	94.2	96.2	92.8	99.2	Operating Expenses	96.7	94.8
.9	6.3	5.8	3.8	7.2	.8	Operating Profit	3.3	5.2
.7	.3	1.2	.4	-1.3	-.7	All Other Expenses (net)	-1.9	1.5
.2	6.0	4.6	3.4	8.5	1.5	Profit Before Taxes	5.2	3.7
						RATIOS		
2.3	5.5	3.2	2.8	3.8	3.3		2.9	2.6
1.2	1.6	1.8	1.9	2.0	2.0	Current	1.7	1.7
.6	1.2	1.2	1.1	1.0	1.3		1.2	1.1
2.2	5.3	2.3	2.5	2.7	3.0		2.5	2.2
.8	1.5	1.3	1.5	1.9	1.6	Quick	1.4	1.3
.4	.9	.8	.9	1.0	1.0		.9	.9
2 153.1	32 11.4	35 10.4	39 9.4	50 7.4	23 15.7		37 9.9	38 9.6
43 8.6	42 8.7	53 6.8	63 5.8	56 6.5	61 6.0	Sales/Receivables	59 6.1	53 6.8
91 4.0	82 4.4	75 4.9	81 4.5	80 4.6	85 4.3		83 4.4	82 4.4
						Cost of Sales/Inventory		
						Cost of Sales/Payables		
10.9	6.7	3.9	4.1	3.0	1.4		4.3	4.5
NM	11.0	7.8	7.8	5.4	5.8	Sales/Working Capital	9.4	9.1
-5.2	26.7	34.1	26.9	NM	17.1		26.8	89.2
11.4	32.0	36.5	92.0		26.3		18.3	16.7
(11) 2.0	(16) 8.8	(38) 9.1	(28) 10.6		(13) 8.8	EBIT/Interest	(113) 5.9	(95) 5.5
-3.0	3.0	.2	.5		.2		1.0	.6
		8.9				Net Profit + Depr., Dep.,	12.5	9.4
		(12) 2.5				Amort./Cur. Mat. L/T/D	(29) 3.2	(30) 3.4
		.1					1.8	1.6
.3	.1	.2	.2	.2	.3		.2	.2
1.9	.5	.5	.5	.5	.5	Fixed/Worth	.5	.5
-1.8	1.7	1.3	1.2	NM	-.6		1.1	1.1
.9	.4	.4	.5	.4	.4		.5	.5
57.1	1.5	1.1	1.1	.6	.7	Debt/Worth	1.0	1.2
-4.9	3.2	3.8	2.2	NM	-5.9		2.1	3.6
	100.0	46.2	44.2		16.0	% Profit Before Taxes/Tangible	36.3	45.5
	(23) 40.9	(55) 17.1	(45) 16.3		(14) 9.6	Net Worth	(143) 12.8	(115) 13.0
	6.4	-.2	-3.6		-6.0		2.3	.6
32.3	24.6	17.9	22.6	14.4	10.9	% Profit Before Taxes/Total	16.7	18.7
5.6	12.0	7.9	7.2	7.6	3.7	Assets	7.0	6.8
-11.2	3.2	-.1	-2.6	5.0	-4.1		.5	-1.6
104.9	37.5	29.1	14.2	18.0	28.1		27.3	27.6
32.5	19.9	13.1	5.2	9.2	10.3	Sales/Net Fixed Assets	8.9	13.2
11.3	12.2	4.6	1.8	1.9	2.7		3.1	3.3
5.7	4.0	2.8	2.4	1.6	1.6		2.8	3.1
3.3	3.2	1.9	1.3	1.1	1.1	Sales/Total Assets	1.8	2.0
1.7	1.7	1.3	.6	.9	.5		.9	.8
	.9	.9	1.1		1.3		1.3	1.2
	(14) 1.8	(47) 2.1	(41) 3.2		(14) 2.4	% Depr., Dep., Amort./Sales	(131) 2.1	(111) 2.1
	3.2	3.7	8.8		5.2		4.8	4.3
						% Officers', Directors',	2.6	2.6
						Owners' Comp/Sales	(34) 5.3	(24) 6.2
							11.1	15.7
14128M	93883M	577805M	1850584M	929039M	3650514M	Net Sales ($)	4863771M	3592086M
3864M	30750M	264096M	1147531M	768208M	3022204M	Total Assets ($)	4253708M	2981389M

M = $ thousand   MM = $ million
See Pages 11 through 21 for Explanation of Ratios and Data

Comparative Historical Data | Current Data Sorted By Sales

4/1/02-3/31/03 ALL	4/1/03-3/31/04 ALL	4/1/04-3/31/05 ALL	Type of Statement	0-1MM	1-3MM	3-5MM	5-10MM	10-25MM	25MM & OVER
70	62	64	Unqualified	1	4	1	10	16	32
27	17	21	Reviewed	1	1	4	7	6	2
16	25	16	Compiled	2	5	4	3	2	
12	18	7	Tax Returns	1	3	1	2		
48	43	66	Other	7	9	4	15	10	21
				55 (4/1-9/30/04)			119 (10/1/04-3/31/05)		
173	165	174	**NUMBER OF STATEMENTS**	12	22	14	37	34	55
%	%	%	**ASSETS**	%	%	%	%	%	%
16.0	19.1	20.0	Cash & Equivalents	12.5	26.1	18.0	19.9	17.0	21.6
30.7	30.4	30.2	Trade Receivables (net)	36.8	33.6	36.6	29.6	27.5	28.0
3.5	2.3	4.7	Inventory	11.1	3.8	6.0	6.2	2.9	3.3
7.5	6.8	6.0	All Other Current	.0	2.0	3.7	7.5	10.2	5.9
57.6	58.7	60.9	Total Current	60.4	65.4	64.3	63.2	57.6	58.8
26.3	26.0	24.0	Fixed Assets (net)	27.1	20.8	32.3	21.7	28.4	21.4
5.1	4.9	5.3	Intangibles (net)	1.2	4.6	.3	2.8	2.9	10.8
10.9	10.4	9.8	All Other Non-Current	10.4	9.1	3.1	12.4	11.1	8.9
100.0	100.0	100.0	Total	100.0	100.0	100.0	100.0	100.0	100.0
			LIABILITIES						
8.0	7.5	7.5	Notes Payable-Short Term	16.7	24.1	7.1	4.8	4.7	2.6
2.6	1.8	1.9	Cur. Mat.-L/T/D	2.3	.7	1.2	2.9	2.0	1.6
9.2	10.2	10.0	Trade Payables	10.7	11.8	9.2	9.3	11.0	9.3
.4	.5	.6	Income Taxes Payable	.0	.6	.0	.5	.7	.9
16.5	17.4	16.8	All Other Current	27.0	10.5	9.2	15.6	15.5	20.6
36.7	37.4	36.8	Total Current	56.6	47.6	26.8	33.2	33.9	35.0
12.6	12.7	10.9	Long-Term Debt	18.2	12.8	23.0	8.2	8.9	8.7
.8	.6	.4	Deferred Taxes	.0	.0	.0	.6	.4	.5
6.7	6.3	6.5	All Other Non-Current	1.6	6.8	6.2	5.0	7.2	8.0
43.2	43.0	45.3	Net Worth	22.5	32.7	43.9	53.1	49.6	47.9
100.0	100.0	100.0	Total Liabilities & Net Worth	100.0	100.0	100.0	100.0	100.0	100.0
			INCOME DATA						
100.0	100.0	100.0	Net Sales	100.0	100.0	100.0	100.0	100.0	100.0
			Gross Profit						
94.4	94.8	95.5	Operating Expenses	99.9	92.5	100.7	94.4	96.3	94.8
5.6	5.2	4.5	Operating Profit	.1	7.5	-.7	5.6	3.7	5.2
2.1	.5	.5	All Other Expenses (net)	1.0	1.4	3.2	.7	-.4	-.4
3.4	4.7	4.0	Profit Before Taxes	-.9	6.1	-3.9	5.0	4.1	5.5
			RATIOS						
2.8	3.7	3.1		2.3	3.8	18.1	3.5	2.8	2.5
1.6	1.7	1.8	Current	1.1	1.6	1.9	2.0	1.9	1.8
1.2	1.1	1.2		.7	1.0	1.4	1.3	1.1	1.1
2.4	3.0	2.5		2.0	2.8	17.5	2.5	2.5	2.4
1.4	1.4	1.4	Quick	.8	1.6	1.8	1.4	1.3	1.5
.9	.9	.9		.4	1.0	1.1	.8	.7	.9
32 11.4	31 11.9	33 11.0		0 UND	19 19.5	34 10.9	33 11.2	37 9.8	38 9.5
56 6.6	52 7.0	55 6.6	Sales/Receivables	76 4.8	46 7.9	44 8.3	52 7.0	56 6.6	61 6.0
81 4.5	76 4.8	79 4.6		106 3.4	84 4.4	80 4.6	85 4.3	67 5.4	77 4.7
			Cost of Sales/Inventory						
			Cost of Sales/Payables						
4.7	4.3	4.1		7.9	3.2	3.1	3.7	4.3	4.2
9.0	8.7	8.5	Sales/Working Capital	NM	8.9	7.4	7.9	8.2	8.4
29.9	34.1	29.8		-5.1	NM	15.6	16.9	22.6	36.8
16.6	28.3	39.5			21.2		57.6	40.2	54.4
(134) 4.9	(118) 5.1	(115) 8.8	EBIT/Interest		(14) 7.9		(22) 11.8	(22) 3.9	(39) 19.2
1.1	1.1	.5			1.9		.4	-3.3	4.2
10.7	7.4	11.7							14.5
(38) 3.9	(27) 2.6	(25) 4.7	Net Profit + Depr., Dep., Amort./Cur. Mat. L/T/D					(13)	6.8
2.6	2.1	1.8							3.4
.2	.2	.2		.1	.3	.1	.2	.3	.2
.5	.5	.5	Fixed/Worth	1.2	.7	.8	.4	.6	.4
1.2	1.4	1.4		-.8	4.9	3.4	.7	1.2	1.6
.5	.5	.4		.4	.8	.1	.4	.4	.6
1.2	1.1	1.1	Debt/Worth	NM	2.1	1.6	.8	.9	1.1
3.4	3.1	3.2		-5.9	39.0	6.8	2.5	2.5	2.7
37.4	37.7	46.2			132.1	32.7	46.2	39.2	42.9
(152) 18.7	(145) 14.0	(153) 17.1	% Profit Before Taxes/Tangible Net Worth	(20) 45.6	(12) -2.3	22.5	(33) 8.8	(45) 25.5	
2.5	.8	.7			8.1	-14.3	-.7	-2.8	9.4
18.3	17.0	16.9		5.3	50.7	17.1	16.4	14.6	16.8
5.4	5.5	7.5	% Profit Before Taxes/Total Assets	-1.2	13.9	.6	8.8	4.4	9.3
-.5	-.1	-1.0		-11.9	4.1	-3.2	-.1	-2.5	2.7
26.7	32.1	30.0		545.2	35.3	31.9	24.7	18.1	31.7
11.0	12.9	12.2	Sales/Net Fixed Assets	23.8	17.9	8.5	13.3	6.5	11.5
3.8	4.2	4.0		3.3	8.2	2.8	5.6	2.1	4.1
3.0	3.1	2.8		2.4	5.3	2.8	3.1	2.7	2.5
2.0	2.0	1.7	Sales/Total Assets	1.4	2.6	1.8	2.0	1.7	1.5
1.0	1.1	1.0		.7	1.3	1.5	1.0	.8	1.0
1.5	1.2	1.3			1.0	.9	.9	1.4	.9
(150) 2.5	(134) 2.5	(131) 2.0	% Depr., Dep., Amort./Sales		(12) 1.9	(11) 3.9	(29) 2.1	(30) 2.7	(44) 1.8
5.1	5.0	5.3			2.2	7.2	4.8	5.9	5.1
6.2	3.5	2.6							
(33) 10.8	(39) 10.6	(25) 3.8	% Officers', Directors', Owners' Comp/Sales						
22.6	16.4	11.3							
5478217M	5203175M	7115953M	Net Sales ($)	6213M	45307M	56219M	267281M	538371M	6202562M
4124902M	3780004M	5236653M	Total Assets ($)	8177M	32710M	68311M	214654M	467084M	4445717M

M = $ thousand   MM = $ million
See Pages 11 through 21 for Explanation of Ratios and Data

Current Data Sorted By Assets							Type of Statement	Comparative Historical Data	
1	2	15	12	1	1		Unqualified	23	17
3	19	39	10		1		Reviewed	82	65
21	32	20	1				Compiled	95	91
47	25	2					Tax Returns	52	36
23	41	48	9	3	1		Other	131	142
	69 (4/1-9/30/04)		308 (10/1/04-3/31/05)					4/1/00-3/31/01	4/1/01-3/31/02
0-500M	500M-2MM	2-10MM	10-50MM	50-100MM	100-250MM			ALL	ALL
95	119	124	32	4	3		NUMBER OF STATEMENTS	383	351
%	%	%	%	%	%		ASSETS	%	%
20.4	14.9	19.2	18.0				Cash & Equivalents	12.8	15.3
28.8	47.0	55.5	47.5				Trade Receivables (net)	47.6	45.9
2.5	4.2	3.1	6.2				Inventory	3.1	2.1
4.2	4.5	3.3	3.3				All Other Current	4.1	4.0
56.0	70.6	81.1	75.0				Total Current	67.6	67.2
28.3	16.1	10.6	7.2				Fixed Assets (net)	18.7	18.8
4.5	4.3	2.6	11.6				Intangibles (net)	5.4	6.3
11.3	9.0	5.8	6.2				All Other Non-Current	8.3	7.7
100.0	100.0	100.0	100.0				Total	100.0	100.0
							LIABILITIES		
25.6	13.9	6.5	3.6				Notes Payable-Short Term	14.2	10.1
5.9	3.9	2.0	1.2				Cur. Mat.-L/T/D	2.5	3.2
22.2	30.8	34.9	38.5				Trade Payables	31.2	32.9
.2	.3	.6	.8				Income Taxes Payable	.5	.4
18.1	15.7	18.5	29.4				All Other Current	17.4	18.8
72.0	64.6	62.5	73.5				Total Current	65.7	65.3
29.4	13.4	5.7	3.2				Long-Term Debt	10.6	11.0
.1	.4	.2	.2				Deferred Taxes	.6	.3
10.1	6.5	5.4	3.3				All Other Non-Current	4.4	4.3
-11.7	15.2	26.2	19.8				Net Worth	18.7	19.2
100.0	100.0	100.0	100.0				Total Liabilities & Net Worth	100.0	100.0
							INCOME DATA		
100.0	100.0	100.0	100.0				Net Sales	100.0	100.0
							Gross Profit		
95.1	96.2	93.9	95.6				Operating Expenses	95.6	97.7
4.9	3.8	6.1	4.4				Operating Profit	4.4	2.3
1.8	.7	.4	.6				All Other Expenses (net)	1.2	1.2
3.0	3.1	5.7	3.8				Profit Before Taxes	3.2	1.1
							RATIOS		
1.9	1.7	1.8	1.1					1.6	1.5
1.1	1.1	1.2	1.0				Current	1.1	1.1
.4	.8	1.1	.9					.9	.8
1.7	1.6	1.6	1.1					1.5	1.3
.9	1.0	1.2	.9				Quick	1.0	1.0
.4	.7	.9	.6					.8	.7
0 UND	34 10.9	40 9.0	45 8.1					32 11.4	28 12.8
20 18.2	46 8.0	64 5.7	72 5.1				Sales/Receivables	51 7.2	49 7.4
39 9.4	69 5.3	87 4.2	107 3.4					78 4.7	74 4.9
							Cost of Sales/Inventory		
							Cost of Sales/Payables		
14.8	12.9	8.0	20.8					12.5	17.3
276.8	50.8	19.2	NM				Sales/Working Capital	57.2	167.8
-11.3	-26.3	123.5	-20.1					-41.4	-27.7
8.2	19.1	54.0	219.8					13.3	8.5
(70) 3.4	(102) 5.3	(95) 12.3	(23) 12.7				EBIT/Interest	(316) 4.2	(281) 2.1
-1.3	1.1	4.2	2.8					1.2	-2.2
	4.1	20.5						11.0	6.8
	(12) 1.5	(23) 4.3					Net Profit + Depr., Dep., Amort./Cur. Mat. L /T/D	(73) 3.2	(57) 2.2
	-.9	1.9						1.7	.3
.2	.2	.1	.2					.3	.3
1.0	.8	.4	.6				Fixed/Worth	.8	1.1
-.7	-5.2	1.2	3.5					7.0	-3.9
.9	1.5	1.5	4.9					1.3	1.7
3.6	4.5	3.5	8.7				Debt/Worth	4.0	5.0
-2.8	-31.4	13.0	125.4					83.5	-18.3
96.9	88.9	83.9	92.8					77.3	65.4
(60) 31.5	(87) 39.8	(108) 39.6	(25) 70.4				% Profit Before Taxes/Tangible Net Worth	(291) 32.2	(243) 19.0
4.3	9.0	12.5	35.7					8.3	-1.6
33.3	20.2	22.6	14.0					17.9	12.3
8.1	6.9	10.2	6.9				% Profit Before Taxes/Total Assets	6.0	2.3
-5.9	.3	2.2	.3					.7	-3.8
141.3	103.1	106.9	99.5					66.3	68.0
31.6	30.1	52.7	36.9				Sales/Net Fixed Assets	29.3	29.5
12.4	13.9	24.1	13.8					13.2	12.8
9.1	4.8	4.5	3.3					5.3	5.2
4.4	3.4	3.3	2.3				Sales/Total Assets	3.5	3.5
3.1	2.2	2.2	1.1					2.3	2.2
.6	.4	.4	.6					.6	.6
(54) 1.6	(95) .9	(101) .7	(23) 1.1				% Depr., Dep., Amort./Sales	(308) 1.2	(281) 1.3
3.2	2.6	1.7	2.3					2.2	2.7
5.7	3.4	2.3						3.6	3.9
(51) 11.2	(53) 6.2	(37) 3.3					% Officers', Directors', Owners' Comp/Sales	(172) 6.3	(149) 7.5
19.6	9.8	7.0						11.6	13.6
141965M	489780M	2016308M	1735006M	603610M	1400400M		Net Sales ($)	6296183M	6422059M
23463M	138783M	580143M	659471M	236038M	504572M		Total Assets ($)	2730871M	2571225M

© RMA 2005

M = $ thousand   MM = $ million
See Pages 11 through 21 for Explanation of Ratios and Data

Comparative Historical Data | Current Data Sorted By Sales

	4/1/02-3/31/03 ALL	4/1/03-3/31/04 ALL	4/1/04-3/31/05 ALL	69 (4/1-9/30/04) 0-1MM	1-3MM	3-5MM	308 (10/1/04-3/31/05) 5-10MM	10-25MM	25MM & OVER
Type of Statement									
Unqualified	17	24	32		2		8	11	11
Reviewed	76	79	72	1	7	12	9	28	15
Compiled	62	98	74	13	17	13	15	10	6
Tax Returns	54	57	74	31	21	12	7	2	1
Other	104	123	125	11	31	16	24	27	16
NUMBER OF STATEMENTS	313	381	377	56	78	53	63	78	49
ASSETS	%	%	%	%	%	%	%	%	%
Cash & Equivalents	16.7	16.0	18.1	22.2	13.9	18.1	16.0	19.3	21.3
Trade Receivables (net)	45.5	46.8	45.1	21.0	43.7	45.4	50.4	55.8	50.6
Inventory	2.9	2.9	3.5	2.3	4.1	3.8	3.2	4.0	3.4
All Other Current	4.4	4.8	4.0	6.4	3.5	5.2	3.2	2.4	4.2
Total Current	69.6	70.4	70.8	51.9	65.2	72.5	72.8	81.6	79.6
Fixed Assets (net)	18.1	14.7	16.6	34.1	19.5	14.1	15.6	8.6	8.8
Intangibles (net)	3.9	4.4	4.4	6.0	4.7	4.4	2.2	4.3	4.9
All Other Non-Current	8.4	10.4	8.3	8.1	10.7	9.0	9.5	5.5	6.7
Total	100.0	100.0	100.0	100.0	100.0	100.0	100.0	100.0	100.0
LIABILITIES									
Notes Payable-Short Term	12.6	14.2	13.4	23.5	16.5	17.1	11.1	8.5	4.1
Cur. Mat.-L/T/D	4.5	3.1	3.5	10.3	3.3	3.0	1.8	1.9	1.2
Trade Payables	32.5	32.7	30.8	19.0	23.9	36.5	31.3	35.7	40.6
Income Taxes Payable	.5	.4	.4	.3	.3	.1	.6	.5	.7
All Other Current	22.2	19.2	18.5	11.6	17.0	17.8	23.9	17.2	24.4
Total Current	72.3	69.7	66.6	64.7	60.9	74.5	68.9	63.8	71.0
Long-Term Debt	11.2	8.5	13.9	39.3	17.4	13.4	8.1	4.0	3.3
Deferred Taxes	.6	.3	.3	.2	.3	.2	.4	.3	.2
All Other Non-Current	3.8	4.7	6.7	11.7	5.7	9.6	3.1	6.0	5.1
Net Worth	12.1	16.7	12.5	-15.9	15.7	2.4	19.6	26.0	20.5
Total Liabilities & Net Worth	100.0	100.0	100.0	100.0	100.0	100.0	100.0	100.0	100.0
INCOME DATA									
Net Sales	100.0	100.0	100.0	100.0	100.0	100.0	100.0	100.0	100.0
Gross Profit									
Operating Expenses	96.6	96.2	95.1	90.7	96.9	96.6	95.3	94.7	96.2
Operating Profit	3.4	3.8	4.9	9.3	3.1	3.4	4.7	5.3	3.8
All Other Expenses (net)	.9	1.0	.9	3.1	.7	.4	.2	.9	.1
Profit Before Taxes	2.6	2.9	4.0	6.2	2.5	3.0	4.5	4.5	3.7
RATIOS									
Current	1.6	1.6	1.7	2.4	2.0	1.7	1.5	1.6	1.3
	1.1	1.1	1.2	1.3	1.2	1.2	1.1	1.2	1.1
	.8	.8	.9	.4	.7	.8	.8	1.0	1.0
Quick	1.4	1.4	1.6	2.4	1.7	1.6	1.3	1.6	1.2
	1.0	1.0	1.1	.9	1.0	1.0	1.0	1.2	1.1
	.7	.7	.7	.4	.6	.7	.8	.9	.8
Sales/Receivables	28 13.0	29 12.6	29 12.8	0 UND	30 12.1	32 11.3	34 10.6	39 9.3	32 11.3
	47 7.8	52 7.0	46 8.0	11 33.4	45 8.1	47 7.8	53 6.8	57 6.4	46 7.9
	71 5.2	76 4.8	72 5.1	38 9.6	69 5.3	78 4.7	94 3.9	82 4.4	67 5.4
Cost of Sales/Inventory									
Cost of Sales/Payables									
Sales/Working Capital	14.1	13.0	11.9	11.2	10.9	8.9	13.5	11.0	15.8
	88.8	93.0	46.0	73.8	93.0	46.6	33.3	27.8	61.4
	-32.1	-24.8	-31.5	-7.2	-17.4	-35.2	-26.3	231.7	-106.8
EBIT/Interest	16.8	19.3	23.8	9.0	15.8	18.1	29.8	74.6	67.6
	(257) 4.3	(304) 4.8	(296) 7.1	(35) 2.9	(68) 4.1	(45) 4.4	(54) 11.6	(61) 11.0	(33) 15.6
	.3	-.7	1.6	.7	.9	1.3	1.1	2.8	7.8
Net Profit + Depr., Dep., Amort./Cur. Mat. L/T/D	7.7	8.5	19.6					21.6	27.7
	(50) 2.0	(52) 3.7	(45) 4.3				(13) 4.3	(10) 19.3	
	.4	.7	1.4					1.4	4.5
Fixed/Worth	.3	.2	.2	.1	.2	.2	.2	.1	.2
	.8	.6	.5	2.2	.8	1.1	.5	.3	.4
	-11.8	46.8	5.7	-.4	-5.0	-1.5	3.5	1.8	1.2
Debt/Worth	1.6	1.7	1.4	1.0	1.0	1.5	1.0	1.7	2.5
	4.6	4.9	4.7	3.5	3.4	5.3	3.4	5.9	5.4
	-57.4	-42.9	271.3	-2.1	-28.8	-13.4	76.7	19.8	15.0
% Profit Before Taxes/Tangible Net Worth	77.6	87.5	89.3	113.5	78.5	72.8	106.2	128.8	92.7
	(228) 27.7	(282) 27.5	(286) 40.8	(33) 47.6	(58) 28.5	(37) 33.3	(49) 45.4	(67) 40.7	(42) 52.2
	3.6	2.5	9.2	9.0	2.2	8.3	13.2	12.2	21.9
% Profit Before Taxes/Total Assets	17.0	16.4	21.0	42.1	20.9	14.2	27.7	25.4	15.4
	5.2	4.5	8.1	10.2	6.9	5.1	8.4	9.1	7.9
	-.5	-1.1	.5	-1.7	.0	.6	1.2	1.9	1.6
Sales/Net Fixed Assets	74.7	97.9	106.2	127.3	78.3	108.7	103.1	117.0	124.9
	34.0	39.5	40.0	20.2	25.5	30.1	30.7	53.6	62.0
	13.7	17.6	15.3	4.6	11.4	13.7	18.6	25.5	34.1
Sales/Total Assets	5.1	5.1	4.9	6.2	4.6	4.6	4.9	5.0	5.8
	3.7	3.5	3.5	3.2	3.5	3.3	3.3	3.8	4.1
	2.4	2.2	2.2	1.2	2.1	2.1	2.4	2.4	2.6
% Depr., Dep., Amort./Sales	.6	.5	.4	1.3	.6	.4	.4	.4	.3
	(260) 1.2	(299) 1.1	(278) 1.1	(29) 2.7	(53) 1.4	(44) .8	(53) 1.1	(65) .7	(34) .6
	2.4	2.3	2.1	9.8	3.0	1.8	2.1	1.5	1.1
% Officers', Directors', Owners' Comp/Sales	3.1	2.8	3.2	8.2	4.5	3.4	2.9	2.2	
	(141) 6.1	(150) 7.4	(143) 6.4	(29) 14.4	(38) 8.7	(27) 4.7	(17) 6.7	(25) 3.1	
	11.0	12.9	11.8	20.8	11.9	7.5	9.7	4.6	
Net Sales ($)	7297368M	10158644M	6387069M	29452M	146834M	204451M	446987M	1228132M	4331213M
Total Assets ($)	1914921M	3183787M	2142470M	14744M	58669M	79039M	171645M	469289M	1349084M

M = $ thousand   MM = $ million
See Pages 11 through 21 for Explanation of Ratios and Data

Current Data Sorted By Assets   **Comparative Historical Data**

0-500M	500M-2MM	2-10MM	10-50MM	50-100MM	100-250MM	Type of Statement	4/1/00-3/31/01 ALL	4/1/01-3/31/02 ALL
1	1	4	3		1	Unqualified	9	7
	4	7	2			Reviewed	19	11
3	6	3				Compiled	15	14
5	1	1			1	Tax Returns	7	9
11	14	3	4		1	Other	22	31
	16 (4/1-9/30/04)			60 (10/1/04-3/31/05)				
20	26	18	9		3	**NUMBER OF STATEMENTS**	72	72
%	%	%	%	%	%	**ASSETS**	%	%
6.9	11.0	11.9				Cash & Equivalents	14.0	15.3
26.5	52.3	52.1				Trade Receivables (net)	47.1	42.6
.4	3.3	4.8				Inventory	3.1	3.0
6.9	5.9	3.4				All Other Current	5.9	3.4
40.8	72.5	72.3				Total Current	70.0	64.3
40.0	14.8	11.1				Fixed Assets (net)	16.4	18.8
5.8	3.1	4.2				Intangibles (net)	1.8	5.6
13.4	9.6	12.4				All Other Non-Current	11.8	11.4
100.0	100.0	100.0				Total	100.0	100.0
			D A T A N O T A V A I L A B L E			**LIABILITIES**		
16.2	18.2	8.4				Notes Payable-Short Term	12.6	29.7
10.7	2.5	.8				Cur. Mat.-L/T/D	3.3	14.9
7.1	18.4	18.4				Trade Payables	16.8	16.5
.0	1.8	1.3				Income Taxes Payable	1.9	2.0
17.8	12.0	14.9				All Other Current	15.8	18.6
51.8	52.9	43.8				Total Current	50.3	81.8
49.2	4.5	3.3				Long-Term Debt	7.2	7.4
.0	.0	.2				Deferred Taxes	.7	.5
7.8	6.9	11.3				All Other Non-Current	4.1	12.7
-8.8	35.8	41.5				Net Worth	37.8	-2.4
100.0	100.0	100.0				Total Liabilities & Net Worth	100.0	100.0
						INCOME DATA		
100.0	100.0	100.0				Net Sales	100.0	100.0
						Gross Profit		
91.4	96.0	93.2				Operating Expenses	92.6	99.7
8.6	4.0	6.8				Operating Profit	7.4	.3
.6	.3	1.2				All Other Expenses (net)	.0	.8
8.1	3.7	5.6				Profit Before Taxes	7.5	-.4
						RATIOS		
2.3	2.8	2.8					2.3	1.7
1.0	1.3	1.6				Current	1.4	1.2
.2	1.0	1.1					1.1	.8
1.6	2.6	2.8					2.0	1.5
.9	1.2	1.5				Quick	1.3	1.0
.1	.8	.9					.9	.6
0 UND	33 11.1	47 7.8					35 10.4	24 15.4
16 23.5	56 6.5	61 6.0				Sales/Receivables	66 5.5	45 8.0
37 9.8	79 4.6	111 3.3					90 4.1	69 5.3
						Cost of Sales/Inventory		
						Cost of Sales/Payables		
16.8	6.8	5.3					6.5	12.0
UND	22.3	9.2				Sales/Working Capital	16.5	38.8
-29.7	218.2	39.4					41.1	-15.7
22.4	70.8	69.0					21.4	9.5
(18) 5.0	(24) 6.1	(14) 12.6				EBIT/Interest	(56) 9.2	(60) 2.4
1.9	.8	3.6					2.3	-3.4
						Net Profit + Depr., Dep.,	9.8	7.6
						Amort./Cur. Mat. L /T/D	(18) 5.2	(15) 1.8
							1.5	-1.1
.2	.2	.1					.1	.2
1.2	.6	.2				Fixed/Worth	.5	.9
UND	1.3	.6					.9	-5.0
.8	.9	.5					.7	1.1
1.5	2.4	1.2				Debt/Worth	1.7	3.7
UND	11.1	4.7					4.2	-17.2
128.5	87.1	77.9				% Profit Before Taxes/Tangible	66.6	45.0
(15) 19.9	(24) 29.8	(16) 12.7				Net Worth	(64) 43.3	(51) 14.5
6.9	.6	8.1					11.4	-15.2
74.1	16.0	20.6				% Profit Before Taxes/Total	26.8	17.4
14.5	8.5	10.3				Assets	12.3	3.0
-.2	-.1	4.5					3.3	-14.7
69.0	47.5	79.4					48.6	54.9
21.4	33.8	33.6				Sales/Net Fixed Assets	25.6	26.3
7.7	17.3	19.9					11.3	13.1
10.1	4.5	3.8					3.8	4.7
5.1	3.3	2.6				Sales/Total Assets	2.8	3.3
3.3	2.5	1.9					1.9	2.5
1.1	1.1	.7					.9	.8
(11) 1.7	(18) 1.4	(14) 1.3				% Depr., Dep., Amort./Sales	(61) 1.4	(57) 1.4
2.9	2.0	2.2					2.8	2.3
10.5							5.8	4.7
(10) 13.5						% Officers', Directors',	(28) 10.6	(29) 9.4
22.6						Owners' Comp/Sales	16.1	17.1
33603M	134560M	220190M	204113M		4434880M	Net Sales ($)	619331M	921592M
4616M	30225M	68799M	190384M		414626M	Total Assets ($)	320436M	466242M

M = $ thousand   MM = $ million
See Pages 11 through 21 for Explanation of Ratios and Data

Comparative Historical Data				**Current Data Sorted By Sales**					
			Type of Statement						
11	6	10	Unqualified	1		1	1	4	3
8	11	13	Reviewed		2	3	5	2	1
18	20	12	Compiled	1	4	5		2	
8	8	8	Tax Returns	2	3			1	2
25	24	33	Other	6	11	5	6	4	1
4/1/02-3/31/03 ALL	4/1/03-3/31/04 ALL	4/1/04-3/31/05 ALL		16 (4/1-9/30/04) 0-1MM	1-3MM	3-5MM	60 (10/1/04-3/31/05) 5-10MM	10-25MM	25MM & OVER
70	69	76	**NUMBER OF STATEMENTS**	10	20	14	12	13	7
%	%	%	**ASSETS**	%	%	%	%	%	%
15.0	13.7	11.0	Cash & Equivalents	10.7	9.2	7.8	8.5	11.9	
45.5	47.2	41.2	Trade Receivables (net)	26.5	33.0	55.6	52.9	48.2	
2.8	2.9	2.5	Inventory	.4	.9	1.5	6.3	5.3	
4.7	3.4	5.8	All Other Current	8.0	8.1	1.6	6.2	4.5	
67.9	67.2	60.5	Total Current	45.6	51.1	66.6	73.8	70.0	
18.7	20.3	20.6	Fixed Assets (net)	46.4	27.8	11.0	11.4	14.6	
4.7	2.9	5.7	Intangibles (net)	.2	5.3	13.4	.5	7.9	
8.6	9.6	13.1	All Other Non-Current	7.8	15.7	9.1	14.2	7.5	
100.0	100.0	100.0	Total	100.0	100.0	100.0	100.0	100.0	
			LIABILITIES						
10.7	20.2	14.1	Notes Payable-Short Term	19.7	15.1	10.3	18.4	8.8	
3.5	2.6	4.2	Cur. Mat.-L/T/D	11.6	6.4	1.5	2.5	1.1	
18.8	16.5	13.5	Trade Payables	10.2	4.4	17.7	16.2	20.1	
.8	1.5	1.0	Income Taxes Payable	.0	.1	2.5	2.7	.5	
24.8	22.0	15.8	All Other Current	5.9	16.4	11.4	14.1	23.2	
58.6	62.8	48.6	Total Current	47.4	42.3	43.4	53.9	53.7	
11.2	12.8	18.2	Long-Term Debt	34.2	36.1	3.4	4.0	16.6	
.5	.4	.0	Deferred Taxes	.0	.0	.2	.0	.0	
7.0	6.9	7.3	All Other Non-Current	14.9	5.0	8.0	5.3	6.2	
22.7	17.1	26.0	Net Worth	3.5	16.5	44.8	36.8	23.5	
100.0	100.0	100.0	Total Liabilities & Net Worth	100.0	100.0	100.0	100.0	100.0	
			INCOME DATA						
100.0	100.0	100.0	Net Sales	100.0	100.0	100.0	100.0	100.0	
			Gross Profit						
96.2	94.2	93.6	Operating Expenses	81.3	96.6	93.3	96.4	96.6	
3.8	5.8	6.4	Operating Profit	18.7	3.4	6.7	3.6	3.4	
1.0	1.6	1.3	All Other Expenses (net)	5.1	1.3	1.1	.5	.3	
2.8	4.2	5.0	Profit Before Taxes	13.6	2.0	5.6	3.0	3.1	
			RATIOS						
2.1	1.8	2.7		2.2	4.2	2.6	2.2	3.0	
1.4	1.3	1.3	Current	1.1	1.3	1.6	1.4	2.6	
.9	.9	.9		.5	.4	1.1	1.1	1.0	
1.8	1.8	2.4		1.5	3.9	2.6	2.1	3.0	
1.2	1.1	1.2	Quick	1.0	.9	1.5	1.2	2.1	
.8	.7	.7		.5	.1	1.1	.7	.7	
28 12.9	30 12.1	24 15.0		0 UND	0 UND	54 6.8	42 8.8	49 7.5	
51 7.1	55 6.6	53 6.8	Sales/Receivables	28 13.0	32 11.5	68 5.3	56 6.5	59 6.2	
73 5.0	77 4.7	76 4.8		70 5.2	68 5.4	122 3.0	78 4.7	69 5.3	
			Cost of Sales/Inventory						
			Cost of Sales/Payables						
8.1	9.1	6.0		8.6	8.5	5.2	6.7	5.0	
17.6	18.2	20.3	Sales/Working Capital	128.8	32.7	9.3	17.5	9.3	
-76.1	-29.9	-179.5		-22.9	-179.5	NM	61.3	NM	
15.0	24.8	36.4			71.5	30.8	14.6	77.5	
(50) 4.9	(57) 5.8	(62) 6.5	EBIT/Interest		(17) 5.9	(13) 6.8	(11) 4.1	(10) 13.6	
.6	1.1	2.2			.7	1.5	2.6	2.0	
6.2	12.3	27.2	Net Profit + Depr., Dep.,						
(11) 1.3	(13) 6.2	(12) 3.4	Amort./Cur. Mat. L/T/D						
-.4	1.5	-.1							
.2	.1	.2		.4	.2	.2	.1	.1	
.5	.5	.5	Fixed/Worth	1.4	.6	.3	.5	.5	
6.0	5.5	1.7		UND	2.1	1.4	.7	NM	
1.2	1.1	.7		.8	.4	.6	.7	.4	
2.5	2.3	2.1	Debt/Worth	6.9	2.0	1.3	2.0	1.9	
22.6	87.1	10.4		UND	6.5	8.6	8.0	NM	
57.6	69.4	84.3	% Profit Before Taxes/Tangible		75.8	31.6	54.8	85.9	
(58) 16.8	(53) 22.4	(66) 19.1	Net Worth		(18) 28.9	(12) 13.3	(11) 15.3	(10) 9.4	
-2.6	4.5	3.6			-2.2	5.4	4.7	-2.7	
19.9	22.0	22.2	% Profit Before Taxes/Total	92.2	28.9	16.9	14.6	19.7	
3.7	7.5	8.9	Assets	13.5	7.7	5.5	6.7	8.1	
-2.1	.3	1.2		1.1	-4.1	1.0	2.8	2.3	
70.5	60.2	62.0		UND	59.6	40.5	62.1	133.5	
27.8	35.1	29.2	Sales/Net Fixed Assets	10.0	29.2	26.8	36.3	61.5	
12.3	14.1	14.2		4.9	10.7	16.1	24.9	16.8	
4.4	4.8	4.9		5.4	7.6	4.1	4.5	4.6	
3.2	3.1	3.1	Sales/Total Assets	3.1	3.5	2.5	3.3	2.7	
2.3	2.4	2.1		1.2	2.5	1.6	2.3	1.8	
.7	.8	1.0			1.3	1.1			
(55) 1.3	(51) 1.4	(51) 1.4	% Depr., Dep., Amort./Sales		(12) 2.1	(12) 1.6			
2.2	2.3	2.3			3.3	2.0			
5.8	5.6	8.4	% Officers', Directors',						
(34) 12.0	(34) 10.0	(28) 12.6	Owners' Comp/Sales						
21.4	20.7	24.4							
998349M	2072571M	5027346M	Net Sales ($)	4253M	41843M	56345M	79364M	192572M	4652969M
424373M	657913M	708650M	Total Assets ($)	14219M	23113M	70143M	25911M	76475M	498789M

M = $ thousand   MM = $ million
See Pages 11 through 21 for Explanation of Ratios and Data

Current Data Sorted By Assets   Comparative Historical Data

						Type of Statement		
	3	1	3			Unqualified	6	6
	5	6	2			Reviewed	4	6
3	5	2	1			Compiled	8	11
4	5	1				Tax Returns	6	6
4	8	6	1	1		Other	17	12
	6 (4/1-9/30/04)		50 (10/1/04-3/31/05)				4/1/00-3/31/01	4/1/01-3/31/02
0-500M	500M-2MM	2-10MM	10-50MM	50-100MM	100-250MM		ALL	ALL
11	21	16	7	1		NUMBER OF STATEMENTS	41	41
%	%	%	%	%	%	**ASSETS**	%	%
14.1	8.4	7.0				Cash & Equivalents	8.6	6.9
30.5	20.4	36.7				Trade Receivables (net)	24.2	19.2
3.5	6.5	12.2				Inventory	6.2	4.1
.0	8.1	3.4				All Other Current	2.4	2.9
48.1	43.4	59.4				Total Current	41.4	33.0
38.0	41.0	30.8				Fixed Assets (net)	50.1	58.3
6.4	5.3	2.4				Intangibles (net)	2.0	1.9
7.5	10.2	7.4				All Other Non-Current	6.5	6.7
100.0	100.0	100.0				Total	100.0	100.0
						LIABILITIES		
15.6	15.0	13.2				Notes Payable-Short Term	3.9	7.1
11.3	4.9	3.8				Cur. Mat.-L/T/D	8.2	6.3
13.1	11.8	17.5				Trade Payables	13.0	8.9
.0	.2	.0				Income Taxes Payable	.3	.1
39.2	7.6	17.8				All Other Current	6.2	8.2
79.4	39.5	52.3				Total Current	31.5	30.5
26.8	21.3	18.7				Long-Term Debt	38.6	40.5
.0	.1	.0				Deferred Taxes	.2	.2
8.5	6.0	4.8				All Other Non-Current	1.8	2.1
-14.7	33.1	24.2				Net Worth	27.8	26.7
100.0	100.0	100.0				Total Liabilities & Net Worth	100.0	100.0
						INCOME DATA		
100.0	100.0	100.0				Net Sales	100.0	100.0
						Gross Profit		
85.5	92.3	93.5				Operating Expenses	84.6	84.2
14.5	7.7	6.5				Operating Profit	15.4	15.8
1.3	2.1	.3				All Other Expenses (net)	5.5	7.4
13.2	5.7	6.2				Profit Before Taxes	9.9	8.3
						RATIOS		
1.1	3.6	1.6					3.0	2.0
.8	.9	1.0				Current	1.6	1.2
.3	.5	.7					.8	.5
1.1	1.7	1.2					2.7	1.5
.8	.5	.8				Quick	1.0	.8
.2	.3	.5					.4	.4
0 UND	0 UND	33 11.0					23 15.8	3 129.3
34 10.7	24 15.1	48 7.6				Sales/Receivables	43 8.5	30 12.2
71 5.1	76 4.8	75 4.9					57 6.4	62 5.9
						Cost of Sales/Inventory		
						Cost of Sales/Payables		
37.0	6.9	9.7					4.3	8.3
-17.1	-98.3	NM				Sales/Working Capital	11.1	28.8
-1.9	-9.5	-15.8					-22.2	-7.2
21.5	8.2	6.2					4.8	4.1
(10) 7.5	(16) 1.8	(14) 3.5				EBIT/Interest	(31) 2.9	(34) 2.1
1.3	-.7	-1.1					1.1	.6
						Net Profit + Depr., Dep., Amort./Cur. Mat. L./T/D		
.0	.4	.4					.5	1.1
2.2	2.5	.8				Fixed/Worth	1.5	2.5
-1.2	NM	2.6					6.3	15.0
1.2	.8	1.7					.7	1.0
-486.0	4.2	3.9				Debt/Worth	1.8	4.1
-2.1	NM	6.6					8.7	42.0
	79.5	81.4				% Profit Before Taxes/Tangible	73.2	67.4
	(16) 26.2	(14) 24.9				Net Worth	(36) 22.4	(33) 14.8
	10.6	-2.0					.9	-4.2
54.1	20.6	14.7				% Profit Before Taxes/Total	19.7	12.5
9.0	6.0	5.7				Assets	6.6	4.4
.4	-3.2	-2.7					-.2	-.7
396.0	26.2	48.0					12.5	7.5
6.6	5.4	12.7				Sales/Net Fixed Assets	3.7	1.6
1.8	1.0	2.9					.5	.5
3.5	3.2	2.8					3.1	1.7
1.9	1.7	2.5				Sales/Total Assets	1.5	1.0
1.0	.6	1.1					.4	.4
	3.5	1.0					1.9	2.1
	(18) 6.5	(13) 5.0				% Depr., Dep., Amort./Sales	(39) 6.3	(36) 7.0
	14.4	9.1					13.4	13.4
	6.9						4.4	4.4
	(10) 9.1					% Officers', Directors', Owners' Comp/Sales	(13) 7.3	(14) 7.2
	14.4						14.0	12.0
5031M	54400M	158512M	136115M	99664M		Net Sales ($)	541626M	347457M
2590M	23868M	69959M	129340M	51955M		Total Assets ($)	417233M	290525M

(In the 100-250MM column: "DATA NOT AVAILABLE" printed vertically.)

M = $ thousand   MM = $ million
See Pages 11 through 21 for Explanation of Ratios and Data

Comparative Historical Data / Current Data Sorted By Sales

	4/1/02-3/31/03 ALL	4/1/03-3/31/04 ALL	4/1/04-3/31/05 ALL	0-1MM	1-3MM	3-5MM	5-10MM	10-25MM	25MM & OVER
Type of Statement									
Unqualified	3	4	4			1	1	2	1
Reviewed	10	8	11		3		3	4	
Compiled	15	11	11	6	3	1	1		
Tax Returns	5	13	10	5	4		1		
Other	14	17	20	7	2	2	5	2	2
				6 (4/1-9/30/04)		50 (10/1/04-3/31/05)			
NUMBER OF STATEMENTS	47	53	56	18	12	4	11	8	3
ASSETS	%	%	%	%	%	%	%	%	%
Cash & Equivalents	7.8	7.3	8.9	7.7	10.2		12.7		
Trade Receivables (net)	21.8	21.9	26.2	19.9	26.3		28.2		
Inventory	5.1	5.9	7.2	3.3	2.1		9.3		
All Other Current	3.4	3.6	4.3	.5	6.8		8.3		
Total Current	38.0	38.6	46.6	31.4	45.4		58.5		
Fixed Assets (net)	48.2	47.6	40.1	53.7	43.1		27.7		
Intangibles (net)	4.4	6.7	4.6	4.4	7.1		3.5		
All Other Non-Current	9.4	7.1	8.7	10.4	4.3		10.4		
Total	100.0	100.0	100.0	100.0	100.0		100.0		
LIABILITIES									
Notes Payable-Short Term	5.3	9.8	12.5	19.5	6.7		9.8		
Cur. Mat.-L/T/D	6.9	5.7	5.8	9.0	4.4		6.4		
Trade Payables	11.9	10.8	12.8	9.2	10.0		11.9		
Income Taxes Payable	.0	.2	.1	.0	.3		.0		
All Other Current	10.9	11.2	17.0	24.7	8.2		9.4		
Total Current	35.0	37.7	48.1	62.4	29.7		37.6		
Long-Term Debt	31.4	31.0	24.1	30.8	25.0		18.2		
Deferred Taxes	.0	.1	.1	.0	.0		.2		
All Other Non-Current	5.1	18.3	5.7	8.1	6.2		1.7		
Net Worth	28.4	12.8	21.9	-1.3	39.1		42.3		
Total Liabilities & Net Worth	100.0	100.0	100.0	100.0	100.0		100.0		
INCOME DATA									
Net Sales	100.0	100.0	100.0	100.0	100.0		100.0		
Gross Profit									
Operating Expenses	86.3	92.8	90.5	83.4	92.5		96.5		
Operating Profit	13.7	7.2	9.5	16.6	7.5		3.5		
All Other Expenses (net)	4.3	4.1	1.7	1.8	2.0		.1		
Profit Before Taxes	9.4	3.1	7.8	14.8	5.5		3.4		
RATIOS									
Current	2.0	1.8	1.6	.9	4.1		3.8		
	1.0	1.0	1.0	.6	1.6		1.3		
	.5	.6	.7	.2	.5		1.1		
Quick	1.6	1.4	1.1	.9	2.1		2.2		
	.8	.9	.8	.5	.9		1.1		
	.5	.4	.4	.2	.4		.8		
Sales/Receivables	21 17.1	19 19.1	7 52.5	0 UND	0 UND		10 36.5		
	41 9.0	37 9.8	43 8.5	32 11.5	40 9.2		32 11.4		
	53 6.9	54 6.8	71 5.2	73 5.0	79 4.6		63 5.8		
Cost of Sales/Inventory									
Cost of Sales/Payables									
Sales/Working Capital	8.0	11.1	9.3	NM	5.1		7.5		
	227.7	UND	200.3	-10.5	7.8		11.6		
	-15.2	-13.4	-12.7	-1.5	-17.8		71.3		
EBIT/Interest	6.8	8.9	9.5	9.2	14.4				
	(40) 2.9	(45) 3.3	(47) 3.0	(16) 4.5	(11) 3.3				
	1.1	.4	.4	.6	1.9				
Net Profit + Depr., Dep., Amort./Cur. Mat. L/T/D									
Fixed/Worth	.4	.8	.4	.6	.6		.1		
	1.3	2.4	1.6	4.9	1.4		.6		
	23.1	-5.9	11.2	-7.4	6.2		1.6		
Debt/Worth	.9	1.2	1.1	1.8	.9		.9		
	2.1	4.7	4.2	10.7	3.6		1.3		
	254.0	-11.5	NM	-6.9	7.8		4.7		
% Profit Before Taxes/Tangible Net Worth	32.3	50.8	77.3	100.6	77.5		52.1		
	(36) 14.3	(35) 26.6	(42) 27.2	(10) 26.2	(11) 45.9		11.4		
	-.4	6.9	9.4	18.0	11.4		2.8		
% Profit Before Taxes/Total Assets	15.3	14.3	19.1	24.0	17.0		18.5		
	6.4	6.1	6.9	6.9	8.8		4.9		
	.1	-2.4	.4	-2.2	2.9		.4		
Sales/Net Fixed Assets	14.3	18.4	29.6	13.8	20.0		123.6		
	2.6	4.7	4.8	1.4	4.6		31.3		
	.9	.8	1.0	.6	2.2		3.4		
Sales/Total Assets	3.4	3.3	2.9	1.6	2.9		5.5		
	1.2	1.9	1.7	.8	1.8		3.2		
	.6	.7	.8	.4	1.0		1.6		
% Depr., Dep., Amort./Sales	2.3	2.0	2.2	9.3	3.2				
	(40) 5.1	(48) 7.2	(47) 7.9	(15) 12.9	5.4				
	14.7	15.2	13.5	24.6	10.4				
% Officers', Directors', Owners' Comp/Sales	3.7	6.2	4.5						
	(16) 9.6	(20) 9.9	(23) 8.5						
	12.5	15.8	12.2						
Net Sales ($)	320380M	257741M	453722M	7507M	23522M	15325M	80186M	116876M	210306M
Total Assets ($)	344187M	194285M	277712M	13564M	15951M	29413M	57203M	70937M	90644M

© RMA 2005

M = $ thousand   MM = $ million
See Pages 11 through 21 for Explanation of Ratios and Data

Current Data Sorted By Assets | Comparative Historical Data

0-500M	500M-2MM	2-10MM	10-50MM	50-100MM	100-250MM	Type of Statement	4/1/00-3/31/01 ALL	4/1/01-3/31/02 ALL
2	9	6	5	2		Unqualified	22	24
	7	15	3			Reviewed	35	26
2	7	5				Compiled	44	42
5		1				Tax Returns	14	12
4	6	11	9	1		Other	33	39
	23 (4/1-9/30/04)			77 (10/1/04-3/31/05)				
13	29	38	17	3		NUMBER OF STATEMENTS	148	143
%	%	%	%	%	%	**ASSETS**	%	%
14.3	10.1	15.8	16.1			Cash & Equivalents	14.6	14.6
38.1	42.8	37.8	29.2			Trade Receivables (net)	37.4	34.0
.8	3.2	2.8	5.9			Inventory	4.7	3.9
1.0	5.6	2.9	8.0			All Other Current	2.7	3.2
54.3	61.7	59.3	59.2			Total Current	59.4	55.7
25.6	24.0	26.8	23.0			Fixed Assets (net)	27.6	29.6
5.0	5.0	3.3	10.1			Intangibles (net)	5.4	7.1
15.1	9.2	10.7	7.7			All Other Non-Current	7.6	7.6
100.0	100.0	100.0	100.0			Total	100.0	100.0
						LIABILITIES		
29.5	10.9	6.9	5.5			Notes Payable-Short Term	9.4	7.3
2.7	5.4	4.6	3.4			Cur. Mat.-L/T/D	5.0	5.4
16.4	14.9	21.3	17.8			Trade Payables	16.5	17.1
1.7	.0	.1	.0			Income Taxes Payable	.4	.1
32.1	16.0	19.4	23.7			All Other Current	23.1	20.4
82.4	47.3	52.3	50.4			Total Current	54.4	50.4
56.6	21.5	13.5	10.2			Long-Term Debt	16.1	17.1
.0	.2	.5	1.2			Deferred Taxes	.4	.2
10.4	13.0	2.6	4.7			All Other Non-Current	5.5	4.4
-49.4	18.2	31.2	33.5			Net Worth	23.6	27.9
100.0	100.0	100.0	100.0			Total Liabilities & Net Worth	100.0	100.0
						INCOME DATA		
100.0	100.0	100.0	100.0			Net Sales	100.0	100.0
						Gross Profit		
94.7	94.8	91.0	97.5			Operating Expenses	95.2	96.1
5.3	5.2	9.0	2.5			Operating Profit	4.8	3.9
3.8	1.8	1.6	.2			All Other Expenses (net)	1.0	2.0
1.5	3.4	7.4	2.3			Profit Before Taxes	3.8	1.9
						RATIOS		
.9	2.0	1.7	1.6				1.6	1.6
.7	1.4	1.0	1.1			Current	1.2	1.1
.4	1.0	.8	.9				.9	.8
.9	2.0	1.5	1.5				1.5	1.5
.7	1.3	.9	.8			Quick	1.1	1.0
.4	.8	.6	.5				.7	.6
0 UND	31 11.9	34 10.7	31 11.9				33 11.1	29 12.6
28 13.2	50 7.4	53 6.9	65 5.6			Sales/Receivables	53 6.9	49 7.5
47 7.8	56 6.5	71 5.2	83 4.4				69 5.3	66 5.5
						Cost of Sales/Inventory		
						Cost of Sales/Payables		
-105.2	9.0	8.6	10.3				9.8	10.0
-42.4	22.8	NM	84.7			Sales/Working Capital	29.4	42.6
-12.0	242.8	-14.0	NM				-42.5	-19.3
	15.9	31.5	21.4				10.2	9.1
(28) 3.4	(35) 10.1	(13) 2.5				EBIT/Interest	(133) 3.1	(125) 2.5
1.3	3.0	1.6					.8	.4
		10.2					2.9	2.7
	(13) 3.4					Net Profit + Depr., Dep., Amort./Cur. Mat. L /T/D	(39) 1.4	(30) 1.5
	1.7						.9	.8
1.0	.5	.2	.4				.5	.4
-1.7	1.1	1.0	1.4			Fixed/Worth	1.1	1.6
-.1	10.8	3.1	2.1				3.5	10.5
3.2	1.5	1.1	1.0				1.3	1.2
-3.7	5.7	2.6	2.8			Debt/Worth	2.8	3.6
-2.1	19.7	7.7	17.6				10.6	51.0
	100.0	73.7	82.3				68.8	56.8
(23) 21.1	(33) 38.7	(14) 15.2				% Profit Before Taxes/Tangible Net Worth	(123) 26.4	(115) 15.8
5.7	13.2	-5.3					5.5	-6.8
35.9	28.2	24.6	14.3				15.7	12.4
8.1	4.1	8.2	3.0			% Profit Before Taxes/Total Assets	6.1	3.7
-11.3	.8	3.1	-1.0				-.6	-2.5
90.6	52.3	31.2	62.4				24.8	23.1
19.2	22.1	13.3	9.9			Sales/Net Fixed Assets	12.1	10.3
15.3	7.6	6.1	4.1				5.8	4.9
9.1	4.8	3.4	2.7				4.1	3.5
5.9	3.5	2.5	2.0			Sales/Total Assets	2.5	2.3
3.9	2.5	1.8	.7				1.8	1.7
	.8	1.2	2.4				.9	1.1
(25) 1.8	(37) 1.9	(13) 4.5				% Depr., Dep., Amort./Sales	(128) 2.5	(124) 2.9
4.1	4.7	8.3					4.3	4.8
2.5	4.7						2.2	2.5
(10) 4.4	(14) 6.2					% Officers', Directors', Owners' Comp/Sales	(64) 4.6	(56) 4.9
20.4	10.0						8.9	7.8
24594M	131188M	503519M	777896M	205676M		Net Sales ($)	2791194M	3359130M
3343M	32447M	193096M	352669M	209871M		Total Assets ($)	1558301M	1702765M

Note: Columns 50-100MM and 100-250MM marked "DATA NOT AVAILABLE" for Assets, Liabilities, Income Data, and Ratios sections.

M = $ thousand   MM = $ million
See Pages 11 through 21 for Explanation of Ratios and Data

	Comparative Historical Data			Type of Statement	Current Data Sorted By Sales					
	26	18	15	Unqualified	2		4	2	7	
	31	27	27	Reviewed		3	6	11	3	
	20	35	14	Compiled	1	5	5	2		
	14	14	13	Tax Returns	1	4	4	1		
	47	43	31	Other	2	5	5	9	7	
	4/1/02-3/31/03	4/1/03-3/31/04	4/1/04-3/31/05			23 (4/1-9/30/04)		77 (10/1/04-3/31/05)		
	ALL	ALL	ALL		0-1MM	1-3MM	3-5MM	5-10MM	10-25MM	25MM & OVER
	138	137	100	NUMBER OF STATEMENTS	6	17	11	24	25	17
	%	%	%	ASSETS	%	%	%	%	%	%
	18.6	15.0	13.6	Cash & Equivalents		11.0	9.5	16.5	16.0	14.1
	35.2	36.2	37.1	Trade Receivables (net)		39.3	53.0	33.5	37.3	30.4
	3.6	3.6	3.3	Inventory		1.9	4.0	2.8	2.9	6.3
	2.2	2.8	4.6	All Other Current		2.4	2.8	6.9	3.0	7.8
	59.5	57.6	58.6	Total Current		54.5	69.3	59.6	59.2	58.7
	27.4	26.1	26.2	Fixed Assets (net)		33.8	19.9	24.1	23.1	27.0
	5.0	7.2	5.1	Intangibles (net)		5.1	4.8	6.0	3.0	9.0
	8.0	9.1	10.1	All Other Non-Current		6.6	5.9	10.3	14.8	5.4
	100.0	100.0	100.0	Total		100.0	100.0	100.0	100.0	100.0
				LIABILITIES						
	8.6	11.4	11.0	Notes Payable-Short Term		19.8	3.3	13.9	7.4	7.4
	6.1	4.6	4.4	Cur. Mat.-L/T/D		5.5	6.0	4.1	4.0	4.3
	19.6	20.0	18.1	Trade Payables		12.0	14.6	17.3	25.9	19.0
	.2	.8	.3	Income Taxes Payable		.1	.0	.0	.0	.3
	19.3	19.3	20.5	All Other Current		24.5	19.6	17.7	20.1	22.4
	53.7	56.0	54.3	Total Current		61.8	43.4	53.1	57.4	53.4
	16.2	18.2	21.5	Long-Term Debt		35.7	15.3	26.2	10.2	13.2
	.2	.3	.4	Deferred Taxes		.3	.0	.9	.2	.8
	6.8	7.5	6.9	All Other Non-Current		16.2	13.9	6.4	1.0	5.1
	23.1	18.0	16.7	Net Worth		−13.9	27.3	13.4	31.1	27.6
	100.0	100.0	100.0	Total Liabilities & Net Worth		100.0	100.0	100.0	100.0	100.0
				INCOME DATA						
	100.0	100.0	100.0	Net Sales		100.0	100.0	100.0	100.0	100.0
				Gross Profit						
	96.5	95.0	93.8	Operating Expenses		94.3	93.0	96.1	93.6	95.5
	3.5	5.0	6.2	Operating Profit		5.7	7.0	3.9	6.4	4.5
	1.8	1.2	1.7	All Other Expenses (net)		4.5	1.0	.9	.9	.9
	1.7	3.8	4.5	Profit Before Taxes		1.2	6.0	3.0	5.4	3.7
				RATIOS						
	1.9	1.6	1.8			1.9	2.3	1.9	1.2	1.6
	1.1	1.0	1.0	Current		1.0	1.5	1.1	1.0	1.0
	.8	.8	.8			.6	1.2	.8	.9	.6
	1.7	1.5	1.6			1.9	2.3	1.7	1.1	1.5
	1.0	.9	.9	Quick		.9	1.5	1.0	.9	.8
	.7	.7	.6			.6	1.0	.6	.7	.4
	31　11.9	24　15.2	28　13.2		26　13.9	38　9.6	26　14.0	36　10.1	22　16.8	
	47　7.8	46　8.0	50　7.3	Sales/Receivables	46　7.9	56　6.5	53　6.9	50　7.3	54　6.7	
	61　5.9	66　5.5	68　5.4		56　6.5	109　3.3	60　6.0	73　5.0	76　4.8	
				Cost of Sales/Inventory						
				Cost of Sales/Payables						
	8.8	13.3	10.3			12.3	6.9	9.3	21.7	12.8
	45.2	102.8	120.0	Sales/Working Capital		638.0	9.5	68.9	999.8	122.5
	−22.7	−25.8	−24.7			−28.4	27.3	−26.0	−17.8	−10.2
	14.8	16.7	28.5			5.6	44.2	14.0	31.5	24.7
	(121)　3.5	(119)　3.3	(88)　4.6	EBIT/Interest	(14)　1.4	2.6	(22)　4.4	(24)　12.0	(14)　3.0	
	1.1	.4	1.6			−.6	1.1	1.9	3.3	2.0
	4.0	3.4	5.3	Net Profit + Depr., Dep.,						
	(35)　1.4	(32)　1.4	(28)　2.1	Amort./Cur. Mat. L/T/D						
	.5	.7	.9							
	.4	.3	.3			1.7	.1	.3	.2	.4
	1.0	1.2	1.3	Fixed/Worth		−1.8	.3	1.2	.8	1.6
	5.5	−9.3	16.1			−.3	15.3	11.7	2.2	4.0
	1.1	1.2	1.2			4.2	.8	1.2	1.1	2.6
	3.5	4.2	3.6	Debt/Worth		−5.9	1.7	4.2	2.5	5.2
	20.3	−34.4	41.6			−2.6	29.4	35.3	7.8	16.0
	63.0	78.4	85.7	% Profit Before Taxes/Tangible			93.2	74.5	114.2	
	(110)　20.5	(100)　27.6	(76)　35.3	Net Worth		(19)　27.6	(22)　38.1	(14)　38.9		
	2.3	5.5	8.7				5.7	12.7	13.2	
	16.0	22.4	24.5	% Profit Before Taxes/Total		13.4	36.2	28.9	29.9	14.3
	4.1	7.1	5.7	Assets		.9	4.1	8.1	11.1	4.0
	−4.1	−.2	.9			−10.3	.7	2.5	2.8	.5
	20.1	34.1	44.1			21.8	70.1	51.7	49.7	62.4
	10.9	14.0	16.4	Sales/Net Fixed Assets		15.5	26.5	17.4	18.8	13.8
	6.0	7.2	6.0			5.5	7.7	6.0	7.2	4.1
	4.0	4.3	4.3			5.8	4.5	4.9	3.8	4.1
	2.4	2.7	2.8	Sales/Total Assets		3.4	3.0	3.0	2.7	2.3
	1.9	2.0	1.9			2.4	2.0	1.9	1.7	1.5
	1.4	1.0	1.0			1.3		.6	.9	1.8
	(122)　3.4	(118)　2.4	(86)　2.3	% Depr., Dep., Amort./Sales	(13)　2.2		(22)　2.1	(23)　1.7	(14)　3.9	
	5.8	4.1	4.6			4.4		4.9	3.8	6.8
	2.7	3.3	1.9	% Officers', Directors',		2.9				
	(62)　4.8	(52)　5.9	(35)　5.9	Owners' Comp/Sales	(12)　7.9					
	8.6	10.5	10.7			18.4				
	2586025M	2450920M	1642873M	Net Sales ($)	3449M	35346M	44338M	169317M	372089M	1018334M
	1243681M	1197720M	791426M	Total Assets ($)	3531M	10656M	16690M	95186M	184927M	480436M

M = $ thousand   MM = $ million
See Pages 11 through 21 for Explanation of Ratios and Data

Current Data Sorted By Assets   Comparative Historical Data

Type of Statement

	0-500M	500M-2MM	2-10MM	10-50MM	50-100MM	100-250MM	Type of Statement	4/1/00-3/31/01 ALL	4/1/01-3/31/02 ALL
		1		3			Unqualified	7	8
		2	5	2			Reviewed	7	8
	3	3	3				Compiled	16	15
	4	2	1				Tax Returns	13	9
	4	11	7	5	2		Other	16	22

9 (4/1-9/30/04) above 500M-2MM; 49 (10/1/04-3/31/05) above 10-50MM.

0-500M	500M-2MM	2-10MM	10-50MM	50-100MM	100-250MM		4/1/00-3/31/01 ALL	4/1/01-3/31/02 ALL
11	19	16	10	2		**NUMBER OF STATEMENTS**	59	62
%	%	%	%	%	%	**ASSETS**	%	%
11.8	9.0	20.6	6.9			Cash & Equivalents	15.0	11.2
9.7	53.1	34.8	35.2			Trade Receivables (net)	40.9	47.7
4.8	7.4	9.4	6.3			Inventory	5.7	5.7
10.1	1.5	3.5	8.3			All Other Current	5.1	3.9
36.4	70.9	68.3	56.7			Total Current	66.7	68.5
47.9	14.5	23.6	10.5			Fixed Assets (net)	19.5	17.3
1.6	5.5	2.3	27.7			Intangibles (net)	4.9	6.3
14.2	9.1	5.8	5.1			All Other Non-Current	8.9	7.8
100.0	100.0	100.0	100.0			Total	100.0	100.0
						LIABILITIES		
12.2	8.7	7.5	1.9			Notes Payable-Short Term	16.1	13.0
5.6	3.1	2.8	4.6			Cur. Mat.-L/T/D	3.8	5.3
18.0	25.7	22.4	20.7			Trade Payables	23.7	23.4
.0	.2	.4	.5			Income Taxes Payable	.8	.4
25.6	16.6	19.8	13.3			All Other Current	23.1	13.5
61.4	54.3	52.8	41.0			Total Current	67.6	55.6
50.8	10.9	13.3	3.5			Long-Term Debt	15.6	16.2
.0	.4	.1	.2			Deferred Taxes	.8	.3
18.8	.5	1.9	6.8			All Other Non-Current	5.5	5.0
−30.3	34.0	31.8	48.5			Net Worth	10.5	23.0
100.0	100.0	100.0	100.0			Total Liabilities & Net Worth	100.0	100.0
						INCOME DATA		
100.0	100.0	100.0	100.0			Net Sales	100.0	100.0
						Gross Profit		
95.6	96.5	88.5	92.0			Operating Expenses	89.6	92.7
4.4	3.5	11.5	8.0			Operating Profit	10.4	7.3
3.0	.5	2.1	.3			All Other Expenses (net)	1.0	1.2
1.4	3.0	9.4	7.8			Profit Before Taxes	9.4	6.1
						RATIOS		
1.3	1.5	2.1	2.0				2.0	2.1
.5	1.4	1.2	1.7			Current	1.2	1.3
.1	1.0	.9	1.3				.8	1.0
1.1	1.3	1.8	1.4				1.7	1.9
.2	1.1	1.2	1.2			Quick	.9	1.1
.1	.9	.8	.4				.6	.7
0 UND	27 13.4	26 13.8	30 12.3				23 16.0	35 10.4
0 UND	47 7.8	43 8.4	52 7.0			Sales/Receivables	50 7.3	50 7.3
20 18.0	54 6.7	85 4.3	70 5.2				91 4.0	81 4.5
						Cost of Sales/Inventory		
						Cost of Sales/Payables		
15.7	11.7	5.1	4.3				7.2	8.3
−26.8	24.1	27.1	10.0			Sales/Working Capital	46.3	16.9
−12.3	−358.4	−38.1	39.3				−32.3	282.7
4.1	22.0	53.8					27.2	15.2
(10) 1.2	(15) 3.9	(12) 19.8				EBIT/Interest	(48) 4.7	(53) 5.2
−7.0	1.3	4.5					2.5	1.8
							6.7	10.5
						Net Profit + Depr., Dep., Amort./Cur. Mat. L /T/D	(13) 2.8	(13) 3.6
							1.0	.6
8.3	.1	.2	.1				.1	.2
−.7	.4	.9	.3			Fixed/Worth	.7	.5
−.5	1.4	4.1	.6				3.7	−11.7
9.3	1.3	1.1	1.0				1.1	1.2
−4.5	2.2	2.4	1.5			Debt/Worth	3.2	3.2
−2.1	20.8	6.4	5.7				−28.7	−27.8
	74.6	92.5				% Profit Before Taxes/Tangible Net Worth	110.6	72.7
	(16) 20.3	(13) 61.8					(44) 54.1	(43) 31.9
	.8	18.7					28.1	5.4
45.0	17.9	27.0	15.7			% Profit Before Taxes/Total Assets	30.2	20.6
1.8	9.9	21.8	8.4				18.0	7.2
−12.5	.4	3.9	3.8				7.4	.6
31.5	257.0	113.1	104.5			Sales/Net Fixed Assets	79.5	63.8
19.4	42.6	18.3	52.0				31.5	27.4
5.6	14.9	7.0	8.3				12.1	11.4
15.7	6.9	3.5	3.1			Sales/Total Assets	4.7	4.6
4.1	4.0	2.0	2.2				2.9	3.2
2.2	3.0	1.5	.5				1.7	1.6
	.3	.3				% Depr., Dep., Amort./Sales	.4	.4
	(16) 1.4	(14) .9					(45) 1.1	(49) 1.4
	2.5	2.5					2.3	2.4
	2.6					% Officers', Directors', Owners' Comp/Sales	5.6	3.8
	(13) 3.3						(27) 10.2	(27) 7.4
	5.5						18.6	14.8
13425M	102222M	159414M	547960M	251036M		Net Sales ($)	617258M	1249413M
2894M	21022M	68044M	218487M	150279M		Total Assets ($)	407742M	840915M

(Columns 50-100MM and 100-250MM marked "DATA NOT AVAILABLE".)

Comparative Historical Data | Current Data Sorted By Sales

			Type of Statement						
14	11	4	Unqualified			2			2
9	11	9	Reviewed			1	2	4	2
9	23	9	Compiled	2	1	3	2	1	
12	12	7	Tax Returns	1	3	3			
20	27	29	Other	3	5	8	3	5	5
4/1/02-3/31/03	4/1/03-3/31/04	4/1/04-3/31/05		9 (4/1-9/30/04)			49 (10/1/04-3/31/05)		
ALL	ALL	ALL		0-1MM	1-3MM	3-5MM	5-10MM	10-25MM	25MM & OVER
64	84	58	**NUMBER OF STATEMENTS**	6	9	14	10	10	9
%	%	%	**ASSETS**	%	%	%	%	%	%
14.2	13.9	12.5	Cash & Equivalents			8.2	11.4	23.2	
33.3	36.3	36.0	Trade Receivables (net)			36.7	48.8	42.6	
6.2	5.4	7.3	Inventory			9.3	10.0	7.2	
9.2	5.8	5.0	All Other Current			7.8	1.5	3.7	
62.9	61.5	60.8	Total Current			62.0	71.7	76.7	
23.0	23.1	22.5	Fixed Assets (net)			20.5	15.6	10.4	
5.8	5.1	8.5	Intangibles (net)			11.5	.8	9.8	
8.2	10.3	8.2	All Other Non-Current			6.0	11.9	3.1	
100.0	100.0	100.0	Total			100.0	100.0	100.0	
			LIABILITIES						
24.1	18.1	7.9	Notes Payable-Short Term			10.8	8.7	4.4	
9.0	6.9	3.8	Cur. Mat.-L/T/D			6.5	1.1	2.4	
17.7	20.6	21.9	Trade Payables			19.7	32.8	24.8	
.3	.2	.2	Income Taxes Payable			.2	.5	.6	
16.7	24.6	18.8	All Other Current			22.2	18.0	15.6	
67.9	70.5	52.7	Total Current			59.4	61.1	47.7	
15.3	16.1	18.3	Long-Term Debt			12.4	9.0	7.4	
.1	.1	.2	Deferred Taxes			.5	.2	.2	
6.5	7.1	5.5	All Other Non-Current			1.9	.8	1.8	
10.3	6.2	23.3	Net Worth			25.9	28.9	42.9	
100.0	100.0	100.0	Total Liabilities & Net Worth			100.0	100.0	100.0	
			INCOME DATA						
100.0	100.0	100.0	Net Sales			100.0	100.0	100.0	
			Gross Profit						
95.4	96.8	93.2	Operating Expenses			94.3	95.2	92.0	
4.6	3.2	6.8	Operating Profit			5.7	4.8	8.0	
1.7	1.1	1.5	All Other Expenses (net)			1.0	−.2	.2	
2.8	2.0	5.3	Profit Before Taxes			4.7	5.0	7.8	
			RATIOS						
1.7	2.1	1.8				1.5	1.5	2.9	
1.1	1.2	1.3	Current			1.1	1.0	2.0	
.7	.8	.9				.8	.9	1.2	
1.3	1.7	1.4				1.2	1.3	2.0	
.8	1.0	1.0	Quick			.9	1.0	1.5	
.5	.6	.7				.3	.9	.8	
17 22.0	29 12.8	18 20.3				29 12.6	16 23.0	39 9.5	
44 8.3	44 8.3	45 8.2	Sales/Receivables			47 7.7	32 11.5	45 8.1	
65 5.6	62 5.9	61 6.0				55 6.6	67 5.5	73 5.0	
			Cost of Sales/Inventory						
			Cost of Sales/Payables						
11.9	8.3	8.7				11.7	11.8	4.2	
49.8	28.0	23.1	Sales/Working Capital			NM	NM	8.5	
−19.6	−32.9	−80.7				−17.3	−72.9	36.6	
18.2	11.7	24.1				21.8			
(58) 5.1	(64) 3.5	(46) 5.9	EBIT/Interest		(12) 3.9				
1.5	−2.6	1.5				2.0			
10.0	6.5	14.6	Net Profit + Depr., Dep.,						
(13) 2.0	(13) 3.3	(12) 4.5	Amort./Cur. Mat. L/T/D						
.7	.4	3.5							
.3	.2	.2				.3	.1	.1	
1.2	.7	.7	Fixed/Worth			1.3	.4	.2	
−4.4	−2.8	−7.3				−3.2	1.2	NM	
1.1	1.0	1.3				1.6	1.5	.6	
7.8	3.5	2.4	Debt/Worth			2.5	2.3	1.4	
−13.4	−17.6	−352.5				−11.6	10.7	NM	
90.6	71.7	80.0	% Profit Before Taxes/Tangible			105.3			
(47) 43.6	(58) 28.1	(43) 34.1	Net Worth			31.7			
9.6	.5	11.8				1.0			
19.9	15.8	22.6	% Profit Before Taxes/Total			16.1	31.9	26.9	
9.6	5.0	8.6	Assets			8.1	8.6	21.8	
1.4	−6.4	2.3				1.4	.3	6.5	
46.1	75.8	94.6				123.8	205.0	171.9	
23.3	22.3	26.9	Sales/Net Fixed Assets			24.1	39.1	73.5	
9.6	8.5	10.2				10.9	11.4	13.5	
5.5	4.4	4.8				4.8	7.9	5.5	
3.4	2.9	3.0	Sales/Total Assets			3.0	4.3	2.7	
1.8	1.7	1.9				1.3	3.0	1.8	
.6	.6	.5						.2	
(54) 2.1	(65) 1.8	(45) 1.6	% Depr., Dep., Amort./Sales					.5	
4.2	3.5	2.9						1.1	
3.2	3.2	2.6	% Officers', Directors',						
(25) 5.1	(32) 5.1	(25) 3.8	Owners' Comp/Sales						
9.3	12.8	8.0							
2958499M	2086754M	1074057M	Net Sales ($)	2734M	17440M	54249M	79072M	144513M	776049M
1136651M	882390M	460726M	Total Assets ($)	8150M	4593M	30681M	34594M	65076M	317632M

© RMA 2005

M = $ thousand   MM = $ million
See Pages 11 through 21 for Explanation of Ratios and Data

Current Data Sorted By Assets   Comparative Historical Data

						Type of Statement		
		1	2		1	Unqualified		
	1	6	2			Reviewed		
6	3	2				Compiled		
3	4	2				Tax Returns		
1	3	5	2		1	Other		
	6 (4/1-9/30/04)		39 (10/1/04-3/31/05)				4/1/00-3/31/01 ALL	4/1/01-3/31/02 ALL
0-500M	500M-2MM	2-10MM	10-50MM	50-100MM	100-250MM			
10	11	16	6		2	NUMBER OF STATEMENTS		
%	%	%	%	%	%	ASSETS	%	%
18.1	21.9	7.7				Cash & Equivalents		
32.3	38.6	36.2		D		Trade Receivables (net)	D	D
9.3	22.0	28.6		A		Inventory	A	A
10.5	2.0	2.2		T		All Other Current	T	T
70.2	84.6	74.7		A		Total Current	A	A
21.2	9.5	13.5				Fixed Assets (net)		
.4	2.8	3.5		N		Intangibles (net)	N	N
8.2	3.1	8.3		O		All Other Non-Current	O	O
100.0	100.0	100.0		T		Total	T	T
				A		LIABILITIES	A	A
19.4	18.9	20.3		V		Notes Payable-Short Term	V	V
12.8	1.1	3.1		A		Cur. Mat.-L/T/D	A	A
14.6	17.3	15.2		I		Trade Payables	I	I
.0	1.3	.0		L		Income Taxes Payable	L	L
28.0	24.5	15.9		A		All Other Current	A	A
74.8	63.1	54.6		B		Total Current	B	B
2.9	5.9	11.8		L		Long-Term Debt	L	L
.0	.0	.3		E		Deferred Taxes	E	E
1.1	3.2	16.2				All Other Non-Current		
21.2	27.8	17.1				Net Worth		
100.0	100.0	100.0				Total Liabilities & Net Worth		
						INCOME DATA		
100.0	100.0	100.0				Net Sales		
						Gross Profit		
97.7	96.2	94.0				Operating Expenses		
2.3	3.8	6.0				Operating Profit		
.0	.6	3.5				All Other Expenses (net)		
2.3	3.2	2.5				Profit Before Taxes		
						RATIOS		
1.7	1.7	2.1						
1.2	1.3	1.4				Current		
.5	1.1	1.1						
1.5	1.5	1.3						
.5	1.1	.8				Quick		
.3	.6	.4						
0 UND	30 12.3	22 16.4						
30 12.2	37 9.9	61 6.0				Sales/Receivables		
41 8.8	46 8.0	70 5.2						
						Cost of Sales/Inventory		
						Cost of Sales/Payables		
16.5	10.7	7.2						
513.6	15.2	13.9				Sales/Working Capital		
-9.0	30.1	48.6						
		19.8						
	(15)	4.0				EBIT/Interest		
		1.2						
						Net Profit + Depr., Dep., Amort./Cur. Mat. L /T/D		
.2	.1	.1						
.7	.2	.5				Fixed/Worth		
NM	1.4	17.7						
1.2	1.3	.9						
2.9	2.1	2.6				Debt/Worth		
NM	10.4	34.4						
		122.0				% Profit Before Taxes/Tangible Net Worth		
	(13)	50.0						
		2.6						
68.5	29.4	27.0				% Profit Before Taxes/Total Assets		
2.1	6.5	6.8						
-11.2	-.9	1.0						
154.2	242.0	239.5						
31.8	45.7	33.6				Sales/Net Fixed Assets		
12.3	24.4	12.6						
6.9	4.0	3.8						
5.0	3.4	2.7				Sales/Total Assets		
3.7	2.8	2.2						
		.8				% Depr., Dep., Amort./Sales		
	(13)	1.6						
		2.5						
						% Officers', Directors', Owners' Comp/Sales		
14601M	38810M	221928M	358034M		379846M	Net Sales ($)		
2154M	10732M	75250M	105457M		338180M	Total Assets ($)		

© RMA 2005

M = $ thousand   MM = $ million
See Pages 11 through 21 for Explanation of Ratios and Data

Comparative Historical Data | **Current Data Sorted By Sales**

		Comparative Historical Data				Current Data Sorted By Sales				
Type of Statement					0-1MM	1-3MM	3-5MM	5-10MM	10-25MM	25MM & OVER
Unqualified	6	3	4					2	3	3
Reviewed	9	12	9			5			2	2
Compiled	16	16	11		2		2	1	2	
Tax Returns	8	7	9		2	3	1	2	1	
Other	14	19	12		1	3	1	3		4
	4/1/02-3/31/03 ALL	4/1/03-3/31/04 ALL	4/1/04-3/31/05 ALL		6 (4/1-9/30/04)		39 (10/1/04-3/31/05)			
NUMBER OF STATEMENTS	53	57	45		5	11	4	8	8	9
	%	%	%		%	%	%	%	%	%
ASSETS										
Cash & Equivalents	15.3	8.3	14.7			20.4				
Trade Receivables (net)	35.6	42.2	35.5			43.2				
Inventory	23.0	20.5	19.8			16.4				
All Other Current	1.9	1.1	5.1			.7				
Total Current	75.8	72.1	75.2			80.6				
Fixed Assets (net)	15.5	18.1	14.9			13.3				
Intangibles (net)	1.1	3.0	2.8			3.0				
All Other Non-Current	7.6	6.8	7.1			3.0				
Total	100.0	100.0	100.0			100.0				
LIABILITIES										
Notes Payable-Short Term	15.5	19.6	16.9			19.4				
Cur. Mat.-L/T/D	3.5	2.9	4.9			1.8				
Trade Payables	19.1	21.7	16.6			18.6				
Income Taxes Payable	.6	.2	.3			.0				
All Other Current	10.5	9.6	23.4			20.2				
Total Current	49.1	54.1	62.1			60.1				
Long-Term Debt	10.0	14.3	8.6			6.6				
Deferred Taxes	.1	.2	.4			.0				
All Other Non-Current	9.4	4.2	9.1			3.2				
Net Worth	31.5	27.1	19.8			30.2				
Total Liabilities & Net Worth	100.0	100.0	100.0			100.0				
INCOME DATA										
Net Sales	100.0	100.0	100.0			100.0				
Gross Profit										
Operating Expenses	94.3	96.5	95.1			96.3				
Operating Profit	5.7	3.5	4.9			3.7				
All Other Expenses (net)	1.1	1.3	1.5			.5				
Profit Before Taxes	4.6	2.2	3.3			3.1				
RATIOS										
Current	3.7 / 1.8 / 1.1	2.1 / 1.4 / 1.1	1.7 / 1.4 / 1.0			1.7 / 1.5 / 1.1				
Quick	2.0 / 1.2 / .6	1.4 / 1.0 / .7	1.4 / .9 / .5			1.7 / 1.3 / .6				
Sales/Receivables	28 13.3 / 34 10.6 / 53 6.9	24 15.3 / 48 7.7 / 67 5.5	27 13.3 / 43 8.6 / 64 5.7			27 13.8 / 37 9.9 / 48 7.6				
Cost of Sales/Inventory										
Cost of Sales/Payables										
Sales/Working Capital	4.5 / 8.7 / 92.7	6.8 / 16.6 / 89.2	9.9 / 16.5 / 269.4			10.7 / 21.3 / 30.1				
EBIT/Interest	(46) 15.2 / 2.5 / -.3	(51) 7.5 / 2.7 / 1.0	(37) 24.9 / 5.3 / 1.3							
Net Profit + Depr., Dep., Amort./Cur. Mat. L/T/D			(13) 11.8 / 3.7 / 1.7							
Fixed/Worth	.1 / .2 / 2.0	.1 / .4 / 2.7	.1 / .4 / 13.4			.1 / .3 / 1.6				
Debt/Worth	.5 / 2.1 / 11.8	1.2 / 2.4 / 6.5	1.3 / 2.3 / 35.9			1.3 / 1.5 / 10.4				
% Profit Before Taxes/Tangible Net Worth	(42) 48.9 / 19.4 / 2.5	(48) 38.5 / 10.6 / -.8	(35) 132.5 / 24.4 / 3.0							
% Profit Before Taxes/Total Assets	20.2 / 6.3 / -.9	10.6 / 2.3 / -1.9	30.0 / 5.5 / -.2			59.2 / 5.5 / -6.2				
Sales/Net Fixed Assets	177.7 / 44.9 / 14.3	98.5 / 44.2 / 15.7	133.0 / 40.5 / 14.0			242.0 / 45.7 / 24.4				
Sales/Total Assets	4.3 / 3.1 / 1.9	4.3 / 3.3 / 2.0	4.5 / 3.4 / 2.5			5.8 / 3.8 / 3.1				
% Depr., Dep., Amort./Sales	(42) .4 / .9 / 2.6	(50) .3 / .7 / 2.1	(33) .5 / 1.1 / 2.5							
% Officers', Directors', Owners' Comp/Sales	(27) 1.7 / 4.4 / 7.4	(28) 1.7 / 3.8 / 6.4	(19) 2.5 / 4.8 / 10.4							
Net Sales ($)	618630M	670617M	1013219M		2498M	23937M	15572M	66258M	128397M	776557M
Total Assets ($)	308307M	283946M	531773M		629M	6418M	5266M	27230M	43879M	448351M

M = $ thousand   MM = $ million
See Pages 11 through 21 for Explanation of Ratios and Data

Current Data Sorted By Assets   Comparative Historical Data

						Type of Statement		
	2	5	10	2	2	Unqualified	24	20
	3	6	2			Reviewed	17	10
1	8	4	1			Compiled	22	20
16	3	1				Tax Returns	7	9
2	15	10	5	2	1	Other	33	37
	11 (4/1-9/30/04)			90 (10/1/04-3/31/05)			4/1/00-3/31/01	4/1/01-3/31/02
0-500M	500M-2MM	2-10MM	10-50MM	50-100MM	100-250MM		ALL	ALL
19	31	26	18	4	3	NUMBER OF STATEMENTS	103	96
%	%	%	%	%	%	ASSETS	%	%
23.6	11.6	14.9	21.6			Cash & Equivalents	14.7	11.5
9.4	50.2	40.1	33.6			Trade Receivables (net)	40.1	44.2
1.3	.8	2.9	1.1			Inventory	1.2	.8
7.5	3.7	5.7	7.9			All Other Current	6.3	6.4
41.8	66.4	63.5	64.2			Total Current	62.4	63.0
35.4	18.2	14.2	14.9			Fixed Assets (net)	19.9	18.8
8.4	2.8	13.8	8.5			Intangibles (net)	5.2	7.4
14.5	12.5	8.5	12.5			All Other Non-Current	12.5	10.8
100.0	100.0	100.0	100.0			Total	100.0	100.0
						LIABILITIES		
18.7	14.3	5.3	9.6			Notes Payable-Short Term	9.9	12.4
9.0	4.3	3.0	.9			Cur. Mat.-L/T/D	2.7	3.5
11.1	22.9	11.3	12.8			Trade Payables	14.5	14.9
.0	.2	.3	.6			Income Taxes Payable	1.1	.3
25.1	20.2	31.4	27.3			All Other Current	16.9	21.5
63.8	61.8	51.3	51.2			Total Current	45.1	52.5
51.4	8.7	7.1	8.6			Long-Term Debt	11.4	13.1
.0	.5	.1	.0			Deferred Taxes	1.0	.7
6.8	11.4	9.7	5.8			All Other Non-Current	4.6	4.4
-21.9	17.5	31.7	34.4			Net Worth	38.0	29.2
100.0	100.0	100.0	100.0			Total Liabilities & Net Worth	100.0	100.0
						INCOME DATA		
100.0	100.0	100.0	100.0			Net Sales	100.0	100.0
						Gross Profit		
97.0	95.7	95.3	92.7			Operating Expenses	91.1	94.8
3.0	4.3	4.7	7.3			Operating Profit	8.9	5.2
2.5	.4	1.0	.0			All Other Expenses (net)	.8	1.7
.5	3.9	3.6	7.3			Profit Before Taxes	8.1	3.5
						RATIOS		
1.8	1.8	1.5	2.1				2.0	1.7
.6	1.5	1.2	1.2			Current	1.4	1.3
.3	.9	.9	.9				1.1	1.0
1.0	1.7	1.4	1.9				1.9	1.5
.6	1.4	1.0	1.2			Quick	1.3	1.1
.2	.9	.8	.7				.9	.8
0 UND	31 11.7	47 7.7	20 18.3				37 9.8	37 9.9
0 UND	57 6.4	55 6.7	65 5.6			Sales/Receivables	63 5.8	64 5.7
0 999.8	68 5.4	75 4.8	76 4.8				86 4.3	79 4.6
						Cost of Sales/Inventory		
						Cost of Sales/Payables		
42.5	7.9	9.4	4.5				6.7	7.3
-38.3	21.2	38.5	67.5			Sales/Working Capital	13.0	23.1
-11.8	-128.5	-54.6	-59.6				45.4	-293.0
12.2	35.0	41.4	28.1				22.7	17.3
(13) 2.2	(27) 4.4	(22) 13.9	(13) 4.6			EBIT/Interest	(72) 7.0	(79) 4.1
-.5	1.2	4.0	1.6				2.3	1.0
						Net Profit + Depr., Dep.,	7.7	4.2
						Amort./Cur. Mat. L /T/D	(20) 4.0 (14) 2.4	
							1.0	.6
.8	.1	.2	.1				.2	.2
-3.8	.4	.5	.8			Fixed/Worth	.5	.6
-.5	2.2	-.8	2.4				1.5	3.0
4.2	.7	1.2	.5				.8	.9
-5.6	1.7	3.3	3.0			Debt/Worth	1.6	2.6
-2.6	7.3	-4.2	82.2				6.7	8.2
	83.1	70.5	34.7			% Profit Before Taxes/Tangible	73.4	51.4
(25) 27.8	(19) 35.7	(15) 23.0				Net Worth	(88) 29.2 (78) 22.4	
6.5	7.9	12.7					9.6	3.4
44.7	24.7	23.1	14.6			% Profit Before Taxes/Total	19.1	16.3
14.7	6.6	12.2	9.1			Assets	9.7	6.9
-11.7	2.1	1.7	.0				2.9	.3
61.1	80.1	53.1	44.2				35.1	39.1
34.1	27.0	30.7	21.7			Sales/Net Fixed Assets	20.4	20.3
9.6	15.2	13.7	13.6				10.0	9.3
10.6	4.3	3.4	2.4				3.5	3.7
6.6	3.7	2.6	1.7			Sales/Total Assets	2.4	2.6
2.8	3.0	1.7	1.3				1.5	1.7
.6	.7	.9	.9				.8	.9
(14) 1.6	(23) 1.3	(21) 1.5	(16) 1.7			% Depr., Dep., Amort./Sales	(81) 1.7	(75) 1.7
3.1	1.8	2.7	3.4				2.8	2.8
6.3	2.6					% Officers', Directors',	4.2	4.2
(13) 9.7	(11) 3.2					Owners' Comp/Sales	(24) 8.8	(29) 8.5
19.0	9.6						20.9	13.6
37915M	134115M	488094M	994141M	509192M	618072M	Net Sales ($)	2971590M	2821343M
4478M	34358M	145364M	463754M	291691M	547785M	Total Assets ($)	1990773M	1983942M

M = $ thousand   MM = $ million
See Pages 11 through 21 for Explanation of Ratios and Data

Comparative Historical Data — Current Data Sorted By Sales

		Comparative Historical Data				Current Data Sorted By Sales				
Type of Statement					0-1MM	1-3MM	3-5MM	5-10MM	10-25MM	25MM & OVER
Unqualified	22	22	21		1		1	1	7	11
Reviewed	11	6	11			1	1	4	3	2
Compiled	8	17	14			1	6	3	2	2
Tax Returns	4	9	20		8	6	1	5		
Other	29	29	35		2	5	5	9	6	8
	4/1/02-3/31/03 ALL	4/1/03-3/31/04 ALL	4/1/04-3/31/05 ALL		11 (4/1-9/30/04)			90 (10/1/04-3/31/05)		
NUMBER OF STATEMENTS	74	83	101		11	13	14	22	18	23
ASSETS	%	%	%		%	%	%	%	%	%
Cash & Equivalents	17.1	16.6	17.8		23.4	19.2	9.1	12.3	16.4	25.8
Trade Receivables (net)	41.2	39.6	35.7		6.5	33.5	47.5	44.5	35.5	35.2
Inventory	2.2	1.3	1.4		2.2	.3	1.9	.2	3.6	.9
All Other Current	3.6	5.6	5.7		3.8	7.0	3.6	6.0	8.0	5.0
Total Current	64.1	63.2	60.5		35.9	60.0	62.1	63.1	63.5	67.0
Fixed Assets (net)	21.5	19.9	19.7		31.1	24.4	21.6	19.6	10.5	17.7
Intangibles (net)	7.0	6.4	8.4		12.2	6.2	.8	10.2	11.5	8.4
All Other Non-Current	7.3	10.5	11.3		20.8	9.5	15.5	7.1	14.5	6.9
Total	100.0	100.0	100.0		100.0	100.0	100.0	100.0	100.0	100.0
LIABILITIES										
Notes Payable-Short Term	9.7	11.9	11.1		19.5	22.1	10.3	10.8	3.7	7.3
Cur. Mat.-L/T/D	3.5	3.4	4.0		3.7	1.9	6.6	8.3	2.0	1.1
Trade Payables	13.2	16.6	15.0		13.6	11.1	12.3	24.3	11.1	13.5
Income Taxes Payable	1.0	.3	.3		.0	.0	.4	.0	.2	.8
All Other Current	21.2	23.8	25.2		14.4	31.4	20.9	24.7	28.2	27.6
Total Current	48.7	56.0	55.5		51.3	66.5	50.5	68.2	45.2	50.3
Long-Term Debt	12.1	9.9	17.2		50.5	21.4	11.6	15.7	5.2	12.9
Deferred Taxes	.4	.3	.2		.2	.0	1.1	.1	.0	.0
All Other Non-Current	8.1	12.5	8.5		3.8	10.5	1.3	15.6	10.9	5.4
Net Worth	30.7	21.3	18.6		-5.6	1.5	35.5	.5	38.7	31.4
Total Liabilities & Net Worth	100.0	100.0	100.0		100.0	100.0	100.0	100.0	100.0	100.0
INCOME DATA										
Net Sales	100.0	100.0	100.0		100.0	100.0	100.0	100.0	100.0	100.0
Gross Profit										
Operating Expenses	95.6	94.4	94.6		98.7	96.8	95.5	95.2	92.0	92.3
Operating Profit	4.4	5.6	5.4		1.3	3.2	4.5	4.8	8.0	7.7
All Other Expenses (net)	.8	1.2	.9		2.0	1.7	.0	1.0	.5	.8
Profit Before Taxes	3.5	4.5	4.5		-.7	1.5	4.5	3.8	7.5	6.9
RATIOS										
Current	2.0	1.8	1.8		3.3	1.8	1.7	1.7	3.4	2.0
	1.4	1.3	1.3		.9	1.0	1.3	1.3	1.2	1.5
	1.1	.9	.9		.3	.7	.9	.7	1.0	1.0
Quick	1.8	1.7	1.6		3.3	1.3	1.5	1.6	1.9	1.8
	1.1	1.2	1.1		.9	.9	1.2	1.1	1.1	1.3
	.9	.8	.7		.0	.6	.8	.6	.7	.9
Sales/Receivables	38 9.5	31 11.9	18 19.9		0 UND	0 UND	37 9.9	29 12.7	34 10.8	29 12.7
	58 6.3	61 6.0	49 7.4		0 UND	29 12.5	55 6.6	51 7.2	57 6.5	62 5.9
	91 4.0	74 4.9	69 5.3		16 22.8	54 6.8	66 5.5	68 5.3	77 4.8	74 4.9
Cost of Sales/Inventory										
Cost of Sales/Payables										
Sales/Working Capital	7.0	8.7	8.2		5.7	19.0	9.2	12.6	3.7	5.7
	16.1	24.7	32.9		-26.6	559.3	108.4	33.3	23.9	11.8
	60.4	-85.5	-53.5		-4.3	-29.2	-54.8	-40.8	-84.3	-244.2
EBIT/Interest	22.3	31.7	28.1			24.4	47.2	33.9	44.0	19.5
	(64) 5.3	(70) 8.2	(81) 7.8			(10) 4.1	(13) 4.4	(18) 10.2	(15) 15.8	(19) 7.8
	1.4	1.6	1.6			-10.6	1.3	2.5	6.6	2.0
Net Profit + Depr., Dep., Amort./Cur. Mat. L/T/D	11.2	15.8	10.1							
	(14) 3.1	(19) 4.2	(17) 4.0							
	.9	1.3	2.0							
Fixed/Worth	.3	.2	.2		.0	.4	.3	.2	.2	.2
	.6	.6	.8		2.2	-11.5	.7	.4	.4	.9
	2.4	1.9	-3.2		-2.5	-.7	2.7	-1.1	NM	4.4
Debt/Worth	1.0	1.1	1.0		.8	1.5	.7	1.4	.4	1.2
	1.9	1.7	3.4		-9.8	-24.1	2.0	3.4	2.5	2.9
	7.2	14.6	-7.5		-1.9	-3.2	5.8	-4.1	NM	35.7
% Profit Before Taxes/Tangible Net Worth	51.9	76.0	76.4				77.2	92.8	57.8	70.7
	(61) 18.6	(69) 30.6	(71) 32.3				(12) 21.1	(15) 41.8	(14) 27.2	(19) 34.7
	2.7	9.9	10.5				1.3	25.6	6.7	19.1
% Profit Before Taxes/Total Assets	16.9	20.7	23.7		4.5	41.9	30.0	24.0	24.3	17.7
	7.3	10.3	10.9		-5.5	17.9	8.2	13.0	13.3	11.6
	.7	.6	1.5		-22.9	-12.7	.6	4.8	2.0	1.5
Sales/Net Fixed Assets	42.0	41.2	50.0		61.1	36.7	56.8	92.7	46.2	43.2
	18.6	21.2	23.4		15.2	23.4	26.0	29.5	22.8	20.2
	8.1	11.3	13.9		2.2	14.2	10.5	21.3	13.6	14.2
Sales/Total Assets	3.3	3.8	4.3		5.6	8.0	4.0	7.1	3.0	3.1
	2.5	2.6	2.9		2.6	3.8	3.7	3.9	2.0	2.0
	1.8	1.9	1.8		.4	2.4	2.9	2.7	1.5	1.5
% Depr., Dep., Amort./Sales	1.0	.9	.8				.8	.4	1.3	.9
	(62) 1.7	(68) 1.7	(80) 1.5			(11) 1.7	(18) 1.0	(16) 1.6	(20) 1.7	
	3.0	3.2	2.4				2.4	2.0	2.3	2.0
% Officers', Directors', Owners' Comp/Sales	3.5	3.1	3.2					2.7		
	(21) 5.8	(22) 6.1	(32) 7.0				(12) 3.2			
	19.7	14.1	14.4					9.1		
Net Sales ($)	2825232M	3025609M	2781529M		5132M	25669M	55388M	149927M	281845M	2263568M
Total Assets ($)	1323344M	1478015M	1487430M		5167M	6251M	16219M	56191M	298272M	1105330M

M = $ thousand   MM = $ million
See Pages 11 through 21 for Explanation of Ratios and Data

		Current Data Sorted By Assets				Type of Statement	Comparative Historical Data	
		1 2	1			Unqualified	2	1
6	3	4			1	Reviewed	8	6
8						Compiled	17	16
2	4	1	1	1	1	Tax Returns	11	11
	9 (4/1-9/30/04)		27 (10/1/04-3/31/05)			Other	13	11
0-500M	500M-2MM	2-10MM	10-50MM	50-100MM	100-250MM		4/1/00- 3/31/01	4/1/01- 3/31/02
							ALL	ALL
16	7	8	1	2	2	NUMBER OF STATEMENTS	51	45
%	%	%	%	%	%	ASSETS	%	%
15.9						Cash & Equivalents	13.9	11.7
10.7						Trade Receivables (net)	11.2	9.7
3.4						Inventory	8.5	7.9
6.8						All Other Current	7.1	.9
36.9						Total Current	40.8	30.2
41.1						Fixed Assets (net)	42.0	47.0
4.3						Intangibles (net)	8.1	13.8
17.7						All Other Non-Current	9.1	9.0
100.0						Total	100.0	100.0
						LIABILITIES		
7.9						Notes Payable-Short Term	7.9	7.8
5.3						Cur. Mat.-L/T/D	7.7	3.9
3.1						Trade Payables	13.6	11.5
.3						Income Taxes Payable	.5	.3
17.4						All Other Current	14.2	21.1
34.1						Total Current	43.8	44.5
43.9						Long-Term Debt	30.5	31.2
.0						Deferred Taxes	.4	.5
1.9						All Other Non-Current	15.4	6.5
20.1						Net Worth	9.9	17.4
100.0						Total Liabilities & Net Worth	100.0	100.0
						INCOME DATA		
100.0						Net Sales	100.0	100.0
						Gross Profit		
95.1						Operating Expenses	94.9	92.7
4.9						Operating Profit	5.1	7.3
1.5						All Other Expenses (net)	.8	2.8
3.5						Profit Before Taxes	4.2	4.5
						RATIOS		
1.9							2.0	1.3
.9						Current	1.0	.6
.5							.6	.3
1.4							1.4	1.1
.7						Quick	(50) .6	(44) .4
.1							.3	.2
0 UND							0 UND	0 UND
0 UND						Sales/Receivables	4 94.8	3 124.0
13 28.3							17 21.5	14 26.1
						Cost of Sales/Inventory		
						Cost of Sales/Payables		
17.6							18.5	42.1
−267.0						Sales/Working Capital	−87.4	−28.7
−15.7							−24.8	−11.6
5.6							10.5	6.0
(13) 3.0						EBIT/Interest	(43) 3.5	(37) 2.7
1.0							1.0	.8
						Net Profit + Depr., Dep.,	14.7	
						Amort./Cur. Mat. L /T/D	(10) 2.1	
							.8	
.2							.8	1.2
1.1						Fixed/Worth	1.9	3.7
NM							−1.2	−1.3
.3							.8	1.0
1.6						Debt/Worth	2.9	4.2
NM							−2.9	−3.4
40.4						% Profit Before Taxes/Tangible	96.6	69.8
(12) 20.3						Net Worth	(35) 35.2	(28) 34.3
6.8							5.1	6.8
24.8						% Profit Before Taxes/Total	19.7	25.3
10.7						Assets	10.0	5.9
2.3							.0	−1.4
38.1							16.8	23.4
8.9						Sales/Net Fixed Assets	10.5	10.3
4.8							6.3	2.5
5.6							5.7	5.1
3.5						Sales/Total Assets	3.3	2.7
2.7							2.2	1.3
1.6							1.6	1.7
(14) 3.7						% Depr., Dep., Amort./Sales	(45) 2.9	(35) 4.4
7.0							4.8	7.6
6.4						% Officers', Directors',	4.6	4.2
(11) 12.2						Owners' Comp/Sales	(28) 9.2	(24) 8.4
16.8							12.4	13.4
12286M	21894M	66930M	51500M	335924M	682603M	Net Sales ($)	779088M	515930M
2974M	6262M	25827M	49500M	104696M	294253M	Total Assets ($)	417760M	219001M

M = $ thousand   MM = $ million
See Pages 11 through 21 for Explanation of Ratios and Data

Comparative Historical Data				Current Data Sorted By Sales					

			Type of Statement						
2	1	2	Unqualified			1	1		1
7	11	2	Reviewed		1				1
13	23	14	Compiled	5	2	2	3	1	1
17	18	8	Tax Returns	7	1				1
13	12	10	Other	4		2	1		3
4/1/02-	4/1/03-	4/1/04-			9 (4/1-9/30/04)		27 (10/1/04-3/31/05)		
3/31/03	3/31/04	3/31/05							
ALL	ALL	ALL		0-1MM	1-3MM	3-5MM	5-10MM	10-25MM	25MM & OVER
52	65	36	NUMBER OF STATEMENTS	16	3	5	5	1	6
%	%	%	ASSETS	%	%	%	%	%	%
18.8	17.7	16.6	Cash & Equivalents	13.8					
6.6	8.2	12.6	Trade Receivables (net)	9.0					
6.4	7.4	6.6	Inventory	2.7					
2.8	4.5	4.6	All Other Current	6.8					
34.6	37.7	40.3	Total Current	32.3					
49.8	46.4	40.6	Fixed Assets (net)	51.0					
8.6	4.3	7.0	Intangibles (net)	3.0					
6.9	11.6	12.1	All Other Non-Current	13.8					
100.0	100.0	100.0	Total	100.0					
			LIABILITIES						
11.3	12.4	10.2	Notes Payable-Short Term	4.5					
4.6	5.0	4.1	Cur. Mat.-L/T/D	6.7					
9.0	7.7	6.3	Trade Payables	3.1					
.1	.2	.8	Income Taxes Payable	.0					
12.0	13.0	13.2	All Other Current	15.3					
37.0	38.4	34.6	Total Current	29.6					
44.0	33.8	30.6	Long-Term Debt	49.8					
.2	.0	.2	Deferred Taxes	.0					
11.5	6.7	14.1	All Other Non-Current	2.4					
7.3	21.1	20.5	Net Worth	18.3					
100.0	100.0	100.0	Total Liabilities & Net Worth	100.0					
			INCOME DATA						
100.0	100.0	100.0	Net Sales	100.0					
			Gross Profit						
95.3	95.7	95.2	Operating Expenses	96.2					
4.7	4.3	4.8	Operating Profit	3.8					
1.7	1.4	2.2	All Other Expenses (net)	1.7					
3.0	2.9	2.6	Profit Before Taxes	2.1					
			RATIOS						
1.8	2.2	2.0		1.9					
.9	1.1	1.0	Current	.7					
.6	.5	.5		.4					
1.5	1.9	1.6		1.4					
.7	.5	.7	Quick	.7					
.3	.2	.2		.1					
0 UND	0 UND	0 UND		0 UND					
1 708.9	1 719.3	2 146.8	Sales/Receivables	1 575.5					
7 53.1	8 46.1	43 8.4		10 36.4					
			Cost of Sales/Inventory						
			Cost of Sales/Payables						
25.8	17.4	9.9		17.6					
−428.7	79.1	−307.0	Sales/Working Capital	−163.6					
−27.6	−16.9	−15.7		−12.5					
7.5	12.4	6.6		4.2					
(44) 1.8	(59) 3.5	(31) 2.3	EBIT/Interest	(14) 2.3					
.5	.6	.7		.8					
			Net Profit + Depr., Dep., Amort./Cur. Mat. L/T/D						
1.2	.7	.5		.5					
2.1	1.8	1.7	Fixed/Worth	1.4					
−3.8	92.3	−4.1		5.2					
.9	.8	.6		.4					
5.0	2.6	2.9	Debt/Worth	2.3					
−6.5	120.7	−7.5		8.0					
72.0	72.0	31.7	% Profit Before Taxes/Tangible	35.7					
(36) 32.2	(50) 27.4	(25) 10.0	Net Worth	(14) 13.0					
.4	−.2	−.3		−4.6					
16.4	22.3	17.4	% Profit Before Taxes/Total	19.9					
3.1	10.6	7.2	Assets	7.4					
−2.9	−.9	−.2		.1					
17.5	21.2	20.8		12.7					
6.7	6.8	8.0	Sales/Net Fixed Assets	6.6					
4.0	3.4	4.6		2.1					
4.3	5.2	4.1		4.8					
3.2	3.1	2.9	Sales/Total Assets	3.3					
2.3	2.0	2.1		1.2					
1.6	1.5	1.6		2.1					
(44) 3.7	(49) 3.1	(30) 3.2	% Depr., Dep., Amort./Sales	(13) 5.2					
5.6	5.9	5.7		10.6					
2.1	4.1	6.9	% Officers', Directors',						
(36) 6.4	(39) 7.1	(16) 11.4	Owners' Comp/Sales						
17.1	12.1	16.3							
1550914M	1875521M	1171137M	Net Sales ($)	7371M	3947M	20643M	30062M	11388M	1097726M
401252M	846879M	483512M	Total Assets ($)	5135M	1478M	7830M	9276M	4937M	454856M

M = $ thousand   MM = $ million
See Pages 11 through 21 for Explanation of Ratios and Data

Current Data Sorted By Assets							Comparative Historical Data	
						Type of Statement		
		1				Unqualified	2	1
	3	2				Reviewed	4	5
	3					Compiled	16	12
6		1				Tax Returns	8	5
4	7	2				Other	6	12
	8 (4/1-9/30/04)		21 (10/1/04-3/31/05)				**4/1/00-3/31/01**	**4/1/01-3/31/02**
0-500M	**500M-2MM**	**2-10MM**	**10-50MM**	**50-100MM**	**100-250MM**		**ALL**	**ALL**
10	13	6				**NUMBER OF STATEMENTS**	36	35
%	%	%	%	%	%	**ASSETS**	%	%
16.8	9.5		DATA NOT AVAILABLE	DATA NOT AVAILABLE	DATA NOT AVAILABLE	Cash & Equivalents	12.2	6.8
17.5	30.2					Trade Receivables (net)	33.4	26.0
10.8	4.5					Inventory	4.1	2.0
1.4	3.5					All Other Current	1.4	4.3
46.5	47.8					Total Current	51.1	39.0
29.7	37.7					Fixed Assets (net)	40.2	44.2
8.9	2.2					Intangibles (net)	2.0	6.5
15.0	12.3					All Other Non-Current	6.7	10.3
100.0	100.0					Total	100.0	100.0
						LIABILITIES		
29.3	12.6					Notes Payable-Short Term	11.3	15.7
1.9	2.9					Cur. Mat.-L/T/D	8.0	6.0
22.6	8.8					Trade Payables	10.0	11.4
.0	.0					Income Taxes Payable	.6	.7
19.2	16.5					All Other Current	10.5	12.8
73.0	40.8					Total Current	40.4	46.6
25.8	22.7					Long-Term Debt	43.9	29.2
.0	.4					Deferred Taxes	.8	.8
5.0	.9					All Other Non-Current	9.9	4.6
-3.9	35.3					Net Worth	5.0	18.9
100.0	100.0					Total Liabilities & Net Worth	100.0	100.0
						INCOME DATA		
100.0	100.0					Net Sales	100.0	100.0
						Gross Profit		
99.5	95.0					Operating Expenses	97.2	95.5
.5	5.0					Operating Profit	2.8	4.5
1.7	.3					All Other Expenses (net)	.1	1.4
-1.2	4.7					Profit Before Taxes	2.7	3.1
						RATIOS		
2.1	2.1						2.3	2.3
1.0	1.6					Current	1.2	1.0
.2	.6						.8	.5
1.7	1.9						2.3	1.8
.5	1.2					Quick	1.0	1.0
.1	.5						.7	.4
0 UND	**23** 16.0						**26** 14.2	**10** 35.5
1 429.9	**45** 8.2					Sales/Receivables	**51** 7.2	**43** 8.4
24 15.3	**91** 4.0						**73** 5.0	**66** 5.5
						Cost of Sales/Inventory		
						Cost of Sales/Payables		
15.6	4.4						7.8	7.1
NM	11.3					Sales/Working Capital	34.9	577.7
-15.7	-11.8						-45.1	-12.2
10.2	36.3						8.3	4.9
1.6	(12) 4.0					EBIT/Interest	(29) 2.7	(29) 2.2
-2.3	-.7						.0	-.2
						Net Profit + Depr., Dep., Amort./Cur. Mat. L /T/D		
.9	.4						.4	.8
NM	.8					Fixed/Worth	1.5	1.7
-.4	3.8						NM	-2.5
.8	.6						1.2	.8
NM	1.2					Debt/Worth	2.3	2.9
-2.5	5.2						NM	-5.1
	46.1						36.9	41.2
	(12) 10.3					% Profit Before Taxes/Tangible Net Worth	(27) 13.4	(25) 9.5
	-12.2						.0	-4.1
43.2	23.2						20.2	17.4
1.5	4.8					% Profit Before Taxes/Total Assets	4.5	6.1
-20.3	-6.2						-4.8	-1.9
60.4	15.4						18.8	12.4
22.4	6.9					Sales/Net Fixed Assets	7.9	6.4
8.4	4.1						3.4	3.1
7.8	3.3						3.8	3.7
5.2	2.7					Sales/Total Assets	2.8	2.6
2.7	1.4						1.8	1.5
	2.3						1.5	1.6
	(10) 5.0					% Depr., Dep., Amort./Sales	(31) 4.3	(27) 5.2
	6.7						6.3	9.1
							5.7	5.6
						% Officers', Directors', Owners' Comp/Sales	(27) 9.6	(20) 10.4
							16.0	15.8
8979M	**38038M**	**62516M**				Net Sales ($)	**130989M**	**104772M**
1970M	**16492M**	**25567M**				Total Assets ($)	**55150M**	**52431M**

M = $ thousand MM = $ million

See Pages 11 through 21 for Explanation of Ratios and Data

Comparative Historical Data | **Current Data Sorted By Sales**

	4/1/02-3/31/03 ALL	4/1/03-3/31/04 ALL	4/1/04-3/31/05 ALL		0-1MM	1-3MM	3-5MM	5-10MM	10-25MM	25MM & OVER
Type of Statement					8 (4/1-9/30/04)			21 (10/1/04-3/31/05)		
Unqualified		2	1					1		
Reviewed	4	5	5			1	1	1	1	1
Compiled	7	11	3		1	2				
Tax Returns	3	6	7		3	3				
Other	13	8	13		4	4	3	2		
NUMBER OF STATEMENTS	27	32	29		8	10	5	4	1	1
ASSETS	%	%	%		%	%	%	%	%	%
Cash & Equivalents	14.1	9.0	10.9		6.7					
Trade Receivables (net)	17.5	26.8	22.0		26.2					
Inventory	3.8	4.8	8.5		3.4					
All Other Current	3.6	4.7	3.9		.2					
Total Current	38.9	45.3	45.4		36.5					
Fixed Assets (net)	44.0	42.4	37.0		40.3					
Intangibles (net)	8.2	2.3	5.8		1.6					
All Other Non-Current	8.8	9.9	11.7		21.6					
Total	100.0	100.0	100.0		100.0					
LIABILITIES										
Notes Payable-Short Term	9.4	14.3	17.1		13.1					
Cur. Mat.-L/T/D	5.4	7.9	3.5		3.5					
Trade Payables	11.8	15.1	15.3		10.4					
Income Taxes Payable	.8	.5	.1		.0					
All Other Current	20.2	13.6	16.0		14.2					
Total Current	47.8	51.4	52.0		41.3					
Long-Term Debt	19.8	22.7	23.2		29.2					
Deferred Taxes	1.3	.9	.3		.0					
All Other Non-Current	10.3	8.2	3.5		1.1					
Net Worth	20.8	16.8	21.1		28.4					
Total Liabilities & Net Worth	100.0	100.0	100.0		100.0					
INCOME DATA										
Net Sales	100.0	100.0	100.0		100.0					
Gross Profit										
Operating Expenses	96.1	97.9	96.6		98.9					
Operating Profit	3.9	2.1	3.4		1.1					
All Other Expenses (net)	1.2	1.2	1.3		1.3					
Profit Before Taxes	2.7	.9	2.1		-.2					
RATIOS										
Current	2.2	2.0	2.0		1.9					
	.8	1.1	1.1		.8					
	.4	.4	.4		.4					
Quick	2.2	1.7	1.6		1.6					
	.6	.9	.6		.7					
	.3	.3	.2		.4					
Sales/Receivables	0 UND	14 27.0	1 275.7		21 17.2					
	29 12.7	41 9.0	26 13.9		46 7.9					
	53 6.8	59 6.2	57 6.4		61 5.9					
Cost of Sales/Inventory										
Cost of Sales/Payables										
Sales/Working Capital	9.6	10.0	10.1		8.4					
	-19.8	42.4	37.1		-154.4					
	-8.0	-10.2	-13.6		-7.7					
EBIT/Interest	(21) 5.6	(26) 4.6	(28) 10.6							
	2.1	1.4	2.7							
	-.9	-3.5	-1.4							
Net Profit + Depr., Dep., Amort./Cur. Mat. L/T/D										
Fixed/Worth	.7	.7	.6		.5					
	2.1	1.2	1.7		1.2					
	-3.5	19.9	NM		3.6					
Debt/Worth	.8	1.1	.9		.7					
	2.8	2.3	2.9		2.1					
	-7.8	34.2	NM		4.2					
% Profit Before Taxes/Tangible Net Worth	(19) 29.8	(25) 45.4	(22) 46.5							
	11.6	6.9	9.8							
	-7.6	-13.9	-7.0							
% Profit Before Taxes/Total Assets	16.7	12.5	23.2		13.5					
	6.5	2.4	4.8		-2.4					
	-4.5	-14.4	-4.5		-10.5					
Sales/Net Fixed Assets	10.8	16.0	28.2		22.3					
	5.0	5.0	9.8		6.9					
	2.8	3.8	4.9		1.9					
Sales/Total Assets	3.2	4.0	4.6		4.0					
	2.2	2.4	3.0		2.7					
	1.3	1.9	1.5		1.0					
% Depr., Dep., Amort./Sales	(20) 2.0	(28) 1.7	(23) 2.2							
	4.6	4.2	4.7							
	9.6	7.5	6.6							
% Officers', Directors', Owners' Comp/Sales	(13) 4.4	(22) 4.4	(17) 5.0							
	8.0	6.8	8.0							
	16.3	10.2	12.7							
Net Sales ($)	113566M	157962M	109533M		3868M	18586M	18103M	26436M	14744M	27796M
Total Assets ($)	45659M	72725M	44029M		2027M	13114M	8674M	11225M	2714M	6275M

© RMA 2005

M = $ thousand   MM = $ million
See Pages 11 through 21 for Explanation of Ratios and Data

Current Data Sorted By Assets   **Comparative Historical Data**

Type of Statement	0-500M	500M-2MM	2-10MM	10-50MM	50-100MM	100-250MM		4/1/00-3/31/01 ALL	4/1/01-3/31/02 ALL
Unqualified	1	1						2	4
Reviewed	1	3	2	1				4	6
Compiled	46	20	2			1		43	52
Tax Returns	112	23	6		2	3		61	51
Other	34	22	6	1				30	53
	33 (4/1-9/30/04)			254 (10/1/04-3/31/05)					
NUMBER OF STATEMENTS	194	69	16	2	3	3		140	166
	%	%	%	%	%	%		%	%
ASSETS									
Cash & Equivalents	21.7	19.0	20.2					17.1	17.5
Trade Receivables (net)	6.9	3.3	11.1					5.8	9.8
Inventory	14.1	6.2	7.7					12.8	11.4
All Other Current	1.7	2.9	5.4					2.5	2.2
Total Current	44.3	31.4	44.4					38.2	40.8
Fixed Assets (net)	31.5	47.7	44.0					40.7	41.3
Intangibles (net)	13.7	12.6	2.8					12.1	10.0
All Other Non-Current	10.4	8.3	8.8					9.0	7.9
Total	100.0	100.0	100.0					100.0	100.0
LIABILITIES									
Notes Payable-Short Term	12.4	5.1	8.3					9.2	7.0
Cur. Mat.-L/T/D	4.5	4.6	3.4					6.6	5.7
Trade Payables	10.8	4.8	9.3					7.5	11.3
Income Taxes Payable	.2	.0	.4					.2	.2
All Other Current	16.9	6.8	11.8					13.3	12.8
Total Current	44.8	21.3	33.1					36.7	37.1
Long-Term Debt	32.2	37.5	37.4					26.5	38.4
Deferred Taxes	.2	.1	.4					.2	.5
All Other Non-Current	8.5	2.5	1.9					5.8	4.7
Net Worth	14.3	38.6	27.2					30.8	19.3
Total Liabilities & Net Worth	100.0	100.0	100.0					100.0	100.0
INCOME DATA									
Net Sales	100.0	100.0	100.0					100.0	100.0
Gross Profit									
Operating Expenses	91.0	84.6	87.5					90.4	91.0
Operating Profit	9.0	15.4	12.5					9.6	9.0
All Other Expenses (net)	1.2	3.6	8.5					1.6	2.8
Profit Before Taxes	7.8	11.8	4.0					7.9	6.3
RATIOS									
Current	2.6	4.4	3.1					2.3	2.5
	1.1	1.6	1.1					1.3	1.4
	.6	.5	.7					.5	.6
Quick	2.0	3.3	1.4					1.5	1.9
	(190) .6	.9	.7					(165) .7	.9
	.3	.3	.4					.2	.3
Sales/Receivables	0 UND	0 UND	0 UND					0 UND	0 UND
	0 UND	0 UND	2 238.1					0 UND	2 231.2
	5 77.9	4 93.1	17 21.7					6 60.4	10 37.9
Cost of Sales/Inventory									
Cost of Sales/Payables									
Sales/Working Capital	20.8	8.2	8.7					20.3	14.8
	183.1	33.2	221.6					83.9	54.8
	-29.2	-26.2	-27.1					-28.8	-38.7
EBIT/Interest	24.2	16.6	25.5					11.0	11.3
	(148) 7.3	(58) 5.5	(11) 6.4					(110) 4.6	(133) 4.4
	1.0	3.0	2.7					1.1	1.4
Net Profit + Depr., Dep., Amort./Cur. Mat. L/T/D								5.8	6.3
								(11) 1.0	(14) 1.4
								.4	-.5
Fixed/Worth	.5	.6	.4					.5	.6
	1.7	2.4	2.1					2.1	2.0
	-.8	15.2	7.9					-7.9	-4.3
Debt/Worth	.7	.6	1.4					.6	.6
	5.4	2.6	6.9					3.4	3.3
	-3.0	17.9	12.6					-12.3	-8.6
% Profit Before Taxes/Tangible Net Worth	194.0	116.9	99.2					154.7	130.6
	(115) 78.8	(54) 50.8	(13) 26.9					(96) 70.9	(113) 52.9
	29.3	23.7	2.0					9.1	15.1
% Profit Before Taxes/Total Assets	77.8	32.6	35.0					60.7	43.9
	26.6	15.4	8.0					16.0	15.0
	.2	4.8	.1					.0	2.1
Sales/Net Fixed Assets	75.3	18.7	46.5					43.5	32.5
	26.3	6.5	15.1					17.4	15.9
	13.6	2.3	1.5					7.7	6.3
Sales/Total Assets	9.6	3.6	4.8					8.1	8.4
	5.8	2.0	3.1					5.0	4.6
	4.0	1.2	1.1					2.7	2.1
% Depr., Dep., Amort./Sales	.8	1.8	1.1					.9	1.0
	(123) 1.5	(56) 2.9	(14) 2.0					(112) 1.8	(132) 1.8
	2.5	5.1	12.9					3.0	3.3
% Officers', Directors', Owners' Comp/Sales	6.9	6.4						7.0	8.1
	(141) 11.4	(44) 9.2						(104) 13.3	(108) 13.9
	16.0	20.6						20.6	20.8
Net Sales ($)	237260M	172889M	286075M	94450M	2644272M	5253728M		205097M	1350608M
Total Assets ($)	39122M	64069M	52036M	24162M	214546M	521821M		61336M	633741M

© RMA 2005

M = $ thousand   MM = $ million
See Pages 11 through 21 for Explanation of Ratios and Data

Comparative Historical Data   Current Data Sorted By Sales

			Type of Statement						
8	8	2	Unqualified	1			1		
12	11	7	Reviewed		3	1	1	1	1
70	68	69	Compiled	22	36	5	4	1	1
97	139	146	Tax Returns	68	57	12	2	1	6
54	74	63	Other	25	28	2	3	4	1
4/1/02-3/31/03 ALL	4/1/03-3/31/04 ALL	4/1/04-3/31/05 ALL		33 (4/1-9/30/04)			254 (10/1/04-3/31/05)		
				0-1MM	1-3MM	3-5MM	5-10MM	10-25MM	25MM & OVER
241	300	287	**NUMBER OF STATEMENTS**	116	124	20	11	7	9
%	%	%	**ASSETS**	%	%	%	%	%	%
20.0	17.8	20.6	Cash & Equivalents	17.7	23.4	22.7	13.4		
9.8	9.3	6.6	Trade Receivables (net)	5.6	5.7	7.8	10.7		
11.2	11.2	12.0	Inventory	11.6	12.0	15.5	2.5		
2.3	3.3	2.2	All Other Current	1.6	2.4	.7	6.3		
43.3	41.5	41.4	Total Current	36.5	43.5	46.7	32.9		
40.8	36.1	36.1	Fixed Assets (net)	36.2	36.2	39.9	41.9		
8.6	13.7	12.5	Intangibles (net)	16.1	11.8	5.2	9.3		
7.2	8.7	10.1	All Other Non-Current	11.2	8.5	8.2	15.9		
100.0	100.0	100.0	Total	100.0	100.0	100.0	100.0		
			LIABILITIES						
8.9	7.5	10.3	Notes Payable-Short Term	13.2	8.7	3.4	13.0		
5.1	6.3	4.4	Cur. Mat.-L/T/D	3.8	4.8	5.9	6.8		
8.7	10.6	9.3	Trade Payables	7.1	10.1	14.8	6.6		
.3	.4	.1	Income Taxes Payable	.2	.1	.0	.0		
14.7	15.2	14.0	All Other Current	11.5	16.3	18.4	6.5		
37.7	40.0	38.2	Total Current	35.8	40.0	42.5	33.0		
27.7	31.9	34.5	Long-Term Debt	44.0	27.8	25.7	27.9		
.2	.3	.2	Deferred Taxes	.4	.0	.0	.4		
6.7	6.9	6.5	All Other Non-Current	4.9	9.3	4.6	3.1		
27.6	20.9	20.7	Net Worth	15.0	22.9	27.2	35.6		
100.0	100.0	100.0	Total Liabilities & Net Worth	100.0	100.0	100.0	100.0		
			INCOME DATA						
100.0	100.0	100.0	Net Sales	100.0	100.0	100.0	100.0		
			Gross Profit						
91.5	90.5	89.3	Operating Expenses	85.7	91.2	93.9	93.7		
8.5	9.5	10.7	Operating Profit	14.3	8.8	6.1	6.3		
2.1	2.2	2.2	All Other Expenses (net)	4.0	1.2	-.3	.6		
6.4	7.3	8.5	Profit Before Taxes	10.2	7.6	6.5	5.7		
			RATIOS						
3.1	2.6	2.9		2.8	3.3	1.9	1.5		
1.4	1.2	1.2	Current	1.2	1.4	1.1	.7		
.7	.5	.6		.4	.6	.4	.7		
2.1	1.8	2.2		2.6	2.5	1.0	1.0		
(240) .9	(298) .8	(283) .7	Quick	(113) .6	(123) .7	.7	.6		
.4	.2	.3		.3	.2	.3	.4		
0 UND	0 UND	0 UND		0 UND	0 UND	0 UND	0 UND		
1 246.9	1 272.5	0 UND	Sales/Receivables	0 UND	0 UND	2 148.9	3 128.8		
11 32.2	9 40.7	5 79.1		4 87.5	4 82.5	6 59.9	6 63.6		
			Cost of Sales/Inventory						
			Cost of Sales/Payables						
14.3	15.8	17.2		17.7	13.9	25.0	715.9		
53.5	99.9	105.2	Sales/Working Capital	75.6	83.2	304.3	-101.8		
-35.2	-24.4	-29.4		-16.8	-35.7	-31.6	-34.1		
12.0	17.6	24.0		15.2	25.0	48.1	31.6		
(182) 4.8	(224) 5.9	(224) 6.6	EBIT/Interest	(80) 4.6	(104) 8.0	(16) 4.0	14.9		
1.7	1.7	1.5		1.7	1.1	-3.3	3.3		
5.9	6.5		Net Profit + Depr., Dep.,						
(16) 3.9	(12) .9		Amort./Cur. Mat. L/T/D						
1.9	.6								
.5	.5	.5		.7	.4	.3	.8		
1.5	2.4	1.9	Fixed/Worth	5.9	1.6	1.3	1.5		
-12.5	-2.6	-2.0		-.5	-2.9	6.1	3.0		
.5	1.0	.7		.9	.6	1.4	1.1		
2.3	4.0	3.8	Debt/Worth	9.7	2.8	3.4	2.3		
-18.4	-4.6	-4.8		-2.6	-6.3	9.9	9.6		
148.8	154.2	159.2	% Profit Before Taxes/Tangible	163.3	143.1	178.4	206.3		
(174) 55.0	(196) 55.4	(188) 73.7	Net Worth	(64) 74.4	(84) 70.1	(17) 53.1	(10) 104.7		
15.8	15.2	23.1		27.0	23.1	6.7	65.1		
44.1	42.2	59.9	% Profit Before Taxes/Total	70.3	45.8	38.6	68.7		
18.1	17.0	21.9	Assets	18.6	23.8	9.3	35.8		
2.4	2.4	1.9		1.9	1.5	-4.2	8.9		
34.3	48.8	55.2		57.0	54.4	79.6	34.3		
15.8	18.0	19.5	Sales/Net Fixed Assets	18.4	18.8	30.1	15.5		
6.8	7.5	7.9		5.3	9.1	8.2	6.2		
7.5	7.0	8.0		6.4	9.1	10.6	9.8		
4.6	4.0	4.8	Sales/Total Assets	3.8	5.4	6.2	6.2		
2.2	2.3	2.6		1.6	2.7	3.8	3.7		
1.2	1.1	.9		1.5	.8	.9	1.1		
(187) 2.3	(211) 2.3	(195) 1.8	% Depr., Dep., Amort./Sales	(72) 2.9	(92) 1.5	(12) 1.5	1.9		
4.2	4.6	3.2		6.9	2.3	2.8	2.5		
7.4	7.2	6.5	% Officers', Directors',	7.4	6.5	5.1			
(154) 12.3	(194) 11.9	(197) 11.3	Owners' Comp/Sales	(76) 11.5	(90) 11.4	(15) 9.1			
17.4	17.2	16.4		15.4	17.4	17.3			
7313822M	4658474M	8688674M	Net Sales ($)	68400M	207542M	77663M	79386M	97874M	8157809M
912449M	881734M	915756M	Total Assets ($)	40301M	56241M	15535M	15056M	22289M	766334M

© RMA 2005   M = $ thousand   MM = $ million
See Pages 11 through 21 for Explanation of Ratios and Data

Current Data Sorted By Assets   **Comparative Historical Data**

Type of Statement	0-500M	500M-2MM	2-10MM	10-50MM	50-100MM	100-250MM		
Unqualified	3	15	50	35	9	8	70	63
Reviewed	3	29	36	7			43	31
Compiled	34	46	30	4			115	83
Tax Returns	123	55	20	4	3		56	49
Other	55	71	68	16	2	7	132	114
	141 (4/1-9/30/04)			592 (10/1/04-3/31/05)			4/1/00-3/31/01 ALL	4/1/01-3/31/02 ALL
	0-500M	500M-2MM	2-10MM	10-50MM	50-100MM	100-250MM		
NUMBER OF STATEMENTS	218	216	204	66	14	15	416	340
ASSETS	%	%	%	%	%	%	%	%
Cash & Equivalents	27.3	16.1	12.4	16.9	18.3	16.5	16.0	14.7
Trade Receivables (net)	18.5	32.3	33.6	23.8	17.2	32.2	26.0	26.8
Inventory	6.0	7.7	7.8	6.8	5.9	12.6	5.8	5.2
All Other Current	5.7	2.9	5.2	5.9	3.8	2.1	4.4	5.5
Total Current	57.5	59.0	59.1	53.4	45.2	63.3	52.1	52.2
Fixed Assets (net)	30.3	27.8	30.0	27.5	25.5	15.9	35.3	32.4
Intangibles (net)	2.7	4.1	3.1	7.2	6.6	8.6	4.5	5.4
All Other Non-Current	9.4	9.2	7.9	11.9	22.7	12.1	8.1	10.1
Total	100.0	100.0	100.0	100.0	100.0	100.0	100.0	100.0
LIABILITIES								
Notes Payable-Short Term	21.2	11.7	9.4	6.7	21.2	6.3	8.9	10.4
Cur. Mat.-L/T/D	6.6	4.7	4.1	3.7	3.9	1.4	4.1	4.5
Trade Payables	10.3	14.1	13.2	11.7	6.1	17.6	11.4	15.8
Income Taxes Payable	.2	.5	.7	.2	.1	1.3	.4	.5
All Other Current	28.7	12.3	12.3	15.2	6.0	11.8	15.6	12.9
Total Current	67.1	43.4	39.9	37.5	37.3	38.4	40.3	44.2
Long-Term Debt	29.8	22.0	16.8	19.4	21.9	9.7	20.6	28.5
Deferred Taxes	.1	.3	.4	.4	.9	2.0	.5	.6
All Other Non-Current	14.5	7.5	4.2	6.2	11.4	7.0	5.9	7.0
Net Worth	-11.5	26.9	38.8	36.5	28.5	43.0	32.7	19.8
Total Liabilities & Net Worth	100.0	100.0	100.0	100.0	100.0	100.0	100.0	100.0
INCOME DATA								
Net Sales	100.0	100.0	100.0	100.0	100.0	100.0	100.0	100.0
Gross Profit								
Operating Expenses	94.4	91.1	88.9	95.1	81.8	82.3	92.5	92.8
Operating Profit	5.6	8.9	11.1	4.9	18.2	17.7	7.5	7.2
All Other Expenses (net)	1.3	2.3	1.6	.6	1.6	3.0	.6	2.5
Profit Before Taxes	4.3	6.6	9.6	4.3	16.7	14.7	6.9	4.7
RATIOS								
Current	3.2	2.8	2.7	2.0	2.2	2.7	2.5	2.9
	1.2	1.6	1.5	1.5	1.5	1.3	1.4	1.4
	.5	.9	1.1	1.0	.5	1.1	.9	.9
Quick	2.3	2.5	2.1	1.9	1.7	2.5	2.2	2.1
	1.0	1.2	1.1	1.0	.9	1.2	1.1	1.1
	.3	.6	.7	.5	.4	.4	.6	.6
Sales/Receivables	0 UND	8 47.5	22 16.4	19 18.8	0 UND	23 16.1	4 101.4	2 161.3
	0 782.2	35 10.5	44 8.3	46 8.0	16 22.8	50 7.3	32 11.4	32 11.3
	27 13.4	60 6.1	82 4.5	63 5.8	44 8.3	75 4.8	62 5.9	59 6.2
Cost of Sales/Inventory								
Cost of Sales/Payables								
Sales/Working Capital	11.8	6.7	5.7	3.5	8.8	6.9	6.0	5.6
	51.8	15.8	13.6	12.1	25.0	13.3	18.2	17.4
	-18.6	-107.8	122.9	NM	-32.7	56.9	-84.8	-65.3
EBIT/Interest	12.8	17.4	19.2	16.4	23.7	53.7	10.5	11.0
	(156) 2.9	(171) 4.9	(158) 6.6	(51) 4.2	(11) 6.0	(10) 16.0	(322) 3.6	(259) 3.1
	-1.0	1.3	2.3	1.3	2.6	4.9	1.0	.8
Net Profit + Depr., Dep., Amort./Cur. Mat. L /T/D		3.8	10.1	17.3			5.9	4.9
		(28) 1.6	(31) 3.2	(19) 1.9			(58) 2.2	(45) 2.5
		.3	1.5	1.0			1.0	1.4
Fixed/Worth	.3	.2	.2	.1	.0	.0	.3	.2
	1.8	.7	.6	.6	1.4	.3	.9	.7
	-.9	4.7	1.9	2.5	NM	2.3	3.3	3.5
Debt/Worth	.7	.8	.6	.9	.6	.5	.7	.6
	7.2	2.4	2.1	2.0	2.5	1.5	2.0	2.1
	-3.5	14.7	5.5	11.7	NM	27.4	8.6	10.8
% Profit Before Taxes/Tangible Net Worth	168.7	64.2	63.7	41.5	84.0	82.3	57.1	56.6
	(132) 53.1	(171) 30.9	(186) 22.5	(57) 20.0	(11) 33.0	(13) 39.2	(349) 21.0	(277) 17.8
	4.0	9.4	7.5	2.2	8.8	25.6	4.0	4.0
% Profit Before Taxes/Total Assets	37.1	21.5	18.6	10.5	36.2	22.7	20.0	17.3
	11.4	9.0	8.4	4.5	8.8	12.0	6.8	5.4
	-5.5	.7	2.6	.4	2.7	8.1	.0	-.4
Sales/Net Fixed Assets	92.5	57.6	45.4	43.1	236.2	392.4	34.6	40.3
	31.7	17.8	12.5	10.8	19.2	22.6	9.8	11.4
	11.9	5.9	2.6	3.3	3.1	6.8	2.6	3.6
Sales/Total Assets	9.7	3.9	3.2	2.7	6.5	3.2	4.0	4.0
	5.3	2.9	2.0	1.5	1.8	1.5	2.1	2.3
	2.8	1.7	1.1	.7	.9	.6	1.0	1.2
% Depr., Dep., Amort./Sales	.8	.9	.7	1.0			.8	.7
	(136) 1.6	(157) 2.1	(166) 1.9	(55) 2.4			(337) 2.4	(270) 2.2
	4.0	4.9	4.9	5.5			5.3	4.5
% Officers', Directors', Owners' Comp/Sales	6.4	2.8	2.0	.6			3.3	3.1
	(111) 11.2	(95) 5.3	(56) 4.3	(11) 1.6			(140) 6.5	(116) 6.3
	18.7	10.4	8.0	2.2			11.7	13.3
Net Sales ($)	282759M	727351M	1956868M	2336930M	6103213M	5646150M	6923313M	6693167M
Total Assets ($)	45636M	234123M	900795M	1440184M	1062165M	2601802M	4974049M	3485632M

© RMA 2005

M = $ thousand   MM = $ million

See Pages 11 through 21 for Explanation of Ratios and Data

Comparative Historical Data			Type of Statement	Current Data Sorted By Sales					
71	114	120	Unqualified	10	11	16	16	30	37
45	78	75	Reviewed	3	14	15	20	18	5
69	159	114	Compiled	27	36	18	19	11	3
75	164	205	Tax Returns	92	70	18	12	7	6
121	191	219	Other	47	53	31	37	29	22
4/1/02-3/31/03	4/1/03-3/31/04	4/1/04-3/31/05		141 (4/1-9/30/04)			592 (10/1/04-3/31/05)		
ALL	ALL	ALL		0-1MM	1-3MM	3-5MM	5-10MM	10-25MM	25MM & OVER
381	706	733	NUMBER OF STATEMENTS	179	184	98	104	95	73
%	%	%	ASSETS	%	%	%	%	%	%
15.6	16.2	18.5	Cash & Equivalents	23.1	19.7	17.5	16.2	12.6	16.9
25.2	26.4	27.5	Trade Receivables (net)	14.2	23.5	37.9	35.2	36.1	34.1
6.3	7.1	7.2	Inventory	4.4	8.0	5.7	7.8	10.7	8.7
4.1	4.9	4.6	All Other Current	4.7	4.3	4.2	3.9	6.2	4.8
51.2	54.6	57.9	Total Current	46.5	55.6	65.2	63.2	65.6	64.4
33.8	31.5	28.8	Fixed Assets (net)	40.0	31.8	24.7	24.8	18.7	18.4
5.9	4.3	3.8	Intangibles (net)	3.5	3.3	2.4	3.6	3.6	8.5
9.1	9.6	9.4	All Other Non-Current	10.0	9.4	7.7	8.4	12.1	8.6
100.0	100.0	100.0	Total	100.0	100.0	100.0	100.0	100.0	100.0
			LIABILITIES						
9.9	11.7	13.5	Notes Payable-Short Term	16.8	13.4	12.3	13.6	11.3	10.3
6.3	4.2	5.0	Cur. Mat.-L/T/D	3.8	7.3	5.4	4.2	4.9	2.6
11.3	11.5	12.4	Trade Payables	7.5	11.0	15.0	13.7	16.3	17.8
.5	.4	.5	Income Taxes Payable	.1	.3	1.0	1.0	.4	.5
13.6	15.6	17.3	All Other Current	18.5	21.3	14.4	16.8	12.2	16.0
41.7	43.4	48.7	Total Current	46.6	53.2	48.1	49.3	45.1	47.2
23.4	20.4	22.4	Long-Term Debt	31.5	28.5	16.7	15.0	13.5	14.1
.4	.4	.3	Deferred Taxes	.1	.3	.5	.3	.6	.5
5.1	5.8	8.6	All Other Non-Current	11.4	9.9	7.0	5.7	7.3	6.3
29.4	30.0	20.0	Net Worth	10.4	8.2	27.8	29.7	33.5	31.9
100.0	100.0	100.0	Total Liabilities & Net Worth	100.0	100.0	100.0	100.0	100.0	100.0
			INCOME DATA						
100.0	100.0	100.0	Net Sales	100.0	100.0	100.0	100.0	100.0	100.0
			Gross Profit						
92.1	91.0	91.5	Operating Expenses	85.7	93.7	94.0	93.8	92.2	92.4
7.9	9.0	8.5	Operating Profit	14.3	6.3	6.0	6.2	7.8	7.6
1.9	2.1	1.7	All Other Expenses (net)	4.5	1.0	.5	.6	.5	1.1
6.0	6.9	6.9	Profit Before Taxes	9.9	5.4	5.5	5.6	7.3	6.6
			RATIOS						
2.5	2.9	2.7		4.3	3.0	2.9	2.6	2.4	2.1
1.3	1.4	1.4	Current	1.4	1.3	1.7	1.5	1.5	1.4
.8	.9	.9		.5	.6	1.0	1.1	1.1	1.0
2.0	2.2	2.2		3.1	2.1	2.7	2.1	1.9	1.7
(380) 1.0	(705) 1.1	1.1	Quick	1.1	.9	1.5	1.1	1.1	1.0
.5	.6	.5		.3	.4	.7	.8	.7	.6
2 174.9	1 504.5	1 626.3		0 UND	0 UND	22 16.3	20 18.1	22 16.2	25 14.6
30 12.0	31 11.7	30 12.1	Sales/Receivables	0 UND	22 16.4	51 7.2	43 8.5	39 9.3	43 14.6
55 6.6	61 6.0	59 6.2		29 12.6	46 8.0	75 4.9	72 5.1	63 5.8	62 5.9
			Cost of Sales/Inventory						
			Cost of Sales/Payables						
6.9	6.7	7.0		6.6	8.2	5.6	6.3	6.9	8.7
26.4	21.3	19.8	Sales/Working Capital	30.8	35.4	10.8	14.4	16.2	17.9
-33.2	-42.8	-47.4		-10.4	-23.4	-196.4	86.4	63.3	200.4
8.2	16.7	17.4		11.3	15.0	19.1	17.9	19.9	19.6
(293) 3.4	(532) 3.7	(557) 4.8	EBIT/Interest	(109) 3.1	(155) 3.5	(74) 5.1	(87) 5.4	(77) 6.0	(55) 7.0
1.0	.8	1.2		.6	.5	.9	2.3	2.2	2.6
5.2	5.3	7.0			2.0	24.2	8.5	8.3	24.4
(58) 2.3	(82) 1.9	(88) 2.8	Net Profit + Depr., Dep., Amort./Cur. Mat. L/T/D		(11) 1.5	(15) 1.6	(15) 2.9	(17) 2.8	(24) 5.1
1.1	.7	1.1			1.0	-.3	1.0	1.2	1.8
.3	.2	.2		.3	.4	.1	.2	.1	.2
.9	.9	.8	Fixed/Worth	1.5	1.8	.4	.5	.5	.5
5.0	4.6	6.3		-10.0	-4.2	1.6	1.9	1.4	2.2
.6	.6	.8		.6	.9	.6	.6	.7	1.0
2.2	2.2	2.5	Debt/Worth	4.3	5.6	1.8	2.1	1.9	2.8
16.7	17.0	30.9		-30.5	-9.5	5.6	5.6	4.7	14.0
56.8	66.1	74.1		102.7	108.3	54.4	63.3	74.0	61.8
(305) 18.2	(563) 23.2	(570) 28.1	% Profit Before Taxes/Tangible Net Worth	(126) 23.3	(124) 39.5	(81) 26.9	(91) 23.6	(87) 25.3	(61) 26.6
1.9	2.9	7.4		4.2	7.1	6.9	6.9	9.5	15.5
16.9	20.7	22.2		21.7	27.1	23.3	20.5	19.5	16.0
5.5	6.9	8.8	% Profit Before Taxes/Total Assets	6.8	9.5	8.8	9.5	9.5	7.8
.0	.0	.5		-1.2	-1.7	.0	2.1	2.5	2.9
43.2	50.6	65.4		46.9	52.3	82.5	61.2	73.4	96.8
12.2	13.4	18.8	Sales/Net Fixed Assets	12.5	18.8	20.4	18.8	28.9	21.6
3.3	4.2	5.6		1.5	5.8	7.3	6.7	8.7	7.8
4.0	4.5	4.8		5.7	5.6	3.9	3.8	4.5	4.1
2.5	2.5	2.8	Sales/Total Assets	2.2	3.3	2.8	2.5	3.0	2.9
1.1	1.2	1.5		.5	2.1	1.7	1.7	1.6	1.5
1.1	1.0	.8		1.5	1.0	.7	.7	.5	.4
(313) 2.7	(528) 2.7	(532) 1.9	% Depr., Dep., Amort./Sales	(116) 3.7	(130) 2.1	(76) 1.7	(78) 1.9	(77) 1.2	(55) 1.3
5.3	5.8	4.8		11.1	5.0	3.3	4.4	2.5	3.0
3.6	3.0	3.1		8.0	3.7	2.8	1.9	1.0	1.1
(118) 6.9	(248) 6.2	(276) 6.5	% Officers', Directors', Owners' Comp/Sales	(66) 12.2	(90) 7.7	(39) 5.2	(42) 3.2	(28) 2.1	(11) 2.7
14.5	12.1	13.0		19.2	12.9	13.4	6.6	6.1	5.5
12312939M	12961305M	17053271M	Net Sales ($)	87788M	350411M	382022M	742870M	1487654M	14002526M
4232885M	5729741M	6284705M	Total Assets ($)	139405M	186502M	229867M	399738M	1061491M	4267702M

M = $ thousand   MM = $ million
See Pages 11 through 21 for Explanation of Ratios and Data

MANAGEMENT OF COMPANIES AND ENTERPRISES

Current Data Sorted By Assets   Comparative Historical Data

	0-500M	500M-2MM	2-10MM	10-50MM	50-100MM	100-250MM	Type of Statement	4/1/00-3/31/01 ALL	4/1/01-3/31/02 ALL
			1	1		2	Unqualified	6	7
							Reviewed	1	1
		4	2	2	1		Compiled	14	8
	1	4					Tax Returns	4	3
	1	3	5	10	1	1	Other	16	21
		3 (4/1-9/30/04)		38 (10/1/04-3/31/05)			NUMBER OF STATEMENTS	41	40
	2	11	8	15	2	3			
	%	%	%	%	%	%	**ASSETS**	%	%
		6.8		6.3			Cash & Equivalents	6.6	10.9
		2.6		4.1			Trade Receivables (net)	3.2	8.0
		.0		3.6			Inventory	.0	1.2
		.0		2.2			All Other Current	2.4	6.6
		9.4		16.2			Total Current	12.3	26.7
		79.4		24.0			Fixed Assets (net)	28.5	35.5
		2.6		2.8			Intangibles (net)	5.2	1.4
		8.6		57.0			All Other Non-Current	53.9	36.4
		100.0		100.0			Total	100.0	100.0
							LIABILITIES		
		11.1		5.8			Notes Payable-Short Term	15.5	8.9
		3.5		3.3			Cur. Mat.-L/T/D	2.6	4.3
		.9		1.5			Trade Payables	2.7	5.5
		.0		.7			Income Taxes Payable	.8	.1
		5.3		9.0			All Other Current	3.7	11.4
		20.8		20.3			Total Current	25.3	30.2
		48.1		22.4			Long-Term Debt	32.5	31.3
		.0		.2			Deferred Taxes	.0	.0
		6.0		.8			All Other Non-Current	2.2	3.2
		25.1		56.3			Net Worth	40.0	35.2
		100.0		100.0			Total Liabilities & Net Worth	100.0	100.0
							INCOME DATA		
		100.0		100.0			Net Sales	100.0	100.0
							Gross Profit		
		59.4		36.1			Operating Expenses	47.0	52.2
		40.6		63.9			Operating Profit	53.0	47.8
		20.9		9.3			All Other Expenses (net)	5.5	17.4
		19.7		54.6			Profit Before Taxes	47.5	30.4
							RATIOS		
		1.1		1.9			Current	1.3	2.1
		.2		.4				.4	1.0
		.1		.1				.1	.2
		1.1		1.9			Quick	1.1	1.3
		.2		.3				.3	.4
		.1		.1				.0	.1
		0 UND		0 UND			Sales/Receivables	0 UND	0 UND
		0 UND		0 UND				0 UND	0 UND
		0 UND		21 17.0				0 UND	9 42.0
							Cost of Sales/Inventory		
							Cost of Sales/Payables		
		74.5		6.5			Sales/Working Capital	7.1	2.9
		-2.1		-3.7				-2.9	NM
		-1.4		-2.3				-.5	-1.6
				32.2			EBIT/Interest	17.7	12.8
				(12) 10.7				(13) 9.1	(13) 6.7
				5.7				4.3	2.5
							Net Profit + Depr., Dep., Amort./Cur. Mat. L /T/D		
		1.0		.0			Fixed/Worth	.0	.0
		2.8		.0				.0	.4
		471.0		3.5				2.8	6.1
		1.4		.2			Debt/Worth	.1	.3
		3.0		.4				.6	4.1
		474.0		5.8				6.3	14.8
				28.6			% Profit Before Taxes/Tangible Net Worth	19.0	23.5
				(14) 14.5				(37) 8.2	(36) 14.0
				6.2				3.1	6.6
		13.4		10.9			% Profit Before Taxes/Total Assets	9.8	7.9
		2.4		6.7				4.4	2.9
		-2.9		4.4				.7	.9
		.4		UND			Sales/Net Fixed Assets	UND	67.7
		.2		15.6				16.0	3.2
		.1		.6				.2	.2
		.4		.4			Sales/Total Assets	.2	.2
		.2		.1				.1	.1
		.1		.1				.1	.1
		13.2					% Depr., Dep., Amort./Sales	9.6	2.1
		(10) 19.8						(17) 13.7	(28) 5.7
		35.6						23.6	13.9
							% Officers', Directors', Owners' Comp/Sales		
Net Sales ($)	201M	7418M	18393M	174056M	7142M	113754M		67102M	259265M
Total Assets ($)	494M	11051M	37419M	294472M	143780M	527410M		509713M	1335854M

M = $ thousand   MM = $ million
See Pages 11 through 21 for Explanation of Ratios and Data

Comparative Historical Data **Current Data Sorted By Sales**

	4/1/02-3/31/03 ALL	4/1/03-3/31/04 ALL	4/1/04-3/31/05 ALL	Type of Statement	0-1MM	1-3MM	3-5MM	5-10MM	10-25MM	25MM & OVER
	9	8	4	Unqualified		1			1	2
		1	2	Reviewed			1		1	
	8	15	9	Compiled	6	2		1		
	2	2	5	Tax Returns	5					
	19	13	21	Other	6	6	5	3		1
					3 (4/1-9/30/04)			38 (10/1/04-3/31/05)		
NUMBER OF STATEMENTS	40	39	41		17	9	6	4	2	3
	%	%	%	**ASSETS**	%	%	%	%	%	%
Cash & Equivalents	14.9	13.7	7.7		4.0					
Trade Receivables (net)	7.0	10.5	6.0		.1					
Inventory	4.1	3.4	2.1		.0					
All Other Current	3.2	5.9	2.2		.1					
Total Current	29.2	33.5	18.1		4.2					
Fixed Assets (net)	36.1	32.6	38.5		61.5					
Intangibles (net)	.6	1.1	2.2		2.2					
All Other Non-Current	34.1	32.8	41.2		32.1					
Total	100.0	100.0	100.0		100.0					
				LIABILITIES						
Notes Payable-Short Term	14.0	10.3	9.5		7.6					
Cur. Mat.-L/T/D	2.2	2.9	5.0		9.1					
Trade Payables	1.3	.6	1.3		.6					
Income Taxes Payable	.0	.1	.3		.0					
All Other Current	16.2	22.8	9.7		1.6					
Total Current	33.7	36.8	25.8		18.8					
Long-Term Debt	37.7	36.3	24.5		35.0					
Deferred Taxes	.2	.0	.1		.0					
All Other Non-Current	.6	1.7	2.1		3.9					
Net Worth	27.7	25.2	47.5		42.3					
Total Liabilities & Net Worth	100.0	100.0	100.0		100.0					
				INCOME DATA						
Net Sales	100.0	100.0	100.0		100.0					
Gross Profit										
Operating Expenses	51.7	53.5	48.3		37.6					
Operating Profit	48.3	46.5	51.7		62.4					
All Other Expenses (net)	18.3	14.5	11.1		19.2					
Profit Before Taxes	30.0	31.9	40.5		43.2					
				RATIOS						
Current	1.9	1.3	1.8		2.5					
	1.0	.8	.4		.2					
	.2	.2	.1		.1					
Quick	1.6	1.1	1.7		2.5					
	.5	.4	.3		.2					
	.1	.1	.1		.1					
Sales/Receivables	0 UND	0 UND	0 UND		0 UND					
	0 UND	0 UND	0 UND		0 UND					
	11 32.4	42 8.8	18 20.4		0 UND					
Cost of Sales/Inventory										
Cost of Sales/Payables										
Sales/Working Capital	3.2	2.1	7.9		9.8					
	NM	-28.2	-8.1		-3.0					
	-2.6	-3.8	-1.7		-1.4					
EBIT/Interest	14.6	23.3	31.5							
	(18) 5.8	(18) 6.0	(26) 12.6							
	1.1	3.6	5.4							
Net Profit + Depr., Dep., Amort./Cur. Mat. L/T/D										
Fixed/Worth	.0	.0	.0		.0					
	.3	.2	.3		2.4					
	9.8	4.0	4.8		243.1					
Debt/Worth	.5	.6	.2		.1					
	5.2	7.1	1.3		1.5					
	14.6	16.6	8.2		244.2					
% Profit Before Taxes/Tangible Net Worth	23.6	26.8	34.1		43.5					
	(35) 10.9	(31) 14.8	(37) 14.2		(14) 14.5					
	5.9	5.5	5.4		4.2					
% Profit Before Taxes/Total Assets	5.8	8.2	12.1		10.4					
	2.3	3.9	5.4		4.0					
	1.2	1.0	1.6		.8					
Sales/Net Fixed Assets	99.3	643.0	UND		375.5					
	2.6	3.7	4.6		.3					
	.3	.4	.2		.1					
Sales/Total Assets	.3	.4	.8		.2					
	.1	.1	.1		.1					
	.1	.1	.1		.1					
% Depr., Dep., Amort./Sales	2.4	3.2	1.9		13.4					
	(21) 7.4	(20) 11.5	(25) 12.1		(11) 18.3					
	18.2	19.3	22.8		34.8					
% Officers', Directors', Owners' Comp/Sales										
Net Sales ($)	372862M	391408M	320964M		5591M	16432M	24197M	28232M	33699M	212813M
Total Assets ($)	1947717M	2088406M	1014626M		51994M	185519M	90460M	265325M	232035M	189293M

© RMA 2005

M = $ thousand   MM = $ million
See Pages 11 through 21 for Explanation of Ratios and Data

Current Data Sorted By Assets							Comparative Historical Data	
1	8	24	35	21	20	**Type of Statement** Unqualified	123	97
4	5	46	20	2	1	Reviewed	100	89
24	74	79	19		1	Compiled	297	284
46	156	100	14		2	Tax Returns	240	227
26	85	99	54	15	10	Other	299	339
	93 (4/1-9/30/04)		898 (10/1/04-3/31/05)				4/1/00-3/31/01	4/1/01-3/31/02
0-500M	500M-2MM	2-10MM	10-50MM	50-100MM	100-250MM		ALL	ALL
101	328	348	142	38	34	**NUMBER OF STATEMENTS**	1059	1036
%	%	%	%	%	%	**ASSETS**	%	%
12.3	6.4	6.2	6.0	7.4	10.1	Cash & Equivalents	5.8	6.3
10.3	4.4	4.3	9.8	12.5	10.7	Trade Receivables (net)	5.2	4.8
4.8	2.2	4.6	13.1	8.1	7.9	Inventory	4.0	4.6
5.1	2.0	2.9	3.9	6.8	5.4	All Other Current	3.8	4.3
32.4	14.9	18.0	32.8	34.8	34.1	Total Current	18.8	20.0
57.5	76.5	66.4	50.6	42.7	35.9	Fixed Assets (net)	68.6	69.0
1.8	2.1	3.0	3.5	8.8	6.9	Intangibles (net)	3.0	2.8
8.4	6.5	12.5	13.0	13.7	23.1	All Other Non-Current	9.5	8.2
100.0	100.0	100.0	100.0	100.0	100.0	Total	100.0	100.0
						LIABILITIES		
9.1	6.8	5.3	10.1	8.0	8.8	Notes Payable-Short Term	5.7	6.3
5.1	3.9	3.6	4.3	3.5	1.7	Cur. Mat.-L/T/D	6.2	5.3
6.3	2.3	2.5	6.1	6.4	8.2	Trade Payables	2.6	2.9
.0	.1	.1	.2	.3	.5	Income Taxes Payable	.1	.1
14.2	3.6	5.8	7.0	7.6	8.2	All Other Current	6.3	6.0
34.6	16.6	17.3	27.7	25.7	27.4	Total Current	21.0	20.7
51.1	59.0	51.2	33.4	33.2	28.5	Long-Term Debt	52.6	54.0
.0	.0	.2	.5	1.1	1.0	Deferred Taxes	.3	.3
5.6	3.6	4.3	5.4	8.3	4.2	All Other Non-Current	3.9	5.6
8.7	20.8	27.0	32.9	31.6	38.9	Net Worth	22.3	19.5
100.0	100.0	100.0	100.0	100.0	100.0	Total Liabilities & Net Worth	100.0	100.0
						INCOME DATA		
100.0	100.0	100.0	100.0	100.0	100.0	Net Sales	100.0	100.0
						Gross Profit		
68.2	51.1	59.0	75.1	82.9	76.7	Operating Expenses	56.6	57.2
31.8	48.9	41.0	24.9	17.1	23.3	Operating Profit	43.4	42.8
10.1	20.7	18.1	9.9	3.8	9.2	All Other Expenses (net)	21.6	23.1
21.8	28.3	22.9	15.0	13.3	14.1	Profit Before Taxes	21.8	19.8
						RATIOS		
2.8	2.1	2.3	1.8	2.0	2.2		1.7	2.1
1.1	.6	.9	1.1	1.3	1.3	Current	.7	.8
.4	.1	.2	.6	.9	.6		.2	.2
1.6	1.6	1.5	1.2	1.3	1.4		1.0	1.3
.6	.4	.5	(141) .6	(37) .7	.8	Quick	(1058) .4	.4
.1	.1	.1	.2	.4	.2		.1	.1
0 UND	0 UND	0 UND	0 UND	5 69.7	5 77.4		0 UND	0 UND
0 UND	0 UND	0 UND	13 29.0	32 11.3	31 11.8	Sales/Receivables	0 UND	0 UND
2 214.5	0 UND	7 50.2	49 7.5	77 4.8	73 5.0		10 36.2	13 29.0
						Cost of Sales/Inventory		
						Cost of Sales/Payables		
6.3	6.2	6.2	6.1	4.2	4.0		7.9	5.4
376.6	-10.9	-20.0	33.3	20.9	9.8	Sales/Working Capital	-15.2	-23.9
-4.8	-2.5	-3.2	-6.7	-47.9	-9.3		-2.6	-2.6
9.2	9.1	6.1	7.9	9.2	15.5		5.7	6.2
(54) 4.4	(149) 4.5	(172) 3.6	(95) 3.5	(30) 3.0	(24) 5.7	EBIT/Interest	(395) 3.5	(391) 3.3
2.1	2.5	1.5	1.1	1.4	1.5		1.8	1.4
	6.0	4.5	4.3	9.2		Net Profit + Depr., Dep.,	3.8	4.1
	(14) 1.5	(31) 1.1	(28) 2.1	(18) 2.3		Amort./Cur. Mat. L./T/D	(98) 1.5	(81) 1.3
	.8	.8	.3	1.2			.7	.6
.4	1.7	1.0	.6	.7	.2		1.4	1.3
2.8	4.3	3.2	1.7	2.2	.9	Fixed/Worth	3.6	3.3
-25.2	27.2	10.7	4.7	11.4	3.8		14.1	23.8
.8	1.3	1.3	1.0	1.3	1.0		1.4	1.4
3.8	4.3	3.3	2.4	3.5	2.5	Debt/Worth	3.8	3.7
-14.6	33.4	12.6	9.6	17.8	5.5		22.2	33.6
120.1	45.7	39.9	29.1	48.1	29.4	% Profit Before Taxes/Tangible	40.6	38.9
(72) 27.6	(257) 22.2	(295) 18.9	(128) 13.8	(32) 21.1	(30) 16.8	Net Worth	(868) 19.3	(819) 17.2
7.7	9.7	4.8	3.7	6.8	4.3		5.6	5.4
23.3	11.4	8.4	6.6	9.5	10.0	% Profit Before Taxes/Total	9.8	8.8
9.0	5.7	4.2	3.8	3.5	5.2	Assets	4.4	4.0
2.3	2.0	.9	.5	1.1	1.0		.9	.8
34.4	.5	2.0	9.4	8.0	30.4		1.3	1.3
1.5	.2	.2	1.9	3.3	4.4	Sales/Net Fixed Assets	.3	.3
.2	.1	.2	.2	.5	.9		.2	.2
4.2	.4	.5	1.5	1.9	1.6		.5	.4
.6	.2	.2	.5	.8	.5	Sales/Total Assets	.2	.2
.2	.1	.1	.1	.3	.2		.1	.1
1.8	10.7	6.9	2.3	2.2	2.0	% Depr., Dep., Amort./Sales	5.7	6.4
(74) 11.8	(291) 16.8	(300) 16.6	(122) 6.1	(31) 4.4	(16) 7.6		(969) 14.4	(927) 14.8
21.3	24.0	26.2	19.4	11.3	18.4		22.0	21.8
5.3	4.3	1.6	1.7			% Officers', Directors',	2.7	2.2
(27) 10.4	(33) 7.0	(43) 4.4	(13) 2.9			Owners' Comp/Sales	(105) 5.6	(108) 5.1
15.4	23.5	9.6	8.1				11.8	11.2
71058M	204282M	1047099M	3517428M	3333591M	5531183M	Net Sales ($)	10148214M	9322781M
29469M	377877M	1561116M	3196963M	2756199M	5250741M	Total Assets ($)	11717285M	11499468M

M = $ thousand   MM = $ million
See Pages 11 through 21 for Explanation of Ratios and Data

Comparative Historical Data

Current Data Sorted By Sales

				Type of Statement						
113		129	109	Unqualified	8	15	8	6	22	50
112		89	78	Reviewed	31	15	4	6	10	12
242		277	197	Compiled	146	25	4	8	10	4
285		300	318	Tax Returns	243	51	10	4	2	8
308		307	289	Other	140	56	19	17	26	31
4/1/02-3/31/03 ALL		4/1/03-3/31/04 ALL	4/1/04-3/31/05 ALL		93 (4/1-9/30/04)			898 (10/1/04-3/31/05)		
1060		1102	991	NUMBER OF STATEMENTS	0-1MM	1-3MM	3-5MM	5-10MM	10-25MM	25MM & OVER
					568	162	45	41	70	105
%		%	%	ASSETS	%	%	%	%	%	%
6.4		6.0	7.0	Cash & Equivalents	5.7	7.5	13.8	8.4	8.3	9.3
5.1		5.9	6.3	Trade Receivables (net)	1.4	7.6	14.6	14.3	17.0	16.8
3.9		4.1	5.3	Inventory	1.3	5.8	7.8	6.4	16.4	16.6
3.6		4.0	3.2	All Other Current	2.6	2.5	3.7	4.6	2.9	7.1
19.0		20.0	21.8	Total Current	11.0	23.3	39.8	33.7	44.7	49.8
69.5		66.3	64.6	Fixed Assets (net)	80.1	57.0	32.5	43.2	41.5	30.2
1.8		2.5	3.0	Intangibles (net)	1.3	3.8	6.0	8.0	3.8	7.1
9.7		11.1	10.6	All Other Non-Current	7.6	15.8	21.7	15.1	10.0	12.9
100.0		100.0	100.0	Total	100.0	100.0	100.0	100.0	100.0	100.0
				LIABILITIES						
5.5		6.4	7.1	Notes Payable-Short Term	4.6	8.5	12.2	7.4	12.6	12.0
5.6		4.5	3.9	Cur. Mat.-L/T/D	3.7	4.9	3.3	2.9	3.8	3.9
3.2		3.4	3.7	Trade Payables	1.0	3.9	6.6	6.0	11.4	10.5
.1		.1	.1	Income Taxes Payable	.0	.0	.2	.6	.4	.3
7.4		8.2	6.2	All Other Current	4.4	6.2	11.3	9.6	7.7	12.0
21.8		22.6	21.0	Total Current	13.8	23.5	33.6	26.5	35.8	38.7
51.1		47.5	49.7	Long-Term Debt	61.8	49.8	21.4	30.8	24.0	21.2
.3		.3	.2	Deferred Taxes	.0	.4	.3	.2	.6	1.1
4.6		6.1	4.5	All Other Non-Current	4.0	3.9	10.8	4.1	3.7	6.4
22.2		23.5	24.5	Net Worth	20.5	22.4	33.9	38.4	35.9	32.7
100.0		100.0	100.0	Total Liabilities & Net Worth	100.0	100.0	100.0	100.0	100.0	100.0
				INCOME DATA						
100.0		100.0	100.0	Net Sales	100.0	100.0	100.0	100.0	100.0	100.0
				Gross Profit						
58.9		59.3	61.1	Operating Expenses	47.2	68.3	77.6	80.0	88.4	92.8
41.1		40.7	38.9	Operating Profit	52.8	31.7	22.4	20.0	11.6	7.2
19.4		17.8	16.1	All Other Expenses (net)	23.2	11.3	5.0	7.4	3.3	1.8
21.7		22.9	22.8	Profit Before Taxes	29.6	20.4	17.4	12.6	8.4	5.4
				RATIOS						
1.6		2.1	2.1		2.1	2.6	2.8	2.9	1.9	1.8
.6		.8	.9	Current	.5	1.0	1.3	1.3	1.2	1.2
.2		.2	.2		.1	.3	.5	.4	1.0	1.0
1.1		1.2	1.5		1.4	1.7	2.4	2.0	1.3	1.2
.4		.4 (989)	.5	Quick (567)	.4	.6	1.0	.7	.8 (104)	.6
.1		.1	.1		.1	.1	.3	.3	.4	.3
0 UND	0 UND	0 UND			0 UND	0 UND	0 945.4	1 472.2	10 35.5	8 48.5
0 UND	0 UND	0 UND		Sales/Receivables	0 UND	0 UND	16 23.4	17 21.3	36 10.2	35 10.5
13 27.6	14 25.5	17 21.2			0 UND	18 20.1	54 6.8	43 8.5	61 6.0	54 6.7
				Cost of Sales/Inventory						
				Cost of Sales/Payables						
8.5		6.9	5.9		6.0	5.7	4.5	6.2	5.9	6.2
-10.6		-22.8	-62.0	Sales/Working Capital	-6.9	NM	18.5	32.4	32.2	16.5
-2.3		-2.4	-3.4		-2.3	-5.9	-9.7	-6.0	-111.5	-75.3
6.9		7.5	7.9		6.9	7.2	18.1	12.1	7.7	12.0
(500) 3.6	(564) 3.8	(524) 4.1	EBIT/Interest	(213) 4.5	(108) 3.2	(30) 5.7	(27) 2.5	(56) 2.3	(90) 3.9
1.5		1.7	1.8		2.7	1.2	1.8	.7	1.1	1.2
3.1		4.0	4.5		1.5	3.2			11.4	9.9
(121) 1.7	(101) 1.7	(100) 1.5	Net Profit + Depr., Dep., Amort./Cur. Mat. L/T/D	(21) 1.0	(13) 1.1		(21)	1.3 (38)	2.5
.8		.8	.8		.8	.8			.2	1.2
1.2		1.1	1.0		1.7	.6	.2	.2	.3	.3
3.1		3.2	2.9	Fixed/Worth	4.3	2.6	.9	.9	1.1	1.1
14.0		14.5	12.4		18.4	15.4	11.0	4.0	2.8	3.5
1.2		1.2	1.2		1.4	1.1	.9	1.1	.9	1.0
3.4		3.6	3.4	Debt/Worth	4.1	3.8	1.9	1.7	2.3	3.1
19.2		21.2	16.5		24.3	18.9	13.6	4.8	5.6	9.2
37.5		43.1	44.1		39.3	59.1	61.7	33.0	34.7	43.0
(882) 17.8	(908) 19.4	(814) 19.4	% Profit Before Taxes/Tangible Net Worth	(457) 19.7	(128) 24.5	(37) 21.1	(37) 8.8	(66) 15.8	(89) 22.7
5.1		7.6	6.4		8.0	5.9	6.7	-.9	2.6	5.5
9.4		9.7	10.0		9.1	12.2	19.8	13.9	10.5	11.3
4.1		4.5	4.8	% Profit Before Taxes/Total Assets	4.7	5.6	7.0	3.4	3.8	5.3
.9		1.1	1.3		1.5	1.2	3.3	-.4	.6	.8
1.6		2.6	4.0		.3	15.9	55.3	24.3	17.9	29.1
.3		.3	.3	Sales/Net Fixed Assets	.2	.6	8.0	4.1	3.6	6.2
.2		.2	.2		.1	.2	1.2	.5	1.0	3.5
.5		.6	.8		.2	1.1	3.2	2.2	2.1	2.6
.2		.2	.2	Sales/Total Assets	.2	.4	.8	1.1	1.2	1.7
.1		.1	.1		.1	.2	.2	.2	.4	1.0
6.8		6.4	5.4		12.7	5.2	.9	2.0	1.3	1.0
(954) 15.1	(958) 15.1	(834) 14.9	% Depr., Dep., Amort./Sales	(513) 18.8	(123) 14.5	(31) 3.2	(31) 3.8	(58) 3.7	(78) 2.7
23.2		22.9	23.0		26.2	22.4	6.1	17.3	6.4	5.4
2.1		2.4	2.4		5.3	3.0	2.2		.9	1.4
(110) 4.9	(126) 5.8	(122) 5.5	% Officers', Directors', Owners' Comp/Sales	(36) 7.9	(39) 9.3	(11) 4.7	(15)	2.5 (14)	2.4
12.2		11.9	13.6		20.8	18.7	12.0		4.3	7.7
10963748M		15766601M	13704641M	Net Sales ($)	193575M	274279M	174858M	282748M	1173625M	11605556M
12591682M		14660347M	13172365M	Total Assets ($)	1199744M	1012337M	572831M	797271M	2131604M	7458578M

M = $ thousand   MM = $ million
See Pages 11 through 21 for Explanation of Ratios and Data

ADMINISTRATIVE AND SUPPORT AND WASTE MANAGEMENT AND REMEDIATION

Current Data Sorted By Assets   **Comparative Historical Data**

0-500M	500M-2MM	2-10MM	10-50MM	50-100MM	100-250MM	Type of Statement	4/1/00-3/31/01 ALL	4/1/01-3/31/02 ALL
4	6	12	13	5	7	Unqualified	66	58
2	14	15	4	1		Reviewed	27	27
9	13	11	3			Compiled	46	46
24	14	6				Tax Returns	27	20
26	16	18	11	3	4	Other	95	86
	34 (4/1-9/30/04)		207 (10/1/04-3/31/05)					
65	63	62	31	9	11	**NUMBER OF STATEMENTS**	261	237
%	%	%	%	%	%	**ASSETS**	%	%
23.3	20.5	16.9	27.5		10.8	Cash & Equivalents	14.7	15.7
20.9	26.7	23.8	24.3		19.3	Trade Receivables (net)	27.6	23.5
.6	1.0	4.1	1.7		5.7	Inventory	2.8	2.5
11.5	5.5	6.1	5.4		3.4	All Other Current	6.5	5.9
56.3	53.7	50.9	59.0		39.1	Total Current	51.6	47.6
17.0	26.8	20.2	21.8		36.6	Fixed Assets (net)	24.2	23.1
11.4	4.1	6.3	11.8		13.1	Intangibles (net)	9.9	8.9
15.4	15.3	22.7	7.4		11.2	All Other Non-Current	14.4	20.5
100.0	100.0	100.0	100.0		100.0	Total	100.0	100.0
						LIABILITIES		
26.4	14.9	8.4	5.0		7.7	Notes Payable-Short Term	10.3	9.4
2.4	4.7	2.2	1.8		3.7	Cur. Mat.-L/T/D	2.9	3.2
10.9	8.2	13.8	11.3		6.5	Trade Payables	15.4	12.3
.2	.5	.6	.7		.0	Income Taxes Payable	.6	.2
32.2	20.3	16.6	16.6		15.7	All Other Current	20.1	18.5
72.1	48.6	41.5	35.4		33.6	Total Current	49.3	43.6
22.4	14.3	19.8	18.7		22.9	Long-Term Debt	16.4	19.1
.0	.1	.7	.4		1.6	Deferred Taxes	.4	.2
6.3	4.7	7.1	3.8		7.2	All Other Non-Current	7.4	7.6
-.8	32.3	30.8	41.8		34.7	Net Worth	26.6	29.6
100.0	100.0	100.0	100.0		100.0	Total Liabilities & Net Worth	100.0	100.0
						INCOME DATA		
100.0	100.0	100.0	100.0		100.0	Net Sales	100.0	100.0
						Gross Profit		
91.3	91.5	85.9	88.3		92.4	Operating Expenses	91.4	91.2
8.7	8.5	14.1	11.7		7.6	Operating Profit	8.6	8.8
.7	1.7	2.9	1.7		.3	All Other Expenses (net)	.6	1.9
8.0	6.8	11.2	9.9		7.3	Profit Before Taxes	8.0	6.9
						RATIOS		
3.0	2.9	2.5	2.8		2.0		2.1	2.0
1.1	1.4	1.2	1.5		1.1	Current	1.2	1.2
.4	.6	.7	1.2		1.0		.7	.6
2.6	2.6	2.2	2.8		1.4		1.7	1.6
(63) .9	1.1	1.2	1.4		1.0	Quick	1.0 (236) 1.0	
.3	.3	.5	1.0		.6		.5	.4
0 UND	0 UND	0 UND	13 28.5		21 17.1		2 190.1	1 493.9
0 999.8	14 25.6	36 10.1	35 10.4		56 6.5	Sales/Receivables	38 9.5	29 12.6
26 13.9	56 6.5	59 6.2	68 5.4		92 4.0		64 5.7	64 5.7
						Cost of Sales/Inventory		
						Cost of Sales/Payables		
9.5	8.2	4.6	3.7		8.0		6.7	8.1
254.0	33.2	28.2	8.9		78.8	Sales/Working Capital	30.9	50.1
-23.9	-14.1	-21.9	24.2		480.1		-22.9	-17.1
21.0	32.0	20.3	34.0		9.9		12.0	12.5
(29) 5.3	(44) 7.8	(52) 6.6	(26) 6.8		4.8	EBIT/Interest	(203) 3.1	(173) 3.3
.5	1.2	1.5	1.1		3.1		1.1	.9
		21.8				Net Profit + Depr., Dep.,	6.8	7.5
		(13) 3.8				Amort./Cur. Mat. L/T/D	(47) 3.0	(39) 4.1
		.6					.9	1.9
.0	.1	.1	.1		.8		.2	.2
.4	.3	.5	.6		1.7	Fixed/Worth	.8	.7
-1.3	1.6	2.4	1.7		-7.4		30.0	6.3
.6	.4	1.1	.5		1.5		.9	.9
3.8	1.4	3.1	3.2		2.5	Debt/Worth	3.5	3.4
-4.1	5.9	10.9	4.6		-16.6		UND	42.0
113.7	68.5	72.1	58.5			% Profit Before Taxes/Tangible	79.5	68.1
(44) 58.9	(55) 23.2	(51) 26.0	(29) 30.7			Net Worth	(197) 30.0	(186) 25.4
22.8	5.5	7.8	5.9				7.7	2.8
47.1	18.8	17.7	14.4		9.2	% Profit Before Taxes/Total	18.7	20.0
20.8	8.5	8.0	7.6		4.3	Assets	7.3	6.2
-.2	.9	2.3	1.2		1.8		.6	-.1
UND	74.4	93.7	51.8		8.4		51.0	65.9
83.5	23.4	24.1	11.7		4.5	Sales/Net Fixed Assets	18.1	18.3
23.7	5.0	6.8	3.0		2.4		5.9	6.3
9.9	4.7	3.5	2.7		2.8		3.8	3.8
5.1	2.9	2.2	1.7		1.3	Sales/Total Assets	2.4	2.1
3.3	1.4	.8	.5		1.1		1.2	1.1
.6	.8	.7	.8				.8	.9
(31) 1.4	(47) 1.8	(51) 1.6	(27) 2.1			% Depr., Dep., Amort./Sales	(212) 1.8	(183) 1.9
2.1	4.2	3.2	5.7				3.6	4.1
4.0	5.1	2.5					3.7	2.5
(20) 12.8	(30) 10.8	(13) 6.4				% Officers', Directors', Owners' Comp/Sales	(63) 9.3	(70) 8.2
25.8	15.8	18.8					18.3	24.0
106818M	280396M	943188M	1293498M	825717M	3480243M	Net Sales ($)	10036108M	6008062M
14521M	70262M	281579M	742761M	701639M	2083933M	Total Assets ($)	5077409M	4004019M

M = $ thousand   MM = $ million

See Pages 11 through 21 for Explanation of Ratios and Data

Comparative Historical Data | Current Data Sorted By Sales

	4/1/02-3/31/03 ALL	4/1/03-3/31/04 ALL	4/1/04-3/31/05 ALL	Type of Statement	0-1MM	1-3MM	3-5MM	5-10MM	10-25MM	25MM & OVER
	64	63	47	Unqualified	2	5	4	5	6	25
	37	33	36	Reviewed	5	3	7	14	5	2
	26	64	36	Compiled	5	12	8	6	3	2
	32	43	44	Tax Returns	21	16	5	1		1
	87	93	78	Other	16	15	15	6	12	14
					34 (4/1-9/30/04)			207 (10/1/04-3/31/05)		
	246	296	241	**NUMBER OF STATEMENTS**	49	51	39	32	26	44
	%	%	%	**ASSETS**	%	%	%	%	%	%
	17.3	18.3	20.4	Cash & Equivalents	16.7	22.5	29.0	12.7	21.9	19.1
	24.3	22.8	23.5	Trade Receivables (net)	13.2	19.8	21.1	40.4	26.1	27.2
	2.7	2.7	2.0	Inventory	.2	1.2	.7	4.7	1.9	3.9
	7.4	8.7	7.0	All Other Current	9.6	8.6	5.1	5.2	8.1	4.8
	51.7	52.6	52.8	Total Current	39.7	52.1	56.0	63.0	57.9	55.0
	26.3	23.2	22.9	Fixed Assets (net)	27.1	24.0	17.6	18.7	21.7	25.3
	6.9	7.7	8.6	Intangibles (net)	14.6	2.1	7.4	5.8	9.8	11.7
	15.2	16.5	15.7	All Other Non-Current	18.7	21.7	19.0	12.5	10.7	8.0
	100.0	100.0	100.0	Total	100.0	100.0	100.0	100.0	100.0	100.0
				LIABILITIES						
	9.9	11.0	14.4	Notes Payable-Short Term	33.1	13.9	3.7	12.3	11.9	6.4
	3.4	3.8	2.9	Cur. Mat.-L/T/D	5.6	2.7	1.2	2.7	2.7	2.1
	11.4	10.7	10.9	Trade Payables	5.3	11.0	9.8	9.7	13.2	17.7
	.6	.4	.4	Income Taxes Payable	.3	.3	.8	.8	.7	.1
	18.2	20.6	21.5	All Other Current	22.2	20.9	20.0	18.7	33.3	18.0
	43.6	46.4	50.2	Total Current	66.5	48.7	35.5	43.9	61.8	44.3
	18.9	18.6	19.8	Long-Term Debt	25.8	22.7	14.6	17.2	15.9	18.6
	.3	.2	.4	Deferred Taxes	.1	.1	.2	.8	.3	1.0
	6.9	9.0	5.7	All Other Non-Current	6.0	5.8	6.4	5.0	7.5	4.3
	30.4	25.8	23.9	Net Worth	1.6	22.7	43.3	33.2	14.5	31.8
	100.0	100.0	100.0	Total Liabilities & Net Worth	100.0	100.0	100.0	100.0	100.0	100.0
				INCOME DATA						
	100.0	100.0	100.0	Net Sales	100.0	100.0	100.0	100.0	100.0	100.0
				Gross Profit						
	91.3	89.3	89.3	Operating Expenses	85.0	88.7	87.5	91.6	91.6	93.3
	8.7	10.7	10.7	Operating Profit	15.0	11.3	12.5	8.4	8.4	6.7
	1.4	2.3	1.8	All Other Expenses (net)	3.9	2.0	.8	1.1	-.1	1.8
	7.3	8.4	8.9	Profit Before Taxes	11.1	9.3	11.7	7.3	8.6	4.8
				RATIOS						
	2.4	2.7	2.6	Current	2.7	2.9	5.8	2.5	2.1	1.8
	1.3	1.3	1.2		.9	1.1	2.5	1.5	1.2	1.2
	.8	.8	.7		.2	.5	1.1	1.0	.7	.9
	2.0	2.0	2.3	Quick	2.5	2.0	5.8	2.2	1.9	1.4
	1.1	1.0 (239)	1.1		(48) .7	(50) 1.0	2.3	1.4	1.0	1.0
	.5	.5	.5		.1	.3	.9	.8	1.0	.7
0 UND / 26 13.8 / 55 6.6		0 UND / 28 13.0 / 57 6.5	0 UND / 21 17.1 / 56 6.5	Sales/Receivables	0 UND / 0 UND / 37 10.0	0 UND / 3 123.8 / 30 12.2	0 UND / 13 28.5 / 65 5.7	14 25.3 / 48 7.7 / 57 6.4	1 377.0 / 40 9.1 / 54 6.7	10 35.6 / 41 9.0 / 70 5.2
				Cost of Sales/Inventory						
				Cost of Sales/Payables						
	7.7	6.2	6.3	Sales/Working Capital	6.5	6.1	3.6	5.7	5.7	10.2
	29.8	22.9	31.1		-271.5	92.2	8.2	20.6	29.7	43.7
	-39.4	-24.5	-26.4		-6.6	-20.8	77.7	NM	-23.3	-234.3
	17.3	15.3	24.5	EBIT/Interest	22.1	10.6	44.1	37.0	15.8	26.0
(183) 4.9		(203) 5.0	(170) 6.2		(26) 5.7	(28) 4.3	(26) 6.3	(30) 8.6	(22) 5.6	(38) 6.2
	1.4	1.5	1.4		1.5	.6	1.3	1.7	.9	2.9
	14.3	11.3	15.6	Net Profit + Depr., Dep., Amort./Cur. Mat. L/T/D						19.2
(38) 4.4		(37) 3.3	(32) 4.2							(12) 4.9
	1.3	1.9	.7							1.5
	.2	.2	.1	Fixed/Worth	.0	.1	.1	.1	.2	.5
	.7	.6	.5		.5	.4	.3	.3	.6	1.0
	3.3	3.7	3.7		NM	3.7	1.1	1.7	88.9	5.7
	.8	.8	.8	Debt/Worth	.7	.5	.3	1.1	1.2	1.6
	2.4	2.5	2.7		3.0	2.1	1.1	1.8	4.3	4.1
	14.8	17.6	15.0		-5.9	8.8	4.6	6.6	-8.4	30.2
	75.0	72.7	82.0	% Profit Before Taxes/Tangible Net Worth	87.0	86.5	66.9	110.6	158.9	63.0
(206) 30.5		(241) 29.8	(193) 27.6		(35) 35.0	(42) 24.7	(34) 26.8	(28) 30.0	(19) 38.2	(35) 27.6
	6.4	7.3	7.8		8.2	6.2	8.5	10.3	7.6	7.1
	20.5	20.6	23.2	% Profit Before Taxes/Total Assets	33.7	23.3	23.1	22.7	21.3	14.7
	8.0	8.9	8.7		12.5	7.8	7.6	12.4	8.4	5.7
	.7	1.2	1.5		-.1	.8	2.3	3.4	1.8	1.7
	56.4	65.9	118.8	Sales/Net Fixed Assets	613.8	234.7	74.4	136.8	81.6	101.4
	15.4	18.5	25.0		30.2	25.5	21.9	40.0	38.6	14.0
	5.0	5.3	6.7		4.8	8.9	4.9	16.6	6.2	4.4
	4.1	4.1	4.8	Sales/Total Assets	4.1	6.5	4.6	5.1	4.2	4.1
	2.3	2.2	2.7		2.0	3.2	1.7	3.3	2.8	2.5
	1.1	1.1	1.3		1.0	1.4	.7	2.2	1.4	1.4
	.8	1.2	.7	% Depr., Dep., Amort./Sales	1.2	.8	.7	.3	.8	.5
(189) 1.8		(209) 2.4	(170) 1.7		(27) 2.6	(34) 1.8	(29) 1.8	(27) 1.3	(20) 1.5	(33) 1.8
	4.8	5.1	3.5		11.0	4.0	3.2	2.4	3.4	3.7
	4.2	3.7	3.5	% Officers', Directors', Owners' Comp/Sales	5.1	2.2	6.4			
(64) 8.6		(67) 8.6	(68) 10.8		(16) 13.4	(22) 12.5	(15) 10.9			
	17.5	16.8	16.1		22.5	16.9	22.2			
	9637337M	2071392M	6929860M	Net Sales ($)	26538M	92374M	154483M	236269M	455108M	5965088M
	4998292M	1507209M	3894695M	Total Assets ($)	27312M	90137M	163869M	113099M	326254M	3174024M

M = $ thousand   MM = $ million
See Pages 11 through 21 for Explanation of Ratios and Data

Current Data Sorted By Assets   **Comparative Historical Data**

						Type of Statement		
	2	8 4	5	2	3	Unqualified	14	11
1	2					Reviewed	5	7
3	3	2	3	1	1	Compiled	3	4
2	7	5		1	1	Tax Returns	2	1
						Other	11	10

0-500M	7 (4/1-9/30/04) 500M-2MM	2-10MM	47 (10/1/04-3/31/05) 10-50MM	50-100MM	100-250MM		4/1/00- 3/31/01 ALL	4/1/01- 3/31/02 ALL
6	14	19	8	4	3	**NUMBER OF STATEMENTS**	35	33
%	%	%	%	%	%	**ASSETS**	%	%
	18.5	9.0				Cash & Equivalents	8.4	6.4
	39.8	49.6				Trade Receivables (net)	41.5	51.2
	4.0	1.5				Inventory	1.7	1.9
	1.0	7.4				All Other Current	8.8	4.8
	63.3	67.6				Total Current	60.4	64.4
	22.2	17.3				Fixed Assets (net)	22.3	19.3
	.2	1.7				Intangibles (net)	9.0	7.3
	14.4	13.5				All Other Non-Current	8.3	9.0
	100.0	100.0				Total	100.0	100.0
						LIABILITIES		
	16.6	13.7				Notes Payable-Short Term	17.7	26.0
	2.9	2.3				Cur. Mat.-L/T/D	3.8	3.4
	18.3	16.4				Trade Payables	14.4	12.1
	.1	1.2				Income Taxes Payable	.2	.6
	11.0	16.4				All Other Current	16.8	15.8
	48.9	50.0				Total Current	53.0	57.9
	13.8	11.6				Long-Term Debt	16.6	17.0
	.0	.4				Deferred Taxes	.2	.3
	5.8	1.6				All Other Non-Current	3.0	6.0
	31.5	36.3				Net Worth	27.2	18.8
	100.0	100.0				Total Liabilities & Net Worth	100.0	100.0
						INCOME DATA		
	100.0	100.0				Net Sales	100.0	100.0
						Gross Profit		
	95.5	93.1				Operating Expenses	93.4	95.5
	4.5	6.9				Operating Profit	6.6	4.5
	3.4	.9				All Other Expenses (net)	1.4	2.0
	1.2	6.1				Profit Before Taxes	5.2	2.5
						RATIOS		
	1.8	2.1					2.0	1.9
	1.2	1.4				Current	1.4	1.3
	.7	1.1					1.0	1.0
	1.8	2.0					1.8	1.7
	1.1	1.3				Quick	1.2	1.1
	.6	.8					.8	.8
	0 UND	32 11.4					34 10.6	39 9.4
	37 9.8	55 6.6				Sales/Receivables	53 6.9	52 7.1
	60 6.1	75 4.8					74 4.9	72 5.1
						Cost of Sales/Inventory		
						Cost of Sales/Payables		
	12.4	6.6					9.9	11.1
	52.4	13.1				Sales/Working Capital	14.2	30.5
	-37.0	135.9					453.9	-149.8
	11.1	24.3					9.2	8.7
	(11) 2.9	(15) 6.6				EBIT/Interest	(28) 3.4	(32) 3.1
	-5.0	1.5					1.8	1.3
						Net Profit + Depr., Dep., Amort./Cur. Mat. L/T/D		
	.0	.1					.2	.2
	.2	.6				Fixed/Worth	.6	.4
	4.4	1.3					5.2	2.5
	.8	.7					.8	1.1
	2.3	2.0				Debt/Worth	2.3	4.2
	15.3	3.4					12.7	-15.4
	96.9	84.1				% Profit Before Taxes/Tangible	73.5	88.2
	(12) 27.1	(17) 29.3				Net Worth	(28) 19.9	(24) 29.3
	-2.4	14.0					12.0	9.2
	17.1	18.0				% Profit Before Taxes/Total	14.2	16.7
	6.0	12.3				Assets	6.1	7.9
	-2.7	1.1					.9	1.4
	577.8	79.7					63.9	76.6
	57.6	24.1				Sales/Net Fixed Assets	34.8	32.3
	13.6	10.7					5.8	10.7
	5.9	4.5					4.3	5.1
	3.4	2.9				Sales/Total Assets	2.8	3.6
	1.6	2.1					1.4	2.3
	.1	.7					.4	.4
	(12) .5	(15) 1.4				% Depr., Dep., Amort./Sales	(25) 1.6	(28) 1.0
	6.8	3.1					3.9	2.6
						% Officers', Directors', Owners' Comp/Sales		
8526M	57391M	303000M	502451M	706077M	1253123M	Net Sales ($)	1476403M	3729224M
1252M	15372M	99369M	199012M	224877M	495114M	Total Assets ($)	700152M	609790M

M = $ thousand   MM = $ million

See Pages 11 through 21 for Explanation of Ratios and Data

Comparative Historical Data | **Current Data Sorted By Sales**

Type of Statement

	4/1/02-3/31/03	4/1/03-3/31/04	4/1/04-3/31/05	Type of Statement	0-1MM	1-3MM	3-5MM	5-10MM	10-25MM	25MM & OVER
	18	26	18	Unqualified			1	3	3	11
	9	3	6	Reviewed	1		1	1	3	
	5	10	3	Compiled	1	2				
		5	9	Tax Returns	1	4	2		1	1
	22	22	18	Other	1	3	2	4	6	2
	ALL	ALL	ALL		7 (4/1-9/30/04)			47 (10/1/04-3/31/05)		
	54	66	54	**NUMBER OF STATEMENTS**	4	9	6	8	13	14

Financial Data

	4/1/02-3/31/03 %	4/1/03-3/31/04 %	4/1/04-3/31/05 %		0-1MM %	1-3MM %	3-5MM %	5-10MM %	10-25MM %	25MM & OVER %
				ASSETS						
	9.2	7.7	13.5	Cash & Equivalents					8.3	11.0
	45.2	48.5	42.0	Trade Receivables (net)					47.1	46.7
	1.9	1.9	2.5	Inventory					.9	1.8
	8.7	8.0	5.3	All Other Current					3.9	7.3
	65.0	66.0	63.3	Total Current					60.2	66.8
	21.5	19.1	20.0	Fixed Assets (net)					13.6	15.6
	7.4	5.4	2.5	Intangibles (net)					.5	5.8
	6.1	9.5	14.2	All Other Non-Current					25.7	11.8
	100.0	100.0	100.0	Total					100.0	100.0
				LIABILITIES						
	18.5	12.9	15.6	Notes Payable-Short Term					14.9	10.2
	4.2	3.8	2.7	Cur. Mat.-L/T/D					1.8	4.3
	12.7	16.6	16.3	Trade Payables					20.7	15.5
	.3	.6	.6	Income Taxes Payable					1.4	.9
	17.4	19.8	15.6	All Other Current					25.7	14.1
	53.1	53.7	50.9	Total Current					64.5	44.9
	14.2	9.6	14.8	Long-Term Debt					5.6	15.7
	.6	.3	.3	Deferred Taxes					.5	.7
	4.1	4.6	3.4	All Other Non-Current					2.3	2.8
	28.0	31.9	30.6	Net Worth					27.1	35.9
	100.0	100.0	100.0	Total Liabilities & Net Worth					100.0	100.0
				INCOME DATA						
	100.0	100.0	100.0	Net Sales					100.0	100.0
				Gross Profit						
	94.5	93.2	92.7	Operating Expenses					94.8	93.2
	5.5	6.8	7.3	Operating Profit					5.2	6.8
	2.1	1.4	2.4	All Other Expenses (net)					.8	1.3
	3.4	5.4	4.9	Profit Before Taxes					4.4	5.5
				RATIOS						
	2.0	1.8	1.9	Current					1.6	2.2
	1.4	1.4	1.3						1.1	1.5
	1.0	1.0	.9						.5	1.0
	1.8	1.6	1.7	Quick					1.6	2.0
	1.1	1.1	1.1						1.0	1.2
	.7	.8	.8						.4	.9
	34 10.7	42 8.6	29 12.6	Sales/Receivables					32 11.5	47 7.8
	56 6.5	63 5.8	50 7.3						51 7.1	56 6.5
	68 5.3	77 4.7	72 5.1						87 4.2	79 4.6
				Cost of Sales/Inventory						
				Cost of Sales/Payables						
	9.1	7.2	8.2	Sales/Working Capital					13.9	8.2
	18.9	16.3	26.6						70.7	20.1
	NM	NM	-123.8						-6.3	483.8
	19.1	20.4	22.2	EBIT/Interest					11.9	56.7
	(48) 5.4	(54) 7.5	(41) 5.9						(11) 5.8	(13) 11.2
	1.9	2.0	1.5						1.5	1.6
	4.9	118.1	12.4	Net Profit + Depr., Dep.,						
	(13) 1.3	(15) 6.0	(15) 4.6	Amort./Cur. Mat. L/T/D						
	.3	1.7	2.3							
	.1	.1	.1	Fixed/Worth					.2	.1
	.7	.4	.4						.4	.4
	2.5	1.4	3.6						1.6	NM
	.9	1.0	1.0	Debt/Worth					1.3	1.0
	3.1	2.3	2.4						2.7	2.5
	18.0	6.7	12.6						8.9	NM
	101.9	82.8	87.3	% Profit Before Taxes/Tangible					87.4	103.0
	(45) 46.5	(55) 40.2	(44) 35.6	Net Worth					(12) 48.3	(11) 62.2
	8.1	12.1	4.8						12.7	21.2
	22.4	22.4	20.7	% Profit Before Taxes/Total					29.0	32.9
	7.9	11.2	9.8	Assets					6.7	13.1
	1.4	2.5	.7						.6	1.9
	118.8	112.0	112.5	Sales/Net Fixed Assets					89.6	62.2
	37.8	40.1	51.0						24.1	45.3
	8.7	11.7	13.0						13.4	14.8
	4.4	3.7	4.8	Sales/Total Assets					4.7	4.5
	2.7	2.7	3.0						3.5	3.2
	1.8	1.6	1.6						2.0	2.2
	.3	.6	.3	% Depr., Dep., Amort./Sales					.5	.3
	(46) 1.2	(52) 1.1	(45) .8						(11) .7	(13) .8
	3.8	2.5	3.2						2.3	1.5
	.8	1.1		% Officers', Directors',						
	(13) 3.1	(17) 6.3		Owners' Comp/Sales						
	4.6	16.6								
	2052429M	3230109M	2830568M	Net Sales ($)	2086M	17614M	22891M	60784M	199664M	2527529M
	943924M	1510231M	1034996M	Total Assets ($)	3164M	11064M	27508M	84224M	117038M	791998M

M = $ thousand   MM = $ million
See Pages 11 through 21 for Explanation of Ratios and Data

Current Data Sorted By Assets   Comparative Historical Data

						Type of Statement		
4	10	23	16	1	3	Unqualified	33	33
2	27	24	3			Reviewed	71	62
12	22	10	3			Compiled	87	92
26	15	4	1			Tax Returns	42	41
28	47	33	11		4	Other	118	125
	38 (4/1-9/30/04)		291 (10/1/04-3/31/05)				4/1/00-3/31/01	4/1/01-3/31/02
0-500M	500M-2MM	2-10MM	10-50MM	50-100MM	100-250MM		ALL	ALL
72	121	94	34	1	7	NUMBER OF STATEMENTS	351	353
%	%	%	%	%	%	ASSETS	%	%
28.4	12.9	10.5	11.4			Cash & Equivalents	13.7	14.6
41.5	56.1	61.9	54.7			Trade Receivables (net)	56.5	49.6
.2	.7	.0	.8			Inventory	.3	.2
4.6	4.7	5.6	9.8			All Other Current	2.8	5.2
74.7	74.5	78.0	76.7			Total Current	73.3	69.7
8.1	8.8	9.7	5.8			Fixed Assets (net)	13.4	13.5
3.1	3.2	3.7	8.8			Intangibles (net)	4.4	6.0
14.1	13.5	8.7	8.7			All Other Non-Current	8.9	10.9
100.0	100.0	100.0	100.0			Total	100.0	100.0
						LIABILITIES		
35.1	23.0	16.0	14.5			Notes Payable-Short Term	22.5	27.7
6.6	2.4	2.3	2.6			Cur. Mat.-L/T/D	3.7	3.1
10.3	7.5	6.8	9.6			Trade Payables	6.5	7.0
.8	1.0	1.7	.5			Income Taxes Payable	.7	1.0
16.1	20.7	23.2	27.9			All Other Current	30.4	21.4
69.0	54.6	49.8	55.1			Total Current	63.9	60.2
9.9	5.7	6.9	3.9			Long-Term Debt	10.5	10.9
.3	.4	.4	.1			Deferred Taxes	.5	.7
13.5	8.8	3.1	10.3			All Other Non-Current	8.9	6.5
7.4	30.5	39.7	30.6			Net Worth	16.2	21.7
100.0	100.0	100.0	100.0			Total Liabilities & Net Worth	100.0	100.0
						INCOME DATA		
100.0	100.0	100.0	100.0			Net Sales	100.0	100.0
						Gross Profit		
97.6	96.6	95.4	97.9			Operating Expenses	96.4	98.8
2.4	3.4	4.6	2.1			Operating Profit	3.6	1.2
.3	.0	1.1	.8			All Other Expenses (net)	-.6	.6
2.0	3.4	3.5	1.3			Profit Before Taxes	4.2	.6
						RATIOS		
2.9	2.3	2.9	1.8				2.6	2.7
1.4	1.5	1.5	1.4			Current	1.6	1.4
.9	1.0	1.2	1.1				1.1	.9
2.4	2.1	2.8	1.7				2.5	2.6
1.3	(120) 1.5	1.4	1.2			Quick	1.5	1.3
.7	.9	1.1	.9				1.0	.8
0 UND	27 13.6	35 10.5	27 13.3				28 12.9	21 17.6
26 13.9	38 9.5	46 7.9	39 9.3			Sales/Receivables	42 8.7	34 10.8
42 8.7	49 7.4	65 5.6	47 7.7				55 6.6	51 7.1
						Cost of Sales/Inventory		
						Cost of Sales/Payables		
12.7	11.9	10.3	14.0				11.5	11.6
47.7	22.0	16.1	26.8			Sales/Working Capital	21.9	29.9
-298.8	-320.0	50.5	89.3				118.3	-162.3
16.1	19.5	31.8	16.0				18.0	10.2
(46) 6.7	(107) 5.6	(84) 7.6	(28) 6.3			EBIT/Interest	(305) 5.8	(300) 2.0
-1.2	1.6	3.7	2.2				1.6	-2.2
		4.7					13.8	14.9
	(15) 3.1					Net Profit + Depr., Dep., Amort./Cur. Mat. L /T/D	(44) 3.7	(40) 1.9
		1.6					1.6	-1.8
.0	.0	.1	.1				.1	.1
.2	.2	.2	.2			Fixed/Worth	.3	.3
UND	1.6	.4	.4				1.1	1.9
1.0	.8	.6	1.5				.7	.7
2.4	1.7	1.6	2.6			Debt/Worth	1.9	2.2
UND	16.4	5.2	6.1				7.5	14.4
124.8	58.4	69.2	57.0				76.2	57.2
(54) 67.2	(95) 36.6	(87) 35.1	(30) 28.3			% Profit Before Taxes/Tangible Net Worth	(294) 41.4	(282) 18.0
2.9	7.8	12.8	16.7				16.4	-15.8
47.8	25.2	24.6	13.0				33.0	21.3
17.4	14.0	10.3	8.5			% Profit Before Taxes/Total Assets	14.3	4.8
-1.7	2.7	4.1	4.0				2.5	-10.6
999.8	523.3	207.0	188.5				157.3	185.3
226.0	133.6	100.7	105.9			Sales/Net Fixed Assets	65.3	69.2
112.0	52.5	52.5	64.0				30.8	30.2
15.1	7.6	6.6	6.8				7.8	8.0
7.4	5.6	5.1	5.5			Sales/Total Assets	5.4	5.3
5.2	4.0	3.2	3.9				4.0	3.9
.1	.1	.2	.1				.3	.2
(29) .3	(82) .3	(70) .3	(27) .3			% Depr., Dep., Amort./Sales	(262) .6	(249) .6
.7	.8	.7	.8				1.2	1.2
2.1	2.8	2.8					2.3	2.0
(35) 3.3	(48) 5.4	(24) 4.4				% Officers', Directors', Owners' Comp/Sales	(143) 5.0	(143) 4.8
7.7	9.0	7.9					10.0	9.1
223189M	1100947M	2491880M	4109719M	170323M	2488922M	Net Sales ($)	10598039M	8571913M
16224M	130895M	425829M	673393M	73681M	946487M	Total Assets ($)	2294685M	1875023M

M = $ thousand   MM = $ million

See Pages 11 through 21 for Explanation of Ratios and Data

© RMA 2005

Comparative Historical Data | **Current Data Sorted By Sales**

Type of Statement	50 55 56 46 121	51 57 82 49 137	57 56 47 46 123	0-1MM	1-3MM	3-5MM	5-10MM	10-25MM	25MM & OVER
Unqualified				3	3	3	8	7	33
Reviewed				1	3	7	21	12	12
Compiled				3	9	9	11	9	6
Tax Returns				7	17	7	8	2	5
Other				8	22	16	23	21	33
	4/1/02-3/31/03 ALL	4/1/03-3/31/04 ALL	4/1/04-3/31/05 ALL	\<— 38 (4/1-9/30/04) —\>		\<— 291 (10/1/04-3/31/05) —\>			
NUMBER OF STATEMENTS	328	376	329	22	54	42	71	51	89
ASSETS	%	%	%	%	%	%	%	%	%
Cash & Equivalents	14.9	12.9	15.5	28.6	19.2	19.5	11.5	10.4	14.1
Trade Receivables (net)	47.8	49.9	53.9	39.9	44.4	51.2	58.0	65.4	54.6
Inventory	.3	.5	.5	.0	.1	.4	1.2	.0	.6
All Other Current	5.8	5.0	5.5	4.7	7.2	5.5	4.0	4.5	6.2
Total Current	68.8	68.3	75.3	73.1	70.9	76.6	74.7	80.3	75.6
Fixed Assets (net)	14.4	12.7	8.9	9.1	11.9	6.0	9.3	7.3	8.9
Intangibles (net)	6.0	7.0	4.2	4.8	4.3	3.5	3.5	4.0	4.8
All Other Non-Current	10.8	12.0	11.6	13.0	12.9	13.9	12.4	8.4	10.6
Total	100.0	100.0	100.0	100.0	100.0	100.0	100.0	100.0	100.0
LIABILITIES									
Notes Payable-Short Term	19.7	22.2	22.5	19.9	30.6	26.4	25.4	21.5	14.7
Cur. Mat.-L/T/D	2.4	2.6	3.3	17.3	1.7	1.3	3.7	2.1	2.1
Trade Payables	7.3	7.1	8.1	15.3	6.6	5.2	10.2	5.4	8.5
Income Taxes Payable	.9	.6	1.1	1.0	2.3	1.2	.5	.6	1.0
All Other Current	22.4	20.6	21.1	13.7	13.3	19.3	21.7	21.0	28.1
Total Current	52.7	53.1	56.1	67.2	54.6	53.4	61.5	50.6	54.4
Long-Term Debt	8.1	10.5	7.0	15.8	11.8	6.2	4.3	6.2	4.9
Deferred Taxes	.6	.5	.3	.0	.4	.2	.5	.1	.4
All Other Non-Current	7.3	8.6	8.3	8.8	7.1	16.4	9.5	7.0	5.0
Net Worth	31.4	27.3	28.3	8.2	26.0	23.8	24.3	36.1	35.4
Total Liabilities & Net Worth	100.0	100.0	100.0	100.0	100.0	100.0	100.0	100.0	100.0
INCOME DATA									
Net Sales	100.0	100.0	100.0	100.0	100.0	100.0	100.0	100.0	100.0
Gross Profit									
Operating Expenses	98.0	96.8	96.6	95.9	94.6	96.9	97.2	96.6	97.5
Operating Profit	2.0	3.2	3.4	4.1	5.4	3.1	2.8	3.4	2.5
All Other Expenses (net)	.9	.9	.5	3.1	-.1	.5	-.2	.8	.4
Profit Before Taxes	1.2	2.3	2.9	1.0	5.5	2.7	3.0	2.5	2.1
RATIOS									
Current	2.3	2.6	2.4	4.1	3.1	2.5	2.2	2.9	2.0
	1.4	1.4	1.5	1.3	1.8	1.5	1.4	1.7	1.4
	.9	1.0	1.1	.9	.9	1.1	.9	1.2	1.1
Quick	2.2	2.4	(328) 2.3	3.9	2.8	2.3	1.9	2.8	1.9
	(327) 1.3	1.3	1.4	1.2	1.6	1.5	1.3	1.6	(88) 1.3
	.8	.8	.9	.7	.8	1.0	.9	1.0	1.0
Sales/Receivables	18 20.3	15 24.5	25 14.6	0 UND	17 21.9	23 16.2	27 13.4	33 10.9	20 17.8
	37 9.9	40 9.1	38 9.5	28 12.9	37 9.9	35 10.5	41 8.9	41 10.9	39 9.3
	50 7.2	54 6.7	53 6.9	82 4.4	46 7.9	48 7.6	55 6.7	64 5.7	52 7.0
Cost of Sales/Inventory									
Cost of Sales/Payables									
Sales/Working Capital	11.3	10.3	11.7	6.7	6.9	10.2	13.4	10.7	15.4
	30.0	28.8	22.2	20.3	15.5	25.7	27.1	15.1	27.5
	-251.9	-571.5	204.7	UND	-139.7	196.5	-172.1	42.2	130.2
EBIT/Interest	14.6	19.7	19.3		16.5	32.2	11.8	18.4	23.5
	(259) 3.3	(317) 4.2	(272) 6.6		(46) 5.1	(33) 7.3	(64) 5.4	(44) 6.1	(77) 9.7
	-.8	.2	2.1		.4	1.0	2.3	1.8	4.6
Net Profit + Depr., Dep., Amort./Cur. Mat. L/T/D	5.3	13.9	6.7						6.7
	(26) 2.4	(39) 3.5	(29) 3.4						(17) 4.3
	.5	.4	1.3						1.6
Fixed/Worth	.1	.1	.0	.0	.0	.0	.0	.1	.1
	.3	.3	.2	.1	.2	.1	.1	.2	.2
	2.0	2.8	1.0	UND	1.9	.4	UND	.4	.5
Debt/Worth	.6	.8	.8	.4	.6	.7	1.0	.6	1.0
	1.7	2.0	1.9	2.1	1.6	1.8	1.9	1.8	2.5
	13.9	22.5	9.2	-91.3	UND	5.1	UND	6.3	6.0
% Profit Before Taxes/Tangible Net Worth	60.6	73.6	71.5	100.0	78.9	87.8	71.3	74.8	57.2
	(269) 22.1	(295) 25.9	(272) 36.3	(16) 66.6	(41) 43.6	(35) 37.0	(54) 34.6	(47) 32.1	(79) 33.4
	-1.7	6.8	10.6	-2.2	9.8	.0	5.4	10.5	16.8
% Profit Before Taxes/Total Assets	19.4	20.5	25.0	29.5	34.5	28.3	25.4	23.2	16.9
	5.3	6.4	11.3	2.2	17.7	20.0	10.8	8.7	10.7
	-3.8	-1.0	2.7	-3.9		-1.2	2.7	2.8	4.5
Sales/Net Fixed Assets	193.3	264.2	417.1	UND	482.8	689.6	514.7	181.1	331.1
	71.7	91.8	129.0	464.0	115.9	187.1	177.8	106.7	115.4
	33.2	37.1	58.2	52.4	26.5	65.4	63.1	66.0	62.4
Sales/Total Assets	7.4	7.6	7.7	8.0	6.7	9.5	7.8	7.3	10.0
	5.3	5.1	5.7	3.7	5.0	5.9	5.6	5.8	6.0
	3.5	3.3	4.0	2.0	2.6	4.0	4.2	4.1	4.7
% Depr., Dep., Amort./Sales	.2	.2	.1		.2	.1	.1	.2	.2
	(246) .5	(279) .4	(216) .3		(31) .7	(26) .3	(45) .2	(39) .3	(69) .3
	1.2	1.1	.8		1.1	1.0	.6	.5	.7
% Officers', Directors', Owners' Comp/Sales	2.0	1.6	2.2		3.2	2.6	2.6	1.4	1.4
	(130) 3.8	(141) 3.3	(114) 4.6		(29) 6.2	(18) 5.5	(29) 4.7	(13) 4.2	(19) 1.7
	7.9	6.7	8.3		10.4	9.5	6.5	5.4	3.5
Net Sales ($)	18439070M	13625838M	10584980M	9336M	103077M	168047M	502364M	781660M	9020496M
Total Assets ($)	2671059M	3537692M	2266509M	4815M	34554M	47017M	217390M	173834M	1788899M

M = $ thousand   MM = $ million

See Pages 11 through 21 for Explanation of Ratios and Data

Current Data Sorted By Assets | Comparative Historical Data

Type of Statement	0-500M	500M-2MM	2-10MM	10-50MM	50-100MM	100-250MM	4/1/00-3/31/01 ALL	4/1/01-3/31/02 ALL
Unqualified	1	3	16	15	4	5	34	39
Reviewed	4	13	32	4			39	39
Compiled	9	25	7				59	61
Tax Returns	12	15	6				21	18
Other	14	32	29	16	4	6	108	87
	33 (4/1-9/30/04)			239 (10/1/04-3/31/05)				
NUMBER OF STATEMENTS	40	88	90	35	8	11	261	244

ASSETS	0-500M %	500M-2MM %	2-10MM %	10-50MM %	50-100MM %	100-250MM %	ALL %	ALL %
Cash & Equivalents	26.0	16.6	9.4	13.5		7.4	9.8	11.5
Trade Receivables (net)	36.0	51.3	62.3	55.6		44.3	58.9	53.4
Inventory	.0	.6	.1	.0		.1	.6	.7
All Other Current	7.1	4.5	7.3	4.7		6.0	3.9	5.2
Total Current	69.1	73.0	79.1	73.8		57.7	73.3	70.8
Fixed Assets (net)	12.0	11.7	8.6	6.9		12.4	10.2	11.5
Intangibles (net)	3.5	4.3	3.8	12.3		18.2	7.6	8.5
All Other Non-Current	15.4	11.0	8.6	7.0		11.7	9.1	9.1
Total	100.0	100.0	100.0	100.0		100.0	100.0	100.0
LIABILITIES								
Notes Payable-Short Term	26.3	22.2	22.7	13.4		2.6	19.7	17.8
Cur. Mat.-L/T/D	16.2	3.8	1.3	3.0		1.6	3.0	4.3
Trade Payables	7.8	8.4	7.2	7.1		6.2	8.1	6.8
Income Taxes Payable	.0	1.1	.1	.3		.8	.5	.5
All Other Current	17.5	16.9	23.5	29.2		16.2	26.1	22.0
Total Current	67.8	52.5	54.9	53.0		27.5	57.4	51.3
Long-Term Debt	21.6	8.0	3.7	4.5		18.9	8.9	8.9
Deferred Taxes	.0	.2	.1	.2		1.5	.4	.3
All Other Non-Current	3.1	5.5	3.3	6.1		14.4	5.9	5.5
Net Worth	7.5	33.9	38.0	36.2		37.7	27.4	34.0
Total Liabilities & Net Worth	100.0	100.0	100.0	100.0		100.0	100.0	100.0
INCOME DATA								
Net Sales	100.0	100.0	100.0	100.0		100.0	100.0	100.0
Gross Profit								
Operating Expenses	98.8	97.0	97.8	96.9		94.0	97.5	98.4
Operating Profit	1.2	3.0	2.2	3.1		6.0	2.5	1.6
All Other Expenses (net)	.2	.5	.1	.3		.2	.2	.4
Profit Before Taxes	1.0	2.5	2.1	2.9		5.8	2.3	1.1

RATIOS	0-500M	500M-2MM	2-10MM	10-50MM	50-100MM	100-250MM	ALL	ALL
Current	2.8	2.3	2.3	1.9		3.0	2.4	2.7
	1.0	1.4	1.4	1.4		1.8	1.4	1.5
	.8	1.0	1.1	1.1		1.5	1.1	1.1
Quick	2.4	2.3	2.2	1.8		3.0	2.2	2.5
	(39) 1.0	1.3	1.3	1.3		1.6	1.3	1.4
	.5	.9	1.0	1.0		1.4	1.0	.9
Sales/Receivables	0 UND	20 17.9	28 13.1	35 10.4		44 8.3	28 13.1	24 15.3
	12 31.7	34 10.8	40 9.0	43 8.6		48 7.5	40 9.1	38 9.6
	30 12.1	46 7.9	53 6.9	58 6.3		53 6.9	56 6.6	50 7.3
Cost of Sales/Inventory								
Cost of Sales/Payables								
Sales/Working Capital	45.7	13.4	13.2	11.2		8.6	11.6	11.5
	999.4	33.5	24.4	27.3		10.8	26.7	25.2
	−58.1	NM	81.0	159.4		21.1	186.9	226.2
EBIT/Interest	11.5	12.7	23.3	21.1			12.2	7.5
	(25) 1.3	(75) 4.2	(80) 6.1	(31) 10.1			(219) 3.7	(211) 2.3
	−12.9	1.4	1.8	3.2			1.3	−.7
Net Profit + Depr., Dep., Amort./Cur. Mat. L/T/D							7.6	4.6
							(34) 2.4	(32) 1.2
							1.3	.0
Fixed/Worth	.1	.1	.1	.1		.2	.1	.1
	.3	.2	.2	.3		.4	.3	.3
	7.3	.7	.5	.8		1.6	1.2	2.0
Debt/Worth	.6	.8	.7	1.1		1.3	.8	.6
	2.9	1.9	1.9	2.7		2.1	2.1	2.0
	−66.2	7.5	5.2	6.2		11.3	7.8	15.1
% Profit Before Taxes/Tangible Net Worth	101.3	59.1	67.5	65.5			59.8	49.8
	(29) 25.0	(74) 33.7	(81) 24.9	(31) 47.5			(211) 32.6	(188) 15.7
	−20.0	10.1	7.7	30.8			12.9	−9.7
% Profit Before Taxes/Total Assets	30.3	22.9	18.7	17.8		16.7	20.5	15.5
	6.8	10.2	9.5	10.3		9.1	9.3	3.8
	−15.4	1.9	1.9	6.3		2.6	1.6	−7.0
Sales/Net Fixed Assets	999.8	350.0	256.7	212.7		85.0	178.0	164.8
	278.5	96.1	119.3	106.0		76.4	81.3	63.1
	68.0	43.0	49.4	57.0		49.1	41.3	35.9
Sales/Total Assets	23.7	8.4	8.3	6.7		4.0	8.0	8.0
	11.0	6.1	5.6	4.5		3.3	5.7	5.3
	5.9	4.6	3.9	3.6		2.0	4.0	3.7
% Depr., Dep., Amort./Sales	.2	.2	.1	.3			.2	.3
	(24) .4	(68) .3	(77) .3	(27) .3			(193) .4	(181) .5
	.7	.8		.6	.6		.8	.9
% Officers', Directors', Owners' Comp/Sales	1.7	2.0	1.2				1.3	1.3
	(19) 3.2	(45) 3.3	(33) 1.9				(88) 2.7	(81) 2.4
	6.1	5.0	3.5				5.8	4.3
Net Sales ($)	157121M	811160M	2696585M	4542059M	1528814M	5478769M	17375546M	16311238M
Total Assets ($)	9060M	95789M	375652M	780301M	575450M	1733296M	3263274M	3626169M

M = $ thousand   MM = $ million
See Pages 11 through 21 for Explanation of Ratios and Data

Comparative Historical Data   **Current Data Sorted By Sales**

Type of Statement									
Unqualified	52	42	44	1	1	2	3	1	37
Reviewed	51	38	53		2	3	13	20	14
Compiled	57	83	41	3	7	10	9	9	3
Tax Returns	14	22	33	4	9	3	10	5	2
Other	88	109	101	3	10	8	16	26	38
	4/1/02-3/31/03 ALL	4/1/03-3/31/04 ALL	4/1/04-3/31/05 ALL	33 (4/1-9/30/04)			239 (10/1/04-3/31/05)		
				0-1MM	1-3MM	3-5MM	5-10MM	10-25MM	25MM & OVER
NUMBER OF STATEMENTS	262	294	272	11	29	26	51	61	94
	%	%	%	%	%	%	%	%	%
ASSETS									
Cash & Equivalents	11.7	14.7	14.6	30.6	16.2	15.2	13.4	12.4	14.2
Trade Receivables (net)	54.8	50.4	52.6	17.0	40.0	55.2	57.1	59.1	53.2
Inventory	.7	.9	.3	.0	.7	.6	.4	.1	.1
All Other Current	6.4	6.9	6.0	13.0	7.1	7.3	3.3	5.0	6.5
Total Current	73.6	72.9	73.4	60.6	63.9	78.2	74.2	76.6	74.1
Fixed Assets (net)	9.6	10.6	10.1	30.4	11.3	6.1	9.4	11.7	7.9
Intangibles (net)	8.3	6.2	6.1	.0	7.3	3.9	4.4	4.4	8.9
All Other Non-Current	8.5	10.2	10.4	9.0	17.5	11.8	11.9	7.3	9.1
Total	100.0	100.0	100.0	100.0	100.0	100.0	100.0	100.0	100.0
LIABILITIES									
Notes Payable-Short Term	22.0	21.8	20.5	28.4	22.8	27.7	27.9	19.4	13.7
Cur. Mat.-L/T/D	5.3	3.3	4.6	1.7	22.9	3.3	3.6	1.8	2.1
Trade Payables	6.7	7.3	7.7	2.8	9.5	8.7	7.7	8.0	7.1
Income Taxes Payable	.5	.5	.5	.0	.6	.2	1.5	.0	.3
All Other Current	22.1	20.7	20.8	12.2	13.8	12.6	12.9	22.8	29.3
Total Current	56.5	53.7	54.1	45.2	69.6	52.5	53.5	52.0	52.6
Long-Term Debt	9.1	11.1	8.6	10.2	16.4	4.0	15.6	5.6	5.5
Deferred Taxes	.2	.2	-.2	.0	.0	.4	.2	.0	.3
All Other Non-Current	7.8	8.7	5.0	4.4	6.6	4.2	1.8	4.0	7.0
Net Worth	26.5	26.3	32.1	40.2	7.4	38.9	28.8	38.3	34.7
Total Liabilities & Net Worth	100.0	100.0	100.0	100.0	100.0	100.0	100.0	100.0	100.0
INCOME DATA									
Net Sales	100.0	100.0	100.0	100.0	100.0	100.0	100.0	100.0	100.0
Gross Profit									
Operating Expenses	98.5	97.0	97.3	91.9	99.7	97.2	97.2	97.9	97.0
Operating Profit	1.5	3.0	2.7	8.1	.3	2.8	2.8	2.1	3.0
All Other Expenses (net)	.6	.7	.3	.4	.5	.5	.2	.2	.3
Profit Before Taxes	.9	2.2	2.4	7.8	-.2	2.3	2.7	1.9	2.7
RATIOS									
Current	2.3	2.4	2.3	12.8	1.9	2.4	2.8	2.5	1.9
	1.5	1.5	1.4	1.3	1.0	1.4	1.3	1.6	1.4
	1.0	1.0	1.0	.6	.7	1.0	1.0	1.1	1.1
Quick	2.0	2.1	2.1	2.8	1.6	2.3	2.6	2.3	1.7
	1.4	1.3 (271)	1.3	1.3	1.0	(25) 1.2	1.3	1.5	1.3
	.9	.9	.9	.4	.6	.9	.9	1.0	1.0
Sales/Receivables	25 14.3	22 16.7	20 17.9	0 UND	7 53.8	22 16.2	26 14.2	25 14.7	20 18.4
	38 9.5	37 10.0	38 9.7	4 97.8	30 12.2	40 9.1	36 10.0	38 9.7	41 8.9
	52 7.0	51 7.2	49 7.5	27 13.7	43 8.4	54 6.8	58 6.3	47 7.7	49 7.4
Cost of Sales/Inventory									
Cost of Sales/Payables									
Sales/Working Capital	11.1	11.0	13.1	11.5	12.9	12.4	13.5	12.7	13.2
	22.8	26.8	30.2	44.2	UND	21.8	29.0	27.0	27.9
	271.7	NM	936.1	-11.8	-49.5	999.8	999.8	120.5	141.9
EBIT/Interest	10.9	18.9	18.3		6.4	12.3	17.0	17.0	24.3
	(226) 2.6	(252) 5.1	(227) 5.2		(22) .8	(20) 2.2	(47) 4.6	(53) 5.2	(80) 8.9
	-.3	.9	1.5		-14.4	-.6	1.7	1.7	3.0
Net Profit + Depr., Dep., Amort./Cur. Mat. L/T/D	3.8	6.7	20.2						29.4
	(37) 1.4	(36) 2.6	(26) 6.3					(17)	10.1
	.1	.5	3.0						4.4
Fixed/Worth	.1	.1	.1	.1	.1	.0	.1	.1	.1
	.2	.2	.2	.7	.3	.1	.2	.2	.2
	1.0	1.2	.7	2.8	NM	.6	1.9	.8	.5
Debt/Worth	.8	.9	.8	.3	1.2	.6	.8	.5	1.2
	2.2	2.4	2.2	1.3	2.4	1.9	1.9	1.5	2.3
	11.4	11.4	7.2	4.1	-3.9	7.3	44.9	5.8	6.1
% Profit Before Taxes/Tangible Net Worth	44.9	61.0	66.9	114.6	98.7	56.9	67.5	58.3	73.9
	(208) 15.9	(237) 25.4	(230) 33.4	(10) 30.6	(20) 20.6	(23) 25.2	(41) 37.4	(52) 20.4	(84) 43.5
	-3.2	3.8	8.4	9.9	-27.3	-6.3	17.3	8.0	22.9
% Profit Before Taxes/Total Assets	14.4	19.4	21.6	26.4	16.2	30.2	22.9	18.9	21.2
	4.5	6.9	9.7	12.2	6.1	5.8	12.1	6.3	11.7
	-3.2	-.1	2.1	5.9	-14.2	-3.8	2.4	2.0	4.4
Sales/Net Fixed Assets	218.9	261.0	318.4	848.0	370.2	598.8	209.8	273.4	351.2
	85.9	90.6	116.0	61.2	134.4	227.4	91.7	119.6	118.0
	38.9	42.2	49.3	3.3	43.8	66.5	45.6	46.4	53.8
Sales/Total Assets	7.7	7.8	8.4	8.1	16.6	7.3	8.4	8.0	9.0
	5.3	5.5	5.7	3.1	6.8	5.2	5.8	6.5	5.4
	3.6	3.6	3.9	.8	3.6	4.0	3.8	4.6	3.6
% Depr., Dep., Amort./Sales	.2	.2	.2		.3	.2	.2	.2	.1
	(202) .5	(227) .5	(210) .3		(19) .4	(17) .3	(42) .3	(51) .3	(74) .3
	1.0	.9	.7		1.6	.7	.8	.7	.6
% Officers', Directors', Owners' Comp/Sales	1.5	1.5	1.6		2.8	1.8	2.4	1.4	.2
	(78) 2.8	(99) 3.1	(99) 2.9		(14) 4.8	(14) 3.3	(28) 3.6	(28) 2.0	(12) 1.0
	4.7	5.5	4.9		9.5	5.0	5.4	3.4	1.4
Net Sales ($)	15867483M	17053670M	15214508M	5904M	61530M	102081M	363300M	962672M	13719021M
Total Assets ($)	3939254M	3551183M	3569548M	3259M	14264M	23578M	69596M	161423M	3297428M

© RMA 2005

M = $ thousand   MM = $ million
See Pages 11 through 21 for Explanation of Ratios and Data

Current Data Sorted By Assets | **Comparative Historical Data**

Type of Statement	0-500M	500M-2MM	2-10MM	10-50MM	50-100MM	100-250MM		4/1/00-3/31/01 ALL	4/1/01-3/31/02 ALL
Unqualified			1	5		1		3	8
Reviewed		5	10	2				14	12
Compiled	3	11	6					26	26
Tax Returns	16	7	2					8	8
Other	5	9	10	3				23	36
		20 (4/1-9/30/04)		76 (10/1/04-3/31/05)				74	90
NUMBER OF STATEMENTS	24	32	29	10	1			74	90
	%	%	%	%	%	%		%	%
ASSETS									
Cash & Equivalents	17.7	9.9	7.1	13.0				7.8	9.4
Trade Receivables (net)	24.1	28.2	33.3	24.3			D	32.7	29.3
Inventory	7.7	12.7	8.3	7.7			A	11.0	10.4
All Other Current	.3	.6	2.0	1.4			T	1.7	1.9
Total Current	49.7	51.4	50.8	46.4			A	53.2	51.0
Fixed Assets (net)	34.2	40.6	37.8	28.3				34.9	35.6
Intangibles (net)	11.6	2.3	4.7	14.6			N	4.0	7.6
All Other Non-Current	4.5	5.8	6.7	10.6			O	7.9	5.8
Total	100.0	100.0	100.0	100.0			T	100.0	100.0
LIABILITIES							A		
Notes Payable-Short Term	11.1	8.0	9.8	6.8			V	10.4	9.0
Cur. Mat.-L/T/D	7.1	7.4	5.6	3.1			A	8.0	7.4
Trade Payables	16.2	11.4	10.5	7.7			I	15.6	15.6
Income Taxes Payable	.0	.2	.4	.2			L	.3	.5
All Other Current	24.6	8.6	10.3	11.2			A	8.2	10.3
Total Current	59.0	35.6	36.7	29.0			B	42.5	42.8
Long-Term Debt	34.4	29.1	21.9	18.4			L	29.3	24.5
Deferred Taxes	.0	.1	1.0	.5			E	.2	.6
All Other Non-Current	14.2	3.0	5.5	7.0				5.9	8.0
Net Worth	-7.7	32.2	34.9	45.0				22.1	24.2
Total Liabilities & Net Worth	100.0	100.0	100.0	100.0				100.0	100.0
INCOME DATA									
Net Sales	100.0	100.0	100.0	100.0				100.0	100.0
Gross Profit									
Operating Expenses	93.4	94.7	95.5	93.6				95.4	97.5
Operating Profit	6.6	5.3	4.5	6.4				4.6	2.5
All Other Expenses (net)	1.9	.5	.8	1.3				2.2	1.0
Profit Before Taxes	4.7	4.8	3.7	5.1				2.4	1.6
RATIOS									
Current	1.4	2.8	2.1	3.8				1.9	2.0
	.9	1.5	1.3	1.6				1.3	1.3
	.6	1.0	1.0	1.3				.9	.9
Quick	1.3	2.3	1.6	2.3				1.4	1.9
	.8	1.2	1.0	1.5				.9	.9
	.4	.7	.8	.9				.6	.6
Sales/Receivables	2 153.3	28 12.9	41 8.9	26 13.8				31 11.7	30 12.1
	27 13.3	33 11.1	49 7.4	45 8.0				45 8.1	41 8.9
	42 8.7	51 7.2	65 5.6	55 6.6				61 6.0	53 6.9
Cost of Sales/Inventory									
Cost of Sales/Payables									
Sales/Working Capital	25.7	6.6	9.1	3.4				9.2	8.8
	UND	15.0	21.3	11.2				17.8	22.6
	-12.8	828.5	NM	29.2				-40.0	-31.1
EBIT/Interest	11.4	12.3	14.8	9.3				4.4	5.3
	(18) 3.4	(31) 3.4	(27) 2.5	4.5				(65) 1.6	(80) 1.6
	-1.5	1.4	.9	2.9				.4	-.2
Net Profit + Depr., Dep., Amort./Cur. Mat. L/T/D								2.5	3.2
								(19) 1.2	(19) 1.4
								.6	.3
Fixed/Worth	2.2	.4	.6	.5				.7	.5
	-7.3	1.4	1.1	1.1				1.5	1.5
	-.6	4.5	3.7	1.6				5.8	10.7
Debt/Worth	5.9	.6	1.0	.9				1.0	.9
	-18.4	2.4	1.9	1.9				2.9	2.6
	-3.4	11.0	5.0	4.1				15.2	20.6
% Profit Before Taxes/Tangible Net Worth	300.0	77.0	45.2	45.5				46.4	43.3
	(11) 37.7	(27) 29.2	(26) 12.2	30.2				(60) 18.3	(69) 11.6
	12.3	10.6	-2.9	17.1				-6.5	-8.9
% Profit Before Taxes/Total Assets	22.9	21.5	18.0	12.6				11.8	13.1
	7.0	8.7	5.2	7.5				3.7	3.0
	-12.6	2.1	-.7	4.5				-3.1	-4.2
Sales/Net Fixed Assets	30.5	11.0	12.2	16.8				16.8	17.3
	14.8	6.0	6.0	9.0				6.2	7.8
	4.2	3.9	3.3	2.5				4.3	4.3
Sales/Total Assets	4.2	3.1	3.1	3.0				3.1	3.4
	3.2	2.6	2.2	1.4				2.3	2.4
	1.9	1.8	1.5	.9				1.8	1.6
% Depr., Dep., Amort./Sales	1.0	2.4	2.7					1.9	2.0
	(16) 2.6	(29) 4.4	(26) 4.9					(67) 4.2	(81) 3.9
	4.3	7.3	6.1					6.4	6.1
% Officers', Directors', Owners' Comp/Sales	3.8	3.3	2.6					4.8	4.2
	(17) 7.2	(19) 4.5	(12) 4.6					(37) 5.8	(48) 5.9
	15.1	9.1	6.7					13.7	7.5
Net Sales ($)	22023M	93352M	272526M	393368M	93652M			823896M	630504M
Total Assets ($)	6534M	35142M	120950M	229798M	81495M			485930M	275784M

M = $ thousand   MM = $ million

See Pages 11 through 21 for Explanation of Ratios and Data

Comparative Historical Data				Current Data Sorted By Sales					
7	6	7	**Type of Statement**						
9	12	17	Unqualified						
17	23	20	Reviewed	1	1	2	1	1	5
11	16	25	Compiled	2	7	6	8	5	2
28	34	27	Tax Returns	9	14	2	3	2	
4/1/02-	4/1/03-	4/1/04-	Other	4	7	3	5	6	2
3/31/03	3/31/04	3/31/05		20 (4/1-9/30/04)			76 (10/1/04-3/31/05)		
ALL	ALL	ALL		0-1MM	1-3MM	3-5MM	5-10MM	10-25MM	25MM & OVER
72	91	96	**NUMBER OF STATEMENTS**	16	29	13	17	14	7
%	%	%	**ASSETS**	%	%	%	%	%	%
10.8	12.2	11.3	Cash & Equivalents	11.6	16.0	8.8	6.1	10.0	
26.5	29.9	28.1	Trade Receivables (net)	20.4	24.3	31.4	33.1	37.4	
9.5	9.2	9.4	Inventory	8.7	12.4	7.6	10.5	6.8	
1.8	2.6	1.0	All Other Current	.2	.8	.1	1.4	2.5	
48.6	53.9	50.0	Total Current	40.8	53.5	48.0	51.1	56.7	
35.8	32.2	36.6	Fixed Assets (net)	40.8	35.8	43.3	39.0	30.7	
5.2	5.3	7.3	Intangibles (net)	16.6	3.0	3.9	3.5	1.6	
10.4	8.5	6.2	All Other Non-Current	1.7	7.7	4.7	6.4	11.0	
100.0	100.0	100.0	Total	100.0	100.0	100.0	100.0	100.0	
			LIABILITIES						
11.9	9.2	9.1	Notes Payable-Short Term	6.4	8.7	11.7	10.2	9.2	
5.9	6.8	6.4	Cur. Mat.-L/T/D	9.0	5.1	10.0	6.0	3.9	
14.8	15.4	11.9	Trade Payables	15.7	11.4	12.2	14.1	7.2	
.2	.3	.2	Income Taxes Payable	.0	.2	.0	.2	.7	
8.9	11.5	13.4	All Other Current	21.2	14.9	5.7	8.9	15.6	
41.8	43.2	40.9	Total Current	52.3	40.2	39.7	39.3	36.5	
24.7	22.6	27.0	Long-Term Debt	38.6	32.6	28.6	19.3	16.4	
.5	.2	.4	Deferred Taxes	.0	.1	.3	1.0	.8	
6.1	7.2	6.9	All Other Non-Current	21.2	3.1	.3	2.1	11.8	
26.8	26.7	24.8	Net Worth	-12.0	23.9	31.2	38.3	34.4	
100.0	100.0	100.0	Total Liabilities & Net Worth	100.0	100.0	100.0	100.0	100.0	
			INCOME DATA						
100.0	100.0	100.0	Net Sales	100.0	100.0	100.0	100.0	100.0	
			Gross Profit						
96.3	94.4	94.5	Operating Expenses	92.3	94.3	98.7	95.5	92.1	
3.7	5.6	5.5	Operating Profit	7.7	5.7	1.3	4.5	7.9	
1.6	1.4	1.0	All Other Expenses (net)	2.4	.3	1.3	1.3	.0	
2.1	4.2	4.5	Profit Before Taxes	5.3	5.4	.0	3.2	7.9	
			RATIOS						
2.1	2.0	2.1		1.4	2.8	1.6	2.0	2.7	
1.3	1.4	1.3	Current	.9	1.8	1.4	1.2	1.5	
.9	1.0	1.0		.6	1.0	.8	.9	1.0	
1.9	1.8	1.7		1.2	2.2	1.5	1.6	2.1	
1.0	1.2	1.0	Quick	.7	1.2	1.2	1.0	1.5	
.6	.7	.7		.3	.7	.7	.7	1.0	
29 12.8	31 11.7	29 12.8		2 153.3	24 15.0	32 11.3	41 8.8	40 9.0	
41 8.9	40 9.1	41 9.0	Sales/Receivables	29 12.5	32 11.5	43 8.4	48 7.7	50 7.2	
53 6.9	50 7.4	52 7.0		42 8.6	45 8.0	54 6.8	60 6.1	66 5.5	
			Cost of Sales/Inventory						
			Cost of Sales/Payables						
11.2	7.6	9.6		17.7	6.9	10.1	9.3	6.2	
22.4	16.1	26.1	Sales/Working Capital	UND	16.5	22.1	36.8	14.3	
-90.4	-318.0	-166.8		-12.8	NM	-261.9	-97.1	548.4	
8.2	10.4	10.8		(12) 13.7	(27) 12.3	(11) 9.4	(16) 15.4	41.3	
(67) 2.5	(83) 5.0	(87) 3.1	EBIT/Interest	2.2	4.1	2.1	3.0	5.4	
-.1	.9	1.2		-2.3	1.9	-1.9	1.0	2.1	
3.5	4.7	3.8							
(20) 2.3	(17) 2.2	(18) 2.3	Net Profit + Depr., Dep., Amort./Cur. Mat. L/T/D						
1.0	1.0	1.1							
.6	.3	.6		2.9	.4	.7	.5	.5	
1.3	1.2	1.5	Fixed/Worth	-4.9	2.1	1.4	1.0	1.1	
6.1	4.9	15.9		-.5	NM	4.1	3.4	2.2	
1.1	1.0	1.0		6.3	.7	1.0	1.0	.9	
2.2	2.3	3.8	Debt/Worth	-14.5	4.0	2.4	1.9	1.9	
13.0	8.8	34.2		-2.2	NM	5.2	5.4	3.5	
60.8	65.0	63.6			87.0	77.0	41.4	68.0	
(56) 14.8	(74) 25.6	(75) 24.8	% Profit Before Taxes/Tangible Net Worth	(22) 34.6	(11) 12.6	14.2	(12) 24.6		
.9	3.4	7.3		13.2	-24.3	.1	7.5		
16.4	20.2	18.1		35.4	17.0	16.8	16.7	27.3	
3.6	8.0	6.4	% Profit Before Taxes/Total Assets	2.3	9.2	4.9	5.2	7.3	
-5.4	-.7	.4		-14.8	4.6	-12.3	.2	3.6	
13.6	25.6	16.4		29.0	20.3	11.2	11.4	20.6	
7.8	10.1	7.0	Sales/Net Fixed Assets	6.2	6.8	8.6	6.2	6.6	
4.1	4.5	3.7		2.4	4.2	3.8	3.1	3.2	
3.1	3.6	3.2		3.4	3.5	3.9	3.2	2.9	
2.3	2.6	2.4	Sales/Total Assets	2.2	2.6	3.1	2.4	2.2	
1.5	1.7	1.6		1.5	1.9	1.9	1.5	1.6	
2.2	1.9	2.3		.7	2.0	2.7	2.6	2.1	
(63) 5.5	(72) 4.7	(81) 4.2	% Depr., Dep., Amort./Sales	(11) 4.3	(24) 4.0	(10) 3.7	4.7	(13) 4.3	
7.3	7.3	6.4		5.4	6.2	8.3	6.8	5.6	
3.7	3.8	3.4		3.8	3.5		2.7		
(32) 6.5	(47) 5.9	(50) 4.9	% Officers', Directors', Owners' Comp/Sales	(11) 7.2	(19) 4.4		(10) 3.7		
11.9	9.0	9.6		15.3	9.3		7.3		
922807M	1494438M	874921M	Net Sales ($)	8049M	56568M	51031M	130149M	211219M	417905M
583415M	790678M	473919M	Total Assets ($)	3779M	23212M	21662M	61471M	110845M	252950M

M = $ thousand MM = $ million
See Pages 11 through 21 for Explanation of Ratios and Data

Current Data Sorted By Assets   Comparative Historical Data

						Type of Statement		
1	4	15	17	7	2	Unqualified	25	18
1	3	6	2			Reviewed	12	10
3	8		1		1	Compiled	18	20
11	11	3	2			Tax Returns	12	14
6	9	11	11	1	3	Other	19	25
	13 (4/1-9/30/04)		126 (10/1/04-3/31/05)				4/1/00- 3/31/01	4/1/01- 3/31/02
0-500M	500M-2MM	2-10MM	10-50MM	50-100MM	100-250MM		ALL	ALL
22	35	35	33	8	6	NUMBER OF STATEMENTS	86	87
%	%	%	%	%	%	ASSETS	%	%
37.0	21.7	26.0	25.8			Cash & Equivalents	19.4	21.8
14.9	35.3	26.7	24.2			Trade Receivables (net)	26.2	22.8
.0	1.9	4.3	3.3			Inventory	1.6	2.7
3.3	5.3	9.9	13.2			All Other Current	5.5	8.2
55.2	64.3	66.9	66.5			Total Current	52.7	55.5
29.7	16.5	14.7	15.9			Fixed Assets (net)	24.2	21.0
7.6	4.0	6.8	10.8			Intangibles (net)	10.0	8.8
7.5	15.2	11.5	6.8			All Other Non-Current	13.0	14.7
100.0	100.0	100.0	100.0			Total	100.0	100.0
						LIABILITIES		
30.5	12.7	8.2	8.7			Notes Payable-Short Term	17.8	11.8
5.4	3.6	6.1	3.9			Cur. Mat.-L/T/D	6.5	13.2
6.3	17.1	9.0	7.0			Trade Payables	8.7	11.2
.2	.3	.4	.1			Income Taxes Payable	.1	1.5
20.8	18.0	19.6	16.8			All Other Current	20.0	19.0
63.1	51.6	43.3	36.5			Total Current	53.1	56.6
16.5	13.4	9.9	13.9			Long-Term Debt	23.7	15.0
.0	.0	.2	.0			Deferred Taxes	.3	.0
7.2	6.7	1.9	5.9			All Other Non-Current	5.0	6.9
13.1	28.2	44.7	43.6			Net Worth	18.0	21.3
100.0	100.0	100.0	100.0			Total Liabilities & Net Worth	100.0	100.0
						INCOME DATA		
100.0	100.0	100.0	100.0			Net Sales	100.0	100.0
						Gross Profit		
94.6	91.3	88.2	83.8			Operating Expenses	87.1	85.6
5.4	8.7	11.8	16.2			Operating Profit	12.9	14.4
1.4	.4	1.5	2.3			All Other Expenses (net)	3.7	1.6
4.0	8.3	10.3	13.9			Profit Before Taxes	9.2	12.7
						RATIOS		
2.5	1.8	3.3	4.3				1.6	2.1
.9	1.2	1.5	1.4			Current	1.1	1.2
.4	.8	.9	1.1				.6	.7
2.5	1.7	2.6	1.8				1.6	1.6
.9	1.1	1.1	1.2			Quick	.9 (86)	1.0
.3	.8	.8	1.0				.4	.4
0 UND	12 31.2	13 28.4	13 27.6				4 94.4	0 UND
0 UND	25 14.6	26 13.9	34 10.8			Sales/Receivables	23 15.8	16 22.4
25 14.7	42 8.7	51 7.2	50 7.4				44 8.3	44 8.2
						Cost of Sales/Inventory		
						Cost of Sales/Payables		
26.2	8.7	2.4	3.6				12.2	6.6
−158.7	34.3	11.8	14.0			Sales/Working Capital	85.5	51.1
−20.8	−51.3	−49.8	42.8				−31.2	−25.0
20.3	38.1	42.9	52.2				14.3	29.9
(18) 4.5	(29) 11.0	(27) 19.6	(29) 9.0			EBIT/Interest	(72) 4.5	(70) 8.2
−2.3	2.0	5.3	4.3				1.6	1.9
						Net Profit + Depr., Dep., Amort./Cur. Mat. L /T/D	13.8	24.7
							(13) 5.6	(12) 9.7
							2.9	3.3
.3	.1	.1	.2				.4	.2
NM	.3	.3	.5			Fixed/Worth	1.0	.9
−.5	1.4	1.1	1.6				6.0	19.4
.9	.9	.7	.4				1.5	.9
NM	2.0	1.3	2.1			Debt/Worth	4.5	3.1
−3.2	10.3	5.1	9.5				25.6	−99.9
64.2	104.4	63.5	143.8			% Profit Before Taxes/Tangible Net Worth	178.1	163.0
(11) 23.9	(29) 58.6	(32) 34.0	(28) 57.9				(67) 49.1	(65) 72.4
−7.4	9.3	13.3	26.0				11.3	21.6
51.1	32.3	21.7	42.3			% Profit Before Taxes/Total Assets	34.0	40.9
11.0	10.7	13.3	15.8				11.3	20.2
−8.2	4.2	5.9	5.1				2.5	3.2
111.4	88.2	58.5	30.2			Sales/Net Fixed Assets	26.5	54.4
38.6	32.9	22.7	15.2				15.3	19.7
20.0	18.6	10.2	9.4				9.4	11.0
9.0	5.1	3.2	3.1			Sales/Total Assets	4.4	5.6
6.5	4.2	2.0	2.0				3.3	2.9
4.0	2.8	1.1	.8				2.0	1.7
.4	.8	1.2	1.3			% Depr., Dep., Amort./Sales	1.6	.9
(13) 1.1	(24) 1.3	(26) 1.6	(25) 2.5				(75) 2.2	(68) 1.8
2.5	2.6	3.3	3.0				3.1	2.6
9.5	3.9					% Officers', Directors', Owners' Comp/Sales	5.5	4.3
(11) 13.8	(18) 7.0						(25) 9.6	(37) 8.0
18.1	12.4						19.9	21.1
36643M	170224M	432557M	2210898M	1005781M	1144560M	Net Sales ($)	1239227M	1492362M
5718M	42171M	186385M	770028M	626161M	957466M	Total Assets ($)	877082M	729063M

M = $ thousand   MM = $ million
See Pages 11 through 21 for Explanation of Ratios and Data

Comparative Historical Data | **Current Data Sorted By Sales**

Type of Statement	'02-03	'03-04	'04-05	0-1MM	1-3MM	3-5MM	5-10MM	10-25MM	25MM & OVER
Unqualified	40	38	46		2	1	12	8	23
Reviewed	21	19	12	1	2		2	6	1
Compiled	11	21	13	2	3	2	4		2
Tax Returns	16	18	27	8	8	7	1	2	1
Other	27	36	41	1	10	5	4	10	11
	4/1/02-3/31/03	4/1/03-3/31/04	4/1/04-3/31/05		13 (4/1-9/30/04)			126 (10/1/04-3/31/05)	
	ALL	ALL	ALL						
NUMBER OF STATEMENTS	115	132	139	12	25	15	23	26	38
ASSETS	%	%	%	%	%	%	%	%	%
Cash & Equivalents	24.6	23.3	26.5	25.9	30.0	28.1	22.2	24.7	27.7
Trade Receivables (net)	22.1	27.6	26.2	17.6	32.3	20.0	30.5	27.6	23.9
Inventory	1.6	.7	2.4	12.4	2.7	.2	4.3	.4	.0
All Other Current	11.8	9.6	8.7	.6	5.5	9.6	6.1	8.4	14.7
Total Current	60.2	61.2	63.8	56.5	70.6	57.9	63.2	61.2	66.3
Fixed Assets (net)	20.5	19.3	17.1	25.8	13.9	26.1	16.3	16.9	13.6
Intangibles (net)	8.1	8.1	8.7	1.3	6.1	6.2	10.2	8.6	13.0
All Other Non-Current	11.2	11.3	10.3	16.4	9.4	9.8	10.3	13.4	7.2
Total	100.0	100.0	100.0	100.0	100.0	100.0	100.0	100.0	100.0
LIABILITIES									
Notes Payable-Short Term	13.1	14.5	12.6	32.6	18.6	19.5	7.4	8.5	5.7
Cur. Mat.-L/T/D	7.7	5.4	4.3	3.5	6.4	3.8	4.7	5.3	2.6
Trade Payables	10.2	10.2	9.8	1.3	9.8	11.5	13.0	10.6	9.1
Income Taxes Payable	.9	.2	.3	.3	.0	.5	.0	.4	.5
All Other Current	19.3	16.0	18.9	15.8	16.0	15.2	18.0	21.6	22.0
Total Current	51.2	46.2	46.0	53.5	50.8	50.6	43.2	46.4	40.0
Long-Term Debt	17.9	14.1	13.3	19.5	16.1	19.7	14.7	6.3	11.0
Deferred Taxes	.5	.3	.1	.0	.0	.0	.0	.3	.2
All Other Non-Current	9.4	6.9	5.2	.3	13.1	.0	5.9	1.8	5.7
Net Worth	21.1	32.6	35.4	26.7	20.0	29.6	36.3	45.2	43.2
Total Liabilities & Net Worth	100.0	100.0	100.0	100.0	100.0	100.0	100.0	100.0	100.0
INCOME DATA									
Net Sales	100.0	100.0	100.0	100.0	100.0	100.0	100.0	100.0	100.0
Gross Profit									
Operating Expenses	90.1	88.0	88.1	85.1	91.5	91.4	88.3	89.5	84.4
Operating Profit	9.9	12.0	11.9	14.9	8.5	8.6	11.7	10.5	15.6
All Other Expenses (net)	2.1	3.2	2.0	4.3	.7	-.4	2.1	1.6	3.3
Profit Before Taxes	7.8	8.8	9.9	10.6	7.8	9.0	9.6	8.9	12.3
RATIOS									
Current	2.2	2.3	2.6	2.3	7.0	1.9	3.3	1.9	3.8
	1.2	1.4	1.3	1.2	1.8	1.6	1.5	1.2	1.3
	.8	.8	.9	.2	.8	.8	.9	1.0	1.1
Quick	1.9	2.0	2.1	1.6	5.4	1.9	1.7	1.4	2.5
	1.0	1.2	1.1	.6	1.4	1.2	1.1	1.1	1.1
	.5	.6	.8	.1	.8	.4	.8	.9	.9
Sales/Receivables	2 208.2	2 184.1	10 36.9	0 UND	0 UND	0 UND	17 21.8	12 30.0	15 24.9
	20 18.3	24 15.1	26 13.9	0 UND	21 17.2	17 21.5	25 14.6	34 10.6	36 10.0
	46 8.0	51 7.1	47 7.8	106 3.4	73 5.0	34 10.6	34 10.8	51 7.2	51 7.1
Cost of Sales/Inventory									
Cost of Sales/Payables									
Sales/Working Capital	6.9	6.3	4.5	1.2	3.5	7.1	4.8	4.9	3.8
	35.8	18.5	19.8	28.5	27.8	18.7	30.3	42.5	16.2
	-35.7	-37.6	-170.4	-20.3	-47.4	-104.6	-51.3	-473.6	48.4
EBIT/Interest	24.8	23.3	36.3		40.9	19.6	36.0	43.8	62.9
	(95) 5.6	(97) 4.4	(115) 9.1		(22) 6.1	(11) 9.4	(21) 14.5	(19) 9.0	(33) 15.4
	1.8	1.4	2.6		.6	2.4	2.5	2.6	5.4
Net Profit + Depr., Dep., Amort./Cur. Mat. L/T/D	6.5	30.8	14.1						20.1
	(12) 3.5	(13) 7.0	(22) 2.9						(11) 3.1
	1.7	1.2	1.4						2.4
Fixed/Worth	.2	.1	.1	.0	.1	.1	.3	.1	.2
	.8	.5	.4	.2	.2	.9	.6	.3	.5
	2.8	2.5	2.1	NM	-.8	3.3	2.4	.8	3.4
Debt/Worth	.8	.9	.8	.7	.6	1.2	.9	.7	.5
	3.6	2.2	1.7	1.2	2.0	2.3	2.1	1.5	1.7
	19.5	11.9	13.4	NM	-5.6	52.0	29.2	4.5	18.0
% Profit Before Taxes/Tangible Net Worth	99.1	94.6	80.7		74.8	94.1	98.1	80.4	117.3
	(89) 56.3	(107) 41.2	(109) 39.5		(16) 25.4	(12) 40.7	(18) 42.6	(24) 35.3	(30) 53.7
	9.9	11.8	17.4		1.8	15.5	11.2	13.7	31.7
% Profit Before Taxes/Total Assets	37.3	26.2	27.1	15.5	30.2	33.5	32.3	35.6	27.4
	12.7	11.4	14.5	8.1	9.0	19.6	8.3	10.1	17.9
	1.9	1.4	4.2	.8	-3.3	7.5	2.4	5.2	7.0
Sales/Net Fixed Assets	50.6	51.3	60.2	209.4	154.4	68.3	35.1	56.1	35.7
	21.1	24.0	24.2	37.1	90.3	23.4	27.4	23.0	15.6
	9.9	11.4	11.4	4.8	17.8	9.7	11.3	9.8	11.8
Sales/Total Assets	5.6	5.1	4.5	4.5	7.0	7.1	4.9	3.4	3.5
	2.8	2.6	2.8	1.7	3.7	4.3	3.4	2.6	2.3
	1.3	1.1	1.3	.4	1.7	1.7	1.5	1.4	1.2
% Depr., Dep., Amort./Sales	1.2	1.0	1.0		.7		1.0	1.1	1.1
	(93) 1.9	(101) 1.9	(101) 1.7		(13) 1.4		(20) 2.0	(19) 1.6	(33) 1.8
	3.1	3.0	2.9		2.3		2.9	3.0	3.3
% Officers', Directors', Owners' Comp/Sales	4.5	4.0	3.7		5.6		3.5		
	(44) 7.9	(44) 8.3	(41) 6.3		(10) 10.9		(10) 5.3		
	13.7	16.7	12.8		14.7		10.8		
Net Sales ($)	2635431M	3475864M	5000663M	7926M	46884M	58119M	168916M	437435M	4281383M
Total Assets ($)	1228924M	2368177M	2587929M	10249M	25254M	26825M	106964M	272497M	2146140M

© RMA 2005

M = $ thousand   MM = $ million

See Pages 11 through 21 for Explanation of Ratios and Data

ADMIN & WASTE MANAGEMENT SERVICES—All Other Business Support Services   NAICS 561499 (SIC 7389)

Current Data Sorted By Assets							Comparative Historical Data	
						Type of Statement	166	146
2	14	56	36	17	17	Unqualified	177	147
9	38	86	16			Reviewed	256	241
33	73	35	3			Compiled	138	138
86	63	26		2		Tax Returns	353	317
54	113	91	42	12	18	Other	4/1/00-	4/1/01-
	154 (4/1-9/30/04)		788 (10/1/04-3/31/05)				3/31/01	3/31/02
0-500M	500M-2MM	2-10MM	10-50MM	50-100MM	100-250MM		ALL	ALL
184	301	294	97	31	35	**NUMBER OF STATEMENTS**	1090	989
%	%	%	%	%	%	**ASSETS**	%	%
25.0	14.4	11.9	11.8	13.0	14.0	Cash & Equivalents	14.0	14.0
26.1	33.9	33.9	31.6	27.0	25.6	Trade Receivables (net)	32.4	32.2
7.0	8.3	8.6	7.5	5.6	2.8	Inventory	7.9	6.9
2.8	4.1	4.5	6.2	11.0	9.1	All Other Current	4.1	4.7
60.8	60.6	58.9	57.0	56.6	51.4	Total Current	58.4	57.8
24.2	24.9	26.7	24.4	14.3	16.9	Fixed Assets (net)	26.7	27.0
4.9	5.7	4.8	8.4	19.7	20.1	Intangibles (net)	5.7	6.6
10.2	8.7	9.6	10.2	9.4	11.6	All Other Non-Current	9.2	8.6
100.0	100.0	100.0	100.0	100.0	100.0	Total	100.0	100.0
						LIABILITIES		
20.6	10.7	9.6	14.7	11.8	6.4	Notes Payable-Short Term	14.2	15.8
5.3	4.1	4.1	4.0	3.3	2.9	Cur. Mat.-L/T/D	6.1	4.9
13.2	15.6	15.9	15.6	10.6	10.2	Trade Payables	14.9	13.7
.1	.4	.6	.3	.3	1.5	Income Taxes Payable	.5	.5
22.5	15.2	14.4	15.1	24.1	21.6	All Other Current	16.7	17.0
61.7	45.9	44.6	49.7	50.0	42.7	Total Current	52.6	51.8
23.5	23.0	15.2	13.1	14.3	16.7	Long-Term Debt	17.4	17.5
.0	.2	.4	.4	.4	.4	Deferred Taxes	.6	.5
8.8	7.1	5.2	6.1	6.5	6.9	All Other Non-Current	8.6	6.6
6.1	23.7	34.7	30.7	28.9	33.3	Net Worth	20.9	23.6
100.0	100.0	100.0	100.0	100.0	100.0	Total Liabilities & Net Worth	100.0	100.0
						INCOME DATA		
100.0	100.0	100.0	100.0	100.0	100.0	Net Sales	100.0	100.0
						Gross Profit		
93.4	89.3	92.6	91.8	88.6	90.9	Operating Expenses	93.6	93.6
6.6	10.7	7.4	8.2	11.4	9.1	Operating Profit	6.4	6.4
1.6	2.2	1.5	2.7	2.1	1.4	All Other Expenses (net)	1.6	1.9
5.0	8.4	6.0	5.5	9.3	7.7	Profit Before Taxes	4.8	4.5
						RATIOS		
2.7	2.5	2.2	1.7	1.7	1.8		2.2	2.3
1.4	1.4	1.3	1.2	1.1	1.2	Current	1.3	1.3
.6	.9	1.0	.8	.9	.9		.9	.8
2.3	2.0	1.7	1.4	1.1	1.6		1.8	1.7
1.2	(300) 1.1	1.1	.8	.8	.9	Quick	(1089) 1.0	1.0
.5	.6	.6	.6	.3	.6		.6	.6
0 UND	11 32.1	24 15.1	29 12.5	32 11.5	34 10.8		18 20.5	17 21.9
17 22.0	37 9.9	46 7.9	52 7.0	43 8.5	54 6.8	Sales/Receivables	43 8.6	40 9.0
43 8.5	55 6.7	68 5.4	67 5.5	73 5.0	73 5.0		68 5.4	64 5.7
						Cost of Sales/Inventory		
						Cost of Sales/Payables		
10.6	7.3	7.0	7.8	9.5	4.3		7.5	7.9
36.3	21.6	19.7	34.4	39.6	22.1	Sales/Working Capital	23.3	25.0
−23.5	−68.6	−93.3	−25.6	−37.3	−25.0		−45.0	−31.9
19.5	21.9	21.3	22.2	23.0	12.3		10.7	10.3
(114) 3.7	(233) 4.8	(255) 5.7	(82) 6.6	(28) 6.8	(30) 5.3	EBIT/Interest	(898) 3.4	(842) 3.2
−.1	1.8	1.9	2.3	2.3	2.0		1.1	.8
	6.6	6.5	17.0		8.3	Net Profit + Depr., Dep.,	6.0	5.9
	(25) 1.9	(56) 2.5	(24) 4.4		(11) 1.6	Amort./Cur. Mat. L /T/D	(200) 2.1	(184) 2.2
	1.0	1.3	2.3		.9		1.0	.8
.1	.2	.2	.2	.2	.4		.3	.2
.5	.7	.8	.7	.9	.9	Fixed/Worth	.9	.9
−9.5	6.2	2.6	2.3	−.6	11.9		5.1	4.6
.6	.8	.9	1.4	1.6	1.4		1.0	.9
2.6	2.0	2.4	3.1	7.3	5.4	Debt/Worth	2.6	2.6
−10.7	21.0	8.0	14.6	−16.7	61.7		16.5	17.4
124.7	77.5	63.4	67.2	116.1	49.0	% Profit Before Taxes/Tangible	68.6	64.8
(128) 46.2	(235) 38.0	(255) 29.9	(84) 29.4	(22) 53.3	(27) 30.9	Net Worth	(873) 31.2	(782) 26.1
9.6	11.6	7.0	10.2	19.8	14.6		6.6	4.4
41.0	27.1	20.0	14.7	21.2	13.7	% Profit Before Taxes/Total	21.0	19.2
12.5	10.7	7.6	6.5	9.5	5.9	Assets	7.2	6.4
−2.6	2.3	1.7	1.6	2.5	1.5		.6	−.4
183.7	62.9	55.8	36.1	58.7	33.4		41.8	44.8
40.3	23.8	16.1	13.5	19.4	10.6	Sales/Net Fixed Assets	15.3	16.4
13.7	6.8	4.5	3.2	6.7	5.8		6.1	6.3
8.2	4.3	3.4	3.3	2.7	2.0		4.0	4.1
4.9	3.0	2.5	2.1	2.0	1.4	Sales/Total Assets	2.6	2.7
2.8	2.0	1.4	1.1	.9	1.0		1.4	1.6
.6	.7	.7	1.0	.6	1.7		.7	.9
(103) 1.6	(216) 1.7	(242) 2.0	(72) 2.2	(23) 1.4	(18) 3.2	% Depr., Dep., Amort./Sales	(876) 2.1	(764) 2.1
3.2	3.7	4.4	4.3	4.6	5.3		4.5	4.5
5.1	2.4	1.5	1.1			% Officers', Directors',	3.2	3.5
(89) 10.3	(126) 4.7	(82) 3.2	(10) 1.5			Owners' Comp/Sales	(409) 6.3	(371) 6.7
18.0	8.7	6.0					12.6	12.4
230708M	1189222M	3787443M	4998692M	4487882M	10419516M	Net Sales ($)	25049185M	23008467M
42107M	347102M	1398331M	2011939M	2215958M	5839546M	Total Assets ($)	15472240M	12198216M

M = $ thousand   MM = $ million

See Pages 11 through 21 for Explanation of Ratios and Data

Comparative Historical Data

Current Data Sorted By Sales

			Type of Statement						
135	146	142	Unqualified	4	12	9	24	32	61
125	150	149	Reviewed	4	16	24	43	47	15
150	236	144	Compiled	24	40	26	38	12	4
116	163	177	Tax Returns	60	60	24	16	13	4
286	340	330	Other	55	67	41	50	52	65
4/1/02-3/31/03 ALL	4/1/03-3/31/04 ALL	4/1/04-3/31/05 ALL		154 (4/1-9/30/04) 0-1MM	1-3MM	3-5MM	788 (10/1/04-3/31/05) 5-10MM	10-25MM	25MM & OVER
812	1035	942	**NUMBER OF STATEMENTS**	147	195	124	171	156	149
%	%	%	**ASSETS**	%	%	%	%	%	%
14.7	14.9	15.4	Cash & Equivalents	19.6	18.1	12.7	13.2	13.8	13.9
32.8	30.6	31.6	Trade Receivables (net)	18.3	26.5	37.8	36.9	37.0	34.4
7.1	8.1	7.8	Inventory	6.2	7.3	8.7	9.8	7.7	6.8
4.8	5.8	4.6	All Other Current	3.2	4.8	4.0	3.3	5.1	7.1
59.5	59.5	59.3	Total Current	47.2	56.7	63.2	63.2	63.6	62.3
25.1	26.6	24.6	Fixed Assets (net)	34.6	27.9	20.6	24.3	23.1	15.9
6.9	6.0	6.5	Intangibles (net)	7.3	4.8	7.1	3.9	4.4	12.7
8.6	8.0	9.6	All Other Non-Current	10.9	10.6	9.1	8.6	8.9	9.1
100.0	100.0	100.0	Total	100.0	100.0	100.0	100.0	100.0	100.0
			LIABILITIES						
12.6	11.3	12.6	Notes Payable-Short Term	13.7	16.7	10.4	12.9	11.2	9.0
4.9	4.3	4.2	Cur. Mat.-L/T/D	3.8	5.3	4.3	4.4	4.6	2.7
15.2	13.4	14.8	Trade Payables	6.8	14.3	16.7	16.7	16.6	18.0
.5	.6	.4	Income Taxes Payable	.0	.3	.6	.5	.6	.6
17.9	16.8	16.9	All Other Current	21.0	16.6	13.0	12.9	17.2	20.7
51.2	46.5	49.0	Total Current	45.3	53.2	45.0	47.4	50.1	51.1
15.9	18.1	19.1	Long-Term Debt	33.7	22.5	16.1	17.8	11.9	11.8
.4	.4	.3	Deferred Taxes	.0	.1	.6	.4	.3	.4
6.6	7.5	6.7	All Other Non-Current	8.3	7.4	8.8	4.6	5.8	5.8
25.8	27.5	24.9	Net Worth	12.7	16.8	29.5	29.7	31.9	30.9
100.0	100.0	100.0	Total Liabilities & Net Worth	100.0	100.0	100.0	100.0	100.0	100.0
			INCOME DATA						
100.0	100.0	100.0	Net Sales	100.0	100.0	100.0	100.0	100.0	100.0
			Gross Profit						
93.4	92.5	91.4	Operating Expenses	82.5	91.2	94.0	93.2	94.2	93.5
6.6	7.5	8.6	Operating Profit	17.5	8.8	6.0	6.8	5.8	6.5
2.1	2.1	1.9	All Other Expenses (net)	5.9	2.2	.7	.9	.7	1.0
4.4	5.4	6.7	Profit Before Taxes	11.7	6.6	5.3	5.9	5.1	5.5
			RATIOS						
1.9	2.3	2.2		3.2	2.8	2.5	2.2	2.0	1.7
1.2	1.3	1.3	Current	1.4	1.4	1.3	1.4	1.3	1.2
.8	.9	.9		.5	.7	1.0	1.0	.9	.9
1.6	1.8	1.8		2.2	2.3	2.1	1.8	1.7	1.4
(810) 1.0	(1034) 1.0	(941) 1.0	Quick	(194) 1.0	1.1	1.1	1.1	1.0	.9
.6	.6	.6		.3	.5	.7	.7	.6	.6
17 21.6	13 28.3	13 27.1		0 UND	0 UND	27 13.4	27 13.7	27 13.3	25 14.4
40 9.1	39 9.3	39 9.4	Sales/Receivables	5 75.0	33 11.1	48 7.7	45 8.2	44 8.4	47 7.7
65 5.6	61 6.0	60 6.1		43 8.6	54 6.8	61 6.0	63 5.8	67 5.5	61 6.0
			Cost of Sales/Inventory						
			Cost of Sales/Payables						
8.8	7.3	7.5		5.4	6.8	6.7	7.6	8.8	10.4
30.4	21.4	25.4	Sales/Working Capital	33.0	29.0	19.2	19.9	25.2	34.4
-33.8	-42.1	-47.0		-9.8	-20.9	-164.0	-135.7	-72.0	-62.5
12.9	13.5	20.8		9.5	21.2	17.9	28.6	23.2	23.1
(672) 3.7	(851) 4.5	(742) 5.2	EBIT/Interest	(76) 3.0	(152) 3.8	(101) 4.5	(142) 7.4	(138) 4.9	(133) 7.2
1.1	1.0	1.6		.4	.5	1.9	2.2	1.7	3.0
5.9	6.6	7.1	Net Profit + Depr., Dep.,		3.5	13.1	6.7	4.9	14.1
(149) 2.2	(156) 2.4	(126) 2.6	Amort./Cur. Mat. L/T/D	(13) 1.5	(18) 2.1	(20) 3.2	(34) 2.3	(41) 4.4	
.9	.9	1.2		1.0	.7	1.6	1.2	1.7	
.2	.2	.2		.1	.1	.2	.2	.1	.2
.9	.8	.7	Fixed/Worth	.8	.8	.5	.6	.8	.8
5.5	5.7	4.3		25.9	-17.5	2.5	2.4	3.2	2.4
1.1	.9	.9		.8	.5	.7	.9	1.0	1.5
2.7	2.5	2.6	Debt/Worth	3.3	2.5	1.9	1.8	2.6	3.7
38.9	21.1	15.9		-12.5	-64.7	9.4	7.6	11.7	21.3
66.0	72.9	78.9	% Profit Before Taxes/Tangible	86.1	100.0	61.9	74.9	68.7	85.5
(626) 25.3	(827) 28.8	(751) 33.9	Net Worth	(106) 31.1	(143) 32.9	(102) 37.2	(149) 33.9	(130) 29.0	(121) 43.2
4.2	5.3	9.8		8.9	10.2	5.2	10.3	6.7	16.0
19.0	20.0	23.8	% Profit Before Taxes/Total	27.3	30.0	25.9	25.7	18.5	19.3
6.9	7.8	8.6	Assets	6.3	9.7	9.3	10.2	6.9	8.6
.1	.2	1.5		.0	-.5	1.9	2.6	1.9	2.6
52.4	51.2	73.2		108.0	70.0	70.2	53.6	95.4	83.7
16.5	16.2	20.1	Sales/Net Fixed Assets	14.8	22.6	23.7	20.8	19.2	19.4
6.8	5.9	6.7		1.4	6.8	8.1	7.4	6.7	9.1
4.2	4.1	4.2		4.5	5.0	4.1	4.2	4.0	4.0
2.7	2.6	2.8	Sales/Total Assets	1.9	2.9	2.6	3.0	2.9	2.7
1.6	1.5	1.6		.5	1.7	2.0	1.9	1.8	1.5
.9	.9	.7		1.4	.8	.8	.7	.5	.5
(629) 2.1	(788) 2.3	(674) 1.8	% Depr., Dep., Amort./Sales	(78) 4.4	(128) 1.9	(94) 2.0	(139) 1.5	(132) 1.5	(103) 1.4
4.6	4.6	4.1		15.5	4.2	3.9	3.6	3.4	3.4
3.2	2.9	2.5	% Officers', Directors',	5.5	3.6	2.8	1.8	1.2	.5
(285) 6.7	(365) 6.1	(315) 5.3	Owners' Comp/Sales	(50) 12.3	(88) 6.3	(53) 5.7	(61) 3.3	(46) 2.1	(17) 1.7
12.1	12.1	11.3		19.5	11.0	.11.0	6.1	5.1	12.6
19760823M 11411081M	29613471M 11992049M	25113463M 11854983M	Net Sales ($) Total Assets ($)	70647M 101703M	366238M 285181M	491701M 233725M	1229489M 610116M	2450430M 1251721M	20504958M 9372537M

© RMA 2005

M = $ thousand   MM = $ million
See Pages 11 through 21 for Explanation of Ratios and Data

Current Data Sorted By Assets   **Comparative Historical Data**

1	4	8 11	3 3	3	1	Type of Statement		
6	8	4				Unqualified	11	10
17	5	1				Reviewed	19	10
10	8	10	2	1	1	Compiled	32	27
						Tax Returns	20	12
						Other	38	26
	28 (4/1-9/30/04)		79 (10/1/04-3/31/05)				4/1/00-3/31/01	4/1/01-3/31/02
0-500M	500M-2MM	2-10MM	10-50MM	50-100MM	100-250MM		ALL	ALL
34	25	34	8	4	2	NUMBER OF STATEMENTS	120	85
%	%	%	%	%	%	ASSETS	%	%
27.8	28.3	30.7				Cash & Equivalents	25.5	28.7
13.7	15.5	28.5				Trade Receivables (net)	25.2	22.3
2.0	.4	.0				Inventory	.9	.9
4.2	5.8	5.4				All Other Current	4.2	6.9
47.6	50.0	64.7				Total Current	55.7	58.9
28.8	24.7	14.1				Fixed Assets (net)	19.2	15.6
10.2	15.2	9.1				Intangibles (net)	11.3	11.6
13.4	10.1	12.1				All Other Non-Current	13.9	14.0
100.0	100.0	100.0				Total	100.0	100.0
						LIABILITIES		
23.4	13.8	5.1				Notes Payable-Short Term	11.6	15.1
5.9	2.4	5.7				Cur. Mat.-L/T/D	6.0	3.5
19.9	20.2	19.5				Trade Payables	18.9	15.2
.0	1.3	.4				Income Taxes Payable	.8	.5
24.2	27.4	32.9				All Other Current	27.3	35.5
73.4	65.1	63.6				Total Current	64.6	69.8
25.2	10.8	4.4				Long-Term Debt	19.8	12.6
.0	.1	.0				Deferred Taxes	.3	.0
14.1	9.7	15.1				All Other Non-Current	10.4	5.4
-12.6	14.2	16.9				Net Worth	4.8	12.2
100.0	100.0	100.0				Total Liabilities & Net Worth	100.0	100.0
						INCOME DATA		
100.0	100.0	100.0				Net Sales	100.0	100.0
						Gross Profit		
97.5	98.0	99.6				Operating Expenses	97.1	98.7
2.5	2.0	.4				Operating Profit	2.9	1.3
.5	.9	-.1				All Other Expenses (net)	-.3	.2
2.0	1.1	.5				Profit Before Taxes	3.2	1.1
						RATIOS		
2.1	1.8	1.5					1.7	1.5
.7	.8	1.1				Current	1.0	1.0
.3	.4	.8					.6	.6
2.1	1.7	1.4					1.6	1.3
.6	.8	1.0				Quick	(119) .9	.9
.2	.3	.7					.6	.5
0 UND	0 UND	3 145.5					2 223.5	1 243.4
1 405.1	4 96.8	20 18.2				Sales/Receivables	10 36.1	12 29.5
9 42.4	13 27.9	51 7.1					32 11.3	32 11.4
						Cost of Sales/Inventory		
						Cost of Sales/Payables		
76.3	43.0	13.1					27.7	23.2
-154.7	-111.7	112.1				Sales/Working Capital	507.7	999.8
-16.6	-10.1	-32.6					-23.7	-16.1
15.6	7.1	35.3					14.0	24.8
(21) 2.9	(18) 3.0	(29) 13.6				EBIT/Interest	(78) 3.6	(63) 3.1
-1.1	.9	2.3					1.1	-1.1
							11.8	4.8
						Net Profit + Depr., Dep., Amort./Cur. Mat. L /T/D	(14) 3.8	(10) 1.2
							1.9	-4.5
.3	.4	.1					.2	.3
2.0	1.8	.6				Fixed/Worth	.7	.7
-1.1	-.8	5.4					-14.3	-2.7
1.2	1.5	1.6					1.1	1.8
10.1	8.9	2.8				Debt/Worth	4.2	3.9
-3.0	-2.8	88.3					-11.5	-14.5
153.2	32.5	74.1					74.6	64.1
(19) 29.5	(15) 19.7	(27) 31.3				% Profit Before Taxes/Tangible Net Worth	(82) 31.8	(57) 19.1
-35.0	10.1	19.8					4.1	-6.0
38.1	11.2	17.9					18.0	11.2
8.3	4.6	6.8				% Profit Before Taxes/Total Assets	8.0	2.9
-4.7	1.0	.5					.5	-5.4
216.7	127.0	151.0					193.3	126.8
82.3	36.5	52.8				Sales/Net Fixed Assets	60.4	47.2
18.8	10.4	24.4					12.9	19.9
32.2	14.9	6.8					18.3	7.8
12.9	5.3	3.6				Sales/Total Assets	5.0	4.7
4.3	2.1	1.8					1.9	2.0
.1	.2	.2					.2	.2
(23) .5	(17) .4	(27) .6				% Depr., Dep., Amort./Sales	(87) .8	(65) .7
1.5	3.1	1.4					2.6	2.2
1.8		.7					1.2	1.5
(22) 3.4	(11) 3.4					% Officers', Directors', Owners' Comp/Sales	(55) 4.2	(31) 5.9
8.6		7.7					10.0	11.2
115810M	297475M	1206034M	777147M	2231514M	420450M	Net Sales ($)	5111736M	3261409M
6326M	28851M	183091M	178461M	285039M	295141M	Total Assets ($)	1062804M	754305M

M = $ thousand   MM = $ million
See Pages 11 through 21 for Explanation of Ratios and Data

Comparative Historical Data · **Current Data Sorted By Sales**

	4/1/02-3/31/03 ALL	4/1/03-3/31/04 ALL	4/1/04-3/31/05 ALL	0-1MM	1-3MM	3-5MM	5-10MM	10-25MM	25MM & OVER
					28 (4/1-9/30/04)			79 (10/1/04-3/31/05)	
Type of Statement									
Unqualified	14	13	16	1	1			3	11
Reviewed	18	18	18		3		4	4	7
Compiled	32	35	18	1	3	3	4	5	2
Tax Returns	20	24	23	7	8	4	2	1	1
Other	41	23	32	2	6	4	9	2	9
NUMBER OF STATEMENTS	125	113	107	11	21	11	19	15	30
ASSETS	%	%	%	%	%	%	%	%	%
Cash & Equivalents	29.1	26.7	30.1	20.2	31.7	28.9	28.3	30.0	34.1
Trade Receivables (net)	21.9	21.7	19.7	9.0	14.8	12.2	12.8	31.1	28.3
Inventory	.7	.6	.7	.0	.3	.0	3.8	.1	.0
All Other Current	4.3	4.7	5.5	5.9	4.8	3.8	2.8	3.9	8.8
Total Current	56.0	53.6	55.9	35.1	51.6	44.9	47.7	65.1	71.2
Fixed Assets (net)	19.0	20.1	20.7	44.4	20.9	19.9	26.4	11.3	13.4
Intangibles (net)	8.0	11.7	11.7	5.9	18.4	17.4	11.6	10.4	7.8
All Other Non-Current	17.0	14.5	11.7	14.6	9.1	17.8	14.3	13.2	7.6
Total	100.0	100.0	100.0	100.0	100.0	100.0	100.0	100.0	100.0
LIABILITIES									
Notes Payable-Short Term	11.1	28.5	12.3	28.7	21.0	10.4	5.3	13.0	4.9
Cur. Mat.-L/T/D	3.4	4.2	4.6	13.7	.5	2.2	1.7	11.8	3.3
Trade Payables	24.6	22.2	20.9	6.9	15.0	20.9	24.1	21.9	27.6
Income Taxes Payable	.5	.5	.5	.0	.0	2.8	.2	.4	.5
All Other Current	27.9	29.9	28.1	13.1	23.4	16.1	42.6	42.0	25.1
Total Current	67.5	85.4	66.4	62.4	60.0	52.4	73.9	89.1	61.4
Long-Term Debt	9.7	9.6	13.2	36.3	9.8	8.8	16.7	11.0	7.6
Deferred Taxes	.1	.3	.0	.0	.1	.0	.1	.0	.0
All Other Non-Current	25.2	10.7	12.1	11.2	4.2	24.6	29.9	8.0	4.0
Net Worth	-2.6	-6.0	8.3	-9.9	26.0	14.2	-20.6	-8.2	27.0
Total Liabilities & Net Worth	100.0	100.0	100.0	100.0	100.0	100.0	100.0	100.0	100.0
INCOME DATA									
Net Sales	100.0	100.0	100.0	100.0	100.0	100.0	100.0	100.0	100.0
Gross Profit									
Operating Expenses	99.5	99.2	98.2	91.0	99.0	101.3	101.8	99.3	96.3
Operating Profit	.5	.8	1.8	9.0	1.0	-1.3	-1.8	.7	3.7
All Other Expenses (net)	.0	.0	.4	1.9	.6	.2	-.2	-.2	.3
Profit Before Taxes	.5	.9	1.4	7.1	.3	-1.6	-1.5	.9	3.4
RATIOS									
Current	1.7	1.5	1.6	1.3	2.2	4.8	1.2	1.7	1.6
	1.0	1.0	1.0	.3	1.1	.7	.6	1.0	1.2
	.5	.4	.6	.1	.5	.3	.4	.7	.9
Quick	1.5	1.5	1.5	1.3	2.1	4.7	1.2	1.7	1.3
	.9	.9	.9	.3	1.1	.7	.6	1.0	1.0
	.5	.3	.4	.0	.4	.3	.3	.7	.8
Sales/Receivables	1 362.9	1 489.0	1 701.8	0 UND	0 UND	0 UND	0 UND	3 137.1	2 177.1
	8 43.1	7 52.3	7 50.2	6 65.0	9 39.4	0 999.8	6 61.7	10 36.9	9 41.5
	30 12.1	26 13.9	33 11.1	13 28.5	33 11.0	6 64.1	17 21.6	53 6.9	39 9.3
Cost of Sales/Inventory									
Cost of Sales/Payables									
Sales/Working Capital	24.0	34.9	25.5	25.2	8.4	83.3	46.2	28.7	17.7
	-315.5	-269.0	UND	-16.8	306.7	-155.8	-63.5	657.7	64.5
	-18.0	-9.5	-17.3	-4.9	-10.5	-13.1	-15.4	-26.5	-413.1
EBIT/Interest	10.2	14.4	22.8		8.3	23.0		100.0	52.8
	(82) 3.4	(83) 4.2	(76) 5.4		(16) 2.0	(15) 3.3	(11) 3.5		(22) 15.9
	-2.0	-2.8	.5		-2.0		-6.1	1.3	7.2
Net Profit + Depr., Dep., Amort./Cur. Mat. L/T/D	21.0	4.4	3.4						
	(17) 6.1	(18) 2.2	(12) 2.0						
	.7	.3	.4						
Fixed/Worth	.2	.3	.3	.1	.3	.4	1.2	.1	.2
	.7	1.3	1.2	2.7	.6	1.5	-4.1	.8	.3
	-1.6	-.7	-1.3	25.1	-3.0	-.5	-.2	-.5	1.4
Debt/Worth	1.2	1.5	1.5	1.5	.7	.7	2.9	2.3	1.6
	4.9	6.5	4.0	5.5	4.0	55.9	-8.9	5.6	2.3
	-7.0	-3.7	-5.4	-2.9	-3.5	-3.2	-3.3	-3.0	5.6
% Profit Before Taxes/Tangible Net Worth	39.9	53.6	73.5		59.0			57.3	68.7
	(80) 17.8	(69) 15.4	(72) 25.0		(12) 19.8		(11) 21.0		(26) 34.1
	.0	-2.8	11.3		10.1			2.1	19.4
% Profit Before Taxes/Total Assets	12.4	14.1	18.1	43.9	8.3	37.4	35.7	10.7	20.8
	4.0	5.0	6.7	4.8	5.1	5.5	5.0	4.7	10.2
	-5.1	-6.6	.7	-1.6	-7.6	-5.2	-4.5	.6	5.9
Sales/Net Fixed Assets	240.1	213.0	149.3	130.2	122.6	172.5	177.0	170.3	188.9
	55.7	40.8	54.9	11.5	36.5	98.3	38.1	86.6	66.3
	15.1	16.2	19.1	3.1	11.1	24.8	11.3	46.0	39.9
Sales/Total Assets	13.7	15.4	15.8	6.6	10.4	33.3	28.2	16.0	24.5
	4.4	5.5	4.4	2.5	3.6	15.7	5.4	4.1	5.6
	2.0	2.4	2.3	1.4	1.3	2.6	1.9	2.4	3.5
% Depr., Dep., Amort./Sales	.2	.2	.2		.2		.1	.1	.2
	(89) .7	(87) .8	(78) .6		(12) 1.1		(15) .5	(11) .9	(26) .4
	2.1	1.9	2.0		4.4		3.5	2.0	.8
% Officers', Directors', Owners' Comp/Sales	1.1	1.0	1.5						
	(50) 2.8	(45) 3.6	(43) 3.4						
	5.9	8.5	7.7						
Net Sales ($)	3623427M	2236549M	5048430M	4753M	42048M	43207M	138732M	241465M	4578225M
Total Assets ($)	1147037M	732848M	976909M	2661M	19193M	7784M	101702M	65924M	779645M

© RMA 2005

M = $ thousand   MM = $ million
See Pages 11 through 21 for Explanation of Ratios and Data

Current Data Sorted By Assets | Comparative Historical Data

	0-500M	500M-2MM	2-10MM	10-50MM	50-100MM	100-250MM	Type of Statement	4/1/00-3/31/01 ALL	4/1/01-3/31/02 ALL
							Unqualified	4	9
							Reviewed		4
		4	4	3	3		Compiled	7	13
	2	2					Tax Returns	5	4
		3	3	3	1		Other	9	20
							Unqualified	1	2	2
							5 (4/1-9/30/04)		34 (10/1/04-3/31/05)	
	6	10	9	9	5		**NUMBER OF STATEMENTS**	25	50

	0-500M	500M-2MM	2-10MM	10-50MM	50-100MM	100-250MM		Hist 1	Hist 2
	%	%	%	%	%	%	**ASSETS**	%	%
	31.8						Cash & Equivalents	35.1	22.8
	4.8					D	Trade Receivables (net)	7.7	6.7
	.2					A	Inventory	1.9	1.4
	2.3					T	All Other Current	3.9	8.4
	39.1					A	Total Current	48.6	39.3
	47.6						Fixed Assets (net)	36.8	43.7
	2.4					N	Intangibles (net)	6.9	4.5
	11.0					O	All Other Non-Current	7.7	12.5
	100.0					T	Total	100.0	100.0
							LIABILITIES		
	4.4					A	Notes Payable-Short Term	14.8	11.7
	13.0					V	Cur. Mat.-L/T/D	3.4	7.3
	17.6					A	Trade Payables	7.1	10.0
	.0					I	Income Taxes Payable	.4	.1
	11.3					L	All Other Current	25.8	21.4
	46.3					B	Total Current	51.5	50.4
	45.2					L	Long-Term Debt	24.2	28.8
	.0					E	Deferred Taxes	.1	.7
	17.7						All Other Non-Current	3.3	14.2
	-9.2						Net Worth	21.0	6.0
	100.0						Total Liabilities & Net Worth	100.0	100.0
							INCOME DATA		
	100.0						Net Sales	100.0	100.0
							Gross Profit		
	94.7						Operating Expenses	97.0	98.2
	5.3						Operating Profit	3.0	1.8
	1.7						All Other Expenses (net)	3.3	1.0
	3.6						Profit Before Taxes	-.3	.8
							RATIOS		
	2.4							1.4	1.6
	1.2						Current	1.2	1.1
	.3							.9	.4
	2.4							1.3	1.2
	1.2						Quick	1.1	.7
	.2							.7	.2
	0 UND							0 UND	0 UND
	0 UND						Sales/Receivables	2 243.1	3 110.5
	7 48.8							35 10.5	21 17.5
							Cost of Sales/Inventory		
							Cost of Sales/Payables		
	14.6							19.5	17.6
	NM						Sales/Working Capital	36.4	141.6
	-26.0							-77.5	-7.2
								14.7	3.3
							EBIT/Interest	(21) 1.6	(38) 1.1
								-.2	-2.0
							Net Profit + Depr., Dep., Amort./Cur. Mat. L./T/D		
	.7							.2	.4
	NM						Fixed/Worth	1.7	1.7
	-.7							NM	-6.4
	.6							.9	1.3
	NM						Debt/Worth	1.9	3.4
	-2.8							NM	-19.5
							% Profit Before Taxes/Tangible Net Worth	48.2 / (19) 27.9 / .5	43.1 / (35) 12.3 / -6.6
	34.4							14.5	14.6
	8.0						% Profit Before Taxes/Total Assets	1.7	2.3
	1.6							-2.4	-9.4
	82.8							72.1	46.0
	6.1						Sales/Net Fixed Assets	21.8	4.2
	3.7							2.3	2.0
	10.0							3.9	3.9
	3.6						Sales/Total Assets	2.7	2.2
	2.0							1.5	1.3
								.4	.9
							% Depr., Dep., Amort./Sales	(20) 2.9	(43) 4.3
								7.8	7.0
									.9
							% Officers', Directors', Owners' Comp/Sales		(16) 4.0
									10.4
	10410M	56550M	123924M	245833M	872572M		Net Sales ($)	934572M	1643478M
	1288M	9374M	44528M	168878M	415656M		Total Assets ($)	454184M	859006M

M = $ thousand   MM = $ million
See Pages 11 through 21 for Explanation of Ratios and Data

Comparative Historical Data | **Current Data Sorted By Sales**

			Type of Statement						
7	7	5	Unqualified		1		1	3	
6	4	4	Reviewed		1	2		1	
13	7	13	Compiled	3	4	1	2	2	1
3	5	4	Tax Returns	2	2	1	2		1
12	24	13	Other			2		5	6
4/1/02- 3/31/03	4/1/03- 3/31/04	4/1/04- 3/31/05			5 (4/1-9/30/04)		34 (10/1/04-3/31/05)		
ALL	ALL	ALL		0-1MM	1-3MM	3-5MM	5-10MM	10-25MM	25MM & OVER
41	47	39	**NUMBER OF STATEMENTS**	5	6	5	4	8	11
%	%	%	**ASSETS**	%	%	%	%	%	%
27.7	29.7	32.5	Cash & Equivalents						38.0
11.2	8.5	11.8	Trade Receivables (net)						8.5
2.1	.8	1.2	Inventory						2.7
7.4	8.2	5.1	All Other Current						9.7
48.5	47.1	50.5	Total Current						58.9
38.4	38.3	29.7	Fixed Assets (net)						17.0
2.6	4.3	2.6	Intangibles (net)						3.4
10.5	10.4	17.2	All Other Non-Current						20.7
100.0	100.0	100.0	Total						100.0
			LIABILITIES						
2.2	3.7	2.1	Notes Payable-Short Term						2.1
4.8	3.6	5.8	Cur. Mat.-L/T/D						1.7
11.1	15.2	12.2	Trade Payables						13.8
.2	.1	.2	Income Taxes Payable						.1
30.2	32.2	33.5	All Other Current						40.2
48.6	54.7	53.7	Total Current						57.9
30.8	22.9	21.9	Long-Term Debt						4.0
.4	.1	.0	Deferred Taxes						.1
3.0	6.4	7.4	All Other Non-Current						5.3
17.2	15.8	16.9	Net Worth						32.7
100.0	100.0	100.0	Total Liabilities & Net Worth						100.0
			INCOME DATA						
100.0	100.0	100.0	Net Sales						100.0
			Gross Profit						
92.8	97.1	96.3	Operating Expenses						95.6
7.2	2.9	3.7	Operating Profit						4.4
2.9	1.0	.3	All Other Expenses (net)						-.3
4.3	1.9	3.4	Profit Before Taxes						4.7
			RATIOS						
1.7	2.1	1.9							2.2
1.1	1.0	1.0	Current						1.0
.8	.5	.7							.3
1.4	1.8	1.7							2.0
1.0	.9	.9	Quick						.7
.7	.4	.6							.2
1 402.4	0 UND	0 UND							1 421.3
8 47.6	4 96.8	3 112.3	Sales/Receivables						2 148.0
29 12.4	14 25.5	22 16.4							3 111.9
			Cost of Sales/Inventory						
			Cost of Sales/Payables						
11.1	14.8	13.2							10.7
36.3	-286.7	-115.3	Sales/Working Capital						-115.3
-46.8	-7.8	-19.6							-7.3
6.6	6.2	15.5							
(29) 1.9	(30) 1.8	(24) 2.6	EBIT/Interest						
.2	-4.0	-.1							
			Net Profit + Depr., Dep., Amort./Cur. Mat. L/T/D						
.5	.5	.3							.1
1.4	2.1	1.5	Fixed/Worth						.5
9.2	-4.6	-5.2							3.3
1.4	1.1	1.0							1.0
3.7	3.7	5.0	Debt/Worth						3.8
35.4	-8.2	-34.8							5.8
68.6	76.1	89.8							118.7
(33) 24.2	(34) 19.7	(29) 22.4	% Profit Before Taxes/Tangible Net Worth					(10) 53.9	
-1.9	-9.1	7.9							9.9
15.8	19.4	20.4							24.3
3.4	4.2	6.3	% Profit Before Taxes/Total Assets						10.0
-1.8	-7.2	.6							2.3
38.1	55.8	66.1							83.6
4.7	11.9	14.8	Sales/Net Fixed Assets						33.3
2.0	2.1	3.3							13.3
4.3	4.6	5.3							5.3
2.0	2.3	2.2	Sales/Total Assets						2.7
1.3	1.2	1.2							1.0
.5	.4	.6							.4
(40) 3.7	(38) 2.2	(30) 2.6	% Depr., Dep., Amort./Sales						.8
7.1	5.8	8.2							2.4
2.3		2.5							
(10) 3.6		(11) 5.6	% Officers', Directors', Owners' Comp/Sales						
4.4		12.0							
913199M	1348737M	1309289M	Net Sales ($)	2391M	12590M	20696M	27718M	146483M	1099411M
441249M	690827M	639724M	Total Assets ($)	1570M	7591M	34784M	9105M	63987M	522687M

Current Data Sorted By Assets   **Comparative Historical Data**

						Type of Statement	4/1/00-3/31/01 ALL	4/1/01-3/31/02 ALL
1		4	5		1	Unqualified		
	4					Reviewed		
2	3	1				Compiled		
1	2	6	1	1	1	Tax Returns		
						Other		
11 (4/1-9/30/04)			22 (10/1/04-3/31/05)					
0-500M	500M-2MM	2-10MM	10-50MM	50-100MM	100-250MM			
4	9	11	6	1	2	**NUMBER OF STATEMENTS**		
%	%	%	%	%	%		%	%
						ASSETS		
		26.5				Cash & Equivalents	D	D
		7.3				Trade Receivables (net)	A	A
		.8				Inventory	T	T
		3.4				All Other Current	A	A
		38.0				Total Current		
		45.0				Fixed Assets (net)	N	N
		3.6				Intangibles (net)	O	O
		13.3				All Other Non-Current	T	T
		100.0				Total		
						LIABILITIES	A	A
		1.4				Notes Payable-Short Term	V	V
		2.6				Cur. Mat.-L/T/D	A	A
		5.4				Trade Payables	I	I
		2.1				Income Taxes Payable	L	L
		10.9				All Other Current	A	A
		22.3				Total Current	B	B
		20.0				Long-Term Debt	L	L
		.9				Deferred Taxes	E	E
		6.5				All Other Non-Current		
		50.3				Net Worth		
		100.0				Total Liabilities & Net Worth		
						INCOME DATA		
		100.0				Net Sales		
						Gross Profit		
		81.3				Operating Expenses		
		18.7				Operating Profit		
		3.4				All Other Expenses (net)		
		15.3				Profit Before Taxes		
						RATIOS		
		10.5				Current		
		2.6						
		1.1						
		10.5				Quick		
		2.2						
		.7						
		2 173.3				Sales/Receivables		
		24 15.2						
		45 8.1						
						Cost of Sales/Inventory		
						Cost of Sales/Payables		
		2.2				Sales/Working Capital		
		4.9						
		45.0						
						EBIT/Interest		
						Net Profit + Depr., Dep., Amort./Cur. Mat. L /T/D		
		.2				Fixed/Worth		
		1.3						
		3.2						
		.3				Debt/Worth		
		1.3						
		2.6						
		45.0				% Profit Before Taxes/Tangible Net Worth		
	(10)	17.5						
		4.7						
		30.1				% Profit Before Taxes/Total Assets		
		7.5						
		2.3						
		15.0				Sales/Net Fixed Assets		
		3.1						
		1.1						
		1.5				Sales/Total Assets		
		.9						
		.6						
						% Depr., Dep., Amort./Sales		
						% Officers', Directors', Owners' Comp/Sales		
2132M	18879M	65307M	205983M	44762M	134160M	Net Sales ($)		
1047M	10612M	43315M	134127M	65981M	237168M	Total Assets ($)		

M = $ thousand   MM = $ million
See Pages 11 through 21 for Explanation of Ratios and Data

Comparative Historical Data					Current Data Sorted By Sales					
10	14	11	Type of Statement							
			Unqualified	1	2	2	2	1	3
3	1		Reviewed						
8	9	4	Compiled	3	1				
5	6	6	Tax Returns	3	2		1		
16	12	12	Other	2	3	2		2	3
4/1/02-	4/1/03-	4/1/04-			11 (4/1-9/30/04)			22 (10/1/04-3/31/05)		
3/31/03	3/31/04	3/31/05								
ALL	ALL	ALL		0-1MM	1-3MM	3-5MM	5-10MM	10-25MM	25MM & OVER
42	42	33	**NUMBER OF STATEMENTS**	9	8	4	3	3	6
%	%	%		%	%	%	%	%	%
			ASSETS						
16.6	20.0	22.0	Cash & Equivalents						
4.4	8.0	10.8	Trade Receivables (net)						
6.9	2.1	2.2	Inventory						
4.2	5.4	7.0	All Other Current						
32.2	35.5	42.1	Total Current						
58.8	52.5	40.5	Fixed Assets (net)						
3.3	2.6	1.4	Intangibles (net)						
5.7	9.4	16.0	All Other Non-Current						
100.0	100.0	100.0	Total						
			LIABILITIES						
2.0	5.9	4.4	Notes Payable-Short Term						
6.3	3.8	3.2	Cur. Mat.-L/T/D						
5.0	5.7	6.7	Trade Payables						
1.0	1.1	1.0	Income Taxes Payable						
7.8	9.4	11.2	All Other Current						
22.1	25.8	26.4	Total Current						
42.1	31.7	22.0	Long-Term Debt						
.0	.6	.5	Deferred Taxes						
4.9	4.5	8.3	All Other Non-Current						
30.9	37.4	42.7	Net Worth						
100.0	100.0	100.0	Total Liabilities & Net Worth						
			INCOME DATA						
100.0	100.0	100.0	Net Sales						
			Gross Profit						
83.7	85.7	85.1	Operating Expenses						
16.3	14.3	14.9	Operating Profit						
7.7	7.4	3.5	All Other Expenses (net)						
8.7	6.9	11.4	Profit Before Taxes						
			RATIOS						
6.0	7.2	5.6							
1.7	1.3	1.8	Current						
.7	.6	.9							
4.1	6.2	5.1							
.9	.9	1.0	Quick						
.4	.2	.3							
0 UND	0 UND	0 UND							
2 161.9	3 140.5	10 34.8	Sales/Receivables						
9 40.3	27 13.4	27 13.6							
			Cost of Sales/Inventory						
			Cost of Sales/Payables						
3.8	2.4	2.4							
10.3	12.0	9.4	Sales/Working Capital						
-21.2	-27.7	-36.1							
6.9	8.6	33.9							
(31) 2.2	(27) 3.7	(25) 4.9	EBIT/Interest						
.7	2.0	1.6							
			Net Profit + Depr., Dep., Amort./Cur. Mat. L/T/D						
.8	.7	.2							
1.8	1.3	1.1	Fixed/Worth						
11.1	4.1	5.3							
.5	.4	.4							
2.3	1.6	1.1	Debt/Worth						
16.0	5.4	16.1							
57.1	39.9	41.3							
(34) 11.7	(35) 13.7	(28) 11.5	% Profit Before Taxes/Tangible Net Worth						
.5	5.2	1.2							
20.2	17.2	23.7							
5.0	6.2	7.8	% Profit Before Taxes/Total Assets						
.2	3.0	1.2							
8.3	12.3	38.6							
2.1	1.9	3.1	Sales/Net Fixed Assets						
.6	.8	1.2							
2.8	1.8	2.0							
1.2	1.0	1.0	Sales/Total Assets						
.5	.5	.6							
2.7	2.9	.9							
(36) 6.4	(32) 5.6	(26) 3.3	% Depr., Dep., Amort./Sales						
10.5	11.3	7.3							
4.5	2.1	3.4							
(13) 11.8	(10) 3.9	(10) 5.2	% Officers', Directors', Owners' Comp/Sales						
17.2	8.4	13.2							
849836M	522091M	471223M	Net Sales ($)	5031M	16273M	14729M	21194M	47402M	366594M
775320M	591694M	492250M	Total Assets ($)	9641M	14284M	36899M	11663M	48230M	371533M

© RMA 2005

M = $ thousand   MM = $ million
See Pages 11 through 21 for Explanation of Ratios and Data

Current Data Sorted By Assets   Comparative Historical Data

0-500M	500M-2MM	2-10MM	10-50MM	50-100MM	100-250MM	Type of Statement	4/1/00-3/31/01 ALL	4/1/01-3/31/02 ALL
	1	3	5	1	3	Unqualified	10	10
	5	15	1			Reviewed	19	17
3	2	8				Compiled	13	17
3	4					Tax Returns	7	9
3	8	12	3	1		Other	25	22
	18 (4/1-9/30/04)		63 (10/1/04-3/31/05)					
9	20	38	9	2	3	**NUMBER OF STATEMENTS**	74	75
%	%	%	%	%	%	**ASSETS**	%	%
	11.7	4.0				Cash & Equivalents	9.7	10.0
	56.8	60.8				Trade Receivables (net)	48.2	48.5
	.0	.9				Inventory	2.4	1.6
	3.1	1.9				All Other Current	3.9	3.4
	71.7	67.5				Total Current	64.2	63.6
	16.7	14.8				Fixed Assets (net)	19.5	21.4
	5.0	3.5				Intangibles (net)	8.3	8.3
	6.7	14.1				All Other Non-Current	8.0	6.8
	100.0	100.0				Total	100.0	100.0
						LIABILITIES		
	10.7	23.1				Notes Payable-Short Term	17.4	17.7
	3.6	3.3				Cur. Mat.-L/T/D	4.4	4.4
	4.4	6.5				Trade Payables	8.3	7.9
	.7	.6				Income Taxes Payable	.7	1.2
	21.4	20.4				All Other Current	19.3	18.4
	40.9	53.9				Total Current	50.1	49.6
	10.5	10.0				Long-Term Debt	13.6	17.5
	.1	.6				Deferred Taxes	.6	.8
	4.2	1.9				All Other Non-Current	5.6	8.6
	44.4	33.6				Net Worth	30.2	23.5
	100.0	100.0				Total Liabilities & Net Worth	100.0	100.0
						INCOME DATA		
	100.0	100.0				Net Sales	100.0	100.0
						Gross Profit		
	94.3	97.2				Operating Expenses	96.3	95.4
	5.7	2.8				Operating Profit	3.7	4.6
	1.1	.2				All Other Expenses (net)	.5	1.1
	4.6	2.6				Profit Before Taxes	3.2	3.5
						RATIOS		
	3.4	1.8					1.9	1.9
	1.7	1.2				Current	1.3	1.2
	1.0	1.0					1.0	1.0
	3.4	1.7					1.7	1.8
	1.7	1.2				Quick	1.2	1.1
	.9	1.0					.9	.8
	29 12.8	40 9.1					33 10.9	28 13.2
	45 8.2	49 7.4				Sales/Receivables	44 8.2	44 8.4
	62 5.9	62 5.9					57 6.4	58 6.3
						Cost of Sales/Inventory		
						Cost of Sales/Payables		
	10.6	14.6					10.2	12.0
	16.0	34.5				Sales/Working Capital	41.7	41.6
	−999.8	999.8					−201.0	633.2
	28.2	8.7					7.2	8.6
	(17) 6.7	(37) 4.0				EBIT/Interest	(67) 3.0	(69) 4.0
	−.2	2.0					1.2	1.6
		9.2				Net Profit + Depr., Dep.,	5.7	7.2
		(13) 4.1				Amort./Cur. Mat. L /T/D	(17) 3.5	(19) 2.8
		1.1					1.5	2.0
	.1	.2					.2	.1
	.3	.4				Fixed/Worth	.6	.7
	1.8	1.1					2.8	9.9
	.6	1.2					1.4	1.3
	1.5	2.6				Debt/Worth	2.7	3.9
	5.3	5.9					NM	−33.6
	70.5	50.9				% Profit Before Taxes/Tangible	69.2	55.9
	(18) 28.5	(36) 26.8				Net Worth	(56) 30.1	(56) 34.6
	−6.5	5.6					9.2	18.1
	23.8	15.0				% Profit Before Taxes/Total	15.7	15.6
	10.5	5.5				Assets	6.7	10.3
	5.6	2.5					1.1	2.2
	72.3	122.6					71.8	81.5
	44.9	56.4				Sales/Net Fixed Assets	33.3	37.9
	28.6	28.7					15.5	19.5
	6.2	5.4					5.5	6.2
	4.5	4.3				Sales/Total Assets	4.4	4.3
	3.4	3.4					2.7	3.0
	.4	.3					.5	.5
	(16) .7	(34) .6				% Depr., Dep., Amort./Sales	(60) 1.1	(60) .9
	1.1	1.6					2.2	2.5
	2.1	1.2					2.1	1.5
	(12) 3.2	(14) 2.0				% Officers', Directors',	(30) 4.7	(34) 4.0
	7.3	5.5				Owners' Comp/Sales	8.3	7.8
18359M	124464M	676379M	569397M	391005M	1265354M	Net Sales ($)	4459378M	3696706M
2122M	25037M	166535M	153186M	125541M	354733M	Total Assets ($)	1807564M	1195896M

M = $ thousand   MM = $ million
See Pages 11 through 21 for Explanation of Ratios and Data

Comparative Historical Data				Current Data Sorted By Sales					
			Type of Statement						
13	11	13	Unqualified	1				1	11
15	17	21	Reviewed		1		6	8	6
13	28	13	Compiled	1	3	1	2	6	
6	3	7	Tax Returns		4	2	1		
24	23	27	Other	1	1	4	8	8	5
4/1/02-	4/1/03-	4/1/04-			18 (4/1-9/30/04)		63 (10/1/04-3/31/05)		
3/31/03	3/31/04	3/31/05		0-1MM	1-3MM	3-5MM	5-10MM	10-25MM	25MM & OVER
ALL	ALL	ALL							
71	82	81	**NUMBER OF STATEMENTS**	3	8	8	17	23	22
%	%	%	**ASSETS**	%	%	%	%	%	%
9.7	7.9	7.4	Cash & Equivalents				7.3	7.8	2.0
49.2	48.3	54.8	Trade Receivables (net)				63.3	60.4	63.0
1.4	.8	.8	Inventory				.0	1.4	.5
7.0	5.8	4.0	All Other Current				2.2	2.1	6.1
67.2	62.7	67.0	Total Current				72.8	71.8	71.7
16.0	18.2	16.5	Fixed Assets (net)				10.4	16.9	7.4
7.8	6.8	4.8	Intangibles (net)				3.3	.7	8.2
8.9	12.2	11.7	All Other Non-Current				13.5	10.6	12.8
100.0	100.0	100.0	Total				100.0	100.0	100.0
			LIABILITIES						
19.1	17.6	19.5	Notes Payable-Short Term				11.7	19.4	23.6
6.2	6.0	5.6	Cur. Mat.-L/T/D				2.3	3.4	2.2
6.2	7.8	5.8	Trade Payables				4.4	6.1	8.2
1.0	1.1	.9	Income Taxes Payable				.7	.4	1.8
22.7	19.8	21.8	All Other Current				22.1	21.6	21.5
55.3	52.3	53.6	Total Current				41.1	50.9	57.3
17.0	19.6	15.8	Long-Term Debt				10.5	9.8	10.8
.5	.7	.5	Deferred Taxes				.0	1.0	.7
6.5	5.8	3.7	All Other Non-Current				5.2	1.3	4.2
20.8	21.7	26.4	Net Worth				43.1	37.1	26.9
100.0	100.0	100.0	Total Liabilities & Net Worth				100.0	100.0	100.0
			INCOME DATA						
100.0	100.0	100.0	Net Sales				100.0	100.0	100.0
			Gross Profit						
96.3	95.6	96.7	Operating Expenses				97.0	98.0	97.0
3.7	4.4	3.3	Operating Profit				3.0	2.0	3.0
.8	1.2	.4	All Other Expenses (net)				.3	.1	.4
2.9	3.1	2.9	Profit Before Taxes				2.7	1.9	2.5
			RATIOS						
1.7	1.8	2.0					3.3	1.9	1.9
1.2	1.2	1.3	Current				1.8	1.3	1.2
1.0	1.0	1.0					1.1	1.1	.9
1.5	1.6	1.8					3.3	1.7	1.6
1.1	1.1	1.2	Quick				1.8	1.2	1.1
.8	.8	.9					1.0	1.0	.9
37 9.9	35 10.4	34 10.8					38 9.7	41 8.9	37 9.9
42 8.7	41 8.8	45 8.1	Sales/Receivables				45 8.1	47 7.8	56 6.5
55 6.6	53 6.8	63 5.8					73 5.0	55 6.7	70 5.2
			Cost of Sales/Inventory						
			Cost of Sales/Payables						
13.9	17.3	13.5					9.7	14.7	12.5
35.8	38.3	28.6	Sales/Working Capital				14.4	28.6	35.1
261.3	-498.0	-999.8					80.7	87.2	-87.2
9.1	7.1	10.0					10.0	9.6	
(65) 3.5	(74) 3.4	(75) 4.5	EBIT/Interest	(15) 6.7	(21) 3.1	(20) 5.0			
1.1	1.4	1.8					3.9	1.5	2.0
4.6	20.8	11.5	Net Profit + Depr., Dep.,				8.5	31.3	
(24) 1.5	(22) 2.4	(25) 4.1	Amort./Cur. Mat. L/T/D	(10) 3.5	(11) 4.3				
.9	1.1	1.6					1.5	1.4	
.2	.2	.2					.1	.2	.1
.7	.6	.4	Fixed/Worth				.2	.3	.4
39.0	2.9	1.3					.8	.8	.9
1.6	1.6	1.1					.5	1.1	2.1
3.9	3.1	2.7	Debt/Worth				1.4	2.0	4.8
141.7	14.1	8.4					5.3	3.0	17.9
83.9	60.2	63.2	% Profit Before Taxes/Tangible				51.9	47.8	95.9
(54) 28.5	(67) 37.4	(70) 28.0	Net Worth	(15) 27.9	(19) 22.0	33.0			
12.5	10.9	8.7					11.1	4.9	13.9
13.5	17.1	15.9	% Profit Before Taxes/Total				21.8	15.0	15.3
5.0	7.9	9.5	Assets				11.5	5.3	9.8
.2	1.4	2.5					6.7	2.0	2.9
94.3	101.4	94.6					82.8	86.9	162.1
45.1	38.4	50.8	Sales/Net Fixed Assets				61.0	43.0	82.5
18.1	17.4	29.3					33.1	32.0	41.7
5.8	5.5	5.6					6.1	5.7	5.0
4.3	4.0	4.3	Sales/Total Assets				4.3	4.2	4.2
2.9	3.0	3.4					3.4	3.9	3.1
.5	.4	.3					.3	.4	.2
(53) 1.1	(63) .9	(71) .6	% Depr., Dep., Amort./Sales	(14) .6	(19) .5	(21) .5			
2.2	2.3	1.1					1.0	1.7	.8
1.7	2.3	1.4	% Officers', Directors',						
(18) 4.8	(28) 3.0	(33) 2.9	Owners' Comp/Sales						
8.6	5.2	6.1							
4114417M	3380297M	3044958M	Net Sales ($)	1452M	14520M	33364M	129895M	371190M	2494537M
1185563M	988903M	827154M	Total Assets ($)	2106M	5305M	10770M	33920M	80079M	694974M

M = $ thousand   MM = $ million
See Pages 11 through 21 for Explanation of Ratios and Data

Current Data Sorted By Assets   **Comparative Historical Data**

						Type of Statement		
	1	9	12	1	3	Unqualified	18	16
	21	18	2			Reviewed	28	26
11	17	5				Compiled	27	24
9	14	5				Tax Returns	10	12
7	15	18	12	4	2	Other	32	29
	32 (4/1-9/30/04)		154 (10/1/04-3/31/05)				4/1/00-3/31/01	4/1/01-3/31/02
0-500M	500M-2MM	2-10MM	10-50MM	50-100MM	100-250MM		ALL	ALL
27	68	55	26	5	5	NUMBER OF STATEMENTS	115	107
%	%	%	%	%	%	ASSETS	%	%
17.0	11.3	8.5	2.9			Cash & Equivalents	10.4	7.7
35.5	42.2	32.8	21.5			Trade Receivables (net)	36.7	34.6
12.4	10.2	9.5	6.2			Inventory	11.1	11.6
.9	2.8	4.4	10.2			All Other Current	3.1	4.3
65.8	66.5	55.1	40.8			Total Current	61.3	58.2
22.4	19.1	15.3	17.1			Fixed Assets (net)	19.2	19.5
2.7	8.7	16.0	28.6			Intangibles (net)	10.5	14.9
9.1	5.7	13.6	13.5			All Other Non-Current	8.9	7.5
100.0	100.0	100.0	100.0			Total	100.0	100.0
						LIABILITIES		
11.4	8.9	13.5	6.9			Notes Payable-Short Term	14.9	11.6
7.4	5.4	8.2	2.6			Cur. Mat.-L/T/D	5.8	4.8
19.0	15.4	10.5	7.6			Trade Payables	14.4	13.3
.0	.2	.3	.2			Income Taxes Payable	.4	.7
24.7	15.1	16.7	18.2			All Other Current	23.9	14.3
62.6	45.0	49.2	35.4			Total Current	59.4	44.6
30.3	17.8	22.9	49.0			Long-Term Debt	21.3	18.2
.0	.5	.3	.3			Deferred Taxes	.4	.8
1.9	6.6	9.6	6.5			All Other Non-Current	5.1	7.6
5.3	30.1	18.1	8.7			Net Worth	13.8	28.7
100.0	100.0	100.0	100.0			Total Liabilities & Net Worth	100.0	100.0
						INCOME DATA		
100.0	100.0	100.0	100.0			Net Sales	100.0	100.0
						Gross Profit		
93.0	94.2	93.3	92.4			Operating Expenses	95.5	93.9
7.0	5.8	6.7	7.6			Operating Profit	4.5	6.1
1.5	.6	2.2	5.3			All Other Expenses (net)	2.4	3.0
5.5	5.2	4.6	2.3			Profit Before Taxes	2.1	3.1
						RATIOS		
1.8	2.4	1.7	2.0				1.7	2.0
1.1	1.6	1.3	1.1			Current	1.2	1.4
.9	1.1	.9	.6				.9	.9
1.6	2.0	1.2	1.3				1.4	1.6
.9	1.2	.9	.6			Quick	.9	1.0
.5	.8	.6	.4				.6	.6
13 28.0	35 10.3	28 13.1	32 11.5				28 13.3	28 13.0
40 9.0	47 7.7	48 7.7	42 8.7			Sales/Receivables	44 8.2	43 8.6
54 6.7	65 5.6	68 5.3	67 5.4				62 5.9	65 5.6
						Cost of Sales/Inventory		
						Cost of Sales/Payables		
13.1	7.0	9.4	10.1				9.4	7.0
79.7	15.3	16.8	45.5			Sales/Working Capital	24.1	14.3
-33.9	55.6	-21.6	-11.7				-57.5	-67.2
11.3	14.9	17.0	5.0				6.7	11.4
(20) 4.8	(60) 6.6	(53) 4.0	(22) 1.7			EBIT/Interest	(106) 2.2	(96) 3.7
1.5	2.0	1.3	.9				1.2	1.4
	4.3	12.6				Net Profit + Depr., Dep.,	8.7	4.5
	(13) 2.2	(19) 3.6				Amort./Cur. Mat. L /T/D	(34) 3.3	(26) 2.9
	1.3	1.8					1.5	.9
.4	.3	.2	.8				.3	.2
4.1	.6	.6	NM			Fixed/Worth	1.0	.7
-.9	-20.2	-.5	-.1				8.7	-5.8
1.2	.8	1.2	3.7				1.4	1.2
9.8	2.0	3.6	NM			Debt/Worth	4.4	3.2
-6.6	-64.8	-4.5	-1.8				-23.0	-13.9
167.2	43.4	78.9	174.8			% Profit Before Taxes/Tangible	56.5	63.9
(17) 60.2	(50) 19.2	(37) 34.1	(13) 29.4			Net Worth	(85) 30.6	(77) 27.3
15.9	3.7	7.4	9.3				12.4	11.7
25.4	21.9	21.8	12.5			% Profit Before Taxes/Total	13.2	17.4
17.3	8.4	6.4	3.4			Assets	4.8	7.5
1.8	1.5	.8	-.5				.6	1.5
75.6	44.6	49.5	54.2				40.5	46.1
25.0	24.6	26.9	15.3			Sales/Net Fixed Assets	19.7	21.1
9.2	13.9	12.5	8.1				9.3	9.7
5.1	3.7	3.0	2.4				4.0	4.0
3.6	3.1	2.4	1.4			Sales/Total Assets	2.7	2.7
2.4	2.4	1.4	.6				1.8	1.5
.4	.8	.8	.9				.9	.6
(20) 1.4	(55) 1.5	(43) 1.3	(15) 2.3			% Depr., Dep., Amort./Sales	(92) 1.9	(78) 1.7
3.7	2.5	2.9	12.4				4.4	3.8
3.5	4.5	2.9				% Officers', Directors',	4.1	3.4
(16) 9.1	(43) 7.4	(14) 3.9				Owners' Comp/Sales	(49) 6.2	(43) 6.9
21.2	11.2	7.9						11.4
29796M	246324M	531321M	897139M	336741M	823491M	Net Sales ($)	1731539M	1089162M
7975M	75034M	237156M	619101M	356742M	652258M	Total Assets ($)	1061486M	969380M

M = $ thousand   MM = $ million
See Pages 11 through 21 for Explanation of Ratios and Data

Comparative Historical Data				Current Data Sorted By Sales					

Hist 1	Hist 2	Hist 3	Type of Statement	0-1MM	1-3MM	3-5MM	5-10MM	10-25MM	25MM & OVER
24	22	26	Unqualified		1		7	9	9
41	44	41	Reviewed		9	9	13	8	2
28	48	33	Compiled	5	16	8	3	1	
24	22	28	Tax Returns	5	14	3	3	3	
39	49	58	Other	3	13	6	14	10	12
4/1/02- 3/31/03 ALL	4/1/03- 3/31/04 ALL	4/1/04- 3/31/05 ALL		32 (4/1-9/30/04)			154 (10/1/04-3/31/05)		
156	185	186	**NUMBER OF STATEMENTS**	13	53	26	40	31	23
%	%	%	**ASSETS**	%	%	%	%	%	%
10.2	9.3	9.7	Cash & Equivalents	17.8	11.1	12.6	7.0	7.8	5.8
35.5	34.1	34.4	Trade Receivables (net)	28.7	37.8	37.8	34.6	31.3	29.7
9.8	11.1	10.0	Inventory	11.9	10.1	8.9	11.1	7.5	11.1
4.4	4.7	4.1	All Other Current	.9	1.7	2.2	5.6	9.1	4.4
59.8	59.2	58.2	Total Current	59.4	60.6	61.5	58.3	55.7	51.0
17.2	19.9	17.9	Fixed Assets (net)	23.3	21.9	14.6	18.6	11.1	17.2
12.9	12.4	14.5	Intangibles (net)	5.2	10.3	13.1	11.4	22.4	25.4
10.0	8.4	9.5	All Other Non-Current	12.1	7.2	10.7	11.7	10.7	6.5
100.0	100.0	100.0	Total	100.0	100.0	100.0	100.0	100.0	100.0
			LIABILITIES						
17.1	13.8	10.0	Notes Payable-Short Term	16.6	10.8	5.0	14.2	7.3	6.2
7.3	5.7	6.1	Cur. Mat.-L/T/D	12.6	4.3	6.4	9.2	4.3	3.1
13.5	14.1	13.0	Trade Payables	10.4	15.1	13.2	14.9	10.0	10.3
.4	.2	.2	Income Taxes Payable	.0	.0	.2	.6	.2	.2
16.9	17.6	17.4	All Other Current	33.6	12.3	17.9	15.0	21.2	18.3
55.2	51.4	46.6	Total Current	73.2	42.4	42.7	53.8	42.9	38.2
20.1	25.1	25.9	Long-Term Debt	34.5	23.1	17.5	23.8	38.2	24.4
.4	.4	.3	Deferred Taxes	.0	.5	.1	.3	.3	.4
6.1	8.8	6.8	All Other Non-Current	1.4	3.3	11.2	10.4	7.0	6.4
18.2	14.3	20.3	Net Worth	-9.1	30.7	28.6	11.7	11.6	30.6
100.0	100.0	100.0	Total Liabilities & Net Worth	100.0	100.0	100.0	100.0	100.0	100.0
			INCOME DATA						
100.0	100.0	100.0	Net Sales	100.0	100.0	100.0	100.0	100.0	100.0
			Gross Profit						
94.4	95.3	93.6	Operating Expenses	90.7	94.0	93.3	93.1	93.8	95.6
5.6	4.7	6.4	Operating Profit	9.3	6.0	6.7	6.9	6.2	4.4
2.8	2.2	2.1	All Other Expenses (net)	2.4	1.4	.9	3.3	2.4	2.1
2.8	2.5	4.3	Profit Before Taxes	6.9	4.6	5.8	3.6	3.8	2.3
			RATIOS						
1.9	1.9	2.2	Current	1.8	2.8	2.2	1.8	1.5	2.0
1.3	1.2	1.3		.9	1.6	1.4	1.4	1.2	1.3
.8	.8	.9		.6	1.0	.8	.8	.8	.9
1.5	1.5	1.5	Quick	1.0	2.5	2.0	1.4	1.1	1.5
.9	.9	1.0		.7	1.3	1.2	.9	.8	.9
.5	.5	.6		.4	.6	.6	.6	.6	.5
26 13.9	27 13.4	31 11.9	Sales/Receivables	0 UND	31 11.9	28 13.1	31 11.7	29 12.7	39 9.2
43 8.4	43 8.5	46 8.0		40 9.0	48 7.5	40 9.0	43 8.4	45 8.2	61 6.0
66 5.5	60 6.1	67 5.4		61 6.0	67 5.4	63 5.8	66 5.6	65 5.7	81 4.5
			Cost of Sales/Inventory						
			Cost of Sales/Payables						
7.6	8.2	7.4	Sales/Working Capital	15.4	7.0	7.0	8.7	12.6	6.3
24.3	27.8	22.5		-69.5	16.0	18.4	28.1	38.8	16.8
-36.8	-21.1	-35.6		-7.4	-309.6	-115.4	-28.7	-22.8	-72.4
10.7	8.0	12.6	EBIT/Interest		7.0	20.1	17.5	14.9	8.4
(136) 3.7	(170) 2.9	(164) 4.7		(44) 3.0	(24) 9.6	(38) 7.6	(30) 2.4	(20) 2.8	
1.4	.5	1.3			.2	4.9	1.4	.9	1.0
4.2	3.3	7.5	Net Profit + Depr., Dep., Amort./Cur. Mat. L/T/D				7.9	19.9	
(42) 2.1	(43) 1.8	(41) 2.4				(14) 3.8	(10) 2.1		
1.2	.8	1.3					1.9	1.1	
.2	.3	.3	Fixed/Worth	.6	.2	.2	.2	.3	.5
.6	1.1	1.1		4.1	1.1	.4	.6	-12.7	1.1
10.9	-.8	-.7		-1.1	-2.4	-1.7	7.2	-.2	-.4
1.2	1.3	1.3	Debt/Worth	2.6	.7	1.1		3.0	2.4
3.9	4.0	4.2		9.8	2.4	2.0	2.9	-53.0	7.3
-13.5	-4.2	-5.4		-5.3	-7.2	-12.8	19.1	-2.7	-3.7
79.9	51.5	72.6	% Profit Before Taxes/Tangible Net Worth		55.0	99.9	55.2	122.9	128.3
(115) 30.7	(120) 19.0	(122) 25.9		(35) 18.4	(17) 34.2	(31) 34.1	(15) 33.1	(15) 23.6	
5.4	1.3	6.0			3.8	3.1	7.9	19.8	1.2
18.1	14.3	21.1	% Profit Before Taxes/Total Assets	24.2	18.0	27.1	22.0	18.0	12.3
6.0	4.3	6.9		20.4	5.8	14.1	8.6	4.3	4.1
.3	-1.7	.8		-5.4	.3	1.4	1.4	.7	.0
43.3	44.1	48.9	Sales/Net Fixed Assets	80.7	37.6	55.9	48.0	66.0	28.8
20.8	21.1	22.1		19.1	19.9	28.3	25.4	28.6	11.2
11.9	10.4	11.2		5.5	9.1	14.5	12.8	15.7	6.0
3.7	3.7	3.5	Sales/Total Assets	4.9	3.6	3.8	3.5	3.5	2.7
2.7	2.7	2.6		2.8	2.6	3.1	2.4	2.4	1.8
1.5	1.7	1.5		1.1	1.8	2.0	1.7	1.2	1.0
.7	.8	.8	% Depr., Dep., Amort./Sales	.4	1.2	.5	1.0	.5	1.0
(113) 1.8	(145) 1.7	(139) 1.5		(11) .9	(40) 1.9	(17) 1.1	(33) 1.4	(20) 1.0	(18) 2.1
3.5	3.3	3.5		4.7	3.8	1.6	3.3	2.1	5.8
3.8	3.5	3.9	% Officers', Directors', Owners' Comp/Sales		4.7	4.2	2.8		
(66) 7.0	(71) 6.6	(74) 6.8		(34) 7.1	(16) 5.5	(13) 5.1			
11.1	10.8	11.6			13.5	8.6	10.5		
2090372M	2563111M	2864812M	Net Sales ($)	6577M	100494M	100273M	281457M	510107M	1865904M
1722376M	1722515M	1948266M	Total Assets ($)	10438M	48464M	42248M	184712M	354499M	1307905M

M = $ thousand   MM = $ million
See Pages 11 through 21 for Explanation of Ratios and Data

Current Data Sorted By Assets   **Comparative Historical Data**

0-500M	500M-2MM	2-10MM	10-50MM	50-100MM	100-250MM	Type of Statement	4/1/00-3/31/01 ALL	4/1/01-3/31/02 ALL
1	2	5	2			Unqualified	4	4
7	9		1			Reviewed	5	6
14	6	3	1			Compiled	22	19
4	8	4	1			Tax Returns	12	8
					1	Other	19	10
14 (4/1-9/30/04)			**55 (10/1/04-3/31/05)**					
26	25	12	5		1	**NUMBER OF STATEMENTS**	62	47
%	%	%	%	%	%	**ASSETS**	%	%
24.4	15.0	7.6				Cash & Equivalents	14.4	12.6
16.5	20.2	32.1				Trade Receivables (net)	23.7	24.4
.8	4.7	4.9				Inventory	4.0	7.1
3.0	3.5	3.8				All Other Current	2.5	2.7
44.8	43.5	48.3				Total Current	44.7	46.8
35.3	39.0	32.1				Fixed Assets (net)	33.0	35.6
7.0	6.6	13.4				Intangibles (net)	9.0	5.7
12.9	10.9	6.2				All Other Non-Current	13.3	11.9
100.0	100.0	100.0				Total	100.0	100.0
						LIABILITIES		
17.0	10.4	2.3				Notes Payable-Short Term	16.1	8.7
8.5	2.7	3.3				Cur. Mat.-L/T/D	5.1	6.3
6.9	8.8	12.4				Trade Payables	9.8	12.1
.1	.7	.6				Income Taxes Payable	.2	.7
10.9	7.1	14.0				All Other Current	16.3	11.8
43.4	29.7	32.6				Total Current	47.5	39.7
40.8	22.9	24.1				Long-Term Debt	17.9	20.6
.2	.7	.2				Deferred Taxes	.6	.5
24.8	.9	3.3				All Other Non-Current	6.2	3.5
-9.2	45.8	39.8				Net Worth	27.8	35.8
100.0	100.0	100.0				Total Liabilities & Net Worth	100.0	100.0
						INCOME DATA		
100.0	100.0	100.0				Net Sales	100.0	100.0
						Gross Profit		
94.7	91.0	92.2				Operating Expenses	93.4	92.8
5.3	9.0	7.8				Operating Profit	6.6	7.2
.4	1.5	4.7				All Other Expenses (net)	1.7	1.0
4.9	7.4	3.1				Profit Before Taxes	5.0	6.2
						RATIOS		
4.0	2.5	2.4					1.7	1.5
.9	1.8	1.3				Current	1.1	1.2
.7	.7	.8					.7	.9
3.8	2.1	1.7					1.4	1.4
.9	1.3	1.0				Quick	.9	1.0
.6	.6	.6					.6	.6
0 UND	11 33.6	23 15.8					16 22.5	11 32.3
0 UND	25 14.8	29 12.4				Sales/Receivables	27 13.3	26 13.8
37 9.7	31 11.9	37 9.9					40 9.2	37 9.9
						Cost of Sales/Inventory		
						Cost of Sales/Payables		
20.4	8.7	10.5					17.6	18.3
-246.9	20.6	41.4				Sales/Working Capital	102.1	66.9
-23.0	-26.9	-60.7					-28.8	-72.4
14.7	15.1	63.3					11.7	10.3
(23) 5.4	(23) 5.3	(11) 9.3				EBIT/Interest	(55) 4.5	(44) 4.3
2.1	3.1	2.2					2.0	1.6
						Net Profit + Depr., Dep.,	7.2	6.4
						Amort./Cur. Mat. L /T/D	(14) 2.3	(12) 2.3
							1.5	.6
.4	.5	.3					.5	.5
1.7	1.0	.9				Fixed/Worth	1.3	1.1
-6.2	1.5	31.6					5.0	1.8
1.1	.5	.7					1.0	1.0
4.9	1.4	2.3				Debt/Worth	1.8	1.8
-4.9	5.7	32.4					NM	4.9
168.3	72.4	73.1				% Profit Before Taxes/Tangible	62.1	50.7
(17) 74.4	(23) 34.1	(10) 21.6				Net Worth	(47) 26.6	(41) 23.9
18.1	9.3	10.0					7.1	9.1
56.9	25.2	17.8				% Profit Before Taxes/Total	20.5	20.5
15.2	13.7	8.0				Assets	9.1	9.1
3.1	5.5	2.7					2.0	2.0
49.4	17.7	30.8					28.4	24.0
15.6	8.8	12.9				Sales/Net Fixed Assets	11.5	10.1
7.2	6.0	7.2					6.7	6.3
8.3	4.0	4.4					4.7	5.5
4.5	3.2	3.7				Sales/Total Assets	3.6	3.7
3.1	2.5	3.0					2.3	1.9
1.5	1.9	.6					1.0	1.1
(17) 2.8	(22) 3.4	(11) 1.8				% Depr., Dep., Amort./Sales	(55) 2.7	(41) 3.2
5.4	6.1	3.0					4.2	4.0
4.6	4.8					% Officers', Directors',	3.7	2.9
(18) 7.5	(15) 10.2					Owners' Comp/Sales	(34) 7.6	(21) 5.9
9.5	16.2						13.8	16.0
41626M	86005M	173928M	278779M		586703M	Net Sales ($)	979209M	585193M
6140M	27018M	50639M	114442M		153117M	Total Assets ($)	345611M	207935M

Note: Columns 10-50MM and 50-100MM marked "DATA NOT AVAILABLE."

M = $ thousand   MM = $ million
See Pages 11 through 21 for Explanation of Ratios and Data

Comparative Historical Data — Current Data Sorted By Sales

			Type of Statement						
6	3	2	Unqualified	1.	2	4	2	4	2
7	6	9	Reviewed	5	5	3	2	2	1
9	15	17	Compiled	5	9	3	2	2	1
13	17	24	Tax Returns	5	2	7	2	1	1
14	13	17	Other	4	2	7	2	1	1
4/1/02-3/31/03	4/1/03-3/31/04	4/1/04-3/31/05		14 (4/1-9/30/04)			55 (10/1/04-3/31/05)		
ALL	ALL	ALL		0-1MM	1-3MM	3-5MM	5-10MM	10-25MM	25MM & OVER
49	54	69	**NUMBER OF STATEMENTS**	15	18	14	8	7	7
%	%	%	**ASSETS**	%	%	%	%	%	%
13.9	13.5	16.6	Cash & Equivalents	14.0	24.0	17.4			
20.5	19.4	20.6	Trade Receivables (net)	12.8	21.3	16.2			
3.7	5.2	3.7	Inventory	.8	1.4	6.4			
2.5	1.9	3.3	All Other Current	3.0	3.3	3.0			
40.7	39.9	44.2	Total Current	30.6	49.9	43.0			
42.9	37.9	37.2	Fixed Assets (net)	49.7	31.5	37.1			
7.7	8.1	7.7	Intangibles (net)	6.5	10.1	4.9			
8.7	14.1	10.9	All Other Non-Current	13.2	8.6	15.0			
100.0	100.0	100.0	Total	100.0	100.0	100.0			
			LIABILITIES						
6.9	10.9	10.7	Notes Payable-Short Term	23.5	10.7	6.3			
6.5	6.7	5.4	Cur. Mat.-L/T/D	8.1	6.7	2.8			
8.3	9.5	8.5	Trade Payables	1.9	11.2	8.6			
.2	.2	.5	Income Taxes Payable	.0	.3	.9			
15.5	17.8	10.4	All Other Current	7.8	11.7	7.2			
37.4	45.0	35.5	Total Current	41.2	40.7	25.8			
27.4	33.2	29.6	Long-Term Debt	47.0	33.4	25.3			
.5	.3	.5	Deferred Taxes	1.5	.0	.0			
3.1	3.2	10.4	All Other Non-Current	37.8	3.4	.7			
31.7	18.3	24.0	Net Worth	-27.6	22.5	48.2			
100.0	100.0	100.0	Total Liabilities & Net Worth	100.0	100.0	100.0			
			INCOME DATA						
100.0	100.0	100.0	Net Sales	100.0	100.0	100.0			
			Gross Profit						
92.9	93.1	92.9	Operating Expenses	86.6	93.9	95.4			
7.1	6.9	7.1	Operating Profit	13.4	6.1	4.6			
1.8	2.9	1.6	All Other Expenses (net)	7.0	-.7	.0			
5.3	3.9	5.6	Profit Before Taxes	6.4	6.7	4.6			
			RATIOS						
1.9	1.4	2.6		1.4	2.4	7.7			
1.1	1.0	1.4	Current	.8	1.4	2.2			
.6	.5	.7		.4	.6	.8			
1.6	1.4	2.2		1.3	2.1	7.2			
1.0	.9	1.0	Quick	.7	1.2	2.0			
.6	.5	.6		.1	.6	.7			
11 32.1	0 UND	0 UND		0 UND	10 35.7	0 UND			
22 16.9	23 15.6	24 15.1	Sales/Receivables	0 UND	25 14.9	19 19.3			
29 12.4	34 10.7	34 10.9		46 8.0	39 9.4	27 13.4			
			Cost of Sales/Inventory						
			Cost of Sales/Payables						
18.0	26.1	10.8		21.6	8.6	10.4			
69.7	137.7	40.3	Sales/Working Capital	-24.3	28.5	30.4			
-19.7	-14.2	-26.6		-7.2	-20.9	-41.2			
18.8	14.3	18.4		6.0	14.9	14.9			
(43) 7.9	(50) 4.6	(63) 5.7	EBIT/Interest	(11) 2.8	(17) 5.7	(13) 5.3			
3.2	1.2	2.6		1.1	2.4	3.4			
9.8	7.9	10.5	Net Profit + Depr., Dep.,						
(13) 2.7	(14) 2.0	(16) 2.2	Amort./Cur. Mat. L/T/D						
2.3	1.5	1.6							
.7	.6	.5		.5	.6	.5			
1.2	1.6	1.1	Fixed/Worth	2.1	1.5	.9			
8.1	21.1	5.5		-10.0	-99.4	1.2			
.9	1.6	.6		1.0	.7	.5			
2.1	3.5	1.9	Debt/Worth	5.1	4.8	1.4			
16.4	33.7	10.0		-5.1	-155.6	3.6			
97.6	118.7	76.4	% Profit Before Taxes/Tangible	91.1	104.4	67.3			
(40) 41.5	(43) 31.4	(56) 34.4	Net Worth	(10) 19.6	(13) 68.3	(13) 32.5			
16.9	7.4	11.0		8.3	17.2	16.0			
24.1	24.5	24.0	% Profit Before Taxes/Total	25.9	23.6	29.9			
14.1	9.2	13.7	Assets	4.9	15.2	13.0			
4.4	.3	3.4		.5	3.0	7.9			
16.9	24.2	24.9		15.5	23.4	32.2			
9.1	10.8	10.4	Sales/Net Fixed Assets	6.5	13.9	10.4			
5.4	5.9	6.5		3.6	7.5	6.9			
4.7	5.0	4.5		4.4	5.1	5.4			
3.6	3.4	3.8	Sales/Total Assets	2.6	3.9	4.0			
2.6	2.0	2.6		1.7	2.6	2.8			
2.3	1.8	1.5			2.4	1.0			
(44) 4.4	(47) 3.3	(55) 2.8	% Depr., Dep., Amort./Sales	(13) 3.4	2.7				
5.4	4.7	4.9		6.4	3.9				
3.5	3.4	4.0			6.5	3.4			
(25) 6.9	(35) 8.1	(43) 7.1	% Officers', Directors', Owners' Comp/Sales	(11) 8.8	(11) 7.1				
13.3	13.0	10.6		24.2	16.2				
798522M	1126511M	1167041M	Net Sales ($)	7475M	29151M	57481M	54945M	108801M	909188M
264689M	390524M	351356M	Total Assets ($)	8892M	8549M	14935M	14659M	26975M	277346M

M = $ thousand   MM = $ million
See Pages 11 through 21 for Explanation of Ratios and Data

Current Data Sorted By Assets   **Comparative Historical Data**

Type of Statement	0-500M	500M-2MM	2-10MM	10-50MM	50-100MM	100-250MM		4/1/00-3/31/01 ALL	4/1/01-3/31/02 ALL
Unqualified	6	7	13	14	6	2		29	18
Reviewed	15	22	26	4				40	41
Compiled	34	14	8					64	74
Tax Returns	12	11	5	1				39	34
Other		17	9	8	4	1		58	69
	44 (4/1-9/30/04)			195 (10/1/04-3/31/05)					
NUMBER OF STATEMENTS	67	71	61	27	10	3		230	236
	%	%	%	%	%	%		%	%
ASSETS									
Cash & Equivalents	14.9	11.0	8.4	10.5	11.9			10.6	10.3
Trade Receivables (net)	29.8	44.7	44.9	45.0	28.7			41.8	37.8
Inventory	1.6	4.7	1.8	3.7	.3			3.4	3.9
All Other Current	3.7	3.9	3.8	2.2	4.7			4.1	4.5
Total Current	49.9	64.3	58.9	61.5	45.6			60.0	56.4
Fixed Assets (net)	29.8	20.7	22.1	18.7	17.6			27.2	27.8
Intangibles (net)	11.7	5.2	3.6	7.4	28.2			4.7	6.9
All Other Non-Current	8.6	9.8	15.5	12.4	8.5			8.1	8.9
Total	100.0	100.0	100.0	100.0	100.0			100.0	100.0
LIABILITIES									
Notes Payable-Short Term	18.9	11.1	12.4	13.2	6.6			13.5	14.5
Cur. Mat.-L/T/D	7.8	3.2	3.1	1.8	2.4			4.6	5.4
Trade Payables	14.6	12.5	11.5	13.0	9.2			11.9	11.2
Income Taxes Payable	.0	.9	.5	.2	.8			.5	.4
All Other Current	19.0	16.8	15.3	21.6	13.6			15.1	14.7
Total Current	60.2	44.5	42.9	49.8	32.6			45.6	46.2
Long-Term Debt	31.8	10.2	15.8	20.3	19.4			13.2	16.7
Deferred Taxes	.0	.3	.5	.5	2.2			.7	.5
All Other Non-Current	2.5	5.1	4.7	13.3	10.7			6.8	5.0
Net Worth	5.5	39.9	36.2	16.0	35.1			33.6	31.6
Total Liabilities & Net Worth	100.0	100.0	100.0	100.0	100.0			100.0	100.0
INCOME DATA									
Net Sales	100.0	100.0	100.0	100.0	100.0			100.0	100.0
Gross Profit									
Operating Expenses	95.0	96.5	95.9	95.3	95.8			95.2	95.7
Operating Profit	5.0	3.5	4.1	4.7	4.2			4.8	4.3
All Other Expenses (net)	.8	.0	.9	.4	.8			.8	1.4
Profit Before Taxes	4.2	3.5	3.2	4.3	3.4			4.0	2.9
RATIOS									
Current	2.1	2.3	2.2	2.1	1.7			2.0	1.9
	.9	1.6	1.3	1.3	1.5			1.4	1.3
	.5	1.1	1.0	.9	1.3			1.0	.9
Quick	1.9	2.2	2.1	1.7	1.4			1.8	1.6
	.6	1.3	1.1	1.2	1.4			1.2	1.1
	.4	.9	.9	.8	1.2			.8	.7
Sales/Receivables	4 91.8	22 16.4	26 13.8	34 10.7	24 15.2			22 16.3	21 17.8
	20 18.4	34 10.7	38 9.5	43 8.5	61 6.0			37 9.8	34 10.8
	30 12.0	50 7.3	58 6.3	62 5.9	66 5.5			57 6.4	51 7.2
Cost of Sales/Inventory									
Cost of Sales/Payables									
Sales/Working Capital	19.2	11.0	8.9	10.3	10.2			11.6	12.5
	−215.1	19.7	37.7	22.9	12.8			28.1	32.2
	−10.5	71.0	786.3	−62.0	266.1			−270.6	−74.5
EBIT/Interest	11.7	25.2	35.8	17.6	12.6			13.1	12.4
	(58) 3.6	(56) 7.8	(54) 7.9	(25) 9.0	7.1			(209) 3.9	(210) 3.5
	1.2	1.9	3.1	2.3	1.4			1.4	1.3
Net Profit + Depr., Dep., Amort./Cur. Mat. L /T/D		3.4	14.6					6.9	5.0
		(16) 2.4	(19) 3.3					(53) 2.9	(50) 2.0
		1.2	1.3					1.4	1.2
Fixed/Worth	.2	.2	.2	.1	.7			.3	.4
	2.7	.5	.6	.4	2.1			.7	.8
	−.7	1.1	1.2	−10.0	−.6			1.6	2.9
Debt/Worth	1.0	.6	.8	1.2	1.7			.9	.9
	8.3	1.6	1.7	3.4	8.3			1.9	2.1
	−2.3	3.6	3.2	−17.3	−3.2			6.2	7.9
% Profit Before Taxes/Tangible Net Worth	142.9	64.3	51.5	62.4				69.3	62.1
	(38) 73.4	(64) 25.0	(54) 29.6	(19) 45.7				(206) 26.6	(193) 22.2
	14.5	7.7	13.8	22.2				6.4	8.9
% Profit Before Taxes/Total Assets	31.1	20.4	21.1	19.5	13.9			21.5	18.0
	13.4	8.9	9.3	11.5	4.6			9.0	8.5
	.0	2.1	3.1	4.1	2.0			1.3	.9
Sales/Net Fixed Assets	115.3	73.2	49.5	90.2	26.2			47.6	47.9
	23.0	24.2	23.2	39.3	14.9			20.6	20.5
	10.1	11.7	10.1	23.1	11.1			9.5	8.8
Sales/Total Assets	7.1	5.7	5.6	5.9	3.1			5.5	5.9
	5.1	4.3	3.6	3.7	2.0			4.1	4.1
	2.9	3.3	2.5	1.9	1.6			2.7	2.5
% Depr., Dep., Amort./Sales	1.3	.6	.8	.5				.8	.7
	(42) 2.4	(56) 1.3	(58) 1.5	(23) .8				(202) 1.4	(204) 1.5
	7.3	2.3	2.5	1.5				3.0	3.3
% Officers', Directors', Owners' Comp/Sales	3.6	2.2	1.2					2.9	2.2
	(37) 6.2	(39) 3.2	(20) 2.6					(125) 5.7	(130) 4.4
	10.8	6.6	5.1					9.5	8.0
Net Sales ($)	86763M	359587M	1100845M	3518487M	1448875M	1322733M		4128240M	4813308M
Total Assets ($)	15203M	80971M	272276M	622398M	670202M	495232M		1456195M	1499028M

© RMA 2005

M = $ thousand   MM = $ million
See Pages 11 through 21 for Explanation of Ratios and Data

Comparative Historical Data | **Current Data Sorted By Sales**

			Type of Statement						
30	22	42	Unqualified	1	2	2	6	6	25
45	58	58	Reviewed	4		7	22	15	10
48	57	37	Compiled	6	12	8	10	1	
40	36	51	Tax Returns	15	21	6	1	1	2
70	66	51	Other	7	9	6	12	4	13
4/1/02- 3/31/03 ALL	4/1/03- 3/31/04 ALL	4/1/04- 3/31/05 ALL		44 (4/1-9/30/04)			195 (10/1/04-3/31/05)		
				0-1MM	1-3MM	3-5MM	5-10MM	10-25MM	25MM & OVER
233	239	239	NUMBER OF STATEMENTS	33	44	29	56	27	50
%	%	%	ASSETS	%	%	%	%	%	%
11.5	12.0	11.5	Cash & Equivalents	15.5	13.5	8.3	11.8	8.1	10.2
39.0	39.6	39.8	Trade Receivables (net)	24.5	28.8	44.6	44.9	47.7	46.6
2.9	2.9	2.8	Inventory	1.1	2.2	7.6	2.4	1.3	2.7
5.1	4.2	3.7	All Other Current	2.3	4.9	4.2	2.5	5.8	3.6
58.6	58.8	57.7	Total Current	43.3	49.5	64.8	61.7	63.0	63.1
24.7	25.0	23.0	Fixed Assets (net)	38.9	26.5	19.5	22.3	17.4	15.5
6.9	5.6	8.1	Intangibles (net)	12.9	10.9	1.9	4.4	5.2	11.9
9.9	10.6	11.1	All Other Non-Current	4.8	13.1	13.8	11.6	14.4	9.5
100.0	100.0	100.0	Total	100.0	100.0	100.0	100.0	100.0	100.0
			LIABILITIES						
15.0	14.4	13.5	Notes Payable-Short Term	9.5	14.0	22.5	11.4	11.1	14.2
4.2	5.8	4.3	Cur. Mat.-L/T/D	9.7	5.2	2.5	4.3	2.4	2.2
12.2	11.3	12.7	Trade Payables	7.8	15.8	11.8	11.4	17.2	12.8
.4	.4	.4	Income Taxes Payable	.0	.1	.6	1.0	.3	.4
17.1	17.2	17.5	All Other Current	25.3	11.5	19.8	14.2	15.4	21.0
48.8	49.1	48.5	Total Current	52.3	46.6	57.1	42.3	46.4	50.5
15.2	14.7	19.2	Long-Term Debt	39.9	24.8	11.1	14.9	8.6	16.0
.4	.5	.4	Deferred Taxes	.3	.1	.0	.3	.8	.8
5.8	6.1	5.6	All Other Non-Current	2.6	5.2	5.1	4.8	1.8	11.1
29.9	29.6	26.3	Net Worth	4.9	23.3	26.6	37.6	42.4	21.6
100.0	100.0	100.0	Total Liabilities & Net Worth	100.0	100.0	100.0	100.0	100.0	100.0
			INCOME DATA						
100.0	100.0	100.0	Net Sales	100.0	100.0	100.0	100.0	100.0	100.0
			Gross Profit						
95.9	96.0	95.8	Operating Expenses	96.1	94.4	95.1	96.1	96.1	96.6
4.1	4.0	4.2	Operating Profit	3.9	5.6	4.9	3.9	3.9	3.4
1.3	.9	.6	All Other Expenses (net)	1.2	1.0	.3	.3	−.3	.6
2.8	3.1	3.7	Profit Before Taxes	2.7	4.6	4.6	3.5	4.2	2.9
			RATIOS						
2.1	2.0	2.1		2.2	2.6	2.8	2.1	2.0	1.8
1.3	1.3	1.4	Current	.6	1.3	1.6	1.5	1.3	1.4
.9	.8	.8		.3	.6	.7	1.1	1.0	1.0
1.9	1.7	2.0		2.1	2.4	2.5	2.1	1.6	1.6
(232) 1.1	1.1	1.2	Quick	.6	1.2	1.1	1.4	1.1	1.2
.7	.7	.6		.3	.5	.6	1.0	.8	.9
19 19.1	21 17.2	20 18.4		4 88.8	3 133.8	19 18.9	23 16.0	29 12.5	28 13.0
32 11.5	35 10.5	33 10.9	Sales/Receivables	22 16.8	21 17.8	31 11.7	35 10.5	39 9.3	42 8.7
47 7.8	51 7.2	51 7.2		36 10.1	41 8.9	48 7.6	51 7.2	59 6.1	61 6.0
			Cost of Sales/Inventory						
			Cost of Sales/Payables						
13.0	12.5	11.7		13.7	13.6	8.0	11.1	14.2	11.1
40.9	34.5	28.8	Sales/Working Capital	−26.8	53.0	19.5	24.5	27.4	24.3
−80.1	−50.8	−67.0		−6.0	−21.9	−21.9	89.5	157.9	NM
12.6	13.0	19.5		10.4	20.5	32.8	20.8	61.3	14.9
(200) 3.4	(209) 5.0	(205) 6.6	EBIT/Interest	(26) 2.9	(38) 5.6	(24) 5.9	(46) 5.9	(24) 10.1	(47) 9.0
1.3	1.9	1.9		.7	1.6	1.8	1.8	4.2	2.2
4.9	6.0	7.0	Net Profit + Depr., Dep.,				2.9	16.5	7.1
(47) 2.1	(63) 2.5	(53) 3.0	Amort./Cur. Mat. L/T/D			(15) 1.7	(10) 5.7	(19) 3.6	
1.1	1.2	1.3					.9	1.3	1.5
.3	.3	.2		.6	.2	.1	.2	.2	.2
.7	.8	.7	Fixed/Worth	4.9	1.2	.3	.8	.4	.6
4.4	3.9	6.3		−.7	−5.1	2.9	1.3	1.0	−14.5
.9	.9	.9		1.6	.6	.5	.7	.7	1.7
2.3	2.3	2.3	Debt/Worth	27.5	1.9	1.5	1.6	1.5	2.8
13.5	12.6	24.5		−2.1	−22.2	6.3	5.9	3.4	−54.3
68.0	61.7	67.8	% Profit Before Taxes/Tangible	157.7	78.1	91.1	56.8	61.3	61.5
(184) 25.5	(192) 26.4	(183) 31.8	Net Worth	(18) 73.5	(30) 23.9	(23) 28.7	(49) 22.9	(26) 31.3	(37) 42.0
8.3	7.4	12.5		9.4	13.1	10.2	3.8	20.5	19.5
19.9	18.6	23.1	% Profit Before Taxes/Total	26.9	26.0	28.1	21.6	18.3	19.8
7.1	7.9	9.3	Assets	14.2	8.8	13.2	8.6	10.3	8.1
1.6	2.0	2.7		−1.2	2.2	2.8	1.2	5.1	3.4
58.4	50.4	69.5		34.7	60.4	160.0	57.0	133.0	77.3
25.3	24.6	25.2	Sales/Net Fixed Assets	12.8	18.3	32.3	24.1	40.4	33.3
12.5	10.7	11.4		3.9	9.1	12.3	10.6	16.1	21.6
6.1	6.0	5.9		5.7	6.3	6.7	6.1	5.7	5.9
4.6	4.0	4.2	Sales/Total Assets	3.2	4.0	4.3	4.3	4.7	4.7
2.9	2.7	2.7		1.9	2.4	2.9	3.3	2.7	2.7
.8	.6	.7		3.0	1.1	.6	.6	.6	.5
(199) 1.3	(193) 1.3	(189) 1.5	% Depr., Dep., Amort./Sales	(20) 7.0	(31) 1.8	(22) 1.9	(48) 1.3	(24) .9	(44) 1.1
2.4	2.4	2.8		10.0	3.2	2.8	2.2	1.9	1.9
2.9	2.6	2.2		5.3	3.3	2.6	2.2	1.0	
(105) 5.5	(108) 4.6	(104) 4.2	% Officers', Directors', Owners' Comp/Sales	(15) 7.9	(26) 5.2	(14) 4.8	(31) 3.2	(10) 2.0	
8.5	8.0	7.3		14.7	10.7	7.4	6.3	3.8	
6138646M	6095485M	7837290M	Net Sales ($)	14493M	73483M	108032M	392607M	436994M	6811681M
1637198M	1737776M	2156282M	Total Assets ($)	8726M	32787M	31876M	123760M	142468M	1816665M

© RMA 2005

M = $ thousand   MM = $ million
See Pages 11 through 21 for Explanation of Ratios and Data

Current Data Sorted By Assets | **Comparative Historical Data**

Type of Statement	0-500M	500M-2MM	2-10MM	10-50MM	50-100MM	100-250MM		4/1/00-3/31/01 ALL	4/1/01-3/31/02 ALL
Unqualified	2	1	9	10	2	4		14	16
Reviewed	23	26	36	3				43	42
Compiled	93	32	12			1		73	74
Tax Returns	38	49	4					41	56
Other		47	19	2		2		68	88
		43 (4/1-9/30/04)	372 (10/1/04-3/31/05)						
NUMBER OF STATEMENTS	156	155	80	15	2	7		239	276
ASSETS	%	%	%	%	%	%		%	%
Cash & Equivalents	15.0	9.9	6.0	5.4				10.1	9.1
Trade Receivables (net)	17.2	25.5	41.2	31.8				28.0	24.0
Inventory	5.7	7.1	9.0	6.9				9.3	9.3
All Other Current	1.5	3.3	3.8	7.0				2.4	3.3
Total Current	39.4	45.7	60.1	51.1				49.8	45.8
Fixed Assets (net)	51.2	43.2	29.9	41.7				43.5	46.0
Intangibles (net)	2.3	3.8	2.4	3.5				2.1	2.6
All Other Non-Current	7.1	7.3	7.6	3.7				4.6	5.6
Total	100.0	100.0	100.0	100.0				100.0	100.0
LIABILITIES									
Notes Payable-Short Term	14.8	12.2	11.5	7.0				9.7	13.8
Cur. Mat.-L/T/D	7.6	7.4	5.7	8.3				7.8	9.7
Trade Payables	10.0	11.1	17.4	11.9				12.2	12.6
Income Taxes Payable	.3	.1	.6	.3				.2	.2
All Other Current	10.0	7.4	8.2	11.8				12.2	20.1
Total Current	42.7	38.2	43.4	39.3				42.2	56.4
Long-Term Debt	51.6	28.3	15.2	26.0				25.4	30.6
Deferred Taxes	.0	.5	1.3	.8				.7	.7
All Other Non-Current	3.9	4.2	5.1	6.1				3.3	5.5
Net Worth	1.8	28.9	35.0	27.7				28.4	6.8
Total Liabilities & Net Worth	100.0	100.0	100.0	100.0				100.0	100.0
INCOME DATA									
Net Sales	100.0	100.0	100.0	100.0				100.0	100.0
Gross Profit									
Operating Expenses	95.6	94.3	95.4	96.5				95.3	95.7
Operating Profit	4.4	5.7	4.6	3.5				4.7	4.3
All Other Expenses (net)	1.1	1.7	.6	.9				1.0	1.3
Profit Before Taxes	3.3	4.0	4.0	2.6				3.7	3.1
RATIOS									
Current	2.2	1.8	2.0	1.6				2.0	1.9
	.9	1.3	1.4	1.3				1.2	1.1
	.4	.8	1.1	1.1				.8	.7
Quick	1.8	1.6	1.6	1.4				1.4	1.4
	.7	1.0	1.1	.9				(238) .9	(274) .8
	.3	.5	.7	.7				.5	.4
Sales/Receivables	0 UND	17 21.7	39 9.4	34 10.9				14 25.4	6 59.6
	7 54.1	29 12.4	54 6.8	50 7.3				32 11.3	25 14.5
	25 14.7	46 7.9	82 4.4	77 4.8				54 6.7	50 7.3
Cost of Sales/Inventory									
Cost of Sales/Payables									
Sales/Working Capital	20.2	11.9	7.9	6.9				11.5	12.7
	−210.8	29.2	17.0	18.9				42.3	56.3
	−19.5	−30.5	40.4	99.4				−47.6	−27.9
EBIT/Interest	(133) 12.3	(142) 8.9	(78) 22.2	6.6				(223) 8.1	(265) 7.1
	4.0	3.9	4.0	3.3				2.8	2.3
	.1	1.0	1.3	2.4				1.2	.9
Net Profit + Depr., Dep., Amort./Cur. Mat. L./T/D		3.1	3.1					3.1	2.7
		(23) 2.1	(26) 1.5					(51) 1.6	(57) 2.0
		1.1	.8					.8	1.1
Fixed/Worth	1.0	.7	.5	.9				.7	.8
	5.5	1.7	.9	1.6				1.2	1.5
	−2.4	4.1	2.0	2.7				3.0	6.4
Debt/Worth	1.3	1.2	.9	2.2				1.0	1.2
	9.7	2.7	1.8	2.7				2.2	2.7
	−5.3	7.7	3.9	3.8				5.2	11.6
% Profit Before Taxes/Tangible Net Worth	(95) 166.7	(130) 68.8	(71) 51.3	(14) 47.7				(200) 53.2	(226) 50.0
	56.9	20.4	27.7	24.2				23.1	20.6
	11.2	3.3	6.1	13.3				5.8	2.1
% Profit Before Taxes/Total Assets	37.9	20.9	22.0	11.9				20.0	17.3
	12.0	6.6	6.6	4.5				7.5	6.1
	−2.7	.0	.9	3.6				.9	−1.0
Sales/Net Fixed Assets	20.1	13.4	13.5	10.2				13.2	13.4
	9.6	7.2	8.9	5.6				7.8	7.6
	5.0	4.3	5.7	2.4				4.4	4.5
Sales/Total Assets	6.7	3.7	3.4	2.6				4.3	4.4
	4.1	2.8	2.8	2.4				3.0	3.0
	2.8	2.0	1.8	1.7				2.2	2.1
% Depr., Dep., Amort./Sales	(109) 2.3	(140) 2.4	(75) 2.3	(13) 3.5				(211) 2.2	(246) 2.2
	4.0	3.6	3.2	6.1				3.7	3.9
	6.8	5.8	4.7	7.1				5.3	6.4
% Officers', Directors', Owners' Comp/Sales	(106) 4.0	(93) 2.7	(44) 1.5					(125) 3.0	(138) 3.1
	6.1	4.7	3.3					5.3	5.3
	9.7	7.6	4.9					9.4	8.1
Net Sales ($)	197056M	480680M	853261M	806169M	246356M	5768554M		2245962M	3138307M
Total Assets ($)	38990M	160613M	310839M	355169M	131503M	1206137M		923373M	1283730M

© RMA 2005

M = $ thousand   MM = $ million

See Pages 11 through 21 for Explanation of Ratios and Data

Comparative Historical Data / Current Data Sorted By Sales

Type of Statement									
	17	20	26	Unqualified			7	5	14
	46	52	67		1	13	14	21	15	3
	73	87	67	Reviewed						
	98	123	147	Compiled	11	31	16	7	2	
	75	86	108	Tax Returns	56	64	18	4	3	2
				Other	22	38	23	12	7	6

Type of Statement (across 6 current columns):

Type of Statement	0-1MM	1-3MM	3-5MM	5-10MM	10-25MM	25MM & OVER
Unqualified				7	5	14
Reviewed	1	13	14	21	15	3
Compiled	11	31	16	7	2	
Tax Returns	56	64	18	4	3	2
Other	22	38	23	12	7	6

Periods: 4/1/02-3/31/03 ALL (309) · 4/1/03-3/31/04 ALL (368) · 4/1/04-3/31/05 ALL (415) · 43 (4/1-9/30/04) · 372 (10/1/04-3/31/05)

	4/1/02-3/31/03 ALL	4/1/03-3/31/04 ALL	4/1/04-3/31/05 ALL	0-1MM	1-3MM	3-5MM	5-10MM	10-25MM	25MM & OVER
NUMBER OF STATEMENTS	309	368	415	90	146	71	51	32	25
ASSETS	%	%	%	%	%	%	%	%	%
Cash & Equivalents	10.5	12.1	11.0	11.7	12.7	10.5	9.6	5.4	9.5
Trade Receivables (net)	22.0	22.1	25.4	14.7	22.6	28.3	34.1	44.4	30.6
Inventory	8.5	7.7	7.0	6.3	7.1	7.0	8.0	8.3	6.1
All Other Current	2.8	2.3	2.8	1.2	2.3	3.9	3.9	2.2	7.0
Total Current	43.8	44.3	46.2	33.9	44.6	49.6	55.7	60.3	53.2
Fixed Assets (net)	47.6	46.3	43.6	53.9	46.6	39.6	33.6	31.1	36.6
Intangibles (net)	2.3	2.2	3.0	4.6	2.0	3.1	2.7	2.4	4.9
All Other Non-Current	6.3	7.2	7.1	7.6	6.7	7.8	8.1	6.2	5.3
Total	100.0	100.0	100.0	100.0	100.0	100.0	100.0	100.0	100.0
LIABILITIES									
Notes Payable-Short Term	11.9	12.5	12.9	13.8	11.6	15.6	14.1	12.3	7.8
Cur. Mat.-L/T/D	7.5	9.1	7.1	6.7	7.9	8.0	6.5	4.4	6.9
Trade Payables	9.9	10.9	11.9	10.2	10.4	12.0	12.0	21.3	14.3
Income Taxes Payable	.3	.5	.3	.2	.3	.1	.9	.0	.3
All Other Current	9.6	10.5	8.7	11.0	7.4	7.4	8.3	10.0	11.5
Total Current	39.3	43.5	41.0	41.8	37.6	43.1	41.8	48.0	40.9
Long-Term Debt	28.4	34.9	34.5	49.1	42.3	26.0	14.9	15.5	25.2
Deferred Taxes	.6	.5	.5	.1	.4	.6	1.0	1.2	.7
All Other Non-Current	4.7	5.6	4.5	7.0	3.1	3.9	3.3	4.6	7.3
Net Worth	27.0	15.5	19.5	2.1	16.5	26.5	39.0	30.7	26.0
Total Liabilities & Net Worth	100.0	100.0	100.0	100.0	100.0	100.0	100.0	100.0	100.0
INCOME DATA									
Net Sales	100.0	100.0	100.0	100.0	100.0	100.0	100.0	100.0	100.0
Gross Profit									
Operating Expenses	95.2	95.0	95.1	94.5	95.2	95.1	95.4	96.0	95.0
Operating Profit	4.8	5.0	4.9	5.5	4.8	4.9	4.6	4.0	5.0
All Other Expenses (net)	1.1	1.3	1.2	3.0	1.0	.3	.5	.5	.9
Profit Before Taxes	3.7	3.7	3.7	2.5	3.8	4.6	4.0	3.5	4.0
RATIOS									
Current	2.0	2.0	1.9	1.8	2.4	1.8	2.0	2.0	1.9
	1.2	1.1	1.3	.8	1.2	1.2	1.3	1.3	1.4
	.7	.7	.7	.3	.6	.8	1.1	.8	1.3
Quick	1.5	1.5	1.6	1.7	1.7	1.4	1.7	1.6	1.5
	.9	.9	.9	.6	.9	.9	1.1	1.0	1.1
	.4	.5	.5	.2	.5	.5	.7	.7	.8
Sales/Receivables	4 96.0	1 421.4	6 56.3	0 UND	6 63.2	14 26.6	24 15.4	31 11.6	18 19.9
	24 15.5	22 16.3	27 13.5	6 64.3	25 14.6	29 12.4	40 9.1	51 7.2	41 8.8
	43 8.4	45 8.2	50 7.3	25 14.3	43 8.4	52 7.1	65 5.6	77 4.8	62 5.9
Cost of Sales/Inventory									
Cost of Sales/Payables									
Sales/Working Capital	12.5	12.9	12.4	19.3	11.0	13.4	9.5	13.6	11.6
	49.6	73.3	32.7	−41.4	32.3	40.4	19.3	20.9	21.9
	−26.1	−23.5	−29.3	−8.1	−29.5	−51.1	64.7	−52.7	33.5
EBIT/Interest	(279) 8.2	(344) 9.2	(377) 10.7	(69) 9.7	(138) 9.7	(67) 12.8	(48) 20.1	(31) 34.0	(24) 11.8
	2.8	3.5	3.9	2.0	3.4	4.7	4.6	6.9	5.0
	1.0	.9	1.1	−.9	1.0	1.3	2.4	1.9	2.5
Net Profit + Depr., Dep., Amort./Cur. Mat. L/T/D	(62) 4.2	(59) 3.5	(56) 3.2		(12) 2.8	(14) 3.4	(15) 3.1		
	2.1	2.0	2.0		1.8	2.1	1.6		
	1.1	1.1	1.2		.5	.8	1.2		
Fixed/Worth	.7	.7	.7	1.2	.8	.7	.5	.5	.5
	1.6	1.9	1.7	UND	1.7	1.7	.8	1.0	1.2
	5.1	55.9	114.0	−1.9	20.3	4.1	2.0	3.2	4.0
Debt/Worth	1.0	1.2	1.2	1.6	1.2	1.4	.9	1.1	1.4
	2.2	2.9	2.9	UND	2.9	2.8	1.7	2.0	2.6
	8.2	315.3	241.0	−3.9	27.8	6.4	4.6	8.3	5.3
% Profit Before Taxes/Tangible Net Worth	(260) 69.3	(278) 71.0	(316) 76.0	(45) 133.3	(115) 82.3	(62) 90.5	(47) 62.7	(26) 63.6	(21) 57.7
	19.8	22.8	29.9	45.4	23.0	33.5	28.8	36.3	33.2
	3.3	1.5	6.5	1.7	5.2	4.3	6.5	17.7	15.1
% Profit Before Taxes/Total Assets	20.7	25.0	24.3	21.1	25.3	24.5	25.7	26.2	22.6
	6.0	6.7	7.2	5.2	6.9	9.8	10.6	9.4	7.1
	.0	−1.4	.2	−6.4	.0	.8	2.5	2.7	4.0
Sales/Net Fixed Assets	13.6	15.4	15.4	14.7	13.5	18.3	13.8	19.8	20.2
	7.8	8.3	8.3	5.3	7.9	9.4	9.2	12.9	10.2
	4.6	4.7	4.8	2.9	4.5	5.6	6.2	8.4	5.1
Sales/Total Assets	4.4	4.8	4.5	4.4	4.9	5.3	3.7	4.0	3.8
	3.2	3.2	3.1	2.9	3.1	3.3	3.0	3.4	2.6
	2.2	2.2	2.1	2.0	2.0	2.3	2.1	2.6	2.0
% Depr., Dep., Amort./Sales	(273) 2.7	(314) 2.4	(340) 2.4	(67) 3.2	(115) 2.2	(65) 2.4	(48) 2.2	(29) 1.5	(16) 2.1
	4.2	4.3	3.6	5.5	3.6	3.6	3.3	2.4	5.2
	7.3	7.3	6.1	9.6	6.8	4.9	4.3	3.6	7.4
% Officers', Directors', Owners' Comp/Sales	(173) 2.6	(230) 2.8	(251) 2.9	(55) 4.3	(100) 3.5	(40) 2.3	(30) 2.3	(18) 1.2	
	5.0	4.9	4.9	7.4	5.3	4.6	3.5	2.2	
	8.8	9.1	7.8	13.3	8.2	6.8	5.1	4.5	
Net Sales ($)	10421222M	5148008M	8352076M	46877M	265529M	275459M	362240M	504561M	6897410M
Total Assets ($)	1933094M	1549961M	2203251M	21827M	99015M	93487M	135152M	171885M	1681885M

M = $ thousand   MM = $ million
See Pages 11 through 21 for Explanation of Ratios and Data

Current Data Sorted By Assets   Comparative Historical Data

0-500M	500M-2MM	2-10MM	10-50MM	50-100MM	100-250MM	Type of Statement	4/1/00-3/31/01 ALL	4/1/01-3/31/02 ALL
						Unqualified	1	1
	3	2				Reviewed	1	2
6	2	3				Compiled	9	4
9	3					Tax Returns	4	13
7	4	2	1			Other	4	8
7 (4/1-9/30/04)			35 (10/1/04-3/31/05)					
22	12	7	1			**NUMBER OF STATEMENTS**	19	28
%	%	%	%	%	%	**ASSETS**	%	%
23.9	7.9					Cash & Equivalents	19.0	16.7
17.6	27.1					Trade Receivables (net)	24.5	16.7
3.0	8.1					Inventory	1.9	5.2
2.3	1.6					All Other Current	4.1	2.1
46.9	44.6					Total Current	49.5	40.7
36.8	29.3		D	D		Fixed Assets (net)	35.2	30.4
10.5	9.2		A	A		Intangibles (net)	9.0	21.9
5.9	16.8		T	T		All Other Non-Current	6.4	7.0
100.0	100.0		A	A		Total	100.0	100.0
			N	N		**LIABILITIES**		
10.3	10.7		O	O		Notes Payable-Short Term	15.7	6.2
6.5	7.9		T	T		Cur. Mat.-L/T/D	7.0	8.1
11.6	21.2					Trade Payables	10.0	6.4
.0	.0		A	A		Income Taxes Payable	.1	.6
9.3	8.3		V	V		All Other Current	9.2	10.8
37.6	48.2		A	A		Total Current	41.9	32.1
35.3	17.8		I	I		Long-Term Debt	22.5	16.5
.0	.3		L	L		Deferred Taxes	.0	.7
5.0	5.1		A	A		All Other Non-Current	3.3	1.2
22.1	28.7		B	B		Net Worth	32.3	49.5
100.0	100.0		L	L		Total Liabilities & Net Worth	100.0	100.0
			E	E		**INCOME DATA**		
100.0	100.0					Net Sales	100.0	100.0
						Gross Profit		
89.8	97.1					Operating Expenses	94.6	89.2
10.2	2.9					Operating Profit	5.4	10.8
1.0	.3					All Other Expenses (net)	-1.1	1.4
9.2	2.7					Profit Before Taxes	6.5	9.4
						RATIOS		
5.4	1.5					Current	2.9	2.9
1.1	.9						1.2	1.4
.5	.5						.7	.5
4.7	1.0					Quick	2.6	2.8
1.0	.7						1.1	.7
.5	.3						.6	.2
0 UND	2 147.0					Sales/Receivables	4 101.2	0 UND
16 23.5	22 16.3						25 14.9	9 39.2
28 13.2	53 6.9						44 8.3	32 11.5
						Cost of Sales/Inventory		
						Cost of Sales/Payables		
8.7	18.6					Sales/Working Capital	10.2	10.8
NM	-149.9						48.3	40.5
-15.9	-11.3						-25.8	-31.8
10.0	12.7					EBIT/Interest	34.0	18.1
(19) 3.7	2.9						(18) 7.6	(24) 6.2
1.2	.4						2.2	1.9
						Net Profit + Depr., Dep., Amort./Cur. Mat. L /T/D		
.5	.5					Fixed/Worth	.6	.5
1.7	1.1						1.1	1.5
-3.7	15.5						3.6	NM
.6	1.4					Debt/Worth	.7	.6
2.2	6.2						2.0	1.6
-5.8	67.0						13.1	NM
125.0	319.4					% Profit Before Taxes/Tangible Net Worth	84.9	107.5
(14) 72.6	(10) 17.5						(15) 41.2	(21) 80.0
31.0	1.1						12.2	5.6
51.1	22.7					% Profit Before Taxes/Total Assets	30.7	50.4
21.6	2.6						19.0	20.8
.4	-.6						5.6	2.6
27.8	35.7					Sales/Net Fixed Assets	23.5	31.7
12.2	13.2						14.6	16.1
6.4	5.0						7.2	7.7
6.7	4.5					Sales/Total Assets	5.2	7.5
4.2	2.9						3.9	3.2
2.4	2.4						2.9	2.2
1.0	1.9					% Depr., Dep., Amort./Sales	1.2	1.4
(14) 1.7	(10) 4.2						(16) 3.4	(17) 2.8
3.1	5.8						5.3	4.7
3.7						% Officers', Directors', Owners' Comp/Sales	5.8	2.7
(12) 7.5							(12) 8.9	(16) 7.5
10.5							14.6	14.5
20840M	35284M	45997M	134219M			Net Sales ($)	2386073M	1459520M
5300M	9899M	28150M	40455M			Total Assets ($)	287980M	333029M

M = $ thousand   MM = $ million
See Pages 11 through 21 for Explanation of Ratios and Data

Comparative Historical Data | Current Data Sorted By Sales

			Type of Statement						
1	1		Unqualified						
3	3	5	Reviewed		2	1	1	1	
9	12	11	Compiled	3	5	2	1		
8	12	12	Tax Returns	7	4		1		
5	6	14	Other	5	5	1	2		1
4/1/02-3/31/03 ALL	4/1/03-3/31/04 ALL	4/1/04-3/31/05 ALL		7 (4/1-9/30/04)			35 (10/1/04-3/31/05)		
				0-1MM	1-3MM	3-5MM	5-10MM	10-25MM	25MM & OVER
26	34	42	NUMBER OF STATEMENTS	15	16	4	5	1	1
%	%	%	ASSETS	%	%	%	%	%	%
12.7	18.2	16.3	Cash & Equivalents	24.8	12.0				
26.0	21.8	21.8	Trade Receivables (net)	18.0	22.5				
4.4	3.2	6.5	Inventory	4.4	4.9				
7.7	3.6	3.5	All Other Current	.0	4.3				
50.8	46.9	48.1	Total Current	47.2	43.6				
30.7	30.4	33.9	Fixed Assets (net)	39.1	31.8				
13.4	17.7	9.3	Intangibles (net)	3.9	16.2				
5.1	5.1	8.7	All Other Non-Current	9.8	8.3				
100.0	100.0	100.0	Total	100.0	100.0				
			LIABILITIES						
20.5	11.2	10.5	Notes Payable-Short Term	11.4	10.7				
7.4	6.5	6.8	Cur. Mat.-L/T/D	8.9	6.0				
8.2	13.8	14.7	Trade Payables	10.6	19.4				
.1	.0	.1	Income Taxes Payable	.0	.0				
11.5	17.2	9.2	All Other Current	8.2	8.1				
47.6	48.8	41.3	Total Current	39.2	44.2				
22.4	27.7	25.8	Long-Term Debt	28.5	32.7				
.1	.0	.2	Deferred Taxes	.0	.2				
6.9	.7	4.7	All Other Non-Current	3.3	7.4				
23.0	22.9	28.0	Net Worth	29.0	15.5				
100.0	100.0	100.0	Total Liabilities & Net Worth	100.0	100.0				
			INCOME DATA						
100.0	100.0	100.0	Net Sales	100.0	100.0				
			Gross Profit						
92.5	99.3	91.8	Operating Expenses	88.6	94.7				
7.5	.7	8.2	Operating Profit	11.4	5.3				
1.3	.9	1.2	All Other Expenses (net)	1.6	.1				
6.2	-.2	7.0	Profit Before Taxes	9.9	5.3				
			RATIOS						
3.5	2.9	2.6		3.9	2.8				
1.1	1.5	1.2	Current	1.0	.9				
.6	.7	.6		.5	.5				
3.3	2.7	1.7		3.9	1.4				
.7	1.2	.9	Quick	1.0	.7				
.3	.5	.5		.5	.4				
0 UND	0 UND	4 98.8		5 73.2	0 UND				
15 23.7	14 25.5	24 15.1	Sales/Receivables	15 23.6	21 17.5				
54 6.7	39 9.3	40 9.2		29 12.8	31 11.9				
			Cost of Sales/Inventory						
			Cost of Sales/Payables						
6.8	9.3	8.8		8.6	10.9				
118.6	31.7	29.2	Sales/Working Capital	-260.5	-539.8				
-31.4	-41.8	-16.2		-15.6	-13.2				
46.7	6.7	13.1		9.5	13.1				
(25) 6.3	(27) 1.6	(39) 4.4	EBIT/Interest	(13) 4.5	(15) 2.5				
1.6	-.1	1.2		1.6	.3				
			Net Profit + Depr., Dep., Amort./Cur. Mat. L/T/D						
.4	.5	.5		.2	.5				
1.4	2.0	1.1	Fixed/Worth	1.0	6.5				
-4.4	-1.7	22.0		-12.6	-11.8				
.6	.7	1.0		.6	1.5				
1.8	2.9	2.5	Debt/Worth	2.6	9.1				
-10.5	-3.5	NM		-24.1	-43.3				
103.3	47.0	111.9		149.4	285.7				
(17) 46.9	(23) 13.9	(32) 53.0	% Profit Before Taxes/Tangible Net Worth	(10) 72.6	(11) 81.5				
22.1	-4.5	7.0		35.6	-8.7				
57.3	12.6	32.1		50.7	28.2				
19.6	1.8	14.1	% Profit Before Taxes/Total Assets	17.6	11.4				
2.3	-5.0	.4		4.2	-4.2				
24.4	33.6	22.1		20.0	33.7				
13.5	12.8	11.8	Sales/Net Fixed Assets	8.5	13.1				
9.4	9.0	4.9		4.5	6.8				
6.3	5.0	5.4		6.4	5.8				
3.9	3.3	3.1	Sales/Total Assets	2.5	3.9				
2.9	2.5	2.2		1.5	2.9				
1.6	1.4	1.1			1.2				
(19) 3.1	(28) 3.6	(32) 2.4	% Depr., Dep., Amort./Sales		(14) 2.4				
4.3	5.4	5.5			5.2				
4.4	3.9	3.3		3.4					
(13) 8.9	(20) 10.3	(21) 4.4	% Officers', Directors', Owners' Comp/Sales	(10) 6.7					
11.7	15.9	9.6		10.2					
2964222M	2032095M	236340M	Net Sales ($)	9091M	29738M	16287M	33116M	13889M	134219M
344498M	299290M	83804M	Total Assets ($)	3684M	8035M	14958M	13125M	3547M	40455M

© RMA 2005

M = $ thousand   MM = $ million
See Pages 11 through 21 for Explanation of Ratios and Data

Current Data Sorted By Assets   **Comparative Historical Data**

						Type of Statement		
	2	1 5 2	1 2	1		Unqualified		
4	5	1				Reviewed		
14	5					Compiled		
11	6	3				Tax Returns		
	5 (4/1-9/30/04)		58 (10/1/04-3/31/05)			Other	4/1/00-3/31/01	4/1/01-3/31/02
0-500M	500M-2MM	2-10MM	10-50MM	50-100MM	100-250MM		ALL	ALL
29	18	12	3	1		NUMBER OF STATEMENTS		
%	%	%	%	%	%	ASSETS	%	%
12.8	7.5	6.6			D	Cash & Equivalents	D	D
22.8	40.9	40.2			A	Trade Receivables (net)	A	A
9.8	3.4	8.2			T	Inventory	T	T
2.4	1.7	2.5			A	All Other Current	A	A
47.8	53.5	57.4				Total Current		
32.4	29.7	32.4			N	Fixed Assets (net)	N	N
6.7	4.7	2.9			O	Intangibles (net)	O	O
13.2	12.2	7.3			T	All Other Non-Current	T	T
100.0	100.0	100.0				Total		
					A	LIABILITIES	A	A
25.0	10.4	11.2			V	Notes Payable-Short Term	V	V
8.7	4.6	4.6			A	Cur. Mat.-L/T/D	A	A
14.4	10.9	20.5			I	Trade Payables	I	I
.0	.0	.5			L	Income Taxes Payable	L	L
13.0	9.2	3.7			A	All Other Current	A	A
61.1	35.1	40.6			B	Total Current	B	B
32.2	16.5	19.9			L	Long-Term Debt	L	L
.0	1.2	1.3			E	Deferred Taxes	E	E
9.4	2.2	4.3				All Other Non-Current		
-2.6	45.0	33.9				Net Worth		
100.0	100.0	100.0				Total Liabilities & Net Worth		
						INCOME DATA		
100.0	100.0	100.0				Net Sales		
						Gross Profit		
92.1	97.1	95.2				Operating Expenses		
7.9	2.9	4.8				Operating Profit		
1.0	.3	2.1				All Other Expenses (net)		
6.9	2.7	2.7				Profit Before Taxes		
						RATIOS		
2.1	2.5	2.6						
.8	1.4	1.3				Current		
.4	1.0	1.1						
.9	2.3	2.3						
.5	1.4	1.1				Quick		
.3	.9	.8						
0 UND	31 11.6	33 11.1						
15 24.0	46 8.0	60 6.1				Sales/Receivables		
33 11.2	59 6.2	86 4.3						
						Cost of Sales/Inventory		
						Cost of Sales/Payables		
14.1	7.1	6.7						
-33.8	24.3	13.4				Sales/Working Capital		
-9.9	NM	61.3						
13.8	9.5	19.7						
(21) 4.3	(17) 6.9	2.8				EBIT/Interest		
.4	1.1	1.2						
						Net Profit + Depr., Dep., Amort./Cur. Mat. L /T/D		
.5	.2	.5						
2.0	.8	1.0				Fixed/Worth		
-2.0	1.3	4.5						
1.4	.7	.6						
6.5	1.4	3.0				Debt/Worth		
-3.8	2.9	6.9						
111.4	40.5	50.0				% Profit Before Taxes/Tangible Net Worth		
(18) 86.0	(17) 16.3	(11) 33.9						
6.8	.9	3.4						
27.4	17.4	14.6				% Profit Before Taxes/Total Assets		
9.2	6.6	6.7						
.3	.3	.7						
49.2	34.9	65.4						
16.8	22.6	11.2				Sales/Net Fixed Assets		
7.8	3.9	3.6						
6.8	4.7	3.1						
3.0	3.0	2.6				Sales/Total Assets		
2.1	2.2	1.4						
1.1	.9	1.8						
(19) 2.0	(13) 2.0	(11) 2.7				% Depr., Dep., Amort./Sales		
4.4	6.5	7.0						
4.9						% Officers', Directors', Owners' Comp/Sales		
(17) 6.8								
10.9								
23335M	55395M	105010M	73490M	89125M		Net Sales ($)		
5862M	16796M	40482M	33131M	64691M		Total Assets ($)		

M = $ thousand   MM = $ million
See Pages 11 through 21 for Explanation of Ratios and Data

Comparative Historical Data   **Current Data Sorted By Sales**

2		4		3	Type of Statement					2	1
7		8		9	Unqualified				5	2	1
9		17		11	Reviewed		1		2		
7		22		20	Compiled	5	2	2	1	1	
15		14		20	Tax Returns	11	6	1	1		
					Other	7	8	3	2		
4/1/02-3/31/03		4/1/03-3/31/04		4/1/04-3/31/05		5 (4/1-9/30/04)			58 (10/1/04-3/31/05)		
ALL		ALL		ALL		0-1MM	1-3MM	3-5MM	5-10MM	10-25MM	25MM & OVER
40		65		63	**NUMBER OF STATEMENTS**	23	17	6	10	5	2
%		%		%	**ASSETS**	%	%	%	%	%	%
9.2		11.4		9.8	Cash & Equivalents	12.6	10.8		5.8		
40.0		32.0		31.5	Trade Receivables (net)	22.4	26.7		47.6		
4.6		4.1		7.3	Inventory	10.3	4.6		5.4		
4.0		2.6		2.1	All Other Current	.2	4.6		1.7		
57.8		50.1		50.8	Total Current	45.5	46.8		60.4		
24.7		29.2		32.7	Fixed Assets (net)	34.2	35.0		25.4		
5.6		9.8		5.4	Intangibles (net)	7.3	4.5		4.4		
11.8		10.8		11.1	All Other Non-Current	13.1	13.7		9.8		
100.0		100.0		100.0	Total	100.0	100.0		100.0		
					LIABILITIES						
18.5		10.9		17.3	Notes Payable-Short Term	17.1	25.2		11.5		
5.6		7.4		6.5	Cur. Mat.-L/T/D	9.7	4.0		5.4		
14.1		13.0		14.3	Trade Payables	14.7	11.5		15.4		
.0		.1		.1	Income Taxes Payable	.0	.0		.6		
10.6		16.7		9.9	All Other Current	9.3	14.8		5.7		
48.7		48.2		48.2	Total Current	50.7	55.6		38.7		
19.0		19.4		25.1	Long-Term Debt	33.1	25.0		19.4		
.1		.2		.7	Deferred Taxes	.0	.0		.7		
2.6		7.4		6.0	All Other Non-Current	10.8	2.9		2.8		
29.6		24.8		20.1	Net Worth	5.4	16.6		38.5		
100.0		100.0		100.0	Total Liabilities & Net Worth	100.0	100.0		100.0		
					INCOME DATA						
100.0		100.0		100.0	Net Sales	100.0	100.0		100.0		
					Gross Profit						
97.9		96.8		94.4	Operating Expenses	91.3	95.4		96.1		
2.1		3.2		5.6	Operating Profit	8.7	4.6		3.9		
.9		.3		1.0	All Other Expenses (net)	1.4	.2		.8		
1.2		2.8		4.6	Profit Before Taxes	7.2	4.4		3.1		
					RATIOS						
1.8		1.7		2.1		2.2	2.0		3.0		
1.3		1.2		1.2	Current	.8	1.1		1.4		
.9		.8		.7		.4	.7		1.2		
1.4		1.6		1.7		.9	1.6		2.8		
1.0		1.0		.9	Quick	.7	.9		1.4		
.8		.6		.5		.3	.5		.9		
25	14.4	7	51.2	15	24.4	0	UND	7	51.6	39	9.3

40	9.1	31	11.9	34	10.8	Sales/Receivables	19	19.2	25	14.5	57	6.4
56	6.5	51	7.1	60	6.1		57	6.4	44	8.2	85	4.3

					Cost of Sales/Inventory						
					Cost of Sales/Payables						
13.0		16.5		12.7	Sales/Working Capital	9.2	14.1		6.9		
34.1		76.5		28.1		-33.8	46.7		18.3		
-118.8		-29.0		-25.6		-9.9	-28.2		41.2		
7.5		11.0		11.0	EBIT/Interest	12.5	11.7		17.5		
2.2	(57)	2.6	(54)	4.2		(16) 3.0	(15) 5.9		5.1		
.2		1.0		1.1		-.1	.0		1.4		
		6.3		6.1	Net Profit + Depr., Dep., Amort./Cur. Mat. L/T/D						
	(11)	2.3	(10)	4.0							
		1.6		1.9							
.3		.5		.5	Fixed/Worth	.2	.7		.2		
.8		1.5		1.0		2.0	1.3		.8		
21.7		-3.8		4.6		-2.4	4.2		2.2		
1.2		1.0		.8	Debt/Worth	.7	1.3		.7		
2.2		3.1		2.7		3.5	2.7		1.5		
30.2		-25.1		10.2		-4.0	11.2		4.7		
37.6		67.5		83.8	% Profit Before Taxes/Tangible Net Worth	91.3	117.1				
(32) 13.8		(48) 30.3		(50) 24.4		(14) 12.6	(15) 49.4				
-4.2		2.8		3.3		1.7	8.0				
16.1		21.6		17.8	% Profit Before Taxes/Total Assets	19.4	33.7		18.0		
2.4		4.2		6.8		5.6	15.0		7.9		
-1.4		-.1		.4		.0	.7		1.1		
43.5		53.6		42.7	Sales/Net Fixed Assets	51.3	36.3		89.3		
23.8		23.8		14.3		10.8	16.8		21.1		
9.4		8.8		4.1		5.8	6.5		5.5		
5.7		6.3		5.2	Sales/Total Assets	3.3	6.8		4.5		
3.5		3.6		2.9		2.2	4.1		3.0		
2.6		2.5		1.9		1.5	2.6		2.0		
1.1		.9		1.3	% Depr., Dep., Amort./Sales	1.3	.9				
(33) 1.6		(48) 1.6		(47) 2.4		(15) 2.0	(12) 3.1				
3.8		3.5		7.0		4.6	8.0				
3.3		2.4		3.6	% Officers', Directors', Owners' Comp/Sales	6.1	3.6				
(24) 5.6		(39) 5.4		(31) 6.1		(11) 8.3	(11) 5.0				
8.4		8.8		12.0		14.3	9.6				
630759M		352022M		346355M	Net Sales ($)	10234M	34487M	21506M	70389M	80642M	129097M
233366M		123145M		160962M	Total Assets ($)	4733M	10661M	8524M	29199M	31272M	76573M

M = $ thousand   MM = $ million
See Pages 11 through 21 for Explanation of Ratios and Data

| Current Data Sorted By Assets | | | | | | | | Comparative Historical Data | |

							Type of Statement		
		10	2	2	2		Unqualified		
	1	2					Reviewed		
2	6	1	1				Compiled		
10	2	3			1		Tax Returns		
3	4	3	4	2	2		Other		
	9 (4/1-9/30/04)		54 (10/1/04-3/31/05)					4/1/00-3/31/01 ALL	4/1/01-3/31/02 ALL
0-500M	500M-2MM	2-10MM	10-50MM	50-100MM	100-250MM		NUMBER OF STATEMENTS		
15	13	19	7	4	5				
%	%	%	%	%	%		ASSETS	%	%
23.3	13.3	10.4					Cash & Equivalents	D	D
21.3	36.7	33.1					Trade Receivables (net)	A	A
7.1	4.4	7.2					Inventory	T	T
5.2	10.3	4.6					All Other Current	A	A
56.9	64.6	55.3					Total Current		
34.4	23.7	32.1					Fixed Assets (net)	N	N
3.9	.6	5.4					Intangibles (net)	O	O
4.8	11.1	7.2					All Other Non-Current	T	T
100.0	100.0	100.0					Total		
							LIABILITIES	A	A
16.9	14.8	8.3					Notes Payable-Short Term	V	V
10.1	.9	4.1					Cur. Mat.-L/T/D	A	A
10.3	17.1	13.3					Trade Payables	I	I
.0	.0	.4					Income Taxes Payable	L	L
12.3	11.2	14.5					All Other Current	A	A
49.7	44.0	40.7					Total Current	B	B
49.4	8.1	18.0					Long-Term Debt	L	L
.0	.0	.6					Deferred Taxes	E	E
15.5	3.0	11.2					All Other Non-Current		
−14.6	44.9	29.5					Net Worth		
100.0	100.0	100.0					Total Liabilities & Net Worth		
							INCOME DATA		
100.0	100.0	100.0					Net Sales		
							Gross Profit		
95.5	92.1	88.8					Operating Expenses		
4.5	7.9	11.2					Operating Profit		
.0	.0	3.8					All Other Expenses (net)		
4.5	7.9	7.4					Profit Before Taxes		
							RATIOS		
2.4	2.8	1.9							
1.2	1.3	1.3					Current		
.5	.9	.8							
2.3	2.3	1.3							
.8	1.1	1.1					Quick		
.3	.6	.7							
0 UND	8 48.3	15 24.3							
1 411.0	43 8.6	43 8.6					Sales/Receivables		
44 8.2	73 5.0	61 5.9							
							Cost of Sales/Inventory		
							Cost of Sales/Payables		
8.6	5.8	10.4							
369.8	23.0	17.8					Sales/Working Capital		
−17.2	−218.9	−35.3							
9.1		31.0							
(13) 2.5		(17) 7.8					EBIT/Interest		
1.4		1.5							
							Net Profit + Depr., Dep., Amort./Cur. Mat. L /T/D		
.2	.2	.1							
1.9	.7	1.4					Fixed/Worth		
−2.5	1.1	3.3							
1.0	.5	1.2							
28.0	1.2	2.1					Debt/Worth		
−3.9	5.2	6.1							
	83.4	79.9							
	(12) 58.1	(17) 36.0					% Profit Before Taxes/Tangible Net Worth		
	19.5	10.9							
33.3	44.5	21.9							
8.1	16.9	11.8					% Profit Before Taxes/Total Assets		
.7	−1.0	.1							
74.6	33.7	141.5							
27.3	25.9	22.1					Sales/Net Fixed Assets		
6.5	6.4	3.5							
6.7	3.6	3.3							
3.8	3.1	2.5					Sales/Total Assets		
3.0	2.4	1.1							
1.8		.9							
(11) 2.8		(14) 2.1					% Depr., Dep., Amort./Sales		
12.1		8.7							
							% Officers', Directors', Owners' Comp/Sales		
18203M	54167M	278401M	383446M	537857M	1731590M		Net Sales ($)		
4303M	15377M	93088M	207668M	283194M	791581M		Total Assets ($)		

M = $ thousand   MM = $ million
See Pages 11 through 21 for Explanation of Ratios and Data

Comparative Historical Data | **Current Data Sorted By Sales**

			Type of Statement						
8	16	16	Unqualified	1	1	1	3	1	9
2	8	3	Reviewed			1	1	1	
7	11	10	Compiled		5	2	1	2	
4	7	16	Tax Returns	6	6	1	1		1
21	16	18	Other	3	2	2	2		9
4/1/02-3/31/03	4/1/03-3/31/04	4/1/04-3/31/05		9 (4/1-9/30/04)			54 (10/1/04-3/31/05)		
ALL	ALL	ALL		0-1MM	1-3MM	3-5MM	5-10MM	10-25MM	25MM & OVER
42	58	63	**NUMBER OF STATEMENTS**	10	14	7	9	4	19
%	%	%	**ASSETS**	%	%	%	%	%	%
13.2	16.7	14.0	Cash & Equivalents	16.8	13.6				10.2
31.8	30.7	31.7	Trade Receivables (net)	13.6	26.3				41.9
7.8	10.9	5.9	Inventory	8.6	6.9				5.2
4.5	4.5	6.0	All Other Current	1.3	8.9				5.2
57.3	62.9	57.6	Total Current	40.4	55.7				62.5
28.0	22.9	28.4	Fixed Assets (net)	59.0	27.4				16.6
9.7	5.0	6.6	Intangibles (net)	.0	4.4				13.2
4.9	9.2	7.3	All Other Non-Current	.6	12.5				7.7
100.0	100.0	100.0	Total	100.0	100.0				100.0
			LIABILITIES						
12.1	13.4	11.0	Notes Payable-Short Term	15.8	6.7				4.7
6.0	1.6	4.3	Cur. Mat.-L/T/D	12.0	3.7				1.6
11.9	21.1	14.2	Trade Payables	7.8	12.8				19.9
1.2	.5	.2	Income Taxes Payable	.0	.0				.3
17.0	18.2	13.9	All Other Current	6.6	12.3				16.5
48.3	54.8	43.6	Total Current	42.2	35.4				43.0
19.8	13.9	22.6	Long-Term Debt	67.4	20.5				9.1
.2	.4	.3	Deferred Taxes	.0	.0				.6
7.0	6.1	10.5	All Other Non-Current	23.3	4.2				12.3
24.6	24.8	22.9	Net Worth	-32.9	39.9				34.9
100.0	100.0	100.0	Total Liabilities & Net Worth	100.0	100.0				100.0
			INCOME DATA						
100.0	100.0	100.0	Net Sales	100.0	100.0				100.0
			Gross Profit						
91.9	92.3	92.4	Operating Expenses	83.1	94.4				93.2
8.1	7.7	7.6	Operating Profit	16.9	5.6				6.8
3.6	.6	1.4	All Other Expenses (net)	5.9	.5				.9
4.5	7.2	6.2	Profit Before Taxes	11.0	5.1				5.9
			RATIOS						
1.6	2.5	2.0	Current	1.6	3.5				1.8
1.2	1.3	1.3		.8	1.6				1.5
.8	.9	.9		.3	.7				.9
1.3	1.9	1.6	Quick	1.4	2.5				1.5
.9	.9	1.1		.5	.9				1.2
.5	.6	.6		.2	.2				.8
10 38.1	3 109.8	4 84.0	Sales/Receivables	0 UND	0 UND				38 9.5
46 8.0	31 11.7	43 8.6		0 UND	25 14.5				50 7.2
80 4.5	59 6.1	69 5.3		6 59.1	49 7.4				73 5.0
			Cost of Sales/Inventory						
			Cost of Sales/Payables						
10.5	7.8	8.0	Sales/Working Capital	7.2	5.0				9.2
73.7	17.7	21.6		-61.5	33.9				12.7
-23.9	-46.7	-25.2		-4.9	-18.3				-35.3
(37) 7.0	(44) 19.2	(53) 18.0	EBIT/Interest		5.9				61.6
2.8	4.6	6.4			(10) 1.4				7.6
.8	1.0	1.6			.1				2.3
(10) 6.4			Net Profit + Depr., Dep., Amort./Cur. Mat. L/T/D						
2.9									
.7									
.3	.2	.2	Fixed/Worth	1.6	.1				.2
.9	.6	1.1		NM	.5				.8
-16.0	3.7	13.5		-2.0	7.5				4.7
1.4	.8	1.0	Debt/Worth	3.2	.5				1.1
3.3	2.0	2.7		NM	1.1				2.1
-24.6	7.7	70.3		-3.8	65.3				13.9
57.5	83.3	82.4	% Profit Before Taxes/Tangible Net Worth		64.8				93.3
(30) 15.9	(46) 21.5	(49) 34.6			(12) 24.7			(16)	28.6
4.5	3.9	8.3			-3.7				21.0
23.5	25.6	21.9	% Profit Before Taxes/Total Assets	19.4	43.8				17.3
3.4	6.8	10.8		7.8	2.7				10.3
-.2	-.3	.7		2.7	-1.5				3.1
46.9	86.1	39.1	Sales/Net Fixed Assets	30.2	92.0				39.1
17.2	26.1	18.5		2.5	26.6				17.3
6.4	6.7	5.8		.8	6.4				6.8
4.3	4.5	3.8	Sales/Total Assets	3.8	5.1				3.3
2.3	3.1	2.9		1.4	3.4				2.3
1.0	2.0	1.4		.6	2.3				1.2
(33) 1.0	(44) .7	(45) 1.2	% Depr., Dep., Amort./Sales					(12)	1.2
2.1	2.0	2.6							2.6
4.9	3.3	5.8							3.1
(10) 2.0	(18) 2.7	(22) 2.2	% Officers', Directors', Owners' Comp/Sales						
4.7	6.6	6.2							
9.7	11.5	12.1							
1315852M	1667690M	3003664M	Net Sales ($)	5351M	26860M	27591M	64520M	58405M	2820937M
971413M	995676M	1395211M	Total Assets ($)	10570M	19654M	9909M	25955M	27466M	1301657M

© RMA 2005

M = $ thousand   MM = $ million

See Pages 11 through 21 for Explanation of Ratios and Data

Current Data Sorted By Assets **Comparative Historical Data**

0-500M	500M-2MM	2-10MM	10-50MM	50-100MM	100-250MM	Type of Statement	4/1/00-3/31/01 ALL	4/1/01-3/31/02 ALL
		5	15	4	4	Unqualified		
	7	10	2	1		Reviewed		
5	14	9				Compiled		
11	8				1	Tax Returns		
4	10	12	6	2	1	Other		
26 (4/1-9/30/04)			105 (10/1/04-3/31/05)					
20	39	36	23	7	6	NUMBER OF STATEMENTS		
%	%	%	%	%	%	ASSETS	%	%
18.3	8.6	7.5	5.4			Cash & Equivalents	D	D
27.0	25.6	24.7	12.6			Trade Receivables (net)	A	A
1.7	2.5	4.1	.5			Inventory	T	T
.1	3.1	4.0	3.0			All Other Current	A	A
47.1	39.9	40.2	21.6			Total Current		
34.4	46.1	46.0	55.8			Fixed Assets (net)		
9.4	6.1	4.8	16.5			Intangibles (net)	N	N
9.0	7.9	9.0	6.2			All Other Non-Current	O	O
100.0	100.0	100.0	100.0			Total	T	T
						LIABILITIES	A	A
30.7	7.8	6.5	2.2			Notes Payable-Short Term	V	V
11.4	9.6	8.7	8.2			Cur. Mat.-L/T/D	A	A
19.1	10.0	13.6	7.5			Trade Payables	I	I
.1	.2	1.1	.2			Income Taxes Payable	L	L
8.9	7.1	7.5	6.8			All Other Current	A	A
70.2	34.6	37.3	25.0			Total Current	B	B
36.5	34.6	29.3	38.5			Long-Term Debt	L	L
.0	.5	.7	3.7			Deferred Taxes	E	E
14.4	11.6	7.0	7.6			All Other Non-Current		
−21.2	18.6	25.6	25.2			Net Worth		
100.0	100.0	100.0	100.0			Total Liabilities & Net Worth		
						INCOME DATA		
100.0	100.0	100.0	100.0			Net Sales		
						Gross Profit		
98.4	96.8	93.9	92.4			Operating Expenses		
1.6	3.2	6.1	7.6			Operating Profit		
−.1	1.3	1.8	2.2			All Other Expenses (net)		
1.7	1.9	4.3	5.4			Profit Before Taxes		
						RATIOS		
1.9	1.8	1.5	1.2			Current		
.8	1.1	1.0	.9					
.4	.9	.7	.6					
1.9	1.4	1.2	1.2			Quick		
.7	1.0	.9	.7					
.4	.6	.6	.4					
0 UND	24 15.5	32 11.4	27 13.5			Sales/Receivables		
22 16.9	36 10.2	42 8.7	34 10.7					
41 8.8	45 8.2	58 6.3	47 7.8					
						Cost of Sales/Inventory		
						Cost of Sales/Payables		
27.5	17.5	20.6	28.4			Sales/Working Capital		
−216.9	90.8	−176.8	−71.1					
−9.8	−54.1	−16.0	−10.7					
8.4	5.5	7.2	4.8			EBIT/Interest		
(16) 2.4	(34) 2.0	(34) 3.0	3.1					
−.9	.7	1.1	1.3					
	1.6	1.7	1.8			Net Profit + Depr., Dep., Amort./Cur. Mat. L /T/D		
	(10) 1.1	(10) 1.5	(12) 1.6					
	.3	1.1	.8					
.7	1.1	.8	2.5			Fixed/Worth		
NM	2.3	1.8	5.8					
−.5	−4.3	3.9	−1.8					
1.5	1.9	1.1	2.8			Debt/Worth		
NM	4.1	2.3	6.1					
−2.1	−9.8	5.6	−5.2					
151.8	64.6	38.8	37.4			% Profit Before Taxes/Tangible Net Worth		
(10) 62.1	(27) 35.9	(28) 14.7	(15) 15.5					
22.3	7.1	7.2	7.6					
38.1	17.8	12.9	8.4			% Profit Before Taxes/Total Assets		
9.7	6.5	5.7	3.8					
−3.7	−.5	.8	1.7					
39.8	18.9	10.1	2.9			Sales/Net Fixed Assets		
14.6	6.4	5.2	1.9					
4.0	2.7	2.3	1.2					
6.9	3.7	2.6	1.4			Sales/Total Assets		
4.2	2.3	2.1	1.1					
2.9	1.7	1.2	.8					
2.3	2.6	2.8	5.4			% Depr., Dep., Amort./Sales		
(11) 9.1	(30) 6.0	5.3	(22) 7.1					
17.0	11.3	9.1	9.8					
3.4	3.4	2.2				% Officers', Directors', Owners' Comp/Sales		
(11) 7.2	(17) 7.5	(13) 2.9						
9.6	9.3	4.9						
18222M	123647M	281201M	780967M	990016M	1041245M	Net Sales ($)		
4920M	45338M	142198M	630960M	536544M	1038583M	Total Assets ($)		

© RMA 2005

M = $ thousand   MM = $ million
See Pages 11 through 21 for Explanation of Ratios and Data

Comparative Historical Data | **Current Data Sorted By Sales**

			Type of Statement						
18	28	28	Unqualified			1	4	10	13
21	27	20	Reviewed	2	2	7	2	6	1
15	29	28	Compiled	3	11	6	5	3	
11	23	20	Tax Returns	6	11	2			1
20	26	35	Other	3	7	7	6	6	6
4/1/02-3/31/03 ALL	4/1/03-3/31/04 ALL	4/1/04-3/31/05 ALL		26 (4/1-9/30/04)			105 (10/1/04-3/31/05)		
				0-1MM	1-3MM	3-5MM	5-10MM	10-25MM	25MM & OVER
85	133	131	**NUMBER OF STATEMENTS**	14	31	23	17	25	21
%	%	%	**ASSETS**	%	%	%	%	%	%
10.4	10.3	8.8	Cash & Equivalents	15.3	11.4	5.6	10.6	7.4	4.5
22.7	20.2	23.0	Trade Receivables (net)	20.3	24.0	23.4	27.8	25.0	16.7
.8	2.2	2.3	Inventory	1.7	.8	4.3	5.0	2.2	.7
4.5	3.9	2.8	All Other Current	.0	2.0	5.2	2.2	3.3	2.8
38.4	36.4	36.9	Total Current	37.4	38.2	38.5	45.6	37.9	24.8
48.7	49.5	45.5	Fixed Assets (net)	51.6	41.0	50.3	38.5	45.7	48.1
3.9	5.4	9.2	Intangibles (net)	4.7	12.2	3.3	4.3	7.7	19.7
9.0	8.7	8.5	All Other Non-Current	6.3	8.6	7.9	11.6	8.7	7.5
100.0	100.0	100.0	Total	100.0	100.0	100.0	100.0	100.0	100.0
			LIABILITIES						
11.5	10.1	9.4	Notes Payable-Short Term	34.6	11.1	5.1	4.2	6.6	2.2
10.0	9.6	9.1	Cur. Mat.-L/T/D	8.4	12.1	9.1	7.0	8.6	7.3
9.1	9.9	11.9	Trade Payables	10.8	11.5	10.9	17.5	10.5	11.3
.3	.2	.4	Income Taxes Payable	.0	.1	.8	1.7	.2	.1
9.6	8.3	7.1	All Other Current	5.5	7.5	8.0	10.1	7.0	4.5
40.5	38.0	37.9	Total Current	59.3	42.2	33.9	40.5	33.0	25.5
36.2	31.8	34.7	Long-Term Debt	46.7	39.0	27.3	34.8	28.1	36.3
.8	.8	1.1	Deferred Taxes	.0	.4	1.4	.3	2.5	1.6
6.2	6.1	9.5	All Other Non-Current	5.3	12.0	16.3	7.5	4.3	8.9
16.3	23.3	16.7	Net Worth	-11.3	6.3	21.1	16.9	32.1	27.7
100.0	100.0	100.0	Total Liabilities & Net Worth	100.0	100.0	100.0	100.0	100.0	100.0
			INCOME DATA						
100.0	100.0	100.0	Net Sales	100.0	100.0	100.0	100.0	100.0	100.0
			Gross Profit						
92.4	94.3	94.3	Operating Expenses	96.6	95.2	96.2	95.4	90.3	93.2
7.6	5.7	5.7	Operating Profit	3.4	4.8	3.8	4.6	9.7	6.8
3.9	1.7	2.0	All Other Expenses (net)	3.5	.9	.8	2.1	3.6	2.1
3.8	4.0	3.7	Profit Before Taxes	-.1	3.9	2.9	2.4	6.1	4.8
			RATIOS						
1.9	1.7	1.5	Current	1.4	1.9	1.5	1.4	1.9	1.2
1.0	1.0	1.0		.6	1.1	1.1	.9	1.0	.9
.6	.6	.6		.2	.5	.9	.7	.6	.7
1.8	1.4	1.2	Quick	1.4	1.8	1.2	1.3	1.8	1.1
.8	.9	.9		.6	1.0	1.0	.7	.8	.8
.5	.5	.5		.2	.5	.7	.5	.5	.5
21 17.6	19 19.7	25 14.5	Sales/Receivables	0 UND	22 16.4	30 12.1	31 11.9	27 13.3	29 12.7
35 10.5	32 11.3	37 10.0		20 18.1	32 11.3	40 9.2	40 9.1	35 10.4	37 10.0
47 7.8	43 8.6	48 7.6		61 6.0	43 8.4	48 7.6	58 6.3	49 7.5	46 8.0
			Cost of Sales/Inventory						
			Cost of Sales/Payables						
11.8	15.0	23.6	Sales/Working Capital	18.9	17.5	12.6	25.0	18.1	31.5
-328.0	999.8	-999.8		-17.0	178.8	117.4	-83.0	341.9	-81.8
-17.0	-16.4	-13.3		-5.2	-11.8	-57.7	-12.7	-11.9	-16.0
4.4	5.4	6.3	EBIT/Interest	3.3	7.8	4.6	7.3	6.5	5.2
(74) 2.2	(119) 2.1	(119) 2.7		(10) .9	(27) 2.3	(21) 2.3	(16) 5.0	(24) 4.1	3.1
.6	1.0	1.1		-1.5	.3	1.3	.1	1.8	1.5
3.1	3.3	1.8	Net Profit + Depr., Dep., Amort./Cur. Mat. L/T/D		1.5				2.4
(22) 1.7	(34) 1.6	(40) 1.5			(10) 1.2				(14) 1.7
1.1	.9	.9			.4				1.4
.8	.8	1.0	Fixed/Worth	.6	1.0	1.4	.7	.7	2.7
2.2	2.5	3.0		-75.2	4.2	1.8	1.9	2.5	6.3
-12.4	37.9	-4.3		-1.6	-1.6	4.4	-21.3	7.4	-3.9
1.2	1.1	1.7	Debt/Worth	2.4	1.5	1.1	1.7	1.0	2.8
3.1	3.6	3.7		-81.0	7.6	2.5	2.5	3.1	7.6
-16.9	112.5	-9.3		-3.4	-3.2	9.7	-83.7	8.3	-9.0
43.3	50.2	59.6	% Profit Before Taxes/Tangible Net Worth		102.7	37.3	43.2	40.0	88.1
(60) 20.6	(105) 20.6	(90) 26.2			(18) 41.8	(19) 25.8	(12) 32.5	(21) 10.3	(14) 20.1
-.3	.5	8.6			5.5	6.6	4.8	8.3	10.8
11.1	10.7	13.9	% Profit Before Taxes/Total Assets	11.8	20.0	13.9	15.0	10.7	10.6
3.1	4.2	6.0		.6	12.1	4.4	6.8	7.2	4.7
-.5	.0	.5		-6.1	-.5	1.3	-1.8	2.1	1.9
10.0	9.9	12.9	Sales/Net Fixed Assets	22.6	21.2	11.0	15.9	9.7	5.3
4.8	4.1	3.9		3.2	6.5	3.5	6.7	3.6	2.3
2.4	1.9	2.1		1.1	3.0	2.2	3.3	1.6	1.4
3.5	3.4	3.3	Sales/Total Assets	5.2	3.7	3.3	3.2	2.9	1.6
2.3	2.1	1.8		1.2	2.3	2.1	2.3	1.5	1.1
1.4	1.1	1.1		.9	1.7	1.3	1.5	1.0	.8
4.2	4.1	3.4	% Depr., Dep., Amort./Sales		4.2	2.9	2.3	1.8	5.4
(74) 6.3	(115) 6.4	(109) 6.4			(21) 8.1	(21) 5.3	(16) 4.0	(24) 5.1	(18) 6.8
9.4	10.9	10.2			12.0	9.5	8.8	7.7	9.0
3.6	1.6	2.7	% Officers', Directors', Owners' Comp/Sales		3.2				
(34) 5.4	(51) 4.3	(44) 5.3			(17) 8.2				
10.1	8.4	8.6			9.2				
1135420M	2103465M	3235298M	Net Sales ($)	6429M	58423M	94392M	131353M	400255M	2544446M
915378M	1420958M	2398543M	Total Assets ($)	6972M	28037M	50563M	143440M	501190M	1668341M

M = $ thousand   MM = $ million
See Pages 11 through 21 for Explanation of Ratios and Data

Current Data Sorted By Assets   **Comparative Historical Data**

						Type of Statement		
		3	3		1	Unqualified		
	4	6	1			Reviewed		
	3	2				Compiled		
	6	1				Tax Returns		
2	2	3	7		1	Other		
	7 (4/1-9/30/04)		38 (10/1/04-3/31/05)				4/1/00-3/31/01	4/1/01-3/31/02
0-500M	500M-2MM	2-10MM	10-50MM	50-100MM	100-250MM		ALL	ALL
2	15	15	11		2	NUMBER OF STATEMENTS		
%	%	%	%	%	%	**ASSETS**	%	%
	10.1	8.8	8.0			Cash & Equivalents		
	33.7	33.8	32.8			Trade Receivables (net)		
	2.6	.6	2.7			Inventory		
	1.4	2.5	6.4			All Other Current		
	47.9	45.7	50.0			Total Current		
	39.5	43.1	35.3			Fixed Assets (net)		
	2.0	.6	9.5			Intangibles (net)		
	10.5	10.6	5.2			All Other Non-Current		
	100.0	100.0	100.0			Total		
						LIABILITIES		
	2.4	6.0	1.9			Notes Payable-Short Term		
	5.3	5.2	3.4			Cur. Mat.-L/T/D		
	18.7	15.2	13.9			Trade Payables		
	.0	.1	.6			Income Taxes Payable		
	10.5	9.1	10.7			All Other Current		
	36.9	35.6	30.6			Total Current		
	35.3	20.6	17.1			Long-Term Debt		
	.1	.6	1.6			Deferred Taxes		
	1.9	5.2	5.6			All Other Non-Current		
	25.9	38.0	45.1			Net Worth		
	100.0	100.0	100.0			Total Liabilities & Net Worth		
						INCOME DATA		
	100.0	100.0	100.0			Net Sales		
						Gross Profit		
	94.8	92.5	92.9			Operating Expenses		
	5.2	7.5	7.1			Operating Profit		
	.3	4.0	2.0			All Other Expenses (net)		
	5.0	3.6	5.1			Profit Before Taxes		
						RATIOS		
	2.9	1.9	2.0					
	1.4	1.3	1.5			Current		
	.9	.6	1.1					
	2.5	1.8	1.8					
	1.1	1.2	1.3			Quick		
	.9	.6	.9					
29	12.6	24 14.9	45 8.1					
44	8.4	40 9.0	54 6.7			Sales/Receivables		
63	5.8	66 5.5	78 4.7					
						Cost of Sales/Inventory		
						Cost of Sales/Payables		
	7.1	9.1	6.9					
	27.9	44.2	10.0			Sales/Working Capital		
	−77.2	−15.0	27.6					
	8.6	72.5	47.6					
(13)	1.7	(13) 9.2	(10) 7.0			EBIT/Interest		
	.0	1.2	1.5					
						Net Profit + Depr., Dep., Amort./Cur. Mat. L /T/D		
	.5	.4	.2					
	1.2	.9	1.0			Fixed/Worth		
	4.8	2.4	3.3					
	.8	.8	.9					
	3.1	2.3	2.0			Debt/Worth		
	20.9	3.0	3.1					
	48.6	60.4	49.2					
(12)	9.0	(14) 26.3	(10) 35.9			% Profit Before Taxes/Tangible Net Worth		
	−4.4	3.7	10.1					
	11.1	20.2	16.9					
	2.4	11.6	10.7*			% Profit Before Taxes/Total Assets		
	−3.9	−.1	2.0					
	17.1	15.5	45.1					
	5.7	7.3	4.4			Sales/Net Fixed Assets		
	3.1	3.4	1.2					
	3.6	3.0	2.5					
	2.3	2.6	1.6			Sales/Total Assets		
	1.8	1.8	.9					
	5.7	1.3						
(12)	6.2	2.9				% Depr., Dep., Amort./Sales		
	9.5	5.4						
	3.7							
(10)	4.9					% Officers', Directors', Owners' Comp/Sales		
	6.9							
901M	47908M	203263M	446641M		119253M	Net Sales ($)		
452M	18052M	81096M	260012M		308445M	Total Assets ($)		

(The 50-100MM, 4/1/00-3/31/01 ALL, and 4/1/01-3/31/02 ALL columns display "DATA NOT AVAILABLE" for all data rows.)

M = $ thousand   MM = $ million
See Pages 11 through 21 for Explanation of Ratios and Data

Comparative Historical Data				Current Data Sorted By Sales					

Comparative Historical Data   **Current Data Sorted By Sales**

			Type of Statement					2	5
3	6	7	Unqualified					3	
3	4	11	Reviewed		2	2	4		
6	4	5	Compiled	1	2	1	1		
4	7	7	Tax Returns		4	2		1	
6	8	15	Other	2	2	1		3	7
4/1/02-3/31/03	4/1/03-3/31/04	4/1/04-3/31/05			7 (4/1-9/30/04)			38 (10/1/04-3/31/05)	
ALL	ALL	ALL		0-1MM	1-3MM	3-5MM	5-10MM	10-25MM	25MM & OVER
22	29	45	**NUMBER OF STATEMENTS**	3	10	6	5	9	12
%	%	%	**ASSETS**	%	%	%	%	%	%
6.4	10.5	9.6	Cash & Equivalents		13.2				10.7
33.3	24.9	33.9	Trade Receivables (net)		25.2				38.5
3.3	1.8	1.8	Inventory		4.0				2.7
5.3	4.2	3.4	All Other Current		1.9				6.7
48.4	41.5	48.7	Total Current		44.2				58.5
37.4	46.0	38.8	Fixed Assets (net)		39.8				32.2
5.6	4.8	3.6	Intangibles (net)		3.1				7.1
8.7	7.8	8.9	All Other Non-Current		13.0				2.2
100.0	100.0	100.0	Total		100.0				100.0
			LIABILITIES						
10.0	6.6	6.1	Notes Payable-Short Term		.8				5.0
3.4	6.2	5.3	Cur. Mat.-L/T/D		7.0				2.8
20.9	16.8	15.2	Trade Payables		11.0				15.2
1.2	.0	.2	Income Taxes Payable		.0				.6
13.0	17.9	11.0	All Other Current		8.8				11.5
48.5	47.5	37.8	Total Current		27.7				35.1
26.9	24.7	27.6	Long-Term Debt		49.0				11.2
.0	.8	.6	Deferred Taxes		.0				1.4
3.5	8.2	4.5	All Other Non-Current		1.2				5.9
21.1	18.7	29.5	Net Worth		22.1				46.3
100.0	100.0	100.0	Total Liabilities & Net Worth		100.0				100.0
			INCOME DATA						
100.0	100.0	100.0	Net Sales		100.0				100.0
			Gross Profit						
90.4	93.1	93.6	Operating Expenses		91.3				93.0
9.6	6.9	6.4	Operating Profit		8.7				7.0
2.5	1.2	2.4	All Other Expenses (net)		2.3				3.7
7.1	5.6	4.0	Profit Before Taxes		6.4				3.3
			RATIOS						
1.8	2.7	2.0			4.0				2.0
1.1	1.3	1.3	Current		2.0				1.5
.4	.6	.9			.9				1.1
1.6	2.5	1.8			3.3				1.8
.8	.8	1.1	Quick		1.3				1.3
.3	.5	.8			.9				.9
16 22.8	16 22.6	29 12.7		0 UND					40 9.2
41 9.0	45 8.1	52 7.1	Sales/Receivables	47 7.8					56 6.5
67 5.4	60 6.1	68 5.4		64 5.7					81 4.5
			Cost of Sales/Inventory						
			Cost of Sales/Payables						
7.6	6.9	8.8			5.3				6.2
63.1	21.5	23.5	Sales/Working Capital		13.4				9.8
−7.2	−14.0	−77.3			−77.4				582.7
13.2	12.0	14.5							41.3
(18) 2.9	(27) 5.1	(40) 4.2	EBIT/Interest					(11)	6.5
1.4	.9	.7							.9
		10.8	Net Profit + Depr., Dep.,						
		(10) 7.8	Amort./Cur. Mat. L/T/D						
		4.2							
.3	.6	.4			.5				.2
1.0	2.1	1.0	Fixed/Worth		1.5				.8
6.7	NM	2.6			−1.9				1.6
1.2	.8	.9			.7				.9
5.1	2.5	2.1	Debt/Worth		2.8				1.8
−9.6	NM	5.3			−4.3				2.3
91.1	85.2	54.5			27.6				54.1
(16) 34.6	(22) 30.0	(38) 20.8	% Profit Before Taxes/Tangible Net Worth		3.5			(11)	20.4
14.4	4.6	1.1			−4.1				−1.8
14.1	16.7	16.4			27.6				19.4
6.4	8.7	6.0	% Profit Before Taxes/Total Assets		3.5				9.0
.9	.0	−.5			−4.1				.0
276.0	7.5	16.3			14.1				38.6
4.2	4.8	5.5	Sales/Net Fixed Assets		4.3				6.4
3.5	2.3	2.5			2.2				1.9
4.0	3.2	3.1			2.6				4.1
1.8	1.9	2.1	Sales/Total Assets		1.8				2.2
1.5	1.2	1.5			1.4				.8
2.3	3.5	1.9							
(17) 4.3	(28) 5.3	(38) 5.5	% Depr., Dep., Amort./Sales						
6.7	8.4	8.6							
		1.7	% Officers', Directors', Owners' Comp/Sales						
		(22) 4.6							
		6.8							
318829M	400706M	817966M	Net Sales ($)	1141M	20874M	23901M	33438M	151118M	587494M
179453M	400970M	668057M	Total Assets ($)	3742M	15892M	21561M	11545M	75749M	539568M

M = $ thousand   MM = $ million
See Pages 11 through 21 for Explanation of Ratios and Data

ADMIN & WASTE MANAGEMENT SERVICES—Solid Waste Landfill NAICS 562212 (SIC 4953)

Current Data Sorted By Assets							Comparative Historical Data	
						Type of Statement		
1	1	16	16	4	8	Unqualified	54	40
4	6	26	8		1	Reviewed	41	38
6	15	7	3		2	Compiled	38	52
4	9	2	1			Tax Returns	20	20
1	9	23	9	2	1	Other	94	82
	36 (4/1-9/30/04)		149 (10/1/04-3/31/05)				4/1/00-3/31/01	4/1/01-3/31/02
0-500M	500M-2MM	2-10MM	10-50MM	50-100MM	100-250MM		ALL	ALL
16	40	74	37	6	12	**NUMBER OF STATEMENTS**	247	232
%	%	%	%	%	%	**ASSETS**	%	%
13.1	13.5	10.0	12.6		8.1	Cash & Equivalents	8.9	8.6
20.9	23.3	19.1	11.9		14.6	Trade Receivables (net)	19.5	20.3
3.6	1.4	2.2	.7		2.1	Inventory	2.4	1.9
3.7	2.1	2.2	2.1		4.5	All Other Current	2.2	2.9
41.3	40.2	33.5	27.3		29.2	Total Current	33.0	33.6
44.7	43.6	50.9	53.8		53.7	Fixed Assets (net)	50.3	51.0
6.7	2.5	5.3	6.3		11.9	Intangibles (net)	6.6	7.2
7.4	13.6	10.3	12.7		5.2	All Other Non-Current	10.1	8.2
100.0	100.0	100.0	100.0		100.0	Total	100.0	100.0
						LIABILITIES		
7.2	9.4	4.3	2.0		5.0	Notes Payable-Short Term	7.5	5.6
7.7	7.8	7.4	5.5		3.0	Cur. Mat.-L/T/D	7.5	8.5
15.8	17.3	11.2	7.5		7.5	Trade Payables	10.5	11.5
.0	.4	.1	.2		.5	Income Taxes Payable	.4	.2
27.7	8.2	10.6	10.1		15.5	All Other Current	8.3	8.2
58.4	43.1	33.6	25.3		31.5	Total Current	34.2	34.0
31.7	37.3	29.8	23.9		32.1	Long-Term Debt	31.0	31.4
.5	.5	.7	1.2		.7	Deferred Taxes	.5	.6
8.6	3.4	6.0	8.9		11.6	All Other Non-Current	9.8	8.2
.8	15.7	29.9	40.7		24.1	Net Worth	24.5	25.8
100.0	100.0	100.0	100.0		100.0	Total Liabilities & Net Worth	100.0	100.0
						INCOME DATA		
100.0	100.0	100.0	100.0		100.0	Net Sales	100.0	100.0
						Gross Profit		
91.8	91.2	91.9	85.9		86.9	Operating Expenses	93.1	93.0
8.2	8.8	8.1	14.1		13.1	Operating Profit	6.9	7.0
.4	2.1	2.6	3.7		6.1	All Other Expenses (net)	1.5	3.1
7.7	6.6	5.5	10.4		7.0	Profit Before Taxes	5.4	4.0
						RATIOS		
2.6	1.9	1.9	1.9		1.6		1.8	1.6
1.0	1.0	1.2	1.1		.9	Current	1.1	1.0
.1	.7	.7	.7		.6		.6	.5
1.7	1.8	1.6	1.8		1.1		1.7	1.5
.7	.9	.9	1.0		.8	Quick	.9	.9
.1	.6	.6	.6		.5		.5	.4
0 UND	18 19.7	29 12.8	29 12.6		34 10.7		23 15.6	28 13.0
5 68.5	34 10.8	38 9.7	37 9.8		43 8.5	Sales/Receivables	37 9.8	39 9.3
48 7.6	51 7.1	49 7.4	61 6.0		52 7.0		58 6.3	55 6.6
						Cost of Sales/Inventory		
						Cost of Sales/Payables		
13.8	15.2	7.8	6.9		15.3		11.5	11.7
UND	NM	38.0	58.8		−334.8	Sales/Working Capital	84.2	−508.8
−5.6	−17.3	−17.1	−14.1		−6.5		−10.0	−8.7
9.6	9.3	9.6	7.9				7.4	6.3
(14) 2.5	(33) 3.6	(71) 4.4	(35) 5.6			EBIT/Interest	(228) 2.8	(210) 2.3
−.1	1.6	1.3	2.0				1.1	.8
		5.0	4.2				4.4	3.4
		(17) 2.7	(13) 1.7			Net Profit + Depr., Dep., Amort./Cur. Mat. L /T/D	(77) 2.2	(60) 1.6
		1.3	1.2				1.3	1.1
.3	.6	.8	1.0		2.4		.8	.9
2.6	2.7	1.9	1.5		3.4	Fixed/Worth	1.7	2.4
−1.3	337.3	8.1	3.1		NM		29.0	72.0
.6	.9	1.2	.7		2.1		.9	1.0
6.6	3.1	2.3	1.2		3.9	Debt/Worth	2.4	3.1
−2.8	NM	10.0	3.9		NM		61.6	99.0
81.3	130.8	58.5	39.2			% Profit Before Taxes/Tangible Net Worth	52.9	51.9
(10) 27.7	(30) 22.3	(61) 27.3	(31) 14.7				(191) 28.2	(176) 22.8
3.5	9.3	5.3	5.3				7.4	1.2
17.7	17.2	14.5	10.3		8.1	% Profit Before Taxes/Total Assets	15.6	15.1
8.2	7.2	4.7	4.6		3.1		6.6	4.7
−3.6	1.4	.6	1.8		.6		.2	−.8
42.0	18.3	5.1	2.8		5.3		6.9	6.6
8.0	6.2	2.8	1.7		1.9	Sales/Net Fixed Assets	3.3	3.1
3.7	2.2	1.8	1.0		.9		1.7	1.6
5.4	3.5	2.3	1.3		1.4		2.5	2.4
2.4	2.4	1.5	.9		.9	Sales/Total Assets	1.6	1.6
1.4	1.0	1.0	.6		.5		.9	.9
	2.2	4.1	5.5				3.3	3.4
	(29) 6.9	(71) 6.8	(36) 8.4			% Depr., Dep., Amort./Sales	(229) 6.2	(211) 6.2
	11.7		10.6	14.4			10.9	10.5
	1.8	1.4					2.6	1.8
	(14) 3.6	(16) 3.9				% Officers', Directors', Owners' Comp/Sales	(83) 4.4	(68) 3.5
	7.3	5.5					8.6	7.5
17477M	119621M	718432M	1064438M	379222M	2215010M	Net Sales ($)	3581526M	3909359M
3879M	49132M	394791M	953508M	424897M	1796423M	Total Assets ($)	3142929M	3664238M

M = $ thousand   MM = $ million
See Pages 11 through 21 for Explanation of Ratios and Data

Comparative Historical Data				Current Data Sorted By Sales					

				Type of Statement						
48	36	46	Unqualified	2	3	5	6	9	21
49	35	45	Reviewed	4	6	6	12	11	6
37	40	33	Compiled	7	8	5	6	4	3
32	25	16	Tax Returns	4	8	2		2	
52	57	45	Other	1	10	6	9	14	5
4/1/02- 3/31/03 ALL	4/1/03- 3/31/04 ALL	4/1/04- 3/31/05 ALL		36 (4/1-9/30/04)			149 (10/1/04-3/31/05)		
				0-1MM	1-3MM	3-5MM	5-10MM	10-25MM	25MM & OVER
218	193	185	NUMBER OF STATEMENTS	18	35	24	33	40	35
%	%	%	ASSETS	%	%	%	%	%	%
8.9	9.7	11.4	Cash & Equivalents	13.4	12.8	14.6	7.8	11.5	9.9
19.6	18.5	18.3	Trade Receivables (net)	18.7	8.9	22.0	20.9	21.6	18.6
1.5	2.6	1.8	Inventory	3.2	2.5	3.1	.3	1.1	1.7
2.0	4.1	2.4	All Other Current	3.2	2.0	3.3	2.0	2.1	2.4
32.0	34.8	33.8	Total Current	38.5	26.2	43.0	30.9	36.3	32.6
53.8	48.8	49.6	Fixed Assets (net)	50.5	54.9	43.9	48.7	48.4	50.1
5.5	7.5	5.7	Intangibles (net)	3.9	3.2	5.3	7.3	4.5	9.4
8.6	8.9	10.9	All Other Non-Current	7.0	15.7	7.9	13.1	10.9	7.9
100.0	100.0	100.0	Total	100.0	100.0	100.0	100.0	100.0	100.0
			LIABILITIES						
7.1	6.7	5.1	Notes Payable-Short Term	3.5	6.7	4.4	5.7	5.7	3.8
7.5	5.0	6.8	Cur. Mat.-L/T/D	6.5	6.5	8.6	10.4	4.8	5.2
11.9	11.8	11.8	Trade Payables	12.3	9.2	17.7	12.6	10.7	10.8
.1	.1	.2	Income Taxes Payable	.0	.2	.4	.1	.1	.4
9.2	11.0	11.6	All Other Current	13.2	13.3	10.5	15.4	6.3	12.4
35.8	34.7	35.6	Total Current	35.5	35.9	41.6	44.1	27.7	32.4
29.1	25.3	30.0	Long-Term Debt	31.2	46.8	28.1	25.4	27.3	21.5
.7	.7	.8	Deferred Taxes	.6	.1	1.2	.9	.8	1.1
5.7	7.4	6.6	All Other Non-Current	.7	8.1	3.2	10.9	5.6	7.5
28.7	32.0	27.0	Net Worth	32.1	9.1	25.8	18.7	38.7	37.5
100.0	100.0	100.0	Total Liabilities & Net Worth	100.0	100.0	100.0	100.0	100.0	100.0
			INCOME DATA						
100.0	100.0	100.0	Net Sales	100.0	100.0	100.0	100.0	100.0	100.0
			Gross Profit						
92.7	92.0	90.0	Operating Expenses	86.3	89.9	87.9	95.6	90.5	87.6
7.3	8.0	10.0	Operating Profit	13.7	10.1	12.1	4.4	9.5	12.4
2.8	2.3	2.6	All Other Expenses (net)	2.3	3.3	1.7	2.2	2.2	3.6
4.5	5.7	7.4	Profit Before Taxes	11.3	6.8	10.4	2.2	7.3	8.8
			RATIOS						
1.4	1.7	1.8		3.8	1.7	1.9	1.3	2.1	1.6
1.0	1.1	1.1	Current	1.3	.9	1.3	1.0	1.3	1.0
.5	.6	.7		.5	.4	.7	.5	.9	.7
1.3	1.4	1.5		3.6	1.5	1.5	1.3	2.1	1.4
(217) .9	(192) .9	.9	Quick	1.0	.8	1.1	.8	1.2	.8
.4	.5	.6		.4	.3	.5	.5	.8	.6
25 14.4	24 15.5	26 13.8		0 UND	8 45.4	25 14.8	27 13.6	29 12.4	32 11.3
38 9.5	39 9.3	37 9.8	Sales/Receivables	32 11.4	30 12.1	41 8.8	38 9.6	36 10.1	43 8.6
59 6.1	55 6.7	53 6.8		61 6.0	48 7.6	58 6.3	48 7.7	52 7.1	57 6.4
			Cost of Sales/Inventory						
			Cost of Sales/Payables						
14.1	10.5	8.3		3.9	7.3	5.5	25.6	7.6	14.6
528.4	80.3	58.8	Sales/Working Capital	21.7	-66.0	33.3	-108.3	24.5	655.5
-10.6	-12.5	-14.3		-11.5	-7.0	-15.7	-10.7	-108.0	-13.0
6.3	8.7	8.4		19.7	5.5	12.3	5.6	13.2	16.4
(205) 2.6	(168) 2.9	(168) 4.1	EBIT/Interest	(15) 3.7	(32) 2.2	(21) 6.8	(32) 2.5	(37) 5.0	(31) 5.5
1.0	.9	1.5		1.0	1.0	2.9	.9	2.2	2.9
4.4	4.5	4.2	Net Profit + Depr., Dep.,					9.3	6.6
(52) 1.8	(31) 2.3	(46) 2.1	Amort./Cur. Mat. L/T/D				(14) 3.2	(12) 3.2 1.7	1.7
1.1	1.3	1.2						1.3	1.0
.9	.9	.9		.4	.8	.8	.9	.8	1.1
2.2	1.9	1.9	Fixed/Worth	1.5	3.2	1.8	2.0	1.1	2.3
8.1	9.8	9.2		7.2	-5.4	NM	94.9	3.3	3.8
1.2	.9	.9		.4	1.1	.8	1.7	.9	.8
2.4	2.4	2.5	Debt/Worth	2.1	4.1	2.3	2.9	1.4	2.7
13.1	12.6	15.1		NM	-8.6	-8.1	112.3	3.8	4.9
46.7	47.1	55.9	% Profit Before Taxes/Tangible	59.3	31.1	155.3	55.3	45.1	62.5
(178) 20.2	(151) 17.7	(147) 21.5	Net Worth	(14) 20.9	(25) 15.2	(17) 47.2	(26) 23.8	(35) 16.9	(30) 26.3
4.4	3.1	6.7		.0	-.6	13.3	6.1	6.7	7.1
12.2	14.6	12.0	% Profit Before Taxes/Total	19.7	9.1	24.8	10.9	15.3	11.1
4.6	4.8	5.2	Assets	5.5	4.4	9.3	4.1	7.2	7.4
.1	-.1	1.0		-.3	.3	3.8	.0	1.0	2.3
5.9	6.2	6.8		15.0	7.1	12.2	7.6	6.2	5.5
3.1	3.1	2.8	Sales/Net Fixed Assets	3.8	1.9	4.4	3.5	3.2	2.3
1.8	1.6	1.4		.9	.9	1.9	2.0	1.7	1.5
2.4	2.3	2.5		2.4	2.1	2.7	2.7	2.6	1.8
1.7	1.5	1.4	Sales/Total Assets	1.4	.9	2.1	1.6	1.5	1.2
1.1	.9	.8		.5	.5	1.0	1.1	.9	.8
4.1	3.5	4.5		7.9	5.8	5.7	4.8	3.4	3.4
(199) 7.6	(166) 7.5	(156) 7.4	% Depr., Dep., Amort./Sales	(13) 10.1	(29) 10.5	(19) 6.8	(28) 7.0	5.8	(27) 6.0
11.1	12.1	12.0		28.8	17.7	12.3	8.8	12.9	9.0
2.1	2.6	1.8	% Officers', Directors',		3.1				
(78) 3.9	(55) 4.8	(42) 4.6	Owners' Comp/Sales	(13)	5.2				
7.5	6.6	7.8			8.9				
3115915M	3624441M	4514200M	Net Sales ($)	9854M	64872M	93894M	243241M	602628M	3499711M
2832190M	3282747M	3622630M	Total Assets ($)	14865M	93699M	84581M	189526M	519390M	2720569M

M = $ thousand   MM = $ million
See Pages 11 through 21 for Explanation of Ratios and Data

Current Data Sorted By Assets   **Comparative Historical Data**

0-500M	500M-2MM	2-10MM	10-50MM	50-100MM	100-250MM	Type of Statement	4/1/00-3/31/01 ALL	4/1/01-3/31/02 ALL
		3	5		1	Unqualified		
2	3	7	2			Reviewed		
	3	1				Compiled		
2	2					Tax Returns		
2	3	1		1		Other		
	8 (4/1-9/30/04)		30 (10/1/04-3/31/05)					
6	11	12	7	1	1	NUMBER OF STATEMENTS		
%	%	%	%	%	%	ASSETS	%	%
	3.3	6.3				Cash & Equivalents	D	D
	58.5	49.1				Trade Receivables (net)	A	A
	2.4	4.6				Inventory	T	T
	10.2	9.5				All Other Current	A	A
	74.5	69.5				Total Current		
	17.6	21.4				Fixed Assets (net)	N	N
	1.1	2.9				Intangibles (net)	O	O
	6.8	6.2				All Other Non-Current	T	T
	100.0	100.0				Total		
						LIABILITIES	A	A
	12.1	11.1				Notes Payable-Short Term	V	V
	5.5	4.7				Cur. Mat.-L/T/D	A	A
	16.4	18.7				Trade Payables	I	I
	.1	1.1				Income Taxes Payable	L	L
	9.2	10.4				All Other Current	A	A
	43.2	46.1				Total Current	B	B
	10.4	12.1				Long-Term Debt	L	L
	.0	.3				Deferred Taxes	E	E
	3.4	.2				All Other Non-Current		
	43.0	41.3				Net Worth		
	100.0	100.0				Total Liabilities & Net Worth		
						INCOME DATA		
	100.0	100.0				Net Sales		
						Gross Profit		
	93.2	92.6				Operating Expenses		
	6.8	7.4				Operating Profit		
	.3	.1				All Other Expenses (net)		
	6.6	7.3				Profit Before Taxes		
						RATIOS		
	3.7	2.3						
	2.0	1.6				Current		
	1.3	1.2						
	2.9	2.1						
	1.7	1.3				Quick		
	1.2	1.0						
54	6.8	63 / 5.8						
89	4.1	77 / 4.8				Sales/Receivables		
124	2.9	107 / 3.4						
						Cost of Sales/Inventory		
						Cost of Sales/Payables		
	4.7	7.4						
	6.8	10.9				Sales/Working Capital		
	16.5	15.9						
	23.2	19.2						
	(10) 5.1	(11) 7.8				EBIT/Interest		
	3.2	1.3						
						Net Profit + Depr., Dep., Amort./Cur. Mat. L /T/D		
	.1	.3						
	.3	.4				Fixed/Worth		
	1.1	1.1						
	.7	.9						
	1.6	1.4				Debt/Worth		
	2.7	2.9						
	68.6	85.0						
	34.4	26.3				% Profit Before Taxes/Tangible Net Worth		
	5.2	4.0						
	23.5	23.5						
	9.9	7.9				% Profit Before Taxes/Total Assets		
	3.9	2.1						
	57.3	27.4						
	19.6	13.0				Sales/Net Fixed Assets		
	10.3	6.8						
	3.3	3.0						
	2.7	2.3				Sales/Total Assets		
	2.0	1.8						
	.8	1.4						
	1.2	(10) 2.6				% Depr., Dep., Amort./Sales		
	3.4	4.7						
						% Officers', Directors', Owners' Comp/Sales		
9925M	32068M	142575M	333121M	91772M	94000M	Net Sales ($)		
1537M	11867M	63226M	178521M	83394M	139000M	Total Assets ($)		

© RMA 2005

M = $ thousand   MM = $ million
See Pages 11 through 21 for Explanation of Ratios and Data

Comparative Historical Data   Current Data Sorted By Sales

				Type of Statement						
2		7	9	Unqualified					3	6
2		8	14	Reviewed	1	3	3	3	3	1
		3	4	Compiled		2	1		1	
1		3	4	Tax Returns		2	1			
5		5	7	Other	2	2	1	1	1	1
4/1/02-		4/1/03-	4/1/04-			8 (4/1-9/30/04)		30 (10/1/04-3/31/05)		
3/31/03		3/31/04	3/31/05		0-1MM	1-3MM	3-5MM	5-10MM	10-25MM	25MM & OVER
ALL		ALL	ALL							
10		26	38	NUMBER OF STATEMENTS	3	9	5	5	8	8
%		%	%	ASSETS	%	%	%	%	%	%
10.3		7.9	6.1	Cash & Equivalents						
52.7		49.8	45.8	Trade Receivables (net)						
.7		2.8	3.2	Inventory						
3.6		8.0	8.5	All Other Current						
67.5		68.5	63.5	Total Current						
23.8		23.5	26.5	Fixed Assets (net)						
.0		1.5	3.2	Intangibles (net)						
8.8		6.9	6.8	All Other Non-Current						
100.0		100.0	100.0	Total						
				LIABILITIES						
15.1		13.7	8.4	Notes Payable-Short Term						
3.3		2.9	4.3	Cur. Mat.-L/T/D						
12.7		15.2	16.4	Trade Payables						
.6		.4	.5	Income Taxes Payable						
8.5		8.1	9.8	All Other Current						
40.1		40.3	39.4	Total Current						
10.7		10.8	14.0	Long-Term Debt						
.0		.2	.6	Deferred Taxes						
1.1		6.2	4.6	All Other Non-Current						
48.1		42.8	41.4	Net Worth						
100.0		100.0	100.0	Total Liabilities & Net Worth						
				INCOME DATA						
100.0		100.0	100.0	Net Sales						
				Gross Profit						
88.9		95.3	92.5	Operating Expenses						
11.1		4.7	7.5	Operating Profit						
1.7		1.3	.8	All Other Expenses (net)						
9.5		3.4	6.7	Profit Before Taxes						
				RATIOS						
2.9		2.5	2.5							
2.0		1.7	1.6	Current						
1.1		1.4	1.2							
2.7		2.0	2.3							
1.9		1.5	1.3	Quick						
1.0		1.0	1.0							
39 9.3	43 8.4		43 8.5							
68 5.4	82 4.4		74 4.9	Sales/Receivables						
92 4.0	107 3.4		106 3.5							
				Cost of Sales/Inventory						
				Cost of Sales/Payables						
5.1		6.1	6.8							
8.4		8.5	10.7	Sales/Working Capital						
NM		14.7	18.0							
		10.3	18.5							
	(20)	4.6	(32) 6.6	EBIT/Interest						
		1.5	2.1							
				Net Profit + Depr., Dep., Amort./Cur. Mat. L/T/D						
.1		.2	.3							
.5		.4	.5	Fixed/Worth						
.9		.9	1.4							
.5		.8	.7							
.9		1.3	1.8	Debt/Worth						
2.8		3.1	3.5							
75.4		33.1	80.6	% Profit Before Taxes/Tangible						
41.1	(25)	10.5	(37) 34.4	Net Worth						
20.9		3.2	6.1							
48.4		10.1	24.4	% Profit Before Taxes/Total						
20.7		3.3	8.6	Assets						
6.5		.9	1.9							
47.8		31.9	29.4							
16.2		13.9	14.4	Sales/Net Fixed Assets						
7.2		5.6	6.6							
4.1		2.9	3.3							
3.1		2.2	2.5	Sales/Total Assets						
1.3		1.8	1.8							
		1.0	1.1							
	(22)	2.0	(30) 2.0	% Depr., Dep., Amort./Sales						
		3.5	3.6							
		2.4	1.0							
	(12)	3.3	(14) 2.4	% Officers', Directors', Owners' Comp/Sales						
		6.9	4.2							
71112M		170830M	703461M	Net Sales ($)	1457M	17204M	19965M	35394M	130884M	498557M
23378M		77228M	477545M	Total Assets ($)	977M	6128M	7090M	18115M	68547M	376688M

M = $ thousand   MM = $ million
See Pages 11 through 21 for Explanation of Ratios and Data

Current Data Sorted By Assets

Comparative Historical Data

						Type of Statement		
	1	1	4			Unqualified		
1	1	3		1		Reviewed		
1	4	2				Compiled		
2	1	1				Tax Returns		
2	4	7	1	1	2	Other		
	9 (4/1-9/30/04)		31 (10/1/04-3/31/05)				4/1/00-3/31/01 ALL	4/1/01-3/31/02 ALL
0-500M	500M-2MM	2-10MM	10-50MM	50-100MM	100-250MM			
6	11	14	5	2	2	NUMBER OF STATEMENTS		
%	%	%	%	%	%	ASSETS	%	%
	12.9	3.6				Cash & Equivalents		
	21.6	18.9				Trade Receivables (net)	D	D
	7.7	6.7				Inventory	A	A
	.7	2.4				All Other Current	T	T
	42.8	31.7				Total Current	A	A
	48.7	57.8				Fixed Assets (net)		
	1.9	2.7				Intangibles (net)	N	N
	6.5	7.8				All Other Non-Current	O	O
	100.0	100.0				Total	T	T
						LIABILITIES	A	A
	5.5	4.9				Notes Payable-Short Term	V	V
	8.6	6.7				Cur. Mat.-L/T/D	A	A
	15.8	11.4				Trade Payables	I	I
	1.6	.1				Income Taxes Payable	L	L
	6.4	15.5				All Other Current	A	A
	37.9	38.7				Total Current	B	B
	30.6	34.6				Long-Term Debt	L	L
	.7	.0				Deferred Taxes	E	E
	4.2	3.7				All Other Non-Current		
	26.6	23.0				Net Worth		
	100.0	100.0				Total Liabilities & Net Worth		
						INCOME DATA		
	100.0	100.0				Net Sales		
						Gross Profit		
	91.8	91.3				Operating Expenses		
	8.2	8.7				Operating Profit		
	3.2	5.3				All Other Expenses (net)		
	5.0	3.4				Profit Before Taxes		
						RATIOS		
	2.0	1.4						
	1.7	.8				Current		
	.9	.5						
	2.0	1.0						
	1.5	.6				Quick		
	.9	.4						
25	14.4	23 15.6						
33	11.1	39 9.4				Sales/Receivables		
43	8.5	73 5.0						
						Cost of Sales/Inventory		
						Cost of Sales/Payables		
	7.6	17.6						
	15.4	-62.2				Sales/Working Capital		
	-145.3	-9.2						
		4.9						
		3.4				EBIT/Interest		
		1.1						
						Net Profit + Depr., Dep., Amort./Cur. Mat. L /T/D		
	.7	1.4						
	.8	2.9				Fixed/Worth		
	-24.5	5.2						
	.5	2.0						
	2.4	4.3				Debt/Worth		
	-34.5	8.3						
		75.4				% Profit Before Taxes/Tangible Net Worth		
	(12)	19.1						
		2.3						
	22.5	13.7				% Profit Before Taxes/Total Assets		
	16.0	3.8						
	-.4	.0						
	7.5	7.3						
	4.1	1.9				Sales/Net Fixed Assets		
	2.8	1.3						
	3.1	2.5						
	2.4	1.2				Sales/Total Assets		
	1.5	.9						
		2.5						
	(13)	7.3				% Depr., Dep., Amort./Sales		
		11.4						
						% Officers', Directors', Owners' Comp/Sales		
5552M	28532M	123560M	182398M	312507M	327055M	Net Sales ($)		
1845M	12842M	60403M	114862M	144727M	415327M	Total Assets ($)		

M = $ thousand　　MM = $ million
See Pages 11 through 21 for Explanation of Ratios and Data

Comparative Historical Data   **Current Data Sorted By Sales**

			Type of Statement						
.11	9	6	Unqualified		1	1	2	1	3
6	8	6	Reviewed	1	2	1	1	1'	
5	11	7	Compiled	1	3	1	1		1
1	5	4	Tax Returns	1	2				
8	13	17	Other		6	4	2	1	4
4/1/02-3/31/03	4/1/03-3/31/04	4/1/04-3/31/05			9 (4/1-9/30/04)		31 (10/1/04-3/31/05)		
ALL	ALL	ALL		0-1MM	1-3MM	3-5MM	5-10MM	10-25MM	25MM & OVER
31	46	40	**NUMBER OF STATEMENTS**	3	14	6	6	3	8
%	%	%	**ASSETS**	%	%	%	%	%	%
7.5	5.7	9.7	Cash & Equivalents		11.3				
18.5	19.8	16.9	Trade Receivables (net)		16.3				
2.4	5.8	7.7	Inventory		6.7				
3.1	3.4	5.6	All Other Current		2.7				
31.5	34.8	39.9	Total Current		37.0				
53.7	49.2	47.8	Fixed Assets (net)		49.8				
7.3	5.3	4.2	Intangibles (net)		3.7				
7.6	10.8	8.2	All Other Non-Current		9.6				
100.0	100.0	100.0	Total		100.0				
			LIABILITIES						
4.4	6.4	4.4	Notes Payable-Short Term		3.5				
7.3	10.7	7.0	Cur. Mat.-L/T/D		6.4				
8.8	12.6	12.3	Trade Payables		8.2				
.0	.2	.5	Income Taxes Payable		.4				
7.0	12.2	11.2	All Other Current		10.5				
27.5	42.1	35.5	Total Current		29.1				
39.0	28.2	31.3	Long-Term Debt		36.6				
.8	.7	.5	Deferred Taxes		.4				
5.2	4.5	6.2	All Other Non-Current		4.4				
27.4	24.5	26.6	Net Worth		29.5				
100.0	100.0	100.0	Total Liabilities & Net Worth		100.0				
			INCOME DATA						
100.0	100.0	100.0	Net Sales		100.0				
			Gross Profit						
91.9	94.6	90.2	Operating Expenses		90.1				
8.1	5.4	9.8	Operating Profit		9.9				
2.5	2.8	4.3	All Other Expenses (net)		3.1				
5.6	2.6	5.5	Profit Before Taxes		6.8				
			RATIOS						
1.7	1.4	2.2			2.3				
1.0	1.0	1.3	Current		1.5				
.5	.6	.8			.9				
1.4	1.0	1.5			1.7				
1.0	.7	.9	Quick		1.3				
.5	.4	.5			.9				
31 11.7	24 15.3	21 17.2			22 16.4				
37 9.9	36 10.2	29 12.5	Sales/Receivables		31 11.8				
61 6.0	53 6.9	43 8.4			44 8.2				
			Cost of Sales/Inventory						
			Cost of Sales/Payables						
16.7	22.3	8.0			7.5				
95.5	NM	29.4	Sales/Working Capital		22.4				
-7.3	-8.5	-17.7			-119.0				
8.4	6.7	10.3			12.2				
(30) 2.8	(43) 3.6	(35) 4.6	EBIT/Interest		(12) 6.4				
1.2	1.5	1.6			1.4				
2.6	3.2		Net Profit + Depr., Dep.,						
(13) 1.3	(16) 1.4		Amort./Cur. Mat. L/T/D						
1.0	1.2								
1.5	1.1	.7			.8				
3.8	2.8	2.1	Fixed/Worth		2.0				
33.0	66.1	NM			-21.6				
1.3	.9	.9			1.0				
5.6	4.2	4.0	Debt/Worth		4.2				
39.3	107.8	NM			-31.9				
87.3	70.9	70.4	% Profit Before Taxes/Tangible		82.3				
(24) 28.0	(36) 22.7	(30) 30.1	Net Worth		(10) 46.7				
9.0	6.9	8.6			10.4				
12.5	12.2	15.9	% Profit Before Taxes/Total		20.8				
6.1	6.0	8.8	Assets		14.7				
.6	.2	1.8			2.6				
8.1	11.8	8.1			8.4				
2.2	3.9	4.1	Sales/Net Fixed Assets		4.1				
1.2	1.7	1.9			1.9				
2.4	2.9	3.0			2.7				
1.3	1.6	1.6	Sales/Total Assets		1.7				
.8	.9	1.2			1.2				
4.7	2.7	1.8			1.5				
(28) 8.2	(40) 5.0	(34) 5.4	% Depr., Dep., Amort./Sales		(11) 5.9				
10.1	7.5	11.2			11.6				
	2.2		% Officers', Directors',						
	(12) 4.8		Owners' Comp/Sales						
	8.5								
5925216M	1002267M	979604M	Net Sales ($)	1619M	25484M	22571M	43321M	52588M	834021M
606269M	885719M	750006M	Total Assets ($)	635M	18658M	13010M	31055M	86361M	600287M

© RMA 2005   M = $ thousand   MM = $ million
See Pages 11 through 21 for Explanation of Ratios and Data

Current Data Sorted By Assets   **Comparative Historical Data**

						Type of Statement		
		9	5	1	2	Unqualified	11	10
2	9	9				Reviewed	11	7
8	9	5				Compiled	15	20
8	10	3				Tax Returns	12	8
5	11	11	5	2		Other	23	25
	18 (4/1-9/30/04)		96 (10/1/04-3/31/05)				4/1/00-3/31/01	4/1/01-3/31/02
0-500M	500M-2MM	2-10MM	10-50MM	50-100MM	100-250MM		ALL	ALL
23	39	37	10	3	2	NUMBER OF STATEMENTS	72	70
%	%	%	%	%	%	ASSETS	%	%
18.2	13.9	9.2	16.4			Cash & Equivalents	12.3	12.0
19.8	22.8	28.9	22.3			Trade Receivables (net)	20.6	21.7
1.7	2.3	2.5	3.9			Inventory	1.5	2.1
1.6	1.9	5.8	4.5			All Other Current	3.0	3.3
41.3	40.9	46.3	47.2			Total Current	37.4	39.0
45.4	48.5	43.3	39.9			Fixed Assets (net)	46.8	49.8
2.0	3.2	3.5	2.4			Intangibles (net)	7.7	4.9
11.2	7.4	6.9	10.4			All Other Non-Current	8.1	6.2
100.0	100.0	100.0	100.0			Total	100.0	100.0
						LIABILITIES		
16.0	8.7	7.1	4.2			Notes Payable-Short Term	11.6	7.0
10.6	6.1	6.7	3.9			Cur. Mat.-L/T/D	6.5	6.8
8.0	10.4	12.5	10.0			Trade Payables	9.3	9.1
.1	.3	.2	.1			Income Taxes Payable	4.6	.2
11.9	5.7	9.3	7.5			All Other Current	7.2	10.8
46.5	31.2	35.7	25.7			Total Current	39.2	33.9
28.8	28.4	29.3	33.2			Long-Term Debt	29.3	26.5
4.6	.5	.9	.7			Deferred Taxes	.4	.4
33.2	8.4	4.5	12.7			All Other Non-Current	5.2	6.6
-13.2	31.5	29.7	27.6			Net Worth	25.9	32.7
100.0	100.0	100.0	100.0			Total Liabilities & Net Worth	100.0	100.0
						INCOME DATA		
100.0	100.0	100.0	100.0			Net Sales	100.0	100.0
						Gross Profit		
93.4	91.1	91.6	93.8			Operating Expenses	94.0	90.4
6.6	8.9	8.4	6.2			Operating Profit	6.0	9.6
1.6	.9	3.1	2.0			All Other Expenses (net)	2.4	2.9
4.9	8.0	5.3	4.2			Profit Before Taxes	3.5	6.7
						RATIOS		
1.4	2.3	2.0	3.2				1.9	2.2
.8	1.3	1.2	1.7			Current	1.1	1.3
.3	.6	.9	1.4				.7	.7
1.4	1.8	1.5	2.2				1.8	1.9
.7	1.0	1.0	1.6			Quick	1.0	1.1
.3	.6	.6	1.1				.6	.6

0	UND	11	33.3	28	12.8	25	14.3			Sales/Receivables	20	18.4	21	17.1
11	31.8	26	14.2	48	7.6	58	6.3				41	8.8	39	9.3
39	9.4	50	7.3	69	5.3	81	4.5				56	6.5	51	7.1

						Cost of Sales/Inventory		
						Cost of Sales/Payables		

27.0	8.1	8.4	3.0				9.8	11.6
-36.1	49.0	29.6	7.0			Sales/Working Capital	66.3	35.3
-6.0	-15.6	-385.2	12.6				-18.2	-17.7

	1.9		21.2		12.2			EBIT/Interest		5.5		12.6
(19)	1.0	(35)	5.4	(35)	5.0				(65)	2.5	(68)	3.5
	-.8		1.5		1.5					.7		1.0

							Net Profit + Depr., Dep.,		3.3		3.2
							Amort./Cur. Mat. L /T/D	(18)	2.2	(16)	1.9
									1.3		1.1

.6	.6	.6	.3				.7	.9
5.9	1.4	1.3	1.6			Fixed/Worth	2.0	1.4
-89.5	7.1	4.0	-15.8				129.8	6.4

1.8	.7	.7	1.2				.9	1.0
18.3	1.9	2.1	2.0			Debt/Worth	2.2	1.8
-15.5	9.7	5.6	-34.3				NM	9.2

	95.8		97.1		52.1			% Profit Before Taxes/Tangible		76.5		56.8
(16)	52.3	(32)	28.7	(31)	25.7			Net Worth	(54)	23.2	(56)	29.9
	-30.0		13.4		6.6					3.1		8.6

24.6	21.4	15.7	11.5				17.2	22.6
4.0	11.1	5.9	6.3			% Profit Before Taxes/Total Assets	5.3	8.2
-9.0	1.7	1.3	-2.6				-1.1	.3

21.2	10.4	9.3	11.2				10.2	7.9
9.1	5.2	5.6	3.3			Sales/Net Fixed Assets	3.9	4.0
2.1	3.1	2.6	1.2				1.5	2.4

5.1	3.5	2.7	1.7				3.3	3.0
3.3	2.4	2.1	1.2			Sales/Total Assets	1.9	2.1
1.9	1.6	1.3	.5				.8	1.3

	3.5		3.3		2.9	2.7		% Depr., Dep., Amort./Sales		2.7		3.1
(16)	5.6	(35)	6.9	(32)	6.0	7.2			(66)	6.7	(64)	6.8
	23.9		9.8		12.9	16.5				11.3		10.3

	2.6		2.2		1.3			% Officers', Directors',		3.5		3.5
(12)	5.1	(19)	3.6	(14)	2.5			Owners' Comp/Sales	(29)	7.0	(30)	4.4
	12.8		7.8		4.5					11.2		9.6

26583M	111405M	329824M	304262M	362091M	181036M	Net Sales ($)	854116M	1239153M
6492M	44651M	157013M	231624M	230282M	359952M	Total Assets ($)	919816M	888591M

M = $ thousand   MM = $ million
See Pages 11 through 21 for Explanation of Ratios and Data

Comparative Historical Data   **Current Data Sorted By Sales**

			Type of Statement						
14	22	17	Unqualified	1	1	2	1	8	5
19	22	20	Reviewed	1	5	7	6	1	
14	24	22	Compiled	7	6	6	1	2	
6	19	21	Tax Returns	7	6	6	1		1
17	18	34	Other	5	10	6	4	5	4
4/1/02-3/31/03	4/1/03-3/31/04	4/1/04-3/31/05		18 (4/1-9/30/04)			96 (10/1/04-3/31/05)		
ALL	ALL	ALL		0-1MM	1-3MM	3-5MM	5-10MM	10-25MM	25MM & OVER
70	105	114	**NUMBER OF STATEMENTS**	20	28	27	13	16	10
%	%	%	**ASSETS**	%	%	%	%	%	%
9.2	10.4	13.5	Cash & Equivalents	17.9	11.2	12.0	8.8	12.9	22.3
20.9	23.3	23.9	Trade Receivables (net)	13.8	18.7	26.5	37.5	28.1	27.4
1.0	2.6	2.6	Inventory	1.7	2.5	1.3	4.9	2.2	6.3
3.2	3.2	3.4	All Other Current	1.9	2.6	2.6	3.2	7.0	5.0
34.3	39.5	43.4	Total Current	35.3	34.9	42.4	54.4	50.1	61.1
50.4	48.5	45.3	Fixed Assets (net)	54.4	51.1	48.7	29.0	41.1	30.0
5.7	4.5	2.9	Intangibles (net)	3.8	2.4	3.7	1.7	2.6	1.8
9.6	7.4	8.4	All Other Non-Current	6.5	11.6	5.3	14.9	6.1	7.0
100.0	100.0	100.0	Total	100.0	100.0	100.0	100.0	100.0	100.0
			LIABILITIES						
4.3	8.4	8.9	Notes Payable-Short Term	16.4	6.0	9.2	9.7	5.8	4.9
11.1	8.2	6.8	Cur. Mat.-L/T/D	12.1	6.4	6.2	4.5	6.4	2.8
10.3	9.3	10.4	Trade Payables	6.2	8.7	9.2	17.9	13.8	12.1
.3	.2	.2	Income Taxes Payable	.1	.1	.4	.0	.2	.1
7.4	7.2	8.4	All Other Current	8.2	6.3	4.0	14.0	9.2	18.0
33.4	33.3	34.7	Total Current	43.0	27.5	29.0	46.2	35.3	37.9
33.9	31.5	29.4	Long-Term Debt	37.6	34.9	30.4	10.9	25.5	25.2
.2	.5	1.5	Deferred Taxes	5.3	.0	1.3	.2	1.2	.3
5.8	6.7	13.2	All Other Non-Current	39.9	6.3	3.3	11.8	8.1	15.9
26.7	28.0	21.3	Net Worth	-25.7	31.3	36.1	31.0	29.9	20.7
100.0	100.0	100.0	Total Liabilities & Net Worth	100.0	100.0	100.0	100.0	100.0	100.0
			INCOME DATA						
100.0	100.0	100.0	Net Sales	100.0	100.0	100.0	100.0	100.0	100.0
			Gross Profit						
91.5	93.1	91.8	Operating Expenses	91.1	92.4	90.5	91.2	94.2	92.2
8.5	6.9	8.2	Operating Profit	8.9	7.6	9.5	8.8	5.8	7.8
3.6	2.8	2.0	All Other Expenses (net)	2.5	2.0	2.6	1.4	1.5	1.3
4.9	4.1	6.2	Profit Before Taxes	6.5	5.6	6.9	7.4	4.3	6.5
			RATIOS						
2.0	2.1	2.1	Current	1.4	2.1	2.5	2.8	2.2	2.1
1.0	1.2	1.3		.6	1.1	1.4	1.3	1.4	1.7
.6	.7	.7		.2	.6	.8	.9	1.1	1.2
1.7	1.7	1.7	Quick	1.4	1.5	2.0	1.8	2.0	1.7
.9	1.0	1.0		.6	.9	1.2	.9	1.1	1.1
.4	.6	.6		.2	.5	.7	.6	.9	1.1
25 14.4	23 15.8	12 30.2	Sales/Receivables	0 UND	0 UND	21 17.2	23 16.1	34 10.7	16 23.5
37 9.8	40 9.1	36 10.1		12 31.5	25 14.5	36 10.1	52 7.1	53 6.9	46 7.9
53 6.9	61 6.0	60 6.1		44 8.3	49 7.4	68 5.4	70 5.2	65 5.7	67 5.5
			Cost of Sales/Inventory						
			Cost of Sales/Payables						
9.4	10.3	7.7	Sales/Working Capital	24.4	8.0	8.1	8.4	5.3	3.0
NM	27.0	27.8		-9.0	108.2	18.1	29.6	10.0	8.6
-15.4	-29.2	-20.9		-3.6	-15.1	-33.9	-178.5	46.7	26.1
(65) 7.4	(97) 10.8	11.4	EBIT/Interest	(16) 1.8	(24) 11.2	(26) 13.9	(12) 23.5	(15) 12.2	
1.9	3.6	3.6		.9	4.2	5.4	2.5	5.9	
.8	1.0	.8		-1.5	1.4	1.5	1.1	1.6	
(19) 3.8	(24) 2.7	(18) 7.3	Net Profit + Depr., Dep., Amort./Cur. Mat. L/T/D						
2.0	1.7	2.5							
1.1	.6	1.6							
.9	.9	.6	Fixed/Worth	3.1	.6	.7	.1	.5	.3
1.7	1.7	1.6		20.0	1.5	1.4	1.0	1.5	1.1
7.9	6.1	15.0		-3.9	3.9	7.1	2.2	4.8	-1.2
.9	1.1	.7	Debt/Worth	5.7	.5	.7	.5	1.0	.5
2.1	2.8	2.1		88.3	1.5	1.4	1.9	2.2	1.3
11.5	12.3	27.9		-5.8	5.9	9.7	3.6	6.9	-43.8
(55) 44.9	(84) 59.4	(90) 61.4	% Profit Before Taxes/Tangible Net Worth	(12) 110.3	(23) 59.0	(23) 99.8	(11) 64.9	(14) 40.7	
21.1	27.3	25.9		35.5	23.8	33.6	24.2	22.6	
1.1	.0	8.1		-135.0	8.6	19.3	4.4	3.2	
16.1	16.3	18.0	% Profit Before Taxes/Total Assets	18.2	20.8	21.4	29.9	11.1	16.6
3.6	6.7	8.7		1.0	10.5	13.7	11.4	3.8	9.9
-1.0	-.7	.0		-9.9	.8	1.2	.8	1.6	-1.8
8.5	10.7	11.6	Sales/Net Fixed Assets	19.7	9.0	10.6	64.3	8.6	66.5
3.5	4.5	5.4		2.5	5.3	5.1	8.4	5.7	6.4
1.6	2.4	2.3		1.2	2.6	2.3	4.7	2.4	3.1
2.7	2.9	3.3	Sales/Total Assets	3.8	3.7	3.5	3.0	2.7	4.6
1.7	2.0	2.1		2.0	2.0	2.3	2.4	2.0	1.7
.8	1.5	1.3		.7	1.3	1.6	2.1	1.2	1.0
(64) 5.3	(93) 3.8	(98) 3.1	% Depr., Dep., Amort./Sales	(16) 4.2	(26) 4.1	(23) 1.7	(10) 1.5	(14) 3.8	
8.6	7.0	6.7		16.5	7.5	5.7	3.3	6.0	
14.5	10.8	13.0		28.7	12.9	12.9	6.9	11.1	
(26) 3.9	(45) 3.0	(46) 2.0	% Officers', Directors', Owners' Comp/Sales		(14) 2.2	(13) 2.3			
6.0	5.3	3.6			5.3	3.6			
9.8	8.7	7.0			12.7	6.7			
813362M	1111920M	1315201M	Net Sales ($)	9747M	54132M	108285M	102162M	223764M	817111M
984964M	988928M	1030014M	Total Assets ($)	7824M	40087M	68530M	47830M	248962M	616781M

EDUCATIONAL
SERVICES

	Current Data Sorted By Assets							Comparative Historical Data	
							Type of Statement		
23	66	224	279	69	26		Unqualified	442	365
1	9	27	7				Reviewed	31	36
6	11	17	2				Compiled	126	151
18	13	7	2				Tax Returns	19	23
25	45	64	56	8	4		Other	154	161
	942 (4/1-9/30/04)			67 (10/1/04-3/31/05)				4/1/00-3/31/01	4/1/01-3/31/02
0-500M	500M-2MM	2-10MM	10-50MM	50-100MM	100-250MM			ALL	ALL
73	144	339	346	77	30		**NUMBER OF STATEMENTS**	772	736
%	%	%	%	%	%		**ASSETS**	%	%
36.7	26.7	20.5	19.5	18.4	17.8		Cash & Equivalents	22.2	20.7
9.6	10.0	7.1	5.3	5.3	5.5		Trade Receivables (net)	6.9	6.3
.1	.2	.3	.3	.2	.4		Inventory	.4	.4
3.6	5.3	4.3	4.4	3.5	2.0		All Other Current	5.0	5.9
50.1	42.2	32.1	29.4	27.4	25.7		Total Current	34.4	33.3
41.0	49.7	57.5	56.0	54.3	55.2		Fixed Assets (net)	48.7	51.2
1.4	.2	1.1	.6	1.2	.2		Intangibles (net)	.8	.9
7.4	7.8	9.2	14.0	17.1	18.9		All Other Non-Current	16.0	14.6
100.0	100.0	100.0	100.0	100.0	100.0		Total	100.0	100.0
							LIABILITIES		
6.8	5.7	2.9	1.7	1.0	2.1		Notes Payable-Short Term	3.6	2.8
10.8	2.8	2.0	1.3	2.1	1.8		Cur. Mat.-L/T/D	1.3	1.2
6.6	6.4	3.4	2.4	2.2	1.9		Trade Payables	3.6	3.2
.4	.0	.0	.0	1.5	.0		Income Taxes Payable	.0	.1
24.4	17.4	11.9	9.0	6.8	8.0		All Other Current	11.5	11.1
49.0	32.2	20.2	14.5	13.7	13.8		Total Current	20.1	18.4
24.3	24.1	26.8	26.6	30.5	35.9		Long-Term Debt	18.9	20.6
2.1	.0	.0	.0	.0	.0		Deferred Taxes	.1	.0
19.8	5.0	6.1	5.8	7.2	2.0		All Other Non-Current	5.8	5.9
4.8	38.7	46.8	53.1	48.6	48.2		Net Worth	55.2	55.1
100.0	100.0	100.0	100.0	100.0	100.0		Total Liabilities & Net Worth	100.0	100.0
							INCOME DATA		
100.0	100.0	100.0	100.0	100.0	100.0		Net Sales	100.0	100.0
							Gross Profit		
96.4	95.2	94.4	91.9	92.9	92.8		Operating Expenses	93.8	94.5
3.6	4.8	5.6	8.1	7.1	7.2		Operating Profit	6.2	5.5
1.3	1.1	.9	–.1	.6	1.0		All Other Expenses (net)	–4.6	1.8
2.3	3.7	4.7	8.2	6.5	6.2		Profit Before Taxes	10.8	3.7
							RATIOS		
5.3	4.3	3.2	4.3	4.1	4.2			4.2	4.9
1.7	1.6	1.7	2.0	2.1	1.6		Current	1.9	2.0
.5	.7	.8	1.1	1.0	1.1			1.0	1.0
5.1	3.8	3.0	3.8	3.6	3.7			3.3	3.7
1.7	1.4	1.4	1.6	1.4	1.3		Quick	(771) 1.5	1.4
.4	.5	.7	.9	.6	1.1			.8	1.2
0 UND	0 UND	2 227.9	2 203.9	1 286.1	6 64.3			2 226.7	1 287.8
1 302.5	5 71.9	7 49.8	8 46.6	10 37.1	13 27.6		Sales/Receivables	7 49.9	6 63.4
10 38.3	24 15.1	27 13.8	34 10.8	33 11.2	49 7.4			27 13.7	23 15.6
							Cost of Sales/Inventory		
							Cost of Sales/Payables		
8.4	5.8	4.1	2.3	2.1	2.8			3.0	2.8
26.8	16.8	11.1	5.8	4.7	9.4		Sales/Working Capital	7.4	7.8
–29.3	–18.5	–24.4	45.3	–341.5	42.7			999.8	–632.2
12.4	7.2	7.5	12.7	6.9	8.2			11.1	4.9
(34) 1.2	(84) 1.5	(230) 2.2	(269) 3.6	(62) 2.4	(23) 2.2		EBIT/Interest	(456) 3.6	(481) 2.1
–3.1	–.2	.5	1.2	1.3	1.0			1.2	.3
							Net Profit + Depr., Dep., Amort./Cur. Mat. L /T/D		
.2	.3	.7	.7	.7	.8			.4	.5
1.1	1.1	1.2	1.0	1.0	1.2		Fixed/Worth	.9	.9
52.0	3.9	2.6	1.6	3.1	2.0			1.4	1.6
.3	.4	.5	.4	.3	.4			.3	.3
2.2	1.4	1.2	.8	.9	1.2		Debt/Worth	.6	.7
–179.0	5.3	2.4	1.9	3.2	2.1			1.6	1.7
56.2	38.2	18.5	13.6	11.9	13.2		% Profit Before Taxes/Tangible Net Worth	19.0	14.3
(54) 16.0	(124) 8.9	(324) 5.8	(334) 6.1	(72) 5.4	4.3			(743) 7.5	(704) 4.5
–2.7	–.7	–1.7	.4	1.1	–2.0			.7	–2.5
23.6	14.9	7.8	6.6	5.8	4.1		% Profit Before Taxes/Total Assets	10.4	7.0
2.5	4.2	2.3	2.8	2.7	2.5			4.2	2.4
–5.5	–3.1	–.8	.2	.7	–.9			.3	–1.6
80.1	20.4	2.9	1.3	1.4	1.6		Sales/Net Fixed Assets	3.3	2.8
20.0	3.6	1.1	.8	.9	.9			1.2	1.1
4.7	1.4	.7	.6	.7	.6			.7	.7
8.2	3.2	1.2	.7	.8	.9		Sales/Total Assets	1.2	1.2
4.3	1.7	.7	.5	.5	.6			.6	.6
2.1	1.0	.5	.4	.3	.2			.4	.4
1.0	1.6	3.1	4.4	3.3	3.0		% Depr., Dep., Amort./Sales	2.0	2.2
(42) 1.5	(99) 2.9	(259) 4.5	(283) 6.0	(62) 4.8	(18) 4.9			(550) 4.0	(544) 4.3
3.6	4.3	6.6	7.5	7.2	8.6			6.0	6.5
6.0	3.1	4.0	2.6				% Officers', Directors', Owners' Comp/Sales	4.0	4.8
(17) 8.2	(18) 5.6	(31) 8.8	(24) 6.7					(96) 7.8	(93) 8.6
11.5	12.7	17.3	13.9					14.3	23.5
81053M	332420M	2035166M	5710101M	3297399M	2918934M		Net Sales ($)	10807584M	8983384M
16245M	162971M	1783617M	8280229M	5286681M	4741304M		Total Assets ($)	18336245M	15552237M

© RMA 2005

M = $ thousand   MM = $ million

See Pages 11 through 21 for Explanation of Ratios and Data

Comparative Historical Data | **Current Data Sorted By Sales**

Hist 1	Hist 2	Hist 3	Type of Statement	0-1MM	1-3MM	3-5MM	5-10MM	10-25MM	25MM & OVER
625	631	687	Unqualified	31	123	70	190	158	115
51	53	44	Reviewed	2	20	12	9	1	
45	153	36	Compiled	11	17	4	3	1	
22	36	40	Tax Returns	17	18	1	2	1	1
216	200	202	Other	23	63	28	42	31	15
4/1/02-3/31/03 ALL	4/1/03-3/31/04 ALL	4/1/04-3/31/05 ALL		942 (4/1-9/30/04)			67 (10/1/04-3/31/05)		
959	1073	1009	NUMBER OF STATEMENTS	84	241	115	246	192	131
%	%	%	**ASSETS**	%	%	%	%	%	%
22.3	22.0	22.0	Cash & Equivalents	22.3	22.5	19.8	21.7	20.1	25.9
5.9	6.1	6.9	Trade Receivables (net)	5.2	6.4	6.8	6.6	6.9	9.5
.2	.3	.3	Inventory	.1	.1	.3	.3	.2	.6
3.9	6.2	4.3	All Other Current	2.0	3.0	4.3	3.5	5.7	7.6
32.3	34.5	33.4	Total Current	29.6	32.0	31.2	32.1	32.9	43.5
52.7	53.7	54.4	Fixed Assets (net)	61.2	59.1	57.6	53.9	48.8	47.4
.6	.7	.8	Intangibles (net)	1.1	1.0	1.0	.3	1.2	.6
14.3	11.0	11.4	All Other Non-Current	8.1	7.9	10.2	13.7	17.1	8.5
100.0	100.0	100.0	Total	100.0	100.0	100.0	100.0	100.0	100.0
			LIABILITIES						
3.3	2.9	3.0	Notes Payable-Short Term	4.0	4.7	3.5	2.3	1.8	2.0
1.4	1.7	2.5	Cur. Mat.-L/T/D	9.9	2.5	1.6	1.4	1.6	2.1
3.3	3.7	3.6	Trade Payables	2.4	3.0	3.4	4.3	2.7	5.5
.1	.1	.2	Income Taxes Payable	.0	.0	.0	.1	.0	.9
12.1	11.5	12.1	All Other Current	11.8	15.0	11.1	10.4	10.7	12.9
20.1	19.9	21.4	Total Current	28.1	25.2	19.5	18.5	16.9	23.4
22.0	23.6	26.7	Long-Term Debt	36.1	30.8	26.7	18.3	24.1	32.9
.0	.1	.2	Deferred Taxes	.0	.1	.0	.6	.1	.0
6.2	6.9	6.8	All Other Non-Current	6.8	8.6	6.9	6.7	4.7	6.4
51.6	49.6	45.0	Net Worth	29.0	35.3	46.8	55.9	54.2	37.3
100.0	100.0	100.0	Total Liabilities & Net Worth	100.0	100.0	100.0	100.0	100.0	100.0
			INCOME DATA						
100.0	100.0	100.0	Net Sales	100.0	100.0	100.0	100.0	100.0	100.0
			Gross Profit						
94.8	94.1	93.7	Operating Expenses	91.9	95.2	94.4	93.6	92.2	93.6
5.2	5.9	6.3	Operating Profit	8.1	4.8	5.6	6.4	7.8	6.4
2.9	1.2	.6	All Other Expenses (net)	3.0	1.5	−.8	−.7	.2	1.7
2.3	4.7	5.7	Profit Before Taxes	5.1	3.3	6.3	7.1	7.7	4.7
			RATIOS						
4.2 / 1.9 / .9	4.7 / 1.8 / 1.0	3.9 / 1.8 / .9	Current	7.0 / 1.6 / .4	3.6 / 1.4 / .7	3.5 / 1.4 / .8	4.4 / 2.0 / 1.0	3.9 / 2.0 / 1.1	3.6 / 1.8 / 1.2
3.6 / 1.6 / .7	3.6 / 1.4 / .7	3.5 / 1.5 / .7	Quick	6.1 / 1.5 / .4	3.3 / 1.2 / .5	3.3 / 1.1 / .6	4.1 / 1.6 / .8	3.4 / 1.6 / .7	3.1 / 1.5 / .9
1 327.9 / 6 62.0 / 24 15.4	1 404.3 / 6 60.7 / 24 14.9	1 296.3 / 7 51.7 / 27 13.3	Sales/Receivables	0 UND / 4 97.5 / 17 21.4	0 UND / 6 62.3 / 22 16.7	3 133.8 / 7 52.0 / 34 10.8	2 222.7 / 6 60.8 / 27 13.4	2 241.7 / 9 42.1 / 40 9.1	2 164.7 / 14 25.3 / 33 11.1
			Cost of Sales/Inventory						
			Cost of Sales/Payables						
3.1 / 8.5 / −50.7	2.8 / 8.8 / 932.2	3.5 / 9.6 / −72.7	Sales/Working Capital	4.8 / 16.3 / −14.2	5.1 / 18.2 / −14.7	3.3 / 14.8 / −35.8	2.8 / 7.1 / NM	2.7 / 6.4 / 53.6	3.8 / 9.1 / 26.9
(635) 5.6 / 1.8 / −.3	(722) 7.4 / 2.2 / .4	(702) 9.0 / 2.7 / .7	EBIT/Interest	(42) 3.2 / 1.0 / .0	(171) 5.2 / 1.6 / −.1	(78) 10.2 / 2.2 / .0	(179) 14.4 / 4.5 / 1.6	(131) 12.8 / 3.5 / .9	(101) 5.2 / 1.9 / 1.1
(13) 6.5 / 2.3 / 2.1	(16) 3.3 / 2.2 / .5	(10) 3.9 / .8 / −.5	Net Profit + Depr., Dep., Amort./Cur. Mat. L/T/D						
.6 / 1.0 / 1.8	.6 / 1.0 / 2.0	.6 / 1.1 / 2.5	Fixed/Worth	.8 / 2.2 / 5.2	.8 / 1.5 / 3.9	.7 / 1.2 / 2.5	.6 / .9 / 1.4	.5 / .9 / 1.5	.5 / 1.3 / 3.3
.4 / .8 / 1.8	.4 / .9 / 2.3	.4 / 1.0 / 2.6	Debt/Worth	.5 / 2.2 / 5.8	.5 / 1.5 / 4.8	.5 / 1.0 / 2.4	.3 / .7 / 1.4	.3 / .7 / 2.0	.6 / 1.6 / 5.2
(911) 12.4 / 2.8 / −3.9	(1026) 13.8 / 4.2 / −2.0	(938) 17.3 / 6.3 / −.1	% Profit Before Taxes/Tangible Net Worth	(74) 28.7 / 8.2 / −2.0	(216) 18.4 / 5.4 / −1.9	(107) 22.3 / 4.8 / −1.7	(237) 15.4 / 6.3 / 1.4	(185) 14.7 / 5.9 / −.4	(119) 19.4 / 7.4 / .2
5.7 / 1.5 / −2.1	6.5 / 1.9 / −1.2	8.1 / 2.6 / −.5	% Profit Before Taxes/Total Assets	13.6 / 2.2 / −1.6	7.4 / 1.7 / −1.6	9.7 / 1.7 / −.8	8.7 / 3.5 / .8	7.4 / 3.1 / −.4	6.9 / 2.7 / .0
2.6 / 1.1 / .7	3.2 / 1.1 / .7	3.4 / 1.1 / .7	Sales/Net Fixed Assets	8.2 / 1.4 / .7	4.3 / 1.0 / .6	2.8 / 1.0 / .7	2.1 / 1.0 / .6	1.9 / 1.0 / .7	5.6 / 1.4 / .9
1.2 / .6 / .4	1.4 / .7 / .4	1.4 / .7 / .4	Sales/Total Assets	2.4 / 1.0 / .5	1.8 / .9 / .5	1.3 / .6 / .4	1.0 / .6 / .3	1.0 / .5 / .3	1.7 / .8 / .6
(712) 3.0 / 4.9 / 7.0	(794) 3.1 / 4.9 / 6.9	(763) 3.1 / 4.7 / 6.8	% Depr., Dep., Amort./Sales	(60) 1.8 / 3.9 / 7.6	(183) 2.2 / 3.7 / 6.3	(97) 3.2 / 4.8 / 7.0	(206) 3.9 / 5.8 / 7.5	(144) 4.2 / 5.6 / 7.2	(73) 2.7 / 3.5 / 5.1
(123) 2.9 / 6.8 / 16.4	(144) 2.9 / 6.6 / 15.0	(100) 3.9 / 7.4 / 12.9	% Officers', Directors', Owners' Comp/Sales	(13) 6.6 / 8.2 / 15.3	(27) 4.3 / 7.0 / 13.1	(15) 3.7 / 5.6 / 9.6	(21) 2.0 / 7.1 / 12.7	(14) .6 / 11.1 / 17.2	2.9 / 4.7 / 8.8
14459644M	15047425M	14375073M	Net Sales ($)	51908M	458985M	451969M	1760610M	2926494M	8725107M
21018518M	21228903M	20271047M	Total Assets ($)	104095M	698968M	752155M	3403568M	6093253M	9219008M

© RMA 2005

M = $ thousand   MM = $ million

See Pages 11 through 21 for Explanation of Ratios and Data

Current Data Sorted By Assets   Comparative Historical Data

						Type of Statement		
	4	7	16	8	4	Unqualified	40	28
						Reviewed		
2			3			Compiled	2	1
						Tax Returns		
		1	3			Other	13	13
	41 (4/1-9/30/04)		7 (10/1/04-3/31/05)				13 4/1/00- 3/31/01	13 4/1/01- 3/31/02
0-500M	500M-2MM	2-10MM	10-50MM	50-100MM	100-250MM		ALL	ALL
2	4	8	22	8	4	NUMBER OF STATEMENTS	55	42
%	%	%	%	%	%	ASSETS	%	%
			16.7			Cash & Equivalents	16.9	19.9
			14.0			Trade Receivables (net)	12.9	7.1
			1.1			Inventory	1.5	1.4
			1.8			All Other Current	4.5	5.6
			33.5			Total Current	35.8	34.0
			46.9			Fixed Assets (net)	47.7	46.8
			1.2			Intangibles (net)	2.1	4.1
			18.4			All Other Non-Current	14.4	15.1
			100.0			Total	100.0	100.0
						LIABILITIES		
			.9			Notes Payable-Short Term	2.3	.7
			2.2			Cur. Mat.-L/T/D	1.4	2.0
			2.7			Trade Payables	4.5	4.2
			.5			Income Taxes Payable	.2	.1
			17.1			All Other Current	18.6	12.9
			23.4			Total Current	27.0	20.0
			24.3			Long-Term Debt	13.3	14.6
			.2			Deferred Taxes	.1	.5
			3.2			All Other Non-Current	6.0	6.3
			49.0			Net Worth	53.6	58.7
			100.0			Total Liabilities & Net Worth	100.0	100.0
						INCOME DATA		
			100.0			Net Sales	100.0	100.0
						Gross Profit		
			83.1			Operating Expenses	95.2	93.7
			16.9			Operating Profit	4.8	6.3
			−.1			All Other Expenses (net)	−1.3	2.5
			17.0			Profit Before Taxes	6.0	3.8
						RATIOS		
			2.3				2.9	3.4
			1.4			Current	1.5	1.9
			.9				.9	1.1
			1.9				2.2	2.7
			1.3			Quick	1.3	1.4
			.9				.8	.7
		10	35.9				6 59.6	4 87.0
		25	14.6			Sales/Receivables	14 25.5	14 26.3
		119	3.1				37 9.9	25 14.3
						Cost of Sales/Inventory		
						Cost of Sales/Payables		
			4.8				4.2	3.3
			13.2			Sales/Working Capital	14.7	6.3
			−35.4				−215.8	37.9
			27.9				21.9	6.9
		(19)	8.2			EBIT/Interest	(35) 6.1	(23) 3.0
			2.5				2.9	.2
						Net Profit + Depr., Dep., Amort./Cur. Mat. L /T/D		
			.7				.6	.6
			1.0			Fixed/Worth	.9	.8
			1.9				1.2	1.1
			.5				.3	.2
			1.2			Debt/Worth	.6	.7
			2.6				2.4	2.0
			36.4				18.2	12.9
			20.6			% Profit Before Taxes/Tangible Net Worth	(53) 6.3	(40) 2.8
			6.3				.3	−1.1
			17.6				8.3	9.1
			9.0			% Profit Before Taxes/Total Assets	3.6	1.7
			2.5				.2	−.3
			3.9				10.0	5.6
			1.5			Sales/Net Fixed Assets	1.6	1.3
			1.0				.8	.7
			1.1				2.1	1.6
			.8			Sales/Total Assets	.8	.7
			.5				.5	.5
			2.2				2.0	3.3
		(21)	4.5			% Depr., Dep., Amort./Sales	(27) 4.7	(22) 4.5
			7.5				6.4	6.9
						% Officers', Directors', Owners' Comp/Sales		
2968M	18934M	57362M	475391M	539543M	358291M	Net Sales ($)	2328712M	1641608M
876M	4612M	40961M	559788M	542411M	617907M	Total Assets ($)	2679610M	2180617M

© RMA 2005

M = $ thousand   MM = $ million
See Pages 11 through 21 for Explanation of Ratios and Data

Comparative Historical Data — Current Data Sorted By Sales

	4/1/02-3/31/03 ALL	4/1/03-3/31/04 ALL	4/1/04-3/31/05 ALL	Type of Statement	0-1MM	1-3MM	3-5MM	5-10MM	10-25MM	25MM & OVER
	32	26	39	Unqualified	1	4	6	3	6	19
	1	2		Reviewed						
	2	3	5	Compiled	1	1		1		2
		1		Tax Returns					1	3
	11	9	4	Other						
						41 (4/1-9/30/04)			7 (10/1/04-3/31/05)	
	46	41	48	**NUMBER OF STATEMENTS**	2	5	6	6	9	21
	%	%	%	**ASSETS**	%	%	%	%	%	%
	19.0	16.3	19.2	Cash & Equivalents						22.2
	12.3	15.1	13.4	Trade Receivables (net)						11.5
	1.0	1.5	1.1	Inventory						1.1
	4.2	5.8	4.1	All Other Current						4.6
	36.5	38.7	37.9	Total Current						39.3
	46.4	45.1	46.8	Fixed Assets (net)						52.4
	5.6	2.8	2.7	Intangibles (net)						4.5
	11.5	13.4	12.7	All Other Non-Current						3.7
	100.0	100.0	100.0	Total						100.0
				LIABILITIES						
	.7	.7	1.9	Notes Payable-Short Term						.6
	2.6	2.4	1.7	Cur. Mat.-L/T/D						2.4
	3.7	4.1	3.5	Trade Payables						2.7
	.4	.1	.3	Income Taxes Payable						.5
	15.7	15.8	14.0	All Other Current						12.4
	23.1	23.1	21.3	Total Current						18.6
	15.7	12.7	18.1	Long-Term Debt						21.0
	.1	.1	.1	Deferred Taxes						.1
	4.7	7.3	6.3	All Other Non-Current						3.8
	56.4	56.7	54.2	Net Worth						56.4
	100.0	100.0	100.0	Total Liabilities & Net Worth						100.0
				INCOME DATA						
	100.0	100.0	100.0	Net Sales						100.0
				Gross Profit						
	90.4	91.1	84.8	Operating Expenses						92.3
	9.6	8.9	15.2	Operating Profit						7.7
	2.5	1.0	-.3	All Other Expenses (net)						.1
	7.1	7.9	15.5	Profit Before Taxes						7.6
				RATIOS						
	3.7	3.8	3.6							3.6
	1.8	2.0	1.6	Current						2.3
	1.0	1.1	1.0							1.4
	2.7	3.1	3.3							3.3
	1.4	1.6	1.4	Quick						1.6
	.7	.9	.9							1.2
	5 75.1	8 46.7	11 33.5							10 36.8
	16 23.4	22 16.7	28 12.9	Sales/Receivables						30 12.3
	35 10.5	66 5.5	74 5.0							59 6.1
				Cost of Sales/Inventory						
				Cost of Sales/Payables						
	3.3	3.3	3.3							2.9
	9.0	8.2	7.5	Sales/Working Capital						4.9
	NM	38.7	269.7							15.5
	13.7	20.4	28.3							28.6
(33)	6.3	(31) 7.3	(37) 8.1	EBIT/Interest					(19)	9.5
	3.2	2.2	3.4							3.6
				Net Profit + Depr., Dep., Amort./Cur. Mat. L/T/D						
	.7	.7	.7							.8
	.9	.8	.9	Fixed/Worth						.9
	1.2	1.2	1.4							2.1
	.4	.4	.3							.2
	.9	.7	.7	Debt/Worth						.7
	2.3	1.8	2.4							2.8
	40.1	37.2	33.7							30.1
(44)	12.7	18.9	(46) 18.0	% Profit Before Taxes/Tangible Net Worth					(20)	8.6
	3.4	2.5	5.8							3.2
	13.4	14.4	17.9							10.5
	5.6	5.1	6.5	% Profit Before Taxes/Total Assets						5.2
	2.7	.9	2.6							2.3
	6.2	7.4	7.2							3.2
	1.6	3.2	1.7	Sales/Net Fixed Assets						1.7
	.9	1.1	1.1							1.2
	1.4	2.0	1.5							1.3
	.9	1.0	.8	Sales/Total Assets						.9
	.5	.6	.5							.7
	3.3	2.3	2.2							3.2
(38)	4.5	(38) 3.9	(42) 3.7	% Depr., Dep., Amort./Sales					(20)	4.0
	5.4	5.5	6.5							5.8
				% Officers', Directors', Owners' Comp/Sales						
	1351832M	1181062M	1452489M	Net Sales ($)	1788M	7678M	22028M	35567M	164730M	1220698M
	1731223M	1409686M	1766555M	Total Assets ($)	2642M	15835M	54528M	53412M	224684M	1415454M

M = $ thousand   MM = $ million
See Pages 11 through 21 for Explanation of Ratios and Data

EDUCATION—Colleges, Universities, and Professional Schools NAICS 611310 (SIC 8221)

Current Data Sorted By Assets							Comparative Historical Data	

Type of Statement

0-500M	500M-2MM	2-10MM	10-50MM	50-100MM	100-250MM	Type of Statement		
3	12	29	176	137	116	Unqualified	390	395
	1		1		1	Reviewed		1
	1		2			Compiled	42	62
1	2	1				Tax Returns		1
5	8	8	35	10	15	Other	83	91
	503 (4/1-9/30/04)		61 (10/1/04-3/31/05)				4/1/00-3/31/01 ALL	4/1/01-3/31/02 ALL
9	24	38	214	147	132	NUMBER OF STATEMENTS	515	550

0-500M	500M-2MM	2-10MM	10-50MM	50-100MM	100-250MM		4/1/00-3/31/01 ALL	4/1/01-3/31/02 ALL
%	%	%	%	%	%	**ASSETS**	%	%
	23.4	19.1	14.7	13.1	16.7	Cash & Equivalents	14.6	15.1
	21.5	11.6	6.3	4.2	3.4	Trade Receivables (net)	5.4	5.0
	2.2	.8	.4	.4	.2	Inventory	.6	.5
	7.5	3.0	4.7	2.5	3.4	All Other Current	3.8	5.1
	54.7	34.5	26.0	20.2	23.6	Total Current	24.4	25.7
	19.0	47.6	50.7	49.1	43.8	Fixed Assets (net)	41.3	44.6
	1.2	3.8	1.1	.8	1.1	Intangibles (net)	.7	.8
	25.1	14.1	22.2	29.8	31.4	All Other Non-Current	33.7	28.8
	100.0	100.0	100.0	100.0	100.0	Total	100.0	100.0
						LIABILITIES		
	6.2	3.2	2.3	1.3	.9	Notes Payable-Short Term	1.6	1.7
	1.9	2.7	1.5	.9	.7	Cur. Mat.-L/T/D	.9	1.1
	7.4	4.0	3.3	2.7	2.2	Trade Payables	2.9	3.2
	.2	.2	.0	.1	.1	Income Taxes Payable	.1	.1
	15.5	16.2	6.9	5.5	4.3	All Other Current	6.2	6.2
	31.1	26.4	14.0	10.5	8.2	Total Current	11.7	12.2
	24.7	21.4	23.8	24.3	23.1	Long-Term Debt	18.2	21.4
	.0	.5	.0	.0	.0	Deferred Taxes	.1	.1
	5.7	3.3	4.5	3.4	3.4	All Other Non-Current	3.8	4.2
	38.4	48.4	57.7	61.8	65.3	Net Worth	66.1	62.0
	100.0	100.0	100.0	100.0	100.0	Total Liabilities & Net Worth	100.0	100.0
						INCOME DATA		
	100.0	100.0	100.0	100.0	100.0	Net Sales	100.0	100.0
						Gross Profit		
	89.7	96.7	91.9	92.0	89.4	Operating Expenses	95.2	95.3
	10.3	3.3	8.1	8.0	10.6	Operating Profit	4.8	4.7
	1.4	-1.5	-.6	-2.8	-3.0	All Other Expenses (net)	-6.1	3.6
	8.9	4.8	8.7	10.8	13.6	Profit Before Taxes	10.9	1.1
						RATIOS		
	3.8	1.8	4.0	3.4	5.3	Current	4.0	3.9
	1.8	1.2	1.9	1.8	2.4		2.0	2.0
	1.1	.8	.8	1.0	1.4		1.0	1.0
	3.0	1.6	2.9	3.0	4.6	Quick	3.3	3.0
	1.6	1.1	1.3	1.4	2.0		1.4	1.4
	.6	.7	.6	.7	.9		.7	.7
	10 37.4	4 87.4	9 41.5	10 36.2	6 63.6	Sales/Receivables	8 46.4	7 50.4
	27 13.4	8 44.7	19 19.6	21 17.5	16 23.0		19 18.9	18 20.2
	53 6.9	21 17.0	41 8.9	35 10.4	36 10.1		43 8.4	41 9.0
						Cost of Sales/Inventory		
						Cost of Sales/Payables		
	5.2	8.3	2.7	3.0	1.7	Sales/Working Capital	2.6	2.5
	8.3	56.3	8.2	8.2	4.6		7.4	7.1
	129.4	-20.1	-45.1	-552.1	15.3		148.0	191.9
	33.7	21.6	11.1	12.2	11.8	EBIT/Interest	9.5	4.2
	(19) 5.3	(30) 4.4	(166) 4.6	(116) 5.0	(110) 5.9		(339) 4.3	(395) 1.6
	1.8	1.4	1.8	2.8	3.2		1.4	-.7
						Net Profit + Depr., Dep., Amort./Cur. Mat. L./T/D	79.8	
							(10) 3.8	
							2.6	
	.2	.3	.6	.6	.5	Fixed/Worth	.4	.5
	.5	1.0	.9	.8	.7		.6	.7
	1.0	1.9	1.3	1.1	.9		.9	1.0
	.4	.3	.4	.4	.3	Debt/Worth	.2	.3
	.9	.8	.7	.6	.5		.4	.5
	2.7	2.7	1.3	1.0	.8		.8	1.0
	58.3	39.2	14.3	11.3	11.9	% Profit Before Taxes/Tangible Net Worth	11.1	7.2
	(22) 26.4	(35) 9.5	(212) 7.5	(146) 7.4	(131) 7.1		(514) 6.1	(543) 1.5
	7.2	1.5	1.3	3.5	4.4		1.3	-2.8
	24.5	12.6	8.2	6.8	7.5	% Profit Before Taxes/Total Assets	7.4	4.3
	9.4	4.3	4.3	4.7	4.8		4.0	.9
	3.0	-.9	.8	2.1	2.4		.7	-1.8
	46.6	10.5	1.8	1.3	1.3	Sales/Net Fixed Assets	1.6	1.5
	15.2	1.7	1.1	1.0	.9		1.0	1.0
	5.9	1.0	.9	.8	.7		.8	.8
	3.4	2.3	.8	.6	.5	Sales/Total Assets	.6	.7
	2.0	1.0	.6	.5	.4		.4	.5
	1.4	.5	.5	.4	.3		.3	.3
	1.4	2.0	3.8	4.4	4.2	% Depr., Dep., Amort./Sales	3.5	3.5
	(19) 2.2	(34) 4.5	(201) 5.4	(137) 5.6	(121) 5.9		(408) 5.0	(486) 5.1
	4.3	6.4	6.6	7.5	8.0		6.5	7.0
			3.8	6.5	7.6	% Officers', Directors', Owners' Comp/Sales	6.4	4.5
			(21) 12.6	(13) 9.8	(14) 16.3		(51) 11.7	(70) 11.0
			28.9	20.7	36.5		19.6	18.7
13568M	76404M	311757M	3890825M	5793472M	8970355M	Net Sales ($)	18341080M	18327979M
2222M	28745M	209472M	6105954M	10795851M	20609716M	Total Assets ($)	38822302M	39666592M

© RMA 2005

M = $ thousand   MM = $ million

See Pages 11 through 21 for Explanation of Ratios and Data

Comparative Historical Data | | | | Current Data Sorted By Sales

			Type of Statement						
494	479	473	Unqualified	-7	13	11	44	155	243
6	3	3	Reviewed				1	1	1
4	56	3	Compiled			1		1	1
2	2	4	Tax Returns		2	1		1	1
91	92	81	Other	5	8	3	9	22	34
4/1/02-3/31/03 ALL	4/1/03-3/31/04 ALL	4/1/04-3/31/05 ALL		0-1MM	1-3MM	3-5MM	5-10MM	10-25MM	25MM & OVER
				503 (4/1-9/30/04)			61 (10/1/04-3/31/05)		
597	632	564	**NUMBER OF STATEMENTS**	12	23	16	54	180	279
%	%	%	**ASSETS**	%	%	%	%	%	%
14.4	15.0	15.7	Cash & Equivalents	21.4	18.1	19.2	15.8	13.6	16.3
5.1	5.6	6.2	Trade Receivables (net)	8.3	8.9	21.9	5.5	5.9	5.3
.5	.6	.5	Inventory	.7	.9	1.5	1.0	.5	.4
4.3	7.5	3.8	All Other Current	2.5	7.6	1.7	5.7	3.6	3.3
24.3	28.7	26.1	Total Current	32.9	35.4	44.3	28.0	23.5	25.4
48.1	47.0	46.9	Fixed Assets (net)	28.8	51.8	36.0	45.4	48.9	46.8
.7	.7	1.3	Intangibles (net)	5.7	.9	.2	1.4	1.4	1.1
26.8	23.5	25.7	All Other Non-Current	32.8	11.8	19.4	25.2	26.1	26.8
100.0	100.0	100.0	Total	100.0	100.0	100.0	100.0	100.0	100.0
			LIABILITIES						
1.6	2.0	2.0	Notes Payable-Short Term	6.2	2.9	6.2	3.6	2.2	1.0
1.2	1.2	1.2	Cur. Mat.-L/T/D	.5	2.2	1.6	1.9	1.2	1.1
3.0	3.0	3.2	Trade Payables	5.0	3.4	6.0	3.1	1.2	1.1
.1	.1	.1	Income Taxes Payable	.0	.1	.0	.0	.1	.1
6.3	6.4	7.4	All Other Current	5.0	15.7	25.5	7.3	5.6	7.0
12.2	12.8	13.9	Total Current	16.8	24.4	39.3	16.0	12.1	12.2
22.3	22.1	23.7	Long-Term Debt	49.0	37.0	12.0	20.7	23.5	22.9
.1	.1	.0	Deferred Taxes	.0	.0	.9	.0	.0	.0
4.1	4.4	3.9	All Other Non-Current	8.7	2.2	1.7	4.4	4.5	3.5
61.3	60.6	58.4	Net Worth	25.9	36.4	46.0	58.9	59.9	61.3
100.0	100.0	100.0	Total Liabilities & Net Worth	100.0	100.0	100.0	100.0	100.0	100.0
			INCOME DATA						
100.0	100.0	100.0	Net Sales	100.0	100.0	100.0	100.0	100.0	100.0
			Gross Profit						
97.1	96.1	91.7	Operating Expenses	90.6	90.6	98.6	90.5	91.6	91.7
2.9	3.9	8.3	Operating Profit	9.4	9.4	1.4	9.5	8.4	8.3
4.6	1.5	-1.7	All Other Expenses (net)	4.7	3.6	-2.8	-1.7	-1.8	-2.3
-1.7	2.4	10.0	Profit Before Taxes	4.8	5.8	4.2	11.1	10.3	10.6
			RATIOS						
3.7	5.0	3.8	Current	4.0	3.4	1.8	3.9	4.3	3.8
1.9	2.1	1.9		1.9	1.3	1.2	1.6	2.0	2.1
1.0	1.1	1.0		.8	.5	.9	.8	1.0	1.1
3.1	3.1	3.1	Quick	3.9	2.5	1.8	3.2	3.4	3.1
1.4	1.4	1.4		1.7	1.1	1.1	1.1	1.4	1.7
.7	.7	.7		.7	.3	.6	.6	.6	.8
8 47.1	8 47.4	8 45.0	Sales/Receivables	1 310.9	0 UND	5 78.3	5 70.8	8 43.0	9 40.5
18 20.1	19 19.7	18 20.0		30 12.2	6 57.1	22 16.9	15 24.6	19 19.0	19 19.2
41 8.9	40 9.2	38 9.5		69 5.3	18 20.3	51 7.2	40 9.1	40 9.2	36 10.2
			Cost of Sales/Inventory						
			Cost of Sales/Payables						
2.5	1.8	2.8	Sales/Working Capital	2.6	5.0	11.9	2.9	2.7	2.6
7.6	5.9	7.4		7.2	14.5	64.7	9.7	7.4	6.6
110.3	45.8	NM		NM	-11.7	-64.2	-19.9	188.8	117.0
4.2	6.4	12.2	EBIT/Interest		14.3	47.5	34.7	10.3	12.4
(437) 1.3	(486) 2.1	(446) 5.1			(18) 1.8	(12) 9.4	(43) 6.2	(137) 4.4	(229) 5.6
-1.5	-.2	2.1			-1.1	2.1	1.3	1.8	2.9
64.1	14.8	76.2	Net Profit + Depr., Dep., Amort./Cur. Mat. L/T/D						
(13) 7.6	(15) 2.7	(15) 6.6							
3.0	.7	2.1							
.5	.5	.6	Fixed/Worth	.3	.4	.2	.3	.6	.6
.8	.8	.8		.6	1.1	.6	.7	.8	.8
1.1	1.1	1.2		NM	18.4	1.2	1.3	1.3	1.1
.3	.3	.4	Debt/Worth	.4	.4	.4	.3	.4	.4
.5	.6	.6		.9	1.3	.8	.8	.6	.6
1.0	1.0	1.1		NM	21.4	2.0	2.1	1.2	1.0
5.5	7.5	13.6	% Profit Before Taxes/Tangible Net Worth		59.3	39.2	14.3	13.6	12.5
(591) .3	(623) 2.4	(551) 7.6			(19) 12.7	(15) 9.5	(51) 6.1	7.4	(277) 7.6
-4.8	-1.7	2.8			-.9	.5	1.5	2.5	3.8
3.2	4.8	8.0	% Profit Before Taxes/Total Assets	5.3	17.7	11.6	9.5	8.0	7.7
.2	1.5	4.6		4.5	1.3	4.0	4.3	4.3	4.9
-3.0	-1.1	1.4		-1.6	-1.5	-.4	.2	1.1	2.4
1.4	1.5	1.7	Sales/Net Fixed Assets	9.9	11.9	22.9	2.6	1.5	1.5
.9	1.0	1.1		1.9	3.4	1.9	1.3	1.0	1.1
.7	.7	.8		.8	.5	1.0	.9	.8	.8
.7	.7	.7	Sales/Total Assets	1.2	2.2	3.6	.9	.7	.7
.5	.5	.5		.6	1.4	.9	.5	.5	.5
.3	.3	.4		.2	.5	.5	.4	.4	.4
4.4	4.3	4.0	% Depr., Dep., Amort./Sales	2.9	1.3	2.1	3.4	4.3	4.1
(539) 6.0	(570) 5.8	(520) 5.4		(10) 4.9	(21) 4.3	(15) 5.6	(51) 4.9	(162) 5.8	(261) 5.3
7.8	7.8	7.1		9.2	7.7	6.1	6.9	7.3	6.9
5.0	4.7	5.2	% Officers', Directors', Owners' Comp/Sales					5.6	5.2
(74) 11.8	(73) 11.5	(58) 13.0						(19) 12.6	(28)
24.3	22.9	23.6						30.2	23.8
19271746M	20472766M	19056381M	Net Sales ($)	4649M	45271M	61689M	422471M	3144737M	15377564M
42748018M	45662964M	37751960M	Total Assets ($)	11845M	126643M	110066M	976554M	7008015M	29518837M

© RMA 2005

M = $ thousand   MM = $ million
See Pages 11 through 21 for Explanation of Ratios and Data

EDUCATION—Other Technical and Trade Schools NAICS 611519 (SIC 8243, 8249, 8299)

		Current Data Sorted By Assets					Comparative Historical Data	
						Type of Statement		
2	11	20	6	5	3	Unqualified	36	32
	1	2				Reviewed	5	2
2	1	1				Compiled	12	10
4	1					Tax Returns	2	1
3	5	7	6	1	1	Other	16	19
	43 (4/1-9/30/04)		39 (10/1/04-3/31/05)				4/1/00-3/31/01	4/1/01-3/31/02
0-500M	500M-2MM	2-10MM	10-50MM	50-100MM	100-250MM		ALL	ALL
11	19	30	12	6	4	NUMBER OF STATEMENTS	71	64
%	%	%	%	%	%	ASSETS	%	%
38.0	29.3	26.0	18.7			Cash & Equivalents	16.5	16.4
19.4	18.4	14.5	14.4			Trade Receivables (net)	25.8	27.8
2.5	1.0	1.0	1.9			Inventory	2.7	1.2
.8	.8	2.7	8.2			All Other Current	4.5	3.4
60.8	49.6	44.2	43.2			Total Current	49.6	48.7
25.6	28.7	46.2	27.4			Fixed Assets (net)	34.8	35.8
1.8	9.0	1.7	5.8			Intangibles (net)	2.4	5.3
11.9	12.8	7.9	23.6			All Other Non-Current	13.2	10.2
100.0	100.0	100.0	100.0			Total	100.0	100.0
						LIABILITIES		
11.8	10.4	3.5	1.4			Notes Payable-Short Term	3.5	5.0
1.7	1.2	2.1	3.0			Cur. Mat.-L/T/D	2.1	1.8
5.0	7.9	4.7	4.3			Trade Payables	4.9	6.3
1.2	.1	1.0	.1			Income Taxes Payable	.2	.3
26.8	31.6	12.6	19.3			All Other Current	17.5	19.7
46.6	51.3	23.9	28.0			Total Current	28.1	33.0
3.1	15.7	19.2	17.1			Long-Term Debt	15.1	17.7
.0	.0	.3	.8			Deferred Taxes	.7	.7
6.5	17.4	5.0	7.0			All Other Non-Current	9.4	7.1
43.8	15.6	51.6	47.1			Net Worth	46.7	41.5
100.0	100.0	100.0	100.0			Total Liabilities & Net Worth	100.0	100.0
						INCOME DATA		
100.0	100.0	100.0	100.0			Net Sales	100.0	100.0
						Gross Profit		
96.0	94.8	90.4	90.3			Operating Expenses	92.1	92.0
4.0	5.2	9.6	9.7			Operating Profit	7.9	8.0
.4	1.4	2.5	.0			All Other Expenses (net)	−1.7	2.4
3.6	3.7	7.2	9.7			Profit Before Taxes	9.6	5.6
						RATIOS		
2.2	3.7	3.8	3.7				4.5	2.6
1.3	1.1	1.9	1.3			Current	2.0	1.6
.7	.8	.9	.9				1.0	1.1
2.2	3.7	3.5	3.3				3.3	2.0
1.3	.9	1.9	1.0			Quick	1.4	1.3
.7	.8	.8	.7				.8	.9
0 UND	8 45.2	5 71.3	14 26.6				6 58.7	8 45.2
0 UND	18 20.8	27 13.8	19 19.1			Sales/Receivables	46 7.9	45 8.1
45 8.0	29 12.7	42 8.6	32 11.4				111 3.3	123 3.0
						Cost of Sales/Inventory		
						Cost of Sales/Payables		
12.7	9.3	5.2	5.0				2.9	4.2
48.5	195.9	8.6	13.6			Sales/Working Capital	7.7	9.8
−24.2	−20.8	−78.7	−43.2				57.5	52.7
	20.1	26.0	88.8				19.0	10.3
	(13) 3.3	(25) 3.4	(10) 8.4			EBIT/Interest	(42) 9.6	(44) 4.1
	1.2	1.5	−6.7				3.4	1.6
						Net Profit + Depr., Dep.,	12.3	8.0
						Amort./Cur. Mat. L /T/D	(11) 4.3	(16) 4.1
							2.4	2.5
.3	.7	.5	.2				.3	.4
.5	1.1	.8	.5			Fixed/Worth	.7	.9
1.1	2.4	1.8	1.7				1.9	2.2
.3	1.3	.5	.2				.3	.6
1.0	2.1	.8	1.6			Debt/Worth	1.5	1.9
282.0	6.2	3.3	4.5				3.5	4.4
378.3	73.9	47.6	128.5			% Profit Before Taxes/Tangible	42.7	38.0
(10) 20.2	(16) 37.4	11.1	(11) 21.1			Net Worth	(66) 15.9	(55) 20.1
−30.3	−3.7	3.0	5.6				3.7	2.1
17.8	20.4	13.0	35.1			% Profit Before Taxes/Total	14.8	14.5
11.7	5.7	5.7	7.0			Assets	5.6	6.4
−.4	−.9	1.3	−3.2				1.8	−.2
75.4	57.0	9.4	23.3				19.8	15.3
18.1	10.4	4.5	4.2			Sales/Net Fixed Assets	5.3	5.4
5.5	6.2	1.4	1.4				1.2	1.7
7.3	3.4	2.3	3.0				1.8	2.3
4.4	2.3	1.5	1.3			Sales/Total Assets	1.1	1.3
2.1	1.3	.7	.5				.5	.8
	1.8	1.6	1.6				1.4	1.6
	(16) 2.7	(28) 3.1	(10) 2.2			% Depr., Dep., Amort./Sales	(56) 3.2	(53) 2.7
	5.0	5.7	5.6				5.4	3.9
						% Officers', Directors',	6.4	3.4
						Owners' Comp/Sales	(14) 12.2	(14) 6.6
							16.9	19.0
11737M	53542M	218824M	546714M	534813M	700046M	Net Sales ($)	741645M	1441900M
2820M	19773M	131011M	325002M	392093M	566004M	Total Assets ($)	858221M	1130897M

M = $ thousand   MM = $ million

© RMA 2005

See Pages 11 through 21 for Explanation of Ratios and Data

Comparative Historical Data | Current Data Sorted By Sales

		Comparative Historical Data		Type of Statement				Current Data Sorted By Sales		
	35	32	47	Unqualified	3	10	9	5	7	13
	3		3	Reviewed		1		2		
	4	9	4	Compiled	3	1				
	2	2	5	Tax Returns	4	1				
	16	22	23	Other	3	5	2	4	3	6
	4/1/02-3/31/03 ALL	4/1/03-3/31/04 ALL	4/1/04-3/31/05 ALL		0-1MM	43 (4/1-9/30/04) 1-3MM	3-5MM	5-10MM	39 (10/1/04-3/31/05) 10-25MM	25MM & OVER
	60	65	82	NUMBER OF STATEMENTS	13	18	11	11	10	19
	%	%	%	ASSETS	%	%	%	%	%	%
	17.8	20.3	26.6	Cash & Equivalents	24.3	25.1	37.6	37.2	19.2	20.9
	27.6	25.7	17.2	Trade Receivables (net)	12.3	16.1	8.9	24.7	17.6	22.0
	2.4	1.8	1.3	Inventory	1.5	1.6	1.2	.6	1.1	1.3
	3.4	6.4	2.9	All Other Current	.4	4.1	1.5	.8	.6	6.6
	51.1	54.2	48.0	Total Current	38.6	46.9	49.2	63.4	38.4	50.8
	31.6	30.0	34.0	Fixed Assets (net)	51.6	34.0	34.2	26.0	36.9	25.0
	4.5	5.0	6.8	Intangibles (net)	1.6	5.5	5.7	3.2	2.4	16.5
	12.9	10.9	11.3	All Other Non-Current	8.2	13.7	10.9	7.4	22.3	7.8
	100.0	100.0	100.0	Total	100.0	100.0	100.0	100.0	100.0	100.0
				LIABILITIES						
	8.1	7.0	5.6	Notes Payable-Short Term	7.1	7.0	3.0	10.8	6.6	1.1
	2.9	2.7	2.0	Cur. Mat.-L/T/D	2.0	2.1	1.1	1.8	1.5	2.6
	9.6	6.3	5.7	Trade Payables	4.3	5.1	3.1	6.7	7.2	7.4
	.4	.6	.6	Income Taxes Payable	.7	.3	.0	.6	2.4	.2
	22.6	23.4	21.8	All Other Current	15.1	19.7	19.4	35.3	14.6	25.5
	43.7	40.1	35.6	Total Current	29.3	34.2	26.5	55.3	32.3	36.8
	17.6	14.1	16.5	Long-Term Debt	21.8	18.6	8.2	8.0	11.6	23.3
	.1	.2	.3	Deferred Taxes	.0	.2	.0	1.0	.2	.5
	10.7	7.5	8.3	All Other Non-Current	8.8	5.5	6.1	17.0	3.5	9.3
	27.9	38.1	39.3	Net Worth	40.1	41.5	59.2	18.7	52.4	30.1
	100.0	100.0	100.0	Total Liabilities & Net Worth	100.0	100.0	100.0	100.0	100.0	100.0
				INCOME DATA						
	100.0	100.0	100.0	Net Sales	100.0	100.0	100.0	100.0	100.0	100.0
				Gross Profit						
	92.1	91.4	91.5	Operating Expenses	88.4	93.8	96.2	94.8	90.1	87.4
	7.9	8.6	8.5	Operating Profit	11.6	6.2	3.8	5.2	9.9	12.6
	3.2	1.2	1.4	All Other Expenses (net)	4.2	1.9	.5	.8	-1.1	1.3
	4.7	7.4	7.1	Profit Before Taxes	7.3	4.3	3.3	4.3	11.1	11.3
				RATIOS						
	2.2	3.0	3.2	Current	4.0	4.5	4.5	4.3	2.0	2.2
	1.3	1.5	1.2		.7	1.1	2.0	2.3	1.3	1.1
	.8	.9	.9		.6	.8	.9	1.2	.8	1.0
	2.0	2.2	3.1	Quick	3.8	4.3	3.9	4.3	2.0	1.4
	1.1	1.2	1.1		.7	.9	1.9	2.3	1.1	1.0
	.7	.7	.8		.4	.8	.9	1.2	.8	.9
	19 19.4	13 29.1	8 45.9	Sales/Receivables	0 UND	3 109.3	6 66.2	13 27.5	10 35.6	18 20.4
	32 11.4	32 11.4	23 16.0		0 UND	22 16.7	14 26.8	23 16.0	29 12.6	35 10.4
	93 3.9	78 4.7	42 8.6		25 14.4	41 8.8	29 12.7	34 10.6	46 7.9	74 4.9
				Cost of Sales/Inventory						
				Cost of Sales/Payables						
	5.6	5.0	6.6	Sales/Working Capital	8.6	7.2	4.5	5.4	7.2	6.7
	14.3	12.5	21.4		-54.0	129.3	7.4	8.1	35.5	45.4
	-28.6	-56.5	-45.7		-17.3	-32.3	-87.1	11.4	-19.6	-177.7
	13.9	21.7	21.0	EBIT/Interest		9.9		45.9		69.9
	(45) 4.6	(45) 7.0	(62) 3.4		(12) 5.2		(10) 26.0		(17) 14.2
	.8	.1	1.2			.9		2.2		1.9
	9.0	10.5	13.6	Net Profit + Depr., Dep., Amort./Cur. Mat. L/T/D						
	(12) 3.1	(16) 3.2	(15) 3.1							
	1.8	1.6	1.2							
	.4	.3	.5	Fixed/Worth	.5	.5	.4	.3	.2	.5
	1.0	.6	.9		1.1	1.1	.9	.5	.8	1.1
	2.8	1.5	2.0		8.7	2.3	1.1	.6	1.9	3.0
	1.0	.3	.6	Debt/Worth	.4	1.0	.2	.4	.4	2.0
	2.4	1.7	1.5		1.0	3.3	.7	.6	1.1	3.3
	12.2	4.3	4.4		145.6	6.0	2.1	1.3	2.5	5.1
	47.6	54.7	77.5	% Profit Before Taxes/Tangible Net Worth	80.0	78.7	46.7	65.7	39.1	144.8
	(49) 16.4	(57) 15.1	(74) 22.4		(11) 16.6	(17) 23.7	10.2	(10) 15.5	12.1	(15) 91.3
	2.4	-.4	3.4		-.8	1.9	-6.2	3.2	2.5	28.1
	15.9	22.0	19.7	% Profit Before Taxes/Total Assets	16.5	14.3	20.4	20.3	26.1	35.2
	6.5	7.8	6.5		5.5	5.5	5.8	9.6	4.2	13.7
	-.6	-.2	1.0		-.3	-.9	-1.5	1.5	.9	2.7
	22.7	18.9	17.1	Sales/Net Fixed Assets	21.0	16.4	113.9	23.1	8.8	20.9
	7.5	7.7	6.8		4.7	8.8	6.2	11.0	4.0	7.7
	3.1	3.0	2.5		.9	1.4	2.0	4.4	2.8	4.3
	2.5	2.7	2.9	Sales/Total Assets	4.3	2.9	2.5	3.7	2.4	3.1
	1.6	1.4	1.8		1.0	1.5	2.0	2.3	2.0	1.7
	.9	.9	.9		.4	.7	1.0	1.3	1.0	1.1
	1.4	1.7	1.7	% Depr., Dep., Amort./Sales	1.6	1.9				1.6
	(52) 2.3	(56) 2.6	(70) 2.7		(11) 4.4	(17) 2.8			(16) 2.2	
	4.6	4.7	4.8		8.8	6.8				4.4
	2.9	3.1	4.1	% Officers', Directors', Owners' Comp/Sales						
	(12) 7.7	(13) 6.8	(15) 6.5							
	13.2	7.6	18.7							
	1362719M	1115152M	2065676M	Net Sales ($)	7730M	34242M	43172M	73633M	140661M	1766238M
	926959M	834141M	1436703M	Total Assets ($)	12348M	30955M	33614M	51339M	138113M	1170334M

						Type of Statement		
	5	4	6	2	1	Unqualified	12	7
	1	1				Reviewed	1	4
1						Compiled	6	8
4						Tax Returns	5	6
3	2			1		Other	6	7
	18 (4/1-9/30/04)			13 (10/1/04-3/31/05)			4/1/00-3/31/01	4/1/01-3/31/02
0-500M	500M-2MM	2-10MM	10-50MM	50-100MM	100-250MM		ALL	ALL
8	8	5	7	2	1	NUMBER OF STATEMENTS	30	32
%	%	%	%	%	%	ASSETS	%	%
						Cash & Equivalents	19.6	16.8
						Trade Receivables (net)	3.6	4.9
						Inventory	2.9	7.4
						All Other Current	3.3	3.8
						Total Current	29.4	32.8
						Fixed Assets (net)	54.3	54.0
						Intangibles (net)	2.6	2.0
						All Other Non-Current	13.7	11.2
						Total	100.0	100.0
						LIABILITIES		
						Notes Payable-Short Term	1.2	4.0
						Cur. Mat.-L/T/D	4.6	4.2
						Trade Payables	9.1	5.4
						Income Taxes Payable	.1	.0
						All Other Current	20.1	9.7
						Total Current	35.0	23.3
						Long-Term Debt	24.4	31.7
						Deferred Taxes	.1	.4
						All Other Non-Current	2.5	6.4
						Net Worth	38.0	38.3
						Total Liabilities & Net Worth	100.0	100.0
						INCOME DATA		
						Net Sales	100.0	100.0
						Gross Profit		
						Operating Expenses	90.3	84.9
						Operating Profit	9.7	15.1
						All Other Expenses (net)	.9	3.8
						Profit Before Taxes	8.7	11.3
						RATIOS		
						Current	4.2	5.3
							1.3	1.7
							.5	.7
						Quick	3.6	4.5
							1.0	.9
							.2	.5
						Sales/Receivables	0 UND	0 UND
							2 150.6	1 243.8
							16 23.3	25 14.7
						Cost of Sales/Inventory		
						Cost of Sales/Payables		
						Sales/Working Capital	6.8	3.2
							36.6	18.9
							−21.1	−25.2
						EBIT/Interest	6.2	8.5
							(19) 2.8	(22) 2.8
							−2.2	1.7
						Net Profit + Depr., Dep., Amort./Cur. Mat. L /T/D		
						Fixed/Worth	.4	.6
							1.0	1.1
							1.9	4.3
						Debt/Worth	.3	.2
							.7	.8
							2.3	4.1
						% Profit Before Taxes/Tangible Net Worth	44.6	46.4
							(26) 20.0	(28) 11.2
							5.7	1.7
						% Profit Before Taxes/Total Assets	24.2	15.0
							9.8	5.3
							−.6	.7
						Sales/Net Fixed Assets	18.5	12.1
							1.9	2.3
							.9	.6
						Sales/Total Assets	3.1	2.8
							1.1	1.2
							.6	.5
						% Depr., Dep., Amort./Sales	1.7	1.5
							(21) 5.1	(24) 3.4
							12.6	10.9
						% Officers', Directors', Owners' Comp/Sales		3.7
								(11) 5.1
								7.2
4125M	13922M	31025M	80198M	54093M	127113M	Net Sales ($)	182598M	123670M
1529M	9129M	25740M	118606M	151974M	193279M	Total Assets ($)	160270M	306184M

© RMA 2005

M = $ thousand   MM = $ million
See Pages 11 through 21 for Explanation of Ratios and Data

Comparative Historical Data　　　　　　　　　　Current Data Sorted By Sales

			Type of Statement					
14	14	18	Unqualified	7	1	4	3	3
			Reviewed					
1	4	3	Compiled	1	1			
2	4	4	Tax Returns	3	1			
7	8	6	Other	3	2		1	
4/1/02-	4/1/03-	4/1/04-			18 (4/1-9/30/04)		13 (10/1/04-3/31/05)	
3/31/03	3/31/04	3/31/05		0-1MM	1-3MM	3-5MM	5-10MM	10-25MM	25MM & OVER
ALL	ALL	ALL						
24	30	31	**NUMBER OF STATEMENTS**	7	11	2	5	3	3
%	%	%	**ASSETS**	%	%	%	%	%	%
14.2	16.6	12.5	Cash & Equivalents		12.3				
6.5	4.0	5.2	Trade Receivables (net)		8.1				
3.8	1.4	6.9	Inventory		3.9				
3.5	2.2	2.2	All Other Current		.2				
27.9	24.2	26.8	Total Current		24.4				
53.1	55.9	55.0	Fixed Assets (net)		59.6				
1.0	2.5	1.7	Intangibles (net)		2.2				
18.0	17.5	16.5	All Other Non-Current		13.8				
100.0	100.0	100.0	Total		100.0				
			LIABILITIES						
7.1	3.8	6.8	Notes Payable-Short Term		13.9				
2.7	.9	2.3	Cur. Mat.-L/T/D		1.5				
5.0	5.3	3.7	Trade Payables		4.6				
.0	.0	.0	Income Taxes Payable		.0				
15.5	18.4	8.0	All Other Current		6.6				
30.3	28.4	20.8	Total Current		26.6				
15.7	22.0	23.8	Long-Term Debt		21.8				
.0	.0	.0	Deferred Taxes		.0				
4.9	6.9	11.2	All Other Non-Current		1.3				
49.1	42.8	44.2	Net Worth		50.3				
100.0	100.0	100.0	Total Liabilities & Net Worth		100.0				
			INCOME DATA						
100.0	100.0	100.0	Net Sales		100.0				
			Gross Profit						
91.0	100.4	85.9	Operating Expenses		91.2				
9.0	-.4	14.1	Operating Profit		8.8				
2.2	.7	2.5	All Other Expenses (net)		3.7				
6.8	-1.1	11.6	Profit Before Taxes		5.0				
			RATIOS						
2.0	3.2	2.3			7.0				
.9	1.0	1.6	Current		1.0				
.4	.6	.7			.7				
1.3	2.7	2.3			6.8				
.6	.8	1.3	Quick		.9				
.2	.5	.3			.3				
0　UND	0　UND	0　UND		4　86.1					
5　80.1	4　100.0	7　54.0	Sales/Receivables	20　18.5					
22　16.9	32　11.6	29　12.5		38　9.7					
			Cost of Sales/Inventory						
			Cost of Sales/Payables						
6.4	8.9	7.3			7.2				
-74.8	NM	11.9	Sales/Working Capital		-95.0				
-10.0	-15.0	-20.8			-34.4				
19.3	7.7	18.4							
(17)　1.5	(19)　.6	(26)　2.5	EBIT/Interest						
-2.6	-3.6	.2							
			Net Profit + Depr., Dep., Amort./Cur. Mat. L/T/D						
.6	.7	.6			.8				
1.1	1.4	1.0	Fixed/Worth		1.1				
2.3	2.4	2.1			2.1				
.3	.3	.4			.2				
1.0	1.3	.8	Debt/Worth		1.2				
2.7	2.8	3.3			3.5				
39.5	18.6	34.7			15.6				
(23)　18.1	(27)　.0	(29)　8.9	% Profit Before Taxes/Tangible Net Worth		9.1				
-5.0	-10.9	.5			-18.4				
16.0	7.8	15.9			11.8				
6.9	-.2	4.2	% Profit Before Taxes/Total Assets		4.3				
-1.8	-9.8	-.2			-4.3				
13.7	18.1	10.3			8.5				
2.5	1.4	1.6	Sales/Net Fixed Assets		1.7				
1.3	.7	.7			1.1				
3.1	2.9	2.3			3.3				
1.5	1.1	1.0	Sales/Total Assets		1.1				
.7	.5	.5			.7				
1.6	1.0	1.6							
(18)　3.1	(25)　4.7	(24)　3.1	% Depr., Dep., Amort./Sales						
5.2	8.6	5.5							
	3.9								
	(10)　8.2		% Officers', Directors', Owners' Comp/Sales						
	18.9								
79364M	89976M	310476M	Net Sales ($)	2448M	15636M	8412M	36577M	54235M	193168M
204386M	145962M	500257M	Total Assets ($)	2440M	17167M	19997M	78555M	94708M	287390M

M = $ thousand　　MM = $ million
See Pages 11 through 21 for Explanation of Ratios and Data

Current Data Sorted By Assets   Comparative Historical Data

						Type of Statement		
2	4	8	10	3		Unqualified		
2		2				Reviewed		
1	1	2	1	1		Compiled		
4	3					Tax Returns		
2	3	6	3	1		Other		
	39 (4/1-9/30/04)		20 (10/1/04-3/31/05)				4/1/00-3/31/01 ALL	4/1/01-3/31/02 ALL
0-500M	500M-2MM	2-10MM	10-50MM	50-100MM	100-250MM			
11	11	18	14	5		NUMBER OF STATEMENTS		
%	%	%	%	%	%	**ASSETS**	%	%
28.0	18.0	18.3	17.9		D	Cash & Equivalents	D	D
18.1	23.1	9.5	7.2		A	Trade Receivables (net)	A	A
.2	3.8	.7	1.8		T	Inventory	T	T
1.8	8.6	7.1	2.3		A	All Other Current	A	A
48.1	53.5	35.7	29.1			Total Current		
31.3	32.2	50.1	50.8		N	Fixed Assets (net)	N	N
10.4	10.9	.4	4.6		O	Intangibles (net)	O	O
10.2	3.4	13.8	15.5		T	All Other Non-Current	T	T
100.0	100.0	100.0	100.0			Total		
					A	**LIABILITIES**	A	A
19.1	11.3	7.9	2.1		V	Notes Payable-Short Term	V	V
2.7	3.0	3.5	1.0		A	Cur. Mat.-L/T/D	A	A
8.1	8.1	8.9	5.3		I	Trade Payables	I	I
.0	.0	.0	.1		L	Income Taxes Payable	L	L
27.6	19.1	6.9	6.9		A	All Other Current	A	A
57.5	41.4	27.2	15.4		B	Total Current	B	B
16.4	24.0	28.8	19.0		L	Long-Term Debt	L	L
.0	.0	.0	.1		E	Deferred Taxes	E	E
4.3	2.9	.4	2.2			All Other Non-Current		
21.5	31.7	43.6	63.3			Net Worth		
100.0	100.0	100.0	100.0			Total Liabilities & Net Worth		
						INCOME DATA		
100.0	100.0	100.0	100.0			Net Sales		
						Gross Profit		
97.0	97.0	96.7	89.8			Operating Expenses		
3.0	3.0	3.3	10.2			Operating Profit		
.6	1.8	.2	–.7			All Other Expenses (net)		
2.4	1.2	3.1	10.9			Profit Before Taxes		
						RATIOS		
3.0	3.6	3.6	4.7					
.7	1.1	1.5	2.2			Current		
.2	.7	.6	.9					
3.0	3.6	3.6	4.4					
.7	1.0	1.0	2.0			Quick		
.2	.4	.4	.5					
0 UND	1 330.0	1 580.3	8 47.4					
3 113.7	29 12.5	6 56.6	22 16.7			Sales/Receivables		
24 15.0	99 3.7	38 9.6	59 6.2					
						Cost of Sales/Inventory		
						Cost of Sales/Payables		
12.2	3.0	4.6	1.8					
–18.4	44.6	9.5	6.7			Sales/Working Capital		
–7.9	–18.0	–15.9	–35.9					
	4.7	5.1	26.2					
	(10) 2.5	(14) 1.7	(12) 5.4			EBIT/Interest		
	.5	–.9	1.3					
						Net Profit + Depr., Dep., Amort./Cur. Mat. L /T/D		
.4	.4	.4	.5					
1.7	1.4	1.2	.8			Fixed/Worth		
–1.2	–1.1	4.1	1.8					
.3	.9	.4	.2					
10.6	2.4	1.1	.5			Debt/Worth		
–3.4	–6.1	4.2	2.1					
		33.4	20.6					
	(16)	6.9	6.6			% Profit Before Taxes/Tangible Net Worth		
		–8.1	3.6					
50.5	8.2	11.8	11.5					
1.3	3.7	4.5	4.0			% Profit Before Taxes/Total Assets		
–11.1	–2.2	–4.1	1.9					
127.5	66.1	13.8	2.8					
19.7	13.1	2.6	1.6			Sales/Net Fixed Assets		
10.7	3.1	1.1	.6					
8.0	4.0	2.1	1.1					
4.8	1.6	1.3	.6			Sales/Total Assets		
3.4	.9	.7	.4					
		1.4	3.1					
	(17)	2.2 (13)	4.1			% Depr., Dep., Amort./Sales		
		4.7	6.6					
						% Officers', Directors', Owners' Comp/Sales		
12979M	23205M	157587M	180627M	400582M		Net Sales ($)		
2632M	11197M	98230M	250297M	346436M		Total Assets ($)		

M = $ thousand   MM = $ million
See Pages 11 through 21 for Explanation of Ratios and Data

Comparative Historical Data				Current Data Sorted By Sales					
			Type of Statement						
14	31	27	Unqualified		8		11	4	4
1	1	4	Reviewed	3			1		
	2	6	Compiled		2	2	2	1	1
		7	Tax Returns	5	2				
6	7	15	Other	3	2	1	3	3	3
4/1/02- 3/31/03	4/1/03- 3/31/04	4/1/04- 3/31/05			39 (4/1-9/30/04)		20 (10/1/04-3/31/05)		
ALL	ALL	ALL		0-1MM	1-3MM	3-5MM	5-10MM	10-25MM	25MM & OVER
21	41	59	**NUMBER OF STATEMENTS**	11	14	3	15	8	8
%	%	%	**ASSETS**	%	%	%	%	%	%
22.7	14.6	21.0	Cash & Equivalents	29.3	16.2		20.2		
6.6	12.6	12.9	Trade Receivables (net)	11.8	20.6		7.7		
.3	1.2	1.8	Inventory	2.5	.1		1.0		
5.2	6.0	4.7	All Other Current	2.1	8.6		6.1		
34.7	34.4	40.4	Total Current	45.7	45.5		35.1		
48.0	50.3	42.3	Fixed Assets (net)	39.6	35.1		51.5		
2.3	3.1	6.3	Intangibles (net)	11.5	8.3		.1		
14.9	12.2	11.1	All Other Non-Current	3.1	11.2		13.4		
100.0	100.0	100.0	Total	100.0	100.0		100.0		
			LIABILITIES						
7.3	6.3	8.6	Notes Payable-Short Term	1.2	23.2		6.5		
2.0	3.2	2.6	Cur. Mat.-L/T/D	2.5	2.1		3.2		
3.0	6.4	7.2	Trade Payables	5.0	9.4		3.6		
.0	.0	.0	Income Taxes Payable	.0	.0		.0		
11.9	15.3	14.3	All Other Current	16.9	20.9		7.3		
24.2	31.3	32.8	Total Current	25.7	55.5		20.6		
18.0	18.1	22.6	Long-Term Debt	26.2	24.8		21.6		
.0	.0	.0	Deferred Taxes	.0	.0		.0		
2.9	4.6	2.7	All Other Non-Current	6.3	.9		1.0		
54.8	45.9	41.8	Net Worth	41.6	18.8		56.8		
100.0	100.0	100.0	Total Liabilities & Net Worth	100.0	100.0		100.0		
			INCOME DATA						
100.0	100.0	100.0	Net Sales	100.0	100.0		100.0		
			Gross Profit						
96.4	98.0	94.8	Operating Expenses	95.7	95.7		92.8		
3.6	2.0	5.2	Operating Profit	4.3	4.3		7.2		
2.2	.0	.7	All Other Expenses (net)	2.2	2.1		-1.5		
1.4	2.0	4.5	Profit Before Taxes	2.1	2.2		8.7		
			RATIOS						
3.0	2.5	3.1		9.3	1.4		3.6		
1.7	1.4	1.4	Current	3.0	1.1		2.5		
.7	.8	.7		.7	.4		.6		
2.4	2.2	3.0		9.3	1.4		3.5		
1.3	1.1	1.4	Quick	3.0	.7		2.0		
.6	.6	.4		.6	.2		.4		
3 116.4	3 126.2	1 306.6		0 UND	0 UND		1 440.5		
13 29.1	19 19.0	16 23.4	Sales/Receivables	1 255.0	12 30.1		10 37.0		
32 11.3	45 8.0	44 8.3		54 6.8	50 7.3		29 12.5		
			Cost of Sales/Inventory						
			Cost of Sales/Payables						
4.6	5.7	4.0		2.3	9.9		3.7		
23.3	16.7	12.2	Sales/Working Capital	4.0	NM		7.6		
-14.3	-17.8	-18.2		-18.2	-14.1		-18.0		
21.0	7.6	6.7			6.0		7.8		
(14) 4.3	(33) 3.7	(47) 2.3	EBIT/Interest		(11) 2.3		(11) 3.8		
-.9	.8	-.2			-.2		-.6		
			Net Profit + Depr., Dep., Amort./Cur. Mat. L/T/D						
.6	.6	.4		.4	.7		.4		
.9	1.0	1.2	Fixed/Worth	1.2	1.6		.9		
1.3	1.8	3.7		-1.1	-1.7		1.4		
.4	.4	.4		.3	2.0		.2		
.7	.7	1.4	Debt/Worth	.9	6.3		.5		
2.1	3.0	8.5		-6.1	-4.6		1.4		
26.4	21.9	26.4	% Profit Before Taxes/Tangible Net Worth		56.6		22.2		
7.6	(37) 6.4	(48) 7.6			(10) 27.7		(14) 9.4		
-4.7	.5	-.7			-10.0		2.4		
9.5	9.1	9.2	% Profit Before Taxes/Total Assets	2.4	26.9		12.3		
5.2	2.6	3.2		-.4	6.8		6.6		
-1.7	-.3	-2.1		-12.1	-2.5		-.7		
9.5	11.2	18.9	Sales/Net Fixed Assets	127.5	29.6		9.1		
1.6	2.1	3.6		10.7	14.0		1.5		
1.0	.8	1.3		.8	1.5		.7		
1.7	2.8	3.4	Sales/Total Assets	4.0	5.2		1.7		
.8	.9	1.4		1.6	3.3		.8		
.6	.5	.6		.6	.9		.5		
1.5	2.0	1.6	% Depr., Dep., Amort./Sales				2.0		
(20) 3.1	(36) 4.3	(49) 3.1					(13) 4.2		
4.9	6.6	4.8					6.5		
		4.5	% Officers', Directors', Owners' Comp/Sales						
		(14) 6.2							
		8.8							
272756M	341404M	774980M	Net Sales ($)	6674M	30028M	11424M	109013M	116873M	500968M
329878M	459163M	708792M	Total Assets ($)	8848M	27951M	17237M	165566M	78909M	410281M

M = $ thousand   MM = $ million
See Pages 11 through 21 for Explanation of Ratios and Data

1334   EDUCATION—Educational Support Services   NAICS 611710   (SIC 8299, 8748)

		Current Data Sorted By Assets						Comparative Historical Data	
						Type of Statement			
10	20	58	50	12	5	Unqualified		131	108
2	4	9	3			Reviewed		8	5
6	9	9				Compiled		51	48
11	9	1			1	Tax Returns		20	15
6	24	23	15		1	Other		60	65
	186 (4/1-9/30/04)		102 (10/1/04-3/31/05)					4/1/00-3/31/01	4/1/01-3/31/02
0-500M	500M-2MM	2-10MM	10-50MM	50-100MM	100-250MM			ALL	ALL
35	66	100	68	13	6	**NUMBER OF STATEMENTS**		270	241
%	%	%	%	%	%	**ASSETS**		%	%
34.1	26.7	19.9	15.7	17.1		Cash & Equivalents		19.5	20.7
22.3	19.7	14.0	11.2	4.8		Trade Receivables (net)		13.3	12.5
2.0	3.7	2.1	2.0	.3		Inventory		2.3	1.3
7.6	4.5	3.5	4.1	4.5		All Other Current		6.5	4.8
65.9	54.5	39.5	33.0	26.8		Total Current		41.5	39.3
21.9	36.0	48.7	45.9	45.8		Fixed Assets (net)		37.8	41.9
7.5	3.1	1.3	.9	3.8		Intangibles (net)		2.3	3.4
4.7	6.4	10.5	20.2	23.6		All Other Non-Current		18.3	15.5
100.0	100.0	100.0	100.0	100.0		Total		100.0	100.0
						LIABILITIES			
13.6	3.4	4.0	3.4	1.7		Notes Payable-Short Term		4.6	4.6
2.5	2.4	1.4	2.1	1.0		Cur. Mat.-L/T/D		1.6	2.7
10.5	8.7	4.8	4.6	3.3		Trade Payables		6.2	5.5
.1	.3	.1	.1	.1		Income Taxes Payable		.1	.1
34.8	17.5	12.3	11.3	16.3		All Other Current		13.8	12.1
61.5	32.3	22.6	21.5	22.5		Total Current		26.3	25.1
18.2	19.0	24.0	21.2	26.5		Long-Term Debt		15.8	21.9
.0	.0	.0	.0	.5		Deferred Taxes		.3	.1
6.2	6.7	5.7	3.2	6.0		All Other Non-Current		6.3	4.2
14.1	42.0	47.6	54.1	44.6		Net Worth		51.3	48.7
100.0	100.0	100.0	100.0	100.0		Total Liabilities & Net Worth		100.0	100.0
						INCOME DATA			
100.0	100.0	100.0	100.0	100.0		Net Sales		100.0	100.0
						Gross Profit			
94.9	92.4	93.5	95.5	91.5		Operating Expenses		93.7	91.1
5.1	7.6	6.5	4.5	8.5		Operating Profit		6.3	8.9
1.8	.7	2.2	−1.4	.8		All Other Expenses (net)		−1.7	1.9
3.3	6.9	4.3	5.9	7.7		Profit Before Taxes		7.9	7.0
						RATIOS			
6.4	3.6	3.1	2.8	2.3				5.0	4.3
1.3	2.0	1.5	1.6	1.3		Current		1.9	1.9
.9	.9	1.0	.9	.7				1.0	1.0
2.2	3.3	2.5	2.2	2.1				4.3	3.7
1.2	1.7	1.3	1.1	1.0		Quick	(269)	1.5	1.5
.8	.8	.7	.7	.6				.7	.7
0 UND	0 999.8	3 116.8	7 55.0	0 UND			4 91.6	1 398.1	
5 68.8	6 56.2	16 22.6	32 11.3	2 158.7		Sales/Receivables	18 19.8	12 30.6	
51 7.1	45 8.1	47 7.8	58 6.3	19 19.6			47 7.7	46 7.9	
						Cost of Sales/Inventory			
						Cost of Sales/Payables			
5.1	3.5	4.2	3.9	8.4				2.9	3.2
19.0	9.9	13.9	9.8	18.9		Sales/Working Capital		8.7	9.2
−79.0	−103.3	562.4	−49.7	−25.5				−81.2	−448.7
12.9	13.7	8.2	25.6					12.8	7.0
(21) 7.0	(44) 3.3	(71) 2.3	(50) 3.3			EBIT/Interest	(179) 3.3	(153) 3.0	
2.2	−3.4	.8	1.0					1.1	1.0
						Net Profit + Depr., Dep.,			7.4
						Amort./Cur. Mat. L /T/D	(10)		3.4
									1.0
.1	.2	.3	.5	.6				.3	.4
.5	.6	1.0	.8	1.0		Fixed/Worth		.8	.8
−.9	2.8	2.6	1.6	4.1				1.5	2.1
.5	.5	.3	.3	.6				.3	.3
1.8	1.1	1.1	.8	1.5		Debt/Worth		.8	1.0
−3.2	5.0	2.8	2.1	4.8				2.4	3.2
79.3	57.2	21.1	16.0	44.8		% Profit Before Taxes/Tangible		27.3	27.3
(22) 29.6	(57) 32.6	(93) 7.1	(66) 6.0	(12) 10.7		Net Worth	(249) 9.0	(220) 9.3	
−9.2	−2.6	.4	.3	5.9				.3	−.1
33.2	23.2	9.7	7.1	8.5		% Profit Before Taxes/Total		12.5	11.1
12.8	6.7	3.2	3.2	4.8		Assets		4.3	3.8
−.7	−2.6	−.3	.2	2.4				−.5	−.1
183.3	52.6	14.9	4.7	8.9				15.2	10.7
21.2	12.1	2.3	1.4	5.6		Sales/Net Fixed Assets		3.6	2.8
8.5	2.1	.8	.7	.7				1.1	1.0
5.4	3.4	2.1	1.3	2.2				2.3	2.5
3.5	2.1	1.0	.6	1.3		Sales/Total Assets		1.1	1.0
2.2	1.1	.5	.4	.5				.5	.5
.7	1.2	1.9	2.7	1.6				.9	1.0
(23) 1.6	(38) 2.9	(80) 4.2	(61) 4.6	(11) 3.0		% Depr., Dep., Amort./Sales	(209) 2.7	(185) 3.0	
2.9	4.7	6.8	6.4	8.0				5.2	5.5
4.3	6.0	1.1						5.0	4.5
(16) 8.1	(17) 6.8	(13) 3.0				% Officers', Directors',	(43) 9.6	(45) 8.9	
20.7	20.7	7.3				Owners' Comp/Sales		19.7	17.2
36048M	172388M	821916M	1462355M	1466021M	2722316M	Net Sales ($)		5630070M	3401231M
9683M	74177M	517245M	1432739M	955868M	1055665M	Total Assets ($)		5062029M	3770022M

M = $ thousand   MM = $ million

© RMA 2005   See Pages 11 through 21 for Explanation of Ratios and Data

Comparative Historical Data | Current Data Sorted By Sales

Hist 1	Hist 2	Hist 3	Type of Statement	0-1MM	1-3MM	3-5MM	5-10MM	10-25MM	25MM & OVER
167	153	155	Unqualified	15	27	23	26	29	35
10	19	18	Reviewed	2	4	1	5	6	
21	50	24	Compiled	7	11	3	2	1	
17	32	22	Tax Returns	6	15				1
88	81	69	Other	9	18	9	15	13	5
4/1/02-3/31/03 ALL	4/1/03-3/31/04 ALL	4/1/04-3/31/05 ALL		186 (4/1-9/30/04)			102 (10/1/04-3/31/05)		
303	335	288	**NUMBER OF STATEMENTS**	39	75	36	48	49	41
%	%	%	**ASSETS**	%	%	%	%	%	%
21.1	20.5	22.4	Cash & Equivalents	29.6	22.3	23.8	20.4	18.9	21.0
15.0	14.6	15.1	Trade Receivables (net)	9.7	15.9	14.5	18.1	19.6	10.1
1.3	1.3	2.3	Inventory	.5	3.4	1.0	2.1	3.2	2.3
4.3	6.1	4.4	All Other Current	7.8	2.6	3.0	2.2	5.4	7.1
41.7	42.5	44.2	Total Current	47.6	44.2	42.3	42.8	47.2	40.6
43.6	42.5	41.1	Fixed Assets (net)	46.0	44.2	46.1	42.1	35.6	31.9
1.8	2.3	2.8	Intangibles (net)	1.5	4.8	1.9	1.6	1.7	3.7
13.0	12.7	11.9	All Other Non-Current	4.9	6.8	9.7	13.5	15.6	23.9
100.0	100.0	100.0	Total	100.0	100.0	100.0	100.0	100.0	100.0
			LIABILITIES						
6.8	5.4	4.7	Notes Payable-Short Term	7.2	5.9	3.8	4.0	5.2	1.2
1.7	4.3	1.9	Cur. Mat.-L/T/D	3.1	1.6	2.8	1.2	2.1	1.0
6.1	6.7	6.2	Trade Payables	4.8	6.8	4.2	8.1	5.1	7.2
.2	.4	.1	Income Taxes Payable	.2	.0	.2	.2	.2	.1
13.3	15.0	16.1	All Other Current	26.6	12.2	17.1	14.3	14.8	16.4
28.0	31.9	29.1	Total Current	41.9	26.5	28.1	27.8	27.5	26.0
22.2	20.3	21.8	Long-Term Debt	28.8	26.1	22.2	16.6	15.5	20.5
.2	.1	.1	Deferred Taxes	.0	.0	.1	.0	.0	.2
4.7	6.4	5.3	All Other Non-Current	1.4	8.1	3.6	6.6	6.5	2.6
44.8	41.3	43.7	Net Worth	27.9	39.3	46.0	49.0	50.5	50.7
100.0	100.0	100.0	Total Liabilities & Net Worth	100.0	100.0	100.0	100.0	100.0	100.0
			INCOME DATA						
100.0	100.0	100.0	Net Sales	100.0	100.0	100.0	100.0	100.0	100.0
			Gross Profit						
94.3	93.0	93.8	Operating Expenses	90.5	94.3	93.1	95.2	94.2	94.5
5.7	7.0	6.2	Operating Profit	9.5	5.7	6.9	4.8	5.8	5.5
1.9	2.0	.8	All Other Expenses (net)	4.6	1.9	.2	-.8	-.6	-.4
3.8	5.0	5.4	Profit Before Taxes	4.9	3.9	6.7	5.5	6.5	5.9
			RATIOS						
3.4	4.2	3.2		9.2	3.1	4.1	3.0	2.6	3.5
1.7	1.8	1.6	Current	1.4	1.6	1.7	1.4	1.7	1.6
.9	.8	.9		.7	.9	.9	.8	1.0	1.0
3.0	3.4	2.7		8.8	2.9	4.1	2.6	2.1	2.7
1.4	1.4	1.3	Quick	1.3	1.4	1.4	1.3	1.4	1.1
.8	.7	.7		.7	.8	.7	.7	.8	.6
2 206.4	1 260.0	2 208.6		0 UND	1 524.7	4 86.5	8 47.8	13 27.7	0 UND
14 27.0	15 23.7	15 23.6	Sales/Receivables	2 161.0	6 59.0	16 22.9	27 13.6	34 10.6	8 44.2
48 7.5	47 7.7	47 7.8		30 12.2	44 8.4	52 7.1	62 5.9	60 6.1	40 9.1
			Cost of Sales/Inventory						
			Cost of Sales/Payables						
4.1	3.8	4.3		2.5	4.2	3.3	5.5	3.9	7.6
12.1	10.3	12.3	Sales/Working Capital	10.1	12.8	12.0	12.5	7.7	14.2
-130.6	-36.5	-130.0		-32.8	-172.4	-62.2	-41.0	83.5	173.4
(206) 9.1	(226) 9.7	(198) 13.6		(23) 10.0	(58) 9.1	(27) 6.2	(30) 17.8	(33) 26.5	(27) 18.4
2.0	3.1	3.4	EBIT/Interest	3.4	2.3	1.4	3.5	4.4	6.8
-.5	.4	1.0		.0	-1.6	-2.0	1.2	1.8	2.1
(16) 9.9	(14) 7.8	(15) 37.4	Net Profit + Depr., Dep.,						
3.8	2.1	5.1	Amort./Cur. Mat. L/T/D						
1.4	.9	1.6							
.4	.3	.3		.2	.3	.5	.4	.1	.1
.9	.9	.8	Fixed/Worth	.9	1.0	1.0	.8	.7	.8
1.8	1.8	2.2		1.8	5.8	2.4	1.7	1.2	1.3
.4	.5	.4		.2	.5	.4	.3	.4	.4
1.0	1.0	1.1	Debt/Worth	1.0	1.7	.9	1.2	.9	.9
2.9	3.1	3.1		6.2	5.5	2.5	2.4	2.2	2.7
21.7	27.7	33.6	% Profit Before Taxes/Tangible	37.6	36.5	40.2	20.0	29.0	28.7
(277) 7.1	(296) 6.6	(255) 9.5	Net Worth	(32) 16.9	(62) 9.6	(32) 2.3	(45) 5.9	(46) 8.4	(38) 16.2
-2.5	-.6	.3		-5.7	-1.2	-2.8	-1.1	4.8	6.0
9.3	11.4	13.1	% Profit Before Taxes/Total	23.6	12.2	19.0	7.9	10.8	17.3
2.6	3.4	4.3	Assets	5.2	4.1	1.0	2.9	4.7	6.0
-2.1	-1.2	.1		-1.2	-.9	-1.6	-.5	1.8	2.5
17.3	19.0	25.9		35.7	27.1	23.4	25.6	24.9	26.8
3.2	3.5	4.1	Sales/Net Fixed Assets	2.9	4.2	2.2	2.3	4.1	6.6
.9	.9	.9		.5	.9	.8	.9	1.4	3.1
2.5	2.4	2.6		3.0	3.1	2.6	2.6	2.0	3.8
1.3	1.2	1.3	Sales/Total Assets	1.2	1.3	.8	1.1	1.3	1.8
.5	.5	.6		.5	.6	.5	.5	.6	1.1
1.6	1.6	1.6		2.3	1.6	3.0	1.3	1.2	1.7
(241) 3.3	(259) 3.4	(218) 3.5	% Depr., Dep., Amort./Sales	(28) 5.5	(56) 3.3	(25) 4.5	(37) 4.6	(41) 3.0	(31) 2.7
5.9	6.0	6.1		15.3	6.3	6.3	6.4	4.7	4.9
4.8	4.3	3.8			4.0				
(59) 9.0	(48) 7.6	(53) 6.7	% Officers', Directors',		(28) 6.5				
13.6	13.1	14.5	Owners' Comp/Sales		13.9				
4589368M	4854012M	6681044M	Net Sales ($)	23469M	143868M	136879M	342258M	738447M	5296123M
4901428M	4210279M	4045377M	Total Assets ($)	42974M	165596M	188451M	443935M	757145M	2447276M

© RMA 2005

M = $ thousand   MM = $ million
See Pages 11 through 21 for Explanation of Ratios and Data

HEALTH CARE AND
SOCIAL ASSISTANCE

Current Data Sorted By Assets   Comparative Historical Data

6	21	68	69	16	13	Type of Statement		111	120
16	48	58	21			Unqualified		79	94
324	198	74	5	3	3	Reviewed		448	533
772	209	58	8	6	9	Compiled		403	429
285	244	188	57	10	8	Tax Returns		390	515
						Other			
	347 (4/1-9/30/04)		2450 (10/1/04-3/31/05)					4/1/00-3/31/01	4/1/01-3/31/02
0-500M	500M-2MM	2-10MM	10-50MM	50-100MM	100-250MM			ALL	ALL
1403	720	446	160	35	33	NUMBER OF STATEMENTS		1431	1691
%	%	%	%	%	%	ASSETS		%	%
35.8	21.8	14.3	13.7	24.1	27.9	Cash & Equivalents		22.1	23.8
3.8	15.9	26.9	26.2	12.6	10.6	Trade Receivables (net)		14.2	12.6
.9	1.0	1.0	1.3	.5	.4	Inventory		.9	1.2
3.3	3.5	3.1	4.3	6.6	3.4	All Other Current		3.6	3.7
43.7	42.3	45.2	45.5	43.8	42.3	Total Current		40.8	41.3
38.1	44.1	41.3	40.4	34.6	38.0	Fixed Assets (net)		44.2	43.7
4.0	3.4	4.4	3.7	8.3	6.5	Intangibles (net)		4.8	4.1
14.1	10.2	9.1	10.3	13.3	13.1	All Other Non-Current		10.1	10.8
100.0	100.0	100.0	100.0	100.0	100.0	Total		100.0	100.0
						LIABILITIES			
32.5	13.6	7.9	4.5	11.2	5.9	Notes Payable-Short Term		21.4	23.4
9.4	7.5	6.2	5.6	9.3	5.8	Cur. Mat.-L/T/D		8.3	8.4
2.8	4.0	4.1	6.1	5.0	6.7	Trade Payables		3.0	3.6
.2	.3	1.0	1.1	1.0	.3	Income Taxes Payable		.5	.4
37.9	21.4	18.2	17.4	22.0	19.2	All Other Current		29.9	32.3
82.8	46.9	37.4	34.6	48.5	38.0	Total Current		63.2	68.1
36.8	32.4	28.8	26.9	27.8	44.1	Long-Term Debt		30.6	32.0
.1	.5	.7	.5	.6	1.4	Deferred Taxes		.6	.5
4.6	4.6	4.8	6.0	8.5	3.3	All Other Non-Current		6.2	5.6
−24.3	15.6	28.3	32.0	14.6	13.2	Net Worth		−.6	−6.2
100.0	100.0	100.0	100.0	100.0	100.0	Total Liabilities & Net Worth		100.0	100.0
						INCOME DATA			
100.0	100.0	100.0	100.0	100.0	100.0	Net Sales		100.0	100.0
						Gross Profit			
91.6	87.9	87.1	87.1	91.4	93.9	Operating Expenses		91.7	91.5
8.4	12.1	12.9	12.9	8.6	6.1	Operating Profit		8.3	8.5
.8	2.0	3.1	2.6	2.4	.7	All Other Expenses (net)		2.0	1.8
7.6	10.1	9.8	10.3	6.2	5.4	Profit Before Taxes		6.3	6.6
						RATIOS			
1.5	2.1	2.6	2.3	1.4	2.9			1.8	1.8
.6	.9	1.2	1.3	1.0	2.0	Current		.8	.9
.2	.4	.6	.9	.8	.7			.3	.3
1.3	1.9	2.4	1.8	1.3	2.5			1.6	1.6
(1399) .5	(719) .8	(442) 1.1	1.2	.8	1.5	Quick		(1426) .7	(1687) .7
.2	.3	.6	.8	.5	.6			.2	.2
0 UND	0 UND	0 UND	21 17.1	0 UND	0 UND			0 UND	0 UND
0 UND	0 UND	31 11.8	44 8.3	24 15.5	9 39.1	Sales/Receivables		0 UND	0 UND
0 UND	34 10.8	57 6.4	60 6.1	49 7.4	48 7.6			36 10.2	28 12.9
						Cost of Sales/Inventory			
						Cost of Sales/Payables			
85.4	15.6	7.9	8.0	17.4	5.8			20.8	23.9
−75.0	−186.0	41.5	24.8	999.8	18.0	Sales/Working Capital		−138.0	−164.6
−19.4	−20.9	−27.4	−68.6	−31.2	−98.2			−22.3	−20.9
18.1	19.5	21.4	16.5	13.4	22.1			8.7	10.6
(1013) 3.1	(580) 4.3	(357) 4.9	(130) 6.4	(30) 5.7	(26) 2.2	EBIT/Interest		(1127) 2.2	(1332) 2.7
.0	.9	1.1	2.0	2.1	.0			.4	.6
3.2	2.4	2.8	3.8	11.9				3.0	3.5
(26) 1.2	(33) 1.5	(59) 1.5	(30) 2.3	(14) 4.1		Net Profit + Depr., Dep., Amort./Cur. Mat. L /T/D		(112) 1.6	(114) 1.7
.3	.9	1.0	1.2	1.9				.8	.8
.5	.6	.6	.6	.4	.2			.7	.7
11.8	3.1	1.7	1.4	2.6	1.1	Fixed/Worth		3.5	3.1
−.8	−5.6	15.3	4.8	−3.9	−8.6			−2.7	−3.4
1.8	1.1	.9	.9	1.3	.9			1.3	1.4
−268.0	6.5	3.2	2.6	4.5	2.7	Debt/Worth		7.8	7.1
−2.6	−10.7	42.6	9.1	−3.6	−10.7			−6.2	−6.1
409.6	176.5	100.6	94.3	35.1	67.0			105.2	146.3
(699) 100.0	(480) 47.7	(349) 31.9	(139) 30.1	(24) 10.8	(23) 14.6	% Profit Before Taxes/Tangible Net Worth		(863) 25.2	(1063) 36.4
11.5	8.2	2.3	6.4	−7.5	4.4			.4	2.2
79.3	38.4	22.4	22.7	21.0	17.2			26.2	33.5
12.4	9.5	6.7	7.7	8.9	4.7	% Profit Before Taxes/Total Assets		4.1	6.2
−3.3	.0	.0	1.6	1.2	−.3			−2.5	−1.6
161.8	36.0	29.1	17.5	68.0	45.6			48.4	56.9
43.7	15.9	12.2	6.3	10.9	10.2	Sales/Net Fixed Assets		19.2	20.0
17.8	6.9	3.4	2.5	3.6	3.2			7.2	7.8
23.1	9.3	5.2	3.4	5.6	17.0			14.4	14.1
11.8	4.9	3.0	2.2	2.5	3.2	Sales/Total Assets		6.0	6.5
6.0	2.4	1.5	1.3	1.5	1.3			2.4	2.7
.6	1.3	1.4	1.7	.9	.6			.8	.7
(837) 1.3	(555) 2.3	(386) 2.4	(143) 2.7	(28) 2.4	(15) 1.9	% Depr., Dep., Amort./Sales		(1186) 1.6	(1339) 1.6
2.4	4.7	5.1	4.5	3.9	4.3			3.3	3.0
15.3	11.9	9.5	7.6	6.9				17.1	16.4
(931) 25.8	(359) 24.8	(149) 25.3	(47) 20.3	(12) 24.3		% Officers', Directors', Owners' Comp/Sales		(726) 28.6	(874) 28.5
35.9	35.8	35.3	34.5	41.0				39.1	38.1
3837293M	4935480M	7511774M	15192288M	13554978M	48107958M	Net Sales ($)		17814452M	42359798M
274591M	761272M	2048797M	3209890M	2446680M	5223077M	Total Assets ($)		7062784M	9516407M

M = $ thousand   MM = $ million

© RMA 2005   See Pages 11 through 21 for Explanation of Ratios and Data

Comparative Historical Data

Current Data Sorted By Sales

			Type of Statement						
163	178	193	Unqualified	9	12	15	29	39	89
136	145	143	Reviewed	14	19	8	31	39	32
551	730	607	Compiled	111	174	99	131	69	23
670	872	1062	Tax Returns	269	403	131	135	83	41
538	671	792	Other	124	163	109	142	140	114
4/1/02- 3/31/03	4/1/03- 3/31/04	4/1/04- 3/31/05		347 (4/1-9/30/04)			2450 (10/1/04-3/31/05)		
ALL	ALL	ALL		0-1MM	1-3MM	3-5MM	5-10MM	10-25MM	25MM & OVER
2058	2596	2797	**NUMBER OF STATEMENTS**	527	771	362	468	370	299
%	%	%	**ASSETS**	%	%	%	%	%	%
25.1	26.9	27.3	Cash & Equivalents	26.5	30.1	31.4	27.1	24.5	19.9
11.6	11.0	12.1	Trade Receivables (net)	5.1	8.4	11.6	14.9	18.5	22.0
.8	.9	.9	Inventory	.5	1.4	.8	.9	.7	1.1
4.0	4.8	3.4	All Other Current	2.7	3.6	3.3	3.0	4.1	4.4
41.6	43.5	43.7	Total Current	34.8	43.4	47.0	45.9	47.8	47.4
43.7	41.8	40.2	Fixed Assets (net)	46.3	39.2	37.2	40.2	39.4	37.0
3.9	3.7	4.0	Intangibles (net)	3.7	4.3	4.9	3.3	3.2	4.6
10.9	11.0	12.1	All Other Non-Current	15.1	13.1	10.9	10.6	9.6	11.0
100.0	100.0	100.0	Total	100.0	100.0	100.0	100.0	100.0	100.0
			LIABILITIES						
23.5	22.6	21.5	Notes Payable-Short Term	29.1	28.1	21.4	17.1	13.5	8.5
8.1	9.0	8.1	Cur. Mat.-L/T/D	8.3	8.5	8.2	9.2	6.4	7.0
3.3	3.2	3.6	Trade Payables	1.9	3.1	3.7	4.1	3.7	6.8
.4	.5	.4	Income Taxes Payable	.2	.2	.5	.3	.7	1.3
28.6	28.1	28.9	All Other Current	22.7	29.4	28.9	35.0	31.5	26.3
63.9	63.4	62.6	Total Current	62.1	69.3	62.7	65.7	55.8	49.8
31.9	32.5	33.8	Long-Term Debt	42.0	39.7	29.7	29.7	25.8	25.5
.3	.2	.3	Deferred Taxes	.0	.2	.5	.3	.6	.8
5.7	6.3	4.7	All Other Non-Current	6.3	4.5	4.1	3.6	4.7	5.2
−1.8	−2.5	−1.5	Net Worth	−10.4	−13.6	3.0	.8	13.0	18.7
100.0	100.0	100.0	Total Liabilities & Net Worth	100.0	100.0	100.0	100.0	100.0	100.0
			INCOME DATA						
100.0	100.0	100.0	Net Sales	100.0	100.0	100.0	100.0	100.0	100.0
			Gross Profit						
91.0	90.1	89.7	Operating Expenses	80.9	90.6	90.9	92.5	93.8	92.3
9.0	9.9	10.3	Operating Profit	19.1	9.4	9.1	7.5	6.2	7.7
1.9	1.6	1.6	All Other Expenses (net)	5.6	1.1	.6	.5	−.4	1.0
7.1	8.3	8.7	Profit Before Taxes	13.6	8.3	8.5	7.0	6.6	6.7
			RATIOS						
1.8	2.0	1.9		2.1	1.9	2.0	1.8	1.9	1.9
.8	.8	.9	Current	.6	.6	.9	.9	1.0	1.1
.3	.3	.3		.2	.3	.4	.3	.4	.6
1.6	1.7	1.7		1.9	1.6	2.0	1.7	1.8	1.6
(2054) .7	(2589) .7	(2788) .8	Quick	(526) .6	(768) .7	(360) .8	(467) .8	(369) .9	(298) .9
.2	.2	.2		.1	.2	.3	.3	.4	.5
0 UND	0 UND	0 UND		0 UND	0 UND	0 UND	0 UND	0 UND	0 UND
0 UND	0 UND	0 UND	Sales/Receivables	0 UND	0 UND	0 UND	0 UND	0 UND	22 16.6
20 18.2	9 39.0	17 21.0		0 UND	0 UND	13 27.5	30 12.3	45 8.1	49 7.5
			Cost of Sales/Inventory						
			Cost of Sales/Payables						
25.2	21.9	23.7		25.0	33.3	23.5	29.4	14.7	15.3
−134.9	−134.5	−148.5	Sales/Working Capital	−35.9	−113.3	−149.0	−112.7	UND	172.7
−21.8	−20.9	−21.6		−6.7	−19.6	−31.4	−25.4	−39.0	−40.5
12.0	18.5	18.8		15.2	18.6	26.3	20.3	15.7	22.2
(1613) 2.7	(2004) 3.8	(2136) 4.1	EBIT/Interest	(322) 4.2	(570) 3.9	(305) 4.4	(381) 4.1	(308) 3.3	(250) 5.1
.2	.6	.7		.8	.3	.2	.9	.7	1.1
3.1	2.7	3.5			2.7	1.5	3.4	2.5	5.1
(159) 1.7	(173) 1.6	(166) 1.6	Net Profit + Depr., Dep., Amort./Cur. Mat. L/T/D	(20)	(11) 1.2	(17) 1.0	(46) 1.5	(63) 1.6	2.4
1.0	.9	.9			.5	.2	.3	1.0	1.3
.7	.7	.6		.4	.5	.6	.7	.6	.5
4.0	4.1	3.2	Fixed/Worth	3.9	5.0	3.4	4.2	2.3	1.9
−3.1	−2.1	−2.2		−1.8	−1.0	−1.3	−2.4	−7.7	47.9
1.4	1.3	1.2		1.2	1.1	1.2	1.5	1.2	1.5
9.2	11.4	9.0	Debt/Worth	7.6	25.6	12.2	12.5	6.0	4.7
−6.4	−5.0	−5.2		−3.9	−3.1	−4.2	−6.0	−14.1	−71.0
160.4	213.1	212.0		217.8	273.8	295.8	206.9	115.8	151.5
(1271) 36.1	(1549) 50.0	(1714) 53.2	% Profit Before Taxes/Tangible Net Worth	(326) 60.0	(423) 80.4	(209) 74.2	(288) 49.6	(248) 30.5	(220) 33.1
.8	4.3	6.6		13.5	5.1	9.7	9.9	.3	3.2
38.3	46.9	49.1		63.9	64.3	64.2	35.2	26.6	27.6
5.7	8.3	9.3	% Profit Before Taxes/Total Assets	10.9	14.7	9.8	8.6	5.4	7.2
−2.6	−1.1	−.8		−.8	−2.8	−1.2	−.4	−.8	.3
59.0	66.7	77.8		72.8	98.9	88.5	76.0	66.5	48.4
20.8	21.7	23.2	Sales/Net Fixed Assets	12.5	29.3	35.1	26.4	22.4	16.3
8.2	8.3	8.8		2.5	10.5	13.0	11.2	11.5	6.9
14.3	14.6	14.5		8.8	16.5	18.1	17.8	15.6	9.9
6.8	6.8	6.6	Sales/Total Assets	3.9	8.2	8.6	7.8	7.3	4.3
2.9	2.9	2.9		1.1	3.8	3.7	3.8	3.1	2.5
.9	.9	.9		1.3	.8	.8	.9	.9	1.0
(1627) 1.9	(1911) 1.9	(1964) 1.9	% Depr., Dep., Amort./Sales	(348) 3.5	(497) 1.6	(256) 1.6	(326) 1.9	(300) 1.8	(237) 1.9
3.7	3.8	3.8		13.6	3.4	3.0	3.6	2.9	2.9
15.4	16.8	14.0		16.5	12.8	13.1	17.4	13.9	12.1
(1097) 26.5	(1440) 27.5	(1506) 25.3	% Officers', Directors', Owners' Comp/Sales	(258) 24.3	(505) 22.5	(198) 27.5	(253) 29.7	(178) 24.5	(114) 26.5
37.0	36.8	35.8		34.0	33.9	39.0	40.2	38.0	35.5
66280356M	86067410M	93139771M	Net Sales ($)	286824M	1474533M	1397701M	3313479M	5732462M	80934772M
10699946M	14702814M	13964307M	Total Assets ($)	261746M	447449M	400319M	812191M	1419531M	10623071M

M = $ thousand   MM = $ million
See Pages 11 through 21 for Explanation of Ratios and Data

Current Data Sorted By Assets **Comparative Historical Data**

	0-500M	500M-2MM	2-10MM	10-50MM	50-100MM	100-250MM	Type of Statement	4/1/00-3/31/01 ALL	4/1/01-3/31/02 ALL
			1	1		1	Unqualified		
			1				Reviewed		
	7	2	3	1			Compiled		
	12	2	2				Tax Returns		
	2	3		1			Other		
				28 (10/1/04-3/31/05)					
	10 (4/1-9/30/04)								
NUMBER OF STATEMENTS	21	7	7	2		1		%	%
	%	%	%	%	%	%	**ASSETS**		
33.5						D	Cash & Equivalents	D	D
3.6						A	Trade Receivables (net)	A	A
.0						T	Inventory	T	T
5.7						A	All Other Current	A	A
42.7							Total Current		
36.3						N	Fixed Assets (net)	N	N
6.1						O	Intangibles (net)	O	O
14.9						T	All Other Non-Current	T	T
100.0							Total		
						A	**LIABILITIES**	A	A
31.2						V	Notes Payable-Short Term	V	V
10.9						A	Cur. Mat.-L/T/D	A	A
.4						I	Trade Payables	I	I
.0						L	Income Taxes Payable	L	L
46.3						A	All Other Current	A	A
88.9						B	Total Current	B	B
57.5						L	Long-Term Debt	L	L
.0						E	Deferred Taxes	E	E
7.9							All Other Non-Current		
-54.4							Net Worth		
100.0							Total Liabilities & Net Worth		
							INCOME DATA		
100.0							Net Sales		
							Gross Profit		
93.6							Operating Expenses		
6.4							Operating Profit		
1.7							All Other Expenses (net)		
4.7							Profit Before Taxes		
							RATIOS		
1.0							Current		
.5									
.1									
.9							Quick		
.4									
.1									
0 UND							Sales/Receivables		
0 UND									
0 UND									
							Cost of Sales/Inventory		
							Cost of Sales/Payables		
NM							Sales/Working Capital		
-61.7									
-16.3									
10.9							EBIT/Interest		
(16) 2.6									
-2.6									
							Net Profit + Depr., Dep., Amort./Cur. Mat. L /T/D		
1.6							Fixed/Worth		
-2.1									
-.2									
13.9							Debt/Worth		
-3.5									
-1.8									
							% Profit Before Taxes/Tangible Net Worth		
68.2							% Profit Before Taxes/Total Assets		
11.7									
-29.4									
140.1							Sales/Net Fixed Assets		
53.9									
23.6									
30.6							Sales/Total Assets		
14.1									
5.8									
.4							% Depr., Dep., Amort./Sales		
(13) 1.0									
1.3									
18.8							% Officers', Directors', Owners' Comp/Sales		
(16) 24.0									
35.1									
43738M	32944M	125512M	21345M		119979M		Net Sales ($)		
2942M	6672M	30045M	21051M		106514M		Total Assets ($)		

M = $ thousand   MM = $ million

See Pages 11 through 21 for Explanation of Ratios and Data

Comparative Historical Data   **Current Data Sorted By Sales**

			Type of Statement						
	4	3	Unqualified				1	1	1
1	1	1	Reviewed					1	
10	8	12	Compiled	2	5	3	3		2
10	14	14	Tax Returns	8	3		3		
5	4	8	Other	2		2	1		1
4/1/02-	4/1/03-	4/1/04-							
3/31/03	3/31/04	3/31/05		10 (4/1-9/30/04)			28 (10/1/04-3/31/05)		
ALL	ALL	ALL		0-1MM	1-3MM	3-5MM	5-10MM	10-25MM	25MM & OVER
26	31	38	**NUMBER OF STATEMENTS**	12	9	6	4	3	4
%	%	%	**ASSETS**	%	%	%	%	%	%
32.5	25.2	28.0	Cash & Equivalents	21.1					
13.5	12.1	6.1	Trade Receivables (net)	8.1					
.6	.1	.4	Inventory	.0					
3.5	3.8	5.3	All Other Current	8.5					
50.1	41.3	39.9	Total Current	37.7					
37.5	44.3	41.2	Fixed Assets (net)	36.9					
7.0	5.0	5.3	Intangibles (net)	16.1					
5.5	9.5	13.6	All Other Non-Current	9.3					
100.0	100.0	100.0	Total	100.0					
			LIABILITIES						
23.5	36.4	23.1	Notes Payable-Short Term	26.4					
9.2	6.1	7.2	Cur. Mat.-L/T/D	2.6					
2.1	4.0	.8	Trade Payables	.8					
.0	.1	.5	Income Taxes Payable	.0					
19.3	20.8	35.3	All Other Current	37.0					
54.0	67.4	66.9	Total Current	66.8					
21.2	29.6	44.2	Long-Term Debt	36.3					
.0	.0	.0	Deferred Taxes	.0					
19.8	13.8	4.4	All Other Non-Current	.0					
5.0	-10.8	-15.5	Net Worth	-3.1					
100.0	100.0	100.0	Total Liabilities & Net Worth	100.0					
			INCOME DATA						
100.0	100.0	100.0	Net Sales	100.0					
			Gross Profit						
83.1	87.9	87.9	Operating Expenses	80.0					
16.9	12.1	12.1	Operating Profit	20.0					
3.4	2.8	3.9	All Other Expenses (net)	10.9					
13.5	9.4	8.1	Profit Before Taxes	9.2					
			RATIOS						
6.7	2.1	1.3		2.5					
1.4	.5	.7	Current	.5					
.4	.2	.2		.1					
6.3	1.8	1.2		1.2					
1.1	.4	.5	Quick	.5					
.4	.2	.2		.0					
0 UND	0 UND	0 UND		0 UND					
0 UND	0 UND	0 UND	Sales/Receivables	0 UND					
6 65.8	35 10.3	4 88.3		0 UND					
			Cost of Sales/Inventory						
			Cost of Sales/Payables						
10.6	11.4	76.1		35.9					
39.2	-41.2	-63.6	Sales/Working Capital	-15.1					
-23.3	-13.8	-16.3		-6.9					
135.3	54.3	9.5							
(20) 11.0	(22) 2.9	(23) 2.8	EBIT/Interest						
1.7	-.6	-2.2							
			Net Profit + Depr., Dep., Amort./Cur. Mat. L/T/D						
.4	.3	1.0		.3					
1.8	6.5	7.1	Fixed/Worth	-25.2					
-1.6	-1.0	-.8		-.4					
.4	1.0	1.7		3.0					
4.0	121.3	80.8	Debt/Worth	-26.6					
-4.1	-2.4	-2.6		-2.3					
241.1	499.1	552.4	% Profit Before Taxes/Tangible						
(15) 126.9	(16) 30.4	(20) 44.8	Net Worth						
25.7	-6.3	6.0							
118.8	76.5	43.8	% Profit Before Taxes/Total	19.3					
21.6	3.0	10.6	Assets	3.9					
.7	-3.0	-1.8		-8.0					
39.3	42.1	73.1		83.9					
18.5	20.8	37.5	Sales/Net Fixed Assets	42.0					
10.0	8.3	10.8		9.0					
12.8	14.0	15.6		12.6					
6.4	9.5	9.4	Sales/Total Assets	4.3					
2.4	2.6	1.9		.4					
.7	.7	.8							
(19) 2.1	(25) 2.4	(26) 1.2	% Depr., Dep., Amort./Sales						
4.8	3.5	3.5							
10.8	9.5	16.5	% Officers', Directors',						
(16) 22.7	(14) 22.9	(22) 24.2	Owners' Comp/Sales						
30.7	33.1	35.3							
1036650M	204516M	343518M	Net Sales ($)	6373M	16615M	23877M	29107M	53895M	213651M
234435M	90311M	167224M	Total Assets ($)	7201M	11615M	13585M	1432M	18802M	114589M

© RMA 2005

M = $ thousand   MM = $ million
See Pages 11 through 21 for Explanation of Ratios and Data

HEALTH CARE—Offices of Dentists NAICS 621210 (SIC 8021)

	Current Data Sorted By Assets						Type of Statement	Comparative Historical Data	
	3	2		6	1	3	Unqualified	10	11
	2	5	1	1	1	1	Reviewed	6	8
	114	38	4	1	1	1	Compiled	119	110
	355	52	5		2		Tax Returns	148	177
	100	35	8	4	1	6	Other	88	115
		68 (4/1-9/30/04)			682 (10/1/04-3/31/05)			4/1/00- 3/31/01	4/1/01- 3/31/02
	0-500M	500M-2MM	2-10MM	10-50MM	50-100MM	100-250MM		ALL	ALL
	574	132	18	11	5	10	NUMBER OF STATEMENTS	371	421
	%	%	%	%	%	%	ASSETS	%	%
	25.1	15.6	14.9	13.2		22.6	Cash & Equivalents	20.7	19.8
	4.3	10.9	8.3	16.8		7.9	Trade Receivables (net)	8.1	8.0
	.3	.4	.4	5.6		.5	Inventory	.7	.7
	2.5	1.5	1.2	3.6		2.7	All Other Current	3.4	2.8
	32.2	28.4	24.8	39.3		33.7	Total Current	33.0	31.4
	42.6	44.3	52.6	24.6		37.4	Fixed Assets (net)	46.3	46.7
	14.9	16.4	14.7	15.5		20.4	Intangibles (net)	12.5	12.2
	10.3	10.8	7.8	20.7		8.4	All Other Non-Current	8.2	9.8
	100.0	100.0	100.0	100.0		100.0	Total	100.0	100.0
							LIABILITIES		
	15.8	9.5	5.3	1.9		14.8	Notes Payable-Short Term	12.9	15.6
	8.8	5.6	4.4	5.1		7.8	Cur. Mat.-L/T/D	8.7	11.9
	2.8	3.4	2.5	7.0		1.2	Trade Payables	2.3	2.8
	.2	.0	.1	.3		.0	Income Taxes Payable	1.3	.4
	21.9	8.4	10.4	32.0		14.5	All Other Current	19.9	22.5
	49.6	27.0	22.6	46.3		38.3	Total Current	45.1	53.3
	44.7	46.5	46.4	15.4		37.1	Long-Term Debt	36.5	46.4
	.0	.2	.1	1.0		.0	Deferred Taxes	.1	.2
	4.1	3.8	2.2	14.0		4.9	All Other Non-Current	13.6	9.3
	1.7	22.6	28.8	23.3		19.7	Net Worth	4.7	-9.2
	100.0	100.0	100.0	100.0		100.0	Total Liabilities & Net Worth	100.0	100.0
							INCOME DATA		
	100.0	100.0	100.0	100.0		100.0	Net Sales	100.0	100.0
							Gross Profit		
	89.1	85.7	88.5	97.7		83.4	Operating Expenses	89.2	89.0
	10.9	14.3	11.5	2.3		16.6	Operating Profit	10.8	11.0
	1.3	3.8	2.4	2.0		1.9	All Other Expenses (net)	1.9	1.9
	9.7	10.5	9.1	.3		14.6	Profit Before Taxes	8.9	9.1
							RATIOS		
	1.9	3.0	3.9	1.6		4.2		1.9	1.8
	.8	.9	1.1	.9		2.1	Current	.9	.6
	.2	.2	.7	.6		.1		.2	.2
	1.9	2.8	3.9	1.4		2.5		1.8	1.6
(571)	.6	(131) .8	1.0	.7		.9	Quick	(370) .7	(417) .5
	.2	.2	.5	.4		.1		.2	.2
0 UND	0 UND	0 UND	0 UND	15 24.3		0 UND		0 UND	0 UND
0 UND	0 UND	0 UND	0 UND	22 16.7		0 UND	Sales/Receivables	0 UND	0 UND
0 UND	26 14.2	32 11.5	46 7.9			0 UND		0 UND	0 UND
							Cost of Sales/Inventory		
							Cost of Sales/Payables		
	38.0	8.3	15.3	5.7		5.2		29.8	32.9
	-90.4	-64.8	NM	-187.6		48.8	Sales/Working Capital	-117.1	-65.9
	-18.7	-11.3	-16.3	-13.4		-21.9		-17.9	-14.4
	18.9	15.3	14.1					10.7	12.6
(429)	4.3	(113) 4.3	(17) 6.3				EBIT/Interest	(299) 3.1	(353) 3.1
	1.0	1.4	1.2					.9	1.0
							Net Profit + Depr., Dep.,	4.2	7.4
							Amort./Cur. Mat. L /T/D	(24) 1.8	(19) 2.5
								1.1	.6
	.9	.9	1.3	.4		.4		1.0	1.1
	48.8	7.4	5.0	1.6		.7	Fixed/Worth	7.0	16.0
	-1.0	-1.9	NM	1.7		-8.2		-1.7	-1.3
	1.5	1.2	1.3	.7		.6		1.5	1.7
	-69.5	13.3	5.2	3.8		1.1	Debt/Worth	12.9	34.2
	-2.6	-4.1	NM	7.2		-10.1		-3.9	-3.0
	406.0	108.6	92.5				% Profit Before Taxes/Tangible	190.0	252.2
(283)	123.4	(77) 52.5	(14) 31.7				Net Worth	(206) 59.0	(226) 74.4
	29.8	7.1	1.3					2.1	8.8
	77.3	36.9	30.3	11.0		113.3	% Profit Before Taxes/Total	49.2	58.4
	22.0	13.1	9.7	1.0		77.8	Assets	10.6	12.3
	.0	1.1	.4	-1.5		23.9		-.2	.0
	43.5	19.7	13.7	10.2		27.2		26.9	30.3
	18.9	7.8	3.4	9.0		13.6	Sales/Net Fixed Assets	12.6	13.5
	8.6	2.8	1.5	6.2		11.3		5.8	5.8
	10.7	3.6	3.0	2.7		9.8		8.7	9.0
	5.9	2.1	1.9	2.0		3.9	Sales/Total Assets	4.4	5.0
	3.3	1.3	1.0	1.5		2.6		2.3	2.7
	1.1	1.9	1.6	3.0				1.1	1.1
(362)	2.4	(97) 3.7	(15) 3.2	(10) 3.7			% Depr., Dep., Amort./Sales	(288) 2.5	(333) 2.4
	4.6	6.6	4.5	6.5				4.7	4.5
	14.0	11.1					% Officers', Directors',	15.4	15.7
(442)	22.0	(81) 16.7					Owners' Comp/Sales	(244) 23.2	(298) 22.6
	29.1	24.9						30.9	30.9
	733435M	355261M	165599M	1137992M	3533802M	7390883M	Net Sales ($)	5062927M	9027610M
	115808M	116238M	73297M	327256M	385461M	1433940M	Total Assets ($)	1924013M	2506276M

M = $ thousand   MM = $ million
See Pages 11 through 21 for Explanation of Ratios and Data

Comparative Historical Data　　　　　　　　　　　　　Current Data Sorted By Sales

	13	14	15	Type of Statement	0-1MM	1-3MM	3-5MM	5-10MM	10-25MM	25MM & OVER
	13	14	15	Unqualified	4				1	10
	10	17	8	Reviewed	1	4		3		3
	153	196	159	Compiled	64	64	12	12	4	3
	295	403	414	Tax Returns	211	169	23	8	1	2
	116	136	154	Other	62	57	12	9	2	12
	4/1/02-3/31/03 ALL	4/1/03-3/31/04 ALL	4/1/04-3/31/05 ALL		68 (4/1-9/30/04) 0-1MM	1-3MM	3-5MM	682 (10/1/04-3/31/05) 5-10MM	10-25MM	25MM & OVER
NUMBER OF STATEMENTS	587	766	750		342	294	47	32	8	27
	%	%	%	**ASSETS**	%	%	%	%	%	%
	20.4	22.3	23.0	Cash & Equivalents	23.1	23.2	27.9	15.2		21.0
	6.8	6.8	5.7	Trade Receivables (net)	4.3	5.6	7.6	13.8		10.6
	.6	.4	.4	Inventory	.2	.5	.2	.4		2.5
	2.4	2.2	2.4	All Other Current	2.4	2.1	2.2	2.9		6.2
	30.2	31.9	31.6	Total Current	30.0	31.5	38.0	32.3		40.3
	47.4	45.3	42.8	Fixed Assets (net)	43.3	41.3	46.9	50.1		32.1
	13.4	12.8	15.2	Intangibles (net)	17.4	15.4	3.9	9.8		15.8
	9.0	10.0	10.4	All Other Non-Current	9.3	11.8	11.3	7.8		11.8
	100.0	100.0	100.0	Total	100.0	100.0	100.0	100.0		100.0
				LIABILITIES						
	14.6	13.3	14.2	Notes Payable-Short Term	14.3	14.3	12.8	17.1		8.7
	9.9	7.7	8.0	Cur. Mat.-L/T/D	6.2	10.6	8.0	8.4		5.0
	2.7	2.6	3.0	Trade Payables	2.5	2.6	4.8	8.1		4.7
	.7	.4	.2	Income Taxes Payable	.2	.1	.1	.1		.2
	19.8	19.0	19.2	All Other Current	18.8	18.4	26.1	20.8		20.6
	47.6	43.1	44.6	Total Current	42.0	45.9	51.8	54.5		39.2
	42.7	41.0	44.2	Long-Term Debt	47.8	44.6	35.4	36.0		22.2
	.1	.1	.1	Deferred Taxes	.0	.0	.3	.0		.4
	5.8	5.7	4.1	All Other Non-Current	4.6	4.0	1.3	1.7		7.6
	3.8	10.1	7.0	Net Worth	5.5	5.5	11.4	7.7		30.6
	100.0	100.0	100.0	Total Liabilities & Net Worth	100.0	100.0	100.0	100.0		100.0
				INCOME DATA						
	100.0	100.0	100.0	Net Sales	100.0	100.0	100.0	100.0		100.0
				Gross Profit						
	89.1	88.2	88.5	Operating Expenses	86.9	89.0	91.4	93.4		90.7
	10.9	11.8	11.5	Operating Profit	13.1	11.0	8.6	6.6		9.3
	2.3	2.2	1.8	All Other Expenses (net)	2.8	.9	.7	.2		1.6
	8.6	9.6	9.7	Profit Before Taxes	10.3	10.1	7.9	6.3		7.7
				RATIOS						
	1.7	1.9	2.1	Current	2.1	2.3	1.5	1.6		2.6
	.7	.7	.8		.8	.8	.6	.5		1.6
	.2	.3	.2		.2	.2	.3	.2		.6
	1.6	1.8	2.0	Quick	2.0	2.1	1.4	1.6		1.9
(584)	.6	(763) .6	(746) .7		(339) .8	.7	.6	(31) .4		1.0
	.2	.2	.2		.2	.1	.3	.2		.3
	0 UND	0 UND	0 UND	Sales/Receivables	0 UND	0 UND	0 UND	0 UND		0 UND
	0 UND	0 UND	0 UND		0 UND	0 UND	0 UND	0 UND		9 41.8
	0 UND	0 UND	0 UND		0 UND	0 UND	0 UND	7 49.5		34 10.8
				Cost of Sales/Inventory						
				Cost of Sales/Payables						
	28.0	28.6	26.8	Sales/Working Capital	23.1	30.6	64.9	55.0		5.7
	-71.1	-85.8	-99.2		-106.0	-97.5	-62.8	-43.2		46.3
	-16.5	-18.4	-17.2		-13.4	-19.6	-28.7	-19.5		-37.6
	12.3	15.7	18.4	EBIT/Interest	13.8	21.2	25.5	24.1		40.0
(483)	3.5	(606) 3.8	(581) 4.5		(248) 3.9	(237) 6.0	(39) 2.4	(27) 7.4	(23)	8.2
	1.0	.9	1.0		1.0	1.1	.3	1.8		1.5
	8.4	6.0	4.9	Net Profit + Depr., Dep., Amort./Cur. Mat. L/T/D						
(27)	2.4	(26) 2.1	(18) 2.1							
	1.3	.7	.5							
	1.3	1.1	.9	Fixed/Worth	1.0	.9	.8	.6		.4
	17.1	10.4	10.8		UND	10.1	5.1	8.4		.8
	-1.3	-1.4	-1.2		-.9	-1.1	-2.0	-5.2		1.7
	1.8	1.5	1.4	Debt/Worth	1.8	1.3	1.1	2.1		.7
	59.0	29.4	71.6		-20.5	26.2	8.9	28.9		1.4
	-3.3	-3.3	-2.9		-2.5	-2.7	-4.6	-6.4		7.2
	266.5	221.1	292.6	% Profit Before Taxes/Tangible Net Worth	327.3	349.7	182.9	253.3		145.1
(309)	75.2	(425) 88.7	(394) 95.9		(160) 104.2	(156) 107.4	(30) 37.6	(20) 22.1	(21)	45.3
	13.2	13.7	16.9		36.4	23.5	-.6	.0		3.6
	56.9	63.0	67.3	% Profit Before Taxes/Total Assets	59.7	77.6	67.4	46.1		90.0
	13.5	15.5	18.1		17.7	24.0	6.1	12.8		14.6
	.0	.0	.3		.9	.3	-2.9	1.2		.8
	33.0	35.0	38.3	Sales/Net Fixed Assets	40.1	36.2	43.5	44.0		24.7
	12.8	13.9	15.3		11.7	18.7	25.9	23.9		10.2
	5.9	6.5	6.9		4.6	9.2	9.2	12.4		7.4
	9.4	8.9	8.9	Sales/Total Assets	7.4	10.1	16.5	13.0		6.0
	4.5	4.8	4.7		3.4	5.9	8.5	6.2		2.7
	2.4	2.7	2.5		2.0	3.4	3.5	3.9		1.9
	1.4	1.3	1.2	% Depr., Dep., Amort./Sales	1.7	1.0	.8	.8		.9
(439)	2.8	(543) 2.7	(491) 2.6		(218) 3.4	(186) 2.2	(39) 1.9	(23) 1.5	(18)	2.8
	5.1	5.2	5.1		8.1	3.9	2.8	2.5		5.0
	14.2	14.8	13.6	% Officers', Directors', Owners' Comp/Sales	12.9	13.6	21.9	8.2		19.3
(406)	20.0	(556) 22.1	(543) 21.4		(248) 20.7	(229) 20.5	(32) 28.1	(19) 24.7	(11)	21.9
	27.9	29.6	28.9		27.8	29.2	35.4	29.6		32.1
	24916966M	12729832M	13316972M	Net Sales ($)	211245M	471470M	183033M	215827M	133193M	12102204M
	3764184M	2651934M	2452000M	Total Assets ($)	84450M	106264M	37864M	42593M	24519M	2156310M

© RMA 2005

M = $ thousand　MM = $ million
See Pages 11 through 21 for Explanation of Ratios and Data

HEALTH CARE—Offices of Chiropractors   NAICS 621310 (SIC 8041)

Current Data Sorted By Assets | **Comparative Historical Data**

Type of Statement	0-500M	500M-2MM	2-10MM	10-50MM	50-100MM	100-250MM		4/1/00-3/31/01 ALL		4/1/01-3/31/02 ALL
Unqualified										
Reviewed	3									
Compiled	14		1					19		24
Tax Returns	44	7		1	1	1		22		15
Other	19	2	1					9		11
		3 (4/1-9/30/04)		90 (10/1/04-3/31/05)						
NUMBER OF STATEMENTS	80	9	2			1		50		50
	%	%	%	%	%	%		%		%
ASSETS										
Cash & Equivalents	25.9							19.2		22.1
Trade Receivables (net)	6.7							7.8		12.5
Inventory	2.2							.5		.7
All Other Current	5.5							6.1		2.6
Total Current	40.3							33.6		37.9
Fixed Assets (net)	42.2							39.1		40.7
Intangibles (net)	7.1							13.5		12.2
All Other Non-Current	10.4							13.8		9.3
Total	100.0							100.0		100.0
LIABILITIES										
Notes Payable-Short Term	17.0							18.8		16.5
Cur. Mat.-L/T/D	9.6							13.9		6.4
Trade Payables	2.3							5.1		1.3
Income Taxes Payable	.1							.2		.3
All Other Current	26.2							17.7		78.0
Total Current	55.2							55.7		102.6
Long-Term Debt	33.4							26.7		39.8
Deferred Taxes	.4							.4		.5
All Other Non-Current	3.8							14.5		3.2
Net Worth	7.2							2.7		−46.1
Total Liabilities & Net Worth	100.0							100.0		100.0
INCOME DATA										
Net Sales	100.0							100.0		100.0
Gross Profit										
Operating Expenses	86.3							91.5		85.2
Operating Profit	13.7							8.5		14.8
All Other Expenses (net)	2.1							.5		2.0
Profit Before Taxes	11.6							8.0		12.8
RATIOS										
Current	2.9 / .8 / .3							2.1 / .7 / .1		2.5 / .9 / .3
Quick	(79) 2.6 / .6 / .2							(49) 1.8 / .6 / .1		(49) 2.5 / .8 / .2
Sales/Receivables	0 UND / 0 UND / 0 UND							0 UND / 0 UND / 0 UND		0 UND / 0 UND / 0 UND
Cost of Sales/Inventory										
Cost of Sales/Payables										
Sales/Working Capital	9.3 / −276.7 / −10.7							37.5 / −44.7 / −8.0		16.3 / UND / −11.8
EBIT/Interest	(58) 27.4 / 3.6 / .3							(36) 14.6 / 2.0 / .7		(36) 16.1 / 4.8 / 1.2
Net Profit + Depr., Dep., Amort./Cur. Mat. L/T/D										
Fixed/Worth	.4 / 7.1 / −1.2							.4 / 2.3 / −1.5		.5 / 2.5 / −1.6
Debt/Worth	.7 / 11.0 / −4.0							1.2 / 9.1 / −2.5		1.3 / 7.1 / −3.4
% Profit Before Taxes/Tangible Net Worth	(48) 554.0 / 83.0 / 13.6							(29) 268.6 / 44.8 / −.6		(33) 243.9 / 85.7 / 28.4
% Profit Before Taxes/Total Assets	67.3 / 19.3 / −3.7							41.0 / 6.4 / −2.6		49.8 / 19.3 / .8
Sales/Net Fixed Assets	42.7 / 16.5 / 5.2							63.0 / 16.4 / 7.1		54.0 / 10.4 / 5.3
Sales/Total Assets	8.1 / 4.0 / 2.1							7.6 / 4.6 / 2.9		5.4 / 2.9 / 1.6
% Depr., Dep., Amort./Sales	(55) 1.3 / 2.6 / 5.0							(34) .9 / 2.2 / 4.7		(36) 1.1 / 2.2 / 4.4
% Officers', Directors', Owners' Comp/Sales	(50) 11.3 / 17.5 / 28.7							(31) 13.4 / 23.0 / 30.7		(26) 14.0 / 26.4 / 34.2
Net Sales ($)	52765M	8765M	6455M	262721M	319341M			60801M		65934M
Total Assets ($)	12153M	6319M	4490M	12918M	116466M			97513M		46758M

M = $ thousand   MM = $ million

See Pages 11 through 21 for Explanation of Ratios and Data

Comparative Historical Data				Current Data Sorted By Sales					
1	1	3	**Type of Statement**						
1			Unqualified	3					
			Reviewed						
17	20	15	Compiled	9	4	2			
44	44	53	Tax Returns	41	9	1			2
20	26	22	Other	19	3				
4/1/02-3/31/03 ALL	4/1/03-3/31/04 ALL	4/1/04-3/31/05 ALL		3 (4/1-9/30/04)			90 (10/1/04-3/31/05)		
				0-1MM	1-3MM	3-5MM	5-10MM	10-25MM	25MM & OVER
83	91	93	**NUMBER OF STATEMENTS**	72	16	3			2
%	%	%	**ASSETS**	%	%	%	%	%	%
24.0	21.2	23.6	Cash & Equivalents	21.1	32.1				
15.2	12.5	8.9	Trade Receivables (net)	9.0	6.9		D	D	
.6	.9	2.0	Inventory	2.0	2.3		A	A	
2.7	5.4	4.8	All Other Current	4.3	8.3		T	T	
42.6	40.0	39.2	Total Current	36.4	49.6		A	A	
42.1	37.0	41.2	Fixed Assets (net)	42.2	38.9				
7.2	13.3	8.5	Intangibles (net)	8.8	4.2		N	N	
8.2	9.7	11.2	All Other Non-Current	12.6	7.3		O	O	
100.0	100.0	100.0	Total	100.0	100.0		T	T	
			LIABILITIES				A	A	
36.1	20.0	15.1	Notes Payable-Short Term	15.2	18.2		V	V	
6.7	10.7	9.6	Cur. Mat.-L/T/D	7.6	20.6		A	A	
5.7	1.8	2.5	Trade Payables	2.5	3.3		I	I	
.8	.3	.1	Income Taxes Payable	.1	.0		L	L	
20.9	13.1	23.5	All Other Current	14.3	65.3		A	A	
70.2	46.0	50.7	Total Current	39.6	107.4		B	B	
29.3	38.0	36.9	Long-Term Debt	35.6	24.4		L	L	
.3	.4	.3	Deferred Taxes	.4	.0		E	E	
7.0	13.1	4.8	All Other Non-Current	4.2	2.3				
-6.8	2.6	7.2	Net Worth	20.1	-34.1				
100.0	100.0	100.0	Total Liabilities & Net Worth	100.0	100.0				
			INCOME DATA						
100.0	100.0	100.0	Net Sales	100.0	100.0				
			Gross Profit						
85.1	84.2	86.7	Operating Expenses	85.7	92.4				
14.9	15.8	13.3	Operating Profit	14.3	7.6				
2.7	2.6	2.8	All Other Expenses (net)	3.4	.3				
12.1	13.2	10.5	Profit Before Taxes	10.9	7.3				
			RATIOS						
5.3	2.8	3.7		4.9	2.4				
1.2	1.1	.9	Current	1.0	.6				
.2	.3	.3		.3	.3				
3.6	2.5	3.3		4.6	2.4				
1.2	1.0	(92) .7	Quick	(71) .7	.6				
.2	.2	.2		.2	.1				
0 UND	0 UND	0 UND		0 UND	0 UND				
0 UND	0 UND	0 UND	Sales/Receivables	0 UND	0 UND				
18 20.3	0 UND	2 173.8		3 137.6	1 482.5				
			Cost of Sales/Inventory						
			Cost of Sales/Payables						
9.5	10.7	8.9		7.1	16.4				
112.0	201.5	-399.0	Sales/Working Capital	UND	-19.1				
-8.8	-23.4	-10.7		-9.8	-11.1				
28.3	23.6	19.0		27.7	10.1				
(62) 4.5	(69) 7.5	(69) 3.5	EBIT/Interest	(51) 3.7	(15) .6				
.7	1.0	-.2		.4	-5.7				
			Net Profit + Depr., Dep., Amort./Cur. Mat. L/T/D						
.4	.5	.3		.2	.9				
2.0	2.6	2.7	Fixed/Worth	3.0	NM				
-1.5	-1.1	-1.2		-1.8	-.4				
.7	1.1	.7		.4	1.2				
5.2	11.5	7.0	Debt/Worth	7.4	NM				
-2.7	-3.6	-4.0		-5.3	-2.0				
295.4	282.0	265.9	% Profit Before Taxes/Tangible Net Worth	185.5					
(53) 121.0	(52) 132.5	(58) 70.8		(46) 63.6					
25.4	13.6	5.4		5.4					
104.2	96.9	58.7	% Profit Before Taxes/Total Assets	60.1	42.3				
28.5	33.9	13.8		12.0	.3				
2.3	.7	-4.1		-1.7	-28.3				
35.3	38.4	40.0		25.6	47.8				
14.7	15.3	16.1	Sales/Net Fixed Assets	11.8	29.0				
6.5	7.2	4.8		4.6	9.1				
8.8	7.0	7.5		6.4	17.5				
4.0	4.1	3.4	Sales/Total Assets	2.9	8.1				
1.9	2.0	1.8		1.5	4.3				
1.4	1.0	1.0		1.3	.7				
(52) 2.8	(60) 2.0	(64) 2.3	% Depr., Dep., Amort./Sales	(49) 2.9	(12) 1.9				
4.9	3.2	4.9		5.9	4.0				
7.9	12.0	12.0	% Officers', Directors', Owners' Comp/Sales	12.3	8.3				
(50) 13.7	(66) 18.3	(56) 18.1		(40) 19.7	(13) 16.8				
25.7	28.8	29.1		29.6	24.2				
706434M	1813990M	650047M	Net Sales ($)	29859M	27020M	11106M			582062M
207685M	328800M	152346M	Total Assets ($)	13590M	6244M	3128M			129384M

Current Data Sorted By Assets   Comparative Historical Data

Type of Statement	0-500M	500M-2MM	2-10MM	10-50MM	50-100MM	100-250MM		ALL	ALL
Unqualified		1	2			1		2	3
Reviewed	1	3	5	1				4	8
Compiled	31	18	4					33	48
Tax Returns	68	16	2			1		41	37
Other	26	16	8	2	1	1		26	34
		16 (4/1-9/30/04)		191 (10/1/04-3/31/05)				4/1/00-3/31/01	4/1/01-3/31/02
NUMBER OF STATEMENTS	126	54	21	3		3		106	130
ASSETS	%	%	%	%	%	%		%	%
Cash & Equivalents	18.9	13.2	10.9					14.3	13.2
Trade Receivables (net)	6.1	13.5	19.8					13.7	11.8
Inventory	15.2	9.9	7.5					14.4	14.1
All Other Current	2.1	3.7	2.2					2.2	2.7
Total Current	42.3	40.1	40.3					44.7	41.8
Fixed Assets (net)	41.9	41.4	44.4					44.1	43.3
Intangibles (net)	6.1	10.2	2.4					4.2	9.5
All Other Non-Current	9.8	8.2	12.9					6.9	5.4
Total	100.0	100.0	100.0					100.0	100.0
LIABILITIES									
Notes Payable-Short Term	16.2	10.3	12.4					10.7	11.4
Cur. Mat.-L/T/D	9.6	8.2	8.4					7.2	8.8
Trade Payables	5.8	5.5	11.3					9.1	6.6
Income Taxes Payable	.1	.9	.8					.8	.1
All Other Current	17.2	11.2	11.8					15.4	20.9
Total Current	48.9	36.1	44.8					43.3	47.7
Long-Term Debt	36.2	40.0	28.9					37.5	31.8
Deferred Taxes	.1	.1	.9					.4	.2
All Other Non-Current	8.3	5.0	3.7					3.4	7.1
Net Worth	6.5	18.8	21.7					15.4	13.0
Total Liabilities & Net Worth	100.0	100.0	100.0					100.0	100.0
INCOME DATA									
Net Sales	100.0	100.0	100.0					100.0	100.0
Gross Profit									
Operating Expenses	89.9	91.2	93.3					92.0	90.9
Operating Profit	10.1	8.8	6.7					8.0	9.1
All Other Expenses (net)	2.1	1.4	.4					1.5	1.8
Profit Before Taxes	8.0	7.4	6.3					6.5	7.2
RATIOS									
Current	2.2	2.4	1.6					2.4	2.1
	1.2	1.4	1.0					1.1	1.2
	.4	.7	.3					.5	.6
Quick	1.4	1.4	1.4					1.7	1.3
	(123) .6	.8	.7					(105) .6	(128) .6
	.2	.3	.3					.2	.3
Sales/Receivables	0 UND	0 UND	0 UND					0 UND	0 UND
	0 UND	6 62.0	22 17.0					1 341.8	4 85.7
	4 101.0	31 11.7	35 10.3					28 13.0	22 16.7
Cost of Sales/Inventory									
Cost of Sales/Payables									
Sales/Working Capital	21.2	10.1	20.4					14.0	15.6
	220.3	36.7	-189.7					124.3	61.8
	-25.6	-60.0	-8.9					-22.7	-30.1
EBIT/Interest	18.1	8.6	18.6					7.6	14.9
	(101) 4.0	(49) 2.9	(20) 8.3					(93) 3.1	(114) 3.1
	.9	.4	1.5					.9	.7
Net Profit + Depr., Dep., Amort./Cur. Mat. L/T/D									
Fixed/Worth	.9	.7	1.0					.7	.5
	3.9	5.6	2.1					3.6	2.5
	-2.2	-2.1	NM					-3.0	-7.8
Debt/Worth	1.2	1.2	1.7					1.7	1.0
	7.1	5.8	3.4					7.2	3.2
	-5.1	-13.3	NM					-6.7	-11.8
% Profit Before Taxes/Tangible Net Worth	387.0	132.2	137.8					124.1	137.7
	(81) 108.1	(33) 34.1	(16) 48.0					(65) 37.2	(84) 53.7
	7.1	1.4	24.5					3.8	14.8
% Profit Before Taxes/Total Assets	78.1	21.1	25.1					24.9	36.3
	15.0	8.6	13.1					8.6	9.5
	.0	-.7	2.7					-.4	-.9
Sales/Net Fixed Assets	42.0	22.2	14.7					28.9	28.5
	17.4	12.6	11.2					12.6	14.1
	9.5	6.5	4.2					4.9	6.6
Sales/Total Assets	12.4	5.6	5.4					7.8	7.0
	6.4	3.3	3.7					4.6	4.7
	3.2	2.1	2.1					2.4	2.7
% Depr., Dep., Amort./Sales	1.3	2.3	1.8					1.5	1.4
	(91) 2.5	(41) 3.1	(20) 2.6					(92) 2.4	(105) 2.6
	4.8	4.6	3.5					3.9	4.1
% Officers', Directors', Owners' Comp/Sales	9.8	7.6						9.4	11.6
	(77) 17.9	(33) 17.0						(76) 18.5	(86) 19.9
	28.2	24.3						27.9	28.9
Net Sales ($)	165110M	215836M	351019M	104789M		4081257M		381088M	1311675M
Total Assets ($)	24421M	48237M	87462M	44252M		542619M		134737M	374327M

© RMA 2005

M = $ thousand   MM = $ million
See Pages 11 through 21 for Explanation of Ratios and Data

Comparative Historical Data					Current Data Sorted By Sales					
9	5	4	Type of Statement Unqualified			1		1	1	1
10	9	10	Reviewed		3		2	3	1
48	56	53	Compiled	14	25	8	4	1	1
65	88	87	Tax Returns	38	33	9	5	1	1
40	42	53	Other	20	13	6	3	7	4
4/1/02-3/31/03 ALL	4/1/03-3/31/04 ALL	4/1/04-3/31/05 ALL		16 (4/1-9/30/04)			191 (10/1/04-3/31/05)			
				0-1MM	1-3MM	3-5MM	5-10MM	10-25MM	25MM & OVER
172	200	207	NUMBER OF STATEMENTS	72	75	24	15	13	8
%	%	%	ASSETS	%	%	%	%	%	%
16.6	17.5	16.7	Cash & Equivalents	10.6	21.1	24.9	18.9	6.6	
10.2	10.9	9.5	Trade Receivables (net)	7.3	9.0	10.1	11.0	19.2	
11.4	13.3	12.7	Inventory	19.0	11.6	5.5	7.1	6.4	
2.6	2.6	2.5	All Other Current	1.8	2.3	2.5	3.3	.2	
40.7	44.4	41.4	Total Current	38.6	43.9	43.0	40.2	32.4	
44.5	40.2	42.1	Fixed Assets (net)	43.0	40.8	40.5	44.6	51.6	
7.6	6.6	6.9	Intangibles (net)	9.0	5.4	6.3	8.5	3.4	
7.2	8.9	9.6	All Other Non-Current	9.4	9.9	10.3	6.6	12.7	
100.0	100.0	100.0	Total	100.0	100.0	100.0	100.0	100.0	
			LIABILITIES						
15.6	15.2	14.5	Notes Payable-Short Term	15.1	12.7	21.5	8.2	12.0	
9.1	7.0	9.0	Cur. Mat.-L/T/D	7.7	9.7	9.1	16.0	6.0	
6.0	7.3	6.4	Trade Payables	5.2	7.1	2.9	7.7	10.5	
.5	.4	.4	Income Taxes Payable	.0	.3	.4	1.8	1.1	
12.9	13.5	14.9	All Other Current	10.3	17.1	18.3	18.3	17.1	
44.0	43.4	45.1	Total Current	38.2	47.0	52.1	52.1	46.7	
34.3	29.1	36.0	Long-Term Debt	50.1	27.8	26.2	41.0	32.5	
.2	.1	.1	Deferred Taxes	.1	.0	.0	.7	.7	
4.6	11.8	6.8	All Other Non-Current	7.4	9.9	.7	5.7	.9	
16.8	15.5	12.0	Net Worth	4.2	15.2	21.0	.5	19.2	
100.0	100.0	100.0	Total Liabilities & Net Worth	100.0	100.0	100.0	100.0	100.0	
			INCOME DATA						
100.0	100.0	100.0	Net Sales	100.0	100.0	100.0	100.0	100.0	
			Gross Profit						
91.7	91.5	90.7	Operating Expenses	88.2	90.4	92.9	92.9	97.2	
8.3	8.5	9.3	Operating Profit	11.8	9.6	7.1	7.1	2.8	
1.3	1.5	1.7	All Other Expenses (net)	3.5	1.2	−.4	1.3	−.2	
7.1	7.0	7.6	Profit Before Taxes	8.3	8.3	7.5	5.8	3.0	
			RATIOS						
2.4	2.3	2.1		2.3	2.9	1.6	1.1	1.6	
1.0	1.1	1.2	Current	1.3	1.2	1.2	1.0	.5	
.4	.5	.5		.5	.5	.4	.5	.3	
1.4	1.3	1.4		1.4	1.8	1.3	1.0	1.3	
(171) .5	(198) .6	(204) .6	Quick	(70) .6	.7	(23) .9	.6	.3	
.2	.3	.2		.1	.2	.5	.2	.2	
0 UND	0 UND	0 UND		0 UND	0 UND	0 UND	0 UND	0 UND	
0 UND	0 UND	0 UND	Sales/Receivables	0 UND	0 UND	0 UND	5 73.8	17 21.2	
21 17.1	18 20.1	18 20.8		15 23.6	13 28.0	19 19.4	24 15.2	33 11.0	
			Cost of Sales/Inventory						
			Cost of Sales/Payables						
19.3	17.2	16.0		13.3	15.1	23.2	66.7	48.1	
−612.7	221.9	141.7	Sales/Working Capital	86.4	123.8	299.3	−189.7	−58.9	
−18.2	−29.1	−28.0		−24.4	−33.1	−55.9	−29.0	−6.9	
10.3	11.9	16.3		11.3	21.1	21.9	17.2	13.4	
(145) 3.7	(158) 3.5	(175) 3.6	EBIT/Interest	(57) 3.3	(65) 4.0	(20) 4.7	(14) 2.2	3.1	
.9	.9	.8		.9	1.0	.8	.7	.7	
2.5	6.9		Net Profit + Depr., Dep.,						
(15) 1.4	(11) 2.6		Amort./Cur. Mat. L/T/D						
.8	1.3								
.7	.6	.9		1.0	.7	.4	2.1	1.3	
2.5	2.8	3.4	Fixed/Worth	7.9	1.8	1.7	−17.2	3.5	
−2.8	−2.5	−2.7		−2.1	−2.2	−7.4	−1.2	NM	
1.0	1.2	1.4		1.7	.8	1.0	3.4	2.3	
5.2	7.9	6.1	Debt/Worth	10.7	4.0	2.4	−33.8	3.1	
−6.5	−6.1	−8.1		−5.1	−16.5	−12.9	−4.2	NM	
113.2	123.8	217.9		371.4	272.1	185.6		123.8	
(112) 44.0	(127) 49.1	(135) 71.3	% Profit Before Taxes/Tangible Net Worth	(45) 121.0	(50) 70.0	(17) 31.0	(10)	40.8	
4.3	2.1	6.7		39.6	2.4	−1.6		−12.0	
39.7	39.1	53.9		55.5	75.7	105.8	35.3	20.7	
8.6	9.2	12.9	% Profit Before Taxes/Total Assets	15.0	12.2	11.3	8.9	6.3	
−.9	−.8	.0		−.4	.0	−1.4	−.9	−.1	
23.5	39.1	31.5		28.3	44.4	42.3	21.9	15.1	
11.5	14.6	13.7	Sales/Net Fixed Assets	10.2	18.1	17.7	12.9	11.5	
6.5	6.9	7.6		3.4	9.7	10.1	6.1	6.9	
7.6	7.9	8.8		6.1	11.6	12.4	10.0	8.3	
4.7	4.6	4.7	Sales/Total Assets	3.4	5.7	6.8	4.6	5.0	
2.7	2.8	2.8		2.0	3.1	4.2	2.8	3.1	
1.9	1.5	1.6		1.3	1.6	1.6	2.4	1.7	
(135) 3.2	(145) 2.7	(157) 2.8	% Depr., Dep., Amort./Sales	(53) 3.0	(54) 2.9	(18) 2.4	(13) 3.0	2.1	
5.3	5.0	4.7		7.4	4.3	4.2	5.0	3.7	
9.9	8.8	9.5		9.4	8.8	14.3			
(108) 19.0	(131) 16.8	(120) 17.3	% Officers', Directors', Owners' Comp/Sales	(41) 13.9	(46) 17.8	(16) 26.5			
28.9	25.9	27.9		20.8	27.2	33.8			
2590254M	4551767M	4918011M	Net Sales ($)	37875M	139798M	94497M	115930M	236428M	4293483M
650312M	1045407M	746991M	Total Assets ($)	14309M	33930M	17635M	33566M	62016M	585535M

© RMA 2005

M = $ thousand   MM = $ million
See Pages 11 through 21 for Explanation of Ratios and Data

Current Data Sorted By Assets   **Comparative Historical Data**

						Type of Statement	4/1/00-3/31/01 ALL	4/1/01-3/31/02 ALL
1	1	5	2			Unqualified		
2	2					Reviewed		
12	2					Compiled		
2	3	1	1			Tax Returns		
2	3					Other		
	11 (4/1-9/30/04)		23 (10/1/04-3/31/05)					
0-500M	500M-2MM	2-10MM	10-50MM	50-100MM	100-250MM			
17	8	6	3			**NUMBER OF STATEMENTS**		
%	%	%	%	%	%	**ASSETS**	%	%
30.2						Cash & Equivalents		
20.3				D	D	Trade Receivables (net)	D	D
.8				A	A	Inventory	A	A
7.2				T	T	All Other Current	T	T
58.5				A	A	Total Current	A	A
35.0						Fixed Assets (net)		
3.3				N	N	Intangibles (net)	N	N
3.2				O	O	All Other Non-Current	O	O
100.0				T	T	Total	T	T
						LIABILITIES		
				A	A		A	A
29.4				V	V	Notes Payable-Short Term	V	V
8.3				A	A	Cur. Mat.-L/T/D	A	A
4.9				I	I	Trade Payables	I	I
2.3				L	L	Income Taxes Payable	L	L
15.8				A	A	All Other Current	A	A
60.8				B	B	Total Current	B	B
14.9				L	L	Long-Term Debt	L	L
.0				E	E	Deferred Taxes	E	E
11.5						All Other Non-Current		
12.8						Net Worth		
100.0						Total Liabilities & Net Worth		
						INCOME DATA		
100.0						Net Sales		
						Gross Profit		
85.8						Operating Expenses		
14.2						Operating Profit		
1.1						All Other Expenses (net)		
13.1						Profit Before Taxes		
						RATIOS		
3.0								
1.1						Current		
.5								
3.0								
(16) .8						Quick		
.4								
0 UND								
0 UND						Sales/Receivables		
42 8.7								
						Cost of Sales/Inventory		
						Cost of Sales/Payables		
9.0								
117.4						Sales/Working Capital		
-52.8								
39.5								
(12) 9.4						EBIT/Interest		
-3.6								
						Net Profit + Depr., Dep., Amort./Cur. Mat. L /T/D		
.2								
1.0						Fixed/Worth		
-18.0								
.7								
37.9						Debt/Worth		
-20.7								
676.7								
(11) 113.3						% Profit Before Taxes/Tangible Net Worth		
30.5								
121.4								
27.3						% Profit Before Taxes/Total Assets		
-20.4								
89.7								
34.1						Sales/Net Fixed Assets		
8.8								
14.8								
5.3						Sales/Total Assets		
2.6								
.6								
(12) 1.0						% Depr., Dep., Amort./Sales		
1.8								
13.0								
(11) 16.1						% Officers', Directors', Owners' Comp/Sales		
28.6								
19149M	34912M	58204M	106333M			Net Sales ($)		
3543M	10838M	35275M	37959M			Total Assets ($)		

M = $ thousand   MM = $ million
See Pages 11 through 21 for Explanation of Ratios and Data

Comparative Historical Data				Current Data Sorted By Sales					
6	8	9	**Type of Statement**						
2	3		Unqualified	1	1	1		3	2
11	5	4	Reviewed						
12	13	14	Compiled	1	1		1	1	
5	5	7	Tax Returns	5	7	2			
			Other	2	2	2		1	
4/1/02-3/31/03	4/1/03-3/31/04	4/1/04-3/31/05			11 (4/1-9/30/04)			23 (10/1/04-3/31/05)	
ALL	ALL	ALL		0-1MM	1-3MM	3-5MM	5-10MM	10-25MM	25MM & OVER
36	34	34	**NUMBER OF STATEMENTS**	9	11	5	2	5	2
%	%	%	**ASSETS**	%	%	%	%	%	%
24.9	22.1	22.6	Cash & Equivalents		28.8				
20.1	20.6	20.6	Trade Receivables (net)		17.5				
.9	.9	.5	Inventory		1.3				
4.5	5.0	6.2	All Other Current		4.5				
50.4	48.6	49.9	Total Current		52.1				
32.3	36.8	38.1	Fixed Assets (net)		39.9				
3.3	4.3	2.0	Intangibles (net)		3.1				
13.9	10.3	10.0	All Other Non-Current		4.9				
100.0	100.0	100.0	Total		100.0				
			LIABILITIES						
24.2	15.9	20.6	Notes Payable-Short Term		30.1				
9.7	14.2	5.1	Cur. Mat.-L/T/D		13.3				
3.8	5.1	6.3	Trade Payables		2.3				
.0	.5	1.2	Income Taxes Payable		3.4				
25.2	19.8	14.3	All Other Current		10.8				
62.9	55.6	47.5	Total Current		60.0				
40.3	17.2	19.3	Long-Term Debt		18.3				
.0	.2	.0	Deferred Taxes		.0				
14.7	1.5	6.9	All Other Non-Current		6.8				
-17.9	25.3	26.3	Net Worth		14.9				
100.0	100.0	100.0	Total Liabilities & Net Worth		100.0				
			INCOME DATA						
100.0	100.0	100.0	Net Sales		100.0				
			Gross Profit						
92.6	92.1	85.7	Operating Expenses		88.0				
7.4	7.9	14.3	Operating Profit		12.0				
-.3	1.6	3.0	All Other Expenses (net)		4.3				
7.7	6.3	11.3	Profit Before Taxes		7.7				
			RATIOS						
2.9	1.9	3.0			3.0				
1.3	1.1	1.5	Current		1.5				
.4	.3	.6			.6				
2.3	1.7	2.7			3.0				
1.1	.9	(33) 1.3	Quick		1.4				
.3	.2	.4			.2				
0 UND	0 UND	0 UND		0 UND					
0 UND	19 19.4	2 183.4	Sales/Receivables	1 395.0					
65 5.6	61 6.0	54 6.7		45 8.1					
			Cost of Sales/Inventory						
			Cost of Sales/Payables						
7.3	9.4	8.8			10.2				
455.6	38.3	17.3	Sales/Working Capital		17.5				
-22.9	-21.8	-60.6			-11.7				
15.4	9.1	37.2							
(28) 1.4	(25) 3.0	(25) 6.2	EBIT/Interest						
.8	-.7	.0							
			Net Profit + Depr., Dep., Amort./Cur. Mat. L/T/D						
.3	.6	.3			.7				
.9	1.6	1.0	Fixed/Worth		31.3				
-4.3	-21.6	UND			-9.4				
.4	.5	.6			.7				
2.9	3.1	3.0	Debt/Worth		54.9				
-5.9	-42.7	UND			-29.7				
96.1	68.4	290.4	% Profit Before Taxes/Tangible Net Worth						
(24) 25.3	(23) 12.2	(26) 47.6							
-2.7	-.2	9.4							
40.5	18.0	55.3	% Profit Before Taxes/Total Assets		82.9				
5.2	3.7	12.4			15.9				
-.9	-1.0	1.4			-2.3				
74.0	40.4	49.7	Sales/Net Fixed Assets		49.0				
17.3	11.7	19.6			25.3				
6.4	7.3	3.8			4.2				
13.5	8.1	6.2	Sales/Total Assets		6.6				
4.3	3.5	2.8			5.2				
2.2	1.6	1.6			2.3				
.9	.8	.8	% Depr., Dep., Amort./Sales		.7				
(32) 1.8	(26) 1.8	(29) 1.1		(10) 1.1					
2.4	2.9	2.1			2.1				
10.8	6.7	11.3	% Officers', Directors', Owners' Comp/Sales						
(17) 17.2	(16) 16.4	(18) 15.8							
31.4	29.4	25.0							
160112M	150744M	218598M	Net Sales ($)	4173M	17783M	18285M	11578M	76487M	90292M
48305M	45891M	87615M	Total Assets ($)	3231M	11994M	6893M	5695M	32799M	27003M

Current Data Sorted By Assets							Comparative Historical Data	

1	3	15	3	2	2	Type of Statement		
1	3	15	3	2	2	Unqualified	14	15
2	5	4	2			Reviewed	8	7
15	7	4	1			Compiled	47	46
57	8	2	1			Tax Returns	33	45
24	12	14	1	1	2	Other	31	40
	29 (4/1-9/30/04)			159 (10/1/04-3/31/05)			4/1/00-3/31/01	4/1/01-3/31/02
0-500M	500M-2MM	2-10MM	10-50MM	50-100MM	100-250MM		ALL	ALL
99	35	39	8	3	4	NUMBER OF STATEMENTS	133	153
%	%	%	%	%	%	ASSETS	%	%
33.7	16.2	15.9				Cash & Equivalents	18.7	25.8
8.9	30.3	33.6				Trade Receivables (net)	20.2	20.6
1.5	1.2	.4				Inventory	.7	.7
1.6	2.7	3.5				All Other Current	4.8	3.5
45.8	50.4	53.3				Total Current	44.4	50.6
39.0	32.7	33.3				Fixed Assets (net)	43.6	37.7
6.0	3.4	3.9				Intangibles (net)	4.8	4.8
9.1	13.4	9.5				All Other Non-Current	7.2	6.9
100.0	100.0	100.0				Total	100.0	100.0
						LIABILITIES		
38.9	13.7	10.8				Notes Payable-Short Term	28.9	20.5
5.1	3.3	3.2				Cur. Mat.-L/T/D	11.6	6.3
4.3	3.5	5.8				Trade Payables	5.0	3.6
.0	.0	.4				Income Taxes Payable	.3	.9
23.5	16.7	19.1				All Other Current	32.9	18.0
71.8	37.3	39.3				Total Current	78.6	49.3
28.0	25.5	17.9				Long-Term Debt	43.0	26.4
.0	.3	.1				Deferred Taxes	.8	.3
11.8	3.1	1.7				All Other Non-Current	2.9	3.6
-11.6	33.8	40.9				Net Worth	-25.3	20.3
100.0	100.0	100.0				Total Liabilities & Net Worth	100.0	100.0
						INCOME DATA		
100.0	100.0	100.0				Net Sales	100.0	100.0
						Gross Profit		
93.0	93.8	93.5				Operating Expenses	90.7	88.5
7.0	6.2	6.5				Operating Profit	9.3	11.5
1.2	1.0	1.1				All Other Expenses (net)	2.0	2.7
5.8	5.2	5.3				Profit Before Taxes	7.3	8.8
						RATIOS		
2.0	2.9	3.1				Current	2.4	2.5
.7	1.4	1.9					1.0	1.3
.3	.9	1.0					.3	.6
1.9	2.5	2.9				Quick	2.1	2.4
.6	1.4	1.8					.9	1.2
.2	.7	.9					.2	.4
0 UND	0 UND	22 16.8				Sales/Receivables	0 UND	0 UND
0 UND	41 9.0	45 8.0					0 UND	0 UND
0 UND	53 6.9	72 5.1					53 6.8	58 6.3
						Cost of Sales/Inventory		
						Cost of Sales/Payables		
26.4	8.4	5.2				Sales/Working Capital	8.0	9.5
-54.3	24.4	13.5					692.8	60.6
-15.4	-88.0	-753.3					-24.4	-33.9
27.0	22.3	24.9				EBIT/Interest	10.7	12.6
(75) 2.7	(33) 8.1	(33) 7.2					(113) 3.3	(124) 5.6
.3	1.5	1.8					.9	1.0
						Net Profit + Depr., Dep., Amort./Cur. Mat. L./T/D	7.7	10.1
							(10) 1.1	(10) 2.1
							-9.7	.3
.6	.3	.3				Fixed/Worth	.4	.3
4.7	.7	.7					1.8	1.3
-.5	4.9	4.6					-20.6	22.1
1.1	.7	.4				Debt/Worth	.7	.8
10.5	2.3	1.1					3.4	2.8
-2.5	8.5	5.4					-21.9	NM
456.6	74.2	35.9				% Profit Before Taxes/Tangible Net Worth	112.7	124.0
(57) 96.4	(28) 26.8	(35) 16.3					(94) 29.5	(115) 46.2
6.1	9.5	2.0					.7	10.6
94.4	29.5	17.1				% Profit Before Taxes/Total Assets	32.2	48.3
15.0	10.2	7.6					7.6	14.0
-1.5	.0	1.4					-.4	1.1
68.8	46.9	27.1				Sales/Net Fixed Assets	37.2	50.5
28.2	20.0	9.5					13.1	18.5
12.4	7.8	3.4					6.1	6.8
14.7	5.5	3.3				Sales/Total Assets	9.7	9.4
8.7	3.6	2.5					4.6	3.8
4.1	1.7	1.4					2.1	2.2
.6	.5	.7				% Depr., Dep., Amort./Sales	.8	.7
(58) 1.3	(29) 1.4	(34) 1.9					(116) 1.6	(121) 1.5
2.4	2.7	2.8					3.2	3.0
12.4	7.9					% Officers', Directors', Owners' Comp/Sales	8.3	8.6
(65) 17.6	(11) 23.1						(62) 15.8	(72) 18.8
27.4	35.4						27.8	26.1
160122M	158872M	409140M	206802M	226007M	690539M	Net Sales ($)	3301296M	1792683M
18447M	35784M	166524M	108352M	178423M	717317M	Total Assets ($)	655687M	497817M

Comparative Historical Data				Current Data Sorted By Sales						
			Type of Statement							
17	24	26	Unqualified	1	1	4	5	11	4	
7	16	13	Reviewed	1	3	3	4		2	
30	45	27	Compiled	7	9	3	5	3		
50	58	68	Tax Returns	29	23	10	2	3	1	
40	53	54	Other	14	13	4	9	10	4	
4/1/02-3/31/03 ALL	4/1/03-3/31/04 ALL	4/1/04-3/31/05 ALL		29 (4/1-9/30/04)			159 (10/1/04-3/31/05)			
				0-1MM	1-3MM	3-5MM	5-10MM	10-25MM	25MM & OVER
144	196	188	**NUMBER OF STATEMENTS**	52	49	24	25	27	11
%	%	%	**ASSETS**	%	%	%	%	%	%
21.6	21.5	24.9	Cash & Equivalents	27.8	28.6	29.4	18.1	22.0	6.8
17.7	22.4	19.3	Trade Receivables (net)	9.7	10.5	25.9	33.9	30.5	29.3
1.1	1.4	1.2	Inventory	1.1	1.1	3.0	.6	.5	2.0
5.1	3.5	2.4	All Other Current	1.3	1.8	2.7	3.4	3.7	3.3
45.4	48.8	47.8	Total Current	39.9	42.1	60.9	56.0	56.7	41.4
41.7	35.4	36.8	Fixed Assets (net)	41.2	41.9	28.2	33.1	31.2	33.6
3.4	6.1	5.3	Intangibles (net)	8.3	4.1	4.0	3.8	1.8	10.8
9.5	9.6	10.2	All Other Non-Current	10.6	11.9	6.9	7.1	10.3	14.2
100.0	100.0	100.0	Total	100.0	100.0	100.0	100.0	100.0	100.0
			LIABILITIES						
22.5	18.4	25.8	Notes Payable-Short Term	35.1	25.3	23.7	34.1	10.0	8.9
5.3	5.9	4.2	Cur. Mat.-L/T/D	5.2	3.8	3.7	4.9	3.4	2.5
4.5	4.4	4.5	Trade Payables	4.1	6.0	1.0	3.4	6.1	5.6
.5	.4	.1	Income Taxes Payable	.0	.0	.0	.5	.1	.5
26.8	21.2	20.2	All Other Current	19.6	16.7	23.1	15.2	33.7	11.2
59.6	50.2	54.8	Total Current	63.9	51.8	51.4	58.1	53.3	28.6
25.2	22.5	25.3	Long-Term Debt	36.3	25.1	24.4	16.8	13.6	24.9
.0	.2	.1	Deferred Taxes	.0	.2	.0	.1	.1	1.1
7.0	6.3	7.3	All Other Non-Current	17.5	5.8	2.0	1.4	2.6	2.0
8.2	20.8	12.4	Net Worth	−17.7	17.1	22.2	23.5	30.4	43.3
100.0	100.0	100.0	Total Liabilities & Net Worth	100.0	100.0	100.0	100.0	100.0	100.0
			INCOME DATA						
100.0	100.0	100.0	Net Sales	100.0	100.0	100.0	100.0	100.0	100.0
			Gross Profit						
92.3	91.6	93.0	Operating Expenses	91.7	90.4	94.2	97.0	94.8	95.3
7.7	8.4	7.0	Operating Profit	8.3	9.6	5.8	3.0	5.2	4.7
.9	1.6	1.2	All Other Expenses (net)	2.8	1.1	−.2	.7	.1	.3
6.8	6.7	5.8	Profit Before Taxes	5.5	8.5	6.0	2.3	5.2	4.4
			RATIOS						
2.4	3.0	2.5		2.6	1.9	4.1	3.2	2.8	2.4
1.2	1.3	1.2	Current	.6	1.1	1.5	1.9	1.2	1.2
.4	.5	.4		.1	.4	.6	.9	.9	1.0
2.1	2.6	2.3		2.5	1.6	3.8	3.1	2.6	1.8
1.0	1.1	1.1	Quick	.5	.8	1.4	1.8	1.1	1.1
.3	.4	.4		.1	.4	.5	.8	.7	.9
0 UND	0 UND	0 UND		0 UND	0 UND	0 UND	0 UND	0 999.8	45 8.1
0 UND	2 209.3	0 UND	Sales/Receivables	0 UND	0 UND	0 UND	45 8.0	34 10.7	55 6.7
44 8.3	58 6.3	46 8.0		0 UND	20 18.5	74 4.9	70 5.2	62 5.9	58 6.3
			Cost of Sales/Inventory						
			Cost of Sales/Payables						
12.7	8.1	10.8		15.1	23.0	7.5	5.6	6.5	6.2
138.0	47.7	91.0	Sales/Working Capital	−44.6	281.5	20.6	22.3	33.9	32.4
−26.8	−24.8	−26.7		−9.2	−23.4	−38.8	NM	−81.0	243.3
15.1	16.4	25.4		25.6	40.5	34.3	24.0	16.0	14.7
(117) 3.2	(156) 4.9	(154) 5.8	EBIT/Interest	(38) 1.8	(39) 5.9	(20) 9.0	(22) 7.5	(25) 6.4	(10) 2.0
−.2	.9	.9		−2.9	2.0	1.8	1.4	1.0	−1.9
	4.9	9.1	Net Profit + Depr., Dep.,						
	(18) 2.4	(13) 1.9	Amort./Cur. Mat. L/T/D						
	.7	.7							
.5	.4	.4		.9	.5	.1	.3	.3	.5
1.6	1.5	1.8	Fixed/Worth	7.1	2.0	.6	.8	.6	1.2
60.1	−7.2	−3.5		−.4	−2.8	NM	14.3	2.1	−64.3
1.0	.8	.7		1.2	.9	.6	.3	.5	.7
3.3	2.4	3.1	Debt/Worth	11.2	2.8	2.0	1.2	2.0	2.3
−59.5	−32.1	−8.8		−1.9	−6.8	NM	31.4	7.0	−999.8
145.5	97.2	107.3	% Profit Before Taxes/Tangible	496.0	143.9	160.1	43.2	39.3	
(106) 42.3	(138) 30.9	(132) 26.0	Net Worth	(29) 74.6	(34) 66.5	(18) 30.0	(20) 19.1	(23) 21.1	
−.4	9.7	3.0		.0	9.4	−.5	8.1	.1	
43.2	38.2	36.5	% Profit Before Taxes/Total	93.4	46.1	40.9	17.7	17.1	19.9
10.7	8.7	9.2	Assets	10.6	18.5	12.2	7.8	7.6	2.3
−3.5	−.6	−.2		−6.4	4.4	−1.5	.6	.0	−4.4
44.5	44.8	62.6		47.8	59.5	100.2	43.4	91.8	17.7
15.1	19.0	21.2	Sales/Net Fixed Assets	19.7	21.1	34.0	23.1	14.9	6.3
6.0	6.0	7.1		7.6	8.2	13.6	9.2	5.4	2.0
8.9	7.5	9.7		9.7	12.3	14.5	9.4	5.4	2.9
4.2	3.7	4.2	Sales/Total Assets	4.3	7.1	6.3	4.2	3.2	1.2
2.3	1.8	1.9		1.7	2.7	2.3	1.8	2.4	.9
1.0	.8	.7		.8	.9	.3	.7	.5	1.1
(102) 2.0	(160) 1.7	(135) 1.6	% Depr., Dep., Amort./Sales	(28) 2.1	(31) 1.7	(23) .7	(18) 1.5	(25) 1.5	(10) 3.1
4.0	3.5	2.9		4.1	3.1	2.1	3.8	2.3	5.6
8.9	10.3	10.5	% Officers', Directors',	12.5	7.8	15.4	9.5		
(73) 16.1	(99) 18.4	(86) 17.0	Owners' Comp/Sales	(32) 17.3	(25) 14.3	(10) 21.7	(12) 16.6		
26.4	29.6	26.5		25.8	25.7	28.4	34.0		
3473354M	6272362M	1851482M	Net Sales ($)	27858M	81292M	91793M	174219M	409188M	1067132M
782077M	1694191M	1224847M	Total Assets ($)	13841M	34065M	25988M	63717M	142655M	944581M

© RMA 2005

M = $ thousand   MM = $ million
See Pages 11 through 21 for Explanation of Ratios and Data

Current Data Sorted By Assets   **Comparative Historical Data**

						Type of Statement		
1	4	15	2			Unqualified		
1	1					Reviewed		
8	5	3	1			Compiled		
29	2	6	1	2	1	Tax Returns		
12	15	6	3	1		Other		
							4/1/00- 3/31/01 ALL	4/1/01- 3/31/02 ALL
29 (4/1-9/30/04)			90 (10/1/04-3/31/05)					
0-500M	500M-2MM	2-10MM	10-50MM	50-100MM	100-250MM			
51	27	30	7	3	1	NUMBER OF STATEMENTS		
%	%	%	%	%	%	ASSETS	%	%
30.8	19.7	12.5				Cash & Equivalents	D	D
10.5	23.5	28.6				Trade Receivables (net)	A	A
1.7	.3	.6				Inventory	T	T
3.3	6.8	3.7				All Other Current	A	A
46.3	50.3	45.4				Total Current		
34.0	38.5	45.1				Fixed Assets (net)	N	N
3.8	6.1	1.2				Intangibles (net)	O	O
15.8	5.1	8.3				All Other Non-Current	T	T
100.0	100.0	100.0				Total		
						LIABILITIES	A	A
16.6	6.6	5.3				Notes Payable-Short Term	V	V
10.9	8.0	7.5				Cur. Mat.-L/T/D	A	A
5.4	4.7	5.6				Trade Payables	I	I
.0	.0	.0				Income Taxes Payable	L	L
40.3	15.8	13.8				All Other Current	A	A
73.2	35.2	32.2				Total Current	B	B
42.9	32.7	24.4				Long-Term Debt	L	L
.1	.2	.0				Deferred Taxes	E	E
14.3	7.6	8.9				All Other Non-Current		
-30.4	24.3	34.5				Net Worth		
100.0	100.0	100.0				Total Liabilities & Net Worth		
						INCOME DATA		
100.0	100.0	100.0				Net Sales		
						Gross Profit		
88.1	87.4	90.5				Operating Expenses		
11.9	12.6	9.5				Operating Profit		
1.7	1.1	1.2				All Other Expenses (net)		
10.2	11.5	8.2				Profit Before Taxes		
						RATIOS		
2.3	3.2	2.4						
.9	1.8	1.5				Current		
.4	.9	.9						
1.8	3.0	2.4						
.8	1.4	1.3				Quick		
.4	.3	.7						
0 UND	0 UND	10 38.1						
0 UND	21 17.7	41 8.8				Sales/Receivables		
7 52.6	46 8.0	67 5.4						
						Cost of Sales/Inventory		
						Cost of Sales/Payables		
27.0	7.5	7.9						
-379.5	15.0	18.3				Sales/Working Capital		
-20.0	-163.9	-42.1						
25.9	25.7	24.2						
(34) 5.0	(21) 9.9	(29) 4.8				EBIT/Interest		
.6	1.8	1.3						
						Net Profit + Depr., Dep., Amort./Cur. Mat. L /T/D		
.3	.3	.5						
2.2	2.3	1.2				Fixed/Worth		
-.8	12.0	2.8						
.7	.8	.7						
24.6	2.6	1.4				Debt/Worth		
-2.2	107.8	3.8						
888.0	163.9	44.2				% Profit Before Taxes/Tangible Net Worth		
(30) 224.8	(21) 53.4	(27) 21.4						
12.9	12.0	3.3						
186.1	27.7	19.0				% Profit Before Taxes/Total Assets		
17.9	17.8	8.4						
-2.3	1.4	.9						
143.2	55.5	10.9						
28.0	13.5	6.8				Sales/Net Fixed Assets		
12.8	3.8	3.1						
17.1	5.6	3.6						
7.7	3.0	2.5				Sales/Total Assets		
4.2	2.1	1.8						
.3	.7	1.4						
(32) 1.0	(20) 2.1	(29) 2.2				% Depr., Dep., Amort./Sales		
4.1	4.5	5.3						
7.4	3.3					% Officers', Directors', Owners' Comp/Sales		
(31) 15.5	(11) 13.2							
25.5	30.9							
92243M	137549M	347924M	167510M	1415386M	1217046M	Net Sales ($)		
10030M	29539M	124501M	96579M	209795M	191941M	Total Assets ($)		

© RMA 2005   M = $ thousand   MM = $ million

See Pages 11 through 21 for Explanation of Ratios and Data

Comparative Historical Data / Current Data Sorted By Sales

Type of Statement					29 (4/1-9/30/04)		90 (10/1/04-3/31/05)			
	1	10	22	Unqualified	3	3	6	10		
		4	2	Reviewed	1	1				
	5	15	17	Compiled	4	7	2	2	2	
	12	26	41	Tax Returns	12	13	5	5	3	3
	16	21	37	Other	6	12	2	6	6	5
	4/1/02-3/31/03 ALL	4/1/03-3/31/04 ALL	4/1/04-3/31/05 ALL		0-1MM	1-3MM	3-5MM	5-10MM	10-25MM	25MM & OVER
NUMBER OF STATEMENTS	34	76	119		22	36	13	19	21	8
ASSETS	%	%	%		%	%	%	%	%	%
Cash & Equivalents	22.5	26.2	23.7		31.3	22.1	19.9	22.0	17.8	
Trade Receivables (net)	22.3	20.7	18.1		10.8	12.7	20.7	27.4	25.6	
Inventory	1.3	2.9	1.0		2.9	.7	.5	.5	.5	
All Other Current	3.3	4.2	4.3		3.9	4.1	2.3	6.2	4.0	
Total Current	49.4	54.0	47.1		48.9	39.7	43.4	56.1	48.0	
Fixed Assets (net)	35.2	34.0	38.0		35.2	43.1	39.5	31.8	40.4	
Intangibles (net)	4.5	3.1	3.6		5.4	4.4	6.4	.9	2.5	
All Other Non-Current	10.9	8.8	11.3		10.5	12.8	10.7	11.3	9.2	
Total	100.0	100.0	100.0		100.0	100.0	100.0	100.0	100.0	
LIABILITIES										
Notes Payable-Short Term	8.2	20.4	10.5		14.5	11.8	8.5	10.0	8.1	
Cur. Mat.-L/T/D	11.8	12.2	8.8		10.1	5.7	3.4	18.6	8.4	
Trade Payables	5.0	3.8	5.4		4.4	4.6	8.2	5.6	5.2	
Income Taxes Payable	.2	.1	.0		.0	.0	.0	.0	.0	
All Other Current	20.0	26.1	25.6		33.5	29.5	14.9	28.7	18.6	
Total Current	45.2	62.7	50.3		62.5	51.6	35.0	62.9	40.4	
Long-Term Debt	21.3	27.8	34.8		26.0	63.7	25.4	11.5	25.1	
Deferred Taxes	.0	.1	.1		.0	.1	.5	.0	.0	
All Other Non-Current	10.8	6.8	10.2		14.2	14.7	5.8	4.7	6.3	
Net Worth	22.7	2.6	4.7		-2.6	-30.1	33.4	20.8	28.2	
Total Liabilities & Net Worth	100.0	100.0	100.0		100.0	100.0	100.0	100.0	100.0	
INCOME DATA										
Net Sales	100.0	100.0	100.0		100.0	100.0	100.0	100.0	100.0	
Gross Profit										
Operating Expenses	92.6	93.3	88.7		79.4	86.2	93.2	94.0	94.9	
Operating Profit	7.4	6.7	11.3		20.6	13.8	6.8	6.0	5.1	
All Other Expenses (net)	.8	1.6	1.3		2.1	2.0	-.2	.0	1.8	
Profit Before Taxes	6.6	5.1	10.1		18.5	11.8	6.9	6.1	3.3	
RATIOS										
Current	3.0	2.5	2.7		3.0	4.3	2.5	2.1	1.9	
	1.2	1.5	1.5		1.7	1.2	1.0	1.5	1.3	
	.4	.5	.6		.7	.5	.8	.5	1.0	
Quick	2.5	2.2	2.6		2.3	3.9	2.4	1.8	1.8	
	(33) 1.2	1.2	1.2		1.2	.8	1.0	1.3	1.3	
	.4	.4	.4		.2	.3	.5	.5	.8	
Sales/Receivables	0 UND	0 UND	0 UND		0 UND	0 UND	0 UND	0 UND	0 UND	
	0 UND	6 61.9	5 75.7		0 UND	0 UND	6 60.4	30 12.2	36 10.0	
	52 7.0	49 7.4	41 8.8		37 9.9	10 35.0	35 10.5	54 6.8	61 6.0	
Cost of Sales/Inventory										
Cost of Sales/Payables										
Sales/Working Capital	15.8	7.8	9.7		8.2	12.2	14.5	8.1	9.6	
	77.2	30.4	36.8		49.8	569.8	UND	19.9	22.8	
	-30.3	-31.1	-31.0		-20.0	-21.8	-193.1	-21.0	NM	
EBIT/Interest	11.8	12.9	24.1		13.8	14.0	65.3	28.3	33.1	
	(26) 2.9	(62) 2.3	(93) 6.3		(13) 9.0	(27) 4.5	(11) 19.1	(15) 6.3	7.5	
	-1.3	-.8	1.3		.8	.6	1.9	1.2	2.0	
Net Profit + Depr., Dep., Amort./Cur. Mat. L/T/D			39.1							
			(10) 5.3							
			1.7							
Fixed/Worth	.2	.3	.3		.2	.7	.6	.3	.3	
	1.1	1.6	1.7		1.4	4.1	1.0	.9	1.2	
	-15.2	-4.0	17.0		-5.9	-1.4	2.6	9.9	3.0	
Debt/Worth	.7	.9	.8		.6	1.1	1.1	.6	.7	
	2.5	2.6	2.8		2.3	19.3	2.6	1.5	1.9	
	-88.6	-11.0	-18.1		-10.0	-3.5	5.1	13.8	3.8	
% Profit Before Taxes/Tangible Net Worth	110.6	105.0	193.8		868.4	374.6	383.4	136.8	49.7	
	(24) 33.7	(50) 20.6	(89) 45.6		(16) 177.3	(20) 83.3	(11) 63.9	(17) 44.2	(17) 24.1	
	6.8	-3.6	8.1		2.9	2.9	7.8	6.6	7.3	
% Profit Before Taxes/Total Assets	38.7	43.3	58.3		116.6	95.0	70.5	33.0	17.6	
	8.1	4.7	9.7		13.0	13.2	8.6	18.6	8.9	
	-2.3	-4.3	.4		-.6	-3.4	2.1	.4	1.9	
Sales/Net Fixed Assets	56.3	115.2	54.4		UND	67.3	85.8	55.5	24.1	
	26.4	21.0	14.7		12.5	17.8	19.7	15.8	8.4	
	8.1	7.1	5.7		6.9	6.4	3.1	6.2	4.2	
Sales/Total Assets	9.3	9.2	7.7		7.3	11.8	10.5	7.7	5.8	
	4.5	3.9	4.0		4.2	5.5	4.4	4.4	3.3	
	2.1	2.2	2.3		1.6	2.3	2.2	2.3	1.8	
% Depr., Dep., Amort./Sales	1.0	.5	.7		.9	.7	.2	.3	1.2	
	(22) 1.5	(61) 1.8	(90) 1.8		(12) 3.8	(25) 2.9	(12) 1.1	(15) 1.3	(20) 2.0	
	5.0	3.2	4.2		5.4	5.4	6.7	2.2	3.0	
% Officers', Directors', Owners' Comp/Sales	7.4	9.1	6.9		13.9	11.0				
	(11) 18.3	(39) 14.1	(54) 14.1		(11) 19.0	(17) 16.1				
	29.5	27.1	23.2		28.8	26.1				
Net Sales ($)	433713M	537762M	3377658M		11540M	61369M	51659M	114681M	366701M	2771708M
Total Assets ($)	146279M	252229M	662385M		7890M	21738M	17876M	29406M	129039M	456436M

M = $ thousand   MM = $ million
See Pages 11 through 21 for Explanation of Ratios and Data

Current Data Sorted By Assets | Comparative Historical Data

0-500M	500M-2MM	2-10MM	10-50MM	50-100MM	100-250MM	Type of Statement	4/1/00-3/31/01 ALL	4/1/01-3/31/02 ALL
2	2	7	1			Unqualified		
	1		1			Reviewed		
						Compiled		
2	3					Tax Returns		
1	2	5	1			Other		
	14 (4/1-9/30/04)		14 (10/1/04-3/31/05)					
5	8	12	3			**NUMBER OF STATEMENTS**		
%	%	%	%	%	%	**ASSETS**	%	%
		19.7				Cash & Equivalents		
		23.1	D	D		Trade Receivables (net)	D	D
		1.5	A	A		Inventory	A	A
		3.8	T	T		All Other Current	T	T
		48.1	A	A		Total Current	A	A
		43.0				Fixed Assets (net)		
		1.9	N	N		Intangibles (net)	N	N
		7.1	O	O		All Other Non-Current	O	O
		100.0	T	T		Total	T	T
						LIABILITIES		
		2.3	A	A		Notes Payable-Short Term	A	A
		1.7	V	V		Cur. Mat.-L/T/D	V	V
		10.0	A	A		Trade Payables	A	A
		.0	I	I		Income Taxes Payable	I	I
		7.5	L	L		All Other Current	L	L
		21.5	A	A		Total Current	A	A
		17.3	B	B		Long-Term Debt	B	B
		.0	L	L		Deferred Taxes	L	L
		.4	E	E		All Other Non-Current	E	E
		60.8				Net Worth		
		100.0				Total Liabilities & Net Worth		
						INCOME DATA		
		100.0				Net Sales		
						Gross Profit		
		91.9				Operating Expenses		
		8.1				Operating Profit		
		−1.4				All Other Expenses (net)		
		9.4				Profit Before Taxes		
						RATIOS		
		3.9						
		2.6				Current		
		1.6						
		3.0						
		2.1				Quick		
		1.6						
		17 21.8						
		46 8.0				Sales/Receivables		
		68 5.4						
						Cost of Sales/Inventory		
						Cost of Sales/Payables		
		4.4						
		8.7				Sales/Working Capital		
		15.0						
						EBIT/Interest		
						Net Profit + Depr., Dep., Amort./Cur. Mat. L /T/D		
		.4						
		.6				Fixed/Worth		
		1.3						
		.3						
		.6				Debt/Worth		
		1.2						
		31.0						
		17.3				% Profit Before Taxes/Tangible Net Worth		
		4.4						
		15.8						
		11.5				% Profit Before Taxes/Total Assets		
		2.3						
		5.6						
		3.7				Sales/Net Fixed Assets		
		3.0						
		2.1						
		1.7				Sales/Total Assets		
		1.4						
		1.2						
		2.3				% Depr., Dep., Amort./Sales		
		3.3						
						% Officers', Directors', Owners' Comp/Sales		
10051M	40996M	97688M	50539M			Net Sales ($)		
1454M	9652M	50673M	56410M			Total Assets ($)		

M = $ thousand   MM = $ million
See Pages 11 through 21 for Explanation of Ratios and Data

Comparative Historical Data   **Current Data Sorted By Sales**

				Type of Statement						
	14	21	12	Unqualified	2	1	4		5	
	1	2		Reviewed						
	4	5	2	Compiled		1			1	
	6	3	5	Tax Returns		2		2	1	
	9	7	9	Other		1	4	2	2	
	4/1/02-3/31/03	4/1/03-3/31/04	4/1/04-3/31/05			14 (4/1-9/30/04)			14 (10/1/04-3/31/05)	
	ALL	ALL	ALL		0-1MM	1-3MM	3-5MM	5-10MM	10-25MM	25MM & OVER
	34	38	28	NUMBER OF STATEMENTS	2	5	8	4	9	
	%	%	%	ASSETS	%	%	%	%	%	%
	13.0	18.3	18.5	Cash & Equivalents						
	24.8	21.0	19.5	Trade Receivables (net)						
	1.2	1.6	2.6	Inventory						
	4.3	6.1	2.9	All Other Current						
	43.4	46.9	43.5	Total Current						
	45.3	41.8	41.6	Fixed Assets (net)						
	2.4	1.8	6.4	Intangibles (net)						
	8.8	9.4	8.5	All Other Non-Current						
	100.0	100.0	100.0	Total						
				LIABILITIES						
	11.7	2.4	2.8	Notes Payable-Short Term						
	5.3	3.4	6.9	Cur. Mat.-L/T/D						
	9.8	8.5	8.7	Trade Payables						
	.0	.4	.3	Income Taxes Payable						
	15.5	12.1	7.3	All Other Current						
	42.5	26.7	26.0	Total Current						
	26.2	26.0	24.4	Long-Term Debt						
	.0	.0	.0	Deferred Taxes						
	2.2	1.4	.2	All Other Non-Current						
	29.2	45.9	49.4	Net Worth						
	100.0	100.0	100.0	Total Liabilities & Net Worth						
				INCOME DATA						
	100.0	100.0	100.0	Net Sales						
				Gross Profit						
	93.4	89.5	85.1	Operating Expenses						
	6.6	10.5	14.9	Operating Profit						
	.5	.5	.7	All Other Expenses (net)						
	6.1	10.0	14.2	Profit Before Taxes						
				RATIOS						
	2.9	2.9	3.3							
	1.5	1.5	1.7	Current						
	.9	1.2	1.0							
	2.7	2.8	2.7							
	1.3	1.4	1.6	Quick						
	.5	1.1	.8							
5	75.8	6 60.1	0 UND							
30	12.3	36 10.1	18 20.8	Sales/Receivables						
61	6.0	57 6.4	65 5.6							
				Cost of Sales/Inventory						
				Cost of Sales/Payables						
	6.0	5.6	5.7							
	24.4	13.6	13.2	Sales/Working Capital						
	−122.4	73.1	162.0							
	16.1	15.5	26.5							
(25)	3.2	(31) 3.7	(18) 16.0	EBIT/Interest						
	.9	1.5	1.9							
				Net Profit + Depr., Dep., Amort./Cur. Mat. L/T/D						
	.5	.5	.3							
	1.1	.9	.6	Fixed/Worth						
	NM	1.7	2.9							
	.5	.7	.4							
	1.5	1.2	.9	Debt/Worth						
	NM	3.4	4.2							
	31.6	49.5	45.7	% Profit Before Taxes/Tangible Net Worth						
(26)	8.3	(37) 15.9	(23) 15.6							
	−1.1	1.5	4.4							
	25.5	38.5	41.6	% Profit Before Taxes/Total Assets						
	5.8	8.0	11.5							
	−.7	.8	2.3							
	29.0	18.6	17.9	Sales/Net Fixed Assets						
	6.0	6.2	6.3							
	2.9	2.5	3.3							
	4.0	4.2	4.2	Sales/Total Assets						
	2.8	2.4	2.1							
	1.6	1.5	1.5							
	1.1	1.8	1.0	% Depr., Dep., Amort./Sales						
(30)	2.2	(34) 2.5	(26) 2.3							
	4.0	3.7	3.4							
	9.2	1.2		% Officers', Directors', Owners' Comp/Sales						
(10)	12.5	(11) 5.0								
	29.3	12.8								
	468518M	652285M	199274M	Net Sales ($)	1103M	9887M	30724M	29495M	128065M	
	120106M	361942M	118189M	Total Assets ($)	1533M	2070M	17188M	9076M	88322M	

(Right-side columns under "Current Data Sorted By Sales" indicate: DATA NOT AVAILABLE)

M = $ thousand   MM = $ million
See Pages 11 through 21 for Explanation of Ratios and Data

Current Data Sorted By Assets **Comparative Historical Data**

0-500M	500M-2MM	2-10MM	10-50MM	50-100MM	100-250MM	Type of Statement	4/1/00-3/31/01 ALL	4/1/01-3/31/02 ALL
		4	15	11	1	Unqualified		
		1	3	1		Reviewed		
1		1				Compiled		
1						Tax Returns		
		1	6	4		Other		
35 (4/1-9/30/04)			14 (10/1/04-3/31/05)					
1	7	24	16	1		**NUMBER OF STATEMENTS**		
%	%	%	%	%	%	**ASSETS**	%	%
		21.6	19.1		D	Cash & Equivalents	D	D
		18.8	13.7		A	Trade Receivables (net)	A	A
		.3	.1		T	Inventory	T	T
		6.5	7.7		A	All Other Current	A	A
		47.3	40.7			Total Current		
		39.3	49.7		N	Fixed Assets (net)	N	N
		1.6	.7		O	Intangibles (net)	O	O
		11.8	8.9		T	All Other Non-Current	T	T
		100.0	100.0			Total		
					A	**LIABILITIES**	A	A
		4.0	2.6		V	Notes Payable-Short Term	V	V
		3.5	2.2		A	Cur. Mat.-L/T/D	A	A
		9.0	4.3		I	Trade Payables	I	I
		.1	.0		L	Income Taxes Payable	L	L
		13.6	12.2		A	All Other Current	A	A
		30.2	21.3		B	Total Current	B	B
		25.7	24.5		L	Long-Term Debt	L	L
		.0	.0		E	Deferred Taxes	E	E
		.9	.1			All Other Non-Current		
		43.2	54.0			Net Worth		
		100.0	100.0			Total Liabilities & Net Worth		
						INCOME DATA		
		100.0	100.0			Net Sales		
						Gross Profit		
		96.9	95.7			Operating Expenses		
		3.1	4.3			Operating Profit		
		-.1	.3			All Other Expenses (net)		
		3.2	4.0			Profit Before Taxes		
						RATIOS		
		3.4	3.0					
		1.5	2.3			Current		
		1.2	1.3					
		2.2	2.9					
		1.4	1.7			Quick		
		1.1	1.0					
		8 46.6	21 17.8					
		22 16.3	25 14.5			Sales/Receivables		
		53 6.8	38 9.6					
						Cost of Sales/Inventory		
						Cost of Sales/Payables		
		5.1	3.7					
		15.4	9.7			Sales/Working Capital		
		28.9	18.2					
		14.2	11.6					
		(18) 2.4	(15) 3.3			EBIT/Interest		
		.5	2.4					
						Net Profit + Depr., Dep., Amort./Cur. Mat. L /T/D		
		.5	.7					
		1.0	.9			Fixed/Worth		
		1.6	1.3					
		.7	.4					
		1.2	.6			Debt/Worth		
		2.9	1.6					
		27.3	16.2					
		(22) 7.9	8.7			% Profit Before Taxes/Tangible Net Worth		
		-3.7	1.8					
		12.3	7.6					
		4.1	5.2			% Profit Before Taxes/Total Assets		
		-.8	1.2					
		18.5	5.0					
		5.6	2.9			Sales/Net Fixed Assets		
		2.4	1.9					
		3.0	2.0					
		1.8	1.3			Sales/Total Assets		
		1.1	1.0					
		1.1	2.3					
		(23) 2.1	(15) 2.8			% Depr., Dep., Amort./Sales		
		3.8	3.7					
						% Officers', Directors', Owners' Comp/Sales		
735M	21312M	301819M	450399M	54869M		Net Sales ($)		
98M	10098M	116971M	274821M	67473M		Total Assets ($)		

© RMA 2005

M = $ thousand   MM = $ million
See Pages 11 through 21 for Explanation of Ratios and Data

Comparative Historical Data | Current Data Sorted By Sales

				Type of Statement						
8	29	31		Unqualified	1	4	4	6	11	5
1	2	5		Reviewed		2			1	2
	4	2		Compiled	1	1				
	5			Tax Returns						
9	10	11		Other		1		4	4	2
4/1/02- 3/31/03	4/1/03- 3/31/04	4/1/04- 3/31/05			35 (4/1-9/30/04)			14 (10/1/04-3/31/05)		
ALL	ALL	ALL			0-1MM	1-3MM	3-5MM	5-10MM	10-25MM	25MM & OVER
18	50	49		**NUMBER OF STATEMENTS**	2	8	4	10	16	9
%	%	%		**ASSETS**	%	%	%	%	%	%
26.4	26.4	20.2		Cash & Equivalents				21.2	19.0	
18.4	16.8	19.1		Trade Receivables (net)				23.4	17.0	
.1	.2	.2		Inventory				.6	.2	
3.4	5.1	6.5		All Other Current				5.3	9.1	
48.3	48.5	46.0		Total Current				50.5	45.3	
43.4	38.9	42.7		Fixed Assets (net)				36.1	47.0	
1.4	.8	1.3		Intangibles (net)				3.1	.8	
6.9	11.8	10.0		All Other Non-Current				10.4	7.0	
100.0	100.0	100.0		Total				100.0	100.0	
				LIABILITIES						
1.0	12.1	3.2		Notes Payable-Short Term				4.3	2.4	
1.0	2.1	3.3		Cur. Mat.-L/T/D				2.2	2.0	
6.3	6.6	6.7		Trade Payables				8.6	6.9	
.0	.2	.0		Income Taxes Payable				.0	.0	
11.5	27.9	16.4		All Other Current				12.2	14.7	
19.9	48.9	29.7		Total Current				27.3	26.1	
20.4	19.5	23.0		Long-Term Debt				17.1	23.6	
.1	.1	.0		Deferred Taxes				.0	.0	
5.6	3.1	.6		All Other Non-Current				1.7	.0	
54.1	28.3	46.8		Net Worth				53.9	50.3	
100.0	100.0	100.0		Total Liabilities & Net Worth				100.0	100.0	
				INCOME DATA						
100.0	100.0	100.0		Net Sales				100.0	100.0	
				Gross Profit						
98.7	97.2	96.2		Operating Expenses				96.3	95.7	
1.3	2.8	3.8		Operating Profit				3.7	4.3	
1.0	.1	.1		All Other Expenses (net)				.8	.8	
.3	2.7	3.7		Profit Before Taxes				3.0	3.5	
				RATIOS						
4.4	2.9	3.3						3.0	3.4	
2.8	1.7	1.7		Current				1.8	1.6	
1.5	1.1	1.2						1.4	1.3	
4.2	2.3	2.9						2.1	3.2	
2.5	1.5	1.5		Quick				1.7	1.3	
1.5	.9	1.0						1.3	1.0	
12 29.3	11 32.0	13 27.5						15 24.2	18 20.7	
30 12.3	32 11.6	24 15.0		Sales/Receivables				27 13.6	27 13.7	
49 7.4	43 8.5	56 6.6						57 6.4	64 5.7	
				Cost of Sales/Inventory						
				Cost of Sales/Payables						
4.4	5.7	4.5						6.0	3.5	
6.9	11.1	12.2		Sales/Working Capital				12.1	12.9	
15.5	55.4	27.1						26.1	21.9	
3.8	7.0	12.2							11.4	
(14) 2.5	(35) 2.5	(41) 3.2		EBIT/Interest					3.0	
-.4	.3	1.0							1.7	
				Net Profit + Depr., Dep., Amort./Cur. Mat. L/T/D						
.3	.4	.6						.3	.7	
.8	.9	.9		Fixed/Worth				.8	.9	
1.7	1.9	1.4						1.3	1.3	
.5	.5	.5						.5	.5	
.7	1.1	1.0		Debt/Worth				.8	1.0	
1.6	4.4	2.1						1.3	1.8	
9.1	20.2	21.7							15.8	
(17) 2.7	(43) 7.1	(46) 9.9		% Profit Before Taxes/Tangible Net Worth					6.9	
-7.1	-2.6	.8							1.6	
7.9	11.4	11.8						14.2	8.8	
1.6	2.9	5.0		% Profit Before Taxes/Total Assets				6.1	3.8	
-4.2	-3.1	.3						-6.7	.7	
19.7	22.3	13.8						24.9	6.9	
3.0	5.7	3.8		Sales/Net Fixed Assets				7.2	2.1	
2.0	2.5	2.1						3.3	1.9	
2.3	3.1	2.6						3.1	2.3	
1.5	1.6	1.5		Sales/Total Assets				2.4	1.3	
1.2	1.3	1.1						1.5	1.0	
.9	1.3	1.4							.8	
2.2	(43) 2.3	(45) 2.7		% Depr., Dep., Amort./Sales					2.7	
2.6	3.3	3.8							3.7	
				% Officers', Directors', Owners' Comp/Sales						
684728M	803204M	829134M		Net Sales ($)	1218M	19582M	16574M	85615M	289959M	416186M
237962M	568148M	469461M		Total Assets ($)	1854M	17143M	16204M	39126M	203398M	191736M

M = $ thousand   MM = $ million
See Pages 11 through 21 for Explanation of Ratios and Data

Current Data Sorted By Assets | Comparative Historical Data

0-500M	500M-2MM	2-10MM	10-50MM	50-100MM	100-250MM	Type of Statement	1	2
		2	4			Unqualified		
		2				Reviewed	1	
1		2				Compiled	2	2
3	3	3				Tax Returns	2	
1	6	8				Other	4	4
							16	16
							4/1/00-3/31/01 ALL	4/1/01-3/31/02 ALL
		2 (4/1-9/30/04)	33 (10/1/04-3/31/05)					
5	9	17	4			NUMBER OF STATEMENTS	25	22
%	%	%	%	%	%	ASSETS	%	%
		11.5		D	D	Cash & Equivalents	12.4	14.2
		24.5		A	A	Trade Receivables (net)	25.3	25.6
		2.1		T	T	Inventory	2.4	5.8
		4.3		A	A	All Other Current	1.5	1.8
		42.3				Total Current	41.5	47.4
		41.6		N	N	Fixed Assets (net)	39.3	33.5
		11.4		O	O	Intangibles (net)	12.0	10.8
		4.6		T	T	All Other Non-Current	7.1	8.3
		100.0				Total	100.0	100.0
				A	A	LIABILITIES		
		4.4		V	V	Notes Payable-Short Term	6.2	6.1
		6.0		A	A	Cur. Mat.-L/T/D	5.3	33.2
		6.5		I	I	Trade Payables	23.3	5.1
		.2		L	L	Income Taxes Payable	.0	.1
		7.1		A	A	All Other Current	8.1	14.7
		24.1		B	B	Total Current	42.9	59.2
		29.8		L	L	Long-Term Debt	31.0	21.8
		.1		E	E	Deferred Taxes	.0	.0
		3.7				All Other Non-Current	7.5	9.0
		42.3				Net Worth	18.6	10.0
		100.0				Total Liabilities & Net Worth	100.0	100.0
						INCOME DATA		
		100.0				Net Sales	100.0	100.0
						Gross Profit		
		76.6				Operating Expenses	90.7	85.4
		23.4				Operating Profit	9.3	14.6
		6.3				All Other Expenses (net)	4.7	4.7
		17.1				Profit Before Taxes	4.6	9.9
						RATIOS		
		3.8				Current	2.3	3.9
		2.2					1.2	2.6
		.7					.5	.4
		3.6				Quick	2.1	3.8
		1.8					.7	1.9
		.6					.5	.4
	0	UND				Sales/Receivables	3 116.9	0 UND
	51	7.1					49 7.4	63 5.8
	68	5.4					72 5.1	78 4.7
						Cost of Sales/Inventory		
						Cost of Sales/Payables		
		5.1				Sales/Working Capital	8.9	4.0
		6.3					15.2	5.7
		-23.9					-8.5	-13.3
		67.2				EBIT/Interest	11.4	71.0
	(14)	23.3					(20) 1.4	(18) 5.8
		2.1					-.2	3.2
						Net Profit + Depr., Dep., Amort./Cur. Mat. L./T/D		
		.4				Fixed/Worth	.7	.3
		1.0					1.3	.8
		NM					-.9	9.8
		.5				Debt/Worth	1.1	.4
		.7					4.3	1.7
		NM					-3.3	NM
		113.8				% Profit Before Taxes/Tangible Net Worth	116.6	81.4
	(13)	88.8					(15) 56.9	(17) 37.4
		28.7					10.5	16.7
		63.4				% Profit Before Taxes/Total Assets	42.3	34.5
		39.5					3.1	14.4
		3.4					-8.2	2.4
		11.8				Sales/Net Fixed Assets	13.4	15.3
		5.8					5.5	5.0
		2.7					2.4	2.9
		2.6				Sales/Total Assets	3.4	3.2
		2.0					1.8	1.7
		1.0					1.1	1.0
		1.7				% Depr., Dep., Amort./Sales	2.1	1.4
		3.1					(20) 4.3	(17) 3.4
		5.6					6.0	5.2
						% Officers', Directors', Owners' Comp/Sales		
9888M	46806M	168031M	137871M			Net Sales ($)	314771M	155230M
1519M	12059M	84978M	55373M			Total Assets ($)	363631M	111044M

© RMA 2005

M = $ thousand   MM = $ million
See Pages 11 through 21 for Explanation of Ratios and Data

Comparative Historical Data

Current Data Sorted By Sales

				Type of Statement						
2	3	6		Unqualified				2	2	2
		2		Reviewed		1		1		
7	4	3		Compiled		1	1	1	1	
1	8	9		Tax Returns	3	1	2	1	1	
22	26	15		Other	3	2	3	4	5	
1					1					

4/1/02-3/31/03 ALL	4/1/03-3/31/04 ALL	4/1/04-3/31/05 ALL			2 (4/1-9/30/04)			33 (10/1/04-3/31/05)		
					0-1MM	1-3MM	3-5MM	5-10MM	10-25MM	25MM & OVER
32	41	35		**NUMBER OF STATEMENTS**	4	3	7	10	9	2
%	%	%		**ASSETS**	%	%	%	%	%	%
15.5	15.0	11.3		Cash & Equivalents				15.2		
27.1	25.1	23.4		Trade Receivables (net)				31.7		
2.4	2.3	1.8		Inventory				2.1		
2.3	3.7	3.7		All Other Current				1.0		
47.3	46.1	40.2		Total Current				49.9		
40.6	34.8	38.8		Fixed Assets (net)				40.2		
6.3	8.5	12.1		Intangibles (net)				8.0		
5.8	10.6	8.9		All Other Non-Current				1.9		
100.0	100.0	100.0		Total				100.0		
				LIABILITIES						
13.3	8.5	17.1		Notes Payable-Short Term				9.6		
3.6	4.1	4.7		Cur. Mat.-L/T/D				7.1		
6.4	7.0	8.7		Trade Payables				15.4		
.5	.0	.1		Income Taxes Payable				.0		
17.2	17.4	21.3		All Other Current				9.3		
41.0	37.0	51.9		Total Current				41.4		
19.3	26.8	32.5		Long-Term Debt				26.3		
.0	.0	.1		Deferred Taxes				.2		
2.3	5.5	2.9		All Other Non-Current				4.2		
37.4	30.7	12.6		Net Worth				27.9		
100.0	100.0	100.0		Total Liabilities & Net Worth				100.0		
				INCOME DATA						
100.0	100.0	100.0		Net Sales				100.0		
				Gross Profit						
88.2	89.3	84.8		Operating Expenses				87.2		
11.8	10.7	15.2		Operating Profit				12.8		
1.4	1.1	3.0		All Other Expenses (net)				.9		
10.4	9.6	12.1		Profit Before Taxes				11.9		
				RATIOS						
3.4	3.6	2.5						3.5		
1.9	2.1	1.5		Current				1.9		
1.0	.8	.3						.6		
3.1	3.2	2.4						3.3		
1.8	1.8	1.0		Quick				1.8		
.8	.7	.3						.6		
0 UND	0 UND	0 UND						0 UND		
54 6.8	45 8.1	47 7.8		Sales/Receivables				55 6.7		
67 5.5	68 5.4	60 6.1						77 4.7		
				Cost of Sales/Inventory						
				Cost of Sales/Payables						
6.5	5.6	6.2						5.7		
14.9	13.1	14.6		Sales/Working Capital				10.8		
NM	-59.8	-23.1						-23.6		
42.0	43.6	57.2								
(27) 10.0	(30) 9.9	(27) 17.8		EBIT/Interest						
4.0	1.7	.9								
				Net Profit + Depr., Dep., Amort./Cur. Mat. L/T/D						
.4	.4	.4						.7		
.9	.8	.9		Fixed/Worth				1.3		
6.3	2.2	-4.3						-1.2		
.4	.5	.6						.4		
1.2	1.5	1.5		Debt/Worth				2.1		
8.4	5.0	-7.1						-3.0		
128.5	102.7	103.6		% Profit Before Taxes/Tangible Net Worth				48.9		
(26) 59.8	(32) 64.6	(24) 55.9								
38.0	16.7	19.0								
43.9	38.8	44.8		% Profit Before Taxes/Total Assets				48.9		
21.7	16.1	15.7						20.9		
6.3	.2	-.4						-6.0		
19.1	19.4	18.7		Sales/Net Fixed Assets				10.4		
7.9	11.6	7.6						6.3		
3.5	3.9	4.1						4.7		
3.8	4.1	4.3		Sales/Total Assets				3.6		
2.5	2.4	2.3						2.1		
1.6	1.5	1.6						1.6		
1.4	1.7	1.7		% Depr., Dep., Amort./Sales				1.7		
(30) 2.1	(38) 2.4	(31) 2.5						2.8		
4.4	3.8	5.0						5.2		
5.3	2.9	5.0		% Officers', Directors', Owners' Comp/Sales						
(10) 7.9	(17) 7.7	(13) 7.2								
46.7	8.2	24.2								
298695M	348230M	362596M		Net Sales ($)	2402M	5898M	26466M	66488M	163906M	97436M
141590M	186803M	153929M		Total Assets ($)	10651M	2375M	14353M	33287M	66765M	26498M

M = $ thousand   MM = $ million
See Pages 11 through 21 for Explanation of Ratios and Data

Current Data Sorted By Assets   **Comparative Historical Data**

						Type of Statement		
	2	10	6	1		Unqualified		
1	5	11	3			Reviewed		
21	15	7				Compiled		
27	7	8				Tax Returns		
8	13	21	3	1	2	Other		
	25 (4/1-9/30/04)		147 (10/1/04-3/31/05)				4/1/00-3/31/01	4/1/01-3/31/02
0-500M	500M-2MM	2-10MM	10-50MM	50-100MM	100-250MM		ALL	ALL
57	42	57	12	2	2	NUMBER OF STATEMENTS		
%	%	%	%	%	%	ASSETS	%	%
39.8	17.9	14.6	6.7			Cash & Equivalents		
2.8	11.3	18.2	25.5			Trade Receivables (net)	D	D
1.0	2.0	2.0	2.5			Inventory	A	A
1.8	3.0	4.5	3.6			All Other Current	T	T
45.5	34.2	39.3	38.3			Total Current	A	A
41.9	48.5	53.2	45.7			Fixed Assets (net)		
7.5	4.6	2.4	4.8			Intangibles (net)	N	N
5.2	12.7	5.0	11.2			All Other Non-Current	O	O
100.0	100.0	100.0	100.0			Total	T	T
						LIABILITIES	A	A
44.3	16.0	3.7	3.2			Notes Payable-Short Term	V	V
7.6	5.5	6.6	4.0			Cur. Mat.-L/T/D	A	A
1.1	4.6	3.7	4.9			Trade Payables	I	I
.7	.0	.1	2.1			Income Taxes Payable	L	L
37.5	13.2	8.5	7.4			All Other Current	A	A
91.3	39.3	22.7	21.6			Total Current	B	B
26.9	29.5	41.3	19.9			Long-Term Debt	L	L
.1	.5	.9	1.5			Deferred Taxes	E	E
8.4	3.2	1.1	2.4			All Other Non-Current		
−26.6	27.5	34.1	54.7			Net Worth		
100.0	100.0	100.0	100.0			Total Liabilities & Net Worth		
						INCOME DATA		
100.0	100.0	100.0	100.0			Net Sales		
						Gross Profit		
88.6	84.3	78.5	84.2			Operating Expenses		
11.4	15.7	21.5	15.8			Operating Profit		
2.2	3.6	5.6	4.9			All Other Expenses (net)		
9.2	12.1	15.9	10.8			Profit Before Taxes		
						RATIOS		
1.2	3.3	3.7	4.1					
.6	.8	1.8	1.8			Current		
.2	.3	.8	1.0					
1.2	3.2	3.4	3.2					
.6	.7	1.5	1.5			Quick		
.1	.2	.6	.8					
0 UND	0 UND	0 UND	29 12.7					
0 UND	0 UND	41 8.9	40 9.1			Sales/Receivables		
0 UND	27 13.4	58 6.2	59 6.2					
						Cost of Sales/Inventory		
						Cost of Sales/Payables		
255.4	14.6	5.0	4.9					
−47.5	−337.7	10.7	9.8			Sales/Working Capital		
−13.0	−11.7	−78.8	NM					
14.7	25.2	30.2	40.4					
(38) 5.6	(39) 6.6	(47) 11.9	(10) 4.6			EBIT/Interest		
.9	.7	1.8	1.2					
						Net Profit + Depr., Dep.,		
						Amort./Cur. Mat. L /T/D		
.9	.5	.8	.4					
−4.9	2.3	1.8	1.0			Fixed/Worth		
−.7	UND	5.9	1.3					
3.1	1.1	.9	.3					
−11.1	4.0	2.2	.9			Debt/Worth		
−2.6	UND	7.2	1.8					
415.0	319.3	140.5	31.5			% Profit Before Taxes/Tangible		
(24) 128.8	(32) 25.9	(52) 53.2	(11) 13.4			Net Worth		
8.2	−7.2	12.9	5.7					
64.3	45.3	51.1	22.4			% Profit Before Taxes/Total		
8.3	7.5	12.3	7.2			Assets		
−1.0	−1.5	3.0	.6					
122.8	28.7	9.3	7.6					
35.6	10.9	3.5	4.4			Sales/Net Fixed Assets		
18.0	4.1	1.6	2.1					
24.3	7.7	2.9	2.6					
13.2	3.6	1.7	1.8			Sales/Total Assets		
6.7	1.8	.8	1.2					
.5	1.3	2.7	2.5					
(36) .9	(36) 3.8	(52) 4.8	(11) 3.5			% Depr., Dep., Amort./Sales		
2.3	7.1	11.7	9.0					
15.1	5.2	.8				% Officers', Directors',		
(37) 25.6	(20) 12.6	(15) 17.2				Owners' Comp/Sales		
36.1	22.8	35.1						
181293M	258762M	537971M	561802M	108448M	360303M	Net Sales ($)		
10940M	48861M	259395M	287963M	145827M	351459M	Total Assets ($)		

© RMA 2005   M = $ thousand MM = $ million
See Pages 11 through 21 for Explanation of Ratios and Data

Comparative Historical Data				Current Data Sorted By Sales					
			Type of Statement						
8	13	19	Unqualified	1	1	2	3	7	5
5	12	20	Reviewed	2	1	1	7	4	5
39	55	43	Compiled	8	12	9	7	6	1
31	39	42	Tax Returns	14	10	8	4	4	2
28	43	48	Other	5	12	8	9	9	5
4/1/02-3/31/03 ALL	4/1/03-3/31/04 ALL	4/1/04-3/31/05 ALL		25 (4/1-9/30/04)		147 (10/1/04-3/31/05)			
				0-1MM	1-3MM	3-5MM	5-10MM	10-25MM	25MM & OVER
111	162	172	**NUMBER OF STATEMENTS**	30	36	28	30	30	18
%	%	%	**ASSETS**	%	%	%	%	%	%
24.1	25.0	23.1	Cash & Equivalents	22.2	27.1	29.5	23.3	22.1	7.6
11.1	10.8	11.9	Trade Receivables (net)	4.8	5.8	7.6	18.8	18.0	20.4
.9	1.3	1.7	Inventory	.6	1.0	2.9	2.8	1.7	1.1
3.2	3.5	3.1	All Other Current	.5	.0	2.1	7.9	4.4	4.9
39.2	40.5	39.7	Total Current	28.2	34.0	42.1	52.7	46.3	34.0
46.2	45.0	47.3	Fixed Assets (net)	56.5	53.6	46.7	35.5	42.8	47.2
5.0	5.3	5.5	Intangibles (net)	10.3	6.1	2.3	3.7	2.1	10.4
9.5	9.2	7.5	All Other Non-Current	5.0	6.3	8.9	8.1	8.9	8.4
100.0	100.0	100.0	Total	100.0	100.0	100.0	100.0	100.0	100.0
			LIABILITIES						
21.7	17.5	20.1	Notes Payable-Short Term	31.4	25.7	24.4	14.9	13.3	3.0
7.7	10.4	6.3	Cur. Mat.-L/T/D	4.5	11.0	3.9	6.9	5.5	4.2
3.3	3.6	3.1	Trade Payables	.5	3.2	4.1	4.7	2.7	4.1
.5	.4	.4	Income Taxes Payable	.0	.0	1.4	.1	.0	1.4
35.2	23.3	19.2	All Other Current	16.3	21.5	23.7	21.4	14.5	16.4
68.5	55.2	49.1	Total Current	52.7	61.5	57.5	48.0	36.0	29.1
31.1	33.9	31.6	Long-Term Debt	57.5	31.9	23.7	23.7	23.3	27.2
.1	.1	.5	Deferred Taxes	.0	.1	.7	1.6	.0	1.1
11.0	6.3	4.2	All Other Non-Current	16.4	1.7	.6	1.0	1.3	4.5
-10.6	4.5	14.6	Net Worth	-26.6	4.8	17.5	25.8	39.4	38.1
100.0	100.0	100.0	Total Liabilities & Net Worth	100.0	100.0	100.0	100.0	100.0	100.0
			INCOME DATA						
100.0	100.0	100.0	Net Sales	100.0	100.0	100.0	100.0	100.0	100.0
			Gross Profit						
94.4	90.8	83.9	Operating Expenses	71.1	92.2	84.0	83.5	85.3	87.2
5.6	9.2	16.1	Operating Profit	28.9	7.8	16.0	16.5	14.7	12.8
.5	1.7	3.7	All Other Expenses (net)	14.8	2.8	.2	1.0	.5	2.9
5.1	7.5	12.3	Profit Before Taxes	14.1	5.1	15.8	15.5	14.2	9.9
			RATIOS						
1.5	2.0	2.6		1.5	2.6	1.8	3.8	3.9	2.4
.7	.9	1.0	Current	.6	.7	.8	1.5	1.5	1.5
.3	.4	.4		.1	.3	.5	.7	.8	.7
1.3	1.8	2.3		1.3	2.5	1.6	3.2	3.5	1.9
.6	.9	.9	Quick	.6	.6	.7	1.2	1.4	1.2
.2	.3	.3		.1	.2	.5	.5	.7	.6
0 UND	0 UND	0 UND		0 UND	0 UND	0 UND	0 UND	0 UND	0 UND
0 UND	0 UND	0 UND	Sales/Receivables	0 UND	0 UND	0 UND	35 10.3	4 92.0	39 9.3
26 13.9	40 9.1	43 8.6		0 UND	40 9.2	23 16.1	51 7.2	56 6.5	59 6.2
			Cost of Sales/Inventory						
			Cost of Sales/Payables						
46.3	15.2	9.9		26.7	18.6	19.5	8.4	5.5	8.4
-52.4	-290.8	NM	Sales/Working Capital	-13.2	-64.9	-46.8	32.4	33.8	31.6
-17.9	-22.1	-21.2		-6.0	-11.0	-22.1	-86.0	-128.2	-237.5
10.8	13.0	23.4		12.9	9.1	37.7	36.2	32.7	35.2
(91) 3.3	(131) 3.5	(137) 6.8	EBIT/Interest	(17) 6.6	(27) 1.0	(23) 8.3	(27) 14.4	(26) 12.4	(17) 5.4
1.0	.7	1.0		1.7	-1.8	.4	2.9	1.0	1.4
5.6	2.9	3.6	Net Profit + Depr., Dep., Amort./Cur. Mat. L/T/D						
(11) 1.5	(13) 2.3	(19) 2.5							
.1	1.4	1.4							
1.2	.9	.8		4.5	.8	.9	.3	.4	.9
5.8	3.7	2.5	Fixed/Worth	29.1	3.1	2.0	1.2	1.1	1.3
-1.3	-2.6	-5.3		-.7	-1.6	NM	NM	8.5	3.6
1.8	1.2	1.0		4.3	.8	1.2	1.0	.5	.9
8.9	7.9	4.0	Debt/Worth	58.0	13.5	4.2	2.4	1.2	2.0
-5.6	-5.5	-12.7		-2.8	-2.9	-9.0	NM	10.7	7.9
203.0	226.6	196.3	% Profit Before Taxes/Tangible Net Worth	323.2	107.4	399.3	312.3	149.4	278.0
(67) 50.9	(104) 42.9	(123) 50.0		(17) 31.6	(21) 27.8	(20) 68.5	(23) 97.6	(26) 48.2	(16) 32.1
6.6	2.6	4.8		15.4	-6.8	-9.7	1.8	9.9	5.1
33.9	35.4	49.3	% Profit Before Taxes/Total Assets	37.0	29.4	94.2	66.4	56.9	28.1
6.1	7.3	8.7		7.5	-.2	18.9	27.2	12.1	7.2
.0	-1.0	-.2		1.0	-13.7	-1.9	1.3	.0	1.1
59.5	33.7	30.6		36.4	35.1	35.3	50.5	19.7	17.8
15.9	11.8	10.0	Sales/Net Fixed Assets	6.4	15.0	13.5	18.2	9.1	6.3
6.1	4.0	3.0		.2	2.0	3.4	4.7	4.1	2.7
14.8	10.2	9.6		6.7	15.5	16.0	10.1	8.4	5.2
5.9	4.3	3.5	Sales/Total Assets	2.7	4.0	6.2	4.1	2.8	2.5
2.6	2.0	1.4		.2	1.3	2.0	1.7	1.7	1.2
.9	1.8	1.6		4.4	.9	.8	.8	2.4	1.6
(81) 1.9	(115) 2.9	(139) 3.5	% Depr., Dep., Amort./Sales	(22) 12.1	(31) 3.0	(20) 3.3	(25) 2.5	(23) 3.1	3.3
5.0	6.9	7.2		21.9	11.0	4.7	4.8	4.9	5.5
4.8	9.5	6.0	% Officers', Directors', Owners' Comp/Sales	15.1	4.5	6.0	4.5	7.0	
(67) 22.7	(89) 24.1	(75) 21.6		(11) 18.0	(19) 15.1	(11) 32.4	(15) 23.5	(14) 16.7	
39.3	33.9	32.8		24.8	27.2	38.3	36.0	30.6	
1195773M	2800292M	2008579M	Net Sales ($)	15916M	71704M	106631M	203504M	456053M	1154771M
551039M	1030121M	1104445M	Total Assets ($)	32321M	40379M	32282M	73125M	171926M	754412M

© RMA 2005

M = $ thousand   MM = $ million
See Pages 11 through 21 for Explanation of Ratios and Data

Current Data Sorted By Assets   **Comparative Historical Data**

0-500M	500M-2MM	2-10MM	10-50MM	50-100MM	100-250MM	Type of Statement	4/1/00-3/31/01 ALL	4/1/01-3/31/02 ALL
2	12	41	26	7	3	Unqualified	80	87
1	7	9	2	2		Reviewed	10	14
5	12	13	2			Compiled	22	45
13	6	7				Tax Returns	9	17
18	29	40	11	3		Other	44	59
	105 (4/1-9/30/04)		164 (10/1/04-3/31/05)					
39	66	110	41	10	3	**NUMBER OF STATEMENTS**	165	222
%	%	%	%	%	%	**ASSETS**	%	%
35.3	18.9	17.0	20.8	10.9		Cash & Equivalents	16.6	17.7
7.2	27.7	20.4	14.3	10.2		Trade Receivables (net)	20.9	21.2
1.5	.7	2.0	.8	1.0		Inventory	1.1	.7
8.8	1.9	4.2	5.9	2.9		All Other Current	3.5	5.2
52.9	49.2	43.5	41.8	24.9		Total Current	42.2	44.8
39.4	45.1	42.9	40.5	37.5		Fixed Assets (net)	44.6	41.8
1.5	1.5	2.7	7.8	18.6		Intangibles (net)	4.1	5.0
6.2	4.2	10.9	9.9	19.0		All Other Non-Current	9.1	8.5
100.0	100.0	100.0	100.0	100.0		Total	100.0	100.0
						LIABILITIES		
23.4	6.0	5.6	1.7	.3		Notes Payable-Short Term	5.3	6.4
6.7	6.7	4.0	4.7	2.1		Cur. Mat.-L/T/D	5.2	3.8
7.5	7.4	7.6	5.3	3.3		Trade Payables	7.7	7.5
1.5	.0	.1	.3	.0		Income Taxes Payable	.6	.1
27.7	16.1	14.4	14.0	8.5		All Other Current	12.8	11.5
66.8	36.1	31.6	26.0	14.1		Total Current	31.7	29.4
19.5	29.3	26.4	23.5	30.4		Long-Term Debt	31.1	25.4
.0	1.5	.0	.2	.1		Deferred Taxes	.3	.1
9.3	.4	2.3	4.9	3.1		All Other Non-Current	4.0	3.0
4.5	32.6	39.6	45.4	52.2		Net Worth	33.0	42.2
100.0	100.0	100.0	100.0	100.0		Total Liabilities & Net Worth	100.0	100.0
						INCOME DATA		
100.0	100.0	100.0	100.0	100.0		Net Sales	100.0	100.0
						Gross Profit		
85.5	78.9	89.0	87.7	82.9		Operating Expenses	92.4	90.6
14.5	21.1	11.0	12.3	17.1		Operating Profit	7.6	9.4
1.6	2.3	2.3	3.1	.8		All Other Expenses (net)	.9	2.6
12.9	18.8	8.8	9.2	16.3		Profit Before Taxes	6.7	6.8
						RATIOS		
4.4	2.8	3.4	2.8	2.8			2.8	3.5
1.2	1.4	1.8	1.8	1.6		Current	1.6	1.8
.2	1.0	1.0	1.2	1.3			1.0	1.0
2.9	2.5	2.8	2.4	2.6			2.5	3.0
1.0	1.4	1.6	1.5	1.4		Quick	1.4	1.6
.2	1.0	.7	.9	.9			.8	.9
0 UND	3 123.6	15 24.0	18 20.0	28 12.9			15 24.3	5 76.4
0 UND	46 7.9	41 8.8	36 10.2	41 8.9		Sales/Receivables	41 8.8	40 9.2
4 85.5	58 6.3	54 6.7	49 7.4	57 6.4			63 5.8	63 5.8
						Cost of Sales/Inventory		
						Cost of Sales/Payables		
13.1	6.4	4.7	5.0	5.3			5.6	4.9
100.0	15.5	10.5	9.1	7.4		Sales/Working Capital	15.2	10.6
-18.2	UND	-126.8	37.5	29.3			-671.9	483.9
95.5	37.3	22.0	15.7				8.4	11.5
(23) 10.9	(51) 11.8	(86) 6.5	(37) 7.6			EBIT/Interest	(129) 3.5	(174) 4.3
1.1	.7	1.6	2.0				1.2	1.5
						Net Profit + Depr., Dep.,	11.1	
						Amort./Cur. Mat. L/T/D	(11) 7.1	
							4.8	
.4	.4	.5	.5	.5			.6	.5
1.0	1.0	1.1	.9	1.1		Fixed/Worth	1.2	1.0
-3.0	4.9	3.2	3.0	4.1			3.6	3.1
.2	.6	.6	.4	.6			.6	.5
3.1	1.5	1.4	1.4	1.4		Debt/Worth	1.5	1.2
-4.7	6.0	5.1	5.0	4.2			8.4	4.5
283.9	215.7	63.2	76.0	94.2		% Profit Before Taxes/Tangible	43.7	49.5
(25) 103.4	(56) 62.0	(96) 10.7	(37) 18.8	37.4		Net Worth	(136) 14.3	(195) 15.3
10.8	12.8	2.7	7.2	11.8			3.2	2.9
127.9	83.9	17.6	19.4	19.6		% Profit Before Taxes/Total	14.3	19.5
31.1	16.3	4.9	7.7	5.4		Assets	4.5	6.0
1.6	1.0	.4	2.5	2.0			.6	.8
58.1	17.6	11.1	10.6	9.2			12.7	16.1
31.6	5.7	4.3	3.4	3.0		Sales/Net Fixed Assets	4.0	5.0
12.1	2.6	1.8	1.7	1.4			2.0	2.2
16.8	3.3	2.4	2.1	1.5			2.8	3.1
10.9	2.2	1.7	1.3	.6		Sales/Total Assets	1.8	1.8
3.9	1.5	.9	.9	.5			1.1	1.1
.5	1.4	1.6	1.9	2.7			1.4	1.3
(27) 1.5	(57) 4.1	(90) 3.4	(40) 2.6	4.7		% Depr., Dep., Amort./Sales	(149) 2.8	(198) 2.4
3.3	9.9	5.9	5.5	10.6			4.8	3.9
6.2		2.8					4.9	5.3
(16) 19.9	(11) 5.8					% Officers', Directors',	(22) 9.5	(38) 9.3
28.9	14.3					Owners' Comp/Sales	13.3	19.0
96329M	204167M	1265264M	1514298M	699989M	917943M	Net Sales ($)	2626520M	3068203M
9446M	76764M	519237M	860209M	667093M	375726M	Total Assets ($)	1905945M	2277980M

M = $ thousand   MM = $ million
See Pages 11 through 21 for Explanation of Ratios and Data

Comparative Historical Data / Current Data Sorted By Sales

			Type of Statement						
100	89	91	Unqualified	3	12	8	24	16	28
17	19	19	Reviewed	1	2	5	9	2	
33	45	32	Compiled	6	8	4	10	3	1
15	28	26	Tax Returns	8	5	10	3		
64	89	101	Other	12	31	15	16	14	13
4/1/02-3/31/03 ALL	4/1/03-3/31/04 ALL	4/1/04-3/31/05 ALL		105 (4/1-9/30/04)			164 (10/1/04-3/31/05)		
				0-1MM	1-3MM	3-5MM	5-10MM	10-25MM	25MM & OVER
229	270	269	**NUMBER OF STATEMENTS**	30	58	42	62	35	42
%	%	%	**ASSETS**	%	%	%	%	%	%
17.1	18.9	20.3	Cash & Equivalents	23.4	22.3	17.3	17.9	18.9	23.1
21.0	20.8	19.1	Trade Receivables (net)	6.7	16.7	20.5	23.8	26.1	17.2
1.3	1.7	1.4	Inventory	.1	.1	3.7	.9	2.8	1.1
5.0	5.2	4.5	All Other Current	3.2	5.1	4.7	4.9	3.5	4.8
44.3	46.6	45.3	Total Current	33.4	44.2	46.3	47.5	51.2	46.2
42.6	41.8	42.1	Fixed Assets (net)	58.7	47.0	39.7	42.6	37.3	29.1
3.9	3.5	3.8	Intangibles (net)	.7	1.2	4.1	2.3	3.3	12.1
9.1	8.2	8.7	All Other Non-Current	7.2	7.5	9.9	7.6	8.1	12.5
100.0	100.0	100.0	Total	100.0	100.0	100.0	100.0	100.0	100.0
			LIABILITIES						
7.1	7.8	7.6	Notes Payable-Short Term	8.3	12.4	6.0	8.5	2.6	4.7
8.1	5.6	5.1	Cur. Mat.-L/T/D	7.4	7.3	5.0	4.0	3.2	3.6
7.2	7.1	7.0	Trade Payables	3.9	4.8	6.2	8.1	8.9	10.0
.3	.4	.3	Income Taxes Payable	1.5	.0	.0	.3	.4	.1
15.5	15.8	16.5	All Other Current	10.0	17.6	17.2	14.3	16.7	22.4
38.1	36.7	36.5	Total Current	31.0	42.1	34.4	35.1	31.9	40.8
30.4	24.6	26.2	Long-Term Debt	35.9	26.4	30.5	25.2	16.3	24.3
.2	.1	.4	Deferred Taxes	.0	1.2	.0	.6	.2	.2
2.9	5.4	3.3	All Other Non-Current	9.9	2.1	.9	1.5	3.7	5.1
28.4	33.2	33.6	Net Worth	23.2	28.3	34.1	37.7	47.9	29.7
100.0	100.0	100.0	Total Liabilities & Net Worth	100.0	100.0	100.0	100.0	100.0	100.0
			INCOME DATA						
100.0	100.0	100.0	Net Sales	100.0	100.0	100.0	100.0	100.0	100.0
			Gross Profit						
91.9	89.7	85.6	Operating Expenses	70.0	80.6	87.1	90.5	91.9	89.8
8.1	10.3	14.4	Operating Profit	30.0	19.4	12.9	9.5	8.1	10.2
1.0	1.5	2.2	All Other Expenses (net)	12.0	1.0	.6	.7	.6	2.3
7.1	8.8	12.1	Profit Before Taxes	18.0	18.4	12.3	8.8	7.5	7.9
			RATIOS						
2.7	3.1	3.0		4.2	4.5	2.7	3.9	2.7	2.4
1.6	1.5	1.6	Current	1.2	1.4	1.6	1.8	1.8	1.5
.8	.9	.9		.2	.9	.7	1.2	1.2	.9
2.4	2.6	2.6		3.9	3.2	2.4	2.9	2.5	1.9
1.4	(269) 1.3	1.4	Quick	1.1	1.4	1.4	1.6	1.6	1.2
.7	.7	.8		.2	.8	.6	.9	1.2	.8
10 38.2	1 269.6	2 239.8		0 UND	0 UND	0 UND	28 13.2	23 15.9	5 71.4
39 9.4	34 10.6	37 9.7	Sales/Receivables	0 UND	40 9.2	51 7.2	44 8.2	37 10.0	30 12.2
59 6.1	57 6.4	53 6.9		34 10.8	56 6.5	64 5.7	58 6.3	53 6.9	46 7.9
			Cost of Sales/Inventory						
			Cost of Sales/Payables						
5.5	6.4	6.1		11.3	6.1	5.0	5.6	7.3	6.7
17.6	16.5	14.8	Sales/Working Capital	78.9	15.1	12.9	10.7	10.4	22.7
-61.2	-126.6	-134.8		-2.0	-89.2	-64.1	125.4	39.6	-111.3
14.5	21.9	28.5		53.9	44.4	12.3	23.1	38.1	40.0
(179) 3.2	(212) 5.5	(207) 7.6	EBIT/Interest	(14) 6.1	(45) 8.5	(36) 4.0	(49) 7.6	(29) 9.0	(34) 9.0
.6	1.2	1.6		-.9	1.2	1.4	1.2	2.7	2.0
8.3	6.2	15.1	Net Profit + Depr., Dep.,						
(22) 2.5	(16) 2.8	(15) 4.1	Amort./Cur. Mat. L/T/D						
1.3	1.3	2.7							
.6	.6	.5		.6	.5	.3	.5	.4	.5
1.3	1.2	1.0	Fixed/Worth	1.7	1.2	.9	1.1	.8	1.3
5.7	3.6	4.0		7.6	4.4	11.1	2.8	1.1	UND
.6	.6	.6		.5	.5	.4	.5	.5	.8
1.8	1.8	1.6	Debt/Worth	2.6	2.0	1.3	1.3	1.0	3.7
17.0	6.4	5.9		8.4	6.7	NM	4.1	3.6	-160.9
60.4	95.9	127.0	% Profit Before Taxes/Tangible	108.3	237.5	152.6	64.1	58.4	87.7
(179) 14.1	(223) 18.5	(224) 26.3	Net Worth	(24) 26.0	(47) 57.4	(32) 46.9	(57) 18.8	(33) 17.5	(31) 28.0
2.4	1.9	3.8		.7	7.1	4.0	1.8	3.1	9.5
19.8	22.2	34.1	% Profit Before Taxes/Total	64.5	83.9	45.0	23.0	19.0	19.7
6.4	7.2	8.1	Assets	4.2	15.6	11.8	7.1	7.8	6.6
-1.1	.2	1.4		-2.2	.6	2.2	.4	1.6	2.5
17.0	26.3	21.4		11.1	22.4	18.0	16.0	17.7	61.0
5.2	5.6	5.3	Sales/Net Fixed Assets	2.7	4.2	6.2	5.7	7.3	5.4
2.3	2.3	2.4		.2	1.8	2.3	2.3	3.5	3.1
3.5	4.0	3.5		4.1	3.4	3.3	3.2	3.9	4.7
2.0	2.0	1.9	Sales/Total Assets	1.4	1.7	2.1	2.1	2.2	1.7
1.1	1.2	1.1		.2	1.0	1.1	1.1	1.6	1.1
1.4	1.4	1.4		2.6	1.2	2.2	1.4	1.4	1.1
(204) 2.6	(226) 3.1	(227) 3.1	% Depr., Dep., Amort./Sales	(22) 9.9	(49) 4.6	(30) 4.5	(55) 2.5	(32) 1.9	(39) 2.2
4.9	5.8	6.7		16.5	12.3	6.7	4.9	3.5	3.7
4.8	4.7	4.0	% Officers', Directors',					3.1	
(40) 14.6	(43) 14.7	(39) 12.7	Owners' Comp/Sales					(12) 14.2	
30.4	34.9	21.5						24.5	
6553622M	8739201M	4697990M	Net Sales ($)	16752M	111774M	171585M	450179M	558288M	3389412M
3490036M	3107400M	2508475M	Total Assets ($)	31327M	104999M	107788M	376389M	274964M	1613008M

M = $ thousand   MM = $ million
See Pages 11 through 21 for Explanation of Ratios and Data

HEALTH CARE—Medical Laboratories NAICS 621511 (SIC 8071)

| | Current Data Sorted By Assets | | | | | | | Comparative Historical Data | |

								4/1/00- 3/31/01	4/1/01- 3/31/02
2	5	7	22	6	6				
6	3	15	3	1	1				
6	10	9			1				
8	11	5			1				
10	20	19	11						
	28 (4/1-9/30/04)			153 (10/1/04-3/31/05)				ALL	ALL
0-500M	500M-2MM	2-10MM	10-50MM	50-100MM	100-250MM				
26	49	55	36	7	8	**NUMBER OF STATEMENTS**		158	145
%	%	%	%	%	%	**ASSETS**		%	%
24.4	16.6	13.0	12.0			Cash & Equivalents		12.4	16.0
19.2	33.2	34.4	27.3			Trade Receivables (net)		28.6	28.8
1.9	3.0	2.0	5.8			Inventory		4.2	4.1
3.6	1.5	4.8	2.8			All Other Current		2.3	2.4
49.1	54.3	54.2	47.9			Total Current		47.5	51.3
37.4	37.0	34.3	34.1			Fixed Assets (net)		38.2	36.1
1.7	3.2	6.6	6.2			Intangibles (net)		4.7	4.6
11.8	5.5	4.9	11.8			All Other Non-Current		9.6	8.0
100.0	100.0	100.0	100.0			Total		100.0	100.0
						LIABILITIES			
18.7	8.8	9.1	5.3			Notes Payable-Short Term		8.9	6.8
7.0	8.6	7.7	5.0			Cur. Mat.-L/T/D		5.7	5.4
15.6	13.8	7.7	8.3			Trade Payables		7.7	7.7
1.4	.1	1.6	1.1			Income Taxes Payable		.7	.6
41.3	9.5	12.7	12.5			All Other Current		15.7	15.4
84.1	41.0	38.6	32.3			Total Current		38.7	35.8
48.2	29.3	18.0	20.3			Long-Term Debt		18.4	24.0
.0	.3	1.2	.5			Deferred Taxes		.9	.7
22.4	6.5	7.3	3.2			All Other Non-Current		3.4	6.8
-54.6	22.9	34.9	43.8			Net Worth		38.7	32.7
100.0	100.0	100.0	100.0			Total Liabilities & Net Worth		100.0	100.0
						INCOME DATA			
100.0	100.0	100.0	100.0			Net Sales		100.0	100.0
						Gross Profit			
94.8	90.4	90.2	89.1			Operating Expenses		87.7	88.5
5.2	9.6	9.8	10.9			Operating Profit		12.3	11.5
.9	3.0	1.3	2.5			All Other Expenses (net)		1.4	1.2
4.2	6.5	8.5	8.4			Profit Before Taxes		10.9	10.3
						RATIOS			
2.5	2.7	2.2	2.7					2.6	3.4
.9	1.2	1.5	1.6			Current		1.4	1.8
.2	.8	.9	1.0					.9	1.1
2.4	2.4	2.1	1.9					2.1	2.9
.6	1.0	1.3	1.3			Quick		1.2	1.5
.1	.7	.6	.8					.7	.9
0 UND	23 15.9	28 13.1	32 11.3					29 12.7	32 11.6
0 UND	52 7.0	48 7.6	56 6.6			Sales/Receivables		55 6.6	53 6.9
35 10.4	99 3.7	78 4.7	95 3.8					74 4.9	69 5.3
						Cost of Sales/Inventory			
						Cost of Sales/Payables			
31.9	6.3	6.2	5.0					5.8	5.1
-131.7	28.0	13.7	11.4			Sales/Working Capital		17.0	9.6
-7.6	-14.2	-56.1	136.0					-50.0	94.1
43.8	10.7	22.8	15.0					15.5	21.3
(17) 4.2	(42) 2.2	(49) 7.1	(32) 7.7			EBIT/Interest		(128) 4.6	(123) 5.8
1.1	1.0	1.3	2.4					1.5	1.5
		5.1				Net Profit + Depr., Dep.,		14.1	6.4
	(12) 2.1					Amort./Cur. Mat. L /T/D		(25) 2.3	(23) 2.9
		.7						1.1	1.0
.4	.3	.3	.3					.4	.4
NM	1.4	1.2	.8			Fixed/Worth		.9	.9
-.4	28.5	2.2	2.2					2.3	2.1
1.2	.7	1.1	.6					.6	.5
-5.3	3.6	1.8	1.2			Debt/Worth		1.6	1.3
-1.6	219.6	5.7	3.7					4.2	4.8
387.3	99.8	68.4	68.3			% Profit Before Taxes/Tangible		68.4	90.1
(12) 124.2	(39) 26.2	(46) 39.6	(32) 29.1			Net Worth		(141) 30.1	(122) 32.4
32.0	2.9	8.3	9.9					5.5	7.9
98.5	29.4	24.4	21.5			% Profit Before Taxes/Total		29.0	37.3
22.1	4.1	10.6	11.3			Assets		11.9	11.3
-.1	-.1	2.4	3.7					1.4	2.0
133.6	34.2	20.8	14.2					16.9	18.6
25.9	11.0	9.9	6.3			Sales/Net Fixed Assets		6.9	8.1
11.7	1.8	4.8	3.0					2.6	2.9
16.7	4.0	3.2	2.3					3.2	3.4
6.2	2.4	2.5	1.6			Sales/Total Assets		2.0	2.2
3.6	1.1	1.4	1.0					1.3	1.5
.7	1.7	1.3	2.3					1.7	1.5
(17) 1.6	(39) 3.7	(49) 2.7	(33) 3.8			% Depr., Dep., Amort./Sales		(140) 3.3	(131) 3.3
4.0	15.2	6.0	4.9					7.0	6.3
	5.7	4.8						5.6	5.1
	(13) 11.0	(17) 11.0				% Officers', Directors',		(33) 9.9	(48) 11.5
	16.7	30.0				Owners' Comp/Sales		21.2	24.2
69887M	167788M	671453M	1780140M	798822M	1130176M	Net Sales ($)		3167893M	2888220M
6326M	56201M	241644M	953782M	496057M	1237364M	Total Assets ($)		2183347M	1932658M

M = $ thousand   MM = $ million
See Pages 11 through 21 for Explanation of Ratios and Data

Comparative Historical Data   Current Data Sorted By Sales

				0-1MM	1-3MM	3-5MM	5-10MM	10-25MM	25MM & OVER
			Type of Statement						
29	38	46	Unqualified	2	1	2	2	11	28
15	20	25	Reviewed	1	1	2	8	7	6
22	38	26	Compiled	2	6	5	9	3	1
22	25	24	Tax Returns	4	9	5	3	3	
66	47	60	Other	7	17	8	7	9	12
4/1/02-3/31/03 ALL	4/1/03-3/31/04 ALL	4/1/04-3/31/05 ALL		28 (4/1-9/30/04)		153 (10/1/04-3/31/05)			
154	168	181	**NUMBER OF STATEMENTS**	16	34	22	29	33	47
%	%	%	**ASSETS**	%	%	%	%	%	%
14.2	14.7	15.4	Cash & Equivalents	15.8	16.9	16.7	16.9	14.9	13.0
26.1	25.4	29.2	Trade Receivables (net)	23.2	29.1	30.8	33.8	31.6	26.0
2.9	4.4	3.3	Inventory	2.0	3.4	.6	2.2	3.9	5.0
2.7	4.2	3.1	All Other Current	1.7	.9	7.1	4.9	2.3	2.7
45.9	48.8	51.0	Total Current	42.8	50.3	55.1	57.8	52.7	46.8
38.7	34.6	35.3	Fixed Assets (net)	42.9	40.4	26.8	31.3	37.7	33.7
6.6	6.7	5.4	Intangibles (net)	3.2	4.5	6.6	4.9	3.7	7.8
8.7	9.9	8.4	All Other Non-Current	11.2	4.7	11.5	6.0	5.9	11.7
100.0	100.0	100.0	Total	100.0	100.0	100.0	100.0	100.0	100.0
			LIABILITIES						
10.0	10.3	9.0	Notes Payable-Short Term	6.9	14.0	16.1	7.4	7.0	5.2
8.3	6.6	7.0	Cur. Mat.-L/T/D	8.7	7.0	5.7	10.4	7.2	4.9
7.6	8.2	10.5	Trade Payables	16.2	18.8	7.8	6.2	8.0	8.4
.8	1.2	.9	Income Taxes Payable	2.3	.0	.4	.6	1.4	1.3
12.3	13.8	15.7	All Other Current	31.5	13.5	19.1	17.6	12.5	11.2
38.9	40.1	43.2	Total Current	65.6	53.4	49.0	42.2	36.1	31.0
26.9	22.2	25.4	Long-Term Debt	30.7	43.1	26.2	18.1	21.6	17.6
.4	.4	.6	Deferred Taxes	.0	.1	.6	2.1	.1	.8
4.0	6.1	8.7	All Other Non-Current	10.2	16.4	4.7	7.5	6.1	6.9
29.8	31.2	22.1	Net Worth	-6.5	-13.0	19.4	30.1	36.1	43.7
100.0	100.0	100.0	Total Liabilities & Net Worth	100.0	100.0	100.0	100.0	100.0	100.0
			INCOME DATA						
100.0	100.0	100.0	Net Sales	100.0	100.0	100.0	100.0	100.0	100.0
			Gross Profit						
89.8	91.7	91.2	Operating Expenses	97.4	90.3	90.1	91.5	87.4	92.7
10.2	8.3	8.8	Operating Profit	2.6	9.7	9.9	8.5	12.6	7.3
2.4	1.9	1.9	All Other Expenses (net)	3.7	2.0	1.5	1.9	3.1	.4
7.8	6.4	7.0	Profit Before Taxes	-1.1	7.7	8.4	6.6	9.5	6.9
			RATIOS						
2.5	2.4	2.6	Current	2.5	3.2	2.7	2.4	2.8	2.5
1.5	1.4	1.5		.8	1.2	1.6	1.4	1.5	1.6
.9	.8	.8		.4	.4	.7	.9	.9	1.0
2.3	2.0	2.1	Quick	2.2	2.5	2.5	2.0	2.3	1.8
1.1	1.1	1.1		.7	.9	1.1	1.3	1.4	1.3
.7	.7	.6		.4	.4	.3	.7	.7	.8
10 35.5	0 UND	20 18.3	Sales/Receivables	0 UND	0 UND	0 UND	0 UND	24 14.9	32 11.3
47 7.7	44 8.3	46 8.0		68 5.4	38 9.7	40 9.1	46 7.9	44 8.4	54 6.7
68 5.4	65 5.6	70 5.2		120 3.1	70 5.2	108 3.4	69 5.3	64 5.7	73 5.0
			Cost of Sales/Inventory						
			Cost of Sales/Payables						
6.9	7.5	6.4	Sales/Working Capital	5.0	6.4	7.7	6.7	6.1	5.7
17.0	22.9	18.2		-10.3	45.5	19.9	18.2	13.7	12.0
-105.1	-32.9	-39.1		-4.1	-9.0	-37.3	-218.6	NM	158.5
15.7	15.8	17.1	EBIT/Interest		19.2	11.8	20.7	26.9	15.4
(135) 5.1	(139) 4.8	(155) 5.1		(29) 2.1	(19) 4.1	(24) 11.0	(30) 5.7	(44) 7.5	
1.4	1.5	1.3			-.3	1.2	1.3	.5	2.5
14.0	11.6	5.5	Net Profit + Depr., Dep., Amort./Cur. Mat. L/T/D						7.1
(29) 4.2	(17) 1.6	(29) 2.9						(13)	3.8
1.6	.2	1.0							2.6
.4	.4	.4	Fixed/Worth	.4	.5	.2	.5	.3	.4
1.1	1.1	1.1		11.7	1.6	1.0	1.0	1.2	.8
7.2	6.4	9.7		-3.8	-.9	-6.5	3.6	2.2	2.1
.7	.7	.7	Debt/Worth	1.6	.7	.6	1.2	.5	.6
2.0	2.1	1.9		297.6	3.1	1.9	2.1	1.8	1.3
22.7	75.7	19.3		-3.5	-2.2	-11.0	8.3	7.0	4.6
86.2	58.1	76.7	% Profit Before Taxes/Tangible Net Worth		146.4	70.9	73.5	116.5	49.6
(122) 29.8	(128) 26.7	(142) 35.6		(23) 44.9	(16) 19.5	(24) 50.4	(29) 12.0	(41) 30.4	
9.2	6.3	6.4			8.9	2.1	10.8	1.5	7.2
22.2	21.9	28.2	% Profit Before Taxes/Total Assets	18.5	37.5	29.4	29.4	20.3	22.9
8.5	7.6	8.5		.6	10.3	11.5	13.1	7.1	9.9
1.0	1.1	.5		-10.3	-1.1	4.3	.5	-.6	3.7
17.2	24.3	24.2	Sales/Net Fixed Assets	65.7	42.9	67.7	32.0	26.5	14.0
6.3	9.8	9.8		6.3	9.7	18.9	11.2	8.7	7.5
2.8	3.0	3.5		.8	3.3	8.2	4.7	3.9	3.0
3.2	3.8	3.7	Sales/Total Assets	3.7	4.3	5.8	4.6	3.4	2.5
2.2	2.1	2.4		1.3	2.6	2.3	3.0	2.6	1.9
1.4	1.3	1.3		.5	1.3	1.3	1.9	1.5	1.1
2.1	1.8	1.6	% Depr., Dep., Amort./Sales	1.4	1.4	1.4	1.7	.8	2.0
(133) 3.7	(144) 3.8	(148) 3.2		(12) 14.1	(25) 5.1	(15) 2.3	(25) 2.7	(30) 2.2	(41) 3.7
7.3	7.1	6.3		38.2	13.1	6.7	6.2	4.7	4.3
5.0	4.3	5.8	% Officers', Directors', Owners' Comp/Sales					3.3	
(41) 11.6	(50) 11.3	(39) 11.5						(12) 8.8	
27.0	23.2	25.2						17.4	
4325226M	4346816M	4618266M	Net Sales ($)	7651M	60848M	86502M	206297M	509935M	3747033M
2777437M	2994866M	2991374M	Total Assets ($)	10270M	31802M	40860M	93725M	310719M	2503998M

© RMA 2005

M = $ thousand   MM = $ million
See Pages 11 through 21 for Explanation of Ratios and Data

Current Data Sorted By Assets

						Type of Statement		
		8	5	1		Unqualified		
	3	5	2			Reviewed		
5	6	5	1			Compiled		
9	6	3				Tax Returns		
1	9	15				Other		
	7 (4/1-9/30/04)		77 (10/1/04-3/31/05)				4/1/00-3/31/01	4/1/01-3/31/02
0-500M	500M-2MM	2-10MM	10-50MM	50-100MM	100-250MM		ALL	ALL
15	24	36	8	1		NUMBER OF STATEMENTS		
%	%	%	%	%	%	ASSETS	%	%
22.9	12.6	13.2				Cash & Equivalents		
7.2	11.0	23.7			D	Trade Receivables (net)	D	D
.0	.0	1.5			A	Inventory	A	A
.4	9.9	2.5			T	All Other Current	T	T
30.5	33.4	40.9			A	Total Current	A	A
49.5	55.6	51.2				Fixed Assets (net)		
3.1	1.9	.6			N	Intangibles (net)	N	N
16.9	9.1	7.3			O	All Other Non-Current	O	O
100.0	100.0	100.0			T	Total	T	T
						LIABILITIES		
35.3	13.7	4.7			A	Notes Payable-Short Term	A	A
5.0	15.0	12.0			V	Cur. Mat.-L/T/D	V	V
2.2	2.7	4.6			A	Trade Payables	A	A
.0	.0	.6			I	Income Taxes Payable	I	I
17.5	12.8	8.4			L	All Other Current	L	L
59.9	44.3	30.3			A	Total Current	A	A
30.8	40.8	37.6			B	Long-Term Debt	B	B
.0	.0	.1			L	Deferred Taxes	L	L
1.0	10.5	6.2			E	All Other Non-Current	E	E
8.2	4.4	25.8				Net Worth		
100.0	100.0	100.0				Total Liabilities & Net Worth		
						INCOME DATA		
100.0	100.0	100.0				Net Sales		
						Gross Profit		
93.3	87.2	86.5				Operating Expenses		
6.7	12.8	13.5				Operating Profit		
1.5	2.0	1.6				All Other Expenses (net)		
5.1	10.8	12.0				Profit Before Taxes		
						RATIOS		
1.9	2.3	2.0						
.5	.7	1.2				Current		
.2	.2	.6						
1.9	1.2	2.0						
.4	.3	1.0				Quick		
.1	.1	.5						
0 UND	0 UND	14 25.3						
0 UND	0 UND	47 7.8				Sales/Receivables		
0 UND	58 6.3	69 5.3						
						Cost of Sales/Inventory		
						Cost of Sales/Payables		
54.1	31.2	7.2						
-76.2	-64.0	19.5				Sales/Working Capital		
-17.7	-6.2	-15.8						
17.1	19.0	22.2						
(11) 2.0	(22) 7.6	(33) 3.1				EBIT/Interest		
-3.0	.2	.8						
						Net Profit + Depr., Dep., Amort./Cur. Mat. L /T/D		
.6	.6	.8						
1.8	2.5	2.1				Fixed/Worth		
-1.8	-2.0	13.7						
.8	.7	1.3						
1.7	3.4	2.5				Debt/Worth		
-3.7	-4.9	17.4						
	117.3	158.1				% Profit Before Taxes/Tangible Net Worth		
	(14) 74.6	(31) 34.5						
	40.1	4.8						
72.5	43.5	24.1				% Profit Before Taxes/Total Assets		
21.9	18.6	8.2						
-33.8	-9.0	-.1						
101.7	8.9	9.8						
17.1	4.4	3.9				Sales/Net Fixed Assets		
11.2	1.8	1.2						
26.5	5.0	2.9						
11.6	2.2	1.8				Sales/Total Assets		
4.5	1.0	.8						
	2.8	3.6				% Depr., Dep., Amort./Sales		
	(18) 6.3	(33) 6.0						
	21.0	13.9						
15.6						% Officers', Directors', Owners' Comp/Sales		
(10) 22.5								
44.5								
60387M	113295M	360050M	276879M	68232M		Net Sales ($)		
3887M	25707M	146914M	196613M	80929M		Total Assets ($)		

M = $ thousand   MM = $ million
See Pages 11 through 21 for Explanation of Ratios and Data

Comparative Historical Data | | | | **Current Data Sorted By Sales**

4	6	14	Type of Statement		2	2	1	4	5
4	6	10	Unqualified		2	3	2	2	2
6	9	17	Reviewed	2	1	3	2	2	1
1	13	18	Compiled	2	5	4	2	3	
12	27	25	Tax Returns	2	10	1	3	2	
			Other	4	6	3	2	8	2
4/1/02-3/31/03	4/1/03-3/31/04	4/1/04-3/31/05			7 (4/1-9/30/04)			77 (10/1/04-3/31/05)		
ALL	ALL	ALL		0-1MM	1-3MM	3-5MM	5-10MM	10-25MM	25MM & OVER
27	61	84	NUMBER OF STATEMENTS	8	24	13	10	19	10
%	%	%	**ASSETS**	%	%	%	%	%	%
15.2	16.9	14.5	Cash & Equivalents		10.4	23.1	10.3	22.7	10.7
24.9	19.2	16.6	Trade Receivables (net)		9.3	12.0	29.5	26.2	15.2
1.7	.3	.7	Inventory		.0	.0	.9	2.0	.8
2.3	6.0	4.3	All Other Current		4.1	1.4	2.9	3.3	6.0
44.1	42.4	36.1	Total Current		23.8	36.5	43.7	54.3	32.7
41.5	44.8	52.6	Fixed Assets (net)		60.8	55.0	49.4	36.6	48.1
6.6	4.6	2.2	Intangibles (net)		3.4	.2	2.3	.1	7.3
7.9	8.2	9.0	All Other Non-Current		12.1	8.2	4.6	9.1	11.9
100.0	100.0	100.0	Total		100.0	100.0	100.0	100.0	100.0
			LIABILITIES						
4.9	11.5	12.8	Notes Payable-Short Term		13.1	11.4	30.7	3.5	3.8
9.6	9.9	11.6	Cur. Mat.-L/T/D		12.4	14.3	7.7	9.4	12.3
4.2	3.6	3.6	Trade Payables		2.0	1.8	7.5	4.8	5.7
.4	.0	.3	Income Taxes Payable		.0	.0	.0	.2	1.8
6.1	18.2	11.3	All Other Current		4.7	6.5	15.0	18.6	19.2
25.2	43.3	39.6	Total Current		32.3	34.0	60.7	36.6	42.7
29.6	31.1	36.6	Long-Term Debt		43.9	46.9	20.3	21.0	28.2
1.7	.2	.1	Deferred Taxes		.0	.0	.4	.0	.0
5.7	4.4	5.9	All Other Non-Current		.7	5.4	.2	15.5	1.4
37.8	21.0	17.9	Net Worth		23.1	13.7	18.4	26.9	27.7
100.0	100.0	100.0	Total Liabilities & Net Worth		100.0	100.0	100.0	100.0	100.0
			INCOME DATA						
100.0	100.0	100.0	Net Sales		100.0	100.0	100.0	100.0	100.0
			Gross Profit						
86.0	90.7	87.5	Operating Expenses		83.3	84.3	95.1	87.9	86.1
14.0	9.3	12.5	Operating Profit		16.7	15.7	4.9	12.1	13.9
3.4	2.1	1.7	All Other Expenses (net)		2.8	1.5	1.0	.3	.4
10.6	7.2	10.8	Profit Before Taxes		13.9	14.2	3.9	11.8	13.5
			RATIOS						
3.7	2.2	2.0	Current		2.3	2.0	1.6	3.7	1.3
1.7	1.2	1.0			.6	.9	1.0	1.6	.9
.8	.5	.4			.2	.3	.2	1.0	.4
2.9	2.0	1.9	Quick		1.7	2.0	1.6	3.4	1.1
1.5	1.0	.8			.6	.9	.9	1.5	.8
.7	.4	.2			.1	.3	.0	.7	.1
31 11.9	0 UND	0 UND	Sales/Receivables	0 UND	0 UND	0 UND	0 UND	0 UND	0 UND
60 6.1	37 9.9	27 13.6			0 UND	13 27.7	56 6.5	41 8.9	40 9.1
87 4.2	69 5.3	63 5.8			79 4.6	56 6.5	77 4.7	58 6.3	47 7.8
			Cost of Sales/Inventory						
			Cost of Sales/Payables						
4.6	8.0	10.9	Sales/Working Capital		31.5	12.6	7.7	7.2	30.3
10.0	47.0	-586.1			-27.6	-72.5	-297.6	16.4	-118.3
-21.6	-18.1	-13.5			-3.8	-14.4	-52.1	-999.8	-35.5
22.7	20.1	17.1	EBIT/Interest		(23) 11.6	(12) 27.2		(14) 45.2	
(21) 8.3	(49) 4.0	(75) 3.5			3.1	3.5		6.1	
1.6	.1	1.0			.0	2.4		.8	
		3.4	Net Profit + Depr., Dep.,						
	(10) 1.1		Amort./Cur. Mat. L/T/D						
		.8							
.3	.8	.9	Fixed/Worth		1.0	1.0	.7	.7	1.0
1.2	2.3	2.2			2.2	2.4	2.2	1.2	2.1
3.5	-11.0	NM			-8.1	14.8	-2.0	59.3	NM
.4	1.1	1.1	Debt/Worth		.7	1.2	1.2	.9	1.3
2.1	3.0	2.4			2.0	2.5	2.7	1.7	3.2
121.4	-21.5	-26.3			-13.0	20.7	-9.8	579.2	NM
82.9	78.5	158.2	% Profit Before Taxes/Tangible		(17) 229.5	(12) 323.3		(15) 196.8	
(21) 45.5	(45) 40.5	(62) 52.9	Net Worth		59.6	72.1		38.2	
11.7	-.8	18.7			16.6	27.1		4.8	
38.5	31.5	40.1	% Profit Before Taxes/Total		61.0	44.6	28.4	51.2	51.8
12.2	7.5	12.3	Assets		17.4	14.3	6.2	7.2	18.2
1.5	-5.5	-.1			-.7	7.1	-12.4	-1.5	.8
18.2	15.5	13.5	Sales/Net Fixed Assets		8.8	40.7	22.5	101.7	30.0
4.5	5.8	5.1			2.4	3.8	10.4	8.4	5.6
1.7	2.3	2.0			1.0	2.3	6.0	4.8	2.9
3.0	3.6	5.0	Sales/Total Assets		3.1	4.9	11.8	6.4	9.2
2.0	2.0	2.4			1.3	1.7	4.4	3.1	2.8
.8	1.0	1.0			.8	1.1	1.9	2.3	1.9
2.4	2.4	3.5	% Depr., Dep., Amort./Sales		(22) 3.7			(14) 3.0	
(25) 7.4	(51) 5.2	(66) 6.1			9.9			4.6	
10.8	11.4	14.3			25.7			13.2	
5.4	11.1	8.5	% Officers', Directors',						
(11) 16.2	(15) 21.5	(24) 20.6	Owners' Comp/Sales						
34.4	28.7	39.5							
344523M	956604M	878843M	Net Sales ($)	4949M	47892M	53216M	62616M	299999M	410171M
319171M	520828M	454050M	Total Assets ($)	7208M	37633M	29287M	24228M	156375M	199319M

M = $ thousand   MM = $ million
See Pages 11 through 21 for Explanation of Ratios and Data

Current Data Sorted By Assets   **Comparative Historical Data**

						Type of Statement		
3	9	46	25	5	3	Unqualified	78	64
	6	12	3			Reviewed	14	12
13	17	4	2			Compiled	36	28
21	12	4				Tax Returns	13	13
18	41	31	15	2	3	Other	67	76
	76 (4/1-9/30/04)			219 (10/1/04-3/31/05)			4/1/00-3/31/01 ALL	4/1/01-3/31/02 ALL
0-500M	500M-2MM	2-10MM	10-50MM	50-100MM	100-250MM			
55	85	97	45	7	6	NUMBER OF STATEMENTS	208	193
%	%	%	%	%	%	ASSETS	%	%
23.2	14.1	17.2	24.8			Cash & Equivalents	14.1	17.0
36.7	44.2	40.8	32.4			Trade Receivables (net)	42.6	38.3
.5	2.2	2.6	.4			Inventory	1.7	2.5
7.2	7.4	3.9	3.3			All Other Current	3.4	3.3
67.5	67.9	64.5	60.9			Total Current	61.8	61.1
20.2	18.1	22.3	22.2			Fixed Assets (net)	22.5	22.6
2.6	1.2	3.2	2.8			Intangibles (net)	4.7	5.7
9.6	12.8	10.0	14.2			All Other Non-Current	11.0	10.6
100.0	100.0	100.0	100.0			Total	100.0	100.0
						LIABILITIES		
21.2	13.7	5.3	6.8			Notes Payable-Short Term	11.0	12.1
3.2	4.8	2.1	1.9			Cur. Mat.-L/T/D	4.0	4.8
12.2	11.3	9.1	8.5			Trade Payables	10.6	10.1
.3	.4	.3	.0			Income Taxes Payable	.3	.2
23.7	21.5	17.3	22.6			All Other Current	24.9	18.5
60.6	51.7	34.0	39.7			Total Current	50.7	45.7
19.2	16.4	12.1	16.0			Long-Term Debt	13.1	15.0
.1	.0	.1	.1			Deferred Taxes	.1	.1
10.0	9.0	3.0	7.2			All Other Non-Current	7.1	3.8
10.2	22.9	50.8	37.0			Net Worth	28.9	35.4
100.0	100.0	100.0	100.0			Total Liabilities & Net Worth	100.0	100.0
						INCOME DATA		
100.0	100.0	100.0	100.0			Net Sales	100.0	100.0
						Gross Profit		
95.2	93.9	94.1	96.9			Operating Expenses	96.9	94.0
4.8	6.1	5.9	3.1			Operating Profit	3.1	6.0
.3	1.4	.0	−.8			All Other Expenses (net)	−.1	.4
4.5	4.7	5.9	3.9			Profit Before Taxes	3.1	5.6
						RATIOS		
3.4	3.1	3.4	3.2				2.3	2.5
1.2	1.5	2.2	1.7			Current	1.4	1.5
.7	.7	1.2	1.1				.9	1.0
2.8	2.8	3.3	3.0				2.1	2.3
(54) 1.0	1.2	1.8	1.6			Quick	(207) 1.3	1.4
.6	.6	1.0	.9				.9	.9
0 UND	25 14.4	38 9.5	44 8.4				37 10.0	31 11.8
23 16.1	41 8.9	51 7.1	54 6.8			Sales/Receivables	56 6.6	52 7.1
49 7.5	68 5.4	79 4.6	69 5.3				74 4.9	75 4.9
						Cost of Sales/Inventory		
						Cost of Sales/Payables		
14.1	6.4	4.4	4.4				7.5	6.1
92.4	15.0	8.4	7.3			Sales/Working Capital	15.0	14.6
−24.6	−18.9	27.7	63.0				−79.6	721.4
54.8	23.0	48.2	24.0				11.3	14.0
(39) 10.0	(62) 5.8	(72) 9.7	(34) 8.4			EBIT/Interest	(175) 3.5	(164) 4.8
.4	.8	2.4	1.4				.0	1.4
						Net Profit + Depr., Dep.,	21.5	12.7
						Amort./Cur. Mat. L /T/D	(14) 6.2 (14) 2.3	
							3.1	.2
.1	.1	.1	.2				.2	.1
.6	.5	.4	.5			Fixed/Worth	.5	.4
−.8	17.4	1.5	1.5				2.7	1.9
.5	.6	.3	.4				.5	.5
2.5	1.8	.8	1.3			Debt/Worth	1.7	1.4
−4.1	60.5	2.8	9.7				12.5	7.5
169.1	90.9	49.3	25.9				50.0	58.6
(35) 75.6	(66) 38.0	(87) 22.1	(39) 13.5			% Profit Before Taxes/Tangible Net Worth	(165) 16.3	(158) 23.6
6.2	10.0	5.2	6.2				.7	4.6
94.3	29.6	22.6	11.4				17.1	24.2
22.3	14.3	8.8	7.5			% Profit Before Taxes/Total Assets	5.9	9.1
−3.8	1.0	3.2	.9				−1.6	1.0
418.1	102.4	72.5	77.3				66.2	57.9
52.2	31.1	16.4	14.2			Sales/Net Fixed Assets	19.9	21.9
23.2	13.8	5.7	3.9				6.8	7.7
10.3	4.9	3.5	3.2				3.8	4.1
6.7	3.4	2.3	1.7			Sales/Total Assets	2.6	2.5
4.0	2.4	1.5	.9				1.7	1.7
.2	.3	.4	.7				.5	.5
(36) .5	(64) .6	(85) 1.6	(39) 1.8			% Depr., Dep., Amort./Sales	(180) 1.2	(160) 1.2
1.2	1.5	3.4	2.2				2.3	2.3
3.1	1.5	2.0					3.2	2.1
(22) 6.4	(24) 3.0	(14) 2.3				% Officers', Directors', Owners' Comp/Sales	(31) 4.1	(32) 5.7
9.8	10.3	5.6					9.7	8.4
119413M	323022M	1084100M	1808312M	832649M	865122M	Net Sales ($)	4441846M	4000051M
13805M	89675M	425370M	884703M	547335M	915018M	Total Assets ($)	2160465M	1693659M

M = $ thousand   MM = $ million
See Pages 11 through 21 for Explanation of Ratios and Data

Comparative Historical Data | Current Data Sorted By Sales

Type of Statement									
	88	97	91	2	8	12	15	32	22	Unqualified
	26	16	21		1	1	12	3	4	Reviewed
	31	49	36	3	17	5	6	5		Compiled
	19	25	37	7	16	7	7	3		Tax Returns
	70	95	110	9	26	19	23	15	18	Other

	4/1/02-3/31/03 ALL	4/1/03-3/31/04 ALL	4/1/04-3/31/05 ALL	0-1MM	1-3MM	3-5MM	5-10MM	10-25MM	25MM & OVER
				76 (4/1-9/30/04)			219 (10/1/04-3/31/05)		
NUMBER OF STATEMENTS	234	282	295	21	68	44	60	58	44
ASSETS	%	%	%	%	%	%	%	%	%
Cash & Equivalents	15.9	17.7	18.5	10.7	18.5	23.8	17.6	16.2	20.8
Trade Receivables (net)	41.7	38.9	38.8	30.2	37.6	37.1	41.6	40.1	41.3
Inventory	3.1	2.1	1.7	1.1	2.2	.9	2.3	2.1	.6
All Other Current	4.3	6.0	5.4	4.1	8.5	5.1	6.2	3.0	3.9
Total Current	64.9	64.7	64.4	46.1	66.8	66.8	67.7	61.5	66.6
Fixed Assets (net)	19.6	19.4	20.6	34.1	18.3	19.9	19.3	26.0	13.1
Intangibles (net)	4.4	4.9	3.6	6.0	1.5	2.9	4.0	1.7	8.3
All Other Non-Current	11.1	10.9	11.4	13.7	13.4	10.4	9.0	10.9	12.1
Total	100.0	100.0	100.0	100.0	100.0	100.0	100.0	100.0	100.0
LIABILITIES									
Notes Payable-Short Term	10.3	11.8	10.7	23.8	12.0	11.2	12.2	4.7	7.9
Cur. Mat.-L/T/D	3.9	3.4	3.2	1.1	3.6	2.2	6.2	2.0	2.2
Trade Payables	9.8	7.9	10.0	10.8	11.3	7.6	11.2	8.1	11.0
Income Taxes Payable	.4	.9	.3	.4	.1	.1	.1	.8	
All Other Current	23.3	23.2	20.3	22.0	20.8	18.2	17.1	19.2	26.4
Total Current	47.6	47.1	44.5	58.1	47.9	39.3	46.9	34.8	47.6
Long-Term Debt	12.2	12.9	15.9	31.5	14.8	16.9	14.6	10.8	17.4
Deferred Taxes	.3	.2	.1	.0	.1	.0	.1	.1	.2
All Other Non-Current	4.2	6.6	6.9	4.5	12.2	5.4	6.5	3.4	6.6
Net Worth	35.8	33.2	32.6	5.7	25.1	38.4	31.9	51.0	28.1
Total Liabilities & Net Worth	100.0	100.0	100.0	100.0	100.0	100.0	100.0	100.0	100.0
INCOME DATA									
Net Sales	100.0	100.0	100.0	100.0	100.0	100.0	100.0	100.0	100.0
Gross Profit									
Operating Expenses	95.3	93.4	94.8	90.0	95.5	91.9	95.3	96.2	96.4
Operating Profit	4.7	6.6	5.2	10.0	4.5	8.1	4.7	3.8	3.6
All Other Expenses (net)	.7	1.1	.5	6.2	.2	.2	-.4	-.2	.5
Profit Before Taxes	4.0	5.5	4.7	3.8	4.3	8.0	5.0	4.0	3.1
RATIOS									
Current	2.7	3.2	3.2	1.5	4.8	4.0	2.9	3.2	2.6
	1.6	1.7	1.7	.8	2.0	2.2	1.7	1.8	1.5
	1.0	1.1	1.0	.4	.8	1.2	1.1	1.1	1.0
Quick	2.5	2.9	3.0	1.5	4.4	3.7	2.7	3.0	2.4
	1.4	1.4	(294) 1.5	.8	(67) 1.4	2.0	1.3	1.7	1.3
	.9	.9	.9	.4	.5	1.1	.8	1.0	.9
Sales/Receivables	33 11.1	30 12.2	28 13.1	0 UND	21 17.8	24 15.1	32 11.5	33 11.1	44 8.3
	50 7.3	47 7.8	48 7.7	17 21.2	37 9.8	49 7.5	49 7.5	48 7.7	54 6.8
	73 5.0	69 5.3	71 5.1	99 3.7	58 6.3	84 4.3	78 4.7	56 6.5	71 5.2
Cost of Sales/Inventory									
Cost of Sales/Payables									
Sales/Working Capital	6.3	5.4	5.5	16.4	6.4	3.7	5.5	5.8	5.3
	13.8	11.9	12.1	-20.4	14.7	8.3	12.6	10.4	10.5
	216.2	86.6	999.8	-6.9	-27.5	46.2	167.6	35.9	106.5
EBIT/Interest	24.6	28.2	33.0	18.0	41.4	39.8	13.6	51.8	34.4
	(183) 6.6	(200) 7.2	(218) 7.9	(11) 7.3	(51) 4.5	(30) 12.8	(48) 4.6	(44) 15.0	(34) 9.0
	1.2	1.7	1.3	-5.1	-.5	4.0	.6	4.6	1.4
Net Profit + Depr., Dep., Amort./Cur. Mat. L/T/D	18.4	11.5	11.5						
	(25) 8.1	(27) 4.2	(25) 1.9						
	2.8	2.1	1.0						
Fixed/Worth	.1	.1	.1	.1	.1	.1	.1	.2	.2
	.5	.4	.5	7.3	.5	.4	.6	.4	.4
	2.2	1.4	3.3	-.5	190.3	1.4	NM	1.2	101.3
Debt/Worth	.6	.4	.4	.8	.5	.2	.6	.4	.5
	1.6	1.3	1.3	17.8	1.4	1.0	1.8	.7	2.5
	9.3	6.0	14.9	-2.5	NM	7.8	NM	2.0	434.6
% Profit Before Taxes/Tangible Net Worth	65.5	60.1	67.4	93.8	104.0	118.3	51.8	51.3	45.5
	(196) 27.1	(232) 24.3	(235) 24.7	(13) 9.8	(51) 42.6	(38) 39.9	(45) 22.5	(54) 19.0	(34) 19.8
	4.7	4.0	6.0	-2.5	4.2	14.4	2.3	8.2	7.4
% Profit Before Taxes/Total Assets	23.6	23.5	26.3	20.5	37.7	32.4	25.3	17.8	15.2
	10.3	10.2	9.5	1.3	7.5	17.8	10.0	9.4	8.2
	1.4	.8	1.2	-16.3	-2.0	5.9	1.0	4.7	1.1
Sales/Net Fixed Assets	79.5	94.5	101.3	80.9	116.5	92.0	125.3	60.9	113.5
	26.6	26.0	26.7	17.3	31.2	28.8	26.3	16.5	37.5
	7.4	7.4	8.1	5.9	12.3	6.8	5.9	5.1	9.7
Sales/Total Assets	4.2	4.2	4.9	5.9	5.5	4.8	5.7	4.9	3.5
	2.6	2.8	2.9	2.2	3.4	2.9	3.0	2.8	2.3
	1.7	1.7	1.6	.6	2.2	1.4	1.8	1.6	1.6
% Depr., Dep., Amort./Sales	.5	.5	.4	.8	.4	.3	.4	.4	.5
	(197) 1.3	(224) 1.2	(235) 1.1	(12) 1.9	(48) .9	(35) .7	(52) .9	(50) 1.8	(38) 1.2
	2.2	2.3	2.2	12.9	1.9	1.8	2.4	2.8	1.9
% Officers', Directors', Owners' Comp/Sales	2.8	3.5	2.0		2.4		2.0		
	(53) 4.4	(56) 5.6	(63) 4.0		(27) 4.9		(11) 2.4		
	9.2	10.9	8.9		11.6		6.6		
Net Sales ($)	7717085M	5663004M	5032618M	10820M	128519M	169181M	409008M	877326M	3437764M
Total Assets ($)	3187405M	2937520M	2875906M	10319M	53504M	180412M	186768M	547296M	1897607M

© RMA 2005

M = $ thousand   MM = $ million
See Pages 11 through 21 for Explanation of Ratios and Data

Current Data Sorted By Assets   **Comparative Historical Data**

0-500M	500M-2MM	2-10MM	10-50MM	50-100MM	100-250MM	Type of Statement	4/1/00-3/31/01 ALL	4/1/01-3/31/02 ALL
	1	1	1			Unqualified		
	2	1				Reviewed		
3		3	1			Compiled		
1	1	3				Tax Returns		
3	6	6			1	Other		
7	10	14	2		1	**NUMBER OF STATEMENTS**		
%	%	%	%	%	%	**ASSETS**	%	%
	17.1	9.4				Cash & Equivalents		
	24.6	39.3	D			Trade Receivables (net)	D	D
	2.9	.9	A			Inventory	A	A
	2.3	5.5	T			All Other Current	T	T
	46.8	55.1	A			Total Current	A	A
	42.0	36.0				Fixed Assets (net)		
	5.3	.7	N			Intangibles (net)	N	N
	5.8	8.3	O			All Other Non-Current	O	O
	100.0	100.0	T			Total	T	T
			A			**LIABILITIES**	A	A
	13.3	7.6	V			Notes Payable-Short Term	V	V
	5.4	12.1	A			Cur. Mat.-L/T/D	A	A
	1.9	10.7	I			Trade Payables	I	I
	.0	.2	L			Income Taxes Payable	L	L
	2.4	3.6	A			All Other Current	A	A
	22.9	34.2	B			Total Current	B	B
	18.3	34.4	L			Long-Term Debt	L	L
	.0	.0	E			Deferred Taxes	E	E
	2.5	7.4				All Other Non-Current		
	56.3	24.0				Net Worth		
	100.0	100.0				Total Liabilities & Net Worth		
						INCOME DATA		
	100.0	100.0				Net Sales		
						Gross Profit		
	83.6	101.5				Operating Expenses		
	16.4	-1.5				Operating Profit		
	1.8	3.8				All Other Expenses (net)		
	14.6	-5.3				Profit Before Taxes		
						RATIOS		
	12.5	3.4						
	3.6	1.7				Current		
	1.3	1.0						
	11.9	3.1						
	3.5	1.6				Quick		
	1.0	.9						
0	UND	49 7.4						
64	5.7	83 4.4				Sales/Receivables		
97	3.8	179 2.0						
						Cost of Sales/Inventory		
						Cost of Sales/Payables		
	2.5	3.4						
	4.1	9.0				Sales/Working Capital		
	85.5	258.5						
		10.1						
	(12)	2.6				EBIT/Interest		
		-11.2						
						Net Profit + Depr., Dep., Amort./Cur. Mat. L /T/D		
	.3	.8						
	.7	1.2				Fixed/Worth		
	2.2	6.3						
	.3	1.0						
	.5	6.0				Debt/Worth		
	3.1	30.2						
	56.0	48.2						
	18.8 (12)	7.8				% Profit Before Taxes/Tangible Net Worth		
	9.7	-310.2						
	37.5	15.8						
	10.8	3.1				% Profit Before Taxes/Total Assets		
	3.3	-32.0						
	8.5	8.4						
	5.9	6.8				Sales/Net Fixed Assets		
	1.3	2.4						
	2.1	2.4						
	1.6	1.5				Sales/Total Assets		
	.7	.8						
		4.4						
		5.6				% Depr., Dep., Amort./Sales		
		7.4						
						% Officers', Directors', Owners' Comp/Sales		
13462M	19642M	108310M	58434M		526603M	Net Sales ($)		
1831M	11544M	63355M	34736M		205241M	Total Assets ($)		

M = $ thousand   MM = $ million
See Pages 11 through 21 for Explanation of Ratios and Data

Comparative Historical Data | Current Data Sorted By Sales

			Type of Statement						
8	10	3	Unqualified			1	1	1	1
4	4	3	Reviewed		1	1	1	1	
6	7	7	Compiled			2	3	1	1
5	6	5	Tax Returns		1	1	2	1	
3	8	16	Other	1	1				2
				4	6	2	2		
4/1/02- 3/31/03	4/1/03- 3/31/04	4/1/04- 3/31/05			6 (4/1-9/30/04)		28 (10/1/04-3/31/05)		
ALL	ALL	ALL		0-1MM	1-3MM	3-5MM	5-10MM	10-25MM	25MM & OVER
26	35	34	NUMBER OF STATEMENTS	5	11	4	7	3	4
%	%	%	ASSETS	%	%	%	%	%	%
6.4	13.3	16.9	Cash & Equivalents		21.3				
31.7	22.9	26.4	Trade Receivables (net)		17.0				
4.0	2.7	1.5	Inventory		.4				
2.8	2.8	3.9	All Other Current		7.1				
44.8	41.7	48.7	Total Current		45.8				
43.2	48.7	41.3	Fixed Assets (net)		42.3				
5.6	3.4	3.5	Intangibles (net)		3.4				
6.4	6.1	6.6	All Other Non-Current		8.5				
100.0	100.0	100.0	Total		100.0				
			LIABILITIES						
12.5	8.9	27.8	Notes Payable-Short Term		52.0				
8.3	6.4	9.9	Cur. Mat.-L/T/D		11.5				
7.9	5.4	6.7	Trade Payables		6.1				
.7	.7	.1	Income Taxes Payable		.0				
10.3	9.5	10.2	All Other Current		6.4				
39.6	30.9	54.6	Total Current		75.9				
33.0	30.5	36.6	Long-Term Debt		28.1				
1.9	.7	.0	Deferred Taxes		.0				
5.0	8.8	6.9	All Other Non-Current		1.8				
20.4	29.0	1.9	Net Worth		-5.8				
100.0	100.0	100.0	Total Liabilities & Net Worth		100.0				
			INCOME DATA						
100.0	100.0	100.0	Net Sales		100.0				
			Gross Profit						
92.6	95.8	95.1	Operating Expenses		99.2				
7.4	4.2	4.9	Operating Profit		.8				
3.3	1.5	2.7	All Other Expenses (net)		3.4				
4.2	2.8	2.2	Profit Before Taxes		-2.6				
			RATIOS						
1.9	3.3	3.5			4.1				
1.2	1.6	1.5	Current		1.1				
.9	1.0	1.0			.5				
1.6	3.1	3.5			4.1				
1.1	1.4	1.2	Quick		.9				
.7	.8	.9			.5				
33 10.9	3 123.0	0 UND			0 UND				
51 7.1	39 9.3	55 6.7	Sales/Receivables		60 6.1				
88 4.2	69 5.3	98 3.7			83 4.4				
			Cost of Sales/Inventory						
			Cost of Sales/Payables						
9.4	7.0	3.4			4.3				
21.4	21.9	10.0	Sales/Working Capital		10.1				
-49.1	-239.0	-171.6			-11.4				
7.3	9.4	13.8							
(25) 3.1	(30) 3.1	(29) 2.3	EBIT/Interest						
.8	.3	-4.5							
			Net Profit + Depr., Dep., Amort./Cur. Mat. L/T/D						
.9	.7	.7			.4				
2.3	1.3	1.5	Fixed/Worth		1.8				
7.3	2.6	NM			-10.6				
1.6	.5	.6			.3				
4.1	1.6	2.9	Debt/Worth		2.7				
23.7	3.9	NM			-31.3				
59.9	43.9	33.6	% Profit Before Taxes/Tangible Net Worth		16.3				
(21) 28.3	(31) 19.3	(26) 15.7			.7				
-5.6	-2.6	-45.2			-30.6				
21.3	17.4	20.2	% Profit Before Taxes/Total Assets		16.3				
4.7	8.0	5.0			.7				
-1.9	-.9	-14.0			-30.6				
10.3	11.0	12.1			10.4				
5.9	5.9	7.6	Sales/Net Fixed Assets		6.9				
1.7	3.2	3.2			5.2				
2.6	3.4	3.9			7.9				
2.0	2.7	1.8	Sales/Total Assets		1.9				
1.1	1.5	1.2			.7				
1.5	1.8	2.7			2.5				
(24) 4.6	(31) 5.2	(30) 4.9	% Depr., Dep., Amort./Sales		4.6				
6.5	6.4	6.9			6.9				
	3.0		% Officers', Directors', Owners' Comp/Sales						
	(10) 5.1								
	10.5								
296196M	826464M	726451M	Net Sales ($)	2931M	18762M	16204M	39696M	34887M	613971M
149331M	342705M	316707M	Total Assets ($)	4071M	15457M	10704M	26632M	12853M	246990M

M = $ thousand   MM = $ million
See Pages 11 through 21 for Explanation of Ratios and Data

Current Data Sorted By Assets   Comparative Historical Data

						Type of Statement	4/1/00-3/31/01 ALL	4/1/01-3/31/02 ALL
	1	15	5		2	Unqualified		
			1			Reviewed		
		1				Compiled		
						Tax Returns		
1	2	1	6			Other		
	15 (4/1-9/30/04)		20 (10/1/04-3/31/05)					
0-500M	500M-2MM	2-10MM	10-50MM	50-100MM	100-250MM			
1	3	17	12		2	NUMBER OF STATEMENTS		
%	%	%	%	%	%	ASSETS	%	%
		21.1	11.1			Cash & Equivalents		
		25.5	17.4			Trade Receivables (net)		
		4.4	5.1			Inventory		
		4.9	3.1			All Other Current		
		55.9	36.7			Total Current		
		32.3	43.7			Fixed Assets (net)		
		4.2	2.4			Intangibles (net)		
		7.6	17.2	DATA NOT AVAILABLE		All Other Non-Current	DATA NOT AVAILABLE	DATA NOT AVAILABLE
		100.0	100.0			Total		
						LIABILITIES		
		2.1	1.7			Notes Payable-Short Term		
		1.7	3.8			Cur. Mat.-L/T/D		
		6.7	9.1			Trade Payables		
		.0	.0			Income Taxes Payable		
		15.3	10.1			All Other Current		
		25.9	24.6			Total Current		
		13.7	23.3			Long-Term Debt		
		.0	.0			Deferred Taxes		
		5.1	4.0			All Other Non-Current		
		55.3	48.0			Net Worth		
		100.0	100.0			Total Liabilities & Net Worth		
						INCOME DATA		
		100.0	100.0			Net Sales		
						Gross Profit		
		91.0	95.2			Operating Expenses		
		9.0	4.8			Operating Profit		
		2.5	.2			All Other Expenses (net)		
		6.5	4.6			Profit Before Taxes		
						RATIOS		
		5.3	2.8					
		2.9	1.6			Current		
		1.2	1.1					
		5.0	2.1					
		2.0	1.4			Quick		
		1.1	1.0					
	15	24.1	33 11.1					
	37	9.8	42 8.6			Sales/Receivables		
	56	6.5	56 6.5					
						Cost of Sales/Inventory		
						Cost of Sales/Payables		
		4.7	5.4					
		6.6	12.2			Sales/Working Capital		
		26.1	NM					
		351.4						
		(13) 19.5				EBIT/Interest		
		1.0						
						Net Profit + Depr., Dep., Amort./Cur. Mat. L /T/D		
		.2	.4					
		.5	1.3			Fixed/Worth		
		1.2	1.8					
		.2	.3					
		.4	1.3			Debt/Worth		
		1.9	1.8					
		26.2	16.8					
		(16) 18.1	(11) 6.7			% Profit Before Taxes/Tangible Net Worth		
		.7	4.3					
		19.8	8.0					
		13.2	3.0			% Profit Before Taxes/Total Assets		
		-1.1	1.1					
		17.7	7.3					
		7.8	3.4			Sales/Net Fixed Assets		
		4.1	1.6					
		2.5	1.8					
		2.1	1.3			Sales/Total Assets		
		1.4	.9					
		.9	1.3					
		(15) 1.9	(10) 2.5			% Depr., Dep., Amort./Sales		
		2.9	3.8					
						% Officers', Directors', Owners' Comp/Sales		
856M	6674M	186453M	357206M		409949M	Net Sales ($)		
84M	2227M	88316M	263020M		335686M	Total Assets ($)		

M = $ thousand   MM = $ million
See Pages 11 through 21 for Explanation of Ratios and Data

Comparative Historical Data / Current Data Sorted By Sales

4/1/02-3/31/03 ALL	4/1/03-3/31/04 ALL	4/1/04-3/31/05 ALL	Type of Statement	0-1MM	1-3MM	3-5MM	5-10MM	10-25MM	25MM & OVER
13	19	23	Unqualified		1		8	9	5
1	3	1	Reviewed					1	
6	2	1	Compiled				1		
	3		Tax Returns						
10	11	10	Other	1	1	1	2	2	3
				15 (4/1-9/30/04)			20 (10/1/04-3/31/05)		
30	38	35	NUMBER OF STATEMENTS	1	2	1	11	12	8
%	%	%	ASSETS	%	%	%	%	%	%
15.9	14.1	19.6	Cash & Equivalents				18.3	17.0	
25.2	25.4	21.3	Trade Receivables (net)				32.6	12.9	
2.0	2.5	4.8	Inventory				4.0	3.3	
7.6	3.1	3.5	All Other Current				1.3	4.8	
50.6	45.1	49.2	Total Current				56.1	38.0	
38.4	33.9	36.4	Fixed Assets (net)				26.8	46.5	
3.3	5.4	2.9	Intangibles (net)				6.6	.2	
7.6	15.6	11.5	All Other Non-Current				10.5	15.3	
100.0	100.0	100.0	Total				100.0	100.0	
			LIABILITIES						
3.4	4.4	4.0	Notes Payable-Short Term				3.3	.0	
1.2	2.6	2.5	Cur. Mat.-L/T/D				1.4	1.7	
7.3	9.4	8.9	Trade Payables				6.0	5.8	
.1	.1	.0	Income Taxes Payable				.0	.0	
10.2	8.6	12.2	All Other Current				10.2	12.5	
22.1	25.0	27.7	Total Current				20.9	20.1	
17.8	19.0	17.6	Long-Term Debt				14.1	19.5	
.1	.1	.0	Deferred Taxes				.0	.0	
2.8	5.7	4.1	All Other Non-Current				4.5	3.2	
57.2	50.2	50.6	Net Worth				60.5	57.2	
100.0	100.0	100.0	Total Liabilities & Net Worth				100.0	100.0	
			INCOME DATA						
100.0	100.0	100.0	Net Sales				100.0	100.0	
			Gross Profit						
92.2	94.0	93.4	Operating Expenses				89.4	95.2	
7.8	6.0	6.6	Operating Profit				10.6	4.8	
1.0	.4	.9	All Other Expenses (net)				3.9	-.7	
6.8	5.6	5.7	Profit Before Taxes				6.7	5.5	
			RATIOS						
4.6	3.5	3.6					7.9	2.9	
2.7	1.8	2.0	Current				3.8	2.1	
1.3	1.2	1.1					1.1	1.4	
3.5	3.0	3.1					7.9	2.1	
2.0	1.7	1.6	Quick				3.1	1.7	
.9	1.1	1.0					1.1	1.3	
29 12.8	35 10.6	28 13.1					37 10.0	29 12.8	
47 7.8	42 8.6	37 9.8	Sales/Receivables				45 8.0	34 10.8	
58 6.3	52 7.0	52 7.0					137 2.7	42 8.7	
			Cost of Sales/Inventory						
			Cost of Sales/Payables						
2.8	5.5	4.5					3.7	6.0	
6.8	8.9	8.7	Sales/Working Capital				5.7	8.3	
31.1	42.2	44.2					31.6	15.9	
37.5	17.2	32.7							
(21) 5.6	(23) 7.8	(25) 8.0	EBIT/Interest						
1.6	2.7	.2							
			Net Profit + Depr., Dep., Amort./Cur. Mat. L/T/D						
.3	.3	.4					.2	.4	
.6	.6	.7	Fixed/Worth				.4	1.2	
1.8	1.3	1.7					.8	1.6	
.2	.4	.2					.2	.2	
.6	.9	1.0	Debt/Worth				.4	.9	
1.8	1.9	1.9					1.8	1.7	
32.1	23.7	23.8					25.4	22.2	
(28) 10.1	(36) 10.6	(33) 9.5	% Profit Before Taxes/Tangible Net Worth				(10) 11.4	13.2	
3.3	1.9	3.4					-1.1	5.5	
16.1	14.1	18.6					19.8	15.2	
8.0	5.8	6.0	% Profit Before Taxes/Total Assets				5.3	7.4	
2.1	.8	-.4					-1.8	2.5	
11.1	15.8	11.1					24.4	6.2	
5.7	4.9	5.5	Sales/Net Fixed Assets				9.1	3.5	
3.1	3.3	3.4					4.3	2.1	
2.7	2.8	2.5					2.5	2.2	
1.7	1.7	1.8	Sales/Total Assets				1.9	1.5	
1.0	1.0	1.2					1.1	1.0	
1.9	1.5	1.4						1.6	
(24) 2.7	(33) 2.4	(30) 2.1	% Depr., Dep., Amort./Sales					(10) 2.4	
3.9	4.2	2.9						3.1	
			% Officers', Directors', Owners' Comp/Sales						
1218875M	1577415M	961138M	Net Sales ($)	856M	3327M	3347M	81976M	200890M	670742M
703289M	964381M	689333M	Total Assets ($)	84M	1654M	573M	77583M	147452M	461987M

M = $ thousand   MM = $ million
See Pages 11 through 21 for Explanation of Ratios and Data

Current Data Sorted By Assets   Comparative Historical Data

						Type of Statement		
1	15	53	45	11	19	Unqualified	152	148
1	6	8	1	1		Reviewed	20	15
10	13	15			1	Compiled	73	68
17	10	4				Tax Returns	35	26
25	30	50	16	5	8	Other	92	115
	135 (4/1-9/30/04)		230 (10/1/04-3/31/05)				4/1/00- 3/31/01	4/1/01- 3/31/02
0-500M	500M-2MM	2-10MM	10-50MM	50-100MM	100-250MM		ALL	ALL
54	74	130	62	17	28	**NUMBER OF STATEMENTS**	372	372
%	%	%	%	%	%	**ASSETS**	%	%
28.9	18.6	15.7	20.0	11.8	15.9	Cash & Equivalents	16.4	17.7
14.5	29.8	31.7	20.9	21.8	16.0	Trade Receivables (net)	25.4	27.4
3.5	3.2	2.1	3.4	6.3	2.3	Inventory	2.2	2.2
6.1	2.7	2.6	3.3	4.0	6.0	All Other Current	4.8	5.3
53.0	54.4	52.0	*47.5	43.9	40.2	Total Current	48.7	52.6
35.2	30.0	35.4	33.0	30.4	24.0	Fixed Assets (net)	33.7	31.7
2.0	5.3	3.4	7.7	9.3	18.1	Intangibles (net)	4.4	4.1
9.9	10.3	9.2	11.7	16.4	17.7	All Other Non-Current	13.1	11.7
100.0	100.0	100.0	100.0	100.0	100.0	Total	100.0	100.0
						LIABILITIES		
29.4	11.8	4.9	3.6	1.9	.8	Notes Payable-Short Term	11.9	10.9
9.5	3.6	4.6	4.1	3.0	3.2	Cur. Mat.-L/T/D	3.9	3.5
6.3	8.6	7.6	7.9	4.7	9.4	Trade Payables	9.5	10.0
.1	.4	.5	.0	.7	.3	Income Taxes Payable	.2	.1
30.0	14.7	15.9	14.2	9.7	8.7	All Other Current	15.8	14.0
75.3	39.1	33.6	29.8	20.1	22.4	Total Current	41.3	38.6
16.0	22.5	19.2	16.3	18.5	23.0	Long-Term Debt	21.8	23.6
.0	.3	.3	.2	.3	.7	Deferred Taxes	.4	.4
15.9	5.2	6.4	4.5	14.6	2.5	All Other Non-Current	5.5	4.2
-7.2	32.9	40.6	49.1	46.5	51.4	Net Worth	31.0	33.2
100.0	100.0	100.0	100.0	100.0	100.0	Total Liabilities & Net Worth	100.0	100.0
						INCOME DATA		
100.0	100.0	100.0	100.0	100.0	100.0	Net Sales	100.0	100.0
						Gross Profit		
90.1	89.8	92.3	91.7	95.6	88.9	Operating Expenses	93.7	92.2
9.9	10.2	7.7	8.3	4.4	11.1	Operating Profit	6.3	7.8
3.4	3.9	1.1	.1	.3	1.4	All Other Expenses (net)	1.5	2.7
6.5	6.3	6.6	8.2	4.1	9.7	Profit Before Taxes	4.8	5.2
						RATIOS		
3.0	2.8	2.7	2.7	2.7	3.0		2.8	3.3
1.2	1.6	1.6	1.6	2.3	1.9	Current	1.7	1.7
.5	.9	1.0	1.1	1.4	1.2		.9	1.0
1.8	2.4	2.3	2.5	2.3	2.6		2.3	2.8
1.0	1.4	1.4	1.4	1.5	1.5	Quick	1.3	1.4
.2	.7	1.0	.9	1.2	1.0		.8	.8
0 UND	0 UND	25 14.9	22 16.5	14 26.7	31 11.7		13 28.2	20 18.1
0 UND	35 10.6	45 8.1	44 8.3	46 7.9	51 7.1	Sales/Receivables	44 8.3	44 8.2
26 14.1	56 6.5	62 5.8	60 6.1	69 5.3	65 5.7		66 5.5	66 5.6
						Cost of Sales/Inventory		
						Cost of Sales/Payables		
11.3	6.0	6.2	4.3	4.6	4.0		5.6	4.5
84.8	15.2	14.1	13.3	9.5	7.4	Sales/Working Capital	13.7	12.3
-17.8	-110.7	132.4	45.7	16.4	29.6		-92.9	163.4
18.8	20.5	14.6	26.6	14.4	9.2		8.6	10.8
(37) 2.0	(49) 7.5	(103) 4.8	(49) 9.2	(14) 4.9	(25) 5.6	EBIT/Interest	(267) 2.7	(275) 3.4
-3.1	1.3	1.7	3.7	1.8	1.9		.5	1.0
			19.1				14.6	11.0
		(14)	7.1			Net Profit + Depr., Dep., Amort./Cur. Mat. L /T/D	(31) 3.3	(28) 3.1
			1.9				1.5	1.0
.4	.1	.3	.3	.4	.4		.3	.2
UND	.6	.8	.7	1.1	.7	Fixed/Worth	.8	.7
-.8	9.9	2.1	2.0	4.8	-2.3		2.8	2.8
1.0	.6	.7	.5	.3	.5		.5	.5
UND	1.5	1.7	1.2	1.2	1.4	Debt/Worth	1.2	1.4
-3.1	NM	3.6	4.0	20.7	-9.1		7.0	5.5
130.0	70.4	50.8	43.8	61.8	23.2		42.5	45.5
(28) 72.9	(56) 19.1	(119) 19.7	(55) 11.8	(14) 11.4	(20) 7.7	% Profit Before Taxes/Tangible Net Worth	(313) 12.6	(315) 14.0
5.0	4.6	4.7	4.5	2.4	3.6		-1.0	.4
60.1	19.9	17.9	15.3	13.4	9.6		14.8	16.5
6.6	6.3	6.4	7.5	5.4	4.7	% Profit Before Taxes/Total Assets	3.6	5.4
-6.7	.6	1.7	2.3	.7	1.4		-1.6	-.4
68.7	74.6	23.6	21.0	19.3	11.3		34.4	30.3
32.5	18.0	8.6	4.5	4.3	4.1	Sales/Net Fixed Assets	7.3	7.7
9.4	4.4	3.3	2.8	2.2	2.4		2.6	3.0
15.2	4.4	3.3	2.1	2.3	1.4		3.3	3.5
4.6	2.5	2.3	1.6	1.5	.9	Sales/Total Assets	1.8	2.0
3.2	1.2	1.4	1.0	.8	.6		1.1	1.1
.6	.7	1.3	1.4	2.3	1.2		.9	.9
(30) 1.2	(59) 2.1	(114) 2.5	(59) 2.8	(14) 3.7	(16) 2.9	% Depr., Dep., Amort./Sales	(316) 2.5	(306) 2.2
4.0	4.8	5.0	3.9	8.8	4.9		4.7	4.2
4.3	3.7	2.2					3.8	5.6
(13) 11.3	(19) 6.4	(20) 8.6				% Officers', Directors', Owners' Comp/Sales	(74) 7.5	(75) 9.5
25.4	13.7	20.2					21.9	18.2
129858M	366594M	1527805M	2398547M	2410726M	4533007M	Net Sales ($)	6734699M	8611782M
12374M	87016M	628941M	1271097M	1201998M	4145359M	Total Assets ($)	5610946M	5674295M

M = $ thousand   MM = $ million
See Pages 11 through 21 for Explanation of Ratios and Data

Comparative Historical Data				Current Data Sorted By Sales					

			Type of Statement						
158	139	144	Unqualified	6	10	9	16	47	56
23	24	17	Reviewed		3	4	3	4	3
26	74	39	Compiled	7	5	8	13	4	2
35	41	31	Tax Returns	8	11	6	4	2	
112	121	134	Other	19	27	16	23	21	28
4/1/02-3/31/03	4/1/03-3/31/04	4/1/04-3/31/05		135 (4/1-9/30/04)			230 (10/1/04-3/31/05)		
ALL	ALL	ALL		0-1MM	1-3MM	3-5MM	5-10MM	10-25MM	25MM & OVER
354	399	365	**NUMBER OF STATEMENTS**	40	56	43	59	78	89
%	%	%	**ASSETS**	%	%	%	%	%	%
19.1	18.1	18.8	Cash & Equivalents	19.5	19.0	22.7	14.1	20.4	18.1
24.2	23.1	25.3	Trade Receivables (net)	11.7	22.4	24.7	34.3	28.8	24.3
2.0	1.8	3.0	Inventory	3.4	2.1	1.0	4.6	2.8	3.4
4.4	6.0	3.6	All Other Current	4.1	3.1	3.0	3.7	2.5	4.8
49.7	49.0	50.6	Total Current	38.7	46.6	51.4	56.7	54.5	50.6
36.5	34.0	32.8	Fixed Assets (net)	47.8	35.4	34.0	31.8	31.3	25.6
3.8	5.8	5.7	Intangibles (net)	4.1	4.2	2.0	4.0	5.9	10.1
10.1	11.3	10.9	All Other Non-Current	9.4	13.8	12.6	7.5	8.3	13.7
100.0	100.0	100.0	Total	100.0	100.0	100.0	100.0	100.0	100.0
			LIABILITIES						
8.5	10.1	9.3	Notes Payable-Short Term	23.0	16.8	11.3	7.9	3.5	3.5
3.6	4.0	4.8	Cur. Mat.-L/T/D	6.9	4.6	7.7	5.9	4.0	2.8
9.5	9.6	7.7	Trade Payables	5.4	6.2	7.3	8.0	8.1	9.2
.4	.3	.3	Income Taxes Payable	.0	.1	.3	.2	.6	.5
17.3	17.3	16.6	All Other Current	12.1	15.8	29.2	14.1	15.3	15.9
39.3	41.3	38.8	Total Current	47.4	43.5	55.8	36.0	31.5	31.8
21.1	21.2	19.2	Long-Term Debt	33.3	20.9	22.2	15.9	14.4	16.5
.1	.3	.3	Deferred Taxes	.0	.4	.4	.1	.1	.4
5.9	5.2	7.3	All Other Non-Current	12.9	10.7	7.6	4.2	7.7	4.2
33.5	32.0	34.5	Net Worth	6.4	24.4	14.0	43.7	46.2	47.1
100.0	100.0	100.0	Total Liabilities & Net Worth	100.0	100.0	100.0	100.0	100.0	100.0
			INCOME DATA						
100.0	100.0	100.0	Net Sales	100.0	100.0	100.0	100.0	100.0	100.0
			Gross Profit						
93.6	92.2	91.3	Operating Expenses	80.4	92.4	88.4	95.5	91.8	93.6
6.4	7.8	8.7	Operating Profit	19.6	7.6	11.6	4.5	8.2	6.4
1.5	1.5	1.8	All Other Expenses (net)	10.6	1.0	1.9	.3	.6	.4
4.8	6.3	6.9	Profit Before Taxes	9.0	6.6	9.7	4.2	7.6	6.0
			RATIOS						
3.0	2.7	2.8		2.9	2.9	2.2	3.3	2.8	2.5
1.5	1.5	1.6	Current	1.4	1.4	1.2	1.6	1.8	1.6
.9	.9	1.0		.5	.7	.6	1.1	1.4	1.1
2.7	2.4	2.4		2.2	2.3	2.1	2.7	2.5	2.2
1.3	1.2	1.4	Quick	1.1	1.1	1.0	1.4	1.6	1.3
.8	.8	.9		.3	.6	.5	.9	1.1	1.0
11 32.4	7 52.3	9 42.8		0 UND	0 UND	0 UND	30 12.3	25 14.6	19 18.9
37 9.7	38 9.6	40 9.2	Sales/Receivables	0 UND	29 12.7	34 10.7	53 6.8	45 8.2	45 8.2
57 6.4	58 6.3	59 6.2		29 12.7	65 5.6	52 7.0	67 5.4	57 6.4	61 6.0
			Cost of Sales/Inventory						
			Cost of Sales/Payables						
5.8	6.0	6.0		3.8	6.5	10.5	5.6	6.0	6.1
15.2	16.7	14.8	Sales/Working Capital	13.8	44.4	43.9	14.8	11.0	14.8
-98.0	-152.0	999.8		-7.0	-25.7	-23.4	59.7	27.4	48.6
10.6	15.1	17.1		14.6	14.2	24.6	16.8	19.2	14.6
(270) 3.4	(299) 4.8	(277) 5.5	EBIT/Interest	(21) 2.8	(40) 2.2	(34) 4.6	(50) 7.2	(57) 7.7	(75) 6.0
1.0	1.4	1.6		-1.7	.2	1.1	1.3	3.3	2.0
5.0	7.0	12.8	Net Profit + Depr., Dep.,						14.7
(32) 2.7	(35) 2.9	(33) 4.8	Amort./Cur. Mat. L/T/D						(17) 2.5
1.2	1.0	1.5							.9
.4	.3	.3		.4	.2	.5	.4	.3	.3
.9	.9	.8	Fixed/Worth	4.9	1.0	1.5	.7	.6	.7
3.6	3.5	5.6		-2.8	-10.9	-1.5	1.8	1.8	2.3
.5	.5	.6		.8	.5	.8	.7	.5	.5
1.4	1.8	1.6	Debt/Worth	4.0	1.9	2.4	1.4	1.2	1.5
7.7	9.6	13.9		-8.4	-69.5	-5.5	2.9	2.5	14.5
39.4	54.9	59.5	% Profit Before Taxes/Tangible	107.2	82.4	89.2	47.2	50.2	43.7
(295) 13.4	(329) 15.9	(292) 16.9	Net Worth	(24) 22.9	(41) 18.5	(28) 47.7	(55) 23.3	(70) 14.5	(74) 11.4
1.1	2.2	4.4		3.1	3.1	8.7	3.5	7.9	3.6
15.0	17.7	16.9	% Profit Before Taxes/Total	19.5	23.7	35.9	19.2	15.0	13.4
4.9	6.6	6.4	Assets	2.9	4.7	8.9	6.4	7.8	6.0
.1	.3	1.0		-4.1	.0	.3	-.4	3.1	1.2
29.7	33.9	37.1		14.7	43.4	63.0	33.2	24.9	39.4
6.3	8.2	9.7	Sales/Net Fixed Assets	5.3	15.4	18.3	8.8	9.0	10.2
2.7	3.0	3.2		.4	2.3	4.7	3.4	3.5	3.1
3.8	3.9	3.9		3.7	4.1	9.5	3.5	3.4	3.6
2.0	2.0	2.1	Sales/Total Assets	1.3	1.9	3.8	2.5	2.3	1.9
1.2	1.2	1.2		.2	1.0	1.4	1.6	1.4	1.0
1.2	1.1	1.1		1.7	1.2	.6	1.0	1.3	.9
(304) 2.6	(326) 2.6	(292) 2.5	% Depr., Dep., Amort./Sales	(29) 6.6	(43) 2.8	(31) 1.6	(50) 2.0	(69) 2.5	(70) 2.5
4.4	4.8	4.7		17.6	4.5	5.4	4.9	3.7	3.8
4.9	4.1	2.1	% Officers', Directors',		5.9		1.4	3.8	1.0
(67) 9.3	(78) 9.3	(62) 6.6	Owners' Comp/Sales	(12) 8.9		(14) 3.6	(10) 25.4	(13) 2.1	
20.9	21.0	19.7		23.9		17.3	41.1	10.0	
11645781M	16542932M	11366537M	Net Sales ($)	17807M	107484M	168500M	443957M	1328800M	9299989M
5962010M	8539660M	7346785M	Total Assets ($)	31491M	90484M	75405M	259834M	1013988M	5875583M

© RMA 2005

M = $ thousand   MM = $ million
See Pages 11 through 21 for Explanation of Ratios and Data

Current Data Sorted By Assets / Comparative Historical Data

Type of Statement	0-500M	500M-2MM	2-10MM	10-50MM	50-100MM	100-250MM	4/1/00-3/31/01 ALL	4/1/01-3/31/02 ALL
Unqualified	3	4	43	115	95	150	309	311
Reviewed		2	5		1	1	9	9
Compiled	7	9	3	2	1	1	45	40
Tax Returns	5	7		1			5	3
Other	6	15	53	41	32	53	189	148
	351 (4/1-9/30/04)			304 (10/1/04-3/31/05)			4/1/00-3/31/01 ALL	4/1/01-3/31/02 ALL
NUMBER OF STATEMENTS	21	37	104	159	129	205	557	511
ASSETS	%	%	%	%	%	%	%	%
Cash & Equivalents	24.8	21.7	13.5	12.1	9.2	9.7	8.7	9.4
Trade Receivables (net)	11.7	21.8	28.1	18.1	15.5	13.3	16.6	17.0
Inventory	1.3	3.0	3.2	2.0	1.7	1.6	2.1	1.9
All Other Current	1.8	6.5	3.5	3.3	3.4	3.0	3.1	3.5
Total Current	39.6	53.0	48.3	35.6	29.7	27.7	30.4	31.8
Fixed Assets (net)	33.2	30.9	44.9	46.0	46.3	44.3	45.2	45.4
Intangibles (net)	3.5	4.5	1.4	1.4	2.0	2.0	2.4	1.7
All Other Non-Current	23.7	11.7	5.5	16.9	22.1	26.0	22.0	21.1
Total	100.0	100.0	100.0	100.0	100.0	100.0	100.0	100.0
LIABILITIES								
Notes Payable-Short Term	20.5	10.3	3.1	.9	1.2	.8	2.0	2.3
Cur. Mat.-L/T/D	3.9	8.7	5.4	2.6	2.9	1.6	2.8	2.2
Trade Payables	11.6	6.7	9.9	6.9	5.5	5.1	5.6	5.8
Income Taxes Payable	.0	.0	.1	.1	.0	.0	.1	.0
All Other Current	42.5	17.5	12.7	10.8	10.2	7.8	9.2	9.5
Total Current	78.5	43.2	31.3	21.3	19.8	15.3	19.7	19.9
Long-Term Debt	25.0	29.5	25.3	25.1	28.1	29.3	27.0	27.8
Deferred Taxes	.0	.0	.0	.1	.1	.0	.1	.1
All Other Non-Current	9.4	8.4	6.9	7.1	4.2	5.6	3.7	2.7
Net Worth	-12.9	18.9	36.6	46.3	47.8	49.6	49.5	49.7
Total Liabilities & Net Worth	100.0	100.0	100.0	100.0	100.0	100.0	100.0	100.0
INCOME DATA								
Net Sales	100.0	100.0	100.0	100.0	100.0	100.0	100.0	100.0
Gross Profit								
Operating Expenses	100.2	84.8	89.3	97.0	96.6	95.9	95.6	95.8
Operating Profit	-.2	15.2	10.7	3.0	3.4	4.1	4.4	4.2
All Other Expenses (net)	.6	2.4	2.2	-.2	.3	.7	.5	1.3
Profit Before Taxes	-.7	12.8	8.4	3.1	3.1	3.5	3.9	2.9
RATIOS								
Current	1.6	2.9	2.8	2.7	2.6	2.5	2.6	2.6
	.6	1.2	1.8	1.7	1.8	1.9	1.8	1.9
	.1	.7	1.0	1.2	1.2	1.4	1.3	1.4
Quick	1.4	2.8	2.3	2.3	2.3	2.1	2.2	2.2
	.6	.8	1.6	1.5	1.5	1.6	1.5	1.6
	.1	.5	.8	1.0	1.0	1.1	1.0	1.1
Sales/Receivables	0 UND	0 UND	34 10.7	43 8.6	45 8.2	42 8.7	49 7.4	49 7.5
	0 UND	13 28.7	52 7.1	51 7.1	54 6.8	50 7.3	62 5.9	61 6.0
	45 8.1	55 6.7	67 5.4	62 5.9	63 5.8	59 6.2	74 4.9	71 5.1
Cost of Sales/Inventory								
Cost of Sales/Payables								
Sales/Working Capital	29.0	7.3	5.5	4.6	5.2	5.4	4.6	5.0
	-68.4	51.5	9.1	8.8	8.0	7.9	8.0	7.7
	-10.0	-17.0	-182.9	30.6	28.5	15.2	20.1	15.5
EBIT/Interest	8.0	66.7	16.8	7.8	6.4	5.7	5.6	5.0
	(15) 1.5	(29) 10.4	(89) 3.2	(153) 2.9	(122) 2.9	(194) 3.2	(503) 2.6	(455) 2.2
	-7.0	2.5	.4	.6	1.6	1.8	.8	.5
Net Profit + Depr., Dep., Amort./Cur. Mat. L /T/D						8.2	10.5	18.5
						(14) 4.9	(18) 4.9	(18) 5.8
						2.2	1.0	2.7
Fixed/Worth	.5	.3	.6	.6	.7	.6	.6	.6
	3.1	.9	1.1	.9	.9	.8	.8	.8
	-.8	NM	2.9	1.6	1.5	1.3	1.4	1.3
Debt/Worth	1.1	1.0	.6	.5	.5	.6	.5	.5
	-22.3	1.6	1.3	1.0	1.0	.9	.9	.9
	-2.3	-10.7	5.9	2.3	1.8	1.5	1.8	1.6
% Profit Before Taxes/Tangible Net Worth	36.3	288.8	75.0	11.6	9.6	10.9	10.8	10.4
	(10) 2.8	(27) 102.0	(91) 18.9	(145) 5.8	(123) 5.9	(198) 7.1	(527) 5.4	(494) 4.7
	-1.9	42.4	.0	-.9	2.1	2.4	.5	-.6
% Profit Before Taxes/Total Assets	11.2	98.0	23.2	6.3	5.4	5.6	5.8	5.2
	.0	29.2	5.5	3.1	2.4	3.6	2.6	2.3
	-22.5	4.3	-.4	-.6	.9	1.2	-.2	-.6
Sales/Net Fixed Assets	65.1	36.4	7.5	3.6	3.0	2.7	2.8	3.0
	23.3	18.8	4.0	2.5	2.3	2.0	2.1	2.2
	7.4	5.4	2.4	1.9	1.7	1.7	1.6	1.7
Sales/Total Assets	12.7	6.1	2.4	1.5	1.3	1.1	1.2	1.2
	7.9	2.9	1.7	1.2	1.0	1.0	.9	1.0
	2.4	2.0	1.2	.9	.8	.8	.7	.8
% Depr., Dep., Amort./Sales	1.0	.7	2.8	3.6	4.1	4.5	4.2	4.2
	(15) 3.2	(30) 2.0	(95) 4.1	(157) 4.9	(128) 4.9	(146) 5.3	(494) 5.6	(448) 5.4
	6.2	4.6	5.8	5.9	6.1	6.3	6.9	6.4
% Officers', Directors', Owners' Comp/Sales				2.1	12.0	8.5	4.5	6.4
				(19) 8.7	(17) 31.0	(17) 38.5	(71) 13.3	(78) 17.2
				32.7	42.5	45.4	35.4	40.3
Net Sales ($)	48734M	168893M	1103213M	5502051M	10103067M	32188906M	38765091M	37950772M
Total Assets ($)	5084M	42090M	598215M	4460955M	9382281M	33035013M	42817213M	39122642M

Comparative Historical Data			Type of Statement	Current Data Sorted By Sales					
427	403	410	Unqualified	9	3	6	18	52	322
11	12	9	Reviewed		1		1	2	3
13	60	23	Compiled	1	6	4	6	2	4
11	15	13	Tax Returns	3	5	3	1		1
206	193	200	Other	5	13	12	21	35	114
4/1/02-3/31/03 ALL	4/1/03-3/31/04 ALL	4/1/04-3/31/05 ALL		351 (4/1-9/30/04) 0-1MM	1-3MM	3-5MM	304 (10/1/04-3/31/05) 5-10MM	10-25MM	25MM & OVER
668	683	655	**NUMBER OF STATEMENTS**	18	28	27	47	91	444
%	%	%	**ASSETS**	%	%	%	%	%	%
11.3	11.4	11.9	Cash & Equivalents	18.1	23.2	13.8	18.3	14.3	9.7
16.8	17.6	17.7	Trade Receivables (net)	9.9	14.8	27.4	22.6	23.4	15.9
1.9	1.8	2.1	Inventory	.4	3.8	2.7	2.4	2.8	1.8
3.6	4.7	3.4	All Other Current	1.3	3.9	6.5	4.7	3.1	3.2
33.5	35.5	35.1	Total Current	29.7	45.9	50.4	48.1	43.5	30.6
45.8	45.4	44.1	Fixed Assets (net)	53.6	39.6	34.0	39.6	43.9	45.1
1.4	1.3	2.0	Intangibles (net)	2.0	1.0	5.2	3.5	.8	1.9
19.3	17.8	18.9	All Other Non-Current	14.7	13.5	10.4	8.8	11.8	22.4
100.0	100.0	100.0	Total	100.0	100.0	100.0	100.0	100.0	100.0
			LIABILITIES						
2.0	3.6	2.4	Notes Payable-Short Term	.9	20.7	.7	4.8	3.7	.9
2.6	3.1	3.2	Cur. Mat.-L/T/D	3.8	5.5	7.3	5.4	4.3	2.3
5.5	6.3	6.7	Trade Payables	4.4	11.1	10.9	6.2	7.1	6.2
.1	.2	.1	Income Taxes Payable	.0	.0	.0	.0	.1	.1
11.9	11.8	11.5	All Other Current	17.8	16.2	16.2	17.9	12.5	9.7
22.1	25.0	23.8	Total Current	26.9	53.5	35.1	34.2	27.7	19.2
27.6	27.6	27.3	Long-Term Debt	26.6	38.3	26.2	26.6	23.4	27.6
.1	.1	.1	Deferred Taxes	.0	.0	.0	.0	.0	.1
3.7	5.2	6.2	All Other Non-Current	10.2	4.9	10.8	4.3	5.6	6.1
46.6	42.1	42.7	Net Worth	36.2	3.2	27.9	34.8	43.3	47.0
100.0	100.0	100.0	Total Liabilities & Net Worth	100.0	100.0	100.0	100.0	100.0	100.0
			INCOME DATA						
100.0	100.0	100.0	Net Sales	100.0	100.0	100.0	100.0	100.0	100.0
			Gross Profit						
94.3	95.2	94.8	Operating Expenses	88.3	93.9	80.4	89.8	94.3	96.6
5.7	4.8	5.2	Operating Profit	11.7	6.1	19.6	10.2	5.7	3.4
1.7	1.5	.7	All Other Expenses (net)	3.9	2.8	2.7	.2	.7	.4
4.0	3.2	4.5	Profit Before Taxes	7.8	3.4	17.0	10.0	4.9	3.0
			RATIOS						
2.7	2.8	2.6		2.1	1.9	4.7	2.6	3.0	2.5
1.9	1.8	1.8	Current	.7	1.1	2.5	1.8	2.0	1.8
1.2	1.2	1.1		.2	.6	.7	.8	1.2	1.2
2.3	2.3	2.2		2.1	1.8	4.5	2.3	2.7	2.1
1.6	(682) 1.5	1.5	Quick	.6	.8	2.0	1.5	1.6	1.5
1.0	1.0	1.0		.2	.3	.4	.8	1.1	1.0
42 8.7	42 8.7	39 9.3		0 UND	0 UND	0 UND	21 17.6	40 9.1	43 8.5
53 6.9	54 6.7	50 7.2	Sales/Receivables	4 90.1	12 31.0	39 9.3	46 7.9	53 6.8	51 7.2
64 5.7	65 5.6	61 6.0		43 8.4	59 6.2	76 4.8	66 5.5	66 5.5	60 6.1
			Cost of Sales/Inventory						
			Cost of Sales/Payables						
4.8	4.7	5.3		9.3	8.0	3.1	5.6	4.4	5.4
7.9	8.6	8.9	Sales/Working Capital	-37.1	NM	6.8	8.9	7.8	8.7
26.6	33.6	33.9		-2.7	-7.2	-18.7	-91.5	23.2	24.0
5.6	6.0	7.5		13.8	8.3	79.9	47.5	13.9	6.3
(594) 2.3	(615) 2.3	(602) 3.2	EBIT/Interest	(10) 2.6	(22) 2.2	(24) 12.0	(39) 5.1	(83) 3.1	(424) 3.1
.5	.3	1.3		-.7	.0	1.6	1.6	.2	1.4
8.7	9.7	8.4	Net Profit + Depr., Dep.,						8.2
(27) 5.3	(26) 4.9	(35) 3.5	Amort./Cur. Mat. L/T/D					(26)	3.3
2.0	1.8	1.3							1.3
.6	.6	.6		.6	.6	.2	.7	.6	.7
.9	.9	.9	Fixed/Worth	1.7	2.1	.9	.9	1.0	.9
1.4	1.6	1.6		5.1	-.9	1.6	5.0	1.7	1.5
.5	.6	.6		.6	1.0	.3	.7	.5	.6
.9	1.1	1.1	Debt/Worth	1.7	4.2	.8	1.5	.9	1.0
1.8	2.5	2.4		77.7	-3.7	-12.1	15.4	2.5	1.8
11.3	12.9	13.8	% Profit Before Taxes/Tangible	42.4	98.4	116.3	130.3	34.8	10.9
(630) 4.5	(624) 5.1	(594) 7.1	Net Worth	(15) 3.3	(18) 18.4	(20) 55.7	(39) 39.0	(84) 7.9	(418) 6.4
-.6	-1.2	1.9		.0	-.9	4.9	3.8	-.5	2.0
5.7	5.5	6.7	% Profit Before Taxes/Total	4.7	21.3	58.2	40.0	13.8	5.6
2.3	2.2	3.5	Assets	1.0	4.0	24.9	6.5	3.7	3.0
-.5	-1.2	.5		-.9	-2.5	1.8	.8	-1.7	.8
3.2	3.4	3.9		27.1	23.8	36.8	20.2	6.0	3.0
2.3	2.3	2.5	Sales/Net Fixed Assets	2.4	7.6	10.8	4.0	3.2	2.3
1.7	1.8	1.8		.2	1.9	3.1	2.1	2.4	1.8
1.4	1.4	1.6		2.9	3.5	3.0	3.3	2.2	1.3
1.1	1.0	1.1	Sales/Total Assets	.7	2.0	1.9	1.6	1.4	1.0
.8	.8	.9		.1	.7	1.3	1.0	1.0	.8
3.9	3.7	3.6		3.4	1.4	1.6	2.8	2.8	4.0
(589) 5.2	(597) 5.0	(571) 4.8	% Depr., Dep., Amort./Sales	(16) 6.4	(20) 4.6	(24) 4.0	(43) 4.3	(84) 4.1	(384) 5.0
6.3	6.3	6.1		30.5	12.4	6.4	5.8	5.7	6.1
5.9	6.9	6.6	% Officers', Directors',					10.2	5.8
(90) 14.9	(84) 18.0	(78) 18.2	Owners' Comp/Sales					(10) 16.6	(49) 27.3
36.2	35.8	39.4						34.3	41.4
46812190M	47474853M	49114864M	Net Sales ($)	8087M	53224M	108969M	360541M	1504193M	47079850M
46198702M	47220859M	47523638M	Total Assets ($)	36500M	48798M	289200M	246842M	1191049M	45711249M

Current Data Sorted By Assets | Comparative Historical Data

Type of Statement counts and date ranges:
147 (4/1-9/30/04) — columns 0-500M, 500M-2MM; 87 (10/1/04-3/31/05) — columns 2-10MM through 100-250MM

0-500M	500M-2MM	2-10MM	10-50MM	50-100MM	100-250MM	Type of Statement	4/1/00-3/31/01 ALL	4/1/01-3/31/02 ALL
1	1	6	67	46	62	Unqualified		11
						Reviewed		
						Compiled		
					1	Tax Returns		
		5	14	18	13	Other		23
2		11	81	64	76	**NUMBER OF STATEMENTS**		34
%	%	%	%	%	%	**ASSETS**	%	%
D	D	17.4	11.8	10.7	9.0	Cash & Equivalents	D	8.4
A	A	21.3	18.1	14.2	13.4	Trade Receivables (net)	A	19.4
T	T	3.3	1.9	1.8	1.6	Inventory	T	2.0
A	A	3.8	3.1	3.8	3.6	All Other Current	A	1.9
		45.7	34.9	30.5	27.5	Total Current		31.7
N	N	50.9	46.2	46.4	42.2	Fixed Assets (net)	N	46.9
O	O	.2	.5	.7	1.0	Intangibles (net)	O	.6
T	T	3.2	18.4	22.4	29.3	All Other Non-Current	T	20.8
		100.0	100.0	100.0	100.0	Total		100.0
A	A					**LIABILITIES**	A	
V	V	.0	1.1	.4	.7	Notes Payable-Short Term	V	1.0
A	A	3.1	2.8	2.3	1.7	Cur. Mat.-L/T/D	A	2.7
I	I	8.1	5.7	4.4	5.6	Trade Payables	I	8.4
L	L	.0	.0	.0	.0	Income Taxes Payable	L	.0
A	A	12.4	10.1	9.0	8.3	All Other Current	A	12.6
B	B	23.7	19.8	16.1	16.3	Total Current	B	24.8
L	L	16.1	21.8	29.3	30.8	Long-Term Debt	L	28.8
E	E	.0	.0	.0	.0	Deferred Taxes	E	.0
		1.0	2.0	5.0	5.3	All Other Non-Current		6.3
		59.2	56.5	49.6	47.6	Net Worth		40.1
		100.0	100.0	100.0	100.0	Total Liabilities & Net Worth		100.0
						INCOME DATA		
		100.0	100.0	100.0	100.0	Net Sales		100.0
						Gross Profit		
		98.4	96.1	96.7	96.9	Operating Expenses		95.6
		1.6	3.9	3.3	3.1	Operating Profit		4.4
		−1.4	.7	.6	.2	All Other Expenses (net)		2.8
		3.0	3.2	2.7	2.9	Profit Before Taxes		1.6
						RATIOS		
		3.2	2.9	2.4	2.4	Current		1.8
		2.0	2.1	2.0	1.8			1.4
		1.2	1.4	1.3	1.3			1.0
		2.5	2.3	2.0	2.0	Quick		1.5
		1.6	1.7	1.6	1.4			1.3
		1.1	1.2	1.1	1.1			1.0
		23 15.6	48 7.7	41 8.9	43 8.5	Sales/Receivables		52 7.0
		42 8.6	56 6.6	51 7.1	50 7.4			59 6.2
		60 6.1	63 5.8	59 6.2	59 6.2			68 5.3
						Cost of Sales/Inventory		
						Cost of Sales/Payables		
		3.8	4.8	5.2	5.3	Sales/Working Capital		8.0
		10.0	7.1	8.4	7.9			13.0
		13.9	15.7	15.5	19.6			177.1
			7.9	5.2	5.5	EBIT/Interest		5.5
			(75) 4.2	(60) 2.7	(75) 2.4			(33) 2.2
			.7	1.5	1.4			1.1
						Net Profit + Depr., Dep., Amort./Cur. Mat. L /T/D		
		.6	.6	.7	.6	Fixed/Worth		.7
		.8	.8	.9	.9			1.0
		1.3	1.2	1.2	1.2			2.2
		.4	.4	.6	.6	Debt/Worth		.6
		.8	.7	.9	1.0			1.0
		1.4	1.3	1.5	1.9			3.0
		14.3	11.2	10.1	9.6	% Profit Before Taxes/Tangible Net Worth		9.1
		2.3	(79) 5.7	(62) 6.0	(72) 4.3			(30) 4.5
		−5.9	.5	1.5	1.6			−.5
		8.0	7.1	4.7	5.0	% Profit Before Taxes/Total Assets		5.4
		1.9	3.9	2.6	2.1			1.8
		−3.7	−.1	.5	.8			−.3
		4.8	3.3	3.0	2.8	Sales/Net Fixed Assets		3.2
		3.4	2.5	2.4	2.2			2.4
		2.4	1.9	1.7	1.8			1.7
		2.1	1.4	1.3	1.2	Sales/Total Assets		1.4
		1.7	1.1	1.0	.9			1.1
		1.3	.9	.8	.8			.8
		2.8	3.8	4.7	4.3	% Depr., Dep., Amort./Sales		4.1
		3.4	4.8	(63) 5.1	(49) 5.1			(31) 5.0
		5.1	5.9	6.3	5.8			5.9
						% Officers', Directors', Owners' Comp/Sales		
	1676M	113556M	2424315M	4904758M	11988364M	Net Sales ($)		2349403M
	1715M	66048M	2140489M	4656167M	12811405M	Total Assets ($)		2362695M

© RMA 2005

M = $ thousand   MM = $ million
See Pages 11 through 21 for Explanation of Ratios and Data

Comparative Historical Data				Current Data Sorted By Sales					
97	149	182	**Type of Statement**		2	1	4	27	148
			Unqualified						
			Reviewed						
		1	Compiled	1					
		1	Tax Returns						1
17	46	50	Other		1	1	2	5	41
4/1/02-	4/1/03-	4/1/04-		147 (4/1-9/30/04)			87 (10/1/04-3/31/05)		
3/31/03	3/31/04	3/31/05							
ALL	ALL	ALL		0-1MM	1-3MM	3-5MM	5-10MM	10-25MM	25MM & OVER
114	195	234	**NUMBER OF STATEMENTS**	1	3	2	6	32	190
%	%	%	**ASSETS**	%	%	%	%	%	%
9.2	9.6	10.8	Cash & Equivalents					15.2	10.1
16.1	16.0	15.6	Trade Receivables (net)					16.5	15.2
1.6	1.6	1.8	Inventory					1.8	1.8
4.2	3.9	3.5	All Other Current					3.3	3.5
31.2	31.1	31.7	Total Current					36.7	30.6
45.1	45.1	45.1	Fixed Assets (net)					48.2	44.4
.7	1.0	.7	Intangibles (net)					.7	.7
23.1	22.9	22.5	All Other Non-Current					14.4	24.3
100.0	100.0	100.0	Total					100.0	100.0
			LIABILITIES						
.6	.7	.7	Notes Payable-Short Term					.4	.5
1.8	2.1	2.3	Cur. Mat.-L/T/D					2.1	2.2
6.4	6.4	5.5	Trade Payables					4.3	5.6
.0	.1	.0	Income Taxes Payable					.0	.0
8.3	7.9	9.3	All Other Current					9.8	9.0
17.0	17.2	17.8	Total Current					16.6	17.3
27.8	26.5	26.6	Long-Term Debt					20.3	27.9
.0	.0	.0	Deferred Taxes					.0	.0
3.1	4.6	3.9	All Other Non-Current					1.5	4.4
52.1	51.7	51.7	Net Worth					61.5	50.4
100.0	100.0	100.0	Total Liabilities & Net Worth					100.0	100.0
			INCOME DATA						
100.0	100.0	100.0	Net Sales					100.0	100.0
			Gross Profit						
97.4	97.2	96.6	Operating Expenses					95.4	97.3
2.6	2.8	3.4	Operating Profit					4.6	2.7
1.2	.2	.4	All Other Expenses (net)					.2	.1
1.3	2.7	3.0	Profit Before Taxes					4.3	2.6
			RATIOS						
2.6	2.9	2.6						3.1	2.5
1.9	2.1	1.9	Current					2.4	1.9
1.4	1.5	1.3						1.6	1.3
2.2	2.3	2.2						2.7	2.1
1.6	1.7	1.5	Quick					2.1	1.5
1.1	1.2	1.1						1.3	1.1
50 7.3	46 8.0	43 8.6					41 8.9		43 8.4
57 6.4	53 6.8	52 7.0	Sales/Receivables				54 6.7		52 7.0
68 5.4	63 5.8	60 6.1					66 5.5		60 6.1
			Cost of Sales/Inventory						
			Cost of Sales/Payables						
5.0	4.5	5.1						3.8	5.3
7.1	7.2	7.9	Sales/Working Capital					6.4	8.0
13.1	15.3	17.2						12.0	18.1
3.8	5.8	6.4						9.6	6.0
(106) 2.0	(183) 2.6	(220) 2.8	EBIT/Interest				(28) 6.4		(183) 2.6
.4	.5	1.3						2.6	1.3
			Net Profit + Depr., Dep., Amort./Cur. Mat. L/T/D						
.7	.6	.6						.5	.6
.8	.9	.9	Fixed/Worth					.8	.9
1.2	1.2	1.2						1.1	1.2
.5	.5	.5						.4	.5
.9	.9	.9	Debt/Worth					.6	.9
1.5	1.4	1.4						1.0	1.4
6.9	9.5	10.5						12.0	9.9
(113) 2.8	(190) 4.1	(226) 5.5	% Profit Before Taxes/Tangible Net Worth					8.6	(183) 5.2
-2.6	-1.5	1.3						2.4	1.5
3.7	4.9	5.6						7.4	5.3
1.4	2.2	2.7	% Profit Before Taxes/Total Assets					5.2	2.4
-1.3	-.9	.5						1.6	.5
2.7	3.1	3.1						3.3	3.0
2.1	2.2	2.4	Sales/Net Fixed Assets					2.5	2.4
1.7	1.7	1.9						1.8	1.9
1.1	1.3	1.3						1.4	1.3
.9	1.0	1.0	Sales/Total Assets					1.1	1.0
.8	.7	.8						.9	.8
4.4	4.2	4.2						4.0	4.3
(93) 5.5	(162) 5.2	(206) 5.0	% Depr., Dep., Amort./Sales					4.8	(162) 5.0
6.6	6.3	6.0						5.8	5.9
	7.9	8.2							
	(11) 29.6	(10) 16.3	% Officers', Directors', Owners' Comp/Sales						
	35.7	37.4							
11248458M	17158235M	19432669M	Net Sales ($)	584M	4698M	7966M	41116M	585044M	18793261M
11908435M	18585177M	19675824M	Total Assets ($)	944M	31087M	6141M	77910M	628272M	18931470M

M = $ thousand   MM = $ million
See Pages 11 through 21 for Explanation of Ratios and Data

Current Data Sorted By Assets   Comparative Historical Data

0-500M	500M-2MM	2-10MM	10-50MM	50-100MM	100-250MM	Type of Statement	4/1/00-3/31/01	4/1/01-3/31/02
1	4	16	19	2		Unqualified	31	32
			1			Reviewed		1
1		1				Compiled	3	4
1	1					Tax Returns	1	
2		6	6	1	1	Other	19	20
	41 (4/1-9/30/04)		21 (10/1/04-3/31/05)				ALL	ALL
5	5	23	25	3	1	NUMBER OF STATEMENTS	54	57
%	%	%	%	%	%	**ASSETS**	%	%
		15.4	14.3			Cash & Equivalents	14.2	14.0
		27.2	17.8			Trade Receivables (net)	24.0	24.2
		.2	.8			Inventory	.4	.3
		3.4	3.6			All Other Current	3.1	4.1
		46.2	36.5			Total Current	41.6	42.6
		46.3	49.2			Fixed Assets (net)	45.1	43.8
		1.3	.6			Intangibles (net)	1.9	3.2
		6.2	13.6			All Other Non-Current	11.4	10.4
		100.0	100.0			Total	100.0	100.0
						LIABILITIES		
		6.2	1.5			Notes Payable-Short Term	3.1	7.4
		5.1	1.1			Cur. Mat.-L/T/D	2.5	2.3
		7.2	5.1			Trade Payables	5.5	8.0
		.0	.0			Income Taxes Payable	.0	.1
		18.2	9.8			All Other Current	12.3	13.2
		36.7	17.5			Total Current	23.5	31.0
		18.7	25.1			Long-Term Debt	21.5	28.9
		.0	.0			Deferred Taxes	.0	.1
		11.2	1.7			All Other Non-Current	2.9	3.4
		33.4	55.7			Net Worth	52.1	36.7
		100.0	100.0			Total Liabilities & Net Worth	100.0	100.0
						INCOME DATA		
		100.0	100.0			Net Sales	100.0	100.0
						Gross Profit		
		97.1	95.5			Operating Expenses	97.3	98.4
		2.9	4.5			Operating Profit	2.7	1.6
		.5	-.8			All Other Expenses (net)	-.2	.6
		2.4	5.3			Profit Before Taxes	2.9	1.0
						RATIOS		
		2.2	3.6			Current	3.5	2.8
		1.4	2.4				1.9	1.5
		1.1	1.3				1.3	.9
		2.0	3.0			Quick	3.2	2.3
		1.4	2.1				1.6	1.2
		1.0	1.1				1.2	.8
		29 12.6	39 9.4			Sales/Receivables	28 13.2	27 13.4
		46 7.9	50 7.3				51 7.1	46 7.9
		67 5.4	64 5.7				66 5.6	59 6.2
						Cost of Sales/Inventory		
						Cost of Sales/Payables		
		6.3	4.1			Sales/Working Capital	5.4	5.7
		17.0	5.7				10.5	13.3
		61.9	24.4				21.9	-76.2
		16.4	26.0			EBIT/Interest	6.9	6.0
		(20) 3.3	(22) 7.4				(45) 3.7	(51) 1.6
		1.2	.9				1.1	-.3
						Net Profit + Depr., Dep., Amort./Cur. Mat. L/T/D		
		.8	.6			Fixed/Worth	.5	.6
		1.0	.9				.9	1.1
		2.0	1.5				1.8	2.8
		.8	.4			Debt/Worth	.5	.5
		1.2	.7				.8	1.1
		2.6	1.4				2.0	4.1
		28.8	21.0			% Profit Before Taxes/Tangible Net Worth	17.5	21.2
		(20) 13.4	(24) 11.4				(51) 5.9	(50) 3.4
		3.4	.5				.1	-3.3
		9.2	10.3			% Profit Before Taxes/Total Assets	10.7	11.6
		5.5	7.3				3.3	1.7
		.3	-.2				.0	-2.5
		9.5	4.7			Sales/Net Fixed Assets	6.9	8.0
		4.1	2.4				3.0	3.7
		2.0	1.8				2.3	2.3
		3.1	1.5			Sales/Total Assets	2.3	2.3
		2.0	1.2				1.6	1.7
		1.2	1.0				1.2	1.2
		1.2	2.2			% Depr., Dep., Amort./Sales	1.6	1.3
		(21) 1.8	(24) 3.1				(51) 2.6	(55) 2.4
		3.1	4.2				3.5	3.1
						% Officers', Directors', Owners' Comp/Sales		
10292M	17692M	275271M	635558M	176502M	180323M	Net Sales ($)	1287719M	1218292M
1219M	5325M	138342M	442978M	216796M	144455M	Total Assets ($)	1015968M	802957M

	Comparative Historical Data			Type of Statement	Current Data Sorted By Sales					
	50	38	42	Unqualified	2	1	4	8	18	9
			1	Reviewed					1	
	1	1	1	Compiled		1				
		4	2	Tax Returns	1	1				
	20	20	16	Other		1	1	2	8	4
	4/1/02-3/31/03 ALL	4/1/03-3/31/04 ALL	4/1/04-3/31/05 ALL		41 (4/1-9/30/04)			21 (10/1/04-3/31/05)		
					0-1MM	1-3MM	3-5MM	5-10MM	10-25MM	25MM & OVER
NUMBER OF STATEMENTS	71	63	62		3	4	5	10	27	13
	%	%	%	**ASSETS**	%	%	%	%	%	%
	13.1	17.7	18.6	Cash & Equivalents				24.7	13.8	13.6
	22.2	21.1	23.1	Trade Receivables (net)				19.0	25.0	19.2
	.3	.8	.7	Inventory				.0	.3	1.4
	4.8	5.0	3.0	All Other Current				2.3	2.7	4.2
	40.4	44.7	45.4	Total Current				46.1	41.7	38.4
	46.9	43.7	44.0	Fixed Assets (net)				48.2	46.9	42.2
	3.1	1.9	1.8	Intangibles (net)				.3	1.1	5.8
	9.5	9.7	8.8	All Other Non-Current				5.4	10.2	13.6
	100.0	100.0	100.0	Total				100.0	100.0	100.0
				LIABILITIES						
	3.7	3.9	5.4	Notes Payable-Short Term				17.1	3.1	2.9
	3.4	1.9	3.1	Cur. Mat.-L/T/D				11.3	1.5	1.2
	6.0	6.9	8.1	Trade Payables				4.5	5.6	9.0
	.0	.1	.1	Income Taxes Payable				.3	.0	.0
	17.6	14.0	13.5	All Other Current				13.3	14.6	11.3
	30.8	26.8	30.2	Total Current				46.6	24.8	24.4
	25.9	21.1	23.1	Long-Term Debt				20.2	21.8	28.0
	.0	.4	.2	Deferred Taxes				.0	.0	.2
	3.5	1.5	5.9	All Other Non-Current				23.6	2.4	3.9
	39.8	50.2	40.7	Net Worth				9.6	51.0	43.5
	100.0	100.0	100.0	Total Liabilities & Net Worth				100.0	100.0	100.0
				INCOME DATA						
	100.0	100.0	100.0	Net Sales				100.0	100.0	100.0
				Gross Profit						
	95.3	96.4	96.0	Operating Expenses				98.5	96.6	95.1
	4.7	3.6	4.0	Operating Profit				1.5	3.4	4.9
	1.7	-.6	.4	All Other Expenses (net)				.5	.2	.0
	3.0	4.2	3.6	Profit Before Taxes				1.0	3.2	4.9
				RATIOS						
	2.7	2.9	2.7					2.8	2.6	3.6
	1.9	2.0	1.5	Current				1.2	1.9	1.3
	1.1	1.2	1.2					.6	1.3	1.1
	2.4	2.5	2.6					2.7	2.6	3.1
	1.5	1.8	1.5	Quick				1.1	1.6	1.2
	.9	.9	1.1					.5	1.2	1.0
	32 11.6	27 13.6	28 13.0					20 17.8	41 9.0	28 12.8
	44 8.3	48 7.5	45 8.1	Sales/Receivables				45 8.0	53 6.9	41 8.8
	58 6.3	64 5.7	63 5.8					68 5.4	69 5.3	56 6.5
				Cost of Sales/Inventory						
				Cost of Sales/Payables						
	4.7	4.9	5.0					5.5	4.9	4.9
	10.7	8.6	12.0	Sales/Working Capital				37.5	8.5	19.8
	69.7	29.7	51.5					-21.0	18.8	60.2
	5.0	9.8	19.8						34.1	14.7
	(60) 1.8	(54) 5.0	(50) 4.7	EBIT/Interest				(21) 9.4	(12) 7.4	
	.3	1.7	1.1						.1	3.1
				Net Profit + Depr., Dep., Amort./Cur. Mat. L/T/D						
	.6	.6	.6					1.0	.6	.6
	1.2	.9	1.0	Fixed/Worth				1.9	.8	1.1
	2.6	1.5	2.0					-1.6	1.4	3.2
	.5	.4	.6					1.0	.4	.5
	1.3	1.0	1.2	Debt/Worth				2.4	.7	1.7
	4.0	2.1	3.1					-4.1	1.5	5.7
	22.9	24.2	28.4	% Profit Before Taxes/Tangible Net Worth					27.0	31.6
	(63) 8.6	(60) 8.4	(54) 12.7						(25) 13.5	(11) 13.4
	-2.1	3.2	4.1						2.4	4.5
	8.5	9.2	11.2	% Profit Before Taxes/Total Assets				9.3	9.9	11.8
	2.8	4.6	7.2					5.8	7.3	8.4
	-1.3	1.3	.3					-5.8	-.7	1.7
	4.4	7.3	7.8					10.7	5.2	6.7
	3.0	3.3	3.5	Sales/Net Fixed Assets				3.3	2.5	4.8
	2.2	2.3	2.0					1.8	1.8	2.6
	2.2	2.4	2.8					2.5	2.0	2.8
	1.5	1.5	1.5	Sales/Total Assets				1.6	1.2	1.7
	1.1	1.1	1.1					1.1	1.0	1.2
	2.0	1.8	1.6						1.6	1.6
	(64) 2.7	(55) 2.7	(56) 2.5	% Depr., Dep., Amort./Sales					(25) 2.8	1.7
	3.7	3.7	3.5						4.1	3.5
			4.0	% Officers', Directors', Owners' Comp/Sales						
		(11)	9.3							
			20.5							
	1896789M	1269551M	1295638M	Net Sales ($)	1713M	7728M	18129M	78015M	420144M	769909M
	1495498M	954704M	949115M	Total Assets ($)	7185M	3750M	15252M	51431M	371542M	499955M

M = $ thousand   MM = $ million
See Pages 11 through 21 for Explanation of Ratios and Data

Current Data Sorted By Assets   **Comparative Historical Data**

0-500M	500M-2MM	2-10MM	10-50MM	50-100MM	100-250MM	Type of Statement	ALL 4/1/00-3/31/01	ALL 4/1/01-3/31/02
	3	10	17	12	7	Unqualified	46	69
6	2	6	1		1	Reviewed	2	6
4	1	2	1			Compiled	20	14
	5	1				Tax Returns	4	
7	9	10	12	2	5	Other	34	56
	47 (4/1-9/30/04)		76 (10/1/04-3/31/05)					
17	20	29	30	14	13	**NUMBER OF STATEMENTS**	106	145
%	%	%	%	%	%	**ASSETS**	%	%
34.0	16.9	14.1	10.7	10.5	8.4	Cash & Equivalents	11.5	13.1
15.6	28.7	31.1	17.4	15.5	13.5	Trade Receivables (net)	17.8	20.1
.2	.8	2.4	1.1	.8	.8	Inventory	1.1	1.6
3.6	.2	3.9	1.2	3.4	5.5	All Other Current	4.4	4.0
53.3	46.6	51.5	30.3	30.2	28.3	Total Current	34.8	38.8
34.4	34.3	37.8	54.3	41.3	38.8	Fixed Assets (net)	46.7	41.9
4.1	7.8	.9	2.6	6.6	1.8	Intangibles (net)	3.9	3.2
8.2	11.3	9.9	12.8	21.8	31.0	All Other Non-Current	14.6	16.1
100.0	100.0	100.0	100.0	100.0	100.0	Total	100.0	100.0
						LIABILITIES		
63.4	11.2	10.1	2.1	.9	1.0	Notes Payable-Short Term	7.4	4.0
7.7	3.5	7.1	3.9	3.3	1.6	Cur. Mat.-L/T/D	4.1	2.6
9.8	6.7	7.4	9.1	4.6	7.4	Trade Payables	6.5	8.4
3.8	.0	.1	1.4	.0	.0	Income Taxes Payable	.0	.2
28.1	18.2	17.7	9.3	9.8	13.1	All Other Current	10.8	13.6
112.8	39.5	42.4	25.9	18.6	23.2	Total Current	28.8	28.7
22.0	28.6	26.2	33.5	28.3	18.7	Long-Term Debt	34.2	29.8
.0	.0	.2	.4	.0	.0	Deferred Taxes	.0	.2
6.6	1.2	2.1	3.5	1.5	3.2	All Other Non-Current	2.1	3.7
-41.4	30.7	29.1	36.8	51.6	54.9	Net Worth	35.0	37.6
100.0	100.0	100.0	100.0	100.0	100.0	Total Liabilities & Net Worth	100.0	100.0
						INCOME DATA		
100.0	100.0	100.0	100.0	100.0	100.0	Net Sales	100.0	100.0
						Gross Profit		
93.3	92.1	88.3	83.2	89.3	88.7	Operating Expenses	94.2	92.1
6.7	7.9	11.7	16.8	10.7	11.3	Operating Profit	5.8	7.9
6.5	1.3	2.4	6.1	2.4	2.7	All Other Expenses (net)	1.0	4.2
.1	6.6	9.3	10.7	8.3	8.6	Profit Before Taxes	4.8	3.7
						RATIOS		
1.7	2.1	2.7	2.7	3.6	2.2	Current	2.9	2.9
.9	1.2	1.5	1.7	2.3	1.3		1.8	1.9
.3	.6	.8	.8	.8	.9		1.0	1.1
1.6	1.9	2.3	2.2	2.9	1.9	Quick	2.6	2.6
.9	1.2	1.2	1.4	1.9	1.2		1.4	1.6
.3	.6	.6	.6	.7	.7		.7	.9
0 UND	0 UND	37 9.9	30 12.3	48 7.6	30 12.2	Sales/Receivables	25 14.7	42 8.7
0 UND	25 14.7	49 7.4	46 8.0	61 6.0	46 8.0		54 6.8	55 6.6
12 31.2	65 5.6	81 4.5	61 6.0	71 5.1	57 6.5		77 4.8	69 5.3
						Cost of Sales/Inventory		
						Cost of Sales/Payables		
44.8	9.1	6.5	5.4	2.8	5.9	Sales/Working Capital	4.8	4.5
-77.0	80.0	16.1	15.7	5.6	19.0		9.2	8.2
-15.9	-11.3	-39.3	-161.5	-19.4	-104.1		435.6	45.7
21.5	19.0	8.6	21.2	9.0	13.7	EBIT/Interest	8.4	7.7
(15) 2.2	(16) 5.6	(27) 5.0	(24) 7.7	3.9	(11) 8.4		(90) 2.9	(127) 2.4
-1.7	1.3	1.5	1.6	2.9	2.2		.5	.8
						Net Profit + Depr., Dep., Amort./Cur. Mat. L/T/D		27.5
							(10)	3.8
								2.1
.5	.1	.5	.8	.5	.6	Fixed/Worth	.5	.5
-7.3	1.1	1.4	2.1	.8	.8		1.3	.9
-.6	NM	NM	5.7	2.5	1.1		6.0	2.3
2.8	.8	.5	.8	.4	.6	Debt/Worth	.5	.5
-24.9	2.4	2.3	2.5	.8	.7		1.2	.9
-3.6	NM	NM	7.9	3.4	1.7		8.1	6.2
	169.7	69.6	84.9	51.6	19.9	% Profit Before Taxes/Tangible Net Worth	30.9	20.7
(15) 20.0	(22) 44.8	(27) 24.4	(13) 8.6		7.4		(84) 7.0	(123) 5.8
.0	5.6	5.8	4.8		1.8		-3.0	-.6
86.1	24.9	21.0	19.0	7.0	13.1	% Profit Before Taxes/Total Assets	11.8	7.8
7.8	5.9	6.3	7.2	5.1	4.5		5.2	2.7
-20.2	-.1	1.4	1.4	2.9	1.1		-2.0	-.5
89.4	36.0	22.9	5.4	4.1	4.6	Sales/Net Fixed Assets	5.9	5.2
46.8	14.4	5.0	3.0	2.0	2.1		2.3	2.3
16.2	3.2	1.9	1.3	1.5	1.8		1.4	1.6
18.4	4.4	2.6	2.5	1.5	1.7	Sales/Total Assets	1.9	1.8
9.8	2.4	1.8	1.3	.8	.9		1.1	1.1
4.1	1.1	1.2	.8	.5	.6		.6	.7
.7	.8	.8	1.9	2.7	1.7	% Depr., Dep., Amort./Sales	1.8	2.3
(12) 1.0	(15) 3.3	(27) 2.9	(29) 3.5	4.6	(10) 3.4		(97) 3.2	(131) 4.5
4.5	11.6	10.7	6.9	5.7	6.5		6.3	5.9
13.1						% Officers', Directors', Owners' Comp/Sales		2.1
(11) 19.0							(12)	11.4
27.8								26.2
44423M	65598M	299219M	4589517M	1014901M	2540903M	Net Sales ($)	2858112M	8775809M
4311M	23376M	152198M	756107M	1039158M	2400293M	Total Assets ($)	3763928M	7904781M

© RMA 2005

M = $ thousand   MM = $ million

See Pages 11 through 21 for Explanation of Ratios and Data

Comparative Historical Data / Current Data Sorted By Sales

			Type of Statement						
61	54	49	Unqualified		3	3	4	11	28
3	3	10	Reviewed		1	3	1	3	2
11	24	9	Compiled	2	4	1	2		
10	7	10	Tax Returns	4	3	1	2		
45	38	45	Other	1	9	7	6	7	15
4/1/02-3/31/03	4/1/03-3/31/04	4/1/04-3/31/05			47 (4/1-9/30/04)			76 (10/1/04-3/31/05)	
ALL	ALL	ALL		0-1MM	1-3MM	3-5MM	5-10MM	10-25MM	25MM & OVER
130	126	123	NUMBER OF STATEMENTS	7	20	15	15	21	45
%	%	%	ASSETS	%	%	%	%	%	%
15.0	11.1	15.5	Cash & Equivalents		24.6	15.9	23.1	15.9	10.1
20.0	21.6	21.6	Trade Receivables (net)		9.8	33.1	26.2	30.7	18.6
1.5	1.8	1.1	Inventory		.4	.8	1.5	1.7	1.1
4.4	6.6	2.7	All Other Current		.8	2.8	3.8	2.8	3.2
41.0	41.1	40.9	Total Current		35.5	52.6	54.7	51.1	33.0
39.6	42.8	41.3	Fixed Assets (net)		47.6	43.8	32.0	33.3	43.7
5.3	3.3	3.6	Intangibles (net)		1.9	1.4	.4	3.2	3.2
14.1	12.7	14.2	All Other Non-Current		15.1	2.2	12.9	12.4	20.1
100.0	100.0	100.0	Total		100.0	100.0	100.0	100.0	100.0
			LIABILITIES						
6.0	5.0	13.7	Notes Payable-Short Term		16.7	23.8	8.4	11.4	1.5
4.0	3.7	4.8	Cur. Mat.-L/T/D		7.1	4.1	8.7	2.3	3.3
6.5	7.2	7.7	Trade Payables		6.6	3.8	4.8	10.5	9.3
.2	.1	.9	Income Taxes Payable		.1	4.2	.1	.0	1.0
23.7	14.0	15.8	All Other Current		11.3	36.6	16.0	15.5	12.7
40.4	29.9	42.9	Total Current		41.8	72.5	37.9	39.6	27.8
24.2	24.6	27.2	Long-Term Debt		35.1	21.6	27.2	18.9	25.4
.2	.1	.1	Deferred Taxes		.4	.0	.0	.2	.1
3.5	3.3	2.9	All Other Non-Current		2.9	1.4	.2	2.9	3.5
31.7	42.1	26.8	Net Worth		19.8	4.5	34.7	38.5	43.1
100.0	100.0	100.0	Total Liabilities & Net Worth		100.0	100.0	100.0	100.0	100.0
			INCOME DATA						
100.0	100.0	100.0	Net Sales		100.0	100.0	100.0	100.0	100.0
			Gross Profit						
91.4	90.9	88.5	Operating Expenses		84.4	85.4	87.2	88.0	90.2
8.6	9.1	11.5	Operating Profit		15.6	14.6	12.8	12.0	9.8
2.6	1.8	3.7	All Other Expenses (net)		8.1	7.4	-.2	1.4	2.4
6.0	7.3	7.8	Profit Before Taxes		7.6	7.2	13.0	10.6	7.4
			RATIOS						
2.4	2.8	2.4			2.4	2.1	3.2	2.8	2.3
1.5	1.7	1.4	Current		1.0	1.5	1.9	1.6	1.3
.8	.9	.7			.4	.7	.9	1.0	.8
2.2	2.2	2.2			1.9	1.7	3.2	2.7	2.0
1.3	1.3	1.2	Quick		.7	1.3	1.7	1.6	1.3
.6	.8	.6			.2	.5	.6	1.0	.7
14 26.0	23 15.6	8 43.8		0 UND	7 49.9	8 43.8	38 9.5	39 9.3	
50 7.3	51 7.2	45 8.1	Sales/Receivables	0 UND	51 7.2	39 9.4	47 7.8	51 7.2	
71 5.1	67 5.5	64 5.7		21 17.5	82 4.4	66 5.5	66 5.5	63 5.8	
			Cost of Sales/Inventory						
			Cost of Sales/Payables						
5.1	5.2	6.3			13.6	7.6	6.7	5.3	5.1
12.9	11.9	27.2	Sales/Working Capital		-999.8	39.1	18.4	7.4	19.0
-52.4	-53.8	-25.8			-11.8	-14.8	-58.6	213.4	-29.9
12.3	13.2	13.7		14.4	9.0	103.6	19.0	12.5	
(113) 3.3	(106) 4.0	(107) 4.9	EBIT/Interest	(15) 5.4	(13) 3.2	(13) 21.5	(17) 5.4	(42) 5.5	
.3	1.1	1.8		-.1	1.4	3.4	1.2	2.6	
	8.6	9.9	Net Profit + Depr., Dep.,						
(10) 4.5	(13) 1.9	Amort./Cur. Mat. L/T/D							
	1.4	.5							
.5	.5	.5			.4	.4	.2	.4	.6
1.1	1.0	1.2	Fixed/Worth		3.9	1.3	.9	.9	.9
4.4	2.7	11.6			NM	-49.5	2.7	NM	2.7
.6	.5	.7			1.0	1.1	.4	.4	.7
1.2	1.3	2.3	Debt/Worth		6.6	2.5	2.4	1.0	1.0
12.5	4.5	24.9			-23.6	-999.8	38.0	NM	5.0
32.1	50.7	84.3		144.8	251.2	162.3	54.8	49.4	
(101) 8.2	(107) 9.3	(97) 20.0	% Profit Before Taxes/Tangible Net Worth	(14) 24.6	(11) 63.9	(12) 40.9	(16) 20.7	(42) 9.8	
-.4	.4	4.5		3.0	20.0	3.0	1.9	4.6	
15.0	15.1	19.1			11.1	33.3	74.9	17.6	13.1
4.2	4.8	6.0	% Profit Before Taxes/Total Assets		5.7	19.6	18.5	6.6	5.2
-1.6	.1	1.3			-1.4	1.5	1.8	.1	2.4
14.1	8.4	22.7			39.5	69.5	49.5	41.4	5.2
3.3	3.0	4.3	Sales/Net Fixed Assets		5.2	22.7	8.9	3.6	3.0
1.6	1.7	1.9			.5	1.7	3.9	2.7	1.8
2.7	2.5	3.0			5.3	12.1	5.2	2.9	2.0
1.4	1.4	1.7	Sales/Total Assets		1.8	3.3	2.4	1.8	1.4
.7	.8	.9			.4	1.1	1.6	1.0	.8
2.1	2.1	1.6			.9	.8	1.4	.8	2.0
(108) 3.7	(113) 3.8	(107) 3.3	% Depr., Dep., Amort./Sales	(16) 7.3	(12) 2.3	(12) 3.0	2.6	(41) 3.5	
6.5	6.8	6.5			19.1	10.9	7.2	3.9	5.3
9.6	10.4	11.0							
(14) 19.1	(11) 17.7	(24) 19.2	% Officers', Directors', Owners' Comp/Sales						
33.4		31.3	27.1						
5535953M	5335563M	8554561M	Net Sales ($)	3956M	36071M	57931M	106835M	358050M	7991718M
4945298M	4687102M	4375443M	Total Assets ($)	3758M	69687M	28069M	58918M	258855M	3956156M

Current Data Sorted By Assets   Comparative Historical Data

Type of Statement									
Unqualified	9	60	186	193	61	41		438	465
Reviewed	12	40	74	17	2	2		113	113
Compiled	16	57	113	17	4	2		238	262
Tax Returns	39	40	33	3				65	63
Other	32	148	215	103	27	10		409	505
	412 (4/1-9/30/04)			1144 (10/1/04-3/31/05)				4/1/00-3/31/01	4/1/01-3/31/02
	0-500M	500M-2MM	2-10MM	10-50MM	50-100MM	100-250MM		ALL	ALL
NUMBER OF STATEMENTS	108	345	621	333	94	55		1263	1408
	%	%	%	%	%	%	ASSETS	%	%
Cash & Equivalents	21.2	11.6	10.9	9.8	9.5	8.9		8.5	9.0
Trade Receivables (net)	28.5	33.5	19.8	12.0	9.3	8.8		17.4	17.4
Inventory	.3	.5	.3	.3	.4	.4		.4	.3
All Other Current	4.2	5.8	3.6	3.1	2.7	4.6		3.0	3.4
Total Current	54.2	51.4	34.7	25.2	21.9	22.6		29.3	30.1
Fixed Assets (net)	29.8	35.5	50.6	54.5	55.8	50.7		53.3	51.8
Intangibles (net)	4.1	3.9	3.9	3.6	3.9	3.8		4.7	4.7
All Other Non-Current	12.0	9.3	10.8	16.7	18.5	22.9		12.8	13.4
Total	100.0	100.0	100.0	100.0	100.0	100.0		100.0	100.0
							LIABILITIES		
Notes Payable-Short Term	18.3	9.3	5.9	2.1	3.0	.6		4.4	6.6
Cur. Mat.-L/T/D	2.9	3.2	3.1	3.2	2.0	5.9		3.2	3.6
Trade Payables	22.9	14.7	8.3	5.1	4.3	5.4		7.4	7.7
Income Taxes Payable	.1	.2	.0	.1	.0	.1		.1	.2
All Other Current	36.4	29.9	14.8	9.5	7.5	6.1		14.7	16.0
Total Current	80.7	57.3	32.1	20.0	16.8	18.0		29.7	34.1
Long-Term Debt	26.3	31.2	47.7	48.5	49.9	48.4		48.0	48.2
Deferred Taxes	.0	.1	.1	.0	.1	.1		.3	.1
All Other Non-Current	6.1	8.9	5.7	7.5	17.4	11.9		7.4	9.3
Net Worth	−13.0	2.6	14.4	23.9	15.8	21.6		14.6	8.3
Total Liabilities & Net Worth	100.0	100.0	100.0	100.0	100.0	100.0		100.0	100.0
							INCOME DATA		
Net Sales	100.0	100.0	100.0	100.0	100.0	100.0		100.0	100.0
Gross Profit									
Operating Expenses	96.2	88.7	87.7	91.5	91.7	91.2		91.8	90.5
Operating Profit	3.8	11.3	12.3	8.5	8.3	8.8		8.2	9.5
All Other Expenses (net)	1.0	4.3	6.5	3.9	4.0	4.3		4.9	6.0
Profit Before Taxes	2.8	7.0	5.8	4.6	4.4	4.5		3.3	3.4
							RATIOS		
Current	1.6	1.8	2.2	2.4	2.2	1.9		1.9	2.0
	.7	1.1	1.3	1.2	1.2	1.4		1.1	1.1
	.4	.6	.7	.8	.9	.9		.7	.6
Quick	1.4	1.6	2.0	1.9	2.0	1.6		1.7	1.7
	.6	1.0	1.1	1.1	1.0	1.1		1.0	.9
	.3	.5	.7	.7	.7	.5		.6	.5
Sales/Receivables	0 UND	9 40.8	19 18.8	23 16.2	17 21.3	20 17.9		15 24.7	14 25.5
	6 58.0	30 12.1	34 10.6	34 10.9	29 12.4	28 12.8		32 11.3	31 11.9
	31 11.8	46 8.0	52 7.0	46 7.9	41 8.9	38 9.5		49 7.4	47 7.8
Cost of Sales/Inventory									
Cost of Sales/Payables									
Sales/Working Capital	52.4	12.4	7.7	6.6	4.1	5.5		9.6	9.1
	−52.0	139.9	28.1	27.9	23.9	14.8		47.2	58.4
	−14.3	−14.3	−18.5	−27.3	−34.9	−41.9		−16.8	−15.0
EBIT/Interest	15.4	15.4	5.7	4.0	3.3	4.8		3.4	3.5
	(66) 1.0	(243) 3.7	(499) 2.6	(295) 2.1	(86) 2.0	(50) 2.0		(1029) 1.5	(1134) 1.6
	−4.7	.5	.9	.9	1.0	1.1		.6	.6
Net Profit + Depr., Dep., Amort./Cur. Mat. L/T/D		33.7	5.5	6.1	5.4			3.9	4.1
		(11) 4.9	(41) 3.0	(19) 2.1	(11) 2.7			(87) 2.1	(80) 2.1
		1.8	1.0	1.0	1.3			.6	1.1
Fixed/Worth	.4	.4	1.0	1.1	1.7	1.1		1.1	1.2
	8.0	3.4	4.6	2.8	5.7	3.3		4.6	4.1
	−.6	−1.8	−5.4	−41.4	−12.3	31.5		−7.4	−6.2
Debt/Worth	1.3	1.3	1.6	1.1	2.2	1.4		1.6	1.6
	UND	7.3	7.2	4.1	9.0	5.5		6.9	6.8
	−3.3	−6.4	−10.7	−61.4	−25.5	42.0		−11.6	−9.4
% Profit Before Taxes/Tangible Net Worth	222.5	100.2	64.0	31.1	36.4	35.8		40.8	50.7
	(54) 46.1	(218) 47.1	(407) 22.8	(243) 10.2	(65) 11.1	(43) 9.8		(838) 9.4	(918) 13.0
	4.9	13.2	5.3	2.1	3.2	.6		−.5	−1.1
% Profit Before Taxes/Total Assets	44.0	24.6	11.8	6.5	6.0	6.4		7.9	9.4
	10.4	9.5	4.8	2.9	1.7	1.8		2.0	2.5
	−9.0	.1	.0	.0	−.2	−.7		−1.8	−1.5
Sales/Net Fixed Assets	163.9	51.6	10.5	2.8	2.3	2.7		7.2	8.4
	34.8	15.8	2.5	1.4	.8	1.0		1.8	2.0
	12.6	3.0	1.2	.8	.4	.5		.8	.8
Sales/Total Assets	14.0	4.9	2.3	1.2	1.3	1.3		2.2	2.4
	6.5	3.1	1.3	.8	.5	.5		1.1	1.1
	3.3	1.5	.7	.5	.3	.2		.5	.5
% Depr., Dep., Amort./Sales	.3	.5	1.5	2.9	3.5	3.2		1.7	1.5
	(71) .9	(298) 1.3	(584) 2.8	(320) 4.7	(93) 7.2	(52) 6.3		(1189) 3.9	(1308) 3.7
	1.8	3.6	5.4	7.5	10.8	12.3		7.1	7.1
% Officers', Directors', Owners' Comp/Sales	3.4	2.5	2.0	2.4				1.6	1.9
	(37) 6.8	(57) 4.4	(90) 4.1	(30) 5.0				(213) 4.5	(198) 4.8
	16.1	9.5	8.0	19.3				9.3	9.4
Net Sales ($)	161225M	1284322M	4487509M	7326749M	5726113M	7745482M		19338070M	21458484M
Total Assets ($)	23916M	410204M	2993871M	7232011M	6484423M	7870866M		22585247M	26301731M

M = $ thousand   MM = $ million
See Pages 11 through 21 for Explanation of Ratios and Data

Comparative Historical Data / Current Data Sorted By Sales

			Type of Statement						
490	478	550	Unqualified	18	41	53	154	163	121
103	138	147	Reviewed	15	14	31	47	32	8
148	272	209	Compiled	28	40	47	56	26	12
77	89	115	Tax Returns	47	41	7	13	6	1
479	478	535	Other	61	99	99	131	83	62
4/1/02-3/31/03 ALL	4/1/03-3/31/04 ALL	4/1/04-3/31/05 ALL		412 (4/1-9/30/04) 0-1MM	1-3MM	3-5MM	1144 (10/1/04-3/31/05) 5-10MM	10-25MM	25MM & OVER
1297	1455	1556	**NUMBER OF STATEMENTS**	169	235	237	401	310	204
%	%	%	**ASSETS**	%	%	%	%	%	%
10.5	10.4	11.4	Cash & Equivalents	10.8	13.3	10.1	12.0	11.3	9.9
17.4	20.1	20.8	Trade Receivables (net)	7.7	16.8	30.9	24.4	19.3	19.5
.3	.4	.3	Inventory	.1	.3	.3	.4	.4	.4
3.2	4.2	4.0	All Other Current	4.8	3.9	4.1	3.8	4.2	3.6
31.4	35.1	36.5	Total Current	23.3	34.3	45.4	40.7	35.2	33.3
51.3	49.4	47.0	Fixed Assets (net)	62.9	49.3	42.2	44.0	44.6	46.0
4.6	3.1	3.8	Intangibles (net)	4.8	4.2	3.3	3.5	3.0	5.0
12.7	12.4	12.7	All Other Non-Current	9.0	12.2	9.1	11.8	17.1	15.6
100.0	100.0	100.0	Total	100.0	100.0	100.0	100.0	100.0	100.0
			LIABILITIES						
5.3	5.0	6.3	Notes Payable-Short Term	3.6	12.1	9.5	5.1	4.6	3.4
3.4	3.7	3.1	Cur. Mat.-L/T/D	3.4	2.2	3.4	3.5	2.4	4.1
7.4	8.3	9.7	Trade Payables	7.1	10.7	12.5	9.7	8.1	10.0
.1	.1	.1	Income Taxes Payable	.0	.1	.2	.2	.0	.1
18.0	17.7	17.8	All Other Current	9.3	22.5	24.6	18.7	13.9	15.3
34.3	34.7	37.1	Total Current	23.5	47.6	50.1	37.1	29.1	32.9
45.5	41.2	42.9	Long-Term Debt	63.8	47.1	38.6	37.3	39.8	41.4
.1	.1	.1	Deferred Taxes	.1	.0	.1	.1	.0	.1
9.6	11.3	7.7	All Other Non-Current	4.6	7.7	9.0	6.9	9.1	8.3
10.5	12.7	12.3	Net Worth	8.1	-2.5	2.1	18.6	22.0	17.3
100.0	100.0	100.0	Total Liabilities & Net Worth	100.0	100.0	100.0	100.0	100.0	100.0
			INCOME DATA						
100.0	100.0	100.0	Net Sales	100.0	100.0	100.0	100.0	100.0	100.0
			Gross Profit						
90.7	91.0	89.7	Operating Expenses	66.6	87.9	92.6	93.4	93.5	94.2
9.3	9.0	10.3	Operating Profit	33.4	12.1	7.4	6.6	6.5	5.8
5.6	5.2	4.8	All Other Expenses (net)	17.4	5.8	3.5	3.3	2.2	2.0
3.7	3.8	5.5	Profit Before Taxes	16.0	6.2	3.9	3.3	4.3	3.8
			RATIOS						
2.0	2.2	2.1	Current	2.8	2.1	1.8	2.0	2.4	1.8
1.1	1.2	1.2		.9	1.0	1.2	1.2	1.3	1.2
.6	.7	.7		.3	.4	.8	.7	.9	.8
1.8	1.8	1.8	Quick	2.0	1.7	1.7	1.9	2.1	1.5
1.0 (1454)	1.0	1.0		.6	.9	1.1	1.1	1.1	1.1
.5	.6	.6		.2	.4	.6	.6	.7	.7
12 29.6	14 25.2	16 23.3	Sales/Receivables	0 UND	0 905.5	21 17.1	26 14.1	25 14.9	28 13.2
31 11.9	33 10.9	32 11.5		0 UND	17 21.5	34 10.7	36 10.0	36 10.3	36 10.2
46 7.9	48 7.5	47 7.8		10 35.5	35 10.3	54 6.7	51 7.1	49 7.5	45 8.1
			Cost of Sales/Inventory						
			Cost of Sales/Payables						
9.0	7.9	8.6	Sales/Working Capital	3.9	9.8	10.8	8.9	6.5	10.4
55.5	37.5	40.9		-140.3	484.3	38.2	29.3	26.3	39.2
-14.8	-16.4	-18.7		-4.3	-11.5	-27.7	-20.3	-48.7	-34.3
(1029) 4.1	(1154) 4.4	(1239) 5.9	EBIT/Interest	(71) 5.3	(182) 6.5	(187) 7.8	(332) 6.7	(274) 5.8	(193) 4.7
1.8	1.8	2.5		2.0	2.0	2.6	2.6	2.5	2.5
.6	.6	.9		.0	.3	.8	.9	.9	1.2
(97) 5.5	(89) 3.6	(91) 6.1	Net Profit + Depr., Dep., Amort./Cur. Mat. L/T/D				(24) 10.0	(19) 4.9	(28) 6.0
2.6	2.0	2.9					3.7	3.1	2.3
1.2	.8	1.2					1.2	1.2	1.4
1.0	.9	.8	Fixed/Worth	1.8	1.0	.6	.6	.8	1.2
3.7	3.7	3.9		15.8	9.8	4.4	2.8	2.2	3.9
-5.6	-6.6	-5.9		-5.7	-2.5	-3.8	-8.0	-12.0	-114.0
1.4	1.4	1.4	Debt/Worth	2.2	1.7	1.8	1.2	.9	1.8
5.9	6.1	6.7		30.1	18.7	7.9	4.3	3.7	6.4
-9.2	-11.7	-11.5		-7.2	-4.4	-7.2	-19.1	-25.5	-154.4
(844) 47.0	(968) 44.4	(1030) 63.8	% Profit Before Taxes/Tangible Net Worth	(99) 65.7	(129) 65.8	(153) 92.8	(281) 66.7	(217) 43.4	(151) 56.4
12.5	13.2	21.1		32.3	19.7	32.0	25.4	10.8	16.6
-.1	-.2	4.3		4.9	2.9	10.4	4.9	2.7	4.7
9.8	9.0	12.1	% Profit Before Taxes/Total Assets	14.2	11.3	18.7	14.7	10.3	8.3
2.6	2.6	4.4		3.8	4.4	7.1	4.8	3.5	4.1
-1.3	-1.6	-.3		-.1	-2.2	-.3	.2	-.3	.5
9.2	12.4	16.8	Sales/Net Fixed Assets	9.2	20.2	34.2	17.1	11.5	8.7
2.2	2.3	2.8		.5	3.0	6.1	3.6	2.2	2.6
.9	.9	1.0		.2	.8	1.5	1.5	1.1	1.3
2.4	2.7	2.9	Sales/Total Assets	1.0	3.6	4.3	3.1	2.4	2.4
1.1	1.2	1.3		.3	1.3	2.0	1.6	1.1	1.3
.6	.6	.6		.2	.5	1.0	.9	.6	.7
(1217) 1.7	(1353) 1.5	(1418) 1.3	% Depr., Dep., Amort./Sales	(137) 6.0	(202) 1.1	(221) .5	(373) 1.2	(293) 1.6	(192) 1.5
3.6	3.5	3.1		14.7	3.5	2.0	2.4	3.4	3.3
7.1	7.2	6.7		25.5	7.8	4.0	4.6	6.6	5.6
(200) 2.0	(190) 2.1	(221) 2.3	% Officers', Directors', Owners' Comp/Sales	(27) 3.8	(51) 3.3	(33) 2.5	(61) 1.6	(34) 1.5	(15) 1.1
4.7	4.6	4.9		10.2	5.2	4.4	2.8	3.8	6.7
10.0	9.4	9.9		27.2	11.4	7.6	5.8	8.9	17.2
20352214M	24244066M	26731400M	Net Sales ($)	87054M	472286M	948441M	2910773M	4673447M	17639399M
22785836M	24200363M	25015291M	Total Assets ($)	337180M	703272M	801296M	3130214M	6727696M	13315633M

M = $ thousand   MM = $ million
See Pages 11 through 21 for Explanation of Ratios and Data

| Current Data Sorted By Assets | | | | | | | Comparative Historical Data | |

0-500M	500M-2MM	2-10MM	10-50MM	50-100MM	100-250MM	Type of Statement	4/1/00-3/31/01 ALL	4/1/01-3/31/02 ALL
1	9	28	13			Unqualified		
	3	1				Reviewed		
						Compiled		
1	3					Tax Returns		
3	4	7	5			Other		
	60 (4/1-9/30/04)		18 (10/1/04-3/31/05)					
5	19	36	18			NUMBER OF STATEMENTS		
%	%	%	%	%	%	**ASSETS**	%	%
	12.5	13.8	9.2	D	D	Cash & Equivalents	D	D
	25.6	15.9	13.5	A	A	Trade Receivables (net)	A	A
	.1	.1	.3	T	T	Inventory	T	T
	10.3	5.9	5.3	A	A	All Other Current	A	A
	48.5	35.8	28.3			Total Current		
	41.3	52.0	58.0	N	N	Fixed Assets (net)	N	N
	.9	1.8	.6	O	O	Intangibles (net)	O	O
	9.3	10.4	13.1	T	T	All Other Non-Current	T	T
	100.0	100.0	100.0			Total		
				A	A	**LIABILITIES**	A	A
	7.7	5.1	1.6	V	V	Notes Payable-Short Term	V	V
	2.0	2.9	2.3	A	A	Cur. Mat.-L/T/D	A	A
	10.2	4.3	5.8	I	I	Trade Payables	I	I
	1.0	.0	.0	L	L	Income Taxes Payable	L	L
	16.6	12.1	10.0	A	A	All Other Current	A	A
	37.4	24.3	19.7	B	B	Total Current	B	B
	26.1	31.3	40.4	L	L	Long-Term Debt	L	L
	.1	.0	.0	E	E	Deferred Taxes	E	E
	6.6	4.5	8.8			All Other Non-Current		
	29.8	39.8	31.1			Net Worth		
	100.0	100.0	100.0			Total Liabilities & Net Worth		
						INCOME DATA		
	100.0	100.0	-100.0			Net Sales		
						Gross Profit		
	93.4	96.9	94.7			Operating Expenses		
	6.6	3.1	5.3			Operating Profit		
	2.3	1.0	3.9			All Other Expenses (net)		
	4.2	2.1	1.4			Profit Before Taxes		
						RATIOS		
	1.7	2.4	2.3					
	1.1	1.5	1.3			Current		
	.9	.9	.9					
	1.6	2.0	2.2					
	1.0	1.2	1.2			Quick		
	.8	.7	.6					
	3 143.8	22 16.9	5 79.3					
	22 16.6	32 11.4	36 10.1			Sales/Receivables		
	35 10.5	38 9.5	43 8.6					
						Cost of Sales/Inventory		
						Cost of Sales/Payables		
	16.2	7.4	5.8					
	156.3	16.9	23.3			Sales/Working Capital		
	-111.0	-95.9	-92.9					
	16.6	7.8	2.9					
	(12) 2.2	(31) 1.3	(14) 1.3			EBIT/Interest		
	1.7	.2	.8					
						Net Profit + Depr., Dep., Amort./Cur. Mat. L /T/D		
	.3	.7	1.0					
	.9	1.5	2.0			Fixed/Worth		
	4.8	4.9	5.0					
	1.3	.6	1.3					
	3.9	1.5	2.4			Debt/Worth		
	33.5	5.8	7.1					
	42.6	12.2	25.5					
	(16) 14.8	(32) 6.4	(17) 5.6			% Profit Before Taxes/Tangible Net Worth		
	1.6	-1.7	.0					
	7.9	6.2	5.7					
	4.6	1.3	1.0			% Profit Before Taxes/Total Assets		
	.7	-1.3	-.3					
	46.2	5.4	3.9					
	11.6	2.9	2.7			Sales/Net Fixed Assets		
	1.3	1.7	1.9					
	4.8	2.4	2.0					
	2.8	1.7	1.3			Sales/Total Assets		
	.8	.9	1.0					
	.8	1.9	2.6					
	(16) 1.8	(35) 2.8	(17) 3.3			% Depr., Dep., Amort./Sales		
	7.7	3.4	5.0					
						% Officers', Directors', Owners' Comp/Sales		
4796M	76175M	344408M	510595M			Net Sales ($)		
1881M	21852M	185637M	351968M			Total Assets ($)		

Comparative Historical Data | Current Data Sorted By Sales

			Type of Statement						
17	39	51	Unqualified	2	8	6	14	13	8
		4	Reviewed	2	2				
	1		Compiled						
1	1	4	Tax Returns	4					
11	6	19	Other	3	2	3	3	6	2
4/1/02-	4/1/03-	4/1/04-			60 (4/1-9/30/04)			18 (10/1/04-3/31/05)	
3/31/03	3/31/04	3/31/05							
ALL	ALL	ALL		0-1MM	1-3MM	3-5MM	5-10MM	10-25MM	25MM & OVER
29	47	78	**NUMBER OF STATEMENTS**	11	10	11	17	19	10
%	%	%	**ASSETS**	%	%	%	%	%	%
11.3	9.9	11.9	Cash & Equivalents	3.7	15.5	10.8	14.1	14.5	9.7
15.1	17.5	17.8	Trade Receivables (net)	1.4	21.8	18.0	22.8	19.2	20.9
.1	.2	.1	Inventory	.1	.0	.2	.0	.3	.2
3.3	6.5	7.8	All Other Current	14.3	4.7	.2	9.0	7.1	11.7
29.8	34.1	37.7	Total Current	19.5	42.0	29.2	45.9	41.1	42.5
56.7	53.9	50.1	Fixed Assets (net)	70.4	40.2	62.9	41.5	46.2	45.4
2.7	1.6	1.3	Intangibles (net)	1.4	.4	1.1	3.5	.4	.4
10.9	10.4	10.9	All Other Non-Current	8.6	17.4	6.7	9.1	12.4	11.7
100.0	100.0	100.0	Total	100.0	100.0	100.0	100.0	100.0	100.0
			LIABILITIES						
5.1	6.6	7.0	Notes Payable-Short Term	13.3	6.8	8.8	8.8	3.5	1.9
5.3	2.7	2.4	Cur. Mat.-L/T/D	1.2	3.0	2.7	2.3	2.2	2.9
5.9	5.6	6.2	Trade Payables	5.1	3.9	4.0	7.8	5.2	11.6
.4	.0	.2	Income Taxes Payable	.0	.0	.0	1.1	.0	.0
12.4	15.5	12.4	All Other Current	1.9	8.5	13.7	17.9	13.8	14.7
29.1	30.4	28.2	Total Current	21.4	22.2	29.1	37.9	24.7	31.1
44.4	32.1	31.7	Long-Term Debt	38.9	29.6	40.5	25.1	28.6	33.5
.0	.0	.0	Deferred Taxes	.0	.0	.1	.0	.0	.0
3.8	4.7	6.7	All Other Non-Current	13.6	7.0	10.7	4.4	4.0	3.3
22.6	32.8	33.3	Net Worth	26.1	41.2	19.6	32.6	42.7	32.0
100.0	100.0	100.0	Total Liabilities & Net Worth	100.0	100.0	100.0	100.0	100.0	100.0
			INCOME DATA						
100.0	100.0	100.0	Net Sales	100.0	100.0	100.0	100.0	100.0	100.0
			Gross Profit						
94.8	96.5	95.1	Operating Expenses	81.8	93.1	94.3	99.6	98.5	98.1
5.2	3.5	4.9	Operating Profit	18.2	6.9	5.7	.4	1.5	1.9
4.1	1.8	2.3	All Other Expenses (net)	7.1	4.1	4.3	.2	.2	.4
1.0	1.7	2.7	Profit Before Taxes	11.1	2.8	1.4	.2	1.3	1.5
			RATIOS						
1.7	1.7	2.4		3.4	4.7	1.3	1.9	2.8	2.5
1.0	1.1	1.3	Current	1.1	2.0	1.0	1.2	1.6	1.1
.9	.8	.9		.7	1.1	.5	.9	1.1	.9
1.5	1.6	1.8		1.6	4.0	1.3	1.8	2.2	1.7
1.0	.8	1.1	Quick	1.0	1.6	1.0	1.0	1.1	1.0
.6	.6	.7		.1	.4	.5	.6	.9	.6
8 47.0	17 21.6	14 26.1		0 UND	6 65.7	15 25.0	21 17.4	23 16.0	20 18.3
26 14.1	34 10.8	30 12.2	Sales/Receivables	1 497.0	34 10.9	29 12.6	29 12.4	33 11.1	35 10.5
40 9.2	43 8.5	40 9.1		20 18.7	54 6.8	32 11.2	45 8.1	43 8.5	40 9.0
			Cost of Sales/Inventory						
			Cost of Sales/Payables						
16.3	10.8	8.0		9.7	3.2	16.2	8.6	7.1	7.9
173.2	117.2	24.4	Sales/Working Capital	115.9	10.1	−999.8	26.0	21.0	103.0
−57.4	−36.1	−98.2		−15.4	NM	−13.0	−83.8	97.4	−49.5
3.2	3.7	5.5				10.6	2.3	17.6	
(27) 1.6	(42) 1.6	(61) 1.7	EBIT/Interest	(10) 1.8	(13) 1.6	(17) 1.2			
.8	.3	.8				.2	.9	.4	
			Net Profit + Depr., Dep.,						
			Amort./Cur. Mat. L/T/D						
1.0	.9	.7		.8	.1	.9	.5	.4	.8
2.8	1.7	1.6	Fixed/Worth	2.7	1.1	5.2	1.5	1.4	1.8
14.7	3.9	4.7		32.3	3.6	−6.1	3.3	2.1	3.6
1.5	.9	.8		.1	.3	1.3	1.0	.7	1.5
5.1	2.4	2.1	Debt/Worth	3.8	1.8	5.3	2.1	1.3	2.1
NM	13.7	6.8		−14.2	8.3	−17.9	10.8	2.8	5.1
23.8	22.5	21.8	% Profit Before Taxes/Tangible				11.8	31.7	25.5
(22) 8.2	(40) 4.8	(68) 6.3	Net Worth			(15) 4.0	8.7	13.8	
.8	−2.4	.1					1.2	−3.4	5.2
4.1	4.8	6.5	% Profit Before Taxes/Total	7.0	5.7	7.9	3.0	9.4	7.2
1.2	1.5	1.5	Assets	4.6	1.1	4.1	1.3	.9	3.2
−.6	−2.3	−.1		−2.0	−.4	−2.2	.0	−.7	1.0
5.0	5.2	7.1		1.8	36.4	5.9	45.4	7.0	16.8
2.6	3.2	3.2	Sales/Net Fixed Assets	1.3	2.8	2.9	3.9	3.4	4.2
.5	1.8	1.8		.2	1.4	.9	2.5	2.4	2.5
2.2	2.8	2.7		1.1	2.3	2.8	4.6	2.6	3.8
1.5	1.7	1.8	Sales/Total Assets	.8	1.2	1.5	2.2	1.9	2.2
.4	1.2	1.0		.2	.8	.7	.9	1.4	1.3
2.7	1.9	1.7		2.6	.9	2.3	1.4	1.8	
(23) 3.9	(43) 2.7	(72) 2.8	% Depr., Dep., Amort./Sales	(10) 6.4	2.4	3.5	(14) 2.4	3.0	
9.7	4.2	3.8		14.1	6.1	11.2	2.9	3.4	
			% Officers', Directors',						
			Owners' Comp/Sales						
898341M	1031530M	935974M	Net Sales ($)	5499M	23799M	43632M	119237M	297847M	445960M
819078M	643025M	561338M	Total Assets ($)	14654M	34668M	63932M	70705M	167318M	210061M

Current Data Sorted By Assets · Comparative Historical Data

0-500M	500M-2MM	2-10MM	10-50MM	50-100MM	100-250MM	Type of Statement	ALL	ALL
5	27	93	53	10	5	Unqualified	179	165
	5	5	1			Reviewed	20	9
1	4	5	4			Compiled	21	36
2	5		1			Tax Returns	14	16
4	10	36	11	1	2	Other	63	81
	183 (4/1-9/30/04)		107 (10/1/04-3/31/05)				4/1/00-3/31/01	4/1/01-3/31/02
12	51	139	70	11	7	NUMBER OF STATEMENTS	297	307
%	%	%	%	%	%	ASSETS	%	%
28.5	16.1	14.4	11.1	10.6		Cash & Equivalents	13.9	12.3
20.4	20.2	14.0	14.6	9.4		Trade Receivables (net)	14.6	15.8
.3	.2	.2	.2	1.4		Inventory	.4	.5
9.2	2.9	1.7	2.8	1.2		All Other Current	2.5	3.5
58.3	39.3	30.2	28.7	22.7		Total Current	31.4	32.0
27.3	52.1	58.3	55.2	59.8		Fixed Assets (net)	52.0	53.1
5.6	1.6	.9	1.2	2.6		Intangibles (net)	2.3	2.5
8.8	7.0	10.5	14.9	14.9		All Other Non-Current	14.3	12.3
100.0	100.0	100.0	100.0	100.0		Total	100.0	100.0
						LIABILITIES		
1.5	3.5	2.9	4.4	1.8		Notes Payable-Short Term	3.2	4.0
1.2	4.2	2.4	3.3	3.6		Cur. Mat.-L/T/D	3.0	2.8
16.6	4.6	5.1	4.3	3.4		Trade Payables	5.5	5.3
.0	.0	.0	.0	.0		Income Taxes Payable	.2	.1
50.0	16.1	9.4	10.5	7.3		All Other Current	11.4	11.0
69.4	28.5	19.8	22.5	16.1		Total Current	23.3	23.1
5.9	34.3	36.9	34.0	31.7		Long-Term Debt	32.3	34.6
.0	.0	.0	.1	.0		Deferred Taxes	.1	.1
30.0	1.2	2.0	6.2	11.0		All Other Non-Current	5.4	5.7
-5.4	36.1	41.2	37.2	41.2		Net Worth	38.8	36.4
100.0	100.0	100.0	100.0	100.0		Total Liabilities & Net Worth	100.0	100.0
						INCOME DATA		
100.0	100.0	100.0	100.0	100.0		Net Sales	100.0	100.0
						Gross Profit		
100.8	93.8	93.1	95.8	98.4		Operating Expenses	96.0	94.2
-.8	6.2	6.9	4.2	1.6		Operating Profit	4.0	5.8
.0	4.0	3.0	.1	-1.7		All Other Expenses (net)	.5	2.6
-.9	2.2	3.9	4.0	3.3		Profit Before Taxes	3.6	3.2
						RATIOS		
3.9	3.2	2.5	2.1	2.4			2.6	2.8
1.4	1.4	1.5	1.4	1.2		Current	1.4	1.5
.7	.8	1.0	1.0	.8			.8	.9
3.9	2.8	2.5	2.0	2.4			2.4	2.4
1.0	1.4	1.5	1.3	1.2		Quick	1.3	1.3
.4	.8	.9	.9	.8			.7	.8
0 UND	0 766.5	10 35.2	20 17.9	3 136.9			8 45.5	10 35.2
5 79.2	24 14.9	30 12.3	36 10.1	38 9.6		Sales/Receivables	30 12.1	31 11.9
24 15.4	41 9.0	42 8.6	60 6.1	57 6.4			46 8.0	49 7.5
						Cost of Sales/Inventory		
						Cost of Sales/Payables		
6.6	7.2	7.9	6.5	2.8			6.4	6.3
81.9	25.6	16.5	16.9	22.0		Sales/Working Capital	20.8	19.0
-66.6	-42.2	208.5	-161.5	-17.9			-42.4	-53.8
	8.1	4.4	5.1				4.6	4.0
	(34) 3.0	(115) 1.9	(62) 1.8			EBIT/Interest	(226) 1.5	(223) 1.7
	.9	.7	.8				.6	.8
						Net Profit + Depr., Dep., Amort./Cur. Mat. L /T/D		
.3	.7	.8	.8	.7			.6	.7
3.4	1.5	1.4	1.6	1.3		Fixed/Worth	1.4	1.5
-1.0	4.9	2.8	3.5	3.9			4.8	4.7
.4	.9	.5	.7	.7			.6	.6
8.8	1.6	1.5	1.8	1.4		Debt/Worth	1.4	1.6
-5.7	6.5	3.5	4.7	5.6			6.4	7.4
	26.3	14.3	13.6				18.9	19.3
	(45) 8.3	(124) 6.0	(61) 4.2			% Profit Before Taxes/Tangible Net Worth	(261) 6.1	(263) 5.3
	-1.4	-.1	-1.1				-1.0	-1.4
8.1	10.0	6.6	6.6	2.3			7.3	6.7
3.3	2.0	2.7	1.7	1.2		% Profit Before Taxes/Total Assets	1.8	1.8
-13.5	-1.0	-.7	-.3	.0			-.7	-.8
546.4	15.9	3.9	3.4	1.9			5.3	5.2
12.4	4.4	2.2	1.9	1.0		Sales/Net Fixed Assets	2.6	2.5
10.7	1.2	1.1	1.0	.7			1.2	1.1
7.9	3.5	2.0	1.6	.9			2.1	2.3
4.5	2.4	1.3	1.0	.7		Sales/Total Assets	1.2	1.4
2.5	1.0	.7	.6	.4			.7	.6
	1.1	2.2	2.1	3.3			1.9	1.6
	(43) 2.2	(132) 3.4	(67) 3.4	6.7		% Depr., Dep., Amort./Sales	(277) 3.4	(280) 3.0
	6.5	5.3	5.4	10.8			5.5	5.8
							5.1	3.7
						% Officers', Directors', Owners' Comp/Sales	(31) 6.8	(38) 6.8
							13.2	12.7
15931M	145507M	1081618M	1568155M	520709M	707549M	Net Sales ($)	2920910M	4356707M
3043M	62855M	720014M	1301127M	737460M	1140104M	Total Assets ($)	3404129M	3964943M

M = $ thousand   MM = $ million
See Pages 11 through 21 for Explanation of Ratios and Data

Comparative Historical Data | Current Data Sorted By Sales

			Type of Statement						
218	184	193	Unqualified	10	30	26	36	63	28
14	11	11	Reviewed	3	3	2	2	1	
9	28	14	Compiled	1	6	2	2	2	1
13	8	8	Tax Returns	3	2	2			1
63	81	64	Other	8	13	9	15	13	6
4/1/02- 3/31/03 ALL	4/1/03- 3/31/04 ALL	4/1/04- 3/31/05 ALL		0-1MM	183 (4/1-9/30/04) 1-3MM	3-5MM	5-10MM	107 (10/1/04-3/31/05) 10-25MM	25MM & OVER
317	312	290	**NUMBER OF STATEMENTS**	25	54	41	55	79	36
%	%	%	**ASSETS**	%	%	%	%	%	%
13.0	13.1	14.3	Cash & Equivalents	16.2	11.8	16.3	15.3	14.4	13.3
16.7	16.4	15.2	Trade Receivables (net)	4.3	11.4	13.3	17.3	18.0	20.8
.4	.3	.2	Inventory	.0	.1	.2	.3	.2	.5
2.9	4.9	2.5	All Other Current	.3	3.2	4.1	1.7	2.6	2.0
33.0	34.6	32.2	Total Current	20.8	26.5	33.9	34.6	35.2	36.6
53.0	52.8	55.3	Fixed Assets (net)	64.8	61.5	54.8	53.1	50.9	53.0
2.1	1.5	1.4	Intangibles (net)	2.6	1.4	2.1	.7	.7	2.3
12.0	11.0	11.1	All Other Non-Current	11.8	10.6	9.2	11.6	13.2	8.1
100.0	100.0	100.0	Total	100.0	100.0	100.0	100.0	100.0	100.0
			LIABILITIES						
4.8	3.5	3.5	Notes Payable-Short Term	.5	2.2	2.3	2.6	5.2	6.6
2.3	2.6	2.9	Cur. Mat.-L/T/D	7.5	2.4	1.9	1.7	3.2	2.6
5.9	5.4	5.2	Trade Payables	3.9	4.9	4.4	4.8	5.8	6.9
.0	.0	.0	Income Taxes Payable	.0	.0	.0	.0	.0	.0
15.6	14.1	12.5	All Other Current	8.5	13.9	13.1	11.8	11.6	15.7
28.6	25.7	24.1	Total Current	20.5	23.4	21.8	21.0	25.8	31.7
34.2	31.3	34.6	Long-Term Debt	48.2	46.2	26.1	31.3	29.7	33.3
.4	.1	.0	Deferred Taxes	.0	.0	.0	.0	.1	.1
2.7	6.4	4.7	All Other Non-Current	14.5	1.1	1.6	5.9	3.3	7.8
34.1	36.5	36.6	Net Worth	16.8	29.3	50.6	41.9	41.2	27.0
100.0	100.0	100.0	Total Liabilities & Net Worth	100.0	100.0	100.0	100.0	100.0	100.0
			INCOME DATA						
100.0	100.0	100.0	Net Sales	100.0	100.0	100.0	100.0	100.0	100.0
			Gross Profit						
96.0	95.4	94.7	Operating Expenses	83.1	90.1	94.8	97.1	97.8	98.9
4.0	4.6	5.3	Operating Profit	16.9	9.9	5.2	2.9	2.2	1.1
4.0	2.5	2.2	All Other Expenses (net)	12.8	4.7	.9	.6	-.3	.7
.0	2.1	3.1	Profit Before Taxes	4.0	5.2	4.3	2.3	2.6	.4
			RATIOS						
2.3	2.5	2.4		7.1	2.5	4.3	2.5	2.0	1.6
1.4	1.4	1.5	Current	1.5	1.3	1.8	1.9	1.4	1.2
.9	.9	.9		.5	.7	1.2	1.2	1.0	.8
2.2	2.0	2.3		7.1	2.3	2.7	2.5	1.9	1.5
1.3	(311) 1.3	1.4	Quick	1.5	1.1	1.7	1.7	1.3	1.1
.7	.8	.8		.4	.5	1.1	.9	.8	.8
13 27.8	13 28.5	10 35.7		0 UND	1 390.2	10 35.1	15 24.3	24 15.0	21 17.5
34 10.8	31 11.6	30 12.3	Sales/Receivables	0 UND	13 27.1	30 12.3	30 12.0	34 10.6	39 9.3
51 7.1	47 7.7	45 8.1		5 79.2	39 9.3	42 8.7	47 7.7	48 7.6	59 6.2
			Cost of Sales/Inventory						
			Cost of Sales/Payables						
6.7	7.2	7.2		4.6	6.2	5.0	6.7	8.9	11.0
19.3	16.1	18.1	Sales/Working Capital	38.7	32.6	11.6	11.3	20.3	24.9
-43.6	-76.8	-84.3		-4.5	-22.2	52.7	52.2	785.3	-40.6
3.7	3.9	4.9		4.5	3.1	6.6	4.9	7.5	4.3
(247) 1.4	(233) 1.8	(226) 1.9	EBIT/Interest	(12) 1.8	(41) 1.3	(30) 2.3	(43) 1.8	(70) 2.0	(30) 1.8
.3	.8	.8		.8	.2	1.2	.7	1.0	1.0
		3.5	Net Profit + Depr., Dep.,						
	(11) 2.1		Amort./Cur. Mat. L/T/D						
		1.0							
.8	.7	.8		1.4	.8	.7	.7	.7	1.0
1.4	1.4	1.5	Fixed/Worth	2.9	2.2	1.2	1.3	1.2	2.0
4.5	4.6	3.8		-9.0	10.4	2.0	2.9	2.5	6.5
.6	.6	.7		1.2	.6	.3	.5	.7	1.2
1.5	1.6	1.6	Debt/Worth	3.3	2.3	1.1	1.2	1.5	2.0
5.9	6.4	4.8		-10.6	23.7	3.2	3.3	3.2	10.3
15.0	18.4	15.4		21.1	16.2	26.3	12.5	15.1	15.2
(276) 2.8	(274) 4.7	(251) 5.1	% Profit Before Taxes/Tangible Net Worth	(18) 3.2	(42) 4.6	(39) 8.1	(51) 3.8	(72) 5.9	(29) 4.2
-4.9	-2.0	-.7		-8.2	-3.4	1.5	-1.5	.6	-2.9
5.2	6.5	6.7		5.1	7.3	7.8	6.5	7.9	5.3
.8	1.6	2.2	% Profit Before Taxes/Total Assets	.1	1.0	4.5	2.6	2.2	1.3
-2.1	-1.0	-.5		-1.7	-2.2	.6	-.7	.2	-.4
4.9	5.9	4.9		2.8	5.9	5.0	5.3	4.7	5.1
2.4	2.6	2.4	Sales/Net Fixed Assets	.5	1.3	2.1	2.8	2.7	3.0
1.1	1.3	1.0		.2	.6	1.4	1.5	1.7	1.5
2.2	2.2	2.2		1.2	1.9	2.7	2.8	2.2	2.3
1.3	1.4	1.3	Sales/Total Assets	.2	.7	1.1	1.4	1.6	1.5
.6	.8	.7		.1	.4	.8	.9	1.0	.9
2.0	2.1	2.0		3.5	1.9	2.1	1.4	1.8	1.9
(299) 3.2	(283) 3.4	(264) 3.2	% Depr., Dep., Amort./Sales	(21) 11.6	(48) 6.0	(35) 3.5	(50) 3.3	(77) 2.9	(33) 2.6
5.6	5.3	5.9		33.8	10.4	5.0	4.5	3.7	4.9
4.4	2.4	1.0							
(40) 8.0	(32) 6.1	(22) 7.2	% Officers', Directors', Owners' Comp/Sales						
15.6	14.5	21.6							
4204164M	4267103M	4039469M	Net Sales ($)	12086M	105508M	168847M	393428M	1231254M	2128346M
4743203M	4628088M	3964603M	Total Assets ($)	43193M	190024M	151768M	381723M	1141985M	2055910M

M = $ thousand   MM = $ million
See Pages 11 through 21 for Explanation of Ratios and Data

Current Data Sorted By Assets							Comparative Historical Data	
1	12	30	58	30	13	Type of Statement Unqualified	32	44
6	3	10	4	1		Reviewed	7	8
3	16	25	4			Compiled	23	31
9	7	6	1			Tax Returns	9	9
10	11	47	37	16	7	Other	40	46
	103 (4/1-9/30/04)			264 (10/1/04-3/31/05)			4/1/00-3/31/01	4/1/01-3/31/02
0-500M	500M-2MM	2-10MM	10-50MM	50-100MM	100-250MM		ALL	ALL
29	49	118	104	47	20	NUMBER OF STATEMENTS	111	138
%	%	%	%	%	%	ASSETS	%	%
19.8	12.7	8.1	9.8	7.8	10.3	Cash & Equivalents	10.3	11.0
17.0	30.9	12.3	6.0	3.8	3.1	Trade Receivables (net)	14.6	15.4
.6	2.2	.2	.3	.2	.3	Inventory	.4	.3
7.0	1.5	1.6	1.6	1.2	4.7	All Other Current	4.2	3.6
44.3	47.3	22.2	17.7	12.9	18.5	Total Current	29.5	30.2
42.8	38.3	67.9	63.1	61.9	54.6	Fixed Assets (net)	57.9	57.6
3.6	2.8	2.1	2.1	1.3	2.2	Intangibles (net)	1.9	2.7
9.3	11.6	7.7	17.1	23.9	24.7	All Other Non-Current	10.7	9.5
100.0	100.0	100.0	100.0	100.0	100.0	Total	100.0	100.0
						LIABILITIES		
22.4	8.3	2.6	3.9	1.2	.6	Notes Payable-Short Term	5.3	5.4
4.4	2.8	3.3	3.4	5.0	.8	Cur. Mat.-L/T/D	4.9	2.6
9.1	13.9	4.8	3.5	1.9	1.7	Trade Payables	7.6	5.5
.0	.4	.2	.0	.0	.0	Income Taxes Payable	.2	.1
54.5	20.2	8.0	5.1	4.1	3.7	All Other Current	10.8	12.0
90.4	45.7	18.9	16.0	12.2	6.9	Total Current	28.7	25.5
32.3	36.0	66.5	49.9	53.8	41.5	Long-Term Debt	43.5	47.5
.0	.3	.0	.1	.5	.1	Deferred Taxes	.1	.2
11.5	5.2	4.7	14.6	18.1	14.7	All Other Non-Current	8.3	13.9
-34.2	12.9	9.8	19.4	15.3	36.7	Net Worth	19.4	13.0
100.0	100.0	100.0	100.0	100.0	100.0	Total Liabilities & Net Worth	100.0	100.0
						INCOME DATA		
100.0	100.0	100.0	100.0	100.0	100.0	Net Sales	100.0	100.0
						Gross Profit		
94.9	92.8	88.2	91.1	96.1	88.3	Operating Expenses	91.5	91.5
5.1	7.2	11.8	8.9	3.9	11.7	Operating Profit	8.5	8.5
1.6	4.3	9.6	5.9	4.1	2.8	All Other Expenses (net)	3.3	6.1
3.5	2.9	2.3	3.0	-.2	8.9	Profit Before Taxes	5.2	2.4
						RATIOS		
2.0	1.8	2.5	2.6	3.0	5.1		2.6	2.8
.8	1.0	1.2	1.3	1.4	2.1	Current	1.4	1.3
.1	.7	.6	.7	.7	.9		.7	.7
2.0	1.8	2.2	2.2	2.8	4.1		2.2	2.3
.7	.9	1.1	1.1	1.2	1.6	Quick	1.2	1.2
.1	.6	.5	.5	.5	.6		.4	.5
0 UND	8 43.2	1 310.4	8 46.5	8 44.6	10 36.5		5 73.4	6 56.5
2 199.3	35 10.5	17 21.2	26 14.2	22 16.4	22 16.9	Sales/Receivables	26 14.3	29 12.7
10 36.4	47 7.7	43 8.6	42 8.8	43 8.5	34 10.8		45 8.1	46 7.9
						Cost of Sales/Inventory		
						Cost of Sales/Payables		
36.6	16.6	7.4	5.0	3.8	1.7		7.4	5.9
-78.1	-182.9	33.9	20.8	18.6	5.8	Sales/Working Capital	24.3	21.1
-8.9	-15.9	-13.0	-15.6	-21.0	-56.6		-24.9	-27.6
15.5	6.1	4.0	3.3	3.2	11.3		4.0	2.9
(21) 2.9	(39) 2.1	(96) 1.8	(90) 1.5	(37) 1.6	(18) 1.8	EBIT/Interest	(96) 2.0	(111) 1.7
-3.0	.9	.8	.8	.8	1.0		1.1	1.0
						Net Profit + Depr., Dep., Amort./Cur. Mat. L./T/D		4.7
							(10) 1.6
								.7
.5	.4	1.6	1.3	1.9	.6		1.1	1.2
2.4	2.2	7.3	3.0	5.7	1.7	Fixed/Worth	3.0	3.9
-.9	-1.1	-5.4	-52.1	-15.4	13.0		163.7	-137.9
1.5	1.2	1.9	1.3	2.0	.5		1.0	1.3
-88.0	3.7	9.6	3.9	3.7	1.7	Debt/Worth	4.5	4.6
-2.4	-6.8	-7.6	-38.1	-19.7	18.1		363.1	-52.1
216.5	84.1	43.7	22.5	16.8	12.0	% Profit Before Taxes/Tangible Net Worth	54.1	36.5
(14) 53.7	(29) 20.9	(71) 14.7	(74) 5.6	(33) 4.1	(16) 6.7		(84) 9.2	(100) 9.3
19.2	4.5	3.8	-1.9	-2.7	-.3		2.3	.2
42.2	14.0	7.5	4.1	3.7	6.1	% Profit Before Taxes/Total Assets	7.7	6.5
23.7	3.8	2.5	1.2	.3	1.7		3.2	2.3
-8.9	-.6	-1.4	-.7	-.8	.0		-.5	-1.2
125.2	48.0	2.7	1.8	.8	1.2		4.9	4.8
21.1	10.8	.8	.8	.4	.7	Sales/Net Fixed Assets	1.8	1.8
10.8	1.2	.4	.5	.3	.3		.6	.6
13.2	4.7	1.3	.8	.5	.5		1.9	2.0
8.2	2.2	.7	.5	.3	.3	Sales/Total Assets	1.1	1.0
5.5	.8	.4	.3	.2	.2		.4	.4
.5	.6	2.9	3.7	7.0	5.6		1.3	1.7
(20) 1.2	(39) 1.7	(112) 6.8	(100) 8.3	10.4	8.8	% Depr., Dep., Amort./Sales	(104) 3.5	(125) 4.0
1.8	6.2	13.2	10.9	15.6	14.3		8.1	8.4
3.4		2.1	2.1				2.7	2.4
(15) 6.8	(23) 6.1	(13) 11.3				% Officers', Directors', Owners' Comp/Sales	(15) 5.9	(17) 5.7
10.7		18.3	30.1				18.4	16.3
36307M	163558M	507487M	1384280M	1414124M	1032888M	Net Sales ($)	1393646M	1819050M
5206M	60165M	572364M	2239376M	3388509M	2625782M	Total Assets ($)	1675008M	2195648M

M = $ thousand   MM = $ million
See Pages 11 through 21 for Explanation of Ratios and Data

Comparative Historical Data | Current Data Sorted By Sales

				Type of Statement						
114	125	144		Unqualified	7	13	18	28	51	27
22	27	24		Reviewed	2	11	4	6	1	
38	59	48		Compiled	3	17	10	15	1	2
17	15	23		Tax Returns	11	8	1	2	1	
91	97	128		Other	11	38	14	24	24	17
4/1/02-3/31/03 ALL	4/1/03-3/31/04 ALL	4/1/04-3/31/05 ALL			103 (4/1-9/30/04) 0-1MM	1-3MM	3-5MM	264 (10/1/04-3/31/05) 5-10MM	10-25MM	25MM & OVER
282	323	367		NUMBER OF STATEMENTS	34	87	47	75	78	46
%	%	%		ASSETS	%	%	%	%	%	%
9.5	10.1	10.2		Cash & Equivalents	12.9	9.6	10.8	10.0	9.0	10.9
12.6	14.4	11.8		Trade Receivables (net)	7.9	8.0	17.2	21.0	7.0	9.3
.6	.4	.5		Inventory	2.9	.3	.3	.2	.2	.7
2.5	3.6	2.1		All Other Current	2.2	2.3	1.6	1.8	1.5	4.1
25.2	28.6	24.7		Total Current	26.0	20.1	29.8	33.1	17.7	25.0
60.2	56.3	59.1		Fixed Assets (net)	62.4	70.0	55.8	50.5	59.2	53.3
1.7	1.9	2.2		Intangibles (net)	5.0	1.3	2.2	2.5	1.9	2.1
12.9	13.2	14.0		All Other Non-Current	6.7	8.6	12.1	14.0	21.2	19.7
100.0	100.0	100.0		Total	100.0	100.0	100.0	100.0	100.0	100.0
				LIABILITIES						
5.1	5.7	5.0		Notes Payable-Short Term	3.6	11.2	5.3	4.3	1.4	1.3
3.0	4.1	3.4		Cur. Mat.-L/T/D	3.6	2.5	3.1	2.9	3.6	5.8
5.9	7.4	5.5		Trade Payables	7.5	5.2	5.1	8.8	2.6	4.0
.0	.1	.1		Income Taxes Payable	.0	.0	.3	.4	.0	.0
13.6	12.4	11.8		All Other Current	20.8	16.6	10.7	12.3	5.5	6.8
27.7	29.7	25.8		Total Current	35.6	35.5	24.6	28.7	13.2	18.0
49.1	45.9	52.0		Long-Term Debt	55.4	69.6	41.6	46.7	49.2	40.6
.3	.1	.1		Deferred Taxes	.0	.2	.0	.0	.3	.2
11.9	11.9	10.4		All Other Non-Current	7.4	6.0	5.4	10.1	19.1	11.6
11.0	12.4	11.6		Net Worth	1.6	−11.4	28.5	14.4	18.2	29.6
100.0	100.0	100.0		Total Liabilities & Net Worth	100.0	100.0	100.0	100.0	100.0	100.0
				INCOME DATA						
100.0	100.0	100.0		Net Sales	100.0	100.0	100.0	100.0	100.0	100.0
				Gross Profit						
90.0	91.8	91.2		Operating Expenses	84.9	87.4	91.3	94.1	93.9	93.1
10.0	8.2	8.8		Operating Profit	15.1	12.6	8.7	5.9	6.1	6.9
7.3	5.0	6.1		All Other Expenses (net)	14.2	10.0	4.7	3.6	3.9	2.2
2.8	3.2	2.7		Profit Before Taxes	.8	2.6	3.9	2.3	2.1	4.6
				RATIOS						
2.0	2.2	2.5			2.0	2.0	2.0	2.6	3.1	2.5
1.2	1.4	1.2		Current	.9	.8	1.3	1.1	1.7	1.5
.6	.7	.6			.2	.3	.9	.8	.8	.9
1.8	1.9	2.2			2.0	1.7	1.8	2.1	2.8	2.2
1.0	1.1	1.0		Quick	.8	.7	1.2	1.0	1.4	1.2
.4	.6	.5			.1	.2	.8	.5	.7	.7
4 88.3	8 44.4	4 97.9			0 UND	0 UND	3 118.2	17 21.7	13 29.1	20 18.1
21 17.6	26 14.0	22 16.9		Sales/Receivables	0 UND	4 101.1	28 13.1	33 11.1	30 12.3	30 12.4
38 9.6	43 8.5	41 8.9			15 24.2	21 17.3	51 7.2	60 6.1	39 9.3	45 8.0
				Cost of Sales/Inventory						
				Cost of Sales/Payables						
8.6	7.7	6.4			23.6	11.8	9.6	7.7	3.7	4.9
37.6	24.8	37.7		Sales/Working Capital	−75.8	−39.2	21.5	131.5	10.1	15.7
−14.7	−24.2	−15.2			−6.8	−6.4	−54.6	−15.7	−28.1	−65.6
3.4	3.3	4.2			7.3	3.1	7.5	5.0	2.8	5.2
(233) 1.6	(265) 1.5	(301) 1.8		EBIT/Interest	(21) 1.6	(64) 1.8	(39) 2.2	(66) 1.9	(69) 1.3	(42) 2.8
.6	.3	.8			.4	.6	1.4	.9	.8	1.1
5.0	4.1	5.4								
(15) 1.5	(21) 2.9	(16) 1.7		Net Profit + Depr., Dep., Amort./Cur. Mat. L/T/D						
.7	2.2	1.1								
1.3	1.1	1.2			1.2	2.2	.7	1.0	1.4	1.0
4.0	3.6	4.1		Fixed/Worth	8.8	−31.9	3.2	3.0	4.0	2.0
−12.8	−22.4	−7.4			−5.4	−2.9	−49.8	−7.5	−48.6	6.5
1.5	1.5	1.4			1.4	4.7	.9	1.4	1.4	1.0
5.6	5.5	5.8		Debt/Worth	NM	−13.6	3.3	4.5	5.8	2.3
−14.8	−26.5	−10.2			−6.6	−4.3	−59.9	−12.9	−61.4	9.4
30.9	38.1	36.7			36.8	93.5	38.3	34.7	13.4	34.2
(195) 10.0	(229) 9.4	(237) 9.7		% Profit Before Taxes/Tangible Net Worth	(17) 8.3	(37) 34.9	(35) 14.7	(53) 10.9	(57) 4.8	(38) 10.4
−.9	−1.8	.0			−2.5	4.1	.5	−.9	−2.5	.6
6.3	6.6	7.0			7.3	9.2	7.9	8.2	3.4	6.9
1.3	1.6	2.0		% Profit Before Taxes/Total Assets	.8	2.1	2.5	3.3	.7	2.8
−1.4	−1.6	−.8			−2.8	−2.9	−1.0	−.5	−.4	.0
4.8	6.3	4.1			23.1	10.5	10.5	9.2	1.7	2.7
1.2	1.4	.9		Sales/Net Fixed Assets	1.1	.6	.9	2.2	.7	1.3
.5	.6	.5			.2	.4	.5	.7	.4	.7
1.9	1.9	1.6			8.1	2.1	2.1	2.4	.9	1.4
.8	.8	.6		Sales/Total Assets	.6	.5	.7	1.0	.4	.6
.3	.4	.3			.1	.3	.4	.5	.2	.3
2.2	2.2	2.7			3.5	2.8	2.7	1.5	5.2	3.3
(267) 5.2	(307) 4.5	(338) 7.0		% Depr., Dep., Amort./Sales	(26) 10.3	(76) 8.8	(43) 6.9	(71) 3.4	(77) 9.5	(45) 5.5
10.5	10.0	11.6			23.0	15.6	10.2	8.2	14.2	8.8
2.5	2.4	2.0				1.7		1.3		
(52) 6.0	(58) 5.1	(65) 6.1		% Officers', Directors', Owners' Comp/Sales	(21) 4.8		(15) 8.2			
12.5	10.9	13.0			9.4		33.2			
3702986M	4453121M	4538644M		Net Sales ($)	17738M	163038M	188104M	558597M	1134503M	2476664M
6171342M	6742938M	8891402M		Total Assets ($)	64261M	385997M	477078M	829964M	3375764M	3758338M

M = $ thousand   MM = $ million
See Pages 11 through 21 for Explanation of Ratios and Data

Current Data Sorted By Assets   **Comparative Historical Data**

	0-500M	500M-2MM 28 (4/1-9/30/04)	2-10MM	10-50MM 50 (10/1/04-3/31/05)	50-100MM	100-250MM		4/1/00-3/31/01 ALL	4/1/01-3/31/02 ALL
Type of Statement									
Unqualified	1	6	13	8	4	2			
Reviewed	6	2	4						
Compiled	5	2							
Tax Returns	1	2	12	9	1				
Other									
NUMBER OF STATEMENTS	13	12	29	17	5	2			
	%	%	%	%	%	%		%	%
ASSETS									
Cash & Equivalents	28.1	14.2	10.7	9.8				D	D
Trade Receivables (net)	6.2	18.9	10.7	5.9				A	A
Inventory	.4	.1	.2	.0				T	T
All Other Current	1.4	2.8	2.5	6.9				A	A
Total Current	36.1	36.0	24.0	22.7					
Fixed Assets (net)	49.6	52.0	64.8	56.1				N	N
Intangibles (net)	1.0	.7	2.1	3.0				O	O
All Other Non-Current	13.3	11.3	9.2	18.1				T	T
Total	100.0	100.0	100.0	100.0					
LIABILITIES								A	A
Notes Payable-Short Term	63.6	.9	3.4	.0				V	V
Cur. Mat.-L/T/D	4.4	4.0	9.5	11.6				A	A
Trade Payables	5.6	7.7	4.1	2.8				I	I
Income Taxes Payable	.2	.2	.0	.0				L	L
All Other Current	15.8	12.2	9.9	6.3				A	A
Total Current	89.5	25.0	27.0	20.6				B	B
Long-Term Debt	53.6	32.8	53.2	46.4				L	L
Deferred Taxes	.0	.7	.1	.1				E	E
All Other Non-Current	12.0	6.7	5.2	9.0					
Net Worth	−55.1	34.8	14.6	23.8					
Total Liabilities & Net Worth	100.0	100.0	100.0	100.0					
INCOME DATA									
Net Sales	100.0	100.0	100.0	100.0					
Gross Profit									
Operating Expenses	93.3	95.6	94.1	92.2					
Operating Profit	6.7	4.4	5.9	7.8					
All Other Expenses (net)	1.4	1.9	5.8	5.0					
Profit Before Taxes	5.3	2.5	.1	2.7					
RATIOS									
Current	1.4	3.5	2.2	3.5					
	.7	.9	1.3	2.5					
	.3	.6	.8	1.6					
Quick	1.4	3.4	2.1	2.5					
	.6	.8	1.3	1.8					
	.1	.3	.5	1.2					
Sales/Receivables	0 UND	1 707.3	4 90.8	4 97.2					
	0 UND	21 17.3	20 18.4	16 23.1					
	9 41.0	36 10.0	31 11.9	38 9.6					
Cost of Sales/Inventory									
Cost of Sales/Payables									
Sales/Working Capital	34.0	6.4	6.4	3.8					
	−115.4	−69.7	25.1	8.4					
	−6.7	−17.1	−32.2	12.6					
EBIT/Interest		13.6	7.6	8.7					
		(10) 2.9	(23) 2.0	(13) 3.0					
		1.3	.5	.6					
Net Profit + Depr., Dep., Amort./Cur. Mat. L/T/D									
Fixed/Worth	.4	.5	1.4	.7					
	1.9	1.7	3.9	1.3					
	−.2	26.5	−15.5	58.7					
Debt/Worth	.3	.4	1.4	.6					
	1.3	1.7	5.7	1.0					
	−4.5	29.8	−20.3	73.1					
% Profit Before Taxes/Tangible Net Worth		43.7	21.5	24.6					
	(10) 8.4	(19) 13.1	(14) 11.4						
	3.5	4.5	2.6						
% Profit Before Taxes/Total Assets	40.3	6.9	6.5	7.9					
	8.5	3.4	2.0	2.1					
	−12.2	.7	−2.2	−.4					
Sales/Net Fixed Assets	75.1	17.9	3.5	3.0					
	19.4	4.3	1.3	1.8					
	4.0	1.2	.5	.5					
Sales/Total Assets	13.1	4.1	1.9	1.3					
	5.7	2.5	.8	.5					
	2.1	.7	.4	.3					
% Depr., Dep., Amort./Sales		1.6	1.8	3.4					
	(11) 2.5	(28) 4.3	(16) 5.7						
	4.8	10.7	11.0						
% Officers', Directors', Owners' Comp/Sales									
Net Sales ($)	11577M	32628M	181173M	366702M	161595M	92225M			
Total Assets ($)	2458M	14758M	154013M	458289M	381192M	377898M			

Comparative Historical Data				Current Data Sorted By Sales					
22	33	33	**Type of Statement** Unqualified	4	3	4	5	12	5
3	3	1	Reviewed		1				
5	8	12	Compiled	6	5	1			
6	12	7	Tax Returns	5	1	1			
11	16	25	Other	1	5	5	5	6	3
4/1/02-3/31/03	4/1/03-3/31/04	4/1/04-3/31/05		28 (4/1-9/30/04)			50 (10/1/04-3/31/05)		
ALL	ALL	ALL		0-1MM	1-3MM	3-5MM	5-10MM	10-25MM	25MM & OVER
47	72	78	**NUMBER OF STATEMENTS**	16	15	11	10	18	8
%	%	%	**ASSETS**	%	%	%	%	%	%
11.7	18.2	13.4	Cash & Equivalents	17.6	16.3	13.8	7.6	11.2	
9.1	9.8	9.4	Trade Receivables (net)	3.8	7.1	7.7	15.9	14.6	
.1	.4	.2	Inventory	.2	.2	.1	.2	.2	
2.0	2.0	3.5	All Other Current	1.3	1.6	.3	11.5	3.8	
22.9	30.5	26.6	Total Current	22.9	25.2	21.9	35.2	29.8	
61.4	54.7	58.8	Fixed Assets (net)	59.6	62.3	62.7	55.5	56.6	
2.7	2.9	1.9	Intangibles (net)	.7	2.2	2.7	1.6	.8	
13.0	11.9	12.8	All Other Non-Current	16.8	10.3	12.7	7.7	12.7	
100.0	100.0	100.0	Total	100.0	100.0	100.0	100.0	100.0	
			LIABILITIES						
3.7	8.3	12.2	Notes Payable-Short Term	50.3	3.7	.0	1.7	3.9	
6.2	5.9	7.6	Cur. Mat.-L/T/D	5.3	15.9	1.4	2.8	9.0	
3.9	5.7	4.4	Trade Payables	1.0	7.1	3.8	4.8	5.4	
.7	.3	.1	Income Taxes Payable	.1	.1	.0	.1	.0	
4.9	17.6	10.5	All Other Current	10.6	8.8	2.8	12.9	15.2	
19.4	37.8	34.7	Total Current	67.3	35.6	8.0	22.3	33.5	
37.4	30.3	49.2	Long-Term Debt	31.2	77.4	65.1	34.9	33.8	
.0	.0	.1	Deferred Taxes	.0	.6	.0	.0	.1	
10.4	13.2	8.1	All Other Non-Current	14.9	1.2	6.0	1.6	12.9	
32.8	18.7	7.8	Net Worth	-13.4	-14.8	20.9	41.2	19.7	
100.0	100.0	100.0	Total Liabilities & Net Worth	100.0	100.0	100.0	100.0	100.0	
			INCOME DATA						
100.0	100.0	100.0	Net Sales	100.0	100.0	100.0	100.0	100.0	
			Gross Profit						
90.2	94.2	92.5	Operating Expenses	94.3	93.2	91.7	99.0	86.6	
9.8	5.8	7.5	Operating Profit	5.7	6.8	8.3	1.0	13.4	
6.0	3.2	4.5	All Other Expenses (net)	2.9	7.4	6.3	-.8	5.6	
3.9	2.5	3.0	Profit Before Taxes	2.8	-.5	2.0	1.8	7.9	
			RATIOS						
3.1	2.4	2.7		1.4	4.6	3.2	14.1	2.6	
1.2	1.1	1.3	Current	.7	1.0	1.6	1.9	1.3	
.7	.6	.6		.3	.1	1.1	.9	.6	
2.5	2.3	2.2		1.4	4.4	3.2	2.0	2.5	
1.2	1.0	1.1	Quick	.6	.8	1.6	1.5	1.3	
.5	.4	.4		.1	.1	1.0	.8	.3	
3 135.0	1 448.4	2 157.3		0 UND	1 447.3	2 150.4	13 28.3	16 23.1	
16 22.9	12 29.2	15 23.6	Sales/Receivables	0 UND	7 51.5	5 75.4	27 13.3	27 13.7	
32 11.4	32 11.5	29 12.7		11 34.0	20 18.4	35 10.5	36 10.0	34 10.8	
			Cost of Sales/Inventory						
			Cost of Sales/Payables						
6.9	9.9	7.0		10.4	22.1	5.7	.7	7.1	
26.9	149.4	27.7	Sales/Working Capital	-73.7	95.7	13.2	12.0	22.6	
-16.6	-10.1	-15.6		-7.2	-6.5	92.3	-63.2	-18.7	
3.2	7.5	8.0		5.3			9.2	9.1	
(38) 1.6	(51) 2.0	(60) 2.4	EBIT/Interest	(12) 1.5			6.4 (14) 3.3		
.9	.5	.9		.4			.5	1.2	
			Net Profit + Depr., Dep., Amort./Cur. Mat. L/T/D						
1.1	.7	1.0		.9	.3	.7	1.0	1.3	
1.8	2.0	1.9	Fixed/Worth	2.4	2.0	7.1	1.3	1.8	
16.4	235.8	-17.4		-6.4	-4.5	-17.7	2.3	NM	
.9	.7	.8		.5	.8	.7	.6	1.8	
3.6	2.5	2.9	Debt/Worth	2.0	1.8	7.9	1.1	5.2	
22.1	-42.5	-26.6		-10.8	-5.7	-21.7	5.0	NM	
19.8	36.9	40.3		54.1				67.2	
(37) 7.3	(53) 15.5	(57) 13.1	% Profit Before Taxes/Tangible Net Worth	(11) 1.8			(14) 20.4		
3.0	1.5	3.2		-15.6				9.5	
7.6	13.1	8.1	% Profit Before Taxes/Total Assets	12.0	9.8	3.7	9.9	8.8	
2.3	3.0	2.4		1.6	.6	2.4	4.7	5.0	
-.4	-2.3	-.6		-2.2	-3.0	.2	-1.0	.8	
3.3	10.5	7.9		26.1	14.4	4.9	5.1	7.9	
.9	2.2	2.0	Sales/Net Fixed Assets	3.4	2.0	.6	2.4	1.9	
.5	.7	.5		.7	.7	.5	.4	.5	
1.9	3.7	2.8		8.4	4.0	1.1	2.5	3.1	
.6	1.4	1.2	Sales/Total Assets	1.3	1.8	.6	1.4	1.1	
.3	.5	.4		.4	.5	.4	.2	.3	
2.6	1.8	1.8		1.5	1.8		1.7	1.4	
(39) 6.6	(62) 3.8	(70) 4.3	% Depr., Dep., Amort./Sales	(12) 4.6	(13) 4.5		3.4	4.2	
10.3	8.4	10.1		6.9	10.2		12.0	10.4	
4.4	5.7	2.8							
(10) 6.6	(16) 11.1	(20) 7.5	% Officers', Directors', Owners' Comp/Sales						
12.4	17.5	15.2							
405093M	689225M	845900M	Net Sales ($)	10388M	29256M	38578M	69458M	292908M	405312M
887969M	945352M	1388608M	Total Assets ($)	25155M	40178M	66197M	134208M	548056M	574814M

M = $ thousand   MM = $ million
See Pages 11 through 21 for Explanation of Ratios and Data

Current Data Sorted By Assets   Comparative Historical Data

0-500M	500M-2MM	2-10MM	10-50MM	50-100MM	100-250MM	Type of Statement	4/1/00-3/31/01 ALL	4/1/01-3/31/02 ALL
						Type of Statement		
1	5	18	7		1	Unqualified		
	1		1			Reviewed		
		3	1			Compiled		
3	3	1				Tax Returns		
4	8	11	3			Other		
	32 (4/1-9/30/04)		39 (10/1/04-3/31/05)					
8	17	33	12		1	**NUMBER OF STATEMENTS**		
%	%	%	%	%	%	**ASSETS**	%	%
	16.1	13.9	18.9	D		Cash & Equivalents	D	D
	27.6	12.1	10.9	A		Trade Receivables (net)	A	A
	.3	.3	.2	T		Inventory	T	T
	4.3	3.9	1.1	A		All Other Current	A	A
	48.4	30.1	31.2			Total Current		
	41.6	57.3	49.2	N		Fixed Assets (net)	N	N
	.3	3.4	.1	O		Intangibles (net)	O	O
	9.7	9.2	19.5	T		All Other Non-Current	T	T
	100.0	100.0	100.0			Total		
				A		**LIABILITIES**	A	A
	5.2	1.3	2.3	V		Notes Payable-Short Term	V	V
	3.3	4.3	1.7	A		Cur. Mat.-L/T/D	A	A
	9.1	4.0	5.2	I		Trade Payables	I	I
	.0	.0	.0	L		Income Taxes Payable	L	L
	35.2	12.1	8.1	A		All Other Current	A	A
	52.8	21.7	17.3	B		Total Current	B	B
	14.0	40.7	21.0	L		Long-Term Debt	L	L
	.0	.1	.0	E		Deferred Taxes	E	E
	1.4	2.3	6.9			All Other Non-Current		
	31.7	35.3	54.8			Net Worth		
	100.0	100.0	100.0			Total Liabilities & Net Worth		
						INCOME DATA		
	100.0	100.0	100.0			Net Sales		
						Gross Profit		
	96.1	87.0	98.4			Operating Expenses		
	3.9	13.0	1.6			Operating Profit		
	-.2	2.8	-.6			All Other Expenses (net)		
	4.1	10.2	2.1			Profit Before Taxes		
						RATIOS		
	3.0	4.5	4.1					
	1.3	2.3	1.4			Current		
	.8	1.2	1.1					
	2.2	4.4	4.0					
	1.1	1.9	1.3			Quick		
	.8	1.1	1.1					
18 20.8	18 20.7	20 18.6						
27 13.7	31 11.7	34 10.7			Sales/Receivables		
35 10.5	47 7.8	54 6.8					
						Cost of Sales/Inventory		
						Cost of Sales/Payables		
	10.3	3.3	3.8					
	29.9	9.1	18.3			Sales/Working Capital		
	-44.8	36.6	74.2					
	84.4	7.9						
	(12) 5.1	(19) 1.2				EBIT/Interest		
	1.7	.4						
						Net Profit + Depr., Dep., Amort./Cur. Mat. L /T/D		
	.6	.8	.4					
	1.1	3.2	1.0			Fixed/Worth		
	9.5	28.4	2.2					
	.1	.4	.2					
	1.0	3.8	.8			Debt/Worth		
	122.8	39.5	2.2					
	99.5	45.8	20.3					
	(14) 12.6	(26) 9.0	3.0			% Profit Before Taxes/Tangible Net Worth		
	.2	-.7	-2.7					
	35.6	16.4	8.4					
	9.1	2.9	1.0			% Profit Before Taxes/Total Assets		
	.3	-.2	-1.8					
	36.0	3.8	3.7					
	6.6	1.6	2.3			Sales/Net Fixed Assets		
	2.5	.7	1.0					
	4.0	1.6	1.8					
	3.1	.9	1.0			Sales/Total Assets		
	1.8	.5	.5					
	.8	2.5	1.8					
	(13) 1.7	(27) 3.6	(11) 2.8			% Depr., Dep., Amort./Sales		
	2.3	6.1	5.7					
						% Officers', Directors', Owners' Comp/Sales		
7829M	66667M	157733M	412554M		65822M	Net Sales ($)		
1561M	20737M	147951M	292687M		148101M	Total Assets ($)		

M = $ thousand   MM = $ million
See Pages 11 through 21 for Explanation of Ratios and Data

Comparative Historical Data				**Current Data Sorted By Sales**					
23	28	32	Type of Statement Unqualified	1	8	6	6	6	5
		2	Reviewed		1		1		
1	5	4	Compiled		3			1	
1	2	7	Tax Returns	2	1	3	1		
5	13	26	Other	4	13	2	4	2	1
4/1/02- 3/31/03	4/1/03- 3/31/04	4/1/04- 3/31/05		32 (4/1-9/30/04)			39 (10/1/04-3/31/05)		
ALL	ALL	ALL		0-1MM	1-3MM	3-5MM	5-10MM	10-25MM	25MM & OVER
30	48	71	NUMBER OF STATEMENTS	7	26	11	12	9	6
%	%	%	ASSETS	%	%	%	%	%	%
14.2	12.7	17.3	Cash & Equivalents		19.7	13.1	18.4		
13.5	13.2	17.0	Trade Receivables (net)		12.9	20.2	17.6		
.1	.1	.3	Inventory		.2	.8	.1		
7.3	5.1	3.2	All Other Current		1.9	.8	7.4		
35.1	31.1	37.8	Total Current		34.7	35.0	43.4		
51.6	53.2	48.0	Fixed Assets (net)		55.9	46.6	46.7		
1.5	3.3	2.8	Intangibles (net)		.3	6.7	2.1		
11.8	12.4	11.4	All Other Non-Current		9.1	11.7	7.9		
100.0	100.0	100.0	Total		100.0	100.0	100.0		
			LIABILITIES						
3.3	3.8	3.9	Notes Payable-Short Term		4.4	5.4	1.9		
3.5	2.4	3.2	Cur. Mat.-L/T/D		1.7	3.2	9.4		
5.3	4.5	6.0	Trade Payables		4.9	4.5	5.2		
.0	.0	.0	Income Taxes Payable		.0	.0	.0		
13.3	7.7	21.4	All Other Current		9.3	26.0	31.1		
25.4	18.5	34.5	Total Current		20.3	39.1	47.5		
36.4	29.8	26.9	Long-Term Debt		39.6	23.9	16.0		
.0	.3	1.1	Deferred Taxes		.0	.0	.2		
14.5	2.7	2.6	All Other Non-Current		.7	1.3	5.1		
23.7	48.7	34.9	Net Worth		39.4	35.8	31.1		
100.0	100.0	100.0	Total Liabilities & Net Worth		100.0	100.0	100.0		
			INCOME DATA						
100.0	100.0	100.0	Net Sales		100.0	100.0	100.0		
			Gross Profit						
92.3	94.0	92.4	Operating Expenses		86.9	91.1	93.5		
7.7	6.0	7.6	Operating Profit		13.1	8.9	6.5		
4.9	1.3	1.2	All Other Expenses (net)		2.3	1.0	1.9		
2.8	4.7	6.4	Profit Before Taxes		10.8	7.9	4.6		
			RATIOS						
4.2	2.8	4.0	Current		5.7	3.2	3.5		
1.9	1.5	1.5			2.7	1.4	1.6		
.9	1.0	1.0			1.1	.8	.6		
2.4	2.7	3.2	Quick		5.1	2.9	3.5		
1.5	1.5	1.3			2.3	1.2	1.2		
.7	.8	.8			1.0	.8	.4		
0 UND	4 96.9	17 21.2	Sales/Receivables		0 UND	27 13.7	17 20.9		
24 15.5	24 15.5	31 11.8			28 13.0	32 11.2	32 11.6		
43 8.5	41 8.9	39 9.4			35 10.4	35 10.5	56 6.5		
			Cost of Sales/Inventory						
			Cost of Sales/Payables						
4.7	5.8	5.7	Sales/Working Capital		3.0	9.7	4.8		
20.9	16.9	15.3			7.8	21.1	24.0		
-244.9	-324.2	999.8			280.4	-36.7	-10.5		
(21) 2.9	(41) 7.2	(45) 11.9	EBIT/Interest	(12) 98.3		(10) 35.8			
1.8	2.0	3.6		2.4		4.7			
.6	.7	.9		.6		.9			
			Net Profit + Depr., Dep., Amort./Cur. Mat. L/T/D						
.6	.6	.6	Fixed/Worth		.8	.7	.5		
1.3	1.1	1.2			1.5	1.1	1.0		
10.6	2.7	14.6			8.7	-36.4	NM		
.4	.4	.3	Debt/Worth		.3	.3	.4		
2.1	1.3	1.9			2.4	.6	1.3		
17.9	4.1	28.3			26.4	-341.8	NM		
(25) 38.1	(43) 23.9	(59) 58.8	% Profit Before Taxes/Tangible Net Worth	(24) 325.3					
6.9	6.3	8.8		14.2					
-.6	-.5	-.7		-1.3					
6.4	7.9	15.9	% Profit Before Taxes/Total Assets		17.1	22.3	16.1		
2.5	3.1	4.1			6.4	10.0	4.5		
-.2	-.6	-.1			-.5	2.0	-.2		
7.3	5.6	13.6	Sales/Net Fixed Assets		10.9	16.8	8.6		
3.4	2.9	2.7			1.6	2.5	2.8		
1.3	1.1	1.1			.6	1.8	1.3		
2.9	2.2	3.1	Sales/Total Assets		2.6	3.3	3.9		
1.6	1.4	1.5			.9	1.4	1.6		
.7	.7	.6			.5	.9	.6		
(27) 2.5	(45) 2.0	(58) 1.6	% Depr., Dep., Amort./Sales	(18) 1.7		(10) .9	(11) 2.1		
2.9	3.6	2.8		3.8		2.7	2.8		
5.0	5.2	4.9		6.7		3.8	3.9		
		(14) 3.1	% Officers', Directors', Owners' Comp/Sales						
		8.2							
		11.5							
487322M	507689M	710605M	Net Sales ($)	4215M	53815M	42365M	87712M	127404M	395094M
425768M	371461M	611037M	Total Assets ($)	3494M	73373M	32725M	85663M	121310M	294472M

M = $ thousand   MM = $ million
See Pages 11 through 21 for Explanation of Ratios and Data

Current Data Sorted By Assets

Comparative Historical Data

						Type of Statement		
8	31	54	12	4	2	Unqualified		
		3				Reviewed		
1	1	1				Compiled		
3	1	2				Tax Returns		
1	8	9	4		1	Other	4/1/00- 3/31/01 ALL	4/1/01- 3/31/02 ALL
	115 (4/1-9/30/04)		31 (10/1/04-3/31/05)					
0-500M	500M-2MM	2-10MM	10-50MM	50-100MM	100-250MM	NUMBER OF STATEMENTS		
13	41	69	16	4	3			
%	%	%	%	%	%	ASSETS	%	%
17.3	23.2	15.5	13.6			Cash & Equivalents	D	D
28.1	31.7	19.7	16.0			Trade Receivables (net)	A	A
.2	.0	.6	.1			Inventory	T	T
5.4	4.5	3.0	1.7			All Other Current	A	A
51.0	59.4	38.8	31.3			Total Current		
41.2	35.4	50.6	51.4			Fixed Assets (net)	N	N
.0	.1	.1	.1			Intangibles (net)	O	O
7.7	5.1	10.6	17.2			All Other Non-Current	T	T
100.0	100.0	100.0	100.0			Total		
						LIABILITIES	A	A
2.8	6.9	2.4	3.8			Notes Payable-Short Term	V	V
.8	2.3	1.7	2.8			Cur. Mat.-L/T/D	A	A
17.0	8.4	7.8	3.2			Trade Payables	I	I
.0	.1	.0	.0			Income Taxes Payable	L	L
16.8	10.8	10.1	6.0			All Other Current	A	A
37.4	28.5	21.9	16.0			Total Current	B	B
19.1	18.0	21.1	28.2			Long-Term Debt	L	L
.0	.0	.0	.0			Deferred Taxes	E	E
6.9	3.0	5.2	2.7			All Other Non-Current		
36.5	50.5	51.8	53.2			Net Worth		
100.0	100.0	100.0	100.0			Total Liabilities & Net Worth		
						INCOME DATA		
100.0	100.0	100.0	100.0			Net Sales		
						Gross Profit		
100.8	98.2	92.9	95.4			Operating Expenses		
-.8	1.8	7.1	4.6			Operating Profit		
.0	.4	1.1	-.6			All Other Expenses (net)		
-.7	1.4	6.0	5.2			Profit Before Taxes		
						RATIOS		
5.3	3.5	3.8	2.8					
1.3	2.1	2.2	2.0			Current		
.8	1.3	1.3	.9					
4.1	3.5	3.6	2.5					
1.3	2.1	1.8	2.0			Quick		
.5	1.2	1.1	.9					
0 UND	23 16.0	13 27.5	28 13.2					
23 15.7	33 11.1	31 11.8	42 8.7			Sales/Receivables		
68 5.4	49 7.5	49 7.5	65 5.6					
						Cost of Sales/Inventory		
						Cost of Sales/Payables		
3.9	5.9	4.9	6.2					
21.3	10.8	10.1	8.0			Sales/Working Capital		
-209.5	31.9	30.0	-76.3					
	26.8	8.4	9.8					
(29) 2.0	(52) 2.9	(13) 2.9				EBIT/Interest		
	-.8	.8	1.7					
						Net Profit + Depr., Dep., Amort./Cur. Mat. L /T/D		
.3	.1	.6	.5					
1.0	.6	.8	1.2			Fixed/Worth		
UND	1.4	1.2	2.0					
.2	.4	.2	.3					
1.6	.8	.5	.8			Debt/Worth		
UND	1.9	1.6	2.5					
316.3	26.4	16.1	17.5			% Profit Before Taxes/Tangible		
(10) 11.0	(37) 4.9	(67) 6.0	9.3			Net Worth		
-3.6	-8.3	-1.1	1.6					
16.9	12.6	8.1	9.0			% Profit Before Taxes/Total		
.8	3.2	2.9	4.2			Assets		
-9.6	-3.9	-.5	.9					
346.1	56.5	6.6	3.4					
5.0	10.4	3.0	2.5			Sales/Net Fixed Assets		
2.3	3.5	1.1	1.1					
4.6	4.2	2.5	1.9					
2.0	2.7	1.5	1.3			Sales/Total Assets		
1.2	1.8	.7	.6					
.3	.6	1.1	1.7					
(11) 1.3	(38) 1.4	(62) 2.4	(14) 2.1			% Depr., Dep., Amort./Sales		
2.9	2.2	3.4	4.3					
						% Officers', Directors', Owners' Comp/Sales		
11045M	146978M	682198M	383573M	343279M	412138M	Net Sales ($)		
3287M	50767M	347515M	336063M	276698M	492411M	Total Assets ($)		

M = $ thousand   MM = $ million
See Pages 11 through 21 for Explanation of Ratios and Data

Comparative Historical Data			Type of Statement	Current Data Sorted By Sales					
76	136	111	Unqualified	9	24	15	26	24	13
	1	3	Reviewed	1	1				1
2	5	3	Compiled	1	1	1			
4	6	6	Tax Returns	3	2	1			
20	25	23	Other	3	3	6	4	4	3
4/1/02-	4/1/03-	4/1/04-		115 (4/1-9/30/04)			31 (10/1/04-3/31/05)		
3/31/03	3/31/04	3/31/05							
ALL	ALL	ALL		0-1MM	1-3MM	3-5MM	5-10MM	10-25MM	25MM & OVER
102	173	146	**NUMBER OF STATEMENTS**	17	31	23	30	28	17
%	%	%	**ASSETS**	%	%	%	%	%	%
18.8	18.3	17.6	Cash & Equivalents	13.8	22.2	14.2	17.0	17.8	18.1
15.4	18.9	23.3	Trade Receivables (net)	14.5	19.3	23.1	27.4	23.3	32.6
.7	.3	.3	Inventory	.1	.9	.1	.1	.1	.0
9.0	6.3	3.6	All Other Current	3.5	1.8	6.7	3.2	3.9	2.7
43.9	43.8	44.7	Total Current	32.0	44.3	44.1	47.7	45.1	53.4
45.6	44.1	45.1	Fixed Assets (net)	62.4	46.0	46.2	41.4	43.0	34.5
.2	.4	.2	Intangibles (net)	.0	.0	.2	.1	.1	1.6
10.2	11.6	9.9	All Other Non-Current	5.6	9.7	9.5	10.9	11.8	10.5
100.0	100.0	100.0	Total	100.0	100.0	100.0	100.0	100.0	100.0
			LIABILITIES						
3.7	4.4	3.9	Notes Payable-Short Term	3.8	4.0	7.0	2.2	2.9	3.9
1.9	2.0	2.0	Cur. Mat.-L/T/D	1.2	1.6	2.6	2.0	1.7	3.0
8.3	8.6	8.1	Trade Payables	9.5	4.9	5.5	9.3	7.9	14.6
.0	.0	.1	Income Taxes Payable	.0	.0	.1	.0	.0	.2
10.0	8.4	10.6	All Other Current	5.1	4.5	10.1	14.5	12.0	18.7
23.9	23.4	24.6	Total Current	19.7	15.0	25.2	28.1	24.5	40.6
19.0	16.4	21.5	Long-Term Debt	22.8	19.5	20.5	23.3	22.0	21.2
.2	.0	.0	Deferred Taxes	.0	.0	.0	.0	.0	.2
4.7	4.1	4.6	All Other Non-Current	5.5	1.0	3.5	1.9	11.0	5.9
52.3	56.0	49.3	Net Worth	52.0	64.6	50.8	46.7	42.6	32.1
100.0	100.0	100.0	Total Liabilities & Net Worth	100.0	100.0	100.0	100.0	100.0	100.0
			INCOME DATA						
100.0	100.0	100.0	Net Sales	100.0	100.0	100.0	100.0	100.0	100.0
			Gross Profit						
92.8	97.0	95.7	Operating Expenses	96.5	91.3	95.2	96.9	97.7	98.0
7.2	3.0	4.3	Operating Profit	3.5	8.7	4.8	3.1	2.3	2.0
2.7	.3	.6	All Other Expenses (net)	3.8	.8	.3	.2	−.9	.4
4.6	2.7	3.7	Profit Before Taxes	−.3	7.9	4.5	2.9	3.3	1.6
			RATIOS						
4.2	4.2	3.6		5.6	6.7	3.8	2.8	2.9	2.4
1.9	2.0	2.0	Current	1.2	3.5	1.7	1.8	1.9	1.1
1.1	1.2	1.1		.5	1.6	1.2	1.4	1.4	1.0
2.6	3.5	3.5		4.8	6.3	3.3	2.5	2.7	2.4
1.5	1.6	1.8	Quick	1.2	3.5	1.5	1.8	1.8	1.1
.8	1.0	1.1		.4	1.6	1.1	1.4	1.4	.9
3 118.6	13 28.3	19 18.9		0 UND	8 48.5	21 17.2	20 18.3	29 12.7	33 11.1
28 13.2	32 11.5	33 11.0	Sales/Receivables	13 27.5	24 15.1	33 11.0	33 11.2	37 9.8	43 8.5
48 7.5	50 7.3	52 7.1		60 6.1	51 7.1	50 7.3	50 7.4	48 7.6	70 5.2
			Cost of Sales/Inventory						
			Cost of Sales/Payables						
4.3	4.2	5.1		3.3	3.9	4.7	6.1	5.6	7.7
12.2	11.0	10.2	Sales/Working Capital	26.5	6.3	11.5	12.6	11.8	36.3
67.0	37.9	40.9		−18.5	15.1	42.1	29.9	32.1	−231.8
	9.8		6.2		8.5					6.4	36.2	8.0	6.6	9.5	4.6
(57) 2.0	(111) 1.8	(107) 2.8	EBIT/Interest	(10) 2.6	(22) 6.9	(20) 2.3	(20) 2.4	(22) 3.0	(13) 2.4
−.7	−.4	.7		−6.3	.9	−.9	.8	.9	.6
			Net Profit + Depr., Dep., Amort./Cur. Mat. L/T/D						
.4	.4	.5		.5	.1	.4	.3	.6	.6
1.0	.8	.9	Fixed/Worth	1.2	.7	.9	.8	.9	1.6
1.8	1.6	1.6		4.2	1.3	1.6	1.5	1.2	2.0
.2	.2	.3		.2	.2	.2	.5	.4	1.3
.9	.7	.7	Debt/Worth	.5	.3	.7	.8	.7	2.2
2.2	1.8	2.1		3.4	1.0	1.8	2.5	1.5	10.9
18.6	14.0	19.0	% Profit Before Taxes/Tangible Net Worth	42.7	31.0	17.4	18.6	12.6	25.2
(97) 8.9	(166) 4.0	(137) 6.0		(16) 4.1	(29) 6.0	(20) 4.1	(28) 7.4	(27) 5.9	15.7
−1.9	−3.5	−1.1		−11.7	−.7	−1.2	−.6	−1.1	3.0
10.1	6.3	8.6	% Profit Before Taxes/Total Assets	6.3	14.4	9.8	10.2	8.2	6.7
2.9	1.6	3.1		.8	5.1	2.6	4.1	3.4	1.2
−2.2	−1.8	−.6		−9.7	−.5	−1.0	−.4	−.5	.5
11.9	10.5	13.4	Sales/Net Fixed Assets	13.4	34.9	13.4	20.5	8.8	138.8
3.7	4.0	3.5		1.4	2.3	3.5	4.0	3.7	3.6
1.3	1.5	1.8		.6	.8	2.6	2.4	2.7	2.4
2.6	2.7	3.2	Sales/Total Assets	2.7	2.7	2.9	4.2	3.0	3.5
1.6	1.7	1.7		1.1	1.2	2.0	1.8	2.0	2.0
.7	.9	.9		.5	.5	1.4	1.3	1.3	1.1
1.3	1.3	1.0	% Depr., Dep., Amort./Sales	1.3	.7	1.3	.9	1.0	.6
(87) 2.3	(152) 2.2	(132) 2.1		(16) 3.2	(24) 2.1	2.1	(28) 2.1	(25) 1.4	(16) 1.8
4.1	3.5	3.4		10.7	5.0	3.0	2.9	3.2	3.4
3.4	4.3	3.5	% Officers', Directors', Owners' Comp/Sales						
(10) 7.4	(19) 6.7	(13) 9.7							
10.9	34.1	13.6							
1561585M	1531419M	1979211M	Net Sales ($)	7518M	67115M	87845M	207926M	444767M	1164040M
1253918M	1153360M	1506741M	Total Assets ($)	12170M	78822M	53591M	162966M	281538M	917654M

M = $ thousand   MM = $ million
See Pages 11 through 21 for Explanation of Ratios and Data

Current Data Sorted By Assets							Comparative Historical Data	
7	9	22	8	2		**Type of Statement**		
			1			Unqualified		
						Reviewed		
2	2	1			1	Compiled		
1	1					Tax Returns		
2	6	9	1	1		Other		
	49 (4/1-9/30/04)		27 (10/1/04-3/31/05)				4/1/00-3/31/01 ALL	4/1/01-3/31/02 ALL
0-500M	500M-2MM	2-10MM	10-50MM	50-100MM	100-250MM			
12	18	32	10	3	1	**NUMBER OF STATEMENTS**		
%	%	%	%	%	%	**ASSETS**	%	%
24.4	15.8	21.2	19.5			Cash & Equivalents	D	D
34.9	23.7	14.2	13.3			Trade Receivables (net)	A	A
.1	.3	1.0	.2			Inventory	T	T
14.5	2.0	5.1	4.2			All Other Current	A	A
73.9	41.8	41.6	37.3			Total Current		
21.9	43.8	49.8	52.5			Fixed Assets (net)	N	N
2.0	.2	.1	.5			Intangibles (net)	O	O
2.1	14.1	8.6	9.7			All Other Non-Current	T	T
100.0	100.0	100.0	100.0			Total		
						LIABILITIES	A	A
30.1	4.6	1.5	2.3			Notes Payable-Short Term	V	V
.4	1.1	3.2	1.9			Cur. Mat.-L/T/D	A	A
12.1	8.2	7.4	9.1			Trade Payables	I	I
.0	.1	.0	.0			Income Taxes Payable	L	L
17.0	17.0	8.5	7.2			All Other Current	A	A
59.6	30.9	20.6	20.5			Total Current	B	B
5.0	15.6	31.3	32.1			Long-Term Debt	L	L
.0	.0	.0	.0			Deferred Taxes	E	E
17.7	3.9	.8	3.8			All Other Non-Current		
17.7	49.6	47.3	43.6			Net Worth		
100.0	100.0	100.0	100.0			Total Liabilities & Net Worth		
						INCOME DATA		
100.0	100.0	100.0	100.0			Net Sales		
						Gross Profit		
93.7	96.1	89.5	96.6			Operating Expenses		
6.3	3.9	10.5	3.4			Operating Profit		
.4	2.9	3.1	.7			All Other Expenses (net)		
5.9	.9	7.5	2.7			Profit Before Taxes		
						RATIOS		
4.3	3.2	3.8	2.9					
2.5	1.6	1.9	1.4			Current		
1.0	1.0	1.1	.8					
2.5	3.1	3.3	2.1					
1.5	1.5	1.9	1.3			Quick		
.8	1.0	1.1	.7					
0 UND	5 66.9	8 48.0	7 51.9					
36 10.0	26 14.1	32 11.3	30 12.1			Sales/Receivables		
54 6.8	56 6.6	49 7.4	45 8.0					
						Cost of Sales/Inventory		
						Cost of Sales/Payables		
5.4	5.5	5.3	5.0					
11.1	21.4	10.9	54.3			Sales/Working Capital		
NM	NM	35.4	−36.1					
	9.6	30.5						
	(11) 1.6	(23) 6.3				EBIT/Interest		
	−4.8	1.3						
						Net Profit + Depr., Dep., Amort./Cur. Mat. L /T/D		
.0	.5	.5	.5					
.4	1.0	1.0	1.3			Fixed/Worth		
1.3	1.7	1.4	3.9					
.4	.4	.3	.6					
.9	1.0	.7	1.1			Debt/Worth		
NM	2.9	1.7	4.7					
	10.2	23.2				% Profit Before Taxes/Tangible Net Worth		
	(17) 1.7	(29) 8.6						
	−13.2	.3						
40.7	5.0	12.2	9.8			% Profit Before Taxes/Total Assets		
8.2	1.3	2.6	4.8					
4.3	−4.6	−.1	−.1					
UND	11.3	9.8	6.8					
41.1	6.5	3.2	2.4			Sales/Net Fixed Assets		
6.4	2.7	1.8	.9					
6.4	3.2	2.3	2.1					
3.7	2.3	1.7	1.6			Sales/Total Assets		
2.5	1.3	.7	.5					
	.5	1.4	1.7					
	(15) 1.2	(27) 2.8	3.2			% Depr., Dep., Amort./Sales		
	2.3	4.5	6.1					
						% Officers', Directors', Owners' Comp/Sales		
10344M	49575M	281854M	298164M	202143M	1026307M	Net Sales ($)		
2559M	20488M	161990M	216917M	165411M	176347M	Total Assets ($)		

M = $ thousand   MM = $ million
See Pages 11 through 21 for Explanation of Ratios and Data

Comparative Historical Data | | | | Current Data Sorted By Sales

			Type of Statement						
17	21	48	Unqualified	6	11	5	10	9	7
1		1	Reviewed						1
	2	6	Compiled	1	2	1		1	1
	1	2	Tax Returns	1	1				
4	12	19	Other	4	3	5	3	4	
4/1/02-3/31/03 ALL	4/1/03-3/31/04 ALL	4/1/04-3/31/05 ALL		49 (4/1-9/30/04) 0-1MM	1-3MM	3-5MM	27 (10/1/04-3/31/05) 5-10MM	10-25MM	25MM & OVER
22	36	76	NUMBER OF STATEMENTS	12	17	11	13	14	9
%	%	%	ASSETS	%	%	%	%	%	%
18.8	12.3	19.5	Cash & Equivalents	22.2	19.4	15.7	21.8	17.1	
25.1	20.1	19.7	Trade Receivables (net)	12.4	22.4	29.4	15.2	15.5	
.0	.3	.5	Inventory	.1	.3	.0	.2	2.3	
2.9	5.7	5.6	All Other Current	13.8	3.2	2.5	5.5	6.3	
46.9	38.5	45.4	Total Current	48.4	45.3	47.7	42.7	41.2	
44.2	49.4	43.1	Fixed Assets (net)	35.1	46.9	48.1	45.0	44.7	
.0	5.1	1.2	Intangibles (net)	2.2	.1	.1	.1	.2	
8.9	7.0	10.4	All Other Non-Current	14.3	7.7	4.2	12.3	14.0	
100.0	100.0	100.0	Total	100.0	100.0	100.0	100.0	100.0	
			LIABILITIES						
4.4	6.3	6.9	Notes Payable-Short Term	11.3	13.8	8.2	1.2	1.4	
1.7	4.3	2.0	Cur. Mat.-L/T/D	.7	.9	5.3	1.5	1.6	
9.0	8.0	8.4	Trade Payables	4.2	9.4	5.5	11.6	4.2	
.0	.0	.0	Income Taxes Payable	.0	.1	.0	.0	.0	
14.4	13.9	11.9	All Other Current	11.7	8.5	24.1	9.9	10.4	
29.5	32.6	29.3	Total Current	27.9	32.6	43.0	24.2	17.5	
19.6	29.0	23.2	Long-Term Debt	20.5	32.1	11.6	23.1	22.7	
.0	.0	.0	Deferred Taxes	.0	.0	.0	.0	.0	
2.8	3.0	4.7	All Other Non-Current	13.4	6.7	.5	1.0	3.5	
48.0	35.4	42.9	Net Worth	38.2	28.6	45.0	51.6	56.3	
100.0	100.0	100.0	Total Liabilities & Net Worth	100.0	100.0	100.0	100.0	100.0	
			INCOME DATA						
100.0	100.0	100.0	Net Sales	100.0	100.0	100.0	100.0	100.0	
			Gross Profit						
98.7	95.9	93.2	Operating Expenses	87.1	93.8	90.2	95.0	95.1	
1.3	4.1	6.8	Operating Profit	12.9	6.2	9.8	5.0	4.9	
.3	4.5	2.2	All Other Expenses (net)	5.5	3.3	−.7	3.7	−.4	
1.0	−.4	4.7	Profit Before Taxes	7.4	2.9	10.5	1.2	5.3	
			RATIOS						
2.8	2.2	3.0		4.3	5.7	2.9	2.7	5.3	
1.6	1.3	1.7	Current	2.7	1.9	1.2	1.8	2.0	
.9	.9	1.1		1.0	1.2	.6	1.2	1.0	
2.7	1.9	2.8		2.8	4.4	2.8	2.6	2.9	
1.5	1.1	1.6	Quick	1.5	1.7	1.2	1.8	1.6	
.8	.6	.8		.6	.9	.6	.9	.7	
13 27.6	11 34.3	7 55.3		0 UND	7 53.2	8 45.5	2 218.8	12 31.4	
31 11.6	32 11.4	31 11.7	Sales/Receivables	10 37.8	21 17.2	53 6.8	26 14.3	34 10.7	
41 8.8	45 8.1	47 7.7		54 6.8	41 8.9	82 4.5	43 8.4	44 8.3	
			Cost of Sales/Inventory						
			Cost of Sales/Payables						
8.0	8.8	5.5		4.8	4.8	5.9	6.2	3.7	
18.2	32.6	14.4	Sales/Working Capital	11.1	11.8	26.7	14.3	10.9	
−122.0	−48.1	88.4		NM	NM	−10.5	35.1	NM	
11.9	4.6	15.3			11.0			44.2	
(13) 2.3	(26) 1.8	(53) 2.6	EBIT/Interest	(10) −.4			(11) 2.6		
.3	.0	.8		−13.0			1.2		
			Net Profit + Depr., Dep., Amort./Cur. Mat. L/T/D						
.2	.7	.4		.1	.2	.7	.5	.4	
.8	1.1	.9	Fixed/Worth	.7	.8	1.2	.9	1.0	
2.2	3.7	1.6		NM	1.7	4.2	1.7	1.3	
.4	.7	.4		.2	.4	.4	.4	.3	
1.1	1.7	1.0	Debt/Worth	.8	.9	.7	1.1	.8	
4.9	7.3	2.9		NM	12.8	4.3	2.1	1.5	
19.1	14.5	24.1			26.8	32.8	15.9	23.4	
9.2	(30) 6.7	(68) 7.3	% Profit Before Taxes/Tangible Net Worth	(14) 2.6	(10) 14.8	(12) 5.0	9.1		
−3.5	2.5	−.7		−7.9	3.0	.0	.5		
8.1	4.9	12.2		28.2	8.2	29.5	4.4	12.9	
2.0	2.4	2.9	% Profit Before Taxes/Total Assets	4.5	.7	5.4	2.0	5.8	
−1.1	−2.7	−.5		−6.3	−7.0	2.5	−1.0	.3	
33.4	10.7	15.0		43.5	80.4	11.1	19.2	11.1	
3.9	3.4	3.9	Sales/Net Fixed Assets	8.6	3.3	5.8	3.3	3.3	
2.2	2.0	2.1		2.5	.8	2.9	2.1	1.1	
3.3	3.3	3.0		3.7	2.9	3.7	2.9	2.2	
1.8	1.9	1.9	Sales/Total Assets	2.0	1.6	2.8	1.7	1.8	
1.6	.9	1.1		.6	.4	1.4	1.2	.6	
1.1	2.5	1.0			.7		1.0	2.3	
(18) 2.5	(30) 3.2	(62) 2.4	% Depr., Dep., Amort./Sales	(14) 2.3		(11) 2.4	(12) 2.9		
3.7	5.0	3.8		9.5		3.5	5.0		
			% Officers', Directors', Owners' Comp/Sales						
249539M	2466820M	1868387M	Net Sales ($)	5621M	30623M	42393M	89034M	201746M	1498970M
160325M	475430M	743712M	Total Assets ($)	8471M	39340M	25990M	62739M	198908M	408264M

HEALTH CARE—Other Individual and Family Services NAICS 624190 (SIC 8322)

	Current Data Sorted By Assets							Comparative Historical Data	
							Type of Statement		
15	88	218	126	11	3		Unqualified	376	417
1	2	6	1				Reviewed	11	8
2	4	4		1	1		Compiled	40	43
9	3	2	1				Tax Returns	13	11
12	26	51	30	6			Other	133	155
	449 (4/1-9/30/04)			174 (10/1/04-3/31/05)				4/1/00-3/31/01 ALL	4/1/01-3/31/02 ALL
0-500M	500M-2MM	2-10MM	10-50MM	50-100MM	100-250MM				
39	123	281	158	18	4		**NUMBER OF STATEMENTS**	573	634
%	%	%	%	%	%		**ASSETS**	%	%
28.4	19.3	16.2	17.4	12.3			Cash & Equivalents	18.4	17.6
24.6	22.4	20.7	14.9	12.0			Trade Receivables (net)	19.6	19.6
2.3	.5	.8	.6	.3			Inventory	.8	.8
2.3	5.1	3.6	3.4	3.6			All Other Current	4.8	5.6
57.6	47.2	41.2	36.4	28.2			Total Current	43.6	43.6
36.6	44.1	47.7	44.5	46.3			Fixed Assets (net)	41.1	43.1
.6	.3	1.1	.6	2.3			Intangibles (net)	1.2	.9
5.1	8.4	10.0	18.6	23.2			All Other Non-Current	14.1	12.4
100.0	100.0	100.0	100.0	100.0			Total	100.0	100.0
							LIABILITIES		
6.3	5.1	4.0	3.6	1.8			Notes Payable-Short Term	5.0	4.5
3.4	2.5	2.8	2.3	.8			Cur. Mat.-L/T/D	2.0	2.0
12.3	8.1	8.6	5.3	3.1			Trade Payables	8.4	7.6
.8	.0	.2	.0	.0			Income Taxes Payable	.0	.0
18.8	12.1	10.0	9.0	12.3			All Other Current	11.1	11.5
41.6	27.8	25.6	20.3	18.0			Total Current	26.5	25.6
18.3	18.6	20.2	19.7	25.7			Long-Term Debt	17.8	19.6
.0	.0	.0	.0	.0			Deferred Taxes	.1	.1
15.9	3.0	3.2	1.8	7.3			All Other Non-Current	4.8	4.6
24.2	50.5	50.9	58.2	49.0			Net Worth	50.7	50.1
100.0	100.0	100.0	100.0	100.0			Total Liabilities & Net Worth	100.0	100.0
							INCOME DATA		
100.0	100.0	100.0	100.0	100.0			Net Sales	100.0	100.0
							Gross Profit		
96.6	99.2	96.1	95.4	96.8			Operating Expenses	95.0	96.0
3.4	.8	3.9	4.6	3.2			Operating Profit	5.0	4.0
.5	.2	.3	−.7	−.7			All Other Expenses (net)	−.9	1.3
2.9	.5	3.6	5.3	3.8			Profit Before Taxes	5.9	2.6
							RATIOS		
4.7	4.8	3.2	3.2	2.4				3.3	3.5
1.9	1.9	1.7	1.9	1.6			Current	1.8	1.9
.7	1.1	1.1	1.1	1.0				1.1	1.1
4.7	4.0	2.9	2.8	2.2				2.8	3.0
1.8	1.6	1.6	1.7	1.5			Quick	1.6	1.6
.7	.9	.9	1.0	.9				.9	.9
1 370.0	10 37.2	14 27.0	14 25.8	23 16.0				13 27.6	11 33.0
19 19.4	28 12.9	34 10.7	34 10.6	37 9.8			Sales/Receivables	33 11.0	32 11.5
35 10.4	41 8.9	50 7.3	57 6.4	54 6.7				52 7.0	51 7.2
							Cost of Sales/Inventory		
							Cost of Sales/Payables		
6.6	4.7	5.5	4.2	5.7				4.6	5.1
17.9	14.6	13.0	8.8	10.2			Sales/Working Capital	10.1	10.7
−25.4	228.4	109.2	93.4	−294.9				71.1	46.2
11.8	4.6	7.9	14.4	7.1				9.8	6.9
(18) 2.5	(75) 1.1	(201) 2.7	(113) 3.9	(13) 2.7			EBIT/Interest	(376) 2.9	(434) 2.1
−6.2	−4.7	.8	1.1	1.6				.7	.1
							Net Profit + Depr., Dep., Amort./Cur. Mat. L /T/D		
.2	.3	.5	.4	.5				.4	.4
.8	.8	.9	.8	.9			Fixed/Worth	.8	.8
7.2	1.5	1.6	1.4	1.8				1.5	1.5
.3	.4	.4	.3	.5				.3	.3
1.5	.8	.8	.7	1.1			Debt/Worth	.8	.9
87.5	2.2	2.2	1.7	1.9				1.9	1.9
53.1	18.4	14.3	15.9	10.9			% Profit Before Taxes/Tangible Net Worth	19.3	16.5
(32) 9.9	(118) 2.6	(271) 5.2	(157) 6.9	(16) 8.7				(551) 7.1	(604) 5.1
−12.2	−12.6	−.4	.9	2.1				.0	−3.0
20.0	9.0	6.9	7.6	6.1			% Profit Before Taxes/Total Assets	11.0	8.5
.9	.9	2.4	3.4	3.8				3.3	2.5
−15.9	−5.9	−.4	.2	.1				−.4	−1.6
45.2	23.3	9.0	5.1	3.8			Sales/Net Fixed Assets	11.9	12.9
16.4	5.0	3.7	2.6	2.2				4.1	3.9
6.6	1.9	1.9	1.4	1.3				1.9	1.9
6.2	3.7	2.6	1.8	1.4			Sales/Total Assets	2.7	2.9
3.6	2.1	1.7	1.1	.8				1.6	1.6
2.0	1.0	1.0	.6	.6				.8	.9
.8	.9	1.2	1.4	2.4			% Depr., Dep., Amort./Sales	1.3	1.2
(25) 1.5	(99) 1.8	(257) 2.0	(149) 2.8	(17) 3.4				(503) 2.1	(560) 2.2
2.4	3.5	3.4	3.9	6.4				3.6	3.7
4.7	1.7	3.4	1.8				% Officers', Directors', Owners' Comp/Sales	3.2	3.4
(11) 16.6	(15) 10.7	(16) 9.6	(14) 4.7					(55) 6.0	(62) 7.1
19.8	29.2	36.4	13.9					18.9	14.4
37693M	353577M	2886222M	4189482M	1505329M	1727698M		Net Sales ($)	6136629M	7656954M
10220M	147414M	1372315M	3063069M	1172210M	613619M		Total Assets ($)	5060948M	6391190M

M = $ thousand   MM = $ million
See Pages 11 through 21 for Explanation of Ratios and Data

Comparative Historical Data   **Current Data Sorted By Sales**

			Type of Statement						
476	437	461	Unqualified	34	77	55	92	132	71
8	8	10	Reviewed	3	3	1	1	1	1
13	51	12	Compiled	1	7	1	2		1
12	17	15	Tax Returns	10	2	1		2	
131	135	125	Other	18	21	17	22	28	19
4/1/02-3/31/03	4/1/03-3/31/04	4/1/04-3/31/05		449 (4/1-9/30/04)			174 (10/1/04-3/31/05)		
ALL	ALL	ALL		0-1MM	1-3MM	3-5MM	5-10MM	10-25MM	25MM & OVER
640	648	623	**NUMBER OF STATEMENTS**	66	110	75	117	163	92
%	%	%	**ASSETS**	%	%	%	%	%	%
18.1	17.1	17.8	Cash & Equivalents	20.3	17.6	16.0	17.9	17.1	18.6
18.3	20.1	19.4	Trade Receivables (net)	9.8	16.7	16.1	19.3	24.2	24.1
.7	.6	.8	Inventory	1.5	.4	.1	.7	.6	1.6
5.2	5.7	3.8	All Other Current	2.1	4.3	6.8	3.0	3.3	4.1
42.2	43.6	41.8	Total Current	33.7	39.0	39.0	40.8	45.2	48.4
44.1	44.3	45.3	Fixed Assets (net)	56.4	49.4	47.8	46.5	41.7	35.7
.9	.7	.8	Intangibles (net)	.5	.6	.3	1.4	.6	1.2
12.8	11.3	12.1	All Other Non-Current	9.5	11.0	13.0	11.4	12.4	14.7
100.0	100.0	100.0	Total	100.0	100.0	100.0	100.0	100.0	100.0
			LIABILITIES						
5.0	4.7	4.2	Notes Payable-Short Term	2.3	5.3	4.3	4.0	3.9	4.7
2.0	2.0	2.6	Cur. Mat.-L/T/D	3.7	2.3	3.7	2.4	2.6	1.4
6.9	7.6	7.7	Trade Payables	5.7	6.4	5.8	6.8	9.2	10.8
.1	.1	.1	Income Taxes Payable	.2	.2	.1	.0	.2	.2
12.4	13.3	10.8	All Other Current	11.8	8.1	7.6	11.6	11.6	13.4
26.4	27.7	25.4	Total Current	23.7	22.4	21.5	24.9	27.5	30.6
19.5	19.6	19.8	Long-Term Debt	25.3	20.2	17.5	21.3	19.7	15.3
.0	.1	.0	Deferred Taxes	.0	.0	.0	.0	.0	.0
3.7	4.9	3.9	All Other Non-Current	2.7	7.3	3.3	2.9	2.7	4.3
50.4	47.6	50.9	Net Worth	48.2	50.1	57.8	50.9	50.1	49.8
100.0	100.0	100.0	Total Liabilities & Net Worth	100.0	100.0	100.0	100.0	100.0	100.0
			INCOME DATA						
100.0	100.0	100.0	Net Sales	100.0	100.0	100.0	100.0	100.0	100.0
			Gross Profit						
97.2	97.2	96.6	Operating Expenses	94.4	96.3	94.2	95.8	98.2	98.7
2.8	2.8	3.4	Operating Profit	5.6	3.7	5.8	4.2	1.8	1.3
1.3	.2	.0	All Other Expenses (net)	2.7	.5	-.3	.0	-.5	-1.2
1.5	2.6	3.4	Profit Before Taxes	2.9	3.3	6.2	4.2	2.4	2.4
			RATIOS						
3.3	3.1	3.3		5.8	5.0	3.9	3.3	2.7	2.6
1.8	1.8	1.8	Current	2.7	2.0	1.8	1.8	1.8	1.5
1.1	1.1	1.1		.6	.8	1.1	1.1	1.2	1.1
2.8	2.7	3.0		5.8	4.6	3.1	3.0	2.4	2.5
1.5	1.6	1.6	Quick	2.1	1.8	1.6	1.6	1.7	1.3
.9	.9	.9		.5	.7	.9	.9	1.0	1.0
15 23.9	14 26.2	13 28.0		0 UND	5 68.1	10 37.9	10 35.9	23 16.2	16 23.3
33 11.1	32 11.3	31 11.8	Sales/Receivables	13 27.3	28 13.2	29 12.7	30 12.1	36 10.1	38 9.6
49 7.4	49 7.5	49 7.4		36 10.1	44 8.3	50 7.3	49 7.5	51 7.2	56 6.5
			Cost of Sales/Inventory						
			Cost of Sales/Payables						
5.0	5.4	5.1		2.6	3.3	4.9	4.8	5.9	6.7
10.9	11.5	12.2	Sales/Working Capital	7.8	11.6	11.2	12.2	10.7	15.4
84.7	90.3	158.5		-12.9	-38.5	60.3	73.6	58.2	98.1
6.8	8.7	9.0		4.8	6.9	11.3	7.3	7.6	14.9
(425) 1.9	(463) 2.4	(423) 2.9	EBIT/Interest	(32) .6	(67) .9	(51) 3.0	(81) 3.0	(126) 2.9	(66) 6.7
-.5	-.2	.3		-2.7	-3.8	-1.1	.5	1.0	1.9
			Net Profit + Depr., Dep., Amort./Cur. Mat. L/T/D						
.4	.4	.4		.3	.4	.4	.5	.5	.3
.9	.9	.9	Fixed/Worth	1.2	.9	.8	.8	.9	.7
1.6	1.6	1.6		2.6	1.9	1.5	1.6	1.4	1.2
.3	.4	.3		.2	.2	.4	.5	.4	.4
.8	.9	.8	Debt/Worth	.7	.7	.7	.9	.9	.8
1.9	2.2	2.1		2.8	2.5	1.8	2.1	2.1	2.1
16.5	15.9	15.8	% Profit Before Taxes/Tangible Net Worth	13.2	14.5	19.5	19.4	12.3	14.0
(611) 3.5	(611) 4.9	(597) 5.9		(61) 1.3	(102) 2.8	(72) 8.3	(114) 5.4	(159) 5.8	(89) 8.2
-5.0	-2.4	-1.9		-7.9	-7.1	-.3	-2.7	.0	1.2
7.6	7.8	7.5	% Profit Before Taxes/Total Assets	6.8	8.0	11.0	8.7	6.5	7.3
1.6	2.3	2.6		.5	1.3	4.5	2.8	2.5	4.1
-2.7	-1.5	-1.3		-5.7	-5.0	-.9	-.9	-.1	.6
10.8	10.4	10.8		12.3	12.4	9.1	8.1	10.2	17.5
3.6	3.8	3.7	Sales/Net Fixed Assets	1.4	3.2	2.7	3.3	4.7	4.6
1.8	1.9	1.7		.3	1.0	1.3	1.9	2.4	2.9
2.6	2.9	2.6		2.0	2.6	2.2	2.5	2.8	3.2
1.6	1.7	1.6	Sales/Total Assets	.7	1.2	1.5	1.6	2.0	1.9
.9	1.0	.8		.3	.6	.7	.9	1.2	1.3
1.4	1.1	1.2		1.8	1.1	1.2	1.3	1.2	.8
(563) 2.3	(586) 2.1	(549) 2.2	% Depr., Dep., Amort./Sales	(45) 4.6	(94) 2.3	(66) 2.8	(105) 2.2	(155) 1.9	(84) 1.7
3.6	3.6	3.6		10.8	4.4	4.4	3.5	3.0	3.0
3.2	3.8	2.9		9.9				4.0	
(68) 7.2	(62) 5.9	(56) 8.3	% Officers', Directors', Owners' Comp/Sales	(14) 15.6				(12) 10.6	
13.8	13.2	18.7		21.2				40.7	
9336058M	10858346M	10700001M	Net Sales ($)	36950M	215325M	303459M	836893M	2551377M	6755997M
6824581M	7133850M	6378847M	Total Assets ($)	88246M	279956M	337156M	823457M	1739170M	3110862M

Current Data Sorted By Assets   Comparative Historical Data

						Type of Statement		
6	34	72	49	5	2	Unqualified	114	112
	1	1	1			Reviewed	4	4
2	2	2	1			Compiled	15	25
5	2	1				Tax Returns	3	4
	9	22	12		1	Other	42	45
	139 (4/1-9/30/04)			91 (10/1/04-3/31/05)			4/1/00-3/31/01 ALL	4/1/01-3/31/02 ALL
0-500M	500M-2MM	2-10MM	10-50MM	50-100MM	100-250MM			
13	48	98	63	5	3	NUMBER OF STATEMENTS	178	190
%	%	%	%	%	%	ASSETS	%	%
22.0	17.0	15.6	19.3			Cash & Equivalents	14.6	15.6
16.0	29.6	15.9	17.5			Trade Receivables (net)	26.6	21.9
2.1	4.6	3.3	3.8			Inventory	2.0	2.5
3.3	5.3	3.0	2.9			All Other Current	3.3	4.6
43.4	56.4	37.7	43.5			Total Current	46.5	44.5
47.7	31.4	50.6	43.1			Fixed Assets (net)	43.4	41.8
3.5	1.6	1.1	1.7			Intangibles (net)	1.4	1.3
5.4	10.5	10.5	11.7			All Other Non-Current	8.7	12.3
100.0	100.0	100.0	100.0			Total	100.0	100.0
						LIABILITIES		
6.6	12.2	2.6	2.6			Notes Payable-Short Term	5.8	5.8
28.6	2.6	1.9	4.1			Cur. Mat.-L/T/D	3.8	2.4
12.8	8.2	7.0	7.6			Trade Payables	8.9	7.8
.2	.0	.1	.1			Income Taxes Payable	.1	.1
27.9	18.4	9.2	12.6			All Other Current	12.5	11.7
76.0	41.4	20.7	26.9			Total Current	31.1	27.7
15.0	15.6	21.5	20.6			Long-Term Debt	20.0	19.4
.0	.0	.0	.0			Deferred Taxes	.0	.0
.8	2.0	2.1	1.9			All Other Non-Current	3.4	3.6
8.2	41.0	55.6	50.6			Net Worth	45.4	49.3
100.0	100.0	100.0	100.0			Total Liabilities & Net Worth	100.0	100.0
						INCOME DATA		
100.0	100.0	100.0	100.0			Net Sales	100.0	100.0
						Gross Profit		
94.1	98.4	97.1	96.5			Operating Expenses	97.1	96.6
5.9	1.6	2.9	3.5			Operating Profit	2.9	3.4
3.2	.6	.3	−.6			All Other Expenses (net)	−.3	.6
2.7	1.0	2.6	4.1			Profit Before Taxes	3.2	2.8
						RATIOS		
2.1	2.8	3.2	3.6				2.7	3.5
.6	1.6	1.9	1.7			Current	1.7	1.9
.1	1.1	1.2	1.1				1.2	1.2
1.3	2.4	2.6	3.0				2.5	2.7
.4	1.3	1.6	1.5			Quick	1.4	1.6
.1	.8						1.0	.9

0	UND	20	18.1	18	20.3	17	21.8				Sales/Receivables	27	13.7	19	19.4
5	74.3	37	9.8	32	11.5	37	9.8					39	9.4	36	10.3
29	12.5	50	7.3	43	8.4	50	7.4					53	7.0	50	7.3

						Cost of Sales/Inventory		

						Cost of Sales/Payables		

14.8	7.4	5.2	4.6				6.3	4.5
−17.4	16.1	10.0	10.5			Sales/Working Capital	12.9	11.7
−5.5	51.5	37.7	45.1				53.3	33.3

	14.0		10.4		11.1		17.3						7.4		6.1
(10)	2.9	(41)	2.9	(83)	3.1	(47)	5.5			EBIT/Interest	(142)	2.9	(146)	2.3
	−9.4		−.1		1.1		2.7					.9		.7

						Net Profit + Depr., Dep., Amort./Cur. Mat. L/T/D		

.6	.3	.6	.6				.4	.5
4.4	.9	1.0	.9			Fixed/Worth	1.0	.8
−.9	1.3	1.5	1.6				1.6	1.4
.7	.6	.4	.5				.5	.4
3.5	1.2	.7	.9			Debt/Worth	1.1	.8
−3.5	2.8	1.5	2.0				2.2	1.8

			31.1		11.7		17.6			% Profit Before Taxes/Tangible Net Worth		19.3		17.3
		(44)	8.3	(95)	4.3	(61)	9.9				(168)	7.5	(175)	5.1
			−2.9		−.1		5.1					−.1		−.9

27.9	12.6	6.0	8.0				9.3	7.8
2.1	3.0	2.3	4.1			% Profit Before Taxes/Total Assets	3.8	2.5
−16.2	−.8	−.1	2.0				−.4	−.8
60.9	21.5	7.0	6.3				12.9	11.4
18.5	12.9	2.7	3.6			Sales/Net Fixed Assets	4.2	4.2
3.2	4.4	1.7	2.0				2.2	2.2
6.9	4.0	2.1	1.9				2.9	2.5
3.3	2.8	1.4	1.5			Sales/Total Assets	1.8	1.7
2.2	1.4	1.0	1.0				1.1	1.1

	.8		1.0		1.8		1.7					1.3		1.4
(12)	1.3	(45)	1.7	(92)	2.7	(58)	3.0			% Depr., Dep., Amort./Sales	(162)	2.6	(174)	2.8
	4.7		3.1		4.8		4.2					3.8		4.0

						% Officers', Directors', Owners' Comp/Sales		2.6		5.6
							(18)	5.2	(23)	11.0
								17.4		19.9

16200M	188850M	866274M	2047637M	668978M	567847M	Net Sales ($)	2875199M	5318253M
3083M	66446M	524918M	1277657M	340579M	447401M	Total Assets ($)	1857754M	1886883M

© RMA 2005

M = $ thousand   MM = $ million
See Pages 11 through 21 for Explanation of Ratios and Data

Comparative Historical Data			Type of Statement	Current Data Sorted By Sales					
153	159	168	Unqualified	9	24	25	33	44	33
1	4	3	Reviewed				2		1
7	21	7	Compiled	1	3	1	1	1	
7	5	8	Tax Returns	3	3		2		
52	54	44	Other	2	4	7	9	14	8
4/1/02-3/31/03	4/1/03-3/31/04	4/1/04-3/31/05		139 (4/1-9/30/04)			91 (10/1/04-3/31/05)		
ALL	ALL	ALL		0-1MM	1-3MM	3-5MM	5-10MM	10-25MM	25MM & OVER
220	243	230	**NUMBER OF STATEMENTS**	15	34	33	47	59	42
%	%	%	**ASSETS**	%	%	%	%	%	%
17.1	15.8	17.3	Cash & Equivalents	12.3	17.2	16.3	17.8	17.0	19.9
20.2	19.3	19.5	Trade Receivables (net)	9.7	17.4	17.1	23.2	18.2	24.3
2.3	2.4	3.5	Inventory	1.0	4.5	4.0	2.9	3.2	4.2
3.6	4.8	3.5	All Other Current	3.6	3.1	4.1	3.2	3.7	3.2
43.3	42.3	43.8	Total Current	26.7	42.2	41.5	47.1	42.2	51.5
45.4	45.4	43.9	Fixed Assets (net)	61.5	44.3	47.1	42.6	44.2	36.0
1.1	1.2	1.5	Intangibles (net)	3.0	1.5	1.2	1.7	.3	2.5
10.3	11.1	10.8	All Other Non-Current	8.8	12.1	10.2	8.7	13.3	10.0
100.0	100.0	100.0	Total	100.0	100.0	100.0	100.0	100.0	100.0
			LIABILITIES						
4.3	5.0	4.8	Notes Payable-Short Term	3.9	5.4	3.9	9.7	2.0	4.0
3.9	2.8	4.1	Cur. Mat.-L/T/D	9.1	3.8	2.3	6.5	2.9	3.2
8.2	6.7	7.8	Trade Payables	10.0	6.7	7.8	6.4	8.0	9.1
.0	.0	.1	Income Taxes Payable	.2	.1	.0	.0	.0	.1
11.4	11.9	13.1	All Other Current	19.1	10.4	7.3	18.0	9.7	17.0
27.9	26.5	29.9	Total Current	42.3	26.4	21.2	40.7	22.7	33.5
21.9	18.4	19.6	Long-Term Debt	20.5	23.7	21.9	17.5	17.9	18.7
.0	.0	.0	Deferred Taxes	.0	.1	.0	.0	.0	.0
2.7	3.9	2.2	All Other Non-Current	1.0	2.7	1.6	2.4	1.4	3.8
47.5	51.2	48.3	Net Worth	36.2	47.1	55.3	39.5	58.0	44.1
100.0	100.0	100.0	Total Liabilities & Net Worth	100.0	100.0	100.0	100.0	100.0	100.0
			INCOME DATA						
100.0	100.0	100.0	Net Sales	100.0	100.0	100.0	100.0	100.0	100.0
			Gross Profit						
96.5	96.2	97.2	Operating Expenses	90.6	97.8	96.0	97.7	98.0	98.0
3.5	3.8	2.8	Operating Profit	9.4	2.2	4.0	2.3	2.0	2.0
2.0	.9	.2	All Other Expenses (net)	4.8	1.1	.4	.2	-1.0	-.7
1.5	2.9	2.6	Profit Before Taxes	4.5	1.0	3.6	2.0	3.1	2.7
			RATIOS						
3.3	3.1	2.9		3.3	3.0	3.6	2.2	4.0	2.1
1.8	1.9	1.7	Current	1.5	2.2	1.9	1.7	2.0	1.6
1.1	1.2	1.1		.4	.9	1.2	.9	1.2	1.1
2.8	2.6	2.6		2.1	2.6	2.8	1.9	3.2	1.8
1.6	1.5	1.5	Quick	.9	1.8	1.6	1.4	1.6	1.4
1.0	.9	.9		.1	.8	1.1	.9	1.0	1.0
19 18.9	17 21.7	17 21.4		0 UND	7 54.4	22 16.8	17 22.0	17 21.8	31 11.8
34 10.8	33 11.0	34 10.8	Sales/Receivables	12 31.4	31 11.8	35 10.4	31 11.6	32 11.5	43 8.6
51 7.1	48 7.7	46 8.0		31 11.6	41 9.0	44 8.3	46 7.9	44 8.4	55 6.6
			Cost of Sales/Inventory						
			Cost of Sales/Payables						
5.3	5.7	5.7		2.8	3.4	4.2	8.2	4.4	7.6
11.3	11.6	11.7	Sales/Working Capital	17.7	9.5	9.0	15.0	11.4	10.5
39.8	30.0	47.8		-8.1	-97.6	29.2	-94.7	39.5	36.7
6.2	9.1	11.0		26.6	6.1	13.8	12.1	10.9	18.5
(174) 2.2	(185) 2.8	(187) 3.5	EBIT/Interest	(10) 2.8	(30) 1.3	(27) 3.0	(42) 3.4	(47) 4.7	(31) 7.8
-.3	.1	1.1		-1.2	-1.2	-.5	1.0	2.2	2.8
			Net Profit + Depr., Dep., Amort./Cur. Mat. L/T/D						
.5	.5	.5		.7	.6	.4	.6	.5	.5
1.0	.9	.9	Fixed/Worth	1.3	1.0	1.0	1.0	.8	.9
1.5	1.4	1.5		UND	1.7	1.5	2.0	1.3	1.6
.4	.4	.5		.5	.6	.2	.5	.4	.7
.8	.8	.9	Debt/Worth	1.4	1.0	.9	.8	.6	1.6
1.9	1.7	2.0		UND	2.0	1.6	2.6	1.5	2.5
14.8	18.5	15.2		41.7	8.6	17.8	15.5	12.1	27.3
(210) 4.7	(233) 4.7	(216) 6.7	% Profit Before Taxes/Tangible Net Worth	(12) 4.8	(32) .9	(41) 8.1	(57) 4.3	(41) 7.0	10.6
-3.8	-2.9	.6		-1.6	-5.2	-4.5	-.2	2.5	5.9
7.4	9.6	8.1		12.9	5.3	9.1	9.4	6.8	8.2
2.4	3.2	3.4	% Profit Before Taxes/Total Assets	2.5	.5	3.8	2.4	4.1	4.8
-2.5	-1.4	.3		-1.3	-1.9	-2.6	-.1	1.4	2.2
8.9	8.7	9.9		9.6	15.7	14.4	16.0	8.1	10.1
3.9	3.5	3.8	Sales/Net Fixed Assets	2.8	3.5	2.5	4.7	3.8	4.4
2.3	1.9	2.0		.4	1.3	1.5	2.1	2.4	2.6
2.4	2.4	2.7		2.4	2.6	2.3	3.3	2.2	2.6
1.8	1.6	1.5	Sales/Total Assets	1.3	1.2	1.3	2.1	1.6	1.8
1.1	1.0	1.1		.4	.6	.8	1.2	1.2	1.4
1.9	1.6	1.6		2.2	1.2	1.7	1.3	1.6	1.5
(201) 2.7	(218) 2.9	(215) 2.5	% Depr., Dep., Amort./Sales	(14) 5.4	(33) 2.3	(31) 3.0	(43) 2.4	(57) 2.5	(37) 2.2
4.1	4.3	4.1		10.9	4.3	4.8	3.9	3.4	3.5
2.8	2.1	4.1							
(25) 9.0	(25) 7.0	(23) 9.1	% Officers', Directors', Owners' Comp/Sales						
29.3	25.5	19.4							
5010836M	4518919M	4355786M	Net Sales ($)	10056M	66526M	130022M	333877M	947170M	2868135M
2340361M	2536540M	2660084M	Total Assets ($)	20088M	85766M	124390M	202715M	625237M	1601888M

© RMA 2005

M = $ thousand   MM = $ million
See Pages 11 through 21 for Explanation of Ratios and Data

Current Data Sorted By Assets

Comparative Historical Data

						Type of Statement		
8	8	30	9	1	1	Unqualified	36	32
1	3	4				Reviewed	8	6
30	16	8				Compiled	39	55
93	38	4	2		1	Tax Returns	57	41
29	17	20	2	2		Other	47	43

0-500M	79 (4/1-9/30/04) 500M-2MM	2-10MM	248 (10/1/04-3/31/05) 10-50MM	50-100MM	100-250MM		4/1/00- 3/31/01 ALL	4/1/01- 3/31/02 ALL
161	82	66	13	3	2	NUMBER OF STATEMENTS	187	177
%	%	%	%	%	%	ASSETS	%	%
24.3	14.1	15.0	17.3			Cash & Equivalents	16.1	18.2
7.2	8.4	12.1	11.2			Trade Receivables (net)	9.2	9.8
.6	.1	.1	.1			Inventory	.4	.8
2.4	1.6	2.8	1.3			All Other Current	3.6	4.1
34.5	24.2	30.1	29.9			Total Current	29.3	32.9
46.8	65.7	58.8	53.9			Fixed Assets (net)	57.5	51.4
7.0	4.9	2.1	10.2			Intangibles (net)	4.9	7.3
11.6	5.2	9.0	6.0			All Other Non-Current	8.3	8.3
100.0	100.0	100.0	100.0			Total	100.0	100.0
						LIABILITIES		
9.4	3.1	3.2	14.8			Notes Payable-Short Term	6.8	8.1
5.6	2.9	2.4	2.4			Cur. Mat.-L/T/D	3.7	4.4
4.5	3.6	7.1	7.4			Trade Payables	5.6	6.3
.3	.1	.5	.0			Income Taxes Payable	.1	.2
25.0	7.5	8.9	16.6			All Other Current	24.9	17.1
44.7	17.3	22.2	41.2			Total Current	41.0	36.1
36.7	50.7	34.1	25.6			Long-Term Debt	33.0	32.3
.0	.2	.1	.6			Deferred Taxes	.1	.1
19.9	4.1	5.7	43.6			All Other Non-Current	17.4	12.4
-1.3	27.7	37.9	-10.9			Net Worth	8.5	19.1
100.0	100.0	100.0	100.0			Total Liabilities & Net Worth	100.0	100.0
						INCOME DATA		
100.0	100.0	100.0	100.0			Net Sales	100.0	100.0
						Gross Profit		
92.7	86.5	92.9	94.9			Operating Expenses	93.7	92.5
7.3	13.5	7.1	5.1			Operating Profit	6.3	7.5
1.3	7.4	2.1	1.3			All Other Expenses (net)	2.8	3.5
6.0	6.0	5.0	3.8			Profit Before Taxes	3.5	4.0
						RATIOS		
3.0	2.2	2.3	1.4				2.5	2.5
1.1	1.1	1.4	1.2			Current	.9	1.1
.3	.4	.8	.4				.2	.3
2.8	2.1	2.2	1.4				2.3	2.1
(159) 1.0	1.0	1.2	.7			Quick	.7 (176)	.8
.3	.2	.4	.4				.2	.2
0 UND	0 UND	1 348.3	2 156.2				0 UND	0 UND
0 UND	0 UND	11 32.4	20 18.7			Sales/Receivables	3 132.5	3 108.8
5 80.3	16 23.1	31 11.6	34 10.7				17 22.0	18 20.5
						Cost of Sales/Inventory		
						Cost of Sales/Payables		
21.7	12.6	10.3	16.3				14.4	12.4
999.8	119.5	31.4	92.7			Sales/Working Capital	-234.3	234.4
-24.2	-16.3	-39.1	-20.8				-14.2	-20.7
10.3	6.3	7.6	7.0				6.7	6.9
(111) 3.9	(60) 2.3	(55) 3.1	(12) 3.9			EBIT/Interest	(136) 2.1	(122) 2.1
-1.0	1.2	1.2	1.1				.8	1.2
						Net Profit + Depr., Dep., Amort./Cur. Mat. L /T/D	8.5	12.1
							(15) 3.2	(19) 2.0
							1.7	.6
.5	1.2	.8	1.0				.8	.5
2.0	3.6	1.4	6.4			Fixed/Worth	2.0	1.5
-2.2	-115.8	3.9	-2.6				21.5	-41.4
.7	1.1	.8	1.2				.6	.5
3.0	3.3	1.7	6.4			Debt/Worth	2.8	2.6
-3.4	-121.8	6.2	-9.0				44.5	-29.9
115.4	66.5	33.9				% Profit Before Taxes/Tangible Net Worth	52.6	52.8
(97) 40.4	(60) 24.8	(63) 10.7					(146) 18.0	(128) 21.7
-.1	7.2	.5					3.0	5.5
51.3	13.3	9.8	9.3			% Profit Before Taxes/Total Assets	16.5	19.2
16.3	6.3	3.5	5.3				5.0	5.4
-5.7	.5	.0	.2				-.6	.2
48.5	9.4	11.2	21.4				15.8	19.6
16.6	1.6	3.0	4.3			Sales/Net Fixed Assets	5.3	7.1
5.5	.8	.9	2.5				1.4	2.0
9.1	2.6	3.3	5.0				5.2	5.4
5.5	1.2	1.6	1.8			Sales/Total Assets	2.4	2.7
2.6	.6	.7	.8				1.0	1.1
.9	1.9	1.3	1.3				1.3	.7
(117) 2.0	(71) 3.8	(57) 2.5	(10) 3.5			% Depr., Dep., Amort./Sales	(156) 2.5	(150) 2.0
3.4	8.8	5.3	5.4				4.1	3.6
2.6	2.2					% Officers', Directors', Owners' Comp/Sales	4.9	3.8
(81) 5.7	(29) 5.6						(69) 7.5	(67) 7.8
11.0	11.3						16.6	16.0
141308M	139460M	614271M	1608725M	266241M	1409587M	Net Sales ($)	1633386M	1855695M
29378M	86906M	277734M	310697M	250981M	338263M	Total Assets ($)	1045107M	1106025M

M = $ thousand   MM = $ million
See Pages 11 through 21 for Explanation of Ratios and Data

© RMA 2005

Comparative Historical Data | Current Data Sorted By Sales

			Type of Statement						
51	70	57	Unqualified	7	9	6	12	12	11
10	18	8	Reviewed	1	5		1	1	
51	82	54	Compiled	28	19	5	2		
89	106	138	Tax Returns	87	41	3	3	1	3
61	54	70	Other	29	20	5		8	3
4/1/02-3/31/03 ALL	4/1/03-3/31/04 ALL	4/1/04-3/31/05 ALL		79 (4/1-9/30/04)		248 (10/1/04-3/31/05)			
				0-1MM	1-3MM	3-5MM	5-10MM	10-25MM	25MM & OVER
262	330	327	**NUMBER OF STATEMENTS**	152	94	19	23	22	17
%	%	%	**ASSETS**	%	%	%	%	%	%
17.6	19.5	19.5	Cash & Equivalents	19.6	19.2	15.2	18.8	27.1	15.2
8.9	9.2	8.6	Trade Receivables (net)	5.1	8.6	14.6	15.2	18.2	11.7
.1	.2	.3	Inventory	.6	.2	.0	.0	.2	.0
4.0	4.0	2.2	All Other Current	1.6	2.1	5.8	3.9	2.6	1.3
30.6	32.8	30.6	Total Current	26.9	30.1	35.6	38.0	48.1	28.3
55.4	53.4	54.3	Fixed Assets (net)	58.4	52.9	53.7	52.7	36.7	51.5
5.9	4.2	5.9	Intangibles (net)	6.0	5.8	5.7	.8	7.6	10.4
8.0	9.6	9.2	All Other Non-Current	8.7	11.2	5.0	8.5	7.7	9.8
100.0	100.0	100.0	Total	100.0	100.0	100.0	100.0	100.0	100.0
			LIABILITIES						
8.2	6.4	6.7	Notes Payable-Short Term	7.7	5.9	4.7	2.8	4.8	11.8
6.5	3.9	4.1	Cur. Mat.-L/T/D	4.9	3.6	4.2	3.7	1.5	4.4
5.0	6.9	4.9	Trade Payables	3.7	2.5	7.4	8.3	14.5	8.7
.1	.1	.3	Income Taxes Payable	.3	.1	.6	.1	1.3	.0
20.7	16.7	16.8	All Other Current	18.4	14.1	31.1	10.1	13.5	15.2
40.5	34.0	32.7	Total Current	34.9	26.0	48.1	25.0	35.7	40.0
34.5	39.3	39.6	Long-Term Debt	42.3	44.0	45.1	26.6	17.2	31.2
.1	.1	.1	Deferred Taxes	.0	.2	.1	.4	.3	.1
15.4	9.1	13.8	All Other Non-Current	19.5	6.2	1.2	5.3	8.0	37.4
9.5	17.5	13.8	Net Worth	3.4	23.5	5.5	42.8	38.8	-8.6
100.0	100.0	100.0	Total Liabilities & Net Worth	100.0	100.0	100.0	100.0	100.0	100.0
			INCOME DATA						
100.0	100.0	100.0	Net Sales	100.0	100.0	100.0	100.0	100.0	100.0
			Gross Profit						
91.8	93.1	91.1	Operating Expenses	87.8	92.8	94.4	93.7	96.2	96.3
8.2	6.9	8.9	Operating Profit	12.2	7.2	5.6	6.3	3.8	3.7
3.6	2.5	3.2	All Other Expenses (net)	4.7	2.2	1.8	1.6	.5	1.4
4.6	4.4	5.8	Profit Before Taxes	7.5	5.0	3.9	4.7	3.3	2.2
			RATIOS						
2.2	2.7	2.5		2.8	3.3	2.3	2.2	2.0	1.4
.9	1.1	1.2	Current	.8	1.2	1.0	1.7	1.3	.7
.3	.4	.4		.3	.4	.5	1.2	1.0	.4
2.0	2.4	2.3		2.5	3.0	2.0	2.0	1.7	1.2
(260) .8	(329) 1.0	(325) 1.0	Quick	(151) .8	(93) 1.1	.8	1.5	1.2	.6
.2	.3	.3		.3	.3	.3	.9	.3	.3
0 UND	0 UND	0 UND		0 UND	0 UND	2 156.7	2 188.8	2 200.6	0 UND
2 187.0	1 302.6	0 999.8	Sales/Receivables	0 UND	0 UND	7 49.0	18 20.4	16 23.5	7 48.7
17 21.8	16 22.2	16 22.7		3 108.3	16 22.5	32 11.4	31 11.8	33 11.0	21 17.2
			Cost of Sales/Inventory						
			Cost of Sales/Payables						
16.9	12.9	16.2		20.4	15.6	10.4	10.2	12.4	56.2
-243.4	152.6	153.2	Sales/Working Capital	-175.2	119.5	209.2	18.7	30.1	-50.2
-13.5	-16.8	-24.8		-13.9	-33.9	-36.3	43.6	NM	-12.8
6.5	5.4	8.0		7.0	9.4	7.0	9.3	9.2	7.6
(184) 2.6	(231) 2.5	(242) 3.2	EBIT/Interest	(96) 2.8	(80) 3.4	(17) 2.3	(18) 5.1	(16) 3.7	(15) 4.7
1.1	1.1	.8		.2	1.2	-.2	1.1	-.1	1.0
5.0	4.1	5.7	Net Profit + Depr., Dep.,		7.8				
(22) 2.0	(24) 1.7	(26) 3.1	Amort./Cur. Mat. L/T/D	(11) 3.6					
1.4	.6	1.7			1.9				
.8	.7	.7		.7	.7	1.3	.7	.4	1.0
2.6	1.9	2.1	Fixed/Worth	3.0	1.9	6.6	1.1	1.1	6.0
-32.5	233.0	-22.1		-9.8	-15.0	-8.1	1.7	2.1	-4.0
.8	.8	.8		.8	.8	.9	.8	.8	1.6
3.7	2.9	2.9	Debt/Worth	3.6	2.5	6.4	1.3	2.1	7.0
-35.1	UND	-14.6		-9.9	-14.4	-26.4	3.2	10.5	-7.5
64.2	60.8	68.0	% Profit Before Taxes/Tangible	97.7	77.9	106.3	25.4	24.2	41.8
(191) 21.1	(248) 17.3	(231) 22.1	Net Worth	(97) 30.4	(69) 31.0	(13) 43.9	(21) 12.3	(19) 11.5	(12) 13.7
4.4	1.5	2.1		-.1	6.0	-4.2	.3	-6.4	.4
19.6	17.2	24.5	% Profit Before Taxes/Total	35.9	26.4	23.0	16.2	11.0	17.6
6.1	5.9	7.7	Assets	8.3	8.7	4.0	4.8	3.2	5.3
.1	.0	-.7		-2.4	1.4	-.7	.3	-2.8	.1
25.3	20.2	25.5		26.5	26.2	33.6	15.5	46.2	22.5
5.6	6.2	6.9	Sales/Net Fixed Assets	5.5	9.5	4.7	5.8	9.7	7.1
1.4	1.5	1.5		1.1	1.5	1.1	1.8	4.1	3.6
5.6	5.8	6.1		6.8	6.6	5.2	3.9	5.9	5.3
2.4	2.5	2.8	Sales/Total Assets	2.5	2.8	2.3	2.8	2.8	3.8
1.1	1.1	1.1		.9	1.1	1.1	1.3	1.9	2.1
1.3	1.3	1.2		1.5	1.1	.7	1.1	1.0	.7
(212) 2.5	(268) 2.7	(259) 2.5	% Depr., Dep., Amort./Sales	(114) 3.1	(78) 2.5	(15) 2.2	(21) 1.6	(17) 1.5	(14) 1.6
5.2	4.4	4.8		6.7	5.3	4.0	3.0	2.3	4.5
3.1	3.4	2.5	% Officers', Directors',	2.8	2.2				
(101) 5.8	(126) 6.1	(120) 5.6	Owners' Comp/Sales	(58) 6.9	(48) 4.7				
12.7	11.4	10.8		12.1	9.0				
3502292M	3749358M	4179592M	Net Sales ($)	79620M	162749M	70637M	164903M	350314M	3351369M
1410504M	1517220M	1293959M	Total Assets ($)	66160M	98929M	46429M	155057M	152673M	774711M

M = $ thousand   MM = $ million
See Pages 11 through 21 for Explanation of Ratios and Data

ARTS, ENTERTAINMENT, AND RECREATION

Current Data Sorted By Assets   Comparative Historical Data

0-500M	500M-2MM	2-10MM	10-50MM	50-100MM	100-250MM	Type of Statement	4/1/00-3/31/01 ALL	4/1/01-3/31/02 ALL
8	5	20	20	5	3	Unqualified	58	47
4	10	9	4			Reviewed	6	9
17	18	11				Compiled	13	12
43	21	4			1	Tax Returns	11	10
26	18	21	10		1	Other	28	27
\<— 85 (4/1-9/30/04) —\>			194 (10/1/04-3/31/05)					
98	72	65	34	6	4	**NUMBER OF STATEMENTS**	116	105
%	%	%	%	%	%	**ASSETS**	%	%
15.5	14.4	12.7	17.8			Cash & Equivalents	18.6	16.1
3.6	5.0	4.0	2.9			Trade Receivables (net)	11.4	11.5
7.5	3.4	3.5	1.1			Inventory	2.9	3.3
2.2	2.3	3.6	2.5			All Other Current	5.0	6.7
28.8	25.1	23.8	24.3			Total Current	38.0	37.6
50.3	55.6	57.0	55.3			Fixed Assets (net)	39.7	40.2
6.8	6.0	4.1	5.0			Intangibles (net)	5.5	5.6
14.0	13.4	15.2	15.4			All Other Non-Current	16.8	16.6
100.0	100.0	100.0	100.0			Total	100.0	100.0
						LIABILITIES		
5.1	5.7	4.2	3.3			Notes Payable-Short Term	9.3	15.1
9.0	4.7	3.2	2.1			Cur. Mat.-L/T/D	2.4	3.9
16.9	9.7	5.9	5.4			Trade Payables	8.4	8.1
.2	.1	.1	.3			Income Taxes Payable	.2	.6
21.1	9.7	14.7	12.5			All Other Current	16.2	17.3
52.3	29.9	28.0	23.6			Total Current	36.5	45.0
35.3	31.2	31.1	26.4			Long-Term Debt	13.5	14.2
.0	.1	.0	.1			Deferred Taxes	.4	.0
13.6	7.9	5.6	2.5			All Other Non-Current	6.0	7.3
-1.3	30.9	35.2	47.5			Net Worth	43.6	33.4
100.0	100.0	100.0	100.0			Total Liabilities & Net Worth	100.0	100.0
						INCOME DATA		
100.0	100.0	100.0	100.0			Net Sales	100.0	100.0
						Gross Profit		
95.4	89.5	95.5	93.1			Operating Expenses	105.4	97.0
4.6	10.5	4.5	6.9			Operating Profit	-5.4	3.0
1.2	3.7	1.2	1.3			All Other Expenses (net)	-15.3	2.6
3.4	6.7	3.3	5.5			Profit Before Taxes	9.9	.4
						RATIOS		
2.6	1.4	1.7	1.7			Current	4.6	2.5
.9	.9	.7	1.0				1.3	1.1
.3	.4	.4	.4				.6	.5
2.2	1.1	1.5	1.2			Quick	3.3	1.7
(93) .4	(71) .6	.5	.7				1.1	.7
.1	.2	.2	.2				.3	.3
0 UND	0 UND	0 UND	0 UND			Sales/Receivables	1 403.7	0 UND
0 UND	0 999.8	1 310.1	2 195.3				12 30.5	10 37.8
1 296.9	4 98.0	11 33.0	13 27.6				45 8.0	35 10.5
						Cost of Sales/Inventory		
						Cost of Sales/Payables		
23.7	40.8	12.0	15.2			Sales/Working Capital	3.1	5.4
UND	-105.2	-59.2	-99.1				19.4	30.8
-17.3	-18.8	-15.6	-13.9				-16.6	-9.4
13.5	11.1	8.7	9.7			EBIT/Interest	13.3	7.5
(74) 2.8	(55) 3.6	(52) 3.3	(23) 5.5				(74) 3.8	(75) 1.0
-.1	.5	-1.9	1.7				.2	-5.3
		5.8	160.6			Net Profit + Depr., Dep.,		
	(13)	3.1	(10) 2.0			Amort./Cur. Mat. L/T/D		
		1.4	.8					
.7	.9	.8	.5			Fixed/Worth	.3	.4
5.4	1.5	1.3	1.4				.8	.9
-1.5	18.0	5.7	3.4				2.5	3.6
.8	.5	.5	.2			Debt/Worth	.2	.4
11.0	1.3	1.9	1.7				.9	1.0
-2.9	17.8	7.2	4.0				3.3	6.0
95.6	68.0	41.5	62.7			% Profit Before Taxes/Tangible	39.3	31.6
(54) 45.8	(57) 18.5	(53) 9.1	(31) 22.5			Net Worth	(97) 13.6	(84) 7.5
10.9	2.8	-2.8	.8				2.7	-11.1
22.0	17.9	14.2	15.4			% Profit Before Taxes/Total	15.5	14.6
6.8	8.2	4.4	5.4			Assets	7.4	1.7
-10.7	-.4	-2.2	.6				.2	-10.8
27.0	11.1	6.2	4.7			Sales/Net Fixed Assets	19.5	23.2
9.6	5.3	3.3	3.2				3.9	6.9
4.1	2.6	1.2	1.5				1.2	1.3
7.6	4.4	2.9	2.6			Sales/Total Assets	2.7	3.0
3.8	2.7	2.0	1.4				1.3	1.4
2.4	1.6	.7	.4				.5	.6
1.1	1.4	2.1	2.3			% Depr., Dep., Amort./Sales	1.3	.9
(76) 2.2	(65) 2.7	(58) 3.7	(33) 3.3				(97) 3.2	(88) 2.6
4.2	4.5	5.9	4.5				6.7	5.2
3.4	2.2	1.0				% Officers', Directors',	6.8	3.4
(49) 5.4	(35) 3.8	(21) 2.2				Owners' Comp/Sales	(24) 8.1	(21) 9.1
9.0	6.6	6.9					13.0	14.1
90888M	218128M	664616M	1314389M	299518M	1290677M	Net Sales ($)	1196931M	1100073M
21619M	74627M	322937M	827958M	372069M	773266M	Total Assets ($)	1741134M	1301663M

M = $ thousand   MM = $ million
See Pages 11 through 21 for Explanation of Ratios and Data

Comparative Historical Data | Current Data Sorted By Sales

Hist 1	Hist 2	Hist 3	Type of Statement	0-1MM	1-3MM	3-5MM	5-10MM	10-25MM	25MM & OVER
57	60	61	Unqualified	11	8	7	8	9	18
16	21	27	Reviewed	3	6	5	1	10	2
31	56	46	Compiled	18	18	3	4	3	
38	40	69	Tax Returns	31	25	7	4	1	1
63	64	76	Other	15	18	12	14	7	10
4/1/02-3/31/03 ALL	4/1/03-3/31/04 ALL	4/1/04-3/31/05 ALL		85 (4/1-9/30/04)			194 (10/1/04-3/31/05)		
205	241	279	**NUMBER OF STATEMENTS**	78	75	34	31	30	31
%	%	%	**ASSETS**	%	%	%	%	%	%
16.4	15.4	14.6	Cash & Equivalents	14.7	12.9	14.1	18.2	13.1	16.6
6.2	5.8	3.9	Trade Receivables (net)	1.6	5.0	5.2	6.0	4.9	2.5
3.8	3.2	4.5	Inventory	5.2	5.3	4.4	1.9	5.8	2.5
5.4	5.6	2.6	All Other Current	1.5	2.5	1.6	4.9	4.4	2.2
31.9	30.0	25.5	Total Current	23.0	25.8	25.2	31.0	28.3	23.8
48.1	50.3	54.1	Fixed Assets (net)	57.4	52.9	59.6	47.3	47.4	56.5
6.3	4.7	5.8	Intangibles (net)	4.9	7.3	3.6	5.5	4.5	8.7
13.7	15.0	14.5	All Other Non-Current	14.7	14.0	11.6	16.2	19.9	11.0
100.0	100.0	100.0	Total	100.0	100.0	100.0	100.0	100.0	100.0
			LIABILITIES						
18.9	15.4	4.7	Notes Payable-Short Term	4.3	4.7	4.7	7.9	3.9	3.4
6.4	5.2	5.6	Cur. Mat.-L/T/D	4.9	8.8	5.3	3.0	3.4	4.6
8.9	6.6	10.7	Trade Payables	7.0	17.6	10.1	9.4	6.7	9.1
.4	.1	.2	Income Taxes Payable	.1	.2	.0	.1	.1	.8
17.8	14.9	15.1	All Other Current	17.5	13.2	9.4	17.6	17.2	15.1
52.4	42.2	36.3	Total Current	33.8	44.5	29.5	38.0	31.2	33.0
23.1	26.8	31.8	Long-Term Debt	44.5	25.2	30.0	24.9	21.4	34.7
.0	.1	.1	Deferred Taxes	.1	.1	.0	.0	.0	.3
7.6	7.8	8.9	All Other Non-Current	10.8	10.3	11.7	3.1	4.6	7.7
16.8	23.0	23.0	Net Worth	10.8	19.9	28.8	34.0	42.8	24.3
100.0	100.0	100.0	Total Liabilities & Net Worth	100.0	100.0	100.0	100.0	100.0	100.0
			INCOME DATA						
100.0	100.0	100.0	Net Sales	100.0	100.0	100.0	100.0	100.0	100.0
			Gross Profit						
95.5	95.2	93.4	Operating Expenses	87.8	96.1	96.8	94.8	95.6	93.4
4.5	4.8	6.6	Operating Profit	12.2	3.9	3.2	5.2	4.4	6.6
1.4	1.6	1.9	All Other Expenses (net)	4.9	.6	1.7	-1.1	.6	1.6
3.1	3.2	4.7	Profit Before Taxes	7.2	3.2	1.5	6.3	3.9	5.0
			RATIOS						
1.7	2.0	1.7		3.1	1.7	1.9	1.7	1.9	1.1
.7	1.0	.9	Current	1.0	.7	1.1	.8	.9	.8
.4	.3	.3		.3	.4	.3	.4	.3	.4
1.3	1.5	1.5		2.7	1.1	1.6	1.5	1.3	1.0
.4 (238)	.7 (273)	.5	Quick	(73) .9	(74) .5	.9	.5	.5	.5
.2	.2	.2		.2	.2	.2	.2	.2	.2
0 UND	0 UND	0 UND		0 UND	0 UND	0 UND	0 999.8	0 UND	0 UND
1 412.4	1 420.2	0 999.8	Sales/Receivables	0 UND	0 UND	1 290.7	2 177.1	1 391.0	1 482.6
12 29.9	14 25.8	4 87.1		0 UND	5 80.2	16 23.2	15 24.1	7 49.0	4 83.9
			Cost of Sales/Inventory						
			Cost of Sales/Payables						
12.8	11.3	21.5		11.0	45.1	11.1	16.7	10.5	95.5
-32.4	999.8	-78.6	Sales/Working Capital	653.0	-35.0	227.6	-62.1	-61.2	-57.3
-11.4	-10.7	-15.8		-19.7	-13.9	-14.0	-18.4	-16.9	-12.3
7.1	6.7	9.4		6.6	16.7	9.4	17.7	8.1	9.0
(150) 2.2	(178) 1.8	(213) 3.4	EBIT/Interest	(52) 2.4	(62) 3.2	(25) 3.5	(22) 3.5	(25) 4.6	(27) 5.5
.2	-.3	.5		.0	-.1	-2.1	-2.1	2.3	1.6
4.3	6.7	4.4	Net Profit + Depr., Dep.,					3.8	5.5
(19) 1.5	(26) 3.0	(35) 2.4	Amort./Cur. Mat. L/T/D				(10) 2.4	(13) 2.5	
.3	1.0	1.0						1.2	1.0
.5	.5	.7		.9	.8	.9	.5	.4	1.5
1.5	1.4	1.7	Fixed/Worth	3.8	1.7	1.9	1.2	1.2	2.9
-12.2	9.4	-49.8		-2.5	-11.0	-13.1	3.7	2.5	25.4
.5	.5	.5		.6	.4	.5	.5	.6	1.7
1.6	1.5	2.5	Debt/Worth	7.4	1.9	2.1	1.0	1.9	3.3
-11.2	16.3	-21.3		-4.0	-12.1	-15.9	5.9	3.6	31.7
47.8	43.7	66.2	% Profit Before Taxes/Tangible	83.7	65.3	58.9	59.1	46.0	80.3
(147) 8.1	(187) 9.4	(203) 21.2	Net Worth	(46) 29.4	(55) 18.5	(25) 14.3	(25) 9.0	(27) 14.1	(25) 58.2
-4.1	-1.5	1.4		-1.6	3.1	-1.0	-6.6	.1	12.8
14.5	13.4	17.0	% Profit Before Taxes/Total	17.3	19.2	14.3	25.1	14.2	20.6
4.0	3.1	6.2	Assets	6.1	6.4	4.6	5.8	5.6	9.0
-3.7	-4.4	-1.1		-3.3	-1.8	-6.1	-2.0	.0	2.4
14.6	13.7	11.7		12.2	19.6	9.5	11.3	10.2	7.8
6.4	4.7	4.6	Sales/Net Fixed Assets	4.0	6.2	3.7	4.2	3.9	3.6
1.9	1.8	2.2		1.0	3.8	1.8	2.2	2.3	1.9
4.7	3.6	4.5		3.4	6.3	5.1	3.8	3.6	3.2
2.3	1.8	2.6	Sales/Total Assets	1.8	3.2	2.6	2.3	2.4	2.4
.9	.8	1.2		.7	2.0	1.1	1.0	1.3	1.3
1.4	1.6	1.6		1.8	1.2	1.8	1.8	1.9	2.0
(174) 3.0	(200) 3.0	(238) 2.8	% Depr., Dep., Amort./Sales	(60) 4.2	(64) 2.3	(31) 3.6	(30) 2.5	(27) 2.7	(26) 3.1
5.5	5.7	4.6		9.1	4.2	4.6	4.3	4.0	4.0
2.3	2.9	2.2	% Officers', Directors',	3.6	2.5	.7	1.8	2.1	
(56) 3.7	(79) 5.6	(111) 4.6	Owners' Comp/Sales	(31) 5.4	(36) 4.4	(15) 5.6	(12) 2.8	(13) 2.4	
9.1	10.9	8.2		9.8	7.1	20.0	3.5	15.9	
3430241M	2553264M	3878216M	Net Sales ($)	39263M	127239M	134261M	216071M	508244M	2853138M
2531480M	2635071M	2392476M	Total Assets ($)	47384M	70402M	130140M	226325M	355963M	1562262M

M = $ thousand   MM = $ million
See Pages 11 through 21 for Explanation of Ratios and Data

Current Data Sorted By Assets   Comparative Historical Data

0-500M	500M-2MM	2-10MM	10-50MM	50-100MM	100-250MM	Type of Statement	4/1/00-3/31/01 ALL	4/1/01-3/31/02 ALL
1	6	8	3	2	3	Unqualified	20	14
1	1			1		Reviewed	1	
2	2	1		1		Compiled	9	9
4	3	1				Tax Returns	2	4
4		2	4	1		Other	11	8
	32 (4/1-9/30/04)			19 (10/1/04-3/31/05)				
12	12	12	7	5	3	**NUMBER OF STATEMENTS**	43	35
%	%	%	%	%	%	**ASSETS**	%	%
34.9	21.5	35.2				Cash & Equivalents	18.2	16.8
22.4	17.5	8.5				Trade Receivables (net)	13.1	9.2
14.4	6.7	2.4				Inventory	5.3	1.2
2.6	4.3	4.3				All Other Current	4.1	8.1
74.4	50.1	50.5				Total Current	40.7	35.3
23.3	28.7	20.8				Fixed Assets (net)	29.5	28.9
.6	1.5	1.0				Intangibles (net)	1.4	7.8
1.7	19.7	27.8				All Other Non-Current	28.4	28.1
100.0	100.0	100.0				Total	100.0	100.0
						LIABILITIES		
5.8	12.5	22.2				Notes Payable-Short Term	16.0	7.1
.9	3.5	.7				Cur. Mat.-L/T/D	1.2	4.0
26.8	8.1	3.5				Trade Payables	14.3	15.8
.0	5.9	.0				Income Taxes Payable	.2	.0
31.6	15.1	7.4				All Other Current	15.2	10.1
65.1	45.1	33.8				Total Current	46.9	37.0
5.6	11.9	16.5				Long-Term Debt	15.6	18.8
.0	.1	.0				Deferred Taxes	1.5	1.7
3.1	5.1	13.1				All Other Non-Current	4.8	20.8
26.1	37.8	36.6				Net Worth	31.2	21.7
100.0	100.0	100.0				Total Liabilities & Net Worth	100.0	100.0
						INCOME DATA		
100.0	100.0	100.0				Net Sales	100.0	100.0
						Gross Profit		
93.0	97.2	97.3				Operating Expenses	102.7	88.4
7.0	2.8	2.7				Operating Profit	-2.7	11.6
.8	.8	-3.2				All Other Expenses (net)	-17.4	2.3
6.3	2.0	5.9				Profit Before Taxes	14.7	9.2
						RATIOS		
6.8	2.9	9.7				Current	2.6	2.1
2.1	1.1	2.0					1.3	1.3
.6	.4	.6					.8	.4
4.7	2.6	9.1				Quick	2.1	1.9
1.4	.9	1.9					.9	.9
.5	.4	.5					.3	.3
0 UND	6 60.5	1 350.6				Sales/Receivables	3 120.8	0 UND
4 86.0	18 20.2	9 38.9					24 15.0	8 47.3
21 17.0	76 4.8	44 8.3					77 4.7	26 14.1
						Cost of Sales/Inventory		
						Cost of Sales/Payables		
6.8	3.5	1.7				Sales/Working Capital	4.5	8.4
36.1	NM	5.5					8.7	32.6
-68.4	-7.3	-9.9					-12.2	-10.2
						EBIT/Interest	14.7 (23)	6.8 (18)
							4.8	-.1
							1.7	-10.0
						Net Profit + Depr., Dep., Amort./Cur. Mat. L /T/D		
.0	.0	.0				Fixed/Worth	.1	.1
.3	.3	.5					.4	.8
3.7	NM	UND					1.5	-1.4
.3	.5	.2				Debt/Worth	.1	.2
1.1	1.0	.6					.4	.9
NM	NM	UND					6.1	-3.3
		27.7				% Profit Before Taxes/Tangible Net Worth	74.3 (39)	36.5 (24)
	(10) 1.3						16.3	10.6
		-7.3					2.3	-2.4
80.0	21.6	9.7				% Profit Before Taxes/Total Assets	17.9	13.7
16.0	1.7	2.0					10.2	3.7
-37.0	-6.4	-4.2					1.2	-6.5
UND	86.7	32.0				Sales/Net Fixed Assets	40.0	82.8
123.9	30.8	19.4					5.9	29.6
9.4	2.8	3.1					1.6	2.6
20.0	2.3	1.7				Sales/Total Assets	2.7	4.8
5.3	1.7	1.0					1.0	1.3
2.5	.9	.4					.4	.5
	.4	.6				% Depr., Dep., Amort./Sales	.4 (37)	.4 (28)
	(11) 1.0	1.0					1.5	.8
	9.5	1.5					5.0	2.2
						% Officers', Directors', Owners' Comp/Sales	2.7 (11)	
							6.3	
							9.4	
17793M	34130M	79304M	110400M	138494M	107040M	Net Sales ($)	637858M	369029M
1950M	16740M	65551M	194723M	311623M	546201M	Total Assets ($)	1183431M	708052M

© RMA 2005

M = $ thousand   MM = $ million

See Pages 11 through 21 for Explanation of Ratios and Data

Comparative Historical Data				Current Data Sorted By Sales					
Type of Statement									
30	28	23	Unqualified	4	4	4	6	2	3
	1	3	Reviewed	1		1			1
12	10	6	Compiled		2	2	1	1	
5	9	8	Tax Returns	5		1	1	1	
26	15	11	Other	2	1	3	1	3	1
4/1/02-3/31/03 ALL	4/1/03-3/31/04 ALL	4/1/04-3/31/05 ALL		32 (4/1-9/30/04)			19 (10/1/04-3/31/05)		
				0-1MM	1-3MM	3-5MM	5-10MM	10-25MM	25MM & OVER
73	63	51	**NUMBER OF STATEMENTS**	12	7	11	9	7	5
%	%	%	**ASSETS**	%	%	%	%	%	%
23.5	26.1	22.7	Cash & Equivalents	45.5		36.1			
13.3	10.3	15.6	Trade Receivables (net)	4.6		18.2			
1.6	4.4	5.9	Inventory	11.8		8.8			
4.7	6.3	6.7	All Other Current	3.4		4.8			
43.1	47.1	50.9	Total Current	65.3		68.0			
27.1	21.8	27.0	Fixed Assets (net)	32.9		25.9			
3.4	4.0	1.7	Intangibles (net)	.1		1.4			
26.4	27.1	20.5	All Other Non-Current	1.7		4.8			
100.0	100.0	100.0	Total	100.0		100.0			
			LIABILITIES						
19.8	17.9	11.3	Notes Payable-Short Term	4.2		7.5			
3.3	2.5	1.5	Cur. Mat.-L/T/D	1.7		2.7			
9.5	10.7	11.4	Trade Payables	25.8		8.6			
.9	1.3	1.4	Income Taxes Payable	.0		1.0			
16.7	30.3	14.7	All Other Current	9.4		29.2			
50.2	62.8	40.4	Total Current	41.1		48.9			
9.7	19.6	15.3	Long-Term Debt	10.5		16.0			
.0	.1	.0	Deferred Taxes	.0		.1			
7.3	12.6	6.0	All Other Non-Current	6.9		1.9			
32.8	4.9	38.2	Net Worth	41.5		33.1			
100.0	100.0	100.0	Total Liabilities & Net Worth	100.0		100.0			
			INCOME DATA						
100.0	100.0	100.0	Net Sales	100.0		100.0			
			Gross Profit						
92.4	91.8	93.2	Operating Expenses	104.7		88.2			
7.6	8.2	6.8	Operating Profit	-4.7		11.8			
2.4	.8	.9	All Other Expenses (net)	-.2		.9			
5.2	7.3	5.9	Profit Before Taxes	-4.4		10.9			
			RATIOS						
2.9	3.5	5.2	Current	10.6		2.9			
1.3	1.3	1.4		6.0		2.4			
.6	.4	.7		1.3		.6			
2.8	2.3	2.7	Quick	9.5		2.7			
(72) 1.0	(62) .9	1.0		3.4		1.7			
.5	.2	.5		1.0		.6			
1 328.2	0 UND	2 232.0	Sales/Receivables	0 UND		2 232.0			
11 32.5	9 42.1	15 24.6		7 55.3		7 55.0			
38 9.6	52 7.0	50 7.3		21 17.0		48 7.7			
			Cost of Sales/Inventory						
			Cost of Sales/Payables						
5.7	3.9	4.0	Sales/Working Capital	.8		3.6			
41.1	80.7	14.3		5.6		6.0			
-16.2	-10.3	-21.2		111.3		-143.6			
15.8	28.6	21.7	EBIT/Interest						
(37) 1.9	(36) 9.1	(29) 2.0							
-8.9	.4	-4.6							
			Net Profit + Depr., Dep., Amort./Cur. Mat. L/T/D						
.0	.0	.0	Fixed/Worth	.0		.0			
.4	.3	.3		.1		1.0			
1.4	4.8	4.6		1.2		-2.2			
.2	.4	.4	Debt/Worth	.2		.5			
.8	1.0	1.0		.7		1.1			
4.9	-10.1	6.0		1.6		-4.6			
70.1	48.8	40.8	% Profit Before Taxes/Tangible Net Worth	8.4		33.6			
(63) 16.3	(47) 21.1	(42) 6.8		(11) -1.9					
-7.6	-3.0	-6.4		-8.2					
25.9	28.8	11.0	% Profit Before Taxes/Total Assets	5.7		33.6			
6.0	7.1	3.8		-1.5		4.8			
-4.9	-4.9	-4.2		-19.0		-5.4			
93.9	327.3	91.7	Sales/Net Fixed Assets	198.1		448.2			
14.5	40.9	21.0		32.9		81.1			
1.8	4.5	2.8		3.1		3.1			
4.3	4.6	3.8	Sales/Total Assets	4.8		24.2			
1.4	1.8	1.3		1.8		2.3			
.5	.6	.4		.4		1.1			
.7	.3	.6	% Depr., Dep., Amort./Sales	.5					
(51) 1.7	(42) 1.0	(40) 1.3		(10) 1.5					
4.7	5.0	2.7		2.4					
4.7	8.4	4.4	% Officers', Directors', Owners' Comp/Sales						
(15) 11.9	(12) 10.5	(11) 8.1							
24.0	19.0	20.8							
721469M	738471M	487161M	Net Sales ($)	6320M	12962M	45921M	70262M	114574M	237122M
1341490M	1037189M	1136788M	Total Assets ($)	10684M	14714M	46201M	208050M	357770M	499369M

© RMA 2005

M = $ thousand   MM = $ million
See Pages 11 through 21 for Explanation of Ratios and Data

Current Data Sorted By Assets   Comparative Historical Data

Type of Statement	0-500M	500M-2MM	2-10MM	10-50MM	50-100MM	100-250MM		
Unqualified	1	3	4	9	13	23	31	36
Reviewed		1	5	1			4	7
Compiled	3	3	3				12	14
Tax Returns	4	4	1				4	3
Other	3	8	5	8	4	7	30	20
		47 (4/1-9/30/04)		66 (10/1/04-3/31/05)			4/1/00- 3/31/01 ALL	4/1/01- 3/31/02 ALL
NUMBER OF STATEMENTS	11	19	18	18	17	30	81	80

ASSETS	%	%	%	%	%	%	%	%
Cash & Equivalents	15.6	16.5	10.3	9.7	8.4	12.8	13.9	10.8
Trade Receivables (net)	14.0	9.4	4.8	12.6	17.8	7.9	12.0	10.6
Inventory	5.4	1.0	1.4	.8	.5	.4	1.6	1.1
All Other Current	.3	4.4	.9	8.1	1.7	2.5	4.2	4.0
Total Current	35.3	31.2	17.5	31.3	28.4	23.5	31.8	26.4
Fixed Assets (net)	45.2	32.6	37.2	31.7	19.5	30.7	21.5	30.1
Intangibles (net)	5.6	18.6	30.3	18.6	35.2	24.0	27.4	24.4
All Other Non-Current	13.8	17.6	15.0	18.4	17.0	21.8	19.3	19.1
Total	100.0	100.0	100.0	100.0	100.0	100.0	100.0	100.0

LIABILITIES								
Notes Payable-Short Term	50.9	18.4	7.8	9.1	7.2	3.5	13.9	10.9
Cur. Mat.-L/T/D	.0	2.4	3.6	3.7	1.3	6.2	4.4	4.7
Trade Payables	5.2	9.8	2.4	7.9	4.3	4.8	8.4	7.2
Income Taxes Payable	.3	.0	.1	.3	.0	.1	1.2	1.2
All Other Current	20.7	16.0	9.0	42.0	25.9	16.3	25.0	17.8
Total Current	77.1	46.5	22.9	63.0	38.7	30.9	52.9	41.8
Long-Term Debt	34.5	21.2	24.9	54.7	49.0	46.8	32.7	38.7
Deferred Taxes	.0	.0	.3	.0	.0	.5	.1	.3
All Other Non-Current	30.6	8.8	7.6	35.1	27.1	22.5	22.3	21.3
Net Worth	-42.3	23.4	44.4	-52.8	-14.8	-.7	-8.1	-2.2
Total Liabilities & Net Worth	100.0	100.0	100.0	100.0	100.0	100.0	100.0	100.0

INCOME DATA								
Net Sales	100.0	100.0	100.0	100.0	100.0	100.0	100.0	100.0
Gross Profit								
Operating Expenses	94.1	96.9	92.7	106.3	95.2	93.0	97.8	95.8
Operating Profit	5.9	3.1	7.3	-6.3	4.8	7.0	2.2	4.2
All Other Expenses (net)	.5	.9	2.3	.3	.8	5.4	3.9	6.1
Profit Before Taxes	5.4	2.2	5.0	-6.6	4.0	1.6	-1.6	-1.9

RATIOS								
Current	2.3	2.8	2.7	1.5	1.4	1.5	1.4	1.3
	1.1	.4	.9	.6	1.0	1.1	.5	.6
	.3	.2	.3	.3	.5	.3	.3	.3
Quick	2.0	2.1	2.5	1.1	1.4	1.3	1.1	1.0
	.4	.4	.7	.5	.9	.8	.4	.4
	.2	.2	.2	.2	.4	.3	.2	.2
Sales/Receivables	0 UND	0 UND	2 221.3	8 45.8	17 21.9	11 34.4	8 48.0	5 73.0
	10 35.5	10 36.4	15 24.4	11 32.5	44 8.4	34 10.6	23 15.7	17 22.1
	23 15.7	27 13.5	45 8.0	37 10.0	98 3.7	62 5.9	50 7.3	46 7.9
Cost of Sales/Inventory								
Cost of Sales/Payables								
Sales/Working Capital	19.3	6.5	5.3	9.4	11.6	9.6	27.5	19.4
	77.7	-25.9	-26.6	-8.4	-66.7	60.7	-5.7	-10.4
	-11.7	-3.4	-5.3	-2.9	-4.1	-3.9	-2.9	-3.3
EBIT/Interest		2.5	6.7	3.8	3.2	4.2	3.7	2.0
	(13) -8.2	(13) 1.7	1.1	.5	(24) 1.8		(64) .3	(62) .1
		-37.5	.2	-11.5	-5.0	-.2	-1.9	-3.6
Net Profit + Depr., Dep., Amort./Cur. Mat. L /T/D								
Fixed/Worth	.8	.6	.4	1.0	-1.3	2.9	.9	.7
	-10.6	5.3	16.2	-.5	-.1	-1.3	-1.4	5.6
	-.1	-.1	-.6	-.1	.0	-.3	-.1	-.1
Debt/Worth	.6	.3	.7	1.0	-4.0	9.5	2.3	2.0
	-12.8	8.9	42.3	-6.1	-2.1	-4.8	-3.2	-12.3
	-2.1	-1.9	-2.0	-1.5	-1.5	-2.3	-1.6	-1.6
% Profit Before Taxes/Tangible Net Worth		98.6	54.6			47.9	68.7	52.1
	(12) 15.3	(11) 22.7			(11) 19.5		(32) 16.6	(39) 10.6
		-4.0	.2			-6.3	.0	-10.0
% Profit Before Taxes/Total Assets	92.9	11.1	19.1	9.8	9.5	6.2	7.8	5.1
	27.0	-2.6	2.4	-.9	-2.2	2.7	-.3	-3.6
	-12.8	-17.7	-2.3	-21.2	-7.8	-3.8	-10.5	-15.1
Sales/Net Fixed Assets	36.0	109.3	11.2	30.5	78.2	11.1	39.5	33.9
	27.7	16.1	4.3	10.3	21.8	2.7	13.9	10.9
	19.1	1.8	.9	.4	2.6	1.2	4.3	1.9
Sales/Total Assets	15.9	4.1	.9	2.3	1.3	.9	1.8	1.9
	5.7	2.0	.7	1.1	1.1	.7	1.1	.9
	2.9	.6	.4	.3	.7	.5	.5	.5
% Depr., Dep., Amort./Sales		1.7	2.5	1.1	1.2	2.3	1.1	.5
	(12) 3.2	(14) 6.6	(15) 2.3	(12) 3.1	(17) 2.9	2.9	(46) 2.4	(52) 2.3
		6.1	9.8	13.5	8.0	11.7	5.9	9.9
% Officers', Directors', Owners' Comp/Sales								4.8	1.1
							(15) 9.9	(10) 4.7
							21.8	7.1
Net Sales ($)	14028M	51625M	89836M	954682M	1255878M	3285679M	3762115M	3515934M
Total Assets ($)	2326M	21171M	88507M	589171M	1249509M	4932334M	4102455M	4256737M

M = $ thousand   MM = $ million
See Pages 11 through 21 for Explanation of Ratios and Data

Comparative Historical Data				Current Data Sorted By Sales					

			Type of Statement						
39	38	53	Unqualified	2	3	2	3	3	40
6	8	7	Reviewed		3		3		1
8	11	9	Compiled	3	5	1			
4	8	9	Tax Returns	3	4	1	1		
35	33	35	Other	5		4	5	3	13
4/1/02-3/31/03 ALL	4/1/03-3/31/04 ALL	4/1/04-3/31/05 ALL		47 (4/1-9/30/04)			66 (10/1/04-3/31/05)		
				0-1MM	1-3MM	3-5MM	5-10MM	10-25MM	25MM & OVER
92	98	113	NUMBER OF STATEMENTS	13	20	8	12	6	54
%	%	%	ASSETS	%	%	%	%	%	%
15.9	10.4	12.1	Cash & Equivalents	17.7	7.9		23.5		10.7
9.1	11.5	10.5	Trade Receivables (net)	7.2	6.2		7.3		13.7
1.3	1.3	1.2	Inventory	1.3	3.0		.4		.6
5.3	5.9	3.1	All Other Current	.2	4.3		1.2		3.9
31.6	29.0	27.0	Total Current	26.4	21.4		32.4		28.9
30.9	30.8	32.0	Fixed Assets (net)	56.0	34.4		30.3		22.7
21.0	23.0	23.1	Intangibles (net)	12.8	25.5		23.0		27.1
16.5	17.2	18.0	All Other Non-Current	4.8	18.7		14.3		21.3
100.0	100.0	100.0	Total	100.0	100.0		100.0		100.0
			LIABILITIES						
6.5	10.0	12.7	Notes Payable-Short Term	17.3	32.5		4.0		7.0
4.6	3.2	3.4	Cur. Mat.-L/T/D	2.0	3.3		2.2		4.8
8.2	5.9	5.7	Trade Payables	3.4	6.2		4.8		6.4
.9	.1	.1	Income Taxes Payable	.0	.2		.1		.1
22.1	17.5	21.0	All Other Current	11.3	12.2		17.8		29.6
42.3	36.7	43.0	Total Current	33.9	54.3		28.9		47.9
36.4	33.9	39.4	Long-Term Debt	22.4	30.6		23.2		53.8
.5	.4	.2	Deferred Taxes	.0	.0		.4		.3
28.3	23.0	21.3	All Other Non-Current	9.5	20.7		9.2		29.5
-7.5	6.0	-3.9	Net Worth	34.3	-5.6		38.3		-31.4
100.0	100.0	100.0	Total Liabilities & Net Worth	100.0	100.0		100.0		100.0
			INCOME DATA						
100.0	100.0	100.0	Net Sales	100.0	100.0		100.0		100.0
			Gross Profit						
94.9	97.0	96.2	Operating Expenses	96.6	97.8		79.4		99.6
5.1	3.0	3.8	Operating Profit	3.4	2.2		20.6		.4
4.9	3.7	2.2	All Other Expenses (net)	1.8	2.1		-.7		2.7
.2	-.7	1.7	Profit Before Taxes	1.6	.0		21.3		-2.3
			RATIOS						
1.8	1.6	2.1		8.3	2.3		3.7		1.3
.8	.9	.9	Current	1.1	.5		1.0		.9
.4	.4	.3		.3	.2		.2		.4
1.4	1.3	1.5		8.2	1.9		3.7		1.1
.7	.7	.7	Quick	.4	.4		1.0		.7
.3	.3	.3		.3	.1		.1		.3
5 77.5	9 41.2	7 49.8		0 UND	0 UND		2 200.7		11 32.3
18 20.4	28 12.9	18 20.6	Sales/Receivables	10 36.4	12 30.0		4 82.7		33 11.2
42 8.6	71 5.2	47 7.7		29 12.4	34 10.8		15 23.8		70 5.2
			Cost of Sales/Inventory						
			Cost of Sales/Payables						
10.8	11.1	10.5		5.7	15.7		3.2		14.0
-14.0	-105.8	-63.3	Sales/Working Capital	77.7	-13.8		NM		-42.7
-4.4	-4.5	-4.2		-6.6	-3.1		-8.4		-3.8
7.1	5.2	4.1			7.5				3.7
(65) 1.0	(75) 1.3	(92) 1.2	EBIT/Interest	(16) .3			(49) 1.1		
-1.9	-1.7	-4.5			-5.5				-4.4
			Net Profit + Depr., Dep., Amort./Cur. Mat. L/T/D						
1.0	.9	1.2		.9	1.1		.4		NM
-2.9	-261.2	-1.6	Fixed/Worth	5.3	NM		1.7		-.5
-.1	-.1	-.1		-.8	-.1		NM		-.1
1.6	1.4	2.2		.3	1.2		.5		-18.2
-6.0	-11.0	-5.3	Debt/Worth	8.9	NM		2.3		-2.5
-1.7	-2.0	-1.8		-3.3	-1.5		NM		-1.6
65.4	12.0	52.9	% Profit Before Taxes/Tangible Net Worth		33.2				52.9
(40) 18.3	(47) .3	(48) 11.7		(10) 1.8			(12) 13.2		
-.5	-13.3	-5.4			-20.7				-43.3
9.1	7.3	10.9	% Profit Before Taxes/Total Assets	19.1	7.7		32.0		7.0
.1	.2	2.0		2.0	-2.0		14.4		1.9
-7.4	-6.6	-6.4		-16.0	-8.7		1.1		-9.9
42.1	24.7	32.2	Sales/Net Fixed Assets	24.2	43.0		100.2		42.7
8.3	7.1	7.3		3.3	29.2		5.3		10.0
1.4	1.8	1.8		.5	1.0		3.0		2.1
1.9	1.8	1.9	Sales/Total Assets	2.9	2.5		4.5		1.4
1.0	.8	.9		1.3	.7		1.1		1.0
.5	.4	.5		.4	.4		.3		.7
.9	1.5	1.4	% Depr., Dep., Amort./Sales	.9	1.4				1.2
(55) 3.0	(65) 3.0	(79) 2.8		(10) 2.4	(14) 2.6				(34) 2.3
5.7	7.4	9.3		6.7	10.4				6.3
1.3	4.0	2.3	% Officers', Directors', Owners' Comp/Sales						
(11) 8.5	(10) 5.9	(15) 6.0							
16.1	18.7	11.5							
5162353M	5017587M	5651728M	Net Sales ($)	6093M	38392M	30301M	83992M	107065M	5385885M
6290681M	6092964M	6883018M	Total Assets ($)	7192M	65089M	33405M	163930M	528067M	6085335M

© RMA 2005

M = $ thousand   MM = $ million
See Pages 11 through 21 for Explanation of Ratios and Data

Current Data Sorted By Assets   **Comparative Historical Data**

0-500M	500M-2MM	2-10MM	10-50MM	50-100MM	100-250MM	Type of Statement	4/1/00-3/31/01 ALL	4/1/01-3/31/02 ALL
1		2	9	5	3	Unqualified	16	17
2	1	1				Reviewed	4	2
7	2	2				Compiled	11	15
1	3	3		3		Tax Returns	3	5
			5			Other	13	13
5 (4/1-9/30/04)			45 (10/1/04-3/31/05)					
11	6	8	14	8	3	**NUMBER OF STATEMENTS**	47	52
%	%	%	%	%	%		%	%
						ASSETS		
15.7			11.9			Cash & Equivalents	14.4	13.0
8.7			6.8			Trade Receivables (net)	7.5	8.0
2.0			.2			Inventory	5.2	2.5
.3			1.1			All Other Current	4.9	5.8
26.8			20.0			Total Current	32.0	29.3
42.5			65.2			Fixed Assets (net)	52.6	56.6
.2			3.6			Intangibles (net)	2.3	4.4
30.6			11.2			All Other Non-Current	13.2	9.7
100.0			100.0			Total	100.0	100.0
						LIABILITIES		
29.5			2.1			Notes Payable-Short Term	6.4	5.8
4.5			3.5			Cur. Mat.-L/T/D	4.3	5.9
19.2			6.9			Trade Payables	9.6	8.4
.0			.1			Income Taxes Payable	.9	.6
25.8			10.7			All Other Current	17.4	15.3
79.0			23.4			Total Current	38.5	36.1
44.0			56.2			Long-Term Debt	23.2	31.2
.0			.4			Deferred Taxes	1.0	.2
4.2			8.7			All Other Non-Current	4.7	3.7
−27.2			11.3			Net Worth	32.6	28.8
100.0			100.0			Total Liabilities & Net Worth	100.0	100.0
						INCOME DATA		
100.0			100.0			Net Sales	100.0	100.0
						Gross Profit		
98.5			95.2			Operating Expenses	93.4	93.1
1.5			4.8			Operating Profit	6.6	6.9
1.8			3.6			All Other Expenses (net)	1.3	2.5
−.3			1.2			Profit Before Taxes	5.2	4.4
						RATIOS		
2.6			1.2				1.6	1.7
.6			.9			Current	.9	.9
.2			.4				.4	.5
2.5			1.1				1.4	1.5
.6			.9			Quick	.6	.7
.1			.4				.2	.4
0 UND			4 99.8				3 111.3	2 189.7
0 UND			7 50.4			Sales/Receivables	8 43.3	11 34.4
17 22.1			36 10.2				25 14.8	23 15.7
						Cost of Sales/Inventory		
						Cost of Sales/Payables		
95.1			11.4				11.5	19.1
−35.8			NM			Sales/Working Capital	−82.6	−148.0
−4.3			−10.1				−6.5	−15.6
			5.1				12.0	13.2
		(12)	1.0			EBIT/Interest	(40) 3.3	(47) 3.1
			−.1				.5	1.0
						Net Profit + Depr., Dep., Amort./Cur. Mat. L/T/D		
1.0			1.7				.8	1.0
181.0			2.7			Fixed/Worth	1.5	2.3
−1.4			NM				7.6	38.4
.9			1.4				.7	1.0
356.0			2.8			Debt/Worth	2.1	3.2
−3.0			NM				11.1	84.8
			17.1				56.8	66.5
		(11)	4.2			% Profit Before Taxes/Tangible Net Worth	(39) 15.8	(40) 27.4
			−4.0				−.6	6.5
38.2			7.2				15.7	23.7
.3			.6			% Profit Before Taxes/Total Assets	4.0	7.8
−7.9			−3.9				−1.5	−.5
22.2			3.0				6.6	6.0
15.6			2.2			Sales/Net Fixed Assets	3.5	3.5
8.5			.7				1.5	1.4
7.6			1.9				2.5	2.8
6.5			1.2			Sales/Total Assets	1.5	1.7
.9			.5				.9	.9
			2.1				.8	.2
		(12)	2.9			% Depr., Dep., Amort./Sales	(43) 3.3	(49) 3.9
			6.8				6.4	9.0
							2.2	2.3
						% Officers', Directors', Owners' Comp/Sales	(10) 4.4	(10) 7.1
							11.2	16.8
13706M	10858M	65305M	455101M	534022M	283974M	Net Sales ($)	1370989M	1642326M
2775M	7764M	38212M	359173M	521875M	682977M	Total Assets ($)	1119054M	1112030M

M = $thousand   MM = $million
See Pages 11 through 21 for Explanation of Ratios and Data

Comparative Historical Data				Current Data Sorted By Sales					
			Type of Statement						
29	17	20	Unqualified		1		5	3	11
3	2		Reviewed						
5	20	4	Compiled	3				1	
3	3	11	Tax Returns	3	5	1	2		
27	18	15	Other	2	2			5	4
4/1/02-3/31/03	4/1/03-3/31/04	4/1/04-3/31/05			5 (4/1-9/30/04)		45 (10/1/04-3/31/05)		
ALL	ALL	ALL		0-1MM	1-3MM	3-5MM	5-10MM	10-25MM	25MM & OVER
67	60	50	**NUMBER OF STATEMENTS**	8	8	3	7	9	15
%	%	%	**ASSETS**	%	%	%	%	%	%
14.1	14.5	10.5	Cash & Equivalents						12.6
6.8	5.8	6.2	Trade Receivables (net)						3.0
3.7	5.4	4.0	Inventory						.3
3.6	5.0	.9	All Other Current						1.0
28.1	30.6	21.7	Total Current						16.8
57.3	55.6	59.5	Fixed Assets (net)						68.5
2.8	6.1	4.3	Intangibles (net)						7.2
11.8	7.8	14.5	All Other Non-Current						7.5
100.0	100.0	100.0	Total						100.0
			LIABILITIES						
4.7	6.7	9.6	Notes Payable-Short Term						2.9
3.0	5.4	4.7	Cur. Mat.-L/T/D						3.1
7.3	7.4	9.2	Trade Payables						5.9
.6	.6	.1	Income Taxes Payable						.1
19.1	15.9	13.9	All Other Current						7.2
34.8	36.0	37.6	Total Current						19.2
26.9	27.2	42.0	Long-Term Debt						25.6
.2	.1	.8	Deferred Taxes						2.3
8.2	5.9	12.4	All Other Non-Current						10.5
29.9	30.9	7.3	Net Worth						42.4
100.0	100.0	100.0	Total Liabilities & Net Worth						100.0
			INCOME DATA						
100.0	100.0	100.0	Net Sales						100.0
			Gross Profit						
94.3	95.6	95.2	Operating Expenses						86.8
5.7	4.4	4.8	Operating Profit						13.2
1.5	1.9	2.9	All Other Expenses (net)						3.8
4.2	2.6	2.0	Profit Before Taxes						9.5
			RATIOS						
1.5	1.8	1.6							1.2
.9	.9	.7	Current						.9
.5	.3	.3							.4
1.3	1.6	1.1							1.2
.6	.6	.6	Quick						.8
.3	.2	.2							.3
1 491.5	1 255.7	1 621.0							6 64.6
6 57.7	9 40.5	8 46.8	Sales/Receivables						8 44.7
26 14.2	18 20.2	18 19.8							12 30.1
			Cost of Sales/Inventory						
			Cost of Sales/Payables						
20.6	8.5	26.9							20.9
-204.0	-53.7	-33.2	Sales/Working Capital						-37.5
-9.2	-5.9	-6.1							-9.1
20.3	13.3	6.0							15.6
(60) 2.8	(53) 1.5	(44) 1.3	EBIT/Interest						2.5
-.3	-1.6	-1.1							1.0
	14.2								
	(10) 1.3		Net Profit + Depr., Dep., Amort./Cur. Mat. L/T/D						
		.7							
.9	.8	1.1							1.1
1.8	1.9	2.7	Fixed/Worth						1.8
5.9	6.0	-6.8							84.3
.7	.7	.9							.6
1.8	1.7	3.0	Debt/Worth						1.7
8.8	6.8	-15.5							96.1
63.5	49.8	39.3							39.3
(57) 20.5	(48) 11.2	(35) 9.0	% Profit Before Taxes/Tangible Net Worth						(12) 25.8
-4.8	-8.4	-4.0							.7
22.8	20.0	10.0							13.4
5.9	1.9	.9	% Profit Before Taxes/Total Assets						6.4
-2.8	-5.7	-4.4							-.1
5.5	7.1	8.9							2.7
2.9	2.8	2.3	Sales/Net Fixed Assets						2.1
2.1	1.2	1.0							.9
2.4	2.3	2.4							1.9
1.7	1.5	1.2	Sales/Total Assets						1.1
1.0	.7	.5							.5
2.1	2.9	2.0							2.4
(61) 3.7	(52) 4.3	(39) 4.9	% Depr., Dep., Amort./Sales						(14) 4.3
7.1	8.3	9.5							7.8
2.4	2.4	1.0							
(15) 8.3	(12) 7.5	(10) 8.0	% Officers', Directors', Owners' Comp/Sales						
17.6	23.4	14.2							
2089023M	1705853M	1362966M	Net Sales ($)	3999M	14692M	13003M	40953M	170369M	1119950M
1612928M	1440323M	1612776M	Total Assets ($)	3732M	9800M	4038M	94765M	258235M	1242206M

© RMA 2005

M = $ thousand   MM = $ million
See Pages 11 through 21 for Explanation of Ratios and Data

Current Data Sorted By Assets   **Comparative Historical Data**

						Type of Statement	4/1/00-3/31/01 ALL	4/1/01-3/31/02 ALL
1		4	5	2	4	Unqualified		
	2	3				Reviewed		
3	2					Compiled		
4	2	1				Tax Returns		
2	3	5	1		1	Other		
23 (4/1-9/30/04)			22 (10/1/04-3/31/05)					
0-500M	500M-2MM	2-10MM	10-50MM	50-100MM	100-250MM			
10	9	13	6	2	5	NUMBER OF STATEMENTS		
%	%	%	%	%	%	ASSETS	%	%
19.4		7.7				Cash & Equivalents	D	D
16.7		7.1				Trade Receivables (net)	A	A
.3		.8				Inventory	T	T
10.6		2.9				All Other Current	A	A
47.0		18.5				Total Current		
36.0		65.5				Fixed Assets (net)	N	N
.2		5.7				Intangibles (net)	O	O
16.9		10.3				All Other Non-Current	T	T
100.0		100.0				Total		
						LIABILITIES	A	A
30.3		2.1				Notes Payable-Short Term	V	V
10.2		1.7				Cur. Mat.-L/T/D	A	A
28.3		3.0				Trade Payables	I	I
.0		.0				Income Taxes Payable	L	L
9.1		16.0				All Other Current	A	A
77.8		22.9				Total Current	B	B
30.7		32.2				Long-Term Debt	L	L
.0		.3				Deferred Taxes	E	E
17.1		.9				All Other Non-Current		
−25.5		43.8				Net Worth		
100.0		100.0				Total Liabilities & Net Worth		
						INCOME DATA		
100.0		100.0				Net Sales		
						Gross Profit		
80.7		74.3				Operating Expenses		
19.3		25.7				Operating Profit		
7.8		7.8				All Other Expenses (net)		
11.5		17.9				Profit Before Taxes		
						RATIOS		
11.8		3.5						
1.9		.8				Current		
.3		.2						
6.1		2.6						
1.9		.5				Quick		
.2		.1						
0 UND		0 UND						
0 UND		1 516.0				Sales/Receivables		
15 24.5		10 38.0						
						Cost of Sales/Inventory		
						Cost of Sales/Payables		
2.9		4.4						
108.4		−45.0				Sales/Working Capital		
−10.5		−3.4						
						EBIT/Interest		
						Net Profit + Depr., Dep., Amort./Cur. Mat. L./T/D		
.0		.9						
1.7		1.7				Fixed/Worth		
−.8		4.5						
1.1		.1						
NM		2.6				Debt/Worth		
−2.4		3.6						
		53.3						
	(11)	26.8				% Profit Before Taxes/Tangible Net Worth		
		2.7						
21.9		21.1						
12.1		9.4				% Profit Before Taxes/Total Assets		
−26.8		−.4						
UND		4.3						
33.6		.3				Sales/Net Fixed Assets		
1.4		.2						
12.8		1.6						
2.7		.3				Sales/Total Assets		
.5		.2						
		5.1						
	(12)	14.0				% Depr., Dep., Amort./Sales		
		18.5						
						% Officers', Directors', Owners' Comp/Sales		
4445M	16944M	54637M	100509M	26022M	339802M	Net Sales ($)		
1792M	10490M	62967M	142196M	151054M	789005M	Total Assets ($)		

© RMA 2005

M = $ thousand   MM = $ million
See Pages 11 through 21 for Explanation of Ratios and Data

Comparative Historical Data | Current Data Sorted By Sales

			Type of Statement						
15	10	16	Unqualified	2	3	2	3	2	4
11	8	5	Reviewed	2	1		1	1	
38	21	5	Compiled	3	1	1			
55	69	7	Tax Returns	5	1	1			
30	30	12	Other	6	2	1	1	1	1
4/1/02-3/31/03	4/1/03-3/31/04	4/1/04-3/31/05		23 (4/1-9/30/04)			22 (10/1/04-3/31/05)		
ALL	ALL	ALL		0-1MM	1-3MM	3-5MM	5-10MM	10-25MM	25MM & OVER
149	138	45	NUMBER OF STATEMENTS	18	8	4	6	4	5
%	%	%	ASSETS	%	%	%	%	%	%
7.0	6.5	10.1	Cash & Equivalents	12.1					
3.8	2.9	7.8	Trade Receivables (net)	6.0					
1.0	.4	.5	Inventory	.1					
1.3	2.4	6.3	All Other Current	4.9					
13.1	12.2	24.6	Total Current	23.1					
77.6	77.6	53.2	Fixed Assets (net)	63.0					
1.4	2.1	7.2	Intangibles (net)	.7					
7.8	8.1	14.9	All Other Non-Current	13.2					
100.0	100.0	100.0	Total	100.0					
			LIABILITIES						
3.4	6.9	8.1	Notes Payable-Short Term	17.7					
4.7	3.2	7.3	Cur. Mat.-L/T/D	2.9					
1.4	1.8	8.0	Trade Payables	12.1					
.1	.0	.1	Income Taxes Payable	.0					
3.4	3.1	11.0	All Other Current	2.2					
13.0	15.1	34.5	Total Current	34.9					
62.1	60.4	31.6	Long-Term Debt	45.8					
.1	.1	.1	Deferred Taxes	.0					
7.2	6.8	6.5	All Other Non-Current	9.5					
17.6	17.6	27.4	Net Worth	9.8					
100.0	100.0	100.0	Total Liabilities & Net Worth	100.0					
			INCOME DATA						
100.0	100.0	100.0	Net Sales	100.0					
			Gross Profit						
52.9	57.0	80.8	Operating Expenses	68.9					
47.1	43.0	19.2	Operating Profit	31.1					
26.1	23.5	7.1	All Other Expenses (net)	13.9					
21.0	19.5	12.1	Profit Before Taxes	17.3					
			RATIOS						
2.9	2.7	2.3		6.2					
.8	.7	.9	Current	.5					
.2	.2	.3		.1					
2.4	2.1	2.0		4.4					
.5	.4	.6	Quick	.5					
.1	.1	.1		.1					
0 UND	0 UND	0 UND		0 UND					
0 UND	0 UND	3 117.7	Sales/Receivables	0 UND					
17 22.1	4 84.7	27 13.8		0 UND					
			Cost of Sales/Inventory						
			Cost of Sales/Payables						
5.3	7.5	4.8		3.3					
-46.7	-15.2	-50.1	Sales/Working Capital	-13.2					
-2.8	-3.3	-4.9		-2.5					
11.0	5.8	13.6							
(44) 3.3	(55) 3.0	(28) 4.1	EBIT/Interest						
2.1	1.8	-1.7							
			Net Profit + Depr., Dep., Amort./Cur. Mat. L/T/D						
1.8	2.0	.7		.4					
4.7	5.1	2.0	Fixed/Worth	3.3					
39.7	-57.6	-11.0		NM					
1.4	1.5	.4		1.1					
4.5	5.6	2.8	Debt/Worth	3.6					
41.3	-63.5	-10.5		-16.2					
41.9	35.6	41.7	% Profit Before Taxes/Tangible Net Worth	53.2					
(120) 16.9	(100) 19.6	(32) 21.5		(13) 26.8					
5.1	3.2	2.0		11.6					
8.1	7.9	15.6	% Profit Before Taxes/Total Assets	11.8					
4.0	3.2	6.2		7.8					
1.4	.9	-.7		-.4					
.6	.6	28.2	Sales/Net Fixed Assets	28.6					
.2	.2	1.6		.3					
.2	.2	.2		.2					
.3	.4	2.6	Sales/Total Assets	2.6					
.2	.2	.4		.3					
.1	.1	.2		.2					
8.8	9.4	4.4	% Depr., Dep., Amort./Sales	7.0					
(137) 16.5	(129) 16.0	(36) 9.6		(14) 14.0					
23.8	22.4	18.5		18.6					
3.0	1.0		% Officers', Directors', Owners' Comp/Sales						
(19) 8.7	(25) 7.4								
13.6	23.7								
633419M	830171M	542359M	Net Sales ($)	6724M	15759M	14906M	39507M	62195M	403268M
1933491M	1254870M	1157504M	Total Assets ($)	25216M	36001M	63159M	210281M	124021M	698826M

M = $ thousand   MM = $ million
See Pages 11 through 21 for Explanation of Ratios and Data

Current Data Sorted By Assets   Comparative Historical Data

0-500M	500M-2MM	2-10MM	10-50MM	50-100MM	100-250MM	Type of Statement	4/1/00-3/31/01 ALL	4/1/01-3/31/02 ALL
	2	29	32	11	8	Unqualified	53	52
1		3	1			Reviewed	3	4
4		2				Compiled	6	14
1		1				Tax Returns	3	4
5	5	6	13		2	Other	32	29
	78 (4/1-9/30/04)		48 (10/1/04-3/31/05)					
11	7	41	46	11	10	**NUMBER OF STATEMENTS**	97	103
%	%	%	%	%	%	**ASSETS**	%	%
39.4		12.3	7.1	18.6	7.6	Cash & Equivalents	13.1	13.1
4.3		3.9	5.5	2.8	2.9	Trade Receivables (net)	5.6	5.3
23.6		7.5	2.3	.4	3.4	Inventory	6.4	9.5
.4		3.1	5.3	2.0	.9	All Other Current	3.9	4.3
67.6		26.8	20.2	23.7	14.8	Total Current	29.0	32.1
21.1		53.0	54.5	42.8	43.8	Fixed Assets (net)	43.9	47.2
.0		.5	1.4	4.7	1.9	Intangibles (net)	4.2	1.1
11.2		19.7	23.9	28.8	39.5	All Other Non-Current	23.0	19.6
100.0		100.0	100.0	100.0	100.0	Total	100.0	100.0
						LIABILITIES		
66.9		7.6	2.1	1.0	1.9	Notes Payable-Short Term	5.0	4.2
5.4		.9	1.4	.3	2.9	Cur. Mat.-L/T/D	2.8	3.8
21.0		5.8	3.0	1.2	1.5	Trade Payables	5.1	5.7
.2		.2	.0	.0	.0	Income Taxes Payable	.0	.0
20.1		5.9	2.6	3.0	1.5	All Other Current	3.9	3.3
113.6		20.4	9.2	5.6	7.9	Total Current	16.9	17.0
3.4		6.2	16.4	16.2	11.2	Long-Term Debt	14.0	13.8
.0		.0	.0	.0	.0	Deferred Taxes	.0	.1
1.8		1.7	.5	.7	2.5	All Other Non-Current	2.0	6.4
-18.8		71.6	73.9	77.5	78.5	Net Worth	67.1	62.8
100.0		100.0	100.0	100.0	100.0	Total Liabilities & Net Worth	100.0	100.0
						INCOME DATA		
100.0		100.0	100.0	100.0	100.0	Net Sales	100.0	100.0
						Gross Profit		
100.7		98.4	85.5	84.5	88.9	Operating Expenses	88.9	87.2
-.7		1.6	14.5	15.5	11.1	Operating Profit	11.1	12.8
2.0		-1.7	.6	3.6	-.7	All Other Expenses (net)	-4.5	4.5
-2.6		3.2	13.9	12.0	11.8	Profit Before Taxes	15.6	8.3
						RATIOS		
2.7		3.5	5.2	11.3	9.7		6.6	6.6
1.5		1.8	1.7	2.4	2.1	Current	2.0	2.2
.2		.8	1.1	1.0	1.4		.9	1.2
2.2		3.1	3.6	9.7	9.6		4.0	4.2
.3		.9	1.1	2.2	1.8	Quick	1.4	1.3
.1		.4	.4	1.0	.5		.4	.4
0 UND		0 UND	1 245.8	0 999.8	2 181.8		2 195.2	1 273.7
0 UND		5 69.8	11 34.3	36 10.1	17 21.1	Sales/Receivables	13 28.8	15 24.0
2 150.0		17 21.2	78 4.7	71 5.1	54 6.8		43 8.5	59 6.2
						Cost of Sales/Inventory		
						Cost of Sales/Payables		
5.2		2.8	2.0	1.7	1.5		1.7	1.8
8.9		5.8	7.8	2.9	3.5	Sales/Working Capital	5.5	4.0
-2.0		-41.3	59.3	533.3	NM		-35.3	35.2
		30.8	10.4				20.0	8.1
	(24)	5.8	(28) 1.5			EBIT/Interest	(57) 4.1	(59) 2.6
		-2.5	-1.1				.5	-2.3
						Net Profit + Depr., Dep., Amort./Cur. Mat. L /T/D		
.0		.4	.3	.2	.1		.3	.3
.1		.9	.8	.6	.6	Fixed/Worth	.6	.7
.8		1.0	1.1	1.0	1.0		1.1	1.0
.4		.1	.1	.0	.1		.1	.1
1.7		.2	.3	.3	.3	Debt/Worth	.3	.3
64.9		.6	.7	.7	.5		.8	1.1
		13.4	13.8	13.5	7.9	% Profit Before Taxes/Tangible Net Worth	15.2	17.7
	(39)	3.5	1.9	6.8	2.1		(92) 5.0	(98) 2.0
		-3.9	-2.1	-2.5	-1.9		-.8	-3.6
3.7		8.6	10.7	11.9	5.8	% Profit Before Taxes/Total Assets	10.2	12.0
.0		2.0	1.1	3.4	1.7		4.1	1.5
-55.6		-3.4	-1.8	-2.5	-1.5		-.5	-2.5
UND		7.2	.9	1.0	1.2		4.0	5.1
17.9		.8	.5	.7	.3	Sales/Net Fixed Assets	.9	.8
7.5		.3	.3	.5	.2		.5	.4
3.8		1.0	.4	.4	.2		.8	1.0
2.3		.5	.3	.3	.2	Sales/Total Assets	.4	.4
1.3		.2	.2	.2	.1		.2	.2
		4.6	5.5	5.1		% Depr., Dep., Amort./Sales	1.9	.9
	(33)	9.6	(38) 9.5	6.9			(81) 4.8	(91) 4.8
		13.3	18.9	21.1			10.2	9.9
						% Officers', Directors', Owners' Comp/Sales	1.3	4.7
							(12) 4.7	(17) 9.5
							14.2	24.7
5387M	6616M	136695M	407333M	267144M	376382M	Net Sales ($)	1331292M	1175501M
2376M	8061M	201266M	1164086M	860301M	1594957M	Total Assets ($)	3134446M	2758919M

M = $ thousand   MM = $ million
See Pages 11 through 21 for Explanation of Ratios and Data

Comparative Historical Data				Current Data Sorted By Sales					

			Type of Statement						
89	86	82	Unqualified	6	16	14	14	23	9
6	4	5	Reviewed	1		2	1	1	
7	12	6	Compiled	4			1	1	
3	3	2	Tax Returns	2					
39	24	31	Other	9	7	3	6	5	1
					78 (4/1-9/30/04)		48 (10/1/04-3/31/05)		
4/1/02-3/31/03	4/1/03-3/31/04	4/1/04-3/31/05		0-1MM	1-3MM	3-5MM	5-10MM	10-25MM	25MM & OVER
ALL	ALL	ALL							
144	129	126	**NUMBER OF STATEMENTS**	22	23	19	22	30	10
%	%	%	**ASSETS**	%	%	%	%	%	%
12.5	14.1	13.8	Cash & Equivalents	27.5	13.8	15.2	8.7	7.0	12.1
4.9	4.2	4.4	Trade Receivables (net)	2.9	1.3	4.7	9.4	4.5	2.3
7.8	5.7	5.7	Inventory	12.5	1.2	5.6	6.2	4.6	3.7
4.4	6.5	3.3	All Other Current	.9	6.1	2.7	3.7	3.4	2.3
29.5	30.5	27.2	Total Current	43.8	22.5	28.3	28.0	19.6	20.3
47.6	48.9	48.4	Fixed Assets (net)	40.9	60.5	42.5	47.1	50.4	45.3
1.0	.7	1.2	Intangibles (net)	.6	.1	.8	2.4	.1	7.1
21.8	19.9	23.1	All Other Non-Current	14.7	17.0	28.4	22.5	29.9	27.3
100.0	100.0	100.0	Total	100.0	100.0	100.0	100.0	100.0	100.0
			LIABILITIES						
3.7	3.6	9.8	Notes Payable-Short Term	33.1	9.8	1.6	7.9	1.6	2.4
1.6	1.8	1.6	Cur. Mat.-L/T/D	1.6	2.2	.5	2.5	.8	3.1
5.8	5.6	5.3	Trade Payables	7.1	6.1	3.5	4.1	6.7	1.5
.0	.1	.1	Income Taxes Payable	.0	.1	.0	.3	.0	.0
3.4	3.1	5.3	All Other Current	7.0	7.0	3.4	3.3	5.7	4.0
14.4	14.2	22.1	Total Current	48.9	25.2	9.0	18.1	14.8	11.0
12.9	11.4	10.8	Long-Term Debt	3.4	10.2	7.6	12.9	15.4	16.0
.0	.0	.0	Deferred Taxes	.0	.0	.0	.0	.0	.0
1.9	2.2	1.2	All Other Non-Current	.9	.6	1.2	.7	1.5	2.8
70.8	72.2	66.0	Net Worth	46.9	64.0	82.2	68.2	68.2	70.2
100.0	100.0	100.0	Total Liabilities & Net Worth	100.0	100.0	100.0	100.0	100.0	100.0
			INCOME DATA						
100.0	100.0	100.0	Net Sales	100.0	100.0	100.0	100.0	100.0	100.0
			Gross Profit						
92.7	94.4	91.2	Operating Expenses	107.4	89.6	85.5	88.4	90.5	78.3
7.3	5.6	8.8	Operating Profit	-7.4	10.4	14.5	11.6	9.5	21.7
5.7	1.7	.1	All Other Expenses (net)	-.6	1.6	.4	-1.5	.6	-.1
1.6	3.9	8.7	Profit Before Taxes	-6.7	8.8	14.1	13.1	8.9	21.8
			RATIOS						
6.5	7.2	4.4		5.6	3.8	7.1	6.8	2.5	7.0
2.2	2.3	1.8	Current	1.9	1.7	3.2	2.2	1.6	2.2
.9	1.1	.9		.5	.6	1.3	1.0	1.0	.8
4.1	4.3	3.5		5.2	3.4	3.6	4.8	2.1	5.6
1.2	1.6	1.1	Quick	.7	1.3	2.8	.9	1.0	2.1
.4	.5	.4		.1	.6	.3	.3	.5	.5
1 436.2	1 420.7	0 999.8		0 UND	0 UND	0 UND	6 63.8	5 70.4	1 650.5
11 34.2	9 39.5	7 49.9	Sales/Receivables	0 UND	3 115.1	2 152.3	33 11.1	10 36.3	7 55.5
45 8.1	46 8.0	47 7.8		5 79.0	17 21.2	64 5.7	192 1.9	51 7.2	45 8.1
			Cost of Sales/Inventory						
			Cost of Sales/Payables						
1.8	1.3	2.2		2.0	2.3	1.3	1.9	3.7	1.9
4.7	4.9	5.7	Sales/Working Capital	5.7	5.9	4.6	5.5	11.6	3.1
-55.6	50.0	-115.4		-7.2	-18.2	39.2	NM	NM	-27.6
6.5	8.5	13.8		5.8	61.6	35.0	11.5	22.9	
(79) 1.4	(69) -.4	(78) 2.4	EBIT/Interest	(11) 1.0	(16) 1.8	(11) 6.9	(10) 8.7	(21) 1.0	
-5.3	-5.8	-1.5		-7.7	-10.2	-.9	-.8	-.8	
			Net Profit + Depr., Dep., Amort./Cur. Mat. L/T/D						
.3	.3	.3		.0	.5	.3	.2	.3	.1
.7	.7	.7	Fixed/Worth	.5	.9	.5	.8	.9	.8
1.1	1.0	1.1		1.0	1.1	.8	1.2	1.1	1.2
.1	.1	.1		.2	.1	.1	.1	.1	.2
.2	.2	.3	Debt/Worth	.4	.2	.2	.3	.3	.4
.8	.7	.6		1.3	.4	.3	.8	1.0	1.0
8.9	8.6	13.2		6.1	7.2	12.2	18.9	14.5	18.5
(139) .5	(125) .0	(122) 2.4	% Profit Before Taxes/Tangible Net Worth	(21) -3.4	(22) 2.5	4.5	(21) 6.3	(29) .7	8.5
-5.9	-3.2	-2.7		-6.8	-3.8	1.3	-3.3	-2.0	.7
4.5	5.1	9.0		3.4	6.1	10.8	11.8	7.2	13.9
.3	-.1	1.3	% Profit Before Taxes/Total Assets	-2.4	1.6	4.1	2.7	.4	4.1
-5.3	-2.7	-2.5		-6.7	-3.4	.9	-3.1	-1.6	.5
3.6	2.3	4.8		67.8	1.0	4.2	2.7	2.9	12.8
.8	.6	.8	Sales/Net Fixed Assets	4.9	.5	.8	.7	.8	.6
.4	.4	.4		.4	.3	.7	.3	.4	.3
.7	.5	.7		2.0	.5	.7	.6	.7	.5
.3	.3	.4	Sales/Total Assets	.7	.2	.5	.4	.4	.4
.2	.2	.2		.2	.2	.2	.2	.2	.2
3.4	4.0	4.0		2.5	7.7	3.8	3.5	3.9	
(116) 6.8	(109) 8.1	(100) 8.7	% Depr., Dep., Amort./Sales	(12) 8.0	(21) 11.2	(16) 6.2	(17) 9.2	(25) 8.7	
12.6	13.9	13.8		15.0	19.0	11.6	21.3	16.1	
4.0	1.4	4.5							
(25) 12.4	(15) 3.5	(13) 10.4	% Officers', Directors', Owners' Comp/Sales						
27.9	22.4	30.6							
1511275M	2787292M	1199557M	Net Sales ($)	11241M	40545M	71848M	147181M	475139M	453603M
4050643M	4465703M	3831047M	Total Assets ($)	33390M	182156M	215888M	539598M	1621536M	1238479M

M = $ thousand   MM = $ million
See Pages 11 through 21 for Explanation of Ratios and Data

Current Data Sorted By Assets   Comparative Historical Data

	0-500M	500M-2MM	2-10MM	10-50MM	50-100MM	100-250MM		4/1/00-3/31/01 ALL	4/1/01-3/31/02 ALL
Type of Statement									
Unqualified		1	2	6	2			10	12
Reviewed		1	8	6	1			15	14
Compiled	6	6	3					14	17
Tax Returns	5	3	6	1				13	13
Other	4	8	6	5		1		25	27
	6 (4/1-9/30/04)			75 (10/1/04-3/31/05)					
NUMBER OF STATEMENTS	15	19	25	18	3	1		77	83
	%	%	%	%	%	%	**ASSETS**	%	%
	18.0	12.8	10.9	5.8			Cash & Equivalents	8.7	8.8
	.6	1.6	1.5	1.0			Trade Receivables (net)	2.4	.5
	4.7	2.2	2.0	2.2			Inventory	2.6	2.9
	.7	1.1	.7	.9			All Other Current	2.1	2.5
	24.1	17.6	15.1	9.9			Total Current	15.9	14.7
	66.3	71.1	63.0	78.4			Fixed Assets (net)	70.4	72.3
	2.4	.8	6.6	2.5			Intangibles (net)	5.0	4.1
	7.2	10.5	15.3	9.1			All Other Non-Current	8.7	8.9
	100.0	100.0	100.0	100.0			Total	100.0	100.0
							LIABILITIES		
	29.1	7.4	9.4	4.4			Notes Payable-Short Term	8.1	8.0
	2.7	11.0	3.9	5.4			Cur. Mat.-L/T/D	5.3	4.8
	5.0	8.4	2.0	1.7			Trade Payables	4.0	2.1
	.0	.4	.0	.0			Income Taxes Payable	.2	.1
	30.3	19.0	10.6	5.9			All Other Current	15.9	18.8
	67.2	46.2	25.9	17.3			Total Current	33.4	33.8
	44.7	46.8	47.3	46.1			Long-Term Debt	42.8	43.5
	.0	.1	1.2	1.9			Deferred Taxes	.4	.2
	23.9	14.9	5.5	2.9			All Other Non-Current	6.2	8.9
	-35.8	-8.0	20.0	31.9			Net Worth	17.2	13.7
	100.0	100.0	100.0	100.0			Total Liabilities & Net Worth	100.0	100.0
							INCOME DATA		
	100.0	100.0	100.0	100.0			Net Sales	100.0	100.0
							Gross Profit		
	101.0	97.2	95.1	83.6			Operating Expenses	93.2	90.7
	-1.0	2.8	4.9	16.4			Operating Profit	6.8	9.3
	4.1	3.8	3.8	9.0			All Other Expenses (net)	3.2	5.7
	-5.1	-1.0	1.1	7.4			Profit Before Taxes	3.6	3.6
							RATIOS		
	.6	1.1	1.9	1.3				1.5	1.2
	.5	.5	.7	.6			Current	.6	.6
	.1	.2	.1	.3				.1	.2
	.5	.9	1.5	.8				1.0	1.0
	.3	.3	.3	.4			Quick	.3	.3
	.0	.1	.1	.1				.1	.1
	0 UND	0 UND	0 UND	0 UND				0 UND	0 UND
	0 UND	0 999.8	1 347.8	2 180.5			Sales/Receivables	0 999.8	0 UND
	0 UND	2 199.6	6 62.5	4 96.1				6 65.5	3 126.2
							Cost of Sales/Inventory		
							Cost of Sales/Payables		
	-35.7	86.6	14.6	33.4				39.0	76.5
	-9.4	-12.8	-32.1	-20.8			Sales/Working Capital	-14.7	-36.9
	-2.6	-6.8	-3.8	-5.9				-3.9	-5.2
	5.8	2.6	3.1	3.6				3.3	4.4
	(10) 1.2	.8	(23) .6	(17) 1.9			EBIT/Interest	(67) 1.6	(70) 1.9
	-1.0	-1.6	-3.7	1.5				.0	.7
							Net Profit + Depr., Dep.,	7.4	2.9
							Amort./Cur. Mat. L/T/D	(15) 1.0	(10) .9
								.2	.1
	2.4	1.6	1.3	1.8				1.4	1.2
	-4.1	4.1	7.5	2.6			Fixed/Worth	2.5	2.1
	-1.1	-2.7	-2.3	21.6				NM	-47.3
	1.5	2.2	.8	1.0				1.0	.7
	-6.5	5.0	11.5	1.9			Debt/Worth	2.1	1.5
	-2.4	-4.2	-4.1	32.3				-9.8	-69.6
		23.3	22.4	27.5			% Profit Before Taxes/Tangible	21.5	33.6
	(13) -3.9	(17) -2.7	(16) 13.9				Net Worth	(56) 9.6	(62) 12.8
		-7.2	-37.6	2.1				.6	-1.6
	3.7	4.5	6.7	7.4			% Profit Before Taxes/Total	8.5	14.0
	.0	-.9	-1.0	4.6			Assets	2.8	3.6
	-16.4	-9.5	-10.2	.7				-6.2	-4.6
	8.8	4.3	3.8	1.3				2.2	2.6
	3.3	2.6	2.3	.9			Sales/Net Fixed Assets	1.3	1.2
	.7	1.1	.9	.5				.7	.8
	5.2	2.7	1.7	1.0				1.4	1.9
	2.1	1.6	1.1	.7			Sales/Total Assets	.9	.9
	.5	1.0	.6	.4				.5	.6
	3.8	6.4	5.8	7.3			% Depr., Dep., Amort./Sales	6.2	5.1
	(14) 6.0	(15) 8.2	(24) 10.5	11.5				(72) 10.6	(80) 10.2
	10.3	16.6	17.5	15.0				16.1	15.6
							% Officers', Directors',	3.1	3.8
							Owners' Comp/Sales	(24) 6.6	(30) 5.8
								10.3	11.2
	14096M	46732M	119398M	302340M	83476M	222417M	Net Sales ($)	981045M	903013M
	3589M	24849M	103198M	410252M	206788M	224102M	Total Assets ($)	1654981M	1309511M

M = $ thousand   MM = $ million
See Pages 11 through 21 for Explanation of Ratios and Data

Comparative Historical Data				Current Data Sorted By Sales					
			Type of Statement						
14	11	11	Unqualified		1		3	4	3
20	22	16	Reviewed		2	3	4	5	2
22	15	15	Compiled	6	4	2	3		
17	15	15	Tax Returns	8	4	2	1		
20	19	24	Other	3	9	5	2	2	3
4/1/02-	4/1/03-	4/1/04-			6 (4/1-9/30/04)		75 (10/1/04-3/31/05)		
3/31/03	3/31/04	3/31/05							
ALL	ALL	ALL		0-1MM	1-3MM	3-5MM	5-10MM	10-25MM	25MM & OVER
93	82	81	**NUMBER OF STATEMENTS**	17	20	12	13	11	8
%	%	%	**ASSETS**	%	%	%	%	%	%
8.8	7.3	11.7	Cash & Equivalents	13.0	15.2	7.5	14.2	6.7	
.5	.6	1.2	Trade Receivables (net)	.5	1.6	1.4	1.4	.9	
2.1	2.2	2.6	Inventory	1.9	3.1	1.2	4.2	1.3	
4.1	2.4	1.0	All Other Current	.4	1.1	1.0	.1	1.5	
15.5	12.6	16.5	Total Current	15.7	21.0	11.1	19.8	10.4	
73.2	72.6	68.7	Fixed Assets (net)	71.6	59.6	75.0	67.0	80.4	
2.7	2.4	3.2	Intangibles (net)	2.3	6.1	4.1	.7	3.2	
8.6	12.4	11.5	All Other Non-Current	10.4	13.3	9.8	12.4	6.0	
100.0	100.0	100.0	Total	100.0	100.0	100.0	100.0	100.0	
			LIABILITIES						
9.1	3.8	11.0	Notes Payable-Short Term	24.2	14.9	2.9	5.0	4.3	
6.8	9.0	5.5	Cur. Mat.-L/T/D	4.9	7.3	3.9	6.9	5.7	
2.3	2.3	4.0	Trade Payables	3.6	4.4	9.3	1.4	2.6	
.3	.0	.1	Income Taxes Payable	.0	.4	.0	.0	.0	
11.5	8.3	14.9	All Other Current	17.8	12.7	21.1	20.4	4.6	
30.1	23.4	35.6	Total Current	50.6	39.7	37.2	33.8	17.2	
36.6	44.9	45.3	Long-Term Debt	57.9	36.9	62.8	41.1	44.3	
.5	1.0	.9	Deferred Taxes	.0	.6	.0	2.2	.0	
13.2	10.7	10.7	All Other Non-Current	13.9	20.2	11.6	.1	3.0	
19.6	20.0	7.6	Net Worth	−22.4	2.6	−11.5	22.8	35.5	
100.0	100.0	100.0	Total Liabilities & Net Worth	100.0	100.0	100.0	100.0	100.0	
			INCOME DATA						
100.0	100.0	100.0	Net Sales	100.0	100.0	100.0	100.0	100.0	
			Gross Profit						
87.5	90.6	94.3	Operating Expenses	91.1	95.8	96.0	98.0	94.9	
12.5	9.4	5.7	Operating Profit	8.9	4.2	4.0	2.0	5.1	
5.9	5.7	4.9	All Other Expenses (net)	11.6	3.3	4.0	2.8	4.0	
6.6	3.7	.8	Profit Before Taxes	−2.7	.9	.0	−.8	1.1	
			RATIOS						
1.2	1.1	1.4		1.0	1.2	1.9	1.3	2.2	
.7	.6	.5	Current	.4	.6	.7	.5	.5	
.2	.2	.2		.1	.2	.1	.4	.2	
1.0	.8	1.0		1.0	.9	1.3	1.1	2.1	
(92) .3	.3	.3	Quick	.3	.3	.3	.4	.3	
.1	.1	.1		.1	.1	.1	.2	.1	
0 UND	0 UND	0 UND		0 UND	0 UND	1 434.4	0 UND	0 UND	
0 UND	0 UND	0 999.8	Sales/Receivables	0 UND	0 UND	2 156.1	1 558.8	2 205.5	
3 108.4	4 96.9	4 101.5		0 UND	3 119.7	5 73.2	4 90.1	4 93.8	
			Cost of Sales/Inventory						
			Cost of Sales/Payables						
37.5	81.2	34.6		NM	71.5	15.2	104.6	14.1	
−27.0	−17.8	−15.4	Sales/Working Capital	−8.9	−17.3	−73.0	−31.8	−13.2	
−7.0	−6.3	−3.9		−2.4	−4.1	−3.1	−8.3	−6.9	
4.1	3.9	3.5		4.5	6.9	3.9	1.9	2.2	
(74) 2.4	(70) 1.4	(72) 1.3	EBIT/Interest	(11) .8	(18) .8	1.1	1.2	1.8	
.7	−.1	−.8		−1.6	−.7	−3.0	−1.0	−.7	
3.3	3.5	2.8	Net Profit + Depr., Dep.,						
(16) 2.2	(17) 2.0	(13) 2.0	Amort./Cur. Mat. L/T/D						
1.1	1.4	1.2							
1.2	1.3	1.4		2.7	1.3	3.4	1.1	1.9	
2.2	2.8	4.0	Fixed/Worth	18.1	13.4	9.4	2.6	2.1	
52.1	−56.3	−3.4		−1.4	−.9	−8.7	NM	2.7	
.7	.8	1.2		3.4	1.9	3.2	.8	1.1	
2.1	2.8	5.0	Debt/Worth	32.0	14.6	9.6	2.1	1.4	
61.1	−63.1	−6.2		−5.0	−2.5	−18.4	NM	2.3	
37.8	28.2	23.3	% Profit Before Taxes/Tangible	14.1	29.7		24.1		
(71) 18.9	(59) 9.0	(57) 6.7	Net Worth	(10) −1.9	(12) .0		(10) 10.7		
2.4	−7.3	−5.4		−77.3	−5.4		−3.2		
13.5	8.0	6.1	% Profit Before Taxes/Total	1.6	5.4	8.1	4.4	5.9	
5.3	1.5	.4	Assets	−.7	−.8	.8	.7	3.5	
−2.4	−5.0	−6.9		−16.2	−7.3	−12.5	−8.0	−1.2	
3.2	2.3	4.1		3.7	8.4	3.3	7.1	1.3	
1.2	1.2	1.6	Sales/Net Fixed Assets	.7	2.9	1.8	2.9	1.1	
.8	.7	.7		.4	1.2	.8	1.1	.5	
1.7	1.6	2.0		2.6	2.1	1.7	2.7	1.1	
.9	.9	1.1	Sales/Total Assets	.5	1.3	1.1	1.4	.9	
.6	.6	.5		.4	.6	.7	.8	.4	
5.4	7.0	5.7		4.6	5.4	7.4	5.6	6.2	
(85) 10.2	(75) 12.0	(74) 10.4	% Depr., Dep., Amort./Sales	(16) 8.8	(17) 8.1	15.3	(11) 11.0	10.8	
15.3	16.5	15.2		18.7	12.3	17.7	13.7	15.8	
3.7	2.9	2.6	% Officers', Directors',						
(30) 7.7	(26) 5.3	(19) 4.8	Owners' Comp/Sales						
12.8	8.9	7.4							
1025267M	1055351M	788459M	Net Sales ($)	6668M	41005M	48387M	88420M	153819M	450160M
1247857M	1411814M	972778M	Total Assets ($)	24269M	36248M	58306M	84341M	281740M	487874M

M = $ thousand   MM = $ million
See Pages 11 through 21 for Explanation of Ratios and Data

Current Data Sorted By Assets   Comparative Historical Data

						Type of Statement		
	1	3	10	4	8	Unqualified	7	19
	2	4				Reviewed	5	3
2	6	2				Compiled	16	14
8	6	4				Tax Returns	10	9
3	2	5	2	2	2	Other	25	36
	26 (4/1-9/30/04)		50 (10/1/04-3/31/05)				4/1/00- 3/31/01	4/1/01- 3/31/02
0-500M	500M-2MM	2-10MM	10-50MM	50-100MM	100-250MM		ALL	ALL
13	17	18	12	6	10	NUMBER OF STATEMENTS	63	81
%	%	%	%	%	%	ASSETS	%	%
25.9	18.3	17.8	15.8		19.2	Cash & Equivalents	15.8	14.4
2.6	3.1	1.9	3.6		.9	Trade Receivables (net)	2.0	3.6
2.0	4.6	4.5	7.5		.6	Inventory	6.8	2.8
8.4	2.6	2.6	2.7		.5	All Other Current	1.7	2.8
38.9	28.6	26.7	29.5		21.2	Total Current	26.3	23.6
52.3	59.8	59.2	60.9		72.7	Fixed Assets (net)	60.0	63.6
1.4	1.5	7.8	5.0		1.2	Intangibles (net)	7.5	6.9
7.4	10.0	6.2	4.6		4.9	All Other Non-Current	6.2	5.9
100.0	100.0	100.0	100.0		100.0	Total	100.0	100.0
						LIABILITIES		
58.2	7.7	4.2	2.5		2.0	Notes Payable-Short Term	3.1	2.8
5.4	4.2	12.4	6.8		4.8	Cur. Mat.-L/T/D	7.3	7.9
15.1	5.4	3.2	3.1		2.5	Trade Payables	6.4	5.5
.0	.0	.0	.0		.0	Income Taxes Payable	.2	.1
19.8	15.6	9.5	9.6		9.0	All Other Current	8.8	11.7
98.5	32.8	29.3	22.0		18.3	Total Current	25.7	28.0
29.3	39.1	29.1	19.9		38.5	Long-Term Debt	32.2	29.8
.0	.0	2.0	.3		.0	Deferred Taxes	.1	.1
32.7	15.3	1.5	.5		.5	All Other Non-Current	5.1	5.3
-60.5	12.8	38.0	57.4		42.6	Net Worth	36.9	36.7
100.0	100.0	100.0	100.0		100.0	Total Liabilities & Net Worth	100.0	100.0
						INCOME DATA		
100.0	100.0	100.0	100.0		100.0	Net Sales	100.0	100.0
						Gross Profit		
103.0	92.3	86.1	80.7		56.0	Operating Expenses	87.4	84.5
-3.0	7.7	13.9	19.3		44.0	Operating Profit	12.6	15.5
3.6	4.3	2.5	1.1		2.7	All Other Expenses (net)	.9	3.5
-6.6	3.5	11.4	18.1		41.3	Profit Before Taxes	11.7	12.0
						RATIOS		
2.3	1.6	2.2	2.0		1.5		1.9	1.5
.3	.8	.9	1.1		1.2	Current	1.0	.9
.1	.2	.3	.6		.9		.5	.4
1.7	.9	2.0	1.5		1.3		1.4	1.1
.1	.7	.7	.7		1.2	Quick	(62) .6	(80) .7
.1	.1	.2	.3		.7		.3	.3
0 UND	0 UND	0 UND	1 466.2		0 UND		0 UND	0 UND
0 UND	0 UND	0 999.8	1 274.2		1 261.5	Sales/Receivables	1 570.9	1 294.1
0 UND	1 479.9	5 77.9	7 52.5		4 93.3		4 87.2	5 72.9
						Cost of Sales/Inventory		
						Cost of Sales/Payables		
14.8	26.0	10.5	9.1		23.9		20.8	31.8
-7.7	-35.4	NM	NM		41.8	Sales/Working Capital	-170.2	-70.1
-3.3	-14.2	-8.5	-19.8		-235.9		-13.7	-11.3
	4.2	28.5	44.2				11.0	12.6
(13) 1.2	(16) 6.6	(11) 8.1				EBIT/Interest	(54) 2.5	(72) 3.7
	-2.1	2.1	3.7				1.1	1.7
						Net Profit + Depr., Dep., Amort./Cur. Mat. L./T/D		
.7	1.0	.7	.7		1.5		.9	1.0
-1.5	7.2	2.7	1.1		1.8	Fixed/Worth	1.9	2.1
-.6	-11.1	-755.7	2.0		2.4		9.4	5.8
3.6	1.2	.5	.3		.8		.6	.7
-4.0	6.4	2.3	.9		1.7	Debt/Worth	2.1	2.1
-1.6	-13.5	-757.4	1.5		2.5		16.0	7.6
	107.4	124.9	81.6		258.8	% Profit Before Taxes/Tangible Net Worth	111.3	127.6
(11) 60.1	(13) 49.6	45.8		143.6		(50) 35.9	(68) 45.5
	-52.8	25.5	21.0		86.3		11.7	13.3
18.1	30.6	46.5	43.1		85.5		39.9	44.0
-21.1	3.0	15.3	16.8		47.5	% Profit Before Taxes/Total Assets	8.9	9.7
-78.5	-11.2	4.3	9.2		33.7		.9	2.3
16.7	13.2	8.6	4.4		2.5		7.0	5.7
4.7	3.9	4.9	2.6		1.8	Sales/Net Fixed Assets	3.7	2.4
2.4	2.1	1.3	1.4		1.5		1.6	1.4
4.7	3.3	3.9	1.9		1.7		3.8	3.0
2.2	1.9	2.3	1.6		1.4	Sales/Total Assets	2.0	1.5
1.6	1.7	.9	1.0		1.1		1.1	1.0
	3.8	3.5	3.9				3.1	3.3
(15) 12.7	7.2	6.0			% Depr., Dep., Amort./Sales	(55) 5.1	(60) 5.3
	19.0	13.7	7.7				12.9	11.3
	4.1						1.3	1.1
(10) 6.6					% Officers', Directors', Owners' Comp/Sales	(23) 2.2	(17) 3.8
	8.2						6.1	10.9
4148M	72914M	271870M	450937M	490966M	2446214M	Net Sales ($)	1544464M	4998468M
1481M	19691M	83490M	312475M	469856M	1666126M	Total Assets ($)	1093987M	3793874M

M = $ thousand   MM = $ million
See Pages 11 through 21 for Explanation of Ratios and Data

Comparative Historical Data / Current Data Sorted By Sales

Type of Statement									
Unqualified	27	30	26					5	21
Reviewed	8	11	6		3		1	1	1
Compiled	18	19	10		5	1	2		
Tax Returns	13	21	18	2	5	1	2	2	2
Other	27	33	16	10	5	1		2	7
				3					
	4/1/02-3/31/03 ALL	4/1/03-3/31/04 ALL	4/1/04-3/31/05 ALL	26 (4/1-9/30/04) 0-1MM	1-3MM	3-5MM	50 (10/1/04-3/31/05) 5-10MM	10-25MM	25MM & OVER
NUMBER OF STATEMENTS	93	114	76	15	14	3	5	10	29
ASSETS	%	%	%	%	%	%	%	%	%
Cash & Equivalents	15.2	16.2	19.3	22.8	8.0			20.8	21.2
Trade Receivables (net)	2.6	3.3	2.3	2.2	3.6			1.9	2.1
Inventory	4.5	4.0	3.8	1.8	5.7			7.3	3.5
All Other Current	3.3	4.1	3.4	7.3	.1			2.3	1.9
Total Current	25.6	27.6	28.8	34.1	17.4			32.3	28.7
Fixed Assets (net)	63.0	60.9	61.2	57.7	67.8			56.5	63.5
Intangibles (net)	4.5	4.3	3.5	1.3	3.9			4.7	3.7
All Other Non-Current	6.9	7.1	6.5	7.0	10.8			6.5	4.1
Total	100.0	100.0	100.0	100.0	100.0			100.0	100.0
LIABILITIES									
Notes Payable-Short Term	4.3	7.0	13.3	50.4	8.6			.3	2.0
Cur. Mat.-L/T/D	8.2	8.4	7.1	4.9	5.5			17.7	6.3
Trade Payables	4.5	4.6	5.6	13.1	5.2			4.2	2.8
Income Taxes Payable	.2	.1	.0	.0	.0			.0	.0
All Other Current	8.7	6.9	12.5	17.2	9.0			16.1	12.2
Total Current	25.9	27.0	38.5	85.7	28.3			38.3	23.3
Long-Term Debt	30.2	30.8	31.1	40.0	44.8			26.3	24.6
Deferred Taxes	.4	.2	.5	.0	.7			2.3	.1
All Other Non-Current	7.2	7.0	9.6	29.7	16.4			1.1	.7
Net Worth	36.2	35.0	20.2	-55.4	9.8			31.9	51.3
Total Liabilities & Net Worth	100.0	100.0	100.0	100.0	100.0			100.0	100.0
INCOME DATA									
Net Sales	100.0	100.0	100.0	100.0	100.0			100.0	100.0
Gross Profit									
Operating Expenses	86.3	86.5	85.6	98.8	97.7			84.9	72.8
Operating Profit	13.7	13.5	14.4	1.2	2.3			15.1	27.2
All Other Expenses (net)	3.6	2.8	2.9	7.1	2.5			2.2	1.6
Profit Before Taxes	10.1	10.7	11.5	-5.9	-.2			12.9	25.7
RATIOS									
Current	1.8 / .9 / .5	2.1 / .9 / .4	1.7 / .9 / .3	3.2 / .3 / .1	1.1 / .5 / .2			2.2 / .7 / .2	1.8 / 1.2 / .8
Quick	1.2 / .7 / .2	1.5 (113) / .7 / .2	1.3 / .7 / .2	2.0 / .1 / .1	.8 / .4 / .1			2.0 / .4 / .2	1.3 / 1.1 / .7
Sales/Receivables	0 UND / 1 704.2 / 4 97.5	0 UND / 1 570.8 / 4 82.2	0 UND / 0 969.7 / 4 102.6	0 UND / 0 UND / 0 UND	0 UND / 0 969.7 / 7 52.6			0 UND / 0 999.8 / 1 260.9	0 887.4 / 1 342.4 / 4 89.1
Cost of Sales/Inventory									
Cost of Sales/Payables									
Sales/Working Capital	21.3 / -82.8 / -10.1	10.6 / -61.2 / -9.6	15.4 / -180.1 / -10.8	15.3 / -7.7 / -3.5	100.9 / -23.3 / -5.4			10.0 / -32.0 / -11.0	12.8 / 52.6 / -39.3
EBIT/Interest	11.4 / (79) 4.3 / 1.1	13.8 / (99) 4.4 / .9	27.7 / (63) 5.0 / 1.3		2.5 / (13) 1.2 / -2.1				45.6 / (26) 12.3 / 5.1
Net Profit + Depr., Dep., Amort./Cur. Mat. L/T/D	10.6 / (11) 4.5 / 1.7	5.0 / (16) 2.7 / 1.5							
Fixed/Worth	.9 / 1.6 / 6.2	.8 / 1.9 / 17.0	.9 / 2.1 / NM	1.1 / -2.4 / -.7	2.0 / 6.7 / -16.2			.7 / 2.6 / NM	.9 / 1.6 / 2.1
Debt/Worth	.6 / 1.5 / 8.7	.6 / 1.9 / 18.3	.8 / 2.1 / -275.3	6.9 / -4.0 / -1.6	2.3 / 6.6 / -22.6			.3 / 2.9 / NM	.4 / 1.2 / 2.0
% Profit Before Taxes/Tangible Net Worth	87.2 / (74) 32.4 / 6.8	96.7 / (87) 32.6 / 3.7	97.5 / (56) 52.6 / 24.9						115.3 / (28) 83.3 / 27.0
% Profit Before Taxes/Total Assets	28.5 / 8.0 / .5	28.7 / 9.7 / -.1	39.4 / 12.1 / 1.0	11.1 / -14.3 / -42.3	6.2 / 1.3 / -14.0			56.9 / 13.8 / 9.0	53.4 / 35.6 / 12.0
Sales/Net Fixed Assets	5.2 / 2.5 / 1.4	5.5 / 2.4 / 1.3	7.0 / 2.8 / 1.5	15.7 / 3.9 / 1.4	3.9 / 2.4 / 1.0			10.0 / 5.2 / 2.6	3.3 / 2.0 / 1.5
Sales/Total Assets	2.4 / 1.5 / 1.1	2.4 / 1.4 / 1.0	3.0 / 1.7 / 1.1	3.9 / 2.1 / 1.3	1.9 / 1.8 / .9			4.3 / 3.0 / 1.7	1.8 / 1.5 / 1.0
% Depr., Dep., Amort./Sales	2.9 / (74) 6.7 / 12.9	3.9 / (94) 7.2 / 12.0	4.1 / (58) 6.9 / 13.7		8.0 / (12) 13.7 / 15.1			3.7 / 5.9 / 7.3	2.6 / (19) 5.2 / 7.9
% Officers', Directors', Owners' Comp/Sales	3.4 / (24) 6.2 / 11.2	3.1 / (38) 5.0 / 10.2	4.1 / (27) 6.6 / 13.0		4.1 / (11) 6.6 / 8.8				
Net Sales ($)	4249972M	5418318M	3737049M	5190M	26974M	11358M	38272M	160361M	3494894M
Total Assets ($)	3338542M	4593314M	2553119M	3891M	22320M	9139M	17273M	67379M	2433117M

M = $ thousand   MM = $ million
See Pages 11 through 21 for Explanation of Ratios and Data

Current Data Sorted By Assets | Comparative Historical Data

0-500M	500M-2MM	2-10MM	10-50MM	50-100MM	100-250MM	Type of Statement	4/1/00-3/31/01 ALL	4/1/01-3/31/02 ALL
	1	2	20	7	10	Unqualified		
	1	1	9	3	1	Reviewed		
5		1				Compiled		
2		3				Tax Returns		
						Other		
18 (4/1-9/30/04)			47 (10/1/04-3/31/05)					
7	1	7	29	10	11	NUMBER OF STATEMENTS		
%	%	%	%	%	%	ASSETS	%	%
			22.0	15.4	18.1	Cash & Equivalents	D	D
			.9	.3	.9	Trade Receivables (net)	A	A
			.6	7.1	.3	Inventory	T	T
			1.9	3.4	1.6	All Other Current	A	A
			25.4	26.2	20.8	Total Current		
			69.2	70.9	71.8	Fixed Assets (net)	N	N
			2.4	1.4	3.2	Intangibles (net)	O	O
			2.9	1.5	4.2	All Other Non-Current	T	T
			100.0	100.0	100.0	Total		
						LIABILITIES	A	A
			.7	.0	.1	Notes Payable-Short Term	V	V
			8.1	3.4	6.3	Cur. Mat.-L/T/D	A	A
			2.4	2.0	2.2	Trade Payables	I	I
			.1	.0	.1	Income Taxes Payable	L	L
			9.7	11.0	9.5	All Other Current	A	A
			21.0	16.4	18.3	Total Current	B	B
			36.6	25.2	25.8	Long-Term Debt	L	L
			.0	.0	.6	Deferred Taxes	E	E
			1.7	.0	3.6	All Other Non-Current		
			40.8	58.4	51.8	Net Worth		
			100.0	100.0	100.0	Total Liabilities & Net Worth		
						INCOME DATA		
			100.0	100.0	100.0	Net Sales		
						Gross Profit		
			76.1	64.0	62.9	Operating Expenses		
			23.9	36.0	37.1	Operating Profit		
			3.7	1.1	2.1	All Other Expenses (net)		
			20.2	34.9	35.0	Profit Before Taxes		
						RATIOS		
			1.7	2.2	1.7			
			1.3	1.0	.9	Current		
			.8	.9	.6			
			1.6	2.0	1.6			
			1.1	.9	.8	Quick		
			.7	.7	.6			
			0 999.8	0 999.8	0 833.2			
			1 589.9	0 818.5	1 375.2	Sales/Receivables		
			3 142.8	1 343.1	3 111.6			
						Cost of Sales/Inventory		
						Cost of Sales/Payables		
			11.0	12.6	14.0			
			42.3	331.2	-77.1	Sales/Working Capital		
			-35.6	-69.3	-25.1			
			51.2		54.1			
			(27) 12.5		24.4	EBIT/Interest		
			5.4		12.9			
						Net Profit + Depr., Dep., Amort./Cur. Mat. L /T/D		
			.9	1.0	1.0			
			1.5	1.1	1.7	Fixed/Worth		
			8.1	1.6	1.9			
			.5	.3	.5			
			1.0	.8	.9	Debt/Worth		
			8.8	1.3	1.7			
			91.4	171.1	259.1			
			(23) 64.3	94.4	91.7	% Profit Before Taxes/Tangible Net Worth		
			15.8	71.1	39.0			
			51.2	127.9	74.9			
			25.3	46.2	47.9	% Profit Before Taxes/Total Assets		
			10.6	26.0	19.6			
			3.1	4.3	2.4			
			2.3	1.9	1.6	Sales/Net Fixed Assets		
			1.6	1.5	1.4			
			2.0	2.5	1.5			
			1.6	1.5	1.4	Sales/Total Assets		
			1.3	.9	1.1			
			4.9	4.0				
			6.0	4.8		% Depr., Dep., Amort./Sales		
			7.2	5.7				
						% Officers', Directors', Owners' Comp/Sales		
17562M	4506M	182203M	1248694M	1180512M	2009263M	Net Sales ($)		
1396M	1980M	48447M	702887M	715582M	1681042M	Total Assets ($)		

© RMA 2005

M = $ thousand   MM = $ million
See Pages 11 through 21 for Explanation of Ratios and Data

Comparative Historical Data / Current Data Sorted By Sales

Type of Statement									
Unqualified	17	33	39					4	35
Reviewed			2					1	1
Compiled	1	1				1			
Tax Returns	3	5	6	2	1	1	1		
Other	12	8	18	1		1	1	5	10
	4/1/02-3/31/03	4/1/03-3/31/04	4/1/04-3/31/05	0-1MM	1-3MM	3-5MM	5-10MM	10-25MM	25MM & OVER
	ALL	ALL	ALL	18 (4/1-9/30/04)			47 (10/1/04-3/31/05)		
NUMBER OF STATEMENTS	33	47	65	3	1	3	2	10	46
	%	%	%	%	%	%	%	%	%
ASSETS									
Cash & Equivalents	21.3	21.4	21.3					15.8	21.4
Trade Receivables (net)	.6	.7	.9					1.9	.7
Inventory	1.1	1.1	1.8					.9	1.9
All Other Current	1.9	3.2	2.2					3.2	2.1
Total Current	25.0	26.3	26.2					21.7	26.0
Fixed Assets (net)	62.8	61.3	64.0					70.1	69.3
Intangibles (net)	9.7	7.6	6.1					3.9	2.0
All Other Non-Current	2.6	4.8	3.7					4.3	2.7
Total	100.0	100.0	100.0					100.0	100.0
LIABILITIES									
Notes Payable-Short Term	2.9	1.3	1.7					2.4	.1
Cur. Mat.-L/T/D	5.6	6.8	7.5					8.2	7.2
Trade Payables	4.3	5.1	3.3					4.9	2.2
Income Taxes Payable	.0	.0	.0					.0	.1
All Other Current	10.6	10.5	10.1					8.3	10.4
Total Current	23.5	23.7	22.6					23.8	20.0
Long-Term Debt	36.0	31.2	31.4					45.4	28.9
Deferred Taxes	.0	.0	.1					.0	.1
All Other Non-Current	1.7	2.4	1.4					1.7	1.6
Net Worth	38.7	42.7	44.6					29.1	49.5
Total Liabilities & Net Worth	100.0	100.0	100.0					100.0	100.0
INCOME DATA									
Net Sales	100.0	100.0	100.0					100.0	100.0
Gross Profit									
Operating Expenses	69.5	76.6	75.0					82.1	69.7
Operating Profit	30.5	23.4	25.0					17.9	30.3
All Other Expenses (net)	4.1	3.0	2.8					3.0	2.7
Profit Before Taxes	26.4	20.4	22.2					14.8	27.6
RATIOS									
Current	1.7	1.8	1.7					1.6	1.7
	1.0	1.1	1.2					1.1	1.2
	.7	.7	.7					.5	.8
Quick	1.5	1.7	1.7					1.4	1.7
	.9	.9	1.0					.8	1.1
	.6	.5	.6					.3	.7
Sales/Receivables	0 UND	0 999.8	0 999.8					0 934.7	0 999.8
	1 497.5	0 735.4	1 635.5					1 381.5	1 594.8
	2 176.1	2 194.7	2 165.8					5 74.0	2 158.7
Cost of Sales/Inventory									
Cost of Sales/Payables									
Sales/Working Capital	21.7	13.3	13.6					23.0	11.9
	164.0	92.9	68.4					NM	43.4
	-42.6	-24.6	-34.6					-13.2	-44.0
EBIT/Interest	-32.1	47.2	65.5						71.8
	(28) 13.0	(38) 12.3	(56) 14.1					(41)	22.9
	3.6	4.5	6.7						9.1
Net Profit + Depr., Dep., Amort./Cur. Mat. L/T/D									
Fixed/Worth	.9	.8	.9					1.0	.9
	1.8	1.5	1.3					3.6	1.3
	NM	5.6	2.9					NM	2.0
Debt/Worth	.4	.4	.5					.6	.4
	1.4	1.0	.9					3.8	.8
	-340.8	5.5	4.5					NM	1.8
% Profit Before Taxes/Tangible Net Worth	228.9	116.8	139.8						121.1
	(24) 92.5	(38) 62.0	(54) 79.1					(41)	77.7
	43.2	27.8	33.9						37.8
% Profit Before Taxes/Total Assets	75.9	51.2	57.1					34.1	57.6
	43.5	26.4	34.0					19.0	45.0
	19.2	7.8	15.1					3.2	19.0
Sales/Net Fixed Assets	5.0	6.6	4.4					5.3	3.2
	2.5	2.7	2.4					2.3	2.2
	1.5	1.8	1.6					1.4	1.6
Sales/Total Assets	3.6	3.5	2.4					2.6	2.0
	1.8	1.9	1.6					1.8	1.5
	1.2	1.4	1.2					1.2	1.1
% Depr., Dep., Amort./Sales	3.4	3.0	4.2					3.5	4.4
	(26) 4.7	(37) 5.1	(54) 5.5					6.2	(40) 5.5
	6.8	6.6	7.0					7.6	6.8
% Officers', Directors', Owners' Comp/Sales									
Net Sales ($)	2241788M	3196556M	4642740M	1697M	2190M	10838M	14670M	179481M	4433864M
Total Assets ($)	1271445M	1920651M	3151334M	419M	62M	2498M	8056M	125006M	3015293M

M = $ thousand   MM = $ million
See Pages 11 through 21 for Explanation of Ratios and Data

Current Data Sorted By Assets | Comparative Historical Data

Type of Statement	0-500M	500M-2MM	2-10MM	10-50MM	50-100MM	100-250MM		4/1/00-3/31/01 ALL	4/1/01-3/31/02 ALL
Unqualified	2	14	132	70	4	6		241	196
Reviewed	8	22	85	19		1		115	101
Compiled	28	65	67	1		1		220	239
Tax Returns	32	31	32	1				62	77
Other	23	54	133	35	3	2		234	253
		183 (4/1-9/30/04)		688 (10/1/04-3/31/05)				4/1/00-3/31/01 ALL	4/1/01-3/31/02 ALL
NUMBER OF STATEMENTS	93	186	449	126	8	9		872	866

ASSETS	%	%	%	%	%	%		%	%
Cash & Equivalents	17.0	6.1	5.2	6.4				7.6	7.5
Trade Receivables (net)	5.2	4.9	5.0	3.6				5.4	5.1
Inventory	7.8	3.5	1.8	.9				2.8	2.7
All Other Current	1.3	.6	1.2	1.6				2.5	3.8
Total Current	31.3	15.1	13.2	12.5				18.4	19.1
Fixed Assets (net)	57.0	77.1	80.1	80.5				73.8	74.3
Intangibles (net)	4.3	1.9	2.1	1.7				1.8	1.4
All Other Non-Current	7.5	6.0	4.7	5.3				6.0	5.2
Total	100.0	100.0	100.0	100.0				100.0	100.0

LIABILITIES									
Notes Payable-Short Term	14.7	5.4	3.0	2.6				3.8	4.4
Cur. Mat.-L/T/D	4.4	4.4	3.1	1.5				3.5	3.5
Trade Payables	10.3	4.3	2.6	1.8				3.9	4.1
Income Taxes Payable	.1	.3	.1	.1				.1	.1
All Other Current	21.1	11.7	7.9	7.4				8.8	8.5
Total Current	50.6	26.1	16.6	13.5				20.0	20.7
Long-Term Debt	25.8	47.6	42.1	30.8				35.6	38.1
Deferred Taxes	.0	.2	.0	.2				.1	.1
All Other Non-Current	11.2	14.0	5.3	5.7				7.0	6.5
Net Worth	12.4	11.9	36.0	49.8				37.3	34.6
Total Liabilities & Net Worth	100.0	100.0	100.0	100.0				100.0	100.0

INCOME DATA									
Net Sales	100.0	100.0	100.0	100.0				100.0	100.0
Gross Profit									
Operating Expenses	98.3	97.1	98.4	98.8				96.7	96.1
Operating Profit	1.7	2.9	1.6	1.2				3.3	3.9
All Other Expenses (net)	1.6	5.2	3.8	2.4				2.4	4.5
Profit Before Taxes	.1	-2.3	-2.3	-1.3				.9	-.5

RATIOS									
Current	2.2	1.5	1.7	1.7				1.9	2.0
	.8	.6	.9	1.1				1.1	1.1
	.2	.3	.5	.6				.5	.6
Quick	1.4	1.2	1.3	1.5				1.5	1.5
	.5	.4	.7	.8				.8	.8
	.1	.1	.3	.4				.3	.3
Sales/Receivables	0 UND	0 UND	3 137.5	12 29.5				1 282.5	1 398.1
	0 UND	2 169.8	24 15.1	24 15.2				19 19.1	19 19.2
	3 121.6	20 18.4	37 9.9	40 9.2				38 9.6	38 9.7
Cost of Sales/Inventory									
Cost of Sales/Payables									
Sales/Working Capital	16.7	20.4	12.1	8.9				9.3	8.2
	-46.7	-18.7	-73.2	71.0				94.5	69.3
	-7.1	-5.6	-6.8	-8.0				-10.6	-10.8
EBIT/Interest	3.3	1.7	1.7	2.4				2.8	2.3
	(62) .6	(156) .6	(377) .7	(91) 1.0				(689) 1.2	(705) 1.0
	-3.2	-.9	-.5	-.5				.2	-.2
Net Profit + Depr., Dep., Amort./Cur. Mat. L/T/D		3.5	4.6	4.9				4.4	4.1
		(13) 1.3	(20) 1.6	(15) 1.7				(82) 2.6	(82) 1.8
		.7	.6	.7				.9	1.0
Fixed/Worth	.8	1.6	1.3	1.2				1.1	1.1
	2.1	3.6	2.2	1.6				1.7	1.8
	-3.8	-18.3	7.7	2.9				4.2	5.6
Debt/Worth	.7	1.2	.6	.3				.5	.5
	3.3	3.4	1.6	.9				1.3	1.4
	-4.0	-19.7	8.4	2.3				4.5	6.0
% Profit Before Taxes/Tangible Net Worth	45.8	8.1	4.7	5.8				11.4	8.8
	(62) 5.5	(132) -.2	(373) -1.7	(115) .2				(748) 2.2	(737) .3
	-7.5	-15.5	-9.6	-5.0				-5.9	-7.8
% Profit Before Taxes/Total Assets	11.0	2.5	1.8	2.8				5.2	3.7
	.6	-.7	-1.0	.0				.7	-.1
	-8.1	-5.3	-4.2	-2.6				-3.1	-3.9
Sales/Net Fixed Assets	15.7	1.9	1.1	.7				1.5	1.4
	4.2	1.0	.7	.5				.9	.9
	1.8	.7	.5	.4				.6	.5
Sales/Total Assets	5.0	1.3	.8	.5				1.0	1.0
	2.6	.9	.6	.4				.7	.6
	1.3	.6	.4	.3				.5	.4
% Depr., Dep., Amort./Sales	3.0	5.6	7.8	7.4				5.7	5.4
	(71) 5.0	(170) 8.8	(416) 9.9	(118) 10.9				(799) 8.8	(798) 8.8
	9.1	13.2	13.6	15.3				11.9	11.8
% Officers', Directors', Owners' Comp/Sales	5.7	5.6	3.9	5.6				4.5	4.4
	(36) 10.3	(52) 9.5	(56) 8.1	(15) 8.2				(160) 8.6	(170) 7.7
	15.0	22.8	29.5	35.2				18.9	15.7
Net Sales ($)	71017M	235754M	1330675M	947496M	237084M	1151331M		4026247M	4081368M
Total Assets ($)	25152M	228089M	2185121M	2218398M	537815M	1656158M		6385857M	5885675M

Note: Quick ratio historical count shown as (871) and (865).

M = $ thousand   MM = $ million
See Pages 11 through 21 for Explanation of Ratios and Data

Comparative Historical Data / Current Data Sorted By Sales

	Type of Statement	Hist 1	Hist 2	Hist 3	0-1MM	1-3MM	3-5MM	5-10MM	10-25MM	25MM & OVER
	Unqualified	283	236	228	6	59	66	74	13	10
	Reviewed	141	126	135	22	61	39	9	4	
	Compiled	155	247	162	69	80	10	2	2	1
	Tax Returns	101	107	96	56	34	4	2	2	
	Other	303	285	250	51	109	45	34	8	3

Historical periods: 4/1/02-3/31/03 ALL | 4/1/03-3/31/04 ALL | 4/1/04-3/31/05 ALL
Current: 183 (4/1-9/30/04)   688 (10/1/04-3/31/05)

Item	Hist 4/1/02-3/31/03	Hist 4/1/03-3/31/04	Hist 4/1/04-3/31/05	0-1MM	1-3MM	3-5MM	5-10MM	10-25MM	25MM & OVER
NUMBER OF STATEMENTS	983	1001	871	204	343	164	121	25	14
ASSETS	%	%	%	%	%	%	%	%	%
Cash & Equivalents	7.6	7.0	6.9	7.4	6.5	6.3	7.6	7.3	10.6
Trade Receivables (net)	5.2	4.9	4.8	2.2	5.2	6.5	5.8	4.3	3.7
Inventory	2.6	2.5	2.6	2.8	2.9	2.7	2.2	1.1	.8
All Other Current	1.4	2.9	1.1	1.3	.8	1.1	1.2	3.8	2.3
Total Current	16.9	17.3	15.5	13.7	15.4	16.5	16.7	16.5	17.5
Fixed Assets (net)	76.9	75.0	76.9	76.6	77.2	77.2	78.0	72.6	68.7
Intangibles (net)	1.5	2.1	2.3	3.3	2.4	1.1	.8	4.9	5.7
All Other Non-Current	4.7	5.6	5.4	6.4	5.1	5.1	4.5	6.0	8.1
Total	100.0	100.0	100.0	100.0	100.0	100.0	100.0	100.0	100.0
LIABILITIES									
Notes Payable-Short Term	3.6	4.4	4.7	8.0	5.0	2.3	1.5	7.1	.9
Cur. Mat.-L/T/D	4.0	3.5	3.3	3.7	3.8	3.2	1.6	1.3	2.7
Trade Payables	3.2	4.2	3.6	3.3	4.6	2.9	2.8	2.5	3.1
Income Taxes Payable	.1	.1	.1	.1	.2	.2	.1	.3	.2
All Other Current	9.5	10.5	10.1	8.6	12.0	8.4	9.6	8.7	13.8
Total Current	20.3	22.7	21.9	23.7	25.5	17.0	15.7	19.9	20.7
Long-Term Debt	38.3	40.6	39.8	46.4	43.3	35.3	26.3	32.6	39.9
Deferred Taxes	.1	.1	.1	.2	.1	.0	.1	1.1	.3
All Other Non-Current	9.6	8.6	7.9	10.0	7.5	5.5	9.0	6.5	9.8
Net Worth	31.6	28.0	30.3	19.7	23.7	42.2	49.0	39.8	29.4
Total Liabilities & Net Worth	100.0	100.0	100.0	100.0	100.0	100.0	100.0	100.0	100.0
INCOME DATA									
Net Sales	100.0	100.0	100.0	100.0	100.0	100.0	100.0	100.0	100.0
Gross Profit									
Operating Expenses	97.9	98.1	98.1	96.1	98.3	100.1	99.4	94.9	90.1
Operating Profit	2.1	1.9	1.9	3.9	1.7	-.1	.6	5.1	9.9
All Other Expenses (net)	4.0	4.2	3.7	7.3	4.1	1.1	.1	3.7	1.3
Profit Before Taxes	-1.9	-2.3	-1.7	-3.4	-2.4	-1.2	.5	1.3	8.6
RATIOS									
Current	1.7	1.7	1.7	2.0	1.5	1.7	2.2	1.8	1.4
	.9	.9	.9	.6	.7	1.0	1.1	1.1	1.0
	.5	.4	.4	.2	.3	.7	.7	.6	.6
Quick	1.4	1.3	1.3	1.1	1.2	1.4	1.8	1.7	1.2
	.7 (981)	.6 (998)	.6	.4	.6	.8	.8	.9	.7
	.3	.2	.2	.1	.2	.5	.5	.3	.4
Sales/Receivables	1 378.2	1 532.3	0 999.8	0 UND	1 510.0	17 21.8	15 24.2	6 65.5	3 123.1
	18 19.7	16 23.2	15 24.1	0 UND	15 24.6	31 12.0	28 13.3	23 16.2	10 37.1
	37 10.0	34 10.7	34 10.8	5 78.9	33 11.0	42 8.8	39 9.3	36 10.2	34 10.8
Cost of Sales/Inventory									
Cost of Sales/Payables									
Sales/Working Capital	11.3	12.4	13.4	18.0	16.8	11.4	7.5	10.9	14.0
	-102.5	-45.4	-49.0	-17.1	-25.3	476.7	27.4	39.7	459.6
	-7.8	-7.1	-6.5	-4.6	-5.2	-12.5	-13.5	-7.1	-6.5
EBIT/Interest	2.1	2.0	1.9	1.3	1.7	2.2	3.0	2.4	6.2
	.9 (807)	.7 (793)	.7 (701)	.2 (152)	.7 (282)	.8 (140)	.9 (96)	1.2 (17)	2.6
	-.4	-.9	-.7	-1.4	-.6	-.7	-.5	.3	1.0
Net Profit + Depr., Dep., Amort./Cur. Mat. L/T/D	3.4	3.1	4.5		3.3	3.6			
	1.7 (98)	1.7 (70)	1.6 (53)		1.6 (14)	1.3 (17)			
	.9	.4	.6		.4	.7			
Fixed/Worth	1.2	1.2	1.2	1.4	1.4	1.2	1.0	1.3	1.3
	2.0	2.2	2.3	3.1	3.2	1.8	1.4	2.1	4.6
	5.3	10.3	11.4	-16.1	146.9	3.5	2.5	4.3	-31.3
Debt/Worth	.5	.6	.6	.9	.7	.5	.3	.7	1.1
	1.5	1.9	1.8	3.2	2.9	1.4	.8	1.8	5.8
	6.0	12.9	12.6	-18.6	174.4	3.3	2.1	5.7	-38.9
% Profit Before Taxes/Tangible Net Worth	6.2	6.2	6.6	7.3	6.7	4.6	5.9	11.6	106.5
	.2 (816)	-.9 (798)	-.4 (695)	-2.0 (144)	-.8 (260)	-.5 (146)	.5 (113)	.4 (22)	7.4 (10)
	-7.9	-8.9	-8.4	-14.0	-11.7	-7.0	-5.3	-6.5	-.8
% Profit Before Taxes/Total Assets	2.6	2.5	2.5	1.9	2.4	1.9	3.2	6.0	12.4
	-.2	-.8	-.6	-1.7	-.7	-.4	.1	.5	2.0
	-4.2	-5.0	-4.3	-6.2	-4.7	-3.3	-2.6	-2.1	.2
Sales/Net Fixed Assets	1.3	1.3	1.4	1.9	1.4	1.2	1.1	1.3	1.4
	.8	.8	.8	.8	.7	.8	.8	.8	.9
	.5	.5	.5	.4	.5	.6	.5	.5	.7
Sales/Total Assets	1.0	1.0	1.0	1.3	1.0	.9	.8	.8	1.0
	.6	.6	.6	.7	.6	.6	.6	.6	.7
	.4	.4	.4	.3	.4	.5	.5	.4	.4
% Depr., Dep., Amort./Sales	7.1	7.1	6.7	5.8	6.8	7.5	6.9	5.5	5.7
	9.9 (901)	10.0 (896)	9.6 (789)	10.0 (179)	9.7 (313)	9.4 (151)	9.0 (113)	9.7 (22)	6.9 (11)
	13.5	13.5	13.4	17.2	13.5	12.5	11.6	13.0	9.7
% Officers', Directors', Owners' Comp/Sales	3.9	5.0	5.3	6.7	4.0	5.8	2.5		
	8.0 (171)	9.7 (180)	9.6 (161)	11.9 (58)	9.0 (66)	9.0 (17)	8.0 (15)		
	16.4	21.4	21.2	19.4	29.4	13.9	35.2		
Net Sales ($)	6340663M	5459001M	3973357M	119483M	659998M	633095M	801341M	364328M	1395112M
Total Assets ($)	8171972M	8448381M	6850733M	256706M	1269380M	1129685M	1451140M	850574M	1893248M

M = $ thousand   MM = $ million
See Pages 11 through 21 for Explanation of Ratios and Data

Current Data Sorted By Assets

Comparative Historical Data

						Type of Statement		
	2	1	8	2	3	Unqualified		
	2	2				Reviewed		
	1	1				Compiled		
						Tax Returns		
		3	4	3		Other		
	23 (4/1-9/30/04)		9 (10/1/04-3/31/05)				4/1/00-3/31/01 ALL	4/1/01-3/31/02 ALL
0-500M	500M-2MM	2-10MM	10-50MM	50-100MM	100-250MM			
	5	7	12	5	3	NUMBER OF STATEMENTS		
%	%	%	%	%	%	ASSETS	%	%
D			2.8			Cash & Equivalents	D	D
A			1.3			Trade Receivables (net)	A	A
T			1.1			Inventory	T	T
A			3.6			All Other Current	A	A
			8.7			Total Current		
N			81.9			Fixed Assets (net)	N	N
O			2.6			Intangibles (net)	O	O
T			6.8			All Other Non-Current	T	T
			100.0			Total		
A						LIABILITIES	A	A
V			1.9			Notes Payable-Short Term	V	V
A			2.2			Cur. Mat.-L/T/D	A	A
I			4.4			Trade Payables	I	I
L			.0			Income Taxes Payable	L	L
A			8.8			All Other Current	A	A
B			17.3			Total Current	B	B
L			27.3			Long-Term Debt	L	L
E			6.3			Deferred Taxes	E	E
			4.8			All Other Non-Current		
			44.4			Net Worth		
			100.0			Total Liabilities & Net Worth		
			100.0			INCOME DATA Net Sales		
						Gross Profit		
			96.7			Operating Expenses		
			3.3			Operating Profit		
			1.9			All Other Expenses (net)		
			1.4			Profit Before Taxes		
						RATIOS		
			.7					
			.5			Current		
			.3					
			.4					
			.3			Quick		
			.1					
		2	181.9					
		5	69.9			Sales/Receivables		
		11	32.3					
						Cost of Sales/Inventory		
						Cost of Sales/Payables		
			−20.8					
			−10.5			Sales/Working Capital		
			−4.9					
			4.0					
		(11)	2.2			EBIT/Interest		
			.1					
						Net Profit + Depr., Dep., Amort./Cur. Mat. L./T/D		
			1.8					
			2.0			Fixed/Worth		
			2.3					
			1.2					
			1.3			Debt/Worth		
			1.9					
			12.2			% Profit Before Taxes/Tangible Net Worth		
			3.7					
			−3.2					
			3.9			% Profit Before Taxes/Total Assets		
			1.5					
			−2.0					
			1.4					
			.8			Sales/Net Fixed Assets		
			.7					
			1.1					
			.6			Sales/Total Assets		
			.6					
			6.6					
		(11)	12.0			% Depr., Dep., Amort./Sales		
			16.0					
						% Officers', Directors', Owners' Comp/Sales		
	6783M	32871M	289026M	172872M	289631M	Net Sales ($)		
	5339M	41861M	411222M	275039M	357086M	Total Assets ($)		

M = $ thousand   MM = $ million
See Pages 11 through 21 for Explanation of Ratios and Data

Comparative Historical Data				Current Data Sorted By Sales					
			Type of Statement						
9	18	14	Unqualified				1	5	8
3	3	4	Reviewed	2		1	1		
	3	3	Compiled		2		1		
	4	1	Tax Returns	1					
7	3	10	Other	1	1	1		3	4
4/1/02-3/31/03 ALL	4/1/03-3/31/04 ALL	4/1/04-3/31/05 ALL		23 (4/1-9/30/04)			9 (10/1/04-3/31/05)		
				0-1MM	1-3MM	3-5MM	5-10MM	10-25MM	25MM & OVER
19	31	32	NUMBER OF STATEMENTS	4	3	2	3	8	12
%	%	%	ASSETS	%	%	%	%	%	%
5.9	4.4	3.1	Cash & Equivalents						1.8
3.5	2.5	.8	Trade Receivables (net)						1.2
1.8	2.1	1.5	Inventory						.9
2.6	2.1	4.9	All Other Current						4.8
13.8	11.2	10.3	Total Current						8.6
78.7	75.5	76.6	Fixed Assets (net)						76.0
2.5	4.7	5.1	Intangibles (net)						6.5
5.0	8.6	7.9	All Other Non-Current						8.9
100.0	100.0	100.0	Total						100.0
			LIABILITIES						
4.4	4.2	5.1	Notes Payable-Short Term						.1
4.2	3.4	3.2	Cur. Mat.-L/T/D						3.8
4.9	5.4	4.7	Trade Payables						4.1
.3	.1	.0	Income Taxes Payable						.0
9.2	7.2	11.7	All Other Current						11.2
22.9	20.3	24.8	Total Current						19.3
29.7	37.9	36.1	Long-Term Debt						26.5
2.2	2.5	3.3	Deferred Taxes						4.2
2.1	7.3	6.4	All Other Non-Current						6.0
43.0	32.1	29.4	Net Worth						44.0
100.0	100.0	100.0	Total Liabilities & Net Worth						100.0
			INCOME DATA						
100.0	100.0	100.0	Net Sales						100.0
			Gross Profit						
92.7	94.3	94.4	Operating Expenses						92.1
7.3	5.7	5.6	Operating Profit						7.9
3.2	6.5	4.5	All Other Expenses (net)						2.9
4.1	-.8	1.2	Profit Before Taxes						5.0
			RATIOS						
1.2	.9	.6	Current						.9
.7	.5	.5							.5
.3	.3	.2							.2
.8	.6	.3	Quick						.4
.4	.3	.2							.2
.1	.1	.0							.0
1 459.2	0 796.0	0 924.7	Sales/Receivables						2 211.6
2 149.1	3 143.1	3 131.7							4 85.3
14 26.9	9 40.6	8 46.1							11 32.8
			Cost of Sales/Inventory						
			Cost of Sales/Payables						
48.8	-68.0	-16.8	Sales/Working Capital						-87.9
-11.5	-11.3	-6.9							-8.0
-6.7	-4.8	-3.7							-3.7
7.7	4.9	5.2	EBIT/Interest						11.3
(18) 2.3	(27) 1.4	(29) 2.2							3.5
1.0	-.3	.3							.7
	114.9	12.5	Net Profit + Depr., Dep., Amort./Cur. Mat. L/T/D						
	(12) 2.6	(12) 2.1							
	1.6	.7							
1.2	1.7	1.6	Fixed/Worth						1.7
1.8	2.2	2.1							1.9
3.1	3.8	9.6							2.3
.5	1.1	1.2	Debt/Worth						1.2
1.2	1.7	1.6							1.3
3.1	3.7	25.2							1.8
27.2	15.0	27.2	% Profit Before Taxes/Tangible Net Worth						26.4
(17) 10.7	(26) 2.0	(25) 9.8						(11)	11.7
1.9	-6.6	-3.1							-1.9
10.2	5.2	8.0	% Profit Before Taxes/Total Assets						9.7
3.9	.6	2.6							3.6
-.4	-3.1	-2.2							-1.1
2.0	1.6	1.6	Sales/Net Fixed Assets						1.3
.9	1.0	.9							.9
.7	.8	.8							.8
1.5	1.2	1.2	Sales/Total Assets						.9
.8	.8	.8							.7
.7	.6	.6							.6
7.2	8.6	9.0	% Depr., Dep., Amort./Sales						8.4
(18) 11.1	(29) 12.7	(28) 11.9						(10)	11.0
14.4	15.1	13.8							12.6
			% Officers', Directors', Owners' Comp/Sales						
387370M	663971M	791183M	Net Sales ($)	3514M	5377M	8038M	22725M	144087M	607442M
524327M	858141M	1090547M	Total Assets ($)	4747M	12509M	13248M	16696M	247326M	796021M

Current Data Sorted By Assets   Comparative Historical Data

Type of Statement	0-500M	500M-2MM	2-10MM	10-50MM	50-100MM	100-250MM		Hist 1	Hist 2
Unqualified		1	4	3				7	3
Reviewed		5	14	2				24	17
Compiled	12	15	10	3				28	38
Tax Returns	13	12	7	3				28	30
Other	6	6	25	4				45	42
	10 (4/1-9/30/04)		132 (10/1/04-3/31/05)					4/1/00-3/31/01 ALL	4/1/01-3/31/02 ALL
NUMBER OF STATEMENTS	31	39	60	12				132	130
ASSETS	%	%	%	%	%	%		%	%
Cash & Equivalents	18.3	10.1	7.5	6.0	D	D		8.6	7.1
Trade Receivables (net)	11.7	6.4	5.2	6.2	A	A		6.5	6.6
Inventory	11.8	22.3	18.5	11.4	T	T		16.3	18.3
All Other Current	2.4	2.7	2.1	1.1	A	A		1.5	2.2
Total Current	44.1	41.6	33.3	24.8				32.8	34.3
Fixed Assets (net)	47.5	50.9	58.5	56.4	N	N		55.5	57.8
Intangibles (net)	3.3	2.8	4.2	8.0	O	O		3.7	2.6
All Other Non-Current	5.2	4.8	4.1	10.8	T	T		8.0	5.3
Total	100.0	100.0	100.0	100.0				100.0	100.0
LIABILITIES					A	A			
Notes Payable-Short Term	6.5	16.7	8.5	9.3	V	V		10.0	9.4
Cur. Mat.-L/T/D	2.5	6.4	8.5	2.3	A	A		2.9	5.1
Trade Payables	6.7	4.2	4.0	2.0	I	I		5.0	4.1
Income Taxes Payable	.1	.1	.0	.0	L	L		.0	.1
All Other Current	28.4	14.2	12.0	3.0	A	A		14.4	12.2
Total Current	44.3	41.5	33.1	16.6	B	B		32.3	30.8
Long-Term Debt	44.9	38.3	47.8	55.8	L	L		43.5	40.9
Deferred Taxes	.1	.2	.0	.0	E	E		.1	.2
All Other Non-Current	12.2	4.2	4.5	4.0				9.5	10.0
Net Worth	-1.4	15.8	14.5	23.6				14.6	18.1
Total Liabilities & Net Worth	100.0	100.0	100.0	100.0				100.0	100.0
INCOME DATA									
Net Sales	100.0	100.0	100.0	100.0				100.0	100.0
Gross Profit									
Operating Expenses	87.8	95.5	87.8	87.6				90.4	87.2
Operating Profit	12.2	4.5	12.2	12.4				9.6	12.8
All Other Expenses (net)	4.3	3.9	5.8	4.6				5.1	6.5
Profit Before Taxes	7.9	.6	6.4	7.8				4.5	6.3
RATIOS									
Current	3.8	2.2	2.1	2.3				2.2	2.8
	1.9	1.3	1.2	1.5				1.2	1.3
	.3	.4	.8	.9				.6	.7
Quick	2.1	1.4	1.5	2.0				1.3	1.5
	.7	.4	.4	1.2				.5	(129) .5
	.1	.1	.1	.2				.2	.2
Sales/Receivables	0 UND	0 UND	5 73.2	6 58.6				4 90.0	2 226.4
	1 452.0	10 38.2	15 24.9	14 25.4				11 32.5	12 29.9
	20 18.4	25 14.4	33 11.0	35 10.4				31 11.6	33 11.1
Cost of Sales/Inventory									
Cost of Sales/Payables									
Sales/Working Capital	7.7	4.8	7.5	6.1				8.8	6.6
	17.6	19.1	18.2	9.3				25.4	21.9
	-3.3	-7.0	-13.5	-258.0				-12.1	-12.7
EBIT/Interest	(19) 3.6	(31) 3.7	(52) 4.4					(111) 3.7	(115) 4.3
	1.5	1.8	2.3					1.7	2.1
	-.2	.5	1.2					1.0	1.1
Net Profit + Depr., Dep., Amort./Cur. Mat. L/T/D								(18) 4.6	(14) 2.8
								3.0	1.4
								1.2	.1
Fixed/Worth	.5	.8	1.3	1.0				1.2	1.3
	4.0	4.1	3.2	4.8				3.3	3.2
	-2.5	-16.0	NM	NM				-13.1	14.7
Debt/Worth	1.8	1.4	1.9	3.0				1.5	1.3
	6.8	6.4	5.7	5.3				4.9	5.2
	-3.1	-18.6	NM	NM				-22.9	115.9
% Profit Before Taxes/Tangible Net Worth	115.0	38.3	44.3					43.2	44.1
	(20) 55.5	(28) 15.2	(45) 20.8					(91) 16.7	(99) 19.0
	-3.0	3.9	3.7					2.9	3.0
% Profit Before Taxes/Total Assets	17.6	5.5	7.9	8.4				7.7	13.1
	8.2	2.5	3.6	2.0				3.1	3.5
	-2.1	-3.4	.5	-.6				-.3	.3
Sales/Net Fixed Assets	15.8	14.0	3.0	2.1				6.8	6.5
	6.2	2.4	1.2	1.1				1.7	1.6
	1.0	.7	.6	.2				.7	.7
Sales/Total Assets	4.5	1.9	1.2	1.1				2.0	2.0
	1.7	1.2	.8	.5				1.0	1.0
	.9	.5	.5	.2				.5	.5
% Depr., Dep., Amort./Sales	1.6	3.1	2.3	4.1				2.0	2.0
	(24) 3.2	(36) 6.3	(56) 6.9	7.2				(124) 5.6	(120) 5.2
	7.7	20.3	13.1	24.6				11.9	11.3
% Officers', Directors', Owners' Comp/Sales	1.4	3.8	1.7					2.8	3.2
	(10) 4.5	(15) 5.8	(17) 3.1					(46) 5.5	(44) 6.6
	15.8	8.8	4.9					13.0	14.2
Net Sales ($)	18456M	58916M	249749M	119148M				408858M	1417814M
Total Assets ($)	8240M	44969M	282777M	211715M				424109M	1076128M

M = $ thousand   MM = $ million
See Pages 11 through 21 for Explanation of Ratios and Data

Comparative Historical Data | Current Data Sorted By Sales

Type of Statement	1	8	8		1	3	3	1	1	1
Unqualified	1	8	8			3	3	1	1	1
Reviewed	19	27	21		1	7	8	1	3	
Compiled	31	38	40		16	17	3	2	2	
Tax Returns	41	43	32		16	9	4	2	1	
Other	39	46	41		12	11	9	8	1	
	4/1/02-3/31/03 ALL	4/1/03-3/31/04 ALL	4/1/04-3/31/05 ALL		0-1MM	1-3MM	3-5MM	5-10MM	10-25MM	25MM & OVER
					10 (4/1-9/30/04)		132 (10/1/04-3/31/05)			
NUMBER OF STATEMENTS	131	162	142		45	47	27	14	8	1
	%	%	%	**ASSETS**	%	%	%	%	%	%
Cash & Equivalents	9.8	8.9	10.4		11.5	11.7	8.6	7.6		
Trade Receivables (net)	6.9	6.5	7.0		6.0	9.5	5.8	2.9		
Inventory	16.9	17.1	17.5		8.0	16.0	12.9	44.6		
All Other Current	3.4	3.0	2.2		2.4	2.3	3.1	.4		
Total Current	37.0	35.6	37.2		28.0	39.5	30.4	55.5		
Fixed Assets (net)	54.9	55.4	53.8		62.8	52.3	56.9	41.2		
Intangibles (net)	3.9	4.1	3.9		5.2	3.2	3.8	1.8		
All Other Non-Current	4.1	5.0	5.1		4.0	4.9	8.9	1.5		
Total	100.0	100.0	100.0		100.0	100.0	100.0	100.0		
				LIABILITIES						
Notes Payable-Short Term	9.4	13.0	10.4		5.1	10.5	10.4	14.1		
Cur. Mat.-L/T/D	6.0	4.1	6.1		3.4	11.8	4.3	2.2		
Trade Payables	4.5	4.1	4.5		3.9	4.2	3.3	4.6		
Income Taxes Payable	.3	.1	.0		.1	.0	.0	.0		
All Other Current	14.4	12.7	15.4		13.0	23.7	9.6	13.5		
Total Current	34.5	34.0	36.4		25.5	50.2	27.6	34.5		
Long-Term Debt	44.0	46.8	45.2		55.5	40.8	44.6	39.6		
Deferred Taxes	.1	.2	.1		.0	.2	.0	.0		
All Other Non-Current	7.9	8.9	6.1		7.5	6.7	4.8	4.5		
Net Worth	13.6	10.0	12.2		11.4	2.0	23.0	21.4		
Total Liabilities & Net Worth	100.0	100.0	100.0		100.0	100.0	100.0	100.0		
				INCOME DATA						
Net Sales	100.0	100.0	100.0		100.0	100.0	100.0	100.0		
Gross Profit										
Operating Expenses	89.5	88.5	89.9		84.3	92.8	91.6	93.0		
Operating Profit	10.5	11.5	10.1		15.7	7.2	8.4	7.0		
All Other Expenses (net)	6.2	5.6	4.9		8.6	3.8	3.3	2.1		
Profit Before Taxes	4.3	5.9	5.2		7.1	3.4	5.1	4.8		
				RATIOS						
Current	2.3	2.3	2.4		2.8	2.9	2.1	3.3		
	1.2	1.2	1.2		1.3	1.1	1.0	1.4		
	.7	.7	.6		.3	.5	.7	1.2		
Quick	1.2	1.3	1.6		1.4	2.1	1.6	.9		
	.4	.5	.5		.7	.5	.5	.3		
	.1	.1	.1		.1	.2	.2	.1		
Sales/Receivables	2 195.0	2 211.3	1 274.6		0 UND	4 84.8	9 39.6	1 324.3		
	12 30.9	12 29.3	11 33.3		1 452.0	16 22.3	23 16.1	6 62.1		
	29 12.4	30 12.3	30 12.1		20 17.8	35 10.6	32 11.5	11 33.5		
Cost of Sales/Inventory										
Cost of Sales/Payables										
Sales/Working Capital	7.4	5.8	7.3		6.8	5.1	9.1	6.5		
	27.0	26.6	17.8		18.0	22.4	366.4	9.8		
	-13.7	-15.3	-6.9		-5.5	-5.1	-6.7	18.3		
EBIT/Interest	4.4	4.0	4.3		3.2	4.1	4.3	7.5		
	(114) 2.0	(143) 2.0	(111) 1.8		(25) 2.2	(42) 1.7	(23) 2.4	(12) 1.5		
	1.2	1.0	.8		.6	.4	.8	.9		
Net Profit + Depr., Dep., Amort./Cur. Mat. L/T/D	5.1	3.7	2.2							
	(20) 2.0	(15) 2.1	(14) 1.6							
	.9	1.2	.1							
Fixed/Worth	1.3	1.0	1.0		1.5	.9	1.3	.7		
	5.0	3.6	3.7		7.0	4.0	3.2	1.4		
	-8.8	-22.0	-15.7		-15.5	-4.6	-7.9	11.5		
Debt/Worth	1.7	1.8	1.8		2.1	1.4	1.1	1.7		
	7.4	7.2	6.2		6.4	6.4	4.5	4.9		
	-11.2	-30.8	-19.3		-19.0	-5.9	-11.8	19.3		
% Profit Before Taxes/Tangible Net Worth	38.8	53.2	49.7		96.3	35.2	42.6	44.2		
	(87) 21.1	(113) 23.3	(102) 16.8		(31) 18.2	(32) 16.0	(20) 14.3	(12) 13.6		
	8.2	2.2	2.7		-2.3	2.6	-.3	4.5		
% Profit Before Taxes/Total Assets	8.5	10.2	9.5		11.0	7.1	11.1	7.6		
	3.4	3.7	3.6		4.3	2.1	3.7	4.0		
	.3	-.1	-.6		-1.1	-3.4	-.8	.1		
Sales/Net Fixed Assets	6.7	6.8	7.1		6.6	6.4	6.2	10.6		
	1.7	1.6	1.6		.9	1.3	1.4	3.9		
	.8	.8	.7		.5	.7	.7	1.7		
Sales/Total Assets	1.9	1.8	1.8		1.8	1.6	2.2	2.0		
	1.0	.9	1.0		.7	.9	.8	1.4		
	.6	.5	.5		.4	.5	.5	1.0		
% Depr., Dep., Amort./Sales	2.1	2.5	2.3		2.5	3.3	3.4	.4		
	(121) 5.5	(145) 6.1	(128) 5.8		(38) 8.3	(41) 6.5	(13) 7.2	1.2		
	11.8	13.2	12.7		18.4	12.7	14.3	6.8		
% Officers', Directors', Owners' Comp/Sales	2.6	2.1	2.5		2.5	3.6				
	(50) 4.0	(58) 4.2	(45) 4.6		(13) 4.8	(13) 5.8				
	8.1	8.2	8.6		15.1	11.2				
Net Sales ($)	571451M	1470371M	446269M		23166M	82826M	103636M	92350M	114064M	30227M
Total Assets ($)	544306M	985260M	547701M		46332M	131790M	185185M	74187M	93888M	16319M

© RMA 2005

M = $ thousand   MM = $ million

See Pages 11 through 21 for Explanation of Ratios and Data

Current Data Sorted By Assets   Comparative Historical Data

Type of Statement	0-500M	500M-2MM	2-10MM	10-50MM	50-100MM	100-250MM	4/1/00-3/31/01 ALL	4/1/01-3/31/02 ALL
Unqualified	6	4	22	27	2		32	30
Reviewed	11	9	20	5			29	19
Compiled	45	23	13				33	51
Tax Returns	26	22	8	2	2	1	35	50
Other		32	42	21	3	2	48	63
	44 (4/1-9/30/04)		304 (10/1/04-3/31/05)					
NUMBER OF STATEMENTS	88	90	105	55	7	3	177	213
ASSETS	%	%	%	%	%	%	%	%
Cash & Equivalents	19.6	10.6	8.3	7.7			10.7	10.7
Trade Receivables (net)	2.5	5.3	3.5	5.1			4.9	3.3
Inventory	1.7	2.0	1.0	2.4			1.5	1.1
All Other Current	2.1	1.6	2.0	1.9			3.5	2.5
Total Current	25.9	19.5	14.7	17.1			20.7	17.5
Fixed Assets (net)	53.9	68.6	72.0	75.6			65.1	67.8
Intangibles (net)	7.8	4.4	3.6	1.9			6.1	6.5
All Other Non-Current	12.4	7.5	9.6	5.4			8.1	8.1
Total	100.0	100.0	100.0	100.0			100.0	100.0
LIABILITIES								
Notes Payable-Short Term	18.0	5.7	4.0	1.3			2.5	4.4
Cur. Mat.-L/T/D	6.5	5.3	3.6	3.2			4.8	4.6
Trade Payables	6.1	2.7	2.5	3.3			4.9	3.9
Income Taxes Payable	.1	.1	.1	.4			.1	.4
All Other Current	15.8	9.7	6.5	5.0			10.1	11.5
Total Current	46.5	23.5	16.7	13.2			22.6	24.8
Long-Term Debt	34.7	40.8	41.1	39.1			39.3	40.5
Deferred Taxes	.0	.0	.1	.3			.0	.1
All Other Non-Current	7.6	11.9	9.7	6.0			10.4	6.9
Net Worth	11.3	23.8	32.4	41.4			27.7	27.7
Total Liabilities & Net Worth	100.0	100.0	100.0	100.0			100.0	100.0
INCOME DATA								
Net Sales	100.0	100.0	100.0	100.0			100.0	100.0
Gross Profit								
Operating Expenses	93.0	90.7	88.3	87.5			88.6	90.3
Operating Profit	7.0	9.3	11.7	12.5			11.4	9.7
All Other Expenses (net)	1.3	3.6	4.5	4.2			4.5	4.6
Profit Before Taxes	5.8	5.7	7.2	8.3			6.9	5.1
RATIOS								
Current	3.0	2.6	2.1	2.6			1.8	1.7
	.8	.6	.8	1.1			.8	.7
	.2	.2	.3	.6			.4	.2
Quick	3.0	2.2	1.7	2.2			1.5	1.4
	.4	.4	(104) .7	.9			(176) .7	.5
	.1	.1	.2	.4			.3	.1
Sales/Receivables	0 UND	0 UND	0 UND	2 180.7			0 UND	0 UND
	0 UND	0 UND	4 88.0	10 36.2			3 142.2	0 UND
	0 UND	10 35.1	15 24.5	25 14.3			16 23.1	8 44.5
Cost of Sales/Inventory								
Cost of Sales/Payables								
Sales/Working Capital	25.0	8.6	11.1	6.0			15.3	21.4
	-59.1	-39.5	-33.6	52.5			-60.7	-37.8
	-9.9	-7.9	-6.8	-13.0			-9.9	-8.3
EBIT/Interest	16.4	11.5	5.2	7.3			6.6	6.3
	(65) 3.0	(82) 3.1	(93) 2.1	(49) 3.2			(140) 2.6	(178) 2.3
	.7	.7	1.0	.9			1.2	1.0
Net Profit + Depr., Dep., Amort./Cur. Mat. L /T/D			10.2	3.1			5.7	4.7
			(14) 5.5	(10) 2.5			(15) 3.4	(15) 2.2
			1.3	2.3			2.3	.9
Fixed/Worth	.7	1.1	1.2	1.1			1.1	1.1
	3.5	2.4	2.5	1.7			2.6	2.8
	-1.9	-73.6	8.0	3.8			14.5	12.8
Debt/Worth	.4	.6	.8	.4			.8	.8
	3.6	2.2	2.2	1.3			2.5	2.8
	-3.8	-84.6	7.9	3.6			30.3	29.1
% Profit Before Taxes/Tangible Net Worth	104.1	58.6	27.6	28.6			66.7	58.1
	(54) 33.1	(65) 27.1	(87) 13.1	(50) 9.4			(139) 19.9	(166) 21.2
	2.7	1.6	-.1	-.1			4.0	2.2
% Profit Before Taxes/Total Assets	45.0	18.7	9.7	9.2			15.6	17.3
	7.5	7.7	3.5	5.4			4.5	5.0
	-1.2	-1.2	-.3	-.5			.4	-.1
Sales/Net Fixed Assets	16.0	4.2	2.0	1.1			5.0	4.8
	7.9	2.2	.9	.7			1.5	1.9
	4.0	1.0	.5	.5			.7	.8
Sales/Total Assets	7.6	2.2	1.1	.8			2.5	2.6
	3.4	1.5	.7	.6			1.0	1.2
	2.1	.8	.4	.4			.5	.6
% Depr., Dep., Amort./Sales	2.4	5.3	4.9	5.5			3.5	3.7
	(66) 4.4	(77) 6.5	(97) 7.1	(50) 8.1			(158) 6.3	(194) 6.4
	7.0	9.8	10.7	9.8			9.6	9.0
% Officers', Directors', Owners' Comp/Sales	5.4	3.4	2.0	5.0			3.7	4.2
	(48) 8.3	(31) 6.3	(25) 3.5	(11) 11.5			(51) 6.4	(72) 6.6
	13.6	12.0		34.4			9.9	13.0
Net Sales ($)	72691M	148413M	450008M	1448047M	1972086M	2454037M	1890227M	1145759M
Total Assets ($)	19894M	90815M	503830M	1200633M	477267M	445446M	1719439M	1447255M

M = $ thousand   MM = $ million
See Pages 11 through 21 for Explanation of Ratios and Data

Comparative Historical Data			Type of Statement	Current Data Sorted By Sales					
46	39	55	Unqualified	2	9	6	24	8	6
30	36	40	Reviewed	7	18	3	9	2	1
58	84	47	Compiled	17	20	8	2		
79	69	80	Tax Returns	47	24	2	4		3
101	98	126	Other	32	42	17	13	13	9
4/1/02-3/31/03	4/1/03-3/31/04	4/1/04-3/31/05		44 (4/1-9/30/04)			304 (10/1/04-3/31/05)		
ALL	ALL	ALL		0-1MM	1-3MM	3-5MM	5-10MM	10-25MM	25MM & OVER
314	326	348	**NUMBER OF STATEMENTS**	105	113	36	52	23	19
%	%	%	**ASSETS**	%	%	%	%	%	%
12.4	10.6	11.7	Cash & Equivalents	13.1	14.0	8.5	8.3	8.4	10.7
3.9	4.8	3.9	Trade Receivables (net)	2.7	3.7	6.4	3.0	7.6	4.9
2.0	2.0	1.7	Inventory	1.4	1.4	1.0	2.0	.3	6.8
2.2	3.4	2.1	All Other Current	1.7	1.9	.7	2.7	3.7	4.8
20.6	20.7	19.4	Total Current	18.8	20.9	16.5	16.1	20.0	27.2
65.5	66.6	66.4	Fixed Assets (net)	63.5	66.0	70.8	72.3	72.5	53.2
4.6	5.3	5.0	Intangibles (net)	7.0	3.7	5.8	2.3	1.2	11.8
9.3	7.4	9.2	All Other Non-Current	10.7	9.3	6.9	9.3	6.4	7.8
100.0	100.0	100.0	Total	100.0	100.0	100.0	100.0	100.0	100.0
			LIABILITIES						
5.8	5.9	7.4	Notes Payable-Short Term	12.9	7.3	7.0	1.7	.6	3.2
4.2	5.2	4.9	Cur. Mat.-L/T/D	6.1	4.5	2.8	4.3	4.0	7.9
5.2	3.9	3.6	Trade Payables	2.1	5.2	2.6	2.7	3.4	7.6
.2	.2	.1	Income Taxes Payable	.1	.0	.3	.1	.9	.2
11.6	14.4	10.5	All Other Current	9.8	10.5	8.5	8.1	6.1	30.6
27.0	29.6	26.7	Total Current	31.0	27.6	21.3	16.9	15.0	49.6
40.8	38.6	38.7	Long-Term Debt	43.1	37.6	37.7	35.0	33.5	38.7
.1	.1	.1	Deferred Taxes	.0	.1	.0	.1	.1	1.3
9.2	12.3	8.9	All Other Non-Current	4.7	14.9	11.7	4.1	7.6	6.4
22.9	19.4	25.6	Net Worth	21.3	19.8	29.3	43.9	43.8	3.9
100.0	100.0	100.0	Total Liabilities & Net Worth	100.0	100.0	100.0	100.0	100.0	100.0
			INCOME DATA						
100.0	100.0	100.0	Net Sales	100.0	100.0	100.0	100.0	100.0	100.0
			Gross Profit						
91.1	90.6	90.1	Operating Expenses	88.5	92.4	90.6	89.0	86.1	91.9
8.9	9.4	9.9	Operating Profit	11.5	7.6	9.4	11.0	13.9	8.1
4.4	4.7	3.3	All Other Expenses (net)	4.4	2.9	3.2	2.9	2.9	1.9
4.5	4.6	6.6	Profit Before Taxes	7.1	4.7	6.2	8.1	11.0	6.2
			RATIOS						
2.4	1.8	2.5		2.7	3.4	1.9	1.8	2.6	1.5
.9	.7	.8	Current	.5	1.2	.9	.7	1.9	.6
.3	.3	.3		.2	.3	.4	.5	.8	.3
1.9	1.3	2.2		2.3	2.9	1.9	1.5	2.3	.8
(312) .7	(324) .5	(346) .6	Quick	(104) .3	.9	.6	.6	1.4	(18) .2
.2	.2	.2		.1	.2	.2	.2	.7	.1
0 UND	0 UND	0 UND		0 UND	0 UND	0 UND	0 UND	4 93.4	0 869.3
1 503.3	1 347.5	1 527.0	Sales/Receivables	0 UND	0 UND	7 53.6	6 62.6	6 60.6	5 80.0
11 33.3	12 29.7	12 31.1		2 148.9	6 60.2	20 17.9	17 21.2	25 14.3	24 15.5
			Cost of Sales/Inventory						
			Cost of Sales/Payables						
12.8	19.1	11.8		20.3	8.8	11.0	12.9	3.3	44.5
−108.4	−39.8	−59.3	Sales/Working Capital	−21.1	171.8	−119.8	−22.6	16.8	−78.4
−9.2	−7.4	−8.2		−6.8	−10.4	−11.5	−11.0	−25.1	−5.9
6.7	7.1	8.3		6.8	9.1	16.1	9.2	15.2	5.5
(264) 2.2	(266) 2.1	(298) 2.4	EBIT/Interest	(82) 1.9	(100) 2.0	(31) 2.7	(46) 3.1	(22) 4.5	(17) 4.0
.8	.8	.9		.6	.8	1.4	1.4	.7	1.3
4.5	5.3	6.2	Net Profit + Depr., Dep.,				13.0		
(25) 2.9	(26) 2.0	(34) 3.0	Amort./Cur. Mat. L/T/D				(11) 5.1		
2.0	1.2	1.6					1.3		
1.1	1.2	1.0		1.0	.9	1.3	1.1	1.0	.8
2.7	2.9	2.3	Fixed/Worth	4.0	1.8	2.6	1.7	1.5	5.6
295.5	−35.6	NM		−7.8	35.7	20.8	3.7	3.8	−4.4
.9	1.0	.5		.8	.4	1.0	.6	.4	1.6
2.9	3.3	2.1	Debt/Worth	4.0	1.8	2.5	1.3	1.3	7.3
NM	−37.3	NM		−11.8	35.9	24.5	3.6	3.1	−6.8
62.4	54.4	42.6	% Profit Before Taxes/Tangible	70.5	40.4	67.5	34.6	31.0	49.2
(236) 15.0	(238) 18.1	(261) 15.5	Net Worth	(67) 16.9	(86) 13.1	(29) 18.0	(49) 13.7	(20) 20.2	(10) 22.9
.6	1.4	.6		1.8	−.2	3.8	.9	4.0	12.3
15.4	14.4	16.2	% Profit Before Taxes/Total	22.8	17.2	19.8	10.1	14.1	13.5
3.9	3.7	5.4	Assets	5.0	3.5	4.8	6.0	10.1	7.1
−1.4	−1.1	−.6		−1.7	−1.2	−.1	.5	−.5	2.9
5.4	5.3	5.8		8.7	6.7	5.0	1.8	1.5	20.7
2.0	1.8	1.9	Sales/Net Fixed Assets	3.0	2.4	2.0	.9	.9	2.8
.8	.7	.8		.9	.8	.6	.6	.7	1.6
2.5	2.7	2.4		3.2	2.9	2.1	1.1	1.0	4.7
1.3	1.2	1.1	Sales/Total Assets	1.7	1.5	1.1	.7	.7	1.4
.6	.5	.6		.6	.6	.5	.5	.5	.8
4.2	4.1	4.4		3.8	4.6	3.9	4.5	5.5	3.8
(281) 7.1	(295) 7.2	(297) 6.5	% Depr., Dep., Amort./Sales	(83) 6.5	(99) 6.5	(28) 6.0	(50) 7.8	(14) 6.3	4.9
10.6	10.1	9.2		10.4	9.2	8.1	9.6	8.6	8.6
3.5	4.3	3.4	% Officers', Directors',	5.3	3.3	1.5	2.4		
(102) 7.1	(108) 7.5	(116) 6.6	Owners' Comp/Sales	(39) 8.7	(47) 6.4	(10) 3.3	(15) 5.0		
13.2	13.2	11.7		15.5	10.6	6.4	8.6		
1940359M	2334628M	6545282M	Net Sales ($)	58267M	202551M	139539M	383484M	363115M	5398326M
1964504M	2050191M	2737885M	Total Assets ($)	66635M	235493M	179541M	609004M	520909M	1126303M

© RMA 2005

M = $ thousand   MM = $ million
See Pages 11 through 21 for Explanation of Ratios and Data

Current Data Sorted By Assets

Comparative Historical Data

						Type of Statement		
4	6	6				Unqualified	3	1
16	22	7	2			Reviewed	15	18
19	21	6				Compiled	53	44
8	13	4				Tax Returns	33	24
			1			Other	15	28
	40 (4/1-9/30/04)		95 (10/1/04-3/31/05)				4/1/00-3/31/01	4/1/01-3/31/02
0-500M	500M-2MM	2-10MM	10-50MM	50-100MM	100-250MM		ALL	ALL
47	62	23	3			NUMBER OF STATEMENTS	119	115
%	%	%	%	%	%	ASSETS	%	%
21.6	10.5	11.1				Cash & Equivalents	12.2	10.9
1.6	1.4	.4				Trade Receivables (net)	2.2	2.7
8.6	2.4	1.4	D	D		Inventory	3.6	4.3
1.4	1.4	1.6	A	A		All Other Current	2.3	1.5
33.1	15.7	14.6	T	T		Total Current	20.1	19.3
53.8	71.7	72.3	A	A		Fixed Assets (net)	64.3	63.3
6.1	4.5	3.2				Intangibles (net)	5.1	4.6
7.0	8.1	9.9	N	N		All Other Non-Current	10.4	12.8
100.0	100.0	100.0	O	O		Total	100.0	100.0
			T	T		LIABILITIES		
4.7	4.1	1.8				Notes Payable-Short Term	8.7	9.5
5.5	7.5	5.4	A	A		Cur. Mat.-L/T/D	4.7	4.7
11.2	2.8	2.6	V	V		Trade Payables	6.8	6.8
.2	.1	.0	A	A		Income Taxes Payable	.1	.0
13.8	11.6	6.0	I	I		All Other Current	16.9	13.1
35.4	26.1	15.8	L	L		Total Current	37.3	34.1
75.5	70.1	78.8	A	A		Long-Term Debt	65.2	54.3
.0	.4	.1	B	B		Deferred Taxes	.2	.3
36.8	12.6	2.6	L	L		All Other Non-Current	11.3	20.0
-47.7	-9.2	2.7	E	E		Net Worth	-14.0	-8.7
100.0	100.0	100.0				Total Liabilities & Net Worth	100.0	100.0
						INCOME DATA		
100.0	100.0	100.0				Net Sales	100.0	100.0
						Gross Profit		
95.1	95.3	83.2				Operating Expenses	92.0	93.7
4.9	4.7	16.8				Operating Profit	8.0	6.3
2.5	4.0	12.0				All Other Expenses (net)	4.2	3.5
2.4	.6	4.8				Profit Before Taxes	3.8	2.8
						RATIOS		
2.2	1.6	1.5					1.5	1.4
.8	.5	.7				Current	.7	.6
.4	.3	.4					.2	.2
1.5	1.0	1.3					1.1	1.0
(46) .6	(61) .3	.4				Quick	(118) .5	(114) .3
.2	.1	.2					.1	.1
0 UND	0 UND	0 UND					0 UND	0 UND
0 UND	0 UND	0 UND				Sales/Receivables	0 UND	0 UND
1 698.0	2 183.1	1 446.1					1 257.8	1 290.5
						Cost of Sales/Inventory		
						Cost of Sales/Payables		
31.4	22.1	9.8					23.8	29.0
-87.3	-15.0	-25.0				Sales/Working Capital	-29.2	-15.1
-12.9	-4.6	-8.1					-6.1	-5.7
6.9	2.8	5.1					3.2	2.9
(34) 2.1	(59) 1.4	(19) 1.5				EBIT/Interest	(108) 1.5	(104) 1.6
.7	.3	.8					.7	.6
						Net Profit + Depr., Dep.,	5.2	3.1
						Amort./Cur. Mat. L./T/D	(16) 2.5	(17) 1.8
							1.7	1.0
1.0	3.5	2.7					2.0	1.8
-1.5	-11.8	9.8				Fixed/Worth	-155.6	999.8
-.6	-2.2	-6.9					-1.8	-2.2
1.6	3.2	3.4					2.1	2.0
-2.7	-15.7	10.3				Debt/Worth	-104.8	-170.0
-1.8	-3.3	-8.7					-3.1	-4.0
59.1	28.5	61.0					58.6	52.7
(18) 18.0	(24) 8.3	(14) 8.8				% Profit Before Taxes/Tangible Net Worth	(58) 13.0	(57) 11.4
-1.9	-15.8	-11.8					-3.4	-.1
17.4	8.5	8.6					11.8	10.3
3.3	2.2	1.9				% Profit Before Taxes/Total Assets	3.7	3.7
-5.7	-5.8	-.5					-1.9	-2.8
17.3	2.4	2.1					6.5	5.5
6.5	1.6	.9				Sales/Net Fixed Assets	2.2	2.6
2.6	1.0	.7					1.2	1.1
5.9	1.8	1.1					2.6	2.4
3.7	1.2	.7				Sales/Total Assets	1.4	1.4
1.7	.7	.6					.9	.8
1.9	5.1	5.9					3.9	3.3
(35) 4.8	(57) 7.9	(22) 9.9				% Depr., Dep., Amort./Sales	(115) 6.6	(110) 6.9
9.8	12.0	14.1					9.9	9.9
2.5	3.2						4.3	3.9
(27) 6.0	(27) 5.3					% Officers', Directors', Owners' Comp/Sales	(48) 8.3	(49) 6.1
12.2	10.1						12.1	9.8
33165M	83719M	69295M	53615M			Net Sales ($)	210654M	348449M
9981M	70193M	88233M	71777M			Total Assets ($)	186674M	247844M

M = $ thousand   MM = $ million
See Pages 11 through 21 for Explanation of Ratios and Data

Comparative Historical Data | | | Current Data Sorted By Sales

				Type of Statement						2
3	5	2		Unqualified						
21	19	16		Reviewed	4	9	1	2		
50	45	45		Compiled	21	19	3	2		
34	49	46		Tax Returns	32	13	1			
25	18	26		Other	10	11	2	2	1	
4/1/02-3/31/03 ALL	4/1/03-3/31/04 ALL	4/1/04-3/31/05 ALL			40 (4/1-9/30/04)			95 (10/1/04-3/31/05)		
					0-1MM	1-3MM	3-5MM	5-10MM	10-25MM	25MM & OVER
133	136	135		NUMBER OF STATEMENTS	67	52	7	6	3	
%	%	%		ASSETS	%	%	%	%	%	%
12.3	11.0	14.3		Cash & Equivalents	14.5	14.9				D
1.3	1.2	1.3		Trade Receivables (net)	1.0	2.0				A
3.4	3.8	4.4		Inventory	5.6	3.5				T
2.0	2.9	1.4		All Other Current	1.7	1.1				A
19.0	18.8	21.4		Total Current	22.8	21.5				
70.3	67.5	65.9		Fixed Assets (net)	62.3	68.6				N
4.6	4.7	4.8		Intangibles (net)	5.9	3.9				O
6.1	8.9	7.9		All Other Non-Current	9.0	6.0				T
100.0	100.0	100.0		Total	100.0	100.0				
				LIABILITIES						A
6.2	5.9	4.0		Notes Payable-Short Term	3.3	4.8				V
6.8	6.2	6.4		Cur. Mat.-L/T/D	5.3	7.8				A
5.0	5.1	5.7		Trade Payables	5.8	6.2				I
.1	.4	.1		Income Taxes Payable	.2	.0				L
20.6	14.9	11.3		All Other Current	10.1	14.0				A
38.7	32.4	27.5		Total Current	24.7	32.8				B
75.8	66.0	73.1		Long-Term Debt	79.3	63.8				L
.2	.1	.2		Deferred Taxes	.0	.3				E
12.4	19.9	19.1		All Other Non-Current	25.5	16.0				
-27.1	-18.5	-19.9		Net Worth	-29.6	-12.9				
100.0	100.0	100.0		Total Liabilities & Net Worth	100.0	100.0				
				INCOME DATA						
100.0	100.0	100.0		Net Sales	100.0	100.0				
				Gross Profit						
91.9	94.2	93.1		Operating Expenses	91.0	95.7				
8.1	5.8	6.9		Operating Profit	9.0	4.3				
5.7	4.5	4.8		All Other Expenses (net)	7.0	2.5				
2.4	1.3	2.1		Profit Before Taxes	1.9	1.7				
				RATIOS						
1.4	1.3	1.7			2.1	1.6				
.5	.6	.7		Current	.7	.7				
.2	.2	.3			.3	.3				
.9	.8	1.2			1.2	1.4				
(131) .3	(135) .3	(133) .4		Quick	(66) .4	(51) .5				
.1	.1	.2			.1	.2				
0 UND	0 UND	0 UND			0 UND	0 UND				
0 UND	0 UND	0 UND		Sales/Receivables	0 UND	0 999.8				
1 265.5	1 284.6	1 292.5			0 UND	2 168.1				
				Cost of Sales/Inventory						
				Cost of Sales/Payables						
30.0	35.1	27.7			22.3	23.0				
-20.6	-17.3	-27.7		Sales/Working Capital	-42.6	-28.9				
-5.5	-5.5	-7.7			-7.8	-7.0				
2.6	2.5	4.7			3.8	5.1				
(111) 1.3	(122) 1.4	(115) 1.6		EBIT/Interest	(49) 1.4	(50) 1.6				
.6	.3	.6			.6	.4				
3.7	3.3	4.4		Net Profit + Depr., Dep.,						
(16) 1.8	(12) 1.4	(14) 1.6		Amort./Cur. Mat. L/T/D						
1.2	.6	1.2								
2.6	3.0	2.4			1.7	2.7				
62.7	-19.7	-23.3		Fixed/Worth	-23.3	-11.8				
-2.1	-1.6	-1.1			-.9	-2.1				
2.7	3.8	3.0			2.3	3.3				
-66.0	-22.7	-16.4		Debt/Worth	-15.8	-16.0				
-3.2	-3.3	-2.5			-2.0	-3.3				
60.7	54.5	43.6		% Profit Before Taxes/Tangible	34.7	59.0				
(66) 14.4	(62) 17.1	(59) 8.8		Net Worth	(29) 6.2	(21) 24.6				
.6	-.1	-4.2			.5	-15.2				
10.7	8.0	10.2		% Profit Before Taxes/Total	9.1	10.2				
2.2	2.2	2.4		Assets	1.9	3.2				
-2.1	-5.2	-2.8			-4.4	-2.5				
4.1	4.4	5.1			7.2	4.8				
1.8	1.9	2.0		Sales/Net Fixed Assets	2.1	2.0				
.9	1.1	1.0			.8	1.3				
2.1	2.3	2.1			3.7	2.1				
1.3	1.2	1.4		Sales/Total Assets	1.4	1.5				
.8	.7	.7			.6	.9				
4.4	4.7	4.6			4.8	4.2				
(124) 7.6	(129) 7.6	(117) 7.7		% Depr., Dep., Amort./Sales	(53) 8.5	(49) 6.9				
11.8	10.9	11.7			13.9	11.4				
4.6	4.0	2.7		% Officers', Directors',	5.0	2.6				
(48) 6.1	(63) 6.0	(64) 5.5		Owners' Comp/Sales	(31) 6.8	(25) 5.2				
11.6	7.9	10.5			12.8	9.9				
424787M	806443M	239794M		Net Sales ($)	38138M	85105M	27796M	35140M	53615M	
349691M	377162M	240184M		Total Assets ($)	46689M	66754M	17947M	37017M	71777M	

© RMA 2005

M = $ thousand   MM = $ million
See Pages 11 through 21 for Explanation of Ratios and Data

Current Data Sorted By Assets							Comparative Historical Data	
						Type of Statement		
1	6	20	19	5	12	Unqualified	58	58
3	9	9	4			Reviewed	28	29
19	23	13	1			Compiled	57	68
47	27	10			1	Tax Returns	39	40
13	22	21	12	6	2	Other	68	108
	67 (4/1-9/30/04)		238 (10/1/04-3/31/05)				4/1/00-3/31/01	4/1/01-3/31/02
0-500M	500M-2MM	2-10MM	10-50MM	50-100MM	100-250MM		ALL	ALL
83	87	73	36	11	15	**NUMBER OF STATEMENTS**	250	303
%	%	%	%	%	%	**ASSETS**	%	%
17.0	9.6	11.3	12.6	8.4	10.6	Cash & Equivalents	12.9	12.4
6.2	3.3	5.5	2.8	2.4	3.4	Trade Receivables (net)	4.0	4.5
8.8	3.0	4.4	3.2	1.7	1.2	Inventory	4.9	4.7
5.0	2.0	4.0	5.5	1.5	2.6	All Other Current	3.8	2.6
37.1	17.9	25.2	24.1	13.9	17.7	Total Current	25.5	24.1
49.6	66.6	63.4	60.2	73.1	65.2	Fixed Assets (net)	63.0	63.7
6.0	3.4	4.7	4.2	6.6	5.3	Intangibles (net)	3.3	3.1
7.3	12.1	6.7	11.5	6.5	11.8	All Other Non-Current	8.2	9.1
100.0	100.0	100.0	100.0	100.0	100.0	Total	100.0	100.0
						LIABILITIES		
13.9	4.1	4.4	7.8	.5	2.1	Notes Payable-Short Term	6.7	4.7
8.1	5.4	7.1	2.4	2.2	6.1	Cur. Mat.-L/T/D	4.3	4.4
7.2	3.7	2.9	4.9	2.8	5.9	Trade Payables	5.9	6.0
.2	.1	.1	.2	.0	.1	Income Taxes Payable	.3	.1
14.1	10.7	9.1	10.3	11.1	14.6	All Other Current	13.7	10.7
43.4	23.9	23.5	25.6	16.6	28.8	Total Current	30.9	25.8
41.0	41.3	32.8	22.6	27.9	26.1	Long-Term Debt	31.3	33.2
.0	.1	.3	.4	2.7	.5	Deferred Taxes	.5	.5
13.4	10.1	7.2	6.2	4.4	2.4	All Other Non-Current	7.6	21.2
2.1	24.6	36.2	45.2	48.4	42.2	Net Worth	29.7	19.2
100.0	100.0	100.0	100.0	100.0	100.0	Total Liabilities & Net Worth	100.0	100.0
						INCOME DATA		
100.0	100.0	100.0	100.0	100.0	100.0	Net Sales	100.0	100.0
						Gross Profit		
93.1	91.6	90.4	93.7	83.7	77.7	Operating Expenses	88.2	88.7
6.9	8.4	9.6	6.3	16.3	22.3	Operating Profit	11.8	11.3
1.8	3.8	4.7	3.4	.5	2.6	All Other Expenses (net)	4.5	5.7
5.0	4.6	4.9	2.9	15.8	19.7	Profit Before Taxes	7.4	5.6
						RATIOS		
3.1	1.5	2.2	2.2	1.8	.7		2.3	1.9
1.0	.9	.9	1.1	1.1	.6	Current	1.0	.9
.4	.2	.2	.5	.6	.2		.4	.4
1.7	1.0	1.8	1.8	1.4	.6		1.4	1.3
(82) .5	.6	.7	.7	.7	.4	Quick	.6	(302) .6
.1	.1	.1	.2	.4	.1		.2	.2
0 UND	0 UND	0 999.8	0 999.8	0 799.7	1 301.6		0 UND	0 UND
0 UND	0 UND	4 103.1	3 128.5	5 80.8	4 83.7	Sales/Receivables	2 213.6	2 232.0
3 128.5	6 58.2	17 22.1	17 21.0	22 16.7	21 17.1		12 30.2	9 41.9
						Cost of Sales/Inventory		
						Cost of Sales/Payables		
12.6	23.9	7.5	9.1	8.6	-19.0		8.3	11.8
-357.5	-55.5	-63.4	144.4	51.9	-8.6	Sales/Working Capital	-199.2	-57.4
-8.1	-8.8	-3.8	-7.5	-23.4	-4.6		-6.3	-9.8
11.4	6.5	5.8	11.1	27.5	22.6		6.2	8.0
(65) 2.1	(67) 2.8	(61) 2.2	(30) 2.3	(10) 8.8	(13) 7.5	EBIT/Interest	(197) 2.0	(248) 2.7
.1	.6	.7	.7	2.5	2.5		.7	.5
						Net Profit + Depr., Dep.,	8.0	5.4
						Amort./Cur. Mat. L/T/D	(37) 2.6	(36) 2.8
							1.5	1.0
.8	1.0	1.1	.7	1.0	1.1		.9	.9
2.4	2.1	2.1	1.2	2.0	1.8	Fixed/Worth	1.9	2.0
-1.4	56.4	5.9	2.6	5.4	3.7		9.8	7.7
.6	.5	.6	.3	.2	1.1		.6	.6
5.0	2.7	1.7	.8	1.5	1.7	Debt/Worth	1.8	1.8
-2.7	-23.0	10.3	2.9	5.3	4.0		10.2	14.6
97.4	46.7	47.8	29.1	131.0	132.4	% Profit Before Taxes/Tangible	44.0	44.9
(55) 33.6	(65) 14.4	(58) 10.3	(33) 5.5	17.4	(14) 42.7	Net Worth	(202) 10.9	(247) 15.7
5.6	-.5	1.1	-1.9	5.7	25.7		-1.3	-1.3
25.9	13.6	10.4	9.1	15.7	49.8	% Profit Before Taxes/Total	15.9	15.7
5.7	4.2	3.6	1.6	6.9	10.9	Assets	3.5	4.8
-8.0	-1.7	-.6	-1.6	3.1	4.9		-1.3	-1.6
23.6	5.1	4.2	3.0	1.9	2.4		4.2	4.3
7.0	2.2	1.2	1.6	1.0	1.6	Sales/Net Fixed Assets	1.6	1.6
2.7	.7	.6	.6	.6	1.2		.7	.8
5.1	2.2	1.7	1.3	1.7	1.4		1.9	2.0
3.0	1.4	.7	.8	.8	1.0	Sales/Total Assets	1.0	1.0
1.4	.6	.5	.5	.4	.7		.5	.5
2.1	3.9	3.4	5.6	5.0			3.3	3.2
(60) 4.7	(72) 6.4	(64) 9.3	(31) 7.7	(10) 8.0		% Depr., Dep., Amort./Sales	(225) 7.1	(267) 6.3
9.2	11.6	14.4	10.3	10.1			11.9	9.8
3.8	3.5	1.8					4.5	2.9
(32) 8.0	(29) 5.9	(19) 5.3				% Officers', Directors',	(66) 7.2	(78) 5.8
13.7	14.9	6.7				Owners' Comp/Sales	19.4	14.5
70435M	150225M	370642M	886607M	824972M	2774012M	Net Sales ($)	4563643M	5070878M
19432M	95599M	357111M	872113M	863016M	2462664M	Total Assets ($)	4551662M	5323556M

© RMA 2005

M = $ thousand   MM = $ million

See Pages 11 through 21 for Explanation of Ratios and Data

Comparative Historical Data				Current Data Sorted By Sales					
			Type of Statement						
67	81	63	Unqualified	2	8	7	11	12	23
29	31	25	Reviewed	5	8	2	4	6	
40	74	56	Compiled	31	12	8	2	3	
62	77	85	Tax Returns	53	22	4	4	1	1
78	84	76	Other	20	19	7	11	7	12
4/1/02-3/31/03 ALL	4/1/03-3/31/04 ALL	4/1/04-3/31/05 ALL		67 (4/1-9/30/04)			238 (10/1/04-3/31/05)		
				0-1MM	1-3MM	3-5MM	5-10MM	10-25MM	25MM & OVER
276	347	305	**NUMBER OF STATEMENTS**	111	69	28	32	29	36
%	%	%	**ASSETS**	%	%	%	%	%	%
13.0	12.1	12.4	Cash & Equivalents	11.3	9.9	16.9	17.1	11.5	13.3
4.7	5.1	4.5	Trade Receivables (net)	3.7	5.5	4.2	6.4	5.5	3.2
5.6	5.4	4.8	Inventory	5.2	4.4	6.7	4.7	5.0	2.8
2.7	4.0	3.7	All Other Current	3.4	3.9	4.0	3.2	5.3	3.3
25.9	26.6	25.4	Total Current	23.6	23.8	31.8	31.5	27.3	22.5
61.2	57.8	60.7	Fixed Assets (net)	64.5	60.3	59.9	47.9	58.0	63.6
2.9	5.1	4.7	Intangibles (net)	4.5	3.7	2.5	10.7	3.5	4.8
10.0	10.5	9.2	All Other Non-Current	7.5	12.3	5.9	9.8	11.2	9.0
100.0	100.0	100.0	Total	100.0	100.0	100.0	100.0	100.0	100.0
			LIABILITIES						
9.7	8.7	7.0	Notes Payable-Short Term	8.7	7.5	5.8	5.3	4.7	5.2
4.2	5.8	6.1	Cur. Mat.-L/T/D	7.4	6.7	4.6	6.2	3.7	4.1
6.3	5.7	4.7	Trade Payables	4.5	4.5	3.6	5.8	3.5	6.4
.2	.1	.1	Income Taxes Payable	.1	.1	.1	.0	.0	.2
12.5	13.1	11.4	All Other Current	12.1	11.9	6.1	11.5	9.2	13.9
32.8	33.5	29.3	Total Current	32.8	30.7	20.2	29.0	21.1	30.0
35.4	32.8	35.8	Long-Term Debt	45.1	40.6	28.4	23.2	21.7	25.9
.2	.6	.3	Deferred Taxes	.0	.1	.5	.2	.2	1.2
14.3	8.3	9.2	All Other Non-Current	11.0	11.6	4.5	9.8	7.6	3.9
17.2	24.8	25.4	Net Worth	11.2	16.9	46.4	37.7	49.4	39.0
100.0	100.0	100.0	Total Liabilities & Net Worth	100.0	100.0	100.0	100.0	100.0	100.0
			INCOME DATA						
100.0	100.0	100.0	Net Sales	100.0	100.0	100.0	100.0	100.0	100.0
			Gross Profit						
91.2	91.5	91.0	Operating Expenses	89.6	94.3	94.9	93.6	94.1	81.4
8.8	8.5	9.0	Operating Profit	10.4	5.7	5.1	6.4	5.9	18.6
4.3	3.9	3.2	All Other Expenses (net)	5.5	1.7	1.2	2.9	.9	3.1
4.5	4.6	5.8	Profit Before Taxes	5.0	4.0	3.8	3.6	5.0	15.6
			RATIOS						
2.0	2.4	2.1	Current	2.0	1.8	3.3	1.9	2.6	1.7
.9	.8	.9		.9	.7	1.3	1.3	1.0	.9
.3	.3	.3		.2	.2	.7	.7	.5	.5
1.5	1.5	1.5	Quick	1.4	.9	1.9	1.7	1.7	1.4
(275) .5	(345) .5	(304) .5		(110) .4	.4	1.1	.9	.5	.6
.2	.1	.1		.1	.1	.5	.3	.1	.3
0 UND	0 UND	0 UND	Sales/Receivables	0 UND	0 UND	0 UND	2 226.9	0 776.3	0 871.1
1 322.5	1 292.9	1 429.6		0 UND	2 192.5	1 696.8	6 56.9	4 101.9	3 145.2
11 33.3	10 38.4	13 27.2		4 91.7	12 31.2	22 17.0	17 21.1	15 24.3	18 20.2
			Cost of Sales/Inventory						
			Cost of Sales/Payables						
12.6	9.9	14.1	Sales/Working Capital	15.0	20.4	13.9	7.8	9.9	12.0
-60.6	-63.6	-88.4		-54.6	-38.0	29.2	115.0	-757.1	-514.7
-8.4	-6.2	-7.7		-5.5	-5.6	-37.6	-15.2	-7.5	-8.9
7.3	8.3	9.2	EBIT/Interest	5.6	7.3	4.9	17.6	10.5	25.6
(215) 2.2	(277) 2.4	(246) 2.6		(83) 1.7	(55) 2.9	(23) 2.9	(26) 5.5	(27) 3.2	(32) 8.8
.3	.1	.7		.0	-.5	1.0	1.2	.9	1.8
7.5	6.9	4.9	Net Profit + Depr., Dep.,						
(26) 3.7	(35) 3.8	(27) 2.0	Amort./Cur. Mat. L/T/D						
1.8	1.6	1.3							
1.0	.9	.9	Fixed/Worth	1.0	1.0	.8	.7	.8	.9
2.0	2.1	1.9		3.5	2.3	1.4	1.2	1.6	1.8
24.2	-40.5	15.0		-2.2	-21.8	3.2	8.4	2.4	3.5
.7	.6	.5	Debt/Worth	.6	.7	.3	.6	.4	.5
1.9	2.5	2.1		3.5	3.2	1.1	1.4	1.0	1.7
NM	-28.4	23.8		-5.3	-17.3	3.9	9.0	4.0	4.1
45.2	47.7	50.9	% Profit Before Taxes/Tangible	43.4	55.5	28.3	67.2	38.8	83.7
(207) 15.2	(254) 14.1	(236) 15.6	Net Worth	(77) 9.5	(48) 15.1	(24) 7.0	(26) 32.0	(28) 6.0	(33) 40.5
.3	-.8	1.5		-4.5	1.8	.7	5.3	.0	14.1
14.4	15.1	14.9	% Profit Before Taxes/Total	12.1	14.7	7.6	19.9	10.2	33.5
3.0	3.4	4.3	Assets	2.2	5.7	3.6	6.2	2.3	10.8
-2.6	-2.1	-1.5		-6.6	-1.9	.0	.1	-.2	3.5
7.2	8.1	6.8	Sales/Net Fixed Assets	7.8	7.7	5.7	13.0	6.4	2.9
1.7	2.0	2.2		1.9	3.1	2.5	3.9	1.9	1.6
.8	.9	.8		.5	1.2	.8	1.1	.8	1.1
2.4	2.5	2.6	Sales/Total Assets	2.8	3.0	2.8	2.6	2.1	1.6
1.1	1.2	1.3		1.1	1.6	1.7	1.4	.9	1.2
.6	.6	.6		.4	.8	.7	.7	.6	.7
3.1	3.5	3.4	% Depr., Dep., Amort./Sales	4.0	2.9	2.8	2.9	3.7	4.3
(231) 7.4	(294) 7.3	(243) 6.7		(86) 8.6	(54) 5.9	(27) 5.5	(24) 5.4	(26) 7.5	(26) 5.9
11.6	12.2	11.5		18.2	13.7	10.2	11.3	10.2	7.6
2.9	3.9	3.5	% Officers', Directors',	4.4	3.4				
(72) 6.6	(92) 7.1	(86) 6.0	Owners' Comp/Sales	(33) 8.9	(30) 5.1				
13.9	12.5	12.9		14.3	15.1				
4921707M	5728054M	5076893M	Net Sales ($)	52313M	124758M	113433M	217358M	434140M	4134891M
3902381M	4809774M	4669935M	Total Assets ($)	81620M	126936M	111511M	205179M	575685M	3569004M

© RMA 2005

M = $ thousand   MM = $ million
See Pages 11 through 21 for Explanation of Ratios and Data

ACCOMMODATION AND FOOD SERVICES

Current Data Sorted By Assets   Comparative Historical Data

0-500M	500M-2MM	2-10MM	10-50MM	50-100MM	100-250MM	Type of Statement	4/1/00-3/31/01 ALL	4/1/01-3/31/02 ALL
2	15	68	55	18	17	Unqualified	147	149
6	31	80	34	2	1	Reviewed	133	142
36	120	137	19	1	1	Compiled	297	309
122	231	251	19	2	4	Tax Returns	287	275
31	92	238	62	10	11	Other	348	428
117 (4/1-9/30/04)		1591 (10/1/04-3/31/05)						
197	489	774	181	33	34	NUMBER OF STATEMENTS	1212	1303
%	%	%	%	%	%	**ASSETS**	%	%
22.3	8.0	5.7	7.1	9.0	12.2	Cash & Equivalents	8.3	8.9
6.1	2.2	1.6	3.0	5.5	4.6	Trade Receivables (net)	2.7	2.4
1.8	.8	.5	.8	3.4	2.6	Inventory	1.5	1.3
3.9	1.8	1.6	2.5	2.4	3.4	All Other Current	2.0	1.6
34.0	12.7	9.3	13.3	20.2	22.8	Total Current	14.5	14.2
49.6	75.8	82.2	73.6	65.3	60.6	Fixed Assets (net)	74.4	75.1
5.6	4.1	2.7	2.0	5.1	2.1	Intangibles (net)	4.1	3.8
10.8	7.4	5.7	11.0	9.3	14.5	All Other Non-Current	7.0	7.0
100.0	100.0	100.0	100.0	100.0	100.0	Total	100.0	100.0
						LIABILITIES		
9.2	3.7	2.6	1.9	2.8	3.3	Notes Payable-Short Term	3.2	3.5
2.7	4.4	3.9	4.3	3.8	4.0	Cur. Mat.-L/T/D	4.3	3.5
9.0	2.3	2.0	2.8	4.1	6.5	Trade Payables	3.7	3.4
.1	.1	.1	.1	.4	.0	Income Taxes Payable	.1	.1
28.4	8.4	6.3	6.0	6.0	26.3	All Other Current	8.6	10.0
49.3	19.0	14.9	15.3	17.1	40.1	Total Current	19.9	20.5
26.1	66.6	73.1	56.5	43.0	33.3	Long-Term Debt	62.3	61.2
.1	.0	.1	.2	.7	1.3	Deferred Taxes	.3	.2
19.8	6.7	4.3	5.8	3.3	11.7	All Other Non-Current	6.4	7.8
4.7	7.7	7.7	22.3	35.9	13.7	Net Worth	11.1	10.4
100.0	100.0	100.0	100.0	100.0	100.0	Total Liabilities & Net Worth	100.0	100.0
						INCOME DATA		
100.0	100.0	100.0	100.0	100.0	100.0	Net Sales	100.0	100.0
						Gross Profit		
92.9	82.9	83.2	87.4	89.1	94.2	Operating Expenses	83.9	85.4
7.1	17.1	16.8	12.6	10.9	5.8	Operating Profit	16.1	14.6
3.6	10.1	11.3	8.6	6.9	4.1	All Other Expenses (net)	10.5	10.8
3.4	7.0	5.5	4.0	4.0	1.8	Profit Before Taxes	5.6	3.8
						RATIOS		
2.6	2.2	1.7	1.5	2.4	2.6		1.7	1.7
.9	.7	.6	.8	.8	.9	Current	.8	.7
.3	.2	.3	.4	.4	.3		.3	.3
2.2	1.8	1.4	1.3	1.0	2.2		1.4	1.4
.7	(486) .6	.5	.5	.5	.6	Quick	(1210) .6	(1299) .5
.2	.1	.2	.2	.3	.2		.2	.2
0 UND	0 UND	1 671.9	4 97.6	5 70.1	4 82.4		0 UND	0 UND
0 UND	2 235.2	5 77.5	8 43.4	15 24.0	11 31.9	Sales/Receivables	5 73.9	4 84.3
5 77.1	7 49.3	10 36.1	13 27.0	24 15.5	27 13.6		11 32.9	10 35.9
						Cost of Sales/Inventory		
						Cost of Sales/Payables		
16.1	14.9	16.8	15.0	4.0	4.6		15.9	18.6
-196.6	-29.7	-20.9	-25.3	-20.6	-120.3	Sales/Working Capital	-41.1	-30.7
-8.8	-5.6	-5.4	-6.9	-6.5	-5.3		-7.7	-6.7
8.9	3.6	2.9	2.8	3.2	5.6		3.0	2.8
(111) 2.0	(375) 1.9	(671) 1.6	(160) 1.7	(29) 1.6	(26) 2.0	EBIT/Interest	(878) 1.8	(973) 1.5
-.4	.9	.9	.8	.9	.4		1.0	.8
	12.5	4.1	5.1			Net Profit + Depr., Dep.,	5.0	4.3
	(16) 4.1	(31) 1.8	(20) 2.4			Amort./Cur. Mat. L /T/D	(99) 2.2	(84) 2.2
	1.3	.5	1.1				1.2	.9
.5	2.7	3.3	1.8	1.4	.9		2.2	2.2
2.2	9.7	10.4	4.5	2.3	2.8	Fixed/Worth	6.0	6.5
-5.6	-8.0	-10.0	48.2	6.5	6.5		-14.6	-13.1
.6	2.5	3.0	1.5	1.4	.8		2.0	2.0
4.9	10.7	11.3	4.7	2.1	3.7	Debt/Worth	6.6	6.9
-8.0	-9.1	-12.0	51.9	6.8	NM		-16.6	-15.1
74.3	58.7	47.5	27.8	25.3	17.5		45.5	44.5
(125) 16.6	(304) 18.8	(493) 19.6	(141) 8.9	(30) 11.8	(26) 5.4	% Profit Before Taxes/Tangible Net Worth	(817) 18.2	(866) 15.5
-6.2	1.9	.8	.0	-3.4	.6		1.7	-.3
25.7	10.1	7.4	6.4	6.8	5.4		9.2	8.4
3.4	3.4	2.7	2.1	3.1	.6	% Profit Before Taxes/Total Assets	3.4	2.1
-7.2	-.6	-1.3	-1.1	-1.9	-3.8		-.8	-2.4
30.3	1.6	.8	1.2	1.2	3.2		1.9	1.7
7.8	.7	.5	.7	.8	.9	Sales/Net Fixed Assets	.7	.7
1.9	.4	.4	.5	.5	.6		.5	.4
7.5	1.0	.6	.8	.8	1.1		1.2	1.1
3.4	.6	.4	.5	.6	.6	Sales/Total Assets	.6	.6
1.3	.4	.3	.3	.4	.4		.4	.4
2.0	6.0	7.6	7.1	6.9	4.6		5.5	5.7
(142) 4.3	(451) 9.2	(725) 10.8	(172) 10.5	(30) 8.5	(22) 8.2	% Depr., Dep., Amort./Sales	(1102) 9.2	(1212) 9.4
8.6	13.4	15.5	14.2	12.0	12.3		13.4	13.7
3.7	2.9	2.5	1.7				2.8	2.3
(79) 5.8	(141) 5.3	(160) 4.8	(27) 4.1			% Officers', Directors', Owners' Comp/Sales	(309) 5.0	(333) 4.5
12.6	10.3	8.3	5.1				9.5	8.4
157392M	537962M	1995449M	2317418M	1802425M	8476619M	Net Sales ($)	10096362M	9441419M
47523M	615296M	3412046M	3810615M	2394565M	4938117M	Total Assets ($)	11783919M	13794660M

© RMA 2005

M = $ thousand   MM = $ million
See Pages 11 through 21 for Explanation of Ratios and Data

Comparative Historical Data   Current Data Sorted By Sales

			Type of Statement						
170	159	175	Unqualified	12	38	19	37	31	38
172	153	154	Reviewed	19	61	23	27	20	4
337	402	314	Compiled	129	128	23	22	9	3
429	603	621	Tax Returns	327	242	24	17	6	5
446	512	444	Other	106	200	40	49	24	25
4/1/02-3/31/03	4/1/03-3/31/04	4/1/04-3/31/05		117 (4/1-9/30/04)			1591 (10/1/04-3/31/05)		
ALL	ALL	ALL		0-1MM	1-3MM	3-5MM	5-10MM	10-25MM	25MM & OVER
1554	1829	1708	**NUMBER OF STATEMENTS**	593	669	129	152	90	75
%	%	%	**ASSETS**	%	%	%	%	%	%
8.6	8.2	8.6	Cash & Equivalents	8.5	8.3	7.2	8.6	11.2	11.2
2.9	2.4	2.6	Trade Receivables (net)	1.2	2.6	1.9	5.7	4.0	5.7
1.2	1.0	.9	Inventory	.4	.7	.9	2.0	1.6	2.3
2.2	2.1	2.1	All Other Current	2.1	1.6	2.0	2.2	3.8	2.6
14.8	13.7	14.1	Total Current	12.2	13.3	12.1	18.6	20.6	21.9
74.4	75.8	74.9	Fixed Assets (net)	76.8	76.3	77.2	69.4	66.6	65.5
4.0	3.6	3.4	Intangibles (net)	4.4	3.4	2.1	1.8	1.7	2.7
6.8	7.0	7.6	All Other Non-Current	6.6	7.0	8.6	10.2	11.1	10.0
100.0	100.0	100.0	Total	100.0	100.0	100.0	100.0	100.0	100.0
			LIABILITIES						
4.2	3.8	3.6	Notes Payable-Short Term	4.4	3.2	4.9	2.9	2.0	2.9
4.0	4.0	4.0	Cur. Mat.-L/T/D	3.4	4.0	3.9	5.1	5.7	4.2
3.6	3.1	3.1	Trade Payables	1.8	3.3	3.7	4.5	4.1	6.6
.1	.1	.1	Income Taxes Payable	.0	.1	.1	.2	.2	.3
11.9	10.9	9.8	All Other Current	10.7	8.1	7.1	10.9	12.8	16.3
23.8	21.8	20.6	Total Current	20.3	18.7	19.8	23.6	24.7	30.2
61.8	61.6	62.7	Long-Term Debt	62.0	65.9	69.0	61.5	53.8	40.7
.1	.1	.1	Deferred Taxes	.0	.1	.0	.1	.3	.9
7.8	7.4	7.1	All Other Non-Current	9.4	6.0	3.0	5.7	6.9	8.2
6.5	9.1	9.6	Net Worth	8.2	9.3	8.1	9.1	14.3	20.0
100.0	100.0	100.0	Total Liabilities & Net Worth	100.0	100.0	100.0	100.0	100.0	100.0
			INCOME DATA						
100.0	100.0	100.0	Net Sales	100.0	100.0	100.0	100.0	100.0	100.0
			Gross Profit						
85.6	86.2	85.0	Operating Expenses	81.7	85.2	85.9	89.2	92.3	91.7
14.4	13.8	15.0	Operating Profit	18.3	14.8	14.1	10.8	7.7	8.3
10.4	10.2	9.5	All Other Expenses (net)	13.0	8.6	8.9	6.4	4.4	4.2
4.0	3.6	5.4	Profit Before Taxes	5.3	6.2	5.2	4.3	3.3	4.2
			RATIOS						
1.8	1.7	1.9		2.2	2.0	1.6	1.3	1.7	1.5
.7	.7	.7	Current	.7	.7	.6	.7	.9	.8
.2	.3	.3		.2	.3	.3	.4	.5	.3
1.4	1.3	1.6		1.8	1.7	1.5	1.1	1.6	1.1
(1551) .5	(1824) .5	(1705) .5	Quick	.5	(666) .6	.5	.5	.5	.6
.2	.2	.2		.1	.2	.2	.2	.3	.2
0 UND	0 UND	0 UND		0 UND	0 999.8	2 158.9	4 84.0	4 96.2	5 80.0
4 94.9	4 98.3	4 90.4	Sales/Receivables	0 UND	5 81.1	6 62.0	8 45.7	8 43.5	12 31.2
10 37.3	10 37.6	10 36.8		5 71.9	10 38.0	11 32.0	13 29.2	15 23.9	24 15.2
			Cost of Sales/Inventory						
			Cost of Sales/Payables						
18.9	18.0	15.4		14.2	16.0	16.8	26.8	12.1	28.2
-28.0	-23.1	-25.6	Sales/Working Capital	-28.1	-29.7	-20.5	-25.6	-50.9	-23.4
-6.0	-5.5	-6.1		-3.9	-7.3	-7.4	-8.5	-8.1	-7.1
2.9	2.8	3.2		3.0	3.2	3.1	3.2	3.2	4.0
(1179) 1.6	(1430) 1.5	(1372) 1.7	EBIT/Interest	(410) 1.6	(561) 1.8	(123) 1.8	(129) 1.5	(86) 1.8	(63) 2.1
.8	.7	.8		.8	.8	1.0	.7	.8	1.0
4.7	3.6	5.6		4.4	7.5		4.3	8.5	6.3
(121) 2.4	(97) 1.9	(82) 2.3	Net Profit + Depr., Dep., Amort./Cur. Mat. L/T/D	(10) 1.7	(17) 3.7		(18) 2.2	(12) 3.4	(17) 2.9
1.1	.9	1.0		.2	.8		.5	1.3	.9
2.3	2.5	2.3		3.0	2.6	2.6	2.0	1.2	1.1
7.5	7.8	7.9	Fixed/Worth	9.7	7.8	10.0	7.4	2.9	2.4
-8.2	-11.9	-11.2		-9.2	-12.2	-8.4	-11.0	-14.7	9.7
2.2	2.4	2.2		2.7	2.5	2.2	1.4	1.4	1.4
8.5	8.5	8.3	Debt/Worth	11.8	8.2	10.1	9.0	3.2	3.3
-9.9	-13.9	-12.4		-10.4	-14.5	-10.5	-13.7	-43.1	10.5
42.2	42.2	47.5		50.0	54.7	33.9	40.2	33.3	28.2
(992) 15.1	(1198) 12.8	(1119) 16.6	% Profit Before Taxes/Tangible Net Worth	(361) 15.2	(447) 21.0	(84) 13.4	(103) 14.1	(64) 11.3	(60) 12.4
.0	-2.5	.3		-1.9	1.8	5.4	-2.8	1.5	1.1
7.7	7.0	8.4		7.1	9.4	8.3	8.3	7.7	7.5
2.2	1.9	2.9	% Profit Before Taxes/Total Assets	2.0	3.6	3.0	2.2	3.1	3.3
-1.8	-2.2	-1.3		-1.5	-1.4	-.1	-1.4	-.4	-1.2
1.6	1.3	1.5		1.1	1.3	1.3	2.6	2.0	2.4
.7	.6	.7	Sales/Net Fixed Assets	.5	.7	.7	1.0	1.1	1.0
.4	.4	.4		.3	.4	.5	.6	.7	.8
1.0	.9	.9		.7	.9	.8	1.4	1.2	1.4
.6	.5	.5	Sales/Total Assets	.4	.5	.5	.8	.8	.8
.4	.3	.4		.3	.4	.4	.5	.5	.6
6.3	6.9	6.3		7.4	6.3	6.6	5.5	5.7	5.0
(1424) 9.7	(1661) 10.3	(1542) 9.6	% Depr., Dep., Amort./Sales	(531) 11.3	(606) 9.3	(118) 9.4	(140) 8.1	(87) 8.2	(60) 7.8
13.9	14.5	14.3		16.8	14.0	14.3	11.8	11.6	10.1
2.5	2.9	2.9		3.4	2.8	2.2	2.1	.5	
(417) 4.8	(457) 5.0	(413) 5.0	% Officers', Directors', Owners' Comp/Sales	(177) 6.3	(165) 4.4	(23) 4.4	(26) 5.5	(15) 3.4	
9.5	9.1	9.6		11.2	8.8	5.2	7.3	6.0	
11037853M	10300865M	15287265M	Net Sales ($)	323184M	1157696M	488969M	1053908M	1391750M	10871758M
13587228M	15285545M	15218162M	Total Assets ($)	888308M	2337254M	1010096M	1688075M	2215072M	7079357M

M = $ thousand   MM = $ million
See Pages 11 through 21 for Explanation of Ratios and Data

RESTAURANT/LODGING—Casino Hotels NAICS 721120 (SIC 7011)

Current Data Sorted By Assets							Comparative Historical Data	
			4	4	9	Type of Statement		
			1			Unqualified		
						Reviewed		
		1				Compiled		
		1	4	6	4	Tax Returns		
						Other		
	12 (4/1-9/30/04)		22 (10/1-04-3/31/05)				4/1/00-3/31/01	4/1/01-3/31/02
0-500M	500M-2MM	2-10MM	10-50MM	50-100MM	100-250MM		ALL	ALL
		2	9	10	13	NUMBER OF STATEMENTS		
%	%	%	%	%	%	ASSETS	%	%
D	D			18.3	13.2	Cash & Equivalents	D	D
A	A			.9	1.1	Trade Receivables (net)	A	A
T	T			.3	.5	Inventory	T	T
A	A			2.2	2.1	All Other Current	A	A
				21.7	16.9	Total Current		
N	N			68.0	77.4	Fixed Assets (net)	N	N
O	O			6.7	1.6	Intangibles (net)	O	O
T	T			3.7	4.0	All Other Non-Current	T	T
				100.0	100.0	Total		
A	A					LIABILITIES	A	A
V	V			4.5	.0	Notes Payable-Short Term	V	V
A	A			3.8	11.4	Cur. Mat.-L/T/D	A	A
I	I			2.5	1.2	Trade Payables	I	I
L	L			.1	.0	Income Taxes Payable	L	L
A	A			8.7	10.7	All Other Current	A	A
B	B			19.6	23.3	Total Current	B	B
L	L			39.9	27.5	Long-Term Debt	L	L
E	E			.2	.4	Deferred Taxes	E	E
				1.2	10.9	All Other Non-Current		
				39.1	38.0	Net Worth		
				100.0	100.0	Total Liabilities & Net Worth		
						INCOME DATA		
				100.0	100.0	Net Sales		
						Gross Profit		
				74.4	84.5	Operating Expenses		
				25.6	15.5	Operating Profit		
				–.6	3.7	All Other Expenses (net)		
				26.3	11.9	Profit Before Taxes		
						RATIOS		
				1.7	1.6			
				.9	.7	Current		
				.7	.6			
				1.6	1.3			
				.8	.6	Quick		
				.5	.5			
			0 849.8	2 193.1				
			2 211.9	3 111.6	Sales/Receivables		
			7 56.0	7 50.5				
						Cost of Sales/Inventory		
						Cost of Sales/Payables		
				15.3	15.9			
				–224.4	–26.5	Sales/Working Capital		
				–23.7	–8.9			
					13.6			
				(12)	2.4	EBIT/Interest		
					1.2			
						Net Profit + Depr., Dep., Amort./Cur. Mat. L /T/D		
				1.0	1.3			
				1.6	1.8	Fixed/Worth		
				NM	10.8			
				.4	.8			
				1.0	1.2	Debt/Worth		
				NM	12.2			
					69.4	% Profit Before Taxes/Tangible		
				(11)	39.7	Net Worth		
					3.9			
				71.0	22.9			
				16.5	10.2	% Profit Before Taxes/Total		
				8.5	.9	Assets		
				2.5	1.6			
				1.4	1.3	Sales/Net Fixed Assets		
				.8	.9			
				2.0	1.2			
				.9	1.1	Sales/Total Assets		
				.6	.7			
				3.9				
				6.5		% Depr., Dep., Amort./Sales		
				8.8				
						% Officers', Directors', Owners' Comp/Sales		
		16923M	335607M	940198M	1812484M	Net Sales ($)		
		15528M	256082M	761274M	1878792M	Total Assets ($)		

M = $ thousand   MM = $ million
See Pages 11 through 21 for Explanation of Ratios and Data

Comparative Historical Data

Current Data Sorted By Sales

				Type of Statement						
17	19	17		Unqualified				1		17
		1		Reviewed						
1	2	1		Compiled			1			
6	6	15		Tax Returns					2	13
4/1/02- 3/31/03	4/1/03- 3/31/04	4/1/04- 3/31/05		Other		12 (4/1-9/30/04)			22 (10/1/04-3/31/05)	
ALL	ALL	ALL			0-1MM	1-3MM	3-5MM	5-10MM	10-25MM	25MM & OVER
24	27	34		NUMBER OF STATEMENTS			1	1	2	30
%	%	%		ASSETS	%	%	%	%	%	%
11.5	9.3	15.5		Cash & Equivalents						15.9
1.0	1.2	1.3		Trade Receivables (net)	D	D				1.2
1.0	.2	.5		Inventory	A	A				.5
2.7	2.8	2.6		All Other Current	T	T				2.7
16.2	13.4	20.0		Total Current	A	A				20.3
78.0	80.3	73.4		Fixed Assets (net)						72.2
2.4	2.7	2.9		Intangibles (net)	N	N				3.3
3.4	3.5	3.8		All Other Non-Current	O	O				4.2
100.0	100.0	100.0		Total	T	T				100.0
				LIABILITIES	A	A				
.4	.3	2.9		Notes Payable-Short Term	V	V				2.7
4.8	6.1	7.3		Cur. Mat.-L/T/D	A	A				7.6
4.9	1.0	2.7		Trade Payables	I	I				2.1
.0	.0	.0		Income Taxes Payable	L	L				.0
5.5	9.3	8.9		All Other Current	A	A				9.5
15.7	16.7	21.9		Total Current	B	B				21.9
41.7	32.9	31.7		Long-Term Debt	L	L				28.7
.4	.2	.2		Deferred Taxes	E	E				.3
3.4	7.3	5.6		All Other Non-Current						5.4
38.8	42.8	40.5		Net Worth						43.7
100.0	100.0	100.0		Total Liabilities & Net Worth						100.0
				INCOME DATA						
100.0	100.0	100.0		Net Sales						100.0
				Gross Profit						
83.6	85.4	82.4		Operating Expenses						81.2
16.4	14.6	17.6		Operating Profit						18.8
4.4	3.6	2.2		All Other Expenses (net)						1.7
12.0	11.0	15.5		Profit Before Taxes						17.0
				RATIOS						
1.5	1.1	1.5								1.6
1.0	.8	.8		Current						.8
.6	.6	.6								.6
1.0	.9	1.2								1.4
.8	.6	.7		Quick						.7
.5	.5	.5								.5
1 251.3	2 146.1	1 250.2								1 300.1
4 103.7	4 88.2	3 108.4		Sales/Receivables						3 116.2
6 56.8	7 49.5	7 53.2								7 53.2
				Cost of Sales/Inventory						
				Cost of Sales/Payables						
26.2	457.0	19.5								17.5
NM	-27.3	-34.7		Sales/Working Capital						-34.7
-16.2	-16.4	-10.6								-10.6
7.5	7.1	12.9								14.5
(23) 4.6	(24) 3.5	(30) 4.5		EBIT/Interest						(26) 5.4
1.2	1.4	1.4								1.4
				Net Profit + Depr., Dep., Amort./Cur. Mat. L/T/D						
1.4	1.3	1.1								1.1
2.6	2.0	1.8		Fixed/Worth						1.7
3.5	4.7	5.4								4.0
.7	.6	.5								.4
2.2	1.4	1.1		Debt/Worth						.9
3.5	4.1	5.3								4.5
77.9	48.4	70.5		% Profit Before Taxes/Tangible						70.5
(22) 33.2	(24) 20.5	(30) 28.1		Net Worth						(26) 32.3
12.8	7.1	8.3								12.5
23.1	15.6	25.3		% Profit Before Taxes/Total						25.3
11.2	9.1	11.3		Assets						13.1
1.8	1.3	1.4								1.9
1.7	1.6	2.0								2.2
1.3	1.2	1.4		Sales/Net Fixed Assets						1.4
1.0	.8	.9								1.0
1.3	1.2	1.5								1.6
1.0	1.0	1.1		Sales/Total Assets						1.1
.7	.7	.7								.7
5.3	5.5	5.1								5.1
(17) 6.5	(22) 7.3	(29) 7.3		% Depr., Dep., Amort./Sales						(25) 7.1
9.2	8.9	8.8								8.5
				% Officers', Directors', Owners' Comp/Sales						
2403472M	2154194M	3105212M		Net Sales ($)			4109M	8483M	35604M	3057016M
2441583M	2185727M	2911676M		Total Assets ($)			6632M	10788M	28228M	2866028M

© RMA 2005

M = $ thousand   MM = $ million
See Pages 11 through 21 for Explanation of Ratios and Data

Current Data Sorted By Assets   Comparative Historical Data

						Type of Statement		
1	1			1	1	Unqualified	5	3
	4	3				Reviewed	4	2
1	16	5				Compiled	18	18
20	18	6				Tax Returns	15	19
1	6	3	4	2		Other	8	13
10 (4/1-9/30/04)			83 (10/1/04-3/31/05)				4/1/00-3/31/01	4/1/01-3/31/02
0-500M	500M-2MM	2-10MM	10-50MM	50-100MM	100-250MM		ALL	ALL
23	45	17	4	3	1	NUMBER OF STATEMENTS	50	55
%	%	%	%	%	%	ASSETS	%	%
16.3	8.1	5.3				Cash & Equivalents	6.1	7.6
.4	1.2	2.4				Trade Receivables (net)	1.5	2.4
10.2	3.7	18.1				Inventory	6.4	6.1
1.6	1.8	1.1				All Other Current	4.7	2.2
28.5	14.8	26.9				Total Current	18.6	18.4
61.7	75.1	58.6				Fixed Assets (net)	68.9	69.7
4.4	2.4	6.5				Intangibles (net)	3.1	4.1
5.5	7.7	8.0				All Other Non-Current	9.3	7.7
100.0	100.0	100.0				Total	100.0	100.0
						LIABILITIES		
35.0	4.5	13.5				Notes Payable-Short Term	6.0	7.6
2.9	4.1	3.5				Cur. Mat.-L/T/D	3.8	4.0
1.7	1.3	1.9				Trade Payables	2.6	2.4
.0	.2	.0				Income Taxes Payable	.1	.1
14.5	4.8	6.1				All Other Current	6.9	11.3
54.2	14.9	25.0				Total Current	19.4	25.4
48.9	57.7	38.8				Long-Term Debt	57.7	51.5
.0	.0	.1				Deferred Taxes	.1	.1
3.7	4.6	11.4				All Other Non-Current	5.6	11.9
-6.7	22.8	24.7				Net Worth	17.3	11.1
100.0	100.0	100.0				Total Liabilities & Net Worth	100.0	100.0
						INCOME DATA		
100.0	100.0	100.0				Net Sales	100.0	100.0
						Gross Profit		
87.9	81.4	90.4				Operating Expenses	81.9	83.1
12.1	18.6	9.6				Operating Profit	18.1	16.9
2.2	9.0	5.4				All Other Expenses (net)	12.2	11.0
9.9	9.7	4.2				Profit Before Taxes	5.9	5.9
						RATIOS		
5.4	2.3	1.7					1.6	2.1
1.0	1.0	.9				Current	.7	.5
.2	.2	.2					.3	.3
4.7	2.3	.9					1.1	1.0
.4	(44) .7	.3				Quick (49)	.3	.4
.1	.1	.0					.1	.2
0 UND	0 UND	0 UND					0 UND	0 UND
0 UND	0 UND	1 535.5				Sales/Receivables	0 UND	0 UND
0 UND	3 142.8	3 120.5					3 108.3	3 121.7
						Cost of Sales/Inventory		
						Cost of Sales/Payables		
12.7	7.6	7.1					14.9	8.4
UND	999.8	-66.4				Sales/Working Capital	-29.0	-15.2
-8.3	-5.0	-6.9					-5.0	-5.6
29.0	8.9	6.1					5.6	3.8
(16) 4.4	(35) 2.5	(16) 2.1				EBIT/Interest (32)	2.7	(42) 1.5
1.1	1.1	1.0					1.2	1.0
						Net Profit + Depr., Dep., Amort./Cur. Mat. L /T/D		
1.0	1.3	1.5					1.1	1.4
2.9	6.7	3.0				Fixed/Worth	4.3	14.2
-1.8	-17.5	NM					-24.4	-6.4
1.3	.9	1.2					1.1	1.4
3.8	6.2	3.7				Debt/Worth	4.4	18.9
-2.8	-31.5	NM					-60.4	-8.8
94.2	41.8	51.5					40.9	96.5
(16) 34.8	(31) 9.3	(13) 14.8				% Profit Before Taxes/Tangible Net Worth (35)	24.1	(33) 30.9
7.2	.4	3.3					4.0	5.2
26.6	10.0	14.2					12.1	10.3
15.3	5.5	4.1				% Profit Before Taxes/Total Assets	5.5	3.2
1.8	.1	.1					-.8	.0
18.0	1.7	3.4					2.2	2.3
3.1	.9	2.0				Sales/Net Fixed Assets	.8	1.1
1.7	.4	.5					.4	.5
3.3	1.0	1.6					1.6	1.3
2.3	.6	.9				Sales/Total Assets	.6	.7
1.3	.4	.5					.3	.4
4.6	4.2	2.7					4.3	4.5
(15) 5.8	(42) 10.4	6.2				% Depr., Dep., Amort./Sales (47)	7.7	(51) 7.4
10.1	16.2	15.3					14.7	14.8
4.7	2.7						2.8	4.1
(10) 9.3	(14) 4.0					% Officers', Directors', Owners' Comp/Sales (20)	6.2	(17) 7.7
15.1	11.4						8.6	11.5
9019M	40733M	74755M	41282M	121796M	13026M	Net Sales ($)	209037M	220824M
4421M	47795M	72072M	105582M	203209M	102604M	Total Assets ($)	272363M	341621M

M = $ thousand   MM = $ million
See Pages 11 through 21 for Explanation of Ratios and Data

Comparative Historical Data   Current Data Sorted By Sales

			Type of Statement						
6	4	4	Unqualified	2				1	1
3	7	7	Reviewed	2	2	1	1	1	
20	17	22	Compiled	14	4		4		
36	33	44	Tax Returns	34	6	4			
12	12	16	Other	4	6		3	2	1
4/1/02- 3/31/03 ALL	4/1/03- 3/31/04 ALL	4/1/04- 3/31/05 ALL		10 (4/1-9/30/04)		83 (10/1/04-3/31/05)			
				0-1MM	1-3MM	3-5MM	5-10MM	10-25MM	25MM & OVER
77	73	93	NUMBER OF STATEMENTS	56	18	5	8	4	2
%	%	%	ASSETS	%	%	%	%	%	%
7.7	7.9	9.7	Cash & Equivalents	10.2	8.8				
1.4	1.7	1.9	Trade Receivables (net)	.4	2.4				
3.8	7.2	8.0	Inventory	6.3	6.5				
1.6	1.6	1.6	All Other Current	1.4	2.4				
14.5	18.4	21.1	Total Current	18.2	20.1				
74.3	66.3	67.6	Fixed Assets (net)	72.2	67.1				
3.7	3.4	3.5	Intangibles (net)	3.0	7.4				
7.4	11.8	7.7	All Other Non-Current	6.6	5.4				
100.0	100.0	100.0	Total	100.0	100.0				
			LIABILITIES						
6.0	7.2	13.4	Notes Payable-Short Term	16.9	4.5				
3.2	5.7	3.5	Cur. Mat.-L/T/D	3.2	5.4				
.9	3.4	1.9	Trade Payables	.8	2.7				
.1	.0	.1	Income Taxes Payable	.2	.0				
10.8	12.3	7.6	All Other Current	7.8	6.9				
21.0	28.6	26.5	Total Current	28.9	19.6				
56.3	54.4	49.8	Long-Term Debt	61.4	37.8				
.1	.2	.1	Deferred Taxes	.0	.0				
10.2	9.3	6.3	All Other Non-Current	2.9	7.9				
12.5	7.5	17.2	Net Worth	6.8	34.8				
100.0	100.0	100.0	Total Liabilities & Net Worth	100.0	100.0				
			INCOME DATA						
100.0	100.0	100.0	Net Sales	100.0	100.0				
			Gross Profit						
83.0	84.2	83.8	Operating Expenses	82.8	88.4				
17.0	15.8	16.2	Operating Profit	17.2	11.6				
10.2	6.8	6.0	All Other Expenses (net)	7.9	3.1				
6.8	9.0	10.1	Profit Before Taxes	9.2	8.5				
			RATIOS						
1.7	1.8	2.3		4.0	1.8				
.7	.8	1.0	Current	1.1	.6				
.2	.2	.2		.2	.1				
1.2	1.0	1.9		3.0	1.0				
.4	.3	(92) .6	Quick	(55) .7	.4				
.1	.1	.1		.1	.1				
0 UND	0 UND	0 UND		0 UND	0 UND				
0 UND	0 UND	0 UND	Sales/Receivables	0 UND	0 UND				
5 75.7	3 105.9	4 98.7		0 UND	15 23.8				
			Cost of Sales/Inventory						
			Cost of Sales/Payables						
16.3	14.3	7.4		6.6	11.6				
-26.0	-28.2	138.5	Sales/Working Capital	UND	-11.5				
-5.0	-7.0	-6.9		-5.5	-4.3				
5.4	6.0	9.1		7.6	11.6				
(59) 1.9	(60) 2.5	(74) 2.9	EBIT/Interest	(42) 2.8	(15) 2.2				
1.0	1.2	1.2		1.0	1.5				
		11.8	Net Profit + Depr., Dep.,						
	(12)	3.9	Amort./Cur. Mat. L/T/D						
		.9							
1.7	1.4	1.2		1.7	.9				
4.5	5.8	4.2	Fixed/Worth	5.9	2.8				
-10.9	-7.9	-42.0		-7.1	-24.7				
1.4	1.5	.9		1.4	.6				
5.2	5.8	4.9	Debt/Worth	6.1	2.3				
-14.7	-10.4	-34.4		-11.0	-28.5				
50.3	48.6	51.2	% Profit Before Taxes/Tangible	52.3	37.6				
(51) 18.9	(49) 18.3	(68) 19.5	Net Worth	(38) 18.5	(13) 8.9				
-1.8	2.7	4.8		.9	6.1				
12.5	12.5	16.9	% Profit Before Taxes/Total	16.5	11.7				
3.3	6.1	5.7	Assets	7.2	3.8				
-1.7	1.2	.9		.0	1.8				
2.0	3.3	3.4		3.1	3.5				
.9	1.4	1.3	Sales/Net Fixed Assets	1.1	1.2				
.5	.6	.5		.4	.8				
1.2	1.9	1.6		1.6	1.5				
.6	.8	.8	Sales/Total Assets	.7	.9				
.4	.4	.4		.4	.6				
4.7	4.6	4.3		5.5	3.6				
(72) 8.4	(68) 8.6	(82) 7.8	% Depr., Dep., Amort./Sales	(46) 10.4	(17) 6.2				
15.6	15.2	15.1		19.0	12.2				
3.8	3.6	3.4		3.5					
(26) 7.7	(24) 7.8	(29) 6.8	% Officers', Directors',	(19) 4.7					
13.4	13.7	12.1	Owners' Comp/Sales	13.3					
300691M	221518M	300611M	Net Sales ($)	24717M	30646M	19724M	60672M	63711M	101141M
390454M	299447M	535683M	Total Assets ($)	38346M	42142M	16925M	108845M	194680M	134745M

© RMA 2005

M = $ thousand   MM = $ million

See Pages 11 through 21 for Explanation of Ratios and Data

Current Data Sorted By Assets   **Comparative Historical Data**

Type of Statement	0-500M	500M-2MM	2-10MM	10-50MM	50-100MM	100-250MM		4/1/00-3/31/01 ALL	4/1/01-3/31/02 ALL
Unqualified		1	4	1				3	4
Reviewed		1	6					9	8
Compiled		6	5					9	7
Tax Returns	10	8	2					7	6
Other	1	4	7	1		1		6	7
	15 (4/1-9/30/04)			43 (10/1/04-3/31/05)					
NUMBER OF STATEMENTS	11	20	24	2		1		34	32
ASSETS	%	%	%	%	%	%		%	%
Cash & Equivalents	17.9	8.8	9.8					7.7	12.3
Trade Receivables (net)	.0	1.5	2.9					2.5	2.0
Inventory	.6	.3	2.1					2.7	1.7
All Other Current	.0	.9	1.9					3.0	3.1
Total Current	18.5	11.6	16.8					15.9	19.1
Fixed Assets (net)	72.8	81.6	67.5					72.0	68.5
Intangibles (net)	2.0	.6	1.3					2.6	3.8
All Other Non-Current	6.7	6.3	14.4					9.5	8.6
Total	100.0	100.0	100.0					100.0	100.0
LIABILITIES									
Notes Payable-Short Term	12.0	5.1	5.2					8.1	3.7
Cur. Mat.-L/T/D	3.4	2.7	3.0					4.5	3.1
Trade Payables	1.5	2.7	3.3					3.3	2.5
Income Taxes Payable	.8	.1	.0					.0	.1
All Other Current	19.6	7.8	5.2					14.1	11.3
Total Current	37.3	18.4	16.6					30.0	20.6
Long-Term Debt	29.5	35.6	34.1					32.0	33.4
Deferred Taxes	.0	.1	.2					.2	.4
All Other Non-Current	2.6	20.3	5.3					10.5	10.9
Net Worth	30.6	25.6	43.7					27.4	34.8
Total Liabilities & Net Worth	100.0	100.0	100.0					100.0	100.0
INCOME DATA									
Net Sales	100.0	100.0	100.0					100.0	100.0
Gross Profit									
Operating Expenses	92.7	92.8	87.0					90.7	90.5
Operating Profit	7.3	7.2	13.0					9.3	9.5
All Other Expenses (net)	1.8	6.4	1.9					3.6	5.3
Profit Before Taxes	5.4	.8	11.2					5.6	4.1
RATIOS									
Current	.8	1.3	1.8					1.6	1.5
	.4	.4	.9					.7	.8
	.1	.2	.3					.2	.3
Quick	.8	1.1	1.6					1.1	1.3
	.4	.3	.4					.4	.6
	.1	.1	.1					.1	.1
Sales/Receivables	0 UND	0 UND	0 UND					0 UND	0 UND
	0 UND	0 UND	0 800.6					1 342.0	0 999.8
	0 UND	4 87.2	5 76.0					11 33.8	3 107.2
Cost of Sales/Inventory									
Cost of Sales/Payables									
Sales/Working Capital	-118.0	NM	7.2					19.8	16.3
	-32.7	-11.6	-106.3					-17.1	-21.2
	-4.2	-3.6	-9.0					-3.8	-7.5
EBIT/Interest		6.9	11.5					4.3	3.9
		(18) 1.4	(23) 4.0					(29) 2.0	(25) 2.4
		-.7	1.6					.6	1.5
Net Profit + Depr., Dep., Amort./Cur. Mat. L./T/D									
Fixed/Worth	1.6	1.3	1.1					1.1	.9
	2.5	3.1	1.7					3.4	2.1
	21.7	NM	3.5					-150.9	5.1
Debt/Worth	1.1	.7	.4					.8	.6
	2.1	2.4	1.5					3.2	2.0
	26.3	NM	5.7					-261.1	8.7
% Profit Before Taxes/Tangible Net Worth	340.0	29.0	25.2					32.3	34.7
	71.5	(15) 7.4	(22) 11.2					(25) 10.3	(28) 12.0
	7.3	-24.0	2.7					1.1	3.7
% Profit Before Taxes/Total Assets	31.3	4.9	13.1					13.2	9.1
	8.9	1.2	4.3					3.2	4.5
	2.7	-7.6	1.3					-1.1	1.4
Sales/Net Fixed Assets	8.1	2.0	1.6					3.1	3.8
	3.5	1.1	1.2					1.6	1.3
	1.6	.4	.7					.8	.8
Sales/Total Assets	4.2	1.6	1.1					2.0	1.4
	2.4	.9	.7					1.1	1.0
	1.6	.3	.5					.7	.5
% Depr., Dep., Amort./Sales		3.6	5.7					4.9	3.7
		(17) 6.7	(21) 6.5					(29) 7.3	(29) 6.7
		11.9	9.8					10.9	9.9
% Officers', Directors', Owners' Comp/Sales								1.5	3.7
							(10)	4.7 (10) 8.8
								6.2	11.0
Net Sales ($)	6323M	22505M	103926M	29568M		64848M		75654M	153014M
Total Assets ($)	2664M	23194M	106478M	47157M		229288M		79415M	142789M

(50-100MM column: DATA NOT AVAILABLE)

© RMA 2005

M = $ thousand   MM = $ million
See Pages 11 through 21 for Explanation of Ratios and Data

Comparative Historical Data | | | | **Current Data Sorted By Sales**

			Type of Statement						
8	8	6	Unqualified	1	1	2		2	
8	7	7	Reviewed		4	2	1		
11	17	11	Compiled	3	4	4			
12	14	20	Tax Returns	13	6		1		
8	12	14	Other	7	2	2	1	1	1
4/1/02-3/31/03	4/1/03-3/31/04	4/1/04-3/31/05		15 (4/1-9/30/04)			43 (10/1/04-3/31/05)		
ALL	ALL	ALL		0-1MM	1-3MM	3-5MM	5-10MM	10-25MM	25MM & OVER
47	58	58	NUMBER OF STATEMENTS	24	17	10	3	3	1
%	%	%	ASSETS	%	%	%	%	%	%
8.8	10.2	10.5	Cash & Equivalents	8.9	17.7	4.3			
1.0	3.3	1.8	Trade Receivables (net)	.5	1.2	1.5			
1.3	1.6	1.2	Inventory	.3	1.3	1.0			
5.1	3.6	1.1	All Other Current	.3	2.0	1.3			
16.2	18.7	14.6	Total Current	10.0	22.2	8.1			
72.3	68.1	74.0	Fixed Assets (net)	81.1	68.4	78.9			
3.3	4.1	1.5	Intangibles (net)	1.2	1.0	1.6			
8.3	9.0	9.9	All Other Non-Current	7.6	8.4	11.4			
100.0	100.0	100.0	Total	100.0	100.0	100.0			
			LIABILITIES						
13.5	13.4	6.2	Notes Payable-Short Term	6.7	4.6	5.1			
4.3	3.7	3.0	Cur. Mat.-L/T/D	3.3	2.4	4.2			
2.3	3.9	2.6	Trade Payables	1.2	3.5	1.4			
.0	.9	.2	Income Taxes Payable	.0	.6	.0			
11.5	11.1	8.7	All Other Current	9.7	9.6	6.3			
31.6	33.0	20.6	Total Current	20.9	20.6	17.0			
35.5	33.7	34.0	Long-Term Debt	32.5	32.1	35.1			
.0	.1	.1	Deferred Taxes	.0	.4	.1			
5.5	8.7	10.4	All Other Non-Current	13.5	8.1	8.1			
27.3	24.5	34.8	Net Worth	33.0	38.8	39.7			
100.0	100.0	100.0	Total Liabilities & Net Worth	100.0	100.0	100.0			
			INCOME DATA						
100.0	100.0	100.0	Net Sales	100.0	100.0	100.0			
			Gross Profit						
91.9	90.2	89.9	Operating Expenses	87.2	97.0	91.2			
8.1	9.8	10.1	Operating Profit	12.8	3.0	8.8			
4.8	5.3	3.9	All Other Expenses (net)	7.5	1.0	.3			
3.3	4.5	6.1	Profit Before Taxes	5.3	2.0	8.5			
			RATIOS						
1.4	1.2	1.3		.7	2.1	1.6			
.6	.7	.5	Current	.3	1.4	.3			
.2	.2	.2		.1	.3	.0			
1.3	.9	1.2		.6	2.1	1.0			
.3	.4	.3	Quick	.3	1.2	.2			
.1	.1	.1		.1	.2	.0			
0 UND	0 UND	0 UND		0 UND	0 UND	0 UND			
0 UND	0 UND	0 UND	Sales/Receivables	0 UND	0 999.8	3 129.0			
2 199.3	6 60.2	3 120.7		0 UND	6 56.4	6 64.9			
			Cost of Sales/Inventory						
			Cost of Sales/Payables						
28.0	64.8	24.3		-39.7	8.8	33.1			
-16.0	-26.4	-22.2	Sales/Working Capital	-10.5	24.0	-9.6			
-3.8	-5.6	-6.0		-3.4	-8.3	-6.2			
5.2	5.5	10.8		5.6	8.6	15.3			
(40) 2.0	(48) 1.7	(52) 2.2	EBIT/Interest	(19) 2.0	3.8	1.9			
.6	.3	.7		-.4	.5	1.6			
			Net Profit + Depr., Dep., Amort./Cur. Mat. L/T/D						
1.2	1.4	1.2		1.5	1.1	1.3			
2.3	2.3	2.1	Fixed/Worth	2.2	1.4	2.6			
-43.4	8.3	6.7		25.9	4.4	7.0			
.6	1.3	.7		.7	.5	.7			
1.9	3.1	1.8	Debt/Worth	1.8	.8	1.8			
-49.8	13.4	7.4		27.3	7.1	7.3			
33.6	30.0	34.7		62.3	30.9				
(35) 10.0	(45) 10.7	(51) 10.5	% Profit Before Taxes/Tangible Net Worth	(20) 8.3	(16) 8.9				
-3.1	.5	2.3		-14.5	-.4				
12.7	8.8	13.6		7.9	14.9	11.3			
1.8	2.4	2.8	% Profit Before Taxes/Total Assets	2.8	2.6	3.6			
-2.0	-3.5	-.3		-5.5	-2.0	1.3			
4.0	3.6	2.2		2.0	2.9	1.4			
1.4	1.7	1.2	Sales/Net Fixed Assets	.9	1.7	1.1			
.6	.8	.6		.3	1.0	.7			
2.2	1.9	1.6		1.6	1.7	1.2			
1.0	1.1	.9	Sales/Total Assets	.5	1.1	.8			
.5	.5	.5		.3	.7	.6			
3.5	3.6	4.7		6.4	3.3	5.3			
(40) 6.2	(54) 5.7	(49) 6.7	% Depr., Dep., Amort./Sales	(18) 10.3	6.3	6.3			
10.1	9.2	10.8		14.4	9.4	7.9			
2.7	3.2	4.9		4.1					
(16) 7.3	(20) 5.6	(21) 8.0	% Officers', Directors', Owners' Comp/Sales	(10) 10.6					
13.6	10.5	13.5		21.7					
85615M	272869M	227170M	Net Sales ($)	11532M	30266M	38416M	19094M	63014M	64848M
99409M	281001M	408781M	Total Assets ($)	27639M	29267M	52531M	21736M	48320M	229288M

© RMA 2005

M = $ thousand   MM = $ million

See Pages 11 through 21 for Explanation of Ratios and Data

Current Data Sorted By Assets   **Comparative Historical Data**

0-500M	500M-2MM	2-10MM	10-50MM	50-100MM	100-250MM	Type of Statement	4/1/00-3/31/01 ALL	4/1/01-3/31/02 ALL
13	28	37	67	19	23	Unqualified	124	142
20	52	60	36			Reviewed	143	156
243	174	90	15		3	Compiled	536	530
629	279	64	5	4	7	Tax Returns	466	489
236	193	167	74	11	17	Other	564	606
\<—— 294 (4/1-9/30/04) ——\>			\<—— 2272 (10/1/04-3/31/05) ——\>					
1141	726	418	197	34	50	**NUMBER OF STATEMENTS**	1833	1923
%	%	%	%	%	%	**ASSETS**	%	%
17.6	12.7	11.3	10.0	13.2	8.6	Cash & Equivalents	12.8	13.1
2.4	2.8	2.7	2.8	2.5	1.9	Trade Receivables (net)	3.5	3.4
9.1	4.7	4.1	3.5	4.1	4.0	Inventory	6.4	6.9
3.3	2.6	2.8	2.9	3.3	3.9	All Other Current	3.0	3.2
32.5	22.7	20.9	19.2	23.1	18.5	Total Current	25.7	26.6
45.3	56.7	59.2	59.8	61.0	52.3	Fixed Assets (net)	54.4	53.5
11.8	7.8	9.9	13.0	8.7	19.5	Intangibles (net)	10.3	9.7
10.3	12.7	10.0	7.9	7.2	9.7	All Other Non-Current	9.6	10.2
100.0	100.0	100.0	100.0	100.0	100.0	Total	100.0	100.0
						LIABILITIES		
12.0	5.5	4.1	2.7	1.6	3.3	Notes Payable-Short Term	6.9	6.1
4.8	4.7	5.4	5.3	3.5	3.4	Cur. Mat.-L/T/D	6.0	5.3
14.2	9.7	8.0	7.1	6.4	4.8	Trade Payables	11.4	11.6
.2	.1	.1	.1	.4	.2	Income Taxes Payable	.3	.3
23.5	15.1	13.0	10.5	12.4	13.5	All Other Current	20.1	18.2
54.8	35.1	30.7	25.7	24.2	25.2	Total Current	44.7	41.5
32.3	39.1	39.7	40.0	35.4	37.3	Long-Term Debt	36.0	36.8
.0	.1	.1	.5	.6	.8	Deferred Taxes	.1	.1
14.9	8.1	5.3	4.7	5.9	19.7	All Other Non-Current	11.7	11.4
-1.9	17.5	24.1	29.1	34.0	17.0	Net Worth	7.5	10.2
100.0	100.0	100.0	100.0	100.0	100.0	Total Liabilities & Net Worth	100.0	100.0
						INCOME DATA		
100.0	100.0	100.0	100.0	100.0	100.0	Net Sales	100.0	100.0
59.0	59.7	59.5	56.2	60.9	54.8	Gross Profit	59.1	58.1
55.6	55.3	55.2	50.2	54.2	49.1	Operating Expenses	55.0	54.2
3.3	4.3	4.3	6.0	6.7	5.7	Operating Profit	4.1	3.9
.9	1.2	1.4	1.4	2.1	2.5	All Other Expenses (net)	1.3	1.6
2.4	3.1	2.8	4.5	4.6	3.2	Profit Before Taxes	2.8	2.3
						RATIOS		
1.7	1.4	1.2	1.2	1.2	1.2		1.4	1.4
.7	.7	.7	.6	.8	.6	Current	.6	.7
.3	.3	.3	.4	.4	.3		.3	.3
1.1	.9	.9	.8	1.0	.6		.9	.9
(1118) .4	(723) .4	.4	(196) .4	(33) .5	.3	Quick	(1803) .4	(1908) .4
.1	.1	.2	.2	.3	.1		.1	.1
0 UND	0 UND	0 UND	0 UND	0 UND	0 UND		0 UND	0 UND
0 UND	0 999.8	1 720.9	1 441.9	3 126.3	2 186.3	Sales/Receivables	0 999.8	0 999.8
0 767.3	2 172.5	3 109.0	5 80.1	6 61.5	7 56.1		3 130.5	3 127.2
4 81.6	6 57.0	7 54.5	6 64.9	9 40.8	5 72.5		7 54.7	6 59.7
9 40.6	10 35.8	10 36.0	9 38.8	12 29.6	12 31.6	Cost of Sales/Inventory	11 34.4	11 34.1
16 23.0	17 21.8	18 20.9	15 24.7	22 16.4	19 19.2		18 20.9	19 19.4
0 UND	8 47.9	13 27.7	13 27.7	16 23.1	5 69.8		7 55.2	7 49.7
11 34.2	22 16.5	25 14.8	26 14.1	30 12.1	20 18.6	Cost of Sales/Payables	21 17.5	22 16.8
30 12.0	42 8.7	43 8.5	42 8.7	50 7.3	37 9.8		40 9.0	40 9.1
54.0	49.4	57.3	66.6	61.0	58.6		44.8	49.5
-57.2	-41.8	-31.6	-30.7	-37.0	-20.5	Sales/Working Capital	-36.6	-44.3
-14.4	-11.8	-12.1	-14.3	-12.3	-11.1		-11.3	-13.6
11.0	8.8	8.4	7.6	9.0	4.6		6.9	6.4
(731) 2.9	(607) 2.9	(382) 3.1	(186) 3.0	(33) 2.7	(41) 2.0	EBIT/Interest	(1527) 2.3	(1588) 2.3
-.5	.6	1.1	1.6	1.4	1.0		.8	.7
7.2	4.2	3.1	8.3	7.3		Net Profit + Depr., Dep.,	5.9	4.2
(20) 2.9	(37) 2.3	(47) 2.3	(65) 2.2	(15) 2.5		Amort./Cur. Mat. L /T/D	(179) 2.2	(179) 2.0
1.5	1.2	1.3	1.5	1.6			1.1	.9
.8	1.1	1.3	1.3	1.3	1.6		1.2	1.1
5.4	4.2	3.8	3.5	3.4	17.9	Fixed/Worth	4.8	4.8
-1.2	-5.0	-7.5	-8.1	10.2	-1.5		-3.1	-3.1
1.1	1.2	1.4	1.2	1.0	1.3		1.3	1.2
16.3	5.0	4.6	3.7	3.1	20.2	Debt/Worth	6.7	6.7
-2.8	-8.0	-10.5	-13.3	11.0	-3.2		-5.2	-5.6
184.8	83.7	66.8	55.4	58.7	68.2	% Profit Before Taxes/Tangible	86.6	81.4
(618) 57.9	(474) 36.3	(285) 25.4	(134) 28.6	(29) 22.1	(27) 21.9	Net Worth	(1138) 34.5	(1189) 30.6
10.4	6.4	7.3	8.9	10.8	11.6		8.4	6.6
38.2	22.3	15.4	13.4	13.2	10.5	% Profit Before Taxes/Total	19.7	20.0
10.5	7.9	5.9	6.8	4.9	5.4	Assets	7.2	6.1
-5.1	-.8	.2	2.2	1.6	.9		-.6	-1.2
39.6	11.9	7.7	5.7	5.0	9.1		13.8	14.8
15.0	5.3	4.3	3.6	3.1	3.6	Sales/Net Fixed Assets	6.2	6.5
6.9	2.8	2.2	2.0	1.8	2.5		3.0	3.1
9.8	4.3	3.4	2.8	2.4	2.8		5.3	5.4
5.9	2.9	2.4	1.9	2.2	1.8	Sales/Total Assets	3.2	3.2
3.7	1.8	1.6	1.4	1.3	1.4		1.9	1.9
1.0	1.6	2.1	2.5	3.0	1.1		1.4	1.3
(886) 1.8	(650) 2.6	(401) 3.1	(193) 3.4	(33) 4.2	(26) 2.8	% Depr., Dep., Amort./Sales	(1634) 2.6	(1725) 2.5
3.3	4.2	4.4	4.5	5.1	3.6		4.1	4.1
2.4	1.9	1.6	.9		1.8		2.4	2.4
(627) 4.7	(331) 3.6	(140) 3.2	(39) 1.8		(13) 5.0	% Officers', Directors',	(802) 4.5	(851) 4.5
7.9	6.5	5.4	4.5		9.3	Owners' Comp/Sales	7.6	7.4
1439635M	2325141M	5040505M	8883007M	6996856M	19709301M	Net Sales ($)	32684125M	36509895M
248001M	725968M	1919679M	4154490M	2398363M	7693584M	Total Assets ($)	12668553M	14947577M

M = $ thousand   MM = $ million

See Pages 11 through 21 for Explanation of Ratios and Data

Comparative Historical Data | | Current Data Sorted By Sales

			Type of Statement						
190	183	187	Unqualified	9	16	18	14	26	104
224	173	168	Reviewed	8	42	19	30	30	39
629	649	525	Compiled	124	211	70	60	46	14
769	941	988	Tax Returns	355	458	90	42	27	16
775	680	698	Other	104	229	80	101	79	105
4/1/02-3/31/03 ALL	4/1/03-3/31/04 ALL	4/1/04-3/31/05 ALL		294 (4/1-9/30/04) 0-1MM	1-3MM	3-5MM	2272 (10/1/04-3/31/05) 5-10MM	10-25MM	25MM & OVER
2587	2626	2566	NUMBER OF STATEMENTS	600	956	277	247	208	278
%	%	%	ASSETS	%	%	%	%	%	%
13.2	12.3	14.4	Cash & Equivalents	15.6	15.1	15.1	13.3	12.9	10.8
2.6	2.8	2.6	Trade Receivables (net)	2.1	2.5	2.9	3.5	3.4	2.5
6.0	6.4	6.5	Inventory	8.1	6.7	6.8	5.2	4.6	4.2
3.3	3.8	3.0	All Other Current	2.9	3.1	3.0	2.9	2.3	3.4
25.1	25.3	26.4	Total Current	28.6	27.4	27.7	24.9	23.2	20.9
54.8	54.6	52.3	Fixed Assets (net)	50.9	50.2	52.5	54.7	56.0	57.2
9.8	9.8	10.6	Intangibles (net)	11.2	10.5	5.8	10.4	12.1	13.4
10.3	10.2	10.7	All Other Non-Current	9.2	12.0	13.9	9.9	8.7	8.5
100.0	100.0	100.0	Total	100.0	100.0	100.0	100.0	100.0	100.0
			LIABILITIES						
5.6	5.0	7.8	Notes Payable-Short Term	11.3	9.1	4.5	6.4	5.1	2.7
5.7	5.0	4.9	Cur. Mat.-L/T/D	4.8	4.5	4.0	6.8	5.4	5.1
10.9	11.3	11.1	Trade Payables	9.4	13.3	12.1	11.6	8.5	7.6
.2	.2	.2	Income Taxes Payable	.2	.2	.2	.1	.2	.2
17.7	19.0	18.1	All Other Current	20.6	18.3	21.4	16.1	13.7	13.6
40.0	40.5	42.1	Total Current	46.2	45.5	42.2	41.0	32.9	29.2
37.9	37.5	36.2	Long-Term Debt	36.0	37.0	31.3	37.5	36.4	37.3
.1	.1	.1	Deferred Taxes	.1	.0	.1	.1	.1	.6
10.3	11.4	10.6	All Other Non-Current	16.7	10.6	9.3	6.0	4.0	7.8
11.7	10.5	11.0	Net Worth	1.0	6.9	17.2	15.4	26.5	25.1
100.0	100.0	100.0	Total Liabilities & Net Worth	100.0	100.0	100.0	100.0	100.0	100.0
			INCOME DATA						
100.0	100.0	100.0	Net Sales	100.0	100.0	100.0	100.0	100.0	100.0
59.7	59.1	59.0	Gross Profit	59.2	59.5	59.0	60.2	57.5	56.7
55.3	56.2	54.9	Operating Expenses	56.9	55.1	55.0	55.2	53.0	51.1
4.4	2.9	4.1	Operating Profit	2.4	4.4	4.0	5.0	4.6	5.6
1.5	1.2	1.2	All Other Expenses (net)	1.4	1.1	.8	.9	1.1	1.5
2.9	1.7	2.9	Profit Before Taxes	1.0	3.2	3.2	4.1	3.4	4.1
			RATIOS						
1.4	1.4	1.4		2.2	1.4	1.4	1.3	1.2	1.1
.7	.6	.7	Current	.7	.6	.7	.7	.7	.6
.3	.3	.3		.3	.3	.3	.3	.4	.4
.9	.8	1.0		1.3	1.0	.9	1.0	.9	.7
(2560) .4	(2594) .3	(2538) .4	Quick	(590) .4	(942) .4	(276) .4	(246) .4	.5	(276) .4
.1	.1	.1		.1	.1	.1	.2	.2	.2
0 UND	0 UND	0 UND		0 UND	0 UND	0 UND	0 UND	0 UND	0 UND
0 999.8	0 UND	0 UND	Sales/Receivables	0 UND	0 UND	0 999.8	1 726.4	1 378.2	1 418.0
2 213.4	2 194.1	2 202.6		0 UND	1 299.8	2 155.9	3 114.4	4 93.6	4 90.0
6 58.8	6 58.7	6 66.0		5 72.5	5 71.9	7 52.2	6 58.1	6 64.0	6 62.2
10 36.4	10 35.8	10 37.9	Cost of Sales/Inventory	10 36.8	9 40.3	11 32.2	10 38.2	9 38.9	10 37.4
16 22.4	18 20.7	16 22.3		19 19.6	15 24.0	18 19.9	17 21.9	15 24.6	15 24.3
7 55.5	6 61.4	4 83.2		0 UND	4 92.4	9 40.0	13 28.6	12 31.0	12 30.0
21 17.6	21 17.7	18 20.2	Cost of Sales/Payables	7 51.5	17 21.2	24 15.2	24 15.1	22 16.9	24 15.0
38 9.6	39 9.3	36 10.0		27 13.5	37 10.0	43 8.6	43 8.5	36 10.3	38 9.6
53.6	54.0	55.8		33.6	56.0	67.3	57.7	64.9	137.8
-39.2	-36.6	-42.3	Sales/Working Capital	-59.1	-45.7	-56.8	-35.1	-41.6	-26.6
-13.1	-12.2	-13.2		-10.7	-13.7	-12.7	-11.8	-15.0	-13.6
8.1	6.9	9.2		6.1	9.2	17.2	8.5	9.1	10.2
(2140) 2.8	(2120) 2.1	(1980) 2.9	EBIT/Interest	(379) 1.6	(715) 2.9	(217) 4.3	(220) 3.7	(194) 3.6	(255) 2.9
.9	.1	.7		-1.3	.3	.9	1.4	1.3	1.5
4.3	4.7	5.3	Net Profit + Depr., Dep.,		4.2	8.4	5.9	3.1	7.9
(245) 2.2	(217) 2.0	(190) 2.3	Amort./Cur. Mat. L/T/D	(26) 2.0	(16) 3.4	(20) 2.5	(31) 2.1	(88) 2.3	
1.3	1.1	1.3			1.1	1.3	1.1	1.5	1.5
1.1	1.1	1.1		.9	.9	.9	1.3	1.2	1.4
3.9	4.3	4.3	Fixed/Worth	8.2	4.3	2.7	4.9	3.0	4.9
-3.2	-2.8	-2.5		-1.3	-2.4	-13.1	-2.5	-6.0	-4.3
1.1	1.2	1.2		1.4	1.1	1.1	1.3	1.3	1.1
5.6	6.5	5.9	Debt/Worth	15.2	7.5	3.8	5.8	3.3	5.6
-5.4	-4.9	-4.8		-3.1	-4.4	-12.9	-5.2	-10.2	-7.9
86.4	73.8	100.3		132.4	125.7	87.0	83.3	66.6	68.2
(1630) 34.4	(1611) 26.1	(1567) 37.7	% Profit Before Taxes/Tangible Net Worth	(331) 39.3	(562) 46.1	(196) 40.1	(150) 30.3	(145) 29.4	(183) 30.6
8.8	2.1	8.1		3.4	8.4	4.9	9.2	10.1	10.3
22.2	17.3	24.3		27.9	28.4	25.5	23.1	15.9	16.7
7.7	4.8	7.6	% Profit Before Taxes/Total Assets	5.5	8.5	9.1	8.2	7.6	6.6
-.3	-3.4	-1.1		-7.4	-2.2	-.7	1.6	1.6	2.2
14.2	14.9	18.6		25.2	24.9	19.1	12.5	10.2	7.8
6.5	6.4	7.3	Sales/Net Fixed Assets	9.2	9.5	8.1	5.5	5.6	4.4
2.9	3.0	3.4		3.6	4.1	3.7	3.1	2.9	2.6
5.4	5.6	6.2		7.6	7.4	6.1	4.7	4.1	3.3
3.2	3.1	3.5	Sales/Total Assets	3.9	4.2	3.9	3.0	2.9	2.3
1.9	1.8	2.0		1.9	2.5	2.5	2.0	1.8	1.6
1.6	1.6	1.4		1.2	1.2	1.3	1.8	1.8	2.1
(2310) 2.8	(2295) 2.8	(2189) 2.5	% Depr., Dep., Amort./Sales	(469) 2.6	(796) 2.2	(251) 2.3	(225) 2.9	(199) 2.9	(249) 3.1
4.3	4.5	4.1		4.9	3.7	3.8	4.1	4.0	4.2
2.2	2.4	2.1		3.2	1.9	1.8	1.8	1.3	1.1
(1109) 4.3	(1135) 4.6	(1155) 4.0	% Officers', Directors', Owners' Comp/Sales	(345) 6.0	(477) 3.6	(109) 3.6	(99) 3.1	(72) 2.2	(53) 3.2
7.9	8.1	7.0		9.9	6.4	6.2	5.4	4.3	5.2
56967854M	55689509M	44394445M	Net Sales ($)	374836M	1712727M	1068763M	1741671M	3296617M	36199831M
21367639M	20469408M	17140085M	Total Assets ($)	152140M	581346M	367840M	728500M	1424375M	13885884M

M = $ thousand   MM = $ million
See Pages 11 through 21 for Explanation of Ratios and Data

Current Data Sorted By Assets   Comparative Historical Data

0-500M	500M-2MM	2-10MM	10-50MM	50-100MM	100-250MM	Type of Statement		
	3	9	9	6	5	Unqualified	46	35
7	10	10	9	1		Reviewed	68	59
49	34	27	5			Compiled	147	101
109	48	12	1		1	Tax Returns	94	77
51	44	39	15			Other	189	151
	49 (4/1-9/30/04)		456 (10/1/04-3/31/05)				4/1/00-3/31/01 ALL	4/1/01-3/31/02 ALL
216	139	97	39	8	6	**NUMBER OF STATEMENTS**	544	423
%	%	%	%	%	%	**ASSETS**	%	%
15.2	14.1	14.4	8.6			Cash & Equivalents	13.4	12.8
1.4	1.5	1.8	1.9			Trade Receivables (net)	1.6	1.6
5.3	2.9	3.0	6.2			Inventory	4.3	4.0
5.0	4.5	2.4	1.1			All Other Current	1.9	2.6
27.0	22.9	21.5	17.7			Total Current	21.3	21.0
49.0	51.3	54.5	56.3			Fixed Assets (net)	55.9	54.7
16.1	13.9	13.0	15.5			Intangibles (net)	13.6	13.3
7.9	11.8	11.0	10.4			All Other Non-Current	9.2	11.0
100.0	100.0	100.0	100.0			Total	100.0	100.0
						LIABILITIES		
10.0	2.8	4.8	11.6			Notes Payable-Short Term	9.8	4.7
7.0	6.3	7.0	4.8			Cur. Mat.-L/T/D	6.3	6.1
9.5	7.5	8.0	5.2			Trade Payables	9.5	9.2
.6	.3	.2	.1			Income Taxes Payable	.2	.2
18.7	12.3	10.7	13.0			All Other Current	15.2	13.9
45.8	29.2	30.8	34.7			Total Current	41.0	34.1
38.4	48.5	42.6	46.1			Long-Term Debt	41.1	40.2
.0	.1	.2	.8			Deferred Taxes	.1	.1
15.9	5.9	3.7	7.7			All Other Non-Current	5.3	4.7
-.1	16.3	22.8	10.7			Net Worth	12.4	20.9
100.0	100.0	100.0	100.0			Total Liabilities & Net Worth	100.0	100.0
						INCOME DATA		
100.0	100.0	100.0	100.0			Net Sales	100.0	100.0
61.8	64.0	59.0	57.8			Gross Profit	62.4	60.3
59.4	59.1	54.8	52.7			Operating Expenses	57.9	56.3
2.4	4.9	4.2	5.1			Operating Profit	4.5	4.0
.9	1.2	.8	2.2			All Other Expenses (net)	1.5	1.3
1.4	3.7	3.4	2.9			Profit Before Taxes	3.0	2.7
						RATIOS		
1.9	1.8	1.1	.9			Current	1.2	1.4
.8	.7	.7	.5				.6	.6
.3	.3	.4	.3				.3	.3
1.3	1.3	.9	.7			Quick	.9	1.0
(214) .4	(135) .4	.4	.3				(541) .4	(418) .4
.1	.1	.2	.2				.1	.1
0 UND	0 UND	0 UND	0 UND			Sales/Receivables	0 UND	0 UND
0 UND	0 UND	0 999.8	0 758.2				0 UND	0 UND
0 UND	0 735.2	1 254.8	2 154.5				1 336.7	1 267.3
6 66.0	5 66.5	5 72.3	7 55.6			Cost of Sales/Inventory	6 58.8	5 66.4
9 42.4	8 45.7	9 40.6	9 41.5				10 37.0	9 41.8
13 28.9	11 32.2	12 30.3	11 33.1				14 26.7	12 29.7
0 UND	6 64.8	10 38.4	12 29.6			Cost of Sales/Payables	10 36.3	7 54.1
9 40.1	20 18.1	20 18.1	23 16.0				22 16.3	20 18.3
21 17.8	35 10.6	37 9.7	38 9.5				38 9.6	34 10.7
45.8	25.2	64.3	-111.2			Sales/Working Capital	56.7	69.4
-85.0	-55.2	-39.4	-26.6				-29.5	-35.1
-13.4	-15.3	-16.2	-13.1				-13.7	-14.5
8.6	8.9	8.1	5.0			EBIT/Interest	5.6	6.2
(161) 2.4	(126) 3.7	(90) 3.0	(37) 2.3				(490) 2.3	(376) 2.2
-1.5	1.4	1.5	1.4				.9	.9
						Net Profit + Depr., Dep., Amort./Cur. Mat. L /T/D	5.0	4.4
							(59) 2.2	(45) 2.0
							1.2	1.1
1.0	1.3	1.3	2.1			Fixed/Worth	1.4	1.3
13.3	8.8	4.9	16.3				5.8	3.7
-1.5	-2.6	-5.9	-1.9				-2.9	-4.8
1.6	1.7	1.4	1.4			Debt/Worth	1.3	1.3
25.6	11.7	4.9	19.7				7.8	4.7
-2.9	-6.0	-9.9	-3.1				-5.1	-7.7
171.2	100.9	71.0	41.9			% Profit Before Taxes/Tangible Net Worth	87.2	86.6
(112) 55.0	(80) 40.3	(63) 32.6	(22) 22.8				(330) 33.7	(276) 28.6
10.8	15.9	11.4	2.9				8.5	7.5
27.9	22.5	15.8	14.9			% Profit Before Taxes/Total Assets	18.7	18.4
6.3	8.9	6.8	7.0				6.7	6.2
-8.7	2.0	1.8	1.3				-.4	.1
23.8	12.6	10.0	7.2			Sales/Net Fixed Assets	11.7	12.5
9.4	6.2	5.1	3.7				5.8	6.4
4.6	3.1	2.6	2.2				2.8	2.8
7.5	4.1	3.8	2.7			Sales/Total Assets	5.0	5.1
4.3	2.9	2.5	2.0				3.1	3.1
2.5	1.7	1.8	1.4				1.8	1.8
1.8	2.0	2.1	2.4			% Depr., Dep., Amort./Sales	2.0	1.9
(178) 3.0	(122) 3.2	(96) 3.2	(37) 3.3				(508) 3.1	(377) 2.8
5.2	4.3	4.6	4.3				4.6	4.4
3.2	1.8	1.1	.8			% Officers', Directors', Owners' Comp/Sales	1.9	1.7
(97) 5.6	(62) 3.6	(38) 2.0	(10) 4.0				(205) 3.3	(171) 3.2
8.1	5.1	4.8	5.9				5.6	5.8
214335M	458509M	1275309M	2730495M	832228M	2270574M	Net Sales ($)	10211746M	8891875M
48995M	145282M	439427M	820541M	532730M	1056656M	Total Assets ($)	4958094M	4384163M

Comparative Historical Data | Current Data Sorted By Sales

4/1/02-3/31/03 ALL	4/1/03-3/31/04 ALL	4/1/04-3/31/05 ALL	Type of Statement	0-1MM	1-3MM	3-5MM	5-10MM	10-25MM	25MM & OVER
16	54	32	Unqualified		2	1	2	6	21
8	57	37	Reviewed	2	6	7	6	7	9
38	126	115	Compiled	26	46	15	11	10	7
66	198	171	Tax Returns	77	58	13	16	5	2
43	154	150	Other	31	49	11	23	5	14
				49 (4/1-9/30/04)		456 (10/1/04-3/31/05)			
171	589	505	**NUMBER OF STATEMENTS**	136	161	47	58	50	53
%	%	%	**ASSETS**	%	%	%	%	%	%
12.4	13.7	14.1	Cash & Equivalents	14.6	14.9	13.9	15.4	13.6	9.4
.9	1.4	1.5	Trade Receivables (net)	1.0	1.8	1.1	1.9	1.2	2.6
3.3	3.8	4.2	Inventory	5.0	3.4	3.7	3.6	3.8	5.6
2.6	3.5	4.0	All Other Current	3.1	6.3	3.4	3.8	2.4	1.5
19.2	22.4	23.8	Total Current	23.7	26.3	22.1	24.7	21.1	19.1
57.0	55.0	51.5	Fixed Assets (net)	54.0	47.0	53.3	52.6	52.3	55.5
14.2	12.6	14.9	Intangibles (net)	16.3	13.8	15.3	12.7	17.5	14.5
9.6	10.0	9.8	All Other Non-Current	6.0	12.9	9.3	10.0	9.2	11.0
100.0	100.0	100.0	Total	100.0	100.0	100.0	100.0	100.0	100.0
			LIABILITIES						
5.6	5.8	6.9	Notes Payable-Short Term	7.0	8.3	2.4	3.9	5.7	10.6
6.0	6.8	6.6	Cur. Mat.-L/T/D	7.0	6.2	7.7	6.6	6.6	6.0
7.4	9.3	8.2	Trade Payables	6.0	9.4	9.4	8.3	10.6	6.8
.2	.3	.4	Income Taxes Payable	1.0	.1	.5	.2	.1	.1
16.9	14.0	14.7	All Other Current	13.7	15.8	16.5	15.7	10.2	15.0
36.1	36.4	36.8	Total Current	34.8	39.9	36.5	34.7	33.1	38.5
45.6	41.9	43.3	Long-Term Debt	45.3	40.8	47.4	41.3	42.0	45.2
.2	.1	.1	Deferred Taxes	.0	.0	.1	.3	.2	.6
8.3	8.7	9.8	All Other Non-Current	12.5	14.2	5.9	2.0	3.7	7.2
9.9	12.9	10.0	Net Worth	7.4	5.1	10.0	21.7	21.0	8.5
100.0	100.0	100.0	Total Liabilities & Net Worth	100.0	100.0	100.0	100.0	100.0	100.0
			INCOME DATA						
100.0	100.0	100.0	Net Sales	100.0	100.0	100.0	100.0	100.0	100.0
60.3	62.1	61.3	Gross Profit	61.7	63.7	62.9	59.4	59.4	55.1
55.6	58.1	57.5	Operating Expenses	59.1	59.9	57.8	55.5	55.8	49.9
4.7	4.0	3.8	Operating Profit	2.6	3.9	5.1	3.9	3.6	5.2
1.6	1.5	1.1	All Other Expenses (net)	2.2	.5	.2	.7	.6	1.9
3.0	2.5	2.7	Profit Before Taxes	.4	3.3	4.9	3.3	3.0	3.3
			RATIOS						
1.5	1.5	1.6	Current	2.3	2.0	1.4	1.1	1.1	.8
.6	.6	.7		.9	.8	.5	.7	.6	.5
.3	.2	.3		.3	.3	.3	.3	.4	.3
1.2	1.1	1.1	Quick	1.8	1.4	.9	.8	.8	.6
(170) .4	(580) .4	(499) .4		(135) .5	(158) .4	(45) .4	.4	.5	.3
.1	.1	.1		.1	.1	.1	.2	.2	.2
0 UND	0 UND	0 UND	Sales/Receivables	0 UND	0 UND	0 UND	0 UND	0 UND	0 UND
0 UND	0 UND	0 UND		0 UND	0 UND	0 999.8	0 999.8	0 999.8	1 685.1
1 599.0	1 446.0	1 587.5		0 UND	0 976.9	1 548.2	1 374.9	1 317.7	3 143.1
5 78.5	6 65.0	5 67.2	Cost of Sales/Inventory	6 60.0	5 75.0	7 55.1	5 71.9	5 74.0	6 63.7
7 49.6	9 40.6	8 43.0		10 35.2	8 47.5	10 36.9	8 45.1	9 42.6	8 45.2
12 31.3	12 29.4	12 30.0		15 24.0	10 35.1	13 29.2	11 32.7	10 35.0	12 31.5
5 75.0	7 55.6	4 83.6	Cost of Sales/Payables	0 UND	7 55.4	6 58.2	9 42.1	10 38.0	13 27.1
16 22.2	18 19.8	16 23.3		5 68.5	18 20.5	19 19.2	21 17.8	22 16.6	20 18.6
30 12.3	34 10.6	31 11.8		16 22.7	31 11.8	35 10.4	33 10.9	41 8.9	37 9.8
50.9	48.0	42.9	Sales/Working Capital	19.4	31.3	37.1	67.3	121.5	-70.0
-46.5	-35.6	-48.9		-221.3	-90.0	-35.0	-40.8	-43.4	-24.1
-14.1	-12.0	-13.7		-11.9	-15.7	-10.2	-16.6	-20.0	-11.9
6.2	7.1	7.8	EBIT/Interest	6.1	6.3	13.0	9.5	9.8	6.4
(149) 2.2	(517) 2.2	(427) 2.8		(105) 2.0	(127) 2.8	(44) 5.2	(53) 3.2	(47) 3.2	(51) 2.4
1.0	.6	1.0		-2.0	.9	1.9	1.5	1.3	1.4
4.7	3.3	3.4	Net Profit + Depr., Dep., Amort./Cur. Mat. L/T/D						5.8
(18) 2.1	(60) 1.6	(33) 1.5							(11) 1.4
1.5	.9	1.0							1.1
1.5	1.4	1.3	Fixed/Worth	1.8	.8	1.3	1.2	1.3	2.2
16.2	5.9	9.6		-83.0	7.3	9.9	4.0	4.7	16.3
-2.6	-3.0	-2.1		-1.8	-2.5	-2.2	-5.8	-2.1	-1.8
1.6	1.5	1.7	Debt/Worth	2.7	1.4	1.3	1.2	1.1	2.2
26.7	8.0	12.7		-93.0	12.7	11.4	4.9	6.3	19.7
-4.4	-4.7	-3.8		-3.3	-4.4	-4.2	-8.6	-3.6	-3.2
118.8	83.3	107.8	% Profit Before Taxes/Tangible Net Worth	157.7	118.9	101.6	53.6	89.6	111.5
(95) 52.6	(345) 30.4	(285) 39.1		(67) 57.6	(94) 39.8	(26) 46.5	(38) 27.7	(29) 32.6	(31) 41.8
8.1	5.7	11.5		3.5	12.2	25.9	10.7	10.4	12.8
20.6	17.5	20.6	% Profit Before Taxes/Total Assets	22.4	20.9	26.2	16.4	18.5	19.4
5.9	6.0	7.2		3.2	7.3	12.9	7.2	10.3	7.0
-.2	-1.4	.0		-10.9	.6	3.0	1.8	1.9	2.2
10.9	12.8	14.4	Sales/Net Fixed Assets	15.6	18.3	12.6	12.9	10.2	9.1
5.5	6.0	6.8		5.2	8.6	6.9	6.1	7.2	4.7
2.8	2.9	3.2		2.0	4.5	3.6	3.0	3.4	2.2
4.6	5.1	5.2	Sales/Total Assets	5.4	6.5	4.9	4.8	4.4	3.8
3.0	3.0	3.1		2.6	3.4	3.1	3.2	3.5	2.4
1.9	1.8	1.9		1.4	2.4	1.9	2.0	2.0	1.5
2.2	2.1	2.0	% Depr., Dep., Amort./Sales	2.2	1.8	1.9	2.0	2.0	2.1
(156) 3.5	(530) 3.2	(444) 3.2		(115) 4.3	(135) 2.7	(43) 3.6	(53) 2.9	2.9	(48) 3.4
5.0	4.6	4.7		6.8	4.2	4.7	4.3	3.9	4.3
1.5	2.0	2.0	% Officers', Directors', Owners' Comp/Sales	3.7	2.7	1.7	1.2	.9	1.2
(64) 4.0	(252) 3.7	(209) 4.1		(66) 6.0	(62) 4.0	(22) 2.5	(30) 2.6	(15) 1.3	(14) 4.0
6.9	6.2	6.7		8.5	6.7	5.1	4.8	3.0	6.7
2941816M	7505302M	7781450M	Net Sales ($)	70192M	268161M	184637M	401610M	861963M	5994887M
1325349M	3802680M	3043631M	Total Assets ($)	38541M	103048M	77290M	148159M	330059M	2346534M

© RMA 2005

M = $ thousand   MM = $ million
See Pages 11 through 21 for Explanation of Ratios and Data

Current Data Sorted By Assets   **Comparative Historical Data**

						Type of Statement		
		1	1	1	1	Unqualified		
1						Reviewed		
1						Compiled		
7	3	1				Tax Returns		
7	3	2				Other		
							4/1/00-3/31/01 ALL	4/1/01-3/31/02 ALL
0-500M	4 (4/1-9/30/04) 500M-2MM	2-10MM	25 (10/1/04-3/31/05) 10-50MM	50-100MM	100-250MM			
16	6	4	1	1	1	NUMBER OF STATEMENTS		
%	%	%	%	%	%	ASSETS	%	%
8.5						Cash & Equivalents	D	D
6.9						Trade Receivables (net)	A	A
5.7						Inventory	T	T
.2						All Other Current	A	A
21.3						Total Current		
64.3						Fixed Assets (net)	N	N
6.8						Intangibles (net)	O	O
7.7						All Other Non-Current	T	T
100.0						Total		
						LIABILITIES	A	A
15.2						Notes Payable-Short Term	V	V
6.5						Cur. Mat.-L/T/D	A	A
5.8						Trade Payables	I	I
.1						Income Taxes Payable	L	L
20.2						All Other Current	A	A
47.7						Total Current	B	B
42.1						Long-Term Debt	L	L
.0						Deferred Taxes	E	E
19.2						All Other Non-Current		
−9.0						Net Worth		
100.0						Total Liabilities & Net Worth		
						INCOME DATA		
100.0						Net Sales		
						Gross Profit		
96.5						Operating Expenses		
3.5						Operating Profit		
1.7						All Other Expenses (net)		
1.8						Profit Before Taxes		
						RATIOS		
2.0						Current		
.8								
.4								
1.7						Quick		
(15) .4								
.1								
0 UND						Sales/Receivables		
0 UND								
0 UND								
						Cost of Sales/Inventory		
						Cost of Sales/Payables		
45.0						Sales/Working Capital		
−527.7								
−9.7								
4.3						EBIT/Interest		
(14) 2.5								
−.7								
						Net Profit + Depr., Dep., Amort./Cur. Mat. L /T/D		
1.3						Fixed/Worth		
−5.0								
−1.1								
.6						Debt/Worth		
−7.0								
−2.3								
						% Profit Before Taxes/Tangible Net Worth		
26.8						% Profit Before Taxes/Total Assets		
10.5								
−6.2								
10.3						Sales/Net Fixed Assets		
5.8								
2.2								
7.1						Sales/Total Assets		
3.5								
1.8								
1.6						% Depr., Dep., Amort./Sales		
(11) 1.9								
4.6								
						% Officers', Directors', Owners' Comp/Sales		
9808M	9472M	60295M	35514M	174789M	163401M	Net Sales ($)		
3047M	5349M	21786M	18200M	72890M	101084M	Total Assets ($)		

M = $ thousand   MM = $ million
See Pages 11 through 21 for Explanation of Ratios and Data

Comparative Historical Data				Current Data Sorted By Sales					
1	5	4	Type of Statement					1	3
2	2	1	Unqualified						
6	8	1	Reviewed	1					
9	22	11	Compiled	1					
2	3	12	Tax Returns	6	4				1
			Other	8	2		2		
4/1/02-3/31/03	4/1/03-3/31/04	4/1/04-3/31/05			4 (4/1-9/30/04)		25 (10/1/04-3/31/05)		
ALL	ALL	ALL		0-1MM	1-3MM	3-5MM	5-10MM	10-25MM	25MM & OVER
20	40	29	**NUMBER OF STATEMENTS**	16	6		2	1	4
%	%	%	**ASSETS**	%	%	%	%	%	%
12.1	9.2	7.9	Cash & Equivalents	8.6					
2.7	2.3	6.4	Trade Receivables (net)	5.3	D				
4.8	4.5	4.5	Inventory	3.7	A				
1.9	.6	1.1	All Other Current	.2	T				
21.4	16.6	19.9	Total Current	17.7	A				
53.7	50.2	59.7	Fixed Assets (net)	68.6					
9.8	17.4	7.2	Intangibles (net)	6.3	N				
15.0	15.8	13.3	All Other Non-Current	7.5	O				
100.0	100.0	100.0	Total	100.0	T				
			LIABILITIES		A				
1.5	5.8	10.6	Notes Payable-Short Term	14.0	V				
9.3	6.9	5.1	Cur. Mat.-L/T/D	5.3	A				
8.3	9.2	7.7	Trade Payables	4.9	I				
.1	.1	.0	Income Taxes Payable	.1	L				
5.4	18.8	14.8	All Other Current	18.8	A				
24.6	40.8	38.2	Total Current	43.0	B				
27.1	51.6	42.2	Long-Term Debt	38.8	L				
.7	.2	.2	Deferred Taxes	.0	E				
6.1	16.8	17.4	All Other Non-Current	19.2					
41.6	-9.3	1.9	Net Worth	-1.0					
100.0	100.0	100.0	Total Liabilities & Net Worth	100.0					
			INCOME DATA						
100.0	100.0	100.0	Net Sales	100.0					
			Gross Profit						
91.0	95.3	94.0	Operating Expenses	93.0					
9.0	4.7	6.0	Operating Profit	7.0					
1.7	4.2	2.4	All Other Expenses (net)	2.9					
7.3	.5	3.6	Profit Before Taxes	4.1					
			RATIOS						
1.3	1.0	1.6		2.1					
.8	.5	.7	Current	.8					
.4	.3	.4		.4					
1.0	.9	.9		1.8					
.6	(39) .3	(28) .4	Quick	(15) .5					
.2	.1	.1		.1					
0 UND	0 UND	0 UND		0 UND					
0 UND	0 UND	0 UND	Sales/Receivables	0 UND					
4 92.4	3 135.7	7 53.3		0 UND					
			Cost of Sales/Inventory						
			Cost of Sales/Payables						
63.1	287.4	60.6		32.8					
-49.4	-33.5	-55.5	Sales/Working Capital	UND					
-20.0	-12.5	-12.0		-9.7					
9.3	7.7	7.1		4.3					
(18) 4.2	(29) 2.0	(26) 2.6	EBIT/Interest	(14) 2.7					
2.0	-2.7	.7		-.7					
			Net Profit + Depr., Dep., Amort./Cur. Mat. L/T/D						
1.2	1.1	1.3		1.4					
1.7	10.5	3.2	Fixed/Worth	NM					
4.1	-1.4	-1.5		-1.7					
.8	1.7	1.0		.6					
1.8	28.0	12.1	Debt/Worth	NM					
5.1	-2.5	-2.9		-3.1					
90.1	100.0	53.2	% Profit Before Taxes/Tangible Net Worth						
(17) 16.9	(22) 46.7	(16) 24.4							
5.7	12.5	5.3							
45.6	20.7	25.9	% Profit Before Taxes/Total Assets	27.3					
12.5	7.1	9.6		9.9					
2.9	-11.6	.2		-6.2					
9.0	12.4	10.1		9.6					
6.0	5.2	5.0	Sales/Net Fixed Assets	4.1					
4.2	3.0	2.4		1.5					
4.3	4.1	4.9		7.1					
3.4	2.7	2.7	Sales/Total Assets	2.5					
2.4	1.8	1.5		1.3					
2.2	2.5	1.7							
(18) 3.4	(36) 4.0	(21) 2.9	% Depr., Dep., Amort./Sales						
4.5	6.8	4.7							
1.9	2.0	2.5							
(14) 3.6	(24) 4.0	(15) 5.3	% Officers', Directors', Owners' Comp/Sales						
9.2	5.7	8.9							
55584M	308910M	453279M	Net Sales ($)	7668M	11612M		13735M	18196M	402068M
18379M	179914M	222356M	Total Assets ($)	4544M	3852M		13722M	2156M	198082M

M = $ thousand   MM = $ million
See Pages 11 through 21 for Explanation of Ratios and Data

RESTAURANT/LODGING—Caterers NAICS 722320 (SIC 5812)

Current Data Sorted By Assets							Comparative Historical Data	
			1	1		Type of Statement		
	1		2			Unqualified		
2	3					Reviewed		
5	3	1				Compiled		
	7					Tax Returns		
						Other		
	7 (4/1-9/30/04)		20 (10/1/04-3/31/05)				4/1/00-3/31/01 ALL	4/1/01-3/31/02 ALL
0-500M	500M-2MM	2-10MM	10-50MM	50-100MM	100-250MM			
8	14	4	1			NUMBER OF STATEMENTS		
%	%	%	%	%	%	ASSETS	%	%
	8.1			D	D	Cash & Equivalents	D	D
	17.7			A	A	Trade Receivables (net)	A	A
	3.2			T	T	Inventory	T	T
	5.6			A	A	All Other Current	A	A
	34.6					Total Current		
	44.5			N	N	Fixed Assets (net)	N	N
	6.1			O	O	Intangibles (net)	O	O
	14.8			T	T	All Other Non-Current	T	T
	100.0					Total		
				A	A	LIABILITIES	A	A
	7.4			V	V	Notes Payable-Short Term	V	V
	3.5			A	A	Cur. Mat.-L/T/D	A	A
	11.7			I	I	Trade Payables	I	I
	.0			L	L	Income Taxes Payable	L	L
	14.4			A	A	All Other Current	A	A
	37.0			B	B	Total Current	B	B
	23.4			L	L	Long-Term Debt	L	L
	.5			E	E	Deferred Taxes	E	E
	5.6					All Other Non-Current		
	33.6					Net Worth		
	100.0					Total Liabilities & Net Worth		
						INCOME DATA		
	100.0					Net Sales		
						Gross Profit		
	94.2					Operating Expenses		
	5.8					Operating Profit		
	1.6					All Other Expenses (net)		
	4.2					Profit Before Taxes		
						RATIOS		
	1.6							
	1.0					Current		
	.2							
	1.4							
	.7					Quick		
	.2							
0	UND							
8	47.5					Sales/Receivables		
20	18.0							
						Cost of Sales/Inventory		
						Cost of Sales/Payables		
	33.9							
	NM					Sales/Working Capital		
	-9.8							
	8.6							
(12)	4.4					EBIT/Interest		
	-1.8							
						Net Profit + Depr., Dep., Amort./Cur. Mat. L /T/D		
	.5							
	2.2					Fixed/Worth		
	18.5							
	.9							
	2.7					Debt/Worth		
	49.9							
	75.7					% Profit Before Taxes/Tangible Net Worth		
(12)	25.1							
	9.9							
	18.4					% Profit Before Taxes/Total Assets		
	5.2							
	-7.9							
	12.7							
	6.4					Sales/Net Fixed Assets		
	2.8							
	3.9							
	3.0					Sales/Total Assets		
	1.1							
						% Depr., Dep., Amort./Sales		
						% Officers', Directors', Owners' Comp/Sales		
9516M	50401M	40200M	37673M			Net Sales ($)		
1459M	15482M	17651M	11932M			Total Assets ($)		

© RMA 2005

M = $ thousand   MM = $ million
See Pages 11 through 21 for Explanation of Ratios and Data

Comparative Historical Data | | | | **Current Data Sorted By Sales**

			Type of Statement						
	1	3	Unqualified		1		1	1	1
	4	3	Reviewed			1		1	
4	6	5	Compiled		4			1	
5	12	9	Tax Returns	4	4		1		
5	7	7	Other	1	4	2			
4/1/02-3/31/03	4/1/03-3/31/04	4/1/04-3/31/05		0-1MM	7 (4/1-9/30/04) 1-3MM	3-5MM	20 (10/1/04-3/31/05) 5-10MM	10-25MM	25MM & OVER
ALL	ALL	ALL							
14	30	27	**NUMBER OF STATEMENTS**	5	13	3	2		1
%	%	%	**ASSETS**	%	%	%	%	%	%
17.1	16.9	13.9	Cash & Equivalents		17.2				
8.6	10.8	19.9	Trade Receivables (net)		20.1				
3.6	6.5	5.9	Inventory		5.7				
1.9	3.7	4.2	All Other Current		1.5				
31.2	37.9	44.0	Total Current		44.5				
51.2	47.4	41.4	Fixed Assets (net)		43.3				
3.9	5.9	5.1	Intangibles (net)		6.3				
13.8	8.8	9.5	All Other Non-Current		5.9				
100.0	100.0	100.0	Total		100.0				
			LIABILITIES						
9.2	4.6	8.3	Notes Payable-Short Term		7.0				
4.4	13.5	2.6	Cur. Mat.-L/T/D		.5				
18.8	18.3	21.1	Trade Payables		20.0				
.1	.1	.0	Income Taxes Payable		.0				
13.6	20.0	17.8	All Other Current		20.6				
46.2	56.5	49.9	Total Current		48.0				
21.4	34.2	19.2	Long-Term Debt		21.2				
.0	.4	.4	Deferred Taxes		.0				
29.1	26.4	25.1	All Other Non-Current		13.7				
3.1	−17.5	5.4	Net Worth		17.1				
100.0	100.0	100.0	Total Liabilities & Net Worth		100.0				
			INCOME DATA						
100.0	100.0	100.0	Net Sales		100.0				
			Gross Profit						
97.5	95.0	96.0	Operating Expenses		96.1				
2.5	5.0	4.0	Operating Profit		3.9				
.8	3.4	1.0	All Other Expenses (net)		1.6				
1.7	1.6	3.0	Profit Before Taxes		2.4				
			RATIOS						
4.5	2.7	1.4			1.8				
.6	.9	1.0	Current		1.0				
.3	.4	.5			.4				
4.0	2.4	1.2			1.3				
.5	.6	.8	Quick		.9				
.2	.3	.3			.2				
0 UND	0 UND	0 UND			0 UND				
5 68.9	2 154.8	7 49.3	Sales/Receivables		2 189.4				
15 23.6	14 26.8	20 18.0			29 12.7				
			Cost of Sales/Inventory						
			Cost of Sales/Payables						
16.7	12.0	15.3			17.4				
−27.6	−137.4	−531.5	Sales/Working Capital		−531.5				
−6.5	−13.9	−11.9			−17.5				
4.1	11.1	8.6							
(11) .4	(21) 4.9	(20) 2.7	EBIT/Interest						
−1.8	−7.0	−1.5							
			Net Profit + Depr., Dep., Amort./Cur. Mat. L/T/D						
.9	1.1	.7			.8				
3.2	4.7	2.5	Fixed/Worth		2.9				
−4.6	−1.1	55.6			−1.0				
.9	1.7	2.2			1.5				
3.7	6.3	3.4	Debt/Worth		3.0				
−7.2	−2.3	177.0			−3.8				
	150.8	86.9							
(19) 61.9	(21) 35.2		% Profit Before Taxes/Tangible Net Worth						
	21.3	10.7							
15.6	30.2	15.4			29.3				
1.3	12.0	4.3	% Profit Before Taxes/Total Assets		8.9				
−9.5	−11.6	−6.5			−11.0				
12.6	21.9	32.3			124.4				
6.8	9.5	12.2	Sales/Net Fixed Assets		8.0				
4.6	3.8	3.1			2.5				
4.3	6.2	4.7			4.7				
3.6	3.6	3.4	Sales/Total Assets		3.3				
2.5	2.0	1.6			1.4				
1.3	.9	.6			.4				
(13) 3.1	(25) 1.7	(20) 1.4	% Depr., Dep., Amort./Sales		(11) 2.2				
5.4	3.6	3.1			4.7				
	2.9	1.6							
	(19) 4.2	(12) 4.6	% Officers', Directors', Owners' Comp/Sales						
	6.9	6.5							
198096M	110173M	137790M	Net Sales ($)	1462M	24378M	10540M	14722M	49015M	37673M
50461M	47126M	46524M	Total Assets ($)	2215M	11264M	5595M	3651M	11867M	11932M

© RMA 2005

M = $ thousand   MM = $ million

See Pages 11 through 21 for Explanation of Ratios and Data

Current Data Sorted By Assets | Comparative Historical Data

0-500M	500M-2MM	2-10MM	10-50MM	50-100MM	100-250MM	Type of Statement	4/1/00-3/31/01 ALL	4/1/01-3/31/02 ALL
		1		1		Unqualified	4	7
1		1				Reviewed	3	2
22	16	2	1			Compiled	51	33
57	19	2	1	1		Tax Returns	50	56
21	19	5	4			Other	38	44
	17 (4/1-9/30/04)		156 (10/1/04-3/31/05)					
101	54	10	6	2		NUMBER OF STATEMENTS	146	142
%	%	%	%	%	%	ASSETS	%	%
16.8	8.5	12.7				Cash & Equivalents	12.9	13.8
1.8	1.1	3.2				Trade Receivables (net)	1.2	1.6
12.5	6.2	2.2				Inventory	9.7	9.2
3.8	6.8	6.8				All Other Current	2.7	2.9
34.9	22.6	24.9				Total Current	26.5	27.5
45.4	55.6	59.0				Fixed Assets (net)	48.4	48.5
13.2	8.5	1.3				Intangibles (net)	13.2	11.7
6.4	13.3	14.8				All Other Non-Current	11.9	12.2
100.0	100.0	100.0				Total	100.0	100.0
						LIABILITIES		
7.7	4.1	8.3				Notes Payable-Short Term	5.9	3.2
2.5	2.4	3.4				Cur. Mat.-L/T/D	4.5	3.8
10.2	5.8	3.0				Trade Payables	6.3	11.1
.1	.1	.0				Income Taxes Payable	.2	.2
26.9	11.1	5.6				All Other Current	26.5	22.8
47.5	23.5	20.2				Total Current	43.4	41.1
38.0	33.2	46.5				Long-Term Debt	31.9	38.3
.0	.0	.0				Deferred Taxes	.1	.0
14.0	12.7	23.9				All Other Non-Current	14.4	13.8
.6	30.6	9.4				Net Worth	10.2	6.7
100.0	100.0	100.0				Total Liabilities & Net Worth	100.0	100.0
						INCOME DATA		
100.0	100.0	100.0				Net Sales	100.0	100.0
57.8	61.9	60.5				Gross Profit	59.3	58.2
55.3	56.3	55.2				Operating Expenses	54.2	53.5
2.4	5.6	5.3				Operating Profit	5.1	4.7
.6	.8	2.5				All Other Expenses (net)	.8	1.6
1.8	4.7	2.8				Profit Before Taxes	4.3	3.1
						RATIOS		
3.4	2.6	3.5				Current	2.2	2.3
1.0	.9	1.3					.9	.8
.4	.4	.7					.3	.3
1.9	1.5	2.5				Quick	1.2	1.1
(100) .4	(53) .3	.7					(144) .4	(140) .4
.1	.1	.3					.1	.1
0 UND	0 UND	0 UND				Sales/Receivables	0 UND	0 UND
0 UND	0 UND	0 UND					0 UND	0 UND
0 UND	2 213.8	4 89.5					1 534.4	1 488.2
8 43.4	10 35.9	8 45.6				Cost of Sales/Inventory	10 36.6	9 39.4
16 23.1	17 21.1	12 29.5					15 24.7	16 22.3
27 13.3	31 11.9	16 22.7					24 14.9	29 12.5
0 UND	1 351.3	0 UND				Cost of Sales/Payables	0 UND	0 UND
4 90.8	12 29.9	7 52.7					7 53.2	14 26.5
26 13.9	35 10.4	22 16.2					34 10.7	38 9.5
14.1	18.9	17.7				Sales/Working Capital	25.7	28.0
262.4	-160.5	47.6					-153.6	-93.3
-25.6	-11.2	-166.1					-18.3	-14.2
8.0	15.7					EBIT/Interest	6.4	7.2
(59) 3.0	(44) 3.2						(110) 2.7	(110) 2.0
.4	.7						1.2	.7
						Net Profit + Depr., Dep., Amort./Cur. Mat. L./T/D		
.5	.9	2.4				Fixed/Worth	.7	.9
2.2	2.2	UND					3.0	2.6
-2.2	-10.9	-4.3					-3.4	-4.1
.7	.6	1.7				Debt/Worth	.7	.8
2.9	3.1	UND					3.4	3.5
-3.6	-16.7	-7.6					-5.3	-7.4
97.2	78.8					% Profit Before Taxes/Tangible Net Worth	73.8	91.3
(60) 28.0	(36) 44.8						(93) 39.0	(92) 40.1
5.3	14.8						14.8	11.1
27.1	29.3	15.3				% Profit Before Taxes/Total Assets	23.6	25.5
8.5	7.6	5.5					8.3	6.6
-3.6	-.9	-2.0					1.6	-2.1
34.4	9.4	7.1				Sales/Net Fixed Assets	17.2	21.5
13.9	4.5	3.8					8.4	8.3
5.4	2.2	1.5					3.9	3.5
8.1	3.1	2.1				Sales/Total Assets	5.4	5.9
3.9	2.3	1.7					3.2	3.2
2.4	1.4	1.1					2.0	1.9
1.0	1.6	2.7				% Depr., Dep., Amort./Sales	1.2	1.3
(74) 2.1	(45) 3.5	4.6					(124) 2.4	(116) 2.5
4.4	6.3	6.5					3.8	4.1
3.3	2.9					% Officers', Directors', Owners' Comp/Sales	3.1	3.7
(49) 6.9	(20) 3.7						(64) 6.9	(64) 6.0
9.8	4.4						9.5	9.3
90697M	129940M	57996M	133521M	1917073M		Net Sales ($)	4042806M	483670M
20869M	52116M	33797M	96870M	130353M		Total Assets ($)	634727M	222806M

Columns 10-50MM, 50-100MM and 100-250MM in the ratio/percentage section are marked **DATA NOT AVAILABLE**.

© RMA 2005

M = $ thousand   MM = $ million
See Pages 11 through 21 for Explanation of Ratios and Data

Comparative Historical Data — **Current Data Sorted By Sales**

Type of Statement				0-1MM	1-3MM	3-5MM	5-10MM	10-25MM	25MM & OVER
Unqualified	6	5	1		1			1	1
Reviewed	2	7	2				1		1
Compiled	37	41	41	13	19	7	1	1	1
Tax Returns	80	85	80	45	28	3	2	1	1
Other	44	38	49	15	20	6	5	1	2
	4/1/02-3/31/03 ALL	4/1/03-3/31/04 ALL	4/1/04-3/31/05 ALL	17 (4/1-9/30/04)			156 (10/1/04-3/31/05)		
NUMBER OF STATEMENTS	169	176	173	73	68	16	8	3	5
	%	%	%	%	%	%	%	%	%
ASSETS									
Cash & Equivalents	16.0	13.1	14.2	14.8	13.7	12.6			
Trade Receivables (net)	1.7	2.2	1.6	.9	2.0	3.6			
Inventory	9.7	9.9	9.5	10.0	10.2	9.9			
All Other Current	4.0	2.4	5.0	3.7	4.7	10.6			
Total Current	31.4	27.6	30.2	29.5	30.5	36.6			
Fixed Assets (net)	48.4	50.5	50.0	48.7	52.0	45.1			
Intangibles (net)	9.6	10.2	10.6	15.0	8.7	5.8			
All Other Non-Current	10.6	11.7	9.2	6.8	8.8	12.5			
Total	100.0	100.0	100.0	100.0	100.0	100.0			
LIABILITIES									
Notes Payable-Short Term	6.3	7.9	6.3	5.6	7.2	9.9			
Cur. Mat.-L/T/D	2.8	5.2	2.6	2.7	2.6	1.2			
Trade Payables	7.1	9.4	8.2	5.3	12.0	7.5			
Income Taxes Payable	.4	.5	.1	.0	.2	.0			
All Other Current	14.3	14.2	19.9	25.4	19.2	9.2			
Total Current	30.8	37.1	37.0	38.9	41.2	27.7			
Long-Term Debt	32.7	33.1	36.8	42.9	34.6	27.1			
Deferred Taxes	.0	.1	.0	.0	.0	.0			
All Other Non-Current	15.5	13.4	14.1	16.9	8.7	21.8			
Net Worth	21.0	16.4	12.1	1.3	15.5	23.4			
Total Liabilities & Net Worth	100.0	100.0	100.0	100.0	100.0	100.0			
INCOME DATA									
Net Sales	100.0	100.0	100.0	100.0	100.0	100.0			
Gross Profit	58.7	58.2	59.2	57.1	62.3	59.1			
Operating Expenses	53.9	55.9	55.5	55.1	57.7	54.5			
Operating Profit	4.8	2.3	3.7	2.0	4.5	4.6			
All Other Expenses (net)	1.2	1.2	.7	.8	.8	.8			
Profit Before Taxes	3.5	1.1	3.0	1.2	3.8	3.8			
RATIOS									
Current	3.5	2.5	3.1	3.9	2.7	3.0			
	1.2	.9	1.0	1.2	.8	1.1			
	.5	.3	.4	.3	.4	.6			
Quick	1.8	1.5	1.8	2.2	1.5	1.0			
	.6 (175)	.3 (171)	.4	.5 (67)	.3	.5			
	.1	.1	.1	.0	.1	.2			
Sales/Receivables	0 UND	0 UND	0 UND	0 UND	0 UND	0 UND			
	0 UND	0 UND	0 UND	0 UND	0 UND	1 585.7			
	0 978.9	1 623.2	1 434.0	0 UND	1 325.9	6 62.3			
Cost of Sales/Inventory	8 43.4	9 41.5	9 41.0	9 41.0	10 36.6	9 42.6			
	18 20.4	16 23.5	16 23.2	17 21.4	16 23.2	12 29.8			
	29 12.6	25 14.5	27 13.4	31 11.9	22 16.6	27 13.4			
Cost of Sales/Payables	0 UND	0 UND	0 UND	0 UND	0 UND	5 77.7			
	8 43.7	14 26.1	8 47.4	0 UND	11 33.0	10 35.5			
	31 11.6	33 11.2	30 12.2	23 16.2	31 11.7	30 12.1			
Sales/Working Capital	15.6	23.4	14.6	11.5	21.1	17.8			
	94.0	-279.0	262.4	79.9	-117.6	181.7			
	-19.1	-12.2	-17.5	-14.2	-13.3	-47.3			
EBIT/Interest	7.6	6.0	10.5	5.8	18.2	30.6			
	2.1 (117)	2.1 (129)	3.1 (119)	1.9 (44)	3.2 (50)	5.2 (11)			
	.6	-.9	.8	.1	.7	.8			
Net Profit + Depr., Dep., Amort./Cur. Mat. L/T/D									
Fixed/Worth	.5	.7	.8	.5	.9	.4			
	2.2	3.2	2.4	3.8	2.2	12.2			
	-5.0	-3.2	-4.8	-2.0	-5.5	-6.2			
Debt/Worth	.5	.9	.7	.8	.8	.5			
	3.1	4.0	2.9	4.0	2.8	16.8			
	-8.2	-4.9	-8.2	-3.5	-8.7	-11.0			
% Profit Before Taxes/Tangible Net Worth	67.4	82.6	85.3	84.2	95.2	73.7			
	30.2 (111)	35.3 (112)	35.7 (109)	24.3 (42)	32.9 (42)	57.8 (11)			
	4.7	.3	7.0	-2.7	9.3	26.2			
% Profit Before Taxes/Total Assets	28.8	20.3	26.3	22.8	30.4	26.8			
	6.5	6.1	8.4	6.1	7.2	12.9			
	-2.3	-5.7	-1.8	-4.2	.2	-2.1			
Sales/Net Fixed Assets	21.6	18.4	22.9	24.0	22.7	28.4			
	7.3	7.4	7.2	7.5	7.9	6.9			
	3.2	3.2	3.0	2.3	3.7	4.2			
Sales/Total Assets	4.9	5.7	5.6	5.1	7.6	5.1			
	3.2	3.3	2.9	2.9	3.1	3.1			
	2.0	1.9	1.8	1.5	2.0	2.3			
% Depr., Dep., Amort./Sales	1.5	1.6	1.4	1.5	.9	1.3			
	2.6 (143)	3.1 (137)	2.9 (136)	2.9 (55)	2.1 (55)	3.5 (13)			
	5.1	4.9	5.0	4.9	5.0	5.1			
% Officers', Directors', Owners' Comp/Sales	2.6	2.8	3.3	3.6	2.6				
	6.0 (74)	5.8 (84)	4.9 (76)	6.7 (33)	4.1 (32)				
	10.5	10.0	8.7	11.0	8.0				
Net Sales ($)	805578M	1667462M	2329227M	37403M	118228M	55858M	58083M	52177M	2007478M
Total Assets ($)	250562M	573966M	334005M	18116M	44799M	19317M	43048M	18980M	189745M

© RMA 2005

M = $ thousand   MM = $ million

See Pages 11 through 21 for Explanation of Ratios and Data

OTHER SERVICES
(EXCEPT PUBLIC
ADMINISTRATION)

OTHER SERVICES—General Automotive Repair NAICS 811111 (SIC 7538)

Current Data Sorted By Assets / Comparative Historical Data

						Type of Statement	4	9
	1	1	4		1	Unqualified	4	9
8	8	11	4			Reviewed	23	19
58	29	11	2	1	2	Compiled	91	95
139	41	7			3	Tax Returns	99	103
43	17	14	5			Other	66	71
	64 (4/1-9/30/04)		346 (10/1/04-3/31/05)				4/1/00-3/31/01	4/1/01-3/31/02
0-500M	500M-2MM	2-10MM	10-50MM	50-100MM	100-250MM		ALL	ALL
248	96	44	15	1	6	NUMBER OF STATEMENTS	283	297

0-500M %	500M-2MM %	2-10MM %	10-50MM %	50-100MM %	100-250MM %		ALL %	ALL %
						ASSETS		
14.9	10.3	8.5	5.1			Cash & Equivalents	10.4	10.7
12.9	14.3	14.2	12.1			Trade Receivables (net)	15.0	13.7
16.6	21.9	19.1	20.1			Inventory	23.6	21.7
2.4	2.0	4.1	1.8			All Other Current	1.5	3.0
46.8	48.5	45.9	39.1			Total Current	50.5	49.0
40.2	37.0	35.7	47.5			Fixed Assets (net)	35.6	37.2
6.4	5.6	6.7	6.4			Intangibles (net)	5.9	6.0
6.7	8.8	11.7	7.1			All Other Non-Current	8.0	7.8
100.0	100.0	100.0	100.0			Total	100.0	100.0
						LIABILITIES		
12.4	7.7	10.2	16.3			Notes Payable-Short Term	12.8	11.1
5.9	3.6	4.3	6.3			Cur. Mat.-L/T/D	5.0	5.4
15.9	11.9	15.2	11.9			Trade Payables	16.4	14.7
.1	.1	.1	.2			Income Taxes Payable	.2	.3
19.2	9.4	8.8	11.4			All Other Current	9.9	11.6
53.5	32.6	38.7	46.1			Total Current	44.3	43.1
42.5	27.9	21.1	32.5			Long-Term Debt	25.6	29.6
.0	.1	.5	.3			Deferred Taxes	.2	.2
11.1	7.4	5.9	5.7			All Other Non-Current	5.8	7.0
-7.2	31.9	33.8	15.4			Net Worth	24.1	20.1
100.0	100.0	100.0	100.0			Total Liabilities & Net Worth	100.0	100.0
						INCOME DATA		
100.0	100.0	100.0	100.0			Net Sales	100.0	100.0
						Gross Profit		
96.1	94.6	95.7	92.1			Operating Expenses	95.8	95.9
3.9	5.4	4.3	7.9			Operating Profit	4.2	4.1
1.2	1.5	-.2	4.7			All Other Expenses (net)	1.4	1.9
2.7	3.8	4.6	3.2			Profit Before Taxes	2.8	2.2
						RATIOS		
2.3	2.9	1.6	1.3			Current	2.4	2.2
1.0	1.5	1.1	.6				1.4	1.2
.5	.9	.7	.4				.8	.7
1.4	1.5	.9	.5			Quick	1.3	1.2
(247) .6	.8	.5	.3				(281) .6	(294) .5
.2	.3	.2	.2				.2	.3
0 UND	2 204.2	4 98.3	2 174.1			Sales/Receivables	2 236.6	2 187.2
6 60.8	13 29.1	18 20.1	15 24.2				9 38.8	10 36.6
16 22.6	28 13.1	31 12.0	38 9.5				27 13.4	24 15.0
						Cost of Sales/Inventory		
						Cost of Sales/Payables		
18.8	8.4	11.0	17.1			Sales/Working Capital	11.2	12.4
643.4	25.6	108.4	-26.6				31.6	46.4
-20.2	-90.1	-23.1	-5.0				-45.3	-28.6
6.5	11.0	7.7	6.8			EBIT/Interest	6.3	7.2
(196) 2.2	(86) 3.9	(40) 2.6	(14) 2.6				(243) 2.5	(254) 2.2
.2	1.4	1.3	.9				1.0	.9
	4.6	3.8				Net Profit + Depr., Dep.,	4.7	3.0
	(17) 2.0	(13) 1.3				Amort./Cur. Mat. L/T/D	(32) 2.1	(40) 1.8
	.5	.9					1.3	.7
.7	.3	.4	.4			Fixed/Worth	.4	.5
4.8	1.2	1.2	1.9				1.4	1.5
-1.2	4.0	2.7	30.4				-20.0	-21.5
1.7	.8	1.0	2.0			Debt/Worth	1.0	1.1
26.6	1.8	2.3	12.9				2.7	3.4
-3.1	13.0	5.6	-19.5				-44.1	-41.3
103.7	57.2	43.5	45.0			% Profit Before Taxes/Tangible	62.8	70.2
(138) 26.7	(79) 22.9	(40) 16.2	(11) 39.0			Net Worth	(208) 20.6	(218) 22.8
1.8	8.9	3.1	19.8				5.8	2.8
23.6	16.2	12.4	7.5			% Profit Before Taxes/Total	16.8	17.8
6.1	7.1	4.1	2.9			Assets	5.7	5.6
-2.9	1.6	.6	1.3				.0	-.7
42.2	29.4	21.9	31.2			Sales/Net Fixed Assets	33.5	29.5
17.6	13.9	12.2	6.5				13.7	13.5
7.1	3.4	2.9	1.5				6.0	5.7
7.5	4.1	4.4	2.8			Sales/Total Assets	5.5	5.3
4.7	2.8	2.7	1.7				3.5	3.5
2.8	1.6	1.3	.9				2.2	2.2
1.3	1.3	1.3	.7			% Depr., Dep., Amort./Sales	.9	1.0
(184) 2.6	(81) 2.1	(40) 2.0	(14) 2.3				(247) 1.8	(255) 1.9
3.9	4.6	3.1	8.4				3.4	3.5
4.7	2.9	1.5				% Officers', Directors',	3.5	3.1
(158) 7.3	(63) 4.8	(21) 3.1				Owners' Comp/Sales	(181) 5.9	(175) 5.9
11.2	7.5	4.6					10.0	9.7
227020M	282201M	583933M	570000M	408318M	3367666M	Net Sales ($)	2358044M	2748927M
51669M	89203M	194119M	304805M	69483M	898899M	Total Assets ($)	727736M	882719M

M = $ thousand   MM = $ million

See Pages 11 through 21 for Explanation of Ratios and Data

Comparative Historical Data | | Current Data Sorted By Sales

10	9	7	Type of Statement						
29	23	31	Unqualified		2				5
100	121	103	Reviewed	1	10	4	4	7	5
147	185	190	Compiled	45	30	17	2	5	4
84	98	79	Tax Returns	110	58	7	7	4	4
4/1/02-	4/1/03-	4/1/04-	Other	28	28	5	6	7	5
3/31/03	3/31/04	3/31/05			64 (4/1-9/30/04)		346 (10/1/04-3/31/05)			
ALL	ALL	ALL		0-1MM	1-3MM	3-5MM	5-10MM	10-25MM	25MM & OVER
370	436	410	**NUMBER OF STATEMENTS**	184	128	33	19	23	23
%	%	%	**ASSETS**	%	%	%	%	%	%
14.0	13.6	12.8	Cash & Equivalents	14.2	13.1	10.0	9.6	9.6	9.7
11.1	12.8	13.2	Trade Receivables (net)	10.3	16.5	16.2	11.7	16.8	12.5
20.0	19.0	18.3	Inventory	14.6	19.5	22.6	25.0	23.9	23.9
2.3	1.8	2.7	All Other Current	1.7	4.0	1.8	1.1	3.0	5.1
47.4	47.3	47.0	Total Current	40.7	53.0	50.6	47.3	53.3	51.2
39.7	40.1	39.1	Fixed Assets (net)	45.2	33.5	35.8	37.0	30.9	37.2
4.4	4.9	6.2	Intangibles (net)	6.3	6.0	5.5	12.0	4.0	5.3
8.5	7.8	7.7	All Other Non-Current	7.8	7.5	8.1	3.7	11.8	6.2
100.0	100.0	100.0	Total	100.0	100.0	100.0	100.0	100.0	100.0
			LIABILITIES						
9.7	9.3	11.3	Notes Payable-Short Term	12.0	10.1	7.3	10.0	15.4	13.8
5.1	6.1	5.1	Cur. Mat.-L/T/D	4.7	5.8	7.4	2.0	5.9	3.1
12.8	17.2	14.6	Trade Payables	12.7	16.6	13.7	15.0	20.2	14.4
.3	.2	.1	Income Taxes Payable	.1	.0	.0	.3	.2	.3
11.8	13.2	15.5	All Other Current	18.0	16.4	7.5	10.3	6.6	14.9
39.7	46.1	46.6	Total Current	47.5	48.9	35.9	37.5	48.2	46.4
28.9	35.0	36.0	Long-Term Debt	47.3	30.8	26.1	21.3	12.8	25.1
.1	.1	.1	Deferred Taxes	.0	.1	.2	.2	.8	.4
7.1	8.6	9.4	All Other Non-Current	12.6	7.6	5.3	9.3	5.3	3.4
24.2	10.2	7.9	Net Worth	−7.5	12.6	32.4	31.8	33.0	24.7
100.0	100.0	100.0	Total Liabilities & Net Worth	100.0	100.0	100.0	100.0	100.0	100.0
			INCOME DATA						
100.0	100.0	100.0	Net Sales	100.0	100.0	100.0	100.0	100.0	100.0
			Gross Profit						
95.8	95.0	95.6	Operating Expenses	94.3	96.6	94.9	98.2	97.9	96.7
4.2	5.0	4.4	Operating Profit	5.7	3.4	5.1	1.8	2.1	3.3
1.5	2.2	1.2	All Other Expenses (net)	2.1	.5	1.0	.1	.1	1.3
2.7	2.8	3.2	Profit Before Taxes	3.6	2.9	4.1	1.7	2.0	1.9
			RATIOS						
2.8	2.5	2.3		2.6	2.6	2.0	1.7	1.7	1.5
1.3	1.2	1.1	Current	1.0	1.2	1.6	1.0	1.0	1.0
.7	.6	.6		.3	.7	1.0	.7	.7	.6
1.7	1.4	1.3		1.5	1.3	1.3	.7	.9	.8
(368) .7	(434) .6	(409) .6	Quick	.6	(127) .6	.8	.4	.5	.5
.3	.2	.2		.2	.3	.4	.1	.2	.2
0 999.8	1 617.8	1 362.9		0 UND	2 227.1	9 39.3	1 246.9	7 54.8	2 240.9
5 66.8	7 53.8	8 47.2	Sales/Receivables	4 81.3	10 37.8	19 19.7	6 65.5	13 27.1	7 56.1
19 19.2	22 16.5	21 17.6		16 22.7	24 15.4	28 13.1	24 15.3	30 12.0	21 17.3
			Cost of Sales/Inventory						
			Cost of Sales/Payables						
10.9	11.5	13.4		15.4	12.2	9.7	8.9	14.8	17.1
47.9	76.7	120.0	Sales/Working Capital	240.2	72.3	17.7	635.9	999.8	586.8
−42.9	−22.5	−22.3		−13.4	−33.2	NM	−43.3	−26.5	−16.8
8.3	6.9	7.2		5.6	7.1	12.2	4.8	10.4	19.9
(303) 2.6	(349) 2.6	(341) 2.7	EBIT/Interest	(136) 1.7	(119) 3.2	(29) 5.3	(17) 2.7	(19) 2.5	(21) 6.3
1.0	.6	.9		.0	1.1	2.2	.7	1.3	1.2
4.9	3.6	4.3	Net Profit + Depr., Dep.,						
(36) 2.5	(43) 1.5	(42) 1.9	Amort./Cur. Mat. L/T/D						
.7	.7	.8							
.4	.5	.5		.7	.5	.4	.3	.4	.6
1.6	2.2	2.2	Fixed/Worth	7.1	1.6	1.0	2.2	.9	1.8
59.0	−5.9	−4.0		−1.2	−9.7	2.5	9.2	2.2	−17.4
.8	1.0	1.3		1.7	1.1	.8	1.0	1.0	1.3
2.6	3.5	5.1	Debt/Worth	50.2	4.0	1.6	2.4	2.5	4.1
UND	−8.4	−6.3		−2.9	−9.1	4.3	9.0	8.8	−19.5
60.5	57.5	64.4	% Profit Before Taxes/Tangible	73.7	75.4	55.8	66.4	40.8	75.5
(282) 19.1	(297) 21.6	(272) 25.4	Net Worth	(99) 25.3	(90) 22.9	(29) 35.5	(16) 9.9	(21) 20.5	(17) 39.0
1.6	2.2	5.5		.0	6.4	11.2	−.5	3.3	25.9
19.3	18.8	18.6	% Profit Before Taxes/Total	19.0	18.2	20.1	19.4	12.8	23.4
5.4	5.2	5.7	Assets	4.6	6.6	10.5	4.5	4.1	6.8
.0	−1.4	.0		−3.6	.9	2.8	−.5	.6	.6
32.0	36.6	34.3		30.1	51.1	26.3	36.8	22.3	31.2
13.7	12.7	15.0	Sales/Net Fixed Assets	12.5	17.5	15.6	16.2	14.9	12.7
5.0	5.1	5.2		2.9	7.6	4.2	2.9	10.2	6.5
6.2	6.2	6.0		6.6	6.1	4.8	6.8	4.9	5.2
3.7	3.8	3.8	Sales/Total Assets	3.6	4.3	3.3	3.1	4.2	3.7
2.2	2.1	2.2		1.8	2.6	2.3	2.3	2.3	1.7
1.1	1.1	1.3		1.6	1.3	1.4	1.3	1.1	.7
(294) 2.1	(344) 2.1	(322) 2.3	% Depr., Dep., Amort./Sales	(136) 2.9	(101) 2.1	(28) 2.1	(17) 1.8	(21) 1.5	(19) 1.3
3.6	3.8	4.4		4.9	3.7	5.7	2.6	2.2	2.3
3.9	3.3	3.6	% Officers', Directors',	5.2	3.4	3.0	1.8	1.0	.7
(236) 6.5	(259) 6.6	(249) 5.7	Owners' Comp/Sales	(107) 8.1	(88) 5.2	(23) 4.2	(12) 4.2	(10) 1.5	
10.3	10.4	9.5		11.8	8.5	7.4	5.2	3.1	
7809240M	7119073M	5439138M	Net Sales ($)	99969M	234612M	126679M	128367M	338703M	4510808M
1671912M	1571474M	1608178M	Total Assets ($)	45100M	96280M	72579M	48936M	123463M	1221820M

M = $ thousand   MM = $ million
See Pages 11 through 21 for Explanation of Ratios and Data

OTHER SERVICES--Automotive Exhaust System Repair   NAICS 811112   (SIC 7533)

Current Data Sorted By Assets							Comparative Historical Data	
				1	1	Type of Statement		
1						Unqualified	1	1
	2	3				Reviewed	3	7
3	3			1		Compiled	19	12
8	4		1			Tax Returns	6	9
4	4.					Other	16	10
	6 (4/1-9/30/04)		29 (10/1/04-3/31/05)				4/1/00-3/31/01	4/1/01-3/31/02
0-500M	500M-2MM	2-10MM	10-50MM	50-100MM	100-250MM		ALL	ALL
16	13	3	1	1	1	NUMBER OF STATEMENTS	45	39
%	%	%	%	%	%	ASSETS	%	%
14.7	6.8					Cash & Equivalents	9.9	10.2
8.5	4.9					Trade Receivables (net)	6.5	5.6
19.7	17.1					Inventory	25.3	29.5
3.1	6.5					All Other Current	3.1	2.8
46.0	35.3					Total Current	44.9	48.1
32.4	41.2					Fixed Assets (net)	30.5	33.1
8.6	7.7					Intangibles (net)	13.7	8.5
13.0	15.9					All Other Non-Current	10.9	10.3
100.0	100.0					Total	100.0	100.0
						LIABILITIES		
5.3	2.9					Notes Payable-Short Term	6.3	6.6
5.6	4.9					Cur. Mat.-L/T/D	4.9	5.2
18.4	16.9					Trade Payables	14.9	19.1
.2	.5					Income Taxes Payable	.9	.6
40.5	7.5					All Other Current	7.8	19.1
70.0	32.7					Total Current	34.7	50.6
11.6	42.4					Long-Term Debt	33.6	29.4
.0	.0					Deferred Taxes	.0	.1
19.0	1.8					All Other Non-Current	6.1	5.6
-.6	23.1					Net Worth	25.5	14.3
100.0	100.0					Total Liabilities & Net Worth	100.0	100.0
						INCOME DATA		
100.0	100.0					Net Sales	100.0	100.0
						Gross Profit		
100.8	91.7					Operating Expenses	94.2	97.1
-.8	8.3					Operating Profit	5.8	2.9
.4	5.0					All Other Expenses (net)	1.6	2.7
-1.3	3.3					Profit Before Taxes	4.2	.2
						RATIOS		
1.5	2.2						1.9	1.6
1.0	.6					Current	1.3	1.0
.7	.5						.9	.6
.7	.8						.7	.5
.4	.2					Quick	(44) .3	.2
.2	.1						.1	.1
1 274.0	0 UND						1 297.8	1 289.6
3 135.6	2 199.9					Sales/Receivables	3 131.3	2 149.4
6 58.0	5 67.5						5 73.9	5 77.7
						Cost of Sales/Inventory		
						Cost of Sales/Payables		
26.0	16.6						15.9	17.1
UND	-23.2					Sales/Working Capital	41.9	999.8
-36.1	-16.3						-82.8	-15.6
3.5	8.8						5.8	3.6
(11) 1.5	(10) 2.0					EBIT/Interest	(37) 2.1	(33) 1.2
-4.2	1.4						.5	-2.0
						Net Profit + Depr., Dep., Amort./Cur. Mat. L./T/D		
.6	1.3						.3	.6
2.4	2.6					Fixed/Worth	1.5	3.6
-5.5	NM						-3.0	-1.4
1.3	2.1						.8	.8
17.5	6.1					Debt/Worth	7.1	3.8
-5.8	NM						-6.3	-3.9
27.8	111.8					% Profit Before Taxes/Tangible	77.6	60.2
(10) 5.6	(10) 41.1					Net Worth	(29) 33.6	(23) 40.3
-16.4	8.4						6.1	5.4
5.7	21.7					% Profit Before Taxes/Total	21.5	20.6
.7	3.9					Assets	6.7	1.5
-10.5	2.2						-1.9	-13.2
52.4	35.9						27.9	36.3
26.1	13.6					Sales/Net Fixed Assets	15.5	13.1
6.2	2.0						6.5	6.7
5.7	4.9						5.1	5.8
4.7	3.7					Sales/Total Assets	3.4	4.0
3.1	1.3						2.1	2.2
1.5	1.2						1.2	.4
(10) 1.9	(10) 2.3					% Depr., Dep., Amort./Sales	(37) 1.9	(34) 1.2
3.3	3.8						3.1	2.9
4.7	2.8					% Officers', Directors',	2.4	3.3
(10) 6.2	(10) 3.8					Owners' Comp/Sales	(25) 5.1	(24) 4.6
8.9	6.4						8.1	8.3
12132M	38085M	56832M	479895M	44066M	44067M	Net Sales ($)	242091M	121494M
2827M	12183M	23488M	42563M	85823M	133975M	Total Assets ($)	110551M	42761M

M = $ thousand   MM = $ million
See Pages 11 through 21 for Explanation of Ratios and Data

Comparative Historical Data / Current Data Sorted By Sales

			Type of Statement						
2	3	3	Unqualified	1					2
1	4	5	Reviewed		2	1	1	1	1
8	10	6	Compiled	2	1	1	2		
10	23	13	Tax Returns	7	5				1
12	8	8	Other	4	3	1			
4/1/02-3/31/03	4/1/03-3/31/04	4/1/04-3/31/05			6 (4/1-9/30/04)		29 (10/1/04-3/31/05)		
ALL	ALL	ALL		0-1MM	1-3MM	3-5MM	5-10MM	10-25MM	25MM & OVER
33	48	35	NUMBER OF STATEMENTS	14	9	4	3	1	4
%	%	%	ASSETS	%	%	%	%	%	%
14.0	11.6	12.0	Cash & Equivalents	12.6					
5.8	5.5	5.9	Trade Receivables (net)	1.9					
21.7	23.1	20.6	Inventory	15.8					
2.2	3.2	4.4	All Other Current	3.3					
43.6	43.4	42.9	Total Current	33.6					
41.0	36.9	34.3	Fixed Assets (net)	51.7					
8.6	8.4	8.3	Intangibles (net)	4.5					
6.8	11.4	14.5	All Other Non-Current	10.1					
100.0	100.0	100.0	Total	100.0					
			LIABILITIES						
5.1	8.8	4.8	Notes Payable-Short Term	5.8					
6.8	4.3	5.1	Cur. Mat.-L/T/D	5.6					
22.3	17.7	15.8	Trade Payables	6.4					
.1	.1	.3	Income Taxes Payable	.0					
33.2	10.8	24.8	All Other Current	43.9					
67.4	41.7	50.8	Total Current	61.7					
34.8	28.2	21.6	Long-Term Debt	30.6					
.0	.0	.1	Deferred Taxes	.0					
.7	7.4	9.4	All Other Non-Current	9.8					
−3.0	22.7	18.0	Net Worth	−2.1					
100.0	100.0	100.0	Total Liabilities & Net Worth	100.0					
			INCOME DATA						
100.0	100.0	100.0	Net Sales	100.0					
			Gross Profit						
95.1	94.7	96.0	Operating Expenses	96.5					
4.9	5.3	4.0	Operating Profit	3.5					
1.9	1.3	2.5	All Other Expenses (net)	4.9					
3.0	3.9	1.5	Profit Before Taxes	−1.4					
			RATIOS						
1.7	2.3	1.5		2.6					
.8	1.0	1.0	Current	1.0					
.4	.6	.6		.2					
.7	1.0	.8		.7					
.3	(47) .2	.4	Quick	.3					
.1	.1	.2		.2					
1 377.3	0 UND	1 387.1		0 UND					
2 149.1	2 172.5	3 143.5	Sales/Receivables	1 244.3					
4 91.4	7 49.9	6 56.5		3 115.9					
			Cost of Sales/Inventory						
			Cost of Sales/Payables						
22.8	9.6	12.8		19.1					
−44.4	184.3	999.8	Sales/Working Capital	NM					
−11.5	−19.8	−17.2		−5.1					
6.6	5.8	3.6							
(24) 1.7	(38) 2.5	(26) 2.0	EBIT/Interest						
1.2	.6	1.2							
			Net Profit + Depr., Dep., Amort./Cur. Mat. L/T/D						
.6	.5	.6		.9					
4.3	2.8	1.8	Fixed/Worth	2.4					
−16.5	−6.6	31.9		NM					
1.3	1.3	1.2		1.3					
6.9	3.5	3.9	Debt/Worth	4.9					
−6.1	−27.9	−31.1		−25.7					
52.4	77.8	55.4	% Profit Before Taxes/Tangible	45.4					
(21) 37.2	(35) 35.5	(26) 21.1	Net Worth	(10) 5.6					
17.1	−3.4	−2.5		−16.4					
22.9	22.3	7.2	% Profit Before Taxes/Total	5.3					
4.4	3.2	2.7	Assets	.6					
−1.7	−2.6	−.3		−8.2					
21.4	27.5	52.2		25.9					
10.8	11.4	14.8	Sales/Net Fixed Assets	6.3					
3.6	5.8	4.3		1.2					
5.1	5.0	5.2		4.8					
3.6	3.2	3.8	Sales/Total Assets	3.2					
2.0	2.1	2.0		1.1					
1.5	1.5	1.4		1.5					
(29) 2.4	(41) 2.6	(24) 2.2	% Depr., Dep., Amort./Sales	(11) 3.2					
3.9	4.0	3.4		3.9					
2.9	3.3	2.4							
(17) 3.9	(32) 5.9	(24) 5.5	% Officers', Directors',						
7.8	9.6	7.4	Owners' Comp/Sales						
270862M	238698M	675077M	Net Sales ($)	6247M	17013M	14761M	19671M	23632M	593753M
98839M	105427M	300859M	Total Assets ($)	3784M	4274M	3929M	10836M	6310M	271726M

M = $ thousand   MM = $ million
See Pages 11 through 21 for Explanation of Ratios and Data

Current Data Sorted By Assets   **Comparative Historical Data**

1 9 6 5	2 4 5 2	1 2 5	1			Type of Statement Unqualified Reviewed Compiled Tax Returns Other	4/1/00-3/31/01	4/1/01-3/31/02
0-500M	9 (4/1-9/30/04) 500M-2MM	2-10MM	10-50MM	34 (10/1/04-3/31/05) 50-100MM	100-250MM		ALL	ALL
21	13	8	1			NUMBER OF STATEMENTS		
%	%	%	%	%	%	ASSETS	%	%
13.4	12.1			D	D	Cash & Equivalents	D	D
18.0	18.1			A	A	Trade Receivables (net)	A	A
17.9	27.6			T	T	Inventory	T	T
4.5	.4			A	A	All Other Current	A	A
53.8	58.2					Total Current		
31.1	27.5			N	N	Fixed Assets (net)	N	N
3.2	7.1			O	O	Intangibles (net)	O	O
11.8	7.2			T	T	All Other Non-Current	T	T
100.0	100.0					Total		
				A	A	LIABILITIES	A	A
15.9	7.5			V	V	Notes Payable-Short Term	V	V
7.8	1.5			A	A	Cur. Mat.-L/T/D	A	A
15.6	14.2			I	I	Trade Payables	I	I
.0	.4			L	L	Income Taxes Payable	L	L
32.5	6.5			A	A	All Other Current	A	A
71.8	30.0			B	B	Total Current	B	B
19.1	22.3			L	L	Long-Term Debt	L	L
.0	2.2			E	E	Deferred Taxes	E	E
14.0	7.7					All Other Non-Current		
-5.0	37.8					Net Worth		
100.0	100.0					Total Liabilities & Net Worth		
						INCOME DATA		
100.0	100.0					Net Sales		
						Gross Profit		
99.2	92.7					Operating Expenses		
.8	7.3					Operating Profit		
.4	1.6					All Other Expenses (net)		
.4	5.8					Profit Before Taxes		
						RATIOS		
2.3	4.4							
1.3	2.0					Current		
.5	1.3							
1.7	2.0							
.9	.8					Quick		
.1	.5							
0 UND	6 57.6							
9 42.2	16 23.1					Sales/Receivables		
17 22.0	30 12.3							
						Cost of Sales/Inventory		
						Cost of Sales/Payables		
16.4	6.4							
41.1	12.3					Sales/Working Capital		
-25.7	33.4							
10.8	24.8							
(20) 1.7	(11) 4.1					EBIT/Interest		
-3.2	2.1							
						Net Profit + Depr., Dep., Amort./Cur. Mat. L /T/D		
.3	.2							
1.0	.5					Fixed/Worth		
UND	3.4							
.9	.4							
3.2	1.5					Debt/Worth		
-18.0	30.1							
114.8	125.8					% Profit Before Taxes/Tangible		
(15) 20.9	(11) 40.9					Net Worth		
12.3	7.2							
18.2	26.0					% Profit Before Taxes/Total		
2.9	16.0					Assets		
-18.9	4.2							
49.3	32.4							
16.7	15.8					Sales/Net Fixed Assets		
9.6	8.4							
7.2	4.0							
4.0	3.7					Sales/Total Assets		
3.1	1.9							
.5	.7							
(18) 1.7	(11) 1.4					% Depr., Dep., Amort./Sales		
2.3	2.6							
2.9	2.9					% Officers', Directors',		
(12) 4.3	(11) 4.1					Owners' Comp/Sales		
6.3	8.5							
29465M	43267M	124494M	82920M			Net Sales ($)		
5352M	14371M	42720M	42904M			Total Assets ($)		

M = $ thousand   MM = $ million
See Pages 11 through 21 for Explanation of Ratios and Data

Comparative Historical Data | | | | | **Current Data Sorted By Sales**

Type of Statement										
	3	2		1	Unqualified	5	2	3	1		1
	6	3		4	Reviewed	2	4	1	2	1	1
	15	12		15	Compiled		6			2	
	16	15		11	Tax Returns		4	1	1		
	7	8		12	Other	3	4		2		1
	4/1/02- 3/31/03 ALL	4/1/03- 3/31/04 ALL		4/1/04- 3/31/05 ALL		0-1MM	9 (4/1-9/30/04) 1-3MM	3-5MM	34 (10/1/04-3/31/05) 5-10MM	10-25MM	25MM & OVER
NUMBER OF STATEMENTS	47	40		43		10	16	5	6	3	3
	%	%		%		%	%	%	%	%	%

ASSETS											
Cash & Equivalents	9.3	11.4	12.6		12.9	13.2				
Trade Receivables (net)	17.9	16.7	18.8		12.2	20.4				
Inventory	24.0	22.9	21.0		16.0	26.3				
All Other Current	3.0	1.6	2.4		3.3	3.6				
Total Current	54.2	52.6	54.8		44.4	63.5				
Fixed Assets (net)	33.9	35.3	30.4		35.8	26.0				
Intangibles (net)	4.4	4.8	6.6		2.0	4.7				
All Other Non-Current	7.6	7.3	8.3		17.8	5.8				
Total	100.0	100.0	100.0		100.0	100.0				

LIABILITIES											
Notes Payable-Short Term	13.4	13.9	11.5		28.8	5.3				
Cur. Mat.-L/T/D	5.6	5.2	5.1		.2	10.7				
Trade Payables	16.1	12.0	15.7		14.0	17.4				
Income Taxes Payable	.6	.0	.1		.0	.0				
All Other Current	30.8	11.8	19.6		51.5	11.1				
Total Current	66.4	42.9	52.0		94.6	44.6				
Long-Term Debt	19.6	28.2	19.9		27.8	20.3				
Deferred Taxes	.5	.7	.7		.0	1.7				
All Other Non-Current	10.4	6.9	9.4		22.8	4.7				
Net Worth	3.1	21.3	17.9		-45.2	28.6				
Total Liabilities & Net Worth	100.0	100.0	100.0		100.0	100.0				

INCOME DATA											
Net Sales	100.0	100.0	100.0		100.0	100.0				
Gross Profit										
Operating Expenses	95.2	94.6	95.6		97.3	97.6				
Operating Profit	4.8	5.4	4.4		2.7	2.4				
All Other Expenses (net)	2.1	2.6	.9		2.1	.6				
Profit Before Taxes	2.7	2.8	3.5		.7	1.9				

RATIOS											
Current	2.0	2.1	2.5		1.7	4.9				
	1.3	1.3	1.3		1.0	2.0				
	.6	.8	.9		.4	1.0				
Quick	1.2	1.3	1.8		1.2	3.1				
	.6	.6	.8		.4	.9				
	.1	.2	.3		.0	.2				
Sales/Receivables	0 999.8	0 807.5	3 112.9		0 UND	6 59.5				
	7 52.8	11 33.4	13 27.5		2 181.5	13 28.3				
	41 8.8	27 13.3	27 13.5		16 23.1	26 14.0				
Cost of Sales/Inventory										
Cost of Sales/Payables										
Sales/Working Capital	8.2	8.1	9.1		17.1	5.7				
	50.5	49.8	26.4		NM	17.3				
	-14.3	-30.5	-78.4		-9.7	NM				
EBIT/Interest	9.0	5.5	10.9		16.3	5.1				
	(40) 2.3	(31) 2.8	(40) 3.9		2.7	(13) 1.7				
	.8	.1	1.3		-2.7	-2.6				
Net Profit + Depr., Dep., Amort./Cur. Mat. L/T/D										
Fixed/Worth	.3	.6	.4		.4	.2				
	1.2	1.6	.8		1.0	1.0				
	-30.9	-6.5	4.7		NM	UND				
Debt/Worth	.7	.9	.8		1.9	.6				
	3.1	3.4	2.3		3.4	1.8				
	-20.1	-16.9	54.6		-5.3	UND				
% Profit Before Taxes/Tangible Net Worth	58.7	82.6	90.0			64.0				
	(32) 13.5	(29) 16.3	(34) 20.9		(12)	31.3				
	-1.7	-5.2	2.8			10.7				
% Profit Before Taxes/Total Assets	21.3	22.5	18.7		24.7	18.1				
	4.8	3.5	5.8		5.0	4.4				
	.0	-3.9	.8		-46.0	.9				
Sales/Net Fixed Assets	33.4	25.6	37.8		54.4	37.9				
	13.0	9.5	16.5		10.8	17.2				
	4.9	4.4	8.0		7.0	12.4				
Sales/Total Assets	5.0	4.5	4.6		4.9	5.3				
	2.7	3.1	3.9		3.3	3.8				
	1.9	1.7	2.7		2.6	3.0				
% Depr., Dep., Amort./Sales	1.2	1.4	.8			.7				
	(35) 2.5	(35) 2.4	(38) 1.7		(15)	1.6				
	3.8	3.8	2.4			2.0				
% Officers', Directors', Owners' Comp/Sales	4.5	2.9	2.9			4.1				
	(25) 7.2	(26) 6.0	(27) 4.1		(11)	6.2				
	10.0	12.4	7.1			7.6				
Net Sales ($)	483558M	164077M	280146M		6172M	28550M	18550M	34224M	49755M	142895M
Total Assets ($)	325397M	90202M	105347M		2591M	10265M	5154M	15913M	16032M	55392M

Current Data Sorted By Assets | **Comparative Historical Data**

Type of Statement	0-500M	500M-2MM	2-10MM	10-50MM	50-100MM	100-250MM		4/1/00-3/31/01 ALL	4/1/01-3/31/02 ALL
Unqualified	1	1	5		1	2		2	2
Reviewed	6	5	5	2				19	17
Compiled	37	22	6					84	77
Tax Returns	84	41	5	2				66	81
Other	44	30	7	2				49	58
		62 (4/1-9/30/04)			246 (10/1/04-3/31/05)				
NUMBER OF STATEMENTS	172	99	28	6	1	2		220	235
	%	%	%	%	%	%		%	%
ASSETS									
Cash & Equivalents	17.7	12.1	9.5					15.9	14.6
Trade Receivables (net)	17.6	13.5	16.6					16.4	15.0
Inventory	11.3	11.5	10.9					14.4	13.5
All Other Current	2.4	1.0	2.9					2.6	2.4
Total Current	49.1	38.2	39.9					49.3	45.4
Fixed Assets (net)	35.7	46.5	43.6					39.2	42.2
Intangibles (net)	5.4	5.1	6.5					4.6	5.0
All Other Non-Current	9.8	10.3	10.0					6.9	7.4
Total	100.0	100.0	100.0					100.0	100.0
LIABILITIES									
Notes Payable-Short Term	9.6	7.3	6.3					9.4	9.7
Cur. Mat.-L/T/D	6.5	3.1	3.4					4.8	5.3
Trade Payables	22.0	13.8	11.6					17.2	13.1
Income Taxes Payable	.6	.2	.4					.4	.4
All Other Current	18.3	8.0	9.9					12.3	9.9
Total Current	57.0	32.3	31.5					44.1	38.4
Long-Term Debt	41.7	32.2	26.7					25.3	42.8
Deferred Taxes	.0	.2	.0					.2	.2
All Other Non-Current	8.2	5.1	9.5					7.4	5.5
Net Worth	-7.0	30.2	32.3					23.1	13.0
Total Liabilities & Net Worth	100.0	100.0	100.0					100.0	100.0
INCOME DATA									
Net Sales	100.0	100.0	100.0					100.0	100.0
Gross Profit									
Operating Expenses	97.6	93.9	88.6					95.2	95.7
Operating Profit	2.4	6.1	11.4					4.8	4.3
All Other Expenses (net)	.9	2.6	4.4					1.1	1.1
Profit Before Taxes	1.5	3.5	7.0					3.8	3.2
RATIOS									
Current	2.1	2.0	2.4					2.1	2.0
	1.2	1.1	1.2					1.2	1.2
	.5	.7	.8					.7	.7
Quick	1.5	1.6	1.8					1.5	1.5
	.7	.8	.8					(219) .7	(233) .7
	.3	.3	.3					.4	.4
Sales/Receivables	0 UND	4 87.1	8 44.2					3 142.9	2 159.3
	8 44.4	11 32.5	16 22.9					13 28.7	10 36.2
	17 20.9	23 15.7	33 11.0					20 18.4	20 18.3
Cost of Sales/Inventory									
Cost of Sales/Payables									
Sales/Working Capital	16.5	16.9	9.9					15.5	16.4
	147.0	91.6	46.2					73.4	82.0
	-21.2	-24.3	-33.0					-40.3	-41.1
EBIT/Interest	9.6	8.5	7.8					11.7	7.2
	(133) 2.1	(83) 2.1	(21) 3.0					(181) 3.6	(192) 3.0
	-.8	.3	1.6					1.5	1.2
Net Profit + Depr., Dep., Amort./Cur. Mat. L/T/D			3.6					3.8	3.3
		(15) 1.6						(27) 2.5	(22) 1.7
		.4						1.4	1.2
Fixed/Worth	.6	.6	1.0					.6	.6
	2.0	2.4	1.9					1.4	1.6
	-.8	21.4	5.4					13.2	12.0
Debt/Worth	1.1	1.1	1.2					.9	.9
	5.9	3.3	3.4					3.2	2.6
	-3.2	25.5	6.9					50.1	39.9
% Profit Before Taxes/Tangible Net Worth	92.5	68.3	33.5					103.4	69.5
	(104) 23.9	(78) 28.5	(25) 18.8					(172) 36.3	(183) 30.5
	2.0	1.3	5.3					8.7	6.7
% Profit Before Taxes/Total Assets	21.3	14.4	8.8					32.5	20.5
	3.1	4.5	5.0					8.5	7.5
	-8.9	-.6	1.4					.8	.5
Sales/Net Fixed Assets	45.5	22.9	17.4					31.9	25.3
	18.8	8.0	9.5					14.6	12.2
	8.7	3.2	2.6					6.9	5.2
Sales/Total Assets	8.5	4.2	4.1					7.2	6.3
	5.3	3.0	2.1					4.2	4.2
	3.6	1.8	1.2					2.7	2.6
% Depr., Dep., Amort./Sales	.7	1.0	1.2					.8	1.1
	(129) 1.4	(90) 2.2	(25) 2.0					(195) 1.7	(208) 1.8
	3.2	3.5	4.8					3.2	3.0
% Officers', Directors', Owners' Comp/Sales	3.4	2.4	1.8					3.1	3.2
	(113) 5.7	(63) 4.2	(12) 3.2					(140) 5.5	(144) 5.6
	10.4	5.9	7.3					8.9	8.5
Net Sales ($)	221684M	306765M	304805M	1754818M	138473M	891060M		1153981M	4382565M
Total Assets ($)	40411M	98126M	121011M	133050M	54123M	267129M		499504M	904297M

M = $ thousand   MM = $ million
See Pages 11 through 21 for Explanation of Ratios and Data

Comparative Historical Data   Current Data Sorted By Sales

7	5	10	Type of Statement						
16	14	18	Unqualified		2			4	4
82	90	65	Reviewed		6	2	6	2	2
85	112	132	Compiled	19	31	11	2	2	
52	68	83	Tax Returns	42	60	21	4	3	2
4/1/02-	4/1/03-	4/1/04-	Other	30	30	13	5	2	3
3/31/03	3/31/04	3/31/05			62 (4/1-9/30/04)			246 (10/1/04-3/31/05)	
ALL	ALL	ALL		0-1MM	1-3MM	3-5MM	5-10MM	10-25MM	25MM & OVER
242	289	308	NUMBER OF STATEMENTS	91	129	47	17	13	11

%	%	%	ASSETS	%	%	%	%	%	%
14.1	13.9	14.8	Cash & Equivalents	11.7	17.9	16.1	12.3	12.7	3.5
14.4	15.9	15.9	Trade Receivables (net)	15.8	15.9	15.0	21.2	18.0	10.3
11.1	12.5	11.3	Inventory	9.2	11.6	14.4	12.1	10.0	13.6
2.4	2.5	2.0	All Other Current	1.3	2.7	.6	3.6	3.1	2.7
42.0	44.9	44.1	Total Current	38.0	48.1	46.0	49.3	43.9	30.1
42.0	39.6	40.3	Fixed Assets (net)	47.5	36.3	35.9	39.8	41.3	47.0
6.6	6.4	5.8	Intangibles (net)	6.4	4.7	5.5	2.9	7.8	17.0
9.5	9.1	9.8	All Other Non-Current	8.1	10.8	12.6	7.9	7.0	5.9
100.0	100.0	100.0	Total	100.0	100.0	100.0	100.0	100.0	100.0
			LIABILITIES						
9.3	9.3	8.5	Notes Payable-Short Term	10.4	7.8	8.7	6.0	4.1	9.5
5.9	5.1	5.0	Cur. Mat.-L/T/D	7.1	4.4	3.3	5.5	3.5	2.9
15.2	15.1	18.1	Trade Payables	20.7	17.4	17.5	15.7	16.2	13.0
.2	.3	.5	Income Taxes Payable	.1	.8	.2	.5	.4	1.7
10.7	12.4	14.1	All Other Current	19.9	10.5	12.9	13.4	14.6	14.3
41.3	42.2	46.2	Total Current	58.2	40.9	42.7	41.1	38.8	41.4
30.8	28.8	36.9	Long-Term Debt	59.4	32.0	20.9	18.4	17.8	28.2
.2	.1	.1	Deferred Taxes	.0	.0	.2	.5	.2	.3
7.0	9.5	7.5	All Other Non-Current	6.8	7.6	8.1	10.6	1.6	12.9
20.7	19.4	9.2	Net Worth	-24.3	19.4	28.1	29.4	41.6	17.3
100.0	100.0	100.0	Total Liabilities & Net Worth	100.0	100.0	100.0	100.0	100.0	100.0
			INCOME DATA						
100.0	100.0	100.0	Net Sales	100.0	100.0	100.0	100.0	100.0	100.0
			Gross Profit						
95.8	96.0	95.6	Operating Expenses	91.5	97.1	97.5	99.3	95.9	98.2
4.2	4.0	4.4	Operating Profit	8.5	2.9	2.5	.7	4.1	1.8
1.6	1.3	1.8	All Other Expenses (net)	4.9	.7	.0	-.2	.4	1.2
2.6	2.7	2.6	Profit Before Taxes	3.6	2.3	2.5	1.0	3.7	.6
			RATIOS						
1.9	2.1	2.1		1.7	2.6	2.0	1.8	2.8	1.1
1.1	1.1	1.1	Current	.9	1.5	1.1	1.1	1.1	.7
.6	.7	.5		.3	.7	.7	.7	.6	.4
1.6	1.7	1.5		1.2	2.0	1.4	1.5	2.4	.5
(240) .7	(285) .7	.7	Quick	.6	.8	.8	.8	.8	.3
.3	.4	.3		.2	.4	.4	.5	.3	.2
2 205.7	1 661.9	1 321.9		0 UND	1 327.6	6 60.7	6 60.0	9 38.7	0 UND
11 33.6	11 32.0	10 37.5	Sales/Receivables	8 45.5	9 40.2	12 29.8	15 25.0	15 24.5	15 24.0
19 18.8	19 18.9	19 19.3		22 16.3	18 19.8	18 20.4	32 11.6	22 16.9	22 16.5
			Cost of Sales/Inventory						
			Cost of Sales/Payables						
17.1	14.9	15.5		25.6	13.6	19.7	20.6	10.8	47.8
216.6	98.6	110.0	Sales/Working Capital	-100.0	39.8	119.9	145.6	104.0	-119.0
-28.2	-33.7	-22.4		-8.7	-33.7	-29.7	-66.1	-44.7	-11.1
9.2	8.3	8.5		6.9	11.3	8.6	5.9	13.5	4.1
(202) 2.6	(231) 2.6	(245) 2.2	EBIT/Interest	(68) 1.4	(104) 2.4	(39) 1.8	(14) 2.8	(10) 7.5	(10) 2.2
.8	.9	-.3		-1.9	.7	.3	-1.3	2.2	.0
4.6	5.3	4.4	Net Profit + Depr., Dep.,		5.7				
(33) 1.9	(26) 1.5	(32) 1.7	Amort./Cur. Mat. L/T/D		(14) 2.0				
.9	.4	.6			.5				
.5	.7	.6		.9	.5	.5	.7	.6	1.3
1.8	2.0	2.1	Fixed/Worth	10.0	1.5	1.5	1.6	1.5	3.2
-10.2	-20.7	-4.9		-.8	-16.9	-6.3	13.3	2.3	-1.1
1.0	1.2	1.1		1.6	.7	.8	1.1	.8	3.2
3.4	4.0	4.1	Debt/Worth	17.8	3.3	2.8	2.4	2.1	8.2
-20.4	-28.9	-9.0		-2.3	-23.4	-20.4	195.2	3.2	-2.9
52.6	73.3	73.4	% Profit Before Taxes/Tangible	74.4	82.4	119.9	67.3	44.4	
(167) 25.5	(210) 23.9	(212) 25.1	Net Worth	(50) 29.9	(95) 21.9	(34) 22.0	(14) 23.0	(12) 22.5	
1.3	1.7	2.4		3.3	.9	-.6	.8	5.7	
20.8	16.8	17.2	% Profit Before Taxes/Total	13.2	18.9	21.2	12.4	17.0	10.3
6.3	6.0	4.0	Assets	1.7	4.7	3.5	4.7	7.8	5.4
-1.0	-.6	-3.3		-12.3	-1.0	-1.5	-5.0	3.3	-1.0
27.7	31.5	32.3		25.1	37.2	38.1	48.7	22.8	18.7
12.0	13.7	15.6	Sales/Net Fixed Assets	8.6	17.5	18.4	15.9	10.6	9.0
5.1	6.5	5.4		3.4	7.2	5.9	5.1	7.6	6.3
6.1	6.4	6.7		6.2	7.1	6.4	7.1	5.9	6.2
4.0	4.5	4.1	Sales/Total Assets	3.6	4.4	4.2	3.5	4.4	2.8
2.4	2.6	2.5		1.8	2.8	2.8	2.0	2.3	2.4
(216) 1.1	(242) .9	(252) .8		1.0	.8	.8	.7	1.5	.9
1.9	1.9	1.8	% Depr., Dep., Amort./Sales	(71) 2.2	(102) 1.8	(40) 1.4	(16) 1.5	1.8	(10) 2.1
3.4	3.5	3.4		5.4	3.1	2.3	3.3	3.3	2.7
3.3	2.9	3.1	% Officers', Directors',	5.2	3.4	2.1	1.6		
(158) 5.5	(200) 4.8	(190) 4.7	Owners' Comp/Sales	(43) 7.8	(96) 4.6	(30) 3.1	(13) 3.8		
8.4	8.0	8.6		12.6	8.0	6.1	5.4		
6595533M	4466555M	3617605M	Net Sales ($)	51654M	228210M	179114M	112388M	200186M	2846053M
1424586M	967171M	713850M	Total Assets ($)	33581M	64987M	46201M	37651M	61403M	470027M

© RMA 2005

M = $ thousand   MM = $ million
See Pages 11 through 21 for Explanation of Ratios and Data

Current Data Sorted By Assets | Comparative Historical Data

	0-500M	500M-2MM	2-10MM	10-50MM	50-100MM	100-250MM		ALL 4/1/00-3/31/01	ALL 4/1/01-3/31/02
	1	1	3			2	Type of Statement		
							Unqualified	1	1
		1	6				Reviewed	7	8
	3	5	3				Compiled	5	4
	14	1	3				Tax Returns	5	4
	2	2	2	1			Other	10	8
	10 (4/1-9/30/04)			36 (10/1/04-3/31/05)				4/1/00-3/31/01	4/1/01-3/31/02
								ALL	ALL
NUMBER OF STATEMENTS	20	9	14	1		2		28	25
	%	%	%	%	%	%	ASSETS	%	%
Cash & Equivalents	12.8		15.3					7.1	11.9
Trade Receivables (net)	30.6		28.3					32.7	34.7
Inventory	12.6		21.9					24.5	18.6
All Other Current	.9		2.0					2.4	2.4
Total Current	56.9		67.6					66.8	67.6
Fixed Assets (net)	35.8		18.1					19.2	19.8
Intangibles (net)	1.6		1.3					6.3	1.8
All Other Non-Current	5.6		13.0					7.6	10.8
Total	100.0		100.0					100.0	100.0
							LIABILITIES		
Notes Payable-Short Term	9.4		7.5					14.2	5.0
Cur. Mat.-L/T/D	.7		2.3					3.2	3.3
Trade Payables	23.3		18.7					24.4	25.4
Income Taxes Payable	.0		.5					.4	.1
All Other Current	5.3		12.2					8.5	10.3
Total Current	45.5		41.2					50.7	44.2
Long-Term Debt	25.5		5.0					16.7	9.9
Deferred Taxes	.0		1.4					.2	.2
All Other Non-Current	15.1		3.8					4.8	1.0
Net Worth	14.0		48.6					27.6	44.7
Total Liabilities & Net Worth	100.0		100.0					100.0	100.0
							INCOME DATA		
Net Sales	100.0		100.0					100.0	100.0
Gross Profit									
Operating Expenses	98.6		98.4					97.9	94.7
Operating Profit	1.4		1.6					2.1	5.3
All Other Expenses (net)	.3		-.6					.3	.2
Profit Before Taxes	1.1		2.2					1.8	5.1
							RATIOS		
Current	2.0 / 1.1 / .7		2.3 / 1.7 / 1.3					3.1 / 1.7 / 1.0	2.2 / 1.6 / 1.2
Quick	1.8 / 1.0 / .5		1.6 / 1.2 / .7					1.7 / 1.0 / .6	1.6 / 1.2 / .7
Sales/Receivables	9 39.3 / 26 14.0 / 32 11.5		17 21.4 / 28 13.2 / 47 7.7					23 16.2 / 27 13.4 / 43 8.5	20 17.8 / 29 12.7 / 40 9.2
Cost of Sales/Inventory									
Cost of Sales/Payables									
Sales/Working Capital	13.4 / 135.7 / -19.6		7.7 / 13.2 / 56.7					7.1 / 11.6 / NM	10.0 / 14.9 / 87.0
EBIT/Interest	9.7 / (15) 3.2 / -.7		48.0 / (13) 11.5 / 2.0					28.7 / (26) 4.4 / .5	46.0 / (21) 6.6 / 1.6
Net Profit + Depr., Dep., Amort./Cur. Mat. L/T/D									
Fixed/Worth	.5 / 3.0 / -4.9		.2 / .3 / .5					.2 / .5 / 2.9	.1 / .3 / 1.1
Debt/Worth	1.8 / 4.0 / -14.2		.6 / 1.1 / 1.8					.5 / 1.6 / 11.8	.5 / 1.2 / 2.4
% Profit Before Taxes/Tangible Net Worth	92.4 / (14) 24.3 / -32.2		49.7 / 21.8 / 3.1					39.4 / (22) 15.0 / 1.4	87.5 / (23) 21.5 / 5.5
% Profit Before Taxes/Total Assets	22.3 / 10.2 / -6.3		16.6 / 7.7 / .6					22.2 / 5.0 / -1.9	49.8 / 11.5 / 1.0
Sales/Net Fixed Assets	25.1 / 16.7 / 7.4		64.6 / 27.4 / 10.7					43.6 / 25.2 / 13.9	63.6 / 25.6 / 11.7
Sales/Total Assets	5.2 / 4.4 / 3.5		4.9 / 3.0 / 2.2					5.1 / 3.2 / 2.1	5.3 / 4.4 / 2.6
% Depr., Dep., Amort./Sales	1.3 / (17) 1.6 / 3.1		.7 / (12) 1.5 / 2.0					.6 / (27) 1.2 / 1.8	.5 / (21) 1.1 / 1.8
% Officers', Directors', Owners' Comp/Sales	3.5 / (15) 5.2 / 10.1								2.4 / (10) 5.3 / 10.0
Net Sales ($)	22282M	38021M	256852M	103845M		307928M		421992M	305606M
Total Assets ($)	5191M	10890M	72154M	29886M		222712M		196225M	98309M

(Columns 10-50MM, 50-100MM, 100-250MM: DATA NOT AVAILABLE for asset, liability, and income sections.)

M = $ thousand   MM = $ million
See Pages 11 through 21 for Explanation of Ratios and Data

Comparative Historical Data				Current Data Sorted By Sales					
			Type of Statement						
8	5	6	Unqualified			1		1	4
1	4	7	Reviewed				2	4	1
5	5	11	Compiled	1	3	3	2	1	1
10	15	15	Tax Returns	8	6	1			
12	15	7	Other	2	1		2	1	1
4/1/02-3/31/03	4/1/03-3/31/04	4/1/04-3/31/05		10 (4/1-9/30/04)		36 (10/1/04-3/31/05)			
ALL	ALL	ALL		0-1MM	1-3MM	3-5MM	5-10MM	10-25MM	25MM & OVER
36	44	46	**NUMBER OF STATEMENTS**	11	10	5	6	7	7
%	%	%	**ASSETS**	%	%	%	%	%	%
9.2	10.3	11.1	Cash & Equivalents	12.7	11.5				
30.9	33.2	29.2	Trade Receivables (net)	22.2	32.0				
14.0	17.1	14.8	Inventory	14.5	13.2				
2.8	1.6	1.7	All Other Current	.8	1.6				
56.9	62.2	56.8	Total Current	50.2	58.3				
28.5	28.1	31.7	Fixed Assets (net)	40.9	37.9				
2.4	2.0	2.1	Intangibles (net)	2.2	1.3				
12.2	7.7	9.3	All Other Non-Current	6.7	2.5				
100.0	100.0	100.0	Total	100.0	100.0				
			LIABILITIES						
9.9	10.9	8.5	Notes Payable-Short Term	9.7	7.4				
4.2	4.0	5.5	Cur. Mat.-L/T/D	8.2	7.4				
21.1	21.1	19.7	Trade Payables	25.7	15.3				
.2	.3	.3	Income Taxes Payable	.0	.1				
10.7	21.1	9.9	All Other Current	4.9	3.1				
46.1	57.4	43.8	Total Current	48.5	33.4				
16.4	26.1	19.7	Long-Term Debt	34.9	24.2				
.1	.2	.4	Deferred Taxes	.0	.0				
10.3	2.1	9.4	All Other Non-Current	10.1	20.7				
27.1	14.2	26.7	Net Worth	6.4	21.7				
100.0	100.0	100.0	Total Liabilities & Net Worth	100.0	100.0				
			INCOME DATA						
100.0	100.0	100.0	Net Sales	100.0	100.0				
			Gross Profit						
97.8	98.6	97.8	Operating Expenses	98.5	94.3				
2.2	1.4	2.2	Operating Profit	1.5	5.7				
.6	.7	.3	All Other Expenses (net)	.6	.8				
1.6	.8	1.9	Profit Before Taxes	.9	4.9				
			RATIOS						
1.8	2.4	2.0		1.9	4.8				
1.4	1.4	1.4	Current	.8	1.4				
.8	.9	.7		.6	.9				
1.5	1.5	1.6		1.7	2.1				
1.1	1.0	.9	Quick	.6	1.0				
.5	.5	.5		.3	.7				
19 19.7	16 22.7	15 23.7		5 66.5	0 UND				
25 14.6	24 15.2	26 13.9	Sales/Receivables	19 19.0	26 13.8				
65 5.7	37 9.9	40 9.1		26 13.9	36 10.2				
			Cost of Sales/Inventory						
			Cost of Sales/Payables						
8.4	8.5	9.0		13.8	6.6				
22.1	22.3	34.9	Sales/Working Capital	-57.4	29.3				
-32.5	-52.8	-19.5		-12.9	-340.4				
13.1	30.9	17.0							
(34) 2.0	(34) 5.1	(38) 6.0	EBIT/Interest						
.3	-.1	-.6							
			Net Profit + Depr., Dep., Amort./Cur. Mat. L/T/D						
.4	.3	.3		1.3	.4				
1.1	1.2	1.2	Fixed/Worth	3.5	2.3				
2.2	NM	NM		-1.1	-5.3				
1.1	1.1	1.0		1.6	1.7				
2.1	3.4	2.4	Debt/Worth	5.7	4.0				
7.3	NM	NM		-5.2	-18.5				
69.9	65.9	59.2	% Profit Before Taxes/Tangible Net Worth						
(30) 9.9	(33) 24.4	(35) 21.0							
-5.7	-1.7	-8.4							
17.2	24.8	20.1	% Profit Before Taxes/Total Assets	37.3	21.8				
3.8	5.5	7.5		10.3	6.4				
-2.2	-4.7	-4.9		-8.1	-5.4				
28.5	28.0	32.1		22.9	32.3				
14.7	17.9	14.5	Sales/Net Fixed Assets	12.2	16.0				
6.1	9.8	6.8		7.0	5.3				
5.0	5.2	5.1		5.0	5.3				
2.9	3.8	3.7	Sales/Total Assets	4.2	3.9				
2.1	2.3	2.4		3.4	2.2				
1.0	1.1	1.2							
(34) 1.9	(40) 1.8	(38) 1.6	% Depr., Dep., Amort./Sales						
3.2	2.7	3.0							
1.3	3.1	2.9							
(11) 2.7	(24) 4.6	(24) 4.8	% Officers', Directors', Owners' Comp/Sales						
4.8	10.0	9.0							
760557M	556689M	728928M	Net Sales ($)	5775M	15566M	19686M	38365M	106143M	543393M
353765M	285852M	340833M	Total Assets ($)	1702M	5154M	4769M	12172M	41220M	275816M

M = $ thousand   MM = $ million
See Pages 11 through 21 for Explanation of Ratios and Data

Current Data Sorted By Assets   Comparative Historical Data

						Type of Statement		
							4	3
1	4	1	4	2	1	Unqualified	13	10
22	40	9	4			Reviewed	67	52
47	57	14	4		1	Compiled	43	60
49	44	11	4	2		Tax Returns	47	63
		28				Other	4/1/00-	4/1/01-
							3/31/01	3/31/02
0-500M	500M-2MM	2-10MM	10-50MM	50-100MM	100-250MM		ALL	ALL
	37 (4/1-9/30/04)		308 (10/1/04-3/31/05)					
119	145	63	12	4	2	NUMBER OF STATEMENTS	174	188
%	%	%	%	%	%	ASSETS	%	%
12.7	8.1	7.0	6.5			Cash & Equivalents	11.8	10.4
6.5	4.9	3.1	5.2			Trade Receivables (net)	2.5	4.2
5.6	2.5	4.3	4.4			Inventory	3.7	4.0
1.5	1.9	1.1	1.1			All Other Current	1.4	2.3
26.4	17.3	15.4	17.2			Total Current	19.3	20.9
58.4	71.0	70.9	72.9			Fixed Assets (net)	66.9	69.2
7.8	5.9	6.2	5.3			Intangibles (net)	7.4	4.3
7.5	5.8	7.5	4.7			All Other Non-Current	6.3	5.6
100.0	100.0	100.0	100.0			Total	100.0	100.0
						LIABILITIES		
3.2	3.3	5.6	8.2			Notes Payable-Short Term	3.0	4.5
5.3	4.4	4.4	4.7			Cur. Mat.-L/T/D	5.9	5.1
6.9	3.1	3.5	3.4			Trade Payables	3.7	4.3
.2	.2	.1	.0			Income Taxes Payable	.2	.2
17.9	4.5	6.4	4.0			All Other Current	15.7	10.7
33.4	15.4	19.9	20.3			Total Current	28.4	24.6
86.6	65.0	59.2	50.9			Long-Term Debt	49.2	55.4
.0	.0	.0	.2			Deferred Taxes	.1	.0
9.0	5.9	4.7	5.0			All Other Non-Current	9.3	21.1
-29.1	13.7	16.2	23.6			Net Worth	12.9	-1.2
100.0	100.0	100.0	100.0			Total Liabilities & Net Worth	100.0	100.0
						INCOME DATA		
100.0	100.0	100.0	100.0			Net Sales	100.0	100.0
						Gross Profit		
95.0	87.2	84.5	89.6			Operating Expenses	86.8	88.1
5.0	12.8	15.5	10.4			Operating Profit	13.2	11.9
6.3	9.7	9.1	2.6			All Other Expenses (net)	6.8	8.3
-1.3	3.1	6.5	7.7			Profit Before Taxes	6.4	3.5
						RATIOS		
2.4	2.9	1.5	1.6			Current	1.9	2.0
1.0	.9	.6	.4				.7	.9
.3	.2	.2	.3				.2	.3
2.1	2.1	1.2	.9			Quick	1.3	1.3
(116) .5	(144) .7	.5	.3				.5	.5
.2	.1	.1	.1				.1	.2
0 UND	0 UND	0 UND	1 368.1			Sales/Receivables	0 UND	0 UND
0 999.8	0 UND	1 527.1	3 117.2				0 UND	0 999.8
5 73.7	3 129.0	4 97.7	20 18.6				4 102.9	4 96.3
						Cost of Sales/Inventory		
						Cost of Sales/Payables		
12.0	10.2	29.1	NM			Sales/Working Capital	18.8	18.4
UND	-54.9	-29.0	-16.4				-34.5	-156.3
-9.1	-5.7	-4.9	-7.5				-6.4	-10.4
2.7	4.0	3.2	4.6			EBIT/Interest	4.9	3.9
(93) 1.1	(117) 1.5	(52) 1.8	3.7				(131) 2.1	(146) 1.7
-.6	.6	.9	2.5				.9	.6
	4.2					Net Profit + Depr., Dep.,	3.8	4.6
	(11) 2.4					Amort./Cur. Mat. L/T/D	(18) 2.4	(17) 1.9
	1.5						.7	.9
2.4	2.2	2.0	1.5			Fixed/Worth	1.3	1.6
-3.9	18.4	7.4	4.0				5.0	7.8
-.8	-4.6	-22.3	20.7				-6.6	-8.7
3.4	2.2	1.8	1.1			Debt/Worth	1.4	1.7
-10.5	25.9	10.3	3.5				6.6	12.1
-2.2	-6.5	-24.7	22.4				-7.8	-9.6
85.3	48.6	58.2	52.5			% Profit Before Taxes/Tangible	78.1	71.2
(49) 23.3	(83) 18.8	(44) 11.6	(10) 27.6			Net Worth	(107) 25.2	(116) 18.2
.0	.3	.8	12.6				7.7	-.7
10.9	9.0	7.7	12.1			% Profit Before Taxes/Total	14.5	11.3
1.4	2.2	2.7	6.4			Assets	5.3	3.3
-7.4	-2.6	.0	4.1				-1.1	-2.8
15.0	3.6	3.2	2.2			Sales/Net Fixed Assets	5.2	6.0
2.3	.8	.8	1.6				1.4	1.4
.9	.4	.3	.9				.7	.6
3.4	1.2	1.9	1.8			Sales/Total Assets	2.3	2.7
1.5	.7	.6	1.0				1.0	1.0
.7	.4	.3	.6				.5	.5
3.2	4.6	2.3	2.7			% Depr., Dep., Amort./Sales	2.9	2.5
(103) 8.5	(134) 11.8	(53) 7.8	5.8				(154) 7.4	(174) 6.8
15.3	22.7	17.2	11.3				16.4	15.6
3.3	2.5	2.9				% Officers', Directors',	3.5	3.1
(37) 8.7	(55) 5.8	(20) 5.9				Owners' Comp/Sales	(66) 6.6	(78) 6.6
14.0	10.4	9.9					9.2	10.2
66828M	171482M	297883M	330655M	314102M	239305M	Net Sales ($)	740650M	736924M
29326M	144248M	239145M	260207M	303559M	209147M	Total Assets ($)	699316M	454698M

© RMA 2005

M = $ thousand   MM = $ million

See Pages 11 through 21 for Explanation of Ratios and Data

Comparative Historical Data | **Current Data Sorted By Sales**

Type of Statement	4/1/02-3/31/03 ALL	4/1/03-3/31/04 ALL	4/1/04-3/31/05 ALL	0-1MM	1-3MM	3-5MM	5-10MM	10-25MM	25MM & OVER
Unqualified	7	12	8		1			3	4
Reviewed	13	18	18	4	5	1	4	4	
Compiled	70	84	76	48	11	10	7		
Tax Returns	76	89	116	88	18	6	2	1	1
Other	83	91	127	80	26	6	5	4	6
				37 (4/1-9/30/04)		308 (10/1/04-3/31/05)			
NUMBER OF STATEMENTS	249	294	345	220	61	23	18	12	11
ASSETS	%	%	%	%	%	%	%	%	%
Cash & Equivalents	10.8	10.1	9.4	7.6	13.7	14.6	10.5	12.8	7.2
Trade Receivables (net)	3.0	4.0	5.1	4.7	3.5	7.8	10.7	5.4	6.3
Inventory	4.0	3.9	4.0	1.8	5.5	11.8	8.6	5.8	11.5
All Other Current	2.4	1.9	1.6	1.3	1.7	1.3	3.9	3.2	1.4
Total Current	20.1	19.9	20.1	15.5	24.4	35.5	33.6	27.2	26.3
Fixed Assets (net)	68.3	67.9	66.6	71.2	61.9	52.3	51.9	61.5	60.5
Intangibles (net)	6.1	6.5	6.7	6.8	6.4	6.6	8.3	2.5	8.4
All Other Non-Current	5.4	5.7	6.6	6.5	7.3	5.6	6.2	8.8	4.7
Total	100.0	100.0	100.0	100.0	100.0	100.0	100.0	100.0	100.0
LIABILITIES									
Notes Payable-Short Term	5.8	5.1	4.0	4.0	1.5	6.0	2.0	2.4	17.2
Cur. Mat.-L/T/D	5.2	4.6	4.7	5.1	4.7	3.1	3.7	3.5	2.7
Trade Payables	5.2	4.8	4.5	3.7	4.2	7.7	7.4	5.5	9.0
Income Taxes Payable	.0	.1	.1	.1	.3	.2	.0	.0	.0
All Other Current	10.3	10.6	9.4	10.5	6.0	12.3	10.8	3.5	4.3
Total Current	26.5	25.2	22.7	23.4	16.8	29.4	23.9	14.9	33.2
Long-Term Debt	54.3	56.5	70.0	83.4	55.2	34.6	48.1	45.8	21.7
Deferred Taxes	.0	.1	.0	.0	.0	.1	.0	.2	.1
All Other Non-Current	6.5	8.6	6.7	6.1	6.6	12.9	5.7	8.1	8.1
Net Worth	12.7	9.6	.6	-12.8	21.4	23.1	22.3	31.0	37.0
Total Liabilities & Net Worth	100.0	100.0	100.0	100.0	100.0	100.0	100.0	100.0	100.0
INCOME DATA									
Net Sales	100.0	100.0	100.0	100.0	100.0	100.0	100.0	100.0	100.0
Gross Profit									
Operating Expenses	86.5	88.0	89.5	88.4	88.1	95.2	94.4	95.7	91.9
Operating Profit	13.5	12.0	10.5	11.6	11.9	4.8	5.6	4.3	8.1
All Other Expenses (net)	8.4	8.5	8.0	10.7	5.2	1.4	1.4	1.6	1.0
Profit Before Taxes	5.0	3.5	2.5	.9	6.7	3.3	4.2	2.7	7.1
RATIOS									
Current	2.1	2.1	2.4	2.3	2.4	3.4	2.7	4.3	1.1
	.8	.7	.8	.6	1.3	1.0	1.3	1.5	.7
	.2	.2	.3	.2	.5	.6	.5	.5	.4
Quick	1.5	1.6	1.8	1.9	1.8	1.3	1.4	3.8	.9
	(248) .5	.5	(341) .6	(216) .4	.9	.6	.8	.8	.2
	.1	.1	.1	.1	.3	.3	.4	.1	.1
Sales/Receivables	0 UND	0 UND	0 UND	0 UND	0 UND	1 598.5	0 732.1	0 931.2	3 133.3
	0 UND	0 UND	0 UND	0 UND	1 375.7	4 83.6	1 305.3	2 154.5	7 50.4
	2 213.7	3 119.6	4 96.4	2 158.1	5 74.5	11 32.6	3 135.1	13 27.5	16 22.6
Cost of Sales/Inventory									
Cost of Sales/Payables									
Sales/Working Capital	18.6	22.0	12.4	12.2	11.5	27.3	11.0	4.1	108.2
	-70.4	-40.4	-54.9	-19.8	82.6	177.3	94.0	48.3	-18.7
	-5.9	-6.2	-7.2	-4.9	-19.1	-15.8	-12.7	-37.4	-7.8
EBIT/Interest	4.6	4.1	3.5	2.4	5.2	4.0	14.4	6.5	
	(186) 1.9	(218) 1.7	(278) 1.5	(168) 1.2	(53) 2.3	(18) 1.3	3.3	3.4	
	.6	.5	.2	.0	.8	-2.8	1.5	1.1	
Net Profit + Depr., Dep., Amort./Cur. Mat. L/T/D	7.4	4.8	4.2						
	(21) 1.3	(23) 2.4	(27) 2.3						
	.8	1.9	1.3						
Fixed/Worth	1.4	1.6	2.2	3.9	1.4	.7	.8	.9	1.1
	9.8	8.8	18.4	-81.2	5.0	14.4	4.3	1.2	1.3
	-7.0	-6.0	-2.6	-1.8	-7.2	-3.9	-6.6	7.3	3.2
Debt/Worth	1.3	1.7	2.0	4.1	1.1	1.0	1.2	.8	.6
	10.1	11.6	21.1	-89.9	5.6	16.2	6.0	1.1	1.7
	-8.8	-7.9	-4.4	-3.4	-12.1	-8.0	-10.1	6.8	20.6
% Profit Before Taxes/Tangible Net Worth	70.2	59.3	54.4	53.8	73.1	51.4	139.9	25.3	133.4
	(152) 19.8	(176) 22.2	(192) 18.4	(106) 18.2	(41) 23.9	(13) 15.3	(12) 45.9	(10) 11.8	(10) 20.6
	4.0	5.6	1.7	-.7	5.9	.0	8.9	9.4	6.5
% Profit Before Taxes/Total Assets	11.4	9.5	9.8	7.8	15.1	12.9	23.4	6.6	14.8
	3.9	3.4	2.4	.9	4.4	2.7	11.7	5.3	7.0
	-1.9	-2.9	-3.1	-4.2	.2	-5.0	2.0	.5	1.2
Sales/Net Fixed Assets	5.0	5.7	4.5	2.4	7.6	21.0	15.1	8.3	5.6
	1.5	1.1	1.2	.8	1.4	5.7	6.0	2.4	2.3
	.5	.5	.5	.4	.6	1.8	2.9	1.3	.9
Sales/Total Assets	2.4	2.2	2.0	1.2	2.6	5.0	4.0	3.1	2.8
	1.0	.8	.8	.6	1.0	2.5	2.6	1.7	1.7
	.5	.4	.4	.3	.6	1.0	2.0	.7	.6
% Depr., Dep., Amort./Sales	3.3	3.6	3.8	6.5	2.3	2.5	1.8	1.6	
	(217) 7.8	(262) 8.6	(306) 9.6	(201) 13.0	(49) 6.3	(19) 3.7	(17) 2.5	3.5	
	18.7	20.4	18.5	22.6	10.8	4.9	4.5	9.4	
% Officers', Directors', Owners' Comp/Sales	3.4	2.9	2.7	4.7	3.0	2.1			
	(86) 6.8	(95) 6.0	(117) 5.9	(68)	(24) 5.1	(10) 3.0			
	11.4	11.9	11.4	14.5	8.0	4.0			
Net Sales ($)	850536M	1460432M	1420255M	87952M	97467M	85876M	125475M	195298M	828187M
Total Assets ($)	838415M	1250513M	1185632M	158459M	121981M	63056M	63244M	157118M	621774M

M = $ thousand   MM = $ million
See Pages 11 through 21 for Explanation of Ratios and Data

Current Data Sorted By Assets | **Comparative Historical Data**

Type of Statement	0-500M	500M-2MM	2-10MM	10-50MM	50-100MM	100-250MM		ALL 4/1/00-3/31/01	ALL 4/1/01-3/31/02
Unqualified		3	2	2	1	1		4	3
Reviewed	17	10	3	2				11	6
Compiled	35	8	1					33	36
Tax Returns	13	13	3	2		1		28	32
Other								15	25
	23 (4/1-9/30/04)			94 (10/1/04-3/31/05)					
NUMBER OF STATEMENTS	65	34	9	6	1	2		91	102

	0-500M %	500M-2MM %	2-10MM %	10-50MM %	50-100MM %	100-250MM %		ALL %	ALL %
ASSETS									
Cash & Equivalents	14.6	11.3						11.2	10.4
Trade Receivables (net)	12.0	24.8						17.2	14.5
Inventory	21.7	16.2						28.1	27.9
All Other Current	1.6	1.7						1.7	1.5
Total Current	49.9	54.0						58.2	54.3
Fixed Assets (net)	31.3	31.7						31.4	35.5
Intangibles (net)	10.0	3.6						2.6	2.8
All Other Non-Current	8.7	10.7						7.9	7.4
Total	100.0	100.0						100.0	100.0
LIABILITIES									
Notes Payable-Short Term	8.4	10.6						9.5	54.3
Cur. Mat.-L/T/D	5.8	4.0						4.3	5.8
Trade Payables	15.0	16.0						16.1	14.8
Income Taxes Payable	.7	.1						.2	.5
All Other Current	22.7	8.9						83.6	16.5
Total Current	52.6	39.5						113.6	91.9
Long-Term Debt	37.7	22.4						119.2	49.2
Deferred Taxes	.0	.1						.0	.0
All Other Non-Current	17.2	10.8						72.5	12.3
Net Worth	-7.5	27.2						-205.4	-53.4
Total Liabilities & Net Worth	100.0	100.0						100.0	100.0
INCOME DATA									
Net Sales	100.0	100.0						100.0	100.0
Gross Profit									
Operating Expenses	96.6	96.4						97.0	95.4
Operating Profit	3.4	3.6						3.0	4.6
All Other Expenses (net)	.4	2.2						.6	1.5
Profit Before Taxes	3.0	1.4						2.4	3.1

RATIOS	0-500M	500M-2MM	2-10MM	10-50MM	50-100MM	100-250MM		ALL	ALL
Current	2.7	2.5						2.3	2.3
	1.2	1.4						1.3	1.3
	.6	.8						.8	.7
Quick	1.3	1.9						1.3	1.1
	(64) .5	.8						(90) .6	(101) .5
	.2	.5						.2	.2
Sales/Receivables	0 UND	6 59.7						2 167.5	1 628.0
	3 124.8	21 17.4						15 24.9	12 31.7
	13 28.9	37 9.9						31 11.9	29 12.6
Cost of Sales/Inventory									
Cost of Sales/Payables									
Sales/Working Capital	18.5	11.2						10.6	8.9
	77.3	28.4						26.8	33.1
	-37.4	-37.3						-102.3	-29.1
EBIT/Interest	8.7	10.6						6.7	4.9
	(52) 1.8	(32) 3.3						(74) 2.0	(85) 2.6
	-2.0	1.1						1.0	1.1
Net Profit + Depr., Dep., Amort./Cur. Mat. L/T/D								5.6	4.2
								(17) 1.9	(12) .9
								.6	.6
Fixed/Worth	.3	.4						.3	.4
	11.1	1.0						1.0	1.6
	-.8	3.5						7.4	-9.9
Debt/Worth	2.6	1.4						.8	.9
	-6.9	2.4						2.3	2.5
	-3.1	9.0						46.0	-21.9
% Profit Before Taxes/Tangible Net Worth	470.7	35.0						46.9	35.7
	(30) 82.8	(29) 19.0						(70) 18.8	(75) 18.5
	4.3	.5						5.2	4.4
% Profit Before Taxes/Total Assets	32.9	14.5						15.2	16.5
	10.0	6.8						5.0	5.7
	-9.5	-.1						.0	.3
Sales/Net Fixed Assets	101.0	40.0						31.5	37.9
	29.9	14.3						14.2	13.9
	8.6	4.7						7.6	5.9
Sales/Total Assets	11.3	4.6						4.7	5.1
	4.3	3.2						3.0	3.3
	2.8	2.4						2.2	2.1
% Depr., Dep., Amort./Sales	.8	1.2						1.1	.9
	(41) 2.0	(26) 2.2						(78) 1.8	(86) 1.9
	4.8	3.4						3.2	3.8
% Officers', Directors', Owners' Comp/Sales	2.8	2.0						2.7	2.7
	(38) 5.6	(19) 2.7						(54) 5.0	(59) 5.2
	10.4	4.3						11.0	10.9
Net Sales ($)	101414M	121491M	76063M	236177M	137991M	854949M		786913M	619115M
Total Assets ($)	14981M	37059M	29625M	148196M	64660M	396927M		472103M	364491M

© RMA 2005

M = $ thousand   MM = $ million

See Pages 11 through 21 for Explanation of Ratios and Data

Comparative Historical Data   **Current Data Sorted By Sales**

Hist 1	Hist 2	Hist 3	Type of Statement	0-1MM	1-3MM	3-5MM	5-10MM	10-25MM	25MM & OVER
7	4	4	Unqualified						4
6	10	7	Reviewed	2	1	1	3		
26	28	30	Compiled	9	10	5	5		1
25	43	44	Tax Returns	19	17	4	4		1
24	36	32	Other	7	10	8	4		3
4/1/02-3/31/03 ALL	4/1/03-3/31/04 ALL	4/1/04-3/31/05 ALL		23 (4/1-9/30/04)			94 (10/1/04-3/31/05)		
88	121	117	**NUMBER OF STATEMENTS**	35	39	18	14	3	8
%	%	%	**ASSETS**	%	%	%	%	%	%
11.8	12.0	12.8	Cash & Equivalents	12.9	13.0	10.9	17.5		
14.8	14.5	16.8	Trade Receivables (net)	4.9	14.7	26.0	37.3		
24.7	25.7	21.2	Inventory	24.2	17.0	23.1	17.1		
2.2	2.3	1.6	All Other Current	1.1	2.1	1.6	1.7		
53.5	54.4	52.3	Total Current	43.1	46.8	61.5	73.6		
33.5	36.1	30.7	Fixed Assets (net)	34.4	35.1	23.8	20.1		
4.2	2.7	7.9	Intangibles (net)	12.0	8.8	4.6	1.7		
8.8	6.7	9.0	All Other Non-Current	10.4	9.3	10.0	4.6		
100.0	100.0	100.0	Total	100.0	100.0	100.0	100.0		
			LIABILITIES						
8.9	11.6	9.9	Notes Payable-Short Term	7.2	9.1	14.7	7.4		
5.7	5.2	4.8	Cur. Mat.-L/T/D	6.8	4.3	3.8	3.5		
21.1	14.5	14.7	Trade Payables	8.3	16.4	19.7	22.9		
.0	.3	.4	Income Taxes Payable	.2	.9	.2	.1		
14.0	17.2	16.4	All Other Current	16.8	25.5	9.9	5.7		
49.7	48.8	46.2	Total Current	39.3	56.2	48.2	39.6		
32.1	31.7	29.2	Long-Term Debt	41.5	30.5	19.9	16.9		
.0	.0	.0	Deferred Taxes	.0	.0	.0	.2		
18.4	11.2	14.6	All Other Non-Current	15.0	17.8	14.9	6.4		
-.2	8.3	10.0	Net Worth	4.1	-4.5	17.0	36.9		
100.0	100.0	100.0	Total Liabilities & Net Worth	100.0	100.0	100.0	100.0		
			INCOME DATA						
100.0	100.0	100.0	Net Sales	100.0	100.0	100.0	100.0		
			Gross Profit						
96.6	96.1	95.1	Operating Expenses	94.8	93.9	97.1	97.0		
3.4	3.9	4.9	Operating Profit	5.2	6.1	2.9	3.0		
1.3	2.0	1.0	All Other Expenses (net)	2.4	.4	.9	.2		
2.0	1.9	3.8	Profit Before Taxes	2.8	5.7	2.0	2.9		
			RATIOS						
2.6	2.5	2.6		1.8	2.8	1.9	3.2		
1.2	1.4	1.4	Current	1.0	1.2	1.5	2.1		
.6	.8	.8		.4	.5	.9	1.4		
1.3	1.4	1.3		.8	2.2	1.3	2.0		
.5 (118)	.7 (116)	.6	Quick	(34) .4	.5	.8	1.7		
.2	.2	.3		.2	.2	.5	.7		
1 272.0	0 UND	0 UND		0 UND	0 UND	6 60.0	10 37.6		
10 35.0	9 39.1	8 42.9	Sales/Receivables	2 239.0	4 103.1	21 17.4	26 14.2		
27 13.4	26 14.0	28 13.1		13 27.9	15 23.7	38 9.7	40 9.2		
			Cost of Sales/Inventory						
			Cost of Sales/Payables						
9.7	8.9	12.0		12.7	20.3	14.2	8.4		
40.8	23.4	34.9	Sales/Working Capital	662.0	77.3	38.6	16.1		
-24.9	-43.4	-40.3		-18.9	-29.3	-41.7	56.9		
4.8	6.5	10.0		4.2	15.9	57.8	7.4		
(77) 2.4	(104) 2.3	(101) 2.5	EBIT/Interest	(28) .6	(32) 3.2	8.8	(12) 3.1		
.1	-.7	-.1		-3.7	-.1	1.0	-1.3		
		2.9	Net Profit + Depr., Dep.,						
	(10)	2.4	Amort./Cur. Mat. L/T/D						
		.8							
.3	.4	.4		.3	.5	.3	.4		
1.5	1.1	1.9	Fixed/Worth	6.9	5.5	1.0	.5		
-10.0	-5.9	-2.1		-1.5	-.6	-7.8	1.0		
1.6	.9	1.4		3.0	.9	1.4	.8		
3.8	3.3	6.0	Debt/Worth	-56.6	10.7	2.8	1.3		
-11.3	-8.1	-5.4		-3.7	-4.1	-32.5	4.3		
57.2	51.7	88.3	% Profit Before Taxes/Tangible	189.3	144.1	69.4	39.3		
(62) 16.8	(85) 15.6	(76) 30.5	Net Worth	(17) 49.3	(23) 38.7	(13) 33.2	(13) 18.8		
1.8	-6.9	1.4		-.5	-11.3	5.6	-6.1		
12.2	17.2	21.8	% Profit Before Taxes/Total	14.3	30.2	24.1	48.2		
3.4	3.9	7.1	Assets	1.2	10.0	7.4	7.0		
-3.5	-4.0	-5.7		-14.5	-8.7	.4	-3.2		
52.1	46.6	60.2		61.6	75.6	78.3	56.0		
16.8	15.9	19.6	Sales/Net Fixed Assets	11.4	29.9	23.7	26.8		
5.1	5.7	6.7		4.7	7.5	8.9	14.7		
5.9	6.7	6.0		4.0	9.8	4.9	11.6		
3.3	3.3	3.4	Sales/Total Assets	2.8	5.0	3.5	4.5		
1.8	2.0	2.4		1.8	2.9	2.9	3.0		
1.2	1.0	1.1		1.7	1.0	1.0	.9		
(70) 2.3	(96) 2.1	(82) 1.9	% Depr., Dep., Amort./Sales	(23) 4.5	(26) 1.9	(11) 1.7	(13) 1.7		
3.5	4.4	4.1		9.7	3.5	2.7	2.0		
1.5	2.9	2.3	% Officers', Directors',	3.0	2.6	1.6			
(41) 4.9	(70) 5.5	(60) 4.1	Owners' Comp/Sales	(20) 4.9	(19) 5.7	(12) 2.7			
3.5	10.0	10.1		13.8	10.3	3.7			
1613417M	3782464M	1528085M	Net Sales ($)	18131M	71027M	69017M	102157M	51644M	1216109M
456703M	769186M	691448M	Total Assets ($)	10974M	18563M	20099M	21848M	28825M	591139M

© RMA 2005

M = $ thousand   MM = $ million
See Pages 11 through 21 for Explanation of Ratios and Data

OTHER SERVICES—Computer and Office Machine Repair and Maintenance   NAICS 811212 (SIC 7378, 7629, 7699)

| Current Data Sorted By Assets | | | | | | | Comparative Historical Data | |

						Type of Statement		
1	2	1	3	1		Unqualified	3	2
	3	2	1			Reviewed	6	3
1	5	1				Compiled	11	12
4	1	1				Tax Returns	6	5
2	5	4				Other	10	13
	8 (4/1-9/30/04)		30 (10/1/04-3/31/05)				4/1/00-3/31/01 ALL	4/1/01-3/31/02 ALL
0-500M	500M-2MM	2-10MM	10-50MM	50-100MM	100-250MM			
8	16	9	4	1		NUMBER OF STATEMENTS	36	35
%	%	%	%	%	%	ASSETS	%	%
14.0						Cash & Equivalents	14.2	9.3
33.2						Trade Receivables (net)	41.2	39.4
23.5						Inventory	13.5	20.2
1.9						All Other Current	3.6	3.1
72.6						Total Current	72.4	72.0
7.9						Fixed Assets (net)	18.3	15.0
3.5						Intangibles (net)	3.3	6.8
16.0						All Other Non-Current	6.0	6.2
100.0						Total	100.0	100.0
						LIABILITIES		
13.3						Notes Payable-Short Term	19.3	13.1
2.6						Cur. Mat.-L/T/D	4.2	3.7
14.2						Trade Payables	23.4	21.1
.7						Income Taxes Payable	.8	.6
14.8						All Other Current	21.2	14.9
45.6						Total Current	68.8	53.4
4.7						Long-Term Debt	11.6	8.9
.0						Deferred Taxes	.2	.2
18.2						All Other Non-Current	6.0	35.1
31.4						Net Worth	13.4	2.4
100.0						Total Liabilities & Net Worth	100.0	100.0
						INCOME DATA		
100.0						Net Sales	100.0	100.0
						Gross Profit		
97.6						Operating Expenses	98.7	93.8
2.4						Operating Profit	1.3	6.2
1.7						All Other Expenses (net)	.4	.6
.7						Profit Before Taxes	.9	5.6
						RATIOS		
4.0							2.2	2.5
1.8						Current	1.3	1.4
1.1							.9	1.0
2.9							1.8	1.8
.9						Quick	1.1	1.0
.5							.6	.6
16 22.8							26 14.3	25 14.4
27 13.6						Sales/Receivables	41 9.0	41 8.8
51 7.2							52 7.0	55 6.7
						Cost of Sales/Inventory		
						Cost of Sales/Payables		
5.4							7.3	8.8
13.4						Sales/Working Capital	23.3	17.3
81.0							−215.1	−96.0
1.9							6.6	18.8
(13) 1.1						EBIT/Interest	(30) 1.7	(31) 5.0
−4.2							.0	1.7
						Net Profit + Depr., Dep.,	3.9	
						Amort./Cur. Mat. L /T/D	(11) 1.5	
							.1	
.1							.2	.2
.2						Fixed/Worth	.5	.5
1.6							1.2	3.2
.8							1.1	.9
2.8						Debt/Worth	2.5	2.7
31.9							7.9	23.0
24.8						% Profit Before Taxes/Tangible	87.2	73.0
(13) 3.0						Net Worth	(31) 7.0	(27) 38.1
−6.1							−9.8	4.8
3.6						% Profit Before Taxes/Total	18.7	28.9
.8						Assets	2.2	10.3
−3.4							−6.5	2.8
233.7							58.0	64.7
102.9						Sales/Net Fixed Assets	28.7	34.6
35.7							15.6	16.4
3.9							4.8	5.7
3.2						Sales/Total Assets	3.9	4.0
2.3							3.1	2.4
.4							.7	.7
(12) .7						% Depr., Dep., Amort./Sales	(31) 1.1	(25) 1.3
1.7							2.2	2.2
						% Officers', Directors',	4.0	2.2
						Owners' Comp/Sales	(16) 5.6	(15) 4.4
							10.2	9.9
9601M	48000M	117443M	301435M	8622M		Net Sales ($)	320279M	473270M
1652M	14409M	37449M	112511M	89475M		Total Assets ($)	96119M	256354M

© RMA 2005

M = $ thousand   MM = $ million
See Pages 11 through 21 for Explanation of Ratios and Data

Comparative Historical Data				Current Data Sorted By Sales					
			Type of Statement	2		1	2		3
3	5	8	Unqualified		3			2	1
6	10	6	Reviewed	1	3	3			
4	12	7	Compiled	2	2		1	1	
4	4	6	Tax Returns	1	3		2	2	3
9	8	11	Other						
4/1/02- 3/31/03	4/1/03- 3/31/04	4/1/04- 3/31/05			**8 (4/1-9/30/04)**		**30 (10/1/04-3/31/05)**		
ALL	ALL	ALL		0-1MM	1-3MM	3-5MM	5-10MM	10-25MM	25MM & OVER
26	39	38	**NUMBER OF STATEMENTS**	6	11	6	5	6	4
%	%	%	**ASSETS**	%	%	%	%	%	%
12.6	10.5	9.7	Cash & Equivalents		17.2				
43.8	37.7	41.4	Trade Receivables (net)		25.2				
14.6	18.1	17.7	Inventory		29.1				
2.4	4.9	2.8	All Other Current		1.1				
73.5	71.3	71.7	Total Current		72.6				
17.1	10.5	12.9	Fixed Assets (net)		11.7				
3.0	5.4	3.1	Intangibles (net)		5.8				
6.5	12.9	12.3	All Other Non-Current		9.9				
100.0	100.0	100.0	Total		100.0				
			LIABILITIES						
18.6	16.3	23.2	Notes Payable-Short Term		16.1				
4.5	2.1	1.7	Cur. Mat.-L/T/D		3.1				
19.5	17.8	16.7	Trade Payables		10.7				
.4	.2	.4	Income Taxes Payable		.4				
17.3	20.9	18.3	All Other Current		7.7				
60.4	57.3	60.4	Total Current		37.9				
10.2	5.9	19.2	Long-Term Debt		6.6				
.0	.1	.5	Deferred Taxes		.0				
10.0	6.3	11.6	All Other Non-Current		18.1				
19.4	30.3	8.4	Net Worth		37.4				
100.0	100.0	100.0	Total Liabilities & Net Worth		100.0				
			INCOME DATA						
100.0	100.0	100.0	Net Sales		100.0				
			Gross Profit						
95.2	94.7	97.0	Operating Expenses		99.5				
4.8	5.3	3.0	Operating Profit		.5				
.9	.9	1.9	All Other Expenses (net)		.5				
3.8	4.4	1.1	Profit Before Taxes		-.1				
			RATIOS						
1.7	2.0	2.0			4.9				
1.4	1.4	1.7	Current		1.9				
1.1	1.0	1.0			1.4				
1.4	1.5	1.7			3.0				
1.1	.9	1.0	Quick		1.6				
.7	.6	.6			.5				
25 14.9	24 15.3	21 17.8			12 30.3				
37 9.8	40 9.2	38 9.5	Sales/Receivables		19 18.9				
58 6.3	54 6.8	59 6.2			47 7.8				
			Cost of Sales/Inventory						
			Cost of Sales/Payables						
11.8	6.4	7.4			5.2				
17.5	14.1	17.7	Sales/Working Capital		15.3				
43.8	-806.3	NM			27.7				
17.2	23.3	12.4							
(24) 3.0	(36) 8.5	(33) 1.8	EBIT/Interest						
1.2	1.3	.4							
			Net Profit + Depr., Dep., Amort./Cur. Mat. L/T/D						
.2	.1	.2			.1				
.5	.4	.5	Fixed/Worth		.6				
2.6	1.2	7.9			2.5				
1.9	1.2	1.1			.8				
3.7	2.9	3.4	Debt/Worth		1.7				
16.9	7.1	95.3			40.5				
56.2	62.0	48.5							
(22) 32.1	(33) 30.3	(30) 11.3	% Profit Before Taxes/Tangible Net Worth						
7.6	5.1	-.9							
23.4	17.6	14.9			3.9				
6.9	9.5	2.7	% Profit Before Taxes/Total Assets		.6				
2.4	.9	-1.0			-1.8				
97.0	83.1	106.1			120.9				
44.7	37.1	47.4	Sales/Net Fixed Assets		37.1				
17.1	21.5	19.6			25.9				
5.6	4.5	5.1			3.9				
3.9	3.3	3.4	Sales/Total Assets		3.0				
3.0	1.8	2.6			2.2				
.5	.5	.5							
(22) 1.0	(30) 1.1	(28) 1.2	% Depr., Dep., Amort./Sales						
1.6	1.6	2.4							
3.8	2.7	2.5							
(15) 6.4	(17) 4.4	(17) 5.9	% Officers', Directors', Owners' Comp/Sales						
12.2	8.0	12.4							
305422M	523151M	485101M	Net Sales ($)	3119M	24105M	24479M	36182M	95781M	301435M
79461M	271508M	255496M	Total Assets ($)	1286M	8190M	6246M	98564M	28699M	112511M

© RMA 2005 **M = $ thousand   MM = $ million**
See Pages 11 through 21 for Explanation of Ratios and Data

Current Data Sorted By Assets   **Comparative Historical Data**

						Type of Statement		
	1	9	9	1	3	Unqualified	22	20
	10	22	6			Reviewed	62	51
8	27	14	1			Compiled	101	89
29	22	5				Tax Returns	48	45
13	27	19	11	2	1	Other	67	67
	46 (4/1-9/30/04)			194 (10/1/04-3/31/05)			4/1/00-3/31/01 ALL	4/1/01-3/31/02 ALL
0-500M	500M-2MM	2-10MM	10-50MM	50-100MM	100-250MM			
50	87	69	27	3	4	**NUMBER OF STATEMENTS**	300	272
%	%	%	%	%	%	**ASSETS**	%	%
16.7	12.7	7.7	4.7			Cash & Equivalents	8.9	10.2
25.2	29.3	34.8	27.1			Trade Receivables (net)	33.3	31.1
16.7	24.6	22.6	24.0			Inventory	18.9	18.4
2.7	1.6	3.3	2.8			All Other Current	2.6	2.9
61.3	68.1	68.3	58.5			Total Current	63.5	62.5
29.3	23.5	23.1	26.6			Fixed Assets (net)	27.0	29.3
3.6	2.9	3.9	8.6			Intangibles (net)	3.7	2.3
5.9	5.6	4.8	6.3			All Other Non-Current	5.7	5.8
100.0	100.0	100.0	100.0			Total	100.0	100.0
						LIABILITIES		
14.8	11.1	13.6	7.8			Notes Payable-Short Term	12.4	9.9
6.2	4.8	3.7	4.1			Cur. Mat.-L/T/D	4.8	5.6
14.8	14.1	13.3	15.4			Trade Payables	16.1	15.0
.1	.3	.4	1.2			Income Taxes Payable	.3	.4
12.1	10.3	11.5	11.3			All Other Current	11.1	9.2
48.0	40.6	42.5	39.8			Total Current	44.8	40.1
30.4	22.2	13.7	24.5			Long-Term Debt	18.8	18.2
.0	.1	.5	1.9			Deferred Taxes	.7	.6
6.8	3.8	8.8	11.2			All Other Non-Current	5.0	5.5
14.8	33.3	34.5	22.6			Net Worth	30.7	35.5
100.0	100.0	100.0	100.0			Total Liabilities & Net Worth	100.0	100.0
						INCOME DATA		
100.0	100.0	100.0	100.0			Net Sales	100.0	100.0
						Gross Profit		
95.1	94.4	96.5	92.3			Operating Expenses	95.5	95.4
4.9	5.6	3.5	7.7			Operating Profit	4.5	4.6
1.6	1.2	.6	2.5			All Other Expenses (net)	1.2	1.3
3.4	4.4	2.9	5.2			Profit Before Taxes	3.3	3.3
						RATIOS		
2.8	2.7	2.5	2.3				2.5	2.7
1.7	1.6	1.6	1.5			Current	1.4	1.5
.8	1.1	1.1	1.0				1.0	1.1
2.3	1.7	1.8	1.1				1.7	1.7
1.0	1.1	.9	.9			Quick	.9	1.0
.3	.6	.7	.6				.5	.6
0 UND	25 14.6	36 10.1	39 9.3				30 12.2	25 14.7
30 12.3	39 9.4	49 7.4	53 6.8			Sales/Receivables	45 8.2	39 9.4
46 7.9	54 6.7	63 5.8	70 5.2				59 6.1	56 6.6
						Cost of Sales/Inventory		
						Cost of Sales/Payables		
7.8	5.4	5.7	5.4				6.5	5.8
24.8	11.6	12.6	16.6			Sales/Working Capital	13.3	13.8
-40.3	87.5	36.9	125.0				300.1	73.7
12.4	11.3	11.1	23.2				6.9	8.7
(42) 3.5	(76) 4.7	(63) 3.8	(26) 3.2			EBIT/Interest	(261) 2.3	(238) 2.8
.4	2.0	1.1	1.3				1.0	1.0
	4.1	4.4	3.9			Net Profit + Depr., Dep.,		4.4	3.6
	(14) 1.9	(18) 2.6	(12) 2.0			Amort./Cur. Mat. L /T/D	(64) 2.1	(53) 1.8
	.9	1.5	1.3				1.2	.6
.3	.2	.2	.5				.3	.3
1.2	.6	.8	1.6			Fixed/Worth	.8	.7
-1.8	3.2	2.2	-2.1				4.1	2.5
.7	.9	1.0	1.5				.8	.7
2.5	2.3	2.3	5.7			Debt/Worth	2.3	2.0
-6.2	9.0	5.1	-10.0				15.5	5.0
76.6	60.2	52.5	73.4			% Profit Before Taxes/Tangible	51.7	44.5
(33) 30.2	(73) 28.1	(59) 17.1	(20) 40.4			Net Worth	(249) 21.2	(240) 17.5
15.6	11.0	4.5	7.5				3.6	1.3
28.7	20.1	16.9	14.4			% Profit Before Taxes/Total	13.6	15.9
11.0	8.4	4.2	7.9			Assets	4.9	5.8
-.8	3.3	.1	.9				.0	.0
81.3	35.8	37.4	23.5				29.4	29.2
22.9	19.4	14.7	12.1			Sales/Net Fixed Assets	12.6	12.8
7.7	7.1	7.0	2.8				6.0	5.6
6.3	3.7	3.3	2.5				3.7	3.6
3.2	2.7	2.4	1.8			Sales/Total Assets	2.6	2.7
2.3	1.9	1.9	1.4				1.7	1.9
1.6	1.0	.8	1.4				1.0	.9
(32) 2.8	(64) 1.7	(61) 1.5	(23) 2.2			% Depr., Dep., Amort./Sales	(259) 2.0	(237) 1.9
4.3	3.2	2.7	5.9				4.1	3.7
4.8	3.3	2.2				% Officers', Directors',	2.9	3.3
(27) 6.8	(49) 6.1	(22) 3.4				Owners' Comp/Sales	(149) 5.5	(128) 6.4
12.6	9.6	6.0					10.5	9.4
51759M	262070M	681564M	1368706M	286128M	1045414M	Net Sales ($)	2926404M	3043916M
13243M	91359M	275492M	597200M	233373M	527074M	Total Assets ($)	1523988M	1522814M

© RMA 2005

M = $ thousand   MM = $ million
See Pages 11 through 21 for Explanation of Ratios and Data

Comparative Historical Data			Type of Statement	Current Data Sorted By Sales					
22	23	23	Unqualified		1	1	3	7	11
58	42	38	Reviewed		4	8	12	12	2
63	82	50	Compiled	6	17	11	9	7	
39	36	56	Tax Returns	26	16	10	3	1	
45	56	73	Other	7	22	11	13	9	11
4/1/02-3/31/03 ALL	4/1/03-3/31/04 ALL	4/1/04-3/31/05 ALL		46 (4/1-9/30/04)		194 (10/1/04-3/31/05)			
				0-1MM	1-3MM	3-5MM	5-10MM	10-25MM	25MM & OVER
227	239	240	**NUMBER OF STATEMENTS**	39	60	41	40	36	24
%	%	%	**ASSETS**	%	%	%	%	%	%
9.9	9.1	11.0	Cash & Equivalents	16.2	12.6	12.1	7.5	8.6	6.3
31.9	31.4	29.7	Trade Receivables (net)	17.5	30.4	30.2	34.3	35.8	30.2
20.4	19.1	22.2	Inventory	20.6	20.1	21.4	25.1	22.3	26.4
2.6	2.9	2.4	All Other Current	2.0	1.9	2.6	3.2	2.7	2.3
64.8	62.6	65.3	Total Current	56.3	65.0	66.2	70.0	69.5	65.1
26.8	26.9	24.8	Fixed Assets (net)	34.6	25.5	24.8	21.1	21.5	18.1
2.1	4.0	4.4	Intangibles (net)	4.6	3.2	4.1	2.6	4.5	10.4
6.2	6.5	5.5	All Other Non-Current	4.5	6.3	4.9	6.2	4.5	6.3
100.0	100.0	100.0	Total	100.0	100.0	100.0	100.0	100.0	100.0
			LIABILITIES						
13.9	13.6	12.1	Notes Payable-Short Term	13.5	10.5	11.2	15.9	13.3	7.2
6.0	4.7	4.6	Cur. Mat.-L/T/D	7.8	4.4	4.2	3.6	4.6	2.7
15.2	15.9	14.4	Trade Payables	9.8	15.5	14.7	13.4	13.8	21.4
.3	.4	.4	Income Taxes Payable	.0	.1	.5	.4	.4	1.4
10.7	11.9	11.2	All Other Current	11.4	8.9	10.8	13.0	14.3	9.3
46.1	46.5	42.7	Total Current	42.5	39.5	41.4	46.3	46.3	42.0
18.4	23.1	21.3	Long-Term Debt	38.0	26.2	18.0	12.3	12.1	16.7
.4	.3	.4	Deferred Taxes	.0	.1	.1	.4	.9	1.5
4.3	5.5	6.7	All Other Non-Current	8.7	4.4	7.0	6.0	7.3	8.9
30.9	24.5	28.9	Net Worth	10.8	29.8	33.5	35.0	33.5	30.9
100.0	100.0	100.0	Total Liabilities & Net Worth	100.0	100.0	100.0	100.0	100.0	100.0
			INCOME DATA						
100.0	100.0	100.0	Net Sales	100.0	100.0	100.0	100.0	100.0	100.0
			Gross Profit						
94.8	94.7	95.0	Operating Expenses	94.1	94.1	96.5	96.4	93.7	95.4
5.2	5.3	5.0	Operating Profit	5.9	5.9	3.5	3.6	6.3	4.6
1.0	1.5	1.2	All Other Expenses (net)	3.0	.9	.7	.4	1.4	1.3
4.2	3.8	3.8	Profit Before Taxes	2.9	5.0	2.8	3.1	5.0	3.3
			RATIOS						
2.6	2.4	2.6		3.6	2.9	2.4	2.3	2.6	2.0
1.4	1.4	1.6	Current	1.7	1.8	1.6	1.5	1.4	1.5
1.0	1.0	1.1		.6	1.0	1.1	1.1	1.1	1.1
1.6	1.5	1.7		1.8	2.2	1.8	1.7	1.4	1.2
.9	(238) .9	.9	Quick	.8	1.1	.9	.8	1.0	.7
.6	.6	.6		.3	.6	.7	.6	.6	.6
24 15.1	28 13.1	26 13.9		0 UND	30 12.3	26 14.2	30 12.1	43 8.5	30 12.0
41 9.0	43 8.4	43 8.6	Sales/Receivables	27 13.6	41 8.9	38 9.5	44 8.3	54 6.7	46 8.0
56 6.5	58 6.3	58 6.3		44 8.3	57 6.4	54 6.7	60 6.0	70 5.2	59 6.2
			Cost of Sales/Inventory						
			Cost of Sales/Payables						
6.0	6.4	6.5		5.8	4.5	7.0	7.8	5.0	6.2
14.2	16.3	13.6	Sales/Working Capital	24.6	10.4	12.8	16.3	14.1	13.5
-839.0	366.5	86.1		-21.9	192.8	56.6	70.0	42.3	136.5
(201) 9.5	(204) 8.5	(213) 12.0		(32) 8.4	(53) 11.2	(38) 12.9	(33) 6.1	(35) 19.3	(22) 50.8
3.7	3.6	4.0	EBIT/Interest	2.6	3.2	5.8	4.4	3.9	6.7
1.1	1.1	1.1		-.9	1.4	1.3	1.0	1.6	1.4
(47) 5.6	(46) 5.5	(48) 4.1	Net Profit + Depr., Dep.,					(16) 3.7	
2.3	2.3	2.1	Amort./Cur. Mat. L/T/D					1.8	
.4	1.0	1.4						1.4	
.3	.3	.2		.3	.3	.2	.2	.2	.3
.8	.9	.8	Fixed/Worth	1.2	.8	.8	.7	.7	.9
3.9	4.5	4.0		-.7	4.2	2.9	1.8	2.1	NM
.8	.9	.9		.6	.7	1.0	.9	1.1	1.4
2.2	2.4	2.3	Debt/Worth	1.8	2.8	2.3	2.4	2.1	3.0
8.8	14.7	30.5		-4.5	33.6	7.3	6.4	4.3	NM
(193) 61.8	(189) 51.1	(190) 59.5	% Profit Before Taxes/Tangible	(24) 51.2	(47) 78.4	(35) 59.3	(35) 61.9	(31) 46.4	(18) 87.1
20.0	23.4	27.0	Net Worth	28.1	28.1	26.2	23.0	24.2	53.3
2.4	5.0	7.2		8.2	8.9	7.5	4.8	7.0	18.4
17.0	16.7	18.7	% Profit Before Taxes/Total	20.0	19.8	22.8	12.8	16.5	18.8
6.0	6.6	7.3	Assets	7.0	10.2	6.0	4.5	7.8	8.0
.4	.5	.7		-1.9	1.5	2.1	.8	1.8	1.2
34.2	28.9	38.2		50.1	31.4	70.4	42.7	46.5	29.8
13.4	13.9	16.5	Sales/Net Fixed Assets	14.7	14.8	18.6	20.2	16.4	16.7
6.9	6.8	6.6		3.6	6.2	6.4	10.4	5.6	6.1
3.7	3.6	3.6		4.6	3.4	4.7	3.8	3.5	2.9
2.8	2.6	2.6	Sales/Total Assets	2.5	2.6	2.9	2.8	2.2	2.1
2.0	1.8	1.8		.9	1.9	1.9	2.3	1.5	1.7
(194) 1.1	(200) .9	(185) 1.0	% Depr., Dep., Amort./Sales	(27) 1.5	(40) 1.3	(32) 1.0	(36) .6	(31) .9	(19) .6
2.2	2.2	1.9		3.0	2.3	1.5	1.5	1.7	1.4
4.2	4.1	3.6		6.6	3.5	4.6	2.3	3.8	2.9
3.5	2.7	3.2	% Officers', Directors',	4.1	4.7	2.5	1.4		
(110) 5.9	(109) 5.6	(101) 5.9	Owners' Comp/Sales	(20) 6.6	(37) 6.3	(21) 6.1	(15) 3.2		
9.0	10.0	9.4		14.1	12.4	7.4	4.2		
3540893M	3238085M	3695641M	Net Sales ($)	22869M	112656M	160886M	288209M	579974M	2531047M
1655672M	1307647M	1737741M	Total Assets ($)	13938M	52151M	70426M	111681M	326686M	1162859M

© RMA 2005

M = $ thousand   MM = $ million
See Pages 11 through 21 for Explanation of Ratios and Data

1478 OTHER SERVICES—Commercial & Industrial Machinery & Equip. (except Automotive & Electronic) Repair & Maintenance   NAICS 811310   (SIC 7623, 7692, 7694)

Current Data Sorted By Assets — **Comparative Historical Data**

	0-500M	500M-2MM	2-10MM	10-50MM	50-100MM	100-250MM	Type of Statement	4/1/00-3/31/01 ALL	4/1/01-3/31/02 ALL
Unqualified	1		7				Unqualified	4	3
Reviewed	16	11	12	5			Reviewed	17	19
Compiled	36	30	11	1	1		Compiled	25	20
Tax Returns		13	2	1			Tax Returns	6	16
Other	9	24	18	3			Other	24	20
		39 (4/1-9/30/04)		162 (10/1/04-3/31/05)					
NUMBER OF STATEMENTS	62	78	50	10	1		**NUMBER OF STATEMENTS**	76	78
	%	%	%	%	%	%	**ASSETS**	%	%
Cash & Equivalents	17.0	8.3	8.1	6.9			Cash & Equivalents	9.3	7.7
Trade Receivables (net)	31.1	32.5	31.0	26.9			Trade Receivables (net)	31.6	35.9
Inventory	11.6	22.2	17.7	15.5			Inventory	14.2	12.8
All Other Current	.7	3.1	3.6	4.3			All Other Current	2.4	1.8
Total Current	60.5	66.1	60.3	53.6			Total Current	57.5	58.1
Fixed Assets (net)	27.4	25.1	30.0	38.4			Fixed Assets (net)	35.2	34.4
Intangibles (net)	3.1	2.3	2.6	4.7			Intangibles (net)	2.1	1.7
All Other Non-Current	9.0	6.5	7.1	3.2			All Other Non-Current	5.3	5.8
Total	100.0	100.0	100.0	100.0			Total	100.0	100.0
					DATA NOT AVAILABLE		**LIABILITIES**		
Notes Payable-Short Term	10.7	12.7	12.6	16.1			Notes Payable-Short Term	11.7	14.4
Cur. Mat.-L/T/D	6.5	4.4	4.7	2.7			Cur. Mat.-L/T/D	5.2	9.6
Trade Payables	15.5	19.2	16.3	9.3			Trade Payables	13.2	14.0
Income Taxes Payable	.3	.2	.4	.0			Income Taxes Payable	.2	.8
All Other Current	12.7	8.5	8.8	7.5			All Other Current	8.0	9.8
Total Current	45.6	45.1	42.8	35.6			Total Current	38.2	48.5
Long-Term Debt	32.0	17.3	18.9	17.7			Long-Term Debt	23.1	20.0
Deferred Taxes	.0	.2	.9	1.7			Deferred Taxes	.4	.2
All Other Non-Current	9.0	7.8	4.9	1.5			All Other Non-Current	5.0	5.3
Net Worth	13.4	29.6	32.5	43.6			Net Worth	33.3	26.1
Total Liabilities & Net Worth	100.0	100.0	100.0	100.0			Total Liabilities & Net Worth	100.0	100.0
							INCOME DATA		
Net Sales	100.0	100.0	100.0	100.0			Net Sales	100.0	100.0
Gross Profit							Gross Profit		
Operating Expenses	93.4	94.6	94.6	95.7			Operating Expenses	95.2	96.4
Operating Profit	6.6	5.4	5.4	4.3			Operating Profit	4.8	3.6
All Other Expenses (net)	1.1	1.1	1.5	-.2			All Other Expenses (net)	1.0	2.0
Profit Before Taxes	5.6	4.3	3.8	4.4			Profit Before Taxes	3.8	1.6
							RATIOS		
Current	3.0	2.5	2.2	3.3			Current	2.9	1.8
	1.3	1.6	1.4	1.5				1.4	1.3
	.7	1.1	1.2	.9				1.1	.9
Quick	2.7	1.6	1.3	1.5			Quick	1.8	1.5
	1.0	(77) 1.0	1.0	1.1				1.0	1.0
	.6	.6	.6	.6				.6	.6
Sales/Receivables	9 41.6	33 11.0	41 9.0	41 8.8			Sales/Receivables	33 10.9	41 8.9
	31 11.6	44 8.3	57 6.4	51 7.2				46 7.9	50 7.2
	47 7.7	57 6.4	71 5.2	72 5.1				62 5.9	64 5.7
Cost of Sales/Inventory							Cost of Sales/Inventory		
Cost of Sales/Payables							Cost of Sales/Payables		
Sales/Working Capital	8.0	6.5	6.0	3.9			Sales/Working Capital	6.3	7.0
	20.9	10.8	13.2	19.9				16.1	17.5
	-46.1	33.3	31.7	-771.8				124.9	-87.7
EBIT/Interest	14.1	12.1	9.0	9.1			EBIT/Interest	6.3	5.4
	(50) 5.9	(66) 3.6	(43) 2.6	5.2				(68) 2.3	(77) 2.9
	.1	1.3	.1	.1				.8	.1
Net Profit + Depr., Dep., Amort./Cur. Mat. L/T/D		7.8	3.3				Net Profit + Depr., Dep., Amort./Cur. Mat. L/T/D	4.2	3.8
	(12)	4.5	(16) 1.6					(19) 1.7	(16) 1.5
		1.9	1.1					.8	-.2
Fixed/Worth	.3	.2	.4	.3			Fixed/Worth	.5	.5
	1.4	.8	1.1	1.0				.9	1.3
	-4.1	2.5	1.9	NM				2.3	4.0
Debt/Worth	.9	.8	1.3	.5			Debt/Worth	.9	1.3
	3.1	2.5	2.5	1.8				1.9	2.8
	-13.4	8.2	7.0	NM				4.0	8.7
% Profit Before Taxes/Tangible Net Worth	102.6	78.9	44.8				% Profit Before Taxes/Tangible Net Worth	41.1	50.8
	(43) 37.0	(66) 27.0	(46) 21.0					(67) 20.8	(67) 15.0
	4.0	6.6	1.9					.2	3.3
% Profit Before Taxes/Total Assets	33.9	22.4	15.5	13.4			% Profit Before Taxes/Total Assets	15.7	15.6
	10.7	6.9	4.8	7.1				6.3	3.3
	-.5	1.4	-1.1	.7				-.8	-6.4
Sales/Net Fixed Assets	56.9	40.9	21.1	54.7			Sales/Net Fixed Assets	17.4	16.9
	22.7	16.3	8.1	6.5				9.8	8.7
	8.4	5.8	3.0	2.8				5.8	4.7
Sales/Total Assets	5.4	3.7	2.4	3.6			Sales/Total Assets	3.7	3.3
	3.7	2.6	2.0	1.9				2.7	2.6
	2.6	1.8	1.4	.9				1.6	1.8
% Depr., Dep., Amort./Sales	1.2	.9	1.2	.7			% Depr., Dep., Amort./Sales	1.4	1.6
	(44) 2.2	(64) 1.5	(46) 2.1	2.1				(69) 2.2	(72) 2.6
	3.6	3.4	3.5	7.3				4.1	4.4
% Officers', Directors', Owners' Comp/Sales	4.5	3.4	1.7				% Officers', Directors', Owners' Comp/Sales	3.0	3.4
	(43) 7.2	(43) 5.1	(21) 3.8					(38) 4.2	(37) 7.2
	10.3	7.9	6.0					6.9	9.7
Net Sales ($)	56591M	230087M	424973M	2100606M	107669M		Net Sales ($)	509629M	575457M
Total Assets ($)	15001M	85610M	214383M	218514M	74396M		Total Assets ($)	238739M	254140M

M = $ thousand   MM = $ million
See Pages 11 through 21 for Explanation of Ratios and Data

Comparative Historical Data				Current Data Sorted By Sales					
3	4	13	Type of Statement						
24	26	24	Unqualified		3	1	2	4	3
37	51	57	Reviewed		2	6	10	5	1
26	56	52	Compiled	11	27	8	7	4	
31	36	55	Tax Returns	27	19	5	•		1
			Other	9	22	8	6	7	3
4/1/02-3/31/03 ALL	4/1/03-3/31/04 ALL	4/1/04-3/31/05 ALL		39 (4/1-9/30/04)			162 (10/1/04-3/31/05)		
				0-1MM	1-3MM	3-5MM	5-10MM	10-25MM	25MM & OVER
121	173	201	NUMBER OF STATEMENTS	47	73	28	25	20	8
%	%	%	ASSETS	%	%	%	%	%	%
10.0	9.5	10.8	Cash & Equivalents	19.1	7.3	9.5	8.9	9.7	
30.5	29.7	31.5	Trade Receivables (net)	26.2	30.7	33.4	39.4	32.3	
16.1	22.3	17.4	Inventory	9.8	20.9	19.1	21.3	15.8	
3.0	2.8	2.5	All Other Current	1.2	1.8	5.8	1.2	4.1	
59.7	64.2	62.3	Total Current	56.2	60.8	67.9	70.9	61.9	
32.3	27.0	27.7	Fixed Assets (net)	29.0	28.6	24.7	22.6	30.9	
2.2	3.1	2.8	Intangibles (net)	4.6	2.4	1.8	2.3	2.6	
5.8	5.6	7.2	All Other Non-Current	10.2	8.2	5.6	4.2	4.6	
100.0	100.0	100.0	Total	100.0	100.0	100.0	100.0	100.0	
			LIABILITIES						
10.9	13.2	12.2	Notes Payable-Short Term	9.8	13.0	11.3	14.7	10.5	
6.5	4.7	5.0	Cur. Mat.-L/T/D	7.3	5.2	3.4	3.2	4.7	
12.4	14.0	16.8	Trade Payables	15.2	16.0	20.3	18.1	18.4	
.3	.2	.3	Income Taxes Payable	.4	.2	.5	.3	.3	
7.3	9.3	9.8	All Other Current	15.1	7.0	10.0	9.6	8.0	
37.3	41.5	44.1	Total Current	47.7	41.4	45.4	45.8	41.8	
25.4	22.2	22.3	Long-Term Debt	35.6	21.1	15.5	15.7	16.4	
.2	.4	.4	Deferred Taxes	.0	.1	.8	1.0	1.0	
6.4	8.4	7.1	All Other Non-Current	6.8	10.0	8.8	3.3	1.0	
30.6	27.5	26.2	Net Worth	9.8	27.4	29.5	34.2	39.7	
100.0	100.0	100.0	Total Liabilities & Net Worth	100.0	100.0	100.0	100.0	100.0	
			INCOME DATA						
100.0	100.0	100.0	Net Sales	100.0	100.0	100.0	100.0	100.0	
			Gross Profit						
96.8	96.4	94.3	Operating Expenses	91.4	95.7	94.1	92.9	97.1	
3.2	3.6	5.7	Operating Profit	8.6	4.3	5.9	7.1	2.9	
1.2	1.1	1.1	All Other Expenses (net)	2.8	.9	.1	1.0	-.3	
2.0	2.5	4.6	Profit Before Taxes	5.8	3.4	5.8	6.1	3.1	
			RATIOS						
2.8	2.6	2.6	Current	3.0	2.6	1.9	2.4	2.4	
1.7	1.6	1.5		1.3	1.6	1.5	1.4	1.2	
1.1	1.1	1.0		.6	1.1	1.2	1.2	1.0	
1.9	1.8	1.6	Quick	2.7	1.7	1.5	1.7	1.4	
(120) 1.2	1.0	(200) 1.0		.9	(72) 1.0	1.1	1.1	1.0	
.7	.6	.6		.4	.6	.6	.8	.7	
31 11.9	23 16.2	27 13.7	Sales/Receivables	0 UND	25 14.7	35 10.3	40 9.1	47 7.8	
50 7.4	41 9.0	45 8.2		38 9.5	42 8.6	45 8.0	55 6.7	61 6.0	
66 5.6	60 6.1	62 5.9		49 7.4	58 6.3	61 6.0	78 4.7	69 5.3	
			Cost of Sales/Inventory						
			Cost of Sales/Payables						
6.3	6.5	6.6	Sales/Working Capital	6.8	6.5	6.3	7.1	6.5	
11.0	12.2	13.3		22.2	11.2	10.5	13.2	16.9	
99.6	50.8	106.7		-12.0	75.6	23.9	22.2	NM	
5.6	7.5	11.8	EBIT/Interest	13.6	9.7	12.7	12.8	14.6	
(108) 2.2	(157) 3.3	(170) 3.8		(36) 1.8	(65) 3.3	(21) 4.0	(23) 6.0	(17) 3.4	
-.4	.9	.9		-2.4	1.1	1.6	2.3	-1.9	
3.5	3.4	6.3	Net Profit + Depr., Dep., Amort./Cur. Mat. L/T/D		8.2				
(20) 1.7	(26) 1.8	(32) 2.5			(11) 1.7				
.4	.7	1.1			1.1				
.3	.3	.3	Fixed/Worth	.3	.3	.3	.3	.3	
1.0	.9	1.0		1.5	.9	1.1	.8	.9	
5.1	3.7	4.2		-3.2	4.4	1.8	1.5	1.8	
.8	1.2	.9	Debt/Worth	.7	.9	.9	1.2	.7	
2.0	2.3	2.6		6.2	2.5	2.8	2.6	1.9	
13.2	11.0	18.3		-8.4	12.6	6.1	8.0	4.5	
28.5	44.1	69.1	% Profit Before Taxes/Tangible Net Worth	96.1	44.4	88.9	84.5	36.0	
(98) 10.8	(139) 21.6	(164) 27.6		(29) 48.8	(61) 23.1	(25) 29.5	(24) 41.0	(18) 24.5	
-1.3	.5	4.8		1.4	4.1	10.4	5.9	3.3	
11.4	16.9	22.1	% Profit Before Taxes/Total Assets	44.4	15.4	26.0	24.3	14.6	
3.0	6.7	6.7		3.6	6.5	9.8	11.8	7.0	
-4.6	.1	.8		-2.9	1.2	1.5	1.8	-.1	
19.4	39.3	35.6	Sales/Net Fixed Assets	40.8	39.5	31.0	34.7	21.0	
9.4	12.8	13.0		12.5	11.9	17.1	14.3	8.1	
4.5	4.9	5.7		5.7	4.8	6.0	7.4	3.1	
3.4	3.8	3.8	Sales/Total Assets	4.1	3.9	3.9	3.7	2.6	
2.4	2.5	2.5		2.9	2.6	2.5	2.7	2.2	
1.8	1.6	1.7		1.4	1.6	1.7	2.0	1.7	
1.4	1.1	1.0	% Depr., Dep., Amort./Sales	1.1	1.1	1.0	.7	1.2	
(99) 2.7	(146) 2.1	(164) 1.9		(30) 2.5	(60) 2.0	(23) 1.4	(24) 1.5	1.9	
4.8	4.1	4.1		5.0	4.0	3.1	2.6	4.8	
3.8	3.0	3.5	% Officers', Directors', Owners' Comp/Sales	4.6	4.3	1.6	1.9		
(65) 6.8	(101) 6.2	(111) 5.2		(28) 7.6	(46) 5.9	(15) 3.5	(12) 3.3		
12.7	11.0	8.1		10.9	8.4	6.3	4.7		
674867M	931349M	2919926M	Net Sales ($)	26532M	138366M	110484M	179294M	302469M	2162781M
306486M	391070M	607904M	Total Assets ($)	15057M	71005M	47244M	77620M	165167M	231811M

© RMA 2005

M = $ thousand   MM = $ million
See Pages 11 through 21 for Explanation of Ratios and Data

Current Data Sorted By Assets   **Comparative Historical Data**

0-500M	500M-2MM	2-10MM	10-50MM	50-100MM	100-250MM		4/1/00-3/31/01 ALL	4/1/01-3/31/02 ALL
						Type of Statement		
						Unqualified	2	
	6	4				Reviewed	23	12
5	8	1	1			Compiled	20	23
9	7	1				Tax Returns	12	12
	5	5	1			Other	13	24
		1	1					
	18 (4/1-9/30/04)		37 (10/1/04-3/31/05)					
14	26	12	3			**NUMBER OF STATEMENTS**	70	71
%	%	%	%	%	%	**ASSETS**	%	%
20.3	11.0	9.1				Cash & Equivalents	13.8	9.0
27.1	32.9	39.6				Trade Receivables (net)	35.0	35.3
18.5	20.9	15.1	D	D		Inventory	16.4	16.2
.9	3.8	7.6	A	A		All Other Current	3.6	4.8
66.7	68.6	71.3	T	T		Total Current	68.8	65.2
23.3	20.5	21.1	A	A		Fixed Assets (net)	22.7	26.0
1.4	5.2	1.8				Intangibles (net)	2.2	2.2
8.5	5.7	5.8	N	N		All Other Non-Current	6.3	6.6
100.0	100.0	100.0	O	O		Total	100.0	100.0
			T	T		**LIABILITIES**		
8.7	10.6	10.7				Notes Payable-Short Term	8.4	24.2
8.2	3.7	4.2	A	A		Cur. Mat.-L/T/D	5.6	5.1
19.8	21.1	22.0	V	V		Trade Payables	16.9	16.0
.0	.3	.2	A	A		Income Taxes Payable	.4	.2
18.5	10.2	20.7	I	I		All Other Current	8.2	10.0
55.2	45.8	57.8	L	L		Total Current	39.5	55.5
20.9	15.0	10.0	A	A		Long-Term Debt	14.2	13.8
.0	.6	.1	B	B		Deferred Taxes	.4	.6
18.6	3.5	6.6	L	L		All Other Non-Current	2.3	9.8
5.3	35.1	25.6	E	E		Net Worth	43.7	20.3
100.0	100.0	100.0				Total Liabilities & Net Worth	100.0	100.0
						INCOME DATA		
100.0	100.0	100.0				Net Sales	100.0	100.0
						Gross Profit		
96.5	95.2	93.7				Operating Expenses	95.8	97.1
3.5	4.8	6.3				Operating Profit	4.2	2.9
.7	.5	1.5				All Other Expenses (net)	.0	.9
2.8	4.2	4.8				Profit Before Taxes	4.2	2.0
						RATIOS		
4.0	1.8	1.7					2.8	2.1
1.1	1.6	1.3				Current	1.6	1.5
.7	1.2	.9					1.2	1.1
1.9	1.4	1.3					2.1	1.6
.8	.9	.8				Quick	1.3	1.1
.5	.6	.4					.7	.6
0 UND	17 21.8	41 9.0					23 15.7	26 14.0
22 16.6	32 11.4	46 7.9				Sales/Receivables	43 8.4	48 7.7
44 8.4	63 5.8	75 4.9					57 6.4	70 5.2
						Cost of Sales/Inventory		
						Cost of Sales/Payables		
14.8	9.9	9.8					6.2	8.4
203.9	15.9	12.6				Sales/Working Capital	11.2	13.4
-14.7	25.8	NM					31.9	84.7
5.9	18.7						17.4	8.7
(12) 3.7	(22) 4.1					EBIT/Interest	(62) 4.0	(68) 2.8
-.2	1.9						1.9	-.1
						Net Profit + Depr., Dep.,	5.2	4.0
						Amort./Cur. Mat. L /T/D	(20) 2.4	(14) 2.2
							1.7	.7
.1	.3	.4					.2	.4
9.7	.7	.6				Fixed/Worth	.5	.7
-1.3	2.5	3.0					1.0	1.9
6.8	1.2	2.0					.7	1.2
NM	2.0	3.1				Debt/Worth	1.5	1.7
-5.2	11.6	14.3					3.2	6.8
	67.3	119.4				% Profit Before Taxes/Tangible	42.0	36.1
	(22) 40.9	(11) 31.5				Net Worth	(65) 18.6	(61) 21.8
	10.1	18.9					8.3	-4.6
29.0	17.5	10.5				% Profit Before Taxes/Total	16.7	15.3
10.4	9.8	8.2				Assets	6.0	5.4
-4.1	2.4	4.5					2.2	-4.1
UND	55.8	34.6					30.6	27.6
30.7	23.3	18.8				Sales/Net Fixed Assets	17.5	18.0
12.6	9.4	12.3					8.8	8.5
6.2	4.5	3.5					3.8	4.1
4.6	3.4	2.7				Sales/Total Assets	2.9	3.2
3.1	2.6	2.2					2.1	2.0
	.6	.8				% Depr., Dep., Amort./Sales	1.2	1.2
	(21) 2.1	1.8					(64) 2.4	(63) 2.0
	2.4	2.8					3.6	3.1
5.4	2.9					% Officers', Directors',	2.7	4.6
(10) 12.0	(16) 5.2					Owners' Comp/Sales	(49) 5.1	(43) 6.2
15.7	9.8						9.4	11.2
14187M	108206M	108880M	242763M			Net Sales ($)	476383M	444999M
3045M	30912M	41560M	60751M			Total Assets ($)	258330M	185893M

M = $ thousand   MM = $ million
See Pages 11 through 21 for Explanation of Ratios and Data

Comparative Historical Data   **Current Data Sorted By Sales**

	4/1/02-3/31/03 ALL	4/1/03-3/31/04 ALL	4/1/04-3/31/05 ALL	Type of Statement	0-1MM	1-3MM	3-5MM	5-10MM	10-25MM	25MM & OVER
	4	4	2	Unqualified				1		1
	8	12	10	Reviewed		1	1	5	3	
	9	12	14	Compiled	2	4	4	4		
	5	14	18	Tax Returns	9	3	3	2		
	20	11	11	Other		4	1	3	2	1
						18 (4/1-9/30/04)		37 (10/1/04-3/31/05)		
NUMBER OF STATEMENTS	46 ALL	53 ALL	55 ALL		11	12	9	15	5	3
	%	%	%	**ASSETS**	%	%	%	%	%	%
Cash & Equivalents	12.5	8.5	13.0		20.9	9.7		11.2		
Trade Receivables (net)	38.8	39.6	33.5		19.8	21.2		40.8		
Inventory	12.1	16.2	18.1		17.9	25.5		20.6		
All Other Current	6.2	5.0	3.9		1.1	.8		4.6		
Total Current	69.6	69.3	68.5		59.7	57.3		77.1		
Fixed Assets (net)	21.5	20.7	21.6		29.5	26.3		11.9		
Intangibles (net)	2.2	2.2	3.6		1.1	5.5		6.4		
All Other Non-Current	6.7	7.8	6.3		9.7	10.9		4.6		
Total	100.0	100.0	100.0		100.0	100.0		100.0		
				LIABILITIES						
Notes Payable-Short Term	10.5	10.7	9.9		8.4	10.8		12.5		
Cur. Mat.-L/T/D	3.4	6.0	4.8		7.6	6.7		4.2		
Trade Payables	21.5	19.8	20.3		12.5	19.3		28.6		
Income Taxes Payable	.8	.2	.2		.0	.2		.4		
All Other Current	16.8	16.0	14.6		21.6	7.4		15.3		
Total Current	53.1	52.6	49.8		50.1	44.4		61.0		
Long-Term Debt	8.1	14.1	15.2		19.7	22.8		8.0		
Deferred Taxes	.3	.5	.3		.0	.0		.6		
All Other Non-Current	4.5	4.6	7.8		17.3	9.7		4.7		
Net Worth	34.0	28.3	26.8		12.8	23.1		25.7		
Total Liabilities & Net Worth	100.0	100.0	100.0		100.0	100.0		100.0		
				INCOME DATA						
Net Sales	100.0	100.0	100.0		100.0	100.0		100.0		
Gross Profit										
Operating Expenses	96.7	97.9	95.3		92.3	93.3		97.8		
Operating Profit	3.3	2.1	4.7		7.7	6.7		2.2		
All Other Expenses (net)	.8	.3	.8		1.7	1.1		.2		
Profit Before Taxes	2.5	1.8	3.9		6.0	5.6		2.0		
				RATIOS						
Current	2.2	2.2	2.0		9.5	1.7		1.8		
	1.3	1.4	1.5		1.0	1.5		1.4		
	1.0	1.0	1.1		.7	1.0		1.0		
Quick	1.7	1.7	1.4		3.6	1.2		1.3		
	1.0	1.0	.9		.8	.7		.8		
	.7	.6	.5		.5	.3		.5		
Sales/Receivables	26 13.8	33 11.2	16 22.3		0 UND	0 UND		26 14.2		
	43 8.6	47 7.7	35 10.4		19 19.5	22 16.8		35 10.4		
	56 6.5	72 5.1	62 5.9		44 8.3	29 12.7		54 6.7		
Cost of Sales/Inventory										
Cost of Sales/Payables										
Sales/Working Capital	9.3	8.5	10.1		16.2	10.5		10.1		
	22.4	17.7	16.2		−105.1	17.5		17.4		
	189.8	UND	343.0		−14.3	656.5		−572.8		
EBIT/Interest	13.0	6.1	14.5			10.2		16.9		
	(38) 3.5	(45) 2.0	(45) 4.1			(11) 4.8		(11) 10.6		
	.9	.4	1.6			2.0		1.5		
Net Profit + Depr., Dep., Amort./Cur. Mat. L/T/D	7.9		5.2							
	(12) 3.0		(12) 2.0							
	.8		1.3							
Fixed/Worth	.3	.3	.4		.0	.5		.2		
	.6	.7	.8		4.8	2.5		.7		
	1.6	3.7	7.3		−2.6	−1.9		−16.6		
Debt/Worth	.8	1.0	1.3		2.3	1.4		1.8		
	1.9	2.6	3.0		23.0	6.7		4.7		
	7.6	24.6	31.4		−5.4	−10.6		−104.8		
% Profit Before Taxes/Tangible Net Worth	54.5	45.1	68.1					166.2		
	(40) 14.0	(44) 8.5	(43) 34.4					(11) 49.0		
	2.2	−.2	10.1					31.5		
% Profit Before Taxes/Total Assets	8.7	9.6	17.1		28.8	24.2		17.1		
	5.0	2.1	9.4		7.4	10.3		10.8		
	.6	−1.9	2.2		−8.3	4.2		2.2		
Sales/Net Fixed Assets	34.5	38.2	60.2		UND	31.6		60.4		
	24.0	20.0	21.6		14.8	14.6		38.6		
	15.4	12.1	12.2		6.4	7.3		17.1		
Sales/Total Assets	4.3	4.1	4.6		4.6	4.8		5.0		
	3.5	3.0	3.4		3.1	3.1		3.7		
	2.5	2.0	2.5		2.1	2.0		3.1		
% Depr., Dep., Amort./Sales	1.1	1.2	.9			2.0		.3		
	(43) 1.7	(46) 1.9	(45) 2.1			(11) 2.2		(13) .6		
	2.6	2.4	2.6			2.5		2.1		
% Officers', Directors', Owners' Comp/Sales	3.2	3.0	3.0							
	(27) 6.2	(35) 5.1	(32) 6.5							
	10.3	10.0	10.3							
Net Sales ($)	403808M	361416M	474036M		6092M	21951M	34433M	103234M	65563M	242763M
Total Assets ($)	137177M	127460M	136268M		4422M	8313M	12382M	28996M	21404M	60751M

M = $ thousand   MM = $ million
See Pages 11 through 21 for Explanation of Ratios and Data

Current Data Sorted By Assets   Comparative Historical Data

0-500M	500M-2MM	2-10MM	10-50MM	50-100MM	100-250MM	Type of Statement	ALL 4/1/00-3/31/01	ALL 4/1/01-3/31/02
1	2		1			Unqualified	8	7
	1	4				Reviewed	9	7
12	9	6				Compiled	22	20
31	14	3				Tax Returns	28	39
14	10	6	2	1	3	Other	23	43
	20 (4/1-9/30/04)			101 (10/1/04-3/31/05)				
58	36	19	4	1	3	NUMBER OF STATEMENTS	90	116
%	%	%	%	%	%	ASSETS	%	%
21.3	16.0	12.4				Cash & Equivalents	19.8	17.5
2.5	7.0	8.7				Trade Receivables (net)	3.1	3.6
11.9	12.4	11.5				Inventory	9.2	11.1
.9	9.0	4.0				All Other Current	1.3	1.9
36.7	44.4	36.6				Total Current	33.5	34.1
51.4	41.8	43.1				Fixed Assets (net)	47.0	48.5
5.3	2.4	9.3				Intangibles (net)	12.2	9.6
6.6	11.4	11.1				All Other Non-Current	7.4	7.9
100.0	100.0	100.0				Total	100.0	100.0
						LIABILITIES		
12.1	3.6	6.0				Notes Payable-Short Term	5.6	9.2
6.9	2.6	3.8				Cur. Mat.-L/T/D	5.6	6.0
7.0	7.9	13.3				Trade Payables	10.4	7.0
.0	.2	.1				Income Taxes Payable	.3	.3
13.2	24.2	16.3				All Other Current	18.9	18.6
39.2	38.5	39.5				Total Current	40.8	41.1
37.5	30.7	18.1				Long-Term Debt	28.9	25.1
.0	.1	.1				Deferred Taxes	.1	.0
9.4	7.4	12.7				All Other Non-Current	10.4	8.0
13.9	23.3	29.6				Net Worth	19.8	25.9
100.0	100.0	100.0				Total Liabilities & Net Worth	100.0	100.0
						INCOME DATA		
100.0	100.0	100.0				Net Sales	100.0	100.0
						Gross Profit		
91.4	94.9	94.5				Operating Expenses	93.9	94.8
8.6	5.1	5.5				Operating Profit	6.1	5.2
2.3	2.2	.3				All Other Expenses (net)	.9	1.0
6.3	2.9	5.2				Profit Before Taxes	5.2	4.2
						RATIOS		
3.5	1.9	1.7					1.9	1.4
1.2	1.2	.9				Current	1.1	.9
.4	.7	.4					.5	.4
2.0	1.1	.8					1.1	1.0
.8	.5	.5				Quick	(89) .7	(115) .3
.2	.2	.1					.2	.2
0 UND	0 UND	0 UND					0 UND	0 UND
0 UND	0 UND	1 437.5				Sales/Receivables	0 UND	0 UND
0 UND	2 223.8	8 47.2					0 UND	2 230.7
						Cost of Sales/Inventory		
						Cost of Sales/Payables		
23.6	13.5	17.0					24.5	27.2
211.0	61.4	-56.7				Sales/Working Capital	258.5	-106.9
-16.0	-22.3	-12.0					-22.4	-12.2
8.1	19.5	17.0					9.0	9.0
(38) 5.1	(30) 4.7	(18) 5.7				EBIT/Interest	(75) 3.8	(94) 3.3
.7	1.4	2.7					1.8	1.3
						Net Profit + Depr., Dep.,	5.1	6.7
						Amort./Cur. Mat. L/T/D	(15) 3.7	(12) 3.3
							2.0	1.3
.7	.7	1.1					.9	.9
2.5	1.6	2.1				Fixed/Worth	3.0	2.2
-2.5	4.2	5.8					-3.1	-9.8
1.0	.8	1.4					.9	1.0
2.8	3.0	4.7				Debt/Worth	4.7	3.4
-4.4	7.4	8.6					-6.4	-13.7
167.9	68.0	71.0				% Profit Before Taxes/Tangible	100.0	83.5
(38) 64.4	(29) 35.1	(17) 38.1				Net Worth	(61) 48.6	(80) 47.1
12.5	13.8	25.2					16.6	10.2
44.8	19.9	19.2				% Profit Before Taxes/Total	39.1	28.6
18.2	7.1	6.9				Assets	13.0	10.4
.0	2.1	4.0					4.0	.3
25.2	14.7	12.0					22.4	20.9
10.3	8.7	9.3				Sales/Net Fixed Assets	10.5	9.2
4.3	4.1	3.7					5.7	4.7
8.7	4.1	3.7					6.2	6.0
6.0	3.1	2.7				Sales/Total Assets	4.3	3.5
2.6	2.2	1.4					2.5	2.4
.9	1.5	1.1					1.1	1.0
(50) 1.8	(33) 2.4	(18) 2.0				% Depr., Dep., Amort./Sales	(78) 2.1	(96) 2.0
3.5	3.2	3.3					3.1	3.1
3.6	2.4					% Officers', Directors',	3.0	3.5
(29) 6.7	(14) 4.6					Owners' Comp/Sales	(45) 5.5	(54) 5.3
11.3	7.1						13.6	11.4
52457M	119589M	209602M	338252M	331699M	960571M	Net Sales ($)	762042M	1440241M
10744M	39777M	78591M	100205M	69632M	547106M	Total Assets ($)	227041M	610369M

© RMA 2005

M = $ thousand   MM = $ million
See Pages 11 through 21 for Explanation of Ratios and Data

Comparative Historical Data · Current Data Sorted By Sales

			Type of Statement						
2	6	4	Unqualified	1	1	1			1
5	4	5	Reviewed			1	1	3	
16	30	27	Compiled	6	13	5	3		
55	62	49	Tax Returns	24	16	3	3	2	1
36	32	36	Other	10	8	2	6	3	7
4/1/02-3/31/03	4/1/03-3/31/04	4/1/04-3/31/05		20 (4/1-9/30/04)			101 (10/1/04-3/31/05)		
ALL	ALL	ALL		0-1MM	1-3MM	3-5MM	5-10MM	10-25MM	25MM & OVER
114	134	121	NUMBER OF STATEMENTS	41	38	12	13	8	9
%	%	%	ASSETS	%	%	%	%	%	%
21.8	20.4	17.9	Cash & Equivalents	22.2	14.7	19.3	14.6		
3.1	2.5	4.8	Trade Receivables (net)	1.3	7.6	10.2	6.3		
10.9	11.0	12.0	Inventory	12.8	11.2	11.7	15.2		
1.0	3.8	3.9	All Other Current	.7	6.7	4.5	5.4		
36.7	37.6	38.7	Total Current	37.0	40.2	45.8	41.5		
48.7	47.1	47.4	Fixed Assets (net)	53.5	44.2	36.5	45.6		
6.9	7.5	5.2	Intangibles (net)	3.7	5.7	9.4	2.1		
7.6	7.8	8.6	All Other Non-Current	5.9	10.0	8.3	10.8		
100.0	100.0	100.0	Total	100.0	100.0	100.0	100.0		
			LIABILITIES						
7.1	10.5	8.4	Notes Payable-Short Term	11.6	7.9	.2	10.7		
6.6	6.8	5.1	Cur. Mat.-L/T/D	7.3	3.4	6.2	2.3		
7.1	5.7	8.5	Trade Payables	7.0	8.8	5.7	8.2		
.3	.2	.1	Income Taxes Payable	.0	.2	.1	.0		
23.6	19.5	17.8	All Other Current	13.7	18.1	24.4	20.2		
44.7	42.8	39.9	Total Current	39.6	38.4	36.5	41.4		
29.4	31.1	33.9	Long-Term Debt	44.7	26.0	36.9	18.4		
.0	.0	.0	Deferred Taxes	.0	.0	.2	.0		
20.6	8.5	9.5	All Other Non-Current	9.5	10.3	4.0	7.3		
5.3	17.6	16.7	Net Worth	6.2	25.3	22.4	33.0		
100.0	100.0	100.0	Total Liabilities & Net Worth	100.0	100.0	100.0	100.0		
			INCOME DATA						
100.0	100.0	100.0	Net Sales	100.0	100.0	100.0	100.0		
			Gross Profit						
95.3	94.4	92.9	Operating Expenses	88.6	95.5	97.0	93.9		
4.7	5.6	7.1	Operating Profit	11.4	4.5	3.0	6.1		
1.2	1.3	2.0	All Other Expenses (net)	4.1	.9	1.1	.1		
3.6	4.2	5.1	Profit Before Taxes	7.3	3.6	1.9	6.0		
			RATIOS						
1.8	2.2	2.2		2.8	3.9	1.6	1.4		
.9	1.0	1.1	Current	1.1	1.2	1.2	1.0		
.4	.5	.5		.4	.5	.8	.6		
1.3	1.3	1.3		1.5	2.0	1.0	1.0		
(112) .5	.6	.6	Quick	.7	.5	.6	.5		
.2	.2	.2		.2	.2	.4	.1		
0 UND	0 UND	0 UND		0 UND	0 UND	0 UND	0 UND		
0 UND	0 UND	0 UND	Sales/Receivables	0 UND	0 UND	0 UND	1 728.6		
0 999.8	1 406.3	1 588.6		0 UND	0 UND	4 83.9	6 66.0		
			Cost of Sales/Inventory						
			Cost of Sales/Payables						
22.1	21.0	22.5		24.2	11.4	20.2	31.2		
-290.8	UND	258.9	Sales/Working Capital	267.0	68.0	61.1	186.9		
-13.7	-16.4	-16.9		-11.9	-16.0	-30.8	-21.5		
6.5	12.0	13.3		6.6	16.6	6.8	20.8		
(84) 2.3	(102) 3.5	(94) 4.7	EBIT/Interest	(24) 4.7	(31) 5.4	(11) 2.6	6.6		
.8	1.5	1.5		.6	.6	1.7	3.3		
		5.5	Net Profit + Depr., Dep.,						
	(15)	2.7	Amort./Cur. Mat. L/T/D						
		1.3							
1.0	.8	.7		.8	.6	1.0	.8		
5.5	2.3	2.3	Fixed/Worth	2.9	2.0	1.5	1.3		
-2.9	-2.9	-5.8		-1.9	-6.3	NM	3.0		
1.4	.8	1.1		1.1	.7	1.4	1.0		
7.3	3.8	3.5	Debt/Worth	4.0	2.6	6.1	2.2		
-5.1	-6.5	-10.8		-3.8	-12.0	NM	5.7		
78.0	105.9	109.2	% Profit Before Taxes/Tangible	212.5	66.2		106.4		
(68) 21.4	(89) 36.8	(87) 50.0	Net Worth	(27) 70.6	(28) 43.6		(12) 46.6		
4.7	7.8	17.2		2.2	17.1		32.3		
30.3	26.9	27.0	% Profit Before Taxes/Total	51.3	23.6	11.9	35.3		
6.9	10.5	10.7	Assets	13.3	14.1	4.4	8.8		
-.4	1.4	1.7		.0	.8	3.1	4.6		
22.6	20.9	17.7		18.3	23.4	15.0	14.5		
9.4	10.5	9.1	Sales/Net Fixed Assets	9.3	8.8	11.4	9.1		
4.4	5.5	3.9		2.8	4.5	8.2	3.7		
6.6	6.7	6.0		8.1	6.1	5.0	5.0		
3.9	4.1	3.4	Sales/Total Assets	5.7	3.5	3.1	3.7		
2.5	2.4	2.1		2.1	2.5	1.9	1.9		
1.2	1.0	1.1		1.1	.7	1.9	.9		
(91) 2.0	(112) 2.1	(106) 2.1	% Depr., Dep., Amort./Sales	(35) 2.4	(35) 1.6	(11) 2.8	(12) 1.5		
4.8	3.7	3.3		4.9	3.0	3.2	2.7		
3.4	3.9	2.5		5.2	2.5				
(61) 5.8	(69) 7.8	(52) 5.4	% Officers', Directors',	(18) 7.3	(19) 5.2				
11.6	13.5	8.5	Owners' Comp/Sales	13.1	8.7				
1411192M	3420298M	2012170M	Net Sales ($)	17958M	74491M	46644M	91674M	125389M	1656014M
478279M	713175M	846055M	Total Assets ($)	7842M	26760M	16612M	33941M	39410M	721490M

M = $ thousand   MM = $ million
See Pages 11 through 21 for Explanation of Ratios and Data

Current Data Sorted By Assets							Comparative Historical Data	
						Type of Statement		
	2	4	3	1		Unqualified	7	11
8	9	9	3	1		Reviewed	35	22
29	52	25	1			Compiled	107	99
51	40	7	1			Tax Returns	46	59
12	25	21	2	2		Other	54	61
86 (4/1-9/30/04)			222 (10/1/04-3/31/05)				**4/1/00-3/31/01**	**4/1/01-3/31/02**
0-500M	**500M-2MM**	**2-10MM**	**10-50MM**	**50-100MM**	**100-250MM**		**ALL**	**ALL**
100	128	66	10	4		**NUMBER OF STATEMENTS**	249	252
%	%	%	%	%	%	**ASSETS**	%	%
11.1	10.4	9.2	4.0			Cash & Equivalents	10.7	9.2
16.3	14.6	10.0	13.4		D	Trade Receivables (net)	14.3	15.7
7.1	4.6	3.6	10.1		A	Inventory	4.6	4.8
1.4	1.2	2.3	.6		T	All Other Current	3.1	2.6
35.9	30.9	25.1	28.2		A	Total Current	32.7	32.3
41.4	47.8	43.7	32.2			Fixed Assets (net)	45.6	46.9
12.5	10.8	5.5	5.7		N	Intangibles (net)	8.1	8.2
10.1	10.6	25.7	33.9		O	All Other Non-Current	13.6	12.6
100.0	100.0	100.0	100.0		T	Total	100.0	100.0
					A	**LIABILITIES**		
7.0	5.1	4.1	5.1		V	Notes Payable-Short Term	5.0	5.7
5.1	3.6	2.4	3.8		A	Cur. Mat.-L/T/D	3.5	4.0
9.6	4.5	3.4	4.9		I	Trade Payables	5.0	6.0
.3	.1	.1	.1		L	Income Taxes Payable	.2	.2
16.5	7.0	9.0	4.7		A	All Other Current	7.5	6.8
38.6	20.4	19.0	18.7		B	Total Current	21.2	22.6
38.1	46.0	37.9	31.8		L	Long-Term Debt	33.0	37.6
.1	.3	1.5	6.7		E	Deferred Taxes	.2	.1
10.3	4.4	14.2	24.5			All Other Non-Current	7.7	7.8
12.9	28.9	27.4	18.2			Net Worth	37.9	31.9
100.0	100.0	100.0	100.0			Total Liabilities & Net Worth	100.0	100.0
						INCOME DATA		
100.0	100.0	100.0	100.0			Net Sales	100.0	100.0
						Gross Profit		
94.9	92.4	89.9	95.8			Operating Expenses	92.8	91.5
5.1	7.6	10.1	4.2			Operating Profit	7.2	8.5
1.8	3.1	3.8	1.5			All Other Expenses (net)	1.0	3.2
3.4	4.6	6.3	2.7			Profit Before Taxes	6.1	5.4
						RATIOS		
2.9	3.5	2.6	4.3				3.1	3.0
1.1	1.9	1.3	1.5			Current	1.6	1.6
.5	.8	.7	1.1				.9	.9
2.1	2.7	2.2	2.5				2.7	2.5
.8	1.4	1.0	1.2			Quick	1.2	1.2
.3	.6	.6	.7				.6	.6
0 UND	**19** 19.6	**21** 17.7	**30** 12.3				**20** 18.0	**18** 20.0
24 15.2	**35** 10.4	**35** 10.5	**43** 8.4			Sales/Receivables	**37** 9.8	**36** 10.2
38 9.6	**47** 7.7	**49** 7.5	**215** 1.7				**54** 6.8	**49** 7.4
						Cost of Sales/Inventory		
						Cost of Sales/Payables		
8.8	5.6	7.0	2.5				4.9	6.2
48.3	11.6	14.7	9.6			Sales/Working Capital	12.5	14.8
−12.1	−22.8	−19.0	NM				−50.1	−66.4
7.2	5.7	4.6	3.8				5.8	5.3
(81) 2.5	(111) 1.9	(55) 1.7	2.2			EBIT/Interest	(205) 2.4	(213) 2.2
.6	.8	1.1	1.5				1.2	1.0
	5.5	5.8				Net Profit + Depr., Dep.,	4.3	4.0
	(20) 1.9	(14) 1.4				Amort./Cur. Mat. L /T/D	(67) 2.2	(42) 1.9
	1.3	.7					1.1	1.2
.7	.7	.8	1.2				.6	.7
2.5	2.4	1.9	1.9			Fixed/Worth	1.4	1.6
−1.0	−15.5	4.7	−2.8				7.0	9.4
.7	.7	1.4	2.0				.5	.7
4.9	2.7	3.8	9.1			Debt/Worth	1.7	2.3
−3.1	−24.4	16.2	−34.0				11.6	13.3
43.3	32.1	20.7				% Profit Before Taxes/Tangible	32.6	43.5
(61) 12.9	(93) 15.3	(56) 8.7				Net Worth	(205) 13.2	(195) 16.6
.0	.9	.9					2.9	2.0
14.0	11.0	6.6	4.8			% Profit Before Taxes/Total	10.4	13.9
4.2	3.1	2.1	2.3			Assets	5.1	5.3
−1.5	−.4	.3	.7				.8	.0
13.9	6.0	4.4	14.9				6.8	7.2
6.3	3.6	1.9	1.9			Sales/Net Fixed Assets	2.9	3.6
3.3	1.6	1.1	.9				1.4	1.6
3.2	2.2	1.1	.9				2.0	2.3
2.2	1.3	.7	.5			Sales/Total Assets	1.2	1.5
1.3	.8	.3	.3				.7	.8
1.8	2.6	3.7	1.8				2.7	2.2
(87) 3.7	(117) 4.8	(60) 5.6	4.0			% Depr., Dep., Amort./Sales	(227) 4.5	(234) 3.6
6.2	7.9	7.7	5.9				6.9	6.1
7.5	7.8	4.6				% Officers', Directors',	6.8	7.5
(67) 12.1	(91) 10.9	(35) 7.6				Owners' Comp/Sales	(155) 11.2	(154) 10.9
18.0	16.4	13.5					16.9	16.6
71892M	**187783M**	**215875M**	**166907M**	**81788M**		Net Sales ($)	**1105969M**	**486911M**
29003M	**133571M**	**279816M**	**217446M**	**238532M**		Total Assets ($)	**1132167M**	**621343M**

M = $ thousand MM = $ million

See Pages 11 through 21 for Explanation of Ratios and Data

Comparative Historical Data			**Type of Statement**	**Current Data Sorted By Sales**					
14	9	10	Unqualified	2	3	1		3	1
24	29	30	Reviewed	9	11	4	5		1
104	130	107	Compiled	40	43	18	5	1	
69	94	99	Tax Returns	63	28	7	1		
59	55	62	Other	24	27	5	3	2	1
4/1/02-3/31/03	4/1/03-3/31/04	4/1/04-3/31/05		86 (4/1-9/30/04)			222 (10/1/04-3/31/05)		
ALL	ALL	ALL		0-1MM	1-3MM	3-5MM	5-10MM	10-25MM	25MM & OVER
270	317	308	**NUMBER OF STATEMENTS**	138	112	35	14	6	3
%	%	%	**ASSETS**	%	%	%	%	%	%
10.9	11.0	10.1	Cash & Equivalents	10.5	9.7	10.9	9.1		
15.3	15.2	14.1	Trade Receivables (net)	11.2	18.5	13.2	10.9		
5.1	4.3	5.5	Inventory	6.2	4.4	4.0	4.3		
2.5	3.1	1.5	All Other Current	1.5	1.1	2.5	2.3		
33.8	33.6	31.2	Total Current	29.4	33.6	30.5	26.7		
42.8	45.0	43.9	Fixed Assets (net)	46.5	42.6	44.3	40.0		
8.2	7.9	10.0	Intangibles (net)	13.3	8.3	5.6	4.9		
15.2	13.5	15.0	All Other Non-Current	10.9	15.5	19.6	28.4		
100.0	100.0	100.0	Total	100.0	100.0	100.0	100.0		
			LIABILITIES						
6.6	4.4	5.4	Notes Payable-Short Term	5.7	5.2	5.2	5.1		
4.0	4.3	3.8	Cur. Mat.-L/T/D	4.0	3.2	5.8	3.4		
4.5	6.0	5.9	Trade Payables	5.1	7.7	3.4	5.3		
.2	.3	.2	Income Taxes Payable	.2	.2	.2	.2		
7.6	9.8	10.5	All Other Current	10.7	12.1	7.8	3.9		
23.0	24.7	25.9	Total Current	25.6	28.5	22.4	17.9		
35.7	37.9	41.0	Long-Term Debt	49.5	32.6	41.5	31.8		
.1	.1	.7	Deferred Taxes	.1	1.7	.2	.1		
11.1	10.4	9.6	All Other Non-Current	9.5	8.6	8.6	13.1		
30.1	26.9	22.8	Net Worth	15.4	28.5	27.4	37.1		
100.0	100.0	100.0	Total Liabilities & Net Worth	100.0	100.0	100.0	100.0		
			INCOME DATA						
100.0	100.0	100.0	Net Sales	100.0	100.0	100.0	100.0		
			Gross Profit						
93.8	92.3	92.8	Operating Expenses	90.1	94.9	95.0	94.8		
6.2	7.7	7.2	Operating Profit	9.9	5.1	5.0	5.2		
2.7	3.2	2.7	All Other Expenses (net)	5.5	.6	.4	-.3		
3.4	4.5	4.6	Profit Before Taxes	4.3	4.5	4.6	5.5		
			RATIOS						
3.2	3.1	3.1	Current	3.5	2.8	4.2	3.6		
1.7	1.5	1.5		1.4	1.4	1.7	1.7		
.9	.8	.7		.5	.8	.7	.9		
2.7	2.6	2.4	Quick	2.5	2.3	3.5	2.1		
1.3	1.2	1.1		.9	1.2	1.4	1.3		
.6	.6	.5		.3	.6	.6	.8		
22 16.7	17 22.0	15 23.6	Sales/Receivables	3 114.5	24 15.4	18 19.8	20 17.9		
36 10.2	34 10.6	32 11.5		26 13.9	37 9.9	29 12.5	37 9.9		
50 7.3	52 7.0	46 8.0		45 8.2	48 7.6	43 8.6	44 8.2		
			Cost of Sales/Inventory						
			Cost of Sales/Payables						
5.5	5.4	6.9	Sales/Working Capital	6.1	7.2	7.5	6.0		
12.4	15.8	15.9		16.6	19.3	12.4	16.0		
-58.1	-34.5	-19.0		-10.2	-21.5	-31.2	-170.5		
4.8	6.0	5.4	EBIT/Interest	4.4	7.5	5.0	5.7		
(221) 2.2	(279) 2.2	(261) 2.0		(110) 1.7	(95) 1.9	(34) 2.4	(13) 3.3		
1.0	.8	.8		.5	1.1	1.2	1.3		
3.0	3.6	4.1	Net Profit + Depr., Dep.,	9.2	3.2				
(51) 1.9	(60) 1.6	(46) 1.9	Amort./Cur. Mat. L/T/D	(10) 1.8	(21) 1.9				
1.2	1.1	.9		-.7	1.2				
.6	.7	.7	Fixed/Worth	.8	.7	.7	.8		
1.6	1.9	2.2		3.7	1.7	1.2	1.1		
17.5	-146.1	-6.7		-2.1	52.5	6.4	2.1		
.7	.8	.9	Debt/Worth	1.0	.7	.7	.8		
2.2	2.9	3.9		8.9	2.2	2.2	1.9		
33.2	-273.5	-18.8		-4.0	107.0	10.2	7.2		
31.9	37.0	32.7	% Profit Before Taxes/Tangible	33.3	36.9	15.6	36.1		
(209) 10.5	(237) 13.0	(219) 10.9	Net Worth	(85) 10.1	(86) 13.0	(29) 6.0	(12) 12.0		
.7	.6	1.0		-3.7	1.8	.7	9.9		
9.6	10.5	10.2	% Profit Before Taxes/Total	10.0	13.1	8.9	7.2		
3.8	3.7	3.1	Assets	2.4	3.2	3.2	5.2		
-.2	-.4	.0		-1.5	.3	.3	.4		
7.6	6.9	8.2	Sales/Net Fixed Assets	7.7	9.1	8.1	6.9		
3.6	3.5	3.8		3.3	4.7	3.6	2.9		
2.0	1.6	1.7		1.5	1.8	2.0	2.0		
2.2	2.2	2.3	Sales/Total Assets	1.8	2.8	2.4	1.6		
1.4	1.2	1.3		1.2	1.8	1.5	1.1		
.8	.7	.7		.6	.9	.8	.9		
2.4	2.6	2.5	% Depr., Dep., Amort./Sales	3.2	2.3	2.7	2.5		
(251) 4.3	(295) 4.7	(278) 4.4		(122) 5.5	(101) 3.6	(32) 3.9	3.6		
7.0	7.8	7.4		9.2	6.7	6.3	4.9		
7.8	6.6	6.9	% Officers', Directors',	8.2	6.7	3.8			
(179) 11.1	(209) 11.5	(196) 10.9	Owners' Comp/Sales	(78) 12.0	(84) 10.9	(25) 7.7			
16.4	15.8	15.7		18.0	15.7	12.0			
1252586M	1463281M	724245M	Net Sales ($)	74942M	192330M	131033M	95386M	93081M	137473M
940782M	1144457M	898368M	Total Assets ($)	94176M	191753M	156617M	102291M	226675M	126856M

© RMA 2005

M = $ thousand   MM = $ million

See Pages 11 through 21 for Explanation of Ratios and Data

Current Data Sorted By Assets | Comparative Historical Data

0-500M	500M-2MM	2-10MM	10-50MM	50-100MM	100-250MM	Type of Statement	4/1/00-3/31/01 ALL	4/1/01-3/31/02 ALL
	1		1		2	Unqualified		
	1	2	1			Reviewed		
1	4	2				Compiled		
5	2	1		1		Tax Returns		
2	4	6				Other		
8	12	11	2	1	2	**NUMBER OF STATEMENTS**		
%	%	%	%	%	%	**ASSETS**	%	%
	7.1	6.5				Cash & Equivalents		
	16.8	9.7				Trade Receivables (net)	D	D
	21.7	3.1				Inventory	A	A
	2.6	.6				All Other Current	T	T
	48.1	19.8				Total Current	A	A
	41.5	34.6				Fixed Assets (net)		
	4.8	4.9				Intangibles (net)	N	N
	5.6	40.7				All Other Non-Current	O	O
	100.0	100.0				Total	T	T
						LIABILITIES	A	A
	10.9	4.1				Notes Payable-Short Term	V	V
	2.5	8.9				Cur. Mat.-L/T/D	A	A
	6.7	3.2				Trade Payables	I	I
	.0	.2				Income Taxes Payable	L	L
	12.5	4.9				All Other Current	A	A
	32.7	21.3				Total Current	B	B
	29.2	20.6				Long-Term Debt	L	L
	.2	.1				Deferred Taxes	E	E
	6.3	20.9				All Other Non-Current		
	31.7	37.1				Net Worth		
	100.0	100.0				Total Liabilities & Net Worth		
						INCOME DATA		
	100.0	100.0				Net Sales		
						Gross Profit		
	87.0	95.8				Operating Expenses		
	13.0	4.2				Operating Profit		
	3.6	-.9				All Other Expenses (net)		
	9.4	5.1				Profit Before Taxes		
						RATIOS		
	4.8	3.5						
	1.6	1.7				Current		
	.7	.6						
	3.6	3.0						
	.5	1.4				Quick		
	.4	.6						
22 16.6		27 13.4						
49 7.5		33 11.0				Sales/Receivables		
126 2.9		59 6.2						
						Cost of Sales/Inventory		
						Cost of Sales/Payables		
	1.7	3.9						
	8.9	6.0				Sales/Working Capital		
	-13.3	-12.5						
	6.5							
	(11) 3.7					EBIT/Interest		
	.0							
						Net Profit + Depr., Dep., Amort./Cur. Mat. L/T/D		
	.5	.2						
	2.0	1.0				Fixed/Worth		
	23.5	5.7						
	.9	.5						
	3.8	2.2				Debt/Worth		
	51.0	-91.7						
	56.0							
	(10) 15.7					% Profit Before Taxes/Tangible Net Worth		
	-11.6							
	6.9	6.3						
	3.4	1.4				% Profit Before Taxes/Total Assets		
	-1.9	-.5						
	8.9	4.3						
	2.2	3.6				Sales/Net Fixed Assets		
	.5	1.3						
	2.3	1.3						
	.6	.5				Sales/Total Assets		
	.2	.3						
	1.6							
	(10) 4.1					% Depr., Dep., Amort./Sales		
	10.4							
						% Officers', Directors', Owners' Comp/Sales		
3578M	17958M	31422M	42218M	9911M	113847M	Net Sales ($)		
1788M	13315M	47938M	46843M	57988M	306286M	Total Assets ($)		

M = $ thousand   MM = $ million
See Pages 11 through 21 for Explanation of Ratios and Data

Comparative Historical Data / Current Data Sorted By Sales

			Type of Statement						
3	5	4	Unqualified	1			1	1	1
6	3	4	Reviewed	2	1				1
15	12	7	Compiled	5	2				
2	14	8	Tax Returns	8					
13	10	13	Other	3	2	4	4		
4/1/02-	4/1/03-	4/1/04-			8 (4/1-9/30/04)		28 (10/1/04-3/31/05)		
3/31/03	3/31/04	3/31/05							
ALL	ALL	ALL		0-1MM	1-3MM	3-5MM	5-10MM	10-25MM	25MM & OVER
39	44	36	**NUMBER OF STATEMENTS**	19	5	4	5	1	2
%	%	%	**ASSETS**	%	%	%	%	%	%
10.4	9.2	8.8	Cash & Equivalents	7.4					
14.3	15.0	14.3	Trade Receivables (net)	12.8					
10.2	13.1	15.0	Inventory	17.0					
1.5	3.5	1.7	All Other Current	.8					
36.5	40.8	39.8	Total Current	37.9					
42.2	35.2	36.9	Fixed Assets (net)	38.1					
6.3	7.4	3.2	Intangibles (net)	2.9					
15.0	16.7	20.0	All Other Non-Current	21.2					
100.0	100.0	100.0	Total	100.0					
			LIABILITIES						
5.4	5.0	8.8	Notes Payable-Short Term	8.9					
3.2	4.3	4.6	Cur. Mat.-L/T/D	7.6					
3.8	7.7	6.0	Trade Payables	4.4					
.3	.1	.2	Income Taxes Payable	.0					
7.7	6.4	10.1	All Other Current	11.4					
20.4	23.5	29.7	Total Current	32.3					
35.6	25.2	24.2	Long-Term Debt	31.0					
.3	.3	.1	Deferred Taxes	.1					
9.6	14.4	10.4	All Other Non-Current	5.1					
34.0	36.5	35.6	Net Worth	31.4					
100.0	100.0	100.0	Total Liabilities & Net Worth	100.0					
			INCOME DATA						
100.0	100.0	100.0	Net Sales	100.0					
			Gross Profit						
87.4	95.5	92.2	Operating Expenses	89.9					
12.6	4.5	7.8	Operating Profit	10.1					
3.5	.7	.8	All Other Expenses (net)	2.1					
9.1	3.7	7.0	Profit Before Taxes	8.1					
			RATIOS						
3.6	3.4	3.4		3.4					
1.8	2.0	1.7	Current	1.5					
.8	1.0	.7		.5					
2.4	2.6	2.6		3.4					
1.2	1.3	.9	Quick	.5					
.4	.4	.4		.4					
19 19.1	19 18.9	21 17.6		18 20.4					
35 10.4	31 11.7	45 8.1	Sales/Receivables	32 11.3					
79 4.6	46 7.9	106 3.4		122 3.0					
			Cost of Sales/Inventory						
			Cost of Sales/Payables						
2.3	4.5	2.4		2.4					
8.1	11.4	6.0	Sales/Working Capital	6.0					
−20.2	233.6	−16.0		−11.9					
8.0	7.4	15.6		6.3					
(33) 2.6	(35) 4.0	(29) 4.5	EBIT/Interest	(16) 4.2					
1.4	2.0	1.0		.7					
	7.2		Net Profit + Depr., Dep.,						
	(11) 2.9		Amort./Cur. Mat. L/T/D						
	2.2								
.4	.5	.4		.3					
1.5	.9	1.0	Fixed/Worth	1.7					
24.2	7.4	5.1		30.2					
.6	.4	.5		.8					
2.0	2.6	2.1	Debt/Worth	3.3					
45.5	21.0	51.0		UND					
27.9	36.9	36.0		38.7					
(31) 12.2	(36) 14.6	(29) 11.0	% Profit Before Taxes/Tangible Net Worth	(15) 11.5					
2.3	3.7	.6		−1.2					
8.4	9.8	9.9		10.8					
4.0	3.4	3.9	% Profit Before Taxes/Total Assets	4.3					
.9	1.0	−.5		−.5					
6.6	10.4	8.3		8.6					
2.1	5.2	3.8	Sales/Net Fixed Assets	4.9					
1.0	2.1	1.2		.8					
1.2	2.7	2.2		2.3					
.7	1.3	.7	Sales/Total Assets	.4					
.4	.6	.3		.2					
2.6	2.0	1.9		2.8					
(32) 3.7	(40) 3.5	(30) 4.1	% Depr., Dep., Amort./Sales	(17) 4.5					
5.5	6.3	6.2		6.7					
3.8	4.1	4.5							
(16) 9.2	(24) 8.8	(16) 9.6	% Officers', Directors', Owners' Comp/Sales						
16.5	13.8	28.5							
238138M	226847M	218934M	Net Sales ($)	8989M	9687M	14182M	35086M	10475M	140515M
507878M	375409M	474158M	Total Assets ($)	21170M	13627M	16260M	86879M	144577M	191645M

© RMA 2005

M = $ thousand   MM = $ million

See Pages 11 through 21 for Explanation of Ratios and Data

Current Data Sorted By Assets | Comparative Historical Data

0-500M	500M-2MM	2-10MM	10-50MM	50-100MM	100-250MM		4/1/00-3/31/01 ALL	4/1/01-3/31/02 ALL
						Type of Statement		
	1		2		1	Unqualified	2	1
1	1	3				Reviewed	6	6
8	7	2	2			Compiled	8	9
18	13	2			2	Tax Returns	7	10
3	7	8	2		1	Other	15	13
10 (4/1-9/30/04)			74 (10/1/04-3/31/05)					
30	29	15	6		4	**NUMBER OF STATEMENTS**	38	39
%	%	%	%	%	%	**ASSETS**	%	%
14.1	10.8	12.6		DATA NOT AVAILABLE		Cash & Equivalents	5.9	8.6
1.2	1.5	4.1				Trade Receivables (net)	4.3	4.9
2.5	2.0	7.6				Inventory	5.0	3.8
1.2	.5	1.2				All Other Current	1.5	1.4
19.0	14.8	25.5				Total Current	16.7	18.8
50.5	68.5	57.9				Fixed Assets (net)	62.8	64.7
14.8	7.4	7.6				Intangibles (net)	15.2	11.5
15.7	9.3	9.1				All Other Non-Current	5.3	5.1
100.0	100.0	100.0				Total	100.0	100.0
						LIABILITIES		
14.6	3.6	5.3				Notes Payable-Short Term	6.7	4.9
7.4	9.3	3.9				Cur. Mat.-L/T/D	6.8	8.5
1.2	2.0	5.6				Trade Payables	4.5	6.4
.0	.0	.0				Income Taxes Payable	.1	.5
15.6	5.3	8.3				All Other Current	4.0	3.8
38.8	20.2	23.2				Total Current	22.2	24.1
40.0	55.4	34.3				Long-Term Debt	50.3	53.4
.0	.0	.3				Deferred Taxes	.6	.2
22.3	3.0	4.0				All Other Non-Current	6.5	7.2
−1.1	21.4	38.2				Net Worth	20.4	15.0
100.0	100.0	100.0				Total Liabilities & Net Worth	100.0	100.0
						INCOME DATA		
100.0	100.0	100.0				Net Sales	100.0	100.0
						Gross Profit		
95.4	90.2	92.1				Operating Expenses	93.3	92.8
4.6	9.8	7.9				Operating Profit	6.7	7.2
4.1	3.2	4.2				All Other Expenses (net)	4.8	5.0
.6	6.6	3.8				Profit Before Taxes	1.9	2.2
						RATIOS		
2.8	3.9	3.7					1.6	1.7
.9	.7	.8				Current	.7	.5
.1	.1	.1					.4	.2
2.1	3.4	2.9					.8	1.3
.4	.7	.5				Quick	.5	.3
.0	.1	.1					.1	.2
0 UND	0 UND	0 UND					0 UND	0 UND
0 UND	0 UND	0 UND				Sales/Receivables	0 999.8	0 UND
0 UND	0 UND	10 35.2					8 47.6	6 58.1
						Cost of Sales/Inventory		
						Cost of Sales/Payables		
31.6	16.1	5.2					20.6	37.3
NM	−55.4	−72.8				Sales/Working Capital	−44.6	−14.2
−5.8	−5.5	−6.8					−10.2	−7.2
5.4	6.7	11.4					2.2	2.3
(24) .5	(27) 1.5	(14) 2.9				EBIT/Interest	(35) 1.5	(34) 1.6
−2.0	.3	1.4					.3	1.0
						Net Profit + Depr., Dep., Amort./Cur. Mat. L /T/D		
.8	1.7	.6					2.1	2.1
6.1	4.6	2.2				Fixed/Worth	8.0	6.4
−.8	−18.7	−15.6					−9.8	−6.9
.3	1.5	.6					2.1	2.4
NM	4.5	3.2				Debt/Worth	9.8	8.5
−2.0	−20.9	−19.8					−12.2	−8.4
57.3	41.7	67.0					47.8	54.2
(15) 30.5	(19) 16.8	(11) 19.3				% Profit Before Taxes/Tangible Net Worth	(25) 22.0	(24) 16.6
.9	−7.6	7.2					−8.0	3.3
17.7	14.7	8.7					7.4	10.0
−.6	3.6	6.2				% Profit Before Taxes/Total Assets	2.3	3.1
−9.3	−2.5	2.7					−2.9	−3.1
16.4	4.7	5.2					4.8	3.4
4.8	1.5	2.7				Sales/Net Fixed Assets	2.0	2.4
2.0	.9	1.3					.9	1.1
4.3	2.0	2.0					1.8	2.1
2.0	1.2	1.7				Sales/Total Assets	1.4	1.6
1.4	.7	.9					.8	.9
2.8	6.8	4.5					5.4	5.1
(25) 6.9	(27) 10.5	(13) 10.9				% Depr., Dep., Amort./Sales	(31) 12.8	(35) 10.4
17.0	13.1	17.3					15.2	15.9
3.5	2.4						1.9	4.2
(20) 6.8	(17) 6.1					% Officers', Directors', Owners' Comp/Sales	(12) 6.5	(20) 7.1
15.5	10.5						10.9	10.3
13753M	40796M	98306M	162422M		1682872M	Net Sales ($)	527425M	245272M
5714M	27004M	68023M	109954M		701881M	Total Assets ($)	540824M	233951M

M = $thousand MM = $million

See Pages 11 through 21 for Explanation of Ratios and Data

Comparative Historical Data				Current Data Sorted By Sales					
Type of Statement									
4	1	4	Unqualified		1			1	2
8	5	5	Reviewed	1	1			1	
17	16	19	Compiled	9	6	2	2	2	2
18	32	35	Tax Returns	24	7	2	4	3	2
14	19	21	Other	7	3	2			
4/1/02- 3/31/03 ALL	4/1/03- 3/31/04 ALL	4/1/04- 3/31/05 ALL		10 (4/1-9/30/04) 0-1MM	1-3MM	74 (10/1/04-3/31/05) 3-5MM	5-10MM	10-25MM	25MM & OVER
61	73	84	**NUMBER OF STATEMENTS**	41	18	6	6	7	6
%	%	%	**ASSETS**	%	%	%	%	%	%
12.3	12.9	11.7	Cash & Equivalents	8.6	20.0				
1.7	4.3	1.8	Trade Receivables (net)	1.0	.3				
1.3	4.8	3.1	Inventory	1.9	.9				
5.1	1.4	1.1	All Other Current	.9	.7				
20.4	23.4	17.7	Total Current	12.5	22.0				
65.0	62.1	59.3	Fixed Assets (net)	60.3	63.3				
8.6	6.0	11.2	Intangibles (net)	12.6	8.2				
5.9	8.5	11.8	All Other Non-Current	14.6	6.5				
100.0	100.0	100.0	Total	100.0	100.0				
			LIABILITIES						
6.9	4.3	7.5	Notes Payable-Short Term	10.6	5.5				
12.1	7.3	7.4	Cur. Mat.-L/T/D	7.9	10.6				
2.8	4.1	2.5	Trade Payables	1.1	.9				
.1	.1	.0	Income Taxes Payable	.0	.0				
8.3	5.8	11.8	All Other Current	13.8	3.3				
30.2	21.6	29.1	Total Current	33.4	20.4				
45.0	42.0	45.8	Long-Term Debt	44.8	56.6				
.3	.3	.3	Deferred Taxes	.0	.0				
8.9	14.2	10.6	All Other Non-Current	15.3	7.2				
15.7	21.8	14.1	Net Worth	6.6	15.8				
100.0	100.0	100.0	Total Liabilities & Net Worth	100.0	100.0				
			INCOME DATA						
100.0	100.0	100.0	Net Sales	100.0	100.0				
			Gross Profit						
93.0	92.5	92.8	Operating Expenses	92.3	93.6				
7.0	7.5	7.2	Operating Profit	7.7	6.4				
3.8	3.4	3.8	All Other Expenses (net)	4.6	2.7				
3.2	4.1	3.4	Profit Before Taxes	3.1	3.8				
			RATIOS						
1.3 / .6 / .3	2.4 / 1.1 / .5	3.1 / .8 / .1	Current	2.8 / .3 / .1	2.8 / 1.4 / .1				
1.1 / .4 / .1	2.0 / .7 / .3	2.1 / .4 / .1	Quick	2.0 / .2 / .0	2.8 / 1.1 / .1				
0 UND / 0 UND / 2 160.0	0 UND / 0 UND / 5 74.4	0 UND / 0 UND / 2 206.2	Sales/Receivables	0 UND / 0 UND / 0 UND	0 UND / 0 UND / 0 UND				
			Cost of Sales/Inventory						
			Cost of Sales/Payables						
61.8 / -25.9 / -9.9	9.7 / 107.8 / -14.8	17.0 / -65.1 / -5.8	Sales/Working Capital	37.8 / -55.4 / -2.7	10.9 / 64.5 / -6.8				
(55) 3.9 / 1.8 / .5	(57) 4.0 / 1.4 / .5	(74) 5.7 / 1.9 / .1	EBIT/Interest	(33) 3.5 / .6 / -1.9	7.2 / 1.6 / .3				
	(10) 7.6 / 2.0 / 1.1	(13) 37.1 / 7.6 / 1.3	Net Profit + Depr., Dep., Amort./Cur. Mat. L/T/D						
1.2 / 4.2 / -7.2	1.0 / 3.3 / -6.8	1.1 / 5.0 / -3.3	Fixed/Worth	1.0 / 5.6 / -1.2	1.7 / -194.2 / -7.9				
.9 / 5.5 / -9.0	.6 / 2.9 / -5.8	1.1 / 5.9 / -3.8	Debt/Worth	.6 / 6.3 / -2.3	1.6 / -385.6 / -9.3				
(38) 60.4 / 18.6 / .0	(51) 32.8 / 15.3 / 1.4	(50) 56.9 / 21.6 / 1.8	% Profit Before Taxes/Tangible Net Worth	(24) 37.5 / 15.3 / -5.9					
18.4 / 4.9 / -.9	14.6 / 3.1 / -1.9	14.3 / 3.4 / -3.5	% Profit Before Taxes/Total Assets	13.1 / -.5 / -5.1	14.5 / 2.7 / -4.1				
7.1 / 2.8 / 1.4	6.6 / 2.4 / 1.1	5.8 / 2.6 / 1.2	Sales/Net Fixed Assets	6.9 / 2.8 / .9	5.2 / 2.2 / 1.1				
3.4 / 1.7 / 1.1	2.7 / 1.6 / .9	2.4 / 1.4 / .9	Sales/Total Assets	2.6 / 1.3 / .7	3.0 / 1.5 / 1.0				
(52) 4.7 / 9.2 / 16.4	(67) 4.0 / 8.6 / 14.2	(71) 4.9 / 10.4 / 15.0	% Depr., Dep., Amort./Sales	(35) 4.7 / 8.9 / 16.4	(17) 6.7 / 11.8 / 13.7				
(29) 4.6 / 9.2 / 12.6	(35) 3.8 / 7.3 / 12.7	(46) 2.5 / 6.1 / 10.5	% Officers', Directors', Owners' Comp/Sales	(24) 3.4 / 8.5 / 14.8	(12) 2.4 / 5.6 / 9.2				
647497M	494440M	1998149M	Net Sales ($)	17229M	31545M	25279M	43834M	97549M	1782713M
504167M	380448M	912576M	Total Assets ($)	15942M	24851M	10253M	30764M	74801M	755965M

© RMA 2005

M = $ thousand   MM = $ million
See Pages 11 through 21 for Explanation of Ratios and Data

Current Data Sorted By Assets   Comparative Historical Data

							Type of Statement		
1	5	4 15	5 1				Unqualified	4	3
14	15	9	2				Reviewed	16	19
30	15	2	1				Compiled	42	33
13	14	15	3		1		Tax Returns	27	22
							Other	24	34
	30 (4/1-9/30/04)		135 (10/1/04-3/31/05)					4/1/00- 3/31/01	4/1/01- 3/31/02
0-500M	500M-2MM	2-10MM	10-50MM	50-100MM	100-250MM			ALL	ALL
58	49	45	12		1		NUMBER OF STATEMENTS	113	111
%	%	%	%	%	%		ASSETS	%	%
13.2	10.3	11.1	7.5				Cash & Equivalents	12.4	12.7
9.4	10.8	10.3	15.5	D			Trade Receivables (net)	11.1	11.3
3.0	5.6	2.8	10.9	A			Inventory	4.0	4.4
6.1	3.5	2.0	.8	T			All Other Current	1.4	1.7
31.7	30.2	26.3	34.8	A			Total Current	29.0	30.0
44.7	53.5	61.0	47.0				Fixed Assets (net)	54.5	50.9
10.6	7.0	5.3	12.5	N			Intangibles (net)	7.4	9.6
13.1	9.3	7.5	5.7	O			All Other Non-Current	9.2	9.5
100.0	100.0	100.0	100.0	T			Total	100.0	100.0
							LIABILITIES		
18.1	8.6	5.3	2.7	A			Notes Payable-Short Term	6.9	5.0
8.4	7.1	6.2	4.6	V			Cur. Mat.-L/T/D	6.8	8.5
13.6	6.3	5.5	16.3	A			Trade Payables	10.8	16.0
.4	.1	.1	.2	I			Income Taxes Payable	.3	.1
10.5	9.5	5.6	6.0	L			All Other Current	10.8	7.5
50.9	31.5	22.7	29.8	A			Total Current	35.5	37.2
44.3	43.7	40.5	24.1	B			Long-Term Debt	44.4	61.4
.1	.2	.6	1.0	L			Deferred Taxes	.3	.4
15.3	4.4	4.4	4.3	E			All Other Non-Current	8.8	5.5
-10.5	20.1	31.8	40.8				Net Worth	11.0	-4.5
100.0	100.0	100.0	100.0				Total Liabilities & Net Worth	100.0	100.0
							INCOME DATA		
100.0	100.0	100.0	100.0				Net Sales	100.0	100.0
							Gross Profit		
95.4	93.1	92.8	96.5				Operating Expenses	95.9	94.0
4.6	6.9	7.2	3.5				Operating Profit	4.1	6.0
1.5	1.9	4.2	-.8				All Other Expenses (net)	2.2	2.8
3.1	5.0	3.0	4.4				Profit Before Taxes	1.9	3.2
							RATIOS		
2.2	2.3	1.7	1.6					1.7	2.0
.9	1.1	1.1	1.2				Current	.8	1.2
.4	.4	.4	.8					.4	.5
1.5	1.5	1.5	1.3					1.2	1.8
.5	.7	.8	.7				Quick	.5	.9
.2	.3	.3	.5					.3	.3
0 UND	0 UND	7 50.6	15 24.9					0 UND	0 999.8
0 UND	10 35.7	22 16.8	31 11.7				Sales/Receivables	11 34.3	12 31.6
16 22.4	27 13.7	36 10.1	42 8.7					23 16.0	28 12.9
							Cost of Sales/Inventory		
							Cost of Sales/Payables		
18.7	14.8	12.1	16.3					20.7	13.6
-191.1	76.9	103.2	NM				Sales/Working Capital	-62.2	100.6
-7.8	-19.4	-8.7	-29.8					-11.4	-16.8
6.8	6.8	6.1	29.1					3.8	4.3
(48) 1.3	(44) 3.2	(40) 2.2	5.1				EBIT/Interest	(102) 1.6	(96) 2.1
-.6	.9	.9	.7					.4	.8
		9.7						3.3	4.1
	(12) 2.5						Net Profit + Depr., Dep., Amort./Cur. Mat. L /T/D	(19) 1.3	(15) 1.8
		1.6						.6	.8
.8	.8	.9	.9					1.1	.9
11.1	2.0	1.9	1.4				Fixed/Worth	2.9	2.4
-.8	-10.5	19.9	NM					-3.0	-4.5
1.2	.8	.8	.8					1.0	1.0
NM	2.6	2.7	1.5				Debt/Worth	4.1	2.5
-2.4	-13.5	22.6	NM					-5.9	-7.7
153.5	49.0	29.7						42.9	43.4
(29) 75.0	(36) 22.8	(36) 11.4					% Profit Before Taxes/Tangible Net Worth	(73) 15.8	(74) 22.1
-4.9	2.6	1.5						1.4	7.0
34.5	17.1	9.4	13.8					12.8	14.5
6.6	5.6	3.1	5.3				% Profit Before Taxes/Total Assets	2.9	5.2
-5.7	.0	-.8	-1.3					-2.0	-.6
23.2	10.4	4.8	9.1					10.0	11.1
7.3	5.1	2.6	4.1				Sales/Net Fixed Assets	5.2	5.3
4.4	2.4	.9	1.6					2.9	2.4
4.8	3.4	2.6	2.8					4.1	3.7
3.4	2.1	1.5	1.5				Sales/Total Assets	2.4	2.3
2.1	1.3	.5	1.1					1.6	1.6
1.7	2.6	4.0	2.3					3.0	2.8
(45) 3.8	(42) 3.9	(42) 6.3	(11) 4.2				% Depr., Dep., Amort./Sales	(110) 4.2	(97) 4.6
7.1	7.1	9.9	6.4					6.5	6.3
4.6	3.2	2.2						3.5	3.3
(38) 8.0	(25) 5.7	(17) 4.4					% Officers', Directors', Owners' Comp/Sales	(58) 5.7	(58) 5.7
11.5	10.3	7.6						8.3	8.8
52597M	128838M	297263M	788559M		903954M		Net Sales ($)	740483M	540157M
14570M	50885M	192394M	197466M		110074M		Total Assets ($)	514157M	275189M

M = $ thousand   MM = $ million
See Pages 11 through 21 for Explanation of Ratios and Data

Comparative Historical Data — Current Data Sorted By Sales

Type of Statement	4/1/02-3/31/03 ALL	4/1/03-3/31/04 ALL	4/1/04-3/31/05 ALL	0-1MM	1-3MM	3-5MM	5-10MM	10-25MM	25MM & OVER
Unqualified	10	8	9				1	6	2
Reviewed	26	23	22	2	3	1	9	6	1
Compiled	53	49	40	11	17	5	5	1	1
Tax Returns	40	56	48	27	14	3	3		1
Other	45	37	46	11	17	5	9	3	1
				30 (4/1-9/30/04)			135 (10/1/04-3/31/05)		
NUMBER OF STATEMENTS	174	173	165	51	51	14	27	16	6
	%	%	%	%	%	%	%	%	%
ASSETS									
Cash & Equivalents	9.9	10.8	11.4	10.5	9.7	9.6	16.1	11.8	
Trade Receivables (net)	9.6	9.9	10.6	6.5	10.3	11.5	12.4	16.0	
Inventory	4.6	3.5	4.4	2.7	4.1	4.4	4.7	5.2	
All Other Current	2.8	2.8	3.8	5.3	4.7	2.3	2.3	1.5	
Total Current	26.8	27.1	30.1	24.9	28.8	27.8	35.4	34.5	
Fixed Assets (net)	56.3	50.7	51.9	54.1	50.7	52.1	55.5	49.4	
Intangibles (net)	6.9	10.4	8.2	11.0	9.8	3.5	2.7	7.7	
All Other Non-Current	10.0	11.8	9.8	10.0	10.7	16.6	6.4	8.3	
Total	100.0	100.0	100.0	100.0	100.0	100.0	100.0	100.0	
LIABILITIES									
Notes Payable-Short Term	8.1	8.1	10.5	16.2	11.2	7.7	6.1	2.3	
Cur. Mat.-L/T/D	7.5	6.6	7.1	7.6	7.0	5.0	9.3	5.3	
Trade Payables	6.0	6.6	9.4	11.4	7.7	7.7	6.7	6.4	
Income Taxes Payable	1.0	.1	.2	.2	.3	.1	.1	.2	
All Other Current	9.6	11.2	8.6	9.4	5.2	14.8	11.7	6.5	
Total Current	32.2	32.7	35.8	44.8	31.3	35.2	34.0	20.7	
Long-Term Debt	51.3	43.8	41.4	49.1	48.8	33.3	34.1	21.8	
Deferred Taxes	.2	.2	.3	.2	.1	.3	.5	1.6	
All Other Non-Current	6.1	7.5	8.2	17.1	4.8	3.4	4.6	.8	
Net Worth	10.2	15.9	14.3	−11.2	15.1	27.8	26.8	55.1	
Total Liabilities & Net Worth	100.0	100.0	100.0	100.0	100.0	100.0	100.0	100.0	
INCOME DATA									
Net Sales	100.0	100.0	100.0	100.0	100.0	100.0	100.0	100.0	
Gross Profit									
Operating Expenses	92.5	93.3	94.1	92.8	92.7	97.1	95.5	95.4	
Operating Profit	7.5	6.7	5.9	7.2	7.3	2.9	4.5	4.6	
All Other Expenses (net)	3.4	3.2	2.2	3.5	3.0	.5	.9	.2	
Profit Before Taxes	4.2	3.5	3.7	3.7	4.3	2.5	3.6	4.4	
RATIOS									
Current	2.0	1.8	1.8	2.3	1.7	2.1	1.9	2.9	
	1.0	.9	1.0	.6	1.1	1.0	1.0	1.5	
	.4	.3	.4	.3	.4	.3	.4	1.0	
Quick	1.4	1.3	1.4	1.7	1.1	1.2	1.6	2.5	
	(173) .6	.7	.7	.4	.5	.8	.9	1.1	
	.3	.3	.3	.1	.4	.3	.4	.7	
Sales/Receivables	0 UND	0 UND	0 UND	0 UND	0 999.8	3 124.9	4 103.0	5 68.1	
	8 47.6	8 46.4	11 33.3	0 UND	12 30.3	18 20.8	16 23.5	34 10.7	
	27 13.5	27 13.6	29 12.4	15 23.6	31 11.8	29 12.5	32 11.4	43 8.6	
Cost of Sales/Inventory									
Cost of Sales/Payables									
Sales/Working Capital	14.3	17.8	16.8	16.5	18.9	16.1	10.7	8.6	
	−612.0	−91.9	−999.8	−28.2	116.7	NM	−191.2	24.5	
	−14.4	−12.0	−13.0	−4.5	−11.7	−6.3	−17.2	NM	
EBIT/Interest	5.0	4.9	7.2	5.5	5.5	6.4	5.9	17.7	
	(157) 2.1	(156) 2.1	(145) 2.2	(38) 1.1	(47) 2.7	2.7	(24) 2.1	6.7	
	1.0	.7	.7	−.7	.7	.5	.8	2.0	
Net Profit + Depr., Dep., Amort./Cur. Mat. L/T/D	3.3	5.3	5.7						
	(31) 1.8	(20) 2.0	(21) 2.3						
	1.4	1.1	1.3						
Fixed/Worth	1.1	1.0	.9	.8	1.3	.9	.7	.9	
	2.9	3.0	2.8	10.1	5.1	2.6	1.3	1.0	
	−5.1	−2.9	−4.0	−1.7	−1.6	13.5	8.4	1.8	
Debt/Worth	1.1	1.1	.9	1.3	1.3	1.1	.5	.5	
	3.6	4.3	4.2	21.0	11.3	3.0	1.3	1.0	
	−6.6	−6.9	−6.0	−2.4	−3.7	16.7	10.3	2.1	
% Profit Before Taxes/Tangible Net Worth	39.6	48.4	58.4	158.0	64.6	126.1	27.0	31.1	
	(113) 18.9	(112) 17.7	(111) 21.1	(28) 44.0	(28) 31.2	(12) 15.5	(24) 9.5	(15) 16.5	
	2.0	1.7	1.4	.5	.5	−6.7	.3	6.8	
% Profit Before Taxes/Total Assets	14.2	13.5	18.8	19.4	19.5	20.0	17.2	13.1	
	5.6	4.3	4.3	.7	5.8	3.3	4.2	7.8	
	.1	−.4	−1.4	−5.8	−1.2	−1.3	.0	2.1	
Sales/Net Fixed Assets	9.3	9.8	11.6	12.0	13.3	9.2	13.2	7.9	
	4.6	5.2	5.1	5.3	4.6	5.5	4.1	5.2	
	1.7	2.6	2.3	2.4	1.6	2.8	1.9	2.9	
Sales/Total Assets	3.6	3.3	3.7	3.4	4.3	3.7	3.5	3.2	
	2.2	2.2	2.2	2.1	2.3	2.7	2.1	2.3	
	1.1	1.4	1.1	1.0	1.1	1.5	1.4	1.4	
% Depr., Dep., Amort./Sales	3.4	3.1	2.6	3.2	2.4	2.6	2.7	2.3	
	(154) 4.8	(154) 5.0	(140) 4.6	(41) 6.1	(44) 4.6	3.8	(21) 4.8	4.0	
	9.0	8.1	7.7	11.5	8.8	6.1	6.9	4.9	
% Officers', Directors', Owners' Comp/Sales	3.4	3.3	3.3	6.4	3.0	2.6	2.6		
	(82) 5.7	(96) 6.6	(82) 6.2	(29) 13.7	(25) 5.2	(10) 4.4	(14) 4.8		
	10.1	10.0	10.3	13.7	9.1	7.8	9.9		
Net Sales ($)	1678947M	2315617M	2171211M	26889M	90870M	54669M	176404M	245322M	1577057M
Total Assets ($)	982496M	714308M	565389M	21315M	76818M	28587M	93434M	123718M	221517M

© RMA 2005

M = $ thousand   MM = $ million

See Pages 11 through 21 for Explanation of Ratios and Data

Current Data Sorted By Assets | **Comparative Historical Data**

0-500M	500M-2MM	2-10MM	10-50MM	50-100MM	100-250MM	Type of Statement	4/1/00-3/31/01 ALL	4/1/01-3/31/02 ALL
	1	11	4	1		Unqualified	11	8
	5	15	2			Reviewed	16	18
3	6	2				Compiled	19	17
	3	2				Tax Returns	4	1
1	1	14	6	2		Other	13	23
28 (4/1-9/30/04)		51 (10/1/04-3/31/05)						
4	16	44	12	3		NUMBER OF STATEMENTS	63	67
%	%	%	%	%	%	**ASSETS**	%	%
	8.4	10.0	9.2		DATA NOT AVAILABLE	Cash & Equivalents	6.0	8.4
	26.8	18.9	19.7			Trade Receivables (net)	21.1	20.1
	6.7	7.7	13.1			Inventory	10.4	11.5
	1.4	2.1	4.2			All Other Current	3.5	3.8
	43.3	38.7	46.1			Total Current	40.9	43.8
	41.5	48.2	37.3			Fixed Assets (net)	45.5	44.6
	7.6	5.0	5.5			Intangibles (net)	7.2	4.9
	7.6	8.1	11.0			All Other Non-Current	6.4	6.5
	100.0	100.0	100.0			Total	100.0	100.0
						LIABILITIES		
	8.8	6.7	7.1			Notes Payable-Short Term	6.4	9.0
	7.1	5.4	5.5			Cur. Mat.-L/T/D	5.7	4.7
	10.4	9.7	10.7			Trade Payables	10.9	10.1
	.0	.3	.6			Income Taxes Payable	.7	.7
	9.0	7.8	6.6			All Other Current	6.7	9.0
	35.4	29.8	30.5			Total Current	30.5	33.5
	36.5	22.0	22.4			Long-Term Debt	27.8	23.0
	1.3	1.0	.0			Deferred Taxes	1.2	.7
	4.1	6.5	3.7			All Other Non-Current	6.3	5.2
	22.7	40.7	43.4			Net Worth	34.3	37.4
	100.0	100.0	100.0			Total Liabilities & Net Worth	100.0	100.0
						INCOME DATA		
	100.0	100.0	100.0			Net Sales	100.0	100.0
						Gross Profit		
	92.1	94.9	96.3			Operating Expenses	93.6	94.7
	7.9	5.1	3.7			Operating Profit	6.4	5.3
	4.1	1.1	.8			All Other Expenses (net)	2.2	2.0
	3.8	4.0	2.9			Profit Before Taxes	4.3	3.3
						RATIOS		
	2.0	2.2	2.1				2.2	2.2
	1.1	1.3	1.4			Current	1.4	1.5
	.8	.9	.9				.8	1.0
	1.3	1.5	1.8				1.4	1.6
	.9	.9	.9			Quick	(62) .9	.9
	.6	.7	.6				.5	.5
	28 12.9	**28** 12.9	**35** 10.5				**31** 11.9	**28** 13.0
	32 11.4	**34** 10.8	**39** 9.4			Sales/Receivables	**37** 9.9	**35** 10.5
	44 8.3	**45** 8.2	**46** 8.0				**46** 7.9	**41** 8.8
						Cost of Sales/Inventory		
						Cost of Sales/Payables		
	12.6	7.5	6.9				7.8	7.6
	80.5	19.7	12.6			Sales/Working Capital	17.7	13.7
	-48.5	-38.2	NM				-49.1	-142.1
	15.6	10.1	4.1				6.7	7.1
	(14) 5.1	(40) 3.9	(11) 2.6			EBIT/Interest	(61) 2.1	(61) 2.7
	1.0	1.3	1.2				.8	.9
		6.7					4.9	3.7
		(18) 2.3				Net Profit + Depr., Dep., Amort./Cur. Mat. L /T/D	(16) 2.3	(17) 1.6
		1.2					.8	.6
	.5	.7	.6				.9	.7
	1.8	1.2	1.1			Fixed/Worth	1.4	1.2
	-21.7	2.4	2.9				5.7	3.4
	.7	.7	.6				.9	.8
	2.8	1.1	2.0			Debt/Worth	2.3	1.5
	-26.4	2.9	4.7				7.0	6.6
	65.7	33.3	32.1				50.3	40.7
	(11) 27.5	(42) 16.3	10.4			% Profit Before Taxes/Tangible Net Worth	(51) 18.9	(57) 11.8
	12.4	.2	5.3				2.2	2.6
	18.7	10.6	6.5				14.1	13.2
	13.0	5.5	3.6			% Profit Before Taxes/Total Assets	4.3	3.3
	.9	.1	.8				-.8	-.5
	11.4	7.3	7.5				7.8	7.1
	9.2	3.9	5.4			Sales/Net Fixed Assets	4.9	4.5
	5.5	2.3	3.5				2.6	3.0
	3.3	2.5	2.1				2.6	2.6
	2.7	1.8	1.9			Sales/Total Assets	2.0	2.0
	2.2	1.3	1.5				1.3	1.3
	2.4	3.5	2.2				2.6	2.3
	(14) 3.2	(37) 4.5	(11) 3.6			% Depr., Dep., Amort./Sales	(57) 4.4	(63) 4.0
	4.7	6.5	5.6				6.5	5.2
		1.9					2.3	2.0
		(18) 3.6				% Officers', Directors', Owners' Comp/Sales	(30) 4.8	(25) 5.3
		10.1					8.5	8.2
2773M	**45823M**	**463759M**	**452065M**	**426653M**		Net Sales ($)	**1442957M**	**1440652M**
918M	**17137M**	**229453M**	**250552M**	**265439M**		Total Assets ($)	**766045M**	**982851M**

M = $ thousand MM = $ million

See Pages 11 through 21 for Explanation of Ratios and Data

Comparative Historical Data			Type of Statement	Current Data Sorted By Sales					
17	19	17	Unqualified	1	5	4	3	4	
20	21	22	Reviewed	1	4	8	7	2	
15	17	11	Compiled	2	5	2	2		
5	7	5	Tax Returns	1	1	1	2		
19	15	24	Other	2	2	8	6	6	
4/1/02- 3/31/03 ALL	4/1/03- 3/31/04 ALL	4/1/04- 3/31/05 ALL		0-1MM	28 (4/1-9/30/04) 1-3MM	3-5MM	51 (10/1/04-3/31/05) 5-10MM	10-25MM	25MM & OVER
76	79	79	NUMBER OF STATEMENTS	3	10	14	24	16	12
%	%	%	ASSETS	%	%	%	%	%	%
8.1	9.9	9.0	Cash & Equivalents	6.1	15.7	9.0	7.6	6.2	
19.4	20.1	20.9	Trade Receivables (net)	22.7	21.7	20.4	20.0	19.4	
13.5	11.5	9.6	Inventory	15.0	6.9	6.6	11.2	13.4	
2.5	3.1	2.2	All Other Current	1.5	2.6	1.3	3.4	3.0	
43.5	44.5	41.6	Total Current	45.3	46.9	37.4	42.2	41.9	
42.0	41.7	44.3	Fixed Assets (net)	45.6	33.5	51.0	43.1	41.1	
4.6	3.6	5.8	Intangibles (net)	5.3	8.0	5.1	4.0	6.5	
10.0	10.3	8.3	All Other Non-Current	3.8	11.5	6.4	10.6	10.6	
100.0	100.0	100.0	Total	100.0	100.0	100.0	100.0	100.0	
			LIABILITIES						
8.0	6.2	6.8	Notes Payable-Short Term	6.8	7.9	6.5	6.3	8.4	
5.7	4.9	5.6	Cur. Mat.-L/T/D	5.8	5.0	7.1	4.4	4.8	
9.5	9.0	9.6	Trade Payables	10.4	9.3	9.3	11.1	9.2	
.5	.4	.3	Income Taxes Payable	.0	.4	.4	.0	.6	
9.5	8.9	8.1	All Other Current	6.1	10.7	7.2	7.2	9.7	
33.2	29.3	30.4	Total Current	29.0	33.2	30.4	29.1	32.8	
25.9	27.5	25.1	Long-Term Debt	24.3	25.4	28.9	20.0	22.1	
	.8	.9	Deferred Taxes	2.1	.9	.9	.5	.7	
7.9	9.1	8.8	All Other Non-Current	5.7	.0	9.5	4.1	7.6	
32.3	33.4	34.8	Net Worth	38.8	40.5	30.4	46.3	36.8	
100.0	100.0	100.0	Total Liabilities & Net Worth	100.0	100.0	100.0	100.0	100.0	
			INCOME DATA						
100.0	100.0	100.0	Net Sales	100.0	100.0	100.0	100.0	100.0	
			Gross Profit						
95.5	96.8	94.8	Operating Expenses	94.0	94.9	93.5	97.1	97.8	
4.5	3.2	5.2	Operating Profit	6.0	5.1	6.5	2.9	2.2	
1.3	1.3	1.7	All Other Expenses (net)	2.4	.5	1.9	.4	1.1	
3.1	1.9	3.5	Profit Before Taxes	3.7	4.7	4.6	2.5	1.1	
			RATIOS						
1.9	2.6	2.2		4.1	2.4	2.2	2.3	2.0	
1.4	1.5	1.3	Current	1.0	1.4	1.3	1.4	1.2	
1.0	1.1	.9		.7	.9	.8	.9	.9	
1.3	1.7	1.6		2.3	1.5	1.5	1.8	1.2	
1.0	1.0	.9	Quick	.7	1.1	.9	.8	.8	
.6	.6	.7		.5	.9	.7	.6	.6	
27 13.7	28 13.1	30 12.4		24 15.0	28 12.9	29 12.8	33 11.1	32 11.3	
35 10.5	34 10.6	35 10.4	Sales/Receivables	36 10.0	32 11.3	32 11.3	38 9.6	36 10.0	
43 8.5	41 9.0	45 8.1		49 7.5	46 7.9	45 8.1	44 8.4	42 8.8	
			Cost of Sales/Inventory						
			Cost of Sales/Payables						
8.6	6.7	7.6		6.6	6.2	8.7	7.8	9.9	
17.6	12.5	19.5	Sales/Working Capital	NM	19.2	18.0	14.4	48.4	
−366.4	73.4	−56.9		−17.7	−84.4	−30.7	−52.9	NM	
6.8	5.8	8.7		29.8	14.1	8.1	10.5	4.0	
(72) 3.4	(74) 2.6	(71) 3.9	EBIT/Interest	11.3	(11) 4.7	(23) 3.6	(15) 4.1	(11) 2.4	
1.2	.4	1.2		3.5	−.6	1.7	1.0	1.2	
5.4	2.7	3.1							
(24) 2.1	(26) 1.5	(26) 2.1	Net Profit + Depr., Dep., Amort./Cur. Mat. L/T/D						
1.2	1.0	1.2							
.7	.6	.7		.4	.4	.8	.5	.8	
1.2	1.2	1.2	Fixed/Worth	1.8	.8	1.5	1.1	1.2	
2.9	2.8	2.9		NM	1.3	8.1	1.4	3.5	
.7	.7	.7		.3	.5	.7	.6	.9	
1.8	1.6	1.4	Debt/Worth	2.3	.9	2.1	1.4	1.8	
4.7	5.8	5.5		NM	2.5	12.5	2.8	7.5	
40.1	32.6	35.6			42.5	37.3	32.8	24.8	
(65) 18.1	(68) 11.8	(70) 19.5	% Profit Before Taxes/Tangible Net Worth	(12) 17.4	(22) 21.4	15.1	(11) 10.8		
7.9	−.7	4.1		−2.3	8.0	.0	4.5		
13.0	12.7	12.7		18.4	20.7	12.2	9.2	6.3	
6.2	3.9	6.4	% Profit Before Taxes/Total Assets	12.4	9.4	5.5	7.0	2.8	
.8	−.9	.1		4.8	−1.0	3.2	.0	.6	
9.7	8.4	8.2		10.0	38.0	8.6	8.0	6.7	
5.4	5.4	4.9	Sales/Net Fixed Assets	6.1	8.3	3.9	4.6	4.4	
3.1	3.7	2.8		3.4	2.3	2.2	2.8	3.5	
2.5	2.6	2.7		3.2	2.5	2.9	2.1	2.3	
2.1	2.1	2.0	Sales/Total Assets	2.7	2.0	2.0	1.9	1.9	
1.4	1.6	1.4		1.6	1.5	1.3	1.4	1.5	
2.4	2.8	3.0			2.4	3.3	2.8	2.3	
(70) 4.1	(69) 4.0	(67) 3.9	% Depr., Dep., Amort./Sales	(10) 3.7	(22) 4.4	(13) 3.9	(10) 3.7		
6.3	6.1	6.1		4.8	7.0	6.2	5.7		
3.0	2.2	1.9				1.9			
(37) 6.1	(37) 3.4	(31) 4.3	% Officers', Directors', Owners' Comp/Sales		(11) 3.0				
10.3	7.5	9.7			8.5				
1513025M	1602253M	1391073M	Net Sales ($)	690M	18622M	55250M	178608M	263198M	874705M
927375M	948669M	763499M	Total Assets ($)	918M	8890M	31504M	107783M	142084M	472320M

© RMA 2005   M = $ thousand   MM = $ million
See Pages 11 through 21 for Explanation of Ratios and Data

Current Data Sorted By Assets · **Comparative Historical Data**

		2	3	1		Type of Statement		
		1				Unqualified	7	5
	3	1	1			Reviewed	7	7
	1	1				Compiled	2	3
	1	5	5			Tax Returns		
						Other	4	9

0-500M	500M-2MM	2-10MM	10-50MM	50-100MM	100-250MM		4/1/00-3/31/01 ALL	4/1/01-3/31/02 ALL
	10 (4/1-9/30/04)		15 (10/1/04-3/31/05)					
	5	10	9	1		NUMBER OF STATEMENTS	20	24
%	%	%	%	%	%	**ASSETS**	%	%
		12.0				Cash & Equivalents	5.8	10.0
		22.5				Trade Receivables (net)	25.9	20.3
		5.9				Inventory	12.1	13.7
D A T A		.1			D A T A	All Other Current	.7	2.2
		40.5				Total Current	44.5	46.1
		48.0				Fixed Assets (net)	44.7	42.6
N O T		6.7			N O T	Intangibles (net)	6.0	6.8
		4.7				All Other Non-Current	4.9	4.5
		100.0				Total	100.0	100.0
A V A I					A V A I	**LIABILITIES**		
		2.8				Notes Payable-Short Term	8.6	5.9
L A B		7.3			L A B	Cur. Mat.-L/T/D	6.8	6.6
		6.7				Trade Payables	12.4	10.1
L E		.0			L E	Income Taxes Payable	.0	.4
		5.3				All Other Current	5.8	5.5
		22.0				Total Current	33.7	28.5
		30.4				Long-Term Debt	26.9	26.5
		.2				Deferred Taxes	1.1	.5
		1.7				All Other Non-Current	7.9	3.4
		45.6				Net Worth	30.4	41.1
		100.0				Total Liabilities & Net Worth	100.0	100.0
						INCOME DATA		
		100.0				Net Sales	100.0	100.0
						Gross Profit		
		91.4				Operating Expenses	93.6	92.4
		8.6				Operating Profit	6.4	7.6
		2.6				All Other Expenses (net)	2.4	2.4
		6.0				Profit Before Taxes	4.1	5.2
						RATIOS		
		3.3					1.8	2.5
		1.6				Current	1.2	1.6
		1.2					.9	1.1
		1.8					1.5	1.7
		1.5				Quick	1.0	1.0
		1.1					.6	.5
		35 10.4					38 9.6	31 11.9
		38 9.6				Sales/Receivables	43 8.5	38 9.6
		49 7.4					48 7.7	42 8.7
						Cost of Sales/Inventory		
						Cost of Sales/Payables		
		5.7					9.0	9.5
		13.8				Sales/Working Capital	30.3	14.3
		121.7					−73.3	32.5
		6.1					4.6	6.7
		2.2				EBIT/Interest	(22) 2.0	3.7
		−.2					1.3	1.8
						Net Profit + Depr., Dep., Amort./Cur. Mat. L/T/D		
		.5					1.0	.9
		1.4				Fixed/Worth	2.1	1.7
		4.6					5.0	3.5
		.5					1.4	.8
		1.4				Debt/Worth	3.8	2.1
		5.9					6.9	5.1
						% Profit Before Taxes/Tangible Net Worth	70.4 / (18) 15.7 / 1.7	71.4 / (21) 27.7 / 4.5
		11.8					10.5	18.2
		2.5				% Profit Before Taxes/Total Assets	3.3	9.1
		−2.4					1.2	2.1
		6.0					7.1	8.6
		4.3				Sales/Net Fixed Assets	3.5	4.3
		2.0					2.8	2.7
		2.3					2.5	2.6
		1.7				Sales/Total Assets	1.7	1.8
		1.3					1.4	1.6
		2.7					3.2	2.7
		5.2				% Depr., Dep., Amort./Sales	(18) 4.7	(20) 4.0
		7.6					6.6	5.6
						% Officers', Directors', Owners' Comp/Sales	1.7 / (10) 2.8 / 6.9	2.0 / (11) 4.6 / 6.7
	17688M	84841M	422529M	106147M		Net Sales ($)	473310M	627358M
	6509M	48772M	268015M	66443M		Total Assets ($)	290097M	375329M

© RMA 2005

M = $ thousand   MM = $ million
See Pages 11 through 21 for Explanation of Ratios and Data

Comparative Historical Data				Current Data Sorted By Sales					

			Type of Statement						
7	5	6	Unqualified			1		1	4
4	2	1	Reviewed				1		
1	3	5	Compiled	1		2	1	1	
2	2	2	Tax Returns		1		1		
5	6	11	Other			1	3	2	5
4/1/02-3/31/03 ALL	4/1/03-3/31/04 ALL	4/1/04-3/31/05 ALL		10 (4/1-9/30/04)			15 (10/1/04-3/31/05)		
				0-1MM	1-3MM	3-5MM	5-10MM	10-25MM	25MM & OVER
19	18	25	NUMBER OF STATEMENTS	1	1	4	6	4	9
%	%	%	ASSETS	%	%	%	%	%	%
9.8	13.7	9.5	Cash & Equivalents						
19.1	16.1	21.5	Trade Receivables (net)						
12.6	8.8	9.7	Inventory						
.3	4.9	.6	All Other Current						
41.8	43.5	41.3	Total Current						
45.2	37.5	42.3	Fixed Assets (net)						
5.8	7.0	8.6	Intangibles (net)						
7.2	12.0	7.8	All Other Non-Current						
100.0	100.0	100.0	Total						
			LIABILITIES						
4.9	5.0	3.1	Notes Payable-Short Term						
6.5	4.7	5.6	Cur. Mat.-L/T/D						
9.8	9.8	10.3	Trade Payables						
.4	.4	.2	Income Taxes Payable						
10.2	11.5	5.4	All Other Current						
31.9	31.4	24.6	Total Current						
21.8	20.6	29.0	Long-Term Debt						
.8	.0	.1	Deferred Taxes						
5.1	9.1	3.9	All Other Non-Current						
40.4	38.9	42.5	Net Worth						
100.0	100.0	100.0	Total Liabilities & Net Worth						
			INCOME DATA						
100.0	100.0	100.0	Net Sales						
			Gross Profit						
94.6	95.4	93.6	Operating Expenses						
5.4	4.6	6.4	Operating Profit						
1.7	.7	1.9	All Other Expenses (net)						
3.7	3.9	4.5	Profit Before Taxes						
			RATIOS						
2.2	2.3	2.3	Current						
1.4	1.5	1.5							
1.0	.8	1.2							
1.4	1.8	1.7	Quick						
.9	.8	1.2							
.5	.3	.8							
35 10.6	30 12.3	33 11.0	Sales/Receivables						
37 9.8	35 10.3	38 9.7							
56 6.5	44 8.2	42 8.8							
			Cost of Sales/Inventory						
			Cost of Sales/Payables						
7.0	5.8	7.7	Sales/Working Capital						
17.5	13.8	16.2							
200.3	−26.4	21.3							
5.3	3.8	4.8	EBIT/Interest						
(18) 3.0	(15) 3.3	(24) 3.2							
.9	2.0	1.5							
			Net Profit + Depr., Dep., Amort./Cur. Mat. L/T/D						
.9	.5	.6	Fixed/Worth						
1.6	1.6	1.3							
2.8	2.0	2.9							
.9	.8	.7	Debt/Worth						
2.6	2.1	1.8							
4.5	7.4	4.7							
40.3	28.9	35.9	% Profit Before Taxes/Tangible Net Worth						
(18) 20.6	(15) 7.1	(22) 13.6							
.4	2.8	1.3							
9.2	8.1	10.1	% Profit Before Taxes/Total Assets						
5.3	3.7	4.5							
−.4	.8	1.8							
6.0	9.2	6.5	Sales/Net Fixed Assets						
3.8	5.7	4.8							
2.7	3.3	3.5							
2.1	2.4	2.5	Sales/Total Assets						
1.6	1.7	1.8							
1.1	.9	1.4							
2.7	2.2	2.5	% Depr., Dep., Amort./Sales						
4.5	(17) 3.3	4.1							
5.6	6.1	6.9							
			% Officers', Directors', Owners' Comp/Sales						
485245M	478218M	631205M	Net Sales ($)	968M	2878M	14542M	42436M	62319M	508062M
307108M	326915M	389739M	Total Assets ($)	797M	1170M	9814M	22350M	41271M	314337M

© RMA 2005

M = $ thousand   MM = $ million

See Pages 11 through 21 for Explanation of Ratios and Data

Current Data Sorted By Assets | Comparative Historical Data

Type of Statement								
						Unqualified	7	5
	1	1				Reviewed	13	8
	3	4				Compiled	19	15
3	6	2				Tax Returns	22	1
2	1					Other	33	24
1		4	1				4/1/00-	4/1/01-
	9 (4/1-9/30/04)		20 (10/1/04-3/31/05)				3/31/01	3/31/02
0-500M	500M-2MM	2-10MM	10-50MM	50-100MM	100-250MM		ALL	ALL
6	11	11	1			NUMBER OF STATEMENTS	94	53
%	%	%	%	%	%	ASSETS	%	%
	12.0	10.3				Cash & Equivalents	14.3	12.1
	34.0	20.8	D	D		Trade Receivables (net)	16.8	21.3
	8.5	7.1	A	A		Inventory	13.9	10.7
	.2	3.3	T	T		All Other Current	2.4	2.0
	54.6	41.6	A	A		Total Current	47.4	46.1
	26.6	48.9				Fixed Assets (net)	44.5	41.9
	6.3	1.0	N	N		Intangibles (net)	2.3	5.7
	12.5	8.5	O	O		All Other Non-Current	5.8	6.3
	100.0	100.0	T	T		Total	100.0	100.0
						LIABILITIES		
	8.9	10.3	A	A		Notes Payable-Short Term	3.7	9.6
	7.2	7.5	V	V		Cur. Mat.-L/T/D	8.3	7.6
	10.2	7.1	A	A		Trade Payables	11.1	13.1
	.4	.2	I	I		Income Taxes Payable	.3	.3
	20.4	11.5	L	L		All Other Current	7.2	11.8
	47.2	36.5	A	A		Total Current	30.7	42.4
	7.4	21.2	B	B		Long-Term Debt	29.4	21.2
	.3	.0	L	L		Deferred Taxes	.5	.6
	4.0	13.1	E	E		All Other Non-Current	9.8	3.8
	41.1	29.3				Net Worth	29.5	32.1
	100.0	100.0				Total Liabilities & Net Worth	100.0	100.0
						INCOME DATA		
	100.0	100.0				Net Sales	100.0	100.0
						Gross Profit		
	97.0	101.0				Operating Expenses	96.3	98.9
	3.0	-1.0				Operating Profit	3.7	1.1
	2.9	.7				All Other Expenses (net)	1.4	1.8
	.1	-1.7				Profit Before Taxes	2.3	-.7
						RATIOS		
	1.9	1.6					3.4	1.8
	1.3	1.1				Current	1.6	1.1
	.8	.8					1.0	.7
	1.8	1.3					2.1	1.4
	.9	.9				Quick	1.1	.9
	.4	.6					.5	.4
19	19.1	25	14.7				6	64.6	9	42.4
39	9.4	36	10.0			Sales/Receivables	20	18.4	28	13.1
64	5.7	50	7.4				40	9.1	47	7.8
						Cost of Sales/Inventory		
						Cost of Sales/Payables		
	9.7	10.1					7.7	11.4
	22.7	35.1				Sales/Working Capital	16.1	112.9
	-25.8	-22.9					514.2	-14.0
	12.1	7.2					4.8	3.4
	2.0 (10)	1.2				EBIT/Interest	(82) 2.0	(48) 1.2
	-1.2	-2.4					.6	-.9
						Net Profit + Depr., Dep.,	3.7	7.9
						Amort./Cur. Mat. L /T/D	(21) 1.3	(15) 2.8
							.8	1.0
	.2	1.1					.6	.7
	.8	1.2				Fixed/Worth	1.3	1.7
	2.4	9.9					3.8	7.2
	.9	1.2					.7	.9
	2.4	1.5				Debt/Worth	1.7	2.2
	6.6	13.7					5.8	10.1
	62.5	19.8				% Profit Before Taxes/Tangible	41.2	21.4
	3.6 (10)	1.6				Net Worth	(78) 8.2	(42) 7.4
	-26.6	-68.4					-.5	-29.1
	9.0	8.2				% Profit Before Taxes/Total	15.6	8.9
	1.7	.8				Assets	3.3	1.3
	-6.5	-11.2					-2.0	-9.6
	27.9	4.6					10.1	11.2
	13.2	4.0				Sales/Net Fixed Assets	5.3	6.9
	9.0	3.0					3.2	3.1
	3.9	2.7					3.0	3.3
	3.2	2.2				Sales/Total Assets	2.3	2.5
	2.5	2.0					1.8	1.6
		4.2					3.3	3.4
	(10)	7.2				% Depr., Dep., Amort./Sales	(84) 4.9	(48) 4.9
		8.1					7.0	7.3
						% Officers', Directors',	4.6	4.2
						Owners' Comp/Sales	(64) 8.2	(20) 4.8
							13.3	7.6
5360M	48072M	109725M	16250M			Net Sales ($)	505183M	344808M
1852M	13738M	48608M	10583M			Total Assets ($)	225228M	165174M

M = $ thousand   MM = $ million
See Pages 11 through 21 for Explanation of Ratios and Data

Comparative Historical Data				Type of Statement	Current Data Sorted By Sales					
5	3		2	Unqualified			1	1		
6	6		7	Reviewed	1	1	3	1	1	
14	7		11	Compiled	2	4	2	2	1	
4	7		3	Tax Returns	2					
19	21		6	Other		2	1	1	2	
4/1/02-	4/1/03-		4/1/04-			9 (4/1-9/30/04)		20 (10/1/04-3/31/05)		
3/31/03	3/31/04		3/31/05							
ALL	ALL		ALL		0-1MM	1-3MM	3-5MM	5-10MM	10-25MM	25MM & OVER
48	44		29	**NUMBER OF STATEMENTS**	4	7	5	7	5	1
%	%		%	**ASSETS**	%	%	%	%	%	%
10.8	11.9		10.4	Cash & Equivalents						
24.4	25.4		30.3	Trade Receivables (net)						
9.5	7.9		6.8	Inventory						
2.4	2.9		1.4	All Other Current						
47.1	48.1		48.9	Total Current						
42.3	42.7		37.7	Fixed Assets (net)						
3.1	2.4		5.1	Intangibles (net)						
7.5	6.8		8.2	All Other Non-Current						
100.0	100.0		100.0	Total						
				LIABILITIES						
11.1	5.8		10.2	Notes Payable-Short Term						
7.0	5.3		6.5	Cur. Mat.-L/T/D						
10.2	11.4		10.5	Trade Payables						
.1	.2		.2	Income Taxes Payable						
9.0	16.3		20.0	All Other Current						
37.3	39.0		47.4	Total Current						
24.7	19.4		14.9	Long-Term Debt						
.3	.2		.1	Deferred Taxes						
3.6	7.0		6.7	All Other Non-Current						
34.2	34.5		30.9	Net Worth						
100.0	100.0		100.0	Total Liabilities & Net Worth						
				INCOME DATA						
100.0	100.0		100.0	Net Sales						
				Gross Profit						
97.2	97.3		99.5	Operating Expenses						
2.8	2.7		.5	Operating Profit						
1.1	.5		1.1	All Other Expenses (net)						
1.6	2.3		-.6	Profit Before Taxes						
				RATIOS						
2.9	2.2		1.6							
1.3	1.2		1.0	Current						
.8	.8		.7							
2.3	1.9		1.4							
.9	.9		.8	Quick						
.5	.5		.6							
18	20.3	20	17.9	23 16.2	Sales/Receivables					
30	12.0	34	10.8	40 9.2						
55	6.6	52	7.0	58 6.3						
				Cost of Sales/Inventory						
				Cost of Sales/Payables						
7.8	8.5		10.8	Sales/Working Capital						
29.7	28.9		431.5							
-22.1	-29.4		-14.3							
8.5	7.1		9.0	EBIT/Interest						
(42) 2.4	(38) 1.9	(27)	1.6							
.6	-.1		-1.5							
				Net Profit + Depr., Dep.,						
				Amort./Cur. Mat. L/T/D						
.6	.7		.8	Fixed/Worth						
1.3	1.2		1.2							
5.1	2.8		7.8							
.8	.8		1.0	Debt/Worth						
1.6	1.4		2.1							
8.2	5.0		11.6							
35.3	33.1		49.8	% Profit Before Taxes/Tangible						
(40) 16.5	(37) 6.5	(25)	3.6	Net Worth						
-1.4	-12.2		-26.8							
16.8	12.9		9.6	% Profit Before Taxes/Total						
4.2	2.3		1.7	Assets						
-1.4	-4.1		-10.3							
10.8	9.7		17.5	Sales/Net Fixed Assets						
5.3	4.5		7.9							
3.1	3.5		3.9							
2.8	2.9		3.1	Sales/Total Assets						
2.2	2.1		2.5							
1.8	1.5		2.1							
2.7	3.5		2.7	% Depr., Dep., Amort./Sales						
(43) 5.3	(38) 5.1	(24)	5.5							
7.3	7.6		7.4							
2.8	4.5		4.1	% Officers', Directors',						
(25) 5.3	(26) 7.0	(10)	5.9	Owners' Comp/Sales						
10.8	12.9		10.7							
242060M	258627M		179407M	Net Sales ($)	2999M	13590M	17070M	48389M	70290M	27069M
99725M	121262M		74781M	Total Assets ($)	1155M	6744M	8795M	19400M	29421M	9266M

M = $ thousand   MM = $ million
See Pages 11 through 21 for Explanation of Ratios and Data

Current Data Sorted By Assets   **Comparative Historical Data**

						Type of Statement		
1	1	3	7	2	2	Unqualified	10	8
2		2	1			Reviewed	3	2
1	2	3				Compiled	6	10
1	4	2				Tax Returns	4	4
1	4	2	3	3	1	Other	6	7
	12 (4/1-9/30/04)		36 (10/1/04-3/31/05)				4/1/00-3/31/01 ALL	4/1/01-3/31/02 ALL
0-500M	500M-2MM	2-10MM	10-50MM	50-100MM	100-250MM	NUMBER OF STATEMENTS		
6	11	12	11	5	3		29	31
%	%	%	%	%	%	**ASSETS**	%	%
	9.6	17.5	11.0			Cash & Equivalents	13.3	18.3
	17.1	9.1	3.9			Trade Receivables (net)	11.5	8.1
	1.2	.6	.0			Inventory	.3	.8
	2.6	2.5	4.1			All Other Current	4.0	6.2
	30.5	29.7	19.0			Total Current	29.1	33.5
	35.0	52.1	61.5			Fixed Assets (net)	56.1	47.9
	15.9	.5	4.0			Intangibles (net)	4.3	6.2
	18.6	17.7	15.5			All Other Non-Current	10.6	12.4
	100.0	100.0	100.0			Total	100.0	100.0
						LIABILITIES		
	22.3	.9	.0			Notes Payable-Short Term	3.5	2.7
	4.2	4.0	9.4			Cur. Mat.-L/T/D	3.8	5.9
	1.4	7.3	3.7			Trade Payables	5.1	8.5
	.1	.2	.2			Income Taxes Payable	.1	.0
	16.0	15.8	10.2			All Other Current	17.5	15.0
	44.1	28.2	23.6			Total Current	30.1	32.1
	23.1	43.8	43.3			Long-Term Debt	38.4	35.9
	.0	.2	.5			Deferred Taxes	.2	.2
	19.6	6.0	9.3			All Other Non-Current	12.6	10.1
	13.1	21.8	23.3			Net Worth	18.8	21.7
	100.0	100.0	100.0			Total Liabilities & Net Worth	100.0	100.0
						INCOME DATA		
	100.0	100.0	100.0			Net Sales	100.0	100.0
						Gross Profit		
	86.7	80.4	77.4			Operating Expenses	86.0	83.4
	13.3	19.6	22.6			Operating Profit	14.0	16.6
	7.0	8.0	11.5			All Other Expenses (net)	2.9	11.2
	6.3	11.6	11.1			Profit Before Taxes	11.1	5.4
						RATIOS		
	1.5	1.1	2.3				1.7	1.7
	.7	.7	.8			Current	.9	.8
	.0	.5	.5				.6	.4
	1.3	.9	1.7				1.6	1.7
	.5	.7	.8			Quick	.9	.5
	.0	.3	.5				.5	.3
0 UND	1 252.9	0 UND					2 153.5	0 UND
12 29.9	10 37.3	9 41.7				Sales/Receivables	11 34.2	4 84.6
24 15.5	18 20.1	23 16.0					27 13.6	17 22.0
						Cost of Sales/Inventory		
						Cost of Sales/Payables		
	33.1	91.7	3.3				9.4	16.5
	-12.7	-27.9	-38.4			Sales/Working Capital	-86.9	-52.9
	-4.6	-8.0	-5.6				-18.0	-8.5
							(22) 7.1	30.8
						EBIT/Interest	3.9	(15) 4.9
							2.0	1.5
						Net Profit + Depr., Dep., Amort./Cur. Mat. L /T/D		
	.6	.5	1.8				1.0	.7
	2.8	1.3	3.7			Fixed/Worth	2.0	3.5
	-1.0	6.4	74.7				10.9	8.2
	2.0	2.2	.8				1.3	2.1
	8.6	3.3	3.8			Debt/Worth	2.5	3.6
	-7.4	255.2	132.1				12.7	28.9
		73.1					72.1	67.0
	(10) 26.0					% Profit Before Taxes/Tangible Net Worth	(24) 15.5	(26) 34.2
		-1.7					10.1	1.9
	14.2	13.3	12.3				13.4	26.6
	2.1	4.0	4.4			% Profit Before Taxes/Total Assets	5.7	4.7
	-.6	-.3	2.2				2.0	.1
	80.6	41.2	4.4				19.7	27.0
	16.4	8.6	.5			Sales/Net Fixed Assets	1.4	9.7
	1.5	.2	.2				.4	.6
	4.9	5.1	2.1				4.5	6.1
	1.4	.4	.3			Sales/Total Assets	.9	2.4
	.3	.1	.2				.3	.2
		1.1	2.5				1.1	.6
	(11) 5.2	8.7				% Depr., Dep., Amort./Sales	(25) 3.5	(26) 3.4
		17.7	22.4				16.5	8.9
							3.0	3.4
						% Officers', Directors', Owners' Comp/Sales	(13) 4.2	(11) 4.9
							6.8	6.9
9852M	34451M	124835M	195613M	284912M	841307M	Net Sales ($)	604925M	746926M
1905M	14367M	62461M	206431M	399100M	521406M	Total Assets ($)	542155M	572381M

© RMA 2005   M = $ thousand   MM = $ million

See Pages 11 through 21 for Explanation of Ratios and Data

Comparative Historical Data | **Current Data Sorted By Sales**

Type of Statement									
14	8	16	Unqualified	2	2	2	1	1	8
5	11	5	Reviewed		4				1
6	9	6	Compiled	2	3		1		
1	9	7	Tax Returns				1	1	
19	20	14	Other	5	4	1	4	1	3

	4/1/02-3/31/03	4/1/03-3/31/04	4/1/04-3/31/05		12 (4/1-9/30/04)		36 (10/1/04-3/31/05)		
	ALL	ALL	ALL	0-1MM	1-3MM	3-5MM	5-10MM	10-25MM	25MM & OVER
NUMBER OF STATEMENTS	45	57	48	10	13	3	7	3	12
	%	%	%	%	%	%	%	%	%
ASSETS									
Cash & Equivalents	12.9	14.3	15.6	18.4	15.5				10.0
Trade Receivables (net)	11.5	11.5	9.4	3.9	6.6				14.3
Inventory	.0	1.0	.4	1.0	.0				.6
All Other Current	4.1	3.2	2.6	1.2	1.1				2.8
Total Current	28.4	30.0	28.0	24.5	23.2				27.7
Fixed Assets (net)	53.7	46.1	48.9	55.0	61.6				31.5
Intangibles (net)	7.7	8.4	8.8	.6	11.1				19.8
All Other Non-Current	10.2	15.6	14.3	19.9	4.1				20.9
Total	100.0	100.0	100.0	100.0	100.0				100.0
LIABILITIES									
Notes Payable-Short Term	3.4	5.9	6.2	8.7	11.6				1.9
Cur. Mat.-L/T/D	4.0	2.3	7.1	2.6	7.8				4.1
Trade Payables	6.9	6.2	4.6	3.3	1.4				12.2
Income Taxes Payable	.3	.5	.1	.0	.1				.2
All Other Current	17.9	18.6	12.9	8.5	10.9				19.9
Total Current	32.5	33.5	31.0	23.1	31.7				38.4
Long-Term Debt	36.6	34.1	38.0	60.2	32.3				29.7
Deferred Taxes	.4	.3	.3	.0	.0				.9
All Other Non-Current	8.8	10.2	9.3	8.2	10.3				13.1
Net Worth	21.7	21.9	21.4	8.5	25.8				17.9
Total Liabilities & Net Worth	100.0	100.0	100.0	100.0	100.0				100.0
INCOME DATA									
Net Sales	100.0	100.0	100.0	100.0	100.0				100.0
Gross Profit									
Operating Expenses	86.2	85.4	80.5	65.4	87.2				91.3
Operating Profit	13.8	14.6	19.5	34.6	12.8				8.7
All Other Expenses (net)	7.9	8.2	8.8	14.7	7.3				3.3
Profit Before Taxes	5.9	6.4	10.7	19.9	5.6				5.4
RATIOS									
Current	1.7	2.0	1.7	2.0	4.1				1.2
	.9	.9	.8	.5	.7				.8
	.6	.4	.5	.2	.5				.5
Quick	1.4	1.9	1.3	1.8	4.0				1.0
	.9	.8	.7	.5	.7				.8
	.5	.3	.5	.2	.5				.5
Sales/Receivables	1 376.0	0 UND	0 781.5	0 UND	0 UND			4 95.1
	10 35.6	7 53.8	10 37.6	0 UND	12 31.1				18 20.0
	33 11.2	22 16.7	23 16.0	18 19.8	23 15.8				31 11.8
Cost of Sales/Inventory									
Cost of Sales/Payables									
Sales/Working Capital	25.7	14.3	26.7	54.6	20.4				73.2
	-86.4	-102.7	-36.7	-7.1	-56.9				-28.9
	-10.4	-7.5	-5.3	-2.2	-6.4				-12.8
EBIT/Interest	6.0	8.3	6.3						8.4
	(31) 2.9	(40) 2.6	(29) 1.8					(10)	3.3
	.8	.3	.7						1.4
Net Profit + Depr., Dep., Amort./Cur. Mat. L/T/D		2.3	4.8						
		(10) 1.8	(13) 1.1						
		.9	.5						
Fixed/Worth	1.0	.7	.7	.5	1.5				1.6
	4.0	2.1	2.9	5.0	4.0				35.5
	-9.3	UND	UND	UND	-3.7				-1.6
Debt/Worth	1.7	1.9	1.9	3.7	1.0				3.3
	5.4	4.0	4.2	15.2	3.2				48.3
	-16.7	UND	UND	UND	-9.9				-8.2
% Profit Before Taxes/Tangible Net Worth	84.2	101.4	73.3						
	(31) 18.7	(43) 20.7	(36) 15.1						
	-1.0	.3	5.6						
% Profit Before Taxes/Total Assets	16.4	12.1	10.5	8.8	7.0				21.5
	2.7	2.9	4.2	1.5	2.1				9.5
	-.4	-.8	.3	-1.0	-3.4				3.0
Sales/Net Fixed Assets	17.5	41.3	19.1	UND	15.7				32.1
	1.2	5.9	4.3	.5	4.3				16.1
	.3	.5	.3	.1	.3				1.8
Sales/Total Assets	3.5	4.7	3.7	.7	4.3				4.7
	.9	1.0	.8	.2	1.4				2.6
	.3	.3	.2	.1	.3				.8
% Depr., Dep., Amort./Sales	1.2	1.4	1.4		2.1				1.2
	(43) 4.2	(47) 3.5	(42) 4.7		(11) 5.2				2.3
	14.7	17.8	12.6		9.0				3.5
% Officers', Directors', Owners' Comp/Sales	2.6	2.1	2.0						
	(14) 8.2	(15) 5.0	(16) 6.4						
	17.1	8.8	9.2						
Net Sales ($)	1128898M	1951651M	1490970M	4813M	24903M	10467M	53649M	39532M	1357606M
Total Assets ($)	1022923M	1166218M	1205670M	25611M	55842M	44846M	191263M	52018M	836090M

© RMA 2005

M = $ thousand   MM = $ million

See Pages 11 through 21 for Explanation of Ratios and Data

Current Data Sorted By Assets   **Comparative Historical Data**

						Type of Statement		
2	5	6	3	1	1	Unqualified	12	8
	4	10	1			Reviewed	8	10
11	15	9			1	Compiled	28	34
68	18	6	1			Tax Returns	31	31
15	20	10	3		2	Other	41	46
	30 (4/1-9/30/04)		182 (10/1/04-3/31/05)				4/1/00-3/31/01	4/1/01-3/31/02
0-500M	500M-2MM	2-10MM	10-50MM	50-100MM	100-250MM		ALL	ALL
96	62	41	8	1	4	NUMBER OF STATEMENTS	120	129
%	%	%	%	%	%	ASSETS	%	%
22.5	15.3	8.2				Cash & Equivalents	14.8	19.0
11.7	25.3	28.9				Trade Receivables (net)	18.9	15.5
5.8	3.8	6.8				Inventory	4.3	5.5
3.6	3.1	3.2				All Other Current	5.1	4.3
43.5	47.5	47.2				Total Current	43.2	44.2
40.1	37.8	35.4				Fixed Assets (net)	40.9	37.1
5.9	4.5	4.8				Intangibles (net)	6.9	6.7
10.5	10.2	12.7				All Other Non-Current	9.0	11.9
100.0	100.0	100.0				Total	100.0	100.0
						LIABILITIES		
29.7	13.8	8.6				Notes Payable-Short Term	10.3	8.3
6.8	6.1	5.0				Cur. Mat.-L/T/D	4.2	6.3
8.3	15.7	12.9				Trade Payables	8.9	10.4
.6	.6	.7				Income Taxes Payable	2.0	.4
36.0	11.7	13.1				All Other Current	20.5	16.9
81.5	48.0	40.3				Total Current	45.9	42.2
29.7	25.9	26.3				Long-Term Debt	26.9	23.5
.0	.1	.2				Deferred Taxes	.5	.3
16.9	6.5	4.2				All Other Non-Current	6.9	5.9
−28.1	19.6	29.0				Net Worth	19.9	28.0
100.0	100.0	100.0				Total Liabilities & Net Worth	100.0	100.0
						INCOME DATA		
100.0	100.0	100.0				Net Sales	100.0	100.0
						Gross Profit		
94.6	90.5	91.1				Operating Expenses	91.7	91.9
5.4	9.5	8.9				Operating Profit	8.3	8.1
1.2	3.2	2.0				All Other Expenses (net)	3.1	3.3
4.2	6.3	7.0				Profit Before Taxes	5.2	4.8
						RATIOS		
2.0	2.5	2.2					2.3	2.1
.8	1.0	1.3				Current	1.2	1.2
.2	.6	.9					.6	.5
1.5	2.2	2.0					1.9	1.8
.5	1.0	1.0				Quick	(119) .9 (128) .8	
.1	.4	.6					.4	.3
0 UND	0 UND	6 60.0					0 UND 0 UND	
0 UND	14 25.3	46 8.0				Sales/Receivables	10 35.9 7 51.5	
7 51.4	41 9.0	69 5.3					38 9.5 35 10.4	
						Cost of Sales/Inventory		
						Cost of Sales/Payables		
15.6	10.7	7.4					11.7	10.7
−141.3	147.5	18.1				Sales/Working Capital	57.0	36.7
−10.0	−12.7	−44.9					−18.0	−16.9
15.2	13.6	12.6					8.9	10.1
(67) 3.5	(45) 3.6	(36) 3.4				EBIT/Interest	(87) 2.8 (95) 3.2	
1.0	1.4	.1					1.4	.8
						Net Profit + Depr., Dep.,		8.6
						Amort./Cur. Mat. L /T/D	(12) 1.8	
								1.5
.3	.2	.3					.4	.4
2.8	1.6	1.0				Fixed/Worth	1.5	1.3
−.8	94.5	19.1					−12.6	UND
1.0	.8	1.0					1.0	.9
31.5	2.5	2.8				Debt/Worth	3.0	2.8
−2.1	174.7	38.6					−67.9	UND
287.0	84.7	46.3					78.9	78.2
(51) 85.7	(48) 30.7	(32) 19.7				% Profit Before Taxes/Tangible Net Worth	(88) 32.2 (97) 26.4	
29.9	6.3	2.3					8.4	7.4
44.5	22.5	12.6					22.0	18.1
22.1	6.7	6.8				% Profit Before Taxes/Total Assets	9.2	6.1
1.4	1.9	−.3					1.9	−.5
116.1	67.6	17.3					49.8	36.6
15.5	8.4	7.0				Sales/Net Fixed Assets	10.0	10.1
6.5	2.1	2.8					3.1	3.1
8.4	4.9	2.4					5.3	4.8
4.6	2.3	2.0				Sales/Total Assets	2.7	2.3
2.6	.9	1.1					1.5	1.3
1.2	1.3	2.5					1.0	.8
(63) 2.8	(43) 3.3	(33) 3.6				% Depr., Dep., Amort./Sales	(92) 3.4 (101) 3.0	
4.6	10.4	7.6					7.6	7.3
4.2	2.6	1.7					5.0	2.5
(51) 7.9	(29) 5.6	(13) 4.6				% Officers', Directors', Owners' Comp/Sales	(51) 7.5 (48) 7.4	
14.6	10.4	8.3					16.2	13.9
104047M	266680M	351425M	107073M	32500M	542881M	Net Sales ($)	6171189M	4762969M
17755M	63650M	186184M	128914M	55108M	533255M	Total Assets ($)	1232265M	1831151M

M = $ thousand   MM = $ million
See Pages 11 through 21 for Explanation of Ratios and Data

Comparative Historical Data				Current Data Sorted By Sales					

			Type of Statement						
14	14	18	Unqualified	3	4	2	3	3	3
10	13	15	Reviewed		1	4	5	5	
30	56	36	Compiled	11	11	3	5	4	2
48	53	93	Tax Returns	54	27	6	4	2	
30	40	50	Other	16	10	4	11	7	2
4/1/02-3/31/03	4/1/03-3/31/04	4/1/04-3/31/05		30 (4/1-9/30/04)			182 (10/1/04-3/31/05)		
ALL	ALL	ALL		0-1MM	1-3MM	3-5MM	5-10MM	10-25MM	25MM & OVER
132	176	212	**NUMBER OF STATEMENTS**	84	53	19	28	21	7
%	%	%	**ASSETS**	%	%	%	%	%	%
14.5	20.2	17.7	Cash & Equivalents	23.0	11.5	21.0	7.2	19.1	
15.6	16.0	19.1	Trade Receivables (net)	6.1	17.5	35.3	38.4	36.4	
3.2	4.6	5.2	Inventory	4.6	7.2	.9	4.8	8.8	
3.9	5.5	3.3	All Other Current	3.1	2.5	4.0	5.6	1.9	
37.3	46.3	45.3	Total Current	36.9	38.8	61.3	55.9	66.1	
44.4	35.9	38.3	Fixed Assets (net)	44.9	45.6	24.0	29.0	22.1	
5.0	5.1	5.7	Intangibles (net)	6.8	4.2	6.6	5.5	2.6	
13.3	12.8	10.7	All Other Non-Current	11.5	11.5	8.2	9.6	9.2	
100.0	100.0	100.0	Total	100.0	100.0	100.0	100.0	100.0	
			LIABILITIES						
11.8	13.8	19.8	Notes Payable-Short Term	26.8	12.6	31.0	15.3	10.9	
7.5	3.9	5.9	Cur. Mat.-L/T/D	3.7	6.2	23.7	3.5	2.4	
9.5	9.9	11.0	Trade Payables	6.0	7.9	16.5	28.6	13.8	
.6	.3	.6	Income Taxes Payable	1.0	.3	.5	.7	.3	
17.6	20.6	23.1	All Other Current	27.7	23.3	19.9	13.2	17.1	
46.9	48.5	60.5	Total Current	65.3	50.3	91.6	61.4	44.4	
27.0	23.4	27.7	Long-Term Debt	33.3	28.9	31.5	17.4	11.3	
.2	.2	.1	Deferred Taxes	.0	.0	.3	.2	.0	
7.0	9.6	10.7	All Other Non-Current	17.3	7.4	1.1	7.1	4.0	
18.9	18.3	1.0	Net Worth	−15.8	13.4	−24.5	13.9	40.2	
100.0	100.0	100.0	Total Liabilities & Net Worth	100.0	100.0	100.0	100.0	100.0	
			INCOME DATA						
100.0	100.0	100.0	Net Sales	100.0	100.0	100.0	100.0	100.0	
			Gross Profit						
91.5	93.1	92.6	Operating Expenses	90.2	92.8	94.4	97.6	94.0	
8.5	6.9	7.4	Operating Profit	9.8	7.2	5.6	2.4	6.0	
4.4	1.8	2.0	All Other Expenses (net)	3.0	2.1	1.1	.2	.4	
4.1	5.1	5.5	Profit Before Taxes	6.8	5.1	4.5	2.2	5.6	
			RATIOS						
2.0	2.1	2.2		3.0	2.0	2.2	2.2	2.3	
.9	1.1	1.1	Current	.8	1.0	1.1	1.0	1.5	
.4	.5	.4		.2	.4	.5	.8	1.0	
1.6	1.8	1.9		1.9	1.4	2.2	2.1	2.1	
.7	(174) .9	.9	Quick	.5	.8	1.0	.9	1.3	
.2	.3	.2		.1	.2	.3	.4	.7	
0 UND	0 UND	0 UND		0 UND	0 UND	3 118.5	18 20.8	9 42.0	
5 78.8	7 56.0	5 68.1	Sales/Receivables	0 UND	2 222.3	36 10.2	42 8.8	37 9.9	
31 11.8	36 10.1	37 9.9		4 99.3	28 12.9	50 7.3	68 5.4	94 3.9	
			Cost of Sales/Inventory						
			Cost of Sales/Payables						
12.1	9.9	10.8		12.7	13.9	9.3	7.8	5.7	
−219.3	210.9	78.0	Sales/Working Capital	−124.8	−999.8	87.9	441.6	11.5	
−9.3	−13.0	−13.0		−4.4	−18.1	−71.7	−25.0	144.4	
9.5	9.0	14.0		15.5	14.2	9.1	10.8	16.9	
(102) 2.9	(123) 3.0	(159) 3.5	EBIT/Interest	(53) 3.1	(44) 3.4	(15) 4.3	(24) 3.4	(18) 6.4	
.2	−.4	1.1		.9	1.2	.9	−.4	3.4	
	4.9	8.1	Net Profit + Depr., Dep.,						
	(14) 2.6	(13) 4.3	Amort./Cur. Mat. L/T/D						
	1.1	1.4							
.6	.2	.3		.2	.7	.2	.3	.1	
2.2	1.3	1.8	Fixed/Worth	3.3	2.0	1.0	1.0	.3	
24.1	−34.2	−2.6		−1.8	−4.9	−.3	−5.4	1.4	
1.3	.8	.9		.9	1.1	1.1	.5	.8	
3.6	2.7	4.0	Debt/Worth	15.4	3.5	5.7	2.8	1.3	
182.2	−25.5	−5.8		−3.1	−9.4	−1.9	−12.4	5.1	
79.3	64.7	104.2	% Profit Before Taxes/Tangible	146.7	98.8	122.1	44.8	85.4	
(101) 24.0	(127) 27.4	(141) 37.5	Net Worth	(49) 73.0	(38) 42.5	(12) 36.6	(19) 14.9	(18) 34.1	
1.5	2.5	12.8		18.3	15.3	13.8	1.9	9.8	
17.6	22.8	29.9	% Profit Before Taxes/Total	39.5	34.8	26.9	12.2	19.6	
5.0	6.8	10.2	Assets	10.7	13.6	19.7	7.4	9.6	
−2.4	−2.7	1.5		−.2	2.7	3.0	−.7	2.3	
24.7	47.5	59.0		43.7	35.5	365.5	33.0	353.4	
7.0	10.8	9.8	Sales/Net Fixed Assets	7.2	8.5	48.1	12.2	13.1	
2.2	3.4	3.7		2.1	3.6	10.9	5.9	4.4	
5.2	5.2	5.6		5.5	5.9	24.2	5.0	5.1	
2.4	2.6	2.7	Sales/Total Assets	2.1	3.5	4.8	2.4	2.4	
1.1	1.1	1.4		.8	1.8	2.4	1.7	1.8	
1.6	1.2	1.5		2.0	1.7	.5	1.9	.8	
(105) 4.1	(137) 3.3	(148) 3.4	% Depr., Dep., Amort./Sales	(55) 4.2	(40) 3.2	(15) 2.0	(20) 3.2	(15) 2.4	
8.6	8.0	6.7		9.7	6.7	5.3	6.3	3.5	
3.6	3.9	3.1		5.2	3.1				
(59) 7.0	(64) 7.2	(94) 6.9	% Officers', Directors', Owners' Comp/Sales	(38) 11.6	(30) 6.4				
11.3	12.2	12.6		20.1	8.5				
1464036M	2486499M	1404606M	Net Sales ($)	39594M	90738M	77049M	202018M	299973M	695234M
927904M	1545469M	984866M	Total Assets ($)	66857M	43357M	39679M	84294M	152554M	598125M

© RMA 2005   M = $ thousand   MM = $ million
See Pages 11 through 21 for Explanation of Ratios and Data

Current Data Sorted By Assets   Comparative Historical Data

						Type of Statement		
11	28	107	110	24	25	Unqualified	211	197
3	13	51	37	1		Reviewed	55	51
18	59	101	19	1		Compiled	135	186
2	2	3				Tax Returns	5	1
80	237	490	115	5	8	Other	445	520
	505 (4/1-9/30/04)		1045 (10/1/04-3/31/05)				4/1/00- 3/31/01	4/1/01- 3/31/02
0-500M	500M-2MM	2-10MM	10-50MM	50-100MM	100-250MM		ALL	ALL
114	339	752	281	31	33	NUMBER OF STATEMENTS	851	955
%	%	%	%	%	%	ASSETS	%	%
43.1	19.3	9.8	14.0	23.9	26.9	Cash & Equivalents	19.0	17.6
3.0	1.5	.9	2.1	3.0	4.7	Trade Receivables (net)	2.4	2.4
.8	.1	.4	.9	.1	.9	Inventory	.5	.3
4.3	1.2	.9	2.2	7.0	3.9	All Other Current	3.1	3.9
51.3	22.2	12.0	19.2	34.0	36.4	Total Current	25.0	24.2
42.2	73.4	83.4	68.8	29.4	31.9	Fixed Assets (net)	64.0	67.4
.1	.1	.2	.3	.1	1.5	Intangibles (net)	.4	.2
6.4	4.3	4.4	11.7	36.5	30.1	All Other Non-Current	10.6	8.1
100.0	100.0	100.0	100.0	100.0	100.0	Total	100.0	100.0
						LIABILITIES		
11.1	3.1	1.6	1.6	2.7	4.5	Notes Payable-Short Term	3.1	2.4
1.1	2.1	1.8	1.7	2.1	.2	Cur. Mat.-L/T/D	2.6	2.2
5.0	1.5	.7	1.5	1.4	1.8	Trade Payables	2.0	1.7
.0	.0	.0	.0	.0	.0	Income Taxes Payable	.0	.0
9.7	4.3	1.8	3.5	12.8	12.0	All Other Current	4.9	4.9
26.8	11.0	5.8	8.3	19.0	18.5	Total Current	12.6	11.1
24.4	37.6	29.8	22.3	10.8	14.8	Long-Term Debt	40.1	24.1
.0	.0	.0	.0	.0	.0	Deferred Taxes	.0	.0
2.5	1.0	.7	4.1	5.5	11.9	All Other Non-Current	3.1	2.8
46.3	50.4	63.7	65.2	64.7	54.8	Net Worth	44.1	62.0
100.0	100.0	100.0	100.0	100.0	100.0	Total Liabilities & Net Worth	100.0	100.0
						INCOME DATA		
100.0	100.0	100.0	100.0	100.0	100.0	Net Sales	100.0	100.0
						Gross Profit		
91.9	85.8	87.6	89.2	91.1	93.5	Operating Expenses	87.0	87.6
8.1	14.2	12.4	10.8	8.9	6.5	Operating Profit	13.0	12.4
1.1	5.4	4.9	2.6	3.4	4.9	All Other Expenses (net)	.3	4.7
7.0	8.8	7.6	8.2	5.6	1.6	Profit Before Taxes	12.6	7.6
						RATIOS		
13.1	14.5	10.5	7.3	4.1	12.8		8.7	10.6
4.0	2.6	2.8	2.4	1.8	2.7	Current	2.7	2.8
1.1	1.0	1.0	1.1	1.0	.7		1.0	1.1
11.6	13.5	9.9	6.6	4.0	10.1		7.6	8.4
3.0	2.5	2.6	2.1	1.3	2.6	Quick	2.3 (954)	2.2
.8	.9	.9	.8	.9	.5		.8	.8
0 UND	0 UND	0 UND	0 UND	4 82.2	0 UND		0 UND	0 UND
0 UND	0 UND	0 UND	0 999.8	22 16.5	25 14.6	Sales/Receivables	0 UND	0 UND
0 UND	0 UND	0 UND	10 35.5	34 10.9	91 4.0		7 49.7	7 50.7
						Cost of Sales/Inventory		
						Cost of Sales/Payables		
3.8	2.9	3.4	2.9	.9	.4		2.3	2.6
13.1	11.3	8.9	7.6	9.0	3.1	Sales/Working Capital	7.2	6.7
107.8	279.0	450.8	77.9	288.4	-4.5		742.8	107.0
7.6	5.5	4.2	7.3	11.7	10.0		6.7	4.5
(41) 2.4	(204) 2.2	(454) 2.1	(200) 2.5	(21) 2.4	(19) 1.4	EBIT/Interest	(458) 2.7	(516) 1.9
.5	1.1	.8	1.0	.0	.7		1.2	.9
						Net Profit + Depr., Dep., Amort./Cur. Mat. L /T/D		
.0	.8	1.0	.7	.1	.1		.5	.7
.6	1.3	1.4	1.1	.2	.5	Fixed/Worth	1.0	1.1
1.4	2.3	1.8	1.5	.9	1.0		1.5	1.6
.1	.2	.2	.2	.1	.3		.2	.2
.5	.7	.5	.5	.6	.7	Debt/Worth	.5	.5
1.5	2.0	1.0	1.1	1.0	2.2		1.1	1.1
29.7	14.7	8.0	9.5	9.9	4.6	% Profit Before Taxes/Tangible	15.0	11.1
(105) 14.2	(322) 5.4	(749) 2.2	(280) 3.1	2.0	(32) .3	Net Worth	(830) 6.0	(933) 2.9
.8	.3	-.3	.0	-2.5	-2.9		.6	-.5
20.6	7.6	4.6	5.7	5.6	2.9	% Profit Before Taxes/Total	8.8	6.3
5.0	2.5	1.4	2.1	1.1	.0	Assets	3.2	1.7
-2.5	.0	-.2	.0	-1.2	-1.3		.3	-.4
UND	1.3	.6	1.1	9.2	2.5		1.5	1.1
10.3	.5	.3	.4	1.3	1.0	Sales/Net Fixed Assets	.6	.5
1.1	.3	.2	.3	.6	.6		.3	.3
4.1	.7	.4	.5	.5	.3		.6	.6
1.7	.4	.3	.3	.3	.2	Sales/Total Assets	.4	.4
.8	.3	.2	.2	.2	.1		.2	.2
1.4	2.9	4.1	3.3	1.5	1.5		2.3	1.7
(37) 2.6	(112) 5.7	(278) 7.1	(197) 6.5	(27) 5.1	(27) 5.1	% Depr., Dep., Amort./Sales	(439) 5.1	(447) 5.0
7.6	10.5	11.5	10.4	9.0	7.4		8.7	8.4
7.1	10.2	6.2	6.4				6.2	8.0
(24) 15.3	(65) 17.8	(119) 12.5	(37) 12.1			% Officers', Directors', Owners' Comp/Sales	(132) 13.6	(155) 14.9
22.1	26.4	27.1	35.2				25.1	27.2
73722M	264931M	1389322M	3604473M	1139326M	1264454M	Net Sales ($)	5665033M	6665701M
28453M	416734M	3625790M	5768086M	2238712M	5176759M	Total Assets ($)	13933699M	15367161M

M = $ thousand   MM = $ million
See Pages 11 through 21 for Explanation of Ratios and Data

Comparative Historical Data			Type of Statement	Current Data Sorted By Sales					
302	303	305	Unqualified	38	73	47	51	56	40
101	96	105	Reviewed	20	41	19	12	11	2
161	292	198	Compiled	108	65	15	7	2	1
2	7	7	Tax Returns	5	1	1			
761	974	935	Other	473	316	68	45	15	18
4/1/02-3/31/03	4/1/03-3/31/04	4/1/04-3/31/05		505 (4/1-9/30/04)			1045 (10/1/04-3/31/05)		
ALL	ALL	ALL		0-1MM	1-3MM	3-5MM	5-10MM	10-25MM	25MM & OVER
1327	1672	1550	**NUMBER OF STATEMENTS**	644	496	150	115	84	61
%	%	%	**ASSETS**	%	%	%	%	%	%
16.7	16.1	15.7	Cash & Equivalents	15.1	14.6	14.5	15.4	23.4	24.5
2.0	1.8	1.5	Trade Receivables (net)	.7	1.2	1.7	2.2	5.2	6.8
.4	.3	.5	Inventory	.2	.1	1.1	1.0	1.1	2.7
1.9	2.6	1.6	All Other Current	1.3	1.2	.9	3.3	2.5	6.0
21.1	20.9	19.4	Total Current	17.3	17.1	18.2	21.9	32.1	40.0
70.5	71.8	73.3	Fixed Assets (net)	78.8	77.6	74.0	65.2	44.3	33.9
.3	.2	.2	Intangibles (net)	.1	.2	.3	.4	1.1	.5
8.1	7.1	7.0	All Other Non-Current	3.8	5.0	7.5	12.5	22.5	25.5
100.0	100.0	100.0	Total	100.0	100.0	100.0	100.0	100.0	100.0
			LIABILITIES						
2.4	2.9	2.7	Notes Payable-Short Term	3.4	2.0	3.1	1.4	1.7	4.1
1.8	1.8	1.8	Cur. Mat.-L/T/D	1.6	2.3	1.9	1.0	1.8	1.0
1.3	1.4	1.4	Trade Payables	1.1	1.2	1.9	1.3	2.3	3.9
.0	.0	.0	Income Taxes Payable	.0	.0	.0	.1	.0	.0
4.2	4.0	3.7	All Other Current	2.4	3.4	3.5	5.6	6.1	11.8
9.7	10.1	9.5	Total Current	8.5	8.8	10.3	9.3	12.0	20.9
26.2	26.7	29.0	Long-Term Debt	31.8	31.8	26.6	22.7	17.5	10.7
.0	.0	.0	Deferred Taxes	.0	.0	.0	.0	.0	.0
2.0	2.6	1.9	All Other Non-Current	.5	1.1	2.1	3.3	8.6	9.6
62.1	60.6	59.6	Net Worth	59.2	58.3	61.0	64.7	61.9	58.8
100.0	100.0	100.0	Total Liabilities & Net Worth	100.0	100.0	100.0	100.0	100.0	100.0
			INCOME DATA						
100.0	100.0	100.0	Net Sales	100.0	100.0	100.0	100.0	100.0	100.0
			Gross Profit						
88.0	88.0	88.0	Operating Expenses	86.3	88.3	89.7	89.7	87.3	97.4
12.0	12.0	12.0	Operating Profit	13.7	11.7	10.3	10.3	12.7	2.6
5.4	4.5	4.3	All Other Expenses (net)	5.8	3.8	3.1	2.5	4.0	-1.4
6.6	7.4	7.7	Profit Before Taxes	7.9	7.9	7.3	7.8	8.7	4.0
			RATIOS						
8.9	10.8	10.8		13.6	11.8	5.3	9.2	7.9	4.6
2.7	2.8	2.7	Current	3.1	2.6	2.0	2.9	2.2	2.3
.9	1.0	1.0		1.0	1.1	1.0	1.3	1.0	.9
8.2	9.5	9.7		12.8	10.5	4.7	9.0	6.1	3.3
2.4	2.3	2.4	Quick	2.8	2.5	2.0	2.2	2.0	1.6
.8	.8	.8		.8	.9	.8	.7	.9	.7
0 UND	0 UND	0 UND		0 UND	0 UND	0 UND	0 UND	0 999.8	0 999.8
0 UND	0 UND	0 UND	Sales/Receivables	0 UND	0 UND	0 UND	0 UND	6 58.5	13 27.2
4 101.3	2 177.1	1 374.5		0 UND	0 UND	5 77.0	9 41.2	40 9.1	36 10.1
			Cost of Sales/Inventory						
			Cost of Sales/Payables						
2.7	2.7	3.1		2.7	3.3	4.4	2.6	1.3	3.2
8.0	8.3	9.1	Sales/Working Capital	10.2	8.6	13.6	6.1	7.7	9.0
-128.5	UND	240.3		UND	109.6	-163.0	23.7	173.0	-25.7
3.9	4.9	5.2		3.7	5.2	6.2	6.7	17.3	18.7
(772) 1.8	(962) 2.1	(939) 2.1	EBIT/Interest	(336) 2.1	(319) 2.0	(101) 2.1	(85) 2.6	(60) 5.0	(38) 3.4
.6	.9	.9		1.0	.9	.7	.6	1.3	.7
			Net Profit + Depr., Dep., Amort./Cur. Mat. L/T/D						
.7	.8	.8		.9	.9	.9	.6	.1	.2
1.2	1.2	1.2	Fixed/Worth	1.4	1.3	1.2	1.1	.6	.5
1.7	1.8	1.8		2.0	1.8	1.7	1.5	1.3	1.0
.2	.2	.2		.2	.2	.2	.2	.2	.3
.5	.6	.6	Debt/Worth	.6	.6	.5	.5	.6	.7
1.1	1.2	1.2		1.3	1.1	1.3	1.1	1.5	1.5
9.8	10.3	10.3		10.1	9.7	11.1	10.3	13.0	11.2
(1306) 2.4	(1632) 2.9	(1519) 3.0	% Profit Before Taxes/Tangible Net Worth	(630) 2.6	(485) 2.9	(147) 3.8	(113) 3.5	(83) 5.4	2.3
-.9	-.4	-.1		-.2	.0	.0	.1	-.8	-2.0
5.7	5.9	5.6		4.8	5.7	6.0	6.0	7.0	7.1
1.4	1.7	1.8	% Profit Before Taxes/Total Assets	1.7	1.7	2.2	2.4	2.9	1.1
-.6	-.3	-.2		-.2	-.1	-.1	.1	-.2	-1.2
1.0	1.0	.9		.7	.8	.9	1.4	5.6	11.5
.5	.4	.4	Sales/Net Fixed Assets	.3	.4	.5	.6	1.3	3.0
.3	.3	.3		.2	.3	.3	.4	.6	.9
.6	.6	.6		.5	.6	.7	.6	.9	2.1
.3	.4	.3	Sales/Total Assets	.3	.4	.4	.4	.5	.8
.2	.2	.2		.2	.2	.3	.3	.3	.4
3.0	3.4	3.0		2.9	4.1	4.3	3.7	1.8	1.2
(638) 6.1	(700) 6.4	(678) 6.3	% Depr., Dep., Amort./Sales	(174) 7.3	(196) 7.2	(99) 7.1	(86) 6.5	(69) 4.1	(54) 2.5
9.5	10.2	10.2		12.8	11.8	11.3	9.3	7.1	5.8
6.7	7.0	7.0		8.6	6.9	5.9	6.0		
(237) 14.7	(296) 14.1	(250) 14.4	% Officers', Directors', Owners' Comp/Sales	(130) 16.3	(74) 13.0	(18) 13.5	(15) 8.0		
27.9	24.5	26.6		24.8	27.6	32.5	22.9		
8720228M	8315481M	7736228M	Net Sales ($)	340691M	863979M	569634M	811581M	1346845M	3803498M
19347756M	19254346M	17254534M	Total Assets ($)	1423230M	2656030M	1596825M	2568174M	4427484M	4582791M

M = $ thousand   MM = $ million
See Pages 11 through 21 for Explanation of Ratios and Data

Current Data Sorted By Assets   Comparative Historical Data

						Type of Statement		
8	14	29	13	1	3	Unqualified		
						Reviewed		
	1					Compiled		
4	4	10	1		1	Tax Returns		
						Other		
	71 (4/1-9/30/04)		18 (10/1/04-3/31/05)				4/1/00-3/31/01 ALL	4/1/01-3/31/02 ALL
0-500M	500M-2MM	2-10MM	10-50MM	50-100MM	100-250MM			
12	19	39	14	2	3	**NUMBER OF STATEMENTS**		
%	%	%	%	%	%	**ASSETS**	%	%
32.9	26.6	19.2	29.2			Cash & Equivalents	D	D
33.2	17.4	13.6	11.2			Trade Receivables (net)	A	A
.6	4.7	.7	2.5			Inventory	T	T
11.8	6.4	3.0	8.7			All Other Current	A	A
78.5	55.1	36.5	51.5			Total Current		
15.9	36.2	48.9	30.6			Fixed Assets (net)	N	N
.0	.0	.1	.0			Intangibles (net)	O	O
5.7	8.8	14.5	17.8			All Other Non-Current	T	T
100.0	100.0	100.0	100.0			Total		
						LIABILITIES	A	A
18.2	2.3	2.6	4.7			Notes Payable-Short Term	V	V
.1	1.0	2.1	.7			Cur. Mat.-L/T/D	A	A
13.0	7.0	4.8	9.0			Trade Payables	I	I
.0	.0	.0	.0			Income Taxes Payable	L	L
22.2	13.1	7.8	14.4			All Other Current	A	A
53.4	23.5	17.3	28.7			Total Current	B	B
3.1	5.7	21.2	17.0			Long-Term Debt	L	L
.0	.0	.0	.0			Deferred Taxes	E	E
6.6	.8	1.6	6.1			All Other Non-Current		
36.8	70.0	59.8	48.2			Net Worth		
100.0	100.0	100.0	100.0			Total Liabilities & Net Worth		
						INCOME DATA		
100.0	100.0	100.0	100.0			Net Sales		
						Gross Profit		
99.4	92.3	99.6	97.2			Operating Expenses		
.6	7.7	.4	2.8			Operating Profit		
.5	.5	−.1	−.5			All Other Expenses (net)		
.1	7.3	.5	3.3			Profit Before Taxes		
						RATIOS		
3.8	7.9	4.0	5.6					
1.6	3.1	2.1	1.6			Current		
1.1	1.2	1.0	1.3					
2.6	5.1	4.0	3.1					
1.6	2.3	2.1	1.4			Quick		
.8	1.1	.7	1.2					
0 UND	0 UND	3 142.3	0 UND					
22 16.6	21 17.1	31 11.9	17 21.0			Sales/Receivables		
47 7.7	35 10.6	51 7.2	61 6.0					
						Cost of Sales/Inventory		
						Cost of Sales/Payables		
4.9	3.3	3.9	2.0					
16.6	10.1	9.7	8.1			Sales/Working Capital		
208.9	31.2	−188.4	22.1					
		5.8						
	(28)	3.0				EBIT/Interest		
		−1.3						
						Net Profit + Depr., Dep., Amort./Cur. Mat. L /T/D		
.0	.0	.4	.0					
.3	.6	.7	.3			Fixed/Worth		
1.0	.9	2.0	1.3					
.8	.1	.2	.3					
1.2	.3	.5	1.3			Debt/Worth		
11.2	1.0	1.6	3.5					
91.8	31.4	13.0	11.5					
(11) −8.3	14.4	4.5	6.8			% Profit Before Taxes/Tangible Net Worth		
−26.8	−.1	−7.3	.5					
51.6	21.1	8.8	6.3					
−1.6	7.3	3.1	2.0			% Profit Before Taxes/Total Assets		
−20.4	−.1	−4.8	.3					
445.7	50.0	6.0	436.9					
47.0	10.9	3.4	5.0			Sales/Net Fixed Assets		
11.8	1.9	1.7	1.5					
6.7	4.2	1.8	3.1					
3.6	2.1	1.4	1.0			Sales/Total Assets		
1.8	1.0	.6	.6					
	.7	1.7	.8					
	(13) 1.5	(35) 2.5	(12) 2.2			% Depr., Dep., Amort./Sales		
	3.9	3.2	4.3					
						% Officers', Directors', Owners' Comp/Sales		
12266M	53955M	250162M	460391M	95596M	520993M	Net Sales ($)		
2915M	19868M	174887M	225469M	157723M	413954M	Total Assets ($)		

© RMA 2005

M = $ thousand   MM = $ million
See Pages 11 through 21 for Explanation of Ratios and Data

Comparative Historical Data   **Current Data Sorted By Sales**

30	50	68	Type of Statement	8	15	10	17	9	9
			Unqualified						
1			Reviewed						
1		1	Compiled						
15	16	20	Tax Returns		1				
			Other	7	6	1		5	1
4/1/02-3/31/03 ALL	4/1/03-3/31/04 ALL	4/1/04-3/31/05 ALL		71 (4/1-9/30/04) 0-1MM	1-3MM	3-5MM	18 (10/1/04-3/31/05) 5-10MM	10-25MM	25MM & OVER
47	66	89	NUMBER OF STATEMENTS	15	22	11	17	14	10
%	%	%	**ASSETS**	%	%	%	%	%	%
19.8	18.1	25.4	Cash & Equivalents	21.4	35.9	19.0	15.8	15.3	45.5
20.0	19.8	16.2	Trade Receivables (net)	11.3	14.3	20.1	23.3	16.4	11.0
1.0	1.0	1.8	Inventory	.5	2.8	1.7	.7	3.1	2.0
4.6	3.6	6.1	All Other Current	10.2	4.8	4.1	4.0	5.3	9.0
45.4	42.6	49.4	Total Current	43.4	57.9	44.9	43.9	40.1	67.6
38.9	45.2	37.8	Fixed Assets (net)	44.1	29.5	38.4	42.3	50.0	21.4
1.0	.5	.1	Intangibles (net)	.0	.0	.2	.0	.1	.0
14.6	11.6	12.7	All Other Non-Current	12.5	12.6	16.4	13.8	9.8	11.0
100.0	100.0	100.0	Total	100.0	100.0	100.0	100.0	100.0	100.0
			LIABILITIES						
3.6	3.3	4.8	Notes Payable-Short Term	7.7	8.3	3.7	1.0	2.7	3.8
1.7	1.1	1.3	Cur. Mat.-L/T/D	1.2	.9	.7	1.4	2.9	.2
7.0	6.9	7.4	Trade Payables	9.2	4.1	4.2	9.3	4.4	16.0
.0	.0	.0	Income Taxes Payable	.0	.0	.0	.0	.0	.0
14.5	10.8	12.0	All Other Current	10.8	13.8	8.4	11.2	9.3	19.0
26.9	22.1	25.4	Total Current	28.8	27.0	17.0	23.0	19.3	38.9
16.0	19.9	14.4	Long-Term Debt	13.0	9.9	17.4	17.0	21.0	9.0
.0	.2	.0	Deferred Taxes	.0	.0	.0	.0	.0	.0
3.4	2.2	2.9	All Other Non-Current	2.1	1.2	5.7	2.5	1.5	7.1
53.7	55.5	57.3	Net Worth	56.1	61.9	59.8	57.5	58.2	45.0
100.0	100.0	100.0	Total Liabilities & Net Worth	100.0	100.0	100.0	100.0	100.0	100.0
			INCOME DATA						
100.0	100.0	100.0	Net Sales	100.0	100.0	100.0	100.0	100.0	100.0
			Gross Profit						
93.3	97.6	97.2	Operating Expenses	97.2	98.8	98.3	95.5	97.7	94.7
6.7	2.4	2.8	Operating Profit	2.8	1.2	1.7	4.5	2.3	5.3
2.3	.7	.1	All Other Expenses (net)	1.7	.1	-1.8	-.5	.4	.3
4.4	1.6	2.7	Profit Before Taxes	1.1	1.1	3.5	5.0	2.0	5.0
			RATIOS						
3.1	4.3	5.2		6.2	9.0	5.6	3.8	5.5	2.9
1.7	1.9	2.1	Current	1.3	3.2	2.3	1.9	2.5	2.0
1.1	1.2	1.1		.5	1.2	1.5	1.1	1.1	1.2
2.5	4.2	4.0		4.5	5.3	5.5	3.6	3.8	2.4
1.4	1.6	1.9	Quick	1.3	2.4	2.1	1.9	1.9	1.4
.9	1.0	1.0		.3	1.0	1.1	.8	1.1	1.1
8 44.5	5 67.5	0 UND		0 UND	0 UND	25 14.6	18 20.4	6 64.3	0 UND
32 11.6	32 11.3	23 16.0	Sales/Receivables	9 41.0	22 16.7	34 10.6	38 9.5	30 12.0	0 UND
47 7.8	63 5.8	40 9.1		30 12.0	36 10.3	69 5.3	60 6.0	36 10.1	17 21.5
			Cost of Sales/Inventory						
			Cost of Sales/Payables						
4.1	4.1	3.3		4.1	2.6	3.1	5.5	6.8	2.6
11.7	8.9	9.6	Sales/Working Capital	20.5	4.2	4.1	10.1	13.1	7.2
55.8	25.0	178.0		-5.1	89.2	26.4	NM	NM	NM
6.7	7.6	16.8			15.0		14.1		
(30) 1.2	(41) 3.2	(54) 5.0	EBIT/Interest		(14) 5.7		(11) 3.9		
-.9	-.3	.4			.7		-1.4		
			Net Profit + Depr., Dep., Amort./Cur. Mat. L/T/D						
.2	.4	.2		.1	.0	.1	.4	.5	.0
.6	.6	.5	Fixed/Worth	.8	.4	.5	.6	1.0	.2
1.4	1.3	1.2		1.4	.9	2.3	1.7	1.7	.8
.3	.3	.2		.2	.1	.3	.2	.2	.4
.6	.7	.7	Debt/Worth	1.1	.4	.4	.5	.9	1.4
1.4	1.8	1.8		1.3	1.2	1.6	2.2	1.7	3.5
16.5	13.7	16.4		25.4	16.8	11.1	23.3	12.4	20.6
(43) 4.9	(65) 4.0	(88) 6.1	% Profit Before Taxes/Tangible Net Worth	-8.3	(21) 4.7	5.6	12.5	6.8	10.2
-5.1	-7.0	-6.2		-27.9	-1.0	-6.5	-5.3	-3.6	3.5
5.5	6.9	9.6		21.1	8.8	8.8	12.6	10.0	12.4
1.3	1.7	3.1	% Profit Before Taxes/Total Assets	-2.9	2.1	3.1	6.9	3.7	5.1
-3.2	-3.0	-2.7		-8.7	-1.8	-.3	-3.8	-1.8	1.8
38.6	7.6	24.8		37.7	120.9	25.6	7.6	7.1	436.9
4.5	3.3	4.4	Sales/Net Fixed Assets	4.1	5.6	3.9	3.7	5.0	11.6
1.6	1.2	1.8		.4	1.8	1.4	2.2	2.3	3.4
2.4	2.4	2.7		2.4	3.1	1.6	2.7	3.3	3.7
1.3	1.3	1.5	Sales/Total Assets	1.0	1.2	1.5	1.7	1.7	2.0
.8	.7	.8		.3	.7	.9	.9	1.0	.7
1.0	1.4	1.4		1.2	.6	.9	1.7	1.5	
(38) 2.3	(55) 2.7	(73) 2.0	% Depr., Dep., Amort./Sales	(11) 7.2	(15) 1.7	(10) 1.6	(14) 2.8	2.1	
4.3	4.2	3.3		12.8	3.3	3.1	3.8	3.3	
		3.0							
		(14) 9.2	% Officers', Directors', Owners' Comp/Sales						
		16.5							
947898M	691960M	1393363M	Net Sales ($)	8246M	35822M	41639M	125286M	197594M	984776M
723533M	652983M	994816M	Total Assets ($)	20527M	39785M	45221M	91920M	121210M	676153M

Current Data Sorted By Assets   **Comparative Historical Data**

0-500M	500M-2MM	2-10MM	10-50MM	50-100MM	100-250MM	Type of Statement	ALL 4/1/00-3/31/01	ALL 4/1/01-3/31/02
11	47	138	67	8	8	Unqualified	244	214
	1	6	2	1		Reviewed	4	6
6	5	5	1			Compiled	34	51
2	6	3	1			Tax Returns	3	5
9	30	31	31	4		Other	76	102
305 (4/1-9/30/04)			118 (10/1/04-3/31/05)				4/1/00-3/31/01	4/1/01-3/31/02
28	89	183	102	13	8	**NUMBER OF STATEMENTS**	361	378
%	%	%	%	%	%	**ASSETS**	%	%
34.5	21.7	19.1	17.5	19.6		Cash & Equivalents	20.0	18.3
27.3	16.8	14.3	13.7	11.9		Trade Receivables (net)	18.3	18.6
1.7	2.4	2.0	1.0	.0		Inventory	1.4	1.4
3.2	4.4	2.9	2.6	2.4		All Other Current	5.3	6.5
66.7	45.4	38.3	34.8	34.0		Total Current	44.9	44.8
25.9	41.0	47.2	45.7	37.7		Fixed Assets (net)	40.7	39.7
.8	1.1	.5	.6	.5		Intangibles (net)	.8	.9
6.5	12.5	14.0	18.9	27.8		All Other Non-Current	13.5	14.6
100.0	100.0	100.0	100.0	100.0		Total	100.0	100.0
						LIABILITIES		
6.3	4.6	2.9	3.2	.6		Notes Payable-Short Term	4.4	3.8
1.2	3.8	1.9	1.0	1.4		Cur. Mat.-L/T/D	1.6	2.0
5.1	6.8	6.8	5.6	7.7		Trade Payables	7.1	7.3
.0	.0	.0	.0	.0		Income Taxes Payable	.0	.1
13.0	8.8	9.7	9.1	12.0		All Other Current	11.4	11.1
25.5	24.0	21.3	18.9	21.8		Total Current	24.5	24.3
6.3	19.2	22.8	23.1	18.0		Long-Term Debt	18.7	18.2
.0	.0	.1	.0	.0		Deferred Taxes	.1	.0
1.6	2.2	3.5	3.5	5.8		All Other Non-Current	2.8	3.3
66.6	54.6	52.3	54.5	54.4		Net Worth	53.9	54.0
100.0	100.0	100.0	100.0	100.0		Total Liabilities & Net Worth	100.0	100.0
						INCOME DATA		
100.0	100.0	100.0	100.0	100.0		Net Sales	100.0	100.0
						Gross Profit		
94.2	96.3	94.3	93.4	94.9		Operating Expenses	94.6	95.0
5.8	3.7	5.7	6.6	5.1		Operating Profit	5.4	5.0
5.6	1.5	1.5	.9	-1.2		All Other Expenses (net)	-2.3	1.8
.2	2.2	4.1	5.8	6.3		Profit Before Taxes	7.7	3.2
						RATIOS		
6.2	5.4	3.4	5.0	3.5			4.9	3.9
3.7	2.0	1.9	1.6	1.7		Current	2.1	2.0
1.6	1.0	1.1	1.0	1.4			1.2	1.1
5.9	4.7	3.2	3.7	2.5			4.2	3.3
3.6	1.8	1.7	1.5	1.6		Quick	1.7	1.6
1.5	.6	1.0	.9	1.3			1.0	.9
1 413.1	1 379.8	5 71.5	9 39.1	0 UND			9 38.6	6 61.7
26 14.2	20 18.6	29 12.7	28 12.9	43 8.5		Sales/Receivables	35 10.6	32 11.6
41 8.9	46 7.9	44 8.4	58 6.3	129 2.8			55 6.6	52 7.0
						Cost of Sales/Inventory		
						Cost of Sales/Payables		
6.0	3.3	4.4	3.1	2.3			3.2	4.1
10.9	9.9	9.9	8.5	8.3		Sales/Working Capital	7.7	9.1
14.9	NM	74.7	-237.3	17.8			36.2	42.3
28.5	10.1	6.9	8.2				8.2	6.0
(12) 9.7	(46) 1.5	(134) 2.1	(72) 2.4			EBIT/Interest	(221) 3.0	(228) 2.0
-5.6	-1.8	-.8	.8				.8	.0
						Net Profit + Depr., Dep., Amort./Cur. Mat. L/T/D		
.1	.1	.4	.4	.2			.3	.3
.3	.6	.8	.8	.7		Fixed/Worth	.7	.7
.6	1.5	1.7	1.5	1.7			1.5	1.5
.1	.2	.4	.3	.2			.3	.3
.3	.9	.8	.8	1.0		Debt/Worth	.8	.7
1.1	2.1	2.0	1.8	1.9			1.7	1.9
34.9	18.7	13.6	12.1	13.5		% Profit Before Taxes/Tangible Net Worth	16.6	15.9
(26) 3.2	(86) 3.2	(177) 4.7	(98) 3.7	6.7			(344) 8.0	(363) 4.1
-40.2	-13.4	-2.5	-.7	2.1			.0	-3.3
36.1	8.7	6.5	5.4	5.6		% Profit Before Taxes/Total Assets	9.3	7.0
2.5	1.1	2.1	2.0	3.1			4.3	1.5
-21.4	-5.5	-1.2	-.3	.4			.0	-1.7
69.5	32.2	8.7	5.6	9.4		Sales/Net Fixed Assets	14.4	17.8
25.6	5.8	2.9	2.3	2.6			3.4	4.4
7.3	1.8	1.0	1.0	1.2			1.5	1.5
5.3	3.0	2.1	1.7	1.3		Sales/Total Assets	2.4	2.6
3.5	1.8	1.1	.8	1.0			1.2	1.4
1.7	.7	.5	.3	.3			.6	.6
.6	.7	1.3	1.6	1.1		% Depr., Dep., Amort./Sales	1.0	.9
(20) 1.3	(66) 1.7	(167) 2.4	(93) 3.1	2.2			(298) 2.2	(311) 2.3
3.0	3.6	5.6	5.8	4.2			4.2	4.4
	2.6	2.5				% Officers', Directors', Owners' Comp/Sales	1.7	1.8
	(11) 6.7	(17)					(21) 9.4	(45) 9.4
	12.5	35.8					34.6	21.5
22178M	272254M	1364130M	2295118M	1326302M	573093M	Net Sales ($)	5212878M	7285091M
7410M	106901M	937349M	2175861M	883329M	1097307M	Total Assets ($)	4788233M	5254868M

© RMA 2005   M = $ thousand   MM = $ million
See Pages 11 through 21 for Explanation of Ratios and Data

Comparative Historical Data / Current Data Sorted By Sales

			Type of Statement						
270	278	279	Unqualified	34	54	49	49	48	45
11	10	10	Reviewed	2	1	1	2	2	2
13	40	17	Compiled	6	6	1	3	1	
9	12	12	Tax Returns	2	6	2	1		1
89	115	105	Other	20	15	22	20	14	14
4/1/02-3/31/03 ALL	4/1/03-3/31/04 ALL	4/1/04-3/31/05 ALL		0-1MM	1-3MM	3-5MM	5-10MM	10-25MM	25MM & OVER
				305 (4/1-9/30/04)			118 (10/1/04-3/31/05)		
392	455	423	NUMBER OF STATEMENTS	64	82	75	75	65	62
%	%	%	ASSETS	%	%	%	%	%	%
19.5	21.1	20.3	Cash & Equivalents	21.1	21.7	18.8	18.4	20.4	21.7
18.9	16.4	15.4	Trade Receivables (net)	10.6	11.1	17.0	15.1	19.1	20.4
1.3	1.2	1.7	Inventory	2.0	1.8	1.1	1.3	1.6	2.8
5.2	5.9	3.1	All Other Current	2.0	3.4	3.1	4.2	4.0	1.7
44.8	44.7	40.6	Total Current	35.8	37.9	40.1	39.0	45.1	46.7
39.9	42.7	43.6	Fixed Assets (net)	48.7	46.0	42.1	45.7	39.4	39.2
1.0	.6	.7	Intangibles (net)	.4	1.3	.6	.6	.3	.8
14.4	12.0	15.1	All Other Non-Current	15.1	14.8	17.2	14.7	15.2	13.4
100.0	100.0	100.0	Total	100.0	100.0	100.0	100.0	100.0	100.0
			LIABILITIES						
4.0	3.6	3.4	Notes Payable-Short Term	3.7	3.1	3.5	3.3	2.7	4.5
1.7	1.9	2.0	Cur. Mat.-L/T/D	2.8	1.4	1.9	3.1	1.5	1.4
7.4	7.4	6.3	Trade Payables	2.9	3.0	5.5	5.9	8.6	13.3
.1	.0	.0	Income Taxes Payable	.0	.0	.0	.0	.1	.0
11.6	10.6	9.6	All Other Current	6.8	6.3	6.6	10.9	14.3	13.7
24.8	23.5	21.4	Total Current	16.3	13.8	17.4	23.3	27.2	32.8
19.3	18.6	21.0	Long-Term Debt	26.8	22.5	18.0	23.2	16.7	18.6
.0	.0	.0	Deferred Taxes	.0	.0	.0	.0	.2	.0
3.6	4.8	3.3	All Other Non-Current	1.5	3.1	2.7	3.4	4.3	5.0
52.3	53.0	54.3	Net Worth	55.4	60.7	61.9	50.1	51.6	43.7
100.0	100.0	100.0	Total Liabilities & Net Worth	100.0	100.0	100.0	100.0	100.0	100.0
			INCOME DATA						
100.0	100.0	100.0	Net Sales	100.0	100.0	100.0	100.0	100.0	100.0
			Gross Profit						
95.8	95.2	94.3	Operating Expenses	88.8	92.9	96.2	93.8	96.5	97.9
4.2	4.8	5.7	Operating Profit	11.2	7.1	3.8	6.2	3.5	2.1
2.0	1.8	1.6	All Other Expenses (net)	6.8	4.3	-.7	-.5	.0	-.4
2.2	3.0	4.1	Profit Before Taxes	4.4	2.8	4.4	6.6	3.5	2.5
			RATIOS						
4.3	4.3	4.5		5.4	7.6	5.4	3.9	2.9	2.1
2.2	2.2	1.9	Current	1.7	3.0	2.3	2.3	1.6	1.3
1.2	1.1	1.1		.8	1.3	1.3	1.4	1.1	1.0
3.6	3.6	3.8		4.9	6.4	4.9	3.6	2.8	1.8
1.7	1.7	1.7	Quick	1.6	2.5	1.9	2.2	1.4	1.2
1.0	.9	1.0		.5	.9	1.2	1.1	1.0	.9
9　41.0	5　79.2	4　86.2		0　UND	2　207.0	11　32.1	10　38.3	10　36.7	16　23.2
32　11.2	28　13.2	27　13.5	Sales/Receivables	2　152.9	17　21.4	31　11.8	30　12.1	31　11.9	33　11.0
56　6.5	55　6.6	47　7.8		41　8.9	44　8.2	61　6.0	44　8.3	44　8.3	54　6.8
			Cost of Sales/Inventory						
			Cost of Sales/Payables						
3.7	3.3	3.9		2.5	2.7	2.9	4.1	5.8	7.9
8.6	8.5	9.3	Sales/Working Capital	12.5	5.5	7.4	9.2	14.7	20.7
34.5	58.0	71.1		-23.4	21.5	27.6	34.8	62.0	-172.5
6.6	7.7	8.6		4.8	10.8	6.4	10.5	15.1	8.3
(249)　2.2	(287)　2.5	(278)　2.2	EBIT/Interest	(33)　1.5	(50)　1.7	(49)　1.2	(59)　2.5	(44)　4.0	(43)　1.8
-1.8	-.3	.1		-1.5	-.9	-3.8	.8	.6	.7
			Net Profit + Depr., Dep., Amort./Cur. Mat. L/T/D						
.3	.3	.3		.2	.2	.2	.5	.4	.4
.7	.8	.8	Fixed/Worth	.8	.7	.7	.8	.7	.9
1.4	1.6	1.5		2.1	1.4	1.1	1.5	1.3	1.8
.3	.3	.3		.2	.2	.2	.4	.4	.7
.8	.8	.8	Debt/Worth	.9	.5	.5	.9	.8	1.3
2.1	2.1	1.9		2.3	1.7	1.5	1.9	1.9	3.2
16.5	12.9	14.1	% Profit Before Taxes/Tangible Net Worth	12.4	18.3	13.3	19.9	12.6	12.6
(377)　4.7	(438)　3.8	(408)　3.9		(61)　2.2	(78)　3.7	(71)　1.9	(62)　6.2	(61)　4.8	(61)　5.2
-6.4	-3.7	-2.6		-15.1	-2.4	-5.0	.0	.6	-.4
7.8	6.5	6.5	% Profit Before Taxes/Total Assets	5.7	7.9	8.1	9.0	5.8	5.5
2.1	1.8	2.0		.8	1.7	.7	3.1	2.5	2.5
-3.4	-2.2	-1.1		-5.2	-1.3	-3.2	-.1	-.3	-.1
16.2	10.9	13.0		20.4	24.6	13.2	7.3	17.1	12.8
3.8	3.2	3.3	Sales/Net Fixed Assets	1.4	1.8	3.2	3.3	4.9	4.8
1.6	1.2	1.1		.3	.6	1.3	1.4	1.9	2.3
2.6	2.3	2.3		1.6	1.7	2.2	2.4	2.9	2.9
1.4	1.2	1.1	Sales/Total Assets	.5	.7	1.1	1.3	1.7	1.8
.7	.6	.5		.2	.3	.6	.7	.8	1.1
1.1	1.4	1.1		1.5	1.0	1.5	1.4	.9	.7
(343)　2.4	(384)　2.7	(366)　2.3	% Depr., Dep., Amort./Sales	(43)　6.2	(68)　3.4	(66)　2.4	(69)　2.7	(60)　1.7	(60)　1.9
4.3	4.8	5.0		18.3	8.2	4.9	3.6	2.9	3.2
1.8	2.1	2.9	% Officers', Directors', Owners' Comp/Sales		4.1				
(35)　9.2	(28)　8.8	(36)　9.0		(10)　5.9					
14.6	26.0	24.8			16.7				
7193031M	7501711M	5853075M	Net Sales ($)	35640M	146994M	286935M	559339M	1007113M	3817054M
6181029M	6691696M	5208157M	Total Assets ($)	121230M	430627M	407188M	716773M	1106094M	2426245M

M = $ thousand　MM = $ million
See Pages 11 through 21 for Explanation of Ratios and Data

Current Data Sorted By Assets						Type of Statement	Comparative Historical Data	
11	25	70	58	4	4	Unqualified	146	117
6	5	1				Reviewed	4	10
3	6	9	2		1	Compiled	37	44
13	10	3	1			Tax Returns	15	15
30	14	24	22	4	2	Other	67	93
172 (4/1-9/30/04)			156 (10/1/04-3/31/05)				4/1/00-3/31/01 ALL	4/1/01-3/31/02 ALL
0-500M	500M-2MM	2-10MM	10-50MM	50-100MM	100-250MM			
63	60	107	83	8	7	NUMBER OF STATEMENTS	269	279
%	%	%	%	%	%	ASSETS	%	%
43.4	31.9	22.9	18.1			Cash & Equivalents	21.9	22.8
10.1	5.9	4.3	6.2			Trade Receivables (net)	6.3	6.6
1.8	2.5	1.3	1.3			Inventory	1.7	1.5
6.9	2.8	2.7	3.5			All Other Current	4.1	4.2
62.2	43.2	31.2	29.0			Total Current	34.0	35.3
31.0	46.8	54.0	56.9			Fixed Assets (net)	48.8	51.0
.3	1.0	.5	.3			Intangibles (net)	.8	.8
6.4	9.0	14.3	13.8			All Other Non-Current	16.3	12.9
100.0	100.0	100.0	100.0			Total	100.0	100.0
						LIABILITIES		
9.4	3.5	2.2	4.3			Notes Payable-Short Term	2.7	2.8
1.9	1.2	1.6	2.3			Cur. Mat.-L/T/D	2.7	2.1
21.3	5.6	2.5	2.6			Trade Payables	3.8	3.9
.2	.1	.0	.0			Income Taxes Payable	.0	.1
14.2	9.4	4.5	5.8			All Other Current	6.3	6.4
47.0	19.8	10.9	15.1			Total Current	15.6	15.4
10.4	18.5	20.0	18.0			Long-Term Debt	16.0	17.5
.0	.0	.0	.0			Deferred Taxes	.0	.0
12.5	3.1	2.6	3.5			All Other Non-Current	2.8	2.9
30.0	58.5	66.5	63.4			Net Worth	65.6	64.3
100.0	100.0	100.0	100.0			Total Liabilities & Net Worth	100.0	100.0
						INCOME DATA		
100.0	100.0	100.0	100.0			Net Sales	100.0	100.0
						Gross Profit		
99.2	94.8	91.3	95.4			Operating Expenses	96.0	94.1
.8	5.2	8.7	4.6			Operating Profit	4.0	5.9
.7	2.9	1.5	−.3			All Other Expenses (net)	−3.5	3.3
.1	2.3	7.2	5.0			Profit Before Taxes	7.5	2.6
						RATIOS		
9.3	8.8	5.9	4.5				5.8	6.7
2.4	2.5	2.6	2.0			Current	2.4	2.6
1.1	.9	1.0	1.0				1.1	1.2
7.8	7.4	5.5	3.0				4.3	5.6
2.2	1.5	2.3	1.6			Quick	1.8	2.1
.6	.6	.8	.8				.8	.9
0 UND	0 UND	0 815.6	5 78.9				2 238.9	0 UND
2 220.0	4 103.0	7 49.5	13 28.7			Sales/Receivables	13 28.4	10 37.1
17 21.5	23 15.7	28 13.2	35 10.4				36 10.2	35 10.5
						Cost of Sales/Inventory		
						Cost of Sales/Payables		
3.0	2.3	2.0	2.7				2.0	2.2
7.1	5.5	5.2	8.8			Sales/Working Capital	5.8	5.8
52.0	−36.2	142.0	130.7				78.6	31.7
6.0	4.9	6.8	14.5				9.5	6.3
(23) −.5	(27) 1.2	(57) 2.4	(63) 1.8			EBIT/Interest	(175) 2.1	(160) 2.0
−11.4	−.8	.0	.2				.4	−.9
						Net Profit + Depr., Dep., Amort./Cur. Mat. L /T/D		
.0	.1	.3	.5				.3	.3
.4	.8	.8	.9			Fixed/Worth	.8	.8
1.3	1.6	1.5	1.5				1.3	1.4
.2	.1	.2	.2				.1	.1
.8	.5	.4	.5			Debt/Worth	.4	.4
2.3	1.7	1.1	1.2				1.0	1.2
21.1	17.3	9.5	10.9				11.3	10.2
(56) 5.0	(53) 3.7	(105) 3.2	(82) 2.2			% Profit Before Taxes/Tangible Net Worth	(266) 3.2	(270) 2.7
−20.6	−5.5	−1.7	−1.6				−2.5	−3.8
11.0	9.7	6.4	6.1				8.4	6.1
.0	.9	1.8	1.6			% Profit Before Taxes/Total Assets	1.9	1.6
−13.1	−6.2	−.9	−1.1				−1.4	−2.8
UND	30.2	3.4	1.6				4.5	4.1
21.6	2.1	1.1	.9			Sales/Net Fixed Assets	1.5	1.4
2.5	.9	.6	.6				.7	.7
3.1	1.7	1.0	.8				1.1	1.2
1.7	1.0	.6	.5			Sales/Total Assets	.6	.7
1.0	.5	.3	.4				.4	.4
.9	1.0	2.3	3.2				2.0	1.7
(28) 2.2	(45) 2.9	(89) 4.7	(78) 5.6			% Depr., Dep., Amort./Sales	(217) 4.8	(215) 4.6
6.6	9.6	8.1	8.6				7.1	7.7
		4.1					5.1	2.4
	(11) 18.9					% Officers', Directors', Owners' Comp/Sales	(30) 9.2	(40) 5.3
	29.2						19.1	20.1
34914M	92983M	391390M	1173908M	214521M	718543M	Net Sales ($)	2548849M	2244130M
16663M	66229M	532026M	1612168M	518116M	959022M	Total Assets ($)	4119979M	3470403M

M = $ thousand   MM = $ million
See Pages 11 through 21 for Explanation of Ratios and Data

Comparative Historical Data						Current Data Sorted By Sales					
			Type of Statement								
172	170	172	Unqualified		24	43	36	29	27	13
11	7	12	Reviewed		8	4				
17	53	21	Compiled		9	6	3	2		1
22	23	27	Tax Returns		22	3			1	1
98	97	96	Other		37	23	8	10	12	6
4/1/02-3/31/03	4/1/03-3/31/04	4/1/04-3/31/05			172 (4/1-9/30/04)			156 (10/1/04-3/31/05)		
ALL	ALL	ALL			0-1MM	1-3MM	3-5MM	5-10MM	10-25MM	25MM & OVER
320	350	328	**NUMBER OF STATEMENTS**		100	79	47	41	40	21
%	%	%	**ASSETS**		%	%	%	%	%	%
23.3	23.0	27.1	Cash & Equivalents		33.1	30.2	20.8	18.7	24.7	21.7
6.5	6.4	6.2	Trade Receivables (net)		5.6	6.1	8.1	5.0	4.1	12.4
1.3	2.0	1.6	Inventory		2.0	1.5	.5	2.0	1.0	2.5
3.4	5.5	3.8	All Other Current		4.8	2.9	3.6	2.4	3.8	5.2
34.5	36.9	38.6	Total Current		45.4	40.6	33.0	28.2	33.6	41.8
52.4	49.7	48.3	Fixed Assets (net)		46.0	49.1	50.9	50.3	51.6	40.3
.6	.4	.5	Intangibles (net)		.5	.2	1.5	.4	.2	.2
12.5	13.1	12.6	All Other Non-Current		8.2	10.2	14.6	21.1	14.6	17.8
100.0	100.0	100.0	Total		100.0	100.0	100.0	100.0	100.0	100.0
			LIABILITIES							
3.4	3.0	4.3	Notes Payable-Short Term		6.5	2.0	4.0	1.3	4.3	8.7
2.5	2.3	1.8	Cur. Mat.-L/T/D		1.6	2.4	2.1	1.1	1.5	.8
6.4	4.5	6.8	Trade Payables		7.9	10.9	4.0	2.8	3.7	6.9
.1	.1	.1	Income Taxes Payable		.1	.1	.0	.0	.0	.1
7.6	7.4	7.7	All Other Current		8.7	7.0	7.6	5.7	6.9	10.4
20.0	17.4	20.6	Total Current		24.8	22.3	17.8	10.9	16.5	27.0
22.1	18.8	17.5	Long-Term Debt		17.6	20.8	15.1	15.2	15.7	17.2
.0	.0	.0	Deferred Taxes		.0	.0	.0	.1	.0	.0
4.5	4.6	4.9	All Other Non-Current		8.6	1.9	2.4	3.6	6.3	4.5
53.4	59.2	57.0	Net Worth		48.9	55.0	64.8	70.2	61.5	51.3
100.0	100.0	100.0	Total Liabilities & Net Worth		100.0	100.0	100.0	100.0	100.0	100.0
			INCOME DATA							
100.0	100.0	100.0	Net Sales		100.0	100.0	100.0	100.0	100.0	100.0
			Gross Profit							
94.9	94.4	94.4	Operating Expenses		93.7	95.9	94.1	92.5	93.2	98.5
5.1	5.6	5.6	Operating Profit		6.3	4.1	5.9	7.5	6.8	1.5
2.3	1.6	1.1	All Other Expenses (net)		2.7	1.0	.4	-1.5	2.3	-1.3
2.8	4.1	4.5	Profit Before Taxes		3.6	3.1	5.6	9.0	4.5	2.7
			RATIOS							
5.0	6.5	6.4			9.6	9.1	4.7	6.4	5.7	2.9
2.2	2.7	2.4	Current		2.9	2.7	1.9	2.0	2.2	1.6
1.0	1.1	1.0			1.1	1.1	.7	1.0	1.0	.9
4.3	5.0	5.4			8.2	6.6	3.7	5.5	3.6	2.4
1.7	1.9	1.9	Quick		2.3	2.2	1.4	1.7	2.0	1.3
.7	.7	.8			.5	.9	.6	.9	.8	.6
0 UND	0 UND	0 UND			0 UND	0 785.3	4 91.5	4 85.2	2 157.0	6 58.0
9 42.4	9 38.5	8 46.9	Sales/Receivables		1 486.0	10 36.4	15 24.4	12 30.6	11 33.8	17 20.9
34 10.8	30 12.1	27 13.3			12 31.1	29 12.8	38 9.7	34 10.6	22 16.9	40 9.0
			Cost of Sales/Inventory							
			Cost of Sales/Payables							
2.8	2.4	2.3			2.3	1.7	2.5	3.3	3.1	4.9
7.0	5.5	6.4	Sales/Working Capital		5.1	6.2	4.5	7.6	10.6	10.5
160.7	82.4	151.1			121.0	34.9	-16.6	208.6	NM	NM
5.2	6.5	8.1			4.3	5.6	7.7	29.5	25.6	7.7
(199) 1.7	(206) 1.8	(177) 1.6	EBIT/Interest		(43) 1.6	(39) 1.2	(25) 1.5	(31) 8.2	(28) .7	(11) 1.6
-1.5	-.8	-.4			-1.4	-.6	.3	.8	-1.2	.6
11.0	5.5									
(13) 3.5	(11) 1.6		Net Profit + Depr., Dep., Amort./Cur. Mat. L/T/D							
.6	-.8									
.4	.3	.3			.0	.3	.5	.4	.4	.3
.9	.8	.8	Fixed/Worth		.8	.9	.8	.6	.9	.9
1.5	1.4	1.5			1.5	1.5	1.5	1.2	1.5	1.4
.2	.2	.2			.1	.2	.2	.1	.2	.5
.5	.4	.5	Debt/Worth		.6	.5	.5	.3	.7	.8
1.4	1.3	1.4			1.7	1.6	1.0	.9	1.5	1.7
9.4	11.4	11.4			16.1	9.3	9.7	11.0	9.5	15.6
(301) 2.2	(331) 3.0	(311) 2.7	% Profit Before Taxes/Tangible Net Worth		(92) 4.1	(74) 1.3	(45) 3.6	3.2	(39) 1.8	(20) 3.7
-3.7	-4.6	-3.0			-6.2	-3.1	-.4	-1.1	-3.3	.6
6.0	6.8	6.9			8.1	5.6	6.2	6.8	6.9	8.2
1.4	1.7	1.5	% Profit Before Taxes/Total Assets		2.1	.4	2.8	2.0	1.0	2.9
-2.7	-3.2	-1.9			-5.6	-1.9	-.4	-.6	-2.4	.3
5.7	6.2	10.9			59.9	10.5	4.9	3.2	4.4	14.5
1.3	1.5	1.4	Sales/Net Fixed Assets		2.0	1.1	1.3	1.3	1.1	4.0
.7	.7	.7			.6	.6	.6	.7	.8	1.0
1.3	1.2	1.3			1.7	1.3	1.0	1.0	1.1	2.8
.7	.7	.7	Sales/Total Assets		.9	.6	.5	.6	.7	1.0
.4	.4	.4			.4	.3	.4	.4	.5	.5
2.5	2.5	2.0			1.5	2.3	3.1	1.9	2.9	.9
(246) 4.8	(267) 4.7	(253) 4.7	% Depr., Dep., Amort./Sales		(54) 4.3	(63) 5.5	(42) 4.6	(39) 4.0	(37) 5.0	(18) 3.6
7.8	7.5	8.1			10.0	10.1	8.1	6.9	7.1	6.3
3.7	4.0	3.0			2.7					
(31) 10.2	(31) 10.5	(28) 10.4	% Officers', Directors', Owners' Comp/Sales		(10) 6.3					
21.4	22.2	27.8			19.7					
3363162M	3077906M	2626259M	Net Sales ($)		45487M	142799M	186925M	289662M	593520M	1367866M
4266314M	4760208M	3704224M	Total Assets ($)		83496M	330529M	377076M	706602M	925195M	1281326M

M = $ thousand   MM = $ million
See Pages 11 through 21 for Explanation of Ratios and Data

| Current Data Sorted By Assets | | | | | | | Comparative Historical Data | |

Type of Statement

0-500M	500M-2MM	2-10MM	10-50MM	50-100MM	100-250MM	Type of Statement	4/1/00-3/31/01 ALL	4/1/01-3/31/02 ALL
7	19	35	32	3	3	Unqualified	100	72
3	6	3	1			Reviewed	6	10
4	4	3	2			Compiled	19	25
4	2	2				Tax Returns	4	1
6	13	20	8		1	Other	37	37
86 (4/1-9/30/04)			**95 (10/1/04-3/31/05)**					
24	44	63	43	3	4	NUMBER OF STATEMENTS	166	145
%	%	%	%	%	%	**ASSETS**	%	%
38.3	38.2	36.1	32.5			Cash & Equivalents	37.5	33.5
14.0	14.7	15.6	13.0			Trade Receivables (net)	13.0	13.1
1.3	.7	1.3	1.9			Inventory	1.6	1.3
8.1	2.8	5.4	3.9			All Other Current	3.4	4.4
61.7	56.4	58.4	51.3			Total Current	55.4	52.3
35.0	33.7	27.8	28.9			Fixed Assets (net)	27.5	31.2
.0	1.0	.7	.8			Intangibles (net)	1.3	1.3
3.2	8.8	13.1	19.1			All Other Non-Current	15.7	15.3
100.0	100.0	100.0	100.0			Total	100.0	100.0
						LIABILITIES		
4.7	4.3	3.2	2.9			Notes Payable-Short Term	2.4	4.2
7.1	2.0	.8	2.6			Cur. Mat.-L/T/D	3.3	2.2
8.6	10.6	12.5	11.2			Trade Payables	11.3	12.9
.0	.3	.2	.2			Income Taxes Payable	.1	.1
31.6	21.3	9.8	16.2			All Other Current	19.3	17.9
52.0	38.5	26.4	33.1			Total Current	36.4	37.3
14.2	12.8	13.5	13.8			Long-Term Debt	17.9	23.4
.2	.1	.3	.1			Deferred Taxes	.3	.0
3.8	3.5	7.3	10.8			All Other Non-Current	7.8	6.9
29.8	45.1	52.5	42.2			Net Worth	37.5	32.3
100.0	100.0	100.0	100.0			Total Liabilities & Net Worth	100.0	100.0
						INCOME DATA		
100.0	100.0	100.0	100.0			Net Sales	100.0	100.0
						Gross Profit		
98.6	94.7	92.2	89.6			Operating Expenses	98.6	95.9
1.4	5.3	7.8	10.4			Operating Profit	1.4	4.1
-.4	.9	.5	3.8			All Other Expenses (net)	-2.8	3.1
1.8	4.4	7.2	6.6			Profit Before Taxes	4.2	1.0
						RATIOS		
4.7	3.5	5.9	2.7			Current	4.1	2.9
1.6	1.5	2.7	1.6				1.9	1.5
.8	.8	1.5	1.0				1.0	1.0
3.3	3.4	5.5	2.6			Quick	3.5	2.8
1.3	1.4	2.2	1.4				1.7	1.3
.6	.7	1.3	.8				.8	.8
0 UND	3 116.8	7 51.0	9 42.3			Sales/Receivables	6 62.1	7 53.8
4 87.1	23 16.2	25 14.9	25 14.8				17 21.3	18 20.8
20 17.9	33 11.0	43 8.5	55 6.6				44 8.3	36 10.3
						Cost of Sales/Inventory		
						Cost of Sales/Payables		
5.6	3.0	2.0	2.5			Sales/Working Capital	2.1	2.9
13.1	18.4	3.3	7.5				6.3	7.9
-70.6	-23.8	10.5	127.5				-82.2	UND
7.0	27.5	12.0	8.5			EBIT/Interest	14.0	5.7
(11) 3.7	(20) 5.9	(29) 3.9	(23) 2.4				(82) 3.3	(74) 2.1
-.4	2.7	1.0	.8				1.3	-1.7
						Net Profit + Depr., Dep., Amort./Cur. Mat. L /T/D		
.1	.1	.1	.2			Fixed/Worth	.1	.1
.6	.6	.5	.5				.5	.6
2.1	1.4	1.1	1.0				1.6	1.4
.2	.4	.3	.7			Debt/Worth	.4	.4
1.5	1.1	.6	1.5				1.0	1.1
26.8	3.8	3.3	2.2				2.8	2.9
61.4	27.2	19.4	14.4			% Profit Before Taxes/Tangible Net Worth	18.9	12.6
(21) 9.5	(39) 8.3	(61) 9.6	(41) 10.2				(150) 7.1	(135) 2.7
-10.7	-5.3	3.2	.8				.1	-11.1
15.2	14.7	9.6	7.6			% Profit Before Taxes/Total Assets	7.4	5.3
3.1	5.3	3.2	4.1				2.6	.6
-2.9	-1.9	1.4	.2				.0	-5.6
62.8	48.3	56.0	16.8			Sales/Net Fixed Assets	39.1	32.8
20.6	11.0	4.6	5.3				7.4	5.7
3.7	1.7	1.7	1.5				2.1	1.8
4.2	2.8	1.9	1.5			Sales/Total Assets	1.8	2.2
2.1	1.4	1.0	.8				1.1	1.1
1.4	.8	.6	.4				.7	.6
.6	.9	1.0	1.4			% Depr., Dep., Amort./Sales	1.1	.9
(13) 2.0	(37) 1.8	(51) 2.3	(34) 3.1				(138) 2.4	(117) 2.8
2.2	3.6	4.3	4.7				4.0	5.0
						% Officers', Directors', Owners' Comp/Sales	6.1	5.8
							(11) 10.2	(12) 12.5
							14.9	17.3
19434M	87501M	517766M	839651M	196389M	2024407M	Net Sales ($)	2767123M	2124706M
5893M	46492M	294758M	943985M	200615M	653754M	Total Assets ($)	2649640M	1911949M

M = $ thousand   MM = $ million
See Pages 11 through 21 for Explanation of Ratios and Data

Comparative Historical Data | Current Data Sorted By Sales

			Type of Statement						
100	95	99	Unqualified	7	23	14	12	24	19
11	11	13	Reviewed	9	2	1			1
10	29	13	Compiled	7	3	1	1		1
6	8	8	Tax Returns	4	1	2		1	
43	58	48	Other	12	16	6	6	5	3
4/1/02-3/31/03	4/1/03-3/31/04	4/1/04-3/31/05		86 (4/1-9/30/04)			95 (10/1/04-3/31/05)		
ALL	ALL	ALL		0-1MM	1-3MM	3-5MM	5-10MM	10-25MM	25MM & OVER
170	201	181	**NUMBER OF STATEMENTS**	39	45	24	19	30	24
%	%	%	**ASSETS**	%	%	%	%	%	%
32.0	31.3	36.0	Cash & Equivalents	31.8	42.7	36.2	37.9	35.6	29.3
15.1	13.7	14.5	Trade Receivables (net)	10.0	7.6	18.3	10.2	17.7	30.7
1.8	2.2	1.3	Inventory	.8	.5	.9	1.7	2.0	2.7
5.2	7.7	4.7	All Other Current	5.7	2.6	6.2	1.9	8.2	3.7
54.1	54.8	56.6	Total Current	48.3	53.4	61.6	51.8	63.5	66.4
30.6	30.0	30.1	Fixed Assets (net)	47.4	33.9	21.0	26.8	22.1	16.9
.8	.7	.7	Intangibles (net)	.1	.5	1.6	1.0	.2	1.3
14.5	14.4	12.5	All Other Non-Current	4.2	12.1	15.7	20.4	14.2	15.4
100.0	100.0	100.0	Total	100.0	100.0	100.0	100.0	100.0	100.0
			LIABILITIES						
3.9	5.7	3.7	Notes Payable-Short Term	4.3	2.1	3.9	3.9	2.6	6.9
2.2	3.0	2.4	Cur. Mat.-L/T/D	3.6	3.9	1.6	1.8	.5	1.1
13.7	10.2	11.2	Trade Payables	4.8	5.7	15.1	6.9	17.3	24.0
.3	.1	.2	Income Taxes Payable	.0	.1	.6	.1	.2	.0
14.0	18.6	17.2	All Other Current	18.9	23.3	12.1	13.1	14.1	15.6
34.2	37.7	34.7	Total Current	31.6	35.0	33.3	25.7	34.8	47.6
12.2	15.7	13.5	Long-Term Debt	22.7	11.2	10.5	14.9	8.0	11.3
.0	.4	.2	Deferred Taxes	.1	.5	.0	.0	.1	.1
6.9	7.7	7.2	All Other Non-Current	3.0	3.3	6.4	10.2	10.3	16.1
46.7	38.6	44.4	Net Worth	42.6	49.9	49.8	49.1	46.9	24.9
100.0	100.0	100.0	Total Liabilities & Net Worth	100.0	100.0	100.0	100.0	100.0	100.0
			INCOME DATA						
100.0	100.0	100.0	Net Sales	100.0	100.0	100.0	100.0	100.0	100.0
			Gross Profit						
98.8	95.6	93.1	Operating Expenses	89.6	93.0	92.8	96.4	92.3	97.9
1.2	4.4	6.9	Operating Profit	10.4	7.0	7.2	3.6	7.7	2.1
1.8	1.2	1.2	All Other Expenses (net)	7.3	−.4	−.4	−.6	−.5	−.7
−.6	3.2	5.7	Profit Before Taxes	3.1	7.4	7.6	4.2	8.2	2.8
			RATIOS						
4.2	4.2	4.2		5.9	5.2	5.3	3.8	4.5	2.4
1.8	2.0	1.8	Current	1.9	1.9	2.2	1.7	2.1	1.4
1.1	1.1	1.1		.7	1.1	1.1	1.2	1.1	1.1
3.5	3.5	3.6		3.3	4.9	3.8	3.8	4.1	2.3
1.5	1.5	1.6	Quick	1.4	1.8	1.8	1.6	1.6	1.3
.9	.8	.9		.6	.8	.8	1.1	1.0	1.1
6 61.3	6 62.0	5 74.6		0 UND	3 117.8	3 136.0	4 87.8	13 27.8	20 18.4
19 19.1	17 21.2	20 17.9	Sales/Receivables	10 37.3	16 23.2	29 12.6	17 21.4	25 14.8	39 9.4
45 8.1	42 8.7	42 8.7		47 7.7	34 10.8	39 9.4	41 8.9	55 6.6	49 7.4
			Cost of Sales/Inventory						
			Cost of Sales/Payables						
2.5	2.3	2.5		2.1	2.0	2.4	2.6	2.0	5.5
6.3	5.9	6.4	Sales/Working Capital	7.0	6.0	4.0	4.3	4.8	16.7
69.6	70.1	118.8		−8.5	260.9	69.9	122.2	24.2	103.6
9.1	8.9	12.4		7.0	11.0	29.8		70.9	17.7
(90) 1.7	(110) 2.2	(88) 4.2	EBIT/Interest	(15) 1.3	(20) 3.3	(12) 5.8	(14) 6.0		(18) 5.6
−2.8	−.7	.9		−.4	.9	2.8		.9	.9
		4.4	Net Profit + Depr., Dep.,						
	(12) 3.4		Amort./Cur. Mat. L/T/D						
		1.8							
.1	.1	.1		.2	.1	.0	.3	.1	.1
.5	.6	.5	Fixed/Worth	1.0	.5	.2	.5	.3	.5
1.2	1.3	1.2		2.3	1.1	1.1	.9	.9	2.2
.4	.5	.4		.2	.3	.4	.6	.4	.9
1.1	1.1	1.1	Debt/Worth	1.2	.6	1.2	1.1	1.3	4.2
2.9	3.5	3.6		5.0	1.7	3.7	1.7	2.1	93.2
14.1	15.4	22.1	% Profit Before Taxes/Tangible	13.2	17.4	37.6	19.4	29.3	22.1
(159) 1.0	(179) 5.2	(166) 9.5	Net Worth	(36) 3.2	(40) 8.4	(23) 15.0	8.9	(29) 13.2	(19) 13.7
−10.4	−1.8	1.0		−2.6	−5.1	5.1	2.3	2.6	8.8
5.8	7.0	9.6		5.0	14.6	19.2	7.3	11.2	8.4
.2	2.1	4.2	% Profit Before Taxes/Total	.9	5.3	7.2	4.2	7.2	3.6
−6.0	−1.8	.2	Assets	−1.9	−1.2	2.0	1.6	.6	.4
20.5	42.2	43.9		25.6	40.4	63.6	16.4	59.8	520.3
5.4	5.1	6.1	Sales/Net Fixed Assets	2.0	4.1	14.5	5.2	12.2	24.4
1.9	1.9	1.7		.7	1.5	3.3	1.6	2.4	4.8
2.0	1.9	2.0		2.0	1.8	2.2	1.7	2.0	4.5
1.1	1.1	1.2	Sales/Total Assets	1.0	1.0	1.1	1.1	1.2	1.6
.6	.6	.6		.4	.6	.6	.7	.7	.9
1.3	1.3	1.0		2.1	.9	.7	1.8	.8	.2
(133) 3.1	(149) 2.5	(139) 2.2	% Depr., Dep., Amort./Sales	(24) 3.1	(38) 2.1	(19) 2.0	(16) 3.6	(26) 1.6	(16) 1.1
4.7	4.7	3.9		7.1	4.0	3.7	5.0	2.6	3.3
5.8	2.9	2.9	% Officers', Directors',						
(14) 11.7	(14) 8.2	(21) 10.8	Owners' Comp/Sales						
14.9	21.1	18.4							
2700835M	2253741M	3685148M	Net Sales ($)	22832M	75865M	90965M	138310M	510864M	2846312M
2425037M	2221787M	2145497M	Total Assets ($)	67600M	112445M	129602M	153985M	566585M	1115280M

© RMA 2005

M = $ thousand   MM = $ million
See Pages 11 through 21 for Explanation of Ratios and Data

| Current Data Sorted By Assets | | | | | | | Comparative Historical Data | |

Type of Statement

0-500M	500M-2MM	2-10MM	10-50MM	50-100MM	100-250MM	Type of Statement		
	11	29	22	4	9	Unqualified	68	59
1		2	1			Reviewed	7	4
2	1	3				Compiled	16	22
1	2					Tax Returns		2
3	5	11	7	1	1	Other	29	32
	62 (4/1-9/30/04)		54 (10/1/04-3/31/05)				4/1/00-3/31/01 ALL	4/1/01-3/31/02 ALL
7	19	45	30	5	10	NUMBER OF STATEMENTS	120	119

ASSETS

0-500M %	500M-2MM %	2-10MM %	10-50MM %	50-100MM %	100-250MM %	ASSETS	%	%
	35.4	38.6	33.4		37.3	Cash & Equivalents	35.0	29.9
	20.2	16.3	4.8		12.3	Trade Receivables (net)	9.7	10.0
	4.4	2.5	2.0		1.0	Inventory	1.6	1.5
	4.3	6.6	2.9		2.2	All Other Current	5.6	4.3
	64.4	63.9	43.0		52.8	Total Current	51.8	45.7
	23.8	30.5	30.5		25.4	Fixed Assets (net)	24.0	29.2
	.3	.3	.7		3.0	Intangibles (net)	1.9	1.6
	11.6	5.3	25.8		18.7	All Other Non-Current	22.4	23.5
	100.0	100.0	100.0		100.0	Total	100.0	100.0

LIABILITIES

0-500M	500M-2MM	2-10MM	10-50MM	50-100MM	100-250MM	LIABILITIES		
	18.7	3.4	2.3		.2	Notes Payable-Short Term	4.2	1.8
	1.3	1.4	.4		.9	Cur. Mat.-L/T/D	1.1	1.4
	9.0	11.6	5.1		5.0	Trade Payables	6.9	6.1
	.0	.1	.0		.5	Income Taxes Payable	.4	.3
	14.6	12.9	13.7		17.9	All Other Current	34.6	16.2
	43.5	29.4	21.5		24.6	Total Current	47.2	25.8
	10.4	11.2	13.7		10.6	Long-Term Debt	9.4	13.0
	.0	.0	.0		.0	Deferred Taxes	.4	.0
	10.6	9.3	10.2		6.3	All Other Non-Current	8.1	8.8
	35.5	50.2	54.7		58.5	Net Worth	34.8	52.4
	100.0	100.0	100.0		100.0	Total Liabilities & Net Worth	100.0	100.0

INCOME DATA

0-500M	500M-2MM	2-10MM	10-50MM	50-100MM	100-250MM	INCOME DATA		
	100.0	100.0	100.0		100.0	Net Sales	100.0	100.0
						Gross Profit		
	91.8	96.3	92.8		91.7	Operating Expenses	98.0	99.2
	8.2	3.7	7.2		8.3	Operating Profit	2.0	.8
	-.6	-.2	.7		-2.3	All Other Expenses (net)	-1.1	1.1
	8.8	3.9	6.6		10.6	Profit Before Taxes	3.1	-.3

RATIOS

0-500M	500M-2MM	2-10MM	10-50MM	50-100MM	100-250MM	RATIOS		
	4.0	4.4	5.3		5.7	Current	4.1	3.7
	2.0	3.3	2.6		2.2		1.8	1.9
	1.0	1.3	.8		1.4		1.0	1.0
	3.8	4.2	3.9		5.4	Quick	3.6	2.9
	1.7	2.6	1.8		1.8		1.6	1.5
	1.0		.6		1.2		.8	.8
0 UND	3 105.2	6 66.3	14 26.5			Sales/Receivables	6 64.0	8 46.9
10 36.1	15 24.4	10 36.4	30 12.0				18 19.9	23 15.7
42 8.6	45 8.2	28 13.2	42 8.7				36 10.1	40 9.2
						Cost of Sales/Inventory		
						Cost of Sales/Payables		
	3.9	2.2	1.9		2.1	Sales/Working Capital	2.5	2.8
	7.9	4.4	3.6		4.8		5.2	6.3
	-999.8	22.8	-20.6		NM		117.4	-999.8
		24.7	23.4			EBIT/Interest	10.1	4.9
	(26) 6.4	(14) 9.0					(64) 2.3	(57) 1.0
	.8	3.0					-1.6	-2.8
						Net Profit + Depr., Dep., Amort./Cur. Mat. L /T/D		
	.0	.1	.1		.3	Fixed/Worth	.1	.2
	.2	.5	.3		.5		.3	.5
	1.7	1.7	1.1		.6		.8	.9
	.5	.4	.3		.4	Debt/Worth	.4	.5
	.9	.7	.7		.7		.8	.8
	4.6	1.9	2.4		1.1		1.7	1.8
	41.4	22.1	13.8			% Profit Before Taxes/Tangible Net Worth	10.7	11.0
(18) 4.0	(42) 8.1	(29) 6.3					(116) 4.0	(117) .1
	-5.5	.2	1.6				-1.3	-10.5
	12.9	9.8	6.1		8.7	% Profit Before Taxes/Total Assets	6.8	5.9
	1.6	2.9	3.7		5.1		2.2	.0
	-2.7	.1	1.1		2.0		-.6	-4.6
	219.0	45.8	14.4		5.7	Sales/Net Fixed Assets	22.9	13.6
	48.6	7.4	4.3		3.3		6.0	3.4
	4.9	2.2	1.6		2.0		2.5	2.4
	3.8	2.5	1.1		1.4	Sales/Total Assets	1.5	1.4
	1.9	1.4	.7		.8		1.0	1.0
	1.1	.7	.4		.5		.6	.6
	.2	1.1	1.8			% Depr., Dep., Amort./Sales	1.3	.6
(14) .8	(38) 2.2	(26) 2.5					(106) 2.2	(104) 2.6
	3.2	3.4	4.5				3.3	4.2
						% Officers', Directors', Owners' Comp/Sales		9.9
							(19)	16.7
								22.4
12122M	76786M	420533M	496820M	625319M	1950477M	Net Sales ($)	1940248M	2442889M
1450M	21712M	229150M	712156M	322981M	1812512M	Total Assets ($)	2655715M	3177079M

© RMA 2005

M = $ thousand   MM = $ million

See Pages 11 through 21 for Explanation of Ratios and Data

Comparative Historical Data   **Current Data Sorted By Sales**

Type of Statement	4/1/02-3/31/03 ALL	4/1/03-3/31/04 ALL	4/1/04-3/31/05 ALL	0-1MM	1-3MM	3-5MM	5-10MM	10-25MM	25MM & OVER
					62 (4/1-9/30/04)		54 (10/1/04-3/31/05)		
Unqualified	75	69	75	3	14	6	14	18	20
Reviewed	2	5	4	1	1		1		1
Compiled	7	26	6	1	2		2	1	
Tax Returns	1	4	3	1	1	1			
Other	35	33	28	4	9	1	2	8	4
NUMBER OF STATEMENTS	120	137	116	10	27	8	19	27	25
	%	%	%	%	%	%	%	%	%
ASSETS									
Cash & Equivalents	31.7	32.2	35.4	20.1	36.9		39.5	38.2	38.8
Trade Receivables (net)	9.0	8.6	12.4	1.1	6.9		19.6	12.9	11.4
Inventory	2.0	1.2	2.6	3.4	2.1		3.9	2.1	2.3
All Other Current	3.0	10.0	4.6	1.4	3.0		6.7	6.1	5.7
Total Current	45.7	52.1	55.1	26.0	48.9		69.7	59.2	58.1
Fixed Assets (net)	30.3	31.8	29.8	60.1	40.5		15.6	20.3	24.0
Intangibles (net)	1.3	1.6	.9	4.3	.2		.2	.9	1.2
All Other Non-Current	22.6	14.4	14.2	9.6	10.4		14.5	19.5	16.6
Total	100.0	100.0	100.0	100.0	100.0		100.0	100.0	100.0
LIABILITIES									
Notes Payable-Short Term	2.0	2.4	10.6	13.0	23.7		18.2	1.6	.6
Cur. Mat.-L/T/D	3.4	1.0	1.2	2.7	2.1		.2	.7	.8
Trade Payables	6.3	6.6	9.1	3.6	3.5		8.6	12.5	14.7
Income Taxes Payable	.5	.2	.2	.0	.0		.2	.0	.6
All Other Current	16.1	15.6	13.3	2.5	7.7		11.0	20.7	19.5
Total Current	28.3	25.7	34.3	21.8	37.0		38.3	35.6	36.2
Long-Term Debt	16.4	11.7	13.2	31.0	24.2		1.4	5.9	9.6
Deferred Taxes	.4	.0	.0	.0	.0		.0	.0	.0
All Other Non-Current	8.6	10.5	9.5	13.4	7.0		6.8	14.4	8.8
Net Worth	46.3	52.0	43.0	33.8	31.7		53.4	44.1	45.4
Total Liabilities & Net Worth	100.0	100.0	100.0	100.0	100.0		100.0	100.0	100.0
INCOME DATA									
Net Sales	100.0	100.0	100.0	100.0	100.0		100.0	100.0	100.0
Gross Profit									
Operating Expenses	97.7	93.6	94.7	94.9	90.0		98.2	95.6	94.4
Operating Profit	2.3	6.4	5.3	5.1	10.0		1.8	4.4	5.6
All Other Expenses (net)	3.2	.4	-.3	1.1	2.6		-2.3	-1.2	-1.5
Profit Before Taxes	-.9	6.0	5.6	4.0	7.3		4.1	5.6	7.1
RATIOS									
Current	3.1 / 1.6 / .9	4.9 / 2.2 / 1.1	4.2 / 2.2 / 1.0	4.5 / .9 / .4	7.2 / 2.6 / .9		4.6 / 3.3 / .8	3.7 / 2.0 / 1.0	3.4 / 2.1 / 1.1
Quick	2.8 / 1.4 / .8	3.5 / 1.7 / .8	3.8 / 1.9 / .9	4.0 / .9 / .2	4.5 / 2.1 / .9		4.3 / 3.0 / .8	3.1 / 1.6 / 1.0	2.8 / 1.7 / 1.0
Sales/Receivables	6 57.6 / 19 19.0 / 34 10.7	5 78.0 / 15 24.2 / 34 10.6	3 136.6 / 11 32.4 / 39 9.4	0 UND / 0 UND / 4 91.3	0 UND / 2 150.3 / 30 12.2		7 49.4 / 25 14.5 / 42 8.6	5 70.5 / 14 26.2 / 41 9.0	9 42.7 / 21 17.2 / 39 9.5
Cost of Sales/Inventory									
Cost of Sales/Payables									
Sales/Working Capital	3.0 / 9.3 / -89.9	2.0 / 5.5 / 38.1	2.5 / 5.3 / -458.5	10.8 / UND / -8.3	2.2 / 4.6 / -39.0		2.6 / 4.4 / -278.0	2.4 / 8.5 / -222.3	2.4 / 4.8 / 42.5
EBIT/Interest	(67) 5.1 / 1.0 / -4.7	(78) 17.6 / 5.4 / .4	(64) 22.5 / 5.0 / 1.0		(14) 3.2 / 1.3 / -1.1		(11) 66.5 / 8.7 / 3.6	(12) 42.2 / 16.7 / 3.9	(15) 42.5 / 9.9 / 2.0
Net Profit + Depr., Dep., Amort./Cur. Mat. L/T/D									
Fixed/Worth	.2 / .6 / 1.1	.2 / .6 / 1.3	.1 / .5 / 1.7	1.4 / 2.0 / 3.4	.1 / .9 / 2.1		.0 / .1 / .5	.1 / .4 / 1.2	.2 / .4 / .7
Debt/Worth	.5 / .9 / 1.8	.4 / .9 / 1.9	.4 / .8 / 2.4	1.1 / 1.9 / 4.1	.4 / .8 / 2.1		.3 / .4 / .8	.5 / 1.1 / 4.7	.6 / .9 / 3.0
% Profit Before Taxes/Tangible Net Worth	(115) 14.4 / -.2 / -12.0	(133) 23.8 / 6.3 / -1.5	(108) 18.9 / 6.5 / .3		(25) 21.8 / 3.6 / -5.2		(18) 19.4 / 5.4 / 1.4	(25) 31.6 / 9.8 / 4.4	(23) 16.1 / 10.3 / 3.1
% Profit Before Taxes/Total Assets	7.3 / -.1 / -6.3	11.9 / 3.6 / -.4	9.0 / 3.5 / .1	10.2 / .2 / -10.0	7.3 / 1.6 / -2.6		16.0 / 3.7 / 1.6	7.8 / 4.0 / 1.4	7.8 / 4.9 / 1.8
Sales/Net Fixed Assets	15.1 / 3.9 / 2.1	17.9 / 4.5 / 2.2	26.3 / 6.4 / 2.3	6.3 / 2.0 / .3	43.2 / 4.9 / .8		72.2 / 19.4 / 7.3	21.7 / 11.5 / 3.8	10.8 / 4.8 / 2.7
Sales/Total Assets	1.5 / 1.0 / .6	1.7 / .9 / .6	2.3 / 1.1 / .7	2.1 / 1.1 / .3	1.9 / .8 / .5		3.0 / 2.2 / 1.3	2.4 / 1.1 / .7	2.1 / 1.0 / .7
% Depr., Dep., Amort./Sales	(103) 1.8 / 2.9 / 4.1	(109) 1.5 / 2.6 / 4.0	(96) 1.1 / 2.3 / 3.8		(22) .7 / 2.4 / 6.0		(16) .4 / 1.2 / 2.2	(24) 1.5 / 2.4 / 3.0	(20) 1.9 / 2.8 / 3.9
% Officers', Directors', Owners' Comp/Sales	(16) 5.3 / 14.8 / 28.6	(13) 8.4 / 15.5 / 40.0	(21) 11.0 / 16.7 / 30.9						
Net Sales ($)	3053712M	2409395M	3582057M	5951M	48168M	29930M	149952M	406814M	2941242M
Total Assets ($)	2894540M	2461146M	3099961M	17682M	112160M	53626M	108487M	398276M	2409730M

M = $ thousand   MM = $ million
See Pages 11 through 21 for Explanation of Ratios and Data

Current Data Sorted By Assets   **Comparative Historical Data**

0-500M	500M-2MM	2-10MM	10-50MM	50-100MM	100-250MM	Type of Statement	4/1/00-3/31/01 ALL	4/1/01-3/31/02 ALL
	2	14	6	1	3	Unqualified	18	18
	2	2				Reviewed	3	
		1				Compiled	4	12
	2	1		1		Tax Returns	1	3
1	6	9	4	2		Other	13	12
	37 (4/1-9/30/04)		20 (10/1/04-3/31/05)					
1	12	27	10	4	3	**NUMBER OF STATEMENTS**	39	45
%	%	%	%	%	%	**ASSETS**	%	%
	32.2	41.1	49.2			Cash & Equivalents	36.6	38.2
	10.2	2.4	4.6			Trade Receivables (net)	10.7	6.3
	.1	.0	.0			Inventory	.3	.6
	5.8	.9	12.6			All Other Current	3.5	5.8
	48.3	44.4	66.4			Total Current	51.2	50.9
	44.1	49.2	24.5			Fixed Assets (net)	30.3	36.2
	.2	.0	.5			Intangibles (net)	6.4	1.0
	7.5	6.4	8.6			All Other Non-Current	12.1	11.9
	100.0	100.0	100.0			Total	100.0	100.0
						LIABILITIES		
	.0	4.6	.0			Notes Payable-Short Term	2.1	.3
	1.2	1.4	6.5			Cur. Mat.-L/T/D	2.0	2.8
	2.8	1.6	7.8			Trade Payables	7.4	4.7
	.0	.0	.2			Income Taxes Payable	.1	.0
	8.1	3.3	14.0			All Other Current	62.8	10.2
	12.1	10.8	28.5			Total Current	74.4	18.0
	22.2	23.8	8.9			Long-Term Debt	12.1	13.8
	.0	.0	.0			Deferred Taxes	.0	.0
	1.3	1.7	.1			All Other Non-Current	5.1	2.4
	64.4	63.7	62.4			Net Worth	8.5	65.7
	100.0	100.0	100.0			Total Liabilities & Net Worth	100.0	100.0
						INCOME DATA		
	100.0	100.0	100.0			Net Sales	100.0	100.0
						Gross Profit		
	98.5	92.4	90.9			Operating Expenses	98.8	94.4
	1.5	7.6	9.1			Operating Profit	1.2	5.6
	.6	3.0	-.3			All Other Expenses (net)	-6.1	-.8
	.8	4.6	9.5			Profit Before Taxes	7.2	6.4
						RATIOS		
	37.7	127.0	105.5				22.2	26.2
	5.0	13.6	10.4			Current	2.4	3.6
	1.8	1.5	1.5				1.5	1.5
	37.6	127.0	104.1				20.4	21.9
	4.5	13.6	10.1			Quick	2.4	2.6
	1.6	1.4	1.4				.9	1.3
	0 UND	0 UND	0 UND				0 UND	0 UND
	0 UND	0 UND	0 UND			Sales/Receivables	1 266.6	3 144.0
	39 9.4	18 19.8	29 12.8				37 10.0	27 13.7
						Cost of Sales/Inventory		
						Cost of Sales/Payables		
	.7	1.1	1.2				1.4	1.9
	5.5	2.4	3.9			Sales/Working Capital	5.1	4.2
	7.4	17.7	NM				20.0	13.0
		8.3					3.7	13.4
		(21) 2.7				EBIT/Interest	(20) 1.4	(26) 3.8
		-1.5					-3.3	1.9
						Net Profit + Depr., Dep., Amort./Cur. Mat. L /T/D		
	.0	.3	.0				.0	.2
	.9	.8	.4			Fixed/Worth	.4	.6
	1.3	1.2	1.1				1.5	1.1
	.1	.2	.0				.0	.1
	.7	.6	.4			Debt/Worth	.7	.4
	1.1	1.1	1.7				2.4	1.1
	9.2	12.7					13.3	26.5
	-1.9	(26) 1.8				% Profit Before Taxes/Tangible Net Worth	(33) 6.0	(44) 6.4
	-5.6	-8.5					-.6	-1.4
	5.4	9.7	12.1				7.6	14.8
	-1.3	4.7	8.6			% Profit Before Taxes/Total Assets	2.2	4.3
	-4.6	-3.4	-3.2				-1.5	-.8
	29.8	9.0	UND				52.0	10.3
	2.5	1.5	4.3			Sales/Net Fixed Assets	5.4	4.3
	.7	.6	2.7				2.1	1.2
	1.7	1.1	1.7				1.5	1.5
	.7	.6	1.1			Sales/Total Assets	1.0	1.3
	.3	.4	.5				.4	.7
		2.1					1.2	1.1
		(24) 3.5				% Depr., Dep., Amort./Sales	(28) 2.1	(41) 1.7
		7.3					4.9	3.9
								14.0
						% Officers', Directors', Owners' Comp/Sales		(13) 26.0
								29.7
466M	15703M	129229M	297208M	219352M	1504978M	Net Sales ($)	859125M	837791M
376M	14478M	130776M	201341M	341653M	666340M	Total Assets ($)	801147M	600245M

M = $ thousand   MM = $ million
See Pages 11 through 21 for Explanation of Ratios and Data

Comparative Historical Data | Current Data Sorted By Sales

			Type of Statement						
34	33	26	Unqualified		9	4	5	2	6
	1	4	Reviewed	1	2			1	
5	9	1	Compiled			1			
3		4	Tax Returns	2		1			1
22	22	22	Other	6	5	2	3	4	2
4/1/02-3/31/03	4/1/03-3/31/04	4/1/04-3/31/05			37 (4/1-9/30/04)		20 (10/1/04-3/31/05)		
ALL	ALL	ALL		0-1MM	1-3MM	3-5MM	5-10MM	10-25MM	25MM & OVER
64	65	57	NUMBER OF STATEMENTS	9	16	8	8	7	9
%	%	%	ASSETS	%	%	%	%	%	%
37.5	39.2	40.7	Cash & Equivalents		37.9				
4.9	4.7	4.9	Trade Receivables (net)		5.5				
.4	.2	.1	Inventory		.1				
1.7	9.3	6.4	All Other Current		1.0				
44.5	53.3	52.1	Total Current		44.4				
39.0	37.5	40.1	Fixed Assets (net)		52.4				
1.2	.2	.1	Intangibles (net)		.0				
15.3	8.9	7.7	All Other Non-Current		3.2				
100.0	100.0	100.0	Total		100.0				
			LIABILITIES						
1.7	1.3	2.4	Notes Payable-Short Term		.6				
2.9	2.7	2.1	Cur. Mat.-L/T/D		1.4				
4.1	5.5	3.9	Trade Payables		2.5				
.1	.0	.0	Income Taxes Payable		.0				
7.1	9.0	7.9	All Other Current		3.0				
16.0	18.5	16.2	Total Current		7.5				
19.6	17.1	18.0	Long-Term Debt		21.3				
.0	.0	.0	Deferred Taxes		.0				
1.6	.7	1.4	All Other Non-Current		1.3				
62.9	63.7	64.5	Net Worth		70.0				
100.0	100.0	100.0	Total Liabilities & Net Worth		100.0				
			INCOME DATA						
100.0	100.0	100.0	Net Sales		100.0				
			Gross Profit						
89.2	90.6	92.0	Operating Expenses		86.7				
10.8	9.4	8.0	Operating Profit		13.3				
5.1	1.3	2.9	All Other Expenses (net)		5.8				
5.6	8.1	5.1	Profit Before Taxes		7.6				
			RATIOS						
11.5	25.4	72.4			148.5				
3.1	4.9	10.5	Current		15.5				
1.3	1.5	1.6			4.2				
11.5	21.3	70.7			148.5				
3.0	4.8	7.6	Quick		15.5				
1.3	1.4	1.4			3.9				
0 UND	0 UND	0 UND			0 UND				
0 UND	1 244.7	0 UND	Sales/Receivables		0 UND				
27 13.7	26 14.0	22 16.3			37 9.8				
			Cost of Sales/Inventory						
			Cost of Sales/Payables						
1.5	1.2	1.1			.7				
6.0	3.3	3.0	Sales/Working Capital		2.6				
25.9	10.1	8.9			5.6				
13.1	5.8	10.2			6.5				
(33) 2.1	(28) 2.1	(35) 3.5	EBIT/Interest		(13) .3				
.3	.6	-1.7			-9.8				
			Net Profit + Depr., Dep., Amort./Cur. Mat. L/T/D						
.1	.1	.1			.3				
.5	.7	.7	Fixed/Worth		.9				
1.4	1.2	1.1			1.2				
.1	.1	.1			.2				
.5	.4	.5	Debt/Worth		.4				
1.5	1.4	1.3			1.2				
13.8	14.1	10.6			9.4				
(61) 5.8	(61) 4.7	(55) .9	% Profit Before Taxes/Tangible Net Worth		5.4				
-4.8	-2.9	-7.0			-9.4				
11.3	10.2	9.6			6.9				
2.9	3.3	.8	% Profit Before Taxes/Total Assets		4.5				
-2.5	-2.4	-5.1			-5.8				
13.0	19.9	14.7			2.6				
3.5	2.9	2.5	Sales/Net Fixed Assets		1.0				
1.2	1.2	1.1			.5				
1.4	1.4	1.3			.8				
1.0	.9	.7	Sales/Total Assets		.5				
.5	.5	.4			.3				
1.4	1.3	1.8			2.5				
(45) 2.9	(49) 3.2	(45) 3.1	% Depr., Dep., Amort./Sales		(14) 4.9				
4.2	5.3	4.9			8.9				
6.6	6.8	6.2							
(21) 23.3	(11) 13.0	(12) 11.8	% Officers', Directors', Owners' Comp/Sales						
31.5	17.0	20.6							
1122726M	698922M	2166936M	Net Sales ($)	4269M	28476M	29480M	57236M	114502M	1932973M
835554M	751396M	1354964M	Total Assets ($)	11574M	68254M	52768M	65981M	198331M	958056M

M = $ thousand   MM = $ million
See Pages 11 through 21 for Explanation of Ratios and Data

Current Data Sorted By Assets   Comparative Historical Data

						Type of Statement		
12	24	36	36	10	5	Unqualified	82	59
2	3	3				Reviewed	3	2
5	3	3				Compiled	32	29
5	3					Tax Returns	8	8
9	16	16	19	6		Other	31	39
	101 (4/1-9/30/04)		115 (10/1/04-3/31/05)				4/1/00-3/31/01	4/1/01-3/31/02
0-500M	500M-2MM	2-10MM	10-50MM	50-100MM	100-250MM		ALL	ALL
33	49	58	55	16	5	**NUMBER OF STATEMENTS**	156	137
%	%	%	%	%	%	**ASSETS**	%	%
49.0	33.0	24.4	18.4	30.9		Cash & Equivalents	23.0	24.7
7.8	5.8	6.3	7.9	6.1		Trade Receivables (net)	7.3	7.9
.1	1.2	1.3	2.8	.4		Inventory	2.8	1.7
1.0	4.3	2.7	3.6	2.3		All Other Current	5.1	5.7
58.0	44.3	34.7	32.7	39.6		Total Current	38.2	39.9
21.9	43.0	49.4	50.2	33.1		Fixed Assets (net)	37.8	44.4
.0	.2	.4	.4	1.3		Intangibles (net)	1.1	.4
20.2	12.6	15.5	16.7	26.0		All Other Non-Current	22.9	15.3
100.0	100.0	100.0	100.0	100.0		Total	100.0	100.0
						LIABILITIES		
19.1	1.7	3.3	1.9	1.4		Notes Payable-Short Term	2.7	3.0
16.6	3.8	1.4	1.6	1.6		Cur. Mat.-L/T/D	1.4	2.2
19.5	4.0	3.2	3.9	27.2		Trade Payables	4.4	7.4
.0	.1	.2	.2	.5		Income Taxes Payable	.0	.0
13.0	10.1	6.2	11.4	12.7		All Other Current	8.4	6.9
68.2	19.7	14.3	19.0	43.4		Total Current	17.0	19.6
20.8	29.1	18.7	18.6	13.9		Long-Term Debt	14.4	19.0
.0	.1	.0	.4	.8		Deferred Taxes	.3	.1
5.0	9.0	8.0	5.4	9.3		All Other Non-Current	6.9	4.5
6.2	42.1	59.0	56.7	32.6		Net Worth	61.4	56.8
100.0	100.0	100.0	100.0	100.0		Total Liabilities & Net Worth	100.0	100.0
						INCOME DATA		
100.0	100.0	100.0	100.0	100.0		Net Sales	100.0	100.0
						Gross Profit		
90.5	91.2	97.1	95.1	93.8		Operating Expenses	96.9	94.6
9.5	8.8	2.9	4.9	6.2		Operating Profit	3.1	5.4
1.9	2.6	.8	.0	2.1		All Other Expenses (net)	-4.3	2.3
7.7	6.2	2.2	5.0	4.1		Profit Before Taxes	7.4	3.1
						RATIOS		
4.9	3.6	6.2	3.3	2.8			5.6	5.7
1.7	2.3	2.8	1.4	1.7		Current	2.4	2.4
.5	1.1	1.4	1.0	.6			1.2	1.1
4.9	3.3	4.6	2.7	2.3			3.6	5.0
1.7	2.1	2.1	1.1	1.5		Quick	1.8	1.7
.5	.7	1.1	.7	.5			.9	.7
0 UND	0 UND	4 97.4	5 70.4	4 94.8			1 250.3	1 435.5
1 302.0	2 211.0	16 22.4	16 22.5	12 31.5		Sales/Receivables	12 30.6	14 25.7
12 30.7	12 29.6	40 9.1	39 9.3	28 12.9			33 10.9	34 10.9
						Cost of Sales/Inventory		
						Cost of Sales/Payables		
3.6	2.9	1.6	3.3	2.4			2.3	2.1
15.9	7.6	5.8	10.1	4.5		Sales/Working Capital	7.2	6.4
-13.2	26.1	13.2	153.7	NM			44.9	46.8
	5.0	10.0	11.3	13.5				15.0	4.5
(17) 1.0	(22) 2.8	(40) 1.8	(36) 5.0			EBIT/Interest	(83) 2.6	(84) 1.4
-4.8	-1.5	-1.8	.7				-.2	-1.1
						Net Profit + Depr., Dep., Amort./Cur. Mat. L /T/D		
.0	.1	.3	.5	.2			.2	.3
.1	.9	.8	.9	.5		Fixed/Worth	.5	.7
.9	1.7	1.3	1.4	.8			1.1	1.3
.2	.2	.3	.4	.3			.1	.2
1.5	.9	.5	.8	.7		Debt/Worth	.5	.5
NM	2.1	1.5	1.4	2.0			1.2	1.3
53.0	16.6	13.3	14.6	19.0		% Profit Before Taxes/Tangible Net Worth	15.7	11.4
(25) 9.2	(42) 4.5	(56) 1.4	5.5	(13) 11.8			(146) 6.9	(129) 2.8
-15.1	-12.6	-4.1	-.8	1.2			.1	-3.8
20.9	9.9	5.4	6.5	9.1			9.2	6.6
7.6	3.1	1.0	2.8	4.2		% Profit Before Taxes/Total Assets	3.9	1.3
-12.0	-5.0	-1.8	-.5	-.8			-.4	-2.9
UND	40.4	4.5	3.4	7.6			10.1	10.9
159.6	3.5	1.3	1.2	3.3		Sales/Net Fixed Assets	2.6	2.0
7.4	.6	.8	.6	.5			1.0	.8
6.0	1.8	1.2	1.1	1.0			1.4	1.5
2.6	.9	.6	.6	.7		Sales/Total Assets	.8	.8
1.3	.5	.4	.5	.2			.4	.5
.3	.8	2.1	2.5	1.4			.7	.6
(15) 1.2	(34) 2.3	(52) 4.5	(45) 6.2	(12) 3.3		% Depr., Dep., Amort./Sales	(130) 2.9	(112) 2.7
2.9	8.0	7.4	9.4	17.5			5.5	6.8
							1.6	2.4
						% Officers', Directors', Owners' Comp/Sales	(26) 8.4	(15) 10.5
							19.4	19.5
24682M	71006M	347471M	989663M	960066M	1669217M	Net Sales ($)	2771895M	2125356M
7184M	54092M	297683M	1265888M	1111497M	866979M	Total Assets ($)	3427450M	2736204M

© RMA 2005

M = $ thousand   MM = $ million
See Pages 11 through 21 for Explanation of Ratios and Data

Comparative Historical Data | Current Data Sorted By Sales

			Type of Statement						
115	125	123	Unqualified	19	37	12	16	17	22
6	10	8	Reviewed	4	4				
10	32	11	Compiled	7	4				
6	11	8	Tax Returns	7		1			
72	79	66	Other	20	12	4	8	12	10
4/1/02-3/31/03	4/1/03-3/31/04	4/1/04-3/31/05		101 (4/1-9/30/04)			115 (10/1/04-3/31/05)		
ALL	ALL	ALL		0-1MM	1-3MM	3-5MM	5-10MM	10-25MM	25MM & OVER
209	257	216	**NUMBER OF STATEMENTS**	57	57	17	24	29	32
%	%	%	**ASSETS**	%	%	%	%	%	%
23.5	28.4	29.8	Cash & Equivalents	38.0	29.8	15.9	18.1	24.0	36.8
7.1	6.7	6.7	Trade Receivables (net)	5.4	4.8	7.3	7.3	7.5	10.6
2.0	1.1	1.4	Inventory	.1	2.8	.7	.6	1.6	1.7
3.7	7.0	3.1	All Other Current	1.5	2.5	6.0	3.0	2.9	5.6
36.3	43.3	41.0	Total Current	45.1	40.0	29.9	29.0	36.1	54.6
48.1	42.2	42.0	Fixed Assets (net)	38.0	43.2	52.4	53.0	48.0	27.9
1.2	.9	.3	Intangibles (net)	.0	.3	.3	.6	.8	.5
14.3	13.6	16.7	All Other Non-Current	16.9	16.5	17.4	17.4	15.0	17.0
100.0	100.0	100.0	Total	100.0	100.0	100.0	100.0	100.0	100.0
			LIABILITIES						
6.0	4.2	4.8	Notes Payable-Short Term	10.8	3.7	2.8	3.6	.7	1.8
2.5	3.6	4.3	Cur. Mat.-L/T/D	6.8	7.0	2.2	1.3	1.7	.7
5.7	5.0	7.8	Trade Payables	8.1	5.7	2.7	7.5	3.2	18.2
.1	.1	.2	Income Taxes Payable	.0	.2	.2	.0	.2	.4
9.0	10.7	9.9	All Other Current	7.9	6.0	3.6	15.6	13.3	16.5
23.3	23.6	27.0	Total Current	33.7	22.5	11.4	27.9	19.1	37.6
19.4	19.7	20.8	Long-Term Debt	25.6	25.2	24.8	14.4	19.1	8.6
.1	.2	.2	Deferred Taxes	.0	.1	.0	.1	.7	.5
7.2	5.2	7.2	All Other Non-Current	2.7	10.2	6.6	4.1	11.1	9.3
50.1	51.3	44.8	Net Worth	38.1	42.0	57.2	53.5	50.0	44.1
100.0	100.0	100.0	Total Liabilities & Net Worth	100.0	100.0	100.0	100.0	100.0	100.0
			INCOME DATA						
100.0	100.0	100.0	Net Sales	100.0	100.0	100.0	100.0	100.0	100.0
			Gross Profit						
94.2	93.2	93.8	Operating Expenses	89.3	95.6	98.5	100.1	93.5	92.0
5.8	6.8	6.2	Operating Profit	10.7	4.4	1.5	-.1	6.5	8.0
3.0	1.8	1.1	All Other Expenses (net)	4.0	.9	-1.7	.0	1.0	-1.0
2.8	5.0	5.0	Profit Before Taxes	6.7	3.5	3.2	-.1	5.5	9.0
			RATIOS						
4.4	5.2	4.7		5.8	4.9	9.1	2.6	4.5	3.3
1.8	2.2	2.1	Current	2.4	2.3	3.0	1.7	2.4	1.7
1.0	1.0	1.1		.8	.9	1.5	1.1	1.1	1.1
3.5	3.9	3.8		5.8	3.4	8.1	2.1	4.0	2.9
1.5	1.5	1.6	Quick	2.3	1.6	3.0	1.2	1.6	1.5
.7	.7	.8		.8	.6	.7	1.0	.8	.9
3 136.1	1 354.0	1 600.3		0 UND	0 857.8	1 453.7	4 95.7	9 42.7	4 95.5
12 29.4	10 36.9	9 41.6	Sales/Receivables	1 359.0	8 48.0	9 41.5	18 20.1	13 28.7	11 32.0
36 10.1	30 12.2	28 13.0		13 28.3	26 14.1	47 7.8	39 9.3	34 10.7	35 10.3
			Cost of Sales/Inventory						
			Cost of Sales/Payables						
2.7	2.3	2.8		2.7	2.0	1.6	3.4	2.7	3.4
7.1	5.8	7.1	Sales/Working Capital	5.4	7.6	7.2	10.9	7.1	7.4
666.9	-146.6	91.0		-60.3	NM	18.4	86.2	94.3	68.7
5.3	9.8	10.9		5.1	6.6	6.3	12.9	20.0	136.7
(126) 1.1	(146) 2.8	(125) 2.2	EBIT/Interest	(26) 1.4	(36) 1.7	(12) 2.8	(16) .6	(17) 2.9	(18) 12.4
-3.0	.6	-.9		-2.3	-2.9	-1.4	-1.4	1.4	5.7
3.3	7.5	10.8	Net Profit + Depr., Dep.,						
(11) 2.4	(13) 3.2	(11) 4.4	Amort./Cur. Mat. L/T/D						
.2	.1	1.2							
.4	.1	.2		.0	.1	.5	.5	.5	.1
.9	.8	.7	Fixed/Worth	.4	.8	.8	.9	.9	.5
1.4	1.3	1.4		1.5	1.7	1.7	1.1	1.6	.9
.2	.2	.3		.2	.3	.2	.2	.4	.4
.7	.7	.7	Debt/Worth	1.1	.6	.5	.5	.9	.8
1.8	1.7	1.8		2.2	2.2	1.1	1.0	1.8	1.5
11.7	15.2	16.0	% Profit Before Taxes/Tangible	21.9	9.1	13.3	5.5	19.0	23.1
(198) 1.2	(235) 5.3	(196) 4.7	Net Worth	(50) 8.9	(50) -.5	(16) 1.7	(23) .3	(26) 6.0	(31) 11.9
-5.5	-1.4	-2.8		-5.9	-10.5	-1.9	-2.9	1.1	6.1
5.4	8.7	8.1	% Profit Before Taxes/Total	10.6	6.2	9.1	3.3	7.5	12.1
.3	2.2	2.3	Assets	3.2	.0	1.0	.1	2.8	7.7
-3.8	-1.3	-1.7		-3.9	-6.7	-1.4	-1.5	.1	3.1
7.3	31.5	21.8		695.0	31.2	5.3	3.1	3.4	26.6
1.5	2.2	2.7	Sales/Net Fixed Assets	7.5	2.5	1.1	1.0	1.9	6.5
.7	.8	.7		.7	.8	.7	.6	.7	3.0
1.3	1.3	1.8		2.2	1.8	.9	.9	1.2	2.6
.7	.8	.8	Sales/Total Assets	.9	.7	.6	.5	.8	1.3
.4	.5	.5		.4	.4	.4	.3	.5	.8
1.9	2.7	1.4		1.2	1.0	2.5	2.0	2.5	.9
(165) 4.4	(184) 4.9	(160) 3.6	% Depr., Dep., Amort./Sales	(31) 2.9	(48) 4.1	(15) 5.1	(19) 7.1	(22) 5.0	(25) 2.4
8.9	8.2	8.2		8.5	8.4	7.9	12.8	9.2	5.1
4.7	5.7	5.7	% Officers', Directors',						
(18) 8.4	(43) 12.3	(24) 10.7	Owners' Comp/Sales						
17.2	31.4	22.4							
2890269M	2917226M	4062105M	Net Sales ($)	29165M	105918M	64202M	183767M	462483M	3216570M
4033363M	3878993M	3603323M	Total Assets ($)	49820M	251222M	110276M	487040M	790605M	1914360M

M = $ thousand   MM = $ million
See Pages 11 through 21 for Explanation of Ratios and Data

OTHER SERVICES—Private Households NAICS 814110 (SIC 8811)

Current Data Sorted By Assets | **Comparative Historical Data**

Type of Statement	0-500M	500M-2MM	2-10MM	10-50MM	50-100MM	100-250MM		
Unqualified	2	2	3	5		2	9	14
Reviewed	1	5	12	5	2		9	10
Compiled	10	10	10	2			15	14
Tax Returns	6	7	3				27	6
Other	9	13	19	15	1	1	26	26
		20 (4/1-9/30/04)		125 (10/1/04-3/31/05)			4/1/00-3/31/01 ALL	4/1/01-3/31/02 ALL
NUMBER OF STATEMENTS	28	37	47	27	3	3	86	70
ASSETS	%	%	%	%	%	%	%	%
Cash & Equivalents	19.7	9.8	10.5	7.9			13.1	13.3
Trade Receivables (net)	14.4	16.8	23.7	21.0			16.8	20.4
Inventory	3.8	9.5	14.7	12.7			12.5	16.6
All Other Current	5.7	3.5	4.9	2.9			3.8	3.2
Total Current	43.6	39.6	53.8	44.5			46.2	53.6
Fixed Assets (net)	34.7	46.7	31.4	33.2			40.4	37.0
Intangibles (net)	6.4	6.3	1.4	4.2			2.4	2.1
All Other Non-Current	15.3	7.4	13.3	18.1			11.0	7.4
Total	100.0	100.0	100.0	100.0			100.0	100.0
LIABILITIES								
Notes Payable-Short Term	29.6	8.5	12.1	28.0			12.1	11.2
Cur. Mat.-L/T/D	2.6	4.4	4.1	2.9			4.8	4.2
Trade Payables	7.5	6.4	7.9	10.8			8.4	11.3
Income Taxes Payable	.0	.0	1.7	.5			.3	.2
All Other Current	25.7	8.0	6.9	12.6			7.2	7.9
Total Current	65.4	27.3	32.7	54.8			32.8	34.9
Long-Term Debt	16.0	48.8	25.5	22.9			25.2	20.9
Deferred Taxes	1.1	.0	.1	.5			.4	.2
All Other Non-Current	18.8	4.0	1.2	4.5			9.2	4.1
Net Worth	−1.3	19.8	40.5	17.2			32.3	39.9
Total Liabilities & Net Worth	100.0	100.0	100.0	100.0			100.0	100.0
INCOME DATA								
Net Sales	100.0	100.0	100.0	100.0			100.0	100.0
Gross Profit								
Operating Expenses	89.6	77.3	83.1	79.9			85.8	87.1
Operating Profit	10.4	22.7	16.9	20.1			14.2	12.9
All Other Expenses (net)	2.1	5.8	2.2	3.9			5.4	5.3
Profit Before Taxes	8.2	16.9	14.7	16.2			8.8	7.6
RATIOS								
Current	1.9	3.1	3.1	1.7			3.8	3.1
	1.0	1.5	1.6	1.2			1.8	1.3
	.2	.9	1.2	.9			.9	.9
Quick	1.6	2.5	2.1	1.3			2.2	2.1
	.7	1.3	1.1	.7			1.1	1.0
	.1	.3	.4	.4			.4	.4
Sales/Receivables	0 UND	0 UND	0 UND	2 165.8			0 UND	2 150.4
	0 UND	1 408.0	34 10.8	41 8.9			9 42.4	28 12.9
	17 21.6	42 8.7	70 5.2	66 5.6			53 6.9	50 7.2
Cost of Sales/Inventory								
Cost of Sales/Payables								
Sales/Working Capital	15.0	7.7	3.1	7.0			5.0	5.0
	NM	18.8	11.0	21.4			14.4	17.3
	−25.5	−70.6	52.0	−44.4			−60.6	−28.9
EBIT/Interest	(21) 21.2	(30) 12.7	(35) 21.1	(21) 11.5			(63) 12.4	(59) 17.5
	3.6	3.8	8.3	6.0			3.0	5.8
	−7.1	.6	2.6	2.9			1.2	1.5
Net Profit + Depr., Dep., Amort./Cur. Mat. L /T/D								14.8
							(12) 2.4
								1.5
Fixed/Worth	.2	.6	.2	.1			.3	.2
	1.4	2.1	.5	1.0			1.0	.9
	−.7	−110.3	2.0	1.8			5.9	2.2
Debt/Worth	.5	1.0	.5	1.1			.7	.5
	2.9	3.5	1.5	1.9			2.1	1.4
	−2.8	−688.3	3.9	7.2			8.7	6.6
% Profit Before Taxes/Tangible Net Worth	(18) 76.8	(27) 58.0	(42) 48.3	(22) 43.0			(69) 63.0	(61) 53.4
	37.9	15.9	20.4	21.3			22.4	23.7
	9.6	−2.5	6.1	12.1			2.2	6.0
% Profit Before Taxes/Total Assets	42.6	18.3	15.9	15.5			20.9	20.5
	13.1	5.9	7.7	7.7			6.1	6.5
	3.7	−2.3	2.6	2.4			.3	2.0
Sales/Net Fixed Assets	120.4	26.4	33.3	47.8			26.8	32.0
	18.9	5.7	10.7	7.8			8.5	10.1
	7.6	1.3	1.5	2.2			1.7	2.4
Sales/Total Assets	7.6	3.1	3.0	2.6			3.9	3.6
	4.2	2.0	1.7	1.2			2.2	2.1
	2.6	.7	.8	.4			1.0	1.1
% Depr., Dep., Amort./Sales	(12) .6	(31) 1.1	(35) .9	(22) 1.2			(71) 1.1	(56) .9
	1.8	4.5	2.5	3.5			3.2	3.2
	8.0	10.6	5.3	6.9			8.2	6.5
% Officers', Directors', Owners' Comp/Sales	(12) 7.4	(13) 2.9	(18) 1.9				(39) 1.9	(20) 1.3
	13.4	7.4	3.9				5.6	4.1
	28.6	10.9	9.2				10.6	11.4
Net Sales ($)	55694M	110570M	420991M	2810268M	197237M	766579M	1640856M	1292890M
Total Assets ($)	6791M	45211M	222956M	667695M	228330M	454224M	800320M	630686M

M = $ thousand   MM = $ million
See Pages 11 through 21 for Explanation of Ratios and Data

Comparative Historical Data — Current Data Sorted By Sales

			Type of Statement						
19	21	14	Unqualified	2	2	1	1	2	6
19	29	25	Reviewed	2	2	3	8	8	2
33	39	32	Compiled	8	8	4	6	4	2
13	16	16	Tax Returns	8	4		2	1	1
45	55	58	Other	13	16	5	8	8	8
4/1/02-3/31/03	4/1/03-3/31/04	4/1/04-3/31/05		20 (4/1-9/30/04)			125 (10/1/04-3/31/05)		
ALL	ALL	ALL		0-1MM	1-3MM	3-5MM	5-10MM	10-25MM	25MM & OVER
129	160	145	NUMBER OF STATEMENTS	33	32	13	25	23	19
%	%	%	ASSETS	%	%	%	%	%	%
12.4	11.6	11.5	Cash & Equivalents	12.7	15.7	10.0	9.7	11.6	5.5
19.0	17.6	19.2	Trade Receivables (net)	7.1	13.4	26.8	32.0	16.6	31.3
13.9	12.8	10.9	Inventory	5.8	4.2	6.9	15.6	19.8	16.9
4.5	5.4	4.3	All Other Current	7.1	3.6	3.2	3.9	2.2	4.2
49.9	47.4	45.9	Total Current	32.7	36.8	47.0	61.3	50.3	57.8
38.2	39.0	36.5	Fixed Assets (net)	49.0	33.5	47.8	28.1	30.5	30.2
3.6	2.5	4.3	Intangibles (net)	5.5	5.4	1.7	2.0	5.9	3.5
8.3	11.1	13.3	All Other Non-Current	12.7	24.3	3.4	8.6	13.4	8.5
100.0	100.0	100.0	Total	100.0	100.0	100.0	100.0	100.0	100.0
			LIABILITIES						
12.3	13.7	17.1	Notes Payable-Short Term	8.9	15.9	10.1	23.4	12.4	35.8
4.9	4.5	3.7	Cur. Mat.-L/T/D	3.5	1.9	3.0	3.7	6.6	3.5
8.0	8.7	8.0	Trade Payables	5.0	5.3	7.9	8.4	10.0	15.2
.3	.9	.7	Income Taxes Payable	.3	.0	.0	1.1	2.3	.4
13.2	12.5	12.1	All Other Current	15.1	10.4	7.5	8.7	11.6	17.4
38.6	40.4	41.5	Total Current	32.7	33.5	28.5	45.4	42.9	72.3
25.0	28.1	28.7	Long-Term Debt	30.4	28.3	38.4	29.3	27.5	20.4
.3	.2	.4	Deferred Taxes	.0	1.0	.0	.1	.2	.6
6.4	6.3	6.4	All Other Non-Current	16.6	3.5	1.4	3.4	3.8	3.8
29.6	25.0	23.1	Net Worth	20.2	33.6	31.7	21.7	25.7	2.9
100.0	100.0	100.0	Total Liabilities & Net Worth	100.0	100.0	100.0	100.0	100.0	100.0
			INCOME DATA						
100.0	100.0	100.0	Net Sales	100.0	100.0	100.0	100.0	100.0	100.0
			Gross Profit						
87.8	83.9	82.0	Operating Expenses	67.6	78.6	82.6	90.3	89.0	92.5
12.2	16.1	18.0	Operating Profit	32.4	21.4	17.4	9.7	11.0	7.5
5.8	3.6	4.3	All Other Expenses (net)	8.6	3.4	1.3	1.2	7.4	.9
6.4	12.6	13.7	Profit Before Taxes	23.8	18.0	16.1	8.4	3.6	6.6
			RATIOS						
2.5	2.6	2.6	Current	3.0	5.1	5.2	2.8	1.6	1.7
1.3	1.2	1.4		1.3	1.6	2.5	1.5	1.2	1.3
.7	.7	.9		.2	.7	1.0	1.2	.8	1.1
1.6	1.7	1.9	Quick	2.0	4.4	3.1	1.7	.8	1.3
.8	.7	.9		.9	1.3	1.9	1.4	.6	.8
.3	.2	.3		.1	.3	.7	.3	.4	.5
0 UND	0 UND	0 UND	Sales/Receivables	0 UND	0 UND	0 UND	4 83.6	1 266.1	26 14.0
15 24.0	15 23.8	17 21.7		0 UND	0 UND	23 16.0	49 7.4	41 8.8	34 10.8
46 8.0	54 6.8	47 7.7		3 110.7	38 9.7	61 6.0	80 4.5	54 6.7	58 6.3
			Cost of Sales/Inventory						
			Cost of Sales/Payables						
6.4	5.1	7.3	Sales/Working Capital	5.4	4.1	6.0	6.7	9.3	9.4
30.2	17.3	16.5		26.1	13.7	16.4	11.0	18.0	21.4
-19.1	-16.5	-49.6		-25.9	-19.1	NM	51.6	-52.3	84.1
(100) 12.7	(124) 11.2	(113) 18.0	EBIT/Interest	(20) 18.1	(26) 15.3	(10) 28.6	(19) 73.6	(20) 12.2	(18) 30.0
3.7	4.4	5.8		3.9	3.6	7.4	8.3	5.2	8.2
1.1	1.6	1.9		.8	1.2	3.0	1.8	.1	2.7
(20) 6.0	(15) 21.5	(16) 9.2	Net Profit + Depr., Dep., Amort./Cur. Mat. L/T/D						
2.7	5.5	6.1							
1.2	2.5	1.9							
.2	.2	.3	Fixed/Worth	.3	.2	.3	.1	.5	.2
1.0	.9	1.0		1.9	.8	2.0	.6	1.0	.6
3.8	4.8	5.2		5.4	3.3	NM	5.4	-3.1	2.2
.8	.7	.7	Debt/Worth	.5	.3	.6	.8	1.1	1.1
1.9	1.7	1.9		2.8	1.4	1.8	2.3	1.6	2.0
7.7	12.5	7.8		7.1	6.3	NM	12.8	-26.1	4.6
(108) 53.3	(127) 44.7	(115) 47.5	% Profit Before Taxes/Tangible Net Worth	(27) 46.8	(25) 35.9	(10) 65.5	(21) 78.5	(17) 38.4	(15) 47.6
16.0	18.2	22.3		30.3	17.8	23.8	40.8	16.4	25.3
.0	3.2	5.9		6.4	4.7	3.2	8.8	-2.6	13.7
18.5	16.9	17.7	% Profit Before Taxes/Total Assets	15.6	17.6	70.7	21.6	14.1	17.1
4.8	6.0	7.7		8.5	6.1	10.1	6.0	6.4	13.0
.0	1.2	2.4		2.9	2.2	3.0	1.0	-3.6	3.3
51.3	27.7	36.5	Sales/Net Fixed Assets	18.9	31.3	25.4	66.2	33.3	100.7
9.9	6.7	9.0		3.2	8.4	6.9	27.3	12.9	19.2
1.7	1.3	2.0		.2	1.9	2.0	4.0	2.3	5.6
3.8	3.3	3.3	Sales/Total Assets	3.3	3.0	3.9	3.5	5.7	3.3
2.2	1.8	2.0		.7	1.5	2.5	2.5	2.1	2.6
.7	.6	.8		.2	.3	1.5	1.4	.8	1.6
(100) 1.0	(124) 1.1	(104) 1.0	% Depr., Dep., Amort./Sales	(19) 5.3	(18) 1.1	(10) 1.7	(21) .7	(21) .7	(15) .5
2.8	3.2	2.7		10.6	4.0	3.7	1.7	1.2	1.7
11.4	9.2	8.4		17.5	8.1	13.1	6.5	4.9	3.6
(31) 2.5	(41) 1.3	(49) 2.5	% Officers', Directors', Owners' Comp/Sales				(13) 1.7	(10) .4	
7.7	5.7	6.7					3.7	4.3	
17.3	9.4	9.4					6.4	13.9	
2201516M	2327211M	4361339M	Net Sales ($)	15195M	55460M	46102M	185548M	413139M	3645895M
1029188M	1290028M	1625207M	Total Assets ($)	46231M	141884M	22628M	133150M	329320M	951994M

© RMA 2005

M = $ thousand   MM = $ million
See Pages 11 through 21 for Explanation of Ratios and Data

PUBLIC
ADMINISTRATION

Current Data Sorted By Assets							Comparative Historical Data	
						Type of Statement		
	9	12	1	1		Unqualified	12	10
						Reviewed		1
						Compiled	1	1
						Tax Returns		
3	2	4		1		Other	1	7
25 (4/1-9/30/04)		8 (10/1/04-3/31/05)					4/1/00-3/31/01	4/1/01-3/31/02
0-500M	500M-2MM	2-10MM	10-50MM	50-100MM	100-250MM		ALL	ALL
3	3	11	16	1	2	**NUMBER OF STATEMENTS**	14	19
%	%	%	%	%	%	**ASSETS**	%	%
		30.6	29.5			Cash & Equivalents	20.8	41.2
		10.9	8.1			Trade Receivables (net)	2.4	6.6
		2.0	.0			Inventory	.3	.6
		4.7	8.8			All Other Current	1.1	4.7
		48.2	46.5			Total Current	24.6	53.1
		39.9	42.2			Fixed Assets (net)	50.0	31.1
		.0	.1			Intangibles (net)	.8	.3
		11.9	11.2			All Other Non-Current	24.6	15.6
		100.0	100.0			Total	100.0	100.0
						LIABILITIES		
		.7	.2			Notes Payable-Short Term	.3	.0
		1.4	2.1			Cur. Mat.-L/T/D	1.3	.9
		4.3	1.9			Trade Payables	1.5	7.1
		.3	.0			Income Taxes Payable	.0	.6
		4.4	5.1			All Other Current	3.9	20.0
		11.0	9.4			Total Current	7.0	28.6
		15.3	24.9			Long-Term Debt	22.2	17.5
		.0	.0			Deferred Taxes	.4	.0
		4.3	7.3			All Other Non-Current	2.5	4.7
		69.4	58.5			Net Worth	67.9	49.1
		100.0	100.0			Total Liabilities & Net Worth	100.0	100.0
						INCOME DATA		
		100.0	100.0			Net Sales	100.0	100.0
						Gross Profit		
		88.8	90.7			Operating Expenses	100.0	96.8
		11.2	9.3			Operating Profit	.0	3.2
		2.6	1.5			All Other Expenses (net)	-3.4	-.9
		8.6	7.8			Profit Before Taxes	3.4	4.1
						RATIOS		
		13.7	8.9				6.2	6.5
		4.0	5.6			Current	3.6	3.5
		2.2	3.3				1.8	1.0
		10.3	8.6				5.9	5.4
		4.0	4.9			Quick	3.3	3.3
		1.6	1.7				1.2	1.0
		8　44.6	8　44.6				6　60.6	2　165.4
		22　16.8	11　32.2			Sales/Receivables	24　15.2	22　16.3
		61　6.0	55　6.7				35　10.5	59　6.2
						Cost of Sales/Inventory		
						Cost of Sales/Payables		
		1.4	1.3				1.0	1.2
		3.1	1.9			Sales/Working Capital	2.5	2.8
		5.5	4.4				8.5	-129.9
							6.7	4.8
						EBIT/Interest	(11)　1.8	(11)　3.0
							-.8	-.5
						Net Profit + Depr., Dep., Amort./Cur. Mat. L /T/D		
		.0	.1				.7	.0
		.4	.8			Fixed/Worth	.8	.5
		1.0	1.0				.9	.7
		.1	.2				.2	.4
		.4	.5			Debt/Worth	.6	.7
		1.1	.8				.7	4.3
		10.5	8.2				4.0	7.0
		8.6	(14)　4.2			% Profit Before Taxes/Tangible Net Worth	.6	(17)　2.0
		-3.6	1.3				-2.1	-3.5
		8.3	6.6				2.5	4.0
		6.2	3.3			% Profit Before Taxes/Total Assets	.4	1.0
		-3.0	1.2				-1.3	-3.2
		UND	UND				.9	UND
		1.7	1.0			Sales/Net Fixed Assets	.6	1.4
		.4	.4				.4	.4
		2.9	1.2				.5	4.1
		.9	.5			Sales/Total Assets	.3	.5
		.3	.3				.2	.2
						% Depr., Dep., Amort./Sales		
						% Officers', Directors', Owners' Comp/Sales		
5360M	77936M	356464M	24070M	69441M		Net Sales ($)	206740M	456688M
3803M	60122M	386215M	86189M	280013M		Total Assets ($)	940397M	1393770M

D A T A　N O T　A V A I L A B L E

Comparative Historical Data				Current Data Sorted By Sales					
26	20	23	**Type of Statement**						
	1		Unqualified	2	2	2	6	7	4
			Reviewed						
			Compiled						
			Tax Returns						
6	7	10	Other	2	2	1	1	2	2
4/1/02- 3/31/03	4/1/03- 3/31/04	4/1/04- 3/31/05			25 (4/1-9/30/04)		8 (10/1/04-3/31/05)		
ALL	ALL	ALL		0-1MM	1-3MM	3-5MM	5-10MM	10-25MM	25MM & OVER
32	28	33	**NUMBER OF STATEMENTS**	4	4	3	7	9	6
%	%	%	**ASSETS**	%	%	%	%	%	%
22.5	23.1	34.6	Cash & Equivalents						
8.9	3.9	8.5	Trade Receivables (net)						
.4	.2	.8	Inventory						
8.2	8.0	6.1	All Other Current						
40.0	35.2	50.0	Total Current						
49.5	54.5	38.9	Fixed Assets (net)						
.1	.9	.1	Intangibles (net)						
10.5	9.4	10.9	All Other Non-Current						
100.0	100.0	100.0	Total						
			LIABILITIES						
.5	.2	.3	Notes Payable-Short Term						
1.0	1.0	1.5	Cur. Mat.-L/T/D						
2.0	2.2	2.9	Trade Payables						
.0	.0	.1	Income Taxes Payable						
6.9	3.5	5.5	All Other Current						
10.4	6.9	10.4	Total Current						
14.8	27.1	18.5	Long-Term Debt						
.9	.0	.0	Deferred Taxes						
6.4	11.3	15.8	All Other Non-Current						
67.5	54.7	55.3	Net Worth						
100.0	100.0	100.0	Total Liabilities & Net Worth						
			INCOME DATA						
100.0	100.0	100.0	Net Sales						
			Gross Profit						
93.7	98.6	90.7	Operating Expenses						
6.3	1.4	9.3	Operating Profit						
5.0	3.3	1.7	All Other Expenses (net)						
1.3	−1.8	7.6	Profit Before Taxes						
			RATIOS						
8.7	6.8	8.9							
4.4	4.4	5.5	Current						
2.6	2.8	2.7							
7.0	5.2	7.5							
4.1	3.2	4.7	Quick						
2.1	2.3	1.7							
11 32.5	5 72.2	8 45.1							
27 13.7	24 15.1	20 18.3	Sales/Receivables						
48 7.7	46 8.0	59 6.2							
			Cost of Sales/Inventory						
			Cost of Sales/Payables						
1.2	1.3	1.3							
2.0	2.4	2.0	Sales/Working Capital						
5.6	3.3	4.9							
6.2	3.6	14.5							
(20) 2.6	(16) .3	(17) 3.5	EBIT/Interest						
.9	−1.0	.9							
			Net Profit + Depr., Dep., Amort./Cur. Mat. L/T/D						
.5	.7	.0							
.7	1.0	.8	Fixed/Worth						
1.0	1.7	1.1							
.2	.2	.2							
.3	.7	.5	Debt/Worth						
1.0	1.6	1.0							
7.9	4.2	9.5	% Profit Before Taxes/Tangible						
1.4	(27) −1.0	(29) 6.1	Net Worth						
−5.9	−6.9	−.1							
4.7	3.2	7.2	% Profit Before Taxes/Total						
1.1	−.2	4.0	Assets						
−3.9	−3.0	−.1							
1.9	1.4	UND							
.5	.5	1.6	Sales/Net Fixed Assets						
.4	.3	.4							
.8	1.1	1.4							
.3	.3	.6	Sales/Total Assets						
.2	.2	.3							
2.9	2.4	1.8							
(15) 6.3	(12) 9.9	(14) 4.6	% Depr., Dep., Amort./Sales						
13.3	24.3	12.7							
			% Officers', Directors', Owners' Comp/Sales						
1087426M	297336M	533271M	Net Sales ($)	3150M	7517M	11851M	48328M	147393M	315032M
1616264M	815213M	816342M	Total Assets ($)	12719M	19273M	40145M	110453M	314050M	319702M

© RMA 2005   **M = $ thousand   MM = $ million**
See Pages 11 through 21 for Explanation of Ratios and Data

	Current Data Sorted By Assets						Comparative Historical Data	

		1	6	7	7	4		
							1	
	1	1		1		1	8	8
	20 (4/1-9/30/04)			10 (10/1/04-3/31/05)			4/1/00-3/31/01	4/1/01-3/31/02
Type of Statement	0-500M	500M-2MM	2-10MM	10-50MM	50-100MM	100-250MM	ALL	ALL
Unqualified		1	6	7	7	4	18	15
Reviewed								
Compiled						1	1	3
Tax Returns								
Other	1		1	1		1	8	8
NUMBER OF STATEMENTS	1	1	7	8	7	6	27	26
	%	%	%	%	%	%	%	%
ASSETS								
Cash & Equivalents							16.6	27.4
Trade Receivables (net)							4.0	2.8
Inventory							.5	.3
All Other Current							6.8	10.5
Total Current							27.8	40.9
Fixed Assets (net)							59.9	48.4
Intangibles (net)							.1	.3
All Other Non-Current							12.3	10.4
Total							100.0	100.0
LIABILITIES								
Notes Payable-Short Term							7.6	8.5
Cur. Mat.-L/T/D							.6	.2
Trade Payables							5.7	3.3
Income Taxes Payable							.0	.0
All Other Current							5.9	8.9
Total Current							19.7	20.9
Long-Term Debt							21.7	16.5
Deferred Taxes							.0	.0
All Other Non-Current							2.2	3.1
Net Worth							56.4	59.4
Total Liabilities & Net Worth							100.0	100.0
INCOME DATA								
Net Sales							100.0	100.0
Gross Profit								
Operating Expenses							100.0	92.7
Operating Profit							.0	7.3
All Other Expenses (net)							−1.1	.8
Profit Before Taxes							1.1	6.5
RATIOS								
Current							4.3	6.0
							2.6	3.8
							1.5	1.9
Quick							3.8	5.0
							1.9	3.1
							.9	1.5
Sales/Receivables							13 28.4	1 300.5
							27 13.4	13 27.2
							37 9.9	33 11.0
Cost of Sales/Inventory								
Cost of Sales/Payables								
Sales/Working Capital							1.2	1.3
							2.9	2.0
							6.6	5.3
EBIT/Interest							2.2	7.1
							(19) .0	(12) 4.3
							−1.8	.5
Net Profit + Depr., Dep., Amort./Cur. Mat. L /T/D								
Fixed/Worth							.8	.2
							.9	.8
							1.2	1.0
Debt/Worth							.3	.2
							.5	.4
							1.0	1.0
% Profit Before Taxes/Tangible Net Worth							1.1	5.5
							(26) −.7	(25) 2.8
							−6.0	−3.6
% Profit Before Taxes/Total Assets							1.4	5.2
							−.4	1.8
							−2.1	−2.0
Sales/Net Fixed Assets							.8	10.3
							.5	.7
							.3	.3
Sales/Total Assets							.6	.7
							.3	.4
							.2	.2
% Depr., Dep., Amort./Sales							4.0	2.9
							(22) 5.5	(15) 5.7
							10.1	6.4
% Officers', Directors', Owners' Comp/Sales								
Net Sales ($)	2778M	6283M	82005M	399535M	504073M	829789M	368103M	615495M
Total Assets ($)	472M	1284M	39362M	219526M	600039M	938232M	1062603M	1340500M

© RMA 2005

M = $ thousand   MM = $ million

See Pages 11 through 21 for Explanation of Ratios and Data

Comparative Historical Data | Current Data Sorted By Sales

Type of Statement

	4/1/02-3/31/03 ALL	4/1/03-3/31/04 ALL	4/1/04-3/31/05 ALL		0-1MM	1-3MM	3-5MM	5-10MM	10-25MM	25MM & OVER
Unqualified	15	27	25				2	1	8	14
Reviewed										
Compiled			1							1
Tax Returns										
Other	7	5	4					1		2
	20 (4/1-9/30/04) →							← 10 (10/1/04-3/31/05)		
NUMBER OF STATEMENTS	22	32	30				3	2	8	17

Columns 0-1MM and 1-3MM: DATA NOT AVAILABLE.

ASSETS (%)

	02-03	03-04	04-05		25MM & OVER
Cash & Equivalents	23.3	20.7	25.8		19.9
Trade Receivables (net)	8.9	1.8	3.4		2.8
Inventory	.5	.8	1.0		.8
All Other Current	4.5	4.2	6.1		5.3
Total Current	37.2	27.5	36.2		28.8
Fixed Assets (net)	53.0	62.7	60.8		67.0
Intangibles (net)	.5	.4	.4		.6
All Other Non-Current	9.3	9.5	2.7		3.6
Total	100.0	100.0	100.0		100.0

LIABILITIES

	02-03	03-04	04-05		25MM & OVER
Notes Payable-Short Term	.2	1.0	1.2		2.1
Cur. Mat.-L/T/D	1.1	1.2	2.6		4.2
Trade Payables	4.1	2.9	4.4		5.5
Income Taxes Payable	.0	.0	.0		.0
All Other Current	9.7	10.7	8.9		8.5
Total Current	15.1	15.8	17.0		20.4
Long-Term Debt	8.9	13.5	19.0		27.9
Deferred Taxes	.0	.0	.0		.0
All Other Non-Current	1.7	2.2	3.7		3.5
Net Worth	74.3	68.4	60.3		48.2
Total Liabilities & Net Worth	100.0	100.0	100.0		100.0

INCOME DATA

	02-03	03-04	04-05		25MM & OVER
Net Sales	100.0	100.0	100.0		100.0
Gross Profit					
Operating Expenses	95.2	75.5	75.3		70.0
Operating Profit	4.8	24.5	24.7		30.0
All Other Expenses (net)	−1.2	1.0	2.5		2.7
Profit Before Taxes	6.0	23.6	22.2		27.3

RATIOS

	02-03	03-04	04-05		25MM & OVER
Current	5.1	3.1	5.3		1.8
	3.3	1.8	1.8		1.0
	1.7	.9	.7		.5
Quick	4.2	2.2	3.7		1.6
	3.0	1.5	1.5		.7
	1.4	.7	.6		.5
Sales/Receivables	3 144.2	0 999.8	0 844.3		0 866.6
	20 18.1	1 300.4	1 269.8		1 367.7
	51 7.2	24 15.0	14 26.0		7 48.8
Cost of Sales/Inventory					
Cost of Sales/Payables					
Sales/Working Capital	1.7	4.0	2.8		8.1
	2.6	13.5	12.1		−218.8
	5.3	−76.5	−29.0		−18.2
EBIT/Interest	(12) 16.3	(18) 46.8	(19) 35.5		(13) 44.8
	4.5	8.6	19.6		20.4
	1.5	2.1	7.0		8.7
Net Profit + Depr., Dep., Amort./Cur. Mat. L/T/D					
Fixed/Worth	.6	.8	.7		.8
	.8	1.0	1.0		1.3
	1.0	1.3	1.6		2.8
Debt/Worth	.1	.2	.3		.3
	.3	.4	.5		1.4
	.7	1.0	1.5		2.8
% Profit Before Taxes/Tangible Net Worth	14.2	133.2	116.7		168.9
	1.0	43.5	45.9		109.5
	−2.3	1.3	2.8		8.3
% Profit Before Taxes/Total Assets	6.5	90.5	68.9		82.9
	.7	26.0	20.4		36.6
	−2.0	.9	1.8		5.0
Sales/Net Fixed Assets	3.9	4.7	4.6		3.9
	.9	2.2	1.8		1.6
	.6	.5	.7		1.1
Sales/Total Assets	1.2	2.4	2.5		2.2
	.5	.9	1.5		1.4
	.3	.4	.4		.8
% Depr., Dep., Amort./Sales	(15) 3.4	(25) 3.5	(19) 3.3		(11) 3.8
	5.4	5.2	4.8		5.2
	9.5	6.7	5.4		7.1
% Officers', Directors', Owners' Comp/Sales					

	02-03	03-04	04-05		3-5MM	5-10MM	10-25MM	25MM & OVER
Net Sales ($)	581874M	1042194M	1824463M		5883M	14626M	132701M	1671253M
Total Assets ($)	943799M	1116997M	1798915M		8759M	6610M	264028M	1519518M

M = $ thousand   MM = $ million
See Pages 11 through 21 for Explanation of Ratios and Data

Current Data Sorted By Assets   Comparative Historical Data

							Type of Statement		
10	9	50	73	29	26		Unqualified	116	78
1					1		Reviewed	1	
	1						Compiled	5	11
							Tax Returns		1
3	5	12	12	7	2		Other	27	50
	176 (4/1-9/30/04)		65 (10/1/04-3/31/05)					4/1/00-3/31/01	4/1/01-3/31/02
0-500M	500M-2MM	2-10MM	10-50MM	50-100MM	100-250MM			ALL	ALL
14	15	62	85	36	29		NUMBER OF STATEMENTS	149	140
%	%	%	%	%	%		ASSETS	%	%
60.0	41.5	42.8	23.5	24.7	23.0		Cash & Equivalents	30.3	25.2
10.6	22.3	9.5	5.7	5.0	6.6		Trade Receivables (net)	5.0	3.8
.0	.2	1.4	.1	.3	.5		Inventory	.6	.4
7.7	4.3	7.6	3.4	6.3	5.0		All Other Current	5.9	8.1
78.3	68.3	61.3	32.8	36.4	35.1		Total Current	41.8	37.5
14.5	29.0	33.3	59.6	53.7	47.9		Fixed Assets (net)	38.3	42.6
.0	.1	.1	.6	.2	2.5		Intangibles (net)	1.4	.9
7.3	2.6	5.3	7.0	9.7	14.5		All Other Non-Current	18.5	19.0
100.0	100.0	100.0	100.0	100.0	100.0		Total	100.0	100.0
							LIABILITIES		
1.3	.0	3.0	1.0	.2	.2		Notes Payable-Short Term	2.0	.9
.5	.4	1.5	1.9	2.0	2.0		Cur. Mat.-L/T/D	.7	1.7
2.3	12.1	4.3	2.9	2.7	2.0		Trade Payables	3.5	2.9
.3	.0	.0	.5	.0	.6		Income Taxes Payable	.0	.4
12.7	18.0	7.2	5.7	5.1	5.5		All Other Current	5.9	5.1
17.1	30.5	16.0	12.0	9.9	10.3		Total Current	12.1	11.0
5.9	8.9	18.7	22.4	22.1	30.9		Long-Term Debt	17.1	20.1
.0	.0	.0	.0	.0	.0		Deferred Taxes	.1	.2
6.2	.7	6.1	2.6	2.7	6.0		All Other Non-Current	6.3	4.9
70.9	60.0	59.2	62.9	65.3	52.8		Net Worth	64.3	63.8
100.0	100.0	100.0	100.0	100.0	100.0		Total Liabilities & Net Worth	100.0	100.0
							INCOME DATA		
100.0	100.0	100.0	100.0	100.0	100.0		Net Sales	100.0	100.0
							Gross Profit		
91.0	99.6	88.6	88.2	89.1	87.2		Operating Expenses	98.6	92.9
9.0	.4	11.4	11.8	10.9	12.8		Operating Profit	1.4	7.1
.5	1.0	3.3	3.9	2.3	5.8		All Other Expenses (net)	-4.3	3.7
8.5	-.6	8.1	7.9	8.6	7.1		Profit Before Taxes	5.7	3.4
							RATIOS		
44.8	28.3	15.2	5.7	6.0	6.9			8.0	9.4
6.7	8.2	5.8	3.3	3.9	3.4		Current	4.1	4.2
3.0	1.1	2.0	1.9	1.9	1.5			2.1	1.9
44.8	15.3	14.3	5.5	5.1	6.8			6.5	7.0
4.8	8.2	4.9	2.9	3.1	2.7		Quick	3.4	3.1
3.0	1.1	1.9	1.6	1.4	1.2			1.7	1.5
0 UND	2 225.1	0 UND	6 60.7	9 42.7	3 107.0			1 243.7	0 810.3
0 UND	12 30.2	18 20.4	27 13.7	28 13.1	25 14.5		Sales/Receivables	16 22.6	12 30.8
25 14.4	53 6.9	42 8.8	54 6.7	50 7.3	71 5.1			38 9.5	40 9.1
							Cost of Sales/Inventory		
							Cost of Sales/Payables		
1.2	1.9	1.3	1.5	1.5	1.0			1.4	1.1
4.4	5.7	3.0	2.4	2.7	1.9		Sales/Working Capital	2.6	2.9
15.0	140.9	5.7	6.7	6.9	5.7			6.8	7.2
		5.7	11.2	13.6	8.3			5.9	4.6
		(38) 1.8	(63) 4.9	(28) 4.6	(22) 3.3		EBIT/Interest	(93) 2.0	(81) 1.4
		-.2	1.1	2.2	2.0			.6	-.8
							Net Profit + Depr., Dep., Amort./Cur. Mat. L./T/D		
.0	.0	.0	.7	.7	.6			.0	.0
.0	.4	.2	1.0	.9	1.0		Fixed/Worth	.7	.7
.3	.9	1.2	1.4	1.4	1.5			1.0	1.0
.0	.1	.2	.2	.2	.4			.2	.2
.4	.2	.5	.6	.4	.9		Debt/Worth	.5	.5
1.1	3.0	1.2	1.0	1.0	2.0			.9	1.0
33.1	37.9	17.7	9.8	8.9	10.7		% Profit Before Taxes/Tangible	7.4	7.5
13.1	(13) -1.0	(60) 5.0	3.6	(35) 4.1	(28) 5.6		Net Worth	(146) 1.5	(137) 1.6
-10.9	-16.7	-1.7	.0	.6	2.1			-1.2	-2.4
19.9	13.2	11.5	5.4	8.6	5.5		% Profit Before Taxes/Total	4.6	5.1
12.7	-.9	2.3	2.2	2.6	2.7		Assets	.9	.9
-5.1	-10.2	-1.4	.0	.6	.6			-.8	-1.5
UND	UND	UND	1.3	1.5	1.2			UND	142.6
UND	158.3	15.5	.4	.7	.7		Sales/Net Fixed Assets	.9	.8
7.8	.8	.6	.3	.4	.4			.4	.4
12.6	5.2	2.4	.7	.8	.5			1.0	.9
2.4	1.9	.9	.3	.4	.4		Sales/Total Assets	.4	.4
.7	.6	.3	.2	.2	.2			.2	.2
		1.2	5.0	3.2	4.2			1.1	1.6
	(27)	5.1	(42) 10.6	(15) 5.3	(15) 6.9		% Depr., Dep., Amort./Sales	(66) 4.7	(63) 6.2
		17.7	17.7	16.1	18.5			9.9	11.8
								6.4	7.5
							% Officers', Directors', Owners' Comp/Sales	(22) 14.6	(24) 16.0
								21.5	27.9
21362M	51879M	471061M	1487826M	1552710M	2408799M		Net Sales ($)	3727064M	3638455M
3877M	16854M	355456M	2120604M	2630710M	4633295M		Total Assets ($)	7408753M	5969670M

M = $thousand   MM = $million
See Pages 11 through 21 for Explanation of Ratios and Data

Comparative Historical Data | Current Data Sorted By Sales

	4/1/02-3/31/03 ALL	4/1/03-3/31/04 ALL	4/1/04-3/31/05 ALL	Type of Statement	0-1MM	1-3MM	3-5MM	5-10MM	10-25MM	25MM & OVER
	194	157	197	Unqualified	17	23	19	36	52	50
	3	2	2	Reviewed	1					1
	5	12	1	Compiled	1					
	1	2		Tax Returns						
	47	38	41	Other	5	7	6	9	7	7
					176 (4/1-9/30/04)			65 (10/1/04-3/31/05)		
	250	211	241	**NUMBER OF STATEMENTS**	24	30	25	45	59	58
	%	%	%	**ASSETS**	%	%	%	%	%	%
	25.6	30.7	31.8	Cash & Equivalents	33.8	25.8	31.5	29.7	33.6	34.2
	6.0	8.5	8.0	Trade Receivables (net)	4.4	5.6	3.1	10.5	9.9	9.1
	.6	.9	.5	Inventory	.0	.1	.2	.1	1.5	.4
	5.6	7.3	5.4	All Other Current	5.4	1.0	7.7	3.6	6.0	7.5
	37.8	47.3	45.8	Total Current	43.6	32.6	42.5	43.9	50.9	51.2
	48.3	43.3	46.0	Fixed Assets (net)	49.9	57.2	52.5	48.1	43.8	36.4
	.4	.4	.6	Intangibles (net)	.3	.4	.1	.1	.2	1.7
	13.5	8.9	7.6	All Other Non-Current	6.2	9.8	4.9	7.9	5.0	10.6
	100.0	100.0	100.0	Total	100.0	100.0	100.0	100.0	100.0	100.0
				LIABILITIES						
	2.1	2.4	1.2	Notes Payable-Short Term	1.0	1.1	.2	.4	2.7	1.0
	1.0	1.6	1.6	Cur. Mat.-L/T/D	1.8	2.2	.9	1.7	1.8	1.4
	3.6	4.1	3.6	Trade Payables	2.0	1.3	1.9	3.7	5.6	4.3
	.1	.0	.3	Income Taxes Payable	.0	.1	.0	.0	.0	1.1
	6.0	8.3	7.1	All Other Current	2.4	4.2	6.8	6.3	11.1	7.4
	12.7	16.4	13.9	Total Current	7.2	8.9	9.8	12.1	21.2	15.2
	20.0	18.9	20.7	Long-Term Debt	26.1	27.4	17.8	19.0	17.0	21.1
	.1	.1	.0	Deferred Taxes	.0	.0	.0	.0	.0	.0
	4.0	5.9	4.0	All Other Non-Current	2.5	4.8	1.0	6.0	3.3	4.8
	63.1	58.8	61.4	Net Worth	64.2	58.9	71.4	62.9	58.5	59.0
	100.0	100.0	100.0	Total Liabilities & Net Worth	100.0	100.0	100.0	100.0	100.0	100.0
				INCOME DATA						
	100.0	100.0	100.0	Net Sales	100.0	100.0	100.0	100.0	100.0	100.0
				Gross Profit						
	91.7	89.7	89.2	Operating Expenses	86.7	83.7	88.2	86.4	95.6	89.1
	8.3	10.3	10.8	Operating Profit	13.3	16.3	11.8	13.6	4.4	10.9
	4.0	3.4	3.4	All Other Expenses (net)	4.5	6.1	3.4	3.5	-.4	5.1
	4.3	6.8	7.5	Profit Before Taxes	8.7	10.2	8.4	10.2	4.8	5.8
				RATIOS						
	8.0	8.2	7.8		26.2	15.0	6.4	12.0	6.7	6.4
	3.8	4.0	4.1	Current	7.3	3.6	4.1	4.1	4.0	3.9
	1.7	1.6	1.9		3.2	1.8	2.1	1.7	1.6	1.9
	6.0	7.3	7.6		18.4	14.8	5.6	10.8	5.8	6.1
	2.9	3.1	3.5	Quick	5.8	3.5	3.5	3.5	3.2	3.1
	1.4	1.3	1.7		2.1	1.6	2.1	1.7	1.2	1.8
	4 84.3	0 972.3	2 149.7		0 UND	0 UND	2 195.1	10 35.5	6 59.7	3 128.2
	21 17.6	20 18.1	23 16.0	Sales/Receivables	12 31.3	14 26.3	18 19.9	30 12.2	25 14.6	19 18.8
	41 8.8	52 7.0	48 7.6		50 7.4	53 6.9	39 9.5	53 6.8	55 6.6	42 8.6
				Cost of Sales/Inventory						
				Cost of Sales/Payables						
	1.2	1.1	1.3		.9	1.0	1.4	1.4	1.5	1.5
	2.6	2.4	2.6	Sales/Working Capital	1.9	2.9	2.1	2.3	3.2	3.6
	7.9	8.8	7.5		7.1	11.4	5.1	9.9	9.3	6.4
	5.7	7.1	10.8		22.3	4.6	7.7	13.1	11.2	13.0
	(177) 2.1	(115) 2.7	(161) 3.5	EBIT/Interest	(10) 1.4	(23) 2.0	(16) 3.6	(32) 3.2	(40) 5.2	(40) 4.0
	-.1	.8	1.0		-.9	-.2	.9	.9	1.1	2.2
				Net Profit + Depr., Dep., Amort./Cur. Mat. L/T/D						
	.4	.0	.0		.0	.4	.0	.0	.0	.0
	.8	.8	.9	Fixed/Worth	.9	1.1	1.0	.9	.8	.8
	1.1	1.2	1.3		1.3	1.5	1.3	1.4	1.2	1.3
	.2	.3	.2		.0	.4	.1	.2	.3	.2
	.5	.6	.5	Debt/Worth	.3	.7	.3	.4	.6	.6
	.9	1.3	1.1		.9	1.3	.8	1.3	1.0	1.5
	6.4	11.2	13.0	% Profit Before Taxes/Tangible	15.6	8.4	10.9	15.7	9.4	16.1
	(246) 2.0	(206) 2.8	(235) 4.1	Net Worth	(22) 1.8	2.2	1.2	(56) 5.5	(57) 3.9	6.1
	-1.9	-.9	-.1		-3.6	-2.1	-.5	-.2	.2	2.1
	3.8	5.7	7.4	% Profit Before Taxes/Total	16.2	3.5	6.7	10.9	6.0	9.5
	1.1	1.7	2.5	Assets	1.6	1.1	.8	3.7	2.3	3.1
	-1.3	-.6	-.2		-1.9	-1.4	-.4	-.1	-1.0	1.0
	11.9	UND	525.1		45.0	3.0	UND	UND	UND	UND
	.6	1.0	.9	Sales/Net Fixed Assets	.7	.5	.4	.6	1.2	1.2
	.3	.3	.4		.2	.2	.2	.3	.4	.6
	.9	1.4	1.2		1.1	.6	1.5	1.0	2.1	1.2
	.4	.5	.5	Sales/Total Assets	.3	.3	.3	.4	.6	.6
	.2	.2	.2		.1	.2	.2	.2	.3	.4
	2.3	1.8	3.3	% Depr., Dep., Amort./Sales	8.3	5.5	5.9	4.7	1.2	1.6
	(139) 6.1	(92) 5.6	(105) 7.8		(14) 20.2	(17) 15.4	(10) 8.6	(18) 9.9	(23) 4.2	(23) 5.1
	10.7	11.5	17.2		29.8	19.2	15.3	17.6	15.6	7.3
	3.1	1.2	2.4	% Officers', Directors',						
	(24) 7.5	(21) 9.3	(20) 6.8	Owners' Comp/Sales						
	19.5	22.2								
	6635311M	7072326M	5993637M	Net Sales ($)	12220M	59308M	100291M	320739M	930392M	4570687M
	11474737M	8741520M	9760796M	Total Assets ($)	55398M	241582M	339792M	998597M	2188301M	5937126M

M = $ thousand   MM = $ million
See Pages 11 through 21 for Explanation of Ratios and Data

Current Data Sorted By Assets   Comparative Historical Data

						Type of Statement		
1	4	16	1			Unqualified	17	9
	1	3				Reviewed	5	3
2	5	1	1			Compiled	4	12
5	4	1				Tax Returns	1	6
2	1	4			1	Other	2	7
	23 (4/1-9/30/04)			30 (10/1/04-3/31/05)			4/1/00-3/31/01	4/1/01-3/31/02
0-500M	500M-2MM	2-10MM	10-50MM	50-100MM	100-250MM		ALL	ALL
10	15	25	2	1		NUMBER OF STATEMENTS	29	37
%	%	%	%	%	%	ASSETS	%	%
40.8	22.2	21.4				Cash & Equivalents	18.1	20.1
19.2	12.0	16.4				Trade Receivables (net)	4.7	9.0
3.0	6.1	2.6				Inventory	2.2	4.0
6.7	2.9	3.7				All Other Current	1.0	3.0
69.6	43.1	44.1				Total Current	26.0	36.1
22.9	53.7	51.5				Fixed Assets (net)	65.0	55.4
.0	.5	1.4				Intangibles (net)	1.1	2.2
7.5	2.7	3.0				All Other Non-Current	7.9	6.3
100.0	100.0	100.0				Total	100.0	100.0
						LIABILITIES		
10.8	.9	3.6				Notes Payable-Short Term	1.3	3.2
81.9	2.1	2.9				Cur. Mat.-L/T/D	2.2	2.0
1.6	7.4	7.8				Trade Payables	2.4	3.9
.0	.0	.2				Income Taxes Payable	.0	.4
10.6	2.0	8.5				All Other Current	1.7	4.0
104.9	12.5	22.8				Total Current	7.6	13.4
5.3	26.1	16.3				Long-Term Debt	18.6	21.5
.0	.0	.0				Deferred Taxes	.1	.0
.0	1.4	2.4				All Other Non-Current	1.6	1.2
−10.2	60.1	58.6				Net Worth	72.2	63.8
100.0	100.0	100.0				Total Liabilities & Net Worth	100.0	100.0
						INCOME DATA		
100.0	100.0	100.0				Net Sales	100.0	100.0
						Gross Profit		
85.8	78.9	89.9				Operating Expenses	94.2	93.1
14.2	21.1	10.1				Operating Profit	5.8	6.9
2.7	2.6	3.4				All Other Expenses (net)	−3.2	3.3
11.5	18.4	6.8				Profit Before Taxes	9.0	3.6
						RATIOS		
86.6	39.5	4.7					12.8	8.0
2.6	6.0	3.0				Current	5.1	5.1
.2	1.8	1.4					2.9	1.7
72.6	33.3	4.6					12.7	7.5
1.6	6.0	2.2				Quick	4.8	3.8
.2	1.2	1.3					2.8	1.2
0 UND	0 UND	0 UND					0 UND	0 UND
0 UND	0 UND	2 215.8				Sales/Receivables	0 UND	0 UND
42 8.7	36 10.1	47 7.8					17 21.9	35 10.6
						Cost of Sales/Inventory		
						Cost of Sales/Payables		
1.3	1.6	3.2					.8	1.1
16.5	5.8	5.0				Sales/Working Capital	2.3	2.1
−6.5	8.8	15.3					4.5	8.8
	56.3	12.1					8.0	6.5
	(13) 11.1	(17) 2.9				EBIT/Interest	(23) 5.0	(27) 3.8
	1.6	.9					.5	1.4
						Net Profit + Depr., Dep., Amort./Cur. Mat. L/T/D		
.1	.2	.3					.7	.6
.5	.9	.9				Fixed/Worth	.9	.9
NM	1.9	2.1					1.1	1.1
.1	.2	.2					.1	.2
.7	.8	.6				Debt/Worth	.3	.3
NM	1.5	2.0					.5	1.2
	28.4	15.5				% Profit Before Taxes/Tangible Net Worth	10.1	9.7
	20.0	(24) 6.0					(28) 5.2	(35) 2.3
	2.7	−1.6					−2.8	−1.7
63.8	23.8	8.1				% Profit Before Taxes/Total Assets	7.6	5.9
23.6	13.1	4.2					4.1	1.8
6.6	1.3	−.4					−3.4	−1.3
UND	19.3	19.9				Sales/Net Fixed Assets	.7	6.7
22.4	.9	1.2					.4	.6
5.0	.3	.5					.3	.3
5.7	2.2	2.7				Sales/Total Assets	.4	1.4
2.6	.6	.8					.3	.4
.9	.3	.4					.2	.2
	1.8	1.2				% Depr., Dep., Amort./Sales	10.8	5.4
	(13) 12.4	(16) 7.2					(14) 17.7	(22) 14.7
	24.2	17.7					23.3	34.3
						% Officers', Directors', Owners' Comp/Sales		
5680M	25885M	153666M	6392M	39498M		Net Sales ($)	66551M	69757M
2322M	21701M	106399M	27758M	64900M		Total Assets ($)	180740M	113711M

M = $ thousand   MM = $ million
See Pages 11 through 21 for Explanation of Ratios and Data

Right-side vertical note in center column: DATA NOT AVAILABLE

Comparative Historical Data   **Current Data Sorted By Sales**

	4/1/02-3/31/03 ALL	4/1/03-3/31/04 ALL	4/1/04-3/31/05 ALL	Type of Statement	0-1MM	1-3MM	3-5MM	5-10MM	10-25MM	25MM & OVER
	11	23	22	Unqualified	5	8	4	4	1	
	6	6	4	Reviewed	2	1				1
	8	13	9	Compiled	5	3	1			
	9	16	10	Tax Returns	7	3				
	10	19	8	Other	1	1	1	2	2	1
					23 (4/1-9/30/04)			**30 (10/1/04-3/31/05)**		
	44	77	53	**NUMBER OF STATEMENTS**	20	15	5	8	3	2
	%	%	%	**ASSETS**	%	%	%	%	%	%
	17.8	17.6	24.8	Cash & Equivalents	31.1	18.5				
	12.7	11.7	15.7	Trade Receivables (net)	4.2	16.3				
	6.0	4.1	3.5	Inventory	1.1	4.4				
	2.7	2.9	3.8	All Other Current	1.8	5.6				
	39.3	36.3	47.8	Total Current	38.1	44.9				
	51.2	52.7	46.2	Fixed Assets (net)	57.6	48.1				
	3.6	3.2	1.4	Intangibles (net)	.2	4.6				
	5.9	7.8	4.5	All Other Non-Current	4.0	2.4				
	100.0	100.0	100.0	Total	100.0	100.0				
				LIABILITIES						
	4.9	5.3	4.0	Notes Payable-Short Term	5.4	.9				
	9.2	11.5	17.5	Cur. Mat.-L/T/D	42.4	2.2				
	4.9	3.8	6.1	Trade Payables	.5	5.7				
	.2	.2	.0	Income Taxes Payable	.0	.0				
	7.0	4.8	7.5	All Other Current	1.1	8.2				
	26.2	25.5	35.2	Total Current	49.4	17.0				
	21.9	20.8	17.8	Long-Term Debt	23.0	21.4				
	.0	.0	.0	Deferred Taxes	.0	.0				
	3.4	3.5	1.5	All Other Non-Current	.0	3.3				
	48.5	50.2	45.5	Net Worth	27.6	58.2				
	100.0	100.0	100.0	Total Liabilities & Net Worth	100.0	100.0				
				INCOME DATA						
	100.0	100.0	100.0	Net Sales	100.0	100.0				
				Gross Profit						
	91.2	90.8	86.2	Operating Expenses	75.1	88.9				
	8.8	9.2	13.8	Operating Profit	24.9	11.1				
	4.3	3.2	2.9	All Other Expenses (net)	4.6	2.1				
	4.5	5.9	10.9	Profit Before Taxes	20.3	8.9				
				RATIOS						
	7.3	9.9	10.3	Current	13.1	39.5				
	3.1	2.3	3.1		3.9	3.9				
	1.2	1.1	1.4		1.4	1.8				
	7.2	9.9	10.3	Quick	13.1	33.3				
	2.7	2.0	2.6		3.8	3.3				
	.8	.8	1.2		.9	1.3				
0	UND	0 UND	0 UND	Sales/Receivables	0 UND	0 UND				
0	UND	0 UND	1 434.6		0 UND	4 94.0				
38	9.7	40 9.1	41 8.9		0 UND	51 7.1				
				Cost of Sales/Inventory						
				Cost of Sales/Payables						
	2.1	1.7	1.7	Sales/Working Capital	1.3	1.9				
	4.8	6.5	5.1		2.4	4.0				
	33.1	75.9	15.1		14.9	14.9				
	7.6	7.5	19.5	EBIT/Interest	14.2	25.3				
(33)	3.6	(58) 2.9	(35) 3.6		(10) 6.1	(11) 6.7				
	.3	-1.3	.9		1.6	.6				
				Net Profit + Depr., Dep., Amort./Cur. Mat. L/T/D						
	.7	.6	.2	Fixed/Worth	.4	.2				
	1.0	.9	.9		1.1	.9				
	2.3	1.6	1.8		2.1	2.0				
	.3	.2	.2	Debt/Worth	.1	.2				
	.5	.5	.8		.5	.8				
	2.2	2.2	2.0		2.7	3.0				
	14.4	11.8	27.2	% Profit Before Taxes/Tangible Net Worth	28.0	32.6				
(40)	6.5	(69) 4.0	(50) 12.4		(18) 20.0	12.5				
	-2.8	-1.3	-.3		2.7	-.2				
	9.5	7.9	18.5	% Profit Before Taxes/Total Assets	24.8	15.2				
	2.3	2.7	7.2		9.1	7.6				
	-3.5	-1.8	-.2		1.2	-.2				
	12.9	9.8	26.0	Sales/Net Fixed Assets	5.5	29.2				
	.8	1.0	2.3		.9	1.2				
	.4	.4	.6		.2	.6				
	2.5	2.1	2.6	Sales/Total Assets	1.2	2.3				
	.6	.5	.8		.4	.6				
	.3	.3	.4		.2	.4				
	2.8	2.2	1.8	% Depr., Dep., Amort./Sales	9.0	1.9				
(27)	7.5	(41) 7.1	(37) 10.8		(14) 14.9	(12) 9.4				
	25.2	17.7	18.9		33.1	17.6				
	3.1	2.6	1.2	% Officers', Directors', Owners' Comp/Sales						
(14)	5.1	(15) 4.7	(15) 3.8							
	20.5	7.4	7.8							
	90581M	169175M	231121M	Net Sales ($)	9268M	27579M	17595M	58811M	47632M	70236M
	113018M	291172M	223080M	Total Assets ($)	30158M	44967M	21109M	38187M	16044M	72615M

© RMA 2005

M = $ thousand   MM = $ million
See Pages 11 through 21 for Explanation of Ratios and Data

Current Data Sorted By Assets   **Comparative Historical Data**

0-500M	500M-2MM	2-10MM	10-50MM	50-100MM	100-250MM	Type of Statement	4/1/00-3/31/01 ALL	4/1/01-3/31/02 ALL
2	3	13	13	4	8	Unqualified	26	28
1			1			Reviewed	1	
		1				Compiled	2	3
	1					Tax Returns		
3	6	6	5		1	Other	7	9
	53 (4/1-9/30/04)		15 (10/1/04-3/31/05)					
6	10	20	19	4	9	NUMBER OF STATEMENTS	36	40
%	%	%	%	%	%		%	%
						ASSETS		
	21.0	27.7	22.7			Cash & Equivalents	31.3	22.8
	9.1	14.1	10.5			Trade Receivables (net)	11.7	13.2
	5.0	2.2	.2			Inventory	.1	.3
	5.4	6.0	5.8			All Other Current	8.4	6.8
	40.6	50.0	39.2			Total Current	51.5	43.1
	35.6	39.4	42.5			Fixed Assets (net)	33.3	39.0
	1.8	.9	4.6			Intangibles (net)	.4	1.3
	22.0	9.7	13.7			All Other Non-Current	14.8	16.6
	100.0	100.0	100.0			Total	100.0	100.0
						LIABILITIES		
	4.7	1.7	.1			Notes Payable-Short Term	.7	2.9
	1.1	2.8	2.2			Cur. Mat.-L/T/D	.5	.9
	6.8	12.1	4.1			Trade Payables	6.3	5.7
	.1	.0	.0			Income Taxes Payable	.0	.0
	20.6	7.2	9.6			All Other Current	14.5	11.2
	33.3	23.7	16.1			Total Current	21.9	20.8
	14.2	15.4	23.3			Long-Term Debt	11.9	14.8
	.0	.0	.0			Deferred Taxes	.0	.0
	1.6	8.4	8.1			All Other Non-Current	9.8	6.0
	50.9	52.5	52.4			Net Worth	56.4	58.4
	100.0	100.0	100.0			Total Liabilities & Net Worth	100.0	100.0
						INCOME DATA		
	100.0	100.0	100.0			Net Sales	100.0	100.0
						Gross Profit		
	99.6	93.7	98.4			Operating Expenses	97.3	96.9
	.4	6.3	1.6			Operating Profit	2.7	3.1
	.4	.3	2.6			All Other Expenses (net)	-4.4	3.5
	.0	6.1	-1.0			Profit Before Taxes	7.1	-.3
						RATIOS		
	2.1	3.9	3.8			Current	4.7	6.1
	1.2	2.6	2.3				2.5	2.2
	.3	1.7	1.6				1.6	1.3
	1.6	3.7	2.8			Quick	4.1	5.2
	.5	2.2	1.9				1.7	1.8
	.1	1.4	1.0				1.1	1.0
0 UND	8 43.3	8 48.2				Sales/Receivables	2 231.2	0 803.1
0 UND	21 17.2	25 14.5					19 19.1	18 20.2
24 15.1	52 7.0	46 7.9					54 6.7	36 10.2
						Cost of Sales/Inventory		
						Cost of Sales/Payables		
	3.2	4.4	3.3			Sales/Working Capital	2.3	2.5
	NM	6.8	5.0				5.3	8.6
	-4.4	15.9	15.3				11.3	43.1
			14.2			EBIT/Interest	42.9	11.8
		(12)	7.0				(13) 3.1	(12) 1.9
			-.3				1.6	.1
						Net Profit + Depr., Dep., Amort./Cur. Mat. L /T/D		
	.1	.3	.4			Fixed/Worth	.1	.2
	.6	.9	.9				.6	.8
	NM	1.1	1.9				.9	1.0
	.3	.4	.3			Debt/Worth	.3	.2
	.6	1.1	.8				.6	.6
	NM	1.8	2.7				1.6	1.5
		23.8	19.4			% Profit Before Taxes/Tangible Net Worth	21.7	6.7
		(18) 5.4	4.0				(34) 6.0	(39) .3
		-2.1	-12.3				.8	-3.6
	7.8	9.9	8.7			% Profit Before Taxes/Total Assets	15.8	3.0
	-.7	2.6	1.0				2.2	.0
	-6.1	-1.4	-7.5				.5	-2.4
	60.5	14.7	10.5			Sales/Net Fixed Assets	43.5	47.8
	4.2	4.5	2.2				2.5	2.8
	.5	1.6	1.5				.9	.9
	1.7	3.1	1.8			Sales/Total Assets	2.3	2.7
	.7	1.5	1.0				.9	.9
	.4	.7	.4				.6	.4
		1.2	1.5			% Depr., Dep., Amort./Sales	.5	.9
		(14) 2.6	(15) 3.1				(19) 1.2	(15) 3.0
		4.9	5.3				5.2	4.9
						% Officers', Directors', Owners' Comp/Sales		
5025M	13361M	201624M	440555M	173508M	1913687M	Net Sales ($)	936419M	848232M
1801M	11568M	102807M	372893M	283251M	1403367M	Total Assets ($)	1478189M	1666965M

M = $ thousand   MM = $ million

See Pages 11 through 21 for Explanation of Ratios and Data

Comparative Historical Data | Current Data Sorted By Sales

Comparative Historical Data			Type of Statement	Current Data Sorted By Sales					
40	75	43	Unqualified	4	3	2	4	13	17
1	1	2	Reviewed	1				1	
	4	1	Compiled			1			
	2	1	Tax Returns	1					
11	14	21	Other	5	5	3	3	3	2
4/1/02-3/31/03 ALL	4/1/03-3/31/04 ALL	4/1/04-3/31/05 ALL		0-1MM	53 (4/1-9/30/04) 1-3MM	3-5MM	5-10MM	15 (10/1/04-3/31/05) 10-25MM	25MM & OVER
52	96	68	**NUMBER OF STATEMENTS**	11	8	6	7	17	19
%	%	%	**ASSETS**	%	%	%	%	%	%
24.0	26.0	24.4	Cash & Equivalents	31.2				22.6	28.8
13.1	11.5	11.6	Trade Receivables (net)	10.9				12.6	13.4
.2	.6	1.6	Inventory	1.9				.1	.7
8.7	6.1	7.1	All Other Current	4.6				8.4	9.3
46.0	44.2	44.6	Total Current	48.7				43.7	52.2
34.8	47.1	39.0	Fixed Assets (net)	39.5				46.9	36.7
1.0	.5	1.8	Intangibles (net)	.1				.1	.1
18.1	8.3	14.6	All Other Non-Current	11.7				9.3	11.1
100.0	100.0	100.0	Total	100.0				100.0	100.0
			LIABILITIES						
1.6	2.8	1.2	Notes Payable-Short Term	1.8				.7	.0
1.3	1.8	2.0	Cur. Mat.-L/T/D	.4				2.1	2.0
4.0	6.5	8.6	Trade Payables	5.1				12.1	7.6
.0	.1	.0	Income Taxes Payable	.0				.0	.0
13.0	9.5	10.7	All Other Current	18.5				7.7	11.2
20.1	20.6	22.5	Total Current	25.7				22.7	20.8
16.9	27.2	18.9	Long-Term Debt	20.1				23.3	19.3
.0	.0	.0	Deferred Taxes	.0				.0	.0
6.0	4.5	5.8	All Other Non-Current	4.1				8.2	4.3
57.1	47.7	52.8	Net Worth	50.1				45.9	55.6
100.0	100.0	100.0	Total Liabilities & Net Worth	100.0				100.0	100.0
			INCOME DATA						
100.0	100.0	100.0	Net Sales	100.0				100.0	100.0
			Gross Profit						
94.0	93.6	96.0	Operating Expenses	92.5				96.9	95.7
6.0	6.4	4.0	Operating Profit	7.5				3.1	4.3
2.4	2.3	.8	All Other Expenses (net)	.3				1.0	.5
3.6	4.1	3.2	Profit Before Taxes	7.3				2.1	3.8
			RATIOS						
4.9	5.4	3.6		4.5				3.1	4.4
2.6	2.1	2.1	Current	2.6				2.0	2.1
1.4	1.3	1.5		.9				1.5	1.5
4.6	4.8	3.0		4.4				2.4	3.2
2.1	1.8	1.8	Quick	2.6				1.7	2.0
1.3	1.0	1.0		.4				1.1	1.4
1 395.6	0 969.3	3 135.2		0 UND				5 73.9	1 352.4
12 30.3	10 37.0	17 22.0	Sales/Receivables	22 16.6				26 13.8	12 30.0
36 10.2	39 9.4	42 8.7		49 7.5				43 8.5	41 8.8
			Cost of Sales/Inventory						
			Cost of Sales/Payables						
2.8	3.1	3.3		1.2				2.8	3.3
10.1	8.6	6.8	Sales/Working Capital	6.5				8.9	5.0
23.0	37.6	19.4		−15.7				18.8	9.0
(19) 5.6	(45) 6.8	(38) 7.5							5.7
2.7	2.4	1.6	EBIT/Interest					(13) 3.0	3.0
1.0	.6	−.4							1.5
			Net Profit + Depr., Dep., Amort./Cur. Mat. L/T/D						
.0	.4	.3		.0				.6	.1
.6	1.0	.8	Fixed/Worth	.9				.9	.8
.9	2.5	1.4		1.6				1.8	1.5
.3	.3	.3		.1				.7	.3
.6	1.1	.9	Debt/Worth	1.2				.9	.8
1.7	3.7	2.3		2.7				3.2	2.2
(49) 23.1	(90) 15.5	(65) 19.4	% Profit Before Taxes/Tangible	(10) 15.0				(16) 17.6	20.1
4.0	3.0	5.3	Net Worth	.3				3.7	9.2
−2.5	−6.6	−3.5		−2.3				−7.3	−6.4
11.7	7.5	8.4	% Profit Before Taxes/Total	9.6				7.4	9.1
2.3	1.1	2.6	Assets	−.3				.2	3.1
−1.3	−3.4	−2.2		−2.3				−3.4	−1.4
112.9	21.9	18.5		57.0				7.7	32.6
3.0	2.3	3.9	Sales/Net Fixed Assets	3.9				2.5	3.9
1.1	1.0	1.5		.4				1.5	1.0
2.7	2.3	2.1		1.9				2.0	2.1
1.0	1.0	1.0	Sales/Total Assets	.4				1.1	.9
.6	.7	.5		.3				.7	.6
(20) .3	(50) .2	(40) 1.4	% Depr., Dep., Amort./Sales					(13) 1.8	
1.9	2.1	2.5						3.0	
4.6	3.9	4.5						6.3	
	3.4		% Officers', Directors',						
	(15) 6.2		Owners' Comp/Sales						
	19.8								
1775918M	3218058M	2747760M	Net Sales ($)	5521M	14419M	25305M	56972M	272719M	2372824M
1907641M	3445137M	2175687M	Total Assets ($)	11982M	21732M	31791M	49273M	318512M	1742397M

M = $ thousand   MM = $ million
See Pages 11 through 21 for Explanation of Ratios and Data

Current Data Sorted By Assets

Comparative Historical Data

0-500M	500M-2MM	2-10MM	10-50MM	50-100MM	100-250MM	Type of Statement	4/1/00-3/31/01 ALL	4/1/01-3/31/02 ALL
2	2	12	11	7	12	Unqualified	35	24
		6				Reviewed	2	4
		1				Compiled	9	9
2	2					Tax Returns	6	2
1	2					Other	12	19
3	4	6	10					
	29 (4/1-9/30/04)		54 (10/1/04-3/31/05)					
8	10	25	21	7	12	NUMBER OF STATEMENTS	64	58
%	%	%	%	%	%	ASSETS	%	%
	8.5	9.1	11.1		19.4	Cash & Equivalents	13.2	12.3
	20.1	24.0	10.2		3.9	Trade Receivables (net)	20.9	21.8
	10.3	1.0	.5		2.2	Inventory	1.6	1.8
	3.2	1.6	1.9		2.6	All Other Current	2.7	2.9
	42.1	35.7	23.8		28.1	Total Current	38.4	38.8
	40.0	58.4	64.8		53.5	Fixed Assets (net)	49.2	47.2
	3.9	2.4	3.8		3.5	Intangibles (net)	2.1	4.4
	13.9	3.6	7.6		14.9	All Other Non-Current	10.2	9.6
	100.0	100.0	100.0		100.0	Total	100.0	100.0
						LIABILITIES		
	3.0	4.9	.7		.0	Notes Payable-Short Term	5.1	3.5
	4.4	3.5	2.6		2.1	Cur. Mat.-L/T/D	5.6	4.7
	11.8	7.7	5.1		2.6	Trade Payables	10.2	11.2
	.1	.1	.8		.0	Income Taxes Payable	.1	.1
	2.3	5.3	4.5		2.7	All Other Current	5.9	5.9
	21.5	21.4	13.7		7.4	Total Current	26.8	25.4
	31.5	30.7	23.7		43.4	Long-Term Debt	31.4	23.8
	.0	.7	.7		.6	Deferred Taxes	.0	.2
	3.7	4.7	3.5		4.9	All Other Non-Current	6.4	2.9
	43.4	42.6	58.4		43.7	Net Worth	35.4	47.6
	100.0	100.0	100.0		100.0	Total Liabilities & Net Worth	100.0	100.0
						INCOME DATA		
	100.0	100.0	100.0		100.0	Net Sales	100.0	100.0
						Gross Profit		
	93.9	88.0	85.3		83.6	Operating Expenses	90.7	88.6
	6.1	12.0	14.7		16.4	Operating Profit	9.3	11.4
	7.1	3.0	1.8		3.9	All Other Expenses (net)	2.5	3.6
	–1.0	8.9	12.8		12.5	Profit Before Taxes	6.8	7.8
						RATIOS		
	4.1	4.0	6.2		5.9		3.6	4.0
	2.5	2.5	2.4		4.1	Current	1.8	1.7
	1.0	1.2	1.2		1.5		.9	1.0
	3.1	3.4	5.6		5.7		3.0	3.7
	1.6	2.1	2.2		3.1	Quick	1.4	1.4
	.7	1.0	1.0		1.1		.7	1.0
22 16.6	34 10.8	26 14.1		20 18.3		31 11.8	26 13.8	
41 8.9	47 7.7	45 8.1		33 10.9	Sales/Receivables	48 7.5	46 7.9	
69 5.3	68 5.4	75 4.9		50 7.2		73 5.0	77 4.7	
						Cost of Sales/Inventory		
						Cost of Sales/Payables		
	2.9	1.4	1.2		.7		1.8	2.4
	7.0	8.6	4.8		2.0	Sales/Working Capital	9.8	7.5
	NM	43.1	24.1		8.2		–40.7	113.8
		22.9	9.0		3.7		2.9	5.2
	(22) 3.5	(17) 6.4		(11) 3.4	EBIT/Interest	(49) 1.7	(50) 2.6	
	1.4	2.5		1.2		.7	1.6	
						Net Profit + Depr., Dep., Amort./Cur. Mat. L /T/D		
	.2	1.1	.9		.8		.7	.6
	.9	1.8	1.0		1.3	Fixed/Worth	1.4	1.3
	39.9	2.8	2.3		2.9		5.2	2.2
	.4	.6	.2		.4		.4	.4
	1.2	1.3	.5		1.1	Debt/Worth	1.4	1.3
	51.4	4.3	2.9		3.2		8.0	3.9
		42.3	23.5		11.1	% Profit Before Taxes/Tangible Net Worth	31.0	45.2
	(23) 10.8	(20) 6.3		(10) 6.3		(53) 5.6	(55) 13.6	
	1.7	1.0		1.2		.5	1.4	
	16.7	11.6	7.1		5.1	% Profit Before Taxes/Total Assets	6.9	13.5
	.5	4.7	4.7		3.9		2.2	4.4
	–3.7	.0	.8		.4		–.1	.8
	17.7	8.1	3.5		1.0	Sales/Net Fixed Assets	10.8	8.5
	9.4	1.7	.4		.3		1.9	2.0
	.3	.2	.2		.2		.3	.4
	2.9	1.9	1.0		.3	Sales/Total Assets	2.5	2.2
	1.4	.9	.2		.2		.8	1.0
	.2	.1	.1		.1		.2	.2
		3.2	3.6		5.2	% Depr., Dep., Amort./Sales	2.8	3.4
	(23) 8.6	(19) 11.5		(11) 12.5		(56) 8.9	(50) 6.5	
	16.9	19.5		19.7		17.1	13.7	
						% Officers', Directors', Owners' Comp/Sales	3.7	2.7
							(13) 7.0	(15) 3.9
							11.9	8.0
6920M	16592M	160389M	242120M	126399M	694778M	Net Sales ($)	567691M	578997M
2178M	10890M	139371M	462947M	485045M	1837038M	Total Assets ($)	2004689M	1201531M

M = $ thousand   MM = $ million
See Pages 11 through 21 for Explanation of Ratios and Data

Comparative Historical Data | | | | **Current Data Sorted By Sales** | | | | |

			Type of Statement						
40	40	46	Unqualified	10	5	1	7	13	10
9	10	6	Reviewed	1			3	1	1
7	8	5	Compiled	3	1			1	
4	5	3	Tax Returns		2	1			
23	25	23	Other	5	8	4	3	3	
4/1/02-3/31/03 ALL	4/1/03-3/31/04 ALL	4/1/04-3/31/05 ALL		0-1MM 29 (4/1-9/30/04)	1-3MM	3-5MM	5-10MM 54 (10/1/04-3/31/05)	10-25MM	25MM & OVER
83	88	83	**NUMBER OF STATEMENTS**	19	16	6	13	18	11
%	%	%	**ASSETS**	%	%	%	%	%	%
13.4	13.2	12.3	Cash & Equivalents	12.9	8.8		6.9	12.3	16.2
15.2	16.4	15.4	Trade Receivables (net)	10.4	16.9		23.9	13.7	17.8
1.7	2.3	2.0	Inventory	.2	4.2		1.8	.1	3.2
2.3	1.7	1.9	All Other Current	.7	2.4		1.1	3.6	1.4
32.6	33.7	31.6	Total Current	24.4	32.3		33.8	29.8	38.6
53.7	52.1	56.6	Fixed Assets (net)	69.4	49.6		59.3	54.3	45.1
4.3	5.8	2.7	Intangibles (net)	.1	2.4		1.2	6.8	3.5
9.3	8.4	9.1	All Other Non-Current	6.2	15.7		5.6	9.1	12.9
100.0	100.0	100.0	Total	100.0	100.0		100.0	100.0	100.0
			LIABILITIES						
5.6	4.7	2.2	Notes Payable-Short Term	.8	1.8		7.2	1.8	.3
5.7	3.9	3.6	Cur. Mat.-L/T/D	5.6	3.2		2.9	3.1	3.6
7.7	7.1	7.0	Trade Payables	6.1	7.1		7.4	6.9	10.1
.1	.2	.2	Income Taxes Payable	.0	.1		.0	1.0	.1
6.9	9.1	4.4	All Other Current	1.3	.8		7.8	4.8	8.7
26.0	25.0	17.4	Total Current	13.8	13.0		25.2	17.5	22.8
25.0	29.5	29.0	Long-Term Debt	38.8	21.9		16.8	29.7	35.9
.3	.8	.5	Deferred Taxes	.0	.0		.8	.9	1.0
6.3	5.3	4.1	All Other Non-Current	2.1	5.5		6.3	2.6	7.8
42.4	39.4	49.0	Net Worth	45.3	59.6		50.8	49.2	32.6
100.0	100.0	100.0	Total Liabilities & Net Worth	100.0	100.0		100.0	100.0	100.0
			INCOME DATA						
100.0	100.0	100.0	Net Sales	100.0	100.0		100.0	100.0	100.0
			Gross Profit						
90.1	88.8	86.5	Operating Expenses	86.3	86.0		85.6	86.8	89.2
9.9	11.2	13.5	Operating Profit	13.7	14.0		14.4	13.2	10.8
3.2	4.1	3.3	All Other Expenses (net)	9.3	1.3		-.7	2.4	2.4
6.7	7.1	10.2	Profit Before Taxes	4.4	12.6		15.0	10.8	8.4
			RATIOS						
4.0	4.8	5.4	Current	6.0	13.3		6.9	3.5	4.2
1.5	1.6	2.5		3.0	3.6		1.2	2.0	1.9
.8	.9	1.2		1.1	1.3		.9	1.2	1.4
3.4	3.7	4.4	Quick	5.9	11.5		5.8	2.6	4.1
1.3	1.5	2.1		2.5	2.3		1.0	1.7	1.4
.6	.8	1.0		1.1	.8		.8	.9	1.0
25 14.7	28 13.0	29 12.7	Sales/Receivables	6 65.7	30 12.3		47 7.8	33 11.2	29 12.7
43 8.5	44 8.3	45 8.1		32 11.6	51 7.1		62 5.9	45 8.0	39 9.5
64 5.7	72 5.0	62 5.9		48 7.6	102 3.6		70 5.2	55 6.6	56 6.5
			Cost of Sales/Inventory						
			Cost of Sales/Payables						
1.5	2.1	1.3	Sales/Working Capital	1.3	1.1		1.1	1.9	1.9
10.4	9.5	6.5		3.3	4.9		19.4	8.5	8.7
-13.9	-309.0	27.9		17.5	16.4		-41.2	18.8	19.5
4.3	7.4	8.4	EBIT/Interest	3.1	20.7		7.1	11.8	11.9
(70) 2.4	(72) 3.4	(70) 2.9		(14) 1.3	(12) 2.5		(10) 3.7	(17) 4.5	3.4
1.2	1.3	1.2		.7	.9		1.3	1.4	2.3
15.9		10.5	Net Profit + Depr., Dep., Amort./Cur. Mat. L/T/D						
(11) 2.1		(12) 1.9							
1.1		1.4							
.8	.9	.8	Fixed/Worth	1.0	.2		.9	.8	.9
1.4	1.4	1.3		1.7	.8		1.3	1.3	1.5
3.1	3.1	2.3		2.8	1.7		2.9	2.7	2.3
.4	.5	.3	Debt/Worth	.3	.2		.2	.5	1.0
1.4	1.5	1.1		1.1	.6		1.0	1.2	1.8
4.0	4.3	3.4		2.4	1.6		7.9	3.5	9.2
23.3	34.2	20.9	% Profit Before Taxes/Tangible Net Worth	7.2	20.9		43.7	32.1	11.4
(71) 7.4	(73) 6.6	(75) 6.3		(16) .0	(15) 3.0		5.0	(16) 8.6	5.1
.6	.5	.3		-6.8	-1.2		1.8	2.1	2.1
7.6	9.9	6.5	% Profit Before Taxes/Total Assets	3.8	8.2		7.4	14.1	11.4
2.7	3.8	3.7		.1	2.0		4.1	4.7	5.1
.2	.1	-.1		-2.8	-1.2		1.4	.8	2.1
8.2	7.3	8.2	Sales/Net Fixed Assets	.7	14.7		8.1	3.3	10.9
1.2	1.7	.5		.2	1.0		.9	.8	2.8
.3	.3	.2		.1	.2		.1	.2	.5
2.0	1.9	1.6	Sales/Total Assets	.7	1.5		2.2	1.6	1.8
.5	.6	.3		.2	.3		.7	.3	.9
.2	.2	.1		.1	.2		.1	.2	.2
4.6	4.2	3.6	% Depr., Dep., Amort./Sales	11.7	5.7		3.3	3.4	2.4
(71) 9.4	(73) 9.5	(73) 10.7		(15) 22.0	(13) 10.3		(12) 7.3	(17) 11.5	4.6
17.7	17.4	20.0		31.9	19.2		21.2	17.2	9.4
2.9	2.9	4.0	% Officers', Directors', Owners' Comp/Sales						
(18) 6.9	(20) 3.7	(13) 6.7							
12.8	6.6	13.3							
1364670M	1585061M	1247198M	Net Sales ($)	8207M	34905M	24338M	93474M	303407M	782867M
2586513M	2724641M	2937469M	Total Assets ($)	47930M	155699M	61843M	391269M	1248341M	1032387M

© RMA 2005

M = $ thousand   MM = $ million

See Pages 11 through 21 for Explanation of Ratios and Data

Current Data Sorted By Assets | | | | | | | **Comparative Historical Data**

0-500M	500M-2MM	2-10MM	10-50MM	50-100MM	100-250MM	Type of Statement	4/1/00-3/31/01 ALL	4/1/01-3/31/02 ALL
2	15	25	22	7	6	Unqualified	42	39
	3					Reviewed	2	
	1	2				Compiled	6	2
1		1				Tax Returns	2	
3	2	11	8	2	1	Other	11	14
	72 (4/1-9/30/04)		40 (10/1/04-3/31/05)				63	55
6	21	39	30	9	7	**NUMBER OF STATEMENTS**		
%	%	%	%	%	%	**ASSETS**	%	%
	10.3	13.7	11.9			Cash & Equivalents	15.5	17.0
	8.9	12.0	3.9			Trade Receivables (net)	8.5	9.8
	2.3	3.3	.8			Inventory	2.9	2.4
	3.3	3.1	5.0			All Other Current	4.9	3.3
	24.8	32.1	21.5			Total Current	31.8	32.5
	51.9	56.1	56.2			Fixed Assets (net)	50.3	49.0
	.4	.7	1.2			Intangibles (net)	1.8	2.4
	23.0	11.1	21.1			All Other Non-Current	16.1	16.2
	100.0	100.0	100.0			Total	100.0	100.0
						LIABILITIES		
	9.8	4.1	1.2			Notes Payable-Short Term	4.2	4.7
	5.5	1.8	1.0			Cur. Mat.-L/T/D	1.3	2.2
	3.3	3.6	2.8			Trade Payables	4.3	3.2
	.0	.0	.0			Income Taxes Payable	.0	.1
	3.3	9.8	2.9			All Other Current	7.1	5.0
	21.8	19.3	8.0			Total Current	16.8	15.2
	32.8	31.4	27.5			Long-Term Debt	33.1	34.5
	3.3	.0	.0			Deferred Taxes	.0	.5
	1.7	2.4	3.7			All Other Non-Current	3.0	3.0
	40.4	46.9	60.8			Net Worth	47.1	46.8
	100.0	100.0	100.0			Total Liabilities & Net Worth	100.0	100.0
						INCOME DATA		
	100.0	100.0	100.0			Net Sales	100.0	100.0
						Gross Profit		
	87.0	89.5	94.2			Operating Expenses	101.1	90.4
	13.0	10.5	5.8			Operating Profit	−1.1	9.6
	12.6	4.4	−1.3			All Other Expenses (net)	−10.3	5.2
	.4	6.0	7.1			Profit Before Taxes	9.2	4.5
						RATIOS		
	3.1	2.8	4.4			Current	5.4	3.8
	.9	1.8	2.5				1.8	1.9
	.2	1.0	1.1				1.0	1.0
	2.5	2.6	3.4			Quick	4.3	2.4
	.9	1.3	1.7				1.4	1.5
	.2	.5	.8				.7	1.0
0 UND	2 209.0	5 73.0				Sales/Receivables	1 243.4	1 302.0
5 73.4	15 24.0	17 21.8					11 34.7	12 29.9
49 7.4	40 9.2	43 8.5					41 9.0	52 7.0
						Cost of Sales/Inventory		
						Cost of Sales/Payables		
	3.1	2.3	2.2			Sales/Working Capital	1.9	3.0
	−52.9	6.9	5.9				6.5	9.2
	−7.0	−177.7	41.3				UND	−488.1
	4.5	8.6	9.2			EBIT/Interest	6.9	3.6
(13) .7	(27) 2.2	(24) 2.6					(33) 2.0	(26) 1.7
	−.7	.4	1.0				.5	−.1
						Net Profit + Depr., Dep., Amort./Cur. Mat. L./T/D		
	.1	.7	.5			Fixed/Worth	.5	.3
	1.1	1.3	.9				1.1	.9
	10.2	2.7	1.6				2.1	2.1
	.3	.5	.2			Debt/Worth	.3	.3
	1.8	1.1	.6				1.2	1.0
	13.0	2.5	1.4				3.5	8.3
	29.9	12.0	8.3			% Profit Before Taxes/Tangible Net Worth	15.2	21.3
(18) .8	(38) 2.8	3.6					(61) 6.7	(49) 4.3
	−7.4	−4.9	−.2				−.4	−1.2
	7.7	5.1	4.1			% Profit Before Taxes/Total Assets	7.9	5.7
	−.6	.6	1.0				1.9	1.1
	−3.6	−2.0	−.2				−.4	−1.3
	4.9	4.5	2.1			Sales/Net Fixed Assets	9.2	13.4
	.9	.8	.8				.7	1.0
	.3	.4	.5				.3	.5
	.8	.9	.7			Sales/Total Assets	1.3	1.2
	.4	.4	.4				.3	.5
	.2	.2	.2				.2	.2
	1.0	2.2	1.9			% Depr., Dep., Amort./Sales	1.5	2.3
(16) 4.5	(34) 5.1	(28) 7.1					(50) 6.1	(43) 6.4
	27.9	13.5	11.8				16.3	13.4
						% Officers', Directors', Owners' Comp/Sales		
1686M	17457M	304120M	429133M	210990M	199751M	Net Sales ($)	565979M	352234M
1729M	25241M	212587M	702880M	520303M	1073037M	Total Assets ($)	1076389M	634484M

© RMA 2005

M = $ thousand   MM = $ million
See Pages 11 through 21 for Explanation of Ratios and Data

Comparative Historical Data / Current Data Sorted By Sales

66	68	77	Type of Statement	20	15	6	5	19	12
1	2	3	Unqualified						
4	4	3	Reviewed	3					
26	35	2	Compiled			1	1		1
		27	Tax Returns	1	1				
4/1/02-	4/1/03-	4/1/04-	Other	7	8	4	4	3	1
3/31/03	3/31/04	3/31/05		72 (4/1-9/30/04)			40 (10/1/04-3/31/05)		
ALL	ALL	ALL		0-1MM	1-3MM	3-5MM	5-10MM	10-25MM	25MM & OVER
97	109	112	**NUMBER OF STATEMENTS**	31	24	11	10	22	14
%	%	%	**ASSETS**	%	%	%	%	%	%
14.0	13.3	12.5	Cash & Equivalents	9.3	12.5	16.4	12.6	13.1	15.4
9.0	8.7	8.9	Trade Receivables (net)	9.0	7.5	15.0	7.9	2.6	16.6
2.2	3.1	2.0	Inventory	3.0	2.2	4.3	.1	1.5	.2
5.0	4.5	3.5	All Other Current	2.9	4.8	1.3	10.7	1.9	2.2
30.2	29.6	26.9	Total Current	24.2	26.9	37.0	31.1	19.0	34.4
49.9	51.1	54.3	Fixed Assets (net)	58.7	53.8	40.7	48.5	62.2	47.6
.5	.5	.8	Intangibles (net)	.2	1.0	1.0	2.2	.5	.8
19.4	18.8	18.0	All Other Non-Current	16.9	18.3	21.2	18.1	18.2	17.2
100.0	100.0	100.0	Total	100.0	100.0	100.0	100.0	100.0	100.0
			LIABILITIES						
4.5	4.2	4.2	Notes Payable-Short Term	9.0	2.9	4.4	1.8	1.1	2.2
1.9	3.9	2.2	Cur. Mat.-L/T/D	4.5	2.1	.9	1.0	1.0	1.3
3.4	2.8	3.0	Trade Payables	2.3	4.1	2.2	5.7	1.7	3.6
.0	.1	.0	Income Taxes Payable	.0	.0	.0	.0	.0	.0
7.4	7.8	5.4	All Other Current	2.9	4.9	7.0	6.9	3.5	12.2
17.3	18.8	14.8	Total Current	18.7	13.9	14.5	15.3	7.3	19.3
27.4	26.8	31.8	Long-Term Debt	37.8	29.7	24.7	27.5	36.3	23.6
.4	.7	.6	Deferred Taxes	.0	1.6	2.8	.0	.0	.0
5.4	4.3	3.2	All Other Non-Current	.7	2.1	1.7	4.6	5.4	7.7
49.5	49.5	49.6	Net Worth	42.9	52.7	56.2	52.5	50.9	49.3
100.0	100.0	100.0	Total Liabilities & Net Worth	100.0	100.0	100.0	100.0	100.0	100.0
			INCOME DATA						
100.0	100.0	100.0	Net Sales	100.0	100.0	100.0	100.0	100.0	100.0
			Gross Profit						
86.8	88.4	88.8	Operating Expenses	81.8	88.7	84.7	95.5	93.7	95.0
13.2	11.6	11.2	Operating Profit	18.2	11.3	15.3	4.5	6.3	5.0
6.1	3.8	4.9	All Other Expenses (net)	13.7	4.3	4.7	-1.7	.6	-2.0
7.2	7.8	6.3	Profit Before Taxes	4.5	6.9	10.6	6.3	5.6	7.0
			RATIOS						
5.4	4.6	3.9		3.4	5.3	3.9	3.7	4.7	3.6
2.4	1.9	2.0	Current	1.0	1.8	2.7	2.3	2.8	2.1
.8	1.0	.9		.5	.7	1.1	.9	1.4	1.1
3.9	3.1	3.2		2.8	2.7	2.8	3.3	4.2	3.5
1.2	1.4	1.4	Quick	.7	1.3	2.2	1.4	2.5	1.8
.6	.7	.6		.4	.4	.8	.6	1.0	.9
1 625.4	1 594.5	2 212.6		0 UND	0 UND	5 67.5	0 UND	4 100.6	4 89.5
12 31.5	16 22.2	10 36.2	Sales/Receivables	10 35.4	4 100.4	19 19.3	20 18.0	7 53.9	11 33.0
45 8.1	45 8.1	42 8.7		47 7.7	41 8.9	89 4.1	67 5.4	19 19.1	44 8.4
			Cost of Sales/Inventory						
			Cost of Sales/Payables						
1.9	2.4	2.3		1.8	1.6	1.7	2.0	2.3	6.9
7.0	7.9	7.4	Sales/Working Capital	132.0	7.8	5.7	3.7	4.3	22.4
-22.2	NM	-57.8		-7.9	-22.0	41.2	-74.7	20.7	NM
5.3	8.9	8.7		5.8	6.8			9.0	12.7
(57) 1.7	(68) 1.9	(78) 2.0	EBIT/Interest	(16) 1.6	(14) 3.2		(19)	1.8	(12) 2.3
.6	.2	.3		-.4	.2			.1	.6
			Net Profit + Depr., Dep., Amort./Cur. Mat. L/T/D						
.2	.3	.4		.2	.5	.0	.6	.7	.3
1.0	.9	1.1	Fixed/Worth	1.4	1.1	.8	.9	1.1	1.0
1.7	2.0	2.1		7.3	2.9	1.2	1.3	2.2	1.4
.3	.3	.4		.3	.3	.4	.5	.2	.4
1.0	.9	.9	Debt/Worth	.9	1.0	.6	.9	.9	1.2
3.0	4.0	3.2		7.2	3.3	1.7	1.2	3.0	3.4
11.1	15.3	12.2		12.7	12.1	10.4	15.1	12.5	11.8
(94) 3.2	(103) 5.4	(106) 3.4	% Profit Before Taxes/Tangible Net Worth	(27) 3.7	(23) 3.2	2.0	(21) 4.2	4.6	4.2
-3.2	-.9	-2.8		-4.9	-5.1	.0	-2.9	-2.6	-2.0
4.3	5.8	5.0		9.9	5.4	5.5	4.2	3.7	4.6
1.3	1.6	1.0	% Profit Before Taxes/Total Assets	.5	.0	.9	1.5	.9	2.2
-1.3	-.8	-1.4		-1.4	-2.6	.0	-1.6	-1.4	-1.0
5.1	4.2	4.3		3.4	3.2	7.6	4.0	2.1	46.0
1.1	1.1	.8	Sales/Net Fixed Assets	.5	.7	1.1	1.2	.7	4.1
.5	.5	.4		.2	.4	.5	.7	.6	.6
1.0	1.0	.7		.4	.7	.6	1.1	.9	4.9
.4	.4	.4	Sales/Total Assets	.2	.4	.2	.5	.4	.9
.3	.2	.2		.1	.2	.2	.3	.3	.4
1.4	1.5	1.4		4.4	3.2	.7	2.6	2.5	.4
(75) 3.8	(88) 4.8	(95) 6.1	% Depr., Dep., Amort./Sales	(21) 18.5	(22) 6.3	(10) 2.3	(20) 5.3	7.2	(12) 1.2
8.9	10.5	12.2		27.2	13.8	12.7	7.1	10.8	6.3
		6.7							
		(11) 15.0	% Officers', Directors', Owners' Comp/Sales						
		26.1							
963925M	1253139M	1163137M	Net Sales ($)	14509M	42515M	42710M	67317M	344470M	651616M
1980763M	2256381M	2535777M	Total Assets ($)	66231M	132720M	241897M	147729M	1003683M	943517M

M = $ thousand   MM = $ million
See Pages 11 through 21 for Explanation of Ratios and Data

Current Data Sorted By Assets | Comparative Historical Data

0-500M	500M-2MM	2-10MM	10-50MM	50-100MM	100-250MM	Type of Statement	4/1/00-3/31/01 ALL	4/1/01-3/31/02 ALL
1	9	12	19	6	2	Unqualified	30	19
		1	1			Reviewed	1	1
	1					Compiled	5	6
			1			Tax Returns	2	3
4	9	5			1	Other	5	8
	55 (4/1-9/30/04)		16 (10/1/04-3/31/05)					
1	14	23	24	6	3	NUMBER OF STATEMENTS	43	37
%	%	%	%	%	%	**ASSETS**	%	%
	20.3	20.3	16.0			Cash & Equivalents	20.7	16.0
	14.5	11.7	7.5			Trade Receivables (net)	9.6	8.4
	1.8	1.1	1.3			Inventory	5.0	10.9
	.8	11.2	5.5			All Other Current	4.5	8.5
	37.4	44.3	30.3			Total Current	39.9	43.8
	48.3	40.6	42.3			Fixed Assets (net)	42.0	40.6
	.2	.8	.9			Intangibles (net)	.4	.6
	14.1	14.3	26.5			All Other Non-Current	17.7	15.0
	100.0	100.0	100.0			Total	100.0	100.0
						LIABILITIES		
	5.6	1.4	6.3			Notes Payable-Short Term	8.7	8.3
	3.9	1.6	2.7			Cur. Mat.-L/T/D	1.5	1.3
	2.7	3.3	2.3			Trade Payables	3.0	6.0
	.0	.3	.0			Income Taxes Payable	.0	.0
	9.2	13.3	2.3			All Other Current	3.9	6.8
	21.3	20.0	13.6			Total Current	17.1	22.4
	45.1	25.8	31.8			Long-Term Debt	32.4	30.1
	.0	.2	.0			Deferred Taxes	.0	.0
	.1	4.7	7.8			All Other Non-Current	5.1	7.0
	33.5	49.2	46.8			Net Worth	45.4	40.5
	100.0	100.0	100.0			Total Liabilities & Net Worth	100.0	100.0
						INCOME DATA		
	100.0	100.0	100.0			Net Sales	100.0	100.0
						Gross Profit		
	82.2	78.9	82.7			Operating Expenses	75.9	84.4
	17.8	21.1	17.3			Operating Profit	24.1	15.6
	7.0	7.5	7.5			All Other Expenses (net)	5.4	9.1
	10.8	13.5	9.8			Profit Before Taxes	18.7	6.6
						RATIOS		
	7.2	12.3	5.6			Current	6.3	3.9
	3.0	1.8	2.8				2.2	1.6
	.9	.7	.7				1.1	1.2
	7.2	8.0	5.2			Quick	3.9	2.2
	2.8	1.5	2.1				1.9	1.1
	.5	.3	.3				1.0	.4
0 UND	0 UND	5 67.0				Sales/Receivables	0 UND	0 UND
0 UND	18 20.3	47 7.8					23 16.2	12 30.1
60 6.1	86 4.2	76 4.8					65 5.6	48 7.5
						Cost of Sales/Inventory		
						Cost of Sales/Payables		
	1.2	1.2	.8			Sales/Working Capital	1.1	1.8
	6.5	2.8	1.7				2.8	3.0
	UND	-13.9	-7.6				14.8	21.7
	11.9	16.4	7.3			EBIT/Interest	6.3	9.1
	(10) 2.9	(12) 4.6	(16) 2.4				(25) 3.4	(22) 2.4
	-1.5	3.4	-.8				.9	.4
						Net Profit + Depr., Dep., Amort./Cur. Mat. L/T/D		
	.3	.1	.2			Fixed/Worth	.2	.1
	1.1	.5	.8				.7	.9
	2.2	2.2	1.6				2.1	2.3
	.4	.3	.6			Debt/Worth	.5	.6
	1.1	.9	1.0				1.0	1.7
	2.9	4.9	2.3				3.4	4.8
	20.1	32.8	19.4			% Profit Before Taxes/Tangible Net Worth	25.5	24.6
	(12) 5.1	(20) 7.8	2.1				(40) 11.5	(34) 8.8
	-7.2	3.5	-1.8				.6	-1.2
	11.0	14.3	4.7			% Profit Before Taxes/Total Assets	11.8	7.9
	3.5	4.6	1.0				3.1	2.5
	-3.9	-1.4	-.7				-.4	-1.5
	44.8	13.0	6.7			Sales/Net Fixed Assets	19.4	30.5
	1.7	2.4	.8				1.0	1.2
	.3	.5	.3				.3	.3
	.8	1.2	.5			Sales/Total Assets	.9	.9
	.5	.4	.2				.3	.6
	.2	.3	.1				.1	.2
		1.0	4.0			% Depr., Dep., Amort./Sales	1.8	.6
	(15)	4.4	(18) 6.5				(29) 3.8	(31) 2.4
		6.4	9.1				12.7	10.3
						% Officers', Directors', Owners' Comp/Sales		
311M	9291M	81601M	148052M	86993M	450107M	Net Sales ($)	137442M	237107M
390M	17376M	105055M	475135M	454614M	411111M	Total Assets ($)	661580M	567788M

M = $thousand   MM = $million
See Pages 11 through 21 for Explanation of Ratios and Data

Comparative Historical Data | Current Data Sorted By Sales

			Type of Statement	0-1MM	1-3MM	3-5MM	5-10MM	10-25MM	25MM & OVER
38	35	49	Unqualified	13	13	8	4	9	2
1	2	1	Reviewed				1		
2	7	1	Compiled	1					
		1	Tax Returns	1					
20	20	19	Other	3	6	2	4	3	1
4/1/02-3/31/03	4/1/03-3/31/04	4/1/04-3/31/05			55 (4/1-9/30/04)			16 (10/1/04-3/31/05)	
ALL	ALL	ALL							
61	64	71	**NUMBER OF STATEMENTS**	18	19	10	9	12	3
%	%	%	**ASSETS**	%	%	%	%	%	%
18.2	14.9	18.9	Cash & Equivalents	23.1	19.5	10.2		24.1	
10.1	11.2	11.6	Trade Receivables (net)	7.7	16.3	2.8		13.0	
.5	1.2	1.2	Inventory	.0	1.3	2.1		.2	
4.5	9.2	6.8	All Other Current	4.5	6.7	3.0		17.0	
33.3	36.6	38.5	Total Current	35.3	43.9	18.1		54.3	
41.0	42.1	41.3	Fixed Assets (net)	52.3	33.7	56.2		25.9	
2.3	1.4	.6	Intangibles (net)	.3	.8	.1		1.5	
23.3	19.9	19.5	All Other Non-Current	12.1	21.6	25.6		18.3	
100.0	100.0	100.0	Total	100.0	100.0	100.0		100.0	
			LIABILITIES						
5.5	4.6	3.7	Notes Payable-Short Term	.9	4.0	3.2		3.2	
3.1	3.4	2.8	Cur. Mat.-L/T/D	4.0	1.8	2.1		3.0	
3.8	3.6	2.6	Trade Payables	.7	2.4	2.0		3.0	
.0	.0	.1	Income Taxes Payable	.0	.0	.0		.0	
6.5	8.4	7.7	All Other Current	5.8	9.9	2.2		16.4	
18.9	20.0	16.9	Total Current	11.3	18.1	9.4		25.5	
28.3	33.8	33.6	Long-Term Debt	47.5	23.0	48.0		26.5	
.0	.0	.1	Deferred Taxes	.0	.0	.0		.0	
5.2	3.3	4.4	All Other Non-Current	4.9	1.9	1.9		6.3	
47.7	42.9	45.1	Net Worth	36.2	57.1	40.6		41.7	
100.0	100.0	100.0	Total Liabilities & Net Worth	100.0	100.0	100.0		100.0	
			INCOME DATA						
100.0	100.0	100.0	Net Sales	100.0	100.0	100.0		100.0	
			Gross Profit						
88.6	85.4	82.6	Operating Expenses	74.9	84.9	68.6		87.7	
11.4	14.6	17.4	Operating Profit	25.1	15.1	31.4		12.3	
7.2	10.2	8.9	All Other Expenses (net)	12.8	6.1	10.0		14.5	
4.2	4.4	8.5	Profit Before Taxes	12.3	9.1	21.5		-2.2	
			RATIOS						
4.3	5.7	5.7		12.1	12.3	5.3		7.6	
1.9	1.7	2.6	Current	3.5	2.6	1.9		4.4	
.9	.7	.9		.9	.6	.8		1.1	
4.2	5.2	5.7		12.1	8.0	5.2		4.5	
1.7	1.1	1.8	Quick	3.5	1.9	1.1		2.9	
.4	.4	.5		.9	.5	.3		.5	
5 71.0	0 UND	0 UND		0 UND	4 81.5	2 161.4		0 UND	
21 17.3	14 25.8	35 10.5	Sales/Receivables	0 UND	50 7.3	28 12.9		47 7.8	
61 6.0	79 4.6	86 4.2		64 5.7	106 3.5	86 4.2		119 3.1	
			Cost of Sales/Inventory						
			Cost of Sales/Payables						
1.4	1.2	1.0		.9	.8	1.1		.5	
4.7	5.0	2.7	Sales/Working Capital	2.1	1.4	2.3		1.9	
-70.5	-11.6	-35.1		UND	-11.4	-12.2		NM	
3.5	4.9	7.4							
(40) 1.5	(42) 1.5	(43) 3.1	EBIT/Interest						
-1.7	-2.4	-.6							
			Net Profit + Depr., Dep., Amort./Cur. Mat. L/T/D						
.1	.1	.1		.0	.0	.7		.0	
.8	.9	.8	Fixed/Worth	1.2	.4	1.2		.3	
1.6	2.2	1.9		3.0	.9	2.3		1.5	
.5	.4	.4		.4	.3	.8		.5	
.9	1.2	1.1	Debt/Worth	.9	.6	1.4		1.4	
2.7	5.4	2.2		11.9	1.9	5.6		5.6	
10.9	14.9	20.9	% Profit Before Taxes/Tangible	9.9	16.6	33.2		22.4	
(56) 1.7	(57) 5.9	(66) 3.9	Net Worth	(15) 4.0	(18) 4.7	8.1		(11) -2.3	
-4.0	-2.6	-2.3		-.3	-3.5	3.0		-6.8	
3.6	5.0	7.6	% Profit Before Taxes/Total	9.0	7.5	14.7		7.9	
1.0	1.4	1.7	Assets	2.6	3.6	2.8		-1.2	
-2.8	-1.3	-1.4		-1.6	-1.5	.5		-2.9	
9.3	11.2	12.6		UND	18.1	2.5		12.9	
1.1	1.1	1.2	Sales/Net Fixed Assets	.4	2.4	.6		8.9	
.5	.4	.3		.1	.3	.3		2.7	
1.1	.6	.8		.4	.8	.5		2.1	
.4	.3	.3	Sales/Total Assets	.2	.4	.3		1.0	
.1	.1	.1		.1	.1	.2		.2	
2.3	1.2	2.0	% Depr., Dep., Amort./Sales	2.7	1.0	2.1			
(46) 5.4	(47) 6.2	(50) 4.4		(10) 6.0	(11) 3.1	5.5			
9.6	11.5	8.3		28.3	9.3	10.0			
			% Officers', Directors', Owners' Comp/Sales						
816350M	348790M	776355M	Net Sales ($)	8811M	34554M	38613M	62799M	160840M	470738M
1428417M	1159264M	1463681M	Total Assets ($)	83454M	147899M	199003M	201704M	449080M	382541M

M = $ thousand   MM = $ million
See Pages 11 through 21 for Explanation of Ratios and Data

Current Data Sorted By Assets   **Comparative Historical Data**

Type of Statement		4/1/00-3/31/01 ALL	4/1/01-3/31/02 ALL
Unqualified	1 8 22 21 3 1	26	24
Reviewed	1 1		2
Compiled	2 3 3 5 1	2	10
Tax Returns	1 1 1	1	4
Other	2 8 12 6 1	7	12
	56 (4/1-9/30/04) 49 (10/1/04-3/31/05)		

	0-500M	500M-2MM	2-10MM	10-50MM	50-100MM	100-250MM		4/1/00-3/31/01 ALL	4/1/01-3/31/02 ALL
NUMBER OF STATEMENTS	6	21	39	33	5	1		36	52
	%	%	%	%	%	%	**ASSETS**	%	%
Cash & Equivalents		16.6	17.8	16.2				23.9	23.6
Trade Receivables (net)		19.4	10.4	6.2				16.9	10.0
Inventory		3.7	5.1	.9				.1	5.1
All Other Current		6.3	5.2	3.6				4.2	5.0
Total Current		46.0	38.5	27.0				45.2	43.7
Fixed Assets (net)		46.3	39.4	39.8				30.2	34.2
Intangibles (net)		.7	1.3	.6				.6	2.5
All Other Non-Current		7.0	20.7	32.6				24.0	19.6
Total		100.0	100.0	100.0				100.0	100.0
							LIABILITIES		
Notes Payable-Short Term		7.9	7.9	1.6				3.4	3.4
Cur. Mat.-L/T/D		1.7	1.8	3.7				1.4	2.7
Trade Payables		9.0	4.1	2.6				5.1	4.7
Income Taxes Payable		.4	.0	.0				.0	.0
All Other Current		11.0	6.8	5.5				6.5	6.0
Total Current		29.9	20.6	13.5				16.4	16.7
Long-Term Debt		23.5	21.9	40.7				32.4	24.8
Deferred Taxes		.0	.0	.0				.0	.0
All Other Non-Current		6.8	5.1	5.3				2.7	4.6
Net Worth		39.8	52.4	40.6				48.5	53.9
Total Liabilities & Net Worth		100.0	100.0	100.0				100.0	100.0
							INCOME DATA		
Net Sales		100.0	100.0	100.0				100.0	100.0
Gross Profit									
Operating Expenses		88.2	84.2	83.9				80.6	76.6
Operating Profit		11.8	15.8	16.1				19.4	23.4
All Other Expenses (net)		7.5	5.3	7.2				5.0	4.9
Profit Before Taxes		4.3	10.5	8.9				14.4	18.5
							RATIOS		
Current		2.7	5.9	5.9				9.5	7.6
		1.5	2.6	1.6				2.4	2.9
		1.0	1.4	.6				1.0	1.5
Quick		2.5	5.3	5.2				8.1	5.1
		1.2	1.8	1.2				1.9	2.2
		.6	.9	.5				.9	1.4
Sales/Receivables	0 UND	0 UND	0 UND	5 76.1				6 59.1	0 UND
	9 39.6		18 20.1	28 12.9				34 10.7	11 34.4
	51 7.2		50 7.4	65 5.6				86 4.2	54 6.7
Cost of Sales/Inventory									
Cost of Sales/Payables									
Sales/Working Capital		5.8	1.9	1.4				.6	1.0
		13.4	3.6	4.1				2.8	2.6
		NM	18.2	-4.9				83.9	10.2
EBIT/Interest		3.4	13.6	4.8				9.4	10.1
	(12)	1.5	(23) 5.3	(22) 1.5			(16)	4.9	(24) 4.7
		-3.9	-.6	-.1				1.2	2.2
Net Profit + Depr., Dep., Amort./Cur. Mat. L./T/D									
Fixed/Worth		.3	.1	.5				.1	.1
		.9	.8	.9				.5	.5
		4.8	1.6	1.4				1.4	1.2
Debt/Worth		.6	.4	.4				.4	.3
		1.2	.9	1.1				1.4	.8
		8.4	2.2	2.2				2.6	2.2
% Profit Before Taxes/Tangible Net Worth		40.7	20.8	10.3				14.6	25.4
	(18)	7.5	(38) 9.0	(31) 1.0			(35)	6.9	(50) 9.1
		-2.3	1.2	-1.5				1.2	1.2
% Profit Before Taxes/Total Assets		9.4	7.6	6.2				7.3	10.2
		2.6	4.0	.4				1.7	4.6
		-1.7	.0	-1.3				.3	.6
Sales/Net Fixed Assets		33.8	34.5	28.3				35.2	24.3
		8.9	1.9	.4				4.3	3.5
		.2	.4	.2				.4	.4
Sales/Total Assets		3.1	1.2	.5				.9	1.1
		2.0	.6	.2				.4	.3
		.2	.2	.1				.2	.1
% Depr., Dep., Amort./Sales		.8	.8	1.1				1.0	.7
	(16)	2.5	(28) 2.1	(22) 6.5			(22)	2.8	(33) 2.1
		17.1	12.9	15.2				6.5	9.2
% Officers', Directors', Owners' Comp/Sales									
Net Sales ($)	9325M	46324M	159489M	563021M	167477M	22592M		259186M	348066M
Total Assets ($)	1393M	25813M	188633M	676285M	340168M	101147M		803537M	911636M

M = $ thousand   MM = $ million
See Pages 11 through 21 for Explanation of Ratios and Data

Comparative Historical Data   **Current Data Sorted By Sales**

			Type of Statement						
56	46	56	Unqualified	9	20	10	9	5	3
8	2	3	Reviewed		1	1	1		
8	23	14	Compiled	5	4	3			2
3	6	3	Tax Returns	1	1			1	
43	30	29	Other	5	9	7	4	4	
4/1/02-3/31/03	4/1/03-3/31/04	4/1/04-3/31/05		56 (4/1-9/30/04)			49 (10/1/04-3/31/05)		
ALL	ALL	ALL		0-1MM	1-3MM	3-5MM	5-10MM	10-25MM	25MM & OVER
118	107	105	NUMBER OF STATEMENTS	20	35	21	14	10	5
%	%	%	ASSETS	%	%	%	%	%	%
15.6	16.4	18.8	Cash & Equivalents	22.8	13.8	16.6	18.3	33.3	
10.7	12.8	10.7	Trade Receivables (net)	.6	9.1	15.6	11.8	19.0	
5.0	5.3	2.9	Inventory	.3	3.8	.4	8.9	.4	
4.8	6.5	5.7	All Other Current	4.3	5.6	5.5	6.9	8.3	
36.0	41.0	38.1	Total Current	28.0	32.3	38.2	46.0	60.9	
42.1	35.6	40.5	Fixed Assets (net)	58.1	47.8	34.5	21.2	25.8	
2.7	2.2	1.1	Intangibles (net)	.1	.7	.0	3.1	1.9	
19.1	21.3	20.3	All Other Non-Current	13.8	19.3	27.3	29.6	11.3	
100.0	100.0	100.0	Total	100.0	100.0	100.0	100.0	100.0	
			LIABILITIES						
5.1	4.5	5.7	Notes Payable-Short Term	1.2	8.0	6.3	7.4	2.4	
3.4	2.4	3.5	Cur. Mat.-L/T/D	3.2	2.5	6.9	2.1	.4	
6.5	4.0	5.6	Trade Payables	1.5	4.0	5.8	7.0	12.6	
.3	.1	.1	Income Taxes Payable	.0	.0	.4	.0	.0	
6.3	7.5	7.1	All Other Current	3.0	7.9	6.8	9.0	11.5	
21.6	18.5	21.9	Total Current	9.0	22.4	26.3	25.4	26.9	
28.6	26.2	28.1	Long-Term Debt	32.7	25.7	22.1	15.7	51.7	
.2	.1	.0	Deferred Taxes	.0	.0	.0	.0	.0	
3.1	4.7	5.0	All Other Non-Current	3.3	3.4	4.3	7.2	12.6	
46.4	50.5	45.0	Net Worth	55.0	48.5	47.3	51.7	8.8	
100.0	100.0	100.0	Total Liabilities & Net Worth	100.0	100.0	100.0	100.0	100.0	
			INCOME DATA						
100.0	100.0	100.0	Net Sales	100.0	100.0	100.0	100.0	100.0	
			Gross Profit						
78.1	80.6	85.2	Operating Expenses	72.6	88.7	83.5	91.3	86.0	
21.9	19.4	14.8	Operating Profit	27.4	11.3	16.5	8.7	14.0	
7.6	8.0	5.8	All Other Expenses (net)	12.7	5.9	3.3	1.6	6.6	
14.3	11.4	8.9	Profit Before Taxes	14.7	5.5	13.2	7.2	7.3	
			RATIOS						
3.8	6.1	5.3		5.4	5.6	6.6	2.7	7.2	
1.9	2.7	1.9	Current	3.4	1.8	2.0	1.7	1.5	
1.1	1.2	1.0		.8	.7	1.0	1.2	1.0	
3.2	4.7	3.9		5.4	4.5	4.8	2.1	6.3	
(117) 1.4	2.1	1.5	Quick	2.5	1.2	1.8	1.0	1.5	
.6	.8	.6		.8	.5	.8	.7	1.0	
1 592.9	0 UND	0 UND		0 UND	1 279.0	4 86.4	1 391.9	0 UND	
21 17.3	16 22.9	19 18.8	Sales/Receivables	0 UND	24 15.2	28 13.0	18 20.9	26 13.8	
60 6.1	46 7.9	51 7.2		24 15.0	54 6.7	64 5.7	68 5.3	36 10.3	
			Cost of Sales/Inventory						
			Cost of Sales/Payables						
1.6	1.3	1.9		1.0	1.9	1.5	3.2	1.7	
6.5	4.1	5.8	Sales/Working Capital	2.8	7.9	3.9	6.5	4.8	
58.8	16.3	186.4		NM	−8.8	NM	36.9	NM	
6.0	9.6	6.8			6.9	5.5			
(62) 3.3	(62) 3.4	(65) 2.1	EBIT/Interest		(26) 1.9	(14) 2.7			
.9	1.4	−.1			−.3	.3			
			Net Profit + Depr., Dep., Amort./Cur. Mat. L/T/D						
.3	.1	.2		.1	.5	.2	.0	.1	
.9	.7	.9	Fixed/Worth	1.1	1.0	.8	.2	1.1	
1.8	1.4	1.8		2.1	1.5	1.4	.8	UND	
.5	.4	.4		.1	.4	.5	.6	.3	
1.0	.8	1.1	Debt/Worth	.8	1.3	1.0	1.1	1.7	
3.9	2.6	2.7		1.5	3.1	2.5	2.4	UND	
21.1	28.4	18.6	% Profit Before Taxes/Tangible	15.1	17.9	15.9	49.2		
(111) 7.0	(103) 9.7	(97) 8.1	Net Worth	(19) 8.1	(33) 6.6	(19) 7.5	7.8		
−.7	.8	−.1		.0	−1.7	.3	−1.0		
7.9	9.5	7.7	% Profit Before Taxes/Total	5.0	7.6	8.8	14.4	16.8	
3.0	3.7	2.6	Assets	2.8	2.5	3.3	3.7	1.4	
−.6	.5	−.8		−.7	−1.5	−.3	−.3	−.1	
18.1	46.2	37.4	Sales/Net Fixed Assets	25.0	8.9	28.0	73.5	UND	
1.5	2.7	2.3		.2	.8	9.5	37.5	45.2	
.2	.4	.3		.1	.2	.4	2.9	.8	
1.2	1.9	1.9		.3	1.1	2.8	3.0	1.9	
.3	.3	.4	Sales/Total Assets	.1	.3	.7	1.1	.9	
.1	.1	.1		.1	.1	.2	.3	.2	
1.3	.9	1.1		6.2	1.5	1.1			
(85) 3.2	(86) 3.3	(75) 2.6	% Depr., Dep., Amort./Sales	(15) 14.3	(27) 2.9	(14) 2.3			
12.4	11.2	13.6		21.9	14.9	8.3			
2.7	1.0	4.4	% Officers', Directors',						
(12) 3.9	(14) 5.3	(14) 5.8	Owners' Comp/Sales						
19.8	9.4	9.1							
1576745M	696019M	968228M	Net Sales ($)	7339M	65221M	79342M	106710M	157338M	552278M
2872566M	1422076M	1333439M	Total Assets ($)	64731M	262644M	300493M	207104M	353247M	145220M

M = $ thousand   MM = $ million
See Pages 11 through 21 for Explanation of Ratios and Data

CONSTRUCTION—
PERCENTAGE OF COMPLETION
BASIS OF ACCOUNTING*

CONSTRUCTION – % OF COMPLETION—Support Activities for Oil and Gas Operations NAICS 213112 (SIC 1382, 1389)

Current Data Sorted By Revenue					Type of Statement	Comparative Historical Data				
1	3	8	18	30	Unqualified	11	14	18	26	30
	2	2		4	Reviewed	4	3	8	7	4
3	20	1		24	Compiled	12	18	29	24	24
3	8			11	Tax Returns	4	5	5	8	11
6	22	13	.6	47	Other	18	31	30	25	47
13 (4/1-9/30/04)			103 (10/1/04-3/31/05)			4/1/00-3/31/01	4/1/01-3/31/02	4/1/02-3/31/03	4/1/03-3/31/04	4/1/04-3/31/05
0-1MM	1-10MM	10-50MM	50 & OVER	ALL	NUMBER OF STATEMENTS	ALL	ALL	ALL	ALL	ALL
13	55	24	24	116		49	71	90	90	116
%	%	%	%	%	ASSETS	%	%	%	%	%
10.3	11.2	8.2	5.4	9.3	Cash & Equivalents	6.9	10.8	8.8	8.2	9.3
17.5	36.2	28.1	22.7	29.6	A/R - Progress Billings	32.3	27.9	30.7	28.3	29.6
.0	.3	.2	.3	.2	A/R - Current Retention	.0	.4	.5	.2	.2
2.5	6.1	6.5	13.2	7.2	Inventory	11.2	7.6	4.7	5.9	7.2
.0	.0	.1	1.2	.3	Cost & Est. Earnings In Excess of Billings	.6	.2	.2	.3	.3
.0	3.4	2.7	2.3	2.7	All Other Current	3.2	4.1	4.2	2.7	2.7
30.3	57.2	45.7	45.1	49.3	Total Current	54.3	50.9	49.2	45.8	49.3
46.0	30.2	44.5	37.6	36.4	Fixed Assets (net)	38.5	41.4	39.7	41.7	36.4
7.9	2.2	.3	2.0	2.4	Joint Ventures & Investments	1.3	.8	3.5	1.2	2.4
.6	3.1	5.3	9.5	4.6	Intangibles (net)	1.3	2.2	3.1	3.3	4.6
15.2	7.3	4.2	5.9	7.2	All Other Non-Current	4.5	4.7	4.5	8.0	7.2
100.0	100.0	100.0	100.0	100.0	Total	100.0	100.0	100.0	100.0	100.0
					LIABILITIES					
7.1	12.1	9.3	5.1	9.5	Notes Payable - Short Term	15.8	9.1	10.3	8.3	9.5
8.6	10.1	9.1	10.0	9.7	A/P - Trade	9.9	10.8	11.3	9.6	9.7
.0	.2	.1	.0	.1	A/P - Retention	.1	.1	.0	.6	.1
.0	.0	.1	.3	.1	Billings in Excess of Costs & Est. Earnings	.6	.2	.2	.1	.1
.0	.0	.1	.6	.2	Income Taxes Payable	.5	.8	.5	.2	.2
2.0	3.7	5.0	3.5	3.8	Cur. Mat.-L/T/D	3.5	4.0	4.2	5.4	3.8
3.8	7.6	5.7	7.1	6.7	All Other Current	8.1	6.8	6.3	6.8	6.7
21.5	33.8	29.4	26.6	30.0	Total Current	38.4	31.9	32.8	31.0	30.0
37.7	16.9	20.0	15.1	19.5	Long-Term Debt	19.8	17.7	19.3	18.3	19.5
.0	.5	1.9	3.2	1.3	Deferred Taxes	.6	.4	.8	.9	1.3
2.5	1.8	7.1	5.0	3.7	All Other Non-Current	6.3	6.6	5.5	7.1	3.7
38.3	46.9	41.6	50.1	45.5	Net Worth	34.9	43.4	41.6	42.8	45.5
100.0	100.0	100.0	100.0	100.0	Total Liabilities & Net Worth	100.0	100.0	100.0	100.0	100.0
					INCOME DATA					
100.0	100.0	100.0	100.0	100.0	Contract Revenues	100.0	100.0	100.0	100.0	100.0
					Gross Profit					
75.5	92.0	85.1	88.9	88.1	Operating Expenses	92.2	86.7	91.2	92.5	88.1
24.5	8.0	14.9	11.1	11.9	Operating Profit	7.8	13.3	8.8	7.5	11.9
5.8	1.5	5.4	1.7	2.8	All Other Expenses (net)	2.3	3.3	2.4	3.0	2.8
18.6	6.6	9.5	9.4	9.1	Profit Before Taxes	5.5	9.9	6.4	4.6	9.1
					RATIOS					
4.0	3.8	2.9	3.2	3.2		2.1	2.4	2.2	2.7	3.2
1.2	1.9	1.3	1.7	1.6	Current	1.3	1.6	1.6	1.5	1.6
.6	1.1	.8	1.2	.9		1.0	1.1	1.1	.9	.9
UND	6.0	11.9	3.9	5.7		6.0	6.0	7.3	8.3	5.7
(11) 1.8	(50) 3.5	2.7	2.6	(109) 2.8	Receivables/Payables	(45) 3.4	(66) 3.1	(86) 2.9	(85) 3.4	(109) 2.8
.0	1.9	1.5	1.9	1.8		1.8	1.4	1.4	1.6	1.8
0 UND	48 7.6	45 8.1	59 6.1	47 7.8		52 7.1	30 12.1	42 8.6	39 9.3	47 7.8
28 12.9	62 5.9	64 5.7	72 5.0	64 5.7	Revenues/Receivables	70 5.2	59 6.2	65 5.6	61 5.9	64 5.7
84 4.3	85 4.3	87 4.2	91 4.0	87 4.2		96 3.8	95 3.8	93 3.9	83 4.4	87 4.2
					Cost of Revenues/Payables					
2.6	4.8	6.4	3.4	4.1		4.6	4.5	5.8	4.9	4.1
41.6	10.3	23.7	5.0	10.6	Revenues/Working Capital	10.2	9.6	11.4	13.4	10.6
-13.9	54.8	-16.0	20.5	-73.3		NM	36.6	58.8	-82.1	-73.3
24.1	22.7	11.0	24.1	15.3		7.3	17.7	11.3	14.6	15.3
(12) 7.0	(51) 4.8	(21) 6.0	(23) 8.0	(107) 5.9	EBIT/Interest	(45) 2.8	(60) 6.5	(83) 3.6	(81) 3.6	(107) 5.9
.9	1.7	4.4	2.3	2.0		1.1	2.4	1.2	.6	2.0
				5.9		25.2	12.6	6.4	4.2	5.9
			(17) 3.0		Net Profit + Depr., Dep., Amort./Cur. Mat. L /T/D	(12) 3.3	(18) 4.2	(14) 4.5	(11) 1.8	(17) 3.0
				1.7		.8	1.9	2.0	-.5	1.7
.6	.2	.6	.4	.3		.4	.4	.4	.3	.3
.9	.4	1.6	.9	.8	Fixed/Worth	.8	.8	1.0	.9	.8
13.5	2.0	7.8	2.0	2.1		2.3	1.6	2.3	2.5	2.1
.5	.4	.6	1.0	.6		.7	.6	.6	.5	.6
1.5	1.3	2.3	1.3	1.4	Debt/Worth	1.8	1.3	1.5	1.4	1.4
47.9	3.2	10.2	2.5	3.1		4.8	2.9	3.1	3.5	3.1
45.7	51.8	72.8	42.5	51.8		42.4	48.6	26.5	41.3	51.8
(11) 25.2	(52) 18.1	(21) 29.9	21.0	(108) 22.9	% Profit Before Taxes/ Tangible Net Worth	(45) 19.5	(66) 29.1	(79) 11.5	(81) 19.5	(108) 22.9
.4	3.4	16.2	7.3	5.7		2.2	11.4	3.7	1.3	5.7
19.4	16.9	20.9	14.8	16.8		16.9	25.1	12.8	15.5	16.8
5.8	6.7	11.6	7.2	8.2	% Profit Before Taxes/ Total Assets	7.2	11.0	4.7	6.0	8.2
-.7	1.7	5.9	2.5	1.9		.4	3.0	.3	-.5	1.9
4.0	1.5	4.0	.3	2.0		1.8	2.1	2.3	2.3	2.0
(12) 5.2	(44) 3.4	(21) 8.4	(10) 1.9	(87) 4.8	% Depr., Dep., Amort./ Revenues	(41) 5.0	(61) 5.0	(67) 5.7	(62) 5.9	(87) 4.8
17.9	9.2	15.7	7.8	12.5		11.5	8.6	9.0	11.6	12.5
	4.6			4.7		2.3	2.8	3.4	2.2	4.7
(26)	6.8		(35)	7.0	% Officers', Directors', Owners' Comp/Revenues	(17) 7.1	(20) 4.4	(31) 6.0	(23) 6.0	(35) 7.0
	10.4			12.6		22.3	13.5	10.0	11.5	12.6
7255M	215930M	498729M	20070465M	20792379M	Contract Revenues ($)	3267187M	3631218M	15895725M	14915619M	20792379M
17088M	510134M	531596M	26403561M	27462379M	Total Assets ($)	7028888M	4966533M	16226053M	16609814M	27462379M

M = $ thousand   MM = $ million
See Pages 11 through 21 for Explanation of Ratios and Data

Current Data Sorted By Revenue · **Comparative Historical Data**

Type of Statement	0-1MM	1-10MM	10-50MM	50 & OVER	ALL	4/1/00-3/31/01 ALL	4/1/01-3/31/02 ALL	4/1/02-3/31/03 ALL	4/1/03-3/31/04 ALL	4/1/04-3/31/05 ALL
Unqualified		1	9	20	30	51	53	54	16	30
Reviewed	2	46	27	10	85	130	124	112	76	85
Compiled	18	73	24	9	124	226	211	181	108	124
Tax Returns	65	185	36	9	295	230	295	302	236	295
Other	11	94	40	7	152	169	169	193	80	152
	90 (4/1-9/30/04)			596 (10/1/04-3/31/05)						
NUMBER OF STATEMENTS	96	399	136	55	686	806	852	842	516	686

ASSETS (%)

	0-1MM	1-10MM	10-50MM	50 & OVER	ALL	4/1/00-3/31/01	4/1/01-3/31/02	4/1/02-3/31/03	4/1/03-3/31/04	4/1/04-3/31/05
Cash & Equivalents	16.5	10.3	7.6	7.5	10.4	9.9	10.7	10.4	10.8	10.4
A/R - Progress Billings	8.6	10.6	8.0	4.3	9.3	11.2	10.0	8.2	8.9	9.3
A/R - Current Retention	.0	.2	.9	.7	.4	.9	.6	.6	.3	.4
Inventory	37.3	46.3	54.2	57.2	47.5	42.6	45.0	49.1	45.5	47.5
Cost & Est. Earnings In Excess of Billings	.6	3.0	5.0	2.4	3.0	4.6	3.7	2.5	3.5	3.0
All Other Current	3.8	6.0	6.4	4.8	5.7	7.2	6.1	5.3	7.1	5.7
Total Current	66.8	76.4	82.0	76.9	76.2	76.4	76.2	76.1	76.0	76.2
Fixed Assets (net)	20.3	13.9	10.1	8.7	13.6	13.2	13.8	14.1	14.1	13.6
Joint Ventures & Investments	2.0	2.2	3.4	3.2	2.5	3.1	2.3	2.1	1.7	2.5
Intangibles (net)	2.4	.4	.4	.8	.7	1.1	1.3	.5	.9	.7
All Other Non-Current	8.6	7.1	4.1	10.3	7.0	6.2	6.4	7.2	7.3	7.0
Total	100.0	100.0	100.0	100.0	100.0	100.0	100.0	100.0	100.0	100.0

LIABILITIES

	0-1MM	1-10MM	10-50MM	50 & OVER	ALL	4/1/00-3/31/01	4/1/01-3/31/02	4/1/02-3/31/03	4/1/03-3/31/04	4/1/04-3/31/05
Notes Payable - Short Term	25.8	32.0	34.1	34.6	31.8	32.6	32.5	30.9	31.1	31.8
A/P - Trade	10.4	13.2	13.5	7.3	12.4	12.8	10.6	10.2	11.4	12.4
A/P - Retention	.7	.5	.2	.3	.4	.3	.5	.4	.4	.4
Billings in Excess of Costs & Est. Earnings	2.7	3.0	2.4	1.0	2.6	2.5	2.3	2.1	2.6	2.6
Income Taxes Payable	.1	.1	.2	.2	.1	.2	.3	.1	.1	.1
Cur. Mat.-L/T/D	2.3	4.9	6.2	2.5	4.6	3.9	5.1	4.8	6.0	4.6
All Other Current	10.1	9.8	7.4	8.6	9.3	9.3	11.9	9.2	11.3	9.3
Total Current	51.9	63.6	64.0	54.5	61.3	61.6	63.1	57.7	62.9	61.3
Long-Term Debt	18.9	13.8	9.2	14.8	13.7	12.3	12.2	12.8	13.4	13.7
Deferred Taxes	.0	.1	.1	.0	.1	.2	.2	.2	.1	.1
All Other Non-Current	17.3	8.4	3.7	4.6	8.4	4.2	5.0	6.5	6.7	8.4
Net Worth	11.9	14.1	22.9	26.1	16.5	21.6	19.4	22.8	16.9	16.5
Total Liabilities & Net Worth	100.0	100.0	100.0	100.0	100.0	100.0	100.0	100.0	100.0	100.0

INCOME DATA

	0-1MM	1-10MM	10-50MM	50 & OVER	ALL	4/1/00-3/31/01	4/1/01-3/31/02	4/1/02-3/31/03	4/1/03-3/31/04	4/1/04-3/31/05
Contract Revenues	100.0	100.0	100.0	100.0	100.0	100.0	100.0	100.0	100.0	100.0
Gross Profit	25.5	18.5	15.7	20.4	19.1	18.3	19.1	19.9	19.9	19.1
Operating Expenses	22.6	14.7	11.1	13.0	15.0	14.5	15.0	15.4	15.9	15.0
Operating Profit	2.9	3.8	4.5	7.4	4.1	3.8	4.1	4.5	4.0	4.1
All Other Expenses (net)	.8	.4	.3	.4	.5	.5	.7	.6	.6	.5
Profit Before Taxes	2.1	3.4	4.2	7.0	3.7	3.3	3.4	3.9	3.4	3.7

RATIOS

	0-1MM	1-10MM	10-50MM	50 & OVER	ALL	4/1/00-3/31/01	4/1/01-3/31/02	4/1/02-3/31/03	4/1/03-3/31/04	4/1/04-3/31/05
Current	3.3	1.7	1.6	2.0	1.8	1.7	1.9	2.1	1.9	1.8
	1.2	1.2	1.2	1.4	1.2	1.2	1.2	1.3	1.2	1.2
	.8	.9	1.1	1.1	1.0	1.0	1.0	1.0	1.0	1.0
Receivables/Payables	3.5	1.4	1.0	.4	1.3	1.4	1.6	1.3	1.4	1.3
	(63) .3	(306) .2	(119) .1	(48) .1	(536) .2	(655) .2	(680) .2	(653) .1	(396) .1	(536) .2
	.0	.0	.0	.0	.0	.0	.0	.0	.0	.0
Revenues/Receivables	0 UND	0 UND	0 UND	0 UND	0 UND	0 UND	0 UND	0 UND	0 UND	0 UND
	0 UND	0 UND	1 656.2	0 999.8	0 UND	0 838.6	0 999.8	0 UND	0 UND	0 UND
	13 28.7	15 25.0	9 38.6	5 73.1	13 28.9	18 20.0	11 31.8	10 37.4	9 39.5	13 28.9
Cost of Revenues/Payables	0 UND	0 UND	2 159.7	1 483.9	0 UND	0 867.5	0 UND	0 UND	0 UND	0 UND
	2 206.3	15 23.9	18 19.9	19 18.9	15 24.5	13 27.6	12 29.5	13 27.3	12 30.9	15 24.5
	31 11.8	32 11.6	34 10.6	33 10.9	32 11.3	31 11.8	29 12.6	31 11.7	31 11.7	32 11.3
Revenues/Working Capital	3.2	6.8	6.7	3.2	5.9	7.7	7.3	5.9	6.5	5.9
	20.6	22.9	13.8	9.2	18.0	22.5	20.2	15.0	18.0	18.0
	-24.4	-68.4	40.1	48.4	-110.3	-99.2	-264.2	UND	-95.6	-110.3
EBIT/Interest	12.8	12.0	18.1	27.3	13.8	12.0	12.8	17.6	18.1	13.8
	(61) 2.4	(304) 4.3	(107) 6.5	(46) 8.7	(518) 5.0	(655) 3.6	(687) 3.6	(661) 5.2	(406) 4.8	(518) 5.0
	-1.4	1.3	2.4	3.7	1.6	1.3	1.3	1.4	1.2	1.6
Net Profit + Depr., Dep., Amort./Cur. Mat. L/T/D		4.4	7.3		6.1	9.1	8.0	7.3	4.9	6.1
		(32) 2.3	(10) 3.3		(48) 2.3	(91) 3.5	(76) 2.2	(76) 3.2	(54) 2.4	(48) 2.3
		.4	.6		.7	1.1	.7	.9	.7	.7
Fixed/Worth	.1	.1	.0	.1	.1	.1	.1	.0	.1	.1
	1.4	.5	.1	.1	.3	.3	.3	.3	.3	.3
	-5.6	3.5	.7	.4	2.6	1.5	1.9	1.9	2.8	2.6
Debt/Worth	1.8	2.0	2.1	1.7	2.0	1.6	1.7	1.6	1.8	2.0
	8.9	6.4	4.3	3.3	5.1	4.5	4.8	4.3	5.1	5.1
	-36.5	47.6	10.7	7.5	33.0	20.1	21.2	21.6	36.3	33.0
% Profit Before Taxes/Tangible Net Worth	95.8	90.8	68.1	74.0	80.4	74.4	82.3	83.1	78.5	80.4
	(64) 42.1	(322) 31.4	(131) 42.0	(53) 39.8	(570) 37.7	(687) 31.2	(723) 34.5	(726) 37.9	(416) 35.5	(570) 37.7
	3.7	8.1	16.4	27.7	10.5	7.9	9.3	11.4	8.8	10.5
% Profit Before Taxes/Total Assets	15.0	14.4	13.2	17.6	14.3	14.1	17.0	15.3	16.3	14.3
	4.3	5.0	6.8	9.5	5.8	5.3	5.4	6.7	5.4	5.8
	-1.7	.6	2.2	4.7	.9	.5	.7	.8	.5	.9
% Depr., Dep., Amort./Revenues	.8	.3	.2	.1	.3	.3	.2	.3	.3	.3
	(56) 1.9	(256) .7	(91) .4	(25) .2	(428) .6	(598) .5	(593) .6	(544) .6	(317) .6	(428) .6
	3.6	1.5	.7	.6	1.5	1.3	1.4	1.4	1.6	1.5
% Officers', Directors', Owners' Comp/Revenues	3.1	1.8	.6	.8	1.4	1.7	1.7	1.8	1.8	1.4
	(48) 5.9	(261) 3.2	(69) 1.2	(19) 2.2	(397) 3.1	(446) 3.2	(464) 3.4	(456) 3.5	(299) 3.7	(397) 3.1
	10.3	5.6	3.3	6.5	6.1	5.9	5.9	7.0	6.7	6.1
Contract Revenues ($)	52954M	1562536M	2807467M	129840118M	134263075M	146145845M	28308103M	84992650M	21762072M	134263075M
Total Assets ($)	52626M	940416M	1529501M	87162402M	89684945M	50957860M	18803027M	41985857M	9493032M	89684945M

© RMA 2005

M = $ thousand   MM = $ million

See Pages 11 through 21 for Explanation of Ratios and Data

Current Data Sorted By Revenue   **Comparative Historical Data**

Current periods: 5 (4/1-9/30/04) and 64 (10/1/04-3/31/05)

0-1MM	1-10MM	10-50MM	50 & OVER	ALL	Type of Statement	4/1/00-3/31/01 ALL	4/1/01-3/31/02 ALL	4/1/02-3/31/03 ALL	4/1/03-3/31/04 ALL	4/1/04-3/31/05 ALL
		2	9	11	Unqualified	27	36	12	11	11
	9	6		15	Reviewed	51	73	32	19	15
2	7			9	Compiled	26	38	20	13	9
3	12	2	1	18	Tax Returns	36	46	33	21	18
4	9	2	1	16	Other	26	37	23	10	16
9	37	12	11	69	**NUMBER OF STATEMENTS**	166	230	120	74	69
%	%	%	%	%	**ASSETS**	%	%	%	%	%
	11.0	13.7	12.2	10.7	Cash & Equivalents	14.6	16.9	14.8	13.6	10.7
	17.6	17.4	18.0	15.8	A/R - Progress Billings	21.6	25.0	20.6	19.5	15.8
	2.2	1.2	4.2	2.1	A/R - Current Retention	3.1	2.8	1.2	2.4	2.1
	33.9	28.6	16.2	32.0	Inventory	20.6	16.1	28.9	27.9	32.0
	2.0	8.3	3.8	3.2	Cost & Est. Earnings In Excess of Billings	3.8	3.3	1.7	3.1	3.2
	3.7	12.2	18.8	9.2	All Other Current	8.3	8.7	8.4	7.6	9.2
	70.4	81.3	73.2	72.9	Total Current	72.0	72.8	75.5	74.0	72.9
	20.5	9.9	16.0	15.9	Fixed Assets (net)	17.5	16.8	15.4	16.8	15.9
	2.1	.1	5.1	3.4	Joint Ventures & Investments	2.2	1.7	1.6	1.4	3.4
	.2	1.8	.0	.4	Intangibles (net)	1.9	.9	.8	.1	.4
	6.8	6.8	5.7	7.3	All Other Non-Current	6.5	7.7	6.7	7.6	7.3
	100.0	100.0	100.0	100.0	Total	100.0	100.0	100.0	100.0	100.0
					LIABILITIES					
	23.4	20.5	20.4	20.8	Notes Payable - Short Term	13.6	11.5	20.7	14.5	20.8
	13.9	16.0	19.4	13.8	A/P - Trade	20.4	22.1	15.9	16.7	13.8
	1.2	.6	2.3	1.1	A/P - Retention	1.7	1.4	1.0	1.0	1.1
	5.5	5.5	5.0	4.8	Billings in Excess of Costs & Est. Earnings	4.9	5.6	3.3	5.2	4.8
	.0	.0	.0	.0	Income Taxes Payable	.5	.2	.4	.1	.0
	2.9	1.4	1.0	2.1	Cur. Mat.-L/T/D	4.3	4.4	4.6	3.6	2.1
	6.0	9.0	13.3	7.3	All Other Current	11.3	11.1	11.9	9.7	7.3
	52.9	53.0	61.6	50.0	Total Current	56.6	56.3	57.9	50.8	50.0
	10.8	8.6	8.6	16.6	Long-Term Debt	10.8	10.7	10.2	17.4	16.6
	.7	.7	.3	.6	Deferred Taxes	.2	.5	.2	.3	.6
	2.7	2.2	2.4	3.9	All Other Non-Current	4.1	4.4	3.2	5.2	3.9
	32.9	35.4	27.2	28.9	Net Worth	28.3	28.1	28.5	26.3	28.9
	100.0	100.0	100.0	100.0	Total Liabilities & Net Worth	100.0	100.0	100.0	100.0	100.0
					INCOME DATA					
	100.0	100.0	100.0	100.0	Contract Revenues	100.0	100.0	100.0	100.0	100.0
	18.8	16.3	20.7	19.9	Gross Profit	17.8	19.0	20.9	19.0	19.9
	13.9	8.4	11.2	13.1	Operating Expenses	14.4	14.6	15.7	15.3	13.1
	4.9	7.9	9.5	6.8	Operating Profit	3.4	4.4	5.2	3.7	6.8
	.6	.6	-.2	1.3	All Other Expenses (net)	.3	.6	.7	.5	1.3
	4.3	7.3	9.7	5.5	Profit Before Taxes	3.2	3.8	4.5	3.2	5.5
					RATIOS					
	1.7	2.5	1.6	2.4	Current	1.8	1.8	1.9	2.4	2.4
	1.3	1.4	1.2	1.4		1.3	1.3	1.3	1.4	1.4
	1.0	1.0	1.1	1.1		1.1	1.1	1.0	1.1	1.1
	1.9	1.4	1.9	1.7	Receivables/Payables	1.9	2.0	2.4	2.4	1.7
	(31) 1.1	(10) 1.1	1.0	(58) 1.0		(154) 1.1	(198) 1.1	(99) 1.1	(65) 1.2	(58) 1.0
	.0	.0	.0	.0		.1	.5	.0	.1	.0
	0 UND	0 UND	1 245.4	0 UND	Revenues/Receivables	0 999.8	0 UND	0 UND	0 UND	0 UND
	4 85.5	15 24.2	33 10.9	2 170.6		15 24.0	22 16.9	5 71.5	11 32.0	2 170.6
	46 8.0	49 7.4	66 5.5	46 8.0		50 7.2	51 7.1	39 9.3	44 8.2	46 8.0
	5 76.1	1 268.1	31 11.9	7 52.3	Cost of Revenues/Payables	6 60.2	7 55.8	0 751.3	7 50.7	7 52.3
	22 16.7	24 15.1	53 6.9	25 14.6		25 14.8	25 14.7	20 18.5	27 13.7	25 14.6
	43 8.6	38 9.6	58 6.2	49 7.5		46 7.9	50 7.3	38 9.7	43 8.5	49 7.5
	8.5	4.9	7.4	5.7	Revenues/Working Capital	10.1	9.1	7.4	5.7	5.7
	15.1	12.7	13.0	13.0		25.0	22.3	14.3	11.8	13.0
	884.3	33.2	76.4	42.1		87.6	100.2	570.9	70.1	42.1
	26.8	47.8	113.5	40.4	EBIT/Interest	21.8	26.9	36.2	32.0	40.4
	(26) 3.8	(10) 28.2	(10) 30.2	(53) 7.9		(136) 5.9	(184) 6.7	(94) 7.3	(60) 5.8	(53) 7.9
	1.7	7.8	12.3	1.9		1.3	2.0	2.5	1.5	1.9
				7.5	Net Profit + Depr., Dep., Amort./Cur. Mat. L /T/D	6.3	7.8	7.3	5.8	7.5
				(10) 1.4		(21) 2.5	(40) 2.5	(20) 2.2	(10) 2.2	(10) 1.4
				-.9		1.4	1.2	1.1	1.0	-.9
	.1	.0	.0	.0	Fixed/Worth	.1	.1	.1	.1	.0
	.4	.2	.3	.2		.4	.3	.3	.4	.2
	1.0	.7	1.4	.9		1.1	1.1	1.4	1.4	.9
	1.1	1.1	1.5	1.5	Debt/Worth	1.3	1.3	1.3	1.2	1.5
	2.5	1.9	3.4	3.2		2.8	2.9	2.4	3.1	3.2
	4.9	7.4	4.4	5.1		8.8	7.7	12.1	8.6	5.1
	58.5	82.9	59.3	60.0	% Profit Before Taxes/Tangible Net Worth	58.7	72.0	66.4	78.6	60.0
	(36) 20.6	47.3	36.5	(65) 26.2		(151) 28.1	(207) 29.9	(110) 31.3	(69) 28.5	(65) 26.2
	7.8	20.3	22.0	8.4		9.6	9.4	12.2	4.3	8.4
	15.4	17.1	18.7	15.9	% Profit Before Taxes/Total Assets	16.6	17.2	21.1	13.0	15.9
	5.4	14.8	6.8	5.4		6.0	7.1	7.4	5.6	5.4
	1.6	4.1	3.5	1.6		1.0	1.6	2.4	1.2	1.6
	.2	.2		.2	% Depr., Dep., Amort./Revenues	.2	.3	.3	.3	.2
	(29) .7	(10) .3		(49) .5		(126) .7	(184) .7	(87) .5	(51) .5	(49) .5
	1.7	1.9		1.6		1.7	1.6	1.3	1.7	1.6
	1.7			.5	% Officers', Directors', Owners' Comp/Revenues	1.3	1.1	1.5	1.5	.5
	(17) 2.7			(27) 2.0		(85) 3.0	(112) 2.4	(60) 2.4	(38) 2.6	(27) 2.0
	4.7			3.9		6.1	6.3	6.1	3.8	3.9
5078M	175289M	288013M	2932256M	3400636M	Contract Revenues ($)	35874627M	39722064M	11567776M	921274M	3400636M
18197M	104405M	221678M	3202006M	3546286M	Total Assets ($)	12797396M	17353390M	11236050M	639806M	3546286M

M = $ thousand   MM = $ million
See Pages 11 through 21 for Explanation of Ratios and Data

Current Data Sorted By Revenue · **Comparative Historical Data**

0-1MM	1-10MM	10-50MM	50 & OVER	ALL	Type of Statement	4/1/00-3/31/01 ALL	4/1/01-3/31/02 ALL	4/1/02-3/31/03 ALL	4/1/03-3/31/04 ALL	4/1/04-3/31/05 ALL
	2	4	9	15	Unqualified	7	6	4	4	15
	20	6	4	30	Reviewed	10	6	4	8	30
2	11	6	1	20	Compiled	6	4	4	7	20
7	32	4		43	Tax Returns	6	4	2	13	43
1	13	6	4	24	Other	5	8	2	15	24
12 (4/1-9/30/04)			120 (10/1/04-3/31/05)							
10	78	26	18	132	NUMBER OF STATEMENTS	34	28	16	47	132
%	%	%	%	%	ASSETS	%	%	%	%	%
18.0	13.0	11.2	5.5	12.0	Cash & Equivalents	12.6	6.4	11.9	11.8	12.0
11.2	14.2	12.5	7.2	12.7	A/R - Progress Billings	22.9	22.6	16.0	12.9	12.7
.0	2.6	4.2	1.3	2.5	A/R - Current Retention	2.7	1.1	.1	.1	2.5
43.7	39.8	51.0	57.4	44.7	Inventory	26.1	42.6	23.5	44.2	44.7
.0	3.5	1.6	1.5	2.6	Cost & Est. Earnings In Excess of Billings	7.2	1.1	1.7	2.7	2.6
5.1	3.0	6.1	5.1	4.1	All Other Current	4.0	3.6	10.8	7.0	4.1
78.0	76.1	86.8	78.0	78.6	Total Current	75.4	77.3	64.0	78.7	78.6
12.2	15.2	7.9	12.4	13.2	Fixed Assets (net)	14.8	13.0	19.8	12.5	13.2
.2	2.0	.9	.6	1.5	Joint Ventures & Investments	1.2	1.2	2.9	1.1	1.5
.0	.1	.4	2.8	.5	Intangibles (net)	.9	.9	.0	1.0	.5
9.6	6.6	4.0	6.3	6.3	All Other Non-Current	7.6	7.5	13.3	6.8	6.3
100.0	100.0	100.0	100.0	100.0	Total	100.0	100.0	100.0	100.0	100.0
					LIABILITIES					
29.2	27.5	28.9	29.0	28.1	Notes Payable - Short Term	16.3	17.5	14.9	32.3	28.1
11.2	13.2	19.3	10.5	13.9	A/P - Trade	20.4	17.2	9.7	14.4	13.9
.0	.0	.6	.2	.2	A/P - Retention	.9	.2	.0	.1	.2
.0	2.1	2.9	.6	1.9	Billings in Excess of Costs & Est. Earnings	4.5	1.8	1.0	2.4	1.9
.0	.1	.1	.3	.1	Income Taxes Payable	.4	.2	.4	.1	.1
18.3	4.6	4.3	3.9	5.5	Cur. Mat.-L/T/D	5.7	5.4	2.9	2.0	5.5
1.0	11.7	11.3	10.1	10.6	All Other Current	5.3	11.6	7.3	8.2	10.6
59.6	59.2	67.3	54.8	60.2	Total Current	53.4	53.8	36.2	59.5	60.2
2.3	11.9	8.3	15.3	10.9	Long-Term Debt	16.7	13.7	35.0	10.9	10.9
.0	.2	.3	.2	.2	Deferred Taxes	.1	.7	1.1	.1	.2
8.2	7.4	1.8	5.4	6.1	All Other Non-Current	5.6	4.4	6.3	5.1	6.1
29.9	21.2	22.3	24.4	22.5	Net Worth	24.2	27.4	21.4	24.4	22.5
100.0	100.0	100.0	100.0	100.0	Total Liabilities & Net Worth	100.0	100.0	100.0	100.0	100.0
					INCOME DATA					
100.0	100.0	100.0	100.0	100.0	Contract Revenues	100.0	100.0	100.0	100.0	100.0
33.5	17.9	12.2	18.0	17.9	Gross Profit	17.9	24.3	25.3	22.5	17.9
28.6	12.9	8.9	10.7	13.0	Operating Expenses	20.3	17.9	20.3	15.8	13.0
4.9	4.9	3.3	7.3	4.9	Operating Profit	-2.4	6.5	5.0	6.8	4.9
1.4	.6	-.2	1.0	.6	All Other Expenses (net)	-5.3	3.2	1.8	.4	.6
3.5	4.3	3.5	6.3	4.4	Profit Before Taxes	2.9	3.3	3.2	6.3	4.4
					RATIOS					
4.9	2.0	1.6	2.3	1.8	Current	2.1	2.6	3.5	1.5	1.8
1.3	1.2	1.3	1.4	1.3		1.4	1.3	1.5	1.2	1.3
.9	1.0	1.1	1.1	1.0		1.1	1.1	1.3	1.0	1.0
	2.3	1.2	1.2	1.6	Receivables/Payables	2.4	2.2	4.3	1.8	1.6
	(61) .7	(25) .4	(17) .1	(110) .6		(31) 1.0	(27) 1.2	(14) 1.4	(37) .4	(110) .6
	.0	.0	.0	.0		.0	.0	.0	.0	.0
0 UND	0 UND	0 999.8	0 UND	0 UND	Revenues/Receivables	0 UND	0 UND	0 UND	0 UND	0 UND
0 UND	3 123.7	4 100.9	2 242.5	2 178.6		7 48.7	19 19.5	10 34.8	1 332.0	2 178.6
64 5.7	30 12.3	48 7.7	17 22.0	31 11.9		41 8.9	64 5.7	68 5.4	24 15.1	31 11.9
0 UND	0 UND	10 36.5	12 29.7	1 329.3	Cost of Revenues/Payables	10 35.0	10 35.6	3 105.8	0 UND	1 329.3
0 UND	16 23.5	35 10.5	21 17.4	19 19.1		22 16.3	41 8.9	20 18.4	18 20.1	19 19.1
93 3.9	38 9.7	47 7.7	27 13.4	40 9.2		47 7.7	70 5.2	62 5.8	39 9.5	40 9.2
1.8	7.0	8.5	4.2	6.7	Revenues/Working Capital	6.6	3.1	3.9	5.8	6.7
9.1	13.7	14.5	9.0	12.2		14.0	13.0	8.6	15.3	12.2
-104.4	-113.5	35.5	21.7	209.8		39.3	63.1	12.4	72.0	209.8
	14.0	29.3	8.7	14.6	EBIT/Interest	22.3	15.4	12.0	57.1	14.6
	(64) 4.9	(20) 10.1	(15) 5.9	(106) 5.3		(28) 5.5	(22) 2.0	(14) 2.5	(35) 4.5	(106) 5.3
	1.9	3.8	3.8	1.9		1.9	.1	.8	2.0	1.9
				5.3	Net Profit + Depr., Dep., Amort./Cur. Mat. L /T/D					5.3
			(10)	2.9					(10)	2.9
				-.5						-.5
.0	.1	.1	.1	.1	Fixed/Worth	.1	.1	.1	.1	.1
.1	.4	.2	.2	.3		.3	.3	.6	.2	.3
1.0	1.8	.6	1.5	1.2		1.8	1.8	3.9	1.1	1.2
1.6	1.2	1.4	2.1	1.5	Debt/Worth	1.4	.8	.9	2.3	1.5
1.9	3.9	4.0	3.8	3.8		3.4	3.8	3.8	4.2	3.8
5.3	27.4	20.5	5.4	17.2		17.3	7.6	8.4	22.8	17.2
	70.8	66.0	60.6	59.6	% Profit Before Taxes/Tangible Net Worth	70.7	45.3	57.5	102.3	59.6
	(65) 28.6	(25) 20.9	(16) 37.9	(115) 29.5		(29) 34.2	(25) 27.7	(15) 14.5	(41) 46.2	(115) 29.5
	9.1	12.6	26.5	10.4		16.9	1.2	-8.4	10.0	10.4
10.6	15.0	9.8	14.1	12.6	% Profit Before Taxes/Total Assets	16.8	12.9	12.7	17.8	12.6
3.9	5.3	5.5	11.0	6.1		8.9	2.5	2.0	9.3	6.1
-3.3	1.2	2.0	3.0	1.5		1.0	-2.5	-1.8	1.1	1.5
	.3	.2	.1	.3	% Depr., Dep., Amort./Revenues	.2	.2	.4	.3	.3
	(58) .8	(20) .7	(10) .3	(91) .7		(26) .6	(21) .9	(13) 1.3	(26) .6	(91) .7
	1.6	1.2	.9	1.4		1.1	3.0	4.8	2.4	1.4
	.9	.6		.8	% Officers', Directors', Owners' Comp/Revenues	2.5	.9		.8	.8
	(50) 2.4	(14) .9		(80) 2.3		(14) 5.2	(16) 3.1		(25) 2.2	(80) 2.3
	4.2	1.6		4.3		8.2	4.3		7.2	4.3
6033M	328171M	513817M	29554673M	30402694M	Contract Revenues ($)	7464190M	14059022M	143460M	6287052M	30402694M
5669M	179182M	287024M	19884995M	20356870M	Total Assets ($)	5057378M	15552412M	172552M	5675309M	20356870M

Current Data Sorted By Revenue

Comparative Historical Data

Type of Statement	0-1MM	1-10MM	10-50MM	50 & OVER	ALL		4/1/00-3/31/01	4/1/01-3/31/02	4/1/02-3/31/03	4/1/03-3/31/04	4/1/04-3/31/05
Unqualified											
Reviewed		2			2					7	2
Compiled	2	4			6					6	6
Tax Returns	6	9			15					16	15
Other	7	7			14					5	14
	6 (4/1-9/30/04)			31 (10/1/04-3/31/05)			ALL	ALL	ALL	ALL	ALL
NUMBER OF STATEMENTS	15	22			37					34	37
	%	%	%	%	%	**ASSETS**	%	%	%	%	%
Cash & Equivalents	20.3	12.0			15.4					10.8	15.4
A/R - Progress Billings	8.6	29.9			21.3					22.5	21.3
A/R - Current Retention	3.1	.0			1.3					1.3	1.3
Inventory	10.4	13.1			12.0					18.0	12.0
Cost & Est. Earnings In Excess of Billings	3.2	3.1			3.2					2.9	3.2
All Other Current	.8	9.9			6.2					10.3	6.2
Total Current	46.5	68.1			59.3					65.8	59.3
Fixed Assets (net)	44.8	16.7			28.0					19.4	28.0
Joint Ventures & Investments	.0	3.9			2.3					4.0	2.3
Intangibles (net)	4.8	1.1			2.6					.4	2.6
All Other Non-Current	4.0	10.2			7.7					10.5	7.7
Total	100.0	100.0			100.0					100.0	100.0
						LIABILITIES					
Notes Payable - Short Term	27.3	14.4			19.6					18.3	19.6
A/P - Trade	9.9	14.8			12.8					12.8	12.8
A/P - Retention	5.6	1.0			2.9					3.1	2.9
Billings in Excess of Costs & Est. Earnings	.0	3.7			2.2					1.9	2.2
Income Taxes Payable	.6	.0			.2					.2	.2
Cur. Mat.-L/T/D	2.7	10.7			7.5					7.7	7.5
All Other Current	7.4	11.4			9.8					7.0	9.8
Total Current	53.4	56.1			55.0					51.0	55.0
Long-Term Debt	20.2	13.1			16.0					17.0	16.0
Deferred Taxes	.2	.5			.4					.1	.4
All Other Non-Current	10.2	4.3			6.7					8.4	6.7
Net Worth	15.9	26.0			21.9					23.4	21.9
Total Liabilities & Net Worth	100.0	100.0			100.0					100.0	100.0
						INCOME DATA					
Contract Revenues	100.0	100.0			100.0					100.0	100.0
Gross Profit	46.8	23.4			32.9					30.9	32.9
Operating Expenses	42.4	19.4			28.8					28.1	28.8
Operating Profit	4.4	4.0			4.1					2.9	4.1
All Other Expenses (net)	.8	-.1			.3					.5	.3
Profit Before Taxes	3.5	4.1			3.9					2.3	3.9
						RATIOS					
Current	2.2	1.9			1.9					2.4	1.9
	.8	1.3			1.2					1.3	1.2
	.5	.9			.7					.9	.7
Receivables/Payables	3.3	3.2			3.0					2.7	3.0
	(10) .8	(18) 2.0		(28) 1.6					(25) 1.5	(28) 1.6
	.2	.4			.3					.3	.3
Revenues/Receivables	0 UND	0 UND		0 UND					0 UND	0 UND
	5 70.4	30 12.1		8 44.4					10 36.6	8 44.4
	29 12.6	48 7.6		43 8.5					47 7.7	43 8.5
Cost of Revenues/Payables	0 UND	2 235.3		0 UND					0 UND	0 UND
	18 20.8	17 21.4		18 20.8					15 23.8	18 20.8
	55 6.7	35 10.5		36 10.0					39 9.4	36 10.0
Revenues/Working Capital	16.5	9.2			11.8					4.8	11.8
	-187.0	35.7			50.8					24.2	50.8
	-13.7	-41.0			-18.9					-45.4	-18.9
EBIT/Interest	8.3	23.4			14.9					10.9	14.9
	(12) 2.4	(17) 6.7		(29) 4.0					(28) 6.1	(29) 4.0
	-2.4	1.3			-.8					.4	-.8
Net Profit + Depr., Dep., Amort./Cur. Mat. L /T/D											
Fixed/Worth	.8	.1			.1					.1	.1
	5.8	.3			.8					.3	.8
	-2.3	2.3			NM					7.6	NM
Debt/Worth	.8	1.1			1.0					1.0	1.0
	5.1	3.4			4.4					2.3	4.4
	-5.3	11.7			NM					64.2	NM
% Profit Before Taxes/ Tangible Net Worth		96.5			96.3					45.6	96.3
	(19) 22.8			(28) 24.3					(27) 11.8	(28) 24.3
		6.3			10.7					6.3	10.7
% Profit Before Taxes/ Total Assets	16.6	23.5			16.6					19.8	16.6
	6.5	3.8			4.2					4.7	4.2
	-15.6	-.7			-2.2					-.9	-2.2
% Depr., Dep., Amort./ Revenues		.5			.6					.2	.6
	(14) .9			(20) 1.3					(23) .7	(20) 1.3
		1.8			2.7					2.3	2.7
% Officers', Directors', Owners' Comp/Revenues		3.2			4.2					2.4	4.2
	(12) 4.9			(21) 6.3					(26) 4.8	(21) 6.3
		6.2			9.8					10.5	9.8
Contract Revenues ($)	8021M	75342M			83363M					103126M	83363M
Total Assets ($)	4319M	40497M			44816M					52693M	44816M

Note: Columns for 10-50MM and 50 & OVER (current) and 4/1/00-3/31/01, 4/1/01-3/31/02, 4/1/02-3/31/03 (historical) are marked "DATA NOT AVAILABLE".

© RMA 2005

M = $ thousand   MM = $ million
See Pages 11 through 21 for Explanation of Ratios and Data

Current Data Sorted By Revenue   **Comparative Historical Data**

Current data periods: 42 (4/1-9/30/04) · 142 (10/1/04-3/31/05)

0-1MM	1-10MM	10-50MM	50 & OVER	ALL	Type of Statement	4/1/00-3/31/01	4/1/01-3/31/02	4/1/02-3/31/03	4/1/03-3/31/04	4/1/04-3/31/05
1	14	24	18	57	Unqualified	165	96	63	55	57
3	40	20	2	65	Reviewed	211	158	105	58	65
2	8	2	1	13	Compiled	39	23	5	12	13
5	15	1		21	Tax Returns	17	13	16	11	21
2	13	6	7	28	Other	60	31	25	14	28

0-1MM	1-10MM	10-50MM	50 & OVER	ALL		4/1/00-3/31/01 ALL	4/1/01-3/31/02 ALL	4/1/02-3/31/03 ALL	4/1/03-3/31/04 ALL	4/1/04-3/31/05 ALL
13	90	53	28	184	**NUMBER OF STATEMENTS**	492	321	214	150	184
%	%	%	%	%	**ASSETS**	%	%	%	%	%
14.6	16.7	18.3	15.3	16.8	Cash & Equivalents	19.3	19.3	20.8	20.7	16.8
36.8	36.3	42.3	39.2	38.5	A/R - Progress Billings	39.9	39.3	38.8	36.6	38.5
.0	1.9	4.8	5.6	3.2	A/R - Current Retention	5.1	4.9	3.9	3.6	3.2
3.4	5.4	1.9	5.3	4.2	Inventory	2.0	1.6	2.1	1.0	4.2
3.4	5.5	5.2	6.9	5.5	Cost & Est. Earnings In Excess of Billings	5.2	4.5	4.8	4.6	5.5
4.1	3.9	5.4	5.6	4.6	All Other Current	4.2	5.3	5.9	8.2	4.6
62.3	69.6	77.8	77.9	72.7	Total Current	75.7	75.0	76.4	74.6	72.7
18.1	21.2	13.9	13.5	17.7	Fixed Assets (net)	14.7	15.5	15.0	16.5	17.7
.0	.7	1.7	2.6	1.2	Joint Ventures & Investments	1.9	1.8	1.1	1.7	1.2
1.4	.8	.3	.8	.7	Intangibles (net)	1.7	1.6	.5	.9	.7
18.1	7.6	6.3	5.2	7.6	All Other Non-Current	5.9	6.2	7.1	6.3	7.6
100.0	100.0	100.0	100.0	100.0	Total	100.0	100.0	100.0	100.0	100.0
					LIABILITIES					
6.4	6.4	4.3	7.0	5.9	Notes Payable - Short Term	5.6	6.4	7.6	5.6	5.9
27.3	24.5	30.6	27.6	26.9	A/P - Trade	30.9	30.1	30.1	28.5	26.9
.3	1.2	2.9	2.5	1.8	A/P - Retention	2.8	2.5	1.8	2.6	1.8
2.1	5.2	7.2	8.9	6.1	Billings in Excess of Costs & Est. Earnings	7.7	7.1	8.1	6.6	6.1
.1	.4	.2	.3	.3	Income Taxes Payable	.5	.4	.4	.3	.3
10.2	3.6	1.8	1.3	3.2	Cur. Mat.-L/T/D	2.4	2.2	2.2	2.4	3.2
14.6	5.8	7.0	12.1	7.7	All Other Current	7.2	7.8	8.9	7.4	7.7
61.0	47.2	54.0	59.8	52.0	Total Current	57.1	56.5	59.0	53.3	52.0
24.5	12.3	5.4	8.1	10.5	Long-Term Debt	6.4	6.8	7.1	8.8	10.5
.0	.7	.8	.8	.7	Deferred Taxes	.8	.5	.2	.5	.7
2.1	3.7	1.1	2.9	2.7	All Other Non-Current	3.2	3.1	2.2	2.7	2.7
12.4	36.2	38.7	28.4	34.0	Net Worth	32.6	33.0	31.5	34.7	34.0
100.0	100.0	100.0	100.0	100.0	Total Liabilities & Net Worth	100.0	100.0	100.0	100.0	100.0
					INCOME DATA					
100.0	100.0	100.0	100.0	100.0	Contract Revenues	100.0	100.0	100.0	100.0	100.0
31.4	18.0	11.9	8.6	15.8	Gross Profit	13.9	15.0	15.4	15.3	15.8
35.1	16.2	9.1	6.8	14.1	Operating Expenses	12.0	12.7	13.9	13.7	14.1
-3.7	1.8	2.8	1.8	1.7	Operating Profit	1.9	2.3	1.5	1.6	1.7
.1	.2	-.2	.2	.0	All Other Expenses (net)	-.1	.0	.3	.0	.0
-3.8	1.6	3.1	1.6	1.6	Profit Before Taxes	2.0	2.4	1.2	1.5	1.6

RATIOS

0-1MM	1-10MM	10-50MM	50 & OVER	ALL		4/1/00-3/31/01	4/1/01-3/31/02	4/1/02-3/31/03	4/1/03-3/31/04	4/1/04-3/31/05
1.5	1.9	1.8	1.6	1.8	Current	1.8	1.8	1.7	2.0	1.8
1.1	1.5	1.4	1.2	1.4		1.3	1.3	1.3	1.4	1.4
.6	1.2	1.2	1.2	1.2		1.1	1.1	1.1	1.1	1.2
2.2	2.8	2.4	2.7	2.6	Receivables/Payables	2.0	2.1	2.2	2.0	2.6
(12) 1.3	(84) 1.6	(27) 1.4	1.6	(176) 1.5		(478) 1.3	(312) 1.4	(207) 1.3	(146) 1.3	(176) 1.5
.2	1.0	1.0	1.0	1.0		1.1	1.0	1.0	1.0	1.0
0 UND	23 16.2	35 10.5	41 9.0	29 12.7	Revenues/Receivables	34 10.8	29 12.6	33 11.1	27 13.7	29 12.7
47 7.8	41 8.8	52 7.1	61 6.0	50 7.3		50 7.3	48 7.6	45 8.1	45 8.1	50 7.3
62 5.9	69 5.3	70 5.2	74 4.9	70 5.2		69 5.3	67 5.5	66 5.6	70 5.3	70 5.2
6 56.3	14 25.3	21 17.2	26 13.8	17 21.9	Cost of Revenues/Payables	25 14.6	23 16.1	22 16.3	21 17.4	17 21.9
43 8.5	29 12.6	39 9.3	37 9.9	33 11.2		42 8.7	38 9.7	38 9.6	38 9.7	33 11.2
73 5.0	62 5.9	51 5.2	58 6.3	58 6.3		58 6.3	57 6.4	55 6.6	59 6.2	58 6.3
16.9	7.1	10.5	9.0	8.8	Revenues/Working Capital	9.5	9.5	9.4	7.2	8.8
28.5	15.0	18.7	21.5	17.1		18.9	20.2	17.5	17.2	17.1
-11.8	33.6	29.3	35.6	33.7		44.4	59.9	47.5	44.2	33.7
	22.9	84.0	23.8	28.4	EBIT/Interest	22.9	19.5	17.3	27.3	28.4
	(70) 4.5	(44) 22.4	(22) 11.9	(145) 8.3		(405) 5.5	(261) 6.3	(167) 6.6	(116) 6.6	(145) 8.3
	.3	6.3	4.4	1.9		1.3	1.9	1.3	.3	1.9
	5.0	12.4	10.3	6.7	Net Profit + Depr., Dep., Amort./Cur. Mat. L /T/D	7.8	8.3	10.8	9.2	6.7
	(23) 3.2	(15) 3.2	(12) 2.5	(50) 3.0		(150) 3.4	(95) 3.1	(70) 3.3	(39) 3.6	(50) 3.0
	.8	.9	2.2	1.1		1.6	.3	1.0	1.3	1.1
.2	.2	.1	.1	.2	Fixed/Worth	.2	.2	.1	.1	.2
.8	.5	.3	.5	.4		.3	.3	.3	.3	.4
-3.3	1.0	.5	.7	.8		.7	.8	.6	.7	.8
1.7	.9	1.0	2.2	1.1	Debt/Worth	1.0	1.1	1.0	.9	1.1
6.5	1.6	1.8	2.7	2.0		2.3	2.3	2.0	1.8	2.0
-5.7	3.8	3.7	3.9	4.0		4.1	4.4	3.8	4.8	4.0
	37.7	38.9	26.4	35.0	% Profit Before Taxes/Tangible Net Worth	40.9	40.3	35.4	32.3	35.0
	(82) 11.7	27.7	(27) 23.3	(171) 18.6		(463) 17.5	(301) 19.5	(196) 13.7	(138) 14.6	(171) 18.6
	-3.3	13.3	6.4	3.2		4.8	4.8	1.9	.1	3.2
6.3	12.2	15.2	6.6	11.2	% Profit Before Taxes/Total Assets	11.1	13.3	9.9	10.9	11.2
-2.6	4.3	8.1	5.0	5.4		5.1	5.0	4.1	3.6	5.4
-18.0	-2.1	3.1	1.4	.2		1.0	.9	.5	-.9	.2
.5	.6	.3	.2	.4	% Depr., Dep., Amort./Revenues	.4	.3	.3	.4	.4
(10) .6	(79) .9	(48) .6	(21) .5	(158) .8		(435) .7	(292) .7	(191) .7	(117) .8	(158) .8
3.1	2.5	1.0	2.3	2.1		1.6	1.4	1.4	2.0	2.1
	1.7	.3		.9	% Officers', Directors', Owners' Comp/Revenues	1.1	1.1	1.2	.9	.9
	(46) 2.7	(20) 1.0		(81) 2.2		(232) 1.9	(169) 2.3	(112) 2.0	(80) 1.7	(81) 2.2
	3.7	2.6		3.5		3.9	4.2	4.4	3.5	3.5
8648M	438403M	1285704M	5930440M	7663195M	Contract Revenues ($)	52677626M	21846236M	5749700M	3685322M	7663195M
3417M	172143M	438994M	2995723M	3610277M	Total Assets ($)	18762339M	7538701M	2173121M	1282195M	3610277M

Current Data Sorted By Revenue   **Comparative Historical Data**

					Type of Statement					
1	20	57	41	119	Unqualified	130	100	124	96	119
10	122	78	4	214	Reviewed	147	135	225	156	214
4	20	5	2	31	Compiled	35	22	48	35	31
17	20	1	2	40	Tax Returns	22	19	49	36	40
5	38	20	9	72	Other	41	44	75	42	72

102 (4/1-9/30/04)   374 (10/1/04-3/31/05)

0-1MM	1-10MM	10-50MM	50 & OVER	ALL		4/1/00-3/31/01 ALL	4/1/01-3/31/02 ALL	4/1/02-3/31/03 ALL	4/1/03-3/31/04 ALL	4/1/04-3/31/05 ALL
37	220	161	58	476	**NUMBER OF STATEMENTS**	375	320	521	365	476
%	%	%	%	%	**ASSETS**	%	%	%	%	%
18.4	19.7	20.4	18.0	19.6	Cash & Equivalents	18.8	19.6	19.1	19.3	19.6
18.1	40.8	45.1	42.7	40.7	A/R - Progress Billings	40.7	39.8	36.6	37.6	40.7
.0	1.9	6.5	7.5	4.0	A/R - Current Retention	5.1	3.5	2.8	3.5	4.0
5.1	3.1	1.4	4.6	2.9	Inventory	1.3	1.3	4.7	4.4	2.9
.7	5.5	5.5	4.2	5.0	Cost & Est. Earnings In Excess of Billings	4.8	4.5	5.0	5.0	5.0
6.1	5.6	6.7	8.4	6.3	All Other Current	6.1	8.2	8.3	7.0	6.3
48.5	76.5	85.5	85.3	78.4	Total Current	76.9	77.0	76.4	76.8	78.4
37.2	15.6	8.9	9.6	14.3	Fixed Assets (net)	14.0	14.9	14.9	15.2	14.3
1.4	1.0	1.5	2.0	1.3	Joint Ventures & Investments	1.8	1.1	1.4	.9	1.3
.9	.6	.2	.3	.5	Intangibles (net)	1.7	2.0	.6	.6	.5
12.0	6.3	3.8	2.8	5.5	All Other Non-Current	5.6	5.0	6.7	6.6	5.5
100.0	100.0	100.0	100.0	100.0	Total	100.0	100.0	100.0	100.0	100.0
					LIABILITIES					
23.6	9.2	3.2	2.0	7.4	Notes Payable - Short Term	6.7	6.1	9.2	9.7	7.4
7.7	29.2	38.1	37.0	31.5	A/P - Trade	32.9	31.6	29.3	29.4	31.5
.0	.8	3.4	8.3	2.6	A/P - Retention	3.5	1.8	1.6	2.0	2.6
2.7	5.7	9.6	10.3	7.3	Billings in Excess of Costs & Est. Earnings	8.6	7.4	7.0	6.7	7.3
.0	.3	.4	.1	.3	Income Taxes Payable	.4	.5	.3	.3	.3
3.2	3.2	1.1	1.2	2.3	Cur. Mat.-L/T/D	2.3	3.3	2.4	2.9	2.3
11.9	7.6	8.3	11.1	8.6	All Other Current	6.7	9.1	10.0	8.3	8.6
49.1	56.1	64.1	70.0	59.9	Total Current	61.1	60.0	59.7	59.3	59.9
26.8	7.8	3.3	4.6	7.4	Long-Term Debt	7.3	7.3	9.4	7.9	7.4
.0	.6	.5	.2	.5	Deferred Taxes	.7	.7	.6	.4	.5
5.6	3.3	2.3	1.7	2.9	All Other Non-Current	1.7	1.8	3.5	2.2	2.9
18.4	32.3	29.8	23.4	29.3	Net Worth	29.2	30.2	26.8	30.1	29.3
100.0	100.0	100.0	100.0	100.0	Total Liabilities & Net Worth	100.0	100.0	100.0	100.0	100.0
					INCOME DATA					
100.0	100.0	100.0	100.0	100.0	Contract Revenues	100.0	100.0	100.0	100.0	100.0
39.1	19.3	11.1	7.7	16.7	Gross Profit	13.9	14.4	15.9	16.1	16.7
35.2	17.2	9.0	6.8	14.6	Operating Expenses	12.0	12.2	13.6	14.7	14.6
3.9	2.1	2.1	.9	2.1	Operating Profit	1.9	2.1	2.2	1.4	2.1
−.5	.0	−.1	−.5	−.1	All Other Expenses (net)	−.2	.1	.3	.1	−.1
4.4	2.1	2.2	1.4	2.2	Profit Before Taxes	2.2	2.0	2.0	1.3	2.2
					RATIOS					
3.1	2.0	1.6	1.3	1.8	Current	1.6	1.7	1.8	1.8	1.8
1.3	1.4	1.3	1.2	1.3		1.3	1.3	1.3	1.3	1.3
.6	1.1	1.2	1.1	1.1		1.1	1.1	1.1	1.1	1.1
7.5	3.1	1.7	1.4	2.2	Receivables/Payables	1.9	2.0	1.9	2.1	2.2
(28) 2.6	(214) 1.4	1.2	1.2	(461) 1.3		(363) 1.3	(311) 1.3	(499) 1.3	(346) 1.3	(461) 1.3
.8	.9	.9	.9	.9		.9	.9	.8	.9	.9
0 UND	29 12.4	37 9.9	47 7.7	31 11.9	Revenues/Receivables	34 10.8	27 13.4	21 17.6	29 12.7	31 11.9
23 15.9	47 7.8	53 6.9	58 6.3	50 7.3		50 7.3	48 7.5	45 8.1	47 7.8	50 7.3
58 6.3	69 5.3	69 5.3	72 5.1	70 5.2		71 5.1	65 5.6	65 5.6	68 5.4	70 5.2
0 UND	19 19.4	31 11.6	44 8.2	24 15.5	Cost of Revenues/Payables	26 14.1	22 16.5	20 18.0	22 16.5	24 15.5
19 18.9	37 9.8	46 8.0	55 6.6	42 8.8		44 8.4	42 8.8	38 9.5	40 9.0	42 8.8
38 9.6	56 6.5	64 5.7	73 5.0	62 5.9		65 5.6	65 5.6	57 6.4	60 6.1	62 5.9
5.4	7.7	10.9	15.3	9.5	Revenues/Working Capital	10.4	10.4	9.4	8.4	9.5
23.2	14.2	17.9	24.7	17.6		21.4	21.3	19.5	16.2	17.6
−17.6	70.1	28.9	46.5	44.5		57.1	61.8	72.1	51.0	44.5
7.7	18.8	56.1	52.5	25.8	EBIT/Interest	26.3	20.0	15.8	21.0	25.8
(31) 2.6	(180) 6.1	(118) 14.8	(37) 9.9	(366) 7.1		(306) 7.6	(251) 6.4	(409) 5.5	(285) 5.9	(366) 7.1
−.3	−.1	3.2	4.1	1.5		2.0	2.0	1.2	.3	1.5
	6.2	11.0	57.8	9.8	Net Profit + Depr., Dep., Amort./Cur. Mat. L/T/D	10.1	8.9	7.9	10.1	9.8
	(53) 2.6	(48) 3.6	(14) 19.5	(119) 3.2		(113) 3.6	(96) 4.0	(146) 3.3	(105) 2.7	(119) 3.2
	.7	2.0	5.0	1.1		1.0	1.6	.9	.4	1.1
.4	.1	.1	.1	.1	Fixed/Worth	.1	.1	.1	.1	.1
1.0	.3	.2	.3	.3		.3	.3	.3	.3	.3
6.6	.9	.5	.5	.7		.7	.9	.8	.8	.7
.9	.9	1.4	2.6	1.2	Debt/Worth	1.4	1.2	1.2	1.1	1.2
2.9	1.8	2.4	3.8	2.4		2.6	2.6	2.6	2.2	2.4
29.5	4.9	4.3	5.8	5.0		5.3	4.9	5.9	4.9	5.0
51.4	41.9	35.9	30.3	37.6	% Profit Before Taxes/Tangible Net Worth	49.2	38.7	41.0	33.4	37.6
(30) 17.7	(196) 14.2	(157) 22.8	23.1	(441) 19.3		(344) 25.8	(291) 18.7	(482) 15.9	(334) 14.8	(441) 19.3
−7.4	−2.5	6.1	8.8	2.2		7.7	6.7	2.0	.9	2.2
22.9	13.8	12.8	6.4	11.9	% Profit Before Taxes/Total Assets	13.8	11.9	11.3	11.0	11.9
6.8	4.5	5.8	3.7	4.7		6.0	5.5	4.1	3.8	4.7
−.3	−1.9	1.8	1.5	.6		1.9	1.3	.4	−.2	.6
1.1	.5	.2	.2	.3	% Depr., Dep., Amort./Revenues	.3	.3	.3	.3	.3
(29) 4.5	(184) .9	(147) .3	(47) .3	(407) .6		(329) .5	(289) .6	(444) .6	(281) .7	(407) .6
8.9	1.5	.7	.5	1.3		1.2	1.4	1.4	1.4	1.3
3.1	1.8	.9	.3	1.2	% Officers', Directors', Owners' Comp/Revenues	1.2	1.2	1.3	1.5	1.2
(17) 6.2	(131) 3.1	(85) 1.7	(18) .5	(251) 2.5		(167) 2.7	(157) 2.7	(265) 2.5	(202) 2.7	(251) 2.5
10.7	5.8	3.1	1.5	4.4		4.7	4.9	4.7	5.3	4.4
20678M	981523M	3270738M	80963947M	85236886M	Contract Revenues ($)	73625045M	10857941M	35950833M	26791082M	85236886M
15651M	336720M	996064M	29704218M	31052653M	Total Assets ($)	22296859M	3526496M	13236457M	8586482M	31052653M

M = $ thousand   MM = $ million
See Pages 11 through 21 for Explanation of Ratios and Data

Current Data Sorted By Revenue   **Comparative Historical Data**

Type of Statement	0-1MM	1-10MM	10-50MM	50 & OVER	ALL		4/1/00-3/31/01	4/1/01-3/31/02	4/1/02-3/31/03	4/1/03-3/31/04	4/1/04-3/31/05
Unqualified		12	11	5	28		74	45	48	34	28
Reviewed	5	44	14	1	64		94	71	71	48	64
Compiled	4	7	2		13		24	18	19	16	13
Tax Returns	5	9			14		11	15	21	9	14
Other	1	11	4		16		21	33	20	16	16

27 (4/1-9/30/04)   108 (10/1/04-3/31/05)

	0-1MM	1-10MM	10-50MM	50 & OVER	ALL		4/1/00-3/31/01 ALL	4/1/01-3/31/02 ALL	4/1/02-3/31/03 ALL	4/1/03-3/31/04 ALL	4/1/04-3/31/05 ALL
NUMBER OF STATEMENTS	15	83	31	6	135		224	182	179	123	135
ASSETS	%	%	%	%	%		%	%	%	%	%
Cash & Equivalents	20.0	18.3	17.1		17.9		13.2	14.4	13.6	14.1	17.9
A/R - Progress Billings	23.0	29.3	32.8		29.4		30.5	28.0	30.1	32.1	29.4
A/R - Current Retention	1.8	2.2	3.2		2.6		2.7	1.9	1.5	1.9	2.6
Inventory	5.7	3.7	.9		3.2		1.5	2.3	2.3	3.1	3.2
Cost & Est. Earnings In Excess of Billings	.1	2.8	5.6		3.3		4.3	3.7	3.1	3.1	3.3
All Other Current	2.0	4.2	7.8		4.7		3.8	4.9	5.1	4.7	4.7
Total Current	52.6	60.5	67.5		61.1		56.0	55.2	55.7	59.0	61.1
Fixed Assets (net)	33.4	32.6	28.6		32.0		34.5	36.3	35.6	32.2	32.0
Joint Ventures & Investments	.0	.6	.3		.6		2.3	1.1	1.7	.7	.6
Intangibles (net)	.1	.5	.4		.4		1.7	1.9	1.4	1.4	.4
All Other Non-Current	13.9	5.7	3.3		5.9		5.5	5.6	5.6	6.7	5.9
Total	100.0	100.0	100.0		100.0		100.0	100.0	100.0	100.0	100.0
LIABILITIES											
Notes Payable - Short Term	10.4	6.5	5.1		6.6		7.3	7.3	7.9	8.6	6.6
A/P - Trade	10.6	14.7	22.2		16.0		14.0	14.0	14.9	17.5	16.0
A/P - Retention	.0	.1	1.2		.5		.6	.2	.1	.5	.5
Billings in Excess of Costs & Est. Earnings	.1	3.2	5.8		3.6		3.1	3.0	2.9	3.0	3.6
Income Taxes Payable	.5	.3	.3		.3		.8	.4	.3	.4	.3
Cur. Mat.-L/T/D	15.7	6.3	4.5		6.8		5.9	6.3	7.0	7.9	6.8
All Other Current	13.6	3.6	5.2		5.4		5.1	5.5	6.1	6.5	5.4
Total Current	51.0	34.7	44.3		39.2		36.8	36.8	39.2	44.4	39.2
Long-Term Debt	37.1	14.6	9.3		16.0		13.4	15.6	19.2	17.8	16.0
Deferred Taxes	.1	1.1	1.8		1.3		1.8	1.4	1.3	1.3	1.3
All Other Non-Current	7.8	2.1	2.0		2.7		3.0	2.7	3.4	3.7	2.7
Net Worth	4.0	47.6	42.6		40.8		45.1	43.5	36.9	32.8	40.8
Total Liabilities & Net Worth	100.0	100.0	100.0		100.0		100.0	100.0	100.0	100.0	100.0
INCOME DATA											
Contract Revenues	100.0	100.0	100.0		100.0		100.0	100.0	100.0	100.0	100.0
Gross Profit	53.4	28.6	15.2		27.7		25.4	28.8	28.8	27.6	27.7
Operating Expenses	47.9	23.5	13.4		23.5		19.8	23.6	25.4	25.0	23.5
Operating Profit	5.5	5.1	1.8		4.2		5.6	5.1	3.3	2.6	4.2
All Other Expenses (net)	1.3	.1	-.1		.2		.1	.5	.5	.8	.2
Profit Before Taxes	4.2	5.0	1.9		4.1		5.5	4.6	2.8	1.8	4.1

RATIOS

	0-1MM	1-10MM	10-50MM	50 & OVER	ALL		4/1/00-3/31/01	4/1/01-3/31/02	4/1/02-3/31/03	4/1/03-3/31/04	4/1/04-3/31/05
Current	2.5 / 1.9 / .6	2.5 / 1.6 / 1.3	2.0 / 1.5 / 1.2		2.3 / 1.6 / 1.2		2.5 / 1.6 / 1.1	2.6 / 1.4 / 1.1	2.5 / 1.5 / 1.1	1.9 / 1.4 / 1.1	2.3 / 1.6 / 1.2
Receivables/Payables	8.4 / (11) 2.7 / 1.5	3.3 / (81) 2.4 / 1.4	2.6 / (30) 1.6 / 1.3		3.2 / (128) 2.2 / 1.4		4.3 / (217) 2.6 / 1.5	4.7 / (173) 2.3 / 1.3	4.4 / (172) 2.1 / 1.3	4.4 / (122) 2.1 / 1.3	3.2 / (128) 2.2 / 1.4
Revenues/Receivables	0 UND / 32 11.5 / 70 5.2	31 11.7 / 53 6.9 / 73 5.0	42 8.8 / 56 6.5 / 75 4.8		31 11.6 / 53 6.9 / 73 5.0		35 10.3 / 53 6.9 / 77 4.8	30 12.2 / 49 7.5 / 71 5.1	27 13.7 / 51 7.2 / 70 5.2	32 11.6 / 55 6.6 / 79 4.6	31 11.6 / 53 6.9 / 73 5.0
Cost of Revenues/Payables	0 UND / 25 14.3 / 100 3.7	14 26.4 / 32 11.6 / 51 7.2	25 14.7 / 46 7.9 / 62 5.9		16 23.4 / 34 10.8 / 55 6.7		12 30.0 / 25 14.5 / 44 8.3	14 26.5 / 28 13.0 / 50 7.3	12 30.3 / 30 12.3 / 48 7.6	14 25.5 / 35 10.5 / 62 5.9	16 23.4 / 34 10.8 / 55 6.7
Revenues/Working Capital	5.9 / 17.7 / -27.8	5.7 / 10.1 / 23.9	6.0 / 12.2 / 30.6		6.2 / 11.1 / 24.8		5.6 / 10.6 / 51.6	6.0 / 12.4 / 66.1	6.2 / 12.2 / 67.6	6.6 / 13.3 / 45.4	6.2 / 11.1 / 24.8
EBIT/Interest	5.0 / (12) 2.2 / -.7	23.2 / (67) 5.2 / 1.7	20.1 / 6.8 / 2.9		18.2 / (116) 5.1 / 1.8		12.7 / (204) 5.3 / 2.1	13.4 / (161) 4.1 / 1.1	9.9 / (159) 3.3 / .6	13.7 / (115) 3.5 / .3	18.2 / (116) 5.1 / 1.8
Net Profit + Depr., Dep., Amort./Cur. Mat. L /T/D		3.8 / (28) 2.3 / .9	4.5 / (18) 2.3 / 1.5		3.8 / (52) 2.2 / 1.1		4.8 / (80) 2.6 / 1.5	5.3 / (61) 2.0 / 1.0	6.0 / (71) 1.9 / 1.0	3.5 / (40) 2.0 / .9	3.8 / (52) 2.2 / 1.1
Fixed/Worth	.3 / 1.9 / -2.5	.3 / .6 / 1.4	.3 / .6 / 1.2		.4 / .7 / 1.4		.5 / .7 / 1.3	.5 / .8 / 1.6	.5 / .9 / 1.7	.4 / .8 / 1.7	.4 / .7 / 1.4
Debt/Worth	.7 / 5.1 / -5.3	.6 / 1.2 / 2.0	1.0 / 1.4 / 2.6		.7 / 1.5 / 2.7		.6 / 1.2 / 2.6	.6 / 1.3 / 3.1	.7 / 1.6 / 3.6	.8 / 1.6 / 3.4	.7 / 1.5 / 2.7
% Profit Before Taxes/Tangible Net Worth	192.5 / (10) 55.3 / 12.7	35.8 / (81) 19.1 / 2.2	34.8 / 13.7 / 2.8		37.1 / (128) 18.0 / 2.3		40.6 / (214) 18.9 / 6.3	39.9 / (173) 17.1 / 1.2	37.6 / (166) 13.6 / 2.1	36.7 / (110) 11.9 / -.2	37.1 / (128) 18.0 / 2.3
% Profit Before Taxes/Total Assets	33.3 / 8.2 / .0	18.5 / 7.7 / 1.1	11.9 / 6.7 / 2.0		15.9 / 6.8 / .9		18.1 / 9.1 / 2.7	17.4 / 6.6 / .4	12.2 / 5.4 / .3	13.5 / 3.8 / -2.4	15.9 / 6.8 / .9
% Depr., Dep., Amort./Revenues		2.6 / (73) 4.2 / 6.3	1.7 / (30) 2.4 / 3.7		2.0 / (117) 3.4 / 5.5		2.0 / (200) 3.8 / 6.1	2.6 / (165) 4.0 / 6.4	2.0 / (158) 3.8 / 6.7	2.2 / (99) 4.9 / 6.9	2.0 / (117) 3.4 / 5.5
% Officers', Directors', Owners' Comp/Revenues	7.2 / (10) 10.0 / 17.0	1.5 / (53) 3.9 / 6.7	.9 / (13) 1.2 / 3.3		1.2 / (79) 3.7 / 7.2		1.8 / (93) 4.0 / 7.0	1.8 / (94) 3.6 / 6.9	1.8 / (89) 3.4 / 7.0	1.4 / (65) 3.1 / 7.4	1.2 / (79) 3.7 / 7.2
Contract Revenues ($)	8041M	383927M	588050M	520975M	1500993M		35114503M	2994279M	2538233M	1212617M	1500993M
Total Assets ($)	3420M	180644M	286363M	353547M	823974M		18785966M	1734394M	1472019M	595632M	823974M

M = $ thousand   MM = $ million
See Pages 11 through 21 for Explanation of Ratios and Data

Current Data Sorted By Revenue   **Comparative Historical Data**

					Type of Statement					
2	3	3	8	16	Unqualified			14	10	16
5	14	5	1	25	Reviewed			26	17	25
9	16	6	3	34	Compiled			24	17	34
43	52	4	1	100	Tax Returns			53	51	100
13	26	13	9	61	Other			59	20	61

19 (4/1-9/30/04)		217 (10/1/04-3/31/05)				4/1/00-3/31/01	4/1/01-3/31/02	4/1/02-3/31/03	4/1/03-3/31/04	4/1/04-3/31/05
0-1MM	1-10MM	10-50MM	50 & OVER	ALL		ALL	ALL	ALL	ALL	ALL
72	111	31	22	236	NUMBER OF STATEMENTS			176	115	236
%	%	%	%	%	ASSETS	%	%	%	%	%
7.7	8.0	6.1	9.3	7.8	Cash & Equivalents	D	D	7.9	6.4	7.8
1.6	3.3	8.0	8.2	3.8	A/R - Progress Billings	A	A	4.8	3.3	3.8
.0	1.1	1.6	.1	.7	A/R - Current Retention	T	T	.2	.7	.7
28.1	49.1	38.6	35.0	40.0	Inventory	A	A	34.0	45.3	40.0
1.3	1.1	.2	1.5	1.1	Cost & Est. Earnings In Excess of Billings			.3	1.8	1.1
3.8	3.1	8.9	2.3	4.0	All Other Current	N	N	4.8	4.0	4.0
42.5	65.7	63.4	56.3	57.5	Total Current	O	O	52.1	61.5	57.5
38.5	18.5	15.3	23.4	24.6	Fixed Assets (net)	T	T	32.5	28.4	24.6
5.6	3.3	3.4	7.3	4.4	Joint Ventures & Investments			5.6	3.1	4.4
.8	.7	.2	2.1	.8	Intangibles (net)	A	A	.5	.4	.8
12.6	11.7	17.7	10.8	12.7	All Other Non-Current	V	V	9.3	6.6	12.7
100.0	100.0	100.0	100.0	100.0	Total	A	A	100.0	100.0	100.0
					LIABILITIES	I	I			
26.5	23.0	24.7	13.3	23.4	Notes Payable - Short Term	L	L	16.1	22.7	23.4
4.4	4.6	6.1	9.8	5.2	A/P - Trade	A	A	8.3	5.4	5.2
.0	.8	.8	.0	.5	A/P - Retention	B	B	1.1	.4	.5
.1	.1	.7	1.4	.3	Billings in Excess of Costs & Est. Earnings	L	L	.5	.8	.3
.1	.1	.0	.3	.1	Income Taxes Payable	E	E	.1	.0	.1
3.6	4.2	1.9	2.8	3.6	Cur. Mat.-L/T/D			2.7	4.5	3.6
5.1	5.9	7.3	4.6	5.7	All Other Current			8.6	6.9	5.7
39.8	38.6	41.5	32.2	38.8	Total Current			37.3	40.7	38.8
32.7	21.9	20.4	24.2	25.2	Long-Term Debt			36.1	26.9	25.2
.0	.1	.4	.9	.1	Deferred Taxes			.2	.3	.1
12.0	8.8	15.5	7.1	10.5	All Other Non-Current			7.4	6.7	10.5
15.5	30.7	22.3	35.6	25.4	Net Worth			19.0	25.4	25.4
100.0	100.0	100.0	100.0	100.0	Total Liabilities & Net Worth			100.0	100.0	100.0
					INCOME DATA					
100.0	100.0	100.0	100.0	100.0	Contract Revenues			100.0	100.0	100.0
					Gross Profit					
78.7	86.4	88.8	85.9	84.3	Operating Expenses			82.6	86.6	84.3
21.3	13.6	11.2	14.1	15.7	Operating Profit			17.4	13.4	15.7
8.7	1.2	2.7	1.4	3.7	All Other Expenses (net)			6.0	5.4	3.7
12.6	12.4	8.5	12.7	12.0	Profit Before Taxes			11.3	8.0	12.0
					RATIOS					
3.1	4.3	2.6	5.4	3.6	Current			3.4	4.4	3.6
1.1	1.6	1.4	1.6	1.4				1.4	1.3	1.4
.1	1.0	1.1	1.1	.8				.8	.8	.8
1.4	1.9	1.9	2.1	1.8	Receivables/Payables			1.3	1.0	1.8
(37) .0	(83) .0	(28) .1	(20) .4	(168) .1		(141) .2	(79) .0			(168) .1
.0	.0	.0	.0	.0				.0	.0	.0
0 UND	0 UND	0 UND	0 UND	0 UND	Revenues/Receivables			0 UND	0 UND	0 UND
0 UND	0 UND	1 482.8	9 40.0	0 UND		1 580.5	0 UND			0 UND
2 226.8	8 46.3	48 7.6	36 10.1	9 40.5		16 22.9	7 49.6			9 40.5
					Cost of Revenues/Payables					
1.2	1.5	1.9	2.0	1.6	Revenues/Working Capital			1.8	1.6	1.6
26.4	4.9	8.0	5.2	7.3				8.5	6.8	7.3
-1.2	-737.0	53.2	NM	-18.9				-11.5	-36.9	-18.9
12.8	12.1	9.4	11.2	11.9	EBIT/Interest			13.9	11.8	11.9
(41) 3.3	(81) 6.3	(25) 3.8	(17) 6.5	(164) 5.1		(119) 4.1	(73) 3.4			(164) 5.1
.9	1.6	1.9	3.2	1.6				1.4	1.3	1.6
				2.6	Net Profit + Depr., Dep., Amort./Cur. Mat. L /T/D					2.6
			(11) 1.6						(11) 1.6	
				1.0						1.0
.0	.0	.0	.0	.0	Fixed/Worth			.0	.0	.0
1.0	.2	.3	.2	.2				.6	.5	.2
17.8	1.0	1.7	1.5	2.6				5.2	4.0	2.6
1.3	.9	2.0	1.4	1.2	Debt/Worth			1.3	1.6	1.2
8.0	3.0	4.3	2.5	3.4				4.5	4.3	3.4
UND	8.5	14.7	5.3	13.5				18.5	21.0	13.5
95.0	68.6	62.5	53.5	66.2	% Profit Before Taxes/ Tangible Net Worth			61.6	65.9	66.2
(55) 25.6	(104) 31.2	(27) 31.6	33.5	(208) 30.4		(147) 24.2	(99) 31.0			(208) 30.4
3.4	10.8	11.9	21.6	10.9				7.3	2.7	10.9
10.2	17.4	12.4	17.3	14.5	% Profit Before Taxes/ Total Assets			13.0	14.2	14.5
3.9	8.1	7.0	10.7	6.7				5.3	3.0	6.7
-.2	1.3	2.3	4.4	1.1				.9	.3	1.1
1.5	.3	.3		.4	% Depr., Dep., Amort./ Revenues			.5	.3	.4
(36) 8.7	(55) 1.0	(17) .6		(116) 1.5		(97) 1.8	(61) 1.4			(116) 1.5
20.5	2.6	1.3		6.0				8.0	8.6	6.0
1.8	2.3			1.8	% Officers', Directors', Owners' Comp/Revenues			1.9	2.2	1.8
(12) 6.1	(31) 3.6		(50)	3.6		(44) 4.6	(29) 3.4		(50)	3.6
21.0	6.9			8.6				8.3	7.8	8.6
30063M	438132M	679061M	28630727M	29777983M	Contract Revenues ($)			26034757M	4611175M	29777983M
100061M	594958M	1460390M	30170897M	32326306M	Total Assets ($)			30382699M	10784244M	32326306M

M = $ thousand   MM = $ million
See Pages 11 through 21 for Explanation of Ratios and Data

Current Data Sorted By Revenue · **Comparative Historical Data**

					Type of Statement					
1	22	52	13	88	Unqualified	182	147	137	78	88
3	37	13		53	Reviewed	95	72	68	54	53
2	7	2		11	Compiled	29	24	19	12	11
4	6		1	11	Tax Returns	15	13	15	9	11
2	19	11	5	37	Other	54	39	27	21	37
0-1MM	1-10MM	10-50MM	50 & OVER	ALL		4/1/00-3/31/01	4/1/01-3/31/02	4/1/02-3/31/03	4/1/03-3/31/04	4/1/04-3/31/05

40 (4/1-9/30/04)   160 (10/1/04-3/31/05)

0-1MM	1-10MM	10-50MM	50 & OVER	ALL		ALL	ALL	ALL	ALL	ALL
12	91	78	19	200	NUMBER OF STATEMENTS	375	295	266	174	200
%	%	%	%	%	ASSETS	%	%	%	%	%
16.1	13.6	15.9	8.9	14.2	Cash & Equivalents	15.7	15.6	16.1	14.0	14.2
29.9	32.1	30.7	22.7	30.5	A/R - Progress Billings	26.6	26.3	25.8	25.5	30.5
1.2	1.6	4.0	2.9	2.6	A/R - Current Retention	3.5	3.0	2.6	3.2	2.6
1.5	4.0	2.7	6.6	3.6	Inventory	2.6	2.5	3.0	4.0	3.6
2.4	3.4	6.0	2.9	4.3	Cost & Est. Earnings In Excess of Billings	3.4	3.1	3.0	3.6	4.3
3.7	3.2	4.8	7.6	4.3	All Other Current	4.2	5.5	5.6	5.3	4.3
54.8	57.8	64.1	51.7	59.5	Total Current	55.9	55.9	56.1	55.5	59.5
28.7	37.1	29.3	39.1	33.8	Fixed Assets (net)	36.0	35.6	36.4	34.7	33.8
.0	.3	2.1	.7	1.1	Joint Ventures & Investments	1.4	1.1	1.5	2.5	1.1
.0	.4	.1	1.4	.4	Intangibles (net)	1.4	1.6	.4	.6	.4
16.5	4.3	4.4	7.1	5.3	All Other Non-Current	5.4	5.8	5.5	6.6	5.3
100.0	100.0	100.0	100.0	100.0	Total	100.0	100.0	100.0	100.0	100.0
					LIABILITIES					
16.7	9.1	3.5	2.3	6.7	Notes Payable - Short Term	6.8	6.2	7.1	7.5	6.7
11.1	16.9	21.5	14.3	18.1	A/P - Trade	17.1	15.4	15.2	16.8	18.1
.0	.1	.4	1.4	.4	A/P - Retention	.8	.8	.6	.8	.4
1.4	2.1	6.1	3.6	3.7	Billings in Excess of Costs & Est. Earnings	3.6	3.7	3.3	2.8	3.7
.0	.2	.1	.5	.2	Income Taxes Payable	.4	.3	.2	.3	.2
5.9	6.9	4.8	4.3	5.8	Cur. Mat.-L/T/D	5.8	5.6	6.3	6.1	5.8
3.4	4.8	5.5	6.5	5.1	All Other Current	4.5	6.6	7.8	6.6	5.1
38.5	40.1	41.9	33.0	40.0	Total Current	39.0	38.6	40.5	40.8	40.0
17.3	19.0	12.3	18.7	16.3	Long-Term Debt	13.8	16.4	15.8	15.2	16.3
.0	2.0	1.7	4.0	2.0	Deferred Taxes	1.7	1.2	1.4	1.4	2.0
7.5	1.9	3.1	1.7	2.7	All Other Non-Current	1.9	2.9	3.0	3.2	2.7
36.7	36.9	41.0	42.7	39.1	Net Worth	43.5	40.8	39.3	39.3	39.1
100.0	100.0	100.0	100.0	100.0	Total Liabilities & Net Worth	100.0	100.0	100.0	100.0	100.0
					INCOME DATA					
100.0	100.0	100.0	100.0	100.0	Contract Revenues	100.0	100.0	100.0	100.0	100.0
38.3	24.6	14.5	16.1	20.7	Gross Profit	18.0	21.3	20.7	19.2	20.7
32.5	21.3	11.3	12.7	17.3	Operating Expenses	14.7	17.8	18.3	16.9	17.3
5.8	3.3	3.2	3.4	3.4	Operating Profit	3.3	3.4	2.4	2.3	3.4
.6	.4	.0	-.2	.2	All Other Expenses (net)	.0	.6	.4	.4	.2
5.2	2.9	3.3	3.6	3.3	Profit Before Taxes	3.3	2.8	2.0	1.9	3.3
					RATIOS					
6.7	2.2	2.1	1.9	2.1	Current	2.1	2.1	2.2	2.0	2.1
1.2	1.4	1.6	1.4	1.5		1.4	1.4	1.4	1.4	1.5
.8	1.0	1.2	1.3	1.2		1.1	1.1	1.1	1.0	1.2
16.2	5.6	2.7	2.3	3.6	Receivables/Payables	2.7	3.3	3.5	2.7	3.6
(10) 2.7	(90) 2.9	(77) 1.6	1.8	(196) 1.9		(371) 1.8	(290) 1.9	(261) 1.9	(168) 1.6	(196) 1.9
1.7	1.4	1.2	.9	1.2		1.2	1.2	1.2	1.2	1.2
1 250.4	29 12.6	39 9.5	25 14.6	30 12.0	Revenues/Receivables	28 13.0	27 13.6	24 15.0	24 15.0	30 12.0
42 8.8	51 7.2	54 6.7	41 9.0	51 7.1		49 7.5	48 7.7	43 8.5	42 8.6	51 7.1
144 2.5	76 4.8	68 5.4	55 6.6	71 5.2		68 5.4	67 5.5	67 5.5	65 5.6	71 5.2
0 UND	9 41.0	22 16.8	20 18.5	14 26.4	Cost of Revenues/Payables	15 24.1	13 27.7	13 28.1	15 24.9	14 26.4
33 11.2	21 17.2	36 10.3	33 11.0	32 11.5		33 11.1	30 12.2	28 13.2	30 12.2	32 11.5
55 6.7	52 7.0	54 6.7	46 7.9	52 7.0		51 7.2	51 7.2	45 8.0	50 7.4	52 7.0
8.4	7.2	6.5	8.7	6.7	Revenues/Working Capital	7.4	7.6	6.8	8.4	6.7
37.7	13.0	9.8	11.8	11.8		13.8	14.1	13.5	15.6	11.8
NM	148.5	22.0	26.5	35.7		47.1	55.3	58.4	281.5	35.7
32.0	12.6	20.6	20.7	17.9	EBIT/Interest	10.6	9.9	10.7	10.5	17.9
(10) 5.1	(86) 3.2	(74) 5.8	(16) 5.2	(186) 4.5		(343) 3.4	(271) 3.7	(240) 3.1	(159) 3.7	(186) 4.5
2.7	1.2	1.7	3.2	1.8		1.3	1.4	1.1	1.5	1.8
	3.4	2.9		3.3	Net Profit + Depr., Dep., Amort./Cur. Mat. L /T/D	4.7	4.3	3.2	3.3	3.3
	(26) 1.7	(32) 1.8		(67) 1.7		(151) 2.2	(112) 1.9	(101) 1.7	(45) 1.6	(67) 1.7
	.9	1.0		1.0		1.1	1.1	.8	.7	1.0
.2	.5	.4	.6	.4	Fixed/Worth	.5	.5	.5	.5	.4
.6	.9	.7	1.2	.8		.8	.8	.8	.8	.8
1.3	1.7	1.1	1.5	1.5		1.4	1.5	1.5	1.5	1.5
.6	.8	.8	.6	.8	Debt/Worth	.7	.8	.7	.9	.8
1.0	1.5	1.3	1.7	1.5		1.3	1.5	1.6	1.7	1.5
4.7	3.9	2.9	2.4	3.2		2.7	3.1	3.1	3.4	3.2
79.7	38.5	31.4	20.3	34.7	% Profit Before Taxes/Tangible Net Worth	30.7	29.2	25.6	26.0	34.7
(10) 18.4	(83) 16.5	(76) 16.9	14.4	(188) 15.5		(361) 13.1	(282) 13.4	(259) 11.9	(168) 10.0	(188) 15.5
5.2	4.6	3.2	7.9	4.5		2.5	3.3	1.9	2.9	4.5
36.9	12.6	14.2	7.2	13.0	% Profit Before Taxes/Total Assets	11.7	11.5	9.7	9.7	13.0
10.9	4.7	5.6	5.6	5.4		4.8	4.8	4.0	3.5	5.4
2.0	.5	1.4	3.2	1.4		.7	1.2	.3	.7	1.4
	2.1	1.8	2.1	1.9	% Depr., Dep., Amort./Revenues	2.2	2.5	1.9	2.1	1.9
	(83) 3.3	(74) 2.9	(11) 4.3	(177) 3.1		(332) 3.5	(261) 4.0	(222) 3.6	(121) 3.3	(177) 3.1
	4.8	4.2	5.0	4.6		5.6	6.0	5.4	5.5	4.6
	1.7	1.0		1.3	% Officers', Directors', Owners' Comp/Revenues	1.2	1.2	1.5	1.5	1.3
	(45) 3.1	(39) 1.9		(96) 2.7		(161) 2.5	(131) 2.5	(122) 2.6	(83) 2.7	(96) 2.7
	6.9	3.1		5.4		4.2	5.2	5.4	5.0	5.4
8210M	412867M	1796266M	5278150M	7495493M	Contract Revenues ($)	25140493M	8637730M	22681338M	11940726M	7495493M
3858M	202233M	822102M	2276707M	3304900M	Total Assets ($)	11876667M	4195980M	8059789M	5430743M	3304900M

© RMA 2005

M = $ thousand   MM = $ million
See Pages 11 through 21 for Explanation of Ratios and Data

Current Data Sorted By Revenue   **Comparative Historical Data**

					Type of Statement					
	5	9		14	Unqualified	47	36	30	12	14
	9	6		15	Reviewed	36	33	21	12	15
	3	1		4	Compiled	6	8	11	5	4
1	1	1		3	Tax Returns	6	9	7	5	3
	3	1		4	Other	13	13	10	11	4
	3 (4/1-9/30/04)		37 (10/1/04-3/31/05)			4/1/00-3/31/01	4/1/01-3/31/02	4/1/02-3/31/03	4/1/03-3/31/04	4/1/04-3/31/05
0-1MM	1-10MM	10-50MM	50 & OVER	ALL		ALL	ALL	ALL	ALL	ALL
1	21	18		40	NUMBER OF STATEMENTS	108	99	79	45	40
%	%	%	%	%	ASSETS	%	%	%	%	%
	10.6	18.1	D	13.8	Cash & Equivalents	15.2	11.6	11.9	18.4	13.8
	25.5	33.2	A	29.6	A/R - Progress Billings	31.8	32.1	27.1	27.8	29.6
	.8	2.5	T	1.6	A/R - Current Retention	1.6	1.6	1.9	3.7	1.6
	2.7	1.7	A	2.2	Inventory	2.2	3.8	4.2	5.2	2.2
	3.4	6.4	N	4.6	Cost & Est. Earnings In Excess of Billings	3.9	3.4	3.7	3.1	4.6
	5.2	9.4	O	6.9	All Other Current	5.3	5.7	8.4	4.8	6.9
	48.1	71.3	T	58.7	Total Current	60.1	58.2	57.1	63.0	58.7
	42.6	24.7		34.6	Fixed Assets (net)	33.1	33.8	34.3	29.2	34.6
	.7	.3	A	.5	Joint Ventures & Investments	1.0	.8	1.6	.5	.5
	.3	.0	V	.1	Intangibles (net)	.8	.9	2.2	1.4	.1
	8.3	3.6	A	6.0	All Other Non-Current	5.1	6.4	4.8	5.9	6.0
	100.0	100.0	I	100.0	Total	100.0	100.0	100.0	100.0	100.0
			L		LIABILITIES					
	7.6	5.8	A	6.6	Notes Payable - Short Term	7.2	6.9	8.8	7.0	6.6
	15.6	28.2	B	21.3	A/P - Trade	18.2	18.4	16.9	16.4	21.3
	.2	.4	L	.3	A/P - Retention	.9	1.6	.7	1.0	.3
	3.4	9.5	E	6.1	Billings in Excess of Costs & Est. Earnings	3.8	4.1	4.3	5.2	6.1
	.4	.2		.3	Income Taxes Payable	.9	.2	.3	.6	.3
	8.2	3.5		5.9	Cur. Mat.-L/T/D	4.7	4.8	4.9	4.1	5.9
	6.2	4.0		5.0	All Other Current	6.4	8.2	7.4	7.7	5.0
	41.5	51.6		45.5	Total Current	42.0	44.1	43.4	42.0	45.5
	18.1	5.8		13.1	Long-Term Debt	14.5	16.8	22.0	17.5	13.1
	1.5	2.0		1.7	Deferred Taxes	1.8	1.2	1.2	1.2	1.7
	3.0	2.5		2.7	All Other Non-Current	4.0	4.0	1.7	6.3	2.7
	35.8	38.0		37.0	Net Worth	37.6	33.9	31.7	33.1	37.0
	100.0	100.0		100.0	Total Liabilities & Net Worth	100.0	100.0	100.0	100.0	100.0
					INCOME DATA					
	100.0	100.0		100.0	Contract Revenues	100.0	100.0	100.0	100.0	100.0
	25.8	14.6		21.7	Gross Profit	21.0	24.6	25.8	23.2	21.7
	22.1	10.9		17.7	Operating Expenses	20.4	20.8	22.5	20.9	17.7
	3.7	3.6		4.0	Operating Profit	.6	3.8	3.3	2.2	4.0
	.4	.1		.2	All Other Expenses (net)	-2.2	1.3	1.2	1.0	.2
	3.4	3.5		3.8	Profit Before Taxes	2.7	2.5	2.1	1.2	3.8
					RATIOS					
	2.0	1.7		1.9		2.1	1.8	1.9	2.1	1.9
	1.1	1.4		1.3	Current	1.4	1.3	1.3	1.5	1.3
	.9	1.1		1.0		1.1	1.0	1.0	1.1	1.0
	3.9	1.7		2.7		3.1	3.3	3.9	4.3	2.7
	2.5	1.4		1.7	Receivables/Payables	(103) 2.0	(95) 1.8	(76) 1.8	(43) 2.1	1.7
	1.4	1.1		1.1		1.3	1.2	1.2	1.3	1.1
28	13.1	34 10.8	33	11.1		34 10.7	34 10.7	31 11.8	35 10.6	33 11.1
42	8.7	46 7.9	46	7.9	Revenues/Receivables	54 6.8	51 7.2	45 8.2	48 7.5	46 7.9
61	6.0	53 6.8	58	6.3		72 5.1	68 5.3	63 5.8	63 5.8	58 6.3
15	24.4	30 12.4	18	20.0		15 24.0	18 20.6	15 24.9	18 19.9	18 20.0
21	17.3	37 10.0	30	12.0	Cost of Revenues/Payables	29 12.6	32 11.5	32 11.5	33 11.2	30 12.0
37	9.8	49 7.4	46	7.9		51 7.2	49 7.5	51 7.2	46 7.9	46 7.9
	11.2	7.9		8.7		5.9	7.1	8.7	6.7	8.7
	66.9	13.5		17.3	Revenues/Working Capital	14.9	18.3	19.6	16.0	17.3
	-21.6	NM		-87.8		53.7	-566.8	300.5	71.3	-87.8
	33.3	29.8		27.8		15.2	12.7	11.1	14.6	27.8
(18)	4.3	13.5	(37)	7.9	EBIT/Interest	(97) 3.6	(92) 4.2	(72) 3.6	(42) 4.0	(37) 7.9
	2.0	6.4		3.3		1.8	1.2	1.0	-.6	3.3
		15.0		10.3		10.6	5.7	3.8	8.9	10.3
	(10)	7.5	(14)	4.9	Net Profit + Depr., Dep., Amort./Cur. Mat. L./T/D	(42) 2.5	(39) 2.3	(22) 1.4	(12) 2.9	(14) 4.9
		3.0		1.3		1.1	1.1	.1	.9	1.3
	.7	.3		.5		.4	.5	.4	.4	.5
	1.1	.6		.9	Fixed/Worth	.8	.8	1.0	.8	.9
	1.9	1.0		1.6		1.3	1.6	2.6	2.2	1.6
	.9	.9		1.0		.8	.9	1.1	1.2	1.0
	1.7	1.8		1.7	Debt/Worth	1.7	1.9	2.6	1.8	1.7
	3.0	2.8		2.7		3.9	3.8	6.8	5.8	2.7
	62.7	29.9		49.6		35.4	49.5	36.3	37.0	49.6
(19)	35.4	(17) 15.8	(37)	20.8	% Profit Before Taxes/ Tangible Net Worth	(102) 19.8	(89) 18.3	(71) 20.3	(41) 13.1	(37) 20.8
	5.4	7.8		6.2		5.2	5.1	1.6	-.2	6.2
	28.8	11.3		16.3		12.8	13.8	12.6	12.7	16.3
	9.4	6.3		7.7	% Profit Before Taxes/ Total Assets	6.2	6.6	4.6	4.6	7.7
	1.5	3.8		2.2		1.9	1.5	.6	-3.3	2.2
	2.2	.6		1.4		1.1	1.2	.7	1.5	1.4
(17)	3.9	(17) 1.9	(35)	2.9	% Depr., Dep., Amort./ Revenues	(97) 2.5	(95) 2.7	(63) 3.0	(31) 3.4	(35) 2.9
	7.1	4.1		5.8		6.4	5.3	9.2	5.7	5.8
	1.7			1.4		1.8	1.7	1.3	2.7	1.4
(11)	3.4		(20)	3.1	% Officers', Directors', Owners' Comp/Revenues	(43) 3.6	(52) 2.6	(31) 3.5	(19) 4.8	(20) 3.1
	5.2			5.1		6.1	5.0	4.8	5.8	5.1
447M	67135M	370298M		437880M	Contract Revenues ($)	3810583M	3699689M	7555027M	1855552M	437880M
351M	35680M	138347M		174378M	Total Assets ($)	2322859M	1710678M	5207717M	1116419M	174378M

M = $ thousand   MM = $ million
See Pages 11 through 21 for Explanation of Ratios and Data

Current Data Sorted By Revenue | **Comparative Historical Data**

0-1MM	1-10MM	10-50MM	50 & OVER	ALL	Type of Statement	4/1/00-3/31/01	4/1/01-3/31/02	4/1/02-3/31/03	4/1/03-3/31/04	4/1/04-3/31/05
	4	2		6	Unqualified	26	14	11	8	6
2	23	11		36	Reviewed	66	47	37	28	36
4	11	1		16	Compiled	33	23	11	11	16
8	16	1		25	Tax Returns	24	27	20	14	25
1	8	3		12	Other	32	36	23	17	12
16 (4/1-9/30/04)			79 (10/1/04-3/31/05)			ALL	ALL	ALL	ALL	ALL
15	62	18		95	**NUMBER OF STATEMENTS**	181	147	102	78	95
%	%	%	%	%	**ASSETS**	%	%	%	%	%
18.8	13.5	9.4		13.6	Cash & Equivalents	12.1	14.1	11.0	12.1	13.6
21.1	37.6	38.3		35.1	A/R - Progress Billings	36.9	33.2	33.7	33.1	35.1
.0	1.1	4.0		1.5	A/R - Current Retention	2.4	1.4	2.0	1.6	1.5
2.2	1.6	1.0		1.6	Inventory	1.3	2.0	1.7	2.5	1.6
1.0	1.3	4.8		1.9	Cost & Est. Earnings In Excess of Billings	2.2	2.1	2.0	2.3	1.9
3.2	5.3	12.3		6.3	All Other Current	3.7	3.8	4.4	5.5	6.3
46.3	60.4	69.8		60.0	Total Current	58.4	56.6	54.8	57.1	60.0
41.2	31.9	23.3		31.7	Fixed Assets (net)	33.5	34.8	38.5	34.6	31.7
.2	.6	.9		.6	Joint Ventures & Investments	1.0	.6	.5	.1	.6
2.6	.9	.5		1.1	Intangibles (net)	1.6	1.1	.6	1.4	1.1
9.7	6.3	5.4		6.6	All Other Non-Current	5.4	6.8	5.5	6.7	6.6
100.0	100.0	100.0		100.0	Total	100.0	100.0	100.0	100.0	100.0
					LIABILITIES					
13.2	9.2	8.1		9.7	Notes Payable - Short Term	8.3	6.5	7.3	8.4	9.7
10.8	18.3	20.1		17.4	A/P - Trade	16.0	16.4	16.9	17.9	17.4
.0	.0	.3		.1	A/P - Retention	.2	.1	.1	.1	.1
.0	2.9	3.7		2.6	Billings in Excess of Costs & Est. Earnings	3.5	1.9	2.3	3.1	2.6
.0	.3	.2		.2	Income Taxes Payable	.4	.2	.4	.4	.2
8.3	8.4	3.9		7.5	Cur. Mat.-L/T/D	5.4	5.4	5.3	6.1	7.5
10.6	4.7	12.0		7.0	All Other Current	6.1	5.1	5.4	6.9	7.0
42.9	43.8	48.3		44.5	Total Current	39.8	35.6	37.7	42.9	44.5
21.2	19.8	7.5		17.7	Long-Term Debt	14.8	18.6	20.2	21.5	17.7
1.4	1.2	1.0		1.2	Deferred Taxes	.9	.6	1.0	.8	1.2
3.9	3.5	2.2		3.3	All Other Non-Current	2.0	5.7	3.4	4.3	3.3
30.6	31.7	40.9		33.3	Net Worth	42.6	39.1	37.8	30.5	33.3
100.0	100.0	100.0		100.0	Total Liabilities & Net Worth	100.0	100.0	100.0	100.0	100.0
					INCOME DATA					
100.0	100.0	100.0		100.0	Contract Revenues	100.0	100.0	100.0	100.0	100.0
43.5	27.6	15.4		27.8	Gross Profit	25.5	28.7	28.7	29.1	27.8
43.5	24.2	11.7		24.9	Operating Expenses	20.1	24.1	24.5	25.8	24.9
.0	3.5	3.7		3.0	Operating Profit	5.3	4.6	4.3	3.3	3.0
1.0	.2	.5		.4	All Other Expenses (net)	.5	.6	.5	1.1	.4
-.9	3.3	3.1		2.6	Profit Before Taxes	4.8	4.0	3.8	2.2	2.6
					RATIOS					
2.6	2.8	1.7		2.4	Current	2.5	2.6	2.3	2.0	2.4
1.1	1.4	1.5		1.4		1.5	1.7	1.7	1.5	1.4
.3	.9	1.2		.9		1.1	1.1	1.0	1.0	.9
4.2	6.2	8.9		6.0	Receivables/Payables	5.7	4.8	4.1	4.9	6.0
(12) 2.0	(58) 2.7	2.3		(88) 2.5		(164) 2.7	(137) 2.5	(91) 2.2	(68) 1.9	(88) 2.5
.5	1.3	1.1		1.2		1.6	1.4	1.5	1.2	1.2
0 UND	27 13.3	38 9.6	22 16.3		Revenues/Receivables	31 11.9	23 15.9	28 12.8	19 19.3	22 16.3
17 21.4	57 6.5	54 6.8	53 6.8			52 7.1	47 7.8	51 7.2	45 8.2	53 6.8
55 6.7	85 4.3	76 4.8	77 4.7			74 4.9	67 5.4	72 5.1	77 4.8	77 4.7
3 121.0	9 42.7	8 47.5	8 48.2		Cost of Revenues/Payables	7 48.7	9 40.1	11 32.9	9 38.6	8 48.2
13 28.0	26 14.0	31 11.8	23 16.2			23 15.7	24 15.3	27 13.7	26 14.3	23 16.2
28 13.0	47 7.7	54 6.8	46 7.9			40 9.1	50 7.3	48 7.7	52 7.0	46 7.9
7.3	6.0	8.3		7.3	Revenues/Working Capital	7.6	6.8	7.5	8.8	7.3
62.4	14.7	15.6		17.4		15.4	14.6	18.0	17.0	17.4
-12.4	-68.6	34.4		-172.8		89.3	72.5	NM	-130.3	-172.8
5.0	10.0	44.8		10.9	EBIT/Interest	15.4	10.8	10.5	14.9	10.9
(11) 1.1	(56) 5.6	(17) 8.0	(84) 5.0			(159) 5.1	(130) 3.4	(93) 4.4	(74) 4.3	(84) 5.0
-2.4	1.9	3.2		1.4		1.7	1.4	1.1	1.5	1.4
	3.5			4.1	Net Profit + Depr., Dep., Amort./Cur. Mat. L /T/D	8.8	3.9	4.3	3.2	4.1
	(18) 2.3		(26) 2.1			(55) 2.2	(36) 2.1	(31) 1.7	(18) 2.3	(26) 2.1
	.8			.8		1.3	.7	1.0	1.5	.8
.4	.5	.3		.4	Fixed/Worth	.3	.4	.4	.6	.4
2.0	.9	.5		.9		.7	.8	1.0	1.1	.9
38.2	2.7	1.2		2.7		1.5	2.2	1.9	2.4	2.7
.6	.8	.8		.8	Debt/Worth	.6	.6	.8	1.1	.8
3.3	2.1	1.6		2.1		1.5	1.3	1.4	2.0	2.1
57.4	6.0	3.0		6.1		3.1	3.5	4.5	5.9	6.1
35.5	52.4	48.9		46.9	% Profit Before Taxes/Tangible Net Worth	47.5	53.2	59.4	40.2	46.9
(12) 10.2	(56) 21.6	(17) 23.2	(85) 17.3			(174) 20.7	(133) 22.3	(96) 21.0	(67) 21.0	(85) 17.3
-66.3	5.1	5.7		4.7		8.7	6.2	6.8	3.1	4.7
10.5	13.9	16.3		14.3	% Profit Before Taxes/Total Assets	22.0	19.8	17.4	13.9	14.3
3.4	7.4	9.7		6.7		10.4	7.8	6.4	6.3	6.7
-9.5	1.8	2.3		1.4		3.0	1.2	1.3	.4	1.4
2.2	1.3	.8		1.3	% Depr., Dep., Amort./Revenues	1.2	1.5	1.3	1.3	1.3
(11) 3.8	(56) 2.5	(17) 1.5	(84) 2.3			(168) 2.2	(130) 3.0	(92) 2.9	(63) 2.9	(84) 2.3
11.4	4.7	2.3		4.2		4.6	4.8	4.7	6.1	4.2
4.5	2.3			2.0	% Officers', Directors', Owners' Comp/Revenues	2.1	2.2	2.5	2.3	2.0
(12) 8.7	(40) 4.0		(59) 4.0			(107) 3.2	(92) 4.2	(71) 3.9	(45) 3.9	(59) 4.0
11.3	7.3			8.7		7.4	7.7	7.5	6.2	8.7
9741M	263431M	302816M		575988M	Contract Revenues ($)	17912948M	2958870M	1084082M	768450M	575988M
3390M	123270M	111393M		238053M	Total Assets ($)	11247191M	1076984M	420024M	305668M	238053M

(The "50 & OVER" current-data column is marked "DATA NOT AVAILABLE.")

M = $ thousand   MM = $ million
See Pages 11 through 21 for Explanation of Ratios and Data

1554 — CONSTRUCTION – % OF COMPLETION—Structural Steel and Precast Concrete Contractors NAICS 238120 (SIC 1791)

Current Data Sorted By Revenue | **Comparative Historical Data**

0-1MM	1-10MM	10-50MM	50 & OVER	ALL	Type of Statement	4/1/00-3/31/01 ALL	4/1/01-3/31/02 ALL	4/1/02-3/31/03 ALL	4/1/03-3/31/04 ALL	4/1/04-3/31/05 ALL
	5	6	5	16	Unqualified	9	15	11	8	16
	14	6		20	Reviewed	20	23	30	17	20
2	8	1		11	Compiled	15	10	13	6	11
2	4			6	Tax Returns	3	6	5	5	6
1	5	1		7	Other	9	10	12	3	7
18 (4/1-9/30/04)			42 (10/1/04-3/31/05)							
5	36	14	5	60	**NUMBER OF STATEMENTS**	56	64	71	39	60
%	%	%	%	%	**ASSETS**	%	%	%	%	%
	10.6	7.1		9.4	Cash & Equivalents	6.5	11.1	12.7	9.9	9.4
	43.8	54.2		44.6	A/R - Progress Billings	43.9	44.1	43.7	43.2	44.6
	2.0	4.3		2.2	A/R - Current Retention	3.0	1.7	1.6	2.3	2.2
	2.1	4.0		2.6	Inventory	3.7	1.8	2.8	4.3	2.6
	3.5	7.7		5.3	Cost & Est. Earnings In Excess of Billings	7.2	4.6	4.9	5.2	5.3
	5.7	1.9		6.2	All Other Current	6.3	4.0	4.2	4.2	6.2
	67.7	79.2		70.4	Total Current	70.5	67.3	69.9	69.1	70.4
	23.3	13.9		21.6	Fixed Assets (net)	23.6	27.0	22.2	22.1	21.6
	1.6	1.4		1.3	Joint Ventures & Investments	1.2	1.1	1.1	1.4	1.3
	1.2	.9		1.0	Intangibles (net)	.6	.3	.8	.4	1.0
	6.2	4.5		5.7	All Other Non-Current	4.1	4.3	6.0	7.0	5.7
	100.0	100.0		100.0	Total	100.0	100.0	100.0	100.0	100.0
					LIABILITIES					
	12.5	9.3		18.6	Notes Payable - Short Term	9.8	9.4	10.8	21.0	18.6
	15.2	16.7		16.5	A/P - Trade	21.0	15.2	13.7	20.7	16.5
	.3	3.2		.9	A/P - Retention	.0	.0	1.0	.0	.9
	3.9	6.2		5.1	Billings in Excess of Costs & Est. Earnings	6.5	6.2	4.2	4.0	5.1
	.3	1.0		.4	Income Taxes Payable	.7	.6	.3	.2	.4
	2.2	.9		2.1	Cur. Mat.-L/T/D	1.6	3.1	2.5	3.0	2.1
	6.0	3.5		7.5	All Other Current	7.1	9.9	9.5	8.3	7.5
	40.4	40.8		51.1	Total Current	46.7	44.4	42.1	57.3	51.1
	11.6	6.1		10.1	Long-Term Debt	7.7	12.2	8.7	8.0	10.1
	1.0	.5		.9	Deferred Taxes	1.6	1.0	.5	.3	.9
	6.2	.2		4.7	All Other Non-Current	1.5	5.3	4.5	4.3	4.7
	40.8	52.4		33.1	Net Worth	42.5	37.1	44.3	30.0	33.1
	100.0	100.0		100.0	Total Liabilities & Net Worth	100.0	100.0	100.0	100.0	100.0
					INCOME DATA					
	100.0	100.0		100.0	Contract Revenues	100.0	100.0	100.0	100.0	100.0
	23.5	12.7		19.8	Gross Profit	19.8	22.6	22.0	16.4	19.8
	20.4	8.9		17.1	Operating Expenses	16.5	18.3	20.0	18.5	17.1
	3.1	3.8		2.7	Operating Profit	3.3	4.2	2.0	-2.1	2.7
	.1	-.6		.0	All Other Expenses (net)	-1.0	.3	.3	.0	.0
	3.0	4.4		2.7	Profit Before Taxes	4.3	3.9	1.7	-2.0	2.7
					RATIOS					
	3.0	3.1		2.8	Current	2.2	2.3	2.6	3.3	2.8
	1.8	2.0		1.8		1.7	1.7	1.6	1.6	1.8
	1.2	1.5		1.3		1.2	1.3	1.2	1.2	1.3
	8.7	5.7		8.0	Receivables/Payables	5.4	7.3	8.7	7.5	8.0
(35)	4.0	3.0	(59)	3.0		2.5	3.8 (70)	3.9 (38)	4.0 (59)	3.0
	1.9	2.0		1.9		1.5	1.8	2.1	1.8	1.9
41	8.8	63 5.8	41	8.9	Revenues/Receivables	40 9.0	46 7.9	46 7.9	46 7.9	41 8.9
69	5.3	84 4.3	67	5.4		65 5.6	65 5.6	71 5.1	65 5.6	67 5.4
89	4.1	106 3.4	90	4.1		85 4.3	87 4.2	88 4.2	84 4.3	90 4.1
9	38.5	18 19.9	12	30.5	Cost of Revenues/Payables	13 27.1	11 33.5	10 35.4	9 40.0	12 30.5
20	18.0	32 11.4	27	13.5		33 11.1	23 15.9	21 17.4	18 20.3	27 13.5
37	9.7	39 9.4	39	9.4		44 8.4	36 10.1	36 10.2	37 9.8	39 9.4
	5.8	4.4		5.6	Revenues/Working Capital	6.3	5.9	5.2	5.6	5.6
	8.3	7.8		8.8		10.0	10.1	8.3	9.3	8.8
	38.7	10.8		20.3		27.2	21.4	27.0	21.8	20.3
	18.3	64.2		25.2	EBIT/Interest	15.1	14.3	8.0	9.0	25.2
(33)	3.8	(12) 25.9	(54)	4.5		(51) 5.6	(57) 3.8	(66) 3.1	(35) 1.6	(54) 4.5
	.5	3.4		1.1		2.8	1.8	-.3	-5.3	1.1
	10.6			11.0	Net Profit + Depr., Dep., Amort./Cur. Mat. L/T/D	15.6	7.3	7.9	5.1	11.0
(12)	2.8		(20)	3.6		(16) 3.3	(17) 3.1	(19) 3.4	(10) 2.1	(20) 3.6
	1.3			1.3		2.1	1.4	1.6	.6	1.3
	.1	.1		.1	Fixed/Worth	.2	.2	.2	.2	.1
	.5	.2		.5		.5	.6	.5	.5	.5
	1.3	.5		1.1		.8	1.1	1.0	.9	1.1
	.6	.4		.6	Debt/Worth	.7	.7	.6	.6	.6
	1.3	1.0		1.4		1.4	1.2	1.3	1.1	1.4
	2.5	1.4		2.5		2.9	2.9	2.6	3.2	2.5
	23.0	29.0		25.1	% Profit Before Taxes/ Tangible Net Worth	43.1	32.0	27.3	12.1	25.1
(32)	10.7	21.9	(53)	12.5		(53) 22.9	(59) 18.1	(66) 11.5	(36) 2.5	(53) 12.5
	-2.6	13.2		1.5		4.4	4.8	-2.9	-25.5	1.5
	14.0	18.2		15.0	% Profit Before Taxes/ Total Assets	18.1	15.1	11.5	7.1	15.0
	4.3	11.3		6.0		8.2	7.5	3.5	.7	6.0
	-.1	5.1		.6		2.1	2.1	-1.9	-13.5	.6
	.6	.4		.4	% Depr., Dep., Amort./ Revenues	.8	.8	.5	.6	.4
(35)	1.5	(13) .5	(56)	1.2		(50) 1.6	(60) 1.8	(65) 1.2	(34) 1.2	(56) 1.2
	3.8	1.3		2.7		3.0	3.5	2.7	2.7	2.7
	2.3			1.9	% Officers', Directors', Owners' Comp/Revenues	1.9	2.8	2.5	2.2	1.9
(14)	3.5		(25)	3.0		(29) 4.1	(33) 4.6	(39) 4.0	(27) 4.1	(25) 3.0
	5.4			5.5		7.4	7.7	7.2	6.3	5.5
3687M	161826M	280259M	863942M	1309714M	Contract Revenues ($)	612372M	618216M	1063677M	276540M	1309714M
1515M	69518M	124012M	397040M	592085M	Total Assets ($)	273428M	267802M	494304M	115540M	592085M

© RMA 2005

M = $ thousand   MM = $ million
See Pages 11 through 21 for Explanation of Ratios and Data

Current Data Sorted By Revenue   **Comparative Historical Data**

0-1MM	1-10MM	10-50MM	50 & OVER	ALL	Type of Statement	4	5	6	7	5
	3	2		5	Unqualified	4	5	6	7	5
	22	4		26	Reviewed	45	32	32	23	26
4	7			11	Compiled	19	9	19	12	11
2	13			15	Tax Returns	7	18	18	15	15
	7	1	1	9	Other	15	12	10	7	9

11 (4/1-9/30/04)   55 (10/1/04-3/31/05)

0-1MM	1-10MM	10-50MM	50 & OVER	ALL		4/1/00-3/31/01 ALL	4/1/01-3/31/02 ALL	4/1/02-3/31/03 ALL	4/1/03-3/31/04 ALL	4/1/04-3/31/05 ALL
6	52	7	1	66	**NUMBER OF STATEMENTS**	90	76	85	64	66
%	%	%	%	%	**ASSETS**	%	%	%	%	%
	13.3			13.7	Cash & Equivalents	14.7	14.1	14.4	10.6	13.7
	42.8			39.5	A/R - Progress Billings	39.1	38.9	37.4	42.1	39.5
	4.6			4.4	A/R - Current Retention	4.5	2.7	1.7	4.8	4.4
	2.2			3.4	Inventory	1.8	3.3	3.4	2.1	3.4
	2.1			2.1	Cost & Est. Earnings In Excess of Billings	2.7	2.2	2.4	1.4	2.1
	5.4			5.3	All Other Current	4.6	5.8	7.1	4.4	5.3
	70.4			68.3	Total Current	67.4	67.0	66.3	65.4	68.3
	23.3			23.6	Fixed Assets (net)	25.2	25.4	24.9	28.5	23.6
	.2			.2	Joint Ventures & Investments	2.2	.8	.5	.3	.2
	.7			2.3	Intangibles (net)	1.2	.9	1.2	1.1	2.3
	5.4			5.6	All Other Non-Current	4.0	5.9	7.2	4.8	5.6
	100.0			100.0	Total	100.0	100.0	100.0	100.0	100.0
					LIABILITIES					
	10.4			11.4	Notes Payable - Short Term	10.4	9.1	9.5	14.3	11.4
	17.3			15.8	A/P - Trade	15.3	14.9	14.7	15.8	15.8
	.0			.0	A/P - Retention	.1	.3	.0	.0	.0
	3.7			4.1	Billings in Excess of Costs & Est. Earnings	4.7	3.5	5.1	4.4	4.1
	.1			.1	Income Taxes Payable	.2	.4	.6	.2	.1
	4.3			4.6	Cur. Mat.-L/T/D	3.9	4.3	3.1	3.6	4.6
	6.5			6.8	All Other Current	8.1	10.3	10.4	9.7	6.8
	42.3			42.8	Total Current	42.8	43.0	43.4	48.0	42.8
	13.5			13.6	Long-Term Debt	10.8	12.1	13.0	21.0	13.6
	.8			.7	Deferred Taxes	1.1	.6	1.0	.6	.7
	2.5			2.0	All Other Non-Current	2.9	9.0	5.5	4.7	2.0
	40.9			41.0	Net Worth	42.4	35.4	37.1	25.7	41.0
	100.0			100.0	Total Liabilities & Net Worth	100.0	100.0	100.0	100.0	100.0
					INCOME DATA					
	100.0			100.0	Contract Revenues	100.0	100.0	100.0	100.0	100.0
	23.4			25.9	Gross Profit	23.7	27.4	26.1	30.5	25.9
	20.1			21.9	Operating Expenses	20.5	23.9	22.9	27.1	21.9
	3.3			3.9	Operating Profit	3.2	3.6	3.3	3.4	3.9
	.4			.4	All Other Expenses (net)	.4	.6	.2	.3	.4
	2.9			3.6	Profit Before Taxes	2.8	3.0	3.0	3.1	3.6
					RATIOS					
	3.2			2.3	Current	2.8	2.8	2.9	2.3	2.3
	1.7			1.7		1.7	1.7	1.7	1.4	1.7
	1.1			1.1		1.1	1.1	1.1	.9	1.1
	5.8			6.1	Receivables/Payables	7.3	6.6	6.1	6.1	6.1
	(49) 2.9		(59)	3.3		(86) 3.9	(72) 3.5	(80) 3.1	(56) 4.0	(59) 3.3
	1.7			1.8		1.8	1.8	1.6	2.1	1.8
36 10.2			28	13.1	Revenues/Receivables	38 9.6	31 11.9	26 14.1	32 11.3	28 13.1
61 6.0			58	6.3		59 6.2	50 7.3	51 7.1	61 6.0	58 6.3
83 4.4			81	4.5		73 5.0	70 5.2	73 5.0	87 4.2	81 4.5
12 31.3			10	35.8	Cost of Revenues/Payables	10 37.4	10 36.3	8 45.7	8 43.2	10 35.8
22 16.5			20	17.9		19 19.7	19 19.6	20 18.1	20 18.4	20 17.9
38 9.5			35	10.5		32 11.3	35 10.3	32 11.3	42 8.6	35 10.5
	5.6			6.4	Revenues/Working Capital	6.0	6.3	5.8	8.6	6.4
	11.0			11.2		11.0	13.5	11.4	15.7	11.2
	82.1			69.7		54.6	34.3	81.5	-108.2	69.7
	10.4			16.0	EBIT/Interest	18.3	14.8	17.2	9.2	16.0
	(44) 4.9		(56)	5.0		(83) 5.3	(70) 4.6	(73) 6.0	(54) 3.9	(56) 5.0
	.8			1.6		1.8	1.9	2.1	-.7	1.6
				5.1	Net Profit + Depr., Dep., Amort./Cur. Mat. L /T/D	9.4	19.1	16.8		5.1
			(11)	2.5		(23) 3.7	(13) 4.6	(18) 5.7		(11) 2.5
				1.8		2.1	1.8	1.3		1.8
	.2			.2	Fixed/Worth	.2	.2	.2	.2	.2
	.7			.5		.5	.6	.6	.6	.5
	2.0			1.9		1.2	1.6	1.6	1.7	1.9
	.6			.6	Debt/Worth	.6	.6	.6	.9	.6
	1.2			1.2		1.3	1.5	1.2	1.8	1.2
	5.1			4.9		4.3	5.5	4.6	4.9	4.9
	46.9			43.4	% Profit Before Taxes/ Tangible Net Worth	45.6	54.0	42.5	52.8	43.4
	(45) 23.6		(57)	23.7		(83) 23.6	(69) 24.2	(72) 16.9	(53) 24.3	(57) 23.7
	1.2			6.2		4.8	9.2	5.2	.5	6.2
	18.5			19.1	% Profit Before Taxes/ Total Assets	20.1	18.2	18.3	20.6	19.1
	9.4			9.4		8.2	7.0	8.5	7.4	9.4
	.5			1.3		1.4	2.4	.9	-1.8	1.3
	1.0			.9	% Depr., Dep., Amort./ Revenues	1.1	1.1	1.0	1.1	.9
	(41) 1.7		(54)	1.7		(87) 2.3	(68) 2.1	(70) 2.1	(45) 2.1	(54) 1.7
	2.8			2.9		3.0	3.2	3.7	3.9	2.9
	2.5			2.5	% Officers', Directors', Owners' Comp/Revenues	2.3	2.7	3.0	3.5	2.5
	(37) 3.9		(45)	4.1		(61) 4.3	(44) 3.8	(56) 4.3	(42) 4.9	(45) 4.1
	5.8			9.0		8.4	6.7	8.3	8.3	9.0
2058M	202430M	135526M	66704M	406718M	Contract Revenues ($)	467651M	394426M	497165M	5086711M	406718M
734M	72657M	41618M	32010M	147019M	Total Assets ($)	168993M	151720M	187526M	2113228M	147019M

M = $ thousand   MM = $ million
See Pages 11 through 21 for Explanation of Ratios and Data

CONSTRUCTION – % OF COMPLETION—Glass and Glazing Contractors   NAICS 238150 (SIC 1793, 1799)

Current Data Sorted By Revenue | **Comparative Historical Data**

0-1MM	1-10MM	10-50MM	50 & OVER	ALL	Type of Statement	4/1/00-3/31/01 ALL	4/1/01-3/31/02 ALL	4/1/02-3/31/03 ALL	4/1/03-3/31/04 ALL	4/1/04-3/31/05 ALL
	2			2	Unqualified	3	4	5	2	2
	16	3		19	Reviewed	16	19	18	14	19
	3			3	Compiled	8	8	9	4	3
4	4			8	Tax Returns	11	9	12	6	8
2	3			5	Other	6	8	7	4	5
7 (4/1-9/30/04)			30 (10/1/04-3/31/05)							
6	28	3		37	**NUMBER OF STATEMENTS**	44	48	51	30	37
%	%	%	%	%	**ASSETS**	%	%	%	%	%
	12.0			10.7	Cash & Equivalents	9.6	10.8	12.1	11.7	10.7
	54.6			51.0	A/R - Progress Billings	50.7	47.8	45.8	47.4	51.0
	1.8			1.8	A/R - Current Retention	3.9	1.9	1.9	1.8	1.8
	6.8			8.7	Inventory	8.6	6.5	7.0	9.8	8.7
	5.0			4.1	Cost & Est. Earnings In Excess of Billings	2.3	2.6	4.1	1.9	4.1
	1.5			2.5	All Other Current	2.5	4.3	3.8	1.7	2.5
	81.6			78.8	Total Current	77.7	73.8	74.7	74.4	78.8
	14.6	(DATA NOT AVAILABLE)		14.9	Fixed Assets (net)	13.6	17.4	18.9	16.4	14.9
	.1			.1	Joint Ventures & Investments	1.2	.7	.7	.1	.1
	.7			2.5	Intangibles (net)	1.8	1.5	1.9	3.4	2.5
	3.0			3.6	All Other Non-Current	5.7	6.7	3.8	5.7	3.6
	100.0			100.0	Total	100.0	100.0	100.0	100.0	100.0
					LIABILITIES					
	9.1			7.6	Notes Payable - Short Term	7.5	10.9	9.0	7.2	7.6
	22.2			22.6	A/P - Trade	25.8	22.0	20.0	21.6	22.6
	.0			.0	A/P - Retention	.1	.5	.2	.0	.0
	5.0			4.9	Billings in Excess of Costs & Est. Earnings	4.7	5.5	3.3	4.5	4.9
	.5			.5	Income Taxes Payable	.3	.3	.1	.0	.5
	1.8			1.8	Cur. Mat.-L/T/D	3.2	3.2	3.3	3.2	1.8
	6.6			6.2	All Other Current	7.1	9.3	9.4	4.3	6.2
	45.3			43.7	Total Current	48.7	51.7	45.3	40.9	43.7
	22.9			23.4	Long-Term Debt	10.3	11.4	17.8	13.0	23.4
	.4			.3	Deferred Taxes	1.3	.5	.7	.5	.3
	6.0			12.7	All Other Non-Current	5.9	6.6	8.5	1.2	12.7
	25.5			19.9	Net Worth	33.8	29.8	27.7	44.3	19.9
	100.0			100.0	Total Liabilities & Net Worth	100.0	100.0	100.0	100.0	100.0
					INCOME DATA					
	100.0			100.0	Contract Revenues	100.0	100.0	100.0	100.0	100.0
	26.2			29.0	Gross Profit	30.5	33.2	35.3	31.0	29.0
	24.5			27.4	Operating Expenses	25.1	29.4	29.4	25.7	27.4
	1.7			1.6	Operating Profit	5.5	3.8	5.9	5.3	1.6
	1.0			.9	All Other Expenses (net)	.2	.3	.7	.5	.9
	.7			.7	Profit Before Taxes	5.3	3.5	5.2	4.9	.7
					RATIOS					
	3.3			2.9	Current	2.5	2.1	2.5	3.0	2.9
	1.7			1.7		1.5	1.5	1.8	1.9	1.7
	1.4			1.4		1.2	1.1	1.3	1.3	1.4
	4.9			4.2	Receivables/Payables	4.2	5.0	4.0	4.1	4.2
	2.6			2.4		2.4	(46) 2.5	(50) 2.8	(29) 2.2	2.4
	1.9			1.6		1.6	1.7	1.5	1.5	1.6
	55 6.6			50 7.3	Revenues/Receivables	41 8.9	38 9.5	31 11.6	36 10.1	50 7.3
	75 4.9			71 5.1		65 5.6	63 5.8	66 5.5	71 5.1	71 5.1
	106 3.4			94 3.9		89 4.1	86 4.2	87 4.2	92 4.0	94 3.9
	21 17.2			24 15.5	Cost of Revenues/Payables	18 19.8	13 28.9	20 18.0	20 17.8	24 15.5
	35 10.4			40 9.2		44 8.2	31 11.7	30 12.3	34 10.8	40 9.2
	47 7.8			53 6.9		64 5.7	57 6.4	49 7.4	59 6.1	53 6.9
	4.1			5.2	Revenues/Working Capital	6.7	8.5	6.2	5.5	5.2
	8.0			8.8		11.2	12.2	8.7	7.4	8.8
	13.9			13.3		21.5	80.5	14.9	14.3	13.3
	47.1			13.0	EBIT/Interest	18.5	16.7	27.8	78.8	13.0
	(24) 4.3			(32) 2.9		(41) 6.8	(42) 5.1	(45) 6.9	(28) 8.8	(32) 2.9
	.1			-.2		2.7	-.7	3.0	2.0	-.2
					Net Profit + Depr., Dep., Amort./Cur. Mat. L /T/D	15.7	24.6	12.8		
						(12) 3.7	(11) 4.2	(12) 3.1		
						1.3	.6	1.0		
	.2			.2	Fixed/Worth	.2	.2	.2	.2	.2
	.3			.3		.4	.4	.4	.4	.3
	1.1			1.7		.7	2.3	1.2	.5	1.7
	.5			.9	Debt/Worth	1.0	1.2	.7	.9	.9
	1.2			1.6		2.0	2.3	1.3	1.4	1.6
	4.5			6.8		5.1	6.4	4.2	2.7	6.8
	28.6			27.9	% Profit Before Taxes/ Tangible Net Worth	72.9	62.1	51.6	47.7	27.9
	(23) 9.6			(29) 9.6		(39) 34.4	(38) 17.0	(44) 30.7	(28) 19.6	(29) 9.6
	.7			-2.0		21.1	-5.4	10.3	5.7	-2.0
	12.5			10.7	% Profit Before Taxes/ Total Assets	21.5	17.8	22.1	24.8	10.7
	4.1			2.4		11.4	4.5	8.8	7.9	2.4
	-1.8			-3.2		6.5	-6.1	4.6	2.3	-3.2
	.7			.7	% Depr., Dep., Amort./ Revenues	.5	.7	.7	.7	.7
	(26) 1.1			(33) 1.1		(42) .9	(38) 1.2	(44) 1.1	(25) 1.0	(33) 1.1
	2.0			2.1		1.4	1.7	1.9	1.7	2.1
	1.8			2.3	% Officers', Directors', Owners' Comp/Revenues	1.4	3.5	2.7	2.8	2.3
	(21) 4.4			(27) 4.4		(37) 6.1	(31) 6.0	(30) 5.7	(21) 4.9	(27) 4.4
	8.6			9.2		9.9	8.5	12.4	9.8	9.2
3469M	125234M	38902M		167605M	Contract Revenues ($)	382300M	632271M	4923991M	146927M	167605M
1602M	53086M	14912M		69600M	Total Assets ($)	159371M	261414M	992970M	57073M	69600M

© RMA 2005

M = $ thousand   MM = $ million
See Pages 11 through 21 for Explanation of Ratios and Data

Current Data Sorted By Revenue · **Comparative Historical Data**

Type of Statement

					Type of Statement					
	4	3		7	Unqualified	27	15	9	4	7
1	43	7		51	Reviewed	98	73	61	37	51
1	22	2		25	Compiled	32	34	27	23	25
4	12			16	Tax Returns	16	17	21	5	16
2	14	1		17	Other	34	31	33	20	17

21 (4/1-9/30/04)   95 (10/1/04-3/31/05)

0-1MM	1-10MM	10-50MM	50 & OVER	ALL		4/1/00-3/31/01 ALL	4/1/01-3/31/02 ALL	4/1/02-3/31/03 ALL	4/1/03-3/31/04 ALL	4/1/04-3/31/05 ALL
8	95	13		116	**NUMBER OF STATEMENTS**	207	170	151	89	116
%	%	%	%	%	**ASSETS**	%	%	%	%	%
	13.7	4.3		13.3	Cash & Equivalents	12.2	12.0	14.1	9.0	13.3
	41.8	50.5		40.4	A/R - Progress Billings	39.9	39.8	37.2	42.0	40.4
	1.5	4.5		1.8	A/R - Current Retention	2.3	.9	1.1	1.7	1.8
	7.3	8.4		7.7	Inventory	6.2	7.4	5.9	5.4	7.7
	4.6	6.2		4.5	Cost & Est. Earnings In Excess of Billings	5.7	3.4	3.9	5.3	4.5
	3.5	4.5		3.4	All Other Current	2.7	4.6	6.5	5.2	3.4
	72.4	78.4		71.1	Total Current	69.0	68.1	68.7	68.6	71.1
	19.2	10.3		19.7	Fixed Assets (net)	21.9	22.7	22.7	21.1	19.7
	1.0	.0		1.0	Joint Ventures & Investments	.7	.3	.5	.6	1.0
	1.0	2.8		1.2	Intangibles (net)	2.1	3.1	1.8	2.4	1.2
	6.4	8.4		7.0	All Other Non-Current	6.2	5.9	6.3	7.4	7.0
	100.0	100.0		100.0	Total	100.0	100.0	100.0	100.0	100.0
					LIABILITIES					
	11.5	6.6		11.2	Notes Payable - Short Term	13.1	11.1	12.4	11.9	11.2
	22.4	23.1		21.6	A/P - Trade	19.5	20.0	18.6	21.4	21.6
	1.0	1.7		1.0	A/P - Retention	.1	.1	.2	.4	1.0
	4.4	5.7		4.2	Billings in Excess of Costs & Est. Earnings	4.2	3.4	3.4	4.4	4.2
	.1	.2		.1	Income Taxes Payable	.4	.3	.8	.2	.1
	4.4	2.2		4.4	Cur. Mat.-L/T/D	2.8	5.5	4.4	4.4	4.4
	8.3	9.1		8.0	All Other Current	8.0	8.6	11.2	7.7	8.0
	52.0	48.5		50.5	Total Current	48.1	49.0	51.1	52.8	50.5
	11.7	5.4		13.1	Long-Term Debt	10.7	13.2	11.1	12.2	13.1
	.7	.6		.6	Deferred Taxes	1.5	.6	.6	.7	.6
	2.0	1.3		3.5	All Other Non-Current	2.4	3.1	3.4	3.0	3.5
	33.6	44.2		32.2	Net Worth	37.3	34.1	33.9	31.3	32.2
	100.0	100.0		100.0	Total Liabilities & Net Worth	100.0	100.0	100.0	100.0	100.0
					INCOME DATA					
	100.0	100.0		100.0	Contract Revenues	100.0	100.0	100.0	100.0	100.0
	27.5	19.1		28.0	Gross Profit	26.2	30.5	30.3	28.9	28.0
	24.1	16.4		24.9	Operating Expenses	23.1	26.6	27.7	25.4	24.9
	3.4	2.6		3.1	Operating Profit	3.1	3.9	2.6	3.6	3.1
	.1	−.8		.1	All Other Expenses (net)	.2	.7	.7	.3	.1
	3.2	3.5		3.0	Profit Before Taxes	2.9	3.2	1.9	3.2	3.0
					RATIOS					
	2.1	2.0		2.1	Current	2.2	2.1	2.1	1.8	2.1
	1.5	1.5		1.5		1.5	1.5	1.4	1.4	1.5
	1.1	1.3		1.1		1.2	1.1	1.1	1.0	1.1
	4.3	2.9		3.6	Receivables/Payables	4.2	4.1	4.6	3.9	3.6
(90)	2.1	2.6	(111)	2.1		(202) 2.4	(168) 2.2	(139) 2.2	(87) 2.6	(111) 2.1
	1.4	1.6		1.3		1.5	1.4	1.2	1.4	1.3
30 12.3	53 6.9		28 13.1		Revenues/Receivables	31 11.9	27 13.4	19 19.4	28 12.8	28 13.1
50 7.3	59 6.2		50 7.2			50 7.3	47 7.8	46 7.9	50 7.3	50 7.2
70 5.2	80 4.5		70 5.2			74 4.9	68 5.3	73 5.0	73 5.0	70 5.2
15 23.9	24 15.2		15 23.9		Cost of Revenues/Payables	16 22.7	17 21.8	12 29.5	15 24.2	15 23.9
25 14.4	33 11.1		26 13.9			27 13.6	29 12.4	27 13.6	27 13.6	26 13.9
52 7.0	55 6.7		52 7.1			43 8.5	51 7.2	48 7.5	53 6.9	52 7.1
	8.1	8.2		8.2	Revenues/Working Capital	7.0	7.7	8.2	8.6	8.2
	15.2	9.4		14.5		14.3	14.3	17.2	16.9	14.5
	56.3	15.4		52.1		41.1	53.9	76.9	NM	52.1
	14.5	17.5		14.7	EBIT/Interest	11.3	14.4	14.9	11.3	14.7
(86)	5.2	(12) 10.1	(105)	5.7		(189) 4.4	(150) 4.6	(133) 4.1	(82) 4.0	(105) 5.7
	1.4	3.5		1.1		1.5	1.4	.4	.3	1.1
	5.6			6.9	Net Profit + Depr., Dep., Amort./Cur. Mat. L /T/D	7.7	6.9	5.3	8.2	6.9
(32)	2.5		(39)	2.5		(64) 3.9	(43) 2.9	(42) 2.2	(21) 3.0	(39) 2.5
	.8			1.2		1.4	1.5	.1	1.2	1.2
	.2	.1		.2	Fixed/Worth	.3	.2	.3	.2	.2
	.5	.3		.5		.5	.5	.5	.6	.5
	1.2	.5		1.2		1.1	1.3	1.2	1.5	1.2
	.9	.8		.9	Debt/Worth	.8	.9	.8	.9	.9
	1.9	1.0		1.9		1.5	1.5	1.8	1.7	1.9
	5.6	2.4		5.8		3.4	4.3	4.1	6.3	5.8
	58.3	38.7		59.4	% Profit Before Taxes/Tangible Net Worth	48.5	48.1	38.2	50.0	59.4
(87)	27.9	21.4	(104)	28.8		(192) 21.7	(152) 19.3	(134) 14.0	(75) 13.0	(104) 28.8
	1.6	6.3		2.2		4.4	4.9	−.1	−.7	2.2
	14.2	17.8		16.0	% Profit Before Taxes/Total Assets	16.4	16.2	14.6	16.0	16.0
	6.1	6.2		6.1		6.6	6.9	5.0	4.7	6.1
	.3	2.6		.2		1.5	.8	−1.7	−1.2	.2
	.6	.5		.6	% Depr., Dep., Amort./Revenues	.9	.9	.9	1.0	.6
(84)	1.4	(12) 1.0	(103)	1.4		(185) 1.6	(150) 1.6	(133) 1.7	(71) 1.5	(103) 1.4
	2.2	1.6		2.2		2.5	2.5	2.8	2.7	2.2
	2.0	1.7		2.0	% Officers', Directors', Owners' Comp/Revenues	2.4	2.6	2.2	2.0	2.0
(60)	3.1	(11) 2.2	(77)	3.4		(114) 4.3	(97) 4.3	(95) 4.4	(61) 4.0	(77) 3.4
	7.1	4.7		7.1		7.4	7.8	7.9	7.3	7.1
4591M	435433M	256382M		696406M	Contract Revenues ($)	30584784M	8295579M	10738454M	6891597M	696406M
1702M	158085M	87030M		246817M	Total Assets ($)	14366245M	3126227M	3532983M	1534313M	246817M

(Columns 0-1MM and 50 & OVER: DATA NOT AVAILABLE for the Assets/Liabilities/Income/Ratios section.)

© RMA 2005

M = $ thousand   MM = $ million
See Pages 11 through 21 for Explanation of Ratios and Data

Current Data Sorted By Revenue   **Comparative Historical Data**

					Type of Statement					
1	19	17	5	42	Unqualified	61	47	42	42	42
8	118	36	3	165	Reviewed	198	168	154	138	165
8	28	1		37	Compiled	88	76	59	50	37
21	33	1	2	57	Tax Returns	31	34	46	43	57
10	31	12	4	57	Other	63	66	64	44	57
93 (4/1-9/30/04)			265 (10/1/04-3/31/05)			4/1/00-3/31/01	4/1/01-3/31/02	4/1/02-3/31/03	4/1/03-3/31/04	4/1/04-3/31/05
0-1MM	1-10MM	10-50MM	50 & OVER	ALL		ALL	ALL	ALL	ALL	ALL
48	229	67	14	358	NUMBER OF STATEMENTS	441	391	365	317	358
%	%	%	%	%	**ASSETS**	%	%	%	%	%
17.1	12.0	9.5	7.9	12.0	Cash & Equivalents	11.8	13.4	13.3	11.2	12.0
32.8	46.3	50.4	37.4	44.9	A/R - Progress Billings	46.0	42.7	44.2	45.8	44.9
.0	1.4	4.3	4.3	1.9	A/R - Current Retention	2.5	1.9	1.6	1.7	1.9
11.0	6.2	4.7	12.0	6.8	Inventory	5.5	5.6	5.5	6.2	6.8
.9	5.6	7.2	4.1	5.2	Cost & Est. Earnings In Excess of Billings	5.2	4.6	4.6	5.0	5.2
3.7	5.2	6.6	9.7	5.4	All Other Current	3.9	5.3	4.9	4.7	5.4
65.4	76.6	82.7	75.5	76.2	Total Current	75.0	73.5	74.1	74.5	76.2
27.4	15.4	11.0	9.7	16.0	Fixed Assets (net)	17.4	18.2	17.9	17.8	16.0
.1	.7	1.3	.0	.7	Joint Ventures & Investments	1.1	.6	.5	.7	.7
1.8	1.0	1.7	3.7	1.3	Intangibles (net)	1.6	2.4	1.2	1.7	1.3
5.3	6.2	3.3	11.2	5.8	All Other Non-Current	4.9	5.3	6.3	5.2	5.8
100.0	100.0	100.0	100.0	100.0	Total	100.0	100.0	100.0	100.0	100.0
					LIABILITIES					
28.0	13.7	9.9	9.1	14.7	Notes Payable - Short Term	10.7	9.9	13.9	13.1	14.7
28.6	21.2	23.6	16.1	22.5	A/P - Trade	19.3	18.5	18.8	19.6	22.5
.1	.2	.3	.0	.2	A/P - Retention	.3	.2	.1	.2	.2
1.1	4.5	7.5	6.2	4.7	Billings in Excess of Costs & Est. Earnings	6.0	5.5	5.1	5.7	4.7
.2	.2	.5	.1	.3	Income Taxes Payable	.6	.5	.3	.3	.3
3.5	3.1	2.1	2.3	3.0	Cur. Mat.-L/T/D	3.5	3.5	4.4	4.8	3.0
5.5	9.5	10.5	9.4	9.2	All Other Current	8.9	10.2	8.5	8.4	9.2
66.9	52.5	54.5	43.2	54.4	Total Current	49.3	48.4	51.1	52.1	54.4
22.4	9.2	6.8	4.1	10.3	Long-Term Debt	9.3	10.3	9.0	10.8	10.3
.0	.7	.3	.1	.5	Deferred Taxes	1.1	.6	.7	.9	.5
14.1	4.0	4.4	9.0	5.7	All Other Non-Current	2.3	2.4	5.1	3.8	5.7
-3.5	33.6	34.0	43.6	29.1	Net Worth	38.1	38.3	34.0	32.4	29.1
100.0	100.0	100.0	100.0	100.0	Total Liabilities & Net Worth	100.0	100.0	100.0	100.0	100.0
					INCOME DATA					
100.0	100.0	100.0	100.0	100.0	Contract Revenues	100.0	100.0	100.0	100.0	100.0
48.7	25.7	19.5	30.6	27.8	Gross Profit	27.1	28.6	27.9	26.6	27.8
45.4	23.4	16.1	26.6	25.1	Operating Expenses	23.5	24.8	26.2	24.3	25.1
3.3	2.3	3.4	4.0	2.7	Operating Profit	3.6	3.7	1.7	2.3	2.7
.6	.2	.3	.6	.3	All Other Expenses (net)	.5	.6	.5	.5	.3
2.7	2.1	3.1	3.4	2.4	Profit Before Taxes	3.1	3.1	1.2	1.8	2.4
					RATIOS					
3.1	2.5	1.9	2.4	2.2	Current	2.2	2.3	2.3	2.3	2.2
1.3	1.7	1.5	1.7	1.6		1.6	1.6	1.5	1.5	1.6
.7	1.2	1.2	1.3	1.2		1.2	1.2	1.2	1.2	1.2
3.8	4.0	3.6	5.9	3.8	Receivables/Payables	4.5	4.9	4.6	4.5	3.8
(40) 2.1	(218) 2.5	2.6	3.3	(339) 2.5		(425) 2.7	(371) 2.8	(352) 2.8	(303) 2.8	(339) 2.5
1.3	1.6	1.7	1.6	1.6		1.8	1.8	1.9	1.8	1.6
0 UND	40 9.2	50 7.3	35 10.3	38 9.5	Revenues/Receivables	42 8.7	33 11.1	40 9.2	40 9.2	38 9.5
39 9.4	59 6.2	63 5.8	58 6.3	59 6.2		60 6.1	56 6.6	56 6.5	61 5.9	59 6.2
70 5.2	82 4.5	84 4.3	66 5.5	82 4.5		79 4.6	76 4.8	78 4.7	84 4.3	82 4.5
8 48.1	18 20.7	21 17.8	16 23.0	18 20.3	Cost of Revenues/Payables	16 22.5	14 25.6	16 23.0	16 22.5	18 20.3
33 11.2	29 12.5	31 11.9	31 11.6	30 12.3		29 12.7	25 14.5	25 14.3	27 13.5	30 12.3
87 4.2	49 7.4	53 6.8	45 8.2	52 7.0		44 8.3	42 8.7	44 8.3	45 8.1	52 7.0
7.5	5.9	8.1	6.4	6.9	Revenues/Working Capital	6.9	6.6	6.5	6.6	6.9
21.4	11.0	11.5	7.8	11.6		10.9	10.9	11.6	11.5	11.6
-21.1	28.7	17.8	20.4	28.6		25.9	27.2	29.4	28.8	28.6
10.1	13.8	20.3	18.7	15.0	EBIT/Interest	14.5	16.6	13.5	12.9	15.0
(40) 4.0	(195) 4.1	(62) 8.1	9.6	(311) 5.0		(391) 4.3	(348) 5.4	(315) 3.2	(288) 4.4	(311) 5.0
-.8	.8	2.7	2.2	1.0		1.4	2.1	-.5	.7	1.0
	6.8	9.3		7.9	Net Profit + Depr., Dep., Amort./Cur. Mat. L./T/D	5.6	7.9	9.1	7.9	7.9
	(73) 2.3	(29) 4.7		(108) 2.6		(140) 2.7	(104) 3.1	(102) 3.0	(79) 2.3	(108) 2.6
	.2	1.6		.5		1.4	1.4	.7	.9	.5
.4	.2	.2	.0	.2	Fixed/Worth	.2	.2	.2	.2	.2
.9	.4	.3	.2	.4		.4	.4	.4	.4	.4
-1.1	.9	.5	.8	1.0		.8	.8	.9	1.0	1.0
1.0	.7	1.1	.7	.8	Debt/Worth	.8	.7	.8	.8	.8
3.4	1.6	1.8	1.6	1.7		1.7	1.5	1.5	1.8	1.7
-5.2	4.7	3.3	4.1	5.0		3.6	3.2	3.7	4.4	5.0
58.1	44.3	51.8	41.3	45.0	% Profit Before Taxes/Tangible Net Worth	52.4	51.7	33.1	42.0	45.0
(33) 19.8	(201) 12.8	(64) 29.1	22.8	(312) 15.3		(412) 22.0	(352) 23.0	(326) 11.9	(279) 16.0	(312) 15.3
-1.8	.8	4.3	4.6	1.3		5.4	7.8	.3	1.2	1.3
33.5	15.2	15.4	15.7	16.0	% Profit Before Taxes/Total Assets	18.1	18.4	12.7	13.9	16.0
9.2	5.3	8.3	8.5	6.1		7.1	8.7	3.4	5.7	6.1
-1.1	-.2	2.0	2.2	.1		1.0	2.3	-2.6	-.7	.1
1.1	.8	.5		.7	% Depr., Dep., Amort./Revenues	.7	.7	.6	.7	.7
(33) 2.4	(203) 1.2	(62) .9		(304) 1.2		(390) 1.3	(345) 1.2	(334) 1.3	(256) 1.3	(304) 1.2
4.3	2.1	1.2		1.9		2.1	2.3	2.3	2.3	1.9
6.0	2.6	.8		2.2	% Officers', Directors', Owners' Comp/Revenues	2.7	2.7	2.8	2.0	2.2
(30) 9.1	(141) 4.7	(34) 1.9		(211) 4.7		(246) 4.7	(230) 4.5	(238) 5.3	(199) 3.7	(211) 4.7
15.8	7.3	5.1		8.1		8.3	8.3	8.5	7.2	8.1
28762M	958339M	1468111M	18557984M	21013196M	Contract Revenues ($)	55857686M	17843272M	31031225M	9379206M	21013196M
12511M	345800M	502728M	6078220M	6939259M	Total Assets ($)	21567310M	8818003M	11872857M	4698327M	6939259M

© RMA 2005   M = $ thousand   MM = $ million
See Pages 11 through 21 for Explanation of Ratios and Data

Current Data Sorted By Revenue | **Comparative Historical Data**

					Type of Statement					
1	10	17	2	30	Unqualified	58	46	43	16	30
2	67	25	3	97	Reviewed	210	189	162	99	97
8	48	2		58	Compiled	83	79	101	47	58
24	40	3	1	68	Tax Returns	65	60	75	39	68
8	33	7	2	50	Other	70	72	82	39	50

73 (4/1-9/30/04) 230 (10/1/04-3/31/05)

0-1MM	1-10MM	10-50MM	50 & OVER	ALL	NUMBER OF STATEMENTS	4/1/00-3/31/01 ALL	4/1/01-3/31/02 ALL	4/1/02-3/31/03 ALL	4/1/03-3/31/04 ALL	4/1/04-3/31/05 ALL
43	198	54	8	303		486	446	463	240	303
%	%	%	%	%	**ASSETS**	%	%	%	%	%
13.7	11.0	11.4		11.5	Cash & Equivalents	11.5	11.4	12.0	11.7	11.5
22.4	42.9	49.1		41.2	A/R - Progress Billings	43.9	41.4	39.9	41.6	41.2
.3	1.2	5.8		1.9	A/R - Current Retention	2.9	3.0	2.2	2.5	1.9
13.5	10.0	4.2		9.4	Inventory	7.8	8.9	9.4	8.2	9.4
.1	3.4	6.2		3.4	Cost & Est. Earnings In Excess of Billings	3.7	3.4	3.5	3.5	3.4
2.6	4.3	5.9		4.3	All Other Current	4.0	4.5	4.8	4.8	4.3
52.6	72.7	82.5		71.7	Total Current	73.8	72.6	71.7	72.4	71.7
28.4	19.1	11.7		19.0	Fixed Assets (net)	19.1	19.6	20.1	19.4	19.0
.3	.6	1.0		.6	Joint Ventures & Investments	.7	.6	.8	.6	.6
3.1	2.2	.4		1.9	Intangibles (net)	1.8	1.8	1.1	1.5	1.9
15.6	5.4	4.4		6.8	All Other Non-Current	4.6	5.3	6.3	6.1	6.8
100.0	100.0	100.0		100.0	Total	100.0	100.0	100.0	100.0	100.0
					LIABILITIES					
22.5	12.8	8.2		13.3	Notes Payable - Short Term	8.8	11.4	10.5	11.9	13.3
21.2	22.6	24.7		22.6	A/P - Trade	23.5	23.2	22.3	21.3	22.6
.0	.2	.8		.2	A/P - Retention	.5	1.6	.4	.2	.2
1.2	3.9	9.9		4.7	Billings in Excess of Costs & Est. Earnings	5.0	5.4	4.8	5.5	4.7
.1	.2	.7		.3	Income Taxes Payable	.6	.4	.4	.3	.3
7.2	3.4	2.3		3.8	Cur. Mat.-L/T/D	3.9	4.1	4.2	3.6	3.8
11.2	10.3	9.0		10.1	All Other Current	7.6	7.9	8.3	11.6	10.1
63.4	53.3	55.6		55.1	Total Current	49.9	54.0	51.0	54.3	55.1
25.8	14.1	5.7		14.2	Long-Term Debt	11.2	11.1	13.0	13.8	14.2
.0	.3	.2		.3	Deferred Taxes	.6	.5	.5	.6	.3
13.8	5.7	2.2		6.2	All Other Non-Current	2.4	4.1	3.6	4.1	6.2
-2.9	26.5	36.2		24.3	Net Worth	35.9	30.3	31.8	27.1	24.3
100.0	100.0	100.0		100.0	Total Liabilities & Net Worth	100.0	100.0	100.0	100.0	100.0
					INCOME DATA					
100.0	100.0	100.0		100.0	Contract Revenues	100.0	100.0	100.0	100.0	100.0
46.5	28.5	17.1		28.8	Gross Profit	26.5	28.2	30.0	29.2	28.8
43.9	26.2	15.1		26.4	Operating Expenses	23.4	25.2	27.8	26.8	26.4
2.6	2.3	2.1		2.3	Operating Profit	3.2	3.0	2.3	2.4	2.3
1.8	.3	.0		.4	All Other Expenses (net)	.3	.6	.5	.5	.4
.8	2.1	2.1		1.9	Profit Before Taxes	2.8	2.4	1.8	1.9	1.9
					RATIOS					
2.1	2.2	1.8		2.1	Current	2.2	2.1	2.3	2.2	2.1
1.1	1.4	1.4		1.4		1.5	1.4	1.5	1.4	1.4
.5	1.1	1.2		1.1		1.1	1.1	1.1	1.1	1.1
2.6	3.3	3.2		3.2	Receivables/Payables	3.4	3.4	3.4	3.6	3.2
(35) 1.2	(192) 2.3	2.1	(289) 2.1			(477) 2.2	(439) 2.1	(442) 2.1	(229) 2.3	(289) 2.1
.3	1.4	1.6		1.3		1.4	1.4	1.3	1.4	1.3
0 UND	28 12.9	51 7.2	27 13.5		Revenues/Receivables	35 10.4	33 11.2	28 13.0	32 11.5	27 13.5
18 19.8	47 7.7	68 5.4	48 7.6			52 7.1	51 7.2	50 7.3	52 7.0	48 7.6
41 8.9	68 5.4	89 4.1	71 5.2			75 4.9	71 5.1	74 5.0	74 4.9	71 5.2
4 89.5	19 19.6	24 15.1	19 19.3		Cost of Revenues/Payables	20 18.4	19 19.0	18 20.6	18 20.1	19 19.3
30 12.1	29 12.7	35 10.6	30 12.1			32 11.6	32 11.3	31 11.9	30 12.3	30 12.1
61 8.2	44 8.2	51 7.1	48 7.6			49 7.5	50 7.3	51 7.2	47 7.8	48 7.6
10.9	8.6	7.5		8.2	Revenues/Working Capital	7.2	7.9	7.1	7.9	8.2
119.0	16.1	14.1		16.5		13.5	15.2	14.7	14.0	16.5
-13.6	97.7	25.0		95.3		43.6	49.8	43.6	37.7	95.3
6.3	12.7	28.6		17.8	EBIT/Interest	13.0	12.1	14.5	17.2	17.8
(35) 3.0	(164) 4.1	(48) 7.0	(255) 4.3			(431) 4.6	(398) 3.8	(404) 4.2	(212) 5.3	(255) 4.3
-1.0	.9	1.5		.7		1.5	1.1	.8	1.3	.7
	4.8	8.9		4.8	Net Profit + Depr., Dep., Amort./Cur. Mat. L /T/D	5.8	6.2	5.7	9.5	4.8
	(50) 2.1	(23) 2.7	(76) 2.5			(152) 3.1	(116) 2.8	(146) 2.1	(62) 3.0	(76) 2.5
	.7	.0		.8		1.5	1.2	.7	1.2	.8
.7	.2	.1		.2	Fixed/Worth	.2	.2	.2	.2	.2
2.1	.6	.3		.6		.4	.5	.5	.5	.6
-1.1	1.5	.6		1.6		1.1	1.2	1.3	1.5	1.6
1.6	.9	1.2		1.1	Debt/Worth	.8	.9	.8	.9	1.1
7.2	2.3	2.0		2.3		1.7	2.2	2.0	2.3	2.3
-4.9	6.1	3.1		6.4		3.9	5.1	5.0	5.2	6.4
90.1	50.3	36.3		46.6	% Profit Before Taxes/ Tangible Net Worth	46.5	46.5	43.5	47.8	46.6
(25) 24.4	(164) 20.2	18.1	(251) 20.3			(442) 18.0	(396) 18.9	(413) 14.8	(206) 18.3	(251) 20.3
2.0	3.3	3.1		3.4		4.8	3.1	.2	3.9	3.4
22.5	15.6	13.7		15.2	% Profit Before Taxes/ Total Assets	16.0	13.8	14.4	15.3	15.2
4.6	5.3	6.9		5.7		6.2	5.4	5.0	5.7	5.7
-7.0	.0	.7		-.2		1.2	.2	-.8	.6	-.2
1.3	.7	.3		.6	% Depr., Dep., Amort./ Revenues	.7	.8	.8	.7	.6
(32) 2.5	(168) 1.2	(47) .6	(251) 1.2			(437) 1.3	(399) 1.4	(409) 1.5	(187) 1.2	(251) 1.2
3.5	2.3	1.3		2.3		2.2	2.3	2.5	2.3	2.3
4.3	2.3	1.1		2.3	% Officers', Directors', Owners' Comp/Revenues	2.4	2.1	2.5	2.3	2.3
(31) 7.1	(135) 4.0	(32) 2.4	(201) 4.1			(287) 4.3	(261) 4.2	(288) 4.5	(156) 4.5	(201) 4.1
11.3	6.8	5.1		7.6		7.7	7.5	7.7	8.8	7.6
24934M	821568M	1033881M	4870674M	6751057M	Contract Revenues ($)	35398122M	25827947M	19010216M	8652715M	6751057M
8450M	270672M	370563M	1249270M	1898955M	Total Assets ($)	13533233M	10433513M	10868176M	3419800M	1898955M

M = $ thousand   MM = $ million
See Pages 11 through 21 for Explanation of Ratios and Data

Current Data Sorted By Revenue   **Comparative Historical Data**

0-1MM	1-10MM	10-50MM	50 & OVER	ALL		4/1/00-3/31/01 ALL	4/1/01-3/31/02 ALL	4/1/02-3/31/03 ALL	4/1/03-3/31/04 ALL	4/1/04-3/31/05 ALL
					Type of Statement					
	1	7	4	12	Unqualified	17	11	16	9	12
	31	15		46	Reviewed	71	55	60	29	46
2	13	1	1	17	Compiled	20	25	26	9	17
2	12			14	Tax Returns	14	19	17	14	14
1	14	4	1	20	Other	17	19	22	11	20
26 (4/1-9/30/04)		83 (10/1/04-3/31/05)								
5	71	27	6	109	**NUMBER OF STATEMENTS**	139	129	141	72	109
%	%	%	%	%	**ASSETS**	%	%	%	%	%
	8.6	10.4		9.7	Cash & Equivalents	11.2	11.8	11.8	9.1	9.7
	54.2	56.8		53.2	A/R - Progress Billings	51.8	50.2	47.1	54.1	53.2
	2.2	3.5		2.3	A/R - Current Retention	4.6	2.2	1.5	3.7	2.3
	7.5	2.0		5.9	Inventory	4.4	4.6	4.2	4.8	5.9
	4.0	5.5		4.1	Cost & Est. Earnings In Excess of Billings	3.6	3.0	4.0	3.7	4.1
	4.1	5.2		4.6	All Other Current	2.5	4.6	5.1	4.7	4.6
	80.5	83.4		79.8	Total Current	78.1	76.4	73.6	80.0	79.8
	13.0	12.2		12.6	Fixed Assets (net)	14.5	15.3	19.3	13.4	12.6
	.4	.3		.3	Joint Ventures & Investments	.9	2.0	.5	.1	.3
	.3	.8		1.8	Intangibles (net)	1.1	.6	.5	1.4	1.8
	5.8	3.4		5.5	All Other Non-Current	5.4	5.7	6.1	5.0	5.5
	100.0	100.0		100.0	Total	100.0	100.0	100.0	100.0	100.0
					LIABILITIES					
	18.4	10.5		16.3	Notes Payable - Short Term	11.5	11.4	10.7	14.0	16.3
	18.7	15.0		16.8	A/P - Trade	16.0	15.0	15.1	20.5	16.8
	.0	.5		.2	A/P - Retention	.2	.4	.7	.2	.2
	4.7	11.1		6.0	Billings in Excess of Costs & Est. Earnings	7.0	6.3	4.0	4.6	6.0
	.3	.3		.3	Income Taxes Payable	.4	.3	.2	.3	.3
	2.0	1.8		1.9	Cur. Mat.-L/T/D	2.4	3.3	3.0	2.4	1.9
	10.6	11.5		10.8	All Other Current	9.4	9.8	10.3	11.2	10.8
	54.9	50.7		52.3	Total Current	46.9	46.4	43.9	53.1	52.3
	11.7	3.5		10.3	Long-Term Debt	7.5	8.8	10.2	9.4	10.3
	.7	1.0		.7	Deferred Taxes	1.2	1.0	.8	.2	.7
	7.7	1.8		5.9	All Other Non-Current	1.7	3.4	4.2	5.6	5.9
	25.1	43.0		30.8	Net Worth	42.7	40.4	40.9	31.7	30.8
	100.0	100.0		100.0	Total Liabilities & Net Worth	100.0	100.0	100.0	100.0	100.0
					INCOME DATA					
	100.0	100.0		100.0	Contract Revenues	100.0	100.0	100.0	100.0	100.0
	23.2	16.5		23.2	Gross Profit	23.9	26.2	24.3	23.0	23.2
	21.6	13.0		21.0	Operating Expenses	19.3	21.2	21.3	19.4	21.0
	1.7	3.6		2.2	Operating Profit	4.6	5.1	3.1	3.5	2.2
	.4	.0		.3	All Other Expenses (net)	.2	.4	.1	.3	.3
	1.2	3.6		1.9	Profit Before Taxes	4.4	4.7	3.0	3.2	1.9
					RATIOS					
	2.6	2.1		2.5	Current	2.4	2.4	2.9	2.6	2.5
	1.5	1.6		1.6		1.7	1.7	1.9	1.6	1.6
	1.1	1.3		1.2		1.3	1.2	1.2	1.3	1.2
	6.4	6.5		6.8	Receivables/Payables	6.7	7.4	7.3	6.3	6.8
(68)	3.6	3.8	(105)	3.8		(135) 4.4	(123) 4.5	(136) 3.9	3.5	(105) 3.8
	2.0	2.8		2.0		2.5	2.5	2.2	2.0	2.0
42 8.6	61 6.0		40 9.1		Revenues/Receivables	46 8.0	40 9.1	37 9.8	47 7.7	40 9.1
63 5.8	74 4.9		66 5.5			66 5.6	62 5.9	54 6.8	64 5.7	66 5.5
86 4.2	90 4.0		86 4.3			86 4.2	81 4.5	79 4.6	83 4.4	86 4.3
11 34.7	14 25.7		11 33.9		Cost of Revenues/Payables	11 33.6	9 39.1	10 36.7	13 28.7	11 33.9
22 16.7	20 18.0		20 18.4			18 20.3	18 20.4	19 19.1	23 15.6	20 18.4
37 9.8	37 9.9		36 10.0			31 11.6	32 11.4	33 11.0	43 8.6	36 10.0
	6.7	6.4		6.7	Revenues/Working Capital	6.6	6.1	6.2	6.1	6.7
	11.0	10.3		11.0		10.9	10.7	9.8	10.6	11.0
	40.7	16.0		28.1		18.8	25.3	30.2	23.7	28.1
	12.5	27.8		15.7	EBIT/Interest	31.6	22.2	20.3	29.8	15.7
(63)	4.1	(21) 9.6	(93)	6.0		(120) 6.2	(112) 8.7	(119) 5.6	(61) 4.6	(93) 6.0
	.3	5.8		1.3		2.4	2.5	1.7	.9	1.3
	5.2			5.6	Net Profit + Depr., Dep., Amort./Cur. Mat. L/T/D	16.2	9.7	4.6	4.3	5.6
(18)	2.1		(29)	3.0		(47) 6.6	(23) 3.5	(43) 2.0	(16) 2.6	(29) 3.0
	-.9			.0		1.9	2.3	.5	.5	.0
	.2	.1		.1	Fixed/Worth	.1	.1	.1	.1	.1
	.3	.2		.3		.3	.3	.3	.3	.3
	1.7	.5		.9		.5	.7	1.0	.7	.9
	1.0	.9		1.0	Debt/Worth	.7	.6	.6	.8	1.0
	2.4	1.3		2.0		1.3	1.6	1.3	1.5	2.0
	10.5	2.5		7.7		3.0	3.0	3.0	3.9	7.7
	66.5	64.5		70.4	% Profit Before Taxes/Tangible Net Worth	55.2	71.1	43.9	36.9	70.4
(64)	25.8	(26) 21.5	(98)	24.4		(134) 31.4	(124) 30.1	(133) 19.8	(63) 16.8	(98) 24.4
	1.7	9.3		3.2		9.9	7.9	5.5	4.2	3.2
	12.3	20.3		14.2	% Profit Before Taxes/Total Assets	24.2	24.4	16.3	19.4	14.2
	6.7	11.6		6.9		9.9	11.6	7.0	4.8	6.9
	-1.2	4.8		.3		3.3	2.5	1.8	.2	.3
	.5	.4		.4	% Depr., Dep., Amort./Revenues	.4	.4	.5	.5	.4
(58)	.8	(24) .8	(88)	.8		(125) .9	(115) .7	(123) 1.0	(51) .9	(88) .8
	1.3	.9		1.2		1.4	1.6	2.1	1.4	1.2
	1.9	1.0		1.8	% Officers', Directors', Owners' Comp/Revenues	2.8	2.1	2.2	2.1	1.8
(44)	2.8	(15) 2.0	(67)	2.7		(86) 4.3	(82) 4.4	(85) 4.2	(51) 3.5	(67) 2.7
	6.2	3.3		7.0		7.7	8.6	8.9	6.8	7.0
2012M	334693M	607690M	4644421M	5588816M	Contract Revenues ($)	1570925M	1163613M	1239190M	882236M	5588816M
840M	110236M	205438M	1087497M	1404011M	Total Assets ($)	518044M	386837M	439446M	296357M	1404011M

M = $ thousand   MM = $ million
See Pages 11 through 21 for Explanation of Ratios and Data

Current Data Sorted By Revenue | **Comparative Historical Data**

0-1MM	1-10MM	10-50MM	50 & OVER	ALL		4/1/00-3/31/01 ALL	4/1/01-3/31/02 ALL	4/1/02-3/31/03 ALL	4/1/03-3/31/04 ALL	4/1/04-3/31/05 ALL
					Type of Statement					
	7	2		9	Unqualified	14	8	18	4	9
3	12	2		17	Reviewed	35	35	53	17	17
3	11			14	Compiled	20	18	37	11	14
7	4			11	Tax Returns	13	15	27	16	11
3	4			7	Other	10	15	29	7	7
15 (4/1-9/30/04)		43 (10/1/04-3/31/05)								
16	38	4		58	**NUMBER OF STATEMENTS**	92	91	164	55	58
%	%	%	%	%	**ASSETS**	%	%	%	%	%
24.4	14.2		DATA NOT AVAILABLE	16.6	Cash & Equivalents	13.0	11.7	13.9	14.5	16.6
26.1	46.4			40.9	A/R - Progress Billings	45.6	43.8	37.0	40.0	40.9
.3	1.8			1.5	A/R - Current Retention	1.3	.7	.9	1.5	1.5
.0	1.2			1.3	Inventory	1.9	3.0	4.5	1.1	1.3
.0	4.7			3.7	Cost & Est. Earnings In Excess of Billings	5.1	4.4	4.4	2.8	3.7
.8	1.9			1.7	All Other Current	2.8	3.2	4.4	4.8	1.7
51.5	70.1			65.7	Total Current	69.6	66.8	65.1	64.6	65.7
35.5	21.4			24.7	Fixed Assets (net)	19.8	23.3	25.4	23.4	24.7
.0	.6			.4	Joint Ventures & Investments	1.8	.4	.5	.5	.4
1.2	.0			.3	Intangibles (net)	.9	.7	.6	.8	.3
11.7	7.9			8.9	All Other Non-Current	8.0	8.7	8.3	10.7	8.9
100.0	100.0			100.0	Total	100.0	100.0	100.0	100.0	100.0
					LIABILITIES					
23.1	19.5			19.9	Notes Payable - Short Term	11.5	21.0	15.0	12.2	19.9
6.7	16.8			14.5	A/P - Trade	13.1	14.9	13.9	16.5	14.5
.0	.0			.0	A/P - Retention	1.2	.3	.2	.0	.0
.0	1.9			1.3	Billings in Excess of Costs & Est. Earnings	2.1	2.5	2.4	2.1	1.3
.0	.8			.5	Income Taxes Payable	1.0	.7	.6	.8	.5
5.0	4.8			4.7	Cur. Mat.-L/T/D	4.7	3.5	6.2	4.1	4.7
7.8	6.5			7.6	All Other Current	10.5	13.2	11.4	9.9	7.6
42.7	50.3			48.5	Total Current	44.1	56.1	49.7	45.6	48.5
33.7	22.6			24.5	Long-Term Debt	10.7	14.7	13.8	16.1	24.5
.0	.6			.4	Deferred Taxes	1.2	.9	.8	.4	.4
4.4	4.3			4.4	All Other Non-Current	7.8	16.6	6.0	6.1	4.4
19.2	22.2			22.2	Net Worth	36.2	11.7	29.7	31.8	22.2
100.0	100.0			100.0	Total Liabilities & Net Worth	100.0	100.0	100.0	100.0	100.0
					INCOME DATA					
100.0	100.0			100.0	Contract Revenues	100.0	100.0	100.0	100.0	100.0
46.7	27.5			32.5	Gross Profit	29.6	31.6	31.2	33.4	32.5
47.7	24.1			30.1	Operating Expenses	26.9	27.7	29.0	29.9	30.1
-1.0	3.4			2.4	Operating Profit	2.8	3.9	2.2	3.6	2.4
-.5	.7			.3	All Other Expenses (net)	.4	.6	.6	.4	.3
-.5	2.8			2.1	Profit Before Taxes	2.4	3.3	1.5	3.1	2.1
					RATIOS					
2.3	2.4			2.4		2.8	2.5	2.3	2.3	2.4
1.2	1.5			1.5	Current	1.7	1.4	1.5	1.5	1.5
.6	1.1			1.0		1.1	1.0	1.1	1.0	1.0
UND	8.2			8.4		6.8	7.3	6.3	7.4	8.4
(10) 5.1	(36) 3.5			(50) 3.7	Receivables/Payables	(86) 3.8	(84) 3.6	(149) 3.8	(47) 3.5	(50) 3.7
3.3	2.2			2.2		2.3	1.9	1.5	1.9	2.2
0 UND	**39** 9.3			**24** 15.2		**44** 8.3	**27** 13.3	**22** 16.2	**16** 22.5	**24** 15.2
31 11.9	**65** 5.7			**60** 6.1	Revenues/Receivables	**64** 5.7	**58** 6.3	**52** 7.0	**55** 6.6	**60** 6.1
71 5.2	**82** 4.5			**81** 4.5		**84** 4.3	**80** 4.6	**76** 4.8	**73** 5.0	**81** 4.5
0 UND	**9** 42.0			**3** 127.1		**9** 38.5	**9** 39.6	**8** 44.7	**2** 176.0	**3** 127.1
0 UND	**24** 15.0			**23** 16.0	Cost of Revenues/Payables	**19** 19.1	**18** 19.9	**20** 18.1	**24** 15.5	**23** 16.0
37 9.8	**40** 9.1			**40** 9.1		**35** 10.4	**43** 8.5	**38** 9.7	**40** 9.0	**40** 9.1
11.2	5.1			5.7		6.0	7.8	7.6	7.5	5.7
40.6	9.5			14.0	Revenues/Working Capital	8.9	17.2	13.9	15.1	14.0
-41.9	49.9			-116.3		51.5	303.0	51.5	999.8	-116.3
20.9	14.2			16.4		8.6	9.0	8.2	21.0	16.4
(12) 3.9	(34) 3.6			(50) 3.9	EBIT/Interest	(76) 3.3	(82) 3.2	(145) 2.8	(43) 7.0	(50) 3.9
.0	.2			.2		-.9	1.2	-.5	2.3	.2
	7.6			5.8		5.3	3.6	4.2	4.8	5.8
	(12) 1.2			(14) 1.2	Net Profit + Depr., Dep., Amort./Cur. Mat. L /T/D	(17) 1.0	(25) 2.3	(49) 1.9	(14) 2.0	(14) 1.2
	.0			-.5		-.2	1.2	.8	.7	-.5
.3	.1			.2		.2	.2	.3	.3	.2
1.2	.3			.5	Fixed/Worth	.3	.5	.5	.5	.5
NM	1.3			1.6		.9	1.7	1.6	1.6	1.6
.9	.8			.9		.6	.9	.8	.7	.9
2.8	1.9			1.9	Debt/Worth	1.2	1.9	1.6	2.0	1.9
NM	3.6			4.9		3.1	6.0	4.7	7.3	4.9
151.8	35.4			63.7		40.3	48.1	41.5	100.4	63.7
(12) 100.0	(33) 9.1			(49) 11.3	% Profit Before Taxes/ Tangible Net Worth	(85) 12.1	(80) 17.4	(147) 12.9	(50) 23.6	(49) 11.3
6.4	-3.6			-.5		-.6	2.3	-2.9	7.6	-.5
44.6	18.0			22.6		15.6	20.6	13.2	20.5	22.6
12.1	5.7			6.3	% Profit Before Taxes/ Total Assets	5.6	5.6	4.7	8.1	6.3
-4.2	-.9			-.9		-2.3	.3	-3.5	2.6	-.9
3.0	.8			.8		.9	.7	.8	.8	.8
(10) 4.7	(29) 1.5			(43) 2.3	% Depr., Dep., Amort./ Revenues	(74) 1.6	(82) 1.6	(145) 1.6	(45) 1.2	(43) 2.3
8.1	2.9			3.8		2.5	2.8	2.8	2.5	3.8
9.2	1.7			2.4		2.6	2.7	2.9	3.2	2.4
(13) 11.1	(23) 3.0			(39) 6.3	% Officers', Directors', Owners' Comp/Revenues	(54) 4.5	(58) 4.7	(104) 5.6	(38) 6.4	(39) 6.3
15.9	7.6			11.0		8.7	9.4	9.2	11.7	11.0
7045M	**151041M**	**73440M**		**231526M**	Contract Revenues ($)	**10134428M**	**334104M**	**11473943M**	**241683M**	**231526M**
3888M	**60519M**	**26354M**		**90761M**	Total Assets ($)	**3127768M**	**123814M**	**5734201M**	**87900M**	**90761M**

M = $ thousand MM = $ million

See Pages 11 through 21 for Explanation of Ratios and Data

Current Data Sorted By Revenue **Comparative Historical Data**

Current columns by revenue size: 0-1MM, 1-10MM, 10-50MM, 50 & OVER, ALL.
Current period split: 8 (4/1-9/30/04) ; 35 (10/1/04-3/31/05).
Columns for 10-50MM and 50 & OVER on the current side show "DATA NOT AVAILABLE" and are left blank below.

Type of Statement	0-1MM	1-10MM	10-50MM	50 & OVER	ALL	4/1/00-3/31/01 ALL	4/1/01-3/31/02 ALL	4/1/02-3/31/03 ALL	4/1/03-3/31/04 ALL	4/1/04-3/31/05 ALL
Unqualified		2			2					2
Reviewed	1	6	3		10	25	23	19	11	10
Compiled	2	8			10	13	16	13	12	10
Tax Returns	3	7	2		12	5	8	5	10	12
Other	1	4		4	9	10	12	14	3	9
NUMBER OF STATEMENTS	7	27	9		43	53	59	51	36	43
ASSETS	%	%	%	%	%	%	%	%	%	%
Cash & Equivalents		9.2			11.7	7.7	8.7	9.9	13.4	11.7
A/R - Progress Billings		55.3			51.5	49.2	44.4	50.5	41.9	51.5
A/R - Current Retention		1.5			.9	1.1	1.0	.9	.5	.9
Inventory		11.7			9.1	14.1	10.8	8.7	11.9	9.1
Cost & Est. Earnings In Excess of Billings		2.3			3.0	3.0	3.8	3.2	3.0	3.0
All Other Current		2.9			4.1	4.1	6.2	5.6	3.1	4.1
Total Current		82.9			80.4	79.2	74.8	78.8	73.9	80.4
Fixed Assets (net)		12.8			12.4	13.0	19.1	12.8	16.0	12.4
Joint Ventures & Investments		.2			.2	1.6	.3	.0	.2	.2
Intangibles (net)		.5			1.0	1.7	1.0	2.1	1.8	1.0
All Other Non-Current		3.5			6.1	4.6	4.8	6.4	8.1	6.1
Total		100.0			100.0	100.0	100.0	100.0	100.0	100.0
LIABILITIES										
Notes Payable - Short Term		21.1			22.6	17.9	14.6	20.9	10.3	22.6
A/P - Trade		23.8			20.7	22.9	18.7	22.9	20.9	20.7
A/P - Retention		.0			.1	.1	1.0	.9	.1	.1
Billings in Excess of Costs & Est. Earnings		2.8			2.0	3.2	1.2	1.3	1.9	2.0
Income Taxes Payable		1.0			.9	.2	.7	1.3	1.2	.9
Cur. Mat.-L/T/D		2.1			2.2	2.6	5.0	3.9	1.8	2.2
All Other Current		5.1			6.6	8.5	11.9	9.3	12.2	6.6
Total Current		55.9			55.0	55.4	53.0	60.6	48.2	55.0
Long-Term Debt		10.4			9.2	7.5	10.7	7.0	10.0	9.2
Deferred Taxes		.0			.1	.4	.8	.6	.2	.1
All Other Non-Current		1.7			4.1	2.9	3.6	3.2	9.3	4.1
Net Worth		32.0			31.6	33.8	31.9	28.7	32.3	31.6
Total Liabilities & Net Worth		100.0			100.0	100.0	100.0	100.0	100.0	100.0
INCOME DATA										
Contract Revenues		100.0			100.0	100.0	100.0	100.0	100.0	100.0
Gross Profit		27.9			29.6	23.7	29.6	26.7	28.9	29.6
Operating Expenses		25.6			26.3	20.7	25.8	24.7	27.3	26.3
Operating Profit		2.4			3.3	3.1	3.8	2.1	1.6	3.3
All Other Expenses (net)		.6			.2	.5	.0	.3	.3	.2
Profit Before Taxes		1.8			3.1	2.5	3.9	1.8	1.3	3.1
RATIOS										
Current		2.0			2.0	2.2	2.2	2.3	2.7	2.0
		1.3			1.4	1.4	1.5	1.4	1.6	1.4
		1.2			1.2	1.1	1.0	1.1	1.2	1.2
Receivables/Payables		4.3			3.9	4.2	5.0	4.8	5.3	3.9
		2.4		(41)	2.8	(50) 2.9	(56) 2.5	(49) 2.4	(35) 2.5	(41) 2.8
		1.4			1.6	1.5	1.4	1.7	1.1	1.6
Revenues/Receivables		38 9.5			38 9.5	30 12.3	23 15.8	32 11.4	15 23.6	38 9.5
		62 5.9			58 6.3	55 6.6	46 8.0	58 6.3	43 8.4	58 6.3
		82 4.4			77 4.7	75 4.9	67 5.5	77 4.7	63 5.8	77 4.7
Cost of Revenues/Payables		19 19.1			15 24.8	14 25.7	12 31.5	14 26.6	9 40.0	15 24.8
		35 10.3			27 13.4	25 14.8	28 13.2	27 13.7	26 14.0	27 13.4
		45 8.1			41 8.9	41 8.9	39 9.3	41 8.8	41 8.8	41 8.9
Revenues/Working Capital		7.8			9.0	8.3	8.1	8.0	6.1	9.0
		21.3			18.1	14.3	14.7	14.4	16.2	18.1
		38.5			39.1	61.0	-999.8	46.4	39.5	39.1
EBIT/Interest		17.2			15.7	10.0	12.9	12.9	21.6	15.7
		(26) 5.5		(40)	5.4	(48) 3.5	(54) 5.3	(46) 3.7	(29) 4.6	(40) 5.4
		.8			.8	1.5	2.0	1.0	1.8	.8
Net Profit + Depr., Dep., Amort./Cur. Mat. L /T/D		8.8			8.8	11.3	9.3	8.0	14.0	8.8
		(13) 4.6			(13) 4.6	(14) 3.5	(20) 3.1	(18) 4.1	(10) 6.3	(13) 4.6
		1.7			1.7	1.6	1.3	1.4	2.0	1.7
Fixed/Worth		.2			.2	.1	.1	.2	.2	.2
		.3			.4	.3	.4	.3	.3	.4
		.7			.6	.7	1.9	1.0	.8	.6
Debt/Worth		1.1			1.2	.9	.9	.7	1.0	1.2
		2.3			2.2	2.1	2.3	3.0	1.6	2.2
		8.4			8.4	5.3	11.3	8.0	4.9	8.4
% Profit Before Taxes/ Tangible Net Worth		67.8			59.8	43.6	52.5	49.1	49.9	59.8
		(25) 17.0		(40)	19.7	(49) 22.8	(50) 31.1	(41) 19.9	(32) 20.8	(40) 19.7
		1.9			4.1	8.2	14.5	5.4	3.0	4.1
% Profit Before Taxes/ Total Assets		21.6			18.5	14.9	23.5	13.6	18.3	18.5
		5.2			6.4	6.3	8.5	5.4	7.3	6.4
		-.5			-.3	2.5	3.3	.2	.0	-.3
% Depr., Dep., Amort./ Revenues		.8			.7	.5	.5	.5	.4	.7
		(22) 1.0		(35)	1.0	(47) .8	(54) .8	(46) 1.0	(32) .9	(35) 1.0
		1.4			1.4	1.5	1.5	1.3	1.7	1.4
% Officers', Directors', Owners' Comp/Revenues		3.7			3.3	2.7	2.6	2.6	3.1	3.3
		(22) 4.5		(33)	4.5	(36) 5.2	(41) 4.6	(38) 4.2	(27) 5.7	(33) 4.5
		5.7			5.9	6.5	6.6	6.5	9.0	5.9
Contract Revenues ($)	4549M	97593M	118891M		221033M	8231863M	423707M	411493M	143003M	221033M
Total Assets ($)	1536M	28934M	36731M		67201M	1855703M	121118M	129439M	37205M	67201M

M = $ thousand   MM = $ million
See Pages 11 through 21 for Explanation of Ratios and Data

Current Data Sorted By Revenue   **Comparative Historical Data**

					Type of Statement					
1	5	27	1	34	Unqualified	53	42	31	23	34
4	57	22	1	84	Reviewed	133	99	119	93	84
5	22	2		29	Compiled	48	54	42	39	29
17	26	1	3	47	Tax Returns	36	28	33	38	47
3	26	11	4	44	Other	34	40	49	31	44
34 (4/1-9/30/04)			204 (10/1/04-3/31/05)			4/1/00-3/31/01	4/1/01-3/31/02	4/1/02-3/31/03	4/1/03-3/31/04	4/1/04-3/31/05
0-1MM	1-10MM	10-50MM	50 & OVER	ALL		ALL	ALL	ALL	ALL	ALL
30	136	63	9	238	NUMBER OF STATEMENTS	304	263	274	224	238
%	%	%	%	%	ASSETS	%	%	%	%	%
8.9	12.1	7.9		10.7	Cash & Equivalents	8.5	8.2	8.0	9.3	10.7
16.3	27.2	35.6		28.2	A/R - Progress Billings	28.8	26.8	27.6	26.2	28.2
.0	1.3	3.9		1.8	A/R - Current Retention	2.3	1.3	1.2	1.3	1.8
6.4	2.4	1.5		2.8	Inventory	1.7	2.3	1.8	2.0	2.8
.8	2.6	5.0		3.0	Cost & Est. Earnings In Excess of Billings	2.8	2.7	2.5	2.6	3.0
.4	3.2	3.8		3.1	All Other Current	2.6	4.4	4.9	4.1	3.1
32.8	48.8	57.6		49.6	Total Current	46.7	45.7	46.0	45.5	49.6
53.7	44.0	36.2		42.7	Fixed Assets (net)	47.1	48.6	46.3	47.3	42.7
.0	.9	1.9		1.0	Joint Ventures & Investments	.7	.7	1.8	1.3	1.0
1.4	.7	.7		.7	Intangibles (net)	.9	.9	.5	.5	.7
12.2	5.6	3.7		5.9	All Other Non-Current	4.6	4.1	5.4	5.4	5.9
100.0	100.0	100.0		100.0	Total	100.0	100.0	100.0	100.0	100.0
					LIABILITIES					
21.3	14.0	6.0		12.5	Notes Payable - Short Term	6.0	7.2	8.1	8.7	12.5
10.1	12.4	18.9		14.0	A/P - Trade	14.0	13.4	13.1	12.2	14.0
.5	.2	.6		.4	A/P - Retention	.2	.2	.4	.3	.4
.2	1.3	5.3		2.3	Billings in Excess of Costs & Est. Earnings	2.5	2.4	2.4	2.0	2.3
.1	.3	.2		.2	Income Taxes Payable	.4	.2	.2	.3	.2
6.9	8.5	8.6		8.3	Cur. Mat.-L/T/D	9.4	9.5	9.0	9.4	8.3
8.7	4.5	5.6		5.4	All Other Current	4.8	4.3	4.8	6.9	5.4
47.8	41.3	45.2		43.1	Total Current	37.2	37.1	38.1	39.7	43.1
37.0	22.3	14.6		21.8	Long-Term Debt	21.7	22.9	20.7	24.2	21.8
.2	.9	1.5		1.0	Deferred Taxes	1.3	1.4	1.4	.9	1.0
8.0	3.5	2.1		4.5	All Other Non-Current	3.3	2.6	3.5	9.0	4.5
6.9	32.0	36.7		29.6	Net Worth	36.5	36.0	36.3	26.1	29.6
100.0	100.0	100.0		100.0	Total Liabilities & Net Worth	100.0	100.0	100.0	100.0	100.0
					INCOME DATA					
100.0	100.0	100.0		100.0	Contract Revenues	100.0	100.0	100.0	100.0	100.0
54.8	34.2	18.8		32.2	Gross Profit	28.6	35.2	31.9	34.8	32.2
53.2	30.3	13.5		28.3	Operating Expenses	24.6	29.3	29.2	31.6	28.3
1.6	3.9	5.3		4.0	Operating Profit	4.1	5.9	2.7	3.2	4.0
2.7	.3	.5		.6	All Other Expenses (net)	1.2	1.3	1.2	1.0	.6
−1.1	3.6	4.8		3.3	Profit Before Taxes	2.9	4.6	1.5	2.2	3.3
					RATIOS					
1.3	2.1	1.4		1.7		1.9	1.7	1.8	1.8	1.7
.7	1.3	1.2		1.3	Current	1.3	1.2	1.2	1.2	1.3
.4	.9	1.1		.9		.9	.9	.8	.9	.9
13.3	4.0	3.6		3.7		4.6	4.1	4.3	4.4	3.7
(22) 1.7	(124) 2.6	2.7	(218)	2.5	Receivables/Payables	(286) 2.4	(244) 2.1	(252) 2.4	(197) 2.3	(218) 2.5
.7	1.3	1.5		1.3		1.4	1.3	1.4	1.4	1.3
0 UND	24 15.1	51 7.2		27 13.6		32 11.4	29 12.6	28 13.1	23 15.9	27 13.6
16 22.6	49 7.4	62 5.9		54 6.8	Revenues/Receivables	54 6.8	49 7.5	47 7.9	48 7.6	54 6.8
66 5.5	76 4.8	78 4.7		75 4.9		75 4.9	71 5.2	73 5.0	74 4.9	75 4.9
0 UND	13 27.9	18 20.6		15 24.0		13 28.6	14 25.7	12 31.2	7 49.6	15 24.0
19 19.5	27 13.4	33 11.2		29 12.8	Cost of Revenues/Payables	28 12.9	29 12.5	26 14.0	28 12.9	29 12.8
98 3.7	47 7.8	55 6.6		54 6.7		47 7.7	50 7.6	48 7.6	46 7.9	54 6.7
17.6	8.4	10.8		9.7		9.1	11.4	8.8	9.8	9.7
−31.5	18.0	21.7		21.5	Revenues/Working Capital	22.0	28.9	24.7	27.9	21.5
−8.0	−167.0	43.6		−72.6		−89.0	−40.3	−44.2	−52.5	−72.6
3.3	8.6	11.8		9.1		6.4	7.7	7.4	7.3	9.1
(27) .8	(126) 3.1	(60) 6.8	(220)	3.3	EBIT/Interest	(288) 3.0	(250) 2.9	(257) 2.5	(211) 2.8	(220) 3.3
−1.7	1.1	1.8		1.0		1.2	1.4	.3	.8	1.0
	2.8	2.3		2.5		2.9	3.2	3.0	2.2	2.5
	(38) 1.7	(26) 1.5	(65)	1.6	Net Profit + Depr., Dep., Amort./Cur. Mat. L /T/D	(106) 1.6	(74) 1.9	(88) 1.6	(50) 1.7	(65) 1.6
	1.1	1.1		1.1		1.1	1.4	.9	.8	1.1
1.0	.7	.7		.7		.7	.8	.7	.9	.7
7.4	1.3	1.0		1.2	Fixed/Worth	1.3	1.4	1.2	1.3	1.2
−4.3	2.4	1.4		2.3		2.3	2.3	2.3	3.1	2.3
.9	.8	1.0		.9		.9	.9	.9	1.0	.9
29.4	1.7	1.9		1.9	Debt/Worth	1.8	2.0	1.7	2.0	1.9
−7.8	4.5	3.3		4.7		3.8	3.8	4.0	5.6	4.7
55.8	37.9	38.6		38.1		36.5	36.8	30.0	32.5	38.1
(17) 10.9	(124) 14.0	(62) 19.0	(211)	15.8	% Profit Before Taxes/ Tangible Net Worth	(280) 17.3	(244) 19.8	(252) 11.3	(196) 14.0	(211) 15.8
−3.2	2.8	4.8		4.1		3.7	5.3	−3.9	1.1	4.1
7.3	14.8	12.8		13.6		11.7	13.3	10.4	11.8	13.6
.6	5.7	8.0		5.9	% Profit Before Taxes/ Total Assets	5.8	5.8	3.7	4.9	5.9
−12.4	.2	1.4		.1		.7	1.2	−2.5	−.6	.1
3.8	4.3	1.2		3.1		3.3	3.4	3.4	3.6	3.1
(24) 10.0	(123) 6.9	(62) 3.9	(213)	5.7	% Depr., Dep., Amort./ Revenues	(285) 5.6	(246) 6.5	(246) 5.8	(179) 7.3	(213) 5.7
16.2	9.1	6.1		8.6		8.7	9.5	9.2	10.3	8.6
4.9	2.2	.8		1.5		2.1	2.3	2.1	2.0	1.5
(20) 6.6	(95) 4.1	(25) 1.3	(143)	3.9	% Officers', Directors', Owners' Comp/Revenues	(169) 4.3	(141) 4.4	(159) 4.4	(136) 4.1	(143) 3.9
9.2	6.9	2.3		6.6		8.4	7.1	6.6	6.3	6.6
14682M	508021M	1207744M	79645199M	81375646M	Contract Revenues ($)	34465773M	7043658M	10434312M	6629549M	81375646M
10740M	283907M	621906M	35665505M	36582058M	Total Assets ($)	13804354M	4719638M	3398247M	2795922M	36582058M

Current Data Sorted By Revenue　　　　　　　　　　　　　　　　**Comparative Historical Data**

0-1MM	1-10MM	10-50MM	50 & OVER	ALL		4/1/00-3/31/01 ALL	4/1/01-3/31/02 ALL	4/1/02-3/31/03 ALL	4/1/03-3/31/04 ALL	4/1/04-3/31/05 ALL
					Type of Statement					
1	1	5		7	Unqualified	17	14	8	8	7
2	34	6	1	43	Reviewed	68	69	64	74	43
6	26			32	Compiled	40	51	32	22	32
20	18		1	39	Tax Returns	25	42	37	44	39
2	22	4	1	29	Other	39	44	22	20	29
28 (4/1-9/30/04)			122 (10/1/04-3/31/05)							
31	101	15	3	150	**NUMBER OF STATEMENTS**	189	220	163	168	150
%	%	%	%	%	**ASSETS**	%	%	%	%	%
19.1	10.1	8.2		11.8	Cash & Equivalents	9.7	11.0	12.0	11.2	11.8
21.3	38.2	51.8		36.0	A/R - Progress Billings	36.1	34.7	35.5	35.8	36.0
.0	.6	1.9		.6	A/R - Current Retention	1.3	.7	.6	.8	.6
8.7	10.0	4.0		8.9	Inventory	9.5	9.5	7.5	9.2	8.9
.1	3.4	3.2		2.7	Cost & Est. Earnings In Excess of Billings	3.8	2.4	2.9	2.7	2.7
2.2	4.6	3.1		3.9	All Other Current	3.6	3.7	4.9	3.2	3.9
51.4	67.0	72.2		63.9	Total Current	64.0	61.9	63.4	62.8	63.9
37.2	23.4	18.3		26.0	Fixed Assets (net)	27.8	27.7	27.2	27.0	26.0
.9	1.0	1.4		1.0	Joint Ventures & Investments	.7	.4	.1	.9	1.0
4.2	2.5	.1		2.5	Intangibles (net)	2.0	2.2	1.8	2.3	2.5
6.3	6.2	7.9		6.5	All Other Non-Current	5.4	7.8	7.5	7.0	6.5
100.0	100.0	100.0		100.0	Total	100.0	100.0	100.0	100.0	100.0
					LIABILITIES					
15.8	15.7	13.3		15.3	Notes Payable - Short Term	10.5	11.5	11.4	13.5	15.3
13.5	19.1	19.7		17.8	A/P - Trade	17.5	17.4	17.8	18.7	17.8
.0	.0	.6		.1	A/P - Retention	.4	.0	.3	.5	.1
4.1	3.0	7.3		3.7	Billings in Excess of Costs & Est. Earnings	2.5	2.2	3.5	3.4	3.7
.1	.1	.3		.1	Income Taxes Payable	.5	.4	.3	.2	.1
8.5	4.0	2.9		4.8	Cur. Mat.-L/T/D	4.8	4.9	5.2	6.9	4.8
14.4	10.7	10.2		11.2	All Other Current	7.8	9.0	7.3	7.2	11.2
56.3	52.6	54.4		53.1	Total Current	44.0	45.4	45.7	50.3	53.1
51.2	17.5	6.0		23.8	Long-Term Debt	13.0	15.6	15.6	22.1	23.8
.0	.5	.8		.4	Deferred Taxes	1.1	.8	.8	.3	.4
8.4	5.4	1.7		5.5	All Other Non-Current	2.6	3.7	4.1	8.0	5.5
−15.9	24.1	37.1		17.2	Net Worth	39.3	34.5	33.9	19.2	17.2
100.0	100.0	100.0		100.0	Total Liabilities & Net Worth	100.0	100.0	100.0	100.0	100.0
					INCOME DATA					
100.0	100.0	100.0		100.0	Contract Revenues	100.0	100.0	100.0	100.0	100.0
44.9	32.8	20.9		34.4	Gross Profit	31.9	34.1	33.3	32.6	34.4
44.2	30.0	18.1		32.0	Operating Expenses	26.8	29.1	29.5	29.7	32.0
.7	2.8	2.8		2.3	Operating Profit	5.1	5.0	3.8	2.9	2.3
1.3	.5	.2		.7	All Other Expenses (net)	.7	.7	1.1	.4	.7
−.6	2.2	2.7		1.7	Profit Before Taxes	4.4	4.3	2.8	2.5	1.7
					RATIOS					
3.3	2.2	1.5		2.0		2.2	2.3	2.1	2.1	2.0
1.0	1.3	1.3		1.3	Current	1.4	1.5	1.4	1.4	1.3
.6	.9	1.2		.9		1.0	1.0	1.0	.9	.9
5.9	4.7	3.7		4.8		4.5	5.7	4.8	4.1	4.8
(21) 1.4	(97) 2.2	3.1		(135) 2.1	Receivables/Payables	(183) 2.4	(207) 2.5	(149) 2.4	(150) 2.0	(135) 2.1
1.0	1.1	1.9		1.1		1.2	1.2	1.2	1.2	1.1
0 UND	23 15.9	44 8.3		15 24.0		23 16.1	23 15.9	23 16.1	15 24.2	15 24.0
15 24.8	46 8.6	76 4.8		41 8.8	Revenues/Receivables	50 7.3	41 8.9	47 7.8	42 8.7	41 8.8
38 9.7	75 4.9	109 3.4		73 5.0		73 5.0	68 5.4	67 5.5	71 5.1	73 5.0
0 UND	12 31.2	25 14.9		8 43.1		13 28.0	10 38.0	13 28.0	10 36.7	8 43.1
5 80.8	28 12.9	31 11.7		25 14.6	Cost of Revenues/Payables	29 12.4	23 15.7	27 13.4	22 16.2	25 14.6
28 13.2	48 7.6	48 7.6		48 7.6		48 7.7	44 8.3	45 8.2	50 7.3	48 7.6
16.9	8.0	9.4		8.6		7.9	6.8	7.2	8.6	8.6
UND	16.9	12.7		19.6	Revenues/Working Capital	14.6	17.1	17.5	18.0	19.6
−22.4	−50.7	23.1		−45.5		173.2	847.6	232.9	−119.0	−45.5
7.6	11.5	36.0		11.5		11.1	12.0	11.1	11.9	11.5
(26) .7	(91) 2.9	(13) 12.4		(131) 2.9	EBIT/Interest	(172) 3.6	(199) 4.5	(146) 3.5	(156) 3.5	(131) 2.9
−3.1	.9	1.7		−.6		1.7	1.7	1.1	.9	−.6
	2.9			3.2	Net Profit + Depr., Dep.,	5.5	5.5	7.6	4.7	3.2
	(12) 2.1			(20) 2.4	Amort./Cur. Mat. L /T/D	(50) 3.4	(52) 3.1	(46) 2.6	(39) 2.6	(20) 2.4
	.8			.8		1.7	1.1	1.2	1.2	.8
.8	.3	.2		.3		.3	.3	.2	.3	.3
UND	.6	.4		.8	Fixed/Worth	.7	.8	.7	.7	.8
−.6	8.6	.7		UND		1.6	1.7	1.6	9.5	UND
1.4	.9	1.4		1.1		.7	.7	.7	1.0	1.1
−166.0	2.8	2.0		3.0	Debt/Worth	1.8	1.7	1.8	2.3	3.0
−3.3	60.1	2.1		−138.3		4.1	5.9	5.7	20.0	−138.3
81.8	54.9	52.8		53.3		46.5	61.0	53.4	51.7	53.3
(15) 35.5	(79) 23.3	16.6		(112) 23.7	% Profit Before Taxes/ Tangible Net Worth	(179) 24.7	(193) 24.6	(145) 21.1	(131) 17.0	(112) 23.7
4.0	1.2	4.0		2.4		6.3	7.4	2.0	2.0	2.4
19.4	15.7	16.8		16.6		17.4	22.9	19.3	15.3	16.6
1.7	5.1	5.6		5.2	% Profit Before Taxes/ Total Assets	8.2	8.3	6.2	4.6	5.2
−10.5	−1.1	1.3		−4.0		2.0	1.6	.0	−.5	−4.0
1.5	.9	.5		.9		.8	.8	.6	1.0	.9
(22) 2.6	(76) 1.8	(13) 1.3		(111) 1.8	% Depr., Dep., Amort./ Revenues	(165) 1.8	(193) 1.9	(137) 1.9	(125) 2.1	(111) 1.8
3.3	3.2	1.7		3.1		3.4	3.4	4.1	4.1	3.1
5.3	2.0			2.2		2.7	2.9	2.5	2.4	2.2
(15) 7.2	(57) 4.0			(77) 5.2	% Officers', Directors', Owners' Comp/Revenues	(99) 4.4	(120) 5.1	(110) 5.5	(103) 4.6	(77) 5.2
11.2	7.9			8.8		7.8	8.5	10.3	8.0	8.8
16347M	366005M	322874M	1308632M	2013858M	Contract Revenues ($)	9681453M	8120118M	15884504M	922872M	2013858M
5575M	131449M	123498M	599689M	860211M	Total Assets ($)	2867026M	3624007M	6166968M	313457M	860211M

© RMA 2005

M = $ thousand　　MM = $ million
See Pages 11 through 21 for Explanation of Ratios and Data

CONSTRUCTION
FINANCIAL MANAGEMENT
ASSOCIATION DATA

About the Construction Financial Management Association (CFMA) Data
Web site: www.cfma.org

Once again, we are delighted to include excerpts from **CFMA's 2005 Construction Industry Annual Financial Survey**. CFMA is **The Source and Resource for Construction Financial Professionals** and has more than 7,000 members in 89 chapters throughout the U.S.

The data presented are based on a survey sent to approximately 4,100 general members employed within U.S. construction firms, plus a small number of other U.S. contractors. Of the 660 total survey participants, 81.5%, or 538 companies, provided detailed financial statement information, with 532 companies being included in the final participant population. 71.1%, or 378 companies, participated in the CFMA survey in 2004. The data submitted was compiled and analyzed by Moss Adams LLP in cooperation with CFMA. Moss Adams was not engaged to and did not audit or review this information and, accordingly, does not express an opinion or any other form of assurance on it.

Almost all companies (87.6%) included in the survey recognize contract revenue and profit in accordance with the percentage of completion method of accounting. Likewise, our Statement Studies contractor data primarily reflects only this method of accounting. It is entirely possible that some of the same contractor companies are included in both the CFMA and Statement Studies data presentations. The inclusion of the CFMA data has not affected our Statement Studies contractor composite data.

Fiscal year-end closing dates reflected in the CFMA survey range from 3/31/04 through 3/31/05. The CFMA data are most comparable to the RMA contractor data from 4/1/04 through 3/31/05 appearing in this edition.

The survey respondents were classified into three categories of construction based on the type of work performed. Classification was based on the level of contract volume reported for various NAICS/SIC codes. A contractor was included in a classification if at least one half of its annual contract revenue was attributable to that classification. CFMA categorized certain NAICS/SIC codes together. The classifications and NAICS/SIC codes included in each are as follows:

NAIC Codes

INDUSTRIAL AND NONRESIDENTIAL CONTRACTORS:

23332	Commercial and Institutional Building Construction (incl. Warehouse, Hotel and Motel Construction)
23331	Manufacturing and Light Industrial Building Construction (Except Warehouse Construction)

HEAVY AND HIGHWAY CONTRACTORS:

23411	Highway and Street Construction
23412	Bridge and Tunnel Construction
23491	Water, Sewer, and Pipeline Construction
23492	Power and Communication Transmission Line Construction
23493	Industrial Non-building Structure Construction
23499	All Other Heavy Construction

SPECIALTY TRADES CONTRACTORS:

23511	Plumbing, Heating, and Air-Conditioning
23521	Painting and Wall Covering Contractors
23531	Electrical Contractors
23541	Masonry and Stone Contractors
23542	Drywall, Plastering, Acoustical, and Insulation Contractors
23543	Tile, Marble, Terrazzo, and Mosaic Contractors
23551	Carpentry Contractors
23552	Floor Laying and Other Floor Contractors
23561	Roofing, Siding, and Sheet Metal Contractors
23571	Concrete Contractors
23581	Water Well Drilling Contractors
23591	Structural Steel Erection Contractors
23592	Glass and Glazing Contractors
23593	Excavation Contractors
23594	Wrecking and Demolition Contractors
23595	Building Equipment and Other Machinery Installation Contractors
23599	All Other Special Trade Contractors
56162	Security Systems Services
56291	Environmental Remediation Services

SIC Codes

1541	General Contractors-Industrial Buildings and Warehouses
1542	General Contractors-Nonresidential Buildings (Other than Industrial Buildings and Warehouses)

1611	Highway and Street Construction (Except Elevated Highways)
1622	Bridge, Tunnel, and Elevated Highway Construction
1623	Water, Sewer, Pipeline, and Communications, Power Line Construction
1629	Heavy Construction, NEC

1711	Plumbing, Heating, and Air-Conditioning Contractors
1721	Painting and Paper Hanging
1731	Electrical Work
1741	Masonry, Stone Setting, and Other Stone Work
1742	Plastering, Drywall, Acoustical, and Insulation Work
1743	Terrazzo, Tile, Marble, and Mosaic Work Contractors
1751	Carpentry Work
1752	Floor Laying and Other Floor Work, NEC
1761	Roofing, Siding, and Sheet Metal Work
1771	Concrete Work Stucco Construction
1781	Water Well Drilling
1791	Structural Steel Erection
1793	Glass and Glazing Work
1794	Excavation Work
1795	Wrecking and Demolition Work
1796	Installation or Erection of Building Equipment
1799	Special Trade Contractors, NEC

The CFMA financial data includes balance sheets, statement of earnings, and financial ratios. The balance sheets and statement of earnings represent a weighted average of all companies included in each classification. Percentages are presented for each dollar amount in the financial statements. Due to rounding, the totals may not agree to the sum of various accounts. Such variations are few and insignificant.

The financial ratios are calculated from the composite balance sheets and statements of earning data. They are not averages of ratios for all companies included in the classification.

If you wish to purchase *CFMA's 2005 Construction Industry Annual Financial Survey* or have questions regarding the data, contact Brian Summers, Chief Operations Officer; Construction Financial Management Association, 29 Emmons Drive F-50, Princeton, NJ 08540; Phone 609-452-8000; Fax 609-452-0474; E-mail bsummers@cfma.org.

Interpretation of the
Construction Financial Management Association (CFMA) Data

CFMA's data should only be regarded as general information. It cannot be used to establish industry norms for a number of reasons, including the following:

(1) The financial statements used in the composite are not selected by any random or statistically reliable method. CFMA members voluntarily submitted financial data pertaining to themselves. Note that contractors' statements have no upper asset/sales limit.
(2) Many companies provide varied services; CFMA includes a contractor in a classification if at least one-half (1/2) of its annual contract revenue was completed within that classification.
(3) Some of the NAIC/SIC group samples may be rather small in relation to the total number of firms in a given industry category. A relatively small sample can increase the chances that some of our composites do not fully represent an industry group.
(4) There is the chance that an extreme statement can be present in a sample, causing a disproportionate influence on the industry composite. This is particularly true in a relatively small sample.
(5) Companies within the same industry may differ in their method of operations, which in turn can directly influence their financial statements. Since such differences affect financial data included in our sample, our composite calculations could be significantly affected.
(6) Other considerations that can result in variation among different companies engaged in the same general line of business are: different labor markets; geographical location; different accounting methods; quality of service rendered; sources and methods of financing; and terms of sale.

The use of CFMA's data may be helpful when considered with other methods of financial analysis. Nevertheless, RMA and CFMA do not recommend the use of CFMA's data to establish norms or parameters for a given industry or grouping, or the industry as a whole. Although CFMA believes that its data is accurate and representative within the confines of the aforementioned reasons, RMA and CFMA specifically make no representations regarding the accuracy of representativeness of the figures printed in this supplement of the RMA Annual Statement Studies.

All Companies
Composite

Balance Sheet

	2005 Participants		2004 Participants	
	Amount	Percent	Amount	Percent
Current assets:				
Cash and cash equivalents	$ 4,818,236	14.6 %	$ 3,849,489	13.7 %
Marketable securities & short-term investments	1,983,264	6.0	1,620,890	5.8
Receivables:				
Contract receivables currently due	12,856,421	38.9	10,741,070	38.1
Retainages on contracts	3,919,134	11.9	3,055,101	10.8
Unbilled work	337,890	1.0	205,744	0.7
Other receivables	419,224	1.3	595,091	2.1
Less allowance for doubtful accounts	(64,638)	(0.2)	(66,026)	(0.2)
Total receivables, net:	17,468,032	52.8	14,530,981	51.6
Inventories	509,170	1.5	382,956	1.4
Costs and recognized earnings in excess of billings on uncompleted contracts	1,735,737	5.3	1,253,584	4.5
Investments in and advances to construction joint ventures	205,853	0.6	169,703	0.6
Income taxes:				
Current/refundable	22,668	0.1	49,688	0.2
Deferred	59,853	0.2	99,384	0.4
Other current assets	705,247	2.1	694,657	2.5
Total current assets	27,508,059	83.2	22,651,333	80.4
Property, plant and equipment	9,304,496	28.2	9,631,053	34.2
Less accumulated depreciation	(5,629,779)	(17.0)	(5,767,700)	(20.5)
Property, plant and equipment, net	3,674,716	11.1	3,863,354	13.7
Noncurrent assets:				
Long-term investments	350,514	1.1	249,691	0.9
Deferred income taxes	92,363	0.3	83,443	0.3
Other assets	1,427,615	4.3	1,317,149	4.7
Total noncurrent assets	1,870,491	5.7	1,650,283	5.9
Total assets	$ 33,053,266	100.0 %	$ 28,164,970	100.0 %

	2005 Participants		2004 Participants	
	Amount	Percent	Amount	Percent
Current liabilities:				
Current maturity on long-term debt	$ 505,428	1.5 %	$ 440,487	1.6 %
Notes payable and lines of credit	549,390	1.7	443,402	1.6
Accounts payable:				
Trade, including currently due to subcontractors	9,779,664	29.6	7,652,838	27.2
Subcontracts retainages	2,774,589	8.4	2,305,985	8.2
Other	203,446	0.6	329,351	1.2
Total accounts payable	12,757,700	38.6	10,288,174	36.5
Accrued expenses	2,117,744	6.4	1,655,309	5.9
Billings in excess of costs and recognized earnings on uncompleted contracts	4,008,261	12.1	3,202,183	11.4
Income taxes:				
Current	47,657	0.1	41,957	0.1
Deferred	41,700	0.1	17,825	0.1
Other current liabilities	374,427	1.1	338,654	1.2
Total current liabilities	20,402,306	61.7	16,427,990	58.3
Noncurrent liabilities				
Long-term debt, excluding current maturities	2,038,046	6.2	2,115,115	7.5
Deferred income taxes	141,937	0.4	127,457	0.5
Other	354,694	1.1	592,959	2.1
Total liabilities	22,936,983	69.4	19,263,522	68.4
Minority interests	45,041	0.1	25,657	0.1
Net worth:				
Common stock, par value	332,075	1.0	332,946	1.2
Preferred stock, stated value	62,793	0.2	39,792	0.1
Additional paid-in capital	1,939,629	5.9	1,393,052	4.9
Retained earnings	7,370,741	22.3	6,954,135	24.7
Treasury stock	(506,391)	(1.5)	(411,600)	(1.5)
Excess value of marketable securities	52,536	0.2	38,396	0.1
Other equity	819,859	2.5	529,071	1.9
Total net worth	10,071,243	30.5	8,875,792	31.5
Total liabilities and net worth	$ 33,053,266	100.0 %	$ 28,164,970	100.0 %

All Companies
Composite

Statement of Earnings

	2005 Participants		2004 Participants	
	Amount	Percent	Amount	Percent
Contract revenue	$ 94,479,099	98.5 %	$ 80,447,035	97.9 %
Other revenue	1,479,664	1.5	1,713,217	2.1
Total Revenue	95,958,762	100.0	82,160,252	100.0
Contract cost	(87,359,593)	(91.0)	(73,912,843)	(90.0)
Other cost	(1,155,465)	(1.2)	(1,558,113)	(1.9)
Total cost	(88,515,059)	(92.2)	(75,470,957)	(91.9)
Gross Profit	7,443,704	7.8	6,689,295	8.1
Selling, general & administrative expenses:				
Payroll	(2,853,533)	(3.0)	(2,878,137)	(3.5)
Professional fees	(192,060)	(0.2)	(182,124)	(0.2)
Sales & marketing costs	(227,170)	(0.2)	(177,599)	(0.2)
Technology costs	(156,413)	(0.2)	(113,352)	(0.1)
Administrative bonuses	(374,451)	(0.4)	(350,325)	(0.4)
Other	(2,040,813)	(2.1)	(1,584,471)	(1.9)
Total SG&A expenses	(5,844,439)	(6.1)	(5,286,009)	(6.4)
Income from operations	1,599,265	1.7	1,403,287	1.7
Interest income	134,207	0.1	111,988	0.1
Interest expense	(130,092)	(0.1)	(144,305)	(0.2)
Other income / (expense), net	100,078	0.1	134,214	0.2
Net earnings / (loss) before income taxes	1,703,457	1.8	1,505,184	1.8
Income tax (expense) / benefit	(175,569)	(0.2)	(181,944)	(0.2)
Net earnings	$ 1,527,888	1.6	$ 1,323,240	1.6

Number of Participants

	Number
2005	532
2004	537

Financial Ratios

	2005 Participants		2004 Participants	
	Average	Median	Average	Median
Liquidity Ratios				
Current Ratio	1.3	1.4	1.4	1.4
Quick Ratio	1.2	1.2	1.2	1.2
Days of Cash	18.1	11.2	16.9	12.6
Working Capital Turnover	13.5	12.9	13.2	12.9
Profitability Ratios				
Return on Assets *	5.2 %	5.3 %	5.3 %	4.8 %
Return on Equity *	16.9 %	18.5 %	17.0 %	15.7 %
Times Interest Earned	14.1	11.5	11.4	8.5
Leverage Ratios				
Debt to Equity	2.3	2.2	2.2	2.1
Revenue to Equity	9.5	9.9	9.3	9.6
Asset Turnover	2.9	3.1	2.9	3.1
Fixed Asset Ratio	36.5 %	25.3 %	43.5 %	29.2 %
Equity to SG&A Expense	1.7	1.2	1.7	1.2
Underbillings to Equity	20.6 %	13.4 %	16.4 %	13.0 %
Backlog to Equity	8.6	5.3	8.5	5.5
Efficiency Ratios				
Backlog to Working Capital	11.8	7.2	12.9	7.4
Months in Backlog	7.7	6.3	8.2	6.9
Days in Accounts Receivable	49.6	51.7	49.4	50.1
Days in Inventory	2.1	2.2	1.8	2.1
Days in Accounts Payable	40.6	33.8	38.1	33.8
Operating Cycle	29.1	33.3	30.0	34.8

* In the CFMA's 2005 Annual Financial Study, Return on Assets (ROA) and Return on Equity (ROE) are calculated using net earnings (loss) before income taxes. Studies conducted in prior years used net earnings (loss) after taxes to calculate ROA and ROE. All references to ROAs and ROEs from prior studies have been updated to reflect this change.

Note: Not all figures will appear to sum due to rounding.

Industrial & Nonresidential Contractors

Composite

Balance Sheet

	2005 Participants		2004 Participants	
	Amount	Percent	Amount	Percent
Current assets:				
Cash and cash equivalents	$ 7,286,579	17.7 %	$ 5,014,225	15.8 %
Marketable securities & short-term investments	3,748,113	9.1	2,967,402	9.4
Receivables:				
Contract receivables currently due	17,039,458	41.4	13,401,900	42.4
Retainages on contracts	5,739,338	13.9	4,195,891	13.3
Unbilled work	231,244	0.6	236,799	0.7
Other receivables	564,447	1.4	402,981	1.3
Less allowance for doubtful accounts	(37,123)	(0.1)	(32,639)	(0.1)
Total receivables, net	23,537,363	57.1	18,204,933	57.5
Inventories	62,318	0.2	97,349	0.3
Costs and recognized earnings in excess of billings on uncompleted contracts	1,771,079	4.3	1,177,625	3.7
Investments in and advances to construction joint ventures	267,770	0.7	145,483	0.5
Income taxes:				
Current/refundable	24,682	0.1	66,405	0.2
Deferred	62,432	0.2	102,552	0.3
Other current assets	848,258	2.1	758,827	2.4
Total current assets	37,608,594	91.3	28,534,801	90.2
Property, plant and equipment	5,129,943	12.5	4,556,042	14.4
Less accumulated depreciation	(3,184,441)	(7.7)	(2,639,877)	(8.3)
Property, plant and equipment, net	1,945,503	4.7	1,916,165	6.1
Noncurrent assets:				
Long-term investments	594,860	1.4	266,187	0.8
Deferred income taxes	152,721	0.4	155,053	0.5
Other assets	890,988	2.2	771,758	2.4
Total noncurrent assets	1,638,569	4.0	1,192,998	3.8
Total assets	$ 41,192,667	100.0 %	$ 31,643,964	100.0 %

	2005 Participants		2004 Participants	
	Amount	Percent	Amount	Percent
Current liabilities:				
Current maturity on long-term debt	$ 192,110	0.5 %	$ 127,990	0.4 %
Notes payable and lines of credit	216,248	0.5	343,526	1.1
Accounts payable:				
Trade, including currently due to subcontractors	15,924,529	38.7	11,983,271	37.9
Subcontracts retainages	5,716,494	13.9	4,257,346	13.5
Other	174,023	0.4	363,707	1.1
Total accounts payable	21,815,045	53.0	16,604,324	52.5
Accrued expenses	2,367,884	5.7	1,631,804	5.2
Billings in excess of costs and recognized earnings on uncompleted contracts	5,128,250	12.4	3,530,668	11.2
Income taxes:				
Current	27,894	0.1	36,395	0.1
Deferred	70,298	0.2	13,661	0.0
Other current liabilities	403,782	1.0	437,455	1.4
Total current liabilities	30,221,513	73.4	22,725,822	71.8
Noncurrent liabilities:				
Long-term debt, excluding current maturities	840,236	2.0	850,318	2.7
Deferred income taxes	35,588	0.1	28,122	0.1
Other	413,410	1.0	564,738	1.8
Total liabilities	31,510,746	76.5	24,169,000	76.4
Minority interests	49,308	0.1	28,270	0.1
Net worth:				
Common stock, par value	267,875	0.7	247,409	0.8
Preferred stock, stated value	134,469	0.3	29,809	0.1
Additional paid-in capital	879,010	2.1	590,023	1.9
Retained earnings	7,614,959	18.5	5,990,736	18.9
Treasury stock	(374,562)	(0.9)	(266,023)	(0.8)
Excess value of marketable securities	98,515	0.2	61,267	0.2
Other equity	1,012,347	2.5	793,473	2.5
Total net worth	9,632,612	23.4	7,446,694	23.5
Total liabilities and net worth	$ 41,192,667	100.0 %	$ 31,643,964	100.0 %

Industrial & Nonresidential Contractors

Composite

Statement of Earnings

	2005 Participants		2004 Participants	
	Amount	Percent	Amount	Percent
Contract revenue	$ 133,182,935	99.9 %	$ 104,304,017	98.9 %
Other revenue	130,634	0.1	1,151,758	1.1
Total Revenue	133,313,569	100.0	105,455,775	100.0
Contract cost	(126,002,256)	(94.5)	(98,195,067)	(93.1)
Other cost	(200,044)	(0.2)	(921,611)	(0.9)
Total cost	(126,202,300)	(94.7)	(99,116,678)	(94.0)
Gross Profit	7,111,269	5.3	6,339,097	6.0
Selling, general & administrative expenses:				
Payroll	(3,002,109)	(2.3)	(2,848,083)	(2.7)
Professional fees	(229,973)	(0.2)	(176,780)	(0.2)
Sales & marketing costs	(283,391)	(0.2)	(178,520)	(0.2)
Technology costs	(224,549)	(0.2)	(93,844)	(0.1)
Administrative bonuses	(445,999)	(0.3)	(365,811)	(0.3)
Other	(1,577,207)	(1.2)	(1,449,629)	(1.4)
Total SG&A expenses	(5,763,229)	(4.3)	(5,112,667)	(4.8)
Income from operations	1,348,040	1.0	1,226,430	1.2
Interest income	221,383	0.2	174,204	0.2
Interest expense	(66,769)	(0.1)	(62,074)	(0.1)
Other income / (expense), net	111,901	0.1	104,770	0.1
Net earnings / (loss) before income taxes	1,614,555	1.2	1,443,331	1.4
Income tax (expense) / benefit	(164,042)	(0.1)	(184,483)	(0.2)
Net earnings	$ 1,450,513	1.1	$ 1,258,848	1.2

Number of Participants

	Number
2005	227
2004	250

Financial Ratios

	2005 Participants		2004 Participants	
	Average	Median	Average	Median
Liquidity Ratios				
Current Ratio	1.2	1.3	1.3	1.3
Quick Ratio	1.1	1.2	1.2	1.2
Days of Cash	19.7	16.3	17.1	16.3
Working Capital Turnover	18.0	18.5	18.2	17.7
Profitability Ratios				
Return on Assets *	3.9 %	4.1 %	4.6 %	4.5 %
Return on Equity *	16.8 %	16.9 %	19.4 %	16.5 %
Times Interest Earned	25.2	14.3	24.3	13.6
Leverage Ratios				
Debt to Equity	3.3	3.1	3.2	2.9
Revenue to Equity	13.8	14.9	14.2	14.6
Asset Turnover	3.2	3.5	3.3	3.6
Fixed Asset Ratio	20.2 %	16.7 %	25.7 %	19.8 %
Equity to SG&A Expense	1.7	1.2	1.5	1.1
Underbillings to Equity	20.8 %	10.6 %	19.0 %	13.1 %
Backlog to Equity	12.4	9.2	13.0	10.1
Efficiency Ratios				
Backlog to Working Capital	16.3	11.9	18.8	12.8
Months in Backlog	8.6	7.3	9.9	7.7
Days in Accounts Receivable	47.4	47.3	47.0	45.0
Days in Inventory	0.2	0.6	0.4	0.6
Days in Accounts Payable	45.9	43.3	44.8	40.4
Operating Cycle	21.4	24.3	19.6	23.9

* In the CFMA's 2005 Annual Financial Study, Return on Assets (ROA) and Return on Equity (ROE) are calculated using net earnings (loss) before income taxes. Studies conducted in prior years used net earnings (loss) after taxes to calculate ROA and ROE. All references to ROAs and ROEs from prior studies have been updated to reflect this change.

Note: Not all figures will appear to sum due to rounding.

Heavy & Highway Contractors
Composite

Balance Sheet

Current assets:	2005 Participants Amount	Percent	2004 Participants Amount	Percent
Cash and cash equivalents	$ 6,230,400	15.4 %	$ 5,527,581	15.0 %
Marketable securities & short-term investments	1,440,197	3.5	604,532	1.6
Receivables:				
Contract receivables currently due	10,507,240	25.9	8,946,371	24.2
Retainages on contracts	3,881,865	9.6	2,853,659	7.7
Unbilled work	863,719	2.1	237,719	0.6
Other receivables	600,087	1.5	914,964	2.5
Less allowance for doubtful accounts	(59,944)	(0.1)	(61,512)	(0.2)
Total receivables, net	15,792,968	38.9	12,891,202	34.9
Inventories	937,194	2.3	1,076,157	2.9
Costs and recognized earnings in excess of billings on uncompleted contracts	2,235,049	5.5	1,625,848	4.4
Investments in and advances to construction joint ventures	419,628	1.0	406,814	1.1
Income taxes:				
Current/refundable	26,004	0.1	37,969	0.1
Deferred	106,147	0.3	203,258	0.6
Other current assets	824,579	2.0	947,122	2.6
Total current assets	28,012,166	69.0	23,320,484	63.1
Property, plant and equipment	23,506,239	57.9	26,097,547	70.7
Less accumulated depreciation	(14,018,135)	(34.5)	(15,425,759)	(41.8)
Property, plant and equipment, net	9,488,103	23.4	10,671,787	28.9
Noncurrent assets:				
Long-term investments	372,452	0.9	496,153	1.3
Deferred income taxes	79,188	0.2	19,878	0.1
Other assets	2,630,588	6.5	2,430,680	6.6
Total noncurrent assets	3,082,228	7.6	2,946,711	8.0
Total assets	$ 40,562,497	100.0 %	$ 36,938,983	100.0 %

Current liabilities:	2005 Participants Amount	Percent	2004 Participants Amount	Percent
Current maturity on long-term debt	$ 1,175,606	2.9 %	$ 1,288,117	3.5 %
Notes payable and lines of credit	468,741	1.2	477,053	1.3
Accounts payable:				
Trade, including currently due to subcontractors	8,432,234	20.8	5,149,105	13.9
Subcontracts retainages	925,713	2.3	1,194,696	3.2
Other	342,847	0.8	272,245	0.7
Total accounts payable	9,700,794	23.9	6,616,046	17.9
Accrued expenses	2,221,762	5.5	2,238,135	6.1
Billings in excess of costs and recognized earnings on uncompleted contracts	4,541,773	11.2	4,061,207	11.0
Income taxes:				
Current	109,226	0.3	71,801	0.2
Deferred	25,941	0.1	32,077	0.1
Other current liabilities	338,119	0.8	284,494	0.8
Total current liabilities	18,581,961	45.8	15,068,929	40.8
Noncurrent liabilities				
Long-term debt, excluding current maturities	5,178,864	12.8	4,890,523	13.2
Deferred income taxes	452,939	1.1	420,844	1.1
Other	616,693	1.5	735,308	2.0
Total liabilities	24,830,458	61.2	21,115,604	57.2
Minority interests	54,805	0.1	9,201	0.0
Net worth:				
Common stock, par value	603,495	1.5	289,699	0.8
Preferred stock, stated value	9,031	0.0	51,984	0.1
Additional paid-in capital	3,733,958	9.2	3,274,592	8.9
Retained earnings	10,831,199	26.7	12,529,731	33.9
Treasury stock	(360,443)	(0.9)	(761,509)	(2.1)
Excess value of marketable securities	20,247	0.0	15,401	0.0
Other equity	859,748	2.1	414,281	1.1
Total net worth	15,697,235	38.7	15,814,179	42.8
Total liabilities and net worth	$ 40,582,497	100.0 %	$ 36,938,983	100.0 %

Heavy & Highway Contractors
Composite

Statement of Earnings

	2005 Participants		2004 Participants	
	Amount	Percent	Amount	Percent
Contract revenue	$ 90,746,172	96.9 %	$ 82,733,602	96.8 %
Other revenue	2,922,353	3.1	2,756,362	3.2
Total Revenue	93,668,525	100.0	85,489,964	100.0
Contract cost	(82,906,467)	(88.5)	(75,283,362)	(88.1)
Other cost	(2,480,502)	(2.6)	(2,269,040)	(2.7)
Total cost	(85,386,969)	(91.2)	(77,552,402)	(90.7)
Gross Profit	8,281,556	8.8	7,937,562	9.3
Selling, general & administrative expenses:				
Payroll	(2,618,696)	(2.8)	(3,135,573)	(3.7)
Professional fees	(175,848)	(0.2)	(257,050)	(0.3)
Sales & marketing costs	(157,591)	(0.2)	(133,979)	(0.2)
Technology costs	(121,201)	(0.1)	(142,244)	(0.2)
Administrative bonuses	(415,481)	(0.4)	(380,150)	(0.4)
Other	(2,120,781)	(2.3)	(1,614,376)	(1.9)
Total SG&A expenses	(5,609,599)	(6.0)	(5,663,373)	(6.6)
Income from operations	2,671,958	2.9	2,274,189	2.7
Interest income	146,619	0.2	104,762	0.1
Interest expense	(246,264)	(0.3)	(303,031)	(0.4)
Other income / (expense), net	70,265	0.1	165,241	0.2
Net earnings / (loss) before income taxes	2,642,577	2.8	2,241,161	2.6
Income tax (expense) / benefit	(220,445)	(0.2)	(361,630)	(0.4)
Net earnings	$ 2,422,132	2.6	$ 1,879,531	2.2

Number of Participants

	Number
2005	106
2004	106

Financial Ratios

	2005 Participants		2004 Participants	
	Average	Median	Average	Median
Liquidity Ratios				
Current Ratio	1.5	1.5	1.5	1.5
Quick Ratio	1.3	1.3	1.3	1.3
Days of Cash	23.9	13.5	23.3	16.2
Working Capital Turnover	9.9	10.5	10.4	11.3
Profitability Ratios				
Return on Assets *	6.5 %	7.8 %	6.1 %	5.8 %
Return on Equity *	16.8 %	19.4 %	14.2 %	14.9 %
Times Interest Earned	11.7	12.5	8.4	8.9
Leverage Ratios				
Debt to Equity	1.6	1.5	1.3	1.4
Revenue to Equity	6.0	5.9	5.4	5.7
Asset Turnover	2.3	2.5	2.3	2.3
Fixed Asset Ratio	60.4 %	68.4 %	67.5 %	64.0 %
Equity to SG&A Expense	2.8	2.1	2.8	2.3
Underbillings to Equity	19.7 %	9.8 %	11.8 %	7.9 %
Backlog to Equity	5.0	3.4	4.4	3.7
Efficiency Ratios				
Backlog to Working Capital	8.8	6.4	10.3	6.8
Months in Backlog	8.6	7.0	8.3	7.3
Days in Accounts Receivable	42.5	42.9	41.3	43.8
Days in Inventory	4.0	3.7	5.0	3.9
Days in Accounts Payable	37.0	26.7	25.2	26.6
Operating Cycle	33.4	38.9	44.4	40.3

Note: Not all figures will appear to sum due to rounding.

* In the CFMA's 2005 Annual Financial Study, Return on Assets (ROA) and Return on Equity (ROE) are calculated using net earnings (loss) before income taxes. Studies conducted in prior years used net earnings (loss) after taxes to calculate ROA and ROE. All references to ROAs and ROEs from prior studies have been updated to reflect this change.

Specialty Trade Contractors
Composite

Balance Sheet

	2005 Participants		2004 Participants	
	Amount	Percent	Amount	Percent
Current assets:				
Cash and cash equivalents	$ 1,088,211	5.7 %	$ 1,201,618	7.0 %
Marketable securities & short-term investments	207,217	1.1	341,095	2.0
Receivables:				
Contract receivables currently due	9,631,845	50.8	8,263,335	48.1
Retainages on contracts	1,897,498	10.0	1,553,333	9.1
Unbilled work	187,032	1.0	128,065	0.7
Other receivables	141,500	0.7	317,591	1.8
Less allowance for doubtful accounts	(104,242)	(0.5)	(109,898)	(0.6)
Total receivables, net	11,753,632	62.0	10,162,476	59.2
Inventories	348,254	1.8	269,500	1.6
Costs and recognized earnings in excess of billings on uncompleted contracts	1,434,561	7.6	1,143,435	6.7
Investments in and advances to construction joint ventures	20,934	0.1	25,425	0.1
Income taxes:				
Current/refundable	10,216	0.1	22,277	0.1
Deferred	38,629	0.2	27,008	0.2
Other current assets	453,047	2.4	460,023	2.7
Total current assets	15,354,703	80.9	13,652,857	79.5
Property, plant and equipment	5,245,272	27.6	5,402,358	31.5
Less accumulated depreciation	(3,248,038)	(17.1)	(3,404,518)	(19.8)
Property, plant and equipment, net	1,997,235	10.5	1,997,840	11.6
Noncurrent assets:				
Long-term investments	68,375	0.4	82,925	0.5
Deferred income taxes	29,033	0.2	17,260	0.1
Other assets	1,522,569	8.0	1,421,347	8.3
Total noncurrent assets	1,619,977	8.5	1,521,532	8.9
Total assets	$ 18,971,914	100.0 %	$ 17,172,230	100.0 %

	2005 Participants		2004 Participants	
	Amount	Percent	Amount	Percent
Current liabilities:				
Current maturity on long-term debt	$ 298,946	1.6 %	$ 260,336	1.5 %
Notes payable and lines of credit	1,000,402	5.3	577,931	3.4
Accounts payable:				
Trade, including currently due to subcontractors	3,243,596	17.1	2,913,802	17.0
Subcontracts retainages	259,732	1.4	219,170	1.3
Other	166,585	0.9	327,121	1.9
Total accounts payable	3,669,913	19.3	3,460,094	20.1
Accrued expenses	1,920,132	10.1	1,332,597	7.8
Billings in excess of costs and recognized earnings on uncompleted contracts	2,501,947	13.2	2,310,444	13.5
Income taxes:				
Current	43,294	0.2	15,065	0.1
Deferred	17,993	0.1	15,189	0.1
Other current liabilities	366,373	1.9	206,059	1.2
Total current liabilities	9,819,000	51.8	8,177,715	47.6
Noncurrent liabilities:				
Long-term debt, excluding current maturities	1,387,425	7.3	2,016,719	11.7
Deferred income taxes	76,990	0.4	67,193	0.4
Other	143,594	0.8	364,493	2.1
Total liabilities	11,427,010	60.2	10,626,120	61.9
Minority interests	15,266	0.1	7,273	0.0
Net worth:				
Common stock, par value	237,508	1.3	482,636	2.8
Preferred stock, stated value	11,663	0.1	45,887	0.3
Additional paid-in capital	2,421,325	12.8	1,421,356	8.3
Retained earnings	5,116,098	27.0	4,744,449	27.6
Treasury stock	(822,400)	(4.3)	(416,361)	(2.4)
Excess value of marketable securities	17,474	0.1	19,881	0.1
Other equity	547,970	2.9	240,989	1.4
Total net worth	7,529,638	39.7	6,538,837	38.1
Total liabilities and net worth	$ 18,971,914	100.0 %	$ 17,172,230	100.0 %

Specialty Trade Contractors
Composite

Statement of Earnings

	2005 Participants		2004 Participants	
	Amount	Percent	Amount	Percent
Contract revenue	$ 52,768,222	97.1 %	$ 44,798,872	97.1 %
Other revenue	1,568,925	2.9	1,358,851	2.9
Total Revenue	54,337,147	100.0	46,157,723	100.0
Contract cost	(45,528,011)	(83.8)	(38,125,762)	(82.6)
Other cost	(1,198,314)	(2.2)	(1,618,423)	(3.5)
Total cost	(46,726,324)	(86.0)	(39,744,185)	(86.1)
Gross Profit	7,610,823	14.0	6,413,537	13.9
Selling, general & administrative expenses:				
Payroll	(2,865,192)	(5.3)	(2,806,534)	(6.1)
Professional fees	(147,747)	(0.3)	(143,587)	(0.3)
Sales & marketing costs	(208,037)	(0.4)	(200,193)	(0.4)
Technology costs	(97,418)	(0.2)	(123,516)	(0.3)
Administrative bonuses	(273,443)	(0.5)	(317,708)	(0.7)
Other	(2,677,039)	(4.9)	(1,725,597)	(3.7)
Total SG&A expenses	(6,268,875)	(11.5)	(5,317,134)	(11.5)
Income from operations	1,341,947	2.5	1,096,403	2.4
Interest income	20,603	0.0	24,404	0.1
Interest expense	(125,746)	(0.2)	(146,426)	(0.3)
Other income / (expense), net	99,088	0.2	162,826	0.4
Net earnings / (loss) before income taxes	1,335,892	2.5	1,137,207	2.5
Income tax (expense) / benefit	(172,942)	(0.3)	(58,383)	(0.1)
Net earnings	$ 1,162,950	2.1	$ 1,078,823	2.3

Number of Participants

	Number
2005	165
2004	171

Financial Ratios

	2005 Participants		2004 Participants	
	Average	Median	Average	Median
Liquidity Ratios				
Current Ratio	1.6	1.6	1.7	1.6
Quick Ratio	1.3	1.3	1.4	1.4
Days of Cash	7.2	4.1	9.4	4.8
Working Capital Turnover	9.8	9.7	8.4	9.7
Profitability Ratios				
Return on Assets *	7.0 %	6.8 %	6.6 %	5.1 %
Return on Equity *	17.7 %	19.9 %	17.4 %	14.9 %
Times Interest Earned	11.6	11.1	8.8	6.4
Leverage Ratios				
Debt to Equity	1.5	1.7	1.6	1.6
Revenue to Equity	7.2	8.4	7.1	7.8
Asset Turnover	2.9	3.0	2.7	2.9
Fixed Asset Ratio	26.5 %	25.8 %	30.6 %	29.5 %
Equity to SG&A Expense	1.2	1.0	1.2	1.0
Underbillings to Equity	21.5 %	20.1 %	19.4 %	15.8 %
Backlog to Equity	6.0	3.4	4.8	3.7
Efficiency Ratios				
Backlog to Working Capital	8.2	4.3	6.7	4.3
Months in Backlog	6.0	5.3	5.9	5.6
Days in Accounts Receivable	64.1	61.8	66.1	62.7
Days in Inventory	2.7	3.0	2.4	2.4
Days in Accounts Payable	26.3	27.4	29.4	26.4
Operating Cycle	47.7	45.7	48.5	49.4

* In the CFMA's 2005 Annual Financial Study, Return on Assets (ROA) and Return on Equity (ROE) are calculated using net earnings (loss) before income taxes. Studies conducted in prior years used net earnings (loss) after taxes to calculate ROA and ROE. All references to ROAs and ROEs from prior studies have been updated to reflect this change.

Note: Not all figures will appear to sum due to rounding.

CFMA Comparative Financial Data

Balance Sheet
Most Recent Year End

	All Companies		Industrial & Nonresidential		Heavy & Highway		Specialty Trade	
	Amount	Percent	Amount	Percent	Amount	Percent	Amount	Percent
Current assets:								
Cash and cash equivalents	$ 4,818,236	14.6 %	$ 7,286,579	17.7 %	$ 6,230,400	15.4 %	$ 1,088,211	5.7 %
Marketable securities & short-term investments	1,983,264	6.0	3,748,113	9.1	1,440,197	3.5	207,217	1.1
Receivables:								
Contract receivables currently due	12,856,421	38.9	17,039,458	41.4	10,507,240	25.9	9,631,845	50.8
Retainages on contracts	3,919,134	11.9	5,739,338	13.9	3,881,865	9.6	1,897,498	10.0
Unbilled work	337,890	1.0	231,244	0.6	863,719	2.1	187,032	1.0
Other receivables	419,224	1.3	564,447	1.4	600,087	1.5	141,500	0.7
Less allowance for doubtful accounts	(64,638)	(0.2)	(37,123)	(0.1)	(59,944)	(0.1)	(104,242)	(0.5)
Total receivables, net:	17,468,032	52.8	23,537,363	57.1	15,792,968	38.9	11,753,632	62.0
Inventories	509,170	1.5	62,318	0.2	937,194	2.3	348,254	1.8
Costs and recognized earnings in excess of billings on uncompleted contracts	1,735,737	5.3	1,771,079	4.3	2,235,049	5.5	1,434,561	7.6
Investments in and advances to construction joint ventures	205,853	0.6	267,770	0.7	419,628	1.0	20,934	0.1
Income taxes:								
Current/refundable	22,668	0.1	24,682	0.1	26,004	0.1	10,216	0.1
Deferred	59,853	0.2	62,432	0.2	106,147	0.3	38,629	0.2
Other current assets	705,247	2.1	848,258	2.1	824,579	2.0	453,047	2.4
Total current assets	27,508,059	83.2	37,608,594	91.3	28,012,166	69.0	15,354,703	80.9
Property, plant and equipment	9,304,496	28.2	5,129,943	12.5	23,506,239	57.9	5,245,272	27.6
Less accumulated depreciation	(5,629,779)	(17.0)	(3,184,441)	(7.7)	(14,018,135)	(34.5)	(3,248,038)	(17.1)
Property, plant and equipment, net	3,674,716	11.1	1,945,503	4.7	9,488,103	23.4	1,997,235	10.5
Noncurrent assets:								
Long-term investments	350,514	1.1	594,860	1.4	372,452	0.9	68,375	0.4
Deferred income taxes	92,363	0.3	152,721	0.4	79,188	0.2	29,033	0.2
Other assets	1,427,615	4.3	890,988	2.2	2,630,588	6.5	1,522,569	8.0
Total noncurrent assets	1,870,491	5.7	1,638,569	4.0	3,082,228	7.6	1,619,977	8.5
Total assets	$ 33,053,266	100.0 %	$ 41,192,667	100.0 %	$ 40,582,497	100.0 %	$ 18,971,914	100.0 %

CFMA Comparative Financial Data

	All Companies		Industrial & Nonresidential		Heavy & Highway		Specialty Trade	
	Amount	Percent	Amount	Percent	Amount	Percent	Amount	Percent
Current liabilities:								
Current maturity on long-term debt	$ 505,428	1.5 %	$ 192,110	0.5 %	$ 1,175,606	2.9 %	$ 298,946	1.6 %
Notes payable and lines of credit	549,390	1.7	216,248	0.5	468,741	1.2	1,000,402	5.3
Accounts payable:								
Trade, including currently due to subcontractors	9,779,664	29.6	15,924,529	38.7	8,432,234	20.8	3,243,596	17.1
Subcontracts retainages	2,774,589	8.4	5,716,494	13.9	925,713	2.3	259,732	1.4
Other	203,446	0.6	174,023	0.4	342,847	0.8	166,585	0.9
Total accounts payable	12,757,700	38.6	21,815,045	53.0	9,700,794	23.9	3,669,913	19.3
Accrued expenses	2,117,744	6.4	2,367,884	5.7	2,221,762	5.5	1,920,132	10.1
Billings in excess of costs and recognized earnings on uncompleted contracts	4,008,261	12.1	5,128,250	12.4	4,541,773	11.2	2,501,947	13.2
Income taxes:								
Current	47,657	0.1	27,894	0.1	109,226	0.3	43,294	0.2
Deferred	41,700	0.1	70,298	0.2	25,941	0.1	17,993	0.1
Other current liabilities	374,427	1.1	403,782	1.0	338,119	0.8	366,373	1.9
Total current liabilities	20,402,306	61.7	30,221,513	73.4	18,581,961	45.8	9,819,000	51.8
Noncurrent liabilities								
Long-term debt, excluding current maturities	2,038,046	6.2	840,236	2.0	5,178,864	12.8	1,387,425	7.3
Deferred income taxes	141,937	0.4	35,588	0.1	452,939	1.1	76,990	0.4
Other	354,694	1.1	413,410	1.0	616,693	1.5	143,594	0.8
Total liabilities	22,936,983	69.4	31,510,746	76.5	24,830,458	61.2	11,427,010	60.2
Minority interests	45,041	0.1	49,308	0.1	54,805	0.1	15,266	0.1
Net worth:								
Common stock, par value	332,075	1.0	267,875	0.7	603,495	1.5	237,508	1.3
Preferred stock, stated value	62,793	0.2	134,469	0.3	9,031	0.0	11,663	0.1
Additional paid-in capital	1,939,629	5.9	879,010	2.1	3,733,958	9.2	2,421,325	12.8
Retained earnings	7,370,741	22.3	7,614,959	18.5	10,831,199	26.7	5,116,098	27.0
Treasury stock	(506,391)	(1.5)	(374,562)	(0.9)	(360,443)	(0.9)	(822,400)	(4.3)
Excess value of marketable securities	52,536	0.2	98,515	0.2	20,247	0.0	17,474	0.1
Other equity	819,859	2.5	1,012,347	2.5	859,748	2.1	547,970	2.9
Total net worth	10,071,243	30.5	9,632,612	23.4	15,697,235	38.7	7,529,638	39.7
Total liabilities and net worth	$ 33,053,266	100.0 %	$ 41,192,667	100.0 %	$ 40,582,497	100.0 %	$ 18,971,914	100.0 %

CFMA Comparative Financial Data

Statement of Earnings
Most Recent Year End

	All Companies		Industrial & Nonresidential		Heavy & Highway		Specialty Trade	
	Amount	Percent	Amount	Percent	Amount	Percent	Amount	Percent
Contract revenue	$ 94,479,099	98.5 %	$ 133,182,935	99.9 %	$ 90,746,172	96.9	$ 52,768,222	97.1 %
Other revenue	1,479,664	1.5	130,634	0.1	2,922,353	3.1	1,568,925	2.9
Total Revenue	95,958,762	100.0	133,313,569	100.0	93,668,525	100.0	54,337,147	100.0
Contract cost	(87,359,593)	(91.0)	(126,002,256)	(94.5)	(82,906,467)	(88.5)	(45,528,011)	(83.8)
Other cost	(1,155,465)	(1.2)	(200,044)	(0.2)	(2,480,502)	(2.6)	(1,198,314)	(2.2)
Total cost	(88,515,059)	(92.2)	(126,202,300)	(94.7)	(85,386,969)	(91.2)	(46,726,324)	(86.0)
Gross Profit	7,443,704	7.8	7,111,269	5.3	8,281,556	8.8	7,610,823	14.0
Selling, general & administrative expenses:								
Payroll	(2,853,533)	(3.0)	(3,002,109)	(2.3)	(2,618,696)	(2.8)	(2,865,192)	(5.3)
Professional fees	(192,060)	(0.2)	(229,973)	(0.2)	(175,848)	(0.2)	(147,747)	(0.3)
Sales & marketing costs	(227,170)	(0.2)	(283,391)	(0.2)	(157,591)	(0.2)	(208,037)	(0.4)
Technology costs	(156,413)	(0.2)	(224,549)	(0.2)	(121,201)	(0.1)	(97,418)	(0.2)
Administrative bonuses	(374,451)	(0.4)	(445,999)	(0.3)	(415,481)	(0.4)	(273,443)	(0.5)
Other	(2,040,813)	(2.1)	(1,577,207)	(1.2)	(2,120,781)	(2.3)	(2,677,039)	(4.9)
Total SG&A expenses	(5,844,439)	(6.1)	(5,763,229)	(4.3)	(5,609,599)	(6.0)	(6,268,875)	(11.5)
Income from operations	1,599,265	1.7	1,348,040	1.0	2,671,958	2.9	1,341,947	2.5
Interest income	134,207	0.1	221,383	0.2	146,619	0.2	20,603	0.0
Interest expense	(130,092)	(0.1)	(66,769)	(0.1)	(246,264)	(0.3)	(125,746)	(0.2)
Other income / (expense), net	100,078	0.1	111,901	0.1	70,265	0.1	99,088	0.2
Net earnings / (loss) before income taxes	1,703,457	1.8	1,614,555	1.2	2,642,577	2.8	1,335,892	2.5
Income tax (expense) / benefit	(175,569)	(0.2)	(164,042)	(0.1)	(220,445)	(0.2)	(172,942)	(0.3)
Net earnings	$ 1,527,888	1.6	$ 1,450,513	1.1	$ 2,422,132	2.6	$ 1,162,950	2.1

Number of Participants

	All Companies	Industrial & Nonresidential	Heavy & Highway	Specialty Trade
	Number	Number	Number	Number
2005	532	227	106	165
2004	537	250	106	171

CFMA Comparative Financial Data

Financial Ratios
Most Recent Year End

	All Companies		Industrial & Nonresidential		Heavy & Highway		Specialty Trade	
	Average	Median	Average	Median	Average	Median	Average	Median
Liquidity Ratios								
Current Ratio	1.3	1.4	1.2	1.3	1.5	1.5	1.6	1.6
Quick Ratio	1.2	1.2	1.1	1.2	1.3	1.3	1.3	1.3
Days of Cash	18.1	11.2	19.7	16.3	23.9	13.5	7.2	4.1
Working Capital Turnover	13.5	12.9	18.0	18.5	9.9	10.5	9.8	9.7
Profitability Ratios								
Return on Assets *	5.2 %	5.3 %	3.9 %	4.1 %	6.5 %	7.8 %	7.0 %	6.8 %
Return on Equity *	16.9 %	18.5 %	16.8 %	16.9 %	16.8 %	19.4 %	17.7 %	19.9 %
Times Interest Earned	14.1	11.5	25.2	14.3	11.7	12.5	11.6	11.1
Leverage Ratios								
Debt to Equity	2.3	2.2	3.3	3.1	1.6	1.5	1.5	1.7
Revenue to Equity	9.5	9.9	13.8	14.9	6.0	5.9	7.2	8.4
Asset Turnover	2.9	3.1	3.2	3.5	2.3	2.5	2.9	3.0
Fixed Asset Ratio	36.5 %	25.3 %	20.2 %	16.7 %	60.4 %	68.4 %	26.5 %	25.8 %
Equity to SG&A Expense	1.7	1.2	1.7	1.2	2.8	2.1	1.2	1.0
Underbillings to Equity	20.6 %	13.4 %	20.8 %	10.6 %	19.7 %	9.8 %	21.5 %	20.1 %
Backlog to Equity	8.6	5.3	12.4	9.2	5.0	3.4	6.0	3.4
Efficiency Ratios								
Backlog to Working Capital	11.8	7.2	16.3	11.9	8.8	6.4	8.2	4.3
Months in Backlog	7.7	6.3	8.6	7.3	8.6	7.0	6.0	5.3
Days in Accounts Receivable	49.6	51.7	47.4	47.3	42.5	42.9	64.1	61.8
Days in Inventory	2.1	2.2	0.2	0.6	4.0	3.7	2.7	3.0
Days in Accounts Payable	40.6	33.8	45.9	43.3	37.0	26.7	26.3	27.4
Operating Cycle	29.1	33.3	21.4	24.3	33.4	38.9	47.7	45.7

* In the CFMA's 2005 Annual Financial Study, Return on Assets (ROA) and Return on Equity (ROE) are calculated using net earnings (loss) before income taxes. Studies conducted in prior years used net earnings (loss) after taxes to calculate ROA and ROE. All references to ROAs and ROEs from prior studies have been updated to reflect this change.

TEXT—KEY WORD INDEX
OF INDUSTRIES APPEARING
IN THE STATEMENT STUDIES

STATEMENT STUDIES KEY WORD INDEX

A complete description of each industry category listed below begins on page 35.

STATEMENT STUDIES KEY WORD INDEX

A complete description of each industry category listed below begins on page 35.

STATEMENT STUDIES KEY WORD INDEX

A complete description of each industry category listed below begins on page 35.

Nonupholstered Wood Household Furniture Manufacturing, 700, 701, mfg

Nursery and Tree Production, 116, 117, ag

Nursery, Garden Center, and Farm Supply Stores, 930, 931, rtl

Nursing Care Facilities, 1384, 1385, HC

O

Office Administrative Services, 1272, 1273, Admin

Office Equipment Merchant Wholesalers, 770, 771, wsle

Office Furniture (except Wood) Manufacturing, 708, 709, mfg

Office Machinery and Equipment Rental and Leasing, 1190, 1191, R/E

Office Supplies and Stationery Stores, 984, 985, rtl

Offices of All Other Miscellaneous Health Practitioners, 1352, 1353, HC

Offices of Bank Holding Companies, 1266, 1267, mgmt

Offices of Certified Public Accountants, 1202, 1203, prof serv

Offices of Chiropractors, 1344, 1345, HC

Offices of Dentists, 1342, 1343, HC

Offices of Lawyers, 1198, 1199, prof serv

Offices of Mental Health Practitioners (except Physicians), 1348, 1349, HC

Offices of Optometrists, 1346, 1347, HC

Offices of Other Holding Companies, 1268, 1269, mgmt

Offices of Physical, Occupational and Speech Therapists, and Audiologists, 1350, 1351, HC

Offices of Physicians (except Mental Health Specialists), 1338, 1339, HC

Offices of Physicians, Mental Health Specialists, 1340, 1341, HC

Offices of Real Estate Agents and Brokers, 1164, 1165, R/E

Oil and Gas Field Machinery and Equipment Manufacturing, 550, 551, mfg

Oil and Gas Pipeline and Related Structures Construction, 188, 189, cons-g

Open-End Investment Funds, 1148, 1149, fin

Ophthalmic Goods Manufacturing, 724, 725, mfg

Ophthalmic Goods Merchant Wholesalers, 778, 779, wsle

Optical Goods Stores, 950, 951, rtl

Optical Instrument and Lens Manufacturing, 564, 565, mfg

Orange Groves, 106, 107, ag

Ornamental and Architectural Metal Work Manufacturing, 506, 507, mfg

Other Accounting Services, 1204, 1205, prof serv

Other Activities Related to Credit Intermediation, 1124, 1125, fin

Other Activities Related to Real Estate, 1170, 1171, R/E

Other Aircraft Parts and Auxiliary Equipment Manufacturing, 684, 685, mfg

Other Airport Operations, 1042, 1043, trans

Other Animal Food Manufacturing, 230, 231, mfg

Other Apparel Accessories and Other Apparel Manufacturing, 320, 321, mfg

Other Automotive Mechanical and Electrical Repair and Maintenance, 1464, 1465, other

Other Building Equipment Contractors, 212, 213, cons-g

Other Building Material Dealers, 926, 927, rtl

Other Business Service Centers (including Copy Shops), 1280, 1281, Admin

Other Chemical and Allied Products Merchant Wholesalers, 864, 865, wsle

Other Clothing Stores, 964, 965, rtl

Other Commercial and Industrial Machinery and Equipment Rental and Leasing, 1192, 1193, R/E

Other Commercial and Service Industry Machinery Manufacturing, 568, 569, mfg

Other Commercial Equipment Merchant Wholesalers, 774, 775, wsle

Other Commercial Printing, 378, 379, mfg

Other Communications Equipment Manufacturing, 618, 619, mfg

Other Computer Peripheral Equipment Manufacturing, 612, 613, mfg

Other Computer Related Services, 1224, 1225, prof serv

Other Concrete Product Manufacturing, 454, 455, mfg

Other Construction Material Merchant Wholesalers, 766, 767, wsle

Other Crushed and Broken Stone Mining and Quarrying, 158, 159, mng

Other Direct Insurance (except Life, Health, and Medical) Carriers, 1144, 1145, fin

Other Direct Selling Establishments, 1002, 1003, rtl

Other Electronic and Precision Equipment Repair and Maintenance, 1476, 1477, other

Other Electronic Component Manufacturing, 632, 633, mfg

Other Electronic Parts and Equipment Merchant Wholesalers, 790, 791, wsle

Other Fabricated Wire Product Manufacturing, 514, 515, mfg

Other Farm Product Raw Material Merchant Wholesalers, 860, 861, wsle

Other Financial Vehicles, 1152, 1153, fin

Other Gasoline Stations, 954, 955, rtl

Other General Government Support, 1526, 1527, pub admin

Other Grocery and Related Products Merchant Wholesalers, 854, 855, wsle

Other Heavy and Civil Engineering Construction, 194, 195, cons-g

Other Heavy and Civil Engineering Construction, 1551, cons-%

Other Hosiery and Sock Mills, 302, 303, mfg

Other Household Textile Product Mills, 296, 297, mfg

Other Individual and Family Services, 1400, 1401, HC

Other Lighting Equipment Manufacturing, 654, 655, mfg

Other Management Consulting Services, 1234, 1235, prof serv

Other Measuring and Controlling Device Manufacturing, 648, 649, mfg

Other Metal Container Manufacturing, 508, 509, mfg

Other Metal Valve and Pipe Fitting Manufacturing, 534, 535, mfg

Other Metalworking Machinery Manufacturing, 586, 587, mfg

Other Millwork (including Flooring), 336, 337, mfg

Other Miscellaneous Durable Goods Merchant Wholesalers, 820, 821, wsle

Other Miscellaneous Nondurable Goods Merchant Wholesalers, 884, 885, wsle

Other Motion Picture and Video Industries, 1090, 1091, info

Other Nonferrous Foundries (except Die-Casting), 488, 489, mfg

Other Nonscheduled Air Transportation, 1010, 1011, trans

Other Professional Equipment and Supplies Merchant Wholesalers, 780, 781, wsle

Other Residential Care Facilities, 1394, 1395, HC

Other Scientific and Technical Consulting Services, 1238, 1239, prof serv

Other Services Related to Advertising, 1252, 1253, prof serv

Other Services to Buildings and Dwellings, 1304, 1305, Admin

Other Similar Organizations (except Business, Professional, Labor, and Political Organizations), 1516, 1517, other

Other Snack Food Manufacturing, 264, 265, mfg

Other Social Advocacy Organizations, 1506, 1507, other

Other Support Activities for Air Transportation, 1044, 1045, trans

Other Support Activities for Road Transportation, 1054, 1055, trans

Other Support Activities for Water Transportation, 1050, 1051, trans

Other Technical and Trade Schools, 1328, 1329, edu

Other Telecommunications, 1102, 1103, info

Other Tobacco Product Manufacturing, 282, 283, mfg

Other Vegetable (except Potato) and Melon Farming, 104, 105, ag

Other Warehousing and Storage, 1070, 1071, trans

Outdoor Power Equipment Stores, 928, 929, rtl

Outerwear Knitting Mills, 304, 305, mfg

Outpatient Mental Health and Substance Abuse Centers, 1356, 1357, HC

Overhead Traveling Crane, Hoist, and Monorail System Manufacturing, 598, 599, mfg

P

Packaged Frozen Food Merchant Wholesalers, 840, 841, wsle

Packaging Machinery Manufacturing, 604, 605, mfg

Packing and Crating, 1058, 1059, trans

Paint and Coating Manufacturing, 408, 409, mfg

Paint and Wallpaper Stores, 922, 923, rtl

Paint, Varnish, and Supplies Merchant Wholesalers, 882, 883, wsle

Painting and Wall Covering Contractors, 216, 217, cons-g

Painting and Wall Covering Contractors, 1560, cons-%

Paper (except Newsprint) Mills, 346, 347, mfg

Paper Industry Machinery Manufacturing, 554, 555, mfg

Parking Lots and Garages, 1498, 1499, other

Passenger Car Leasing, 1174, 1175, R/E

Passenger Car Rental, 1172, 1173, R/E

Periodical Publishers, 1076, 1077, info

Pesticide and Other Agricultural Chemical Manufacturing, 402, 403, mfg

Petroleum and Petroleum Products Merchant Wholesalers (except Bulk Stations and Terminals), 868, 869, wsle

Petroleum Bulk Stations and Terminals, 866, 867, wsle

Petroleum Lubricating Oil and Grease Manufacturing, 388, 389, mfg

Petroleum Refineries, 384, 385, mfg

Pharmaceutical Preparation Manufacturing, 406, 407, mfg

Pharmacies and Drug Stores, 946, 947, rtl

Photofinishing Laboratories (except One-Hour), 1496, 1497, other

Photographic and Photocopying Equipment Manufacturing, 566, 567, mfg

Photographic Equipment and Supplies Merchant Wholesalers, 768, 769, wsle

Photography Studios, Portrait, 1256, 1257, prof serv

Piece Goods, Notions, and Other Dry Goods Merchant Wholesalers, 830, 831, wsle

Plastics and Rubber Industry Machinery Manufacturing, 552, 553, mfg

Plastics Bottle Manufacturing, 434, 435, mfg

Plastics Material and Resin Manufacturing, 396, 397, mfg

Plastics Materials and Basic Forms and Shapes Merchant Wholesalers, 862, 863, wsle

Plastics Pipe and Pipe Fitting Manufacturing, 428, 429, mfg

STATEMENT STUDIES KEY WORD INDEX

A complete description of each industry category listed below begins on page 35.

STATEMENT STUDIES INDEX FOR PARTS I-IV

A complete description of each industry category listed below begins on page 35.

NOTES

NOTES

NOTES

NOTES

NOTES

NOTES

NOTES

NOTES

NOTES

NOTES

NOTES

NOTES

NOTES

NOTES

NOTES

NOTES